The 79 Radicals (v...
79 の部首 (異...

2

亻 a	人 (a)	𠆢 (a)	冫 b	丶 (b)	子 c				
刀 (f)	力 g	又 h	冖 i	宀 j	艹 k	十 (k)	卜 m	⺊ (m)	n / o
八 (o)	八 (o)	厂 p	辶 q	辶 (q)	廴 (q)	冂 r	刀 (r)	几 (r)	匚 t

3

氵 a	水 (a)	永 (a)	氺 (a)	土 b	土 (b)	扌 c	手 (c)	口 d	口 (d)	女 e
巾 f	犭 g	犬 (g)	弓 h	彳 (4k)	忄 j	彡 k	艹 m	宀 n	⺌ (n)	
⺍ (n)	屮 o	土 p	夊 (4i)	广 q	尸 r	辶 (2q)	夂 (4i)	弋 (4n)	匚 (2t)	口 s

4

木 a	月 b	日 c	火 d	灬 (d)	礻 e	示 (e)	王 f	玉 (f)	牛 g	方 h
水 (3a)	手 (3c)	犬 (3g)	攵 i	夂 (i)	夂 (i)	欠 j	心 k	心 (k)	忄 (k)	⺗ (k)
戸 m	戸 (m)	戈 n	弋 (n)							

5

石 a	立 b	立 (b)	目 c	禾 d	礻 e	衣 (e)	玉 (4f)	罒 f	罒 g	皿 h
氺 (3a)	示 (4e)	疒 i								

6

糸 a	米 b	舟 c	虫 d	耳 e	竹 f	竹 (f)	衣 (5e)	襾	

7

言 a	貝 b	車 c	⻊	足 (d)	酉 e

8

金 a	食 b	食 (b)	𩙿 (b)	隹 c	雨 d	雨 (d)	襾 (d)	門 e	鬥 (e)

9

食 (8b)	𩙿 (8b)	頁 a

10 馬 a

11 魚 a | 鳥 b

Characters which have no radical are listed under the pseudo-radical 0a.
部首をもたない漢字は疑似部首の 0a 部に収録。

The Kanji Dictionary

Mark Spahn

Wolfgang Hadamitzky

with

Kumiko Fujie -Winter

漢字熟語字典

CHARLES E. TUTTLE COMPANY
Rutland, Vermont & Tokyo, Japan

This book has been typeset by Seiko Harada and Rainer Weihs, Berlin, Germany, on a Macintosh® computer, using the Japanese PageMaker®.

*Published by the Charles E. Tuttle Company, Inc.
of Rutland, Vermont & Tokyo, Japan
with editorial offices at
Suido 1-chome, 2-6, Bunkyo-ku, Tokyo 112*

*LCC Card No. 95-61609
ISBN 0-8048-2058-9
ISBN 4-8053-0545-2 (in Japan)*

First edition, 1996

Printed in Singapore

TABLE OF CONTENTS
目　次

List of Tables
図　表

付録   **Appendices**

Preface

The purpose of this dictionary is to make it as easy as possible to look up the readings and meanings of Japanese words written in Chinese characters (kanji). It includes, as either main entries or variants, all the kanji in the JIS X 0208-1990 character set titled Code of the Japanese Graphic Character Set for Information Interchange established on September 1, 1990, plus hundreds more. This revised and enlarged edition includes about 1,000 new entries not found in the first edition, bringing the total to 5,910 characters (7,062 counting variants) and over 48,000 multi-character compounds. In addition, various tables, maps, and other supplements have been added for the user's edification and entertainment.

Each character entry lists all of the character's important Chinese-derived *on* and native-Japanese *kun* readings, meanings, and variant forms. Old forms and variants of characters are listed with a cross-reference to their standard form.

We have tried to include all compounds which commonly occur in the modern language, including the names of all the prefectures and major cities, all the emperor and era names, and various surnames whose reading cannot easily be inferred from the readings of their component characters, such as 服部 *(Hattori)* and 長谷川 *(Hase-gawa)*. Also listed are a number of kanji-katakana and katakana-kanji compounds like 生ビール *(namabīru)* and アル中 *(aruchū)*.

What makes this dictionary different from other character dictionaries is that every compound is listed under each of its constituent characters. This multiple listing feature enables the user to look up the desired compound under whichever of its kanji he finds easiest to locate quickly. It is also a big help in deciphering blurry faxes and handwriting.

Entries are arranged according to a radical-based lookup system of the same type used in virtually all character dictionaries, but with certain significant improvements which make it considerably easier to learn and use.

With the alphabetically arranged readings index one can look up a character via any of its readings, without having to determine its radical or count strokes.

Hundreds of books and countless articles were evaluated in compiling this dictionary. Also consulted for the selection of characters and compounds were the newer domestic Japanese dictionaries and character dictionaries as well as the frequency count research in *Gendai Shinbun no Kanji* (1976) of the *Kokuritsu Kokugo Kenkyū-jo*. Meanings listed for characters and compounds likewise follow modern domestic and Japanese-English dictionaries. Many words not found in comparable dictionaries

have been incorporated, such as 端末機 *(tanmatsuki)*, サラ金 *(sarakin)*, 宅配便 *(takuhaibin)*, 光ファイバー *(hikarifaibā)*, and 人間工学 *(ningen kōgaku)*. A sampling of the compounds newly added in this edition includes ながら族 *(nagarazoku)*, マイクロ波 *(maikuroha)*, 電子レンジ *(denshi renji)*, 燃費 *(nenpi)*, and 酸性雨 *(sanseiu)*, and abbreviations like 販促 *(hansoku)*, 減俸 *(genpō)*, 損保 *(sonpo)*, 日電 *(Nichiden)*, and 経団連 *(Keidanren)*.

We welcome user's comments about any errors or omissions, so that this dictionary can be kept always accurate and up to date.

We thank Junko Bauermeister and Kimi Mizonobe-Knopf for their assistance in the selection of compounds. We are grateful to Jörg Ruminski for his preparation of the database, and especially to Seiko Harada and Rainer Weihs for conversion of the data and the layout.

MARK SPAHN
WOLFGANG HADAMITZKY

How to Use This Dictionary

How to Look Up a Character

The characters in this dictionary are arranged according to the same general scheme adopted by virtually all character dictionaries used by Japanese: a set of character components called "radicals" is prescribed, and each character is classified according to the radical it contains, with rules for determining which radical to take when a character contains more than one.

The radicals are listed inside the front cover, arranged in groups according to the number of strokes in which they are written. Within each stroke-count group the radicals are arranged according to their usual position within a character, in the order: left side, right side, top, bottom, enclosure (on two or more sides). Each radical is identified by a number-letter name (like "3k" for radical ⁺⁺ *(kusa-kanmuri)* or "7a" for radical 訁 *(gon-ben))*, where the number indicates its stroke-count. (In naming radicals, the letter "I" is skipped, lest it be confused with the digit "1".)

A character will usually contain two or more radicals, and it must be decided which radical to take. The general rule is: if the character consists of a left and right side and the left side is a radical, take the left-side radical; if the character naturally divides itself into a top and bottom and the top part is a radical, take the radical on the top. The detailed rules are given on page xii in "How to Determine the Radical of a Character", and a summary of them is given inside the back cover.

Having determined the radical of a character, then you count number of strokes in the rest of the character (its "residual stroke-count"); the radical and residual stroke-count of the character specify where in the dictionary the character will be found. For example, the radical of the character 諸 *(SHO)* is 訁 *(gon-ben)* 7a and its non-radical part 者 consists of 8 strokes. This character will therefore be found within group 7a8, the group of all characters whose radical is 7a and whose residual stroke-count is 8. The characters within this group are numbered sequentially 7a8.1, 7a8.2, 7a8.3, etc. These "descriptor" appearing at the top of each page indicate which characters are listed on that page.

Once the search has been narrowed down this far, it is usually just a matter of flipping a few pages until the desired character is found. When there are many characters with the same radical and same stroke-count, scanning for the desired character goes faster if you keep in mind that they are ordered according to the position of the radical within the character (left, right, top, bottom, elsewhere) and subordered according to the form of the residual part of the character (indivisible, divisible left

and right, divisible into a top and bottom, divisible into an enclosure and an enclosed part); observe for example the order of the characters within the group 4k10: 慨、慎、慓、愴、愾、態.

When you know the radical and the residual stroke-count of the character you are looking for, you can locate it quickly with the help of the "trailer" printed in the outer margin of each page. The trailer consists of a stroke-count number followed by all the radicals having that stroke-count. The radical of the characters which appear on the page is highlighted, and a numeral indicates their residual stroke-count.

There are two other ways to locate a character. Knowing only a character's radical, the character can be found without stroke counting by scanning the "overview list" which appears at the beginning of each radical section and includes all the characters (as well as variants and cross-reference entries) which are listed under that radical. Or, if one of the readings of a character is known, it can be located via the readings index at the back of the dictionary, without having to determine its radical or count strokes. (In the readings index, a kanji can almost always be found more quickly under its *kun* reading than under its *on* reading, since few kanji share the same *kun* reading but some *on* readings are shared by many kanji.)

How to Look Up a Compound

Under each character (the "head character") are listed, first, all compounds beginning with the head character. These compounds are arranged in increasing order of the stroke-count (and then the radical) of their second character. This is followed by a section of all compounds whose second character is the head character; these compounds are arranged in increasing order of the stroke-count of their first character. Next comes a section of all compounds whose third character is the head character, likewise arranged in increasing order of the stroke-count of their first character. That is, each head character entry is followed by a list of all the compounds in which that character entry is followed by a list of all the compounds in which that character occurs in first, second, third, and subsequent position.

A consequence of this scheme is that each compound appears in several places in the dictionary, namely, under each of its characters. So to find the entry for a compound, just look in the proper section following whichever of its characters you can locate the most quickly and easy.

To take an example, you have a choice of about eight different ways to look up the compound 殺虫剤 *(satchūzai)*. It is listed under the kanji 殺, which may be located directly by the radical system (explained below) or via its *on* reading *SATSU* or its *kun* reading *koro(su)* in the alphabetical readings index. This compound is also listed under its second kanji 虫, which may be found either directly via its radical or indi-

rectly via its *on* reading *CHŪ* or its *kun* reading *mushi*. A third copy of this compound will be found under its third kanji 剤, whose location in the dictionary can be determined either via its radical or via its sole reading *ZAI*.

A Word about Stroke Counting

The way in which a character is actually written with pen or pencil is the criterion which we adopt for counting strokes. We count as a single stroke any line which is drawn with the pen or pencil in continuous contact with the paper, no matter how the line may cusp and curve.

Taking the character 艮 as an example, the leftmost stroke is drawn by starting at the top, changing its direction at the lower left corner of the character, and continuing the stroke toward the upper right, to the center of the character. In printed versions of this character (良), however, this single stroke usually looks like two separate strokes.

When counting strokes, be aware that in this dictionary we consider the following components to consist of the following number of strokes: 了 (1), 子 (2), 阝 (2), 辶 (2), 比 (4), 灬 (4), 臣 (7).

Explanation of Sample Entries

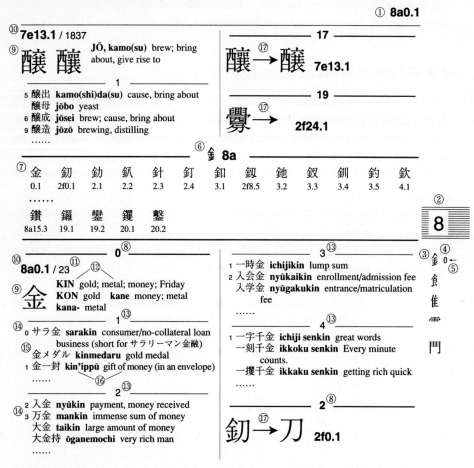

① The range of characters on the double-page spread, identified by the descriptor of the first character on the left-hand page and the last on the right-hand page (8a0.1, in this case).

② Trailer header, indicating that this is the section of the dictionary where characters are listed whose radical consists of (in this example) 8 strokes.

③ Trailer; a string of all radicals (without variants) of a given stroke count (8, in this case).

④ Number indicating the residual stroke-count of the first character whose entry starts on this page (or of the last character if it is a right-hand page).

⑤ Mark indicating that this is the radical of the characters which appear on this page.

⑥ The header beginning the section where all the characters having a given radical are listed. The radical is shown, along with the number-letter descriptor which identifies it.

⑦ The overview list, which presents in compact form all the characters listed under a given radical, either as main entries or as cross-references to an entry under another radical. Below each character in the overview list is printed the tail of its descriptor (or its full descriptor, if the entry is a variant or is listed under some other radical).

x

⑧ Number within a column-wide divider indicating that here begins the section which lists those characters under the current radical which have a given residual stroke-count.

⑨ The character ("head character"). Following the character are listed its pre-Second World War form and its variants, if any.

⑩ The character's "descriptor", a name by which the character is identified and referred to. A descriptor (example: (8a0.1) consisting of the character's radical (8a, in this example), the number of strokes in its non-radical part (0, in this example), and, separated by a decimal point, its sequential number (1, in this example) within the group of characters having the same radical and same residual stroke-count.

⑪ The serial number of this character in the book *Kanji & Kana* and in the computer program *SUNRISE Script*.* Since *Kanji & Kana* includes only the 1,945 *Jōyō Kanji*, which are officially recommended for general use, the presence of a *K&K* number indicates that the character is one of the *Jōyō Kanji*, and in general, the lower the *K&K* number, the greater the frequency of the character's occurrence. The cross-reference to Kanji & Kana may be used to check the brush and pen-written forms of the character and the sequence in which its strokes are written.

⑫ Readings and meanings of the character. *On* readings are given in all uppercase bold letters, and *kun* readings are given in lowercase bold letters, with *okurigana* indicated within parentheses.

⑬ Number giving the position of the head character within the following group of compounds; that is, whether the head character is the first, second, third, etc. kanji.

⑭ Stroke count of the second character of compounds beginning with the head character (or, if in a section of compounds where the head kanji occurs in other than first position, the stroke count of the first character). Listed under "stroke-count zero" are compounds consisting only of the head character and a word written in kana.

⑮ Compound containing the head character. Compounds are arranged in increasing order of the stroke-count (then radical) of their second character (or, if the head character occurs in other than first position, of their first character). *Okurigana* are not indicated.

⑯ Reading(s) and meaning(s) of the compound. *Okurigana* are indicated within parentheses. Only the most important meanings of each compound are listed. Many Japanese words can, depending on context and grammatical ending, be used as either noun, verb, or adjective, but in general the English translation includes only one part of speech.

⑰ Cross-reference showing that this character is listed elsewhere. Cross-references are provided for kanji whose radical or stroke-count might be mistaken or miscounted, as well as for variant and pre-Second World War forms of kanji.

---

* Kanji & Kana
English-language edition: Tuttle (Tokyo and Rutland, Vermont)
German editions: Langenscheidt (Berlin, Vienna, Zurich) and Enderle (Tokyo)
French edition: Maisonneuve (Paris)

SUNRISE Script (Seven-language edition on CD-ROM) JAPAN Media (Berlin)

How to Determine the Radical of a Character

The term "radical" is used with either of two meanings: (1) any of the character components included in some specified list (in this book, in the Radical Table inside the front cover), or (2) that particular radical under which a given character is listed in a given character dictionary. Context usually makes it clear which meaning is intended (for example, "a radical" for the first meaning and "the radical" or "its radical" for the second meaning).

To determine under which radical any given character is listed in this dictionary, go through the following checklist, stopping at the first step which applies. Look for any radicals which appear within the character.

Consider as radicals only those which consists of complete strokes not crossed by a line which is not part of the radical (for example, 寺 does not contain radical 龹 because the short vertical line at the top is only part of a stroke, and 本 does not contain the radical 木 because the 木 is crossed by the short horizontal stroke). It sometimes happens that one radical is part of another radical; in such cases, consider only the more inclusive radical.

0. **All** 🄰 If the entire character is itself a radical (or a variant of a radical), then that is its radical.
   Examples: 十 → 龹 2k, 手 → 扌 3c, 金 → 釒 8a.
   (金 contains radical 2a, but remember that we always take the more inclusive radical.)

1. **Left** 🄱 If the left side of the character is a radical, then that is the character's radical. Here we do not merely mean a radical which appears somewhere on the left side of the character (as 龹 and 田 do in 畝), but rather one which forms the entire left side of the character and can be separated from the rest of the character by a straight (or nearly straight) vertical line.
   Examples: 協 → 龹 2k, 休 → 亻 2a, 明 → 日 4c, 情 → 忄 4k.
   About half of all characters divide themselves in a natural way into a left side and a right side, with the left side being the radical.

2. **Right** 🄲 If the right side of the character is a radical (but the left side is not), then that is the character's radical.
   Examples: 教 → 攵 4i, 別 → 刂 2f, 外 → 卜 2m, 郎 → 阝 2d.
   Notice that the rule is "left before right": if both the left side and the right side of a character are radicals, as in 明, we take the left-side radical (in this example, 日 4c).

3. **Up** 🄳 If the upper part of the character is a radical, then that is the character's radical. Here the radical must form the whole top part of the character, and it may

embrace the rest of the character symmetrically like the overhanging eaves of a roof.

Examples: 芯 → ⁺⁺ 3k, 虎 → ⌐ 2m, 急 → ⌒ 2n, 企 → 𠆢 2a, 前 → ˇ 2o, 父 → 𠆢 2o, 翁 → 𠆢 2o.

Note that some radicals (in this case "2o") may appear in different shapes as shown in the table "The 79 Radicals (with variants)" (front end paper).

4. **Down** ▱ If the lower part of the character is a radical (but not the upper part), then that is the character's radical.

Examples: 想 → 心 4k, 無 → 灬 4d, 攀 → 𢦏 5a, 呉 → 八 2o.

(Observe that in the last example the radical cannot be 口 because it does not "cap" the bottom part of the character and cannot be separated from the rest of the character by a horizontal line.) Notice that the rule is "top before bottom": If both the upper part and the lower part of the character are radicals, as in 共, we take the upper-part radical (⁺⁺ 3k in this example).

5. **Around** ▱▱▱▱▱▱ If the character contains a radical which encloses the rest of the character on two or more sides, then that is the character's radical.

Examples: 進 → 辶 2q, 式 → 弋 4n, 原 → 厂 2p, 区 → 匚 2t, 同 → 冂 2r, 国 → 囗 3s.

6. **Everywhere** ? If no radical appears in any of the positions checked so far, then look for a radical anywhere in the character.

(a) **only one** ① If the character contains only one radical, then there is nothing to decide; the character's sole radical is the only possible radical under which it could be classified.

Examples: 契 → 刂 2f, 止 → ⌐ 4m, 友 → 又 2h, 缶 → ⌐ 2k, 矩 → 匚 2t.

(b) **greater stroke-count** ⊳ If the character contains two (or more) radicals, take the radical which consists of more strokes.

Examples: in 向 take the 3-stroke radical 冂 3d in preference to the 2-stroke radical 冂 2r; in 者 take the 4-stroke radical 耂 4c rather than the 2-stroke radical ⁺ 2k; in 鞘 take the 4-stroke radical 刂 4b instead of the 3-stroke radical ⁺⁺ 3k or ⁰ 3n; in 哉 the radical is the 4-stroke 弋 4n, not the 3-stroke 冂 3d or the 2-stroke ⁺ 2k.

(c) **leftmost** ⊟ If the character contains two (or more) radicals of equally greatest stroke-count, take the one whose leftmost point is farther left.

Examples: in 喪 the radicals 土 3b and 冂 3d are of equally high stroke-count, but since the 土 3b protrudes farther left, the radical of this character is 土 3b; in 鼻, 5-stroke radical 田 5f extends farther left than 5-stroke radical 刂 5c, so we look for this character under radical 田 5f; in 叛 the only possibilities are 厂 2p and 又 2h (the ˇ 2o in the upper left is considered destroyed as a radical by the stroke which crossed it, separating its two parts), and since the 厂 2p ex-

tends farther left, 厂 2p is the radical of this character.

(d) **highest** ⊤ If the character contains two (or more) radicals of equally leftmost point, then take whichever has the higher highest point.

Examples: 舖 → 土 3b, 栽 → 戈 4n, 段 → 几 2s.

The steps of this whole search procedure can be neatly summarized in the mnemonic slogan "Look <u>left</u>, <u>right</u>, <u>up</u>, <u>down</u>, <u>all</u> <u>around</u> <u>everywhere</u>". (The "all" is out of sequence but the changed order yields the same result.)

7. **Nowhere** ⓪ If the character contains no radical at all, then it will be found in the section at the beginning of the book labeled "0a", in which such characters are listed in increasing order of stroke-count. Among these radicalless characters, characters having the same stroke-count are arranged in increasing order of number of points at which strokes intersect (then subclassified in increasing order of number of points at which strokes only touch one another; observe the progression in "0a11": 疎、野、爽、肅、彗).

(If you find it convenient, you may think of 0a as the "none of the above" radical which consists of zero strokes, thereby making it invisible and making the residual stroke-count of the character the same as its total stroke-count. For example, it is a matter of personal preference whether you think of 本 as a 5-stroke character having no radical, or as a character which "contains" the null radical 0a plus 5 strokes; in either case it will be found in group 0a5.)

Once you have understood these rules, a quick glance at the summary of them listed inside the back cover will refresh your memory should you ever be in doubt about how to apply them in a particular case.

These rules for determining the radical of a character may at first seem complex, but it takes much less time to apply them than to state them explicitly. Notice that the one-stroke radicals found in many character dictionaries are absent. This has the advantage that a meaning-bearing radical (usually the same as the traditional radical) is thereby selected, eliminating such counterintuitive results as classifying 彫 under a radical 丿 instead of under radical 彡 3j, or 悪 under a radical 一 instead of under radical 心 4k.

How to Use Other Character Dictionaries

The arrangement of characters in most character dictionaries is based on the classification scheme of the Kangxi zidian (康熙字典). Published in China in 1716, this 42-volume work arranged some 42,000 Chinese characters according to a system using a set of 214 radicals.

It may be argued that the compilers of the Kangxi zidian had to have so many radicals

in order to classify so many characters into groups of manageable size, but a smaller set of radicals suffices for the no more than 5,000–6,000 characters of modern Japanese. Nevertheless, Japanese character dictionaries have usually been arranged according to the 214 traditional radicals. Indeed, to keep up with the orthographic reforms made since the Second World War, by which many characters were simplified and lost their former radical, Japanese dictionary publishers added new radicals to the traditional set, so that today many dictionaries recognize even more than 214 radicals.

To determine the radical of a character, most Japanese character dictionaries use more or less the same rule as the Kangxi zidian: the radical is usually that part of the character (or, in many cases, of its pre-1946 form) which is associated with its meaning. This presents the user with the paradoxical predicament of having to know the meaning of a character in order to locate it in a dictionary and look up its meaning. For about 85% of all characters, the traditional radical is the same as that given by the rules of the present dictionary.

Thus, the user of this dictionary who should have occasion to refer to a dictionary which is based on the historical radicals need only familiarize himself with the particular set of radicals which it uses, and be aware that the rules for determining a character's radical are somewhat different. The accompanying table "The 214 Historical Radicals in Comparison with the 79 Radicals" will be of help in making this transition (see page 1674).

この字典の使い方

1. この字典の特徴

　この字典は、漢字及び熟語の読み方やその英語の意味が簡単に引けるように構成したものである。

　最大の特徴は、従来の字典と異なり、すべての熟語がそれを構成している漢字(見出し字)それぞれの元で引けるようになっているので、熟語中の一つの漢字の部首か読みがわかりさえすれば、先頭の漢字からはもちろん、2字目以降のどの漢字からでも求める熟語が引けることである。

2. 収録範囲

1)　見出し字5,910字(異体字を含めると7,062字)及び、熟語48,000語を収録した。

2)　漢字、熟語の選択にあたっては、最新の国内の国語辞典や漢和辞典、さらに国立国語研究所の「現代新聞の漢字(1976)」中の頻度調査なども参考にした。

　漢字と熟語の意味についても、上記のもののほか和英辞典を参考にした。

3)　熟語の範囲は、現在使用されている一般的な熟語を中心に下記のものも収録した。

- 都道府県名と大きな都市名
- 元号名、天皇名
- 読み方が難しい姓　　　　　　　　(例) 服部、長谷川
- カタカナ混じりの言葉　　　　　　(例) 生ビール、アル中、サラ金
- 日常生活で使われる特殊用語や専門用語

　　　　　　　　　　　　(例) 端末機、宅配便、人間工学、光ファイバー

3. 配列方法

1) 見出し字

　見出し字の部首の画数順とし、同部首の場合は部首以外の部分の画数順。同一画数の中では、その部首の位置が、左、右、上、下、囲みの順とした。(巻末の部首チェックリスト参照)

　この字典に使用している部首は従来の「康熙字典」の214部首のなかから選んだ、検索しやすい形の部首78と新しく採用した〝の79部首である。(従来の部首との比較は巻末の一覧表を参照願いたい。)

　なお、どの部首でもとらえられない漢字は、0aとして先頭におき、画数順とした。

　部首が不明の場合は、漢字の読みから見出し字を検索できる音訓索引を利用していただきたい。

2) 熟語

　　見出し字を1字目に含む熟語、2字目に含む熟語、3字目…と、見出し字の
ある位置で分けた。

　　同じ位置の場合、見出し字が1字目にあれば2字目の漢字の画数順、見出し
字が2字目以降にあれば1字目の画数順とし、同画の場合はその部首順とし
た。

　　カタカナ混じりの熟語などは、これらの先頭においた。

4. 各項目内容

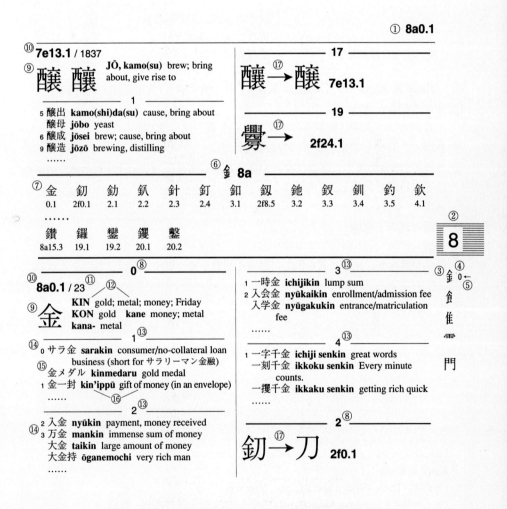

① 当該ページの最初の見出し字(偶数ページ)か、最後の見出し字(奇数ページ)をデスクリプタ(→ ⑩)で示す。

② 部首の画数、③ 同画の部首一覧、④ 部首を除く画数、⑤ 矢印
　　(当該ページの部首を矢印で示し、さらに部首を除く画数を示すことにより、
　　求める漢字が探せる。)

⑥ 部首とその番号

⑦ 同部首の漢字一覧

⑧ 部首を除いた画数

⑨ 漢字(見出し字)
　　旧字、異体字は右2字目、3字目…に示す。

⑩ デスクリプタ(漢字の番号)

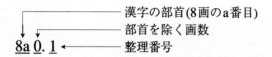

　　　　　　　　　　　　　　漢字の部首(8画のa番目)
　　　　　　　　　　　　　　部首を除く画数
　　　8a 0. 1 ◄────────── 整理番号

⑪ 「Kanji & Kana」*や「Sunrise Script」*での漢字番号(常用漢字1,945字)

⑫ 漢字の読みと意味
　　音読みは大文字、訓読みは小文字。送り仮名は(　)で囲んだ。

⑬ 熟語中、見出し字を何番目に含むかを示す。

⑭ 熟語の2字目の漢字の画数(1字目が見出し字の場合)、または1字目の漢字の画数
　　(2字目以降が見出し字の場合)

⑮ 熟語

⑯ 熟語の読みと意味

⑰ 参照
　　旧字や異体字、またまぎらわしい部首や画数を持つ漢字などは、参照を入れた。

* *Kanji & Kana*
　(英語版) Tuttle (Tokyo and Rutland, Vermont)
　(ドイツ語版) Langenscheidt (Berlin, Wien, Zürich) and Enderle (Tokyo)
　(フランス語版) Maisonneuve (Paris)

Sunrise Script (CD-ROM七か国語版) JAPAN Media (Berlin)

THE KANJI DICTIONARY

漢字と熟語

─────────────────────── **0a1** ───────────────────────

一	ノ	丶	亅	乙	了	⺃
1.1	1.2	1.3	1.4	1.5	2c0.3	0a2.12

0a1.1 / 2

ICHI, ITSU, hito(tsu), hito- one, a

一

──────────── 1 ────────────

1 一一 **ichi-ichi** one by one; in full detail
hito(tsu)-hito(tsu) one by one
2 一入 **hitoshio** all the more, especially
一丁 **itchō** one block (of tofu), one serving (of food), one city block
一丁字 **itteiji** (can't read) a single letter
一人 **hitori, ichinin** one person
一人一人 **hitori-hitori, hitori-bitori** one by one
一人子 **hitorikko, hitorigo** an only child
一人芝居 **hitori shibai** one-man show
一人当 **hitoria(tari)** per person/capita
一人歩 **hitoriaru(ki)** walking alone; walking/existing on one's own
一人者 **hitorimono** someone alone; unmarried/single person
一人物 **ichijinbutsu** a person of consequence
一人乗 **ichininno(ri)** single-seater
一人前 **ichininmae, hitorimae** one portion/serving; full adulthood
一人残 **hitori noko(razu)** everyone
一人娘 **hitori musume** an only daughter
一人旅 **hitoritabi** traveling alone
一人息子 **hitori musuko** an only son
一人称 **ichininshō** first person (in grammar)
一人舞台 **hitori butai** unrivaled
一子 **isshi** a child; an only child
hitorigo an only child
一子相伝 **isshi sōden** (secret) handed down from father to son
一刀 **ittō** (a single stroke of) a sword/blade
一八 **ichi(ka)bachi(ka)** sink or swim
3 一己 **ikko** oneself
一夕 **isseki** one evening; some evening
一寸 **issun** one *sun*/inch (3.03 cm)
chotto a little; just a minute
一寸先 **issun saki** an inch ahead; the immediate future
一寸見 **chottomi** a glance/glimpse
一寸逃 **issunnoga(re)** quibbling, putting off
一寸法師 **issunbōshi** dwarf, midget, Tom Thumb
一大事 **ichidaiji** a serious matter
一丸 **ichigan** a lump, (rolled into) one
一口 **hitokuchi** a mouthful; a unit; a word
一山 **hitoyama** a pile (of bananas); the

whole mountain
4 一元 **ichigen** unitary
一元化 **ichigenka** unification, centralization
一元論 **ichigenron** monism
一天 **itten** the (whole) sky
一夫一婦 **ippu-ippu** monogamy
一夫多妻 **ippu-tasai** polygamy
一毛作 **ichimōsaku** one crop a year
一介 **ikkai** mere, only
一切 **issai** all, everything; entirely, absolutely
hitoki(re) a piece/slice
一切合財 **issai-gassai** everything, the whole shebang
一切経 **Issaikyō** complete collection of Buddhist scriptures
一双 **issō** a pair (of screens)
一六勝負 **ichiroku shōbu** gambling; a gamble
一文 **ichimon** one-thousandth of a yen
ichibun a sentence
一文字 **ichimonji** a straight line
一文惜 **ichimon'oshi(mi)** stinginess; miser
一文無 **ichimonna(shi)** penniless
一片 **ippen** a piece/bit
一分 **ippun** a minute **ichibu** one tenth; one hundredth, one percent; one quarter *ryō* (an old coin) **ichibun** duty, honor
一分別 **hitofunbetsu** (careful) consideration
一辺倒 **ippentō** complete partiality to one side
一円 **ichien** the whole area; one yen
一区 **ikku** a district/ward; a section/division
一匹 **ippiki** one animal; 20-m bolt of cloth
一匹狼 **ippiki ōkami** lone wolf
一手 **itte** a move (in a game); sole, exclusive (agent) **hitote** by one's own effort
一手販売 **itte hanbai** sole agency
一木 **ichiboku** one tree
一月 **ichigatsu** January **ik(ka)getsu, hitotsuki, ichigetsu** one month
一日 **tsuitachi** the 1st (day of the month)
ichinichi, ichijitsu one/a day
一日千秋 **ichinichi-senshū, ichijitsu-senshū** days seeming like years
一日中 **ichinichi-jū** all day long
一日長 **ichijitsu (no) chō** superior, a little better
一方 **ippō** one side; on one hand, on the other hand; one party, the other party; nothing but, only **hitokata(narazu)** greatly, immensely
一方交通 **ippō kōtsū** one-way traffic

一方的 **ippōteki** one-sided, unilateral
一方通行 **ippō tsūkō** one-way traffic
一心 **isshin, hito(tsu)kokoro** one mind; the whole heart, wholehearted
一心同体 **isshin-dōtai** one flesh; one in body and spirit
一戸 **ikko** a house; a household
5 一矢報 **isshi (o) muku(iru)** shoot back, retort
一半 **ippan** a half; a part
一本 **ippon** one (long object); a book; one version; a blow; a full-fledged geisha
一本立 **ipponda(chi)** independence
一本気 **ippongi** one-track mind
一本杉 **ipponsugi** a solitary cedar tree
一本道 **ipponmichi** straight road; road with no turnoffs
一本調子 **ipponchōshi/jōshi** monotony
一本橋 **ipponbashi** log bridge
一失 **isshitsu** a disadvantage; a defect; an error
一生涯 **isshōgai** a lifetime, one's (whole) life
一生懸命 **isshōkenmei** with all one's might
一世 **issei** a lifetime; a generation; the First; first-generation (Japanese-American)
isse a lifetime
一世一元 **issei ichigen** one era name per emperor's reign
一世一代 **isse ichidai** once in a lifetime
一世紀 **isseiki** a century; first century
一冊 **issatsu** one copy (of a book)
一代 **ichidai** one generation; a lifetime; an age
一代記 **ichidaiki** a biography
一存 **ichizon** at one's own discretion
一巡 **hitomegu(ri)** a turn/round; one full year
ichijun a round/patrol
一汁一菜 **ichijū-issai** a simple meal
一打 **hitou(chi), ichida** a blow
一号 **ichigō** number one
一句 **ikku** a phrase/verse; (counter for haiku)
一字 **ichiji** a character/letter
一字千金 **ichiji senkin** great words
一穴 **hito(tsu)ana** the same hole/den; one gang
一札 **issatsu** a document/bond
一札入 **issatsu i(reru)** give a signed statement/I.O.U.
一旦 **ittan** once
一礼 **ichirei** a bow/greeting
一石二鳥 **isseki nichō** killing two birds with one stone
一目 **hitome, ichimoku** a glance/look
hito(tsu)me one-eyed (goblin)
一目惚 **hitomebo(re)** love at first sight
一目散 **ichimokusan** at top speed
一目瞭然 **ichimoku ryōzen** clear at a glance, obvious

一皿 **hitosara** a plate/dish (of food)
6 一気 **ikki** in one breath; straight through, without a break, at a stroke
一気呵成 **ikki kasei** in one breath/stroke/stretch
一両 **ichiryō** one vehicle; one *ryō* (an old coin)
一両日 **ichiryōjitsu** a day or two
一年 **ichinen** one year
hitotose one year, some time ago
一年中 **ichinen-jū** all year long
一年生 **ichinensei** first-year student; annual (plant)
一再 **issai** once or twice
issai(narazu) again and again
一曲 **ikkyoku** a tune/melody
一休 **hitoyasu(mi)** a rest
一件 **ikken** a matter, an item
一任 **ichinin** entrust
一合目 **ichigōme** first station (of ten up a mountain)
一次 **ichiji** first; primary; linear (equation)
一次元 **ichijigen** one-dimensional
一列 **ichiretsu** a row/line
一考 **ikkō** consideration, a thought
一同 **ichidō** all concerned, all of us
一先 **hitoma(zu)** for the present
一向 **ikkō** (not) at all
一名 **ichimei** one person; another name
一如 **ichinyo** oneness
一行 **ichigyō** a line (of text)
ikkō party, group; troupe
一安心 **hitoanshin** feeling relieved for a while
一回 **ikkai** once, one time; a game; an inning
hitomawa(ri) a turn/round
一回分 **ikkaibun** a dose; an installment
一回忌 **ikkaiki** first anniversary of a death
一回転 **ikkaiten, ichikaiten** one revolution/rotation
一回戦 **ikkaisen** first game/round (of tennis)
一因 **ichiin** a cause
一団 **ichidan** a group
一肌脱 **hitohada nu(gu)** pitch in and help
一式 **isshiki** a complete set; all, the whole
一衣帯水 **ichii taisui** narrow strait
一糸 **isshi** a string
一糸乱 **isshi mida(renai)** not a thread out of place, airtight (argument)
7 一身 **isshin** oneself, one's own interests
一身上 **isshinjō** personal (affairs)
一束 **issoku, hitotaba** a bundle; a hundred
一里 **ichiri** one *ri*, 3.9 km
一里塚 **ichirizuka** milestone
一位 **ichii** first place/rank
一体 **ittai** one body; (what) in the world, (how) the devil; properly speaking; generally

一卵性双生児 **ichiransei sōseiji** identical twins
一別 **ichibetsu** parting
一助 **ichijo** a help
一対 **ittsui** a pair
一対一 **ittaiichi** one-to-one
一角 **ikkaku** a corner/section; narwhal; apparently, seemingly
　hitokado full-fledged, respectable
一角獣 **ikkakujū** unicorn
一決 **ikketsu** be agreed/settled
一走 **hitohashi(ri), hito(p)pashi(ri)** a run/spin
一呑 **hitono(mi)** drinking at one draft/gulp
一役 **ichiyaku** an (important) office
　hitoyaku a role
一役買 **hitoyaku ka(u)** take on a role/task
一花 **hitohana** a flower; success
一芸 **ichigei** an art
一声 **issei, hitokoe** a voice/cry
一応 **ichiō** once; tentatively; in outline
一条 **ichijō** a line/streak; a matter; a passage (from a book)
　Ichijō (emperor, 986–1011)
一見 **ikken** take a look at, glance at
一利 **ichiri** one advantage
一利一害 **ichiri ichigai** advantages and disadvantages
一私人 **isshijin, ichishijin** a private individual
一系 **ikkei** single-family lineage
一言 **hitokoto, ichigen, ichigon** a word
一言二言 **hitokoto futakoto** a word or two
一足 **issoku** a pair (of shoes)
　hitoashi a step
一足飛 **issokuto(bi)** at one bound
一長一短 **itchō ittan** advantages and disadvantages
一事 **ichiji** one thing
　hito(tsu)koto the same thing
一例 **ichirei** one example, an instance
一念 **ichinen** a determined purpose
一命 **ichimei** a life; a command
一刻 **ikkoku** a minute/moment; stubborn, hotheaded
一刻千金 **ikkoku senkin** Every minute counts.
一刹那 **issetsuna** an instant, a moment
一夜 **ichiya, hitoyo, hitoya** one night; all night
一夜漬 **ichiyazuke** pickled just overnight; hastily prepared
一斉 **issei** all at once, simultaneously
一斉射撃 **issei shageki** volley, fusillade
一版 **ippan** an edition
一直線 **itchokusen** a straight line
一周 **isshū** once around, a revolution/tour/lap
一周年 **isshūnen** one full year, anniversary
一周忌 **isshūki** first anniversary of a death
一周期 **isshūki** a period (in astronomy)

一波 **ippa** a school/sect
一泊 **ippaku** an overnight stay
一泊二食付 **ippaku nishoku-tsu(ki)** with overnight lodging and two meals
一泡吹 **hitoawa fu(kaseru)** confound, upset (someone's plans)
一抹 **ichimatsu** a touch/tinge of
一抱 **hitokaka(e)** an armful
一味 **ichimi** an ingredient; a touch/tinge of; conspirators, gang
一味違 **hitoaji chiga(u)** with a unique flavor
一知半解 **itchi hankai** superficial knowledge
一妻多夫 **issai-tafu** polyandry
一昔 **hitomukashi** about ten years ago
一定 **ittei** fixed, prescribed, regular, definite; fix, settle; standardize
　ichijō definitely settled
一定不変 **ittei fuhen** invariable, permanent
一歩 **ippo** a step
一国 **ikkoku** stubborn, hotheaded; the whole country
一国一党主義 **ikkoku-ittō shugi** one-party system
一枚 **ichimai** one sheet
一枚看板 **ichimai kanban** one's only suit; leading actor; sole issue, slogan
一杯 **ippai** a cup of; a drink; full; to the upmost
一杯機嫌 **ippai kigen** slight intoxication
一服 **ippuku** a dose; a smoke; a rest/break; a lull, calm market
一物 **ichimotsu** an article, a thing; ulterior motive, designs
一所 **ik(ka)sho, issho, hitotokoro** one place; the same place
一所懸命 **isshokenmei** with all one's might
一雨 **hitoame** a shower/rainfall
一門 **ichimon** a family/clan
一発 **ippatsu** a shot
一巻 **ikkan** one volume　**hitomaki** one roll
一重 **hitoe** one layer; single
　hitokasa(ne) a suit (of clothes); a set (of nested boxes)
一院制 **ichiinsei** unicameral system
一郭 **ikkaku** a city block, quarter
一変 **ippen** a complete change
一点 **itten** a point; speck, dot, particle
一点張 **ittenba(ri)** persistence
一首 **isshu** a poem
一連 **ichiren** a series; a ream (of paper)
一途 **ichizu** wholeheartedly
　itto way, course; the only way
一通 **hitotō(ri)** in general, briefly
　ittsū one copy (of a document)
一風変 **ippū kawa(tta)** eccentric, queer; unconventional, original

一段 **ichidan** one stage/step, all the more

一段落 **ichidanraku** a pause

一封 **ippū** a sealed letter/document; an enclosure

一括 **ikkatsu** one lump/bundle; summing up

一指 **isshi** a finger

一挺 **itchō** (counter for guns, ink sticks, oars, candles, palanquins, rickshaws)

一品 **ippin** an article/item; a dish/course

一品料理 **ippin ryōri** dishes à la carte

一律 **ichiritsu** uniform, even, equal

一荒 **hitoa(re)** a squall; a burst of anger

一度 **ichido, hitotabi** once, one time

一面 **ichimen** one side/phase; the whole surface; first page (of a newspaper)

一面観 **ichimenkan** one-sided view

一面識 **ichimenshiki** knowing someone by sight, a passing acquaintance

一昨日 **issakujitsu, ototoi, ototsui** the day before yesterday

一昨年 **issakunen, ototoshi** the year before last

一昨昨日 **issakusakujitsu, sakiototoi, sakiototsui** three days ago

一昨昨年 **issakusakunen, sakiototoshi** three years ago

一昨昨夜 **issakusakuya** three nights ago

一神教 **isshinkyō** monotheism

一音節 **ichionsetsu** one syllable

一思 **hitoomo(i)** with one effort, once and for all, resolutely

一級 **ikkyū** one grade; first class

一計 **ikkei** a plan

一食 **isshoku** a meal

10 一倍 **ichibai** the same number/amount; double

一俵 **ippyō** a straw-bagful

一個人 **ichikojin, ikkojin** a private individual

一部 **ichibu** a part; a copy (of a publication)

一部分 **ichibubun** a part

一部始終 **ichibu shijū** full particulars

一進一退 **isshin-ittai** advance and retreat, fluctuating

一週 **isshū** a week

一週間 **isshūkan** a week

一流 **ichiryū** a school (of art); first-rate, top-notch; unique

一員 **ichiin** a person; a member

一姫二太郎 **ichi-hime ni-Tarō** It's good to have a girl first and then a boy.

一帯 **ittai** a region/zone; the whole place

一家 **ikka, ikke** a house/family/household; one's family; a style

一家団欒 **ikka danran** happy family circle, happy home

一家言 **ikkagen** one's own opinion, a personal view

一宮 **Ichinomiya** (city, Aichi-ken)

一案 **ichian** a plan, idea

一挙 **ikkyo** one effort, a single action

一挙一動 **ikkyo-ichidō** one's every action

一挙手一投足 **ikkyoshu-ittōsoku** a slight effort, the least trouble

一挙両得 **ikkyo ryōtoku** killing two birds with one stone

一座 **ichiza** all present, the company; a troupe

一席 **isseki** a speech/story/feast

一桁 **hitoketa** single digit

一脈 **ichimyaku** vein, thread, connection

一時 **ichiji** a time; at one time; for a time
ittoki twelfth part of a day
hitotoki a little while, a short period
ichidoki at a/one time

一時払 **ichijibara(i)** lump-sum payment

一時的 **ichijiteki** temporary

一時金 **ichijikin** lump sum

一時預場 **ichiji azukarijō** baggage safe-keeping area

一致 **itchi** agree

一致点 **itchiten** point of agreement

一息 **hitoiki** a breath; a pause/break; (a little more) effort

一眠 **hitonemu(ri)** a short sleep, a nap

一病息災 **ichibyō-sokusai** One who has an illness is careful of his health and lives long.

一般 **ippan** general

一般人 **ippannin, ippanjin** an ordinary person

一般化 **ippanka** generalization, popularization

一般的 **ippanteki** general

一般性 **ippansei** generality

一笑 **isshō** a laugh/smile

一軒 **ikken** a house

一軒家 **ikken'ya** isolated/freestanding/detached house

一隻 **isseki** one ship/boat

一隻眼 **issekigan** discerning eye

一閃 **issen** a flash

11 一陽来復 **ichiyō-raifuku** return of spring

一階 **ikkai** first/ground floor

一毫 **ichigō** an iota, one bit

一遍 **ippen** once

一過性 **ikkasei** transient, temporary

一掃 **issō** a clean sweep

一掬 **ikkiku** one scoop (of water)

一喝 **ikkatsu** a thundering cry, a roar

一帳羅 **itchōra** one's only good clothes

一張羅 **itchōra** one's only good clothes

一得 **ittoku** one advantage, a merit

一得一失 **ittoku isshitsu** advantages and disadvantages

一堂 **ichidō** a building/hall; a temple/shrine; a room

一票 **ippyō** a vote
一視同仁 **isshi-dōjin** impartiality, universal brotherhood
一理 **ichiri** a principle, a reason
一望千里 **ichibō-senri** vast, boundless
一族 **ichizoku** a family/household
一眼 **ichigan** one eye; single lens
一盛 **hitomo(ri)** a pile
　　　 hitosaka(ri) temporary prosperity
一組 **hitokumi, ichikumi** one set, one class
一絃琴 **ichigenkin** one-stringed instrument
一粒 **hitotsubu** a grain
一粒種 **hitotsubudane** an only child
一敗 **ippai** one defeat
一貫 **ikkan** consistency, coherence; (3.75 kg)
一転 **itten** a turn, complete change
一問一答 **ichimon-ittō** question-and-answer session
一頃 **hitokoro** once, some time ago
12 一割 **ichiwari** ten percent
一着 **itchaku** first arrival; first (in a race); a suit (of clothes)
一場 **ichijō** one time, one place
一報 **ippō** a report, information
一揆 **ikki** riot, insurrection
一揃 **hitosoro(i)** a set, a suit
一握 **hitonigi(ri), ichiaku** a handful
一幅 **ippuku** a scroll
一葉 **ichiyō** a leaf; a page; a copy (of a photo)
一喜一憂 **ikki ichiyū** alternation of joy and sorrow, hope and fear
一期 **ichigo** one's lifespan
　　　 ikki a term, a half year, a quarter
一朝 **itchō** a time, a short period
一朝一夕 **itchō-isseki** in a day, in a short time
一晩 **hitoban** a night, one evening; all night
一斑 **ippan** a part, a glimpse, an outline
一散 **issan** at top speed
一塁 **ichirui** first base
一畳 **ichijō** one mat
一番 **ichiban** number one, the first; most, best; a game/bout
一番鶏 **ichibandori** first cockcrowing
一統 **ittō** a lineage; bringing under one rule; all (of you)
一筆 **ippitsu, hitofude** a stroke of the pen, a few lines
一策 **issaku** an idea, a plan, a measure
一筋 **hitosuji** a line; earnestly, wholeheartedly
一筋道 **hitosujimichi** straight road, road with no turnoffs
一筋縄 **hitosujinawa** a piece of rope; ordinary means
一等 **ittō** first class/rank, the most/best

一等兵 **ittōhei** private first-class
一等車 **ittōsha** first-class coach
一等国 **ittōkoku** a first-class power
一等星 **ittōsei** first-magnitude star
一等賞 **ittōshō** first prize
一等親 **ittōshin** first-degree relative, immediate family
一飲 **hitono(mi)** a mouthful; a swallow/sip; an easy prey
一閑張 **ikkanba(ri)** lacquered papier-mâché
一間 **ikken** (1.8 m)
一項 **ikkō** an item; a paragraph
13 一際 **hitokiwa** conspicuously; still more, especially
一義 **ichigi** a reason; a principle; a meaning; the first principle/consideration
一義的 **ichigiteki** unambiguous
一塊 **hitokatama(ri)** a lump, a group
　　　 ikkai a lump
一塩 **hitoshio** slightly salted
一群 **hitomu(re), ichigun** a group; a flock, a crowd
一献 **ikkon** a cup (of saké)
一幕 **hitomaku** one act
一幕物 **hitomakumono** one-act play
一蓮托生 **ichiren-takushō** sharing fate with another
一廉 **hitokado, ikkado** superior, uncommon, full-fledged, respectable
一戦 **issen** a battle, a game/bout
一歳 **issai** one year old
一意 **ichii** unambiguous; single-minded
一意専心 **ichii-senshin** wholeheartedly
一新 **isshin** complete change, reform, renovation
一新紀元 **isshin kigen** a new era
一睡 **issui** a short sleep, a nap
一置 **hito(tsu)o(ki)** every other one
一触即発 **isshoku sokuhatsu** touch-and-go, hair-trigger, explosive (situation)
一節 **issetsu** a (Bible) verse, a stanza/passage
一話 **hito(tsu)banashi** anecdote, common talk
一路 **ichiro** one road; straight
14 一滴 **itteki** a drop
一掴 **hitotsuka(mi)** a handful; a grasp
一髪 **ippatsu** a hair, a hair's-breadth
一層 **issō** still more, all the more
一概 **ichigai** unconditionally, sweepingly
一様 **ichiyō** uniformity, evenness; equality, impartiality
一旗 **hitohata** a flag; an undertaking
一端 **ittan** a part; a general idea
一種 **isshu** a kind, a species; one kind
一緒 **issho** together
一網打尽 **ichimō dajin** a large catch, roundup; wholesale arrest

一箇 **ikko** one; a piece
一語 **ichigo** one word
一語一語 **ichigo-ichigo** word for word
一読 **ichidoku** a perusal/reading
一説 **issetsu** one/another view
一酸化炭素 **issanka tanso** carbon monoxide
15 一億 **ichioku** one hundred million
一撃 **ichigeki** a blow/hit
一徹 **ittetsu** obstinate, stubborn
一徹者 **ittetsumono** stubborn person
一審 **isshin** first instance/trial
一線 **issen** a line
一艘 **issō** a ship/vessel
一輪 **ichirin** a flower; a wheel
一輪車 **ichirinsha** unicycle
一輪挿 **ichirinza(shi)** a vase for one flower
16 一興 **ikkyō** amusement, fun
一獲 **ikkaku** one grab
一樹 **ichiju** one tree, the same tree
一樹蔭 **ichiju (no) kage** preordained fate
一膳 **ichizen** a bowl (of rice); a pair (of chopsticks)
一膳飯屋 **ichizen meshiya** eatery, diner
一頭 **ittō** a head (of cattle)
一頭地抜 **ittōchi (o) nu(ku)** stand head and shoulders above others
17 一臂 **ippi** a (helping) hand, one's bit
一環 **ikkan** a link, a part
一瞥 **ichibetsu** a glance/look
一覧 **ichiran** a look/glance; a summary; catalog
一覧表 **ichiranhyō** table, list
一縷 **ichiru** a thread, a ray (of hope)
18 一儲 **hitomōke** money-making
一瀉千里 **issha-senri** in a rush, at full gallop
一瞬 **isshun** a moment, an instant
一瞬間 **isshunkan** a moment, an instant
一癖 **hitokuse** trait, peculiarity; slyness
一難 **ichinan** one difficulty, one danger
一類 **ichirui** same kind; accomplices, companions
一騎 **ikki** one horseman
一騎打 **ikkiu(chi)** man-to-man combat
一騎当千 **ikki-tōsen** matchless, mighty
19 一蹴 **isshū** kick; reject
20 一齣 **hitokoma** a frame (of a film); a scene
一議 **ichigi** a word, an opinion, an objection
21 一躍 **ichiyaku** one bound; in one leap
一顧 **ikko** (take no) notice of
22 一纏 **hitomato(me)** a bunch/bundle
一驚 **ikkyō** surprise, amazement
23 一攫 **ikkaku** one grab
一攫千金 **ikkaku senkin** getting rich quick

———— 2 ————

1 一一 **ichi-ichi** one by one; in full detail
hito(tsu)-hito(tsu) one by one

2 人一倍 **hito-ichibai** uncommon, more than others
力一杯 **chikara-ippai** with all one's might
十一月 **jūichigatsu** November
3 万一 **man'ichi** (if) by any chance, should happen to
千一夜 **Sen'ichiya** Thousand and One Nights
4 不一致 **fuitchi** disagreement, incompatibility
今一 **ima hito(tsu)** leaving something to be desired, not quite perfect
片一方 **kata-ippō** one side/party, the other side/party
手一杯 **te-ippai** hands full; barely making ends meet
5 好一対 **kōittsui** well-matched (couple)
6 全一 **zen'itsu** a complete whole
合一 **gōitsu** unification, union
同一 **dōitsu** the same, identical, equal
同一人 **dōitsunin** the same person
同一人物 **dōitsu jinbutsu** the same person
同一視 **dōitsushi** consider alike, put in the same category
7 均一 **kin'itsu** uniform
択一 **takuitsu** choosing an alternative
初一念 **shoichinen** one's original intention
男一匹 **otoko ippiki** full-grown man
8 画一 **kakuitsu** uniform, standard
画一主義 **kakuitsu shugi** standardization
画一的 **kakuitsuteki** uniform, standard
刻一刻 **koku-ikkoku** moment by moment, hour by hour
斉一 **seiitsu** uniform, all alike
歩一歩 **ho-ippo** step by step
金一封 **kin'ippū** gift of money (in an envelope)
9 専一 **sen'itsu, sen'ichi** concentration; best care; utmost importance
逐一 **chikuichi** one by one, in detail
通一片 **tō(ri)-ippen** passing, casual, perfunctory
通一遍 **tō(ri)-ippen** passing, casual, perfunctory
後一条 **Goichijō** (emperor, 1016–1036)
単一 **tan'itsu** single, simple, individual
紅一点 **kōitten** one red flower in the foliage; the only woman in the group
10 随一 **zuiichi** No. 1, most, greatest
帰一 **kiitsu** be united into one, be reduced to one
真一文字 **ma-ichimonji** in a straight line
桐一葉 **kiri hitoha** falling paulownia leaf (a sign of the arrival of autumn or of the beginning of the end)
純一 **jun'itsu** purity, homogeneity
紙一重 **kami hitoe** paper-thin (difference)
11 唯一 **yuiitsu, tada hito(tsu)** the only, sole

第一 **dai-ichi** No. 1, first, best, main
第一人者 **dai-ichininsha** foremost/leading person
第一人称 **dai-ichininshō** first person (in grammar)
第一次 **dai-ichiji** first
第一流 **dai-ichiryū** first-rate
第一義 **dai-ichigi** original meaning; first principles
第一線 **dai-issen** the first/front line
12 御一新 **goisshin** the Meiji restoration
無一文 **muichimon** penniless
無一物 **muichibutsu, muichimotsu** penniless
統一 **tōitsu** unity, unification, uniformity
統一的 **tōitsuteki** unified, uniform
間一髪 **kan ippatsu** a hair's breadth
13 腹一杯 **hara ippai** full stomach; to one's heart's content
裸一貫 **hadaka ikkan** with no property but one's body
14 精一杯 **sei-ippai** with all one's might
15 誰一人 **dare hitori (mo)** (with negative) no one
16 壁一重 **kabe hitoe** (separated by) just a wall
20 鐚一文 **bita ichimon** (not even) a farthing/cent
21 鶴一声 **tsuru (no) hitokoe** the voice of authority

--------- 3 ---------

1 一人一人 **hitori-hitori/-bitori** one by one
一夫一婦 **ippu-ippu** monogamy
一世一代 **issei ichidai** once in a lifetime
一汁一菜 **ichijū-issai** a simple meal
一対一 **ittaiichi** one-to-one
一利一害 **ichiri ichigai** advantages and disadvantages
一長一短 **itchō ittan** advantages and disadvantages
一国一党主義 **ikkoku-ittō shugi** one-party system
一進一退 **isshin-ittai** advance and retreat, fluctuating
一挙一動 **ikkyo-ichidō** one's every action
一得一失 **ittoku isshitsu** advantages and disadvantages
一問一答 **ichimon-ittō** question-and-answer session
一喜一憂 **ikki ichiyū** alternation of joy and sorrow, hope and fear
一朝一夕 **itchō-isseki** in a day, in a short time
一語一語 **ichigo-ichigo** word for word
2 九死一生得 **kyūshi (ni) isshō (o) e(ru)** narrowly escape death
八紘一宇 **hakkō-ichiu** universal brotherhood
3 三位一体 **Sanmi-ittai** the Trinity
三国一 **sangoku-ichi** unparalleled in Japan, China, and India
万分一 **manbun (no) ichi** one ten-thousandth

万世一系 **bansei ikkei** unbroken (imperial) lineage
千載一遇 **senzai-ichigū** a rare experience, chance of a lifetime
4 不統一 **futōitsu** disunity
天下一 **tenka-ichi** unique, matchless
天下一品 **tenka ippin** best article under heaven
日本一 **Nihon/Nippon-ichi** Japan's best
心機一転 **shinki-itten** change of attitude
5 世界一 **sekai-ichi** best in the world
世界一周 **sekai isshū** round-the-world trip, circumnavigation
6 全会一致 **zenkai-itchi** unanimous
危機一髪 **kiki-ippatsu** imminent/hairbreadth danger
百人一首 **hyakunin-isshu** 100 poems by 100 poets (a collection of 100 *tanka*; basis for the popular card game *uta karuta*)
百姓一揆 **hyakushō ikki** peasants' uprising
百聞一見如 **hyakubun (wa) ikken (ni) shi(kazu)** Seeing for oneself once is better than hearing 100 accounts.
7 言文一致 **genbun itchi** unification of the written and spoken language
9 首尾一貫 **shubi-ikkan** logically consistent, coherent
面目一新 **menboku isshin** take on a completely new aspect
10 挙国一致 **kyokoku-itchi** national unity
破顔一笑 **hagan-isshō** break into a grin
11 乾坤一擲 **kenkon-itteki** risking everything, all or nothing
祭政一致 **saisei-itchi** theocracy
終始一貫 **shūshi-ikkan** constant, consistent
頂門一針 **chōmon (no) isshin** stinging reproach/admonition (like a needle plunged into the top of one's head)
12 満場一致 **manjō-itchi** unanimous
尋常一様 **jinjō-ichiyō** common, mediocre
衆口一致 **shūkō-itchi** unanimous
衆議一決 **shūgi-ikketsu** decided unanimously
15 窮余一策 **kyūyo (no) issaku** last resort
緊褌一番 **kinkon-ichiban** gird/brace oneself for
霊肉一致 **reiniku itchi** oneness of body and soul
18 鎧袖一触 **gaishū-isshoku** easy victory

--------- 4 ---------

1 一挙手一投足 **ikkyoshu-ittōsoku** a slight effort, the least trouble
2 二者択一 **nisha-takuitsu** an alternative
九仞功一簣欠 **kyūjin (no) kō (o) ikki (ni) ka(ku)** failure on the verge of success

0a1

6 安全第一 **anzen dai-ichi** Safety First

──────── 6 ────────

3 大山鳴動鼠一匹 **taizan meidō (shite)**
nezumi ippiki The mountains have
brought forth a mouse. Much ado about
nothing much.

0a1.2

HETSU curve

ノ

0a1.3

CHU mark, dot

丶

0a1.4

KETSU hook

亅

0a1.5 / 983

OTSU second (in a series), "B"; strange,
queer; stylish, spicy
kinoto second calendar sign

乙

──────── 1 ────────

3 乙女 **otome** virgin, maiden
10 乙姫 **otohime** younger princess

──────── 2 ────────

5 甲乙 **kō-otsu** A and B; make distinctions,
rank, grade
甲乙丙 **kō-otsu-hei** A, B, C; No. 1, 2, 3
6 早乙女 **saotome** rice-planting girl

──────── 3 ────────

4 天津乙女 **amatsuotome** celestial maiden
5 甲論乙駁 **kōron-otsubaku** pros and cons

了 → **2c0.3**

乄 → 乂 **0a2.12**

─────────────── **0a2** ───────────────

二	儿	入	丁	厶	匚	凵	勹	之	乃	乂	乄	七
2.1	2.2	2.3	2.4	2.5	2.6	2.7	2.8	2.9	2.10	2.11	2.12	2.13

匕	九
2.14	2.15

0a2.1 / 3

NI, futa(tsu), futa- two

二

──────── 1 ────────

2 二人 **futari, ninin** two persons, pair, couple
二人三脚 **ninin-sankyaku** three-legged race
二人共 **futaritomo** both (persons)
二人前 **futarimae, nininmae** enough for two,
two servings
二人連 **futarizu(re)** a party of two, couple
二人殺 **futarigoro(shi)** double murder
二人称 **nininshō** second person (in grammar)
二人組 **niningumi** twosome, duo
二子 **futago** twins, a twin
二十日 **hatsuka** the 20th (day of the month);
twenty days
二十日大根 **hatsuka daikon** radish
二十日鼠 **hatsuka nezumi** mouse

二十世紀 **nijisseiki, nijusseiki** the twentieth
century
二十代 **nijūdai** in one's twenties
二十年代 **nijūnendai** the '20s
二十歳 **hatachi** 20 years old, age 20
二八 **nippachi** slack season for business
(February and August)
3 二三 **nisan** two or three
二大政党主義 **nidaiseitō shugi** the two-party
system
4 二元的 **nigenteki** dual(istic), two-element
二元論 **nigenron** dualism
二毛作 **nimōsaku** two crops a year
二分 **nifun** two minutes **nibun** halve, bisect
二分音符 **nibun onpu** half note
二手 **futate** two groups/bands
二月 **nigatsu** February
futatsuki two months
二日 **futsuka** the 2nd (day of the month);
two days

二日酔 **futsukayo(i)** a hangover

二王 **Niō** fierce-looking temple-guarding Deva Kings

二王門 **Niōmon** temple gate guarded by Deva statues

二方 **futakata** both people

二心 **futagokoro** duplicity, double-dealing

5 二本立 **nihonda(te)** double feature (movie)

二本建 **nihonda(te)** dual system; double standard

二本差 **nihonza(shi)** two-sworded (samurai)

二世 **nisei** (Elizabeth) II, the Second; second-generation (Japanese-American)
nise two existences, present and future

二世契 **nise (no) chigi(ri)** marriage vows

二号 **nigō** No. 2; mistress, concubine

二句 **ni (no) ku** another word, rejoinder

二字 **niji** two characters; name

二目 **futame** for a/the second time

6 二次 **niji** second(ary); quadratic, second degree (in math)
ni (no) tsugi secondary, subordinate

二次元 **nijigen** two-dimensional

二次方程式 **niji hōteishiki** quadratic equation

二次会 **nijikai** after-party party

二次的 **nijiteki** secondary

二次配列 **niji hairetsu** secondary arrange-ment, arrangement on second level

二列 **niretsu** two rows, double file

二色刷 **nishokuzu(ri)** two-color printing

二返事 **futa(tsu)henji** immediate reply, readily, most willingly

二共 **futa(tsu) tomo** both

二百二十日 **nihyaku hatsuka** 220th day from the first day of spring, about September 10 (a time of typhoons)

二百十日 **nihyaku tōka** 210th day from the first day of spring, the "storm day"

7 二束三文 **nisoku-sanmon** a dime a dozen, dirt cheap

二位 **nii** second place

二伸 **nishin** postscript, P.S.

二役 **futayaku** double role

二言 **futakoto** two words
nigon double-dealing

二言目 **futakotome** second word; the topic one's talk constantly turns to

二足 **nisoku** two legs/feet, biped; two pairs (of shoes)

二足三文 **nisoku-sanmon** a dime a dozen, dirt cheap

二足踏 **ni (no) ashi (o) fu(mu)** hesitate, think twice

8 二拍子 **nibyōshi** double/two-part time

二枚目 **nimaime** (role of a) handsome man/beau

二枚舌 **nimaijita** forked tongue, duplicity

二股 **futamata** bifurcation, fork, parting of the ways

二者 **nisha** two things/persons

二者択一 **nisha-takuitsu** an alternative

9 二重 **nijū** double   **futae** two-fold, two-ply, double

二重人格 **nijū jinkaku** double/split person-ality

二重写 **nijū utsu(shi)** double exposure

二重否定 **nijū hitei** double negative

二重底 **nijūzoko** double bottom/sole

二重国籍 **nijū kokuseki** dual nationality

二重奏 **nijūsō** instrumental duet

二重道徳 **nijū dōtoku** double standard of morality

二重唱 **nijūshō** vocal duet

二重窓 **nijū mado** double/storm window

二重結婚 **nijū kekkon** bigamy

二重橋 **Nijūbashi** the Double Bridge (at the Imperial Palace)

二乗 **nijō** square (a number), multiply by itself

二乗根 **nijōkon** square root

二院制 **niinsei** bicameral system

二連式 **nirenshiki** double, duplex

二連発 **nirenpatsu** double-barreled gun

二連銃 **nirenjū** double-barreled gun

二通 **nitsū** two copies
futatō(ri) two ways/kinds, duplicate

二度 **nido** two times

二度目 **nidome** for the second time, again

二食 **nishoku, nijiki** two meals (a day)

10 二倍 **nibai** double, twice, twofold

二部 **nibu** two parts/copies; the second part

二進法 **nishinhō** binary notation/system

二週間 **nishūkan** two weeks, fortnight

二流 **niryū** second-rate, inferior

二桁 **futaketa** two digits, double-digit

二軒建 **nikenda(te)** duplex, semidetached (house)

11 二階 **nikai** second floor, upstairs

二階建 **nikaida(te)** two-story

二道 **futamichi** forked road, crossroads, two ways (to go)

12 二割 **niwari** 20 percent
futa(tsu)wa(ri) half; cutting in two

二着 **nichaku** second (in a race); two suits

二葉 **niyō** two leaves **futaba** bud, sprout

二期 **niki** two terms; twice a year

二塁 **nirui** second base

二番 **niban** No. 2, second

二番目 **nibanme** No. 2, second

二番煎 **nibansen(ji)** second brew of tea; rehash

二番線 **nibansen** track No. 2

二筋道 **futasujimichi** forked road, crossroads

二等 **nitō** second class; second
二等分 **nitōbun** bisect
二等辺三角形 **nitōhen sankakkei/ sankakukei** isosceles triangle
二等賞 **nitōshō** second prize
二等親 **nitōshin** a second-degree relative
13 二義的 **nigiteki** secondary
14 二様 **niyō** two ways
15 二舞 **ni (no) mai** a repetition
二輪 **nirin** two wheels/flowers
16 二膳 **ni (no) zen** (tray with) side-dishes
二親 **futaoya** (both) parents
二頭立 **nitōda(te)** two-horse (cart)
二頭筋 **nitōkin** biceps

──────── 2 ────────
2 十二支 **jūnishi** the twelve horary signs
十二分 **jūnibun** more than enough
jūnifun twelve minutes
十二月 **jūnigatsu** December
十二使徒 **jūni shito** the Twelve Apostles
十二指腸 **jūnishichō** the duodenum
十二指腸虫 **jūnishichōchū** hookworm
4 不二 **fuji** one, only
中二階 **chūnikai** mezzanine
6 瓜二 **uri-futa(tsu)** alike as two halves of a split-open melon, the spitting image of each other
羽二重 **habutae** *habutae* silk
7 良二千石 **ryōnisenseki** good local official
8 青二才 **aonisai** callow youth, stripling
10 真二 **ma(p)puta(tsu)** (split) right in two
11 第二人称 **dai-nininshō** second person (in grammar)
第二次 **dai-niji** second
第二次的 **dai-nijiteki** secondary
第二組合 **dai-ni kumiai** rival labor union
第二義 **dai-nigi** secondary meaning
第二義的 **dai-nigiteki** of secondary importance
12 無二 **muni** peerless, unequaled
無二無三 **muni-musan** like mad, furiously; forcibly
14 総二階 **sōnikai** full two-story house

──────── 3 ────────
1 一石二鳥 **isseki nichō** killing two birds with one stone
一言二言 **hitokoto futakoto** a word or two
一泊二食付 **ippaku nishoku-tsu(ki)** with overnight lodging and two meals
一姫二太郎 **ichi-hime ni-Tarō** It's good to have a girl first and then a boy.
2 二百二十日 **nihyaku hatsuka** 220th day from the first day of spring, about September 10 (a time of typhoons)
10 紋羽二重 **mon habutae** figured habutae

0a2.2

儿 **JIN, NIN** man

0a2.3 / 52

入 **NYŪ, JU, hai(ru), i(ru)** go/come in, enter **i(reru)** put/let in

──────── 1 ────────
2 入子 **i(re)ko** nested boxes
3 入口 **iriguchi** entrance
4 入内 **judai** imperial bride's entry into court
入水 **nyūsui, jusui** suicide by drowning
入手 **nyūshu** obtain, get
入日 **i(ri)hi** the setting sun
5 入母屋 **irimoya** roof with eaves below the gables
入用 **nyūyō, i(ri)yō** need, demand
入札 **nyūsatsu** tender, bid, bidding
入札者 **nyūsatsusha** bidder
6 入会 **nyūkai** enrollment, admission
入会者 **nyūkaisha** new member
入会金 **nyūkaikin** enrollment/admission fee
入廷 **nyūtei** admission to the courtroom
入江 **i(ri)e** inlet, cove
入団 **nyūdan** join, enlist
7 入来 **nyūrai** incoming, arrival, visit
入牢 **nyūrō** imprisonment
入学 **nyūgaku** admission into school, matriculation
入学生 **nyūgakusei** new student
入学式 **nyūgakushiki** entrance ceremony
入学金 **nyūgakukin** entrance/matriculation fee
入学試験 **nyūgaku shiken** entrance exams
入学難 **nyūgakunan** difficulty of getting into a school
入学願書 **nyūgaku gansho** application for admission
入社 **nyūsha** joining a company
8 入念 **nyūnen** careful, scrupulous
入知恵 **i(re)jie** suggestion, hint
入国 **nyūkoku** entering a country, immigration
入物 **i(re)mono** receptacle, container
入所 **nyūsho** entrance, admission; imprisonment
入金 **nyūkin** payment, money received
入門 **nyūmon** admission, entrance; introduction, handbook, primer
9 入信 **nyūshin** come to believe in, be converted
入院 **nyūin** be admitted to hospital
入洛 **juraku, nyūraku** visit to Kyōto

入海 **i(ri)umi** bay, inlet
入城 **nyūjō** entry into the fortress of the enemy
入室 **nyūshitsu** enter a room; become a member
入相 **i(ri)ai** sunset
入神 **nyūshin** inspired, divine
10 入浸 **i(ri)bita(ru)** be steeped in water; stay long
入浴 **nyūyoku** take a bath
入荷 **nyūka** fresh supply of goods
入党 **nyūtō** join a political party
入庫 **nyūko** warehousing, storage; entering the car barn
入校 **nyūkō** entering school, matriculation
入梅 **nyūbai** beginning of the rainy season
入貢 **nyūkō** pay tribute
11 入隊 **nyūtai** enlist (in the army)
入道 **nyūdō** entering the priesthood; priest
入道雲 **nyūdōgumo** thunderhead, cumulonimbus cloud
入混 **i(ri)maji(ru)** be mixed together
入寂 **nyūjaku** death of a saint, entering Nirvana
入寇 **nyūkō** invasion, encroachment
入眼 **i(re)me** artificial/glass eye
入組 **i(ri)ku(mu)** become complicated
12 入違 **i(re)chiga(i)** passing each other
入港 **nyūkō** entering port
入湯 **nyūtō** take a bath
入場 **nyūjō** entrance, admission
入場券 **nyūjōken** admission/platform ticket
入場者 **nyūjōsha** visitors, attendance
入場門 **nyūjōmon** admission gate
入場料 **nyūjōryō** admission fee
入超 **nyūchō** excess of imports over exports, unfavorable balance of trade (short for 輸入超過)
入婿 **i(ri)muko** man who takes his wife's name
入営 **nyūei** enlist (in the army)
入棺 **nyūkan** placing into the coffin
入植 **nyūshoku** settlement, immigration
入朝 **nyūchō** visit Japan, arrive in Japan
入替 **i(re)ka(eru)** replace, substitute
入歯 **i(re)ba** artificial tooth, dentures
13 入滅 **nyūmetsu** death of a saint, entering Nirvana
入試 **nyūshi** entrance exam (short for 入学試験)
入電 **nyūden** message/telegram received
14 入選 **nyūsen** be chosen (in a competition)
入選者 **nyūsensha** winner, successful competitor
入墨 **i(re)zumi** tattooing; tattoo
入獄 **nyūgoku** imprisonment
入魂 **jikkon, jukon** intimacy, familiarity

入閣 **nyūkaku** enter/join the cabinet
15 入賞 **nyūshō** win a prize
入賞者 **nyūshōsha** prizewinner
入質 **nyūshichi** pawning
20 入籍 **nyūseki** have one's name entered on the family register

─────────── 2 ───────────

1 一入 **hitoshio** all the more, especially
3 大入 **ōi(ri)** full house, capacity audience
大入道 **ōnyūdō** large bald-shaven monster/specter
口入 **kuchii(re)** act as go-between
口入屋 **kuchii(re)ya** employment agency
4 不入 **fui(ri)** sparse audience, box-office flop
中入 **nakai(ri)** intermission
介入 **kainyū** intervention
刈入 **ka(ri)i(re)** harvest, reaping
収入 **shūnyū** income, receipts, revenue, earnings
収入役 **shūnyūyaku** treasurer
収入源 **shūnyūgen** source of income
分入 **wa(ke)i(ru)** make one's way through
込入 **ko(mi)i(ru)** be complicated
水入 **mizui(re)** water jug, pitcher
mizui(razu de) privately, among ourselves
手入 **tei(re)** repairs; care, tending
日入 **hi(no)i(ri)** sunset
火入 **hii(re)** first lighting (of a furnace); heating (to prevent spoilage); setting brush afire
5 出入口 **deiriguchi** entrance/exit
出入国 **shutsunyūkoku** emigration and immigration
申入 **mō(shi)i(reru)** propose, suggest
仕入 **shii(re)** laying in stock
付入 **tsu(ke)i(ru)** take advantage of
召入 **me(shi)i(reru)** call in
加入金 **kanyūkin** entrance/initiation fee
圧入 **atsunyū** press fit, press in
立入 **ta(chi)i(ru)** enter, trespass, pry into
立入禁止 **tachiiri kinshi** Keep Out
6 気入 **ki (ni) i(ru)** like, be pleased with
再入学 **sainyūgaku** readmission (to a school)
再入国 **sainyūkoku** re-entry (into a country)
仮入学 **karinyūgaku** provisional enrollment, admission on probation
肉入 **nikui(re)** ink-pad case
迎入 **muka(e)i(reru)** usher in, welcome
汲入 **ku(mi)i(reru)** fill up (with water)
先入主 **sennyūshu** preconception, preoccupation, prejudice
先入観 **sennyūkan** preconception, preoccupation, prejudice
吸入 **kyūnyū** inhale

吸入器 **kyūnyūki** inhaler, respirator
糸入 **itoi(ri)** (silk/paper) with cotton threads
7 没入 **botsunyū** be immersed/absorbed in
折入 **o(ri)i(tte)** earnestly
投入 **tōnyū** throw into, commit (resources); invest **na(ge)i(reru)** throw into **na(ge)i(re)** free-style flower arrangement
乱入 **rannyū** intrusion
乱入者 **rannyūsha** intruder, trespasser
花入 **hanai(re)** vase
床入 **tokoi(ri)** consummation of marriage
肝入 **kimoi(ri)** sponsorship, good offices
攻入 **se(me)i(ru)** invade, penetrate
忍入 **shino(bi)i(ru)** steal/sneak into, slip in
見入 **mii(ru)** gaze at, scrutinize; captivate
足入婚 **ashii(re)kon** tentative marriage
8 念入 **nen'i(ri)** careful, scrupulous, conscientious
受入 **u(ke)i(re)** receiving, accepting
注入 **chūnyū** injection; pour into, infuse
押入 **o(shi)i(re)** closet, wall cupboard **o(shi)i(ru)** break into **o(shi)i(ri)** burglar
呼入 **yo(bi)i(reru)** call in
帙入 **chitsui(ri)** book kept in a Japanese-style book cover
参入 **sannyū** enter (a market), participate in
実入 **mii(ri)** crop; earnings, gains
突入 **totsunyū** rush/plunge into
底入 **sokoi(re)** (prices) bottoming out
国入 **(o)kunii(ri)** daimyō's return (from Edo); celebrity's homecoming
物入 **monoi(ri)** expenses
肩入 **katai(re)** support, assistance
取入 **to(ri)i(reru)** take in, accept, adopt; harvest **to(ri)i(ru)** win (someone's) favor
金入 **kanei(re)** purse, wallet; till
9 飛入 **to(bi)i(ri)** joining in (on the spur of the moment); speckled with a different color **to(bi)i(ru)** jump/dive/fly into
飛入勝手 **tobii(ri) katte** open to all comers
乗入 **no(ri)i(reru)** ride/drive into; extend (a train line) into (a city)
侵入 **shinnyū** invade, raid, break into
侵入者 **shinnyūsha** invader, intruder
陥入 **kannyū** subside, cave in, collapse
風入 **kazai(re)** airing, ventilation
封入 **fūnyū** enclose, seal in
挺入 **tekoi(re)** shore/prop up, bolster
草入水晶 **kusai(ri)zuishō** crystal with impurities forming grass-blade patterns
思入 **omo(i)i(ru)** consider, ponder **omo(i)i(re)** meditation, reverie; to one's heart's content
食入 **ku(i)i(ru)** eat into; encroach upon
10 都入 **miyakoi(ri)** arrive in the capital

差入 **sa(shi)i(reru)** insert; send in to a prisoner
進入 **shinnyū** enter, penetrate, go/come in
流入 **ryūnyū** influx, flow in
消入 **ki(e)i(ru)** vanish, fade away
挿入 **sōnyū** insert
屑入 **kuzui(re)** trash can/receptacle
書入 **ka(ki)i(reru)** write/fill in, enter
書入時 **ka(ki)i(re)doki** the busiest season
恐入 **oso(re)i(ru)** be overwhelmed (with gratitude/shame), be astonished, be sorry to trouble, beg pardon; be defeated, yield; plead guilty
悟入 **gonyū** attain (Buddhist) enlightenment
紙入 **kamii(re)** purse, wallet
納入 **nōnyū** pay, deliver, supply
恥入 **ha(ji)i(ru)** feel ashamed
討入 **u(chi)i(ru)** break into, raid
記入 **kinyū** entry (in a form/ledger)
11 運入 **hako(bi)i(reru)** carry/bring in
混入 **konnyū** mix in, adulterate
深入 **fukai(ri)** go/get deep into
密入国 **mitsunyūkoku** smuggle oneself into a country
移入 **inyū** bring in, import
袋入 **fukuroi(ri)** in bags, sacked, pouched
組入 **ku(mi)i(reru)** include, insert
貫入 **kannyū** penetrate
転入 **tennyū** move in, be transferred
12 湾入 **wannyū** inlet, gulf, bight
婿入 **mukoi(ri)** marry into one's bride's family
焼入 **ya(ki)i(re)** hardening, tempering
斑入 **fui(ri)** spotted, mottled, variegated
雇入 **yato(i)i(reru)** employ, hire; charter
買入 **ka(i)i(reru)** purchase, stock up on
痛入 **ita(mi)i(ru)** be grateful
絵入 **ei(ri)** illustrated, pictorial
歯入 **hai(re)** repairing clogs/geta
筆入 **fudei(re)** writing-brush holder
13 鼠入 **nezumii(razu)** mouseproof cupboard
滅入 **mei(ru)** feel depressed
塩入 **shioi(re)** salt shaker
搬入 **hannyū** carry/send in
嫁入 **yomei(ri)** marriage, wedding
嫁入支度 **yomei(ri)-jitaku** trousseau
寝入 **nei(ri)** fall asleep
感入 **kan(ji)i(ru)** be deeply impressed
歳入 **sainyū** annual revenue
新入 **shinnyū** new, incoming, entering
新入生 **shinnyūsei** new student, freshman
蛸入道 **takonyūdō** octopus; bald-headed man
預入 **azu(ke)i(reru)** make a deposit
14 導入 **dōnyū** bring in, introduce
綿入 **watai(re)** padded, quilted
総入歯 **sōi(re)ba** full set of dentures

算入 **sannyū** count in, include
誘入 **saso(i)i(reru), obi(ki)i(reru)** entice, lure into
銭入 **zenii(re)** purse
聞入 **ki(ki)i(reru)** accede to, comply with
     ki(ki)i(ru) listen attentively
15 潮入 **shioi(ri)** coming in of the tide
潜入 **sennyū** infiltrate
蔵入 **kurai(re)** warehousing
編入 **hennyū** entry, incorporation
箱入 **hakoi(ri)** boxed, in cases
箱入娘 **hakoi(ri) musume** girl who has led a sheltered life
請入 **shō(jI)I(reru)** invite/usher in
質入 **shichii(re)** pawning
踏入 **fu(mi)i(reru)** set foot in, tread on
16 積入 **tsu(mi)i(reru)** take on (board)
輸入 **yunyū** import
輸入品 **yunyūhin** imports
輸入港 **yunyūkō** port of entry
輸入税 **yunyūzei** import duties/tariff
頼入 **tano(mi)i(ru)** earnestly request
17 輿入 **koshii(re)** bride's entry into the groom's home; bridal procession; wedding
購入 **kōnyū** purchase
購入者 **kōnyūsha** purchaser, buyer
鍬入 **kuwai(re)** ground-breaking
18 濫入 **rannyū** enter without permission
鎌入 **kamai(re)** harvesting
闖入 **chinnyū** intrusion, forced entry
闖入者 **chinnyūsha** intruder, trespasser
19 繰入 **ku(ri)i(reru)** transfer (money)
繰入金 **kuriirekin** money/balance transferred
22 彎入 **wannyū** bay, gulf, bight
驚入 **odoro(ki)i(ru)** be filled with amazement

———————— 3 ————————

1 一札入 **issatsu i(reru)** give a signed statement/I.O.U.
3 土俵入 **dohyōi(ri)** display of sumo wrestlers in the ring
4 不介入 **fukainyū** noninvolvement, nonintervention
不可入性 **fukanyūsei** impenetrability
5 本腰入 **hongoshi (o) i(reru)** make an earnest effort, get down to business
6 再輸入 **saiyunyū** reimportation
仲間入 **nakama-i(ri)** become one of the group
名刺入 **meishii(re)** card case
7 弟子入 **deshii(ri)** becoming a pupil, entering an apprenticeship
8 直輸入 **chokuyunyū, jikiyunyū** direct import
逆輸入 **gyakuyunyū** reimportation
泣寝入 **na(ki)ne-i(ri)** cry oneself to sleep
定収入 **teishūnyū** fixed income
空寝入 **sorane-i(ri)** pretend to be asleep

9 狐嫁入 **kitsune (no) yome-i(ri)** a line of foxfire; a light rain during sunshine
胡椒入 **koshōi(re)** pepper skaker
10 狸寝入 **tanuki ne-i(ri)** pretending to be an old woman
荷受入 **niu(ke)nin** consignee
11 副収入 **fukushūnyū** additional/side income
密輸入 **mitsuyunyū** smuggling
12 御国入 **okunii(ri)** victor's return (home)
筋金入 **sujiganei(ri)** hardcore, dyed-in-the-wool
間髪入 **kanhatsu (o) i(rezu)** imminently; immediately
13 煙草入 **tabako-i(re)** tobacco pouch, cigarette case
14 雑収入 **zatsushūnyū, zasshūnyū** miscellaneous income
16 輸出入 **yushutsunyū** export and import
輸出入品 **yushutsunyūhin** exports and imports

———————— 4 ————————

5 四捨五入 **shisha-gonyū** rounding off
9 単刀直入 **tantō-chokunyū** getting straight to the point
10 家宅侵入 **kataku shinnyū** trespassing
15 窮鳥懐入 **kyūchō futokoro (ni) hai(ru)** (like a) bird in distress seeking refuge

0a2.4 / 184

丁 **CHŌ** city block-size area (used in addresses); two-page leaf of paper; (counter for dishes of food, blocks of tofu, guns) **TEI** fourth (in a series), "D"; adult man; servant **hinoto** fourth calendar sign

———————— 1 ————————

5 丁半 **chōhan** even and odd numbers; dice game; heads-or-tails gamble
丁付 **chōzu(ke)** pagination, foliation
丁字形 **teijikei** T-shaped
丁字路 **teijiro** T-junction of roads/streets
丁目 **chōme** city block-size area (used in addresses)
6 丁年 **teinen** age of majority, adulthood
丁年者 **teinensha** adult
8 丁抹 **Denmāku** Denmark
9 丁度 **chōdo** exactly
13 丁数 **chōsū** number of pages; even numbers
丁稚 **detchi** apprentice
丁稚奉公 **detchi bōkō** apprenticeship
14 丁寧 **teinei** polite, courteous; careful, meticulous

———————— 2 ————————

1 一丁 **itchō** one block (of tofu), one serving (of food), one city block
一丁字 **itteiji** (can't read) a single letter

0a2

2 八丁 **hatchō** skillfulness
5 包丁 **hōchō** kitchen knife; cooking
6 壮丁 **sōtei** a youth, able-bodied man
廷丁 **teitei** court attendant/clerk
7 沈丁花 **jinchōge, chinchōge** (sweet-smelling) daphne
乱丁 **ranchō** mixed-up collation/pagination
8 長丁場 **nagachōba** long stretch/scene
使丁 **shitei** servant, messenger
拉丁 **Raten** Latin
拉丁語 **Ratengo** Latin
庖丁 **hōchō** kitchen knife
10 馬丁 **batei** groom, footman, stable hand
11 符丁 **fuchō** mark, symbol, code
12 落丁 **rakuchō** missing pages
装丁 **sōtei** binding
13 園丁 **entei** gardener

——————— 3 ———————

3 口八丁 **kuchihatchō** eloquent, talkative

——————— 4 ———————

5 出刃庖丁 **debabōchō** pointed kitchen knife
6 肉切庖丁 **nikuki(ri)bōchō** butcher knife
8 刺身庖丁 **sashimi-bōchō** fish-slicing knife
10 胸突八丁 **munatsu(ki) hatchō** steepest part of the path up the mountain

0a2.5

SHI I, me; private (not public)

0a2.6

KEI conceal

0a2.7

KAN open mouth

0a2.8

HŌ wrap

0a2.9

SHI, kore this
no (the possessive particle), of
yu(ku) go

——————— 1 ———————

18 之繞掛 **shinnyū (o) ka(keru)** emphasize, exaggerate

0a2.10

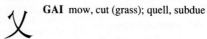

DAI, NAI your sunawa(chi) whereupon, accordingly no (the possessive particle), of

——————— 2 ———————

4 木乃伊 **miira** mummy

0a2.11

GAI mow, cut (grass); quell, subdue

0a2.12

shime closing; seal; total; ream
shime(te) totaling

——————— 1 ———————

4 〆切 **shimeki(ri)** deadline, closing date

0a2.13 / 9

SHICHI, nana(tsu), nana, nano- seven

——————— 1 ———————

2 七十 **nanajū, shichijū** seventy
3 七夕 **tanabata** Star Festival (July 7)
4 七不思議 **nanafushigi** the seven wonders
七五三 **shichi-go-san** the lucky numbers 7, 5, and 3; festival for children 7, 5, and 3 years old
七五調 **shichigochō** seven-and-five-syllable meter
七分三分 **shichibu-sanbu** split 70–30
七分袖 **shichibusode** three-quarter sleeves
七月 **shichigatsu** July
七日 **nanoka, nanuka** the 7th (day of the month); seven days
5 七生 **shichishō** seven lives
6 七曲 **nanama(gari)** winding, tortuous
七色 **nanairo** the colors of the rainbow
七光 **nanahikari** enjoying advantages because of one's parent's/lord's fame or authority
七回忌 **shichikaiki** seventh anniversary of a death
8 七宝 **shippō** the seven treasures (gold, silver, lapis lazuli, pearls, crystal, agate, and coral); cloisonné
七宝焼 **shippōyaki** cloisonné
9 七重 **nanae** seven-fold, seven-ply
七草 **nanakusa** the seven plants (of spring/ autumn)
七面倒 **shichimendō** great trouble, difficulty
七面鳥 **shichimenchō** turkey

11 七転八倒 **shichiten-battō, shitten-battō**
writhing in agony
　七転八起 **nanakoro(bi)ya(oki)** ups and
downs of life, Fall seven times and get
up eight.
13 七福神 **Shichifukujin** the Seven Gods of
Good Fortune
15 七輪 **shichirin** earthen charcoal brazier (for
cooking)
16 七賢 **shichiken** the seven wise men (of
ancient Greece)

─────── 2 ───────

3 三七日 **minanoka, minanuka,**
sanshichinichi 21st day after a death
7 初七日 **shonanoka, shonanuka** (religious
service on) the seventh day after
someone's death
9 春七草 **haru (no) nanakusa** the seven herbs
of spring
　秋七草 **aki (no) nanakusa** the seven flowers
of autumn

─────── 3 ───────

5 北斗七星 **Hokuto Shichisei** the Big Dipper

0a2.14

匕 匕

HI, saji spoon

─────── 1 ───────

9 匕首 **hishu, aikuchi** dagger, dirk

0a2.15 / 11

九

KYŪ, KU, kokono(tsu), kokono- nine

─────── 1 ───────

2 九九 **kuku** the multiplication table
　九十九折 **tsuzurao(ri)** winding, meandering,
zigzag
　九十九髪 **tsukumogami** old woman's hair
4 九分 **kubu** nine out of ten; nine percent
　kyūfun nine minutes
　九分九厘 **kubu-kurin** 99 cases out of 100,
in all probability
　九月 **kugatsu** September **kyū(ka)getsu,**
ku(ka)getsu nine months
　九日 **kokonoka** the 9th (day of the month);
nine days
5 九仞功一簣欠 **kyūjin (no) kō (o) ikki (ni)**
ka(ku) failure on the verge of success
6 九死一生得 **kyūshi (ni) isshō (o) e(ru)**
narrowly escape death
　九州 **Kyūshū** (island)
9 九星術 **kyūseijutsu** astrology
15 九輪 **kurin** nine-ring pagoda spire

─────── 2 ───────

2 九九 **kuku** the multiplication table
16 薬九層倍 **kusuri-kusōbai** the high markup
on drug prices

─────── 3 ───────

2 九十九折 **tsuzurao(ri)** winding, meandering,
zigzag
　九十九髪 **tsukumogami** old woman's hair
　九分九厘 **kubu-kurin** 99 cases out of 100,
in all probability
3 三々九度 **sansankudo** exchange of nuptial
cups
　三拝九拝 **sanpai kyūhai** three kneelings and
nine prostrations, kowtowing, bowing
repeatedly

─────── **0a3** ───────

三	川	丫	巛	乞	勹	ケ	工	ヨ	々	久	万	兀
3.1	3.2	3.3	0a3.2	3.4	3.5	6f8.15	3.6	0a3.15	2n1.1	3.7	3.8	3.9
幺	圣	乏	己	已	夕	互	巳	寸	大	屮	于	叉
3.10	0a3.6	3.11	3.12	3.13	3.14	3.15	3.16	3.17	3.18	3.19	3.20	2h0.1
尢	门	刃	与	及	廾	丈	才	丸	也	夊		
3.21	8e0.1	3.22	3.23	3.24	3.25	3.26	3.27	3.28	3.29	3.30		

0a3.1 / 4

三

SAN, mit(tsu), mi(tsu), mi- three

─────── 1 ───────

2 三七日 **minanoka, minanuka,**
sanshichinichi 21st day after a death
　三人 **sannin** three people

三人称 **sanninshō** third person (in grammar)
三人組 **sanningumi** trio, threesome
三子 **mi(tsu)go** triplets; a three-year-old
三十六計 **sanjūrokkei** many plans/
strategies
三十六計逃 **sanjūrokkei ni(geru ni**
shikazu) It's wisest here to run away./
Discretion is the better part of valor.

三十日 **sanjūnichi** the 30th (day of the month); 30 days **misoka** the last day of the month
三十路 **misoji** age 30
3 三寸舌 **sanzun (no) shita** eloquent tongue
三叉 **sansa, mi(tsu)mata** three-pronged fork
三叉路 **sansaro** Y-junction of roads
三千 **sanzen** 3,000; many
三千世界 **sanzen sekai** the whole world, the universe
三々九度 **sansankudo** exchange of nuptial cups
三々五々 **sansan-gogo** in small groups, by twos and threes
三口 **mi(tsu)kuchi** harelip
4 三毛作 **sanmōsaku** three crops a year
三毛猫 **mikeneko** white-black-and-brown cat
三文 **sanmon** farthing; cheap
三文小説 **sanmon shōsetsu** cheap novel
三文文士 **sanmon bunshi** hack writer
三文判 **sanmonban** ready-made seal
三分 **sanpun** three minutes **sanbun** divide into three, trisect
三尺 **sanjaku** three (Japanese) feet; waistband, obi; loincloth
三月 **sangatsu** March **san(ka)getsu, mitsuki** three months
三日 **mikka** the 3rd (day of the month); three days
三日三晩 **mikka miban** three days and three nights
三日天下 **mikka tenka** short-lived reign
三日月 **mikazuki** crescent moon
三日坊主 **mikka bōzu** one who can stick to nothing, "three-day monk"
三方 **sanbō** three sides; small stand for placing an offering on
5 三世 **sansei** the Third; third-generation (Japanese-American) **sanze** past, present, and future existences
三号雑誌 **sangō zasshi** short-lived magazine
6 三曲 **sankyoku** instrumental trio
三次元 **sanjigen** three dimensions
三次配列 **sanji hairetsu** tertiary arrangement, arrangement on third level
三羽烏 **sanbagarasu** triumvirate
三色 **sanshoku** three colors
三色版 **sanshokuban** three-color printing
三色菫 **sanshoku sumire** pansy
三色旗 **sanshokuki** tricolor flag
三行 **sangyō** three lines (of text)
三行広告欄 **sangyō kōkokuran** classified ads
三行半 **mikudarihan** letter of divorce **sangyōhan** three and a half lines (of text)
三百 **sanbyaku** 300; many
三百代言 **sanbyaku daigen** shyster lawyer, pettifogger
7 三位 **san'i, sanmi** third rank/place
三位一体 **Sanmi-ittai** the Trinity
三体 **santai** the three kanji handwriting styles (square, semicursive, and "grass")
三助 **sansuke** male bathhouse attendant
三角 **sankaku** triangular **mi(tsu)kado** Y-junction of streets
三角巾 **sankakukin** triangular bandage
三角州 **sankakusu** delta
三角帆 **sankakuho** jib sail
三角形 **sankakkei, sankakukei** triangle
三角函数 **sankaku kansū** trigonometric function
三角法 **sankakuhō** trigonometry
三角洲 **sankakusu** delta
三角旗 **sankakuki** pennant
三角関係 **sankaku kankei** love triangle
三角錐 **sankakusui** triangular-base pyramid
三折 **mi(tsu)o(ri)** folded in three
三役 **san'yaku** the three highest sumo ranks under *yokozuna*; the three top-ranking officials
三条 **Sanjō** (emperor, 1011–1016)
三男 **sannan** third son; three men
8 三河 **Mikawa** (ancient kuni, Aichi-ken)
三拝 **sanpai** worshiping three times
三拝九拝 **sanpai kyūhai** three kneelings and nine prostrations, kowtowing, bowing repeatedly
三拍子 **sanbyōshi** triple time (in music); three important requisites, triple-threat
三味線 **shamisen, samisen** samisen (three-stringed instrument)
三味線弾 **shamisenhi(ki), samisenhi(ki)** samisen player
三弦 **sangen** three-stringed instrument; samisen
三宝 **sanbō** the three treasures of Buddhism (Buddha, the sutras, and the priesthood)
三国 **sangoku** three countries
三国一 **sangoku-ichi** unparalleled in Japan, China, and India
三枚 **sanmai** three sheets
三枚目 **sanmaime** comedian
三者会談 **sansha kaidan** three-party conference
三門 **sanmon** large three-door gate
9 三重 **sanjū, mie** three-fold, three-ply, triple
三重奏 **sanjūsō** instrumental trio
三重冠 **sanjūkan** tiara
三重県 **Mie-ken** (prefecture)
三重唱 **sanjūshō** vocal trio
三乗 **sanjō** cube (in math)
三乗根 **sanjōkon** cube root
三軍 **sangun** a great army, the whole army

三途川 **Sanzu (no) Kawa** the River Styx
三段跳 **sandanto(bi)** hop, step, and jump
三段構 **sandangama(e)** thorough preparation with fall-back options should anything go wrong
三面 **sanmen** three sides/faces; page 3 (of a newspaper)
三面六臂 **sanmen roppi** as if having three faces and six arms, versatile, all-around, doing the work of many
三面記事 **sanmen kiji** page-3 news, police news, human-interest stories
三相 **sansō** three-phase (current)
三昧 **sanmai** concentration, absorption
三省 **sansei** introspection, reflection (three times a day)
三思 **sanshi** reflect on, think seriously
三界 **sangai** past, present, and future existences
三食 **sanshoku** three meals (a day)
10 三倍 **sanbai** threefold, three times
三部 **sanbu** three parts; three copies (of a publication)
三部合奏 **sanbu gassō** instrumental trio
三原色 **sangenshoku** the three primary colors
三流 **sanryū** third-rate
三振 **sanshin** strikeout (in baseball)
三桁 **miketa** three digits
三校 **sankō** third proof
11 三唱 **sanshō** three cheers; sing three times
三菱 **Mitsubishi** (company name)
三脚 **sankyaku** tripod; three legs
三脚架 **sankyakuka** tripod
三組 **sankumi, mikumi, mi(tsu)gumi** set of three
三絃 **sangen** three-stringed instrument; samisen
12 三揃 **mi(tsu)zoro(i)** three-piece suit
三寒四温 **sankan shion** alternation of three cold then four warm days
三景 **sankei** three famous scenic spots
三塁 **sanrui** third base
三塁手 **sanruishu** third baseman
三塁打 **sanruida** three-base hit, triple
三等 **santō** third class
三等分 **santōbun** trisect
13 三業 **sangyō** a business consisting of restaurant, waiting room, and geisha house
三業地 **sangyōchi** licensed red-light district
三嘆 **santan** admire, praise, extol
三猿 **mizaru, san'en** the three see-not, hear-not, speak-not monkeys
三幕物 **sanmakumono** three-act play
14 三徳 **santoku** the three primary virtues (wisdom, benevolence, and valor)

三種神器 **Sanshu (no) Jingi** the Three Sacred Treasures (mirror, sword, and jewels)
三箇日 **sanganichi** the first three days of the new year
15 三権分立 **sanken bunritsu** separation of powers (legislative, executive, and judicial)
三輪車 **sanrinsha** tricycle, three-wheeled vehicle
16 三頭政治 **santō seiji** triumvirate
21 三顧礼 **sanko (no) rei** special confidence (in someone)

─────── 2 ───────

2 二三 **nisan** two or three
十三夜 **jūsan'ya** 13th night of a lunar month (especially a moonlit September 13)
3 三三九度 **sansankudo** exchange of nuptial cups
三三五五 **sansan-gogo** in small groups, by twos and threes
口三味線 **kuchijamisen, kuchizamisen** humming a samisen tune; cajolery
4 六三制 **roku-sansei** the 6-3(-3-year) education system
5 正三角形 **seisankakkei, seisankakukei** equilateral triangle
6 両三日 **ryōsannichi** two or three days
再三 **saisan** again and again, repeatedly
再三再四 **saisan-saishi** over and over again
10 胸三寸 **munesanzun** heart, mind, feelings
11 第三人称 **dai-sanninshō** third person (in grammar)
第三火 **dai-san (no) hi** nuclear energy
第三国 **dai-sangoku** third country/power
第三国人 **dai-sangokujin** third-country national
第三者 **dai-sansha** third person/party
第三紀 **dai-sanki** the Tertiary (geological) period
第三階級 **dai-san kaikyū** the third estate, the bourgeoisie
12 御三家 **Gosanke** the three branch families of the Tokugawas
朝三暮四 **chōsan-boshi** being deceived by immediate gain (like the monkey who did not realize that being given four chestnuts in the morning and three in the evening amounts to the same as three in the morning and four in the evening)

─────── 3 ───────

2 二人三脚 **ninin-sankyaku** three-legged race
二束三文 **nisoku-sanmon** a dime a dozen, dirt cheap
二足三文 **nisoku-sanmon** a dime a dozen, dirt cheap

0a3

七五三 **shichi-go-san** the lucky numbers 7, 5, and 3; festival for children 7, 5, and 3 years old

七分三分 **shichibu-sanbu** split 70–30

3 三日三晩 **mikka miban** three days and three nights

4 五十三次 **gojūsan tsugi** the 53 stages on the Tōkaidō

日本三景 **Nihon sankei** Japan's three noted scenic sights (Matsushima, Miyajima, Amanohashidate)

6 舌先三寸 **shitasaki-sanzun** eloquence

12 等辺三角形 **tōhen sankakkei, tōhen sankakukei** equilateral triangle

等脚三角形 **tōkyaku sankakkei, tōkyaku sankakukei** isosceles triangle

───────── 4 ─────────

2 二等辺三角形 **nitōhen sankakkei, nitōhen sankakukei** isosceles triangle

12 無二無三 **muni-musan** like mad, furiously; forcibly

0a3.2 / 33

川 巛   SEN, kawa river

───────── 1 ─────────

3 川上 **kawakami** upstream

川下 **kawashimo** downstream

川口 **kawaguchi** mouth of a river
Kawaguchi (city, Saitama-ken)

4 川辺 **kawabe** riverside

5 川尻 **kawajiri** lower stream; mouth of a river

7 川床 **kawadoko** riverbed

8 川沿 **kawazo(i)** along the river

川岸 **kawagishi** riverbank

9 川風 **kawakaze** river breeze

川柳 **kawayanagi** purple willow

10 川原 **kawahara, kawara** dry riverbed; river beach

川遊 **kawaaso(bi)** go boating/swimming in a river

11 川崎 **Kawasaki** (city, Kanagawa-ken)

川魚 **kawauo** river fish

12 川幅 **kawahaba** width of a river

川蒸汽/気 **kawajōki** river steamboat

川越 **kawago(e/shi)** crossing a river
Kawagoe (city, Saitama-ken)

川筋 **kawasuji** course of a river

川開 **kawabira(ki)** river festival

13 川路 **kawaji** course of a river

14 川端 **kawabata** riverside
Kawabata (surname)

15 川縁 **kawabuchi** riverside

川蝦 **kawaebi** river shrimp, crawfish

19 川瀬 **kawase** shallows, rapids

川獺 **kawauso** otter

川藻 **kawamo** river/freshwater plants

川霧 **kawagiri** river fog/mist

───────── 2 ─────────

3 大川 **ōkawa** large river

大川端 **ōkawabata** banks of the Sumida River (in Tōkyō)

小川 **ogawa** brook, creek
Ogawa (surname)

4 天川 **Ama(no)kawa** the Milky Way

5 市川 **Ichikawa** (city, Chiba-ken)

石川県 **Ishikawa-ken** (prefecture)

田川 **Tagawa** (city, Fukuoka-ken)

6 旭川 **Asahikawa** (city, Hokkaidō)

7 谷川 **tanigawa** river in a valley, mountain stream

8 河川 **kasen** rivers

河川工事 **kasen kōji** river improvement, riparian works

9 荒川 **Arakawa** (river in Tōkyō)

香川県 **Kagawa-ken** (prefecture)

11 淀川 **Yodogawa** (river, Ōsaka-fu)

堀川 **horikawa** canal

13 滝川 **takigawa** rapids

溝川 **mizogawa** ditch/trench with running water

14 徳川 **Tokugawa** (shogun family during Edo period)

───────── 3 ─────────

3 三途川 **Sanzu (no) Kawa** the River Styx

大井川 **Ōigawa** (river, Shizuoka-ken)

4 天龍川 **Tenryūgawa** (river, Shizuoka-ken)

木曾川 **Kisogawa** (river, Gifu-ken)

5 北上川 **Kitakamigawa** (river, Miyagi-ken)

石狩川 **Ishikari-gawa** (river, Hokkaidō)

6 多摩川 **Tamagawa** (river, Tōkyō-to/Kanagawa-ken)

江戸川 **Edogawa** (river, Chiba-ken)

7 利根川 **Tone-gawa** (river, Chiba-ken)

8 長良川 **Nagaragawa** (river, Gifu-ken)

長谷川 **Hasegawa** (surname)

9 相模川 **Sagami-gawa** (river, Kanagawa-ken)

神奈川県 **Kanagawa-ken** (prefecture)

11 隅田川 **Sumida-gawa** (river, Tōkyō-to)

球磨川 **Kumagawa** (river, Kumamoto-ken)

12 富士川 **Fuji-kawa** (river, Shizuoka-ken)

最上川 **Mogamigawa** (river, Yamagata-ken)

0a3.3

Ｙ   **A** crotch, fork, Y-shape

〈〈〈 → 川 **0a3.2**

0a3.4
乞 **KOTSU, KITSU, ko(u)** ask for, beg

———————— 1 ————————
9 乞食 **kojiki** beggar
———————— 2 ————————
8 物乞 **monogo(i)** begging
雨乞 **amago(i)** praying for rain
13 暇乞 **itomago(i)** leave-taking, farewell visit
———————— 3 ————————
8 河原乞食 **kawara kojiki** actors (and beggars; a term of opprobrium)

0a3.5 / 1903
勺 **SHAKU** (unit of volume, about 18 ml)

ケ → 箇 **6f8.15**
0 1ケ年 **ikkanen** one year
3ケ所 **sankasho** three places
りんご1ケ **ringo ikko** one apple
13 鳩ケ谷 **Hatogaya** (city, Saitama-ken)

0a3.6 / 139
工 互 **KŌ, KU** artisan; manufacturing, construction **takumi** craftsman, workman

———————— 1 ————————
2 工人 **kōjin** worker, craftsman
3 工大 **kōdai** engineering/technical college
工女 **kōjo** factory girl
4 工夫 **kufū** device, invention, contrivance; means **kōfu** coolie, workman, laborer
工手 **kōshu** workman
6 工合 **guai** condition, state; convenience; state of health
工匠 **kōshō** artisan, craftsman
7 工作 **kōsaku** construction, engineering; handicraft; maneuver, scheme
工作物 **kōsakubutsu** a building; manufactured goods
工作品 **kōsakuhin** handicrafts
工作機械 **kōsaku kikai** machine tools
工兵 **kōhei** military engineer, sapper
工芸 **kōgei** technical arts
工芸学 **kōgeigaku** technology, polytechnics
工芸美術 **kōgei bijutsu** applied fine arts
工芸品 **kōgeihin** industrial-art objects

工学 **kōgaku** engineering
工学士 **kōgakushi** Bachelor of Engineering
工学者 **kōgakusha** engineer
8 工事 **kōji** construction
工事中 **kōjichū** Under Construction
工事場 **kōjiba** construction site
工房 **kōbō** studio, atelier
工具 **kōgu** tool, implement
9 工面 **kumen** contrive, manage, make do; raise (funds); (pecuniary) circumstances
工科 **kōka** engineering course
工科大学 **kōka daigaku** engineering college
10 工員 **kōin** factory worker, machine operator
11 工率 **kōritsu** rate of production
工商 **kōshō** industry and commerce; artisans and merchants
工務 **kōmu** engineering
工務店 **kōmuten** engineering firm
工務所 **kōmusho** engineering office
12 工場 **kōjō, kōba** factory, workshop, mill
工程 **kōtei** process; progress of the work
工費 **kōhi** cost of construction
13 工業 **kōgyō** industry
工業大学 **kōgyō daigaku** technical college
工業化 **kōgyōka** industrialization
工業用 **kōgyōyō** for industrial use
工業地 **kōgyōchi** industrial area
工業地帯 **kōgyō chitai** industrial area
工業国 **kōgyōkoku** industrial nation
工業界 **kōgyōkai** industrial circles, industry
工業都市 **kōgyō toshi** industrial city, factory town
工業家 **kōgyōka** industrialist, manufacturer
工賃 **kōchin** wages, labor costs
14 工銀 **kōgin** wages, pay
15 工廠 **kōshō** arsenal

———————— 2 ————————
2 人工 **jinkō** artificial
人工林 **jinkōrin** planted forest
人工的 **jinkōteki** artificial
人工雨 **jinkōu** artificial rain, rainmaking
刀工 **tōkō** swordsmith
3 大工 **daiku** carpenter
土工 **dokō** earthwork; construction laborer
女工 **jokō** woman factory worker
4 天工 **tenkō** a work of nature
分工場 **bunkōjō** branch plant/factory
手工 **shukō** manual arts, handicraft
手工芸 **shukōgei** handicraft(s)
手工業 **shukōgyō** manual industry, handicrafts
木工 **mokkō** woodworking; carpenter
5 加工 **kakō** processing
加工品 **kakōhin** processed goods
石工 **sekkō, ishiku** stone mason/cutter
6 同工異曲 **dōkō-ikyoku** superficially different but essentially the same

0a3

名工 **meikō** master craftsman
7 良工 **ryōkō** skilled artisan
技工 **gikō** artisan, craftsman, technician
完工 **kankō** completion (of construction)
図工 **zukō** draftsman
男工 **dankō** male worker
8 画工 **gakō** painter, artist
拙工 **sekkō** poor workman
金工 **kinkō** metalwork; metalsmith
9 重工業 **jūkōgyō** heavy industry
施工 **sekō, shikō** construct, build, execute
10 陶工 **tōkō** potter
高工 **kōkō** higher technical school (short for
　　高等工業学校)
起工 **kikō** start construction
起工式 **kikōshiki** ground-breaking ceremony
11 商工 **shōkō** commerce and industry
商工会議所 **Shōkō Kaigisho** Chamber of
　　Commerce and Industry
商工業 **shōkōgyō** commerce and industry
細工 **saiku** work(manship); artifice, trick
細工人 **saikunin** craftsman, artisan
12 着工 **chakkō** start of construction
竣工 **shunkō** completion (of construction)
竣工式 **shunkōshiki** completion ceremony
軽工業 **keikōgyō** light industry
13 農工 **nōkō** agriculture and industry
農工業 **nōkōgyō** agriculture and industry
塗工 **tokō** painter; painting
新工夫 **shinkufū** new device/gadget
鉄工 **tekkō** ironworker, blacksmith
鉄工場 **tekkōjō** ironworks
鉛工 **enkō** plumber
鉱工業 **kōkōgyō** mining and manufacturing
電工 **denkō** electrician
14 漆工 **shikkō** lacquer work(er)
17 鍛工 **tankō** metalworker, smith
鍛工所 **tankōjo, tankōsho** foundry
18 織工 **shokkō** weaver, textile worker
職工 **shokkō** (factory) worker
19 蟹工船 **kanikōsen** crab-canning ship

――――――――― 3 ―――――――――

2 人間工学 **ningen kōgaku** ergonomics
3 小細工 **kozaiku** handiwork; tricks, wiles
士農工商 **shinōkōshō** samurai-farmers-
　　artisans-merchants, the military,
　　agricultural, industrial, and mercantile
　　classes
4 不細工 **busaiku** awkward, clumsy, botched;
　　homely, plain-looking
文選工 **bunsenkō** typesetter
水力工学 **suiryoku kōgaku** hydraulic
　　engineering
手細工 **tezaiku** handicraft, handmade
5 半加工品 **hankakōhin** semiprocessed goods
皮細工 **kawazaiku** leatherwork
叩大工 **tata(ki)daiku** clumsy carpenter

石細工 **ishizaiku** masonry
6 竹細工 **takezaiku** bamboo handicrafts
7 角細工 **tsunozaiku** horn work/carving
見習工 **minara(i)kō** apprentice
貝細工 **kaizaiku** shellwork
車大工 **kuruma daiku** cartwright
8 治水工事 **chisui kōji** riverbank works
河川工事 **kasen kōji** river improvement,
　　riparian works
取付工事 **to(ri)tsu(ke) kōji** installation work
金細工 **kinzaiku** goldwork, gold ware
金属工業 **kinzoku kōgyō** metalworking
　　industry
9 俄細工 **niwakazaiku** hastily prepared
軍事工場 **gunji kōjō** war plant
軍需工業 **gunju kōgyō** munitions industry
美術工芸 **bijutsu kōgei** artistic handicrafts,
　　arts and crafts
革細工 **kawazaiku** leathercraft
10 修理工 **shūrikō** repairman
家内工業 **kanai kōgyō** home/cottage industry
時計工 **tokeikō** watchmaker
紡績工 **bōsekikō** spinner
紙細工 **kamizaiku** paper handicrafts
11 旋盤工 **senbankō** lathe operator, turner
組立工 **kumita(te)kō** assembler, fitter
組立工場 **kumita(te) kōjō** assembly/
　　knockdown plant
船大工 **funadaiku** boatbuilder, shipwright
13 電子工学 **denshi kōgaku** electronics
14 漆細工 **urushizaiku** lacquerware
熟練工 **jukurenkō** skilled workman/
　　craftsman
製缶工場 **seikan kōjō** cannery
製材工 **seizaikō** sawyer
網細工 **amizaiku** filigree
銀細工 **ginzaiku** silverwork
銀細工師 **ginzaikushi** silversmith
銅細工 **dōzaiku** copperwork
16 機械工 **kikaikō** mechanic, machinist
機械工学 **kikai kōgaku** mechanical
　　engineering
機械工業 **kikai kōgyō** the machine industry
蹄鉄工 **teitetsukō** horseshoer
18 鎔接工 **yōsetsukō** welder
20 護岸工事 **gogan kōji** riparian works
21 籐細工 **tōzaiku** rattanwork, canework

――――――――― 4 ―――――――――

12 象牙細工 **zōgezaiku** ivory work/carving
嵌木細工 **ha(me)kizaiku** inlaid woodwork
14 遺伝子工学 **idenshi kōgaku** genetic
　　engineering

ヨ → 彑 **0a3.15**

々 →　　**2n1.1**

0a3.7 / 1210

久　KYŪ, KU, hisa(shii) long (time)

─────── 1 ───────

3 久々 **hisabisa** (for the first time in) a long time
4 久方振 **hisakatabu(ri)** (for the first time in) a long time
6 久安 **Kyūan** (era, 1145–1151)
7 久寿 **Kyūju** (era, 1154–1156)
10 久振 **hisa(shi)bu(ri)** (for the first time in) a long time
久留米 **Kurume** (city, Fukuoka-ken)
12 久遠 **kuon, kyūen** eternity
17 久闊 **kyūkatsu** neglecting to keep in touch
久闊叙 **kyūkatsu (o) jo(su)** greet for the first time in a long time

─────── 2 ───────

4 元久 **Genkyū** (era, 1204–1206)
文久 **Bunkyū** (era, 1861–1864)
5 永久 **eikyū** permanence, perpetuity, eternity
Eikyū (era, 1113–1118)
永久歯 **eikyūshi** permanent tooth
7 承久 **Jōkyū** (era, 1219–1222)
延久 **Enkyū** (era, 1069–1074)
8 長久 **chōkyū** eternity, permanence
Chōkyū (era, 1040–1044)
建久 **Kenkyū** (era, 1190–1199)
9 耐久 **taikyū** endurance, persistence, permanence, durability
耐久力 **taikyūryoku** durability, endurance
耐久性 **taikyūsei** durability
持久 **jikyū** hold out, endure, persist
持久力 **jikyūryoku** endurance, stamina
持久策 **jikyūsaku** dilatory tactics
持久戦 **jikyūsen** war of attrition, endurance contest
恒久 **kōkyū** permanence, perpetuity
恒久化 **kōkyūka** perpetuation
恒久的 **kōkyūteki** permanent
恒久性 **kōkyūsei** permanence
11 悠久 **yūkyū** eternity, perpetuity

─────── 4 ───────

4 天長地久 **tenchō-chikyū** coeval with heaven and earth
19 曠日弥久 **kōjitsu bikyū** idle away one's time/years

0a3.8 / 16

万 萬　MAN ten thousand, myriad
BAN countless, myriad; all
yorozu ten thousand; all sorts of, everything

─────── 1 ───────

1 万一 **man'ichi** (if) by any chance, should happen to
2 万人 **bannin, banjin** all people, everybody
万人向 **banninmu(ki)** for everyone, suiting all tastes
万力 **manriki** vise
3 万丈 **banjō** great height
万才 **banzai** hurrah
万々 **banban** very much, fully; (with negative) never
4 万分一 **manbun (no) ichi** one ten-thousandth
万引 **manbi(ki)** shoplifting; shoplifter
5 万民 **banmin** all the people/nation
万世 **bansei** all ages, eternity
yorozuyo thousands of years
万世一系 **bansei ikkei** unbroken (imperial) lineage
万世不易 **bansei fueki** everlasting, eternal
万代 **bandai** all ages, eternity
yorozuyo thousands of years
万古 **banko** perpetuity, eternity
6 万年 **mannen** ten thousand years; perpetual, perennial
万年床 **mannendoko** bedding/futon left spread out on the floor during the daytime
万年青 **omoto** (a plant in the lily family)
万年雪 **mannen'yuki** perpetual snow
万年筆 **mannenhitsu** fountain pen
万全 **banzen** perfect, sure, prudent
万全策 **banzen (no) saku** carefully thought-out plan, prudent policy
万邦 **banpō** all nations
万梁 **banda** many branches
万有 **ban'yū** all things, all creation; universal
万有神教 **ban'yū shinkyō** pantheism
万灯 **mandō** votive lanterns hung in a row
万灯会 **mandōe** Buddhist lantern festival
7 万里 **banri** thousands of miles
万里長城 **Banri (no) Chōjō** Great Wall of China
万寿 **Manju** (era, 1024–1028)
万延 **Man'en** (era, 1860–1861)
8 万事 **banji** all, everything
万事休 **banji kyū(su)** It's all over. Nothing more can be done.
万治 **Manji** (era, 1658–1661)
万国 **bankoku** all nations
万国博覧会 **bankoku hakurankai** world's fair
万国旗 **bankokuki** flags of all nations
万物 **banbutsu, banmotsu** all things, all creation

万物霊長 **banbutsu (no) reichō** man, the lord of creation
万金 **mankin** immense sum of money
9 万屋 **yorozuya** general merchant/store
万祝 **maiwai** fisherman's coat (given by the shipowner to his crew to congratulate them on a big catch, from 1800s to mid-1940s)
10 万華鏡 **mangekyō, bankakyō** kaleidoscope
万骨 **bankotsu** thousands of lives
万能 **bannō** omnipotent, all-around, all-purpose **mannō** all-purpose
万能薬 **bannōyaku** cure-all, panacea
万病 **manbyō** all diseases, any kind of illness
万般 **banpan** all, every(thing)
11 万遍 **manben(naku)** equally, uniformly, without exception
12 万博 **banpaku** world's fair (short for 万国博覧会)
万象 **banshō** all creation
万葉仮名 **man'yōgana** kanji used phonetically
万葉集 **Man'yōshū** (Japan's oldest anthology of poems)
万策 **bansaku** every means
13 万障 **banshō** all obstacles
万福 **banpuku** all health and happiness
万感 **bankan** flood of emotions
万歳 **banzai** hurrah
万雷 **banrai** thunderous (applause)
14 万端 **bantan** everything, all
16 万機 **banki** state affairs
18 万難 **bannan** innumerable difficulties, all obstacles

───────── 2 ─────────

3 万万 **banban** very much, fully; (with negative) never
千万 **senman, chiyorozu** ten million; countless **senban** exceedingly, very much, indeed
千万無量 **senman-muryō** innumerable
5 巨万 **kyoman** millions, immense amount
永万 **Eiman** (era, 1165–1166)
6 百万 **hyakuman** million
百万長者 **hyakumanchōja** (multi-) millionaire
百万遍 **hyakumanben** (praying) a million times
9 拾万円 **jūman'en** 100,000 yen
12 幾万 **ikuman** tens of thousands
13 数万 **sūman** tens of thousands
15 億万長者 **okumanchōja** multimillionaire, billionaire

───────── 3 ─────────

2 八百万 **yaoyorozu** myriads, countless
3 千辛万苦 **senshin-banku** countless hardships

千変万化 **senpen-banka** innumerable/kaleidoscopic changes, immense variety
千客万来 **senkaku-banrai, senkyaku-banrai** thronged with customers/visitors
千思万考 **senshi-bankō** deep meditation, careful deliberation
千差万別 **sensa-banbetsu** infinite variety
千紫万紅 **senshi-bankō** dazzling variety of colors
4 天地万物 **tenchi-banbutsu** the whole universe, all creation
6 気炎万丈 **kien-banjō** high spirits
気焰万丈 **kien-banjō** high spirits
8 波瀾万丈 **haran-banjō** full of ups and downs, stormy, checkered
12 森羅万象 **shinra-banshō** all creation, the universe
15 諸事万端 **shoji-bantan** everything

───────── 4 ─────────

10 笑止千万 **shōshi-senban** ridiculous, absurd

0a3.9

KOTSU rising high; bald; unstable

兀

0a3.10

YŌ very young

幺

互 → 工 **0a3.6**

0a3.11 / 754

BŌ, tobo(shii) meager, scanty, scarce

乏

───────── 2 ─────────

4 欠乏 **ketsubō** lack, scarcity, shortage, deficiency
11 貧乏 **binbō** poor
貧乏人 **binbōnin** poor man, pauper
貧乏性 **binbōshō** destined to poverty
貧乏神 **binbōgami** god of poverty
貧乏揺 **binbōyu(suri)** absent-minded shaking of knee or foot
貧乏暮 **binbōgu(rashi)** living in poverty
15 窮乏 **kyūbō** poverty

───────── 4 ─────────

15 器用貧乏 **kiyō-binbō** Jack of all trades but master of none

0a3.12 / 370

己

KO, onore oneself
KI sixth (in a series), "F"
tsuchinoto sixth calendar sign

——————— 2 ———————

1 一己 **ikko** oneself
6 自己 **jiko** self-, oneself, one's own
自己主義 **jiko shugi** egoism, selfishness
自己紹介 **jiko shōkai** introduce oneself
7 克己 **kokki** self-denial, self-control
克己心 **kokkishin** spirit of self-denial
利己 **riko** self-interest
利己主義 **riko shugi** selfishness
利己的 **rikoteki** selfish
8 知己 **chiki** acquaintance, friend

0a3.13

已

I already   **ya(mu), ya(meru)** stop

——————— 1 ———————

11 已得 **ya(mu o) e(nai)** unavoidable

0a3.14 / 81

夕

SEKI, yū, yū(be) evening

——————— 1 ———————

4 夕化粧 **yūgeshō** evening makeup
夕月 **yūzuki** evening moon
夕月夜 **yūzukiyo** moonlit evening
夕日 **yūhi** the setting sun
夕方 **yūgata** evening
5 夕刊 **yūkan** evening paper/edition
夕刊紙 **yūkanshi** evening paper/edition
夕立 **yūdachi** sudden afternoon shower
6 夕凪 **yūnagi** evening calm
8 夕刻 **yūkoku** evening
夕波 **yūnami** evening waves
9 夕風 **yūkaze** evening breeze
夕映 **yūba(e)** evening/sunset glow
夕食 **yūshoku** supper, evening meal
10 夕時雨 **yūshigure** evening shower
11 夕陽 **sekiyō** the setting sun
夕涼 **yūsuzu(mi)** enjoy the evening cool
夕張 **Yūbari** (city, Hokkaidō)
12 夕晴 **yūba(re)** clearing up in the evening
夕景色 **yūgeshiki** evening scene/view
夕焼 **yūya(ke)** red/glowing sunset
夕飯 **yūhan, yūmeshi** evening meal
夕飯時 **yūhandoki** suppertime
14 夕暮 **yūgu(re)** evening
15 夕餉 **yūge** evening meal
17 夕霞 **yūgasumi** evening mist

夕闇 **yūyami** dusk, twilight
18 夕顔 **yūgao** bottle gourd, calabash; moonflower
19 夕霧 **yūgiri** evening mist
24 夕靄 **yūmoya** evening haze

——————— 2 ———————

1 一夕 **isseki** one evening; some evening
2 七夕 **tanabata** Star Festival (July 7)
4 日夕 **nisseki** day and night
5 旦夕 **tanseki** morning and evening, day and night
6 毎夕 **maiyū** every evening
9 昨夕 **sakuyū** last/yesterday evening
12 朝夕 **chōseki, asayū** morning and/till evening, day and night, constantly

——————— 4 ———————

1 一朝一夕 **itchō-isseki** in a day, in a short time

0a3.15

互 彐

KEI pig's head

0a3.16

巳

SHI, mi sixth horary sign (serpent)

0a3.17 / 1894

寸

SUN small amount, just a little; (unit of length, about 3 cm, an inch); measure

——————— 1 ———————

3 寸土 **sundo** an inch of land
4 寸分 **sunbun** a bit, a little
寸心 **sunshin** a little token (of one's gratitude)
6 寸地 **sunchi** an inch of land
7 寸志 **sunshi** a little token (of one's appreciation)
寸言 **sungen** pithy remark, epigram
8 寸刻 **sunkoku** brief time
寸法 **sunpō** measurements, dimensions; plan, arrangement
9 寸前 **sunzen** just before
寸秒 **sunbyō** moment, second
10 寸進 **sunshin** inch along
寸時 **sunji** moment, minute
寸書 **sunsho** brief note, a line
11 寸描 **sunbyō** brief/thumbnail description
寸断 **sundan** cut/tear to pieces
12 寸隙 **sungeki** a moment's leisure, spare moments
寸評 **sunpyō** brief review/commentary

0a3

0a3

13 寸暇 **sunka** a moment's leisure, spare moments
寸鉄 **suntetsu** small weapon; pithy remark, epigram
15 寸劇 **sungeki** short dramatic performance, skit

──────── 2 ────────

1 一寸 **issun** one *sun*/inch (3.03 cm)
chotto a little; just a minute
一寸先 **issun saki** an inch ahead; the immediate future
一寸見 **chottomi** a glance/glimpse
一寸逃 **issunnoga(re)** quibbling, putting off
一寸法師 **issunbōshi** dwarf, midget, Tom Thumb
3 三寸舌 **sanzun (no) shita** eloquent tongue
4 五寸釘 **gosun kugi** long nail, spike
尺寸 **sekisun, shakusun** a bit/little
方寸 **hōsun** square *sun*; one's mind/intentions
10 原寸 **gensun** actual size
原寸大 **gensundai** actual size
17 燐寸 **matchi** matches

──────── 3 ────────

10 胸三寸 **munesanzun** heart, mind, feelings

──────── 4 ────────

6 舌先三寸 **shitasaki-sanzun** eloquence

0a3.18 / 26

大

DAI big, large, great; (university, short for 大学); (as suffix) the size of ...
TAI, ō(kii), ō(inaru), ō- big, large, great
ō(i ni) very, much, greatly

──────── 1 ────────

0 大した **tai(shita)** much; important, serious, of great consequence
大して **tai(shite)** very, much, greatly
大それた **dai(soreta)** audacious; outrageous
大あり **ō(ari)** there sure is, indeed exist
大びら/っぴら **ō(bira/ppira)** openly, publicly
大きさ **ō(kisa)** size
大わらわ **ō(warawa)** feverish activity, great effort
大ざっぱ/まか **ō(zappa/maka)** rough (estimate); generous
2 大入 **ōi(ri)** full house, capacity audience
大入道 **ōnyūdō** large bald-shaven monster/specter
大人 **otona** adult **otona(shii)** gentle, quiet
taijin giant; adult; man of virtue
大人気 **otonage(nai)** childish, puerile
大人物 **daijinbutsu** great man
大刀 **daitō** long sword
大力 **dairiki, tairiki** great strength
大八車 **daihachiguruma** large wagon
3 大川 **ōkawa** large river

大川端 **ōkawabata** banks of the Sumida River (in Tōkyō)
大工 **daiku** carpenter
大丈夫 **daijōbu** alright, safe, secure
大上段 **daijōdan** raising a sword (to kill)
大々的 **daidaiteki** great, grand, on a large scale
大凡 **ōyoso** approximately
大口 **ōguchi, ōkuchi** large mouth; bragging, exaggeration; large amount
大口径 **daikōkei** large-caliber
大巾 **ōhaba** by a large margin, substantial
大弓 **daikyū** bow; archery
大小 **daishō** large and/or small size; (relative) size; long sword and short sword
dai(nari) shō(nari) more or less
大小便 **daishōben** defecation and urination
大山 **taizan** large mountain
Daisen (mountain, Shimane-ken)
大山鳴動鼠一匹 **taizan meidō (shite) nezumi ippiki** The mountains have brought forth a mouse. Much ado about nothing much.
4 大元帥 **daigensui** generalissimo
大太鼓 **ōdaiko** large drum, bass drum
大凶 **daikyō** very bad luck; atrocity, brutality
大夫 **taifu** high steward
大井川 **Ōigawa** (river, Shizuoka-ken)
大仏 **daibutsu** huge image of Buddha
大仏殿 **daibutsuden** temple with a huge image of Buddha
大化 **Taika** (era, 645–650)
大切 **taisetsu** important; valuable, precious
大文字 **ōmoji** capital letter **daimonji** large character; the character 大
大分 **daibu, daibun** much, greatly, considerably **Ōita** (city, Ōita-ken)
大分県 **Ōita-ken** (prefecture)
大公 **taikō** grand duke
大円 **daien** large circle; great circle
大水 **ōmizu** flood, inundation
大手 **ōte** large, major (companies); front castle gate **ōde** both arms
大手門 **ōtemon** front gate of a castle
大手柄 **ōtegara** great exploit
大手筋 **ōtesuji** big traders, major companies
大木 **taiboku** large tree
大日本 **Dai-Nippon/-Nihon** (Great) Japan
大火 **taika** large fire, conflagration
大火傷 **ōyakedo** severe burn
大王 **daiō** great king
大方 **ōkata** probably; almost, mostly; people in general
大欠伸 **ōakubi** big yawn
5 大巧 **taikō** great skill
大出来 **ōdeki** a great success, well done

大半 **taihan** majority, greater part; mostly
大本 **ōmoto, taihon** foundation, base
大本山 **daihonzan** headquarters temple (of a sect)
大本営 **daihon'ei** imperial headquarters
大仕掛 **ōjika(ke)** on a grand scale
大功 **taikō** great merit, distinguished service
大正 **Taishō** (era, 1912–1926)
大永 **Daiei** (era, 1521–1528)
大司教 **daishikyō** archbishop, cardinal (Catholic)
大好 **daisu(ki)** very fond of, love
大好物 **daikōbutsu** a favorite food
大字 **ōaza** major section of a village
　　dai(no)ji the character 大
大穴 **ōana** gaping hole; huge deficit; (make) a killing; (bet on) a long shot
大広間 **ōhiroma** grand hall
大旦那 **ōdanna** benefactor (of a temple); proprietor, man of the house
大白 **taihaku** large cup, goblet
大礼 **tairei** state ceremony; enthronement
大礼服 **taireifuku** court dress, full-dress uniform
大主教 **daishukyō** archbishop (Protestant)
大目玉 **ōmedama** big eyes; a scolding, dressing-down
大目見 **ōme (ni) mi(ru)** overlook (faults), let go, view with tolerance
6 大臼歯 **daikyūshi** molar
大多数 **daitasū** the great majority
大気 **taiki** atmosphere, the air
大気圧 **taikiatsu** atmospheric pressure
大気圏 **taikiken** the atmosphere
大年増 **ōtoshima** woman in her 40's
大西洋 **Taiseiyō** Atlantic Ocean
大任 **tainin** great task, important responsibility
大仰 **ōgyō** exaggeration
大全 **taizen** complete works, encyclopedia
大会 **taikai** large/general meeting, conference, convention; tournament, meet
大会堂 **daikaidō** cathedral
大阪 **Ōsaka** (city, Ōsaka-fu)
大阪府 **Ōsaka-fu** (prefecture)
大老 **tairō** chief minister
大同 **Daidō** (era, 806–810)
大同小異 **daidō-shōi** substantially the same, not much different
大同団結 **daidō danketsu** merger, combination
大凪 **ōnagi** dead calm
大汗 **ōase** profuse sweating
大地 **daichi** the ground, the (solid) earth
大地主 **ōjinushi** large landowner
大地震 **ōjishin, daijishin** major earthquake

大寺院 **daijiin** large temple
大名 **daimyō** feudal lord, daimyo
　　taimei renown
大名旅行 **daimyō ryokō** spendthrift tour, junket
大名領 **daimyōryō** fief
大行 **taikō** great undertaking
大行天皇 **taikō tennō** the late emperor
大安 **taian** lucky day
大安日 **taiannichi** lucky day
大安売 **ōyasuu(ri)** big (bargain) sale
大宇宙 **daiuchū** the great universe
大当 **ōa(tari)** big hit, great success; (make) a killing; bumper crop
大吉 **daikichi** splendid luck
大尽 **daijin** millionaire, magnate; lavish spender
大尽風吹 **daijinkaze (o) fu(kasu)** display one's wealth
大回 **ōmawa(ri)** the long way around, circuitous route
大団円 **daidan'en** end, denouement, finale
大旨 **ōmune** the main idea, gist
大牟田 **Ōmuta** (city, Fukuoka-ken)
大成 **taisei** complete, accomplish; compile; attain greatness
大自然 **daishizen** Mother Nature
7 大身 **taishin** man of rank/wealth
大束 **ōtaba** large bundle
大体 **daitai** generally, on the whole; outline, summary; in substance; originally
大伯父 **ōoji** great-uncle, granduncle
大伯母 **ōoba** great-aunt, grandaunt
大佐 **taisa** colonel; (navy) captain
大作 **taisaku** masterpiece, a monumental work
大判 **ōban** (large old gold coin); large size (paper/book), folio
大別 **taibetsu** broad classification
大兵 **taihei** large army **daihyō** big (stature)
大臣 **daijin** cabinet member, minister
大医 **taii** great physician
大乱 **tairan** serious disturbance, rebellion
大豆 **daizu** soybean
大君 **ōkimi, ōgimi** sovereign
大役 **taiyaku** important task/role
大形 **ōgata** large size **ōgyō** exaggeration
大学 **daigaku** university, college
大学生 **daigakusei** university/college student
大学院 **daigakuin** graduate school
大志 **taishi** ambition, aspiration
大売出 **ōu(ri)da(shi)** big sale
大声 **ōgoe** loud voice **taisei** loud voice; sonorous voice
大尾 **taibi** end, finale
大局 **taikyoku** the general/total situation
大社 **taisha** grand shrine; Izumo Shrine

大麦 **ōmugi** barley
大見得 **ōmie** ostentatious display, grand posture
大男 **ōotoko** tall/large man
大系 **taikei** outline, overview, survey
大言壮語 **taigen sōgo** boasting, exaggeration
大車輪 **daisharin** hectic activity; large wheel; giant swing (in gymnastics)
大足 **ōashi** large feet
8 大東亜 **Dai-Tōa** Greater East Asia
大事 **daiji** important, precious; great thing; serious matter **ōgoto** serious matter
大使 **taishi** ambassador
大使館 **taishikan** embassy
大供 **ōdomo** grownups
大命 **taimei** imperial mandate
大叔父 **ōoji** great-uncle, granduncle
大叔母 **ōoba** great-aunt, grandaunt
大受 **ōu(ke)** great popularity, a hit
大卒 **daisotsu** college/university graduate (short for 大学卒業(者))
大典 **taiten** state ceremony; important law, canon
大逆 **taigyaku, daigyaku** hideous wickedness; treason; parricide
大逆無道 **daigyaku-mudō** high treason
大逆罪 **taigyakuzai, daigyakuzai** treason; parricide
大波 **ōnami** big wave, billow, swell
大法 **taihō** fundamental law
大治 **Daiji** (era, 1126−1131)
大河 **taiga** large river
大抵 **taitei** generally, usually; probably
大味 **ōaji** flat-tasting, flavorless
大呼 **taiko** cry aloud, shout
大往生 **daiōjō** a peaceful death
大英帝国 **Dai-Ei Teikoku** the British Empire
大英断 **daieidan** bold decision
大昔 **ōmukashi** remote antiquity, long long ago
大宗 **taisō** originator; leading figure; main items
大宝 **Taihō** (era, 701−704)
大官 **taikan** high-ranking official
大空 **ōzora, taikū** the sky
大国 **taikoku** large country; major nation
大枚 **taimai** large amount of money
大杯 **taihai** large cup, goblet
大物 **ōmono** big thing; great man, big shot; big game
大所 **ōdokoro** rich family; important person/company
大和 **Yamato** ancient Japan
大和絵 **Yamato-e** medieval picture in Japanese rather than Chinese style
大和歌 **Yamato-uta** 31-syllable poem, tanka

大和魂 **Yamato-damashii** the Japanese spirit
大和撫子 **Yamato nadeshiko** daughter/woman of Japan
大金 **taikin** large amount of money
大金持 **ōganemochi** very rich man
大雨 **ōame, taiu** heavy rainfall, downpour
大門 **daimon** large outer gate (of a Buddhist temple) **ōmon** front gate
9 大乗仏教 **Daijō Bukkyō** Mahayana Buddhism, Great-Vehicle Buddhism
大乗的 **daijōteki** broad-minded
大便 **daiben** feces, excrement
大降 **ōbu(ri)** heavy rainfall/snowfall
大勇 **taiyū** great courage
大軍 **taigun** large army **ōikusa** great battle; great war
大帝 **taitei** great emperor
大変 **taihen** serious; terrible, awful, huge, very
大負 **ōma(ke)** a crushing defeat; big price reduction
大急 **ōiso(gi)** in a big hurry/rush
大前提 **daizentei** major premise
大通 **ōdō(ri)** a main street, thoroughfare
大風 **ōkaze** strong wind, gale
大津 **Ōtsu** (city, Shiga-ken)
大洪水 **Daikōzui** the Flood/Deluge
大活躍 **daikatsuyaku** great/energetic activity
大洋 **taiyō** ocean
大洋州 **Taiyōshū** Oceania
大海 **taikai** the ocean
大海原 **ōunabara** the ocean, the vast sea
大型 **ōgata** large size
大要 **taiyō** summary, outline
大度 **taido** magnanimous
大屋 **ōya** landlord
大相撲 **ōzumō** grand sumo tournament; exciting match
大柄 **ōgara** large build; large pattern (on a kimono)
大胆 **daitan** bold, daring
大胆不敵 **daitan-futeki** audacious, daredevil
大神宮 **Daijingū** the Grand Shrine (at Ise)
大政 **taisei** administration of a country; imperial rule
大政奉還 **taisei hōkan** restoration of imperial rule
大威張 **ōiba(ri)** bragging
大音声 **daionjō** loud/stentorian voice
大計 **taikei** long-range plan, farsighted policy
大食 **taishoku, ōgu(i)** gluttony, voracity; glutton
10 大将 **taishō** general; admiral; head, leader, boss
大将軍 **taishōgun** generalissimo
大陸 **tairiku** continent

大陸棚 **tairikudana** continental shelf
大都会 **daitokai** big city
大部分 **daibubun** a large part, most; for the most part, mostly
大部屋 **ōbeya** large room; actors' common room
大差 **taisa** wide difference/margin, great disparity
大酒 **ōzake, taishu** heavy drinking
大酒飲 **ōzakeno(mi)** heavy drinker
大流行 **dairyūkō, ōhayari** the fashion/rage
大振 **ōbu(ri)** big swing; large size
大師 **daishi** great (Buddhist) teacher, saint
大家 **taika** mansion; illustrious/wealthy family; past master, authority
     taike illustrious/wealthy family
     ōya landlord; main building
大家族 **daikazoku** large family
大宮 **Ōmiya** (city, Saitama-ken)
大宮司 **daigūji** high priest of a grand shrine
大宮御所 **Ōmiya gosho** Empress Dowager's Palace
大宮様 **ōmiya-sama** the empress dowager
大挙 **taikyo** en masse, in full force
大島 **Ōshima** (frequent name for an island)
大株主 **ōkabunushi** large shareholder
大根 **daikon** daikon, Japanese radish
大根役者 **daikon yakusha** ham actor
大根卸 **daikon oro(shi)** grated daikon; daikon grater
大根漬 **daikonzu(ke)** pickled daikon
大祓 **ōharai** exorcism; Shinto purification ceremony
大息 **taisoku** sigh
大恐慌 **daikyōkō** great panic
大恩 **daion, taion** great debt of gratitude
大悟 **taigo, daigo** great wisdom; (Buddhist) enlightenment
大破 **taiha** serious damage, havoc, ruin
大砲 **taihō** cannon, gun, artillery
大病 **taibyō** serious illness
大笑 **ōwara(i), taishō** a big laugh
大釘 **ōkugi** large nail, spike
大馬鹿 **ōbaka** big fool
11 大野 **ōno** big field   **Ōno** (surname)
大隅 **Ōsumi** (ancient kuni, Kagoshima-ken)
大隊 **daitai** battalion
大動脈 **daidōmyaku** aorta
大商人 **daishōnin** great merchant
大商店 **daishōten** emporium
大道 **daidō** highway, main street; great moral principle
大道具 **ōdōgu** stage setting, scenery
大過 **taika** serious mistake/error
大過去 **daikako** past perfect tense, pluperfect

大掛 **ōgaka(ri)** large-scale
大掃除 **ōsōji** general house-cleaning, spring/fall cleaning
大喝 **taikatsu, daikatsu** bellow, roar, thunder, yell
大婚 **taikon** imperial wedding
大猟 **tairyō** a large catch
大著 **taicho** voluminous work; great work
大麻 **taima** marijuana; Shinto paper amulet
     ōasa hemp
大脳 **dainō** the cerebrum
大晦 **ōtsugomori** last day of the year
大晦日 **Ōmisoka** last day of the year; New Year's Eve
大黒 **Daikoku** god of wealth
大黒柱 **daikokubashira** central pillar; pillar, mainstay
大祭 **taisai, ōmatsu(ri)** grand festival
大尉 **taii** captain; lieutenant
大理石 **dairiseki** marble
大望 **taimō, taibō** ambition, aspirations
大赦 **taisha** amnesty; plenary indulgence
大欲 **taiyoku** greed, avarice, covetousness
大悪人 **daiakunin** utter scoundrel
大患 **taikan** serious illness; great cares
大規模 **daikibo** large-scale
大袈裟 **ōgesa** exaggerated
大略 **tairyaku** summary, outline; great plan; roughly, approximately
大組 **ōgu(mi)** making up (a newspaper)
大粒 **ōtsubu** a large drop/grain
大船 **ōbune** big ship
大蛇 **daija, orochi** monster serpent; large snake
大敗 **taihai** a crushing defeat
大酔 **taisui** drunken stupor
大雪 **ōyuki, taisetsu** heavy snow
大雪山 **Daisetsuzan** (mountain, Hokkaidō)
12 大違 **ōchiga(i)** big difference
大揺 **ōyu(re)** upheaval
大喧嘩 **ōgenka** big quarrel
大幅 **ōhaba** by a large margin, substantial
大幅物 **ōhabamono** full-width yard goods, broadcloth
大御所 **ōgosho** retired *shōgun*; influential figure, doyen
大葬 **taisō** imperial funeral
大募集 **daiboshū** wholesale hiring/solicitation
大寒 **daikan** coldest season, midwinter
大嵐 **ōarashi** big storm
大喜 **ōyoroko(bi)** great joy
大圏 **taiken** great circle
大圏航路 **taiken kōro** great-circle route
大勝 **taishō** decisive victory
大勝利 **daishōri** decisive victory

大暑 **taisho** midsummer day (about July 24)
大量 **tairyō** large quantity
大量生産 **tairyō seisan** mass production
大童 **ōwarawa** feverish activity, great effort
大衆 **taishū** a crowd; the masses, the general public
大衆化 **taishūka** popularization
大衆文化 **taishūbunka** popular/mass culture
大衆向 **taishūmu(ki)** for the general public, popular
大衆性 **taishūsei** popularity
大統領 **daitōryō** president
大奥 **ōoku** inner palace; harem
大筒 **ōzutsu** cannon
大評判 **daihyōban** sensation, smash
大詔 **taishō** imperial rescript
大間違 **ōmachiga(i)** big mistake
大順 **ō(kii) jun** decreasing order, largest first
13 大業 **taigyō** a great undertaking/achievement
大僧正 **daisōjō** high priest, cardinal
大傷 **ōkizu** serious injury, deep gash
大勢 **ōzei** large number of people
　　taisei the general trend
大慈大悲 **daiji-daihi** mercy and compassion
大義 **taigi** a great cause
大義名分 **taigi-meibun** proper relationship between sovereign and subjects; justification, just cause
大農 **dainō** large-scale farming; wealthy farmer
大塊 **taikai** large chunk, great mass
大損 **ōzon** heavy loss
大群 **taigun** large crowd/herd
大嫌 **daikira(i)** hate, abhor, detest
大蒜 **ninniku** garlic
大腿 **daitai** thigh, femur
大腸 **daichō** large intestine, colon
大腸炎 **daichōen** colitis
大福 **daifuku** great fortune, good luck
大禍 **taika** great disaster
大聖 **taisei** great sage
大聖堂 **daiseidō** cathedral
大数 **taisū** large number; round numbers
大戦 **taisen** great/world war
大意 **taii** gist, outline, summary
大罪 **daizai** heinous crime, grave sin
大罪人 **daizainin** great criminal
大詰 **ōzu(me)** finale, final scene
大路 **ōji** highway, main thoroughfare
大鉈 **ōnata** big hatchet, ax
14 大漁 **tairyō** a large catch (of fish)
大演習 **daienshū** large-scale maneuvers, war games
大摑 **ōzuka(mi)** big handful; summary
大嘘 **ōuso** big lie
大嘗祭 **daijōsai, ōname-matsuri** first harvest festival after an emperor's

enthronement
大概 **taigai** in general; mostly; probably; moderate, reasonable
大様 **ōyō** magnanimous; lordly
大静脈 **daijōmyaku** the vena cava
大綱 **ōzuna** hawser, cable **taikō** general principles; outline, general features
大雑把 **ōzappa** rough (guess); generous
大関 **ōzeki** sumo wrestler of second-highest rank
15 大儀 **taigi** national ceremony; laborious, troublesome; wearisome, listless
大潮 **ōshio** flood tide, spring tide
大器 **taiki** large container; great talent
大器晩成 **taiki bansei** Great talent blooms late.
大蔵大臣 **ōkura daijin** Minister of Finance
大蔵省 **Ōkurashō** Ministry of Finance
大蔵経 **Daizōkyō** The collection of Classic Buddhist Scriptures
大慶 **taikei** great happiness
大権 **taiken** supreme power/authority
大敵 **taiteki** archenemy; formidable opponent
大監督 **daikantoku** archbishop (Anglican)
大盤石 **daibanjaku** large stone, huge rock
大輪 **tairin** large wheel; large flower
大震災 **daishinsai** great earthquake; the 1923 Tōkyō earthquake
16 大憲章 **Daikenshō** Magna Carta
大樹 **taiju** large tree
大賢 **taiken** man of great wisdom, sage
大鋸 **ōnokogiri** large saw
大鋸屑 **ogakuzu** sawdust
大頭 **ōatama** large head; leader, boss
17 大鼾 **ōibiki** loud snoring
大霜 **ōshimo** heavy frost
18 大儲 **ōmō(ke)** large profit
大観 **taikan** comprehensive view, general survey; philosophical outlook
大鎌 **ōgama** scythe
大難 **tainan** great misfortune, calamity
大騒 **ōsawa(gi)** clamor, uproar
19 大蟻食 **ōariku(i)** great anteater
大願 **taigan** ambition, aspiration; earnest wish
大鯛 **ōdai** red sea bream
21 大艦 **taikan** large warship
24 大鷹 **ōtaka** goshawk

─────── 2 ───────

1 一大事 **ichidaiji** a serious matter
2 二大政党主義 **nidaiseitō shugi** the two-party system
3 工大 **kōdai** engineering/technical college
大大的 **daidaiteki** great, grand, on a large scale
干大根 **ho(shi) daikon** dried daikon
下大根 **o(roshi) daikon** grated daikon

4 内大臣 **naidaijin** Lord Keeper of the Privy
　　Seal
五大州 **godaishū** the five continents
六大州 **rokudaishū** the six continents
5 北大西洋 **Kita Taiseiyō** the North Atlantic
左大臣 **sadaijin** Minister of the Left
巨大 **kyodai** huge, gigantic, enormous
叩大工 **tata(ki)daiku** clumsy carpenter
右大臣 **udaijin** Minister of the Right
広大 **kōdai** vast, extensive, huge
広大無辺 **kōdai-muhen** boundless,
　　immeasurable, vast
6 多大 **tadai** much, great amount
壮大 **sōdai** grand, magnificent, spectacular
老大家 **rōtaika** veteran authority
至大 **shidai** greatest possible, enormous
7 医大 **idai** medical university
尨大 **bōdai** enormous, extensive, bulky
宏大 **kōdai** vast, extensive, grand
私大 **shidai** private college
　　(short for 私立大学)
車大工 **kuruma daiku** cartwright
8 長大 **chōdai** tall and stout
長大息 **chōtaisoku** a long sigh
事大 **jidai** subservience to the stronger
事大主義 **jidai shugi** worship of the powerful
並大抵 **namitaitei** ordinary
拡大 **kakudai** magnification, expansion
拡大率 **kakudairitsu** magnifying power
拡大鏡 **kakudaikyō** magnifying glass
肥大 **hidai** fleshiness, corpulence
青大将 **aodaishō** (a nonpoisonous green
　　snake)
9 甚大 **jindai** very great, immense, serious
重大 **jūdai** important, serious
重大視 **jūdaishi** regard as important/serious
尨大 **bōdai** enormous, huge
洪大 **kōdai** immense, vast, huge
10 倍大 **baidai** double size, twice as large
莫大 **bakudai** vast, immense, enormous
莫大小 **meriyasu** knitted goods
党大会 **tōtaikai** (political) convention
特大 **tokudai** extra large
11 副大統領 **fukudaitōryō** vice president
商大 **shōdai** commercial college
　　(short for 商科大学)
過大 **kadai** excessive, too much, unreasonable
強大 **kyōdai** powerful, mighty
盛大 **seidai** thriving, grand, magnificent
細大 **saidai** great and small
粗大 **sodai** coarse, rough, bulky
粗大ゴミ **sodai gomi** large-item trash
　　(discarded washing machines, TV sets,
　　etc.)
船大工 **funadaiku** boatbuilder, shipwright
12 偉大 **idai** great, grand, mighty

博大 **hakudai** extensive
尊大 **sondai** haughty, arrogant, self-important
遠大 **endai** far-reaching, grand
短大 **tandai** junior college
　　(short for 短期大学)
御大 **ontai** the boss/chief
御大葬 **gotaisō** imperial funeral
掌大 **shōdai** palm-size
極大 **kyokudai** maximum
最大 **saidai** maximum, greatest, largest
最大限 **saidaigen** maximum
最大限度 **saidai gendo** maximum
絶大 **zetsudai** greatest, immense
雄大 **yūdai** grand, magnificent
集大成 **shūtaisei** compilation
13 寛大 **kandai** magnanimous, tolerant, lenient
誇大 **kodai** exaggeration
14 増大 **zōdai** increase
増大号 **zōdaigō** enlarged number/issue
総大将 **sōdaishō** commander-in-chief
16 膨大 **bōdai** swelling; large, enormous

──────── 3 ────────

3 工科大学 **kōka daigaku** engineering college
工業大学 **kōgyō daigaku** technical college
大慈大悲 **daiji-daihi** mercy and compassion
大蔵大臣 **ōkura daijin** Minister of Finance
女子大生 **joshi daisei** a coed
4 不拡大 **fukakudai** nonexpansion,
　　nonaggravation, localization
天照大神 **Amaterasu Ōmikami** the Sun
　　Goddess
内務大臣 **naimu daijin** (prewar) Home
　　Minister
五輪大会 **Gorin taikai** Olympic games
文部大臣 **monbu daijin** Minister of
　　Education
水泳大会 **suiei taikai** swimming meet
水産大学 **suisan daigaku** fisheries college
5 世界大戦 **sekai taisen** World War
外務大臣 **gaimu daijin** Minister of Foreign
　　Affairs
外様大名 **tozama daimyō** non-Tokugawa
　　daimyo
司法大臣 **shihō daijin** Minister of Justice
6 伊勢大神宮 **Ise Daijingū** the Grand Shrines
　　of Ise
全権大使 **zenken taishi** ambassador
　　plenipotentiary
7 伴食大臣 **banshoku daijin** figurehead
　　minister
医科大学 **ika daigaku** medical university/
　　school
8 奄美大島 **Amami Ōshima** (island,
　　Kagoshima-ken)
厚生大臣 **kōsei daijin** Minister of Health
　　and Welfare

法務大臣 **hōmu daijin** Minister of Justice
征夷大将軍 **seii taishōgun** general in command of expeditionary forces to subjugate the barbarians
実物大 **jitsubutsudai** actual size
9 海軍大臣 **kaigun daijin** Minister of the Navy
独活大木 **udo (no) taiboku** large and useless
後生大事 **goshō daiji** religiously, earnestly
砂糖大根 **satō daikon** sugar beet
10 原寸大 **gensundai** actual size
特筆大書 **tokuhitsu-taisho** write large, single out
12 短期大学 **tanki daigaku** junior college
無限大 **mugendai** infinity
14 練馬大根 **Nerima daikon** daikon (grown in Nerima, Tōkyō); woman's fat legs
総合大学 **sōgō daigaku** university
総理大臣 **sōri daijin** prime minister
15 餓鬼大将 **gaki-daishō** dominant child among playmates
19 譜代大名 **fudai daimyō** hereditary daimyo

———————— 4 ————————

2 二十日大根 **hatsuka daikon** radish
4 公明正大 **kōmei-seidai** just, fair
6 気宇広大 **kiu-kōdai** magnanimous, big-hearted
9 重厚長大 **jūkō-chōdai** large and heavy, bulky (cf. 軽薄短小)
10 針小棒大 **shinshō-bōdai** exaggeration
12 無任所大臣 **muninsho daijin** minister without portfolio

———————— 5 ————————

13 農林水産大臣 **nōrinsuisan daijin** Minister of Agriculture, Forestry and Fisheries

———————— 7 ————————

6 全国人民代表大会 **Zenkoku Jinmin Daihyō Taikai** (Chinese) National People's Congress

0a3.19

屮

TETSU bud, sprout   **SŌ** grass

0a3.20

于

U at, from, than; (exclamation)

又 → 又 **2h0.1**

0a3.21

尢

Ō crooked legs, cripple, hunchback

门 → 門 **8e0.1**

0a3.22 / 1413

刃 双

JIN, NIN, ha, yaiba blade

———————— 1 ————————

6 刃先 **hasaki** edge of a blade
刃向 **hamu(kau)** strike at; turn on, rise against, oppose, defy
8 刃物 **hamono** edged tool, cutlery
12 刃渡 **hawata(ri)** length of a blade
13 刃傷 **ninjō** bloodshed
刃傷沙汰 **ninjōzata** bloodshed

———————— 2 ————————

2 刀刃 **tōjin** sword blade
4 凶刃 **kyōjin** assassin's dagger
切刃 **ki(ri)ha** cutting blade/edge
片刃 **kataha** single-edged (blade)
5 出刃 **deba** pointed kitchen knife
出刃庖丁 **debabōchō** pointed kitchen knife
氷刃 **hyōjin** keenly honed sword
白刃 **hakujin, shiraha** naked blade, drawn sword
6 両刃 **ryōba** double-edged
兇刃 **kyōjin** assassin's blade
自刃 **jijin** suicide by sword
7 利刃 **rijin** sharp sword
8 毒刃 **dokujin** assassin's dagger
12 焼刃 **ya(ki)ba** tempered blade
15 諸刃 **moroha** double-edged
16 薄刃 **usuba** thin blade(d kitchen knife)

———————— 3 ————————

5 付焼刃 **tsu(ke)yakiba** affectation, pretension

0a3.23 / 539

与 與

YO give; together **ata(eru)** give **kumi(suru)** take part in; side with

———————— 1 ————————

4 与太 **yota** nonsense, idle talk, bunk; fool, liar
yota(ru) talk rot; live a wicked life
与太郎 **yotarō** fool, liar
与太者 **yotamono, yotamon** a good-for-nothing
与太話 **yotabanashi** idle gossip
9 与信 **yoshin** granting/extending credit, lending

10 与党 **yotō** party in power, ruling party
11 与野党 **yoyatō** governing and opposition parties
14 与奪 **yodatsu** (the power to) give or take away

—————— 2 ——————

3 干与 **kan'yo** participation
4 天与 **ten'yo** a gift from heaven, God-given
　分与 **bun'yo** distribute, apportion
5 付与 **fuyo** give, grant, confer
7 投与 **tōyo** give (medicine), dose
　　na(ge)ata(eru) throw (a bone) to (a dog)
8 供与 **kyōyo** grant, furnish, provide
　参与 **san'yo** participate; councilor
　参与者 **san'yosha** participant
10 党与 **tōyo** companions, confederates
　恵与 **keiyo** give, present, bestow
11 授与 **juyo** conferring, awarding
　授与式 **juyoshiki** presentation ceremony
　寄与 **kiyo** contribute to, be conducive to
12 給与 **kyūyo** allowance, grant, wages
　給与金 **kyūyokin** allowance, grant
14 関与 **kan'yo** participation
15 賞与 **shōyo** bonus, reward
　賞与金 **shōyokin** bonus
　賦与 **fuyo** grant, give
18 贈与 **zōyo** gift, donation
　贈与者 **zōyosha** donor
　贈与物 **zōyobutsu** gift, present
20 譲与 **jōyo** cede, transfer

—————— 3 ——————

5 生殺与奪 **seisatsu-yodatsu** (the power to) kill or let live

0a3.24 / 1257

及

KYŪ, oyo(bu) reach, amount to, extend to, match, equal **oyo(bosu)** exert **oyo(bi)** and, as well as

—————— 1 ——————

11 及第 **kyūdai** passing (an exam), make the grade
　及第点 **kyūdaiten** passing grade
12 及落 **kyūraku** passing or failure (in an exam)
13 及腰 **oyo(bi)goshi** a bent back

—————— 2 ——————

5 可及的 **kakyūteki** as ... as possible
6 企及 **kikyū** attempt
7 言及 **genkyū, i(i)oyo(bu)** refer to, mention
8 追及 **tsuikyū** pursue, get to the bottom of
　波及 **hakyū** extend to, affect, have repercussions
9 思及 **omo(i)oyo(bu)** think of, hit upon
10 埃及 **Ejiputo** Egypt
12 普及 **fukyū** diffusion, dissemination, wide use/ownership, popularization
　普及版 **fukyūban** popular edition

13 溯及 **sokyū, sakkyū** be retroactive
　溯及的 **sokyūteki** retroactive
14 説及 **to(ki)oyo(bu)** refer to, mention
　聞及 **ki(ki)oyo(bu)** hear about, learn of
15 論及 **ronkyū** mention, refer to

—————— 3 ——————

11 過不及 **kafukyū** excess or deficiency

0a3.25

丼

KYŌ present, offer, hold in both hands

0a3.26 / 1325

丈 丈

JŌ (unit of length, about 3 m); (as suffix) (title of respect, used on kabuki actor's stage name) **take** height, length

—————— 1 ——————

4 丈夫 **jōbu** strong and healthy; strong and durable **jōfu, masurao** manly man, hero; gentleman
7 丈余 **jōyo** more than three meters, over ten feet

—————— 2 ——————

2 八丈島 **Hachijōjima** (island, Tōkyō-to)
3 万丈 **banjō** great height
　大丈夫 **daijōbu** alright, safe, secure
　女丈夫 **jojōfu** heroic woman
4 方丈 **hōjō** ten feet square; chief priest('s quarters)
　心丈夫 **kokorojōbu** secure, reassured
6 気丈 **kijō** stout-hearted
　気丈夫 **kijōbu** reassuring
　気丈者 **kijōmono** stout-hearted fellow
　有丈 **a(rit)take** all there is
7 身丈 **mitake, mi(no)take** one's height
8 其丈 **sore dake** that much; only that; only that much **sore dake (ni)** all the more because
　居丈高 **itakedaka** overbearing, domineering
9 草丈 **kusatake** height of a (rice) plant
　背丈 **setake** one's height
　威丈高 **itakedaka** domineering, overbearing
10 袖丈 **sodetake** sleeve length
　軒丈 **nokitake** height of the eaves
11 裄丈 **yukitake** sleeve length and dress length
12 偉丈夫 **ijōfu** great man
　着丈 **kitake** dress length
13 頑丈 **ganjō** solid, firm, robust

—————— 3 ——————

11 黒八丈 **kurohachijō** (a type of thick black silk)

—————— 4 ——————

6 気炎万丈 **kien-banjō** high spirits
　気焔万丈 **kien-banjō** high spirits
8 波瀾万丈 **haran-banjō** full of ups and downs, stormy, checkered

0a3.27 / 551

才 SAI ability, talent; (unit of volume or area); (as suffix) years old

――――――― 1 ―――――――

2 才人 **saijin** talented/accomplished person
才子 **saishi** talented/clever person
才力 **sairyoku** ability, talent
3 才女 **saijo** talented woman
4 才分 **saibun** (natural) talent
6 才気 **saiki** talent, resourcefulness
才気煥発 **saiki-kanpatsu** brilliant, wise
才色 **saishoku** wit and beauty
7 才走 **saibashi(ru)** be sharp-witted, be a smart aleck
才芸 **saigei** talent and accomplishment
才学 **saigaku** ability and learning
8 才知 **saichi** wit, intelligence
10 才能 **sainō** talent, ability
11 才略 **sairyaku** wise planning, resourcefulness
12 才媛 **saien** talented woman
才覚 **saikaku** ready wit; raise (money); a plan
才腕 **saiwan** ability, skill
才智 **saichi** wit and intelligence
13 才筆 **saihitsu** literary talent, brilliant style
才槌 **saizuchi** small wooden mallet
才槌頭 **saizuchi atama** head with protruding forehead and occiput, hammerhead
才幹 **saikan** ability, talent
14 才徳 **saitoku** talent and virtue
15 才器 **saiki** talent, ability
19 才藻 **saisō** talent as a poet

――――――― 2 ―――――――

2 人才 **jinzai, jinsai** man of talent
3 万才 **banzai** hurrah
凡才 **bonsai** run-of-the-mill ability, mediocre talent
小才 **kosai, shōsai** clever, smart
4 不才 **fusai** lack of talent, incompetence
天才 **tensai** genius, natural gift
天才児 **tensaiji** child prodigy
文才 **bunsai** literary talent
5 弁才 **bensai** oratorical talent, eloquence
6 多才 **tasai** many-talented, versatile
如才 **josai(nai)** sharp, shrewd, adroit, tactful
7 学才 **sakusai** academic ability
秀才 **shūsai** talented man, bright boy/girl
8 非才 **hisai** lack of ability, incompetence
画才 **gasai** artistic talent
奇才 **kisai** genius, wizard, prodigy
英才 **eisai** gifted, talented
9 俊才 **shunsai** genius, man of exceptional talent
俗才 **zokusai** worldly wisdom

10 鬼才 **kisai** genius, man of remarkable talent
11 商才 **shōsai** business ability
非才 **hisai** lack of ability
庸才 **yōsai** mediocre talent
異才 **isai** genius, prodigy
12 偉才 **isai** great man, man of extraordinary talent
短才 **tansai** lacking in talent
無才 **musai** untalented, incompetent
幾才 **ikusai** how old, what age
鈍才 **donsai** dull-witted
13 微才 **bisai** (my) meager talent
楽才 **gakusai** musical talent
詩才 **shisai** poetic genius
14 漫才 **manzai** comic dialog
16 機才 **kisai** quick-wittedness
賢才 **kensai** man of ability
穎才 **eisai** gifted, talented

――――――― 3 ―――――――

8 青二才 **aonisai** callow youth, stripling

――――――― 4 ―――――――

3 士魂商才 **shikon-shōsai** samurai in spirit and merchant in business acumen
8 和魂漢才 **wakon-kansai** Japanese spirit and Chinese learning

0a3.28 / 644

丸 GAN, maru circle; entire, complete, full (month); (suffix for names of ships)
maru(i), maru(kkoi) round
maru (de) quite, utterly, completely; just like, as it were **maru(meru)** make round, form into a ball

――――――― 1 ―――――――

3 丸々 **marumaru** completely
marumaru (to) plump
4 丸太 **maruta** log
丸太小屋 **marutagoya** log cabin
丸天井 **marutenjō** arched ceiling, vault
丸内 **Maru(no)uchi** (area of Tōkyō)
丸切 **maru(k)ki(ri), maruki(ri)** completely, utterly
丸込 **maru(me)ko(mu)** cajole, coax, seduce
丸木 **maruki** log
丸木舟 **marukibune** dugout canoe
丸木船 **marukibune** dugout canoe
丸木橋 **marukibashi** log bridge
7 丸坊主 **marubōzu** close-cropped, shaven (head)
丸呑 **maruno(mi)** swallowing whole
丸形 **marugata** round shape, circle
8 丸味 **marumi** roundness
9 丸洗 **maruara(i)** washing (a kimono) without taking it apart
丸括弧 **marugakko** parentheses

10 丸帯 **maruobi** one-piece sash
11 丸彫 **marubo(ri)** carving in the round
丸窓 **marumado** circular window
12 丸勝 **maruga(chi)** complete/overwhelming victory
丸焼 **maruya(ki)** barbecue **maruya(ke)** totally destroyed by fire
13 丸損 **maruzon** total loss
丸腰 **marugoshi** swordless, unarmed
丸暗記 **maruanki** learn by heart/rote
丸裸 **maru hadaka** naked
16 丸髷 **marumage** married woman's hairdo
丸薬 **gan'yaku** pill
丸鋸 **marunoko** circular/buzz saw
18 丸儲 **marumō(ke)** clear gain/profit

———————— 2 ————————

1 一丸 **ichigan** a lump, (rolled into) one
3 丸丸 **marumaru** completely **marumaru (to)** plump
4 日丸 **hi(no)maru** the Japanese/red-sun flag
10 真丸 **ma(n)maru, ma(n)maru(i)** perfectly round
砲丸 **hōgan** cannonball

砲丸投 **hōganna(ge)** the shot put
12 弾丸 **dangan** projectile, bullet, shell
14 睾丸 **kōgan** testicle, testes
銃丸 **jūgan** bullet

———————— 4 ————————

16 親方日丸 **oyakata hi(no)maru** "the government will foot the bill" attitude, budgetary irresponsibility

0a3.29

也

YA, nari to be, is (classical)

廿→  **0a4.36**

0a3.30

夊

SUI (walking) slowly/unhurriedly

———————————————— 0a4 ————————————————

气	不	斤	云	元	幻	比	勹	勾	爪	片	爿	勿
4.1	4.2	4.3	4.4	4.5	4.6	2m3.5	4.7	4.8	4.9	2j2.5	4.10	4.11
予	允	歹	互	巴	斗	斗	犬	太	才	凶	尤	天
4.12	4.13	4.14	4.15	4.16	8e10.2	4.17	3g0.1	4.18	6f5.5	4.19	4.20	4.21
夭	内	內	无	氏	卍	内	五	牙	旡	爻	夫	升
4.22	4.23	0a4.23	4.24	4.25	2k4.7	4.26	4.27	4.28	4.29	4.30	4.31	4.32
毛	丹	屯	廿	夬	夂	丑	中	丹	弔	卅	丰	尹
4.33	4.34	4.35	4.36	4.37	4.38	4.39	4.40	0a4.34	4.41	4.42	4.43	4.44
冊	井	母										
4.45	4.46	4.47										

以→ **0a5.1**

0a4.1

气

KI spirit; air; disposition
KITSU beg

0a4.2 / 94

不

FU, BU not, un-

———————— 1 ————————

1 不一致 **fuitchi** disagreement, incompatibility

2 不二 **fuji** one, only
不入 **fui(ri)** sparse audience, box-office flop
不人気 **funinki** unpopular
不人情 **funinjō** unfeeling, callous
不十分 **fujūbun** insufficient, inadequate
3 不才 **fusai** lack of talent, incompetence
不干渉 **fukanshō** nonintervention
4 不予 **fuyo** (emperor's) illness, indisposition
不毛 **fumō** barren, unproductive
不仁 **fujin** heartlessness
不介入 **fukainyū** noninvolvement, nonintervention
不文 **fubun** unwritten; illiterate, unlettered
不文律 **fubunritsu** unwritten law/rule
不公平 **fukōhei** unfair, unjust

不公正 **fukōsei** unfair, unjust
不手際 **futegiwa** clumsy, unskilled, inept
不日 **fujitsu** at an early date, before long
不心得 **fukokoroe** imprudent, indiscreet
5 不必要 **fuhitsuyō** unnecessary
不出来 **fudeki** poorly made, unsatisfactory
不本意 **fuhon'i** reluctant, unwilling, to one's regret
不生産的 **fuseisanteki** unproductive
不世出 **fuseishutsu** rare, extraordinary, unparalleled
不仕合 **fushia(wase)** misfortune, unhappiness, ill luck
不平 **fuhei** discontent, dissatisfaction, complaint
不平等 **fubyōdō** unequal
不正 **fusei** improper, unjust, wrong, false
不正行為 **fusei kōi** an unfair practice, wrongdoing, malpractice, cheating, foul play
不正直 **fushōjiki** dishonest
不正確 **fuseikaku** inaccurate
不用 **fuyō** unused, useless, waste
不用心 **buyōjin, fuyōjin** unsafe, insecure; careless
不用品 **fuyōhin** useless article, castoff
不用意 **fuyōi** unprepared, unguarded, careless
不払 **fubara(i), fuhara(i)** nonpayment, default
不可 **fuka** wrong, bad, improper, disapproved
不可入性 **fukanyūsei** impenetrability
不可分 **fukabun** indivisible, inseparable
不可欠 **fukaketsu** indispensable, essential
不可抗力 **fukakōryoku** force majeure, beyond one's control, unavoidable
不可知 **fukachi** unknowable
不可知論 **fukachiron** agnosticism
不可侵 **fukashin** nonaggression; inviolable
不可思議 **fukashigi** mystery, wonder, miracle
不可能 **fukanō** impossible
不可解 **fukakai** mysterious, baffling
不可避 **fukahi** inescapable, unavoidable, inevitable
6 不死 **fushi** immortal
不死身 **fujimi** insensible to pain, invulnerable, immortal
不死鳥 **fushichō** phoenix
不気味 **bukimi** uncanny, weird, eerie, ominous
不仲 **funaka** discord, on bad terms with
不全 **fuzen** partial, incomplete, imperfect
不合格 **fugōkaku** failure (in an exam), rejection, disqualification
不合理 **fugōri** unreasonable, irrational
不充分 **fujūbun** insufficient, inadequate
不孝 **fukō** disobedience to parents, lack of filial piety

不老 **furō** eternal youth
不老不死 **furō-fushi** eternal youth
不同 **fudō** not uniform, unequal, uneven, not in order
不同化 **fudōka** nonassimilation
不同意 **fudōi** disagreement, dissent, objection
不在 **fuzai** absence
不向 **fumu(ki)** unsuitable, unfit
不名誉 **fumeiyo** dishonor, disgrace
不如意 **funyoi** contrary to one's wishes, hard up (for money)
不行状 **fugyōjō** misconduct, immorality
不行届 **fuyu(ki)todo(ki)** negligent, remiss, careless, incompetent
不行跡 **fugyōseki** misconduct, immorality
不行儀 **fugyōgi** bad manners, rudeness
不安 **fuan** uneasiness, apprehension; unsettled, precarious; suspenseful, fearful
不安心 **fuanshin** uneasiness, apprehension
不安気 **fuange** uneasy, apprehensive
不安定 **fuantei** unstable, shaky
不当 **futō** improper, unfair, wrongful
不当(たり) **fua(tari)** unpopularity, failure
不吉 **fukitsu** inauspicious, unlucky
不朽 **fukyū** immortal, everlasting
不成功 **fuseikō** failure
不成立 **fuseiritsu** failure, rejection
不成績 **fuseiseki** poor results/performance
不自由 **fujiyū** inconvenience, discomfort; privation; disability, handicap
不自然 **fushizen** unnatural
7 不良 **furyō** bad, substandard, delinquent
不良導体 **furyō dōtai** nonconductor, poor conductor
不身持 **fumimo(chi)** profligate, dissolute, licentious, loose
不承 **fushō** dissent, disagreement, noncompliance
不承不承 **fushō-bushō** reluctant, grudging
不承知 **fushōchi** dissent, disagreement, noncompliance
不承諾 **fushōdaku** nonconsent, refusal
不束 **futsutsuka** ill-bred, inexperienced, inept, stupid
不体裁 **futeisai** in bad form, unseemly, improper
不作 **fusaku** bad harvest, crop failure
不作法 **busahō** bad manners, discourtesy
不似合 **funia(i)** unbecoming, unsuitable, ill-matched
不即不離 **fusoku-furi** neutral, noncommittal
不決断 **fuketsudan** indecisive, vacillating, irresolute
不均斉 **fukinsei** asymmetrical, lop-sided
不均衡 **fukinkō** imbalance, disequilibrium
不抜 **fubatsu** firm, steadfast

不妊 **funin** sterile, barren
不妊症 **funinshō** sterility, barrenness
不完全 **fukanzen** incomplete, imperfect, faulty, defective
不肖 **fushō** unlike one's father; I (humble)
不労所得 **furō shotoku** unearned/investment income
不図 **futo** suddenly, unexpectedly, by chance
不条理 **fujōri** unreasonable, irrational
不快 **fukai** unpleasant, uncomfortable; displeased
不利 **furi** (to one's) disadvantage, handicap
不利益 **furieki** (to one's) disadvantage
不言不語 **fugen-fugo** silence
不足 **fusoku** shortage, lack
8 不例 **furei** indisposition, illness
不夜城 **fuyajō** nightless city, city that never sleeps
不斉 **fusei** not uniform, uneven, asymmetrical
不退転 **futaiten** determination, firm resolve
不注意 **fuchūi** carelessness
不法 **fuhō** unlawful, illegal, wrongful
不況 **fukyō** recession, business slump
不治 **fuji, fuchi** incurable
不幸 **fukō** unhappiness, misfortune
不拡大 **fukakudai** nonexpansion, nonaggravation, localization
不知 **fuchi** ignorance
不知火 **shiranui, shiranuhi** sea fire/luminescence
不始末 **fushimatsu** mismanagement, carelessness; lavish, spendthrift
不参加 **fusanka** nonparticipation
不実 **fujitsu** unfaithful, inconstant; false, untrue
不定 **futei, fujō** uncertain, indefinite, changeable
不定期 **futeiki** at irregular intervals, for an indefinite term
不定詞 **futeishi** an infinitive
不届 **futodo(ki)** insolent, rude
不屈 **fukutsu** indomitable
不服 **fufuku** dissatisfaction, protest
不服従 **fufukujū** insubordination
不明 **fumei** unclear, unknown; ignorance
不明朗 **fumeirō** gloomy; dubious; dishonest
不明瞭 **fumeiryō** unclear, indistinct
不易 **fueki** immutable
不忠 **fuchū** disloyalty, infidelity
不忠実 **fuchūjitsu** disloyal, unfaithful
不所存 **fushozon** imprudence, indiscretion
不具 **fugu, katawa** physical deformity/disability
不具者 **fugusha** cripple, disabled person
不和 **fuwa** discord, trouble, strife
9 不発 **fuhatsu** misfire

不発弾 **fuhatsudan** unexploded shell/bomb, dud
不信 **fushin** unfaithfulness; unbelief; distrust
不信心 **fushinjin** lack of faith, nonbelief
不信用 **fushin'yō** discredit, distrust
不信任 **fushinnin** nonconfidence
不信任案 **fushinnin'an** nonconfidence motion
不信仰 **fushinkō** lack of faith, unbelief
不信者 **fushinja** unbeliever
不信義 **fushingi** faithlessness, insincerity
不便 **fuben** inconvenient, inexpedient
不侵略 **fushinryaku** nonaggression
不変 **fuhen** invariable, constant, immutable, permanent
不貞 **futei** (marital) infidelity
不貞寝 **futene** stay in bed out of spite
不貞腐 **futekusa(reru)** become sulky/spiteful
不急 **fukyū** not urgent, nonessential
不首尾 **fushubi** failure; disgrace, disfavor
不連続 **furenzoku** discontinuity
不透明 **futōmei** opaque
不風流 **bufūryū** lacking refinement, prosaic
不活発 **fukappatsu** inactive, sluggish
不浄 **fujō** unclean, filthy, tainted, defiled
不品行 **fuhinkō** loose moral conduct, profligacy
不要 **fuyō** of no use, unneeded, waste
不面目 **fumenboku** shame, disgrace
不相応 **fusōō** out of proportion to, unsuited, inappropriate, undue
不恰好 **bukakkō** unshapely, clumsy
不思議 **fushigi** wonder, mystery, marvel
不軌 **fuki** lawlessness, rebellion
10 不倶戴天 **fugutaiten** irreconcilable (enemies)
不倫 **furin** immoral, illicit
不健全 **fukenzen** unhealthy, unsound
不健康 **fukenkō** unhealthy, unhealthful
不凍剤 **futōzai** antifreeze
不凍液 **futōeki** antifreeze
不凍港 **futōkō** ice-free port
不随 **fuzui** paralysis
不随意 **fuzuii** involuntary
不随意筋 **fuzuiikin** involuntary muscle
不都合 **futsugō** inconvenience, trouble, harm; impropriety, misconduct
不帰 **fuki** returning no more; dying
不真面目 **fumajime** not serious-minded, insincere
不勉強 **fubenkyō** idleness, failure to study
不逞 **futei** insubordinate, rebellious, lawless
不消化 **fushōka** indigestion
不消化物 **fushōkabutsu** indigestible food
不埒 **furachi** rude, insolent, outrageous, reprehensible

0a4

不起訴 **fukiso** nonprosecution, nonindictment
不振 **fushin** dullness, slump, stagnation
不従順 **fujūjun** disobedience
不案内 **fuannai** ignorant of, unfamiliar with
不能 **funō** impossible; impotent
不時 **fuji** unforeseen, emergency
不時着 **fujichaku** emergency landing
不祥 **fushō** inauspicious; disgraceful, deplorable
不敏 **fubin** not clever, untalented, inept
不眠 **fumin** sleeplessness
不眠不休 **fumin-fukyū** without sleep or rest, day and night
不眠症 **fuminshō** insomnia
不純 **fujun** impure
不純物 **fujunbutsu** impurities, foreign matter
不納 **funō** nonpayment, default
不粋 **busui** lacking in polish, inelegant
11 不偏 **fuhen** impartial, fair, neutral
不偏不党 **fuhen-futō** nonpartisan
不動 **fudō** immovable, fixed
不動産 **fudōsan** immovable property, real estate
不動産屋 **fudōsan'ya** real estate agent
不遇 **fugū** misfortune, adversity; obscurity
不運 **fuun** misfortune, bad luck
不道理 **fudōri** unreasonable; immoral
不道徳 **fudōtoku** immoral
不猟 **furyō** poor catch
不得手 **fuete** unskillful, poor at, weak in
不得要領 **futoku-yōryō** vague, ambiguous
不得策 **futokusaku** unwise, bad policy, ill-advised
不得意 **futokui** one's weak point
不規律 **fukiritsu** irregular, disorganized
不規則 **fukisoku** irregular, unsystematic
不細工 **busaiku** awkward, clumsy, botched; homely, plain-looking
不経済 **fukeizai** poor economy, waste
不断 **fudan** constant, ceaseless; usually
不断着 **fudangi** everyday clothes
不敗 **fuhai** invincible, undefeated
不釣合 **futsuria(i)** unbalanced, disproportionate, ill-matched
12 不備 **fubi** deficiency, defect, inadequacy; Yours in haste
不着 **fuchaku** nonarrival, nondelivery
不善 **fuzen** evil, vice, sin
不遜 **fuson** arrogant, presumptuous
不測 **fusoku** unexpected; immeasurable
不満 **fuman** dissatisfaction, displeasure, discontent
不満足 **fumanzoku** dissatisfaction, displeasure, discontent

不渡 **fuwata(ri)** nonpayment, dishonoring (a bill)
不換 **fukan** inconvertible
不揃 **fuzoro(i), fusoro(i)** not uniform, uneven, odd, unsorted
不覚 **fukaku** imprudence, failure, mistake
不覚涙 **fukaku (no) namida** crying in spite of oneself
不検束 **fukensoku** unrestrained
不景気 **fukeiki** business slump, recession; cheerless, gloomy
不量見 **furyōken** indiscretion; evil intent
不敬 **fukei** disrespect, irreverence, blasphemy, profanity
不敬罪 **fukeizai** lese majesty
不惑 **fuwaku** age 40
不愉快 **fuyukai** unpleasant, disagreeable
不結果 **fukekka** failure, poor results
不統一 **futōitsu** disunity
不等 **futō** inequality
不等辺 **futōhen** unequal sides
不評 **fuhyō** bad reputation, disrepute, unpopularity
不評判 **fuhyōban** bad reputation, disrepute, unpopularity
不間 **buma** awkward, clumsy, bungling
不順 **fujun** irregularity; unseasonable
13 不義 **fugi** immorality; injustice; impropriety, misconduct, adultery
不義理 **fugiri** dishonesty, injustice; dishonor; ingratitude
不適 **futeki** unsuited, unfit, inappropriate
不適切 **futekisetsu** unsuitable, inappropriate
不適任 **futekinin** unfit, incompetent
不適当 **futekitō** unsuited, unfit, inappropriate
不適格 **futekikaku** unqualified, unacceptable
不溶性 **fuyōsei** insoluble
不滅 **fumetsu** immortal, indestructible
不摂生 **fusessei** neglect of one's health
不寝番 **fushinban** night watch
不感症 **fukanshō** sexual frigidity
不戦 **fusen** renunciation of war
不意 **fui** sudden, unexpected
不意打 **fuiu(chi)** surprise attack
不節制 **fusessei** intemperance, excesses
不誠実 **fuseijitsu** insincere, unfaithful, dishonest
不誠意 **fuseii** insincere, unfaithful, dishonest
不詳 **fushō** unknown, unidentified
不馴 **funa(re)** inexperienced in, unfamiliar with
14 不漁 **furyō** poor catch (of fish)
不徳 **futoku** lack of virtue, immorality, depravity
不様 **buzama** unshapely, unsightly, awkward, clumsy, uncouth

不熟練 **fujukuren** unskilled
不慣 **funa(re)** inexperienced in, unfamiliar with
不導体 **fudōtai** nonconductor
不精 **bushō** lazy, indolent
不精髭 **bushōhige** stubbly beard
不認可 **funinka** disapproval, rejection
15 不慮 **furyo** unforeseen, unexpected
不養生 **fuyōjō** neglect of one's health
不潔 **fuketsu** filthy, dirty
不撓不屈 **futō-fukutsu** inflexible, unyielding, indefatigable
不器用 **bukiyō** clumsy, unskillful
不器量 **bukiryō** ugly, homely
不徹底 **futettei** not thorough, halfway, unconvincing, inconclusive
不審 **fushin** dubious, suspicious; strange
不審訊問 **fushin jinmon** questioning (by a policeman)
不履行 **furikō** nonperformance, default
不熱心 **funesshin** unenthusiastic, indifferent, halfhearted
不敵 **futeki** bold, daring, fearless
不憫 **fubin** pitiful, poor
不確 **futashi(ka)** uncertain, unreliable, indefinite
不確実 **fukakujitsu** uncertain, unreliable
不縁 **fuen** divorce; dim marriage prospects; unrealized marriage
不調 **fuchō** failure to agree; out of sorts
不調法 **buchōhō** impoliteness; carelessness; misconduct; awkward, inexperienced
不調和 **fuchōwa** disharmony, disagreement
不賛成 **fusansei** disapproval, disagreement
不銹鋼 **fushūkō** stainless steel
16 不興 **fukyō** displeasure, ill-humor
不衛生 **fueisei** unsanitary, unhygienic
不機嫌 **fukigen** ill humor, sullenness
不燃性 **funensei** nonflammable, incombustible
不躾 **bushitsuke** ill-breeding, bad manners
不整脈 **fuseimyaku** irregular pulse
不親切 **fushinsetsu** unkind, unfriendly
不穏 **fuon** unrest, disquiet
不穏当 **fuontō** improper
17 不謹慎 **fukinshin** imprudent, rash
不鮮明 **fusenmei** indistinct, blurred
24 不羈 **fuki** freedom, independence

——————— 2 ———————

2 七不思議 **nanafushigi** the seven wonders
3 土不踏 **tsuchifumazu** the arch of the foot
口不調法 **kuchi-buchōhō** awkward in expressing oneself
4 手不足 **tebusoku** shorthanded, understaffed
5 出不精 **debushō** stay-at-home
6 汗不知 **aseshirazu** prickly-heat/baby powder

7 良不良 **ryō-furyō** (whether) good or bad
役不足 **yakubusoku** dissatisfaction with one's role
8 幸不幸 **kōfukō** good or ill fortune, happiness or misery
11 過不及 **kafukyū** excess or deficiency
過不足 **kafusoku** excess or deficiency
理不尽 **rifujin** unreasonable, unjust
12 御不浄 **gofujō** lavatory
筆不精 **fudebushō** negligent in corresponding
13 適不適 **teki-futeki** fitness, suitability
寝不足 **nebusoku** lack of sleep
16 親不孝 **oyafukō** lack of filial piety

——————— 3 ———————

1 一定不変 **ittei fuhen** invariable, permanent
3 万世不易 **bansei fueki** everlasting, eternal
大胆不敵 **daitan-futeki** audacious, daredevil
4 不老不死 **furō-fushi** eternal youth
不承不承 **fushō-bushō** reluctant, grudging
不即不離 **fusoku-furi** neutral, noncommital
不言不語 **fugen-fugo** silence
不眠不休 **fumin-fukyū** without sleep or rest, day and night
不偏不党 **fuhen-futō** nonpartisan
不撓不屈 **futō-fukutsu** inflexible, unyielding, indefatigable
5 半身不随 **hanshin fuzui** paralyzed on one side
6 全身不随 **zenshin fuzui** total paralysis
老少不定 **rōshō-fujō** Death comes to old and young alike.
行方不明 **yukue-fumei** missing
8 直立不動 **chokuritsu-fudō** standing at attention
9 前後不覚 **zengo-fukaku** unconscious
面向不背 **menkō-fuhai** beautiful from every angle, flawless
神変不思議 **shinpen-fushigi** miracle, marvel
音信不通 **onshin-futsū, inshin-futsū** no news of, haven't heard from
食思不振 **shokushi fushin** loss of appetite
10 原因不明 **gen'in fumei** of unknown cause/origin
消化不良 **shōka furyō** indigestion
11 運動不足 **undō-busoku** lack of exercise
欲求不満 **yokkyū fuman** frustration
12 勝手不如意 **katte-funyoi** hard up (for money), bad off
13 傲岸不遜 **gōgan-fuson** arrogant, insolent, presumptuous
14 練習不足 **renshū-busoku** out/lack of training
15 摩可不思議 **maka-fushigi** profound mystery
摩訶不思議 **maka-fushigi** profound mystery
霊魂不滅 **reikon fumetsu** immortality of the soul
17 優柔不断 **yūjū-fudan** indecisiveness

0a4

18 難攻不落 **nankō-furaku** impregnable
20 轗軻不遇 **kanka-fugū** ill fortune and lack of
public recognition, obscurity

0a4.3 / 1897

斤

KIN (unit of weight, about 600 g); ax

───────── 1 ─────────

5 斤目 **kinme** weight
12 斤量 **kinryō** weight

0a4.4

云

UN, i(u) say

───────── 1 ─────────

3 云々 **unnun, shikajika** and so forth, and so
on, and the like

0a4.5 / 137

元

GEN origin; yuan (Chinese monetary
unit); Mongol (dynasty) **GAN** origin
moto origin, basis; (as prefix) former,
ex-

───────── 1 ─────────

3 元久 **Genkyū** (era, 1204–1206)
元々 **motomoto** from the first, originally; by
nature, naturally
4 元凶 **genkyō** ringleader
元中 **Genchū** (era, 1384–1390)
元仁 **Gennin** (era, 1224–1225)
元文 **Genbun** (era, 1736–1741)
元手 **motode** capital, funds
元木阿弥 **moto (no) mokuami** losing what
was gained, no better of
元日 **ganjitsu** New Year's Day
5 元本 **ganpon** the principal, capital
元正 **Genshō** (empress, 715–724)
元永 **Gen'ei** (era, 1118–1120)
元号 **gengō** era name
元弘 **Genkō** (era, 1331–1334)
元旦 **gantan** New Year's Day
6 元気 **genki** vigor, energy, health, vitality,
spirit, courage, pep
元兇 **genkyō** ringleader
元年 **gannen** first year (of an era)
元老 **genrō** elder statesman, veteran
7 元来 **ganrai** originally, primarily, by nature,
properly speaking
元享 **Genkō** (era, 1321–1324)
元応 **Gen'ō** (era, 1319–1321)
元利 **ganri** principal and interest
8 元治 **Genji** (era, 1864–1865)

元服 **genpuku** ceremony of attaining
manhood
元明 **Genmei** (empress, 707–715)
元和 **Genna** (era, 1615–1624)
元金 **gankin, motokin** the principal, capital
9 元首 **genshu** ruler, sovereign
元通 **motodō(ri)** as before
元帥 **gensui** field marshal, general of the
army, admiral of the fleet
元祖 **ganso** originator, founder, inventor,
pioneer
10 元値 **motone** cost
元素 **genso** (chemical) element
11 元亀 **Genki** (era, 1570–1573)
元寇 **Genkō** the Mongol invasions 1274 and
1281
12 元禄 **Genroku** (era, 1688–1704)
元結 **motoyu(i)** paper cord for tying the hair
14 元暦 **Genryaku** (era, 1184–1185)
元徳 **Gentoku** (era, 1329–1331)
15 元慶 **Gangyō** (era, 877–885)
元締 **motoji(me)** manager, boss

───────── 2 ─────────

1 一元 **ichigen** unitary
一元化 **ichigenka** unification, centralization
一元論 **ichigenron** monism
2 二元的 **nigenteki** dual(istic), two-element
二元論 **nigenron** dualism
3 大元帥 **daigensui** generalissimo
口元 **kuchimoto** (shape of the) mouth; near
the entrance
4 元元 **motomoto** from the first, originally; by
nature, naturally
天元 **Tengen** (era, 978–983)
中元 **chūgen** 15th day of the seventh lunar
month; midyear gift-giving
手元 **temoto** at hand; in one's care; ready
cash
火元 **himoto** origin of a fire
5 正元 **Shōgen** (era, 1259–1260)
6 多元論 **tagenron** pluralism
次元 **jigen** dimension (in math)
孝元 **Kōgen** (emperor, 214–158 B.C.)
地元 **jimoto** local
安元 **Angen** (era, 1175–1177)
耳元 **mimimoto** close to one's ear
7 身元 **mimoto** one's identity; one's character
身元保証 **mimoto hoshō** personal references
承元 **Jōgen** (era, 1207–1211)
延元 **Engen** (era, 1336–1340)
改元 **kaigen** change to a new era (name)
8 長元 **Chōgen** (era, 1028–1037)
版元 **hanmoto** publisher
空元気 **karagenki** mere bravado
枕元 **makuramoto** bedside
9 保元 **Hōgen** (era, 1156–1159)

単元 **tangen** unit (of academic credit)
紀元 **kigen** era (of year reckoning)
紀元前 **kigenzen** B.C.
紀元後 **kigengo** A.D.
紀元節 **kigensetsu** Empire Day
10 家元 **iemoto** (head of a) school (of an art)
座元 **zamoto** theater manager, producer
根元 **kongen** root, origin, cause
     nemoto part near the root, base
胸元 **munamoto** the solar plexus; breast
11 道元 **Dōgen** (Zen priest, 1200–1253)
清元 **kiyomoto** (type of ballad drama)
帳元 **chōmoto** manager, promoter; bookie
康元 **Kōgen** (era, 1256–1257)
乾元 **Kengen** (era, 1302–1303)
12 湯元 **yumoto** source of a hot spring
喉元 **nodomoto** throat
復元 **fukugen** restoration (to the original state)
貸元 **ka(shi)moto** financier; boss gambler
13 隠元 **ingen** kidney bean
隠元豆 **ingenmame** kidney bean
寛元 **Kangen** (era, 1243–1247)
腰元 **koshimoto** lady's maid
14 嘉元 **Kagen** (era, 1303–1306)
鼻元思案 **hanamoto-jian** superficial view
網元 **amimoto** head of a fishing crew
15 還元 **kangen** restore; reduce, deoxidize
蔵元 **kuramoto** warehouse superintendent; saké brewer
窯元 **kamamoto** place where pottery is made
膝元 **hizamoto** at the knees (of one's parents)
諸元 **shogen** equipment performance figures, specifications
諸元表 **shogenhyō** list of equipment performance figures
16 親元 **oyamoto** one's parents' home
18 襟元 **erimoto** front of the neck
織元 **o(ri)moto** textile manufacturer

——————— 3 ———————

1 一次元 **ichijigen** one-dimensional
2 二次元 **nijigen** two-dimensional
3 三次元 **sanjigen** three dimensions
5 四次元 **yojigen, shijigen, yonjigen** fourth dimension, four dimensions
6 同位元素 **dōi genso** isotope
11 販売元 **hanbaimoto** selling agency
12 勝手元 **kattemoto** one's financial circumstances
13 勧進元 **kanjinmoto** promoter, sponsor
新紀元 **shinkigen** new ear/epoch
14 製造元 **seizōmoto** the manufacturer

——————— 4 ———————

1 一新紀元 **isshin kigen** a new era

0a4.6 / 1227

 GEN, maboroshi illusion, vision, dream, apparition

——————— 1 ———————

5 幻出 **genshutsu** appear as a phantom, appear dimly
幻世 **gensei** this fleeting world
6 幻灯 **gentō** magic lantern, slides
8 幻怪 **genkai** strange, mysterious
11 幻術 **genjutsu** magic, sorcery, witchcraft
幻視 **genshi** visual hallucination
12 幻覚 **genkaku** hallucination
幻惑 **genwaku** fascination, bewitching
13 幻滅 **genmetsu** disillusionment
幻夢 **genmu** dreams, visions
幻想 **gensō** fantasy, illusion
幻想曲 **gensōkyoku** fantasy, fantasia
14 幻像 **genzō** illusion, phantom
15 幻影 **gen'ei** illusion, phantom
17 幻聴 **genchō** auditory hallucination

——————— 2 ———————

9 変幻 **hengen** transformation
変幻自在 **hengen-jizai** ever-changing
13 夢幻 **mugen** dreams and fantasies

 2m3.5

0a4.7

 nio(u), nio(i) smell

——————— 1 ———————

11 匂袋 **nioibukuro** sachet

0a4.8

 KŌ be bent, slope; capture

——————— 1 ———————

4 勾引 **kōin** arrest, take into custody
勾引状 **kōinjō** arrest warrant, summons
5 勾玉 **magatama** comma-shaped jewels
10 勾留 **kōryū** detention, custody
勾配 **kōbai** slope, incline, gradient

——————— 2 ———————

9 急勾配 **kyūkōbai** steep slope

0a4.9

 SŌ, tsume, tsuma- nail, claw, talon; plectrum

——————— 1 ———————

4 爪切 **tsumeki(ri)** nail clippers

0a4

---

5 爪皮 **tsumakawa** toe cover, mud guard (on a clog)
6 爪印 **tsumein** thumbprint
爪先 **tsumasaki** tip of the toe, tiptoe
9 爪革 **tsumakawa** toe cover, mud guard (on a clog)
11 爪痕 **tsumeato** scratch; pinch mark
13 爪楊枝 **tsumayōji** toothpick
爪跡 **tsumeato** scratch; pinch mark
19 爪繰 **tsumagu(ru)** to finger

_____ 2 _____

3 小爪 **kozume** root of a fingernail
5 生爪 **namazume** the quick (of a fingernail)
11 深爪 **fukazume** cutting to the quick (of a fingernail)
鹿爪 **shikatsume(rashii)** formal, solemn
12 琴爪 **kotozume** plectrum
19 蹴爪 **kezume** spur (on a chicken's foot)

片 → **2j2.5**

0a4.10

SHŌ, ZŌ left half of a split tree

0a4.11

MOCHI, BUTSU, **naka(re)** must not, be not

_____ 1 _____

7 勿体 **mottai** (over)emphasis
勿体振 **mottaibu(ru)** put on airs, act self-important
勿体無 **mottaina(i)** more than one deserves, too good for; wasteful
勿忘草 **wasurenagusa** forget-me-nots
8 勿怪幸 **mokke (no) saiwa(i)** stroke of good luck
15 勿論 **mochiron** of course, naturally

_____ 2 _____

8 事勿主義 **kotonaka(re) shugi** hoping that all turns out well

0a4.12 / 393

YO previously, beforehand; I, myself **arakaji(me)** previously, in advance
kane(te) previously, already

_____ 1 _____

5 予示 **yoji** show signs of, foreshadow

---

6 予防 **yobō** prevent, protect against
予防法 **yobōhō** precautionary measures
予防接種 **yobō sesshu** inoculation
予防策 **yobōsaku** precautionary measures
予防線張 **yobōsen (o) ha(ru)** guard against
予防薬 **yobōyaku** a preventive/prophylactic medicine
予行 **yokō** rehearsal
7 予告 **yokoku** advance notice; (movie) preview
予見 **yoken** foresee, foreknow
予言 **yogen** prediction **kanegoto** prediction; promise
予言者 **yogensha** prophet
8 予知 **yochi** foresee, foretell, predict
予定 **yotei** plan, prearrangement, expectation
予定日 **yoteibi** scheduled date, expected date (of birth)
予定案 **yoteian** program, schedule
9 予後 **yogo** recuperation, convalescence
予科 **yoka** preparatory course
予約 **yoyaku** reservations, booking, advance order, subscription, contract
予約者 **yoyakusha** subscriber
11 予習 **yoshū** lesson preparation
予断 **yodan** guess, predict, conclude
12 予備 **yobi** preparatory, preliminary, in reserve, spare
予備兵 **yobihei** reservists
予備知識 **yobi chishiki** preliminary knowledge, background
予備金 **yobikin** reserve/emergency fund
予備品 **yobihin** spares, reserve supply
予備員 **yobiin** reserve men
予備校 **yobikō** preparatory school
予備隊 **yobitai** reserve corps
予備費 **yobihi** preliminary expenses; reserve/emergency fund
予備選挙 **yobi senkyo** preliminary election, a primary
予測 **yosoku** forecast, estimate
予報 **yohō** forecast, preannouncement
予覚 **yokaku** premonition, hunch
予期 **yoki** expect, anticipate
13 予想 **yosō** expect, anticipate, conjecture, imagine; estimate
予想外 **yosōgai** unexpected, unforeseen
予想通 **yosōdō(ri)** as expected
予想高 **yosōdaka** estimated amount
予感 **yokan** premonition, hunch
予鈴 **yorei** first bell
14 予選 **yosen** preliminary selection/screening, elimination round
予算 **yosan** budget, estimate
予算外 **yosangai** outside the budget, off-budget

予算案 **yosan'an** proposed budget
15 予審 **yoshin** preliminary examination,
     pretrial hearing
   予震 **yoshin** foreshock, preliminary tremor
17 予餞会 **yosenkai** farewell party (before
     graduation is completed)
───────── 2 ─────────
4 不予 **fuyo** (emperor's) illness, indisposition
6 伊予 **Iyo** (ancient kuni, Ehime-ken)
12 猶予 **yūyo** postponement, deferment
   猶予期間 **yūyo kikan** grace period
───────── 3 ─────────
4 収穫予想 **shūkaku yosō** crop estimate
───────── 4 ─────────
11 執行猶予 **shikkō yūyo** stay of execution,
     suspended sentence

0a4.13

允 **IN** sincere; permit

───────── 1 ─────────
11 允許 **inkyo** permission, license

瓦 → 0a5.11

0a4.14

歹 **GATSU** broken bone

0a4.15 / 907

互 **GO, taga(i)** mutual, reciprocal,
   together

───────── 1 ─────────
7 互助会 **gojokai** a mutual-aid society
   互角 **gokaku** equal, evenly-matched
10 互恵 **gokei** reciprocity, mutual benefit
12 互違 **taga(i)chiga(i)** alternating
   互換性 **gokansei** compatibility, interchange-
     ability
14 互選 **gosen** co-optation, mutual election
20 互譲 **gojō** mutual concession, compromise,
     conciliation
───────── 2 ─────────
9 相互 **sōgo** mutual, reciprocal
   相互作用 **sōgo sayō** interaction
───────── 3 ─────────
9 相身互 **aimitaga(i)** mutual sympathy/help

0a4.16

巴 **HA** vortex, whirlpool, spiral
   tomoe swirling-commas design

───────── 1 ─────────
5 巴旦杏 **hatankyō, hadankyō** almond tree;
     plum
7 巴里 **Pari** Paris
───────── 2 ─────────
6 卍巴 **manji-tomoe** (snow falling) in swirls
11 淋巴液 **rinpaeki** lymph
   淋巴腺 **rinpasen** lymph gland
───────── 3 ─────────
8 欧羅巴 **Yōroppa** Europe

斗 → 闘 8e10.2

0a4.17 / 1899

斗 **TO** (unit of volume, 18 liters); ladle,
   dipper

───────── 1 ─────────
10 斗酒 **toshu** kegs/gallons of saké
───────── 2 ─────────
5 北斗七星 **Hokuto Shichisei** the Big Dipper
   北斗星 **Hokutosei** the Big Dipper
8 抽斗 **hikidashi** drawer
9 星斗 **seito** stars
10 泰斗 **taito** an authority, leading figure
14 漏斗 **rōto, jōgo** funnel
   漏斗状 **rōtojō** funnel-shaped
15 熨斗 **noshi** decorative paper strip attached to
     a gift
   熨斗目 **noshime** samurai's ceremonial robe
───────── 3 ─────────
4 火熨斗 **hinoshi** an iron (for ironing clothes)

犬 → 3g0.1

0a4.18 / 629

太 **TAI, TA** big **futo(i)** fat **futo(ru)**
   get fat

───────── 1 ─────────
2 太子 **taishi** crown prince
   太刀 **tachi** (long) sword
   太刀打 **tachiu(chi)** cross swords with;
     contend, vie

0a4

太刀先 **tachisaki** tip of a sword; force of tongue
太刀魚 **tachiuo** hairtail, scabbard fish
4 太夫 **tayū, taifu** chief actor in a Noh play; entertainer; kabuki female-role actor; courtesan
5 太古 **taiko** antiquity, prehistoric times
太平 **taihei** peace, tranquility
太平洋 **Taiheiyō** the Pacific Ocean
太平洋戦争 **Taiheiyō Sensō** the Pacific War, World War II
太平楽 **taiheiraku** idle/irresponsible talk
太字 **futoji** bold-face lettering
太白 **taihaku** Venus; refined sugar; thick silk thread
6 太后 **taikō** empress dowager, queen mother
太守 **taishu** governor-general, viceroy
7 太初 **taisho** the beginning of the world
8 太宗 **taisō** imperial ancestor ranking highest in achievement after the founder of the dynasty
太股 **futomomo** thigh
太物 **futomono** dry/piece goods
9 太祖 **taiso** first emperor (of a dynasty), founder
10 太陰 **taiin** the moon, lunar
太陰暦 **taiinreki** the lunar calendar
太宰府 **Dazaifu** (ancient) Kyūshū government headquarters
11 太陽 **taiyō** the sun, solar
太陽年 **taiyōnen** solar year
太陽系 **taiyōkei** the solar system
太陽神 **taiyōshin** sun god
太陽暦 **taiyōreki** the solar calendar
太陽熱 **taiyōnetsu** solar heat
太虚 **taikyo** the sky; the universe
12 太筋 **futosuji** thick line, bar
13 太鼓 **taiko** drum
太鼓判 **taikoban** large seal
太鼓持 **taikomo(chi)** professional jester; flatterer
太鼓腹 **taikobara** paunch, potbelly
太腹 **futo(p)para** generous; bold
14 太綱 **futozuna** cable, hawser
太閤 **taikō** the father of an imperial adviser; Toyotomi Hideyoshi
18 太織 **futoo(ri)** coarse silk cloth

───────────── 2 ─────────────

3 大太鼓 **ōdaiko** large drum, bass drum
与太 **yota** nonsense, idle talk, bunk; fool, liar
yota(ru) talk rot; live a wicked life
与太郎 **yotarō** fool, liar
与太者 **yotamono, yotamon** a good-for-nothing
与太話 **yotabanashi** idle gossip
丸太 **maruta** log

丸太小屋 **marutagoya** log cabin
4 木太刀 **kidachi** wooden sword
心太 **tokoroten** gelidium jelly (pushed through a screen to make a spaghetti-like food)
5 白太 **shirata** sapwood
立太子 **rittaishi** investiture of the crown prince
立太子式 **rittaishi-shiki** investiture of the crown prince
6 伊太利 **Itaria, Itarii** Italy
肉太 **nikubuto** bold-faced (type)
汎太平洋 **han-Taiheiyō** pan-Pacific
先太 **sakibuto** thicker toward the end, club-shaped
7 図太 **zubuto(i)** impudent, audacious
肝太 **kimo (ga) futo(i)** bold, courageous
8 受太刀 **u(ke)dachi** on the defensive
9 陣太鼓 **jindaiko** war drum
南太平洋 **Minami Taiheiyō** the South Pacific
皇太子 **kōtaishi** crown prince
皇太后 **kōtaikō, kōtaigō** empress dowager, queen mother
皇太孫 **kōtaison** emperor's eldest direct-line grandson
皇太神宮 **Kōtai Jingū** the Ise Shrine
10 根太 **neda** joist **nebuto** a boil
脂太 **aburabuto(ri)** obese, fat
骨太 **honebuto** large-boned, stoutly built
11 悪太郎 **akutarō** bad/naughty boy
12 堅太 **katabuto(ri)** solidly built (person)
焼太 **ya(ke)buto(ri)** becoming richer after a fire
焼太刀 **ya(ki)tachi** tempered-bladed sword
筆太 **fudebuto** bold strokes/lettering
13 義太夫 **gidayū** (a form of ballad-drama)
触太鼓 **fu(re)daiko** drum beating (to herald the start of sumo wrestling)
14 樺太 **Karafuto** Sakhalin
15 横太 **yokobuto(ri)** pudgy, stocky
16 墺太利 **Ōsutoria** Austria
17 濠太剌利 **Ōsutoraria** Australia
環太平洋 **kan-Taiheiyō** pan-Pacific, circum-Pacific
環太平洋造山帯 **kan-Taiheiyō zōzantai** circum-Pacific orogeny
環太平洋地震帯 **kan-Taiheiyō jishintai** circum-Pacific seismic zone
環太平洋火山帯 **kan-Taiheiyō kazantai** circum-Pacific volcanic belt

───────────── 4 ─────────────

1 一姫二太郎 **ichi-hime ni-Tarō** It's good to have a girl first and then a boy.

 **6f5.5**

0a4.19 / 1280

 KYŌ evil, bad luck, misfortune; disaster; bad harvest

———————— 1 ————————

3 凶刃 **kyōjin** assassin's dagger
4 凶手 **kyōshu** (the work of an) evil person
　凶日 **kyōjitsu** unlucky day
6 凶年 **kyōnen** bad year; year of bad harvest
　凶兆 **kyōchō** evil omen
　凶行 **kyōkō** violence, murder
7 凶作 **kyōsaku** bad harvest, crop failure
　凶状 **kyōjō** crime, offense
8 凶事 **kyōji** tragic accident, calamity, misfortune
9 凶変 **kyōhen** disaster; assassination
　凶荒 **kyōkō** crop failure; famine
10 凶猛 **kyōmō** fierce
　凶徒 **kyōto** murderer, rioter, rebel, outlaw
11 凶悪 **kyōaku** heinous, brutal, fiendish
12 凶報 **kyōhō** bad news
　凶弾 **kyōdan** assassin's bullet
13 凶漢 **kyōkan** scoundrel, outlaw, assassin
14 凶聞 **kyōbun** bad news
15 凶器 **kyōki** lethal weapon
　凶暴 **kyōbō** ferocity, brutality, savagery

———————— 2 ————————

3 大凶 **daikyō** very bad luck; atrocity, brutality
4 元凶 **genkyō** ringleader
6 吉凶 **kikkyō** (good or ill) fortune
13 豊凶 **hōkyō** rich or poor harvest

0a4.20

 YŪ superb, outstanding **motto(mo)** admittedly, although, but, of course **motto(mo-rashii)** plausible, likely-sounding

0a4.21 / 141

天 **TEN** sky, the heavens; heaven, nature, God **ame** sky, heaven **ama-** heavenly **amatsu-** heavenly, imperial

———————— 1 ————————

2 天人 **tennin** heavenly being
　　　 tenjin nature/God and man
　天子 **tenshi** the emperor
3 天川 **Ama(no)kawa** the Milky Way
　天工 **tenkō** a work of nature
　天与 **ten'yo** a gift from heaven, God-given
　天才 **tensai** genius, natural gift
　天才児 **tensaiji** child prodigy
　天上 **tenjō** the heavens
　天上界 **tenjōkai** the celestial world, heaven
　天下 **amakuda(ri)** descent from heaven;

employment of retired officials by companies they used to regulate **tenka, tenga, ame(ga)shita** under heaven; the whole country, the public/world; the reins of government; having one's own way

天下一 **tenka-ichi** unique, matchless
天下一品 **tenka ippin** best article under heaven
天下分目 **tenka-wa(ke)me** decisive, fateful
天下無双 **tenka-musō** unique, unequaled
天下無比 **tenka-muhi** unique, incomparable
天女 **tennyo** celestial nymph, goddess
4 天元 **Tengen** (era, 978–983)
天井 **tenjō** ceiling
天井灯 **tenjōtō** ceiling light
天井板 **tenjō ita** ceiling boards
天井桟敷 **tenjō sajiki** the upper gallery
天井裏 **tenjōura** between ceiling and roof
天仁 **Tennin** (era, 1108–1110)
天文 **tenmon** astronomy
　　　 Tenbun (era, 1532–1555)
天文台 **tenmondai** observatory
天文学 **tenmongaku** astronomy
天分 **tenbun** one's nature; one's natural talents; one's sphere of activity, one's mission
天水 **tensui** rainwater
天水桶 **tensui oke** rain barrel
天手古舞 **tentekoma(i)** hectic activity
天引 **tenbi(ki)** deduction (of interest) in advance
天日 **tenpi, tenjitsu** the sun
天火 **tenpi** oven; (waffle) iron
　　 tenka fire caused by lightning
天王星 **Tennōsei** Uranus
天心 **tenshin** zenith; divine will, providence
5 天丼 **tendon** bowl of rice and tempura
天平 **Tenpyō** (era, 729–749)
天平宝字 **Tenpyō Hōji** (era, 757–765)
天平神護 **Tenpyō Jingo** (era, 765–767)
天平勝宝 **Tenpyō Shōhō** (era, 749–757)
天平感宝 **Tenpyō Kanpō** (era, 749)
天外 **tengai** beyond the heavens; farthest regions
天正 **Tenshō** (era, 1573–1592)
天永 **Ten'ei** (era, 1110–1113)
天台 **Tendai** (a Buddhist sect)
天主 **Tenshu** Lord of Heaven, God
天主教 **Tenshukyō** Roman Catholicism
6 天瓜粉 **tenkafun** talcum powder
天気 **tenki** the weather; good weather
天気図 **tenkizu** weather map
天気模様 **tenki moyō** weather conditions
天刑 **tenkei** divine punishment
天刑病 **tenkeibyō** leprosy

天地 **tenchi, ametsuchi** heaven and earth, all nature; top and bottom; world, realm, sphere
天地人 **tenchijin** heaven, earth, and man
天地万物 **tenchi-banbutsu** the whole universe, all creation
天地神明 **tenchi-shinmei** the gods of heaven and earth
天地創造 **tenchi sōzō** the Creation
天安 **Tennan** (era, 857–859)
天安門 **Ten'anmon** Tiananmon, Gate of Heavenly Peace (in Beijing)
天守閣 **tenshukaku** castle tower
天成 **tensei** natural, born (musician)
天成美 **tensei (no) bi** natural beauty
天衣無縫 **ten'i-muhō** flawless, perfect
7 天来 **tenrai** heavenly, divine
天承 **Tenjō** (era, 1131–1132)
天寿 **tenju** natural lifespan
天体 **tentai** heavenly body
天体学 **tentaigaku** uranology
天体図 **tentaizu** celestial map, star chart
天佑 **ten'yū** divine favor/providence
天邪鬼 **amanojaku** devil being trampled by temple guardian deities; a contrary/cranky person
天助 **tenjo** divine help/providence
天延 **Ten'en** (era, 973–976)
天花粉 **tenkafun** talcum powder
天応 **Ten'ō** (era, 781–782)
天災 **tensai** natural disaster
8 天長 **Tenchō** (era, 824–834)
天長地久 **tenchō-chikyū** coeval with heaven and earth
天長節 **Tenchōsetsu** Emperor's Birthday
天使 **tenshi, ten (no) tsuka(i)** angel
天命 **tenmei** God's will, fate, destiny; one's life
天治 **Tenji** (era, 1124–1126)
天河 **Ama(no)gawa** the Milky Way
天狗 **tengu** long-nosed goblin; braggart
天空 **tenkū** the sky/air
天岩戸 **Ama(no)iwato** Gate of the Celestial Rock Cave
天国 **tengoku** paradise, heaven
天明 **tenmei** dawn, daybreak
　　Tenmei (era, 1781–1789)
天性 **tensei** natural, born (musician)
天武 **Tenmu** (emperor, 673–686)
天和 **Tenna** (era, 1681–1684)
天竺 **Tenjiku** India
天金 **tenkin** gilt-topped (book)
9 天保 **Tenpō** (era, 1830–1844)
天孫 **tenson** descendant of the gods
天降 **amakuda(ru)** descend from heaven
天帝 **Tentei** Lord of Heaven, God

天変 **tenpen** cataclysm, natural disaster
天変地異 **tenpen-chii** cataclysm
天津乙女 **amatsuotome** celestial maiden
天草 **tengusa** agar-agar
天為 **ten'i** providential, natural
天神 **tenjin** the heavenly gods; Michizane's spirit **amatsukami** the heavenly gods
天皇 **tennō** Emperor of Japan
天皇制 **tennōsei** the emperor system
天皇杯 **Tennōhai** the Emperor's Trophy
天皇陛下 **Tennō Heika** His Majesty the Emperor
天皇家 **tennōke** the imperial family
天皇旗 **tennōki** the imperial standard
天則 **tensoku** nature's law
10 天候 **tenkō** the weather
天険 **tenken** natural defenses, steep place
天真 **tenshin** naive
天真爛漫 **tenshin-ranman** naive, simple and innocent, unaffected
天原 **ama(no)hara** the sky/heavens
天狼星 **Tenrōsei** Sirius, the Dog Star
天宮図 **tenkyūzu** horoscope
天恵 **tenkei** gift of nature, natural advantages
天恩 **ten'on** benevolence of the emperor; the grace of heaven
天秤 **tenbin** a balance, pair of scales; carrying pole, yoke
天馬 **tenba** flying horse, Pegasus
11 天動説 **tendōsetsu** the Ptolemaic theory
天道 **tendō** the way of heaven, destiny
　　tentō heaven, providence; the sun
天道虫 **tentōmushi** ladybug, ladybird beetle
天道様 **tentōsama** the sun; heaven
天涯 **tengai** horizon; distant land
天授 **tenju** natural gifts
　　Tenju (era, 1375–1381)
天窓 **tenmado** skylight
天堂 **tendō** heaven, paradise
天理 **tenri** the law of nature, rule of heaven
天理教 **Tenrikyō** the Tenriism sect (founded 1838)
天球 **tenkyū** the celestial sphere
天球儀 **tenkyūgi** a celestial globe
天産物 **tensanbutsu** natural products
天眼通 **tengantsū** clairvoyance
天頂 **tenchō** zenith
天頂点 **tenchōten** zenith
12 天象 **tenshō** astronomical phenomenon; the weather
天象儀 **tenshōgi** planetarium
天測 **tensoku** astronomical observations
天喜 **Tengi** (era, 1053–1058)
天極 **tenkyoku** the celestial poles
天晴 **appa(re)** admirable, splendid, bravo!
天智 **Tenji** (emperor, 668–671)

天然 **tennen** natural
天然色 **tennenshoku** natural color, technicolor
天然記念物 **tennen kinenbutsu** natural monument
天然痘 **tennentō** smallpox
天然資源 **tennen shigen** natural resources
天禄 **Tenroku** (era, 970–973)
天童 **tendō** cherub; gods disguised as children
天軸 **tenjiku** celestial axis
13 天稟 **tenpin** natural talents
天蓋 **tengai** canopy, baldachin
天幕 **tenmaku** curtain; tent
天照大神 **Amaterasu Ōmikami** the Sun Goddess
天福 **tenpuku** blessing of heaven
　　　 Tenpuku (era, 1233–1234)
天意 **ten'i** divine will, providence
天誅 **tenchū** heaven's punishment; well-deserved punishment
天資 **tenshi** nature, natural talents
14 天暦 **Tenryaku** (era, 947–957)
天徳 **Tentoku** (era, 957–961)
天罰 **tenbatsu** divine punishment
天網 **tenmō** heaven's net/vengeance
15 天養 **Ten'yō** (era, 1144–1145)
天慶 **Tengyō** (era, 938–947)
天敵 **tenteki** natural enemy
天麩羅 **tenpura** tempura, Japanese-style fried foods
天賦 **tenpu** natural, inborn
16 天壌無窮 **tenjō mukyū** eternal as heaven and earth
天機 **tenki** profound secret; the emperor's health
天龍川 **Tenryūgawa** (river, Shizuoka-ken)
17 天覧 **tenran** inspection by the emperor
18 天職 **tenshoku** vocation, calling, lifework
天顔 **tengan** the emperor's countenance
天鵞絨 **birōdo** velvet
21 天魔 **tenma** evil spirit, demon

——————— 2 ———————
1 一天 **itten** the (whole) sky
3 丸天井 **marutenjō** arched ceiling, vault
干天 **kanten** dry weather, drought
上天 **jōten** heaven; God
上天気 **jōtenki** fine weather
女天下 **onnadenka** a woman who is boss
小天地 **shōtenchi** small world, microcosm
4 中天 **chūten** midair; the zenith
水天彷彿 **suiten-hōfutsu** sea and sky merging into each other
5 北天 **hokuten** the northern sky
半天 **hanten** half the sky; midair
弁天 **Benten** Sarasvati, an Indian goddess of music, eloquence, and fortune
好天気 **kōtenki** fine weather

四天王 **shitennō** the four Deva kings; the big four
冬天 **tōten** wintry weather/sky
6 両天秤 **ryōtenbin** two alternatives
仰天 **gyōten** be astounded
先天的 **sententeki** inborn, congenital, hereditary
先天性 **sentensei** congenital, hereditary
在天 **zaiten** in heaven, heavenly
吊天井 **tsu(ri)tenjō** suspended ceiling
回天 **kaiten** herculean task, moving heaven and earth
早天 **sōten** dawn, early morning
7 伴天連 **Bateren** Portuguese Jesuit missionaries; Christianity
別天地 **bettenchi** another world
沖天 **chūten** rising skyward
旱天 **kanten** drought, dry weather
8 青天 **seiten** the blue sky
青天井 **aotenjō** the blue sky
青天白日 **seiten-hakujitsu** clear weather; cleared of suspicion, proved innocent
青天霹靂 **seiten (no) hekireki** a bolt from the blue
炎天 **enten** hot weather, blazing sun
雨天 **uten** rainy weather
雨天順延 **uten-jun'en** in case of rain postponed to the next fair day
9 信天翁 **ahōdori** albatross
南天 **nanten** the southern sky
独天下 **hito(ri)tenka, hito(ri)denka** sole figure, unchallenged master
後天 **kōten** not inborn, a posteriori
後天的 **kōtenteki** acquired, cultivated
後天性 **kōtensei** acquired trait
荒天 **kōten** stormy weather
則天去私 **sokuten-kyoshi** selfless devotion to justice
10 高天原 **Takamagahara** the heavens, the abode of the gods
唐天 **tōten** velveteen
唐天竺 **Kara-Tenjiku** China and India
格天井 **gōtenjō** coffered ceiling
烏天狗 **karasu tengu** crow-billed goblin
破天荒 **hatenkō** unprecedented
11 野天 **noten** the open air
梵天 **Bonten** Brahma, the Creator
脳天 **nōten** crown of the head
悪天候 **akutenkō** bad weather
組天井 **ku(mi)tenjō** fretwork ceiling
釣天井 **tsu(ri) tenjō** ceiling rigged to fall onto and kill someone
12 満天 **manten** the whole sky
満天下 **mantenka** the whole world
寒天 **kanten** agar-agar, gelatin; cold weather, wintry sky

暁天 **gyōten** dawn, daybreak
晴天白日 **seiten-hakujitsu** clear weather; proved innocent
13 溥天 **futen** the whole world
滔天 **tōten** overwhelming, irresistible
楽天 **rakuten** optimism
楽天主義 **rakuten shugi** optimism
楽天地 **rakutenchi** a paradise; amusement center
楽天的 **rakutenteki** optimistic, cheerful
楽天家 **rakutenka** optimist
14 総天然色 **sōtennenshoku** in full (natural) color
15 衝天 **shōten** in high spirits
摩天楼 **matenrō** skyscraper
震天動地 **shinten-dōchi** (heaven-and-)earth-shaking
16 曇天 **donten** cloudy/overcast sky
17 嬶天下 **kakādenka** the wife being boss
21 露天 **roten** outdoor, open-air
露天商 **rotenshō** stall/booth keeper
露天掘 **rotenbo(ri)** strip mining
22 驚天動地 **kyōten-dōchi** earth-shaking, astounding

———————— 3 ————————

3 三日天下 **mikka tenka** short-lived reign
大行天皇 **taikō tennō** the late emperor
6 吉祥天 **Kichijōten** Sri-mahadevi, goddess of fortune
有頂天 **uchōten** ecstasy, rapture
8 奇想天外 **kisō-tengai** original concept
9 怒髪天突 **dohatsu ten (o) tsu(ku)** be infuriated
10 俯仰天地 **fugyōtenchi** (nothing to be ashamed of) before God or man
韋駄天 **Idaten** Skanda, the fleet-footed god
11 野暮天 **yaboten** unrefined, rustic; stupid, senseless; stale, trite
運否天賦 **unpu-tenpu** trusting to chance

———————— 4 ————————

4 不倶戴天 **fugutaiten** irreconcilable (enemies)
6 旭日昇天 **kyokujitsu-shōten** the rising sun
8 歩行者天国 **hokōsha tengoku** street temporarily closed to vehicles, mall
9 毘沙門天 **Bishamon-ten** Vaisravana, god of treasure
15 摩利支天 **Marishiten** Marici, Buddhist god of war

0a4.22

夭 **YŌ** young; death at a young age

———————— 1 ————————

6 夭死 **yōshi** premature death

7 夭折 **yōsetsu** premature death
9 夭逝 **yōsei** premature death

0a4.23 / 84

 NAI, DAI inside; within; between, among **uchi** inside; house, one's home; within; between, among

———————— 1 ————————

0 内ゲバ **uchigeba** internecine violence (from the German *Gewalt*, violence)
3 内大臣 **naidaijin** Lord Keeper of the Privy Seal
内々 **uchiuchi** private, informal
nainai private, secret, confidential
4 内分 **naibun** secret, confidential
内分泌 **naibunpitsu, naibunpi** internal secretion, endocrine
内心 **naishin** one's heart/mind, inward thoughts
5 内包 **naihō** contain, involve, connote
内出血 **naishukketsu** internal bleeding/hemorrhage
内弁慶 **uchi-Benkei** tough-acting at home (but meek before outsiders)
内申 **naishin** unofficial report
内申書 **naishinsho** student's school record
内玄関 **uchigenkan** side entrance
内外 **naigai** inside and outside; domestic and foreign; approximately
uchi-soto inside and out
内圧 **naiatsu** internal pressure
内用 **naiyō** for internal use; private business
内払 **uchibara(i)** partial payment
内示 **naiji** unofficial announcement
6 内気 **uchiki** bashful, diffident, timid
内争 **naisō** internal strife
内廷 **naitei** inner court
内地 **naichi** inland; homeland; mainland
内地人 **naichijin** homelanders; people on Honshū
内地米 **naichimai** homegrown rice
内在 **naizai** immanence, inherence, indwelling
内在的 **naizaiteki** immanent, inherent, intrinsic
内向性 **naikōsei** introverted
内因 **naiin** internal cause
内旨 **naishi** secret orders
内耳 **naiji** the inner ear
内耳炎 **naijien** inflammation of the inner ear
7 内助 **naijo** one's wife's help
内角 **naikaku** interior angle; inside corner (in baseball)
内弟子 **uchideshi** apprentice living in his master's home

内乱 **nairan** civil war, rebellion
内応 **naiō** secret understanding, collusion
内局 **naikyoku** bureau (within a ministry)
内攻 **naikō** (disease) attacking internal organs
内見 **naiken** private viewing, preview
8 内事 **naiji** personal affairs; internal affairs
内侍 **naishi** lady-in-waiting, maid of honor
内命 **naimei** private/secret orders
内法 **uchinori** interior dimensions
内治 **naiji, naichi** domestic/internal affairs
内妻 **naisai** common-law wife
内径 **naikei** inside diameter
内苑 **naien** inner garden/park
内実 **naijitsu** the facts
内定 **naitei** informal/tentative decision
内国 **naikoku** home country, domestic
内国産 **naikokusan** domestically produced
内服 **naifuku** take (medicine) internally
内服薬 **naifukuyaku** medicine to be taken internally
内股 **uchimomo, uchimata** inner thigh
uchimata (ni) (walking) pigeon-toed
内股膏薬 **uchimata-kōyaku** duplicity, double-dealing; double-dealer, fence-sitter
内的 **naiteki** inner, intrinsic
内金 **uchikin** partial payment, earnest money
9 内奏 **naisō** secret report to the emperor
内陣 **naijin** inner temple, sanctuary
内院 **naiin** inner sanctuary of a shrine
内通 **naitsū** secret understanding, collusion
内海 **uchiumi, naikai** inland sea, inlet, bay
内室 **naishitsu** one's wife
内庭 **uchiniwa, naitei** inner court, courtyard
内面 **naimen** inside, interior, inner
内面的 **naimenteki** internal, inside, inner
内相 **naishō** (prewar) Home Minister
内祝 **uchiiwa(i)** family celebration; small present on the occasion of a family celebration
内祝言 **naishūgen** private wedding
内政 **naisei** domestic/internal affairs
内省 **naisei** introspection, reflection
内科 **naika** internal medicine
内科医 **naikai** physician, internist
内界 **naikai** inner world, inward
内約 **naiyaku** private/secret agreement
10 内借 **uchiga(ri)** drawing an advance on one's salary
内陸 **nairiku** inland
内陸国 **nairikukoku** landlocked country
内部 **naibu** interior, inside, internal
内挿 **naisō** interpolation
内宴 **naien** private dinner/banquet
内宮 **Naigū, Naikū** Inner Shrine of Ise

内容 **naiyō** content(s), substance
内紛 **naifun** internal discord
内訓 **naikun** private/secret instructions
11 内野 **naiya** infield (in baseball)
内野手 **naiyashu** infielder, baseman
内側 **uchigawa** inside, interior, inner
内偵 **naitei** scouting, reconnaissance; private inquiry
内達 **naitatsu** unofficial notice
内済 **naisai** settlement out of court
内接 **naisetsu** inscribed (circle)
内探 **naitan** private inquiry, secret investigation
内掘 **uchibori** inner moat, moat within the castle walls
内密 **naimitsu** private, secret, confidential
内視鏡 **naishikyō** endoscope
内務 **naimu** internal/domestic affairs
内務大臣 **naimu daijin** (prewar) Home Minister
内務省 **Naimushō** (prewar) Ministry of Home Affairs
内患 **naikan** internal/domestic trouble
内情 **naijō** internal conditions; true state of affairs
内規 **naiki** private rules, bylaws
内訳 **uchiwake** itemization, breakdown
12 内勤 **naikin** indoor/office work
内港 **naikō** inner harbor
内渡 **uchiwata(shi)** partial delivery/payment
内報 **naihō** advance/confidential information
内証 **naishō** secret; internal evidence; one's circumstances
内証事 **naishōgoto** a secret
内証話 **naishōbanashi** confidential talk, whispering
内診 **naishin** internal/pelvic examination
内貸 **uchiga(shi)** advancing part of a salary
13 内債 **naisai** internal/domestic loan
内裏 **dairi** imperial palace
内裏様 **(o)dairi-sama** emperor and empress dolls
内幕 **uchimaku** inside information
内蒙古 **Uchi Mōko** Inner Mongolia
内殿 **naiden** inner shrine
内戦 **naisen** civil war
内意 **naii** intention; personal opinion
14 内膜 **naimaku** lining membrane
内緒 **naisho** secret
内緒事 **naishogoto** a secret
内緒話 **naishobanashi** confidential talk, whispering
内製 **naisei** make in one's own factory (cf. 外注)
内需 **naiju** domestic demand
内聞 **naibun** secret, private

内閣 **naikaku** the cabinet
15 内儀 **naigi** wife; landlady
内憂 **naiyū** internal/domestic discord
内線 **naisen** (telephone) extension; indoor wiring; inner line
内縁 **naien** common-law marriage
内謁 **naietsu** private audience
内談 **naidan** private conversation
内諾 **naidaku** informal consent
内輪 **uchiwa** family circle, the inside; moderate, conservative (estimate)
内輪揉 **uchiwamo(me)** internal dissension, family trouble
内閲 **naietsu** private perusal/inspection
16 内壁 **naiheki** inside wall
内燃機関 **nainen kikan** internal-combustion engine
内懐 **uchibutokoro** inside pocket; one's true intention
内親王 **naishinnō** imperial/royal princess
17 内濠 **uchibori** inner moat, moat within the castle walls
内覧 **nairan** private viewing, preview
18 内観 **naikan** introspection
内職 **naishoku** at-home work, side job, cottage industry
19 内臓 **naizō** internal organs

——————— 2 ———————

2 入内 **judai** imperial bride's entry into court
3 丸内 **Maru(no)uchi** (area of Tōkyō)
口内炎 **kōnaien** stomatitis
4 内内 **uchiuchi** private, informal **nainai** private, secret, confidential
区内 **kunai** in the ward/borough
手内 **te(no)uchi** palm; skill, capacity; (secret) intentions
手内職 **tenaishoku** manual piecework at home
5 以内 **inai** within, not more than
市内 **shinai** (within the) city
6 年内 **nennai** within the year, before the end of the year
西内 **nishi(no)uchi** (a type of strong Japanese paper)
州内 **shūnai** intrastate
廷内 **teinai** in the court
宇内 **udai** the whole world
7 身内 **miuchi** relations, family, friends
体内 **tainai** inside the body, internal
邸内 **teinai** grounds, premises
対内 **tainai** domestic, internal
坑内 **kōnai** in the mine
学内 **gakunai** intramural, on-campus, school (newspaper)
社内 **shanai** in the company/shrine
町内 **chōnai** (in the) town, neighborhood

車内 **shanai** inside the car
8 其内 **so(no) uchi** before long, some day
河内 **Kawachi** (ancient kuni, Ōsaka-fu)
参内 **sandai** palace visit
国内 **kokunai** domestic
松内 **matsu(no)uchi** New Year's Week
枠内 **wakunai** within the limits
青内障 **aosokohi** glaucoma
9 院内 **innai** within the House/congress
海内 **kaidai** the whole country
城内 **jōnai** inside the castle
室内 **shitsunai** indoor(s), interior
室内音楽 **shitsunai ongaku** chamber music
室内遊戯 **shitsunai yūgi** indoor/parlor games
室内装飾 **shitsunai sōshoku** interior decorating
室内楽 **shitsunaigaku** chamber music
屋内 **okunai** indoor(s)
胎内 **tainai** in the womb
10 都内 **tonai** within the capital
部内 **bunai** within the department, (government) circles
家内 **kanai** my wife; family, home
家内工業 **kanai kōgyō** home/cottage industry
宮内庁 **Kunaichō** Imperial Household Agency
宮内省 **Kunaishō** Imperial Household Department
案内 **annai** guidance, information
案内状 **annaijō** letter of invitation
案内図 **annaizu** information map
案内者 **annaisha** guide
案内所 **annaijo** information office/booth
案内書 **annaisho** guidebook
案内嬢 **annaijō** (girl) guide
党内 **tōnai** intra-party
校内 **kōnai** in the school (grounds), intramural
11 黒内障 **kokunaishō** black cataract, amaurosis
12 港内 **kōnai** in the harbor
湾内 **wannai** inside the bay
場内 **jōnai** within the premises/grounds/hall
圏内 **kennai** within the range/orbit of
極内 **gokunai** top-secret, confidential
13 幕内 **makuuchi** senior-rank sumo wrestler
maku(no)uchi rice-ball lunch; senior-rank sumo wrestler
14 境内 **keidai** precincts, grounds
獄内 **gokunai** in prison
構内 **kōnai** premises, grounds, precincts
鼻内 **binai** in the nose
緑内障 **ryokunaishō** glaucoma
管内 **kannai** (area of) jurisdiction
閣内 **kakunai** within the cabinet
領内 **ryōnai** (within the) territory
15 畿内 **Kinai** the five home provinces around Kyōto

16 機内 **kinai** inside the airplane
　館内 **kannai** within the building

─────── 3 ───────

4 不案内 **fuannai** ignorant of, unfamiliar with
9 連立内閣 **renritsu naikaku** coalition cabinet
　独案内 **hito(ri)annai** teach-yourself book
11 道案内 **michi annai** guidance; guide; road
　　marker
12 超然内閣 **chōzen naikaku** non-party
　　government
15 範囲内 **han'inai** within the limits of
19 瀬戸内海 **Setonaikai** the Inland Sea

─────── 4 ───────

4 水先案内 **mizusaki annai** pilot; piloting
　水先案内人 **mizusaki annainin** (harbor) pilot

內 → 内　0a4.23

0a4.24

无

MU, BU, na(i) not be, without

0a4.25 / 566

氏

SHI Mr.; family, clan; surname
uji clan; lineage, birth; surname

─────── 1 ───────

2 氏人 **ujihito, ujiudo, ujindo** clansman
　氏子 **ujiko** shrine parishoner
6 氏寺 **ujidera** clan temple
　氏名 **shimei** surname and given name, (full)
　　name
9 氏神 **ujigami** patron deity
11 氏族 **shizoku** family, clan
　氏族制度 **shizoku seido** the family/clan
　　system
19 氏譜 **shifu** a genealogy

─────── 2 ───────

6 両氏 **ryōshi** both men
　列氏 **resshi** Réaumur (thermometer)
　同氏 **dōshi** the same person, said person, he,
　　she
8 姓氏 **seishi** surname
　彼氏 **kareshi** he; boyfriend, lover
9 某氏 **bōshi** a certain person
10 華氏 **kashi** Fahrenheit
13 源氏 **Genji** Genji, the Minamoto family
　源氏物語 **Genji Monogatari** The Tale of
　　Genji
　摂氏 **sesshi** Celsius, centigrade
15 諸氏 **shoshi** you all

─────── 3 ───────

5 失名氏 **shitsumeishi** unknown/anonymous
　　person
12 無名氏 **mumeishi** anonymous person

卍 → 　2k4.7

0a4.26

内

JŪ footprint

0a4.27 / 7

五

GO, itsu(tsu), itsu- five

─────── 1 ───────

2 五人組 **goningumi** five-family unit; five-
　　man group
　五人囃子 **goninbayashi** five court-musician
　　dolls
　五子 **itsu(tsu)go** quintuplets
　五十三次 **gojūsan tsugi** the 53 stages on the
　　Tōkaidō
　五十歩百歩 **gojippo-hyappo** not much
　　different
　五十音図 **gojūonzu** the kana syllabary table
　五十音順 **gojūonjun** in *aiueo* order of the
　　kana alphabet
　五十嵐 **Igarashi** (surname)
　五十路 **isoji** 50 years; age 50
3 五寸釘 **gosun kugi** long nail, spike
　五大州 **godaishū** the five continents
4 五分 **gofun** five minutes　**gobu** fifty
　　percent, half; five percent
　五分五分 **gobu-gobu** evenly matched; a tie
　五分刈 **gobuga(ri)** close-cropped haircut
　五分試 **gobudame(shi)** killing by inches
　五辺形 **gohenkei** pentagon
　五月 **gogatsu** May　**satsuki** fifth month of
　　the lunar calendar
　五月人形 **gogatsu ningyō** Boys' Festival
　　dolls
　五月雨 **samidare, satsuki ame** early-
　　summer rain
　五月晴 **satsukiba(re)** fine weather during
　　the rainy season
　五日 **itsuka** the 5th (day of the month); five
　　days
5 五目 **gomoku** hodgepodge
　五目並 **gomokunara(be)** five-in-a-row game
　五目飯 **gomokumeshi** a rice, fish, and
　　vegetable dish

0a4

0a4

6 五色 **goshiki** the five colors (red, yellow, blue, black, white); multicolored

五行 **gogyō** the five elements (fire, wood, earth, metal, water)

7 五里霧中 **gori-muchū** in a fog, groping in the dark

五体 **gotai** the whole body

五角形 **gokakkei, gokakukei** pentagon

8 五官 **gokan** the five sense organs (eye, ear, nose, tongue, skin)

9 五重 **gojū, itsue** five-fold, quintuplicate

五重塔 **gojū (no) tō** five-storied pagoda

五指 **goshi** the five fingers

10 五倫 **gorin** the five human relationships of Confucianism (lord-vassal, father-son, husband-wife, old-young, friend-friend)

五桁 **goketa** five digits

11 五常 **gojō** the five cardinal virtues of Confucianism (benevolence, justice, politeness, wisdom, fidelity)

五経 **Gokyō** the five classics (of Confucianism)

13 五感 **gokan** the five senses

14 五徳 **gotoku** the five cardinal virtues of Confucianism)

五種競技 **goshu kyōgi** pentathlon

五穀 **gokoku** the five grains (rice, wheat, *awa* millet, *kibi* millet, beans)

15 五線紙 **gosenshi** music paper

五線譜 **gosenfu** staff notation, score (in music)

五輪大会 **Gorin taikai** Olympic games

五輪聖火 **Gorin seika** Olympic torch

五輪旗 **Gorinki** Olympic flag

19 五臓 **gozō** the five viscera (lungs, heart, spleen, liver, kidneys)

五臓六腑 **gozō-roppu** the five viscera and six entrails

——————— 2 ———————

2 七五三 **shichi-go-san** the lucky numbers 7, 5, and 3; festival for children 7, 5, and 3 years old

七五調 **shichigochō** seven-and-five-syllable meter

十五夜 **jūgoya** 15th night of a lunar month (especially a moonlit August 15)

11 第五列 **dai-goretsu** fifth column

——————— 3 ———————

3 三々五々 **sansan-gogo** in small groups, by twos and threes

4 五分五分 **gobu-gobu** evenly matched; a tie

5 四分五裂 **shibun-goretsu** disruption, disintegration

四捨五入 **shisha-gonyū** rounding off

6 近代五種 **kindai goshu** the modern pentathlon

0a4.28

GA, GE, kiba fang, canine tooth, tusk

——————— 1 ———————

9 牙城 **gajō** stronghold, inner citadel

——————— 2 ———————

8 毒牙 **dokuga** poison fang

12 象牙 **zōge** ivory

象牙海岸 **Zōge Kaigan** Ivory Coast

象牙細工 **zōgezaiku** ivory work/carving

象牙塔 **zōge (no) tō** ivory tower

歯牙 **shiga** teeth

——————— 3 ———————

6 西班牙 **Supein** Spain

0a4.29

无

KI, muse(bu) be choked, choke on (food)

0a4.30

爻

KŌ divination-stick pattern; intersect

0a4.31 / 315

夫

FU, FŪ husband; man

otto husband

so(re) that

——————— 1 ———————

2 夫人 **fujin** wife, married woman, Mrs.

4 夫夫 **so(re)zo(re)** each, respectively

7 夫君 **fukun** (your) husband

8 夫妻 **fusai** husband and wife, Mr. and Mrs.

11 夫婦 **fūfu, meoto, myōto** husband and wife, couple

夫婦喧嘩 **fūfu-genka** domestic quarrel

15 夫権 **fuken** husband's rights

——————— 2 ———————

1 一夫一婦 **ippu-ippu** monogamy

一夫多妻 **ippu-tasai** polygamy

2 人夫 **ninpu** coolie, laborer

3 工夫 **kufū** device, invention, contrivance, means **kōfu** coolie, workman, laborer

大夫 **taifu** high steward

丈夫 **jōbu** strong and healthy; strong and durable **jōfu, masurao** manly man, hero; gentleman

亡夫 **bōfu** one's late husband

凡夫 **bonpu** ordinary man

4 太夫 **tayū, taifu** chief actor in a Noh play; entertainer; kabuki female-role actor; courtesan
夫夫 **so(re)zo(re)** each, respectively
匹夫 **hippu** a man; man of humble position
匹夫匹婦 **hippu-hippu** humble men and women, common people
水夫 **suifu** sailor, seaman
火夫 **kafu** stoker, fireman
5 令夫人 **reifujin** Mrs., Lady, Madam; your wife
田夫 **denpu** peasant
田夫野人 **denpu-yajin** a rustic, country bumpkin, yokel
6 壮夫 **sōfu** able-bodied man
老夫 **rōfu** old man
有夫 **yūfu** married (woman)
7 坑夫 **kōfu** miner
役夫 **ekifu** laborer, coolie
村夫子 **sonpūshi** educated person in the country
車夫 **shafu** rickshaw puller
8 炊夫 **suifu** a (male) cook
牧夫 **bokufu** herder, ranch hand
9 前夫 **zenpu** one's former husband
姦夫 **kanpu** adulterer
10 烈夫 **reppu** patriot, hero
11 情夫 **jōfu** lover, paramour
13 農夫 **nōfu** farmer, farmhand
農夫症 **nōfushō** farmer's syndrome
鉱夫 **kōfu** miner
14 僕夫 **bokufu** ostler
漁夫 **gyofu** fisherman
漁夫利 **gyofu (no) ri** profiting while others fight over a prize
駅夫 **ekifu** station hand, porter
16 樵夫 **shōfu** woodcutter
賢夫人 **kenpujin** wise wife
17 懦夫 **dafu** weakling, coward

─────────── 3 ───────────

3 大丈夫 **daijōbu** alright, safe, secure
女丈夫 **jojōfu** heroic woman
4 公爵夫人 **kōshaku fujin** princess, duchess
心丈夫 **kokorojōbu** secure, reassured
6 気丈夫 **kijōbu** reassuring
9 侯爵夫人 **kōshaku fujin** marchioness
炭坑夫 **tankōfu** coal miner
11 清掃夫 **seisōfu** garbage man/collector
掃除夫 **sōjifu** cleaner, janitor
12 偉丈夫 **ijōfu** great man
13 義太夫 **gidayū** (a form of ballad-drama)
新工夫 **shinkufū** new device/gadget
14 雑役夫 **zatsuekifu** handyman
15 潜水夫 **sensuifu** diver

─────────── 4 ───────────

1 一妻多夫 **issai-tafu** polyandry

0a4.32 / 1898

升 **SHŌ** (unit of volume, 1.8 liters)
masu square measuring box

0a4.33 / 287

毛 **MŌ** hair; tiny amount; 1/10,000 yen
ke hair, fur, wool

─────────── 1 ───────────

3 毛孔 **keana** pores
5 毛生薬 **keha(e)gusuri** hair restorer
毛皮 **kegawa** fur, skin, pelt
毛皮商 **kegawashō** furrier
毛布 **mōfu** blanket
毛穴 **keana** pores
6 毛羽 **keba** fuzz, nap, pile
毛色 **keiro** color of the hair; disposition
毛糸 **keito** wool yarn, worsted, woolen
毛虫 **kemushi** caterpillar
7 毛抜 **kenu(ki)** tweezers
8 毛並 **kena(mi)** the lie of the hair; color of the hair; disposition; lineage
9 毛染 **kezo(me)** hair coloring/dyeing
毛染薬 **kezo(me)gusuri** hair dye
10 毛唐 **ketō** hairy barbarian, foreigner
毛唐人 **ketōjin** hairy barbarian, foreigner
毛根 **mōkon** hair root
11 毛深 **kebuka(i)** hairy
毛脛 **kezune** hairy legs
毛細血管 **mōsai kekkan** capillaries
12 毛焼 **keya(ki)** singe
毛程 **kehodo(mo)** (not) a bit
毛筆 **mōhitsu** writing/painting brush
毛筋 **kesuji** hairline; a hair
13 毛裏 **keura** fur lining
毛嫌 **kegira(i)** antipathy, aversion, prejudice
毛鈎 **kebari** (fishing) fly
14 毛髪 **mōhatsu** hair
毛製品 **mōseihin** woolen goods
毛管 **mōkan** capillary
15 毛編 **kea(mi)** knitting; knitted (from wool)
16 毛頭 **mōtō** (not) at all
17 毛氈 **mōsen** rug, carpet
18 毛織 **keo(ri)** woolen goods
毛織物 **keorimono** woolen goods

─────────── 2 ───────────

1 一毛作 **ichimōsaku** one crop a year
2 二毛作 **nimōsaku** two crops a year
3 三毛作 **sanmōsaku** three crops a year
三毛猫 **mikeneko** white-black-and-brown cat
4 不毛 **fumō** barren, unproductive
木毛 **mokumō, mokuge** wood wool (for packing)

0a4

5 立毛 **ta(chi)ge** crops yet to be harvested
6 多毛 **tamō** hairy, hirsute
羽毛 **umō** feathers, plumage, down
羊毛 **yōmō** wool
7 身毛 **mi(no)ke** body hair
赤毛 **akage** red hair, red-headed
赤毛布 **akagetto** red blanket; country bumpkin
抜毛 **nu(ke)ge** hair falling out, molting
8 兎毛 **u(no)ke** just a hair
逆毛 **sakage** hair standing on end
房毛 **fusage** lock, tuft, tassel
9 巻毛 **ma(ki)ge** curl, ringlet
厘毛 **rinmō** a trifle, insignificant
後毛 **oku(re)ge** loose strands of hair, stray lock
染毛剤 **senmōzai** hair dye
眉毛 **mayuge** eyebrows
紅毛 **kōmō** red hair
10 陰毛 **inmō** pubic hair
剛毛 **gōmō** bristle
原毛 **genmō** raw wool
起毛 **kimō** nap raising
栗毛 **kurige** chestnut-color/bay/sorrel (horse)
胸毛 **munage** chest hair; breast down
紡毛 **bōmō** carded wool
純毛 **junmō** all-wool
恥毛 **chimō** pubic hair
11 脱毛 **datsumō, nu(ke)ge** falling-out/removal of hair
脱毛剤 **datsumōzai** a depilatory
脱毛症 **datsumōshō** alopecia, baldness
旋毛 **tsumuji** whorl of hair on the head
旋毛曲 **tsumujima(gari)** cranky person
産毛 **ubuge** downy hair, fluff, fuzz
細毛 **saimō** cilia
軟毛 **nanmō** soft hairs, down
12 短毛 **tanmō** short hair
短毛種 **tanmōshu** short-haired
腋毛 **wakige** underarm hair
無毛 **mumō** hairless
絨毛 **jūmō** (intestinal) villi; (peach) fuzz
13 葦毛 **ashige** gray(-dappled) horse
睫毛 **matsuge** eyelashes
14 髪毛 **kami (no) ke** hair (on the head)
鼻毛 **hanage** nostril hairs
綿毛 **watage** down, fluff, nap
総毛立 **sōkeda(tsu)** hair stand on end, have goose flesh
15 養毛剤 **yōmōzai** hair tonic
16 獣毛 **jūmō** animal hair, fur
17 鴻毛 **kōmō** goose feathers; a trifle
繊毛 **senmō** fine hairs, cilia
縮毛 **chiji(re)ge** curly/kinky/wavy hair
18 癖毛 **kusege** curly/kinky hair

――――――― 3 ―――――――
15 膝栗毛 **hizakurige** go on foot, hike it

――――――― 4 ―――――――
7 牡丹刷毛 **botanbake** (powder) puff, down pad

0a4.34 / 1093

丹 丹 **TAN** red; red lead; (suffix for medicines) **ni** red; red earth

――――――― 1 ―――――――
4 丹心 **tanshin** sincerity
8 丹毒 **tandoku** erysipelas
丹念 **tannen** painstaking, elaborate
丹波 **Tanba** (ancient kuni, Kyōto-fu and Hyōgo-ken)
丹青 **tansei** red and blue; a painting
9 丹前 **tanzen** large padded kimono
丹後 **Tango** (ancient kuni, Kyōto-fu)
13 丹誠 **tansei** sincerity; diligence
14 丹精 **tansei** diligence

――――――― 2 ―――――――
7 牡丹 **botan** peony (shrub)
牡丹杏 **botankyō** plum
牡丹刷毛 **botanbake** (powder) puff, down pad
牡丹雪 **botan yuki** large snowflakes
牡丹餅 **botamochi** rice cake covered with bean jam
12 雲丹 **uni** sea urchin

――――――― 3 ―――――――
4 切支丹 **Kirishitan** (early) Japanese Christianity/Christian
12 葉牡丹 **habotan** ornamental kale
18 臍下丹田 **seika-tanden** center of the abdomen

0a4.35 / 1936

屯 **TON** ton; garrison **tamuro** garrison

――――――― 1 ―――――――
5 屯田 **tonden** colonization
屯田兵 **tondenhei** farmer-soldiers, colonizers
8 屯所 **tonsho** post, garrison; police station
12 屯営 **ton'ei** military camp, barracks, garrison

――――――― 2 ―――――――
15 駐屯 **chūton** be stationed/quartered
駐屯地 **chūtonchi** (army) post

0a4.36

廿 **JŪ, nijū** twenty

0a4.37

KAI decide, determine
KETSU archery glove

0a4.38 / 1902

monme (unit of weight, about 3.75 g)

甘 → 　　**0a5.32**

0a4.39

丑　CHŪ, ushi second horary sign (cow)

0a4.40 / 28

中　CHŪ middle; China　-chū, -jū throughout, during, within　naka inside, midst
uchi among

───────── 1 ─────────

0 アル中 aruchū alcoholism (short for アルコール中毒)
2 中二階 chūnikai mezzanine
中入 nakai(ri) intermission
中子 nakago tang, blade; core
3 中小企業 chūshō kigyō small business(es)
4 中元 chūgen 15th day of the seventh lunar month; midyear gift-giving
中天 chūten midair; the zenith
中支 Chūshi central China
中支那 Naka-Shina central China
中止 chūshi discontinue, suspend, stop, call off, cancel
中分 chūbun halve
中手 nakate mid-season rice/vegetables
中日 Chū-Nichi China and Japan　chūnichi day of the equinox　nakabi, chūnichi the middle day (of a sumo tournament)
中火 chūbi medium heat (in cooking)
中心 chūshin center
中心人物 chūshin jinbutsu central figure, key person
中心地 chūshinchi center, metropolis
中心点 chūshinten center
5 中生代 chūseidai the Mesozoic era
中央 chūō center, middle
中央集権 chūō shūken centralization of government
中甲板 chūkōhan, chūkanpan main deck

中世 chūsei the Middle Ages, medieval
中古 chūko secondhand; the Middle Ages
chūburu secondhand
中古史 chūkoshi medieval history
中古車 chūkosha used/secondhand car
中古品 chūkohin secondhand goods
中外 chūgai domestic and foreign, home and abroad
中正 chūsei inpartial, fair
中打 nakau(chi) middle third of a fish sliced lengthwise into three
中立 chūritsu neutrality
中立労連 Chūritsu Rōren Federation of Independent Unions of Japan (short for 中立労働組合連絡会議)
中立国 chūritsukoku neutral country
6 中気 chūki paralysis
中年 chūnen middle age
中年者 chūnenmono middle-aged person; late starter
中西部 Chūseibu the Midwest
中休 nakayasu(mi) take a break
中肉 chūniku medium build; meat of medium quality
中肉中背 chūniku-chūzei medium height and build
中次 nakatsugi joint; relay, entrepôt, transit
中州 nakasu sandbank/shoal in the middle of a river
中老 chūrō age about 65–70
中近東 Chūkintō the Near and Middle East
中弛 nakadaru(mi) a slump
中共 Chūkyō Chinese Communists, Communist China (short for 中国共産党)
中旬 chūjun middle ten days of a month, mid-(May)
中米 Chūbei Central America
中耳 chūji the middle ear
中耳炎 chūjien otitis media, tympanitis
7 中身 nakami contents
中位 chūi medium, average　chūgurai, chūkurai about medium/average
中佐 chūsa lieutenant colonel; commander (navy)
中低 nakabiku, nakahiku concave, hollow
中判 chūban medium size
中折 nakao(ri) folded in the middle
中折帽 nakao(re)bō felt hat, fedora
中形 chūgata medium size
中学 chūgaku junior high school
中学生 chūgakusei junior-high-school student
中学校 chūgakkō junior high school
中売 nakau(ri) walking around selling snacks and drinks to the audience in a theater or spectators in a stadium; walk-around vendor

0a4

8 中表 **nakaomote** folding cloth so that the facing is inside and the lining outside

中東 **Chūtō** the Middle East, Mideast

中毒 **chūdoku** poisoning

中卒 **chūsotsu** junior-high-school graduate (short for 中学卒業(者))

中京 **Chūkyō** Nagoya

中退 **chūtai** leaving school before graduation, dropping out

中波 **chūha** medium wave (100–1500 kHz)

中波帯 **chūhatai** medium-wave band, AM radio

中味 **nakami** contents

中実 **chūjitsu** solid, not hollow

中空 **chūkū** midair; hollow
nakazora midair

中国 **Chūgoku** China; Western tip of Honshū, comprising Hiroshima, Okayama, Shimane, Tottori, and Yamaguchi prefectures

中国人 **chūgokujin** a Chinese

中国地方 **Chūgoku chihō** the Chūgoku region (Hiroshima, Okayama, Shimane, Tottori, and Yamaguchi prefectures)

中枢 **chūsū** center, pivot, nucleus

中欧 **Chūō** central Europe

中性 **chūsei** neuter; (chemically) neutral; sterile

中性子 **chūseishi** neutron

中和 **chūwa** neutralize

9 中巻 **chūkan** middle volume (of three)

中南米 **Chūnanbei** Central and South America

中点 **chūten** midpoint

中途 **chūto** midway, halfway

中途半端 **chūto-hanpa** half finished, incomplete

中通 **chūdō(ri)** medium quality
nakadō(ri) intermediate street

中風 **chūbū, chūbu** paralysis, palsy

中段 **chūdan** halfway up a stairway/slope; center column (of print)

中洲 **nakasu** sandbank/shoal in the middle of a river

中型 **chūgata** medium size

中指 **nakayubi, chūshi** middle finger

中庭 **nakaniwa** courtyard

中柄 **chūgara** medium size, medium pattern, medium stature

中柱 **nakabashira** pillar in the middle of a room

中背 **chūzei** average height

中秋 **chūshū** 15th day of the eighth lunar month; mid-autumn

10 中値 **nakane** medium price, bid-and-asked price

中将 **chūjō** lieutenant general; vice-admiral

中陰 **chūin** seven-week mourning period

中部 **chūbu** central part **Chūbu** the central Honshū region

中高 **nakadaka** convex

中高音部 **chūkōonbu** alto, mezzo-soprano

中原 **chūgen** middle of a field; middle of a country; field of contest

中流 **chūryū** middle class; middle part of a river

中華 **Chūka** China

中華人民共和国 **Chūka Jinmin Kyōwakoku** People's Republic of China

中華民国 **Chūka Minkoku** Republic of China (Taiwan)

中華料理 **chūka ryōri** Chinese cooking/food

中宮 **chūgū** palace of the empress; empress; emperor's second consort

中島 **nakajima** island in a river or lake

中座 **chūza** leave before (a meeting) is over

中席 **nakaseki** the entertainment (scheduled by a music hall) for the second ten days of the month

中核 **chūkaku** kernel, core, nucleus

11 中隊 **chūtai** company, squadron

中道 **chūdō** middle-of-the-road

中道派 **chūdōha** centrists, middle-of-the-roaders

中庸 **chūyō** the golden mean, middle path, moderation

中脳 **chūnō** the midbrain

中黒 **nakaguro** the centered-dot punctuation mark (·)

中尉 **chūi** first lieutenant; lieutenant junior grade

中産階級 **chūsan kaikyū** middle class

中略 **chūryaku** omission of a part, ellipsis (…)

中断 **chūdan** break off, interrupt, suspend

中頃 **nakagoro** about the middle

12 中着 **nakagi** singlet worn between undershirt and outer clothing

中堅 **chūken** main body (of troops), center, backbone, mainstay, main-line

中堅企業 **chūken kigyō** medium-size business/company

中幅 **chūhaba** medium width

中葉 **chūyō** about the middle (of an era)

中期 **chūki** middle period

中越 **Chū-Etsu** China and Vietnam

中程 **nakahodo** middle, halfway

中絶 **chūzetsu** interruption, discontinuation, termination; abortion

中等 **chūtō** medium/secondary grade, average quality

中軸 **chūjiku** axis, pivot, central figure, key man

中距離 **chūkyori** medium-range, middle-distance
中飯 **chūhan** midday meal, lunch
中間 **chūkan** middle, midway, intermediate; midterm, interim
中間子 **chūkanshi** meson
中間層 **chūkansō** middle stratum/class
中間駅 **chūkan eki** intermediate station
13 中傷 **chūshō** slander, defamation
中農 **chūnō** middle-class farmer
中塗 **nakanu(ri)** second/next-to-last coating (of lacquer)
中幕 **nakamaku** middle performance (of a three-item kabuki program)
中腰 **chūgoshi** half-sitting/half-standing posture
中腹 **chūfuku** mountain side, halfway up
　　chū(p)para offended, in a huff
中数 **chūsū** arithmetic mean, average
中継 **chūkei** (remote broadcast) relay
15 中敷 **nakaji(ki)** spread inside, lay in the middle
中盤戦 **chūbansen** the middle game (in chess and other board games); the midst of an election campaign
中編 **chūhen** second volume; medium-length (novel)
中篇 **chūhen** second volume; medium-length (novel)
16 中興 **chūkō** restoration, revival
中衛 **chūei** middle guard (in volleyball); halfback (in soccer)

─────────── 2 ───────────

2 人中 **hitonaka** society, company, public
3 上中下 **jō-chū-ge** good-fair-poor; first-second-third class; volumes/parts 1, 2, 3 (of a 3-volume/3-part series)
口中 **kōchū** (interior of) the mouth
女中 **jochū** maid
山中 **yamanaka, sanchū** in the mountains
山中湖 **Yamanaka-ko** Lake Yamanaka
4 元中 **Genchū** (era, 1384–1390)
文中 **Bunchū** (era, 1372–1375)
水中 **suichū** underwater, in the water
日中 **Nit-Chū** Japan and China
　　nitchū during the day
　　hinaka broad daylight, daytime
火中 **kachū** in the fire, midst of the flames
心中 **shinjū** lovers' double suicide; murder-suicide **shinchū** in one's heart
5 生中継 **namachūkei** live (remote) broadcast
世中 **yo(no)naka** the world, life, the times
市中 **shichū** in the city; open market
正中 **seichū** the exact middle
　　Shōchū (era, 1324–1326)
正中線 **seichūsen** median line
6 年中 **nenjū** all year, year-round

年中行事 **nenjū gyōji** an annual event
老中 **rōjū** member of the shogun's council of elders
地中 **chichū** underground, subterranean
地中海 **Chichūkai** the Mediterranean Sea
在中 **zaichū** within
在中物 **zaichūbutsu** contents
忙中 **bōchū** during the busyness of work
米中 **Bei-Chū** America and China
7 身中 **shinchū** one's heart, inmost thoughts
対中 **tai-Chū** toward/with China
社中 **shachū** office staff; troupe
忌中 **kichū** in mourning
車中 **shachū** in the car/vehicle
車中談 **shachūdan** train interview
8 侍中 **jichū** imperial political adviser
命中 **meichū** hit, on-target impact
夜中 **yonaka** midnight, dead of night
　　yachū at night **yojū** all night
卒中 **sotchū** cerebral stroke, apoplexy
泥中 **deichū** in the mud
空中 **kūchū** in the air/sky, aerial
空中戦 **kūchūsen** air battle, aerial warfare
空中線 **kūchūsen** antenna
居中 **kyochū** standing in-between
居中調停 **kyochū-chōtei** mediation, arbitration
国中 **kokuchū, kunijū** the whole country
的中 **tekichū** hit the mark, come true, guess right
房中 **bōchū** in the room/bedroom
9 陣中 **jinchū** in the field, at the front
連中 **renchū, renjū** companions, party, company, crowd, clique
途中 **tochū** on the way, en route
途中下車 **tochū gesha** stopover, layover
途中計時 **tochū keiji** lap time (in races)
洛中 **rakuchū** in Kyōto
海中 **kaichū** in the sea
胎中 **taichū** in the womb
背中 **senaka** one's back
背中合 **senakaa(wase)** back to back
食中 **shokuata(ri)** food poisoning, stomach upset
食中毒 **shokuchūdoku** food poisoning
10 陸中 **Rikuchū** (ancient kuni, Iwate-ken)
華中 **Kachū** central China
家中 **iejū** the whole family; all over the house **kachū** the whole family; retainer
宮中 **kyūchū** imperial court
座中 **zachū** in the room; member of the troupe
胸中 **kyōchū** one's bosom, heart, feelings
胴中 **dōnaka** torso
書中 **shochū** in the letter/document/book
病中 **byōchū** during an illness
11 野中 **nonaka** in a field

道中 **dōchū** travel, journey
道中記 **dōchūki** traveler's journal
術中 **jutchū** trick, strategem, ruse
脳中 **nōchū** in one's head
眼中 **ganchū** in one's eyes/consideration
船中 **senchū** in/aboard the ship
雪中 **setchū** in/through the snow
12 備中 **Bitchū** (ancient kuni, Okayama-ken)
渦中 **kachū** maelstrom, vortex
喪中 **mochū** period of mourning
就中 **nakanzuku** especially
御中 **onchū** To: (name of addressee organization), Dear Sirs:
寒中 **kanchū** the cold season
掌中 **shōchū** in the hand; pocket (edition)
掌中玉 **shōchū (no) tama** apple of one's eye
暑中 **shochū** midsummer, hot season
暑中見舞 **shochū mima(i)** inquiry after (someone's) health in the hot season
最中 **saichū, sanaka** the midst/height of
monaka middle; bean-jam-filled wafers
越中 **Etchū** (ancient kuni, Toyama-ken)
集中 **shūchū** concentration
閑中 **kanchū** during one's free time
13 豊中 **Toyonaka** (city, Ōsaka-fu)
夢中 **muchū** rapture; absorption, intentness; frantic
腹中 **fukuchū** in one's heart
暗中 **anchū** in the dark; in secret
暗中飛躍 **anchū hiyaku** secret maneuvering
暗中摸索 **anchū mosaku** groping in the dark
禁中 **kinchū** the court, the imperial household
戦中 **senchū** during the war
意中 **ichū** one's mind/thoughts
意中人 **ichū (no) hito** the one in one's thoughts, one's beloved
話中 **hana(shi)chū** in the midst of speaking; (phone is) busy
鉛中毒 **enchūdoku** lead poisoning
14 獄中 **gokuchū** in prison
15 履中 **Richū** (emperor, 400–405)
熱中 **netchū** be enthusiastic/crazy about, be engrossed/absorbed in
敵中 **tekichū** midst of the enemy
16 懐中 **kaichū** one's pocket
懐中物 **kaichūmono** pocketbook, wallet
懐中時計 **kaichū-dokei** pocket watch
懐中電灯 **kaichū dentō** flashlight
懐中鏡 **kaichūkagami** pocket mirror
磧中 **sekichū** in the desert
17 講中 **kōjū, kōchū** religious association
18 難中難 **nanchū (no) nan** the hardest of all
19 霧中 **muchū** in the fog
霧中信号 **muchū shingō** fog signal
22 嚢中 **nōchū** in the bag; in one's purse
嚢中錐 **nōchū (no) kiri** Talent will show.

───────── 3 ─────────

1 一日中 **ichinichi-jū** all day long
一年中 **ichinen-jū** all year long
3 工事中 **kōjichū** Under Construction
上京中 **jōkyōchū** in the capital
下女中 **shimojochū** kitchen maid
小夜中 **sayonaka** midnight
4 中肉中背 **chūniku-chūzei** medium height and build
日本中 **Nihonjū, Nipponjū** all over Japan
午前中 **gozenchū** all morning
5 世界中 **sekaijū** all over the world
外出中 **gaishutsuchū** while away/out, out (of the office)
6 在日中 **zai-Nichichū** while in Japan
在任中 **zaininchū** while in office
在京中 **zaikyōchū** while in the capital
在官中 **zaikanchū** while in office
在獄中 **zaigokuchū** while in prison
自家中毒 **jika chūdoku** autotoxemia
7 妊娠中 **ninshinchū** during pregnancy
妊娠中絶 **ninshin chūzetsu** abortion
局外中立 **kyokugai chūritsu** neutrality
見習中 **minara(i)chū** in training
9 昼日中 **hiruhinaka** daytime, broad daylight
食事中 **shokujichū** during a meal
10 修理中 **shūrichū** under repair
真只中 **ma(t)tadanaka** right in the middle of
真夜中 **mayonaka** dead of night, midnight
真唯中 **ma(t)tadanaka** right in the middle of
真最中 **ma(s)saichū** right in the midst/ middle of, at the height of
進軍中 **shingunchū** on the march
留守中 **rusuchū** during one's absence
11 脳卒中 **nōsotchū** cerebral apoplexy
12 開会中 **kaikaichū** during the session
開催中 **kaisaichū** in session
13 滞在中 **taizaichū** during one's stay
数日中 **sūjitsuchū** within a few days
戦争中 **sensōchū** during the war
戦時中 **senjichū** during the war, wartime
16 薬籠中物 **yakurōchū (no) mono** at one's beck and call

───────── 4 ─────────

4 五里霧中 **gori-muchū** in a fog, groping in the dark
5 四六時中 **shirokujichū** 24 hours a day, constantly
6 年百年中 **nenbyaku-nenjū** all year round
百発百中 **hyappatsu-hyakuchū** on target every time
12 御多忙中 **gotabōchū** while you are so busy
無我夢中 **muga-muchū** total absorption, ecstasy
無理心中 **muri shinjū** murder-suicide
13 獅子身中虫 **shishi-shinchū (no) mushi** treacherous friend

丹 → 丹 0a4.34

0a4.41 / 1796

弔 **CHŌ, tomura(u)** mourn
tomura(i) funeral

──────── 1 ────────

4 弔文 **chōbun** funeral address
6 弔合戦 **tomura(i) gassen** battle to avenge a death
10 弔砲 **chōhō** artillery funeral salute
11 弔問 **chōmon** condolence call/visit
12 弔詞 **chōshi** message of condolence, memorial address
13 弔意 **chōi** condolences, sympathy
弔辞 **chōji** message of condolence, memorial address
弔電 **chōden** telegram of condolence
14 弔旗 **chōki** flag draped in black, flag at half-staff
弔歌 **chōka** dirge
15 弔慰 **chōi** condolences, sympathy
弔慰金 **chōikin** condolence money
20 弔鐘 **chōshō** funeral bell

──────── 2 ────────

8 追弔 **tsuichō** mourning
15 慶弔 **keichō** congratulations and condolences

0a4.42

卅 **SŌ** thirty

0a4.43

丰 **BŌ, FU** beautiful

世 → 0a5.37

0a4.44

尹 **IN** (an ancient government rank)

0a4.45

毌 **KAN** pierce

0a4.46 / 1193

井 **SEI, SHŌ, i** (water) well

──────── 1 ────────

3 井上 **Inoue** (surname)
4 井水 **seisui** well water
井戸 **ido** (water) well
井戸端 **idobata** well side
井戸端会議 **idobata kaigi** well-side gossip
12 井筒 **izutsu** well curb/wall
16 井頭 **I(no)kashira** (park in Tōkyō)

──────── 2 ────────

3 大井川 **Ōigawa** (river, Shizuoka-ken)
4 天井 **tenjō** ceiling
天井灯 **tenjōtō** ceiling light
天井板 **tenjō ita** ceiling boards
天井桟敷 **tenjō sajiki** the upper gallery
天井裏 **tenjōura** between ceiling and roof
5 市井 **shisei** the streets; the town
古井戸 **furuido** old unused well
7 車井戸 **kuruma ido** well with a pulley and rope
8 油井 **yusei** oil well
油井戸 **aburaido** oil well/spring
11 掘井戸 **ho(ri)ido** a well
12 筒井 **tsutsui** round well
筒井筒 **tsutsuizutsu** wall/curb of a round well
13 福井 **Fukui** (city, Fukui-ken)
福井県 **Fukui-ken** (prefecture)
28 鑿井 **sakusei** well drilling

──────── 3 ────────

3 丸天井 **marutenjō** arched ceiling, vault
6 吊天井 **tsu(ri)tenjō** suspended ceiling
8 青天井 **aotenjō** the blue sky
10 格天井 **gōtenjō** coffered ceiling
11 掘抜井戸 **ho(ri)nu(ki) ido** a well
組天井 **ku(mi)tenjō** fretwork ceiling
釣天井 **tsu(ri) tenjō** ceiling rigged to fall onto and kill someone

0a4.47

毋 **MU, BU** not, do not

──────── 0a5 ──────────

以	丞	丕	癶	夘	北	矛	巧	叵	包	正	乍	瓦
5.1	2c4.3	5.2	5.3	5.4	5.5	5.6	5.7	5.8	5.9	2m3.3	5.10	5.11

0a4

互	丘	凸	凹	且	必	乎	斥	矢	左	丙	出	民
0a6.2	5.12	5.13	5.14	5.15	5.16	5.17	5.18	5.19	5.20	5.21	5.22	5.23
半	本	末	未	失	生	弁	勿	甘	央	甲	由	母
5.24	5.25	5.26	5.27	5.28	5.29	5.30	5.31	5.32	5.33	5.34	5.35	5.36
世	史	申	丼	冊	冊	冉	冊	弗				
5.37	5.38	5.39	5.40	5.41	5.42	5.43	0a5.43	5.44				

0a5.1 / 46

以

I, mot(te) with, by (means of); because of; in view of

――――――― 1 ―――――――

3 以上 **ijō** or more, more than, over, above, beyond; the above; since, so long as; that is all
以下 **ika** or less, less than; under, below; the following
4 以内 **inai** within, not more than
以心伝心 **ishin-denshin** telepathy, tacit understanding
5 以外 **igai** except, other than
7 以来 **irai** since
9 以降 **ikō** on and after, beginning ...
以前 **izen** ago; formerly
以後 **igo** from now/then on, (t)henceforth
12 以遠 **ien** farther than, beyond

――――――― 2 ―――――――

8 尚以 **naomo(tte)** still more, all the more
所以 **yuen** the reason, why
9 前以 **maemot(te)** beforehand, previously

――――――― 3 ―――――――

6 有史以来 **yūshi irai** since the dawn of history

瓜 → **0a6.3**

丞 → **2c4.3**

0a5.2

不

HI big, grand

0a5.3

癶

HATSU, HACHI stand back-to-back; go

0a5.4

卯

KAN young (child)

0a5.5 / 73

北

HOKU, kita north

――――――― 1 ―――――――

3 北大西洋 **Kita Taiseiyō** the North Atlantic
北上 **hokujō** go north
北上川 **Kitakamigawa** (river, Miyagi-ken)
4 北斗七星 **Hokuto Shichisei** the Big Dipper
北斗星 **Hokutosei** the Big Dipper
北天 **hokuten** the northern sky
北支 **Hokushi** North China
北支事変 **Hokushi jihen** the Marco Polo Bridge incident
北方 **hoppō** north, northward, northern
5 北北西 **hokuhokusei** north-northwest
北北東 **hokuhokutō** north-northeast
北半球 **Kita Hankyū** Northern Hemisphere
北氷洋 **Hoppyōyō, Hokuhyōyō** the Arctic Ocean
6 北西 **hokusei** northwest
北向 **kitamu(ki)** facing north
北光 **hokkō** the northern lights, aurora borealis
北回帰線 **Kita Kaikisen** the Tropic of Cancer
北米 **Hokubei** North America
7 北宋 **Hokusō** early Sung dynasty (960–1127)
8 北東 **hokutō** northeast
北京 **Pekin** Peking, Beijing
北岸 **hokugan** north coast, north bank
北国 **hokkoku, kitaguni** northern provinces, northern countries
北枕 **kitamakura** sleeping with one's head toward the north
北欧 **Hokuō** Northern Europe
北欧人 **Hokuōjin** a Northern European, a Scandinavian
9 北風 **kitakaze, hokufū** north wind

北洋 **hokuyō** northern sea
北海 **hokkai** northern sea
     Hokkai the North Sea
     北海道 **Hokkaidō** (prefecture)
10 北陸地方 **Hokuriku chihō** the Hokuriku
     region (Fukui, Ishikawa, Toyama,
     Niigata prefectures)
北部 **hokubu** north, northern part
北進 **hokushin** advance northward
11 北側 **kitagawa, hokusoku** north side
北清事変 **Hokushin jihen** the North China
     incident, the Boxer uprising
12 北極 **hokkyoku** the North Pole
北極光 **hokkyokukō** the northern lights,
     aurora borealis
北極海 **Hokkyokukai** the Arctic Ocean
北極星 **hokkyokusei** the North Star, Polaris
北極圏 **hokkyokuken** the Arctic Circle, the
     Arctic
北極熊 **hokkyokuguma** polar bear
北朝 **Hokuchō** the Northern Dynasty
北朝鮮 **Kita Chōsen** North Korea
14 北境 **hokkyō** northern boundary/frontier
北端 **hokutan** northern extremity/tip
16 北緯 **hokui** north latitude
17 北鮮 **Hokusen** North Korea

———————— 2 ————————

5 北北西 **hokuhokusei** north-northwest
北北東 **hokuhokutō** north-northeast
正北 **seihoku** due north
台北 **Taipei, Taihoku** Taipei (capital of
     Taiwan)
6 西北 **seihoku** northwest
江北 **kōhoku** north of the (Yangtze/Yangzi)
     river
8 東北 **tōhoku** northeast   **Tōhoku** (northeast-
     ern Honshū)
河北 **kahoku** north of the (Yellow) river
9 南北 **nanboku** north and south
南北朝 **Nanbokuchō** the Northern and
     Southern Dynasties (439–589 in China,
     1336–1392 in Japan)
南北戦争 **Nanboku Sensō** the War Between
     the States, the (U.S.) Civil War
10 華北 **Kahoku** north China
朔北 **sakuhoku** north
11 敗北 **haiboku** defeat
12 極北 **kyokuhoku** the far north, North Pole

———————— 3 ————————

9 南船北馬 **nansen-hokuba** constant travel-
     ing, restless wandering

———————— 4 ————————

8 東西南北 **tōzainanboku** north, south, east,
     and west

0a5.6 / 773

矛

     MU, hoko halberd

———————— 1 ————————

6 矛先 **hokosaki** point of a spear; aim of an
     attack
9 矛盾 **mujun** contradiction

0a5.7 / 1627

巧

     KŌ, taku(mi) skill

———————— 1 ————————

4 巧手 **kōshu** a skill; skilled worker
7 巧技 **kōgi** skilled workmanship
巧妙 **kōmyō** skillful, clever, deft
巧言 **kōgen** flattery
巧言令色 **kōgen-reishoku** ingratiating
     geniality
8 巧拙 **kōsetsu** skill, proficiency
巧知 **kōchi** skilled and knowledgeable
巧者 **kōsha** skillful, adept, tactful
16 巧緻 **kōchi** elaborate, finely wrought

———————— 2 ————————

3 大巧 **taikō** great skill
6 老巧 **rōkō** veteran, experienced
7 技巧 **gikō** art, craftsmanship, technique
技巧的 **gikōteki** skillful
9 便巧 **benkō** flatter, curry favor
11 悪巧 **warudaku(mi)** wiles, scheme, plot,
     machinations
13 傾巧 **keikō** flatter, toady, curry favor
14 精巧 **seikō** exquisite (workmanship),
     sophisticated (equipment)
16 機巧 **kikō** contrivance; cleverness
17 繊巧 **senkō** detailed workmanship

———————— 3 ————————

3 小利巧 **korikō** clever, smart
12 無技巧 **mugikō** artless

0a5.8

卮 卮

     SHI large winecup; apt, fitting

0a5.9 / 804

包 包

     HŌ, tsutsu(mu) wrap; cover,
     envelop; conceal   **tsutsu(mi)**
     package   **kuru(mu)** wrap up,
     tuck in   **kuru(meru)** lump
     together

———————— 1 ————————

2 包丁 **hōchō** kitchen knife; cooking

4 包込 **tsutsu(mi)ko(mu)** wrap up
5 包皮 **hōhi** the foreskin
　包皮切断 **hōhi setsudan** circumcision
7 包含 **hōgan** include, comprehend; imply
　包囲 **hōi** surround, encircle, besiege
8 包直 **tsutsu(mi)nao(su)** rewrap
　包茎 **hōkei** phimosis
9 包括 **hōkatsu** include, comprehend
　包括的 **hōkatsuteki** inclusive, comprehensive
10 包帯 **hōtai** bandage, dressing
　包容 **hōyō** comprehend, embrace, imply; tolerate
　包紙 **tsutsu(mi)gami** wrapping paper
12 包装 **hōsō** packaging, packing, wrapping
13 包隠 **tsutsu(mi)kaku(shi)** concealment
　包摂 **hōsetsu** connotation
　包飾 **tsutsu(mi)kaza(ri)** ostentation
15 包蔵 **hōzō** contain, comprehend; imply; entertain (an idea)

――――― 2 ―――――

3 上包 **uwazutsu(mi)** cover, wrapper, envelope
　小包 **kozutsumi** parcel, package
4 内包 **naihō** contain, involve, connote
8 空包 **kūhō** a blank (cartridge)
10 紙包 **kamizutsu(mi)** wrapped in paper
11 梱包 **konpō** packing, packaging
16 薬包 **yakuhō** gun cartridge
　薬包紙 **yakuhōshi** a paper wrapping for a dose of medicine
　薦包 **komozutsu(mi)** wrapped in straw matting

正 → **2m3.3**

0a5.10

乍

SA, -naga(ra) while, although; while, during

――――― 2 ―――――

8 居乍 **inaga(ra)** as one sits, without stirring
10 恐乍 **oso(re)naga(ra)** most humbly/respectfully
8 然乍 **shika(shi)naga(ra)** however
15 憚乍 **habaka(ri)naga(ra)** I dare say, Excuse me, but ...

0a5.11

瓦

GA, kawara tile
guramu gram

――――― 1 ―――――

8 瓦版 **kawaraban** tile engraving, tile block print

9 瓦屋 **kawaraya** tilemaker; tiler; tile-roofed house
　瓦屋根 **kawara yane** tiled roof
10 瓦家 **kawaraya** tile-roofed house
12 瓦斯 **gasu** gas
13 瓦解 **gakai** collapse, fall to pieces
20 瓦礫 **gareki** rubble; rubbish

――――― 2 ―――――

8 青瓦台 **Seigadai** the Blue House (South Korean presidential palace)
10 鬼瓦 **onigawara** (gargoyle-like) ridgepole-end tile
12 棟瓦 **munagawara** ridge tile
13 煉瓦 **renga** brick

――――― 3 ―――――

4 木煉瓦 **mokurenga** wooden blocks/bricks
15 敷煉瓦 **shi(ki)renga** paving bricks

――――― 4 ―――――

9 耐火煉瓦 **taika renga** firebrick

互 → 瓦 **0a6.2**

0a5.12 / 1357

丘

KYŪ, oka hill

――――― 1 ―――――

10 丘陵 **kyūryō** hill

――――― 2 ―――――

4 片丘 **kataoka** a rise, hill steeper on one side
5 比丘 **biku** Buddhist priest
　比丘尼 **bikuni** Buddhist priestess
9 段丘 **dankyū** terrace, bench
　砂丘 **sakyū** dune

0a5.13 / 1892

凸

TOTSU protrusion, bulge

――――― 1 ―――――

5 凸凹 **dekoboko** uneven, bumpy, jagged
7 凸角 **tokkaku** a salient (angle)
8 凸版 **toppan** letterpress, relief (printing)
9 凸面 **totsumen** convex (surface)
　凸面鏡 **totsumenkyō** convex mirror/lens
19 凸鏡 **tokkyō** convex lens

――――― 2 ―――――

5 凹凸 **ōtotsu** uneven, irregular, jagged; concavo-convexy

0a5.14 / 1893

凹 Ō indentation, depression **heko(mu)** be dented, sink, collapse, give in, cave in; be daunted **heko(masu)** dent in; humiliate, put down **kubo** hollow, depression

――――――――― 1 ―――――――――
5 凹凸 **ōtotsu** uneven, irregular, jagged; concavo-convex
6 凹地 **ōchi** hollow, basin, depression
7 凹形 **ōkei** concavity; intaglio
8 凹版 **ōhan, ōban** intaglio (printing)
　凹所 **ōsho** concavity, hollow, depression
9 凹面 **ōmen** concave (surface)
　凹面鏡 **ōmenkyō** concave mirror/lens
11 凹眼鏡 **ōgankyō** concave-lens eyeglasses
13 凹溜 **kubotama(ri)** a hollow; a pond formed in a hollow

――――――――― 2 ―――――――――
5 凸凹 **dekoboko** uneven, bumpy, jagged

0a5.15 / 1926

且 SHO, ka(tsu) and

――――――――― 1 ―――――――――
2 且又 **ka(tsu)mata** and, moreover

――――――――― 2 ―――――――――
8 尚且 **naoka(tsu)** furthermore; and yet

0a5.16 / 520

 HITSU certain, sure **kanara(zu)** surely, be sure to, without fail, invariably

――――――――― 1 ―――――――――
6 必死 **hisshi** certain death; desperate, frantic
9 必要 **hitsuyō** necessary
　必要物 **hitsuyōbutsu** necessities
　必要品 **hitsuyōhin** necessities
　必要悪 **hitsuyōaku** a necessary evil
10 必修 **hisshū** required (subject)
　必修科目 **hisshū kamoku** required subject
12 必須 **hissu** indispensable, essential, compulsory
　必須科目 **hissu kamoku** required subject
　必勝 **hisshō** sure victory
　必然 **hitsuzen** inevitability, necessity
　必然性 **hitsuzensei** inevitability, necessity
13 必滅 **hitsumetsu** doomed to perish, mortal
　必携 **hikkei** indispensable; handbook, manual
14 必読 **hitsudoku** required reading, a must read
　必需 **hitsuju** necessary
　必需品 **hitsujuhin** necessities, essentials

4 不必要 **fuhitsuyō** unnecessary
――――――――― 3 ―――――――――
9 信賞必罰 **shinshō-hitsubatsu** sure punishment and sure reward

0a5.17

乎 KO, ka, ya (question-mark particle)

――――――――― 1 ―――――――――
5 乎古止点 **okototen** marks to aid in reading Chinese classics
――――――――― 2 ―――――――――
7 牢乎 **rōko** firm, solid, inflexible
11 断乎 **danko** firm, resolute
15 確乎 **kakko** firm, determined
――――――――― 3 ―――――――――
11 断々乎 **dandanko** firm, resolute

0a5.18 / 1401

斥 SEKI repel, repulse; scout, reconnoiter **shirizo(keru)** repel, repulse; reject

――――――――― 1 ―――――――――
2 斥力 **sekiryoku** repulsion, repulsive force
10 斥候 **sekkō** scout, patrol, spy
――――――――― 2 ―――――――――
9 除斥 **joseki** exclude, expel, reject
11 排斥 **haiseki** exclude, expel, ostracize, boycott
17 擯斥 **hinseki** reject, disdain, ostracize

0a5.19 / 213

矢 SHI, ya arrow

――――――――― 1 ―――――――――
4 矢文 **yabumi** letter tied to an arrow
5 矢玉 **yadama** arrows and bullets
　矢立 **yata(te)** portable brush-and-ink case
6 矢羽 **yabane** arrow feathers
　矢印 **yajirushi** arrow
　矢先 **yasaki** arrowhead; moment, point
　矢叫 **yasake(bi)** archers' shout (upon loosing a volley of arrows)
7 矢来 **yarai** picket fence, palisade, stockade
9 矢飛白 **yagasuri** arrow-feather pattern
　矢庭 **yaniwa (ni)** suddenly, immediately
　矢面 **yaomote** facing incoming arrows, brunt
　矢柄 **yagara** arrow shaft
10 矢師 **yashi** arrow maker, fletcher
　矢根 **ya(no)ne** arrowhead

12 矢場 **yaba** archery ground/range
矢絣 **yagasuri** arrow-feather pattern
矢筈 **yahazu** nock, notch of an arrow
矢筒 **yazutsu** quiver
13 矢継早 **yatsu(gi)baya (ni)** rapid-fire, in quick succession
14 矢種 **yadane** remaining arrows

————————— 2 —————————

1 一矢報 **isshi (o) muku(iru)** shoot back, retort
3 弓矢 **yumiya** bow and arrow
弓矢八幡 **yumiya hachiman** god of war
4 火矢 **hiya** flaming/incendiary arrow
6 竹矢来 **takeyarai** bamboo palisade
7 吹矢 **fu(ki)ya** blowgun, dart
8 毒矢 **dokuya** poisoned arrow
9 通矢 **tō(shi)ya** long-distance archery
10 逸矢 **so(re)ya** stray arrow
流矢 **naga(re)ya** stray arrow
徒矢 **adaya** arrow which misses the target
11 掛矢 **ka(ke)ya** large mallet
12 遠矢 **tōya** long-distance arrow/archery
16 嚆矢 **kōshi** arrow rigged to buzz as it flies (shot at start of battle); beginning, kickoff
19 鏑矢 **kaburaya** arrow rigged to buzz as it flies

————————— 3 —————————

5 白羽矢立 **shiraha (no) ya (ga) ta(tsu)** be selected (for a task/post)
石火矢 **ishibiya** (ancient) cannon
12 無理矢理 **muriyari** forcibly, under compulsion
13 滅多矢鱈 **mettayatara** indiscriminate, frantic

0a5.20 / 75

左

SA, hidari left

————————— 1 —————————

3 左大臣 **sadaijin** Minister of the Left
4 左辺 **sahen** left side
左手 **hidarite** left hand
左方 **sahō** the left
左心房 **sashinbō** the left auricle
左心室 **sashinshitsu** the left ventricle
5 左右 **sayū** left and right; control, dominate, govern, influence
6 左回 **hidarimawa(ri)** counterclockwise
左団扇 **hidari uchiwa** (living in) ease and luxury
7 左折 **sasetsu** left turn
左利 **hidariki(ki)** left-handed; left-hander; a drinker
8 左官 **sakan** plasterer
左岸 **sagan** left bank
9 左巻 **hidarima(ki)** counterclockwise; eccentric, crazy

左前 **hidarimae** the wrong way, folding the left side of a kimono over the right side; adversity
左派 **saha** leftists
10 左党 **satō** leftists, opposition party; drinker
左記 **saki** the following
11 左側 **hidarigawa** left side
左側通行 **hidarigawa tsūkō** Keep Left
左寄 **hidariyo(ri)** leaning toward the left
左眼 **sagan** left eye
左舷 **sagen** port (not starboard)
12 左腕 **hidariude** left arm **sawan** left-handed pitcher
13 左傾 **sakei** leftist, radical
14 左遷 **sasen** demotion
左様 **sayō** such, like that; yes, indeed; well, let me see
17 左翼 **sayoku** left wing, leftist; left field (in baseball)
21 左顧右眄 **sako-uben** irresolution, vacillation

————————— 2 —————————

3 土左衛門 **dozaemon** drowned person
5 右左 **migi-hidari** right and left
7 言左右託 **gen (o) sayū (ni) taku(suru)** equivocate, be noncommittal
12 極左 **kyokusa** ultraleft
最左翼 **saisayoku** ultraleft
証左 **shōsa** evidence, proof

————————— 3 —————————

5 右往左往 **uō-saō** go hither and thither
右顧左眄 **uko-saben** look right and left; vacillate, waver
9 前後左右 **zengo-sayū** in all directions

0a5.21 / 984

丙

HEI third in a series, "C"
hinoe third calendar sign

————————— 3 —————————

5 甲乙丙 **kō-otsu-hei** A, B, C; No. 1, 2, 3

0a5.22 / 53

出

SHUTSU, SUI, de(ru), ide(ru) go/come out, appear, emerge **de** turnout; one's turn; flow; origin **da(su), ida(su)** put/take out; send; (as verb suffix) begin to **da(shi)** broth; pretext

————————— 1 —————————

0 お出で, お出 **(o)i(de), (o)ide** come; go; be
2 出入口 **deiriguchi** entrance/exit
出入国 **shutsunyūkoku** emigration and immigration
出力 **shutsuryoku** output

3 出刃 **deba** pointed kitchen knife
出刃庖丁 **debabōchō** pointed kitchen knife
出口 **deguchi** exit; outlet
4 出不精 **debushō** stay-at-home
出水 **shussui, demizu** flood, inundation, freshet
出火 **shukka** (outbreak of) fire
出方 **dekata** attitude; a move
出欠 **shukketsu** attendance or absence
5 出生 **shusshō, shussei** birth
出生年月日 **shusshō nengappi, shussei nengappi** date of birth
出生地 **shusshōchi, shusseichi** birthplace
出生届 **shusseitodoke** report of birth
出生率 **shusshōritsu, shusseiritsu** birth rate
出生数 **shusseisū, shusshōsū** number of live births
出世 **shusse** succeed in life, get ahead
出汁 **da(shi)jiru, dashi** broth, (soup) stock
出払 **dehara(u)** be all out of, have none left
出札 **shussatsu** issuing tickets
出札口 **shussatsuguchi** ticket window
出処 **shussho, dedokoro** source, origin
出目 **deme** protruding eyes, goggle-eyed
6 出任 **demaka(se)** saying whatever comes to mind
出合 **dea(u)** happen to meet, run into; rendezvous **da(shi)a(u)** contribute jointly, share the expenses
出合頭 **dea(i)gashira** upon running into each other, upon happening to meet
出廷 **shuttei** appear in court
出迎 **demuka(eru)** (go/come to) meet (someone upon his arrival)
出先 **desaki** destination
出向 **demu(ku)** go to, leave for, repair to **shukkō** repair to; be on loan (to a subsidiary), be seconded (to another company), temporary transfer
出向社員 **shukkō shain** employee on loan to a subsididary/another company
出帆 **shuppan** set sail, depart
出光 **Idemitsu** (surname; company name)
出回 **demawa(ru)** appear on the market
出血 **shukketsu** bleeding, hemorrhage
7 出身 **shusshin** (as suffix) originally from ...
出身地 **shusshinchi** native place, birthplace
出来 **deki(ru)** can, be able to, be possible; be done, be finished, be ready; be made of; be formed; come into being
出来上 **dekia(garu)** be finished, be ready; be cut out for
出来心 **dekigokoro** sudden impulse, whim
出来合 **dekia(u)** be ready-made; become intimate with
出来事 **dekigoto** incident, event, happenings

出来物 **dekimono** skin eruption, rash, pimple, boil, a growth
出来具合 **dekiguai** workmanship, result, performance
出来映 **dekiba(e)** result, effect, workmanship, performance
出来値 **dekine** selling price
出兵 **shuppei** dispatch/send troops
出没 **shutsubotsu** frequently appear (then disappear)
出抜 **da(shi)nu(ku)** forestall, anticipate, get the jump on, circumvent **da(shi)nu(ke ni)** all of a sudden, unexpectedly
出花 **debana** the first brew (of tea), fresh-brewed tea
出社 **shussha** go/come to the office
出戻 **demodo(ri)** divorced woman (back at her parents' home)
出初 **dezome** first appearance, debut; firemen's New Year's demonstrations
出初式 **dezomeshiki** firemen's New Year's demonstrations
出足 **deashi** start
8 出版 **shuppan** publishing
出版社 **shuppansha** publishing house, publisher
出版物 **shuppanbutsu** a publication
出版費 **shuppanhi** publishing costs
出版業 **shuppangyō** the publishing business
出奔 **shuppon** run away/off, abscond
出典 **shutten** source, authority
出征 **shussei** depart for the front, go to war
出芽 **shutsuga** germinate, sprout
出店 **demise** branch store **shutten** open a new store
出国 **shukkoku** departure from a country
出物 **demono** rash, boil; secondhand article **da(shi)mono** performance, program
出放題 **dehōdai** free flow; saying whatever comes to mind
出所 **shussho** source, origin; be released from prison **dedokoro** source, origin
出金 **shukkin** defray, pay; invest money
9 出発 **shuppatsu** departure
出発点 **shuppatsuten** starting point, point of departure
出陣 **shutsujin** depart for the front
出前 **demae** cooked-food home delivery **da(shi)mae** one's share (of the expenses)
出城 **dejiro** branch castle
出品 **shuppin** exhibit, display
出品者 **shuppinsha** exhibitor
出品物 **shuppinbutsu** an exhibit
10 出郷 **shukkyō** leave one's home town
出捐 **shutsuen** donate, contribute, bestow
出荷 **shukka** shipment, consignment

出家 **shukke** become a priest/monk; priest, monk
出席 **shusseki** attendance
出席者 **shussekisha** those present, the attendance
出席率 **shussekiritsu** percentage of attendance
出席簿 **shussekibo** roll book, attendance record
出格子 **degōshi** projecting lattice, latticed bay window
出納 **suitō** receipts and disbursements
出納係 **suitōgakari** cashier; teller
出納簿 **suitōbo** account book
出航 **shukkō** departure, sailing
出馬 **shutsuba** ride into battle; go in person; run for election
11 出動 **shutsudō** be sent/called out, take the field
出遅 **deoku(re), da(shi)oku(re)** off to a late start, belated
出涸 **degara(shi)** thin (tea), insipid
出掛 **deka(keru)** go out, set out **de(gake)** about to go out
出猟 **shutsuryō** going hunting
出張 **shutchō** business trip **deba(ri)** projection, ledge
出張店 **shutchōten** branch store
出張所 **shutchōjo** branch office
出張員 **shutchōin** agent, representative, dispatched official
出窓 **demado** bay window
出殻 **da(shi)gara** used tea leaves, (coffee) grounds
出現 **shutsugen** appear, show up
出産 **shussan** childbirth
出盛 **desaka(ri)** best time for, season for **desaka(ru)** appear in abundance
出船 **defune, debune** setting sail; outgoing ship
12 出勤 **shukkin** go/come to work
出勤日 **shukkinbi** workday
出勤簿 **shukkinbo** work attendance record
出港 **shukkō** leave port, put out to sea
出場 **shutsujō** appear on stage, perform; participate in, enter (a competition)
出超 **shutchō** excess of exports over imports, favorable balance of trade (short for 輸出超過)
出揃 **desoro(u)** appear all together, be all present
出棺 **shukkan** carry a coffin out
出塁 **shutsurui** get on base (in baseball)
出番 **deban** one's turn
出歯 **deba, de(p)pa** protruding tooth, buckteeth

出費 **shuppi** expenses, disbursements
出雲 **Izumo** (ancient kuni, Shimane-ken)
13 出際 **degiwa** the time of setting out
出損 **desoko(nau)** fail to go/come
出資 **shusshi** investment, financing, contribution
出資金 **shusshikin** investment, capital
14 出演 **shutsuen** appear on stage, play, perform
出獄 **shutsugoku** release from prison
出精 **shussei** diligence, industriousness
15 出撃 **shutsugeki** sortie, sally
出穂 **shussui** (grain) coming into ears
出稼 **dekase(gi)** working away from home
16 出稽古 **degeiko** giving lessons at the students' homes
出頭 **shuttō** appear, attend, be present
18 出藍 **shutsuran** excelling one's teacher
出題 **shutsudai** propose a question, set a problem
19 出願 **shutsugan** application

--------- 2 ---------

2 人出 **hitode** turnout, crowd
3 大出来 **ōdeki** a great success, well done
上出来 **jōdeki** good performance, well done
口出 **kuchida(shi)** meddling, butting in
小出 **koda(shi)** (take/dole out) in small quantities, bit by bit
山出 **yamada(shi)** bumpkin, from the country
4 不出来 **fudeki** poorly made, unsatisfactory
幻出 **genshutsu** appear as a phantom, appear dimly
内出血 **naishukketsu** internal bleeding/hemorrhage
切出 **ki(ri)da(su)** cut and carry out (timber); broach, bring up (a subject) **ki(ri)da(shi)** pointed knife; logging; (meat) scraps; broaching (a subject)
支出 **shishutsu** expenditure, disbursement
支出額 **shishutsugaku** (amount of) expenditures
手出 **teda(shi)** interfere, have a hand in; strike the first blow
引出 **hi(ki)da(shi)** (desk) drawer
日出 **hi(no)de** sunrise
5 生出 **u(mi)da(su)** bring forth, produce, yield
申出 **mō(shi)de(ru)** offer, submit, report, request **mō(shi)i(de)** proposal; request, application, claim; report, notice
仕出 **shida(shi)** catering
他出 **tashutsu** going out
外出 **gaishutsu, sotode** go/step out
外出中 **gaishutsuchū** while away/out, out (of the office)
外出好 **gaishutsuzu(ki)** gadabout
外出嫌 **gaishutsugira(i)** a stay-at-home

払出 **hara(i)da(su)** pay out, disburse; drive away

打出 **u(chi)da(su)** begin to beat; open fire; hammer out; end, be over   **u(tte)de(ru), u(chi)de(ru)** sally forth, come forward **u(chi)da(shi)** close (of a show); embossing; delivery (of a ball)

叩出 **tata(ki)da(su)** begin to beat; drive out; dismiss

6 死出旅 **shide (no) tabi** journey to the next world

再出 **saishutsu** reappear, re-emerge

再出発 **saishuppatsu** start over, make a fresh start

仮出所 **karishussho** release on parole, out on bail

仮出獄 **karishutsugoku** release on parole, out on bail

考出 **kanga(e)da(su)** think/work out, devise; recall, remember; begin to think

汲出 **ku(mi)da(su)** bail/scoop/pump out

吐出 **ha(ki)da(su)** vomit, disgorge, spew out

吸出 **su(i)da(su)** suck/pump out

吊出 **tsu(ri)da(su)** pull out (a fish); lure out

早出 **hayade** early arrival (at the office)

百出 **hyakushutsu** arise in great numbers

7 助出 **tasu(ke)da(su)** help out of

走出 **hashi(ri)de(ru)** run out of (a house), pull out (from a station) **hashi(ri)da(su)** start running

抜出 **nu(ki)da(su)** select, extract, pull out **nu(ke)da(su)** slip out, sneak away; excel; choose the best   **nu(kin)de(ru), nu(ki)de(ru)** be outstanding, excel

抄出 **shōshutsu** take excerpts

投出 **na(ge)da(su)** throw/fling out; give up, renounce

吹出 **fu(ki)da(su)** begin to blow; breathe out; burst out laughing

吹出物 **fu(ki)demono** skin rash, pimple

芯出 **shinda(shi)** aligning/determining the central axis, centering, aligning

岐出 **waka(re)de(ru)** branch off, diverge

売出 **u(ri)da(shi)** sale

見出 **miida(su)** find, discover, pick out **mida(shi)** heading, caption, headline

見出語 **mida(shi)go** headword, entry word

初出 **shoshutsu** first appearance/occurrence

言出 **i(i)da(su)** begin to speak, broach

言出屁 **i(i)da(ship)pe, i(i)da(shi)be** The one who brought up the subject must act first. The one who says "What's that smell?" is the one who farted.

8 供出 **kyōshutsu** delivery

併出 **heishutsu** go/put out side by side

退出 **taishutsu** leave, withdraw

追出 **o(i)da(su)** chase/turn away, kick out, eject

逃出 **ni(ge)da(su), noga(re)de(ru)** run off/away

送出 **oku(ri)da(su)** send out; see (someone) out, send forth

泣出 **na(ki)da(su)** burst into tears, start crying

押出 **o(shi)da(shi)** presence, appearance; pushing out, extrusion   **o(shi)da(su)** push/squeeze out; crowd out; set out all together

抽出 **chūshutsu** extraction, sampling

拠出 **kyoshutsu** contribute, donate

呼出 **yo(bi)da(su)** call out/up/forth, summon

呼出状 **yo(bi)da(shi)jō** summons, subpoena

芽出度 **medeta(i)** happy, congratulatory

突出 **tsu(ki)da(su)** thrust/push/stick out **tsu(ki)de(ru)** jut/stick out, protrude **tosshutsu** projection, protrusion

届出 **todokeide, todokede** report, notification

析出 **sekishutsu** be deposited, precipitate; educe, extract

炊出 **ta(ki)da(shi)** emergency group cooking

放出 **hōshutsu** release, discharge, emit **hō(ri)da(su)** throw out; expel; abandon

取出 **to(ri)da(su)** take/pick out

門出 **kadode** depart, set out

9 飛出 **to(bi)da(su)** fly/jump/dart out **to(bi)de(ru)** protrude

乗出 **no(ri)da(su)** set out, embark on; lean forward

降出 **fu(ri)da(su)** begin to rain/snow

連出 **tsu(re)da(su)** lead out, entice, abduct

洗出 **ara(i)da(su)** (inquire into and) identify

派出 **hashutsu** dispatch, send out

派出所 **hashutsujo** police box; branch office

派出婦 **hashutsufu** visiting maid

挟出 **hasa(mi)da(su)** clamp onto and take out

持出 **mo(chi)da(su)** take out; run off with; propose, bring up

拾出 **hiro(i)da(su)** pick/single out, select

咲出 **sa(ki)da(su), sa(ki)de(ru)** begin to bloom, come out

狩出 **ka(ri)da(su)** hunt/round up

染出 **so(me)da(su)** dye

肺出血 **haishukketsu** discharge of blood from the lungs

神出鬼没 **shinshutsu-kibotsu** elusive, phantom

思出 **omo(i)de** memory, remembrance **omo(i)da(su)** remember

思出笑 **omo(i)da(shi)wara(u)** smile over a memory

思出話 **omo(i)da(shi)banashi** reminiscences

食出 **ha(mi)da(su), ha(mi)de(ru)** protrude, project, jut/bulge out, overflow

10 射出 **shashutsu** shoot out, emit, extrude, radiate, catapult
剔出 **tekishutsu** cut/gouge out, remove
剥出 **mu(ki)da(su)** show, bare
mu(ki)da(shi) bare, open, frank, blunt
差出 **sa(shi)da(su)** present, submit; send; hold out (one's hand)
差出人 **sashidashinin** sender, return address
差出口 **sa(shi)deguchi** uncalled-for remark
差出者 **sa(shi)demono** intruder, meddler, busybody
這出 **ha(i)de(ru), ha(i)da(su)** crawl out
進出 **shinshutsu** advance, march, inroads, push **susu(mi)de(ru)** step forward
逸出 **isshutsu** escape; excel
流出 **ryūshutsu, naga(re)de(ru), naga(re)da(su)** flow out
浸出 **shinshutsu** exuding, oozing out, percolation
捜出 **saga(shi)da(su)** find out, discover, locate
振出 **fu(ri)da(su)** shake out; draw (a bill), issue (a check); infuse, decoct
fu(ri)da(shi) start; draft, issuing
振出人 **furidashinin** remitter, issuer
振出局 **furidashikyoku** the issuing (post) office (for a money order)
家出 **iede** leave home; run away from home
案出 **anshutsu** contrive, devise
書出 **ka(ki)da(su)** begin to write; make an excerpt; make out a bill
ka(ki)da(shi) opening paragraph/words
特出 **tokushutsu** superior, excellent
旅出 **tabide** departure
笑出 **wara(i)da(su)** burst out laughing
11 運出 **hako(bi)da(su)** carry out
排出 **haishutsu** discharge, exhaust; excretion
排出物 **haishutsubutsu** excreta
探出 **sagu(ri)da(su)** spy/sniff out (a secret)
描出 **ega(ki)da(su)** portray, depict
掃出 **ha(ki)da(su)** sweep out
捻出 **nenshutsu** contrive, work out, raise (money) **hine(ri)da(su)** squeeze out; work/crank out, devise
掘出 **ho(ri)da(su)** dig out, unearth
掘出物 **ho(ri)da(shi)mono** treasure trove; lucky find, bargain
掬出 **suku(i)da(su)** bail/ladle out
萌出 **mo(e)de(ru)** sprout, bud
庶出 **shoshutsu** illegitimate birth
脳出血 **nōshukketsu** cerebral hemorrhage
脱出 **dasshutsu** escape from; prolapse
nu(ke)da(su) slip away
現出 **genshutsu, ara(ware)de(ru)** appear, emerge
救出 **kyūshutsu** rescue
suku(i)da(su) rescue from, help out of

産出 **sanshutsu** production, yield, output
産出物 **sanshutsubutsu** product
産出高 **sanshutsudaka** output, yield, production
移出 **ishutsu** ship out, export
船出 **funade** set sail, put to sea
訳出 **yakushutsu** translate
転出 **tenshutsu** move out, be transferred
釣出 **tsu(ri)da(su)** fish/draw out
12 割出 **wa(ri)da(su)** calculate; infer
遣出 **ya(ri)da(su)** begin, set about, take up
遠出 **tōde** going far away
湧出 **wa(ki)de(ru), yūshutsu** gush forth/out, well/bubble up
揉出 **mo(mi)da(su)** squeeze out
提出 **teishutsu** presentation, filing
提出者 **teishutsusha** proposer, mover
揺出 **yu(rugi)de(ru)** wiggle out
弾出 **haji(ki)da(su)** snap out; expel; calculate; squeeze out (the money needed)
検出 **kenshutsu** detect
焼出 **ya(ke)da(sareru)** be burned out/homeless
煮出 **nida(su)** boil down, decoct
煮出汁 **nida(shi)jiru** soup stock, broth
買出 **ka(i)da(shi)** buy (wholesale), lay in (supplies)
絞出 **shibo(ri)da(su)** press/squeeze out
貼出 **ha(ri)da(su)** put up (a notice)
貸出 **ka(shi)da(su)** lend/hire out
13 傑出 **kesshutsu** excel, be pre-eminent
煎出 **sen(ji)da(su)** extract by boiling, decoct, infuse
滑出 **sube(ri)da(su)** start sliding; get underway
塩出 **shioda(shi)** steep out the salt
搬出 **hanshutsu** carry/take out
搾出 **shibo(ri)da(su)** press/squeeze out
搔出 **ka(i)da(su)** bail/ladle out
嗅出 **ka(gi)da(su)** sniff out, get wind of
煙出 **kemuda(shi)** chimney
歳出 **saishutsu** annual expenditures
裸出 **rashutsu** exposure, denudation
続出 **zokushutsu** appear one after another
触出 **fu(re)da(shi)** announcement, professing to be
跳出 **ha(ne)da(su), ha(ne)de(ru), to(bi)de(ru)** spring out
14 選出 **senshutsu, era(bi)da(su), e(ri)da(su)** select, pick out
漕出 **ko(gi)da(su)** row out; begin to row
演出 **enshutsu** production, performance
演出者 **enshutsusha** producer, director
演出家 **enshutsuka** producer, director
滲出 **shinshutsu** exude, ooze/seep out
滲出性 **shinshutsusei** weeping/exudative (eczema)

漏出　**rōshutsu** leak out, escape
摘出　**tekishutsu** pluck out, extract; expose
攫出　**tsuka(mi)da(su)** take out by handfuls
嫡出子　**chakushutsushi** legitimate child
総出　**sōde** all together, in full force
精出　**seida(su)** work hard
算出　**sanshutsu** computation, calculation
誘出　**saso(i)da(su), obi(ki)da(su)** decoy, lure away
踊出　**odo(ri)da(su)** begin to dance; dance out (into the limelight)
聞出　**ki(ki)da(su)** hear, find out about
駆出　**ka(ke)da(su)** rush out, start running
　　ka(ke)da(shi) beginner
　　ka(ri)da(su) round up, muster
15 撥出　**ha(ne)da(su)** eliminate, reject
撮出　**tsuma(mi)da(su)** pick out, drag/throw out
噴出　**funshutsu** eruption, gushing, spouting
　　fu(ki)da(su) spew/gush/spurt out, discharge
蔵出　**kurada(shi)** delivery from a warehouse
暴出　**aba(re)da(su)** get rowdy, go on a rampage
罷出　**maka(ri)de(ru)** report to, appear before; leave, withdraw
締出　**shi(me)da(su)** shut/lock out
編出　**a(mi)da(su)** work out, devise
請出　**u(ke)da(su)** redeem, pay off
輩出　**haishutsu** appear one after another
踏出　**fu(mi)da(su)** step forward, go forth
16 燃出　**mo(e)da(su)** begin to burn, ignite
親出　**oyada(shi)** first character (of a dictionary entry) protruding into the margin; main entry
積出　**tsu(mi)da(su)** send, ship, forward
積出人　**tsu(mi)da(shi)nin** shipper
輸出　**yushutsu** export
輸出入　**yushutsunyū** export and import
輸出入品　**yushutsunyūhin** exports and imports
輸出品　**yushutsuhin** exports
輸出港　**yushutsukō** exporting port
輸出税　**yushutsuzei** export duties/tax
輸出業　**yushutsugyō** export business
17 頻出　**hinshutsu** frequent appearance
18 濫出　**ranshutsu** publish in great quantity, flood the market
織出　**o(ri)da(su)** weave designs into
顔出　**kaoda(shi)** put in an appearance, visit
19 艶出　**tsuyada(shi)** polishing, glazing, burnishing, calendering, mercerizing
繰出　**ku(ri)da(su)** pay out (rope); call out (troops); sally forth
繰出梯子　**ku(ri)da(shi)bashigo** extension ladder

蹴出　**keda(su)** kick out
願出　**nega(i)de(ru)** apply for
20 醸出　**kamo(shi)da(su)** cause, bring about
醵出　**kyoshutsu** donation, contribution
21 露出　**roshutsu** (indecent/film) exposure
露出計　**roshutsukei** light meter

───────── 3 ─────────

3 大売出　**ōu(ri)da(shi)** big sale
小見出　**komida(shi)** subheading, subtitle
4 不世出　**fuseishutsu** rare, extraordinary, unparalleled
手繰出　**tagu(ri)da(su)** pay out (a line); trace (a clue)
引摺出　**hi(ki)zu(ri)da(su)** drag out
5 立身出世　**risshin-shusse** success in life
田舎出　**inakade** from the country
6 再輸出　**saiyushutsu** re-exportation
自費出版　**jihi shuppan** publishing at one's own expense, vanity press
7 学校出　**gakkōde** school graduate, educated person
初日出　**hatsuhi(no)de** New Year's Day sunrise
8 直輸出　**chokuyushutsu, jikiyushutsu** direct export
逆輸出　**gyakuyushutsu** re-exportation
金輸出　**kin yushutsu** export of gold
11 密輸出　**mitsuyushutsu** smuggle out/abroad
眼底出血　**gantei shukketsu** hemorrhage in the fundus of the eye
14 総支出　**sōshishutsu** gross expenditures
16 親見出　**oyamida(shi)** heading, main entry

0a5.23 / 177

MIN, tami people, nation

───────── 1 ─────────

2 民力　**minryoku** national strength
4 民心　**minshin** popular sentiment
5 民本主義　**minpon shugi** democracy
民生　**minsei** the people's livelihood, welfare
民生委員　**minsei iin** district welfare officer
民主　**minshu** democratic
民主化　**minshuka** democratization
民主主義　**minshu shugi** democracy
民主国　**minshukoku** democratic country, a democracy
民主的　**minshuteki** democratic
民主党　**Minshutō** Democratic Party
6 民有　**min'yū** privately owned
7 民兵　**minpei** militia(man)
民芸　**mingei** folkcraft, folk art
8 民事　**minji** civil affairs; civil (law)
民事裁判　**minji saiban** civil trial

0a5

民事訴訟 **minji soshō** civil suit
民法 **minpō** civil law/code
9 民俗 **minzoku** ethnic/folk customs
民俗学 **minzokugaku** folklore
民活 **minkatsu** private-sector vitality
民草 **tamikusa, tamigusa** the people, populace
民政 **minsei** civil/civilian government
民約説 **min'yakusetsu** the social-contract theory
10 民家 **minka** private house
11 民族 **minzoku** race, a people
民族学 **minzokugaku** ethnology
民族性 **minzokusei** racial/national trait
民情 **minjō** the people's situation
12 民営 **min'ei** private management, privately run
民営化 **min'eika** privatization, denational-ization
民衆 **minshū** people, populace, masses
民衆化 **minshūka** popularization
民間 **minkan** private (not public)
民間人 **minkanjin** private citizen
13 民業 **mingyō** a private business
民福 **minpuku** national welfare
民意 **min'i** will of the people
民話 **minwa** folk tale, folklore
14 民選 **minsen** popular election
民需 **minju** private/civilian demand
15 民権 **minken** civil rights
16 民謡 **min'yō** folk song

——————— 2 ———————

2 人民 **jinmin** the people
人民投票 **jinmin tōhyō** plebiscite, referen-dum
人民戦線 **jinmin sensen** popular front
3 万民 **banmin** all the people/nation
土民 **domin** natives, aborigines
4 文民 **bunmin** civilian
公民権 **kōminken** civil rights, citizenship
公民館 **kōminkan** public hall, community center
5 生民 **seimin** the people, subjects
市民 **shimin** citizen
市民権 **shiminken** citizenship, civil rights
平民 **heimin** the common people
四民 **shimin** the four classes (samurai, farmers, artisans, merchants)
6 全民衆 **zenminshū** all the people
自民党 **Jimintō** LDP, Liberal Democratic Party (short for 自由民主党)
7 良民 **ryōmin** good/law-abiding citizens
佚民 **itsumin** retired person
住民 **jūmin** residents, inhabitants
住民登録 **jūmin tōroku** resident registration
住民税 **jūminzei** inhabitants tax
臣民 **shinmin** subject, national

乱民 **ranmin** insurgents, rioters, mob
村民 **sonmin** villagers
町民 **chōmin** townspeople
8 官民 **kanmin** government and people, public and private
国民 **kokumin** the/a people, a national; national
国民化 **kokuminka** nationalization
国民服 **kokuminfuku** national uniform (for civilians)
国民的 **kokuminteki** national
国民性 **kokuminsei** national character
国民軍 **kokumingun** national army
牧民 **bokumin** governing
9 烝民 **jōmin** the common people, the masses
10 都民 **tomin** Tōkyō citizens/residents
遊民 **yūmin** idlers; the unemployed
逸民 **itsumin** retired person, recluse
流民 **ryūmin** drifting people, displaced persons
島民 **tōmin** islanders
11 貧民 **hinmin** the poor
貧民街 **hinmingai** slums
貧民窟 **hinminkutsu** slums
済民 **saimin** relieving people's suffering
庶民 **shomin** the (common) people
救民 **kyūmin** aiding disaster victims
移民 **imin** immigration, emigration; immi-grant, emigrant, settler
細民 **saimin** the poor
12 蛮民 **banmin** a barbarous people
植民 **shokumin** colonization, settlement; colonist, settler
植民地 **shokuminchi** colony
植民地化 **shokuminchika** colonization
13 義民 **gimin** public-spirited man
農民 **nōmin** peasants, farmers
漢民族 **Kan minzoku** the Han/Chinese people
愚民 **gumin** ignorant people, rabble
14 選民 **senmin** chosen people, the elect
漁民 **gyomin** fishermen
15 窮民 **kyūmin** the needy
暴民 **bōmin** mob, rioters
賤民 **senmin** the lowly
18 難民 **nanmin** refugees

——————— 3 ———————

3 土着民 **dochakumin** natives, aborigines
小市民 **shōshimin** petty bourgeois, lower middle class
小国民 **shōkokumin** rising generation
4 中華民国 **Chūka Minkoku** Republic of China (Taiwan)
少数民族 **shōsū minzoku** minority nationali-ties, ethnic minorities
5 他国民 **takokumin** other nations/peoples
6 全市民 **zenshimin** all the citizens of the city

全国民 **zenkokumin** the entire nation
先住民族 **senjū minzoku** aborigines
在留民 **zairyūmin** residents
7 社会民主主義 **shakai minshu shugi** social
    democracy
8 非国民 **hikokumin** unpatriotic person
官尊民卑 **kanson-minpi** exalting the
    government at the expense of the people
居留民 **kyoryūmin** residents
国利民福 **kokuri-minpuku** the national
    interest and the welfare of the people
10 部落民 **burakumin** (lowly class of people
    historically engaged in butchery and
    tanning)
原住民 **genjūmin** natives, aborigines
教区民 **kyōkumin** parishoners
14 漂流民 **hyōryūmin** persons adrift; castaways
15 避難民 **hinanmin** refugees, evacuees

———————— 4 ————————

4 中華人民共和国 **Chūka Jinmin Kyōwakoku**
    People's Republic of China
5 半官半民 **hankan-hanmin** semigovernmental
主権在民 **shuken-zaimin** sovereignty
    resides with the people
6 全国人民代表大会 **Zenkoku Jinmin Daihyō**
    Taikai (Chinese) National People's
    Congress

0a5.24 / 88

半

HAN half, semi-; odd number
naka(ba) half, semi-; middle, halfway;
partly

———————— 1 ————————

2 半人前 **hanninmae** half portion; half a man
3 半口 **hankuchi** half-share
半弓 **hankyū** small bow
4 半天 **hanten** half the sky; midair
半分 **hanbun** half   **hanpun** half a minute
半円 **han'en** semicircle
半円形 **han'enkei** semicircular
半月 **hantsuki** half a month
    hangetsu half moon, semicircle
半月刊 **hangekkan** a semimonthly
半月形 **hangetsugata** semicircular
半日 **hannichi** half day
5 半母音 **hanboin** semivowel
半世紀 **hanseiki** half century
半加工品 **hankakōhin** semiprocessed goods
半句 **hanku** a brief word
半玉 **hangyoku** child geisha, apprentice
    entertainer
半田 **handa** solder
6 半死半生 **hanshi-hanshō** half dead
半年 **hantoshi, hannen** half year, six months
半休 **hankyū** half-day holiday

7 半身 **hanshin** half the body
半身不随 **hanshin fuzui** paralyzed on one side
半狂乱 **hankyōran** half-crazed
8 半価 **hanka** half price
半盲 **hanmō** half blind
半周 **hanshū** go halfway around
半径 **hankei** radius
半官半民 **hankan-hanmin** semigovernmental
半官的 **hankanteki** semiofficial
半官報 **hankanpō** semiofficial paper
半金 **hankin** half the amount
9 半信半疑 **hanshin-hangi** incredulous, half
    doubting
半途 **hanto** halfway; unfinished
半面 **hanmen** half the face; one side, half;
    the other side
半神 **hanshin** demigod
半音 **han'on** half tone, half step (in music)
半衿 **han'eri** (kimono) neckpiece
10 半値 **hanne** half price
半島 **hantō** peninsula
半殺 **hangoro(shi)** half killed
半夏 **hange** eleventh day after the summer
    solstice, final day for seed-sowing
半袖 **hansode** short sleeves
半病人 **hanbyōnin** sickly person
半紙 **hanshi** common Japanese writing
    paper, rice paper
11 半過去 **hankako** imperfect tense
半球 **hankyū** hemisphere
12 半減 **hangen** reduction by half
半減期 **hangenki** halflife (in physics)
半期 **hanki** half term, half year
半焼 **han'ya(ke)** half-burnt; half-done, rare
半煮 **hanni(e)** parboiled
半畳 **hanjō** half mat; heckling
半開 **hankai, hanbira(ki)** semicivilized; half
    open   **hanbira(ki)** half open
13 半農 **hannō** part-time farming
半搗米 **hantsu(ki)mai** half-polished rice
半数 **hansū** half the number
半裸体 **hanratai** seminude
14 半熟 **hanjuku** half-boiled, soft-boiled; half-
    ripe
半旗 **hanki** flag at half-staff
半端 **hanpa** fragment; incomplete set;
    fraction; remnant; incomplete
半導体 **handōtai** semiconductor
半製品 **hanseihin** semiprocessed goods
15 半影 **han'ei** penumbra
16 半濁音 **handakuon** semivoiced sound,
    p-sound
半諧音 **hankaion** assonance
18 半襟 **han'eri** (kimono) neckpiece
半額 **hangaku** half the amount/price
20 半鐘 **hanshō** fire bell/alarm

22 半纏 **hanten** short coat

--------- 2 ---------

1 一半 **ippan** a half; a part

2 丁半 **chōhan** even and odd numbers; dice game; heads-or-tails gamble

3 大半 **taihan** majority, greater part; mostly

上半 **jōhan** first/upper half

上半身 **jōhanshin, kamihanshin** upper half of the body

上半期 **kamihanki** the first half (of the year)

下半 **kahan** lower half

下半身 **kahanshin, shimohanshin** lower half of the body

下半期 **kahanki, shimohanki** the latter half (of the year)

小半日 **kohannichi** about half a day

小半年 **kohannen** about six months

小半時 **kohantoki** about half an hour

5 北半球 **Kita Hankyū** Northern Hemisphere

生半尺 **namahanjaku** half-done, unfinished

生半可 **namahanka** superficial, half-baked

四半分 **shihanbun** quarter, fourth

四半期 **shihanki** quarter (of a year)

6 西半球 **nishi hankyū** Western Hemisphere

7 折半 **seppan** dividing into halves

8 東半球 **higashi hankyū** Eastern Hemisphere

夜半 **yowa, yahan** midnight, dead of night

苗半作 **naehansaku** The seedlings determine the harvest.

9 南半球 **minami hankyū** the Southern Hemisphere

前半 **zenpan** first half

後半 **kōhan** latter half

後半生 **kōhansei** the latter half of one's life

後半戦 **kōhansen** the latter half of a game

約半分 **yaku hanbun** about half

10 遊半分 **aso(bi)hanbun** half in fun

11 過半 **kahan** the greater part

過半数 **kahansū** majority, more than half

脚半 **kyahan** leggings, gaiters

13 話半分 **hanashi-hanbun** taking a story at half its face value

15 慰半分 **nagusa(mi)hanbun** partly for pleasure

17 藁半紙 **warabanshi** (a low-grade paper)

--------- 3 ---------

1 一知半解 **itchi hankai** superficial knowledge

3 三行半 **mikudarihan** letter of divorce
sangyōhan three and a half lines (of text)

4 中途半端 **chūto-hanpa** half finished, incomplete

5 半死半生 **hanshi-hanshō** half dead

半官半民 **hankan-hanmin** semigovernmental

半信半疑 **hanshin-hangi** incredulous, half doubting

6 伊豆半島 **Izu-hantō** Izu Peninsula (Shizuoka-ken)

行動半径 **kōdō hankei** radius of action, range

9 面白半分 **omoshiro-hanbun** half in fun, jokingly

10 能登半島 **Noto-hantō** (peninsula, Ishikawa-ken)

0a5.25 / 25

本 本 **HON** book; this; main; origin; (counter for long objects)
moto origin

--------- 1 ---------

2 本人 **honnin** the person himself, the said person, the principal

3 本土 **hondo** mainland

本山 **honzan** head temple; this temple

4 本文 **honbun, honmon** (main) text, body

本文批評 **honmon hihyō** textual criticism

本月 **hongetsu** this month

本日 **honjitsu** today

本心 **honshin** one's right mind, one's senses; real intention/motive, true sentiment; conscience

5 本末 **honmatsu** cause and effect, means and end, substance and shadow, beginning and end

本代 **hondai** price/bill for books

本号 **hongō** current number (of a publication)

6 本気 **honki** serious, in earnest

本気違 **hon kichiga(i)** bibliomania; bibliomaniac

本年 **honnen** this year

本年度 **honnendo** this fiscal/business year

本州 **Honshū** (Japan's main island)

本色 **honshoku** one's real character, true quality

本名 **honmyō, honmei** one's real name

本宅 **hontaku** principal residence

本当 **hontō** true, real

本旨 **honshi** the main purpose

本式 **honshiki** regular, orthodox

7 本来 **honrai** properly speaking; in essence, naturally; originally, primarily

本位 **hon'i** standard, basis, principle

本体論 **hontairon** ontology

本邸 **hontei** principal residence

本決 **hongima(ri)** final decision

本局 **honkyoku** main/central office

本社 **honsha** head office; main shrine; this shrine

8 本命 **honmei** probable winner, favorite (to win)

本拠 **honkyo** base, headquarters

本姓 **honsei** real/original surname

本官 **honkan** one's permanent post, principal assignment; I, the present official

本店 **honten** head office; main store; this store

本国 **hongoku** one's own country

本物 **honmono** genuine article, the real thing

本性 **honshō, honsei** true nature/character

9 本陣 **honjin** troop headquarters; daimyo's inn; stronghold

本院 **hon'in** this institution; main institution

本通 **hondō(ri)** main street, boulevard

本草 **honzō** plants, (medicinal) herbs

本屋 **hon'ya** bookstore

本音 **honne** real intention, underlying motive

本食虫 **honku(i)mushi** bookworm

10 本俸 **honpō** basic/regular salary

本部 **honbu** headquarters

本流 **honryū** mainstream

本家 **honke** main family; originator

本案 **hon'an** this proposal/plan

本島 **hontō** main island; this island

本格的 **honkakuteki** full-scale, genuine, in earnest

本能 **honnō** instinct

本書 **honsho** the text/script; this book

本紙 **honshi** this newspaper

11 本隊 **hontai** main body (of troops)

本堂 **hondō** main temple building

本望 **honmō** long-cherished desire; satisfaction

12 本尊 **honzon** main image (of worship), idol; the man himself

本場 **honba** home, habitat, the best place for

本営 **hon'ei** headquarters

本棚 **hondana** bookshelf

本然 **honzen, honnen** natural, inborn, inherent

本塁 **honrui** base, stronghold; home plate

本塁打 **honruida** home run

本番 **honban** the actual performance (not a dry run)

本給 **honkyū** basic/regular salary

本筋 **honsuji** plot, main thread (of a story)

13 本業 **hongyō** one's principal occupation

本義 **hongi** true meaning, basic principle

本源 **hongen** origin, root, cause, principle

本殿 **honden** main/inner shrine

本腰入 **hongoshi (o) i(reru)** make an earnest effort, get down to business

本意 **hon'i** one's real intention

本署 **honsho** police headquarters; this office

本絹 **honken** pure silk

14 本管 **honkan** main (pipe)

本誌 **honshi** this magazine

本読 **hon'yo(mi)** good reader; reading the script

本領 **honryō** characteristic; specialty; duty; proper function; fief

15 本線 **honsen** main (railway) line

本箱 **honbako** bookcase

本論 **honron** main subject/discussion; this subject

本調子 **honchōshi** proper key (of an instrument); one's regular form

本質 **honshitsu** essence

本質的 **honshitsuteki** in substance, essential

16 本曇 **hongumo(ri)** rain-threatening overcast

本館 **honkan** main building; this building

18 本職 **honshoku** one's regular occupation; an expert; I

本題 **hondai** the main issue/subject

19 本願 **hongan** long-cherished desire; Amida Buddha's original vow

20 本籍 **honseki** one's legal domicile

本籍地 **honsekichi** one's legal domicile

--- 2 ---

1 一本 **ippon** one (long object); a book; one version; a blow; a full-fledged geisha

一本立 **ipponda(chi)** independence

一本気 **ippongi** one-track mind

一本杉 **ipponsugi** a solitary cedar tree

一本道 **ipponmichi** straight road; road with no turnoffs

一本調子 **ipponchōshi, ipponjōshi** monotony

一本橋 **ipponbashi** log bridge

2 二本立 **nihonda(te)** double feature (movie)

二本建 **nihonda(te)** dual system; double standard

二本差 **nihonza(shi)** two-sworded (samurai)

人本主義 **jinpon shugi** humanism

3 大本 **ōmoto, taihon** foundation, base

大本山 **daihonzan** headquarters temple (of a sect)

大本営 **daihon'ei** imperial headquarters

4 不本意 **fuhon'i** reluctant, unwilling, to one's regret

元本 **ganpon** the principal, capital

円本 **enpon** one-yen book

手本 **tehon** model, example, pattern

日本 **Nihon, Nippon** Japan

日本一 **Nihon-ichi, Nippon-ichi** Japan's best

日本中 **Nihonjū, Nipponjū** all over Japan

日本人 **Nihonjin, Nipponjin** a Japanese

日本刀 **nihontō** Japanese sword

日本三景 **Nihon sankei** Japan's three noted scenic sights (Matsushima, Miyajima, Amanohashidate)

日本化 **nihonka** Japanization, Nipponization

日本犬 **nihonken** Japanese dog

日本史 **Nihonshi** Japanese history

日本主義 **Nihon shugi** Japanism

日本学 **nihongaku** Japanology

日本画 **nihonga** Japanese-style painting/drawing

0a5

日本的 **nihonteki** (very) Japanese
日本風 **nihonfū** Japanese style
日本海 **Nihonkai** the Sea of Japan
日本酒 **nihonshu** saké
日本紙 **nohonshi** Japanese paper
日本脳炎 **Nihon nōen** Japanese encephalitis
日本訳 **nihon'yaku** Japanese translation
日本晴 **nihonba(re)** clear cloudless sky, beautiful weather
日本間 **nihonma** Japanese-style room
日本髪 **nihongami** Japanese hairdo
日本製 **nihonsei** made in Japan
日本語 **nihongo** the Japanese language
欠本 **keppon** missing volume
5 民本主義 **minpon shugi** democracy
写本 **shahon** manuscript, handwritten copy, codex
古本 **furuhon** used/secondhand book
　　 kohon secondhand book; ancient book
古本屋 **furuhon'ya** used/secondhand book store
正本 **seihon, shōhon** an attested copy; the original (of a document)　**shōhon** playbook, script; unabridged book
台本 **daihon** script, screenplay, libretto
禾本科 **kahonka** grasses
6 西本願寺 **Nishi Honganji** (main temple, in Kyōto, of Jōdo sect)
合本 **gappon** bound volumes
返本 **henpon** books/magazines returned unsold
守本尊 **mamo(ri)honzon** guardian deity
7 赤本 **akahon** cheap storybook/novel
折本 **o(ri)hon** folding book; folder
抜本 **bappon** eradication; radical
抄本 **shōhon** excerpt, abridged transcript
豆本 **mame-hon** miniature book, pocket edition
完本 **kanpon** complete works/set
見本 **mihon** sample, specimen
見本市 **mihon ichi** sample/trade fair
見本組 **mihongu(mi)** specimen page
8 刷本 **su(ri)hon** printed (but not yet bound) book
版本 **hanpon** printed book; book printed by engraved wood blocks
送本 **sōhon** deliver books
拓本 **takuhon** a rubbing (of an inscription)
官本 **kanpon** government publication
定本 **teihon** the authentic/standard text
底本 **teihon** the original text
国本 **kokuhon** foundations of the nation
松本 **Matsumoto** (city, Nagano-ken)
物本 **mono (no) hon** (in some) book
和本 **wahon** book bound in Japanese style
金本位 **kinhon'i** the gold standard

金本位制 **kinhon'isei** the gold standard
9 院本 **inpon** script, playbook of *jōruri* text
美本 **bihon** beautifully bound book
造本 **zōhon** making books
洋本 **yōhon** Western book
草本 **sōhon** herbs; draft, manuscript
春本 **shunpon** pornographic book
珍本 **chinpon** rare book
10 残本 **zanpon** unsold copies (of a book); remainders
原本 **genpon** the original (work/copy)
唐本 **tōhon** books from China
根本 **konpon** root, cause; basis
　　 nemoto part near the root, base
根本主義 **konpon shugi** fundamentalism
根本法 **konponhō** fundamental law
根本的 **konponteki** fundamental, radical
校本 **kōhon** complete/annotated text
教本 **kyōhon** textbook
秘本 **hihon** treasured/secret book
納本 **nōhon** book delivery; presentation copy
粉本 **funpon** a copy, sketch
配本 **haihon** book distribution
11 副本 **fukuhon** duplicate, copy
基本 **kihon** basic, fundamental, standard
基本的 **kihonteki** basic, fundamental
基本金 **kihonkin** endowment fund
基本給 **kihonkyū** basic salary, base pay
張本人 **chōhonnin** ringleader
脚本 **kyakuhon** script, play
異本 **ihon** different edition
訳本 **yakuhon** a translation (of a book)
12 猥本 **waihon** pornographic book
絵本 **ehon** picture book
貸本 **ka(shi)hon** book for lending out
貸本屋 **ka(shi)hon'ya** lending library
13 農本主義 **nōhon shugi** agriculture-first policy, physiocracy
献本 **kenpon** presentation (copy)
絹本 **kenpon** silk cloth/canvas for painting
資本 **shihon** capital
資本主義 **shihon shugi** capitalism
資本金 **shihonkin** capital
資本家 **shihonka** capitalist, financier
資本財 **shihonzai** capital goods
14 摺本 **surihon** printed (but unbound) book
熊本 **Kumamoto** (city, Kumamoto-ken)
熊本県 **Kumamoto-ken** (prefecture)
旗本 **hatamoto** direct vassal of the shogun
端本 **hahon** odd volume, incomplete set
種本 **tanehon** source book, manual
製本 **seihon** bookbinding
複本 **fukuhon** a duplicate, copy
複本位 **fukuhon'i** double standard
複本位制 **fukuhon'isei** bimetalism
綴本 **to(ji)hon** bound book

総本山 **sōhonzan** (sect's) head temple
総本店 **sōhonten** head office
総本家 **sōhonke** head family
読本 **tokuhon** reader, book of readings
銀本位 **ginhon'i** the silver standard
15 蔵本 **zōhon** one's library
標本 **hyōhon** specimen, sample
敵本主義 **tekihon shugi** feint, pretense,
　　having ulterior motives
稿本 **kōhon** manuscript
諸本 **shohon** various books
16 謡本 **utaibon** Noh libretto
17 謄本 **tōhon** transcript, copy
18 贈本 **zōhon** gift book, complimentary copy
類本 **ruihon** similar book

―――――――― 3 ――――――――

3 大日本 **Dai-Nippon/-Nihon** (Great) Japan
4 文庫本 **bunkobon** small paperback book
　　(page size 14.8 x 10.5 cm)
手沢本 **shutakubon** a favorite book
木版本 **mokuhanbon** xylographic book
5 古写本 **koshahon** ancient manuscript, codex
好色本 **kōshokubon** erotic story
6 西日本 **Nishi Nihon** western Japan
全日本 **zen-Nihon, zen-Nippon** all Japan
全日本空輸 **Zen Nippon Kūyu** All Nippon
　　Airways
自力本願 **jiriki hongan** salvation by works
7 束見本 **tsuka-mihon** pattern volume, dummy
　　(of a book to be printed)
8 表日本 **Omote Nihon** Pacific side of Japan
9 活字本 **katsujibon** printed book
活版本 **kappanbon** printed book
単行本 **tankōbon** separate volume, in book
　　form
10 帰巣本能 **kisō honnō** homing instinct
進呈本 **shinteihon** complimentary copy
流布本 **rufubon** popular edition
教則本 **kyōsokubon** (music) practice book
袖珍本 **shūchinbon** pocket-size book
純日本風 **jun-Nihon-fū** classical Japanese
　　style
12 無資本 **mushihon** without capital/funds
稀覯本 **kikōbon** rare book
集注本 **shūchūbon** variorum edition
13 裏日本 **ura-Nihon, ura-Nippon** Sea-of-
　　Japan side of Japan
滑稽本 **kokkeibon** comic book (Edo period)
18 覆刻本 **fukkokubon** reissued book
贈呈本 **zōteihon** presentation copy

―――――――― 4 ――――――――

4 戸籍抄本 **koseki shōhon** extract from a
　　family register
戸籍謄本 **koseki tōhon** copy of a family
　　register

10 遊休資本 **yūkyū shihon** idle capital

0a5.26 / 305

末　　**MATSU, BATSU** end; powder
　　sue end; youngest child; descendant;
　　the future; trivialities

―――――――― 1 ――――――――

2 末子 **sue(k)ko, basshi, masshi** youngest
　　child
4 末日 **matsujitsu** last day (of a month)
5 末世 **sue(no)yo, masse** future ages, last days
末代 **matsudai** all ages to come, eternity
末広 **suehiro** folding fan　**suehiro(gari)**
　　spreading/widening out toward the end;
　　prospering as time goes on
6 末寺 **matsuji** branch temple
7 末弟 **battei, mattei** youngest brother; last
　　disciple
末尾 **matsubi** end, last, final
末社 **massha** subordinate shrine; profes-
　　sional jester
8 末法 **mappō** latter days (of Buddhism), age
　　of decadence
末法思想 **mappō shisō** pessimism due to the
　　decadent-age theory
9 末派 **mappa** sect; underling
末茶 **matcha** powdered tea
末枯 **uraga(reru)** (leaves) wither (as winter
　　approaches)
10 末流 **matsuryū** descendants
末席 **masseki, basseki** lowest-ranking seat
11 末梢 **masshō** tip of a twig; periphery;
　　nonessentials, trifles
末梢神経 **masshō shinkei** peripheral nerves
12 末葉 **matsuyō** end, close
末期 **makki** closing years, last stage
　　matsugo hour of death, deathbed
13 末裔 **matsuei** descendant
末節 **massetsu** trifles, minor details
末路 **matsuro** last days, end
14 末端 **mattan** end, tip, terminal
末端価格 **mattan kakaku** end-user price,
　　street value
15 末輩 **mappai** underling; rank and file

―――――――― 2 ――――――――

4 木末 **konure** twigs, treetops
月末 **getsumatsu, tsukizue** end of the month
5 本末 **honmatsu** cause and effect, means and
　　end, substance and shadow, beginning
　　and end
6 年末 **nenmatsu** the end of the year, year-end
行末 **yu(ku)sue** the future
7 季末 **kimatsu** end of the term
8 始末 **shimatsu** circumstances; manage,
　　dispose of, take care of; economize

0a5

始末屋 **shimatsuya** frugal person
始末書 **shimatsusho** written explanation/
  apology
9 巻末 **kanmatsu** end of a book
10 週末 **shūmatsu** weekend
粉末 **funmatsu** powder
11 野末 **nozue** farthest corners of a field
毫末 **gōmatsu** iota, slightest bit
細末 **saimatsu** trivia; powder
終末 **shūmatsu** end, conclusion
終末観 **shūmatsukan** eschatology
粗末 **somatsu** coarse, plain, crude, rough, rude
断末魔 **danmatsuma** one's dying moments
12 場末 **basue** outskirts, suburbs
葉末 **hazue** leaf tip
期末 **kimatsu** end of the term/period
結末 **ketsumatsu** end, conclusion, upshot
13 幕末 **bakumatsu** latter days of the Tokugawa
  government
歳末 **saimatsu** year's end
14 端末機 **tanmatsuki** (computer) terminal
語末 **gomatsu** word ending
19 顛末 **tenmatsu** circumstances, facts
23 巓末 **tenmatsu** details, full particulars

―――――――― 3 ――――――――

4 不始末 **fushimatsu** mismanagement,
  carelessness; lavish, spendthrift
7 亜鉛末 **aenmatsu** zinc dust
学期末 **gakkimatsu** end of the term/semester
8 枝葉末節 **shiyō-massetsu** branches and
  leaves; unimportant details
9 後始末 **atoshimatsu** settle, wind/finish up
11 強弩末 **kyōdo (no) sue** a once strong but
  now spent force
13 跡始末 **atoshimatsu** winding-up, settlement,
  straightening up (afterwards)

0a5.27 / 306

未 **MI** not yet, un- **ima(da)** still, as yet,
to this day, ever **mada** still, not yet
hitsuji eighth horary sign (sheep)

―――――――― 1 ――――――――

1 未了 **miryō** unfinished
3 未亡人 **mibōjin** widow
4 未公表 **mikōhyō** not yet officially announced
5 未刊 **mikan** unpublished
未払 **mihara(i)** unpaid
未処置 **mishochi** untreated
6 未成年 **miseinen** minority, not of age
未成年者 **miseinensha** a minor
未成品 **miseihin** unfinished goods
7 未来 **mirai** future; future tense
未来完了 **mirai kanryō** future perfect tense
未来派 **miraiha** futurist (artists)
未決 **miketsu** pending, unsettled

未決囚 **miketsushū** unconvicted prisoner
未決済 **mikessai** outstanding (accounts)
未決算 **mikessan** outstanding (accounts)
未完 **mikan** incomplete, unfinished
未完成 **mikansei** incomplete, unfinished
未見 **miken** unacquainted, unknown
8 未到 **mitō** unexplored
未知 **michi** unknown, strange
未定 **mitei** undecided, pending
未届 **mitodo(ke)** failing to report
未明 **mimei** (pre-)dawn
9 未発 **mihatsu** before anything happens
未発行 **mihakkō** unissued
未発見 **mihakken** undiscovered, unexplored
未発表 **mihappyō** not yet made public
未発達 **mihattatsu** undeveloped
10 未帰還者 **mikikansha** person still not
  repatriated
未納 **minō** nonpayment, default, arrears
11 未済 **misai** unpaid, unsettled, outstanding
未婚 **mikon** unmarried
未婚者 **mikonsha** unmarried person
未経験 **mikeiken** unexperienced
未経験者 **mikeikensha** person having no
  experience
未設 **misetsu** yet unbuilt, projected
12 未着 **michaku** nonarrival
未満 **miman** less than, below
未然 **mizen** before (it) happens, beforehand
未開 **mikai** uncivilized, barbarous
未開拓 **mikaitaku** undeveloped, unexploited
未開発 **mikaihatsu** undeveloped
未開墾 **mikaikon** uncultivated
13 未解決 **mikaiketsu** unsolved, unsettled
未詳 **mishō** unknown, unidentified
14 未製品 **miseihin** unfinished goods
未練 **miren** lingering affection
未聞 **mimon** not yet heard, unheard of
14 未熟 **mijuku** not yet ripe; premature;
  immature, inexperienced
15 未確定 **mikakutei** unsettled, pending
未踏 **mitō** untrodden, unexplored

―――――――― 2 ――――――――

6 尽未来 **jinmirai** forever

―――――――― 3 ――――――――

2 人跡未到 **jinseki-mitō** unexplored
人跡未踏 **jinseki-mitō** unexplored
6 自殺未遂 **jisatsu misui** attempted suicide
9 前人未到 **zenjin-mitō** untrodden, unexplored
前代未聞 **zendai-mimon** unprecedented

0a5.28 / 311

失 **SHITSU** lose; err **shis(suru)** lose, miss,
forget; be excessive **ushina(u)** lose
u(seru) disappear, vanish

─────── 1 ───────

4 失火 **shikka** an accidental fire
　失心 **shisshin** faint, lose consciousness
5 失礼 **shitsurei** rudeness, discourtesy
6 失地 **shitchi** lost territory
　失名 **shitsumei** nameless, anonymous
　失名氏 **shitsumeishi** unknown/anonymous person
　失当 **shittō** improper, unfair, wrongful
　失血 **shikketsu** loss of blood
7 失言 **shitsugen** verbal slip/impropriety
8 失効 **shikkō** lapse, lose effect, become null and void
　失明 **shitsumei** lose one's eyesight, go blind
　失物 **u(se)mono** lost article
9 失陥 **shikkan** surrender, fall
　失神 **shisshin** faint, lose consciousness
　失政 **shissei** misgovernment, misrule
10 失恋 **shitsuren** unrequited love
　失格 **shikkaku** disqualification
　失笑 **shisshō** laugh, burst out laughing
11 失脚 **shikkyaku** lose one's standing, be overthrown, fall
　失望 **shitsubō** disappointment, despair
　失敗 **shippai** failure, blunder, mistake
12 失敬 **shikkei** rudeness, disrespect
　失策 **shissaku** blunder, slip, error
　失費 **shippi** expenses, expenditures
13 失業 **shitsugyō** unemployment
　失業者 **shitsugyōsha** unemployed person
　失禁 **shikkin** incontinence (of urine/feces)
　失意 **shitsui** despair, disappointment; adversity
　失跡 **shisseki** disappear, be missing
14 失墜 **shittsui** lose, fall
　失態 **shittai** blunder, mismanagement; disgrace
　失語 **shitsugo** inability to speak correctly, forgetting words
15 失権 **shikken** forfeiture of rights, disenfranchisement
　失調 **shitchō** malfunction, lack of coordination
　失踪 **shissō** disappear, be missing
18 失職 **shisshoku** unemployment

─────── 2 ───────

1 一失 **isshitsu** a disadvantage; a defect; an error
3 亡失 **bōshitsu** loss
　凡失 **bonshitsu** common error, muff, flub
4 火失 **kashitsu** accidental fire
6 気失 **ki (o) ushina(u)** faint, pass out
　自失 **jishitsu** be dazed/absent-minded
7 見失 **miushina(u)** lose sight of, miss
10 流失 **ryūshitsu** be washed away
　消失 **shōshitsu, ki(e)u(seru)** disappear, vanish, die out/away

紛失 **funshitsu** loss, be missing
11 過失 **kashitsu** error, mistake; accident; negligence
　過失致死 **kashitsu chishi** accidental homicide, manslaughter
　過失致死罪 **kashitsu chishizai** accidental homicide, manslaughter
　得失 **tokushitsu** advantages and disadvantages
12 喪失 **sōshitsu** loss
　焼失 **shōshitsu** be destroyed by fire
　散失 **sanshitsu** be scattered and lost
13 損失 **sonshitsu** loss
14 遺失 **ishitsu** loss
　遺失物 **ishitsubutsu** lost article
　遺失品 **ishitsuhin** lost article
　漂失 **hyōshitsu** drift away

─────── 3 ───────

12 無過失 **mukashitsu** no-fault (liability)

─────── 4 ───────

1 一得一失 **ittoku isshitsu** advantages and disadvantages
4 心神喪失 **shinshin sōshitsu** not of sound mind
7 利害得失 **rigai-tokushitsu** pros and cons
9 茫然自失 **bōzen-jishitsu** abstraction, stupefaction, entrancement

0a5.29 / 44

生 **SEI** birth; life; (as suffix) student **SHŌ** birth; life **i(kiru)** live, be alive **i(ki)** living; fresh; stet. **i(keru)** living, alive; arrange flowers **i(kasu)** let live, revive; make best use of **nama** raw, fresh, unprocessed **u(mu)** give birth to **u(mareru)** be born **ha(eru)** grow (intr.) **ha(yasu)** grow (tr.) **o(u)** grow

─────── 1 ───────

0 生じる/ずる **shō(jiru/zuru)** produce, bring about; be produced, come about
　生ゴミ **namagomi** biodegradable/wet garbage, kitchen scraps
　生ゴム **namagomu** latex
　生コン **namakon** mixed concrete ready for pouring
　生データ **namadēta** raw data
　生テープ **namatēpu** blank/unrecorded tape
　生ビール **namabīru** draft beer
　生フィルム **namafirumu** unexposed film
　生ワクチン **namawakuchin** live-virus vaccine
2 生人形 **i(ki)ningyō** lifelike doll; living doll
3 生干 **namabi, namabo(shi)** half-dried
　生々 **namanama(shii)** fresh, vivid **seisei** lively

4 生爪 **namazume** the quick (of a fingernail)
生中継 **namachūkei** live (remote) broadcast
生仏 **i(ki)botoke** a living Buddha, incarnation of Buddha
生化学 **seikagaku** biochemistry
生分解性 **seibunkaisei** biodegradable
生水 **namamizu** unboiled water
生木 **namaki** living tree; unseasoned wood
生牛乳 **namagyūnyū** unprocessed milk (not powdered or condensed)
生欠伸 **namaakubi** slight yawn
5 生出 **u(mi)da(su)** bring forth, produce, yield
生民 **seimin** the people, subjects
生半尺 **namahanjaku** half-done, unfinished
生半可 **namahanka** superficial, half-baked
生甲斐 **i(ki)gai** something worth living for
生母 **seibo** one's (biological) mother
生存 **seizon** existence, life, survival
生存者 **seizonsha** survivor
生存権 **seizonken** right to live
生写 **i(ki)utsu(shi)** close resemblance
生字引 **i(ki)jibiki** walking dictionary
生白 **namajiro(i), namatchiro(i)** pale, pallid
生石灰 **seisekkai, kisekkai** quicklime
生立 **u(mi)ta(te)** fresh-laid (eggs)
　　u(mare)ta(te) newborn
　　o(i)ta(chi) one's childhood, growing up
6 生死 **seishi** life or/and death
生気 **seiki** animation, life, vitality
生年 **seinen, u(mare)doshi** year of birth, age
生年月日 **seinengappi** date of birth
生仲 **na(sanu) naka** no blood relation
生肉 **seiniku** raw meat
生色 **seishoku** animated look
生返 **i(ki)kae(ru)** revive, be resuscitated
生返事 **namahenji** vague answer
生汗 **namaase** a tense sweat
生地 **seichi** birthplace　**kiji** cloth, material; one's true colors; unadorned
生地獄 **i(ki)jigoku** a living hell
生先 **o(i)saki** one's future career, remaining years
生成 **seisei** creation, formation, generation
生血 **i(ki)chi** lifeblood, blood of a living man/animal　**namachi** blood just shed, blood of a living man/animal
生糸 **kiito** raw silk
7 生身 **i(ki)mi** living body; fresh fish
　　namami flesh and blood; living flesh; raw meat/fish
生来 **seirai, shōrai** by nature, inborn, congenital
生体 **seitai** living body
生卵 **namatamago** raw egg
生別 **i(ki)waka(re), seibetsu** lifelong separation

生兵法 **namabyōhō** untried tactics; smattering of knowledge
生延 **i(ki)no(biru)** live on, live long, survive
生没 **seibotsu** (year of one's) birth and death
生抜 **ha(e)nu(ki)** native-born
生花 **i(ke)bana** flower arrangement
　　seika flower arrangement; natural flower
生学者 **namagakusha** dilettante, dabbler
生学門 **namagakumon** superficial knowledge
生貝 **namagai** raw shellfish
8 生長 **i(ki)naga(raeru)** live on, live long, survive
生命 **seimei** life
生命保険 **seimei hoken** life insurance
生限 **i(kiru) kagi(ri)** as long as life continues
生育 **seiiku** growth, development
　　ha(e)soda(tsu) spring up
生直 **kisu(gu)** well-behaved and straightforward
生茂 **o(i)shige(ru)** grow luxuriantly
生国 **shōkoku** one's native country/place
生易 **namayasa(shii)** easy, simple
生物 **seibutsu, i(ki)mono** living creature, life　**namamono** uncooked food, unbaked cake
生物学 **seibutsugaku** biology
生物界 **seibutsukai** plants and animals, life
生放送 **namahōsō** live broadcast
9 生保 **seiho** life insurance (short for 生命保険)
生変 **u(mare)ka(waru)** be born again, start life afresh, be reincarnated
　　ha(e)ka(waru) grow in a place of previous growth, grow in again
生首 **namakubi** freshly severed head
生前 **seizen** during one's lifetime
生活 **seikatsu** life, livelihood
生活力 **seikatsuryoku** vitality; earning power
生活苦 **seikatsuku** economic distress, hard times
生活圏 **seikatsuken** Lebensraum
生活費 **seikatsuhi** living expenses
生活難 **seikatsunan** economic distress, hard times
生垣 **i(ke)gaki** hedge
生後 **seigo** after birth
生茹 **namayu(de)** half-boiled
生面 **seimen** new field; first meeting
生神 **i(ki)gami** a living god
生神様 **i(ki)gamisama** a living god
生故郷 **u(mare)kokyō** one's birthplace, native place
生臭 **namagusa(i)** smelling of fish/blood
生臭坊主 **namagusa bōzu** worldly priest, corrupt monk
生臭物 **namagusamono** raw foods (forbidden to monks)

生計 **seikei** livelihood, living
生計費 **seikeihi** living expenses
10 生残 **i(ki)noko(ru)** survive   **seizan** survival
生残者 **seizansha** survivor
生原稿 **namagenkō** raw manuscript (not yet typeset)
生酒 **kizake** pure saké
生埋 **i(ki)u(me)** burying alive
生起 **seiki** occur, arise
生捕 **i(ke)do(ru)** capture alive
生娘 **kimusume** virgin; innocent girl
生徒 **seito** student, pupil
生家 **seika** house of one's birth
生害 **shōgai** be killed; commit suicide
生梅 **namaume** fresh-picked plum
生殺 **seisatsu** life and death
　　namagoro(shi) half-kill; keep in suspense
生殺与奪 **seisatsu-yodatsu** (the power to) kill or let live
生息 **seisoku** live, multiply, inhabit
生息子 **kimusuko** unsophisticated young man
生紙 **kigami** unsized paper
生粋 **kissui** pure, true
生恥 **i(ki)haji** living in dishonor, shame
生馬 **i(ki)uma** (sharp and wily enough to pluck the eyes out of) a living horse
11 生動 **seidō** being full of life
生涯 **shōgai** life, lifetime, career; for life, lifelong
生得 **seitoku, shōtoku** by nature, innate
生彩 **seisai** luster, brilliance, vividness
生菓子 **namagashi** unbaked cake
生乾 **namagawa(ki)** damp-dry
生理 **seiri** physiology; menstruation
生理学 **seirigaku** physiology
生理的 **seiriteki** physiological
生理的食塩水 **seiriteki shokuensui** saline solution
生産 **seisan** production
生産力 **seisanryoku** (productive) capacity, productivity
生産地 **seisanchi** producing region
生産物 **seisanbutsu** product, produce
生産性 **seisansei** productivity
生産高 **seisandaka** output, production, yield
生産財 **seisanzai** producer's goods
生産量 **seisanryō** amount produced, output, production
生産費 **seisanhi** production costs
生酔 **namayo(i)** half-drunk, tipsy
生魚 **namazakana, seigyo** raw/fresh fish
12 生揚 **namaa(ge)** fried tofu
生落 **u(mare)o(chiru)** be born
　　u(mi)o(tosu) give birth to

生焼 **namaya(ke)** half-cooked, underdone, rare
生煮 **namani(e)** half-cooked, underdone
生硬 **seikō** crude, immature, unrefined
生殖 **seishoku** reproduction, procreation
生殖器 **seishokki, seishokuki** reproductive organs
生番組 **namabangumi** live program
13 生業 **seigyō** occupation, calling
生傷 **namakizu** unhealed wound, fresh bruise
生際 **ha(e)giwa** one's hairline
生滅 **shōmetsu** birth and death, appearance and disappearance
生損 **u(mi)soko(nau)** miscarry
生暖 **namaatataka(i)** lukewarm
生意気 **namaiki** conceited, impertinent, smart-alecky
生新 **namaatara(shii)** brand new
生節 **namabushi** half-dried bonito
14 生態 **seitai** mode of life, ecology
生態学 **seitaigaku** ecology
生憎 **ainiku** unfortunately
生誕 **seitan** birth
生聞 **namagi(ki)** smattering of knowledge
15 生還 **seikan** come back alive; cross home plate
生還者 **seikansha** survivor
生蕎麦 **kisoba** buckwheat noodles
生蕃 **seiban** wild tribesmen
生麩 **shōfu** wheat starch
生餌 **i(ki)e** live bait
生霊 **i(ki)ryō** apparition of a living person, wraith
16 生壁 **namakabe** undried wall
生薬 **kigusuri** herb medicine
生薬屋 **kigusuriya** drugstore, apothecary
生薑 **shōga** ginger
生親 **u(mi no) oya** one's biological father; originator, creator
17 生鮮 **seisen** fresh
生鮮度 **seisendo** freshness
18 生贄 **i(ke)nie** sacrificial offering
生醬油 **kijōyu** raw/pure soy sauce
生類 **shōrui, seirui** living creatures
21 生齧 **namakaji(ri)** superficial knowledge

――――――― 2 ―――――――

1 一生涯 **isshōgai** a lifetime, one's (whole) life
一生懸命 **isshōkenmei** with all one's might
2 七生 **shichishō** seven lives
人生 **jinsei** life, human existence
人生派 **jinseiha** humanists
人生観 **jinseikan** one's philosophy of life
3 下生 **shitaba(e)** underbrush, undergrowth
女生 **josei** schoolgirl, coed
女生徒 **joseito** schoolgirl, coed
小生 **shōsei** I, me

0a5

小生意気 **konamaiki** conceit, impudence
4 不生産的 **fuseisanteki** unproductive
毛生薬 **keha(e)gusuri** hair restorer
中生代 **chūseidai** the Mesozoic era
化生 **kasei** metaplasia, metamorphosis
今生 **konjō** this life/world
双生 **sōsei** growing in pairs
双生児 **sōseiji** twins
公生活 **kōseikatsu** public life
水生 **suisei** aquatic (plant)
5 出生 **shusshō, shussei** birth
出生年月日 **shusshō nengappi, shussei nengappi** date of birth
出生地 **shusshōchi, shusseichi** birthplace
出生届 **shusseitodoke** report of birth
出生率 **shusshōritsu, shusseiritsu** birth rate
出生数 **shusseisū, shusshōsū** number of live births
民生 **minsei** the people's livelihood, welfare
民生委員 **minsei iin** district welfare officer
生生 **namanama(shii)** fresh, vivid **seisei** lively
他生 **tashō** previous existence
存生 **zonjō** be alive
写生 **shasei** draw from life, sketch, portray
古生物 **koseibutsu** extinct plants and animals
古生物学 **koseibutsugaku** paleontology
平生 **heizei** usual, everyday, ordinary
永生 **eisei** eternal life, immortality
芝生 **shibafu** lawn
6 死生 **shisei** life and death
両生 **ryōsei** amphibious (animal)
再生 **saisei** (as if) alive/born again; reclamation, regeneration, recycling; reproduction, playback
再生産 **saiseisan** reproduction
全生涯 **zenshōgai** one's entire life
老生 **rōsei** I (word used by old men)
先生 **sensei** teacher, master, doctor
早生 **hayau(mare)** born between January 1 and April 1 **wase** early-ripening (rice); precocious
早生児 **sōseiji** prematurely born baby
自生 **jisei** spontaneous generation; grow in the wild
7 更生 **kōsei** rebirth, resuscitation; making over, rehabilitation, reorganization
更生品 **kōseihin** reconditioned article
余生 **yosei** the remainder of one's life
対生 **taisei** (leaves) growing in opposing pairs
抗生 **kōsei** antibiotic
抗生物質 **kōsei busshitsu** an antibiotic
花生 **hanai(ke)** vase
学生 **gakusei** student
学生服 **gakuseifuku** school uniform
学生帽 **gakuseibō** school cap

学生証 **gakuseishō** student I.D.
私生子 **shiseishi** illegitimate child
私生児 **shiseiji** illegitimate child
私生活 **shiseikatsu** one's private life
初生 **shosei** newborn **hatsuna(ri)** first fruits
初生児 **shoseiji** newborn baby
8 非生産的 **hiseisanteki** nonproductive, unproductive
長生 **nagai(ki), chōsei** long life, longevity
厚生 **kōsei** public welfare
厚生大臣 **kōsei daijin** Minister of Health and Welfare
厚生年金 **kōsei nenkin** welfare pension
厚生省 **Kōseishō** Ministry of Health and Welfare
弥生 **yayoi** third lunar month; spring **Yayoi** (archaelogical period, 200 B.C.-250 A.D.)
往生 **ōjō** die (and be reborn in paradise); give in; be at one's wit's end
往生際悪 **ōjōgiwa (ga) waru(i)** accept defeat with bad grace
芽生 **meba(e)** bud, sprout
実生 **mishō, miba(e)** seedling
実生活 **jisseikatsu** real/practical life
性生活 **sei seikatsu** sex life
9 発生 **hassei** occurrence, outbreak; genesis; generation; growth, rise, development
発生学 **hasseigaku** embryology
発生器 **hasseiki** generator
院生 **insei** graduate student
派生 **hasei** derive from, originate with
派生的 **haseiteki** derivative, secondary
派生語 **haseigo** a derivative
後生 **kōsei** born later, younger, junior **goshō** the next world
後生大事 **goshō daiji** religiously, earnestly
相生 **aio(i)** growing from the same root
胎生 **taisei** viviparous
胎生学 **taiseigaku** embryology
紅生姜 **beni shōga** red pickled ginger
食生活 **shokuseikatsu** eating/dietary habits
10 残生 **zansei** one's remaining years
陸生 **rikusei** (living on) land
畜生 **chikushō** beast, brute; Dammit!
畜生道 **chikushōdō** incest
原生 **gensei** primitive, primeval, proto-
原生林 **genseirin** primeval/virgin forest
桐生 **Kiryū** (city, Gunma-ken)
殺生 **sesshō** destroy life, kill (animals)
殺生戒 **sesshōkai** Buddhist precept against killing
殺生禁断 **sesshō kindan** hunting and fishing prohibited
書生 **shosei** student; student-houseboy
書生論 **shoseiron** impractical argument

教生 **kyōsei** student teacher
11 野生 **yasei** wild
　偸生 **tōsei** continue living when one should die
　遅生 **osouma(re)** born after April 1 (school entrance date)
　済生 **saisei** life saving
　密生 **missei** grow thick/luxuriantly
　寄生 **kisei** parasitic
　寄生木 **yadorigi** mistletoe; parasitic plant
　寄生虫 **kiseichū** parasitic insects, parasite
　寄生物 **kiseibutsu** parasite
　庶生 **shosei** illegitimate birth
　現生 **gennama** hard cash
　畢生 **hissei** lifelong
　終生 **shūsei** all one's life, lifelong
　酔生夢死 **suisei-mushi** idle one's life away
12 着生 **chakusei** insertion
　晩生 **okute** late(-maturing) rice; late crops
　無生 **musei** lifeless, inanimate
　無生物 **museibutsu** inanimate object
　衆生 **shujō** all living things; mankind
　筆生 **hissei** copyist, amanuensis
　筍生活 **takenoko seikatsu** living by selling off one's personal effects
13 塾生 **jukusei** cram-school student
　摂生 **sessei** taking care of one's health
　群生 **gunsei** grow gregariously, grow in crowds
　微生物 **biseibutsu** microorganism, microbe
　微生物学 **biseibutsugaku** microbiology
　新生 **shinsei** new life
　新生児 **shinseiji** newborn baby
　新生命 **shinseimei** new life
　新生活 **shinseikatsu** a new life
　新生面 **shinseimen** new aspect/field
　新生涯 **shinshōgai** a new life/career
　鈴生 **suzuna(ri)** grow in clusters/abundance
14 誕生 **tanjō** birth
　誕生日 **tanjōbi** birthday
　誕生石 **tanjōseki** birthstone
　誕生祝 **tanjō iwa(i)** birthday celebration
15 養生 **yōjō** take care of one's health; curing (of concrete)
　養生法 **yōjōhō** hygiene, rules of health
　寮生 **ryōsei** dormitory student
　諸生 **shosei** students
16 儒生 **jusei** Confucian scholar, student of Confucianism
　衛生 **eisei** hygiene, sanitation
　衛生上 **eiseijō** hygienic, sanitary
　衛生兵 **eiseihei** (military) medic
　衛生学 **eiseigaku** hygiene, hygienics
　衛生法 **eiseihō** hygiene, hygienics
　衛生的 **eiseiteki** hygienic, sanitary
　衛生係 **eiseigakari** health officer

衛生班 **eiseihan** a sanitation detail
衛生隊 **eiseitai** medical corps
17 優生学 **yūseigaku** eugenics
　優生保護法 **Yūsei Hogo Hō** Eugenic Protection Law
　簇生 **zokusei, sōsei** grow in clusters
19 蘇生 **sosei** revival, resuscitation; resurrection

──────── 3 ────────

1 一年生 **ichinensei** first-year student; annual (plant)
2 入学生 **nyūgakusei** new student
3 大学生 **daigakusei** university/college student
　大往生 **daiōjō** a peaceful death
　大量生産 **tairyō seisan** mass production
　上級生 **jōkyūsei** upperclassman
　下級生 **kakyūsei** underclassman
　女学生 **jogakusei** girl student
　小学生 **shōgakusei** elementary-school student
4 不摂生 **fusessei** neglect of one's health
　不養生 **fuyōjō** neglect of one's health
　不衛生 **fueisei** unsanitary, unhygienic
　中学生 **chūgakusei** junior-high-school student
　水上生活者 **suijō seikatsusha** seafarer
5 立往生 **ta(chi)ōjō** be at a standstill, be stalled/stranded; stand speechless (without a rejoinder)
6 多年生 **tanensei** perennial
　同級生 **dōkyūsei** classmate
　同窓生 **dōsōsei** schoolmate, fellow student, alumnus
　同期生 **dōkisei** (former) classmate
　在学生 **zaigakusei** student
　在校生 **zaikōsei** present students
　竹園生 **take (no) sonoo** bamboo garden; the imperial family
7 医学生 **igakusei** medical student
8 非衛生的 **hieiseiteki** unsanitary, unhygienic
　受講生 **jukōsei** trainee, seminar participant
　受験生 **jukensei** student preparing for exams
　苦学生 **kugakusei** self-supporting student
　実習生 **jisshūsei** trainee, apprentice
　官費生 **kanpisei** government-supported student
　性衛生 **sei eisei** sexual hygiene
　門下生 **monkasei** one's pupil
9 通学生 **tsūgakusei** day student
　浮遊生物 **fuyū seibutsu** plankton
　後半生 **kōhansei** the latter half of one's life
　食養生 **shokuyōjō** taking nourishing food, dietary cure
10 候補生 **kōhosei** cadet
　高校生 **kōkōsei** senior-high-school student
　校外生 **kōgaisei** extension/correspondence course student
　特待生 **tokutaisei** scholarship student

0a5

留学生 **ryūgakusei** student studying abroad
11 寄宿生 **kishukusei** dormitory student
12 落花生 **rakkasei** peanuts
落第生 **rakudaisei** student who failed
給費生 **kyūhisei** student on scholarship
貸費生 **taihisei** loan-scholarship student
13 適者生存 **tekisha seizon** survival of the fittest
奨学生 **shōgakusei** student on a scholarship
新入生 **shinnyūsei** new student, freshman
14 選科生 **senkasei** nonregular student
模範生 **mohansei** model student
17 優等生 **yūtōsei** honors student
聴講生 **chōkōsei** auditing student

———————— 4 ————————

1 一蓮托生 **ichiren-takushō** sharing fate with another
2 九死一生得 **kyūshi (ni) isshō (o) e(ru)** narrowly escape death
3 女子大生 **joshi daisei** a coed
5 半死半生 **hanshi-hanshō** half dead
6 自力更生 **jiriki kōsei** be saved by one's own efforts
10 起死回生 **kishi kaisei** resuscitation, revival
烏有先生 **Uyū-sensei** fictitious person
12 極楽往生 **gokuraku ōjō** a peaceful death
無理往生 **muri-ōjō** forced compliance

———————— 5 ————————

1 一卵性双生児 **ichiransei sōseiji** identical twins

0a5.30 / 711

弁 辯瓣辨辧

BEN speech, dialect, oratory; valve; petal; distinguish between; braid, bind
wakima(eru) discern, understand, bear in mind

———————— 1 ————————

0 弁じる **ben(jiru)** speak, talk, argue for; attend to, carry out
3 弁才 **bensai** oratorical talent, eloquence
弁士 **benshi** speaker, orator; movie "explainer"
4 弁天 **Benten** Sarasvati, an Indian goddess of music, eloquence, and fortune
6 弁舌 **benzetsu** speech, eloquence
弁当 **bentō** (box) lunch
弁当屋 **bentōya** lunch vendor
弁当箱 **bentōbako** lunch box
7 弁別 **benbetsu** distinguish, discriminate
8 弁明 **benmei** explanation, justification
弁者 **bensha** speaker, orator
11 弁済 **bensai** (re)payment, settlement
弁理 **benri** management

弁理士 **benrishi** patent attorney
弁務官 **benmukan** commissioner
12 弁証法 **benshōhō** dialectic, dialectics
弁証論 **benshōron** apologetics; dialectics
13 弁解 **benkai** explanation, vindication, justification, defense, excuse, apology
14 弁髪 **benpatsu** pigtail, queue
弁膜 **benmaku** valve (in internal organs)
弁駁 **benpaku** refutation
15 弁論 **benron** argument, debate; oral proceedings, pleading
弁慶 **Benkei** (legendary warrior-monk, ?–1189)
17 弁償 **benshō** indemnification
弁償金 **benshōkin** indemnity, reparations
20 弁護 **bengo** defend, plead for
弁護人 **bengonin** counsel, defender, advocate
弁護士 **bengoshi** lawyer, attorney
弁護士会 **bengoshikai** bar association
弁護依頼人 **bengo irainin** client
弁護者 **bengosha** defender, advocate
弁護料 **bengoryō** attorney's fees

———————— 2 ————————

4 内弁慶 **uchi-Benkei** tough-acting at home (but meek before outsiders)
支弁 **shiben** pay, defray
手弁当 **tebentō** bringing/buying one's own lunch
5 代弁 **daiben** pay by proxy; act for another; speak for another
6 多弁 **taben** talkative
気弁 **kiben** air valve
合弁 **gōben** joint management/venture
合弁会社 **gōben-gaisha** joint venture (company)
自弁 **jiben** paying one's own expenses
7 佞弁 **neiben** flattery, cajolery
抗弁 **kōben** plea, defense, protest, demurral
花弁 **hanabira, kaben** petal
快弁 **kaiben** eloquence
8 武弁 **buben** soldier
9 通弁 **tsūben** interpreter, interpreting
活弁 **katsuben** silent-movie interpreter/explainer (short for 活動写真の弁士)
思弁 **shiben** speculation
10 陳弁 **chinben** explain oneself, justify, defend, vindicate
陰弁慶 **kage-Benkei** a lion at home but meek before outsiders
能弁 **nōben** eloquence, oratory
能弁家 **nōbenka** good speaker, orator
11 勘弁 **kanben** pardon, forgive, tolerate
達弁 **tatsuben** eloquent, glib, fluent
強弁 **kyōben** quibble, chop logic
訥弁 **totsuben** slow/awkward of speech
12 堪弁 **kanben** pardon, forgive

答弁 **tōben** reply, explanation, defense
雄弁 **yūben** eloquence
13 滑弁 **katsuben** slide valve
腰弁 **koshiben** petty official, low-salaried worker
腰弁当 **koshibentō** lunch tied to one's belt; lunch-carrying worker
詭弁 **kiben** sophistry, logic-chopping
詭弁家 **kibenka** sophist, quibbler
14 駄弁 **daben** foolish talk, bunk
駅弁 **ekiben** box lunch sold at a train station
15 熱弁 **netsuben** fervent speech
論弁 **ronben** argument

———————— 3 ————————
6 安全弁 **anzenben** safety valve
7 汽車弁当 **kisha bentō** railway lunch
8 空気弁 **kūkiben** air valve
国選弁護人 **kokusen bengonin** court-appointed defense counsel

0a5.31
匆 **SŌ** in a flurry/hurry

0a5.32 / 1492
甘 **KAN** sweet; good-tasting; contented; indulgent **ama(i)** sweet; honeyed (words); lenient; easygoing, overoptimistic; sugary, sentimental **ama(eru), ama(ttareru)** act like a spoiled child, coax **ama(yakasu)** be indulgent, pamper, coddle **ama(nzuru), ama(njiru)** be content with, be resigned to **uma(i)** good tasting

———————— 1 ————————
2 甘子 **ama(ttarek)ko** spoiled child
3 甘口 **amakuchi** mild, light (flavor); sweet tooth; flattery
4 甘心 **kanshin** contentment, satisfaction
7 甘汞 **kankō** calomel, mercurous chloride
甘言 **kangen** honeyed words, flattery, blarney
8 甘受 **kanju** submit meekly to, resign oneself to
甘味 **kanmi, amami** sweetness
甘味料 **kanmiryō** sweetener
9 甘美 **kanbi** sweet
甘草 **kanzō** licorice
甘茶 **amacha** hydrangea tea
10 甘酒 **amazake** sweet saké
甘党 **amatō** person with a sweet tooth
甘栗 **amaguri** roasted sweet chestnuts
甘納豆 **amanattō** adzuki-bean candy
13 甘塩 **amajio** slightly salted
14 甘蔗 **kansho** sugar cane
甘蔗糖 **kanshotō** cane sugar, sucrose
17 甘薯 **kansho** sweet potato

19 甘藷 **kansho** sweet potato
21 甘露 **kanro** syrup, nectar, sweetness
甘露煮 **kanroni** sweet dish of boiled fish or shellfish

0a5.33 / 351
央 **Ō** center, middle

———————— 2 ————————
4 中央 **chūō** center, middle
中央集権 **chūō shūken** centralization of government
15 震央 **shin'ō** epicenter

0a5.34 / 982
甲 **KŌ** first in a series, "A"; (turtle's) shell, carapace; armor; back (of the hand), top (of the foot) **KAN** high-pitched **kinoe** first calendar sign

———————— 1 ————————
1 甲乙 **kō-otsu** A and B; make distinctions, rank, grade
甲乙丙 **kō-otsu-hei** A, B, C; No. 1, 2, 3
6 甲虫 **kabutomushi, kōchū** beetle
7 甲状腺 **kōjōsen** thyroid gland
8 甲府 **Kōfu** (city, Yamanashi-ken)
甲板 **kanpan, kōhan** deck
9 甲冑 **katchū** armor (and helmet)
10 甲高 **kandaka(i)** high-pitched, shrill
kōdaka having a high instep
11 甲殻 **kōkaku** shell, carapace
甲殻類 **kōkakurui** crustaceans
12 甲斐 **kai** effect, result; worth, avail, use
Kai (ancient kuni, Yamanashi-ken)
甲斐性 **kaishō** resourcefulness, competence
14 甲種 **kōshu** grade A
15 甲論乙駁 **kōron-otsubaku** pros and cons
19 甲羅 **kōra** (turtle's) shell

———————— 2 ————————
3 上甲板 **jōkanpan** upper deck
4 中甲板 **chūkōhan, chūkanpan** main deck
手甲 **te(no)kō** the back of the hand
tekkō covering for the back of the hand
5 生甲斐 **i(ki)gai** something worth living for
正甲板 **seikanpan** main deck
7 言甲斐 **i(i)gai** worth mentioning
8 肩甲骨 **kenkōkotsu** shoulder blade
10 華甲 **kakō** age 60
破甲弾 **hakōdan** armor-piercing shell
11 亀甲 **kikkō, kame (no) kō** tortoise shell
12 腑甲斐無 **fugaina(i)** faint-hearted, feckless
装甲 **sōkō** armor, armor plating
装甲車 **sōkōsha** armored car

13 鉄甲 **tekkō** iron armor/helmet
16 機甲 **kikō** armored
24 鼈甲 **bekkō** tortoiseshell
　鼈甲色 **bekkō-iro** amber color

0a5.35 / 363

由

YU, YŪ, YUI, yo(ru) be based on, be due to, depend on　**yoshi** purport, it is said that; reason, cause, significance; means, way

─────────── 1 ───────────

3 由々 **yuyu(shii)** grave, serious
7 由来 **yurai** origin, derivation, how it came about; originally, by nature
　由来書 **yuraisho** history, memoirs
14 由緒 **yuisho** history, lineage
15 由縁 **yuen** relationship, reason, way

─────────── 2 ───────────

6 因由 **in'yu** cause
　自由 **jiyū** freedom, liberty; free
　自由化 **jiyūka** liberalization
　自由主義 **jiyū shugi** liberalism
　自由刑 **jiyūkei** punishment by confinement, imprisonment
　自由自在 **jiyū-jizai** free, unrestricted
　自由形 **jiyūgata** freestyle (swimming)
　自由労働者 **jiyū rōdōsha** casual laborer
　自由国 **jiyūkoku** free/independent nation
　自由放任 **jiyū hōnin** nonintervention, laissez-faire
　自由型 **jiyūgata** freestyle (wrestling)
　自由党 **jiyūtō** liberal party
　自由訳 **jiyūyaku** free translation
　自由港 **jiyūkō** free port
　自由営業 **jiyū eigyō** nonrestricted trade
　自由業 **jiyūgyō** freelance occupation, self-employed
　自由意志 **jiyū ishi** free will
　自由詩 **jiyūshi** free verse
8 事由 **jiyū** reason, cause
11 理由 **riyū** reason, cause
　経由 **keiyu** via, by way of
15 縁由 **en'yu** relationship

─────────── 3 ───────────

4 不自由 **fujiyū** inconvenience, discomfort; privation; disability, handicap

0a5.36 / 112

母

BO, haha, (o)kā(san) mother

─────────── 1 ───────────

2 母子 **boshi, hahako** mother and child
　母子草 **hahakogusa** cottonweed

母子家庭 **boshi katei** fatherless home
母子寮 **boshiryō** home for mothers and children
3 母上 **hahaue** mother (polite)
4 母方 **hahakata** the mother's side (of the family)
6 母后 **bokō** empress dowager
7 母体 **botai** the mother('s body); parent organization
　母君 **hahagimi** mother (polite)
　母乳 **bonyū** mother's milk
　母系 **bokei** maternal line
　母系制度 **bokei seido** matriarchal system
　母系家族 **bokei kazoku** matriarchal family
8 母国 **bokoku** one's mother/native country
　母国語 **bokokugo** one's mother/native tongue
　母性 **bosei** motherhood, maternal
　母性愛 **boseiai** a mother's love, maternal affection
9 母型 **bokei** matrix (in printing)
　母屋 **omoya** main building
　母胎 **botai** womb, uterus
　母音 **boin** vowel
10 母校 **bokō** one's alma mater
11 母堂 **bodō** mother (polite)
　母船 **bosen** mother ship
12 母港 **bokō** home port
　母御 **hahago** mother (polite)
　母御前 **hahagoze, hahagozen** mother (polite)
　母斑 **bohan** birthmark
14 母様 **(o)kāsama** mother, mama
15 母権 **boken** maternal authority
16 母親 **hahaoya** mother
21 母艦 **bokan** mother ship, tender

─────────── 2 ───────────

2 入母屋 **irimoya** roof with eaves below the gables
3 亡母 **bōbo** one's late mother
4 分母 **bunbo** denominator
　父母 **fubo, chichihaha** father and mother
　水母 **kurage** jellyfish
5 半母音 **hanboin** semivowel
　生母 **seibo** one's (biological) mother
　字母 **jibo** letter; printing type
6 老母 **rōbo** one's aged mother
7 伯母 **oba, hakubo** aunt
　乳母 **uba** wet nurse
　乳母車 **ubaguruma** baby carriage/buggy
8 叔母 **oba, shukubo** aunt
　実母 **jitsubo** one's biological mother
　空母 **kūbo** aircraft carrier (short for 航空母艦)
　国母 **kokubo** empress, empress dowager
9 保母 **hobo** kindergarten teacher
　祖母 **sobo** grandmother
10 酒母 **shubo** rice-malt-yeast culture (from which saké is made)

教母 **kyōbo** godmother, sponsor
病母 **byōbo** one's invalid mother
11 異母 **ibo** different mother
12 雲母 **unmo, kirara** mica, isinglas
13 慈母 **jibo** affectionate mother
義母 **gibo** mother-in-law; foster mother; stepmother
聖母 **Seibo** the Holy Mother
酵母 **kōbo** yeast
酵母菌 **kōbokin** yeast fungus
14 複母音 **fukuboin** diphthong
15 養母 **yōbo** adoptive/foster mother
寮母 **ryōbo** dormitory matron
16 賢母 **kenbo** wise mother
20 醸母 **jōbo** yeast

─────── 3 ───────

3 大伯母 **ōoba** great-aunt, grandaunt
大叔母 **ōoba** great-aunt, grandaunt
4 公分母 **kōbunbo** common denominator
9 祖父母 **sofubo** grandparents
10 高祖母 **kōsobo** great-great-grandmother
鬼子母神 **Kishibojin, Kishimojin** (goddess of children)
航空母艦 **kōkū bokan** aircraft carrier
11 曽祖母 **sōsobo, hiibaba** great-grandmother
15 養父母 **yōfubo** adoptive/foster parents
養祖母 **yōsobo** foster grandmother
潜水母艦 **sensui bokan** submarine tender

─────── 4 ───────

7 良妻賢母 **ryōsai-kenbo** good wife and wise mother

0a5.37 / 252

世 丗 丗 丗

SEI, SE generation; the world, society
yo the world, society, life; age, era, generation

─────── 1 ───────

2 世人 **sejin** people, the public/world
3 世上 **sejō** the world
4 世中 **yo(no)naka** the world, life, the times
5 世代 **sedai** generation
8 世事 **seji** worldly affairs
世直 **yonao(shi)** reform of the world
9 世俗 **sezoku** common customs; the world; common, mundane, vulgar
世俗化 **sezokuka** secularization
世俗的 **sezokuteki** worldly
世相 **sesō** phase of life, the times, world conditions
世界 **sekai** the world
世界一 **sekai-ichi** best in the world
世界一周 **sekai isshū** round-the-world trip, circumnavigation

世界人 **sekaijin** citizen of the world, cosmopolitan
世界大戦 **sekai taisen** World War
世界中 **sekaijū** all over the world
世界史 **sekaishi** world history
世界観 **sekaikan** world view
世紀 **seiki** century
10 世帯 **setai, shotai** household, home
世帯主 **setainushi** head of a household
11 世捨人 **yosu(te)bito** recluse, hermit
世務 **seimu** public/worldly affairs
世情 **sejō** world conditions; human nature
12 世渡 **yowata(ri)** get on in the world, make one's living
世智辛 **sechigara(i)** hard (times), tough (life)
世評 **sehyō** popular opinion; reputation; rumor
世間 **seken** the world, people, the public, society, life; rumor, gossip
世間体 **sekentei** decency, respectability, appearances
世間並 **sekenna(mi)** average, ordinary, common
世間知 **sekenshi(razu)** ignorant of the ways of the world
世間的 **sekenteki** worldly, earthly
世間話 **sekenbanashi** small-talk, chat, gossip
世間離 **sekenbana(re)** strange, uncommon; unworldly
13 世辞 **seji** flattery, compliment
世継 **yotsu(gi)** heir, successor
世話 **sewa** help, assistance; good offices, recommendation; take care of; everyday life
世話人 **sewanin** go-between, intermediary; sponsor; caretaker
世話役 **sewayaku** go-between, intermediary; sponsor; caretaker
世馴 **yona(reru)** get used to the world, become worldly-wise
14 世態 **setai** social conditions, the world
世慣 **yona(reru)** get used to the world, become worldly-wise
世銀 **Segin** the World Bank (short for 世界銀行)
15 世論 **seron, yoron** public opinion
世論調査 **seron chōsa, yoron chōsa** (public-opinion) poll
22 世襲 **seshū** hereditary (right)

─────── 2 ───────

1 一世 **issei** a lifetime; a generation; the First; first generation (Japanese-American) **isse** a lifetime
一世一代 **issei ichidai** once in a lifetime
一世紀 **isseiki** a century; first century

2 二世 **nisei** (Elizabeth) II, the Second; second-generation (Japanese-American)
　　nise two existences, present and future
二世契 **nise (no) chigi(ri)** marriage vows
人世 **jinsei** this world, life
3 三世 **sansei** the Third; third generation (Japanese-American)　**sanze** past, present, and future existences
万世 **bansei** all ages, eternity
　　yorozuyo thousands of years
万世一系 **bansei ikkei** unbroken (imperial) lineage
万世不易 **bansei fueki** everlasting, eternal
女世帯 **onnajotai** household of women
4 不世出 **fuseishutsu** rare, extraordinary, unparalleled
幻世 **gensei** this fleeting world
中世 **chūsei** the Middle Ages, medieval
月世界 **gessekai** the lunar world, the moon
5 出世 **shusse** succeed in life, get ahead
半世紀 **hanseiki** half century
末世 **sue(no)yo, masse** future ages, last days
永世 **eisei** permanence, eternity
旧世界 **kyūsekai** the Old World
処世 **shosei** conduct of life, getting on
処世訓 **shoseikun** rules for living
処世術 **shoseijutsu** how to get on in life
6 全世界 **zensekai** the whole world
次世代 **jisedai** next-generation (product)
近世 **kinsei** recent times, modern age
近世史 **kinseishi** modern history
当世 **tōsei** modern times, nowadays
当世風 **tōseifū** latest fashion, up-to-date
早世 **sōsei** early death
7 佐世保 **Sasebo** (city, Nagasaki-ken)
別世界 **bessekai** another world
乱世 **ransei** tumultuous times
希世 **kisei** rare
見世物 **misemono** show, exhibition
男世帯 **otokojotai** all-male household
8 治世 **chisei** reign, rule
実世界 **jissekai** the real/outside world
実世間 **jisseken** the real/everyday world
空世辞 **karaseji** flattery, empty compliments
9 俗世 **zokuse, zokusei** this world, earthly existence
俗世界 **zokusekai** the everyday world
俗世間 **zokuseken** this world, secular society
奕世 **ekisei** generation after generation
前世 **zense** previous existence
前世界 **zensekai** prehistoric ages
前世紀 **zenseiki** last century; prehistoric times
浮世 **u(ki)yo** this transitory world
浮世草子 **ukiyozōshi** realistic novel (Edo period)

浮世絵 **ukiyoe** (type of Japanese woodblock print)
浮世絵師 **ukiyoeshi** ukiyoe artist
後世 **kōsei** later ages, posterity
　　gose the next world
10 時世 **jisei** the times
11 済世 **saisei** social reform
済世事業 **saisei jigyō** public-welfare work
常世国 **tokoyo (no) kuni** far-off land; heaven; hades
現世 **gense, gensei, genze, utsu(shi)yo** this present world
現世的 **genseteki, genseiteki** worldly, temporal
現世紀 **genseiki** this century
救世 **kyūsei** salvation of the world
救世主 **Kyūseishu** the Savior/Messiah
救世軍 **Kyūseigun** the Salvation Army
累世 **ruisei** successive generations; from generation to generation
終世 **shūsei** all one's life, lifelong
経世 **keisei** administration, statecraft
経世家 **keiseika** statesman, administrator
12 隔世 **kakusei** a distant age
創世 **sōsei** creation of the world
創世記 **Sōseiki** Genesis
遁世 **tonsei** seclusion
遁世者 **tonseisha** recluse, hermit
渡世 **tosei** livelihood; occupation, trade
渡世人 **toseinin** gambler, gangster
御世 **miyo** reign, period
絶世 **zessei** peerless, unequaled
13 慨世 **gaisei** concern for the public
新世界 **shinsekai** new world; the New World
新世帯 **shinjotai** new home/household
辞世 **jisei** passing away; deathbed poem
14 厭世 **ensei** weariness with life, pessimism
厭世主義 **ensei shugi** pessimism
厭世的 **enseiteki** world-weary, pessimistic
厭世家 **enseika** pessimist
厭世観 **enseikan** pessimistic view of life, Weltschmerz
痩世帯 **ya(se)jotai** poor household
銀世界 **ginsekai** vast silvery/snowy scene
16 濁世 **dakuse** (this) corrupt world
18 観世音 **Kanzeon** the Goddess of Mercy
観世音菩薩 **Kanzeon Bosatsu** the Goddess of Mercy
19 曠世 **kōsei** unprecedented, unmatched
警世 **keisei** warning to the world/public
警世家 **keiseika** prophet, seer

――――――― 3 ―――――――

2 二十世紀 **nijisseiki, nijusseiki** the twentieth century
3 三千世界 **sanzen sekai** the whole world, the universe

₈ 夜見世 **yomise** night fair; night stall

——————— 4 ———————

₅ 立身出世 **risshin-shusse** success in life

0a5.38 / 332

史 史

SHI history, chronicles, record; (as suffix) (title of respect)

——————— 1 ———————

₃ 史上 **shijō** in history; historical
₆ 史伝 **shiden** history and biography; historical records
₇ 史学 **shigaku** (study of) history
₈ 史実 **shijitsu** historical fact
　史的 **shiteki** historical
₉ 史乗 **shijō** history, annals
₁₀ 史家 **shika** historian
　史書 **shisho** history book, a history
　史料 **shiryō** historical materials/records
₁₁ 史眼 **shigan** historical view, sense of history
　史略 **shiryaku** a brief history
₁₃ 史跡 **shiseki** historical landmark
₁₅ 史劇 **shigeki** historical drama
　史論 **shiron** historical essay
₁₈ 史観 **shikan** view of history
　史蹟 **shiseki** historical landmark
₂₀ 史籍 **shiseki** history book, historical work

——————— 2 ———————

₃ 女史 **joshi** Mrs., Miss, Madam
　小史 **shōshi** a brief history
₅ 外史 **gaishi** unofficial history
　正史 **seishi** authentic history
₆ 先史学 **senshigaku** prehistory
　有史 **yūshi** historical, in recorded history
　有史以来 **yūshi irai** since the dawn of history
₈ 侍史 **jishi** private secretary; respectfully
　国史 **kokushi** national/Japanese history
　青史 **seishi** history, annals
₉ 哀史 **aishi** tragic story
　前史 **zenshi** history of the early part of a period; prehistory
　通史 **tsūshi** outline of history
₁₀ 修史 **shūshi** compilation of a history
　秘史 **hishi** secret history
₁₁ 野史 **yashi** an unofficial history
　偽史 **gishi** falsified history
　情史 **jōshi** love story
　略史 **ryakushi** brief history
₁₂ 詠史 **eishi** historical poem, epic
₁₃ 戦史 **senshi** military/war history
₁₄ 歴史 **rekishi** history
　歴史学 **rekishigaku** (the study of) history
　歴史的 **rekishiteki** historic(al)
　歴史劇 **rekishigeki** historical drama

歴史観 **rekishikan** philosophy/view of history

——————— 3 ———————

₃ 上古史 **jōkoshi** ancient history
₄ 中古史 **chūkoshi** medieval history
　文化史 **bunkashi** cultural history
　文学史 **bungakushi** history of literature
　文明史 **bunmeishi** history of civilization
　日本史 **Nihonshi** Japanese history
₅ 世界史 **sekaishi** world history
　古代史 **kodaishi** ancient history
　比較史 **hikakushi** comparative history
₆ 近世史 **kinseishi** modern history
₈ 宗教史 **shūkyōshi** history of religion
₉ 美術史 **bijutsushi** art history
　政治史 **seijishi** political history
₁₀ 郷土史 **kyōdoshi** local history
　教会史 **kyōkaishi** church history
₁₁ 唯物史観 **yuibutsu shikan** materialistic interpretation of history
₁₅ 編年史 **hennenshi** chronicle, annals

——————— 4 ———————

₈ 国文学史 **kokubungakushi** history of Japanese literature

0a5.39 / 309

申

SHIN, mō(su) say (humble); be named (humble) **saru** ninth horary sign (monkey)

——————— 1 ———————

₂ 申入 **mō(shi)i(reru)** propose, suggest
　申子 **mō(shi)go** child born in answer to one's prayers
₃ 申上 **mō(shi)a(geru)** say, tell (humble)
₄ 申分 **mō(shi)bun** something to say (against), objection, shortcomings
　申込 **mō(shi)ko(mu)** propose, file, apply for, book
　申込書 **mōshikomisho** an application
　申込順 **mōshiko(mi)jun** in order of applications received
₅ 申出 **mō(shi)de(ru)** offer, submit, report, request **mō(shi)i(de)** proposal; request, application, claim; report, notice
　申付 **mō(shi)tsu(keru)** tell, order, instruct
　申立 **mō(shi)ta(teru)** state, declare
₆ 申合 **mō(shi)a(waseru)** arrange, agree upon
₇ 申告 **shinkoku** report, declaration, notification, filing
₈ 申受 **mō(shi)u(keru)** accept; ask for, charge (a price)
　申送 **mō(shi)oku(ru)** send word, write to; transfer (a matter to someone else)
₁₀ 申兼 **mō(shi)ka(neru)** I'm sorry to trouble you(, but ...)

0a5

11 申遅 **mō(shi)oku(reru)** be late in saying
申添 **mō(shi)so(eru)** add (to what has been said)
申訳 **mō(shi)wake** excuse, apology
12 申渡 **mō(shi)wata(su)** tell, declare
申開 **mō(shi)hira(ku)** explain, justify
15 申請 **shinsei** application, petition
申請書 **shinseisho** application, petition

————————— 2 —————————

3 上申 **jōshin** report (to a superior)
上申書 **jōshinsho** written report/statement
4 内申 **naishin** unofficial report
内申書 **naishinsho** student's school record
8 具申 **gushin** (full) report (to a superior)
12 復申 **fukushin** reply; report
答申 **tōshin** report
答申書 **tōshinsho** report, findings

0a5.40

丼

TAN, TON, **donburi** bowl

————————— 1 —————————

11 丼勘定 **donburi kanjō** paying money into and out of a pot, keeping no records of revenues and expenditures, slipshod accounting, rough estimate

————————— 2 —————————

4 天丼 **tendon** bowl of rice and tempura
22 鰻丼 **unagi donburi, unadon** bowl of eel and rice

————————— 3 —————————

16 親子丼 **oyako donburi** bowl of rice topped with chicken and egg

0a5.41

卌

SHŪ, **shijū** forty

0a5.42 / 1158

SATSU, SAKU book, letter; (counter for books)

————————— 1 —————————

2 冊子 **sasshi** booklet, pamphlet
sōshi storybook
13 冊数 **sassū** number of books

————————— 2 —————————

1 一冊 **issatsu** one copy (of a book)
3 小冊 **shōsatsu** booklet, pamphlet
小冊子 **shōsasshi** booklet, pamphlet
4 分冊 **bunsatsu** separate volume
7 別冊 **bessatsu** separate volume, supplement
10 書冊 **shosatsu** books
12 短冊 **tanzaku** strip of paper for writing a poem on

0a5.43

冄 冄

ZEN, NEN advancing; supple; bushy (beard)

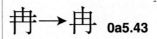 **0a5.43**

0a5.44

弗

FUTSU not, non- **doru** dollar

————————— 1 —————————

10 弗素 **fusso** fluorine

————————————— 0a6 —————————————

州	釆	互	羽	瓜	臼	多	彐	死	艮	弍	气	夸
2f4.1	6.1	6.2	2b4.5	6.3	6.4	6.5	0a6.5	6.6	6.7	4n3.3	6.8	6.9

匈	両	兇	朱	艸	束	年	舛	异	两	西	乇	耒
6.10	6.11	6.12	6.13	6.14	6.15	6.16	6.17	6.18	6.19	6.20	3p9.1	0a7.6

耒	臾	吏	曳	夷	毎	再	曲	聿
6.21	2a7.23	6.22	6.23	6.24	6.25	6.26	6.27	6.28

州 → **2f4.1**

0a6.1

SHŪ assemble, gather

0a6.2

互 互

KŌ, wata(ru) range/extend over, span

羽 → 羽 **2b4.5**

0a6.3

瓜

KA, uri melon

─────── 1 ───────

2 瓜二 **uri-futa(tsu)** alike as two halves of a split-open melon, the spitting image of each other
8 瓜実顔 **urizanegao** oval/classic face

─────── 2 ───────

4 天瓜粉 **tenkafun** talcum powder
6 西瓜 **suika** watermelon
　糸瓜 **hechima** sponge gourd, loofah
9 南瓜 **kabocha, tōnasu** pumpkin, squash
　胡瓜 **kyūri** cucumber
10 烏瓜 **karasuuri** snake gourd
　破瓜 **haka** age 16 (for girls); age 64 (for men); deflowering

0a6.4

臼

KYŪ, usu mortar, hand mill

─────── 1 ───────

10 臼砲 **kyūhō** mortar
12 臼歯 **kyūshi, usuba** molar

─────── 2 ───────

3 大臼歯 **daikyūshi** molar
5 石臼 **ishiusu** stone mill/mortar
11 脱臼 **dakkyū** become dislocated
13 搗臼 **tsu(ki)usu** mortar (for pounding rice)

凸 → **0a5.13**

凹 → **0a5.14**

0a6.5 / 229

多 彡

TA, ō(i) many, much, multi-, poly-

2 多人数 **taninzū** a large number of people
3 多大 **tadai** much, great amount
　多才 **tasai** many-talented, versatile
　多孔 **takō** porous, open (weave)
　多孔性 **takōsei** porosity
　多士済々 **tashi-seisei** many able people
4 多元論 **tagenron** pluralism
　多毛 **tamō** hairy, hirsute
　多分 **tabun** probably, maybe, likely, presumably; a great deal/many
　多辺形 **tahenkei** polygon
　多辺的 **tahenteki** multilateral
　多方面 **tahōmen** various, different, many-sided, versatile
5 多弁 **taben** talkative
　多用 **tayō** busyness
6 多年 **tanen** many years
　多年生 **tanensei** perennial
　多肉 **taniku** fleshy
　多肉果 **tanikuka** pulpy fruit
　多肉質 **tanikushitsu** fleshy, pulpy, succulent
　多汗症 **takanshō** excessive sweating
　多忙 **tabō** busy
　多血 **taketsu** sanguine, full-blooded
　多血質 **taketsushitsu** sanguine, hot-blooded
7 多作 **tasaku** prolific writing
　多作家 **tasakuka** prolific writer
　多角 **takaku** many-sided, diversified, multilateral
　多角的 **takakuteki** many-sided, versatile, diversified, multilateral
　多角経営 **takaku keiei** diversified management
　多形 **takei** multiform, polymorphous
　多芸 **tagei** versatility, varied accomplishments
　多岐 **taki** many branches/digressions/ramifications
　多売 **tabai** large sales volume
　多足 **tasoku** many-legged
8 多事多端 **taji-tatan** eventful, busy
　多幸 **takō** great happiness, good fortune
　多妻 **tasai** many wives
　多雨 **tau** heavy rain
9 多発式 **tahatsushiki** multi-engined
　多発性 **tahatsusei** multiple (sclerosis)
　多発機 **tahatsuki** multi-engine airplane
　多重 **tajū** multiplex, multiple
　多重放送 **tajū hōsō** multiplex broadcasting
　多段式 **tadanshiki** multistage
　多面 **tamen** many sides/facets
　多面体 **tamentai** polyhedron
　多神教 **tashinkyō** polytheism
　多神教的 **tashinkyōteki** polytheistic
　多神論 **tashinron** polytheism

0a6

多恨 **takon** many regrets, great discontent
多音節 **taonsetsu** polysyllable
10 多座機 **tazaki** multi-seated airplane
多能 **tanō** versatile
多病 **tabyō** sickly, in frail health
11 多過 **ōsu(giru)** be too many/much
多淫 **tain** lascivious, lustful
多彩 **tasai** colorful, multicolored
多望 **tabō** promising, with bright prospects
多欲 **tayoku** avarice, greed, covetousness
多情 **tajō** inconstant, wanton, flirty; senti-
mentalism
多情仏心 **tajō-busshin** tenderheartedness
多情多恨 **tajō-takon** taking everything to
heart
多情多感 **tajō-takan** emotional, sentimental
多産 **tasan** multiparous; fecund, prolific
多産系 **tasankei** the type that bears many
children
12 多量 **taryō** large quantity, a great deal
多項式 **takōshiki** polynomial expression
13 多勢 **tazei** great numbers, numerical
superiority
多義 **tagi** various meanings
多福 **(o)tafuku** ugly/homely woman
多福風邪 **(o)tafuku kaze** mumps
多数 **tasū** a large number; majority
多数決 **tasūketsu** decision by the majority
多数党 **tasūtō** majority party
多感 **takan** sensitive, sentimental, emotional
14 多寡 **taka** quantity, number, amount
多様 **tayō** diverse, varied
多様性 **tayōsei** diversity, variety
多端 **tatan** many items; busyness
多種多様 **tashu-tayō** various, diversified
多読 **tadoku** extensive reading
多読家 **tadokuka** voracious reader, well-
read person
15 多摩川 **Tamagawa** (river, Tōkyō-to/
Kanagawa-ken)
多慾 **tayoku** avarice, greed, covetousness
多趣味 **tashumi** many-sided interests
16 多頭 **tatō** many-headed
17 多謝 **tasha** many thanks; a thousand apologies
18 多難 **tanan** full of difficulties, thorny
多額 **tagaku** large sum/amount
19 多識 **tashiki** well-informed, knowledgeable

———————— 2 ————————
3 大多数 **daitasū** the great majority
6 宇多 **Uda** (emperor, 887–897)
7 阿多福 **otafuku** ugly/homely woman
9 畏多 **oso(re)ō(i)** gracious, august, awe-
inspiring
10 恐多 **oso(re)ō(i)** gracious, august
11 過多 **kata** excess, overabundance
12 御多忙中 **gotabōchū** while you are so busy

最多数 **saitasū** greatest number, plurality
幾多 **ikuta** many, various
13 滅多 **metta (ni)** (with negative) seldom, rarely
滅多切 **mettagi(ri)** hacking to pieces
滅多矢鱈 **mettayatara** indiscriminate, frantic
滅多打 **mettau(chi)** random shooting
煩多 **hanta** so many as to be a nuisance
数多 **kazuō(ku), amata** many, great
numbers of
14 夥多 **kata** in abundance, many
雑多 **zatta** various, all kinds of
16 繁多 **hanta** busy
18 穢多 **eta** old term for *burakumin* (Japanese
minority group)

———————— 3 ————————
1 一夫多妻 **ippu-tasai** polygamy
一妻多夫 **issai-tafu** polyandry
6 多事多端 **taji-tatan** eventful, busy
多情多恨 **tajō-takon** taking everything to
heart
多情多感 **tajō-takan** emotional, sentimental
多種多様 **tashu-tayō** various, diversified
14 歌留多 **karuta** playing cards
16 薄利多売 **hakuri-tabai** large-volume sales at
low profit margin

———————— 4 ————————
9 胃酸過多症 **isankatashō** gastric hyperacidity
12 滋養過多 **jiyōkata** hypertrophy
14 種々雑多 **shuju-zatta** various, every sort of

弖 → 多 **0a6.5**

0a6.6 / 85

死 **SHI, shi(nu)** die

———————— 1 ————————
0 死する **shi(suru)** die
2 死人 **shinin** dead person, the dead
死力 **shiryoku** desperate effort
3 死亡 **shibō** die
死亡届 **shibō todo(ke)** report of a death
死亡者 **shibōsha** the deceased, fatalities
死亡者欄 **shibōsharan** obituary column
死亡率 **shibōritsu** death rate, mortality
死亡数 **shibōsū** number of deaths
4 死文 **shibun** dead letter, mere scrap of paper
死水 **shi(ni)mizu** water given to a dying
person
死火山 **shikazan** extinct volcano
死方 **shi(ni)kata** how to die, how one died
5 死出旅 **shide (no) tabi** journey to the next
world

死生　**shisei**　life and death
死去　**shikyo**　die
死処　**shisho**　where to die, where one died
死目　**shi(ni)me**　the moment of death
6 死肉　**shiniku**　dead flesh, carrion
死刑　**shikei**　capital punishment
死刑囚　**shikeishū**　criminal sentenced to die
死刑執行　**shikei shikkō**　execution
死刑場　**shikeijō**　place of execution
死刑罪　**shikeizai**　capital offense
死色　**shishoku**　deathly pallor
死灰　**shikai**　dead embers, ashes
死地　**shichi**　the jaws of death, fatal situation
死守　**shishu**　desperately fought defense
死因　**shiin**　cause of death
7 死体　**shitai**　corpse, remains
死体解剖　**shitai kaibō**　autopsy
死体置場　**shitai o(ki)ba**　morgue
死別　**shibetsu**　separation by death
死角　**shikaku**　dead/unseen angle
死没　**shibotsu**　death
死花咲　**shi(ni)bana (o) sa(kaseru)**　do something just before one's death to win glory
死児　**shiji**　dead child; stillborn child
8 死命　**shimei**　life or death, fate
死歿　**shibotsu**　death
死法　**shihō**　a dead law
死苦　**shiku**　agony of death
死者　**shisha**　dead person, the dead
死物　**shibutsu**　lifeless thing, inanimate object
死物狂　**shi(ni)monoguru(i)**　struggle to the death; desperation, frantic efforts
死所　**shisho**　where to die, where one died
死金　**shi(ni)gane**　wastefully spent money; idle capital
9 死活　**shikatsu**　life or death
死活問題　**shikatsu mondai**　a matter of life and death
死海　**Shikai**　the Dead Sea
死後　**shigo**　after death, posthumous **shi(ni)oku(reru)**　outlive, survive
死後強直　**shigo kyōchoku**　rigor mortis
死後硬直　**shigo kōchoku**　rigor mortis
死屍　**shishi**　corpse
死面　**shimen**　death mask
死相　**shisō**　shadow of death
死胎　**shitai**　dead fetus
死神　**shi(ni)gami**　god of death; death
10 死脈　**shimyaku**　fatal pulse; exhausted ore vein
死時　**shi(ni)doki**　the time to die
死病　**shibyō**　fatal disease
死恥　**shi(ni)haji**　shameful death; disgrace not erased by death
11 死球　**shikyū**　dead ball (in baseball)

死産　**shizan**　stillbirth
死産児　**shisanji**　stillborn baby
12 死場　**shi(ni)ba**　place to die, place of death
死期　**shiki**　time of death, one's last hour
死絶　**shizetsu**　extinction　**shi(ni)ta(eru)**　die out, become extinct
13 死傷　**shishō**　casualties, killed and injured
死傷者　**shishōsha**　casualties, killed and wounded
死際　**shi(ni)giwa**　the hour of death
死滅　**shimetsu**　extinction, destruction
死損　**shi(ni)soko(nau)**　fail to die **shi(ni)zoko(nai)**　would-be suicide; one who has outlived his time
死戦　**shisen**　death struggle
死罪　**shizai**　capital punishment
14 死様　**shi(ni)zama**　manner of death
死語　**shigo**　dead language; obsolete word
15 死蔵　**shizō**　hoard
死線　**shisen**　prison perimeter which one may be shot dead for crossing; the brink of death
死霊　**shiryō**　spirit of a dead person
16 死骸　**shigai**　corpse
18 死闘　**shitō**　life-and-death struggle
死顔　**shi(ni)gao**　face of a dead person

———————— 2 ————————

2 九死一生得　**kyūshi (ni) isshō (o) e(ru)**　narrowly escape death
人死　**hitoji(ni)**　loss of life
4 不死　**fushi**　immortal
不死身　**fujimi**　insensible to pain, invulnerable, immortal
不死鳥　**fushichō**　phoenix
夭死　**yōshi**　premature death
水死　**suishi**　drowning
犬死　**inuji(ni)**　die in vain
5 必死　**hisshi**　certain death; desperate, frantic
半死半生　**hanshi-hanshō**　half dead
生死　**seishi**　life or/and death
圧死　**asshi**　be crushed to death
6 仮死　**kashi**　suspended animation, apparent death
刑死　**keishi**　execution
刎死　**funshi**　suicide by self-decapitation
老死　**rōshi**　die of old age
安死術　**anshijutsu**　euthanasia
早死　**hayaji(ni)**　die young/prematurely
7 即死　**sokushi**　die instantly
即死者　**sokushisha**　persons killed instantly
決死　**kesshi**　desperate, do-or-die
決死隊　**kesshitai**　suicide corps
狂死　**kyōshi, kuru(i)ji(ni)**　death from madness
牢死　**rōshi**　die in prison
8 若死　**wakaji(ni)**　die young

0a6

空死 **soraji(ni)** feign death
怪死 **kaishi** mysterious death
9 変死 **henshi** accidental death
急死 **kyūshi** sudden/untimely death
客死 **kakushi, kyakushi** die abroad
枯死 **koshi** wither, die
10 倒死 **tōshi** collapse and die
凍死 **tōshi, kogo(e)ji(nu), kogo(e)ji(ni)** freeze to death
凍死者 **tōshisha** person frozen to death
起死 **kishi** saving from the jaws of death
起死回生 **kishi kaisei** resuscitation, revival
徒死 **toshi** die in vain
殉死 **junshi** kill oneself on the death of one's lord
致死 **chishi** fatal, lethal, deadly, mortal
致死量 **chishiryō** lethal dose
病死 **byōshi** death from illness, natural death
討死 **u(chi)ji(ni)** fall in battle
飢死 **u(e)ji(ni)** starve to death
11 窒死 **chisshi** death from suffocation/asphyxiation
脳死 **nōshi** brain death
黒死病 **kokushibyō** bubonic plague, black death
惨死 **zanshi** tragic/violent death
惨死体 **zanshitai** mangled corpse
惨死者 **zanshisha** mangled corpse
情死 **jōshi** lovers' double suicide
12 検死 **kenshi** coroner's inquest, autopsy
焼死 **shōshi, ya(ke)ji(ni)** be burned to death
焼死体 **shōshitai** charred body/remains
焼死者 **shōshisha** person burned to death
無死 **mushi** no outs (and bases loaded)
焦死 **ko(gare)ji(ni)** die from love, pine away
悶死 **monshi** die in agony
13 溺死 **dekishi, obo(re)ji(ni)** drowning
溺死体 **dekishitai** drowned body
溺死者 **dekishisha** drowned person
愧死 **kishi** die of shame/humiliation
戦死 **senshi** death in battle, killed in action
戦死者 **senshisha** fallen soldier
頓死 **tonshi** sudden death
14 墜死 **tsuishi** fall to one's death
獄死 **gokushi** die in prison
15 窮死 **kyūshi** a miserable death
横死 **ōshi** violent death
憤死 **funshi** die in a fit of anger; be put out (with men on base)
餓死 **gashi** starve to death
16 縊死 **ishi** death by strangulation
諫死 **kanshi** commit suicide in protest against
17 擬死 **gishi** feigning death, playing possum
18 斃死 **heishi** fall dead, perish
19 瀕死 **hinshi** on the verge of death
爆死 **bakushi** death from bombing

22 轢死 **rekishi** be run over and killed

――――― 3 ―――――

6 安楽死 **anrakushi** euthanasia
自然死 **shizenshi** natural death
11 野垂死 **nota(re)ji(ni)** die by the roadside
窒息死 **chissokushi** death from suffocation/asphyxiation
12 無駄死 **mudaji(ni)** die in vain
13 戦病死 **senbyōshi** death from disease contracted at the front

――――― 4 ―――――

4 不老不死 **furō-fushi** eternal youth
11 過失致死 **kashitsu chishi** accidental homicide, manslaughter
過失致死罪 **kashitsu chishizai** accidental homicide, manslaughter
酔生夢死 **suisei-mushi** idle one's life away

0a6.7

艮

GON (one of the eight *hakke* divination signs)

弐 → **4n3.3**

0a6.8 / 134

気 氣

KI, KE spirit, mind, heart; intention; mood; temperament; disposition; attention; air, atmosphere; flavor, smell

――――― 1 ―――――

2 気入 **ki (ni) i(ru)** like, be pleased with
気力 **kiryoku** energy, vitality, mettle
3 気丈 **kijō** stout-hearted
気丈夫 **kijōbu** reassuring
気丈者 **kijōmono** stout-hearted fellow
気孔 **kikō** pores, stomata
4 気化 **kika** vaporize
気化器 **kikaki** carburetor
気分 **kibun** feeling, mood
気分転換 **kibun tenkan** a (refreshing) change, diversion
気心 **kigokoro** disposition, temperament
5 気失 **ki (o) ushina(u)** faint, pass out
気弁 **kiben** air valve
気付 **kizu(ku)** notice, find out
kitsu(ke) encouragement; resuscitation
-**kizuke** in care of **ki (o) tsu(keru)** be careful, watch out **ki (ga) tsu(ku)** notice, realize
気圧 **kiatsu** atmospheric pressure
気圧計 **kiatsukei** barometer

気立 **kida(te)** disposition, temperament
6 気休 **kiyasu(me)** to ease one's mind
気任 **kimaka(se)** at one's pleasure/fancy
気合 **kia(i)** spiritedness; a yell
気合負 **kia(i)ma(ke)** be overawed
気合術 **kia(i)jutsu** hypnotism
気色 **kishiki, kishoku** one's mood, disposition; (facial) expression
  keshiki(bamu) get angry
気宇広大 **kiu-kōdai** magnanimous, big-hearted
気団 **kidan** air mass
気早 **kibaya** quick-tempered
気忙 **kizewa(shii)** restless, fidgety
7 気位 **kigurai** feelings about oneself, self-esteem
気体 **kitai** gas (not solid or liquid)
気体力学 **kitai rikigaku** aerodynamics
気体化 **kitaika** gasify, vaporize
気状 **kijō** gaseous
気迫 **kihaku** spirit, vigor
気折 **kio(re)** depression, dejection
気抜 **kinu(ke)** lackadaisical; dispirited
気狂 **ki (ga) kuru(u)** go mad/crazy
気利 **ki (ga) ki(ku)** be clever, be considerate; be stylish
8 気長 **kinaga** leisurely, patient
気毒 **ki(no)doku** pitiable, regrettable, too bad
気受 **kiu(ke)** popularity, favor
気迷 **kimayo(i)** hesitation, wavering
気泡 **kihō** (air) bubble
気味 **kimi** feeling, sensation; a touch, tinge
気味悪 **kimi (no) waru(i)** eerie, ominous, weird
気苦労 **kigurō** worry, cares, anxiety
気炎 **kien** big talk; high spirits
気炎万丈 **kien-banjō** high spirits
気性 **kishō** disposition, temperament, spirit
気取 **kido(ru)** make an affected pose
  kedo(ru) suspect, sense
気取屋 **kido(ri)ya** affected person, poseur
9 気重 **kiomo(i)** heavy-hearted, depressed
気乗 **kino(ri)** take an interest in
気保養 **kihoyō** recreation, diversion
気変 **kiga(wari)** change one's mind, be fickle
気負 **kio(u)** rouse oneself, get psyched up
気負立 **kio(i)ta(tsu)** rouse oneself, get psyched up
気前 **kimae** generosity
気風 **kifū, kippu** character, disposition, temper; morale, spirit
気海 **kikai** the atmosphere
気持 **kimo(chi)** feeling, mood
気品 **kihin** dignity
気後 **kioku(re)** diffidence, timidity
気荒 **kiara** violent-tempered

気室 **kishitsu** air chamber
気音 **kion** an aspirate
気食 **ki (ni) kuwa(nu)** go against the grain, be disagreeable
10 気候 **kikō** climate
気候学 **kikōgaku** climatology
気随 **kizui** willful, self-indulgent
気随気儘 **kizui-kimama** as one pleases
気高 **kedaka(i)** noble, exalted
気兼 **kiga(ne)** feel constraint, be afraid of giving trouble
気流 **kiryū** air current
気振 **kebu(ri)** look, air, bearing; indications
気弱 **kiyowa** timid, fainthearted
気根 **kikon** energy, perseverance; aerial root
気格 **kikaku** dignity
気脈通 **kimyaku (o) tsū(jiru)** have a secret understanding with, be in collusion with
気胸 **kikyō** pneumothorax
気骨 **kikotsu** spirit, mettle, backbone
  kibone mental effort
気骨折 **kibone (ga) o(reru)** nerve-wracking
気息 **kisoku** breathing
気息奄々 **kisoku-en'en** gasping for breath, dying
気疲 **kizuka(re)** mental fatigue, nervous strain
気病 **ki (no) yamai** illness caused by anxiety, neurosis **ki (ni) ya(mu)** worry about, brood over
気紛 **kimagu(re)** whimsical, capricious
気恥 **kiha(zukashii)** embarrassed, ashamed, bashful
気配 **kehai** sign, indication **kihai** market trend **kikuba(ri)** vigilance, attentiveness
11 気運 **kiun** trend, tendency
気遅 **kioku(re)** timidity, diffidence
気済 **ki (ga) su(mu)** be satisfied
気掛 **kiga(kari)** anxiety
気張 **kiba(ru)** exert oneself, make an effort; be extravagant, treat oneself to
気強 **kizuyo(i)** reassuring; stout-hearted, resolute
気密 **kimitsu** airtight
気密室 **kimitsushitsu** airtight chamber
気球 **kikyū** (hot-air/helium) balloon
気移 **kiutsu(ri)** fickleness
気組 **kigu(mi)** readiness, ardor, attitude
気転 **kiten** wits, quick-wittedness
12 気象 **kishō** weather; disposition, temperament
気象台 **kishōdai** weather station
気象庁 **Kishōchō** Meteorological Agency
気象学 **kishōgaku** meteorology
気象図 **kishōzu** weather map
気象観測 **kishō kansoku** meteorological observations

0a6

気遣 **kizuka(i)** anxiety, fear, worry
気違 **kichiga(i)** insanity; mania, craze; lunatic; enthusiast, fan
気温 **kion** the (air) temperature
気揉 **ki (o) mo(mu)** worry, be anxious
気短 **kimijika** short-tempered, impatient
気落 **kio(chi)** discouragement, despondency
気圏 **kiken** the atmosphere
気晴 **kiba(rashi)** diversion, pastime, recreation
気焔 **kien** big talk; high spirits
気焔万丈 **kien-banjō** high spirits
気無精 **kibushō** laziness
気散 **kisan(ji)** diversion, recreation, amusement
気絶 **kizetsu** faint, pass out
気軽 **kigaru** lightheartedly, readily, feel free to
13 気障 **ki (ni) sawa(ru)** have one's feelings hurt, take offense **kizawa(ri)** disagreeable feeling
気勢 **kisei** spirit, ardor, élan
気楽 **kiraku** feeling at ease, easygoing, comfortable
気慨 **kigai** spirit, mettle, pluck
気触 **kabu(reru)** have a skin rash; be influenced by, become infected with
気詰 **kizu(mari)** feeling of awkwardness, ill at ease
14 気構 **kigama(e)** readiness, anticipation
気魂 **kikon** spirit
気管 **kikan** windpipe, trachea
気管支 **kikanshi** bronchial tubes
気管支炎 **kikanshien** bronchitis
気管炎 **kikan'en** tracheitis
15 気魄 **kihaku** spirit, vigor
気質 **katagi, kishitsu** disposition, temperament, spirit
気鋭 **kiei** spirited, energetic
16 気儘 **kimama** having one's own way
18 気難 **kimuzuka(shii)** hard to please, grouchy
19 気韻 **kiin** grace, elegance
20 気懸 **kigaka(ri)** anxiety
22 気嚢 **kinō** air sac/bladder
29 気鬱 **kiutsu** gloom, melancholy, depression
気鬱症 **kiutsushō** melancholia, depression

─────── 2 ───────

1 一気 **ikki** in one breath; straight through, without a break, at a stroke
一気呵成 **ikki kasei** in one breath/stroke/stretch
2 人気 **ninki** popularity; popular feeling; business conditions **hitoke** signs of life (in a place)
人気者 **ninkimono** popular person, a favorite
人気取 **ninkito(ri)** grandstanding, bid for popularity

人気商売 **ninki shōbai** occupation dependent on public favor
3 大気 **taiki** atmosphere, the air
大気圧 **taikiatsu** atmospheric pressure
大気圏 **taikiken** the atmosphere
才気 **saiki** talent, resourcefulness
才気煥発 **saiki-kanpatsu** brilliant, wise
上気 **jōki** rush of blood to the head, dizziness
土気色 **tsuchike-iro** earth color
口気 **kōki** bad breath; way of talking
小気味 **kokimi** feeling, sentiment
山気 **sanki** mountain air **yamagi, yamake** speculative spirit, venturesomeness
士気 **shiki** morale
4 不気味 **bukimi** uncanny, weird, eerie, ominous
元気 **genki** vigor, energy, health, vitality, spirit, courage, pep
天気 **tenki** the weather; good weather
天気図 **tenkizu** weather map
天気模様 **tenki moyō** weather conditions
内気 **uchiki** bashful, diffident, timid
中気 **chūki** paralysis
水気 **mizuke** moisture, juiciness **suiki** dropsy; moisture, humidity, vapor
火気 **kaki** fire **hi(no)ke** heat of fire
火気厳禁 **kaki genkin** Danger: Flammable
心気 **shinki** mind, mood
5 本気 **honki** serious, in earnest
本気違 **hon kichiga(i)** bibliomania; bibliomaniac
生気 **seiki** animation, life, vitality
平気 **heiki** calm, cool, unconcerned, nonchalant
外気 **gaiki** the open/outside air
好気 **i(i) ki** easygoing, happy-go-lucky; conceited
6 色気 **iroke** sexiness, sexuality, amorousness, romance
色気抜 **irokenu(ki)** without female companionship
色気違 **irokichiga(i)** sex mania
同気 **dōki** of like disposition/mind
吐気 **ha(ki)ke** nausea
安気 **anki** ease of mind, at ease
有気音 **yūkion** an aspirate
血気 **kekki** vigor, hot blood **chi(no)ke** -bloodedness, complexion
血気盛 **kekkizaka(ri)** the prime of one's vigor
虫気 **mushike** bowel complaint, nervous weakness
7 低気圧 **teikiatsu** low (atmospheric) pressure
何気無 **nanigena(ku)** unintentionally; nonchalantly
冷気 **reiki** cold, chill, cold weather

邪気 **jaki** miasma, noxious vapor; malice, evil; a cold
呆気 **akke** blank amazement
呆気無 **akkena(i)** unsatisfying, not enough
呑気 **nonki** easygoing, free and easy, optimistic
呑気者 **nonkimono** happy-go-lucky person
妖気 **yōki** ghostly, weird
狂気 **kyōki** madness, insanity
志気 **shiki** will, enthusiasm
辛気 **shinki** fretfulness
辛気臭 **shinkikusa(i)** fretful
男気 **otokogi** chivalrous spirit
　　 otoko(k)ke male, man
8 毒気 **dokuke, dokki** poisonous nature, noxious air; malice, spite
侍気質 **samurai katagi** samurai spirit
夜気 **yaki** the night air/stillness/cool
送気管 **sōkikan** air pipe/duct
油気 **aburake** oiliness, greasiness
沼気 **shōki** marsh gas, methane
味気無 **ajikena(i)** irksome, wearisome, dreary
呼気 **koki** exhalation
英気 **eiki** energetic spirit, enthusiasm
若気 **wakage** youthful vigor
昔気質 **mukashi-katagi** old-time spirit, old-fashioned
空気 **kūki** air, atmosphere; pneumatic
空気弁 **kūkiben** air valve
空気抜 **kūkinu(ki)** vent(ilator)
空気室 **kūkishitsu** air chamber
空気銃 **kūkijū** air gun/rifle
底気味悪 **sokokimi waru(i)** eerie, ominous
怖気 **o(ji)ke, ozoke** fear, timidity, nervousness
怪気 **aya(shi)ge** suspicious, questionable, shady; faltering
和気 **waki** harmony, peacefulness
疝気 **senki** lower-abdominal pain, lumbago
金気 **kanake** metalic taste; money
雨気 **amake** signs of rain
9 乗気 **no(ri)ki** eagerness, interest
侠気 **kyōki** chivalrous spirit
俗気 **zokke, zokuke, zokki** vulgarity, worldly ambition
勇気 **yūki** courage
負気 **ma(ken)ki** unyielding/competitive spirit
通気 **tsūki** ventilation
通気孔 **tsūkikō** vent, air hole
風気 **kazeke, kazake, kaza(k)ke** a slight cold
浮気 **uwaki** (marital) infidelity, cheating, fickle
活気 **kakki** liveliness, activity, vigor
活気付 **kakkizu(keru)** enliven, invigorate
海気 **kaiki** sea air/breeze
客気 **kakki** youthful ardor, rashness

神気 **shinki** energy, spirits; mind
怒気 **doki** (fit of) anger
臭気 **shūki** offensive odor, stink, stench
秋気 **shūki** the autumn air
香気 **kōki** fragrance, aroma
食気 **ku(i)ke, ku(i)ki** appetite
10 健気 **kenage** manly, heroic; admirable
陰気 **inki** gloomy, dreary
陰気臭 **inkikusa(i)** gloomy-looking
剛気 **gōki** brave, indomitable
高気圧 **kōkiatsu** high atmospheric pressure
酒気 **sakake, shuki** the smell of liquor
娘気質 **musume katagi** the nature of a young woman
弱気 **yowaki** faintheartedness; bearishness
根気 **konki** patience, perseverance
根気負 **konkima(ke)** be outpersevered
殺気 **sakki** bloodthirstiness
殺気立 **sakkida(tsu)** grow excited/menacing
脂気 **aburake** oily, greasy
悋気 **rinki** jealousy, envy
眠気 **nemuke** sleepiness, drowsiness
眠気覚 **nemukeza(mashi)** something to wake one up
鬼気 **kiki** ghastly, eerie
病気 **byōki** sickness, illness; sick, ill
素気 **sokke(nai)** curt, brusque
笑気 **shōki** laughing gas
11 陽気 **yōki** cheerful, gay, convivial; season, weather
勘気 **kanki** displeasure, disfavor
運気 **unki** fate, fortune
涼気 **ryōki** the cool (air)
排気 **haiki** exhaust (fumes)
排気量 **haikiryō** (piston) displacement
排気管 **haikikan** exhaust pipe
強気 **tsuyoki** bullish (market)
　　 gōgi great, powerful, grand
衒気 **genki** affectation, ostentation, vanity
脚気 **kakke** beriberi
悪気 **warugi** evil intent, malice, ill will
惚気 **noroke(ru)** speak fondly of one's beloved
惜気 **o(shi)ge** regret
産気 **sanke** labor pains
産気付 **sankezu(ki)** beginning of labor
眼気 **ganki** eye disease
移気 **utsu(ri)gi** fickle, capricious
粘気 **neba(ri)ke** stickiness
12 湿気 **shikke, shikki** moisture, humidity
湯気 **yuge** steam, vapor
堅気 **katagi** honest, decent, straight
換気 **kanki** ventilation
換気扇 **kankisen** ventilation fan
短気 **tanki** short temper, touchiness, hastiness

0a6

蒸気 **jōki** vapor, steam; steamship
蒸気力 **jōkiryoku** steam power
蒸気船 **jōkisen** steamship, steamer
寒気 **kanki, samuke** the cold
勝気 **ka(chi)ki** determined to succeed
暑気 **atsuke, shoki** the heat; heatstroke
景気 **keiki** business conditions
景気付 **keikizu(ku)** become active, pick up
無気力 **mukiryoku** spiritless, flabby, gutless
無気味 **bukimi** ominous, eerie
然気無 **sa(ri)gena(i)** nonchalant, casual
斑気 **muragi, muraki** capricious
惰気 **daki** inactivity, dullness
買気 **ka(i)ki** buying mood, bullishness
軽気球 **keikikyū** (hot-air/helium) balloon
雲気 **unki** the look of the sky
13 義気 **giki** chivalrous spirit, public-spiritedness
塩気 **shioke** saltiness
嫌気 **iyake, iyaki** aversion, repugnance
腰気 **koshike** leucorrhea, vaginal discharge
暖気 **danki** warmth, warm weather
瑞気 **zuiki** good omen
意気 **iki** spirits, morale
意気込 **ikigo(mu)** be enthusiastic about
意気地 **ikuji (no nai), ikiji (no nai)** weak, spineless, helpless
意気投合 **iki-tōgō** sympathy, mutual understanding
意気消沈 **iki-shōchin** dejected, despondent
意気揚々 **iki-yōyō** exultant, triumphant
稚気 **chiki** childlike state of mind
蜃気楼 **shinkirō** mirage
飾気 **kaza(ri)ke** affectation, love of display
電気 **denki** electricity; electric light
電気版 **denkiban** electrotype
電気炉 **denkiro** electric furnace
電気屋 **denkiya** electrical appliance store/dealer
電気浴 **denkiyoku** electric bath
電気量 **denkiryō** amount of electricity
電気銅 **denkidō** electrolytic copper
14 豪気 **gōki** stouthearted
漆気触 **urushikabure** lacquer poisoning
暢気 **nonki** easygoing, happy-go-lucky
憎気 **nikuge** hatred, ill will
磁気 **jiki** magnetism, magnetic
磁気学 **jikigaku** magnetics
磁気嵐 **jikiarashi** magnetic storm
磁気圏 **jikiken** magnetosphere
精気 **seiki** vitality, spirit
語気 **goki** tone of voice
15 潮気 **shioke** salt air
熱気 **nekki** hot air; heat; enthusiasm
netsuke feverishness
鋭気 **eiki** spirit, mettle, energy
霊気 **reiki** feeling of mystery

16 噯気 **okubi** belch, burp
薄気味悪 **usukimiwaru(i)** weird, eerie
瘴気 **shōki** miasma
19 覇気 **haki** ambition, aspirations
20 朧気 **oboroge** hazy, vague, faint
29 鬱気 **ukki** gloom, melancholy

─────── 3 ───────

1 一本気 **ippongi** one-track mind
3 川蒸気 **kawajōki** river steamboat
大人気 **otonage(nai)** childish, puerile
上天気 **jōtenki** fine weather
上昇気流 **jōshō kiryū** rising air current, updraft
上景気 **jōkeiki** boom, prosperity, a brisk economy
上層気流 **jōsō kiryū** upper-air currents
小意気 **koiki** stylish, tasteful
4 不人気 **funinki** unpopular
不安気 **fuange** uneasy, apprehensive
不景気 **fukeiki** business slump, recession; cheerless, gloomy
水蒸気 **suijōki** water vapor; steam
心意気 **kokoroiki** disposition, spirit, sentiment
5 生意気 **namaiki** conceited, impertinent, smart-alecky
好天気 **kōtenki** fine weather
好景気 **kōkeiki** business prosperity, boom
芝居気 **shibaigi** striving for dramatic effect
6 気随気儘 **kizui-kimama** as one pleases
地磁気 **chijiki** the earth's magnetism
光磁気ディスク **hikari-jiki disuku** magnetic-optical disk (MOD)
7 阻塞気球 **sosai kikyū** barrage balloon
乱痴気騒 **ranchiki sawa(gi)** boisterous merrymaking, spree
8 空元気 **karagenki** mere bravado
空景気 **karageiki** false economic prosperity
9 俄景気 **niwakageiki** temporary boom
前景気 **maegeiki** prospects, outlook
風邪気 **kazeke, kaza(k)ke** a slight cold
洒落気 **share(k)ke** a bent for witticism; vanity in dress
茶目気 **chame(k)ke** waggish, playful
10 陰電気 **indenki** negative electricity
洒落気 **share(k)ke** a bent for witticism; vanity in dress
浩然気 **kōzen (no) ki** spirits, morale
11 野球気違 **yakyū kichiga(i)** baseball fan
陽電気 **yōdenki** positive electricity
商売気 **shōbaigi** business-mindedness, profit motive
商売気質 **shōbai katagi** mercenary spirit
得意気 **tokuige** proud, elated
12 無邪気 **mujaki** innocent, ingenuous
雰囲気 **fun'iki** atmosphere, ambience

13 電磁気 **denjiki** electromagnetic
頓痴気 **tonchiki** nincompoop, dope
14 静電気 **seidenki** static electricity
静電気学 **seidenkigaku** electrostatics
16 親切気 **shinsetsugi** kindliness

──────── 4 ────────

3 小生意気 **konamaiki** conceit, impudence
6 糸偏景気 **itohen keiki** textile boom
8 金偏景気 **kanehen keiki** metal-industry boom
9 軍需景気 **gunju keiki** war prosperity
12 跛行景気 **hakō keiki** spotty boom/prosperity
17 鍋底景気 **nabezoko keikl** prolonged recession

0a6.9

       KO, hoko(ru) boast

0a6.10

       KYŌ turmoil; Hungary

──────── 1 ────────

5 匈奴 **Kyōdo** the Huns

0a6.11 / 200

両 兩   **RYŌ** both; two; (obsolete Japanese coin); (counter for vehicles)

──────── 1 ────────

2 両刀 **ryōtō** two swords
両刀使 **ryōtōtsuka(i)** two-sword fencer; expert in two fields
両刀遣 **ryotōtsuka(i)** two-sword fencer; expert in two fields
3 両三日 **ryōsannichi** two or three days
両刃 **ryōba** double-edged
両々 **ryōryō** both
4 両天秤 **ryōtenbin** two alternatives
両氏 **ryōshi** both men
両分 **ryōbun** bisect, cut in two
両手 **ryōte** both hands
両手花 **ryōte (ni) hana** have a double advantage; sit between two pretty women
両日 **ryōjitsu** both days; two days
両方 **ryōhō** both
5 両生 **ryōsei** amphibious (animal)
両立 **ryōritsu** coexist, be compatible
6 両全 **ryōzen** advantageous for both sides
両舌 **ryōzetsu** sowing discord by saying different things to different people, double-dealing

──────────

両成敗 **ryōseibai** punishing both parties
7 両足 **ryōashi, ryōsoku** both feet/legs
8 両岸 **ryōgan** both banks (of a river)
両者 **ryōsha** both persons; both things
両性 **ryōsei** both sexes
両性花 **ryōseika** bisexual flower
両性的 **ryōseiteki** bisexual, androgynous
9 両便 **ryōben** urination and defecation
両陛下 **Ryōheika** Their Majesties
両院 **ryōin** both houses (of parliament/congress)
両洋 **ryōyō** orient and occident; two-ocean
両面 **ryōmen** both faces/sides
両面刷 **ryōmenzu(ri)** printing on both sides
10 両家 **ryōke** both families
両党 **ryōtō** both (political) parties, bipartisan
両袖 **ryōsode** both sleeves
11 両側 **ryōgawa** both sides
両得 **ryōtoku** double advantage
両脚規 **ryōkyakuki** compass (for drawing circles)
両眼 **ryōgan** both eyes
両断 **ryōdan** bisect, break in two
12 両極 **ryōkyoku** both extremities; both poles
両極端 **ryōkyokutan** both extremes
両棲 **ryōsei** amphibious (animal)
両腕 **ryōude** both arms
両替 **ryōgae** money exchange
両替人 **ryōgaenin** money changer
両替屋 **ryōgaeya** money-exchange shop
両雄 **ryōyū** two great men
両開 **ryōbira(ki)** double(-leafed door)
13 両義 **ryōgi** double meaning, two meanings
両損 **ryōzon** loss for both sides
14 両様 **ryōyō** both ways, two ways
両端 **ryōtan, ryōhashi** both ends, both edges; sitting on the fence
15 両論 **ryōron** both arguments, both theories
両輪 **ryōrin** two wheels
16 両親 **ryōshin** (both) parents
両頭 **ryōtō** double-headed
17 両翼 **ryōyoku** both wings; both flanks
20 両議院 **ryōgiin** both houses (of parliament/congress)

──────── 2 ────────

1 一両 **ichiryō** one vehicle; one *ryō* (an old coin)
一両日 **ichiryōjitsu** a day or two
3 千両役者 **senryō yakusha** great actor, star
千両箱 **senryōbako** chest containing a thousand pieces of gold
6 両両 **ryōryō** both
7 車両 **sharyō** vehicles, cars, rolling stock

──────── 3 ────────

1 一挙両得 **ikkyo ryōtoku** killing two birds with one stone

0a6

4 文武両道 **bunbu-ryōdō** both soldierly and scholarly arts
12 衆参両院 **shū-san ryōin** both Houses of the Diet

0a6.12

兇
KYŌ evil

——————— 1 ———————

3 兇刃 **kyōjin** assassin's blade
4 兇手 **kyōshu** (work of an) evil person
6 兇行 **kyōkō** violence, murder
7 兇状 **kyōjō** crime, offense
兇状持 **kyōjōmo(chi)** criminal at large
9 兇変 **kyōhen** disaster; assassination
10 兇猛 **kyōmō** fierce
兇徒 **kyōto** murder, rioter, rebel, outlaw
12 兇弾 **kyōdan** assassin's bullet
13 兇漢 **kyōkan** scoundrel, assailant, assassin
兇賊 **kyōzoku** bandit, a rowdy
15 兇器 **kyōki** lethal weapon
兇暴 **kyōbō** ferocity, brutality, savagery

——————— 2 ———————

4 元兇 **genkyō** ringleader

 0a5.23

0a6.13 / 1503

朱
SHU red

——————— 1 ———————

2 朱子学 **Shushigaku** teachings of the Confucian philosopher Zhuzi (1130–1200), Neo-Confucianism
6 朱肉 **shuniku** red ink pad
朱印 **shuin** red seal
朱印状 **shuinjō** official document with a red seal
朱印船 **shuinsen, shuinbune** shogunate-licensed trading ship
朱色 **shuiro** scarlet, vermilion
8 朱門 **shumon** red-lacquered gate
11 朱雀 **Suzaku** (emperor, 930–946)
朱鳥 **Shuchō** (era, 686–701)
13 朱塗 **shunu(ri)** red-lacquered

——————— 2 ———————

9 後朱省 **Gosuzaku** (emperor, 1036–1045)
12 御朱印 **goshuin** sealed letter issued by a shogun
御朱印船 **goshuinsen** shogunate-licensed trading ship

0a6.14

SŌ, kusa grass

0a6.15

SHI thorn

0a6.16 / 45

年
NEN, toshi year

——————— 1 ———————

2 年子 **toshigo** children (of the same mother) born within a year of each other
3 年上 **toshiue** older, senior
年下 **toshishita** younger, junior
年々 **nennen, toshidoshi** year by year, every year
4 年内 **nennai** within the year, before the end of the year
年中 **nenjū** all year, year-round
年中行事 **nenjū gyōji** an annual event
年収 **nenshū** annual income
年分 **nenbun** yearly amount
年少 **nenshō** young
年月 **nengetsu, toshitsuki** months and years, time
年月日 **nengappi** date
5 年末 **nenmatsu** the end of the year, year-end
年代 **nendai** age, period, era; date
年代記 **nendaiki** chronicle
年代順 **nendaijun** chronological order
年令 **nenrei** age
年功 **nenkō** long service
年市 **toshi (no) ichi** year-end market (cf. 節季市)
年号 **nengō** era name
年玉 **toshidama** New Year's gift
6 年会 **nenkai** annual meeting/convention
年次 **nenji** annual
年回 **toshimawa(ri)** luck associated with one's age
年百年中 **nenbyaku-nenjū** all year round
7 年来 **nenrai** for (some) years
年忘 **toshiwasu(re)** year-end drinking party
年忌 **nenki** anniversary of a death
年利 **nenri** annual interest
年初 **nensho** beginning of the year
年男 **toshiotoko** lucky-bean scatterer (at Setsubun festival)
8 年長 **nenchō** seniority
年長者 **nenchōsha** a senior, older person

0a6

年表 **nenpyō** chronological table
年限 **nengen** term, length of time
年始 **nenshi** beginning of the year, New Year's
年金 **nenkin** annuity, pension
9 １９９６年型 **1996nen-gata** the 1996 model
年度 **nendo** fiscal/business year
年恰好 **toshi kakkō** approximate age
10 年俸 **nenpō** annual salary
年差 **nensa** annual variation
年益 **nen'eki** annual profit
年弱 **toshiyowa** child born in the last half of the year
年貢 **nengu** land tax
年貢米 **nengumai** annual rice tax
年配 **nenpai** age
11 年商 **nenshō** annual sales
年強 **toshizuyo** child born in the first half of the year
年寄 **toshiyo(ri)** old person
年祭 **nensai** anniversary
年産 **nensan** annual production
年盛 **toshizaka(ri)** the prime of life
年頃 **toshigoro** age; marriageable age
12 年割 **nenwa(ri)** annual installment
年報 **nenpō** annual report
年期 **nenki** term of service, apprenticeship; experience
年期奉公 **nenki bōkō** apprenticeship
年税 **nenzei** annual tax
年給 **nenkyū** annual salary
年賀 **nenga** New Year's greetings/visit
年賀状 **nengajō** New Year's card
年間 **nenkan** period of a year; during the year
13 年嵩 **toshikasa** senior, older
年数 **nensū** number of years
14 年増 **toshima** mature/older woman
年端 **toshiha** age, years
15 年賦 **nenpu** annual installment
年輪 **nenrin** annular (tree) ring
年輩 **nenpai** age; elderly age
16 年頭 **nentō** beginning of the year
 toshigashira the oldest person
17 年齢 **nenrei** age
18 年額 **nengaku** annual amount
19 年瀬 **toshi(no)se** end of year
年譜 **nenpu** chronological record
23 年鑑 **nenkan** yearbook

———— 2 ————

1 一年 **ichinen** one year **hitotose** one year, some time ago
一年中 **ichinen-jū** all year long
一年生 **ichinensei** first-year student; annual (plant)
2 丁年 **teinen** age of majority, adulthood
丁年者 **teinensha** adult

3 万年 **mannen** ten thousand years; perpetual, perennial
万年床 **mannendoko** bedding/futon left spread out on the floor during the daytime
万年青 **omoto** (a plant in the lily family)
万年雪 **mannen'yuki** perpetual snow
万年筆 **mannenhitsu** fountain pen
大年増 **ōtoshima** woman in her 40's
4 元年 **gannen** first year (of an era)
凶年 **kyōnen** bad year; year of bad harvest
中年 **chūnen** middle age
中年者 **chūnenmono** middle-aged person; late starter
今年 **kotoshi** this year
厄年 **yakudoshi** unlucky age, one's critical year
少年 **shōnen** boy
少年法 **shōnenhō** juvenile law
少年院 **shōnen'in** reform school
少年感化院 **shōnen kankain** reform school
5 半年 **hantoshi, hannen** half year, six months
本年 **honnen** this year
本年度 **honnendo** this fiscal/business year
生年 **seinen, u(mare)doshi** year of birth, age
生年月日 **seinengappi** date of birth
他年 **tanen** some other year, some day
幼年 **yōnen** infancy, childhood (up to age 7)
幼年時代 **yōnen jidai** childhood
幼年期 **yōnenki** childhood
平年 **heinen** average/normal year; non-leap year
平年作 **heinensaku** normal harvest
永年 **einen, naganen** many years, a long time
去年 **kyonen, kozo** last year
旧年 **kyūnen** the old year, last year
6 多年 **tanen** many years
多年生 **tanensei** perennial
年年 **nennen, toshidoshi** year by year, every year
毎年 **mainen, maitoshi** every year, annually
壮年 **sōnen** the prime of manhood
老年 **rōnen** old age
老年者 **rōnensha** old people, the aged
近年 **kinnen** in recent years
同年 **dōnen** that (same) year; same age
同年輩 **dōnenpai** persons of the same age
先年 **sennen** former years; a few years ago
行年 **gyōnen, kōnen** one's age at death
光年 **kōnen** light-year
当年 **tōnen** the current year; that year
 a(tari)doshi a good/abundant year
百年祭 **hyakunensai** a centennial
成年 **seinen** (age of) majority, adulthood
成年式 **seinenshiki** coming-of-age ceremony
7 来年 **rainen** next year

更年期 **kōnenki** menopause
何年 **nannen** how many years; what year
享年 **kyōnen** one's age at death
忘年会 **bōnenkai** year-end party
延年 **ennen** longevity
没年 **botsunen** one's age at death; year of death
学年 **gakunen** school year, grade in school
初年 **shonen** first year, early years
初年兵 **shonenhei** new soldier, raw recruit
初年級 **shonenkyū** beginners' class
8 長年 **naganen** many years, a long time
例年 **reinen** normal/average year; every year
周年 **shūnen** whole year, anniversary
往年 **ōnen** in years gone by
若年 **jakunen** youth
若年寄 **waka-doshiyo(ri)** young person who looks/acts old
昔年 **sekinen** (many) years ago
定年 **teinen** age limit, retirement age
青年 **seinen** young man/people, a youth
青年会 **seinenkai** young (wo)men's association
青年団 **seinendan** young men's association
9 前年 **zennen** the preceding year, last year
前年度 **zennendo** the preceding business/fiscal year
連年 **rennen** every year
逐年 **chikunen** year by year, annually
逝年 **yu(ku) toshi** (ring out) the old year
後年 **kōnen** in later/future years, afterward
客年 **kakunen** last year
某年 **bōnen** a certain year
昨年 **sakunen** last year
10 高年 **kōnen** old age
高年者 **kōnensha** elderly person
流年 **ryūnen** the passing years
弱年 **jakunen** youth, young
11 停年 **teinen** age limit, retirement age
過年度 **kanendo** past fiscal/business year
翌年 **yokunen, yokutoshi** the following year
累年 **ruinen** successive years; from year to year
盛年 **seinen** the prime of life
12 隔年 **kakunen** every other year
晩年 **bannen** latter part of one's life
越年 **etsunen** tide over the year end; pass the winter, hibernate
幾年 **ikunen, ikutose** how many years
閏年 **urūdoshi** leap year
13 豊年 **hōnen** year of abundance
数年 **sūnen** several years **kazo(e)doshi** one's calendar-year age (reckoned racehorse-style)
新年 **shinnen** the New Year
14 暦年 **rekinen** calendar (not fiscal) year; time

歴年 **rekinen** year after year
15 億年 **okunen** hundred million years
編年史 **hennenshi** chronicle, annals
編年体 **hennentai** chronological order
16 積年 **sekinen** (many) years

───────── 3 ─────────

1 一ヶ年 **ikkanen** one year
1 一周年 **isshūnen** one full year, anniversary
一昨年 **issakunen, ototoshi** the year before last
2 二十年代 **nijūnendai** the '20s
3 小半年 **kohannen** about six months
4 太陽年 **taiyōnen** solar year
5 出生年月日 **shusshō nengappi, shussei nengappi** date of birth
未成年 **miseinen** minority, not of age
未成年者 **miseinensha** a minor
6 年百年中 **nenbyaku-nenjū** all year round
再来年 **sarainen** the year after next
7 低学年 **teigakunen** elementary school grades 1 and 2
8 厚生年金 **kōsei nenkin** welfare pension
服務年限 **fukumu nengen** tenure of office
青少年 **seishōnen** young people, the young
9 美少年 **bishōnen** a handsome youth
耐用年数 **taiyō nensū** useful lifetime, life
10 高学年 **kōgakunen** upper (5th and 6th) grades in elementary school
11 翌翌年 **yokuyokunen** two years later/after

───────── 4 ─────────

1 一昨昨年 **issakusakunen, sakiototoshi** three years ago
10 恭賀新年 **kyōga shinnen** Happy New Year
17 謹賀新年 **kinga shinnen** Happy New Year

0a6.17

舛 **SEN, somu(ku), taga(u)** go against, be contrary to

0a6.18

异 **I** be different

0a6.19

襾 **A** cover, place on top of

0a6.20 / 72

西 **SEI** west; Spain **SAI, nishi** west

—————————— 1 ——————————

0 西ドイツ **Nishi Doitsu** West Germany, FRG
2 西人 **seijin** a Westerner
3 西下 **saika** go west from Tōkyō (to Kansai)
　西土 **seido** western lands
4 西内 **nishi(no)uchi** (a type of strong Japanese paper)
　西日 **nishibi** the afternoon sun
　西日本 **Nishi Nihon** western Japan
　西方 **seihō** west, western, westward
　西方浄土 **Saihō Jōdo** (Buddhist) Western Paradise
5 西北 **seihoku** northwest
　西半球 **nishi hankyū** Western Hemisphere
　西本願寺 **Nishi Honganji** (main temple, in Kyōto, of Jōdo sect)
6 西瓜 **suika** watermelon
　西向 **nishimu(ki)** facing west
8 西郊 **seikō** western suburbs
　西京 **Saikyō** the western capital, Kyōto
　西岸 **seigan** west coast; west bank
　西国 **saigoku** the western countries; western Japan
　西明 **nishi a(kari)** evening twilight, afterglow
　西欧 **Seiō** Western Europe, the West
　西欧人 **Seiōjin** Westerner, European
　西欧化 **Seiōka** Westernization
　西武 **Seibu** (company name)
9 西陣 **nishijin** Nishijin brocade
　西陣織 **nishijin'o(ri)** Nishijin brocade
　西南 **seinan** southwest
　西風 **nishikaze, seifū** west wind
　西洋 **seiyō** the West, the occident
　西洋人 **seiyōjin** a Westerner
　西洋化 **seiyōka** Westernization
　西洋式 **seiyōshiki** Western-style
　西洋画 **seiyōga** Western painting, oil painting
　西洋風 **seiyofū** Western-style
　西洋紙 **seiyōshi** Western-style (machine-made) paper
　西独 **Seidoku** West Germany
　西紀 **seiki** A.D., Christian Era
10 西部 **seibu** western part, the west
　西部劇 **seibugeki** a Western (movie)
　西高東低 **seikō-tōtei** high (barometric pressure) in the west and low in the east
　西遊 **seiyū, saiyū** trip to the west/West
　西哲 **seitetsu** Western philosopher
　西宮 **Nishinomiya** (city, Hyōgo-ken)
　西班牙 **Supein** Spain
11 西側 **nishigawa** the western side; the West
　西域 **seiiki** lands to the west of China
　西経 **seikei** west longitude
14 西暦 **seireki** Christian Era, A.D.
　西漸 **seizen** westward advance
15 西蔵 **Chibetto** Tibet

—————————— 2 ——————————

3 大西洋 **Taiseiyō** Atlantic Ocean
4 中西部 **Chūseibu** the Midwest
5 北西 **hokusei** northwest
6 江西 **Kōsei** Jiangxi (province)
8 東西 **tōzai** east and west; Orient and Occident; Ladies and gentlemen!
　東西南北 **tōzainanboku** north, south, east, and west
9 南西 **nansei** southwest
10 真西 **manishi** due west
　泰西 **taisei** the occident/West
　泰西名画 **taisei meiga** famous Western painting
12 最西 **saisei** westernmost
13 瑞西 **Suisu** Switzerland
14 墨西哥 **Mekishiko** Mexico
　関西 **Kansai** (region including Ōsaka and Kyōto)
21 露西亜 **Roshia** Russia

—————————— 3 ——————————

4 仏蘭西 **Furansu** France
5 北大西洋 **Kita Taiseiyō** the North Atlantic
　北北西 **hokuhokusei** north-northwest
7 伯剌西爾 **Burajiru** Brazil
8 東奔西走 **tōhon-seisō** busy oneself, take an active interest in
9 南南西 **nannansei** south-southwest
12 普魯西 **Puroshia** Prussia

—————————— 4 ——————————

5 古今東西 **kokon-tōzai** all ages and places

咤 → 喜 **3p9.1**

耒 → 来 **0a7.6**

0a6.21

耒   **RAI, suki** spade, plow

臾 → 臾 **2a7.23**

0a6.22 / 1007

吏 吏   **RI** an official

—————————— 1 ——————————

10 吏員 **riin** an official

0a6

--- 2 ---
3 下吏 **kari** low-ranking official
小吏 **shōri** petty official
4 公吏 **kōri** public servant, official
6 老吏 **rōri** veteran official
廷吏 **teiri** court attendant/clerk
7 良吏 **ryōri** good/capable official
8 官吏 **kanri** government official
9 俗吏 **zokuri** petty official
10 能吏 **nōri** capable official
12 属吏 **zokuri** subordinate official
税吏 **zeiri** customs collector/officer
13 幕吏 **bakuri** shogunate official
廉吏 **renri** an honest official
14 獄吏 **gokuri** jailer
酷吏 **kokuri** exacting official

--- 3 ---
4 収税吏 **shūzeiri** tax collector
8 官公吏 **kankōri** public officials
11 執行吏 **shikkōri** bailiff, court officer
12 税関吏 **zeikanri** customs officer/inspector

0a6.23

EI, hi(ku) pull

曳 曳

--- 1 ---
6 曳光弾 **eikōdan** tracer bullet, illumination round
10 曳航 **eikō** tow (a ship)
11 曳船 **hikifune, hikibune, eisen** tugboat
14 曳網 **hikiami** seine, dragnet

--- 2 ---
6 地曳 **jibi(ki)** seine fishing
地曳網 **jibi(ki)ami** dragnet, seine
8 底曳網 **sokobi(ki)ami** dragnet, trawlnet
12 揺曳 **yōei** flutter, tremble; drag; linger

0a6.24

I barbarian **ebisu** barbarian, savage; Ainu

夷

--- 1 ---
7 夷狄 **iteki** barbarians, aliens

--- 2 ---
7 辛夷 **kobushi** cucumber tree (a magnolia-like tree whose large white blossoms resemble fists)
8 東夷 **tōi** eastern barbarians
征夷 **seii** pacifying the barbarians
征夷大将軍 **seii taishōgun** general in command of expeditionary forces to subjugate the barbarians
12 焼夷弾 **shōidan** incendiary shell, firebomb

15 蝦夷 **Ezo** Ainu; Hokkaidō
蝦夷松 **Ezo-matsu** silver fir, spruce
蝦夷菊 **Ezo-giku** China aster
20 攘夷 **jōi** exclusion/expulsion of foreigners
攘夷論 **jōiron** anti-alien policy

--- 4 ---
12 尊王攘夷 **sonnō-jōi** Revere the emperor and expel the barbarians.

0a6.25 / 116

MAI, -goto every, each

--- 1 ---
3 毎夕 **maiyū** every evening
4 毎月 **maigetsu, maitsuki** every month, monthly
毎日 **mainichi** every day, daily
5 毎号 **maigō** every issue (of a magazine)
6 毎年 **mainen, maitoshi** every year, annually
毎次 **maiji** every time
毎回 **maikai** every time
8 毎夜 **maiyo** every evening, nightly
9 毎度 **maido** each time; frequently; always
10 毎週 **maishū** every week, weekly
毎時 **maiji** every hour, per hour
12 毎期 **maiki** every term
毎朝 **maiasa** every morning
毎晩 **maiban** every evening, nightly

--- 2 ---
4 月毎 **tsukigoto (ni)** every month
日毎 **higoto (ni)** every day, daily
戸毎 **kogoto (ni)** at every house, door to door
8 事毎 **kotogoto (ni)** in everything, always
夜毎 **yogoto** every night
門毎 **kadogoto** at every gate, door-to-door
10 家毎 **iegoto** at every house/door

0a6.26 / 782

SAI, SA again, re-, twice, second **futata(bi)** again, twice

再

--- 1 ---
2 再入学 **sainyūgaku** readmission (to a school)
再入国 **sainyūkoku** re-entry (into a country)
3 再三 **saisan** again and again, repeatedly
再三再四 **saisan-saishi** over and over again
再上映 **saijōei** reshowing (of a movie)
再下付 **saikafu** regrant, reissue, renewal
再々 **saisai** often, frequently
4 再分配 **saibunpai** redistribution
5 再出 **saishutsu** reappear, re-emerge
再出発 **saishuppatsu** start over, make a fresh start

再生 **saisei** (as if) alive/born again; reclamation, regeneration, recycling; reproduction, playback
再生産 **saiseisan** reproduction
再刊 **saikan** reprint, republication
再犯 **saihan** second offense
再犯者 **saihansha** second offender
6 再再 **saisai** often, frequently
再任 **sainin** reappoint
再会 **saikai** meeting again, reunion
再交付 **saikōfu** regrant, reissue
再考 **saikō** reconsider
7 再来 **sairai** second coming
再来月 **saraigetsu** the month after next
再来年 **sarainen** the year after next
再来週 **saraishū** the week after next
再吟味 **saiginmi** re-examine, review
8 再使用 **saishiyō** reuse
再版 **saihan** reprint; second printing/edition
再建 **saiken** reconstruction, rebuilding
再注 **saichū** reorder
再注文 **saichūmon** reorder
再拝 **saihai** bowing twice
再放送 **saihōsō** rebroadcast
再武装 **saibusō** rearmament
9 再発 **saihatsu** recurrence, relapse
再発足 **saihossoku** start again
再保険 **saihoken** reinsurance
再軍備 **saigunbi** rearmament
再変 **saihen** second change; second disaster
再度 **saido** twice, a second time, again
再思 **saishi** reconsider
再訂 **saitei** second revision
10 再帰 **saiki** recursive
再帰熱 **saikinetsu** recurrent fever
再遊 **saiyū** return visit, second trip
再起 **saiki** comeback; recovery
再案 **saian** revised plan/draft
再挙 **saikyo** second attempt
再校 **saikō** second proof
再教育 **saikyōiku** retraining
再配置 **saihaichi** reallocate, rearrange
11 再婚 **saikon** remarry
再現 **saigen** reappearance, return; revival
再組織 **saisoshiki** reorganization
12 再割引 **saiwaribiki** rediscount
再検査 **saikensa** re-examination
再検討 **saikentō** re-examination, reappraisal, review
再勝 **saishō** another win
再評価 **saihyōka** reassessment, re-evaluation
再開 **saikai** reopen, resume, reconvene
13 再嫁 **saika** remarriage
再試合 **saishiai** rematch, resumption of a game
再試験 **saishiken** make-up exam, retesting

14 再選 **saisen** re-election
再選挙 **saisenkyo** re-election
再演 **saien** repeat performance
再製 **saisei** remanufacture, recondition
再読 **saidoku** reread
15 再審 **saishin** re-examination, review, retrial
再審査 **saishinsa** re-examination
再確認 **saikakunin** reaffirmation
再縁 **saien** remarriage
再編成 **saihensei** reorganization, reshuffle
再調査 **saichōsa** reinvestigation
再鋳 **saichū** recast
16 再興 **saikō** revive, restore, re-establish
再燃 **sainen** reignite, revive
再輸入 **saiyunyū** reimportation
再輸出 **saiyushutsu** re-exportation
18 再臨 **sairin** the Second Coming
20 再議 **saigi** reconsideration, redeliberation

——————— 2 ———————
1 一再 **issai** once or twice
   issai(narazu) again and again
6 再再 **saisai** often, frequently

——————— 3 ———————
6 再三再四 **saisan-saishi** over and over again

0a6.27 / 366

KYOKU curve; melody
ma(garu) bend, curve, be crooked
ma(geru) bend, distort

——————— 1 ———————
7 曲角 **ma(gari)kado** (street) corner
曲折 **kyokusetsu** winding, twists and turns; vicissitudes, complications
曲芸 **kyokugei** acrobatics
曲芸師 **kyokugeishi** acrobat, tumbler
8 曲易 **ma(ge)yasu(i)** easy to bend, supple, pliant, flexible
9 曲乗 **kyokuno(ri)** trick riding
10 曲馬 **kyokuba** equestrian feats; circus
曲馬団 **kyokubadan** circus troupe
曲馬師 **kyokubashi** circus stunt rider
11 曲率 **kyokuritsu** curvature
13 曲解 **kyokkai** strained interpretation, distortion
曲路 **ma(gari)michi** roundabout road; winding road
15 曲線 **kyokusen** a curve
曲線美 **kyokusenbi** beautiful curves
曲論 **kyokuron** sophistry

——————— 2 ———————
1 一曲 **ikkyoku** a tune/melody
2 七曲 **nanama(gari)** winding, tortuous
3 三曲 **sankyoku** instrumental trio
小曲 **shōkyoku** short musical piece
4 双曲線 **sōkyokusen** hyperbola

5 古曲 **kokyoku** old tune, ancient melody
6 名曲 **meikyoku** famous music
7 作曲 **sakkyoku** musical composition
作曲家 **sakkyokuka** composer
邪曲 **jakyoku** wickedness, injustice
折曲 **o(ri)ma(geru)** bend, turn up/down
妙曲 **myōkyoku** fine music
序曲 **jokyoku** overture, prelude
私曲 **shikyoku** corrupt practices, graft
8 夜曲 **yakyoku** nocturne
屈曲 **kukkyoku** crookedness; refraction; curvature
委曲 **ikyoku** details, full particulars
9 俗曲 **zokkyoku** folk song
歪曲 **waikyoku** distortion
神曲 **Shinkyoku** (Dante's) Divine Comedy
音曲 **ongyoku, onkyoku** song with samisen accompaniment; musical performances
紆曲 **ukyoku** meander
10 浪曲 **rōkyoku** samisen-accompanied recital of ancient tales
秘曲 **hikyoku** secret/esoteric music
11 捩曲 **ne(ji)ma(geru)** bend by twisting
婉曲 **enkyoku** euphemistic, circumlocutory
組曲 **kumikyoku** suite (in music)
終曲 **shūkyoku** finale
12 湾曲 **wankyoku** curve, curvature, bend
悲曲 **hikyoku** plaintive melody
13 楽曲 **gakkyoku** musical composition/piece
新曲 **shinkyoku** new tune/composition
14 歌曲 **kakyoku** (art) song, lied
箏曲 **sōkyoku** koto music
雑曲 **zakkyoku** medley; popular song
15 舞曲 **bukyoku** music and dancing; dance music
戯曲 **gikyoku** drama, play
編曲 **henkyoku** (musical) arrangement
16 褶曲 **shūkyoku** bend into folds, flex

謡曲 **yōkyoku** Noh song/chant
18 臍曲 **hesoma(gari)** cranky person, grouch
難曲 **nankyoku** piece which is hard to play/sing
22 彎曲 **wankyoku** curve, bend, curvature

───────── 3 ─────────
3 小夜曲 **sayokyoku** serenade
4 幻想曲 **gensōkyoku** fantasy, fantasia
6 合唱曲 **gasshōkyoku** chorus, choral, part-song
交響曲 **kōkyōkyoku** symphony
行進曲 **kōshinkyoku** a (musical) march
7 即興曲 **sokkyōkyoku** an impromptu
狂想曲 **kyōsōkyoku** rhapsody
8 夜想曲 **yasōkyoku** nocturne
協奏曲 **kyōsōkyoku** concerto
9 変奏曲 **hensōkyoku** a variation (in music)
前奏曲 **zensōkyoku** prelude, overture
連弾曲 **rendankyoku** piano piece for four hands
後奏曲 **kōsōkyoku** postlude
紆余曲折 **uyo-kyokusetsu** meandering, twists and turns, complications
11 旋毛曲 **tsumujima(gari)** cranky person
12 間奏曲 **kansōkyoku** interlude
14 演奏曲目 **ensō kyokumoku** musical program
歌謡曲 **kayōkyoku** popular song
綺想曲 **kisōkyoku** capriccio
18 鎮魂曲 **chinkonkyoku** requiem

───────── 4 ─────────
6 同工異曲 **dōkō-ikyoku** superficially different but essentially the same

───────── 5 ─────────
12 葬送行進曲 **sōsō kōshinkyoku** funeral march

0a6.28

聿 **ITSU** writing brush; finally

─────────────── 0a7 ───────────────

巫	豕	豸	艮	卮	良	求	矣	身	来	承	束	帚
2a5.26	7.1	7.2	0a7.3	0a5.8	7.3	2b5.5	7.4	7.5	7.6	7.7	7.8	2m6.3

里	我	甫	曳	更	串	亜	寿	事
7.9	7.10	7.11	0a6.23	7.12	7.13	7.14	7.15	0a8.15

───────────────────────────────

巫 → **2a5.26**

0a7.1

豕 **SHI, inoko** hog

0a7.2

豸 **CHI, TAI** legless insects, worms

艮 → 良  **0a7.3**

厄→厄 **0a5.8**

0a7.3 / 321

RYŌ, i(i), yo(i) good

良 良

───── 1 ─────

2 良二千石 **ryōnisenseki** good local official
3 良工 **ryōkō** skilled artisan
4 良不良 **ryō-furyō** (whether) good or bad
　良友 **ryōyū** good friend
　良心 **ryōshin** conscience
　良心的 **ryōshinteki** conscientious
5 良民 **ryōmin** good/law-abiding citizens
　良好 **ryōkō** good, favorable, satisfactory
　良田 **ryōden** fertile rice field
6 良吏 **ryōri** good/capable official
7 良医 **ryōi** good doctor, skilled physician
　良否 **ryōhi** (whether) good or bad
　良材 **ryōzai** good timber; people of ability
8 良夜 **ryōya** moonlit night
　良法 **ryōhō** good method
　良知 **ryōchi** intuition
　良妻 **ryōsai** good wife
　良妻賢母 **ryōsai-kenbo** good wife and wise mother
　良性 **ryōsei** benign (tumor)
9 良俗 **ryōzoku** good custom
　良風 **ryōfū** good custom
　良風美俗 **ryōfū-bizoku** good customs
　良品 **ryōhin** article of superior quality
　良計 **ryōkei** good plan, clever scheme
10 良剤 **ryōzai** effective medicine
　良師 **ryōshi** good teacher
　良家 **ryōka** good family
　良案 **ryōan** good idea
　良能 **ryōnō** natural ability
　良書 **ryōsho** good book
11 良過 **yosu(giru)** be too good
　良貨 **ryōka** good money
12 良港 **ryōkō** good harbor
　良策 **ryōsaku** good plan/policy
14 良導体 **ryōdōtai** good conductor
　良種 **ryōshu** good breed, thoroughbred
15 良縁 **ryōen** good (marital) match
　良質 **ryōshitsu** good quality
16 良薬 **ryōyaku** effective medicine
19 良識 **ryōshiki** good sense

───── 2 ─────

4 不良 **furyō** bad, substandard, delinquent
　不良導体 **furyō dōtai** nonconductor, poor conductor

6 仲良 **nakayo(ku)** on friendly terms
　　nakayo(shi) good friends
　色良 **iroyo(i)** favorable (answer)
7 体良 **teiyo(ku)** gracefully, politely
　改良 **kairyō** improvement, reform
8 長良川 **Nagaragawa** (river, Gifu-ken)
　佳良 **karyō** excellent, good
　奈良 **Nara** (city, Nara-ken)
　奈良県 **Nara-ken** (prefecture)
　奈良漬 **narazu(ke)** pickles seasoned in saké lees
　忠良 **chūryō** loyal
10 純良 **junryō** pure, genuine
11 野良 **nora** the fields; laziness
　野良犬 **norainu** stray dog
　野良仕事 **nora shigoto** farm/field work
　野良猫 **noraneko** stray cat
　野良着 **noragi** clothes for working in the fields
　運良 **un'yo(ku)** fortunately, luckily
12 善良 **zenryō** good, good-natured, virtuous
　温良 **onryō** gentle, amiable
　最良 **sairyō** best
　程良 **hodoyo(i)** good, favorable, proper; moderate; vague, noncommittal
　飲良 **no(mi)yo(i)** pleasant to drink
　順良 **junryō** peaceful, law-abiding
14 選良 **senryō** an elite; member of parliament
17 優良 **yūryō** superior, excellent

───── 3 ─────

7 良不良 **ryō-furyō** (whether) good or bad
9 首尾良 **shubiyo(ku)** successfully
10 都合良 **tsugōyo(ku)** fortunately, successfully, satisfactorily

───── 4 ─────

2 人種改良 **jinshu kairyō** eugenics
10 消化不良 **shōka furyō** indigestion

求→ **2b5.5**

0a7.4

I (sentence particle)

0a7.5 / 59

SHIN body **mi** body, one's person; one's station in life; heart, mind; flesh, meat

───── 1 ─────

0 身じろぎ **mi(jirogi)** slight movement, stirring

3 身丈 **mitake, mi(no)take** one's height
身上 **shinjō** merit, strong point **shinshō** one's fortune/property; household **mi(no)ue** one fortune/future; one's circumstances; one's background
身上判断 **mi(no)ue handan** telling a person's fortune
身上持 **shinshōmo(chi)** rich man; house-keeping
身上話 **mi(no)uebanashi** one's life story
4 身元 **mimoto** one's identity; one's character
身元保証 **mimoto hoshō** personal references
身内 **miuchi** relations, family, friends
身毛 **mi(no)ke** body hair
身中 **shinchū** one's heart, inmost thoughts
身支度 **mijitaku** grooming, outfit, prepara-tions
身分 **mibun** social standing, status; one's circumstances
身辺 **shinpen** one's person
身方 **mikata** friend, ally, supporter
身欠鰊 **mika(ki) nishin** dried herring
身心 **shinshin** body and mind
5 身仕舞 **mijimai** grooming, outfit, prepara-tions
身代 **shindai** fortune, property, estate **migawa(ri)** substitute, vicarious **mi(no)shiro** ransom money
身代限 **shindaikagi(ri)** bankruptcy
身代金 **mi(no)shirokin** ransom money
6 身近 **mijika** familiar, close to one
身共 **midomo** I, we
7 身体 **shintai, karada** the body
身体障害者 **shintai shōgaisha** physically handicapped person
身抜 **minu(ke)** get away from, get out of (one's circumstances)
身投 **mina(ge)** drown oneself
身形 **minari** one's personal appearance
身売 **miu(ri)** selling oneself (into bondage)
8 身長 **shinchō** one's height
身長順 **shinchō-jun** in order of height
身命 **shinmei** (risk) one's life
身受 **miu(ke)** redeem, ransom
身拵 **migoshira(e)** dress/outfit oneself; makeup
身知 **mishi(razu)** not knowing one's place, self-conceit
身空 **misora** one's lot/circumstaces
身性 **mijō** one's background; one's personal conduct
9 身重 **miomo** pregnant
身持 **mimo(chi)** one's personal conduct; pregnant
身柄 **migara** one's person
10 身振 **mibu(ri)** gesture, gesticulation

11 身動 **miugo(ki)** move about, stir
身過 **misu(gi)** living, livelihood
12 身幅 **mihaba** width (of a garment)
身勝手 **migatte** selfishness, having one's own way
身程 **mi(no)hodo** one's place, social standing
身程知 **mi(no)hodo shi(razu)** not knowing one's place
身軽 **migaru** light, agile, nimble
身悶 **mimoda(e)** writhe
13 身嗜 **midashina(mi)** personal grooming
14 身構 **migama(e)** stand ready, be on guard
身銭 **mizeni** one's own money
15 身罷 **mimaka(ru)** die, pass away
身請 **miu(ke)** redeem, ransom
身震 **miburu(i)** shiver, tremble, shudder
18 身繕 **mizukuro(i)** dress up, groom oneself
21 身贔屓 **mibiiki** nepotism
22 身籠 **migomo(ru)** become pregnant

─────────── 2 ───────────

1 一身 **isshin** oneself, one's own interests
一身上 **isshinjō** personal (affairs)
2 人身 **jinshin** the human body; one's person
人身売買 **jinshin baibai** slave trade
人身攻撃 **jinshin kōgeki** personal attack
人身保護 **jinshin hogo** habeas corpus
人身御供 **hitomi gokū** human sacrifice, victim
刀身 **tōshin** sword blade
3 大身 **taishin** man of rank/wealth
小身 **shōshin** humble position/rank
4 不身持 **fumimo(chi)** profligate, dissolute, licentious, loose
中身 **nakami** contents
化身 **keshin** incarnation, embodiment, manifestation
切身 **ki(ri)mi** slice, chop, cutlet
文身 **bunshin** tattooing
片身 **katami** one side of the body
分身 **bunshin** parturition, delivery; one's child; branch, offshoot; one's alter ego
心身 **shinshin** mind and body, psychosomatic
5 出身 **shusshin** (as suffix) originally from ...
出身地 **shusshinchi** native place, birthplace
半身 **hanshin** half the body
半身不随 **hanshin fuzui** paralyzed on one side
生身 **i(ki)mi** living body; fresh fish **namami** flesh and blood; living flesh; raw meat/fish
平身低頭 **heishin-teitō** prostrate oneself
打身 **u(chi)mi** bruise
白身 **shiromi** whiteness; white meat; white of an egg
立身 **risshin** success in life, getting ahead
立身出世 **risshin-shusse** success in life

6 全身 **zenshin** the whole body
全身不随 **zenshin fuzui** total paralysis
全身麻酔 **zenshin masui** general anasthesia
老身 **rōshin** aged body
当身 **a(te)mi** a knockdown blow
肌身 **hadami** the body, one's person
自身 **jishin** oneself, itself
自身番 **jishinban** (Edo-era) guardhouses
7 我身 **wa(ga)mi** oneself
即身成仏 **sokushin jōbutsu** attaining Buddhahood while still alive
赤身 **akami** lean meat; heartwood
抜身 **nu(ki)mi** drawn sword
投身 **tōshin** suicide by throwing oneself (into a river, from a building, in front of a train)
8 長身 **chōshin** tall
刺身 **sashimi** sliced raw fish, sashimi
刺身庖丁 **sashimi-bōchō** fish-slicing knife
受身 **ukemi** being acted upon; passivity; passive (in grammar)
法身 **hosshin** highest form of existence, soul (in Buddhism)
空身 **karami** without luggage, (traveling) light
肩身 **katami** face, honor
9 保身 **hoshin** self-protection
保身術 **hoshinjutsu** the art of self-protection
変身 **henshin** transformation
前身 **zenshin** antecedents, predecessor
浮身 **u(ki)mi** floating on one's back
挺身 **teishin** come forward, volunteer
独身 **dokushin, hito(ri)mi** unmarried
独身者 **dokushinsha** unmarried/single person
単身 **tanshin** alone, unaided, away from home
単身銃 **tanshinjū** single-barreled gun
相身互 **aimitaga(i)** mutual sympathy/help
10 修身 **shūshin** morals, ethics; moral training
随身 **zuishin** have on one's person; attend on; attendant **zuijin** bodyguard (historical)
剥身 **mu(ki)mi** shellfish removed from the shell **su(ki)mi** sliced very thin
差身 **sa(shi)mi** sliced raw fish, sashimi
捕身 **to(raware no) mi** a captive, taken prisoner
脂身 **aburami** fat (on meat)
骨身 **honemi** flesh and bones; marrow
砲身 **hōshin** gun barrel
病身 **byōshin** sickly constitution, poor health
馬身 **bashin** a horse's length
11 捨身 **su(te)mi** desperation
shashin renounce the flesh; die
黄身 **kimi** (egg) yolk
移身 **utsu(ri)mi** nimble, quick, adroit
細身 **hosomi** narrow blade, slender build
終身 **shūshin** for life, lifelong, lifetime

終身刑 **shūshinkei** life sentence
終身官 **shūshinkan** official appointed for life
転身 **tenshin** changing (jobs)
12 着身着儘 **ki(no)mi-ki(no)mama** with only the clothes one happens to be wearing
満身 **manshin** the whole body
渾身 **konshin** one's whole body
御身 **onmi, omi** you
装身具 **sōshingu** personal accessories
艇身 **teishin** boat length
等身 **tōshin** life-size
等身像 **tōshinzō** life-size statue
13 献身 **kenshin** self-sacrifice, dedication
献身的 **kenshinteki** self-sacrificing, devoted
裸身 **rashin** nakedness
14 痩身 **sōshin** slender body, thin build
総身 **sōmi** the whole body
銃身 **jūshin** gun barrel
15 膚身 **hadami** the body
膚身離 **hadami-hana(sazu)** always kept on one's person, highly treasured
影身 **kagemi** person's shadow
憂身 **u(ki)mi (o yatsusu)** be utterly/slavishly devoted to
16 樹身 **jushin** (tree) trunk
親身 **shinmi** blood relation; kind, cordial
20 護身 **goshin** personal protection
護身術 **goshinjutsu** art of self-defense

———————— 3 ————————

3 上半身 **jōhanshin, kamihanshin** upper half of the body
下半身 **kahanshin, shimohanshin** lower half of the body
4 不死身 **fujimi** insensible to pain, invulnerable, immortal
7 私自身 **watakushi jishin** personally, as for me
13 獅子身中虫 **shishi-shinchū (no) mushi** treacherous friend

———————— 4 ————————

6 自分自身 **jibun-jishin** oneself
7 低頭平身 **teitō heishin** prostrate oneself
10 粉骨砕身 **funkotsu-saishin** do one's utmost

0a7.6 / 69

来 未 來 徠   **RAI** come; (as prefix) next (week); (as suffix) since

ku(ru) come   **ki(taru)** come, this coming (Sunday); be due to   **ki(tasu)** cause, bring about

———————— 1 ————————

4 来月 **raigetsu** next month
来日 **rainichi** come to Japan
6 来年 **rainen** next year
来合 **kia(waseru)** happen to come along

来迎 **raigō** the coming of Amida Buddha to welcome the spirits of the dead
9 来信 **raishin** letter received
来客 **raikyaku** visitor, caller
来春 **raishun** next spring
10 来遊 **raiyū** visit
来週 **raishū** next week
来航 **raikō** arrival of ships; arrival by ship
11 来訪 **raihō** visit, call
12 来着 **raichaku** arrival
来場 **raijō** attendance
来朝 **raichō** visit to Japan, arrival in Japan
来診 **raishin** doctor's visit, house call
13 来意 **raii** purpose of one's visit
来電 **raiden** incoming telegram
14 来歴 **raireki** personal history, background, career
15 来賓 **raihin** guest, visitor
来賓席 **raihinseki** visitors' seats/gallery
17 来聴 **raichō** attend (a lecture)
18 来臨 **rairin** one's attendance, presence
来観 **raikan** inspection visit
来観者 **raikansha** visitor (to an exhibit)
22 来襲 **raishū** attack, raid, invasion

─────── 2 ───────

2 入来 **nyūrai** incoming, arrival, visit
4 元来 **ganrai** originally, primarily, by nature, properly speaking
天来 **tenrai** heavenly, divine
5 以来 **irai** since
矢来 **yarai** picket fence, palisade, stockade
出来 **deki(ru)** can, be able to, be possible; be done, be finished, be ready; be made of; be formed; come into being
出来上 **dekia(garu)** be finished, be ready; be cut out for
出来心 **dekigokoro** sudden impulse, whim
出来合 **dekia(u)** be ready-made; become intimate with
出来事 **dekigoto** incident, event, happenings
出来物 **dekimono** skin eruption, rash, pimple, boil, a growth
出来具合 **dekiguai** workmanship, result, performance
出来映 **dekiba(e)** result, effect, workmanship, performance
出来値 **dekine** selling price
本来 **honrai** properly speaking; in essence, naturally; originally, primarily
未来 **mirai** future; future tense
未来完了 **mirai kanryō** future perfect tense
未来派 **miraiha** futurist (artists)
生来 **seirai, shōrai** by nature, inborn, congenital
由来 **yurai** origin, derivation, how it came about; originally, by nature

由来書 **yuraisho** history, memoirs
古来 **korai** from ancient times, time-honored
外来 **gairai** foreign, imported
外来者 **gairaisha** person from abroad
外来患者 **gairai kanja** outpatient
外来語 **gairaigo** word of foreign origin, loanword
旧来 **kyūrai** from old times, traditional
6 年来 **nenrai** for (some) years
再来 **sairai** second coming
再来月 **saraigetsu** the month after next
再来年 **sarainen** the year after next
再来週 **saraishū** the week after next
伝来 **denrai** be transmitted, be handed down; be imported
老来 **rōrai** since growing old
近来 **kinrai** recently
在来 **zairai, a(ri)ki(tari)** usual, customary
如来 **nyorai** a Buddha
行来 **yu(ki)ki** come and go, associate with
7 言来 **i(i)ki(tari)** legend, tradition
8 到来 **tōrai** arrival, advent
到来物 **tōraimono** something received as a gift
夜来 **yarai** since last night, overnight
招来 **shōrai** bring about, invite, incur
往来 **ōrai** coming and going, traffic; road, street; fluc
往来止 **ōraido(me)** Road Closed
取来 **to(tte) ku(ru)** go get, fetch
9 飛来 **hirai** come flying; come by airplane
風来坊 **fūraibō** wanderer, vagabond, hobo
持来 **mo(tte) ku(ru)** bring (along)
　　 mo(tte)ko(i) ideal, excellent, just right
客来 **kyakurai** arrival of visitors
神来 **shinrai** inspiration
10 将来 **shōrai** future
将来性 **shōraisei** future, possibilities, prospects
帰来 **kirai** come back
従来 **jūrai** up to now, usual, conventional
家来 **kerai** vassal, retainer, retinue
11 舶来 **hakurai** imported
舶来品 **hakuraihin** imported goods
12 遠来 **enrai** from afar
渡来 **torai** introduction, influx; visit
御来光 **goraikō** sunrise viewed from a mountaintop
朝来 **chōrai** since morning
13 新来 **shinrai** newcomer
置来 **o(ite) ku(ru)** leave behind
14 爾来 **jirai** since then
22 襲来 **shūrai** invasion, raid, attack

─────── 3 ───────

1 一陽来復 **ichiyō-raifuku** return of spring

3 大出来 **ōdeki** a great success, well done
上出来 **jōdeki** good performance, well done
4 不出来 **fudeki** poorly made, unsatisfactory
6 尽未来 **jinmirai** forever
竹矢来 **takeyarai** bamboo palisade
9 故事来歴 **koji-raireki** origin and history
11 過般来 **kahanrai** for some time
13 数日来 **sūjitsurai** for the last few days

───────── 4 ─────────

3 千客万来 **senkaku-banrai, senkyaku-banrai** thronged with customers/visitors
5 古往今来 **koō-konrai** in all ages, since antiquity
6 有史以来 **yūshi irai** since the dawn of history
11 捲土重来 **kendo-chōrai, kendo-jūrai** comeback (from a defeat with renewed vigor)
釈迦如来 **Shaka Nyorai** Sakyamuni
16 薬師如来 **yakushi nyorai** a buddha who can cure any ailment

兎→ **0a8.5**

0a7.7 / 942

承 **SHŌ, JŌ, uketamawa(ru)** hear, listen to, be informed

───────── 1 ─────────

3 承久 **Jōkyū** (era, 1219–1222)
4 承元 **Jōgen** (era, 1207–1211)
5 承平 **Shōhei** (era, 931–938)
6 承安 **Jōan** (era, 1171–1175)
7 承応 **Jōō** (era, 1652–1655)
8 承知 **shōchi** consent to; know, be aware of
承服 **shōfuku** compliance, consent, submission
承和 **Shōwa** (era, 834–848)
9 承保 **Jōhō** (era, 1074–1077)
14 承暦 **Jōryaku** (era, 1077–1081)
承徳 **Jōtoku** (era, 1097–1099)
承認 **shōnin** approval
15 承諾 **shōdaku** consent

───────── 2 ─────────

1 了承 **ryōshō** acknowledge, understand
3 口承 **kōshō** word of mouth, oral tradition
4 不承 **fushō** dissent, disagreement, noncompliance
不承不承 **fushō-bushō** reluctant, grudging
不承知 **fushōchi** dissent, disagreement, noncompliance
不承諾 **fushōdaku** nonconsent, refusal
天承 **Tenjō** (era, 1131–1132)

5 永承 **Eijō** (era, 1046–1053)
6 伝承 **denshō** transmit, hand down (folklore)
8 長承 **Chōjō** (era, 1132–1135)
治承 **Jijō** (era, 1177–1181)
拝承 **haishō** I am informed that ...
10 起承転結 **ki-shō-ten-ketsu** introduction, development, turn, and conclusion (rules for composing a Chinese poem)
13 継承 **keishō** succession, inheritance
継承者 **keishōsha** successor
14 嘉承 **Kajō** (era, 1106–1108)
領承 **ryōshō** understand, acknowledge, estimate
15 諒承 **ryōshō** acknowledge, understand, note

───────── 3 ─────────

8 事後承諾 **jigo shōdaku** approval after the fact

───────── 4 ─────────

4 不承不承 **fushō-bushō** reluctant, grudging

0a7.8 / 501

束 **SOKU** bundle, sheaf, ream (of paper) **taba** bundle, bunch, sheaf **taba(neru)** bundle, tie in a bundle; govern, manage, control **tsuka** handbreadth; brief time; (book's) thickness **tsuka(neru)** tie in bundles; fold (one's arms)

───────── 1 ─────────

7 束見本 **tsuka-mihon** pattern volume, dummy (of a book to be printed)
9 束柱 **tsuka-bashira** supporting post between beam and roof ridge
束帯 **sokutai** full traditional court dress
12 束間 **tsuka(no)ma** brief time, moment
14 束髪 **sokuhatsu** bun hairdo
16 束縛 **sokubaku** restraint, constraint, shackles

───────── 2 ─────────

1 一束 **issoku, hitotaba** a bundle; a hundred
2 二束三文 **nisoku-sanmon** a dime a dozen, dirt cheap
3 大束 **ōtaba** large bundle
4 不束 **futsutsuka** ill-bred, inexperienced, inept, stupid
収束 **shūsoku** bring together; converge (in math)
5 札束 **satsutaba** wad of money, bundle/roll of bills
6 光束 **kōsoku** beam/flux of light
7 花束 **hanataba** bouquet
8 拘束 **kōsoku** restriction, constraint
拘束力 **kōsokuryoku** binding force (of a rule)
拘束者 **kōsokusha** person who restrains, captor
9 約束 **yakusoku** promise; appointment
約束手形 **yakusoku tegata** promissory note

0a7

約束事 **yakusokugoto** promise
12 覚束 **obotsuka(nai)** uncertain, dubious, well-nigh hopeless, precarious
検束 **kensoku** detention, custody, arrest
装束 **shōzoku** attire, dress
結束 **kessoku** band together, be united
14 磁束 **jisoku** magnetic flux
15 幣束 **heisoku** Shinto offerings of cloth, rope, or cut paper
16 鍵束 **kagitaba** bunch of keys

───────── 3 ─────────

3 口約束 **kuchi yakusoku** oral agreement/promise
4 不検束 **fukensoku** unrestrained
5 白装束 **shiroshōzoku** (clothed) all in white
6 衣冠束帯 **ikan-sokutai** full court dress; Shinto priest's vestments
11 黒装束 **kuroshōzoku** black clothes

庨→虍 2m6.3

0a7.9 / 142

里 **RI** village; (old unit of distance, about 3.9 km) **sato** village; one's parents' home

───────── 1 ─────────

2 里人 **satobito** villagers, countryfolk
里子 **satogo** child put out to nurse, foster child
4 里方 **satokata** one's wife's family
里心 **satogokoro** honesickness, nostalgia
6 里芋 **satoimo** taro
7 里扶持 **satobuchi** child-fostering expenses
里言葉 **sato kotoba** rural dialect; courtesans' language
9 里神楽 **sato kagura** sacred dance performance in a Shinto shrine
10 里帰 **satogae(ri)** bride's first visit to her old home
12 里程 **ritei** mileage, distance
里程標 **riteihyō** milepost
13 里数 **risū** mileage, distance
15 里標 **rihyō** milestone
16 里親 **sato oya** foster parent

───────── 2 ─────────

1 一里 **ichiri** one *ri*, 3.9 km
一里塚 **ichirizuka** milestone
2 人里 **hitozato** village, habitation
3 万里 **banri** thousands of miles
万里長城 **Banri (no) Chōjō** Great Wall of China
千里 **senri** a thousand leagues, a long distance

千里眼 **senrigan** clairvoyant
山里 **yamazato** mountain village, hilly district
4 巴里 **Pari** Paris
五里霧中 **gori-muchū** in a fog, groping in the dark
片里 **katazato** out-of-the-way village
方里 **hōri** square *ri*
5 古里 **furusato** native place, home town, home
6 色里 **irozato** red-light district
9 海里 **kairi** nautical mile
10 郷里 **kyōri** one's native place, home (town)
遊里 **yūri** red-light district
16 親里 **oyazato** one's parents' home
21 露里 **rori** Russian mile, *verst* (1066 m)

───────── 3 ─────────

4 片山里 **katayamazato** remote mountain village
12 遠山里 **tōyamazato** remote mountain village

───────── 4 ─────────

1 一望千里 **ichibō-senri** vast, boundless
一瀉千里 **issha-senri** in a rush, at full gallop

0a7.10 / 1302

我 **GA, wa** self **wa(ga)** my, our, one's own **ware** I, oneself

───────── 1 ─────────

3 我々 **wareware** we, us, our
5 我田引水 **gaden insui** drawing water for one's own field, promoting one's own interests
7 我身 **wa(ga)mi** oneself
我我 **wareware** we, us, our **ware(mo)-ware(mo)** vying with one another
我利 **gari** one's own interests, self-interest
8 我事 **wagakoto** one's own affair/concern, (take it) personally
我国 **wa(ga)kuni** our country
我物 **wa(ga)mono** one's own (property)
我物顔 **wa(ga)monogao** as if one's own
我武者羅 **gamushara** reckless, daredevil
10 我流 **garyū** self-taught, one's own way
我家 **wa(ga)ya** our home/house
11 我執 **gashū** egoistic attachment; obstinacy
我張 **ga (o) ha(ru)** be self-willed, insist on having one's own way
我欲 **gayoku** selfishness
12 我勝 **warega(chi ni)** everyone for himself
我等 **warera** we
13 我意 **gai** self-will, obstinacy
14 我慢 **gaman** put up with, bear, endure, be patient
15 我輩 **wagahai** I
16 我儘 **wagamama** selfish, capricious, wanting to have one's own way

─────────── 2 ───────────

3 小我 **shōga** the self/ego
5 主我 **shuga** ego, self
主我主義 **shuga shugi** egoism, love of self
6 自我 **jiga** self, ego
自我実現 **jiga jitsugen** self-realization
7 我我 **wareware** we, us, our **ware(mo)-ware(mo)** vying with one another
忘我 **bōga** self-oblivion, trance, ecstasy
没我 **botsuga** self-effacement, selflessness
8 彼我 **higa** oneself and others, each other
怪我 **kega** injury, wound; accident, chance
怪我人 **keganin** injured person, the wounded
11 唯我独尊 **yuiga-dokuson** self-conceit, vainglory
唯我論 **yuigaron** solipsism
12 無我 **muga** selflessness, self-forgetfulness
無我夢中 **muga-muchū** total absorption, ecstasy
14 瘦我慢 **ya(se)gaman** endure for sake of pride

0a7.11

甫 **HO, FU** (eulogistic male name suffix); for the first time

曳 → 曳 **0a6.23**

0a7.12 / 1008

更 更 **KŌ** (two-hour) night watch; anew **sara** new thing/matter **sara (ni)** anew, again, furthermore **sara(naru)** (even) more, further **fu(kasu)** stay up till late **fu(keru)** grow late

─────────── 1 ───────────

5 更生 **kōsei** rebirth, resuscitation; making over, rehabilitation, reorganization
更生品 **kōseihin** reconditioned article
更正 **kōsei** correct, rectify
6 更年期 **kōnenki** menopause
更衣 **kōi** changing one's clothes; lady court attendant **koromogae** seasonal change of clothing
更衣室 **kōishitsu** clothes-changing room
7 更迭 **kōtetsu** change, reshuffle, shake-up
更改 **kōkai** renovate, renew, reform
13 更新 **kōshin** renew, renovate

─────────── 2 ───────────

4 今更 **imasara** now, at this late date
7 初更 **shokō** first watch (8–10 p.m.)
8 夜更 **yofuka(shi)** staying up late
yofuke late at night, the small hours

尚更 **naosara** still more, all the more
9 変更 **henkō** change, alteration, amendment
10 殊更 **kotosara** especially, particularly; intentionally
11 深更 **shinkō** the dead of night, late at night
12 満更 **manzara** (not) wholly/altogether

─────────── 3 ───────────

3 小夜更 **sayofu(kete)** late a night
6 自力更生 **jiriki kōsei** be saved by one's own efforts

─────────── 4 ───────────

4 日付変更線 **hizuke henkōsen** the international date line

0a7.13

串 **KAN** pierce **kushi** spit, skewer

─────────── 1 ───────────

8 串刺 **kushiza(shi)** skewering
9 串柿 **kushigaki** persimmons dried on skewers
12 串焼 **kushiya(ki)** spit-roasted

─────────── 2 ───────────

12 焼串 **ya(ki)gushi** skewer, spit

0a7.14 / 1616

亜 亞 **A** rank next, come after, sub-; -ous (in acids); Asia

─────────── 1 ───────────

6 亜成層圏 **asei sōken** substratosphere
亜米利加 **Amerika** America
9 亜炭 **atan** lignite, brown coal
亜砒酸 **ahisan** arsenious acid, … arsenite
亜音速 **aonsoku** subsonic (speed)
10 亜流 **aryū** adherent, follower, imitator
11 亜麻 **ama** flax, linen
亜麻仁 **amani** linseed, flaxseed
亜麻仁油 **amaniyu** linseed oil
亜麻布 **amanuno** linen
亜麻製 **amasei** flaxen, linen
亜麻織物 **ama orimono** flax fabrics, linen
亜族 **azoku** subtribe
亜細亜 **Ajia** Asia
12 亜寒帯 **akantai** subarctic zone
亜属 **azoku** subgenus
亜硫酸 **aryūsan** sulfurous acid, … sulfite
13 亜鉛 **aen** zinc
亜鉛引 **aenbi(ki)** galvanized
亜鉛末 **aenmatsu** zinc dust
亜鉛版 **aenban** zinc etching
亜鉛板 **aenban** zinc plate
亜鉛華 **aenka** flowers of zinc, zinc oxide
亜鉛鉄 **aentetsu** galvanized iron

0a7

0a7

14 亜種 **ashu** subspecies
15 亜熱帯 **anettai** subtropics

─────── 2 ───────

3 小亜細亜 **Shō-Ajia** Asia Minor
5 白亜 **hakua** chalk
白亜層 **hakuasō** chalk bed/stratum
白亜館 **Hakuakan** the White House
6 次亜 **jia-** hypo- (in chemicals)
8 東亜 **Tōa** East Asia
東亜諸国 **Tōa shokoku** the countries of East Asia
欧亜 **Ō-A** Europe and Asia

─────── 3 ───────

3 大東亜 **Dai-Tōa** Greater East Asia
7 亜細亜 **Ajia** Asia
21 露西亜 **Roshia** Russia

─────── 4 ───────

3 小亜細亜 **Shō-Ajia** Asia Minor

0a7.15 / 1550

寿　壽

JU, SU age; lifespan; longevity; congratulations
kotobuki congratulations; long life **kotoho(gu)** congratulate

─────── 1 ───────

5 寿永 **Juei** (era, 1182–1184)

寿司 **sushi** sushi (raw fish and other delicacies with vinegared rice)
8 寿命 **jumyō** life, lifespan
17 寿齢 **jurei** long life

─────── 2 ───────

3 久寿 **Kyūju** (era, 1154–1156)
万寿 **Manju** (era, 1024–1028)
4 天寿 **tenju** natural lifespan
仁寿 **Ninju** (era, 851–854)
6 米寿 **beiju** one's 88th birthday
7 延寿 **enju** prolongation of life
8 長寿 **chōju** long life, longevity
10 高寿 **kōju** advanced age
12 喜寿 **kiju** one's 77th birthday
13 福寿 **fukuju** happiness and longevity
福寿草 **fukujusō** Amur adonis
聖寿 **seiju** the emperor's age
頌寿 **shōju** (congratulations on) one's 60th, 70th, 80th, etc. birthday

─────── 3 ───────

13 福禄寿 **Fukurokuju** (tall-headed god of happiness, wealth, and longevity)
14 稲荷寿司 **inarizushi** fried tofu stuffed with vinegared rice

事 → 事 **0a8.15**

─────────────── 0a8 ───────────────

函	些	非	長	兒	爬	亞	兩	妖	乖	兎	表	画
2b6.3	2m6.4	8.1	8.2	4c3.3	8.3	0a7.14	0a6.11	8.4	2k6.4	8.5	8.6	8.7

果	東	奄	秉	垂	奉	毒	事
8.8	8.9	8.10	8.11	8.12	8.13	8.14	8.15

函 → **2b6.3**

些 → **2m6.4**

0a8.1 / 498

非

HI non-, un-; wrong
ara(zu) not, not so

─────── 1 ───────

2 非人 **hinin** beggar; outcast
非人道 **hijindō** inhumanity
非人情 **hininjō** inhuman, unfeeling
非人間的 **hiningenteki** inhuman, impersonal
非力 **hiriki** powerless; incompetent

3 非才 **hisai** lack of ability, incompetence
非凡 **hibon** extraordinary, unusual
4 非文明 **hibunmei** uncivilized
非公式 **hikōshiki** unofficial
非公開 **hikōkai** closed (meeting), closed-door (session)
非日 **hi-Nichi** un-Japanese
5 非生産的 **hiseisanteki** nonproductive, unproductive
非礼 **hirei** impolite
非立憲的 **hirikkenteki** unconstitutional
6 非合法 **higōhō** illegal
非合理的 **higōriteki** unreasonable, irrational
非行 **hikō** misdeed, misconduct, delinquency
非米 **hi-Bei** un-American
7 非芸術的 **higeijutsuteki** inartistic
非売同盟 **hibai dōmei** sellers' strike
非売品 **hibaihin** article not for sale

非社会的 **hishakaiteki** antisocial
非社交的 **hishakōteki** unsociable, retiring
8 非命 **himei** untimely (death)
非法 **hihō** illegal, unlawful, lawless
非実用品 **hijitsuyōhin** unessential items
非実際的 **hijissaiteki** impractical
非国民 **hikokumin** unpatriotic person
非武装 **hibusō** demilitarized (zone),
    unarmed (neutrality)
非金属 **hikinzoku** nonmetallic
9 非科学的 **hikagakuteki** unscientific
10 非党派的 **hitōhateki** nonpartisan
非能率的 **hinōritsuteki** inefficient
11 非運 **hiun** misfortune, bad luck
非道 **hidō** inhuman, unjust, cruel, tyrranical
非常 **hijō** emergency; extraordinary; very,
    exceedingly, extremely
非常口 **hijōguchi** emergency exit
非常時 **hijōji** emergency, crisis
非常勤 **hijōkin** part-time work
非常線 **hijōsen** cordon
非常識 **hijōshiki** lacking common sense,
    absurd
非理 **hiri** unreasonable, absurd
非現実的 **higenjitsuteki** unrealistic
非現業 **higengyō** clerical/non-field work
非現業員 **higengyōin** office/desk worker
非望 **hibō** inordinate ambition
非情 **hijō** inanimate; unfeeling
非紳士的 **hishinshiteki** ungentlemanly
12 非違 **hii** lawlessness, unlawfulness
非営利的 **hieiriteki** nonprofit
非番 **hiban** off duty
非買同盟 **hibai dōmei** boycott
非統制 **hitōsei** noncontrolled (goods)
13 非業 **higō** untimely (death)
非愛国的 **hiaikokuteki** unpatriotic, disloyal
非戦論 **hisenron** pacificism
非戦闘員 **hisentōin** noncombatant
非鉄金属 **hitetsu kinzoku** nonferrous metals
15 非課税 **hikazei** tax exemption
非論理的 **hironriteki** illogical, irrational
16 非衛生的 **hieiseiteki** unsanitary, unhygienic
18 非職 **hishoku** retired
非難 **hinan** criticize, denounce
20 非議 **higi** criticize, blame

————————— 2 —————————

2 人非人 **ninpinin** man of brutal nature
6 先非 **senpi** past error/sins
7 似非 **ni(te)hi(naru)** alike only in appearance
    ese- false, would-be, pseudo-
9 前非 **zenpi** one's past error
昨非今是 **sakuhi-konze** reversing one's way
    of thinking
是非 **zehi** right and wrong; by all means

11 理非 **rihi** the rights and wrongs, relative
    merits
————————— 3 —————————
7 似而非 **ese-** false, would-be, pseudo-
9 是々非々 **zeze-hihi** fair and unbiased

0a8.2 / 95

CHŌ long; (especially as suffix) head,
chief, director **naga(i)** long **naga-**
(tarashii) lengthy, long and boring
naga(raeru) live long, live on
ta(keru) excel in; grow older **osa** head, chief
tokoshi(e) forever

————————— 1 —————————

0 長じる/ずる **chō(jiru/zuru)** grow up; be
    older; excel in
2 長丁場 **nagachōba** long stretch/scene
長子 **chōshi** eldest son; first child
長刀 **naginata** halberd
3 長久 **chōkyū** eternity, permanence
    Chōkyū (era, 1040–1044)
長大 **chōdai** tall and stout
長大息 **chōtaisoku** a long sigh
長上 **chōjō** one's elder, a superior
長々 **naganaga(shii)** long-drawn-out
長女 **chōjo** eldest daughter
4 長元 **Chōgen** (era, 1028–1037)
長文 **chōbun** long sentence/article/letter
長円 **chōen** ellipse, oval
長円形 **chōenkei** ellipse, oval
長手 **nagate** long(ish), longitudinal;
    a stretcher (in bricklaying)
長引 **nagabi(ku)** be prolonged, drag on
長尺物 **chōjakumono, chōshakumono** long/
    lengthy item (film)
長月 **nagatsuki** ninth lunar month
長火鉢 **nagahibachi** oblong brazier
長方形 **chōhōkei** rectangle
5 長生 **nagai(ki), chōsei** long life, longevity
長幼 **chōyō** young and old
長幼序 **chōyō (no) jo** Elders first.
長兄 **chōkei** eldest brother
長穴 **nagaana** slot
長広舌 **chōkōzetsu** loquacity, long(-winded)
    talk
長尻 **nagajiri** overstaying one's welcome
長石 **chōseki** feldspar
6 長年 **naganen** many years, a long time
長老 **chōrō** an elder
長老教会 **Chōrō Kyōkai** Presbyterian
    Church
長芋 **nagaimo** yam
7 長良川 **Nagaragawa** (river, Gifu-ken)
長身 **chōshin** tall
長承 **Chōjō** (era, 1132–1135)

長寿 **chōju** long life, longevity
長享 **Chōkyō** (era, 1487–1489)
長谷 **Hase** (surname)
長谷川 **Hasegawa** (surname)
長男 **chōnan** eldest son
長足 **chōsoku** rapid/giant strides
8 長長 **naganaga(shii)** long-drawn-out
長命 **chōmei** long life, longevity
長夜 **chōya** long night
長岡 **Nagaoka** (city, Niigata-ken)
長波 **chōha** long wave
長波長 **chōhachō** long wavelength
長治 **Chōji** (era, 1104–1106)
長征 **chōsei** long march
長官 **chōkan** director, head, chief, secretary, administrator
長居 **nagai** stay too long
長枕 **nagamakura** bed bolster
長者 **chōja** millionaire, rich person
長物 **chōbutsu** useless item, white elephant
長物語 **nagamonogatari** a tedious talk
長所 **chōsho** one's strong point, advantages
長和 **Chōwa** (era, 1012–1017)
長雨 **nagaame** rain lasting several days
長門 **Nagato** (ancient kuni, Yamaguchi-ken)
9 長保 **Chōhō** (era, 999–1004)
長逝 **chōsei** die, pass away
長途 **chōto** a long way/distance
長持 **nagamo(chi)** oblong chest; be durable, last
長屋 **nagaya** tenement building
長柄 **nagae** long handle; spear
長音 **chōon** a long sound/vowel, long tone, dash
長音階 **chōonkai** major scale
長音符 **chōonpu** long-vowel mark, macron
10 長射程砲 **chōshateihō** long-range gun/artillery
長唄 **nagauta** song accompanied on the samisen
長座 **chōza** stay long
長時間 **chōjikan** a long time
長旅 **nagatabi** long journey
長袖 **nagasode** long sleeves
長針 **chōshin** the long/minute hand
11 長野 **Nagano** (city, Nagano-ken)
長野県 **Nagano-ken** (prefecture)
長崎 **Nagasaki** (city, Nagasaki-ken)
長崎県 **Nagasaki-ken** (prefecture)
長患 **nagawazura(i)** a long/protracted illness
長蛇 **chōda** long snake; long line of people, long queue
12 長湯 **nagayu** a long bath
長短 **chōtan** (relative) length; merits and demerits, advantages and disadvantages
長須鯨 **nagasu kujira** razorback whale

長椅子 **nagaisu** sofa, couch
長期 **chōki** long-term, long-range
長期戦 **chōkisen** prolonged/protracted war
長禄 **Chōroku** (era, 1457–1460)
長軸 **chōjiku** major axis
長距離 **chōkyori** long-distance, long-range
長閑 **nodo(ka)** tranquil, mild, balmy
13 長嘆 **chōtan** a long sigh
長靴 **nagagutsu** boots
長寛 **Chōkan** (era, 1163–1165)
長煩 **nagawazura(i)** a long/protracted illness
長話 **nagabanashi** a long/tedious talk
14 長暦 **Chōryaku** (era, 1037–1040)
長徳 **Chōtoku** (era, 995–999)
長髪 **chōhatsu** long hair
長歌 **chōka, nagauta** long epic poem
長駆 **chōku** ride a great distance, make a long march
15 長編 **chōhen** long (article), full-length (novel), feature-length (movie)
長談議 **nagadangi** a long-winded speech
長調 **chōchō** major key, in (C) major
17 長講 **chōkō** a long talk/lecture
18 長軀 **chōku** tall stature
19 長襦袢 **nagajuban** long underwear

──────── 2 ────────
1 一長一短 **itchō ittan** advantages and disadvantages
3 上長 **jōchō** one's superior, a senior, an elder
4 天長 **Tenchō** (era, 824–834)
天長地久 **tenchō-chikyū** coeval with heaven and earth
天長節 **Tenchōsetsu** Emperor's Birthday
冗長 **jōchō** verbose, redundant
区長 **kuchō** head of the ward
手長 **tenaga** long-armed person; kleptomaniac
手長猿 **tenagazaru** long-armed ape, gibbon
月長石 **getchōseki** moonstone
心長閑 **kokoronodoka** peaceful, at ease
5 生長 **i(ki)naga(raeru)** live on, live long, survive
市長 **shichō** mayor
正長 **Shōchō** (era, 1428–1429)
永長 **Eichō** (era, 1096–1097)
弘長 **Kōchō** (era, 1261–1264)
6 気長 **kinaga** leisurely, patient
年長 **nenchō** seniority
年長者 **nenchōsha** a senior, older person
伍長 **gochō** corporal, staff sergeant
全長 **zenchō** overall length
会長 **kaichō** chairman, president
次長 **jichō** deputy director, assistant chief
舌長 **shitanaga** talkative
団長 **danchō** leader (of a group)
亘長 **kōchō** span, interval, distance
成長 **seichō** growth

7 身長 **shinchō** one's height
身長順 **shinchō-jun** in order of height
伸長 **shinchō** extension, expansion
助長 **jochō** promote, further, encourage
延長 **enchō** extension, continuation, prolongation, elongation
　　　Enchō (era, 923–930)
医長 **ichō** head doctor
学長 **gakuchō** dean, rector
応長 **Ōchō** (era, 1311–1312)
尾長鳥 **onagadori** blue magpie; long-tailed bird
尾長猿 **onagazaru** long-tailed monkey
局長 **kyokuchō** bureau chief, director, postmaster
村長 **sonchō** village mayor
社長 **shachō** company president
町長 **chōchō** town mayor
足長 **ashinaga(-ojisan)** Daddy Longlegs
8 長長 **naganaga(shii)** long-drawn-out
夜長 **yonaga** long night
建長 **Kenchō** (era, 1249–1255)
波長 **hachō** wavelength
店長 **tenchō** store/shop manager
所長 **shochō** director, head, manager
9 係長 **kakarichō** chief clerk
院長 **inchō** head of the hospital/school/institute
酋長 **shūchō** chief(tain)
首長 **shuchō** leader, head, chief
室長 **shitsuchō** senior roommate; section chief
面長 **omonaga** elongated/oval face
科長 **kachō** department head
級長 **kyūchō** head/president of the class
10 部長 **buchō** department head
消長 **shōchō** rise and fall
家長 **kachō** family head, patriarch, matriarch
座長 **zachō** chairman, moderator; troupe leader
校長 **kōchō** principal, headmaster
胴長 **dōnaga** long-torsoed
班長 **hanchō** group leader
特長 **tokuchō** distinctive feature, characteristic; strong point, forte, merit
11 隊長 **taichō** unit commander, captain, leader
深長 **shinchō** profound, deep, abstruse
婦長 **fuchō** head nurse
曹長 **sōchō** sergeant major, master sergeant
族長 **zokuchō** patriarch
悠長 **yūchō** leisurely, slow, easygoing
細長 **hosonaga(i)** long and thin
組長 **kumichō** group leader, foreman
船長 **senchō** (ship's) captain
12 最長 **saichō** longest
艇長 **teichō** coxswain; skipper
13 裏長屋 **uranagaya** back-street tenement

塾長 **jukuchō** cram-school principal
園長 **enchō** head of a kindergarten/zoo
楽長 **gakuchō** band leader, conductor
署長 **shochō** government office chief, police precinct head
14 増長 **zōchō** grow presumptuous, get too big for one's britches
総長 **sōchō** (university) president
管長 **kanchō** superintendent priest
駅長 **ekichō** stationmaster
15 寮長 **ryōchō** dormitory director
慶長 **Keichō** (era, 1596–1615)
横長 **yokonaga** oblong
課長 **kachō** section chief
霊長 **reichō** crown of creation, mankind
霊長類 **reichōrui** primates
16 機長 **kichō** (airplane) captain
館長 **kanchō** director, curator
17 優長 **yūchō** leisurely, easygoing
18 職長 **shokuchō** foreman
20 議長 **gichō** chairman, president
21 艦長 **kanchō** the captain (of a warship)

────────── 3 ──────────

1 一日長 **ichijitsu (no) chō** superior, a little better
2 八百長 **yaochō** rigged affair, fixed game
3 万里長城 **Banri (no) Chōjō** Great Wall of China
4 支局長 **shikyokuchō** branch manager
支部長 **shibuchō** branch manager
6 百万長者 **hyakumanchōja** (multi-)millionaire
百薬長 **hyakuyaku (no) chō** (saké is) the best medicine
7 技師長 **gishichō** chief engineer
学部長 **gakubuchō** dean of a university department
学校長 **gakkōchō** school principal
8 長波長 **chōhachō** long wavelength
事務長 **jimuchō** head official; manager
事務長官 **jimuchōkan** chief secretary
参謀長 **sanbōchō** chief of staff
官房長官 **kanbō chōkan** Chief Cabinet Secretary
国務長官 **kokumu chōkan** (U.S.) Secretary of State
委員長 **iinchō** chairman
9 重厚長大 **jūkō-chōdai** large and heavy, bulky (cf. 軽薄短小)
変ロ長調 **hen-ro chōchō** B-flat major
連隊長 **rentaichō** regimental commander
10 部隊長 **butaichō** commanding officer
師団長 **shidanchō** division commanderg
書記長 **shokichō** chief secretary
鬼課長 **onikachō** hard-driving boss/section-chief

11 副会長 **fukukaichō** (company) vice president
   副議長 **fukugichō** vice president/chairman
   理事長 **rijichō** chairman, president
12 短波長 **tanpachō** short wavelength
   棟割長屋 **munewa(ri) nagaya** long tene-
      ment/partitioned building
   無用長物 **muyō (no) chōbutsu** useless
      obstruction
   税関長 **zeikanchō** director of customs
   裁判長 **saibanchō** presiding judge
13 幹事長 **kanjichō** executive secretary,
      secretary-general
14 鼻下長 **bikachō** amorous man   **hana (no)
      shita (ga) naga(i)** easily charmed by
      women
   総務長官 **sōmu chōkan** director-general
15 億万長者 **okumanchōja** multimillionaire,
      billionaire
   編集長 **henshūchō** editor-in-chief

————————— 4 —————————

3 万物霊長 **banbutsu (no) reichō** man, the
      lord of creation
7 図書館長 **toshokanchō** head librarian
9 看護婦長 **kangofuchō** head nurse
10 書記官長 **shokikanchō** chief secretary
13 意味深長 **imi-shinchō** full of meaning
14 総務部長 **sōmu buchō** head of the general
      affairs department

兒 → 児　4c3.3

0a8.3

爬
HA scratch; crawl

————————— 1 —————————

6 爬行 **hakō** crawl, creep
   爬虫類 **hachūrui** reptiles

————————— 2 —————————

13 搔爬 **sōha** curettage, scraping out

亞 → 亜　0a7.14

兩 → 両　0a6.11

0a8.4

殀
YŌ dying young

乖 → 　2k6.4

0a8.5

兎 兔 兔 菟
TO, usagi rabbit

————————— 1 —————————

4 兎毛 **u(no)ke** just a hair
9 兎狩 **usagiga(ri)** rabbit hunting
10 兎唇 **toshin, mitsukuchi, iguchi** harelip
   兎馬 **usagiuma** donkey

————————— 2 —————————

5 白兎 **shirousagi** white rabbit
11 野兎 **nousagi** hare, jackrabbit
   脱兎 **datto** dashing away, fast as a rabbit

0a8.6 / 272

表
HYŌ table, chart; surface; expression
arawa(su) express, manifest **arawa-
(reru)** be expressed   **omote** surface,
face; front; heads (of a coin); first half
(of an inning)

————————— 1 —————————

0 表する **hyō(suru)** express, manifest
3 表口 **omoteguchi** front entrance/door
4 表日本 **Omote Nihon** Pacific side of Japan
5 表皮 **hyōhi** epidermis; bark, rind, peel, husk
   表玄関 **omote genkan** front entrance/door
   表札 **hyōsatsu** nameplate, doorplate
   表示 **hyōji** indicate, express, display
   表立 **omoteda(tsu)** become public/known
7 表沙汰 **omotezata** making public; lawsuit
   表芸 **omotegei** one's principal accomplish-
      ment
8 表表紙 **omotebyōshi** front cover
   表明 **hyōmei** state, express, announce
   表具屋 **hyōguya** picture mounter/framer
   表具師 **hyōgushi** picture mounter/framer
9 表面 **hyōmen** surface
   表面化 **hyōmenka** come to the surface/fore,
      become an issue
   表面的 **hyōmenteki** on the surface, out-
      wardly
   表面張力 **hyōmen chōryoku** surface tension
   表音文字 **hyōon moji** phonetic symbol/script
   表看板 **omote-kanban** sign out in front;
      figurehead, mask
   表計算 **hyōkeisan** spreadsheet
10 表紙 **hyōshi** cover, binding
   表記 **hyōki** inscription, indication, declara-
      tion; orthography
11 表側 **omotegawa** the front
   表現 **hyōgen** expression

表情 **hyōjō** (facial) expression
12 表象 **hyōshō** symbol, emblem
表替 **omotega(e)** refacing tatami mats
表装 **hyōsō** mount (a picture); bind (a book)
13 表裏 **hyōri** inside and outside; duplicity
表意文字 **hyōi moji** ideograph
14 表彰 **hyōshō** commendation
表構 **omotegama(e)** facade
15 表編 **omoteami** plain knitting, stockinet stitch
18 表題 **hyōdai** title, heading, caption

──────── 2 ────────
3 上表紙 **uwabyōshi** outer cover, (book) jacket
4 中表 **nakaomote** folding cloth so that the facing is inside and the lining outside
公表 **kōhyō** official announcement
5 代表 **daihyō** representation, typical; a delegate
代表団 **daihyōdan** delegation, mission
代表作 **daihyōsaku** masterpiece, most important work
代表的 **daihyōteki** representative, typical
代表者 **daihyōsha** a representative
付表 **fuhyō** attached table
右表 **uhyō** the chart at the right
布表紙 **nunobyōshi** cloth binding
6 年表 **nenpyō** chronological table
地表 **chihyō** surface of the earth
7 別表 **beppyō** the attached table/list
図表 **zuhyō** chart, table, graph
言表 **i(i)ara(wasu)** express
8 表表紙 **omotebyōshi** front cover
9 発表 **happyō** announce
革表紙 **kawabyōshi** leather cover/binding
10 書表 **ka(ki)ara(wasu)** express/describe in writing
紙表紙 **kamibyōshi** paper cover, paperback
11 黄表紙 **kibyōshi** Edo-period comic book
黒表 **kokuhyō** blacklist
12 無表情 **muhyōjō** expressionless
税表 **zeihyō** tariff (schedule)
畳表 **tatami omote** tatami facing
賀表 **gahyō** congratulatory card (to the emperor)
雲表 **unpyō** above the clouds
13 裏表 **ura-omote** both sides; reverse, inside out; two-faced
墓表 **bohyō** grave marker/post
意表 **ihyō** surprise, something unexpected
辞表 **jihyō** (letter of) resignation
15 儀表 **gihyō** model, paragon
19 譜表 **fuhyō** staff (in music)

──────── 3 ────────
1 一覧表 **ichiranhyō** table, list
4 分類表 **bunruihyō** table of classifications
5 未公表 **mikōhyō** not yet officially announced
未発表 **mihappyō** not yet made public

正誤表 **seigohyō** errata
6 考課表 **kōkahyō** personnel/service record; business report
早見表 **hayamihyō** chart, table
成績表 **seisekihyō** report/score card
8 価格表 **kakakuhyō** price list
定価表 **teikahyō** price list
9 通知表 **tsūchihyō** report card
10 時刻表 **jikokuhyō** timetable, schedule
時間表 **jikanhyō** timetable, schedule
12 換算表 **kansanhyō** conversion table
統計表 **tōkeihyō** statistical table
13 献立表 **kondatehyō** menu
15 諸元表 **shogenhyō** list of equipment performance figures

──────── 4 ────────
7 利益代表 **rieki daihyō** representing (another country's) diplomatic interests

──────── 5 ────────
12 貸借対照表 **taishakutaishōhyō** balance sheet

──────── 6 ────────
6 全国人民代表大会 **Zenkoku Jinmin Daihyō Taikai** (Chinese) National People's Congress

0a8.7 / 343

画　畫　**GA** picture, drawing, painting
KAKU stroke (of a kanji)
ega(ku) draw, paint, describe

──────── 1 ────────
0 画する **kaku(suru)** draw, mark off; plan
1 画一 **kakuitsu** uniform, standard
画一主義 **kakuitsu shugi** standardization
画一的 **kakuitsuteki** uniform, standard
3 画工 **gakō** painter, artist
画才 **gasai** artistic talent
5 画仙紙 **gasenshi** drawing paper
画用紙 **gayōshi** drawing paper
画布 **gafu** a canvas
6 画会 **gakai** artist's patrons association
7 画伯 **gahaku** (great) artist, (master) painter
8 画法 **gahō** art of drawing/painting
画板 **gaban** drawing/drafting board
9 画風 **gafū** style of painting/drawing
画室 **gashitsu** artist's studio, atelier
画面 **gamen** scene, picture, (TV etc.) screen
画架 **gaka** easel
10 画家 **gaka** painter, artist
画竜点晴 **garyō-tensei** completing the eyes of a painted dragon; the finishing touches
画素 **gaso** picture element, pixel, dot
11 画商 **gashō** picture dealer
画廊 **garō** picture gallery
12 画報 **gahō** illustrated magazine, news in pictures

画期的 **kakkiteki** epoch-making, revolutionary
画然 **kakuzen (to)** distinctly, sharply
画筆 **gahitsu** artist's brush
画策 **kakusaku** plan, map out; maneuver, scheme
13 画数 **kakusū** number of strokes (of a kanji)
14 画像 **gazō** portrait, picture, image
15 画稿 **gakō** a sketch
画賛 **gasan** legend written over a picture
画鋲 **gabyō** thumbtack
画餅 **gabei** failure, fiasco, (come to) nought
16 画壇 **gadan** the artists' world
画龍点晴 **garyō-tensei** completing the eyes of a painted dragon; the finishing touches
18 画題 **gadai** subject/title of a painting
19 画譜 **gafu** picture book/album
22 画讃 **gasan** legend written over a picture

─────── 2 ───────

4 仏画 **butsuga** Buddhist painting
区画 **kukaku** division, section
区画整理 **kukaku seiri** land readjustment, readjustment of town lots
5 古画 **koga** old painting, ancient picture
字画 **jikaku** strokes (of a kanji)
6 企画 **kikaku** plan, planning
邦画 **hōga** Japanese movie/painting
印画 **inga** (photographic) print
名画 **meiga** famous picture, masterpiece
自画 **jiga** picture painted by oneself
自画像 **jigazō** self-portrait
自画賛 **jigasan** praising one's own picture
7 図画 **zuga** drawing
8 版画 **hanga** woodcut print
参画 **sankaku** participate (in the planning)
参画者 **sankakusha** person participating in the planning
9 盆画 **bonga** tray landscape
洋画 **yōga** Western painting/movie
洋画家 **yōgaka** painter of Western-type pictures
映画 **eiga** movie, film
映画化 **eigaka** make a movie version of
映画界 **eigakai** the cinema/screen world
映画劇 **eigageki** film drama
映画館 **eigakan** movie theater
春画 **shunga** obscene picture, pornography
計画 **keikaku** plan, project
計画的 **keikakuteki** planned, systematic, intentional
計画者 **keikakusha** planner
10 俳画 **haiga** haiku-like picture, sketch
陰画 **inga** a negative
原画 **genga** the original picture
挿画 **sa(shi)e, sōga** illustration (in a book)

唐画 **tōga** Chinese(-style) painting
席画 **sekiga** impromptu drawing
書画 **shoga** pictures and writings
11 陽画 **yōga** a positive (photographic print)
動画 **dōga** animation
描画 **byōga** drawing, painting
彩画 **saiga** colored painting/picture
密画 **mitsuga** detailed drawing
略画 **ryakuga** rough sketch
12 童画 **dōga** pictures for children
絵画 **kaiga** pictures, paintings, drawings
絵画界 **kaigakai** the world of painting
絵画館 **kaigakan** art gallery
13 聖画像 **seigazō** sacred image, icon
14 漫画 **manga** cartoon, comic book/strip
漫画家 **mangaka** cartoonist
墨画 **bokuga** India-ink drawing
総画 **sōkaku** total stroke-count (of a kanji)
15 戯画 **giga** a caricature
線画 **senga** line drawing
16 壁画 **hekiga** fresco, mural
録画 **rokuga** (videotape) recording
18 題画 **daiga** picture bearing a poem or phrase

─────── 3 ───────

2 人物画 **jinbutsuga** portrait
3 山水画 **sansuiga** landscape painting; a landscape
4 文人画 **bunjinga** painting in the literary artist's style
水彩画 **suisaiga** a watercolor
水彩画家 **suisai gaka** watercolor painter
水墨画 **suibokuga** India-ink painting
木版画 **mokuhanga** wood-block print
木炭画 **mokutanga** charcoal drawing
日本画 **nihonga** Japanese-style painting/drawing
5 用器画 **yōkiga** mechanical drawing
石版画 **sekibanga** lithograph
6 西洋画 **seiyōga** Western painting, oil painting
自在画 **jizaiga** freehand drawing
7 肖像画 **shōzōga** portrait
8 抽象画 **chūshōga** abstract painting
宗教画 **shūkyōga** religious picture
具象画 **gushōga** representational painting
9 透視画法 **tōshigahō** perspective (drawing)
風俗画 **fūzokuga** painting depicting customs
風景画 **fūkeiga** landscape painting
活人画 **katsujinga** costumed people posing in a tableau vivant
11 彩色画 **saishikiga** colored painting/picture
12 無計画 **mukeikaku** unplanned, haphazard
13 裸体画 **rataiga** nude picture
14 静止画 **seishiga** still life
静物画 **seibutsuga** still-life picture, still life

15 劇映画 **gekieiga** movie/film drama
16 諷刺画 **fūshiga** caricature, cartoon

———————— 4 ————————

10 泰西名画 **taisei meiga** famous Western
painting
12 無声映画 **musei eiga** silent movie

0a8.8 / 487

KA fruit; result **ha(tasu)** carry out,
accomplish **ha(tashite)** as was
expected; really; ever **ha(teru)** come
to an end, be exhausted; die, perish
ha(te), ha(teshi) end, limit; result, outcome
ō(seru) succeed in doing

———————— 1 ————————

5 果汁 **kajū** fruit juice
6 果肉 **kaniku** the flesh/pulp of fruit
8 果実 **kajitsu** fruit
果実酒 **kajitsushu** fruit wine
果物 **kudamono** fruit
12 果報 **kahō** good fortune, luck
果報者 **kahōmono** lucky person
果敢 **haka(nai)** fleeting, transitory; vain,
hopeless **kakan** resolute, determined,
bold
16 果樹 **kaju** fruit tree
果樹園 **kajuen** orchard
果糖 **katō** fruit sugar, fructose

———————— 2 ————————

6 因果 **inga** cause and effect; fate; misfortune
因果応報 **inga-ōhō** reward according to
deeds, retribution
因果者 **ingamono** unlucky/ill-fated person
因果律 **ingaritsu** principle of causality
朽果 **ku(chi)ha(teru)** rot away
成果 **seika** result, fruit **na(ri)ha(teru)**
become, be reduced to **na(re) (no)**
ha(te) the wreck of one's former self
7 呆果 **aki(re)ha(teru)** be astonished
困果 **koma(ri)ha(teru)** be greatly troubled/
nonplussed
見果 **miha(teru)** see till the end
8 使果 **tsuka(i)hata(su)** use up, squander
効果 **kōka** effect, effectiveness
効果的 **kōkateki** effective
青果 **seika** vegetables and fruits
青果物 **seikabutsu** vegetables and fruits
9 変果 **ka(wari)ha(teru)** change completely
美果 **bika** good fruit/results
荒果 **a(re)ha(teru)** be dilapidated/desolate
10 消果 **ki(e)ha(teru)** disappear, vanish
疲果 **tsuka(re)ha(teru)** get tired out, be
exhausted
討果 **u(chi)hata(su)** slay

11 毬果 **kyūka** (pine) cone
12 善果 **zenka** good results
堅果 **kenka** nut
結果 **kekka** result, consequence, effect
絶果 **ta(e)ha(teru)** die out, become extinct
13 蒴果 **sakuka** seed pod
戦果 **senka** war results
14 摘果 **tekika** thinning out fruit
暮果 **ku(re)ha(teru)** get completely dark
15 漿果 **shōka** berry

———————— 3 ————————

4 不結果 **fukekka** failure, poor results
5 好結果 **kōkekka** good results, success
6 多肉果 **tanikuka** pulpy fruit
7 見下果 **misa(ge)ha(teru)** look down on, scorn
misa(ge)ha(teta) contemptible, low-
down
8 逆効果 **gyakukōka** opposite effect, counter-
productive
12 無花果 **ichijiku** fig

———————— 4 ————————

11 悪因悪果 **akuin-akka** Evil breeds evil.
12 善因善果 **zen'in-zenka** Good actions lead to
good results.

0a8.9 / 71

東

TŌ, **higashi** east **azuma** east; eastern
Japan (east of old capital Kyōto)

———————— 1 ————————

0 東ドイツ **Higashi Doitsu** East Germany,
GDR
3 東上 **tōjō** go east to Tōkyō
東下 **azuma kuda(ri)** journey to the
provinces east of the old capital Kyōto
東口 **higashiguchi** east exit/entrance
4 東支那海 **Higashi Shinakai** East China Sea
東方 **tōhō** east, eastward, eastern
5 東北 **tōhoku** northeast **Tōhoku** (northeast-
ern Honshū)
東半球 **higashi hankyū** Eastern Hemisphere
東芝 **Tōshiba** (company name)
6 東西 **tōzai** east and west; Orient and
Occident; Ladies and gentlemen!
東西南北 **tōzainanboku** north, south, east,
and west
東夷 **tōi** eastern barbarians
東邦 **tōhō** an eastern country; the Orient
東印度会社 **Higashi Indo Gaisha** East India
Company
東向 **higashimu(ki)** facing east
7 東亜 **Tōa** East Asia
東亜諸国 **Tōa shokoku** the countries of East
Asia

0a8

東男 **azuma otoko** man from eastern Japan
8 東京 **Tōkyō** (city, capital of Japan)
東京都 **Tōkyō-to** the Metropolis of Tōkyō
東奔西走 **tōhon-seisō** busy oneself, take an
active interest in
東岸 **tōgan** eastern coast; east bank
東欧 **Tōō** Eastern Europe
9 東南 **tōnan** southeast
東風 **tōfū, kochi** east wind; spring wind
東洋 **tōyō** the Orient
東洋人 **tōyōjin** an Oriental
東海 **tōkai** eastern sea
東海道 **Tōkaidō** the Tōkaidō highway
東独 **Tōdoku** East Germany
東屋 **azumaya** arbor, bower, summerhouse
10 東宮 **tōgū** crown prince
東宮御所 **Tōgū gosho** the Crown Prince's
Palace
11 東側 **higashigawa** east side
東経 **tōkei** east longitude
12 東雲 **shinonome** dawn, daybreak
14 東漸 **tōzen** advance eastward

──────── 2 ────────

3 大東亜 **Dai-Tōa** Greater East Asia
4 中東 **Chūtō** the Middle East, Mideast
5 北東 **hokutō** northeast
6 近東 **Kintō** the Near East
8 河東 **katō** east of the (Yellow) river
9 南東 **nantō** southeast
10 真東 **mahigashi** due east
12 極東 **kyokutō** the Far East
最東 **saitō** easternmost
14 関東 **Kantō** (region including Tōkyō)

──────── 3 ────────

4 中近東 **Chūkintō** the Near and Middle East
5 北北東 **hokuhokutō** north-northeast
古今東西 **kokon-tōzai** all ages and places
6 西高東低 **seikō-tōtei** high (barometric
pressure) in the west and low in the east
9 南南東 **nannantō** south-southeast
10 馬耳東風 **bajitōfū** utter indifference, turn a
deaf ear

0a8.10

奄
EN cover; sudden

──────── 1 ────────

3 奄々 **en'en** gasping
9 奄美大島 **Amami Ōshima** (island,
Kagoshima-ken)

──────── 3 ────────

6 気息奄々 **kisoku-en'en** gasping for breath,
dying

0a8.11

秉
HEI take; cherish; sheaf; (unit of
volume)

0a8.12 / 1070

垂
SUI, ta(reru), ta(rasu) (intr./tr.) hang
down, dangle, drip **tare** hanging,
straw curtain; tassel, flap
nanna(n to suru) be close to

──────── 1 ────────

3 垂下 **suika, ta(re)sa(garu)** hang down,
dangle, droop
4 垂仁 **Suinin** (emperor, 29 B.C.–70 A.D.)
6 垂耳 **ta(re)mimi** droopy ears, flop-eared
8 垂直 **suichoku** vertical; perpendicular
垂直線 **suichokusen** a perpendicular
9 垂迹 **suijaku** manifestations of Buddha to
save men
垂涎 **suizen** watering at the mouth
13 垂幕 **ta(re)maku** hanging screen, curtain
14 垂髪 **suberakashi** hair tied at the back and
hanging down **ta(re)gami** long
flowing hair
15 垂線 **suisen** a perpendicular
22 垂籠 **ta(re)ko(meru)** lie/hang over; seclude
oneself inside

──────── 2 ────────

3 下垂 **kasui** hang down, droop
6 虫垂 **chūsui** the (vermiform) appendix
虫垂炎 **chūsuien** appendicitis
耳垂 **mimida(re)** ear discharge
8 枝垂柳 **shida(re)yanagi** weeping willow
枝垂桜 **shida(re)zakura** droopy-branch
cherry tree
雨垂 **amada(re)** raindrops, eavesdrops
雨垂石 **amada(re) ishi** dripstone (to catch
roof runoff)
9 前垂 **maeda(re)** apron
洟垂小僧 **hanata(re) kozō** drippy-nosed
little boy, snot-nose kid
11 野垂死 **nota(re)ji(ni)** die by the roadside
頂垂 **unada(reru)** hang down one's head
15 潮垂 **shiota(reru)** shed copious tears
17 糞垂 **kusota(re), kuso(t)ta(re)** (shit-dripping)
son-of-a-bitch
20 懸垂 **kensui** suspension, dangling; chin-ups
懸垂運動 **kensui undō** chin-ups

──────── 3 ────────

3 口蓋垂 **kōgaisui** the uvula
11 脳下垂体 **nōkasuitai** pituitary gland
20 懸壅垂 **ken'yōsui** the uvula

0a8.13 / 1541

奉 **HŌ, BU** present, dedicate; obey, follow, believe in; serve
tatematsu(ru) offer, present; revere

───── 1 ─────

0 奉じる/ずる **hō(jiru/zuru)** present, dedicate; obey, follow, believe in; serve
4 奉公 **hōkō** service
奉公先 **hōkōsaki** employer
5 奉仕 **hōshi** service
奉加帳 **hōgachō** subscription/contributions list
6 奉迎 **hōgei** welcome
奉迎門 **hōgeimon** welcome arch
奉行 **bugyō** magistrate, prefect
10 奉書 **hōsho** thick high-quality paper
奉納 **hōnō** dedication, offering
奉納物 **hōnōbutsu** votive offering
奉納額 **hōnōgaku** votive tablet
13 奉献 **hōken** dedicate, offer, consecrate
18 奉職 **hōshoku** be in the service of, hold a post

───── 2 ─────

5 只奉公 **tadabōkō** serving without pay
7 町奉行 **machi-bugyō** town magistrate
8 供奉 **kyōhō, gubu** be in attendance on, accompany
9 信奉 **shinpō** belief, faith
信奉者 **shinpōsha** adherent, believer, devotee
12 渡奉公 **wata(ri)bōkō** working as a servant at one place after another
14 遵奉 **junpō** observe, adhere to, abide by

───── 3 ─────

2 丁稚奉公 **detchi bōkō** apprenticeship
3 大政奉還 **taisei hōkan** restoration of imperial rule
6 年期奉公 **nenki bōkō** apprenticeship
12 勤労奉仕 **kinrō hōshi** labor service
13 滅私奉公 **messhi hōkō** selfless patriotic service

0a8.14 / 522

毒 毒 **DOKU** poison

───── 1 ─────

0 毒する **doku(suru)** poison, corrupt
毒づく **doku(zuku)** curse, revile
毒あたり **doku(atari)** poisoning
2 毒人参 **doku ninjin** poison hemlock
3 毒刃 **dokujin** assassin's dagger
毒々 **dokudoku(shii)** poisonous-looking; malicious, vicious; heavy, gross
毒口 **dokuguchi** venomous tongue, abusive remarks
4 毒牙 **dokuga** poison fang
毒手 **dokushu** the clutches of
毒心 **dokushin** malice, spite
5 毒矢 **dokuya** poisoned arrow
毒汁 **dokujū** poisonous juices
6 毒気 **dokuke, dokki** poisonous nature, noxious air; malice, spite
毒舌 **dokuzetsu** stinging tongue, blistering remarks
毒虫 **dokumushi** poisonous insect
7 毒見 **dokumi** tasting for poison
毒言 **dokugen** abusive language
8 毒々 **dokudoku(shii)** poisonous-looking; malicious, vicious; heavy, gross
毒味 **dokumi** tasting for poison
毒味役 **dokumiyaku** taster for poison
毒炎 **dokuen** flame producing poisonous fumes
毒物 **dokubutsu** poisonous substance
毒物学 **dokubutsugaku** toxicology
毒性 **dokusei** virulence, toxicity
9 毒除 **dokuyo(ke)** protection against poisoning
毒草 **dokusō** poisonous plant
10 毒酒 **dokushu** poisoned saké
毒消 **dokuke(shi)** antidote
毒害 **dokugai** poisoning
毒殺 **dokusatsu** a poisoning
毒素 **dokuso** toxin
11 毒液 **dokueki** poisonous liquid
毒婦 **dokufu** wicked woman
毒悪 **dokuaku** great wickedness
毒蛇 **dokuhebi, dokuja** poisonous snake
12 毒筆 **dokuhitsu** spiteful/poison pen
13 毒蛾 **dokuga** Oriental tussock moth
15 毒質 **dokushitsu** poisonous nature/ingredient
16 毒薬 **dokuyaku** a poison

───── 2 ─────

4 丹毒 **tandoku** erysipelas
中毒 **chūdoku** poisoning
5 目毒 **me(no)doku** something tempting
6 気毒 **ki(no)doku** pitiable, regrettable, too bad
防毒 **bōdoku** anti-poison, gasproof
防毒面 **bōdokumen** gas mask
有毒 **yūdoku** poisonous
7 抗毒素 **kōdokuso** antitoxin, antidote
尿毒症 **nyōdokushō** uremia
8 毒毒 **dokudoku(shii)** poisonous-looking; malicious, vicious; heavy, gross
服毒 **fukudoku** take poison
9 胎毒 **taidoku** congenital eczema
10 酒毒 **shudoku** alcoholism, alcohol poisoning
消毒 **shōdoku** disinfect, sterilize
消毒液 **shōdokueki** antiseptic solution
消毒器 **shōdokuki** sterilizer
消毒薬 **shōdokuyaku** disinfectant, antiseptic

0a8

猛毒 **mōdoku** virulent poison
害毒 **gaidoku** an evil (influence), harm
梅毒 **baidoku** syphilis
梅毒性 **baidokusei** syphilitic
病毒 **byōdoku** virus, germ
11 蛇毒 **jadoku** snake poison/venom
12 無毒 **mudoku** nonpoisonous
13 煙毒 **endoku** smoke pollution
解毒剤 **gedokuzai** antidote
鉛毒 **endoku** lead poisoning
鉱毒 **kōdoku** mine pollution, copper poisoning
15 劇毒 **gekidoku** deadly poison
22 蠹毒 **todoku** worm damage, being eaten away from within
23 黴毒 **baidoku** syphilis

―――――― 3 ――――――
9 食中毒 **shokuchūdoku** food poisoning
13 鉛中毒 **enchūdoku** lead poisoning

―――――― 4 ――――――
6 自家中毒 **jika chūdoku** autotoxemia

0a8.15 / 80

事 事

JI, ZU, koto thing, matter

―――――― 1 ――――――
3 事大 **jidai** subservience to the stronger
事大主義 **jidai shugi** worship of the powerful
事々 **kotogoto(shii)** exaggerated, pretentious
事々物々 **jiji-butsubutsu** everything
4 事勿主義 **kotonaka(re) shugi** hoping that all turns out well
事切 **kotoki(reru)** breath one's last, die
事欠 **kotoka(ku)** lack, be in need of
5 事由 **jiyū** reason, cause
6 事毎 **kotogoto (ni)** in everything, always
事件 **jiken** case, affair, incident
7 事局 **jikyoku** circumstances
事足 **kotota(riru), kotota(ru)** suffice
8 事例 **jirei** example; precedent
事典 **jiten** encyclopedia, dictionary
事実 **jijitsu** fact
事実上 **jijitsujō** in fact, actually
事実無根 **jijitsu mukon** contrary to fact, unfounded
事物 **jibutsu** things, affairs
9 事変 **jihen** accident, mishap; incident, uprising, emergency
事前 **jizen** before the fact, prior, pre-
事後 **jigo** after the fact, ex post facto, post-
事後承諾 **jigo shōdaku** approval after the fact
事相 **jisō** aspect, phase, phenomenon

事柄 **kotogara** matters, affairs, circumstances
事故 **jiko** accident; unavoidable circumstances
11 事寄 **kotoyo(sete)** under the pretext of
事理 **jiri** reason, facts, sense
事務 **jimu** business, clerical work
事務当局 **jimu tōkyoku** the authorities in charge
事務局 **jimukyoku** secretariat, executive office
事務長 **jimuchō** head official; manager
事務長官 **jimuchōkan** chief secretary
事務官 **jimukan** administrative official, secretary, commissioner
事務服 **jimufuku** office clothes
事務的 **jimuteki** businesslike, practical
事務所 **jimusho** office
事務取扱 **jimu toriatsuka(i)** acting director
事務室 **jimushitsu** office
事務員 **jimuin** clerk, office staff
事務家 **jimuka** man of business, practical man
事情 **jijō** circumstances, reasons
事細 **kotokoma(ka ni)** minutely, in detail
12 事象 **jishō** matter, aspect, phenomenon, event
事無 **koto(mo)na(ge)** careless, casual, nonchalant **kotona(ku)** without incident, uneventfully
事項 **jikō** matters, facts, items
13 事業 **jigyō** undertakings, business, activities
事業化 **jigyōka** industrialization
事業界 **jigyōkai** industrial/business world
事業部 **jigyōbu** operations department
事業家 **jigyōka** entrepreneur; businessman, industrialist
事業税 **jigyōzei** business tax
事跡 **jiseki** evidence, trace, vestige
14 事態 **jitai** situation, state of affairs
17 事績 **jiseki** achievements, exploits
18 事蹟 **jiseki** evidence, trace, vestige

―――――― 2 ――――――
1 一事 **ichiji** one thing **hito(tsu)koto** the same thing
2 人事 **jinji** personal/personnel affairs **hitogoto** other people's affairs
3 工事 **kōji** construction
工事中 **kōjichū** Under Construction
工事場 **kōjiba** construction site
万事 **banji** all, everything
万事休 **banji kyū(su)** It's all over. Nothing more can be done.
大事 **daiji** important, precious; great thing; serious matter **ōgoto** serious matter
小事 **shōji** small matter, trifle

4 凶事 **kyōji** tragic accident, calamity, misfortuneg
内事 **naiji** personal affairs; internal affairs
仏事 **butsuji** Buddhist memorial service
文事 **bunji** civil affairs, literary matters
公事 **kōji** public affairs, official business
火事 **kaji** fire, conflagration
火事見舞 **kaji mima(i)** sympathy visit after a fire
火事泥 **kajidoro** thief at a fire
火事場 **kajiba** scene of a fire
王事 **ōji** the emperor's/king's cause
心事 **shinji** one's mind/motives
5 民事 **minji** civil affairs; civil (law)
民事裁判 **minji saiban** civil trial
民事訴訟 **minji soshō** civil suit
世事 **seji** worldly affairs
仕事 **shigoto** work
他事 **taji** other matters; other people's affairs
古事 **koji** ancient/historical events
古事記 **Kojiki** (Japan's) Ancient Chronicles
外事 **gaiji** foreign affairs
用事 **yōji** business, errand, something to attend to
只事 **tadagoto** trivial/common matter
兄事 **keiji** regard as one's senior
好事 **kōji** happy event; good act
　　kōzu curiosity, dilettantism
好事家 **kōzuka** dilettante, amateur
主事 **shuji** manager, director
6 多事多端 **taji-tatan** eventful, busy
刑事 **keiji** (police) detective; criminal case
刑事上 **keijijō** criminal, penal
刑事犯 **keijihan** criminal offense
刑事処分 **keiji shobun** criminal punishment
刑事事件 **keiji jiken** criminal case
刑事被告 **keiji hikoku** the accused, defendant
刑事訴訟 **keiji soshō** criminal action/suit
考事 **kanga(e)goto** something to think about, thinking; concern, worry, preoccupation
色事 **irogoto** love affair; love scene
色事師 **irogotoshi** lady-killer, Don Juan
近事 **kinji** recent events
返事 **henji** reply
同事 **dōji** the same thing; no change
行事 **gyōji** event, function, observance
当事 **tōji** related matters
当事者 **tōjisha** the parties (concerned)
吉事 **kichiji, kitsuji** auspicious event
有事 **yūji** emergency
式事 **shikiji** ceremony, observance
7 我事 **wagakoto** one's own affair/concern, (take it) personally
作事 **tsuku(ri)goto** fiction, fabrication
何事 **nanigoto** what, whatever

余事 **yoji** other matters
判事 **hanji** a judge
別事 **betsuji** another affair; mishap
兵事 **heiji** military affairs
臣事 **shinji** service as a retainer
芸事 **geigoto** accomplishments
学事 **gakuji** educational affairs; studies
快事 **kaiji** gratifying matter, pleasure
見事 **migoto** beautiful, splendid
私事 **shiji, watakushigoto** personal affairs
8 事事 **kotogoto(shii)** exaggerated, pretentious
事事物物 **jiji-butsubutsu** everything
法事 **hōji** (Buddhist) memorial service
拵事 **koshira(e)goto** fabrication, made-up story
知事 **chiji** governor
往事 **ōji** the past
参事 **sanji** councilor
参事会 **sanjikai** council
参事官 **sanjikan** councilor
官事 **kanji** government business
国事 **kokuji** affairs of state
国事犯 **kokujihan** political offense, treason
杯事 **sakazukigoto** drinking feast; exchange of nuptial cups; pledging over cups of wine
炊事 **suiji** cooking
炊事婦 **suijifu** a (female) cook
炊事場 **suijiba** kitchen, cookhouse
物事 **monogoto** things, matters
怪事 **kaiji** mystery, wonder, scandal
怪事件 **kaijiken** strange/mystery case
房事 **bōji** sexual intercourse
9 俗事 **zokuji** worldly affairs; workaday routine
叙事 **joji** narration, description
叙事文 **jojibun** description, a narrative
叙事詩 **jojishi** epic poem/poetry
軍事 **gunji** military affairs; military
軍事力 **gunjiryoku** military strength
軍事工場 **gunji kōjō** war plant
軍事上 **gunjijō** military, strategic
軍事公債 **gunji kōsai** war bonds
軍事犯 **gunjihan** military offense
軍事会議 **gunji kaigi** council of war
軍事協定 **gunji kyōtei** military pact
軍事的 **gunjiteki** military
軍事通 **gunjitsū** military expert
軍事面 **gunjimen** military aspects
軍事施設 **gunji shisetsu** military installations
軍事教練 **gunji kyōren** military training
軍事基地 **gunji kichi** military base
軍事裁判 **gunji saiban** court-martial
軍事費 **gunjihi** military expenditures

0a8

軍事輸送 **gunji yusō** military transport
軍事警察 **gunji keisatsu** military police
軍事顧問 **gunji komon** military adviser
変事 **henji** accident, mishap, disaster
美事 **migoto** splendid **biji** commendable act
通事 **tsūji** interpreter
海事 **kaiji** maritime affairs
後事 **kōji** future affairs; affairs after one's death
荒事 **aragoto** bravado posturing
荒事師 **aragotoshi** actor who plays the part of a ruffian
神事 **shinji** Shinto rituals
祝事 **iwa(i)goto** auspicious/festive occasion
珍事 **chinji** rare event, singular incident
政事 **seiji** political/administrative affairs
故事 **koji** historical event
故事来歴 **koji-raireki** origin and history
恨事 **konji** regrettable/deplorable matter
思事 **omo(i)goto** one's wishes/prayer
食事 **shokuji** meal, dining
食事中 **shokujichū** during a meal
食事時 **shokujidoki** mealtime
10 陰事 **inji** secret
逸事 **itsuji** anecdote
徒事 **tadagoto** trivial matter
従事 **jūji** engage in, carry on
家事 **kaji** housework; domestic affairs
能事 **nōji** one's work
時事 **jiji** current events
秘事 **hiji** secret; mystery **hi(me)goto** secret
笑事 **wara(i)goto** laughing matter
記事 **kiji** article, report
記事文 **kijibun** descriptive composition
11 商事 **shōji** commercial affairs (short for 商事会社)
商事会社 **shōji-gaisha** business company
執事 **shitsuji** steward; deacon
密事 **mitsuji** secret
常事 **jōji** everyday affair/occurrence
習事 **nara(i)goto** practice, training, drill
祭事 **saiji** festival, ritual, rites
理事 **riji** director, trustee
理事会 **rijikai** board of directors/trustees
理事長 **rijichō** chairman, president
悪事 **akuji** evil deed
惨事 **sanji** disaster, tragic accident
情事 **jōji** love affair
盛事 **seiji** grand undertaking/event
細事 **saiji** trivia, details
12 善事 **zenji** good thing/deed
揉事 **mo(me)goto** trouble, discord
喜事 **yoroko(bi)goto** happy event
検事 **kenji** public procurator/prosecutor
検事局 **kenjikyoku** prosecutor's office
無事 **buji** safe and sound

無事故 **mujiko** without accident/trouble
痛事 **itagoto** hard blow, misfortune
軼事 **itsuji** unknown fact
飯事 **mamagoto** (children) playing house
閑事業 **kanjigyō** useless work
13 隠事 **kaku(shi)goto, inji** secret
農事 **nōji** agriculture, farming
椿事 **chinji** accident; sudden occurrence
幹事 **kanji** manager, secretary
幹事長 **kanjichō** executive secretary, secretary-general
禍事 **magagoto** evil, disaster, mishap
歳事 **saiji** the year's events
14 瑣事 **saji** petty/trivial matter
雑事 **zatsuji** miscellaneous affairs
聞事 **ki(ki)goto** something worth listening to
領事 **ryōji** consul
領事館 **ryōjikan** consulate
15 慶事 **keiji** happy event, matter for congratualtions
監事 **kanji** inspector, supervisor, auditor
諸事 **shoji** various matters/affairs
諸事万端 **shoji-bantan** everything
16 薬事法 **yakujihō** the Pharmaceutical Affairs Law
賭事 **kakegoto** betting, gambling
17 濡事 **nu(re)goto** love affair
18 難事 **nanji** difficult matter
19 艶事 **tsuyagoto** love affair, romance
韻事 **inji** artistic pursuits
願事 **nega(i)goto** one's wish/prayer
20 議事 **giji** proceedings
議事堂 **gijidō** assembly hall, parliament/diet building
議事録 **gijiroku** minutes, proceedings

——————— 3 ———————
1 一大事 **ichidaiji** a serious matter
2 二返事 **futa(tsu)henji** immediate reply, readily, most willingly
力仕事 **chikara shigoto** physical labor
3 下仕事 **shitashigoto** preliminary work; subcontracted work
山火事 **yamakaji** forest fire
4 内証事 **naishōgoto** a secret
内緒事 **naishogoto** a secret
公共事業 **kōkyō jigyō** public works, utilities
水仕事 **mizu shigoto** scrubbing and washing
手仕事 **teshigoto** hand work, manual labor
心配事 **shinpaigoto** cares, worries, troubles
5 北支事変 **Hokushi jihen** the Marco Polo Bridge incident
北清事変 **Hokushin jihen** the North China incident, the Boxer uprising
出来事 **dekigoto** incident, event, happenings
生返事 **namahenji** vague answer

6 刑事事件 **keiji jiken** criminal case
百科事典 **hyakka jiten** encyclopedia
7 判検事 **hankenji** judges and prosecutors/
    procurators
決議事項 **ketsugi jikō** agenda, resolutions
8 注意事項 **chūi jikō** matter requiring
    attention; N.B.
奇麗事 **kireigoto** glossing over, whitewash-
    ing
府知事 **fuchiji** urban-prefectural governor
物見事 **mono(no)migoto (ni)** splendidly
所作事 **shosagoto** dance drama, posture
    dance
取込事 **toriko(mi)goto** confusion, busyness
9 海外事情 **kaigai jijō** foreign news
荒仕事 **arashigoto** heavy work, hard labor
茶飯事 **sahanji** everyday occurrence
県知事 **kenchiji** prefectural governor
約束事 **yakusokugoto** promise
10 既成事実 **kisei jijitsu** fait accompli
真似事 **manegoto** sham, semblance, pretense
針仕事 **hari shigoto** needlework, sewing
11 済世事業 **saisei jigyō** public-welfare work
船火事 **funakaji** a fire aboard ship
12 満州事変 **Manshū Jihen** the Manchurian
    Incident
勝負事 **shōbugoto** game of skill/chance
痛恨事 **tsūkonji** matter for deep regret

13 慈善事業 **jizen jigyō** charity work, philan-
    thropy
賃仕事 **chinshigoto** piecework
14 綺麗事 **kireigoto** glossing over, whitewashing
総領事 **sōryōji** consul-general
総領事館 **sōryōjikan** consulate-general
関心事 **kanshinji** matter of concern
15 隣保事業 **rinpo jigyō** welfare work, social
    services
18 儲仕事 **mō(ke)shigoto** lucrative work

———————— 4 ————————

3 三面記事 **sanmen kiji** page-3 news, police
    news, human-interest stories
4 手間仕事 **tema shigoto** tedious work;
    piecework
6 年中行事 **nenjū gyōji** an annual event
8 治水工事 **chisui kōji** riverbank works
河川工事 **kasen kōji** river improvement,
    riparian works
取付工事 **to(ri)tsu(ke) kōji** installation work
9 後生大事 **goshō daiji** religiously, earnestly
11 野良仕事 **nora shigoto** farm/field work
13 腰掛仕事 **koshika(ke) shigoto** temporary
    work
20 護岸工事 **gogan kōji** riparian works

———————— 5 ————————

4 日常茶飯事 **nichijō sahanji** an everyday
    occurrence

0a9

———————————— 0a9 ————————————

歪	幽	韭	彖	癸	兓	矩	飛	巷	発	疕	虘	舁
2m7.4	3o6.6	3k9.2	9.1	9.2	9.3	2t7.1	9.4	3k6.17	9.5	9.6	2a7.24	9.7
殃	袤	甚	巻	柬	匍	禹	禺	専	拜	毒	奏	革
9.8	9.9	9.10	9.11	9.12	9.13	9.14	9.15	9.16	3c5.3	0a8.14	9.17	3k6.2
重	乗											
9.18	9.19											

歪→ 2m7.4

幽→ 3o6.6

韭→韮 3k9.2

0a9.1
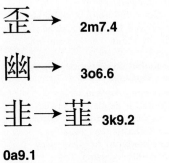
彖
TAN divination

0a9.2
癸
KI tenth in a series, "J"
mizunoto tenth calendar sign

0a9.3
兓
ton ton, 1000 kg

矩→ 2t7.1

0a9.4 / 530

飛

HI, to(bu) fly; jump; skip over
to(basu) let fly; drive fast; skip over, omit

——————— 1 ———————

2 飛入 **to(bi)i(ri)** joining in (on the spur of the moment); speckled with a different color
to(bi)i(ru) jump/dive/fly into
飛入勝手 **tobii(ri) katte** open to all comers
3 飛上 **to(bi)a(garu)** fly/jump up
飛下 **tobio(ri)** jumping off
4 飛切 **tobiki(ri)** superfine, choicest, beyond compare
飛込 **to(bi)ko(mu)** jump/dive/rush in
飛込台 **tobikomidai** diving board
飛込自殺 **tobiko(mi) jisatsu** suicide by jumping in front of an oncoming train
飛込板 **tobikomiita** diving board
飛火 **to(bi)hi** flying sparks, leaping flames
5 飛出 **to(bi)da(su)** fly/jump/dart out
to(bi)de(ru) protrude
飛付 **to(bi)tsu(ku)** jump/leap/snatch at
飛去 **to(bi)sa(ru)** fly away/off
飛札 **hisatsu** urgent letter
飛白 **kasuri** splashed pattern
飛石 **to(bi)ishi** stepping-stones
飛石伝 **to(bi)ishizuta(i)** following stepping-stones
飛立 **to(bi)ta(tsu)** take wing; jump up
6 飛交 **to(bi)ka(u)** fly/flit about
飛地 **to(bi)chi** detached land/territory, enclave
飛行 **hikō** flight, flying, aviation
飛行士 **hikōshi** aviator
飛行服 **hikōfuku** flying suit, flight uniform
飛行便 **hikōbin** airmail
飛行家 **hikōka** aviator
飛行隊 **hikōtai** flying/air corps
飛行船 **hikōsen** airship, dirigible, blimp
飛行場 **hikōjō** airport, airfield
飛行帽 **hikōbō** aviator's cap, flight helmet
飛行艇 **hikōtei** flying boat, seaplane
飛行機 **hikōki** airplane
飛行機雲 **hikōkigumo** vapor trail, contrail
飛回 **to(bi)mawa(ru)** fly/jump/rush around
7 飛来 **hirai** come flying; come by airplane
8 飛退 **to(bi)no(ku)** jump back/aside
飛沫 **himatsu** splash, spray
飛歩 **to(bi)aru(ku)** run around, gad about
9 飛飛 **to(bi)to(bi)** desultory, sporadic
飛乗 **to(bi)no(ru)** jump on (a horse/train)
飛降 **tobio(ri)** jumping off
飛泉 **hisen** waterfall
10 飛将棋 **to(bi)shōgi** halma
飛起 **to(bi)o(kiru)** jump out of bed; leap to one's feet

11 飛道具 **to(bi)dōgu** projectile weapon, firearms
飛掛 **to(bi)ka(karu)** pounce on, lunge for
飛脚 **hikyaku** express messenger, courier
飛球 **hikyū** fly ball
飛移 **to(bi)utsu(ru)** jump from one thing to another
飛魚 **to(bi)uo** flying fish
飛鳥 **hichō** flying bird, bird on the wing
Asuka (era, 593–710)
12 飛翔 **hishō** flying, soaring
飛違 **to(bi)chiga(u)** fly/dodge about
飛報 **hihō** urgent message
飛揚 **hiyō** flying, flight
飛弾 **hidan** flying bullet
飛散 **hisan, to(bi)chi(ru)** scatter, disperse
飛越 **to(bi)ko(su)** jump over, fly across
飛雲 **hiun** fleeting cloud
13 飛跳 **to(bi)hane(ru)** jump up and down, hop
飛電 **hiden** urgent telegram
14 飛語 **higo** false report, wild rumor
飛読 **to(bi)yo(mi)** read desultorily, skim through
15 飛蝗 **batta** grasshopper, locust
16 飛燕 **hien** flying swallow, swallow on the wing
18 飛瀑 **hibaku** waterfall
飛離 **to(bi)hana(reru)** fly apart; tower above; out of the ordinary
20 飛礫 **tsubute** stone throwing; thrown stone
21 飛躍 **hiyaku** leap; activity; rapid progress
飛躍的 **hiyakuteki** rapid, by leaps and bounds
22 飛騨 **Hida** (ancient kuni, Gifu-ken)

——————— 2 ———————

5 矢飛白 **yagasuri** arrow-feather pattern
叱飛 **shika(ri)to(basu)** blow up at, bawl out
立飛 **ta(chi)to(bi)** standing plunge
7 投飛 **na(ge)to(basu)** fling away
吹飛 **fu(ki)to(basu)** blow away
売飛 **u(ri)to(basu)** sell off
8 逆飛込 **sakato(bi)ko(mi)** headlong plunge
突飛 **toppi** wild, fantastic, reckless, eccentric
tsu(ki)to(basu) knock down, send flying
空飛 **sorato(bu)** flying (saucer/carpet) (short for 空飛ぶ円盤)
雨飛 **uhi** coming down like rain
9 飛飛 **to(bi)to(bi)** desultory, sporadic
10 高飛車 **takabisha** high-handed, domineering
振飛 **fu(ri)to(basu)** fling away
笑飛 **wara(i)to(basu)** laugh off/away
12 幅飛 **habato(bi)** longjump
雄飛 **yūhi** leap, soar; embark on, launch out into
14 鳴飛 **na(kazu)-to(bazu)** inactive, lying low

15 撥飛 **ha(ne)to(basu)** send (something)
        flying; spatter, splash
   縄飛 **nawato(bi)** jumping/skipping rope
19 蹴飛 **keto(basu)** kick away/out, reject

————————— 3 —————————

1 一足飛 **issokuto(bi)** at one bound
4 水上飛行機 **suijō hikōki** hydroplane,
         seaplane
6 宇宙飛行士 **uchū hikōshi** astronaut
7 低空飛行 **teikū hikō** low-level flying
9 造言飛語 **zōgen-higo** false report, wild rumor
10 流言飛語 **ryūgen-higo** rumor, gossip
11 軟式飛行船 **nanshiki hikōsen** dirigible,
         balloon
12 棒高飛 **bōtakato(bi)** pole vault
13 暗中飛躍 **anchū hiyaku** secret maneuvering

巷→巷 3k6.17

0a9.5 / 96

発 發   **HATSU, HOTSU** departure;
        shot, discharge; emit, give forth
        aba(ku) divulge, bring to
        light, open up

————————— 1 —————————

0 発する **has(suru)** fire (a gun); emit, ema-
        nate, issue; send forth; leave
4 発火 **hakka** ignition, combustion; discharge,
        firing
   発火点 **hakkaten** ignition/flash point
   発心 **hosshin** religious awakening; resolution
5 発生 **hassei** occurrence, outbreak; genesis;
        generation; growth, rise, development
   発生学 **hasseigaku** embryology
   発生器 **hasseiki** generator
   発令 **hatsurei** announce officially, issue
   発刊 **hakkan** publish, issue
   発句 **hokku** first line (of a *renga*); haiku
   発布 **happu** promulgation, proclamation
6 発会 **hakkai** open a meeting
   発会式 **hakkaishiki** opening ceremony
   発汗 **hakkan** sweating
   発向 **hakkō** departure
   発行 **hakkō** publish, issue
   発行日 **hakkōbi** date of issue
   発行者 **hakkōsha** publisher
   発行所 **hakkōsho** publishing house
   発光 **hakkō** luminous
   発光体 **hakkōtai** luminous body, corona
7 発作 **hossa** fit, spasm, an attack of
   発作的 **hossateki** spasmodic, fitful
   発走 **hassō** start; first race
   発狂 **hakkyō** madness, insanity

発売 **hatsubai** sale
発声 **hassei** utterance, speaking
発声法 **hasseihō** vocalization, enunciation
発声器 **hasseiki** vocal organs
発条 **hatsujō** a spring
発見 **hakken** discover
発見者 **hakkensha** discoverer
発言 **hatsugen** utterance, speaking; proposal
発言力 **hatsugenryoku** a voice, a say
発言者 **hatsugensha** speaker
発言権 **hatsugenken** right to speak, a voice
発車 **hassha** start, departure (of a train)
発足 **hossoku, hassoku** start, inauguration
8 発表 **happyō** announce
   発券 **hakken** issuance of bank notes
   発効 **hakkō** come into effect
   発育 **hatsuiku** growth, development
   発育盛 **hatsuikuzaka(ri)** period of rapid
        growth
   発送 **hassō** send, ship, forward
   発注 **hatchū** order (goods)
   発泡 **happō** foaming
   発芽 **hatsuga** germination, sprouting
   発明 **hatsumei** invention
   発明者 **hatsumeisha** inventor
   発明品 **hatsumeihin** an invention
   発明家 **hatsumeika** inventor
9 発信 **hasshin** send (a message)
   発音 **hatsuon** pronunciation
   発音学 **hatsuongaku** phonetics
10 発射 **hassha** firing, launching; emanation,
        radiation
   発射管 **hasshakan** torpedo tube
   発進 **hasshin** takeoff, blast-off
   発起 **hokki** propose, promote, initiate
   発起人 **hokkinin** promoter, originator
   発振器 **hasshinki** oscillator
   発案 **hatsuan** proposal
   発展 **hatten** expansion, growth, development
   発展性 **hattensei** growth potential
   発展途上国 **hattentojōkoku** developing
        country
   発展家 **hattenka** man about town, playboy
   発祥 **hasshō** origin, beginnings
   発祥地 **hasshōchi** cradle, birthplace
   発破 **happa** blasting
   発砲 **happō** firing, discharge, shooting
   発病 **hatsubyō** be taken ill
   発疱 **happō** blister
   発疹 **hasshin, hosshin** (break out in) a rash
   発航 **hakkō** departure, sailing
11 発動 **hatsudō** put into motion, exercise,
        invoke
   発動力 **hatsudōryoku** motive power
   発動的 **hatsudōteki** active
   発達 **hattatsu** development, progress

0a9

0a9

発掘 **hakkutsu** excavation; disinterment
発現 **hatsugen** revelation, manifestation
発情 **hatsujō** sexual arousal, (in) heat
発情期 **hatsujōki** puberty; mating season
12 発着 **hatchaku** departures and arrivals
発喪 **hatsumo** death announcement
発揚 **hatsuyō** exalt, enhance, promote
発揮 **hakki** exhibit, demonstrate, make manifest
発覚 **hakkaku** be detected, come to light
発散 **hassan** give forth, emit, exhale, radiate, evaporate; divergent
発給 **hakkyū** issue
13 発煙 **hatsuen** emitting smoke, fuming
発想 **hassō** conception; expression (in music)
発意 **hatsui** initiative, suggestion, original idea
発酵 **hakkō** fermentation
発酵素 **hakkōso** a ferment, yeast
発電 **hatsuden** generation of electricity; sending a telegram
発電子 **hatsudenshi** armature
発電力 **hatsudenryoku** power
発電所 **hatsudensho** power plant, generating station
発電機 **hatsudenki** generator, dynamo
14 発端 **hottan** origin, beginning
発語 **hatsugo** speech, utterance; introductory word like *Sate*, ...
発駅 **hatsueki** starting station
15 発熱 **hatsunetsu** generation of heat; have a fever
発憤 **happun** be roused to action
16 発奮 **happun** be roused to action
発頭人 **hottōnin** ringleader, originator
17 発癌 **hatsugan** cancer-causing, carcinogenic
20 発議 **hatsugi** proposal, motion
21 発露 **hatsuro** expression, manifestation

──── 2 ────

1 一発 **ippatsu** a shot
4 不発 **fuhatsu** misfire
不発弾 **fuhatsudan** unexploded shell/bomb, dud
双発機 **sōhatsuki** twin-engine airplane
反発 **hanpatsu** repel; rebound, recover; oppose
反発力 **hanpatsuryoku** repellent force, resiliency
5 出発 **shuppatsu** departure
出発点 **shuppatsuten** starting point, point of departure
未発 **mihatsu** before anything happens
未発行 **mihakkō** unissued
未発見 **mihakken** undiscovered, unexplored
未発表 **mihappyō** not yet made public

未発達 **mihattatsu** undeveloped
6 多発式 **tahatsushiki** multi-engined
多発性 **tahatsusei** multiple (sclerosis)
多発機 **tahatsuki** multi-engine airplane
再発 **saihatsu** recurrence, relapse
再発足 **saihossoku** start again
先発 **senpatsu** start in advance, go ahead of
先発隊 **senpatsutai** advance party
早発性痴呆症 **sōhatsusei chihōshō** schizophrenia
百発百中 **hyappatsu-hyakuchū** on target every time
自発 **jihatsu** spontaneous
自発的 **jihatsuteki** spontaneous, voluntary
自発性 **jihatsusei** spontaneousness
7 告発 **kokuhatsu** prosecution, indictment, accusation
告発状 **kokuhatsujō** bill of indictment
告発者 **kokuhatsusha** prosecutor, accuser, informant
乱発 **ranpatsu** random/reckless shooting
利発 **rihatsu** cleverness, intelligence
初発 **shohatsu** first, initial, incipient
8 併発 **heihatsu** break out at the same time, be complicated by
勃発 **boppatsu** outbreak, sudden occurrence
始発 **shihatsu** first (train) departure
突発 **toppatsu** occur suddenly, break out
空発 **kūhatsu** random shooting; detonation which does not achieve the purpose
9 連発 **renpatsu** fire/shoot in rapid succession
連発銃 **renpatsujū** repeating firearm
活発 **kappatsu** active, lively
挑発 **chōhatsu** arouse, excite, provoke
挑発的 **chōhatsuteki** provocative, suggestive
後発 **kōhatsu** start out late, lag behind
単発 **tanpatsu** single-engine (plane), single-shot (rifle)
10 倶発 **guhatsu** concurrence
原発 **genpatsu** (generating electricity from) nuclear power (short for 原子力発電)
進発 **shinpatsu** march off, start
特発 **tokuhatsu** special (train); idiopathic
11 偶発 **gūhatsu** happen unforeseen, come about by chance
偶発的 **gūhatsuteki** accidental, incidental, occasional
遅発 **chihatsu** delayed start/action
啓発 **keihatsu** enlightenment, edification
12 着発 **chakuhatsu** arrivals and departures
渙発 **kanpatsu** proclamation
揮発 **kihatsu** volatile, vaporize
揮発油 **kihatsuyu** volatile oils, gasoline
揮発性 **kihatsusei** volatility
蒸発 **jōhatsu** evaporate; disappear
蒸発熱 **jōhatsunetsu** heat of evaporation

散発 **sanpatsu** scattered shots/hits
散発的 **sanpatsuteki** sporadic
開発 **kaihatsu** development
13 煥発 **kanpatsu** blaze, glitter
新発売 **shinhatsubai** new(ly marketed) product
新発見 **shinhakken** new discovery
新発足 **shinhossoku** a fresh start
新発明 **shinhatsumei** new invention
続発 **zokuhatsu** occur one after another
続発症 **zokuhatsushō** deuteropathy
触発 **shokuhatsu** detonation upon contact
触発水雷 **shokuhatsu suirai** contact (sea) mine
14 増発 **zōhatsu** put on an extra train; increased issue (of bonds)
増発列車 **zōhatsu ressha** extra train
摘発 **tekihatsu** expose, unmask, uncover
摘発者 **tekihatsusha** exposer, informer
嘘発見器 **uso hakkenki** lie detector
徴発 **chōhatsu** commandeer, requisition, press into service
徴発令 **chōhatsurei** requisition orders
誘発 **yūhatsu** induce, give rise to
15 撃発 **gekihatsu** percussion (fuse)
暴発 **bōhatsu** accidental/spontaneous firing
熱発 **neppatsu** have a fever
16 激発 **gekihatsu** outburst, fit (of anger), explosion
奮発 **funpatsu** exertion, strenuous effort; splurge
17 頻発 **hinpatsu** frequency, frequent occurrence
18 濫発 **ranpatsu** overissue (of money)
19 爆発 **bakuhatsu** explosion
爆発力 **bakuhatsuryoku** explosive force
爆発的 **bakuhatsuteki** explosive (popularity)
爆発物 **bakuhatsubutsu** explosives
爆発性 **bakuhatsusei** explosive (bullets)

———————— 3 ————————

2 二連発 **nirenpatsu** double-barreled gun
4 不活発 **fukappatsu** inactive, sluggish
六連発 **roku renpatsu** six-chambered (revolver)
水力発電所 **suiryoku hatsudensho** hydro-electric plant
5 未開発 **mikaihatsu** undeveloped
6 再出発 **saishuppatsu** start over, make a fresh start
7 低開発国 **teikaihatsukoku** less-developed countries
9 海外発展 **kaigai hatten** overseas expansion
春機発動期 **shunki hatsudōki** puberty

———————— 4 ————————

1 一触即発 **isshoku sokuhatsu** touch-and-go, hair-trigger, explosive (situation)

3 才気煥発 **saiki-kanpatsu** brilliant, wise
10 原子力発電所 **genshiryoku hatsudensho** nuclear power plant
15 談論風発 **danron-fūhatsu** animated conversation

0a9.6

毢 **miriguramu** milligram, thousandth of a gram

俎→俎 **2a7.24**

0a9.7

舁 **YO, ka(ku)** bear, carry (a palanquin)

0a9.8

殃 **Ō** disaster, misfortune

0a9.9 / 1677

衷 衷 **CHŪ** heart, mind; inside

———————— 1 ————————

4 衷心 **chūshin** one's inmost heart/feelings
11 衷情 **chūjō** one's inmost feelings

———————— 2 ————————

7 折衷 **setchū** compromise, cross, blending
折衷主義 **setchū shugi** eclecticism
8 苦衷 **kuchū** anguish, distress
和衷 **wachū** harmony, concord
13 微衷 **bichū** one's true feelings

———————— 4 ————————

8 和洋折衷 **wayō setchū** blending of Japanese and Western styles

0a9.10 / 1501

甚 **JIN, hanaha(da), hanaha(dashii)** very much, extreme, great, enormous, intense **ita(ku)** very, greatly

———————— 1 ————————

3 甚大 **jindai** very great, immense, serious
4 甚六 **jinroku** simpleton, blockhead

———————— 2 ————————

8 幸甚 **kōjin** very happy, much obliged
11 深甚 **shinjin** profound, deep

0a9

15 劇甚 **gekijin** intense, fierce, keen, severe
16 激甚 **gekijin** intense, fierce

0a9.11 / 507

巻 卷

KAN, KEN, maki roll, reel; volume, book
ma(ku) roll up, wind, coil

——————— 1 ———————

3 巻上 **ma(ki)a(geru)** roll/wind up, raise; take away, rob
4 巻毛 **ma(ki)ge** curl, ringlet
巻込 **ma(ki)ko(mu)** roll up, enfold; entangle, drag into, involve in
巻尺 **ma(ki)jaku** (roll-up) tape measure
5 巻末 **kanmatsu** end of a book
巻付 **ma(ki)tsu(ku)** coil/wind around
6 巻返 **ma(ki)kae(shi)** rollback, fight back (from a losing position)
巻舌 **ma(ki)jita** rolling one's tongue, trill
7 巻尾 **kanbi** end of a book
巻戻 **ma(ki)modo(shi)** rewind (a tape)
8 巻物 **ma(ki)mono** scroll
巻取紙 **ma(ki)to(ri)gami, ma(ki)to(ri)shi** roll of paper
9 巻首 **kanshu** beginning of a book
10 巻起 **ma(ki)o(kosu)** stir up, create (a sensation)
巻紙 **makigami** paper on a roll
11 巻添 **ma(ki)zo(e)** involvement, entanglement
12 巻揚 **ma(ki)a(geru)** roll/wind up, hoist
巻揚機 **ma(ki)a(ge)ki** hoist, winch, windlass
巻軸 **kanjiku, ma(ki)jiku** scroll
巻雲 **ma(ki)gumo, ken'in** cirrus clouds
13 巻煙草 **ma(ki)tabako** cigarette
14 巻層雲 **kensōun** cirrostratus clouds
16 巻積雲 **kensekiun** cirrocumulus clouds
巻頭 **kantō** beginning of a book

——————— 2 ———————

1 一巻 **ikkan** one volume   **hitomaki** one roll
3 上巻 **jōkan** first volume (of two or three)
下巻 **gekan** last volume (of two or three)
4 中巻 **chūkan** middle volume (of three)
手巻 **tema(ki)** hand-rolled (cigarettes), wind-up (clock)
5 左巻 **hidarima(ki)** counterclockwise; eccentric, crazy
圧巻 **akkan** best part/one, highlight
右巻 **migima(ki)** clockwise
6 全巻 **zenkan** the whole volume; the whole reel (of a movie)
全１０巻 **zen-jikkan** ten volumes in all
糸巻 **itoma(ki)** spool, reel, bobbin
8 虎巻 **tora(no)maki** pony, answer book; (trade) secrets
逆巻 **sakama(ku)** surge, roll, rage, seethe

取巻 **to(ri)ma(ku)** surround, encircle
to(ri)ma(ki) follower, hanger-on
取巻連 **to(ri)ma(ki)ren** one's entourage
9 首巻 **kubima(ki)** (neck) muffler
荒巻 **aramaki** leaf-wrapped fish; salted salmon (New Year's gift)
春巻 **haruma(ki)** egg roll
10 席巻 **sekken** sweeping conquest
胴巻 **dōma(ki)** money belt
息巻 **ikima(ku)** be in a rage, fume
紙巻 **kamima(ki)** (cigarette) wound in paper
12 遠巻 **tōma(ki)** surround at a distance, form a wide circle around
湯巻 **yuma(ki)** loincloth
渦巻 **uzuma(ki)** eddy, vortex, whirlpool; spiral, coil
葉巻 **hamaki** cigar
絵巻 **ema(ki)** picture scroll
絵巻物 **emakimono** picture scroll
開巻 **kaikan** opening of a book
13 掻巻 **ka(i)ma(ki)** sleeved quilt
寝巻 **nema(ki)** nightclothes
腰巻 **koshima(ki)** underskirt, waistband; book wrapper
腹巻 **harama(ki)** waistband, bellyband
詩巻 **shikan** a collection of poems
鉢巻 **hachima(ki)** cloth tied around one's head
14 管巻 **kuda (o) ma(ku)** drunkenly babble on
16 頸巻 **kubima(ki)** muffler
18 襟巻 **erima(ki)** muffler, scarf
19 蟻巻 **arimaki** ant cow, aphid

——————— 3 ———————

6 伊達巻 **datema(ki)** under-sash; rolled omelet
向鉢巻 **mu(kō) hachimaki** rolled towel tied around the head
自動巻 **jidōma(ki)** self-winding (watch)
9 海苔巻 **norima(ki)** (vinegared) rice rolled in seaweed
後鉢巻 **ushi(ro) hachimaki** twisted towel tied around one's head and knotted behind
11 捩鉢巻 **neji(ri)/ne(ji)hachima(ki)** twisted towel tied around one's head
13 鉄火巻 **tekkama(ki)** seaweed-wrapped tuna sushi

0a9.12

束

KAN select, pick out

0a9.13

HO crawl, creep, lie/fall face-down

——————— 1 ———————
11 匍匐 **hofuku** crawl, creep

0a9.14

禹 **U** (name of a Chinese emperor)

0a9.15

禺 **GU** long-tailed monkey

0a9.16 / 600

専 専 **SEN, moppa(ra)** exclusively

——————— 1 ———————
1 専一 **sen'itsu, sen'ichi** concentration; best care; utmost importance
4 専心 **senshin** concentration, undivided attention, singleness of purpose
5 専用 **sen'yō** private/personal use, exclusively for
　専用車 **sen'yōsha** personal car
　専用機 **sen'yōki** personal airplane
6 専任 **sennin** exclusive duty, full-time
　専行 **senkō** acting on one's own authority/discretion
　専有 **sen'yū** exclusive possession
　専有権 **sen'yūken** exclusive right, monopoly
7 専決 **senketsu** decide/act on one's own
　専売 **senbai** monopoly
　専売品 **senbaihin** monopoly goods
　専売特許 **senbai tokkyo** patent
　専売権 **senbaiken** monopoly
　専攻 **senkō** academic specialty, one's major
8 専念 **sennen** undivided/close attention
　専制 **sensei** absolutism, despotism
　専制主義 **sensei shugi** absolutism, despotism
　専制君主 **sensei kunshu** absolute monarch, despot
　専制的 **senseiteki** despotic, autocratic, arbitrary
　専制政治 **sensei seiji** despotic government, autocracy
　専門 **senmon** specialty
　専門化 **senmonka** specialization
　専門用語 **senmon yōgo** technical term
　専門医 **senmon'i** (medical) specialist
　専門学校 **senmon gakkō** professional school
　専門店 **senmonten** specialty store
　専門的 **senmonteki** professional, technical
　専門家 **senmonka** specialist, expert

専門書 **senmonsho** technical books
9 専政 **sensei** absolutism, despotism
　専科 **senka** special course
10 専修 **senshū** specialize in
　専従 **senjū** full-time (work)
11 専務 **senmu** special duty; principal business; managing/executive (director)
　専断 **sendan** deciding/acting on one's own
12 専属 **senzoku** belong exclusively to, be attached to
13 専業 **sengyō** specialty, monopoly, main occupation
15 専横 **sen'ō** arbitrary, high-handed, tyrannical
　専権 **senken** exclusive right; arbitrary power

——————— 3 ———————
1 一意専心 **ichii-senshin** wholeheartedly
9 独断専行 **dokudan-senkō** arbitrary action

拝→拝 **3c5.3**

毒→毒 **0a8.14**

0a9.17 / 1544

 SŌ play (a musical instrument); present, report (to a superior); take effect **kana(deru)** play (a musical instrument)

——————— 1 ———————
0 奏する **sō(suru)** report (to the emperor); play, perform; take effect
3 奏上 **sōjō** report to the emperor
5 奏功 **sōkō** be effective
8 奏効 **sōkō** be effective
13 奏楽 **sōgaku** instrumental music
14 奏聞 **sōmon** report to the emperor
15 奏請 **sōsei** petition the emperor for approval

——————— 2 ———————
3 上奏 **jōsō** report to the throne
4 内奏 **naisō** secret report to the emperor
6 伏奏 **fukusō** report to the throne
　伝奏 **densō** deliver a message to the emperor
　合奏 **gassō** concert, ensemble
7 伴奏 **bansō** (musical) accompaniment
　吹奏 **suisō** blow/play (a flute)
　吹奏者 **suisōsha** wind-instrument player
　吹奏楽 **suisōgaku** wind-instrument music, brass
　序奏 **josō** introduction (in music)
8 劾奏 **gaisō** investigate and report an official's offense to the emperor
　協奏曲 **kyōsōkyoku** concerto

0a9

9 重奏 **jūsō** instrumental ensemble
変奏曲 **hensōkyoku** a variation (in music)
前奏 **zensō** prelude (in music)
前奏曲 **zensōkyoku** prelude, overture
連奏 **rensō** performance by two or more
  musicians
独奏 **dokusō** instrumental solo
独奏会 **dokusōkai** instrumental recital
後奏 **kōsō** postlude
後奏曲 **kōsōkyoku** postlude
12 弾奏 **dansō** play (guitar/piano)
弾奏者 **dansōsha** (guitar/piano) player
間奏曲 **kansōkyoku** interlude
13 節奏 **sessō** rhythm
14 演奏 **ensō** (musical) performance
演奏曲目 **ensō kyokumoku** musical program
演奏会 **ensōkai** concert, recital
演奏法 **ensōhō** (musical) execution, interpretation
18 覆奏 **fukusō** reinvestigate and report

———————— 3 ————————

2 二重奏 **nijūsō** instrumental duet
3 三重奏 **sanjūsō** instrumental trio
4 六重奏 **rokujūsō** sextet
5 四重奏 **shijūsō** (instrumental) quartet

———————— 4 ————————

3 三部合奏 **sanbu gassō** instrumental trio
5 四部合奏 **shibu gassō** (instrumental) quartet

革 → 3k6.2

0a9.18 / 227

重

JŪ, CHŌ heavy; serious; lie/pile on top
of one another **omo(i/tai)** heavy; serious
omo(sa) weight **omo(mi)** weight,
  importance **omo(njiru/nzuru)** attach
importance to, honor, respect **kasa(naru/neru)**
lie/pile on top of one another **-e** -fold, -ply

———————— 1 ————————

2 重力 **jūryoku** gravity
3 重工業 **jūkōgyō** heavy industry
重大 **jūdai** important, serious
重大視 **jūdaishi** regard as important/serious
重々 **omoomo(shii)** serious, grave, solemn
  jūjū repeated; very much
4 重水 **jūsui** heavy water
重水素 **jūsuiso** heavy hydrogen, deuterium
重火器 **jūkaki** heavy weapons
重心 **jūshin** center of gravity
5 重圧 **jūatsu** pressure
重用 **jūyō** appoint to an important post
重立 **omoda(tta)** principal, leading, prominent

6 重任 **jūnin** heavy responsibility; re-election,
  reappointment
重合 **jūgō** polymerization **kasa(nari)a(u)**
  lie on top of each other, overlap; pile up
重合体 **jūgōtai** polymer
重刑 **jūkei** severe punishment/sentence
7 重役 **jūyaku** (company) director
重労働 **jūrōdō** heavy/hard labor
重労働者 **jūrōdōsha** heavy laborer
重囲 **jūi, chōi** close siege
8 重厚 **jūkō** profoundness, depth, seriousness
重厚長大 **jūkō-chōdai** large and heavy,
  bulky (cf. 軽薄短小)
重油 **jūyu** heavy/crude oil
重味 **omomi** weight; importance; emphasis;
  dignity
重苦 **omokuru(shii)** heavy, ponderous,
  oppressive, awkward (expression)
重宝 **chōhō** convenient, handy, useful
重金属 **jūkinzoku** heavy metals
9 重奏 **jūsō** instrumental ensemble
重重 **kasa(ne)gasa(ne)** repeatedly, frequently
  omoomo(shii) serious, grave, solemn
  jūjū repeated; very much
重点 **jūten** important point, priority,
  emphasis
重要 **jūyō** important
重要性 **jūyōsei** importance, gravity
重要視 **jūyōshi** regard as important
10 重荷 **omoni** heavy burden **jūka** heavy
  load; heavy responsibility
重砲 **jūhō** heavy gun/artillery
重病 **jūbyō** serious illness
重症 **jūshō** serious illness
11 重商主義 **jūshō shugi** mercantilism
重婚 **jūkon** bigamy
重婚者 **jūkonsha** bigamist
重曹 **jūsō** sodium bicarbonate, baking soda
重視 **jūshi** attach great importance to
重患 **jūkan** serious illness
重責 **jūseki** heavy responsibility
12 重着 **kasa(ne)gi** wear one garment over
  another
重湯 **omoyu** thin rice gruel
重復 **chōfuku, jūfuku** duplication, repetition, overlapping, redundancy
重量 **jūryō** weight
重量感 **jūryōkan** massiveness, heft
重税 **jūzei** heavy tax
重畳 **chōjō** one atop another; splendid
  jūjō superimposed
13 重傷 **jūshō, omode** serious wound, major
  injury
重傷者 **jūshōsha** seriously injured person
重農主義 **jūnō shugi** physiocracy
重罪 **jūzai** serious crime, felony

14 重態 **jūtai** in serious/critical condition
   重複 **chōfuku, jūfuku** duplication, repetition, overlapping, redundancy
15 重箱 **jūbako** nest of boxes
16 重機関銃 **jūkikanjū** heavy machine gun
   重篤 **jūtoku** serious (illness)
18 重鎮 **jūchin** leader, authority, mainstay
19 重爆撃機 **jūbakugekiki** heavy bomber

─────────── 2 ───────────

1 一重 **hitoe** one layer; single
   hitokasa(ne) a suit (of clothes); a set (of nested boxes)
2 二重 **nijū** double   **futae** two-fold, two-ply, double
   二重人格 **nijū jinkaku** double/split personality
   二重写 **nijū utsu(shi)** double exposure
   二重否定 **nijū hitei** double negative
   二重底 **nijūzoko** double bottom/sole
   二重国籍 **nijū kokuseki** dual nationality
   二重奏 **nijūsō** instrumental duet
   二重道徳 **nijū dōtoku** double standard of morality
   二重唱 **nijūshō** vocal duet
   二重窓 **nijū mado** double/storm window
   二重結婚 **nijū kekkon** bigamy
   二重橋 **Nijūbashi** the Double Bridge (at the Imperial Palace)
   七重 **nanae** seven-fold, seven-ply
   十重 **toe** ten-fold, ten layers
   八重 **yae** double(-petaled); eightfold
   八重咲 **yaeza(ki)** double-flowering
   八重歯 **yaeba** double tooth, snaggletooth
   八重桜 **yaezakura** double-flowering cherry tree
3 三重 **sanjū, mie** three-fold, three-ply, triple
   三重奏 **sanjūsō** instrumental trio
   三重冠 **sanjūkan** tiara
   三重県 **Mie-ken** (prefecture)
   三重唱 **sanjūshō** vocal trio
   口重 **kuchiomo** slow of speech; prudent
4 五重 **gojū, itsue** five-fold, quintuplicate
   五重塔 **gojū (no) tō** five-storied pagoda
   六重奏 **rokujūsō** sextet
5 加重 **kajū** weighted (average), aggravated (assault)
   比重 **hijū** specific gravity; relative importance
   尻重 **shiriomo** slow-moving person
   四重奏 **shijūsō** (instrumental) quartet
6 多重 **tajū** multiplex, multiple
   多重放送 **tajū hōsō** multiplex broadcasting
   気重 **kiomo(i)** heavy-hearted, depressed
   自重 **jijū** (truck's) weight when empty
   jichō self-esteem; taking care of oneself; prudence, caution

7 身重 **miomo** pregnant
   体重 **taijū** one's weight
   折重 **o(ri)kasa(naru)** overlap; telescope
9 重重 **kasa(ne)gasa(ne)** repeatedly, frequently
   omoomo(shii) serious, grave, solemn
   jūjū repeated; very much
   荘重 **sōchō** solemn, sublime, impressive
   度重 **tabikasa(naru)** repeatedly
   珍重 **chinchō** value highly, prize
10 起重機 **kijūki** crane, derrick
   荷重 **kajū** load
11 偏重 **henchō** overemphasis
   過重 **kajū** overweight
12 尊重 **sonchō** respect, esteem
   落重 **o(chi)kasa(naru)** fall one upon another
   無重力 **mujūryoku** weightlessness
   無重量 **mujūryō** weightlessness
   幾重 **ikue** how many folds/ply; repeatedly; earnestly
   貴重 **kichō** valuable, precious
   貴重品 **kichōhin** valuables
   軽重 **keichō, keijū** relative weight, importance
13 慎重 **shinchō** cautious
14 鄭重 **teichō** courteous
   総重量 **sōjūryō** gross weight
15 輜重 **shichō** military supplies, logistics
16 積重 **tsu(mi)kasa(naru)** be piled/stacked up
   頭重 **zuomo** top-heavy; undeferential
17 厳重 **genjū** strict, stringent, rigid

─────────── 3 ───────────

6 羽二重 **habutae** *habutae* silk
10 紙一重 **kami hitoe** paper-thin (difference)
11 捲土重来 **kendo-chōrai, kendo-jūrai** comeback (from a defeat with renewed vigor)
12 然諾重 **zendaku (o) omo(njiru)** keep one's word
16 壁一重 **kabe hitoe** (separated by) just a wall

─────────── 4 ───────────

10 紋羽二重 **mon habutae** figured habutae

0a9.19 / 523

乗 乘   **JŌ** ride; multiply, raise to a power (in math) **no(ru), no(kkaru)** ride; get on, mount; join in; be deceived, be taken in
no(seru) give a ride, take aboard; place, put, load; let join in; deceive, take in

─────────── 1 ───────────

0 乗じる/ずる **jō(jiru/zuru)** take advantage of; multiply
2 乗入 **no(ri)i(reru)** ride/drive into; extend (a train line) into (a city)

0a9

3 乗上 **no(ri)a(geru)** run aground
4 乗切 **no(ri)ki(ru)** ride through/out, weather (a crisis)
乗込 **no(ri)ko(mu)** get into/aboard; ride into, enter
乗手 **no(ri)te** (horse) rider; passenger
乗心地 **no(ri)gokochi** riding comfort
5 乗出 **no(ri)da(su)** set out, embark on; lean forward
乗付 **no(ri)tsu(keru)** ride up to; get used to riding
乗用車 **jōyōsha** passenger car
6 乗気 **no(ri)ki** eagerness, interest
乗合 **no(ri)a(wasu)** happen to ride together **no(ri)a(i)** riding together; fellow passenger; partnership; bus, stagecoach
乗回 **no(ri)ma(wasu/waru)** drive/ride around
7 乗車 **jōsha** get on (a train)
乗車券 **jōshaken** (train) ticket
乗車賃 **jōshachin** (train) fare
8 乗法 **jōhō** multiplication
乗物 **no(ri)mono** vehicle
乗取 **no(t)to(ru)** hijack, commandeer, capture, occupy
9 乗降 **jōkō, no(ri)o(ri)** getting on and off
乗除 **jōjo** multiplication and division
乗客 **jōkyaku** passenger
10 乗馬 **jōba, no(ri)uma** horseback riding; riding horse
乗馬靴 **jōbagutsu** riding boots
11 乗遅 **no(ri)oku(reru)** miss (a train)
乗掛 **no(ri)ka(keru)** be about to board; be riding on; get on top of, lean over; set about; collide with
乗捨 **no(ri)su(teru)** get off; abandon (a ship), leave (a rented car) at the destination (of a one-way trip)
乗務員 **jōmuin** train/plane crew
乗移 **no(ri)utsu(ru)** change (vehicles), transfer; possess, inspirit
乗組員 **norikumiin** crew
乗船 **jōsen** get on board, embark
12 乗場 **no(ri)ba** (taxi) stand, bus stop, platform
乗換 **no(ri)ka(e)** change conveyances, transfer
乗換券 **norikaeken** ticket for transfer
乗越 **no(ri)ko(su)** ride past, pass
13 乗溢 **no(ri)kobo(reru)** be packed to overflowing with passengers
乗損 **no(ri)soko(nau)** miss (a train)
乗継 **no(ri)tsu(gu)** change conveyances, make connections, transfer
乗馴 **no(ri)na(rasu)** break in (a horse)
14 乗算 **jōzan** multiplication (in math)

―――――― 2 ――――――

2 二乗 **nijō** square (a number), multiply by itself
二乗根 **nijōkon** square root
3 三乗 **sanjō** cube (in math)
三乗根 **sanjōkon** cube root
大乗仏教 **Daijō Bukkyō** Mahayana Buddhism, Great-Vehicle Buddhism
大乗的 **daijōteki** broad-minded
下乗 **gejō** get off (a horse), get out of (a car)
小乗仏教 **Shōjō bukkyō** Hinayana/Lesser-vehicle Buddhism
小乗的 **shōjōteki** narrow-minded
4 分乗 **bunjō** ride separately
5 史乗 **shijō** history, annals
只乗 **tadano(ri)** free/stolen ride
玉乗 **tamano(ri)** balancing on a ball; dancer on a ball
6 気乗 **kino(ri)** take an interest in
曲乗 **kyokuno(ri)** trick riding
同乗 **dōjō** ride together
名乗 **nano(ru)** call oneself, profess to be
自乗 **jijō** square (of a number)
自乗根 **jijōkon** square root
8 波乗 **namino(ri)** surfing
宙乗 **chūno(ri)** suspended above the stage
岩乗 **ganjō** robust, solid, firm
9 飛乗 **to(bi)no(ru)** jump on (a horse/train)
便乗 **binjō** get aboard; take advantage of
相乗 **aino(ri)** riding together **sōjō** multiply together
10 陪乗 **baijō** riding in the same car (with a superior)
座乗 **zajō** be aboard
馬乗 **umano(ri)** horseback riding
11 添乗員 **tenjōin** tour conductor
球乗 **tamano(ri)** balancing/dancer on a ball
移乗 **ijō** change vehicles, transfer
累乗 **ruijō** raising a number to a power
船乗 **funano(ri)** seaman, sailor
12 遠乗 **tōno(ri)** long ride
搭乗 **tōjō** board, get on
搭乗券 **tōjōken** boarding pass
13 試乗 **shijō** trial ride, test drive
15 箱乗 **hakono(ri)** riding in the same train car (as the one one wishes to interview)
輪乗 **wano(ri)** riding in a circle
18 騎乗 **kijō** mounted, on horseback
19 警乗 **keijō** police (a train)
警乗警察 **keijō keisatsu** railway police

―――――― 3 ――――――

1 一人乗 **ichininno(ri)** single-seater
5 加減乗除 **kagenjōjo** addition, subtraction, multiplication, and division
尻馬乗 **shiriuma (ni) no(ru)** imitate/follow blindly

四人乗 **yoninno(ri)** four-seater
11 梯子乗 **hashigono(ri)** acrobatic ladder-top
stunts
12 勝名乗 **ka(chi)nano(ri)** be declared winner

無賃乗車 **muchin jōsha** free/stolen ride
13 煙管乗 **kiseruno(ri)** ride a train with tickets
only for the first and last stretches of the
route

0a10

幽	豹	邕	乘	套	矩	豺	既	剢	歪	殊	射	耘
3o6.6	10.1	10.2	0a9.19	10.3	2t7.1	10.4	10.5	10.6	0a8.12	10.7	10.8	10.9

耙	残	耗	耕	畢	菁
10.10	10.11	10.12	10.13	5f6.6	10.14

幽→ 3o6.6

0a10.1

豹　　**HYŌ** leopard, panther, jaguar

—————— 1 ——————
9 豹変 **hyōhen** sudden change
—————— 2 ——————
9 海豹 **azarashi, kaihyō** seal

0a10.2

邕　　**CHŌ** tumeric

乘→乘 0a9.19

0a10.3

套　　**TŌ** cover; timeworn, trite

—————— 2 ——————
5 外套 **gaitō** overcoat
11 常套 **jōtō** commonplace, conventional
常套手段 **jōtō shudan** well-worn device, old
trick
常套句 **jōtōku** stock phrase, cliché
常套語 **jōtōgo** hackneyed expression, trite
saying

矩→ 2t7.1

0a10.4

豺 豺　　**SAI** wild dog, hyena, jackal

—————— 1 ——————
10 豺狼 **sairō** jackals and wolves; cruel/
rapacious person

0a10.5 / 1458

既 旡　　**KI, sude (ni)** already,
previously

—————— 1 ——————
5 既存 **kison** existing
既刊 **kikan** already published
既刊号 **kikangō** back numbers
6 既成 **kisei** existing, established
既成事実 **kisei jijitsu** fait accompli
7 既述 **kijutsu** aforesaid
既決 **kiketsu** decided, settled
既決囚 **kiketsushū** a convict
8 既知 **kichi** (already) known
既知数 **kichisū** known quantity
既往 **kiō** the past
既往症 **kiōshō** previous illness, medical
history
既往歴 **kiōreki** patient's medical history
既定 **kitei** predetermined, prearranged, fixed
10 既記 **kiki** aforesaid, the above
11 既遂 **kisui** consummated
既済 **kisai** paid-up, already settled
既婚 **kikon** (already) married
既婚者 **kikonsha** married person
既得 **kitoku** already acquired
既得権 **kitokuken** vested rights/interests
既習 **kishū** already learned
既視感 **kishikan** (feeling of) déjà vu
既望 **kibō** 16th night of a lunar month
既設 **kisetsu** already built, established, existing
既設線 **kisetsusen** lines in operation
12 既報 **kihō** previous report
13 既電 **kiden** previous message
14 既製 **kisei** ready-made
既製服 **kiseifuku** ready-made clothing
既製品 **kiseihin** manufactured/ready-made
goods, goods in stock

─────── 2 ───────

9 皆既 **kaiki** total eclipse, totality
皆既食 **kaikishoku** total eclipse, totality
皆既蝕 **kaikishoku** total eclipse, totality

0a10.6

窻 蒭
SŪ hay, straw, fodder; mowing hay

─────── 2 ───────

4 反芻 **hansū** chewing the cud, rumination

埀 → 垂 **0a8.12**

0a10.7 / 1505

殊
SHU, koto (ni) especially, in particular

─────── 1 ───────

5 殊功 **shukō** meritorious deed
殊外 **koto(no)hoka** exceedingly, exceptionally
7 殊更 **kotosara** especially, particularly; intentionally
10 殊恩 **shuon** special favor
11 殊遇 **shugū** special favor, cordial treatment
12 殊勝 **shushō** admirable, praiseworthy, commendable
15 殊勲 **shukun** distinguished service

─────── 2 ───────

10 特殊 **tokushu** special
特殊性 **tokushusei** peculiarity, characteristic
特殊鋼 **tokushukō** special steel

0a10.8 / 900

射
SHA, i(ru) shoot (an arrow)
sa(su) shine into/upon

─────── 1 ───────

3 射干玉 **nubatama** pitch-black, darkness
4 射止 **ito(meru)** shoot (an animal) dead; win (a girl)
射手 **ite, shashu** archer, bowman
5 射出 **shashutsu** shoot out, emit, extrude, radiate, catapult
6 射返 **ikae(su)** shoot back; reflect
射当 **ia(teru)** hit the target
7 射角 **shakaku** angle of fire
射利 **shari** love of money
射利心 **sharishin** mercenary spirit
8 射幸 **shakō** speculation

射幸心 **shakōshin** speculative spirit
射的 **shateki** target shooting
射的場 **shatekijō** rifle/shooting range
9 射通 **itō(su)** shoot through
10 射倒 **itao(su)** shoot down/dead
射倖心 **shakōshin** mercenary spirit
射殺 **shasatsu, ikoro(su)** shoot to death
11 射掛 **ika(keru)** attack with arrows
12 射場 **shajō** shooting/rifle range; archery ground
射落 **io(tosu)** shoot down
射竦 **isuku(meru)** shoot and make (the enemy) take cover, pin down
射程 **shatei** range (of a gun/missile)
射距離 **shakyori** range (of a gun/missile)
13 射損 **isoko(nau), ison(jiru)** miss (the target)
14 射精 **shasei** ejaculation, discharge of semen
15 射撃 **shageki** shooting, firing
射撃場 **shagekijō** shooting/rifle range
射影 **shaei** projection (in math)

─────── 2 ───────

4 反射 **hansha** reflection, reflex
反射的 **hanshateki** reflecting, reflective(ly), reflexive(ly)
反射炉 **hansharo** reverberatory furnace
日射病 **nisshabyō** sunstroke
5 立射 **rissha** firing from a standing position
6 伏射 **fukusha** shoot lying prone
7 投射 **tōsha** projection (in math); incidence (in physics); throwing (spears)
投射角 **tōshakaku** angle of incidence
投射物 **tōshabutsu** projectile
投射機 **tōshaki** projector
乱射 **ransha** random shooting
乱射乱撃 **ransha-rangeki** random shooting
応射 **ōsha** return fire
8 長射程砲 **chōshateihō** long-range gun/artillery
斉射 **seisha** volley, fusillade
直射 **chokusha** direct fire/rays
注射 **chūsha** injection, shot
注射針 **chūshabari** hypodermic needle
注射液 **chūshaeki** injection (the liquid)
注射器 **chūshaki** hypodermic syringe, injector
放射 **hōsha** radiation, emission, discharge
放射学 **hōshagaku** radiology
放射性 **hōshasei** radioactive
放射能 **hōshanō** radioactivity, radiation
放射雲 **hōshaun** radioactive cloud
放射線 **hōshasen** radiation
9 発射 **hassha** firing, launching; emanation, radiation
発射管 **hasshakan** torpedo tube
速射 **sokusha** rapid fire
速射砲 **sokushahō** rapid-fire gun/cannon

10 高射砲 **kōshahō** antiaircraft gun
   猛射 **mōsha** heavy gunfire
11 掃射 **sōsha** sweeping fire, strafing
13 照射 **shōsha** irradiation
   試射 **shisha** test firing
15 噴射 **funsha** jet, spray, injection
   熱射病 **nesshabyō** heatstroke, sunstroke
16 縦射 **jūsha** raking fire, enfilade
   輻射 **fukusha** radiate
18 騎射 **kisha** equestrian archery

————————— 3 —————————

1 一斉射撃 **issei shageki** volley, fusillade
7 乱反射 **ranhansha** diffused reflection
8 逆噴射 **gyakufunsha** retro-firing
15 膝反射 **shitsuhansha** knee-jerk reaction
21 艦砲射撃 **kanpō shageki** shelling from a
   naval vessel

————————— 4 —————————

5 皮下注射 **hika chūsha** hypodermic injection
16 機銃掃射 **kijū sōsha** machine-gunning

————————— 5 —————————

15 膝蓋腱反射 **shitsugaiken hansha** knee-jerk
   reaction

0a10.9

耘
    UN, **kusagi(ru)** weed

————————— 2 —————————

10 耕耘機 **kōunki** cultivator, tiller

0a10.10

耙
    HA rake, hoe

0a10.11 / 650

残 殘
    ZAN remain **noko(ru)** remain,
    be left over; stay, linger
    noko(su) leave behind
    noko(ri) remainder, remnant

————————— 1 —————————

3 残亡 **zanbō** be defeated and perish; be
   defeated and flee
4 残片 **zanpen** remaining fragment
   残月 **zangetsu** the moon in the morning sky
   残火 **zanka** remaining fire, embers
5 残本 **zanpon** unsold copies (of a book);
   remainders
   残生 **zansei** one's remaining years
   残存 **zanzon, zanson** survive, remain
   残存者 **zansonsha** survivor, holdover
6 残光 **zankō** afterglow

7 残余 **zan'yo** remainder, residual, remnant,
   balance
   残余額 **zan'yogaku** balance, remainder
   残兵 **zanpei** the remnants (of a defeated
   army), survivors
   残花 **zanka** a flower still in bloom
   残忍 **zannin** cruel, brutal, ruthless
   残忍性 **zanninsei** cruelty, brutality
8 残念 **zannen** regrettable, too bad
   残念賞 **zannenshō** consolation prize
   残物 **zanbutsu, noko(ri)mono** remnants,
   scraps, leftovers
   残金 **zankin** balance, surplus
9 残虐 **zangyaku** cruelty, atrocity, brutality
   残品 **zanpin** remaining stock, unsold
   merchandise
   残品整理 **zanpin seiri** clearance sale
   残春 **zanshun** the last days of spring
   残秋 **zanshū** the last days of autumn
   残香 **zankō** lingering scent
10 残部 **zanbu** remainder, what is left
   残高 **zandaka** balance, remainder
   残党 **zantō** the remnants (of a defeated party)
   残夏 **zanka** the last days of summer
   残留 **zanryū** remain behind
11 残陽 **zan'yō** the setting sun
   残務 **zanmu** unfinished business
   残惜 **noko(ri)o(shii)** regrettable, reluctant
   残雪 **zansetsu** lingering snow
12 残渣 **zansa** residue, dregs
   残期 **zanki** remaining period, unexpired term
   残暑 **zansho** the lingering summer heat
   残塁 **zanrui** runners left on base
   残飯 **zanpan** left-over rice/food, leftovers
13 残業 **zangyō** overtime
   残業手当 **zangyō teate** overtime pay
   残滓 **zanshi, zansai** remnants, residue, dregs
   残照 **zanshō** afterglow
14 残像 **zanzō** afterimage
   残酷 **zankoku** cruel, brutal
15 残影 **zan'ei** traces, relics
   残熱 **zannetsu** the lingering summer heat
   残敵 **zanteki** enemy survivors/stragglers
   残編 **zanpen** remaining/extant books
16 残骸 **zangai** remains, corpse, wreckage
18 残類 **zanrui** those remaining
   残額 **zangaku** remaining amount, balance

————————— 2 —————————

4 心残 **kokoronoko(ri)** regret, reluctance
5 生残 **i(ki)noko(ru)** survive **seizan** survival
   生残者 **seizansha** survivor
   払残 **hara(i)noko(ri)** arrears, balance due
6 名残 **nago(ri)** farewell; remembrance,
   keepsake; relics, vestiges
   名残惜 **nago(ri)o(shii)** reluctant to part

0a10

7 売残 **u(re)noko(ri)** goods left unsold; unmarried woman

見残 **minoko(su)** leave without seeing

言残 **i(i)noko(su)** leave word; leave unsaid

8 使残 **tsuka(i)noko(ri)** those left unused, remnants, odds and ends

居残 **inoko(ru)** remain behind, work overtime

取残 **to(ri)noko(su)** leave behind/out

9 咲残 **sa(ki)noko(ru)** be still in bloom

思残 **omo(i)noko(su)** look back on with regret

食残 **ta(be)noko(su), ku(i)noko(su)** leave half-eaten

10 衰残 **suizan** emaciated, decrepit, worn out

書残 **ka(ki)noko(su)** leave (a will) behind; omit, leave out; leave half-written

11 採残 **to(ri)noko(su)** leave behind

敗残 **haizan** survival after defeat; failure, ruin

敗残兵 **haizanhei** remnants of a defeated army

12 勝残 **ka(chi)noko(ru)** make the finals

焼残 **ya(ke)noko(ru)** remain unburned, escape the fire

無残 **muzan** cruel, ruthless; pitiful

飲残 **no(mi)noko(ri)** leftover drinks

16 燃残 **mo(e)noko(ri)** embers

積残 **tsu(mi)noko(su)** omit from a shipment

————— 3 —————

1 一人残 **hitori noko(razu)** everyone

0a10.12 / 1197

耗 耗   **MŌ, KŌ** decrease

————— 2 —————

10 消耗 **shōmō** consumption, attrition, wear and tear

消耗品 **shōmōhin** supplies, expendables

消耗戦 **shōmōsen** war of attrition

12 減耗 **genmō, genkō** decrease, shrinkage

13 損耗 **sonmō** wear and tear, loss

16 磨耗 **mamō** wear and tear, abrasion

0a10.13 / 1196

耕 畊   **KŌ, tagaya(su)** till, plow, cultivate

————— 1 —————

3 耕土 **kōdo** arable soil

6 耕地 **kōchi** arable/cultivated land

7 耕作 **kōsaku** cultivation, farming

耕作地 **kōsakuchi** arable/cultivated land

耕作者 **kōsakusha** tiller, plowman, farmer

耕作物 **kōsakubutsu** farm products

10 耕耘機 **kōunki** cultivator, tiller

14 耕種 **kōshu** tilling and planting

————— 2 —————

4 水耕 **suikō** hydroponics

水耕法 **suikōhō** hydroponics

8 退耕 **taikō** retire (to the country) from public office

10 帰耕 **kikō** return to the farm/land

馬耕 **bakō** tilling with a horse-drawn harrow

11 深耕 **shinkō** deep plowing

12 晴耕雨読 **seikō-udoku** tilling the fields when the sun shines and reading at home when it rains

筆耕 **hikkō** copy, stencil

筆耕料 **hikkōryō** copying fee

13 農耕 **nōkō** agriculture, farming

畢→   **5f6.6**

0a10.14

冓   **KŌ** put together; inner palace

═══════════════ 0a11 ═══════════════

犹	匏	將	巢	耜	疎	野	春	爽	肅	專	彗
11.1	11.2	2b8.3	3n8.1	11.3	11.4	11.5	11.6	11.7	11.8	0a9.16	11.9

0a11.1

犹 貔   **HI** ferocious leopard-like animal; brave warrior

————— 1 —————

13 犹狄 **hikyū** ferocious beast; brave warrior

0a11.2

匏   **HŌ, hisago** gourd

將→将   **2b8.3**

巣 → 巣 **3n8.1**

0a11.3

耜   **SHI, suki** plow

0a11.4 / 1514

疎 疎   **SO** pass through; estrangement; sparseness; shun, neglect **uto(i)** distant, estranged; be unfamiliar with, know little of
uto(mu), uto(njiru) shun, neglect, estrange
uto(mashii) disagreeable   **oroso(ka)** negligent, remiss   **maba(ra)** sparse, scattered

——————— 1 ———————
4 疎水 **sosui** drainage; canal
5 疎外 **sogai** shun, avoid someone's company, estrange
9 疎通 **sotsū** mutual understanding
疎音 **soin** long silence, neglecting to keep in touch
11 疎密 **somitsu** sparseness or denseness, density
疎略 **soryaku** coarse, crude
12 疎隔 **sokaku** estrangement, alienation
疎遠 **soen** estrangement; long silence
疎開 **sokai** dispersal, removal, evacuation
疎開者 **sokaisha** evacuee
14 疎漏 **sorō** carelessness, oversight

——————— 2 ———————
8 空疎 **kūso** empty, without substance
16 親疎 **shinso** degree of intimacy

——————— 3 ———————
11 強制疎開 **kyōsei sokai** forced evacuation/removal, eviction

0a11.5 / 236

野 埜   **YA** field; the opposition (parties); rustic; wild **no** field

——————— 1 ———————
0 野ばら **no(bara)** wild rose
2 野人 **yajin** a rustic, bumpkin, uncouth person; private citizen
3 野山 **noyama** hills and fields
4 野天 **noten** the open air
野中 **nonaka** in a field
野分 **nowaki, nowake** wind storm in autumn
野辺 **nobe** fields
野辺送 **nobeoku(ri)** bury one's remains

野犬 **yaken** stray dog
野火 **nobi** brush/prairie fire
野心 **yashin** ambition
野心的 **yashinteki** ambitious
野心家 **yashinka** ambitious person
野心満々 **yashin-manman** full of ambition
5 野末 **nozue** farthest corners of a field
野生 **yasei** wild
野史 **yashi** an unofficial history
野外 **yagai** the open air, outdoor
6 野合 **yagō** illicit cohabitation
7 野良 **nora** the fields; laziness
野良犬 **norainu** stray dog
野良仕事 **nora shigoto** farm/field work
野良猫 **noraneko** stray cat
野良着 **noragi** clothes for working in the fields
8 野兎 **nousagi** hare, jackrabbit
野垂死 **nota(re)ji(ni)** die by the roadside
野郎 **yarō** fellow, guy, bastard
野育 **nosoda(chi)** wild; ill-bred
野放 **nobana(shi)** putting to pasture; leaving things to themselves
野放図 **nohōzu** wild, unbridled
野性 **yasei** wild nature, uncouthness
野性味 **yaseimi** wildness, roughness
野性的 **yaseiteki** wild, rough
野武士 **nobushi** wandering samurai, free lance
9 野陣 **nojin** bivouac
野草 **yasō** wild grass/plants   **nogusa** grass in a field
野卑 **yahi** vulgar, coarse, boorish
10 野原 **nohara** field, plain
野遊 **noaso(bi)** picnic, outing
野師 **yashi** showman; charlatan, quack
野党 **yatō** opposition party
野晒 **nozara(shi)** weather-beaten
野砲 **yahō** field gun/artillery
野砲兵 **yahōhei** field artilleryman
野馬 **nouma** wild horse
11 野道 **nomichi** path across a field
野菜 **yasai** vegetables
野菜畑 **yasaibatake** vegetable garden
野菊 **nogiku** wild chrysanthemum; aster
野宿 **nojuku** camping out
野球 **yakyū** baseball
野球気違 **yakyū kichiga(i)** baseball fan
野球狂 **yakyūkyō** baseball fan
野球場 **yakyūjō** baseball park/stadium
野球熱 **yakyūnetsu** baseball fever/mania
野鳥 **yachō** wild birds
12 野禽 **yakin** wild birds
野蛮 **yaban** savage, barbarous
野蛮人 **yabanjin** savage, barbarian
野蛮国 **yabankoku** uncivilized country

野葡萄 **nobudō** wild grapes
野営 **yaei** camp, bivouac
野営地 **yaeichi** camping ground
野焼 **noya(ki)** winter burning of the fields
13 野鼠 **nonezumi** field mouse
野猿 **yaen** wild monkey
野戦 **yasen** open warfare, field operations
野路 **noji** path across a field
14 野暮 **yabo** unrefined, rustic; stupid, sense-less; stale, trite
野暮天 **yaboten** unrefined, rustic; stupid, senseless; stale, trite
15 野趣 **yashu** rural beauty, rustic air
16 野獣 **yajū** wild animal/beast
野獣主義 **yajū shugi** Fauvism
野獣派 **yajūha** Fauvists
野獣狩 **yajūga(ri)** wild animal hunt
野薔薇 **nobara** wild rose

───────── 2 ─────────

3 大野 **ōno** big field **Ōno** (surname)
与野党 **yoyatō** governing and opposition parties
上野 **Ueno** (section of Tōkyō)
　　 Kōzuke (ancient kuni, Gunma-ken)
下野 **geya** retire from public life
　　 Shimotsuke (ancient kuni, Tochigi-ken)
小野 **ono** field **Ono** (proper name)
山野 **san'ya** fields and mountains
4 内野 **naiya** infield (in baseball)
内野手 **naiyashu** infielder, baseman
分野 **bun'ya** field, sphere, area, division
5 平野 **heiya** a plain, open field
外野 **gaiya** outfield
外野手 **gaiyashu** outfielder
外野席 **gaiyaseki** bleachers
広野 **kōya** open field/country
田野 **den'ya** cultivated fields
6 在野 **zaiya** out of office/power
吉野 **Yoshino** (proper name); common cherry tree; (a type of thin high-quality paper)
7 沃野 **yokuya** fertile field/plain
花野 **hanano** field of flowers
花野菜 **hanayasai** cauliflower
8 長野 **Nagano** (city, Nagano-ken)
長野県 **Nagano-ken** (prefecture)
郊野 **kōya** suburban fields
林野 **rin'ya** forests and fields, woodlands
林野庁 **Rin'yachō** Forestry Agency
牧野 **bokuya** pasture land, ranch
9 草野球 **kusa-yakyū** sandlot baseball
荒野 **a(re)no, arano, kōya** wilderness, wasteland
枯野 **ka(re)no** desolate fields
10 高野山 **Kōyasan** (mountain, Wakayama-ken)
高野豆腐 **kōyadōfu** frozen tofu

原野 **gen'ya** wasteland, wilderness, field, plain
11 視野 **shiya** field of vision/view
粗野 **soya** rustic, loutish, vulgar
12 朝野 **chōya** government and people, the whole nation
焼野 **ya(ke)no** burnt field
焼野原 **ya(ke)nohara** burned-out area
13 裾野 **susono** foot of a mountain
14 緑野 **ryokuya** green field
19 曠野 **kōya** broad plain, prairie

───────── 3 ─────────

5 田夫野人 **denpu-yajin** a rustic, country bumpkin, yokel
11 軟式野球 **nanshiki yakyū** softball

0a11.6

春   **SHŌ, usutsu(ku)** pound (grain in a mortar)

0a11.7

爽   **SŌ, sawa(yaka)** refreshing, bracing; clear, resonant, fluent

───────── 1 ─────────

7 爽快 **sōkai** thrilling, exhilarating

───────── 2 ─────────

14 颯爽 **sassō** dashing, smart, gallant

0a11.8 / 1695

粛　肅   **SHUKU** rectify, admonish; reverential; solemn; quiet

───────── 1 ─────────

3 粛々 **shukushuku** in hushed silence; solemnly
5 粛正 **shukusei** strictly rectify, enforce (discipline)
10 粛党 **shukutō** purge (of a political party)
11 粛清 **shukusei** purge, cleanup, liquidation
12 粛然 **shukuzen** solemnly

───────── 2 ─────────

6 自粛 **jishuku** self-restraint
10 振粛 **shinshuku** strict enforcement
14 静粛 **seishuku** silent, still, quiet
17 厳粛 **genshuku** grave, serious, solemn

───────── 3 ─────────

14 綱紀粛正 **kōki shukusei** enforcement of discipline among officials

専 → 專 0a9.16

0a11.9

彗

SUI comet; broom, sweep

―――――――――――――― 1 ――――――――――――――

9 彗星 **suisei, hōkiboshi** comet

――――――――――――― **0a12-19** ―――――――――――――

黹	瓟	躰	棘	棗	毳	甦	鼠	黽	業	參	斠	蕭
12.1	12.2	2a5.6	12.3	12.4	12.5	12.6	13.1	13.2	13.3	13.4	13.5	0a11.8

肆	肄	翡	夥	貍	爾	奬	貌	舞	耦	舉	瓬	戳
13.6	13.7	14.1	14.2	3g7.2	14.3	3n10.4	3g8.2	15.1	15.2	3n7.1	16.1	17.1

艱	斷	鼬	黼
3k14.7	6b5.6	18.1	19.1

――――――――――――― 12 ―――――――――――――

0a12.1

黹

CHI, nu(u) embroider

0a12.2

瓟

KO, hisago gourd
KAKU dilapidated

躰 → 体 **2a5.6**

0a12.3

棘

KYOKU thorns, brambles; halberd
ibara brier, brambles, jujube

―――――――――――――― 2 ――――――――――――――

9 荊棘 **keikyoku** thorns, brier; nettlesome situation

0a12.4

棗

SŌ, natsume jujube tree, Chinese date

0a12.5

毳

ZEI, keba nap, shag, fluff, fuzz
mukuge down, fluff

―――――――――――――― 1 ――――――――――――――

5 毳立 **kebada(tsu)** be fluffy/plush

0a12.6

甦

SO, yomigae(ru) come back to life, be revived

――――――――――――― 13 ―――――――――――――

0a13.1

鼠 鼡

SO, SHU, nezumi rat, mouse

―――――――――――――― 1 ――――――――――――――

2 鼠入 **nezumii(razu)** mouseproof cupboard
5 鼠穴 **nezumiana** rathole, mousehole
6 鼠色 **nezumiiro** dark gray, slate
8 鼠取 **nezumito(ri)** rat poison; mousetrap, rattrap
9 鼠咬症 **sokōshō** rat-bite fever
14 鼠算 **nezumizan** geometrical progression, multiplying like rats

―――――――――――――― 2 ――――――――――――――

5 白鼠 **shironezumi** white rat/mouse
9 海鼠 **namako** trepang, sea slug
畑鼠 **hatanezumi** field mouse
10 栗鼠 **risu** squirrel
11 野鼠 **nonezumi** field mouse
15 窮鼠 **kyūso** a cornered mouse/rat
17 濡鼠 **nu(re)nezumi** (like a) drowned rat
23 鼴鼠 **mogura** mole

―――――――――――――― 3 ――――――――――――――

21 麝香鼠 **jakōnezumi** muskrat

―――――――――――――― 4 ――――――――――――――

2 二十日鼠 **hatsuka nezumi** mouse

―――――――――――――― 5 ――――――――――――――

3 大山鳴動鼠一匹 **taizan meidō (shite) nezumi ippiki** The mountains have brought forth a mouse. Much ado about nothing much.

0a13.2

BIN, BEN, BŌ frog; diligence

0a13.3 / 279

業 GYŌ business, trade, industry; undertaking GŌ karma **waza** a work, deed, act, performance, trick

——————— 1 ———————

4 業火 **gōka** hell fire
9 業界 **gyōkai** the business world, industry, the trade
業界紙 **gyōkaishi** trade paper/journal
11 業務 **gyōmu** business, work, operations, duties
13 業腹 **gōhara** resentment, spite, vexation
14 業種 **gyōshu** type of industry, category of business
17 業績 **gyōseki** (business) performance, results, achievement

——————— 2 ———————

2 力業 **chikarawaza** heavy labor; feat of strength
3 三業 **sangyō** a business consisting of restaurant, waiting room, and geisha house
三業地 **sangyōchi** licensed red-light district
工業 **kōgyō** industry
工業大学 **kōgyō daigaku** technical college
工業化 **kōgyōka** industrialization
工業用 **kōgyōyō** for industrial use
工業地 **kōgyōchi** industrial area
工業地帯 **kōgyō chitai** industrial area
工業国 **kōgyōkoku** industrial nation
工業界 **kōgyōkai** industrial circles, industry
工業都市 **kōgyō toshi** industrial city, factory town
工業家 **kōgyōka** industrialist, manufacturer
大業 **taigyō** a great undertaking/achievement
4 分業 **bungyō** division of labor, specialization
手業 **tewaza** hand work, skill
5 民業 **mingyō** a private business
本業 **hongyō** one's principal occupation
失業 **shitsugyō** unemployment
失業者 **shitsugyōsha** unemployed person
生業 **seigyō** occupation, calling
仕業 **shiwaza** act, deed
正業 **seigyō** legitimate occupation, honest business
巡業 **jungyō** tour (of a troupe/team)
立業 **ta(chi)waza** (judo) standing techniques
6 休業 **kyūgyō** suspension of business, Shop Closed
休業日 **kyūgyōbi** business holiday
企業 **kigyō** enterprise, corporation
企業家 **kigyōka** industrialist, entrepreneur
近業 **kingyō** a recent work
同業 **dōgyō** the same trade/business
因業 **ingō** heartless, cruel
早業 **hayawaza** quick work; sleight of hand

成業 **seigyō** completion of one's work/studies
自業自得 **jigō-jitoku** reaping what one sows
7 作業 **sagyō** work, operations
作業衣 **sagyōi** work clothes
作業服 **sagyōfuku** work clothes
余業 **yogyō** remaining work; avocation, sideline
別業 **betsugyō** another line of work; villa
医業 **igyō** medical practice
投業 **na(ge)waza** throwing trick/technique
学業 **gakugyō** schoolwork, scholastic achievement
社業 **shagyō** the company's business
足業 **ashiwaza** footwork; foot tricks
8 非業 **higō** untimely (death)
事業 **jigyō** undertakings, business, activities
事業化 **jigyōka** industrialization
事業界 **jigyōkai** industrial/business world
事業部 **jigyōbu** operations department
事業家 **jigyōka** entrepreneur; businessman, industrialist
事業税 **jigyōzei** business tax
夜業 **yagyō** night work/shift
卒業 **sotsugyō** graduation
協業 **kyōgyō** cooperative undertaking
始業 **shigyō** begin work, open
始業式 **shigyōshiki** opening ceremony
実業 **jitsugyō** industry, business
実業学校 **jitsugyō gakkō** vocational school
実業家 **jitsugyōka** industrialist, businessman
官業 **kangyō** government/state enterprise
定業 **teigyō** regular occupation
林業 **ringyō** forestry
所業 **shogyō** deed, act, work
9 専業 **sengyō** specialty, monopoly, main occupation
茶業 **chagyō** the tea industry/business
神業 **kamiwaza** the work of God; superhuman feat
祖業 **sogyō** family business of many generations
怠業 **taigyō** work stoppage, slow-down strike
10 残業 **zangyō** overtime
残業手当 **zangyō teate** overtime pay
修業 **shūgyō** pursuit of knowledge
兼業 **kengyō** side business
起業 **kigyō** start a business, organize an undertaking
徒業 **adawaza** useless thing
従業 **jūgyō** be employed
従業員 **jūgyōin** employee
家業 **kagyō** one's trade
座業 **zagyō** sedentary work
蚕業 **sangyō** sericulture
11 副業 **fukugyō** side business, sideline
商業 **shōgyō** commerce, trade, business

商業化 **shōgyōka** commercialization
商業文 **shōgyōbun** business correspondence
商業主義 **shōgyō shugi** commercialism
商業地 **shōgyōchi** business district
商業国 **shōgyōkoku** mercantile nation
商業界 **shōgyōkai** the business world
商業組合 **shōgyō kumiai** trade association
商業港 **shōgyōkō** trading port
商業街 **shōgyōgai** shopping street/area
授業 **jugyō** teaching, instruction
授業料 **jugyōryō** tuition
得業士 **tokugyōshi** special-school graduate
宿業 **shukugō** karma, fate
現業 **gengyō** work-site operations
現業員 **gengyōin** outdoor/field worker
悪業 **akugyō** evil, wickedness
　　　akugō evil karma
産業 **sangyō** industry
産業界 **sangyōkai** (the) industry
終業 **shūgyō** close of work/school
終業式 **shūgyōshiki** closing ceremony
転業 **tengyō** change occupations
12 偉業 **igyō** great achievement, feat
創業 **sōgyō** found, establish
創業者 **sōgyōsha** founder
善業 **zengō** good deed
就業 **shūgyō** employment
就業日数 **shūgyō nissū** days worked
就業率 **shūgyōritsu** percentage of employment
復業 **fukugyō** return to work
営業 **eigyō** (running a) business
営業費 **eigyōhi** operating expenses
廃業 **haigyō** going out of business
悲業 **higō** misfortune, unnatural (death)
軽業 **karuwaza** acrobatics
軽業師 **karuwazashi** acrobat, tumbler
開業 **kaigyō** opening/starting a business
開業医 **kaigyōi** doctor in private practice
13 勧業 **kangyō** encouragement of industry; industry
農業 **nōgyō** agriculture
農業国 **nōgyōkoku** agricultural country
適業 **tekigyō** suitable occupation
聖業 **seigyō** sacred work; imperial achievements
罪業 **zaigō** sin
鉱業 **kōgyō** mining
14 遺業 **igyō** unfinished work (of the deceased)
漁業 **gyogyō** fishery, fishing industry
漁業権 **gyogyōken** fishing rights
15 窯業 **yōgyō** ceramics (industry)
稼業 **kagyō** one's trade/occupation
罷業 **higyō** strike, walkout
課業 **kagyō** lessons, schoolwork
賤業 **sengyō** lowly/shameful occupation

質業 **shichigyō** the pawn business
16 興業 **kōgyō** promotion of industry
操業 **sōgyō** operation, work
操業率 **sōgyōritsu** percentage of capacity in operation
操業短縮 **sōgyō tanshuku** curtailed operations
操業費 **sōgyōhi** operating expenses
機業 **kigyō** the textile industry
機業界 **kigyōkai** the textile world
機業家 **kigyōka** textile manufacturer, weaver
糖業 **tōgyō** the sugar industry
17 醜業 **shūgyō** shameful calling, prostitution
醜業婦 **shūgyōfu** prostitute
18 職業 **shokugyō** occupation, profession
職業安定所 **shokugyō anteisho/jo** (public) employment security office
職業的 **shokugyōteki** professional
職業病 **shokugyōbyō** occupational disease
離業 **hana(re)waza** stunt, feat
19 覇業 **hagyō** domination, hegemony

────────── 3 ──────────

2 人間業 **ningenwaza** the work of man
3 下請業者 **shitauke gyōsha** subcontractor
土建業 **dokengyō** civil engineering and construction
小企業 **shōkigyō** small enterprises/business
4 片手業 **katate waza** side job
水産業 **suisangyō** fisheries, marine products industry
手工業 **shukōgyō** manual industry, handicrafts
5 出版業 **shuppangyō** the publishing business
代理業 **dairigyō** business of an agent, agency
広告業 **kōkokugyō** advertising business
6 光産業 **hikari sangyō** optronics industry
自由業 **jiyūgyō** freelance occupation, self-employed
7 売文業 **baibungyō** hack writing
8 非現業 **higengyō** clerical/non-field work
非現業員 **higengyōin** office/desk worker
建築業者 **kenchiku gyōsha** builder
周旋業 **shūsengyō** brokerage, commission agency
牧畜業 **bokuchikugyō** stock farming, ranching
取次業 **toritsugigyō** agency/commission business
9 重工業 **jūkōgyō** heavy industry
造酒業 **zōshugyō** saké brewing industry
造船業 **zōsengyō** shipbuilding industry
海運業 **kaiungyō** shipping, maritime trade
宣伝業 **sendengyō** publicity/advertising businessg
宣伝業者 **senden gyōsha** publicist
10 酒造業 **shuzōgyō** brewery business

0a13

流作業 **naga(re)sagyō** (assembly-)line operation
書籍業 **shosekigyō** bookselling and publishing business
旅館業 **ryokangyō** the hotel business
蚕糸業 **sanshigyō** the silk-reeling industry
11 商工業 **shōkōgyō** commerce and industry
運送業 **unsōgyō** transport business
運送業者 **unsōgyōsha** carrier, forwarding agent
接客業 **sekkyakugyō** hotel and restaurant trade
著述業 **chojutsugyō** the literary profession
宿屋業 **yadoyagyō** the hotel business
船舶業 **senpakugyō** shipping industry
12 貿易業 **bōekigyō** the trading business
軽工業 **keikōgyō** light industry
閑事業 **kanjigyō** useless work
13 農工業 **nōkōgyō** agriculture and industry
新聞業 **shinbungyō** the newspaper business
鉄鋼業 **tekkōgyō** the steel industry
鉱工業 **kōkōgyō** mining and manufacturing
鉱山業 **kōzangyō** mining
14 製糸業 **seishigyō** the silk industry
製造業 **seizōgyō** manufacturing industry
製革業 **seikakugyō** the tanning industry
製茶業 **seichagyō** the tea manufacturing industry
製炭業 **seitangyō** the charcoal industry
製陶業 **seitōgyō** the ceramics industry
製紙業 **seishigyō** the paper industry
製菓業 **seikagyō** the confectionery industry
製塩業 **seiengyō** the salt industry
製靴業 **seikagyō** the shoemaking industry
製鉄業 **seitetsugyō** the iron industry
製糖業 **seitōgyō** the sugar industry
総罷業 **sōhigyō** general strike
15 養蚕業 **yōsangyō** silkworm raising, sericulture
養鶏業 **yōkeigyō** poultry farming
請負業 **ukeoigyō** contracting business
16 獣医業 **jūigyō** veterinary practice/business
輸出業 **yushutsugyō** export business
18 鞣皮業 **jūhigyō** tannery
織物業 **orimonogyō** the textile business
20 醸造業 **jōzōgyō** brewing industry

─────────── 4 ───────────
4 中小企業 **chūshō kigyō** small business(es)
中堅企業 **chūken kigyō** medium-size business/company
公共事業 **kōkyō jigyō** public works, utilities
6 有畜農業 **yūchiku nōgyō** diversified farming
自由営業 **jiyū eigyō** nonrestricted trade
8 沿岸漁業 **engan gyogyō** coastal fishing
泥水稼業 **doromizu kagyō** shameful occupation

武者修業 **musha shugyō** knight-errantry
金属工業 **kinzoku kōgyō** metalworking industry
9 軍需工業 **gunju kōgyō** munitions industry
通商産業省 **Tsūshōsangyōshō** Ministry of International Trade and Industry
10 家内工業 **kanai kōgyō** home/cottage industry
11 済世事業 **saisei jigyō** public-welfare work
13 慈善事業 **jizen jigyō** charity work, philanthropy
戦時産業 **senji sangyō** wartime industry
15 隣保事業 **rinpo jigyō** welfare work, social services
16 機械工業 **kikai kōgyō** the machine industry
─────────── 5 ───────────
14 総同盟罷業 **sōdōmei higyō** general strike

0a13.4

篆

KEN, KAN (raising) domestic animals

0a13.5

斟

SHIN dip, ladle, pour; conjecture

─────────── 1 ───────────
10 斟酌 **shinshaku** take into consideration

肅 → 粛 **0a11.8**

0a13.6

肆

SHI put in a row, line up; expose; shop; as one pleases; four

─────────── 2 ───────────
8 放肆 **hōshi** self-indulgent, licentious
10 書肆 **shoshi** bookstore

0a13.7

肄

I learn; striving, effort

─────────── 14 ───────────

0a14.1

翡

HI male kingfisher

─────── 1 ───────

14 翡翠 **hisui** green jadeite, jade; kingfisher
kawasemi kingfisher

0a14.2

夥 **KA, obitada(shii)** much, many, immense, numerous

─────── 1 ───────

6 夥多 **kata** in abundance, many

貍 → 狸 **3g7.2**

0a14.3

爾 尒 **JI, NI** thou, you; so, in that way; only; since, from

─────── 1 ───────

7 爾来 **jirai** since then
9 爾後 **jigo** thereafter

─────── 2 ───────

10 莞爾 **kanji (to shite)** with a smile

─────── 4 ───────

7 伯剌西爾 **Burajiru** Brazil

獎 → 奨 **3n10.4**

─────── 15 ───────

貌 → 狼 **3g8.2**

0a15.1 / 810

舞 **BU, ma(u)** dance; flutter about
mai dance

─────── 1 ───────

2 舞子 **maiko** dancing girl
3 舞上 **ma(i)a(garu)** fly up, soar
4 舞込 **ma(i)ko(mu)** drop in, visit; befall
舞手 **ma(i)te** dancer
5 舞台 **butai** stage
舞台負 **butaima(ke)** stage fright
舞台姿 **butaisugata** in stage costume
舞台面 **butaimen** scene, scenery
舞台裏 **butaiura** backstage
舞台劇 **butaigeki** stage play
舞台稽古 **butai geiko** dress rehearsal
6 舞曲 **bukyoku** music and dancing; dance music

7 舞妓 **maiko** dancing girl
舞狂 **ma(i)kuru(u)** dance wildly, dance in a frenzy
舞戻 **ma(i)modo(ru)** find one's way back, return
10 舞姫 **maihime** dancing girl
舞扇 **maiōgi** dancer's fan
13 舞楽 **bugaku** old Japanese court-dance music
14 舞踊 **buyō** dancing; dance
ma(i)odo(ru) dance
舞踊劇 **buyōgeki** dance drama
15 舞踏 **butō** dancing
舞踏会 **butōkai** ball, dance
舞踏病 **butōbyō** St. Vitus's dance, chorea
舞踏場 **butōjō** dance hall
21 舞鶴 **Maizuru** (city, Kyōto-fu)

─────── 2 ───────

2 二舞 **ni (no) mai** a repetition
4 円舞 **enbu** waltz
木舞 **komai** lath
5 仕舞 **shima(u)** finish, end; put away; close, wind up
6 回舞台 **mawa(ri)butai** revolving stage
7 乱舞 **ranbu** boisterous dance
見舞 **mima(u)** inquire after (someone's health), visit (someone in hospital)
見舞人 **mima(i)nin** sympathizer, visitor
見舞状 **mima(i)jō** how-are-you/get-well card
見舞金 **mima(i)kin** money gift to a sick person
見舞品 **mima(i)hin** gift to a sick person
見舞客 **mima(i)kyaku** hospital visitor
初舞台 **hatsubutai** one's stage debut
8 京舞 **kyōmai** a traditional Kyōto dance performed to the accompaniment of *jiuta*
9 前舞台 **maebutai** apron stage, proscenium
独舞台 **hito(ri)butai** having the stage to oneself
10 剣舞 **kenbu** sword dance
振舞 **furuma(u)** behave, conduct oneself; entertain, treat
振舞酒 **furuma(i)zake** a saké treat
13 群舞 **gunbu** group dance
鼓舞 **kobu** encouragement, inspiration
14 演舞場 **enbujō** playhouse, theater
歌舞 **kabu** singing and dancing, entertainment
歌舞伎 **kabuki** kabuki
15 輪舞 **rinbu** round dance
17 檜舞台 **hinoki butai** cypress-floored

─────── 3 ───────

1 一人舞台 **hitori butai** unrivaled
4 手仕舞 **tejima(i)** clearing of accounts, clearance (sale)
5 立振舞 **ta(chi)buruma(i)** farewell dinner
ta(chi)furuma(i) demeanor

0a15

6 仮装舞踏会 **kasō butōkai** masquerade ball
地唄舞 **jiutamai** a traditional Kyōto dance performed to the accompaniment of *jiuta*
早仕舞 **hayajimai** early closing
7 身仕舞 **mijimai** grooming, outfit, preparations
8 店仕舞 **misejima(i)** close shop (for the day); go out of business
9 後仕舞 **atojimai** straightening up afterwards, winding up
10 酒振舞 **sakaburuma(i)** wining and dining
13 獅子舞 **shishimai** lion-mask dance
14 総仕舞 **sōjimai** closing up, selling out

———————— 4 ————————

4 天手古舞 **tentekoma(i)** hectic activity
火事見舞 **kaji mima(i)** sympathy visit after a fire
10 起居振舞 **ta(chi)i furuma(i)** deportment, manners
12 暑中見舞 **shochū mima(i)** inquiry after (someone's) health in the hot season
13 節季仕舞 **sekki-jimai** year-end closeout

0a15.2

耦 **GŪ, GŌ** one's wife/husband, mate, consort, partner; kind, sort, match, equal; a pair (plowing together); face each other

———————— 1 ————————

8 耦刺 **gūshi** killing each other with swords/ knives

———————— 16 ————————

舉 → 挙 3n7.1

0a16.1

甎 **SEN, shikigawara** floor tiles

———————— 17 ————————

0a17.1

黻 **FUTSU** lap robe; embroidery pattern

艱 → 3k14.7

———————— 18 ————————

斷 → 断 6b5.6

0a18.1

鼬 **YŪ, itachi** weasel

———————— 19 ————————

0a19.1

黼 **FU, HO** embroidery

———————— イ 2a ————————

人	从	个	个	仔	仂	什	仆	仇	仏	化	仍	仁
0.1	3i7.3	2a8.36	6f8.15	2.1	2a11.1	2.2	2.3	2.4	2.5	2.6	2.7	2.8
分	公	介	今	久	仙	仕	代	伵	他	仗	付	仟
2o2.1	2o2.2	2.9	2.10	0a3.7	3.1	3.2	3.3	2a3.8	3.4	3.5	3.6	3.7
仞	以	仝	令	勾	伏	休	仿	件	伐	伊	住	仲
3.8	0a5.1	2r4.2	3.9	3.10	4.1	4.2	4.3	4.4	4.5	4.6	2a5.19	4.7
伍	任	仰	价	优	伎	伜	伝	仮	全	企	合	会
4.8	4.9	4.10	4.11	4.12	4.13	2a8.29	4.14	4.15	4.16	4.17	4.18	4.19
肉	耒	朱	位	佃	佛	伸	伴	佚	体	伯	佑	佐
4.20	0a7.6	0a6.13	5.1	5.2	2a2.5	5.3	5.4	5.5	5.6	5.7	5.8	5.9
作	似	伽	攸	但	低	佗	佇	伶	估	住	佞	何
5.10	5.11	5.12	5.13	5.14	5.15	2a6.14	5.16	5.17	5.18	5.19	5.20	5.21
佝	伺	余	含	巫	夾	依	使	価	侠	侏	侑	侈
5.22	5.23	5.24	5.25	5.26	5.27	6.1	6.2	6.3	2a7.7	6.4	6.5	6.6

例 6.7	挑 6.8	俘 6.9	佳 6.10	侍 6.11	侃 6.12	供 6.13	侘 6.14	倭 2a5.20	佶 6.15	佼 6.16	併 6.17	伴 6.18
佰 6.19	侮 6.20	侭 2a14.2	佩 6.21	個 6.22	舍 6.23	舎 2a6.23	念 6.24	侖 6.25	命 6.26	來 0a7.6	信 7.1	俥 7.2
促 7.3	俄 7.4	侮 2a6.20	便 7.5	俚 7.6	俠 7.7	俐 4k7.2	係 7.8	俔 7.9	俊 7.10	保 7.11	俣 7.12	侶 7.13
俏 7.14	侵 7.15	俛 7.16	俗 7.17	俤 7.18	俟 7.19	俑 7.20	侯 7.21	臥 7.22	俞 4b5.11	赴 3b6.14	起 3b7.11	臾 7.23
俎 7.24	矜 7.25	乗 0a9.19	們 8.1	健 8.2	倆 8.3	俾 8.4	倒 8.5	俶 8.6	做 8.7	俳 8.8	倂 2a6.17	倏 8.9
候 8.10	修 8.11	倪 8.12	倦 8.13	倍 8.14	俱 8.15	倭 8.16	倥 8.17	俸 8.18	倡 8.19	倩 8.20	俵 8.21	借 8.22
倖 8.23	倘 8.24	俺 8.25	倚 8.26	倹 8.27	倫 8.28	倅 8.29	値 8.30	倨 8.31	倬 8.32	倔 8.33	健 8.34	俯 8.35
個 8.36	倉 8.37	拿 3c5.30	衾 8.38	偶 9.1	偽 9.2	偖 9.3	假 2a4.15	側 9.4	做 9.5	倦 2a8.13	條 4i4.1	脩 9.6
偲 9.7	偬 9.8	偟 9.9	偈 9.10	偕 9.11	修 9.12	偸 9.13	停 9.14	偵 9.15	偏 9.16	偓 9.17	偃 9.18	猷 5f5.5
盒 9.19	貪 9.20	超 3b9.18	越 4n8.2	麥 4i4.2	剱 2f8.5	斜 9.21	敘 2h7.1	肅 0a11.8	疎 0a11.4	傲 10.1	博 10.2	傀 10.3
備 10.4	僅 2a11.13	偉 10.5	傍 10.6	傘 10.7	禽 10.8	翁 10.9	超 3b9.18	越 4n8.2	幾 4n8.4	疎 0a11.4	働 11.1	傲 11.2
傾 11.3	條 11.4	傳 2a4.14	僂 11.5	傑 11.6	僧 11.7	僄 11.8	傯 11.9	傷 11.10	債 11.11	催 11.12	僅 11.13	傭 11.14
偏 11.15	會 2a4.19	愈 11.16	僉 11.17	猷 4a9.9	越 4n8.2	業 0a13.3	靴 3k10.34	僕 12.1	僭 12.2	僮 12.3	僚 12.4	僑 12.5
僞 2a9.2	僥 12.6	僖 12.7	像 12.8	僧 2a11.7	趣 6e9.1	疑 2m12.1	僻 13.1	儁 13.2	儂 13.3	價 2a6.3	儀 13.4	僵 13.5
億 13.6	儚 13.7	儈 13.8	儉 2a8.27	趣 6e9.1	麪 4i17.1	麩 4i12.2	齒 6b6.11	儒 14.1	儘 14.2	儔 14.3	儕 14.4	趨 3b14.5
儲 2a16.1	優 15.1	儡 15.2	儡 15.3	償 15.4	龠 15.5	趨 3b14.5	齔 15.6	儲 16.1	鞭 3k15.8	離 18.1	齡 6b11.5	儺 19.1
儷 19.2	齦 19.3	蠥 19.4	儻 20.1	儼 20.2	龕 20.3	齲 22.1						

2

イ ィ 子 阝 卩 力 刂 又 宀 亠 艹 夂 冖 厂 辶 冂 八 匚　0←

— 0 —

2a0.1 / 1

人 **JIN, NIN, hito** man, person, human being

— 1 —

0 アメリカ人 **Amerikajin** an American
1 人一倍 **hito-ichibai** uncommon, more than others

2 人力 **jinriki** human power, man-powered
　　jinryoku human power/efforts
　人力車 **jinrikisha** rickshaw
3 人工 **jinkō** artificial
　人工林 **jinkōrin** planted forest
　人工的 **jinkōteki** artificial
　人工雨 **jinkōu** artificial rain, rainmaking
　人才 **jinzai, jinsai** man of talent
　人々 **hitobito** people, everybody

人口 **jinkō** population; common talk
人山 **hitoyama** crowd of people
4 人夫 **ninpu** coolie, laborer
人中 **hitonaka** society, company, public
人文 **jinmon, jinbun** humanity, civilization
人文主義 **jinbun shugi** humanism
人文地理 **jinbun chiri, jinmon chiri** anthropogeography
人文科学 **jinbun kagaku** cultural sciences
人込 **hitogo(mi)** crowd of people
人手 **hitode** worker, hand, help
人心 **jinshin** people's hearts
人心地 **hitogokochi** consciousness
5 人出 **hitode** turnout, crowd
人民 **jinmin** the people
人民投票 **jinmin tōhyō** plebiscite, referendum
人民戦線 **jinmin sensen** popular front
人本主義 **jinpon shugi** humanism
人生 **jinsei** life, human existence
人生派 **jinseiha** humanists
人生観 **jinseikan** one's philosophy of life
人世 **jinsei** this world, life
人付合 **hitozu(ki)a(i)** sociability
人払 **hitobara(i)** clear (the room) of people
人好 **hitozu(ki)** amiability, attractiveness
人目 **hitome** notice, attention
6 人死 **hitoji(ni)** loss of life
人気 **hinki** popularity; popular feeling; business conditions **hitoke** signs of life (in a place)
人気者 **ninkimono** popular person, a favorite
人気取 **ninkito(ri)** grandstanding, bid for popularity
人気商売 **ninki shōbai** occupation dependent on public favor
人件費 **jinkenhi** personnel expenses
人任 **hitomaka(se)** leaving it to others
人伝 **hitozu(te)** hearsay; message
人肉 **jinniku** human flesh
人名 **jinmei** person's name
人名録 **jinmeiroku** name list, directory
人名簿 **jinmeibo** name list, directory
人当 **hitoa(tari)** manners, demeanor
人肌 **hitohada** (warmth of) the skin
7 人身 **jinshin** the human body; one's person
人身売買 **jinshin baibai** slave trade
人身攻撃 **jinshin kōgeki** personal attack
人身保護 **jinshin hogo** habeas corpus
人身御供 **hitomi gokū** human sacrifice, victim
人里 **hitozato** village, habitation
人位 **jin'i** one's rank
人体 **jintai** the human body
人助 **hitodasu(ke)** kind deed
人君 **jinkun** sovereign, ruler

人形 **ningyō** doll, puppet
人形芝居 **ningyō shibai** puppet show
人声 **hitogoe** voice
人材 **jinzai** man of talent, personnel
人材登用 **jinzai tōyō** selection of people for higher positions
人見知 **hitomishi(ri)** be bashful before strangers
人足 **hitoashi** pedestrian traffic
ninsoku coolie, laborer
8 人非人 **ninpinin** man of brutal nature
人事 **jinji** personal/personnel affairs
hitogoto other people's affairs
人使 **hitozuka(i)** how one handles one's workers
人命 **jinmei** (human) life
人並 **hitona(mi)** average, ordinary
人泣 **hitona(kase)** nuisance to others
人波 **hitonami** surging crowd
人知 **jinchi** human intellect/knowledge
hitoshi(renu), hitoshi(rezu) unknown to others, hidden, secret
人妻 **hitozuma** (someone else's) wife
人参 **ninjin** carrot
人的 **jinteki** human, personal
人物 **jinbutsu** person; one's character; character (in a story); man of ability
人物画 **jinbutsuga** portrait
人物像 **jinbutsuzō** statue, picture
人性 **jinsei** human nature; humanity
人怖 **hitooji** (child's) fear of strangers
9 人前 **hitomae** before others, in public
人造 **jinzō** artificial, synthetic, imitation
人造米 **jinzōmai** artificial rice
人通 **hitodō(ri)** pedestrian traffic
人垣 **hitogaki** human wall, crowd, throng
人品 **jinpin** personal bearing/appearance, character
人待顔 **hitoma(chi)gao** look of expectation
人後 **jingo** not as good as others
人面獣心 **jinmen-jūshin** human face but brutal heart
人相 **ninsō** facial features, physiognomy
人相占 **ninsō urana(i)** divination by facial features
人相学 **ninsōgaku** physiognomy
人相見 **ninsōmi** physiognomist
人相書 **ninsōga(ki)** description of one's looks
人柄 **hitogara** character, personality; personal appearance
人柱 **hitobashira** human sacrifice
人為 **jin'i** human agency, artifice
人為的 **jin'iteki** artificial
人食 **hitoku(i)** man-eating, cannibalism
人食人種 **hitoku(i) jinshu** cannibals

10 人倫 **jinrin** human relations, morality
人畜 **jinchiku** men and animals
人真似 **hitomane** mimicry, imitations
人差指 **hitosa(shi) yubi** index finger
人員 **jin'in** personnel, staff, crew
人員整理 **jin'in seiri** personnel cutback
人家 **jinka** a human habitation, dwelling
人格 **jinkaku** character, personality
人格化 **jinkakuka** personification
人格者 **jinkakusha** man of character
人殺 **hitogoro(shi)** murder; murderer
人脈 **jinmyaku** (network of) personal connections
人骨 **jinkotsu** human bones
人称 **ninshō** person, personal (in grammar)
人笑 **hitowara(ware)** laughingstock
人馬 **jinba** men and horses
11 人達 **hitotachi** people
人道 **jindō** humanity; sidewalk
人道主義 **jindō shugi** humanitarianism
人探 **hitosaga(shi)** searching for someone
人寄 **hitoyo(se)** an attraction, a draw
人望 **jinbō** popularity
人情 **ninjō** human feelings, humanity, kindness
人情味 **ninjōmi** human interest, kindness
人魚 **ningyo** mermaid, merman
12 人違 **hitochiga(i)** mistaken identity
人喰 **hitoku(i)** man-eating, cannibalism
人喰人種 **hitoku(i) jinshu** cannibals
人智 **jinchi** human intellect, knowledge
人買 **hitoka(i)** slave trading/trader
人間 **ningen** human being, man
人間工学 **ningen kōgaku** ergonomics
人間学 **ningengaku** anthropology
人間並 **ningenna(mi)** like most people, average, common
人間味 **ningenmi** humanity, human touch
人間性 **ningensei** human nature, humanity
人間界 **ningenkai** the world of mortals
人間業 **ningenwaza** the work of man
人間嫌 **ningengira(i)** misanthropy; misanthrope
人間愛 **ningen'ai** human love
人間離 **ningenbana(re)** unworldly, superhuman
13 人傑 **jinketsu** great man
人嫌 **hitogira(i)** avoiding others' company; misanthrope
人数 **ninzū, ninzu, hitokazu** number of people
人意 **jin'i** public sentiment
人絹 **jinken** artificial silk, rayon
人跡 **jinseki** human traces/footsteps
人跡未到 **jinseki-mitō** unexplored
人跡未踏 **jinseki-mitō** unexplored

人馴 **hitona(re)** be used to people
14 人選 **jinsen** personnel selection
人徳 **jintoku, nintoku** natural/personal virtue
人様 **hitosama** other people
人種 **jinshu** race (of people)
人種改良 **jinshu kairyō** eugenics
人魂 **hitodama** spirit of a dead person; will-o'-the-wisp
人聞 **hitogi(ki)** reputation, respectability
15 人膚 **hitohada** (warmth of) the skin
人影 **hitokage, jin'ei** person's shadow, human form
人権 **jinken** human rights
人権蹂躙 **jinken jūrin** infringement of human rights
人質 **hitojichi** hostage
16 人寰 **jinkan** the world, people
人懐 **hitonatsu(koi), hitonatsu(kkoi)** amiable, sociable, friendly **hitonatsu(kashii)** lonesome (for)
人頼 **hitodano(mi)** relying on others
人頭 **jintō** number of people, population
人頭税 **jintōzei** poll tax
17 人擦 **hitozu(re)** sophistication
人糞 **jinpun** human feces, night soil
18 人類 **jinrui** mankind, man
人類学 **jinruigaku** anthropology
人類猿 **jinruien** anthropoid ape
人類愛 **jinruiai** love for mankind
人騒 **hitosawa(gase)** false alarm

———————— 2 ————————

1 一人 **hitori, ichinin** one person
一人一人 **hitori-hitori/-bitori** one by one
一人子 **hitorikko, hitorigo** an only child
一人芝居 **hitori shibai** one-man show
一人当 **hitoria(tari)** per person/capita
一人歩 **hitoriaru(ki)** walking alone; walking/existing on one's own
一人者 **hitorimono** someone alone; unmarried/single person
一人物 **ichijinbutsu** a person of consequence
一人乗 **ichininno(ri)** single-seater
一人前 **ichininmae, hitorimae** one portion/serving; full adulthood
一人残 **hitori noko(razu)** everyone
一人娘 **hitori musume** an only daughter
一人旅 **hitoritabi** traveling alone
一人息子 **hitori musuko** an only son
一人称 **ichininshō** first person (in grammar)
一人舞台 **hitori butai** unrivaled
2 二人 **futari, ninin** two persons, pair, couple
二人三脚 **ninin-sankyaku** three-legged race
二人共 **futaritomo** both (persons)
二人前 **futarimae, nininmae** enough for two, two servings

2

→ 0

二人連 **futarizu(re)** a party of two, couple
二人殺 **futarigoro(shi)** double murder
二人称 **nininshō** second person (in grammar)
二人組 **niningumi** twosome, duo
人人 **hitobito** people, everybody
十人力 **jūninriki** the strength of ten
十人十色 **jūnin-toiro** Tastes differ. To each his own.
十人並 **jūninna(mi)** average, ordinary
3 三人 **sannin** three people
三人称 **sanninshō** third person (in grammar)
三人組 **sanningumi** trio, threesome
工人 **kōjin** worker, craftsman
万人 **bannin, banjin** all people, everybody
万人向 **banninmu(ki)** for everyone, suiting all tastes
大人 **otona** adult **otona(shii)** gentle, quiet **taijin** giant; adult; man of virtue
大人気 **otonage(nai)** childish, puerile
大人物 **daijinbutsu** great man
才人 **saijin** talented/accomplished person
亡人 **na(ki)hito** deceased person, the dead
千人力 **senninriki** strength of a thousand
千人針 **senninbari** soldier's good-luck waistband sewn one stitch each by a thousand women
上人 **shōnin** (Buddhist) saint, holy priest
凡人 **bonjin** ordinary person, man of mediocre ability
土人 **dojin** native, aborigine
土人形 **tsuchi ningyō** clay figure/doll
女人 **nyonin** woman
女人禁制 **nyonin kinsei** closed to women
小人 **kobito** dwarf, midget **shōnin** child **shōjin** insignificant/small-minded person
小人物 **shōjinbutsu** stingy/base person
小人数 **koninzū** small number of people
山人 **yamabito** mountain folk; hermit
4 不人気 **funinki** unpopular
不人情 **funinjō** unfeeling, callous
天人 **tennin** heavenly being **tenjin** nature/God and man
氏人 **ujihito, ujiudo, ujindo** clansman
五人組 **goningumi** five-family unit; five-man group
五人囃子 **goninbayashi** five court-musician dolls
夫人 **fujin** wife, married woman, Mrs.
仁人 **jinnin** man of benevolence
友人 **yūjin** friend
文人 **bunjin** literary man
文人画 **bunjinga** painting in the literary artist's style
公人 **kōjin** a public figure
5 半人前 **hanninmae** half portion; half a man

本人 **honnin** the person himself, the said person, the principal
生人形 **i(ki)ningyō** lifelike doll; living doll
世人 **sejin** people, the public/world
仙人 **sennin** mountain-dwelling wizard; hermit-like otherworldly man
仙人掌 **saboten** cactus
代人 **dainin** proxy, deputy, substitute
他人 **tanin** someone else, others, outsider
付人 **tsu(ke)bito** attendant, assistant, chaperone
玄人 **kurōto** expert, professional
玄人筋 **kurōtosuji** professionals
外人 **gaijin** foreigner
用人 **yōnin** steward, factotum
巨人 **kyojin** giant
好人物 **kōjinbutsu** good-natured person
犯人 **hannin** criminal, culprit, offender
囚人 **shūjin** prisoner, convict
四人 **yonin** four people
四人乗 **yoninno(ri)** four-seater
四人組 **yoningumi** group/gang of four, foursome
白人 **hakujin** a white, Caucasian
白人種 **hakujinshu** white race
主人 **shujin** master; one's husband
主人公 **shujinkō** main character, hero (of a story)
主人役 **shujin'yaku** host(ess)
6 多人数 **taninzū** a large number of people
死人 **shinin** dead person, the dead
西人 **seijin** a Westerner
仲人 **nakōdo, chūnin** go-between, matchmaker
全人 **zenjin** well-balanced person
全人代 **Zenjindai** (Chinese) National People's Congress (short for 全国人民代表大会)
全人格 **zenjinkaku** one's whole personality
全人教育 **zenjin kyōiku** well-rounded education, education for the whole man
全人類 **zenjinrui** all mankind
防人 **sakimori** soldiers garrisoned in Kyūshū (historical)
邦人 **hōjin** fellow countryman; a Japanese
老人 **rōjin** old man/person, the old/aged
同人 **dōjin, dōnin** the same person, said person; clique, fraternity, coterie
同人雑誌 **dōjin zasshi** literary coterie magazine, small magazine
至人 **shijin** man of utmost spiritual/moral cultivation
先人 **senjin** predecessor
扱人 **atsuka(i)nin** person in charge
名人 **meijin** master, expert, virtuoso
名人肌 **meijinhada** artist's

temperamentalness
名人芸 **meijingei** virtuosity
行人 **kōjin** passerby
当人 **tōnin** the one concerned, the said
 person, the person himself
有人 **yūjin** manned
百人一首 **hyakunin-isshu** 100 poems by
 100 poets (a collection of 100 *tanka*;
 basis for the popular card game *uta
 karuta*)
各人 **kakujin** each person, everyone
成人 **seijin** adult
成人式 **seijinshiki** Coming-of-Age-Day (Jan.
 15) ceremony
米人 **beijin** an American
舟人 **funabito** boatman, sailor; passenger
7 里人 **satobito** villagers, countryfolk
伶人 **reijin** musician
住人 **jūnin** resident, inhabitant
佞人 **neijin** sycophant, flatterer
何人 **nannin** how many people
 nanpito(mo) everyone, all
余人 **yojin, yonin** others, other people
求人 **kyūjin** seeking workers, Help Wanted
求人広告 **kyūjin kōkoku** help-wanted ad
別人 **betsujin** different person; changed man
対人 **taijin** personal
吾人 **gojin** we
豆人形 **mame-ningyō** miniature doll
狂人 **kyōjin** insane person, lunatic
役人 **yakunin** public official
役人風 **yakunin kaze** air of official dignity
役人根性 **yakunin konjō** bureaucratism
芸人 **geinin** artiste, performer
杣人 **somabito** woodcutter, woodsman
村人 **murabito** villager
私人 **shijin** private individual
町人 **chōnin** merchant
8 非人 **hinin** beggar; outcast
非人道 **hijindō** inhumanity
非人情 **hininjō** inhuman, unfeeling
非人間的 **hiningenteki** inhuman, impersonal
毒人参 **doku ninjin** poison hemlock
佳人 **kajin** beautiful woman
供人 **tomobito** companion
盲人 **mōjin** blind person
法人 **hōjin** juridical person, legal entity,
 corporation
法人税 **hōjinzei** corporation tax
知人 **chijin** an acquaintance
奇人 **kijin** an eccentric
英人 **eijin** Briton, Englishman
若人 **wakōdo** young person, a youth
官人 **kanjin** an official
牧人 **bokujin** herder, ranch hand
怪人物 **kaijinbutsu** mystery man

或人 **a(ru) hito** somebody, a certain person
武人 **bujin** military man
門人 **monjin** pupil, disciple, follower
9 俗人 **zokujin** layman; worldly-minded
 person
俑人 **yōjin** doll, effigy
軍人 **gunjin** soldier, military man
変人 **henjin** an eccentric
前人 **zenjin** predecessor, former people
前人未到 **zenjin-mitō** untrodden, unexplored
美人 **bijin** beautiful woman
通人 **tsūjin** man about town
活人 **katsujin** a living person
活人画 **katsujinga** costumed people posing
 in a tableau vivant
海人 **ama, kaijin** fisherman
指人形 **yubi ningyō** finger/glove puppet
要人 **yōjin** important person, leading figure
狩人 **karyūdo, kariudo** hunter
後人 **kōjin** those coming later, posterity
茶人 **chajin, sajin** tea-ceremony expert;
 an eccentric
客人 **kyakujin, marōdo** visitor, guest
県人 **kenjin** native/resident of a prefecture
県人会 **kenjinkai** an association of people
 from the same prefecture
神人 **shinjin** gods and men; demigod
故人 **kojin** the deceased
科人 **toganin** criminal, offender
思人 **omo(i)bito** sweetheart, lover
食人種 **shokujinshu** a cannibal race
10 俳人 **haijin** haiku poet
倚人 **kijin** deformed/maimed person, cripple
個人 **kojin** private person, individual
個人主義 **kojin shugi** individualism
個人的 **kojinteki** individual, personal, self-
 centered
個人差 **kojinsa** differences between
 individuals
個人教授 **kojin kyōju** private lessons
都人 **miyakobito, tojin** people of the capital;
 townspeople
都人士 **tojinshi** people of the capital
恋人 **koibito** sweetheart, boyfriend, girlfriend
真人 **shinjin** true man
真人間 **maningen** honest man, good citizen
原人 **genjin** primitive/early man
遊人 **aso(bi)nin** gambler; jobless person
浦人 **urabito** seaside dweller
浪人 **rōnin** lordless samurai; unaffiliated/
 jobless person, high-school graduate
 studying to pass a university entrance
 exam
流人 **runin** an exile
捕人 **to(raware)bito** captives
哲人 **tetsujin** wise man, philosopher

徒人 **adabito** fickle person
家人 **kajin** the family **kenin** retainer
宮人 **miyabito** courtier
党人 **tōjin** party member, partisan
島人 **tōjin** islander
唐人 **Tōjin, karabito** a Chinese/foreigner
殺人 **satsujin** murder
殺人犯 **satsujinhan** (the crime of) murder
殺人的 **satsujinteki** murderous, deadly,
　　　terrific, hectic, cutthroat
殺人鬼 **satsujinki** bloodthirsty killer
殺人罪 **satsujinzai** murder
時人 **jijin** contemporaries
旅人 **tabibito, tabinin, ryojin** traveler,
　　　wayfarer
恩人 **onjin** benefactor, patron
病人 **byōnin** sick person, patient, invalid
素人 **shirōto** amateur, layman
素人下宿 **shirōto geshuku** boarding house
素人目 **shirōtome** untrained eye
素人芸 **shirōtogei** amateur's skill
素人臭 **shirōtokusa(i)** amateurish
素人離 **shirōtobana(re)** free of amateurish-
　　　ness
粋人 **suijin** man of refined tastes
11 野人 **yajin** a rustic, bumpkin, uncouth
　　　person; private citizen
偶人 **gūjin** puppet, doll
偏人 **henjin** an eccentric
商人 **shōnin** merchant, trader, shopkeeper
達人 **tatsujin** expert, master
婦人 **fujin** lady, woman
婦人用 **fujin'yō** for ladies, women's
婦人会 **fujinkai** ladies' society
婦人科 **fujinka** gynecology
婦人科医 **fujinkai** gynecologist
婦人病 **fujinbyō** women's diseases/disorders
婦人警官 **fujin keikan** policewoman
猟人 **kariudo, karyūdo, ryōjin** hunter
菊人形 **kiku ningyō** chrysanthemum-
　　　decorated doll
常人 **jōjin** ordinary person
黒人 **kokujin** a black, Negro
悪人 **akunin** evildoer, scoundrel, the wicked
情人 **jōjin** lover, sweetheart
異人 **ijin** foreigner; different person
異人種 **ijinshu** different race
盗人 **nusubito, nusutto** thief
船人 **funabito** seaman; passenger
鳥人 **chōjin** birdman, aviator
12 偉人 **ijin** great man
傍人 **bōjin** bystander
勤人 **tsuto(me)nin** office/white-collar worker
蛮人 **banjin** barbarian, savage
善人 **zennin** virtuous man, good people
満人 **Manjin** a Manchurian

堅人 **katajin** honest/serious person
超人 **chōjin** superman
超人的 **chōjinteki** superhuman
尋人 **tazu(ne)bito** person being sought,
　　　missing person
落人 **ochibito, ochiudo, ochūdo** refugee;
　　　fugitive; deserter
廃人 **haijin** a cripple/invalid
無人 **mujin, munin** uninhabited; unmanned
　　　bunin shortage of help
無人地帯 **mujin chitai** no man's land
無人島 **mujintō** uninhabited island
雇人 **yato(i)nin** employee; servant
幾人 **ikunin** how many people
番人 **bannin** watchman, guard
衆人 **shūjin** the people/public
訴人 **sonin** suer, plaintiff
証人 **shōnin** witness
証人台 **shōnindai** the witness stand/box
証人席 **shōninseki** the witness stand/box
貴人 **kijin** nobleman, dignitary
閑人 **kanjin, himajin** man of leisure
13 傑人 **ketsujin** outstanding person
傭人 **yōnin** employee
義人 **gijin** righteous/public-spirited man
漢人 **Kanjin** a Chinese
猿人 **enjin** ape-man
楽人 **gakujin** musician, minstrel
　　　rakujin person living at ease
聖人 **seijin** sage, saint, holy man
数人 **sūnin** several persons
愛人 **aijin** lover
愚人 **gujin** fool, idiot
新人 **shinjin** newcomer, new face
矮人 **waijin** dwarf, midget
罪人 **zainin** criminal **tsumibito** sinner
痴人 **chijin** fool, idiot
詩人 **shijin** poet
雅人 **gajin** man of refined taste
預人 **azu(kari)nin** person with whom
　　　something is entrusted, possessor
14 厭人 **enjin** misanthropy
厭人者 **enjinsha** misanthrope
厭人癖 **enjinheki** misanthropy
寡人 **kajin** I (used by royalty)
歌人 **kajin** poet
読人 **yo(mi)bito** author of a poem
読人知 **yo(mi)bito shi(razu)** anonymous
　　　(poem)
15 隣人 **rinjin** neighbor
隣人愛 **rinjin'ai** love of one's fellow man
蔵人 **kurōdo, kurando** imperial-archives
　　　keeper
稼人 **kase(gi)nin** breadwinner; hard worker
諸人 **morobito** everyone
請人 **u(ke)nin** guarantor

16 操人形 **ayatsu(ri)ningyō** puppet, marionette
   賢人 **kenjin** wise man, sage, the wise
17 擬人 **gijin** personification
   擬人化 **gijinka** personification
   擬人法 **gijinhō** personification
   藁人形 **wara ningyō** straw effigy
   癈人 **haijin** a cripple
18 韓人 **Kanjin** a Korean (historical)
   職人 **shokunin** craftsman, workman
   雛人形 **hina ningyō** (Girls' Festival) doll
   類人猿 **ruijin'en** anthropoid ape
   騒人 **sōjin** man of letters, poet
19 麗人 **reijin** beautiful woman
21 蠟人形 **rōningyō** wax figure

────────── 3 ──────────

1 一私人 **isshijin, ichishijin** a private individual
   一個人 **ichikojin, ikkojin** a private individual
   一般人 **ippannin, ippanjin** an ordinary
   person
2 二重人格 **nijū jinkaku** double/split personality
   人非人 **ninpinin** man of brutal nature
   人食人種 **hitoku(i) jinshu** cannibals
   人喰人種 **hitoku(i) jinshu** cannibals
3 大商人 **daishōnin** great merchant
   大悪人 **daiakunin** utter scoundrel
   大罪人 **daizainin** great criminal
   下手人 **geshunin** perpetrator, culprit, criminal
   下宿人 **geshukunin** lodger, boarder
   小作人 **kosakunin** tenant farmer
   小役人 **koyakunin** petty/minor official
4 天地人 **tenchijin** heaven, earth, and man
   内地人 **naichijin** homelanders; people on
   Honshū
   五月人形 **gogatsu ningyō** Boys' Festival
   dolls
   毛唐人 **ketōjin** hairy barbarian, foreigner
   中心人物 **chūshin jinbutsu** central figure,
   key person
   中華人民共和国 **Chūka Jinmin Kyōwakoku**
   People's Republic of China
   中国人 **chūgokujin** a Chinese
   文化人 **bunkajin** man of culture
   支払人 **shiharainin** payer
   支配人 **shihainin** manager
   止宿人 **shishukunin** lodger
   公証人 **kōshōnin** notary public
   引受人 **hikiukenin** guarantor, acceptor (of a
   bill), underwriter
   引取人 **hikitorinin** claimant; caretaker
   日本人 **Nihonjin, Nipponjin** a Japanese
   火星人 **kaseijin** a Martian
5 北欧人 **Hokuōjin** a Northern European, a
   Scandinavian

民間人 **minkanjin** private citizen
半病人 **hanbyōnin** sickly person
未亡人 **mibōjin** widow
弁護人 **bengonin** counsel, defender, advocate
世界人 **sekaijin** citizen of the world,
   cosmopolitan
世捨人 **yosu(te)bito** recluse, hermit
世話人 **sewanin** go-between, intermediary;
   sponsor; caretaker
仕掛人 **shika(ke)nin** intriguer, schemer,
   plotter
代理人 **dairinin** agent, proxy, substitute,
   representative
他国人 **takokujin** foreigner, stranger
令夫人 **reifujin** Mrs., Lady, Madam; your wife
外国人 **gaikokujin** foreigner
犯罪人 **hanzainin** criminal, offender, convict
穴居人 **kekkyojin** caveman
立会人 **tachiainin** observer, witness
6 両替人 **ryōgaenin** money changer
   西欧人 **Seiōjin** Westerner, European
   西洋人 **seiyōjin** a Westerner
   仲裁人 **chūsainin** arbitrator, mediator
   仲買人 **nakaga(i)nin** broker, agent
   全国人民代表大会 **Zenkoku Jinmin Daihyō
   Taikai** (Chinese) National People's
   Congress
   近代人 **kindaijin** modern person
   同一人 **dōitsunin** the same person
   同一人物 **dōitsu jinbutsu** the same person
   同居人 **dōkyonin** person living with the
   family, lodger
   名宛人 **naatenin** addressee
   行商人 **gyōshōnin** peddler, traveling
   salesman
   有名人 **yūmeijin** celebrity
   有罪人 **yūzaijin** guilty person
   自然人 **shizenjin** natural (uncultured)
   person; natural (not juridical) person
7 赤他人 **aka (no) tanin** a perfect/total
   stranger
   告訴人 **kokusonin** complainant
   花盗人 **hananusubito** one who steals
   flowers or cherry-blossom branches
   芸能人 **geinōjin** an entertainment personality, star
   牢役人 **rōyakunin** jailer
   社会人 **shakaijin** full member of society
   見物人 **kenbutsunin** spectator, sightseer
   見舞人 **mima(i)nin** sympathizer, visitor
8 東洋人 **tōyōjin** an Oriental
   使用人 **shiyōnin** employee
   受取人 **uketorinin** recipient, payee
   受信人 **jushinnin** addressee
   知識人 **chishikijin** an intellectual
   参考人 **sankōnin** person to consult

2
亻 0 ←
冫
孑
阝
卩
刂
力
又
亠
十
厂
辶
冂
几
匸

2

→0 亻 冫 孑 阝 卩 力 刀 刂 又 亠 亠 十 卜 勹 冖 冫 厂 辶 冂 几 匚

参観人 **sankannin** visitor
英国人 **Eikokujin** Briton, Englishman
苦労人 **kurōnin** worldly-wise man
怪我人 **keganin** injured person, the wounded
所持人 **shojinin** holder, bearer
取扱人 **toriatsukainin** agent, person in charge
9 発起人 **hokkinin** promoter, originator
発頭人 **hottōnin** ringleader, originator
保証人 **hoshōnin** guarantor
南蛮人 **nanbanjin** southern barbarians, the early Europeans
急病人 **kyūbyōnin** emergency patient/case
通行人 **tsūkōnin** passer-by, pedestrian
浮浪人 **furōnin** vagrant, street bum
持参人 **jisannin** bearer (of a check)
後見人 **kōkennin** (legal) guardian; assistant
面会人 **menkainin** visitor, caller
相続人 **sōzokunin** heir
看護人 **kangonin** male nurse
10 都会人 **tokaijin** city resident, urban dweller
帰化人 **kikajin** naturalized citizen
差出人 **sashidashinin** sender, return address
差配人 **sahainin** landlord's agent
原始人 **genshijin** primitive man
振出人 **furidashinin** remitter, issuer
荷送人 **nioku(ri)nin** shipper
旅芸人 **tabigeinin** itinerant performer
旅商人 **tabishōnin, tabiakindo** peddler, traveling salesman
被告人 **hikokunin** defendant
素町人 **suchōnin** common townspeople
素浪人 **surōnin** (mere) lordless retainer
料理人 **ryōrinin** a cook
財界人 **zaikaijin** financier, businessman
配達人 **haitatsunin** deliveryman
11 野蛮人 **yabanjin** savage, barbarian
商売人 **shōbainin** merchant; professional
貧乏人 **binbōnin** poor man, pauper
運搬人 **unpannin** porter, carrier
掃除人 **sōjinin** cleaner, janitor
張本人 **chōhonnin** ringleader
黄色人種 **ōshoku jinshu** the yellow race
宿泊人 **shukuhakunin** lodger, boarder, guest
現代人 **gendaijin** people today
産婦人科 **sanfujinka** obstetrics and gynecology
異邦人 **ihōjin** foreigner, stranger
細工人 **saikunin** craftsman, artisan
経済人 **keizaijin** economic man
第一人者 **dai-ichininsha** foremost/leading person
第一人称 **dai-ichininshō** first person (in grammar)
第二人称 **dai-nininshō** second person (in grammar)
第三人称 **dai-sanninshō** third person (in grammar)
販売人 **hanbainin** seller, agent
12 傍聴人 **bōchōnin** hearer, auditor, audience
普通人 **futsūjin** average person
渡世人 **toseinin** gambler, gangster
媒妁人 **baishakunin** matchmaker, go-between
媒酌人 **baishakunin** matchmaker, go-between
御家人 **gokenin** a lower-grade vassal
落札人 **rakusatsunin** successful bidder
極悪人 **gokuakunin** utter scoundrel
朝鮮人 **Chōsenjin** a Korean
朝鮮人参 **Chōsen ninjin** ginseng
訴訟人 **soshōnin** plaintiff
訴願人 **sogannin** petitioner, appellant
証拠人 **shōkonin** witness
貴婦人 **kifujin** lady
集金人 **shūkinnin** bill collector
集配人 **shūhainin** postman
雲上人 **unjōbito** a court noble
間借人 **maga(ri)nin** lodger, roomer
13 虞美人草 **gubijinsō** field poppy
義理人情 **giri-ninjō** duty versus/and human feelings
蒙古人 **Mōkojin** a Mongol(ian)
殿上人 **tenjōbito, denjōbito** court noble
意中人 **ichū (no) hito** the one in one's thoughts, one's beloved
褐色人種 **kasshoku jinshu** the brown races
賃借人 **chinshakunin** lessee
賃貸人 **chintainin** lessor
14 選挙人 **senkyonin** voter, elector
管財人 **kanzainin** trustee, administrator
管理人 **kanrinin** manager, superintendent
読書人 **dokushojin** (avid) book reader
15 器量人 **kiryōjin** talented person
監守人 **kanshunin** custodian, (forest) ranger
誰一人 **dare hitori (mo)** (with negative) no one
請負人 **ukeoinin** contractor
調理人 **chōrinin** a cook
16 積出人 **tsu(mi)da(shi)nin** shipper
謀反人 **muhonnin** rebel, conspirator
謀叛人 **muhonnin** rebel, conspirator
賢夫人 **kenpujin** wise wife
17 闇商人 **yamishōnin** black marketeer
20 競売人 **kyōbainin** auctioneer
譲渡人 **jōtonin** assignor, grantor
23 鑑定人 **kanteinin** appraiser, expert (witness)

──────── 4 ────────

1 一人一人 **hitori-hitori, hitori-bitori** one by one
2 八方美人 **happō bijin** one who is affable to everybody
4 公爵夫人 **kōshaku fujin** princess, duchess

月下氷人 **gekka hyōjin** matchmaker, go-
between, cupid
5 白系露人 **hakkei rojin** a White Russian,
Byelorussian
田夫野人 **denpu-yajin** a rustic, country
bumpkin, yokel
6 同名異人 **dōmei-ijin** different person of the
same name
在外邦人 **zaigai hōjin** Japanese living
abroad
在留外人 **zairyū gaijin** foreign residents
在留邦人 **zairyū hōjin** Japanese residing
abroad
7 吟遊詩人 **gin'yū shijin** troubadour, minstrel
社団法人 **shadan hōjin** corporate juridical
person
9 侯爵夫人 **kōshaku fujin** marchioness
10 桂冠詩人 **keikan shijin** poet laureate
被選挙人 **hisenkyonin** person eligible for
election
財団法人 **zaidan hōjin** (incorporated)
foundation
11 第三国人 **dai-sangokujin** third-country
national
12 傍若無人 **bōjaku-bujin** arrogant, insolent
御用商人 **goyō shōnin** purveyor to the
government
14 総支配人 **sōshihainin** general manager

───────── 5 ─────────
4 水先案内人 **mizusaki annainin** (harbor) pilot
5 弁護依頼人 **bengo irainin** client
8 国選弁護人 **kokusen bengonin** court-
appointed defense counsel

从 → 従 **3i7.3**

───────── 1 ─────────

个 → 個 **2a8.36**

个 → 箇 **6f8.15**

───────── 2 ─────────

2a2.1
仔
SHI, ko (animal) offspring

───────── 1 ─────────
4 仔犬 **koinu** puppy
11 仔細 **shisai** reasons, circumstances; significance; details

仂 → 働 **2a11.1**

2a2.2
什
JŪ utensil; ten

───────── 1 ─────────
8 什宝 **jūhō** treasured article
什物 **jūmotsu** utensil; furniture, fixtures;
treasure
15 什器 **jūki** utensil, appliance, furniture

2a2.3
仆
FU fall down, collapse, overturn

2a2.4
仇
KYŪ, ada, kataki enemy; enmity;
revenge; harm, evil, ruin; invasion

───────── 1 ─────────
10 仇討 **adau(chi)** vendetta, revenge
15 仇敵 **kyūteki** bitter enemy

───────── 2 ─────────
10 恋仇 **koigataki** one's rival in love
12 復仇 **fukkyū, fukukyū** revenge

2a2.5 / 583
仏 佛
BUTSU Buddha, Buddhism
FUTSU France, French
hotoke Buddha; Buddhist
image; the dead

───────── 1 ─────────
2 仏力 **butsuriki** the power of Buddha
4 仏文 **Futsubun** French, French literature
仏心 **busshin, hotokegokoro** Buddha's heart
6 仏印 **Futsu-In** French Indochina
仏寺 **butsuji** Buddhist temple
仏名 **butsumyō** a Buddha's name
仏式 **busshiki** Buddhist rites
7 仏陀 **Butsuda, Budda** Buddha
8 仏画 **butsuga** Buddhist painting
仏事 **butsuji** Buddhist memorial service
仏舎利 **busshari** Buddha's ashes
仏典 **butten** Buddhist literature/scriptures
仏法 **buppō** Buddhism
仏法僧 **buppōsō** Buddha, doctrine, and
priesthood; broad-billed roller, Japanese
scops owl
仏者 **bussha** a Buddhist; Buddhist priest

仏具 **butsugu** Buddhist altar articles
仏門 **butsumon** Buddhism, priesthood
9 仏前 **butsuzen** before Buddha, before the tablet of the deceased
10 仏徒 **butto** a Buddhist
仏家 **bukke** Buddhist temple/priest
仏座 **butsuza** seat of a Buddhist idol
仏書 **bussho** Buddhist literature/scriptures
仏教 **bukkyō** Buddhism
11 仏道 **butsudō** Buddhism
仏堂 **butsudō** Buddhist temple
仏経 **bukkyō** Buddhist sutras
仏頂面 **butchōzura** sour face, pout, scowl
12 仏葬 **bussō** Buddhist funeral
仏間 **butsuma** Buddhist altar room
13 仏僧 **bussō** Buddhist priest
仏滅 **butsumetsu** Buddha's death; unlucky day
仏殿 **butsuden** Buddhist temple
14 仏像 **butsuzō** image of Buddha
仏様 **hotoke-sama** a Buddha; deceased person
仏説 **bussetsu** Buddha's teachings
仏閣 **bukkaku** Buddhist temple
仏領 **Futsuryō** French possession/territory
16 仏壇 **butsudan** household Buddhist altar
19 仏蘭西 **Furansu** France

─────── 2 ───────

3 大仏 **daibutsu** huge image of Buddha
大仏殿 **daibutsuden** temple with a huge image of Buddha
小仏 **kobotoke** small image of Buddha
4 木仏 **kibotoke, kibutsu** wooden Buddha
日仏 **Nichi-Futsu** Japan and France
5 生仏 **i(ki)botoke** a living Buddha, incarnation of Buddha
石仏 **ishibotoke, sekibutsu** stone image of Buddha
6 成仏 **jōbutsu** attain Nirvana; die
米仏 **Bei-Futsu** America and France
8 念仏 **nenbutsu** Buddhist invocation (of Amitabha)
金仏 **kanabutsu** a metal Buddha
9 独仏 **Doku-Futsu** Germany and France
神仏 **shinbutsu** gods and Buddha; Shinto and Buddhism
10 秘仏 **hibutsu** Buddhist image kept hidden
12 普仏 **Fu-Futsu** Franco-Prussian (War)
渡仏 **to-Futsu** going to France
喉仏 **nodobotoke** Adam's apple
13 滞仏 **tai-Futsu** staying in France
15 駐仏 **chū-Futsu** resident/stationed in France
16 儒仏 **jubutsu** Confucianism and Buddhism
17 濡仏 **nu(re)botoke** Buddhist image exposed to the weather

20 灌仏会 **kanbutsue** Buddha's-birthday
21 露仏 **Ro-Futsu** Russia and France

─────── 3 ───────

3 大乗仏教 **Daijō Bukkyō** Mahayana Buddhism, Great-Vehicle Buddhism
小乗仏教 **Shōjō bukkyō** Hinayana/Lesser-vehicle Buddhism
6 多情仏心 **tajō-busshin** tenderheartedness
8 空念仏 **karanenbutsu** perfunctory praying, empty/fruitless talk
12 御陀仏 **odabutsu** dead man
無縁仏 **muenbotoke** a deceased having no one to tend his grave

─────── 4 ───────

7 即身成仏 **sokushin jōbutsu** attaining Buddhahood while still alive

─────── 6 ───────

9 南無阿弥陀仏 **Namu Amida Butsu** Hail Amida Buddha

2a2.6 / 254

化 **KA** make into, transform, -ization
KE, ba(kasu) bewitch, enchant, deceive **ba(keru)** take the form of, disguise oneself as

─────── 1 ───────

0 グローバル化 **gurōbaruka** globalization
5 化生 **kasei** metaplasia, metamorphosis
化石 **kaseki** fossil
6 化合 **kagō** chemical combination
化合物 **kagōbutsu** chemical compound
化成 **kasei** transformation, chemical synthesis
7 化身 **keshin** incarnation, embodiment, manifestation
化学 **kagaku** chemistry (sometimes pronounced *bakegaku* to avoid confusion with 科学, science)
化学式 **kagaku shiki** chemical formula
化学者 **kagakusha** chemist
8 化物 **ba(ke)mono** ghost, spook
12 化粧 **keshō** makeup
化粧品 **keshōhin** cosmetics, makeup
17 化膿 **kanō** suppurate, fester
化膿菌 **kanōkin** suppurative germ
化繊 **kasen** synthetic fiber

─────── 2 ───────

3 夕化粧 **yūgeshō** evening makeup
大化 **Taika** (era, 645–650)
4 文化 **bunka** culture, civilization
Bunka (era, 1804–1818)
文化人 **bunkajin** man of culture
文化日 **Bunka (no) Hi** Culture Day (November 3)

文化史 **bunkashi** cultural history
文化的 **bunkateki** cultural
文化財 **bunkazai** cultural asset
文化祭 **bunkasai** cultural festival
分化 **bunka** specialization, differentiation
水化物 **suikabutsu** a hydrate
王化 **ōka** emperor's benevolent influence
5 生化学 **seikagaku** biochemistry
弘化 **Kōka** (era, 1844–1848)
石化 **sekka** petrify, fossilize
6 気化 **kika** vaporize
気化器 **kikaki** carburetor
羽化 **uka** grow wings
孵化 **fuka** hatch, incubate (eggs)
同化 **dōka** assimilation, adaptation
光化学 **kōkagaku** photochemistry
光化学スモッグ **kōkagaku sumoggu** photochemical smog
光化学反応 **kōkagaku hannō, hikari kagaku hannō** photochemical reaction
劣化 **rekka** deterioration, degradation
7 赤化 **sekka** communization
乳化 **nyūka** emulsification
8 厚化粧 **atsugeshō** heavy makeup
退化 **taika** retrogression, degeneration
青化物 **seikabutsu** a cyanide
欧化 **ōka** Europeanization, Westernization
9 俗化 **zokka** vulgarization, popularization
変化 **henka** change **henge** goblin, apparition
美化 **bika** beautification; glorification
造化 **zōka** creation, nature
風化 **fūka** weathering; efflorescence
浄化 **jōka** purification
茶化 **chaka(su)** make fun of
宣化 **Senka** (emperor, 535–539)
炭化 **tanka** carbonization
炭化水素 **tanka suiso** hydrocarbon
炭化物 **tankabutsu** carbide
神化 **shinka** deification, apotheosis
10 帰化 **kika** become naturalized
帰化人 **kikajin** naturalized citizen
進化 **shinka** evolution
進化論 **shinkaron** theory of evolution
進化論者 **shinkaronsha** evolutionist
消化 **shōka** digest
消化不良 **shōka furyō** indigestion
消化剤 **shōkazai** aid to digestion
消化液 **shōkaeki** digestive fluid/juices
消化腺 **shōkasen** digestive glands
消化管 **shōkakan** alimentary canal, digestive tract
消化器 **shōkaki** digestive organs
骨化 **kokka** ossification
時化 **shike(ru)** be stormy; be badly off; be gloomy
教化 **kyōka** culture, education, enlightenment

純化 **junka** purification
11 道化 **dōke** clowning
道化方 **dōkekata** clown
道化役 **dōkeyaku** clown
道化者 **dōkemono** jester, joker, wag
道化師 **dōkeshi** clown
深化 **shinka** deepening
液化 **ekika** liquefy
強化 **kyōka** strengthen, fortify
理化学 **rikagaku** physics and chemistry
悪化 **akka** worsening, deterioration
軟化 **nanka** softening
転化 **tenka** change, be transformed
転化糖 **tenkatō** inverted sugar
12 硬化 **kōka** hardening
硬化油 **kōkayu** hydrogenated oil
硬化症 **kōkashō** sclerosis
開化 **kaika** civilization, enlightenment **Kaika** (emperor, 158–98 B.C.)
順化 **junka** acclimate
13 溶化 **yōka** melt
塩化ビニル **enka biniru** vinyl chloride
寝化粧 **negeshō** makeup/toilet before retiring
孵化 **fuka** incubation, hatching
感化 **kanka** influence, inspiration, reform
感化院 **kankain** reformatory
電化 **denka** electrification
馴化 **junka** acclimate
14 遷化 **senge** death/demise (of a high priest)
徳化 **tokka** moral influence/reform
磁化 **jika** magnetization
緑化 **ryokka** tree planting
酸化 **sanka** oxidation
酸化物 **sankabutsu** oxide
醇化 **junka** refine, purify
15 劇化 **gekika** dramatization
権化 **gonge** incarnation, embodiment
膠化 **kōka** gelatinize, change into a colloid
霊化 **reika** spiritualization
16 激化 **gekka, gekika** intensification, aggravation
濃化 **nōka** thicken, concentrate
薄化粧 **usugeshō** light makeup
糖化 **tōka** convert to sugar
融化 **yūka** deliquesce, soften
18 類化 **ruika** assimilate, incorporate

───────── 3 ─────────
1 一元化 **ichigenka** unification, centralization
一般化 **ippanka** generalization, popularization
一酸化炭素 **issanka tanso** carbon monoxide
2 人格化 **jinkakuka** personification
3 工業化 **kōgyōka** industrialization
大衆化 **taishūka** popularization
女性化 **joseika** feminization

2

→2

亻
⺆
�) 孑
阝
卩
刂
力
又
⼇
⼗
⼞
⼃
⼅
⼂
厂
⻌
冂
几
匚

4 不同化 **fudōka** nonassimilation
不消化 **fushōka** indigestion
不消化物 **fushōkabutsu** indigestible food
水酸化物 **suisankabutsu** a hydroxide
日本化 **nihonka** Japanization, Nipponization
5 民主化 **minshuka** democratization
民営化 **min'eika** privatization, denationalization
民衆化 **minshūka** popularization
世俗化 **sezokuka** secularization
正常化 **seijōka** normalization
白熱化 **hakunetsuka** heat up, reach a climax
6 気体化 **kitaika** gasify, vaporize
西欧化 **Seiōka** Westernization
西洋化 **seiyōka** Westernization
合理化 **gōrika** rationalization, streamlining
近代化 **kindaika** modernization
尖鋭化 **sen'eika** become acute/radicalized
有機化学 **yūki kagaku** organic chemistry
成文化 **seibunka** put in writing, codify
自由化 **jiyūka** liberalization
7 体系化 **taikeika** systematize, organize
形式化 **keishikika** formalization
局地化 **kyokuchika** localization
社会化 **shakaika** socialization
初期化 **shokika** initialization
8 表面化 **hyōmenka** come to the surface/fore, become an issue
事業化 **jigyōka** industrialization
法文化 **hōbunka** enact into law
実体化 **jittaika** substantiate
官僚化 **kanryōka** bureaucratization
定型化 **teikeika** standardization
空洞化 **kūdōka** hollowing out, deindustrialization
国民化 **kokuminka** nationalization
国有化 **kokuyūka** nationalization
国営化 **kokueika** nationalization
国際化 **kokusaika** internationalization
明文化 **meibunka** state explicitly, stipulate
具体化 **gutaika** embodiment, materialization
具象化 **gushōka** make concrete
9 専門化 **senmonka** specialization
通俗化 **tsūzokuka** popularization
単純化 **tanjunka** simplification
炭水化物 **tansuikabutsu** carbohydrates
映画化 **eigaka** make a movie version of
神格化 **shinkakuka** deification
恒久化 **kōkyūka** perpetuation
省力化 **shōryokuka** labor saving
10 弱体化 **jakutaika** weakening
骨軟化症 **kotsunankashō** osteomalacia
11 偶像化 **gūzōka** idolize
商業化 **shōgyōka** commercialization
過酸化 **kasanka** (hydrogen) peroxide
淡水化 **tansuika** desalin(iz)ation

深刻化 **shinkokuka** intensification, aggravation
脳軟化症 **nōnankashō** encephalomalacia
理想化 **risōka** idealize
現代化 **gendaika** modernization
現実化 **genjitsuka** realize, turn (dreams) into reality
現金化 **genkinka** convert to cash, cash (a check)
情報化社会 **jōhōka shakai** information-oriented society
規格化 **kikakuka** standardization
14 概念化 **gainenka** generalization
慢性化 **manseika** become chronic
複雑化 **fukuzatsuka** complication
誤魔化 **gomaka(su)** cheat, deceive; gloss over; tamper with, doctor
15 標準化 **hyōjunka** standardization
16 機動化 **kidōka** mechanization
機械化 **kikaika** mechanization, mechanized
17 擬人化 **gijinka** personification

――――――――――― 4 ―――――――――――
3 千変万化 **senpen-banka** innumerable/kaleidoscopic changes, immense variety
4 文明開化 **bunmei kaika** civilization and enlightenment
少年感化院 **shōnen kankain** reform school
6 有声音化 **yūseionka** vocalization, voicing
11 動脈硬化 **dōmyaku kōka** hardening of the arteries
動脈硬化症 **dōmyaku kōkashō** arteriosclerosis
経時変化 **keiji henka** change with the passage of time, aging
12 植民地化 **shokuminchika** colonization
無形文化財 **mukei-bunkazai** intangible cultural asset
14 語尾変化 **gobi henka** inflection

2a2.7

仍   **JŌ** due to, therefore, moreover

2a2.8 / 1619

仁   **JIN, NI** virtue, benevolence; man
NIN kernel

――――――――――― 1 ―――――――――――
2 仁人 **jinnin** man of benevolence
4 仁王 **Niō** Deva kings (guarding temple gate)
仁王門 **Niōmon** temple gate guarded by two fierce Deva king statues
仁心 **jinshin** benevolence, humanity
5 仁平 **Ninpei** (era, 1151–1154)

仁兄 **jinkei** (term of address for a friend)
6 仁安 **Nin'an** (era, 1166–1169)
7 仁寿 **Ninju** (era, 851–854)
仁君 **jinkun** benevolent ruler
8 仁治 **Ninji** (era, 1240–1243)
仁明 **Ninmyō** (emperor, 833–850)
仁者 **jinsha** man of virtue
仁和 **Ninna** (era, 885–889)
9 仁政 **jinsei** benevolent rule
10 仁恵 **jinkei** graciousness, benevolence, mercy
11 仁術 **jinjutsu** benevolent act; healing art
13 仁慈 **jinji** benevolence
仁義 **jingi** humanity and justice; duty; moral code (of a gang)
仁愛 **jin'ai** benevolence, charity, love
14 仁徳 **jintoku** benevolence, graciousness
Nintoku (emperor, 313–399)
16 仁賢 **Ninken** (emperor, 488–498)

——————— 2 ———————
4 不仁 **fujin** heartlessness
元仁 **Gennin** (era, 1224–1225)
天仁 **Tennin** (era, 1108–1110)
5 永仁 **Einin** (era, 1293–1299)
弘仁 **Kōnin** (era, 810–824)
6 同仁 **dōjin** impartial benevolence
光仁 **Kōnin** (emperor, 770–781)
7 応仁 **Ōnin** (era, 1467–1469)
8 垂仁 **Suinin** (emperor, 29 B.C.–70 A.D.)
建仁 **Kennin** (era, 1201–1204)
10 淳仁 **Junnin** (emperor, 758–764)
13 寛仁 **kanjin** magnanimous
Kannin (era, 1017–1020)
14 暦仁 **Ryakunin** (era, 1238–1239)
16 親仁方 **oyajikata** role of an old man

——————— 3 ———————
6 朴念仁 **bokunenjin** unsociable close-mouthed person
7 亜麻仁 **amani** linseed, flaxseed
亜麻仁油 **amaniyu** linseed oil

——————— 4 ———————
1 一視同仁 **isshi-dōjin** impartiality, universal brotherhood

分 → 分 **2o2.1**

公 → 公 **2o2.2**

2a2.9 / 453
介 **KAI** be in between, mediate; concern oneself with; shell, shellfish

——————— 1 ———————
2 介入 **kainyū** intervention
6 介在 **kaizai** lie between
8 介抱 **kaihō** nurse, care for
11 介添 **kaizo(e)** helper, assistant
13 介意 **kaii** care about, concern oneself with
16 介錯 **kaishaku** assist at harakiri

——————— 2 ———————
1 一介 **ikkai** mere, only
4 不介入 **fukainyū** noninvolvement, nonintervention
厄介 **yakkai** troublesome, burdensome; help, care
厄介払 **yakkaibara(i)** good riddance
厄介者 **yakkaimono** a dependent; nuisance
厄介物 **yakkaimono** burden, nuisance
6 仲介 **chūkai** intermediation, agency
仲介者 **chūkaisha** mediator, intermediary, middleman
10 狷介 **kenkai** obstinate, unyielding
11 紹介 **shōkai** introduction, presentation
紹介状 **shōkaijō** letter of introduction
紹介者 **shōkaisha** introducer
魚介 **gyokai** fish and shellfish, sea food
12 媒介 **baikai** mediation; matchmaking
媒介物 **baikaibutsu** medium, agency; carrier (of a disease)
14 蒋介石 **Shō Kaiseki** Chiang Kai-shek

——————— 3 ———————
10 荷厄介 **niyakkai** burden, encumbrance

——————— 4 ———————
6 自己紹介 **jiko shōkai** introduce oneself

2a2.10 / 51
今 **KON, KIN** now, the present, this
ima, ima(ya) now

——————— 1 ———————
1 今一 **ima hito(tsu)** leaving something to be desired, not quite perfect
3 今上 **kinjō** the present/reigning emperor
4 今月 **kongetsu** this month
今日 **kyō, konnichi** today
今方 **imagata** a moment ago
5 今生 **konjō** this life/world
今古 **kinko** now and in ancient times
6 今年 **kotoshi** this year
今次 **konji** present, new, recent
今回 **konkai** this time, lately
7 今更 **imasara** now, at this late date
8 今夜 **kon'ya** tonight
今昔 **konjaku** past and present
9 今風 **imafū** present/modern style
今後 **kongo** after this, henceforth

イ 2←
冫
孑
阝
卩
刂
力
又
亠
十
ト
夂
丷
厂
辷
冂
几
匸

2   今度 **kondo** this time; next time
10   今週 **konshū** this week
        今宵 **koyoi** this evening
        今時 **imadoki** today, nowadays; this time of
        day
11   今頃 **imagoro** at about this time
12   今期 **konki** the present/current term
        今朝 **kesa, konchō** this morning
        今朝方 **kesagata** this morning
        今晩 **konban** this evening, tonight
        今程 **imahodo** recently
13   今際 **imawa** one's dying hour
14   今様 **imayō** present/modern style

──────────── 2 ────────────

4   方今 **hōkon** at present, nowadays
5   古今 **kokon** ancient and modern times, all
        ages
        古今東西 **kokon-tōzai** all ages and places
        古今和歌集 **Kokinwakashū** (poetry
        anthology, early tenth century)
        古今集 **Kokinshū** (see preceding entry)
        只今 **tadaima** just now
        目今 **mokkon** at present, now
6   当今 **tōkon** at present, nowadays
        自今 **jikon** henceforth
7   即今 **sokkon** at the moment, now
9   昨今 **sakkon** nowadays, recently
11   唯今 **tadaima** right/just now
        現今 **genkon** now, today

──────────── 3 ────────────

5   古往今来 **koō-konrai** in all ages, since
        antiquity
9   昨非今是 **sakuhi-konze** reversing one's way
        of thinking

久 →   **0a3.7**

──────────── 3 ────────────

2a3.1 / 1891

仙   **SEN** hermit; wizard

──────────── 1 ────────────

2   仙人 **sennin** mountain-dwelling wizard;
        hermit-like otherworldly man
        仙人掌 **saboten** cactus
3   仙女 **sennyo, senjo** fairy, nymph
5   仙台 **Sendai** (city, Miyagi-ken)
9   仙界 **senkai** dwelling place of hermits; pure
        land away from the world
10   仙郷 **senkyō** fairyland, enchanted land
        仙骨 **senkotsu** philosophic turn of mind

11   仙術 **senjutsu** wizardry
14   仙境 **senkyō** fairyland, enchanted land
16   仙薬 **sen'yaku** panacea, elixir

──────────── 2 ────────────

4   水仙 **suisen** daffodil; narcissus
8   画仙紙 **gasenshi** drawing paper
9   神仙 **shinsen** hermit-wizard
10   酒仙 **shusen** heavy drinker
12   登仙 **tōsen** die; become a saint
        雲仙岳 **Unzendake** (mountain, Nagasaki-ken)
13   詩仙 **shisen** great poet
14   鳳仙花 **hōsenka** a balsam
        歌仙 **kasen** great poet
        銘仙 **meisen** (a type of silk)

2a3.2 / 333

仕   **SHI, JI, tsuka(eru)** serve, work for

──────────── 1 ────────────

2   仕入 **shii(re)** laying in stock
3   仕上 **shia(ge)** finish, finishing touches
4   仕切 **shiki(ri)** partition; settlement of
        accounts; toeing the mark (in sumo)
        仕分 **shiwa(keru)** sort, classify
        仕込 **shiko(mu)** train, bring up; fit into; stock
        up on
        仕手 **shite** protagonist; speculator
        仕方 **shikata** way, method, means, how to
5   仕出 **shida(shi)** catering
        仕付 **shitsu(ke)** tacking, basting
        仕付糸 **shitsu(ke)ito** tacking, basting (thread)
        仕打 **shiu(chi)** treatment; behavior, conduct
        仕立 **shita(te)** sewing, tailoring; outfitting
6   仕返 **shikae(shi)** get even, give tit for tat; do
        over again
        仕向 **shimu(keru)** treat, act toward; dispatch
8   仕事 **shigoto** work
        仕送 **shioku(ri)** allowance, remittance
        仕始 **shihaji(meru)** begin, start
        仕官 **shikan** enter government/samurai's
        service
        仕放題 **shihōdai** have one's own way
9   仕草 **shigusa** treatment, behavior, manner-
        isms
10   仕兼 **shika(neru)** cannot do, be reluctant to
        do
        仕留 **shito(meru)** kill, shoot down (a plane)
11   仕掛 **shikaka(ri)** beginning
        shika(ke) contrivance, device; scale,
        size; half finished
        仕掛人 **shika(ke)nin** intriguer, schemer,
        plotter
        仕組 **shiku(mi)** construction; contrivance,
        mechanism; plan

13 仕業 **shiwaza** act, deed
仕損 **shisoko(nau), shison(jiru)** make a
    mistake, fail, blunder
仕置 **shio(ki)** punishment; execution
14 仕様 **shiyō** specifications; way, method
15 仕舞 **shima(u)** finish, end; put away; close,
    wind up
仕儀 **shigi** circumstances, developments

───────── 2 ─────────

2 力仕事 **chikara shigoto** physical labor
3 大仕掛 **ōjika(ke)** on a grand scale
下仕事 **shitashigoto** preliminary work;
    subcontracted work
4 不仕合 **fushia(wase)** misfortune, unhappi-
    ness, ill luck
水仕事 **mizu shigoto** scrubbing and washing
手仕事 **teshigoto** hand work, manual labor
手仕舞 **tejima(i)** clearing of accounts,
    clearance (sale)
6 仲仕 **nakashi** longshoreman, stevedore
色仕掛 **irojika(ke)** feigned affection
早仕舞 **hayajimai** early closing
7 身仕舞 **mijimai** grooming, outfit, prepara-
    tions
8 奉仕 **hōshi** service
泥仕合 **dorojiai** mudslinging
店仕舞 **misejima(i)** close shop (for the day);
    go out of business
取仕切 **to(ri)shiki(ru)** run the whole
    (business)
9 俄仕込 **niwakajiko(mi)** hasty preparation
俄仕立 **niwakajita(te)** improvised, extempo-
    raneous
後仕舞 **atojimai** straightening up afterwards,
    winding up
荒仕事 **arashigoto** heavy work, hard labor
10 宮仕 **miyazuka(e)** court/temple service
針仕事 **hari shigoto** needlework, sewing
12 給仕 **kyūji** wait on; waiter, waitress, bellhop
13 賃仕事 **chinshigoto** piecework
14 総仕舞 **sōjimai** closing up, selling out
18 儲仕事 **mō(ke)shigoto** lucrative work

───────── 3 ─────────

4 手間仕事 **tema shigoto** tedious work;
    piecework
7 沖仲仕 **okinakashi** stevedore, longshoreman
10 時計仕掛 **tokei-jika(ke)** clockwork
11 野良仕事 **nora shigoto** farm/field work
13 腰掛仕事 **koshika(ke) shigoto** temporary
    work
節季仕舞 **sekki-jimai** year-end closeout
16 機械仕掛 **kikai-jika(ke)** mechanism

───────── 4 ─────────

12 勤労奉仕 **kinrō hōshi** labor service

2a3.3 / 256

代

DAI, TAI generation, age, era; charge,
fee **ka(eru)** change, exchange, replace,
substitute **ka(waru)** take the place of
yo generation **shiro** price; substitu-
tion; materials

───────── 1 ─────────

0 のり代 **norishiro** flap to put glue onto
2 代人 **dainin** proxy, deputy, substitute
3 代々 **daidai, yoyo** from generation to
    generation
5 代弁 **daiben** pay by proxy; act for another;
    speak for another
代代 **daidai, yoyo** from generation to
    generation **ka(waru)ga(waru),**
    ka(wari)ga(wari) by turns, alternately
代用 **daiyō** substitute
代用品 **daiyōhin** a substitute
代用食 **daiyōshoku** substitute food
代打 **daida** pinch-hitting
6 代休 **daikyū** compensatory day off (for work
    on a holiday)
代任 **dainin** acting for another; deputy
代印 **daiin** signing by proxy
代返 **daihen** answer roll call for another
代名詞 **daimeishi** pronoun
代行 **daikō** acting for another
代行者 **daikōsha** agent, proxy
7 代作 **daisaku** ghostwriting
代役 **daiyaku** substitute, stand-in, understudy
代言 **daigen** speaking for another; lawyer
8 代表 **daihyō** representation, typical; a delegate
代表団 **daihyōdan** delegation, mission
代表作 **daihyōsaku** masterpiece, most
    important work
代表的 **daihyōteki** representative, typical
代表者 **daihyōsha** a representative
代価 **daika** price, cost
代官 **daikan** local governor, chief magistrate
代金 **daikin** price, charge, the money/bill
9 代品 **daihin** a substitute
代栄 **ka(wari)ba(e)** change for the better
代映 **ka(wari)ba(e)** change for the better
10 代案 **daian** alternate plan/proposal
代書 **daisho** scribe, amanuensis
代納 **dainō** pay for another; pay in kind
11 代理 **dairi** representation, agency, proxy,
    agent, alternate, acting (minister)
代理人 **dairinin** agent, proxy, substitute,
    representative
代理店 **dairiten** agent, agency
代理業 **dairigyō** business of an agent,
    agency
代理権 **dairiken** right of representation,
    power of attorney

2

亻 3←
冫
孑
阝
卩
刂
力
又
宀
⼇
十
ⴑ
⽅
丷
厂
辶
冂
八
匸

2

→3

亻
⺡
子
阝
卩
刂
力
又
一
亠
十
ケ
ソ
厂
辶
冂
几
匸

代務 **daimu** management for another
12 代替 **daitai, daiga(e)** substitute, alternative
代替物 **daitaibutsu** a substitute
代筆 **daihitsu** write (a letter) for another
代診 **daishin** doctor's assistant
13 代数 **daisū** algebra
代署 **daisho** sign for another
代置 **daichi** replace
14 代演 **daien** substitute for another actor
代読 **daidoku** read on behalf of another
16 代稽古 **daigeiko** act as a substitute teacher
17 代償 **daishō** compensation, indemnification
代謝 **taisha** metabolism
代講 **daikō** act as a substitute lecturer
20 代議士 **daigishi** member of parliament/congress/diet
代議員 **daigiin** representative, delegate

──────── 2 ────────

1 一代 **ichidai** one generation; a lifetime; an age
一代記 **ichidaiki** a biography
2 十代 **jūdai** the teens, teenage
3 万代 **bandai** all ages, eternity **yorozuyo** thousands of years
千代 **chiyo** a thousand years/ages
千代紙 **chiyogami** colored paper
上代 **jōdai** ancient times
4 手代 **tedai** (sales) clerk
5 本代 **hondai** price/bill for books
末代 **matsudai** all ages to come, eternity
世代 **sedai** generation
代代 **daidai, yoyo** from generation to generation **ka(waru)ga(waru), ka(wari)ga(wari)** by turns, alternately
古代 **kodai** ancient times, antiquity
古代史 **kodaishi** ancient history
立代 **ta(chi)ka(wari)** taking turns
6 年代 **nendai** age, period, era; date
年代記 **nendaiki** chronicle
年代順 **nendaijun** chronological order
次代 **jidai** the coming/rising generation
交代 **kōtai** take turns, alternate, relieve, work in shifts
近代 **kindai** modern
近代人 **kindaijin** modern person
近代五種 **kindai goshu** the modern pentathlon
近代化 **kindaika** modernization
近代主義 **kindai shugi** modernism
近代的 **kindaiteki** modern
地代 **jidai** land rent
先代 **sendai** predecessor (in the family line); previous age/generation
舌代 **zetsudai** notice, circular
名代 **myōdai** proxy, deputy, representative **nadai** well-known

当代 **tōdai** the present generation/day; those days; the present head of the family
成代 **na(ri)ka(waru)** take the place of (someone)
米代 **komedai** money for rice
7 身代 **shindai** fortune, property, estate **migawa(ri)** substitute, vicarious **mi(no)shiro** ransom money
身代限 **shindaikagi(ri)** bankruptcy
身代金 **mi(no)shirokin** ransom money
何代目 **nandaime** what ordinal number
君代 **Kimi(ga)yo** (Japan's national anthem)
希代 **kitai, kidai** uncommon, singular
形代 **katashiro** paper image (used in purification ceremony)
花代 **hanadai** price for flowers; geisha fee
宋代 **Sōdai** Sung dynasty/era
売代 **u(ri)shiro** sales
初代 **shodai** the first generation; the founder
車代 **kurumadai** fare; cartage charge
足代 **ashidai** transportation expenses, carfare
8 其代 **so(no) ka(wari)** (but) on the other hand
苗代 **nawashiro, naeshiro** bed for rice seedlings
岩代 **Iwashiro** (ancient kuni, Fukushima-ken)
肩代 **kataga(wari)** change of palanquin bearers; takeover, transfer (of a business)
取代 **to(tte)ka(waru)** take the place of, supersede
9 前代 **zendai** previous generation; former ages
前代未聞 **zendai-mimon** unprecedented
城代 **jōdai** castle warden
後代 **kōdai** future generations, posterity
茶代 **chadai** charge for tea; tip
神代 **jindai** age/era of the gods
神代文字 **jindai moji** ancient Japanese characters
神代杉 **jindaisugi** lignitized cedar
食代 **ku(i)shiro** food/board bill
10 酒代 **sakadai, sakashiro** drink money, tip
時代 **jidai** era, period, age
時代物 **jidaimono** an antique; a historical drama
時代相 **jidaisō** trend of the times
時代劇 **jidaigeki** period/costume drama
11 現代 **gendai** the present age, today, modern times
現代人 **gendaijin** people today
現代化 **gendaika** modernization
現代版 **gendaiban** modern edition
現代語 **gendaigo** modern language
累代 **ruidai** successive generations; from generation to generation
盛代 **seidai** era of prosperity
12 場代 **badai** admission fee
御代 **miyo** reign, period

無代　**mudai** free, without charge
稀代　**kidai, kitai** uncommon, rare
飲代　**no(mi)shiro** drinking money
間代　**madai** room rent
13 聖代　**seidai** glorious reign
14 歴代　**rekidai** successive generations
綴代　**to(ji)shiro** binding margin
総代　**sōdai** representative, delegate
網代　**ajiro** wickerwork
誌代　**shidai** price of a magazine
15 縫代　**nu(i)shiro** margin left for a seam
16 薬代　**kusuridai, yakudai** charge for medicine
親代　**oyaga(wari)** (one who is) acting as a parent, guardian
19 譜代　**fudai** successive generations; hereditary vassal
譜代大名　**fudai daimyō** hereditary daimyo

─────── 3 ───────
2 二十代　**nijūdai** in one's twenties
八千代　**yachiyo** thousands of years
3 三百代言　**sanbyaku daigen** shyster lawyer, pettifogger
4 中生代　**chūseidai** the Mesozoic era
6 全人代　**Zenjindai** (Chinese) National People's Congress (short for 全国人民代表大会)
次世代　**jisedai** next-generation (product)
同時代　**dōjidai** contemporaneous
7 利益代表　**rieki daihyō** representing (another country's) diplomatic interests
車馬代　**shabadai** traveling expenses
8 治療代　**chiryōdai** medical fees/bill
10 部屋代　**heyadai** room rent
11 現時代　**genjidai** the present age
13 新陳代謝　**shinchintaisha** metabolism
新時代　**shinjidai** new era
新聞代　**shinbundai** newspaper subscription charge
14 疑問代名詞　**gimon daimeishi** interrogative pronoun
関係代名詞　**kankei daimeishi** relative pronoun
15 線香代　**senkōdai** (geisha's) time charge

─────── 4 ───────
1 一世一代　**issei ichidai** once in a lifetime
2 二十年代　**nijūnendai** the '20s
5 幼年時代　**yōnen jidai** childhood
石器時代　**sekki jidai** the Stone Age
8 参勤交代　**sankin kōtai** daimyo's alternate-year residence in Edo
13 戦国時代　**sengoku jidai** era of civil wars

─────── 5 ───────
6 全国人民代表大会　**Zenkoku Jinmin Daihyō Taikai** (Chinese) National People's Congress

伢 → 仞　**2a3.8**

2a3.4 / 120

他　**TA, hoka** another, other

─────── 1 ───────
2 他人　**tanin** someone else, others, outsider
他力　**tariki** outside help; salvation by faith
3 他山　**tazan** another mountain/temple
他山石　**tazan (no) ishi** object lesson
4 他日　**tajitsu** some (other) day
他方　**tahō** another side/direction; on the other hand
5 他出　**tashutsu** going out
他生　**tashō** previous existence
6 他年　**tanen** some other year, some day
他行　**tagyō, takō** going out
7 他見　**taken** showing to others
他言　**tagon, tagen** tell others, divulge
8 他事　**taji** other matters; other people's affairs
他念　**tanen** thinking about something else
他姓　**tasei** another surname
他国　**takoku** foreign country; another province
他国人　**takokujin** foreigner, stranger
他国民　**takokumin** other nations/peoples
他国者　**takokumono** stranger, person from another place
他物　**tabutsu, ta(no)mono** the other thing; another's property
他所　**tasho** another place
9 他律　**taritsu** heteronomy; non-autonomous
他面　**tamen** the other side, on the other hand
他界　**takai** the next world; die
10 他郷　**takyō** foreign country, strange land
他流　**taryū** another style, another school (of thought)
他家　**take** another family
他殺　**tasatsu** murder
11 他動詞　**tadōshi** transitive verb
12 他覚的　**takakuteki** objective (symptoms)
13 他愛　**taai** altruism
他意　**tai** another intention, ulterior motive, malice

─────── 2 ───────
6 自他　**jita** self and others; transitive and intransitive
7 赤他人　**aka (no) tanin** a perfect/total stranger
利他　**rita** altruism
8 其他　**so(no)ta** and others, and so forth
11 排他　**haita** exclusion
排他的　**haitateki** exclusive
13 愛他　**aita** altruism
愛他主義　**aita shugi** altruism

2
イ 3 ←
冫
孑
阝
卩
刂
力
又
宀
亠
十
卜
ケ
丶
厂
辶
冂
几
匚

2a3.5

仗 **JŌ** soldier; weapon, stick

───── 2 ─────

15 儀仗 **gijō** cortege, guard
儀仗兵 **gijōhei** honor guard, military escort

2a3.6 / 192

付 **FU** attach, affix, set; refer, submit
tsu(keru) attach **tsu(ku)** be attached/
connected; be in luck

───── 1 ─────

2 付入 **tsu(ke)i(ru)** take advantage of
付人 **tsu(ke)bito** attendant, assistant, chaperone
3 付与 **fuyo** give, grant, confer
付上 **tsu(ke)a(garu)** be overproud/spoiled/elated; take advantage of
4 付文 **tsu(ke)bumi** love letter
付込 **tsu(ke)ko(mu)** take advantage of; make an entry
付火 **tsu(ke)bi** arson
5 付加 **fuka** an addition **tsu(ke)kuwa(eru)** add
付加価値税 **fuka-kachi zei** value-added tax
付加税 **fukazei** surtax
付札 **tsu(ke)fuda** tag, label
付目 **tsu(ke)me** purpose; weak point to take advantage of
6 付合 **tsu(ki)a(u)** keep company with, associate with **tsu(ke)a(wase)** vegetables added as relish
付近 **fukin** vicinity, neighborhood
付回 **tsu(ke)mawa(ru)** follow around, tag after
7 付図 **fuzu** attached diagram
付言 **fugen** additional remark, postscript
付足 **tsu(ke)ta(su)** add on, append
8 付表 **fuhyō** attached table
付注 **fuchū** annotation
付狙 **tsu(ke)nera(u)** prowl after, keep watch on
付届 **tsu(ke)todo(ke)** tip, present; bribe
付和 **fuwa** blindly follow others
付和雷同 **fuwa-raidō** follow blindly, echo
9 付保 **fuho** cover (by insurance), carry (insurance)
付則 **fusoku** supplementary provisions, bylaws
10 付値 **tsu(ke)ne** the price offered, bid
付随 **fuzui** incidental, concomitant, collateral
付帯 **futai** incidental, accessory, ancillary, secondary
付徒 **tsu(ki)shitaga(u)** follow, accompany

付根 **tsu(ke)ne** root, joint, base, crotch
付託 **futaku** refer/submit (to a committee)
付記 **fuki** additional remark, supplementary note
11 付添 **tsu(ki)so(u)** attend on, accompany, escort
12 付着 **fuchaku** adhere, stick to
付換 **tsu(ke)ka(eru)** replace (with a new one)
付属 **fuzoku** attached, associated, auxiliary
付焼刃 **tsu(ke)yakiba** affectation, pretension
14 付箋 **fusen** tag, label
16 付髭 **tsu(ke)hige** false mustache/beard
付薬 **tsu(ke)gusuri** medicine for external application, ointment
付録 **furoku** supplement, appendix
20 付議 **fugi** bring up, submit, discuss
22 付纒 **tsu(ki)mato(u)** follow about, shadow, tag after

───── 2 ─────

2 丁付 **chōzu(ke)** pagination, foliation
人付合 **hitozu(ki)a(i)** sociability
3 下付 **kafu** grant, issue
口付 **kuchizu(ke)** kiss **kuchitsu(ki)** (shape of one's) mouth; manner of speech; mouthpiece (of a cigarette)
4 片付 **katazu(keru)** put in order; put away; settle, dispose of; marry off
katazu(ku) be put in order; be settled, be disposed of; get married off
手付 **tetsu(ke)** earnest money, deposit
tetsu(ki) way of using one's hands
手付金 **tetsu(ke)kin** earnest money, deposit
日付 **iwa(ku)tsu(ki)** (someone) with a past
日付 **hizuke** day, dating
日付変更線 **hizuke henkōsen** the international date line
火付 **hitsu(ke)** arson; instigator, firebrand
hitsu(ki) kindling
心付 **kokorozu(ke)** tip, gratuity
5 申付 **mō(shi)tsu(keru)** tell, order, instruct
仕付 **shitsu(ke)** tacking, basting
仕付糸 **shitsu(ke)ito** tacking, basting (thread)
打付 **u(chi)tsu(keru)** stroke, knock, dash against, nail to **u(chi)tsu(ke ni)** bluntly, flatly **u(tte)tsu(ke)** just right
叱付 **shika(ri)tsu(keru)** scold/rebuke severely
叩付 **tata(ki)tsu(keru)** beat, thrash; throw at
札付 **fudatsu(ki)** tagged (with a brand name), marked; notorious
立付 **ta(te)tsu(ke)** how smoothly (a sliding door) opens and shuts; continuously, at a stretch
目付 **metsu(ki)** a look, expression of the eyes

6 気付 **kizu(ku)** notice, find out   **kitsu(ke)** encouragement; resuscitation   **-kizuke** in care of   **ki (o) tsu(keru)** be careful, watch out   **ki (ga) tsu(ku)** notice, realize

仰付 **ō(se)tsu(keru)** tell (someone to do); appoint

肉付 **nikuzu(ki)** fleshiness, build   **nikuzu(ke)** fleshing out, modeling (clay)

交付 **kōfu** deliver, furnish with

考付 **kanga(e)tsu(ku)** think of/up, hit upon; remember

色付 **irozu(ku)** take on color   **irotsu(ke)** coloring, painting

近付 **chikazu(ku)** come/go near, approach   **chikazu(ki)** acquaintance

返付 **henpu** return, give back

吸付 **su(i)tsu(keru)** attract; light (a cigarette) from (another); be used to smoking (a pipe)   **su(i)tsu(ku)** cling/stick to

名付 **nazu(ke)** naming; fiancé(e)   **nazu(keru)** name, call, entitle

名付主 **nazu(ke)nushi** person who names the newborn, godparent

名付祝 **nazu(ke)iwa(i)** naming ceremony, christening

名付親 **nazu(ke) oya** godparent

回付 **kaifu** transmit, pass on to, refer to

7 体付 **karadatsu(ki)** one's build, figure

作付 **sakutsu(ke), sakuzu(ke)** planting

決付 **ki(me)tsu(keru)** take to task, scold

抑付 **osa(e)tsu(keru)** hold down, curb, control

投付 **na(ge)tsu(keru)** throw at/against/down

吹付 **fu(ki)tsu(keru)** blow against

役付 **yakuzu(ke)** allotment of roles, casting

売付 **u(ri)tsu(keru)** sell to; foist, palm off

見付 **mitsu(keru)** find   **mitsu(karu)** be found

見付門 **mitsukemon** castle lookout gate

利付 **ritsu(ki)** interest-bearing

言付 **i(i)tsu(keru)** tell (someone to do something); tell on (someone), tattle   **kotozu(ke)** message

足付 **ashitsu(ki)** gait; having legs

8 受付 **uketsuke** receipt, acceptance; reception desk; receptionist

受付係 **uketsukegakari** receptionist, usher

追付 **o(i)tsu(ku)** catch up with

送付 **sōfu** send, forward, remit

段付 **nagu(ri)tsu(keru)** strike, beat, thrash

泣付 **na(ki)tsu(ku)** entreat, implore

押付 **o(shi)tsu(keru)** press against; force upon   **o(shi)tsu(kegamashii)** importunate

抱付 **da(ki)tsu(ku)** embrace, cling to

味付 **ajitsu(ke)** seasoning

呼付 **yo(bi)tsu(keru)** call, send for, summon

突付 **tsu(ki)tsu(keru)** thrust before, point (a gun) at

委付 **ifu** abandonment (of rights)

取付 **to(ri)tsu(keru)** install; patronize   **to(ri)tsu(ke)** (store) which one patronizes; installing; run on a bank   **to(ri)tsu(ku)** hold fast to, catch hold of; possess, haunt   **to(ri)/to(t)tsu(ki)** the beginning, the first you come to; first impression

取付工事 **to(ri)tsu(ke) kōji** installation work

9 飛付 **to(bi)tsu(ku)** jump/leap/snatch at

巻付 **ma(ki)tsu(ku)** coil/wind around

乗付 **no(ri)tsu(keru)** ride up to; get used to riding

造付 **tsuku(ri)tsu(keru)** fasten firmly, build into

浮付 **uwatsu(ku)** be fickle/flippant

括付 **kuku(ri)tsu(keru)** tie up/together, tie down to

狐付 **kitsunetsu(ki)** possessed by a fox/spirit

面付 **tsuratsu(ki)** expression, look

染付 **so(me)tsu(keru)** dye in   **shi(mi)-tsu(ku)** be dyed in deeply, be stained

思付 **omo(i)tsu(ki)** idea, thought that comes to mind

食付 **ta(be)tsu(keru)** be used to eating   **ku(i)tsu(ku)** bite at/into; hold fast to

10 差付 **sa(shi)tsu(keru)** point (a gun at); put right under one's nose

振付 **fu(ri)tsu(ke)** choreography

家付 **ietsu(ki)** attached to the house; daughter who brings in a husband as joint heir

座付 **zatsu(ki)** (actor) attached to a theater

根付 **netsu(ke)** ornamental button for suspending a pouch from a belt

格付 **kakuzu(ke)** grading, rating

書付 **ka(ki)tsu(keru)** note down   **ka(ki)tsu(ke)** note; bill

病付 **ya(mi)tsu(ku)** be taken ill; be confirmed in a habit

紐付 **himotsu(ki)** with strings attached

納付 **nōfu** payment, delivery

納付金 **nōfukin** contribution

紋付 **montsu(ki)** clothing bearing one's family crest

配付 **haifu** distribution, apportionment

釘付 **kugizu(ke)** nailing (down); pegging (a price)

11 勘付 **kanzu(ku)** suspect, sense, scent

添付 **tenpu** attach, append

据付 **su(e)tsu(keru)** set into position, install

帳付 **chōtsu(ke)** bookkeeping; bookkeeper

2

イ 3←
冫
孑
阝
卩
刂
力
又
宀
亠
艹
⼂
勹
广
辶
冂
几
匚

2

→ 3

亻
冫
子
阝
卩
刂
力
又
宀
十
ト
ケ
丶
厂
辶
冂
几
匚

寄付 **kifu** contribution, donation **yo(se)tsu-(keru)** let come near **yo(ri)tsu(ku)** come near; open (the day's trading)

寄付金 **kifukin** contributions

脚付 **ashitsu(ki)** with legs; gait

盛付 **mo(ri)tsu(keru)** dish up

疵付 **kizutsu(keru)** wound, injure; mar; besmirch

組付 **ku(mi)tsu(ku)** grapple with, seize hold of

粘付 **nebatsu(ku)** be sticky

責付 **se(me)tsu(keru)** denounce scathingly

12 備付 **sona(e)tsu(keru)** provide, equip, install **sona(e)tsu(ke)** equipment, provision

割付 **wa(ri)tsu(keru)** allot, apportion, allocate **wa(ri)tsu(ke)** layout

着付 **kitsu(ke)** dress (someone); fitting

遣付 **ya(ri)tsu(keru)** be accustomed/used to

極付 **ki(me)tsu(keru)** take to task, reprimand

植付 **u(e)tsu(keru)** plant, implant

焼付 **ya(ki)tsu(keru)** bake onto, bake (china), fuse **ya(ki)tsu(ku)** be burned/seared onto

焚付 **ta(ki)tsu(keru)** light, kindle; instigate

煮付 **nitsu(ke)** vegetables/fish boiled hard with soy sauce

番付 **banzu(ke)** graded list, ranking

買付 **ka(i)tsu(ke)** buying, purchase

痛付 **ita(me)tsu(keru)** rebuke, reprimand

結付 **musu(bi)tsu(keru)** tie together, link

絡付 **kara(mi)tsu(ku)** coil around, cling to

給付 **kyūfu** present, pay, provide

奥付 **okuzu(ke)** colophon

筆付 **fudetsu(ki)** brushwork

貼付 **chōfu, tenpu, ha(ri)tsu(keru)** stick, paste, affix

貸付 **ka(shi)tsu(keru)** lend

貸付金 **kashitsukekin** a loan, advance

焦付 **ko(ge)tsu(ku)** get burned/scorched; become uncollectible

13 傷付 **kizutsu(keru)** injure, damage

裏付 **urazu(keru)** support, endorse, substantiate

煎付 **i(ri)tsu(keru)** parch, roast, broil, scorch

塗付 **nu(ri)tsu(keru)** smear, daub

嗅付 **ka(gi)tsu(keru)** scent, smell out, detect

蒔付 **ma(ki)tsu(ke)** sowing, seeding

腰付 **koshitsu(ki)** gait, carriage, posture

照付 **te(ri)tsu(keru)** shine down on

感付 **kanzu(ku)** suspect, sense

睨付 **nira(mi)tsu(keru), ne(me)tsu(keru)** glare/scowl at

節付 **fushizu(ke)** setting to music

飾付 **kaza(ri)tsu(ke)** decoration

14 墨付 **sumitsu(ki)** handwriting, signed certificate

様付 **samazu(ke)** address (someone) with -*sama*

種付 **tanetsu(ke)** mating, stud service

説付 **to(ki)tsu(keru)** persuade, talk into

聞付 **ki(ki)tsu(keru)** hear (the sound of); learn of

駆付 **ka(ke)tsu(keru)** rush/hurry to

15 隣付合 **tonarizu(ki)a(i)** neighborliness

還付 **kanpu** return, restore, refund

撫付 **na(de)tsu(keru)** comb/smooth down **na(de)tsu(ke)** smoothed-down hair

撥付 **ha(ne)tsu(keru)** refuse, turn down

横付 **yokozu(ke)** bring alongside

瘤付 **kobutsu(ki)** wen; nuisance; with a child along

縁付 **enzu(ku)** get married **enzu(keru)** give in marriage

締付 **shi(me)tsu(keru)** bind, tighten, throttle; press hard

縋付 **suga(ri)tsu(ku)** cling to, depend on

縫付 **nu(i)tsu(keru)** sew on

糊付 **noritsu(ke)** starching; pasting

踏付 **fu(mi)tsu(keru)** trample; oppress; despise

餌付 **ezu(ku)** (birds) begin to eat/feed

震付 **furu(i)tsu(ku)** hug with affection

16 燃付 **mo(e)tsu(ku)** catch fire, ignite

縛付 **shiba(ri)tsu(keru)** tie/fasten to

錆付 **sabitsu(ku)** rust (together/fast)

17 擦付 **su(ri)tsu(keru)** rub on/against, strike (a match) **nasu(ri)tsu(keru)** attribute to, blame on; rub on, smear

18 噛付 **ka(mi)tsu(ku)** bite/snap at

顔付 **kaotsu(ki)** face, look(s), expression

額付 **hitaitsu(ki)** (form of one's) brow, forehead

21 齧付 **kaji(ri)tsu(ku)** bite at and not let go; stick to

––––––––– 3 –––––––––

6 再下付 **saikafu** regrant, reissue, renewal

再交付 **saikōfu** regrant, reissue

先日付 **sakihizu(ke)** postdating, dating forward

7 折紙付 **o(ri)gamitsu(ki)** certified, genuine

尾頭付 **okashiratsu(ki)** whole fish

条件付 **jōkentsu(ki)** conditional

言葉付 **kotobatsu(ki)** way of speaking

8 取片付 **to(ri)katazu(keru)** clear away, tidy up

9 保証付 **hoshōtsu(ki)** guaranteed

造作付 **zōsakutsu(ki)** furnished (house)

活気付 **kakkizu(keru)** enliven, invigorate

後片付 **atokatazu(ke)** straightening up afterwards, putting things in order

11 牽強付会 **kenkyō-fukai** farfetched, distorted

運命付 **unmeizu(keru)** destine, doom

産気付 **sankezu(ki)** beginning of labor

12 景気付 **keikizu(ku)** become active, pick up
番号付 **bangōtsu(ke)** numbering
13 隠目付 **kaku(shi)metsuke** spy, detective (historical)
愚図付 **guzutsu(ku)** dawdle, be irresolute
意味付 **imizu(keru)** give meaning to
跡片付 **atokatazu(ke)** straightening up (afterwards)
14 総裏付 **sōuratsu(ki)** fully lined (coat)
15 調子付 **chōshizu(ku)** warm up to, be elated by, be in high spirits
16 親類付合 **shinrui-zu(ki)a(i)** association among relatives; intimate association
26 驥尾付 **kibi (ni) fu(su)** follow (another's) lead

— 4 —

8 武者振付 **mushabu(ri)tsu(ku)** pounce upon, devour

— 5 —

1 一泊二食付 **ippaku nishoku-tsu(ki)** with overnight lodging and two meals

2a3.7

仟 **SEN** leader of a thousand men; thousand; north-south path between paddies

— 1 —

8 仟佰 **senpaku** many; paths between paddies

2a3.8

仞 仭 **JIN** fathom

— 2 —

2 九仞功一簣欠 **kyūjin (no) kō (o) ikki (ni) ka(ku)** failure on the verge of success

以→ **0a5.1**

仝→同 **2r4.2**

2a3.9 / 831

令 **REI** order, command; good; (honorific prefix) **RYŌ** law

— 1 —

4 令夫人 **reifujin** Mrs., Lady, Madam; your wife
6 令色 **reishoku** servile look
令名 **reimei** fame, reputation, renown
7 令状 **reijō** warrant, writ
9 令室 **reishitsu** your wife
10 令息 **reisoku** your son
14 令聞 **reibun** good reputation, renown
16 令嬢 **reijō** your daughter, young lady

— 2 —

5 号令 **gōrei** command, order
司令 **shirei** command, control; commander
司令官 **shireikan** commanding officer
司令部 **shireibu** headquarters, the command
司令塔 **shireitō** control/conning tower
布令 **furei** official notice, proclamation
6 年令 **nenrei** age
伝令 **denrei** message; messenger
7 改令 **kairei** countermand an order
条令 **jōrei** law, ordinance, rule, regulation
8 使令 **shirei** a directive
命令 **meirei** command, order
命令形 **meireikei** imperative form
制令 **seirei** regulations
法令 **hōrei** laws and (cabinet or ministerial) orders
府令 **furei** urban-prefectural ordinance
9 発令 **hatsurei** announce officially, issue
勅令 **chokurei** imperial edict
軍令 **gunrei** military command
指令 **shirei** order, instructions
律令 **ritsuryō, ritsurei** laws and orders (of Nara and Heian period)
県令 **kenrei** prefectural ordinance
政令 **seirei** government ordinance, cabinet order
威令 **irei** authority
省令 **shōrei** ministerial order
10 家令 **karei** steward, butler
訓令 **kunrei** instructions, directive
訓令式 **kunreishiki** (a system of romanization which differs from Hepburn romanization in such syllables as *shi/si*, *tsu/tu*, *cha/tya*)
12 朝令暮改 **chōrei-bokai** issuing an order in the morning and changing it in the evening, lack of constancy/principle
13 禁令 **kinrei** prohibition, ban, interdict
辞令 **jirei** written appointment/order; wording, phraseology
14 閣令 **kakurei** cabinet order

— 3 —

5 巧言令色 **kōgen-reishoku** ingratiating geniality
召集令 **shōshūrei** draft call
7 戒厳令 **kaigenrei** martial law
9 軍司令部 **gunshireibu** military headquarters
軍司令官 **gunshireikan** army commander
11 動員令 **dōinrei** mobilization order
13 禁止令 **kinshirei** prohibition (decree), ban

2
亻 3←
冫
子
阝
卩
刂
力
又
亠
亠
十
卜
⺈
丷
厂
辶
冂
几
匚

2a3.10

14 徴発令 **chōhatsurei** requisition orders
徴集令 **chōshūrei** order calling up draftees
総司令 **sōshirei** general headquarters, supreme command
箝口令 **kankōrei** gag law/order

——————— 4 ———————

6 至上命令 **shijō meirei** supreme/inviolable command; categorical imperative

2a3.10

囪 **KAI** beg

——————— 4 ———————

2a4.1 / 1356

伏 **FUKU, fu(su)** bend down, prostrate oneself **fu(seru)** turn downward; cover; lay (pipes); conceal **fu(shite)** bowing down; respectfully

——————— 1 ———————

5 伏字 **fu(se)ji** characters (like ○ or ×) to indicate an unprintable word
6 伏在 **fukuzai** lie hidden
7 伏兵 **fukuhei** an ambush
8 伏拝 **fu(shi)oga(mu)** kneel down and worship
9 伏奏 **fukusō** report to the throne
伏屋 **fu(se)ya** humble cottage, hovel
10 伏射 **fukusha** shoot lying prone
13 伏罪 **fukuzai** plead guilty
15 伏線 **fukusen** foreshadowing; precautionary measures
伏縫 **fu(se)nu(i)** hemming
21 伏魔殿 **fukumaden** abode of demons

——————— 2 ———————

3 山伏 **yamabushi** mountain/itinerant priest
5 平伏 **heifuku, hirefu(su)** prostrate oneself
圧伏 **appuku** overpower, subdue
叩伏 **tata(ki)fu(seru)** knock down; utterly defeat
7 言伏 **i(i)fu(seru)** argue down, confute
8 泣伏 **na(ki)fu(su)** throw oneself down crying
屈伏 **kuppuku** submit/yield/surrender to
9 降伏 **kōfuku** surrender
待伏 **ma(chi)bu(se)** ambush, lying in wait
面伏 **omobu(se)** shame-faced
10 俯伏 **utsubu(su)** lie face down
fufuku lie prostrate
帰伏 **kifuku** surrender, submission
埋伏 **maifuku** lie hidden; bury (to hide); impacted (tooth)
起伏 **kifuku** ups and downs, relief (map)
o(ki)fu(shi) getting up and lying down;

morning and evening, daily life
11 捩伏 **ne(ji)fu(seru)** throw/hold (someone) down
組伏 **ku(mi)fu(seru)** pin/hold (someone) down
14 慴伏 **shōfuku** fear and prostrate oneself before; fear and obey
説伏 **to(ki)fu(seru)** confute, argue down, convince **seppuku** persuade, convince
雌伏 **shifuku** remain in obscurity, lie low
15 潜伏 **senpuku** hide, be hidden; be dormant/latent
潜伏性 **senpukusei** latent (disease)
潜伏期 **senpukuki** incubation period
調伏 **chōbuku** exorcise; curse
17 蟄伏 **chippuku** hibernate, lie dormant

——————— 3 ———————

12 腕立伏 **udeta(te)fu(se)** push-ups

2a4.2 / 60

休 **KYŪ, yasu(mu)** rest; take the day off
yasu(meru) rest, set at ease
yasu(maru) be rested, feel at ease
yasu(mi) rest, break, vacation, absence

——————— 1 ———————

4 休止 **kyūshi** pause, suspension, dormancy
休止符 **kyūshifu** rest (in music)
休日 **kyūjitsu** holiday, day off
休火山 **kyūkazan** dormant volcano
休心 **kyūshin** feel at ease, rest assured
5 休刊 **kyūkan** suspend publication
6 休会 **kyūkai** adjourn, go into recess
休廷 **kyūtei** adjourn court
7 休学 **kyūgaku** absence from school
8 休泊所 **kyūhakujo** place for resting and sleeping
10 休校 **kyūkō** school closing
休息 **kyūsoku** rest
休息所 **kyūsokujo** resting room, lounge
休航 **kyūkō** suspension of ship or airline service
12 休診 **kyūshin** see no patients, Clinic Closed
休閑 **kyūkan** fallowing
休閑地 **kyūkanchi** land lying fallow
13 休業 **kyūgyō** suspension of business, Shop Closed
休業日 **kyūgyōbi** business holiday
休暇 **kyūka** holiday, vacation, leave of absence
休戦 **kyūsen** truce, cease-fire
休載 **kyūsai** not be published, not carry
休電 **kyūden** electricity cut-off, power outage

14 休演 **kyūen** suspend performances
15 休養 **kyūyō** rest, recreation
16 休憩 **kyūkei** recess, break, intermission
休憩所 **kyūkeijo** resting room, lounge, lobby
休憩室 **kyūkeishitsu** resting room, lounge, lobby
17 休講 **kyūkō** lecture cancelled
18 休職 **kyūshoku** temporary retirement from office, layoff

——————— 2 ———————
1 一休 **hitoyasu(mi)** a rest
3 小休止 **shōkyūshi** brief recess, short break
4 中休 **nakayasu(mi)** take a break
公休日 **kōkyūbi** legal holiday
手休 **teyasu(mi)** rest, pause, break
5 半休 **hankyū** half-day holiday
代休 **daikyū** compensatory day off (for work on a holiday)
冬休 **fuyuyasu(mi)** winter vacation
6 気休 **kiyasu(me)** to ease one's mind
8 定休日 **teikyūbi** regular holiday, Closed (Tuesday)s
9 連休 **renkyū** consecutive holidays
昼休 **hiruyasu(mi)** lunch/noontime break
食休 **shokuyasu(mi)** an after-meal rest
10 帰休 **kikyū** (soldier's) leave, furlough
遊休 **yūkyū** idle, unused
遊休資本 **yūkyū shihon** idle capital
週休 **shūkyū** weekly day off
骨休 **honeyasu(me)** relaxation, recreation
夏休 **natsuyasu(mi)** summer vacation
息休 **kyūsoku** a rest, breather
11 運休 **unkyū** (train) cancelled, not running
12 無休 **mukyū** no holidays, always open (shop)
13 盟休 **meikyū** (students') strike
電休日 **denkyūbi** a no-electricity day
18 臨休 **rinkyū** special holiday (short for 臨時休校 or 臨時休業)

——————— 3 ———————
3 万事休 **banji kyū(su)** It's all over. Nothing more can be done.
6 有給休暇 **yūkyū kyūka** paid vacation
10 振替休日 **furikae kyūjitsu** substitute holiday (for one falling on a Sunday)

——————— 4 ———————
4 不眠不休 **fumin-fukyū** without sleep or rest, day and night

2a4.3
仿 **HŌ** wander

——————— 1 ———————
11 仿徨 **hōkō** wander, roam

2a4.4 / 732
件 **KEN** case, matter, item
kudan, kudari the aforesaid

——————— 1 ———————
13 件数 **kensū** number of cases/items

——————— 2 ———————
1 一件 **ikken** a matter, an item
2 人件費 **jinkenhi** personnel expenses
5 用件 **yōken** business, things to be done
7 条件 **jōken** condition, stipulation
条件付 **jōkentsu(ki)** conditional
8 事件 **jiken** case, affair, incident
物件 **bukken** thing, article, physical object, a property
9 要件 **yōken** requisite, essentials
10 案件 **anken** matter, case, item
12 訴件 **soken** (legal) case
14 雑件 **zakken** miscellaneous matters
18 難件 **nanken** difficult matter/case

——————— 3 ———————
8 怪事件 **kaijiken** strange/mystery case
11 悪条件 **akujōken** unfavorable conditions, handicap
12 無条件 **mujōken** unconditional

——————— 4 ———————
6 刑事事件 **keiji jiken** criminal case

2a4.5 / 1509
伐 **BATSU, u(tsu)** strike, attack; punish; cut

——————— 1 ———————
4 伐木 **batsuboku** felling, cutting, logging
11 伐採 **bassai** felling, deforestation, cutting

——————— 2 ———————
7 乱伐 **ranbatsu** indiscriminate deforestation
攻伐 **kōbatsu** subjugation
8 征伐 **seibatsu** subjugate, conquer, punish, exterminate
10 殺伐 **satsubatsu** bloodthirsty, brutal, savage
討伐 **tōbatsu** subjugation, suppression
討伐隊 **tōbatsutai** punitive force
11 採伐 **saibatsu** timbering, felling
盗伐 **tōbatsu** illegal logging, timber theft
12 間伐 **kanbatsu** thinning out (a forest)
15 輪伐 **rinbatsu** lumbering area by area
18 濫伐 **ranbatsu** reckless deforestation

2a4.6
伊 **I** that one; Italy

——————— 1 ———————
4 伊予 **Iyo** (ancient kuni, Ehime-ken)

伊太利 **Itaria, Itarii** Italy

7 伊呂波 **i-ro-ha** the Japanese alphabet; ABC's, rudiments

伊豆 **Izu** (ancient kuni, Shizuoka-ken)

伊豆半島 **Izu-hantō** Izu Peninsula (Shizuoka-ken)

11 伊達 **date** foppish, ostentatious

伊達男 **dateotoko** a dandy, fop

伊達巻 **datema(ki)** under-sash; rolled omelet

12 伊賀 **Iga** (ancient kuni, Mie-ken)

13 伊勢大神宮 **Ise Daijingū** the Grand Shrines of Ise

伊勢参 **Ise-mai(ri)** Ise pilgrimage

伊勢蝦 **ise-ebi** spiny lobster

14 伊語 **Igo** Italian language

────────── 2 ──────────

4 日伊 **Nichi-I** Japan and Italy

9 紀伊 **Kii** (ancient kuni, Wakayama-ken)

13 滞伊 **tai-I** staying in Italy

────────── 3 ──────────

4 木乃伊 **miira** mummy

住 → 住 2a5.19

2a4.7 / 1347

仲 **CHŪ, naka** relationship

────────── 1 ──────────

2 仲人 **nakōdo, chūnin** go-between, match-maker

4 仲介 **chūkai** intermediation, agency

仲介者 **chūkaisha** mediator, intermediary, middleman

5 仲仕 **nakashi** longshoreman, stevedore

仲好 **nakayo(shi)** good friends

仲冬 **chūtō** mid-winter, December

仲立 **nakada(chi)** intermediation; agent, broker; go-between

7 仲良 **nakayo(ku)** on friendly terms

nakayo(shi) good friends

8 仲直 **nakanao(ri)** reconciliation, make up

仲居 **nakai** waitress

9 仲哀 **Chūai** (emperor, 192–200)

仲春 **chūshun** mid-spring, March

仲秋 **chūshū** mid-autumn, September

10 仲夏 **chūka** mid-summer, June

12 仲違 **nakataga(i)** quarrel, discord

仲裁 **chūsai** arbitration, mediation

仲裁人 **chūsainin** arbitrator, mediator

仲裁者 **chūsaisha** arbitrator, mediator

仲買 **nakaga(i)** broking, brokerage

仲買人 **nakaga(i)nin** broker, agent

仲間 **nakama** member of a group, mate, fellow **chūgen** samurai's attendant

仲間入 **nakama-i(ri)** become one of the group

仲間外 **nakamahazu(re)** being left out

仲間割 **nakamawa(re)** split among friends, internal discord

────────── 2 ──────────

4 不仲 **funaka** discord, on bad terms with

5 生仲 **na(sanu) naka** no blood relation

7 伯仲 **hakuchū** be evenly matched

沖仲仕 **okinakashi** stevedore, longshoreman

10 恋仲 **koinaka** love relationship, love

遊仲間 **aso(bi)nakama** playmate

11 釣仲間 **tsu(ri) nakama** fishing buddies

12 飲仲間 **no(mi)nakama** drinking buddy

────────── 3 ──────────

4 犬猿仲 **ken'en (no) naka** hating each other

2a4.8

伍 **GO** five; five-man squad; file, line; rank/associate with

────────── 1 ──────────

0 伍する **go(suru)** rank/associate with

8 伍長 **gochō** corporal, staff sergeant

────────── 2 ──────────

11 隊伍 **taigo** (lined up in) ranks, array, (parade) formation

12 落伍 **rakugo** fall out, straggle, drop behind

2a4.9 / 334

任 **NIN** duties, responsibility; tenure **maka(seru), maka(su)** entrust to, leave it to

────────── 1 ──────────

0 任じる/ずる **nin(jiru/zuru)** appoint; assume (responsibility); profess to be

5 任用 **nin'yō** appoint

6 任地 **ninchi** one's post, place of appointment

8 任命 **ninmei** appoint, nominate

任免 **ninmen** appointments and dismissals

任官 **ninkan** appointment, installation

9 任侠 **ninkyō** chivalry

11 任務 **ninmu** duty, task, function

12 任期 **ninki** term of office, tenure

13 任意 **nin'i** optional, voluntary, discretionary, arbitrary

────────── 2 ──────────

1 一任 **ichinin** entrust

2 人任 **hitomaka(se)** leaving it to others

力任 **chikaramaka(se)** with all one's might

3 大任 **tainin** great task, important responsibility

口任 **kuchimaka(se)** random talk
5 出任 **demaka(se)** saying whatever comes to mind
代任 **dainin** acting for another; deputy
主任 **shunin** person in charge
6 気任 **kimaka(se)** at one's pleasure/fancy
再任 **sainin** reappoint
先任 **sennin** seniority
先任者 **senninsha** predecessor
在任 **zainin** hold office, be in office
在任中 **zaininchū** while in office
自任 **jinin** fancy/regard oneself as
7 初任 **shonin** first appointment
初任給 **shoninkyū** starting salary
足任 **ashimaka(se)** go where one fancies, with no set destination; walk till one's legs tire
8 受任 **junin** be appointed
退任 **tainin** retire from office
担任 **tannin** charge, responsibility
昇任 **shōnin** be promoted, advance
放任 **hōnin** nonintervention
委任 **inin** trust, mandate, authorization
委任状 **ininjō** power of attorney
委任者 **ininsha** mandator
委任統治 **inin tōchi** mandate
9 専任 **sennin** exclusive duty, full-time
重任 **jūnin** heavy responsibility; re-election, reappointment
信任 **shinnin** confidence, trust
信任状 **shinninjō** credentials
叙任 **jonin** appointment, investiture
前任 **zennin** former (official)
前任地 **zenninchi** one's former post
前任者 **zenninsha** one's predecessor
赴任 **funin** proceed to one's new post
赴任地 **funinchi** one's place of appointment
赴任先 **funinsaki** one's place of appointment
後任 **kōnin** successor
背任 **hainin** breach of trust
背任罪 **haininzai** breach of trust
10 帰任 **kinin** return to one's post/duties
兼任 **kennin** concurrent post
留任 **ryūnin** remain in office
11 運任 **unmaka(se)** trusting to luck
常任委員会 **jōnin iinkai** standing committee
現任 **gennin** present post, incumbent
責任 **sekinin** responsibility, liability
責任者 **sekininsha** person in charge
責任感 **sekininkan** sense of responsibility
転任 **tennin** change of assignments/personnel
12 着任 **chakunin** arrival at one's post
就任 **shūnin** assumption of office
就任式 **shūninshiki** inauguration, installation
復任 **fukunin** reappointment, reinstatement
無任所大臣 **muninsho daijin** minister without portfolio

補任 **honin** appoint
13 適任 **tekinin** fit, suited, competent
適任者 **tekininsha** well-qualified person
適任証 **tekininshō** certificate of competence
解任 **kainin** dismissal, release
新任 **shinnin** new appointment
辞任 **jinin** resign
14 歴任 **rekinin** successively holding various posts
選任 **sennin** select, appointment
16 親任 **shinnin** personal appointment by the emperor
親任式 **shinninshiki** ceremony of investiture by the emperor
親任官 **shinninkan** official personally appointed by the emperor
18 離任 **rinin** quit one's office

─────── 3 ───────
4 不信任 **fushinnin** nonconfidence
不信任案 **fushinnin'an** nonconfidence motion
不適任 **futekinin** unfit, incompetent
12 無責任 **musekinin** irresponsibility

─────── 4 ───────
6 自由放任 **jiyū hōnin** nonintervention, laissez-faire

2a4.10 / 1056

仰   **GYŌ, KŌ, ao(gu)** look up; look up to, respect; ask for, depend on; drink **os(haru)** say (polite) **ōse** what you say (polite)

─────── 1 ───────
3 仰々 **gyōgyō(shii)** grandiloquent, grandiose, ostentatious
仰山 **gyōsan** many, much; grandiose
4 仰天 **gyōten** be astounded
5 仰付 **ō(se)tsu(keru)** tell (someone to do); appoint
6 仰向 **aomu(keru)** turn to face upward
7 仰角 **gyōkaku** angle of elevation
9 仰臥 **gyōga** lie face up
11 仰視 **gyōshi** look up

─────── 2 ───────
3 大仰 **ōgyō** exaggeration
9 信仰 **shinkō** religious faith, belief in
信仰告白 **shinkō kokuhaku** profession of faith
10 俯仰 **fugyō** looking up and down; one's actions
俯仰天地 **fugyōtenchi** (nothing to be ashamed of) before God or man
11 渇仰 **katsugō, katsugyō** adore, admire, idolize

2

イ 4 ←
彳
孑
阝
卩
刂
力
又
宀
亠
十
卜
ク
ゝ
厂
辶
冂
八
匚

12 景仰 **keigyō** adoration, admiration; love of virtue **keikō** love of virtue

――――――― 3 ―――――――

4 不信仰 **fushinkō** lack of faith, unbelief

似 → **2a5.11**

2a4.11

价 **KAI** good; large; servant; man in armor

2a4.12

伉 **KŌ** same kind; high spirits

2a4.13

伎 **GI** deed; skill

――――――― 1 ―――――――

13 伎楽 **gigaku** (an ancient mask show)

――――――― 3 ―――――――

14 歌舞伎 **kabuki** kabuki

伜 → 倅 **2a8.29**

2a4.14 / 434

伝 傳 **DEN, TEN** transmit; legend, tradition **tsuta(eru)** tell, convey, transmit **tsuta(waru)** be conveyed transmitted; be handed down **tsuta(u)** go/walk along

――――――― 1 ―――――――

5 伝令 **denrei** message; messenger
7 伝来 **denrai** be transmitted, be handed down; be imported
 伝承 **denshō** transmit, hand down (folklore)
 伝述 **denjutsu** pass on, relay
 伝言 **dengon** message
 伝言板 **dengonban** message/bulletin board
8 伝受 **denju** be told, hear
 伝送 **densō** transmit, relay
 伝法 **denpō, denbō** affected bravado
 伝奇 **denki** romance (fiction)
9 伝奏 **densō** deliver a message to the emperor
 伝染 **densen** contagion, infection
 伝染病 **densenbyō** contagious/communi-

cable disease
10 伝家 **denka** heirloom; trump card, last resort
 伝書鳩 **denshobato** carrier pigeon
 伝記 **denki** biography
 伝記物 **denkimono** biographical literature
 伝馬 **tenma, denba** post-horse
 伝馬船 **tenmasen** a lighter, jolly (boat)
11 伝達 **dentatsu** transmit, convey, propagate
 伝道 **dendō** evangelism, proselytizing, missionary work
 伝道師 **dendōshi** evangelist
 伝授 **denju** instruct, initiate into
 伝唱 **denshō** advocate, espouse
 伝習 **denshū** learn, be instructed
 伝票 **denpyō** slip of paper
12 伝統 **dentō** tradition
 伝統的 **dentōteki** traditional
14 伝導 **dendō** conduction
 伝説 **densetsu** legend
 伝聞 **denbun** hearsay, report, rumor
15 伝播 **denpa** propagation, dissemination

――――――― 2 ―――――――

2 人伝 **hitozu(te)** hearsay; message
3 口伝 **kuchizute, kuchizuta(e)** word of mouth, oral tradition
 小伝 **shōden** brief biography/account
5 史伝 **shiden** history and biography; historical records
 古伝 **koden** legend, tradition
 外伝 **gaiden** lateral biography; anecdote
 正伝 **seiden** authentic/official biography
6 列伝 **retsuden** series of biographies
 列伝体 **retsudentai** biographical style
 自伝 **jiden** autobiography
7 言伝 **i(i)tsuta(eru)** hand down (a legend), spread (a rumor) **kotozu(te)** hearsay; message
8 直伝 **jikiden** handed down directly, initiation into
 其伝 **so(no) den** that way/trick
9 宣伝 **senden** propaganda; advertising, publicity
 宣伝係 **sendengakari** public relations man
 宣伝屋 **senden'ya** propagandist, publicist
 宣伝部 **sendenbu** publicity department
 宣伝隊 **sendentai** propaganda squad
 宣伝費 **sendenhi** publicity/advertising expenses
 宣伝業 **sendengyō** publicity/advertising business
 宣伝業者 **senden gyōsha** publicist
 宣伝戦 **sendensen** propaganda/advertising campaign
 宣伝機関 **senden kikan** propaganda organ
 相伝 **sōden** inheritance, handed down

皆伝 **kaiden** initiation into all the mysteries (of an art)

10 家伝 **kaden** family tradition, handed down within the family

書伝 **ka(ki)tsuta(eru)** set forth in writing (for posterity)

秘伝 **hiden** secret, esoteric mysteries

11 虚伝 **kyoden** false rumor

略伝 **ryakuden** brief biography

経伝 **keiden** writings of saints and sages

12 超伝導 **chōdendō** superconductivity

喧伝 **kenden** bruit about, circulate

評伝 **hyōden** critical biography

13 詳伝 **shōden** detailed biography

14 遺伝 **iden** heredity

遺伝子 **idenshi** gene

遺伝子工学 **idenshi kōgaku** genetic engineering

遺伝因子組替 **iden'inshi kumika(e)** recombinant gene splicing

遺伝学 **idengaku** genetics

遺伝法 **idenhō** laws of heredity

遺伝病 **idenbyō** hereditary disease

誤伝 **goden** false report

聞伝 **ki(ki)tsuta(e)** hearsay

駅伝 **ekiden** post horse, stagecoach; long-distance relay race

駅伝競走 **ekiden kyōsō** long-distance relay race

———————— 3 ————————

5 以心伝心 **ishin-denshin** telepathy, tacit understanding

立志伝 **risshiden** success story

6 自叙伝 **jijoden** autobiography

8 逆宣伝 **gyakusenden** counterpropaganda

武勇伝 **buyūden** story of marital heroics

9 飛石伝 **to(bi)ishizuta(i)** following stepping-stones

屋根伝 **yanezuta(i)** from roof to roof

14 銘々伝 **meimeiden** lives, biographies

———————— 4 ————————

1 一子相伝 **isshi sōden** (secret) handed down from father to son

2a4.15 / 1049

仮假   **KA, KE, kari** temporary, provisional; supposing; assumed (name), false

———————— 1 ————————

2 仮入学 **karinyūgaku** provisional enrollment, admission on probation

3 仮小屋 **karigoya** temporary shed, booth

4 仮分数 **kabunsū** improper fraction

5 仮出所 **karishussho** release on parole, out on bail

仮出獄 **karishutsugoku** release on parole, out on bail

仮処分 **karishobun** provisional disposition

6 仮死 **kashi** suspended animation, apparent death

仮名 **kana** kana, Japanese syllabary character

kamei, kemyō, karina pseudonym, alias, pen name

仮名草紙 **kanazōshi** story book written in kana

仮名遣 **kanazuka(i)** kana orthography

7 仮作 **kasaku** fiction

仮条約 **karijōyaku** provisional treaty

仮初 **karisome** temporary; trivial

8 仮免状 **karimenjō** temporary license; provisional diploma

仮泊 **kahaku** temporary anchoring

仮拵 **karigoshira(e)** makeshift

仮定 **katei** supposition, assumption, hypothesis

仮定法 **kateihō** subjunctive mood

仮枕 **karimakura** nap

仮性 **kasei** false (symptoms)

9 仮屋 **kariya** temporary shelter

仮面 **kamen** mask, disguise

仮相 **kasō** appearance, phenomenon

仮政府 **kariseifu** provisional government

10 仮借 **kashaku, kasha** pardon, be lenient; using a kanji for another having the same reading

仮眠 **kamin** nap

仮称 **kashō** tentative/provisional/working name

仮病 **kebyō** feigned illness

仮託 **kataku** pretext

11 仮勘定 **karikanjō** suspense account

仮宿 **kari (no) yado** temporary dwelling; this transient world

仮庵 **kariio** booth, tabernacle, temporary dwelling

仮釈放 **karishakuhō** release on parole

仮設 **kasetsu** temporary construction; (legal) fiction

12 仮普請 **karibushin** temporary building

仮寓 **kagū** temporary residence

仮装 **kasō** disguise, fancy dress; converted (cruiser)

仮装舞踏会 **kasō butōkai** masquerade ball

仮歯 **kashi** false tooth

13 仮寝 **karine** nap; stay at an inn

仮想 **kasō** imaginary, supposed, virtual (mass), hypothetical

仮睡 **kasui** nap

14 仮綴 **karito(ji)** temporary binding; paperback

仮説 **kasetsu** hypothesis, tentative theory

2

イ 4 ←
冫
子
阝
刂
力
又
宀
十
卜
⺮
⺌
厂
辶
冂
几
匸

15 仮縫 **karinu(i)** temporary sewing, basting
仮調印 **karichōin** initialing (a treaty)
16 仮橋 **karibashi** temporary bridge

——————— 2 ———————

4 片仮名 **katakana** katakana, the non-cursive syllabary
5 平仮名 **hiragana** (the cursive syllabary)
8 送仮名 **oku(ri)gana** suffixed kana showing inflection
9 草仮名 **sōgana** hiragana
10 振仮名 **fu(ri)gana** (small kana written above or beside a kanji to show its pronunciation)
11 虚仮 **koke** fool, idiot
虚仮威 **kokeodo(shi)** empty threat, mere show, bluff
虚仮猿 **kokezaru** idiotic monkey
13 寛仮 **kanka** be tolerant toward

——————— 3 ———————

3 万葉仮名 **man'yōgana** kanji used phonetically
9 変体仮名 **hentai-gana** anomalous (obsolete) kana

2a4.16 / 89

全 全

ZEN all **matta(ku)** completely; truly, indeed **matto(u suru)** accomplish, fulfill

——————— 1 ———————

1 全一 **zen'itsu** a complete whole
2 全人 **zenjin** well-balanced person
全人代 **Zenjindai** (Chinese) National People's Congress (short for 全国人民代表大会)
全人格 **zenjinkaku** one's whole personality
全人教育 **zenjin kyōiku** well-rounded education, education for the whole man
全人類 **zenjinrui** all mankind
全力 **zenryoku** one's every effort, full capacity
3 全土 **zendo** the whole country
4 全文 **zenbun** full text; whole sentence
全日本 **zen-Nihon, zen-Nippon** all Japan
全日本空輸 **Zen Nippon Kūyu** All Nippon Airways
全日制 **zennichisei** full-time (school) system
全日空 **Zennikkū** ANA = All Nippon Airways (short for 全日本空輸)
5 全民衆 **zenminshū** all the people
全生涯 **zenshōgai** one's entire life
全世界 **zensekai** the whole world
全市 **zenshi** the whole city
全市民 **zenshimin** all the citizens of the city
6 全会一致 **zenkai-itchi** unanimous

全地方 **zenchihō** the whole region
全米 **zen-Bei** all-America(n), pan-American
7 全身 **zenshin** the whole body
全身不随 **zenshin fuzui** total paralysis
全身麻酔 **zenshin masui** general anasthesia
全体 **zentai** the whole, in all
全体主義 **zentai shugi** totalitarianism
全形 **zenkei** the whole shape
全乳 **zennyū** whole milk
全局 **zenkyoku** the whole situation
全図 **zenzu** complete map; whole view
全快 **zenkai** complete recovery, full cure
8 全長 **zenchō** overall length
全治 **zenchi, zenji** fully recover, heal completely
全知 **zenchi** onmiscience
全知全能 **zenchi-zennō** all-knowing and all-powerful
全店 **zenten** the whole store, all the stores
全国 **zenkoku, zengoku** the whole country, nationwide, national
全国人民代表大会 **Zenkoku Jinmin Daihyō Taikai** (Chinese) National People's Congress
全国民 **zenkokumin** the entire nation
全国的 **zenkokuteki** nationwide
全欧 **zen-Ō** all Europe
9 全巻 **zenkan** the whole volume; the whole reel (of a movie)
全１０巻 **zen-jikkan** ten volumes in all
全院 **zen'in** the whole house/institution
全院委員会 **zen'in iinkai** committee of the whole house
全軍 **zengun** the whole army/team
全速力 **zensokuryoku** full/top speed
全通 **zentsū** be opened to through traffic
全段 **zendan** the whole page
全面 **zenmen** the whole surface; full-scale, all-out
全面的 **zenmenteki** all-out, full, general
全音 **zen'on** whole tone (in music)
全音符 **zen'onpu** whole note
全科 **zenka** complete course/curriculum
全級 **zenkyū** the whole class
10 全都 **zento** the whole capital, all of Tōkyō
全部 **zenbu** all, whole; entirely
全員 **zen'in** all the members, the whole staff/crew
全家 **zenka** the whole family
全容 **zen'yō** the full picture/story
全島 **zentō** the whole island, all the islands
全校 **zenkō** the whole school, all the schools
全能 **zennō** omnipotence
全書 **zensho** complete book, compendium
全紙 **zenshi** the whole sheet/newspaper

全納 **zennō** payment in full
全般 **zenpan** whole, general, overall
全般的 **zenpanteki** general, overall, across-the-board
11 全隊 **zentai** the entire force, all units
全域 **zen'iki** the whole area
全盛 **zensei** height of prosperity
全盛期 **zenseiki** golden age, heyday
全船 **zensen** the whole ship, all the ships
全訳 **zen'yaku** complete translation
全敗 **zenpai** complete defeat
12 全備 **zenbi** fully equipped, complete, perfect
全幅 **zenpuku** overall width; utmost
全廃 **zenpai** total abolition
全勝 **zenshō** complete victory
全景 **zenkei** complete view, panorama
全量 **zenryō** the whole quantity
全智 **zenchi** onmiscience
全焼 **zenshō** be totally destroyed by fire
全然 **zenzen** entirely, utterly, (not) at all
全集 **zenshū** complete works
全開 **zenkai** open fully
13 全滅 **zenmetsu** annihilation
全損 **zenson** total loss
全数 **zensū** the whole number, all
全裸 **zenra** stark naked, nude
14 全貌 **zenbō** the full picture/story
全製品 **zenseihin** manufactured product
15 全潰 **zenkai** complete collapse/destruction
全権 **zenken** full authority
全権大使 **zenken taishi** ambassador plenipotentiary
全線 **zensen** the whole line, all lines
全編 **zenpen** the whole book
全篇 **zenpen** the whole book
16 全壊 **zenkai** complete destruction
17 全優 **zen'yū** straight A's
18 全癒 **zen'yu** complete healing
全額 **zengaku** the full amount

───────── 2 ─────────

2 十全 **jūzen** perfection, consummation; absolute safety
3 万全 **banzen** perfect, sure, prudent
万全策 **banzen (no) saku** carefully thought-out plan, prudent policy
大全 **taizen** complete works, encyclopedia
4 不全 **fuzen** partial, incomplete, imperfect
6 両全 **ryōzen** advantageous for both sides
安全 **anzen** safety
安全弁 **anzenben** safety valve
安全地帯 **anzen chitai** safety zone/island
安全保障 **anzen hoshō** (national) security
安全率 **anzenritsu** safety factor
安全第一 **anzen dai-ichi** Safety First

安全装置 **anzen sōchi** safety device
安全感 **anzenkan** sense of security
7 完全 **kanzen** complete, perfect
完全性 **kanzensei** completeness, perfection
完全無欠 **kanzen-muketsu** flawlessly perfect
完全雇傭 **kanzen koyō** full employment
完全数 **kanzensū** whole number, integer
9 保全 **hozen** preservation
10 健全 **kenzen** healthy, sound

───────── 3 ─────────

4 不完全 **fukanzen** incomplete, imperfect, faulty, defective
不健全 **fukenzen** unhealthy, unsound
六法全書 **roppō zensho** the statute books
6 全知全能 **zenchi-zennō** all-knowing and all-powerful
百科全書 **hyakka zensho** encyclopedia

2a4.17 / 481

企 **KI, kuwada(teru)** plan, scheme, intend; attempt, undertake **taku(ramu)** scheme, devise, contrive, plot

───────── 1 ─────────

3 企及 **kikyū** attempt
7 企図 **kito** plan, project, undertaking
8 企画 **kikaku** plan, planning
13 企業 **kigyō** enterprise, corporation
企業家 **kigyōka** industrialist, entrepreneur

───────── 2 ─────────

3 小企業 **shōkigyō** small enterprises/business

───────── 3 ─────────

4 中小企業 **chūshō kigyō** small business(es)
中堅企業 **chūken kigyō** medium-size business/company

2a4.18 / 159

合 **GŌ, GA', KA'** together; total; (unit of area, 0.33 square meters); (unit of volume, 180 ml); one of ten stations up a mountain; total **a(u)** fit, match, agree with, be correct **a(waseru), a(wasu)** put together, combine, compare

───────── 1 ─────────

0 合する **gas(suru)** combine, meet, accord with
合カギ **aikagi** duplicate key; passkey; Keys Made
1 合一 **gōitsu** unification, union
2 合子 **a(ino)ko** cross, hybrid, half-breed
合力 **gōryoku** resultant force; cooperation; alms-giving, assistance
4 合切 **gassai** all, all together

合手 **a(ino)te** interlude; musical accompaniment; sideshow
5 合本 **gappon** bound volumes
合弁 **gōben** joint management/venture
合弁会社 **gōben-gaisha** joint venture (company)
合札 **a(i)fuda** check, tally
合目 **a(wase)me** joint, seam
6 合羽 **kappa** raincoat
合印 **a(i)jirushi** comradeship badge; tally marks **aiin** tally marks
合同 **gōdō** combined, joint
合名会社 **gōmei-gaisha** unlimited partnership
合成 **gōsei** synthetic, composite, combined
合成物 **gōseibutsu** a compound/synthetic
合成語 **gōseigo** a compound (word)
合成樹脂 **gōsei jushi** synthetic resin, plastic
合成繊維 **gōsei sen'i** synthetic fiber
7 合体 **gattai** amalgamation, combination, union
合作 **gassaku** joint work, collaboration
合判 **a(i)ban, a(i)han, gōhan** medium size (paper)
合図 **aizu** signal, sign
合言葉 **a(i)kotoba** password, watchword
8 合併 **gappei** merger, consolidation
合法 **gōhō** legality, lawfulness
合法的 **gōhōteki** legal, lawful
合板 **gōhan, gōban** plywood
合服 **a(i)fuku** between-season clothing, spring or fall wear
合祀 **gōshi** enshrine together
合性 **a(i)shō** compatibility, affinity
合金 **gōkin** alloy
9 合奏 **gassō** concert, ensemble
合点 **gaten, gatten** understand, comprehend; consent to
合計 **gōkei** total
10 合流 **gōryū** confluence; join
合従連衡 **gasshō-renkō** multi-party alliance (against a powerful enemy)
合格 **gōkaku** pass (an exam/inspection)
合致 **gatchi** agreement, concurrence, conforming to
11 合唱 **gasshō** chorus
合唱曲 **gasshōkyoku** chorus, choral, part-song
合唱団 **gasshōdan** chorus, choir
合唱隊 **gasshōtai** chorus, choir
合著 **gōcho** joint authorship
合宿 **gasshuku** lodging together
合理 **gōri** rationality
合理化 **gōrika** rationalization, streamlining
合理主義 **gōri shugi** rationalism
合理的 **gōriteki** rational, reasonable, logical

合理性 **gōrisei** rationality, reasonableness
12 合着 **a(i)gi** between-season clothing, spring or fall wear
合掌 **gasshō** join one's hands (in prayer)
合衆国 **Gasshūkoku** United States
合評 **gappyō** joint review/criticism
合間 **a(i)ma** interval
13 合戦 **kassen** battle
合意 **gōi** mutual consent, agreement
合資 **gōshi** partnership
合資会社 **gōshi-gaisha** limited partnership
14 合算 **gassan** add up, total
15 合歓 **gōkan** enjoy together
合歓木 **nemunoki** silk tree
16 合壁 **kappeki, gappeki** next-door house just a wall away
合憲性 **gōkensei** constitutionality
合鍵 **aikagi** duplicate key; passkey; Keys Made
20 合議 **gōgi** consultation, conference
合議制 **gōgisei** parliamentary system

———— 2 ————

1 一合目 **ichigōme** first station (of ten up a mountain)
3 工合 **guai** condition, state; convenience; state of health
4 不合格 **fugōkaku** failure (in an exam), rejection, disqualification
不合理 **fugōri** unreasonable, irrational
弔合戦 **tomura(i) gassen** battle to avenge a death
化合 **kagō** chemical combination
化合物 **kagōbutsu** chemical compound
切合 **ki(ri)a(i)** crossing swords, fighting with swords, cutting each other
六合 **rikugō** the universe/cosmos
分合 **wa(ke)a(u), wa(kachi)a(u)** share
込合 **ko(mi)a(u)** be crowded
手合 **tea(i)** fellow, chap **tea(wase)** game, contest; sale, transaction
5 出合 **dea(u)** happen to meet, run into; rendezvous **da(shi)a(u)** contribute jointly, share the expenses
出合頭 **dea(i)gashira** upon running into each other, upon happening to meet
申合 **mō(shi)a(waseru)** arrange, agree upon
付合 **tsu(ki)a(u)** keep company with, associate with **tsu(ke)a(wase)** vegetables added as relish
巡合 **megu(ri)a(u)** chance to meet
打合 **u(chi)a(u)** hit each other, exchange blows **u(chi)a(waseru)** strike (one thing) against (another); prearrange **u(chi)a(wase)** previous arrangement, appointed (hour)

叩合 **tata(ki)a(u)** fight, exchange blows
示合 **shime(shi)a(u)** inform/show each other
石合戦 **ishi gassen** stone-throwing fight
6 気合 **kia(i)** spiritedness; a yell
気合負 **kia(i)ma(ke)** be overawed
気合術 **kia(i)jutsu** hypnotism
会合 **kaigō** meeting, assembly
交合 **kōgō** copulation
色合 **iroa(i)** coloring, shade, tint
迎合 **geigō** flattery, ingratiation
地合 **jia(i)** texture, weave, fabric
向合 **mu(kai)a(u)** face each other
光合成 **kōgōsei** photosynthesis
回合 **megu(ri)/mawa(ri)a(wase)** turn of fate, chance
肌合 **hadaa(i)** disposition, temperament
有合 **a(ri)a(u)** happen to be on hand
　　　a(ri)a(wase) what is on hand
早合点 **hayagaten** hasty conclusion
百合 **yuri** lily
百合根 **yurine** lily bulb
血合 **chia(i)** meat of bloody color
7 来合 **kia(waseru)** happen to come along
似合 **nia(u)** befit, go well with, be becoming
　　　nia(washii) suitable, becoming, well-matched
助合 **tasu(ke)a(u)** help one another
励合 **hage(mi)a(u)** vie with one another
沖合 **okia(i)** open sea, offshore
折合 **o(ri)a(u)** come to an agreement
抜合 **nu(ki)a(waseru)** unsheathe (swords) at the same time
投合 **tōgō** coincide, agree with, meet
吻合 **fungō** coincidence; inosculation
花合 **hanaa(wase)** floral playing cards
見合 **mia(u)** look at each other; offset
　　　mia(i) arranged-marriage interview
　　　mia(waseru) exchange glances; set off against; postpone, abandon
言合 **i(i)a(u)** quarrel; exchange words
　　　i(i)a(waseru) arrange beforehand
8 非合法 **higōhō** illegal
非合理的 **higōriteki** unreasonable, irrational
併合 **heigō** annexation, amalgamation, merger
受合 **u(ke)a(i)** guarantee, assurance
押合 **o(shi)a(u)** jostle one another
抱合 **da(ki)a(u)** embrace each other
　　　da(ki)a(waseru) cause to embrace
　　　hōgō combination; embrace
抱合売 **da(ki)a(wase) u(ri)** selling poorly selling articles in a tie-up with articles which sell well
知合 **shi(ri)a(i)** an acquaintance
　　　shi(ri)a(u) know each other
茂合 **shige(ri)a(u)** grow luxuriantly

突合 **tsu(ki)a(u)** poke/jab each other
　　　tsu(ki)a(waseru) bring face to face; compare with
空合 **soraa(i)** weather
歩合 **buai** rate, percentage; commission
　　　ayu(mi)a(u) compromise
歩合算 **buaizan** calculation of percentage
居合 **ia(waseru)** happen to be present
居合抜 **ia(i)nu(ki)** swordplay exhibition
和合 **wagō** harmony, concord
取合 **to(ri)a(u)** take each other's (hand); scramble for; take notice of　**to(ri)a(waseru)** put together, assort, match
雨合羽 **amagappa** raincoat
9 重合 **jūgō** polymerization　**kasa(nari)a(u)** lie on top of each other, overlap; pile up
重合体 **jūgōtai** polymer
乗合 **no(ri)a(wasu)** happen to ride together
　　　no(ri)a(i) riding together; fellow passenger; partnership; bus, stagecoach
係合 **keigō** engage/mesh with, fit into
　　　kaka(ri)a(u) have to do with, be implicated in
連合 **rengō** union, league, federation, alliance, combination　**tsu(re)a(i)** spouse, mate
連合国 **rengōkoku** allied nations, allies
連合軍 **rengōgun** allied armies
造合 **tsuku(ri)a(waseru)** make and join together; make a duplicate
通合 **tō(ri)a(waseru)** happen to come along
　　　tsū(ji)a(u) plot together
風合 **fūai** the feel, texture
独合点 **hito(ri)gaten** hasty conclusion
待合 **ma(chi)a(waseru)** wait for (as previously arranged)　**ma(chi)a(i)** waiting room; geisha entertainment place
待合室 **machiaishitsu** waiting room
度合 **doa(i)** degree, extent, rate
相合傘 **aia(i)gasa (de)** under the same umbrella
香合 **kōgō** incense container
思合 **omo(i)a(u)** love each other
　　　omo(i)a(waseru) consider together
糾合 **kyūgō** rally, muster
食合 **ku(i)a(waseru)** combining foods
　　　ku(i)a(u) bite each other; fit together exactly, mesh
10 都合 **tsugō** circumstances; one's convenience; opportunity; arrangements
都合上 **tsugōjō** for convenience
都合良 **tsugōyo(ku)** fortunately, successfully, satisfactorily
兼合 **ka(ne)a(i)** equilibrium, balance, poise
差合 **sa(shi)a(i)** hindrance, impediment
埋合 **u(me)a(waseru)** make up for, compensate for

2

→4 亻
　ノ
　孑
　阝
　卩
　刂
　力
　又
　一
　十
　卜
　ケ
　マ
　厂
　辶
　冂
　几
　匚

振合 **fu(ri)a(i)** balancing, comparison, consideration, relationship
烏合衆 **ugō(no)shū** disorderly crowd, mob
配合 **haigō** arrangement, combination
11 野合 **yagō** illicit cohabitation
勘合貿易 **kangō bōeki** licensed trade
混合 **kongō** mixture, mixed, compound **ma(ze)a(waseru)** mix, blend, compound
混合物 **kongōbutsu** mixture, compound
混合酒 **kongōshu** mixed drink, blended liquor
混合語 **kongōgo** word derived/combined from two other words
混合機 **kongōki** mixer
掛合 **ka(ke)a(u)** negotiate/bargain with **ka(ke)a(wasu)** multiply together; cross, interbreed **ka(kari)a(i)** involvement, implication in
接合 **setsugō** joining, union **ha(gi)a(waseru)** join/patch together
接合剤 **setsugōzai** glue, adhesive
探合 **sagu(ri)a(i)** probing each other's feelings
啀合 **iga(mi)a(u)** snarl at each other, bicker, feud
帳合 **chōa(i)** balancing/keeping accounts
張合 **ha(ri)a(u)** vie/compete with
寄合 **yo(ri)a(i)** meeting, get-together
組合 **ku(mi)a(u)** form a partnership; grapple with **kumiai** association, union **ku(mi)a(waseru)** combine; fit together **ku(mi)a(wase)** combination
符合 **fugō** coincidence, agreement, correspondence
訳合 **wakea(i)** circumstances, matter
斬合 **ki(ri)a(i)** crossing swords, fighting with swords
釣合 **tsu(ri)a(u)** be in balance, match **tsu(ri)a(i)** balance, equilibrium, proportion
雪合戦 **yuki gassen** snowball fight
問合 **to(i)a(waseru), to(i)a(wasu)** inquire
頃合 **koroa(i)** suitable time; propriety; moderation
12 割合 **wariai** rate, proportion, percentage; comparatively
遣合 **ya(ri)a(u)** do to each other, argue, compete
渡合 **wata(ri)a(u)** cross swords, argue
場合 **baai** case, occasion, circumstances
落合 **o(chi)a(u)** come together, meet
嵌合 **kangō, hamea(i)** fit into, engage
廃合 **haigō** abolition and amalgamation, reorganization
程合 **hodoa(i)** extent, limit

結合 **ketsugō** union, combination **musu-(bi)a(waseru)** tie together, combine
結合組織 **ketsugō soshiki** connective tissue
絡合 **kara(mi)a(u)** intertwine
統合 **tōgō** unify, integrate, combine
筋合 **sujia(i)** reason
軽合金 **keigōkin** light alloy
集合 **shūgō** gathering, meeting; set (in math)
集合名詞 **shūgō meishi** collective noun
集合的 **shūgōteki** collective
雲合 **kumoa(i)** the look of the sky
間合 **ma (ni) a(u)** be in time for; serve the purpose, suffice
13 適合 **tekigō** conform to, suit, fit
溶合 **to(ke)a(u)** melt together, fade into
搗合 **ka(chi)a(u)** clash
搔合 **ka(ki)a(waseru)** adjust, arrange
夢合 **yumea(wase)** interpretation of dreams
幕合 **makua(i)** intermission (between acts)
腹合 **haraa(wase)** facing each other
暗合 **angō** coincidence
煉合 **ne(ri)a(waseru)** knead together, compound
照合 **te(rashi)a(waseru)** check by comparison **shōgō** check against, verify
睨合 **nira(mi)a(u)** glare at each other **nira(mi)a(waseru)** take (something) for comparison
継合 **tsu(gi)a(waseru), tsu(gi)a(wasu)** join/patch/splice together
触合 **fu(re)a(u)** touch, come in contact with
詰合 **tsu(me)a(waseru)** pack an assortment of
話合 **hana(shi)a(u)** talk over, discuss
試合 **shiai** game, match
鉢合 **hachia(wase)** bump heads; run into
馴合 **na(re)a(u)** collude; become intimate with
14 摑合 **tsuka(mi)a(u)** grapple, tussle
歌合 **utaawa(se)** poetry contest
憎合 **niku(mi)a(u)** hate one another
複合 **fukugō** composite, compound, complex
複合語 **fukugōgo** compound word
練合 **ne(ri)a(waseru)** knead together
綴合 **tsuzu(ri)a(waseru)** bind/sew together, fasten, file
綜合 **sōgō** comprehensive, composite, synthetic
綜合的 **sōgōteki** comprehensive, overall
総合 **sōgō** synthesis, comprehensive
総合大学 **sōgō daigaku** university
総合的 **sōgōteki** comprehensive, overall
語合 **kata(ri)a(u)** talk together, chat
読合 **yo(mi)a(waseru)** read and compare
奪合 **uba(i)a(u)** scramble/struggle for
聞合 **ki(ki)a(wase)** inquiry

15 隣合 **tona(ri)a(u)** adjoin, be next to each other
潮合 **shioa(i)** (waiting for) the tide, opportunity
横合 **yokoa(i)** (from the) side
編合 **a(mi)a(wasu), a(mi)a(waseru)** knit together
縫合 **nu(i)a(waseru)** sew up, stitch together
     hōgō a suture, stitch
談合 **dan(ji)a(u)** confer/negotiate with
     dangō consultation, conference
請合 **u(ke)a(u)** undertake; guarantee, vouch for   **u(ke)a(i)** sure, certain, guaranteed
調合 **chōgō** compounding, mixing
調合剤 **chōgōzai** preparation, concoction
16 整合 **seigō** adjust, coordinate
融合 **yūgō** fusion
諜合 **shime(shi)a(waseru)** prearrange, collude, conspire
17 擦合 **su(re)a(u)** rub/chafe against each other, be at variance with
聯合 **rengō** combination, league, coalition
18 噛合 **ka(mi)a(u)** bite each other; (gears) engage, mesh with   **ka(mi)a(waseru)** clench (one's teeth); engage (gears), mesh with
癒合 **yugō** agglutination, adhesion, knitting
織合 **o(ri)a(waseru)** interweave
離合 **rigō** meeting and parting
顔合 **kaoa(wase)** meeting; appearing together
19 繰合 **ku(ri)a(waseru)** manage, find the time
繋合 **tsuna(gi)a(waseru)** join/tie together
蹴合 **kea(u)** kick each other   **kea(i)** cock-fighting
騙合 **dama(shi)a(i)** cheating each other
20 競合 **kyōgō** competition, rivalry
     se(ri)a(u) compete with, vie for
譲合 **yuzu(ri)a(u)** defer/yield to each other, compromise

———————— 3 ————————

1 一切合財 **issai-gassai** everything, the whole shebang
2 人付合 **hitozu(ki)a(i)** sociability
3 三部合奏 **sanbu gassō** instrumental trio
小百合 **sayuri** lily
小競合 **kozeria(i)** skirmish; bickering, quarrel
4 不仕合 **fushia(wase)** misfortune, unhappiness, ill luck
不似合 **funia(i)** unbecoming, unsuitable, ill-matched
不都合 **futsugō** inconvenience, trouble, harm; impropriety, misconduct
不釣合 **futsuria(i)** unbalanced, disproportionate, ill-matched
公武合体 **kōbu gattai** union of imperial court and shogunate

5 出来合 **dekia(u)** be ready-made; become intimate with
好都合 **kōtsugō** favorable, good
四部合奏 **shibu gassō** (instrumental) quartet
四部合唱 **shibu gasshō** (vocal) quartet
白百合 **shirayuri** Easter lily
6 再試合 **saishiai** rematch, resumption of a game
近所合壁 **kinjo gappeki** immediate neighborhood
安請合 **yasuu(ke)a(i)** be too ready to make a promise/commitment
7 角突合 **tsunotsu(ki)a(i)** bickering, wrangling
初顔合 **hatsukaoa(wase)** first meeting
8 泥仕合 **dorojiai** mudslinging
泥試合 **dorojiai** mudslinging
取組合 **to(k)ku(mi)a(u)** grapple, tussle
9 背中合 **senakaa(wase)** back to back
10 核融合 **kakuyūgō** nuclear fusion
書具合 **ka(ki)guai** the feel of the pen against the paper as one writes
鬼百合 **oniyuri** tiger lily
11 混声合唱 **konsei gasshō** mixed chorus
黒百合 **kuroyuri** (a variety of dark-purple lily)
12 御都合 **gotsugō** your convenience
御都合主義 **gotsugō shugi** opportunism
間尺合 **mashaku (ni) a(wanai)** not be worth it
13 義理合 **giria(i)** social relationship
腹具合 **haraguai** condition of one's bowels
意味合 **imia(i)** meaning, implications
14 語呂合 **goroa(wase)** play on words, pun
語路合 **goroa(wase)** play on words, pun
15 隣付合 **tonarizu(ki)a(i)** neighborliness
16 懐具合 **futokoro guai** one's financial circumstances
17 鍔迫合 **tsubazeria(i)** close fighting

———————— 4 ————————

4 公定歩合 **kōtei buai** official bank rate, rediscount rate
5 出来具合 **dekiguai** workmanship, result, performance
6 共済組合 **kyōsai kumiai** mutual aid society
7 対校試合 **taikō-jiai** interschool match
労働組合 **rōdō kumiai** labor union
8 国際連合 **Kokusai Rengō** United Nations
9 信用組合 **shin'yō kumiai** credit union
11 商業組合 **shōgyō kumiai** trade association
情意投合 **jōi-tōgō** mutual sentiment/understanding
第二組合 **dai-ni kumiai** rival labor union
12 御用組合 **goyō kumiai** company union
13 意気投合 **iki-tōgō** sympathy, mutual understanding
16 親類付合 **shinrui-zu(ki)a(i)** association among relatives; intimate association
17 購買組合 **kōbai kumiai** a co-op

2a4.19 / 158

会 會

KAI meeting; society, association E understanding
a(u) meet

─────── 1 ───────

4 会心 **kaishin** congeniality, satisfaction
6 会合 **kaigō** meeting, assembly
会同 **kaidō** assembly, meeting
7 会社 **kaisha** company, corporation
会社員 **kaishain** company employee
会見 **kaiken** interview
8 会長 **kaichō** chairman, president
会所 **kaisho** meeting place; club
9 会計 **kaikei** accounting; the bill
会計士 **kaikeishi** accountant
会則 **kaisoku** rules of a society
会食 **kaishoku** dining together; mess
10 会陰 **ein** the perineum
会員 **kaiin** member
会員証 **kaiinshō** membership certificate/card
会席 **kaiseki** meeting place; poetry meeting; group dinner
会席料理 **kaiseki ryōri** banquet food served on individual trays
会席膳 **kaisekizen** dinner tray
11 会商 **kaishō** negotiations, talks
会得 **etoku** understanding, comprehension, appreciation
会堂 **kaidō** church, chapel; assembly hall
会規 **kaiki** rules of a society
会釈 **eshaku** salutation, greeting, bow
12 会場 **kaijō** meeting place; grounds
会報 **kaihō** bulletin, report, transactions (of a society)
会葬 **kaisō** attend a funeral
会期 **kaiki** term, session (of a legislature)
会衆 **kaishū** audience, congregation
会費 **kaihi** membership fee, dues
13 会戦 **kaisen** battle
会意 **kaii** formation of a kanji from meaningful components (e.g., 人 + 言 = 信)
会話 **kaiwa** conversation
14 会読 **kaidoku** reading-and-discussion meeting
15 会談 **kaidan** conversation, conference
16 会稽 **kaikei** revenge, vendetta
会館 **kaikan** (assembly) hall
会頭 **kaitō** president of a society
20 会議 **kaigi** conference, meeting
会議所 **kaigisho** meeting hall, site of a conference
会議室 **kaigishitsu** meeting/conference room
会議場 **kaigijō** meeting hall, place of assembly
会議録 **kaigiroku** minutes, proceedings

─────── 2 ───────

2 入会 **nyūkai** enrollment, admission
入会者 **nyūkaisha** new member
入会金 **nyūkaikin** enrollment/admission fee
子会社 **kogaisha** a subsidiary
3 大会 **taikai** large/general meeting, conference, convention; tournament, meet
大会堂 **daikaidō** cathedral
小会 **shōkai** small gathering
4 分会 **bunkai** branch, (local) chapter
公会 **kōkai** public meeting
公会堂 **kōkaidō** public hall, civic center
区会 **kukai** ward assembly
5 市会 **shikai** city council
正会員 **seikaiin** full/regular member
句会 **kukai** a haiku meeting
司会 **shikai** preside over, officiate
司会者 **shikaisha** emcee, chairman
立会 **ta(chi)a(i)** attendance, presence, witnessing; (trading) session
立会人 **tachiainin** observer, witness
立会演説 **ta(chi)a(i) enzetsu** campaign speech in a joint meeting of candidates, debate
6 年会 **nenkai** annual meeting/convention
再会 **saikai** meeting again, reunion
休会 **kyūkai** adjourn, go into recess
全会一致 **zenkai-itchi** unanimous
次会 **jikai** the next meeting
行会 **yu(ki)a(u), i(ki)a(u)** meet, come upon
7 延会 **enkai** adjournment
学会 **gakkai** academic society
村会 **sonkai** village assembly
社会 **shakai** society, social
社会人 **shakaijin** full member of society
社会化 **shakaika** socialization
社会民主主義 **shakai minshu shugi** social democracy
社会主義 **shakai shugi** socialism
社会学 **shakaigaku** sociology
社会的 **shakaiteki** social
社会性 **shakaisei** social nature
社会面 **shakaimen** local-news page
社会科 **shakaika** social studies, civics
社会部 **shakaibu** local-news section, city desk
社会党 **shakaitō** socialist party
社会悪 **shakaiaku** social evils
社会福祉 **shakai fukushi** social welfare
忍会 **shino(bi)a(i)** clandestine/secret meeting, rendezvous, tryst
町会 **chōkai** town council, town-block association
8 画会 **gakai** artist's patrons association
例会 **reikai** regular meeting
夜会 **yakai** evening party, ball

夜会服 **yakaifuku** evening dress
協会 **kyōkai** society, association
退会 **taikai** withdraw from membership
参会 **sankai** attendance (at a meeting)
参会者 **sankaisha** those present
英会話 **eikaiwa** English conversation
府会 **fukai** urban-prefectural assembly
府会議員 **fukai giin** urban-prefectural assemblyman
国会 **kokkai** national assembly, parliament, diet, congress
9 発会 **hakkai** open a meeting
発会式 **hakkaishiki** opening ceremony
茶会 **chakai** tea party/ceremony
県会 **kenkai** prefectural assembly
面会 **menkai** interview, meeting
面会人 **menkainin** visitor, caller
面会日 **menkaibi** one's at-home day
10 都会 **tokai** city　**Tokai** Tōkyō Assembly
都会人 **tokaijin** city resident, urban dweller
部会 **bukai** sectional meeting, department
流会 **ryūkai** adjourn, call off (for lack of a quorum)
宴会 **enkai** banquet, dinner party
宴会場 **enkaijō** banquet hall
教会 **kyōkai** church
教会史 **kyōkaishi** church history
教会法 **kyōkaihō** canon law
教会員 **kyōkaiin** church member
教会堂 **kyōkaidō** church, place of worship
教会暦 **kyōkaireki** church calendar
納会 **nōkai** the last meeting (of the year/month)
11 停会 **teikai** suspension of a meeting, adjournment, recess
副会長 **fukukaichō** (company) vice president
商会 **shōkai** company, firm
密会 **mikkai** clandestine meeting
常会 **jōkai** regular meeting/session
脱会 **dakkai** withdrawal (from an organization)
盛会 **seikai** succesful meeting
閉会 **heikai** closing, adjournment
12 散会 **sankai** adjourn, break up
集会 **shūkai** meeting, assembly
集会所 **shūkaijo** meeting place, assembly hall
集会室 **shūkaishitsu** meeting room/hall
開会 **kaikai** opening a meeting
開会中 **kaikaichū** during the session
開会日 **kaikaibi** opening day
開会式 **kaikaishiki** opening ceremony
13 際会 **saikai** meet, face, confront
準会員 **junkaiin** associate member
農会 **nōkai** agricultural association
照会 **shōkai** inquiry
碁会 **gokai** go club/meet

碁会所 **gokaisho, gokaijo** go club
節会 **sechie** court banquet
詩会 **shikai** poetry-writing meeting
14 歌会 **kakai, utakai** poetry party/competition
総会 **sōkai** general meeting, plenary session
読会 **dokkai** reading (of a bill)
領会 **ryōkai** understanding, consent
16 機会 **kikai** opportunity, occasion, chance
機会均等 **kikai kintō** equal opportunity
親会社 **oyagaisha** parent company
20 議会 **gikai** parliament, diet, congress

────── 3 ──────

2 二次会 **nijikai** after party party
3 三者会談 **sansha kaidan** three-party conference
万灯会 **mandōe** Buddhist lantern festival
大都会 **daitokai** big city
小都会 **shōtokai** small city/town
4 予餞会 **yosenkai** farewell party (before graduation is completed)
互助会 **gojokai** a mutual-aid society
文学会 **bungakukai** literary society
午餐会 **gosankai** luncheon
公教会 **Kōkyōkai** Catholic Church
公聴会 **kōchōkai** public hearing
父兄会 **fukeikai** parents' association
円卓会議 **entaku kaigi** round-table conference
5 正教会 **Seikyōkai** Greek Orthodox Church
好機会 **kōkikai** good opportunity, the right moment
弘済会 **kōsaikai** benefit association
主脳会談 **shunō kaidan** summit conference
主脳会議 **shunō kaigi** summit conference
6 合弁会社 **gōben-gaisha** joint venture (company)
合名会社 **gōmei-gaisha** unlimited partnership
合資会社 **gōshi-gaisha** limited partnership
壮行会 **sōkōkai** farewell party
同好会 **dōkōkai** association of like-minded people
同志会 **dōshikai** association of like-minded people
同窓会 **dōsōkai** alumni association/meeting
共進会 **kyōshinkai** competitive exhibition, prize show
有限会社 **yūgen-gaisha** limited liability company, Ltd.
7 即売会 **sokubaikai** exhibition and spot sale
忘年会 **bōnenkai** year-end party
医師会 **ishikai** medical association/society
役員会 **yakuinkai** board meeting
学友会 **gakuyūkai** alumni association
学芸会 **gakugeikai** (school) literary program

2

イ 4 ←
ハ
子
阝
卩
刂
力
又
宀
亠
十
卜
厂
ㇴ
丶
厂
辶
冂
几
匸

8 非社会的 **hishakaiteki** antisocial
協議会 **kyōgikai** conference, council
追悼会 **tsuitōkai** memorial services
送行会 **sōkōkai** going-away/farewell party
送別会 **sōbetsukai** going-away/farewell party
披露会 **hirōkai** (wedding) reception
参事会 **sanjikai** council
実社会 **jisshakai** the real world, actual society
府議会 **fugikai** urban-prefectural assembly
青年会 **seinenkai** young (wo)men's association
委員会 **iinkai** committee
9 保険会社 **hoken-gaisha** insurance company
軍事会議 **gunji kaigi** council of war
軍法会議 **gunpō kaigi** court-martial
首脳会談 **shunō kaidan** summit conference
持株会社 **mo(chi)kabu-gaisha** holding company
品評会 **hinpyōkai** competitive exhibition
独奏会 **dokusōkai** instrumental recital
独演会 **dokuenkai** solo recital/performance
狩猟会 **shuryōkai** hunting party
後援会 **kōenkai** supporters' association
茶話会 **sawakai, chawakai** tea party
県人会 **kenjinkai** an association of people from the same prefecture
県議会 **kengikai** prefectural assembly
査問会 **samonkai** (court of) inquiry, hearing
祝賀会 **shukugakai** a celebration
音楽会 **ongakkai, ongakukai** concert
10 都議会 **Togikai** Tōkyō Assembly
涅槃会 **nehan'e** anniversary of Buddha's death
党大会 **tōtaikai** (political) convention
座談会 **zadankai** round-table discussion, symposium
展示会 **tenjikai** show, exhibition
展覧会 **tenrankai** exhibition
展覧会絵 **Tenrankai (no) e** Pictures from an Exhibition (Mussorgsky, 1874)
株式会社 **kabushiki-gaisha, kabushiki kaisha** corporation, Co., Ltd.
校友会 **kōyūkai** alumni association
教育会 **kyōikukai** educational association
航空会社 **kōkū-gaisha** airline (company)
討論会 **tōronkai** forum, debate, discussion
記者会見 **kisha kaiken** news/press conference
11 商工会議所 **Shōkō Kaigisho** Chamber of Commerce and Industry
商事会社 **shōji-gaisha** business company
運送会社 **unsō-gaisha** transport/express company
運動会 **undōkai** athletic meet
婦人会 **fujinkai** ladies' society

理事会 **rijikai** board of directors/trustees
12 博覧会 **hakurankai** exhibition, exposition, fair
御前会議 **gozen kaigi** council held in the presence of the emperor
晩餐会 **bansankai** dinner party, banquet
無教会主義 **mukyōkai shugi** Nondenominationalism (a Japanese Christian sect)
評議会 **hyōgikai** council, commission
貿易会社 **bōeki-gaisha** trading firm
13 園遊会 **en'yūkai** garden party
禁酒会 **kinshukai** temperance society
聖公会 **Seikōkai** Episcopal/Anglican Church
14 演芸会 **engeikai** an entertainment, variety show
演奏会 **ensōkai** concert, recital
製薬会社 **seiyaku-gaisha** pharmaceutical company
読書会 **dokushokai** reading club
15 舞踏会 **butōkai** ball, dance
審議会 **shingikai** deliberative assembly, commission, council
歓迎会 **kangeikai** welcoming meeting, reception
歓送会 **kansōkai** farewell party, send-off
慰安会 **iankai** recreational get-together
慰労会 **irōkai** dinner/party given in appreciation of someone's services
16 親睦会 **shinbokukai** social get-together
17 懇話会 **konwakai** social get-together
懇談会 **kondankai** get-together, friendly discussion
懇親会 **konshinkai** social gathering
聴聞会 **chōmonkai** public hearing
謝恩会 **shaonkai** thank-you party, testimonial dinner
講習会 **kōshūkai** short course, class, training conference
講演会 **kōenkai** lecture meeting
18 観桜会 **kan'ōkai** cherry-blossom viewing party
20 灌仏会 **kanbutsue** Buddha's-birthday
競技会 **kyōgikai** athletic meet, contest

───── 4 ─────

3 小委員会 **shōiinkai** subcommittee
4 五輪大会 **Gorin taikai** Olympic games
井戸端会議 **idobata kaigi** well-side gossip
水泳大会 **suiei taikai** swimming meet
5 弁護士会 **bengoshikai** bar association
8 長老教会 **Chōrō Kyōkai** Presbyterian Church
東印度会社 **Higashi Indo Gaisha** East India Company
泥水社会 **doromizu shakai** red-light districts

国連総会 **Kokuren Sōkai** UN General Assembly
盂蘭盆会 **Urabon'e** o-Bon festival
9 通常国会 **tsūjō kokkai** ordinary Diet session
11 牽強付会 **kenkyō-fukai** farfetched, distorted

———————— 5 ————————

3 万国博覧会 **bankoku hakurankai** world's fair
6 全院委員会 **zen'in iinkai** committee of the whole house
仮装舞踏会 **kasō butōkai** masquerade ball
11 常任委員会 **jōnin iinkai** standing committee
情報化社会 **jōhōka shakai** information-oriented society

———————— 8 ————————

6 全国人民代表大会 **Zenkoku Jinmin Daihyō Taikai** (Chinese) National People's Congress

2a4.20 / 223

肉 NIKU meat, flesh

———————— 1 ————————

2 肉入 **nikui(re)** ink-pad case
4 肉太 **nikubuto** bold-faced (type)
肉切庖丁 **nikuki(ri)bōchō** butcher knife
肉牛 **nikugyū** beef cattle
5 肉付 **nikuzu(ki)** fleshiness, build
nikuzu(ke) fleshing out, modeling (clay)
肉用種 **nikuyōshu** breed of animal raised for meat
肉汁 **nikujū** meat juice, gravy, broth
6 肉交 **nikukō** sexual intercourse
肉色 **nikuiro** flesh color
肉池 **nikuchi** ink-pad case
7 肉体 **nikutai** the body/flesh
肉体的 **nikutaiteki** sensual, corporal
肉体美 **nikutaibi** physical beauty
肉豆蔲 **nikuzuku** nutmeg
肉声 **nikusei** natural voice (not via microphone)
8 肉厚 **nikuatsu** (wall) thickness
肉芽 **nikuga** granulation, proud flesh
肉的 **nikuteki** fleshly, physical
9 肉屋 **nikuya** butcher (shop)
肉界 **nikukai** the physical/sensual world
肉食 **nikushoku** meat eating
10 肉桂 **nikkei** cinnamon
肉粉 **nikufun** powdered meat
11 肉欲 **nikuyoku** carnal desires
肉情 **nikujō** carnal desire
肉眼 **nikugan** the naked/unaided eye
肉細 **nikuboso** light-faced (type)
12 肉弾 **nikudan** human bullet

肉弾戦 **nikudansen** human-wave warfare
肉筆 **nikuhitsu** one's own handwriting, autograph
13 肉塊 **nikkai** piece of meat; the body
肉腫 **nikushu** sarcoma
肉感 **nikkan** sexual feeling, sensuality
肉感的 **nikkanteki** suggestive, voluptuous
14 肉製品 **niku seihin** meat products
15 肉質 **nikushitsu** flesh, pulp
16 肉薄 **nikuhaku** press hard, close in on
肉親 **nikushin** blood relationship/relative
17 肉鍋 **niku nabe** meat pot; meat served in a pot
18 肉類 **nikurui** meats
19 肉襦袢 **nikujuban** tights, leotards
20 肉饅頭 **niku manjū** meat-filled bun

———————— 2 ————————

2 人肉 **jinniku** human flesh
4 中肉 **chūniku** medium build; meat of medium quality
中肉中背 **chūniku-chūzei** medium height and build
牛肉 **gyūniku** beef
5 生肉 **seiniku** raw meat
皮肉 **hiniku** irony, sarcasm
6 多肉 **taniku** fleshy
多肉果 **tanikuka** pulpy fruit
多肉質 **tanikushitsu** fleshy, pulpy, succulent
死肉 **shiniku** dead flesh, carrion
朱肉 **shuniku** red ink pad
印肉 **inniku** inkpad, stamp pad
羊肉 **yōniku** mutton
血肉 **ketsuniku** flesh and blood
7 冷肉 **reiniku** cold meat, cold cuts
8 果肉 **kaniku** the flesh/pulp of fruit
苦肉 **kuniku** (desperate measure) at personal sacrifice
股肉 **momoniku** (ground) round, ham
9 食肉 **shokuniku** (edible) meat; flesh-eating
食肉獣 **shokunikujū** a carnivore
食肉類 **shokunikurui** carnivorous animals
10 凍肉 **tōniku** frozen meat
隆肉 **ryūniku** hunch (back), (camel's) hump
酒肉 **shuniku** saké and meat
挽肉 **hi(ki)niku** ground meat
弱肉強食 **jakuniku-kyōshoku** survival of the fittest
桜肉 **sakuraniku** horsemeat
骨肉 **kotsuniku** one's flesh and blood, kin
馬肉 **baniku** horsemeat
11 鹿肉 **shikaniku** venison
豚肉 **butaniku** pork
魚肉 **gyoniku** fish (meat)
鳥肉 **toriniku** chicken (meat)
12 焼肉 **ya(ki)niku** roast/broiled meat
歯肉 **haniku, shiniku** the gums

2
イ 4 ←
冫
孑
阝
卩
刂
力
又
亠
丷
广
廴
冂
凡
匸

筋肉 **kinniku** muscle
13 腰肉 **koshiniku** loin, sirloin
14 腐肉 **funiku** tainted meat; carrion; gangrene
精肉 **seiniku** meat
15 霊肉一致 **reiniku itchi** oneness of body and soul
16 獣肉 **jūniku** flesh of animals, meat
薄肉 **usuniku** light red, pinkish
薄肉彫 **usunikubo(ri)** low relief, bas-relief
17 謝肉祭 **shanikusai** carnival
鮮肉 **senniku** fresh meat
18 贅肉 **zeiniku** excess fat
19 髀肉嘆 **hiniku (no) tan** lamenting the lack of opportunity to show one's skill
鯨肉 **geiniku** whale meat
鶏肉 **keiniku** chicken (meat)

――――――― 3 ―――――――
7 冷凍肉 **reitōniku** frozen meat
10 酒池肉林 **shuchi-nikurin** sumptuous feast

――――――― 4 ―――――――
6 羊頭狗肉 **yōtō-kuniku** advertising mutton but selling dog meat

耒→来 **0a7.6**

朱→ **0a6.13**

――――――― 5 ―――――――

2a5.1 / 122

位

I rank, place, grade **kurai** rank; dignity; be located; throne, crown; (decimal) place **-kurai, -gurai** to the extent of, about

――――――― 1 ―――――――
6 位次 **iji** seating according to rank
8 位官 **ikan** rank and official position
位取 **kuraido(ri)** positioning of the ones digit within a number
9 位相 **isō** phase
10 位記 **iki** diploma of court rank
11 位階 **ikai** court rank
12 位牌 **ihai** Buddhhist mortuary tablet
13 位置 **ichi** position, location
15 位勲 **ikun** rank and order of merit

――――――― 2 ―――――――
1 一位 **ichii** first place/rank
2 二位 **nii** second place
人位 **jin'i** one's rank
3 三位 **san'i, sanmi** third rank/place
三位一体 **Sanmi-ittai** the Trinity

上位 **jōi** high rank, precedence
下位 **kai** low rank, subordinate
4 中位 **chūi** medium, average **chūgurai, chūkurai** about medium/average
水位 **suii** water level
水位標 **suiihyō** watermark
王位 **ōi** the throne, the crown
方位 **hōi** direction, bearing, azimuth
5 本位 **hon'i** standard, basis, principle
主位 **shui** leading position, first place
6 気位 **kigurai** feelings about oneself, self-esteem
次位 **jii** second rank/place
同位 **dōi** the same rank/position, coordinate
同位元素 **dōi genso** isotope
地位 **chii** position, status
在位 **zaii** be on the throne, reign
各位 **kakui** gentlemen, you all
7 体位 **taii** physical standard, physique; body position
即位 **sokui** accession to the throne
即位式 **sokuishiki** enthronement ceremony, coronation
対位法 **taiihō** counterpoint
学位 **gakui** academic degree
8 退位 **taii** abdication
官位 **kan'i** office and rank; official rank
定位 **teii** orientation; normal position
空位 **kūi** vacant post, interregnum
9 冠位 **kan'i** system indicating court ranks by headgear colors
帝位 **teii** the throne/crown
首位 **shui** top place, leading position
風位 **fūi** wind direction
品位 **hin'i** grade, quality, fineness; dignity
栄位 **eii** exalted position, high rank
単位 **tan'i** unit, denomination
皇位 **kōi** imperial throne
10 部位 **bui** region, part (of the body)
高位 **kōi** high rank, honors
座位 **zai** seating order, precedence
11 階位 **kaii** rank, grade
虚位 **kyoi** nominal rank, titular post
転位 **ten'i** transposition, displacement
12 御位 **mikurai** the throne
復位 **fukui** restoration, reinstatement
廃位 **haii** depose, dethrone
無位 **mui** without rank, commoner
等位 **tōi** rank, grade
順位 **jun'i** ranking, standing
13 電位 **den'i** (electrical) potential
零位 **reii** zero (point)
14 層位学 **sōigaku** stratigraphy
銀位 **gin'i** silver fineness/quality
15 横位 **ōi** transverse presentation (of a fetus)
勲位 **kun'i** order of merit

霊位 **reii** (Buddhist) mortuary tablet
17 優位 **yūi** ascendance, predominance
爵位 **shakui** peerage, court rank
18 贈位 **zōi** confer a posthumous court rank
20 譲位 **jōi** abdication

——————— 3 ———————

8 金本位 **kinhon'i** the gold standard
金本位制 **kinhon'isei** the gold standard
10 高品位テレビ **kōhin'i terebi** high-definition television
12 最下位 **saikai** lowest rank
14 複本位 **fukuhon'i** double standard
複本位制 **fukuhon'isei** bimetalism
銀本位 **ginhon'i** the silver standard
15 熱単位 **netsutan'i** heat/thermal unit

2a5.2

佃

TEN, DEN, tsukuda cultivated field

——————— 1 ———————

12 佃煮 **tsukudani** (boiled dish of small fish, shellfish, soy sauce, etc.)

佛 → 仏 **2a2.5**

2a5.3 / 1108

伸

SHIN stretch **no(biru)** stretch, extend (intr.); grow **no(basu)** stretch, extend (tr.) **no(su)** stretch, spread, smooth out; gain influence **no(biyaka)** comfortable, carefree

——————— 1 ———————

3 伸上 **no(shi)a(garu)** rise in the world, move up **no(shi)a(geru)** give a sound thrashing; run aground **no(bi)a(garu)** stretch, stand on tiptoes
7 伸伸 **no(bi)no(bi)** feel at ease, feel refreshed
8 伸長 **shinchō** extension, expansion
9 伸度 **shindo** elasticity, ductility
10 伸展 **shinten** extension, stretching
伸悩 **no(bi)naya(mu)** be sluggish, stagnate, level off, mark time
11 伸率 **no(bi)ritsu** rate of growth
伸張 **shinchō** extension, expansion
12 伸筋 **shinkin** protractor/extensor muscle
17 伸縮 **shinshuku, no(bi)chiji(mi)** expansion and contraction; elastic, flexible
伸縮自在 **shinshuku-jizai** elastic, flexible, telescoping
伸縮性 **shinshukusei** elasticity

——————— 2 ———————

2 二伸 **nishin** postscript, P.S.

4 引伸 **hi(ki)noba(su)** stretch/pad out, enlarge
欠伸 **akubi** yawn
7 伸伸 **no(bi)no(bi)** feel at ease, feel refreshed
8 追伸 **tsuishin** postscript, P.S.
屈伸 **kusshin** extension and contraction; bending and stretching
9 背伸 **seno(bi)** stretch oneself, stand on tiptoes
10 差伸 **sa(shi)no(beru)** hold out, extend (a hand)
15 皺伸 **shiwano(bashi)** smoothing out wrinkles; diversion, recreation

——————— 3 ———————

3 大欠伸 **ōakubi** big yawn
5 生欠伸 **namaakubi** slight yawn

2a5.4 / 1027

伴

BAN, HAN, tomona(u) accompany, be accompanied by

——————— 1 ———————

4 伴天連 **Bateren** Portuguese Jesuit missionaries; Christianity
9 伴奏 **bansō** (musical) accompaniment
伴侶 **hanryo** companion
伴食 **banshoku** eating at the same table
伴食大臣 **banshoku daijin** figurehead minister
13 伴僧 **bansō** assistant priest, acolyte

——————— 2 ———————

6 同伴 **dōhan** accompany, go with
同伴者 **dōhansha** companion
10 随伴 **zuihan** attend on, accompany
随伴者 **zuihansha** attendant, follower, retinue
11 接伴 **seppan** receive, entertain

2a5.5

佚

ITSU, TETSU flee, hide; enjoy

——————— 1 ———————

5 佚民 **itsumin** retired person
10 佚書 **issho** lost book
13 佚楽 **itsuraku** idle pleasure

——————— 2 ———————

11 淫佚 **in'itsu** debauchery

2a5.6 / 61

体 體 躰 軆

TAI body; object, thing; style, form
TEI appearance; condition, state **karada** body

——————— 1 ———————

0 体する **tai(suru)** obey, heed

2
イ 5←
冫
子
阝
卩
刂
力
又
一
十
卜
宀
丷
厂
辶
冂
八
匚

2

→ 5 亻
⺡
子
阝
⻖
刂
力
又
一
亠
十
卜
勹
⼴
⻍
冂
几
匚

2 体力 **tairyoku** physical strength
4 体内 **tainai** inside the body, internal
5 体付 **karadatsu(ki)** one's build, figure
6 体刑 **taikei** corporal punishment; penal servitude
体当 **taia(tari)** hurl oneself against
7 体良 **teiyo(ku)** gracefully, politely
体位 **taii** physical standard, physique; body position
体技 **taigi** competitive physical sports; strength and skill
体形 **taikei** form, figure
体系 **taikei** system, organization
体系化 **taikeika** systematize, organize
体系的 **taikeiteki** systematic
体言 **taigen** uninflected word
8 体制 **taisei** structure, system, order; the establishment
体育 **taiiku** physical education, athletics
体育館 **taiikukan** gymnasium
9 体重 **taijū** one's weight
体要 **taiyō** gist, main point
体面 **taimen** honor, prestige, appearances
体臭 **taishū** body odor; a characteristic
10 体格 **taikaku** physique, constitution
11 体液 **taieki** body fluids
体得 **taitoku** realization, experience; comprehension, mastery
体現 **taigen** embody, personify
12 体温 **taion** body temperature
体温計 **taionkei** (clinical) thermometer
体腔 **taikō, taikū** body cavity
体量 **tairyō** one's weight
体裁 **teisai** decency, form, appearance, effect
体裁上 **teisaijō** for sake of appearances
体裁振 **teisaibu(ru)** put on airs, pose
13 体感 **taikan** bodily sensation
14 体罰 **taibatsu** corporal punishment
15 体熱 **tainetsu** body heat
体質 **taishitsu** physical constitution
16 体操 **taisō** calisthenics, gymnastics
体操場 **taisōjō** gymnasium, exercise grounds
体積 **taiseki** volume
18 体軀 **taiku** body; height; physique
体験 **taiken** experience
体験談 **taikendan** story of one's personal experiences

——————— 2 ———————

1 一体 **ittai** one body; (what) in the world, (how) the devil; properly speaking; generally
2 人体 **jintai** the human body
八体 **hattai** the eight styles of writing kanji
3 三体 **santai** the three kanji handwriting styles (square, semicursive, and "grass")

大体 **daitai** generally, on the whole; outline, summary; in substance; originally
上体 **jōtai** upper part of the body
女体 **nyotai, jotai** woman's body
4 不体裁 **futeisai** in bad form, unseemly, improper
勿体 **mottai** (over)emphasis
勿体振 **mottaibu(ru)** put on airs, act self-important
勿体無 **mottaina(i)** more than one deserves, too good for; wasteful
天体 **tentai** heavenly body
天体学 **tentaigaku** uranology
天体図 **tentaizu** celestial map, star chart
五体 **gotai** the whole body
文体 **buntai** (literary) style
分体 **buntai** fission
5 本体論 **hontairon** ontology
生体 **seitai** living body
母体 **botai** the mother('s body); parent organization
古体 **kotai** old form, ancient style
正体 **shōtai** one's true nature/character; in one's right mind, senses
巨体 **kyotai** large body/build
字体 **jitai** form of a character, typeface
旧体制 **kyūtaisei** the old regime/establishment
玉体 **gyokutai** the emperor's person/presence
主体 **shutai** the subject; main part
主体性 **shutaisei** subjectivity, independence
立体 **rittai** a solid (body), three-dimensional
立体的 **rittaiteki** three-dimensional
立体美 **rittaibi** beauty of sculpture
立体派 **rittaiha** cubists
立体感 **rittaikan** sense of depth
立体戦 **rittaisen** three-dimensional warfare
立体鏡 **rittaikyō** stereoscope
6 死体 **shitai** corpse, remains
死体解剖 **shitai kaibō** autopsy
死体置場 **shitai o(ki)ba** morgue
気体 **kitai** gas (not solid or liquid)
気体力学 **kitai rikigaku** aerodynamics
気体化 **kitaika** gasify, vaporize
全体 **zentai** the whole, in all
全体主義 **zentai shugi** totalitarianism
合体 **gattai** amalgamation, combination, union
肉体 **nikutai** the body/flesh
肉体的 **nikutaiteki** sensual, corporal
肉体美 **nikutaibi** physical beauty
老体 **rōtai** old body, aged person
近体 **kintai** recent/up-to-date style
近体詩 **kintaishi** modern-style poem
同体 **dōtai (ni)** as one, together
行体 **gyōtai** semicursive form (of kanji)

光体 **kōtai** luminous body
団体 **dantai** group, organization
有体 **a(ri)tei** the plain truth, like it is
有体物 **yūtaibutsu** something tangible
成体 **seitai** (insect's) adult form
　　　na(ri)katachi appearance
自体 **jitai** itself; one's own body
7 身体 **shintai, karada** the body
身体障害者 **shintai shōgaisha** physically
　　　handicapped person
抗体 **kōtai** antibody
形体 **keitai** form, shape, configuration
　　　narikatachi one's appearance
図体 **zūtai** one's body/frame
車体 **shatai** body, chassis
8 実体 **jittai** substance, entity; three-dimen-
　　　sional
実体化 **jittaika** substantiate
実体論 **jittairon** substantialism,
　　　noumenalism
国体 **kokutai** national structure/essence/
　　　polity **Kokutai** (short for 国民体育大
　　　会) National Athletic Meet
固体 **kotai** a solid
肢体 **shitai** limbs; body and limbs
物体 **buttai** body, object, substance
具体 **gutai** concrete, specific, definite
具体化 **gutaika** embodiment, materialization
具体的 **gutaiteki** concrete, specific, definite
具体策 **gutaisaku** specific measures
9 変体 **hentai** anomaly
変体仮名 **hentai-gana** anomalous (obsolete)
　　　kana
連体形 **rentaikei** a participial adjective
風体 **fūtei, fūtai** appearance, looks, attitude
浮体 **futai** floating body (in physics)
客体 **kyakutai, kakutai** object
屍体 **shitai** corpse
面体 **mentei** face, looks
神体 **shintai** relic in a Shinto shrine
政体 **seitai** form/system of government
10 個体 **kotai** an individual
剛体 **gōtai** rigid body (in physics)
流体 **ryūtai** a fluid (in physics)
流体力学 **ryūtai rikigaku** fluid dynamics
弱体 **jakutai** weak, effete
弱体化 **jakutaika** weakening
容体 **yōdai** (patient's) condition
　　　yōdai(buru) put on airs, act important
胴体 **dōtai** the body, torso; fuselage
書体 **shotai** style of calligraphy/type
病体 **byōtai** sickly constitution, poor health
11 動体 **dōtai** moving body
液体 **ekitai** liquid
得体 **etai** nature, character
球体 **kyūtai** sphere

略体 **ryakutai** simplified form (of a character)
異体 **itai** different form, variant
異体同心 **itai-dōshin** of one mind, perfect
　　　accord
船体 **sentai** hull, ship
蛇体 **jatai** serpentine
軟体動物 **nantai dōbutsu** mollusk
12 尊体 **sontai** your health; image of Buddha
媒体 **baitai** medium (in physics)
落体 **rakutai** falling body
無体 **mutai** forcible; intangible (assets)
筐体 **kyōtai** housing, case, cabinet, enclosure
13 群体 **guntai** colony (of coral)
解体 **kaitai** dismantle
新体 **shintai** new form/style
新体制 **shintaisei** new system/order
新体詩 **shintaishi** new-style poem/poetry
裸体 **ratai** naked body, nudity
裸体主義 **ratai shugi** nudism
裸体画 **rataiga** nude picture
継体 **Keitai** (emperor, 507–531)
14 遺体 **itai** corpse, remains
様体 **yōtai** situation, condition
導体 **dōtai** conductor (of electricity/heat)
総体 **sōtai** on the whole
16 機体 **kitai** fuselage
21 艦体 **kantai** the hull (of a warship)

──────── 3 ────────

3 口語体 **kōgotai** colloquial style, colloquialism
4 不導体 **fudōtai** nonconductor
文語体 **bungotai** literary style
水晶体 **suishōtai** lens (of the eye)
5 半導体 **handōtai** semiconductor
半裸体 **hanratai** seminude
世間体 **sekentei** decency, respectability,
　　　appearances
立方体 **rippōtai** a cube
6 多面体 **tamentai** polyhedron
列伝体 **retsudentai** biographical style
行草体 **gyōsōtai** semicursive and cursive
　　　forms/styles
共同体 **kyōdōtai** community
有機体 **yūkitai** organism
自治体 **jichitai** self-governing body,
　　　municipality
7 良導体 **ryōdōtai** good conductor
8 直方体 **chokuhōtai** rectangular parallelepiped
固形体 **kokeitai** a solid
肥満体 **himantai** plump/roly-poly physique
9 発光体 **hakkōtai** luminous body, corona
重合体 **jūgōtai** polymer
美容体操 **biyō taisō** calisthenics
透明体 **tōmeitai** transparent body/medium
単量体 **tanryōtai** monomer
染色体 **senshokutai** chromosome

2

亻 5←
冫
孑
阝
卩
刂
力
又
一
丷
卜
勹
亅
广
辶
門
八
匚

10 健康体 **kenkōtai** healthy body
這々体 **hōhō(no)tei** hurriedly, precipitously
流動体 **ryūdōtai** a fluid
帯電体 **taidentai** charged body
徒手体操 **toshu taisō** calisthenics without apparatus
被写体 **hishatai** subject/object photographed
病原体 **byōgentai** pathogen
11 清朝体 **seichōtai** (a type of printed kanji resembling brush writing)
蛍光体 **keikōtai** fluorescent body
惨死体 **zanshitai** mangled corpse
12 焼死体 **shōshitai** charred body/remains
絶縁体 **zetsuentai** insulator, nonconductor
13 溺死体 **dekishitai** drowned body
戦時体制 **senji taisei** war footing
新字体 **shinjitai** new form of a character
電文体 **denbuntai** telegram-like style
14 導電体 **dōdentai** conductor (of electricity)
誘導体 **yūdōtai** (chemical) derivative
15 編年体 **hennentai** chronological order
談話体 **danwatai** colloquial style
16 機械体操 **kikai taisō** gymnastics using equipment
親団体 **oyadantai** parent organization
駢儷体 **benreitai** flowery ancient Chinese prose style

—————— 4 ——————

1 一心同体 **isshin-dōtai** one flesh; one in body and spirit
3 三位一体 **Sanmi-ittai** the Trinity
4 不良導体 **furyō dōtai** nonconductor, poor conductor
公共団体 **kōkyō dantai** public body/organization
公武合体 **kōbu gattai** union of imperial court and shogunate
5 外郭団体 **gaikaku dantai** auxiliary organization
右翼団体 **uyoku dantai** right-wing group
11 脳下垂体 **nōkasuitai** pituitary gland
12 無理無体 **muri-mutai** forcible

—————— 5 ——————

8 欧州共同体 **Ōshū Kyōdōtai** the European Community

—————— 6 ——————

5 立憲君主政体 **rikken kunshu seitai** constitutional monarchy

2a5.7 / 1176

伯

HAKU count, earl; eldest brother; uncle; chief official; Brazil

—————— 1 ——————

4 伯父 **oji, hakufu** uncle

5 伯母 **oba, hakubo** aunt
伯兄 **hakkei** eldest brother
6 伯仲 **hakuchū** be evenly matched
8 伯林 **Berurin** Berlin
9 伯剌西爾 **Burajiru** Brazil
10 伯耆 **Hōki** (ancient kuni, Tottori-ken)
13 伯楽 **hakuraku, hakurō, bakurō** horse expert/dealer
17 伯爵 **hakushaku** count, earl

—————— 2 ——————

3 大伯父 **ōoji** great-uncle, granduncle
大伯母 **ōoba** great-aunt, grandaunt
8 画伯 **gahaku** (great) artist, (master) painter
9 風伯 **fūhaku** god of the wind

2a5.8

佑

YŪ, U help

—————— 2 ——————

4 天佑 **ten'yū** divine favor/providence

2a5.9 / 1744

佐

SA help

—————— 1 ——————

5 佐世保 **Sasebo** (city, Nagasaki-ken)
8 佐官 **sakan** field officer
9 佐保姫 **saohime** goddess of spring
12 佐渡 **Sado** (ancient kuni, Niigata-ken)
佐渡島 **Sado(ga)shima** (island, Niigata-ken)
佐賀 **Saga** (city, Saga-ken)
佐賀県 **Saga-ken** (prefecture)
13 佐幕 **sabaku** adherence to the shogunate
14 佐様 **sayō** such; yes, indeed; well...

—————— 2 ——————

3 大佐 **taisa** colonel; (navy) captain
土佐 **Tosa** (ancient kuni, Kōchi-ken)
4 中佐 **chūsa** lieutenant colonel; commander (navy)
少佐 **shōsa** major, lieutenant commander
12 補佐 **hosa** aide, adviser
14 輔佐 **hosa** assistance; assistant, adviser

2a5.10 / 360

作

SAKU, SA a work/production; tillage; harvest, crop **tsuku(ru)** make

—————— 1 ——————

2 作力 **saryoku** effort, effective force
4 作文 **sakubun** composition, writing
作手 **tsuku(ri)te** maker, builder; tiller, cultivator

作方 **tsuku(ri)kata** how to make; style of
  building, construction, workmanship
5 作付 **sakutsu(ke), sakuzu(ke)** planting
  作用 **sayō** action, function, effect
6 作曲 **sakkyoku** musical composition
  作曲家 **sakkyokuka** composer
  作当 **sakua(tari)** good crop
  作成 **sakusei** draw up, prepare
7 作声 **tsuku(ri)goe** disguised voice
  作図 **sakuzu** drawing figures, construction
  (in geometry)
  作男 **sakuotoko** farm hand
  作言 **tsuku(ri)goto** fabrication, lie, fiction
8 作事 **tsuku(ri)goto** fiction, fabrication
  作例 **sakurei** model of writing
  作法 **sahō** manners, etiquette
  作者 **sakusha** author
  作物 **sakumotsu** crops **tsuku(ri)mono**
  artificial product; decoration; fake; crop
9 作風 **sakufū** literary style
  作品 **sakuhin** a work
  作柄 **sakugara** crop conditions; quality (of
  art)
  作為 **sakui** artificiality; commission (of a
  crime)
10 作酒屋 **tsuku(ri)zakaya** saké brewer(y)
  作家 **sakka** writer, novelist
  作笑 **tsuku(ri)wara(i)** forced laugh
13 作業 **sagyō** work, operations
  作業衣 **sagyōi** work clothes
  作業服 **sagyōfuku** work clothes
  作戦 **sakusen** (military) operation, tactics
  作意 **sakui** central theme, motif; intention
  作詩 **sakushi** writing poetry
  作話 **tsuku(ri)banashi** made-up story,
  fabrication, fable
14 作歌 **sakka** writing songs/poems
  作製 **sakusei** manufacture
16 作興 **sakkō** promote, arouse
18 作顔 **tsuku(ri)gao** affected look; made-up
  face

—————————— 2 ——————————

2 力作 **rikisaku** masterpiece, tour de force
3 工作 **kōsaku** construction, engineering;
  handicraft; maneuver, scheme
  工作物 **kōsakubutsu** a building; manufactured goods
  工作品 **kōsakuhin** handicrafts
  工作機械 **kōsaku kikai** machine tools
  大作 **taisaku** masterpiece, a monumental
  work
  上作 **jōsaku** good crop; masterpiece
  下作 **gesaku** poorly made, of inferior quality
  凡作 **bonsaku** mediocre writing
  小作 **kosaku** tenant farming **kozuku(ri)** of
  small build, small size

小作人 **kosakunin** tenant farmer
小作地 **kosakuchi** tenant farm land
小作米 **kosakumai** rent paid in rice
小作料 **kosakuryō** farm rent
小作農 **kosakunō** tenant farming
4 不作 **fusaku** bad harvest, crop failure
  不作法 **busahō** bad manners, discourtesy
  凶作 **kyōsaku** bad harvest, crop failure
  反作用 **hansayō** reaction
  手作 **tezuku(ri)** handmade, homemade
5 代作 **daisaku** ghostwriting
  皮作 **kawatsuku(ri)** making sashimi without
  cutting away the fish's skin
  平作 **heisaku** normal harvest/crop
6 多作 **tasaku** prolific writing
  多作家 **tasakuka** prolific writer
  仮作 **kasaku** fiction
  合作 **gassaku** joint work, collaboration
  近作 **kinsaku** a recent work
  名作 **meisaku** literary masterpiece
  自作 **jisaku** made/grown/written by oneself
  自作農 **jisakunō** (non-tenant) owner-farmer
  米作 **beisaku** rice cultivation/crop
7 述作 **jussaku** write (a book)
  抜作 **nu(ke)saku** dunce, nincompoop
  形作 **katachizuku(ru)** form, shape, make
  花作 **hanazuku(ri)** floriculture; florist
  労作 **rōsaku** toil, labor; laborious task
  改作 **kaisaku** adaptation (of a play)
  麦作 **mugisaku** wheat cultivation
8 佳作 **kasaku** an excellent work
  制作 **seisaku** a work, production
  逆作用 **gyakusayō** adverse effect, reaction
  拙作 **sessaku** (my) poor/clumsy work
  若作 **wakazuku(ri)** made up to look young
  所作 **shosa** conduct, bearing
  所作事 **shosagoto** dance drama, posture dance
9 発作 **hossa** fit, spasm, an attack of
  発作的 **hossateki** spasmodic, fitful
  美作 **Mimasaka** (ancient kuni, Okayama-ken)
  連作 **rensaku** plant (a field) with the same
  crop year after year; story written by
  several writers in turn
  造作 **zōsaku** house fixtures; facial features
  zōsa trouble, difficulty **zōsa(nai)** easy,
  simple
  造作付 **zōsakutsu(ki)** furnished (house)
  後作 **atosaku** second crop
  単作 **tansaku** single crop
  畑作 **hatasaku** dry-field farming
  秋作 **akisaku** crops sown/harvested in
  autumn
10 耕作 **kōsaku** cultivation, farming
  耕作地 **kōsakuchi** arable/cultivated land
  耕作者 **kōsakusha** tiller, plowman, farmer
  耕作物 **kōsakubutsu** farm products

2

亻 5←
冫
子
阝
卩
刂
力
又
宀
亠
十
ㅏ
勹
丶
厂
廴
冂
几
匚

2

→5　亻
　　冫
　　子
　　阝
　　卩
　　刂
　　力
　　又
　　宀
　　亠
　　十
　　ト
　　⺈
　　丶
　　厂
　　辶
　　冂
　　几
　　匚

原作 **gensaku** the original work
原作者 **gensakusha** the original author (of a translated work)
流作業 **naga(re)sagyō** (assembly-)line operation
振作 **shinsaku** encouragement
荷作 **nizuku(ri)** packing
家作 **kasaku** house for rent
11 偶作 **gūsaku** something accidentally accomplished
偽作 **gisaku** a spurious work, a forgery
動作 **dōsa** action, movements, motion; bearing, behavior
混作 **konsaku** mixed crops
著作 **chosaku** writing, authorship
著作者 **chosakusha** author, writer
著作物 **chosakubutsu** a (literary) work, book
著作家 **chosakka, chosakuka** author, writer
著作権 **chosakuken** copyright
菊作 **kikuzuku(ri)** chrysanthemum growing/ grower
習作 **shūsaku** a study, étude
黒作 **kurozuku(ri)** salted cuttlefish mixed with their ink
盗作 **tōsaku** plagiarism
12 創作 **sōsaku** a creation/work
創作力 **sōsakuryoku** creative power, originality
創作的 **sōsakuteki** creative
創作家 **sōsakuka** writer, novelist
満作 **mansaku** bumper crop
減作 **gensaku** short crop, lower yield
無作法 **busahō** bad manners, rudeness
無作為 **musakui** random (sample)
間作 **kansaku** intercropping, a catch crop
13 傑作 **kessaku** masterpiece
裏作 **urasaku** second crop
農作 **nōsaku** cultivation, tillage, farming
農作物 **nōsakubutsu** crops, farm produce
適作 **tekisaku** suitable crop
豊作 **hōsaku** abundant harvest
愚作 **gusaku** a poor work, trash
新作 **shinsaku** a new work/composition
罪作 **tsumitsuku(ri)** sinfulness; sinner
詩作 **shisaku** write poetry
試作 **shisaku** trial manufacture
14 遺作 **isaku** (deceased's) unpublished works
寡作 **kasaku** low production
稲作 **inasaku** rice crop
製作 **seisaku** manufacturing, production
製作者 **seisakusha** manufacturer, producer
製作所 **seisakujo** factory, works, workshop
駄作 **dasaku** poor work, worthless stuff
15 劇作家 **gekisakka** playwright, dramatist
戯作 **gesaku** light literature, popular fiction

輪作 **rinsaku** crop rotation
16 操作 **sōsa** operation, handling, control
18 濫作 **ransaku** overproduction
顔作 **kaozuku(ri)** makeup
19 贋作 **gansaku** counterfeit, sham

――――――― 3 ―――――――

1 一毛作 **ichimōsaku** one crop a year
2 二毛作 **nimōsaku** two crops a year
3 三毛作 **sanmōsaku** three crops a year
5 代表作 **daihyōsaku** masterpiece, most important work
平年作 **heinensaku** normal harvest
永小作 **eikosaku** perpetual (land) lease
永小作権 **eikosakuken** perpetual (land) lease
礼儀作法 **reigisahō** etiquette, courtesy, propriety
処女作 **shojosaku** one's first (published) work
6 自浄作用 **jijō-sayō** self-purification
自壊作用 **jikai sayō** disintegration
8 苗半作 **naehansaku** The seedlings determine the harvest.
9 相互作用 **sōgo sayō** interaction
12 超特作 **chōtokusaku** super production, feature film
無造作 **muzōsa** with ease; simple, artless
14 閨秀作家 **keishū sakka** woman writer
19 贋金作 **niseganezuku(ri)** counterfeiter

――――――― 4 ―――――――

14 選外佳作 **sengai kasaku** honorable mention

2a5.11 / 1486

似

JI, ni(ru) be similar, resemble
ni(seru) imitate; counterfeit

――――――― 1 ―――――――

0 似つかわしい **ni(tsukawashii)** suitable, appropriate
6 似合 **nia(u)** befit, go well with, be becoming
　　nia(washii) suitable, becoming, well-matched
似而非 **ese-** false, would-be, pseudo-
8 似非 **ni(te)hi(naru)** alike only in appearance
　　ese- false, would-be, pseudo-
9 似通 **nikayo(u)** resemble closely
18 似顔 **nigao** portrait, likeness
似顔絵 **nigaoe** portrait, likeness

――――――― 2 ―――――――

4 不似合 **funia(i)** unbecoming, unsuitable, ill-matched
6 近似 **kinji** approximation, convergence
近似値 **kinjichi** an approximation
8 空似 **sorani** chance resemblance
9 相似 **sōji** resemblance, similarity, analogy
相似形 **sōjikei** similar figures (in geometry)

10 真似 **mane** imitation, mimicry; behavior; pretense
真似事 **manegoto** sham, semblance, pretense
13 猿似 **saruni** a chance resemblance
14 疑似 **giji-** suspected, sham, pseudo-, dummy, simulated
酷似 **kokuji** close resemblance
18 類似 **ruiji** similarity, resemblance
類似点 **ruijiten** points of similarity
類似品 **ruijihin** an imitation

3

2 人真似 **hitomane** mimicry, imitations
3 口真似 **kuchimane** mimicry
4 手真似 **temane** gesture, hand signals
8 泣真似 **na(ki)mane** crocodile tears
物真似 **monomane** doing imitations, mimicry
13 猿真似 **sarumane** monkey-see monkey-do

仰 → 2a4.10

2a5.12

伽 **KYA, GA, KA, togi** nursing, nurse; attend on, keep entertained; attendant

1

5 伽芝居 **(o)togi shibai** fairy play, play for children
8 伽国 **(o)togi (no) kuni** fairyland, never-never land
9 伽草子 **(o)togizōshi** fairy-tale book
13 伽話 **(o)togibanashi** fairy tale
18 伽藍 **garan** Buddhist temple, monastery
19 伽羅 **kyara** aloes wood (tree or fragrance)

2

12 御伽 **otogi** keep company, entertain (guests); attend on, nurse
御伽国 **otogi (no) kuni** fairyland
御伽話 **otogibanashi** fairy tale
13 瑜伽 **yuga** yoga
16 閼伽 **aka** (Buddhist) holy water

2a5.13

攸 **YŪ** relaxed, at ease; place
tokoro place

2a5.14 / 1927

但 **tada(shi)** but, however, provided

1

10 但書 **tada(shi)ga(ki)** proviso
但馬 **Tajima** (ancient kuni, Hyōgo-ken)

2a5.15 / 561

低 低 **TEI, hiku(i)** low
hiku(meru) lower
hiku(maru) become low(er)

1

3 低下 **teika** decline, go down, fall
4 低木 **teiboku** shrub
5 低圧 **teiatsu** low pressure/voltage
低目 **hikume** on the low side
6 低気圧 **teikiatsu** low (atmospheric) pressure
低地 **teichi** low-lying ground, lowlands
低劣 **teiretsu** low grade; base, vulgar
低回 **teikai** loiter, linger
低回趣味 **teikai shumi** dilettantism
7 低吟 **teigin** sing in a low voice, hum
低学年 **teigakunen** elementary school grades 1 and 2
低声 **teisei** low voice, whisper
低利 **teiri** low interest
8 低迷 **teimei** hang low, be sluggish
低周波 **teishūha** low frequency
低空 **teikū** low altitude
低空飛行 **teikū hikō** low-level flying
低物価 **teibukka** low prices
低性能 **teiseinō** low efficiency
低金利 **teikinri** low interest
9 低俗 **teizoku** vulgar
低徊 **teikai** loiter, linger
低徊趣味 **teikai shumi** dilettantism
低度 **teido** low degree
低音 **teion** bass (in music); low voice, sotto voce
低級 **teikyū** low-grade, lowbrow, vulgar
10 低能 **teinō** low intelligence, mentally deficient
低能児 **teinōji** retarded child; backward pupil
11 低率 **teiritsu** low rate
低唱 **teishō** hum, sing softly
12 低温 **teion** low temperature
低減 **teigen** decline, decrease, reduce
低落 **teiraku** fall, decline, slump
低開発国 **teikaihatsukoku** less-developed countries
13 低廉 **teiren** low-priced
低賃金 **teichingin** low wages
15 低潮 **teichō** low tide
低調 **teichō** low-pitched; dull, inactive, sluggish (market)
16 低頭平身 **teitō heishin** prostrate oneself
18 低額 **teigaku** small amount

2

4 中低 **nakabiku, nakahiku** concave, hollow

2 亻5← 冫 子 阝 卩 刂 力 又 冖 亠 十 卜 ⺈ 丷 厂 辶 冂 八 匚

10 高低 **kōtei, takahiku** highs and lows, unevenness, fluctuations; height, pitch
12 最低 **saitei** lowest, minimum
15 熱低 **nettei** tropical depression, cyclone

——————— 3 ———————

5 平身低頭 **heishin-teitō** prostrate oneself

——————— 4 ———————

6 西高東低 **seikō-tōtei** high (barometric pressure) in the west and low in the east

佗→侘 **2a6.14**

2a5.16

佇 **CHO, tatazu(mu)** stop, linger **tatazu(mai)** appearance, shape, form

——————— 1 ———————

5 佇立 **choritsu** stand still

2a5.17

伶 **REI** entertainer, musician; clever

——————— 1 ———————

2 伶人 **reijin** musician
9 伶俐 **reiri** clever

2a5.18

估 **KO** price; selling; merchant

——————— 2 ———————

8 依估地 **ikoji, ekoji** obstinacy, stubbornness
依估贔屓 **ekohiiki** favoritism, bias

2a5.19 / 156

住 住 **JŪ** dwelling, residing, living **su(mu), su(mau)** live, reside **su(mai)** residence

——————— 1 ———————

2 住人 **jūnin** resident, inhabitant
4 住友 **Sumitomo** (company name)
住込 **su(mi)ko(mu)** live in/with
住心地 **su(mi)gokochi** livability, comfort
5 住民 **jūmin** residents, inhabitants
住民登録 **jūmin tōroku** resident registration
住民税 **jūminzei** inhabitants tax
6 住宅 **jūtaku** dwelling, residence, house, housing
住宅地 **jūtakuchi** residential area/land

住宅難 **jūtakunan** housing shortage
8 住居 **jūkyo, sumai** residence, dwelling
住所 **jūsho, su(mi)dokoro** address; residence, domicile
住所録 **jūshoroku** address book
9 住持 **jūji** chief priest of a temple
10 住家 **sumika** where one lives, residence
18 住職 **jūshoku** chief priest of a temple

——————— 2 ———————

5 永住 **eijū** permanent residence
6 先住民族 **senjū minzoku** aborigines
先住者 **senjūsha** former occupant
在住 **zaijū** reside, dwell, live
在住者 **zaijūsha** resident
行住坐臥 **gyōjū-zaga** walking, stopping, sitting, and lying down; daily life
安住 **anjū** live in peace
7 町住 **machizuma(i)** town life
8 侘住 **wa(bi)zu(mai)** wretched abode; solitary life
定住 **teijū** settle down/permanently
定住地 **teijūchi** fixed/permanent abode
定住者 **teijūsha** permanent resident
居住 **kyojū** reside   **izuma(i)** one's sitting posture
居住地 **kyojūchi** place of residence
居住者 **kyojūsha** resident, inhabitant
居住費 **kyojūhi** housing expenses
居住権 **kyojūken** right of residence
9 独住居 **hito(ri)zumai** living alone
10 都住居 **miyakozumai** city life
原住民 **genjūmin** natives, aborigines
旅住 **tabizuma(i)** one's stopping place on a trip
11 常住 **jōjū** everlasting; always; permanently residing
現住所 **genjūsho** present address
移住 **ijū** migration, moving
移住者 **ijūsha** emigrant, immigrant
転住 **tenjū** move, migrate to
12 無住 **mujū** (temple) without a resident priest

——————— 3 ———————

6 衣食住 **ishokujū** food, clothing, and shelter
10 部屋住 **heyazu(mi)** dependent, hanger-on; heir who has not yet taken over
11 組立住宅 **kumita(te) jūtaku** prefab housing

——————— 4 ———————

3 下駄履住宅 **getaba(ki) jūtaku** apartment building whose first floor is occupied by stores and businesses

2a5.20

佞 侫 **NEI** flattery, glibness, wiliness

——————— 1 ———————
2 佞人 **neijin** sycophant, flatterer
5 佞弁 **neiben** flattery, cajolery
6 佞奸 **neikan** wily, treacherous
7 佞臣 **neishin** crafty courtier, treacherous retainer

2a5.21 / 390

何

KA, nani, nan what
izu(re), do(re) which

——————— 1 ———————
2 何人 **nannin** how many people
　　 nanpito(mo) everyone, all
3 何千 **nanzen** (how) many thousands
4 何分 **nanibun** anyway; please **nanpun** how many minutes **nanbun** what fraction
　 何月 **nangatsu** what month
　　 nan(ka)getsu how many months
　 何日 **nannichi** how many days; what day of the month
　 何方 **donata** who **dochira** where, what place; which **izukata** which, which-ever
5 何代目 **nandaime** what ordinal number
　 何奴 **doitsu** who
　 何処 **izuko, izuku, doko** where
　 何処迄 **doko made** how far
6 何気無 **nanigena(ku)** unintentionally; nonchalantly
　 何年 **nannen** how many years; what year
　 何如 **ikan** what, how
　 何回 **nankai** how many times
8 何事 **nanigoto** what, whatever
　 何卒 **nanitozo** please
　 何者 **nanimono** who
　 何物 **nanimono** what
9 何度 **nando** how many times; how many degrees
　 何屋 **nan(demo)ya** jack-of-all-trades, handyman
　 何某 **nanigashi** a certain person; a certain amount
　 何故 **naze, naniyue** why
　 何食顔 **naniku(wanu) kao** innocent look
10 何個 **nanko** how many (pieces)
　 何時 **nanji** what time, when
　 何時迄 **itsu made** till when, how soon/long
　 何時間 **nanjikan** how many hours
11 何遍 **nanben** how many times
12 何期 **nanki** how many periods; what period
　 何程 **nanihodo** to what extent, how much
　 何番 **nanban** what number
　 何等 **nanra** what, whatever
13 何歳 **nansai** how many years old

14 何様 **nanisama** who (polite); indeed, truly
　 何箇 **nanko** how many (pieces)
　 何箇月 **nankagetsu** how many months
18 何曜日 **nan'yōbi, naniyōbi** what day of the week
——————— 2 ———————
6 如何 **ikaga, ika (ni)** how
　 如何物 **ikamono** spurious article, a fake
　 如何許 **ikabaka(ri)** how much
　 如何程 **ikahodo** how much/many
　 如何様 **ikayō** how, what kind **ikasama** bogus, fraud, swindle; how; I see
　 如何様師 **ikasamashi** swindler, sharpie
12 無何有郷 **mukau (no) sato** an unspoiled paradise, utopia
　 幾何 **kika** geometry
　 幾何学 **kikagaku** geometry
　 幾何学的 **kikagakuteki** geometrical
15 誰何 **suika** challenge, Who goes there?

2a5.22

佝

KŌ, KU foolish; stooped over

——————— 1 ———————
13 佝僂 **kuru** hunchback; rickets

2a5.23 / 1761

伺

SHI, ukaga(u) visit; ask, inquire; hear, be told **ukaga(i)** visit; inquiry

——————— 1 ———————
10 伺候 **shikō** wait upon; pay a courtesy call
　 伺書 **ukaga(i)sho** written request for instructions

2a5.24 / 1063

余 餘

YO remainder, the rest; other; more than, upward of; I, myself, this writer **ama(ri)** remainder, surplus; more than, upward of; (not) very **ama(ru)** remain left over, be more than enough; be beyond, exceed **ama(su)** let remain, leave; save

——————— 1 ———————
2 余人 **yojin, yonin** others, other people
　 余力 **yoryoku** remaining strength; surplus energy; money to spare
4 余分 **yobun** extra, excess
　 余日 **yojitsu** days left, remaining time
5 余生 **yosei** the remainder of one's life
　 余白 **yohaku** blank space, margin
6 余色 **yoshoku** complementary color
　 余地 **yochi** room, place, margin, scope

2

亻 5←
冫
孑
阝
卩
刂
力
又
宀
亠
十
ト
宀
厂
辶
冂
几
匸

余光 **yokō** afterglow, remaining light
7 余角 **yokaku** complementary angle
余沢 **yotaku** blessings, benefits
余技 **yogi** avocation, hobby
8 余事 **yoji** other matters
余念 **yonen** thinking of other matters
余命 **yomei** the remainder of one's life
余波 **yoha** aftereffects, secondary effects, aftermath, consequences
余弦 **yogen** cosine
余所 **yoso** another place; other, strange
余所目 **yosome** someone else's eye, casual observer
余所行 **yosoyu(ki), yosoi(ki)** going out, formal (manners), one's best (attire)
余所見 **yosomi** look away
余所者 **yosomono** stranger
9 余風 **yofū** surviving custom, holdover
余栄 **yoei** posthumous honors
余音 **yoin** lingering tone, reverberation; aftertaste, suggestiveness
余臭 **yoshū** lingering smell
余香 **yokō** lingering fragrance
余計 **yokei** more than enough, extra; unneeded, uncalled-for
10 余党 **yotō** remnants of a political party
余病 **yobyō** secondary disease, complications
余財 **yozai** available funds, spare cash; remaining fortune
11 余剰 **yojō** surplus
余得 **yotoku** additional gain, extra benefit
余情 **yojō** suggestiveness, lingering charm
12 余寒 **yokan** the lingering cold
余程 **yohodo, yo(p)podo** very, much, to a great degree
余裕 **yoyū** surplus, leeway, room, margin
13 余業 **yogyō** remaining work; avocation, sideline
余勢 **yosei** surplus energy, momentum
余暇 **yoka** spare time, leisure
余罪 **yozai** other crimes
14 余塵 **yojin** trailing dust; aftereffects
余算 **yosan** one's remaining years
余聞 **yobun** rumor, gossip
15 余儀 **yogi(naku)** unavoidable, be obliged to
余熱 **yonetsu** remaining heat
余弊 **yohei** a lingering evil
余憤 **yofun** pent-up anger, rage
余談 **yodan** digression
余震 **yoshin** aftershock
16 余興 **yokyō** entertainment, sideshow
17 余齢 **yorei** one's remaining years
18 余燼 **yojin** embers, smoldering fire
余類 **yorui** remnants of a party/gang
19 余韻 **yoin** lingering tone, reverberation; aftertaste, suggestiveness

───── 2 ─────
3 丈余 **jōyo** more than three meters, over ten feet
4 手余 **teama(su)** have/be too much to handle
手余者 **teama(shi)mono** someone hard to handle
尺余 **shakuyo** more than a foot (long/high)
5 字余 **jiama(ri)** hypermetric
6 刑余 **keiyo** previous conviction
有余 **a(ri)ama(ru)** be superfluous, be more than enough **yūyo** more than
自余 **jiyo** the others/rest
8 雨余 **uyo** after a rainfall
9 持余 **mo(te)ama(su)** have more than one can manage
持余者 **mo(te)ama(shi)mono** nuisance, black sheep
思余 **omo(i)ama(ru)** not know what to do, be unable to contain oneself
紆余 **uyo** meandering; abundant talent
紆余曲折 **uyo-kyokusetsu** meandering, twists and turns, complications
食余 **ta(be)ama(su)** not finish one's meal
10 残余 **zan'yo** remainder, residual, remnant, balance
残余額 **zan'yogaku** balance, remainder
11 剰余 **jōyo** a surplus
剰余金 **jōyokin** a surplus
酔余 **suiyo** drunken
13 歳余 **saiyo** longer than a year
睡余 **suiyo** after awakening
15 窮余 **kyūyo** desperate
窮余一策 **kyūyo (no) issaku** last resort

───── 3 ─────
5 四百余州 **shihyakuyoshū** all China

2a5.25 / 1249

含 **GAN, fuku(mu)** contain, include; hold in the mouth; bear in mind, understand; imply, involve **fuku(meru)** include; give instructions

───── 1 ─────
4 含水炭素 **gansuitanso** carbohydrate
6 含有 **gan'yū** contain
含有量 **gan'yūryō** quantity of a constituent substance, content
7 含声 **fuku(mi)goe** muffled voice
8 含味 **ganmi** taste, relish, appreciate
10 含浸 **ganshin** impregnation
含笑 **fuku(mi)wara(i)** suppressed laugh, chuckle, giggle
13 含蓄 **ganchiku** implication, significance
含意 **gan'i** implication

───── 2 ─────
5 包含 **hōgan** include, comprehend; imply

7 言含 **i(i)fuku(meru)** instruct/brief thoroughly

2a5.26

巫   **FU** sorcerer, sorceress

———————— 1 ————————

2 巫子 **miko** medium, sorceress; shrine maiden
3 巫女 **miko, fujo** medium, sorceress; shrine maiden
巫山戯 **fuzake(ru)** frolic, be playful, jest; flirt
11 巫術 **fujutsu** divination, sorcery, witchcraft

———————— 2 ————————

11 悪巫山戯 **warufuzake** prank, practical joke

2a5.27

夾   **KYŌ** insert/pinch between

———————— 1 ————————

6 夾竹桃 **kyōchikutō** oleander, phlox
14 夾雑物 **kyōzatsubutsu** admixture, impurities

———————— 6 ————————

2a6.1 / 678

依   **I, E, yo(ru)** depend on, be due to

———————— 1 ————————

5 依存 **ison, izon** depend on, be dependent on
7 依怙地 **ikoji, ekoji** obstinacy, stubbornness
依怙贔屓 **ekohiiki** favoritism, bias
8 依拠 **ikyo** dependence
10 依託 **itaku** request, entrust
12 依然 **izen (to shite)** still, as ever
15 依嘱 **ishoku** entrust with, commission
16 依頼 **irai** request; entrust; rely on
依頼心 **iraishin** spirit of dependence
19 依願免官 **igan menkan** retirement at one's own request

———————— 2 ————————

10 帰依 **kie** become a believer in, embrace, convert to

———————— 3 ————————

5 弁護依頼人 **bengo irainin** client

2a6.2 / 331

使 使   **SHI** use; messenger
tsuka(u) use
tsuka(i) mission, errand; messenger; trainer, tamer

———————— 1 ————————

2 使丁 **shitei** servant, messenger

4 使分 **tsuka(i)wa(ke)** proper use
使込 **tsuka(i)ko(mu)** embezzle; accustom oneself to using
使手 **tsuka(i)te** user, consumer; employer; spendthrift; (fencing) master
使方 **tsuka(i)kata** how to use, management
5 使令 **shirei** a directive
使古 **tsuka(i)furu(su)** wear out
使用 **shiyō** use, employ, utilize
使用人 **shiyōnin** employee
使用法 **shiyōhō** use, directions
使用者 **shiyōsha** user, consumer; employer
使用料 **shiyōryō** rental fee
使用量 **shiyōryō** amount used
使用権 **shiyōken** right to use
6 使先 **tsuka(i)saki** the place one is sent to on an errand
使尽 **tsuka(i)tsuku(su)** use up, exhaust
7 使臣 **shishin** envoy
使役 **shieki** employ, use, set to work
8 使果 **tsuka(i)hata(su)** use up, squander
使命 **shimei** mission, appointed task
使者 **shisha** messenger, envoy
9 使途 **shito** purpose for which money is spent
10 使残 **tsuka(i)noko(ri)** those left unused, remnants, odds and ends
使徒 **shito** apostle
11 使道 **tsuka(i)michi** use
使過 **tsuka(i)su(giru)** use too much, work (someone) too hard
13 使節 **shisetsu** envoy; mission, delegation
使節団 **shisetsudan** mission, delegation
使賃 **tsuka(i)chin** tip for a messenger, errand charge
14 使嗾 **shisō** instigate
使様 **tsuka(i)yō** how to use
使慣 **tsuka(i)na(reru)** get accustomed to using, get used to

———————— 2 ————————

2 人使 **hitozuka(i)** how one handles one's workers
3 大使 **taishi** ambassador
大使館 **taishikan** embassy
小使 **kozuka(i)** handyman, errand boy
4 天使 **tenshi, ten (no) tsuka(i)** angel
公使 **kōshi** minister (of a legation)
公使館 **kōshikan** legation
5 召使 **me(shi)tsuka(i)** servant
正使 **seishi** senior envoy, chief delegate
6 再使用 **saishiyō** reuse
扱使 **ko(ki)tsuka(u)** work (someone) hard
行使 **kōshi** use, exercise (rights), put (money) into circulation
7 走使 **hashi(ri)zuka(i)** errand boy, messenger
労使 **rōshi** labor and management

8 追使 **o(i)tsuka(u)** work (someone) hard
苦使 **kushi** overwork, exploit
国使 **kokushi** envoy
金使 **kanezuka(i)** way of spending money
9 勅使 **chokushi** imperial messenger
虐使 **gyakushi** overwork (someone), drive too hard, exploit, give rough use
急使 **kyūshi** express messenger, courier
10 特使 **tokushi** special envoy/messenger
11 密使 **misshi** secret messenger/agent
蛇使 **hebitsuka(i)** snake charmer
12 棒使 **bōtsuka(i)** pole fighting/fighter
14 酷使 **kokushi** work (someone) hard
駆使 **kushi** have at one's command

—————————— 3 ——————————

2 十二使徒 **jūni shito** the Twelve Apostles
3 小間使 **komazuka(i)** chambermaid
6 両刀使 **ryōtōtsuka(i)** two-sword fencer; expert in two fields
10 猛獣使 **mōjūzuka(i)** wild-animal tamer
12 遣唐使 **kentōshi** Japanese envoy to Tang-dynasty China
答礼使節 **tōrei shisetsu** envoy sent to return courtesies
21 魔法使 **mahōtsuka(i)** magician, wizard

—————————— 4 ——————————

6 全権大使 **zenken taishi** ambassador plenipotentiary

2a6.3 / 421

価 價

KA, atai price, cost; value, worth

—————————— 1 ——————————

10 価値 **kachi** value, merit
価格 **kakaku** price, cost, value
価格表 **kakakuhyō** price list
18 価額 **kagaku** value, amount, price

—————————— 2 ——————————

2 力価 **rikika** potency; titer
4 円価 **enka** value of the yen
5 半価 **hanka** half price
代価 **daika** price, cost
市価 **shika** market/current price
平価 **heika** par, parity
正価 **seika** (net) price
比価 **hika** parity
6 同価 **dōka** equivalent
地価 **chika** land value/prices
安価 **anka** low price
有価 **yūka** valuable, negotiable
有価物 **yūkabutsu** valuables
有価証券 **yūka shōken** (negotiable) securities

糸価 **shika** price of (silk) thread
米価 **beika** (government-set) rice price
7 対価 **taika** equivalent value, a compensation
売価 **baika** selling price
声価 **seika** reputation, fame, popularity
8 実価 **jikka** real/intrinsic value; actual/cost price
定価 **teika** (fixed/set) price
定価表 **teikahyō** price list
物価 **bukka** (commodity) prices
物価指数 **bukka shisū** price index
物価高 **bukkadaka** high prices
物価騰貴 **bukka tōki** rise in prices
9 単価 **tanka** unit cost/price; univalent
10 高価 **kōka** high price
真価 **shinka** true value
原価 **genka** cost price, cost
株価 **kabuka** share price, stock prices
時価 **jika** current/market price
特価 **tokka** special/reduced price
特価品 **tokkahin** bargain goods
紙価 **shika** the price of paper
12 減価 **genka** price reduction, discount
換価 **kanka** realize, convert into money
無価 **muka** priceless
無価値 **mukachi** worthless
等価 **tōka** equivalence, parity
評価 **hyōka** appraisal
13 廉価 **renka** low price
廉価版 **renkaban** cheap/popular edition
廉価品 **renkahin** low-priced goods
16 薬価 **yakuka, yakka** drug charge/prices

—————————— 3 ——————————

5 末端価格 **mattan kakaku** end-user price, street value
付加価値税 **fuka-kachi zei** value-added tax
6 再評価 **saihyōka** reassessment, re-evaluation
7 低物価 **teibukka** low prices
9 栄養価 **eiyōka** food value
10 原子価 **genshika** valence

侠→俠 2a7.7

2a6.4

侏

SHU short, dwarf; actor

2a6.5

侑

YŪ give, offer (food and drink)

2a6.6

SHI extravagance; arbitrariness

—————— 2 ——————
12 奢侈 **shashi** luxury, extravagance

2a6.7 / 612

例

REI example; custom, practice, precedent **tato(eru)** compare, liken **tato(eba)** for example **tameshl** instance, example, precedent; experience

—————— 1 ——————
4 例文 **reibun** illustrative sentence
例月 **reigetsu** every month
例日 **reijitsu** weekday
5 例外 **reigai** exception
例示 **reiji** give an example of
6 例年 **reinen** normal/average year; every year
例会 **reikai** regular meeting
例式 **reishiki** regular ceremony; established form
7 例言 **reigen** explanatory notes
8 例刻 **reikoku** the usual hour
11 例祭 **reisai** regular/annual festival
例規 **reiki** established rule
12 例証 **reishō** example, illustration
13 例解 **reikai** example, illustration
例話 **reiwa** illustration
18 例題 **reidai** example, exercise (in a textbook)

—————— 2 ——————
1 一例 **ichirei** one example, an instance
3 凡例 **hanrei** explanatory notes; legend (on a map/diagram)
4 不例 **furei** indisposition, illness
文例 **bunrei** model sentence/writing
引例 **inrei** quotation, citation
月例 **getsurei** monthly
5 古例 **korei** old custom, established practice
比例 **hirei** proportion, ratio; proportional (representation)
用例 **yōrei** example, illustration
好例 **kōrei** good example, case in point
旧例 **kyūrei** old custom, tradition
6 先例 **senrei** precedent
吉例 **kichirei, kitsurei** (annual festive) custom
7 作例 **sakurei** model of writing
判例 **hanrei** (judicial) precedent
条例 **jōrei** regulation, law, ordinance, rule
8 事例 **jirei** example; precedent
佳例 **karei** good example
法例 **hōrei** the conflict-of-laws law

実例 **jitsurei** example, illustration
定例 **teirei, jōrei** established usage, precedent; regular (meeting)
9 前例 **zenrei** precedent
通例 **tsūrei** usual(ly)
活例 **katsurei** living example
恒例 **kōrei** established practice, custom
10 特例 **tokurei** special case, exception
症例 **shōrei** a case (of cholera)
11 常例 **jōrei** custom, conventional practice
悪例 **akurei** bad example/precedent
異例 **irei** exceptional case; indisposition
13 適例 **tekirei** good example, case in point
新例 **shinrei** new example/precedent
14 遺例 **irei** surviving example
慣例 **kanrei** custom, precedent
慣例上 **kanreijō** conventionally, traditionally
15 範例 **hanrei** example
18 類例 **ruirei** similar example, a parallel

—————— 3 ——————
4 反比例 **hanpirei** in inverse proportion to
5 正比例 **seihirei** in direct proportion/ratio
8 逆比例 **gyakuhirei** inversely proportional to
9 除外例 **jogairei** an exception

—————— 4 ——————
8 治安条例 **chian jōrei** public-order regulations
9 按分比例 **anbun hirei** proportionately, prorated

2a6.8

CHŌ shallow, frivolous

—————— 2 ——————
12 軽佻 **keichō** frivolous, flippant
軽佻浮薄 **keichō-fuhaku** frivolous, flippant

2a6.9

俘

FU, **toriko** captive

—————— 1 ——————
13 俘虜 **furyo** captive, prisoner of war
17 俘馘 **fukaku** sever a captive's left ear

2a6.10 / 1462

佳

KA beautiful; good **yo(i)** good

—————— 1 ——————
2 佳人 **kajin** beautiful woman
5 佳句 **kaku** beautiful passage, literary gem

2

亻6←
冫
孑
阝
卩
刂
力
又
宀
亠
十
卜
勹
厂
辶
冂
几
匚

7 佳良 **karyō** excellent, good
佳作 **kasaku** an excellent work
佳言 **kagen** good words
8 佳例 **karei** good example
9 佳品 **kahin** choice article
佳客 **kakyaku, kakaku** welcome guest; valued customer
12 佳景 **kakei** beautiful view
13 佳節 **kasetsu** auspicious occasion
14 佳境 **kakyō** interesting part, climax (of a story)
19 佳麗 **karei** beautiful

————————— 2 —————————

12 絶佳 **zekka** superb

————————— 3 —————————

14 選外佳作 **sengai kasaku** honorable mention

2a6.11 / 571

侍

JI, habe(ru) wait upon, serve **samurai** warrior, samurai

————————— 1 —————————

0 侍する **ji(suru)** wait upon, serve
3 侍女 **jijo** lady in waiting
4 侍中 **jichū** imperial political adviser
5 侍史 **jishi** private secretary; respectfully
6 侍気質 **samurai katagi** samurai spirit
7 侍臣 **jishin** courtier, attendant
侍医 **jii** court physician
8 侍者 **jisha** attendant, valet; altar boy
10 侍従 **jijū** chamberlain
17 侍講 **jikō** imperial tutor

————————— 2 —————————

4 内侍 **naishi** lady-in-waiting, maid of honor
犬侍 **inuzamurai** shameless/cowardly samurai
6 近侍 **kinji** attendant, entourage
8 典侍 **tenji** maid of honor, lady in waiting

2a6.12

侃

KAN moral strength, integrity

————————— 1 —————————

3 侃々諤々 **kankan-gakugaku** outspoken

2a6.13 / 197

供

KYŌ, KU, GU offer, submit; serve (a meal); supply **sona(eru)** make an offering, dedicate **tomo** attendant, servant, retinue

————————— 1 —————————

0 供する **kyō(suru)** offer, submit; serve (a meal); supply

2 供人 **tomobito** companion
3 供与 **kyōyo** grant, furnish, provide
5 供出 **kyōshutsu** delivery
6 供米 **kyōmai** delivery of rice (to the government) **kumai** offering of rice to a god
7 供応 **kyōō** treat, banquet, dinner
8 供奉 **kyōhō, gubu** be in attendance on, accompany
供物 **kumotsu, sona(e)mono** votive offering
10 供託 **kyōtaku** deposit
12 供給 **kyōkyū** supply
供給者 **kyōkyūsha** supplier
供給源 **kyōkyūgen** source of supply
15 供養 **kuyō, kyōyō** memorial service
17 供覧 **kyōran** display, show

————————— 2 —————————

2 子供 **kodomo** child
kodomo(rashii) childlike
子供心 **kodomogokoro** a child's mind/heart
子供好 **kodomozu(ki)** fond of children
子供扱 **kodomoatsuka(i)** treating (someone) like a child
子供向 **kodomomu(ki)** for children
子供服 **kodomofuku** children's wear
子供部屋 **kodomo-beya** children's room, nursery
子供騙 **kodomodama(shi)** childish trick
3 大供 **ōdomo** grownups
口供 **kōkyō** affidavit, deposition
口供書 **kōkyōsho** affidavit, deposition
6 自供 **jikyō** confession
7 花供養 **hanakuyō** Buddha's-birthday commemoration
12 提供 **teikyō** offer, present
13 節供 **sekku** seasonal festival

————————— 3 —————————

8 追善供養 **tsuizen-kuyo** (Buddhist) memorial service

————————— 4 —————————

2 人身御供 **hitomi gokū** human sacrifice, victim

2a6.14

侘 侘

TA lonely; other **wa(bi)** taste for the simple and quiet **wa(biru)** live a lonely life; be worried **wa(bishii)** lonely, forlorn, wretched

————————— 1 —————————

7 侘住 **wa(bi)zu(mai)** wretched abode; solitary life

————————— 2 —————————

9 待侘 **ma(chi)wa(biru)** get anxious from long waiting

佞 → 佞 2a5.20

2a6.15

佶   KITSU healthy; correct

2a6.16

佼   KŌ beautiful; sly

2a6.17 / 1162

併 併   HEI, awa(seru) put together

———————— 1 ————————
- 5 併出 heishutsu go/put out side by side
- 併用 heiyō use together, use in combination
- 6 併合 heigō annexation, amalgamation, merger
- 併行 heikō go by twos, go together
- 併有 heiyū own together, combine
- 7 併呑 heidon annexation, absorption
- 9 併発 heihatsu break out at the same time, be complicated by
- 10 併起 heiki occur simultaneously
- 併殺 heisatsu double play (in baseball)
- 併称 heishō rank with, classify together
- 併記 heiki write side by side, print together
- 13 併置 heichi juxtapose, place side by side

———————— 2 ————————
- 6 合併 gappei merger, consolidation

2a6.18

佯   YŌ, itsuwa(ru) feign

———————— 1 ————————
- 7 佯狂 yōkyō feigned madness

———————— 2 ————————
- 10 倘佯 shōyō wandering about

2a6.19

佰   HAKU leader of 100 men; hundred; east-west path between paddies

———————— 2 ————————
- 5 仟佰 senpaku many; paths between paddies

2a6.20 / 1736

侮 侮   BU, anado(ru) despise, hold in contempt

———————— 1 ————————
- 7 侮弄 burō ridicule
- 侮言 bugen an insult
- 10 侮辱 bujoku insult
- 侮笑 bushō derision
- 14 侮蔑 bubetsu contempt, scorn, slight
- 侮慢 buman insult, contempt

———————— 2 ————————
- 12 軽侮 keibu contempt, disdain

侭 → 儘 2a14.2

2a6.21

佩   HAI wear at one's side, gird on

———————— 1 ————————
- 2 佩刀 haitō sword worn at one's side; wear a sword
- 10 佩剣 haiken sword worn at one's side; wear a sword

2a6.22

佪   KAI go/wander around

2a6.23 / 791

舍 舍   SHA building; inn

———————— 1 ————————
- 6 舍宅 shataku house
- 7 舍利 shari Buddha's bones; a saint's bones
- 12 舍営 shaei billeting, quarters
- 15 舍監 shakan dormitory superintendent, housemaster

———————— 2 ————————
- 4 仏舍利 busshari Buddha's ashes
- 犬舍 kensha kennel, doghouse
- 牛舍 gyūsha cowshed, barn
- 5 庁舍 chōsha government-office building
- 田舍 inaka the country, rural areas
- 田舍出 inakade from the country
- 田舍回 inakamawa(ri) tour of the country, provincial tour
- 田舍育 inakasoda(chi) country-bred

2

亻 6 ←
冫
孑
阝
卩
刂
力
又
亠
十
卜
勹
丷
厂
辶
冂
八
匸

田舎者 **inakamono** person from the country, rustic, rube
田舎風 **inakafū** rustic, country-style
田舎染 **inakajimi(ru)** be countrified
田舎娘 **inakamusume** country girl
田舎家 **inakaya** country house
田舎道 **inakamichi** country road
7 兵舎 **heisha** barracks
坊舎 **bōsha** priests' quarters
学舎 **gakusha** school (building)
8 官舎 **kansha** official residence
9 客舎 **kakusha, kyakusha** hotel, inn
10 倶舎 **Kusha** (a Buddhist sect)
校舎 **kōsha** school building
旅舎 **ryosha** hotel, inn
病舎 **byōsha** infirmary, hospital
11 宿舎 **shukusha** lodgings, quarters, billet
豚舎 **tonsha** pigsty, pigpen
12 禽舎 **kinsha** aviary, birdhouse
営舎 **eisha** barracks
13 幕舎 **bakusha** barracks, camp
鳩舎 **kyūsha** dovecote
14 厩舎 **kyūsha** barn
獄舎 **gokusha** prison, jail
精舎 **shōja** monastery, convent
駅舎 **ekisha** station building
19 鶏舎 **keisha** chicken coop, henhouse

———— 3 ————
4 片田舎 **kata-inaka** backwoods, boondocks
11 寄宿舎 **kishukusha** dormitory

———— 4 ————
13 蒲鉾兵舎 **kamaboko heisha** Quonset hut

舎 → 舍 **2a6.23**

2a6.24 / 579

念 **NEN** idea, thought, sense; desire; concern, care

———— 1 ————
0 念じる **nen(jiru)** have in mind; pray for
2 念入 **nen'i(ri)** careful, scrupulous, conscientious
念力 **nenriki** will power, faith
3 念々 **nennen** continually thinking about something
4 念仏 **nenbutsu** Buddhist invocation (of Amitabha)
10 念珠 **nenju** rosary
14 念誦 **nenju** Buddhist invocation
15 念慮 **nenryo** thought, consideration
16 念頭 **nentō** mind

19 念願 **nengan** one's heart's desire, earnest wish

———— 2 ————
1 一念 **ichinen** a determined purpose
2 入念 **nyūnen** careful, scrupulous
4 丹念 **tannen** painstaking, elaborate
5 他念 **tanen** thinking about something else
存念 **zonnen** thought, idea, concept
正念場 **shōnenba** the crucial/now-or-never moment
6 妄念 **mōnen** irrelevant thoughts, distracting ideas
朴念仁 **bokunenjin** unsociable close-mouthed person
7 余念 **yonen** thinking of other matters
邪念 **janen** sinister intent, evil designs
8 念念 **nennen** continually thinking about something
実念論 **jitsunenron** realism
空念仏 **karanenbutsu** perfunctory praying, empty/fruitless talk
祈念 **kinen** a prayer
放念 **hōnen** feel at ease, relax
9 専念 **sennen** undivided/close attention
信念 **shinnen** faith, belief, conviction
俗念 **zokunen** worldliness, earthly desires
通念 **tsūnen** common(ly accepted) idea
怨念 **onnen** grudge, malice, hatred
思念 **shinen** thought
10 残念 **zannen** regrettable, too bad
残念賞 **zannenshō** consolation prize
記念 **kinen** commemoration, remembrance
記念切手 **kinen kitte** commemorative stamp
記念日 **kinenbi** memorial day, anniversary
記念号 **kinengō** commemorative issue (of a magazine)
記念物 **kinenbutsu** souvenir, memento
記念品 **kinenhin** souvenir, memento
記念祭 **kinensai** commoration, anniversary
記念碑 **kinenhi** monument
記念館 **kinenkan** memorial hall
11 道念 **dōnen** moral sense; priest's wife
執念 **shūnen** tenacity of purpose, vindictiveness
執念深 **shūnenbuka(i)** tenacious; vengeful, spiteful
理念 **rinen** idea, doctrine, ideology
欲念 **yokunen** desire, wishes, passions
悪念 **akunen** evil thought
情念 **jōnen** sentiment, passions
断念 **dannen** abandon, relinquish
12 無念 **munen** regret, resentment, vexation
無念無想 **munen-musō** blank state of mind
軫念 **shinnen** (emperor's) anxiety
13 想念 **sōnen** idea, conception
14 疑念 **ginen** doubt, suspicion, misgivings

概念 **gainen** general idea, concept
概念化 **gainenka** generalization
概念的 **gainenteki** general, conceptual
雑念 **zatsunen** idle/worldly thoughts
15 黙念 **mokunen** silent, mute, tacit
16 憶念 **okunen** something always kept in mind
18 観念 **kannen** idea; sense (of duty)
観念的 **kannenteki** ideal, ideological
観念論 **kannenron** idealism (in philosophy)
20 懸念 **kenen** fear, apprehension

———————— 3 ————————

7 初一念 **shoichinen** one's original intention
18 類概念 **ruigainen** genus, generic concept

———————— 4 ————————

4 天然記念物 **tennen kinenbutsu** natural monument
11 強迫観念 **kyōhaku kannen** obsession

2a6.25

命

RIN, RON, omo(u) think

2a6.26 / 578

命

MEI, MYŌ command, order; life; fate
inochi life   mikoto lord, prince

———————— 1 ————————

0 命じる **mei(jiru)** command; appoint
4 命中 **meichū** hit, on-target impact
命日 **meinichi** anniversary of a death
5 命令 **meirei** command, order
命令形 **meireikei** imperative form
6 命名 **meimei** name, christen, call
8 命知 **inochishi(razu)** recklessness; daredevil
命取 **inochito(ri)** fatal
9 命拾 **inochibiro(i)** narrow escape from death
10 命冥加 **inochi-myōga** miraculous escape from death
命脈 **meimyaku** life
11 命運 **meiun** fate
命婦 **myōbu, meifu** woman official (historical)
13 命数 **meisū** one's natural lifespan; destiny
14 命綱 **inochizuna** lifeline
18 命題 **meidai** proposition, thesis
20 命懸 **inochiga(ke)** life-or-death, risky, desperate

———————— 2 ————————

1 一命 **ichimei** a life; a command
2 人命 **jinmei** (human) life
3 大命 **taimei** imperial mandate
亡命 **bōmei** flee one's country
亡命者 **bōmeisha** exile, emigré

下命 **kamei** order, command
4 天命 **tenmei** God's will, fate, destiny; one's life
内命 **naimei** private/secret orders
5 本命 **honmei** probable winner, favorite (to win)
生命 **seimei** life
生命保険 **seimei hoken** life insurance
存命 **zonmei** be alive
用命 **yōmei** order, command
立命 **ritsumei** philosophical peace of mind
6 死命 **shimei** life or death, fate
任命 **ninmei** appoint, nominate
7 身命 **shinmei** (risk) one's life
寿命 **jumyō** life, lifespan
余命 **yomei** the remainder of one's life
助命 **jomei** spare (someone's) life
延命 **enmei** prolongation of life
社命 **shamei** company orders
8 非命 **himei** untimely (death)
長命 **chōmei** long life, longevity
使命 **shimei** mission, appointed task
受命 **jumei** (official's) commission
拝命 **haimei** receive an official appointment
知命 **chimei** age 50
官命 **kanmei** official orders/mission
定命 **teimei** fate; (predetermined) lifespan
jōmyō normal/alloted lifespan
9 勅命 **chokumei** imperial order/command
急命 **kyūmei** urgent orders
待命 **taimei** awaiting orders
革命 **kakumei** revolution
革命的 **kakumeiteki** revolutionary, radical
革命家 **kakumeika** a revolutionary
革命歌 **kakumeika** revolutionary song
宣命 **senmyō** imperial edict
10 特命 **tokumei** specially appointed
致命的 **chimeiteki** fatal, lethal, deadly, mortal
致命傷 **chimeishō** fatal wound/injury
恩命 **onmei** gracious words/command
11 運命 **unmei** fate, destiny
運命付 **unmeizu(keru)** destine, doom
運命的 **unmeiteki** fateful
運命論 **unmeiron** fatalism
宿命 **shukumei** fate, destiny
宿命的 **shukumeiteki** fatal
宿命論 **shukumeiron** fatalism
宿命論者 **shukumeironsha** fatalist
救命 **kyūmei** lifesaving
救命具 **kyūmeigu** life preserver
救命索 **kyūmeisaku** lifeline
救命帯 **kyūmeitai** life belt
救命袋 **kyūmeibukuro** escape chute
救命艇 **kyūmeitei** lifeboat
救命網 **kyūmeimō** safety net

2

→ 7

亻
⺅
孑
阝
阝
刂
力
又

亠
土
十
⺊
ク

⼍
厂
辶
冂
几
匸

12 短命 **tanmei** short-lived
復命 **fukumei** report
落命 **rakumei** die
絶命 **zetsumei** death
貴命 **kimei** your orders/instructions
13 幕命 **bakumei** shogunate orders
電命 **denmei** telegraphed instructions
14 遺命 **imei** will, dying instructions
16 薄命 **hakumei** ill-fated, unfortunate
17 厳命 **genmei** strict orders
懇命 **konmei** kind words
20 懸命 **kenmei** eager, going all-out; risking
one's life
21 露命 **romei** transient life

————————— 3 —————————

4 反革命 **hankakumei** counterrevolution
6 至上命令 **shijō meirei** supreme/inviolable
command; categorical imperative
10 祥月命日 **shōtsuki meinichi** anniversary of
one's death
13 新生命 **shinseimei** new life

————————— 4 —————————

1 一生懸命 **isshōkenmei** with all one's might
一所懸命 **isshokenmei** with all one's might
6 安心立命 **anshin-ritsumei** spiritual peace
and enlightenment
安神立命 **anshin-ritsumei** spiritual peace
and enlightenment
12 絶対絶命 **zettai-zetsumei** desperate situation

來→来 0a7.6

————————— 7 —————————

2a7.1 / 157

信

SHIN sincerity, trust, reliability;
message, communication, signal
makoto sincerity, fidelity

————————— 1 —————————

0 信じる/ずる **shin(jiru/zuru)** believe,
believe in
3 信女 **shinnyo** (title affixed to woman's
posthumous Buddhist name)
信士 **shinshi** (title affixed to man's posthumous Buddhist name)
4 信天翁 **ahōdori** albatross
信心 **shinjin** faith, belief, piety
5 信玄袋 **shingenbukuro** cloth bag
信用 **shin'yō** trust, confidence; credit;
reputation
信用状 **shin'yōjō** letter of credit
信用取引 **shin'yō torihiki** credit transaction
信用組合 **shin'yō kumiai** credit union

信号 **shingō** signal
信号灯 **shingōtō** signal light, blinker
信号塔 **shingōtō** signal tower
信号旗 **shingōki** signal/code flag
信号機 **shingōki** signal
6 信任 **shinnin** confidence, trust
信任状 **shinninjō** credentials
信仰 **shinkō** religious faith, belief in
信仰告白 **shinkō kokuhaku** profession of
faith
7 信条 **shinjō** article of faith, creed
8 信奉 **shinpō** belief, faith
信奉者 **shinpōsha** adherent, believer,
devotee
信念 **shinnen** faith, belief, conviction
信実 **shinjitsu** sincerity, honesty
信服 **shinpuku** be convinced
信者 **shinja** believer, adherent, the faithful
10 信徒 **shinto** believer, follower, the faithful
信書 **shinsho** letter, correspondence
信教 **shinkyō** religion, religious belief
信託 **shintaku** trust, entrusting
信託統治 **shintaku tōchi** trusteeship
11 信望 **shinbō** confidence and popularity,
prestige
信販 **shinpan** credit sales (short for 信用販売)
12 信証 **shinshō** evidence, sign
13 信義 **shingi** faith, fidelity, loyalty
信愛 **shin'ai** love and believe in
14 信疑 **shingi** belief or doubt
信管 **shinkan** fuse
信認 **shinnin** trust and accept, acknowledge
15 信賞必罰 **shinshō-hitsubatsu** sure punishment and sure reward
16 信濃 **Shinano** (ancient kuni, Nagano-ken)
信憑性 **sinpyōsei** credibility, authenticity
信頼 **shinrai** reliance, trust, confidence
信頼性 **shinraisei** reliability
信頼感 **shinraikan** feeling of trust

————————— 2 —————————

2 入信 **nyūshin** come to believe in, be
converted
3 与信 **yoshin** granting/extending credit,
lending
4 不信 **fushin** unfaithfulness; unbelief; distrust
不信心 **fushinjin** lack of faith, nonbelief
不信用 **fushin'yō** discredit, distrust
不信任 **fushinnin** nonconfidence
不信任案 **fushinnin'an** nonconfidence
motion
不信仰 **fushinkō** lack of faith, unbelief
不信者 **fushinja** unbeliever
不信義 **fushingi** faithlessness, insincerity
5 半信半疑 **hanshin-hangi** incredulous, half
doubting

平信 **heishin** peaceful tidings/news
外信部 **gaishinbu** foreign-news department
6 妄信 **mōshin, bōshin** blind acceptance, credulity
返信 **henshin** reply
返信料 **henshinryō** return postage
自信 **jishin** confidence (in oneself)
自信満々 **jishin-manman** full of confidence
7 来信 **raishin** letter received
赤信号 **akashingō** red (traffic) light
狂信 **kyōshin** fanaticism
狂信的 **kyōshinteki** fanatical
狂信者 **kyōshinsha** fanatic, faddist
狂信性 **kyoshinsei** fanaticism
芳信 **hōshin** your kind/esteemed letter
花信 **kashin** news of how the flowers are blooming
応信 **ōshin** answer signal, countersignal
私信 **shishin** private message
8 受信 **jushin** receipt of a message, (radio) reception
受信人 **jushinnin** addressee
受信料 **jushinryō** (NHK TV) reception fee
受信機 **jushinki** (radio) receiver
盲信 **mōshin** blind acceptance, credulity
迷信 **meishin** superstition
迷信家 **meishinka** superstitious person
送信 **sōshin** transmission of a message
送信機 **sōshinki** transmitter
往信 **ōshin** letter/message requesting a reply
青信号 **aoshingō** green (traffic) light
忠信 **chūshin** loyalty, faithfulness, devotion
所信 **shoshin** one's belief, conviction, opinion
9 発信 **hasshin** send (a message)
急信 **kyūshin** urgent message
逓信 **teishin** communications
通信 **tsūshin** (tele)communications, correspondence, message, news, dispatch, report
通信社 **tsūshinsha** news agency
通信制 **tsūshinsei** system of education by correspondence
通信員 **tsūshin'in** correspondent, reporter
通信教育 **tsūshin kyōiku** education by correspondence
通信販売 **tsūshin hanbai** mail order
通信費 **tsūshinhi** postage, communications expenses
通信網 **tsūshinmō** communications network
通信簿 **tsūshinbo** report card
通信欄 **tsūshinran** correspondence column
風信子 **fūshinshi** hyacinth
風信器 **fūshinki** weather vane
背信 **haishin** breach of faith, betrayal, infidelity

神信心 **kami-shinjin** piety, devoutness
威信 **ishin** prestige, dignity
音信 **onshin, inshin, otozure** a communication, letter, news
音信不通 **onshin-futsū, inshin-futsū** no news of, haven't heard from
10 家信 **kashin** news from home
書信 **shoshin** letter, message
11 過信 **kashin** put too much confidence in
混信 **konshin** jamming, interference, crosstalk
12 着信 **chakushin** arrival of mail/message
着信局 **chakushinkyoku** destination post office
堅信礼 **kenshinrei** (Christian) confirmation
短信 **tanshin** brief note/message
無信心 **mushinjin** impiety, unbelief, infidelity
13 電信 **denshin** telegraph, telegram, cable
電信局 **denshinkyoku** telegraph office
電信柱 **denshinbashira** telegraph pole
電信料 **denshinryō** telegram charges
電信術 **denshinjutsu** telegraphy
電信線 **denshinsen** telegraph line
電信機 **denshinki** a telegraph
14 旗信号 **hatashingō** semaphore, flag signal
誤信 **goshin** mistaken belief
15 確信 **kakushin** firm belief, conviction
16 興信所 **kōshinjo** detective/investigative agency
興信録 **kōshinroku** directory
篤信 **tokushin** devotion
頼信紙 **raishinshi** telegram form/blank

———————— 3 ————————

4 手旗信号 **tebata shingō** flag signaling, semaphore
6 光通信 **hikari tsūshin** optical communication
8 送受信機 **sōjushinki** transceiver
12 腕木信号 **udegi shingō** semaphore
19 霧中信号 **muchū shingō** fog signal

———————— 4 ————————

12 無線電信 **musen denshin** radiotelegraph

2a7.2

kuruma rickshaw

俥

2a7.3 / 1557

SOKU, unaga(su) urge, promote, prompt

———————— 1 ————————

6 促成 **sokusei** growth promotion

促成栽培 **sokusei saibai** forcing culture, hothouse cultivation
9 促音 **sokuon** assimilated sound (represented by a small つ or, in romanization, a doubled letter)
10 促進 **sokushin** promote, encourage
促進剤 **sokushinzai** accelerator, accelerant

——————— 2 ———————
11 偓促 **akuseku, akusoku** fussily, busily
販促 **hansoku** sales promotion (short for 販売促進)
13 催促 **saisoku** urge, press for, demand
催促状 **saisokujō** dunning letter
督促 **tokusoku** urge, press, dun

——————— 3 ———————
8 居催促 **izaisoku** not leave till (a debt is) paid
11 販売促進 **hanbai sokushin** sales promotion

2a7.4

俄 GA, niwa(ka), niwaka sudden, unexpected

——————— 1 ———————
5 俄仕込 **niwakajiko(mi)** hasty preparation
俄仕立 **niwakajita(te)** improvised, extemporaneous
6 俄成金 **niwakanarikin** overnight millionaire
7 俄狂言 **niwakakyōgen** mime, farce
8 俄盲 **niwakamekura** sudden loss of eyesight; person who has unexpectedly become blind
俄雨 **niwakaame** (sudden) shower
9 俄造 **niwakazuku(ri)** makeshift, improvised
10 俄勉強 **niwakabenkyō** cramming
11 俄細工 **niwakazaiku** hastily prepared
12 俄景気 **niwakageiki** temporary boom
俄然 **gazen** all of a sudden, all at once

侮 → 侮 2a6.20

2a7.5 / 330

便 便 BEN convenience, facilities; excrement, feces BIN mail; transport, flight; opportunity tayo(ri) news, tidings yosuga a means

——————— 1 ———————
3 便々 **benben(taru)** protuberant, paunchy **benben (to)** idly
便口 **benkō** fair-spoken, smooth-tongued
5 便巧 **benkō** flatter, curry favor
6 便衣 **ben'i** ordinary clothes

7 便状 **binjō** letter, written communication
便利 **benri** convenient, handy
便利屋 **benriya** handyman
8 便法 **benpō** easier method, shortcut
便宜 **bengi** convenience, expediency
便宜上 **bengijō** for convenience
便服 **benpuku** civilian clothes
便易 **ben'i** easy, convenient
便所 **benjo** toilet, lavatory
9 便乗 **binjō** get aboard; take advantage of
便便 **benben(taru)** protuberant, paunchy **benben (to)** idly
便通 **bentsū** bowel movement
10 便益 **ben'eki** convenience, benefit, advantage
便秘 **benpi** constipation
11 便捷 **binshō** nimble, agile; sharp, shrewd
便船 **binsen** available ship
13 便殿 **binden, benden** imperial resting room
便意 **ben'i** urge to go to the toilet, call of nature
14 便箋 **binsen** stationery, notepaper
15 便器 **benki** toilet, urinal, bedpan
17 便覧 **benran** manual, handbook

——————— 2 ———————
3 大便 **daiben** feces, excrement
小便 **shōben** urine, urination
小便所 **shōbenjo** urinal
4 不便 **fuben** inconvenient, inexpedient
片便 **katabin, katadayo(ri)** one-way correspondence
方便 **hōben** expedient, means, instrument
5 用便 **yōben** going to the toilet
用便後 **yōbengo** after stool
6 両便 **ryōben** urination and defecation
至便 **shiben** very convenient
先便 **senbin** previous letter
血便 **ketsuben** bloody stools
7 別便 **betsubin** by separate mail
花便 **hanadayo(ri)** news of how the flowers are blooming
快便 **kaiben** a refreshing defecation
利便 **riben** convenience
8 幸便 **kōbin** favorable opportunity
空便 **karabin, a(ki)bin** flight with no passengers
9 便便 **benben(taru)** protuberant, paunchy **benben (to)** idly
前便 **zenbin** one's last letter
後便 **kōbin** next letter, later mail
音便 **onbin** (for sake of) euphony
10 郵便 **yūbin** mail
郵便局 **yūbinkyoku** post office
郵便車 **yūbinsha** mail car
郵便物 **yūbinbutsu** mail
郵便船 **yūbinsen** mail boat

郵便箱 **yūbinbako** mailbox
11 排便 **haiben** evacuation, defecation
宿便 **shukuben** long-retained feces, coprostasis
船便 **funabin** sea mail; ship transportation
軟便 **nanben** soft/loose stools
12 検便 **kenben** examination of stools
軽便 **keiben** convenient, handy, simple
軽便鉄道 **keiben tetsudō** narrow-gauge railroad
14 緑便 **ryokuben** green stools
16 穏便 **onbin** gentle, quiet, amicable
17 糞便 **funben** excrement, night soil
18 簡便 **kanben** simple, easy, convenient

—————— 3 ——————

3 大小便 **daishōben** defecation and urination
4 水洗便所 **suisen benjo** flush toilet
5 立小便 **ta(chi)shōben** urinate outdoors
6 汲取便所 **ku(mi)to(ri) benjo** hole-in-the-floor/non-flush toilet
至急便 **shikyūbin** express mail
宅配便 **takuhaibin** parcel delivery business
7 汽車便 **kishabin** (sent) by rail
8 固形便 **kokeiben** (normal) firm feces
9 飛行便 **hikōbin** airmail
急行便 **kyūkōbin** express mail
10 航空便 **kōkūbin** airmail
13 寝小便 **neshōben** bedwetting
鉄道便 **tetsudōbin** transport by rail

2a7.6

俚

RI uncouth, boorish

—————— 1 ——————

6 俚耳 **riji** the ears of the rabble/public
7 俚言 **rigen** dialect, slang
9 俚俗 **rizoku** vulgarity, base manners
14 俚語 **rigo** slang, dialect
16 俚諺 **rigen** folk saying, proverb

2a7.7

俠　侠

KYŌ chivalry
(o)kyan, kyan tomboy

—————— 1 ——————

6 俠気 **kyōki** chivalrous spirit
9 俠客 **kyōkaku** chivalrous man, a gallant
10 俠骨 **kyōkotsu** chivalrous spirit

—————— 2 ——————

6 任俠 **ninkyō** chivalry
10 遊俠 **yūkyō** chivalrous man
13 義俠 **gikyō** chivalry, generosity, heroism
義俠心 **gikyōshin** chivalrous spirit, public-spiritedness

俐→悧 4k7.2

2a7.8 / 909

係

KEI, kakari duty, person in charge
kaka(waru), kaka(ru) have to do with, be involved with

—————— 1 ——————

6 係合 **keigō** engage/mesh with, fit into
kaka(ri)a(u) have to do with, be implicated in
係争 **keisō** dispute, contention
8 係長 **kakarichō** chief clerk
係官 **kakarikan** official in charge
10 係員 **kakariin** clerk in charge
係留 **keiryū** moor, anchor
11 係累 **keirui** dependents, encumbrances
係船 **keisen** mooring, berthing
13 係嗣 **keishi** successor, heir
係数 **keisū** coefficient

—————— 2 ——————

9 連係 **renkei** connection, liaison, contact
14 関係 **kankei** relation(ship), connection
関係代名詞 **kankei daimeishi** relative pronoun
関係者 **kankeisha** interested party, those concerned
関係副詞 **kankei fukushi** relative adverb

—————— 3 ——————

5 出納係 **suitōgakari** cashier; teller
7 売場係 **u(ri)bagakari** sales clerk
8 受付係 **uketsukegakari** receptionist, usher
9 宣伝係 **sendengakari** public relations man
計時係 **keijigaka(ri)** timekeeper
計算係 **keisangaka(ri)** accountant
10 進行係 **shinkōgakari** person to expedite the proceedings, steering committee
校正係 **kōseigakari** proofreader
記録係 **kirokugakari** recording secretary
11 接客係 **sekkyakugakari** receptionist
12 無関係 **mukankei** unrelated, irrelevant
集札係 **shūsatsugakari** ticket collector
16 操車係 **sōshagakari** train dispatcher
衛生係 **eiseigakari** health officer
17 醜関係 **shūkankei** illicit liaison

—————— 4 ——————

3 三角関係 **sankaku kankei** love triangle
7 利害関係 **rigai kankei** interests

2a7.9

俔

KEN, tato(eru) compare
ukaga(u) spy on

2a7.10 / 1845

俊 **SHUN** excellence, genius

────────── 1 ──────────

3 俊才 **shunsai** genius, man of exceptional talent
7 俊抜 **shunbatsu** uncommon, above average
俊秀 **shunshū** genius, man of exceptional talent
8 俊英 **shun'ei** talent, genius, gifted person
10 俊逸 **shun'itsu** excellence, genius
俊敏 **shunbin** keen, quick-witted
俊馬 **shunme, shunba** fine horse
13 俊傑 **shunketsu** outstanding man, hero, genius
14 俊徳 **shuntoku** great virtue

────────── 2 ──────────

8 英俊 **eishun** genius, prodigy, gifted person

2a7.11 / 489

保 **HO, HŌ, tamo(tsu)** keep, preserve, maintain

────────── 1 ──────────

4 保元 **Hōgen** (era, 1156–1159)
5 保母 **hobo** kindergarten teacher
保存 **hozon** preservation
6 保全 **hozen** preservation
保安 **hoan** preservation of public peace, security **Hōan** (era, 1120–1124)
保安官 **hoankan** sheriff
保守 **hoshu** conservative
保守主義 **hoshu shugi** conservatism
保守的 **hoshuteki** conservative
保守党 **hoshutō** conservative party
保有 **hoyū** possess, hold, maintain
保有者 **hoyūsha** possessor, holder, owner
7 保身 **hoshin** self-protection
保身術 **hoshinjutsu** the art of self-protection
保延 **Hōen** (era, 1135–1141)
8 保育 **hoiku** nurture, childcare, rearing
保育所 **hoikujo** nursery school
保育園 **hoikuen** nursery school
9 保持 **hoji** maintain, preserve
保持者 **hojisha** holder (of a record)
10 保健 **hoken** health preservation, hygiene
保健医 **hoken'i** public-health physician
保健所 **hokenjo** health center
保健婦 **hokenfu** public-health nurse
保険 **hoken** insurance
保険会社 **hoken-gaisha** insurance company
保険金 **hokenkin** insurance money
保険料 **hokenryō** insurance premium

保留 **horyū** reserve, defer
11 保菌者 **hokinsha** carrier (of a disease)
保釈 **hoshaku** bail
保釈金 **hoshakukin** bail
12 保温 **hoon** keeping warm
保証 **hoshō** guarantee
保証人 **hoshōnin** guarantor
保証付 **hoshōtsu(ki)** guaranteed
保証金 **hoshōkin** security deposit, key money
13 保障 **hoshō** guarantee, security
14 保管 **hokan** custody, deposit, storage
保管料 **hokanryō** custody/storage fee
15 保養 **hoyō** preservation of health; recuperation; recreation
保養地 **hoyōchi** health resort
保養所 **hoyōsho/jo** sanitarium, rest home
20 保護 **hogo** protect, shelter, take care of
保護色 **hogoshoku** protective coloration
保護国 **hogokoku** protectorate
保護者 **hogosha** protector, guardian
保護委員 **hogoiin** rehabilitation worker
保護鳥 **hogochō** protected bird
保護貿易 **hogo bōeki** protectionistic trade
保護領 **hogoryō** protectorate

────────── 2 ──────────

4 天保 **Tenpō** (era, 1830–1844)
文保 **Bunpō** (era, 1317–1319)
5 生保 **seiho** life insurance (short for 生命保険)
付保 **fuho** cover (by insurance), carry (insurance)
正保 **Shōhō** (era, 1644–1648)
永保 **Eihō** (era, 1081–1084)
6 気保養 **kihoyō** recreation, diversion
再保険 **saihoken** reinsurance
安保 **anpo** (national) security (short for 安全保障)
安保条約 **anpo jōyaku** security treaty
7 承保 **Jōhō** (era, 1074–1077)
佐保姫 **saohime** goddess of spring
享保 **Kyōhō** (era, 1716–1736)
応保 **Ōhō** (era, 1161-1163)
8 長保 **Chōhō** (era, 999–1004)
建保 **Kenpō** (era, 1213–1219)
担保 **tanpo** a security, guarantee
10 健保 **kenpo** health insurance (short for 健康保険)
酒保 **shuho** canteen, military base exchange
被保険物 **hihokenbutsu** insured property
被保護国 **hihogokoku** protectorate, dependency
被保護者 **hihogosha** ward
留保 **ryūho** reserve, withhold
11 康保 **Kōhō** (era, 964–968)
13 損保 **sonpo** casualty/nonlife insurance (short for 損害保険)

寛保 **Kanpō** (era, 1741–1743)
14 嘉保 **Kahō** (era, 1094–1096)
15 隣保 **rinpo** neighborhood
隣保事業 **rinpo jigyō** welfare work, social services
隣保館 **rinpokan** settlement house
確保 **kakuho** secure, ensure

——————— 3 ———————

2 人身保護 **jinshin hogo** habeas corpus
4 火災保険 **kasai hoken** fire insurance
5 生命保険 **seimei hoken** life insurance
6 安全保障 **anzen hoshō** (national) security
7 身元保証 **mimoto hoshō** personal references
佐世保 **Sasebo** (city, Nagasaki-ken)
労災保険 **rōsai hoken** workman's accident compensation insurance
災害保険 **saigai hoken** accident insurance
10 健康保険 **kenkō hoken** health insurance
12 無担保 **mutanpo** unsecured, without collateral
13 損害保険 **songai hoken** casualty/nonlife insurance
17 優生保護法 **Yūsei Hogo Hō** Eugenic Protection Law
18 簡易保険 **kan'i hoken** post-office life insurance

2a7.12

俣 **mata** crotch, thigh, groin

2a7.13

侶 **RYO, RO, tomo** companion, follower

——————— 2 ———————

7 伴侶 **hanryo** companion
13 僧侶 **sōryo** (Buddhist) priest, monk, bonze

2a7.14

俏 **SHŌ, yatsu(su)** disguise oneself as; dress up; pine away

2a7.15 / 1077

侵 **SHIN, oka(su)** invade, raid; violate, infringe

——————— 1 ———————

2 侵入 **shinnyū** invade, raid, break into
侵入者 **shinnyūsha** invader, intruder
5 侵犯 **shinpan** invasion, violation

7 侵攻 **shinkō** invasion
9 侵食 **shinshoku** encroachment; erosion; pitting corrosion
10 侵害 **shingai** infringement, violation
11 侵掠 **shinryaku** aggression, invasion
侵略 **shinryaku** aggression, invasion
侵略的 **shinryakuteki** aggressive
侵略者 **shinryakusha** aggressor, invader
14 侵奪 **shindatsu** disseizin, usurpation
15 侵撃 **shingeki** invade and attack
侵蝕 **shinshoku** encroachment; erosion; pitting corrosion

——————— 2 ———————

4 不侵略 **fushinryaku** nonagression

——————— 3 ———————

4 不可侵 **fukashin** nonaggression; inviolable
10 家宅侵入 **kataku shinnyū** trespassing

2a7.16

俛 **FU** hang one's head, look down
BEN diligent

2a7.17 / 1126

俗 **ZOKU** customs, manners; worldliness; laymen; vulgarity **zoku(ppoi)** lowbrow, common, vulgar

——————— 1 ———————

2 俗人 **zokujin** layman; worldly-minded person
3 俗才 **zokusai** worldly wisdom
4 俗化 **zokka** vulgarization, popularization
俗文 **zokubun** colloquial style
俗文学 **zokubungaku** popular literature
5 俗世 **zokuse, zokusei** this world, earthly existence
俗世界 **zokusekai** the everyday world
俗世間 **zokuseken** this world, secular society
俗用 **zokuyō** worldly matters
俗字 **zokuji** popular form of a kanji
6 俗気 **zokke, zokuke, zokki** vulgarity, worldly ambition
俗吏 **zokuri** petty official
俗曲 **zokkyoku** folk song
俗向 **zokumu(ki)** popular (literature)
俗名 **zokumei** common name; secular name
zokumyō secular name
俗耳 **zokuji** vulgar ears, attention of the masses
7 俗学 **zokugaku** shallow learning
俗見 **zokken** layman's opinion, popular view
俗言 **zokugen** colloquial language
8 俗事 **zokuji** worldly affairs; workaday routine
俗念 **zokunen** worldliness, earthly desires
俗受 **zokuu(ke)** popular appeal

2

イ 7 ←
冫
子
阝
卩
刂
力
又
宀
亠
卜
ケ
丷
厂
辶
冂
八
匸

俗姓 **zokusei** (priest's) secular surname
俗物 **zokubutsu** worldly-minded person, person of vulgar tastes
9 俗臭 **zokushū** vulgarity, worldly-mindedness
俗界 **zokkai** the workaday/secular world
10 俗流 **zokuryū** the common throng, the vulgar masses
俗骨 **zokkotsu** vulgar temperament; lowly person
俗書 **zokusho** cheap fiction; unrefined handwriting
俗称 **zokushō** popular/vernacular name
11 俗習 **zokushū** (popular) custom
俗務 **zokumu** worldly concerns, daily routine
俗悪 **zokuaku** vulgar, coarse
俗情 **zokujō** mundane affairs; worldly-mindedness
俗眼 **zokugan** layman's eye, popular opinion
12 俗衆 **zokushū** the mass public, the common herd
俗筆 **zokuhitsu** crude handwriting
俗間 **zokkan** the world/public
13 俗僧 **zokusō** worldly priest
俗楽 **zokugaku** popular/vulgar music
俗解 **zokkai** popular interpretation
俗話 **zokuwa** gossip, town talk
14 俗境 **zokkyō** the lay world
俗塵 **zokujin** the world, earthly affairs
俗歌 **zokka** popular/folk song, ditty
俗語 **zokugo** colloquial language, slang
俗説 **zokusetsu** common saying; folklore
15 俗縁 **zokuen** worldly ties
俗談 **zokudan** chit-chat, gossip
俗論 **zokuron** popular opinion, conventional wisdom
俗調 **zokuchō** popular melody, vulgar music
俗輩 **zokuhai** the vulgar throng, the crowd
16 俗謡 **zokuyō** popular/folk song
20 俗議 **zokugi** popular opinion

──── 2 ────

3 凡俗 **bonzoku** mediocre, common, vulgar
土俗 **dozoku** local customs
土俗学 **dozokugaku** folklore, ethnography
5 民俗 **minzoku** ethnic/folk customs
民俗学 **minzokugaku** folklore
世俗 **sezoku** common customs; the world; common, mundane, vulgar
世俗化 **sezokuka** secularization
世俗的 **sezokuteki** worldly
7 良俗 **ryōzoku** good custom
低俗 **teizoku** vulgar
9 俚俗 **rizoku** vulgarity, base manners
美俗 **bizoku** beautiful/admirable custom
通俗 **tsūzoku** popular, conventional
通俗化 **tsūzokuka** popularization

通俗的 **tsūzokuteki** popular
風俗 **fūzoku** manners, customs, morals
風俗画 **fūzokuga** painting depicting customs
卑俗 **hizoku** vulgar, coarse
10 時俗 **jizoku** customs/ways of the times
11 道俗 **dōzoku** priests and laity
脱俗 **datsuzoku** withdraw from the world, become a hermit
脱俗的 **datsuzokuteki** unworldly, saintly
習俗 **shūzoku** manners and customs, usages
異俗 **izoku** strange custom
12 超俗 **chōzoku** unworldly, aloof from the world
13 僧俗 **sōzoku** clergy and laity
雅俗 **gazoku** the refined and the vulgar
15 還俗 **genzoku** return to secular life, quit the priesthood

──── 4 ────

7 良風美俗 **ryōfū-bizoku** good customs
14 醇風美俗 **junpū bizoku** good morals and manners

2a7.18

俤 **omokage** face; traces, vestiges

2a7.19

俟 竢 **SHI, ma(tsu)** wait for

──── 2 ────

9 相俟 **aima(tte)** coupled with, in cooperation with

2a7.20

俑 **YŌ** effigy

──── 1 ────

2 俑人 **yōjin** doll, effigy

2a7.21 / 1924

侯 **KŌ** marquis; lord, daimyo

──── 1 ────

17 侯爵 **kōshaku** marquis, marquess
侯爵夫人 **kōshaku fujin** marchioness

──── 2 ────

4 王侯 **ōkō** princes, royalty
6 列侯 **rekkō** many feudal lords
15 諸侯 **shokō** lords, daimyos

18 藩侯 **hankō** feudal lord, daimyo

2a7.22

臥 臥 **GA, fu(su), fu(seru)** lie down, go to bed

—————— 1 ——————
7 臥床 **gashō** be confined to bed
8 臥所 **fushido** place to sleep, bed
10 臥竜 **garyō** reclining dragon; great man in obscurity
16 臥薪嘗胆 **gashin-shōtan** perseverance and determination

—————— 2 ——————
5 平臥 **heiga** lie down; be laid up (ill)
6 仰臥 **gyōga** lie face up
安臥 **anga** lie quiet in bed
9 草臥 **kutabi(reru)** be tired/exhausted
10 起臥 **kiga** daily life
座臥 **zaga** sitting and lying down
病臥 **byōga** be sick in bed, be bedridden
11 添臥 **so(i)bushi** sleeping together
15 横臥 **ōga** lie on one's side

—————— 3 ——————
12 着草臥 **kikutabi(re)** worn out

—————— 4 ——————
6 行住坐臥 **gyōjū-zaga** walking, stopping, sitting, and lying down; daily life

俞 → 4b5.11

赴 → 3b6.14

起 → 3b7.11

2a7.23

臾 臾 **YU, YO, YŌ** a little while

—————— 2 ——————
12 須臾 **shuyu** instant, moment

2a7.24

俎 俎 **SO** sacrificial altar **manaita** cutting board, chopping block

—————— 1 ——————
3 俎上 **sojō** on the chopping block

7 俎豆 **sotō** altar (for offerings)

2a7.25

矜 **KYŌ, KIN** pride; pity; respect

—————— 1 ——————
9 矜持 **kyōji, kinji** dignity, pride
矜恃 **kyōji, kinji** dignity, pride

乗 → 0a9.19

—————— 8 ——————

2a8.1

們 **MON** (plural suffix)

2a8.2

健 **SHŌ** speedy; healthy

2a8.3

倆 **RYŌ** skill

—————— 2 ——————
7 技倆 **giryō** skill, ability

2a8.4

俾 **HI** do, make

2a8.5 / 905

倒 **TŌ, tao(reru), ko(keru)** fall, collapse, break down **tao(su)** bring down, topple

—————— 1 ——————
5 倒句 **tōku** inversion (of normal word order)
6 倒死 **tōshi** collapse and die
11 倒産 **tōsan** bankruptcy
13 倒幕 **tōbaku** overthrowing the shogunate
倒置 **tōchi** turning upside down; inversion (of normal word order)
倒置法 **tōchihō** inversion (of normal word order)
14 倒閣 **tōkaku** overthrowing the cabinet
15 倒影 **tōei** reflection

16 倒壊 **tōkai** collapse, be destroyed
倒錯 **tōsaku** perversion

――――― 2 ―――――

4 切倒 **ki(ri)tao(su)** cut/chop down, fell
引倒 **hi(ki)tao(su)** pull/drag down
5 圧倒 **attō** overwhelm
圧倒的 **attōteki** overwhelming
打倒 **datō** overthrow **u(chi)tao(su)** knock down; overthrow
6 行倒 **i(ki)dao(re), yu(ki)dao(re)** lying dead on the road
共倒 **tomodao(re)** mutual ruin
7 技倒 **gitō** technical knockout, TKO
投倒 **na(ge)tao(su)** throw (someone) down
吹倒 **fu(ki)tao(su)** blow down
8 送倒 **oku(ri)tao(su)** push down from behind (in sumo)
拝倒 **oga(mi)tao(su)** entreat into consenting
押倒 **o(shi)tao(su)** push down
突倒 **tsu(ki)tao(su)** knock down
昏倒 **kontō** faint, swoon
9 前倒 **maetao(shi), maedao(shi)** spending (part of next year's budget) ahead of time
面倒 **mendō** trouble, difficulty; taking care of, tending to
面倒臭 **mendōkusa(i)** troublesome, a big bother
食倒 **ku(i)tao(su)** sponge off (someone), eat out of house and home
ku(i)dao(re) wasting one's money on fine foods
10 射倒 **itao(su)** shoot down/dead
借倒 **ka(ri)tao(su)** fail to repay
11 率倒 **sottō** faint, swoon
掛倒 **ka(ke)dao(re)** bad debt; earnings not covering expenses
張倒 **ha(ri)tao(su)** knock down
転倒 **tentō** fall down violently, turn upside down, reverse
12 着倒 **kidao(re)** extravagance in dress
棒倒 **bōtao(shi)** topple-the-other-team's-pole game
絶倒 **zettō** convulsed with laughter
貸倒 **ka(shi)dao(re)** bad debts
飲倒 **no(mi)tao(su)** not pay one's bar bill
13 傾倒 **keitō** devote oneself to; admire, idolize
睨倒 **nira(mi)tao(su)** stare (someone) down, outstare
15 横倒 **yokodao(shi)** topple sideways
罵倒 **batō** denunciation, condemnation
踏倒 **fu(mi)tao(su)** kick over; evade payment
19 蹴倒 **ketao(su)** kick down/over
顚倒 **tentō** fall down; turn upside down
22 轢倒 **hi(ki)tao(su)** knock down (someone with a car)

驚倒 **kyōtō** be astounded/amazed

――――― 3 ―――――

1 一辺倒 **ippentō** complete partiality to one side
2 七面倒 **shichimendō** great trouble, difficulty
7 見掛倒 **mika(ke)dao(shi)** mere show
10 将棋倒 **shōgidao(shi)** falling like a row of dominoes

――――― 4 ―――――

2 七転八倒 **shichiten-battō, shitten-battō** writhing in agony
5 主客顚倒 **shukaku-tentō** reverse order, putting the cart before the horse
8 抱腹絶倒 **hōfuku-zettō** convulsed with laughter
11 捧腹絶倒 **hōfuku-zettō** convulsed with laughter

2a8.6

俶

SHUKU beginning; good
TEKI excel

――――― 1 ―――――

22 俶儻 **tekitō** remarkable talent, genius; free and independent

2a8.7 / 1776

倣

HŌ, nara(u) imitate, follow, emulate

――――― 2 ―――――

14 模倣 **mohō** copy, imitation
24 鑾倣 **hiso(mi ni) nara(u)** slavishly imitate

2a8.8 / 1035

俳

HAI actor

――――― 1 ―――――

2 俳人 **haijin** haiku poet
4 俳文 **haibun** haiku-style prose
5 俳号 **haigō** haiku poet's pen name
俳句 **haiku** haiku
6 俳名 **haimei** haiku poet's pen name
8 俳画 **haiga** haiku-like picture, sketch
俳味 **haimi** subdued haiku-like taste
俳徊 **haikai** loiter, saunter, wander about
16 俳壇 **haidan** the haiku world
俳諧 **haikai** joke; *haikai*, haiku
俳諧師 **haikaishi** *haikai* poet
俳謔 **haigyaku** joke, funny story
17 俳優 **haiyū** actor, actress

――――― 2 ―――――

14 雑俳 **zappai** playful literature originating from haiku

併→併 **2a6.17**

2a8.9

候 SHUKU quick, prompt

2a8.10 / 944

候 KŌ season, weather; wait for
-sōrō (classical verb ending equivalent to -*masu*)

——————— 1 ———————

4 候文 **sōrōbun** epistolary style
11 候鳥 **kōchō** bird of passage, migratory bird
12 候補 **kōho** candidacy
候補生 **kōhosei** cadet
候補地 **kōhochi** proposed site
候補者 **kōhosha** candidate

——————— 2 ———————

4 天候 **tenkō** the weather
5 斥候 **sekkō** scout, patrol, spy
立候補 **rikkōho** stand/run for office, announce one's candidacy
6 気候 **kikō** climate
気候学 **kikōgaku** climatology
兆候 **chōkō** sign, indication
7 伺候 **shikō** wait upon; pay a courtesy call
季候 **kikō** climate
季候帯 **kikōtai** climatic zone
8 居候 **isōrō** hanger-on, dependent, sponger
10 時候 **jikō** season, time of year; weather
時候外 **jikōhazu(re)** unseasonable
症候 **shōkō** symptom
12 測候 **sokkō** meteorological observation
測候所 **sokkōjo** weather station
14 徴候 **chōkō** sign, indication, symptom
15 潮候 **chōkō** tide period, time of the tide

——————— 3 ———————

11 悪天候 **akutenkō** bad weather

2a8.11 / 945

修 SHŪ, SHU, **osa(maru)** govern oneself, conduct oneself well   **osa(meru)** order (one's life); study, cultivate, master

——————— 1 ———————

1 修了 **shūryō** completion (of a course)
3 修士 **shūshi** master's degree, M.A., M.S.
5 修史 **shūshi** compilation of a history
修正 **shūsei** amendment, revision, alteration, correction
修正案 **shūseian** proposed amendment

修好 **shūkō** amity, friendship
6 修交 **shūkō** amity, friendship
修行 **shūgyō, shugyō, shūkō** training, study, ascetic practices
修行者 **shugyōsha** practitioner of (Buddhist) austerities
7 修身 **shūshin** morals, ethics; moral training
修学 **shūgaku** learning
修学旅行 **shūgaku ryokō** school excursion, field trip
11 修道 **shūdō** living a religious life
修道女 **shūdōjo** (Catholic) nun
修道士 **shūdōshi** monk, friar
修道院 **shūdōin** monastery, convent, cloister
修得 **shūtoku** learning, acquirement
修理 **shūri** repair
修理工 **shūrikō** repairman
修理中 **shūrichū** under repair
12 修復 **shūfuku** repair
修補 **shūho** repair
13 修業 **shūgyō** pursuit of knowledge
修辞 **shūji** figure of speech, rhetoric
修辞学 **shūjigaku** rhetoric
修辞法 **shūjihō** rhetoric
修飾 **shūshoku** decorate, adorn; modify (in grammar)
修飾語 **shūshokugo** modifier
14 修熟 **shūjuku** developing skill
修練 **shūren** training, discipline, drill
15 修養 **shūyō** cultivation of the mind, character-building
16 修整 **shūsei** retouching (in photography)
修築 **shūchiku** repair (a house)
18 修繕 **shūzen** repair
修験者 **shugenja** ascetic mountain-dwelling monk
19 修羅 **shura** Asura (battle-loving Buddhist demon); fighting
修羅場 **shurajō, shuraba** scene of carnage

——————— 2 ———————

5 必修 **hisshū** required (subject)
必修科目 **hisshū kamoku** required subject
6 自修 **jishū** teaching oneself, self-study
7 学修 **gakushū** learning, study
改修 **kaishū** repair, improvement
8 逆修 **gyakushu** hold memorial services for oneself before one's death; hold memorial services for a younger predeceased person
官修 **kanshū** government editing
9 専修 **senshū** specialize in
独修 **dokushū** self-study
研修 **kenshū** study and training
研修所 **kenshūjo** training institute/center
10 兼修 **kenshū** study an additional subject

2

亻 8←
冫
孑
阝
卩
刂
力
又
一
十
卜
ク
丷
厂
辶
冂
八
匚

12 補修 **hoshū** repair
13 新修 **shinshū** new compilation
15 撰修 **senshū** writing, editing
履修 **rishū** study, complete (a course)
監修 **kanshū** (editorial) supervision
編修 **henshū** editing, compilation

─────── 3 ───────
8 武者修業 **musha shugyō** knight-errantry

2a8.12

倪

GEI young child; limit

2a8.13

倦 倦

KEN, a(kiru), agu(mu), u(mu) get tired of

─────── 1 ───────
9 倦怠 **kentai** fatigue, weariness
倦怠期 **kentaiki** period of weariness
倦怠感 **kentaikan** fatigue
10 倦疲 **u(mi)tsuka(reru)** get tired of, get fed up

─────── 2 ───────
7 攻倦 **se(me)agu(mu)** become disheartened in conducting a siege
9 待倦 **ma(chi)agu(mu)** be tired of waiting

2a8.14 / 87

倍

BAI double, twice; times, -fold

─────── 1 ───────
0 倍する **bai(suru)** double, be doubled; increased
3 倍大 **baidai** double size, twice as large
5 倍加 **baika** to double
倍旧 **baikyū** redoubled, increased
11 倍率 **bairitsu** magnifying power, magnification
13 倍数 **baisū** a multiple
14 倍増 **baizō, baima(shi)** to double
18 倍額 **baigaku** double the amount

─────── 2 ───────
1 一倍 **ichibai** the same number/amount; double
2 二倍 **nibai** double, twice, twofold
十倍 **jūbai** tenfold, ten times
3 三倍 **sanbai** threefold, three times
4 公倍数 **kōbaisū** common multiple
6 百倍 **hyakubai** a hundredfold
7 阿倍 **Abe** (surname)
13 数倍 **sūbai** several times as (large), several-fold

─────── 3 ───────
2 人一倍 **hito-ichibai** uncommon, more than others

─────── 4 ───────
16 薬九層倍 **kusuri-kusōbai** the high markup on drug prices

2a8.15

俱

KU, GU, tomo together

─────── 1 ───────
8 俱舎 **Kusha** (a Buddhist sect)
9 俱発 **guhatsu** concurrence
13 俱楽部 **kurabu** club

─────── 2 ───────
4 不俱戴天 **fugutaiten** irreconcilable (enemies)

2a8.16

倭

WA, Yamato ancient Japan

─────── 1 ───────
11 倭寇 **wakō** Japanese pirates

2a8.17

倥

KŌ foolish; busy; distressed; blunder, slip

─────── 1 ───────
11 倥偬 **kōsō** busy; grieve, suffer

2a8.18 / 1542

俸

HŌ salary

─────── 1 ───────
6 俸米 **hōmai** rice given in payment for services
12 俸禄 **hōroku** stipend, pay, salary
俸禄米 **hōrokumai** rice given in payment for services
俸給 **hōkyū** salary
俸給日 **hōkyūbi** payday

─────── 2 ───────
4 月俸 **geppō** monthly salary
5 本俸 **honpō** basic/regular salary
加俸 **kahō** additional allowance, extra pay
6 年俸 **nenpō** annual salary
11 現俸 **genpō** present salary
12 減俸 **genpō** salary reduction
14 増俸 **zōhō** salary increase
罰俸 **bappō** docking of salary

2a8.19

倡

SHŌ singer, entertainer; advocate

———————— 1 ————————

8 倡和 **shōwa** singing in harmony
11 倡道 **shōdō** herald, lead

2a8.20

倩

SEN beautiful
SEI son-in-law; hire
tsuratsura profoundly

2a8.21 / 1890

俵

HYŌ bag, bale, sack; (counter for bags)
tawara straw bag

———————— 1 ————————

8 俵物 **tawaramono, hyōmotsu** (marine) products in straw bags
13 俵数 **hyōsū** number of straw bags

———————— 2 ————————

1 一俵 **ippyō** a straw-bagful
3 土俵 **dohyō** the sumo ring; sandbag
   土俵入 **dohyōi(ri)** display of sumo wrestlers in the ring
   土俵際 **dohyōgiwa** at the brink, critical moment
6 米俵 **komedawara** straw rice bag
9 炭俵 **sumidawara** charcoal sack
10 桟俵 **sandawara** round straw lid (on the ends of a rice bag)

2a8.22 / 766

借

SHAKU, SHA, ka(riru), ka(ru)
borrow, rent **ka(ri)** borrowing, debt, loan

———————— 1 ————————

4 借手 **ka(ri)te** borrower, lessee, tenant
   借方 **ka(ri)kata** debit, debtor side; way of borrowing
5 借用 **shakuyō** borrowing, loan
   借用者 **shakuyōsha** borrower
   借用証書 **shakuyō shōsho** bond of debt
   借主 **ka(ri)nushi** borrower, renter
6 借地 **shakuchi, ka(ri)chi** leased land
8 借受 **ka(ri)u(keru)** borrow
   借逃 **ka(ri)ni(ge)** run away leaving unpaid debts
   借店 **ka(ri)dana** rented shop
   借物 **ka(ri)mono** something borrowed
   借放 **ka(rip)pana(shi)** borrowing without returning

借金 **shakkin** debt
借金取 **shakkinto(ri)** bill collection/collector
10 借倒 **ka(ri)tao(su)** fail to repay
   借家 **shakuya, shakka, ka(ri)ie, ka(ri)ya** rented house, house for rent
   借料 **shakuryō** rental fee
   借財 **shakuzai** debt
11 借問 **shamon, shakumon** inquire
12 借着 **ka(ri)gi** borrowed/rented clothes
   借換 **ka(ri)ka(e)** conversion, refunding, renewal
   借款 **shakkan** loan
   借越 **ka(ri)ko(su)** overdraw
   借越金 **ka(ri)ko(shi)kin** overdraft, debt balance
   借貸 **ka(ri)ka(shi)** borrowing and lending, loan
   借間 **ka(ri)ma** rented room
13 借賃 **ka(ri)chin** the rent
17 借覧 **shakuran** borrow and read

———————— 2 ————————

2 又借 **mataga(ri)** borrow secondhand, sublease
4 内借 **uchiga(ri)** drawing an advance on one's salary
6 仮借 **kashaku, kasha** pardon, be lenient; using a kanji for another having the same reading
8 拝借 **haishaku** borrow
   押借 **o(shi)ga(ri)** having to borrow
   店借 **tanaga(ri)** renting a house, tenancy
9 前借 **maega(ri), zenshaku** getting an advance, a loan
   連借 **renshaku** joint debt
10 家借 **kashaku** renting a house
   租借 **soshaku** lease (land)
   租借地 **soshakuchi** leased territory
   租借権 **soshakuken** lease, leasehold
11 宿借 **yadoka(ri)** hermit crab
   転借 **tenshaku** sublease
12 貸借 **taishaku, ka(shi)ka(ri)** lending and borrowing, debit and credit, loan
   貸借対照表 **taishakutaishōhyō** balance sheet
   間借 **maga(ri)** renting a room
   間借人 **maga(ri)nin** lodger, roomer
13 賃借 **chinshaku, chinga(ri)** lease, rent, hire
   賃借人 **chinshakunin** lessee
   賃借料 **chinshakuryō** rent

———————— 3 ————————

13 賃貸借 **chintaishaku** leasing, renting

2a8.23

倖

KŌ, shiawa(se) happiness, good fortune

———————— 2 ————————

10 射倖心 **shakōshin** mercenary spirit

14 僥倖 **gyōkō** good fortune, stroke of luck
16 薄倖 **hakkō** misfortune, bad luck

2a8.24

倘

SHŌ wander

→8

───── 1 ─────

8 倘佯 **shōyō** wandering about

2a8.25

俺

EN, ore I, me

2a8.26

倚

I, yo(ru) depend/lean on
KI strange; deformed, crippled

───── 1 ─────

2 倚人 **kijin** deformed/maimed person, cripple
8 倚門望 **imon (no) bō** a mother's love (leaning on the gate longing for her child's return home)
10 倚託 **itaku** entrust to

2a8.27 / 878

倹 儉

KEN thrift **tsuma(shii)** thrifty, frugal **tsuzuma(yaka)** neat and small; frugal; unpretentious; concise

───── 1 ─────

7 倹客 **kenrin** miserliness, stinginess
9 倹約 **ken'yaku** thrift, frugality
倹約家 **ken'yakuka** thrifty person, economizer
10 倹素 **kenso** frugal and simple

───── 2 ─────

10 恭倹 **kyōken** deference, respectfulness
12 勤倹 **kinken** industriousness and thrift
13 節倹 **sekken** economizing, thrift

2a8.28 / 1163

倫

RIN road to take; sequence **tagui** kind, sort; an equal

───── 1 ─────

11 倫理 **rinri** ethics, morals
倫理学 **rinrigaku** ethics, moral philosophy
倫理的 **rinriteki** ethical
倫敦 **Rondon** London

───── 2 ─────

2 人倫 **jinrin** human relations, morality

4 不倫 **furin** immoral, illicit
五倫 **gorin** the five human relationships of Confucianism (lord-vassal, father-son, husband-wife, old-young, friend-friend)
5 比倫 **hirin** peer, match, equal, rival
7 乱倫 **ranrin** immorality
10 破倫 **harin** immorality
12 絶倫 **zetsurin** excellence, superiority

2a8.29

倅 伜

SAI, segare my son

2a8.30 / 425

値

CHI, ne, atai price, cost, value

───── 1 ─────

0 値する **atai (suru)** be worthy of
3 値上 **nea(ge)** price hike **nea(gari)** higher price
値下 **nesa(ge)** price reduction **nesa(gari)** price decline, lower prices
値巾 **nehaba** price range/fluctuations
4 値切 **negi(ru)** haggle, bargain
値引 **nebi(ki)** discount
値打 **neu(chi)** value, worth; dignity
6 値安 **neyasu** low-priced
9 値段 **nedan** price
11 値頃 **negoro** reasonable price
12 値幅 **nehaba** price range, change in price
15 値踏 **nebu(mi)** appraisal, valuation
16 値鞘 **nezaya** margin, spread (in prices)

───── 2 ─────

3 上値 **uwane** higher price
下値 **shitane** lower price
4 元値 **motone** cost
中値 **nakane** medium price, bid-and-asked price
5 半値 **hanne** half price
付値 **tsu(ke)ne** the price offered, bid
6 安値 **yasune** low price
7 沖値 **okine** free-overside price
売値 **u(ri)ne** selling price
初値 **hatsune** first price (of a stock in the new year)
言値 **i(i)ne** seller's price
8 価値 **kachi** value, merit
建値 **tatene** officially quoted price
呼値 **yo(bi)ne** nominal price, price asked
底値 **sokone** rock-bottom price
9 卸値 **oroshine** wholesale price
指値 **sa(shi)ne** (buying/selling-)price limits

10 高値 **takane** high price
11 掛値 **ka(ke)ne** overcharge
捨値 **su(te)ne** giveaway price
唱値 **tona(e)ne** asking price
寄値 **yo(ri)ne** opening price
12 買値 **ka(i)ne** purchase/bid price
等値 **tōchi** equal value
13 数値 **sūchi** numerical value
新値 **shinne** new price
裸値 **hadakane** net price
15 潰値 **tsubu(shi)ne** scrap value
16 閾値 **ikichi** threshold (value)
17 闇値 **yamine** black-market price

───────── 3 ─────────

5 出来値 **dekine** selling price
6 近似値 **kinjichi** an approximation
血糖値 **kettōchi** blood-sugar level
8 固有値 **koyūchi** eigenvalue
12 落札値 **rakusatsune** contract/highest-bid price
無価値 **mukachi** worthless
絶対値 **zettaichi** absolute value (in math)

───────── 4 ─────────

5 付加価値税 **fuka-kachi zei** value-added tax

2a8.31

侮

KYO proud; sitting with legs outstretched

───────── 1 ─────────

13 倨傲 **kyogō** proud, arrogant

2a8.32

倬

TAKU large; clear; remarkable

2a8.33

倔

KUTSU stubborn

───────── 1 ─────────

11 倔強 **kukkyō** stubborn

2a8.34 / 893

健

KEN health, strength
suko(yaka) healthy

───────── 1 ─────────

6 健気 **kenage** manly, heroic; admirable
健全 **kenzen** healthy, sound
健在 **kenzai** in good health
7 健忘 **kenbō** forgetfulness

健忘症 **kenbōshō** forgetfulness, amnesia
健児 **kenji** vigorous boy
9 健保 **kenpo** health insurance (short for 健康保険)
健胃剤 **ken'izai** stomach medicine
11 健啖 **kentan** hearty appetite, voracity, gluttony
健啖家 **kentanka** hearty eater, trencherman, glutton
健康 **kenkō** health; healthy, sound
健康体 **kenkōtai** healthy body
健康児 **kenkōji** healthy child
健康法 **kenkōhō** how to keep fit, hygiene
健康的 **kenkōteki** healthful
健康保険 **kenkō hoken** health insurance
健康美 **kenkōbi** healthy beauty
健康診断 **kenkō shindan** medical examination, physical checkup
健脚 **kenkyaku** strong legs
健脚家 **kenkyakuka** good walker
12 健勝 **kenshō** healthy, robust, hale and hearty
健筆 **kenpitsu** powerful pen
18 健闘 **kentō** put up a good fight, make strenuous efforts

───────── 2 ─────────

4 不健全 **fukenzen** unhealthy, unsound
不健康 **fukenkō** unhealthy, unhealthful
6 壮健 **sōken** healthy, hale and hearty
9 保健 **hoken** health preservation, hygiene
保健医 **hoken'i** public-health physician
保健所 **hokenjo** health center
保健婦 **hokenfu** public-health nurse
勇健 **yūken** sound health
10 剛健 **gōken** strong and sturdy, virile
11 強健 **kyōken** robust health
12 雄健 **yūken** virile, vigorous
13 頑健 **ganken** strong and robust, in excellent health
16 穏健 **onken** moderate
穏健派 **onkenha** the moderates

───────── 4 ─────────

15 質実剛健 **shitsujitsu-gōken** rough-hewn and robust

2a8.35

俯

FU, fu(seru) lay face down
fu(su) prostrate oneself
utsumu(ku/keru) look/turn downward

───────── 1 ─────────

6 俯伏 **utsubu(su)** lie face down **fufuku** lie prostrate
俯仰 **fugyō** looking up and down; one's actions
俯仰天地 **fugyōtenchi** (nothing to be ashamed of) before God or man

2

亻 8 ←
冫
孑
阝
卩
刂
力
又
宀
亠
十
ト
ク
丷
厂
辶
門
八
匚

俯向 **utsumu(keru)** turn upside down, turn downward **utsumu(ku)** look downward

7 俯角 **fukaku** angle of depression

17 俯瞰 **fukan** overlook, have a bird's-eye view

俯瞰図 **fukanzu** bird's-eye/overhead view

2a8.36 / 973

個 个

KO individual; (counter for objects) **KA** (counter)

─────── 1 ───────

2 個人 **kojin** private person, individual

個人主義 **kojin shugi** individualism

個人的 **kojinteki** individual, personal, self-centered

個人差 **kojinsa** differences between individuals

個人教授 **kojin kyōju** private lessons

3 個々 **koko** individual, separate, one by one

7 個体 **kotai** an individual

個別 **kobetsu** indivudual by individual

8 個性 **kosei** individuality, idiosyncrasy

個性的 **koseiteki** personal, individual

10 個展 **koten** one-man exhibition

13 個数 **kosū** number of objects/articles

─────── 2 ───────

1 一個人 **ichikojin, ikkojin** a private individual

5 好個 **kōko** fine, good, ideal

6 各個 **kakko** each, individual, one by one

7 何個 **nanko** how many (pieces)

別個 **bekko** separate, different

10 個個 **koko** individual, separate, one by one

13 数個 **sūko** several (objects)

2a8.37 / 1307

倉

SŌ, kura warehouse, storehouse

─────── 1 ───────

5 倉主 **kuranushi** warehouse owner

8 倉卒 **sōsotsu** sudden; hurried, busy

10 倉荷 **kurani** warehouse goods

倉庫 **sōko** warehouse

15 倉敷 **kurashiki** storage place; storage charges **Kurashiki** (city, Okayama-ken)

倉敷料 **kurashikiryō** storage charges

─────── 2 ───────

3 土倉 **tsuchigura** underground storehouse

小倉 **kokura** duck cloth **Kokura** (city, Fukuoka-ken)

6 米倉 **komegura** rice granary

10 校倉 **azekura** ancient log storehouse

校倉造 **azekura-zuku(ri)** (ancient architectural style using triangular logs which interlace and protrude at the building's corners)

胸倉 **munagura** the lapels

11 船倉 **sensō** (ship's) hold, hatch

12 営倉 **eisō** guardhouse, brig

14 穀倉 **kokusō, kokugura** granary, grain elevator

18 鎌倉 **Kamakura** (city, Kanagawa-ken); (era, 1185–1333)

─────── 3 ───────

8 武器倉 **bukigura** armory

11 常平倉 **jōheisō** granary

拿 → 挐 3c5.30

2a8.38

衾

KIN, fusuma quilt, bedding

─────── 2 ───────

6 同衾 **dōkin** sleep together

14 槍衾 **yaribusuma** line of spears held ready to attack

─────── 9 ───────

2a9.1 / 1639

偶

GŪ even number; couple, man and wife; same kind; doll **tama (ni)** occasionally, rarely **tamatama** by chance, unexpectedly

─────── 1 ───────

2 偶人 **gūjin** puppet, doll

3 偶々 **tamatama** by chance, unexpectedly

4 偶日 **gūjitsu** even-numbered day of the month

5 偶処 **gūsho** be/live together

6 偶因 **gūin** contingent cause

偶成 **gūsei** contingent, fortuitous

7 偶作 **gūsaku** something accidentally accomplished

9 偶発 **gūhatsu** happen unforeseen, come about by chance

偶発的 **gūhatsuteki** accidental, incidental, occasional

12 偶然 **gūzen** by chance, happen to ...

13 偶数 **gūsū** even number

偶感 **gūkan** random thoughts

14 偶像 **gūzō** image, idol

偶像化 **gūzōka** idolize

偶像崇拝 **gūzō sūhai** idol worship, idolatry

偶像視 **gūzōshi** idolize

─────────── 2 ───────────

3 土偶 **dogū** clay figure
4 木偶坊 **deku(no)bō** wooden doll, dummy
7 対偶 **taigū** contrapositive; pair
8 奇偶 **kigū** odd or even
10 時偶 **tokitama** once in a while, on rare occasions
11 偶偶 **tamatama** by chance, unexpectedly

2a9.2 / 1485

偽 僞

GI, itsuwa(ru) lie, misrepresent; feign; deceive
nise fakc, counterfeit

─────────── 1 ───────────

5 偽史 **gishi** falsified history
偽札 **nisesatsu** counterfeit paper money
6 偽名 **gimei** assumed name, alias
7 偽作 **gisaku** a spurious work, a forgery
偽君子 **gikunshi, nisekunshi** hypocrite, snob
8 偽版 **gihan** pirated edition
偽者 **itsuwa(ri)mono** imposter, liar
偽物 **gibutsu, nisemono** a counterfeit/fake
9 偽造 **gizō** forgery
10 偽称 **gishō** misrepresentation
11 偽悪 **giaku** pretending to be evil
12 偽善 **gizen** hypocrisy
偽善者 **gizensha** hypocrite
偽報 **gihō** false report, canard
偽装 **gisō** camouflage
偽筆 **gihitsu** forged handwriting/picture
偽証 **gishō** false testimony, perjury
偽証罪 **gishōzai** perjury

─────────── 2 ───────────

10 真偽 **shingi** true or false, whether genuine or spurious
11 虚偽 **kyogi** false, untrue

2a9.3

偖

SHA (split) open
sate well, now

假 → 仮 2a4.15

2a9.4 / 609

側

SOKU, kawa, -gawa side
soba side, vicinity
hata side, edge

─────────── 1 ───────────

4 側辺 **sokuhen** side
5 側目 **sokumoku** watch for attentively
6 側近 **sokkin** close associate
側近(く) **sobachika(ku)** nearby

側近者 **sokkinsha** close associate
7 側役 **sobayaku** personal attendant
側杖 **sobazue** blow received by a bystander
8 側泳 **sokuei** sidestroke
9 側室 **sokushitsu** noble's concubine
側面 **sokumen** side, flank
側面図 **sokumenzu** side view
側面観 **sokumenkan** side view
10 側部 **sokubu** side, lateral
14 側聞 **sokubun** hear tell, be told
15 側線 **sokusen** siding, sidetrack; sideline (in field sports)
16 側壁 **sokuheki** side wall

─────────── 2 ───────────

4 内側 **uchigawa** inside, interior, inner
片側 **katagawa, katakawa** one side
片側通行 **katagawa tsūkō** One Way (Traffic)
5 北側 **kitagawa, hokusoku** north side
左側 **hidarigawa** left side
左側通行 **hidarigawa tsūkō** Keep Left
外側 **sotogawa** outside, exterior
右側 **migigawa, usoku** right side
6 両側 **ryōgawa** both sides
西側 **nishigawa** the western side; the West
向側 **mu(kō)gawa** the opposite side, across from
8 表側 **omotegawa** the front
東側 **higashigawa** east side
金側 **kingawa** gold case
9 南側 **minamigawa, nansoku** south side
11 偏側 **hensoku** not according to regulations, nonstandard
船側 **sensoku** side of a ship
船側渡 **sensoku-wata(shi)** Free Alongside Ship, ex-ship
舷側 **gensoku** ship's side, broadside
13 裏側 **uragawa** the back side
14 銀側 **gingawa** silver case
15 敵側 **tekigawa** the enemy's side
縁側 **engawa** veranda, porch, balcony

─────────── 3 ───────────

4 反対側 **hantaigawa** the opposite side
9 政府側 **seifugawa** the government (side)
15 権力側 **kenryokugawa** the more powerful side

─────────── 4 ───────────

17 輾転反側 **tenten-hansoku** tossing about (in bed)

2a9.5

做

SA, -na(su) make, do

─────────── 2 ───────────

7 見做 **mina(su)** regard as, consider, deem
9 看做 **mina(su)** regard as, consider, deem

→ 9

倦 → 倦 2a8.13

條 → 条 4i4.1

2a9.6

脩 SHŪ dried meat; long; put in order

2a9.7

偲 SHI, SAI, shino(bu) recollect, remember

─────── 1 ───────
9 偲草 shino(bu)gusa hare's-foot fern

2a9.8

偬 SŌ busy, flurried, upset

─────── 2 ───────
10 倥偬 kōsō busy; grieve, suffer

2a9.9

偟 KŌ wander; leisure

─────── 2 ───────
6 仿偟 hōkō wander, roam

2a9.10

偈 GE verse in praise of Buddha
KETSU fast; healthy
KEI rest

2a9.11

偕 KAI together

2a9.12

傸 GEN, GAN fake, counterfeit

2a9.13

偸 TŌ, CHŪ, nusu(mu) steal

─────── 1 ───────
5 偸生 tōsei continue living when one should die
6 偸安 tōan steal a moment of pleasure/rest; stall for time
11 偸盗 chūtō theft; thief

2a9.14 / 1185

停 TEI, todo(maru), todo(meru), to(maru) stop

─────── 1 ───────
4 停止 teishi suspension, stop, halt, cessation
6 停年 teinen age limit, retirement age
停会 teikai suspension of a meeting, adjournment, recess
7 停学 teigaku suspension from school
停車 teisha stopping a vehicle
停車場 teishajō, teishaba railway station; taxi stand
8 停泊 teihaku anchorage, mooring
10 停留 teiryū stop, halt
停留所 teiryūjo stopping place, (bus) stop
11 停船 teisen stopping (a ship), heave to, quarantine
13 停滞 teitai be stagnant, accumulate; fall into arrears
停戦 teisen cease-fire, armistice
停電 teiden cutoff of electricity, power outage
停頓 teiton standstill, deadlock, stalemate
18 停職 teishoku suspension from office

─────── 2 ───────
9 急停車 kyūteisha sudden stop
12 無停車 muteisha nonstop
13 電停 dentei streetcar stop
15 調停 chōtei arbitration, mediation, conciliation
調停裁判 chōtei saiban court arbitration

─────── 3 ───────
6 各駅停車 kakuekiteisha local train

─────── 4 ───────
8 居中調停 kyochū-chōtei mediation, arbitration

2a9.15 / 1928

偵 TEI spy

─────── 1 ───────
14 偵察 teisatsu reconnaissance
偵察隊 teisatsutai reconnoitering party, patrol, scouts
偵察機 teisatsuki reconnaissance/spotter plane

———————— 2 ————————
4 内偵 **naitei** scouting, reconnaissance; private inquiry
11 探偵 **tantei** (private) detective, investigator, spy
探偵小説 **tantei shōsetsu** detective story
密偵 **mittei** spy, undercover agent

2a9.16 / 1159

偏 偏

HEN inclining; left-side part of a kanji **katayo(ru)** lean toward, be biased
hitoe (ni) earnestly; humbly; solely

———————— 1 ————————
0 偏する **hen(suru)** lean toward, be biased
2 偏人 **henjin** an eccentric
5 偏平 **henpei** flat
偏平足 **henpeisoku** flat feet
6 偏在 **henzai** uneven distribution, maldistribution
偏向 **henkō** leanings, deviation; deflection
偏光 **henkō** polarized light, polarization
7 偏狂 **henkyō** monomania; monomaniac
偏見 **henken** biased view, prejudice
8 偏屈 **henkutsu** eccentric, bigoted, narrow-minded
9 偏重 **henchō** overemphasis
偏狭 **henkyō** narrow-minded, intolerant, parochial
偏食 **henshoku** unbalanced diet
10 偏差 **hensa** deviation, deflection, declination
偏流 **henryū** drift
11 偏側 **hensoku** not according to regulations, nonstandard
偏執 **henshū** bigotry, obstinacy
13 偏愛 **hen'ai** partiality, favoritism
14 偏頗 **henpa** partiality, unfair discrimination
16 偏頭痛 **henzutsū, hentōtsu** migraine headache

———————— 2 ————————
4 不偏 **fuhen** impartial, fair, neutral
不偏不党 **fuhen-futō** nonpartisan
6 糸偏景気 **itohen keiki** textile boom
8 金偏景気 **kanehen keiki** metal-industry boom
無偏 **muhen** unbiased, impartial

2a9.17

偓

AKU fuss, fretfulness

———————— 1 ————————
9 偓促 **akuseku, akusoku** fussily, busily

2a9.18

偃

EN lie/fall down; wave, bend, yield; cease, quit; dam up

———————— 1 ————————
4 偃月刀 **engetsutō** scimitar
8 偃武 **enbu** cease hostilities

歃 → **5f5.5**

2a9.19

盒

KŌ lidded container

———————— 2 ————————
12 飯盒 **hangō** mess kit, eating utensils

2a9.20

貪

DON, TAN, musabo(ru) covet, be voracious; indulge in

———————— 1 ————————
9 貪食 **donshoku, musabo(ri)ku(u/rau)** eat voraciously, devour
11 貪婪 **donran, tanran** covetousness, greed
貪欲 **don'yoku** avaricious, rapacious, covetous
15 貪慾 **don'yoku** avaricious, rapacious, covetous

超 → **3b9.18**

越 → **4n8.2**

麥 → 麦 **4i4.2**

劔 → 剣 **2f8.5**

2a9.21 / 1069

斜

SHA, nana(me), hasu slanting, diagonal, oblique, askew

———————— 1 ————————
4 斜辺 **shahen** slanting side; hypotenuse

斜方形 **shahōkei** rhombus
6 斜交 **hasukai** diagonal, oblique
7 斜角 **shakaku** oblique angle, bevel
9 斜面 **shamen** slope, inclined plane
11 斜陽 **shayō** setting sun
斜陽族 **shayōzoku** impoverished aristocracy
斜視 **shashi** strabismus (cross-eye or walleye), squint
斜視図 **shashizu** perspective view
12 斜塔 **shatō** leaning tower (of Pisa)
15 斜影 **shaei** obliquely cast shadow
斜線 **shasen** oblique line

──────── 2 ────────

9 急斜面 **kyūshamen** steep slope/incline
13 傾斜 **keisha** inclination, slant, slope
傾斜角 **keishakaku** angle of inclination, dip
傾斜度 **keishado** gradient
傾斜面 **keishamen** inclined plane

──────── 3 ────────

9 急傾斜 **kyūkeisha** steep slope/incline

敍→叙 **2h7.1**

肅→ **0a11.8**

疎→ **0a11.4**

──────── 10 ────────

2a10.1

倣 **KŌ, nara(u)** imitate, emulate

2a10.2

傅 **FU** tutor
kashizu(ku), tsu(ku) attend, wait upon, watch over

──────── 1 ────────

8 傅育 **fuiku** bring up, tutor

2a10.3

傀 **KAI** large; strange; doll

──────── 1 ────────

17 傀儡 **kairai** puppet

偕→ **2a9.11**

2a10.4 / 768

備 **BI, sona(eru)** provide, furnish; provide for, make preparations; be endowed with, possess   **sona(waru)** be provided/endowed with, possess

──────── 1 ────────

4 備中 **Bitchū** (ancient kuni, Okayama-ken)
5 備付 **sona(e)tsu(keru)** provide, equip, install
sona(e)tsu(ke) equipment, provision
6 備考 **bikō** note, remarks
7 備忘 **bibō** reminder
備忘録 **bibōroku** memorandum, notebook
9 備前 **Bizen** (ancient kuni, Okayama-ken)
備品 **bihin** fixtures, furnishings, equipment
備後 **Bingo** (ancient kuni, Hiroshima-ken)
備荒 **bikō** provision against famine
13 備蓄 **bichiku** store (for emergencies), reserve

──────── 2 ────────

4 不備 **fubi** deficiency, defect, inadequacy; Yours in haste
予備 **yobi** preparatory, preliminary, in reserve, spare
予備兵 **yobihei** reservists
予備知識 **yobi chishiki** preliminary knowledge, background
予備金 **yobikin** reserve/emergency fund
予備品 **yobihin** spares, reserve supply
予備員 **yobiin** reserve men
予備校 **yobikō** preparatory school
予備隊 **yobitai** reserve corps
予備費 **yobihi** preliminary expenses; reserve/emergency fund
予備選挙 **yobi senkyo** preliminary election, a primary
6 全備 **zenbi** fully equipped, complete, perfect
防備 **bōbi** defensive preparations
守備 **shubi** defense
守備兵 **shubihei** guards, garrison
守備隊 **shubitai** garrison, guards
7 完備 **kanbi** fully equipped/furnished
8 武備 **bubi** armaments, defenses
具備 **gubi** have, possess, be endowed with
9 軍備 **gunbi** military preparations, preparedness
10 兼備 **kenbi** have both, combine
配備 **haibi** deployment, disposition
11 常備 **jōbi** standing, permanent, regular
常備兵 **jōbihei** regular/standing army
常備金 **jōbikin** reserve fund
常備軍 **jōbigun** regular/standing army
常備薬 **jōbiyaku** household remedy
設備 **setsubi** equipment, facilities, accommodations
12 装備 **sōbi** equipment
13 準備 **junbi** preparations, provision, reserve
準備金 **junbikin** reserve fund

戦備 **senbi** military preparedness
16 整備 **seibi** make/keep ready for use, maintain, equip
19 警備 **keibi** security, guard, defense
　警備兵 **keibihei** guard
　警備艦 **keibikan** guard ship

――――――― 3 ―――――――

3 下準備 **shitajunbi** preliminary arrangements
6 再軍備 **saigunbi** rearmament
8 金準備 **kin junbi** gold reserves
12 無防備 **mubōbi** defenseless, unfortified

僅 → 僅 **2a11.13**

2a10.5 / 1053

偉

I, era(i) great
era(garu) be self-important

――――――― 1 ―――――――

2 偉人 **ijin** great man
　偉力 **iryoku** great power, mighty force
3 偉大 **idai** great, grand, mighty
　偉丈夫 **ijōfu** great man
　偉才 **isai** great man, man of extraordinary talent
5 偉功 **ikō** great deed, meritorious service
8 偉効 **ikō** great/marked effect
10 偉容 **iyō** magnificent appearance
　偉挙 **ikyo** great deeds
13 偉業 **igyō** great achievement, feat
15 偉勲 **ikun** great achievement, distinguished service
17 偉績 **iseki** glorious achievements
18 偉観 **ikan** grand sight

――――――― 2 ―――――――

12 雄偉 **yūi** imposing, grand, magnificent
14 魁偉 **kaii** imposing, formidable

2a10.6 / 1183

傍

BŌ, HŌ, katawara, soba, hata side

――――――― 1 ―――――――

2 傍人 **bōjin** bystander
5 傍目 **okame, hatame** looking on by an outsider, kibitzing
　傍目八目 **okame-hachimoku** Lookers-on see more than the players.
7 傍杖 **sobazue** blow received by a bystander
　傍系 **bōkei** collateral family line; affiliated, subsidiary
8 傍受 **bōju** intercept, monitor, tap
　傍注 **bōchū** marginal notes

傍若無人 **bōjaku-bujin** arrogant, insolent
11 傍視 **bōshi** look on from the side
12 傍証 **bōshō** supporting evidence, corroboration
　傍註 **bōchū** marginal notes
15 傍線 **bōsen** sideline, underline
　傍輩 **hōbai** colleagues under the same teacher or lord, companions
17 傍聴 **bōchō** hearing, attendance, auditing
　傍聴人 **bōchōnin** hearer, auditor, audience
　傍聴席 **bōchōseki** seats for the public, visitors' gallery
18 傍観 **bōkan** look on, remain a spectator
　傍観者 **bōkansha** onlooker, bystander

――――――― 2 ―――――――

6 近傍 **kinbō** neighborhood, vicinity
13 路傍 **robō** roadside, wayside

――――――― 3 ―――――――

9 拱手傍観 **kyōshu bōkan** stand idly by
10 袖手傍観 **shūshu-bōkan** look on with arms folded

2a10.7 / 790

傘

SAN, kasa umbrella

――――――― 1 ―――――――

3 傘下 **sanka** affiliated, subsidiary
5 傘立 **kasata(te)** umbrella stand
9 傘屋 **kasaya** umbrella shop

――――――― 2 ―――――――

4 日傘 **higasa** parasol
8 雨傘 **amagasa** umbrella
9 洋傘 **yōgasa** Western umbrella
10 唐傘 **karakasa** paper umbrella
12 番傘 **bangasa** coarse oilpaper umbrella
13 置傘 **o(ki)gasa** spare umbrella kept at one's workplace

――――――― 3 ―――――――

9 相々傘 **aiaigasa (de)** under the same umbrella
　相合傘 **aia(i)gasa (de)** under the same umbrella
11 蛇目傘 **ja(no)megasa** umbrella with a bull's-eye design
12 落下傘 **rakkasan** parachute
　落下傘兵 **rakkasanhei** paratrooper
15 蝙蝠傘 **kōmorigasa** umbrella

2a10.8

禽

KIN bird; captive, capture
tori bird

――――――― 1 ―――――――

8 禽舎 **kinsha** aviary, birdhouse

2

亻 10 ←
冫
孑
阝
卩
刂
力
又
宀
亠
艹
⺮
⼅
厂
辶
冂
几
匸

2

→10 亻
⺅
孑
阝
卩
力
又
一
二
十
⺧
丶
厂
辶
门
八
匸

16 禽獣 **kinjū** birds and beasts, animals

——— 2 ———

3 小禽 **shōkin** small birds
4 水禽 **suikin** waterfowl
10 猛禽 **mōkin** bird of prey
　家禽 **kakin** domestic fowl, poultry
11 野禽 **yakin** wild birds
　渉禽類 **shōkinrui** wading birds
13 愛禽 **aikin** favorite bird
　愛禽家 **aikinka** bird lover
14 鳴禽 **meikin** songbird

2a10.9

翕

KYŪ gather; all at once

——— 1 ———

12 翕然 **kyūzen** with one accord

超 → **3b9.18**

越 → **4n8.2**

幾 → **4n8.4**

疎 → **0a11.4**

——— 11 ———

2a11.1 / 232

働 仂

DŌ, hatara(ku) work
hatara(ki) work, function

——— 1 ———

3 働口 **hatara(ki)guchi** job opening, employment
4 働手 **hatara(ki)te** worker, breadwinner; able man
8 働者 **hatara(ki)mono** hard worker
10 働振 **hatara(ki)bu(ri)** how one works, discharge of one's duty
11 働掛 **hatara(ki)ka(keru)** work on (someone), influence, appeal to; begin to work
　働盛 **hatara(ki)zaka(ri)** prime of one's working life
13 働蜂 **hatara(ki)bachi** worker bee

——— 2 ———

3 下働 **shitabatara(ki)** subordinate work; assistant, servant

5 只働 **tadabatara(ki)** working without pay
　立働 **ta(chi)hatara(ku)** work
6 共働 **tomobatara(ki)** (husband and wife) both working, dual income
7 別働隊 **betsudōtai** flying column, detached force
　労働 **rōdō** labor, work, toil
　労働力 **rōdōryoku** labor, manpower, workforce
　労働者 **rōdōsha** worker, laborer
　労働省 **Rōdōshō** Ministry of Labor
　労働党 **rōdōtō** labor/Labour party
　労働祭 **rōdōsai** Labor Day; May Day
　労働組合 **rōdō kumiai** labor union
15 稼働 **kadō** operation, work
17 糠働 **nukabatara(ki)** fruitless effort

——— 3 ———

8 実労働 **jitsurōdō** actual labor
9 重労働 **jūrōdō** heavy/hard labor
　重労働者 **jūrōdōsha** heavy laborer
12 軽労働 **keirōdō** light work
13 節句働 **sekkubatara(ki)** working on a holiday (to make up for lost time)

——— 4 ———

6 自由労働者 **jiyū rōdōsha** casual laborer

2a11.2

傲

GŌ be proud

——— 1 ———

8 傲岸 **gōgan** arrogant, haughty
　傲岸不遜 **gōgan-fuson** arrogant, insolent, presumptuous
12 傲然 **gōzen(taru)** proud, arrogant, haughty
14 傲慢 **gōman** proud, arrogant, haughty
　傲慢無礼 **gōman-burei** arrogant and insolent

——— 2 ———

10 倨傲 **kyogō** proud, arrogant
22 驕傲 **kyōgō** arrogance, pride

2a11.3 / 1441

傾

KEI, katamu(ku), kashi(gu) (intr.) lean, incline, tilt **katamu(keru), kashi(geru), kata(geru)** (tr.) lean

——— 1 ———

5 傾巧 **keikō** flatter, toady, curry favor
6 傾向 **keikō** tendency, trend; inclination, leanings
8 傾注 **keichū** devotion, concentration
　傾国 **keikoku** a beauty, siren; courtesan, prostitute
9 傾城 **keisei** courtesan, prostitute; an infatuating beauty

傾度　**keido**　inclination, gradient
10 傾倒　**keitō**　devote oneself to; admire, idolize
11 傾斜　**keisha**　inclination, slant, slope
傾斜角　**keishakaku**　angle of inclination, dip
傾斜度　**keishado**　gradient
傾斜面　**keishamen**　inclined plane
17 傾聴　**keichō**　listen (attentively) to

─────── 2 ───────
5 左傾　**sakei**　leftist, radical
右傾　**ukei**　leaning to the right, rightist
9 急傾斜　**kyūkeisha**　steep slope/incline

2a11.4

條

JŌ　braid

─────── 1 ───────
6 條虫　**jōchū**　tapeworm

傳→伝 **2a4.14**

2a11.5

僂

RŌ, RU　bend over, stoop

─────── 2 ───────
7 佝僂　**kuru**　hunchback; rickets
13 僂僂　**uru, semushi**　bent over, hunchbacked

2a11.6 / 1731

傑 杰

KETSU, sugu(reru)　excel

─────── 1 ───────
2 傑人　**ketsujin**　outstanding person
5 傑出　**kesshutsu**　excel, be pre-eminent
7 傑作　**kessaku**　masterpiece
8 傑物　**ketsubutsu**　great man, outstanding figure
12 傑然　**ketsuzen**　resolute, decisive, determined

─────── 2 ───────
2 人傑　**jinketsu**　great man
3 女傑　**joketsu**　outstanding woman
8 英傑　**eiketsu**　great man, hero
怪傑　**kaiketsu**　extraordinary man
9 俊傑　**shunketsu**　outstanding man, hero, genius
14 豪傑　**gōketsu**　hero, great man

2a11.7 / 1366

僧 僧

SŌ　monk, priest

─────── 1 ───────
5 僧正　**sōjō**　(Buddhist) bishop
僧号　**sōgō**　Buddhist name
僧尼　**sōni**　monks and nuns
6 僧衣　**sōi**　priest's vestment
7 僧兵　**sōhei**　monk soldier
僧坊　**sōbō**　priests' living quarters
8 僧房　**sōbō**　priests' living quarters
僧門　**sōmon**　priesthood
9 僧侶　**sōryo**　(Buddhist) priest, monk, bonze
僧俗　**sōzoku**　clergy and laity
僧院　**sōin**　temple; monastery
10 僧都　**sōzu**　Buddhist priest
僧徒　**sōto**　priests, monks
僧家　**sōka**　Buddhist temple; Buddhist priest
11 僧庵　**sōan**　monk's cell, hermitage
14 僧綱　**sōgō**　(ancient Buddhist ecclesiastical authority); monk's collar
18 僧職　**sōshoku**　(Buddhist) priesthood
20 僧籍　**sōseki**　priesthood

─────── 2 ───────
3 大僧正　**daisōjō**　high priest, cardinal
下僧　**gesō**　lowly priest
女僧　**nyosō**　Buddhist nun
小僧　**kozō**　young Buddhist priest; errand boy; youngster, kid
4 仏僧　**bussō**　Buddhist priest
5 尼僧　**nisō**　nun
尼僧院　**nisōin**　convent
6 老僧　**rōsō**　old/aged priest
名僧　**meisō**　famous priest
7 伴僧　**bansō**　assistant priest, acolyte
役僧　**yakusō**　sexton; assistant priest
学僧　**gakusō**　learned priest
社僧　**shasō**　priest residing at a shrine
9 俗僧　**zokusō**　worldly priest
客僧　**kyakusō**　traveling priest
10 高僧　**kōsō**　high priest, prelate; virtuous priest
旅僧　**tabisō**　traveling priest
11 悪僧　**akusō**　dissolute priest
12 貴僧　**kisō**　you (referring to a priest)
13 禅僧　**zensō**　Zen priest
愚僧　**gusō**　this foolish priest

─────── 3 ───────
4 仏法僧　**buppōsō**　Buddha, doctrine, and priesthood; broad-billed roller, Japanese scops owl
6 行脚僧　**angyasō**　itinerant priest
11 虚無僧　**komusō**　mendicant flute-playing Zen priest
15 膝小僧　**hizakozō**　one's knees, kneecap
17 聴聞僧　**chōmonsō**　confessor

─────── 4 ───────
9 洟垂小僧　**hanata(re) kozō**　drippy-nosed little boy, snot-nose kid

2

イ 11←
彳
子
阝
卩
刂
力
又
亠
宀
十
艹
竹
ク
厂
辶
門
几
匸

2a11.8

儦 **HYŌ** fast, nimble

2a11.9

僊 **SEN** hermit, wizard; jumping up and down

2a11.10 / 633

傷 **SHŌ, kizu** wound, injury **ita(mu)** hurt, suffer pain/injury/damage; go bad (food) **ita(meru)** hurt, cause pain/injury/damage to

──────── 1 ────────

3 傷口 **kizuguchi** wound
4 傷心 **shōshin** heartbreak, sorrow
5 傷付 **kizutsu(keru)** injure, damage
7 傷兵 **shōhei** wounded soldier
8 傷者 **shōsha** injured person
　傷物 **kizumono** damaged goods
9 傷神 **shōshin** heartbreak, sorrow
10 傷害 **shōgai** injury, bodily harm
　傷病 **shōbyō** injury or illness
　傷病兵 **shōbyōhei** the sick and wounded (soldiers)
11 傷痍 **shōi** wound, injury
　傷痕 **shōkon, kizuato** scar
12 傷創 **shōsō** wound, injury
13 傷嘆 **shōtan** crying in pain
　傷跡 **kizuato** scar
16 傷薬 **kizugusuri** salve, ointment

──────── 2 ────────

3 大傷 **ōkizu** serious injury, deep gash
　刃傷 **ninjō** bloodshed
　刃傷沙汰 **ninjōzata** bloodshed
4 中傷 **chūshō** slander, defamation
　切傷 **ki(ri)kizu** cut, gash, scar
　手傷 **tekizu** wound, injury
　火傷 **kashō, yakedo** a burn
5 生傷 **namakizu** unhealed wound, fresh bruise
　古傷 **furukizu** old wound
　外傷 **gaishō** external wound, visible injury
　打傷 **u(chi)kizu** bruise
6 死傷 **shishō** casualties, killed and injured
　死傷者 **shishōsha** casualties, killed and wounded
8 受傷 **jushō** be injured
　突傷 **tsu(ki)kizu** stab wound
9 重傷 **jūshō, omode** serious wound, major injury
　重傷者 **jūshōsha** seriously injured person
　哀傷 **aishō** sorrow, grief

負傷 **fushō** sustain an injury, get hurt
負傷兵 **fushōhei** wounded soldier
負傷者 **fushōsha** injured person, the wounded
咬傷 **kōshō** a bite (wound)
食傷 **shokushō** be fed up with; suffer food poisoning
10 凍傷 **tōshō** frostbite, chilblains
挫傷 **zashō** sprain, fracture, bruise
殺傷 **sasshō** killing or wounding, casualties
破傷風 **hashōfū** tetanus, lockjaw
11 掠傷 **kasu(ri)kizu** scratch, bruise
12 創傷 **sōshō** a wound, trauma
無傷 **mukizu** uninjured, undamaged, unblemished
悲傷 **hishō** be sad/distressed
裂傷 **resshō** laceration
軽傷 **keishō** minor injury
13 毀傷 **kishō** injury, damage
損傷 **sonshō** damage, injury
微傷 **bishō** slight wound, minor injury, scratch
愁傷 **shūshō** grief, sorrow
愁傷様 **(go)shūshō-sama** My heartfelt sympathy.
感傷 **kanshō** sentimentality
感傷的 **kanshōteki** sentimental
戦傷 **senshō** war wound
14 銃傷 **jūshō** gunshot wound
17 擦傷 **su(ri)kizu** abrasion, scratch
螫傷 **sa(shi)kizu** (insect) bite, sting
18 嚙傷 **ka(mi)kizu** a bite (wound)
19 爆傷 **bakushō** blast damage

──────── 3 ────────

3 大火傷 **ōyakedo** severe burn
10 致命傷 **chimeishō** fatal wound/injury
13 鉄砲傷 **teppō kizu** gunshot wound
17 擦過傷 **sakkashō** abrasion, scratch

2a11.11 / 1118

債 **SAI** debt, loan

──────── 1 ────────

5 債主 **saishu** creditor
8 債券 **saiken** bond, debenture
10 債鬼 **saiki** cruel creditor, bill collector
11 債務 **saimu** debt, liabilities
　債務者 **saimusha** debtor
15 債権 **saiken** credit, claims
　債権者 **saikensha** creditor

──────── 2 ────────

4 内債 **naisai** internal/domestic loan
　公債 **kōsai** public debt, government bond
5 市債 **shisai** municipal loan/bond
　外債 **gaisai** foreign loan/bond/debt

旧債 **kyūsai** an old debt
7 社債 **shasai** (company) bonds, debentures
8 国債 **kokusai** national debt/bonds
9 負債 **fusai** debt, liabilities
10 起債 **kisai** issue bonds, float a loan
12 減債 **gensai** partial payment of a debt
募債 **bosai** floating a loan
13 戦債 **sensai** war debts/bonds

――――――― 3 ―――――――
5 外国債 **gaikokusai** foreign loan
外貨債 **gaikasai** foreign-currency bond

――――――― 4 ―――――――
9 軍事公債 **gunji kōsai** war bonds

2a11.12 / 1317

催 **SAI, moyō(su)** bring about, hold (a meeting); feel (sick)

――――――― 1 ―――――――
7 催告 **saikoku** notification, admonition
8 催物 **moyō(shi)mono** public event, show
9 催促 **saisoku** urge, press for, demand
催促状 **saisokujō** dunning letter
10 催涙弾 **sairuidan** tear-gas bomb/grenade
催眠 **saimin** hypnosis
催眠剤 **saiminzai** sleep-inducing drug
催眠術 **saiminjutsu** hypnotism
催眠薬 **saimin'yaku** sleep-inducing drug
催馬楽 **saibara** (type of *gagaku* song)

――――――― 2 ―――――――
5 主催 **shusai** sponsor, promote
主催者 **shusaisha** sponsor, organizer
6 共催 **kyōsai** joint sponsorship
8 居催促 **izaisoku** not leave till (a debt is) paid
雨催 **amamoyo(i), amemoyo(i)** signs of rain
11 雪催 **yukimoyo(i)** threatening to snow
12 開催 **kaisai** hold (a meeting)
開催中 **kaisaichū** in session

2a11.13

僅 僅 **KIN, wazu(ka)** few, little

――――――― 1 ―――――――
3 僅々 **kinkin** only, merely, no more than
4 僅少 **kinshō** few, little

2a11.14

傭 **YŌ, yato(u)** employ, hire

――――――― 1 ―――――――
2 傭人 **yōnin** employee

7 傭兵 **yōhei, yato(i)hei** mercenary soldier
11 傭船 **yōsen** chartered ship; chartering a vessel

――――――― 2 ―――――――
12 雇傭 **koyō** employment, hiring

――――――― 4 ―――――――
7 完全雇傭 **kanzen koyō** full employment

2a11.15

傴 **U** bend over, stoop, bow

――――――― 1 ―――――――
13 傴僂 **uru, semushi** bent over, hunchbacked

會 → 会 2a4.19

2a11.16

愈 愈 **YU** be superior; heal **iyoiyo** more and more, increasingly; finally; beyond doubt

――――――― 1 ―――――――
3 愈々 **iyoiyo** more and more, increasingly; finally; beyond doubt

2a11.17

僉 **SEN, mina** all

越 → 4n8.2

業 → 0a13.3

靴 → 3k10.34

貐 → 4a9.9

――――――― 12 ―――――――

2a12.1 / 1888

僕 **BOKU** I, me; manservant
shimobe manservant

――――――― 1 ―――――――
4 僕夫 **bokufu** ostler

2

→12 亻 ⺅ 孑 阝 卩 刂 力 又 宀 亠 十 ⼘ ⺀ ⼍ 厂 辶 冂 八 匚

10 僕従 **bokujū** servant
11 僕婢 **bokuhi** male and female servants

――――― 2 ―――――

3 下僕 **geboku** servant
4 公僕 **kōboku** public servant
6 老僕 **rōboku** old manservant
7 学僕 **gakuboku** servant-student
8 忠僕 **chūboku** faithful (man)servant
10 従僕 **jūboku** male servant, attendant
　家僕 **kaboku** manservant, houseboy
　校僕 **kōboku** school servant; student-servant
11 婢僕 **hiboku** servants, menials
13 義僕 **giboku** loyal servant

2a12.2

僭 僣　SEN have pretentions to, usurp

――――― 1 ―――――

3 僭上 **senjō** presumption, effrontery
10 僭称 **senshō** pretend to, assume a title
12 僭越 **sen'etsu** insolent, presumptuous

2a12.3

僮　DŌ child; servant; ignorant, foolish; respectful

2a12.4 / 1324

僚　RYŌ colleague; an official

――――― 1 ―――――

4 僚友 **ryōyū** colleague, co-worker
8 僚官 **ryōkan** a (fellow) official
16 僚機 **ryōki** consort plane
21 僚艦 **ryōkan** consort ship

――――― 2 ―――――

3 下僚 **karyō** subordinates, petty official
6 同僚 **dōryō** colleague, associate
8 官僚 **kanryō** bureaucracy, officialdom
　官僚化 **kanryōka** bureaucratization
　官僚主義 **kanryō shugi** bureaucracy
　官僚制 **kanryōsei** bureaucracy
　官僚的 **kanryōteki** bureaucratic
12 属僚 **zokuryō** subordinates
13 幕僚 **bakuryō** staff, aide, adviser
14 閣僚 **kakuryō** cabinet members

2a12.5

僑　KYŌ temporary home; person living outside his home country

――――― 2 ―――――

10 華僑 **Kakyō** overseas Chinese

偽 → 偽 **2a9.2**

2a12.6

僥　GYŌ good fortune; seeking gain

――――― 1 ―――――

10 僥倖 **gyōkō** good fortune, stroke of luck

2a12.7

僖　KI joy, enjoyment, pleasure

2a12.8 / 740

像　ZŌ, SHŌ, katachi image, statue, portrait

――――― 1 ―――――

9 像型 **zōkei** mold for cast images

――――― 2 ―――――

3 小像 **shōzō** small statue, figurine
4 幻像 **genzō** illusion, phantom
　仏像 **butsuzō** image of Buddha
　木像 **mokuzō** wooden image
　心像 **shinzō** mental image
5 巨像 **kyozō** huge statue/image
　石像 **sekizō** stone image/statue
　立像 **ritsuzō** (standing) statue
7 肖像 **shōzō** portrait
　肖像画 **shōzōga** portrait
8 画像 **gazō** portrait, picture, image
　受像 **juzō** receive television pictures
　受像機 **juzōki** television set
　実像 **jitsuzō** real image
9 映像 **eizō** image, reflection
10 残像 **zanzō** afterimage
　原像 **genzō** original statue (not a replica)
　座像 **zazō** seated image
　胸像 **kyōzō** (sculptured) bust
11 偶像 **gūzō** image, idol
　偶像化 **gūzōka** idolize
　偶像崇拝 **gūzō sūhai** idol worship, idolatry
　偶像視 **gūzōshi** idolize
　虚像 **kyozō** virtual image
　彫像 **chōzō** carved statue, sculpture
　現像 **genzō** developing (film)
　現像液 **genzōeki** developing solution
12 尊像 **sonzō** your portrait
　結像 **ketsuzō** image formation

結像面 **ketsuzōmen** focal plane
絵像 **ezō** portrait, likeness, picture
13 塑像 **sozō** clay figure, plastic image
群像 **gunzō** group of people (in an artwork)
聖像 **seizō** sacred image, icon
解像 **kaizō** (image) resolution, definition
想像 **sōzō** imagine
想像力 **sōzōryoku** (powers of) imagination
想像上 **sōzōjō** imaginary
裸像 **razō** nude statue
14 銅像 **dōzō** bronze statue
15 影像 **eizō** image
鋳像 **chūzō** cast image

——————— 3 ———————
2 人物像 **jinbutsuzō** statue, picture
6 自画像 **jigazō** self-portrait
血液像 **ketsuekizō** hemogram
12 等身像 **tōshinzō** life-size statue
13 聖画像 **seigazō** sacred image, icon

僧 → 僧 **2a11.7**

趣 → **6e9.1**

疑 → **2m12.1**

——————— 13 ———————

2a13.1

僻 HEKI distorted; remote **katayo(ru)** be one-sided, be biased **higa(mu)** be prejudiced against **higa-** evil; erroneous

——————— 1 ———————
5 僻目 **higame** squint; error; bias; misjudgment
6 僻地 **hekichi** remote place
7 僻村 **hekison** remote village
12 僻遠 **hekien** remote, out-of-the-way, outlying

——————— 3 ———————
3 山間僻地 **sankan-hekichi** secluded mountain recesses

2a13.2

僖 SHUN excel

2a13.3

儂 DŌ, NŌ I, my; he, his
washi I, me

價 → 価 **2a6.3**

2a13.4 / 727

儀 GI rule; ceremony; model; affair, matter

——————— 1 ———————
2 儀刀 **gitō** ceremonial sword
4 儀文 **gibun** formalistic style, officialese
5 儀仗 **gijō** cortege, guard
儀仗兵 **gijōhei** honor guard, military escort
儀礼 **girei** etiquette, courtesy
儀礼的 **gireiteki** formal, courtesy (call)
6 儀式 **gishiki** ceremony
8 儀表 **gihyō** model, paragon
儀典 **giten** ceremony, rites
儀法 **gihō** rule, commandment
9 儀型 **gikei** model, pattern
10 儀容 **giyō** mien, bearing, manners
12 儀装 **gisō** ceremonial equipment

——————— 2 ———————
3 大儀 **taigi** national ceremony; laborious, troublesome; wearisome, listless
4 内儀 **naigi** wife; landlady
公儀 **kōgi** court, shogunate, authorities; official
5 仕儀 **shigi** circumstances, developments
古儀 **kogi** ancient rite
礼儀 **reigi** courtesy, politeness, propriety
礼儀正 **reigitada(shii)** polite, courteous
礼儀作法 **reigisahō** etiquette, courtesy, propriety
6 行儀 **gyōgi** manners, deportment, behavior
7 余儀 **yogi(naku)** unavoidable, be obliged to
役儀 **yakugi** one's duty, role
8 其儀 **so(no) gi** such is the case
9 風儀 **fūgi** manners; (sexual) morality
律儀 **richigi** honesty, integrity, loyalty
律儀者 **richigimono** honest hardworking man
祝儀 **shūgi** (wedding) celebration
威儀 **igi** dignity, majesty, solemnity
10 流儀 **ryūgi** school (of thought), style, system, method
容儀 **yōgi** deportment, demeanor
11 婚儀 **kongi** wedding
密儀 **mitsugi** secret rites, mysteries
祭儀 **saigi** festival
略儀 **ryakugi** informal
盛儀 **seigi** grand ceremony
12 葬儀 **sōgi** funeral
葬儀社 **sōgisha** funeral home, undertaker's
葬儀屋 **sōgiya** undertaker, funeral home
葬儀場 **sōgijō** funeral home

13 辞儀 **jigi** bow, greeting; decline, refuse
17 謝儀 **shagi** expression of gratitude
18 難儀 **nangi** difficult, trying

——————— 3 ———————

4 不行儀 **fugyōgi** bad manners, rudeness
天球儀 **tenkyūgi** a celestial globe
天象儀 **tenshōgi** planetarium
六分儀 **rokubungi** sextant
6 地球儀 **chikyūgi** a globe of the world
回転儀 **kaitengi** gyroscope
11 経緯儀 **keiigi** theodolite, altazimuth
12 測距儀 **sokkyogi** range finder
御辞儀 **ojigi** bow, greeting
19 羅針儀 **rashingi** compass

——————— 5 ———————

9 神変不思儀 **shinpen-fushigi** miracle, marvel

2a13.5

僵 **KYŌ** fall down, collapse

2a13.6 / 382

億 億 **OKU** hundred million, 100,000,000

——————— 1 ———————

3 億万長者 **okumanchōja** multimillionaire, billionaire
6 億年 **okunen** hundred million years
億兆 **okuchō** people, multitude, masses
7 億劫 **okkū** bothersome, troublesome
okukō, okugō, okkō unimaginable long time

——————— 2 ———————

1 一億 **ichioku** one hundred million
13 数億 **sūoku** hundreds of millions

2a13.7

儚 **BŌ** dark; lost
hakana(i) vain, empty, hopeless

2a13.8

儈 **KAI** middleman, broker

儉 → 倹 2a8.27

趣 → 6e9.1

麪 → 麺 4i17.1

麩 → 麸 4i12.2

齒 → 歯 6b6.11

——————— 14 ———————

2a14.1 / 1417

儒 **JU** Confucianism

——————— 1 ———————

4 儒仏 **jubutsu** Confucianism and Buddhism
5 儒生 **jusei** Confucian scholar, student of Confucianism
7 儒学 **jugaku** Confucianism
儒学者 **jugakusha** Confucianist, Confucian scholar
儒学界 **jugakkai** Confucianists
8 儒官 **jukan** official Confucian teacher
儒者 **jusha** a Confucianist
10 儒家 **juka** a Confucianist
儒書 **jusho** Confucianist writings
儒教 **jukyō** Confucianism
11 儒道 **judō** Confucianism

——————— 2 ———————

4 犬儒学派 **kenjugakuha** the Cynics
6 老儒 **rōju** old Confucian scholar
13 漢儒 **kanju** Chinese/Han-dynasty Confucian scholar
14 腐儒 **fuju** worthless scholar, pedant
18 藩儒 **hanju** scholar retained by a daimyo

2a14.2

儘 侭 **JIN, mama** as is, as one likes

——————— 2 ———————

6 気儘 **kimama** having one's own way
此儘 **ko(no)mama** as is
7 我儘 **wagamama** selfish, capricious, wanting to have one's own way
8 其儘 **so(no) mama** as is, without modification

——————— 4 ———————

6 気随気儘 **kizui-kimama** as one pleases
12 着身着儘 **ki(no)mi-ki(no)mama** with only the clothes one happens to be wearing

2a14.3

儔

CHŪ same kind, companions

2a14.4

儕

SEI, SAI companions

──────── 1 ────────

15 儕輩 **saihai** colleagues, comrades

趨→ **3b14.5**

──────── 15 ────────

儲→儲 **2a16.1**

2a15.1 / 1033

優

YŪ superior; gentle; actor
sugu(reru), masa(ru) excel, surpass
yasa(shii) gentle   yasa- gentle
yasa(shige) gentle-looking

──────── 1 ────────

0 優に **yū (ni)** fully, more than, well over, easily; gracefully
　マル優 **maruyū** (tax exemption for savings-account interest)
3 優女 **yasa-onna** gentle woman
5 優生学 **yūseigaku** eugenics
　優生保護法 **Yūsei Hogo Hō** Eugenic Protection Law
6 優先 **yūsen** preference, priority
　優先的 **yūsenteki** preferential
　優先株 **yūsenkabu** preferred shares
　優先権 **yūsenken** (right of) priority
　優劣 **yūretsu** superiority or inferiority, relative merits　**masa(ru tomo) oto(ranai)** in no way inferior to, at least so good as
7 優良 **yūryō** superior, excellent
　優位 **yūi** ascendance, predominance
　優形 **yasagata** slender figure
　優秀 **yūshū** superior, excellent
　優男 **yasa-otoko** mild-mannered man, man of delicate features
8 優長 **yūchō** leisurely, easygoing
　優者 **yūsha** superior individual
　優性 **yūsei** dominant (gene)
9 優美 **yūbi** graceful, elegant
　優姿 **yasasugata** graceful figure
　優待 **yūtai** treat with consideration, receive hospitably

優待券 **yūtaiken** complimentary ticket
優柔 **yūjū** indecisiveness
優柔不断 **yūjū-fudan** indecisiveness
11 優遇 **yūgū** warm welcome, hospitality, favorable treatment
優婉 **yūen** elegant, graceful
12 優勝 **yūshō** victory, championship
優勝劣敗 **yūshō-reppai** survival of the fittest
優勝杯 **yūshōhai** championship cup
優勝者 **yūshōsha** winner, champion, title-holder
優勝旗 **yūshōki** championship pennant
優越 **yūetsu** superiority, supremacy
優越感 **yūetsukan** superiority complex
優等 **yūtō** excellence, superiority
優等生 **yūtōsei** honors student
優等賞 **yūtōshō** honor prize
13 優勢 **yūsei** predominance, superiority, the advantage
優雅 **yūga** elegant, graceful, refined
16 優曇華 **udonge** udumbara plant (said to blossom once in 3,000 years); insect eggs (laid by a lacewing in a flower-like pattern whose shape portends good or ill fortune)
19 優艶 **yūen** beautiful and refined, charming

──────── 2 ────────

3 女優 **joyū** actress
4 心優 **kokoroyasa(shii)** kind, considerate
6 全優 **zen'yū** straight A's
　老優 **rōyū** old actor/actress
　名優 **meiyū** great actor, star
7 声優 **seiyū** radio actor/actress, dubber
　男優 **dan'yū** actor
10 俳優 **haiyū** actor, actress

2a15.2

儖

RAN ugly

2a15.3

儡

RAI doll, puppet; defeat

──────── 2 ────────

12 傀儡 **kairai** puppet

2a15.4 / 971

償

SHŌ, tsuguna(u) make up for, recompense

──────── 1 ────────

7 償却 **shōkyaku** repayment, redemption, amortization

2

亻 15←
冫
孑
阝
卩
刂
力
又
一
亠
十
卜
ク
ヽ
厂
廴
冂
几
匚

2 →15

亻 冫 孑 阝 卩 刂 力 又 亠 十 匕 夂 宀 厂 辶 冂 几 匚

8 償金 **shōkin** indemnities, reparations, damages
15 償還 **shōkan** repayment, redemption, amortization

――――― 2 ―――――
5 弁償 **benshō** indemnification
弁償金 **benshōkin** indemnity, reparations
代償 **daishō** compensation, indemnification
6 有償 **yūshō** for a consideration/compensation
9 要償 **yōshō** claim for damages
12 報償 **hōshō** compensation, reward, remuneration
無償 **mushō** free, gratuitous
無償行為 **mushō kōi** gratuitous act, volunteer service
補償 **hoshō** compensation, indemnification
補償金 **hoshōkin** indemnity, compensation (money)
15 賠償 **baishō** reparation, indemnification
賠償金 **baishōkin** indemnities, reparations, damages

――――― 3 ―――――
9 皆勤償 **kaikinshō** reward for perfect attendance

――――― 4 ―――――
13 損害賠償 **songai baishō** restitution, indemnification, (pay) damages

2a15.5

侖 YAKU, **fue** flute

趰 → 3b14.5

2a15.6

齔 SHIN losing one's baby teeth; child

――――― 16 ―――――

2a16.1

儲 儲 CHO, **mō(karu)** be profitable **mō(keru)** gain, earn, make (money) **mō(ke)** profits

――――― 1 ―――――
3 儲口 **mō(ke)guchi** profitable job
5 儲仕事 **mō(ke)shigoto** lucrative work
儲主義 **mō(ke)shugi** moneymaking
7 儲役 **mō(ke)yaku** lucrative position
8 儲物 **mō(ke)mono** good bargain, windfall

――――― 2 ―――――
1 一儲 **hitomōke** money-making
3 大儲 **ōmō(ke)** large profit
丸儲 **marumō(ke)** clear gain/profit
8 金儲 **kanemō(ke)** moneymaking
14 銭儲 **zenimō(ke)** money-making

鞭 → 3k15.8

――――― 18 ―――――

2a18.1

齟 SO bite; malocclusion

――――― 1 ―――――
22 齟齬 **sogo** inconsistency, discrepancy, contradiction, conflict; go awry, fail in

齡 → 齢 6b11.5

――――― 19 ―――――

2a19.1

儺 DA, NA exorcism

――――― 2 ―――――
8 追儺 **tsuina** exorcism

2a19.2

儷 REI pair off

――――― 2 ―――――
16 駢儷体 **benreitai** flowery ancient Chinese prose style

2a19.3

齦 GIN the gums

――――― 2 ―――――
12 歯齦 **shigin** the gums
歯齦炎 **shigin'en** gingivitis

2a19.4

齧 嚙 GETSU, **kaji(ru)** gnaw, nibble at

———————— 1 ————————

5 齧付 **kaji(ri)tsu(ku)** bite at and not let go; stick to

———————— 2 ————————

5 生齧 **namakaji(ri)** superficial knowledge

———————— 20 ————————

2a20.1

儼   **GEN** solemn, grave

———————— 1 ————————

12 儼然 **genzen** solemn, august

———————— 2 ————————

10 俶儻 **tekitō** remarkable talent, genius; free and independent

2a20.2

儸   **GEN** solemn

2a20.3

龕   **GAN** cabinet for Buddhist accouterments

———————— 1 ————————

6 龕灯 **gandō** altar lamp; hand lantern
龕灯返 **gandōgae(shi)** apparatus for changing stage scenery

———————— 22 ————————

2a22.1

齲   **U, mushiba** decayed tooth, cavity

———————— 1 ————————

12 齲歯 **ushi, mushiba** decayed tooth, caries

———————— 冫 2b ————————

冫	冰	冴	冲	次	壮	決	冱	兆	羽	状	冴	況
0.1	3a1.2	2b5.2	3a4.5	4.1	4.2	3a4.6	4.3	4.4	4.5	5.1	5.2	3a5.21

冷	冶	求	冽	隷	函	飛	准	凍	将	凄	凌	涼
5.3	5.4	5.5	6.1	6.2	6.3	0a9.4	8.1	8.2	8.3	8.4	8.5	3a8.31

凋	涸	毬	馮	奬	斟	凛	凝	鏊
8.6	3a8.36	9.1	10.1	3n10.4	0a13.5	13.1	14.1	3p15.1

———————— 0 ————————

2b0.1

冫   **HYŌ** freeze

———————— 4 ————————

冰 → 氷   **3a1.2**

冴 → 冴   **2b5.2**

冲 → 沖   **3a4.5**

2b4.1 / 384

次   **JI, SHI, tsugi** next
tsu(gu) rank next to, come after

0 4次 **yonji, shiji** fourth-degree (equation)
2 次子 **jishi** second child
3 次々 **tsugitsugi** one by one, one after another
次女 **jijo** second daughter
4 次元 **jigen** dimension (in math)
5 次世代 **jisedai** next-generation (product)
次代 **jidai** the coming/rising generation
次兄 **jikei** one's second-oldest elder brother
次号 **jigō** the next issue
6 次会 **jikai** the next meeting
次回 **jikai** next time
7 次亜 **jia-** hypo- (in chemicals)
次位 **jii** second rank/place
次序 **jijo** order, system, arrangement
次条 **jijō** the following article
次男 **jinan** second son
次男坊 **jinanbō** second son
8 次長 **jichō** deputy director, assistant chief
次官 **jikan** vice-minister, undersecretary
9 次点 **jiten** runner-up
10 次席 **jiseki** associate, junior, assistant; runner-up

11 次第 **shidai** order, precedence; circumstances; as soon as; according to; gradually
12 次善 **jizen** second best
次期 **jiki** next term
13 次数 **jisū** degree (in math)

──────── 2 ────────

1 一次 **ichiji** first; primary; linear (equation)
一次元 **ichijigen** one-dimensional
2 二次 **niji** second(ary); quadratic, second degree (in math)
ni (no) tsugi secondary, subordinate
二次元 **nijigen** two-dimensional
二次方程式 **niji hōteishiki** quadratic equation
二次会 **nijikai** after-party party
二次的 **nijiteki** secondary
二次配列 **niji hairetsu** secondary arrangement, arrangement on second level
3 三次元 **sanjigen** three dimensions
三次配列 **sanji hairetsu** tertiary arrangement, arrangement on third level
4 中次 **nakatsugi** joint; relay, entrepôt, transit
今次 **konji** present, new, recent
月次 **getsuji** monthly **tsukinami** every month; commonplace, trite
日次 **nichiji** day, date
5 四次元 **yojigen, shijigen, yonjigen** fourth dimension, four dimensions
目次 **mokuji** table of contents
6 年次 **nenji** annual
毎次 **maiji** every time
次次 **tsugitsugi** one by one, one after another
列次 **retsuji** order, sequence
式次 **shikiji** the program of a ceremony
7 位次 **iji** seating according to rank
序次 **joji** order, sequence
8 弥次 **yaji** cheering; jeering; hecklers, spectators
弥次馬 **yajiuma** bystanders, spectators, crowd of onlookers
取次 **to(ri)tsu(gu)** act as agent; transmit, convey
取次店 **toritsugiten** agency, distributor
取次業 **toritsugigyō** agency/commission business
9 逐次 **chikuji** one by one, in sequence
造次顛沛 **zōji-tenpai** a moment
途次 **toji** on the way, en route
相次 **aitsu(gu)** follow in succession
10 高次 **kōji** higher-order, meta-
席次 **sekiji** seating order, precedence
11 副次的 **fukujiteki** secondary
望次第 **nozo(mi) shidai** as desired, on demand
累次 **ruiji** successive, repeated
12 腕次第 **ude-shidai** according to one's ability
順次 **junji** in order, successively; gradually
13 数次 **sūji** for a number of times

歳次 **saiji** year
路次 **roji** on the road/way
14 漸次 **zenji** gradually

──────── 3 ────────

4 手当次第 **tea(tari) shidai** (whatever is) within reach, haphazardly
9 政務次官 **seimu jikan** parliamentary vice-minister
11 第一次 **dai-ichiji** first
第二次 **dai-niji** second
第二次的 **dai-nijiteki** secondary
12 勝手次第 **katte-shidai** having one's own way

──────── 4 ────────

4 五十三次 **gojūsan tsugi** the 53 stages on the Tōkaidō

2b4.2 / 1326

壮 壯

SŌ manhood; strength; prosperity **saka(n)** prosperous

──────── 1 ────────

2 壮丁 **sōtei** a youth, able-bodied man
3 壮大 **sōdai** grand, magnificent, spectacular
壮士 **sōshi** swashbuckler; ruffian
4 壮夫 **sōfu** able-bodied man
6 壮年 **sōnen** the prime of manhood
壮行 **sōkō** rousing send-off
壮行会 **sōkōkai** farewell party
7 壮志 **sōshi** ambition
壮図 **sōto** grand undertaking
壮快 **sōkai** exhilarating, thrilling
壮言 **sōgen** spirited words
8 壮者 **sōsha** man in his prime
9 壮美 **sōbi** splendor, magnificence
10 壮健 **sōken** healthy, hale and hearty
壮挙 **sōkyo** daring undertaking, heroic attempt
壮烈 **sōretsu** heroic, brave
12 壮絶 **sōzetsu** sublime, magnificent
14 壮語 **sōgo** boasting, grandiloquence
17 壮齢 **sōrei** prime of life
18 壮観 **sōkan** grand/awe-inspiring sight
19 壮麗 **sōrei** splendor, glory

──────── 2 ────────

5 広壮 **kōsō** grand, magnificent, imposing
6 老壮 **rōsō** young and old
7 宏壮 **kōsō** grand, imposing, magnificent
9 勇壮 **yūsō** brave, heroic, stirring
11 強壮 **kyōsō** strong, robust, sturdy
強壮剤 **kyōsōzai** a tonic
12 悲壮 **hisō** tragic heroism
雄壮 **yūsō** heroic, valiant
14 豪壮 **gōsō** splendor, grandeur

──────── 3 ────────

3 大言壮語 **taigen sōgo** boasting, exaggeration

決 → 決 3a4.6

2b4.3

洦 洦
GO, KO freeze, be cold
sae(ru) be clear/bright; attain skill

2b4.4 / 1562

兆 兆
CHŌ sign, indication; trillion, 1,000,000,000,000
kiza(shi) signs, omen, symptoms kiza(su) show signs of

―――――― 1 ――――――
10 兆候 chōkō sign, indication

―――――― 2 ――――――
4 凶兆 kyōchō evil omen
6 吉兆 kitchō good/lucky omen
9 前兆 zenchō portent, omen, sign
13 瑞兆 zuichō good omen
15 億兆 okuchō people, multitude, masses
慶兆 keichō good omen

2b4.5 / 590

羽 羽
U, ha feather hane feather, wing; (propeller) blade
-wa, -ba (counter for birds)

―――――― 1 ――――――
2 羽二重 habutae habutae silk
羽子板 hagoita battledore, pingpong-like paddle
4 羽毛 umō feathers, plumage, down
羽化 uka grow wings
5 羽目 hame situation, predicament; panel, wainscoting
羽目板 hameita paneling, wainscoting
羽田 Haneda (airport in Tōkyō)
6 羽交 haga(i) pinion, wings
羽交締 haga(i)ji(me) pin, full nelson
羽衣 hagoromo robe of feathers
7 羽抜 hanu(ke) molting
8 羽突 hanetsu(ki) battledore and shuttlecock (badminton-like game)
9 羽前 Uzen (ancient kuni, Yamagata-ken)
羽風 hakaze breeze caused by flapping wings
羽後 Ugo (ancient kuni, Akita-ken)
羽音 haoto flapping of wings
10 羽振 habu(ri) influence, power
13 羽裏 haura underside of a wing
羽搏 habata(ki) flapping of wings, flutter
羽蒲団 hanebuton feather-filled futon, down quilt
羽飾 hanekaza(ri) a feather (in one's lapel)

14 羽箒 habōki, hanebōki feather duster
15 羽撃 habata(ki) flapping of wings
17 羽翼 uyoku wings; assistance
18 羽織 haori Japanese half-coat
hao(ru) put on
19 羽蟻 haari winged ant

―――――― 2 ――――――
3 三羽烏 sanbagarasu triumvirate
4 毛羽 keba fuzz, nap, pile
切羽 ki(ri)ha (mine tunnel) cutting/working face
切羽詰 seppa-tsu(maru) be driven to the wall, be at one's wit's end, be cornered
木羽 koba shingles
5 矢羽 yabane arrow feathers
白羽 shiraha white feather
白羽矢立 shiraha (no) ya (ga) ta(tsu) be selected (for a task/post)
6 合羽 kappa raincoat
7 尾羽 oha tail feathers
8 追羽根 o(i)bane battledore and shuttlecock
9 陣羽織 jinbaori sleeveless coat worn over armor
10 烏羽玉 ubatama jet/raven/pitch black
夏羽織 natsubaori summer haori coat
紋羽二重 mon habutae figured habutae
11 鳥羽 Toba (emperor, 1107–1124)
12 絵羽 eba figured haori coat
絵羽織 ebaori figured haori coat
13 腰羽目 koshibame hip-high wainscoting
鳩羽色 hatoba-iro bluish gray

―――――― 3 ――――――
8 雨合羽 amagappa raincoat
9 風切羽 kazaki(ri)ba flight feathers

―――――― 5 ――――――

2b5.1 / 626

状 狀
JŌ condition, circumstances; form, appearance; letter

―――――― 1 ――――――
8 状況 jōkyō circumstances
9 状挟 jōbasa(mi) letter clip/file
10 状差 jōsa(shi) letter file/rack
11 状袋 jōbukuro envelope
14 状貌 jōbō looks, appearance
状態 jōtai state of affairs, situation

―――――― 2 ――――――
3 弓状 kyūjō bow-shaped, arched
4 凶状 kyōjō crime, offense
5 甲状腺 kōjōsen thyroid gland
令状 reijō warrant, writ
召状 shōjō letter of invitation
白状 hakujō confess, admit

2

亻 5←
冫
子
阝
卩
刂
力
又
宀
亠
廾
⺾
⺇
⺀
厂
辶
冂
几
匸

礼状 **reijō** letter of thanks
6 気状 **kijō** gaseous
兇状 **kyōjō** crime, offense
兇状持 **kyōjōmo(chi)** criminal at large
近状 **kinjō** recent situation, present state
舌状 **zetsujō** tongue-shaped
名状 **meijō** describe
行状 **gyōjō** behavior, conduct, deportment
糸状 **shijō** threadlike, filament
7 別状 **betsujō** anything wrong, mishap
形状 **keijō** form, shape
乳状 **nyūjō** milky
8 免状 **menjō** diploma; license
送状 **oku(ri)jō** invoice
油状 **yujō** oily
波状 **hajō** wave, undulation
泥状 **deijō** muddy, pasty
実状 **jitsujō** actual state of affairs
性状 **seijō** properties, characteristics
具状 **gujō** (full) report (to a superior)
9 便状 **binjō** letter, written communication
冠状 **kanjō** coronary
弧状 **kojō** arc-shaped
柱状 **chūjō** pillar-shaped, columnar
悔状 **ku(yami)jō** letter of condolence
10 原状 **genjō** original state
帯状 **obijō** (in the shape of a) narrow strip
脈状 **myakujō** veinlike
書状 **shojō** letter
扇状 **senjō** fan-shaped
扇状地 **senjōchi** alluvial fan, delta
病状 **byōjō** patient's condition
症状 **shōjō** symptoms
粉状 **funjō** powder(ed)
針状 **harijō** needle-like
11 添状 **so(e)jō** accompanying letter
液状 **ekijō** liquid state, liquefied
桿状 **kanjō** rod-shaped
梯状 **teijō** trapezoid; echelon formation
現状 **genjō** present situation, current state of affairs
惨状 **sanjō** miserable state, disastrous scene
情状 **jōjō** circumstances, conditions
異状 **ijō** something wrong, abnormality
粒状 **ryūjō** granular, granulated
12 渦状 **kajō** spiral, whirled
掌状 **shōjō** hand-shaped, palmate
棒状 **bōjō** cylindrical
歯状 **shijō** tooth-shaped
訴状 **sojō** petition, (written) complaint
賀状 **gajō** greeting card
雲状 **unjō** cloudlike
13 塊状 **kaijō** massive
感状 **kanjō** (letter of) commendation
罪状 **zaijō** nature of the offense, charges
詫状 **wa(bi)jō** written apology

14 層状 **sōjō** in layers, stratified
網状 **mōjō, amijō** netlike, reticular
管状 **kanjō** tubular
15 褒状 **hōjō** certificate of merit, commendation
窮状 **kyūjō** distress, dire straits
賞状 **shōjō** certificate of merit
暴状 **bōjō** outrage, atrocity, violence
穂状 **suijō** shaped like a head of grain
輪状 **rinjō** circular, ring-shaped
16 蹄状 **teijō** horseshoe/U shape
錘状 **suijō** spindle-shaped
17 翼状 **yokujō** wing-shaped
環状 **kanjō** ring, loop, annulation
環状線 **kanjōsen** loop/belt line
謝状 **shajō** letter of thanks/apology
醜状 **shūjō** disgraceful state of affairs
18 鎖状 **sajō** chainlike
20 譲状 **yuzu(ri)jō** deed of assignment
24 鱗状 **rinjō** scale-like, scaly

——————— 3 ———————

4 不行状 **fugyōjō** misconduct, immorality
勾引状 **kōinjō** arrest warrant, summons
公開状 **kōkaijō** open letter
6 朱印状 **shuinjō** official document with a red seal
年賀状 **nengajō** New Year's card
仮免状 **karimenjō** temporary license; provisional diploma
考課状 **kōkajō** personnel/service record; business report
7 告発状 **kokuhatsujō** bill of indictment
見舞状 **mima(i)jō** how-are-you/get-well card
8 免許状 **menkyojō** license, certificate, permit
招待状 **shōtaijō** (written) invitation
拘引状 **kōinjō** arrest warrant, summons
拘留状 **kōryūjō** warrant for detention
呼出状 **yo(bi)da(shi)jō** summons, subpoena
委任状 **ininjō** power of attorney
9 信用状 **shin'yōjō** letter of credit
信任状 **shinninjō** credentials
連判状 **renpanjō, renbanjō** jointly sealed compact
挑戦状 **chōsenjō** written challenge
10 脅迫状 **kyōhakujō** threatening letter
逮捕状 **taihojō** arrest warrant
起訴状 **kisojō** (written) indictment
案内状 **annaijō** letter of invitation
特許状 **tokkyojō** charter, special license
11 推薦状 **suisenjō** letter of recommendation
控訴状 **kōsojō** petition of appeal
赦免状 **shamenjō** (letter of) pardon
紹介状 **shōkaijō** letter of introduction
斬奸状 **zankanjō** statement of reasons for slaying (a traitor)
12 葡萄状鬼胎 **budōjō kitai** vesicular/ hydatid(iform) mole

葡萄状菌 **budōjōkin** staphylococcus
葡萄状球菌 **budōjōkyūkin** staphylococcus
無症状 **mushōjō** without symptoms
絶交状 **zekkōjō** letter breaking off a
　　relationship
13 催促状 **saisokujō** dunning letter
感謝状 **kanshajō** letter of thanks
14 遺言状 **yuigonjō** will, testament
漏斗状 **rōtojō** funnel-shaped
15 慰問状 **imonjō** letter of condolence
16 鋸歯状 **kyōshijō** sawtooth, serrated
18 離縁状 **rienjō** letter of divorce

────────── 4 ──────────

6 自覚症状 **jikaku shōjō** subjective symp-
　　toms, patient's complaints
12 無封書状 **mufū shojō** unsealed letter

2b5.2

冴　冴

GO, sa(eru) be clear; be cold;
become skilled

────────── 1 ──────────

6 冴返 **sa(e)kae(ru)** be exceedingly clear; be
　　keenly cold
12 冴渡 **sa(e)wata(ru)** get cold; freeze over

況 → 況　3a5.21

2b5.3 / 832

冷

REI, tsume(tai) cold　**hi(eru)** get cold
hi(yasu) cool, refrigerate　**hi(yakasu)**
banter, tease; window-shop, browse;
cool in water or ice　**hi(ya)** cold water/
saké/rice　**sa(meru)** get cold, cool down
sa(masu) let cool; put a damper on

────────── 1 ──────────

4 冷込 **hi(e)ko(mu)** get colder/chilly
冷水 **reisui, hi(ya)mizu** cold water
冷水浴 **reisuiyoku** cold bath/shower
冷水摩擦 **reisui masatsu** rubdown with a
　　cold wet towel
5 冷奴 **hi(ya)yakko** iced tofu
6 冷気 **reiki** cold, chill, cold weather
冷肉 **reiniku** cold meat, cold cuts
冷汗 **hi(ya)ase, reikan** a cold sweat
冷光 **reikō** cold light, luminescence
冷血 **reiketsu** cold-blooded; coldhearted
冷血漢 **reiketsukan** coldhearted person
7 冷却 **reikyaku** cooling (off), refrigeration
冷却器 **reikyakuki** refrigerator, freezer,
　　cooler, (car) radiator
冷麦 **hi(ya)mugi** iced noodles
8 冷性 **hi(e)shō** oversensitivity to cold

冷房 **reibō** air conditioning
冷房車 **reibōsha** air-conditioned car
冷雨 **reiu** chilly rain
9 冷泉 **reisen** cold mineral springs
　　Reizei (emperor, 967–969)
10 冷凍 **reitō** freezing, refrigeration
冷凍肉 **reitōniku** frozen meat
冷凍車 **reitōsha** refrigerator car
冷凍食品 **reitō shokuhin** frozen foods
冷凍剤 **reitōzai** refrigerant
冷凍船 **reitōsen** refrigerator ship
冷凍魚 **reitōgyo** frozen fish
冷凍器 **reitōki** freezer
冷酒 **hi(ya)zake** cold saké
冷害 **reigai** cold-weather damage
冷笑 **reishō** derisive smile, scornful laugh,
　　sneer
11 冷遇 **reigū** cold reception/treatment
冷淡 **reitan** indifferent, apathetic; cold,
　　coldhearted
12 冷湿布 **reishippu** cold compress
冷然 **reizen** cold, indifferent, coldhearted
冷評 **reihyō** sarcasm, sneer
冷飯 **hi(ya)meshi** cold rice
13 冷戦 **reisen** cold war
冷罨法 **reianpō** cold compress/pack
14 冷静 **reisei** calm, cool, unruffled
冷酷 **reikoku** cruel, callous
15 冷蔵 **reizō** cold storage, refrigeration
冷蔵室 **reizōshitsu** cold-room, cold-storage
　　locker
冷蔵庫 **reizōko** refrigerator
冷罵 **reiba** sneer, abuse, revilement
17 冷厳 **reigen** grim, stark, stern

────────── 2 ──────────

4 水冷式 **suireishiki** water-cooled
7 肝冷 **kimo (o) hiya(su)** be startled/frightened
8 空冷式 **kūreishiki** air-cooled
底冷 **sokobi(e)** chilled to the bone
9 後冷泉 **Goreizei** (emperor, 1045–1068)
秋冷 **shūrei** the chill/cold of autumn
12 湯冷 **yuza(me)** after-bath chill
　　yuza(mashi) boiled water cooled for
　　drinking
寒冷 **kanrei** cold, chilly
寒冷前線 **kanrei zensen** cold front
13 寝冷 **nebi(e)** catching cold while sleeping
15 熱冷 **netsusa(mashi)** an antipyretic
16 燗冷 **kanza(mashi)** leftover warmed saké

2b5.4

冶

YA smelting; captivating

────────── 1 ──────────

8 冶金 **yakin** metallurgy

冶金学 **yakingaku** metallurgy

——————— 2 ———————
10 陶冶 **tōya** training, cultivation, education
17 鍛冶 **kaji** blacksmith
鍛冶屋 **kajiya** blacksmith

2b5.5 / 724

求

KYŪ, moto(meru/mu) want, seek, request, demand

——————— 1 ———————
2 求人 **kyūjin** seeking workers, Help Wanted
求人広告 **kyūjin kōkoku** help-wanted ad
4 求心力 **kyūshinryoku** centripetal force
6 求刑 **kyūkei** sentence sought (by prosecutor)
11 求道 **kyūdō** seeking after truth
求婚 **kyūkon** proposal of marriage
求婚者 **kyūkonsha** suitor
13 求愛 **kyūai** courting, courtship
18 求職 **kyūshoku** job hunting, Situation Wanted

——————— 2 ———————
7 希求 **kikyū** desire, seek, aspire to
8 追求 **tsuikyū, o(i)moto(meru)** pursue
9 要求 **yōkyū** require, demand
10 捜求 **saga(shi)moto(meru)** seek
11 探求 **tankyū** quest, pursuit
欲求 **yokkyū** wants, desires
欲求不満 **yokkyū fuman** frustration
15 請求 **seikyū** demand, request
請求書 **seikyūsho** application, claim, bill
請求額 **seikyūgaku** the amount claimed/billed
17 購求 **kōkyū** purchase

——————— 6 ———————
2b6.1

冽

RETSU cold; lonely

——————— 2 ———————
11 清冽 **seiretsu** clear, limpid

2b6.2

隷

TAI pursue; slave

2b6.3

函 凾

KAN, hako box

——————— 1 ———————
13 函数 **kansū** function (in math)
16 函館 **Hakodate** (city, Hokkaidō)

——————— 2 ———————
7 投函 **tōkan** mail (a letter)

——————— 3 ———————
3 三角函数 **sankaku kansū** trigonometric function

——————— 7 ———————

飛→ 0a9.4

——————— 8 ———————

2b8.1 / 1232

准

JUN quasi-, semi-, associate

——————— 1 ———————
3 准士官 **junshikan** warrant officer
7 准決勝 **junkesshō** semifinals
10 准将 **junshō** brigadier general; commodore
11 准尉 **jun'i** warrant officer

——————— 2 ———————
7 批准 **hijun** ratification
批准書 **hijunsho** instrument of ratification

2b8.2 / 1205

凍

TŌ, kō(ru), kogo(eru), shi(miru), i(teru) freeze (intr.) kō(rasu) freeze (tr.) kogo(eru) be frozen, be chilled

——————— 1 ———————
3 凍土 **tōdo** frozen soil, tundra
6 凍死 **tōshi, kogo(e)ji(nu), kogo(e)ji(ni)** freeze to death
凍死者 **tōshisha** person frozen to death
凍肉 **tōniku** frozen meat
10 凍原 **tōgen** frozen field, tundra
凍害 **tōgai** frost damage
12 凍結 **tōketsu** freeze
13 凍傷 **tōshō** frostbite, chilblains
15 凍瘡 **tōsō** frostbite, chilblains

——————— 2 ———————
4 不凍剤 **futōzai** antifreeze
不凍液 **futōeki** antifreeze
不凍港 **futōkō** ice-free port
7 冷凍 **reitō** freezing, refrigeration
冷凍肉 **reitōniku** frozen meat
冷凍車 **reitōsha** refrigerator car
冷凍食品 **reitō shokuhin** frozen foods
冷凍剤 **reitōzai** refrigerant
冷凍船 **reitōsen** refrigerator ship

冷凍魚 **reitōgyo** frozen fish
冷凍器 **reitōki** freezer

2b8.3 / 627

将 将

SHŌ commander, general
masa (ni) just about to, on the verge of

———————— 1 ————————

3 将士 **shōshi** officers and men
7 将来 **shōrai** future
将来性 **shōraisei** future, possibilities, prospects
将兵 **shōhei** officers and men
8 将卒 **shōsotsu** officers and men
将官 **shōkan** general, admiral
9 将軍 **shōgun** general, commander, shogun
将軍家 **shōgunke** family to inherit the shogunate
将軍職 **shōgunshoku** shogunate
将帥 **shōsui** commander
将星 **shōsei** general, commander
10 将校 **shōkō** (commissioned) officer
12 将棋 **shōgi** *shōgi*, Japanese chess
将棋倒 **shōgidao(shi)** falling like a row of dominoes
将棋盤 **shōgiban** *shōgi* board, chessboard

———————— 2 ————————

3 大将 **taishō** general; admiral; head, leader, boss
大将軍 **taishōgun** generalissimo
女将 **joshō, okami** landlady, proprietress
4 中将 **chūjō** lieutenant general; vice-admiral
少将 **shōshō** major general, rear admiral
5 尼将軍 **ama shōgun** woman general
主将 **shushō** commander-in-chief; captain (of a team)
冬将軍 **Fuyu Shōgun** Gen. Winter, Jack Frost
6 老将 **rōshō** old general
名将 **meishō** famous commander
8 武将 **bushō** military commander
9 飛将棋 **to(bi)shōgi** halma
勇将 **yūshō** brave general
軍将 **gunshō** army commander
首将 **shushō** commander-in-chief
挟将棋 **hasa(mi) shōgi** (a piece-capturing board game)
10 准将 **junshō** brigadier general; commodore
部将 **bushō** a general
猛将 **mōshō** brave general, strong contender
鬼将軍 **onishōgun** brave/tough general
11 副将 **fukushō** adjutant general, second in command
強将 **kyōshō** strong/brave general
宿将 **shukushō** veteran general
敗将 **haishō** defeated general
13 賊将 **zokushō** insurgent army leader

15 敵将 **tekishō** enemy general
18 闘将 **tōshō** brave fighter/leader

———————— 3 ————————

8 青大将 **aodaishō** (a nonpoisonous green snake)
14 総大将 **sōdaishō** commander-in-chief

———————— 4 ————————

8 征夷大将軍 **seii taishōgun** general in command of expeditionary forces to subjugate the barbarians
15 餓鬼大将 **gaki-daishō** dominant child among playmates

2b8.4

凄 凄

SEI, **sugo(i), susa(majii)** awful, tremendous, terrible, enormous
sugo(mu) threaten

———————— 1 ————————

4 凄文句 **sugomonku** menacing language
8 凄味 **sugomi** dreadfulness, ghastliness, weirdness
11 凄惨 **seisan** ghastly, gruesome, lurid
12 凄絶 **seizetsu** ghastly, gruesome
13 凄愴 **seisō** desolate, dreary
19 凄艶 **seien** bewitchingly beautiful

———————— 2 ————————

8 物凄 **monosugo(i)** awful, terrific, tremendous

2b8.5

凌

RYŌ, **shino(gu)** withstand; stave off, keep out; tide over, pull through; surpass, outdo

———————— 1 ————————

10 凌辱 **ryōjoku** insult, affront; rape
12 凌雲 **ryōun** rising high
15 凌駕 **ryōga** surpass, excel, outdo

———————— 2 ————————

3 口凌 **kuchishino(gi)** hand-to-mouth living
12 暑凌 **atsu(sa)shino(gi)** relief from the heat

———————— 3 ————————

8 其場凌 **so(no)ba-shino(gi)** makeshift, muddling through
退屈凌 **taikutsu-shino(gi)** killing time

凉 → 涼 **3a8.31**

2b8.6

凋 凋

CHŌ, **shibo(mu)** wither, wilt

———————— 1 ————————

12 凋落 **chōraku** wither, decline, wane

2

亻
彳
孑
阝
卩
刂
力
又
宀
亠
艹
⺣
⺮
丶
厂
辶
門
八
匸

2

→ 9

イ 冫 子 阝 卩 力 又 一 亠 十 ヒ ㄏ 厂 辶 冂 几 匸

涸 → 涸 **3a8.36**

━━━━━━━━━ 9 ━━━━━━━━━

2b9.1

毬

KYŪ, iga burr mari ball

━━━━━━━━━ 1 ━━━━━━━━━

7 毬投 marina(ge) play ball/catch
8 毬果 kyūka (pine) cone
10 毬栗 igaguri chestnuts in burrs
毬栗頭 igaguri atama close-cropped head, burr haircut
19 毬藻 marimo aegagropila

━━━━━━━━━ 2 ━━━━━━━━━

4 手毬 temari (traditional cloth) handball
手毬歌 temari uta handball song
8 松毬 matsukasa pinecone

━━━━━━━━━ 10 ━━━━━━━━━

2b10.1

馮

HYŌ displeasure FŪ (proper name)

━━━━━━━━━ 11 ━━━━━━━━━

奬 → **3n10.4**

斟 → **0a13.5**

━━━━━━━━━ 13 ━━━━━━━━━

2b13.1

凛 凜

RIN cold; chilling

━━━━━━━━━ 1 ━━━━━━━━━

3 凛々 rinrin severe, intense, biting; awe-inspiring riri(shii) gallant, imposing

12 凛然 rinzen(taru) awe-inspiring, commanding

━━━━━━━━━ 14 ━━━━━━━━━

2b14.1 / 1518

凝

GYŌ, ko(ru) get stiff; be absorbed in, be a fanatic; to elaborate ko(tta) elaborate, exquisite ko(rasu) concentrate, devote, apply, strain kogo(ru) congeal, freeze shiko(ru) stiffen, harden

━━━━━━━━━ 1 ━━━━━━━━━

5 凝立 gyōritsu stand absolutely still
6 凝血 gyōketsu coagulated blood, bloot clot
7 凝乳 gyōnyū curdled milk, curds
8 凝固 gyōko solidify, congeal, coagulate
ko(ri)kata(maru) coagulate; be fanatical
凝固点 gyōkoten freezing point
凝性 ko(ri)shō single-minded enthusiasm, fastidiousness
10 凝脂 gyōshi solidified fat; beautiful white skin
11 凝視 gyōshi stare, steady gaze, fixation
12 凝着 gyōchaku adhesion
凝結 gyōketsu coagulation, curdling, settling, congealing, freezing, condensation, solidification
凝集 gyōshū cohesion, condensation, agglutination
凝集力 gyōshūryoku cohesive force, cohesion
13 凝滞 gyōtai delay
凝塊 gyōkai a clot
17 凝縮 gyōshuku condensation
20 凝議 gyōgi deliberation, consultation

━━━━━━━━━ 2 ━━━━━━━━━

12 煮凝 nikogo(ri) jellied/congealed fish (broth)

蟞 → **3p15.1**

━━━━━━━━━ 子 2c ━━━━━━━━━

子	子	了	孔	孕	存	孜	孚	孝	丞	孟	孥	承
0.1	0.2	0.3	1.1	2.1	3.1	4.1	4.2	2k4.3	4.3	5.1	5.2	0a7.7

孩	孤	香	孫	孵	學	孺
6.1	6.2	6.3	7.1	3n10.5	3n4.2	14.1

─────────── 0 ───────────

2c0.1 / 103

子
SHI, SU child; (male name suffix)
ko child, offspring; (female name suffix)
ne first horary sign (rat)

─────────── 1 ───────────

3 子々孫々 **shishi-sonson** descendants, posterity
子女 **shijo** children
4 子午線 **shigosen** the meridian
子午環 **shigokan** meridian circle
子分 **kobun** follower, protégé, henchman, hanger-on
6 子会社 **kogaisha** a subsidiary
子守 **komori** baby tending/sitting; nursemaid, baby sitter
子守歌 **komoriuta** lullaby
7 子弟 **shitei** children
子沢山 **kodakusan** many children (in the family)
子役 **koyaku** child's role; child actor/actress
8 子供 **kodomo** child
　　 kodomo(rashii) childlike
子供心 **kodomogokoro** a child's mind/heart
子供好 **kodomozu(ki)** fond of children
子供扱 **kodomoatsuka(i)** treating (someone) like a child
子供向 **kodomomu(ki)** for children
子供服 **kodomofuku** children's wear
子供部屋 **kodomo-beya** children's room, nursery
子供騙 **kodomodama(shi)** childish trick
子宝 **kodakara** the treasure that is children
9 子孫 **shison** descendants
子持 **komo(chi)** a mother, maternity; pregnancy
子音 **shiin** consonant
10 子宮 **shikyū** the uterus, womb
子宮口 **shikyūkō** the cervix
子宮炎 **shikyūen** uteritis
子宮癌 **shikyūgan** cancer of the uterus
子株 **kokabu** new shares of stock
子殺 **kogoro(shi)** infanticide
子息 **shisoku** son
12 子葉 **shiyō** the first leaves of a sprouting seed, cotyledon
13 子煩悩 **kobonnō** fond of one's children
子福 **kobuku** blessed with many children
子福者 **kobukusha** person blessed with many children
子飼 **koga(i)** raising from infancy
14 子種 **kodane** issue, children, descendants
17 子爵 **shishaku** viscount
子癇 **shikan** eclampsia, pregnancy-caused convulsions

22 子嚢 **shinō** ascus, seed pod

─────────── 2 ───────────

1 一子 **isshi** a child; an only child
　　 hitorigo an only child
一子相伝 **isshi sōden** (secret) handed down from father to son
2 二子 **futago** twins, a twin
入子 **i(re)ko** nested boxes
子子孫孫 **shishi-sonson** descendants, posterity
3 三子 **mi(tsu)go** triplets; a three-year-old
才子 **saishi** talented/clever person
孔子 **Kōshi** Confucius (Chinese philosopher, 551–479 B.C.)
女子 **joshi** woman; women's **onna(no)-ko** girl **onago** girl, woman, maid
女子大生 **joshi daisei** a coed
4 太子 **taishi** crown prince
天子 **tenshi** the emperor
氏子 **ujiko** shrine parishoner
五子 **itsu(tsu)go** quintuplets
中子 **nakago** tang, blade; core
切子 **ki(ri)ko** facet
双子 **futago** twins, a twin
双子葉 **sōshiyō** dicotyledonous
分子 **bunshi** molecule; numerator; elements, faction
分子量 **bunshiryō** molecular weight
分子説 **bunshisetsu** molecular theory
公子 **kōshi** young nobleman
父子 **fushi** father and child
日子 **nisshi** (number of) days, time
王子 **ōji** prince
5 末子 **sue(k)ko, basshi, masshi** youngest child
甘子 **ama(ttarek)ko** spoiled child
母子 **boshi, hahako** mother and child
母子草 **hahakogusa** cottonweed
母子家庭 **boshi katei** fatherless home
母子寮 **boshiryō** home for mothers and children
申子 **mō(shi)go** child born in answer to one's prayers
冊子 **sasshi** booklet, pamphlet **sōshi** storybook
幼子 **osanago** little child, baby
布子 **nunoko** padded cotton clothes
穴子 **anago** conger eel
四子 **yo(tsu)go** quadruplets
白子 **shirako** milt, soft roe; albino **shiroko** albino **shirasu** young sardines
白子干 **shirasubo(shi)** dried young sardines
白子鳩 **shirakobato** collared dove
玉子 **tamago** egg
石子詰 **ishikozu(me)** execution by burying alive under stones

2

亻 冫 子 阝 卩 刂 力 又 一 十 卜 ⼍ ⼄ 厂 辶 冂 几 匚

目子勘定 **me(no)ko kanjō** measuring by eye; mental arithmetic

目子算 **me(no)kozan** measuring by eye; mental arithmetic

6 朱子学 **Shushigaku** teachings of the Confucian philosopher Zhuzi (1130–1200), Neo-Confucianism

年子 **toshigo** children (of the same mother) born within a year of each other

合子 **a(ino)ko** cross, hybrid, half-breed

次子 **jishi** second child

羽子板 **hagoita** battledore, pingpong-like paddle

孝子 **kōshi** dutiful/devoted child

老子 **Rōshi** Laozi, Lao-tzu (founder of Taoism)

寺子屋 **terakoya** temple primary school

光子 **kōshi** photon

因子 **inshi** factor (in math); gene

団子 **dango** dumpling

団子鼻 **dangobana** flat/pug nose

竹子 **take(no)ko** bamboo shoots

7 里子 **satogo** child put out to nurse, foster child

巫子 **miko** medium, sorceress; shrine maiden

孟子 **Mōshi** Mencius (Chinese philosopher, 372–289 B.C.)

卵子 **ranshi** ovum, egg cell

判子 **hanko** one's seal

弟子 **deshi, teishi** pupil, disciple, adherent, apprentice

弟子入 **deshii(ri)** becoming a pupil, entering an apprenticeship

臣子 **shinshi** retainer or child, retainers and children

赤子 **akago** baby　**sekishi** baby; subjects

君子 **kunshi** gentleman, wise man

芥子 **karashi** mustard　**keshi** poppy

芥子泥 **karashidei** mustard plaster

芥子菜 **karashina** mustard plant, rape

芥子粒 **keshitsubu** poppy seed; something tiny

芥子漬 **karashizu(ke)** mustard pickles

芸子 **geiko** geisha

売子 **u(rek)ko** popular person　**u(ri)ko** salesclerk

杓子 **shakushi** dipper, ladle, scoop

杓子定規 **shakushi-jōgi** hard-and-fast rule

利子 **rishi** interest (on a loan)

初子 **hatsugo** one's first child

男子 **danshi** man, male, boy, son　**otoko(no)ko** boy

男子用 **danshiyō** for men, men's

8 長子 **chōshi** eldest son; first child

刺子 **sa(shi)ko** quilted coat (worn in judo)

刷子 **sasshi, hake** brush

虎子 **tora (no) ko** tiger cub; one's treasure　**omaru** chamber pot, bedpan

迷子 **maigo, mayo(i)go** lost child

逆子 **sakago** breech baby/presentation

拍子 **hyōshi** time, tempo, beat; chance, moment

拍子木 **hyōshigi** wooden clappers

拍子抜 **hyōshinu(ke)** disappointment

担子 **tanshi** sedan-chair (carried on shoulders); load, cargo, baggage

担子胞子 **tanshi hōshi** basidiospore

担子菌類 **tanshi kinrui** basidiomycetes

呼子 **yo(bi)ko** (police) whistle

妻子 **saishi** wife and child(ren)

茄子 **nasu, nasubi** eggplant

実子 **jisshi** one's biological child

店子 **tanako** tenant

板子 **itago** floor planks (in a small boat)

金子 **kinsu** money, funds

9 孫子 **magoko** children and grandchildren, descendants

連子 **tsure(k)ko** child brought by a second wife/husband

連子窓 **renjimado** lattice window

風子 **kaze (no) ko** (children are) outdoor creatures

挺子 **teko** lever

独子 **hito(rik)ko, hito(ri)go** an only child

単子葉 **tanshiyō** monocotyledonous

面子 **mentsu** face, honor　**menko** cardboard game doll

柚子 **yuzu** citron

胞子 **hōshi** spore

皇子 **kōshi, ōji** imperial prince

砂子 **sunago** sand; gold/silver dust

思子 **omo(i)go** a favorite child

10 原子 **genshi** atom

原子力 **genshiryoku** atomic energy, nuclear power

原子力発電所 **genshiryoku hatsudensho** nuclear power plant

原子価 **genshika** valence

原子核 **genshikaku** atomic nucleus

原子病 **genshibyō** radiation sickness

原子量 **genshiryō** atomic weight

原子雲 **genshiun** atomic/mushroom cloud

原子爆弾 **genshi bakudan** atom bomb

逗子 **Zushi** (city, Kanagawa-ken)

遊子 **yūshi** wanderer, traveler

振子 **fu(ri)ko** pendulum

家子郎党 **ie(no)ko rōtō** one's followers

根子 **nekko** root; stump

格子 **kōshi** lattice, bars, grating, grille

格子戸 **kōshido** lattice door

格子造 **kōshi-zuku(ri)** latticework

格子窓 **kōshi mado** latticed window

格子縞 **kōshijima** checkered pattern
梃子 **teko** lever
骨子 **kosshi** bones; essentials, gist
教子 **oshi(e)go** one's (former) student, disciple
息子 **musuko** son
扇子 **sensu** folding fan
鬼子 **onigo** child born with teeth or dark hair; unruly child; child unlike its parents
鬼子母神 **Kishibojin, Kishimojin** (goddess of children)
紙子 **kamiko** paper garment
素子 **soshi** (electronic) element
馬子 **mago** passenger/pack horse tender
11 陽子 **yōshi** proton
亀子 **kame(no)ko** young turtle/tortoise
捻子 **neji** screw; (wind-up toy) spring
捨子 **su(te)go** abandoned child, foundling
捩子 **neji** screw; (wind-up toy) spring
帷子 **katabira** light kimono
張子 **ha(ri)ko** papier-mâché
菓子 **(o)kashi** candy, confection, pastry
菓子皿 **kashizara** cake plate
菓子屋 **kashiya** candy store, confectionery shop
菓子器 **kashiki** cake-serving bowl
庶子 **shoshi** illegitimate child
梯子 **hashigo** ladder; barhopping, pub-crawling
梯子車 **hashigosha** (firefighting) ladder truck
梯子乗 **hashigono(ri)** acrobatic ladder-top stunts
梯子段 **hashigodan** step, stair
梯子酒 **hashigozake** barhopping, pub-crawling
梔子 **kuchinashi** Cape jasmine, gardenia
黒子 **kuroko** black-clad stagehand
  kokushi (facial) mole; miniscule thing
  hokuro (facial) mole
組子 **ku(mi)ko** member of a squad (of firemen)
粒子 **ryūshi** (atomic) particle; grain (in film)
12 厨子 **zushi** miniature shrine
揚子江 **Yōsukō** the Yangtze/Yangzi river
帽子 **bōshi** hat, cap
帽子屋 **bōshiya** hat shop
御子 **miko** child of the king/emperor
落子 **o(toshi)go** illegitimate child
椰子 **yashi** palm/coconut tree
椅子 **isu** chair, seat, couch
量子 **ryōshi** quantum
量子論 **ryōshiron** quantum theory
硝子 **garasu** glass
童子 **dōji** child, boy
筋子 **sujiko** salmon roe

貰子 **mora(i)go** adoption; adopted child
間子 **ai(no)ko** a cross between, halfbreed
13 障子 **shōji** sliding door with translucent paper panes
障子紙 **shōjigami** shōji paper
隠子 **kaku(shi)go** illegitimate child
勢子 **seko** beater (on a hunt)
義子 **gishi** adopted child
嗣子 **shishi** heir
獅子 **shishi** lion
獅子王 **shishiō** the king of beasts
獅子吼 **shishiku** lion's roar; impassioned speech
獅子身中虫 **shishi-shinchū (no) mushi** treacherous friend
獅子鼻 **shishibana, shishi(p)pana** pug nose
獅子舞 **shishimai** lion-mask dance
獅子奮迅 **shishi funjin** great power and speed
獅子頭 **shishigashira** lion-head mask
楊子江 **Yōsukō** the Yangzi/Yangtze river
腹子 **harako** fish eggs
数子 **kazu(no)ko** herring roe
碍子 **gaishi** insulator
裸子植物 **rashi shokubutsu** gymnospermous plant
継子 **keishi** stepchild
賊子 **zokushi** rebel, traitor; rebellious child
鉗子 **kanshi** forceps
雉子 **kiji, kigisu** pheasant
電子 **denshi** electron
電子レンジ **denshi renji** microwave oven
電子工学 **denshi kōgaku** electronics
電子式 **denshishiki** electronic
14 遺子 **ishi** posthumous child; orphan
鳴子 **naruko** clapper
嫡子 **chakushi** legitimate child
様子 **yōsu** situation, aspect, appearance
骰子 **sai** dice
憎子 **niku(marek)ko** bad/naughty boy
端子 **tanshi** (electrical) terminal
種子 **shushi** seed, pit
種子島 **tane(ga)shima** matchlock gun, harquebus **Tanegashima** (island, Kagoshima-ken)
綸子 **rinzu** figured satin
精子 **seishi** sperm
踊子 **odo(ri)ko** dancer, dancing girl
15 舞子 **maiko** dancing girl
養子 **yōshi, yashina(i)go** adopted child
養子先 **yōshisaki** one's adopted home
養子縁組 **yōshi engumi** adopting an heir
撫子 **nadeshiko** a pink, a baby's breath
暴子 **aba(rek)ko** unruly child
緞子 **donsu** damask
諸子 **shoshi** you all
調子 **chōshi** tone; mood; condition

2
イ
冫
子 0 ←
阝
卩
刂
力
又
宀
亠
十
ト
勹
ソ
厂
辶
冂
几
匸

2

亻 冫 →0 子 阝 卩 刂 力 又 宀 亠 十 卜 夂 冖 厂 辶 冂 几 匚

調子付 **chōshizu(ku)** warm up to, be elated by, be in high spirits
調子外 **chōshihazu(re)** discord, out of tune
調子者 **chōshimono** person easily elated
餃子 **gyōza** potsticker (pan-fried dumplings stuffed with minced pork and vegetables)
16 親子 **oyako, shinshi** parent and child
親子丼 **oyako donburi** bowl of rice topped with chicken and egg
鍵子 **kagi(k)ko** latchkey child (who carries a key to school because no one will be home when he returns)
17 螺子 **neji** screw; stopcock; (wind-up) spring
簀子 **su(no)ko** rough-woven mat; slat curtain/blind
餡子 **anko** bean jam
18 織子 **o(ri)ko** weaver, textile worker
20 繻子 **shusu** satin
21 囃子 **hayashi** (percussion) accompaniment
櫺子 **renji** latticework
26 鑷子 **sesshi** forceps, tweezers

———————— 3 ————————

1 一人子 **hitorikko, hitorigo** an only child
2 二拍子 **nibyōshi** double/two-part time
又弟子 **matadeshi** indirect pupil, disciple of a disciple
八王子 **Hachiōji** (city, Tōkyō-to)
3 三拍子 **sanbyōshi** triple time (in music); three important requisites, triple-threat
干菓子 **higashi** dry candies
上調子 **uwachōshi, uwajōshi** high pitch, higher key **uwa(t)chōshi** flippant, frivolous, shallow
土団子 **tsuchidango** mud pie
小冊子 **shōsasshi** booklet, pamphlet
小楊子 **koyōji** toothpick
山梔子 **kuchinashi** Cape jasmine, gardenia
士君子 **shikunshi** man of learning and virtue, gentleman
4 内弟子 **uchideshi** apprentice living in his master's home
中性子 **chūseishi** neutron
中間子 **chūkanshi** meson
手拍子 **tebyōshi** beating time; carelessly
父無子 **chichina(shi)go, tetena(shi)go** fatherless/illegitimate child
水菓子 **mizugashi** fruit
犬張子 **inuha(ri)ko** papier-mâché dog
引菓子 **hi(ki)gashi** ornamental gift cakes
戸障子 **toshōji** doors and shōji (translucent-paper-paned sliding doors)
5 出格子 **degōshi** projecting lattice, latticed bay window
本調子 **honchōshi** proper key (of an instrument); one's regular form

生息子 **kimusuko** unsophisticated young man
生菓子 **namagashi** unbaked cake
氷菓子 **kōrigashi** a frozen sweet
打菓子 **u(chi)gashi** molded confections
兄弟子 **anideshi** senior fellow student/apprentice
好男子 **kōdanshi** handsome man
白拍子 **shirabyōshi** female dancer (historical); prostitute
立太子 **rittaishi** investiture of the crown prince
立太子式 **rittaishi-shiki** investiture of the crown prince
6 江戸子 **Edo(k)ko** true Tōkyōite
名調子 **meichōshi** eloquence
光梃子 **hikari teko** optical lever
牝獅子 **mejishi** lioness
7 伽草子 **(o)togizōshi** fairy-tale book
没食子 **mosshokushi, bosshokushi** gallnut
赤茄子 **akanasu** tomato
乱調子 **ranchōshi** discord, disorder, confusion; wild (market) fluctuations
乳呑子 **chinomigo** suckling child, infant
乳飲子 **chino(mi)go** suckling infant, babe in arms
村夫子 **sonpūshi** educated person in the country
快男子 **kaidanshi** agreeable/straightforward chap
私生子 **shiseishi** illegitimate child
車椅子 **kurumaisu** wheelchair
足拍子 **ashibyōshi** beating time with one's foot
8 長椅子 **nagaisu** sofa, couch
直弟子 **jikideshi** immediate pupil, direct disciple
油障子 **aburashōji** translucent oilpapered sliding doors
妻格子 **tsumagōshi** latticework
突拍子 **toppyōshi (mo nai)** out of tune, exorbitant, very
板硝子 **itagarasu** plate glass
炉格子 **rogōshi** (furnace) grate
炒玉子 **i(ri)tamago** scrambled eggs
和菓子 **wagashi** Japanese-style confections
金杓子 **kanajakushi** metal ladle, dipper
9 発電子 **hatsudenshi** armature
孫弟子 **magodeshi** one's disciples' disciples
美男子 **bidanshi, binanshi** handsome man
風信子 **fūshinshi** hyacinth
浮塵子 **unka** leafhopper, rice insect
洋菓子 **yōgashi** Western candies
茹玉子 **yu/u(de)tamago** boiled egg
茶菓子 **chagashi** teacakes
相弟子 **aideshi** fellow pupil/apprentice
皇太子 **kōtaishi** crown prince

10 陰電子 **indenshi** negatron, electron
高調子 **takachōshi** high pitch; rising stockmarket tone
消息子 **shōsokushi** (surgical) probe
案山子 **kakashi** scarecrow; figurehead
唐辛子 **tōgarashi** cayenne/red pepper
唐獅子 **kara shishi** lion
烏帽子 **eboshi** noble's court headgear
夏帽子 **natsubōshi** summer/straw hat
竜落子 **tatsu (no) o(toshi)go** sea horse
素粒子 **soryūshi** (subatomic) particle
11 偽君子 **gikunshi, nisekunshi** hypocrite, snob
陽電子 **yōdenshi** positron
婦女子 **fujoshi** woman; woman and child
異分子 **ibunshi** foreign elements, outsider
盛菓子 **mo(ri)gashi** cakes heaped in a basket
船梯子 **funabashigo** gangway
釣梯子 **tsu(ri)bashigo** rope ladder
12 婿養子 **muko-yōshi** son-in-law adopted as an heir
蒸菓子 **mu(shi)gashi** steamed cake
焼団子 **ya(ki)dango** toasted dumpling
無利子 **murishi** non-interest-bearing
黍団子 **kibidango** millet-flour dumpling
貴公子 **kikōshi** young noble
13 煎玉子 **i(ri)tamago** scrambled eggs
微分子 **bibunshi** particle, atom, molecule
微粒子 **biryūshi** tiny particle, fine-grained
蓖麻子油 **himashiyu** castor oil
寝椅子 **neisu** sofa, lounge chair
愛弟子 **manadeshi** favorite pupil
鉄格子 **tetsugōshi** iron bars, grating
電機子 **denkishi** armature
14 遺伝子 **idenshi** gene
遺伝子工学 **idenshi kōgaku** genetic engineering
嫡出子 **chakushutsushi** legitimate child
綿帽子 **watabōshi** bride's silk-floss veil
綱梯子 **tsunabashigo** rope ladder
銀砂子 **ginsunago** silver dust
駄々子 **dada(k)ko** peevish/spoiled child
駄菓子 **dagashi** cheap candy
駄駄子 **dada(k)ko** peevish/spoiled child
15 膝拍子 **hizabyōshi** beating time on one's knee
縄梯子 **nawabashigo** rope ladder
16 整流子 **seiryūshi** commutator
親分子分 **oyabun-kobun** boss and underlings
親無子 **oyana(shi)go** orphan
18 藪柑子 **seiryūshi** commutator
槟榔子 **binrōji** betel palm tree
覆面子 **fukumenshi** anonymous writer
襖障子 **fusuma shōji** opaque paper sliding door
21 籐椅子 **tōisu** rattan/wickerwork chair

────── 4 ──────

1 一人息子 **hitori musuko** an only son

一本調子 **ipponchōshi, ipponjōshi** monotony
3 大和撫子 **Yamato nadeshiko** daughter/woman of Japan
4 五人囃子 **goninbayashi** five court-musician dolls
5 圧着端子 **atchaku tanshi** crimp contact
6 安楽椅子 **anraku isu** easy chair
尖鋭分子 **sen'ei bunshi** radical elements
8 放蕩息子 **hōtō musuko** prodigal son
担子胞子 **tanshi hōshi** basidiospore
9 浮世草子 **ukiyozōshi** realistic novel (Edo period)
11 道楽息子 **dōraku musuko** prodigal son
13 腰高障子 **koshidaka shōji** sliding door with hip-high paneling
14 遺伝子組替 **idenshi kumika(e)** recombinant gene splicing
構成分子 **kōsei bunshi** components
19 繰出梯子 **ku(ri)da(shi)bashigo** extension ladder

2c0.2

子 **KETSU, GETSU** be left over, remain; alone; mosquito larva; halberd

────── 1 ──────

3 孑々 **ketsuketsu, getsugetsu** standing alone
bōfura mosquito larva

2c0.3 / 941

了 **RYŌ** complete, finish; understand

────── 1 ──────

7 了承 **ryōshō** acknowledge, understand
了見 **ryōken** idea; intention; decision, discretion; forgive
8 了知 **ryōchi** understand, appreciate
13 了解 **ryōkai** understand, comprehend; Roger!
18 了簡 **ryōken** idea; intention; decision, discretion; forgive
了簡違 **ryōkenchiga(i)** mistaken idea; an imprudence

────── 2 ──────

5 未了 **miryō** unfinished
7 完了 **kanryō** complete, finish, conclude
完了形 **kanryōkei** perfect tense
10 修了 **shūryō** completion (of a course)
校了 **kōryō** proofreading completed
11 終了 **shūryō** end, conclusion, completion, expiration
訳了 **yakuryō** finish translating
12 満了 **manryō** expiration

2

亻
冫
子 0←
阝
卩
刂
力
又
亠
宀
冖
厶
⺈
厂
辶
冂
几
匸

結了 **ketsuryō** end, be completed
14 読了 **dokuryō** finish reading
15 魅了 **miryō** charm, captivate, hold spellbound
20 議了 **giryō** finish discussion, close debate

——————— 3 ———————
13 暗黙了解 **anmoku (no) ryōkai** tacit understanding

——————— 4 ———————
5 未来完了 **mirai kanryō** future perfect tense
11 過去完了 **kako kanryō** past perfect tense

——————— 1 ———————

2c1.1 / 940

孔 **KŌ, KU** hole; Confucius; huge
ana hole

——————— 1 ———————
2 孔子 **Kōshi** Confucius (Chinese philosopher, 551–479 B.C.)
5 孔穴 **kōketsu** hole
7 孔孟 **Kō-Mō** Confucius and Mencius
8 孔門 **Kōmon** the Confucian school
11 孔雀 **kujaku** peacock

——————— 2 ———————
4 毛孔 **keana** pores
6 多孔 **takō** porous, open (weave)
多孔性 **takōsei** porosity
気孔 **kikō** pores, stomata
有孔質 **yūkōshitsu** porous
10 穿孔 **senkō** perforation; punching, boring
穿孔機 **senkōki** perforator, drill, (key)punch
11 眼孔 **gankō** eyehole; eye socket
細孔 **saikō** small hole, pore
14 鼻孔 **bikō** nostril
17 瞳孔 **dōkō** pupil (of the eye)
23 鑽孔機 **sankōki** boring machine

——————— 3 ———————
9 通気孔 **tsūkikō** vent, air hole
通風孔 **tsūfūkō** vent, air hole
12 覘視孔 **tenshikō** peephole

——————— 2 ———————

2c2.1

孕 **YŌ, hara(mu)** become pregnant; be filled with

——————— 3 ———————

2c3.1 / 269

存 **SON, ZON** be, exist

——————— 1 ———————
0 存じる **zon(jiru)** know, be aware of; think, feel

存する **son(suru)** exist, remain; retain
3 存亡 **sonbō** life or death
4 存分 **zonbun (ni)** to one's heart's content, as much as one wants, without reserve
5 存生 **zonjō** be alive
存外 **zongai** contrary to expectations; beyond expectations
存立 **sonritsu** existence, subsistence
6 存在 **sonzai** exist
存在論 **sonzairon** ontology
7 存否 **sonpi** existence, whether alive or dead
8 存念 **zonnen** thought, idea, concept
存命 **zonmei** be alive
12 存廃 **sonpai** continuation or abolition, existence
13 存置 **sonchi** retain, maintain
存続 **sonzoku** continued existence, duration

——————— 2 ———————
1 一存 **ichizon** at one's own discretion
5 生存 **seizon** existence, life, survival
生存者 **seizonsha** survivor
生存権 **seizonken** right to live
6 共存 **kyōson, kyōzon** coexistence
自存 **jison** exist of itself
8 依存 **ison, izon** depend on, be dependent on
並存 **heizon** coexistence
実存 **jitsuzon** existence
実存主義 **jitsuzon shugi** existentialism
所存 **shozon** thought, opinion
9 保存 **hozon** preservation
恒存 **kōzon** conservation (of energy)
思存分 **omo(u) zonbun** as much as one pleases
10 既存 **kison** existing
残存 **zanzon, zanson** survive, remain
残存者 **zansonsha** survivor, holdover
11 現存 **genson, genzon** living, existing, extant
異存 **izon** objection
12 温存 **onzon** keep, preserve, retain
御存 **gozon(ji)** (as) you know
15 賦存 **fuson** existence, presence (of resources)
17 厳存 **genson** exist; be in full force

——————— 3 ———————
4 不所存 **fushozon** imprudence, indiscretion
6 危急存亡 **kikyū-sonbō** life-or-death situation, crisis

——————— 4 ———————
13 適者生存 **tekisha seizon** survival of the fittest

——————— 4 ———————

2c4.1

孜 **SHI** industrious

——————— 1 ———————
3 孜々 **shishi (to shite)** assiduously, diligently

2c4.2

孚   FU sincere; nourish; wrap, encase

――――― 1 ―――――
4 孚化 **fuka** hatch, incubate (eggs)

孝→ **2k4.3**

2c4.3

丞   JŌ, SHŌ help

――――― 5 ―――――

2c5.1

孟   MŌ beginning; leader; Mencius

――――― 1 ―――――
2 孟子 **Mōshi** Mencius (Chinese philosopher, 372–289 B.C.)
――――― 2 ―――――
3 孔孟 **Kō-Mō** Confucius and Mencius

2c5.2

孥   DO child; wife and children; servant, slave

――――― 1 ―――――
15 孥戮 **doriku** executing wife and children together with the criminal

承→ **0a7.7**

――――― 6 ―――――

2c6.1

孩   GAI baby, infant

2c6.2 / 1480

孤   KO alone; orphan

――――― 1 ―――――
3 孤山 **kozan** lone mountain

5 孤立 **koritsu** be isolated
6 孤帆 **kohan** solitary sailboat
孤灯 **kotō** a solitary light
孤舟 **koshū** a single/solitary boat
7 孤児 **koji, minashigo** orphan
孤児院 **kojiin** orphanage
9 孤軍 **kogun** isolated/unsupported army
孤城 **kojō** isolated/besieged castle
孤独 **kodoku** solitary, isolated, lonely
孤客 **kokaku, kokyaku** a lone traveler
10 孤高 **kokō** splendid/proud isolation, aloofness
孤島 **kotō** solitary/desert island
15 孤影 **koei** a lone figure

――――― 2 ―――――
14 遺孤 **iko** orphan

2c6.3

盉   KIN cup

――――― 7 ―――――

2c7.1 / 910

孫   SON descendants; **mago** grandchild

――――― 1 ―――――
2 孫子 **magoko** children and grandchildren, descendants
4 孫手 **mago(no)te** back scratcher
孫引 **magobi(ki)** quoting secondhand, reference to secondary sources
7 孫弟子 **magodeshi** one's disciples' disciples
10 孫娘 **magomusume** granddaughter
――――― 2 ―――――
2 子孫 **shison** descendants
4 天孫 **tenson** descendant of the gods
7 児孫 **jison** children and grandchildren, descendants
初孫 **uimago, hatsumago** one's first grandchild
9 皇孫 **kōson** imperial grandchild/descendant
11 曽孫 **sōson, hiimago, himago** great-grandchild
13 愛孫 **aison** beloved grandchild
14 嫡孫 **chakuson** eldest son of one's son and heir
――――― 3 ―――――
2 子々孫々 **shishi-sonson** descendants, posterity
9 皇太孫 **kōtaison** emperor's eldest direct-line grandson
――――― 4 ―――――
2 子子孫孫 **shishi-sonson** descendants, posterity

— 10 —

孵→ **3n10.5**

— 13 —

學→学 **3n4.2**

— 14 —

2c14.1

孺 JU young child

┌ **2d** ──────────────

阡	防	阯	阬	阮	阪	陁	那	邦	邯	阻	阼	陂
3.1	4.1	3b4.3	4.2	4.3	4.4	4.5	4.6	4.7	4a3.11	5.1	5.2	5.3
附	陀	阿	邯	邪	邱	邸	邵	限	陏	陌	陋	郎
5.4	5.5	5.6	5.7	5.8	5.9	5.10	5.11	6.1	6.2	6.3	6.4	6.5
郁	郛	郊	陣	陏	陜	陝	陞	陛	降	陟	院	除
6.6	6.7	6.8	7.1	7.2	7.3	7.4	7.5	7.6	7.7	7.8	7.9	7.10
陷	郎	郡	郢	郭	郤	陲	陳	陪	陸	陵	隆	陰
7.11	2d6.5	7.12	7.13	7.14	7.15	8.1	8.2	8.3	8.4	8.5	8.6	8.7
険	陥	阪	随	陶	郵	都	郷	部	隅	隈	隋	隍
8.8	2d7.11	8.9	8.10	8.11	8.12	8.13	8.14	8.15	9.1	9.2	9.3	9.4
陽	階	隆	隊	郷	都	鄂	隗	隔	隕	隙	隘	郷
9.5	9.6	2d8.6	9.7	2d8.14	2d8.13	9.8	10.1	10.2	10.3	10.4	10.5	2d8.14
鄒	隙	際	障	隠	鄙	隨	隧	鄧	鄯	鄭	鄲	
10.6	2d10.4	11.1	11.2	11.3	11.4	2d8.10	12.1	12.2	12.3	2d12.4	12.4	12.5
隣	鄰	険	隰	隱	隴	隴						
13.1	2d13.1	2d8.8	14.1	2d11.3	14.2	16.1						

— 3 —

2d3.1

阡 SEN thousand; north-south path between paddies

— 1 —

8 阡陌 **senpaku** paths between paddies

— 4 —

2d4.1 / 513

防 BŌ protect against, prevent; (as prefix) anti-, -proof, -resistant **fuse(gu)** defend, protect against, prevent, resist

— 1 —

2 防人 **sakimori** soldiers garrisoned in Kyūshū (historical)

4 防止 **bōshi** prevention

防水 **bōsui** waterproof, watertight; flooding prevention

防水布 **bōsuifu** waterproof cloth, tarpaulin, oilskin

防火 **bōka** fire prevention, fire fighting, fireproof

防火戸 **bōkado** fire door

防火用水 **bōka yōsui** water for putting out fires

防火栓 **bōkasen** fire hydrant

防火壁 **bōkaheki** fire wall

5 防犯 **bōhan** crime prevention

6 防共 **bōkyō** anticommunist

防守 **bōshu** defense, the defensive

防虫剤 **bōchūzai** insecticide

7 防材 **bōzai** boom, fender (to block a harbor entrance)

8 防毒 **bōdoku** anti-poison, gasproof

防毒面 **bōdokumen** gas mask

防波提 **bōhatei** breakwater

防空 **bōkū** air defense

防空壕 **bōkūgō** air-raid/bomb shelter

9 防風 **bōfū** protection/shelter against the wind

防風林 **bōfūrin** windbreak (forest)
防砂林 **bōsarin** trees planted to arrest shifting sand
防砂提 **bōsatei** barricade to arrest shifting sand
防音 **bōon** sound-deadening, soundproof(ing)
防臭 **bōshū** deodorization
防臭剤 **bōshūzai** deodorant, deodorizer
防疫 **bōeki** prevention of epidemics
11 防雪 **bōsetsu** protect against snow
防雪林 **bōsetsurin** snowbreak (forest)
12 防備 **bōbi** defensive preparations
防湿 **bōshitsu** dampproof
防弾 **bōdan** bulletproof; bombproof
防御 **bōgyo** defense
防御率 **bōgyoritsu** earned run average
防寒 **bōkan** protection against the cold
防寒服 **bōkanfuku** winter/arctic clothes
防寒具 **bōkangu** cold-protection/arctic outfit
防寒靴 **bōkangutsu** arctic boots
13 防塞 **bōsai** roadblock, barricade
防戦 **bōsen** a defensive fight
14 防腐 **bōfu** preservation against decay
防腐剤 **bōfuzai** a preservative, antiseptic
防塵 **bōjin** dustproof
15 防蝕 **bōshoku** corrosion-resistant
防蝕剤 **bōshokuzai** an anticorrosive
16 防壁 **bōheki** barrier, bulwark
防衛 **bōei** defense
防衛庁 **Bōeichō** Defense Agency
防諜 **bōchō** counterintelligence
17 防禦 **bōgyo** defense
19 防蟻 **bōgi** termite-proof
20 防護 **bōgo** protection, custody

————————— 2 —————————
4 予防 **yobō** prevent, protect against
予防法 **yobōhō** precautionary measures
予防接種 **yobō sesshu** inoculation
予防策 **yobōsaku** precautionary measures
予防線張 **yobōsen (o) ha(ru)** guard against
予防薬 **yobōyaku** a preventive/prophylactic medicine
水防 **suibō** flood prevention
7 攻防 **kōbō** offense and defense
8 周防 **Suō** (ancient kuni, Yamaguchi-ken)
国防 **kokubō** national defense
国防色 **kokubōshoku** khaki
国防軍 **kokubōgun** national defense forces
国防費 **kokubōhi** defense expenditures
9 海防 **kaibō** coastal defense
砂防 **sabō** prevention of sand erosion
砂防林 **sabōrin** erosion-control forest
10 消防 **shōbō** fire fighting, firemen
消防士 **shōbōshi** fireman
消防隊 **shōbōtai** fire brigade

消防組 **shōbōgumi** fire brigade
消防署 **shōbōsho** fire station
破防法 **Habōhō** the Subversive Activities Prevention Law (short for 破壊活動防止法)
12 堤防 **teibō** embankment, dike, levee
無防備 **mubōbi** defenseless, unfortified
19 警防 **keibō** preserving order
警防団 **keibōdan** civil defense corps

————————— 3 —————————
4 水害防止 **suigai bōshi** flood prevention
5 正当防衛 **seitō bōei** legitimate self-defense

阯 → 址 3b4.3

2d4.2
阬 **KŌ** hole, pit; bury

2d4.3
阮 **GEN** (place name)

2d4.4
阪 **HAN** slope; embankment; Ōsaka
     saka slope

————————— 1 —————————
9 阪神 **Han-Shin** Ōsaka-Kōbe area

————————— 2 —————————
3 大阪 **Ōsaka** (city, Ōsaka-fu)
大阪府 **Ōsaka-fu** (prefecture)
8 京阪神 **Kei-Han-Shin** Kyōto-Ōsaka-Kōbe
松阪 **Matsuzaka** (city, Mie-ken)

2d4.5
阨 **YAKU** obstruct; distress
     AI narrow

2d4.6
那 那 **NA** what, which

————————— 1 —————————
4 那辺 **nahen** where, whither
19 那覇 **Naha** (city, Okinawa-ken)

————————— 2 —————————
4 支那 **Shina** China

2

亻
冫
孑
阝
阝 ← 4
刂
力
又
宀
亠
艹
勹
冖
丷
厂
辶
冂
八
匸

支那海 **Shinakai** the China Sea
5 旦那 **danna** master; husband; gentleman
旦那芸 **dannagei** amateurism
旦那様 **danna-sama** master; husband; gentleman
8 刹那 **setsuna** moment, instant
刹那主義 **setsuna shugi** living only for (the pleasures of) the moment
刹那的 **setsunateki** momentary, ephemeral
10 旃那 **senna** senna
17 檀那寺 **dannadera** one's family's temple

━━━━━━━ 3 ━━━━━━━

1 一刹那 **issetsuna** an instant, a moment
3 大旦那 **ōdanna** benefactor (of a temple); proprietor, man of the house
4 中支那 **Naka-Shina** central China
8 東支那海 **Higashi Shinakai** East China Sea
若旦那 **wakadanna** young master/gentleman
9 南支那海 **Minami Shinakai** the South China Sea

2d4.7 / 808

邦

HŌ country; our country
kuni country

━━━━━━━ 1 ━━━━━━━

2 邦人 **hōjin** fellow countryman; a Japanese
3 邦土 **hōdo** country, territory
4 邦文 **hōbun** Japanese language, vernacular
5 邦字 **hōji** Japanese characters
邦字新聞 **hōji shinbun** Japanese-language newspaper
8 邦画 **hōga** Japanese movie/painting
邦国 **hōkoku** country, nations
10 邦家 **hōka** one's country
11 邦域 **hōiki** country's borders/territory
邦訳 **hōyaku** translation into Japanese
邦貨 **hōka** Japanese currency; yen
13 邦楽 **hōgaku** (traditional) Japanese music
14 邦語 **hōgo** vernacular; Japanese language

━━━━━━━ 2 ━━━━━━━

3 万邦 **banpō** all nations
4 友邦 **yūhō** friendly nation, ally
8 東邦 **tōhō** an eastern country; the Orient
9 連邦 **renpō** federation; federal
11 異邦 **ihō** foreign country
異邦人 **ihōjin** foreigner, stranger
13 盟邦 **meihō** ally
15 隣邦 **rinpō** neighboring country

━━━━━━━ 3 ━━━━━━━

6 在外邦人 **zaigai hōjin** Japanese living abroad
在留邦人 **zairyū hōjin** Japanese residing abroad

郝 → 村 **4a3.11**

━━━━━━━ 5 ━━━━━━━

2d5.1 / 1085

阻

SO, haba(mu) obstruct, prevent, impede, block, hamper

━━━━━━━ 1 ━━━━━━━

4 阻止 **soshi** obstruct, hinder, deter, check
10 阻害 **sogai** impede, check, hinder, retard
12 阻隔 **sokaku** alienation, estrangement
13 阻塞気球 **sosai kikyū** barrage balloon

━━━━━━━ 2 ━━━━━━━

10 険阻 **kenso** steep
11 悪阻 **tsuwari, oso** morning sickness

2d5.2

阼

SO eastern stairway; throne

2d5.3

陂

HI, tsutsumi levee, embankment
HA hill, slope

2d5.4 / 1843

附

FU attached **tsu(ku)** be attached
tsu(keru) attach

━━━━━━━ 1 ━━━━━━━

12 附属 **fuzoku** attached, affiliated, ancillary

━━━━━━━ 2 ━━━━━━━

7 見附 **mitsuke** the approach to a castle gate
11 寄附 **kifu** contribution, donation
寄附行為 **kifu kōi** act of endowment, donation

2d5.5

陀

DA slanting

━━━━━━━ 2 ━━━━━━━

4 仏陀 **Butsuda, Budda** Buddha
7 吠陀 **Bēda** the Vedas
8 弥陀 **Mida** Amitabha
11 曼陀羅 **mandara** mandala, picture of Buddha
12 御陀仏 **odabutsu** dead man
16 頭陀袋 **zudabukuro** (pilgrim's) holdall-bag
5 加奈陀 **Kanada** Canada

—————— 3 ——————

7 阿弥陀 **Amida** Amida Buddha; lottery;
wearing a hat on the back of the head
阿弥陀経 **Amidakyō** the Sukhavati sutra
阿蘭陀 **Oranda** Holland

—————— 5 ——————

9 南無阿弥陀仏 **Namu Amida Butsu** Hail
Amida Buddha

2d5.6

阿 **A, O** (used phonetically)
omone(ru) be obsequious

—————— 1 ——————

4 阿片 **ahen** opium
阿片窟 **ahenkutsu** opium den
5 阿古屋貝 **akoyagai** pearl oyster
阿比 **abi** loon
6 阿多福 **otafuku** ugly/homely woman
7 阿呆 **ahō** fool, jackass
阿呆臭 **ahōkusa(i)** foolish, dumb, stupid
8 阿波 **Awa** (ancient kuni, Tokushima-ken)
阿弥陀 **Amida** Amida Buddha; lottery;
wearing a hat on the back of the head
阿弥陀経 **Amidakyō** the Sukhavati sutra
10 阿倍 **Abe** (surname)
阿部 **Abe** (surname)
11 阿亀 **okame** ugly/homely woman
阿婆擦 **abazu(re)** wicked woman, hussy
13 阿媽 **ama** amah, nurse
14 阿漕 **akogi** insatiable; cruel, harsh
阿鼻叫喚 **abikyōkan** (two of Buddhism's
eight hells)
16 阿諛 **ayu** flattery
19 阿蘇山 **Asosan** (mountain, Kumamoto-ken)
阿蘭陀 **Oranda** Holland
阿羅漢 **arakan** arhat

—————— 2 ——————

5 四阿 **azumaya** arbor, bower, gazebo

—————— 3 ——————

4 元木阿弥 **moto (no) mokuami** losing what
was gained, no better off
9 南無阿弥陀仏 **Namu Amida Butsu** Hail
Amida Buddha

2d5.7

邯 **KAN** (place name); tree cricket

—————— 1 ——————

14 邯鄲 **Kantan** (an ancient Chinese capital)
kantan tree cricket
邯鄲步 **Kantan (no) ayu(mi)** like the young
man who tried to learn how to walk

stylishly like the people in Kantan, gave
up his study before mastering it, and
forgot how to walk at all
邯鄲師 **kantanshi** bedroom thief
邯鄲夢 **Kantan (no) yume** vain dream of
splendor and wealth

2d5.8 / 1457

邪 邪 **JA** evil, unjust, wicked
yokoshima wicked, evil,
dishonest, unjust

—————— 1 ——————

4 邪心 **jashin** wicked heart, evil intent
5 邪正 **jasei** right and wrong
6 邪気 **jaki** miasma, noxious vapor; malice,
evil; a cold
邪曲 **jakyoku** wickedness, injustice
邪行 **jakō** wickedness; go diagonally
7 邪見 **jaken** wrong view
8 邪念 **janen** sinister intent, evil designs
邪法 **jahō** sorcery, witchcraft; heresy
邪知 **jachi** perverted talent, guile, cunning
邪宗 **jashū** heretical sect; evil (foreign)
religion
邪宗門 **jashūmon** heretical religion
9 邪神 **jashin** evil deity, demon, false god
10 邪険 **jaken** harsh, cruel
邪教 **jakyō** heretical religion, heathenism
邪鬼 **jaki** a devil, imp, evil spirit
11 邪道 **jadō** evil course; heresy
邪淫 **jain** lewdness, adultery, incest
邪推 **jasui** unjust suspicion, mistrust
邪婬 **jain** lewdness, adultery, incest
邪欲 **jayoku** evil/carnal passion
邪悪 **jaaku** wicked, malicious, sinister
14 邪説 **jasetsu** heretical doctrine
15 邪慾 **jayoku** evil/carnal passion
邪樫 **jaken** harsh, cruel
21 邪魔 **jama** hinder, obstruct, get in the way,
interfere, bother, disturb
邪魔者 **jamamono** person who gets in the
way
邪魔物 **jamamono** obstacle, impediment,
nuisance

—————— 2 ——————

4 天邪鬼 **amanojaku** devil being trampled by
temple guardian deities; a contrary/
cranky person
5 正邪 **seija** right and wrong
9 風邪 **kaze, fūja** a cold
風邪気 **kazeke, kaza(k)ke** a slight cold
風邪声 **kazagoe** hoarseness from a cold
風邪薬 **kazegusuri, kazagusuri** medicine/
remedy for a cold
10 破邪 **haja** defeating evil

破邪顕正 **haja-kenshō** smiting evil and spreading the truth
12 無邪気 **mujaki** innocent, ingenuous
———————— 3 ————————
14 鼻風邪 **hanakaze** head cold
———————— 4 ————————
6 多福風邪 **(o)tafuku kaze** mumps

2d5.9

邱 **KYŪ, oka** hill

2d5.10 / 563

邸 **TEI, yashiki** mansion, residence

———————— 1 ————————
4 邸内 **teinai** grounds, premises
6 邸宅 **teitaku** mansion, residence
———————— 2 ————————
4 公邸 **kōtei** official residence
5 本邸 **hontei** principal residence
7 別邸 **bettei** villa, separate residence
　私邸 **shitei** private residence
8 官邸 **kantei** official residence
18 藩邸 **hantei** daimyo's estate
———————— 3 ————————
12 御用邸 **goyōtei** imperial villa

2d5.11

邵 **SHŌ** (place name)

———————— 6 ————————

2d6.1 / 847

限 **GEN, kagi(ru)** limit, restrict
kagi(ri) limit(s); as far/much as possible; (as suffix) only; no later than

———————— 1 ————————
5 限外 **gengai** outside the limits, excess, extra
8 限定 **gentei** limit, qualify, modify; define, determine
　限定版 **genteiban** limited edition
9 限度 **gendo** limit
　限界 **genkai** limit, boundary; marginal; critical
12 限無 **kagi(ri)na(i)** boundless, endless, unlimited
———————— 2 ————————
4 分限 **bungen, bugen** social standing; wealthy man

分限者 **bugensha** wealthy man
日限 **nichigen** time limit, date, term
5 生限 **i(kiru) kagi(ri)** as long as life continues
6 年限 **nengen** term, length of time
有限 **yūgen** limited, finite **a(ru) kagi(ri)** as long as there is/are any
有限会社 **yūgen-gaisha** limited liability company, Ltd.
7 局限 **kyokugen** localize, limit
見限 **mikagi(ru)** abandon, forsake
8 制限 **seigen** restriction, limitation
刻限 **kokugen** time, appointed time
定限 **teigen** limit, restrict
門限 **mongen** closing time
10 時限 **jigen** time limit; time (bomb)
12 象限 **shōgen** quadrant
極限 **kyokugen** limit, extremity
期限 **kigen** term, period, due date, deadline
無限 **mugen** infinite
無限大 **mugendai** infinity
無限小 **mugenshō** infinitesimal
無限遠 **mugen'en** (focused) at infinity
13 際限 **saigen** limits, bounds, end
14 精限根限 **seikagi(ri)-konkagi(ri)** with all one's might
15 権限 **kengen** authority, power, jurisdiction
———————— 3 ————————
7 身代限 **shindaikagi(ri)** bankruptcy
8 其場限 **so(no)ba-kagi(ri)** makeshift, rough-and-ready
12 最大限 **saidaigen** maximum
　最大限度 **saidai gendo** maximum
　最小限 **saishōgen** minimum
　最小限度 **saishō gendo** minimum
　無制限 **museigen** unlimited, unrestricted
　無期限 **mukigen** indefinite, without time limit
———————— 4 ————————
8 服務年限 **fukumu nengen** tenure of office
14 精限根限 **seikagi(ri)-konkagi(ri)** with all one's might

2d6.2

陏 **DA** melon; wrap

2d6.3

陌 **HAKU** east-west path between paddies; road

———————— 2 ————————
5 阡陌 **senpaku** paths between paddies

2d6.4

陋 　RŌ　narrow; mean, base, lowly

────────── 1 ──────────
6 陋劣 **rōretsu** mean, base, low, nasty, sneaky
9 陋屋 **rōoku** squalid hut, hovel; my humble abode
11 陋習 **rōshū** evil practice/custom, abuse

────────── 2 ──────────
8 固陋 **korō** narrow-minded, hidebound, extremely conservative
9 卑陋 **hirō** despicable, vulgar

2d6.5 / 980

郎 郎 　RŌ　man; husband; (ending for male names)

────────── 1 ──────────
10 郎党 **rōtō, rōdō** vassals, retainers
12 郎等 **rōdō** vassals, retainers

────────── 2 ──────────
3 女郎 **jorō** prostitute
　女郎花 **ominaeshi** (a yellow-flowered plant)
　女郎屋 **jorōya** brothel
5 外郎 **uirō** (a rice-jelly confection)
11 野郎 **yarō** fellow, guy, bastard
13 新郎 **shinrō** bridegroom
　新郎新婦 **shinrō-shinpu** the bride and groom

────────── 3 ──────────
3 与太郎 **yotarō** fool, liar
10 家子郎党 **ie(no)ko rōtō** one's followers
11 悪太郎 **akutarō** bad/naughty boy
　雪女郎 **yukijorō** snow fairy

────────── 5 ──────────
1 一姫二太郎 **ichi-hime ni-Tarō** It's good to have a girl first and then a boy.

2d6.6

郁 　IKU　culturally advanced; fragrant

────────── 2 ──────────
18 馥郁 **fukuiku** fragrant, balmy

2d6.7

郛 　FU, kuruwa　earthwork enclosure around a castle

2d6.8 / 817

郊 　KŌ　suburbs; the country(side)

────────── 1 ──────────
5 郊外 **kōgai** suburbs, outskirts
11 郊野 **kōya** suburban fields

────────── 2 ──────────
6 西郊 **seikō** western suburbs
　近郊 **kinkō** suburbs
9 秋郊 **shūkō** fields in autumn
11 断郊競走 **dankō kyōsō** cross-country race

────────── 7 ──────────

2d7.1 / 1404

陣 　JIN　battle array, ranks; camp; brief time, sudden

────────── 1 ──────────
4 陣太鼓 **jindaiko** war drum
　陣中 **jinchū** in the field, at the front
5 陣立 **jinda(te)** battle array/formation
6 陣羽織 **jinbaori** sleeveless coat worn over armor
　陣列 **jinretsu** troop disposition, battle formation
　陣地 **jinchi** position, encampment
　陣地戦 **jinchisen** position/stationary warfare
7 陣没 **jinbotsu** be killed in action
　陣形 **jinkei** battle array/formation
8 陣取 **jindo(ru)** encamp, take up positions
9 陣風 **jinpū** squall, gust
　陣屋 **jin'ya** encampment
10 陣容 **jin'yō** battle array, lineup
11 陣笠 **jingasa** (ancient) soldier's helmet; rank and file (of a party)
12 陣営 **jin'ei** camp
　陣痛 **jintsū** labor (pains)
13 陣幕 **jinmaku** camp enclosure
16 陣頭 **jintō** at the head of an army

────────── 2 ──────────
4 内陣 **naijin** inner temple, sanctuary
　円陣 **enjin** (people standing in a) circle
　方陣 **hōjin** square formation, phalanx; magic square
5 出陣 **shutsujin** depart for the front
　本陣 **honjin** troop headquarters; daimyo's inn; stronghold
　布陣 **fujin** lineup, (troop) disposition
6 西陣 **nishijin** Nishijin brocade
　西陣織 **nishijin'o(ri)** Nishijin brocade
　先陣 **senjin** vanguard, advance guard
7 対陣 **taijin** encamp opposite the enemy; confront each other
　初陣 **uijin** one's first campaign, baptism of fire
8 退陣 **taijin** decampment; retirement

9 後陣 **kōjin** rear guard
10 殺陣 **tate** swordplay
11 野陣 **nojin** bivouac
12 着陣 **chakujin** take up positions
堅陣 **kenjin** stronghold
筆陣 **hitsujin** verbal battle; lineup of writers
13 滞陣 **taijin** encampment
戦陣 **senjin** the front, battlefield
15 敵陣 **tekijin** enemy camp/position/lines
論陣 **ronjin** argument, stating one's case
16 縦陣 **jūjin** column (of soldiers)

———————— 3 ————————

9 背水陣 **haisui (no) jin** last stand
12 報道陣 **hōdōjin** the press corps

2d7.2

陦 **TŌ** island

2d7.3

陝 **KYŌ** narrow

2d7.4

陝 **SEN** (place name)

2d7.5

陞 **SHŌ** go up, rise, climb

———————— 1 ————————

9 陞叙 **shōjo** promotion, advancement
10 陞進 **shōshin** promotion, advancement

2d7.6 / 589

陛 **HEI, kizahashi** steps (of the throne)

———————— 1 ————————

3 陛下 **Heika** His/Her Majesty

———————— 2 ————————

6 両陛下 **Ryōheika** Their Majesties

———————— 3 ————————

4 天皇陛下 **Tennō Heika** His Majesty the Emperor
9 皇后陛下 **Kōgō Heika** Her Majesty the Empress

2d7.7 / 947

降 **KŌ** come/go down; surrender
fu(ru) fall, come down (rain, etc.)
o(riru) come/go down, get off (a vehicle)
o(rosu) take/get down (from a shelf); let (someone) alight, drop (someone) off
kuda(ru) surrender **kuda(su)** defeat
kuda(tte) (from then) on down; as for me

———————— 1 ————————

3 降下 **kōka** descend, fall, drop
降口 **o(ri)guchi, o(ri)kuchi** exit (from a station)
4 降止 **fu(ri)ya(mu)** stop raining/snowing
降込 **fu(ri)ko(mu)** rain in on
降水 **kōsui** precipitation
降水量 **kōsuiryō** (amount of) precipitation
5 降出 **fu(ri)da(su)** begin to rain/snow
6 降伏 **kōfuku** surrender
7 降車 **kōsha** get off (a train)
降車口 **kōshaguchi** gateway for arriving passengers, exit
8 降注 **fu(ri)soso(gu)** rain/pour onto
降参 **kōsan** surrender; be nonplussed
降服 **kōfuku** surrender
降雨 **kōu** rain(fall)
降雨量 **kōuryō** (amount of) rainfall
9 降神術 **kōshinjutsu** spiritualism
11 降掛 **fu(ri)ka(karu)** fall on; befall, happen to; hang over; impend
降雪 **kōsetsu** snow, a snowfall
13 降続 **fu(ri)tsuzu(ku)** continue to rain/snow
降雹 **kōhyō** hailstorm
14 降旗 **kōki** white flag (of surrender)
降誕 **kōtan** birth, nativity
16 降壇 **kōdan** leave the rostrum
降機 **kōki** deplane
17 降霜 **kōsō** a frost
18 降臨 **kōrin** advent, descent

———————— 2 ————————

3 大降 **ōbu(ri)** heavy rainfall/snowfall
上降 **a(gari)o(ri)** going up and down
下降 **kakō** descend, fall, sink
下降線 **kakōsen** downward curve
4 天降 **amakuda(ru)** descend from heaven
5 以降 **ikō** on and after, beginning ...
7 沈降 **chinkō** sedimentation, precipitation
投降 **tōkō** surrender
8 昇降 **shōkō** rise and fall, ascend and descend
昇降口 **shōkōguchi** (ship) entrance, hatchway
昇降場 **shōkōjō** (station) platform
昇降機 **shōkōki** elevator
雨降 **amefu(ri)** rainfall, rainy weather
9 飛降 **tobio(ri)** jumping off
乗降 **jōkō, no(ri)o(ri)** getting on and off
急降下 **kyūkōka** drop rapidly; dive, swoop

神降 **kamio(roshi)** spiritualism; séance
10 帰降 **kikō** surrender, submission
11 雪降 **yukifu(ri)** snowfall
13 滑降 **kakkō** slide/ski down
14 漸降 **zenkō** gradual decline
15 横降 **yokobu(ri)** a driving rain
17 霜降 **shimofu(ri)** marbled (meat), salt-and-pepper pattern

——————— 3 ———————
3 土砂降 **doshabu(ri)** downpour
7 臣籍降下 **shinseki kōka** (royalty) becoming subjects

2d7.8

陟 **CHOKU** climb, rise

2d7.9 / 614

院 **IN** institution, palace, temple, hospital, school, house (of a legislature); ex-emperor

——————— 1 ———————
4 院内 **innai** within the House/congress
5 院本 **inpon** script, playbook of *jōruri* text
院生 **insei** graduate student
院外 **ingai** outside congress/parliament, outside the institution
院外団 **ingaidan** lobbying group
院外者 **ingaisha** lobbyist; persons outside congress/parliament
院庁 **inchō** retired emperor's office
8 院長 **inchō** head of the hospital/school/institute
9 院政 **insei** government by an ex-emperor
20 院議 **ingi** decision of the House/congress/parliament

——————— 2 ———————
1 一院制 **ichiinsei** unicameral system
2 二院制 **niinsei** bicameral system
入院 **nyūin** be admitted to hospital
3 上院 **jōin** the Upper House (of a legislature), Senate
下院 **kain** the Lower House (of a legislature)
4 内院 **naiin** inner sanctuary of a shrine
分院 **bun'in** branch (of a hospital)
5 本院 **hon'in** this institution; main institution
6 両院 **ryōin** both houses (of parliament/congress)
全院 **zen'in** the whole house/institution
全院委員会 **zen'in iinkai** committee of the whole house
寺院 **jiin** temple
7 別院 **betsuin** branch temple
医院 **iin** doctor's office, clinic, hospital

学院 **gakuin** academy
8 退院 **taiin** leave the hospital
参院 **San'in** House of Councilors (short for 参議院)
門院 **mon'in** empress dowager
9 通院 **tsūin** go to hospital regularly (as an outpatient)
10 書院 **shoin** writing alcove with a window; a study; drawing room; publishing house
書院造 **shoinzuku(ri)** (a traditional architectural style)
病院 **byōin** hospital
病院船 **byōinsen** hospital ship
11 産院 **san'in** maternity hospital
閉院 **heiin** adjourn the assembly/parliament
12 登院 **tōin** attend the diet/parliament
奥院 **oku(no)in** inner sanctuary
開院 **kaiin** opening of a session of parliament; opening of a new hospital/institute
13 僧院 **sōin** temple; monastery
20 議院 **giin** house of a legislature, diet

——————— 3 ———————
3 大寺院 **daijiin** large temple
大学院 **daigakuin** graduate school
女学院 **jogakuin** girls' academy
4 少年院 **shōnen'in** reform school
5 尼僧院 **nisōin** convent
6 両議院 **ryōgiin** both houses (of parliament/congress)
7 助産院 **josan'in** maternity hospital
芸術院 **Geijutsuin** Academy of Art
学士院 **gakushiin** academy
8 孤児院 **kojiin** orphanage
参議院 **Sangiin** House of Councilors
枢密院 **Sūmitsuin** Privy Council
9 美容院 **biyōin** beauty parlor, hairdresser's
美術院 **bijutsuin** academy of art
美粧院 **bishōin** beauty parlor, hairdresser's
10 修道院 **shūdōin** monastery, convent, cloister
11 控訴院 **kōsoin** court of appeal
脳病院 **nōbyōin** hospital for brain diseases
救貧院 **kyūhin'in** poorhouse
12 衆議院 **Shūgiin** the House of Representatives
貴族院 **Kizokuin** the House of Peers/Lords
13 感化院 **kankain** reformatory
15 養老院 **yōrōin** old-folks home
養育院 **yōikuin** orphanage
避病院 **hibyōin** isolation/quarantine hospital
16 翰林院 **kanrin'in** academy, institute

——————— 4 ———————
12 衆参両院 **shū-san ryōin** both Houses of the Diet

——————— 5 ———————
4 少年感化院 **shōnen kankain** reform school

2

亻
⺅
孑
阝 7←
卩
刂
力
又
一
亠
艹
匕
夂
丷
厂
辶
門
八
匸

2d7.10 / 1065

除

JO, JI exclude, remove; division (in math) **nozo(ku)** exclude, except; remove, abolish, cancel **no(keru)** remove, clear out of the way, get rid of; omit **nozo(ite)** except **-yo(ke)** protection against, charm

———————— 1 ————————

0 除する **jo(suru)** divide (in math)
5 除斥 **joseki** exclude, expel, reject
除外 **jogai** exception
除外例 **jogairei** an exception
除去 **jokyo** remove, eliminate
除号 **jogō** division sign
6 除名 **jomei** expel, drop from membership
除虫菊 **jochūgiku** Dalmatian pyrethrum
8 除夜 **joya** New Year's Eve
除夜鐘 **joya (no) kane** New Year's midnight bells
除法 **johō** division (in math)
除者 **no(ke)mono** outcast
9 除草 **josō** weeding
除草器 **josōki** weeder
11 除隊 **jotai** be discharged from the military
除雪 **josetsu** snow removal
13 除幕式 **jomakushiki** unveiling (ceremony)
除数 **josū** divisor
14 除算 **josan** division (in math)
17 除霜 **josō** defrosting, deicing
20 除籍 **joseki** remove a name (from the family register); decommission (a warship)

———————— 2 ————————

4 切除 **setsujo** cut off/out, remove, excise
厄除 **yakuyo(ke)** warding off evil
日除 **hiyo(ke)** sunshade, awning, blind
火除 **hiyo(ke)** protection against fire
欠除 **ketsujo** remove, eliminate
5 加除 **kajo** insertion and deletion
6 扣除 **kōjo** deduction, subtraction
虫除 **mushiyo(ke)** insect repellent, charm against insects
8 毒除 **dokuyo(ke)** protection against poisoning
免除 **menjo** exemption
波除 **namiyo(ke)** breakwater, sea wall
泥除 **doroyo(ke)** mudguards, mudflaps
突除 **tsu(ki)no(keru)** push aside, elbow out
取除 **to(ri)nozo(ku)** remove, get rid of
to(ri)no(keru) clear away; make an exception of; set aside
9 乗除 **jōjo** multiplication and division
削除 **sakujo** delete, eliminate
風除 **kazayo(ke)** windbreak
10 剔除 **tekijo** excise, cut out, remove
11 排除 **haijo** exclude, remove, eliminate
控除 **kōjo** deduct, subtract

掃除 **sōji** cleaning, clean-up
掃除人 **sōjinin** cleaner, janitor
掃除夫 **sōjifu** cleaner, janitor
掃除婦 **sōjifu** cleaning lady/woman
掃除機 **sōjiki** vacuum cleaner
雪除 **yukiyo(ke)** barrier against snow
12 弾除 **tamayo(ke)** protection against bullets, bulletproof
廃除 **haijo** remove, exclude
13 解除 **kaijo** cancel, rescind; release from
裾除 **susoyo(ke)** underskirt
14 塵除 **chiriyo(ke)** dust cloth/cover
駆除 **kujo** exterminate
駆除剤 **kujozai** expellent; insecticide
15 撥除 **ha(ne)no(keru)** push/brush aside
16 整除 **seijo** divide exactly
21 魔除 **mayo(ke)** charm against evil, talisman

———————— 3 ————————

3 大掃除 **ōsōji** general house-cleaning, spring/fall cleaning
4 水難除 **suinan'yo(ke)** charm against drowning
火難除 **kanan'yo(ke)** charm against fire
9 拭掃除 **fu(ki)sōji** cleaning (a house)
11 掃掃除 **ha(ki)sōji** sweeping and cleaning

———————— 4 ————————

5 加減乗除 **kagenjōjo** addition, subtraction, multiplication, and division
10 真空掃除機 **shinkū sōjiki** vacuum cleaner
14 徴兵免除 **chōhei menjo** draft exemption

2d7.11 / 1218

陥 陥

KAN, ochii(ru) fall/get into, sink, cave in; fall (to the enemy) **otoshii(reru)** entrap, ensnare; capture (a town)

———————— 1 ————————

2 陥入 **kannyū** subside, cave in, collapse
9 陥穽 **kansei** pitfall, trap
12 陥落 **kanraku** fall, surrender (of a city); sinking, a cave-in

———————— 2 ————————

4 欠陥 **kekkan** defect, deficiency, shortcoming
5 失陥 **shikkan** surrender, fall

郎 → 郎 2d6.5

2d7.12 / 193

郡

GUN county, district

1

7 郡役所 **gun'yakusho** county office
9 郡県 **gunken** counties and prefectures
10 郡部 **gunbu** rural districts

郷→ **2d8.14**

2d7.13

郢 EI (place name)

2d7.14 / 1673

郭 **KAKU** enclosure; town wall
kuruwa area enclosed by earthwork, fortification; quarter, district; red-light district

---

1

4 郭公 **kakkō** cuckoo
郭公鳥 **kakkōdori** cuckoo
11 郭清 **kakusei** purify, clean up

2

1 一郭 **ikkaku** a city block, quarter
5 外郭 **gaikaku** outer wall; contour, outlines
外郭団体 **gaikaku dantai** auxiliary organization
9 城郭 **jōkaku** castle; castle walls
10 遊郭 **yūkaku** red-light district
胸郭 **kyōkaku** the chest, thorax
15 輪郭 **rinkaku** outline, contours

2d7.15

郤 GEKI crevice, interstice

8

2d8.1

陲 SUI, hotori vicinity

2d8.2 / 1405

陳 **CHIN** state, explain; line up; old
no(beru) state, mention, explain

1

5 陳弁 **chinben** explain oneself, justify, defend, vindicate
陳皮 **chinpi** dried mikan peels
6 陳列 **chinretsu** exhibit, display

陳列室 **chinretsushitsu** showroom
陳列棚 **chinretsudana** display rack/case
7 陳述 **chinjutsu** state, set forth, declare
陳述書 **chinjutsusho** statement, declaration
11 陳情 **chinjō** petition, appeal, lobbying
陳情書 **chinjōsho** petition, representation
14 陳腐 **chinpu** out-of-date, commonplace, trite, worn out, threadbare
17 陳謝 **chinsha** apology

2

8 具陳 **guchin** formal statement
9 前陳 **zenchin** the above-mentioned
12 開陳 **kaichin** statement
13 新陳代謝 **shinchintaisha** metabolism

2d8.3 / 1943

陪 **BAI** follow, accompany, attend on

1

7 陪臣 **baishin** undervassal
9 陪乗 **baijō** riding in the same car (with a superior)
陪食 **baishoku** dining with a superior
10 陪従 **baijū** wait upon, accompany
陪席 **baiseki** sitting as an associate (judge)
15 陪審 **baishin** jury
18 陪観 **baikan** view with one's superior

2d8.4 / 647

陸 **RIKU, ROKU, oka** land

1

3 陸上 **rikujō** on shore, land
陸上機 **rikujōki** land-based airplane
4 陸中 **Rikuchū** (ancient kuni, Iwate-ken)
5 陸生 **rikusei** (living on) land
6 陸地 **rikuchi** land
陸行 **rikkō** go by land, travel overland
7 陸兵 **rikuhei** land troops/forces
9 陸軍 **rikugun** army
陸軍省 **Rikugunshō** Ministry of War
陸前 **Rikuzen** (ancient kuni, Miyagi-ken)
陸風 **rikufū** land(-to-sea) breeze
陸海 **rikukai** land and sea
陸海軍 **rikukaigun, rikkaigun** army and navy
陸屋根 **rokuyane** flat roof
陸相 **rikushō** War Minister
11 陸運 **rikuun** land transport
陸産 **rikusan** land products
陸産物 **rikusanbutsu** land products
陸軟風 **rikunanpū** land(-to-sea) breeze

陸釣 **okazu(ri)** fishing from the shore
12 陸揚 **rikua(ge)** land, unloading
陸蒸汽 **okajōki** steam train
陸棚 **rikudana** continental shelf
陸棲 **rikusei** (living on) land
陸奥 **Mutsu** (ancient kuni, Aomori-ken)
13 陸戦 **rikusen** land combat/warfare
陸戦隊 **rikusentai** landing forces
陸続 **rikuzoku** continuously, successively
陸路 **rikuro** (over)land route
14 陸稲 **rikutō, okabo** dry-land rice
16 陸橋 **rikkyō** bridge over land, overpass,
viaduct
18 陸離 **rikuri** dazzling, brilliant

——————— 2 ———————

3 大陸 **tairiku** continent
大陸棚 **tairikudana** continental shelf
上陸 **jōriku** landing, going ashore
4 内陸 **nairiku** inland
内陸国 **nairikukoku** landlocked country
水陸 **suiriku** water and land, amphibious
5 北陸地方 **Hokuriku chihō** the Hokuriku
region (Fukui, Ishikawa, Toyama,
Niigata prefectures)
8 空陸 **kūriku** land and air (forces)
9 海陸 **kairiku** land and sea, amphibious
11 常陸 **Hitachi** (ancient kuni, Ibaraki-ken)
12 着陸 **chakuriku** (airplane) landing
着陸地 **chakurikuchi** landing zone
揚陸 **yōriku** landing, unloading
18 離陸 **ririku** (airplane) takeoff

——————— 3 ———————

11 軟着陸 **nanchakuriku** soft landing
12 無着陸 **muchakuriku** nonstop (flight)
18 離着陸 **richakuriku** takeoff and landing

2d8.5 / 1844

陵

RYŌ, misasagi imperial tomb

——————— 1 ———————

10 陵辱 **ryōjoku** insult; rape
13 陵墓 **ryōbo** imperial tomb

——————— 2 ———————

3 山陵 **sanryō** mountains and hills; imperial
tomb
5 丘陵 **kyūryō** hill
9 帝陵 **teiryō** imperial mausoleum
12 御陵 **goryō** imperial tomb

2d8.6 / 946

隆 隆

RYŪ high; noble; flourishing

——————— 1 ———————

3 隆々 **ryūryū** prosperous, thriving; muscular
6 隆肉 **ryūniku** hunch (back), (camel's) hump
10 隆起 **ryūki** protuberance, bulge, rise,
elevation
11 隆盛 **ryūsei** prosperous, flourishing, thriving
14 隆鼻術 **ryūbijutsu** nasal plastic surgery

——————— 2 ———————

16 興隆 **kōryū** rise, prosperity

2d8.7 / 867

陰

IN, ON the yin principle; negative;
shadow, hidden, back, dark, secret; sex
organs; indebtedness, favor; hades
kage(ru) darken; cloud up; be obscured
kage shade; back　**(o)kage** indebtedness, favor

——————— 1 ———————

3 陰干 **kagebo(shi)** drying in the shade
陰口 **kageguchi** malicious gossip
4 陰毛 **inmō** pubic hair
陰文 **inbun** engraved/intaglio lettering
5 陰日向 **kage-hinata** light and shade
陰弁慶 **kage-Benkei** a lion at home but
meek before outsiders
6 陰気 **inki** gloomy, dreary
陰気臭 **inkikusa(i)** gloomy-looking
7 陰忍 **innin** endure, be patient, put up with
8 陰画 **inga** a negative
陰事 **inji** secret
陰茎 **inkei** penis
陰性 **insei** negative; dormant
陰門 **inmon** the vulva
10 陰険 **inken** tricky, wily, treacherous
陰部 **inbu** the pubic region, the genitals
陰唇 **inshin** the labia
陰核 **inkaku** the clitoris
11 陰陽 **in'yō, on'yō** yin and yang, positive and
negative, active and passive, male and
female, sun and moon, light and shade
in (ni) yō (ni) overtly and covertly,
explicitly and implicitly
陰陽師 **on'yōji** fortuneteller, diviner
陰乾 **kagebo(shi)** drying in the shade
陰惨 **insan** dreary, dismal, gloomy
12 陰極 **inkyoku** negative pole, cathode
陰極線 **inkyokusen** cathode rays
13 陰電子 **indenshi** negatron, electron
陰電気 **indenki** negative electricity
陰電荷 **indenka** negative charge
14 陰暦 **inreki** the lunar calendar
陰徳 **intoku** secret act of charity
15 陰影 **in'ei** shadow; shading; gloom
陰蔽 **inpei** conceal, cover up
16 陰謀 **inbō** conspiracy, plot, intrigue
陰謀家 **inbōka** schemer

17 陰翳 **in'ei** shadow; shading; gloom
22 陰囊 **innō** the scrotum
29 陰鬱 **in'utsu** gloomy, dismal, melancholy

———————— 2 ————————
3 山陰 **san'in, yamakage** mountain recesses; northern slopes
4 太陰 **taiin** the moon, lunar
太陰暦 **taiinreki** the lunar calendar
中陰 **chūin** seven-week mourning period
片陰 **katakage** shade
木陰 **kokage** tree shade
日陰 **hikage** the shade
日陰者 **hikagemono** one who keeps out of the public eye
6 会陰 **ein** the perineum
光陰 **kōin** time
8 夜陰 **yain** darkness of night
物陰 **monokage** cover, hiding; a form, shape
12 葉陰 **hakage** under the leaves
14 緑陰 **ryokuin** the shade of trees
16 樹陰 **juin, kokage** shade of a tree

2d8.8 / 533

険 險

KEN steep; fearsome
kewa(shii) steep; stern

———————— 1 ————————
7 険阻 **kenso** steep
9 険相 **kensō** forbidding/sinister look
10 険峻 **kenshun** steep
11 険悪 **ken'aku** dangerous, threatening, serious
13 険路 **kenro** steep path
18 険難 **kennan** steep; fraught with danger

———————— 2 ————————
4 天険 **tenken** natural defenses, steep place
6 危険 **kiken** danger, risk
危険物 **kikenbutsu** hazardous articles, explosives and combustibles
危険性 **kikensei** riskiness, danger
7 邪険 **jaken** harsh, cruel
9 保険 **hoken** insurance
保険会社 **hoken-gaisha** insurance company
保険金 **hokenkin** insurance money
保険料 **hokenryō** insurance premium
冒険 **bōken** adventure
冒険好 **bōkenzu(ki)** venturesome
冒険的 **bōkenteki** adventurous, risky
冒険談 **bōkendan** account of one's adventures
10 陰険 **inken** tricky, wily, treacherous
11 探険 **tanken** exploration, expedition

———————— 3 ————————
6 再保険 **saihoken** reinsurance
10 被保険物 **hihokenbutsu** insured property

———————— 4 ————————
4 火災保険 **kasai hoken** fire insurance
5 生命保険 **seimei hoken** life insurance
7 労災保険 **rōsai hoken** workman's accident compensation insurance
災害保険 **saigai hoken** accident insurance
10 健康保険 **kenkō hoken** health insurance
13 損害保険 **songai hoken** casualty/nonlife insurance
18 簡易保険 **kan'i hoken** post-office life insurance

陷 → 陥 **2d7.11**

2d8.9

陬

SŪ corner

———————— 2 ————————
4 辺陬 **hensū** remote rural area

2d8.10 / 1741

随 隨

ZUI, shitaga(u) follow
manimani at the mercy of, with (the wind)

———————— 1 ————————
1 随一 **zuiichi** No. 1, most, greatest
4 随分 **zuibun** very
5 随処 **zuisho** everywhere, anywhere
6 随行 **zuikō** attend on, accompany
随行員 **zuikōin** attendants, entourage, retinue
7 随身 **zuishin** have on one's person; attend on; attendant **zuijin** bodyguard (historical)
随伴 **zuihan** attend on, accompany
随伴者 **zuihansha** attendant, follower, retinue
8 随所 **zuisho** everywhere, anywhere
9 随神道 **Kannagara (no) Michi** Shintoism
10 随員 **zuiin** attendants, retinue
随従 **zuijū** follow the lead of, play second fiddle to
随従者 **zuijūsha** henchman, follower, satellite
随時 **zuiji** at any time, whenever required
12 随筆 **zuihitsu** essay, miscellaneous writings
13 随想 **zuisō** occasional thoughts
随想録 **zuisōroku** occasional thoughts, essays
随感 **zuikan** random thoughts/impressions
随意 **zuii** voluntary, optional **manimani** at the mercy of, with (the wind)
随意筋 **zuiikin** voluntary muscle

———————— 2 ————————
4 不随 **fuzui** paralysis
不随意 **fuzuii** involuntary

8 ←

不随意筋 **fuzuiikin** involuntary muscle
5 付随 **fuzui** incidental, concomitant, collateral
6 気随 **kizui** willful, self-indulgent
気随気侭 **kizui-kimama** as one pleases
8 追随 **tsuizui** follow (in the footsteps of)

——— 3 ———
8 服装随意 **fukusō zuii** informal attire

——— 4 ———
5 半身不随 **hanshin fuzui** paralyzed on one side
6 全身不随 **zenshin fuzui** total paralysis

2d8.11 / 1650

陶

TŌ porcelain, pottery

——— 1 ———
3 陶工 **tōkō** potter
陶土 **tōdo** potter's clay, kaolin
7 陶冶 **tōya** training, cultivation, education
陶芸 **tōgei** ceramic art
11 陶酔 **tōsui** intoxication; fascination, rapture
12 陶棺 **tōkan** earthenware coffin
陶然 **tōzen** pleasantly drunk; enraptured
14 陶磁器 **tōjiki** ceramics, china and porcelain
陶製 **tōsei** ceramic, earthen
15 陶器 **tōki** china, ceramics, pottery
陶器商 **tōkishō** crockery dealer, chinashop

——— 2 ———
14 製陶 **seitō** porcelain manufacturing
製陶業 **seitōgyō** the ceramics industry
16 薫陶 **kuntō** discipline, training, education
29 鬱陶 **uttō(shii)** gloomy, depressing

2d8.12 / 524

郵

YŪ mail

——— 1 ———
8 郵券 **yūken** postage stamp
郵送 **yūsō** to mail
郵送料 **yūsōryō** postage
9 郵便 **yūbin** mail
郵便局 **yūbinkyoku** post office
郵便車 **yūbinsha** mail car
郵便物 **yūbinbutsu** mail
郵便船 **yūbinsen** mail boat
郵便箱 **yūbinbako** mailbox
郵政 **yūsei** postal system
郵政省 **Yūseishō** Ministry of Posts and Telecommunications
11 郵袋 **yūtai** mailbag
郵船 **yūsen** mail boat
12 郵税 **yūzei** postage

2d8.13 / 188

都 都

TO, TSU, miyako capital, metropolis

——— 1 ———
2 都入 **miyakoi(ri)** arrive in the capital
都人 **miyakobito, tojin** people of the capital; townspeople
都人士 **tojinshi** people of the capital
3 都下 **toka** in the capital
4 都内 **tonai** within the capital
都心 **toshin** heart of the city, midtown
5 都民 **tomin** Tōkyō citizens/residents
都市 **toshi** city
都庁 **Tochō** Tōkyō Government Office
都立 **toritsu** metropolitan, municipal
6 都合 **tsugō** circumstances; one's convenience; opportunity; arrangements
都合上 **tsugōjō** for convenience
都合良 **tsugōyo(ku)** fortunately, successfully, satisfactorily
都会 **tokai** city Tokai Tōkyō Assembly
都会人 **tokaijin** city resident, urban dweller
7 都住居 **miyakozumai** city life
8 都制 **tosei** metropolitan government
都育 **miyakosoda(chi)** city-bred
9 都度 **tsudo** each time, whenever
11 都道府県 **to-dō-fu-ken** prefectures
都鳥 **miyakodori** plover; gull
12 都落 **miyakoo(chi)** leave the capital, rusticate
都営 **toei** city-run, metropolitan
都税 **tozei** metropolitan tax
13 都鄙 **tohi** town and country
都雅 **toga** elegant, urbane, refined
20 都議会 **Togikai** Tōkyō Assembly

——— 2 ———
3 大都会 **daitokai** big city
小都市 **shōtoshi** small city/town
小都会 **shōtokai** small city/town
4 不都合 **futsugō** inconvenience, trouble, harm; impropriety, misconduct
水都 **suito** city on the water's edge
5 古都 **koto** ancient city; former capital
好都合 **kōtsugō** favorable, good
6 全都 **zento** the whole capital, all of Tōkyō
宇都宮 **Utsunomiya** (city, Tochigi-ken)
8 京都 **Kyōto** (city, Kyōto-fu)
京都府 **Kyōto-fu** (prefecture)
国都 **kokuto** national capital
9 帝都 **teito** imperial capital
首都 **shuto** capital
12 港都 **kōto** port city
御都合 **gotsugō** your convenience
御都合主義 **gotsugō shugi** opportunism
13 僧都 **sōzu** Buddhist priest

14 遷都 **sento** transfer of the capital

——————— 3 ———————

3 工業都市 **kōgyō toshi** industrial city, factory
town
8 東京都 **Tōkyō-to** the Metropolis of Tōkyō
16 衛星都市 **eisei toshi** satellite towns

2d8.14 / 855

郷 郷   **KYŌ, GŌ** village, place, native place

——————— 1 ———————

3 郷土 **kyōdo** one's native place; local
郷土文学 **kyōdo bungaku** local literature
郷土史 **kyōdoshi** local history
郷土色 **kyōdoshoku** local color
郷土愛 **kyōdoai** love for one's home province
郷士 **gōshi** country samurai
7 郷里 **kyōri** one's native place, home (town)
郷社 **gōsha** village shrine
8 郷国 **kyōkoku** one's native land
10 郷党 **kyōtō** people of/from one's home town
13 郷愁 **kyōshū** homesickness, nostalgia
14 郷関 **kyōkan** one's native place, home town

——————— 2 ———————

5 出郷 **shukkyō** leave one's home town
仙郷 **senkyō** fairyland, enchanted land
他郷 **takyō** foreign country, strange land
6 近郷 **kingō** neighboring districts
同郷 **dōkyō** the same village/province
在郷 **zaikyō, zaigō** (in the) country(side)
9 故郷 **kokyō, furusato** birthplace, home town
10 帰郷 **kikyō** return home, return to one's
home town
家郷 **kakyō** one's old home, one's birthplace
11 望郷 **bōkyō** homesickness, nostalgia
異郷 **ikyō** foreign country
13 滞郷 **taikyō** living in one's native place
愛郷 **aikyō** love for one's home town
愛郷心 **aikyōshin** home-town pride
16 懐郷 **kaikyō** nostalgic reminiscence
懐郷病 **kaikyōbyō** nostalgia, homesickness
18 離郷 **rikyō** leaving one's home town

——————— 3 ———————

5 生故郷 **u(mare)kokyō** one's birthplace,
native place
10 桃源郷 **tōgenkyō** Shangri-La, paradise
11 理想郷 **risōkyō** ideal land, Shangri-La,
utopia
12 温泉郷 **onsenkyō** hot-springs town

——————— 4 ———————

12 無何有郷 **mukau (no) sato** an unspoiled
paradise, utopia

2d8.15 / 86

部   **BU** department; part, category; (counter for copies of a newspaper or magazine)
be clan engaged in a certain occupation

——————— 1 ———————

3 部下 **buka** a subordinate, the people working
under one
4 部内 **bunai** within the department, (government) circles
部分 **bubun** part   **buwa(ke)** classification
部分的 **bubunteki** partial, here and there
部分品 **bubunhin** parts, components
部分食 **bubunshoku** partial eclipse
5 部外 **bugai** outside
部外秘 **bugaihi** to be kept secret from
outsiders, Restricted
部外者 **bugaisha** outsider
6 部会 **bukai** sectional meeting, department
7 部位 **bui** region, part (of the body)
部局 **bukyoku** department, bureau
部材 **buzai** (structural) member
8 部長 **buchō** department head
部厚 **buatsu** thick, bulky
部門 **bumon** field, branch, line; division,
section; class, category
9 部首 **bushu** radical (of a kanji)
部品 **buhin** parts
部屋 **heya** room, apartment
部屋代 **heyadai** room rent
部屋住 **heyazu(mi)** dependent, hanger-on;
heir who has not yet taken over
部屋割 **heyawa(ri)** assignment of rooms
部屋着 **heyagi** house dress, dressing gown
部面 **bumen** phase, aspect, field, side
10 部将 **bushō** a general
部員 **buin** staff, staff member
11 部隊 **butai** unit, corps, detachment, squad
部隊長 **butaichō** commanding officer
部族 **buzoku** tribe
12 部落 **buraku** community, settlement, village
部落民 **burakumin** (lowly class of people
historically engaged in butchery and
tanning)
部属 **buzoku** section, division
13 部数 **busū** number of copies, circulation
部署 **busho** one's post, duty station
18 部類 **burui** class(ification), category
部類分 **buruiwa(ke)** classification, grouping

——————— 2 ———————

1 一部 **ichibu** a part; a copy (of a publication)
一部分 **ichibubun** a part
一部始終 **ichibu shijū** full particulars
2 二部 **nibu** two parts/copies; the second part
3 三部 **sanbu** three parts; three copies (of a
publication)

2

→8

亻 冫 孑 阝 卩 刂 力 又 宀 亠 亡 亅 勹 亠 厂 辶 冂 几 匸

三部合奏 **sanbu gassō** instrumental trio
大部分 **daibubun** a large part, most; for the most part, mostly
大部屋 **ōbeya** large room; actors' common room
上部 **jōbu** upper part/side, top surface
下部 **kabu** lower part, subordinate
4 内部 **naibu** interior, inside, internal
中部 **chūbu** central part **Chūbu** the central Honshū region
文部大臣 **monbu daijin** Minister of Education
文部省 **Monbushō** Ministry of Education
支部 **shibu** a branch (office), local chapter
支部長 **shibuchō** branch manager
5 北部 **hokubu** north, northern part
本部 **honbu** headquarters
市部 **shibu** urban districts
外部 **gaibu** the outside, external
四部合奏 **shibu gassō** (instrumental) quartet
四部合唱 **shibu gasshō** (vocal) quartet
主部 **shubu** main part; subject (in grammar)
石部金吉 **Ishibe Kinkichi** man of strict morals
6 西部 **seibu** western part, the west
西部劇 **seibugeki** a Western (movie)
全部 **zenbu** all, whole; entirely
宇部 **Ube** (city, Yamaguchi-ken)
各部 **kakubu** every part/department, various parts
式部 **shikibu** master of ceremony/protocol
式部官 **shikibukan** master of court ceremony
式部省 **Shikibushō** Ministry of Ceremony
7 阿部 **Abe** (surname)
学部 **gakubu** academic department, faculty
学部長 **gakubuchō** dean of a university department
局部 **kyokubu** part, section; local; the affected region; one's private parts
局部麻酔 **kyokubu masui** local anesthetic
足部 **sokubu** the foot
8 空部屋 **a(ki)beya** vacant room
服部 **Hattori** (surname)
9 郡部 **gunbu** rural districts
軍部 **gunbu** the military
南部 **nanbu** southern part, the South
前部 **zenbu** front part, front
要部 **yōbu** principal/essential part
後部 **kōbu** back part, rear, stern
後部灯 **kōbutō** taillight
面部 **menbu** face, facial region
背部 **haibu** the back, posterior
音部記号 **onbu kigō** (G) clef
胃部 **ibu** stomach region
10 残部 **zanbu** remainder, what is left

陰部 **inbu** the pubic region, the genitals
胸部 **kyōbu** the chest
恥部 **chibu** the private parts
11 側部 **sokubu** side, lateral
基部 **kibu** base, foundation
脚部 **kyakubu** leg
患部 **kanbu** diseased part, the affected area
細部 **saibu** details, particulars
12 貸部屋 **ka(shi)beya** room for rent
13 腰部 **yōbu** the pelvic region, waist, hips, loins
腹部 **fukubu** abdomen, belly
幹部 **kanbu** (top) executives, management
14 語部 **kata(ri)be** family of professional reciters
15 鞍部 **anbu** col, saddle (between mountains)
16 頸部 **keibu** the neck
頭部 **tōbu** the head
17 臀部 **denbu** the buttocks, posterior
19 警部 **keibu** police inspector

——————— 3 ———————

2 子供部屋 **kodomo-beya** children's room, nursery
3 下腹部 **kafukubu** abdomen
4 中西部 **Chūseibu** the Midwest
文学部 **bungakubu** literature department/faculty
心臓部 **shinzōbu** the heart of
5 外信部 **gaishinbu** foreign-news department
司令部 **shireibu** headquarters, the command
弘報部 **kōhōbu** public relations department
広告部 **kōkokubu** publicity department
広報部 **kōhōbu** public relations department
7 兵站部 **heitanbu** supply/logistical department
医学部 **igakubu** medical department/school
社会部 **shakaibu** local-news section, city desk
8 事業部 **jigyōbu** operations department
空挺部隊 **kūtei butai** airborne troops, paratroops
9 首脳部 **shunōbu** leaders, top management
前頭部 **zentōbu** front of the head, forehead
後頭部 **kōtōbu** the back of the head
宣伝部 **sendenbu** publicity department
10 倶楽部 **kurabu** club
11 道具部屋 **dōgu-beya** toolroom; prop room
情報部 **jōhōbu** information bureau
12 港務部 **kōmubu** harbor department/office
14 総務部長 **sōmu buchō** head of the general affairs department
16 整理部 **seiribu** (newspaper's) copy desk
17 購買部 **kōbaibu** cooperative store

——————— 4 ———————

4 中高音部 **chūkōonbu** alto, mezzo-soprano
9 軍司令部 **gunshireibu** military headquarters

9

2d9.1 / 1640

隅

GŪ corner
sumi, sumi(kko) corner, nook

---1---

3 隅々 **sumizumi** every nook and cranny
5 隅石 **sumiishi** cornerstone
隅田川 **Sumida-gawa** (river, Tōkyō-to)

---2---

3 大隅 **Ōsumi** (ancient kuni, Kagoshima-ken)
4 片隅 **katasumi** corner, nook
5 四隅 **yosumi** four corners

2d9.2

隈

WAI, kuma corner, nook; indentation, bend, turn; shade, shading; makeup

---1---

0 隈なく **kuma(naku)** in every nook and cranny, everywhere
8 隈取 **kumado(ru)** tint, shade; make up (one's face) **kumado(ri)** shading; makeup
12 隈無 **kumana(ku)** in every nook and cranny, everywhere

---2---

9 界隈 **kaiwai** neighborhood, vicinity

2d9.3

隋

ZUI (name of a Chinese dynasty)

2d9.4

隍

KŌ, hori (dry) moat

2d9.5 / 630

陽

YŌ the yang principle; positive; the sun
hi the sun

---1---

0 陽に **yō (ni)** explicitly, openly
2 陽子 **yōshi** proton
6 陽気 **yōki** cheerful, gay, convivial; season, weather
陽光 **yōkō** sunshine, sunlight
陽当 **hia(tari)** exposure to the sun
陽成 **Yōzei** (emperor, 876–884)
8 陽画 **yōga** a positive (photographic print)
陽炎 **yōen, kagerō** heat shimmer

陽物 **yōbutsu** the phallus
陽性 **yōsei** positive
11 陽転 **yōten** positive (reaction to a medical test)
12 陽報 **yōhō** open reward (for a secret act of charity)
陽極 **yōkyoku** positive pole, anode
13 陽電子 **yōdenshi** positron
陽電気 **yōdenki** positive electricity
陽電荷 **yōdenka** positive charge
14 陽暦 **yōreki** the solar calendar

---2---

1 一陽来復 **ichiyō-raifuku** return of spring
3 夕陽 **sekiyō** the setting sun
4 太陽 **taiyō** the sun, solar
太陽年 **taiyōnen** solar year
太陽系 **taiyōkei** the solar system
太陽神 **taiyōshin** sun god
太陽暦 **taiyōreki** the solar calendar
太陽熱 **taiyōnetsu** solar heat
9 春陽 **shun'yō** (warm) spring sunshine
10 残陽 **zan'yō** the setting sun
陰陽 **in'yō, on'yō** yin and yang, positive and negative, active and passive, male and female, sun and moon, light and shade
in (ni) yō (ni) overtly and covertly, explicitly and implicitly
陰陽師 **on'yōji** fortuneteller, diviner
11 斜陽 **shayō** setting sun
斜陽族 **shayōzoku** impoverished aristocracy
12 落陽 **rakuyō** setting sun
紫陽花 **ajisai** hydrangea
19 艶陽 **en'yō** balmy late spring

2d9.6 / 588

階

KAI stairs; step, grade; floor, story
kizahashi steps, stairway

---1---

3 階上 **kaijō** upper floor, upstairs
階下 **kaika** lower floor, downstairs
7 階位 **kaii** rank, grade
9 階段 **kaidan** steps, stairs, stairway
階級 **kaikyū** (social) class; (military) rank
11 階梯 **kaitei** step, stairs, ladder; threshold, steppingstone; guide, primer, manual
14 階層 **kaisō** tier; social stratum, class

---2---

1 一階 **ikkai** first/ground floor
2 二階 **nikai** second floor, upstairs
二階建 **nikaida(te)** two-story
6 各階 **kakkai, kakukai** each/every floor
7 位階 **ikai** court rank
9 段階 **dankai** stage, phase, step; rank, grade
音階 **onkai** (musical) scale

18 職階 **shokkai** (civil-service) grade
職階制 **shokkaisei** job-rank system

─────────── 3 ───────────

4 中二階 **chūnikai** mezzanine
中産階級 **chūsan kaikyū** middle class
6 有産階級 **yūsan kaikyū** the propertied class
有閑階級 **yūkan kaikyū** the leisure class
8 長音階 **chōonkai** major scale
11 第三階級 **dai-san kaikyū** the third estate, the bourgeoisie
第四階級 **dai-shi kaikyū** the fourth estate, the proletariat
12 短音階 **tan'onkai** minor scale
無産階級 **musan kaikyū** the proletariat
14 総二階 **sōnikai** full two-story house

隆→隆 2d8.6

2d9.7 / 795

隊 隊

TAI squad, band

─────────── 1 ───────────

6 隊伍 **taigo** (lined up in) ranks, array, (parade) formation
隊列 **tairetsu** (in serried) ranks, file
7 隊形 **taikei** (troop) formation, order
8 隊長 **taichō** unit commander, captain, leader
10 隊員 **taiin** member of a brigade/team
11 隊商 **taishō** caravan
隊商宿 **taishōjuku** caravansary
14 隊旗 **taiki** flag of a unit

─────────── 2 ───────────

2 入隊 **nyūtai** enlist (in the army)
3 大隊 **daitai** battalion
小隊 **shōtai** platoon
4 中隊 **chūtai** company, squadron
分隊 **buntai** squad
5 本隊 **hontai** main body (of troops)
6 全隊 **zentai** the entire force, all units
7 兵隊 **heitai** soldier; sailor
8 枝隊 **shitai** detachment (of troops)
9 除隊 **jotai** be discharged from the military
軍隊 **guntai** army, troops, corps
連隊 **rentai** regiment
連隊長 **rentaichō** regimental commander
連隊旗 **rentaiki** regimental standard/colors
10 部隊 **butai** unit, corps, detachment, squad
部隊長 **butaichō** commanding officer
帰隊 **kitai** return to one's unit
11 船隊 **sentai** fleet
12 艇隊 **teitai** flotilla
13 楽隊 **gakutai** band, orchestra

解隊 **kaitai** disband, demobilize
戦隊 **sentai** corps, squadron
15 横隊 **ōtai** rank, line
編隊 **hentai** (fly in) formation
16 縦隊 **jūtai** column (of soldiers)
17 聯隊 **rentai** regiment
21 艦隊 **kantai** fleet, squadron

─────────── 3 ───────────

4 予備隊 **yobitai** reserve corps
6 合唱隊 **gasshōtai** chorus, choir
先発隊 **senpatsutai** advance party
守備隊 **shubitai** garrison, guards
自衛隊 **Jieitai** Self Defense Forces
7 別動隊 **betsudōtai** flying column, detached force
別働隊 **betsudōtai** flying column, detached force
決死隊 **kesshitai** suicide corps
8 突撃隊 **totsugekitai** shock troops
9 飛行隊 **hikōtai** flying/air corps
軍楽隊 **gungakutai** military band
海兵隊 **kaiheitai** the Marine Corps
派遣隊 **hakentai** contingent, detachment
挺進隊 **teishintai** advance corps
宣伝隊 **sendentai** propaganda squad
音楽隊 **ongakutai** band, orchestra
10 陸戦隊 **rikusentai** landing forces
遊動隊 **yūdōtai** mobile corps
遊撃隊 **yūgekitai** flying column, commando unit
消防隊 **shōbōtai** fire brigade
捜索隊 **sōsakutai** search party
特科隊 **tokkatai** technical corps
航空隊 **kōkūtai** air force
討伐隊 **tōbatsutai** punitive force
11 偵察隊 **teisatsutai** reconnoitering party, patrol, scouts
商船隊 **shōsentai** merchant fleet
探検隊 **tankentai** exploration party
救助隊 **kyūjotai** rescue party
12 遠征隊 **enseitai** expeditionary forces, invaders; visiting team
補充隊 **hojūtai** the reserves
13 鼓笛隊 **kotekitai** drum-and-bugle corps, fife-and-drum band
禁衛隊 **kin'eitai** the imperial guards
聖歌隊 **seikatai** choir
愚連隊 **gurentai** hooligans, street gang
戦車隊 **senshatai** tank corps
督戦隊 **tokusentai** supervising unit
15 敵艦隊 **teki kantai** enemy fleet
16 衛生隊 **eiseitai** medical corps
機動隊 **kidōtai** riot squad
親衛隊 **shin'eitai** bodyguard troops
19 警官隊 **keikantai** police force/squad

—————— 4 ——————
8 空挺部隊 **kūtei butai** airborne troops,
   paratroops

鄉 → 郷 **2d8.14**

都 → 都 **2d8.13**

2d9.8
鄂
   GAKU (place name); frankly

—————— 10 ——————

2d10.1
陦
   KAI high, steep

—————— 1 ——————
8 陦始 **Kai (yori) haji(meyo)** He who suggests
   it should go first.

2d10.2 / 1589
隔 隔
   KAKU every other, alternate;
   distance between
   heda(teru) separate, interpose,
   screen off; estrange, alienate
heda(taru) be distant/separated from; become
estranged

—————— 1 ——————
4 隔月 **kakugetsu** every other month
   隔日 **kakujitsu** every other day, alternate
      days
5 隔世 **kakusei** a distant age
6 隔年 **kakunen** every other year
10 隔週 **kakushū** every other week
12 隔晩 **kakuban** every other evening
   隔番 **kakuban** alternation, taking turns
   隔絶 **kakuzetsu** be isolated/separated
13 隔靴搔痒 **kakka-sōyō** irritation, impatience
      (like trying to scratch an itchy foot
      through the shoe)
   隔意 **kakui** reserve, estrangement
16 隔壁 **kakuheki** partition, bulkhead, septum
18 隔離 **kakuri** isolate, segregate

—————— 2 ——————
4 心隔 **kokoroheda(te)** unconfiding
7 阻隔 **sokaku** alienation, estrangement
   別隔 **wa(ke)heda(te)** make distinctions,
      discriminate

11 疎隔 **sokaku** estrangement, alienation
12 遠隔 **enkaku** distant, remote (control)
   間隔 **kankaku** space, spacing; interval
15 横隔膜 **ōkakumaku** the diaphragm
18 離隔 **rikaku** isolation, segregation
20 懸隔 **kenkaku** disparity, gap **ka(ke)-
      heda(taru)** be far apart, differ widely
      ka(ke)heda(teru) estrange

2d10.3
隕
   IN fall

—————— 1 ——————
5 隕石 **inseki** meteorite

2d10.4
隙 隙
   GEKI crevice; spare time;
   discord **suki** opening, crack,
   crevice, space; chance,
   opportunity; unguarded
   moment **hima** (spare) time

—————— 1 ——————
12 隙間 **sukima** crevice, opening, gap, space
   隙間風 **sukimakaze** a draft

—————— 2 ——————
3 寸隙 **sungeki** a moment's leisure, spare
      moments
4 手隙 **tesuki** leisure, spare/idle time
8 空隙 **kūgeki** gap, opening
12 間隙 **kangeki** gap, opening, crevice
13 塡隙 **tengeki** caulking, filling

—————— 3 ——————
4 手間隙 **temahima** labor and time, trouble

2d10.5
隘
   AI narrow

—————— 1 ——————
13 隘路 **airo** defile, narrow path; bottleneck,
      impasse

—————— 2 ——————
9 狭隘 **kyōai** narrow, cramped, too small

鄉 → 郷 **2d8.14**

2d10.6
鄒
   SŪ (place name)

2

イ 亻 子 阝 阝 刂 力 又 亠 十 ト 宀 丷 厂 辶 門 几 匸

→ 11

─────── 11 ───────

隙 → 隙 **2d10.4**

2d11.1 / 618

際 **SAI** time, occasion, when; (as suffix)
inter- **kiwa** side, edge, verge
kiwa(doi) dangerous, critical, risky;
venturous; risqué

─────── 1 ───────

5 際立 **kiwada(tsu)** be conspicuous/prominent
6 際会 **saikai** meet, face, confront
8 際限 **saigen** limits, bounds, end
際物 **kiwamono** seasonal goods
11 際涯 **saigai** extremity, limits

─────── 2 ───────

1 一際 **hitokiwa** conspicuously; still more,
especially
3 山際 **yamagiwa** by the mountains; skyline
4 今際 **imawa** one's dying hour
分際 **bunzai** social standing
水際 **mizugiwa, migiwa** water's edge, shore
水際立 **mizugiwada(tta)** splendid, fine
手際 **tegiwa** performance, execution; skill,
deftness, workmanship
5 出際 **degiwa** the time of setting out
生際 **ha(e)giwa** one's hairline
6 死際 **shi(ni)giwa** the hour of death
州際 **shūsai** interstate
交際 **kōsai** associate with, keep company
with, be friends with
交際費 **kōsaihi** entertainment expenses
此際 **ko(no)sai** on this occasion, now
7 学際的 **gakusaiteki** interdisciplinary
8 実際 **jissai** actual(ly), real(ly)
実際的 **jissaiteki** practical
実際家 **jissaika** practical man; expert
空際 **kūsai** edge of the sky, horizon
国際 **kokusai** international
国際化 **kokusaika** internationalization
国際主義 **kokusai shugi** internationalism
国際法 **kokusaihō** international law
国際的 **kokusaiteki** international
国際連合 **Kokusai Rengō** United Nations
国際間 **kokusaikan** international
国際語 **kokusaigo** international language
9 海際 **umigiwa** seaside, beach
10 根際 **negiwa** area around the root
12 覚際 **sa(me)giwa** on the verge of awaking
間際 **magiwa** on the verge of, just before
13 寝際 **negiwa** just before going to bed
14 髪際 **kamigiwa** the hairline
16 壁際 **kabegiwa** by/near the wall
18 額際 **hitaigiwa** hairline

─────── 3 ───────

3 土俵際 **dohyōgiwa** at the brink, critical
moment
4 不手際 **futegiwa** clumsy, unskilled, inept
8 非実際的 **hijissaiteki** impractical
波打際 **namiu(chi)giwa** shore
往生際悪 **ōjōgiwa (ga) waru(i)** accept
defeat with bad grace
金輪際 **konrinzai** never, by no means
12 無辺際 **muhensai** limitless, boundless,
infinite
19 瀬戸際 **setogiwa** crucial moment, crisis, brink

2d11.2 / 858

障 **SHŌ, sawa(ru)** hinder, interfere with;
affect, hurt, harm

─────── 1 ───────

2 障子 **shōji** sliding door with translucent
paper panes
障子紙 **shōjigami** shōji paper
10 障害 **shōgai** obstacle, hindrance, impediment, handicap
障害物 **shōgaibutsu** obstacle, obstruction
16 障壁 **shōheki** barrier

─────── 2 ───────

3 万障 **banshō** all obstacles
4 支障 **shishō** hindrance, impediment, difficulty
戸障子 **toshōji** doors and shōji (translucent-
paper-paned sliding doors)
5 目障 **mezawa(ri)** eyesore, offensive sight
6 気障 **ki (ni) sawa(ru)** have one's feelings hurt,
take offense **kizawa(ri)** disagreeable
feeling
当障 **a(tari)sawa(ri ga nai)** inoffensive,
harmless, noncommittal
耳障 **mimizawa(ri)** offensive to the car
8 油障子 **aburashōji** translucent oilpapered
sliding doors
9 保障 **hoshō** guarantee, security
故障 **koshō** out of order, breakdown, trouble,
accident, hindrance, obstacle; objection
故障車 **koshōsha** disabled car
10 高障害 **kōshōgai** high hurdles
差障 **sa(shi)sawa(ri)** obstacle, hindrance;
offense
13 罪障 **zaishō** sins
罪障消滅 **zaishō shōmetsu** expiation of
one's sins
18 襖障子 **fusuma shōji** opaque paper sliding
door

─────── 3 ───────

7 身体障害者 **shintai shōgaisha** physically
handicapped person
8 青内障 **aosokohi** glaucoma

11 黒内障 **kokunaishō** black cataract,
   amaurosis
13 腰高障子 **koshidaka shōji** sliding door with
   hip-high paneling
14 緑内障 **ryokunaishō** glaucoma

─────────── 4 ───────────

6 安全保障 **anzen hoshō** (national) security

2d11.3 / 868

隠 隠
　　IN, ON, kaku(reru) (intr.)
　　hide　kaku(su) (tr.) hide

─────────── 1 ───────────

2 隠子 **kaku(shi)go** illegitimate child
3 隠女 **kaku(shi)onna** a mistress
　隠士 **inshi** hermit, recluse
4 隠元 **ingen** kidney bean
　隠元豆 **ingenmame** kidney bean
　隠文 **kaku(shi)bumi** secret/anonymous letter
5 隠立 **kaku(shi)da(te)** keep secret
　隠目付 **kaku(shi)metsuke** spy, detective
　　(historical)
　隠田 **kaku(shi)da** unregistered paddy
7 隠坊 **kaku(ren)bō** hide-and-seek
　　onbō crematory worker
　隠芸 **kaku(shi)gei** parlor trick, hidden talent
　隠岐 **Oki** (ancient kuni, Shimane-ken)
　隠岐諸島 **Oki shotō** (group of islands,
　　Shimane-ken)
　隠忍 **innin** patience, endurance
　隠見 **inken** appear then disappear (repeat-
　　edly)
　隠男 **kaku(shi)otoko** lover, paramour
　隠言葉 **kaku(shi)kotoba** secret language,
　　argot
8 隠事 **kaku(shi)goto, inji** secret
　隠退 **intai** retire
　隠泣 **kaku(shi)na(ki)** crying in secret
　隠岩 **kaku(re)iwa** sunken rock, reef
　隠居 **inkyo** retirement; retired person; old
　　person
10 隠遊 **kaku(re)aso(bi)** clandestine visit to a
　　red-light district
　隠匿 **intoku** concealment
　隠家 **kaku(re)ga** retreat, refuge, hideout
　隠釘 **kaku(shi)kugi** concealed nail
11 隠道 **kaku(re)michi** secret passage
　隠密 **onmitsu** privacy, secrecy; detective,
　　spy, secret agent
12 隠遁 **inton** retirement, seclusion
　隠場 **kaku(re)ba** refuge, hiding place
　隠場所 **kaku(re)basho** refuge, hiding place
　隠喩 **in'yu** metaphor
　隠棲 **insei** live in seclusion
　隠然 **inzen** latent, hidden

13 隠微 **inbi** hidden, escoteric, abstruse
　隠蓑 **kaku(re)mino** cloak that makes the
　　wearer invisible
14 隠語 **ingo** secret language; argot, jargon
15 隠蔽 **inpei** conceal, suppress, cover up
　隠縫 **kaku(shi)nu(i)** sewing concealed seams
18 隠顕 **inken** appear then disappear (repeatedly)

─────────── 2 ───────────

4 木隠 **kogaku(re)** hidden behind trees
5 包隠 **tsutsu(mi)kaku(shi)** concealment
　目隠 **mekaku(shi)** blindfold; screen
6 耳隠 **mimikaku(shi)** ear-covering hairdo
7 角隠 **tsunokaku(shi)** bride's wedding hood
　見隠 **mi(e)gaku(re)** now in and now out of
　　view
8 退隠 **taiin** retirement
　逃隠 **ni(ge)kaku(reru)** flee and hide
　若隠居 **waka-inkyo** early retirement
9 神隠 **kamikaku(shi)** be spirited away
　　kamigaku(re) (gods') hiding
11 雪隠 **setchin** toilet
　雪隠詰 **setchinzu(me)** to (force into a) corner
12 葉隠 **hagaku(re)** hide in the leaves
　惻隠情 **sokuin (no) jō** pity, compassion
　雲隠 **kumogaku(re)** be hidden behind
　　clouds; disappear
13 楽隠居 **rakuinkyo** comfortable retirement
　照隠 **te(re)kaku(shi)** covering up one's
　　embarrassment

2d11.4

鄙
　　HI lowly; the country(side)
　　hina the country(side)
　　hina(biru) be countrified

─────────── 1 ───────────

6 鄙劣 **hiretsu** base, sordid, dirty
7 鄙見 **hiken** my humble opinion
12 鄙猥 **hiwai** indecent, obscene
14 鄙語 **higo** vulgar word/expression

─────────── 2 ───────────

4 辺鄙 **henpi** remote, secluded
10 都鄙 **tohi** town and country

─────────── 12 ───────────

隨 → 随 2d8.10

2d12.1

隧
　　SUI, ZUI tunnel

─────────── 1 ───────────

11 隧道 **suidō, zuidō** tunnel

2

亻
⺅
孑
阝 12←
卩
刂
力
又
⼇
亠
艹
⺍
⺋

厂
廴
冂
八
匸

2d12.2

鄧

TŌ (an ancient Chinese province)

2d12.3

鄯

ZEN (proper name)

鄭 → 鄭 **2d12.4**

2d12.4

鄭　鄭

TEI, JŌ courteous

――――――― 1 ―――――――

9 鄭重 **teichō** courteous

2d12.5

鄲

TAN (place name)

――――――― 2 ―――――――

7 邯鄲 **Kantan** (an ancient Chinese capital)
kantan tree cricket
邯鄲步 **Kantan (no) ayu(mi)** like the young man who tried to learn how to walk stylishly like the people in Kantan, gave up his study before mastering it, and forgot how to walk at all
邯鄲師 **kantanshi** bedroom thief
邯鄲夢 **Kantan (no) yume** vain dream of splendor and wealth

――――――― 13 ―――――――

2d13.1 / 809

隣　鄰

RIN, tona(ru) be neighboring/ adjacent, adjoin
tonari next-door, adjoining

――――――― 1 ―――――――

2 隣人 **rinjin** neighbor
隣人愛 **rinjin'ai** love of one's fellow man
5 隣付合 **tonarizu(ki)a(i)** neighborliness
6 隣合 **tona(ri)a(u)** adjoin, be next to each other
隣邦 **rinpō** neighboring country

隣近所 **tonarikinjo** neighborhood
7 隣村 **tonarimura, rinson** neighboring village
8 隣国 **ringoku** neighboring country
9 隣保 **rinpo** neighborhood
隣保事業 **rinpo jigyō** welfare work, social services
隣保館 **rinpokan** settlement house
隣室 **rinshitsu** the next/adjoining room
10 隣家 **rinka** neighboring house, next door
隣席 **rinseki** the seat next to one
11 隣接 **rinsetsu** border on, be contiguous, adjoin
隣組 **tonarigumi** neighborhood association

――――――― 2 ―――――――

2 又隣 **matadonari** two doors away
5 比隣 **hirin** vicinity
四隣 **shirin** the whole neighborhood, the surrounding countries
6 近隣 **kinrin** neighborhood, vicinity
先隣 **sakidonari** next door but one
15 横隣 **yokodonari** nextdoor, to one's side

鄰 → 隣 **2d13.1**

險 → 険 **2d8.8**

――――――― 14 ―――――――

2d14.1

隰

SHITSU be moist/wet

隱 → 隠 **2d11.3**

2d14.2

隲

CHOKU, SHITSU stallion; climb; make

――――――― 16 ―――――――

2d16.1

隴

RŌ hill, mound

――――――― 阝 2e ―――――――

冂	印	卯	夘	印	即	卵	却	卹	卽	卸	卻	卿
0.1	2.1	3.1	2e3.1	4.1	5.1	5.2	5.3	6.1	2e5.1	7.1	2e5.3	2e10.1

卿	孵
10.1	3n10.5

0

2e0.1

冂 **SETSU** mark, handprint

2

2e2.1

印 **GYŌ** look upward; await

3

2e3.1

卯 夘 **BŌ, u** fourth horary sign (rabbit)

1

4 卯月 **uzuki** fourth lunar month
7 卯花 **u(no)hana** deutzia (a flower); tofu lees/dregs

夘 → 卯 **2e3.1**

4

2e4.1 / 1043

印 **IN** seal, stamp; India
shirushi sign, mark, symbol

1

0 印する **in(suru)** imprint, impress
5 印加 **inka** apply/impress (a voltage)
印字 **inji** printing, typing
6 印肉 **inniku** inkpad, stamp pad
7 印判 **inban** seal, stamp
印判師 **inbanshi** seal engraver
8 印画 **inga** (photographic) print
印刻 **inkoku** engrave/cut a seal
印刷 **insatsu** printing
印刷者 **insatsusha** printer
印刷物 **insatsubutsu** printed matter
印刷所 **insatsujo** press, print shop
印刷機 **insatsuki** printing press
9 印度 **Indo** India
12 印象 **inshō** impression
印象主義 **inshō shugi** impressionism
印象的 **inshōteki** impressive, graphic
印象派 **inshōha** impressionist school
印税 **inzei** royalties
19 印璽 **inji** imperial/state seal
22 印籠 **inrō** medicine case, pillbox; seal case

23 印鑑 **inkan** one's seal; seal impression

2

4 爪印 **tsumein** thumbprint
仏印 **Futsu-In** French Indochina
日印 **Nichi-In** Japan and India
5 矢印 **yajirushi** arrow
代印 **daiin** signing by proxy
好印象 **kōinshō** good impression
目印 **mejirushi** mark, sign
6 朱印 **shuin** red seal
朱印状 **shuinjō** official document with a red seal
朱印船 **shuinsen, shuinbune** shogunate-licensed trading ship
合印 **a(i)jirushi** comradeship badge; tally marks **aiin** tally marks
糸印 **itojirushi** thread to make seams conspicuous
7 改印 **kaiin** change one's seal
私印 **shiin** personal seal
8 東印度会社 **Higashi Indo Gaisha** East India Company
刻印 **kokuin** carved seal; stamp into
拇印 **boin** thumbprint
押印 **ōin** affixing a seal
実印 **jitsuin** one's registered seal
官印 **kan'in** official seal
9 封印 **fūin** (stamped) seal
10 消印 **keshiin** postmark, cancellation stamp
烙印 **rakuin** branding iron; brand, mark, stigma
馬印 **umajirushi** (ancient) commander's standard
11 捺印 **natsuin** seal (a document)
12 極印 **gokuin** hallmark, stamp, impress
検印 **ken'in** stamp of approval
焼印 **ya(ki)in** branding iron; brand, mark, stigma
奥印 **okuin** seal of approval
証印 **shōin** seal on a document
14 旗印 **hatajirushi** the design on a flag; banner, slogan
認印 **mito(me)in** personal seal, signet
15 調印 **chōin** signing (of a treaty)
調印国 **chōinkoku** a signatory
18 職印 **shokuin** official seal

3

6 仮調印 **karichōin** initialing (a treaty)
12 御朱印 **goshuin** sealed letter issued by a shogun
御朱印船 **goshuinsen** shogunate-licensed trading ship

4

13 署名捺印 **shomei-natsuin** signature and seal

2

亻 冫 孑 阝 卩 4←
刂 力 又 ㄅ 亠 亠 卜 ⺁ ヽ 厂 辶 冂 几 匚

───────────── 5 ─────────────

2e5.1 / 463

即 卽

SOKU immediate, as is, on the spot **sunawa(chi)** namely, i.e. **tsu(ku)** ascend (a throne)

───────────── 1 ─────────────

0 即する **soku(suru)** conform to
4 即今 **sokkon** at the moment, now
即日 **sokujitsu** on the same day
即日速達 **sokujitsu sokutatsu** same-day special delivery
5 即功 **sokkō** immediate effect
6 即死 **sokushi** die instantly
即死者 **sokushisha** persons killed instantly
即行 **sokkō** carry out immediately
7 即身成仏 **sokushin jōbutsu** attaining Buddhahood while still alive
即位 **sokui** accession to the throne
即位式 **sokuishiki** enthronement ceremony, coronation
即決 **sokketsu** prompt decision
即決裁判 **sokketsu saiban** summary trial
即吟 **sokugin** improvisation, impromptu poem
即妙 **sokumyō** ready wit
即売 **sokubai** sale on the spot
即売会 **sokubaikai** exhibition and spot sale
即応 **sokuō** conform/adapt to, meet
8 即刻 **sokkoku** immediately, at once
即効 **sokkō** immediate effect
即効薬 **sokkōyaku** quick remedy
即夜 **sokuya** on the same night
即物的 **sokubutsuteki** matter-of-fact
即金 **sokkin** (payment in) cash
10 即座 **sokuza** prompt, on the spot
即席 **sokuseki** extemporaneous, impromptu, instant (foods)
即席料理 **sokuseki ryōri** quick meal
即時 **sokuji** immediately, on the spot
即時払 **sokujibara(i)** immediate payment, at sight
即時渡 **sokujiwata(shi)** spot delivery
即納 **sokunō** prompt payment/delivery
11 即断 **sokudan** prompt decision
12 即答 **sokutō** prompt reply
14 即製 **sokusei** manufacture on the spot
15 即諾 **sokudaku** ready consent
16 即興 **sokkyō** improvised, ad-lib
即興曲 **sokkyōkyoku** an impromptu
即興詩 **sokkyōshi** improvised poem
18 即題 **sokudai** subject for improvisation; impromptu composition; (math) problem for immediate solution

───────────── 4 ─────────────

4 不即不離 **fusoku-furi** neutral, noncommittal
6 色即是空 **shikisoku-zekū** Matter is void.

All is vanity.
8 空即是色 **kūsoku-zeshiki** void matter as tangible

───────────── 3 ─────────────

1 一触即発 **isshoku sokuhatsu** touch-and-go, hair-trigger, explosive (situation)
6 当意即妙 **tōi-sokumyō** ready wit, repartee
9 速戦即決 **sokusen-sokketsu** all-out surprise offensive, blitzkrieg

2e5.2 / 1058

卵

RAN, tamago egg

───────────── 1 ─────────────

2 卵子 **ranshi** ovum, egg cell
5 卵白 **ranpaku** white of an egg, albumin
6 卵色 **tamago-iro** yellowish color
7 卵形 **tamagogata, rankei** egg-shaped, oval
11 卵黄 **ran'ō** yolk
卵巣 **ransō** ovary
卵殻 **rankaku** eggshell
卵細胞 **ransaibō** egg cell, ovum
12 卵焼 **tamagoyaki** fried eggs; square frypan
14 卵管 **rankan** Fallopian tubes, oviduct

───────────── 2 ─────────────

1 一卵性双生児 **ichiransei sōseiji** identical twins
5 生卵 **namatamago** raw egg
8 抱卵 **hōran** brooding over eggs, incubation
抱卵期 **hōranki** incubation period
9 茹卵 **yu(de)tamago, u(de)tamago** boiled egg
10 蚕卵 **sanran** silkworm egg
11 排卵 **hairan** ovulation
採卵 **sairan** egg raising
産卵 **sanran** egg laying, spawning
産卵期 **sanranki** breeding/spawning season
累卵危 **ruiran (no) aya(uki)** imminent peril
魚卵 **gyoran** fish eggs, roe, spawn
12 落卵 **o(toshi)tamago** poached egg
寒卵 **kantamago** winter eggs
13 煎卵 **i(ri)tamago** scrambled eggs
孵卵 **furan** incubation, hatching
孵卵器 **furanki** incubator
14 腐卵 **furan** bad egg
16 輸卵管 **yurankan** oviduct, Fallopian tubes
19 鶏卵 **keiran** chicken egg

───────────── 3 ─────────────

12 無精卵 **museiran** unfertilized egg

2e5.3 / 1783

却 卻

KYAKU reject; contrary **kae(tte)** on the contrary, instead; rather, all the more

───────────── 1 ─────────────

3 却下 **kyakka** reject, dismiss

——————— 2 ———————

6 返却 **henkyaku** return, repayment
7 冷却 **reikyaku** cooling (off), refrigeration
  冷却器 **reikyakuki** refrigerator, freezer, cooler, (car) radiator
  忘却 **bōkyaku** forget, be oblivious to
  没却 **bokkyaku** ignore, forget
  売却 **baikyaku** sell off, dispose of
  困却 **konkyaku** embarrassment, dilemma
8 退却 **taikyaku** retreat
10 消却 **shōkyaku** efface, erase, extinguish (a debt)
11 脱却 **dakkyaku** free oneself from, slough off
12 焼却 **shokyaku** destroy by fire, incinerate
  閑却 **kankyaku** neglect, ignore, overlook
13 棄却 **kikyaku** reject, dismiss
  滅却 **mekkyaku** extinguish, destroy, efface
17 償却 **shōkyaku** repayment, redemption, amortization

——————— 3 ———————

14 総退却 **sōtaikyaku** general retreat

——————— 6 ———————

2e6.1

卹 JUTSU pity, succor

——————— 7 ———————

卽 → 即 **2e5.1**

2e7.1 / 707

卸 **oro(su)** sell at wholesale
   oroshi wholesale

——————— 1 ———————

7 卸売 **oroshiu(ri)** wholesale
10 卸値 **oroshine** wholesale price

11 卸商 **oroshishō** wholesaler
   卸問屋 **oroshiton'ya** wholesaler

——————— 2 ———————

8 店卸 **tanaoroshi** taking inventory; fault-finding
10 荷卸 **nioro(shi)** unloading, discharge
12 棚卸 **tanaoroshi** inventory, stock-taking
16 積卸 **tsu(mi)oro(shi)** loading and unloading; unloading; cargo handling

——————— 3 ———————

3 大根卸 **daikon oro(shi)** grated daikon; daikon grater

卻 → 却 **2e5.3**

——————— 8 ———————

卿 → 卿 **2e10.1**

——————— 10 ———————

2e10.1

卿 卿 KEI you; state minister
        KYŌ (as suffix) Lord, Sir

——————— 1 ———————

9 卿相 **keishō** court nobles and state ministers

——————— 2 ———————

4 公卿 **kugyō, kuge** court noble

——————— 3 ———————

8 枢機卿 **sūkikei** (Catholic) cardinal

——————— 11 ———————

孵 → **3n10.5**

——————— 刂 2f ———————

刀	刈	切	分	刊	刋	召	州	刑	刔	刎	列	删
0.1	2.1	2.2	2o2.1	3.1	3.2	3.3	4.1	4.2	3c4.3	4.3	4.4	5.1
判	刧	刦	免	別	叛	制	刺	封	到	刮	刴	刻
5.2	2g5.2	2g5.2	2n6.1	5.3	2o7.8	6.1	6.2	6.3	6.4	6.5	6.6	6.7
刹	刷	兔	券	刺	到	荊	削	剃	契	剖	剔	剳
6.8	6.9	0a8.5	6.10	7.1	7.2	7.3	7.4	7.5	7.6	8.1	8.2	8.3
剥	剝	剣	剤	剛	帰	剰	副	剳	剩	割	剴	創
2f8.4	8.4	8.5	8.6	8.7	8.8	9.1	9.2	9.3	2f9.1	10.1	10.2	10.3
靭	剽	剿	劃	劂	劍	劉	劇	劈	劒	劑	釁	
10.4	11.1	11.2	12.1	12.2	2f8.5	13.1	13.2	13.3	2f8.5	2f8.6	24.1	

0

2f0.1 / 37

TŌ, katana sword

刀 釖

左側部首: 亻 冫 孑 阝 卩 →0 刂 力 又 宀 亠 十 卜 夂 丷 厂 辶 冂 几 匸

1

3 刀工 **tōkō** swordsmith
刀刃 **tōjin** sword blade
6 刀匠 **tōshō** swordsmith
刀圭 **tōkei** medicine
刀圭家 **tōkeika** physician
刀自 **tōji** lady, matron, Madam
7 刀身 **tōshin** sword blade
10 刀剣 **tōken** swords
11 刀痕 **tōkon** sword/saber scar

2

1 一刀 **ittō** (a single stroke of) a sword/blade
3 大刀 **daitō** long sword
小刀 **shōtō** shorter sword
　　 kogatana (pocket)knife
山刀 **yamagatana** woodsman's hatchet
4 太刀 **tachi** (long) sword
太刀打 **tachiu(chi)** cross swords with; contend, vie
太刀先 **tachisaki** tip of a sword; force of tongue
太刀魚 **tachiuo** hairtail, scabbard fish
木刀 **bokutō** wooden sword
牛刀 **gyūtō** butcher knife
5 古刀 **kotō** old sword
6 両刀 **ryōtō** two swords
両刀使 **ryōtōtsuka(i)** two-sword fencer; expert in two fields
両刀遣 **ryōtōtsuka(i)** two-sword fencer; expert in two fields
名刀 **meitō** famed sword, fine blade
守刀 **mamo(ri)gatana** sword for self-defense
血刀 **chigatana** bloodstained sword
竹刀 **shinai** bamboo sword (for kendo)
7 抜刀 **battō** draw one's sword; drawn sword
8 長刀 **naginata** halberd
佩刀 **haitō** sword worn at one's side; wear a sword
宝刀 **hōtō** treasured sword
9 剃刀 **kamisori** razor
軍刀 **guntō** military sword, saber
洋刀 **yōtō** saber
単刀直入 **tantō-chokunyū** getting straight to the point
秋刀魚 **sanma** mackerel/saury pike
10 帯刀 **taitō** wear a sword
馬刀貝 **mategai** razor clam
11 執刀 **shittō** performance of a surgical operation
猟刀 **ryōtō** hunting knife

12 短刀 **tantō** short sword, dagger
廃刀 **haitō** abolish the wearing of swords
13 腰刀 **koshigatana** short sword
新刀 **shintō** newly-forged/modern sword
15 儀刀 **gitō** ceremonial sword
16 懐刀 **futokoro-gatana** dagger; confidant

3

4 木太刀 **kidachi** wooden sword
日本刀 **nihontō** Japanese sword
8 受太刀 **u(ke)dachi** on the defensive
9 指揮刀 **shikitō** saber, parade sword
11 偃月刀 **engetsutō** scimitar
彫刻刀 **chōkokutō** chisel, graver
12 焼太刀 **ya(ki)tachi** tempered-bladed sword

2

2f2.1 / 1282

刈

KAI, GAI, ka(ru) cut, clip, shear, reap, prune

1

2 刈入 **ka(ri)i(re)** harvest, reaping
3 刈干 **ka(ri)ho(su)** cut and (sun-)dry
4 刈込 **ka(ri)ko(mi)** haircut, shearing, pruning
刈手 **ka(ri)te** reaper, mower
8 刈取 **ka(ri)to(ru)** mow, cut down, reap
刈取機 **ka(ri)to(ri)ki** reaper, harvester
10 刈株 **ka(ri)kabu** stubble
15 刈穂 **ka(ri)ho** harvested ears of rice

2

3 下刈 **shitaga(ri)** weeding
5 芝刈 **shibaka(ri)** lawn mowing
芝刈機 **shibaka(ri)ki** lawn mower
7 角刈 **kakuga(ri)** square-cut hair, crewcut
8 虎刈 **toraga(ri)** unevenly cropped, close-cropped (head)
9 草刈 **kusaka(ri)** grass cutting, mowing
13 裾刈 **susoga(ri)** trim (someone's) hair just above the nape
14 稲刈 **ineka(ri)** rice mowing/reaping

3

4 五分刈 **gobuga(ri)** close-cropped haircut
7 坊主刈 **bōzuga(ri)** close-cropped haircut

2f2.2 / 39

切

SETSU, SAI, ki(ru) cut **-ki(ru)** finish, do completely, be able to **-ki(ri)** all there is, only; since **ki(ri)** limit, end, place to leave off **-ki(tte no)** the most ... in the (whole place) **ki(reru)** cut well, be sharp **ki(re)** piece, cut, slice, scrap **ki(rasu)** run out of, be short of **setsu (na)** earnest, ardent; keen, acute **setsu(nai)** oppressive, suffocating; painful, distressing

—————————— 1 ——————————

2 切子 **ki(ri)ko** facet
3 切刃 **ki(ri)ha** cutting blade/edge
切干 **kiribo(shi)** dried strips of daikon
切上 **ki(ri)a(ge)** end, conclusion; rounding up (to the nearest integer); revalue, up-value (a currency)
切下 **ki(ri)sa(ge)** reduction, devaluation
切々 **setsusetsu** ardent, earnest
切口 **ki(ri)kuchi** cut end, opening
切口上 **ki(ri)kōjō** stiff and formal language
4 切切 **ki(re)gi(re)** pieces, scraps, fragments
setsusetsu ardent, earnest
切片 **seppen** cut-off pieces
切支丹 **Kirishitan** (early) Japanese Christianity/Christian
切分法 **setsubunhō** syncopation
切込 **ki(ri)ko(mu)** cut into; attack
ki(ri)ko(mi) cut, notch, incision
切手 **kitte** (postage) stamp
切火 **ki(ri)bi** flint sparks; purification by fire
切欠 **kirika(ki)** notch
切戸 **ki(ri)do** low gate, side entrance
5 切出 **ki(ri)da(su)** cut and carry out (timber); broach, bring up (a subject)
ki(ri)da(shi) pointed knife; logging; (meat) scraps; broaching (a subject)
切払 **ki(ri)hara(u)** clear/chop away, lop off
切札 **ki(ri)fuda** trump card
切石 **ki(ri)ishi** hewn/quarried stone
切立 **ki(ri)ta(tsu)** rise perpendicularly
ki(ri)ta(te) freshly cut
切目 **ki(re)me** rift, gap, break; end, pause, interruption **ki(ri)me** cut; conclusion
6 切合 **ki(ri)a(i)** crossing swords, fighting with swords, cutting each other
切羽 **ki(ri)ha** (mine tunnel) cutting/working face
切羽詰 **seppa-tsu(maru)** be driven to the wall, be at one's wit's end, be cornered
切返 **ki(ri)kae(shi)** cutback; counterattack
切地 **ki(re)ji** fabric, cloth, material
切先 **ki(s)saki** the point of a sword
切回 **ki(ri)mawa(su)** run around killing; manage, run, control
7 切身 **ki(ri)mi** slice, chop, cutlet
切迫 **seppaku** draw near, impend, be imminent; become acute, grow tense
切抜 **ki(ri)nu(ku)** cut/clip out
kirinu(ki) a (newspaper) clipping
切抜帳 **kirinu(ki)chō** scrapbook
切狂言 **ki(ri)kyōgen** last act
切花 **ki(ri)bana** cut flowers
切売 **ki(ri)u(ri)** sell by the piece
切言 **setsugen** urging, earnest persuasion
8 切刻 **ki(ri)kiza(mu)** chop up, hack

切味 **ki(re)aji** sharpness
切妻 **ki(ri)zuma** gable
切実 **setsujitsu** acute, keen, urgent; earnest
切放 **ki(ri)hana(su)** cut off/apart, sever, separate
切取 **ki(ri)to(ru)** cut off/out
切取線 **ki(ri)to(ri)sen** perforated line
9 切除 **setsujo** cut off/out, remove, excise
10 切倒 **ki(ri)tao(su)** cut/chop down, fell
切屑 **ki(ri)kuzu** scraps, chips, shavings
切株 **ki(ri)kabu** stump, stubble
切殺 **ki(ri)koro(su)** slay, put to the sword
切紙 **ki(ri)kami** cut paper **kirigami** cutting folded paper into figures
11 切捨 **ki(ri)su(teru)** cut down, slay; discard, cast away
切張 **ki(ri)ba(ri)** patching (a paper screen)
切崩 **ki(ri)kuzu(su)** level (a hill), cut through (a mountain); break (a strike), split (the opposition)
切望 **setsubō** earnest desire, yearning
切盛 **ki(ri)mo(ri)** manage, administer, run
切疵 **ki(ri)kizu** cut, gash, scar
切痔 **ki(re)ji** hemorrhoid, anal fistula
切断 **setsudan** cutting, section; cut, sever, amputate
切断面 **setsudanmen** section, cutting plane
切断機 **setsudanki** cutter, cutting machine
切符 **kippu** ticket
12 切換 **ki(ri)ka(eru)** change, exchange, convert; renew; replace; switch over
切落 **ki(ri)oto(su)** cut down, lop off
切替 **ki(ri)ka(eru)** change, exchange, convert; renew; replace; switch over
切歯 **sesshi** an incisor; gnashing of teeth
切歯扼腕 **sesshi-yakuwan** gnash one's teeth and clench one's arms on the chest (in vexation)
切貼 **ki(ri)ba(ri)** patching (a paper screen)
切間 **ki(re)ma** interval, break, opening
切開 **sekkai** incision, section, operation; clear (land) **ki(ri)hira(ku)** clear (land), hack out (a path)
13 切傷 **ki(ri)kizu** cut, gash, scar
切腹 **seppuku** disembowelment, harakiri
切愛 **setsuai** deep love
切詰 **ki(ri)tsu(meru)** shorten; reduce, economize, curtail, retrench
14 切髪 **ki(ri)gami** cut hair; widow's hair style (historical)
切端 **ki(re)hashi** cut-off piece/end, scraps
15 切磋琢磨 **sessa-takuma** work hard/assiduously
切線 **sessen** a tangent (in geometry)
18 切離 **ki(ri)hana(su)** cut off/apart, sever, separate

2

亻
冫
子
阝
卩
刂 2←
力
又
亠
十
卜
宀
ン
厂
辶
冂
几
匚

19 切願 **setsugan** entreaty, supplication, appeal

──────── 2 ────────

1 一切 **issai** all, everything; entirely, absolutely
hitoki(re) a piece/slice
一切合財 **issai-gassai** everything, the whole shebang
一切経 **Issaikyō** complete collection of Buddhist scriptures

2 〆切 **shimeki(ri)** deadline, closing date
八切 **ya(tsu)gi(ri)** cut into eight parts; octavo

3 大切 **taisetsu** important; valuable, precious
丸切 **maru(k)ki(ri), maruki(ri)** completely, utterly
千切 **chigi(ru)** tear up/off; pluck
sengiri thin strips of vegetables
口切 **kuchiki(ri)** broach, break the silence
小切手 **kogitte** check, cheque

4 爪切 **tsumeki(ri)** nail clippers
切切 **ki(re)gi(re)** pieces, scraps, fragments
setsusetsu ardent, earnest
区切 **kugi(ru)** punctuate; partition
手切 **tegi(re)** sever connections with, break up with
手切金 **tegi(re)kin** solatium for severing relations
手切話 **tegi(re)banashi** talk of separation
引切無 **hi(k)ki(ri)na(shi ni)** incessantly
木切 **kigi(re)** piece/chip of wood
日切 **higi(ri)** fixed date; setting the date

5 仕切 **shiki(ri)** partition; settlement of accounts; toeing the mark (in sumo)
皮切 **kawaki(ri)** beginning, start
打切 **u(chi)ki(ru)** end, close
叩切 **tata(ki)ki(ru)** hack down, chop off
句切 **kugi(ru)** punctuate; mark off, partition
尻切 **shiriki(re)** left unfinished
四切 **yo(tsu)gi(ri)** cut into four pieces, quarter; 30.5 by 25.5 cm (photo size)
石切 **ishiki(ri)** stonecutting, quarrying
石切場 **ishiki(ri)ba** quarry, stone pit
立切 **ta(te)ki(ru)** close/shut up

6 合切 **gassai** all, all together
肉切庖丁 **nikuki(ri)bōchō** butcher knife
缶切 **kanki(ri)** can opener
共切 **tomogi(re)** the same cloth
有切 **a(ri)ki(re)** remnants (of cloth), unsold leftovers
糸切歯 **itoki(ri)ba** eyetooth, canine tooth

7 赤切符 **akagippu** third-class ticket
抜切 **nu(ke)ki(ru)** get rid of, be free from
売切 **u(ri)ki(re)** sold out
困切 **koma(ri)ki(ru)** be in a fix, be at a loss
見切 **miki(ru)** see all; abandon, sell at a sacrifice
見切品 **miki(ri)hin** bargain goods

言切 **i(i)ki(ru)** state positively, declare; tell everything

8 事切 **kotoki(reru)** breath one's last, die
厚切 **atsugi(ri)** sliced thick
押切 **o(shi)ki(ru)** have one's own way, push through
知切 **shi(re)ki(tta)** obvious
苦切 **niga(ri)ki(ru)** look sour, scowl
金切声 **kanaki(ri)goe** shrill voice, shriek

9 飛切 **tobiki(ri)** superfine, choicest, beyond compare
乗切 **no(ri)ki(ru)** ride through/out, weather (a crisis)
哀切 **aisetsu** pathetic
首切 **kubiki(ri)** decapitation, execution; dismissal, firing
途切 **togi(reru)** be interrupted, break off
途切途切 **togi(re)togi(re)** disconnected, intermittent
通切符 **tō(shi)kippu** through ticket
耐切 **ta(e)ki(reru)** be able to endure, can stand
風切羽 **kazaki(ri)ba** flight feathers
封切 **fūki(ri)** new release, first run (of a movie)
挟切 **hasa(mi)ki(ru)** snip/clip (off)
持切 **mo(chi)ki(ru)** continue to hold, keep; hold all; maintain; talk of nothing else
指切 **yubiki(ri)** hooking each other's little finger (as a sign of a pledge)
品切 **shinagi(re)** out of stock, sold out
思切 **omo(i)ki(ru)** resolve, make up one's mind; resign oneself, give up
omo(i)ki(tta) radical, drastic
計切 **haka(ri)ki(ru)** give exact measure/weight
食切 **ku(i)ki(ru)** bite off/through; eat (it) all up

10 値切 **negi(ru)** haggle, bargain
挽切 **hi(ki)ki(ru)** saw off
振切 **fu(ri)ki(ru)** shake off, break free of
根切 **negi(ri)** pit excavation
息切 **ikigi(re)** shortness of breath
疲切 **tsuka(re)ki(ru)** get tired out, be exhausted
紙切 **kamiki(re)** scrap of paper
紋切形 **monki(ri)gata** conventional
紋切型 **monki(ri)gata** conventional

11 捩切 **ne(ji)ki(ru)** twist/wrench off
張切 **ha(ri)ki(ru)** stretch tight; be tense/eager
盛切 **mo(ri)ki(ri)** single helping
細切 **komagi(re)** small pieces of cloth; chopped meat
断切 **ta(chi)ki(ru)** cut off, sever

12 割切 **wa(ri)ki(ru)** divide; give a clear explanation

剴切 **gaisetsu** appropriate, apt
着切雀 **ki(ta)ki(ri) suzume** person having only the clothes he is wearing
遣切 **ya(ri)ki(renai)** cannot stand, cannot go on
極切 **kima(ri)ki(tta)** fixed, definite; stereotyped; self-evident
焼切 **ya(ke)ki(ru)** burn itself out
　　　ya(ki)ki(ru) burn out/off
煮切 **ni(e)ki(ranai)** undercooked; indecisive
散切 **zangi(ri)** regular haircut (no topknot)
散切頭 **zangi(ri) atama** cropped head
買切 **ka(i)ki(ru)** buy up, reserve, charter
痛切 **tsūsetsu** keen, acute
歯切 **hagi(re)** the feel when biting; articulation
　　　hagi(ri) grinding one's teeth; file for cutting cogs
貸切 **ka(shi)ki(ri)** reservations, booking
貸切車 **ka(shi)ki(ri)sha** reserved car
間切 **magi(ri)** tacking (in sailing)
13 裏切 **uragi(ru)** betray
　　　uragi(ri) betrayal, treachery
裏切者 **uragi(ri)mono** betrayer, traitor
適切 **tekisetsu** appropriate, pertinent
搔切 **ka(ki)ki(ru)** cut (off)
幕切 **makugi(re)** fall of the curtain (in a play)
腹切 **haraki(ri)** suicide by disembowelment
数切 **kazo(e)kire(nai)** countless
継切 **tsu(gi)gi(re)** patch
詰切 **tsu(me)ki(ru)** be always on hand
跡切 **togi(reru)** break off, stop, be interrupted
跡切跡切 **togi(re)-togi(re)** intermittent, off-and-on
14 摘切 **tsu(mi)ki(ru)** pick/nip/pluck off
髪切虫 **kamiki(ri) mushi** long-horned beetle
種切 **tanegi(re)** running out of seeds/materials
読切 **yo(mi)ki(ru)** read it through
15 澄切 **su(mi)ki(ru)** become perfectly clear
横切 **yokogi(ru)** cross, traverse, intersect
縁切 **enki(ri)** severing of a relationship
締切 **shi(me)ki(ru)** close
　　　shi(me)ki(ri) closing (date), deadline
緊切 **kinsetsu** urgent, pressing
輪切 **wagi(ri)** round slices
踏切 **fu(mi)ki(ru)** cross; take the plunge, take action, make bold to
　　　fumikiri railroad (grade) crossing
踏切番 **fumikiriban** railroad crossing gateman
16 薄切 **usugi(ri)** sliced thin
燃切 **mo(e)ki(ru)** burn (itself) out
親切 **shinsetsu** kind, friendly
親切気 **shinsetsugi** kindliness
積切 **tsu(mi)ki(ru)** ship/load completely
縡切 **kotoki(reru)** breathe one's last, die
17 擦切 **su(ri)ki(reru)** wear out, be frayed

懇切 **konsetsu** cordial, exhaustive, detailed
18 嚙切 **ka(mi)ki(ru)** bite off, gnaw through
―――――― 3 ――――――
3 巾着切 **kinchakuki(ri)** cutpurse, pickpocket
4 不適切 **futekisetsu** unsuitable, inappropriate
不親切 **fushinsetsu** unkind, unfriendly
火蓋切 **hibuta (o) ki(ru)** open fire; commence
5 包皮切断 **hōhi setsudan** circumcision
8 往復切符 **ōfuku kippu** round trip ticket
取仕切 **to(ri)shiki(ru)** run the whole (business)
9 帝王切開 **teiō sekkai** Caesarean section
10 息急切 **ikise(ki)ki(ru)** pant, gasp
記念切手 **kinen kitte** commemorative stamp
13 滅多切 **mettagi(ri)** hacking to pieces
―――――― 4 ――――――
9 途切途切 **togi(re)togi(re)** disconnected, intermittent
13 跡切跡切 **togi(re)-togi(re)** intermittent, off-and-on

分→分 2o2.1

―――――― 3 ――――――

2f3.1 / 585

刊　　**KAN** publish; carve, engrave

―――――― 1 ――――――
6 刊行 **kankō** publish
刊行物 **kankōbutsu** a publication
―――――― 2 ――――――
3 夕刊 **yūkan** evening paper/edition
夕刊紙 **yūkanshi** evening paper/edition
4 月刊 **gekkan** monthly publication
日刊 **nikkan** a daily (newspaper)
5 未刊 **mikan** unpublished
6 再刊 **saikan** reprint, republication
休刊 **kyūkan** suspend publication
近刊 **kinkan** recent/forthcoming publication
旬刊 **junkan** published every ten days
7 季刊 **kikan** quarterly publication
季刊誌 **kikanshi** a quarterly (magazine)
8 追刊 **tsuikan** additional publication
9 発刊 **hakkan** publish, issue
10 既刊 **kikan** already published
既刊号 **kikangō** back numbers
週刊 **shūkan** (published) weekly
週刊誌 **shūkanshi** a weekly (magazine)
11 終刊 **shūkan** ceasing publication
終刊号 **shūkangō** final issue
12 創刊 **sōkan** start a magazine; first issue

創刊号 **sōkangō** first issue/number
復刊 **fukkan** republication, reissue
廃刊 **haikan** discontinue publication
朝刊 **chōkan** morning paper/edition
13 新刊 **shinkan** new publication
新刊書 **shinkansho** a new publication
続刊 **zokkan** continue publication
14 増刊 **zōkan** special edition, extra number

───────── 3 ─────────

5 半月刊 **hangekkan** a semimonthly

2f3.2

刊

SEN, kezu(ru) cut, whittle

2f3.3 / 995

召

SHŌ summon **me(su)** summon, call for; (honorific) eat, drink, put on, wear, take (a bath/bus), buy

───────── 1 ─────────

2 召入 **me(shi)i(reru)** call in
3 召上 **me(shi)a(garu)** (polite) eat, drink, have
me(shi)a(geru) confiscate
7 召状 **shōjō** letter of invitation
8 召使 **me(shi)tsuka(i)** servant
召抱 **me(shi)kaka(eru)** employ
召物 **me(shi)mono** (polite) food, drink, clothing
10 召捕 **me(shi)to(ru)** arrest, apprehend
12 召換 **me(shi)ka(e)** change of clothes
召喚 **shōkan** summons
召集 **shōshū** call together, convene
召集令 **shōshūrei** draft call
15 召還 **shōkan** recall, order to return

───────── 2 ─────────

7 応召 **ōshō** be drafted
応召兵 **ōshōhei** draftee
9 思召 **obo(shi)me(shi)** your wishes/opinion; liking, fancy
14 聞召 **ki(koshi)me(su)** hear; drink, eat; go

───────── 4 ─────────

2f4.1 / 195

州 馴

SHŪ state, province
su sandbank, shoals

───────── 1 ─────────

4 州内 **shūnai** intrastate
13 州際 **shūsai** interstate

───────── 2 ─────────

2 九州 **Kyūshū** (island)
4 中州 **nakasu** sandbank/shoal in mid-river
5 本州 **Honshū** (Japan's main island)

加州 **Kashū** California
8 欧州 **Ōshū** Europe
欧州同盟 **Ōshū Dōmei** the European Union
欧州共同体 **Ōshū Kyōdōtai** the European Community
9 神州 **shinshū** land of the gods, Japan
砂州 **sasu** sandbar, sandbank
10 座州 **zasu** run aground, be beached
12 満州 **Manshū** Manchuria
満州事変 **Manshū Jihen** the Manchurian Incident
満州国 **Manshūkoku** Manchukuo
14 豪州 **Gōshū** Australia
17 濠州 **Gōshū** Australia

───────── 3 ─────────

3 三角州 **sankakusu** delta
大洋州 **Taiyōshū** Oceania
4 五大州 **godaishū** the five continents
六大州 **rokudaishū** the six continents
8 沿海州 **enkaishū** maritime provinces
9 南満州 **Minami Manshū** South Manchuria

───────── 4 ─────────

5 四百余州 **shihyakuyoshū** all China

2f4.2 / 887

刑

KEI penalty, punishment, criminal (law)

───────── 1 ─────────

6 刑死 **keishi** execution
7 刑余 **keiyo** previous conviction
8 刑事 **keiji** (police) detective; criminal case
刑事上 **keijijō** criminal, penal
刑事犯 **keijihan** criminal offense
刑事処分 **keiji shobun** criminal punishment
刑事事件 **keiji jiken** criminal case
刑事被告 **keiji hikoku** the accused, defendant
刑事訴訟 **keiji soshō** criminal action/suit
刑法 **keihō** criminal law, the Criminal Code
11 刑務所 **keimusho** prison
12 刑場 **keijō** place of execution
刑期 **keiki** prison term
14 刑罰 **keibatsu** punishment, penalty

───────── 2 ─────────

4 天刑 **tenkei** divine punishment
天刑病 **tenkeibyō** leprosy
火刑 **kakei** execution by fire, burning at the stake
5 主刑 **shukei** principal penalty
処刑 **shokei** punish, execute
処刑台 **shokeidai** the gallows
6 死刑 **shikei** capital punishment
死刑囚 **shikeishū** criminal sentenced to die
死刑執行 **shikei shikkō** execution

死刑場 **shikeijō** place of execution
死刑罪 **shikeizai** capital offense
7 体刑 **taikei** corporal punishment; penal servitude
求刑 **kyūkei** sentence sought (by prosecutor)
私刑 **shikei** taking the law into one's own hand, lynch law
8 受刑 **jukei** serve a sentence
受刑者 **jukeisha** a convict
実刑 **jikkei** (prison) sentence with no stay of execution
9 重刑 **jūkei** severe punishment/sentence
10 流刑 **ryūkei** deportation, exile, banishment
流刑地 **ryūkeichi** penal colony
流刑者 **ryūkeisha** an exile
徒刑 **tokei** penal servitude
宮刑 **kyūkei** castration
11 笞刑 **chikei** flogging
12 減刑 **genkei** reduction of penalty/sentence
極刑 **kyokkei** capital punishment; maximum penalty
絞刑 **kōkei** (execution by) hanging
14 酷刑 **kokkei** severe punishment
銃刑 **jūkei** execution by firing squad
16 磔刑 **haritsuke, takkei** crucifixion
17 厳刑 **genkei** severe punishment

————————— 3 —————————

6 有期刑 **yūkikei** penal servitude for a stated term
自由刑 **jiyūkei** punishment by confinement, imprisonment
11 終身刑 **shūshinkei** life sentence
12 無期刑 **mukikei** life imprisonment
絞首刑 **kōshukei** (execution by) hanging

刔 → 抉 3c4.3

2f4.3

刎 **FUN, ha(neru)** behead, decapitate

————————— 1 —————————

6 刎死 **funshi** suicide by self-decapitation
16 刎頸交 **funkei (no) maji(wari)** devoted/ lifelong friendship

2f4.4 / 611

列 **RETSU** row, line; queue
tsura(neru) put in a row
tsura(naru) lie in a row

————————— 1 —————————

0 列する **res(suru)** attend; rank with

4 列氏 **resshi** Réaumur (thermometer)
列王 **retsuō** chronicles of the kings
6 列伝 **retsuden** series of biographies
列伝体 **retsudentai** biographical style
列次 **retsuji** order, sequence
7 列車 **ressha** train
8 列国 **rekkoku** the powers, all nations
9 列侯 **rekkō** many feudal lords
10 列挙 **rekkyo** enumerate, list
列島 **rettō** archipelago
列座 **retsuza** presence, attendance
列席 **resseki** attend, be present
列席者 **ressekisha** those present
列記 **rekki** enumeration, listing
11 列強 **rekkyō** the great/world powers
13 列聖式 **resseishiki** canonization
18 列藩 **reppan** the various clans

————————— 2 —————————

1 一列 **ichiretsu** a row/line
2 二列 **niretsu** two rows, double file
3 上列車 **nobo(ri) ressha** train going toward the capital, up train
下列車 **kuda(ri) ressha** train going away from the capital, down train
4 分列 **bunretsu** filing off
分列式 **bunretsushiki** march-past, military review
6 同列 **dōretsu** same row; same rank; company, attendance
行列 **gyōretsu** queue, procession, parade; matrix (in math)
7 序列 **joretsu** order, sequence, rank
系列 **keiretsu** system, series; ownership affiliation, corporate group
8 直列 **chokuretsu** series (circuit)
並列 **heiretsu** arrange in a row; parallel (circuit)
参列 **sanretsu** attendance, presence
参列者 **sanretsusha** those present
9 陣列 **jinretsu** troop disposition, battle formation
前列 **zenretsu** front row
後列 **kōretsu** the back row, rear rank
10 陳列 **chinretsu** exhibit, display
陳列室 **chinretsushitsu** showroom
陳列棚 **chinretsudana** display rack/case
砲列 **hōretsu** gun battery, emplacement
配列 **hairetsu** arrangement, grouping
11 隊列 **tairetsu** (in serried) ranks, file
排列 **hairetsu** arrangement, configuration
終列車 **shūressha** last train
13 数列 **sūretsu** series (in math)
戦列 **senretsu** line of battle
16 整列 **seiretsu** stand in a row, line up
縦列 **jūretsu** file, column, queue
19 羅列 **raretsu** marshal, enumerate, cite

2

4 ←

4 ←

2

→ 5

亻 宀 子 阝 卩 刂 力 又 一 亠 十 卜 ケ 丷 厂 辶 冂 几 匚

21 艦列 **kanretsu** column of warships

――――――― 3 ―――――――

3 千島列島 **Chishima-rettō** the Kurile Islands
11 第五列 **dai-goretsu** fifth column
12 最前列 **saizenretsu** the front lines
14 増発列車 **zōhatsu ressha** extra train
　旗行列 **hata gyōretsu** flag procession

――――――― 4 ―――――――

2 二次配列 **niji hairetsu** secondary arrange-
　ment, arrangement on second level
3 三次配列 **sanji hairetsu** tertiary arrange-
　ment, arrangement on third level

――――――― 5 ―――――――

2f5.1

冊 SAN cut away, delete; anthologize

2f5.2 / 1026

判 HAN, BAN one's seal; judgment
waka(ru) understand, be clear
-ban size (of paper or books)

――――――― 1 ―――――――

0 判じる **han(jiru)** judge, decide; solve,
　decipher, interpret
A 6 判 **ērokuban** 148 x 257 mm paper/book
　size (A1 = 841 x 594 mm, A2 = 594 x
　420 mm, etc.)
B 4 判 **bīyonban** 364 x 257 mm paper size
　(B1 = 1030 x 728 mm, B2 = 728 x 515
　mm, etc.)
2 判子 **hanko** one's seal
7 判別 **hanbetsu** distinguish, discriminate
　判決 **hanketsu** judgment, (judicial) decision
8 判事 **hanji** a judge
　判例 **hanrei** (judicial) precedent
　判官 **hangan** judge, magistrate
　判定 **hantei** judgment, decision, verdict
　判定勝 **hanteiga(chi)** win by a decision
　判明 **hanmei** become clear, be ascertained
　判取 **hanto(ri)** getting someone to stamp his
　seal (for receipt or approval)
　判取帳 **hanto(ri)chō** receipt/chit book
11 判断 **handan** judgment
　判断力 **handanryoku** judgment, discernment
12 判検事 **hankenji** judges and prosecutors/
　procurators
　判然 **hanzen** clear, distinct, definite
14 判読 **handoku** decipher, read, make out

――――――― 2 ―――――――

3 大判 **ōban** (large old gold coin); large size
　(paper/book), folio

小判 **koban** small size (paper); (obsolete oval
　gold coin)
小判形 **kobangata** oval, elliptical
4 中判 **chūban** medium size
　公判 **kōhan** public trial/hearing
6 合判 **a(i)ban, a(i)han, gōhan** medium size
　(paper)
　印判 **inban** seal, stamp
　印判師 **inbanshi** seal engraver
　血判 **keppan** seal with one's blood
7 批判 **hihan** criticism, critique, comment
　批判的 **hihanteki** critical
8 盲判 **mekuraban** stamp one's seal without
　reading the document, rubber-stamp
9 連判 **renpan, renban** joint signature/seal
　連判状 **renpanjō, renbanjō** jointly sealed
　compact
10 原判決 **genhanketsu** the original decision/
　judgment
　書判 **ka(ki)han** written seal, signature
11 菊判 **kikuban** 22-by-15 cm size
12 焼判 **ya(ki)han, ya(ki)ban** branding iron;
　brand, mark, stigma
　裁判 **saiban** trial, hearing
　裁判長 **saibanchō** presiding judge
　裁判官 **saibankan** the judge
　裁判所 **saibansho** (law) court
　裁判権 **saibanken** jurisdiction
　評判 **hyōban** fame, popularity; rumor, gossip
　評判記 **hyōbanki** book of commentary on
　artists or celebrities
13 夢判断 **yume handan** interpretation of dreams
14 誤判 **gohan** mistrial, miscarriage of justice
15 審判 **shinpan, shinban** decision, judgment,
　refereeing
　審判官 **shinpankan** judge, umpire, referee
　談判 **danpan** negotiation, talks
　請判 **u(ke)han** surety seal
　論判 **ronpan** argument, discussion

――――――― 3 ―――――――

3 三文判 **sanmonban** ready-made seal
　大評判 **daihyōban** sensation, smash
4 不評判 **fuhyōban** bad reputation, disrepute,
　unpopularity
　太鼓判 **taikoban** large seal
　区裁判所 **kusaibansho** local court
5 四六判 **shirokuban** duodecimo, 12mo
7 身上判断 **mi(no)ue handan** telling a person's
　fortune
10 原裁判 **gensaiban** the original decision/
　judgment
12 無批判 **muhihan** uncritical
　無罪判決 **muzai hanketsu** acquittal

――――――― 4 ―――――――

5 民事裁判 **minji saiban** civil trial

7 即決裁判 **sokketsu saiban** summary trial
8 宗教裁判 **shūkyō saiban** the Inquisition
9 軍事裁判 **gunji saiban** court-martial
10 家庭裁判所 **katei saibansho** Family Court
12 最高裁判所 **Saikō Saibansho** Supreme Court
15 膝詰談判 **hizazu(me) danpan** direct/knee-to-knee negotiations
　調停裁判 **chōtei saiban** court arbitration
18 簡易裁判所 **kan'i saibansho** summary court

刧 → 劫 **2g5.2**

刼 → 劫 **2g5.2**

兔 → 免 **2n6.1**

2f5.3 / 267

別 **BETSU** different, separate, another; special; parting, farewell; (as suffix) classified by ... **waka(reru)** part, bid farewell, part company with; get divorced; diverge, branch off; disperse **wa(keru), waka(tsu)** divide, separate, distinguish **wa(kete)** above all, especially, all the more **waka(chi)** distinction, discrimination, differentiation

───── 1 ─────

0 別に, 別して **betsu (ni), bes(shite)** (not) particularly, especially
2 別人 **betsujin** different person; changed man
3 別々 **betsubetsu** separate, individual
　別口 **betsukuchi** different kind/item/lot
4 別天地 **bettenchi** another world
　別戸 **bekko** separate house
5 別世界 **bessekai** another world
　別冊 **bessatsu** separate volume, supplement
　別目 **waka(re)me** turning point, junction, parting of the ways
6 別名 **betsumei** another name, alias, pseudonym
　別宅 **bettaku** second residence
　別当 **bettō** groom, footman, horsekeeper; steward, attendant
7 別状 **betsujō** anything wrong, mishap
　別邸 **bettei** villa, separate residence
　別売 **betsuuri** sold separately, optional
　別条 **betsujō** anything wrong, mishap
8 別表 **beppyō** the attached table/list
　別事 **betsuji** another affair; mishap

別刷 **betsuzu(ri)** offprint
別送 **bessō** by separate mail, under separate cover
別法 **beppō** different method
別府 **Beppu** (city, Ōita-ken)
別居 **bekkyo** (legal) separation, living apart
別杯 **beppai** farewell cup/dinner
別物 **betsumono** something else, exception, special case
9 別便 **betsubin** by separate mail
別院 **betsuin** branch temple
別途 **betto** special
別段 **betsudan** special, particular
別派 **beppa** different sect/party/school
別封 **beppū** under separate cover
別品 **beppin** beautiful woman (slang)
別後 **betsugo** since parting, since we last saw each other
別荘 **bessō** villa, country place
別室 **besshitsu** separate/special room
別珍 **betchin** velveteen
別科 **bekka** special course
別盃 **beppai** farewell cup/dinner
10 別個 **bekko** separate, different
別家 **bekke** branch family
別宴 **betsuen** farewell dinner
別席 **besseki** different/special seat, separate room
別格 **bekkaku** special, exceptional
別時 **betsuji** another time; time of separation
別書 **waka(chi)ga(ki)** write leaving a space between words
別称 **besshō** another name, alias, pseudonym
別紙 **besshi** attached sheet, enclosure
別納 **betsunō** another method of payment
別記 **bekki** separate paragraph, stated elsewhere
11 別動隊 **betsudōtai** flying column, detached force
別勘定 **betsukanjō** separate account
別道 **waka(re)michi** forked road, branch-off, crossroads, parting of the ways
別問題 **betsumondai** another question, a different story
12 別隔 **wa(ke)heda(te)** make distinctions, discriminate
別報 **beppō** another report
別棟 **betsumune** another building, annex
別間 **betsuma** separate/special room
別項 **bekkō** separate/another paragraph
13 別業 **betsugyō** another line of work; villa
別働隊 **betsudōtai** flying column, detached force
別殿 **betsuden** palace/shrine annex
別意 **betsui** different opinion; malice; intention to part

2

2

別辞 **betsuji** parting words, farewell address
別誂 **betsuatsura(e)** special order, custom-made
14 別種 **besshu** another kind, distinct species
別製 **bessei** special make
16 別館 **bekkan** annex
17 別嬪 **beppin** beautiful woman (slang)
別懇 **bekkon** intimacy
18 別離 **betsuri** parting, separation

────── 2 ──────

1 一別 **ichibetsu** parting
3 大別 **taibetsu** broad classification
4 分別 **funbetsu** discretion, good judgment
分別 **bunbetsu** classification, separation, discrimination
分別盛 **funbetsuzaka(ri)** age of discretion, mature judgment
区別 **kubetsu** distinguish between
戸別 **kobetsu** every house, door to door
5 生別 **i(ki)waka(re), seibetsu** lifelong separation
弁別 **benbetsu** distinguish, discriminate
6 死別 **shibetsu** separation by death
7 判別 **hanbetsu** distinguish, discriminate
別別 **betsubetsu** separate, individual
告別 **kokubetsu** leave-taking, farewell
告別式 **kokubetsushiki** funeral service
8 送別 **sōbetsu** farewell, send-off
送別会 **sōbetsukai** going-away/farewell party
国別 **kunibetsu** classified by countries
物別 **monowaka(re)** rupture, failure (to reach agreement)
性別 **seibetsu** sex, whether male or female
9 哀別 **aibetsu** sad parting
段別 **tanbetsu** land area, acreage
派別 **habetsu** division (into factions)
咾別 **Ikanbetsu** (place name, Hokkaidō)
10 個別 **kobetsu** indivudual by individual
差別 **sabetsu** discrimination
差別界 **sabetsukai** world of inequality
峻別 **shunbetsu** sharp distinction
格別 **kakubetsu** particularly, exceptionally
特別 **tokubetsu** special, extraordinary
特別号 **tokubetsugō** special number
特別機 **tokubetsuki** special airplane
留別 **ryūbetsu** farewell to those staying
軒別 **kenbetsu** house-to-house
11 惜別 **sekibetsu** reluctuant parting
産別 **sanbetsu** industry-by-industry (unions)
細別 **saibetsu** subdivide, itemize
訣別 **ketsubetsu** parting, farewell
13 聖別 **seibetsu** consecrate, sanctify
愛別離苦 **aibetsuriku** parting from loved ones
14 選別 **senbetsu** sort, grade
種別 **shubetsu** classification, assortment
総別 **sōbetsu** in general

17 餞別 **senbetsu** farewell gift
18 離別 **ribetsu** separation, divorce
類別 **ruibetsu** classify
19 識別 **shikibetsu** discrimination, recognition
23 鑑別 **kanbetsu** discrimination, differentiation

────── 3 ──────

1 一分別 **hitofunbetsu** (careful) consideration
8 性差別 **sei sabetsu** sex discrimination
12 無分別 **mufunbetsu** imprudent, thoughtless, rash
無差別 **musabetsu** indiscriminate
14 種類別 **shuruibetsu** classification, assortment

────── 4 ──────

3 千差万別 **sensa-banbetsu** infinite variety

────── 6 ──────

叛→ 2o7.8

2f6.1 / 427

制 **SEI** system, organization; regulate, control

────── 1 ──────

0 制する **sei(suru)** control, suppress
4 制止 **seishi** control, restrain, keep in check
5 制令 **seirei** regulations
7 制作 **seisaku** a work, production
8 制限 **seigen** restriction, limitation
制定 **seitei** enact, establish
制空権 **seikūken** mastery of the air, air superiority
制服 **seifuku** uniform
制服制帽 **seifuku-seibō** cap and uniform
9 制海権 **seikaiken** control of the seas, naval superiority
制度 **seido** system
制約 **seiyaku** restriction, limitation, condition
11 制動 **seidō** braking, damping
制動機 **seidōki** brake
制球 **seikyū** (pitcher's) control
制欲 **seiyoku** control of one's passions
12 制帽 **seibō** regulation/school cap
制御 **seigyo** control
制裁 **seisai** sanctions, punishment
19 制覇 **seiha** mastery, supremacy; championship

────── 2 ──────

5 市制 **shisei** organization as a municipality
古制 **kosei** ancient system/precepts
圧制 **assei** oppression, tyranny
圧制的 **asseiteki** oppressive, repressive
圧制者 **asseisha** oppressor, despot, tyrant
6 自制 **jisei** self-control, self-restraint

自制心 **jiseishin** self-control
7 体制 **taisei** structure, system, order; the establishment
兵制 **heisei** military system
抑制 **yokusei** control, restrain, suppress, inhibit
抑制力 **yokuseiryoku** restraint, control
学制 **gakusei** educational system
町制 **chōsei** town organization
8 法制 **hōsei** legislation, laws
宗制 **shūsei** religious institutions
官制 **kansei** government organization
服制 **fukusei** dress regulations, uniform
9 専制 **sensei** absolutism, despotism
専制主義 **sensei shugi** absolutism, despotism
専制君主 **sensei kunshu** absolute monarch, despot
専制的 **senseiteki** despotic, autocratic, arbitrary
専制政治 **sensei seiji** despotic government, autocracy
軍制 **gunsei** military system/organization
帝制 **teisei** imperial rule
10 都制 **tosei** metropolitan government
時制 **jisei** tense (in grammar)
11 牽制 **kensei** check, restrain; diversion, feint
控制 **kōsei** checking, controlling
強制 **kyōsei** compulsory, forced
強制力 **kyōseiryoku** compelling/legal force
強制処分 **kyōsei shobun** disposition by legal compulsion
強制労働 **kyōsei rōdō** forced labor
強制的 **kyōseiteki** compulsory, forced
強制疎開 **kyōsei sokai** forced evacuation/removal, eviction
現制 **gensei** present system
規制 **kisei** regulation, control
12 無制限 **museigen** unlimited, unrestricted
税制 **zeisei** tax system
統制 **tōsei** control, regulation
統制力 **tōseiryoku** control over, power
統制品 **tōseihin** controlled goods
13 禁制 **kinsei** prohibition, ban
禁制品 **kinseihin** contraband
新制 **shinsei** new system
節制 **sessei** moderation, temperance
14 遺制 **isei** institution originating in the past
管制 **kansei** control
管制塔 **kanseitō** control tower
15 幣制 **heisei** monetary system
編制 **hensei** organize, put together
17 擬制 **gisei** (legal) fiction, fictitious
18 職制 **shokusei** office organization

——————— 3 ———————

1 一院制 **ichiinsei** unicameral system
2 二院制 **niinsei** bicameral system

4 不節制 **fusessei** intemperance, excesses
天皇制 **tennōsei** the emperor system
氏族制度 **shizoku seido** the family/clan system
六三制 **roku-sansei** the 6-3(-3-year) education system
5 母系制度 **bokei seido** matriarchal system
旧体制 **kyūtaisei** the old regime/establishment
6 全日制 **zennichisei** full-time (school) system
合議制 **gōgisei** parliamentary system
共和制 **kyōwasei** republican form of government
自治制 **jichisei** self-governing system
自動制御 **jidō seigyo** servocontrol
8 非統制 **hitōsei** noncontrolled (goods)
制服制帽 **seifuku-seibō** cap and uniform
官僚制 **kanryōsei** bureaucracy
定時制 **teijisei** part-time (school) system
9 通信制 **tsūshinsei** system of education by correspondence
封建制 **hōkensei** feudalism
独裁制 **dokusaisei** dictatorship
11 許可制 **kyokasei** license system
12 無統制 **mutōsei** uncontrolled
無節制 **musessei** intemperate
13 新体制 **shintaisei** new system/order
鉄拳制裁 **tekken seisai** the law of the fist
14 徴兵制 **chōheisei** conscription system
15 輪番制 **rinbansei** rotation system
16 機先制 **kisen (o) sei(suru)** forestall, beat (someone) to it
18 職階制 **shokkaisei** job-rank system

——————— 4 ———————

3 女人禁制 **nyonin kinsei** closed to women
6 灯火管制 **tōka kansei** lighting control, blackout, brownout
8 金本位制 **kinhon'isei** the gold standard
13 戦時体制 **senji taisei** war footing
14 複本位制 **fukuhon'isei** bimetalism

2f6.2 / 881

刺   **SHI** stab, pierce; name card
sa(su) stab, pierce, sting; sew, stitch
sa(saru) stick, be stuck   **toge** thorn, barb

——————— 1 ———————

2 刺子 **sa(shi)ko** quilted coat (worn in judo)
7 刺身 **sashimi** sliced raw fish, sashimi
刺身庖丁 **sashimi-bōchō** fish-slicing knife
刺抜 **togenu(ki)** tweezers
8 刺股 **sasumata** two-pronged weapon for catching criminals (historical)
刺青 **shisei, irezumi** tattooing
9 刺通 **sa(shi)tō(su)** stab through, pierce
刺客 **shikaku** assassin

10 刺殺 **sa(shi)koro(su)** stab to death
shisatsu stab to death; put out (a runner)
12 刺戟 **shigeki** stimulus, stimulation
14 刺網 **sa(shi)ami** gill net
16 刺激 **shigeki** stimulus, stimulation
刺激的 **shigekiteki** stimulating
刺激剤 **shigekizai** a stimulant, irritant
19 刺繡 **shishū** embroidery

――――――― 2 ―――――――

5 目刺 **meza(shi)** dried sardines (tied together with a string through their eyes)
6 名刺 **meishi** business card
名刺入 **meishii(re)** card case
有刺 **yūshi** thorny, barbed
有刺鉄線 **yūshi tessen** barbed wire
米刺 **komesa(shi)** rice-sampling tool
7 串刺 **kushiza(shi)** skewering
8 突刺 **tsu(ki)sa(su)** stab, pierce
9 風刺 **fūshi** satire, sarcasm
10 穿刺 **senshi** puncture (with a hypodermic needle), paracentesis, (spinal) tap
針刺 **harisa(shi)** pincushion
11 鳥刺 **torisa(shi)** bird catcher; chicken sashimi
15 𦥑刺 **gūshi** killing each other with swords/knives
16 諷刺 **fūshi** satire, sarcasm, lampoon
諷刺画 **fūshiga** caricature, cartoon

2f6.3

刲 **KEI** cut, stab; kill

2f6.4 / 904

到 **TŌ, ita(ru)** arrive, reach

――――――― 1 ―――――――

7 到来 **tōrai** arrival, advent
到来物 **tōraimono** something received as a gift
8 到底 **tōtei** (cannot) possibly, (not) at all, utterly, absolutely
11 到達 **tōtatsu** reach, attain
到達点 **tōtatsuten** destination
12 到着 **tōchaku** arrival
到着港 **tōchakukō** port of arrival
到着駅 **tōchakueki** arrival/destination station
16 到頭 **tōtō** at last, finally, after all

――――――― 2 ―――――――

5 未到 **mitō** unexplored
8 周到 **shūtō** meticulous, careful, thorough
10 殺到 **sattō** rush, stampede
13 想到 **sōtō** think of, consider, hit upon

――――――― 4 ―――――――

2 人跡未到 **jinseki-mitō** unexplored
5 用意周到 **yōi-shūtō** very careful, thoroughly prepared
9 前人未到 **zenjin-mitō** untrodden, unexplored

2f6.5

刮 **KATSU** rub

――――――― 1 ―――――――

5 刮目 **katsumoku** watch eagerly/closely

2f6.6

剞 **KO, egu(ru), ku(ru)** gouge, hollow out, bore, excavate

――――――― 1 ―――――――

7 剞抜 **ku(ri)nu(ku)** gouge out, bore a hole
剞形 **ku(ri)kata** molding

2f6.7 / 1211

刻 **KOKU** time; carve, engrave
kiza(mu) cut fine, chop up; carve, engrave; notch, score, mark off
kiza(mi) notch, nick; shredded tobacco

――――――― 1 ―――――――

1 刻一刻 **koku-ikkoku** moment by moment, hour by hour
3 刻下 **kokka** the present
刻々 **kokukoku, kokkoku** moment by moment, hour by hour
5 刻目 **kiza(mi)me** notch, nick
6 刻印 **kokuin** carved seal; stamp into
8 刻限 **kokugen** time, appointed time
刻苦 **kokku** hard work
13 刻煙草 **kiza(mi) tabako** shredded tobacco

――――――― 2 ―――――――

1 一刻 **ikkoku** a minute/moment
一刻千金 **ikkoku senkin** Every minute counts.
3 夕刻 **yūkoku** evening
寸刻 **sunkoku** brief time
小刻 **kokiza(mi)** mincing, in small bits
4 切刻 **ki(ri)kiza(mu)** chop up, hack
6 印刻 **inkoku** engrave/cut a seal
先刻 **senkoku** already, a while ago
7 即刻 **sokkoku** immediately, at once
8 例刻 **reikoku** the usual hour
刻刻 **kokukoku, kokkoku** moment by moment, hour by hour
定刻 **teikoku** the scheduled/appointed time
9 後刻 **gokoku** afterwards, later

10 時刻 **jikoku** time, hour
時刻表 **jikokuhyō** timetable, schedule
11 遅刻 **chikoku** be late/tardy
遅刻届 **chikoku todo(ke)** tardiness report
遅刻者 **chikokusha** latecomer
深刻 **shinkoku** serious, grave, acute
深刻化 **shinkokuka** intensification, aggravation
彫刻 **chōkoku** sculpture, carving, engraving
ho(ri)kiza(mu) engrave, carve
彫刻刀 **chōkokutō** chisel, graver
彫刻師 **chōkokushi** engraver, carver, sculptor
彫刻家 **chōkokuka** engraver, carver, sculptor
12 復刻 **fukkoku** republication, reissue
13 数刻 **sūkoku** several hours
14 漏刻 **rōkoku** water clock
腐刻 **fukoku** etching
15 篆刻 **tenkoku** seal engraving
18 覆刻 **fukkoku** reproduce, republish
覆刻本 **fukkokubon** reissued book
瞬刻 **shunkoku** instant, moment
翻刻 **honkoku** reprint

――――― 3 ―――――
8 刻一刻 **koku-ikkoku** moment by moment,
hour by hour
10 時々刻々 **jiji-kokukoku** hourly, minute by
minute

――――― 4 ―――――
10 時時刻刻 **jiji-kokukoku** hourly, minute by
minute

2f6.8

刹

SETSU, SATSU temple

――――― 1 ―――――
6 刹那 **setsuna** moment, instant
刹那主義 **setsuna shugi** living only for (the
pleasures of) the moment
刹那的 **setsunateki** momentary, ephemeral
――――― 2 ―――――
1 一刹那 **issetsuna** an instant, a moment
5 古刹 **kosatsu** old/ancient temple
6 名刹 **meisatsu** famous temple
11 梵刹 **bonsetsu** (Buddhist) temple

2f6.9 / 1044

刷

SATSU, su(ru) print

――――― 1 ―――――
2 刷子 **sasshi, hake** brush
3 刷上 **su(ri)a(garu)** be off the press, be
printed

5 刷本 **su(ri)hon** printed (but not yet bound)
book
刷立 **su(ri)ta(te)** fresh/hot off the presses
8 刷直 **su(ri)nao(su)** reprint (to correct
mistakes)
刷物 **su(ri)mono** printed matter
13 刷新 **sasshin** reform, renovation

――――― 2 ―――――
3 下刷 **shitazu(ri)** proof printing
4 手刷 **tezu(ri)** hand-printing
6 印刷 **insatsu** printing
印刷者 **insatsusha** printer
印刷物 **insatsubutsu** printed matter
印刷所 **insatsujo** press, print shop
印刷機 **insatsuki** printing press
色刷 **irozu(ri)** color printing
7 別刷 **betsuzu(ri)** offprint
抜刷 **nu(ki)zu(ri)** offprint
13 試刷 **shisatsu** proof printing
14 増刷 **zōsatsu** additional printing, reprints
17 縮刷 **shukusatsu** print in reduced size
縮刷版 **shukusatsuban** small-size edition

――――― 3 ―――――
2 二色刷 **nishokuzu(ri)** two-color printing
4 木版刷 **mokuhanzu(ri)** wood engraving
5 石版刷 **sekibanzu(ri)** lithography
6 両面刷 **ryōmenzu(ri)** printing on both sides
7 牡丹刷毛 **botanbake** (powder) puff, down
pad
10 校正刷 **kōseizu(ri)** (galley) proofs

兔 → 兎 0a8.5

2f6.10 / 506

券 劵

KEN ticket, certificate

――――― 1 ―――――
9 券面 **kenmen** the face of a banknote/
cetificate
――――― 2 ―――――
7 車券 **shaken** bicycle-race betting ticket
8 沽券 **koken** credit, dignity, reputation
金券 **kinken** gold certificate, paper money
9 発券 **hakken** issuance of bank notes
食券 **shokken** meal ticket
10 郵券 **yūken** postage stamp
株券 **kabuken** share/stock certificate
旅券 **ryoken** passport
竜券 **tatsuma(ki)** tornado
馬券 **baken** horse-race betting ticket
12 証券 **shōken** securities
13 債券 **saiken** bond, debenture

2 入場券 **nyūjōken** admission/platform ticket

15 質券 **shichiken** pawn ticket

———————— 3 ————————

2 入場券 **nyūjōken** admission/platform ticket
4 引替券 **hikika(e)ken** exchange ticket
6 回数券 **kaisūken** (train) coupon tickets
8 周遊券 **shūyūken** excursion ticket
抽選券 **chūsenken** lottery/raffle ticket
抽籤券 **chūsenken** lottery/raffle ticket
招待券 **shōtaiken** complimentary ticket
定期券 **teikiken** (train) pass, commuting ticket
9 乗車券 **jōshaken** (train) ticket
乗換券 **norikaeken** ticket for transfer
急行券 **kyūkōken** express ticket
前売券 **maeu(ri)ken** ticket sold in advance
10 特待券 **tokutaiken** complimentary ticket
航空券 **kōkūken** flight/airplane ticket
11 商品券 **shōhinken** gift certificate
12 割引券 **waribikiken** discount coupon
搭乗券 **tōjōken** boarding pass
診察券 **shinsatsuken** consultation ticket
13 寝台券 **shindaiken** sleeping-car ticket
福引券 **fukubi(ki)ken** lottery ticket
14 銀行券 **ginkōken** bank note
17 優待券 **yūtaiken** complimentary ticket
聴講券 **chōkōken** lecture admittance ticket
18 観覧券 **kanranken** admission ticket

———————— 4 ————————

6 有価証券 **yūka shōken** (negotiable) securities
11 船荷証券 **funani shōken** bill of lading

———————— 7 ————————

2f7.1

刺

RATSU go against, be contrary to

———————— 2 ————————

7 伯剌西爾 **Burajiru** Brasil
15 潑剌 **hatsuratsu** lively, animated

———————— 3 ————————

17 濠太剌利 **Ōsutoraria** Australia

2f7.2

剄

KEI, kubiki(ru) behead, decapitate

2f7.3

荊 荊

KEI thorny shrub; whip, switch, cane **ibara** thorny shrub, brier, brambles

———————— 1 ————————

8 荊妻 **keisai** my wife (deprecatory)

9 荊冠 **keikan** crown of thorns
12 荊棘 **keikyoku** thorns, brier; nettlesome situation

2f7.4 / 1611

削 削

SAKU, kezu(ru) whittle down, sharpen (a pencil); curtail; delete **so(gu), so(geru)** slice off; detract from, dampen

———————— 1 ————————

4 削片 **sakuhen** splinter, chip
5 削氷機 **sakuhyōki** ice-shaving machine
9 削除 **sakujo** delete, eliminate
10 削屑 **kezu(ri)kuzu** shavings
12 削減 **sakugen** reduction, cutback
13 削節 **kezu(ri)bushi** flaked shavings of dried bonito

———————— 2 ————————

5 氷削機 **hyōsakuki** ice-shaving machine
9 荒削 **arakezu(ri)** rough planing/hewing
11 添削 **tensaku** correct (a composition)
掘削 **kussaku** excavation
粗削 **arakezu(ri)** rough-planed, rough-hewn
12 開削 **kaisaku** building a road/canal
18 鎬削 **shinogi (o) kezu(ru)** fight fiercely

———————— 3 ————————

23 鰹節削 **katsuobushi kezu(ri)** plane for making bonito shavings

2f7.5

剃

TEI, so(ru), su(ru) shave

———————— 1 ————————

2 剃刀 **kamisori** razor
5 剃立 **so(ri)ta(te)** freshly shaven
14 剃髪 **teihatsu** tonsure, shaving the head

———————— 2 ————————

8 逆剃 **sakazo(ri)** shaving against the grain

2f7.6 / 565

契

KEI, chigi(ru) pledge, vow, promise

———————— 1 ————————

9 契約 **keiyaku** contract, agreement
契約書 **keiyakusho** contract
16 契機 **keiki** opportunity, chance

———————— 2 ————————

15 黙契 **mokkei** a tacit understanding

———————— 3 ————————

2 二世契 **nise (no) chigi(ri)** marriage vows
4 双務契約 **sōmu keiyaku** bilateral contract

─────── 8 ───────

2f8.1 / 1830

剖 剖　　BŌ　divide, cut

─────── 2 ───────

13 解剖　**kaibō**　dissection, autopsy; analysis
解剖学　**kaibōgaku**　anatomy
解剖室　**kaibōshitsu**　dissecting room

─────── 4 ───────

6 死体解剖　**shitai kaibō**　autopsy

2f8.2

剔　　TEKI　gouge out, cut away

─────── 1 ───────

5 剔出　**tekishutsu**　cut/gouge out, remove
7 剔抉　**tekketsu**　gouge out
9 剔除　**tekijo**　excise, cut out, remove

2f8.3

劂　　KI　carve

剥 → 剝　**2f8.4**

2f8.4

剝 剝　　HAKU, ha(geru) come/peel off, be worn off; fade, discolor ha(gu), ha(gasu) tear/peel/strip off; deprive of
mu(keru) come/peel off　mu(ku) peel, pare
hezu(ru) decrease by stealing, pilfer

─────── 1 ───────

5 剝出　**mu(ki)da(su)**　show, bare
　　mu(ki)da(shi)　bare, open, frank, blunt
7 剝身　**mu(ki)mi**　shellfish removed from the shell　**su(ki)mi**　sliced very thin
8 剝取　**ha(gi)to(ru)**　strip/tear off; rob of
11 剝脱　**hakudatsu**　come/peel off
12 剝落　**hakuraku**　peel/fall off
14 剝暦　**ha(gashi)goyomi**　calendar pad
剝製　**hakusei**　stuffing, stuffed/mounted specimen
剝奪　**hakudatsu**　deprive/divest of
18 剝離　**hakuri**　come/peel off

─────── 2 ───────

4 引剝　**hi(ki)ha(gu)**　pull/strip off

7 赤剥　**akamu(ke)**　red skin, rubbed raw
8 追剥　**o(i)ha(gi)**　highway robber, hijacker
逆剥　**sakamu(ke)**　hangnail
13 継剥　**tsu(gi)ha(gi)**　patching; a patch
17 擦剥　**su(ri)mu(ku)**　abrade, chafe

2f8.5 / 879

剣 劍劔劒剱釼　KEN, tsurugi　sword

─────── 1 ───────

3 剣山　**kenzan**　frog (in ikebana)
剣士　**kenshi**　swordsman, fencer
5 剣玉　**kendama**　ball-and-cup toy
6 剣先　**kensaki**　point of a sword/bayonet
7 剣呑　**kennon**　dangerous, risky
9 剣客　**kenkaku**　swordsman, fencer
11 剣道　**kendō**　Japanese fencing, kendo
剣術　**kenjutsu**　fencing
12 剣戟　**kengeki**　sword and halberd, arms, weapons
13 剣幕　**kenmaku**　angry/menacing look, glare
14 剣豪　**kengō**　master fencer
15 剣舞　**kenbu**　sword dance
剣劇　**kengeki**　swordplay/samurai drama

─────── 2 ───────

2 刀剣　**tōken**　swords
4 木剣　**bokken**　wooden sword
7 抜剣　**bakken**　draw one's sword
8 佩剣　**haiken**　sword worn at one's side; wear a sword
宝剣　**hōken**　sacred/treasured sword
9 神剣　**shinken**　sacred/divine sword
10 真剣　**shinken**　serious
真剣勝負　**shinken-shōbu**　fighting with real swords; game played in earnest
帯剣　**taiken**　sword at one's side; wear a sword
12 着剣　**chakken**　fixed bayonet
短剣　**tanken**　dagger; hour hand
14 銃剣　**jūken**　bayonet
銃剣術　**jūkenjutsu**　bayonet fencing
15 撃剣　**gekken**　fencing, kendō
霊剣　**reiken**　wondrous sword
16 懐剣　**kaiken**　dagger

─────── 3 ───────

4 手裏剣　**shuriken**　throwing-knife

2f8.6 / 550

剤 劑　　ZAI　medicine, preparation

─────── 2 ───────

3 下剤　**gezai**　laxative

2

亻冫子阝卩刂力又宀亠十卜夂丷厂辶冂几匚

8 ←

6 吐剤 **tozai** an emetic
7 良剤 **ryōzai** effective medicine
　乳剤 **nyūzai** an emulsion
9 洗剤 **senzai** detergent
10 配剤 **haizai** compounding (a prescription); (heaven's) disposition
11 液剤 **ekizai** liquid medicine
12 寒剤 **kanzai** (ice-salt) mixture for cooling
13 滑剤 **katsuzai** lubricant
　溶剤 **yōzai** a solvent
　試剤 **shizai** reagent
　鉄剤 **tetsuzai** iron-containing preparation
15 調剤 **chōzai** compounding medicines
　調剤師 **chōzaishi** pharmacist
16 薬剤 **yakuzai** medicine, drugs
　薬剤学 **yakuzaigaku** pharmacology
　薬剤師 **yakuzaishi** pharmacist
　錠剤 **jōzai** tablet, pill
18 鎔剤 **yōzai** flux

———— 3 ————

4 不凍剤 **futōzai** antifreeze
　止血剤 **shiketsuzai** hemostatic drug, styptic agent
　止痛剤 **shitsūzai** painkiller
6 防虫剤 **bōchūzai** insecticide
　防臭剤 **bōshūzai** deodorant, deodorizer
　防腐剤 **bōfuzai** a preservative, antiseptic
　防蝕剤 **bōshokuzai** an anticorrosive
　吸収剤 **kyūshūzai** an absorbent
7 冷凍剤 **reitōzai** refrigerant
　対症剤 **taishōzai** specific medicine
　利尿剤 **rinyōzai** a diuretic
8 刺激剤 **shigekizai** a stimulant, irritant
　定着剤 **teichakuzai** fixing agent
9 促進剤 **sokushinzai** accelerator, accelerant
　造血剤 **zōketsuzai** blood-making medicine
　栄養剤 **eiyōzai** nutritional supplement, tonic
　染毛剤 **senmōzai** hair dye
　染髪剤 **senpatsuzai** hair dye
10 健胃剤 **ken'izai** stomach medicine
　消化剤 **shōkazai** aid to digestion
　消炎剤 **shōenzai** an antiphlogistic, balm
　起爆剤 **kibakuzai** priming/triggering explosive
　峻下剤 **shungezai** powerful laxative
　殺虫剤 **satchūzai** insecticide
　殺菌剤 **sakkinzai** germicide, disinfectant
11 混和剤 **konwazai** a compound/blend
　清凉剤 **seiryōzai** refrigerant
　接合剤 **setsugōzai** glue, adhesive
　接着剤 **setchakuzai** adhesive, glue
　強心剤 **kyōshinzai** heart stimulant
　強壮剤 **kyōsōzai** a tonic
　脱毛剤 **datsumōzai** a depilatory
　脱臭剤 **dasshūzai** deodorant, deodorizer
　乾燥剤 **kansōzai** desiccant

12 覚醒剤 **kakuseizai** stimulant drugs
　補血剤 **hoketsuzai** an antianemic
13 催眠剤 **saiminzai** sleep-inducing drug
　塗擦剤 **tosatsuzai** liniment
　解毒剤 **gedokuzai** antidote
　解熱剤 **genetsuzai** an antipyretic
　睡眠剤 **suiminzai** sleeping drug/pills
14 漂白剤 **hyōhakuzai** bleach
　駆虫剤 **kuchūzai** vermicide, insect repellent
　駆除剤 **kujozai** expellent; insecticide
15 養毛剤 **yōmōzai** hair tonic
　撒布剤 **sanpuzai, sappuzai** dusting powder
　膠着剤 **kōchakuzai** glue, binder
　緩下剤 **kangezai** laxative
　調合剤 **chōgōzai** preparation, concoction
　賦形剤 **fukeizai** exipient, vehicle
16 興奮剤 **kōfunzai** stimulant
18 燻蒸剤 **kunjōzai** fumigant
　鎔接剤 **yōsetsuzai** welding flux
　鎮痛剤 **chintsūzai** painkiller
　鎮静剤 **chinseizai** tranquilizer, sedative

2f8.7 / 1610

剛

GŌ strong, hard, rigid

———— 1 ————

2 剛力 **gōriki** great physical strength; mountain porter-guide
4 剛毛 **gōmō** bristle
6 剛気 **gōki** brave, indomitable
7 剛体 **gōtai** rigid body (in physics)
8 剛直 **gōchoku** unbending, of integrity
　剛性 **gōsei** rigidity, stiffness
9 剛勇 **gōyū** valor, bravery
10 剛健 **gōken** strong and sturdy, virile
12 剛愎 **gōfuku** magnanimous; obstinate
13 剛腹 **gōfuku** magnanimous; obstinate
15 剛毅 **gōki** hardy, stout-hearted

———— 2 ————

8 金剛 **kongō** diamond; strong man; emery powder
　金剛力 **kongōriki** Herculean strength
　金剛石 **kongōseki** diamond
　金剛砂紙 **kongōshashi** emery paper
11 強剛 **kyōgō** strong, robust, forceful

———— 3 ————

15 質実剛健 **shitsujitsu-gōken** rough-hewn and robust

2f8.8 / 317

帰 歸皈

KI, kae(ru) return **kae(su)** let (someone) return, send (someone) back

——————— 1 ———————

0 帰する **ki(suru)** come to, result in; be attributable/due to, impute/ascribe to
1 帰一 **kiitsu** be united into one, be reduced to one
4 帰化 **kika** become naturalized
　帰化人 **kikajin** naturalized citizen
　帰支度 **kae(ri)jitaku** preparations to return
　帰心 **kishin** longing for home
5 帰田 **kiden** (an official) returning to the farm
6 帰伏 **kifuku** surrender, submission
　帰休 **kikyū** (soldier's) leave, furlough
　帰任 **kinin** return to one's post/duties
　帰向 **kikō** hearken back to
　帰帆 **kihan** sail back
　帰宅 **kitaku** return/come home
7 帰来 **kirai** come back
　帰村 **kison** return to one's village
8 帰依 **kie** become a believer in, embrace, convert to
　帰京 **kikyō** return to Tōkyō
　帰参 **kisan** return to one's former service/master
　帰国 **kikoku** return to one's country
　帰服 **kifuku** surrender, submission
9 帰降 **kikō** surrender, submission
　帰途 **kito** homeward journey
　帰省 **kisei** returning to one's home town (for the holidays)
10 帰耕 **kikō** return to the farm/land
　帰郷 **kikyō** return home, return to one's home town
　帰従 **kijū** surrender
　帰荷 **kae(ri)ni** return cargo
　帰校 **kikō** return to school
　帰納 **kinō** induction, recursion
　帰納法 **kinōhō** inductive method
　帰納的 **kinōteki** inductive (reasoning)
　帰航 **kikō** homeward trip/voyage
11 帰隊 **kitai** return to one's unit
　帰道 **kae(ri)michi** the way back/home
　帰掛 **kae(ri)ga(ke)** upon leaving, on one's way back
　帰巣本能 **kisō honnō** homing instinct
　帰船 **kisen** return to one's ship
12 帰着 **kichaku** return; conclusion, consequence
　帰雁 **kigan** returning wild geese
　帰港 **kikō** return to port
　帰営 **kiei** return to barracks
　帰属 **kizoku** revert to, belong to, be ascribed to
　帰朝 **kichō** return from abroad
　帰結 **kiketsu** conclusion, result, consequence

　帰順 **kijun** submission, (rebels') return to allegiance
13 帰農 **kinō** going back to the soil
　帰路 **kiro** the way home/back, return route
15 帰還 **kikan** return, repatriation; feedback
　帰還兵 **kikanhei** repatriated soldiers
　帰還者 **kikansha** a repatriate
17 帰趨 **kisū** trend, tendency; consequence
21 帰艦 **kikan** return to one's warship

——————— 2 ———————

4 不帰 **fuki** returning no more; dying
　日帰 **higae(ri)** a one-day (trip)
5 未帰還者 **mikikansha** person still not repatriated
6 再帰 **saiki** recursive
　再帰熱 **saikinetsu** recurrent fever
　回帰 **kaiki** recurrent; regression (coefficient)
　回帰熱 **kaikinetsu** recurrent fever
　回帰線 **kaikisen** the tropics (of Cancer and Capricorn); regression line
7 里帰 **satogae(ri)** bride's first visit to her old home
8 逃帰 **ni(ge)kae(ru)** run back, flee home
9 連帰 **tsu(re)kae(ru)** bring (someone) back/home
　持帰 **mo(tte) kae(ru), mo(chi)kae(ru)** bring back, take home　**mo(chi)kae(ri)** (two burgers) to go
11 転帰 **tenki** crisis (of an illness)
12 復帰 **fukki** return, comeback, reinstatement
　朝帰 **asagae(ri)** returning home in the morning after an all-night stay
13 適帰 **tekki** lead to, follow

——————— 3 ———————

5 北回帰線 **Kita Kaikisen** the Tropic of Cancer
9 南回帰線 **Minami Kaikisen** the Tropic of Capricorn
10 烏有帰 **uyū (ni) ki(suru)** be reduced to ashes

——————— 9 ———————

2f9.1 / 1068

剰 剰　**JŌ** surplus
　　　amatsusa(e) besides

——————— 1 ———————

7 剰余 **jōyo** a surplus
　剰余金 **jōyokin** a surplus
10 剰員 **jōin** superfluous personnel, overstaffing
14 剰語 **jōgo** redundancy

——————— 2 ———————

7 余剰 **yojō** surplus
11 過剰 **kajō** excess, surplus

2f9.2 / 714

副 **FUKU** accompany; vice-, deputy, assistant **so(u)** accompany; marry; meet, suit, satisfy, fulfill

───────── 1 ─────────

3 副大統領 **fukudaitōryō** vice president
4 副収入 **fukushūnyū** additional/side income
5 副本 **fukuhon** duplicate, copy
6 副会長 **fukukaichō** (company) vice president
副次的 **fukujiteki** secondary
副因 **fukuin** secondary cause
8 副官 **fukukan, fukkan** adjutant, aide
9 副食 **fukushoku** side dish; supplementary food
副食物 **fukushokubutsu** side dish; supplementary food
10 副将 **fukushō** adjutant general, second in command
11 副産物 **fukusanbutsu** by-product
12 副葬品 **fukusōhin** articles buried with the dead
副詞 **fukushi** adverb
13 副業 **fukugyō** side business, sideline
副腎 **fukujin** adrenal gland
副署 **fukusho** countersignature
15 副審 **fukushin** sub-umpire, assistant referee
副賞 **fukushō** extra prize
18 副題 **fukudai** subtitle, subheading
20 副議長 **fukugichō** vice president/chairman

───────── 2 ─────────

5 正副 **seifuku** original and copy; chief and vice-chief

───────── 3 ─────────

14 関係副詞 **kankei fukushi** relative adverb

2f9.3

剳 **TŌ** hook; sickle; layer of paper

───────── 10 ─────────

剰 → 剰 **2f9.1**

2f10.1 / 519

割 **KATSU, wa(ru)** divide, separate, split; break, crack; dilute; drop below **wa(reru)** break, crack/split apart **sa(ku)** cut up; separate; spare (time)
wari rate; ten percent; comparatively, in comparison with

───────── 1 ─────────

4 割切 **wa(ri)ki(ru)** divide; give a clear explanation
割込 **wa(ri)ko(mu)** wedge oneself in, cut/butt in **wariko(mi)** an interrupt (in computers)
割引 **waribiki** discount
wa(ri)bi(ku) give a discount
割引券 **waribikiken** discount coupon
5 割出 **wa(ri)da(su)** calculate; infer
割付 **wa(ri)tsu(keru)** allot, apportion, allocate **wa(ri)tsu(ke)** layout
割礼 **katsurei** circumcision
割目 **wa(re)me** crack, crevice
6 割合 **wariai** rate, proportion, percentage; comparatively
割安 **wariyasu** comparatively cheap, a good buy
割当 **wa(ri)a(teru)** allocate, allot, divide/distribute among
割当額 **wariategaku** allotment
7 割戻 **wa(ri)modo(su)** rebate
割戻金 **wa(ri)modo(shi)kin** a rebate
8 割拠 **kakkyo** each a leader in his own sphere
割易 **wa(re)yasu(i)** fragile
割物 **wa(re)mono** broken article; fragile article
9 割前 **wa(ri)mae** share, quota
10 割烹 **kappō** cooking
割烹店 **kappōten** restaurant
割烹着 **kappōgi** cook's apron
割高 **waridaka** comparatively expensive
割振 **wa(ri)fu(ru)** allocate, allot, divide/distribute among
割栗石 **wa(ri)guriishi** broken stones, macadam
11 割勘 **wa(ri)kan** Dutch treat
割符 **wa(ri)fu** tally, check
13 割腹 **kappuku** disembowelment, harakiri
割愛 **katsuai** part with (reluctantly), give up, spare, share
14 割増 **warima(shi)** extra (charge/payment)
割算 **wa(ri)zan** division (in math)
15 割箸 **wa(ri)bashi** half-split chopsticks
割賦 **kappu, wa(p)pu** paying in installments
20 割譲 **katsujō** cede (territory)

───────── 2 ─────────

1 一割 **ichiwari** ten percent
2 二割 **niwari** 20 percent
futa(tsu)wa(ri) half; cutting in two
3 干割 **hiwa(re)** cracking due to drying
口割 **kuchi (o) wa(ru)** (break down and) confess
4 片割 **katawa(re)** fragment; one of the group, accomplice

分割 **bunkatsu** partition, division
分割払 **bunkatsubara(i)** payment in
  installments
水割 **mizuwa(ri)** (whiskey) diluted with water
月割 **tsukiwa(ri)** per month, monthly
  installments
日割 **hiwa(ri)** daily/per-diem rate
5 打割 **u(chi)wa(ru)** divide, split
叩割 **tata(ki)wa(ru)** break to pieces, smash
四割 **yonwari, shiwari** forty percent
  yo(tsu)wa(ri) divide into four, quarter
6 年割 **nenwa(ri)** annual installment
再割引 **saiwaribiki** rediscount
地割 **jiwa(re)** fissure, crack in the ground
  jiwa(ri) allotment of land
7 役割 **yakuwa(ri)** role
8 押割麦 **o(shi)wa(ri) mugi** rolled barley/oats
歩割 **buwa(ri)** proportion; commission
底割 **sokowa(re)** (prices) falling through the
  floor, the bottom dropping out
  soko (o) wa(tte) (speaking) frankly,
  holding nothing back
10 書割 **ka(ki)wa(ri)** setting, background
笑割 **e(mi)wa(reru)** crack/split open
11 堀割 **horiwari** canal, waterway
掘割 **ho(ri)wa(ri)** canal, ditch
断割 **ta(chi)wa(ru)** cut apart, split open
12 棟割長屋 **munewa(ri) nagaya** long tene-
  ment/partitioned building
15 踏割 **fu(mi)wa(ru)** step on and break
16 縦割 **tatewa(ri)** slivers
頭割 **atamawa(ri)** per capita

——————— 3 ———————

6 仲間割 **nakamawa(re)** split among friends,
  internal discord
9 胡桃割 **kurumiwa(ri)** nutcracker
10 部屋割 **heyawa(ri)** assignment of rooms
11 採算割 **saisanwa(re)** below cost
13 群雄割拠 **gun'yū kakkyo** rivalry of local
  barons
碁盤割 **gobanwa(ri)** partitioned like a
  checkerboard

2f10.2

剴

GAI scythe; be appropriate

——————— 1 ———————

4 剴切 **gaisetsu** appropriate, apt

2f10.3 / 1308

創

SŌ create, originate, make; wound,
injury

——————— 1 ———————

5 創世 **sōsei** creation of the world
創世記 **Sōseiki** Genesis
創刊 **sōkan** start a magazine; first issue
創刊号 **sōkangō** first issue/number
創立 **sōritsu** establishment, founding
創立者 **sōritsusha** founder
7 創作 **sōsaku** a creation/work
創作力 **sōsakuryoku** creative power,
  originality
創作的 **sōsakuteki** creative
創作家 **sōsakuka** writer, novelist
創見 **sōken** original view, originality
8 創建 **sōken** found, establish
創始 **sōshi** originate, create, found
創始者 **sōshisha** originator, founder
9 創造 **sōzō** creation
創造力 **sōzōryoku** creative power
創造的 **sōzōteki** creative
10 創案 **sōan** original idea
創案者 **sōansha** originator, inventor
11 創痍 **sōi** a wound
創設 **sōsetsu** establishment, founding
13 創業 **sōgyō** found, establish
創業者 **sōgyōsha** founder
創傷 **sōshō** a wound, trauma
創意 **sōi** original idea, inventiveness
14 創製 **sōsei** invent, create, originate

——————— 2 ———————

9 独創 **dokusō** originality, creativity
独創力 **dokusōryoku** creative talent,
  originality
独創的 **dokusōteki** original, creative
独創性 **dokusōsei** originality, inventiveness
草創 **sōsō** inauguration, inception
草創期 **sōsōki** initial/early period
10 挫創 **zasō** contusion, fracture
11 絆創膏 **bansōkō** adhesive plaster
13 傷創 **shōsō** wound, injury
14 銃創 **jūsō** gunshot wound

——————— 3 ———————

4 天地創造 **tenchi sōzō** the Creation

2f10.4

靭 靭 靫 靫

JIN tough,
supple and strong
utsubo quiver

——————— 1 ———————

10 靭帯 **jintai** ligament

——————— 2 ———————

11 強靭 **kyōjin** tough, tenacious

─────────── 11 ───────────

2f11.1

剽 HYŌ threaten

─────────── 1 ───────────

9 剽窃 **hyōsetsu** plagiarism, pirating
10 剽悍 **hyōkan** fierce; daring
11 剽盗 **hyōtō** (highway) robbery
12 剽軽 **hyōkin** funny, droll
　剽軽者 **hyōkinmono** jokester, wag

2f11.2

剿 SHŌ, SŌ destroy; steal

─────────── 1 ───────────

13 剿滅 **sōmetsu** annihilate

─────────── 12 ───────────

2f12.1

劃 KAKU cut, split; boundary
　　kagi(ru) delimit, partition

─────────── 2 ───────────

4 区劃 **kukaku** division, section

2f12.2

劂 KETSU carve, sculpt

─────────── 13 ───────────

劍 → 剣 2f8.5

2f13.1

劉 RYŪ kill; line up; battle-ax

2f13.2 / 797

劇 GEKI drama, play; intense

─────────── 1 ───────────

4 劇化 **gekika** dramatization
　劇文学 **gekibungaku** dramatic literature
6 劇団 **gekidan** troupe, theatrical company

7 劇作家 **gekisakka** playwright, dramatist
8 劇毒 **gekidoku** deadly poison
　劇的 **gekiteki** dramatic
9 劇甚 **gekijin** intense, fierce, keen, severe
　劇通 **gekitsū** drama expert
　劇映画 **gekieiga** movie/film drama
　劇界 **gekikai** the theatrical world, the stage
12 劇場 **gekijō** theater
13 劇詩 **gekishi** dramatic poem/poetry
15 劇談 **gekidan** talk on drama; intense
　　negotiating
16 劇壇 **gekidan** the stage/theater
　劇薬 **gekiyaku** powerful medicine; deadly
　　poison

─────────── 2 ───────────

3 寸劇 **sungeki** short dramatic performance,
　　skit
　小劇場 **shōgekijō** little theater
5 史劇 **shigeki** historical drama
　旧劇 **kyūgeki** kabuki
9 活劇 **katsugeki** action scene/movie
10 剣劇 **kengeki** swordplay/samurai drama
　笑劇 **shōgeki** farce
11 惨劇 **sangeki** tragedy, tragic event
12 喜劇 **kigeki** a comedy
　悲劇 **higeki** tragedy
　悲劇的 **higekiteki** tragic
13 楽劇 **gakugeki** opera, musical drama
　新劇 **shingeki** new drama
　詩劇 **shigeki** a play in verse
14 演劇 **engeki** drama, play
　演劇的 **engekiteki** dramatic, theatrical
　演劇界 **engekikai** (the world of) the theater
　演劇術 **engekijutsu** dramatics
　演劇場 **engekijō** theater, stage
　歌劇 **kageki** opera
15 黙劇 **mokugeki** pantomime
16 繁劇 **hangeki** busyness
18 観劇 **kangeki** theatergoing

─────────── 3 ───────────

6 西部劇 **seibugeki** a Western (movie)
8 受難劇 **junangeki** Passion play
　宗教劇 **shūkyōgeki** religious drama
9 茶番劇 **chabangeki** farce, low comedy
　映画劇 **eigageki** film drama
　神秘劇 **shinpigeki** mystery drama
10 時代劇 **jidaigeki** period/costume drama
12 喜歌劇 **kikageki** comic opera
　無言劇 **mugongeki** pantomime
　悲喜劇 **hikigeki** tragicomedy
　童話劇 **dōwageki** a play for children
　軽演劇 **keiengeki** light comedy
14 歴史劇 **rekishigeki** historical drama
15 舞台劇 **butaigeki** stage play
　舞踊劇 **buyōgeki** dance drama

2f13.3

劈 **HEKI, HYAKU, sa(ku), tsunza(ku)**
split, break, rend

─────── 1 ───────

12 劈開 **hekikai** cleavage (of a gemstone)
16 劈頭 **hekitō** the first, outset

─────── 14 ───────

劒 → 剣 2f8.5

劑 → 剤 **2f8.6**

─────── 24 ───────

2f24.1

釁 **KIN, chinu(ru)** smear with blood

─────── 1 ───────

14 釁端 **kintan** origin of a dispute

─────── 力 2g ───────

力	加	功	幼	劣	助	劫	劭	励	劬	努	劾	効
0.1	3.1	3.2	3.3	3n3.4	5.1	5.2	5.3	5.4	5.5	5.6	6.1	6.2

勃	劼	劵	券	勅	勁	勇	勍	脅	動	勒	勘	勖
6.3	6.4	6.5	2f6.10	7.1	7.2	7.3	8.1	8.2	9.1	9.2	9.3	4c7.6

勤	勞	勧	勰	勠	勣	勦	勢	舅	勲	勵	黜	勸
10.1	3n4.3	11.1	11.2	11.3	11.4	11.5	11.6	11.7	4d11.3	2g5.4	15.1	2g11.1

─────── 0 ───────

2g0.1 / 100

力 **RYOKU, RIKI, chikara** power, force, strength **riki(mu)** exert one's strength, strain, bear down; brag, bluff, boast

─────── 1 ───────

1 力一杯 **chikara-ippai** with all one's might
3 力士 **rikishi** sumo wrestler
5 力仕事 **chikara shigoto** physical labor
6 力任 **chikaramaka(se)** with all one's might
  力行 **rikkō** strenuous efforts, exertion
  力自慢 **chikara jiman** boasting of one's strength
7 力作 **rikisaku** masterpiece, tour de force
  力走 **rikisō** run as fast as one can, sprint
  力投 **rikitō** powerful pitching
  力学 **rikigaku** dynamics, mechanics
8 力価 **rikika** potency; titer
  力泳 **rikiei** powerful swimming
9 力点 **rikiten** fulcrum; emphasis
  力負 **chikarama(ke)** be defeated by misapplication of one's own strength
  力持 **chikaramo(chi)** strong man
11 力動的 **rikidōteki** dynamic
  力率 **rikiritsu** power factor
  力添 **chikarazo(e)** assistance
  力強 **chikarazuyo(i)** forceful, vigorous, emboldened
12 力落 **chikarao(toshi)** discouragement, disappointment
  力量 **rikiryō** physical strength; ability, capacity

力無 **chikarana(ge)** feebly, dejectedly
13 力業 **chikarawaza** heavy labor; feat of strength
  力戦 **rikisen** hard fighting
  力試 **chikaradame(shi)** test of strength/ability
14 力説 **rikisetsu** emphasis, stress
15 力瘤 **chikarakobu** flexed biceps

─────── 2 ───────

2 人力 **jinriki** human power, man-powered
  jinryoku human power/efforts
  人力車 **jinrikisha** rickshaw
3 万力 **manriki** vise
  大力 **dairiki, tairiki** great strength
  才力 **sairyoku** ability, talent
4 仏力 **butsuriki** the power of Buddha
  分力 **bunryoku** component force
  水力 **suiryoku** water/hydro power
  水力工学 **suiryoku kōgaku** hydraulic engineering
  水力学 **suiriki/suiryokugaku** hydraulics
  水力発電所 **suiryoku hatsudensho** hydroelectric plant
  引力 **inryoku** gravitation, attraction
  火力 **karyoku** caloric force, thermal/steam-generated power
  心力 **shinryoku** mental power, faculties
5 斥力 **sekiryoku** repulsion, repulsive force
  出力 **shutsuryoku** output
  民力 **minryoku** national strength
  他力 **tariki** outside help; salvation by faith
  外力 **gairyoku** external force
  圧力 **atsuryoku** pressure

2

亻 冫 子 阝 卩 刂 力 又 一 亠 十 夂 宀 厂 辶 門 儿 匚

2

亻
冫
孑
阝
卩
刂
→0 力
又
一
十
卜
勹
ン
厂
辶
冂
几
匚

圧力計 **atsuryokukei** pressure gauge
打力 **daryoku** batting power
主力 **shuryoku** main force/strength
6 死力 **shiryoku** desperate effort
気力 **kiryoku** energy, vitality, mettle
全力 **zenryoku** one's every effort, full capacity
合力 **gōryoku** resultant force; cooperation; alms-giving, assistance
地力 **chiryoku** fertility
光力 **kōryoku** intensity of light
尽力 **jinryoku** efforts, exertions; assistance
有力 **yūryoku** influential, powerful
有力者 **yūryokusha** influential/powerful person
自力 **jiryoku** one's own strength/efforts
jiriki one's own strength/efforts; (Buddhist) salvation by works
自力本願 **jiriki hongan** salvation by works
自力更生 **jiriki kōsei** be saved by one's own efforts
7 体力 **tairyoku** physical strength
作力 **saryoku** effort, effective force
余力 **yoryoku** remaining strength; surplus energy; money to spare
助力 **joryoku** help, assistance
助力者 **joryokusha** helper, supporter
努力 **doryoku** effort, endeavor
努力家 **doryokuka** hard worker
角力 **sumō** sumo
兵力 **heiryoku** military force; troop strength
迫力 **hakuryoku** (dramatic) force, intensity, appeal
学力 **gakuryoku** scholastic ability, scholarship
労力 **rōryoku** trouble, effort; labor
応力 **ōryoku** stress
車力 **shariki** cartman, dray driver
8 非力 **hiriki** powerless; incompetent
念力 **nenriki** will power, faith
効力 **kōryoku** effectiveness, effect, validity
協力 **kyōryoku** cooperation
協力者 **kyōryokusha** collaborator, coworker
法力 **hōriki** the merits/power of Buddhism
知力 **chiryoku** mental capacity, intellect
実力 **jitsuryoku** actual ability, competence; arms, force
実力者 **jitsuryokusha** powerful person
実力派 **jitsuryokuha** powerful group
底力 **sokojikara** latent energy/strength
国力 **kokuryoku** national strength/resources
怪力 **kairiki** superhuman strength
武力 **buryoku** military force
金力 **kinryoku** the power of money
9 重力 **jūryoku** gravity
歪力 **wairyoku** stress
速力 **sokuryoku** speed, velocity
通力 **tsūriki** supernatural power

風力 **fūryoku** wind power/force
浮力 **furyoku** buoyancy, lift
活力 **katsuryoku** vitality, vigor
独力 **dokuryoku** one's own efforts, single-handed
胆力 **tanryoku** courage, mettle
神力 **shinryoku, shinriki** divine power
威力 **iryoku** power, might, authority, influence
省力化 **shōryokuka** labor saving
10 剛力 **gōriki** great physical strength; mountain porter-guide
能力 **nōryoku** ability, capacity, talent
財力 **zairyoku** financial resources
馬力 **bariki** horsepower
11 動力 **dōryoku** power, motive force
動力学 **dōrikigaku** kinetics, dynamics
動力源 **dōryokugen** power source
堕力 **daryoku** inertia, force of habit
推力 **suiryoku** thrust
張力 **chōryoku** tension, tensile strength
強力 **kyōryoku** strength, power **gōriki** great physical strength; mountain carrier-guide
強力犯 **gōrikihan** crime of violence
脚力 **kyakuryoku** walking ability
脱力 **datsuryoku** be drained of strength
脱力感 **datsuryokukan** feeling of exhaustion
視力 **shiryoku** visual acuity, eyesight
眼力 **ganriki** insight, discernment, observation
粘力 **nenryoku** viscosity; tenacity
12 偉力 **iryoku** great power, mighty force
蛮力 **banryoku** brute force
揚力 **yōryoku** (dynamic) lift
握力 **akuryoku** grasping power, grip
弾力 **danryoku** elasticity
弾力性 **danryokusei** elasticity, resilience, flexibility
富力 **furyoku** wealth, resources
極力 **kyokuryoku** to the utmost, to the best of one's ability, as much as possible
腕力 **wanryoku** physical strength
智力 **chiryoku** intelligence
無力 **muryoku** powerless, ineffectual, feeble; incompetent
惰力 **daryoku** inertia
筆力 **hitsuryoku** power of the pen
筋力 **kinryoku** physical strength
13 勢力 **seiryoku** influence, force
勢力下 **seiryokuka** under the influence/power of
微力 **biryoku** (my) poor ability, what little (I) can do
戦力 **senryoku** war-fighting capacity
意力 **iryoku** will power
資力 **shiryoku** means, resources, funds
電力 **denryoku** electric power
14 膂力 **ryoryoku** strength, brawn

静力学 **seirikigaku** statics
磁力 **jiryoku** magnetic force, magnetism
総力 **sōryoku** all one's might, all-out
総力戦 **sōryokusen** total war
精力 **seiryoku** energy, vigor, vitality
精力家 **seiryokuka** energetic person
15 権力 **kenryoku** power, authority, influence
権力主義 **kenryoku shugi** authoritarianism
権力争 **kenryoku araso(i)** struggle for
supremacy/power
権力者 **kenryokusha** powerful person
権力家 **kenryokuka** powerful person
権力側 **kenryokugawa** the more powerful side
暴力 **bōryoku** violence, force
暴力団 **bōryokudan** gangster organization
熱力学 **netsurikigaku** thermodynamics
魅力 **miryoku** charm, appeal, fascination
魅力的 **miryokuteki** attractive, charming,
captivating
16 鋳力 **buriki** tin (plate/sheet)
17 糞力 **kusojikara** brute force, great strength
聴力 **chōryoku** hearing ability
19 願力 **ganriki** the power of prayer
21 魔力 **maryoku** magical power, charm

───────────── 3 ─────────────

2 十人力 **jūninriki** the strength of ten
3 千人力 **senninriki** strength of a thousand
4 収容力 **shūyōryoku** (seating) capacity
支配力 **shihairyoku** one's control/hold over
反発力 **hanpatsuryoku** repellent force,
resiliency
5 生活力 **seikatsuryoku** vitality; earning power
生産力 **seisanryoku** (productive) capacity,
productivity
6 気体力学 **kitai rikigaku** aerodynamics
全速力 **zensokuryoku** full/top speed
自然力 **shizenryoku** forces of nature
7 求心力 **kyūshinryoku** centripetal force
判断力 **handanryoku** judgment, discernment
決断力 **ketsudanryoku** resolution, determination
抑制力 **yokuseiryoku** restraint, control
労働力 **rōdōryoku** labor, manpower,
workforce
8 注意力 **chūiryoku** attentiveness
治癒力 **chiyuryoku** healing/recuperative
power
抵抗力 **teikōryoku** (power of) resistance
拘束力 **kōsokuryoku** binding force (of a rule)
実行力 **jikkōryoku** executive ability, action
金剛力 **kongōriki** Herculean strength
9 発言力 **hatsugenryoku** a voice, a say
発動力 **hatsudōryoku** motive power
発電力 **hatsudenryoku** power
軍事力 **gunjiryoku** military strength

透視力 **tōshiryoku** penetration; clairvoyant
powers
耐久力 **taikyūryoku** durability, endurance
耐火力 **taikaryoku** fire resistance
海軍力 **kaigunryoku** naval power
洞察力 **dōsatsuryoku** insight
持久力 **jikyūryoku** endurance, stamina
独創力 **dokusōryoku** creative talent,
originality
背筋力 **haikinryoku** back-muscle strength
神通力 **jintsūriki, jinzūriki** supernatural
power
政治力 **seijiryoku** political influence
思考力 **shikōryoku** mental faculties
10 原子力 **genshiryoku** atomic energy, nuclear
power
原子力発電所 **genshiryoku hatsudensho**
nuclear power plant
原動力 **gendōryoku** motive force, prime
mover
流体力学 **ryūtai rikigaku** fluid dynamics
消費力 **shōhiryoku** consumer buying power
起電力 **kidenryoku** electromotive force
殺菌力 **sakkinryoku** germicidal effect
破壊力 **hakairyoku** destructive power
航続力 **kōzokuryoku** cruising/flying range
記憶力 **kiokuryoku** memory (ability)
11 牽引力 **ken'inryoku** pulling power, traction
推進力 **suishinryoku** thrust, impulse
強制力 **kyōseiryoku** compelling/legal force
理解力 **rikairyoku** comprehension
経済力 **keizairyoku** economic strength
粘着力 **nenchakuryoku** adhesion, viscosity
12 創作力 **sōsakuryoku** creative power,
originality
創造力 **sōzōryoku** creative power
遠心力 **enshinryoku** centrifugal force
蒸気力 **jōkiryoku** steam power
無気力 **mukiryoku** spiritless, flabby, gutless
無重力 **mujūryoku** weightlessness
無能力 **munōryoku** incompetent; impotent
無能力者 **munōryokusha** an incompetent
無資力 **mushiryoku** without funds
統制力 **tōseiryoku** control over, power
順応力 **junnōryoku** adaptability
13 溶解力 **yōkairyoku** solubility
想像力 **sōzōryoku** (powers of) imagination
戦闘力 **sentōryoku** fighting strength
意志力 **ishiryoku** will power
電動力 **dendōryoku** electromotive force
14 精神力 **seishinryoku** force of will
読書力 **dokushoryoku** reading ability
説得力 **settokuryoku** persuasiveness
15 潜勢力 **senseiryoku** latent power, potential
影響力 **eikyōryoku** effect, influence
16 凝集力 **gyōshūryoku** cohesive force, cohesion

2

亻
冫
孑
阝
卩
刂
力 0 ←
又
⺊
亠
十
⻌
⺈
ヽ
厂
⻌
冂
八
匸

機動力 **kidōryoku** mobility, maneuverability
親和力 **shinwaryoku** (chemical) affinity
17 購買力 **kōbairyoku** purchasing power
18 観察力 **kansatsuryoku** power of observation
19 爆発力 **bakuhatsuryoku** explosive force
警察力 **keisatsuryoku** police force
23 鑑賞力 **kanshōryoku** ability to appreciate
鑑識力 **kanshikiryoku** discernment

─────────── 4 ───────────

4 不可抗力 **fukakōryoku** force majeure, beyond one's control, unavoidable
6 光起電力 **hikari-kidenryoku** photoelectromotive force
8 表面張力 **hyōmen chōryoku** surface tension

─────────── 3 ───────────

2g3.1 / 709

加 **KA** add, apply; Canada; California
kuwa(eru) add, increase; give, inflict
kuwa(waru) increase; join in

─────────── 1 ───────────

2 加入金 **kanyūkin** entrance/initiation fee
3 加工 **kakō** processing
加工品 **kakōhin** processed goods
4 加水分解 **kasui bunkai** hydrolysis
5 加圧 **kaatsu** apply pressure
加号 **kagō** addition/plus sign
6 加州 **Kashū** California
8 加法 **kahō** addition (in math)
加担 **katan** assistance, support; conspiracy, complicity
加味 **kami** flavoring, seasoning
加奈陀 **Kanada** Canada
9 加重 **kajū** weighted (average), aggravated (assault)
加除 **kajo** insertion and deletion
加速度 **kasokudo** acceleration
加持 **kaji** incantation, faith-healing
10 加俸 **kahō** additional allowance, extra pay
加害 **kagai** do harm to, assault
加害者 **kagaisha** assailant, perpetrator
12 加減 **kagen** addition and subtraction; degree, extent, condition; adjust, keep within bounds; state of health; seasoning, flavor; allow for
加減乗除 **kagenjōjo** addition, subtraction, multiplication, and division
加硫 **karyū** vulcanization
加給 **kakyū** raising salaries
加筆 **kahitsu** correct, revise, retouch
加賀 **Kaga** (ancient kuni, Ishikawa-ken)
13 加勢 **kasei** assistance, support
加盟 **kamei** join, be affiliated with
加盟国 **kameikoku** member nation, signatory

14 加算 **kasan** addition (in math)
15 加熱 **kanetsu** heating
20 加護 **kago** divine protection

─────────── 2 ───────────

4 手加減 **tekagen** use discretion, make allowances; knack, tact, skill
日加 **Nik-Ka** Japan and Canada
火加減 **hikagen** condition of the fire
5 半加工品 **hankakōhin** semiprocessed goods
付加 **fuka** an addition   **tsu(ke)kuwa(eru)** add
付加価値税 **fuka-kachi zei** value-added tax
付加税 **fukazei** surtax
好加減 **i(i) kagen** moderate, temperate, suitable; haphazard, irresponsible, not thorough, halfhearted
6 印加 **inka** apply/impress (a voltage)
8 奉加帳 **hōgachō** subscription/contributions list
追加 **tsuika** addition, supplement
参加 **sanka** participate, take part
参加者 **sankasha** participant
10 倍加 **baika** to double
冥加 **myōga** divine protection
冥加金 **myōgakin** votive offering; forced contributions (Edo era)
書加 **ka(ki)kuwa(eru)** add (a postscript)
11 添加 **tenka** annex, append, affix, add
添加物 **tenkabutsu** additives
匙加減 **saji kagen** dosage, prescription; consideration, discretion, making allowances for
累加 **ruika** acceleration, progressive increase
12 湯加減 **yukagen** temperature of the bath water
煮加減 **ni(e)kagen** amount of boiling
13 塩加減 **shiokagen** seasoning with salt
掻加 **ka(tete) kuwa(ete)** besides, to make matters worse
14 漸加 **zenka** gradual increase, cumulative
増加 **zōka** increase, addition, rise, growth
15 糅加 **ka(tete) kuwa(ete)** besides, to make matters worse

─────────── 3 ───────────

4 不参加 **fusanka** nonparticipation
8 命冥加 **inochi-myōga** miraculous escape from death

─────────── 4 ───────────

7 亜米利加 **Amerika** America

2g3.2 / 818

功 **KŌ** merit, meritorious deed; success; credit   **KU, isao** merit, meritorious deed

─────────── 1 ───────────

5 功田 **kōden** rice-field reward (historical)
6 功名 **kōmyō, kōmei** great achievement
功名心 **kōmyōshin** ambition, love of fame

7 功労 **kōrō** meritorious service
功労者 **kōrōsha** man of distinguished service
功利 **kōri** utility; utilitarian
功利主義 **kōri shugi** utilitarianism
功利的 **kōriteki** utilitarian, businesslike
11 功過 **kōka** merits and demerits
13 功罪 **kōzai** merits and demerits
14 功徳 **kudoku, kōtoku** charity, virtuous acts, merit
15 功勲 **kōkun** meritorious service
17 功績 **kōseki** meritorious service

───────── 2 ─────────

3 大功 **taikō** great merit, distinguished service
6 年功 **nenkō** long service
有功 **yūkō** merit(orious)
有功章 **yūkōshō** medal for merit
成功 **seikō** success
7 即功 **sokkō** immediate effect
8 奇功 **kikō** singular/phenomenal success
武功 **bukō** military exploits
9 奏功 **sōkō** be effective
軍功 **gunkō** meritorious military service
神功 **Jingū** (empress, 201–269)
10 殊功 **shukō** meritorious deed
特功 **tokkō** special efficacy
12 偉功 **ikō** great deed, meritorious service
竣功 **shunkō** completion (of construction)
13 微功 **bikō** minor achievement
戦功 **senkō** military exploits, distinguished war service
15 勲功 **kunkō** distinguished service, merits
論功 **ronkō** evaluation of merit
論功行賞 **ronkō kōshō** conferring of honors

───────── 3 ─────────

2 九仞功一簣欠 **kyūjin (no) kō (o) ikki (ni) ka(ku)** failure on the verge of success
4 不成功 **fuseikō** failure
11 蛍雪功 **keisetsu (no) kō** the fruits of diligent study

2g3.3 / 1229

幼

YŌ, osana(i), itokena(i), ito- very young, infant, small child

───────── 1 ─────────

2 幼子 **osanago** little child, baby
3 幼女 **yōjo** little/baby girl
4 幼友達 **osana tomodachi** childhood friend
幼少 **yōshō** infancy, childhood
幼心 **osanagokoro** child's mind/heart
6 幼年 **yōnen** infancy, childhood (up to age 7)
幼年時代 **yōnen jidai** childhood
幼年期 **yōnenki** childhood
幼名 **yōmei, yōmyō** one's childhood/infant name

幼虫 **yōchū** larva
7 幼君 **yōkun** young master
幼児 **yōji** small child, tot, baby
幼児食 **yōjishoku** baby food
幼児期 **yōjiki** young childhood, infancy
8 幼芽 **yōga** germ (in grains)
幼者 **yōsha** child, infant
10 幼弱 **yōjaku** young and weak
幼宮 **itomiya** infant prince
幼時 **yōji** childhood, infancy
11 幼魚 **yōgyo** young fish
幼鳥 **yōchō** young bird, fledgling
12 幼童 **yōdō** small child
13 幼稚 **yōchi** infantile, immature
幼稚園 **yōchien** kindergarten
幼馴染 **osana najimi** childhood playmate
16 幼樹 **yōju** young tree
17 幼齢 **yōrei** young age
18 幼顔 **osanagao** what one looked like as a baby/tot

───────── 2 ─────────

6 老幼 **rōyō** old people and children
7 乳幼児 **nyūyōji** infant
8 長幼 **chōyō** young and old
長幼序 **chōyō (no) jo** Elders first.

───────── 4 ─────────

劣 → 3n3.4

───────── 5 ─────────

2g5.1 / 623

助

JO help; (as prefix) assistant, auxiliary **tasu(keru)** help, rescue **tasu(karu)** be helped/rescued **suke** assistance; moll, broad, dame; (suffix of personification)

───────── 1 ─────────

2 助力 **joryoku** help, assistance
助力者 **joryokusha** helper, supporter
3 助上 **tasu(ke)a(geru)** help up; pick up, bring safely to land
4 助手 **joshu** helper, assistant
5 助出 **tasu(ke)da(su)** help out of
6 助合 **tasu(ke)a(u)** help one another
助成 **josei** foster, promote, aid
助成金 **joseikin** subsidy, grant
7 助役 **joyaku** assistant official
助言 **jogen** advice
助言者 **jogensha** adviser, counselor
8 助長 **jochō** promote, further, encourage
助命 **jomei** spare (someone's) life
10 助起 **tasu(ke)oko(su)** help (someone) up

2
イ
冫
子
阝
卩
刂
力 5←
又
宀
十
ト
夂
丷
厂
辶
冂
八
匚

助教授 **jokyōju** assistant professor
11 助動詞 **jodōshi** auxiliary verb
助祭 **josai** (Catholic) deacon
助産 **josan** midwifery
助産院 **josan'in** maternity hospital
助産婦 **josanpu** midwife
助船 **tasu(ke)bune** lifeboat
12 助詞 **joshi** a particle (in grammar)
13 助勢 **josei** encouragement, backing
14 助演 **joen** play a supporting role, co-star

———————— 2 ————————

1 一助 **ichijo** a help
2 人助 **hitodasu(ke)** kind deed
3 三助 **sansuke** male bathhouse attendant
4 互助会 **gojokai** a mutual-aid society
天助 **tenjo** divine help/providence
内助 **naijo** one's wife's help
手助 **tedasu(ke)** help
6 自助 **jijo** self-help, self-reliance
7 扶助 **fujo** aid, support, relief
扶助料 **fujoryō** pension
9 神助 **shinjo** divine aid
11 救助 **kyūjo** rescue, relief, aid
救助米 **kyūjomai** dole rice
救助法 **kyūjohō** lifesaving
救助者 **kyūjosha** rescuer
救助隊 **kyūjotai** rescue party
救助船 **kyūjosen** rescue ship, lifeboat
救助網 **kyūjoami** (streetcar) cowcatcher; safety net
12 援助 **enjo** assistance, aid
幇助 **hōjo** aid and abet, support
補助 **hojo** assistance, supplement, subsidy
補助金 **hojokin** subsidy, grant
飲助 **no(mi)suke** heavy drinker, a souse
雲助 **kumosuke** (cheating) palanquin bearer
13 福助 **fukusuke** large-headed dwarf who brings good luck
15 権助 **gonsuke** manservant
賛助 **sanjo** support, backing

2g5.2

劫 刧 刦 **KYŌ, GŌ** threat; long ages **KŌ** (a certain type of situation in the game go) **obiya(kasu)** threaten

———————— 1 ————————

4 劫火 **gōka** world-destroying conflagration

———————— 2 ————————

5 永劫 **eigō** eternal, forever
15 億劫 **okkū** bothersome, troublesome **okukō, okugō, okkō** unimaginable long time

2g5.3

劭 **SHŌ** recommend; work hard; beautiful

2g5.4 / 1340

励 勵 **REI** encouragement; diligence **hage(mu)** be diligent **hage(masu)** encourage, urge on

———————— 1 ————————

6 励合 **hage(mi)a(u)** vie with one another
励行 **reikō** strict enforcement
10 励起 **reiki** excitation

———————— 2 ————————

10 勉励 **benrei** diligence, industriousness
13 奨励 **shōrei** encourage, promote, give incentive
督励 **tokurei** encourage, urge
14 精励 **seirei** diligence
16 激励 **gekirei** urge on, encourage
奮励 **funrei** strenuous effort

2g5.5

劬 **KU** become tired; work busily

2g5.6 / 1595

努 **DO, tsuto(meru)** make efforts, exert oneself, strive

———————— 1 ————————

2 努力 **doryoku** effort, endeavor
努力家 **doryokuka** hard worker

———————— 6 ————————

2g6.1 / 1939

劾 **GAI** investigate, prosecute

———————— 1 ————————

9 劾奏 **gaisō** investigate and report an official's offense to the emperor

———————— 2 ————————

12 弾劾 **dangai** impeachment, censure, denunciation

2g6.2 / 816

効 效 **KŌ, ki(ku)** be effective

———————— 1 ————————

2 効力 **kōryoku** effectiveness, effect, validity

5 効用 **kōyō** use, utility, effect
効目 **ki(ki)me** effect, efficacy
8 効果 **kōka** effect, effectiveness
効果的 **kōkateki** effective
10 効能 **kōnō** efficacy, effect
11 効率 **kōritsu** efficiency
18 効験 **kōken** efficacy

— 2 —

5 失効 **shikkō** lapse, lose effect, become null and void
6 有効 **yūkō** effective, valid
7 即効 **sokkō** immediate effect
即効薬 **sokkōyaku** quick remedy
8 逆効果 **gyakukōka** opposite effect, counter-productive
奇効 **kikō** remarkable effect
実効 **jikkō** practical effect
9 発効 **hakkō** come into effect
奏効 **sōkō** be effective
速効 **sokkō** quick effect
10 時効 **jikō** prescription, statute of limitations
特効 **tokkō** special efficacy
特効薬 **tokkōyaku** specific remedy
12 偉効 **ikō** great/marked effect
無効 **mukō** null, void, invalid, ineffective
16 薬効 **yakkō** efficacy of a drug

— 3 —

5 主治効能 **shuji kōnō** chief efficacy (of a drug)
16 薬石効無 **yakusekikō na(ku)** all remedies having proved unavailing

2g6.3

勃 **BOTSU** sudden; active

— 1 —

3 勃々 **botsubotsu** spirited, energetic
9 勃発 **boppatsu** outbreak, sudden occurrence
10 勃起 **bokki** an erection
12 勃然 **botsuzen (to)** suddenly; in a fit of anger
16 勃興 **bokkō** sudden rise to power

2g6.4

劼 **KATSU** be careful; hard; strive

2g6.5

劵

券→ **2f6.10**

— 7 —

2g7.1 / 1886

勅 敕 **CHOKU, mikotonori** imperial decree

— 1 —

5 勅令 **chokurei** imperial edict
6 勅旨 **chokushi** imperial order/wishes
8 勅使 **chokushi** imperial messenger
勅命 **chokumei** imperial order/command
10 勅書 **chokusho** imperial rescript
12 勅裁 **chokusai** imperial decision/approval
勅答 **chokutō** reply from/to the emperor
14 勅語 **chokugo** imperial rescript
15 勅撰 **chokusen** compilation for the emperor
勅撰集 **chokusenshū** emperor-commissioned anthology of poems
16 勅諭 **chokuyu** imperial instructions
18 勅題 **chokudai** theme of the New Year's Imperial Poetry Competition
19 勅願 **chokugan** imperial prayer

— 2 —

11 密勅 **mitchoku** secret decree
12 違勅 **ichoku** disobeying an imperial decree
詔勅 **shōchoku** imperial proclamation

2g7.2

勁 **KEI** strong

— 1 —

9 勁草 **keisō** (strong and constant as a) plant that resists the changing winds

— 2 —

12 雄勁 **yūkei** pithy, vigorous (style)

2g7.3 / 1386

勇 **YŪ** brave, courageous
isa(mu) be in high spirits
isa(mashii) brave, courageous, stirring

— 1 —

3 勇士 **yūshi** brave warrior
6 勇気 **yūki** courage
勇壮 **yūsō** brave, heroic, stirring
8 勇退 **yūtai** retire voluntarily, step down
勇者 **yūsha** brave/courageous man
10 勇健 **yūken** sound health
勇将 **yūshō** brave general
勇進 **yūshin** march bravely onward
勇猛 **yūmō** dauntless, intrepid, fearless
勇猛心 **yūmōshin** intrepid spirit
勇烈 **yūretsu** brave, valiant, intrepid
11 勇断 **yūdan** resolute decision

12 勇敢 **yūkan** courageous, brave, heroic
13 勇鼓 **yū (o) ko(su)** muster one's courage
 勇戦 **yūsen** brave/desperate fight
21 勇躍 **yūyaku** be in high spirits

─────── · 2 ───────

3 大勇 **taiyū** great courage
 小勇 **shōyū** mere brute courage
7 沈勇 **chin'yū** calm courage
8 知勇 **chiyū** wisdom and valor
 忠勇 **chūyū** loyalty and bravery
 武勇 **buyū** bravery, valor
 武勇伝 **buyūden** story of marital heroics
9 胆勇 **tan'yū** courage, pluck, dauntlessness
10 剛勇 **gōyū** valor, bravery
 真勇 **shin'yū** true courage
 猛勇 **mōyū** dauntless courage
12 蛮勇 **ban'yū** brute courage, reckless valor
 喜勇 **yoroko(bi)isa(mu)** be in high spirits
13 義勇 **giyū** loyalty and courage, heroism
 義勇兵 **giyūhei** volunteer soldier
 義勇軍 **giyūgun** volunteer army
22 驍勇 **gyōyū** bravery, valor

─────── 8 ───────

2g8.1

勍 **KEI** strong, fierce

2g8.2 / 1263

脅 **KYŌ, obiya(kasu), odo(kasu), odo(su)** threaten

─────── 1 ───────

4 脅文句 **odo(shi)monku** threating words, menacing language
7 脅迫 **kyohaku** threat, intimidation
 脅迫状 **kyōhakujō** threatening letter
 脅迫的 **kyōhakuteki** threatening, menacing
9 脅威 **kyōi** threat, menace
11 脅喝 **kyōkatsu** threaten, intimidate

─────── 9 ───────

2g9.1 / 231

動 **DŌ, ugo(ku)** (intr.) move
 ugo(kasu) (tr.) move

─────── 1 ───────

0 動じる/ずる **dō(jiru/zuru)** be perturbed
2 動力 **dōryoku** power, motive force
 動力学 **dōrikigaku** kinetics, dynamics
 動力源 **dōryokugen** power source
6 動向 **dōkō** trend, attitude

 動名詞 **dōmeishi** gerund
7 動体 **dōtai** moving body
 動作 **dōsa** action, movements, motion; bearing, behavior
 動乱 **dōran** upheaval, disturbance, riot
8 動画 **dōga** animation
 動的 **dōteki** dynamic, kinetic
 動物 **dōbutsu** animal
 動物学 **dōbutsugaku** zoology
 動物性 **dōbutsusei** animal (protein)
 動物相 **dōbutsusō** fauna
 動物界 **dōbutsukai** animal kingdom
 動物園 **dōbutsuen** zoo
 動物愛 **dōbutsuai** love for animals
 動物愛護 **dōbutsu aigo** being kind to animals, animal welfare
 動物誌 **dōbutsushi** fauna, zoography
10 動員 **dōin** mobilization
 動員令 **dōinrei** mobilization order
 動脈 **dōmyaku** artery
 動脈硬化 **dōmyaku kōka** hardening of the arteries
 動脈硬化症 **dōmyaku kōkashō** arteriosclerosis
 動悸 **dōki** palpitation, throbbing (of the heart)
11 動産 **dōsan** movable/personal property
 動転 **dōten** be surprised/stunned; transition
12 動揺 **dōyō** shaking, pitching, rolling; excitement, commotion, unrest
 動植物 **dōshokubutsu** plants and animals, flora and fauna
 動詞 **dōshi** verb
 動軸 **dōjiku** live spindle, drive shaft
13 動滑車 **dōkassha** movable pulley, running block
14 動静 **dōsei** movements, conditions
15 動輪 **dōrin** driving wheel
16 動機 **dōki** motive
20 動議 **dōgi** a (parliamentary) motion

─────── 2 ───────

2 力動的 **rikidōteki** dynamic
3 大動脈 **daidōmyaku** aorta
4 不動 **fudō** immovable, fixed
 不動産 **fudōsan** immovable property, real estate
 不動産屋 **fudōsan'ya** real estate agent
 天動説 **tendōsetsu** the Ptolemaic theory
 反動 **handō** reaction; recoil
 反動主義者 **handō shugisha** a reactionary
 反動的 **handōteki** reactionary
 反動家 **handōka** a reactionary
 手動 **shudō** manual, hand-operated
 手動式 **shudōshiki** manual, hand-operated
 手動車 **shudōsha** handcar
5 出動 **shutsudō** be sent/called out, take the field

生動 **seidō** being full of life
他動詞 **tadōshi** transitive verb
可動 **kadō** movable, mobile
可動性 **kadōsei** mobility
可動橋 **kadōkyō** movable bridge
主動 **shudō** leadership
主動的 **shudōteki** autonomous
6 妄動 **mōdō, bōdō** act blindly
地動説 **chidōsetsu** heliocentric/Copernican theory
行動 **kōdō** action, conduct, behavior, operations
行動半径 **kōdō hankei** radius of action, range
行動主義 **kōdō shugi** behaviorism
回動 **kaidō** rotate
自動 **jidō** automatic
自動式 **jidōshiki** automatic
自動車 **jidōsha** motor vehicle, automobile
自動制御 **jidō seigyo** servocontrol
自動的 **jidōteki** automatic
自動巻 **jidōma(ki)** self-winding (watch)
自動連結機 **jidō renketsuki** automatic coupler
自動販売機 **jidō hanbaiki** vending machine
自動詞 **jidōshi** intransitive verb
7 身動 **miugo(ki)** move about, stir
別動隊 **betsudōtai** flying column, detached force
助動詞 **jodōshi** auxiliary verb
言動 **gendō** speech and conduct
8 制動 **seidō** braking, damping
制動機 **seidōki** brake
受動 **judō** passivity
受動的 **judōteki** passive
受動態 **judōtai** passive voice
盲動 **mōdō** act blindly
波動 **hadō** wave, undulatory motion
始動 **shidō** starting (a machine)
実動 **jitsudō** actual work
9 発動 **hatsudō** put into motion, exercise, invoke
発動力 **hatsudōryoku** motive power
発動的 **hatsudōteki** active
変動 **hendō** fluctuations
連動 **rendō** gears, linkage, drive
浮動 **fudō** floating, fluctuating
活動 **katsudō** activity
活動写真 **katsudō shashin** moving pictures, movie
活動的 **katsudōteki** active, dynamic
活動家 **katsudōka** energetic person; activist
律動 **ritsudō** rhythm, rhythmic movement
胎動 **taidō** fetal movement, quickening
胎動期 **taidōki** the quickening period
10 原動力 **gendōryoku** motive force, prime mover
遊動 **yūdō** not stationary, movable, mobile

遊動円木 **yūdō enboku** suspended horizontal log, swinging pole (playground equipment)
遊動隊 **yūdōtai** mobile corps
流動 **ryūdō** flowing, liquid (assets), current (liabilities)
流動体 **ryūdōtai** a fluid
流動物 **ryūdōbutsu** fluid, liquid
流動食 **ryūdōshoku** liquid diet/food
起動 **kidō** starting
起動機 **kidōki** starter, starting motor
振動 **shindō** vibration, oscillation
     fu(ri)ugo(ku) swing, shake, oscillate
荷動 **niugo(ki)** movement of goods
挙動 **kyodō** behavior, movements
脈動 **myakudō** pulsation
能動 **nōdō** activity
能動的 **nōdōteki** active
能動態 **nōdōtai** active voice (in grammar)
扇動 **sendō** incitement, instigation, agitation
扇動者 **sendōsha** instigator, agitator
11 運動 **undō** motion, movement; exercise, sports; a movement, campaign
運動不足 **undō-busoku** lack of exercise
運動用具 **undō yōgu** sporting goods
運動会 **undōkai** athletic meet
運動服 **undōfuku** sportswear, uniform
運動界 **undōkai** the sporting world, sports
運動員 **undōin** campaigner, canvasser
運動家 **undōka** athlete, sportsman
運動場 **undōjō** playing/athletic field
運動帽 **undōbō** sports cap
運動費 **undōhi** campaign expenses
運動靴 **undōgutsu** athletic shoes, sneakers
運動欄 **undōran** the sports page/columns
移動 **idō** moving, migration
異動 **idō** change, reshuffling
12 渦動 **kadō** vortex
揺動 **yu(ri)ugo(kasu)** (tr.) shake
     yu(re)ugo(ku) (intr.) shake
策動 **sakudō** manipulation, maneuvering
策動家 **sakudōka** schemer
13 微動 **bidō** slight tremor, quiver
鼓動 **kodō** (heart) beat
感動 **kandō** impression, inspiration, emotion, excitement
電動 **dendō** electric (not manual)
電動力 **dendōryoku** electromotive force
電動式 **dendōshiki** electric (not manual)
電動機 **dendōki** electric motor
14 摺動 **shūdō, shōdō** sliding
鳴動 **meidō** rumbling
煽動 **sendō** instigate, abet, agitate, incite
総動員 **sōdōin** general mobilization
15 衝動 **shōdō** impulse, urge, drive
衝動的 **shōdōteki** impulsive

2

亻 冫
孑 阝
阝 刂
力 9←
又 宀
亠 艹
ⴑ 夂
 丷
厂 辶
门 几
匸

暴動 **bōdō** riot, disturbance, uprising
暴動者 **bōdōsha** rioter, rebel, insurgent
震動 **shindō** tremor, vibration
16 激動 **gekidō** violent shaking; excitement, stir
機動 **kidō** mechanized, mobile
機動力 **kidōryoku** mobility, maneuverability
機動化 **kidōka** mechanization
機動隊 **kidōtai** riot squad
機動演習 **kidō enshū** maneuvers
頸動脈 **keidōmyaku** the carotid artery
17 聳動 **shōdō** electrify, startle, shock
18 騒動 **sōdō** disturbance, riot
20 蠕動運動 **zendō undō** vermicular motion, peristalsis
21 蠢動 **shundō** wriggling, squirming; maneuvering, scheming
躍動 **yakudō** lively motion

——————— 3 ———————

3 上下動 **jōgedō** up-and-down/vertical motion
4 円運動 **en undō** circular motion
6 有袋動物 **yūtai dōbutsu** a marsupial
米騒動 **kome sōdō** rice riot
7 形容動詞 **keiyōdōshi** quasi-adjective used with -na (e.g., *shizuka*, *kirei*)
花自動車 **hana jidōsha** flower-bedecked automobile
9 食指動 **shokushi (ga) ugo(ku)** feel a craving for, want
10 哺乳動物 **honyū dōbutsu** mammal
脊椎動物 **sekitsui dōbutsu** vertebrates
11 軟体動物 **nantai dōbutsu** mollusk
12 貸自動車 **ka(shi)-jidōsha** rental car
軽自動車 **keijidōsha** light car
15 震天動地 **shinten-dōchi** (heaven-and-)earth-shaking
蹠行動物 **shokō dōbutsu** plantigrade (animal that walks on the whole sole of its foot, as man or bear)
20 蠕形動物 **zenkei dōbutsu** legless animal
22 驚天動地 **kyōten-dōchi** earth-shaking, astounding

——————— 4 ———————

1 一挙一動 **ikkyo-ichidō** one's every action
3 大山鳴動鼠一匹 **taizan meidō (shite) nezumi ippiki** The mountains have brought forth a mouse. Much ado about nothing much.
8 直立不動 **chokuritsu-fudō** standing at attention
9 単独行動 **tandoku kōdō** acting on one's own
春機発動期 **shunki hatsudōki** puberty
11 強制労働 **kyōsei rōdō** forced labor
12 御家騒動 **oie sōdō** family quarrel
軽挙妄動 **keikyo-mōdō** act rashly
15 課外活動 **kagai katsudō** extracurricular activities

20 懸垂運動 **kensui undō** chin-ups
蠕動運動 **zendō undō** vermicular motion, peristalsis

2g9.2

勒 **ROKU** halter and bit; engrave

——————— 2 ———————

8 弥勒 **Miroku** Maitreya

2g9.3 / 1502

勘 **KAN** perception, intuition, sixth sense; think over; censure

——————— 1 ———————

5 勘弁 **kanben** pardon, forgive, tolerate
勘付 **kanzu(ku)** suspect, sense, scent
6 勘気 **kanki** displeasure, disfavor
勘合貿易 **kangō bōeki** licensed trade
勘考 **kankō** consideration, deliberation
勘当 **kandō** disinheritance
8 勘定 **kanjō** calculation; account; settling an account
勘定日 **kanjōbi** settlement day
勘定高 **kanjōdaka(i)** calculating, mercenary
勘定書 **kanjōsho** bill, one's account
勘定違 **kanjōchiga(i)** miscalculation
勘所 **kandokoro** the point (on a violin string) to press to get the desired tone; vital point, crux
9 勘亭流 **Kantei-ryū** (style of calligraphy used in kabuki and sumo programs)
10 勘案 **kan'an** take into consideration
12 勘違 **kanchiga(i)** misunderstanding, mistaken idea
19 勘繰 **kangu(ru)** be suspicious of

——————— 2 ———————

3 山勘 **yamakan** speculation, guesswork
5 丼勘定 **donburi kanjō** paying money into and out of a pot, keeping no records of revenues and expenditures, slipshod accounting, rough estimate
6 仮勘定 **karikanjō** suspense account
7 別勘定 **betsukanjō** separate account
9 前勘定 **maekanjō** paying in advance
12 割勘 **wa(ri)kan** Dutch treat
14 総勘定 **sōkanjō** final settlement
16 懐勘定 **futokoro kanjō** counting one's pocket money; one's financial situation

——————— 3 ———————

5 目子勘定 **me(no)ko kanjō** measuring by eye; mental arithmetic
10 差引勘定 **sashihiki kanjō** account balance

勖 → 勗 4c7.6

──────────── 10 ────────────

2g10.1 / 559

勤 勤
KIN work GON Buddhist religious services
tsuto(meru) work for, be employed by, serve
tsuto(maru) be fit/competent for

──────────── 1 ────────────

2 勤人 **tsuto(me)nin** office/white-collar worker
3 勤上 **tsuto(me)a(geru)** do one's time of service
  勤口 **tsuto(me)guchi** position, place of employment
4 勤王 **kinnō** loyalty to the emperor/king
  勤王家 **kinnōka** loyalist, royalist
6 勤先 **tsuto(me)saki** place of work, employer
  勤行 **gongyō** Buddhist religious services
7 勤労 **kinrō** labor, work
  勤労奉仕 **kinrō hōshi** labor service
  勤労者 **kinrōsha** worker, laborer
  勤労所得 **kinrō shotoku** earned income
9 勤皇 **kinnō** loyalty to the emperor
  勤皇家 **kinnōka** loyalist
10 勤倹 **kinken** industriousness and thrift
  勤勉 **kinben** industrious, hard-working
  勤振 **tsuto(me)bu(ri)** how well one works, one's conduct
11 勤務 **kinmu** service, work, duty
  勤務先 **kinmusaki** place of employment, employer
  勤務評定 **kinmu hyōtei** job performance appraisal
12 勤惰 **kinda** (degree of) diligence or indolence
13 勤続 **kinzoku** long service
  勤続者 **kinzokusha** person of long service, senior worker

──────────── 2 ────────────

4 内勤 **naikin** indoor/office work
  日勤 **nikkin** daily work
  欠勤 **kekkin** absence (from work)
  欠勤届 **kekkin todo(ke)** report of absence
  欠勤者 **kekkinsha** absentee
  欠勤率 **kekkinritsu** rate of absenteeism
5 出勤 **shukkin** go/come to work
  出勤日 **shukkinbi** workday
  出勤簿 **shukkinbo** work attendance record
  外勤 **gaikin** outside duty, outdoor work
6 在勤 **zaikin** serve, hold office
8 夜勤 **yakin** night duty/shift
  参勤交代 **sankin kōtai** daimyō's alternate-year residence in Edo

忠勤 **chūkin** faithful service
9 通勤 **tsūkin** commute to work
  皆勤 **kaikin** perfect attendance
  皆勤償 **kaikinshō** reward for perfect attendance
  恪勤 **kakkin, kakugon** working earnestly
10 兼勤 **kenkin** additional post
11 常勤 **jōkin** full-time (employment)
  転勤 **tenkin** be transferred (to another office)
14 精勤 **seikin** diligence, good attendance

──────────── 3 ────────────

8 非常勤 **hijōkin** part-time work

勞 → 労 3n4.3

──────────── 11 ────────────

2g11.1 / 1051

勧 勸
KAN, susu(meru) recommend, advise, encourage; offer

──────────── 1 ────────────

7 勧告 **kankoku** recommendation, advice
10 勧進 **kanjin** soliciting religious contributions
  勧進元 **kanjinmoto** promoter, sponsor
  勧進帳 **kanjinchō** subscription book
12 勧善懲悪 **kanzen-chōaku** rewarding good and punishing evil, didactic/morality (play)
13 勧業 **kangyō** encouragement of industry; industry
  勧奨 **kanshō** encouragement, promotion
14 勧誘 **kan'yū** solicitation, invitation, canvassing

──────────── 2 ────────────

14 説勧 **to(ki)susu(meru)** persuade, urge

2g11.2

耡
JO, su(ku) plow
suki plow, spade

2g11.3

勠
RIKU combine, join forces

2g11.4

勣
SEKI, SHAKU merit, achievement

2g11.5

勣

SŌ destroy; steal

———————— 1 ————————

13 勣滅 **sōmetsu** annihilate, eradicate

2g11.6 / 646

勢

SEI, SE, ikio(i) force, energy, vigor

———————— 1 ————————

2 勢子 **seko** beater (on a hunt)
勢力 **seiryoku** influence, force
勢力下 **seiryokuka** under the influence/ power of
12 勢揃 **seizoro(i)** array, full lineup

———————— 2 ————————

3 大勢 **ōzei** large number of people
　　　 taisei the general trend
弓勢 **yunzei** strength put forth in drawing a bow
小勢 **kozei** small force, small number of people
4 文勢 **bunsei** force of style
水勢 **suisei** force of water, current
手勢 **tezei** troops under one's command
火勢 **kasei** force of the flames
5 加勢 **kasei** assistance, support
市勢 **shisei** city conditions; municipal census
去勢 **kyosei** castrate
6 多勢 **tazei** great numbers, numerical superiority
気勢 **kisei** spirit, ardor, élan
伊勢大神宮 **Ise Daijingū** the Grand Shrines of Ise
伊勢参 **Ise-mai(ri)** Ise pilgrimage
伊勢蝦 **ise-ebi** spiny lobster
同勢 **dōzei** party, company
地勢 **chisei** geographical features
守勢 **shusei** (on the) defensive
劣勢 **ressei** numerical inferiority
7 余勢 **yosei** surplus energy, momentum
助勢 **josei** encouragement, backing
形勢 **keisei** situation, conditions, prospects
攻勢 **kōsei** the offensive
8 退勢 **taisei** deteriorating position, decline
国勢 **kokusei** strength/condition of a country
国勢調査 **kokusei chōsa** (national) census
9 軍勢 **gunzei** number of troops, forces
姿勢 **shisei** posture, stance
威勢 **isei** power, influence; high spirits
10 衰勢 **suisei** declining fortunes, deteriorating position

党勢 **tōsei** strength of a party
時勢 **jisei** the times/Zeitgeist
病勢 **byōsei** condition of a disease
11 虚勢 **kyosei** bluff, false show of strength
運勢 **unsei** one's fate, fortune, luck
現勢 **gensei** present state; actual strength
情勢 **jōsei** situation, condition, circumstances
12 無勢 **buzei** numerical inferiority
筆勢 **hissei** brushwork, penmanship
14 豪勢 **gōsei** grand, luxurious, magnificent
寡勢 **kazei** small force
態勢 **taisei** preparedness, stance
総勢 **sōzei** the whole army/group
語勢 **gosei** stress, emphasis
15 潜勢力 **senseiryoku** latent power, potential
権勢 **kensei** power, influence
敵勢 **tekizei** the enemy's strength/forces
16 頽勢 **taisei** one's declining fortunes
17 優勢 **yūsei** predominance, superiority, the advantage
趨勢 **sūsei** trend, tendency
擬勢 **gisei** sham display of forces, bluff
20 騰勢 **tōsei** rising/upward trend

———————— 3 ————————

10 高姿勢 **kōshisei** high posture/profile, aggressive attitude
18 騎虎勢 **kiko (no) ikio(i)** unable to stop/quit

2g11.7

舅

KYŪ, shūto father-in-law

———————— 2 ————————

3 小舅 **kojūto** one's spouse's brother

———————— 14 ————————

勳 → 勲　4d11.3

厲 → 励　2g5.4

———————— 15 ————————

2g15.1

黝

YŪ black

———————— 17 ————————

勸 → 勧　2g11.1

又 2h

又	叉	双	収	友	圣	皮	叔	受	殳	版	叙	叚
0.1	1.1	2.1	2.2	2.3	6a5.11	3.1	6.1	6.2	6.3	2j6.8	7.1	7.2

叟	桑	皰	敍	皺	叡	燮	雙	叢	皨	鬢
7.3	8.1	8.2	10.1	13.1	14.1	15.1	2h2.1	6e12.3	18.1	19.1

─────── 0 ───────

2h0.1 / 1593

又 又

mata again; also, moreover
mata(wa) or

─────── 1 ───────

3 又々 **matamata** once again
7 又弟子 **matadeshi** indirect pupil, disciple of
a disciple
10 又借 **mataga(ri)** borrow secondhand, sublease
又従兄弟 **mataitoko** second cousin
又従姉妹 **mataitoko** second cousin
12 又貸 **mataga(shi)** lend what one has
borrowed, sublet, sublease
14 又聞 **matagi(ki)** hearsay, secondhand
information
15 又隣 **matadonari** two doors away
16 又頼 **matadano(mi)** ask for through another

─────── 2 ───────

2 又々 **matamata** once again
5 且又 **ka(tsu)mata** and, moreover

─────── 1 ───────

2h1.1

叉

SA, SHA, mata crotch (of a tree), fork
(in a road)

─────── 1 ───────

4 叉木 **matagi** forked tree/branch

─────── 2 ───────

3 三叉 **sansa, mi(tsu)mata** three-pronged fork
三叉路 **sansaro** Y-junction of roads
6 交叉 **kōsa** cross, intersect
交叉点 **kōsaten** crossing, intersection
7 角叉 **tsunomata** red algae
8 夜叉 **yasha** she-devil, female demon
9 音叉 **onsa** tuning fork

─────── 4 ───────

8 金色夜叉 **konjiki yasha** usurer

─────── 2 ───────

2h2.1 / 1594

双 雙

SŌ, futa pair, both

─────── 1 ───────

2 双子 **futago** twins, a twin
双子葉 **sōshiyō** dicotyledonous
4 双六 **sugoroku** (a parcheesi-like dice game)
双手 **sōshu** both hands
双方 **sōhō** both parties/sides
5 双生 **sōsei** growing in pairs
双生児 **sōseiji** twins
6 双曲線 **sōkyokusen** hyperbola
双成 **futana(ri)** androgynous, hermaphrodite
8 双肩 **sōken** one's shoulders
9 双発機 **sōhatsuki** twin-engine airplane
10 双胴機 **sōdōki** twin-fuselage airplane
11 双殻類 **sōkakurui** bivalves
双務契約 **sōmu keiyaku** bilateral contract
双眼 **sōgan** both eyes; binocular
双眼鏡 **sōgankyō** binoculars
双眸 **sōbō** (the pupils of) both eyes
12 双葉 **futaba** bud, sprout
16 双頭 **sōtō** double-headed
17 双翼 **sōyoku** both wings/flanks

1 一双 **issō** a pair (of screens)
9 草双紙 **kusazōshi** storybook with pictures
12 無双 **musō** unequaled, unparalleled
無双窓 **musōmado** openable panel in a door
絵双紙 **ezōshi** picture book

─────── 3 ───────

10 娑羅双樹 **shara sōju** sal tree

─────── 4 ───────

1 一卵性双生児 **ichiransei sōseiji** identical
twins
4 天下無双 **tenka-musō** unique, unequaled

2h2.2 / 757

収 収

SHŪ, osa(meru) obtain, collect
osa(maru) be obtained; end

─────── 1 ───────

2 収入 **shūnyū** income, receipts, revenue,
earnings
収入役 **shūnyūyaku** treasurer
収入源 **shūnyūgen** source of income
4 収支 **shūshi** revenues and expenditures
5 収用 **shūyō** expropriation

7 収束 **shūsoku** bring together; converge (in math)
8 収受 **shūju** receive
9 収拾 **shūshū** control, cope with
10 収差 **shūsa** aberration
収益 **shūeki** earnings, proceeds
収容 **shūyō** accommodate, admit, receive
収容力 **shūyōryoku** (seating) capacity
収容所 **shūyōjo** home, asylum, camp
収納 **shūnō** receipts; harvest; put in, store
11 収得 **shūtoku** keep for one's own
12 収税 **shūzei** tax collection
収税吏 **shūzeiri** tax collector
13 収賄 **shūwai** accepting bribes, graft
15 収蔵 **shūzō** to store
収監 **shūkan** imprison
16 収縛 **shūbaku** arrest and tie up
収録 **shūroku** collect, record
17 収斂 **shūren** convergent; astringent
収覧 **shūran** grasp; win over
収縮 **shūshuku** contraction, constriction
収縮期血圧 **shūshukuki ketsuatsu** systolic blood pressure
18 収穫 **shūkaku** harvest
収穫予想 **shūkaku yosō** crop estimate
収穫物 **shūkakubutsu** harvest, crop, yield
収穫高 **shūkakudaka** yield, crop
収穫時 **shūkakuji** time of harvest
収穫祭 **shūkakusai** harvest festival
収穫期 **shūkakuki** harvest time
25 収攬 **shūran** grasp; win over

――――― 2 ―――――

6 年収 **nenshū** annual income
吸収 **kyūshū** absorb
吸収性 **kyūshūsei** absorbency
吸収剤 **kyūshūzai** an absorbent
回収 **kaishū** recover, reclaim, collect, withdraw from circulation
米収 **beishū** rice crop/harvest
7 没収 **bosshū** confiscate
見収 **miosa(me)** last/farewell look
8 押収 **ōshū** confiscation
実収 **jisshū** actual income, take-home pay
定収入 **teishūnyū** fixed income
10 純収益 **junshūeki** net earnings
11 副収入 **fukushūnyū** additional/side income
接収 **sesshū** requisition, take over
12 減収 **genshū** decrease in income
検収 **kenshū** (inspection and) acceptance
税収 **zeishū** tax revenues
買収 **baishū** purchase; buy off, bribe
14 増収 **zōshū** increased income/yield
徴収 **chōshū** collect, levy, charge
雑収入 **zatsushūnyū, zasshūnyū** miscellaneous income

領収 **ryōshū** receipt
領収者 **ryōshūsha** receiver, recipient
領収書 **ryōshūsho** receipt
領収証 **ryōshūshō** receipt
15 撤収 **tesshū** withdraw, remove
18 贈収賄 **zōshūwai** bribery

――――― 4 ―――――

13 源泉徴収 **gensen chōshū** collecting (taxes) at the source, withholding

2h2.3 / 264

YŪ, tomo friend

友

――――― 1 ―――――

2 友人 **yūjin** friend
5 友好 **yūkō** friendship, amity
友好的 **yūkōteki** friendly, amicable
6 友邦 **yūhō** friendly nation, ally
8 友宜 **yūgi** friendship, friendly relations
9 友軍 **yūgun** allied army, friendly troops
友垣 **tomogaki** friend
10 友党 **yūtō** allied (political) party
11 友達 **tomodachi** friend
友情 **yūjō** friendship, fellowship
友釣 **tomozu(ri)** fishing using decoys
13 友愛 **yūai** friendship, brotherly love
15 友誼 **yūgi** friendship, friendly relations

――――― 2 ―――――

5 幼友達 **osana tomodachi** childhood friend
旧友 **kyūyū** an old friend
6 老友 **rōyū** old/aged friend
血友病 **ketsuyūbyō** hemophilia
7 良友 **ryōyū** good friend
住友 **Sumitomo** (company name)
学友 **gakuyū** schoolmate, alumnus
学友会 **gakuyūkai** alumni association
社友 **shayū** friend of the firm; colleague
8 知友 **chiyū** acquaintance, friend
尚友 **shōyū** become close to ancient authors (by reading their works)
朋友 **hōyū** friend, companion
9 政友 **seiyū** political ally
畏友 **iyū** esteemed friend
級友 **kyūyū** classmate
10 益友 **ekiyū** good/useful friend
校友 **kōyū** schoolmate, alumnus
校友会 **kōyūkai** alumni association
病友 **byōyū** sick friend; hospital ward-mate
11 清友 **seiyū** refined friend
悪友 **akuyū** bad companion(s)
13 戦友 **sen'yū** comrade-in-arms, fellow soldier
盟友 **meiyū** sworn friend, staunch ally
詩友 **shiyū** one's friend in poetry
14 僚友 **ryōyū** colleague, co-worker

誌友　**shiyū**　fellow subscriber/reader
16　親友　**shin'yū**　close friend

─────── 3 ───────
6　竹馬友　**chikuba (no) tomo**　childhood playmate
9　茶飲友達　**chano(mi) tomodachi**　crony, pal
10　莫逆友　**bakugyaku (no) tomo**　steadfast friend

─────── 3 ───────

収→　**2h2.2**

圣→経　**6a5.11**

2h3.1 / 975

皮　HI, **kawa**　skin, hide, leather, pelt, bark, rind

─────── 1 ───────
3　皮下　**hika**　subcutaneous
　皮下注射　**hika chūsha**　hypodermic injection
4　皮切　**kawaki(ri)**　beginning, start
6　皮肉　**hiniku**　irony, sarcasm
7　皮作　**kawatsuku(ri)**　making sashimi without cutting away the fish's skin
9　皮革　**hikaku**　hides, leather
　皮相　**hisō**　superficial, outward
11　皮細工　**kawazaiku**　leatherwork
14　皮層　**hisō**　the cortex
　皮膜　**himaku**　membrane, integument, skin
　皮算用　**kawazan'yō, kawasan'yō**　counting one's pelts before catching the raccoons
15　皮膚　**hifu**　skin
　皮膚科　**hifuka**　dermatology
　皮膚病　**hifubyō**　skin disease
22　皮癬　**hizen**　itch, scabies, mange

─────── 2 ───────
3　上皮　**jōhi**　epidermis　**uwakawa**　epidermis, outer skin, film, crust
4　爪皮　**tsumakawa**　toe cover, mud guard (on a clog)
　毛皮　**kegawa**　fur, skin, pelt
　毛皮商　**kegawashō**　furrier
　木皮　**mokuhi**　bark
　牛皮　**gyūhi**　cowhide
5　包皮　**hōhi**　the foreskin
　包皮切断　**hōhi setsudan**　circumcision
　外皮　**gaihi**　outer cover, crust, shell, husk, skin
6　羊皮　**yōhi**　sheepskin
　羊皮紙　**yōhishi**　parchment
　竹皮　**take(no)kawa**　bamboo sheath
7　杉皮　**sugikawa**　sugi bark
8　表皮　**hyōhi**　epidermis; bark, rind, peel, husk

9　面皮　**menpi**　countenance
　面皮厚　**tsura (no) kawa (no) atsu(i)**　brazen-faced, impudent, nervy
10　陳皮　**chinpi**　dried mikan peels
　帯皮　**obikawa**　leather belt
　桂皮　**keihi**　cassia bark, cinnamon
11　渋皮　**shibukawa**　astringent skin (of a chestnut)
　鹿皮　**shikagawa**　deerskin
　脱皮　**dappi**　shedding, molting, emergence
　粗皮　**arakawa**　bark, hull; untanned hide
　蛇皮　**hebikawa**　snakeskin
12　象皮病　**zōhibyō**　elephantiasis
　雁皮紙　**ganpishi**　(a type of high-quality paper)
　植皮　**shokuhi**　skin grafting
13　腹皮　**harakawa**　skin of a fish's abdomen
14　種皮　**shuhi**　seed coat
　総皮　**sōhi, sōgawa**　full-leather binding
15　敷皮　**shi(ki)gawa**　fur cushion, bearskin rug
16　獣皮　**jūhi**　animal skin, hide, pelt
　薄皮　**usukawa**　thin skin/layer, film
　樹皮　**juhi**　(tree) bark
17　檜皮　**hiwada**　cypress bark
　檜皮葺　**hiwadabu(ki)**　cypress-bark roofing
　鮫皮　**samegawa**　sharkskin
18　鞣皮　**jūhi, name(shi)gawa**　leather
　鞣皮業　**jūhigyō**　tannery
20　鰐皮　**wanigawa**　alligator skin

─────── 3 ───────
13　鉄面皮　**tetsumenpi**　brazen, impudent
17　擬羊皮紙　**giyōhishi**　parchment paper

─────── 4 ───────
9　草根木皮　**sōkon-mokuhi**　medicinal herb roots and tree barks

─────── 6 ───────

2h6.1 / 1667

叔　SHUKU　younger sibling of a parent

─────── 1 ───────
4　叔父　**oji, shukufu**　uncle
5　叔母　**oba, shukubo**　aunt

─────── 2 ───────
3　大叔父　**ōoji**　great-uncle, granduncle
　大叔母　**ōoba**　great-aunt, grandaunt

2h6.2 / 260

受　JU, **u(keru)**　receive, catch (a ball), undergo (an operation), take (an exam), sustain (injuries); be well received, be a hit　**u(ke)**　receiving; receptacle; support, prop; popularity　**u(karu)**　pass (an exam)

─────── 1 ───────
2　受入　**u(ke)i(re)**　receiving, accepting

3 受口 **u(ke)guchi** receiving window; notch, socket **u(ke)kuchi, u(ke)guchi** mouth with a protruding lower jaw
4 受太刀 **u(ke)dachi** on the defensive
受止 **u(ke)to(meru)** stop, catch; parry, ward off
受手 **u(ke)te** receiver (of a message)
受引 **u(ke)hi(ku)** accept, consent
受木 **u(ke)gi** a support
5 受付 **uketsuke** receipt, acceptance; reception desk; receptionist
受付係 **uketsukegakari** receptionist, usher
受払 **u(ke)hara(i)** receipts and disbursements
受皿 **u(ke)zara** saucer
6 受任 **junin** be appointed
受合 **u(ke)a(i)** guarantee, assurance
受刑 **jukei** serve a sentence
受刑者 **jukeisha** a convict
受血者 **juketsusha** blood recipient
7 受身 **ukemi** being acted upon; passivity; passive (in grammar)
受売 **u(ke)u(ri)** retailing; second-hand (knowledge)
受戻 **u(ke)modo(su)** redeem
受戒 **jukai** Buddhist confirmation
8 受命 **jumei** (official's) commission
受注 **juchū** receive an order for
受取 **u(ke)to(ru)** receive, accept, take **uketo(ri)** receipt, acknowledgment
受取人 **uketorinin** recipient, payee
受取済 **uketorizu(mi)** (payment) received
受取帳 **uketorichō** receipt book
受取証 **uketorishō** receipt, voucher
9 受信 **jushin** receipt of a message, (radio) reception
受信人 **jushinnin** addressee
受信料 **jushinryō** (NHK TV) reception fee
受信機 **jushinki** (radio) receiver
受洗 **jusen** baptism
受洗者 **jusensha** person baptized
受持 **u(ke)mo(tsu)** have/take charge of
受胎 **jutai** conception, fertilization
10 受益 **jueki** benefit by
受益者 **juekisha** beneficiary
受流 **u(ke)naga(su)** parry, turn aside
受容 **juyō** receive, accept
受納 **junō** receipt, acceptance
受粉 **jufun** pollination, fertilization
受託 **jutaku** be entrusted with
受配者 **juhaisha** recipient of an allotment
11 受動 **judō** passivity
受動的 **judōteki** passive
受動態 **judōtai** passive voice
受理 **juri** accept
12 受渡 **u(ke)wata(shi)** delivery, transfer
受検 **juken** undergo investigation

受給 **jukyū** receive (payments)
受給者 **jukyūsha** pensioner
受答 **u(ke)kota(e)** reply, response
受訴 **juso** (court's) acceptance of a lawsuit
受診 **jushin** receive a medical examination
受註 **juchū** receive an order for
13 受傷 **jushō** be injured
受損 **u(ke)soko(nau)** fail to catch/parry
受腰 **u(ke)goshi** stance for catching
受継 **u(ke)tsu(gu)** inherit, succeed to
受話器 **juwaki** (telephone) receiver
14 受像 **juzō** receive television pictures
受像機 **juzōki** television set
受精 **jusei** fertilization, pollination
受領 **juryō** receive, accept
受領者 **juryōsha** recipient
受領高 **juryōdaka** amount received, receipts
受領書 **juryōsho** receipt
受領証 **juryōshō** receipt
15 受賞 **jushō** receive a prize
受賞者 **jushōsha** prizewinner
受箱 **u(ke)bako** box for receiving (mail/milk)
受諾 **judaku** accept, agree to
17 受講 **jukō** take lectures
受講生 **jukōsei** trainee, seminar participant
18 受贈 **juzō** receive a gift
受贈者 **juzōsha** recipient (of a gift)
受難 **junan** ordeal, sufferings; (Jesus's) Passion
受難日 **junanbi** Good Friday
受難者 **junansha** sufferer
受難週 **junanshū** Passion Week
受難節 **junansetsu** Lent
受難劇 **junangeki** Passion play
受験 **juken** take an examination
受験生 **jukensei** student preparing for exams
受験者 **jukensha** examinee
受験科 **jukenka** exam-coaching course
受験料 **jukenryō** examination fee
受験票 **jukenhyō** examination admission ticket

— 2 —

3 大受 **ōu(ke)** great popularity, a hit
4 収受 **shūju** receive
引受 **hi(ki)u(keru)** undertake, consent to, accept responsibility for, guarantee
引受人 **hikiukenin** guarantor, acceptor (of a bill), underwriter
5 甘受 **kanju** submit meekly to, resign oneself to
申受 **mō(shi)u(keru)** accept; ask for, charge (a price)
6 気受 **kiu(ke)** popularity, favor
伝受 **denju** be told, hear
灰受 **haiu(ke)** ashpan, ashtray
7 身受 **miu(ke)** redeem, ransom

享受 **kyōju** enjoy, have, be given
見受 **miu(keru)** see, come across; judge from the appearance
初受賞 **hatsujushō** winning a prize for the first time
8 送受信機 **sōjushinki** transceiver
拝受 **haiju** receive, accept
9 俗受 **zokuu(ke)** popular appeal
待受 **ma(chi)u(keru)** await, expect
10 借受 **ka(ri)u(keru)** borrow
荷受 **niu(ke)** receipt of goods
荷受入 **niu(ke)nin** consignee
納受 **nōju** receipt, acceptance
11 接受 **setsuju** receive, intercept
授受 **juju** giving and receiving, transfer
12 傍受 **bōju** intercept, monitor, tap
買受 **ka(i)u(keru)** acquire by purchase
軸受 **jikuu(ke)** bearing
13 感受 **kanju** (radio) reception, susceptibility
感受性 **kanjusei** sensibility, sensitivity
継受 **keiju** inheritance
15 請受 **ko(i)u(keru)** ask and receive
20 譲受 **yuzu(ri)u(keru)** obtain by transfer, take over, inherit

────── 3 ──────
5 玉軸受 **tamajikuu(ke)** ball bearing
6 自花受粉 **jika jufun** self-pollination
　自家受精 **jika jusei** self-fertilization
11 異花受精 **ika jusei** cross-pollination

2h6.3

殁

BOTSU, shi(nu) die

────── 2 ──────
6 死殁 **shibotsu** death
10 病殁 **byōbotsu** death from illness, natural death
13 戦殁 **senbotsu** death in battle, killed in action
　戦殁者 **senbotsusha** fallen soldier

版→ 2j6.8

────── 7 ──────

2h7.1 / 1067

叙 敍 敘

JO narrate, describe; confer (a rank)

────── 1 ──────
0 叙する **jo(suru)** depict, relate; confer (a rank)
6 叙任 **jonin** appointment, investiture
7 叙述 **jojutsu** description, narration

8 叙事 **joji** narration, description
　叙事文 **jojibun** description, a narrative
　叙事詩 **jojishi** epic poem/poetry
11 叙情 **jojō** description of feelings, lyricism
　叙情詩 **jojōshi** lyric poem/poetry
12 叙景 **jokei** description of scenery
15 叙勲 **jokun** confer a decoration
17 叙爵 **joshaku** conferring a peerage

────── 2 ──────
6 自叙 **jijo** writing one's own story
　自叙伝 **jijoden** autobiography
9 陞叙 **shōjo** promotion, advancement
11 略叙 **ryakujo** brief account, outline

────── 3 ──────
3 久闊叙 **kyūkatsu (o) jo(su)** greet for the first time in a long time

2h7.2

叹

KAN, KEN hard; wise

2h7.3

叟

SŌ old person

────── 8 ──────

2h8.1 / 1873

桑

SŌ, kuwa mulberry tree

────── 1 ──────
5 桑田 **sōden** mulberry orchard
8 桑門 **sōmon** Buddhist priest/monk
9 桑畑 **kuwabatake** mulberry field
10 桑原桑原 **kuwabara-kuwabara** Heaven forbid! Thank God!
13 桑園 **sōen** mulberry farm/orchard
14 桑摘 **kuwatsu(mi)** picking mulberry leaves

────── 2 ──────
7 扶桑 **Fusō** Japan

────── 3 ──────
10 桑原桑原 **kuwabara-kuwabara** Heaven forbid! Thank God!

2h8.2

皰

HŌ, BYŌ, nikibi pimple

────── 2 ──────
9 面皰 **nikibi** pimple

──────── 10 ────────

2h10.1

皴 **SHUN** wrinkles, cracking, creases

──────── 13 ────────

2h13.1

皺 **SŪ, SHŪ, shiwa** wrinkles, lines (on the face); creases, rumples

──── 1 ────

7 皺伸 **shiwano(bashi)** smoothing out wrinkles; diversion, recreation
11 皺寄 **shiwayo(se)** shifting (the burden) to
13 皺腹 **shiwabara** wrinkled abdomen, old belly

──── 2 ────

3 小皺 **kojiwa** little wrinkles, crow's feet

──────── 14 ────────

2h14.1

叡 睿 **EI** wise; imperial

──── 1 ────

12 叡智 **eichi** wisdom, intelligence; intellect

──── 2 ────

5 比叡山 **Hieizan** (mountain, Kyōto-fu)

──────── 15 ────────

2h15.1

燮 **SHŌ** moderate, alleviate; boil over low heat

──────── 16 ────────

雙 → 双 **2h2.1**

叢 → **6e12.3**

──────── 18 ────────

2h18.1

矍 **KAKU** look at in amazement

──── 1 ────

23 矍鑠 **kakushaku** (old but) vigorous, hale and hearty

──────── 19 ────────

2h19.1

鬘 **MAN, katsura** wig, hairpiece

──────── ⼍ 2i ────────

⼍	冗	写	罕	軍	冠	冢	冥	冤	寇	冨	冕	彙
0.1	2.1	3.1	5.1	7.1	7.2	8.1	8.2	8.3	3m8.10	3m9.5	2i8.3	11.1

| 寫 | 冪 | 囊 | | | | | | | | | | |
| 2i3.1 | 13.1 | 3d19.3 | | | | | | | | | | |

──────── 0 ────────

2i0.1

⼍ **BEKI** cover, covering

──────── 2 ────────

2i2.1 / 1614

冗 冗宂 **JŌ** uselessness

──── 1 ────

4 冗文 **jōbun** redundancy, pleonasm
5 冗句 **jōku** redundant phrase
8 冗長 **jōchō** verbose, redundant

冗官 **jōkan** superfluous official, overstaffing
冗物 **jōbutsu** redundancy
10 冗員 **jōin** superfluous personnel, overstaffing
12 冗費 **jōhi** unnecessary expenses
14 冗漫 **jōman** verbose, rambling
冗語 **jōgo** a redundancy, wordiness
15 冗談 **jōdan** a joke
冗談口 **jōdanguchi** a joke

──────── 3 ────────

2i3.1 / 540

写 寫 冩 **SHA, utsu(ru)** be photographed, be projected (on a screen) **utsu(su)** copy, transcribe, duplicate, photograph

—————— 1 ——————

5 写本 **shahon** manuscript, handwritten copy, codex
写生 **shasei** draw from life, sketch, portray
写字 **shaji** copying, transcription
8 写実 **shajitsu** objective portrayal; realism
写実主義 **shajitsu shugi** realism, literalism
写実的 **shajitsuteki** realistic, true to life, graphic
10 写真 **shashin** photograph
写真版 **shashinban** photographic plate
写真屋 **shashin'ya** photographer, photo studio
写真帳 **shashinchō** photo album
写真術 **shashinjutsu** photography
写真植字 **shashin shokuji** photocomposition, phototypesetting
写真結婚 **shashin kekkon** marriage arranged after seeing photos of each other
写真嫌 **shashingira(i)** camera shy
写真機 **shashinki** camera
写真館 **shashinkan** photo studio
12 写象 **shazō** image
写植 **shashoku** photocomposition, phototypesetting (short for 写真植字)
写絵 **utsu(shi)e** magic-lantern picture; copy picture; shadowgraph

—————— 2 ——————

4 手写 **shusha** copy/transcribe by hand
引写 **hi(ki)utsu(shi)** tracing, copy
5 生写 **i(ki)utsu(shi)** close resemblance
古写本 **koshahon** ancient manuscript, codex
7 抜写 **nu(ki)utsu(shi)** excerpt, extract
抄写 **shōsha** excerpt, quotation
8 実写 **jissha** on-the-spot pictures
空写 **karautsu(shi)** clicking the camera shutter without taking a photo (because the film is improperly loaded or to advance the film)
青写真 **aojashin, aoshashin** blueprints
9 速写 **sokusha** quick copying; take a snapshot
透写 **tōsha** trace (out)
透写紙 **tōshashi** tracing paper
浄写 **jōsha** clean copy
映写 **eisha** project (a picture onto a screen)
映写幕 **eishamaku** (projection) screen
映写機 **eishaki** projector
10 書写 **ka(ki)utsu(su)** transcribe, trace
shosha transcribing; penmanship
特写 **tokusha** special/exclusive photo
被写体 **hishatai** subject/object photographed
11 描写 **byōsha** depiction, portrayal, description
組写真 **ku(mi)shashin** composite photograph
転写 **tensha** transcribe, transfer, copy
12 筆写 **hissha** copy, transcribe
13 試写 **shisha** preview, private showing

14 模写 **mosha** copy, replica
複写 **fukusha** copying, duplication; a copy, facsimile
複写紙 **fukushashi** copying paper
複写器 **fukushaki** copier
誤写 **gosha** error in copying
15 敷写 **shi(ki)utsu(shi)** tracing
17 謄写 **tōsha** copy, duplication
謄写版 **tōshaban** mimeograph
謄写料 **tōsharyō** copying charge
謄写機 **tōshaki** mimeograph machine, copier
縮写 **shukusha** reduced copy, miniature reproduction
18 臨写 **rinsha** copying

—————— 3 ——————

2 二重写 **nijū utsu(shi)** double exposure
6 早取写真 **hayato(ri) shashin** snapshot
9 活動写真 **katsudō shashin** moving pictures, movie
10 航空写真 **kōkū shashin** aerial photo
13 電送写真 **densō shashin** telephoto

—————— 4 ——————

7 声帯模写 **seitai mosha** vocal mimicry

—————— 5 ——————

2i5.1

罕 **KAN** bird-catching net
mare rare

—————— 7 ——————

2i7.1 / 438

軍 **GUN** army, military
ikusa war, battle

—————— 1 ——————

2 軍人 **gunjin** soldier, military man
軍刀 **guntō** military sword, saber
4 軍手 **gunte** (thick white cotton) work gloves
軍犬 **gunken** army/military dog
5 軍令 **gunrei** military command
軍功 **gunkō** meritorious military service
軍用 **gun'yō** for military use
軍用犬 **gun'yōken** army/military dog
軍用金 **gun'yōkin** war funds; campaign funds
軍用品 **gun'yōhin** military supplies, munitions, materiel
軍用鳩 **gun'yōbato** carrier pigeon
軍用機 **gun'yōki** warplane
軍司令部 **gunshireibu** military headquarters
軍司令官 **gunshireikan** army commander
6 軍団 **gundan** army corps
軍衣 **gun'i** military clothes, uniform
7 軍医 **gun'i** military surgeon

2

亻
冫
孑
阝
卩
刂
力
又
—7←
亠
十
卜
⼏
丶

厂
辶
冂
几
匸

軍役 **gun'eki** military service
軍学 **gungaku** military science, tactics, strategy
8 軍事 **gunji** military affairs; military
軍事力 **gunjiryoku** military strength
軍事工場 **gunji kōjō** war plant
軍事上 **gunjijō** military, strategic
軍事公債 **gunji kōsai** war bonds
軍事犯 **gunjihan** military offense
軍事会議 **gunji kaigi** council of war
軍事協定 **gunji kyōtei** military pact
軍事的 **gunjiteki** military
軍事通 **gunjitsū** military expert
軍事面 **gunjimen** military aspects
軍事施設 **gunji shisetsu** military installations
軍事教練 **gunji kyōren** military training
軍事基地 **gunji kichi** military base
軍事裁判 **gunji saiban** court-martial
軍事費 **gunjihi** military expenditures
軍事輸送 **gunji yusō** military transport
軍事警察 **gunji keisatsu** military police
軍事顧問 **gunji komon** military adviser
軍制 **gunsei** military system/organization
軍法 **gunpō** military law; martial law; tactics, strategy
軍法会議 **gunpō kaigi** court-martial
軍拡 **gunkaku** military buildup
軍拡競争 **gunkaku kyōsō** arms race
軍国 **gunkoku** militaristic nation, a belligerent
軍国主義 **gunkoku shugi** militarism
軍服 **gunpuku** military uniform
9 軍律 **gunritsu** martial law; articles of war; military discipline
軍神 **gunshin** god of war; war hero
軍政 **gunsei** military government/administration
軍政府 **gunseifu** military government
軍紀 **gunki** military discipline
10 軍将 **gunshō** army commander
軍部 **gunbu** the military
軍師 **gunshi** tactician, strategist; schemer
軍容 **gun'yō** military equipment; troop formation
軍書 **gunsho** military book, war history
軍記 **gunki** war chronicle
軍記物語 **gunki monogatari** war chronicle
軍配 **gunbai** strategem, tactics; (ancient) military leader's fan; sumo referee's fan
軍馬 **gunba** warhorse, charger
11 軍隊 **guntai** army, troops, corps
軍曹 **gunsō** sergeant
軍務 **gunmu** military affairs
軍規 **gunki** military regulations
軍略 **gunryaku** strategy, tactics
軍船 **gunsen** warship

12 軍備 **gunbi** military preparations, preparedness
軍港 **gunkō** naval port/station
軍帽 **gunbō** military cap
軍営 **gun'ei** military camp
軍属 **gunzoku** civilian employee of the military
軍装 **gunsō** soldier's equipment
軍費 **gunpi** military expenditures
13 軍勢 **gunzei** number of troops, forces
軍靴 **gunka** military shoes, combat boots
軍楽 **gungaku** military/martial music
軍楽隊 **gungakutai** military band
軍資 **gunshi** war funds/materiel; campaign funds
軍資金 **gunshikin** war funds; campaign funds
14 軍旗 **gunki** battle flag, colors, ensign
軍歌 **gunka** military song
軍管区 **gunkanku** military district
軍需 **gunju** military demand/supplies
軍需工業 **gunju kōgyō** munitions industry
軍需品 **gunjuhin** military supplies, materiel
軍需景気 **gunju keiki** war prosperity
軍閥 **gunbatsu** military clique, militarist party
15 軍談 **gundan** war story
16 軍機 **gunki** military secret
17 軍縮 **gunshuku** arms reduction, disarmament
18 軍職 **gunshoku** military profession
20 軍籍 **gunseki** military register, muster roll
軍議 **gungi** war council
21 軍艦 **gunkan** warship, battleship

——————— 2 ———————

3 三軍 **sangun** a great army, the whole army
大軍 **taigun** large army
　ōikusa great battle; great war
4 友軍 **yūgun** allied army, friendly troops
6 再軍備 **saigunbi** rearmament
全軍 **zengun** the whole army/team
行軍 **kōgun** march, marching
米軍 **beigun** U.S. armed forces
7 赤軍 **Sekigun** Red Army
乱軍 **rangun** melee, free-for-all fight
8 孤軍 **kogun** isolated/unsupported army
退軍 **taigun** decamp, withdraw
官軍 **kangun** government/imperial troops
空軍 **kūgun** air force
9 叛軍 **hangun** rebel army, mutinous troops
海軍 **kaigun** navy
海軍力 **kaigunryoku** naval power
海軍大臣 **kaigun daijin** Minister of the Navy
海軍国 **kaigunkoku** a naval power
海軍省 **Kaigunshō** Admiralty, Navy Department

海軍旗 **kaigunki** navy flag
海軍機 **kaigunki** navy plane
後軍 **kōgun** rear guard, reserves
皇軍 **kōgun** imperial army
10 将軍 **shōgun** general, commander, shogun
将軍家 **shōgunke** family to inherit the shogunate
将軍職 **shōgunshoku** shogunate
陸軍 **rikugun** army
陸軍省 **Rikugunshō** Ministry of War
進軍 **shingun** a march, an advance
進軍中 **shingunchū** on the march
遊軍 **yūgun** reserve corps, flying column
従軍 **jūgun** serve in a war
従軍記者 **jūgun kisha** war correspondent
11 敗軍 **haigun** defeated army
12 援軍 **engun** reinforcements
13 義軍 **gigun** righteous army
幕軍 **bakugun** shogunate army
賊軍 **zokugun** rebel army, rebels
14 総軍 **sōgun** the whole army
15 敵軍 **tekigun** enemy army, hostile forces
21 露軍 **rogun** the Russian army

─────────── 3 ───────────

2 十字軍 **Jūjigun** the Crusades, Crusaders
3 大将軍 **taishōgun** generalissimo
5 占領軍 **senryōgun** army of occupation
正規軍 **seikigun** regular army
尼将軍 **ama shōgun** woman general
冬将軍 **Fuyu Shōgun** Gen. Winter, Jack Frost
6 同盟軍 **dōmeigun** allied armies
地上軍 **chijōgun** ground forces
7 赤衛軍 **Sekieigun** the Red Guards
攻撃軍 **kōgekigun** attacking army/force
8 国民軍 **kokumingun** national army
国防軍 **kokubōgun** national defense forces
国連軍 **Kokurengun** UN troops
9 連合軍 **rengōgun** allied armies
派遣軍 **hakengun** expeditionary army
10 陸海軍 **rikukaigun, rikkaigun** army and navy
進駐軍 **shinchūgun** army of occupation
鬼将軍 **onishōgun** brave/tough general
11 強行軍 **kyōkōgun** forced march
常備軍 **jōbigun** regular/standing army
救世軍 **Kyūseigun** the Salvation Army
救援軍 **kyūengun** reinforcements
13 義勇軍 **giyūgun** volunteer army
15 駐留軍 **chūryūgun** stationed/occupying troops

─────────── 5 ───────────

8 征夷大将軍 **seii taishōgun** general in command of expeditionary forces to subjugate the barbarians

---

2i7.2 / 1615

冠

KAN, kanmuri crown

─────────── 1 ───────────

0 冠する **kan(suru)** crown, cap; name, entitle
冠たる **kan(taru)** foremost, first, top
4 冠水 **kansui** be submerged/flooded
冠木門 **kabukimon** gate with overhead crossbar
7 冠位 **kan'i** system indicating court ranks by headgear colors
冠状 **kanjō** coronary
8 冠者 **kanja, kaja** young man come of age
11 冠婚葬祭 **kankonsōsai** ceremonial occasions
12 冠絶 **kanzetsu** be unique, have no peer
冠詞 **kanshi** article (in grammar)

─────────── 2 ───────────

4 王冠 **ōkan** crown; bottle cap
6 光冠 **kōkan** corona
衣冠 **ikan** nobleman's kimono and headdress
衣冠束帯 **ikan-sokutai** full court dress; Shinto priest's vestments
7 花冠 **kakan** corolla (of a flower)
8 宝冠 **hōkan** crown, diadem
定冠詞 **teikanshi** definite article
金冠 **kinkan** gold crown (on a tooth)
9 荊冠 **keikan** crown of thorns
帝冠 **teikan** imperial crown
栄冠 **eikan** laurels, crown, garland
10 弱冠 **jakkan** age 20; youth
桂冠 **keikan** crown of laurel
桂冠詩人 **keikan shijin** poet laureate
12 無冠 **mukan** uncrowned
歯冠 **shikan** crown of a tooth
17 戴冠式 **taikanshiki** coronation
19 鶏冠 **keikan** cockscomb

─────────── 3 ───────────

3 三重冠 **sanjūkan** tiara
4 月桂冠 **gekkeikan** crown of laurel, laurels

─────────── 8 ───────────

2i8.1

冢

CHŌ mound; head, chief

2i8.2

冥

MEI, MYŌ dark

─────────── 1 ───────────

3 冥土 **meido** hades, realm of the dead

2

亻 冫 子 阝 卩 刂 力 又 一 二 亠 十 卜 厶 丶 厂 辶 冂 几 匚

4 冥王星 **Meiōsei** Pluto
5 冥加 **myōga** divine protection
冥加金 **myōgakin** votive offering; forced contributions (Edo era)
7 冥利 **myōri** divine favor, providence, luck
8 冥府 **meifu** hades, realm of the dead
9 冥途 **meido** hades, realm of the dead
冥界 **meikai** hades, realm of the dead
13 冥福 **meifuku** happiness in the next world, repose of someone's soul
冥想 **meisō** meditation, contemplation

————— 2 —————

8 命冥加 **inochi-myōga** miraculous escape from death
9 幽冥 **yūmei** semidarkness; realm of the dead
11 晦冥 **kaimei** darkness
13 頑冥 **ganmei** bigoted, obstinate

2i8.3

冤 冤 冤 宛　**EN** false charge; grudge

————— 1 —————

13 冤罪 **enzai** false charge

————— 2 —————

11 雪冤 **setsuen** vindication, exoneration

寇 → 寇 3m8.10

————— 9 —————

冨 → 富 3m9.5

冤 → 冤 2i8.3

————— 11 —————

2i11.1

彙　**I** classify and compile

————— 1 —————

12 彙報 **ihō** collection of reports, bulletin

————— 2 —————

13 辞彙 **jii** dictionary
14 語彙 **goi** vocabulary

————— 12 —————

寫 → 写 2i3.1

————— 13 —————

2i13.1

冪 冪　**BEKI** cover; cloth, curtain; raising to a power (in math)

————— 16 —————

囊 → 囊 3d19.3

————— 亠 2j —————

亠	亡	之	卞	六	亢	文	片	乏	主	市	玄	亥
0.1	1.1	0a2.9	2.1	2.2	2.3	2.4	2.5	0a3.11	4f1.1	3.1	3.2	4.1
亨	交	孝	亦	衣	充	妄	享	辛	弃	吝	肓	忘
4.2	4.3	3n4.2	4.4	5e0.1	4.5	4.6	5.1	5b2.2	2j11.5	5.2	5.3	5.4
対	夜	卒	京	育	齐	盲	氓	版	亰	帝	奕	弯
5.5	6.1	6.2	6.3	6.4	6.5	6.6	6.7	6.8	2j6.3	7.1	7.2	3h19.1
変	哀	亭	亮	彦	奇	彦	衰	衷	离	恋	旁	亳
7.3	7.4	7.5	7.6	5b4.4	3d5.17	5b4.4	8.1	0a9.9	8c10.3	8.2	8.3	8.4
烹	高	畜	紊	殺	率	袤	牵	毫	衮	斎	産	産
8.5	8.6	8.7	8.8	8.9	9.1	9.2	9.3	9.4	9.5	9.6	5b6.4	5b6.4
商	髙	疏	蛮	啻	牌	斐	雍	裏	稟	亶	棄	齊
9.7	2j8.6	9.8	10.1	10.2	10.3	10.4	11.1	11.2	11.3	11.4	11.5	2j6.5

膏	裹	豪	毓	褒	稾	壅	齋	褻	褒	襄	甕	罋
12.1	12.2	12.3	2j6.4	13.1	5d10.5	14.1	2j9.6	15.1	2j13.1	15.2	16.1	2j21.1

贏	贏	齋	囊	龥
17.1	18.1	19.1	3d19.3	21.1

━━━━━━━━ 0 ━━━━━━━━

2j0.1

止 **TŌ** (used as an abbreviation for various characters)

━━━━━━━━ 1 ━━━━━━━━

2j1.1 / 672

亡 亡

BŌ, MŌ dead
na(kunaru) die, pass away
na(ki) the late, deceased
horo(biru) perish, come to ruin
horo(bosu) destroy, bring to ruin

━━━━━━━ 1 ━━━━━━━

2 亡人 **na(ki)hito** deceased person, the dead
4 亡夫 **bōfu** one's late husband
　亡父 **bōfu** one's late father
5 亡失 **bōshitsu** loss
　亡母 **bōbo** one's late mother
　亡兄 **bōkei** one's deceased elder brother
7 亡君 **bōkun** one's deceased lord
8 亡命 **bōmei** flee one's country
　亡命者 **bōmeisha** exile, emigré
　亡妻 **bōsai** one's late wife
　亡国 **bōkoku** ruined country, national ruin
　亡者 **mōja** the dead; ghost
9 亡後 **na(ki)ato** after one's death
14 亡魂 **bōkon** departed soul, spirit
15 亡霊 **bōrei** departed soul, ghost
16 亡骸 **na(ki)gara** one's remains, corpse

━━━━━━━ 2 ━━━━━━━

5 未亡人 **mibōjin** widow
　存亡 **sonbō** life or death
6 死亡 **shibō** die
　死亡届 **shibō todo(ke)** report of a death
　死亡者 **shibōsha** the deceased, fatalities
　死亡者欄 **shibōsharan** obituary column
　死亡率 **shibōritsu** death rate, mortality
　死亡数 **shibōsū** number of deaths
8 逃亡 **tōbō** escape, flight, desertion
　逃亡者 **tōbōsha** runaway, fugitive, deserter
10 残亡 **zanbō** be defeated and perish; be defeated and flee
　衰亡 **suibō** decline (and fall), downfall, ruin
　流亡 **ryūbō** wander about far from home
11 敗亡 **haibō** defeat

13 滅亡 **metsubō** downfall, destruction
　損亡 **sonmō** loss
16 興亡 **kōbō** rise and fall, vicissitudes

━━━━━━━━ 4 ━━━━━━━━

6 危急存亡 **kikyū-sonbō** life-or-death situation, crisis

之 → **0a2.9**

━━━━━━━━ 2 ━━━━━━━━

2j2.1

卞 **BEN, HEN** law, rule; rash, hasty

2j2.2 / 8

六 **ROKU, RIKU, mut(tsu), mu(tsu), mu, mui** six

━━━━━━━ 1 ━━━━━━━

3 六三制 **roku-sansei** the 6-3(-3-year) education system
　六大州 **rokudaishū** the six continents
4 六分儀 **rokubungi** sextant
　六辺形 **rokuhenkei** hexagon
　六尺 **rokushaku** six feet (tall); palanquin bearer
　六月 **rokugatsu** June
　六日 **muika** the sixth (day of the month); six days
6 六合 **rikugō** the universe/cosmos
7 六角 **rokkaku** hexagon
　六角形 **rokkakukei, rokkakkei** hexagon
8 六法 **roppō** the six directions; the six law codes
　六法全書 **roppō zensho** the statute books
9 六重奏 **rokujūsō** sextet
　六連発 **roku renpatsu** six-chambered (revolver)
10 六書 **rikusho** the six types of kanji
12 六腑 **roppu** the six entrails (large intestine; small intestine; gallbladder; stomach; organs of ingestion, digestion, and excretion; urinary bladder)
13 六感 **rokkan** the six senses; sixth sense

2

1 一六勝負 **ichiroku shōbu** gambling; a gamble

2 十六夜 **izayoi** 16th night of a lunar month

4 双六 **sugoroku** (a parcheesi-like dice game)

5 四六判 **shirokuban** duodecimo, 12mo

四六時中 **shirokujichū** 24 hours a day, constantly

9 甚六 **jinroku** simpleton, blockhead

11 宿六 **yadoroku** my hubby, my old man

第六感 **dai-rokkan** sixth sense

14 暮六 **ku(re)mu(tsu)** 6 p.m. (bell)

3

2 八面六臂 **hachimen roppi** eight faces and six arms; versatile talent

3 三十六計 **sanjūrokkei** many plans/strategies

三十六計逃 **sanjūrokkei ni(geru ni shikazu)** It's wisest here to run away.

三面六臂 **sanmen roppi** as if having three faces and six arms, versatile, all-around, doing the work of many

4 五臓六腑 **gozō-roppu** the five viscera and six entrails

5 四分六 **shiburoku** six-to-four (ratio/chance)

2j2.3

亢 **KŌ** high spirits, excitement

1

10 亢進 **kōshin** rise, become exacerbated

16 亢奮 **kōfun** excitement

3

4 心悸亢進 **shinki kōshin** palpitations

2j2.4 / 111

文 文 **BUN** writing, composition, sentence, text, style; literature **MON** character, word; design; (ancient unit of money); (unit of length, about 2.4 cm) **fumi** letter, note **aya** design; figure of speech; plan, plot

1

2 文人 **bunjin** literary man

文人画 **bunjinga** painting in the literary artist's style

3 文久 **Bunkyū** (era, 1861–1864)

文才 **bunsai** literary talent

文士 **bunshi** literary man

4 文中 **Bunchū** (era, 1372–1375)

文化 **bunka** culture, civilization

Bunka (era, 1804–1818)

文化人 **bunkajin** man of culture

文化日 **Bunka (no) Hi** Culture Day (November 3)

文化史 **bunkashi** cultural history

文化的 **bunkateki** cultural

文化財 **bunkazai** cultural asset

文化祭 **bunkasai** cultural festival

文月 **fuzuki, fumizuki** July (of lunar calendar)

5 文民 **bunmin** civilian

文正 **Bunshō** (era, 1466–1467)

文永 **Bun'ei** (era, 1264–1275)

文句 **monku** phrase, expression; complaint, objection; excuse

文字 **moji, monji** character, letter

文字通 **mojidō(ri)** literal(ly)

文字盤 **mojiban** (clock) dial, (typewriter) keyboard

文目 **ayame** designs, patterns; distinction

6 文安 **Bunnan** (era, 1444–1449)

7 文身 **bunshin** tattooing

文体 **buntai** (literary) style

文芸 **bungei** literary arts

文芸学 **bungeigaku** the science of literature

文芸欄 **bungeiran** literary column

文学 **bungaku** literature

文学上 **bungakujō** literary

文学士 **bungakushi** Bachelor of Arts

文学史 **bungakushi** history of literature

文学会 **bungakukai** literary society

文学的 **bungakuteki** literary

文学者 **bungakusha** literary man, man of letters

文学界 **bungakukai** the literary world

文学部 **bungakubu** literature department/faculty

文学書 **bungakusho** a literary work

文学賞 **bungakushō** literary award

文応 **Bun'ō** (era, 1260–1261)

8 文事 **bunji** civil affairs, literary matters

文例 **bunrei** model sentence/writing

文盲 **monmō** illiteracy

文典 **bunten** a grammar

文法 **bunpō** grammar

文法上 **bunpōjō** grammatically

文治 **bunchi, bunji** civilian administration **Bunji** (era, 1185–1190)

文官 **bunkan** civil official

文明 **bunmei** civilization, culture **Bunmei** (era, 1469–1487)

文明史 **bunmeishi** history of civilization

文明国 **bunmeikoku** civilized country

文明病 **bunmeibyō** a disease of civilization

文明開化 **bunmei kaika** civilization and enlightenment

文物 **bunbutsu** civilization

文房具 **bunbōgu** writing materials, stationery

文房具屋 **bunbōguya** stationery store

文武 **bunbu** literary and military arts, pen and sword   **Monmu** (emperor, 697–707)

文武両道 **bunbu-ryōdō** both soldierly and scholarly arts

文武百官 **bunbu hyakkan** civil and military officials

文和 **Bunna** (era, 1352–1356)

9 文保 **Bunpō** (era, 1317–1319)

文通 **buntsū** correspondence

文面 **bunmen** text, wording, purport

文相 **bunshō** Education Minister

文政 **bunsei** educational administration   **Bunsei** (era, 1818–1830)

文科 **bunka** liberal arts

10 文部大臣 **monbu daijin** Minister of Education

文部省 **Monbushō** Ministry of Education

文弱 **bunjaku** effeminate

文案 **bun'an** draft

文庫 **bunko** stationery box; bookcase; library

文庫本 **bunkobon** small paperback book (page size 14.8 x 10.5 cm)

文脈 **bunmyaku** context

文書 **monjo, bunsho** document; correspondence; records

文教 **bunkyō** education, culture

11 文亀 **Bunki** (era, 1501–1503)

文運 **bun'un** cultural progress, enlightenment

文理 **bunri** context, line of thought; science and literature

文理学 **bunrigaku** humanities and sciences

文章 **bunshō** composition, writing; article, essay

文章語 **bunshōgo** literary language

文章論 **bunshōron** syntax, grammar

文責 **bunseki** responsibility for the wording (of an article)

文鳥 **bunchō** Java sparrow, paddy bird

12 文博 **bunhaku** Doctor of Literature (short for 文学博士)

文禄 **Bunroku** (era, 1592–1596)

文筆 **bunpitsu** literary activity, writing

文筆家 **bunpitsuka** literary man, writer

文集 **bunshū** anthology

13 文勢 **bunsei** force of style

文献 **bunken** literature (on a subject), bibliography

文献学 **bunkengaku** bibliography, philology

文楽 **bunraku** puppet theater

文意 **bun'i** meaning (of a passage)

文飾 **bunshoku** rhetorical embellishment

文雅 **bunga** elegant, refined, artistic

14 文豪 **bungō** literary master

文暦 **Bunryaku** (era, 1234–1235)

文選 **bunsen** anthology; typesetting

文選工 **bunsenkō** typesetter

文徳 **Montoku** (emperor, 850–858)

文様 **mon'yō** pattern

文語 **bungo** literary language

文語文 **bungobun** literary language

文語体 **bungotai** literary style

15 文範 **bunpan** model compositions

文箱 **fubako, fumibako** box/case for letters

16 文壇 **bundan** the literary world; literary column

18 文鎮 **bunchin** paperweight

文題 **bundai** theme, subject

19 文藻 **bunsō** literary talent

────── **2** ──────

1 一文 **ichimon** one-thousandth of a yen   **ichibun** a sentence

一文字 **ichimonji** a straight line

一文惜 **ichimon'oshi(mi)** stinginess; miser

一文無 **ichimonna(shi)** penniless

2 人文 **jinmon, jinbun** humanity, civilization

人文主義 **jinbun shugi** humanism

人文地理 **jinbun chiri, jinmon chiri** anthropogeography

人文科学 **jinbun kagaku** cultural sciences

十文字 **jūmonji** cross

八文字 **hachimonji** the shape of the kanji 八 hachi (eight)

3 三文 **sanmon** farthing; cheap

三文小説 **sanmon shōsetsu** cheap novel

三文文士 **sanmon bunshi** hack writer

三文判 **sanmonban** ready-made seal

大文字 **ōmoji** capital letter   **daimonji** large character; the character 大

上文 **jōbun** the foregoing/above

女文字 **onna moji** woman's handwriting; hiragana

小文字 **komoji** small/lowercase letters

4 不文 **fubun** unwritten; illiterate, unlettered

不文律 **fubunritsu** unwritten law/rule

元文 **Genbun** (era, 1736–1741)

天文 **tenmon** astronomy   **Tenbun** (era, 1532–1555)

天文台 **tenmondai** observatory

天文学 **tenmongaku** astronomy

弔文 **chōbun** funeral address

仏文 **Futsubun** French, French literature

冗文 **jōbun** redundancy, pleonasm

公文 **kōbun** official document/dispatch

公文所 **kumonjo** government office (historical)

公文書 **kōbunsho** official document

手文庫 **tebunko** small bookcase

欠文 **ketsubun** missing part, lacuna, gap

5 矢文 **yabumi** letter tied to an arrow

本文 **honbun, honmon** (main) text, body

本文批評 **honmon hihyō** textual criticism

付文 **tsu(ke)bumi** love letter
古文 **kobun, komon** ancient writings
古文書 **komonjo, kobunsho** ancient documents
正文 **seibun** the (official) text
弘文 **Kōbun** (emperor, 671–672)
白文 **hakubun** unpunctuated Chinese text
主文 **shubun** the text
石文 **ishibumi** (inscribed) stone monument
6 死文 **shibun** dead letter, mere scrap of paper
全文 **zenbun** full text; whole sentence
邦文 **hōbun** Japanese language, vernacular
色文 **irobumi** love letter
同文同種 **dōbun-dōshu** same script and same race
地文学 **chimongaku, chibungaku** physical geography
名文 **meibun** excellent composition, fine prose
名文句 **meimonku** fine expression, famous words
名文家 **meibunka** fine writer
行文 **kōbun** writing, style, diction
行文流麗 **kōbun-ryūrei** fluent style/writing
回文 **kaibun** palindrome; a circular
成文 **seibun** composition, writing
成文化 **seibunka** put in writing, codify
成文法 **seibunhō** statute/written law
成文律 **seibunritsu** statute/written law
7 作文 **sakubun** composition, writing
延文 **Enbun** (era, 1356–1361)
決文句 **ki(mari)monku** set phrase, conventional expression
告文 **kokubun** written appeal of a case
　　 kōmon imperial proclamation
狂文 **kyōbun** humorous composition
花文字 **hanamoji** capital letter; flowers planted to form characters
芸文 **geibun** art and literature
売文 **baibun** hack writing
売文業 **baibungyō** hack writing
序文 **jobun** preface, foreword, introduction
杓文字 **shamoji** dipper, ladle, scoop
条文 **jōbun** the text, provisions
私文書 **shibunsho** private document
言文一致 **genbun itchi** unification of the written and spoken language
8 非文明 **hibunmei** uncivilized
長文 **chōbun** long sentence/article/letter
例文 **reibun** illustrative sentence
注文 **chūmon** order, commission
注文先 **chūmonsaki** where one places an order
注文取 **chūmonto(ri)** taking orders
注文品 **chūmonhin** goods ordered
注文書 **chūmonsho** order form

注文帳 **chūmonchō** order book
注文聞 **chūmonki(ki)** taking orders; order taker
法文 **hōbun** (text of) the law; law and literature
法文化 **hōbunka** enact into law
拙文 **setsubun** (my) poor writing
呪文 **jumon** spell, curse, magic formula
英文 **eibun** English, English composition
英文学 **eibungaku** English literature
空文 **kūbun** dead letter, mere scrap of paper
国文 **kokubun** Japanese-language; Japanese literature
国文学 **kokubungaku** Japanese literature
国文学史 **kokubungakushi** history of Japanese literature
国文法 **kokubunpō** Japanese grammar
国文科 **kokubunka** Japanese literature course
明文 **meibun** express provision
明文化 **meibunka** state explicitly, stipulate
欧文 **ōbun** European language, roman script
怪文書 **kaibunsho** defamatory literature of unknown source
和文 **wabun** Japanese (writing)
金文字 **kinmoji** gold/gilt letters
9 俗文 **zokubun** colloquial style
俗文学 **zokubungaku** popular literature
前文 **zenbun** the above statement; preamble
美文 **bibun** elegant prose
美文調 **bibunchō** ornate style
律文 **ritsubun** legal provisions; verse
衍文 **enbun** a redundancy
単文 **tanbun** simple sentence
祝文 **shukubun** congratulatory message
約文 **yakubun** summarize, condense
10 俳文 **haibun** haiku-style prose
候文 **sōrōbun** epistolary style
凄文句 **sugomonku** menacing language
陰文 **inbun** engraved/intaglio lettering
脅文句 **odo(shi)monku** threating words, menacing language
恋文 **koibumi** love letter
原文 **genbun** the text/original
逸文 **itsubun** lost writings
案文 **anbun** draft
殺文句 **koro(shi) monku** "killing" words, cajolery, clincher
能文 **nōbun** skilled in writing
能文家 **nōbunka** skilled writer
時文 **jibun** contemporary/modern writing
秘文 **himon** magic formula, incantation
純文学 **junbungaku** pure literature, belles lettres
11 達文 **tatsubun** clearly written composition
添文 **so(e)bumi** accompanying letter
脱文 **datsubun** missing passage, lacuna

黒文字 **kuromoji** spicebush; toothpick
祭文 **saimon, saibun** Shinto funeral prayer; address to the gods
悪文 **akubun** poor writing style
異文 **ibun** variant reading
経文 **kyōmon** sutras
訳文 **yakubun** a translation
軟文学 **nanbungaku** light literature
12 湯文字 **yumoji** loincloth
短文 **tanbun** short sentence/composition
落文 **o(toshi)bumi** letter purposely left behind
散文 **sanbun** prose
散文的 **sanbunteki** prosaic
散文詩 **sanbunshi** prose poem
結文 **ketsubun** epilog, conclusion
絵文字 **emoji** pictograph
証文 **shōmon** deed, bond, in writing
軽文学 **keibungaku** light literature
13 隠文 **kaku(shi)bumi** secret/anonymous letter
漢文 **kanbun** Chinese writing/classics
漢文学 **kanbungaku** Chinese literature
寛文 **Kanbun** (era, 1661–1672)
触文 **fu(re)bumi** announcement
詩文 **shibun** poetry and prose, literature
雅文 **gabun** elegant/classic style
電文 **denbun** telegram
電文体 **denbuntai** telegram-like style
14 遺文 **ibun** (deceased's) unpublished works
漫文 **manbun** rambling essay
構文 **kōbun** sentence construction, syntax
碑文 **hibun** epitaph, inscription
複文 **fukubun** complex sentence
説文 **setsumon** etymology of Chinese characters (short for 説文解字)
説文解字 **Setsumon Kaiji** (oldest Chinese character dictionary)
誓文 **seimon** written oath
誓文払 **seimonbara(i)** bargain sale
雑文 **zatsubun** literary miscellany
駄文 **dabun** poor piece of writing
15 儀文 **gibun** formalistic style, officialese
劇文学 **gekibungaku** dramatic literature
横文字 **yokomoji** European/horizontal writing
縄文 **jōmon** (ancient Japanese) straw-rope pattern
論文 **ronbun** thesis, essay
16 親文字 **oyamoji** capital letter
繁文縟礼 **hanbun-jokurei** tedious formalities, red tape
諺文 **onmon, onmun** Korean script, Hangul
頭文字 **kashiramoji** initials; capital letter
17 檄文 **gekibun** manifesto
18 難文 **nanbun** hard-to-understand passage/ style
闕文 **ketsubun** lacuna

19 韻文 **inbun** verse, poetry

——————— 3 ———————

3 三文文士 **sanmon bunshi** hack writer
口語文 **kōgobun** colloquial language
4 文語文 **bungobun** literary language
公用文 **kōyōbun** writing in the officially prescribed way
引用文 **in'yōbun** quotation
6 再注文 **saichūmon** reorder
7 決議文 **ketsugibun** (written) resolution
抗議文 **kōgibun** (written) protest
否定文 **hiteibun** negative sentence
8 表音文字 **hyōon moji** phonetic symbol/script
表意文字 **hyōi moji** ideograph
肯定文 **kōteibun** affirmative sentence
金石文 **kinsekibun** inscription on a stone monument
9 叙事文 **jojibun** description, a narrative
神代文字 **jindai moji** ancient Japanese characters
音標文字 **onpyō moji** phonetic characters
紀行文 **kikōbun** account of a journey
10 郷土文学 **kyōdo bungaku** local literature
真一文字 **ma-ichimonji** in a straight line
流行文句 **haya(ri)monku** popular phrase
消息文 **shōsokubun** personal letter
起請文 **kishōmon** written pledge, personal contract
従属文 **jūzokubun** subordinate clause
書簡文 **shokanbun** epistolary style
記事文 **kijibun** descriptive composition
11 商用文 **shōyōbun** business correspondence
商業文 **shōgyōbun** business correspondence
12 象形文字 **shōkei moji** hieroglyphics
無一文 **muichimon** penniless
無形文化財 **mukei-bunkazai** intangible cultural asset
13 楔形文字 **kusabigata moji, sekkei moji** cuneiform writing
暗号文 **angōbun** coded message, cryptogram
感想文 **kansōbun** (written) description of one's impressions
14 疑問文 **gimonbun** interrogative sentence
説明文 **setsumeibun** (written) explanation
16 機械文明 **kikai bunmei** machine civilization
17 擬古文 **gikobun** (pseudo)classical style
19 蟹行文字 **kaikō moji, kaikō monji** horizontal/Western writing
20 懸想文 **kesōbumi, kesōbun** love letter
錙一文 **bita ichimon** (not even) a farthing/cent

——————— 4 ———————

2 二束三文 **nisoku-sanmon** a dime a dozen, dirt cheap
二足三文 **nisoku-sanmon** a dime a dozen, dirt cheap
20 懸賞論文 **kenshō ronbun** prize essay

2

イ
マ
子
阝
阝
刂
力
又
宀
丷
十
卜
ケ
ン
厂
辶
冂
几
匚

2j2.5 / 1045

片 HEN one (of two); fragment; just a little
kata one (of two), one-sided, single
hira leaf, sheet, petal, flake

———————— 1 ————————

1 片一方 **kata-ippō** one side/party, the other side/party
3 片刃 **kataha** single-edged (blade)
片々 **henpen** pieces, fragments
片口 **katakuchi** lipped bowl; one side of a story
片山里 **katayamazato** remote mountain village
4 片手 **katate** one hand, one-handed
片手桶 **katate oke** bucket with handle on one side
片手落 **katateo(chi)** partial, one-sided
片手間 **katatema** in one's spare time, on the side
片手業 **katate waza** side job
片方 **katahō, katappō, katakata** one side/party, the other side/party
片戸 **katado** one-leaf door, single-swing door
5 片丘 **kataoka** a rise, hill steeper on one side
片付 **katazu(keru)** put in order; put away; settle, dispose of; marry off
katazu(ku) be put in order; be settled, be disposed of; get married off
片白 **katahaku** a liquor brewed from rice and malt
片目 **katame** one eye, one-eyed
片田舎 **kata-inaka** backwoods, boondocks
6 片仮名 **katakana** katakana, the non-cursive syllabary
片帆 **kataho** reefed sail
片肌脱 **katahada nu(gu)** bare one shoulder; help out
片耳 **katamimi** one ear
7 片身 **katami** one side of the body
片里 **katazato** out-of-the-way village
片肘 **katahiji** one elbow
片町 **katamachi** town with buildings on one side of a road only
片言 **katakoto** baby talk, broken (English)
hengen few words
片言交 **katakotoma(jiri)** babbling; broken (English)
片言隻句 **hengen-sekku** few words
片言隻語 **hengen-sekigo** few words
片足 **kataashi** one leg/foot
9 片便 **katabin, katadayo(ri)** one-way correspondence
片前 **katamae** single-breasted (suit)
片面 **katamen/tsura/omote** one side
片為替 **katagawase** exchange imbalance

片恨 **kataura(mi)** one-sided grudge
片思 **kataomo(i)** unrequited love
10 片陰 **katakage** shade
片恋 **katakoi** unrequited love
片流 **katanaga(re)** (roof) sloping one way only
片荷 **katani** one-sided/lop-sided load
片栗粉 **katakuriko** dogtooth-violet starch
片脇 **katawaki** one's side, under one's arm; one side, aside
片時 **katatoki, henji** moment, instant
11 片側 **katagawa, katakawa** one side
片側通行 **katagawa tsūkō** One Way (Traffic)
片隅 **katasumi** corner, nook
片道 **katamichi** one way
片寄 **katayo(ru)** lean to one side; be biased
片脳 **hennō** (refined) camphor
片脳油 **hennōyu** camphor oil
片務的 **henmuteki** unilateral, one-sided
片眼 **katame** one eye, one-eyed
12 片割 **katawa(re)** fragment; one of the group, accomplice
片棒 **katabō (o katsugu)** take part, have a hand in
片腕 **kataude** one arm; right-hand man
片貿易 **katabōeki** one-way/unbalanced trade
片跛 **katachinba** mismatched (pair of socks); a limp
片雲 **hen'un** a (speck of) cloud **katagumo** clouds on one side of the sky only
13 片寝 **katane** sleep on one's side
片腹 **katahara** one side (of the body)
片腹痛 **katahara-ita(i)** ridiculous, absurd
片意地 **kata-iji** stubborn, bigoted
14 片端 **katahashi, kata(p)pashi** one end, one side; small piece **katawa** deformed/disabled person; deformed, unbalanced **kata(p)pashi (kara)** one by one, one after another
15 片膚脱 **katahada nu(gu)** bare one shoulder; help out
片影 **hen'ei** shadow, sign, glimpse
片膝 **katahiza** one knee
片輪 **katawa** deformed, maimed, crippled
16 片親 **kataoya** one parent
片頬 **katahō** one cheek
17 片臂 **katahiji** one elbow
22 片聾 **katatsunbo** deaf in one ear
24 片鱗 **henrin** small part; glimpse, indication

———————— 2 ————————

1 一片 **ippen** a piece/bit
3 小片 **shōhen** fragment, piece
4 切片 **seppen** cut-off pieces
片片 **henpen** pieces, fragments
木片 **mokuhen** block/chip/splinter of wood

火片 **kahen** sparks
欠片 **kakera** broken piece, fragment
5 石片 **sekihen** piece of stone
7 阿片 **ahen** opium
阿片窟 **ahenkutsu** opium den
8 取片付 **to(ri)katazu(keru)** clear away, tidy up
9 削片 **sakuhen** splinter, chip
後片付 **atokatazu(ke)** straightening up afterwards, putting things in order
砕片 **saihen** fragment, splinter
10 残片 **zanpen** remaining fragment
骨片 **koppen** pieces of bone
破片 **hahen** broken piece, fragment, splinter
紙片 **shihen** scrap of paper
11 細片 **saihen** chip, splinters
断片 **danpen** fragment, snippet
断片的 **danpenteki** fragmentary
12 弾片 **danpen** shell splinter, shrapnel
13 跡片付 **atokatazu(ke)** straightening up (afterwards)
鉄片 **teppen** piece/scrap of iron
16 薄片 **hakuhen** thin leaf/layer, flake

——————— 3 ———————
9 通一片 **tō(ri)-ippen** passing, casual, perfunctory

乏 → **0a3.11**

——————— 3 ———————
主 → 主 **4f1.1**

2j3.1 / 181

市

SHI city, town; market
ichi market; fair

——————— 1 ———————
3 市川 **Ichikawa** (city, Chiba-ken)
4 市内 **shinai** (within the) city
市中 **shichū** in the city; open market
市井 **shisei** the streets; the town
市区 **shiku** municipal district; streets
5 市民 **shimin** citizen
市民権 **shiminken** citizenship, civil rights
市外 **shigai** outside the city limits; suburbs
市庁 **shichō** municipal office
市立 **shiritsu** municipal, city(-run)
6 市会 **shikai** city council
市有 **shiyū** city-owned
7 市役所 **shiyakusho** city hall
市町 **shichō** cities and towns

市町村 **shichōson** cities, towns, and villages; municipalities
8 市長 **shichō** mayor
市価 **shika** market/current price
市制 **shisei** organization as a municipality
市況 **shikyō** market conditions
市松 **ichimatsu** checkered (pattern)
9 市政 **shisei** city government, municipal administration
10 市部 **shibu** urban districts
11 市販 **shihan** marketing; commercially available (product)
12 市場 **shijō** market **ichiba** marketplace
市街 **shigai** the streets; city, town
市街地 **shigaichi** urban district
市街戦 **shigaisen** street-to-street fighting
市営 **shiei** run by the city, municipal
市税 **shizei** city tax
13 市債 **shisai** municipal loan/bond
市勢 **shisei** city conditions; municipal census
市電 **shiden** municipal railway, trolley

——————— 2 ———————
3 上市 **jōshi** put (a new product) on the market
小市民 **shōshimin** petty bourgeois, lower middle class
6 年市 **toshi (no) ichi** year-end market
全市 **zenshi** the whole city
全市民 **zenshimin** all the citizens of the city
7 花市 **hanaichi** flower market
酉市 **tori (no) ichi** year-end fair
8 夜市 **yoichi** night market
9 城市 **jōshi** castle/walled town
草市 **kusa ichi** market selling flowers for the Obon festival
某市 **bōshi** a certain city
10 都市 **toshi** city
馬市 **umaichi** horse market
11 魚市場 **uoichiba** fish market
12 朝市 **asaichi** morning market/fair
13 歳市 **toshi (no) ichi** year-end market
17 闇市 **yamiichi** black market
20 競市 **se(ri)ichi** an auction (house)

——————— 3 ———————
3 小都市 **shōtoshi** small city/town
5 四日市 **Yokkaichi** (city, Mie-ken)
7 見本市 **mihon ichi** sample/trade fair
8 青空市場 **aozora ichiba** open-air market
門前市 **monzen'ichi** throngs of callers outside the gate
10 株式市場 **kabushiki shijō** stock market
13 節季市 **sekki-ichi** year-end fair

——————— 4 ———————
3 工業都市 **kōgyō toshi** industrial city, factory town
16 衛星都市 **eisei toshi** satellite towns

2j3.2 / 1225

玄 GEN black, mysterious, occult

——————— 1 ———————

2 玄人 **kurōto** expert, professional
玄人筋 **kurōtosuji** professionals
5 玄冬 **gentō** winter
6 玄米 **genmai** unpolished/unmilled rice
7 玄妙 **genmyō** abstruse, recondite, profound
11 玄理 **genri** abstruse theory, esoteric mystery
14 玄関 **genkan** entranceway, vestibule, front door
玄関払 **genkanbara(i)** refusal to see a visitor
玄関先 **genkansaki** entrance, front door
玄関番 **genkanban** doorkeeper, porter

——————— 2 ———————

4 内玄関 **uchigenkan** side entrance
8 表玄関 **omote genkan** front entrance/door
9 信玄袋 **shingenbukuro** cloth bag
幽玄 **yūgen** the profound, occult

——————— 4 ———————

2j4.1

亥 GAI, i twelfth horary sign (boar)

2j4.2

亨 KŌ pass through
KYŌ offer
HŌ boil, cook

2j4.3 / 114

交 KŌ intersect; coming and going; associate with **ma(jiru), ma(zaru)** (intr.) mix **maji(eru), ma(zeru)** (tr.) mix **maji(waru)** associate with **ka(wasu)** exchange (greetings) **-ka(u)** go past each other

——————— 1 ———————

3 交叉 **kōsa** cross, intersect
交叉点 **kōsaten** crossing, intersection
5 交代 **kōtai** take turns, alternate, relieve, work in shifts
交付 **kōfu** deliver, furnish with
6 交合 **kōgō** copulation
7 交尾 **kōbi** copulation, mating
9 交通 **kōtsū** traffic, transport, communication
交通公社 **Kōtsū Kōsha** Japan Travel Bureau
交通費 **kōtsūhi** transportation expenses
交通機関 **kōtsū kikan** transportation facilities
10 交差 **kōsa** cross, intersect

交差点 **kōsaten** crossing, intersection
交流 **kōryū** alternating current, AC; (cultural) exchange
交配 **kōhai** mating, crossbreeding
11 交渉 **kōshō** negotiations
交接 **kōsetsu** copulation
12 交換 **kōkan** exchange
交換手 **kōkanshu** switchboard operator
交替 **kōtai** take turns, alternate, relieve, work in shifts
交番 **kōban** police box/stand; alternation
kawa(ri)ban(ko ni) taking turns
13 交際 **kōsai** associate with, keep company with, be friends with
交際費 **kōsaihi** entertainment expenses
交戦 **kōsen** war, hostilities, combat
16 交錯 **kōsaku** mixture, jumble
19 交響曲 **kōkyōkyoku** symphony
交響楽団 **kōkyō gakudan** symphony orchestra

——————— 2 ———————

4 手交 **shukō** hand over, deliver
5 外交 **gaikō** diplomacy, foreign relations
外交上 **gaikōjō** diplomatic
外交団 **gaikōdan** diplomatic corps
外交官 **gaikōkan** diplomat
外交的 **gaikōteki** diplomatic
外交界 **gaikōkai** diplomatic circles
外交員 **gaikōin** canvasser, door-to-door/ traveling salesman
外交術 **gaikōjutsu** diplomacy, diplomatic skill
外交筋 **gaikōsuji** diplomatic sources
旧交 **kyūkō** an old friendship
立交 **ta(chi)ma(jiru)** join
6 再交付 **saikōfu** regrant, reissue
肉交 **nikukō** sexual intercourse
羽交 **haga(i)** pinion, wings
羽交締 **haga(i)ji(me)** pin, full nelson
行交 **yu(ki)ka(u)** come and go
団交 **dankō** collective bargaining (short for 団体交渉)
7 没交渉 **bokkōshō** unrelated, independent
乱交 **rankō** orgy
社交 **shakō** society, social life
社交服 **shakōfuku** party clothes, evening dress
社交的 **shakōteki** social, sociable
社交性 **shakōsei** sociability
社交界 **shakōkai** (high) society
社交家 **shakōka** sociable person
見交 **mika(wasu)** exchange glances
言交 **i(i)kawa(su)** exchange vows/remarks
8 国交 **kokkō** diplomatic relations

物交 **bukkō, butsukō** barter (short for 物々交換)
性交 **seikō** sexual intercourse
取交 **to(ri)kawa(su)** exchange
to(ri)ma(zeru) mix, put together
9 飛交 **to(bi)ka(u)** fly/flit about
通交 **tsūkō** diplomatic relations
10 修交 **shūkō** amity, friendship
差交 **sa(shi)ka(wasu)** cross (swords)
酌交 **ku(mi)ka(wasu)** pour (saké) for each other
11 斜交 **hasukai** diagonal, oblique
混交 **konkō** mix up, confuse, jumble together
深交 **shinkō** close friendship
情交 **jōkō** intimacy
断交 **dankō** break off relations with
雪交 **yukima(jiri)** (rain) mixed with snow
12 遠交近攻 **enkō-kinkō** befriending distant countries and antagonizing neighbors
復交 **fukkō** restoration of diplomatic relations
絶交 **zekkō** sever one's relationship with
絶交状 **zekkōjō** letter breaking off a relationship
筋交 **sujika(i)** diagonal; brace
14 雑交 **zakkō** crossing (in biology)
15 霊交術 **reikōjutsu** spiritualism
16 親交 **shinkō** friendship, intimacy
17 醜交 **shūkō** immoral intercourse

――――― 3 ―――――
1 一方交通 **ippō kōtsū** one-way traffic
4 片言交 **katakotoma(jiri)** babbling; broken (English)
水魚交 **suigyo (no) maji(wari)** intimate friendship
6 刎頸交 **funkei (no) maji(wari)** devoted/lifelong friendship
8 非社交的 **hishakōteki** unsociable, retiring
参勤交代 **sankin kōtai** daimyo's alternate-year residence in Edo
物々交換 **butsubutsu kōkan** barter

孛 → 学 3n4.2

2j4.4

亦 **EKI, YAKU, mata** also, again

――――― 2 ―――――
7 吾亦紅 **waremokō** burnet (a flowering herb)

衣 → 5e0.1

2j4.5 / 828

充 **JŪ** fill **a(teru)** allocate **mi(tasu)** fulfill, satisfy

――――― 1 ―――――
4 充分 **jūbun** enough, sufficient; thoroughly
6 充当 **jūtō** allot, allocate, appropriate
充血 **jūketsu** become congested/bloodshot
7 充足 **jūsoku** sufficiency
8 充実 **jūjitsu** repletion, completion, beefing up, making substantial
12 充満 **jūman, michimichi(te iru)** be full of, be replete/teeming with
13 充溢 **jūitsu** overflow, abundance
充填 **jūten** filling
充塞 **jūsoku** plug, fill up; be stopped/clogged up
充電 **jūden** recharge (a battery)
充電器 **jūdenki** charger

――――― 2 ―――――
4 不充分 **fujūbun** insufficient, inadequate
8 拡充 **kakujū** expansion, amplification
11 脳充血 **nōjūketsu** brain congestion
12 補充 **hojū** supplement, replacement
補充兵 **hojūhei** reservists
補充隊 **hojūtai** the reserves
13 填充 **tenjū** fill (up), plug

2j4.6 / 1376

妄 **BŌ, MŌ** incoherent, reckless, false **mida(ri ni)** without authority; without good reason; indiscriminately, recklessly

――――― 1 ―――――
8 妄念 **mōnen** irrelevant thoughts, distracting ideas
9 妄信 **mōshin, bōshin** blind acceptance, credulity
11 妄動 **mōdō, bōdō** act blindly
妄執 **mōshū** deep-seated delusion/obsession
12 妄評 **bōhyō, mōhyō** unfair/savage criticism, excoriation
13 妄想 **mōsō, bōsō** wild fantasy, delusion
14 妄語 **mōgo, bōgo** lie, falsehood
妄説 **bōsetsu, mōsetsu** fallacy, false report

――――― 2 ―――――
7 狂妄 **kyōbō, kyōmō** mad, crazy
8 迷妄 **meimō** illusion, delusion
11 虚妄 **kyomō** false, fallacious, groundless
20 譫妄 **senmō** delirium

――――― 3 ―――――
12 軽挙妄動 **keikyo-mōdō** act rashly

──────── 5 ────────

2j5.1 / 1672

享

KYŌ enjoy; receive
u(keru) receive

──────── 1 ────────

6 享年 **kyōnen** one's age at death
享有 **kyōyū** enjoy, possess
8 享受 **kyōju** enjoy, have, be given
享和 **Kyōwa** (era, 1801–1804)
9 享保 **Kyōhō** (era, 1716–1736)
12 享禄 **Kyōroku** (era, 1528–1532)
13 享楽 **kyōraku** enjoyment
享楽主義 **kyōraku shugi** epicureanism
14 享徳 **Kyōtoku** (era, 1452–1454)

──────── 2 ────────

4 元享 **Genkō** (era, 1321–1324)
5 永享 **Eikyō** (era, 1429–1441)
7 延享 **Enkyō** (era, 1744–1748)
8 長享 **Chōkyō** (era, 1487–1489)
9 貞享 **Jōkyō** (era, 1684–1688)

辛 → **5b2.2**

弃 → 棄 **2j11.5**

2j5.2

吝

RIN, yabusa(ka), shiwa(i) miserly,
stingy, unwilling, sparing of

──────── 1 ────────

13 吝嗇 **rinshoku** miserly, stingy
吝嗇家 **rinshokuka** miser, niggard

──────── 2 ────────

10 倹吝 **kenrin** miserliness, stinginess

2j5.3

肓

KŌ interior region of the body above
the diaphragm too deep to be reached by
acupuncture needles

──────── 2 ────────

14 膏肓 **kōkō** the inmost part, region between
heart and diaphragm too deep to be
reached by acupuncture needles

──────── 3 ────────

10 病膏肓 **yamaikōkō** incurable; incorrigible

2j5.4 / 1374

忘 忘

BŌ, wasu(reru) forget

──────── 1 ────────

6 忘年会 **bōnenkai** year-end party
7 忘我 **bōga** self-oblivion, trance, ecstasy
忘却 **bōkyaku** forget, be oblivious to
忘形見 **wasu(re)gatami** memento, keepsake;
posthumous child
8 忘物 **wasu(re)mono** something forgotten
10 忘恩 **bōon** ingratitude

──────── 2 ────────

4 勿忘草 **wasurenagusa** forget-me-nots
6 年忘 **toshiwasu(re)** year-end drinking party
7 見忘 **miwasu(reru)** forget, fail to recognize
8 物忘 **monowasu(re)** forgetfulness
9 度忘 **dowasu(re)** forget for the moment, slip
one's mind
面忘 **omowasu(re)** fail to recognize
10 健忘 **kenbō** forgetfulness
健忘症 **kenbōshō** forgetfulness, amnesia
胴忘 **dōwasu(re)** have a lapse of memory,
forget for the moment
12 備忘 **bibō** reminder
備忘録 **bibōroku** memorandum, notebook
13 寝忘 **newasu(re)** oversleep
置忘 **o(ki)wasu(reru)** mislay, forget
14 聞忘 **ki(ki)wasu(reru)** forget to ask about;
forget what one hears

2j5.5 / 365

対 對

TAI against, vis-à-vis, versus,
anti-, counter-
TSUI pair, set

──────── 1 ────────

0 対する **tai(suru)** be opposite to, face; toward;
as opposed to; in response to
2 対人 **taijin** personal
4 対内 **tainai** domestic, internal
対中 **tai-Chū** toward/with China
対辺 **taihen** opposite side (in geometry)
対日 **tai-Nichi** toward/with Japan
5 対生 **taisei** (leaves) growing in opposing pairs
対外 **taigai** foreign, international, overseas
対外的 **taigaiteki** external
対比 **taihi** contrast, comparison, opposition,
analogy
対句 **tsuiku** couplet, distich; antithesis
対処 **taisho** deal/cope with
対立 **tairitsu** confrontation, opposing
6 対当 **taitō** corresponding, equivalent
対米 **tai-Bei** toward/with America
7 対位法 **taiihō** counterpoint
対角 **taikaku** opposite angle
対角線 **taikakusen** a diagonal
対決 **taiketsu** confrontation, showdown
対坐 **taiza** sit facing each other
対抗 **taikō** oppose, counter

対抗馬 **taikōba** rival horse; rival candidate
対抗策 **taikōsaku** (counter)measures
対応 **taiō** correspond to, be equivalent to; cope with
対応策 **taiōsaku** (counter)measures
対局 **taikyoku** play a game (of go)
8 対価 **taika** equivalent value, a compensation
対英 **tai-Ei** toward/with Britain
対空 **taikū** antiaircraft
対岸 **taigan** opposite shore
対物鏡 **taibutsukyō** objective lens
対欧 **tai-Ō** toward/with Europe
9 対陣 **taijin** encamp opposite the enemy; confront each other
対独 **tai-Doku** toward/with Germany
対峙 **taiji** confront each other, hold one's own against
対面 **taimen** interview, meeting; facing each other
10 対流 **tairyū** convection
対華 **tai-Ka** toward/with China
対案 **taian** counterproposal
対座 **taiza** sit facing each other
対校 **taikō** interschool, intercollegiate
対校試合 **taikō-jiai** interschool match
対称 **taishō** symmetry; second person (in grammar)
対称的 **taishōteki** symmetrical
対称軸 **taishōjiku** axis of symmetry
対症剤 **taishōzai** specific medicine
対症薬 **taishōyaku** specific medicine
対馬 **Tsushima** (island and ancient kuni, Nagasaki-ken)
対馬海峡 **Tsushima-kaikyō** Tsushima Strait (between Tsushima and Iki Island)
11 対偶 **taigū** contrapositive; pair
対訳 **taiyaku** bilingual text (with Japanese and English side by side)
12 対象 **taishō** object, subject, target
対象的 **taishōteki** objective
対象物 **taishōbutsu** object, subject, target
対策 **taisaku** (counter)measures
対等 **taitō** equality, parity
13 対照 **taishō** contrast
対照的 **taishōteki** (sharply) contrasting
対数 **taisū** logarithm
対戦 **taisen** wage war, compete
対置 **taichi** set opposite/against
対話 **taiwa** conversation, dialog
15 対敵 **taiteki** toward/with the enemy
対談 **taidan** face-to-face talk, conversation, interview
対論 **tairon** argue face to face
対質 **taishitsu** confront (with a witness)
18 対蹠地 **taisekichi** the antipodes
対蹠点 **taisekiten** antipode, nadir

対顔 **taigan** face, meet
21 対露 **tai-Ro** toward/with Russia

───────── 2 ─────────

1 一対 **ittsui** a pair
一対一 **ittaiichi** one-to-one
4 反対 **hantai** opposition, against; opposite, reverse, contrary
反対党 **hantaitō** opposition party
反対訊問 **hantai jinmon** cross-examination
反対側 **hantaigawa** the opposite side
反対語 **hantaigo** antonym
反対論 **hantairon** counterargument, opposing view
7 応対 **ōtai** receive (visitors), wait on (customers)
初対面 **shotaimen** first meeting
9 相対 **sōtai** relativity　**aitai** facing each other, directly
相対主義 **sōtai shugi** relativism
相対的 **sōtaiteki** relative
相対性 **sōtaisei** relativity
12 絶対 **zettai** absolute
絶対主義 **zettai shugi** absolutism
絶対的 **zettaiteki** absolute
絶対者 **zettaisha** the Absolute
絶対値 **zettaichi** absolute value (in math)
絶対量 **zettairyō** absolute amount
絶対絶命 **zettai-zetsumei** desperate situation
15 敵対 **tekitai** hostility, antagonism
敵対心 **tekitaishin** enmity, animosity
敵対的 **tekitaiteki** hostile, antagonistic

───────── 3 ─────────

4 水害対策 **suigai taisaku** flood control/relief measures
5 正反対 **seihantai** the exact opposite
好一対 **kōittsui** well-matched (couple)
12 貸借対照表 **taishakutaishōhyō** balance sheet
15 熱電対 **netsudentsui** thermocouple

───────── 6 ─────────

2j6.1 / 471

夜

YA, yo, yoru night

───────── 1 ─────────

3 夜叉 **yasha** she-devil, female demon
4 夜中 **yonaka** midnight, dead of night
　　yachū at night　**yojū** all night
夜分 **yabun** night, evening
5 夜半 **yowa, yahan** midnight, dead of night
夜市 **yoichi** night market
夜目 **yome** in the dark
6 夜気 **yaki** the night air/stillness/cool
夜毎 **yogoto** every night
夜曲 **yakyoku** nocturne

2

夜会 **yakai** evening party, ball
夜会服 **yakaifuku** evening dress
夜色 **yashoku** shades of night, night scene
夜行 **yakō** night travel; night train
夜光 **yakō** glowing in the dark
夜光虫 **yakōchū** night-glowing insect
夜光時計 **yakō-dokei** luminous-dial watch
夜光塗料 **yakō toryō** luminous paint
7 夜来 **yarai** since last night, overnight
夜更 **yofuka(shi)** staying up late
　　 yofuke late at night, the small hours
夜汽車 **yogisha** night train
夜学 **yagaku** evening classes, night school
夜学校 **yagakkō** night school
夜尿症 **yanyōshō** bed-wetting
夜見世 **yomise** night fair; night stall
夜見国 **yomi (no) kuni** hades, abode of the dead
8 夜長 **yonaga** long night
夜夜 **yo(na)yo(na)** night after night
夜盲症 **yamōshō** night blindness
夜逃 **yoni(ge)** fly by night, give (creditors) the slip
夜空 **yozora** night sky
夜歩 **yoaru(ki)** walk about at night
夜店 **yomise** night stall; night fair
夜明 **yoa(kashi)** stay up all night
　　 yoa(ke) dawn, daybreak
夜具 **yagu** bedding
夜雨 **yau** night rain
9 夜前 **yazen** last night
夜通 **yodō(shi)** all night long
夜風 **yokaze** night wind
夜昼 **yoru-hiru** day and night
夜食 **yashoku** supper, night meal
10 夜陰 **yain** darkness of night
夜這 **yobai** creep in to see a woman
夜遊 **yoaso(bi)** nighttime amusements
夜桜 **yozakura** cherry trees at night
夜討 **you(chi)** night attack
11 夜道 **yomichi** night journey
夜盗 **yatō** nighttime burglar
夜釣 **yozu(ri)** fishing at night
夜鳥 **yachō** nocturnal bird
12 夜勤 **yakin** night duty/shift
夜着 **yogi** bedclothes; bedding
夜寒 **yosamu, yozamu** the night cold
夜営 **yaei** camp(ing), bivouac
夜嵐 **yoarashi** night storm
夜景 **yakei** night view
夜番 **yoban, yaban** night watch(man)
夜間 **yakan** night, nighttime
13 夜業 **yagyō** night work/shift
夜想曲 **yasōkyoku** nocturne
夜話 **yobanashi, yawa** light talk after the day's work is done

15 夜稼 **yokase(gi)** night work; burglary
19 夜警 **yakei** night watch(man)
夜霧 **yogiri** night fog
21 夜露 **yotsuyu** evening dew
22 夜襲 **yashū** night attack
夜籠 **yogomo(ri)** praying all night (in a temple)
24 夜鷹 **yotaka** nighthawk; prostitute

──────── 2 ────────

1 一夜 **ichiya, hitoyo, hitoya** one night; all night
一夜漬 **ichiyazuke** pickled just overnight; hastily prepared
3 小夜 **sayo** night
小夜中 **sayonaka** midnight
小夜曲 **sayokyoku** serenade
小夜更 **sayofu(kete)** late a night
4 不夜城 **fuyajō** nightless city, city that never sleeps
今夜 **kon'ya** tonight
月夜 **tsukiyo** moonlit night
日夜 **nichiya** day and night, constantly
5 白夜 **hakuya, byakuya** bright (arctic) night
6 毎夜 **maiyo** every evening, nightly
夙夜 **shukuya** from morning till night
先夜 **sen'ya** the other night
当夜 **tōya** that night; tonight
7 良夜 **ryōya** moonlit night
即夜 **sokuya** on the same night
初夜 **shoya** first night; wedding night; first watch (8–10 p.m.)
8 長夜 **chōya** long night
夜夜 **yo(na)yo(na)** night after night
9 除夜 **joya** New Year's Eve
除夜鐘 **joya (no) kane** New Year's midnight bells
前夜 **zen'ya** last night, the previous night
前夜祭 **zen'yasai** (Christmas) Eve
連夜 **ren'ya** night after night, nightly
通夜 **tsuya** wake, vigil
昨夜 **sakuya, yūbe** last night/evening
昼夜 **chūya** day and night
昼夜兼行 **chūya-kenkō** 24 hours a day, around the clock
昼夜帯 **chūyaobi** a two-faced obi
10 真夜中 **mayonaka** dead of night, midnight
逮夜 **taiya** eve of a death anniversary
11 深夜 **shin'ya** late at night, the dead of night
常夜 **tokoyo** endless night
終夜 **shūya, yomosugara** all night long
終夜灯 **shūyatō** nightlight
12 短夜 **miji(ka)yo** short (summer) night
幾夜 **ikuyo** how many nights; many a night
13 暗夜 **an'ya** dark night
聖夜 **seiya** Christmas Eve

14 暮夜 **boya** evening, night
　　静夜 **seiya** quiet night
15 徹夜 **tetsuya** stay up all night
17 霜夜 **shimoyo** frosty night
　　闇夜 **yamiyo, an'ya** dark night

───────── 3 ─────────

2 十三夜 **jūsan'ya** 13th night of a lunar month
　　　(especially a moonlit September 13)
　　十五夜 **jūgoya** 15th night of a lunar month
　　　(especially a moonlit August 15)
　　十六夜 **izayoi** 16th night of a lunar month
3 夕月夜 **yūzukiyo** moonlit evening
　　千一夜 **Sen'ichiya** Thousand and One Nights
5 白河夜船 **Shirakawa yofune** fast asleep
6 百鬼夜行 **hyakki-yakō, hyakki-yagyō** all
　　　sorts of demons roaming about at night;
　　　rampant evil, scandal, pandemonium
8 金色夜叉 **konjiki yasha** usurer
9 星月夜 **hoshizukiyo** starlit night
15 熱帯夜 **nettaiya, nettaiyo** a night during
　　　which the temperature never falls below
　　　25 degrees Celsius

───────── 4 ─────────

1 一昨昨夜 **issakusakuya** three nights ago

2j6.2 / 787

卒 卆

SOTSU soldier, private;
sudden; come to an end; die;
graduate

───────── 1 ─────────

0 卒する **sos(suru)** die, pass away
4 卒中 **sotchū** cerebral stroke, apoplexy
8 卒直 **sotchoku** frank, openhearted
12 卒塔婆 **sotoba** wooden grave tablet, stupa
13 卒業 **sotsugyō** graduation

───────── 2 ─────────

3 大卒 **daisotsu** college/university graduate
　　　(short for 大学卒業(者))
　　士卒 **shisotsu** a private, soldier
4 中卒 **chūsotsu** junior-high-school graduate
　　　(short for 中学卒業(者))
6 戍卒 **jusotsu** border guard
7 何卒 **nanitozo** please
　　兵卒 **heisotsu** private, enlisted man
8 歩卒 **hosotsu** infantryman
9 忽卒 **sōsotsu** hurried, hasty, sudden
10 倉卒 **sōsotsu** sudden; hurried, busy
　　将卒 **shōsotsu** officers and men
　　高卒 **kōsotsu** high-school graduate (short for
　　　高等学校卒業(者))
　　弱卒 **jakusotsu** cowardly soldier
　　従卒 **jūsotsu** soldier-servant, orderly
11 脳卒中 **nōsotchū** cerebral apoplexy
14 獄卒 **gokusotsu** prison guards; hell's
　　tormenting devils
16 輸卒 **yusotsu** transport soldier

2j6.3 / 189

京 京 錆

KYŌ, KEI capital,
metropolis; Kyōto;
Tōkyō; ten quadrillion,
10,000,000,000,000,000

miyako capital, metropolis

───────── 1 ─────────

6 京阪神 **Kei-Han-Shin** Kyōto-Ōsaka-Kōbe
　　京成 **Kei-Sei** Tōkyō-Narita
9 京城 **Keijō** Seoul
10 京都 **Kyōto** (city, Kyōto-fu)
　　京都府 **Kyōto-fu** (prefecture)
　　京浜 **Kei-Hin** Tōkyō-Yokohama
12 京葉 **Kei-Yō** Tōkyō-Chiba
15 京舞 **kyōmai** a traditional Kyōto dance per-
　　　formed to the accompaniment of *jiuta*

───────── 2 ─────────

3 上京 **jōkyō** go/come to the capital
　　上京中 **jōkyōchū** in the capital
4 中京 **Chūkyō** Nagoya
5 北京 **Pekin** Peking, Beijing
6 西京 **Saikyō** the western capital, Kyōto
　　在京 **zaikyō** residing in the capital, in Tōkyō
　　在京中 **zaikyōchū** while in the capital
8 東京 **Tōkyō** (city, capital of Japan)
　　東京都 **Tōkyō-to** the Metropolis of Tōkyō
　　退京 **taikyō** leave the capital, leave Tōkyō
　　英京 **Eikyō** London, the British capital
9 南京 **Nankin** Nanking
　　南京虫 **nankinmushi** bedbugs
　　南京豆 **nankinmame** peanuts
　　南京町 **Nankinmachi** Chinatown
　　南京袋 **nankinbukuro** gunny sack
10 帰京 **kikyō** return to Tōkyō
13 滞京 **taikyō** staying in the capital
18 離京 **rikyō** leaving the capital

───────── 3 ─────────

5 平安京 **Heiankyō** ancient Kyōto
　　平城京 **Heijōkyō** ancient Nara

2j6.4 / 246

育 毓

IKU, soda(teru), haguku(mu)
raise, rear, bring up
soda(te) bringing up, raising
soda(tsu) be raised, be brought
up, grow up　**soda(chi)** upbringing; growth

───────── 1 ─────────

6 育成 **ikusei** rearing, training
7 育児 **ikuji** care/raising of children
8 育英 **ikuei** education

2

亻 ⺅
冫
孑
阝
卩
刂
力
又
宀
十 6 ←
卄
⺮
丷

厂
辶
门
几
匸

14 育種 **ikushu** (plant) breeding
16 育親 **soda(te no) oya** foster parent

───────── 2 ─────────

3 山育 **yamasoda(chi)** mountain-bred
5 生育 **seiiku** growth, development
　　 ha(e)soda(tsu) spring up
6 成育 **seiiku** growth, development
7 体育 **taiiku** physical education, athletics
　体育館 **taiikukan** gymnasium
　扶育 **fuiku** bring up, tutor
8 知育 **chiiku** mental training
　肥育 **hiiku** fattening (livestock)
9 発育 **hatsuiku** growth, development
　発育盛 **hatsuikuzaka(ri)** period of rapid growth
　保育 **hoiku** nurture, childcare, rearing
　保育所 **hoikujo** nursery school
　保育園 **hoikuen** nursery school
　美育 **biiku** esthetic culture
10 都育 **miyakosoda(chi)** city-bred
　哺育 **hoiku** suckle, nurse
　島育 **shimasoda(chi)** island-bred
　教育 **kyōiku** education
　教育上 **kyōikujō** educationwise
　教育会 **kyōikukai** educational association
　教育学 **kyōikugaku** pedagogy, education
　教育法 **kyōikuhō** teaching method
　教育的 **kyōikuteki** educational, instructive
　教育者 **kyōikusha** educator
　教育界 **kyōikukai** (the world of) education
　教育家 **kyōikuka** educator
　教育費 **kyōikuhi** school/education expenses
　紐育 **Nyūyōku** New York
　訓育 **kun'iku** education, discipline
11 野育 **nosoda(chi)** wild; ill-bred
12 傅育 **fuiku** bring up, tutor
13 愛育 **aiiku** tender loving care
　飼育 **shiiku** raising, breeding
　飼育者 **shiikusha** raiser, breeder
14 徳育 **tokuiku** moral education
15 養育 **yōiku** bring up, rear; support
　養育者 **yōikusha** rearer, guardian
　養育院 **yōikuin** orphanage
　撫育 **buiku** care, tending

───────── 3 ─────────

5 田舎育 **inakasoda(chi)** country-bred
6 再教育 **saikyōiku** retraining
　早教育 **sōkyōiku** early education
8 性教育 **sei kyōiku** sex education
12 無教育 **mukyōiku** uneducated

───────── 4 ─────────

6 全人教育 **zenjin kyōiku** well-rounded education, education for the whole man
9 通信教育 **tsūshin kyōiku** education by correspondence
13 義務教育 **gimu kyōiku** compulsory education

2j6.5 / 1477

斉 齊　SEI in order, all together; alike
　　 hito(shii) equal, similar

───────── 1 ─────────

1 斉一 **seiitsu** uniform, all alike
8 斉明 **Saimei** (empress, 655–661)
10 斉射 **seisha** volley, fusillade
11 斉唱 **seishō** sing in unison
16 斉衡 **Saikō** (era, 854–857)

───────── 2 ─────────

1 一斉 **issei** all at once, simultaneously
　一斉射撃 **issei shageki** volley, fusillade
4 不斉 **fusei** not uniform, uneven, asymmetrical
7 均斉 **kinsei** symmetry, balance

───────── 3 ─────────

4 不均斉 **fukinsei** asymmetrical, lop-sided

2j6.6 / 1375

盲 盲　MŌ, BŌ, **mekura**, **meshii** blind

───────── 1 ─────────

2 盲人 **mōjin** blind person
5 盲打 **mekura-u(chi)** hitting blindly
　盲目 **mōmoku** blindness
　盲目的 **mōmokuteki** blind (devotion)
7 盲判 **mekuraban** stamp one's seal without reading the document, rubber-stamp
　盲学校 **mōgakkō** school for the blind
9 盲信 **mōshin** blind acceptance, credulity
　盲点 **mōten** blind spot
10 盲進 **mōshin** advance recklessly, plunge headlong
　盲従 **mōjū** blind obedience
11 盲動 **mōdō** act blindly
　盲啞 **mōa** blind and mute
　盲啞学校 **mōa gakkō** school for the blind and mute
　盲断 **mōdan** arbitrary judgment, hasty conclusion
12 盲買 **mekuraga(i)** buying sight-unseen
13 盲滅法 **mekura meppō** recklessly, at random
　盲腸 **mōchō** appendix
　盲腸炎 **mōchōen** appendicitis
　盲愛 **mōai** blind love
14 盲導犬 **mōdōken** seeing-eye dog
15 盲撃 **mekura-u(chi)** random shooting
19 盲爆 **mōbaku** indiscriminate bombing

───────── 2 ─────────

4 文盲 **monmō** illiteracy
5 半盲 **hanmō** half blind
6 色盲 **shikimō** color blindness
8 夜盲症 **yamōshō** night blindness

明盲 **a(ki)mekura** blind; illiterate
9 俄盲 **niwakamekura** sudden loss of eyesight; person who has unexpectedly become blind
11 雪盲 **setsumō** snow blindness
13 群盲 **gunmō** blind populace, illiterates

2j6.7

氓

BŌ, tami a people (who came from elsewhere)

2j6.8 / 1046

版

HAN printing block/plate; printing, edition, impression; board; roster

———————— 1 ————————

3 版下 **hanshita** art boards, mechanicals, camera-ready copy
4 版元 **hanmoto** publisher
版木 **hangi** printing/engraving block, woodcut
5 版本 **hanpon** printed book; book printed by engraved wood blocks
6 版行 **hankō** publication; one's seal
7 版図 **hanto** territory, dominion
8 版画 **hanga** woodcut print
14 版摺 **hansu(ri)** printing from woodcuts
15 版権 **hanken** copyright
版権法 **hankenhō** copyright law
20 版籍 **hanseki** (register of) land and people

———————— 2 ————————

1 一版 **ippan** an edition
4 木版 **mokuhan** wood-block print(ing)
木版本 **mokuhanbon** xylographic book
木版画 **mokuhanga** wood-block print
木版刷 **mokuhanzu(ri)** wood engraving
5 瓦版 **kawaraban** tile engraving, tile block print
凸版 **toppan** letterpress, relief (printing)
凹版 **ōhan, ōban** intaglio (printing)
出版 **shuppan** publishing
出版社 **shuppansha** publishing house, publisher
出版物 **shuppanbutsu** a publication
出版費 **shuppanhi** publishing costs
出版業 **shuppangyō** the publishing business
古版 **kohan** old edition
旧版 **kyūhan** old edition
石版 **sekiban** lithograph(y)
石版画 **sekibanga** lithograph
石版刷 **sekibanzu(ri)** lithography
6 再版 **saihan** reprint; second printing/edition
7 図版 **zuhan** plate, figure, illustration
改版 **kaihan** revised edition

私版 **shihan** private publication
初版 **shohan** first edition
9 活版 **kappan** movable-type printing
活版本 **kappanbon** printed book
活版所 **kappanjo** print shop
活版屋 **kappan'ya** print ship; printer
10 原版 **genban** original edition
11 偽版 **gihan** pirated edition
12 絶版 **zeppan** out of print
13 解版 **kaihan** distribute/unset type
新版 **shinpan** new publication/edition
鉛版 **enban** stereotype, printing plate
14 製版 **seihan** platemaking (in printing)
製版所 **seihanjo** platemaking shop
網版 **amihan** halftone (printing)
銅版 **dōban** copperplate
15 蔵版 **zōhan** copyrighted by
16 整版 **seihan** block printing, plate making

———————— 3 ————————

3 三色版 **sanshokuban** three-color printing
4 日曜版 **nichiyōban** Sunday edition
5 写真版 **shashinban** photographic plate
6 地方版 **chihōban** local edition
7 亜鉛版 **aenban** zinc etching
決定版 **ketteiban** definitive edition
改訂版 **kaiteiban** revised edition
8 限定版 **genteiban** limited edition
英語版 **eigoban** English-language edition
9 海外版 **kaigaiban** overseas edition
海賊版 **kaizokuban** pirate edition
10 校訂版 **kōteiban** revised edition
特装版 **tokusōban** specially bound edition
11 現代版 **gendaiban** modern edition
12 普及版 **fukyūban** popular edition
13 廉価版 **renkaban** cheap/popular edition
新訂版 **shinteiban** newly revised edition
電気版 **denkiban** electrotype
14 豪華版 **gōkaban** deluxe edition
17 謄写版 **tōshaban** mimeograph
縮刷版 **shukusatsuban** small-size edition

———————— 4 ————————

6 自費出版 **jihi shuppan** publishing at one's own expense, vanity press

———————— 7 ————————

京 → 京 **2j6.3**

2j7.1 / 1179

帝　帝

TEI emperor
mikado emperor (of Japan)

———————— 1 ————————

4 帝王 **teiō** monarch, emperor

帝王切開 **teiō sekkai** Caesarean section
7 帝位 **teii** the throne/crown
8 帝制 **teisei** imperial rule
帝国 **teikoku** empire
帝国主義 **teikoku shugi** imperialism
9 帝冠 **teikan** imperial crown
帝室 **teishitsu** the imperial household
帝政 **teisei** imperial government/rule
10 帝陵 **teiryō** imperial mausoleum
帝都 **teito** imperial capital

——————— 2 ———————

3 大帝 **taitei** great emperor
上帝 **jōtei** God
女帝 **jotei** empress
4 天帝 **Tentei** Lord of Heaven, God
反帝国主義 **han-teikoku shugi** anti-imperialism
6 先帝 **sentei** the late emperor
9 皇帝 **kōtei** emperor
12 廃帝 **haitei** deposed emperor, ex-king

——————— 3 ———————

3 大英帝国 **Dai-Ei Teikoku** the British Empire

2j7.2

奕 **EKI, YAKU** large; beautiful; flourishing; sparkling

——————— 1 ———————

5 奕世 **ekisei** generation after generation

——————— 2 ———————

12 博奕 **bakuchi** gambling
博奕打 **bakuchiu(chi)** gambler

弯 → 彎 **3h19.1**

2j7.3 / 257

変 變 **HEN** change; strange; flat (in musical keys); mishap; disturbance **ka(waru)** change (intr.); be different **ka(eru)** change (tr.)

——————— 1 ———————

0 変じる/ずる **hen(jiru/zuru)** change
変ロ長調 **hen-ro chōchō** B-flat major
2 変人 **henjin** an eccentric
4 変幻 **hengen** transformation
変幻自在 **hengen-jizai** ever-changing
変化 **henka** change **henge** goblin, apparition
変心 **henshin** change of mind, fickleness
5 変圧 **hen'atsu** transform (voltage)
変圧器 **hen'atsuki** transformer

変目 **ka(wari)me** change, turning point, transition
6 変死 **henshi** accidental death
変色 **henshoku** change of color, discoloration
変名 **henmei, henmyō** assumed name, alias
変成 **hensei** metamorphosis
7 変身 **henshin** transformation
変更 **henkō** change, alteration, amendment
変体 **hentai** anomaly
変体仮名 **hentai-gana** anomalous (obsolete) kana
変形 **henkei** transformation, metamorphosis, modification, deformation
変声期 **henseiki** age of puberty/voice-cracking
8 変果 **ka(wari)ha(teru)** change completely
変事 **henji** accident, mishap, disaster
変易 **ka(wari)yasu(i)** changeable, inconstant
変者 **ka(wari)mono** an eccentric
変性 **hensei** degenerate, denature
9 変奏曲 **hensōkyoku** a variation (in music)
変速 **hensoku** change speeds, shift gears
変造 **henzō** alter, deface, falsify, forge
変通 **hentsū** versatility, flexibility
変革 **henkaku** change, reform, revolution
変則 **hensoku** irregular, abnormal
10 変流器 **henryūki** current transformer
変哲 **hentetsu(mo nai)** commonplace
変容 **hen'yō** changed appearance
変容期 **hen'yōki** period of changing appearance
変格 **henkaku** irregular (inflection)
11 変動 **hendō** fluctuations
変移 **hen'i** change, alteration, mutation
変異 **hen'i** mishap, unforeseen event; variation
変転 **henten** changes, vicissitudes
12 変換 **henkan** change, conversion, transformation (in math)
変装 **hensō** disguise
13 変数 **hensū** a variable (in math)
変節 **hensetsu** defection, apostasy, changing sides
変電所 **hendensho** transformer substation
14 変遷 **hensen** changes, vicissitudes, transition
変貌 **henbō** transformation
変態 **hentai** metamorphosis; abnormal, perverted
変種 **henshu** variety, strain; freak of nature **ka(wari)dane** a novelty, exceptional case
15 変調 **henchō** change of tone/key; irregular, abnormal; modulation (in radio)
変質 **henshitsu** deterioration, degeneration
変質者 **henshitsusha** a pervert/deviant

—————— 2 ——————

1 一変 **ippen** a complete change
3 大変 **taihen** serious; terrible, awful, huge, very
千変万化 **senpen-banka** innumerable/ kaleidoscopic changes, immense variety
小変 **shōhen** a slight change; minor incident
4 不変 **fuhen** invariable, constant, immutable, permanent
凶変 **kyōhen** disaster; assassination
天変 **tenpen** cataclysm, natural disaster
天変地異 **tenpen-chii** cataclysm
心変 **kokoroga(wari)** change of mind, inconstancy
6 生変 **u(mare)ka(waru)** be born again, start life afresh, be reincarnated
ha(e)ka(waru) grow in a place of previous growth, grow in again
打変 **u(tte)kawa(ru)** change completely
可変 **kahen** variable, changeable
6 気変 **kiga(wari)** change one's mind, be fickle
兇変 **kyōhen** disaster; assassination
再変 **saihen** second change; second disaster
色変 **irogawa(ri)** discoloration; different color/kind
地変 **chihen** natural calamity
光変調 **hikari henchō** optical modulation
早変 **hayaga(wari)** quick change (of costume)
7 声変 **koega(wari)** change/cracking of voice
応変 **ōhen** expediency
改変 **kaihen** change, alter, renovate
見変 **mika(eru)** prefer; forsake for another
8 事変 **jihen** accident, mishap; incident, uprising, emergency
逆変 **gyakuhen** adverse change; vary inversely
9 急変 **kyūhen** sudden change; emergency
風変 **fūgawa(ri)** eccentric, peculiar
面変 **omoga(wari)** change in one's looks
相変 **aikawa(razu)** as usual
神変 **shinpen** immeasurable/mysterious change
神変不思儀 **shinpen-fushigi** miracle, marvel
政変 **seihen** change of government
10 豹変 **hyōhen** sudden change
唐変木 **tōhenboku** blockhead, oaf
病変 **byōhen** become morbid
11 黄変米 **ōhenmai** discolored/spoiled rice
移変 **utsu(ri)kawa(ri)** changes, transition
異変 **ihen** accident, disaster, unforeseen occurrence
転変 **tenpen** change, vicissitudes
13 腹変 **haraga(wari)** born of a different mother but having the same father; changing one's mind, going back on one's word
14 様変 **samaga(wari)** change in the situation

種変 **tanegawa(ri)** half-brother/half-sister by a different father; new strain, hybrid variety
15 権変 **kenpen** meeting the situation as it arises; trickery
16 激変 **gekihen** sudden change, upheaval
機変 **kihen** adaptation to circumstances

—————— 3 ——————

1 一風変 **ippū kawa(tta)** eccentric, queer; unconventional, original
4 日付変更線 **hizuke henkōsen** the international date line
7 肝硬変 **kankōhen** cirrhosis of the liver
8 突然変異 **totsuzen hen'i** mutation
11 経時変化 **keiji henka** change with the passage of time, aging
14 語尾変化 **gobi henka** inflection

—————— 4 ——————

1 一定不変 **ittei fuhen** invariable, permanent
5 北支事変 **Hokushi jihen** the Marco Polo Bridge incident
北清事変 **Hokushin jihen** the North China incident, the Boxer uprising
6 有為転変 **ui-tenpen** vicissitudes of life
12 満州事変 **Manshū Jihen** the Manchurian Incident
13 暖冬異変 **dantō ihen** abnormally warm winter
18 臨機応変 **rinki-ōhen** adaptation to circumstances

2j7.4 / 1675

哀 **AI, awa(remu)** pity, feel compassion
awa(re) pitiable, wretched, sorrowful, piteous

—————— 1 ——————

4 哀切 **aisetsu** pathetic
5 哀史 **aishi** tragic story
哀号 **aigō** moan, wailing
7 哀別 **aibetsu** sad parting
11 哀情 **aijō** sadness
哀惜 **aiseki** grief, sorrow
哀悼 **aitō** condolence, sympathy, mourning
12 哀訴 **aiso** appeal, entreat, implore
13 哀傷 **aishō** sorrow, grief
哀楽 **airaku** grief and pleasure
哀愁 **aishū** sadness, sorrow, grief
哀感 **aikan** sadness, pathos
哀詩 **aishi** elegy
哀話 **aiwa** sad story
14 哀歌 **aika** plaintive song, elegy, lament
15 哀歓 **aikan** joys and sorrows
哀調 **aichō** mournful melody; minor key
16 哀憐 **airen** pity, compassion
19 哀願 **aigan** entreat, implore, petition

―――――― 2 ――――――
5 可哀相 **kawaisō** poor, pitiable, pathetic
6 仲哀 **Chūai** (emperor, 192–200)
8 物哀 **mono (no) awa(re)** pathos, esthetic sense
12 悲哀 **hiai** sorrow, grief, sadness

―――――― 3 ――――――
12 喜怒哀楽 **kidoairaku** joy-anger-sorrow-
pleasure, emotions

2j7.5 / 1184

亭 **TEI** restaurant; arbor, pavilion, summer
house; vaudeville theater; lofty

―――――― 1 ――――――
3 亭々 **teitei(taru)** lofty, towering
5 亭主 **teishu** husband; master, host
亭主関白 **teishu kanpaku** autocratic husband

―――――― 2 ――――――
10 料亭 **ryōtei** restaurant
11 勘亭流 **Kantei-ryū** (style of calligraphy used
in kabuki and sumo programs)
13 園亭 **entei** arbor, bower, gazebo
14 旗亭 **kitei** inn; restaurant

2j7.6

亮 **RYŌ** clear; help

彦→ **5b4.4**

竒→奇 **3d5.17**

彦→彦 **5b4.4**

―――――― 8 ――――――

2j8.1 / 1676

衰 **SUI, otoro(eru)** become weak, wither,
ebb, go into decline

―――――― 1 ――――――
3 衰亡 **suibō** decline (and fall), downfall, ruin
8 衰退 **suitai** decline, degeneration
10 衰残 **suizan** emaciated, decrepit, worn out
衰弱 **suijaku** grow weak, become feeble
11 衰運 **suiun** declining fortunes
13 衰勢 **suisei** declining fortunes, deteriorating
position

衰滅 **suimetsu** decline, downfall, ruin
衰微 **suibi** decline, fall into decay, wane
16 衰頹 **suitai** decline, waning, decay

―――――― 2 ――――――
6 老衰 **rōsui** infirmity of old age
11 盛衰 **seisui** rise and fall, ups and downs
12 減衰 **gensui** decrease, dampen, attenuate
14 痩衰 **ya(se)otoro(eru)** become emaciated,
waste away

―――――― 4 ――――――
9 栄枯盛衰 **eiko-seisui** prosperity and decline,
rise and fall

衷→衷 **0a9.9**

离→離 **8c10.3**

2j8.2 / 258

恋 戀 **REN, koi** love
ko(u) be in love
koi(shii) dear, beloved

―――――― 1 ――――――
2 恋人 **koibito** sweetheart, boyfriend, girlfriend
3 恋々 **renren (to suru)** be fondly attached to
4 恋仇 **koigataki** one's rival in love
恋文 **koibumi** love letter
恋心 **koigokoro** (awakening of) love
6 恋仲 **koinaka** love relationship, love
9 恋風 **koikaze** zephyr of love
11 恋情 **renjō** love, affection
恋情 **koinasake** lovesickness
12 恋着 **renchaku** love, attachment
恋焦 **ko(i)ko(gareru)** pine for, be desperately
in love
13 恋煩 **koiwazura(i)** lovesickness
恋愛 **ren'ai** love
恋愛至上主義 **ren'ai-shijō shugi** love for
love's sake
恋愛観 **ren'aikan** philosophy of love
恋路 **koiji** love's pathway, romance
14 恋慕 **renbo** fall in love with
ko(i)shita(u) yearn for, miss
恋歌 **koiuta, koika, renka** love song/poem
15 恋敵 **koigataki** one's rival in love

―――――― 2 ――――――
4 片恋 **katakoi** unrequited love
5 失恋 **shitsuren** unrequited love
6 色恋 **irokoi** love
7 初恋 **hatsukoi** one's first love
8 妻恋 **tsumagoi** love for one's wife

10 恋恋 **renren (to suru)** be fondly attached to
11 眷恋 **kenren** strong attachment, deep affection
12 悲恋 **hiren** disappointed love
15 横恋慕 **yokorenbo** illicit love

2j8.3

旁

BŌ, katawa(ra) side
tsukuri right half of a kanji

─────── 1 ───────

3 旁々 **katagata** at the same time, combined with

2j8.4

亳

HAKU (an ancient Chinese capital)

2j8.5

烹

HŌ boil, cook

─────── 2 ───────

12 割烹 **kappō** cooking
割烹店 **kappōten** restaurant
割烹着 **kappōgi** cook's apron

2j8.6 / 190

高 髙

KŌ high **taka(i)** high; expensive **taka(maru)** rise, increase **taka(meru)** raise, heighten **taka** amount
taka(buru) be proud/haughty; grow excited
(o)taka(ku) haughty, stuck up **taka(raka)** loud
taka(ga) only, at most, after all

─────── 1 ───────

0 高じる **kō(jiru)** increase; be proud
ドル高 **dorudaka** strong dollar (relative to other currencies)
3 高工 **kōkō** higher technical school (short for 高等工業学校)
高上 **takaa(gari)** climb high; occupy a seat of honor; more expensive than expected
高下 **kōge** rise and fall, fluctuations; rank, grade, quality
高下駄 **takageta** high clogs/geta
高々 **takadaka** at most; high, aloft, loudly
高々指 **takatakayubi** the middle finger
高々度 **kōkōdo** high-altitude
高山 **kōzan** high mountain, alpine
高山病 **kōzanbyō** mountain/altitude sickness
高士 **kōshi** man of noble character
4 高天原 **Takamagahara** the heavens, the abode of the gods

高手小手 **takate-kote** (bound) hand and foot
高木 **kōboku** tall tree **Takagi** (surname)
5 高圧 **kōatsu** high voltage/pressure; high-handedness
高圧的 **kōatsuteki** high-handed, coercive
高圧線 **kōatsusen** high-voltage power lines
高台 **takadai** high ground, elevation
高札 **kōsatsu** bulletin board; highest bid
高目 **takame** high, on the high side
6 高気圧 **kōkiatsu** high atmospheric pressure
高年 **kōnen** old age
高年者 **kōnensha** elderly person
高次 **kōji** higher-order, meta-
高地 **kōchi** high ground, highlands, plateau
高名 **kōmyō** fame, renown; your name
　　　kōmei fame, renown
高血圧 **kōketsuatsu** high blood pressure
7 高寿 **kōju** advanced age
高位 **kōi** high rank, honors
高低 **kōtei, takahiku** highs and lows, unevenness, fluctuations; height, pitch
高角 **kōkaku** altitude, high-angle
高角砲 **kōkakuhō** high-angle/antiaircraft gun
高弟 **kōtei** one's best student, leading disciple
高坏 **takatsuki** serving table
高批 **kōhi** your valued criticism
高吟 **kōgin** recite (a poem) aloud
高学年 **kōgakunen** upper (5th and 6th) grades in elementary school
高声 **kōsei** loud voice
高見 **kōken** your (esteemed) opinion/views
高利 **kōri** high interest (rate)
高利貸 **kōriga(shi)** usury; usurer
高言 **kōgen** boasting
高足 **kōsoku** best student, leading disciple
高足駄 **takaashida** high clogs/geta
高足蟹 **takaashigani** giant spider crab
8 高価 **kōka** high price
高卒 **kōsotsu** high-school graduate (short for 高等学校卒業(者))
高周波 **kōshūha** high-frequency
高岡 **Takaoka** (city, Toyama-ken)
高波 **takanami** high wave/seas
高知 **Kōchi** (city, Kōchi-ken)
高知県 **Kōchi-ken** (prefecture)
高官 **kōkan** high official/office
高空 **kōkū, takazora** high altitude
高尚 **kōshō** lofty, refined, advanced
高松 **Takamatsu** (city, Kagawa-ken)
高炉 **kōro** blast furnace
高性能 **kōseinō** high-performance
高所 **kōsho** elevation, height; altitude; broad view
9 高飛車 **takabisha** high-handed, domineering
高点 **kōten** high score
高速 **kōsoku** high-speed; expressway

2

亻 丿 子 阝 卩 刂 力 又 一 亠 十 卜 宀 ⺌ 厂 辶 冂 几 匸

→ 8

高速度 **kōsokudo** high speed
高風 **kōfū** noble mien/character
高浮彫 **takau(ki)bo(ri)** high relief
高品位テレビ **kōhin'i terebi** high-definition television
高姿勢 **kōshisei** high posture/profile, aggressive attitude
高度 **kōdo** high(ly developed), advanced, sophisticated; altitude
高度計 **kōdokei** altimeter
高架 **kōka** elevated, overhead
高祖 **kōso** founder of a dynasty/sect
高祖父 **kōsofu** great-great-grandfather
高祖母 **kōsobo** great-great-grandmother
高音 **kōon, takane** high-pitched tone/key, loud sound
高級 **kōkyū** high-grade, high-class; high rank
高級車 **kōkyūsha** luxury car
高級品 **kōkyūhin** high-grade goods
10 高射砲 **kōshahō** antiaircraft gun
高値 **takane** high price
高高 **takadaka** at most; high, aloft, loudly
高高指 **takatakayubi** the middle finger
高高度 **kōkōdo** high-altitude
高原 **kōgen** plateau, highlands
高峰 **kōhō** lofty peak
高島田 **takashimada** (a traditional hairdo)
高座 **kōza** platform, dais, stage; upper seat
高校 **kōkō** senior high school (short for 高等学校)
高校生 **kōkōsei** senior-high-school student
高教 **kōkyō** your instructions/suggestions
高恩 **kōon** great benevolence/blessings
高笑 **takawara(i)** loud/boisterous laughter
高配 **kōhai** your trouble/assistance
11 高野山 **Kōyasan** (mountain, Wakayama-ken)
高野豆腐 **kōyadōfu** frozen tofu
高率 **kōritsu** high rate
高唱 **kōshō** sing loudly; advocate; emphasize
高著 **kōcho** your (literary) work
高菜 **takana** (a leaf mustard)
高崎 **Takasaki** (city, Gunma-ken)
高望 **takanozo(mi)** aim (too) high, be ambitious
12 高遠 **kōen** lofty, exalted
高温 **kōon** high temperature
高揚 **kōyō** heighten, enhance, exalt, promote
高禄 **kōroku** high salary
高裁 **kōsai** High Court
高給 **kōkyū** high salary
高歯 **takaba** (clogs/geta with) high supports
高等 **kōtō** high-grade, high-class
高等学校 **kōtō gakkō** senior high school
高等官 **kōtōkan** senior official
高評 **kōhyō** your (esteemed) opinion/criticism
高貴 **kōki** noble, exalted; valuable

13 高僧 **kōsō** high priest, prelate; virtuous priest
高障害 **kōshōgai** high hurdles
高義 **kōgi** high morality; great kindness/favor
高蒔絵 **takamakie** embossed gilt lacquerwork
高殿 **takadono** stately mansion
高楼 **kōrō** tall building, skyscraper
高話 **takabanashi** loud talking
高雅 **kōga** refined, elegant
14 高鳴 **takana(ru)** ring loud, clang, throb/beat audibly
高徳 **kōtoku** eminent virtue
高察 **kōsatsu** your idea
高層 **kōsō** high-altitude, high-rise (building)
高層雲 **kōsōun** altostratus clouds
高歌 **kōka** loud singing
高慢 **kōman** proud, haughty, supercilious
高説 **kōsetsu** (your) valuable opinion/suggestions
高閣 **kōkaku** high building/shelf
15 高邁 **kōmai** lofty, exalted
高潮 **takashio** high tide
　　 kōchō high tide; climax, peak
高潮時 **kōchōji** time of high tide
高潔 **kōketsu** high-minded, noble, upright
高熱 **kōnetsu** high fever
高談 **kōdan** (your) lofty discourse
高論 **kōron** (your) exalted opinion
高調 **kōchō** high pitch/spirits
高調子 **takachōshi** high pitch; rising stockmarket tone
高踏 **kōtō** transcending the mundane
高踏的 **kōtōteki** transcendent
高踏派 **kōtōha** the transcendentalists
16 高曇 **takagumo(ri)** overcast with wispy high-altitude clouds
高積雲 **kōsekiun** altocumulus clouds
高緯度 **kōido** high/cold latitudes
17 高嶺 **takane** lofty peak
高嶺花 **takane (no) hana** flower on an inaccessible height; the unattainable
高燥 **kōsō** elevated, high and dry
高覧 **kōran** your perusal
高鼾 **takaibiki** loud snoring
高齢 **kōrei** advanced age
高齢者 **kōreisha** elderly person
18 高額 **kōgaku** large amount
19 高瀬 **takase** shallows
高瀬舟 **takasebune** flatboat, riverboat
高麗 **Kōrai** (an ancient Korean kingdom)
20 高欄 **kōran** balustrade, bannister, handrail
高騰 **kōtō** steep rise (in prices)

———————— 2 ————————

3 上高 **a(gari)daka** revenue, income, receipts, yield
小高 **kodaka(i)** slightly elevated

山高帽 **yamatakabō** derby hat, bowler
4 中高 **nakadaka** convex
中高音部 **chūkōonbu** alto, mezzo-soprano
円高 **endaka** strong yen (exchange rate)
5 甲高 **kandaka(i)** high-pitched, shrill
　　 kōdaka having a high instep
石高 **kokudaka** crop, yield; stipend
6 気高 **kedaka(i)** noble, exalted
西高東低 **seikō-tōtei** high (barometric
　　 pressure) in the west and low in the east
至高 **shikō** supreme, sublime, highest
至高善 **shikōzen** the highest good
先高 **sakidaka** higher quotations for future
　　 months
名高 **nadaka(i)** famous, renowned
光高温計 **hikari-kōonkei** optical pyrometer
有高 **a(ri)daka** amount/goods on hand
7 走高跳 **hashi(ri)takato(bi)** running high jump
売高 **u(re)daka** (amount of) sales
声高 **kowadaka** (in a) loud voice
8 孤高 **kokō** splendid/proud isolation, aloofness
波高 **hakō** height of a wave
金高 **kindaka** amount of money
9 背高 **seitaka** tall
秋高 **akidaka** large fall harvest; high rice
　　 price due to poor fall harvest
10 残高 **zandaka** balance, remainder
高高 **takadaka** at most; high, aloft, loudly
高高指 **takatakayubi** the middle finger
高高度 **kōkōdo** high-altitude
座高 **zakō** one's height when seated
胸高 **munadaka** (wearing an obi) high
特高 **tokkō** political-control police (short for
　　 特別高等警察)
疳高 **kandaka(i)** high-pitched, shrill
軒高 **kenkō** rising high; in high spirits
11 崇高 **sūkō** lofty, sublime, noble
現高 **gendaka** the present amount
12 割高 **waridaka** comparatively expensive
超高速度 **chōkōsokudo** superhigh-speed
登高 **tōkō** climbing a height
棒高飛 **bōtakato(bi)** pole vault
棒高跳 **bōtakato(bi)** pole vault
最高 **saikō** maximum, best; great
最高点 **saikōten** highest point/score
最高裁 **Saikōsai** Supreme Court
最高裁判所 **Saikō Saibansho** Supreme Court
最高潮 **saikōchō** highwater mark; climax,
　　 peak
禄高 **rokudaka** (amount of a samurai's)
　　 stipend/salary
等高線 **tōkōsen** contour line
13 嵩高 **kasadaka** bulky, voluminous; high-
　　 handed
腰高 **koshidaka** hip-high; high-hipped
　　 (unstable sumo stance), haughty

腰高障子 **koshidaka shōji** sliding door with
　　 hip-high paneling
14 鼻高々 **hanatakadaka** proudly, triumphantly
総高 **sōdaka** total (amount)
15 標高 **hyōkō** height above sea level
稼高 **kase(gi)daka** earnings
締高 **shi(me)daka** total

——————— 3 ———————

4 予想高 **yosōdaka** estimated amount
収穫高 **shūkakudaka** yield, crop
5 生産高 **seisandaka** output, production, yield
6 自慢高慢 **jiman-kōman** with great pride
7 売上高 **uria(ge)daka** amount sold, sales
8 受領高 **juryōdaka** amount received, receipts
居丈高 **itakedaka** overbearing, domineering
物見高 **monomidaka(i)** burning with
　　 curiosity
物価高 **bukkadaka** high prices
放歌高吟 **hōka-kōgin** loud singing
取引高 **torihikidaka** volume of business,
　　 turnover
9 造石高 **zōkokudaka** brew, brewage
威丈高 **itakedaka** domineering, overbearing
10 消費高 **shōhidaka** (amount of) consumption
11 勘定高 **kanjōdaka(i)** calculating, mercenary
現在高 **genzaidaka** amount on hand
産出高 **sanshutsudaka** output, yield,
　　 production
13 損害高 **songaidaka** (amount of) damage

2j8.7 / 1223

畜　　CHIKU (keep) domestic animals

——————— 1 ———————

4 畜犬 **chikken, chikuken** keeping a dog;
　　 domestic dog
畜犬税 **chikkenzei** dog tax
5 畜生 **chikushō** beast, brute; Dammit!
畜生道 **chikushōdō** incest
11 畜産 **chikusan** livestock raising
18 畜類 **chikurui** (domestic) animals, livestock

——————— 2 ———————

2 人畜 **jinchiku** men and animals
6 有畜 **yūchiku** with livestock
有畜農業 **yūchiku nōgyō** diversified farming
8 牧畜 **bokuchiku** livestock/cattle raising
牧畜業 **bokuchikugyō** stock farming,
　　 ranching
10 家畜 **kachiku** domestic animals, livestock
鬼畜 **kichiku** devil, brutal man
12 屠畜 **tochiku** butchering, slaughter
無畜 **muchiku** without livestock
14 種畜 **shuchiku** breeding stock

2j8.8

紊

BIN, BUN disturb, throw into confusion

──────── 1 ────────

7 紊乱 **binran, bunran** disturb, derange, put into disorder

2j8.9

毇

KAI laughter

──────── 9 ────────

2j9.1 / 788

率

RITSU rate, percentage, porportion, coefficient **SOTSU** obey; lead; all; light, easy; sudden **hiki(iru)** lead, be in command of

──────── 1 ────────

6 率先 **sossen** take the initiative, be the first
8 率直 **sotchoku** straightforward, frank, forthright
10 率倒 **sottō** faint, swoon
12 率然 **sotsuzen** suddenly, unexpectedly

──────── 2 ────────

2 力率 **rikiritsu** power factor
3 工率 **kōritsu** rate of production
4 引率 **insotsu** lead, head up
　引率者 **insotsusha** leader
5 比率 **hiritsu** ratio, percentage
　打率 **daritsu** batting average
6 曲率 **kyokuritsu** curvature
7 伸率 **no(bi)ritsu** rate of growth
　低率 **teiritsu** low rate
　利率 **riritsu** rate of interest
8 効率 **kōritsu** efficiency
　定率 **teiritsu** fixed/flat rate
10 倍率 **bairitsu** magnifying power, magnification
　高率 **kōritsu** high rate
　真率 **shinsotsu** simple, honest, frank
　能率 **nōritsu** efficiency
　能率的 **nōritsuteki** efficient
12 勝率 **shōritsu** percentage of wins
　税率 **zeiritsu** tax rate, tariff
　統率 **tōsotsu** command, lead
　統率者 **tōsotsusha** commander, leader
　軽率 **keisotsu** rash, hasty
15 確率 **kakuritsu** probability

──────── 3 ────────

3 千分率 **senbunritsu** rate per thousand
4 円周率 **enshūritsu** ratio of circumference to diameter, pi, π

欠勤率 **kekkinritsu** rate of absenteeism
5 出生率 **shusshōritsu, shusseiritsu** birth rate
　出席率 **shussekiritsu** percentage of attendance
　打撃率 **dagekiritsu** batting average
6 死亡率 **shibōritsu** death rate, mortality
　防御率 **bōgyoritsu** earned run average
　安全率 **anzenritsu** safety factor
　百分率 **hyakubunritsu** percentage
7 投票率 **tōhyōritsu** (rate of) voter turnout
8 非能率的 **hinōritsuteki** inefficient
　拡大率 **kakudairitsu** magnifying power
11 視聴率 **shichōritsu** (TV show popularity) rating
12 就業率 **shūgyōritsu** percentage of employment
14 導電率 **dōdenritsu** conductivity
　関税率 **kanzeiritsu** customs rates/tariff
15 課税率 **kazeiritsu** tax rate
16 操業率 **sōgyōritsu** percentage of capacity in operation

2j9.2

裒

BŌ (north-south) length, extent

──────── 2 ────────

5 広裒 **kōbō** area, expanse

2j9.3

牽

KEN, hi(ku) pull

──────── 1 ────────

4 牽引 **ken'in** drag, tow, haul, pull
　牽引力 **ken'inryoku** pulling power, traction
　牽引車 **ken'insha** tractor
8 牽制 **kensei** check, restrain; diversion, feint
11 牽強付会 **kenkyō-fukai** farfetched, distorted

2j9.4

毫

GŌ a fine hair; minute amount; writing brush **gō(mo)** (not) in the least

──────── 1 ────────

5 毫末 **gōmatsu** iota, slightest bit

──────── 2 ────────

1 一毫 **ichigō** an iota, one bit
12 揮毫 **kigō** writing, painting, drawing

2j9.5

袞

KON imperial (dragon-pattern) robes

2j9.6 / 1478

斎　齋   SAI religious purification; abstinence, fasting; Buddhist food; a room; equal **imi, monoimi** fasting, abstinence

——————— 1 ———————

4 斎日 **saijitsu** fast day
5 斎主 **saishu** presiding priest
7 斎戒 **saikai** purification
8 斎服 **saifuku** vestments
9 斎垣 **igaki** shrine fence
12 斎場 **saijō** site of a religious/funeral service
18 斎藤 **Saitō** (surname)

——————— 2 ———————

10 書斎 **shosai** study, library, den
15 潔斎 **kessai** abstinence, purification

產 → 産 **5b6.4**

産 → **5b6.4**

2j9.7 / 412

商   SHŌ trade, merchant; quotient (in math) **akina(u)** sell, deal in, handle

——————— 1 ———————

2 商人 **shōnin** merchant, trader, shopkeeper
3 商工 **shōkō** commerce and industry
　商工会議所 **Shōkō Kaigisho** Chamber of Commerce and Industry
　商工業 **shōkōgyō** commerce and industry
　商大 **shōdai** commercial college (short for 商科大学)
　商才 **shōsai** business ability
5 商用 **shōyō** business
　商用文 **shōyōbun** business correspondence
　商用語 **shōyōgo** commercial term
　商号 **shōgō** corporate name
6 商会 **shōkai** company, firm
　商行為 **shōkōi** business transaction
7 商売 **shōbai** business, trade, transaction; occupation
　商売人 **shōbainin** merchant; professional
　商売気 **shōbaigi** business-mindedness, profit motive
　商売気質 **shōbai katagi** mercenary spirit
　商売柄 **shōbaigara** in one's line of business
　商売道具 **shōbai dōgu** tools of the trade
　商売替 **shōbaiga(e)** change one's occupation
　商売筋 **shōbaisuji** business connections
　商売敵 **shōbaigataki** business competitor

　商社 **shōsha** trading company, business firm
　商利 **shōri** commercial profit
8 商事 **shōji** commercial affairs; (short for 商事会社)
　商事会社 **shōji-gaisha** trading company
　商法 **shōhō** way of doing business; commercial law/code
　商況 **shōkyō** business conditions
　商店 **shōten** store, shop
　商店街 **shōtengai** shopping area
　商取引 **shōtorihiki** business transaction
9 商品 **shōhin** goods, merchandise
　商品券 **shōhinken** gift certificate
　商科 **shōka** business course
10 商家 **shōka** store; merchant family
11 商運 **shōun** business fortunes
　商務 **shōmu** commercial affairs
　商務官 **shōmukan** commercial attaché
　商略 **shōryaku** business policy
　商経 **shōkei** commerce and economics
　商船 **shōsen** merchant ship
　商船隊 **shōsentai** merchant fleet
　商船旗 **shōsenki** merchant flag
12 商港 **shōkō** trading port
　商量 **shōryō** consideration, deliberation
　商策 **shōsaku** business policy
13 商業 **shōgyō** commerce, trade, business
　商業化 **shōgyōka** commercialization
　商業文 **shōgyōbun** business correspondence
　商業主義 **shōgyō shugi** commercialism
　商業地 **shōgyōchi** business district
　商業国 **shōgyōkoku** mercantile nation
　商業界 **shōgyōkai** the business world
　商業組合 **shōgyō kumiai** trade association
　商業港 **shōgyōkō** trading port
　商業街 **shōgyōgai** shopping street/area
　商戦 **shōsen** commercial competition, sales battle
14 商慣習 **shōkanshū** commercial practices
　商魂 **shōkon** commercial spirit, salesmanship
15 商舗 **shōho** store, shop
　商標 **shōhyō** trademark
　商標権 **shōhyōken** trademark rights
　商権 **shōken** commercial rights
　商談 **shōdan** business talks/negotiations
16 商機 **shōki** business opportunity
　商館 **shōkan** trading house, firm
20 商議 **shōgi** conference, consultation

——————— 2 ———————

3 工商 **kōshō** industry and commerce; artisans and merchants
　大商人 **daishōnin** great merchant
　大商店 **daishōten** emporium
　小商 **koakina(i)** small trade, retail business
4 水商売 **mizu shōbai** trades dependent on public patronage (bars, restaurants, entertainment)

犬商 **inushō** dog fancier, kennelman
5 外商 **gaishō** foreign merchant
6 年商 **nenshō** annual sales
会商 **kaishō** negotiations, talks
奸商 **kanshō** dishonest merchant
行商 **gyōshō** itinerant trade, peddling
行商人 **gyōshōnin** peddler, traveling salesman
米商 **beishō** rice dealer
8 画商 **gashō** picture dealer
協商 **kyōshō** entente, an understanding, agreement
協商国 **kyōshōkoku** allies
9 重商主義 **jūshō shugi** mercantilism
卸商 **oroshishō** wholesaler
通商 **tsūshō** commerce, trade
通商産業省 **Tsūshōsangyōshō** Ministry of International Trade and Industry
海商 **kaishō** maritime commerce
客商売 **kyakushōbai** a service/public-patronage trade
政商 **seishō** businessman with political ties
10 華商 **kashō** overseas-Chinese merchant
旅商人 **tabishōnin, tabiakindo** peddler, traveling salesman
11 隊商 **taishō** caravan
隊商宿 **taishōjuku** caravansary
掛商 **ka(ke)akina(i)** selling on credit
紳商 **shinshō** merchant prince
12 富商 **fushō** wealthy merchant
14 豪商 **gōshō** wealthy merchant
15 質商 **shichishō** pawnshop
17 闇商人 **yamishōnin** black marketeer

───── 3 ─────

2 人気商売 **ninki shōbai** occupation dependent on public favor
3 小売商 **kou(ri)shō** retail trade
士魂商才 **shikon-shōsai** samurai in spirit and merchant in business acumen
4 毛皮商 **kegawashō** furrier
5 古物商 **kobutsushō** curio/secondhand dealer
石材商 **sekizaishō** stone dealer
目玉商品 **medama shōhin** bargain item to attract customers, loss leader
7 材木商 **zaimokushō** lumber business/dealer
9 美術商 **bijutsushō** art dealer
10 陶器商 **tōkishō** crockery dealer, chinashop
唐物商 **tōbutsushō** foreign-goods store
書籍商 **shosekishō** bookseller, bookstore
12 御用商人 **goyō shōnin** purveyor to the government
貿易商 **bōekishō** trader
14 種物商 **tanemonoshō** seed seller/store
雑貨商 **zakkashō** general store
雑穀商 **zakkokushō** grain merchant
18 織物商 **orimonoshō** draper

21 露天商 **rotenshō** stall/booth keeper
露店商 **rotenshō** stall keeper/vendor

───── 4 ─────

3 士農工商 **shinōkōshō** samurai-farmers-artisans-merchants, the military, agricultural, industrial, and mercantile classes
9 食料品商 **shokuryōhinshō** grocer

髙 → 高 **2j8.6**

2j9.8

疏 SO pass through; note, commentary

───── 1 ─────

4 疏水 **sosui** drainage; canal
9 疏通 **sotsū** mutual understanding

───── 2 ─────

12 註疏 **chūso** notes, commentary

───── 10 ─────

牽 → **2j9.3**

2j10.1 / 1879

蛮 蠻 BAN barbarian

───── 1 ─────

2 蛮人 **banjin** barbarian, savage
蛮力 **banryoku** brute force
5 蛮民 **banmin** a barbarous people
6 蛮地 **banchi** barbaric region
蛮行 **bankō** barbarity, savagery
7 蛮声 **bansei** raucous voice
9 蛮勇 **ban'yū** brute courage, reckless valor
蛮風 **banpū** barbarous customs
10 蛮骨 **bankotsu** brute courage, recklessness
11 蛮習 **banshū** barbarous custom
蛮族 **banzoku** savage tribe
14 蛮境 **bankyō** land of barbarians
蛮語 **bango** barbarian language

───── 2 ─────

9 南蛮 **nanban** southern barbarians; cayenne pepper
南蛮人 **nanbanjin** southern barbarians, the early Europeans
11 野蛮 **yaban** savage, barbarous
野蛮人 **yabanjin** savage, barbarian
野蛮国 **yabankoku** uncivilized country

2j10.2

齊

SHI, tada (not) only

棄→ **2j11.5**

2j10.3

牌 牌

HAI label, sign; medal
pai mahjong playing tiles

——————— 2 ———————
7 位牌 **ihai** Buddhhist mortuary tablet
8 金牌 **kinpai** gold medal
10 骨牌 **koppai, karuta** (Japanese-style) playing cards
14 銀牌 **ginpai** silver medal
銅牌 **dōhai** bronze medal
15 賞牌 **shōhai** medal, medallion

疏→ **2j9.8**

2j10.4

斐

HI beautiful; bend, yield

——————— 2 ———————
5 甲斐 **kai** effect, result; worth, avail, use
Kai (ancient kuni, Yamanashi-ken)
甲斐性 **kaishō** resourcefulness, competence
——————— 3 ———————
5 生甲斐 **i(ki)gai** something worth living for
7 言甲斐 **i(i)gai** worth mentioning
12 腑甲斐無 **fugaina(i)** faint-hearted, feckless

——————— 11 ———————

2j11.1

雍

YŌ softening, mitigation

2j11.2 / 273

裏 裡

RI, ura reverse side, opposite, rear; palm, sole; last half (of an inning)

——————— 1 ———————
0 裏ビデオ **ura bideo** an under-the-counter (porno) videotape
3 裏口 **uraguchi** back door, rear entrance

裏山 **urayama** hill at the back
4 裏切 **uragi(ru)** betray
uragi(ri) betrayal, treachery
裏切者 **uragi(ri)mono** betrayer, traitor
裏手 **urate** at the back, rear
裏木戸 **urakido** back door
裏日本 **ura-Nihon, ura-Nippon** Sea-of-Japan side of Japan
裏方 **urakata** lady consort; stagehand
5 裏付 **urazu(keru)** support, endorse, substantiate
裏打 **urau(chi)** lining; backing
裏目 **urame** the reverse (of the intended outcome)
6 裏返 **uragae(su)** turn the other way, turn inside out, turn over **uragae(shi)** inside out, upside down **uragae(ru)** be turned inside out; turn against (someone)
裏地 **uraji** lining (cloth)
7 裏作 **urasaku** second crop
裏声 **uragoe** falsetto
裏町 **uramachi** back street, alley
8 裏長屋 **uranagaya** back-street tenement
裏表 **ura-omote** both sides; reverse, inside out; two-faced
裏店 **uradana** house in an alley
裏門 **uramon** back gate
9 裏通 **uradō(ri)** alley, side street
裏庭 **uraniwa** back garden/yard
裏屋 **uraya** back-street house, slum
裏面 **rimen** back, reverse side; background, behind the scenes
裏衿 **uraeri** neckband lining
10 裏書 **uraga(ki)** endorsement; certificate of genuineness; proof
裏紋 **uramon** informal family crest
11 裏側 **uragawa** the back side
裏道 **uramichi** back lane, secret path
13 裏腹 **urahara** the contrary, opposite
裏話 **urabanashi** inside story, story behind the story
18 裏襟 **uraeri** neckband lining

——————— 2 ———————
4 内裏 **dairi** imperial palace
内裏様 **(o)dairi-sama** emperor and empress dolls
毛裏 **keura** fur lining
手裏 **te (no) ura, shuri** palm of the hand
手裏剣 **shuriken** throwing-knife
6 羽裏 **haura** underside of a wing
7 抜裏 **nu(ke)ura** bypass
8 表裏 **hyōri** inside and outside; duplicity
10 庫裏 **kuri** priests' quarters; temple kitchen
胸裏 **kyōri** one's inmost heart
11 麻裏 **asaura** hemp-soled straw sandals
脳裡 **nōri** the brain, one's mind

12 葉裏 **haura** underside of a leaf
13 禁裏 **kinri** the imperial palace/court
禁裏様 **kinrisama** the emperor
裾裏 **susoura** hem lining
14 総裏 **sōura** full lining
総裏付 **sōuratsu(ki)** fully lined (coat)

———————— 3 ————————

4 天井裏 **tenjōura** between ceiling and roof
7 囲炉裏 **irori** sunken hearth
15 舞台裏 **butaiura** backstage

2j11.3

稟 稟 **RIN, HIN** salary paid in rice; receive; inborn

———————— 1 ————————

7 稟告 **rinkoku** notice, notification
8 稟性 **rinsei, hinsei** nature, character
20 稟議 **ringi** decision-making by circular letter (instead of holding a meeting)

———————— 2 ————————

4 天稟 **tenpin** natural talents

2j11.4

亶 **TAN, SEN** truly, wholly, cordial

牌→ **2j10.3**

2j11.5 / 962

棄 弃 **KI, su(teru)** throw away, abandon, renounce

———————— 1 ————————

7 棄却 **kikyaku** reject, dismiss
9 棄約 **kiyaku** break a promise
15 棄権 **kiken** abstain from voting; renounce one's rights, withdraw
棄権者 **kikensha** nonvoter

———————— 2 ————————

6 自棄 **yake, jiki** desperation, despair
自棄酒 **yakezake** drowning one's cares in saké
7 投棄 **tōki** abandon, give up
8 拋棄 **hōki** waive, abandon
放棄 **hōki** abandon, renounce, waive, forfeit
委棄 **iki** abandonment, desertion
10 破棄 **haki** annulment, repudiation, abrogation, reversal
11 唾棄 **daki** spit out; detest, abhor

12 廃棄 **haiki** do away with, scrap, rescind
廃棄物 **haikibutsu** waste matter, wastes
13 毀棄 **kiki** (willful) destruction
14 遺棄 **iki** abandon, leave unattended

———————— 4 ————————

6 自暴自棄 **jibō-jiki** desperation, despair

———————— 12 ————————

齊→斉 **2j6.5**

2j12.1

膏 **KŌ** ointment, grease
abura fat, grease, tallow

———————— 1 ————————

6 膏血 **kōketsu** blood and sweat
7 膏肓 **kōkō** the inmost part, region between heart and diaphragm too deep to be reached by acupuncture needles
16 膏薬 **kōyaku** salve, ointment, plaster

———————— 2 ————————

5 石膏 **sekkō** gypsum, plaster (of Paris)
10 病膏肓 **yamaikōkō** incurable; incorrigible
11 軟膏 **nankō** ointment, salve

———————— 3 ————————

4 内股膏薬 **uchimata-kōyaku** duplicity, double-dealing; double-dealer, fence-sitter
11 絆創膏 **bansōkō** adhesive plaster

2j12.2

裹 **KA** wrap

2j12.3 / 1671

豪 **GŌ** strength, power; splendor, magnificence; Australia

———————— 1 ————————

3 豪士 **gōshi** samurai-farmer
4 豪戸 **gōko** ancient administrative clan unit of about two dozen persons
5 豪句 **gōku** grandiloquence
6 豪気 **gōki** stouthearted
豪壮 **gōsō** splendor, grandeur
豪州 **Gōshū** Australia
7 豪快 **gōkai** exciting, stirring, heroic
8 豪放 **gōhō** manly and openhearted
豪雨 **gōu** heavy rain, downpour
9 豪胆 **gōtan** stouthearted, dauntless
10 豪遊 **gōyū** extravagant merrymaking, spree

豪華 **gōka** luxurious, splendid, gorgeous
豪華版 **gōkaban** deluxe edition
豪家 **gōka** wealthy and powerful family
11 豪商 **gōshō** wealthy merchant
豪族 **gōzoku** powerful family/clan
豪盛 **gōsei** great, grand, magnificent
12 豪奢 **gōsha** luxurious, grand, sumptuous
豪飲 **gōin** heavy drinking, carousing
13 豪傑 **gōketsu** hero, great man
豪勢 **gōsei** grand, luxurious, magnificent
豪農 **gōnō** wealthy farmer
14 豪語 **gōgo** boasting, bombast, big talk

————— 2 —————

4 文豪 **bungō** literary master
日豪 **Nichi-Gō** Japan and Australia
5 古豪 **kogō** veteran, old campaigner
10 剣豪 **kengō** master fencer
酒豪 **shugō** heavy drinker
11 強豪 **kyōgō** strong (contender), champion
12 富豪 **fugō** wealthy man, millionaire

毓 → 育   2j6.4

————— 13 —————

2j13.1 / 803

褒 褒褒   HŌ, ho(meru) praise

————— 1 —————

0 褒めたたえる **ho(metataeru)** laud, praise, admire
褒めちぎる **ho(mechigiru)** praise very highly
3 褒上 **ho(me)a(geru)** praise very highly
5 褒立 **ho(me)ta(teru)** praise, applaud
7 褒状 **hōjō** certificate of merit, commendation
褒言葉 **ho(me)kotoba** words of praise, laudatory remarks
9 褒美 **hōbi** reward, prize
10 褒称 **ho(me)tata(eru)** laud, praise, admire
褒貶 **hōhen** praise and censure, criticism
11 褒章 **hōshō** medal
12 褒詞 **ho(me)kotoba** words of praise
13 褒辞 **hōji** words of praise
15 褒賞 **hōshō** prize, reward

————— 3 —————

13 毀誉褒貶 **kiyo-hōhen** praise and/or criticism
18 藍綬褒章 **ranju hōshō** blue ribbon medal

槀 → 稿   5d10.5

————— 14 —————

2j14.1

壅   YŌ plug/shut/dam up; cultivate, grow

————— 2 —————

20 懸壅垂 **ken'yōsui** the uvula

————— 15 —————

齋 → 斎   2j9.6

2j15.1

褻   SETSU dirty; get used to, everyday

————— 2 —————

12 猥褻 **waisetsu** obscene, lewd

褒 → 褒   2j13.1

2j15.2

襄   JŌ rise; raise

————— 16 —————

2j16.1

甕   Ō, YŌ, kame jar, urn

————— 17 —————

甕 → 籬   2j21.1

2j17.1

羸   RUI thin, weak

————— 1 —————

10 羸弱 **ruijaku** delicate, frail

————— 18 —————

2j18.1

贏   EI more than enough, surplus

————— 2 —————

16 輸贏 **shuei, yuei** victory or defeat

2

亻 ⺕
⻌ ⼦
⻏ ⻖
卩 力
又 冖
⺍ ←18
⺒ ⺮
⺨ ⺤
⼚ ⻌
冂 八
匸

2

─────────── 19 ───────────

2j19.1

齎

SEI bring
SHI goods, valuables
motara(su) bring

─────────── 20 ───────────

囊 → 3d19.3

─────────── 21 ───────────

2j21.1

齏 齏

SEI, a(eru) dress (dishes with vinegar, miso, sesame seeds, etc.)

─── 1 ───

8 齏物 aemono dishes dressed with vinegar, miso, sesame seeds, etc.

───────── ⼗ 2k ─────────

十	干	千	支	午	卆	古	卉	芐	本	尤	平	平
0.1	1.1	1.2	2.1	2.2	2j6.2	3.1	3.2	0a5.37	0a5.25	3.3	2k3.4	3.4
李	卋	开	孝	考	老	缶	卍	克	求	砒	協	幸
4.1	0a5.37	4.2	4.3	4.4	4.5	4.6	4.7	5.1	2b5.5	5.2	6.1	3b5.9
堯	直	阜	乖	奔	卑	旺	南	卑	缸	豺	真	盍
3b9.3	6.2	6.3	6.4	6.5	5f4.8	6.6	7.1	5f4.8	7.2	0a10.4	8.1	3b7.9
索	翠	皋	毳	翅	缺	皐	博	悳	辜	準	覃	賁
8.2	2k12.2	4c7.12	8.3	8.4	4j0.1	4c7.12	10.1	3i11.3	10.2	2k11.1	10.3	7b5.6
喪	準	献	瓶	睾	翠	罇	矗	蘳				
3b9.20	11.1	3g9.6	2o9.6	12.1	12.2	15.1	22.1	9a15.1				

─────────── 0 ───────────

2k0.1 / 12

十

JŪ, JI', tō, to- ten

─── 1 ───

1 十一月 jūichigatsu November
2 十二支 jūnishi the twelve horary signs
 十二分 jūnibun more than enough
  jūnifun twelve minutes
 十二月 jūnigatsu December
 十二使徒 jūni shito the Twelve Apostles
 十二指腸 jūnishichō the duodenum
 十二指腸虫 jūnishichōchū hookworm
 十人力 jūninriki the strength of ten
 十人十色 jūnin-toiro Tastes differ. To each his own.
 十人並 jūninna(mi) average, ordinary
 十八番 jūhachiban Kabuki repertoire of 18 classical pieces; one's forte/hobby, one's favorite (song/topic) ohako one's forte/hobby, one's favorite (song/topic)
3 十三夜 jūsan'ya 13th night of a lunar month (especially a moonlit September 13)
 十干 jikkan the ten calendar signs
4 十五夜 jūgoya 15th night of a lunar month (especially a moonlit August 15)

十六夜 izayoi 16th night of a lunar month
十文字 jūmonji cross
十分 jūbun enough, satisfactory; thorough
 jippun ten minutes
十月 jūgatsu October
十日 tōka the tenth (day of the month); ten days
5 十代 jūdai the teens, teenage
十字 jūji cross
十字火 jūjika crossfire
十字形 jūjikei cross, cross-shaped
十字軍 Jūjigun the Crusades, Crusaders
十字架 jūjika cross, crucifix
十字路 jūjiro crossroads, intersection
6 十全 jūzen perfection, consummation; absolute safety
7 十戒 jikkai the ten Buddhist precepts
9 十重 toe ten-fold, ten layers
十指 jisshi the ten fingers
10 十倍 jūbai tenfold, ten times
十進 jisshin decimal
十進法 jisshinhō decimal/base-10 notation
13 十数 jūsū ten-odd, a dozen or so
14 十種競技 jisshu kyōgi decathlon
十誡 jikkai the Ten Commandments
16 十薬 jūyaku (a foul-smelling herb; also known as dokudami)

———————— 2 ————————

2 二十日 **hatsuka** the 20th (day of the month); 20 days

二十日大根 **hatsuka daikon** radish

二十日鼠 **hatsuka nezumi** mouse

二十世紀 **nijisseiki, nijusseiki** the twentieth century

二十代 **nijūdai** in one's twenties

二十年代 **nijūnendai** the '20s

二十歳 **hatachi** 20 years old, age 20

七十 **nanajū, shichijū** seventy

九十九折 **tsuzurao(ri)** winding, meandering, zigzag

九十九髪 **tsukumogami** old woman's hair

八十路 **yasoji** eighty years old

3 三十六計 **sanjūrokkei** many plans/strategies

三十六計逃 **sanjūrokkei ni(geru ni shikazu)** It's wisest here to run away.

三十日 **sanjūnichi** the 30th (day of the month); 30 days   **misoka** the last day of the month

三十路 **misoji** age 30

4 不十分 **fujūbun** insufficient, inadequate

五十三次 **gojūsan tsugi** the 53 stages on the Tōkaidō

五十歩百歩 **gojippo-hyappo** not much different

五十音図 **gojūonzu** the kana syllabary table

五十音順 **gojūonjun** in *aiueo* order of the kana alphabet

五十嵐 **Igarashi** (surname)

五十路 **isoji** 50 years; age 50

5 四十 **yonjū, shijū** forty

白十字 **hakujūji** white cross

7 赤十字 **sekijūji** Red Cross

赤十字社 **Sekijūjisha** Red Cross Society

9 南十字星 **minami jūjisei** the Southern Cross

13 数十 **sūjū** dozens/scores of

14 複十字 **fukujūji** double-crosspiece cross (tuberculosis prevention symbol)

———————— 3 ————————

2 二百十日 **nihyaku tōka** 210th day from the first day of spring, the "storm day"

十人十色 **jūnin-toiro** Tastes differ. To each his own.

———————— 4 ————————

2 二百二十日 **nihyaku hatsuka** 220th day from the first day of spring, about September 10 (a time of typhoons)

———————— 1 ————————

2k1.1 / 584

干

KAN, **ho(su)** dry **hi(ru)** become dry/parched; ebb, recede

———————— 1 ————————

3 干大根 **ho(shi) daikon** dried daikon

干与 **kan'yo** participation

干上 **hia(garu)** dry up, parch; ebb away

4 干天 **kanten** dry weather, drought

干支 **kanshi, eto** the sexagenary cycle

干戈 **kanka** shield and halberd; weapons; war

8 干拓 **kantaku** reclaim (land) by drainage

干拓地 **kantakuchi** reclaimed land, innings

干物 **himono** dried fish   **ho(shi)mono** laundry (hung up) to be dried

9 干城 **kanjō** bulwark, defender

干草 **ho(shi)gusa, ho(shi)kusa** dry grass, hay

10 干害 **kangai** drought damage

11 干渉 **kanshō** intervention; interference

干菓子 **higashi** dry candies

干乾 **hibo(shi)** starved to death

干魚 **ho(shi)uo, ho(shi)zakana** dried fish

12 干割 **hiwa(re)** cracking due to drying

干満 **kanman** ebb and flow, tide

干場 **ho(shi)ba** a drying-ground

干葉 **hiba** dried daikon leaves

干葡萄 **ho(shi)budō** raisins

干飯 **hoshii** (sun-)dried boiled rice

15 干潮 **kanchō, hishio, hikishio** ebb tide

干潟 **higata** dry beach (at ebb tide), tideland

干魃 **kanbatsu** drought

17 干瓢 **kanpyō** dried gourd shavings

22 干鱈 **hidara** dried codfish

———————— 2 ————————

2 十干 **jikkan** the ten calendar signs

4 不干渉 **fukanshō** nonintervention

刈干 **ka(ri)ho(su)** cut and (sun-)dry

切干 **kiribo(shi)** dried strips of daikon

日干 **hibo(shi)** sun-dried

火干 **hibo(shi)** drying by fire; fire-dried

5 生干 **namabi, namabo(shi)** half-dried

6 汲干 **ku(mi)ho(su)** drain, pump/bail out

汐干狩 **shiohiga(ri)** shell gathering at low tide

虫干 **mushibo(shi)** airing out (clothes)

8 若干 **jakkan** some, a number of

物干 **monoho(shi)** (frame for) drying clothes

物干竿 **monoho(shi)zao** washline pole

物干場 **monoho(shi)ba** place for drying

10 射干玉 **nubatama** pitch-black, darkness

陰干 **kagebo(shi)** drying in the shade

梅干 **umebo(shi)** pickled plums

素干 **subo(shi)** drying in the shade

11 乾干 **karabo(shi)** sun-dried fish/vegetables

12 満干 **mankan, mi(chi)hi** ebb and flow

無干渉 **mukanshō** nonintervention

煮干 **nibo(shi)** dried sardines

飲干 **no(mi)ho(su)** drink (the cup) dry

15 潮干 **shiohi** low/ebb tide

潮干狩 **shiohiga(ri)** shell gathering (at low tide)

17 闌干 **rankan** railing, bannister
20 欄干 **rankan** railing, banister

——————— 3 ———————

3 土用干 **doyōbo(shi)** summer airing (of clothes)
5 白子干 **shirasubo(shi)** dried young sardines

2k1.2 / 15

千 **SEN, chi** thousand

——————— 1 ———————

1 千一夜 **Sen'ichiya** Thousand and One Nights
2 千人力 **senninriki** strength of a thousand
千人針 **senninbari** soldier's good-luck waistband sewn one stitch each by a thousand women
3 千万 **senman, chiyorozu** ten million; countless
senban exceedingly, very much, indeed
千々 **chiji** a great many; variety
4 千切 **chigi(ru)** tear up/off; pluck
sengiri thin strips of vegetables
千分 **senbun** thousandth
千分率 **senbunritsu** rate per thousand
千木 **chigi** ornamental upward-projecting rafters on a shrine roof
5 千代 **chiyo** a thousand years/ages
千代紙 **chiyogami** colored paper
千古 **senko** all ages, eternity; remote antiquity
千石船 **sengokubune** large junk (Edo period)
6 千両役者 **senryō yakusha** great actor, star
千両箱 **senryōbako** chest containing a thousand pieces of gold
7 千里 **senri** a thousand leagues, a long distance
千里眼 **senrigan** clairvoyant
千辛万苦 **senshin-banku** countless hardships
8 千枚通 **senmaidō(shi)** awl
9 千変万化 **senpen-banka** innumerable/ kaleidoscopic changes, immense variety
千草 **chigusa** great variety of flowering plants
千客万来 **senkaku-banrai, senkyaku-banrai** thronged with customers/ visitors
千秋 **senshū** a thousand years, many years
千秋楽 **senshūraku** the last day (of a play's run)
千思万考 **senshi-bankō** deep meditation, careful deliberation
10 千差万別 **sensa-banbetsu** infinite variety
千島列島 **Chishima-rettō** the Kurile Islands
11 千鳥 **chidori** plover; zigzag
千鳥足 **chidori-ashi** tottering steps

千鳥掛 **chidoriga(ke)** catch/cross stitch; crossing
12 千葉 **Chiba** (city, Chiba-ken)
千葉県 **Chiba-ken** (prefecture)
千紫万紅 **senshi-bankō** dazzling variety of colors
13 千歳 **chitose** a thousand years
千載 **senzai** a thousand years
千載一遇 **senzai-ichigū** a rare experience, chance of a lifetime

——————— 2 ———————

2 八千代 **yachiyo** thousands of years
八千草 **yachigusa** many plants
3 三千 **sanzen** 3,000; many
三千世界 **sanzen sekai** the whole world, the universe
千千 **chiji** a great many; variety
5 四千 **yonsen** four thousand
7 何千 **nanzen** (how) many thousands
9 海千山千 **umisen-yamasen** experienced and shrewd, wily veteran, sly old dog
12 幾千 **ikusen** thousands
13 群千鳥 **mura chidori** flock of plovers
数千 **sūsen** several thousand

——————— 3 ———————

1 一日千秋 **ichinichi-senshū, ichijitsu-senshū** days seeming like years
一字千金 **ichiji senkin** great words
一刻千金 **ikkoku senkin** Every minute counts.
一望千里 **ichibō-senri** vast, boundless
一瀉千里 **issha-senri** in a rush, at full gallop
一攫千金 **ikkaku senkin** getting rich quick
7 良二千石 **ryōnisenseki** good local official
10 笑止千万 **shōshi-senban** ridiculous, absurd

——————— 4 ———————

1 一騎当千 **ikki-tōsen** matchless, mighty
9 海千山千 **umisen-yamasen** experienced and shrewd, wily veteran, sly old dog

——————— 2 ———————

2k2.1 / 318

支 **SHI** support, branch **sasa(eru)** support, prop; check, stem **tsuka(eru)** be obstructed, be blocked, break down, get caught (in one's throat) **ka(u)** prop up

——————— 1 ———————

5 支出 **shishutsu** expenditure, disbursement
支出額 **shishutsugaku** (amount of) expenditures
支弁 **shiben** pay, defray ·
支払 **shihara(u)** pay
支払人 **shiharainin** payer
支払日 **shiharaibi** pay day
支払済 **shiharaizu(mi)** paid

支払期日 **shiharaikijitsu** due date, maturity
支庁 **shichō** (government) branch office
6 支那 **Shina** China
支那海 **Shinakai** the China Sea
7 支局 **shikyoku** a branch (office)
支局長 **shikyokuchō** branch manager
支社 **shisha** a branch (office)
8 支店 **shiten** a branch (store/office)
支所 **shisho** branch office, substation
9 支点 **shiten** fulcrum
支持 **shiji** support
支度 **shitaku** preparation, arrangements
支柱 **shichū** prop, support, fulcrum, under-
pinnings
10 支部 **shibu** a branch (office), local chapter
支部長 **shibuchō** branch manager
支流 **shiryū** tributary, branch
支脈 **shimyaku** spur, feeder, branch
支配 **shihai** management, control, rule
支配人 **shihainin** manager
支配力 **shihairyoku** one's control/hold over
支配下 **shihaika** under the control of
支配的 **shihaiteki** dominant, overriding
支配者 **shihaisha** ruler, administrator
支配層 **shihaisō** the ruling class
支配権 **shihaiken** control, supremacy
12 支援 **shien** support, backing, aid
支給 **shikyū** provide, furnish, issue, grant
13 支障 **shishō** hindrance, impediment, difficulty
支署 **shisho** branch office, substation
15 支線 **shisen** branch/feeder line
18 支離滅裂 **shiri-metsuretsu** incoherent,
inconsistent, chaotic

─────── 2 ───────
3 干支 **kanshi, eto** the sexagenary cycle
4 中支 **Chūshi** central China
中支那 **Naka-Shina** central China
切支丹 **Kirishitan** (early) Japanese Chris-
tianity/Christian
収支 **shūshi** revenues and expenditures
日支 **Nis-Shi** Japan and China
心支度 **kokorojitaku** mental readiness/
attitude
5 北支 **Hokushi** North China
北支事変 **Hokushi jihen** the Marco Polo
Bridge incident
冬支度 **fuyujitaku** preparations for winter;
winter clothing
7 身支度 **mijitaku** grooming, outfit, preparations
8 東支那海 **Higashi Shinakai** East China Sea
逃支度 **ni(ge)jitaku** make ready to flee
突支 **tsukkai** prop, strut, support
突支棒 **tsukkaibō** prop, strut, support
雨支度 **amajitaku** preparing for rain

9 南支那海 **Minami Shinakai** the South China
Sea
10 帰支度 **kae(ri)jitaku** preparations to return
差支 **sa(shi)tsuka(enai)** no impediment,
justifiable, allowable, may
旅支度 **tabijitaku** travel preparations/outfit
14 総支出 **sōshishutsu** gross expenditures
総支配人 **sōshihainin** general manager

─────── 3 ───────
2 十二支 **jūnishi** the twelve horary signs
6 気管支 **kikanshi** bronchial tubes
気管支炎 **kikanshien** bronchitis
13 嫁入支度 **yomei(ri)-jitaku** trousseau
15 摩利支天 **Marishiten** Marici, Buddhist god
of war

2k2.2 / 49

午 **GO, uma** seventh horary sign (horse),
noon

─────── 1 ───────
9 午前 **gozen** morning, a.m.
午前中 **gozenchū** all morning
午後 **gogo** afternoon, p.m.
13 午睡 **gosui** nap, siesta
16 午餐 **gosan** luncheon
午餐会 **gosankai** luncheon

─────── 2 ───────
2 子午線 **shigosen** the meridian
子午環 **shigokan** meridian circle
5 正午 **shōgo** noon
14 端午 **tango** Boys' Day (May 5)

卆 → 卒 **2j6.2**

─────── 3 ───────

2k3.1 / 172

古 **KO, furu(i)** old -**furu(su)** wear out
furu(biru) become old
furu(bokeru) look old; wear out
furu(mekashii) old, from long ago
inishie ancient times

─────── 1 ───────
2 古刀 **kotō** old sword
4 古井戸 **furuido** old unused well
古今 **kokon** ancient and modern times, all
ages
古今東西 **kokon-tōzai** all ages and places
古今和歌集 **Kokinwakashū** (poetry
anthology, early tenth century)
古今集 **Kokinshū** (see preceding entry)
古文 **kobun, komon** ancient writings

2

亻 冫
孑 阝
卩 刂
力 又 一
亠 十
卜 ク
丷
厂 辶
冂 几
匸

古文書 **komonjo, kobunsho** ancient documents
古手 **furute** used/secondhand article; ex-, retired
古木 **koboku** old tree
5 古本 **furuhon** used/secondhand book
kohon secondhand book; ancient book
古本屋 **furuhon'ya** used/secondhand book store
古生物 **koseibutsu** extinct plants and animals
古生物学 **koseibutsugaku** paleontology
古代 **kodai** ancient times, antiquity
古代史 **kodaishi** ancient history
古写本 **koshahon** ancient manuscript, codex
6 古曲 **kokyoku** old tune, ancient melody
古伝 **koden** legend, tradition
古老 **korō** old person
古色 **koshoku** ancient appearance
古色蒼然 **koshoku-sōzen** antique-looking, hoary
古池 **furuike** old pond
古寺 **koji, furudera** old temple
古式 **koshiki** old style, ancient ritual
古米 **komai** old/long-stored rice
7 古来 **korai** from ancient times, time-honored
古里 **furusato** native place, home town, home
古体 **kotai** old form, ancient style
古兵 **kohei, furutsuwamono** old soldier, veteran
古希 **koki** age 70
8 古画 **koga** old painting, ancient picture
古事 **koji** ancient/historical events
古事記 **Kojiki** (Japan's) Ancient Chronicles
古例 **korei** old custom, established practice
古制 **kosei** ancient system/precepts
古刹 **kosatsu** old/ancient temple
古版 **kohan** old edition
古典 **koten** the classics, classic
古典主義 **koten shugi** classicism
古典的 **kotenteki** classical
古典派 **kotenha** the classical school
古典語 **kotengo** a classical language
古往今来 **koō-konrai** in all ages, since antiquity
古参 **kosan** seniority
古参者 **kosansha** senior, old hand
古服 **furufuku** old clothes
古物 **furumono, kobutsu** old things, secondhand goods, curios, antiques
古物商 **kobutsushō** curio/secondhand dealer
9 古美術品 **kobijutsuhin** old/ancient art object
古風 **kofū** old custom, old style
古城 **kojō** old castle
古狐 **furugitsune** sly old fox

古茶 **kocha** tea picked last year
古臭 **furukusa(i)** old, musty, outdated, trite, stale
10 古都 **koto** ancient city; former capital
古酒 **furuzake** old saké, last year's saké
koshu well-cured saké
古流 **koryū** old style; old school (of art)
古狸 **furudanuki** old raccoon dog, veteran, old-timer
古家 **furuie** old house
古株 **furukabu** old-timer
古書 **kosho** old/rare book
古訓 **kokun** ancient precept; old reading (of a character)
11 古道 **kodō** ancient road; ancient ways/morality
古道具 **furudōgu** secondhand goods, used furniture
古道具屋 **furudōguya** secondhand store
古巣 **furusu** old nest, one's former haunt
12 古着 **furugi** old/secondhand clothes
古稀 **koki** age 70
古筆 **kohitsu** old writings
13 古傷 **furukizu** old wound
古義 **kogi** old/original meaning
古戦場 **kosenjō** ancient battlefield
古跡 **koseki, furuato** historic spot, ruins
古鉄 **furutetsu** scrap iron
古雅 **koga** classical elegance/grace
14 古豪 **kogō** veteran, old campaigner
古歌 **furuuta** old song/poem
古語 **kogo** archaic/obsolete word; old saying
古銭 **kosen** old coin
古銭学 **kosengaku** numismatics
15 古儀 **kogi** ancient rite
古墳 **kofun** ancient burial mound
16 古義真言宗 **Kogi Shingon shū** the "old meaning" sect of Esoteric Buddhism
古諺 **kogen** old proverb/adage
18 古蹟 **koseki** historic spot, ruins
古顔 **furugao** familiar face, old-timer

──────── 2 ────────

3 万古 **banko** perpetuity, eternity
千古 **senko** all ages, eternity; remote antiquity
上古 **jōko** ancient times
上古史 **jōkoshi** ancient history
4 太古 **taiko** antiquity, prehistoric times
中古 **chūko** secondhand; the Middle Ages
chūburu secondhand
中古史 **chūkoshi** medieval history
中古車 **chūkosha** used/secondhand car
中古品 **chūkohin** secondhand goods
今古 **kinko** now and in ancient times
5 乎古止点 **okototen** marks to aid in reading Chinese classics

好古　**kōko**　love of antiquities
好古癖　**kōkoheki**　antiquarianism
6 考古　**kōko**　study of antiquities
考古学　**kōkogaku**　archeology (cf. 考現学)
近古　**kinko**　early modern age
名古屋　**Nagoya**　(city, Aichi-ken)
7 阿古屋貝　**akoyagai**　pearl oyster
言古　**i(i)furu(shita)**　hackneyed, stale
8 使古　**tsuka(i)furu(su)**　wear out
往古　**ōko**　ancient times
尚古　**shōko**　esteem for olden days
10 穿古　**ha(ki)furu(shi)**　worn-out (shoes)
11 推古　**Suiko**　(empress, 592–628)
12 着古　**kifuru(su)**　wear out
復古　**fukko**　restoration (of the old regime)
復古調　**fukkochō**　reactionary/revival mood
最古　**saiko**　oldest
閑古鳥　**kankodori**　cuckoo
13 蒙古　**Mōko**　Mongolia
蒙古人　**Mōkojin**　a Mongol(ian)
蒙古斑　**mōkohan**　Mongolian spot
14 聞古　**ki(ki)furu(shita)**　hackneyed, trite
16 懐古　**kaiko**　nostalgia
懐古談　**kaikodan**　reminiscences
稽古　**keiko**　practice, training, drill, rehearsal
稽古台　**keikodai**　something/someone to practice on
稽古着　**keikogi**　practice/gym suit
17 擬古　**giko**　imitating classical style
擬古文　**gikobun**　(pseudo)classical style
擬古主義　**giko shugi**　classicism
擬古的　**gikoteki**　classical, pseudoarchaic
19 曠古　**kōko**　unprecedented, historic

――――― 3 ―――――
3 下稽古　**shitageiko**　rehearsal, run-through
土耳古　**Toruko**　Turkey
4 天手古舞　**tentekoma(i)**　hectic activity
内蒙古　**Uchi Mōko**　Inner Mongolia
5 出稽古　**degeiko**　giving lessons at the students' homes
代稽古　**daigeiko**　act as a substitute teacher
外蒙古　**Gaimōko, Soto Mōko**　Outer Mongolia
立稽古　**ta(chi)geiko**　rehearsal
12 寒稽古　**kangeiko**　winter (judo) exercises

――――― 4 ―――――
15 舞台稽古　**butai geiko**　dress rehearsal

2k3.2

卉

KI　grass

――――― 2 ―――――
7 花卉　**kaki**　flowering plants

乴 → 世　**0a5.37**

本 → 本　**0a5.25**

2k3.3

朮

JUTSU, mochiawa　(a type of millet)
okera　(a type of herb)

平 → 平　**2k3.4**

2k3.4 / 202

平　平

HEI, BYŌ　flat, level; common, ordinary, average; peaceful
tai(ra), hira(tai)　flat, level
hira-　common, ordinary, average

――――― 1 ―――――
0 平らげる　**tai(rageru)**　subjugate, quell; gobble, eat up, devour
3 平々凡々　**heihei-bonbon**　commonplace, ordinary
平凡　**heibon**　common, ordinary
平土間　**hiradoma**　pit, orchestra (in a theater)
4 平分　**heibun**　bisect, divide equally
平手　**hirate**　palm; (play) equally, with no handicap
平日　**heijitsu**　weekday; everyday
平方　**heihō**　square (of a number); square (meter)
平方形　**heihōkei**　a square
平方根　**heihōkon**　square root
5 平民　**heimin**　the common people
平生　**heizei**　usual, everyday, ordinary
6 平気　**heiki**　calm, cool, unconcerned, nonchalant
平年　**heinen**　average/normal year; non-leap year
平年作　**heinensaku**　normal harvest
平伏　**heifuku, hirefu(su)**　prostrate oneself
平仮名　**hiragana**　(the cursive syllabary)
平地　**heichi, hirachi**　flatland, level ground, plain
平行　**heikō**　parallel
平行四辺形　**heikōshihenkei**　parallelogram
平行棒　**heikōbō**　parallel bars
平行線　**heikōsen**　parallel line
平安　**heian**　peace, tranquility; the Heian period (794–1185)

2

亻
冫
孑
阝
卩
刂
力
又
一
亠
→ 3 十
ﾄ
夂
丷
广
辶
冂
几
匚

平安京 **Heiankyō** ancient Kyōto
平安朝 **Heianchō** the Heian period (794–1185)
平成 **Heisei** (era, 1989–)
7 平身低頭 **heishin-teitō** prostrate oneself
平作 **heisaku** normal harvest/crop
平均 **heikin** average, mean; balance, equilibrium
平均点 **heikinten** average mark/grade
8 平価 **heika** par, parity
平泳(ぎ) **hiraoyo(gi)** breaststroke
平治 **Heiji** (era, 1159–1160)
平坦 **heitan** even, flat, level
平定 **heitei** suppress, subdue
平底 **hirazoko** flat bottom
平底船 **hirazokobune** flat-bottomed boat
平板 **heiban** flat board, slat; monotonous
平服 **heifuku** ordinary clothes, out of uniform
平明 **heimei** plain, clear, simple
平易 **heii** easy; plain, simple
平和 **heiwa** peace
平和主義 **heiwa shugi** pacificism
平和条約 **heiwa jōyaku** peace treaty
9 平信 **heishin** peaceful tidings/news
平臥 **heiga** lie down; be laid up (ill)
平城 **Heizei** (emperor, 806–809)
平城京 **Heijōkyō** ancient Nara
平庭 **hiraniwa** garden with no hills
平屋 **hiraya** one-story house
平屋根 **hirayane** flat roof
平面 **heimen** plane, level surface
平面図 **heimenzu** plane view, floor plan
平面鏡 **heimenkyō** plane mirror
10 平原 **heigen** plain, prairie
平家 **hiraya** one-story house
     Heike the Taira family/clan
平脈 **heimyaku** normal pulse
平時 **heiji** normal times, peacetime
平袖 **hirasode** wide sleeves
平素 **heiso** ordinarily; in the past
11 平野 **heiya** a plain, open field
平淡 **heitan** plain, simple, light
平常 **heijō** normal; normally, usually
12 平温 **heion** the usual temperature
平然 **heizen** calm, composed, unruffled
平歯車 **hirahaguruma** spur gear/wheel
平等 **byōdō** equality, impartiality
13 平滑 **heikatsu** smooth, level, flat, even
14 平静 **heisei** calm, serene, tranquil
15 平熱 **heinetsu** normal temperature
16 平壌 **Heijō** Pyongyang
平衡 **heikō** equilibrium, balance
平穏 **heion** calm, peaceful, tranquil
17 平謝 **hiraayama(ri)** humble/profuse apology
平鍋 **hiranabe** pan
18 平癒 **heiyu** convalescence

平織 **hiraori** plain weave (fabric)

— 2 —

4 不平 **fuhei** discontent, dissatisfaction, complaint
不平等 **fubyōdō** unequal
太平 **taihei** peace, tranquility
太平洋 **Taiheiyō** the Pacific Ocean
太平洋戦争 **Taiheiyō Sensō** the Pacific War, World War II
太平楽 **taiheiraku** idle/irresponsible talk
天平 **Tenpyō** (era, 729–749)
天平宝字 **Tenpyō Hōji** (era, 757–765)
天平神護 **Tenpyō Jingo** (era, 765–767)
天平勝宝 **Tenpyō Shōhō** (era, 749–756)
天平感宝 **Tenpyō Kanpō** (era, 749)
仁平 **Ninpei** (era, 1151–1154)
公平 **kōhei** fair, just
公平無私 **kōhei-mushi** fair and disinterested
水平 **suihei** horizontal
水平面 **suiheimen** horizontal plane/surface
水平線 **suiheisen** the horizon; horizontal line
手平 **te (no) hira** palm
5 平平凡凡 **heihei-bonbon** commonplace, ordinary
正平 **Shōhei** (era, 1346–1370)
6 地平面 **chiheimen** horizontal plane
地平線 **chiheisen** the horizon
行平 **yukihira** earthenware casserole
行平鍋 **yukihiranabe** earthenware casserole
7 承平 **Shōhei** (era, 931–938)
8 治平 **chihei** peace and tranquility
和平 **wahei** peace
9 段平 **danbira** broadsword, sword
扁平 **henpei** flat
扁平足 **henpeisoku** flat feet
10 真平 **mappira** (not) by any means; humbly
泰平 **taihei** peace, tranquility
泰平期 **taiheiki** period of peace
11 偏平 **henpei** flat
偏平足 **henpeisoku** flat feet
常平倉 **jōheisō** granary
康平 **Kōhei** (era, 1058–1065)
12 開平 **kaihei** determining the square root
13 源平 **Gen-Pei** Genji and Heike clans, the Minamoto and Taira families
寛平 **Kanpyō** (era, 889–897)
16 衡平 **kōhei** equitable

— 3 —

4 不公平 **fukōhei** unfair, unjust
6 汎太平洋 **han-Taiheiyō** Pan-Pacific
7 低頭平身 **teitō heishin** prostrate oneself
9 南太平洋 **Minami Taiheiyō** the South Pacific
17 環太平洋 **kan-Taiheiyō** pan-Pacific, circum-Pacific

環太平洋火山帯 **kan-Taiheiyō kazantai**
circum-Pacific volcanic belt
環太平洋地震帯 **kan-Taiheiyō jishintai**
circum-Pacific seismic zone
環太平洋造山帯 **kan-Taiheiyō zōzantai**
circum-Pacific orogeny

———————— 4 ————————

6 至公至平 **shikō-shihei** utterly just

———————— 4 ————————

2k4.1

李

HAI comet; dark, obscure

昔 → 世 **0a5.37**

2k4.2

开

KEN flat

2k4.3 / 542

孝

KŌ filial piety

———————— 1 ————————

2 孝子 **kōshi** dutiful/devoted child
3 孝女 **kōjo** dutiful/devoted daughter
4 孝元 **Kōgen** (emperor, 214–158 B.C.)
孝心 **kōshin** filial devotion
6 孝行 **kōkō** filial piety
孝安 **Kōan** (emperor, 392–291 B.C.)
9 孝昭 **Kōshō** (emperor, 475–393 B.C.)
11 孝道 **kōdō** filial piety
12 孝順 **kōjun** obedience, filial piety
14 孝徳 **Kōtoku** (emperor, 645–654)
15 孝養 **kōyō** discharge of filial duties
孝霊 **Kōrei** (emperor, 290–215 B.C.)
17 孝謙 **Kōken** (empress, 749–758)

———————— 2 ————————

4 不孝 **fukō** disobedience to parents, lack of
filial piety
6 至孝 **shikō** utmost filial piety
光孝 **Kōkō** (emperor, 884–887)
8 忠孝 **chūkō** loyalty and filial piety
16 親孝行 **oyakōkō** filial piety

———————— 3 ————————

16 親不孝 **oyafukō** lack of filial piety

2k4.4 / 541

考 攷

KŌ, kanga(eru) think, consider
kanga(e) thought, idea

———————— 1 ————————

4 考込 **kanga(e)ko(mu)** be deep in thought,
meditate
考方 **kanga(e)kata** way of thinking, viewpoint
5 考出 **kanga(e)da(su)** think/work out, devise;
recall, remember; begin to think
考付 **kanga(e)tsu(ku)** think of/up, hit upon;
remember
考古 **kōko** study of antiquities
考古学 **kōkogaku** archeology (cf. 考現学)
7 考究 **kōkyū** investigation, inquiry, research
8 考事 **kanga(e)goto** something to think about,
thinking; concern, worry, preoccupation
考直 **kanga(e)nao(su)** reconsider, rethink
考物 **kanga(e)mono** puzzle, problem
9 考査 **kōsa** consideration; test, exam
10 考案 **kōan** idea, conception; plan, project;
design, contrivance
11 考現学 **kōgengaku** study of modern
phenomena (cf. 考古学)
12 考違 **kanga(e)chiga(i)** mistaken idea, wrong
impression
考量 **kōryō** consider, weigh
考証 **kōshō** historical research
14 考察 **kōsatsu** consideration, examination,
study
考様 **kanga(e)yō** way of thinking, viewpoint
15 考慮 **kōryo** consideration, careful thought
考課 **kōka** evaluation of someone's record
考課状 **kōkajō** personnel/service record;
business report
考課表 **kōkahyō** personnel/service record;
business report

———————— 2 ————————

1 一考 **ikkō** consideration, a thought
6 再考 **saikō** reconsider
先考 **senkō** one's late father
7 私考 **shikō** personal opinion
8 追考 **tsuikō** second thoughts
参考 **sankō** reference, consultation
参考人 **sankōnin** person to consult
参考品 **sankōhin** reference materials
参考書 **sankōsho** reference book/work
9 皇考 **kōkō** the late emperor
思考 **shikō** thinking, thought
思考力 **shikōryoku** mental faculties
11 勘考 **kankō** consideration, deliberation
推考 **suikō** infer, conjecture, deliberate
12 備考 **bikō** note, remarks
無考 **mukanga(e)** thoughtless, rash
13 愚考 **gukō** my humble opinion

14 選考 **senkō** selection, screening
熟考 **jukkō** mature reflection, due deliberation
銓考 **senkō** selection, screening
15 黙考 **mokkō** contemplation, meditation
論考 **ronkō** a study

────────── 4 ──────────

3 千思万考 **senshi-bankō** deep meditation, careful deliberation

2k4.5 / 543

老

RŌ old age
o(iru), fu(keru) grow old
oi(raku) old age o(i) old age; old man

────────── 1 ──────────

2 老人 **rōjin** old man/person, the old/aged
老子 **Rōshi** Laozi, Lao-tzu (founder of Taoism)
3 老大家 **rōtaika** veteran authority
老女 **rōjo** old woman; senior lady-in-waiting
4 老夫 **rōfu** old man
老中 **rōjū** member of the shogun's council of elders
老友 **rōyū** old/aged friend
老公 **rōkō** elderly nobleman (polite)
老父 **rōfu** one's aged father
老込 **o(i)ko(mu)** grow old, become decrepit/senile
老手 **rōshu** old hand, past master, veteran, expert
老少 **rōshō** young and old
老少不定 **rōshō-fujō** Death comes to old and young alike.
老木 **rōboku, o(i)ki** old tree
5 老巧 **rōkō** veteran, experienced
老生 **rōsei** I (word used by old men)
老母 **rōbo** one's aged mother
老幼 **rōyō** old people and children
6 老死 **rōshi** die of old age
老年 **rōnen** old age
老年者 **rōnensha** old people, the aged
老吏 **rōri** veteran official
老壮 **rōsō** young and old
老先 **o(i)saki** one's remaining years
老朽 **rōkyū** age, decrepitude
老成 **rōsei** mature
7 老身 **rōshin** aged body
老来 **rōrai** since growing old
老体 **rōtai** old body, aged person
老兵 **rōhei** old soldier, veteran
老臣 **rōshin** senior vassal
老妓 **rōgi** old geisha
老役 **fu(ke)yaku** role of an old person
8 老妻 **rōsai** one's old wife
老若 **rōjaku, rōnyaku** young and old

老実 **rōjitsu** loyal, faithful
老松 **o(i)matsu, rōshō** old pine tree
9 老後 **rōgo** one's old age
老荘 **Rō-Sō** Laozi and Zhongzi, Lao-tzu and Chung-tzu; Taoism
10 老将 **rōshō** old general
老衰 **rōsui** infirmity of old age
老耄 **o(i)bo(re)** dotage; dotard, senile old man
老翁 **rōō** old man
老酒 **rōshu** old wine
老師 **rōshi** aged teacher/priest
老弱 **rōjaku** infirmity/feebleness of old age
老骨 **rōkotsu** one's old bones
老病 **rōbyō** infirmities of old age
老馬 **rōba** old horse
11 老婦 **rōfu** old woman
老婆 **rōba** old woman
老婆心 **rōbashin** old-womanish solicitude
老眼 **rōgan** farsightedness
老眼鏡 **rōgankyō** eyeglasses for farsightedness
12 老廃 **rōhai** old, superannuated
老廃物 **rōhaibutsu** waste matter/products
老雄 **rōyū** old hero
13 老僧 **rōsō** old/aged priest
老農 **rōnō** old/experienced farmer
14 老僕 **rōboku** old manservant
老境 **rōkyō** old age
老熟 **rōjuku** mature skill, maturity, mellowness
老練 **rōren** experienced, veteran
老練家 **rōrenka** expert, veteran
15 老舗 **rōho, shinise** long-established shop/store
老輩 **rōhai** the aged, old people
16 老儒 **rōju** old Confucian scholar
老嬢 **rōjō** old maid, spinster
老獪 **rōkai** crafty, astute, wily
老樹 **rōju** old tree
17 老優 **rōyū** old actor/actress
老齢 **rōrei** old age
老齢艦 **rōreikan** old warship
18 老軀 **rōku** one's old bones, old age

────────── 2 ──────────

3 大老 **tairō** chief minister
4 不老 **furō** eternal youth
不老不死 **furō-fushi** eternal youth
元老 **genrō** elder statesman, veteran
中老 **chūrō** age about 65–70
父老 **furō** elders, the old
5 古老 **korō** old person
6 早老 **sōrō** premature old age
7 初老 **shorō** early old age (formerly 40, now about 60)
8 長老 **chōrō** an elder

長老教会 **Chōrō Kyōkai** Presbyterian
　　Church
9 海老 **ebi** shrimp, prawn; lobster
　海老色 **ebi-iro** reddish brown
　海老茶 **ebicha** brownish red, maroon
　海老腰 **ebigoshi** stooped over, bent with age
　海老錠 **ebijō** padlock
　故老 **korō** an elder, old-timer
10 家老 **karō** chief retainer
11 宿老 **shukurō** elders, seniors
12 敬老 **keirō** respect for the aged
15 養老 **yōrō** provision for old age
　　Yōrō (era, 717–724)
　養老金 **yōrōkin** old-age pension
　養老院 **yōrōin** old-folks home
18 藩老 **hanrō** clan elder

2k4.6 / 1649

缶 罐 鑵
　　　KAN, FU can
　　　kama steam boiler

——————— 1 ———————
4 缶切 **kanki(ri)** can opener
13 缶詰 **kanzume** canned goods
——————— 2 ———————
4 牛缶 **gyūkan** canned beef
7 汽缶 **kikan** boiler
　汽缶室 **kikanshitsu** boiler room
8 空缶 **a(ki)kan** empty can
14 製缶 **seikan** making cans/boilers
　製缶工場 **seikan kōjō** cannery
19 蟹缶 **kanikan** canned crab

2k4.7

卍
　　BAN, MAN, manji fylfot, gammadion,
　　swastika

——————— 1 ———————
4 卍巴 **manji-tomoe** (snow falling) in swirls

——————— 5 ———————
2k5.1 / 1372

克
　　KOKU, ka(tsu) conquer, overcome
　　yo(ku) well, skillfully

——————— 1 ———————
3 克己 **kokki** self-denial, self-control
　克己心 **kokkishin** spirit of self-denial
8 克服 **kokufuku** conquest, subjugation
　克明 **kokumei** faithful, conscientious
12 克復 **kokufuku** be restored, return

——————— 2 ———————
3 下克上 **gekokujō** the lower dominating the
　　upper
12 超克 **chōkoku** overcome, surmount

求 →　　　**2b5.5**

2k5.2

础
　　dekaguramu decagram, ten grams

——————— 6 ———————
2k6.1 / 234

協
　　KYŌ cooperation

——————— 1 ———————
2 協力 **kyōryoku** cooperation
　協力者 **kyōryokusha** collaborator, coworker
6 協会 **kyōkai** society, association
　協同 **kyōdō** cooperation, collaboration,
　　partnership
8 協定 **kyōtei** agreement, accord
　協和 **kyōwa** harmony, concord, concert
9 協奏曲 **kyōsōkyoku** concerto
　協約 **kyōyaku** agreement, convention, pact
11 協商 **kyōshō** entente, an understanding,
　　agreement
　協商国 **kyōshōkoku** allies
13 協業 **kyōgyō** cooperative undertaking
15 協調 **kyōchō** cooperation, conciliation
　協賛 **kyōsan** approve, support, assist
20 協議 **kyōgi** consultation, conference
　協議会 **kyōgikai** conference, council
　協議所 **kyōgisho** conference site
　協議員 **kyōgiin** delegate, conferee

——————— 2 ———————
7 妥協 **dakyō** compromise
8 和協 **wakyō** harmony and cooperation
13 農協 **nōkyō** agricultural cooperative, co-op
　　(short for 農業共同組合)

——————— 3 ———————
9 軍事協定 **gunji kyōtei** military pact
11 紳士協定 **shinshi kyōtei** gentleman's
　　agreement

幸 →　　　**3b5.9**

尭 → 堯　　**3b9.3**

2k6.2 / 423

直 **CHOKU, JIKI** straight, immediate, direct, correct **nao(su)** fix, correct; revise; convert into; (as suffix) re-, do over **nao(ru)** return to normal, be fixed/corrected, recover **tada(chi ni)** immediately **su(gu)** immediately; readily, easily; right (near) **jika (ni)** directly, in person

――――――― 1 ―――――――

3 直上 **chokujō** immediately above
直々 **jikijiki** personal, direct
4 直方体 **chokuhōtai** rectangular parallelepiped
5 直払 **jikibara(i)** cash payment
直立 **chokuritsu** stand erect/upright, rise perpendicularly
直立不動 **chokuritsu-fudō** standing at attention
6 直伝 **jikiden** handed down directly, initiation into
直列 **chokuretsu** series (circuit)
直行 **chokkō** going straight, direct, nonstop
7 直角 **chokkaku** right angle
直弟子 **jikideshi** immediate pupil, direct disciple
直売 **chokubai** direct sales
直系 **chokkei** lineal descendant, direct line
直言 **chokugen** plain speaking, straight talk
8 直送 **chokusō** direct delivery
直径 **chokkei** diameter
直参 **jikisan** immediate vassal/retainer
直取引 **jikitorihiki** spot/cash transaction
9 直前 **chokuzen** just before
直通 **chokutsū** direct communication, nonstop service
直後 **chokugo** immediately after
直面 **chokumen** be faced with, confront
10 直射 **chokusha** direct fire/rays
直進 **chokushin** advance/go straight ahead
直流 **chokuryū** direct current, DC
直航 **chokkō** nonstop flight, direct voyage
11 直接 **chokusetsu** direct
直接法 **chokusetsuhō** direct method; indicative mood
直接税 **chokusetsuzei** direct tax
直接話法 **chokusetsu wahō** direct quotation
直視 **chokushi** look straight at, face squarely
直球 **chokkyū** straight ball/pitch
直情 **chokujō** straightforward, impulsive
直情径行 **chokujō keikō** straightforward, impulsive
直訳 **chokuyaku** literal translation
12 直渡 **jikawata(shi)** direct delivery
直喩 **chokuyu** simile
直営 **chokuei** direct management
直覚 **chokkaku** intuition

直覚的 **chokkakuteki** intuitive
直属 **chokuzoku** under the direct control of
直結 **chokketsu** direct connection
直筆 **jikihitsu** in one's own handwriting
chokuhitsu write with brush held upright; write plainly/frankly
直答 **chokutō, jikitō** prompt answer, direct/personal answer
直訴 **jikiso** direct appeal/petition
13 直腸 **chokuchō** the rectum
直感 **chokkan** intuition
直感的 **chokkanteki** intuitive
直話 **jikiwa** one's own account, firsthand story
14 直説法 **chokusetsuhō** indicative mood
15 直撃 **chokugeki** direct hit
直撃弾 **chokugekidan** direct hit
直線 **chokusen** straight line
16 直輸入 **chokuyunyū, jikiyunyū** direct import
直輸出 **chokuyushutsu, jikiyushutsu** direct export
17 直轄 **chokkatsu** direct control/jurisdiction
18 直観 **chokkan** intuition
直観的 **chokkanteki** intuitive

――――――― 2 ―――――――

1 一直線 **itchokusen** a straight line
3 口直 **kuchinao(shi)** kill the aftertaste
4 手直 **tenao(shi)** adjust afterwards, readjust
引直 **hi(ki)nao(su)** restore to, bring back to
5 包直 **tsutsu(mi)nao(su)** rewrap
生直 **kisu(gu)** well-behaved and straightforward
世直 **yonao(shi)** reform of the world
正直 **shōjiki** honest, upright, straightforward
正直者 **shōjikimono** honest person, man of integrity
司直 **shichoku** judicial authorities
立直 **ta(te)nao(ru)** recover, rally, pick up
6 仲直 **nakanao(ri)** reconciliation, make up
考直 **kanga(e)nao(su)** reconsider, rethink
色直 **ironao(shi)** changing wedding dress for ordinary clothes; redyeing
安直 **anchoku** cheap, inexpensive
当直 **tōchoku** on duty
朴直 **bokuchoku** simple and honest, ingenuous
7 吹直 **fu(ki)nao(shi)** smelting, recoinage
見直 **minao(su)** take another look at, reevaluate; think better of; get better
言直 **i(i)nao(su)** rephrase, correct
8 垂直 **suichoku** vertical; perpendicular
垂直線 **suichokusen** a perpendicular
刷直 **su(ri)nao(su)** reprint (to correct mistakes)
卒直 **sotchoku** frank, openhearted

直直 **jikijiki** personal, direct
建直 **ta(te)nao(ru)** be rebuilt
　　 ta(te)nao(su) rebuild
拵直 **koshira(e)nao(su)** remake, remodel
実直 **jitchoku** honest, steadfast
居直 **inao(ru)** sit up straight; change one's attitude, come on strong; turn violent, resort to threat
取直 **to(rimo)nao(sazu)** namely, in other words **to(ri)nao(su)** recover; retake, regrasp
9 造直 **tsuku(ri)nao(su)** remake, rebuild
持直 **mo(chi)nao(su)** improve, rally, recover; change one's grip/hold
染直 **so(me)nao(su)** redye
思直 **omo(i)nao(su)** reconsider, change one's mind
計直 **haka(ri)nao(su)** remeasure, reweigh
10 剛直 **gōchoku** unbending, of integrity
真直 **ma(s)su(gu)** straight; honest, upright, frank
起直 **o(ki)nao(ru)** sit up
書直 **ka(ki)nao(su)** rewrite
素直 **sunao** gentle, meek, docile; frank, honest
11 率直 **sotchoku** straightforward, frank, forthright
強直 **kyōchoku, gōchoku** rigidity, stiffness; honesty, integrity
宿直 **shukuchoku** night duty/watch
12 遣直 **ya(ri)nao(su)** do over again, redo, start over
量直 **haka(ri)nao(su)** measure again, reweigh
焼直 **ya(ki)nao(su)** rebake; rehash, adapt
硬直 **kōchoku** rigid, firm, inflexible
畳直 **tata(mi)nao(su)** refold
飲直 **no(mi)nao(su)** drink again
開直 **hira(ki)nao(ru)** become defiant; turn serious
13 靴直 **kutsunao(shi)** shoe repairing; shoe-maker
廉直 **renchoku** integrity, honesty
数直 **kazo(e)nao(su)** do a recount, count over
愚直 **guchoku** simple honesty, tactless frankness
置直 **o(ki)nao(su)** replace, transpose, rearrange
鉛直 **enchoku** perpendicular, plumb
14 練直 **ne(ri)nao(su)** polish up, work over
綴直 **to(ji)nao(su)** rebind
読直 **yo(mi)nao(su)** reread
聞直 **ki(ki)nao(su)** ask/inquire again
15 撮直 **to(ri)nao(su)** retake (a photo)
縫直 **nu(i)nao(su)** resew, remake
調直 **shira(be)nao(su)** reinvestigate, reexamine
鋳直 **inao(su)** recast, recoin

16 樸直 **bokuchoku** simple and honest
積直 **tsu(mi)nao(su)** reload, pile up again
17 矯直 **ta(me)nao(su)** set up again, correct, reform, cure
謹直 **kinchoku** conscientious
18 癖直 **kusenao(shi)** straightening out one's hair

――― 3 ―――
4 不正直 **fushōjiki** dishonest
9 急転直下 **kyūten-chokka** sudden change, sudden turn (toward a solution)
単刀直入 **tantō-chokunyū** getting straight to the point
10 真正直 **ma(s)shōjiki** perfectly honest
15 縁起直 **enginao(shi)** a change of luck

――― 4 ―――
6 死後強直 **shigo kyōchoku** rigor mortis
死後硬直 **shigo kōchoku** rigor mortis

2k6.3
阜　**FU** hill, mound
――― 1 ―――
16 阜頭 **futō** wharf
――― 2 ―――
7 岐阜 **Gifu** (city, Gifu-ken)
岐阜県 **Gifu-ken** (prefecture)

2k6.4
乖　**KAI, somu(ku)** go against, disobey
――― 1 ―――
18 乖離 **kairi** estranged, disparate

2k6.5 / 1659
奔　**HON, hashi(ru)** run
――― 1 ―――
7 奔走 **honsō** running about, efforts
8 奔放 **honpō** wild, extravagant, uninhibited
10 奔流 **honryū** rushing current, torrent
奔馬 **honba** galloping/runaway horse
――― 2 ―――
5 出奔 **shuppon** run away/off, abscond
7 狂奔 **kyōhon** rush madly about
8 東奔西走 **tōhon-seisō** busy oneself, take an active interest in
11 淫奔 **inpon** wanton, loose, lewd

卑 → 卑 **5f4.8**

2k6.6

瓩 **kiroguramu** kilogram, thousand grams

───────── 7 ─────────

2k7.1 / 74

南 **NAN, NA, minami** south

───────── 1 ─────────

0 南ア **Nan'a** South Africa
2 南十字星 **minami jūjisei** the Southern Cross
3 南下 **nanka** go south
南口 **minamiguchi** south exit/entrance
4 南太平洋 **Minami Taiheiyō** the South Pacific
南天 **nanten** the southern sky
南支那海 **Minami Shinakai** the South China Sea
南方 **nanpō** south, southern, southward
5 南北 **nanboku** north and south
南北朝 **Nanbokuchō** the Northern and Southern Dynasties (439–589 in China, 1336–1392 in Japan)
南北戦争 **Nanboku Sensō** the War Between the States, the (U.S.) Civil War
南半球 **minami hankyū** the Southern Hemisphere
南氷洋 **Nanpyōyō** the Antarctic Ocean
6 南瓜 **kabocha, tōnasu** pumpkin, squash
南西 **nansei** southwest
南向 **minamimu(ki)** facing south
南回帰線 **Minami Kaikisen** the Tropic of Capricorn
南米 **Nanbei** South America
7 南宋 **Nansō** the Southern Songs (1127–1279)
8 南東 **nantō** southeast
南京 **Nankin** Nanking
南京虫 **nankinmushi** bedbugs
南京豆 **nankinmame** peanuts
南京町 **Nankinmachi** Chinatown
南京袋 **nankinbukuro** gunny sack
南欧 **Nan'ō** Southern Europe
9 南南西 **nannansei** south-southwest
南南東 **nannantō** south-southeast
南風 **nanpū, minamikaze** south wind
南洋 **Nan'yō** the South Seas
南洋諸島 **Nan'yō-shotō** the South Sea Islands
南海 **nankai** southern sea
10 南部 **nanbu** southern part, the South
南進 **nanshin** advance south
南航 **nankō** sail south
11 南側 **minamigawa, nansoku** south side
南寄 **minamiyo(ri)** southerly (wind)
南船北馬 **nansen-hokuba** constant travel-

ing, restless wandering
12 南蛮 **nanban** southern barbarians; cayenne pepper
南蛮人 **nanbanjin** southern barbarians, the early Europeans
南満 **Nanman** South Manchuria
南満州 **Minami Manshū** South Manchuria
南極 **Nankyoku** the South Pole
南極光 **nankyokukō** the aurora australis, the southern lights
南極海 **Nankyokukai** the Antarctic Ocean
南極圏 **Nankyokuken** the Antarctic Circle, the Antarctic
南無阿弥陀仏 **Namu Amida Butsu** Hail Amida Buddha
南無妙法蓮華経 **Namu Myōhō Rengekyō** Hail Lotus Sutra
14 南端 **nantan** southern extremity/tip
16 南緯 **nan'i** south latitude

───────── 2 ─────────

4 中南米 **Chūnanbei** Central and South America
5 石南花 **shakunage** rhododendron
6 西南 **seinan** southwest
江南 **kōnan** south of the (Yangtze/Yangzi) river
8 東南 **tōnan** southeast
河南 **Kanan** Henan (province; south of the Yellow river)
9 南南西 **nannansei** south-southwest
南南東 **nannantō** south-southeast
指南 **shinan** instruction, guidance
指南役 **shinan'yaku** instructor, teacher
指南車 **shinansha** (ancient Chinese) compass vehicle
指南番 **shinanban** instructor, teacher
10 真南 **maminami** due south
12 最南 **sainan** southernmost
越南 **Etsunan, Betonamu** Vietnam

───────── 3 ─────────

8 東西南北 **tōzainanboku** north, south, east, and west

卑 → **5f4.8**

2k7.2

缸 **KŌ, kame** urn

───────── 8 ─────────

豹 → **0a10.4**

2k8.1 / 422

真 眞

SHIN true, genuine **makoto** true, sincere **ma-** just, right, due (north); pure, genuine, true

———————— 1 ————————

1 真一文字 **ma-ichimonji** in a straight line
2 真二 **ma(p)puta(tsu)** (split) right in two
  真人 **shinjin** true man
  真人間 **maningen** honest man, good citizen
3 真丸 **ma(n)maru, ma(n)maru(i)** perfectly round
  真上 **maue** right over, directly above
  真下 **mashita** right under, directly below
5 真平 **mappira** (not) by any means; humbly
  真正 **shinsei** genuine, authentic, true
  真正直 **ma(s)shōjiki** perfectly honest
  真正面 **ma(s)shōmen** directly opposite, right in front
  真打 **shin'u(chi)** star performer
  真只中 **ma(t)tadanaka** right in the middle of
  真四角 **mashikaku** square
  真白 **ma(s)shiro** pure white
  真冬 **mafuyu** dead of winter, midwinter
  真田虫 **sanada mushi** tapeworm
  真田紐 **sanada himo** braid
6 真西 **manishi** due west
  真向 **mamuka(i)** just opposite, right across from, face to face **ma(k)kō** forehead; front
  真如 **shinnyo** the absolute, absolute reality
  真帆 **maho** spread-out sail
  真因 **shin'in** true cause/reason
  真竹 **madake** (common) bamboo
7 真似 **mane** imitation, mimicry; behavior; pretense
  真似事 **manegoto** sham, semblance, pretense
  真赤 **ma(k)ka** deep red, crimson
  真否 **shinpi** true or false
8 真東 **mahigashi** due east
  真価 **shinka** true value
  真夜中 **mayonaka** dead of night, midnight
  真直 **ma(s)su(gu)** straight; honest, upright, frank
  真味 **shinmi** a real taste
  真実 **shinjitsu** truth, reality, the facts
  真実性 **shinjitsusei** truth, authenticity, credibility
  真空 **shinkū** vacuum
  真空掃除機 **shinkū sōjiki** vacuum cleaner
  真空管 **shinkūkan** vacuum tube
  真青 **ma(s)sao** deep blue; ghastly pale
  真性 **shinsei** inborn nature
9 真勇 **shin'yū** true courage
  真南 **maminami** due south
  真前 **ma(n)mae** right in front of

真後 **maushi(ro)** right behind
真面目 **majime** serious-minded, earnest, honest **shinmenmoku** one's true self/character; seriousness, earnestness
真相 **shinsō** the truth/facts, the real situation
真昼 **mahiru** broad daylight, midday
真昼間 **ma(p)piruma** broad daylight
真砂 **masago** sand
真紅 **shinku** crimson
10 真剣 **shinken** serious
真剣勝負 **shinken-shōbu** fighting with real swords; game played in earnest
真珠 **shinju** pearl
真珠色 **shinju-iro** pearl gray
真珠貝 **shinjugai** pearl oyster
真珠取 **shinjuto(ri)** pearl fishing; pearl diver
真珠湾 **Shinju-wan** Pearl Harbor
真珠層 **shinjusō** mother-of-pearl
真夏 **manatsu** midsummer
真症 **shinshō** true case (of a disease)
11 真偽 **shingi** true or false, whether genuine or spurious
真率 **shinsotsu** simple, honest, frank
真唯中 **ma(t)tadanaka** right in the middle of
真黒 **ma(k)kuro** jet-black, coal-black
真理 **shinri** truth
真情 **shinjō** one's feelings/heart
真盛 **ma(s)saka(ri)** the middle/height of, in full bloom
12 真最中 **ma(s)saichū** right in the midst/middle of, at the height of
真筆 **shinpitsu** autograph, one's own handwriting
13 真暗 **makkura** pitch-dark
真暗闇 **makkurayami** utter darkness
真意 **shin'i** real intention, true motive; true meaning
真新 **maatara(shii)** brand new
真裸 **ma(p)padaka** stark naked
真跡 **shinseki** one's genuine handwriting
14 真綿 **mawata** silk floss/wadding
15 真摯 **shinshi** earnest, sincere
真影 **shin'ei** portrait, photograph
16 真鴨 **magamo** mallard duck
17 真鍮 **shinchū** brass
18 真髄 **shinzui** essence, spirit, soul
真顔 **magao** serious look, straight face
真鯉 **magoi** black carp
19 真贋 **shingan** whether genuine or counterfeit
真鯛 **madai** red sea bream, porgy

———————— 2 ————————

2 人真似 **hitomane** mimicry, imitations
3 口真似 **kuchimane** mimicry
4 不真面目 **fumajime** not serious-minded, insincere

天真 **tenshin** naive
天真爛漫 **tenshin-ranman** naive, simple and innocent, unaffected
手真似 **temane** gesture, hand signals
5 写真 **shashin** photograph
写真版 **shashinban** photographic plate
写真屋 **shashin'ya** photographer, photo studio
写真帳 **shashinchō** photo album
写真術 **shashinjutsu** photography
写真植字 **shashin shokuji** photocomposition, phototypesetting
写真結婚 **shashin kekkon** marriage arranged after seeing photos of each other
写真嫌 **shashingira(i)** camera shy
写真機 **shashinki** camera
写真館 **shashinkan** photo studio
正真正銘 **shōshin-shōmei** genuine, authentic
7 迫真 **hakushin** true to life, realistic
迫真性 **hakushinsei** true to life, realistic
8 泣真似 **na(ki)mane** crocodile tears
物真似 **monomane** doing imitations, mimicry
10 純真 **junshin** ingenuous, sincere
12 御真影 **goshin'ei** emperor's portrait
13 猿真似 **sarumane** monkey-see monkey-do
17 糞真面目 **kusomajime** humorless earnestness

——————— 3 ———————

5 古義真言宗 **Kogi Shingon shū** the "old meaning" sect of Esoteric Buddhism
8 青写真 **aojashin, aoshashin** blueprints
9 浄土真宗 **Jōdo Shinshū** (a Buddhist sect, offshoot of the Jodo sect)
11 組写真 **ku(mi)shashin** composite photograph
13 新義真言宗 **Shingi Shingon shū** New Shingon religion

——————— 4 ———————

6 早取写真 **hayato(ri) shashin** snapshot
9 活動写真 **katsudō shashin** moving pictures, movie
10 航空写真 **kōkū shashin** aerial photo
13 電送写真 **densō shashin** telephoto

盍 → **3b7.9**

2k8.2 / 1059

索 **SAKU** rope, cord; search for

——————— 1 ———————

4 索引 **sakuin** index
7 索条 **sakujō** cable, rope
8 索具 **sakugu** rigging, gear, tackle
10 索莫 **sakubaku** bleak, desolate

15 索敵 **sakuteki** searching for the enemy
20 索麺 **sōmen** vermicelli, noodles

——————— 2 ———————

9 思索 **shisaku** thinking, speculation, meditation
思索的 **shisakuteki** speculative, meditative
10 捜索 **sōsaku** search
捜索隊 **sōsakutai** search party
11 探索 **tansaku** search; inquiry, investigation
12 検索 **kensaku** retrieval, lookup, reference
13 摸索 **mosaku** groping
詮索 **sensaku** search, inquiry
鉄索 **tessaku** cable
14 模索 **mosaku** groping, trial and error
総索引 **sōsakuin** general index
16 鋼索 **kōsaku** cable

——————— 3 ———————

11 救命索 **kyūmeisaku** lifeline

——————— 4 ———————

10 家宅捜索 **kataku sōsaku** domiciliary search
13 暗中摸索 **anchū mosaku** groping in the dark

翆 → 翠 **2k12.2**

皋 → 皐 **4c7.12**

2k8.3

耄 **MŌ, BŌ** senility

——————— 1 ———————

13 耄碌 **mōroku** senility, dotage

——————— 2 ———————

6 老耄 **o(i)bo(re)** dotage; dotard, senile old man

2k8.4

翅 **SHI** wings; fly; merely
hane wings

——————— 2 ———————

10 展翅板 **tenshiban** setting board (for spreading butterfly-specimen wings)

缺 → 欠 **4j0.1**

——————— 9 ———————

皐 → **4c7.12**

────────── 10 ──────────

2k10.1 / 601

博 博   HAKU broad, extensive; gambling; (as suffix) Ph.D.; (as suffix) exposition, fair, exhibition   BAKU gambling

────────── 1 ──────────

0 博する **haku(suru)** gain, achieve, win
3 博大 **hakudai** extensive
   博士 **hakase, hakushi** Ph.D.
   博士号 **hakasegō** doctor's degree, Ph.D.
5 博打 **bakuchi** gambling
   博打打 **bakuchiu(chi)** gambler
7 博学 **hakugaku** broad knowledge, erudition
   博労 **bakurō** horse trader
8 博物学 **hakubutsugaku** natural history
   博物館 **hakubutsukan** museum
9 博奕 **bakuchi** gambling
   博奕打 **bakuchiu(chi)** gambler
10 博徒 **bakuto** gambler
13 博愛 **hakuai** philanthropy
   博愛家 **hakuaika** philanthropist
17 博覧 **hakuran** extensive reading/knowledge; open to the public
   博覧会 **hakurankai** exhibition, exposition, fair
   博覧強記 **hakuran-kyōki** extensive reading and retentive memory
19 博識 **hakushiki** extensive knowledge

────────── 2 ──────────

3 万博 **banpaku** world's fair (short for 万国博覧会)
4 文博 **bunhaku** Doctor of Literature (short for 文学博士)
10 脈博 **myakuhaku** pulse (rate)
13 節博士 **fushi hakase** chanting intonation marks
   該博 **gaihaku** profound, vast (learning)
16 賭博 **tobaku** gambling

────────── 3 ──────────

3 万国博覧会 **bankoku hakurankai** world's fair

悳 → 徳   3i11.3

2k10.2

辜   KO sin, crime, fault

────────── 2 ──────────

12 無辜 **muko** innocent, harmless

準 → 準   2k11.1

2k10.3

覃   TAN stretch, extend; deep; large

賈 →   7b5.6

喪 →   3b9.20

────────── 11 ──────────

2k11.1 / 778

準   JUN quasi-, semi-; level; aim **nazora(eru)** model after, liken to, imitate

────────── 1 ──────────

0 準じる/ずる **jun(jiru/zuru)** correspond to, be porportionate to, conform to
5 準用 **jun'yō** apply (mutatis mutandis)
6 準会員 **junkaiin** associate member
7 準決勝 **junkesshō** semifinals
   準社員 **junshain** junior employee, associate member
8 準拠 **junkyo** conform to, be pursuant to, be based on
9 準急 **junkyū** local express (train)
   準則 **junsoku** rule, criterion
10 準教員 **junkyōin** assistant teacher
12 準備 **junbi** preparations, provision, reserve
   準備金 **junbikin** reserve fund
13 準禁治産 **junkinchisan** quasi-incompetence (in law)
   準禁治産者 **junkinchisansha** a quasi-incompetent (person)
15 準縄 **junjō** a level and an inked string; norm, criterion

────────── 2 ──────────

3 下準備 **shitajunbi** preliminary arrangements
4 水準 **suijun** water level; level, standard
   水準器 **suijunki** (carpenter's) level
8 金準備 **kin junbi** gold reserves
11 基準 **kijun** standard, criterion, basis
   規準 **kijun** standard, criterion
13 照準 **shōjun** aiming, sights
15 標準 **hyōjun** standard, norm, criterion
   標準化 **hyōjunka** standardization
   標準型 **hyōjungata** standard type
   標準時 **hyōjunji** standard/universal time
   標準語 **hyōjungo** the standard language

2

亻 冫 子 阝 卩 刂 力 又 宀 冖 十 11← ⼬ 夂 丷 厂 辶 冂 几 匸

献→ 3g9.6

瓶→甁 2o9.6

— 12 —

2k12.1

睾 **KŌ** high; vast; testicle

— 1 —

3 睾丸 **kōgan** testicle, testes

2k12.2

翠 翠翠 **SUI** female kingfisher; green **midori** green

— 1 —

6 翠色 **suishoku** green

— 2 —

14 翡翠 **hisui** green jadeite, jade; kingfisher
kawasemi kingfisher

— 15 —

2k15.1

罅 **KA, hibi** crack, fissure

— 1 —

12 罅焼 **hibiya(ki)** crackleware

— 22 —

2k22.1

矗 **CHIKU** standing straight/tall

顰→ 9a15.1

ト 2m

卜	上	下	支	止	丐	外	占	正	疋	比	乍	虍
0.1	1.1	1.2	2.1	2.2	2.3	3.1	3.2	3.3	3.4	3.5	0a5.10	4.1
臼	此	步	卦	卓	奌	虎	兒	些	長	臥	貞	点
0a6.4	4.2	3n5.3	6.1	6.2	2m7.2	6.3	4c3.3	6.4	0a8.2	2a7.22	7.1	7.2
虐	昇	歪	韭	虔	虚	處	鹵	埜	套	舂	虛	疎
7.3	0a9.7	7.4	3k9.2	8.1	9.1	4i2.2	9.2	9.3	0a10.3	0a11.6	2m9.1	0a11.4
疏	豼	虞	虜	鼠	觜	睿	翡	疑	膚	慮	貌	盧
2j9.8	0a11.1	11.1	11.2	0a13.1	2n11.2	2h14.1	0a14.1	12.1	13.1	13.2	3g8.2	14.1
罅	鼬											
2k15.1	0a18.1											

— 0 —

2m0.1

卜 **BOKU, urana(u)** tell fortunes, divine, augur

— 1 —

0 卜する **boku(suru)** tell fortunes, predict; fix, choose, settle
13 卜筮 **bokuzei** fortunetelling, divination

— 1 —

2m1.1 / 32

上 **JŌ** upper, top, above; first volume/part (of a series); top-grade; emperor, sovereign; (as suffix) from the viewpoint of **SHŌ** upper, above **ue** up, upper part, top, above, over; besides, on top of; upon, after **uwa-** upper, outer **kami** upper part, top; upstream; emperor, the authorities, a superior **a(geru)** raise, lift up, elevate, increase; give **-a(gezu)** every (three days) or less **a(garu)** go/come up, rise; enter (someone's home), call on; come to an end **a(gari)** rise, ascent; completion, finish; receipts, profit; tea (in a restaurant); (as suffix) ex-, former; (as suffix) (just) after (a rainfall/bath/illness) **a(gattari)** out of business, ruined, done for **nobo(ru)** go/come up, ascend, climb; go/come to the capital; reach, amount to **nobo(ri)** ascent; Tōkyō-bound (train)

— 1 —

0 お上りさん **(o)nobo(ri-san)** country visitor (to Tōkyō)
2 上人 **shōnin** (Buddhist) saint, holy priest

2 亻 冫 子 阝 卩 刂 力 又 冖 十 →12 ト ⺈ ⺌ 厂 辶 冂 八 匚

3 上下 **jōge** top and bottom, upper and lower; volumes 1 and 2 (of a two-volume set), parts 1 and 2 (of a two-part serialization); inbound (toward Tōkyō) and outbound; rise and fall, go up and down; the high and the low, ruler and ruled; government and people **shōka** ruler and ruled **kamishimo** the high and the low, government and people; the upper and lower halves of the body **a(gari)sa(gari)** rise and fall, fluctuations **a(ge)sa(ge)** raising and lowering; praising and blaming; rising and falling, intonation **a(ge)o(roshi)** raising and lowering; loading and unloading

上下水道 **jōgesuidō** water and sewer service

上下動 **jōgedō** up-and-down/vertical motion

上々 **jōjō** the (very) best

4 上天 **jōten** heaven; God

上天気 **jōtenki** fine weather

上中下 **jō-chū-ge** good-fair-poor; first-second-third class; volumes/parts 1, 2, 3 (of a 3-volume/3-part series)

上文 **jōbun** the foregoing/above

上辺 **uwabe** exterior, surface, outside; outward appearance

上込 **a(gari)ko(mu)** enter, step in

上水 **jōsui** water supply, tap water

上水道 **jōsuidō** piped/city water

上手 **jōzu** skillful, good at **uwate** better at, superior to; upper part, upstream **kamite** upper part; upstream; right side of the stage (as seen from the audience)

上方 **jōhō** upper part, above, upward **kamigata** Kyōto-Ōsaka area

上戸 **jōgo** drinker (of alcohol)

5 上包 **uwazutsu(mi)** cover, wrapper, envelope

上出来 **jōdeki** good performance, well done

上半 **jōhan** first/upper half

上半身 **jōhanshin, kamihanshin** upper half of the body

上半期 **kamihanki** the first half (of the year)

上甲板 **jōkanpan** upper deck

上申 **jōshin** report (to a superior)

上申書 **jōshinsho** written report/statement

上代 **jōdai** ancient times

上皮 **jōhi** epidermis **uwakawa** epidermis, outer skin, film, crust

上市 **jōshi** put (a new product) on the market

上古 **jōko** ancient times

上古史 **jōkoshi** ancient history

上句 **kami(no)ku** the first pàrt of a poem

上司 **jōshi** one's superior(s)

上玉 **jōdama** fine jewel; best article

上目 **uwame** upward glance, upturned eyes **a(gari)me** slanting eyes (temple side higher than nose side)

6 上気 **jōki** rush of blood to the head, dizziness

上列車 **nobo(ri) ressha** train going toward the capital, up train

上向 **uwamu(ku)** look/turn upward, rise

上回 **uwamawa(ru)** be more than, exceed

上旬 **jōjun** the first ten days of a month

上衣 **uwagi** coat, jacket

7 上位 **jōi** high rank, precedence

上体 **jōtai** upper part of the body

上作 **jōsaku** good crop; masterpiece

上述 **jōjutsu** the above-mentioned

上坂 **nobo(ri)zaka** upward slope, uphill

上告 **jōkoku** appeal (to a higher court)

上役 **uwayaku** senior official, one's superior

上図 **jōzu** the upper diagram/illustration

8 上長 **jōchō** one's superior, a senior, an elder

上表紙 **uwabyōshi** outer cover, (book) jacket

上京 **jōkyō** go/come to the capital

上京中 **jōkyōchū** in the capital

上弦 **jōgen** first quarter (phase of the moon)

上官 **jōkan** senior official, one's superior

上空 **jōkū** the sky/air, high-altitude **uwa(no)sora** inattentive, absent-minded

上底 **a(ge)zoko** raised/false bottom

上板 **a(ge)ita** movable floorboards; trap door

上肢 **jōshi** upper limbs, arms

上昇 **jōshō** rise, ascend, climb

上昇気流 **jōshō kiryū** rising air current, updraft

上物 **jōmono** high-quality article **uwamono** buildings on a plot of land

9 上巻 **jōkan** first volume (of two or three)

上奏 **jōsō** report to the throne

上降 **a(gari)o(ri)** going up and down

上院 **jōin** the Upper House (of a legislature), Senate

上帝 **jōtei** God

上首尾 **jōshubi** a (great) success, satisfactory result

上前 **uwamae** outer skirt; commission, rake-off

上段 **jōdan** upper row; raised portion of a floor, dais; seats of honor **a(gari)dan** stairs, doorstep

上洛 **jōraku** go/come to the capital

上海 **Shanhai** Shanghai

上品 **jōhin** refined, elegant, genteel; first-class article

上草履 **uwazōri** indoor sandals

上客 **jōkyaku** guest of honor; good customer

上屋 **uwaya** a shed

上屋敷 **kamiyashiki** (daimyo's) main residence

上面 **jōmen** surface, top, exterior **uwatsura, uwa(t)tsura** surface, appearances

2

亻 冫 子 阝 卩 刂 力 又 宀 亠 十 ├ 1 ← 丿 丶 厂 辶 門 几 匚

2

上背 **uwazei** height, stature
上映 **jōei** screen, show, play (a movie)
上皇 **jōkō** ex-emperor
上級 **jōkyū** upper grade, senior
上級生 **jōkyūsei** upperclassman
10 上値 **uwane** higher price
上陸 **jōriku** landing, going ashore
上部 **jōbu** upper part/side, top surface
上高 **a(gari)daka** revenue, income, receipts, yield
上流 **jōryū** upstream; upper-class
上唇 **uwakuchibiru, jōshin** upper lip
上帯 **uwaobi** outer sash
上座 **kamiza, jōza** top seat, place of honor
上席 **jōseki** seniority, precedence; place of honor
上書 **uwaga(ki)** the writing on the outside, the address
上紙 **uwagami** paper cover/wrapping
上納 **jōnō** payment (to the government)
上記 **jōki** the above-mentioned/aforesaid
11 上野 **Ueno** (section of Tōkyō)
　　 Kōzuke (ancient kuni, Gunma-ken)
上達 **jōtatsu** make progress, become proficient
上張 **uwaba(ri)** face, coat, veneer
　　 uwa(p)pa(ri) overalls, duster, smock
上梓 **jōshi** publishing; wood-block printing
12 上着 **uwagi** coat, jacket
上湯 **a(gari)yu** hot bath water (for rinsing oneself)
上棟式 **jōtōshiki** ridgepole-raising/roof-laying ceremony
上腕 **jōwan** the upper arm
上期 **kamiki** the first half (of the year)
上景気 **jōkeiki** boom, prosperity, a brisk economy
上智 **jōchi** supreme wisdom
　　 Jōchi Sophia (University)
上程 **jōtei** introduce (a bill), put on the agenda
上番 **jōban** on duty
上歯 **uwaba** upper teeth
上策 **jōsaku** good plan, wisest policy
上等 **jōtō** first-rate, superior
上等品 **jōtōhin** top-quality goods
上訴 **jōso** appeal (to a higher court)
13 上滑 **uwasube(ri)** superficial, shallow; inattentive
上塗 **uwanu(ri)** final coat(ing)
上靴 **uwagutsu** house shoes, slippers, overshoes
上腿 **jōtai** thigh
上意 **jōi** the emperor's wishes
上意下達 **jōi katatsu** conveying the will of those in authority to those who are governed

14 上演 **jōen** play, stage, perform
上層 **jōsō** upper layer/stratum
上層気流 **jōsō kiryū** upper-air currents
上層雲 **jōsōun** upper clouds
上様 **uesama** (title of respect)
上膊 **jōhaku** the upper arm
上端 **jōtan** upper end, top, tip
上製 **jōsei** superior manufacture/binding
上総 **Kazusa** (ancient kuni, Chiba-ken)
15 上澄 **uwazu(mi)** (clear) supernatant (liquid)
上履 **uwabaki** slippers
上敷 **uwaji(ki)** carpet
上調子 **uwachōshi, uwajōshi** high pitch, higher key **uwa(t)chōshi** flippant, frivolous, shallow
上質 **jōshitsu** fine quality
16 上機嫌 **jōkigen** good humor, high spirits
上積 **uwazu(mi)** load/pile on top of
17 上擦 **uwazu(ru)** sound nervous/tense
上覧 **jōran** imperial inspection
18 上瞼 **uwamabuta** upper eyelid
上顎 **jōgaku, uwaago** upper jaw; the palate
20 上欄 **jōran** top/preceding column
上騰 **jōtō** rise, jump, advance

───────── 2 ─────────

3 川上 **kawakami** upstream
大上段 **daijōdan** raising a sword (to kill)
干上 **hia(garu)** dry up, parch; ebb away
上上 **jōjō** the (very) best
口上 **kōjō** oral (statement)
口上手 **kuchijōzu** fair-spoken, glib
口上書 **kōjōsho** verbal note
山上 **sanjō** mountaintop
4 天上 **tenjō** the heavens
天上界 **tenjōkai** the celestial world, heaven
井上 **Inoue** (surname)
今上 **kinjō** the present/reigning emperor
切上 **ki(ri)a(ge)** end, conclusion; rounding up (to the nearest integer); revalue, up-value (a currency)
父上 **chichiue** father (polite)
込上 **ko(mi)a(geru)** well up, feel about to gush forth (vomit, tears, anger)
水上 **suijō** (on the) water, aquatic
　　 minakami headwaters, source
水上生活者 **suijō seikatsusha** seafarer
水上飛行機 **suijō hikōki** hydroplane, seaplane
水上警察 **suijō keisatsu** water/harbor police
水上競技 **suijō kyōgi** water sports
引上 **hi(ki)a(geru)** raise, increase; withdraw, leave
5 以上 **ijō** or more, more than, over, above, beyond; the above; since, so long as; that is all
北上 **hokujō** go north

北上川 **Kitakamigawa** (river, Miyagi-ken)
母上 **hahaue** mother (polite)
世上 **sejō** the world
史上 **shijō** in history; historical
申上 **mō(shi)a(geru)** say, tell (humble)
仕上 **shia(ge)** finish, finishing touches
付上 **tsu(ke)a(garu)** be overproud/spoiled/ elated; take advantage of
召上 **me(shi)a(garu)** (polite) eat, drink, have
　　me(shi)a(geru) confiscate
打上 **u(chi)a(geru)** shoot up, launch (a rocket), cast up on shore, wash ashore; finish, close (a performance)
打上花火 **u(chi)a(ge) hanabi** skyrocket, fireworks
叩上 **tata(ki)a(geru)** work one's way up
兄上 **aniue** elder brother
右上 **migi ue** upper right
尻上 **shiria(gari)** rising (intonation)
立上 **ta(chi)a(garu)** stand up; start
　　ta(chi)nobo(ru) rise, ascend
目上 **meue** one's superior/senior
6 年上 **toshiue** older, senior
再上映 **saijōei** reshowing (of a movie)
此上 **ko(no)ue** furthermore; above this, better
　　ko(no)ue(mo nai) best, unsurpassed
返上 **henjō** send back, go without
同上 **dōjō** same as above, ditto
汲上 **ku(mi)a(geru)** pump/scoop/draw up
地上 **chijō** (on the) ground/surface; in this world
地上軍 **chijōgun** ground forces
至上 **shijō** supreme, highest
至上命令 **shijō meirei** supreme/inviolable command; categorical imperative
至上権 **shijōken** supremacy, sovereignty
吸上 **su(i)a(geru)** suck/pump up
吊上 **tsu(ri)a(geru)** hang up, suspend, hoist
　　tsuru(shi)a(ge) kangaroo court
向上 **kōjō** improvement, advancement
安上 **yasua(gari)** cheap, economical
机上 **kijō** desk-top, academic, theoretical, armchair
成上 **na(ri)a(garu)** rise to prominence
成上者 **na(ri)a(gari)mono** upstart, parvenu
7 身上 **shinjō** merit, strong point **shinshō** one's fortune/property; household
　　mi(no)ue one fortune/future; one's circumstances; one's background
身上判断 **mi(no)ue handan** telling a person's fortune
身上持 **shinshōmo(chi)** rich man; house-keeping
身上話 **mi(no)uebanashi** one's life story
伸上 **no(shi)a(garu)** rise in the world, move up
　　no(shi)a(geru) give a sound thrashing;

run aground **no(bi)a(garu)** stretch, stand on tiptoes
助上 **tasu(ke)a(geru)** help up; pick up, bring safely to land
走上 **hashi(ri)a(garu)** run up
抜上 **nu(ke)a(garu)** be bald in front
投上 **na(ge)a(garu)** toss/throw up
吹上 **fu(ki)a(geru)** blow up(ward); wash (ashore)
呈上 **teijō** present, offer
売上 **u(ri)a(ge)** sales
売上高 **uria(ge)daka** amount sold, sales
床上 **yukaue** on the floor, (flooded) above floor level **tokoa(ge)** recovery from illness
尾上 **o(no)e** mountain ridge/top
村上 **Murakami** (surname); (emperor, 946–967)
見上 **mia(geru)** look up at/to, admire
利上 **ria(ge)** raising the interest rate
禿上 **ha(ge)a(garu)** go bald, recede (hairline)
言上 **gonjō** tell, inform (a superior)
車上 **shajō** aboard (the train/vehicle)
車上荒 **shajōara(shi)** theft from a parked car
8 長上 **chōjō** one's elder, a superior
東上 **tōjō** go east to Tōkyō
刷上 **su(ri)a(garu)** be off the press, be printed
直上 **chokujō** immediately above
卓上 **takujō** table-top, desk-top
其上 **so(no) ue** on top of that, in addition
追上 **o(i)a(geru)** catch up to
逆上 **gyakujō** rush of blood to the head, dizziness, frenzy
泣上戸 **na(ki)jōgo** maudlin drinker
押上 **o(shi)a(geru)** push/force up, raise
抱上 **da(ki)a(geru)** take up in one's arms
呼上 **yo(bi)a(geru)** call out, call the roll
姉上 **aneue** elder sister
弥上 **iya(ga)ue (ni mo)** all the more
参上 **sanjō** visit, call on
突上 **tsu(ki)a(geru)** push/toss up; press/urge from below
炎上 **enjō** go up in flames, burst into flames
肩上 **kataa(ge)** shoulder tuck (in clothes)
取上 **to(ri)a(geru)** take up, adopt; take away
雨上 **amea(gari), amaa(gari)** after the rain
9 飛上 **to(bi)a(garu)** fly/jump up
巻上 **ma(ki)a(geru)** roll/wind up, raise; take away, rob
奏上 **sōjō** report to the emperor
乗上 **no(ri)a(geru)** run aground
俎上 **sojō** on the chopping block
造上 **tsuku(ri)a(geru)** make, build up, complete
途上 **tojō** on the way/road
風上 **kazakami** windward

2

亻亻子阝卩刂力又一宀十
→1 卜
ケ
ソ
厂辶冂几匚

浮上 **fujō** flotation, (submarine) surfacing; rise (in rank); (magnetic) levitation
洋上 **yōjō** on the ocean, seagoing, floating
海上 **kaijō** ocean, seagoing, marine
海上権 **kaijōken** sea power
持上 **mo(chi)a(geru)** raise, lift up; extol **mo(chi)a(garu)** be lifted; arise, happen
拾上 **hiro(i)a(geru)** pick up, pick out
咳上 **se(ki)a(geru)** have a fit of coughing; sob convulsively
屋上 **okujō** roof, rooftop
面上 **menjō** (expressed) on one's face
怒上戸 **oko(ri) jōgo** one who gets angry when drunk
砂上 **sajō** (built) on the sand
音上 **ne (o) a(geru)** give in, cry uncle
思上 **omo(i)a(garu)** be conceited
計上 **keijō** add up; appropriate
食上 **ku(i)a(geru)** eat (it) all up
10 値上 **nea(ge)** price hike **nea(gari)** higher price
陸上 **rikujō** on shore, land
陸上機 **rikujōki** land-based airplane
高上 **takaa(gari)** climb high; occupy a seat of honor; more expensive than expected
真上 **maue** right over, directly above
差上 **sa(shi)a(geru)** give; raise up
差上物 **sa(shi)a(ge)mono** gift
這上 **ha(i)a(garu)** crawl up
進上 **shinjō** give, present
起上 **o(ki)a(garu)** get up, rise
起上小法師 **o(ki)a(gari) koboshi** self-righting toy
捏上 **de(tchi)a(geru)** fabricate, trump/frame up
振上 **fu(ri)a(geru)** swing/lift up
席上 **sekijō** at the meeting, on the occasion
格上 **kakua(ge)** promotion, upgrading
胴上 **dōa(ge)** hoist (someone) shoulder-high
骨上 **kotsua(ge)** gathering (the deceased's) ashes
書上 **ka(ki)a(geru)** finish writing; write out
特上 **tokujō** finest, choicest
病上 **ya(mi)a(gari)** convalescence
紙上 **shijō** on paper; by letter; in the newspapers
笑上戸 **wara(i)jōgo** one who gets jolly when drunk; one who laughs readily
馬上 **bajō** on horseback, mounted
11 階上 **kaijō** upper floor, upstairs
運上 **hako(bi)a(geru)** carry/bring up
捲上 **maku(ri)a(geru)** roll up; drive up (the enemy onto the hill) **maku(shi)a(geru)** roll up **ma(ki)a(geru)** wind up, roll up; weigh (anchor); fling up (dust); cheat (money) out of (a person)
捩上 **ne(ji)a(geru)** screw up, twist

掬上 **suku(i)a(geru)** scoop/dip up
張上 **ha(ri)a(geru)** raise/strain (one's voice)
堂上 **dōjō** on the roof; court nobles
税上 **udatsu (ga) a(garanai)** have no hope of being a success in the world
祭上 **matsu(ri)a(geru)** exalt (someone)
救上 **suku(i)a(geru)** rescue, pick up
盛上 **mo(ri)a(geru)** heap/pile up
組上 **ku(mi)a(geru)** compose, make up (a page)
経上 **hea(garu)** climb up, rise
釣上 **tsu(ri)a(geru)** fish out, land; raise (one's eyes); keep/jack up (prices)
雪上 **setsujō** on the snow
雪上車 **setsujōsha** snowmobile
頂上 **chōjō** summit, peak, top, climax
12 勤上 **tsuto(me)a(geru)** do one's time of service
湖上 **kojō** on the lake
湯上 **yua(gari)** just after a bath
揉上 **mo(mi)a(ge)** sideburns
御上 **okami** the emperor; the government/authorities; one's lord; madam, the Mrs.
街上 **gaijō** on the street(s)
棟上 **munea(ge)** ridgepole raising
棟上式 **munea(ge)shiki** roof-raising ceremony
棚上 **tanaa(ge)** put on the shelf, shelve
極上 **gokujō** finest, top-quality
晴上 **ha(re)a(garu)** clear up
最上 **saijō** best, highest
最上川 **Mogamigawa** (river, Yamagata-ken)
焼上 **ya(ki)a(geru)** burn up; bake
無上 **mujō** supreme, greatest, highest
煮上 **ni(e)a(garu), nia(garu)** boil up, be thoroughly cooked
買上 **ka(i)a(geru)** buy (up/out)
買上品 **ka(i)a(ge)hin** purchases
絞上 **shibo(ri)a(geru)** gather up (a curtain); squeeze (money) out of
雲上 **unjō** above the clouds; the imperial court
雲上人 **unjōbito** a court noble
13 献上 **kenjō** presentation
殿上人 **tenjōbito, denjōbito** court noble
楼上 **rōjō** upper story, balcony
腫上 **ha(re)a(garu)** swell up
腰上 **koshia(ge)** tuck at the waist
照上 **te(ri)a(garu)** clear up after a rain
聖上 **seijō** the emperor
数上 **kazo(e)a(geru)** count up, enumerate
賃上 **chin'a(ge)** raise in wages
跳上 **ha(ne)a(garu), to(bi)a(garu)** jump up
路上 **rojō** on the road
14 僭上 **senjō** presumption, effrontery
誌上 **shijō** in a magazine
読上 **yo(mi)a(geru)** read aloud/out; finish reading

聞上手 **ki(ki)jōzu** a good listener
駆上 **ka(ke)a(garu)** run up(stairs)
15 舞上 **ma(i)a(garu)** fly up, soar
褒上 **ho(me)a(geru)** praise very highly
撫上 **na(de)a(geru)** comb back, stroke upward
締上 **shi(me)a(geru)** tie up
編上 **a(mi)a(ge)** lace up (boots)
編上靴 **a(mi)a(ge)gutsu** lace-up boots
縫上 **nu(i)a(ge)** a tuck (in a dress)
震上 **furu(e)a(garu)** tremble, shudder
16 壇上 **danjō** on the platform/stage/altar
磨上 **miga(ki)a(geru)** polish up
機上 **kijō** aboard the airplane
燃上 **mo(e)a(garu)** blaze up, burst into flames
積上 **tsu(mi)a(geru)** heap up
縛上 **shiba(ri)a(geru)** tie/truss up
築上 **kizu(ki)a(geru)** build up
頭上 **zujō** overhead
17 縮上 **chiji(mi)a(garu)** shrink, quail, wince
鍛上 **kita(e)a(geru)** become highly trained
19 繰上 **ku(ri)a(geru)** advance, move up (a date)
蹴上 **kea(geru)** kick up
20 競上 **se(ri)a(geru)** bid up (the price)
21 艦上 **kanjō** aboard (a warship)
躍上 **odo(ri)a(garu)** jump up, dance for joy
22 鰻上 **unaginobo(ri)** rise steadily

――――――― 3 ―――――――

1 一身上 **isshinjō** personal (affairs)
3 下克上 **gekokujō** the lower dominating the upper
下剋上 **gekokujō** the lower dominating the upper
下意上達 **kai jōtatsu** conveying the will of those who are governed to those in authority
4 切口上 **ki(ri)kōjō** stiff and formal language
文学上 **bungakujō** literary
文法上 **bunpōjō** grammatically
5 出来上 **dekia(garu)** be finished, be ready; be cut out for
外交上 **gaikōjō** diplomatic
立法上 **rippōjō** legislative
6 刑事上 **keijijō** criminal, penal
名義上 **meigijō** nominal, titular
7 体裁上 **teisaijō** for sake of appearances
技術上 **gijutsujō** technically
形而上 **keijijō** metaphysical
形而上学 **keijijōgaku** metaphysics
8 事実上 **jijitsujō** in fact, actually
其者上 **soreshaa(gari)** former geisha/prostitute
逃口上 **ni(ge)kōjō** excuse, evasion
法律上 **hōritsujō** legally
宗教上 **shūkyōjō** from the standpoint of religion

突立上 **tsu(t)ta(chi)a(garu)** jump to one's feet
9 便宜上 **bengijō** for convenience
軍事上 **gunjijō** military, strategic
前口上 **maekōjō** introductory remarks, prolog
政治上 **seijijō** political
10 都合上 **tsugōjō** for convenience
教育上 **kyōikujō** educationwise
財政上 **zaiseijō** fiscal
11 道徳上 **dōtoku-jō** from a moral viewpoint
経済上 **keizaijō** economically, financially
13 数字上 **sūjijō** numerically, in figures
数理上 **sūrijō** mathematically
想像上 **sōzōjō** imaginary
戦略上 **senryakujō** strategic
14 徳義上 **tokugijō** morally, ethically
構造上 **kōzōjō** structurally
慣用上 **kan'yōjō** by usage
慣例上 **kanreijō** conventionally, traditionally
15 論理上 **ronrijō** logically (speaking)
16 衛生上 **eiseijō** hygienic, sanitary

――――――― 4 ―――――――

7 芸術至上主義 **geijutsushijō shugi** art for art's sake
9 発展途上国 **hattentojōkoku** developing country
10 恋愛至上主義 **ren'ai-shijō shugi** love for love's sake

2m1.2 / 31

下 **KA, GE** low, lower; below, under **shita** lower part, below, under **shimo** lower part; downstream; the lower classes, the servants; lower part of the body **moto** under **sa(geru)** hang, suspend; lower, bring down; demote; move back; remove **sa(garu)** hang down; fall, go/come down; leave, withdraw; step back **kuda(ru)** come/go/get/step down; be given; be less than; have diarrhea **kuda(ranai)** trifling, worthless, absurd, inane **kuda(saru)** give, bestow **kuda(sai)** (indicator for polite imperative), please **kuda(su)** let down, lower; give, bestow, issue (an order), render (a judgment); have diarrhea **o(riru)** come/go/get/step down, get off (a train), get out of (a car); be discharged (from the body); be granted

――――――― 1 ―――――――

3 下大根 **o(roshi) daikon** grated daikon
下々 **shimojimo, shitajita** the lower classes, the common people
下女 **gejo** maidservant, (house)maid
下女下男 **gejo-genan** servants
下女中 **shimojochū** kitchen maid
下山 **gezan** come/go down a mountain; leave a temple

下士 **kashi** noncommissioned officer

下士官 **kashikan** noncommissioned officer

4 下刈 **shitaga(ri)** weeding

下水 **gesui** sewer, drain, drainage

下水道 **gesuidō** drainage/sewer system, drain

下水管 **gesuikan** sewer/drain (pipe)

下手 **heta** unskillful, poor at **shimote** lower part; left side of the stage (as seen from the audience) **shitate, shitade** humble position; alee

下手人 **geshunin** perpetrator, culprit, criminal

下手物 **getemono** low-quality article; strange things

下火 **shitabi** burning low; waning

下方 **kahō** lower part, downward, below

下心 **shitagokoro** ulterior motive

下戸 **geko** nondrinker, teetotaler

5 下半 **kahan** lower half

下半身 **kahanshin, shimohanshin** lower half of the body

下半期 **kahanki, shimohanki** the latter half (of the year)

下生 **shitaba(e)** underbrush, undergrowth

下仕事 **shitashigoto** preliminary work; subcontracted work

下付 **kafu** grant, issue

下句 **shimo(no)ku** the last part of a poem

下札 **sa(ge)fuda** tag, label

下目 **shitame** downward glance; look down on **saga(rì)me** on the decline; drooping eyes (temple side lower than nose side)

6 下吏 **kari** low-ranking official

下列車 **kuda(ri) ressha** train going away from the capital, down train

下地 **shitaji** groundwork; aptitude for; first coat(ing)

下向 **shitamu(ki)** downward look; downturn, decline

下名 **kamei** the undermentioned/undersigned

下劣 **geretsu** base, sordid, vulgar

下回 **shitamawa(ru)** be less than, fall short of **shitamawa(ri)** subordinate work; underling; utility actor

下旬 **gejun** 21st through last day of a month

7 下位 **kai** low rank, subordinate

下作 **gesaku** poorly made, of inferior quality

下克上 **gekokujō** the lower dominating the upper

下臣 **kashin** lowly retainer

下坂 **kuda(ri)zaka** downward slope, downhill

下役 **shitayaku** subordinate official, underling

下図 **shitazu** rough sketch **kazu** the lower illustration

下見 **shitami** preliminary inspection, preview; clapboard, siding

下町 **shitamachi** part of the city near the sea or river, downtown

下男 **genan** manservant

下車 **gesha** get off (a train/bus)

下足 **gesoku** footwear

下足料 **gesokuryō** footwear-checking charge

8 下垂 **kasui** hang down, droop

下命 **kamei** order, command

下刷 **shitazu(ri)** proof printing

下押 **shitao(su)** decline, sag, drop

下拵 **shitagoshira(e)** preliminary arrangements

下弦 **kagen** last quarter (phase of the moon)

下肥 **shimogoe** night soil, manure

下肢 **kashi** lower limbs, legs

下物 **o(ri)mono** uterine discharge, menstruation; afterbirth

下取 **shitado(ri)** trade-in

9 下巻 **gekan** last volume (of two or three)

下乗 **gejō** get off (a horse), get out of (a car)

下降 **kakō** descend, fall, sink

下降線 **kakōsen** downward curve

下院 **kain** the Lower House (of a legislature)

下段 **gedan, kadan** lowest step/tier, lower column/part

下品 **gehin** vulgar, coarse, gross

下剋上 **gekokujō** the lower dominating the upper

下草 **shitakusa, shitagusa** grass/weeds growing in the shade of a tree

下屋敷 **shimoyashiki** (daimyo's) villa

下相談 **shitasōdan** preliminary talks/arrangements

下界 **gekai** this world, here below

下卑 **gebi** vulgar, coarse

下級 **kakyū** lower grade/class, junior, subordinate

下級生 **kakyūsei** underclassman

下級審 **kakyūshin** lower court

下級職 **kakyūshoku** subordinate post

10 下値 **shitane** lower price

下部 **kabu** lower part, subordinate

下剤 **gezai** laxative

下流 **karyū** downstream; lower-class

下唇 **shitakuchibiru, kashin** lower lip

下帯 **shitaobi** loincloth, waistcloth

下座 **geza** squat, kneel **shimoza** lower seat

下書 **shitaga(ki)** rough draft

下疳 **gekan** chancre

下紐 **shitahimo** undersash, belt

下記 **kaki** the following

下馬 **geba** dismount

下馬評 **gebahyō** outsiders' irresponsible talk, rumor

11 下野 **geya** retire from public life **Shimotsuke** (ancient kuni, Tochigi-ken)

下宿 **geshuku** lodging, room and board; boarding house
下宿人 **geshukunin** lodger, boarder
下宿屋 **geshukuya** boardinghouse
下宿料 **geshukuryō** room-and-board charge
下情 **kajō** conditions of the common people
下略 **geryaku** the rest omitted, ... (in quoting)
下船 **gesen** disembark, go ashore
下問 **kamon** inquire, consult
12 下着 **shitagi** underwear
下渡 **sa(ge)wata(su)** grant; release
下場 **o(ri)ba** place to get off, disembarking point
下落 **geraku** fall, decline, deteriorate
下葉 **shitaba** lower leaves
下検分 **shitakenbun** preliminary examination
下検査 **shitakensa** preliminary inspection
下脹 **shimobuku(re)** swelling on the lower part of the face/body
下期 **shimoki** the latter/second half (of the year)
下痢 **geri** diarrhea
下絵 **shitae** rough sketch
下歯 **shitaba** lower teeth
下等 **katō** low, lower (animals/plants), inferior, base, vulgar
13 下働 **shitabatara(ki)** subordinate work; assistant, servant
下僧 **gesō** lowly priest
下準備 **shitajunbi** preliminary arrangements
下塗 **shitanu(ri)** undercoat(ing)
下幕 **sa(ge)maku** drop curtain
下腹 **shitabara, shitahara, shita(p)para** abdomen, belly
下腹部 **kafukubu** abdomen
下意上達 **kai jōtatsu** conveying the will of those who are governed to those in authority
下馴 **shitanara(shi)** training, warming up
14 下僕 **geboku** servant
下僚 **karyō** subordinates, petty official
下獄 **gegoku** be sent to prison
下髪 **sa(ge)gami** hair hanging down the back
下層 **kasō** lower layer, substratum; lower classes
下端 **katan** lower end
shita(p)pa lower position; underling
下種 **gesu** person of lowly rank, mean person
下種根性 **gesu konjō** mean feelings
下緒 **sageo** sword cord
下総 **Shimousa** (ancient kuni, Chiba-ken)
下関 **Shimonoseki** (city, Yamaguchi-ken)
下駄 **geta** clogs
下駄履住宅 **getaba(ki) jūtaku** apartment building whose first floor is occupied by stores and businesses

下駄箱 **getabako** shoe cabinet
15 下履 **shitaba(ki)** footwear; underpants
下敷 **shitaji(ki)** mat, desk pad; pinned under, crushed beneath; model, pattern
下請 **shitauke** subcontract
下請負 **shitaukeoi** subcontract
下請業者 **shitauke gyōsha** subcontractor
下調 **shitashira(be)** preliminary investigation; prepare (lessons)
下賜 **kashi** imperial grant/gift
下賤 **gesen** humble birth/origin
16 下薬 **geyaku, kuda(shi)gusuri** laxative **o(roshi)gusuri** an abortifacient
下膨 **shimobuku(re)** swelling of the lower part of the face/body
下稽古 **shitageiko** rehearsal, run-through
下積 **shitazu(mi)** goods piled underneath; lowest social classes
18 下瞼 **shitamabuta** lower eyelid
下顎 **shitaago, kagaku** lower jaw

――――― 2 ―――――

3 川下 **kawashimo** downstream
上下 **jōge** top and bottom, upper and lower; volumes 1 and 2 (of a two-volume set), parts 1 and 2 (of a two-part serialization); inbound (toward Tōkyō) and outbound; rise and fall, go up and down; the high and the low, ruler and ruled, government and people **shōka** ruler and ruled **kamishimo** the high and the low, government and people; the upper and lower halves of the body **a(gari)sa(gari)** rise and fall, fluctuations **a(ge)sa(ge)** raising and lowering; praising and blaming; rising and falling, intonation **a(ge)o(roshi)** raising and lowering; loading and unloading
上下水道 **jōgesuidō** water and sewer service
上下動 **jōgedō** up-and-down/vertical motion
下下 **shimojimo, shitajita** the lower classes, the common people
土下座 **dogeza** bow while kneeling
口下手 **kuchibeta** awkward tongue, poor talker
4 天下 **amakuda(ri)** descent from heaven; employment of retired officials by companies they used to regulate **tenka, tenga, ame(ga)shita** under heaven; the whole country, the public/world; the reins of government; having one's own way
天下一 **tenka-ichi** unique, matchless
天下一品 **tenka ippin** best article under heaven
天下分目 **tenka-wa(ke)me** decisive, fateful
天下無双 **tenka-musō** unique, unequaled

天下無比 **tenka-muhi** unique, incomparable
切下 **ki(ri)sa(ge)** reduction, devaluation
手下 **teshita** subordinate, follower
引下 **hi(ki)sa(garu)** withdraw, leave
　　 hi(ki)o(rosu) pull down
木下 **Kinoshita** (surname)
月下 **gekka** in the moonlight
月下氷人 **gekka hyōjin** matchmaker, go-between, cupid
5 以下 **ika** or less, less than; under, below; the following
皮下 **hika** subcutaneous
皮下注射 **hika chūsha** hypodermic injection
払下 **hara(i)sa(geru)** sell, dispose of
払下品 **hara(i)sa(ge)hin** articles sold off by the government
打下 **u(chi)o(rosu)** bring (a club) down on, strike a blow
右下 **migi shita** lower right
好下物 **kōkabutsu** favorite dish/snack
尻下 **shirisa(gari)** falling off toward the end
白下 **shiroshita** treacle, molasses
目下 **meshita** one's subordinate/junior
　　 mokka at present, now
6 年下 **toshishita** younger, junior
西下 **saika** go west from Tōkyō (to Kansai)
再下付 **saikafu** regrant, reissue, renewal
地下 **chika** underground; basement
地下水 **chikasui** underground water
地下牢 **chikarō** underground dungeon
地下足袋 **jika tabi** split-toed heavy-cloth work shoes
地下茎 **chikakei** rhizome
地下室 **chikashitsu** basement, cellar
地下道 **chikadō** underground passage
地下街 **chikagai** underground shopping mall
地下鉄 **chikatetsu** subway
地下線 **chikasen** underground cable/wire
扱下 **ko(ki)oro(su)** excoriate, criticize severely
吐下 **ha(ki)kuda(shi)** vomiting and purging
吊下 **tsu(ri)sa(garu)** hang, dangle, be suspended
灯下 **tōka** beneath the lamp, (read) by lamplight
成下 **na(ri)sa(garu)** come down in the world, be reduced to
虫下 **mushikuda(shi)** medicine for intestinal worms
7 低下 **teika** decline, go down, fall
却下 **kyakka** reject, dismiss
臣下 **shinka** subject, retainer, vassal
沈下 **chinka** sinking, subsidence, settling
走下 **hashi(ri)kuda(ru), hashi(ri)o(riru)** run down
投下 **tōka** throw down, drop; invest

吹下 **fu(ki)o(rosu)** blow down(ward)
床下 **yukashita** below the floor
見下 **mio(rosu)** command a view of
　　 mikuda(su) look down on, despise
　　 misa(geru) look down on, despise
見下果 **misa(ge)ha(teru)** look down on, scorn
　　 misa(ge)ha(teta) contemptible, low-down
利下 **risa(ge)** lowering the interest rate
言下 **genka** promptly, readily
足下 **ashimoto** gait, pace; at one's feet; (watch your) step　**sokka** at one's feet
8 垂下 **suika, ta(re)sa(garu)** hang down, dangle, droop
東下 **azuma kuda(ri)** journey to the provinces east of the old capital Kyōto
刻下 **kokka** the present
版下 **hanshita** art boards, mechanicals, camera-ready copy
治下 **chika** under the rule of
押下 **o(shi)sa(geru)** push/force down, depress
　　 ōka press (a key)
空下手 **karaheta, kara(p)peta** utterly inept
府下 **fuka** suburban districts
取下 **to(ri)sa(geru)** withdraw, dismiss
　　 to(ri)o(rosu) take down
門下 **monka** one's pupil
門下生 **monkasei** one's pupil
9 飛下 **tobio(ri)** jumping off
陛下 **Heika** His/Her Majesty
降下 **kōka** descend, fall, drop
南下 **nanka** go south
前下 **maesa(gari)** front low(er than back)
風下 **kazashimo** leeward
泉下 **senka** hades; the next world
城下 **jōka** castle town; seat of a daimyo's government
城下町 **jōkamachi** castle town
宣下 **senge** imperial proclamation
県下 **kenka** in the prefecture
庭下駄 **niwageta** garden clogs
昼下 **hirusa(gari)** early afternoon
卑下 **hige** humble oneself
食下 **ku(i)sa(garu)** hang on to, refuse to relent
10 値下 **nesa(ge)** price reduction
　　 nesa(gari) price decline, lower prices
都下 **toka** in the capital
部下 **buka** a subordinate, the people working under one
高下 **kōge** rise and fall, fluctuations; rank, grade, quality
高下駄 **takageta** high clogs/geta
真下 **mashita** right under, directly below
這下 **ha(i)o(riru)** crawl down
荷下 **nio(roshi)** unloading, discharge
峻下剤 **shungezai** powerful laxative

格下 **kakusa(ge)** demotion, downgrading
脇下 **waki (no) shita** armpit; armhole
脂下 **yanisa(garu)** put on airs, be self-complacent
時下 **jika** now, at present
書下 **ka(ki)kuda(su)** write down
ka(ki)o(rosu) write a new novel/play
軒下 **nokishita** under the eaves
配下 **haika** followers, subordinates
11 階下 **kaika** lower floor, downstairs
掘下 **ho(ri)sa(geru)** dig down, delve into
猊下 **geika** Your/His Holiness, Right Reverend
廊下 **rōka** corridor, hall
梧下 **goka** To: (addressee)
脚下 **kyakka** at one's feet
脳下垂体 **nōkasuitai** pituitary gland
現下 **genka** the present time
眼下 **ganka** below one's eyes
組下 **kumishita** group member; one's subordinates
雪下 **yukio(roshi)** clearing snow off a roof; snowy wind blowing down a mountain
12 傘下 **sanka** affiliated, subsidiary
御下問 **gokamon** emperor's question
落下 **rakka** fall, descend, drop
落下傘 **rakkasan** parachute
落下傘兵 **rakkasanhei** paratrooper
腋下 **ekika, waki(no)shita** armpit
最下 **saika** lowest; worst
最下位 **saikai** lowest rank
最下層 **saikasō** lowest class (of people)
無下 **muge (ni)** (refuse) flatly, (denounce) roundly
貴下 **kika** you
貸下 **ka(shi)sa(geru)** lend
飲下 **no(mi)kuda(su)** swallow, gulp down
13 幕下 **makushita** junior-rank sumo wrestler
bakka vassal; staff; follower
靴下 **kutsushita** socks, stockings
靴下止 **kutsushitado(me)** garters
靴下留 **kutsushitado(me)** garters
殿下 **Denka** His/Your Highness
腹下 **harakuda(shi)** diarrhea; laxative
跳下 **to(bi)o(ri)** jumping off
零下 **reika** below zero, subzero
14 滴下 **tekika** drip, trickle down
旗下 **kika** under the banner of
種下 **taneo(roshi)** sowing, seeding, planting
鼻下 **bika** under the nose　**hana (no) shita** area between nose and mouth, upper lip
鼻下長 **bikachō** amorous man　**hana (no) shita (ga) naga(i)** easily charmed by women
管下 **kanka** under the jurisdiction of
読下 **yo(mi)kuda(su)** read it through

聞下手 **ki(ki)beta** a poor listener
閣下 **kakka** Your Excellency
駆下 **ka(ke)o(riru), ka(ke)kuda(ru)** run down(stairs)
15 撫下 **na(de)o(rosu)** stroke down
麾下 **kika** under one's command
膝下 **shikka** at the knees (of one's parents)
緩下剤 **kangezai** laxative
縁下 **en(no)shita** under the floor
駒下駄 **komageta** low clogs
18 臍下丹田 **seika-tanden** center of the abdomen
19 嚥下 **enge, enka** swallowing
繰下 **ku(ri)sa(geru)** move ahead, defer
願下 **nega(i)sa(geru)** withdraw a request

──────── 3 ────────

3 上中下 **jō-chū-ge** good-fair-poor; first-second-third class; volumes/parts 1, 2, 3 (of a 3-volume/3-part series)
上意下達 **jōi katatsu** conveying the will of those in authority to those who are governed
下女下男 **gejo-genan** servants
女天下 **onnadenka** a woman who is boss
4 支配下 **shihaika** under the control of
5 氷点下 **hyōtenka** below the freezing point, below zero (Celsius)
6 両陛下 **Ryōheika** Their Majesties
妃殿下 **hidenka** Her Highness
7 形而下 **keijika** physical, material
形而下学 **keijikagaku** the physical sciences
9 急降下 **kyūkōka** drop rapidly; dive, swoop
途中下車 **tochū gesha** stopover, layover
指揮下 **shikika** under one's command
独天下 **hito(ri)tenka, hito(ri)denka** sole figure, unchallenged master
10 素人下宿 **shirōto geshuku** boarding house
11 軟性下疳 **nansei gekan** soft chancre
12 満天下 **mantenka** the whole world
渡廊下 **wata(ri) rōka** covered passageway
13 勢力下 **seiryokuka** under the influence/power of
溜飲下 **ryūin (ga) sa(garu)** feel satisfaction
戦時下 **senjika** during the war, wartime
15 影響下 **eikyōka** under the influence of
監督下 **kantokuka** under the jurisdiction of
鞶穀下 **renkoku (no) moto** the imperial capital
17 嬶天下 **kakādenka** the wife being boss

──────── 4 ────────

3 三日天下 **mikka tenka** short-lived reign
4 天皇陛下 **Tennō Heika** His Majesty the Emperor
7 臣籍降下 **shinseki kōka** (royalty) becoming subjects

2

亻
冫
子
阝
卩
刂
力
又
宀
亠
十
卜 1
夕
丷
厂
辶
門
几
匚

9 急転直下 **kyūten-chokka** sudden change, sudden turn (toward a solution)

皇后陛下 **Kōgō Heika** Her Majesty the Empress

────────── 2 ──────────

2m2.1

BOKU hit, tap

支

2m2.2 / 477

止

SHI stop **to(maru)** (come to a) stop **to(meru)** (bring/put to a) stop
todo(maru) (come to a) stop; be limited to **todo(meru)** (bring/put to a) stop; limit oneself to **todo(me)** finishing blow
ya(mu) stop, (come to an) end, be over
ya(meru) stop, (put to an) end, discontinue
yo(su) stop, desist from, cut it out

────────── 1 ──────────

4 止水 **shisui** still water
止木 **to(mari)gi** perch, roost
5 止処 **to(me)do** termination, end
6 止血 **shiketsu** stopping/stanching bleeding
止血剤 **shiketsuzai** hemostatic drug, styptic agent
7 止役 **to(me)yaku** role of stopping a quarrel, peacemaker
8 止金 **to(me)gane** clasp, latch
9 止音器 **shionki** (piano) damper
11 止宿 **shishuku** lodging
止宿人 **shishukunin** lodger
12 止痛剤 **shitsūzai** painkiller
止間 **ya(mi)ma** lull
18 止難 **ya(mi)gata(i)** hard to stop, compelling

────────── 2 ──────────

3 口止 **kuchido(me)** forbid to speak of
口止料 **kuchido(me)ryō** hush money
4 中止 **chūshi** discontinue, suspend, stop, call off, cancel
5 打止 **u(chi)to(meru)** kill, shoot/bring down **u(chi)do(me)** end (of an entertainment/ match) **u(chi)ya(mu)** stop
札止 **fudado(me)** Sold Out
立止 **ta(chi)do(maru)** stop, halt, stand still
6 休止 **kyūshi** pause, suspension, dormancy
休止符 **kyūshifu** rest (in music)
防止 **bōshi** prevention
色止 **irodo(me)** color fixing
行止 **yu(ki)do(mari), i(ki)do(mari)** dead end, impasse
血止 **chido(me)** a styptic
7 阻止 **soshi** obstruct, hinder, deter, check

抑止 **yokushi** deter stave off
売止 **u(ri)do(me)** suspension of sales
車止 **kurumado(me)** Closed to Vehicles; railway buffer stop
足止 **ashido(me)** keep indoors; induce to stay
8 制止 **seishi** control, restrain, keep in check
受止 **u(ke)to(meru)** stop, catch; parry, ward off
泣止 **na(ki)ya(mu)** stop crying
波止場 **hatoba** wharf, pier
押止 **o(shi)to(meru)** stop, check, prevent
抱止 **da(ki)to(meru)** hold (someone) back
突止 **tsu(ki)to(meru)** ascertain
底止 **teishi** come to an end
9 降止 **fu(ri)ya(mu)** stop raining/snowing
咳止 **sekido(me)** cough medicine/lozenge
客止 **kyakudo(me)** turning away customers, full house
食止 **ku(i)to(meru)** check, stem, curb, hold back
10 射止 **ito(meru)** shoot (an animal) dead; win (a girl)
差止 **sa(shi)to(meru)** prohibit, forbid, ban
挙止 **kyoshi** bearing, carriage, demeanor
笑止 **shōshi** laughable, ludicrous
笑止千万 **shōshi-senban** ridiculous, absurd
11 停止 **teishi** suspension, stop, halt, cessation
終止 **shūshi** come to an end
終止符 **shūshifu** full stop, period, end
雪止 **yukido(me)** barrier against snow, snowshed
12 堰止 **se(ki)to(meru)** dam up; check, stem
廃止 **haishi** abolition, abrogation
痛止 **ita(mi)do(me)** painkiller
歯止 **hado(me)** pawl; brake
13 滑止 **sube(ri)do(me)** tire chains; nonskid heels
禁止 **kinshi** prohibition
禁止令 **kinshirei** prohibition (decree), ban
14 静止 **seishi** still, standstill, at rest, stationary, static state
静止画 **seishiga** still life
静止衛星 **seishi eisei** stationary satellite
煽止 **ao(ri)do(me)** doorstop
15 撃止 **u(chi)to(meru)** kill, bring down
黙止 **mokushi** remain silent, leave as is
輪止 **wado(me)** wheel block; linchpin
踏止 **fu(mi)todo(maru)** stand one's ground, hold one's own
16 諫止 **kanshi** dissuade from
錆止 **sabido(me)** anticorrosive, rust preventive
18 鎖止 **kusarido(me)** sprocket
19 繋止 **tsuna(gi)to(meru)** connect; save (a life)
23 黴止 **kabido(me)** anti-mildew preparation, fungicide

─────────── 3 ───────────

3 小休止 **shōkyūshi** brief recess, short break
5 乎古止点 **okototen** marks to aid in reading
 Chinese classics
8 往来止 **ōraido(me)** Road Closed
 明鏡止水 **meikyō-shisui** serene state of mind
9 通行止 **tsūkōdo(me)** Road Closed, No
 Thoroughfare
13 靴下止 **kutsushitado(me)** garters

─────────── 4 ───────────

4 水害防止 **suigai bōshi** flood prevention
5 立入禁止 **tachiiri kinshi** Keep Out
11 張紙禁止 **ha(ri)gami kinshi** Post No Bills

─────────── 5 ───────────

15 諸車通行止 **Shosha Tsūkōdo(me)** No
 Thoroughfare

2m2.3

丐 KAI, ko(u) ask for, beg

─────────── 3 ───────────

2m3.1 / 83

外
GAI outside, external; foreign
GE outside, external **soto** outside;
outdoors **hoka** other **hazu(su)** take
off, remove, disconnect; miss, fail in;
avoid, leave (one's desk) **hazu(reru)** come/slip
off, be/get out of place, be disconnected; miss
(the target)

─────────── 1 ───────────

2 外人 **gaijin** foreigner
 外力 **gairyoku** external force
4 外辺 **gaihen** environs, outskirts
 外方 **gaihō** outward
 soppo (look) the other way
 外心 **gaishin** center of the circumscribed
 circle; double-mindedness
5 外出 **gaishutsu, sotode** go/step out
 外出中 **gaishutsuchū** while away/out, out
 (of the office)
 外出好 **gaishutsuzu(ki)** gadabout
 外出嫌 **gaishutsugira(i)** a stay-at-home
 外史 **gaishi** unofficial history
 外皮 **gaihi** outer cover, crust, shell, husk, skin
 外圧 **gaiatsu** external/outside pressure
 外用 **gaiyō** for external use/application
 外用薬 **gaiyōyaku** medicine to be applied
 externally (rather than ingested or
 injected)
 外字 **gaiji** kanji not officially recognized for
 everyday use; foreign letters/language
 外字紙 **gaijishi** foreign-language newspaper

外字新聞 **gaiji shinbun** foreign-language
 newspaper
6 外気 **gaiki** the open/outside air
 外伝 **gaiden** lateral biography; anecdote
 外交 **gaikō** diplomacy, foreign relations
 外交上 **gaikōjō** diplomatic
 外交団 **gaikōdan** diplomatic corps
 外交官 **gaikōkan** diplomat
 外交的 **gaikōteki** diplomatic
 外交界 **gaikōkai** diplomatic circles
 外交員 **gaikōin** canvasser, door-to-door/
 traveling salesman
 外交術 **gaikōjutsu** diplomacy, diplomatic skill
 外交筋 **gaikōsuji** diplomatic sources
 外地 **gaichi** overseas (territory)
 外向 **gaikō** extroverted, outgoing
 外向性 **gaikōsei** extroverted, outgoing
 外向型 **gaikōgata** outgoing type, extrovert
 外因 **gaiin** external cause, exogenous
 外米 **gaimai** foreign/imported rice
 外耳 **gaiji** external/outer ear
 外耳炎 **gaijien** inflammation of the outer ear,
 otitis externa
7 外来 **gairai** foreign, imported
 外来者 **gairaisha** person from abroad
 外来患者 **gairai kanja** outpatient
 外来語 **gairaigo** word of foreign origin,
 loanword
 外角 **gaikaku** external angle; outside (corner)
 外形 **gaikei** external form, appearance
 外形的 **gaikeiteki** external, outward
 外局 **gaikyoku** bureau whose director has
 authority independent of the ministry
 外囲 **sotogako(i)** outer fence
 外見 **gaiken** external/outward appearance
 外車 **gaisha** foreign car
8 外事 **gaiji** foreign affairs
 外郎 **uirō** (a rice-jelly confection)
 外泊 **gaihaku** overnight stay
 外注 **gaichū** order from outside suppliers (cf.
 内製)
 外征 **gaisei** foreign expedition/campaign
 外径 **gaikei** outside diameter
 外苑 **gaien** outer garden/park
 外国 **gaikoku** foreign country; foreign
 外国人 **gaikokujin** foreigner
 外国風 **gaikokufū** foreign style/manners
 外国船 **gaikokusen** foreign ship
 外国債 **gaikokusai** foreign loan
 外国語 **gaikokugo** foreign language
 外的 **gaiteki** external, outward
 外物 **gaibutsu** external object, foreign matter
9 外信部 **gaishinbu** foreign-news department
 外郭 **gaikaku** outer wall; contour, outlines
 外郭団体 **gaikaku dantai** auxiliary organization

2

外洋 **gaiyō** ocean, open sea
外海 **gaikai, sotoumi** open sea, the high seas
外客 **gaikyaku** foreign visitor, tourist
外面 **gaimen** exterior, outward appearance, surface
外相 **gaishō** the Foreign Minister
外為法 **Gaitamehō** Foreign Exchange (and Foreign Trade) Control Law (short for 外国為替及び外国貿易管理法)
外科 **geka** surgery
外科医 **gekai** surgeon
外界 **gaikai** outside world; physical world; externals
外食 **gaishoku** eating out
10 外套 **gaitō** overcoat
外部 **gaibu** the outside, external
外遊 **gaiyū** foreign travel/trip
外挿 **gaisō** extrapolation
外宮 **Gekū, Gegū** Outer Shrine of Ise
外紙 **gaishi** foreign-language newspaper
11 外野 **gaiya** outfield
外野手 **gaiyashu** outfielder
外野席 **gaiyaseki** bleachers
外側 **sotogawa** outside, exterior
外商 **gaishō** foreign merchant
外道 **gedō** heresy; heretic
外堀 **sotobori** outer moat
外接 **gaisetsu** be circumscribed (in geometry)
外接円 **gaisetsuen** circumscribed circle
外殻 **gaikaku** shell, crust
外務 **gaimu** foreign affairs
外務大臣 **gaimu daijin** Minister of Foreign Affairs
外務省 **Gaimushō** Ministry of Foreign Affairs
外患 **gaikan** foreign/external troubles
外船 **gaisen** foreign ship
外貨 **gaika** foreign currency; imported goods
外貨債 **gaikasai** foreign-currency bond
12 外勤 **gaikin** outside duty, outdoor work
外塀 **sotobei** outer wall
13 外傷 **gaishō** external wound, visible injury
外債 **gaisai** foreign loan/bond/debt
外蒙 **Gaimō** Outer Mongolia
外蒙古 **Gaimōko, Soto Mōko** Outer Mongolia
外資 **gaishi** foreign capital
外電 **gaiden** foreign cable/dispatch
14 外層 **gaisō** outer layer
外構 **sotogama(e)** exterior, outward appearance
外様 **tozama** outside the group; non-Tokugawa daimyo
外様大名 **tozama daimyō** non-Tokugawa daimyo
外貌 **gaibō** external appearance, exterior, one's looks

外語 **gaigo** foreign language
外聞 **gaibun** reputation, respectability
15 外敵 **gaiteki** foreign enemy
外線 **gaisen** outside (telephone) line; outside wiring
外輪 **gairin** outer wheel; hubcap
外輪山 **gairinzan** the outer crater, somma
外輪船 **gairinsen** paddlewheel steamer
16 外壁 **gaiheki** outer wall
17 外濠 **sotobori** outer moat
18 外観 **gaikan** external appearance
外題 **gedai** title (of a play); play, piece
20 外鰐 **sotowani** walking with the feet pointing outward, frog-footed

———————————— 2 ————————————

3 口外 **kōgai** divulge, reveal, tell
4 天外 **tengai** beyond the heavens; farthest regions
内外 **naigai** inside and outside; domestic and foreign; approximately **uchi-soto** inside and out
中外 **chūgai** domestic and foreign, home and abroad
分外 **bungai** inordinate, excessive
心外 **shingai** unexpected; regrettable
戸外 **kogai** outdoor, open-air
5 以外 **igai** except, other than
存外 **zongai** contrary to expectations; beyond expectations
市外 **shigai** outside the city limits; suburbs
号外 **gōgai** an extra (edition of a newspaper)
6 在外 **zaigai** overseas, abroad
在外邦人 **zaigai hōjin** Japanese living abroad
当外 **a(tari)hazu(re)** hit or miss, risk **a(te)hazu(re)** a disappointment
7 対外 **taigai** foreign, international, overseas
対外的 **taigaiteki** external
赤外線 **sekigaisen** infrared rays
学外 **gakugai** outside the school, off-campus
局外 **kyokugai** the outside
局外中立 **kyokugai chūritsu** neutrality
局外者 **kyokugaisha** outsider, onlooker
社外 **shagai** outside the company
社外船 **shagaisen** tramp steamer/vessel
町外 **machihazu(re)** outskirts of town
言外 **gengai** unexpressed, implied
車外 **shagai** outside the car/vehicle
8 例外 **reigai** exception
限外 **gengai** outside the limits, excess, extra
郊外 **kōgai** suburbs, outskirts
並外 **namihazu(re)** out of the ordinary
法外 **hōgai** exorbitant, preposterous
治外法権 **chigaihōken** extraterritoriality
国外 **kokugai** outside the country, abroad
枠外 **wakugai** beyond the limits

的外 **matohazu(re)** wide of the mark; out of focus

取外 **to(ri)hazu(su)** remove, dismantle

門外 **mongai** outside the gate; outside one's specialty

門外漢 **mongaikan** outsider; layman

9 院外 **ingai** outside congress/parliament, outside the institution

院外団 **ingaidan** lobbying group

院外者 **ingaisha** lobbyist; persons outside congress/parliament

除外 **jogai** exception

除外例 **jogairei** an exception

海外 **kaigai** overseas, abroad

海外事情 **kaigai jijō** foreign news

海外版 **kaigaiban** overseas edition

海外発展 **kaigai hatten** overseas expansion

海外渡航 **kaigai tokō** foreign travel

城外 **jōgai** outside the castle

室外 **shitsugai** outdoor(s)

県外 **kengai** outside the prefecture

度外 **dohazu(re)** extraordinary, excessive

度外視 **dogaishi** disregard, ignore

屋外 **okugai** outdoor(s)

思外 **omo(ino)hoka** unexpectedly, more than expected

10 殊外 **koto(no)hoka** exceedingly, exceptionally

部外 **bugai** outside

部外秘 **bugaihi** to be kept secret from outsiders, Restricted

部外者 **bugaisha** outsider

埒外 **rachigai** beyond the pale, beyond bounds

員外 **ingai** nonmembership

案外 **angai** unexpectedly

桁外 **ketahazu(re)** extraordinary

格外 **kakuhazu(re)** ungraded, irregular

格外品 **kakugaihin** nonstandard goods

校外 **kōgai** outside the school, off-campus, extra-curricular

校外生 **kōgaisei** extension/correspondence course student

時外 **tokihazu(re)** unseasonable, untimely, inopportune

11 疎外 **sogai** shun, avoid someone's company, estrange

野外 **yagai** the open air, outdoor

渉外 **shōgai** public relations, liaison

域外 **ikigai** outside the area

掛外 **ka(ke)hazu(shi)** hanging up and taking down, engaging and disengaging (gears)

排外 **haigai** anti-foreign

窓外 **sōgai** out(side) the window

理外 **rigai** transcendental, supernatural

望外 **bōgai** unexpected

船外機 **sengaiki** outboard motor

12 遣外 **kengai** sent abroad

港外 **kōgai** outside the harbor

場外 **jōgai** outside the premises/grounds/hall

圏外 **kengai** outside the range/orbit of

番外 **bangai** extra; oversize

紫外線 **shigaisen** ultraviolet rays

等外 **tōgai** non-winner, also-ran, offgrade

13 意外 **igai** unexpected, surprising

14 選外 **sengai** left out, not chosen

選外佳作 **sengai kasaku** honorable mention

構外 **kōgai** outside the premises

管外 **kangai** outside the jurisdiction of

聞外 **ki(ki)hazu(su)** not hear it all, mishear

閣外 **kakugai** outside the cabinet

15 慮外 **ryogai** unexpected; rude

課外 **kagai** extracurricular

課外活動 **kagai katsudō** extracurricular activities

諸外国 **shogaikoku** foreign countries

論外 **rongai** irrelevant

踏外 **fu(mi)hazu(su)** miss one's footing

20 欄外 **rangai** margin (of a page)

───── 3 ─────

3 口腔外科 **kōkō geka** oral surgery

4 予想外 **yosōgai** unexpected, unforeseen

予算外 **yosangai** outside the budget, off-budget

5 正課外 **seikagai** extracurricular

6 仲間外 **nakamahazu(re)** being left out

在留外人 **zairyū gaijin** foreign residents

10 時候外 **jikōhazu(re)** unseasonable

11 問題外 **mondaigai** beside the point, irrelevant

13 意想外 **isōgai** unexpected, surprising

15 調子外 **chōshihazu(re)** discord, out of tune

16 整形外科 **seikei geka** plastic surgery

───── 4 ─────

8 奇想天外 **kisō-tengai** original concept

2m3.2 / 1706

占

SEN, shi(meru) occupy, hold
urana(u) tell fortunes

───── 1 ─────

6 占有 **sen'yū** exclusive possession, occupancy

8 占拠 **senkyo** occupation

占者 **uranaisha** fortuneteller

占取 **senshu** pre-occupation, preoccupancy

9 占星術 **senseijutsu** astrology

10 占師 **uranaishi** fortuneteller

14 占領 **senryō** occupation, capture; have all to oneself

占領地 **senryōchi** occupied territory

占領軍 **senryōgun** army of occupation

——————— 2 ———————

4 辻占 **tsujiura** fortunetelling slips of paper, omen

9 独占 **dokusen** exclusive possession; monopoly

独占的 **dokusenteki** monopolistic

星占 **hoshiurana(i)** astrology, horoscope

12 買占 **ka(i)shi(meru)** buy up, corner (the market)

13 夢占 **yume urana(i)** fortunetelling by dreams

14 寡占 **kasen** oligopoly

——————— 3 ———————

2 人相占 **ninsō urana(i)** divination by facial features

2m3.3 / 275

正 **SEI, SHŌ** correct, right, just; straight; principal, original; positive (number)
tada(shii) correct, right, proper
tada(su) correct, rectify
masa (ni) surely, indeed, truly; precisely
masa(shiku) surely, indeed, truly

——————— 1 ———————

3 正三角形 **seisankakkei, seisankakukei** equilateral triangle

正々堂々 **seisei-dōdō** fair and square, open and aboveboard

4 正元 **Shōgen** (era, 1259–1260)

正中 **seichū** the exact middle **Shōchū** (era, 1324–1326)

正中線 **seichūsen** median line

正文 **seibun** the (official) text

正午 **shōgo** noon

正反対 **seihantai** the exact opposite

正月 **shōgatsu** the New Year; January

正方形 **seihōkei** square

5 正北 **seihoku** due north

正本 **sei/shōhon** an attested copy; the original (of a document) **shōhon** playbook, script; unabridged book

正甲板 **seikanpan** main deck

正史 **seishi** authentic history

正平 **Shōhei** (era, 1346–1370)

正比例 **seihirei** in direct proportion/ratio

正号 **seigō** plus sign (+)

正犯 **seihan** principal offense/offender

正犯者 **seihansha** principal offender

正字 **seiji** correct form of a kanji

正字法 **seijihō** orthography

正札 **shōfuda** price tag, label

正目 **masame** straight grain (in wood)

6 正伝 **seiden** authentic/official biography

正会員 **seikaiin** full/regular member

正安 **Shōan** (era, 1299–1302)

正当 **seitō** proper, just, justifiable, right, fair, reasonable, legitimate

正当防衛 **seitō bōei** legitimate self-defense

正式 **seishiki** formal, official

7 正体 **shōtai** one's true nature/character; in one's right mind, senses

正邪 **seija** right and wrong

正否 **seihi** right and wrong

正応 **Shōō** (era, 1288–1293)

正社員 **seishain** regular employee, full member of the staff

正攻法 **seikōhō** frontal assault/attack

正系 **seikei** legitimate lineage, direct descent

8 正長 **Shōchō** (era, 1428–1429)

正使 **seishi** senior envoy, chief delegate

正価 **seika** (net) price

正念場 **shōnenba** the crucial/now-or-never moment

正直 **shōjiki** honest, upright, straightforward

正直者 **shōjikimono** honest person, man of integrity

正治 **Shōji** (era, 1199–1201)

正味 **shōmi** net (weight)

正妻 **seisai** one's legal wife

正弦 **seigen** sine

正服 **seifuku** a uniform

正和 **Shōwa** (era, 1312–1317)

正金 **shōkin** specie, bullion; cash

正門 **seimon** front gate, main entrance

9 正保 **Shōhō** (era, 1644–1648)

正負 **seifu** positive and negative, plus and minus

正客 **shōkyaku** guest of honor

正室 **seishitsu** one's legal wife

正面 **shōmen** front, head-on **matomo** front, head-on; honest

正面図 **shōmenzu** front view

正面衝突 **shōmen shōtotsu** head-on collision

正則 **seisoku** regular, systematic, normal, correct, proper

10 正真正銘 **shōshin-shōmei** genuine, authentic

正員 **seiin** full/regular member

正座 **seiza** sit straight (on one's heels) **shōza** seat of honor

正格 **seikaku** orthodox

正教 **seikyō** orthodoxy; Greek Orthodox Church

正教会 **Seikyōkai** Greek Orthodox Church

正教員 **seikyōin** regular/licensed teacher

11 正副 **seifuku** original and copy; chief and vice-chief

正道 **seidō** the right(eous) path

正常 **seijō** normal

正常化 **seijōka** normalization

正規 **seiki** regular, normal, formal, legal

正規軍 **seikigun** regular army

12 正帽 **seibō** cap of a uniform
正覚坊 **shōgakubō** large sea turtle; heavy drinker
正装 **seisō** full dress/uniform
正統 **seitō** orthodox, traditional
正統派 **seitōha** orthodox school, fundamentalists
13 正業 **seigyō** legitimate occupation, honest business
正義 **seigi** justice, right(eousness); correct meaning
正義感 **seigikan** sense of justice
正夢 **masayume** dream which later comes true
正腹 **seifuku** legitimate (child)
正解 **seikai** correct interpretation/solution, the right answer
正数 **seisū** positive number
正路 **seiro** life's path; escape route
14 正暦 **Shōryaku** (era, 990–995)
正嫡 **seichaku** legal wife; legitimate child
正徳 **Shōtoku** (era, 1711–1716)
正嘉 **Shōka** (era, 1257–1259)
正誤 **seigo** correction
正誤表 **seigohyō** errata
15 正賓 **seihin** guest of honor
正慶 **Shōkei** (era, 1332–1338)
正確 **seikaku** exact, precise, accurate
正編 **seihen** main part (of a book)
正課 **seika** regular curriculum/course
正課外 **seikagai** extracurricular
正論 **seiron** fair/sound argument
正調 **seichō** traditional tune
16 正餐 **seisan** formal dinner, banquet
18 正鵠 **seikoku, seikō** the bull's eye, the mark

─────── 2 ───────

3 大正 **Taishō** (era, 1912–1926)
小正月 **koshōgatsu** Little New Year's, 14th–16th of first lunar month
4 不正 **fusei** improper, unjust, wrong, false
不正行為 **fusei kōi** an unfair practice, wrongdoing, malpractice, cheating, foul play
不正直 **fushōjiki** dishonest
不正確 **fuseikaku** inaccurate
元正 **Genshō** (empress, 715–724)
天正 **Tenshō** (era, 1573–1592)
中正 **chūsei** inpartial, fair
文正 **Bunshō** (era, 1466–1467)
公正 **kōsei** fair, just
反正 **Hanzei** (emperor, 406–410)
方正 **hōsei** correct behavior
5 正正堂堂 **seisei-dōdō** fair and square, open and aboveboard
永正 **Eishō** (era, 1504–1521)
叱正 **shissei** correction

旧正月 **kyūshōgatsu** the lunar New Year
7 更正 **kōsei** correct, rectify
邪正 **jasei** right and wrong
改正 **kaisei** revision, amendment; improvement
8 斧正 **fusei** correction, revision
9 是正 **zesei** correct, rectify
訂正 **teisei** correction, revision
10 修正 **shūsei** amendment, revision, alteration, correction
修正案 **shūseian** proposed amendment
真正 **shinsei** genuine, authentic, true
真正直 **ma(s)shōjiki** perfectly honest
真正面 **ma(s)shōmen** directly opposite, right in front
校正 **kōsei** proofreading
校正刷 **kōseizu(ri)** (galley) proofs
校正係 **kōseigakari** proofreader
純正 **junsei** pure, genuine
純正科学 **junsei kagaku** pure science
11 粛正 **shukusei** strictly rectify, enforce (discipline)
康正 **Kōshō** (era, 1455–1457)
規正 **kisei** regulate, control, readjust
12 補正 **hosei** revision, compensation
賀正 **gashō** New Year's greetings
13 僧正 **sōjō** (Buddhist) bishop
適正 **tekisei** proper, appropriate, right
寛正 **Kanshō** (era, 1460–1465)
廉正 **rensei** pure-hearted
較正 **kōsei** calibration
14 端正 **tansei** correct, right, proper
醇正 **junsei** pure, proper
17 矯正 **kyōsei** correct, reform
厳正 **gensei** exact, strict, impartial
18 顕正 **kenshō** spreading the (religious) truth

─────── 3 ───────

3 大僧正 **daisōjō** high priest, cardinal
4 不公正 **fukōsei** unfair, unjust
公明正大 **kōmei-seidai** just, fair
5 正真正銘 **shōshin-shōmei** genuine, authentic
礼儀正 **reigitada(shii)** polite, courteous
7 折目正 **o(ri)metada(shii)** good-mannered; ceremonious
10 秩序正 **chitsujo-tada(shii)** in good order
14 暦改正 **koyomi kaisei** calendar reform

─────── 4 ───────

9 品行方正 **hinkō-hōsei** respectable, irreproachable
10 破邪顕正 **haja-kenshō** smiting evil and spreading the truth
14 綱紀粛正 **kōki shukusei** enforcement of discipline among officials
15 撥乱反正 **hatsuran hansei** restoration of public order

亻
冫
孑
阝
卩
刂
力
又
冖
亠
十
�ト 3 ←
ケ
ソ
厂
辶
冂
八
匸

2m3.4

正
HIKI, HITSU (counter for lengths of cloth, about 9 m); (counter for animals) **SHO, SO** leg **GA** correct **hiki** (counter for lengths of cloth, about 21 m)

2m3.5 / 798

比
HI compare; ratio; the Philippines **kura(beru)** compare **tagui** kind, sort, class

――――――― 1 ―――――――

0 比する **hi(suru)** compare
比べっこ **kura(bekko)** race, contest
5 比丘 **biku** Buddhist priest
比丘尼 **bikuni** Buddhist priestess
8 比価 **hika** parity
比例 **hirei** proportion, ratio; proportional (representation)
比況 **hikyō** comparison, likening
比物 **kura(be)mono** comparison, match
比肩 **hiken** rank with, be comparable to
9 比重 **hijū** specific gravity; relative importance
10 比倫 **hirin** peer, match, equal, rival
11 比率 **hiritsu** ratio, percentage
12 比喩 **hiyu** simile, metaphor, allegory
比喩的 **hiyuteki** figurative
13 比較 **hikaku** compare; comparative (literature)
比較史 **hikakushi** comparative history
比較的 **hikakuteki** relative(ly), comparative(ly)
比較級 **hikakukyū** the comparative degree (in grammar)
15 比隣 **hirin** vicinity
比熱 **hinetsu** specific heat
16 比叡山 **Hieizan** (mountain, Kyōto-fu)
17 比翼 **hiyoku** wings abreast; (short for 比翼仕立て) garment folded double at edges, fly front
比翼塚 **hiyokuzuka** lovers' double grave
18 比類 **hirui** a parallel, an equal

――――――― 2 ―――――――

4 反比例 **hanpirei** in inverse proportion to
日比 **Nip-Pi** Japan and the Philippines
5 正比例 **seihirei** in direct proportion/ratio
7 阿比 **abi** loon
対比 **taihi** contrast, comparison, opposition, analogy
見比 **mikura(beru)** compare (by eying)
8 逆比 **gyakuhi** inverse ratio
逆比例 **gyakuhirei** inversely proportional to
金比羅 **Konpira** (the god of seafarers)
9 背比 **seikura(be)** comparing heights

10 根比 **konkura(be)** endurance contest
恵比須 **Ebisu** (a god of wealth)
恵比須顔 **ebisugao** smiling/beaming face
12 腕比 **udekura(be)** contest of strength/skill
無比 **muhi** incomparable, matchless, unrivaled
等比 **tōhi** equal ratio
等比級数 **tōhi kyūsū** geometric progression
18 類比 **ruihi** analogy, comparison
19 櫛比 **shippi** stand close together in a long row

――――――― 3 ―――――――

6 百分比 **hyakubunhi** percentage
9 按分比例 **anbun hirei** proportionately, prorated

――――――― 4 ―――――――

4 天下無比 **tenka-muhi** unique, incomparable

乍→ **0a5.10**

――――――― 4 ―――――――

2m4.1

虍
KO tiger stripes

臼→ **0a6.4**

2m4.2

此
SHI, ko(no), ko(re) this

――――――― 1 ―――――――

3 此上 **ko(no)ue** furthermore; above this, better
ko(no)ue(mo nai) best, unsurpassed
此々 **korekore** this and that, such and such
4 此方 **ko(no)hō** this one; I, we
ko(no) kata since; this person
kochira, kotchi, konata here, this side
5 此奴 **koitsu** this guy/fellow
此処 **koko** here, this place
此処迄 **koko made** to this point, up to now
6 此此 **ko(re)ko(re)** this and that, such and such
此迄 **ko(re)made** until now, thus far
7 此見 **ko(re)mi(yogashi ni)** ostentatiously, flauntingly, to attract attention
9 此度 **ko(no) tabi** at this time
11 此許 **ko(re)baka(ri)** only this, only this much
此頃 **ko(no)goro** these days, lately
12 此程 **ko(no)hodo** the other day, recently
此間 **ko(no) aida** the other day, recently
13 此際 **ko(no)sai** on this occasion, now

此節 **ko(no)setsu** now, at present
14 此樣 **ko(no) yō** such, this kind of, in this way
16 此儘 **ko(no)mama** as is

─────── 5 ───────

步→歩 **3n5.3**

─────── 6 ───────

2m6.1

卦 **KA, KE** divination sign (one of a set of eight signs, each consisting of a triplet of bars or bar-pairs; seen on the South Korean flag)

─────── 2 ───────
2 八卦 **hakke** the eight divination signs; fortunetelling
6 有卦 **uke** lucky period

2m6.2 / 1679

卓 **TAKU** table, desk; excel

─────── 1 ───────
3 卓上 **takujō** table-top, desk-top
7 卓抜 **takubatsu** excellence, (pre)eminence
卓見 **takken** farsighted, incisive, broad vision
11 卓球 **takkyū** table tennis, ping-pong
12 卓越 **takuetsu** be superior, excel, surpass
14 卓説 **takusetsu** excellent opinion, enlightened views
15 卓論 **takuron** sound argument
─────── 2 ───────
4 円卓会議 **entaku kaigi** round-table conference
9 食卓 **shokutaku** dining table
食卓用 **shokutakuyō** for table use
13 電卓 **dentaku** (desktop) calculator (short for 電子式卓上計算機)

奌→点 **2m7.2**

2m6.3

虎 **KO, tora** tiger; drunkard

─────── 1 ───────
2 虎子 **tora (no) ko** tiger cub; one's treasure
omaru chamber pot, bedpan
3 虎口 **kokō** tiger's mouth; dangerous situation

4 虎刈 **toraga(ri)** unevenly cropped, close-cropped (head)
5 虎穴 **koketsu** tiger's den; dangerous situation
9 虎巻 **tora(no)maki** pony, answer book; (trade) secrets
虎狩 **toraga(ri)** tiger hunt
10 虎狼 **korō** tigers and wolves; wild beasts; cruel man, brute
11 虎視眈々 **koshi-tantan** with hostile vigilance, waiting one's chance (to pounce)
虎視耽々 **koshi-tantan** with hostile vigilance, waiting one's chance (to pounce)
12 虎落 **mogari** bamboo palisade/drying-rack; extortion
虎落笛 **mogaribue** sound of the winter wind whistling through a fence
22 虎鬚 **torahige** bristly mustache/beard
─────── 2 ───────
10 猛虎 **mōko** ferocious tiger
竜虎 **ryūko** dragon and tiger, titans
11 猟虎 **rakko** sea otter
18 騎虎勢 **kiko (no) ikio(i)** unable to stop/quit

兒→児 **4c3.3**

2m6.4

些 **SA, isasaka, chi(to), chit(to)** a little, a bit, slight

─────── 1 ───────
4 些少 **sashō** slight, trifling, little, few
11 些細 **sasai** trifling, trivial, slight, insignificant

長→ **0a8.2**

─────── 7 ───────

臥→臥 **2a7.22**

2m7.1 / 1681

貞 **TEI, JŌ** chastity, fidelity, virtue

─────── 1 ───────
3 貞女 **teijo** chaste woman, faithful wife
5 貞永 **Jōei** (era, 1232–1233)
7 貞享 **Jōkyō** (era, 1684–1688)
貞応 **Jōō** (era, 1222–1224)
8 貞治 **Jōji** (era, 1362–1368)

2

イ
ン
扌
阝
卩
刂
力
又
宀
亠
十
⼘ 7 ←
𠂉
⼍
厂
辶
冂
几
匸

2

貞実 **teijitsu** faithful, devoted
貞和 **Jōwa** (era, 1345–1350)
10 貞烈 **teiretsu** very virtuous/chaste
11 貞淑 **teishuku** chastity, modesty
貞婦 **teifu** virtuous woman, faithful wife
13 貞節 **teisetsu** fidelity, chastity
15 貞潔 **teiketsu** chaste and pure
18 貞観 **Jōgan** (era, 859–877)

—————————— 2 ——————————

4 不貞 **futei** (marital) infidelity
不貞寝 **futene** stay in bed out of spite
不貞腐 **futekusa(reru)** become sulky/spiteful
6 安貞 **Antei** (era, 1227–1229)
8 忠貞 **chūtei** fidelity
12 童貞 **dōtei** (male) virgin

2m7.2 / 169

点 點 桌

TEN point **tomo(ru)**
burn, be lighted
tomo(su) burn, light,
turn on (a lamp)
tsu(ku) catch (fire), be lit, (lights) come on

—————————— 1 ——————————

0 点じる **ten(jiru)** drop (eyedrops); light, kindle; make (tea)
3 点々 **tenten** dots, spots; here and there, scattered
4 点火 **tenka** ignite
5 点字 **tenji** Braille
6 点在 **tenzai** be dotted with
点光 **tenkō** spotlight
点灯 **tentō** light (a lamp) (cf. 消灯)
8 点呼 **tenko** roll call
点取 **tento(ri)** competition for marks; keeping score
点取虫 **tento(ri)mushi** student who studies just to get good marks, a grind
9 点茶 **tencha** preparing tea (in tea ceremony)
11 点眼 **tengan** apply eyedrops/eyewash
12 点検 **tenken** inspection
点晴 **tensei** adding the eyes and other finishing touches to a painting (of a dragon)
点景 **tenkei** human-interest details in a picture
13 点滅 **tenmetsu** switch/flash on and off
点滅器 **tenmetsuki** a switch
点数 **tensū** points, marks, score
14 点滴 **tenteki** falling drops, raindrops; intravenous drip
点綴 **tentei, tentetsu** be scattered/interspersed here and there
15 点線 **tensen** dotted/perforated line
16 点頭 **tentō** nod

—————————— 2 ——————————

1 一点 **itten** a point; speck, dot, particle

一点張 **ittenba(ri)** persistence
2 力点 **rikiten** fulcrum; emphasis
4 中点 **chūten** midpoint
支点 **shiten** fulcrum
分点 **bunten** equinox
欠点 **ketten** defect, flaw, faults
5 氷点 **hyōten** the freezing point
氷点下 **hyōtenka** below the freezing point, below zero (Celsius)
打点 **daten** runs batted in, RBI
句点 **kuten** period (the punctuation mark)
6 合点 **gaten, gatten** understand, comprehend; consent to
次点 **jiten** runner-up
争点 **sōten** point of contention, issue
返点 **kae(ri)ten** marks indicating the Japanese word order in reading Chinese classics
同点 **dōten** a tie/draw
汚点 **oten** stain, smudge, blot, disgrace
地点 **chiten** spot, point, position
至点 **shiten** solstice/equinoctial point
光点 **kōten** luminous point
百点 **hyakuten** 100 points, perfect score
7 批点 **hiten** correction marks (in a manuscript); emphasis marks; points to be criticized
灸点 **kyūten** moxa-treatment points
利点 **riten** advantage, point in favor
8 盲点 **mōten** blind spot
沸点 **futten** boiling point
拠点 **kyoten** (military) base, position
定点 **teiten** fixed point
9 重点 **jūten** important point, priority, emphasis
点点 **tenten** dots, spots; here and there, scattered
美点 **biten** good point, virtue, merit
要点 **yōten** main point(s), gist
10 高点 **kōten** high score
原点 **genten** starting point
起点 **kiten** starting point
弱点 **jakuten** weak point, a weakness
班点 **hanten** spot, dot, fleck, speck
特点 **tokuten** special favor, privilege
訓点 **kunten** punctuation marks
11 基点 **kiten** cardinal point
採点 **saiten** marking, grading, scoring
採点者 **saitensha** marker, grader, scorer
得点 **tokuten** one's score, points made
黒点 **kokuten** black/dark spot; sunspot
視点 **shiten** center of one's field of view; viewpoint
終点 **shūten** end of the line, last stop, terminus
頂点 **chōten** zenith, peak, climax
12 満点 **manten** perfect score
減点 **genten** demerit mark

寒点 **kanten** points on the skin sensitive to the cold
極点 **kyokuten** highest/lowest point
斑点 **hanten** spot, speck
痛点 **tsūten** point of pain, where it hurts
評点 **hyōten** examination marks
焦点 **shōten** focal point, focus
13 零点 **reiten** (a score/temperature of) zero
14 疑点 **giten** doubtful point
罰点 **batten** demerit marks
総点 **sōten** total points/marks
読点 **tōten** comma
15 論点 **ronten** point at issue
16 濁点 **dakuten** voiced-consonant mark
融点 **yūten** melting point
18 観点 **kanten** viewpoint
鎔点 **yōten** melting point
難点 **nanten** difficult point
21 露点 **roten** the dew point

———————— 3 ————————
1 一致点 **itchiten** point of agreement
3 及第点 **kyūdaiten** passing grade
小数点 **shōsūten** decimal point
4 天頂点 **tenchōten** zenith
中心点 **chūshinten** center
分岐点 **bunkiten** branch/ramification/turning point, fork, junction
引火点 **inkaten** flash point
5 出発点 **shuppatsuten** starting point, point of departure
平均点 **heikinten** average mark/grade
句読点 **kutōten** punctuation mark
主眼点 **shuganten** main point/purpose
立脚点 **rikkyakuten** position, standpoint
6 交叉点 **kōsaten** crossing, intersection
交差点 **kōsaten** crossing, intersection
近日点 **kinjitsuten** perihelion
近地点 **kinchiten** perigee
共通点 **kyōtsūten** something in common
早合点 **hayagaten** hasty conclusion
自責点 **jisekiten** earned run (in baseball)
7 対蹠点 **taisekiten** antipode, nadir
決勝点 **kesshōten** goal, finish line
折返点 **o(ri)kae(shi)ten** (marathon) turn-back point
8 画竜点晴 **garyō-tensei** completing the eyes of a painted dragon; the finishing touches
画龍点晴 **garyō-tensei** completing the eyes of a painted dragon; the finishing touches
到達点 **tōtatsuten** destination
沸騰点 **futtōten** boiling point
9 発火点 **hakkaten** ignition/flash point
独合点 **hito(ri)gaten** hasty conclusion
春分点 **shunbunten** the vernal equinoctal point

紅一点 **kōitten** one red flower in the foliage; the only woman in the group
11 接触点 **sesshokuten** point of contact/tangency
転向点 **tenkōten** turning point
問題点 **mondaiten** the point at issue
12 着眼点 **chakuganten** viewpoint
遠日点 **enjitsuten, ennichiten** aphelion
弾着点 **danchakuten** point of impact
落第点 **rakudaiten** failing mark
最高点 **saikōten** highest point/score
無得点 **mutokuten** scoreless (game)
13 溶解点 **yōkaiten** melting point
飽和点 **hōwaten** saturation point
16 凝固点 **gyōkoten** freezing point
融解点 **yūkaiten** melting point
18 鎔融点 **yōyūten** melting point
類似点 **ruijiten** points of similarity

———————— 4 ————————
5 乎古止点 **okototen** marks to aid in reading Chinese classics

———————— 5 ————————
13 損益分岐点 **son'eki bunkiten** break-even point

2m7.3 / 1574
虐 虐   **GYAKU, shiita(geru)** oppress, tyrannize over

———————— 1 ————————
8 虐使 **gyakushi** overwork (someone), drive too hard, exploit, give rough use
9 虐待 **gyakutai** treat cruelly, mistreat
虐政 **gyakusei** oppressive government, tyranny
10 虐殺 **gyakusatsu** massacre

———————— 2 ————————
10 残虐 **zangyaku** cruelty, atrocity, brutality
15 暴虐 **bōgyaku** outrage, atrocity, violence

舁→   **0a9.7**

2m7.4
歪   **WAI, E, yuga(mu)** be distorted/warped **yuga(mi)** distortion **yuga(meru)** distort, bend **hizu(mu)** be strained, warp **hizu(mi)** strain, deformation
ibitsu oval, elliptical; distorted, warped

———————— 1 ————————
2 歪力 **wairyoku** stress
6 歪曲 **waikyoku** distortion

韭 → 韮 3k9.2

2

──────── 8 ────────

2m8.1

虔

KEN respect; hard; kill

──────── 2 ────────

12 敬虔 **keiken** piety, devotion, reverence

──────── 9 ────────

2m9.1 / 1572

虚 虚

KYO, KO empty
muna(shii) empty, vain, futile
uro cavity, hollow, hole

──────── 1 ────────

3 虚々実々 **kyokyo-jitsujitsu** clever fighting, trying every strategy
4 虚心 **kyoshin** disinterested, unbiased
虚心坦懐 **kyoshin-tankai** frank, open-minded
5 虚字 **kyoji** kanji representing a verb or adjective
虚礼 **kyorei** empty formalities
6 虚伝 **kyoden** false rumor
虚仮 **koke** fool, idiot
虚仮威 **kokeodo(shi)** empty threat, mere show, bluff
虚仮猿 **kokezaru** idiotic monkey
虚妄 **kyomō** false, fallacious, groundless
虚名 **kyomei** false reputation, publicity
7 虚位 **kyoi** nominal rank, titular post
虚言 **kyogen** lie, falsehood
8 虚実 **kyojitsu** truth or falsehood; clever fighting, trying every strategy
虚空 **kokū** empty space, the air
9 虚栄 **kyoei** vanity, vainglory
虚栄心 **kyoeishin** vanity, vainglory
10 虚弱 **kyojaku** weak, feeble, frail
11 虚偽 **kyogi** false, untrue
虚虚実実 **kyokyo-jitsujitsu** clever fighting, trying every strategy
虚脱 **kyodatsu** prostration, collapse
12 虚報 **kyohō** flase report, groundless rumor
虚無 **kyomu** nothingness
虚無主義 **kyomu shugi** nihilism
虚無的 **kyomuteki** nihilistic
虚無党 **kyomutō** nihilists
虚無僧 **komusō** mendicant flute-playing Zen priest
13 虚勢 **kyosei** bluff, false show of strength
虚数 **kyosū** imaginary number
虚辞 **kyoji** lie, falsehood

虚飾 **kyoshoku** ostentation, affectation
14 虚像 **kyozō** virtual image
虚構 **kyokō** fabricated, false, unfounded
虚説 **kyosetsu** baseless rumor, false report
虚誕 **kyotan** false, trumped-up
虚聞 **kyobun** false rumor

──────── 2 ────────

4 太虚 **taikyo** the sky; the universe
8 空虚 **kūkyo** empty, hollow; inane
9 盈虚 **eikyo** wax and wane
11 虚虚実実 **kyokyo-jitsujitsu** clever fighting, trying every strategy
17 謙虚 **kenkyo** modest, humble

處 → 処 4i2.2

2m9.2

鹵

RO salty/barren soil; natural salt; plunder; foolish

──────── 1 ────────

16 鹵獲 **rokaku** capture, plunder
鹵獲物 **rokakubutsu** booty, spoils, trophy
19 鹵簿 **robo** imperial procession

2m9.3

禁

fumoto foot/base (of a mountain)

套 → 0a10.3

春 → 0a11.6

──────── 10 ────────

虚 → 虚 2m9.1

疎 → 0a11.4

疏 → 2j9.8

貔 → 0a11.1

———————— 11 ————————

2m11.1 / 1941

虞 虞

GU, osore fear, concern, risk

———————— 1 ————————

9 虞美人草 **gubijinsō** field poppy

2m11.2 / 1385

虜 虜

RYO captive, prisoner of war; barbarian
toriko captive, slave

———————— 1 ————————

5 虜囚 **ryoshū** captive, prisoner (of war)

———————— 2 ————————

8 俘虜 **furyo** captive, prisoner of war
10 捕虜 **horyo** prisoner of war, captive

鼠→ **0a13.1**

觜→ **2n11.2**

———————— 12 ————————

睿→叡 **2h14.1**

翡→ **0a14.1**

2m12.1 / 1516

疑

GI, utaga(u), utagu(ru) doubt, distrust, be suspicious of
utaga(washii) doubtful, suspicious

———————— 1 ————————

4 疑心 **gishin** suspicion, fear, apprehension
疑心暗鬼 **gishin-anki** Suspicion creates monsters in the dark. Suspicion feeds on itself.
7 疑似 **giji-** suspected, sham, pseudo-, dummy, simulated
8 疑念 **ginen** doubt, suspicion, misgivings
9 疑点 **giten** doubtful point
11 疑深 **utaga(i)buka(i)** doubting, distrustful
疑問 **gimon** question, doubt
疑問文 **gimonbun** interrogative sentence
疑問代名詞 **gimon daimeishi** interrogative pronoun

疑問符 **gimonfu** question mark
疑問詞 **gimonshi** interrogative word
12 疑惑 **giwaku** suspicion, distrust, misgivings
疑雲 **giun** cloud of suspicion/doubt
13 疑義 **gigi** doubt
14 疑獄 **gigoku** scandal

———————— 2 ————————

9 信疑 **shingi** belief or doubt
狐疑 **kogi** doubt, indecision
10 容疑 **yōgi** suspicion
容疑者 **yōgisha** a suspect
被疑者 **higisha** a suspect
11 遅疑 **chigi** hesitate, vacillate
猜疑 **saigi** suspicion, jealousy
猜疑心 **saigishin** suspicion, jealousy
13 嫌疑 **kengi** suspicion
嫌疑者 **kengisha** a suspect
15 質疑 **shitsugi** question, inquiry
質疑応答 **shitsugi-ōtō** question-and-answer (session)
16 懐疑 **kaigi** doubt, skepticism
懐疑心 **kaigishin** doubt, skepticism
懐疑説 **kaigisetsu** skepticism
懐疑論 **kaigiron** skepticism

———————— 4 ————————

5 半信半疑 **hanshin-hangi** incredulous, half doubting

———————— 13 ————————

2m13.1 / 1269

膚

FU, hada skin

———————— 1 ————————

6 膚色 **hada-iro** flesh-colored
7 膚身 **hadami** the body
膚身離 **hadami-hana(sazu)** always kept on one's person, highly treasured
11 膚脱 **hadanu(gi)** bare to the waist
12 膚着 **hadagi** underwear
膚寒 **hadasamu(i), hadazamu(i)** chilly
13 膚触 **hadazawa(ri)** the touch, the feel
19 膚襦袢 **hadajuban** underwear

———————— 2 ————————

2 人膚 **hitohada** (warmth of) the skin
3 山膚 **yamahada** mountain's surface
4 片膚脱 **katahada nu(gu)** bare one shoulder; help out
5 皮膚 **hifu** skin
皮膚科 **hifuka** dermatology
皮膚病 **hifubyō** skin disease
15 諸膚 **morohada** stripped to the waist
餅膚 **mochihada** smooth white skin
17 鮫膚 **samehada** fishskin, dry/scaly skin

2m13.2 / 1384

慮 **RYO** thought, consideration
omonpaka(ri) thought, consideration, prudence; fear, apprehension

――――― 1 ―――――

5 慮外 **ryogai** unexpected; rude

――――― 2 ―――――

3 凡慮 **bonryo** ordinary minds/men
4 不慮 **furyo** unforeseen, unexpected
6 考慮 **kōryo** consideration, careful thought
8 念慮 **nenryo** thought, consideration
   知慮 **chiryo** foresight
   苦慮 **kuryo** worry over
9 浅慮 **senryo** indiscreet, imprudent
   神慮 **shinryo** divine will, decree of heaven
   思慮 **shiryo** thoughtfulness, prudence
10 配慮 **hairyo** consideration, care
11 深慮 **shinryo** thoughtfulness, deliberateness, prudence
12 遠慮 **enryo** reserve, restraint, diffidence; refrain from **enryo(naku)** frankly
   遠慮深 **enryobuka(i)** reserved, bashful
   短慮 **tanryo** quick/hot temper
   無慮 **muryo** as many as, approximately
   焦慮 **shōryo** impatience, anxiousness
13 聖慮 **seiryo** imperial wishes
14 熟慮 **jukuryo** mature consideration
   熟慮断行 **jukuryo-dankō** deliberate and decisive

15 憂慮 **yūryo** anxiety, apprehension, cares
16 賢慮 **kenryo** (your) wise consideration
21 顧慮 **koryo** regard, consideration

――――― 3 ―――――

12 無思慮 **mushiryo** thoughtless, imprudent
   無遠慮 **buenryo** unreserved, forward, impertinent

――――― 4 ―――――

11 深謀遠慮 **shinbō-enryo** farsighted planning

貌 → 犲 **3g8.2**

――――― 14 ―――――

2m14.1

盧 **RO** rice coffer; black; liquor-selling place

――――― 15 ―――――

罅 → **2k15.1**

――――― 16 ―――――

鼬 → **0a18.1**

ク **2n**

々	久	夕	色	争	危	角	兔	免	負	急	奐	勉
1.1	0a3.7	0a3.14	4.1	4.2	4.3	5.1	0a8.5	6.1	7.1	7.2	7.3	8.1

亀	魚	斛	晁	象	觝	麁	解	觚	觧	觜	复	豫
9.1	11a0.1	9.2	4c7.9	10.1	10.2	3q30.1	4g9.1	11.1	4g9.1	11.2	12.1	0a4.12

龜
2n9.1

――――― 1 ―――――

2n1.1

々 ("odoriji", "kurikaeshi kigō") (kanji repetition symbol)

――――― 2 ―――――

2 人々 **hitobito** people, everybody
   子々孫々 **shishi-sonson** descendants, posterity
   孑々 **ketsuketsu, getsugetsu** standing alone
      bōfura mosquito larva
   又々 **matamata** once again
3 三々九度 **sansankudo** exchange of nuptial cups
   三々五々 **sansan-gogo** in small groups, by twos and threes
   久々 **hisabisa** (for the first time in) a long time
   万々 **banban** very much, fully; (with negative) never
   大々的 **daidaiteki** great, grand, on a large scale
   丸々 **marumaru** completely
      marumaru (to) plump
   千々 **chiji** a great many; variety
   上々 **jōjō** the (very) best
   下々 **shimojimo, shitajita** the lower classes, the common people
   口々 **kuchiguchi** each entrance/mouth
   女々 **meme(shii)** effeminate, unmanly
   山々 **yamayama** mountains; very much

4 云々 **unnun, shikajika** and so forth, and so on, and the like

元々 **motomoto** from the first, originally; by nature, naturally

内々 **uchiuchi** private, informal
nainai private, secret, confidential

切々 **setsusetsu** ardent, earnest

片々 **henpen** pieces, fragments

仄々 **honobono** dimly, faintly

区々 **kuku** various, diverse, mixed; petty

少々 **shōshō** a little, a few, slightly

月々 **tsukizuki** every month

日々 **hibi** daily; days
nichi-nichi daily, every day

方々 **katagata** people, ladies and gentlemen
hōbō every direction

戸々 **koko** at every house, door to door

5 生々 **namanama(shii)** fresh, vivid
seisei lively

由々 **yuyu(shii)** grave, serious

代々 **daidai, yoyo** from generation to generation

平々凡々 **heihei-bonbon** commonplace, ordinary

正々堂々 **seisei-dōdō** fair and square, open and aboveboard

好々爺 **kōkōya** good-natured old man

白々 **shirojiro** pure white **shirajira** dawning
shirajira(shii) feigning ignorance; barefaced (lie) **hakuhaku** very clear

6 両々 **ryōryō** both

年々 **nennen, toshidoshi** year by year, every year

再々 **saisai** often, frequently

仰々 **gyōgyō(shii)** grandiloquent, grandiose, ostentatious

次々 **tsugitsugi** one by one, one after another

孜々 **shishi (to shite)** assiduously, diligently

此々 **korekore** this and that, such and such

色々 **iroiro** various

近々 **chikajika, kinkin** before long

汲々 **kyūkyū (to shite)** diligently, industriously

先々 **sakizaki** the distant future; places one goes to; beforehand

先々月 **sensengetsu** the month before last

共々 **tomodomo** together with

安々 **yasuyasu** very peaceful; easily

早々 **sōsō** early, immediately; Hurriedly yours, **hayabaya** early, immediately

各々 **onoono** each, every, respectively

7 我々 **wareware** we, us, our

別々 **betsubetsu** separate, individual

角々 **kadokado (ni)** on every corner
kadokado(shii) angular; unaffable

延々 **en'en** repeatedly postponed, protracted, interminable

赤々 **aka-aka** brightly

折々 **oriori** from time to time

抑々 **somosomo** in the first place; well, now

吶々 **totsu-totsu** falteringly

否々 **iya-iya** grudgingly; by no means

芬々 **funpun** fragrant

図々 **zūzū(shii)** impudent, brazen, cheeky

忌々 **imaima(shii)** vexing, provoking

辛々 **karagara** barely

初々 **uiui(shii)** innocent, naive, unsophisticated

言々 **gengen** every word

8 長々 **naganaga(shii)** long-drawn-out

奄々 **en'en** gasping

毒々 **dokudoku(shii)** poisonous-looking; malicious, vicious; heavy, gross

事々 **kotogoto(shii)** exaggerated, pretentious

事々物々 **jiji-butsubutsu** everything

侃々諤々 **kankan-gakugaku** outspoken

念々 **nennen** continually thinking about something

刻々 **kokukoku, kokkoku** moment by moment, hour by hour

勃々 **botsubotsu** spirited, energetic

直々 **jikijiki** personal, direct

並々 **naminami** ordinary, commonplace

泌々 **shimijimi** keenly, deeply, thoroughly

坦々 **tantan** level, even; uneventful, peaceful

呵々 **kaka** ha ha (sound of laughter)

奇々怪々 **kiki-kaikai** very strange, fantastic

狒々 **hihi** baboon

往々 **ōō** sometimes, occasionally, often

若々 **wakawaka(shii)** youthful

苦々 **niganiga(shii)** unpleasant, disgusting, scandalous

昔々 **mukashi mukashi** Once upon a time ...

空々 **sorazora(shii)** feigned, false, empty, transparent (lie) **kūkū** emptiness, nothing; absence of fleshly passions

空々漠 **kūkū-bakubaku** vast and empty

国々 **kuniguni** countries, nations

青々 **aoao(shita)** fresh and green, verdant

明々白々 **meimei-hakuhaku** perfectly clear

易々 **ii(taru), yasuyasu** easy, simple

昏々 **konkon (to)** dead to the world, fast (asleep)

炎々 **en'en** blazing, fiery

物々 **monomono(shii)** showy, imposing, elaborate

物々交換 **butsubutsu kōkan** barter

怏々 **ōō** despondent, in low spirits

房々 **fusafusa** tufty, bushy, profuse (hair)

所々 **tokorodokoro, shosho** here and there

所々方々 **shosho-hōbō** everywhere

9 重々 **omoomo(shii)** serious, grave, solemn
jūjū repeated; very much

便々 **benben(taru)** protruberant, paunchy
benben (to) idly
亭々 **teitei(taru)** lofty, towering
点々 **tenten** dots, spots; here and there, scattered
美々 **bibi(shii)** beautiful, resplendent
段々 **dandan** steps, terrace; gradually, increasingly
段々畑 **dandanbatake** terraced fields
津々 **shinshin** brimfull
津々浦 **tsutsu-uraura** throughout the land, the entire country
品々 **shinajina** various articles
後々 **atoato, nochinochi** the future
茫々 **bōbō** vague; vast
草々 **sōsō** in haste; (closing words of a letter)
荒々 **araara(shii)** rough, rude, harsh, wild, violent
茶々 **chacha** interruption
度々 **tabitabi** often, frequently
面々 **menmen** every one, all
相々傘 **aiaigasa (de)** under the same umbrella
柔々 **yawayawa** softly, gently; gradually
是々非々 **zeze-hihi** fair and unbiased
皆々様 **minaminasama** everyone, all of you
炯々 **keikei** glaring, penetrating
神々 **kōgō(shii)** divine, sublime, awe-inspiring
kamigami gods
忽々 **sōsō** hurry, flurry, rush; Yours in haste
恢々 **kaikai** broad, extensive
香々 **kōkō** pickled vegetables
10 個々 **koko** individual, separate, one by one
隆々 **ryūryū** prosperous, thriving; muscular
恋々 **renren (to suru)** be fondly attached to
旁々 **katagata** at the same time, combined with
高々 **takadaka** at most; high, aloft, loudly
高々指 **takatakayubi** the middle finger
高々度 **kōkōdo** high-altitude
益々 **masumasu** increasingly, more and more
這々 **hōhō** confusedly, in consternation
這々体 **hōhō(no)tei** hurriedly, precipitously
殷々 **in'in(to)** roaring, booming, pealing, reverberating
捗々 **hakabaka(shii)** rapid, expeditious, active; satisfactory
猛々 **takedake(shii)** fierce, ferocious; audacious
弱々 **yowayowa(shii)** weak-looking, frail, delicate
徐々 **jojo** slowly, gradually
華々 **hanabana(shii)** glorious, brilliant, resplendent
峨々 **gaga(taru)** rugged, craggy
島々 **shimajima** (many) islands
脈々 **myakumyaku** continuous, unbroken
朗々 **rōrō** clear, sonorous
時々 **tokidoki** sometimes

時々刻々 **jiji-kokukoku** hourly, minute by minute
烈々 **retsuretsu** ardent, fierce, fervent
恐々 **kyōkyō** respect (in letters)
kowagowa timidly
悄々 **shōshō** anxious, worried; quiet
紛々 **funpun** in confusion, conflicting
粉々 **konagona** into tiny pieces
11 粛々 **shukushuku** in hushed silence; solemnly
偶々 **tamatama** by chance, unexpectedly
隅々 **sumizumi** every nook and cranny
虚々実々 **kyokyo-jitsujitsu** clever fighting, trying every strategy
孳々 **shishi** diligently
道々 **michimichi** on the way, while walking
遅々 **chichi** slow, lagging
淡々 **tantan(taru)** unconcerned, indifferent; plain, light
清々 **seisei** feel refreshed/relieved
渋々 **shibushibu** reluctantly, grudgingly
深々 **fukabuka** deeply
shinshin getting late, silently (falling show), piercingly (cold)
淙々 **sōsō** murmuring, babbling
唯々諾々 **ii-dakudaku** quite willing, readily, obediently
得々 **tokutoku** proudly, triumphantly
密々 **mitsumitsu** secretly, privately
常々 **tsunezune** always, constantly
堂々巡 **dōdōmegu(ri)** circle a temple in worship; going round and round (without getting anywhere); roll-call vote
黒々 **kuroguro** dark black
悠々 **yūyū** calm, composed, leisurely
略々 **hobo** roughly, approximately
累々 **ruirui(taru)** piled up, in heaps
細々 **komagoma** in pieces, in detail
hosoboso slender; scanty (livelihood)
粒々 **ryūryū** assiduously
tsubutsubu lumps, grains
粗々 **araara** roughly, not in detail
粘々 **nebaneba** sticky, gooey
断々乎 **dandanko** firm, resolute
転々 **tenten** roll; keep changing (jobs), change hands often
12 着々 **chakuchaku** steadily
湛々 **tantan** brimming, overflowing
温々 **nukunuku** comfortably warm, snug; brazen
満々 **manman** full of, brimming with
喋々 **chōchō** chatter on, be long-winded
喧々囂々 **kenken-gōgō** pandemonium
猩々 **shōjō** orangutan; heavy drinker
猩々緋 **shōjōhi** scarlet
営々 **eiei (to)** strenuously, eagerly, busily
焔々 **en'en** blazing, fiery
然々 **shikajika** such and such; and so on

2
亻 冫 子 阝 卩 刂 力 又 一 十 卜
→1 ク
ヾ
厂 辶 冂 几 匚

犇々 **hishihishi** firmly, tightly; thronging

散々 **sanzan** thoroughly, scathingly, to the full

程々 **hodohodo** moderately, not overdoing it

痛々 **itaita(shii)** pitiful, pathetic

等々 **tōtō** etc., and so forth

軽々 **karugaru(shii)** frivolous, rash, thoughtless   **karugaru (to)** with ease

雄々 **oo(shii)** manly, virile, valiant

間々 **mama** often, occasionally

悶々 **monmon** discontent, anguish

順々 **junjun** in order, by turns

13 僅々 **kinkin** only, merely, no more than

愈々 **iyoiyo** more and more, increasingly; finally; beyond doubt

遙々 **harubaru** from afar, at a great distance

滔々 **tōtō** flowing (swiftly) along; fluently, eloquently

漠々 **bakubaku** vast, boundless; vague, obscure

微々 **bibi(taru)** slight, tiny, insignificant

楽々 **rakuraku** comfortably, with great ease

楚々 **soso(taru)** tasteful, graceful

暗々 **an'an** darkness; covertly

暗々裡 **an'anri** tacitly; covertly

煌々 **kōkō** bright, brilliant

福々 **fukubuku(shii)** (fat and) happy-looking

瑞々 **mizumizu(shii)** young and vivacious

数々 **kazukazu** many

戦々恐々 **sensen-kyōkyō** with fear and trembling; with trepidation

戦々競々 **sensen-kyōkyō** with fear and trembling; with trepidation

歳々 **saisai** annual, every year

碌々 **rokuroku** in idleness; sufficiently, decently

続々 **zokuzoku** successively, one after another

節々 **fushibushi** joints; points (in a talk)

電々 **Denden** Telegraph and Telephone (Co., Ltd.) (short for 電信電話)

14 歴々 **rekireki, (o)rekireki** VIPs, big shots **rekireki(taru)** clear, obvious

漫々 **manman** vast, boundless

滾々 **konkon** gushingly, copiously

赫々 **kakkaku, kakukaku** brilliant, glorious, distinguished

兢々 **kyōkyō** with fear (and trembling)

寥々 **ryōryō** lonesome, quiet; few, rare

様々 **samazama** various, varied

静々 **shizushizu** quietly, calmly, gently

瑣々 **sasa** trifling; tedious; tinkling

態々 **wazawaza** on purpose, deliberately

憎々 **nikuniku(shii)** hateful, loathsome, malicious

端々 **hashibashi** odds and ends, parts

颯々 **sassatsu** rustling, soughing

種々 **shuju, kusagusa** various

種々相 **shujusō** various phases/aspects

種々様々 **shuju-samazama** all kinds of, diverse

種々雑多 **shuju-zatta** various, every sort of

複々々線 **fukufukufukusen** six-track rail line

複々線 **fukufukusen** four-track rail line

綿々 **menmen(taru)** endless, unabating

精々 **seizei** to the utmost; at most

管々 **kudakuda(shii)** verbose, tedious

諄々 **junjun** painstakingly, earnestly

賑々 **niginigi(shii)** thriving; merry, gay

銘々 **meimei** each, apiece

銘々伝 **meimeiden** lives, biographies

駄々 **dada (o koneru)** wheedle, ask for the impossible

駄々子 **dada(k)ko** peevish/spoiled child

15 凛々 **rinrin** severe, intense, biting; awe-inspiring   **riri(shii)** gallant, imposing

黙々 **mokumoku** silent, mute, tacit

蝶々 **chōchō** butterfly

諸々 **moromoro** various, all, every sort of

諾々 **dakudaku** quite willingly

16 濛々 **mōmō** thick (fog), dim

薄々 **usuusu** thinly, dimly, vaguely, hazily

錚々 **sōsō** eminent, outstanding

霏々 **hihi** (falling) thick and fast

17 翼々 **yokuyoku** careful, prudent

嚇々 **kakukaku(taru), kakkaku(taru)** brilliant, glorious

朦々 **mōmō** dimly lit, gloomy

燦々 **sansan** bright, brilliant, radiant

懇々 **konkon (to)** earnestly, repeatedly

縷々 **ruru** minutely, in detail; continuously

闇々 **yamiyami** without one's knowledge, suddenly, easily

頻々 **hinpin** frequent, repeated

駸々 **shinshin** rapidly, in great strides

18 騒々 **sōzō(shii), zawazawa** noisy, clamorous

19 麗々 **reirei** ostentatious, pretentious

20 兢々 **kyōkyō** fear and trepidation

飄々 **hyōhyō** buoyantly; wandering

21 巍々 **gigi** lofty, towering

爛々 **ranran** glaring, fiery

飈々 **hyōhyō** soughing

轟々 **gōgō (to)** thunderously, with a rumble

29 鬱々 **utsuutsu** gloomily, cheerlessly

3

6 行先々 **yu(ku) sakisaki (de)** wherever one goes

7 赤裸々 **sekirara** stark naked; frank, outspoken

11 黒猩々 **kuroshōjō** chimpanzee

14 複々々線 **fukufukufukusen** six-track rail line

鼻高々 **hanatakadaka** proudly, triumphantly

2

亻
冫
子
阝
卩
刂
力
又
宀
十
卜
ケ 1 ←
丷
厂
辶
冂
八
匚

2

イ
ヲ
子
阝
卩
力
又
宀
亠
卜
→4 ケ
ソ
厂
辶
冂
匸

———— 4 ————

2 子々孫々 **shishi-sonson** descendants, posterity
3 三々五々 **sansan-gogo** in small groups, by twos and threes
小心翼々 **shōshin-yokuyoku** very timid/cautious
5 平々凡々 **heihei-bonbon** commonplace, ordinary
正々堂々 **seisei-dōdō** fair and square, open and aboveboard
6 多士済々 **tashi-seisei** many able people
気息奄々 **kisoku-en'en** gasping for breath, dying
自信満々 **jishin-manman** full of confidence
8 事々物々 **jiji-butsubutsu** everything
侃々諤々 **kankan-gakugaku** outspoken
虎視眈々 **koshi-tantan** with hostile vigilance, waiting one's chance (to pounce)
虎視眈々 **koshi-tantan** with hostile vigilance, waiting one's chance (to pounce)
奇々怪々 **kiki-kaikai** very strange, fantastic
空々漠々 **kūkū-bakubaku** vast and empty
明々白々 **meimei-hakuhaku** perfectly clear
所々方々 **shosho-hōbō** everywhere
9 津々浦々 **tsutsu-uraura** throughout the land, the entire country
是々非々 **zeze-hihi** fair and unbiased
威風堂々 **ifū dōdō** pomp and circumstance
音吐朗々 **onto-rōrō** in a clear/ringing voice
10 時々刻々 **jiji-kokukoku** hourly, minute by minute
11 野心満々 **yashin-manman** full of ambition
虚々実々 **kyokyo-jitsujitsu** clever fighting, trying every strategy
唯々諾々 **ii-dakudaku** quite willing, readily, obediently
12 喧々囂々 **kenken-gōgō** pandemonium
13 戦々恐々 **sensen-kyōkyō** with fear and trembling; with trepidation
戦々競々 **sensen-kyōkyō** with fear and trembling; with trepidation
意気揚々 **iki-yōyō** exultant, triumphant
14 種々様々 **shuju-samazama** all kinds of, diverse
18 闘志満々 **tōshi-manman** full of fighting spirit

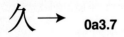 **→ 0a3.7**

 **→ 0a3.14**

———— 4 ————

2n4.1 / 204

 SHOKU, SHIKI, iro color; erotic passion

———— 1 ————

0 色めく **iro(meku)** take on color, be tinged; liven up, grow agitated, waver
色づく **iro(zuku)** take on color
色っぽい **iro(ppoi)** sexy, seductive, fascinating
3 色々 **iroiro** various
色女 **ironna** mistress
4 色文 **irobumi** love letter
色止 **irodo(me)** color fixing
色分 **irowa(ke)** classification (by color), color coding
5 色仕掛 **irojika(ke)** feigned affection
色付 **irozu(ku)** take on color
irotsu(ke) coloring, painting
色好 **irogono(mi)** sensuality, lust
色白 **irojiro** light-complexioned, fair-skinned
色立 **iro(meki)ta(tsu)** become excited/enlivened
色目 **irome** amorous glance
6 色気 **iroke** sexiness, sexuality, amorousness, romance
色気抜 **irokenu(ki)** without female companionship
色気違 **irokichiga(i)** sex mania
色合 **iroa(i)** coloring, shade, tint
色色 **iroiro** various
色糸 **iroito** colored thread
7 色良 **iroyo(i)** favorable (answer)
色里 **irozato** red-light district
色即是空 **shikisoku-zekū** Matter is void. All is vanity.
色抜 **ironu(ki)** decolor
色狂 **iroguru(i)** sex mania
色町 **iromachi** red-light district
色男 **irootoko** lover, paramour; lady-killer
8 色事 **irogoto** love affair; love scene
色事師 **irogotoshi** lady-killer, Don Juan
色刷 **irozu(ri)** color printing
色盲 **shikimō** color blindness
色直 **ironao(shi)** changing wedding dress for ordinary clothes; redyeing
色物 **iromono** colored fabrics
色取 **irodo(ru)** add color, paint, makeup
9 色変 **irogawa(ri)** discoloration; different color/kind
色柄 **irogara** colored pattern
色染 **irozo(me)** dyeing
色香 **iroka** color and scent; beauty, loveliness
10 色恋 **irokoi** love

色消 **iroke(shi)** achromatic; unromantic, prosaic
色弱 **shikijaku** slight color blindness
色留 **irodo(me)** color fixing
色紙 **irogami** colored paper
　　 shikishi (a type of calligraphy paper)
色素 **shikiso** pigment, coloring matter
11 色道 **shikidō** sexual passion
色彩 **shikisai** color, coloration
色黒 **iroguro** dark-complexioned, dark-skinned
色欲 **shikiyoku** sexual desire, lust
色悪 **iroaku** handsome villain
色情 **shikijō** sexual desire, lust
色情狂 **shikijōkyō** sex mania
色眼鏡 **iromegane** colored glasses; prejudiced view
色盛 **irozaka(ri)** a woman's most (sexually) attractive age
12 色揚 **iroa(ge)** redye, restore the original color
色覚 **shikikaku** color sense/vision
色絵 **iroe** colored picture
13 色感 **shikikan** color sense/vision
色鉛筆 **iroenpitsu** colored pencil
14 色模様 **iromoyō** color pattern; love scene
15 色調 **shikichō** color tone
19 色艶 **irotsuya** (facial) color, complexion; luster
21 色魔 **shikima** lady-killer, libertine

────── 2 ──────

2 二色刷 **nishokuzu(ri)** two-color printing
七色 **nanairo** the colors of the rainbow
3 三色 **sanshoku** three colors
三色版 **sanshokuban** three-color printing
三色菫 **sanshoku sumire** pansy
三色旗 **sanshokuki** tricolor flag
才色 **saishoku** wit and beauty
土色 **tsuchi-iro** earth-color, ashen
女色 **joshoku** feminine charms, sensuality
4 五色 **goshiki** the five colors (red, yellow, blue, black, white); multicolored
毛色 **keiro** color of the hair; disposition
水色 **mizu-iro** sky blue, turquoise
火色 **hi-iro** flame color
5 本色 **honshoku** one's real character, true quality
生色 **seishoku** animated look
令色 **reishoku** servile look
古色 **koshoku** ancient appearance
古色蒼然 **koshoku-sōzen** antique-looking, hoary
好色 **kōshoku** sensuality, eroticism, lust
好色本 **kōshokubon** erotic story
好色家 **kōshokuka** sensualist, lecher
好色漢 **kōshokukan** sensualist, lecher

白色 **hakushoku** white
主色 **shushoku** predominant color
目色 **me (no) iro** color of one's eyes; one's facial/eye expression
6 死色 **shishoku** deathly pallor
気色 **kishiki, kishoku** one's mood, disposition; (facial) expression
　　 keshiki(bamu) get angry
朱色 **shuiro** scarlet, vermilion
肉色 **nikuiro** flesh color
色色 **iroiro** various
灰色 **hai-iro** gray
同色 **dōshoku** the same color
地色 **ji-iro** ground-color
肌色 **hada-iro** flesh-colored
有色 **yūshoku** colored (race)
血色 **kesshoku** complexion, color
血色素 **kesshikiso** hemoglobin
7 余色 **yoshoku** complementary color
卵色 **tamago-iro** yellowish color
赤色 **aka-iro, sekishoku** red
呈色 **teishoku** coloration
花色 **hana-iro** light blue
声色 **seishoku** voice and countenance; songs and women **kowairo** tone of voice; vocal mimicry
男色 **danshoku, nanshoku** sodomy
8 夜色 **yashoku** shades of night, night scene
退色 **taishoku** fading; faded color
空色 **sora-iro** sky blue; weather
青色 **seishoku** blue
明色 **meishoku** bright color
物色 **busshoku** look for; select
金色 **kinshoku, kin-iro, konjiki** golden color
金色夜叉 **konjiki yasha** usurer
9 変色 **henshoku** change of color, discoloration
負色 **ma(ke)iro** signs of defeat
茜色 **akane-iro** madder red, crimson
草色 **kusa-iro** dark/emerald green
茶色 **cha-iro** (light) brown
単色 **tanshoku** single color, monochrome
面色 **menshoku** complexion, expression
柚色 **yuzu-iro** lemon yellow
染色 **senshoku** dyeing, staining
染色体 **senshokutai** chromosome
春色 **shunshoku** spring scenery
神色 **shinshoku** mind and countenance
神色自若 **shinshoku-jijaku** calm and composed, unruffled
音色 **neiro, onshoku** tone quality, timbre
秋色 **shūshoku** autumn colors/scenery
紅色 **kōshoku** red
10 原色 **genshoku** primary color
酒色 **shushoku** wine and women
容色 **yōshoku** looks, personal appearance
党色 **tōshoku** partisan coloring

2

亻
冫
子
阝
卩
刂
力
又
宀
一十
├
→ 4 ⺧
⺎
厂
辶
冂
几
匚

桃色 **momo-iro** pink
桃色遊戯 **momo-iro yūgi** sex play
桜色 **sakura-iro** pink, cerise
特色 **tokushoku** characteristic, distinguishing feature, peculiarity
純色 **junshoku** pure color
配色 **haishoku** color scheme/arrangement
11 淡色 **tanshoku** light color
渋色 **shibuiro** tan color
基色 **kishoku** (back)ground color
猟色 **ryōshoku** lechery, debauchery
猟色家 **ryōshokuka** lecher, libertine
彩色 **saishiki** coloring, coloration
彩色画 **saishikiga** colored painting/picture
黄色 **ki-iro** yellow
黄色人種 **ōshoku jinshu** the yellow race
脚色 **kyakushoku** dramatization, stage/film adaptation
脚色者 **kyakushokusha** dramatizer, adapter
脱色 **dasshoku** decoloration, bleaching
黒色 **kokushoku** black
異色 **ishoku** different color; unique, novel
紺色 **kon'iro** dark/navy blue
敗色 **haishoku** signs of impending defeat
12 着色 **chakushoku** to color, tint
遜色 **sonshoku** inferior
温色 **onshoku** warm color; calm facial expression
寒色 **kanshoku** a cold color
喜色 **kishoku** joyful look, all smiles
景色 **keshiki** scenery
無色 **mushoku** colorless, achromatic
補色 **hoshoku** complementary color
紫色 **murasaki-iro** purple
鈍色 **nibu-iro, nibi-iro** dark gray
間色 **kanshoku** a compound color
13 鼠色 **nezumiiro** dark gray, slate
暗色 **anshoku** dark color
愁色 **shūshoku** worried/sorrowful look
辞色 **jishoku** words and looks
褐色 **kasshoku** brown
褐色人種 **kasshoku jinshu** the brown races
鉄色 **tetsu-iro** reddish black, iron blue
鉛色 **namari-iro** lead color, gray
14 翠色 **suishoku** green
漁色 **gyoshoku** debauchery
漁色家 **gyoshokuka** lecher
墨色 **sumi-iro** shade of India ink
暮色 **boshoku** evening twilight
旗色 **hatairo** the tide of war; things, the situation
褪色 **taishoku** fade, lose color; faded color
緑色 **midori-iro, ryokushoku** green
銀色 **gin-iro, ginshoku** silver color
銅色 **dōshoku** copper-colored
飴色 **ame-iro** amber, light brown

雑色 **zasshoku** various colors
鳶色 **tobi-iro** brown, auburn
15 膚色 **hada-iro** flesh-colored
潤色 **junshoku** embellishment
憂色 **yūshoku** worried look, gloom
調色 **chōshoku** mixing colors, toning
調色板 **chōshokuban** palette
16 薄色 **usuiro** light/pale color
橙色 **daidai-iro** orange (color)
錆色 **sabi-iro** rust color
17 濡色 **nu(re)iro** wet/glossy color
18 藤色 **fuji-iro** light purple, lilac, lavender
織色 **o(ri)iro** color as woven (undyed)
難色 **nanshoku** unwillingness, opposition
顔色 **kaoiro, ganshoku** complexion; expression

———— 3 ————

3 三原色 **sangenshoku** the three primary colors
夕景色 **yūgeshiki** evening scene/view
土気色 **tsuchike-iro** earth color
小麦色 **komugi-iro** cocoa brown
山吹色 **yamabuki-iro** orangish/golden yellow
4 天然色 **tennenshoku** natural color, technicolor
5 玉虫色 **tamamushi-iro** iridescent; ambiguous
石竹色 **sekichiku-iro** pink (the color)
6 灰緑色 **kairyokushoku** greenish gray
地方色 **chihōshoku** local color
自然色 **shizenshoku** natural color
7 赤茶色 **akacha-iro** reddish brown
赤紫色 **aka-murasaki-iro** purplish red
赤褐色 **sekkasshoku** reddish brown
赤銅色 **shakudō-iro** brown, bronze, tanned
乳白色 **nyūhakushoku** milky white
8 退紅色 **taikōshoku** pink
国防色 **kokubōshoku** khaki
青銅色 **seidōshoku** bronze-color
9 保護色 **hogoshoku** protective coloration
海老色 **ebi-iro** reddish brown
茶褐色 **chakasshoku** brown
春景色 **haru-geshiki** spring scenery
10 郷土色 **kyōdoshoku** local color
真珠色 **shinju-iro** pearl gray
流行色 **ryūkōshoku** fashionable/prevailing color
11 淡赤色 **tansekishoku** rose color
淡紅色 **tankōshoku** rose/salmon pink
淡黄色 **tankōshoku** light yellow, straw color
淡紫色 **tanshishoku** light purple
淡褐色 **tankasshoku** light brown
淡緑色 **tanryokushoku** light green
深紅色 **shinkōshoku** deep/ruby red
萌黄色 **moegi-iro** yellowish/light green
黄金色 **ōgonshoku, kogane-iro** gold color

黄緑色 **ōryokushoku** yellowish green, olive
黄銅色 **kōdōshoku** brass yellow
黒褐色 **kokkasshoku** blackish brown
雪景色 **yukigeshiki** snowy landscape
12 葡萄色 **budō-iro** dark purple
極彩色 **gokusaishiki** brilliant coloring, full color (illustrations)
焦茶色 **ko(ge)cha-iro** dark brown, umber
13 暗赤色 **ansekishoku** dark red
暗紫色 **anshishoku** dark purple
暗褐色 **ankasshoku** dark brown
暗緑色 **anryokushoku** dark green
戦時色 **senjishoku** wartime look/aspect
鉄褐色 **tekkasshoku** iron gray
鳩羽色 **hatoba-iro** bluish gray
14 瑠璃色 **ruri-iro** sky blue, azure
褪紅色 **taikōshoku** light pink
緑黄色 **ryokuōshoku** greenish yellow
16 濃青色 **nōseishoku** deep/dark blue
濃紅色 **nōkōshoku** deep red, crimson
濃紫色 **nōshishoku** deep purple
濃褐色 **nōkasshoku** dark brown
薄茶色 **usucha-iro** light brown, buff
19 警戒色 **keikaishoku** warning color
20 臙脂色 **enji-iro** deep red
24 鼈甲色 **bekkō-iro** amber color
29 鬱金色 **ukon-iro** saffron color

—————— 4 ——————
2 十人十色 **jūnin-toiro** Tastes differ. To each his own.
5 巧言令色 **kōgen-reishoku** ingratiating geniality
8 空即是色 **kūsoku-zeshiki** void matter as tangible
14 総天然色 **sōtennenshoku** in full (natural) color

2n4.2 / 302

争　争　**SŌ, araso(u)** dispute, argue, contend for
araso(i) dispute, altercation

—————— 1 ——————
5 争好 **araso(i)zu(ki)** quarrelsome, contentious
7 争乱 **sōran** rioting, disturbance
9 争点 **sōten** point of contention, issue
14 争端 **sōtan** beginning of a dispute
争奪 **sōdatsu** contend/scramble for
争奪戦 **sōdatsusen** contest/scramble/struggle for
15 争論 **sōron** dispute, argument, controversy
18 争闘 **sōtō** struggle
19 争覇 **sōha** contend for supremacy
20 争議 **sōgi** dispute, strife, conflict

—————— 2 ——————
4 内争 **naisō** internal strife

水争 **mizu araso(i)** irrigation/water-rights dispute
7 抗争 **kōsō** dispute; resistance
言争 **i(i)araso(i)** quarrel, altercation
9 係争 **keisō** dispute, contention
政争 **seisō** political dispute
10 党争 **tōsō** party rivalry, factionalism
紛争 **funsō** dispute, strife
13 戦争 **sensō** war
戦争中 **sensōchū** during the war
15 論争 **ronsō** dispute, controversy
18 闘争 **tōsō** struggle, conflict; strike
19 繋争 **keisō** dispute, contention
20 競争 **kyōsō** competition
競争者 **kyōsōsha** competitor, rival

—————— 3 ——————
3 山猫争議 **yamaneko sōgi** wildcat strike
9 相続争 **sōzoku araso(i)** inheritance dispute
12 無競争 **mukyōsō** without competition, unopposed
15 権力争 **kenryoku araso(i)** struggle for supremacy/power
縄張争 **nawaba(ri) araso(i)** jurisdictional dispute, turf battle

—————— 4 ——————
7 局地戦争 **kyokuchi sensō** limited war
9 軍拡競争 **gunkaku kyōsō** arms race
南北戦争 **Nanboku Sensō** the War Between the States, the (U.S.) Civil War

—————— 5 ——————
4 太平洋戦争 **Taiheiyō Sensō** the Pacific War, World War II

2n4.3 / 534

危　**KI, abu(nai), ayau(i)** dangerous
aya(bumu) fear, have misgivings about, be apprehensive about

—————— 1 ——————
6 危地 **kichi** dangerous position, peril
9 危急 **kikyū** emergency, crisis
危急存亡 **kikyū-sonbō** life-or-death situation, crisis
危殆 **kitai** danger, peril, jeopardy
10 危険 **kiken** danger, risk
危険物 **kikenbutsu** hazardous articles, explosives and combustibles
危険性 **kikensei** riskiness, danger
危害 **kigai** injury, harm
11 危惧 **kigu** fear, misgivings, apprehension
16 危機 **kiki** crisis
危機一髪 **kiki-ippatsu** imminent/hairbreadth danger
危篤 **kitoku** critically ill, near death
18 危難 **kinan** danger, distress

2

亻 冫 子 阝 卩 刂 力 又 宀 冖 十 卜 厂 4←

ノ 厂 辶 冂 几 匚

─────── 2 ───────
6 安危 **anki** safety (or danger), fate, welfare
─────── 3 ───────
11 累卵危 **ruiran (no) aya(uki)** imminent peril

─────── 5 ───────

2n5.1 / 473

角 KAKU angle; corner; (animal's) horn; compare, compete **tsuno** horn, antlers **kado** corner, angle **sumi** corner, nook

─────── 1 ───────
2 角力 **sumō** sumo
3 角叉 **tsunomata** red algae
角々 **kadokado (ni)** on every corner
kadokado(shii) angular; unaffable
4 角刈 **kakuga(ri)** square-cut hair, crewcut
5 角石 **kakuishi** square stone
角立 **kadoda(tsu)** be pointed/sharp, be rough; sound harsh
角目立 **tsunomeda(tsu)** be pointed/sharp, be rough; sound harsh
6 角行 **kakkō** (one of the "chessmen" in shōgi)
7 角形 **kakugata** squared-off, angular
角材 **kakuzai** rectangular timber/lumber
8 角突合 **tsunotsu(ki)a(i)** bickering, wrangling
角店 **kadomise** corner store
9 角盆 **kakubon** square tray
角逐 **kakuchiku** compete, contend, vie
角通 **kakutsū** sumo expert
角度 **kakudo** angle
角屋敷 **kadoyashiki** corner house
角柱 **kakuchū** square pillar; prism (in geometry)
角砂糖 **kakuzatō** sugar cubes
10 角帯 **kakuobi** man's stiff obi/sash
角書 **tsunoga(ki)** two-line subtitle
角袖 **kakusode** square/bag sleeves; plainclothes policeman (in Meiji period)
11 角瓶 **kakubin** square bottle
角張 **kakuba(ru), kado(baru)** be angular; be stiff and formal
角細工 **tsunozaiku** horn work/carving
角笛 **tsunobue** huntsman's horn, bugle
12 角帽 **kakubō** square college cap
13 角隠 **tsunokaku(shi)** bride's wedding hood
14 角膜 **kakumaku** cornea
角膜炎 **kakumakuen** inflammation of the cornea
15 角質 **kakushitsu** horny substance, keratin
角質物 **kakushitsubutsu** horny/keratinous material
16 角錐 **kakusui** pyramid
─────── 2 ───────
1 一角 **ikkaku** a corner/section; narwhal;

apparently, seemingly **hitokado** full-fledged, respectable
一角獣 **ikkakujū** unicorn
3 三角 **sankaku** triangular
mi(tsu)kado Y-junction of streets
三角巾 **sankakukin** triangular bandage
三角州 **sankakusu** delta
三角帆 **sankakuho** jib sail
三角形 **sankakkei, sankakukei** triangle
三角函数 **sankaku kansū** trigonometric function
三角法 **sankakuhō** trigonometry
三角洲 **sankakusu** delta
三角旗 **sankakuki** pennant
三角関係 **sankaku kankei** love triangle
三角錐 **sankakusui** triangular-base pyramid
口角 **kōkaku** corners of the mouth
4 互角 **gokaku** equal, evenly-matched
内角 **naikaku** interior angle; inside corner (in baseball)
五角形 **gokakkei, gokakukei** pentagon
六角 **rokkaku** hexagon
六角形 **rokkakukei, rokkakkei** hexagon
方角 **hōgaku** direction
5 凸角 **tokkaku** a salient (angle)
外角 **gaikaku** external angle; outside (corner)
好角家 **kōkakuka** sumo fan
広角 **kōkaku** wide-angle (lens)
四角 **shikaku** square; quadrilateral **yo(tsu)kado** four corners; intersection
四角号碼 **shikaku gōma** (an encoding scheme which assigns to each kanji a four-digit number based on its four corners)
四角四面 **shikaku-shimen** methodical, prim
四角形 **shikakukei** quadrilateral, square
四角張 **shikakuba(ru)** be formal/stiff
目角 **mekado** corner of the eye; sharp look
6 多角 **takaku** many-sided, diversified, multilateral
多角的 **takakuteki** many-sided, versatile, diversified, multilateral
多角経営 **takaku keiei** diversified management
死角 **shikaku** dead/unseen angle
曲角 **ma(gari)kado** (street) corner
仰角 **gyōkaku** angle of elevation
同角 **dōkaku** equal angles
7 余角 **yokaku** complementary angle
対角 **taikaku** opposite angle
対角線 **taikakusen** a diagonal
角角 **kadokado (ni)** on every corner **kadokado(shii)** angular; unaffable
折角 **sekkaku** going to (much) trouble, on purpose, expressly; kindly
8 直角 **chokkaku** right angle
突角 **tokkaku** convex angle

底角 **teikaku** base angle
9 海角 **kaikaku** promontory, cape
10 射角 **shakaku** angle of fire
俯角 **fukaku** angle of depression
高角 **kōkaku** altitude, high-angle
高角砲 **kōkakuhō** high-angle/antiaircraft gun
11 斜角 **shakaku** oblique angle, bevel
接角 **sekkaku** adjacent angles
視角 **shikaku** angle of vision; viewpoint
頂角 **chōkaku** vertical angle
12 街角 **machikado** street corner
補角 **hokaku** supplementary angle
等角 **tōkaku** equal angles
鈍角 **donkaku** obtuse angle
13 触角 **shokkaku** feeler, antenna, tentacle
15 鋭角 **eikaku** acute angle
16 錯角 **sakkaku** alternate angles
頭角現 **tōkaku (o) ara(wasu)** be preeminent

—————— 3 ——————
5 正三角形 **seisankakkei, seisankakukei**
    equilateral triangle
7 投射角 **tōshakaku** angle of incidence
10 真四角 **mashikaku** square
13 傾斜角 **keishakaku** angle of inclination, dip

—————— 4 ——————
12 等辺三角形 **tōhen sankakkei, tōhen**
    sankakukei equilateral triangle
等脚三角形 **tōkyaku sankakkei, tōkyaku**
    sankakukei isosceles triangle

—————— 5 ——————
2 二等辺三角形 **nitōhen sankakkei, nitōhen**
    sankakukei isosceles triangle

—————— 6 ——————

兔 → 兔　**0a8.5**

2n6.1 / 733

免　免　**MEN** exemption; permission;
dismissal **manuka(reru)**
escape from; be saved; avoid,
evade; be exempted/spared

—————— 1 ——————
0 免じる **men(jiru)** dismiss; exempt
7 免状 **menjō** diploma; license
免役 **men'eki** exemption from military
    service; release from prison
8 免官 **menkan** dismissal
9 免除 **menjo** exemption
免疫 **men'eki** immunity (from a disease)
免疫性 **men'ekisei** immunity (from a disease)
10 免租 **menso** tax exemption
11 免許 **menkyo** license, permission

免許状 **menkyojō** license, certificate, permit
免許証 **menkyoshō** license, certificate, permit
免責 **menseki** exemption from responsibility
12 免税 **menzei** tax exemption
免税品 **menzeihin** duty-free goods
免訴 **menso** dismissal (of a case), acquittal
13 免罪 **menzai** acquittal, pardon; papal
    indulgence
免罪符 **menzaifu** an indulgence
18 免職 **menshoku** dismissal, discharge

—————— 2 ——————
6 任免 **ninmen** appointments and dismissals
仮免状 **karimenjō** temporary license;
    provisional diploma
8 放免 **hōmen** release, acquittal
10 特免 **tokumen** special license; dispensation
11 赦免 **shamen** pardon, clemency
赦免状 **shamenjō** (letter of) pardon
12 減免 **genmen** reduction of or exemption
    from (taxes), mitigation and remission
    (of punishment)
御免 **gomen** (I beg) your pardon; no thankyou,
    not me; permission
無免許 **mumenkyo** without a license
15 罷免 **himen** dismissal (from one's post)

—————— 3 ——————
8 依願免官 **igan menkan** retirement at one's
    own request
14 徴兵免除 **chōhei menjo** draft exemption

—————— 7 ——————

2n7.1 / 510

負　**FU** bear, carry; be defeated; negative
(number) **ma(keru)** be defeated/beaten,
lose; be outdone by, fall behind; lower
the price **(o)ma(ke)** a little extra
thrown in; in addition, besides **ma(kasu)** defeat,
beat **ma(karu)** reduce the price **o(u)** carry
(on the back), bear (responsibility/expenses), owe,
sustain (an injury) **o(waseru)** make (someone)
carry, make (someone) bear (the responsibility/
expenses), inflict (injury) **o(nbu), o(buu)** carry
(a baby) on one's back **o(busaru)** be carried
piggyback; be dependent on

—————— 1 ——————
4 負犬 **ma(ke)inu** loser
5 負号 **fugō** minus sign (–)
負目 **o(i)me** debt
6 負気 **ma(ken)ki** unyielding/competitive spirit
負色 **ma(ke)iro** signs of defeat
負劣 **ma(kezu)-oto(razu)** keeping up with
    (each other)
8 負担 **futan** burden, load, responsibility,
    liability

9 負革 **o(i)kawa** sling, carrying strap (on a rifle)

負星 **ma(ke)boshi** mark indicating a loss

10 負荷 **fuka** burden, load (electricity)

負託 **futaku** mandate, trust

11 負惜 **ma(ke)o(shimi)** unwillingness to admit defeat

12 負量 **furyō** negative/minus quantity

負越 **ma(ke)ko(shi)** more losses than wins

13 負傷 **fushō** sustain an injury, get hurt

負傷兵 **fushōhei** wounded soldier

負傷者 **fushōsha** injured person, the wounded

負債 **fusai** debt, liabilities

負嫌 **ma(kezu)gira(i)** unyielding, determined to win

負腹立 **ma(ke)bara (o) ta(teru)** get angry upon losing

負数 **fusū** negative number

14 負魂 **ma(keji)damashii** unyielding spirit, striving to keep ahead of others

――――――― 2 ―――――――

2 力負 **chikarama(ke)** be defeated by misapplication of one's own strength

3 大負 **ōma(ke)** a crushing defeat; big price reduction

4 手負 **teo(i)** wounded

5 正負 **seifu** positive and negative, plus and minus

打負 **u(chi)ma(kasu)** beat, defeat

6 気負 **kio(u)** rouse oneself, get psyched up

気負立 **kio(i)ta(tsu)** rouse oneself, get psyched up

自負 **jifu** be proud of oneself, be conceited

7 言負 **i(i)ma(keru)** lose an argument

i(i)ma(kasu) confute

8 抱負 **hōfu** aspiration, ambition

9 背負 **seo(u), sho(u)** carry on one's back, shoulder, be burdened with

背負投 **shio(i)na(ge), seo(i)na(ge)** throw over one's shoulder; betrayal

10 荷負 **nio(i)** shouldering a load

根負 **konma(ke)** be outperservered

夏負 **natsuma(ke)** succumb to the summer heat

12 勝負 **shōbu** victory or defeat; match, showdown

勝負事 **shōbugoto** game of skill/chance

勝負師 **shōbushi** gambler

14 漆負 **urushima(ke)** lacquer poisoning

15 請負 **u(ke)o(u)** contract for, undertake

ukeoi contracting

請負人 **ukeoinin** contractor

請負師 **ukeoishi** contractor

請負業 **ukeoigyō** contracting business

18 顔負 **kaoma(ke)** be put to shame, be outdone

――――――― 3 ―――――――

3 下請負 **shitaukeoi** subcontract

6 気合負 **kia(i)ma(ke)** be overawed

10 根気負 **konkima(ke)** be outperservered

12 無勝負 **mushōbu** a tie/draw, undecided

15 舞台負 **butaima(ke)** stage fright

――――――― 4 ―――――――

1 一六勝負 **ichiroku shōbu** gambling; a gamble

10 真剣勝負 **shinken-shōbu** fighting with real swords; game played in earnest

2n7.2 / 303

急 急 **KYŪ** urgent, sudden, emergency; steep, sharp (turn) **iso(gu)** (be in a) hurry **se(ku)** be in a hurry, be impatient

――――――― 1 ―――――――

4 急勾配 **kyūkōbai** steep slope

急込 **se(ki)ko(mu)** get agitated, be in a hurry, become impatient

急火 **kyūka** a sudden fire; a nearby fire

5 急用 **kyūyō** urgent business

6 急死 **kyūshi** sudden/untimely death

急行 **kyūkō** an express (train)

急行券 **kyūkōken** express ticket

急行便 **kyūkōbin** express mail

7 急迫 **kyūhaku** be imminent/pressing, grow acute

急坂 **kyūhan** steep hill

急告 **kyūkoku** urgent notice

急足 **iso(gi)ashi** brisk pace, hurried steps

8 急使 **kyūshi** express messenger, courier

急命 **kyūmei** urgent orders

急追 **kyūtsui** hot pursuit

急送 **kyūsō** send by express, rush

急歩 **kyūho** fast walking

急性 **kyūsei** acute (not chronic)

急性病 **kyūseibyō** acute illness

急所 **kyūsho** vital point, vulnerable spot; crux, key (to)

9 急信 **kyūshin** urgent message

急降下 **kyūkōka** drop rapidly; dive, swoop

急変 **kyūhen** sudden change; emergency

急速 **kyūsoku** prompt, swift, fast, speedy

急速度 **kyūsokudo** high speed

急逝 **kyūsei** sudden/untimely death

急造 **kyūzō** build in a hurry

急派 **kyūha** dispatch, rush, expedite

10 急進 **kyūshin** rapid progress; radical, extreme

急進主義 **kyūshin shugi** radicalism

急進的 **kyūshinteki** radical, extreme

急進派 **kyūshinha** radicals

急進党 **kyūshintō** radical party, radicals

急流 **kyūryū** swift current; rapids
急峻 **kyūshun** steep
急病 **kyūbyō** sudden illness
急病人 **kyūbyōnin** emergency patient/case
急症 **kyūshō** sudden illness; emergency case
11 急停車 **kyūteisha** sudden stop
急斜面 **kyūshamen** steep slope/incline
急務 **kyūmu** urgent business, pressing need
急患 **kyūkan** emergency patient/case
急設 **kyūsetsu** speedy installation
急転 **kyūten** sudden change
急転直下 **kyūten-chokka** sudden change, sudden turn (toward a solution)
急転換 **kyūtenkan** sudden change, rapid switchover
12 急場 **kyūba** emergency, crisis
急報 **kyūhō** urgent message, alarm
急須 **kyūsu** teapot
急落 **kyūraku** sudden/sharp decline
急募 **kyūbo** urgent recruiting, immediate hiring
13 急傾斜 **kyūkeisha** steep slope/incline
14 急増 **kyūzō** sudden increase
15 急撃 **kyūgeki** surprise attack, raid
16 急遽 **kyūkyo** hastily, hurriedly
急激 **kyūgeki** sudden, abrupt, drastic
18 急難 **kyūnan** impending danger; sudden disaster
20 急騰 **kyūtō** sudden rise (in prices)
22 急襲 **kyūshū** surprise attack, raid

──────── 2 ────────

3 大急 **ōiso(gi)** in a big hurry/rush
4 不急 **fukyū** not urgent, nonessential
火急 **kakyū** urgent, emergency
6 危急 **kikyū** emergency, crisis
危急存亡 **kikyū-sonbō** life-or-death situation, crisis
至急 **shikyū** urgent
至急便 **shikyūbin** express mail
至急報 **shikyūhō** urgent telegram/call
早急 **sōkyū, sakkyū** urgently, without delay
7 売急 **u(ri)iso(gu)** be eager to sell, sell in haste
応急 **ōkyū** emergency, temporary, stopgap
応急手当 **ōkyū tea(te)** first aid
応急策 **ōkyūsaku** emergency/stopgap measure
8 性急 **seikyū** impetuous, impatient
取急 **to(ri)iso(gu)** hurry
10 特急 **tokkyū** limited express (train)
息急切 **ikise(ki)ki(ru)** pant, gasp
11 救急 **kyūkyū** emergency (relief)
救急車 **kyūkyūsha** ambulance
救急法 **kyūkyūhō** first aid
救急策 **kyūkyūsaku** emergency measures
救急箱 **kyūkyūbako** first-aid kit

救急薬 **kyūkyūyaku** first-aid medicine
13 準急 **junkyū** local express (train)
15 緩急 **kankyū** fast or/and slow; emergency
緊急 **kinkyū** emergency
19 警急 **keikyū** alarm, emergency

──────── 3 ────────

12 超特急 **chōtokkyū** superexpress (train)
短兵急 **tanpeikyū** impetuous, sudden

2n7.3

奐   **KAN** clear, bright

──────── 8 ────────

2n8.1 / 735

勉 勉   **BEN** diligence
tsuto(meru) make efforts, work hard, be diligent

──────── 1 ────────

7 勉励 **benrei** diligence, industriousness
勉学 **bengaku** study
11 勉強 **benkyō** studying; diligence; sell cheap
勉強家 **benkyōka** diligent student, hard worker

──────── 2 ────────

4 不勉強 **fubenkyō** idleness, failure to study
9 俄勉強 **niwakabenkyō** cramming
12 勤勉 **kinben** industrious, hard-working
17 糞勉強 **kusobenkyō** cramming

──────── 9 ────────

2n9.1

亀 龜   **KI, kame** turtle, tortoise

──────── 1 ────────

2 亀子 **kame(no)ko** young turtle/tortoise
5 亀甲 **kikkō, kame (no) kō** tortoise shell
12 亀裂 **kiretsu** crack, fissure
16 亀頭 **kitō** the glans (penis)
23 亀鑑 **kikan** pattern, model, exemplar

──────── 2 ────────

4 元亀 **Genki** (era, 1570–1573)
文亀 **Bunki** (era, 1501–1503)
7 阿亀 **okame** ugly/homely woman
8 宝亀 **Hōki** (era, 770–781)
9 海亀 **umigame** sea turtle
神亀 **Jikki** (era, 724–728)
15 霊亀 **Reiki** (era, 715–717)
21 鶴亀 **tsurukame** crane and tortoise; congratulations

2

亻 冫 子 阝 卩 刂 力 又 宀 亠 十 卜
夕 9 ←
ⁿ
厂 辶 冂 几 匚

鶴亀算 **tsurukamezan** solving a system of linear equations (example: How many cranes and how many turtles, given a total of 11 animals and 36 legs?)

魚→ **11a0.1**

2n9.2

斛 **KOKU** (unit of volume, about 180 liters)

冕 → 冕 **4c7.9**

─────── 10 ───────

2n10.1 / 739

象 **SHŌ** image, shape
ZŌ elephant
katado(ru) pattern after, imitate

─────── 1 ───────

4 象牙 **zōge** ivory
象牙海岸 **Zōge Kaigan** Ivory Coast
象牙細工 **zōgezaiku** ivory work/carving
象牙塔 **zōge (no) tō** ivory tower
5 象皮病 **zōhibyō** elephantiasis
6 象虫 **zōmushi** weevil, snout beetle
7 象形 **shōkei** hieroglyphic; type of kanji resembling what it represents
象形文字 **shōkei moji** hieroglyphics
8 象限 **shōgen** quadrant
11 象眼 **zōgan** inlay, damascene
12 象嵌 **zōgan** inlay, damascene
14 象徴 **shōchō** symbol
象徴主義 **shōchō shugi** symbolism
象徴的 **shōchōteki** symbolic
象徴詩 **shōchōshi** symbolical/symbolist poetry

─────── 2 ───────

3 万象 **banshō** all creation
4 天象 **tenshō** astronomical phenomenon; the weather
天象儀 **tenshōgi** planetarium
心象 **shinshō** mental image
5 写象 **shazō** image
6 気象 **kishō** weather; disposition, temperament
気象台 **kishōdai** weather station
気象庁 **Kishōchō** Meteorological Agency
気象学 **kishōgaku** meteorology
気象図 **kishōzu** weather map

気象観測 **kishō kansoku** meteorological observations
印象 **inshō** impression
印象主義 **inshō shugi** impressionism
印象的 **inshōteki** impressive, graphic
印象派 **inshōha** impressionist school
有象無象 **uzō-muzō** all things tangible and intangible; the rabble, riffraff
7 対象 **taishō** object, subject, target
対象的 **taishōteki** objective
対象物 **taishōbutsu** object, subject, target
形象 **keishō** shape, figure, phenomenon
8 表象 **hyōshō** symbol, emblem
事象 **jishō** matter, aspect, phenomenon, event
抽象 **chūshō** abstraction
抽象画 **chūshōga** abstract painting
抽象的 **chūshōteki** abstract
抽象論 **chūshōron** abstract argument/discussion
物象 **busshō** object; material phenomenon
具象化 **gushōka** make concrete
具象画 **gushōga** representational painting
具象的 **gushōteki** concrete, not abstract
金象眼 **kinzōgan** inlaying with gold
金象嵌 **kinzōgan** inlaying with gold
9 海象 **kaishō** ocean conditions
seiuchi walrus
11 捨象 **shashō** abstraction; disregard, ignore
現象 **genshō** phenomenon
現象界 **genshōkai** the phenomenal world
14 穀象虫 **kokuzō-mushi** rice weevil
雌象 **mezō** cow elephant
18 観象 **kanshō** meterological observation

─────── 3 ───────

5 好印象 **kōinshō** good impression
9 珍現象 **chingenshō** strange phenomenon
11 釈迦象 **shakazō** image of Buddha

─────── 4 ───────

6 有象無象 **uzō-muzō** all things tangible and intangible; the rabble, riffraff
12 森羅万象 **shinra-banshō** all creation, the universe

2n10.2

觝 **TEI** touch, feel; collide/conflict with

─────── 11 ───────

麀 → 麀 麀 **3q30.1**

解 → **4g9.1**

2n11.1

舐　　**KO** goblet; wooden writing tablet

解→解　**4g9.1**

2n11.2

觜　　**SHI** (bird's) bill; horns

— 12 —

2n12.1

夐　　**KEI** far, distant

豫→予　**0a4.12**

— 14 —

龜→亀　**2n9.1**

— 16 —

イ ヽ 孑 阝 卩 刂 力 又 亠 亠 ⺍ ⺅ ケ ヽ 0←
广 辶 冂 几 匚

— ˇ 2o —

八	分	公	父	兮	半	乎	羊	并	共	弟	兌	谷
0.1	2.1	2.2	2.3	2.4	0a5.24	0a5.17	4.1	4.2	3k3.3	5.1	5.2	5.3
坌	岔	兵	呉	来	並	羌	忿	斧	具	典	其	券
5.4	5.5	5.6	5.7	0a7.6	6.1	6.2	6.3	6.4	5c3.1	6.5	6.6	2f6.10
莽	氛	酋	盆	首	前	美	姜	盆	瓮	剏	朏	叛
2f6.10	6.7	2o7.1	7.1	7.2	7.3	7.4	7.5	7.6	7.7	7.8	7.9	2p7.3
巻	巷	釜	兼	羔	恙	差	拳	益	翁	釜	眞	恭
0a9.11	3k6.17	2o8.7	8.1	8.2	8.3	8.4	3c6.18	8.5	8.6	8.7	2k8.1	3k7.16
剪	孳	曽	盖	羞	貧	黄	瓶	質	羝	羚	粛	着
9.1	9.2	9.3	3k10.15	9.4	9.5	3k8.16	9.6	7b8.7	9.7	9.8	0a11.8	10.1
善	尊	尊	奠	普	曾	爺	巽	巽	翔	斯	期	黹
10.2	10.3	2o10.3	10.4	10.5	2o9.3	10.6	2o10.7	10.7	10.8	10.9	4b8.11	0a12.1
慈	煎	義	羨	與	業	粂	爾	冀	養	羹	躾	羲
11.1	11.2	11.3	11.4	0a3.23	0a13.3	0a13.4	0a14.3	2o9.1	13.1	2o17.1	4f12.2	14.1
興	冀	輿	糞	翼	戴	叢	羮	黼	囍	爨		
14.2	14.3	15.1	6b11.3	15.2	0a17.1	6e12.3	17.1	0a19.1	2o10.2	23.1		

— 0 —

2o0.1 / 10

八　八　　**HACHI, yat(tsu), ya(tsu), ya, yō-** eight

— 1 —

2 八丁 **hatchō** skillfulness
八十路 **yasoji** eighty years old
3 八丈島 **Hachijōjima** (island, Tōkyō-to)
八千代 **yachiyo** thousands of years
八千草 **yachigusa** many plants

4 八切 **ya(tsu)gi(ri)** cut into eight parts; octavo
八文字 **hachimonji** the shape of the kanji 八 *hachi* (eight)
八分目 **hachibunme, hachibume** eight-tenths; moderation
八分音符 **hachibu onpu** an eighth note (♪)
八辺形 **hachihenkei** octagon
八月 **hachigatsu** August
八日 **yōka** eight days; the eighth (of the month)
八王子 **Hachiōji** (city, Tōkyō-to)
八方 **happō** all sides/directions

八方美人 **happō bijin** one who is affable to everybody

八方塞 **happō fusa(gari)** blocked in every direction, stymied

八戸 **Hachinohe** (city, Aomori-ken)

5 八字 **hachi (no) ji** figure eight

6 八百万 **yaoyorozu** myriads, countless

八百長 **yaochō** rigged affair, fixed game

八百屋 **yaoya** vegetable store; jack-of-all-trades

7 八体 **hattai** the eight styles of writing kanji

8 八卦 **hakke** the eight divination signs; fortunetelling

八苦 **hakku** the eight pains (Buddhism)

9 八重 **yae** double(-petaled); eightfold

八重咲 **yaeza(ki)** double-flowering

八重歯 **yaeba** double tooth, snaggletooth

八重楼 **yaezakura** double-flowering cherry tree

八面 **hachimen** eight faces; all sides

八面六臂 **hachimen roppi** eight faces and six arms; versatile talent

八面玲瓏 **hachimen-reirō** beautiful from all sides; perfect serenity, affability

10 八紘一宇 **hakkō-ichiu** universal brotherhood

12 八景 **hakkei** the eight beautiful sights (of a region)

八裂 **ya(tsu)za(ki)** tear limb from limb

15 八幡 **Hachiman** the god of war
Yahata (city, Fukuoka-ken)

八幡宮 **Hachimangū** shrine of the god of war

16 八橋 **ya(tsu)hashi** zigzag bridge

────────── 2 ──────────

1 一八 **ichi(ka)bachi(ka)** sink or swim

2 二八 **nippachi** slack season for business (February and August)

十八番 **jūhachiban** Kabuki repertoire of 18 classical pieces; one's forte/hobby, one's favorite (song/topic) **ohako** one's forte/hobby, one's favorite (song/topic)

3 大八車 **daihachiguruma** large wagon

口八丁 **kuchihatchō** eloquent, talkative

4 尺八 **shakuhachi** bamboo flute/recorder

5 目八分 **mehachibu** (hold an offering) a little below eye level; most respectfully; about eight-tenths full

7 村八分 **murahachibu** ostracism

11 黒八丈 **kurohachijō** (a type of thick black silk)

12 御八 **oyatsu** afternoon snack

13 腹八分 **hara hachibu** eating to only 80 percent of stomach capacity

14 嘘八百 **usohappyaku** a pack of lies

────────── 3 ──────────

2 七転八倒 **shichiten-battō, shitten-battō** writhing in agony

七転(び)八起(き) **nanakoro(bi)ya(oki)** ups and downs of life, Fall seven times and get up eight.

3 弓矢八幡 **yumiya hachiman** god of war

5 四方八方 **shihō-happō** in every direction, far and wide

四苦八苦 **shiku-hakku** agony, dire distress

10 胸突八丁 **munatsu(ki) hatchō** steepest part of the path up the mountain

12 傍目八目 **okame-hachimoku** Lookers-on see more than the players.

────────── 2 ──────────

2o2.1 / 38

分　分

BUN dividing, portion
FUN minute (of time or arc); (unit of weight, about 375 mg)
BU rate, percentage; one percent; thickness; (unit of length, about 3.03 cm)
wa(karu) understand **wa(keru/katsu)** divide, split up; separate, isolate; distribute; distinguish
wa(kareru) part, leave; branch off; be divided

────────── 1 ──────────

2 分入 **wa(ke)i(ru)** make one's way through

分子 **bunshi** molecule; numerator; elements, faction

分子量 **bunshiryō** molecular weight

分子説 **bunshisetsu** molecular theory

分力 **bunryoku** component force

3 分工場 **bunkōjō** branch plant/factory

分与 **bun'yo** distribute, apportion

4 分化 **bunka** specialization, differentiation

分水界 **bunsuikai** watershed, (continental) divide

分水線 **bunsuisen** watershed, (continental) divide

分水嶺 **bunsuirei** watershed, (continental) divide

5 分母 **bunbo** denominator

分冊 **bunsatsu** separate volume

分目 **wa(kare)me** turning point, junction, parting of the ways

分外 **bungai** inordinate, excessive

分布 **bunpu** distribution

分立 **bunritsu** separation (of powers), independence

6 分合 **wa(ke)a(u), wa(kachi)a(u)** share

分会 **bunkai** branch, (local) chapter

分列 **bunretsu** filing off

分列式 **bunretsushiki** march-past, military review

分光 **bunkō** diffraction of light into a spectrum
分光学 **bunkōgaku** spectroscopy
分光器 **bunkōki** spectroscope
分団 **bundan** branch, (local) chapter
7 分身 **bunshin** parturition, delivery; one's child; branch, offshoot; one's alter ego
分体 **buntai** fission
分別 **funbetsu** discretion, good judgment
　　 bunbetsu classification, separation, discrimination
分別盛 **funbetsuzaka(ri)** age of discretion, mature judgment
分岐 **bunki** branch off, fork, ramify, diverge
分岐点 **bunkiten** branch/ramification/turning point, fork, junction
分局 **bunkyoku** branch office
分社 **bunsha** branch shrine
分利 **bunri** crisis (of an illness), critical
8 分限 **bungen, bugen** social standing; wealthy man
分限者 **bugensha** wealthy man
分厚 **buatsu** thick
分泌 **bunpitsu** secretion
分泌物 **bunpitsubutsu** a secretion
分担 **buntan** apportionment, sharing
分店 **bunten** branch store
分析 **bunseki** analysis
分明 **bunmei, bunmyō** clear, distinct
分取 **bunshu** taking a sample
　　 wa(ke)do(ri) apportionment
9 分乗 **bunjō** ride separately
分院 **bun'in** branch (of a hospital)
分点 **bunten** equinox
分前 **wa(ke)mae** share, portion
分派 **bunpa** branch, offshoot, sect, faction
分室 **bunshitsu** isolated room, detached office
分県地図 **bunken chizu** maps grouped by prefecture
分度器 **bundoki** protractor
分秒 **funbyō** a moment
分科 **bunka** department, section, branch, course
分界 **bunkai** demarcation, boundary, border
分界線 **bunkaisen** line of demarcation
分級 **bunkyū** classify
10 分流 **bunryū** tributary
分捕 **bundo(ru)** capture, seize, plunder
分捕品 **bundo(ri)hin** botty, loot, spoils
分娩 **bunben** childbirth, delivery
分家 **bunke** branch family
分党 **buntō** secession from a party
分校 **bunkō** branch school
分骨 **bunkotsu** bury parts of a person's ashes in separate places
分書 **wa(kachi)ga(ki)** writing with a space between words

分教場 **bunkyōjō** detached classroom
分納 **bunnō** payment/delivery in installments
分配 **bunpai** division, sharing, allotment
11 分野 **bun'ya** field, sphere, area, division
分隊 **buntai** squad
分宿 **bunshuku** billeting, lodging separately
12 分割 **bunkatsu** partition, division
分割払 **bunkatsubara(i)** payment in installments
分遣 **bunken** detachment, detail
分極 **bunkyoku** polarization
分量 **bunryō** quantity, amount
分散 **bunsan** breakup, dispersion, variance
分裂 **bunretsu** dissolution, breakup, division
分詞 **bunshi** participle
13 分業 **bungyō** division of labor, specialization
分際 **bunzai** social standing
分解 **bunkai** analysis, breakdown, decomposition, disassembly, disintegration
分数 **bunsū** fraction
分署 **bunsho** substation, branch
14 分銅 **fundō** (counter)weight
15 分権 **bunken** decentralization of authority
分課 **bunka** subdivision, section, department
分蝕 **bunshoku** partial eclipse
16 分館 **bunkan** annex
17 分轄 **bunkatsu** separate jurisdiction
18 分離 **bunri** separation, division
分離主義者 **bunri shugisha** separatist, secessionist
分類 **bunrui** classification
分類学 **bunruigaku** taxonomy
分類表 **bunruihyō** table of classifications
分類法 **bunruihō** system of classification
20 分蘖 **bunketsu, bungetsu** offshoot
分譲 **bunjō** selling (land) in lots
分譲地 **bunjōchi** a subdivision

--------- 2 ---------

1 一分 **ippun** a minute **ichibu** one tenth; one hundredth, one percent; one quarter *ryō* (an old coin) **ichibun** duty, honor
一分別 **hitofunbetsu** (careful) consideration
2 二分 **nifun** two minutes **nibun** halve, bisect
二分音符 **nibun onpu** half note
七分三分 **shichibu-sanbu** split 70-30
七分袖 **shichibusode** three-quarter sleeves
九分 **kubu** nine out of ten; nine percent **kyūfun** nine minutes
九分九厘 **kubu-kurin** 99 cases out of 100, in all probability
子分 **kobun** follower, protégé, henchman, hanger-on
十分 **jūbun** enough, satisfactory; thorough **jippun** ten minutes
八分目 **hachibunme, hachibume** eight-tenths; moderation

八分音符 **hachibu onpu** an eighth note (♪)

3 三分 **sanpun** three minutes
sanbun divide into three, trisect

万分一 **manbun (no) ichi** one ten-thousandth

寸分 **sunbun** a bit, a little

大分 **daibu, daibun** much, greatly, considerably **Ōita** (city, Ōita-ken)

大分県 **Ōita-ken** (prefecture)

才分 **saibun** (natural) talent

千分 **senbun** thousandth

千分率 **senbunritsu** rate per thousand

口分 **kuchiwa(ke)** assort, itemize

小分 **kowa(ke)** subdivide, classify

山分 **yamawa(ke)** dividing equally

4 天分 **tenbun** one's nature; one's natural talents; one's sphere of activity, one's mission

内分 **naibun** secret, confidential

内分泌 **naibunpitsu, naibunpi** internal secretion, endocrine

五分 **gofun** five minutes
gobu fifty percent, half; five percent

五分五分 **gobu-gobu** evenly matched; a tie

五分刈 **gobuga(ri)** close-cropped haircut

五分試 **gobudame(shi)** killing by inches

中分 **chūbun** halve

切分法 **setsubunhō** syncopation

六分儀 **rokubungi** sextant

公分母 **kōbunbo** common denominator

区分 **kubun, kuwa(ke)** division, partition; classification

水分 **suibun** moisture, water content

手分 **tewa(ke)** dividing up the work

引分 **hi(ki)wa(ke)** tie, draw, standoff

5 半分 **hanbun** half **hanpun** half a minute

生分解性 **seibunkaisei** biodegradable

申分 **mō(shi)bun** something to say (against), objection, shortcomings

仕分 **shiwa(keru)** sort, classify

存分 **zonbun (ni)** to one's heart's content, as much as one wants, without reserve

平分 **heibun** bisect, divide equally

可分 **kabun** divisible, separable

可分性 **kabunsei** divisibility

四分五裂 **shibun-goretsu** disruption, disintegration

四分六 **shiburoku** six-to-four (ratio/chance)

四分音符 **shibu onpu, shibun onpu** quarter note

処分 **shobun** disposal, disposition; punishment

目分量 **mebunryō** measuring by eye

6 多分 **tabun** probably, maybe, likely, presumably; a great deal/many

気分 **kibun** feeling, mood

気分転換 **kibun tenkan** a (refreshing) change, diversion

両分 **ryōbun** bisect, cut in two

年分 **nenbun** yearly amount

再分配 **saibunpai** redistribution

仮分数 **kabunsū** improper fraction

充分 **jūbun** enough, sufficient; thoroughly

色分 **irowa(ke)** classification (by color), color coding

名分 **meibun** moral duty; justice

当分 **tōbun** for now, for a while

早分 **hayawa(kari)** quick understanding; guide, handbook

百分比 **hyakubunhi** percentage

百分率 **hyakubunritsu** percentage

成分 **seibun** composition, content, ingredient, component

自分 **jibun** oneself, one's own

自分自身 **jibun-jishin** oneself

自分勝手 **jibun-katte** having one's own way, selfish

7 身分 **mibun** social standing, status; one's circumstances

何分 **nanibun** anyway; please **nanpun** how many minutes **nanbun** what fraction

余分 **yobun** extra, excess

弟分 **otōtobun** one treated as a younger brother

均分 **kinbun** divide equally

応分 **ōbun** appropriate, fitting

見分 **miwa(keru)** tell apart, distinguish between, recognize; judge, identify

言分 **i(i)bun** one's say; objection

8 使分 **tsuka(i)wa(ke)** proper use

夜分 **yabun** night, evening

追分 **oiwake** forked road, parting of the ways; packhorse driver's song

追分節 **oiwakebushi** packhorse driver's song

押分 **o(shi)wa(keru)** push apart, work one's way through

国分寺 **kokubunji** (ancient) state-established provincial temple

物分 **monowa(kari)** understanding

性分 **shōbun** nature, disposition

取分 **to(ri)wa(ke)** especially
to(ri)wa(keru) divide, portion out
to(ri)bun share, portion

9 通分 **tsūbun** reduction (of fractions) to a common denominator

持分 **mo(chi)bun** share, quota; holdings, interest in

按分 **anbun** proportional division

按分比例 **anbun hirei** proportionately, prorated

咲分 **sa(ki)wa(keru)** bloom in various colors
sa(ki)wa(ke) variegated flowering

品分 **shinawa(ke)** assort

草分 **kusawa(ke)** pioneer

客分　**kyakubun** guest, honorary member
染分　**so(me)wa(ke)** dyed in various colors
春分　**shunbun** the vernal equinox
春分日　**shunbun (no) hi** the vernal equinox
　　(a holiday, about March 21)
春分点　**shunbunten** the vernal equinoctial
　　point
秋分　**shūbun** fall equinox
約分　**yakubun** reduce (a fraction to lowest
　　terms)
10 随分　**zuibun** very
部分　**bubun** part　**buwa(ke)** classification
部分的　**bubunteki** partial, here and there
部分品　**bubunhin** parts, components
部分食　**bubunshoku** partial eclipse
振分　**fu(ri)wa(keru)** divide in two, distribute
振分髪　**fu(ri)wa(ke)gami** hair parted and
　　hanging down
株分　**kabuwa(ke)** spread of a plant by
　　sending out branching roots
根分　**newa(ke)** divide the roots (and
　　transplant)
核分裂　**kakubunretsu** nuclear fission
時分　**jibun** time, hour, season
書分　**ka(ki)wa(keru)** distinguish in writing
純分　**junbun** fineness (of gold)
純分度　**junbundo** fineness (of gold)
配分　**haibun** distribution, allocation
11 野分　**nowaki, nowake** wind storm in autumn
過分　**kabun** excessive, undeserved
得分　**tokubun** profits, winnings, one's share
異分子　**ibunshi** foreign elements, outsider
細分　**saibun** subdivide
組分　**kumiwa(ke)** sorting, grouping
12 検分　**kenbun** inspect, examine
無分別　**mufunbetsu** imprudent, thoughtless,
　　rash
幾分　**ikubun** some, a portion
痛分　**ita(mi)wa(ke)** tie due to injury (sumo)
等分　**tōbun** (division into) equal parts
13 塩分　**enbun** salt content, salinity
搔分　**ka(ki)wa(keru)** push aside
嗅分　**ka(gi)wa(keru)** tell/differentiate by
　　scent
微分　**bibun** differential (calculus)
微分子　**bibunshi** particle, atom, molecule
微分学　**bibungaku** differential calculus
微分積分　**bibun-sekibun** differential and
　　integral calculus
数分間　**sūfunkan** for a few minutes, several
　　minutes
裾分　**susowa(ke)** sharing (of a gift)
節分　**setsubun** last day of winter
鉄分　**tetsubun** iron content
14 選分　**yo(ri)wa(keru), e(ri)wa(keru)** sort/
　　single/pick out, winnow, cull

精分　**seibun** nourishment; vitality
説分　**to(ki)wa(keru)** explain carefully
聞分　**ki(ki)wa(keru)** listen to reason;
　　distinguish between by hearing
領分　**ryōbun** territory; domain, sphere
15 養分　**yōbun** nourishment
線分　**senbun** line segment
踏分　**fu(mi)wa(keru)** push one's way through
16 親分　**oyabun** boss, chief
親分子分　**oyabun-kobun** boss and underlings
積分　**sekibun** integral calculus
積分学　**sekibungaku** integral calculus
糖分　**tōbun** sugar content
篩分　**furu(i)wa(keru)** screen, sift out
頭分　**kashirabun** leader, boss, chief
18 噛分　**ka(mi)wa(keru)** understand, appreciate
職分　**shokubun** one's duties

──────── 3 ────────

1 一回分　**ikkaibun** a dose; an installment
一部分　**ichibubun** a part
2 二等分　**nitōbun** bisect
十二分　**jūnibun** more than enough
　　jūnifun twelve minutes
3 三等分　**santōbun** trisect
三権分立　**sanken bunritsu** separation of
　　powers (legislative, executive, and
　　judicial)
大部分　**daibubun** a large part, most; for the
　　most part, mostly
下検分　**shitakenbun** preliminary examination
4 不十分　**fujūbun** insufficient, inadequate
不可分　**fukabun** indivisible, inseparable
不充分　**fujūbun** insufficient, inadequate
天下分目　**tenka-wa(ke)me** decisive, fateful
5 加水分解　**kasui bunkai** hydrolysis
兄弟分　**kyōdaibun** sworn brother, buddy, pal
四半分　**shihanbun** quarter, fourth
主成分　**shuseibun** main ingredient
目八分　**mehachibu** (hold an offering) a little
　　below eye level; most respectfully; about
　　eight-tenths full
6 仮処分　**karishobun** provisional disposition
尖鋭分子　**sen'ei bunshi** radical elements
因数分解　**insū bunkai** factorization
7 形見分　**katamiwa(ke)** distribution of
　　mementos (of the deceased)
村八分　**murahachibu** ostracism
8 定性分析　**teisei bunseki** qualitative analysis
定量分析　**teiryō bunseki** quantitative analysis
9 栄養分　**eiyōbun** a nutrient
思存分　**omo(u) zonbun** as much as one
　　pleases
約半分　**yaku hanbun** about half
10 部類分　**buruiwa(ke)** classification, grouping
遊半分　**aso(bi)hanbun** half in fun

2

亻
⺅
孑
阝
刂
力
又
宀
十
卜
ケ
ソ 2 ←
厂
辶
冂
几
匚

12 滋養分 **jiyōbun** nutrient
無痛分娩 **mutsū bunben** painless childbirth
13 損益分岐点 **son'eki bunkiten** break-even point
微積分 **bisekibun** differential and integral calculus
腹八分 **hara hachibu** eating to only 80 percent of stomach capacity
話半分 **hanashi-hanbun** taking a story at half its face value
14 遺留分 **iryūbun** heir's legal portion
構成分子 **kōsei bunshi** components
精神分析 **seishin bunseki** psychoanalysis
精神分裂症 **seishin bunretsushō** schizophrenia
15 慰半分 **nagusa(mi)hanbun** partly for pleasure

──────── 4 ────────

2 七分三分 **shichibu-sanbu** split 70-30
3 大義名分 **taigi-meibun** proper relationship between sovereign and subjects; justification, just cause
4 五分五分 **gobu-gobu** evenly matched; a tie
6 刑事処分 **keiji shobun** criminal punishment
9 面白半分 **omoshiro-hanbun** half in fun, jokingly
11 強制処分 **kyōsei shobun** disposition by legal compulsion
13 滞納処分 **tainō shobun** disposition for failure to pay (taxes)
→2 微分積分 **bibun-sekibun** differential and integral calculus
16 親分子分 **oyabun-kobun** boss and underlings

2o2.2 / 126

公公 **KŌ** public; unbiased, fair; in common; prince, lord; (title of familiarity or contempt, used like -*kun*) **KU, oyake** public

──────── 1 ────────

0 ポリ公 **porikō** cop
2 公人 **kōjin** a public figure
公子 **kōshi** young nobleman
4 公文 **kōbun** official document/dispatch
公文所 **kumonjo** government office (historical)
公文書 **kōbunsho** official document
公分母 **kōbunbo** common denominator
公方 **kubō** imperial court; shogun, warlord
5 公民権 **kōminken** civil rights, citizenship
公民館 **kōminkan** public hall, community center
公生活 **kōseikatsu** public life
公平 **kōhei** fair, just
公平無私 **kōhei-mushi** fair and disinterested
公正 **kōsei** fair, just

公用 **kōyō** official business; public use; public expense
公用文 **kōyōbun** writing in the officially prescribed way
公司 **kōshi, konsu** company, firm (in China)
公布 **kōfu** promulgation
公庁 **kōchō** government office
公示 **kōji** public announcement
公立 **kōritsu** public (institution)
公田 **kōden, kuden** public paddy (historical)
6 公吏 **kōri** public servant, official
公休日 **kōkyūbi** legal holiday
公会 **kōkai** public meeting
公会堂 **kōkaidō** public hall, civic center
公共 **kōkyō** public society, community
公共心 **kōkyōshin** public spirit, community-mindedness
公共団体 **kōkyō dantai** public body/organization
公共事業 **kōkyō jigyō** public works, utilities
公安 **kōan** public order/safety
公安官 **kōankan** (railway) police
公団 **kōdan** public (housing) corporation
公有 **kōyū** publicly owned
公有地 **kōyūchi** public land
公有林 **kōyūrin** public forest
公式 **kōshiki** formula, formality
7 公邸 **kōtei** official residence
公判 **kōhan** public trial/hearing
公沙汰 **ōyakezata** public affair
公告 **kōkoku** public notice
公役 **kōeki** public service, conscription
公売 **kōbai** public auction
公社 **kōsha** public corporation
公私 **kōshi** public and private
公言 **kōgen** declaration, avowal
8 公表 **kōhyō** official announcement
公事 **kōji** public affairs, official business
公使 **kōshi** minister (of a legation)
公使館 **kōshikan** legation
公法 **kōhō** public law
公知 **kōchi** (well/widely) known
公定 **kōtei** official(ly set)
公定歩合 **kōtei buai** official bank rate, rediscount rate
公国 **kōkoku** duchy, principality
公明 **kōmei** just, fair
公明正大 **kōmei-seidai** just, fair
公明党 **Kōmeitō** (a political party)
公的 **kōteki** public, official
公武 **kōbu** nobles and soldiers; imperial court and shogunate
公武合体 **kōbu gattai** union of imperial court and shogunate
公取委 **Kōtorii** Fair Trade Commission (short for 公正取引委員会)

公金 **kōkin** public funds
9 公海 **kōkai** international waters
公約 **kōyaku** public commitment/pledge
公約数 **kōyakusū** common divisor
10 公倍数 **kōbaisū** common multiple
公差 **kōsa** allowable margin of error, tolerance
公益 **kōeki** public benefit/interest
公家 **kuge** imperial court; court noble
公害 **kōgai** pollution
公庫 **kōko** municipal treasury; finance corporation
公教 **kōkyō** Roman Catholicism
公教会 **Kōkyōkai** Catholic Church
公租 **kōso** tax
公称 **kōshō** nominal
11 公達 **kindachi** young nobleman
公道 **kōdō** highway; justice
公娼 **kōshō** licensed prostitute
公理 **kōri** axiom
公務 **kōmu** public service, official business
公務員 **kōmuin** government employee
公許 **kōkyo** official permission, authorization
公設 **kōsetsu** public
公魚 **wakasagi** pond smelt
12 公卿 **kugyō, kuge** court noble
公報 **kōhō** official bulletin, communiqué
公葬 **kōsō** public funeral
公募 **kōbo** public appeal/solicitation
公営 **kōei** public, government-run
公然 **kōzen** open, public
公裁 **kōsai** judicial decision
公衆 **kōshū** public (telephone, toilet, etc.)
公訴 **kōso** arraignment, accusation, charge
公評 **kōhyō** fair appraisal; public's opinion
公証 **kōshō** authentication, notarization
公証人 **kōshōnin** notary public
公開 **kōkai** open to the public
公開状 **kōkaijō** open letter
13 公債 **kōsai** public debt, government bond
公園 **kōen** park
公署 **kōsho** government office
公電 **kōden** official telegram/dispatch
14 公僕 **kōboku** public servant
公選 **kōsen** public election
公演 **kōen** public performance
公徳 **kōtoku** public morality
公徳心 **kōtokushin** public-spiritedness
公算 **kōsan** probability
公認 **kōnin** officially authorized, certified
公領 **kōryō** duchy, principality
15 公儀 **kōgi** court, shogunate, authorities; official
公器 **kōki** public institution
公敵 **kōteki** public enemy
公憤 **kōfun** public indignation
公課 **kōka** taxes

公論 **kōron** public opinion; just view
16 公館 **kōkan** official residence
17 公爵 **kōshaku** prince, duke
公爵夫人 **kōshaku fujin** princess, duchess
公聴会 **kōchōkai** public hearing
18 公職 **kōshoku** public official
20 公議 **kōgi** public opinion; just view

———————— 2 ————————
3 大公 **taikō** grand duke
4 不公平 **fukōhei** unfair, unjust
不公正 **fukōsei** unfair, unjust
5 未公表 **mikōhyō** not yet officially announced
6 老公 **rōkō** elderly nobleman (polite)
至公 **shikō** utmost fairness
至公至平 **shikō-shihei** utterly just
8 非公式 **hikōshiki** unofficial
非公開 **hikōkai** closed (meeting), closed-door (session)
奉公 **hōkō** service
奉公先 **hōkōsaki** employer
官公庁 **kankōchō** government and municipal agencies
官公吏 **kankōri** public officials
官公署 **kankōsho** government and municipal offices
9 郭公 **kakkō** cuckoo
郭公鳥 **kakkōdori** cuckoo
12 貴公 **kikō** you
貴公子 **kikōshi** young noble
13 蒲公英 **tanpopo** dandelion
聖公会 **Seikōkai** Episcopal/Anglican Church
雷公 **raikō** the god of thunder

———————— 3 ————————
5 只奉公 **tadabōkō** serving without pay
主人公 **shujinkō** main character, hero (of a story)
6 交通公社 **Kōtsū Kōsha** Japan Travel Bureau
9 軍事公債 **gunji kōsai** war bonds
12 渡奉公 **wata(ri)bōkō** working as a servant at one place after another

———————— 4 ————————
2 丁稚奉公 **detchi bōkō** apprenticeship
6 年期奉公 **nenki bōkō** apprenticeship
13 滅私奉公 **messhi hōkō** selfless patriotic service

2o2.3 / 113

FU, chichi, (o)tō(san) father

父

———————— 1 ————————
2 父子 **fushi** father and child
3 父上 **chichiue** father (polite)
4 父日 **Chichi (no) Hi** Father's Day

父方 **chichikata** on the father's side, paternal
5 父母 **fubo, chichihaha** father and mother
父兄 **fukei** parents and older brothers, guardians
父兄会 **fukeikai** parents' association
6 父老 **furō** elders, the old
7 父君 **chichigimi, fukun** father (polite)
父系 **fukei** male line, patriarchal (family)
9 父祖 **fuso** forefathers, ancestors
12 父御 **chichigo, tetego** your father
父無子 **chichina(shi)go, tetena(shi)go** fatherless/illegitimate child
15 父権 **fuken** paternal rights
16 父親 **chichioya, teteoya** father

———————— 2 ————————

3 亡父 **bōfu** one's late father
6 老父 **rōfu** one's aged father
7 伯父 **oji, hakufu** uncle
8 叔父 **oji, shukufu** uncle
実父 **jippu** one's biological father
岳父 **gakufu** father of one's wife
9 神父 **shinpu** (Catholic) priest, Father
祖父 **sofu** grandfather
祖父母 **sofubo** grandparents
10 家父 **kafu** my father
教父 **kyōfu** church father; godfather, sponsor
病父 **byōfu** one's invalid father
11 異父 **ifu** different father
13 慈父 **jifu** affectionate father
義父 **gifu** father-in-law; foster father; stepfather
農父 **nōfu** farmer
継父 **keifu** stepfather
15 養父 **yōfu** adoptive/foster father
養父母 **yōfubo** adoptive/foster parents
16 親父 **oyaji** one's father; the old man, the boss
17 厳父 **genpu** strict father; your esteemed father

———————— 3 ————————

3 大伯父 **ōoji** great-uncle, granduncle
大叔父 **ōoji** great-uncle, granduncle
10 高祖父 **kōsofu** great-great-grandfather
11 曽祖父 **sōsofu, hiijiji** great-grandfather
15 養祖父 **yōsofu** foster grandfather

2o2.4

今 **KEI** (auxiliary word for euphony or emphasis)

———————— 3 ————————

半 → **0a5.24**

乎 → **0a5.17**

———————— 4 ————————

2o4.1 / 288

羊 **YŌ, hitsuji** sheep

———————— 1 ————————

3 羊小屋 **hitsujigoya** sheep pen, sheepfold
4 羊毛 **yōmō** wool
羊水 **yōsui** amniotic fluid
5 羊皮 **yōhi** sheepskin
羊皮紙 **yōhishi** parchment
6 羊肉 **yōniku** mutton
12 羊歯 **shida, yōshi** fern
羊歯類 **shidarui, yōshirui** ferns
13 羊群 **yōgun** flock of sheep
羊腸 **yōchō(taru)** winding, zigzag, meandering
羊飼 **hitsujika(i)** shepherd, sheepherder
16 羊頭狗肉 **yōtō-kuniku** advertising mutton but selling dog meat
19 羊羹 **yōkan** sweet adzuki-bean jelly

———————— 2 ————————

3 小羊 **kohitsuji** lamb
山羊 **yagi** goat
山羊鬚 **yagihige** goatee
6 牝羊 **mehitsuji** female sheep, ewe
8 牧羊 **bokuyō** sheep raising
牧羊地 **bokuyōchi** sheep meadow
11 羚羊 **kamoshika** serow **reiyō** antelope
13 群羊 **gun'yō** flock of sheep
煉羊羹 **ne(ri)yōkan** bean jelly
14 綿羊 **men'yō** sheep
15 緬羊 **men'yō** sheep
17 擬羊皮紙 **giyōhishi** parchment paper

2o4.2

并 **HEI, nara(bu/beru)** line up in a row **awa(seru)** put together, combine

共 → **3k3.3**

———————— 5 ————————

2o5.1 / 405

弟 **TEI, DAI, DE** younger brother; pupil, disciple **otōto** younger brother

———————— 1 ————————

2 弟子 **deshi, teishi** pupil, disciple, adherent, apprentice
弟子入 **deshii(ri)** becoming a pupil, entering an apprenticeship

4 弟分 **otōtobun** one treated as a younger brother
8 弟妹 **teimai** younger brothers and sisters
12 弟御 **otōtogo** your younger brother
13 弟嫁 **otōtoyome** younger brother's wife

———————— 2 ————————
2 子弟 **shitei** children
又弟子 **matadeshi** indirect pupil, disciple of a disciple
4 内弟子 **uchideshi** apprentice living in his master's home
5 末弟 **battei, mattei** youngest brother; last disciple
兄弟 **kyōdai, ani-otōto** brothers (and sisters)
兄弟子 **anideshi** senior fellow student/ apprentice
兄弟分 **kyōdaibun** sworn brother, buddy, pal
兄弟愛 **kyōdaiai** brotherly love
8 直弟子 **jikideshi** immediate pupil, direct disciple
実弟 **jittei** one's biological younger brother
門弟 **montei** pupil, disciple
9 孫弟子 **magodeshi** one's disciples' disciples
相弟子 **aideshi** fellow pupil/apprentice
10 高弟 **kōtei** one's best student, leading disciple
師弟 **shitei** master and pupil
徒弟 **totei** apprentice
従弟 **jūtei** younger male cousin
13 義弟 **gitei** younger brother-in-law
愛弟子 **manadeshi** favorite pupil
愚弟 **gutei** my (foolish) younger brother
16 賢弟 **kentei** (wise) younger son/friend

———————— 3 ————————
7 乳兄弟 **chikyōdai** foster brother(s and sisters)
10 従兄弟 **itoko, jūkeitei** male cousin
13 義兄弟 **gikyōdai** brother-in-law; stepbrother; sworn brother
16 親兄弟 **oya-kyōdai** one's parents and brothers and sisters

———————— 4 ————————
2 又従兄弟 **mataitoko** second cousin

2o5.2
兌 DA exchange

———————— 1 ————————
12 兌換 **dakan** convert(ible), non-fiat (paper money)

2o5.3 / 653
谷 KOKU, tani, -ya valley

———————— 1 ————————
3 谷川 **tanigawa** river in a valley, mountain stream
8 谷底 **tanizoko, tanisoko** bottom of a valley/ ravine
9 谷風 **tanikaze** valley wind
12 谷間 **tanima, taniai** valley, ravine

———————— 2 ————————
8 長谷 **Hase** (surname)
長谷川 **Hasegawa** (surname)
宗谷海峡 **Sōya-kaikyō** (strait between Hokkaidō and Sakhalin)
空谷 **kūkoku** lonely valley
9 峡谷 **kyōkoku** gorge, ravine, canyon
幽谷 **yūkoku** (deep) ravine, narrow valley
11 渓谷 **keikoku** ravine, gorge, valley
17 蟀谷 **komekami** the temple (of the head)
20 櫨谷 **Kataragai** (place name, Shimane-ken)

———————— 3 ————————
13 鳩ヶ谷 **Hatogaya** (city, Saitama-ken)

2o5.4
坌 FUN come together; dust

2o5.5
岔 TA fork in a road

2o5.6 / 784
兵 HEI, HYŌ soldier; warfare
tsuwamono soldier

———————— 1 ————————
2 兵力 **heiryoku** military force; troop strength
3 兵士 **heishi** soldier
6 兵団 **heidan** army corps
7 兵役 **heieki** military service
兵学 **heigaku** military science, tactics, strategy
8 兵事 **heiji** military affairs
兵舎 **heisha** barracks
兵制 **heisei** military system
兵卒 **heisotsu** private, enlisted man
兵法 **heihō** tactics, strategy
9 兵威 **heii** military power
兵科 **heika** branch of the army
10 兵員 **heiin** military personnel/strength
兵家 **heika** soldier; tactician, strategist
兵庫県 **Hyōgo-ken** (prefecture)
兵書 **heisho** book on military science
兵站 **heitan** military supplies, logistics
兵站部 **heitanbu** supply/logistical department

11 兵隊 **heitai** soldier; sailor
兵曹 **heisō** warrant officer
12 兵営 **heiei** barracks
14 兵端 **heitan** (commencement of) hostilities
15 兵器 **heiki** weapon, arms
18 兵糧 **hyōrō** provisions, victuals
20 兵籍 **heiseki** military register, army roll

———————— 2 ————————

3 工兵 **kōhei** military engineer, sapper
大兵 **taihei** large army **daihyō** big (stature)
女兵 **johei** woman soldier
小兵 **kohyō** short (stature)
4 水兵 **suihei** (navy) sailor
水兵服 **suiheifuku** sailor's uniform;
(schoolgirl's) sailor suit
手兵 **shuhei** troops under one's command
5 出兵 **shuppei** dispatch/send troops
民兵 **minpei** militia(man)
生兵法 **namabyōhō** untried tactics; smattering of knowledge
古兵 **kohei, furutsuwamono** old soldier,
veteran
用兵 **yōhei** tactics
白兵戦 **hakuheisen** hand-to-hand fighting
6 伏兵 **fukuhei** an ambush
老兵 **rōhei** old soldier, veteran
守兵 **shuhei** guards, garrison
尖兵 **senpei** point man, advance guard
米兵 **beihei** U.S. soldier/sailor
7 呑兵衛 **no(n)bē** heavy drinker
私兵 **shihei** private army
8 奇兵 **kihei** shock troops, commandos
官兵 **kanpei** government troops
歩兵 **hohei** foot soldier, infantry
9 造兵 **zōhei** ordnance, arms manufacture
造兵廠 **zōheishō** arms factory, arsenal, armory
海兵 **kaihei** marines
海兵隊 **kaiheitai** the Marine Corps
派兵 **hahei** dispatch/send troops
城兵 **jōhei** castle garrison
恤兵 **juppei** soldiers' relief
10 残兵 **zanpei** the remnants (of a defeated
army), survivors
将兵 **shōhei** officers and men
陸兵 **rikuhei** land troops/forces
哨兵 **shōhei** sentry, sentinel
挙兵 **kyohei** raise an army
核兵器 **kakuheiki** nuclear weapons
砲兵 **hōhei** artillery; artilleryman, gunner
病兵 **byōhei** sick soldier
11 強兵 **kyōhei** powerful army, military buildup
敗兵 **haihei** routed troops
12 援兵 **enpei** reinforcements
短兵急 **tanpeikyū** impetuous, sudden
募兵 **bohei** recruiting, enlistment, drafting

廃兵 **haihei** disabled soldier
散兵 **sanpei** skirmisher
番兵 **banpei** sentry, guard
飲兵衛 **no(n)bē** heavy drinker
13 僧兵 **sōhei** monk soldier
傷兵 **shōhei** wounded soldier
傭兵 **yōhei, yato(i)hei** mercenary soldier
義兵 **gihei** loyal soldier, volunteer
農兵 **nōhei** farmer-soldiers
幕兵 **bakuhei** shogunate soldiers
新兵 **shinpei** new soldier, recruit
14 増兵 **zōhei** reinforcements
徴兵 **chōhei** conscription; draftee
徴兵忌避 **chōhei kihi** draft evasion
徴兵制 **chōheisei** conscription system
徴兵免除 **chōhei menjo** draft exemption
徴兵検査 **chōhei kensa** examination for
conscription
寡兵 **kahei** small army/force
練兵 **renpei** (military) drill
練兵場 **renpeijō** parade ground
精兵 **seihei, seibyō** elite troops, crack corps
雑兵 **zappei, zōhyō** common soldiers
15 撤兵 **teppei** withdraw troops, disengage
敵兵 **tekihei** enemy soldier
閲兵 **eppei** inspection of troops, parade, review
駐兵 **chūhei** station troops
16 衛兵 **eihei** guards, sentinel
憲兵 **kenpei** military police, MP's
17 癈兵 **haihei** disabled soldier
18 観兵式 **kanpeishiki** military review, parade
騎兵 **kihel** cavalry(man)

———————— 3 ————————

1 一等兵 **ittōhei** private first-class
4 予備兵 **yobihei** reservists
屯田兵 **tondenhei** farmer-soldiers, colonizers
6 近衛兵 **konoehei** imperial guards; bodyguards
守備兵 **shubihei** guards, garrison
7 応召兵 **ōshōhei** draftee
初年兵 **shonenhei** new soldier, raw recruit
8 狙撃兵 **sogekihei** sniper, sharpshooter
9 負傷兵 **fushōhei** wounded soldier
看護兵 **kangohei** military nurse, medic
紅衛兵 **Kōeihei** the Red Guards (in China)
10 帰還兵 **kikanhei** repatriated soldiers
特科兵 **tokkahei** technical soldier
11 野砲兵 **yahōbē** field artilleryman
常備兵 **jōbihei** regular/standing army
脱走兵 **dassōhei** deserter
現役兵 **gen'ekihei** soldier on active duty
敗残兵 **haizanhei** remnants of a defeated
army
12 復員兵 **fukuinhei** demobilized soldier
補充兵 **hojūhei** reservists
軽騎兵 **keikihei** light cavalry(man)

13 傷病兵 **shōbyōhei** the sick and wounded (soldiers)

義勇兵 **giyūhei** volunteer soldier

蒲鉾兵舎 **kamaboko heisha** Quonset hut

14 槍騎兵 **sōkihei** lancer

15 儀仗兵 **gijōhei** honor guard, military escort

16 衛生兵 **eiseihei** (military) medic

親衛兵 **shin'eihei** bodyguard

19 警備兵 **keibihei** guard

20 護衛兵 **goeihei** guard, military escort

_____ 4 _____

12 落下傘兵 **rakkasanhei** paratrooper

富国強兵 **fukoku-kyōhei** national wealth and military strength

2o5.7 / 1436

呉 吳   **GO** (region/dynasty of ancient China); China **Kure** (ancient name for China); (city, Hiroshima-ken) **ku(reru)** give; do (something) for

_____ 1 _____

8 呉服 **gofuku** cloth/dry goods, draperies

呉服屋 **gofukuya** dry-goods store

9 呉音 **goon** Wu-dynasty *on* reading of a kanji (e.g., 男 read as *nan*)

12 呉越同舟 **Go-Etsu dōshū** enemies in the same boat

来→   **0a7.6**

_____ 6 _____

美→   **2o7.4**

2o6.1 / 1165

並 竝   **HEI, nara(bu)** be in a row; rank with   **nara(bi ni)** and, as well as   **nara(beru)** arrange, put side by side, marshal

na(mi) average, common, ordinary

_____ 1 _____

3 並大抵 **namitaitei** ordinary

並々 **naminami** ordinary, commonplace

4 並木 **namiki** row of trees; roadside tree

並木路 **namiki michi** tree-lined street

5 並存 **heizon** coexistence

並外 **namihazu(re)** out of the ordinary

6 並列 **heiretsu** arrange in a row; parallel (circuit)

並行 **heikō** parallel

7 並足 **namiashi** walking pace, slow step

9 並型 **namigata** ordinary/standard size

12 並幅 **namihaba** standard-width cloth (about 36 cm)

13 並置 **heichi** place side by side, juxtapose

_____ 2 _____

2 人並 **hitona(mi)** average, ordinary

4 毛並 **kena(mi)** the lie of the hair; color of the hair; disposition; lineage

手並 **tena(mi)** skill, performance

月並 **tsukina(mi)** every month; commonplace, trite

5 立並 **ta(chi)nara(bu)** stand in a row; be equal to

7 杉並木 **suginamiki** avenue of sugi trees

町並 **machinami** row of stores and houses along a street

足並 **ashina(mi)** pace, step

8 並並 **naminami** ordinary, commonplace

押並 **o(shi)na(bete)** generally

居並 **inara(bu)** sit in a row, be arrayed

松並木 **matsunamiki** avenue/row of pines

門並 **kadona(mi)** row of houses; door to door, at every door

10 家並 **iena(mi)** row of houses; every house

軒並 **nokina(mi), nokinara(bi)** row of houses

12 歯並 **hanara(bi), hana(mi)** row of teeth, dentition

15 穂並 **honami** standing grain

16 鮎並 **ainame** rock trout

_____ 3 _____

2 人間並 **ningenna(mi)** like most people, average, common

十人並 **jūninna(mi)** average, ordinary

4 五目並 **gomokunara(be)** five-in-a-row game

5 世間並 **sekenna(mi)** average, ordinary, common

2o6.2

羌   **KYŌ** barbarian

2o6.3

忿   **FUN, ika(ru)** be angry/indignant

2o6.4

斧   **FU, ono** ax

_____ 1 _____

5 斧正 **fusei** correction, revision

2

イ
冫
孑
阝
卩
刂
力
又
宀
亠
十
卜
ケ
ソ 6
厂
辶
冂
几
匚

13 斧鉞 **fuetsu** ax

――――― 2 ―――――
4 手斧 **chōna, teono** adz, hatchet
5 石斧 **sekifu** stone ax

――――― 3 ―――――
19 蟷螂斧 **tōrō (no) ono** (valiant but) hopeless resistance (like a praying mantis lifting its front legs to block a man's path)

具 → 具 **5c3.1**

2o6.5 / 367

典 TEN rule; ceremony; writing, book; pledge, pawn; model
nori rule, law

――――― 1 ―――――
5 典礼 **tenrei** ceremony
8 典侍 **tenji** maid of honor, lady in waiting
典拠 **tenkyo** authority
典物 **tenbutsu** article to pawn
9 典型 **tenkei** type, pattern, model
典型的 **tenkeiteki** typical
典則 **tensoku** regulations
13 典雅 **tenga** refined, elegant, classic
14 典獄 **tengoku** prison warden
15 典範 **tenpan** model, standard; law
19 典麗 **tenrei** graceful, elegant
20 典籍 **tenseki** books

――――― 2 ―――――
3 大典 **taiten** state ceremony; important law, canon
4 仏典 **butten** Buddhist literature/scriptures
文典 **bunten** a grammar
5 出典 **shutten** source, authority
古典 **koten** the classics, classic
古典主義 **koten shugi** classicism
古典的 **kotenteki** classical
古典派 **kotenha** the classical school
古典語 **kotengo** a classical language
字典 **jiten** character dictionary
礼典 **reiten** ceremony, ritual, rites
6 成典 **seiten** law code; established rites
式典 **shikiten** ceremonies
8 事典 **jiten** encyclopedia, dictionary
法典 **hōten** law code
宝典 **hōten** valued book; handbook
国典 **kokuten** national lawcode; state ceremony; national literary classic
9 祝典 **shukuten** celebration, festival
香典 **kōden** condolence gift
香典返 **kōdengae(shi)** return present for a condolence gift

10 特典 **tokuten** special favor, privilege
教典 **kyōten** scriptures
恩典 **onten** favor, privilege, grace
11 祭典 **saiten** festival, ritual
盛典 **seiten** grand/imposing ceremony
経典 **kyōten, keiten** scriptures, sacred books, sutras
12 掌典 **shōten** ritualist
13 寛典 **kanten** leniency, clemency
楽典 **gakuten** rules of musical composition
瑞典 **Suēden** Sweden
聖典 **seiten** sage's writings; holy book, scriptures
辞典 **jiten** dictionary
15 儀典 **giten** ceremony, rites
16 操典 **sōten** drill book/manual
19 羅典 **Raten** Latin

――――― 3 ―――――
10 華燭典 **kashoku (no) ten** wedding ceremony

――――― 4 ―――――
6 百科事典 **hyakka jiten** encyclopedia
百科辞典 **hyakka jiten** encyclopedia
11 康熙字典 **Kōki Jiten** the Kangxi zidian (a 42-volume 47,216-entry character dictionary published in China in 1716)
13 漢和辞典 **Kan-Wa jiten** kanji dictionary

2o6.6

其 **so(no)** that
sore that, it

――――― 1 ―――――
3 其丈 **sore dake** that much; only that; only that much **sore dake (ni)** all the more because
其上 **so(no) ue** on top of that, in addition
4 其内 **so(no) uchi** before long, some day
其辺 **so(no) hen** thereabouts, in the neighborhood
其手 **so(no) te** that trick/move/way
其日 **so(no) hi** that (very) day
其日暮 **so(no)hi-gura(shi)** living from day to day, hand-to-mouth existence
其日稼 **so(no)hi-kase(gi)** day labor
5 其代 **so(no) ka(wari)** (but) on the other hand
其他 **so(no)ta** and others, and so forth
其処 **soko** that place, there **soredokoro(ka)** on the contrary, far from it
其処許 **sokomoto** you
6 其伝 **so(no) den** that way/trick
其式 **soreshiki** only that much
8 其実 **so(no)jitsu** in reality
其者 **so(no)mono** himself, herself
soresha professional; geisha, prostitute

其者上 **soreshaa(gari)** former geisha/
    prostitute
其物 **so(no)mono** (in) itself
9 其後 **so(no)go** thereafter, later, since then
其相応 **sore sōō** in its own way
其故 **soreyue** therefore
11 其道 **so(no) michi** line of business, field
其許 **sorebakari** only that, about that much
12 其場 **so(no) ba** the place, on the spot, the
    occasion/situation
其場限 **so(no)ba-kagi(ri)** makeshift, rough-
    and-ready
其場逃 **so(no)ba-noga(re)** temporizing,
    stopgap
其場凌 **so(no)ba-shino(gi)** makeshift,
    muddling through
其程 **sorehodo** so, so much, to that extent
其筋 **so(no) suji** the authorities concerned
其筈 **so(no) hazu** reasonable, to be expected
其間 **so(no) aida** (in) the meantime/interim
    so(no) kan the situation
13 其節 **so(no) setsu** at that time
14 其様 **so(no) yō** that kind of, (in) that way
15 其儀 **so(no) gi** such is the case
16 其儘 **so(no) mama** as is, without modification
18 其癖 **so(no) kuse** and yet, nevertheless

券→ **2f6.10**

劵→券 **2f6.10**

2o6.7

FUN air, atmosphere, weather

氛

——— 7 ———

酉→酋 **2o7.1**

2o7.1

SHŪ chief(tain)

酋 酉

——— 1 ———

8 酋長 **shūchō** chief(tain)

2o7.2 / 148

首

SHU head, neck; beginning, first;
(counter for poems and songs)
kubi neck, head　**kōbe** the head

——— 1 ———

4 首切 **kubiki(ri)** decapitation, execution;
    dismissal, firing
首引 **kubi(p)pi(ki)** tug of war using necks;
    constantly referring to (a dictionary)
5 首玉 **kubi(t)tama, kubitama** neck
6 首吊 **kubitsu(ri)** hang oneself
7 首位 **shui** top place, leading position
首尾一貫 **shubi-ikkan** logically consistent,
    coherent
首尾良 **shubiyo(ku)** successfully
首足 **shusoku** head and feet
8 首長 **shuchō** leader, head, chief
首実検 **kubi jikken** inspection of a severed
    head; identification of a suspect
首府 **shufu** capital
首肯 **shukō** assent/agree to
9 首巻 **kubima(ki)** (neck) muffler
首狩 **kubiga(ri)** headhunting
首相 **shushō** prime minister
首枷 **kubikase** pillory; encumbrance
首級 **shukyū** (enemy's) decapitated head
10 首将 **shushō** commander-in-chief
首都 **shuto** capital
首席 **shuseki** head, chief, chairman
首班 **shuhan** head, leader
11 首唱 **shushō** advocate, suggest
首唱者 **shushōsha** advocate, proponent
首脳 **shunō** leader
首脳会談 **shunō kaidan** summit conference
首脳部 **shunōbu** leaders, top management
12 首無 **kubina(shi)** headless
首筋 **kubisuji** nape/scruff of the neck
13 首飾 **kubikaza(ri)** necklace
14 首魁 **shukai** (ring)leader
首領 **shuryō** leader, head, chief, boss
15 首輪 **kubiwa** necklace; collar
16 首縊 **kubikuku(ri)** hang oneself
首謀 **shubō** plotting; ringleader
首謀者 **shubōsha** ringleader, mastermind
18 首題 **shudai** first topic

——— 2 ———

1 一首 **isshu** a poem
2 匕首 **hishu, aikuchi** dagger, dirk
3 上首尾 **jōshubi** a (great) success, satisfactory
    result
小首 **kokubi** neck; head
4 不首尾 **fushubi** failure; disgrace, disfavor
元首 **genshu** ruler, sovereign
手首 **tekubi** wrist
5 生首 **namakubi** freshly severed head
打首 **u(chi)kubi** beheading, decapitation
6 自首 **jishu** surrender (to the police)
7 投首 **na(ge)kubi** dropping one's head
花首 **hanakubi** the part where the flower
    joins the stem

2

亻 冫
孑 阝
卩 刂
力 又
宀
亠 十
卜 厃
⺈
⺍ 冖
厂
辶 冂
几 匸

2

亻
冫
孑
阝
卩
刂
力
又
亠
十
卜
ク
→ 7 ゝ
厂
廴
冂
几
匚

乳首 **chikubi** nipple
足首 **ashikubi** ankle
9 巻首 **kanshu** beginning of a book
10 部首 **bushu** radical (of a kanji)
起首 **kishu** beginning
党首 **tōshu** party leader
晒首 **sara(shi)kubi** gibbeted severed head
素首 **sokubi, so(k)kubi** one's head
馬首 **bashu** horse's head
11 猪首 **ikubi** short and thick neck, bull neck
船首 **senshu** bow, prow
貫首 **kanju** head priest
斬首 **zanshu** decapitation
　　 ki(ri)kubi a severed head
12 雁首 **gankubi** bowl of a pipe; gooseneck
喉首 **nodokubi** neck, throat
落首 **rakushu** lampoon, satirical poem
腕首 **udekubi** the wrist
期首 **kishu** beginning of the term/period
絞首 **kōshu** strangulation, hanging
絞首台 **kōshudai** gallows
絞首刑 **kōshukei** (execution by) hanging
艇首 **teishu** the bow (of a boat)
13 寝首搔 **nekubi (o) ka(ku)** chop off someone's head while he is asleep
歳首 **saishu** beginning of the year
頓首 **tonshu** bow low, kowtow; Your Humble Servant
鳩首 **kyūshu** go into a huddle
16 機首 **kishu** nose of an airplane
稽首 **keishu** bowing to the floor
縛首 **shiba(ri)kubi** (execution by) hanging
頭首 **tōshu** leader, chief, head of
17 馘首 **kakushu** decapitate; dismissal
18 襟首 **erikubi** nape/scruff of the neck
鎌首 **kamakubi** gooseneck
19 贋首 **nisekubi** falsified severed head
21 艦首 **kanshu** the bow (of a warship)
鶴首 **kakushu** stretching one's neck

—————— 3 ——————

18 轆轤首 **rokurokubi** long-necked monster

—————— 4 ——————

6 百人一首 **hyakunin-isshu** 100 poems by 100 poets (a collection of 100 *tanka*; basis for the popular card game *uta karuta*)

2o7.3 / 47

前

ZEN, mae before; front

—————— 1 ——————

2 前人 **zenjin** predecessor, former people
前人未到 **zenjin-mitō** untrodden, unexplored
3 前下 **maesa(gari)** front low(er than back)

前口上 **maekōjō** introductory remarks, prolog
4 前夫 **zenpu** one's former husband
前文 **zenbun** the above statement; preamble
前日 **zenjitsu** the day before
前方 **zenpō** front **maekata** before; immature
5 前以 **maemot(te)** beforehand, previously
前半 **zenpan** first half
前世 **zense** previous existence
前世界 **zensekai** prehistoric ages
前世紀 **zenseiki** last century; prehistoric times
前史 **zenshi** history of the early part of a period; prehistory
前代 **zendai** previous generation; former ages
前代未聞 **zendai-mimon** unprecedented
前払 **maebara(i)** advance payment
前号 **zengō** preceding issue
前立腺 **zenritsusen** prostate gland
6 前年 **zennen** the preceding year, last year
前年度 **zennendo** the preceding business/fiscal year
前任 **zennin** former (official)
前任地 **zenninchi** one's former post
前任者 **zenninsha** one's predecessor
前兆 **zenchō** portent, omen, sign
前列 **zenretsu** front row
前向 **maemu(ki)** forward-looking
前行 **zenkō** one's former conduct; preceding
前回 **zenkai** last time
7 前身 **zenshin** antecedents, predecessor
前述 **zenjutsu** the above-mentioned
前売 **maeu(ri)** advance sale
前売券 **maeu(ri)ken** ticket sold in advance
前条 **zenjō** preceding article
前言 **zengen** one's previous remarks
前車 **zensha** the car ahead
前足 **maeashi** forefoot, front leg
8 前非 **zenpi** one's past error
前垂 **maeda(re)** apron
前例 **zenrei** precedent
前夜 **zen'ya** last night, the previous night
前夜祭 **zen'yasai** (Christmas) Eve
前知 **zenchi** prescience
前官 **zenkan** one's former post
前屈 **zenkutsu** bend forward
　　 maekaga(mi) slouch
前肢 **zenshi** forelimbs, front leg
前者 **zensha** the former
前金 **maekin, zenkin** advance payment
前門 **zenmon** front gate
9 前奏 **zensō** prelude (in music)
前奏曲 **zensōkyoku** prelude, overture
前便 **zenbin** one's last letter
前途 **zento** the road ahead, one's future prospects
前途有望 **zento yūbō** having a promising future

前段　**zendan** the preceding paragraph/portion
前後　**zengo** about, approximately; front and back, longitudinal; order, sequence
　　　maeushi(ro) front and back
前後不覚　**zengo-fukaku** unconscious
前後左右　**zengo-sayū** in all directions
前庭　**zentei, maeniwa** front yard/garden
前面　**zenmen** front, front side
前祝　**maeiwa(i)** advance celebration
前科者　**zenkamono** person with a criminal record
前科…犯　**zenka …-han/…-pan** (a criminal record of three) previous convictions
前約　**zen'yaku** previous commitment/engagement
10 前倒　**maetao(shi), maedao(shi)** spending (part of next year's budget) ahead of time
前借　**maega(ri), zenshaku** getting an advance, a loan
前陳　**zenchin** the above-mentioned
前部　**zenbu** front part, front
前進　**zenshin** advance, drive, progress
前週　**zenshū** last week, the week before
前哨　**zenshō** outpost
前哨戦　**zenshōsen** preliminary skirmish
前哨線　**zenshōsen** scouting line
前座　**zenza** opening performance; minor performer
前書　**maega(ki)** preface, foreword
前納　**zennō** prepayment, advance payment
前記　**zenki** the above-mentioned
11 前勘定　**maekanjō** paying in advance
前掛　**maeka(ke)** apron
前掲　**zenkei** the above-mentioned
前著　**zencho** the above-cited publication, ibid.
前菜　**zensai** hors d'oeuvres
前脚　**zenkyaku, maeashi** forelegs, front leg
前脳　**zennō** the forebrain
前章　**zenshō** the preceding chapter
前略　**zenryaku** first part omitted; (salutation in a letter)
12 前渡　**maewata(shi)** advance payment/delivery
前場　**zenba** the morning (trading) session
前提　**zentei** premise, prerequisite
前葉　**zen'yō** the preceding page
前期　**zenki** the first/preceding term
前景　**zenkei** foreground
前景気　**maegeiki** prospects, outlook
前歯　**maeba, zenshi** front tooth
前貸　**maega(shi)** advance payment
前項　**zenkō** the preceding/foregoing paragraph
13 前照灯　**zenshōtō** headlights
前置　**maeo(ki)** preface, introduction
前置詞　**zenchishi** preposition

前触　**maebu(re)** advance notice/warning
14 前歴　**zenreki** one's personal history
前髪　**maegami** forelock, bangs
前説　**zensetsu** one's former opinion
前駆　**zenku** vanguard, forerunner, precursor
15 前舞台　**maebutai** apron stage, proscenium
前線　**zensen** front lines, the front; a (cold) front
前篇　**zenpen** the first volume/part
前輪　**zenrin, maewa** front wheel
16 前衛　**zen'ei** advance guard, vanguard
前橋　**Maebashi** (city, Gunma-ken)
前頭部　**zentōbu** front of the head, forehead
18 前額　**zengaku** forehead

─────────── 2 ───────────

2 人前　**hitomae** before others, in public
3 寸前　**sunzen** just before
大前提　**daizentei** major premise
上前　**uwamae** outer skirt; commission, rake-off
小前提　**shōzentei** minor premise
4 丹前　**tanzen** large padded kimono
仏前　**butsuzen** before Buddha, before the tablet of the deceased
片前　**katamae** single-breasted (suit)
午前　**gozen** morning, a.m.
午前中　**gozenchū** all morning
分前　**wa(ke)mae** share, portion
手前　**temae** you; this side of, toward oneself; out of consideration for; tea-ceremony procedures; oneself
手前勝手　**temae-gatte** selfish
5 以前　**izen** ago; formerly
左前　**hidarimae** the wrong way, folding the left side of a kimono over the right side; adversity
出前　**demae** cooked-food home delivery
　　　da(shi)mae one's share (of the expenses)
生前　**seizen** during one's lifetime
弘前　**Hirosaki** (city, Aomori-ken)
立前　**ta(te)mae** principle, policy, official stance
目前　**me (no) mae, mokuzen** before one's eyes; immediate (gain)
6 気前　**kimae** generosity
羽前　**Uzen** (ancient kuni, Yamagata-ken)
名前　**namae** name
帆前船　**homaesen** sailing vessel
当前　**a(tari)mae** a matter of course, natural, usual
自前　**jimae** paying one's own expenses, independent (geisha)
7 男前　**otokomae** good looks, handsome
足前　**ta(shi)mae** supplement; help
8 事前　**jizen** before the fact, prior, pre-

2

亻
冫
孑
阝
卩
刂
力
又
一
亠
十
ⵏ
ク
→7 ⺍
厂
辶
冂
几
匸

夜前 **yazen** last night
直前 **chokuzen** just before
建前 **ta(te)mae** principle, official position; erection of the framework
空前 **kūzen** unprecedented
空前絶後 **kūzen-zetsugo** the first ever and probably last ever
板前 **itamae** a cook
肥前 **Hizen** (ancient kuni, Nagasaki-ken)
取前 **to(ri)mae** share, portion
門前 **monzen** before the gate
門前市 **monzen'ichi** throngs of callers outside the gate
門前払 **monzenbara(i)** turning (someone) away at the gate, refusing to see (someone)
9 風前 **fūzen** exposed to the wind
風前灯 **fūzen (no) tomoshibi** (like a) candle in the wind, precarious situation
持前 **mo(chi)mae** nature, property, characteristic
後前 **ushi(ro)-mae** with front and back reversed
面前 **menzen** in the presence of, before
昼前 **hirumae** forenoon; just before noon
神前 **shinzen** before God, at the shrine
神前結婚 **shinzen kekkon** Shinto wedding
食前 **shokuzen** before a meal
10 陸前 **Rikuzen** (ancient kuni, Miyagi-ken)
真前 **ma(n)mae** right in front of
差前 **sa(shi)mae** sword worn at one's side
従前 **jūzen** previous, former, hitherto
11 現前 **genzen** before one's eyes
産前 **sanzen** before childbirth/delivery
眼前 **ganzen** before one's eyes
12 備前 **Bizen** (ancient kuni, Okayama-ken)
割前 **wa(ri)mae** share, quota
御前 **omae** you **mimae** before (God) **gozen** before an exalted person; your excellency
御前会議 **gozen kaigi** council held in the presence of the emperor
落前 **o(toshi)mae** money which changes hands (in settlement of a fight)
極前線 **kyokuzensen** polar front
腕前 **udemae** ability, skill
最前 **saizen** forefront; a little while ago
最前列 **saizenretsu** the front lines
最前線 **saizensen** forefront, front lines
越前 **Echizen** (ancient kuni, Fukui-ken)
筑前 **Chikuzen** (ancient kuni, Fukuoka-ken)
13 豊前 **Buzen** (ancient kuni, Fukuoka-ken)
墓前 **bozen** before the grave
戦前 **senzen** before the war, prewar
戦前派 **senzenha** prewar generation

14 駅前 **ekimae** in front of the station
15 敵前 **tekizen** before/facing the enemy
霊前 **reizen** before the (deceased's) spirit
16 錠前 **jōmae** a lock
錠前屋 **jōmaeya** locksmith

──────── 3 ────────

1 一人前 **ichininmae, hitorimae** one portion/serving; full adulthood
2 二人前 **futarimae, nininmae** enough for two, two servings
4 日没前 **nichibotsuzen** before sunset
5 半人前 **hanninmae** half portion; half a man
母御前 **hahagoze, hahagozen** mother (polite)
6 江戸前 **Edomae** Edo-style (cooking)
9 紀元前 **kigenzen** B.C.
12 寒冷前線 **kanrei zensen** cold front
朝飯前 **asameshimae** (easy enough to do) before breakfast

2o7.4 / 401

美

BI beauty
utsuku(shii) beautiful

──────── 1 ────────

2 美人 **bijin** beautiful woman
3 美々 **bibi(shii)** beautiful, resplendent
美女 **bijo** beautiful woman
美女桜 **bijozakura** verbena
4 美化 **bika** beautification; glorification
美文 **bibun** elegant prose
美文調 **bibunchō** ornate style
美少年 **bishōnen** a handsome youth
5 美本 **bihon** beautifully bound book
美田 **biden** good rice field
6 美名 **bimei** good/reputable name
7 美作 **Mimasaka** (ancient kuni, Okayama-ken)
美妙 **bimyō** exquisite, elegant
美妓 **bigi** beautiful geisha
美形 **bikei** beautiful form/woman
美学 **bigaku** esthetics
美学的 **bigakuteki** esthetic
美声 **bisei** beautiful voice
美男 **binan** handsome man
美男子 **bidanshi, binanshi** handsome man
8 美果 **bika** good fruit/results
美事 **migoto** splendid **biji** commendable act
美育 **biiku** esthetic culture
美味 **oi(shii)** good-tasting, delicious **bimi** good flavor; delicacies
美服 **bifuku** fine clothes
美的 **biteki** esthetic
9 美俗 **bizoku** beautiful/admirable custom
美点 **biten** good point, virtue, merit
美美 **bibi(shii)** beautiful, resplendent

美風 **bifū** beautiful/admirable custom
美音 **bion** beautiful voice
美食 **bishoku** delicious food, lavish diet
美食家 **bishokuka** epicure, gourmet
10 美酒 **bishu** excellent saké
美容 **biyō** beauty culture
美容体操 **biyō taisō** calisthenics
美容室 **biyōshitsu** beauty parlor, hairdresser's
美容院 **biyōin** beauty parlor, hairdresser's
美容師 **biyōshi** beautician
美容術 **biyōjutsu** beauty treatment, cosmetology
美挙 **bikyo** commendable act
美称 **bishō** euphemism
11 美術 **bijutsu** art, fine arts
美術工芸 **bijutsu kōgei** artistic handicrafts, arts and crafts
美術史 **bijutsushi** art history
美術的 **bijutsuteki** artistic
美術院 **bijutsuin** academy of art
美術品 **bijutsuhin** work of art
美術界 **bijutsukai** the art world
美術家 **bijutsuka** artist
美術商 **bijutsushō** art dealer
美術館 **bijutsukan** art gallery
12 美景 **bikei** beautiful view
美装 **bisō** fine dress, rich attire
美粧 **bishō** beautiful makeup
美粧院 **bishōin** beauty parlor, hairdresser's
13 美感 **bikan** sense of beauty
美意識 **biishiki** esthetic awareness
美辞 **biji** flowery language
美辞麗句 **biji-reiku** flowery language
14 美徳 **bitoku** virtue, noble attribute
美髪 **bihatsu** beautiful hair
美貌 **bibō** good looks
15 美談 **bidan** praisworthy anecdote/story
16 美濃 **Mino** (ancient kuni, Gifu-ken)
17 美醜 **bishū** beauty or ugliness, appearance
18 美観 **bikan** fine view, beautiful sight
美顔 **bigan** beautiful face
美顔水 **bigansui** face lotion
美顔術 **biganjutsu** facial treatment
19 美麗 **birei** beautiful

─── 2 ───

5 甘美 **kanbi** sweet
古美術品 **kobijutsuhin** old/ancient art object
6 壮美 **sōbi** splendor, magnificence
7 快美 **kaibi** sweet, mellow, pleasant
8 奄美大島 **Amami Ōshima** (island, Kagoshima-ken)
9 美美 **bibi(shii)** beautiful, resplendent

10 華美 **kabi** splendor, pomp, gorgeousness
称美 **shōbi** praise, admiration
純美 **junbi** unalloyed beauty
耽美 **tanbi** estheticism
耽美主義 **tanbi shugi** estheticism
耽美的 **tanbiteki** esthetic
耽美派 **tanbiha** the esthetic school
11 唯美主義 **yuibi shugi** estheticism
唯美的 **yuibiteki** esthetic
婉美 **enbi** beauty, charm
12 善美 **zenbi** the good and the beautiful; sumptuous
絶美 **zetsubi** of surpassing beauty
13 虞美人草 **gubijinsō** field poppy
嘆美 **tanbi** admire, extol
嘆美者 **tanbisha** admirer, adorer
14 精美 **seibi** exquisite beauty
15 褒美 **hōbi** reward, prize
審美 **shinbi** esthetic appreciation
審美的 **shinbiteki** esthetic
賞美 **shōbi** admire, appreciate, prize
賛美 **sanbi** praise, glorification
賛美歌 **sanbika** hymn
17 優美 **yūbi** graceful, elegant
19 艶美 **enbi** beauty, charm
22 讃美 **sanbi** praise, glorification
讃美歌 **sanbika** hymn

─── 3 ───

2 八方美人 **happō bijin** one who is affable to everybody
3 工芸美術 **kōgei bijutsu** applied fine arts
女性美 **joseibi** womanly beauty
4 天成美 **tensei (no) bi** natural beauty
5 立体美 **rittaibi** beauty of sculpture
6 曲線美 **kyokusenbi** beautiful curves
肉体美 **nikutaibi** physical beauty
有終美 **yūshū (no) bi** crowning glory, splendid finish
自然美 **shizenbi** natural beauty
7 良風美俗 **ryōfū-bizoku** good customs
形式美 **keishikibi** beauty of form
男性美 **danseibi** masculine beauty
9 造形美術 **zōkei bijutsu** the plastic arts
10 健康美 **kenkōbi** healthy beauty
11 脚線美 **kyakusenbi** leg beauty/shapeliness
14 醇風美俗 **junpū bizoku** good morals and manners

2o7.5

姜 **KYŌ** (a Chinese surname); ginger

─── 3 ───

9 紅生姜 **beni shōga** red pickled ginger

2o7.6 / 1099

盆 盆 **BON** Lantern Festival, Festival of the Dead; tray

──────── 1 ────────

5 盆石 **bonseki** miniature landscape on a tray
6 盆地 **bonchi** basin, round valley
8 盆画 **bonga** tray landscape
10 盆栽 **bonsai** bonsai, potted dwarf tree
11 盆祭 **Bon-matsu(ri)** Bon Festival
12 盆提灯 **bonjōchin** Bon Festival lantern
盆景 **bonkei** tray landscape
14 盆暮 **Bon-kure** Bon and year-end seasons
盆踊 **Bon odo(ri)** Bon Festival dancing

──────── 2 ────────

7 角盆 **kakubon** square tray
初盆 **hatsubon** first o-Bon festival after someone's death
9 茶盆 **chabon** tea tray
13 塗盆 **nu(ri)bon** lacquered tray
新盆 **niibon** first Obon festival after one's death

──────── 3 ────────

8 盂蘭盆 **Urabon** o-Bon festival
盂蘭盆会 **Urabon'e** o-Bon festival
13 煙草盆 **tabakobon** tobacco tray
18 覆水盆返 **fukusui bon (ni) kae(razu)** No use crying over spilt milk.

2o7.7

瓷 **Ō, motai** jar, jug, container

2o7.8

瓻 **SŌ, SHŌ** begin; be damaged, break, fail

2o7.9

瓰 **deshiguramu** decigram, one-tenth gram

叛→ **2p7.3**

卷→ **0a9.11**

巷→ **3k6.17**

──────── 8 ────────

釜 → 釜 **2o8.7**

2o8.1 / 1081

兼 **KEN** and, in addition, concurrently
ka(neru) combine, double as; hold an additional post; (as suffix) cannot

──────── 1 ────────

5 兼用 **ken'yō** combined use, serving two purposes
6 兼任 **kennin** concurrent post
兼合 **ka(ne)a(i)** equilibrium, balance, poise
兼行 **kenkō** doing both
兼有 **ken'yū** having both
8 兼官 **kenkan** additional post
10 兼修 **kenshū** study an additional subject
兼帯 **kentai** combined use, holding two posts
11 兼務 **kenmu** additional post
12 兼備 **kenbi** have both, combine
兼勤 **kenkin** additional post
兼営 **ken'ei** manage both, run two businesses
13 兼業 **kengyō** side business
18 兼職 **kenshoku** concurrent post
兼題 **kendai** subject for a poem

──────── 2 ────────

5 申兼 **mō(shi)ka(neru)** I'm sorry to trouble you(, but ...)
仕兼 **shika(neru)** cannot do, be reluctant to do
6 気兼 **kiga(ne)** feel constraint, be afraid of giving trouble
有兼 **a(ri)ka(nenai)** not impossible, possible
7 見兼 **mika(neru)** be unable to just idly watch
9 待兼 **ma(chi)ka(neru)** can't stand the wait

──────── 3 ────────

9 昼夜兼行 **chūya-kenkō** 24 hours a day, around the clock

2o8.2

羔 **KŌ, kohitsuji** lamb

2o8.3

恙 **YŌ, tsutsuga** (a type of parasitic mite); illness, misfortune

──────── 1 ────────

0 恙なく **tsutsuga(naku)** safe and sound, without mishap, in good health
6 恙虫病 **tsutsugamushibyō** scrub typhus

2o8.4 / 658

差 SA difference **sa(su)** hold (an umbrella); wear (a sword); extend (a hand); offer; thrust; insert **sa(shi)-** (emphatic verb prefix) **sa(shi de)** between two persons

———————— 1 ————————

2 差入 **sa(shi)i(reru)** insert; send in to a prisoner
3 差上 **sa(shi)a(geru)** give; raise up
差上物 **sa(shi)a(ge)mono** gift
差土 **sa(shi)tsuchi** (adding) flowerbed soil
4 差支 **sa(shi)tsuka(enai)** no impediment, justifiable, allowable, may
差止 **sa(shi)to(meru)** prohibit, forbid, ban
差込 **sa(shi)ko(mu)** insert, plug in
差水 **sa(shi)mizu** (adding) water
差手 **sa(shi)te** (not) very
差引 **sa(shi)hi(ku)** deduct
差引勘定 **sashihiki kanjō** account balance
5 差出 **sa(shi)da(su)** present, submit; send; hold out (one's hand)
差出人 **sashidashinin** sender, return address
差出口 **sa(shi)deguchi** uncalled-for remark
差出者 **sa(shi)demono** intruder, meddler, busybody
差付 **sa(shi)tsu(keru)** point (a gun at); put right under one's nose
差立 **sa(shi)ta(teru)** send, forward
6 差合 **sa(shi)a(i)** hindrance, impediment
差交 **sa(shi)ka(wasu)** cross (swords)
差向 **sa(shi)mu(keru)** send around; point (a light) toward **sa(shi)muka(i)** face to face
差当 **sa(shi)a(tari)** for the time being
差回 **sa(shi)mawa(su)** send (a car) around
7 差身 **sa(shi)mi** sliced raw fish, sashimi
差伸 **sa(shi)no(beru)** hold out, extend (a hand)
差別 **sabetsu** discrimination
差別界 **sabetsukai** world of inequality
差延 **sa(shi)no(beru)** extend (a hand)
差迫 **sa(shi)sema(ru)** be imminent/impending
差乳 **sa(shi)jichi** breast full of milk; breast with protruding nipple
差戻 **sa(shi)modo(su)** send/refer back
差足 **sa(shi)ashi** stealthy steps
8 差送 **sa(shi)oku(ru)** send
差油 **sa(shi)abura** lubricating oil; oil (a machine)
差押 **sa(shi)osa(eru)** attach, seize, impound
差押品 **sa(shi)osa(e)hin** attached/seized goods
差担 **sa(shi)nina(i)** carry on the shoulders between two persons

差招 **sa(shi)mane(ku)** beckon to; take command of
差固 **sa(shi)kata(meru)** shut tight; warn sternly
差肥 **sa(shi)goe** (spreading) fertilizer
差物屋 **sashimonoya** cabinetmaker
差物師 **sashimonoshi** cabinetmaker
差金 **sakin** difference, margin **sa(shi)kin** partial payment; difference **sa(shi)gane** carpenter's square; instigation; suggestion
9 差前 **sa(shi)mae** sword worn at one's side
差挟 **sa(shi)hasa(mu)** insert, put between, put in (a word); harbor, entertain
10 差益 **saeki** marginal profit
差紙 **sa(shi)gami** summons, official order
差配 **sahai** conduct of business; management; agency, agent
差配人 **sahainin** landlord's agent
11 差添 **sa(shi)zo(e)** one's shorter sword **sa(shi)zo(i)** assistance
差掛 **sa(shi)ka(karu)** hang over, overhang; be urgent; be imminent; approach, come near **sa(shi)ka(keru)** hold (an umbrella) over (someone)
差掛小屋 **sa(shi)ka(ke)goya** penthouse, lean-to
差控 **sa(shi)hika(eru)** be moderate in; withhold, refrain from
差異 **sai** difference, disparity
差許 **sa(shi)yuru(su)** permit, allow
12 差遣 **saken** dispatch
差違 **sa(shi)chiga(eru)** err in refereeing (in sumo); make a bad move (in chess) **sai** difference
差湯 **sa(shi)yu** (adding) hot water
差渡 **sa(shi)wata(ru)** cross in a boat **sa(shi)wata(shi)** distance across, diameter
差換 **sa(shi)ka(eru)** replace, change
差替 **sa(shi)ka(eru)** replace, change
差越 **sa(shi)ko(eru)** go out of turn, jump the queue **sa(shi)ko(su)** go out of turn; cross; send, give
差歯 **sa(shi)ba** clog supports; post crown, capped tooth
差等 **satō** gradation; difference
13 差障 **sa(shi)sawa(ri)** obstacle, hindrance; offense
差置 **sa(shi)o(ku)** leave, let alone; ignore
差詰 **sa(shi)zu(me)** for the present
差詰引詰 **sa(shi)tsu(me)-hi(ki)tsu(me)** shooting a flurry of arrows
15 差潮 **sa(shi)shio** rising tide
16 差薬 **sa(shi)gusuri** eye drops; injection
19 差響 **sa(shi)hibi(ku)** affect, influence

差繰 **sa(shi)ku(ru)** manage skillfully

──────── 2 ────────

2 人差指 **hitosa(shi) yubi** index finger
3 大差 **taisa** wide difference/margin, great disparity
　千差万別 **sensa-banbetsu** infinite variety
　小差 **shōsa** slight difference, narrow margin
4 収差 **shūsa** aberration
　公差 **kōsa** allowable margin of error, tolerance
　水差 **mizusa(shi)** water jug, pitcher
　日差 **hiza(shi)** sunlight
5 目差 **meza(su)** aim at
6 年差 **nensa** annual variation
　交差 **kōsa** cross, intersect
　交差点 **kōsaten** crossing, intersection
　自差 **jisa** deviation (of a compass needle) .
7 状差 **jōsa(shi)** letter file/rack
　抜差 **nu(ki)sa(shi)** insertions and deletions
　　nu(ki)sa(shinaranu) impossible, sticky (dilemma)
　言差 **i(i)sa(su)** stop short (in mid-sentence)
8 油差 **aburasa(shi)** oil can, oiler
　物差 **monosa(shi)** ruler, measure, yardstick
　性差別 **sei sabetsu** sex discrimination
9 段差 **dansa** difference in level/ranking
　指差 **yubisa(su)** point to
　面差 **omoza(shi)** looks, features
　紅差指 **benisa(shi)yubi** the ring finger
10 根差 **neza(su)** take root; stem from
　格差 **kakusa** gap, differential
　脇差 **wakiza(shi)** short sword
　時差 **jisa** time difference, staggered
　　jisa(boke) jet lag
11 偏差 **hensa** deviation, deflection, declination
　視差 **shisa** parallax
　眼差 **manaza(shi)** a look, expression
12 落差 **rakusa** water level, head
　無差別 **musabetsu** indiscriminate
　等差 **tōsa** equal difference; graduated
　等差級数 **tōsa kyūsū** arithmetic progression
14 誤差 **gosa** error, aberration
15 潮差 **chōsa** tide range
　輪差 **wasa** loop
16 燃差 **mo(e)sa(shi)** embers

──────── 3 ────────

2 二本差 **nihonza(shi)** two-sworded (samurai)
6 地域差 **chiikisa** regional differences
　光行差 **kōkōsa** aberration (in astronomy)
7 抜足差足 **nu(ki)ashi-sa(shi)ashi (de)** stealthily
　学校差 **gakkōsa** scholastic disparity among schools
10 個人差 **kojinsa** differences between individuals
12 雲泥差 **undei (no) sa** a great difference

拳→　　**3c6.18**

2o8.5 / 716

益　**EKI, YAKU** gain, benefit, profit, advantage, use
　ma(su) increase

──────── 1 ────────

3 益々 **masumasu** increasingly, more and more
4 益友 **ekiyū** good/useful friend
6 益虫 **ekichū** beneficial insect
11 益鳥 **ekichō** beneficial bird

──────── 2 ────────

4 収益 **shūeki** earnings, proceeds
　公益 **kōeki** public benefit/interest
5 用益権 **yōekiken** usufruct
6 年益 **nen'eki** annual profit
　共益 **kyōeki** common benefit
　有益 **yūeki** beneficial, profitable
7 利益 **rieki** profit, gain; benefit, advantage
　　(go)riyaku divine favor
　利益代表 **rieki daihyō** representing (another country's) diplomatic interests
　私益 **shieki** personal gain, self-interest
8 受益 **jueki** benefit by
　受益者 **juekisha** beneficiary
　実益 **jitsueki** net profit, practical benefit
　国益 **kokueki** national interests/benefit
9 便益 **ben'eki** convenience, benefit, advantage
10 差益 **saeki** marginal profit
　益益 **masumasu** increasingly, more and more
　純益 **jun'eki** net profit
12 無益 **mueki** useless, futile
13 損益分岐点 **son'eki bunkiten** break-even point
　損益計算書 **son'eki keisansho** income/profit-and-loss statement
　裨益 **hieki** benefit/profit by
14 総益 **sōeki** gross profit
　総益金 **sōekikin** gross profit
15 権益 **ken'eki** (rights and) interests

──────── 3 ────────

4 不利益 **furieki** (to one's) disadvantage
10 純収益 **junshūeki** net earnings

──────── 4 ────────

6 有害無益 **yūgai-mueki** harmful, more harm than good

2o8.6 / 1930

翁 翁　**Ō, okina** old man

6 老翁 **rōō** old man
14 漁翁 **gyoō** old fisherman
——————— 3 ———————
9 信天翁 **ahōdori** albatross

2o8.7

釜 釜

FU, kama kettle, cooking pot

——————— 1 ———————
0 お釜 **(o)kama** a male homosexual
3 釜山 **Fuzan, Pusan** Pusan
9 釜茹 **kamayu(de)** boiling in a kettle
12 釜飯 **kamameshi** rice dish served in a small pot
15 釜敷 **kamashi(ki)** pad to set a kettle on
——————— 2 ———————
9 後釜 **atogama** successor
茶釜 **chagama** teakettle
12 湯釜 **yugama** cauldron, kettle
蒸釜 **mu(shi)gama** steaming kettle

眞 → 真 **2k8.1**

瓶 → **2o9.6**

恭 → **3k7.16**

——————— 9 ———————

2o9.1

剪 翦

SEN, hasa(mu) snip, clip, shear

——————— 1 ———————
8 剪定 **sentei** pruning
剪定鋏 **sentei-basami** pruning shears
12 剪裁 **sensai** shear, cut, trim, prune
剪裁機 **sensaiki** shearing machine

2o9.2

孳

JI, SHI bear children, increase, multiply

——————— 1 ———————
3 孳々 **shishi** diligently

2o9.3

曽 曾

SO, SŌ, katsu(te) once, formerly, before; ever; former, ex-

——————— 1 ———————
9 曽孫 **sōson, hiimago, himago** great-grand-child
曽祖父 **sōsofu, hiijiji** great-grandfather
曽祖母 **sōsobo, hiibaba** great-grandmother
10 曽遊 **sōyū** previous visit

蓋 → 蓋 **3k10.15**

2o9.4

羞

SHŪ, ha(jiru) feel ashamed

——————— 1 ———————
10 羞恥 **shūchi** shame
羞恥心 **shūchishin** sense of shame

2o9.5 / 753

貧 貧

HIN, BIN, mazu(shii) poor

——————— 1 ———————
3 貧乏 **binbō** poor
貧乏人 **binbōnin** poor man, pauper
貧乏性 **binbōshō** destined to poverty
貧乏神 **binbōgami** god of poverty
貧乏揺 **binbōyu(suri)** absent-minded shaking of knee or foot
貧乏暮 **binbōgu(rashi)** living in poverty
5 貧民 **hinmin** the poor
貧民街 **hinmingai** slums
貧民窟 **hinminkutsu** slums
6 貧血 **hinketsu** anemia
貧血症 **hinketsushō** anemia
7 貧困 **hinkon** poverty; lack
8 貧苦 **hinku** hardships of poverty
貧者 **hinja** poor man, pauper
9 貧相 **hinsō** poor-looking, seedy
10 貧弱 **hinjaku** poor, meager, scanty
貧家 **hinka** poor home
貧素 **hinso** dire poverty
12 貧富 **hinpu** rich and poor, wealth and poverty
13 貧農 **hinnō** poor farmer, needy peasant
15 貧窮 **hinkyū** dire poverty
——————— 2 ———————
7 赤貧 **sekihin** abject poverty
11 清貧 **seihin** honorable poverty

脳貧血 **nōhinketsu** cerebral anemia
救貧 **kyūhin** poverty assistance
救貧院 **kyūhin'in** poorhouse
12 寒貧 **kanpin** very poor
極貧 **gokuhin** dire poverty

——— 3 ———

10 素寒貧 **sukanpin** poverty; pauper
15 器用貧乏 **kiyō-binbō** Jack of all trades but master of none

黄→ **3k8.16**

2o9.6 / 1161

瓶 瓶

BIN, HEI bottle, jar
kame jar, jug, vase, vat, urn

——— 1 ———

0 ビール瓶 **bīrubin** beer bottle
13 瓶詰 **binzu(me)** bottling; bottled

——— 2 ———

3 土瓶 **dobin** earthen teapot
小瓶 **kobin** small bottle
4 水瓶 **mizugame** water jar/jug
7 角瓶 **kakubin** square bottle
花瓶 **kabin, hanagame** vase
尿瓶 **shibin** pisspot, bedpan
8 空瓶 **a(ki)bin** empty bottle
9 茶瓶 **chabin** teapot, tea urn
茶瓶頭 **chabin atama** bald head
11 釣瓶 **tsurube** well bucket
釣瓶打 **tsurubeu(chi)** firing in rapid succession
13 溲瓶 **shibin** piss pot/bottle
鉄瓶 **tetsubin** iron kettle
16 薬瓶 **kusuribin** medicine bottle, vial

——— 3 ———

4 火炎瓶 **kaenbin** firebomb, Molotov cocktail
10 哺乳瓶 **honyūbin** baby bottle
15 撥釣瓶 **ha(ne)tsurube** a well sweep
21 魔法瓶 **mahōbin** thermos bottle

質→質 **7b8.7**

2o9.7

羝

TEI, ohitsuji male sheep, ram

——— 1 ———

7 羝乳 **teinyū** impossible

2o9.8

羚

REI serow, antelope

——— 1 ———

6 羚羊 **kamoshika** serow   **reiyō** antelope

粛→ **0a11.8**

——— 10 ———

2o10.1 / 657

着

CHAKU, JAKU arrive at; put on, wear; (counter for suits) **tsu(ku)** arrive at **ki(ru), tsu(keru)** put on, wear **ki(seru)** clothe, dress, put on

——— 1 ———

0 着こなす **ki(konasu)** wear (stylishly), dress (well)
3 着工 **chakkō** start of construction
着丈 **kitake** dress length
着々 **chakuchaku** steadily
4 着切雀 **ki(ta)ki(ri) suzume** person having only the clothes he is wearing
着込 **kiko(mu)** wear extra clothes, dress warmly
着水 **chakusui** landing on water, splashdown
着手 **chakushu** start, commence, proceed with
着尺 **kijaku** standard length of cloth for a kimono
着尺地 **kijakuji** standard-length kimono cloth
着火 **chakka** ignition, combustion
着心地 **kigokochi** fit and feel (of clothes)
5 着生 **chakusei** insertion
着付 **kitsu(ke)** dress (someone); fitting
着古 **kifuru(su)** wear out
着用 **chakuyō** have on, wear
着氷 **chakuhyō** ice up, icing
着払 **chakubarai** payment upon delivery, COD
着目 **chakumoku** notice, observe
6 着任 **chakunin** arrival at one's post
着色 **chakushoku** to color, tint
着地 **chakuchi** landing (in gymnastics)
着衣 **chakui** dressing (oneself); one's clothes
7 着身着儘 **ki(no)mi-ki(no)mama** with only the clothes one happens to be wearing
着床 **chakushō** become implanted
着初 **kizo(me)** first wearing (of a suit)
着車 **chakusha** arrival (of a train)
8 着呼 **chakko** incoming (telephone) call
着実 **chakujitsu** steady, solid, trustworthy
着岸 **chakugan** reach the shore

着服 **chakufuku** put on clothes; embezzle
着物 **kimono** clothes, kimono
9 着発 **chakuhatsu** arrivals and departures
着信 **chakushin** arrival of mail/message
着信局 **chakushinkyoku** destination post office
着陣 **chakujin** take up positions
着通 **kidō(shi)** wearing (the same clothes) all the time
着草臥 **kikutabi(re)** worn out
10 着倒 **kidao(re)** extravagance in dress
着陸 **chakuriku** (airplane) landing
着陸地 **chakurikuchi** landing zone
着剣 **chakken** fixed bayonet
着流 **kinaga(shi)** everyday clothes, dishabille
着帯 **chakutai** wear a maternity belt
着荷 **chakuni, chakka** goods arrived
着座 **chakuza** take a seat
着席 **chakuseki** take a seat
11 着道楽 **kidōraku** love of fine clothes
着崩 **kikuzu(re)** worn out of shape
着眼 **chakugan** notice, observe
着眼点 **chakuganten** viewpoint
着船 **chakusen** arrival (of a ship)
着雪 **chakusetsu** accumulation of snow
12 着着 **chakuchaku** steadily
着港 **chakkō** arrival in port
着帽 **chakubō** put on one's cap
着弾距離 **chakudan kyori** range (of a gun)
着替 **kiga(e)** changing clothes; change of clothes
着装 **chakusō** put on, install, attach
着筆 **chakuhitsu** begin to write; manner of writing
着順 **chakujun** in order of arrival
13 着想 **chakusō** idea, conception
着意 **chakui** conception; caution
着飾 **kikaza(ru)** dress up
着電 **chakuden** telegram received
14 着駅 **chakueki** destination station
16 着膨 **kibuku(re)** wear thick clothes, bundle up
18 着類 **kirui** clothing

———————— 2 ————————

1 一着 **itchaku** first arrival; first (in a race); a suit (of clothes)
2 二着 **nichaku** second (in a race); two suits
3 上着 **uwagi** coat, jacket
下着 **shitagi** underwear
土着 **dochaku** native, indigenous
土着民 **dochakumin** natives, aborigines
巾着 **kinchaku** moneybag, purse
巾着切 **kinchakuki(ri)** cutpurse, pickpocket
4 不着 **fuchaku** nonarrival, nondelivery
中着 **nakagi** singlet worn between undershirt and outer clothing

水着 **mizugi** bathing suit, swimwear
5 未着 **michaku** nonarrival
付着 **fuchaku** adhere, stick to
古着 **furugi** old/secondhand clothes
圧着端子 **atchaku tanshi** crimp contact
冬着 **fuyugi** winter clothing
6 合着 **a(i)gi** between-season clothing, spring or fall wear
辿着 **tado(ri)tsu(ku)** make it to, grope/ trudge along to
近着 **kinchaku** recently/just arrived
先着 **senchaku** first arrival, first-come(-first-served)
先着順 **senchakujun** by order of arrival, in the order of receipt, (on a) first-come-first-served basis
吸着 **kyūchaku** adsorb
行着 **i(ki)tsu(ku), yu(ki)tsu(ku)** arrive at, reach
安着 **anchaku** arrive safely
肌着 **hadagi** underwear
7 来着 **raichaku** arrival
延着 **enchaku** delayed arrival
決着 **ketchaku** conclusiveness, settlement
沈着 **chinchaku** composed, calm
初着 **hatsugi** first dress-up clothes worn in the new year; new clothing worn for the first time
8 到着 **tōchaku** arrival
到着港 **tōchakukō** port of arrival
到着駅 **tōchakueki** arrival/destination station
夜着 **yogi** bedclothes; bedding
厚着 **atsugi** wearing thick/heavy clothing
参着 **sanchaku** arrival; payable on sight
参着払 **sanchakubara(i)** payment on demand/sight
定着 **teichaku** fix, fasten, anchor
定着物 **teichakubutsu** fixtures
定着剤 **teichakuzai** fixing agent
定着液 **teichakueki** fixing solution
居着 **itsu(ku)** settle down
固着 **kochaku** adhere/stick to
金着 **kinki(se)** gold-plated
雨着 **amagi** raincoat
9 発着 **hatchaku** departures and arrivals
重着 **kasa(ne)gi** wear one garment over another
逢着 **hōchaku** encounter, face
春着 **harugi** spring/New-Year's clothes
10 借着 **ka(ri)gi** borrowed/rented clothes
帰着 **kichaku** return; conclusion, consequence
恋着 **renchaku** love, attachment
流着 **naga(re)tsu(ku)** drift to, be washed ashore
胴着 **dōgi** undergarment; chest protector (worn in kendo)

2

亻
冫
子
阝
卩
刂
力
又
宀
亠
十
ㅏ
夂

ㅛ 10←

厂
辶
冂
几
匸

夏着 **natsugi** summer wear/clothes
11 遅着 **chichaku** late arrival
執着 **shūchaku** attachment to, tenacity
押着 **monchaku** trouble, dispute
接着 **setchaku** adhesion
接着剤 **setchakuzai** adhesive, glue
密着 **mitchaku** adhere to, stick fast
産着 **ubugi** newborn baby's first clothes
装着 **sōchaku** equip, fit, put, place
終着駅 **shūchakueki** terminal station
粘着 **nenchaku** adhesion
　　　neba(ri)tsu(ku) be sticky
粘着力 **nenchakuryoku** adhesion, viscosity
船着場 **funatsu(ki)ba** harbor, wharf
軟着陸 **nanchakuriku** soft landing
12 着着 **chakuchaku** steadily
換着 **ka(e)gi** change of clothes
弾着点 **danchakuten** point of impact
弾着距離 **danchaku kyori** range (of a gun)
落着 **o(chi)tsu(ku)** calm down
　　　rakuchaku be settled
落着払 **o(chi)tsu(ki)hara(u)** be quite unperturbed
晴着 **ha(re)gi** one's best clothes
替着 **ka(e)gi** a change of clothing
無着陸 **muchakuriku** nonstop (flight)
装着 **sōchaku** equip, install, fit with
結着 **ketchaku** conclusion, settlement
悶着 **monchaku** trouble; dispute
13 愛着 **aichaku, aijaku** attachment, affection
新着 **shinchaku** newly arrived
新着荷 **shinchakuni** newly arrived goods
頓着 **tonchaku** be mindful of, care, heed
14 漕着 **ko(gi)tsu(keru)** row up to, reach
漂着 **hyōchaku** drift ashore
15 膚着 **hadagi** underwear
撞着 **dōchaku** inconsistency
横着 **ōchaku** dishonest; cunning; impudent; lazy; selfish
膠着 **kōchaku** agglutination; stalemate
膠着剤 **kōchakuzai** glue, binder
膠着語 **kochakugo** an agglutinative language
16 凝着 **gyōchaku** adhesion
薄着 **usugi** lightly/thinly dressed
瞞着 **manchaku** deceive, trick, dupe
18 癒着 **yuchaku** adhere, knit together, heal up; too close a relationship (with an organization)
離着 **richaku** takeoff and landing
離着陸 **richakuriku** takeoff and landing

———— 3 ————
4 不時着 **fujichaku** emergency landing
不断着 **fudangi** everyday clothes
水泳着 **suieigi** swimming suit
9 海水着 **kaisuigi** bathing/swimming suit

10 部屋着 **heyagi** house dress, dressing gown
11 野良着 **noragi** clothes for working in the fields
訪問着 **hōmongi** woman's semi-formal kimono
12 割烹着 **kappōgi** cook's apron
着身着儘 **ki(no)mi-ki(no)mama** with only the clothes one happens to be wearing
普段着 **fudangi** everyday clothes
無頓着 **mutonjaku, mutonchaku** indifferent/unattentive to
間祝着 **maiwa(i)gi** festive fisherman's kimono
13 寝間着 **nemaki** nightclothes
腰巾着 **koshiginchaku** belt purse; one's shadow/follower-around
16 稽古着 **keikogi** practice/gym suit
17 濡衣着 **nu(re)ginu (o) ki(serareru)** be falsely accused
糞落着 **kusoo(chi)tsu(ki)** provokingly calm

2o10.2 / 1139

善 譱

ZEN, yo(i), i(i) good

———— 1 ————
2 善人 **zennin** virtuous man, good people
3 善女 **zennyo** woman Buddhist
4 善心 **zenshin** virtue, conscience, moral sense
5 善用 **zen'yō** put to good use
善玉 **zendama** good guy
善処 **zensho** take appropriate action; (as an official's term of art) do nothing for the present
6 善行 **zenkō** good conduct/deed
善因善果 **zen'in-zenka** Good actions lead to good results.
7 善良 **zenryō** good, good-natured, virtuous
善男善女 **zennan-zennyo** devout men and women
8 善果 **zenka** good results
善事 **zenji** good thing/deed
善性 **zensei** innate goodness of human nature
9 善美 **zenbi** the good and the beautiful; sumptuous
善後策 **zengosaku** remedial measures
善政 **zensei** good government
善哉 **zenzai** Well done!; thick bean-jam soup
10 善根 **zenkon** good deed, act of charity
11 善道 **zendō** path of virtue, righteousness
善悪 **zen'aku** good and evil
yo(shi)waru(shi), yo(shi)a(shi) good and bad, good or bad
yo(kare)a(shikare) right or wrong, for better or worse

13 善業 **zengō** good deed
善感 **zenkan** successful vaccination, positive reaction
善戦 **zensen** put up a good fight
善意 **zen'i** good faith; well-intentioned; favorable sense
14 善導 **zendō** proper guidance

——————— 2 ———————

3 小善 **shōzen** a small kindness
4 不善 **fuzen** evil, vice, sin
6 次善 **jizen** second best
至善 **shizen** the highest good
7 改善 **kaizen** improvement
8 追善 **tsuizen** (Buddhist) memorial service
追善供養 **tsuizen-kuyō** (Buddhist) memorial service
性善説 **seizensetsu** the view that human nature is basically good
9 独善 **hito(ri)yo(gari), dokuzen** self-righteous, complacent, smug
独善的 **dokuzenteki** self-righteous, complacent, smug
11 偽善 **gizen** hypocrisy
偽善者 **gizensha** hypocrite
12 最善 **saizen** (do one's) best
13 勧善懲悪 **kanzen-chōaku** rewarding good and punishing evil, didactic/morality (play)
慈善 **jizen** charity
慈善事業 **jizen jigyō** charity work, philanthropy
慈善家 **jizenka** charitable person, philanthropist
慈善鍋 **jizennabe** charity pot
16 親善 **shinzen** friendship, amity, goodwill
積善 **sekizen** accumulation of good deeds

——————— 3 ———————

6 至高善 **shikōzen** the highest good
12 善因善果 **zen'in-zenka** Good actions lead to good results.
善男善女 **zennan-zennyo** devout men and women

2o10.3 / 704

SON, tatto(bu), tōto(bu/mu) esteem, value, respect
tatto(i), tōto(i) valuable, precious; noble, exalted
mikoto lord, prince

——————— 1 ———————

3 尊大 **sondai** haughty, arrogant, self-important
4 尊王 **sonnō** reverence for the emperor, advocacy of imperial rule
尊王党 **Sonnōtō** Imperialists
尊王攘夷 **sonnō-jōi** Revere the emperor and expel the barbarians.
5 尊号 **songō** honorific title
7 尊体 **sontai** your health; image of Buddha
8 尊者 **sonja** Buddhist saint; one's superior
9 尊重 **sonchō** respect, esteem
尊卑 **sonpi** high and low, aristocrat and plebian
10 尊称 **sonshō** honorific title
11 尊崇 **sonsū** reverence, veneration
12 尊属 **sonzoku** ancestor
尊敬 **sonkei** respect, esteem, honor
尊貴 **sonki** exalted person
14 尊像 **sonzō** your portrait
17 尊厳 **songen** dignity
20 尊攘 **sonjō** Revere the emperor and expel the barbarians. (short for 尊王攘夷)

——————— 2 ———————

3 女尊 **joson** respect for women
女尊男卑 **joson-danpi** putting women above men
5 本尊 **honzon** main image (of worship), idol; the man himself
6 至尊 **shison** His Majesty the Emperor
自尊 **jison** self-esteem; conceit
自尊心 **jisonshin** self-esteem; conceit
7 男尊女卑 **danson-johi** predominance of men over women
8 官尊民卑 **kanson-minpi** exalting the government at the expense of the people
11 釈尊 **Shakuson** Gautama, Buddha

——————— 3 ———————

6 守本尊 **mamo(ri)honzon** guardian deity

——————— 4 ———————

9 独立自尊 **dokuritsu-jison** independence and self-respect
11 唯我独尊 **yuiga-dokuson** self-conceit, vainglory

寏 → 尊 2o10.3

2o10.4

TEN, DEN decide; accouterment

——————— 2 ———————

9 香奠 **kōden** condolence gift
香奠返 **kōdengae(shi)** return present for a condolence gift

2o10.5 / 1166

普 **FU** everywhere, general; Prussia
amane(ku) widely, generally

——— 1 ———
3 普及 **fukyū** diffusion, dissemination, wide use/ownership, popularization
普及版 **fukyūban** popular edition
4 普仏 **Fu-Futsu** Franco-Prussian (War)
9 普通 **futsū** ordinary, common, usual
普通人 **futsūjin** average person
普通選挙 **futsū senkyo** universal suffrage
普段 **fudan** usual, ordinary; constant, ceaseless
普段着 **fudangi** everyday clothes
11 普遍 **fuhen** universal, general
普遍的 **fuhenteki** universal, general
14 普選 **fusen** universal suffrage
15 普請 **fushin** building, construction
普請場 **fushinba** construction site
普魯西 **Puroshia** Prussia

——— 2 ———
6 仮普請 **karibushin** temporary building
安普請 **yasubushin** flimsy building, jerry-built
11 道普請 **michi bushin** road repair
16 橋普請 **hashi-bushin** bridge construction

曾→曽 **2o9.3**

2o10.6

爺 **YA, jijii, jiji, jii(ya)** old man, geezer

——— 1 ———
9 爺臭 **jijikusa(i)** old-mannish
——— 3 ———
5 好々爺 **kōkōya** good-natured old man

巽→巽 **2o10.7**

2o10.7

巽 巽 **SON, tatsumi** southeast

2o10.8

翔 **SHŌ, ka(keru)** fly, soar, spread one's wings

——— 2 ———
9 飛翔 **hishō** flying, soaring

2o10.9

斯 **SHI** this
ka(karu) such
ka(ku/kute/kushite) thus, in this way

——— 1 ———
9 斯界 **shikai** this field (of endeavor)
14 斯様 **kayō** such
——— 2 ———
5 瓦斯 **gasu** gas
8 波斯 **Perusha** Persia
12 然斯 **so(u)ko(u)** this and that

期→期 **4b8.11**

粭→ **0a12.1**

——— 11 ———

2o11.1 / 1547

慈 慈 **JI, itsuku(shimu)** love, be affectionate to; pity

——— 1 ———
4 慈父 **jifu** affectionate father
5 慈母 **jibo** affectionate mother
慈兄 **jikei** affectionate elder brother
8 慈姑 **kuwai** arrowhead (an edible tuber)
慈雨 **jiu** beneficial/welcome rain
10 慈恵 **jikei** charity
12 慈善 **jizen** charity
慈善事業 **jizen jigyō** charity work, philanthropy
慈善家 **jizenka** charitable person, philanthropist
慈善鍋 **jizennabe** charity pot
慈悲 **jihi** compassion, mercy, charity
慈悲心 **jihishin** benevolence
13 慈愛 **jiai** affection, kindness, love

——— 2 ———
3 大慈大悲 **daiji-daihi** mercy and compassion
4 仁慈 **jinji** benevolence
12 無慈悲 **mujihi** merciless, ruthless

2o11.2

煎 **SEN** boil, decoct
i(ru) roast, parch, broil, boil down

——— 1 ———
0 煎じる **sen(jiru)** boil, decoct
5 煎出 **sen(ji)da(su)** extract by boiling, decoct, infuse

煎付 **i(ri)tsu(keru)** parch, roast, broil, scorch
煎玉子 **i(ri)tamago** scrambled eggs
7 煎卵 **i(ri)tamago** scrambled eggs
煎豆腐 **i(ri)dōfu** bean curd boiled dry and seasoned
9 煎茶 **sencha** green tea
13 煎詰 **sen(ji)tsu(meru)** boil down
15 煎餅 **senbei** (rice) cracker
煎餅布団 **senbei-buton** thinly stuffed futon/bedding
16 煎薬 **sen(ji)gusuri, sen'yaku** medical decoction, herb tea

————————— 2 —————————

7 肝煎 **kimoi(ri)** sponsorship, good offices
12 湯煎 **yusen** boiling, decoction

————————— 3 —————————

2 二番煎 **nibansen(ji)** second brew of tea; rehash

2o11.3 / 291

義 **GI** justice, righteousness; loyalty; non-blood family relationship; meaning, significance; substitute, artificial

————————— 1 —————————

2 義人 **gijin** righteous/public-spirited man
義子 **gishi** adopted child
3 義士 **gishi** loyal retainer; righteous person; martyr
4 義太夫 **gidayū** (a form of ballad-drama)
義父 **gifu** father-in-law; foster father; stepfather
義手 **gishu** artificial arm/hand
義心 **gishin** chivalrous/public spirit
5 義民 **gimin** public-spirited man
義母 **gibo** mother-in-law; foster mother; stepmother
義兄 **gikei** elder brother-in-law
義兄弟 **gikyōdai** brother-in-law; stepbrother; sworn brother
6 義気 **giki** chivalrous spirit, public-spiritedness
7 義弟 **gitei** younger brother-in-law
義兵 **gihei** loyal soldier, volunteer
義足 **gisoku** artificial leg
8 義妹 **gimai** younger sister-in-law
義姉 **gishi** elder sister-in-law
義姉妹 **gishimai** sister-in-law; stepsister
義肢 **gishi** artificial limb
義和団 **Giwadan** the Boxers
義金 **gikin** donation, contribution
9 義侠 **gikyō** chivalry, generosity, heroism
義侠心 **gikyōshin** chivalrous spirit, public-spiritedness
義勇 **giyū** loyalty and courage, heroism
義勇兵 **giyūhei** volunteer soldier

義勇軍 **giyūgun** volunteer army
義軍 **gigun** righteous army
10 義捐 **gien** donation, contribution
義捐金 **gienkin** donation, contribution
義挙 **gikyo** worthy undertaking; heroic deed
義烈 **giretsu** nobility of soul, heroism
11 義理 **giri** sense of duty/honor, decency, courtesy, debt of gratitude
義理人情 **giri-ninjō** duty versus/and human feelings
義理立 **girida(te)** do one's duty
義理合 **giria(i)** social relationship
義理知 **girishi(razu)** ungrateful person
義理堅 **girigata(i)** having a strong sense of duty
義務 **gimu** obligation, duty
義務心 **gimushin** sense of duty
義務的 **gimuteki** obligatory, compulsory
義務者 **gimusha** debtor, obligor, responsible person
義務教育 **gimu kyōiku** compulsory education
義眼 **gigan** artificial eye
12 義援 **gien** donation, contribution
義援金 **gienkin** donation, contribution
義絶 **gizetsu** disown, break off the relationship
義歯 **gishi** artificial/false tooth, dentures
13 義塾 **gijuku** private school
義戦 **gisen** holy war, crusade
義賊 **gizoku** chivalrous robber
14 義僕 **giboku** loyal servant
義旗 **giki** flag/banner of righteousness
15 義憤 **gifun** righteous indignation

————————— 2 —————————

1 一義 **ichigi** a reason; a principle; a meaning; the first principle/consideration
一義的 **ichigiteki** unambiguous
2 二義的 **nigiteki** secondary
3 大義 **taigi** a great cause
大義名分 **taigi-meibun** proper relationship between sovereign and subjects; justification, just cause
4 不義 **fugi** immorality; injustice; impropriety, misconduct, adultery
不義理 **fugiri** dishonesty, injustice; dishonor; ingratitude
仁義 **jingi** humanity and justice; duty; moral code (of a gang)
5 本義 **hongi** true meaning, basic principle
古義 **kogi** old/original meaning
古義真言宗 **Kogi Shingon shū** the "old meaning" sect of Esoteric Buddhism
正義 **seigi** justice, right(eousness); correct meaning
正義感 **seigikan** sense of justice
字義 **jigi** meaning of a word

2

广义 **kōgi** broad sense
主義 **shugi** -ism, principle
主義者 **shugisha** -ist, advocate (of a theory/doctrine)
6 多義 **tagi** various meanings
両義 **ryōgi** double meaning, two meanings
同義 **dōgi** the same meaning
同義語 **dōgigo** synonym
名義 **meigi** name; moral duty
名義上 **meigijō** nominal, titular
8 定義 **teigi** definition
忠義 **chūgi** loyalty
忠義立 **chūgida(te)** act of loyalty
9 信義 **shingi** faith, fidelity, loyalty
通義 **tsūgi** universal principle; the usual interpretation
要義 **yōgi** essence, digest, outline
狭義 **kyōgi** narrow sense
律義 **richigi** honesty, integrity, loyalty
律義者 **richigimono** honest hardworking man
10 高義 **kōgi** high morality; great kindness/favor
原義 **gengi** original/primary meaning
教義 **kyōgi** doctrine, dogma, tenet
教義学 **kyōgigaku** dogmatics
教義的 **kyōgiteki** doctrinal
恩義 **ongi** favor, debt of gratitude
訓義 **kungi** reading and meaning (of a kanji)
11 道義 **dōgi** moral principles
道義心 **dōgishin** moral sense, scruples
異義 **igi** different meaning
釈義 **shakugi** explication, commentary
釈義学 **shakugigaku** exegesis
転義 **tengi** figurative/extended meaning
12 奥義 **okugi, ōgi** secrets, esoteric mysteries
13 意義 **igi** meaning, significance
意義深 **igibuka(i)** full of meaning
新義 **shingi** new meaning　**Shingi** (short for 新義真言宗) New Shingon religion
新義派 **Shingi-ha** New Shingon religion
新義真言宗 **Shingi Shingon shū** New Shingon religion
節義 **setsugi** fidelity to one's principles
14 疑義 **gigi** doubt
演義 **engi** amplification, commentary, popular adaptation
徳義 **tokugi** morality, integrity
徳義上 **tokugijō** morally, ethically
徳義心 **tokugishin** sense of morality/honor
精義 **seigi** exact meaning; detailed exposition
語義 **gogi** meaning of a word
15 談義 **dangi** sermon; lecture, scolding
17 講義 **kōgi** lecture
講義録 **kōgiroku** lecture transcripts; correspondence course
18 類義語 **ruigigo** words of similar meaning

───────── 3 ─────────

4 不信義 **fushingi** faithlessness, insincerity
5 白耳義 **Berugī** Belgium
6 同意義 **dōigi** the same meaning
有意義 **yūigi** significant
11 第一義 **dai-ichigi** original meaning; first principles
第二義 **dai-nigi** secondary meaning
第二義的 **dai-nigiteki** of secondary importance
12 無意義 **muigi** meaningless, not significant
18 儲主義 **mō(ke)shugi** moneymaking

───────── 4 ─────────

2 人文主義 **jinbun shugi** humanism
人本主義 **jinpon shugi** humanism
人道主義 **jindō shugi** humanitarianism
4 分離主義者 **bunri shugisha** separatist, secessionist
反動主義者 **handō shugisha** a reactionary
日本主義 **Nihon shugi** Japanism
5 民本主義 **minpon shugi** democracy
民主主義 **minshu shugi** democracy
功利主義 **kōri shugi** utilitarianism
写実主義 **shajitsu shugi** realism, literalism
古典主義 **koten shugi** classicism
平和主義 **heiwa shugi** pacificism
主我主義 **shuga shugi** egoism, love of self
主知主義 **shuchi shugi** intellectualism
主観主義 **shukan shugi** subjectivism
6 全体主義 **zentai shugi** totalitarianism
合理主義 **gōri shugi** rationalism
印象主義 **inshō shugi** impressionism
近代主義 **kindai shugi** modernism
同音異義 **dōon-igi** the same pronunciation but different meanings
汎愛主義 **han'ai shugi** philanthropism
行動主義 **kōdō shugi** behaviorism
共産主義 **kyōsan shugi** communism
自己主義 **jiko shugi** egoism, selfishness
自由主義 **jiyū shugi** liberalism
自然主義 **shizen shugi** naturalism
7 享楽主義 **kyōraku shugi** epicureanism
折衷主義 **setchū shugi** eclecticism
形式主義 **keishiki shugi** formalism; red-tapism
社会主義 **shakai shugi** socialism
快楽主義 **kairaku shugi** hedonism, epicureanism
利己主義 **riko shugi** selfishness
8 画一主義 **kakuitsu shugi** standardization
事大主義 **jidai shugi** worship of the powerful
事勿主義 **kotonaka(re) shugi** hoping that all turns out well
刹那主義 **setsuna shugi** living only for (the pleasures of) the moment

拝金主義 **haikin shugi** mammonism
英雄主義 **eiyū shugi** heroism
実存主義 **jitsuzon shugi** existentialism
実用主義 **jitsuyō shugi** pragmatism
実利主義 **jitsuri shugi** utilitarianism,
　　materialism
実証主義 **jisshō shugi** positivism
官能主義 **kannō shugi** sensualism
官僚主義 **kanryō shugi** bureaucracy
国家主義 **kokka shugi** nationalism
国粋主義 **kokusui shugi** ultranationalism
国際主義 **kokusai shugi** internationalism
9 専制主義 **sensei shugi** absolutism, despotism
重商主義 **jūshō shugi** mercantilism
重農主義 **jūnō shugi** physiocracy
保守主義 **hoshu shugi** conservatism
軍国主義 **gunkoku shugi** militarism
帝国主義 **teikoku shugi** imperialism
急進主義 **kyūshin shugi** radicalism
封建主義 **hōken shugi** feudalism
客観主義 **kyakkan shugi, kakkan shugi**
　　objectivism
相対主義 **sōtai shugi** relativism
神秘主義 **shinpi shugi** mysticism
10 個人主義 **kojin shugi** individualism
進歩主義 **shinpo shugi** progressivism
浪漫主義 **rōman shugi** romanticism
根本主義 **konpon shugi** fundamentalism
破壊主義 **hakai shugi** vandalism
耽美主義 **tanbi shugi** estheticism
11 野獣主義 **yajū shugi** Fauvism
商業主義 **shōgyō shugi** commercialism
虚無主義 **kyomu shugi** nihilism
過激主義 **kageki shugi** radicalism, extremism
唯物主義 **yuibutsu shugi** materialism
唯美主義 **yuibi shugi** estheticism
菜食主義 **saishoku shugi** vegetarianism
理想主義 **risō shugi** idealism
現実主義 **genjitsu shugi** realism
12 象徴主義 **shōchō shugi** symbolism
温情主義 **onjō shugi** paternalism
無妻主義 **musai shugi** celibacy
絶対主義 **zettai shugi** absolutism
13 農本主義 **nōhon shugi** agriculture-first
　　policy, physiocracy
楽天主義 **rakuten shugi** optimism
楽観主義 **rakkan shugi** optimism
禁欲主義 **kin'yoku shugi** asceticism,
　　stoicism
愛他主義 **aita shugi** altruism
愛国主義 **aikoku shugi** patriotism
裸体主義 **ratai shugi** nudism
詰込主義 **tsu(me)ko(mi) shugi** education
　　emphasizing cramming and memoriza-
　　tion rather than understanding
資本主義 **shihon shugi** capitalism

14 厭世主義 **ensei shugi** pessimism
構造主義 **kōzō shugi** structuralism
熟柿主義 **jukushi shugi** wait-and-see policy
15 権力主義 **kenryoku shugi** authoritarianism
権威主義 **ken'i shugi** authoritarianism
敵本主義 **tekihon shugi** feint, pretense,
　　having ulterior motives
16 積読主義 **tsu(n)doku shugi** acquiring books
　　without reading them
17 擬古主義 **giko shugi** classicism

———————— 5 ————————
4 反帝国主義 **han-teikoku shugi** anti-
　　imperialism
12 超国家主義 **chōkokka shugi** ultranationalism
超現実主義 **chōgenjitsu shugi** surrealism
御都合主義 **gotsugō shugi** opportunism
無政府主義 **museifu shugi** anarchism
無政府主義者 **museifushugisha** anarchist
無教会主義 **mukyōkai shugi**
　　Nondenominationalism (a Japanese
　　Christian sect)

———————— 6 ————————
1 一国一党主義 **ikkoku-ittō shugi** one-party
　　system
2 二大政党主義 **nidaiseitō shugi** the two-
　　party system
7 芸術至上主義 **geijutsushijō shugi** art for
　　art's sake
社会民主主義 **shakai minshu shugi** social
　　democracy
10 恋愛至上主義 **ren'ai-shijō shugi** love for
　　love's sake

2o11.4

羨 **SEN, uraya(mu/mashigaru)** envy, be
envious of **uraya(mashii)** enviable

———————— 1 ————————
11 羨望 **senbō** envy

與 → 与　**0a3.23**

業 → 　**0a13.3**

豢 → 　**0a13.4**

———————— 12 ————————
爾 → 　**0a14.3**

─────────── 13 ───────────

翦 → 剪 2o9.1

2o13.1 / 402

養

YŌ, yashina(u) nurture, bring up, rear; adopt, foster; support; promote (health); cultivate, develop

─────────── 1 ───────────

2 養子 **yōshi, yashina(i)go** adopted child
養子先 **yōshisaki** one's adopted home
養子縁組 **yōshi engumi** adopting an heir
3 養女 **yōjo** adopted daughter; stepdaughter; daughter-in-law
4 養毛剤 **yōmōzai** hair tonic
養分 **yōbun** nourishment
養父 **yōfu** adoptive/foster father
養父母 **yōfubo** adoptive/foster parents
養手 **yashina(i)te** supporter, provider
5 養生 **yōjō** take care of one's health; curing (of concrete)
養生法 **yōjōhō** hygiene, rules of health
養母 **yōbo** adoptive/foster mother
6 養老 **yōrō** provision for old age
Yōrō (era, 717–724)
養老金 **yōrōkin** old-age pension
養老院 **yōrōin** old-folks home
養成 **yōsei** train, educate, cultivate
8 養育 **yōiku** bring up, rear; support
養育者 **yōikusha** rearer, guardian
養育院 **yōikuin** orphanage
養和 **Yōwa** (era, 1181–1182)
9 養祖父 **yōsofu** foster grandfather
養祖母 **yōsobo** foster grandmother
10 養家 **yōka** adoptive family
養蚕 **yōsan** silkworm raising/culture
養蚕地 **yōsanchi** silkworm-raising district
養蚕業 **yōsangyō** silkworm raising, sericulture
11 養豚 **yōton** hog raising
養豚者 **yōtonsha** hog raiser, pig farmer
養豚場 **yōtonjō** hog/pig farm
養魚 **yōgyo** fish farming/breeding
養魚池 **yōgyochi** fish/breeding pond
養魚場 **yōgyojō** fish farm/hatchery
12 養殖 **yōshoku** raising, culture, cultivation
13 養蜂 **yōhō** beekeeping
養蜂植物 **yōhō shokubutsu** plants for bees
16 養樹園 **yōjuen** tree nursery, arboretum
養親 **yōshin, yashina(i)oya** adoptive/foster parents
19 養鶏 **yōkei** poultry farming
養鶏家 **yōkeika** poultry farmer
養鶏場 **yōkeijō** poultry farm

養鶏業 **yōkeigyō** poultry farming
20 養護 **yōgo** protection, care
養護学級 **yōgo gakkyū** class for the handicapped
養護学校 **yōgo gakkō** school for the handicapped

─────────── 2 ───────────

4 不養生 **fuyōjō** neglect of one's health
天養 **Ten'yō** (era, 1144–1145)
6 休養 **kyūyō** rest, recreation
孝養 **kōyō** discharge of filial duties
7 扶養 **fuyō** support (a family)
扶養者 **fuyōsha** supporter, breadwinner
扶養家族 **fuyō kazoku** family dependents
8 供養 **kuyō, kyōyō** memorial service
9 保養 **hoyō** preservation of health; recuperation; recreation
保養地 **hoyōchi** health resort
保養所 **hoyōsho/jo** sanitarium, rest home
栄養 **eiyō** nutrition, nourishment
栄養分 **eiyōbun** a nutrient
栄養学 **eiyōgaku** (science of) nutrition, dietetics
栄養価 **eiyōka** food value
栄養剤 **eiyōzai** nutritional supplement, tonic
栄養素 **eiyōso** a nutrient
食養生 **shokuyōjō** taking nourishing food, dietary cure
10 修養 **shūyō** cultivation of the mind, character-building
教養 **kyōyō** culture, education, refinement
素養 **soyō** grounding in, attainments
11 涵養 **kan'yō** cultivate, foster, develop
培養 **baiyō** cultivation, culture
培養液 **baiyōeki** culture fluid/solution
培養基 **baiyōki** culture medium
12 滋養 **jiyō** nourishment
滋養分 **jiyōbun** nutrient
滋養物 **jiyōbutsu** nourishing food, sustenance
滋養過多 **jiyōkata** hypertrophy
婿養子 **muko-yōshi** son-in-law adopted as an heir
給養 **kyūyō** supplies, provisions
13 摂養 **setsuyō** taking care of one's health
飼養 **shiyō** breeding, raising
14 静養 **seiyō** rest, recuperate
17 療養 **ryōyō** medical treatment/care
療養所 **ryōyōjo** sanitarium

─────────── 3 ───────────

6 気保養 **kihoyō** recreation, diversion
7 花供養 **hanakuyō** Buddha's-birthday commemoration

─────────── 4 ───────────

8 追善供養 **tsuizen-kuyō** (Buddhist) memorial service

11 転地療養 **tenchi ryōyō** getting away for a
   change of climate for one's health

羹 → 羹 **2o17.1**

躾 → **4f12.2**

───────── 14 ─────────

2o14.1

義
   GI, KI (used in proper names)

2o14.2 / 368

興
   KŌ, KYŌ interest; entertainment;
   prosperity **oko(ru)** rise, flourish
   oko(su) revive, resuscitate, retrieve
   (fortunes)

───────── 1 ─────────

0 興がる **kyō(garu)** be amused, find pleasure in
  興じる/ずる **kyō(jiru/zuru)** amuse oneself,
   make merry
3 興亡 **kōbō** rise and fall, vicissitudes
6 興行 **kōgyō** entertainment industry
  興行主 **kōgyōnushi, kōgyōshu** promoter,
   showman, producer
  興行師 **kōgyōshi** impresario, show manager
8 興味 **kyōmi** interest
  興味津津 **kyōmi-shinshin(taru)** very
   interesting, absorbing
  興味深 **kyōmibuka(i)** very interesting
  興国 **kōkoku** making a country prosperous;
   prosperous country
   Kōkoku (era, 1340–1346)
9 興信所 **kōshinjo** detective/investigative
   agency
  興信録 **kōshinroku** directory
10 興隆 **kōryū** rise, prosperity
  興起 **kōki** rise, ascendancy
12 興廃 **kōhai** rise and fall, destiny
13 興業 **kōgyō** promotion of industry
15 興趣 **kyōshu** interest
16 興奮 **kōfun** get excited
  興奮剤 **kōfunzai** stimulant
  興醒 **kyōza(mashi), kyōza(me)** dampening
   the fun, wet blanket

───────── 2 ─────────

1 一興 **ikkyō** amusement, fun
4 不興 **fukyō** displeasure, ill-humor
  中興 **chūkō** restoration, revival
6 再興 **saikō** revive, restore, re-establish
7 作興 **sakkō** promote, arouse

余興 **yokyō** entertainment, sideshow
即興 **sokkyō** improvised, ad-lib
即興曲 **sokkyōkyoku** an impromptu
即興詩 **sokkyōshi** improvised poem
初興行 **hatsukōgyō** first performance,
   premiere
8 勃興 **bokkō** sudden rise to power
9 昼興行 **hirukōgyō** matinée
10 遊興 **yūkyō** pleasure seeking, merrymaking
  遊興者 **yūkyōsha** carouser, reveler
  遊興税 **yūkyōzei** entertainment tax
  遊興費 **yūkyōhi** amusement expenses
  逸興 **ikkyō** very interesting/amusing
  酒興 **shukyō** conviviality, merrymaking
  振興 **shinkō** promotion, encouragement
  座興 **zakyō** for the amusement/entertainment
   of those present
  旅興行 **tabikōgyō** road show
11 清興 **seikyō** refined amusement
12 復興 **fukkō** reconstruction, revival
13 感興 **kankyō** interest, pleasure
  新興 **shinkō** new, rising
  新興国 **shinkōkoku** emerging nation
  詩興 **shikyō** poetic inspiration

2o14.3

冀
   KI, koinega(u) request, entreat, wish

───────── 15 ─────────

2o15.1

輿
   YO, koshi palanquin; bier

───────── 1 ─────────

2 輿入 **koshii(re)** bride's entry into the groom's
   home; bridal procession; wedding
11 輿望 **yobō** popularity, esteem; trust, confidence
15 輿論 **yoron** public opinion
  輿論調査 **yoron chōsa** public-opinion survey,
   poll

───────── 2 ─────────

9 神輿 **mikoshi** (Shinto) palanquin shrine
12 御輿 **mikoshi** portable/palanquin shrine

糞 → **6b11.3**

2o15.2 / 1062

翼 翼
   YOKU wing; help
   tsubasa wing

───────── 1 ─────────

3 翼々 **yokuyoku** careful, prudent

7 翼状 **yokujō** wing-shaped
15 翼賛 **yokusan** support, approval

─────── 2 ───────

4 双翼 **sōyoku** both wings/flanks
5 左翼 **sayoku** left wing, leftist; left field (in baseball)
比翼 **hiyoku** wings abreast; single garment made to look double
比翼塚 **hiyokuzuka** lovers' double grave
右翼 **uyoku** right wing, rightists; right flank
右翼団体 **uyoku dantai** right-wing group
主翼 **shuyoku** main wing (of an airplane)
6 両翼 **ryōyoku** both wings; both flanks
羽翼 **uyoku** wings; assistance
7 扶翼 **fuyoku** aid, support
尾翼 **biyoku** tail (of an airplane)
14 銀翼 **gin'yoku** silvery wings
16 機翼 **kiyoku** airplane wing
17 翼翼 **yokuyoku** careful, prudent

─────── 3 ───────

3 小心翼々 **shōshin-yokuyoku** very timid/cautious
12 最左翼 **saisayoku** ultraleft
最右翼 **saiuyoku** ultraright

斁 → 0a17.1

─────── 16 ───────

叢 → 6e12.3

─────── 17 ───────

2o17.1

羹 羮   **KŌ, KAN, atsumono** hot soup

─────── 2 ───────

6 羊羹 **yōkan** sweet adzuki-bean jelly

─────── 3 ───────

13 煉羊羹 **ne(ri)yōkan** bean jelly

繡 → 0a19.1

─────── 18 ───────

譱 → 善 2o10.2

─────── 23 ───────

2o23.1

黌   **KŌ** school

─────────── 厂 2p ───────────

厂	厂	仄	反	厄	圧	灰	辰	厚	厓	版	厘	厖
0.1	2p12.4	2.1	2.2	2.3	3.1	4.1	5.1	6.1	6.2	2j6.8	7.1	7.2

叛	原	唇	辱	厠	厨	厥	厩	雁	厦	鴈	農	厭
7.3	8.1	3d7.12	8.2	9.1	10.1	10.2	2p12.2	10.3	3q10.2	2p10.3	11.1	12.1

厩	厰	暦	歴	厲	厘	鴈	耨	壓	曆	贋	鬠	醫
12.2	3q12.1	12.3	12.4	12.5	12.6	2p10.3	14.1	2p3.1	17.1	17.2	21.1	4c19.1

魘	黶
22.1	4d22.1

─────── 0 ───────

2p0.1

厂   **KAN** cliff; shore

厂 → 歴 2p12.4

─────── 2 ───────

2p2.1

仄   **SOKU, honoka** dim, faint, indistinct
hono(meku) be seen dimly
hono(mekasu) hint at, intimate

─────── 1 ───────

3 仄々 **honobono** dimly, faintly
13 仄暗 **honogura(i)** dim(ly lit)

14 仄聞 **sokubun** hear (by chance)

2p2.2 / 324

反 **HAN, HON** against, opposite, anti-
TAN (unit of cloth measurement, about 34 cm by 10.6 m), (unit of land area, 300 tsubo or about 992 square meters)
so(ru/rasu) (intr./tr.) warp, bend back

──────── 1 ────────

4 反日 **han-Nichi** anti-Japanese
5 反正 **Hanzei** (emperor, 406–410)
反比例 **hanpirei** in inverse proportion to
6 反返 **so(ri)ka(eru)** bend backward; throw back the head/shoulders
反共 **hankyō** anticommunist
反米 **han-Bei** anti-American
7 反作用 **hansayō** reaction
反対 **hantai** opposition, against; opposite, reverse, contrary
反対党 **hantaitō** opposition party
反対訊問 **hantai jinmon** cross-examination
反対側 **hantaigawa** the opposite side
反対語 **hantaigo** antonym
反対論 **hantairon** counterargument, opposing view
反抗 **hankō** resistance, opposition, rebellion
反抗的 **hankōteki** rebellious, defiant, antagonistic
反乱 **hanran** rebellion, revolt
反乱者 **hanransha** rebel, insurgents
反応 **hannō** reaction, response
反攻 **hankō** counteroffensive, counterattack
8 反逆 **hangyaku** treason, treachery, revolt
反英 **han-Ei** anti-British
反物 **tanmono** dry/piece goods, textiles
反物屋 **tanmonoya** dry-goods store
9 反発 **hanpatsu** repel; rebound, recover; oppose
反発力 **hanpatsuryoku** repellent force, resiliency
反帝国主義 **han-teikoku shugi** anti-imperialism
反独 **han-Doku** anti-German
反革命 **hankakumei** counterrevolution
反面 **hanmen** the other side, on the other hand
反映 **han'ei** reflect, mirror
反政府 **hanseifu** antigovernment
反故 **hogo, hogu** wastepaper, mere scrap of paper
反省 **hansei** reflection, introspection; reconsideration
反則 **hansoku** violation of the rules, a foul
10 反芻 **hansū** chewing the cud, rumination
反射 **hansha** reflection, reflex

反射的 **hanshateki** reflecting, reflective(ly), reflexive(ly)
反射炉 **hansharo** reverberatory furnace
反徒 **hanto** rebels, insurgents
11 反動 **handō** reaction; recoil
反動主義者 **handō shugisha** a reactionary
反動的 **handōteki** reactionary
反動家 **handōka** a reactionary
反転 **hanten** turn/roll over, reverse directions, invert
反問 **hanmon** ask in return; cross-examine
12 反復 **hanpuku** repetition
反落 **hanraku** reactionary fall (in stock prices)
反歯 **soppa** protruding front tooth, buckteeth
反訴 **hanso** countersuit, counterclaim
反証 **hanshō** counterevidence
反間 **hankan** seeking to cause dissension among the enemy
13 反感 **hankan** antipathy, animosity
反戦 **hansen** antiwar
反意語 **han'igo** antonym
14 反旗 **hanki** standard/banner of revolt
反歌 **hanka** short poem appended to a long poem
反語 **hango** rhetorical question; irony
反駁 **hanbaku, hanpaku** refutation, rebuttal
15 反撃 **hangeki** counterattack
反撥 **hanpatsu** repel; rebound, recover; oppose
反論 **hanron** counterargument, refutation
16 反橋 **so(ri)hashi, so(ri)bashi** arched bridge
18 反覆 **hanpuku** repeat; reverse oneself
19 反響 **hankyō** echo, reverberation; repercussions, reaction
20 反騰 **hantō** reactionary rise (in stock prices), rally

──────── 2 ────────

5 正反対 **seihantai** the exact opposite
7 乱反射 **ranhansha** diffused reflection
9 背反 **haihan** revolt, rebel
悖反 **haihan** run counter to, violate
10 猛反撃 **mōhangeki** fierce counterattack
核反応 **kakuhannō** nuclear reaction
核反応炉 **kakuhannōro** nuclear reactor
12 違反 **ihan** violation
減反 **gentan** acreage reduction
15 膝反射 **shitsuhansha** knee-jerk reaction
16 謀反 **muhon** rebellion, insurrection
謀反人 **muhonnin** rebel, conspirator
18 離反 **rihan** estrangement, alienation, breakaway

──────── 3 ────────

9 連鎖反応 **rensa hannō** chain reaction
15 撥乱反正 **hatsuran hansei** restoration of public order

17 輾転反側 **tenten-hansoku** tossing about (in
   bed)
———————— 4 ————————
6 光化学反応 **kōkagaku hannō, hikari kagaku
   hannō** photochemical reaction
15 膝蓋腱反射 **shitsugaiken hansha** knee-jerk
   reaction
16 憲法違反 **kenpō ihan** unconstitutionality

2p2.3 / 1341

厄

YAKU misfortune, disaster

———————— 1 ————————
4 厄介 **yakkai** troublesome, burdensome; help,
   care
  厄介払 **yakkaibara(i)** good riddance
  厄介者 **yakkaimono** a dependent; nuisance
  厄介物 **yakkaimono** burden, nuisance
  厄日 **yakubi** unlucky/critical day
5 厄払 **yakubara(i)** exorcism
6 厄年 **yakudoshi** unlucky age, one's critical
   year
9 厄除 **yakuyo(ke)** warding off evil
12 厄落 **yakuo(toshi)** escape from evil, exorcism
———————— 2 ————————
7 災厄 **saiyaku** misfortune, disaster, accident
9 後厄 **atoyaku** the year following one's critial
   year
10 荷厄介 **niyakkai** burden, encumbrance

———————— 3 ————————

2p3.1 / 1342

圧 壓

ATSU pressure
o(su) press, push

———————— 1 ————————
0 圧する **as(suru)** press, weigh on, overpower
2 圧入 **atsunyū** press fit, press in
  圧力 **atsuryoku** pressure
  圧力計 **atsuryokukei** pressure gauge
6 圧死 **asshi** be crushed to death
  圧伏 **appuku** overpower, subdue
7 圧延 **atsuen** rolling (steel)
  圧延機 **atsuenki** rolling machine/mill
  圧延鋼 **atsuenkō** rolled steel
  圧迫 **appaku** pressure, oppression, compulsion
8 圧制 **assei** oppression, tyranny
  圧制的 **asseiteki** oppressive, repressive
  圧制者 **asseisha** oppressor, despot, tyrant
  圧服 **appuku** overpower, keep down
9 圧巻 **akkan** best part/one, highlight
10 圧倒 **attō** overwhelm

圧倒的 **attōteki** overwhelming
12 圧着端子 **atchaku tanshi** crimp contact
  圧覚 **akkaku** sensation of pressure
  圧勝 **asshō** overwhelming victory
13 圧搾 **assaku** pressure, compression, compressed (air)
  圧搾機 **assakuki** a press, compressor
17 圧縮 **asshuku** compression, compressed (air)
  圧縮機 **asshukuki** compressor
———————— 2 ————————
4 内圧 **naiatsu** internal pressure
  水圧 **suiatsu** water/hydraulic pressure
  水圧計 **suiatsukei** water-pressure gauge
  水圧機 **suiatsuki** hydraulic press
5 加圧 **kaatsu** apply pressure
  外圧 **gaiatsu** external/outside pressure
6 気圧 **kiatsu** atmospheric pressure
  気圧計 **kiatsukei** barometer
  血圧 **ketsuatsu** blood pressure
  血圧計 **ketsuatsukei** sphygmomanometer
7 低圧 **teiatsu** low pressure/voltage
  汽圧 **kiatsu** steam pressure
  均圧 **kin'atsu** equal pressure
  抑圧 **yokuatsu** suppress, restrain
8 油圧 **yuatsu** oil pressure; hydraulic
9 重圧 **jūatsu** pressure
  変圧 **hen'atsu** transform (voltage)
  変圧器 **hen'atsuki** transformer
  風圧 **fūatsu** wind pressure
  指圧 **shiatsu** finger pressure
  指圧療法 **shiatsu ryōhō** finger-pressure
   treatment, chiropractic
  威圧 **iatsu** coercion
  威圧的 **iatsuteki** coercive, domineering
10 高圧 **kōatsu** high voltage/pressure; high-
   handedness
  高圧的 **kōatsuteki** high-handed, coercive
  高圧線 **kōatsusen** high-voltage power lines
  被圧迫 **hiappaku** oppressed
11 強圧 **kyōatsu** pressure, coercion
12 減圧 **gen'atsu** pressure reduction
  弾圧 **dan'atsu** pressure, oppression, suppression
  検圧 **ken'atsu** measuring pressure
  検圧器 **ken'atsuki** pressure gauge
  等圧 **tōatsu** equal pressure
  等圧線 **tōatsusen** isobar
13 禁圧 **kin'atsu** suppress, ban, prohibit
  電圧 **den'atsu** voltage
  電圧計 **den'atsukei** voltmeter
18 鎮圧 **chin'atsu** suppression, quelling

———————— 3 ————————
3 大気圧 **taikiatsu** atmospheric pressure
7 低気圧 **teikiatsu** low (atmospheric) pressure
10 高気圧 **kōkiatsu** high atmospheric pressure

高血圧 **kōketsuatsu** high blood pressure

───────── 5 ─────────
4 収縮期血圧 **shūshukuki ketsuatsu** systolic blood pressure

───────── 4 ─────────

2p4.1 / 1343

灰

KAI, hai ash, ashes

───────── 1 ─────────
6 灰汁 **aku** lye; harsh taste
灰白 **kaihaku** light gray, ashen
灰皿 **haizara** ashtray
6 灰色 **hai-iro** gray
8 灰受 **haiu(ke)** ashpan, ashtray
11 灰殻 **haigara** ashes
12 灰落 **haio(toshi)** ashpan, ashtray
13 灰滅 **kaimetsu** burn up, be destroyed
14 灰塵 **kaijin** ashes and dust
灰緑色 **kairyokushoku** greenish gray
16 灰篩 **haifurui** ash sieve/sifter
18 灰燼 **kaijin** (reduced to) ashes

───────── 2 ─────────
4 木灰 **kibai** wood ashes
5 石灰 **sekkai, ishibai** lime
石灰水 **sekkaisui** limewater
石灰石 **sekkaiseki** limestone
石灰乳 **sekkainyū** milk of lime
石灰岩 **sekkaigan** limestone
石灰洞 **sekkaidō** limestone cave
石灰窯 **ishibaigama** limekiln
6 死灰 **shikai** dead embers, ashes
8 取灰 **to(ri)bai** ashes removed (from an oven)
10 骨灰 **kotsubai** bone ashes
12 焼灰 **ya(ke)bai** ashes
17 藁灰 **warabai** straw ash

───────── 3 ─────────
4 火山灰 **kazanbai** volcanic ash
5 生石灰 **seisekkai, kisekkai** quicklime
10 消石灰 **shōsekkai** slaked lime, calcium hydroxide
16 懐炉灰 **kairobai** pocket-heater fuel
20 護摩灰 **goma(no)hai** thief posing as a fellow traveler

───────── 5 ─────────

2p5.1

辰

SHIN, tatsu fifth horary sign (dragon)

───────── 1 ─────────
9 辰砂 **shinsha** cinnabar

───────── 6 ─────────

2p6.1 / 639

厚

KŌ, atsu(i) thick; kind, cordial

───────── 1 ─────────
0 厚ぼったい **atsu(bottai)** very thick, heavy
厚かましい **atsu(kamashii)** shameless, brazen, impudent
4 厚化粧 **atsugeshō** heavy makeup
厚切 **atsugi(ri)** sliced thick
厚手 **atsude** thick (paper)
5 厚生 **kōsei** public welfare
厚生大臣 **kōsei daijin** Minister of Health and Welfare
厚生年金 **kōsei nenkin** welfare pension
厚生省 **Kōseishō** Ministry of Health and Welfare
6 厚地 **atsuji** thick cloth/fabric
7 厚志 **kōshi** kindness, good wishes
8 厚板 **atsuita** thick board, plank, plate (glass), heavy (metal) sheet; heavy brocaded obi
9 厚相 **kōshō** Welfare Minister
10 厚恩 **kōon** great kindness/favor
厚紙 **atsugami** thick paper, cardboard
11 厚遇 **kōgū** warm welcome, hospitality
厚情 **kōjō** kindness, good wishes, hospitality
12 厚着 **atsugi** wearing thick/heavy clothing
13 厚意 **kōi** kindness, favor, courtesy
15 厚誼 **kōgi** (your) kindness
16 厚薄 **kōhaku** (relative) thickness; partiality
18 厚顔 **kōgan** impudence, effrontery

───────── 2 ─────────
4 分厚 **buatsu** thick
手厚 **teatsu(i)** warm, cordial, hospitable; generous
6 肉厚 **nikuatsu** (wall) thickness
8 肥厚 **hikō** thickening (of the skin)
肥厚性鼻炎 **hikōsei bien** hypertrophic rhinitis
9 重厚 **jūkō** profoundness, depth, seriousness
重厚長大 **jūkō-chōdai** large and heavy, bulky (cf. 軽薄短小)
10 部厚 **buatsu** thick, bulky
11 深厚 **shinkō** deep, heartfelt, sincere
12 温厚 **onkō** gentle, courteous
13 寛厚 **kankō** generous, largehearted
16 濃厚 **nōkō** thickness, richness, strength

───────── 3 ─────────
9 面皮厚 **tsura (no) kawa (no) atsu(i)** brazen-faced, impudent, nervy

2p6.2

崖

GAI cliff, precipice; shore; glare at; outer corner of the eye

2
イ 冫 孑 阝 卩 刂 力 又 宀 亠 十 ㅏ ク ハ 厂 6← 辶 冂 几 匚

版→ **2j6.8**

亻冫孑阝卩刂力又宀亠十卜勹丷→7厂辶冂凡匚

———————— 7 ————————

2p7.1 / 1900

厘
RIN (old unit of currency, 1/1,000 yen), (unit of length, about 0.3 mm), (unit of weight, about 3.75 mg)

———————— 1 ————————

4 厘毛 **rinmō** a trifle, insignificant

———————— 4 ————————

2 九分九厘 **kubu-kurin** 99 cases out of 100, in all probability

2p7.2

厖
BŌ large; mix

———————— 1 ————————

3 厖大 **bōdai** enormous, huge

2p7.3

叛
HAN, HON rebellion
somu(ku) go against, disobey, rebel

———————— 1 ————————

7 叛乱 **hanran** rebellion, revolt
8 叛逆 **hangyaku** treason, treachery, revolt
9 叛軍 **hangun** rebel army, mutinous troops
10 叛徒 **hanto** rebels, insurgents
14 叛旗 **hanki** standard/banner of revolt

———————— 2 ————————

16 謀叛 **muhon** rebellion, insurrection
謀叛人 **muhonnin** rebel, conspirator

———————— 8 ————————

2p8.1 / 136

原
GEN original, fundamental; a plain
hara field, plain; wilderness

———————— 1 ————————

2 原人 **genjin** primitive/early man
原子 **genshi** atom
原子力 **genshiryoku** atomic energy, nuclear power
原子力発電所 **genshiryoku hatsudensho** nuclear power plant
原子価 **genshika** valence
原子核 **genshikaku** atomic nucleus
原子病 **genshibyō** radiation sickness
原子量 **genshiryō** atomic weight

原子雲 **genshiun** atomic/mushroom cloud
原子爆弾 **genshi bakudan** atom bomb
3 原寸 **gensun** actual size
原寸大 **gensundai** actual size
4 原毛 **genmō** raw wool
原文 **genbun** the text/original
原水爆 **gensuibaku** atomic and hydrogen bombs, nuclear bombs
5 原本 **genpon** the original (work/copy)
原生 **gensei** primitive, primeval, proto-
原生林 **genseirin** primeval/virgin forest
6 原色 **genshoku** primary color
原因 **gen'in** cause
原因不明 **gen'in fumei** of unknown cause/origin
原成岩 **genseigan** primary rocks
原虫 **genchū** a protozoan
7 原作 **gensaku** the original work
原作者 **gensakusha** the original author (of a translated work)
原住民 **genjūmin** natives, aborigines
原状 **genjō** original state
原判決 **genhanketsu** the original decision/judgment
原告 **genkoku** plaintiff
原形 **genkei** original form
原形質 **genkeishitsu** protoplasm
原図 **genzu** the original drawing
原材料 **genzairyō** raw materials
8 原画 **genga** the original picture
原価 **genka** cost price, cost
原版 **genban** original edition
原油 **gen'yu** crude oil
原注 **genchū** the original annotations
原始 **genshi** origin; primitive
原始人 **genshijin** primitive man
原始的 **genshiteki** primitive, primeval, original
原物 **genbutsu** the original
9 原発 **genpatsu** (generating electricity from) nuclear power (short for 原子力発電)
原点 **genten** starting point
原型 **genkei** prototype, model
原品 **genpin** the original article
原音 **gen'on** the fundamental tone (in physics)
原則 **gensoku** principle, general rule
原則的 **gensokuteki** in principle/general
10 原案 **gen'an** original proposal, draft
原書 **gensho** the original document
原料 **genryō** raw materials
11 原野 **gen'ya** wasteland, wilderness, field, plain
原動力 **gendōryoku** motive force, prime mover
原著 **gencho** the original work (not a translation)

原著者 **genchosha** the author
原理 **genri** principle, theory
原産地 **gensanchi** place of origin, home, habitat
原産物 **gensanbutsu** primary products
12 原裁判 **gensaiban** the original decision/judgment
原註 **genchū** the original annotations
13 原義 **gengi** original/primary meaning
原意 **gen'i** original/primary meaning
原罪 **genzai** original sin
原鉱 **genkō** (raw) ore
14 原像 **genzō** original statue (not a replica)
原種 **genshu** pure breed, germ
原語 **gengo** original word/language
15 原潜 **gensen** nuclear(-powered) sub(marine) (short for 原子力潜水艦)
原稿 **genkō** manuscript
原稿用紙 **genkō yōshi** manuscript paper
原稿料 **genkōryō** payment for a manuscript
原論 **genron** theory, principles
16 原薄 **genbo** ledger, original register
19 原爆 **genbaku** atomic bomb (short for 原子爆弾)
原爆症 **genbakushō** illnesses caused by atomic-bomb radiation
20 原籍 **genseki** domicile, permanent address

––––––––––––––– 2 –––––––––––––––

3 三原色 **sangenshoku** the three primary colors
川原 **kawahara, kawara** dry riverbed; river beach
4 天原 **ama(no)hara** the sky/heavens
中原 **chūgen** middle of a field; middle of a country; field of contest
5 生原稿 **namagenkō** raw manuscript (not yet typeset)
平原 **heigen** plain, prairie
氷原 **hyōgen** ice field/floe
広原 **kōgen** wide plain, open country
6 吉原 **Yoshiwara** (proper name); (a former red-light district in Tōkyō)
7 抗原 **kōgen** antigen
8 河原 **kawara** dry river bed
河原乞食 **kawara kojiki** actors (and beggars; a term of opprobrium)
河原物 **kawaramono** actors (a term of opprobrium)
始原 **shigen** origin, inception
松原 **matsubara** pine grove
9 海原 **unabara** the (vast) ocean
草原 **sōgen** grassy plain, grasslands
kusahara meadow, a green
荒原 **kōgen** wilderness, wasteland
砂原 **sunahara** sandy plain
10 凍原 **tōgen** frozen field, tundra

桑原桑原 **kuwabara-kuwabara** Heaven forbid! Thank God!
高原 **kōgen** plateau, highlands
起原 **kigen** origin, beginning
病原 **byōgen** cause of a disease, etiology
病原体 **byōgentai** pathogen
病原菌 **byōgenkin** pathogenic bacteria, germ
11 野原 **nohara** field, plain
菅原 **Sugawara** (surname)
雪原 **setsugen** field/expanse of snow
12 復原 **fukugen** restoration (to the original state)
14 語原 **gogen** derivation, etymology
語原学 **gogengaku** etymology
15 権原 **kengen** title (to territory)
16 楢原 **Tsusahara** (place name, Fukushima-ken)
燎原 **ryōgen (no) hi** prairie fire, wildfire

––––––––––––––– 3 –––––––––––––––

3 大海原 **ōunabara** the ocean, the vast sea
小田原 **Odawara** (city, Kanagawa-ken)
小田原提灯 **odawara-jōchin** collapsible cylindrical paper lantern
小田原評定 **odawara hyōjō** endless debate, fruitless conference
小笠原諸島 **Ogasawara-shotō** the Bonin Islands
8 若殿原 **wakatonobara** young samurais
青海原 **aounabara** blue expanse of water
10 高天原 **Takamagahara** the heavens, the abode of the gods
12 焼野原 **ya(ke)nohara** burned-out area
13 豊葦原 **Toyoashihara** (ancient) Japan
14 種起原 **shu (no) kigen** (Darwin's) The Origin of Species
関ヶ原 **Sekigahara** decisive battle
16 機雷原 **kiraigen** minefield

––––––––––––––– 4 –––––––––––––––

10 桑原桑原 **kuwabara-kuwabara** Heaven forbid! Thank God!

唇→   **3d7.12**

2p8.2 / 1738

辱   **JOKU, hazukashi(meru)** humiliate, disgrace **katajike(nai)** grateful

––––––––––––––– 1 –––––––––––––––

8 辱知 **jokuchi** an acquaintance

––––––––––––––– 2 –––––––––––––––

6 汚辱 **ojoku** disgrace, dishonor, obloquy
8 侮辱 **bujoku** insult
屈辱 **kutsujoku** humiliation, indignity
屈辱的 **kutsujokuteki** humiliating, disgraceful

2

亻
彳
孑
阝
卩
刂
力
又
宀
亠
十
ﾄ
夂
ﾉ
→9
厂
辶
冂
几
匸

国辱 **kokujoku** national disgrace
9 栄辱 **eijoku** honor or/and disgrace
10 凌辱 **ryōjoku** insult, affront; rape
陵辱 **ryōjoku** insult; rape
恥辱 **chijoku** disgrace, humiliation
11 雪辱 **setsujoku** vindication, clearing one's name; revenge
雪辱戦 **setsujokusen** return match, a fight for vindication

——————— 9 ———————

2p9.1

廁 厠

SHI, kawaya toilet

——————— 10 ———————

2p10.1

厨 廚 厨

CHŪ, ZU, kuriya kitchen

——————— 1 ———————

2 厨子 **zushi** miniature shrine
7 厨芥 **chūkai** (kitchen) garbage
8 厨房 **chūbō** kitchen, galley

2p10.2

厥

KETSU that; dizziness, chills

厩 → 厩 2p12.2

2p10.3

雁 鴈 鳫

GAN, kari, karigane wild goose

——————— 1 ———————

4 雁木 **gangi** steps on a pier; toothing gear, escapement; zigzag; covered alley
5 雁皮紙 **ganpishi** (a type of high-quality paper)
雁字搦 **ganjigarame** (bind) firmly, (bound) hand and foot
6 雁行 **gankō** go/fly in echelon formation (like geese); keeping abreast (of each other)
8 雁金 **karigane** (cry/honk of a) wild goose
9 雁首 **gankubi** bowl of a pipe; gooseneck
雁音 **kari(ga)ne** (cry/honk of a) wild goose

——————— 2 ———————

10 帰雁 **kigan** returning wild geese

厦 → 廈 3q10.2

——————— 11 ———————

鳫 → 雁 2p10.3

2p11.1 / 369

農

NŌ agriculture, farming

——————— 1 ———————

3 農工 **nōkō** agriculture and industry
農工業 **nōkōgyō** agriculture and industry
農山村 **nōsanson** agricultural and mountain villages
4 農夫 **nōfu** farmer, farmhand
農夫症 **nōfushō** farmer's syndrome
農父 **nōfu** farmer
5 農民 **nōmin** peasants, farmers
農本主義 **nōhon shugi** agriculture-first policy, physiocracy
農奴 **nōdo** serf
6 農会 **nōkai** agricultural association
農地 **nōchi** farmland
農地改革 **nōchi kaikaku** agrarian reform
7 農作 **nōsaku** cultivation, tillage, farming
農作物 **nōsakubutsu** crops, farm produce
農兵 **nōhei** farmer-soldiers
農芸 **nōgei** (the art of) agriculture, husbandry
農学 **nōgaku** (the science of) agriculture
農学士 **nōgakushi** agricultural expert, agronomist
農村 **nōson** farm village, rural community
8 農事 **nōji** agriculture, farming
農協 **nōkyō** agricultural cooperative, co-op (short for 農業協同組合)
農法 **nōhō** farming methods
農林 **nōrin** agriculture and forestry
農林水産大臣 **nōrinsuisan daijin** Minister of Agriculture, Forestry and Fisheries
農林水産省 **Nōrinsuisanshō** Ministry of Agriculture, Forestry and Fisheries
農牧 **nōboku** raising crops and livestock, general farming
農牧地 **nōbokuchi** crop and grazing land
農具 **nōgu** farm implements
9 農相 **nōshō** Agriculture (, Forestry and Fisheries) Minister
農政 **nōsei** agricultural administration
農科 **nōka** agriculture department; agricultural course
10 農耕 **nōkō** agriculture, farming

農家 **nōka** farmhouse; farm household; farmer
11 農道 **nōdō** farm road
農婦 **nōfu** farm woman
農務 **nōmu** agricultural affairs
農産 **nōsan** agricultural products
農産物 **nōsanbutsu** agricultural products
12 農場 **nōjō** farm, ranch, plantation
農期 **nōki** farming season
農閑期 **nōkanki** farmers' slack season
13 農業 **nōgyō** agriculture
農業国 **nōgyōkoku** agricultural country
農園 **nōen** farm, plantation
16 農薬 **nōyaku** agricultural chemicals
農機具 **nōkigu** farm equipment
農繁 **nōhan** farmers' busy season
農繁期 **nōhanki** farmers' busy season

――――――――― 2 ―――――――――

3 大農 **dainō** large-scale farming; wealthy farmer
小農 **shōnō** small farmer, peasant
士農工商 **shinōkōshō** samurai-farmers-artisans-merchants, the military, agricultural, industrial, and mercantile classes
4 中農 **chūnō** middle-class farmer
5 半農 **hannō** part-time farming
6 老農 **rōnō** old/experienced farmer
7 労農 **rōnō** workers and farmers
労農党 **rōnōtō** labor-farmer party
9 重農主義 **jūnō shugi** physiocracy
10 帰農 **kinō** going back to the soil
11 貧農 **hinnō** poor farmer, needy peasant
12 富農 **funō** prosperous farmer
13 酪農 **rakunō** dairy farming
酪農家 **rakunōka** dairy farmer
酪農場 **rakunōjo** dairy farm
14 豪農 **gōnō** wealthy farmer
精農 **seinō** hard-working farmer
16 篤農 **tokunō** exemplary farmer

――――――――― 3 ―――――――――

3 小作農 **kosakunō** tenant farming
6 有畜農業 **yūchiku nōgyō** diversified farming
自作農 **jisakunō** (non-tenant) owner-farmer
13 零細農 **reisainō** poor peasant

――――――――― 12 ―――――――――

2p12.1

厭 **EN, YŌ, a(kiru)** get tired of, get fed up with **ito(u)** dislike, hate; be unwilling; grudge (effort), spare (pains); take (good) care of **i(ya)** disagreeable, detestable, hated, unwelcome

――――――――― 1 ―――――――――

2 厭人 **enjin** misanthropy

厭人者 **enjinsha** misanthrope
厭人癖 **enjinheki** misanthropy
5 厭世 **ensei** weariness with life, pessimism
厭世主義 **ensei shugi** pessimism
厭世的 **enseiteki** world-weary, pessimistic
厭世家 **enseika** pessimist
厭世観 **enseikan** pessimistic view of life, Weltschmerz
8 厭味 **iyami** offensiveness, disagreeableness
厭性 **a(ki)shō** fickleness, flighty temperament
11 厭悪 **en'o** dislike, detest, abhor

2p12.2

厩 厩 厩 厩   **KYŪ, umaya** barn, stable

――――――――― 1 ―――――――――

8 厩舎 **kyūsha** barn

廠 → 廠   **3q12.1**

2p12.3 / 1534

暦 曆   **REKI, RYAKU, koyomi** calendar

――――――――― 1 ―――――――――

4 暦仁 **Ryakunin** (era, 1238–1239)
暦日 **rekijitsu** calendar, time
6 暦年 **rekinen** calendar (not fiscal) year; time
7 暦応 **Ryakuō** (era, 1338–1342)
暦改正 **koyomi kaisei** calendar reform
8 暦法 **rekihō** calendar making
13 暦数 **rekisū** calendar; one's fate; number of years

――――――――― 2 ―――――――――

4 元暦 **Genryaku** (era, 1184–1185)
天暦 **Tenryaku** (era, 947–957)
文暦 **Bunryaku** (era, 1234–1235)
5 正暦 **Shōryaku** (era, 990–995)
永暦 **Eiryaku** (era, 1160)
旧暦 **kyūreki** the old (lunar) calendar
6 西暦 **seireki** Christian Era, A.D.
7 承暦 **Jōryaku** (era, 1077–1081)
延暦 **Enryaku** (era, 782–806)
花暦 **hanagoyomi** calendar with information about flower blooming seasons
改暦 **kaireki** new year; calendar reform
8 長暦 **Chōryaku** (era, 1037–1040)
建暦 **Kenryaku** (era, 1211–1213)
治暦 **Jiryaku** (era, 1065–1069)
宝暦 **Hōreki** (era, 1751–1764)
明暦 **Meireki** (era, 1655–1657)

9 柱暦 **hashiragoyomi** wall calendar
10 陰暦 **inreki** the lunar calendar
剥暦 **ha(gashi)goyomi** calendar pad
梅暦 **umegoyomi** plum blossoms as a harbinger of spring
11 陽暦 **yōreki** the solar calendar
13 新暦 **shinreki** new/Gregorian calendar
14 嘉暦 **Karyaku** (era, 1326–1329)
15 還暦 **kanreki** one's 60th birthday

――――――― 3 ―――――――

4 太陰暦 **taiinreki** the lunar calendar
太陽暦 **taiyōreki** the solar calendar
10 教会暦 **kyōkaireki** church calendar

2p12.4 / 480

歴 歴 **REKI** continuation, passage of time; successive; clear
he(ru) pass, elapse

――――――― 1 ―――――――

3 歴々 **rekireki, (o)rekireki** VIPs, big shots
rekireki(taru) clear, obvious
5 歴史 **rekishi** history
歴史学 **rekishigaku** (the study of) history
歴史的 **rekishiteki** historic(al)
歴史劇 **rekishigeki** historical drama
歴史観 **rekishikan** philosophy/view of history
歴代 **rekidai** successive generations
6 歴年 **rekinen** year after year
歴任 **rekinin** successively holding various posts
10 歴遊 **rekiyū** tour
11 歴訪 **rekihō** round/tour of visits
12 歴朝 **rekichō** successive reigns/dynasties
歴然 **rekizen** clear, unmistakable

――――――― 2 ―――――――

5 巡歴 **junreki** tour
7 来歴 **raireki** personal history, background, career
学歴 **gakureki** one's academic background
8 披歴 **hireki** express (one's opinion)
実歴 **jitsureki** actual experience
官歴 **kanreki** one's official career
9 前歴 **zenreki** one's personal history
活歴 **katsureki** historical drama
10 遊歴 **yūreki** tour, pleasure trip
病歴 **byōreki** patient's case history
11 遍歴 **henreki** travels, pilgrimage
略歴 **ryakureki** brief personal history, résumé
経歴 **keireki** personal history, career
13 戦歴 **senreki** war experience, combat record
14 歴歴 **rekireki, (o)rekireki** VIPs, big shots
rekireki(taru) clear, obvious
15 履歴 **rireki** one's background, career; hysteresis

履歴書 **rirekisho** personal history, vita
閲歴 **etsureki** career, personal history
18 職歴 **shokureki** one's occupational history

――――――― 3 ―――――――

10 既往歴 **kiōreki** patient's medical history

――――――― 4 ―――――――

9 故事来歴 **koji-raireki** origin and history

2p12.5

厲 **REI** whetstone; strict; encourage

2p12.6

甅 **senchiguramu** centigram, hundredth of a gram

――――――― 13 ―――――――

鴈 → 雁 2p10.3

――――――― 14 ―――――――

2p14.1

耨 **DŌ** hoe

――――――― 15 ―――――――

2p15

壓 → 圧 2p3.1

――――――― 17 ―――――――

2p17.1

靨 **EN, heta** operculum (of a conch)

2p17.2

贋 **GAN** counterfeit
nise fake, counterfeit, forgery, imitation, false

――――――― 1 ―――――――

5 贋札 **nisesatsu, gansatsu** counterfeit currency
7 贋作 **gansaku** counterfeit, sham
8 贋物 **ganbutsu, nisemono** imitation, counterfeit, forgery
贋金 **nisegane** counterfeit money
贋金作 **niseganezuku(ri)** counterfeiter

9 贋首 **nisekubi** falsified severed head
　贋造 **ganzō** counterfeiting, forgery, fabrication
　贋造者 **ganzōsha** counterfeiter, forger
　贋造紙幣 **ganzō shihei** counterfeit currency

―――――― 2 ――――――
10 真贋 **shingan** whether genuine or counterfeit

―――――― 21 ――――――
2p21.1

饜

EN, **a(kiru)** be satiated

饜 → 4c19.1

―――――― 22 ――――――
2p22.1

魘

EN, **unasa(reru)** have a nightmare

―――――― 24 ――――――

饜 → 4d22.1

―――――――――― 辶 **2q** ――――――――――

㐄	辶	辺	辻	込	辿	迂	巡	迄	迅	迪	廷	近
0.1	1.1	2.1	2.2	2.3	3.1	3.2	3.3	3.4	3.5	4.1	4.2	4.3

迎	返	迪	㢠	迭	述	延	迫	迦	迯	迢	迠	迯
4.4	4.5	2q5.1	5.1	5.2	5.3	5.4	5.5	5.6	2q6.5	5.7	5.8	2q14.1

迩	迥	廻	迷	建	退	追	逃	迹	迸	逆	送	迺
2q14.1	5.9	2q6.13	6.1	6.2	6.3	6.4	6.5	6.6	6.7	6.8	6.9	2q6.10

酒	逅	迴	廻	這	連	逋	速	逼	逎	逐	逑	逝
6.10	6.11	6.12	6.13	7.1	7.2	7.3	7.4	7.5	2q9.15	7.6	7.7	7.8

迯	透	造	逡	逕	逞	逍	逢	途	浴	通	逗	進
7.9	7.10	7.11	7.12	3i5.5	7.13	7.14	7.15	7.16	7.17	7.18	7.19	8.1

逮	遊	逶	逵	達	逸	週	遇	遁	退	遯	遜	遑
8.2	8.3	8.4	8.5	2q9.8	8.6	8.7	9.1	9.2	9.3	2q9.2	9.4	9.5

遏	逼	遥	達	逾	運	逾	遉	遂	道	遒	遍	遅
9.6	9.7	2q10.3	9.8	9.9	9.10	9.11	9.12	9.13	9.14	9.15	9.16	9.17

過	遡	遡	遘	遣	遙	遠	違	蓮	遞	遨	遯	遭
9.18	3a10.2	3a10.2	10.1	10.2	10.3	10.4	10.5	3k10.31	2q7.5	11.1	2q9.2	11.2

適	遮	遷	遶	選	遺	遼	遑	邁	遵	遲	導	邀
11.3	11.4	12.1	12.2	12.3	12.4	12.5	12.6	12.7	12.8	2q9.17	5c9.3	13.1

邂	避	澷	還	邃	邇	邃	邀	邊	邏			
13.2	13.3	2q2.1	13.4	13.5	14.1	14.2	15.1	2q2.1	19.1			

―――――――― 0 ――――――――
2q0.1

㐄

IN **pull**

―――――――― 1 ――――――――
2q1.1

辶

sube(ru) slip, slide

―――――――― 2 ――――――――
6 地辷 **jisube(ri)** landslide

―――――――― 2 ――――――――
2q2.1 / 775

辺 邊 邉

HEN side; boundary, border; vicinity
ata(ri), hoto(ri), -be vicinity

―――――――― 1 ――――――――
3 辺土 **hendo** remote region

亻 冫 孑 阝 阝 刂 力 又 丶 丶 厂 辶 冂 几 匚

6 辺地 **henchi** remote/out-of-the-way place
10 辺陬 **hensū** remote rural area
12 辺幅 **henpuku** one's personal appearance
13 辺鄙 **henpi** remote, secluded
14 辺境 **henkyō** frontier, outlying region

——————— 2 ———————

1 一辺倒 **ippentō** complete partiality to one side
2 八辺形 **hachihenkei** octagon
3 川辺 **kawabe** riverside
　上辺 **uwabe** exterior, surface, outside; outward appearance
　山辺 **yamabe** the vicinity of a mountain
4 五辺形 **gohenkei** pentagon
　水辺 **suihen** water's edge, shore
5 左辺 **sahen** left side
　外辺 **gaihen** environs, outskirts
　右辺 **uhen** right side
6 多辺形 **tahenkei** polygon
　多辺的 **tahenteki** multilateral
　那辺 **nahen** where, whither
　近辺 **kinpen** neighborhood, vicinity
　机辺 **kihen** near the desk
7 身辺 **shinpen** one's person
　対辺 **taihen** opposite side (in geometry)
　沖辺 **okibe** the offing, offshore
8 其辺 **so(no) hen** thereabouts, in the neighborhood
　周辺 **shūhen** periphery, environs, outskirts
　知辺 **shi(ru)be** acquaintance, friend
　官辺 **kanpen** government, official
　官辺筋 **kanpensuji** government/official sources
　底辺 **teihen** base (in geometry)
　枕辺 **makurabe, chinpen** bedside
　炉辺 **rohen, robata** fireside, hearth
　武辺 **buhen** military affairs
　武辺者 **buhenmono** warrior
9 海辺 **umibe** seashore, beach
10 浦辺 **urabe** seacoast
　浜辺 **hamabe** beach, seashore
11 野辺 **nobe** fields
　野辺送 **nobeoku(ri)** bury one's remains
　側辺 **sokuhen** side
　斜辺 **shahen** slanting side; hypotenuse
　寄辺 **yo(ru)be** friend, protector, helper
12 無辺 **muhen** limitless, boundless, infinite
　無辺際 **muhensai** limitless, boundless, infinite
　等辺 **tōhen** equal sides
　等辺三角形 **tōhen sankakkei, tōhen sankakukei** equilateral triangle
13 路辺 **rohen** roadside
15 縁辺 **enpen** kin; edge, margin
17 磯辺 **isobe** (rocky) beach, seashore

——————— 3 ———————

2 二等辺三角形 **nitōhen sankakkei, nitōhen**

　sankakukei isosceles triangle
4 不等辺 **futōhen** unequal sides

——————— 4 ———————

5 平行四辺形 **heikōshihenkei** parallelogram
　広大無辺 **kōdai-muhen** boundless, immeasurable, vast

2q2.2

辻 辻　**tsuji** crossroad, intersection, street corner, roadside

——————— 1 ———————

5 辻占 **tsujiura** fortunetelling slips of paper, omen
　辻札 **tsujifuda** street-corner bulletin board
7 辻君 **tsujigimi** streetwalker, prostitute
9 辻待 **tsujima(chi)** (rickshaw) waiting to be hired
10 辻馬車 **tsujibasha** cab, hansom
11 辻強盗 **tsujigōtō** highway robbery/holdup
　辻堂 **tsujidō** wayside shrine
　辻斬 **tsujigi(ri)** murder of a passer-by (to try out a new sword)
12 辻番 **tsujiban** watchman, guard
13 辻褄 **tsujitsuma** coherence, consistency
14 辻説法 **tsujiseppō** street preaching
15 辻駕籠 **tsujikago** palanquin/litter for hire

2q2.3 / 776

込 込　**ko(mu)** be crowded, be included; (as verb suffix) in, into **-ko(mi)** including, inclusive of **ko(meru)** include; load (a gun); concentrate, devote oneself to

——————— 1 ———————

2 込入 **ko(mi)i(ru)** be complicated
3 込上 **ko(mi)a(geru)** well up, feel about to gush forth (vomit, tears, anger)
6 込合 **ko(mi)a(u)** be crowded

——————— 2 ———————

2 人込 **hitogo(mi)** crowd of people
3 丸込 **maru(me)ko(mu)** cajole, coax, seduce
　上込 **a(gari)ko(mu)** enter, step in
4 刈込 **ka(ri)ko(mi)** haircut, shearing, pruning
　切込 **ki(ri)ko(mu)** cut into; attack **ki(ri)ko(mi)** cut, notch, incision
　手込 **te (no) kon(da)** elaborate **tego(me)** rape
　引込 **hi(ki)ko(mu)** bring around, win over **hi(k)ko(mu)** draw back, retire; sink, cave in; stand back; disappear
　引込思案 **hi(k)ko(mi)jian** conservative, retiring
5 包込 **tsutsu(mi)ko(mu)** wrap up

申込 **mō(shi)ko(mu)** propose, file, apply for, book

申込書 **mōshikomisho** an application

申込順 **mōshiko(mi)jun** in order of applications received

仕込 **shiko(mu)** train, bring up; fit into; stock up on

付込 **tsu(ke)ko(mu)** take advantage of; make an entry

払込 **hara(i)ko(mu)** pay in/up, pay an installment

打込 **u(chi)ko(mu)** drive/pound in, shoot into; fall madly in love, put (one's heart) into

叩込 **tata(ki)ko(mu)** drive/throw into; hammer in, inculcate

尻込 **shirigo(mi)** flinch, shrink back, hesitate

立込 **ta(chi)ko(mu)** be crowded
　　　ta(chi)ko(meru) hang over, envelop

6 考込 **kanga(e)ko(mu)** be deep in thought, meditate

老込 **o(i)ko(mu)** grow old, become decrepit/senile

汲込 **ku(mi)ko(mu)** fill up (with water)

吸込 **su(i)ko(mu)** inhale; suck in; swallow up

7 住込 **su(mi)ko(mu)** live in/with

冷込 **hi(e)ko(mu)** get colder/chilly

走込 **hashi(ri)ko(mu)** run into (a house)

折込 **o(ri)ko(mu)** tuck in, insert
　　　o(ri)ko(mi) an insert

投込 **na(ge)ko(mu)** throw/dump into

吹込 **fu(ki)ko(mu)** blow in; record (a song); inspire

呑込 **no(mi)ko(mu)** swallow; understand

売込 **u(ri)ko(mu)** sell (aggressively), push

忍込 **shino(bi)ko(mu)** steal/sneak into, slip in

見込 **miko(mi)** prospects, promise, hope, possibility

見込違 **miko(mi)chiga(i)** miscalculation

言込 **i(i)ko(meru)** argue (someone) into silence, confute

8 使込 **tsuka(i)ko(mu)** embezzle; accustom oneself to using

建込 **ta(te)ko(mu)** be densely built up

追込 **o(i)ko(mu)** corner, drive into; strike inward (a disease); make an extra effort at the end; run on (a line of print)

送込 **oku(ri)ko(mu)** see (someone) home, usher/escort in

殴込 **nagu(ri)ko(mi)** attack, raid

押込 **o(shi)ko(mu)** push in, crowd into
　　　o(shi)ko(mi) closet; burglar
　　　o(shi)ko(meru) shut up, imprison

押込強盗 **o(shi)ko(mi) gōtō** burglar(y)

抱込 **da(ki)ko(mu)** win (someone) over
　　　kaka(e)ko(mu) hold/carry in one's arms

呼込 **yo(bi)ko(mu)** call in

突込 **tsu(ki)ko(mu), tsu(k)ko(mu)** thrust/poke/plunge into

取込 **to(ri)ko(mu)** take in; embezzle; win favor

取込事 **tori(ko)(mi)goto** confusion, busyness

9 飛込 **to(bi)ko(mu)** jump/dive/rush in

飛込台 **tobikomidai** diving board

飛込自殺 **tobiko(mi) jisatsu** suicide by jumping in front of an oncoming train

飛込板 **tobikomiita** diving board

巻込 **ma(ki)ko(mu)** roll up, enfold, entangle, drag into, involve in

乗込 **no(ri)ko(mu)** get into/aboard; ride into, enter

降込 **fu(ri)ko(mu)** rain in on

急込 **se(ki)ko(mu)** get agitated, be in a hurry, become impatient

連込 **tsu(re)ko(mu)** take (a lover) into (a hotel)

連込宿 **tsu(re)ko(mi)yado** hotel catering to lovers, love/rendezvous hotel

封込 **fū(ji)ko(meru)** confine, contain, seal up

挟込 **hasa(mi)ko(mu)** put between, insert

持込 **mo(chi)ko(mu)** bring in; propose, lodge (a complaint)

拭込 **fu(ki)ko(mu)** shine up, polish, wipe thoroughly

咳込 **se(ki)ko(mu)** have a fit of coughing

狩込 **ka(ri)ko(mi)** roundup, mass arrest

染込 **shi(mi)ko(mu)** soak into, permeate; be instilled with **so(me)ko(mu)** dye in

思込 **omo(i)ko(mu)** have the idea that, be convinced that; set one's heart on

計込 **haka(ri)ko(mu)** give overmeasure/overweight

食込 **ku(i)ko(mu)** eat into, erode, be deep-rooted **ku(rai)ko(mu)** be put in jail; be forced to bear

10 差込 **sa(shi)ko(mu)** insert, plug in

這込 **ha(i)ko(mu)** crawl into

流込 **naga(re)ko(mu)** flow/drift into
　　　naga(shi)ko(mu) wash down, pour into

振込 **fu(ri)ko(mu)** pay in, transfer (funds into an account)

座込 **suwa(ri)ko(mu)** sit down, stage a sit-in

書込 **ka(ki)ko(mu)** write/fill in, enter

教込 **oshi(e)ko(mu)** inculcate

紛込 **magi(re)ko(mu)** be lost among, disappear among

11 運込 **hako(bi)ko(mu)** carry/bring in

捩込 **ne(ji)ko(mu)** screw in; thrust into; protest to

掘込 **ho(ri)ko(mu)** dig in(to)

張込 **ha(ri)ko(mu)** be on the lookout for, stake out; splurge

習込 **nara(i)ko(mu)** learn thoroughly, master

祭込 **matsu(ri)ko(mu)** give (someone) a sinecure; recommend a fool for a post

惚込 **ho(re)ko(mu)** fall in love, be charmed

組込 **ku(mi)ko(mu)** cut in (in printing)

転込 **koro(gari)ko(mu), koro(ge)ko(mu)** roll in, come one's way

釣込 **tsu(ri)ko(mu)** lure into, entice

閉込 **to(ji)ko(meru)** shut in, confine

12 割込 **wa(ri)ko(mu)** wedge oneself in, cut/ butt in   **wariko(mi)** an interrupt (in computers)

着込 **kiko(mu)** wear extra clothes, dress warmly

遣込 **ya(ri)ko(meru)** refute, argue down

減込 **me(ri)ko(mu)** sink/cave in, stick into

弾込 **tamago(me)** loading (a gun)

落込 **o(chi)ko(mu)** fall/sink/cave in, (prices) decline

覚込 **obo(e)ko(mu)** learn, master

嵌込 **ha(me)ko(mu)** fit into, insert, inlay

植込 **u(e)ko(mi)** thick growth of plants, shrubbery

量込 **haka(ri)ko(mu)** measure liberally, give overweight

煮込 **niko(mu)** boil well, stew, cook together

覗込 **nozo(ki)ko(mu)** look/peek/peer into

税込 **zeiko(mi)** including tax

買込 **ka(i)ko(mu)** buy, stock up on

飲込 **no(mi)ko(mu)** swallow; understand; consent to

13 滑込 **sube(ri)ko(mu)** slide into (second base)

溜込 **ta(me)ko(mu)** save up, amass

搔込 **ka(ki)ko(mu)** rake/shovel in

寝込 **neko(mu)** fall asleep; oversleep; be sick in bed

照込 **te(ri)ko(mi)** sunshine; drought

触込 **fu(re)ko(mi)** announcement, professing to be

詰込 **tsu(me)ko(mu)** cram, stuff, pack in

詰込主義 **tsu(me)ko(mi) shugi** education emphasizing cramming and memorization rather than understanding

話込 **hana(shi)ko(mu)** have a long talk with

14 漬込 **tsu(ke)ko(mu)** pickle

滲込 **shinnyū** permeate, infiltrate, sink in

練込 **ne(ri)ko(mu)** knead into

綴込 **to(ji)ko(mu)** file away, insert

誑込 **tara(shi)ko(mu)** coax into

踊込 **odo(ri)ko(mu)** jump/rush into

聞込 **ki(ki)ko(mu)** hear about, learn

駆込 **ka(ke)ko(mu)** rush into, seek refuge in

15 舞込 **ma(i)ko(mu)** drop in, visit; befall

潜込 **mogu(ri)ko(mu)** get/crawl/slip in; hide

暴込 **aba(re)ko(mu)** storm/burst into

黙込 **dama(ri)ko(mu)** fall silent, say no more

締込 **shi(me)ko(mu)** shut/lock in

縫込 **nu(i)ko(mu)** sew in, tuck

踏込 **fu(mi)ko(mu)** step/rush into

鋳込 **iko(mu)** cast (in a mold)

16 積込 **tsu(mi)ko(mu)** load, take on (board)

頼込 **tano(mi)ko(mu)** earnestly request

頽込 **nada(re)ko(mu)** rush/surge into

17 擦込 **su(ri)ko(mu)** rub/mix in

18 織込 **o(ri)ko(mu)** weave into

19 繰込 **ku(ri)ko(mu)** stream into; count in, round up

蹴込 **keko(mi)** riser (of a step/entranceway)

騙込 **dama(shi)ko(mu)** take in, deceive, defraud

21 躍込 **odo(ri)ko(mu)** jump/rush into

29 鬱込 **fusa(gi)ko(mu)** be depressed, feel low, mope

─────────── 3 ───────────

4 手繰込 **tagu(ri)ko(mu)** haul in

引摺込 **hi(ki)zu(ri)ko(mu)** drag in

6 早呑込 **hayano(mi)ko(mi)** hasty conclusion

8 逆飛込 **sakato(bi)ko(mi)** headlong plunge

9 俄仕込 **niwakajiko(mi)** hasty preparation

13 意気込 **ikigo(mu)** be enthusiastic about

─────────── 3 ───────────

2q3.1

辿 辿

TEN, tado(ru) walk along, follow (a course), trace, follow up

─────────── 1 ───────────

12 辿着 **tado(ri)tsu(ku)** make it to, grope/ trudge along to

14 辿読 **tado(ri)yo(mi)** read with difficulty

2q3.2

迂 迂

U roundabout; unrealistic

─────────── 1 ───────────

6 迂回 **ukai** detour

12 迂遠 **uen** roundabout; circumlocutory

13 迂愚 **ugu** silly, stupid

17 迂闊 **ukatsu** careless, stupid

2q3.3 / 777

巡

JUN, megu(ru) go around
megu(rasu) surround
(o)mawa(ri-san) policeman

─────────── 1 ───────────

5 巡礼 **junrei** pilgrimage; pilgrim

巡礼者 **junreisha** pilgrim

6 巡合 **megu(ri)a(u)** chance to meet

巡行 **junkō** patrol, tour, one's beat/rounds

巡回 **junkai** tour, patrol, one's rounds

8 巡幸 **junkō** imperial tour
巡拝 **junpai** circuit pilgrimage
巡歩 **megu(ri)aru(ku)** walk around
9 巡洋 **jun'yō** cruise
巡洋艦 **jun'yōkan** cruiser
巡査 **junsa** patrolman, cop
10 巡遊 **jun'yū** tour
巡航 **junkō** cruise
巡航船 **junkōsen** cruiser
11 巡視 **junshi** inspection tour, patrol
巡視艇 **junshitei** patrol boat
12 巡検 **junken** inspection tour
13 巡業 **jungyō** tour (of a troupe/team)
14 巡歴 **junreki** tour
巡察 **junsatsu** patrol, one's rounds
15 巡閲 **jun'etsu** inspection tour
16 巡錫 **junshaku** preaching tour
17 巡覧 **junran** tour, sightseeing
19 巡警 **junkei** patrolman
22 巡邏 **junra** patrol, one's beat/rounds

──────── 2 ────────

1 一巡 **hitomegu(ri)** a turn/round; one full year
ichijun a round/patrol
5 立巡 **ta(chi)megu(ru)** stand/move about
6 血巡 **chi (no) megu(ri)** circulation of the blood; (quick/slow)-wittedness
9 逡巡 **shunjun** hesitate, be reluctant
思巡 **omo(i)megu(rasu)** recall, recollect; think over
10 島巡 **shimamegu(ri)** tour of the island(s)
11 経巡 **hemegu(ru)** wander/travel about
14 駆巡 **ka(ke)megu(ru)** run around

──────── 3 ────────

11 堂々巡 **dōdōmegu(ri)** circle a temple in worship; going round and round (without getting anywhere); roll-call vote

2q3.4

迄 迄

KITSU, made until, up to, as far as, to the extent of

──────── 2 ────────

6 此迄 **ko(re)made** until now, thus far
12 然迄 **samade** to that extent, so much
13 飽迄 **a(ku) made, a(ku) made (mo)** to the last, throughout, strictly

──────── 3 ────────

6 此処迄 **koko made** to this point, up to now
7 何処迄 **doko made** how far
何時迄 **itsu made** till when, how soon/long

2q3.5 / 1798

迅

JIN fast

──────── 1 ────────

9 迅速 **jinsoku** quick, prompt, speedy
13 迅雷 **jinrai** thunderclap; sudden and forceful

──────── 2 ────────

16 奮迅 **funjin** furious/vigorous activity

──────── 3 ────────

10 疾風迅雷 **shippū-jinrai** lightning speed

──────── 4 ────────

13 獅子奮迅 **shishi funjin** great power and speed

──────── 4 ────────

2q4.1

迚

tote(mo) very

2q4.2 / 1111

廷

TEI imperial court; law court

──────── 1 ────────

2 廷丁 **teitei** court attendant/clerk
4 廷内 **teinai** in the court
6 廷吏 **teiri** court attendant/clerk
7 廷臣 **teishin** court official, courtier

──────── 2 ────────

2 入廷 **nyūtei** admission to the courtroom
4 内廷 **naitei** inner court
5 出廷 **shuttei** appear in court
6 休廷 **kyūtei** adjourn court
8 退廷 **taitei** leave the court
法廷 **hōtei** (law) court, courtroom
10 宮廷 **kyūtei** the court/place
11 閉廷 **heitei** adjourn court
12 朝廷 **chōtei** imperial court
開廷 **kaitei** opening/holding court

2q4.3 / 445

近

KIN, chika(i) near

──────── 1 ────────

0 近づく **chika(zuku)** come/go near, approach
近づき **chika(zuki)** acquaintance
3 近々 **chikajika, kinkin** before long
4 近辺 **kinpen** neighborhood, vicinity
近日 **kinjitsu** soon, in a few days
近日点 **kinjitsuten** perihelion
近火 **kinka, chikabi** a fire in one's neighborhood
5 近世 **kinsei** recent times, modern age

2

亻
冫
孑
阝
卩
刂
力
又
一
十
卜
勹
丷
厂
辶
冂
八
匸
→ 4

近世史 **kinseishi** modern history
近代 **kindai** modern
近代人 **kindaijin** modern person
近代五種 **kindai goshu** the modern pentathlon
近代化 **kindaika** modernization
近代主義 **kindai shugi** modernism
近代的 **kindaiteki** modern
近付 **chikazu(ku)** come/go near, approach
　　　chikazu(ki) acquaintance
近刊 **kinkan** recent/forthcoming publication
近古 **kinko** early modern age
近目 **chikame** nearsighted; shortsighted
6 近年 **kinnen** in recent years
近江 **Ōmi** (ancient kuni, Shiga-ken)
近地点 **kinchiten** perigee
近在 **kinzai** neighboring villages, suburbs
近回 **chikamawa(ri)** neighborhood, vicinity; short cut
近因 **kin'in** proximate cause
7 近来 **kinrai** recently
近体 **kintai** recent/up-to-date style
近体詩 **kintaishi** modern-style poem
近作 **kinsaku** a recent work
近似 **kinji** approximation, convergence
近似値 **kinjichi** an approximation
近状 **kinjō** recent situation, present state
近臣 **kinshin** trusted vassal, personal attendant
近村 **kinson** neighboring villages
8 近東 **Kintō** the Near East
近事 **kinji** recent events
近侍 **kinji** attendant, entourage
近郊 **kinkō** suburbs
近況 **kinkyō** recent situation, present state
近国 **kingoku** neighboring country/province
近所 **kinjo** neighborhood, vicinity
近所合壁 **kinjo gappeki** immediate neighborhood
9 近海 **kinkai** coastal waters, adjoining seas
近海魚 **kinkaigyo** coastal/shore fish
近県 **kinken** neighboring prefectures
10 近郷 **kingō** neighboring districts
近時 **kinji** recent, modern
近称 **kinshō** (in grammar) denoting nearness to the speaker
11 近道 **chikamichi** short cut
近接 **kinsetsu** neighboring, contiguous, close-by
近著 **kincho** a recent work
近寄 **chikayo(ru)** go/come near, approach
近視 **kinshi** nearsightedness
近視眼 **kinshigan** myopia
近情 **kinjō** recent conditions, present state
近眼 **kingan, chikame** nearsighted; shortsighted
近眼者 **kingansha** nearsighted person

近眼鏡 **kingankyō** eyeglasses for nearsightedness
近頃 **chikagoro** recently, nowadays
12 近傍 **kinbō** neighborhood, vicinity
近着 **kinchaku** recently/just arrived
近詠 **kin'ei** recent poem
近距離 **kinkyori** short distance/range
近間 **chikama** neighborhood, vicinity
13 近業 **kingyō** a recent work
15 近隣 **kinrin** neighborhood, vicinity
近影 **kin'ei** recent portrait/photograph
近畿 **Kinki** the Ōsaka-Kyōto area
16 近衛 **konoe** imperial guards; bodyguards
近衛兵 **konoehei** imperial guards; bodyguards
近親 **kinshin** close relative
近親者 **kinshinsha, kinshinja** close relative
近親相姦 **kinshin sōkan** incest
18 近藤 **Kondō** (surname)

──────── 2 ────────

4 中近東 **Chūkintō** the Near and Middle East
手近 **tejika** close by, handy, familiar
5 付近 **fukin** vicinity, neighborhood
6 近近 **chikajika, kinkin** before long
至近 **shikin** very near
至近弾 **shikindan** near miss
7 身近 **mijika** familiar, close to one
9 昵近 **jikkin** intimate, familiar
11 側近 **sokkin** close associate
　　　sobachika(ku) nearby
側近者 **sokkinsha** close associate
接近 **sekkin** approach, draw near
12 遠近 **enkin** far and/or near, distance
遠近法 **enkinhō** (law of) perspective
最近 **saikin** recently; latest, newest
最近親者 **saikinshinsha** nearest relative, next of kin
程近 **hodochika(i)** nearby
間近 **majika** nearby, close, affecting one personally
14 漸近 **zenkin** approach asymptotically, asymptotic (line/value)
端近 **hashijika** near the edge/threshold
15 隣近所 **tonarikinjo** neighborhood
輓近 **bankin** recent, modern
16 親近 **shinkin** familiarity
親近性 **shinkinsei** familiarity
親近相姦 **shinkin sōkan** incest
親近感 **shinkinkan** feeling of familiarity

──────── 3 ────────

12 遠交近攻 **enkō-kinkō** befriending distant countries and antagonizing neighbors

2q4.4 / 1055

迎　**GEI, muka(eru)** go to meet, receive, greet, invite, send for

——————————— 1 ———————————

2 迎入 **muka(e)i(reru)** usher in, welcome
4 迎水 **muka(e)mizu** pump-priming
迎火 **muka(e)bi** fire to welcome departed souls home
6 迎合 **geigō** flattery, ingratiation
9 迎春 **geishun** welcoming the new year
迎春花 **geishunka** flowers which bloom around New Year's time
10 迎酒 **muka(e)zake** a drink to cure a hangover
11 迎接 **geisetsu** meeting and entertaining
15 迎撃 **geigeki, muka(e)u(tsu)** intercept (and attack)
迎賓 **geihin** welcoming guests
迎賓館 **geihinkan** reception hall, residence for guests

——————————— 2 ———————————

5 出迎 **demuka(eru)** (go/come to) meet (someone upon his arrival)
7 来迎 **raigō** the coming of Amida Buddha to welcome the spirits of the dead
8 奉迎 **hōgei** welcome
奉迎門 **hōgeimon** welcome arch
送迎 **sōgei, oku(ri)muka(e)** seeing (someone) off and meeting upon return, dropping off and picking up (passengers)
呼迎 **yo(bi)muka(eru)** send for
14 魂迎 **tamamuka(e)** welcoming the spirits of the dead
15 歓迎 **kangei** welcome
歓迎会 **kangeikai** welcoming meeting, reception

2q4.5 / 442

返 HEN, kae(su) (tr.) return
HEN, kae(ru) (intr.) return

——————————— 1 ———————————

3 返上 **henjō** send back, go without
5 返本 **henpon** books/magazines returned unsold
返付 **henpu** return, give back
返礼 **henrei** return gift, in return for
6 返返 **kae(su)gae(su)** repeatedly, really, indeed
返血 **kae(ri)chi** blood spurted back (from a stabbing victim onto the assailant)
7 返却 **henkyaku** return, repayment
返花 **kae(ri)bana** flower blooming out of season, flower blooming for a second time
8 返事 **henji** reply
返送 **hensō** send back, return
返杯 **henpai** offer the cup in return
返忠 **kae(ri)chū** switching loyalties, betrayal
返金 **henkin** repayment
9 返信 **henshin** reply

返信料 **henshinryō** return postage
返点 **kae(ri)ten** marks indicating the Japanese word order in reading Chinese classics
返咲 **kae(ri)za(ki)** second blooming; comeback
返品 **henpin** returned goods, returns
返盃 **henpai** offer the cup in return
10 返書 **hensho** reply
返納 **hennō** return, restoration
返討 **kae(ri)u(chi)** killing a would-be avenger
11 返済 **hensai** repayment
12 返報 **henpō** in return/retaliation for
返答 **hentō** reply
13 返照 **henshō** evening glow; reflected light
返辞 **henji** reply
返電 **henden** reply telegram
14 返歌 **henka** poem in reply
15 返還 **henkan** return; repayment

——————————— 2 ———————————

2 二返事 **futa(tsu)henji** immediate reply, readily, most willingly
4 切返 **ki(ri)kae(shi)** cutback; counterattack
反返 **so(ri)ka(eru)** bend backward; throw back the head/shoulders
引返 **hi(ki)kae(su)** turn back
5 生返 **i(ki)kae(ru)** revive, be resuscitated
生返事 **namahenji** vague answer
仕返 **shikae(shi)** get even, give tit for tat; do over again
代返 **daihen** answer roll call for another
打返 **u(chi)kae(su)** hit back
立返 **ta(chi)kae(ru)** return to
6 返返 **kae(su)gae(su)** repeatedly, really, indeed
行返 **yu(ki)kae(ru)** go and return
7 冴返 **sa(e)kae(ru)** be exceedingly clear; be keenly cold
折返 **o(ri)kae(su)** fold back; double back
o(ri)kae(shi) immediate (reply)
折返点 **o(ri)kae(shi)ten** (marathon) turn-back point
投返 **na(ge)kae(su)** throw back
呆返 **aki(re)ka(eru)** be flabbergasted
見返 **mikae(ru)** look back at
mikae(shi) inside the cover
見返物資 **mikae(ri) busshi** collateral goods
言返 **i(i)kae(su)** talk back, retort
8 追返 **o(i)kae(su)** repulse, drive back, turn away
送返 **oku(ri)kae(su)** send back
沸返 **wa(ki)kae(ru)** seethe, be in an uproar
押返 **o(shi)kae(su)** push back
呼返 **yo(bi)kae(su)** call back, recall
若返 **wakagae(ru)** be rejuvenated
宙返 **chūgae(ri)** somersault
突返 **tsu(ki)kae(su)** thrust back; refuse to accept

2
イ
冫
孑
阝
卩
刂
力
又
一
亠
十
卜
宀
厂
辶
門
几
匸
4 ←

2

亻 宀 子 阝 卩 刂 力 又 亠 十 ├ 夂 ⿱ 广 ⻌ 冂 几 匸

→5⻌

取返 **to(ri)kae(su)** get back, regain, recover, recoup, catch up on
to(tte)kae(su) hurry/double back
9 巻返 **ma(ki)kae(shi)** rollback, fight back (from a losing position)
染返 **so(me)kae(su)** redye
祝返 **iwa(i)gae(shi)** return gift
思返 **omo(i)kae(su)** think over, reconsider
10 射返 **ikae(su)** shoot back; reflect
捏返 **ko(ne)kae(su)** knead, mix; be muddy
振返 **fu(ri)kae(ru)** turn one's head, look back
恩返 **ongae(shi)** repayment of a favor
病返 **ya(mi)kae(shi)** relapse
納返 **osa(mari)kae(ru)** be content/nonchalant
馬返 **umagae(shi)** the place on a mountain road too steep to go further on horseback
11 混返 **ma(ze)kae(su), ma(zek)kae(su)** stir up; interrupt, butt in
掘返 **ho(ri)kae(su)** dig up
盛返 **mo(ri)kae(su)** rally, recover
12 遣返 **ya(ri)kae(su)** try again, do over; retort, refute
揺返 **yu(ri)kae(shi)** aftershock
蒸返 **mu(shi)kae(su)** reheat; repeat, rehash
煮返 **ni(e)kae(su)** reboil, cook over again
13 裏返 **uragae(su)** turn the other way, turn inside out, turn over **uragae(shi)** inside out, upside down **uragae(ru)** be turned inside out; turn against (someone)
寝返 **negae(ri)** tossing about while sleeping; switching sides
照返 **te(ri)kae(su)** reflect
睨返 **nira(mi)kae(su), ne(me)kae(su)** glare back
跳返 **ha(ne)kae(su)** bounce back, repel
14 静返 **shizu(mari)kae(ru)** become perfectly quiet
読返 **yo(mi)kae(su)** reread
奪返 **uba(i)kae(su)** recapture, take back
聞返 **ki(ki)kae(su)** ask back
15 撥返 **ha(ne)kae(su)** repulse, repel
縫返 **nu(i)kae(su)** resew, remake
鋤返 **su(ki)kae(su)** plow up, turn over
19 繰返 **ku(ri)kae(su)** repeat
蹴返 **kekae(su)** kick back

――― 3 ―――

4 引繰返 **hi(k)ku(ri)kae(ru)** be overturned, capsize, collapse; be reversed
hi(k)ku(ri)kae(su) overturn, turn upside down, turn inside out
6 竹箆返 **shippeigae(shi)** retaliation, tit for tat
9 香典返 **kōdengae(shi)** return present for a condolence gift
香奠返 **kōdengae(shi)** return present for a condolence gift

12 煮繰返 **ni(e)ku(ri)kae(ru)** boil, seethe
13 意趣返 **ishugae(shi)** revenge
14 蜻蛉返 **tonbogae(ri)** somersault
22 龕灯返 **gandōgae(shi)** apparatus for changing stage scenery
28 鸚鵡返 **ōmugae(shi)** parroting

――― 4 ―――

18 覆水盆返 **fukusui bon (ni) kae(razu)** No use crying over spilt milk.

――― 5 ―――

迪→廸 **2q5.1**

2q5.1

廸 迪

TEKI, michi path, way
michibi(ku) guide, lead
susu(mu) proceed, advance
ita(ru) reach, arrive

2q5.2 / 1507

迭

TETSU alternate

――― 2 ―――

7 更迭 **kōtetsu** change, reshuffle, shake-up

2q5.3 / 968

述

JUTSU, no(beru) state, mention, refer to, explain

――― 1 ―――

7 述作 **jussaku** write (a book)
14 述語 **jutsugo** predicate
16 述懐 **jukkai** reminiscences

――― 2 ―――

3 上述 **jōjutsu** the above-mentioned
口述 **kōjutsu** oral statement, dictation
6 伝述 **denjutsu** pass on, relay
9 叙述 **jojutsu** description, narration
前述 **zenjutsu** the above-mentioned
後述 **kōjutsu** discussed below
祖述 **sojutsu** expound/propagate one's master's doctrines
祖述者 **sojutsusha** exponent
10 既述 **kijutsu** aforesaid
陳述 **chinjutsu** state, set forth, declare
陳述書 **chinjutsusho** statement, declaration
記述 **kijutsu** description, account
11 著述 **chojutsu** write (books)
著述家 **chojutsuka** writer, author
著述業 **chojutsugyō** the literary profession

略述 **ryakujutsu** brief account, outline
訳述 **yakujutsu** translate
13 詳述 **shōjutsu** detailed explanation, full account
14 説述 **setsujutsu** explanation, exposition
15 撰述 **senjutsu** write, author, compile
論述 **ronjutsu** state, enunciate, set forth

2q5.4 / 1115

延 EN stretch **no(basu)** (tr.) stretch, lengthen, extend, prolong, postpone **no(beru)** (tr.) lengthen, extend **no(biru)** (intr.) stretch, extend, grow, be prolonged/delayed/postponed **no(be)** total, aggregate; futures transaction

——————— 1 ———————
3 延久 **Enkyū** (era, 1069–1074)
延々 **en'en** repeatedly postponed, protracted, interminable
4 延元 **Engen** (era, 1336–1340)
延文 **Enbun** (era, 1356–1361)
延引 **en'in, ennin** delay
延日数 **no(be)nissū** total number of days
5 延払 **no(be)bara(i)** deferred payment
6 延年 **ennen** longevity
延会 **enkai** adjournment
7 延寿 **enju** prolongation of life
延享 **Enkyō** (era, 1744–1748)
延延 **no(bi)no(bi), en'en** repeatedly postponed, long delayed, interminable
延応 **En'ō** (era, 1239–1240)
8 延長 **enchō** extension, continuation, prolongation, elongation **Enchō** (era, 923–930)
延命 **enmei** prolongation of life
延岡 **Nobeoka** (city, Miyazaki-ken)
延坪 **no(be)tsubo** total floor space
延宝 **Enpō** (era, 1673–1681)
延板 **no(be)ita** board for making udon, etc.; hammered-out metal
延性 **ensei** ductility
延金 **no(be)gane** sheet/hammered-out metal; sword, dagger
9 延音 **en'on** elongated (vowel) sound
10 延紙 **no(be)gami** paper handkerchief (Edo period)
延納 **ennō** deferred payment
12 延着 **enchaku** delayed arrival
延喜 **Engi** (era, 901–923)
延棒 **no(be)bō** (metal) bar
延期 **enki** postpone, defer, prolong
延焼 **enshō** spread of a fire
13 延滞 **entai** arrears, overdue (payment)
14 延暦 **Enryaku** (era, 782–806)
延徳 **Entoku** (era, 1489–1492)

15 延慶 **Enkei** (era, 1308–1311)
18 延髄 **enzui** the hindbrain

——————— 2 ———————
3 万延 **Man'en** (era, 1860–1861)
4 天延 **Ten'en** (era, 973–976)
引延 **hi(ki)noba(su)** stretch out; enlarge; defer
日延 **hino(be)** postponement
5 生延 **i(ki)no(biru)** live on, live long, survive
圧延 **atsuen** rolling (steel)
圧延機 **atsuenki** rolling machine/mill
圧延鋼 **atsuenkō** rolled steel
永延 **Eien** (era, 987–989)
打延 **u(chi)no(be)** hammer out
7 延延 **no(bi)no(bi), en'en** repeatedly postponed, long delayed, interminable
8 逃延 **ni(ge)no(biru)** make good one's escape, get away
9 保延 **Hōen** (era, 1135–1141)
食延 **ku(i)no(basu)** stretch out (one's rations), make (supplies) last
10 差延 **sa(shi)no(beru)** extend (a hand)
11 遅延 **chien** delay
12 落延 **o(chi)no(biru)** make good one's escape
間延 **mano(bi)** slow, dull-witted
順延 **jun'en** postpone, defer
13 寛延 **Kan'en** (era, 1748–1750)
14 遷延 **sen'en** delay
蔓延 **man'en** spread, be widespread
15 熱延 **netsuen** hot rolling
19 繰延 **ku(ri)no(be)** postponement, deferment

——————— 3 ———————
12 無期延期 **muki enki** indefinite postponement

——————— 4 ———————
8 雨天順延 **uten-jun'en** in case of rain postponed to the next fair day

2q5.5 / 1175

迫 HAKU, **sema(ru)** press (someone) for, urge; approach, draw near

——————— 1 ———————
2 迫力 **hakuryoku** (dramatic) force, intensity, appeal
10 迫真 **hakushin** true to life, realistic
迫真性 **hakushinsei** true to life, realistic
迫害 **hakugai** persecution
迫害者 **hakugaisha** persecutor, oppressor
15 迫撃 **hakugeki** attack at close quarters
迫撃砲 **hakugekihō** mortar

——————— 2 ———————
4 切迫 **seppaku** draw near, impend, be imminent; become acute, grow tense
5 圧迫 **appaku** pressure, oppression, compulsion

6 気迫 **kihaku** spirit, vigor
8 押迫 **o(shi)sema(ru)** press hard
9 急迫 **kyūhaku** be imminent/pressing, grow acute
10 脅迫 **kyōhaku** threat, intimidation
脅迫状 **kyōhakujō** threatening letter
脅迫的 **kyōhakuteki** threatening, menacing
差迫 **sa(shi)sema(ru)** be imminent/impending
11 強迫 **kyōhaku** compel, coerce
強迫観念 **kyōhaku kannen** obsession
12 逼迫 **hippaku** (money) stringency, austerity
15 窮迫 **kyūhaku** financial distress, poverty
緊迫 **kinpaku** tension
17 鍔迫合 **tsubazeria(i)** close fighting

──────── 3 ────────
10 被圧迫 **hiappaku** oppressed

2q5.6

迦 迦   **KA** (used phonetically)

──────── 2 ────────
11 釈迦 **Shaka** Gautama, Buddha
釈迦如来 **Shaka Nyorai** Sakyamuni
釈迦牟尼 **Shakamuni** Sakyamuni, Gautama, Buddha
釈迦象 **shakazō** image of Buddha

逈 → 逃 2q6.5

2q5.7

迢   **CHŌ** far off, distant

2q5.8

迨   **SHŌ, made** until

迱 → 邐 2q14.1

迻 → 邐 2q14.1

2q5.9

迥   **KEI** far, distant

廻 → 迴 2q6.13

──────── 6 ────────

2q6.1 / 967

迷   **MEI, mayo(u)** go astray, get lost, be perplexed **mayo(i)** perplexity, doubt, delusion **mayo(wasu)** perplex; lead astray; charm, seduce

──────── 1 ────────
2 迷子 **maigo, mayo(i)go** lost child
6 迷妄 **meimō** illusion, delusion
9 迷信 **meishin** superstition
迷信家 **meishinka** superstitious person
10 迷宮 **meikyū** maze, labyrinth
11 迷彩 **meisai** camouflage
12 迷惑 **meiwaku** trouble, annoyance, inconvenience
13 迷夢 **meimu** illusion, delusion
迷想 **meisō** illusion, fallacy
迷路 **meiro** maze, labyrinth
15 迷論 **meiron** fallacy

──────── 2 ────────
5 立迷 **ta(chi)mayo(u)** float along, drift
6 気迷 **kimayo(i)** hesitation, wavering
血迷 **chimayo(u)** lose control of oneself, run amok
7 低迷 **teimei** hang low, be sluggish
8 昏迷 **konmei** be stupefied/bewildered
11 混迷 **konmei** be stupefied/befuddled/confused
13 頑迷 **ganmei** bigoted, obstinate
15 踏迷 **fu(mi)mayo(u)** lose one's way

──────── 3 ────────
6 有難迷惑 **a(ri)gata-meiwaku** unwelcome favor

2q6.2 / 892

建   **KEN, KON, ta(teru)** build **ta(tsu)** be built **-da(te)** built in the form of (two stories); (yen)-denominated (loan)

──────── 1 ────────
3 建久 **Kenkyū** (era, 1190–1199)
4 建仁 **Kennin** (era, 1201–1204)
建込 **ta(te)ko(mu)** be densely built up
建方 **ta(te)kata** architectural style; how to build
5 建永 **Ken'ei** (era, 1206–1207)
建白 **kenpaku** memorial, petition
建白書 **kenpakusho** memorial, petition
建立 **konryū** erection, building
7 建売 **ta(te)u(ri)** build (houses) to sell; ready-built (house)
建材 **kenzai** construction materials

建言 **kengen** petition, proposal
8 建長 **Kenchō** (era, 1249–1255)
建直 **ta(te)nao(ru)** be rebuilt
     ta(te)nao(su) rebuild
建治 **Kenji** (era, 1275–1278)
建坪 **tatetsubo** floor space
建国 **kenkoku** founding of a country
建物 **tatemono** a building
建武 **Kenmu** (era, 1334–1336)
建具 **tategu** household fittings, fixtures
建具屋 **tateguya** cabinetmaker
9 建保 **Kenpō** (era, 1213–1219)
建前 **ta(te)mae** principle, official position; erection of the framework
建造 **kenzō** build, construct
建造物 **kenzōbutsu** a building, structure
10 建値 **tatene** officially quoted price
11 建設 **kensetsu** construction
建設的 **kensetsuteki** constructive
建設者 **kensetsusha** builder
建設省 **Kensetsushō** Ministry of Construction
12 建替 **ta(te)ka(e)** rebuilding, reconstruction
14 建暦 **Kenryaku** (era, 1211–1213)
建増 **tatema(shi)** extension, annex
建徳 **Kentoku** (era, 1370–1372)
建碑 **kenpi** erection of a monument
建網 **ta(te)ami** set net
16 建築 **kenchiku** building, construction, architecture
建築学 **kenchikugaku** architecture
建築者 **kenchikusha** builder
建築物 **kenchikubutsu** a building, structure
建築師 **kenchikushi** builder
建築家 **kenchikuka** architect, building contractor
建築術 **kenchikujutsu** architecture
建築費 **kenchikuhi** construction costs
建築業者 **kenchiku gyōsha** builder
20 建議 **kengi** proposal
建議者 **kengisha** proposer
建議案 **kengian** proposition
21 建艦 **kenkan** naval construction

──────── 2 ────────

3 土建屋 **doken'ya** contractor
土建業 **dokengyō** civil engineering and construction
5 打建 **u(chi)ta(teru)** erect, build
6 再建 **saiken** reconstruction, rebuilding
8 金建 **kinda(te), kinta(te)** gold basis, quotations in gold
9 封建 **hōken** feudalism
封建主義 **hōken shugi** feudalism
封建制 **hōkensei** feudalism
封建的 **hōkenteki** feudal(istic)
12 創建 **sōken** found, establish

──────── 3 ────────

2 二本建 **nihonda(te)** dual system; double standard
二軒建 **nikenda(te)** duplex, semidetached (house)
二階建 **nikaida(te)** two-story

2q6.3 / 846

退

TAI, shirizo(ku) retreat
shirizo(keru) drive away, repel
no(ku), do(ku) get out of the way, go away **no(keru), do(keru)** get rid of, remove **hi(ku)** retreat; subside

──────── 1 ────────

4 退化 **taika** retrogression, degeneration
退引 **no(p)piki(naranu)** unavoidable, inescapable
5 退出 **taishutsu** leave, withdraw
退去 **taikyo** leave, withdraw, evacuate
退庁 **taichō** leaving the office
6 退任 **tainin** retire from office
退会 **taikai** withdraw from membership
退色 **taishoku** fading; faded color
退廷 **taitei** leave the court
退行 **taikō** regression, degeneration
7 退位 **taii** abdication
退却 **taikyaku** retreat
退役 **taieki** retirement from military service
退学 **taigaku** leave school, drop out
退社 **taisha** retirement from a company; leaving the office
8 退京 **taikyō** leave the capital, leave Tōkyō
退治 **taiji** subjugation; extermination, (pest) control
退官 **taikan** retire from office
退歩 **taiho** retrogress, backward step; degeneration
退屈 **taikutsu** boring, dull
退屈凌 **taikutsu-shino(gi)** killing time
9 退陣 **taijin** decampment; retirement
退院 **taiin** leave the hospital
退軍 **taigun** decamp, withdraw
退紅色 **taikōshoku** pink
10 退耕 **taikō** retire (to the country) from public office
退席 **taiseki** leave one's seat; withdraw, retire
退校 **taikō** leaving school
11 退転 **taiten** distraction, backsliding
12 退場 **taijō** leave, exit, walk out
退廃 **taihai** corruption, decadence
退廃的 **taihaiteki** corrupt, decadent
退散 **taisan** (intr.) disperse, break up
13 退隠 **taiin** retirement
退勢 **taisei** deteriorating position, decline
退路 **tairo** path of retreat

15 退避 **taihi** taking refuge, evacuation
　　退潮 **taichō** ebb/low tide
　　退蔵 **taizō** hoard
　　退蔵品 **taizōhin** hoarded goods, cache
17 退嬰 **taiei** conservatism, retrogression
　　退嬰的 **taieiteki** conservative, retiring (disposition)
18 退職 **taishoku** retirement
　　退職金 **taishokukin** retirement allowance
20 退譲 **taijō** humility

――――――――― 2 ―――――――――

3 凡退 **bontai** (batter) be put out easily
4 不退転 **futaiten** determination, firm resolve
　　中退 **chūtai** leaving school before graduation, dropping out
　　引退 **intai** retire
5 立退 **ta(chi)no(ku)** move out (of the premises)
6 早退 **sōtai** leave early
9 飛退 **to(bi)no(ku)** jump back/aside
　　勇退 **yūtai** retire voluntarily, step down
　　後退 **kōtai** retreat, back up
　　　　atozusa(ri) move/shrink/hold back
10 衰退 **suitai** decline, degeneration
　　進退 **shintai** advance or retreat, movement; course of action, attitude; resigning or staying on
11 脱退 **dattai** secede, withdraw
　　敗退 **haitai** defeat, setback
12 減退 **gentai** decline, ebb
13 隠退 **intai** retire
　　搔退 **ka(ki)no(keru)** push aside, scratch away
　　辞退 **jitai** decline, refuse
14 総退却 **sōtaikyaku** general retreat
15 撃退 **gekitai** repulse, drive back, dislodge
　　撤退 **tettai** withdraw, pull out, retreat

――――――――― 4 ―――――――――

1 一進一退 **isshin-ittai** advance and retreat, fluctuating

2q6.4 / 1174

追

TSUI, o(u) pursue, chase after; drive (cattle); shoo away (flies)
o(tte) later on, afterward

――――――――― 1 ―――――――――

3 追及 **tsuikyū** pursue, get to the bottom of
　　追上 **o(i)a(geru)** catch up to
4 追弔 **tsuichō** mourning
　　追分 **oiwake** forked road, parting of the ways; packhorse driver's song
　　追分節 **oiwakebushi** packhorse driver's song
　　追込 **o(i)ko(mu)** corner, drive into; strike inward (a disease); make an extra effort at the end; run on (a line of print)
　　追手 **otte, o(i)te** pursuer

5 追出 **o(i)da(su)** chase/turn away, kick out, eject
　　追付 **o(i)tsu(ku)** catch up with
　　追刊 **tsuikan** additional publication
　　追加 **tsuika** addition, supplement
　　追払 **o(p)para(u), o(i)hara(u)** drive away
　　　　o(i)bara(i) later payment
　　追号 **tsuigō** posthumous title
　　追白 **tsuihaku** postscript, P.S.
　　追立 **o(i)ta(teru)** send/drive away, pack off, evict
6 追羽根 **o(i)bane** battledore and shuttlecock
　　追考 **tsuikō** second thoughts
　　追返 **o(i)kae(su)** repulse, drive back, turn away
　　追回 **o(i)mawa(su)** chase/follow around; order about
7 追伸 **tsuishin** postscript, P.S.
　　追求 **tsuikyū, o(i)moto(meru)** pursue
　　追抜 **o(i)nu(ku)** overtake
　　追究 **tsuikyū** pursuit, inquiry
　　追尾 **tsuibi** pursuit, tracking
8 追使 **o(i)tsuka(u)** work (someone) hard
　　追追 **o(i)o(i ni)** gradually, by and by
　　追送 **tsuisō** send in addition
　　追突 **tsuitotsu** rear-end collision
　　追肥 **tsuihi, o(i)goe** supplementary fertilizer/manuring
　　追炊 **o(i)da(ki)** boil some more (rice)
　　追放 **tsuihō** banishment; purge
　　追放者 **tsuihōsha** purgee, deportee
9 追風 **o(i)kaze, o(i)te** tailwind
10 追随 **tsuizui** follow (in the footsteps of)
　　追剝 **o(i)ha(gi)** highway robber, hijacker
　　追従 **tsuijū** follow, imitate; be servile to
　　　　tsuishō flattery, boot-licking
　　追書 **o(tte)ga(ki)** postscript, P.S.
　　追納 **tsuinō** supplementary payment
　　追討 **tsuitō** liquidate rebels
　　　　o(i)u(chi) attack the routed enemy
　　追記 **tsuiki** postscript, P.S.
11 追掛 **o(i)ka(keru)** chase, run after
　　追悼 **tsuitō** mourning; memorial (address)
　　追悼会 **tsuitōkai** memorial services
　　追悼歌 **tsuitōka** dirge
12 追善 **tsuizen** (Buddhist) memorial service
　　追善供養 **tsuizen-kuyō** (Buddhist) memorial service
　　追落 **o(i)o(tosu)** capture (a fort)
　　追散 **o(i)chi(rasu)** disperse, scatter, put to rout
　　追越 **o(i)ko(su)** overtake
　　追訴 **tsuiso** supplementary lawsuit/indictment
13 追腹 **tsuifuku, o(i)bara** committing harakiri to follow one's dead master
　　追福 **tsuifuku** memorial service
　　追想 **tsuisō** recollection, reminiscences

追詰 **o(i)tsu(meru)** corner, drive to the wall, hunt down
追試 **tsuishi** follow-up experiment/test; makeup exam
追試験 **tsuishiken** supplementary/makeup exam
追跡 **tsuiseki** pursue, track, stalk
追跡者 **tsuisekisha** pursuer
14 追徴 **tsuichō** additional collection, supplementary charge
追徴金 **tsuichōkin** additional collection, supplementary charge
追徴税 **tsuichōzei** supplementary/penalty tax
追慕 **tsuibo** cherish the memory of
追認 **tsuinin** ratification, confirmation
追銭 **o(i)sen** additional payment, throwing good money after bad
15 追撃 **tsuigeki, o(i)u(chi)** pursuit, follow-up attack
追撃戦 **tsuigekisen** pursuit battle, running fight
追撃機 **tsuigekiki** pursuit/chase plane
追縋 **o(i)suga(ru)** close in on, be hot on the heels of
16 追憶 **tsuioku** recollection, reminiscences
追懐 **tsuikai** recollection, reminiscences
追録 **tsuiroku** supplement, postscript, addendum
18 追贈 **tsuizō** posthumous conferment of court rank
21 追儺 **tsuina** exorcism

─────── 2 ───────
4 犬追物 **inuoumono** (noisy martial arts event of Kamakura period in which 36 mounted archers pursue and shoot at 150 dogs)
8 追追 **o(i)o(i ni)** gradually, by and by
9 急追 **kyūtsui** hot pursuit
10 馬追 **umao(i)** horse driver; katydid
11 鳥追 **torio(i)** shooing birds away; New Year's minstrel girl
12 訴追 **sotsui** prosecution, indictment
15 窮追 **kyūtsui** drive into a corner

─────── 3 ───────
7 貝殻追放 **kaigara tsuihō** ostracism

2q6.5 / 1566

逃 逃 **TŌ, ni(geru)** flee, run away, escape **noga(reru)** escape **ni(gasu), no(gasu)** let go/ escape, set free

─────── 1 ───────
3 逃亡 **tōbō** escape, flight, desertion
逃亡者 **tōbōsha** runaway, fugitive, deserter
逃口 **ni(ge)guchi** way of escape, loophole

逃口上 **ni(ge)kōjō** excuse, evasion
4 逃支度 **ni(ge)jitaku** make ready to flee
逃水 **ni(ge)mizu** mirage of water
5 逃出 **ni(ge)da(su), noga(re)de(ru)** run off/away
逃去 **ni(ge)sa(ru)** flee, disappear
6 逃回 **ni(ge)mawa(ru)** run around trying to escape, dodge
7 逃延 **ni(ge)no(biru)** make good one's escape, get away
逃走 **tōsō** flight, escape, desertion **ni(ge)hashi(ru)** run away
逃足 **ni(ge)ashi** flight; preparation for flight
9 逃後 **ni(ge)oku(reru)** fail to escape
10 逃帰 **ni(ge)kae(ru)** run back, flee home
11 逃道 **ni(ge)michi** way of escape, way out
12 逃場 **ni(ge)ba** place of refuge; means of escape
逃散 **ni(ge)chi(ru)** flee in all directions, scatter, be routed **chōsan, tōsan** serfs' fleeing
逃惑 **ni(ge)mado(u)** run about trying to escape
13 逃隠 **ni(ge)kaku(reru)** flee and hide
逃損 **ni(ge)sokona(u)** fail to escape
逃腰 **ni(ge)goshi** preparation to flee; evasive attitude
逃路 **ni(ge)michi** way of escape, loophole
15 逃避 **tōhi** escape, flight, evasion
逃避行 **tōhikō** runaway trip, flight
逃避的 **tōhiteki** escapist, evasive

─────── 2 ───────
7 見逃 **minoga(su)** overlook
言逃 **i(i)noga(re)** evasion, excuse
8 夜逃 **yoni(ge)** fly by night, give (creditors) the slip
取逃 **to(ri)ni(gasu)** fail to catch, miss
9 持逃 **mo(chi)ni(ge)** make off with, abscond with
食逃 **ku(i)ni(ge)** run off without paying for what one has eaten
10 借逃 **ka(ri)ni(ge)** run away leaving unpaid debts
12 勝逃 **ka(chi)ni(ge)** quit while one is ahead
飲逃 **no(mi)ni(ge)** running off without paying for one's drinks
22 轢逃 **hi(ki)ni(ge)** hit-and-run
23 籤逃 **kujinoga(re)** elimination by lottery

─────── 3 ───────
1 一寸逃 **issunnoga(re)** quibbling, putting off
8 其場逃 **so(no)ba-noga(re)** temporizing, stopgap

─────── 5 ───────
3 三十六計逃 **sanjūrokkei ni(geru ni shikazu)** It's wisest here to run away.

2q6.6

迹 SEKI, ato mark, vestige

——————— 2 ———————

8 垂迹 suijaku manifestations of Buddha to save men

2q6.7

迸 HŌ, hotobashi(ru) gush out, spout forth tobashi(ru) splash tobatchi(ri) splash; by-blow, unsought involvement in

2q6.8 / 444

逆 GYAKU, GEKI reverse, inverse, opposite; treason saka- reverse, inverse saka(rau) be contrary to

——————— 1 ———————

0 逆さ/しま saka(sa/shima) reverse, inverted, upside down
2 逆子 sakago breech baby/presentation
3 逆上 gyakujō rush of blood to the head, dizziness, frenzy
4 逆毛 sakage hair standing on end
逆手 gyakute foul/dirty trick
sakate underhand/backhand (grip)
逆心 gyakushin treachery
5 逆比 gyakuhi inverse ratio
逆比例 gyakuhirei inversely proportional to
逆用 gyakuyō reverse (of the intended) use
逆立 sakada(chi) handstand, standing on one's head sakada(tsu) stand on end sakada(teru) set on end, bristle/ruffle up
逆目 sakame against the grain
6 逆行 gyakkō go back, move backward, run counter to
逆光 gyakkō backlighting
逆光線 gyakkōsen backlighting
7 逆作用 gyakusayō adverse effect, reaction
逆臣 gyakushin rebellious retainer, traitor
逆児 sakago breech baby/presentation
逆攻撃 gyakukōgeki counterattack
逆戻 gyakumodo(ri) turn/go back, revert, relapse
逆言葉 sakakotoba word of opposite meaning; word pronounced backwards
8 逆効果 gyakukōka opposite effect, counter-productive
逆送 gyakusō send back
逆波 sakanami head/choppy seas
逆茂木 sakamogi abatis
逆性石鹸 gyakusei sekken antiseptic soap
9 逆飛込 sakato(bi)ko(mi) headlong plunge
逆巻 sakama(ku) surge, roll, rage, seethe

逆剃 sakazo(ri) shaving against the grain
逆変 gyakuhen adverse change; vary inversely
逆風 gyakufū adverse wind, headwind
逆宣伝 gyakusenden counterpropaganda
逆恨 sakaura(mi) requited resentment; resentment based on a misunderstanding
10 逆修 gyakushu hold memorial services for oneself before one's death; hold memorial services for a younger predeceased person
逆剥 sakamu(ke) hangnail
逆進 gyakushin backward movement
逆浪 sakanami, gyakurō head/choppy sea
逆流 gyakuryū backward flow, reverse current, regurgitation
逆徒 gyakuto rebel, traitor, insurgent
11 逆運 gyakuun reversal of fortunes
逆接 gyakusetsu contrary conjunction, "but" relationship
逆振食 sakane(ji o) ku(waseru) retort, criticize in return
逆寄 sakayo(se) counterattack
逆産 gyakuzan, gyakusan foot presentation, breech birth
逆転 gyakuten reversal
12 逆落 sakao(toshi) headlong fall; downhill rush
逆富士 saka(sa) Fuji inverted reflection of Mt. Fuji
逆結 gyakumusu(bi) granny knot
逆順 gyakujun in reverse order
13 逆夢 sakayume dream which is the opposite of what comes true
逆数 gyakusū a reciprocal
逆睫 saka(sa)matsuge, sakamatsuge turned-in eyelashes
逆賊 gyakuzoku rebel, traitor, insurgent
14 逆境 gyakkyō adversity
逆様 sakasama upside-down, reverse, backwards
逆算 gyakusan counting backwards/down
逆語 saka(sa)kotoba word of opposite meaning; word pronounced backwards
逆説 gyakusetsu paradox
逆説的 gyakusetsuteki paradoxical
15 逆潮 sakashio, gyakuchō head tide, countertide, weather tide, crosstide, adverse current
逆撫 sakana(de) rub against the grain
逆噴射 gyakufunsha retro-firing
逆縁 gyakuen irony of fate
逆調 gyakuchō adverse, unfavorable
16 逆輸入 gyakuyunyū reimportation
逆輸出 gyakuyushutsu re-exportation
22 逆襲 gyakushū counterattack
24 逆鱗 gekirin the emperor's wrath

—————— 2 ——————

3 大逆 **taigyaku, daigyaku** hideous wickedness; treason; parricide
大逆無道 **daigyaku-mudō** high treason
大逆罪 **taigyakuzai, daigyakuzai** treason;
parricide
4 反逆 **hangyaku** treason, treachery, revolt
6 吃逆 **kitsugyaku, shakkuri** hiccups
9 叛逆 **hangyaku** treason, treachery, revolt
10 莫逆 **bakugyaku** firm friendship
莫逆友 **bakugyaku (no) tomo** steadfast
friend
11 悪逆 **akugyaku** heinous, treacherous
12 弑逆 **shiigyaku** murder (of one's lord/parent),
regicide
順逆 **jungyaku** obedience and disobedience,
right and wrong
15 横逆 **ōgyaku** perverse, obstinate, unreasonable
暴逆 **bōgyaku** outrage, atrocity, violence

2q6.9 / 441

SŌ, oku(ru) send

—————— 1 ——————

4 送込 **oku(ri)ko(mu)** see (someone) home,
usher/escort in
送手 **oku(ri)te** sender
送火 **oku(ri)bi** bonfire for speeding home the
spirits of the dead
5 送出 **oku(ri)da(su)** send out; see (someone)
out, send forth
送本 **sōhon** deliver books
送付 **sōfu** send, forward, remit
送主 **oku(ri)nushi** sender
6 送気管 **sōkikan** air pipe/duct
送仮名 **oku(ri)gana** suffixed kana showing
inflection
送迎 **sōgei, oku(ri)muka(e)** seeing (someone)
off and meeting upon return, dropping
off and picking up (passengers)
送返 **oku(ri)kae(su)** send back
送先 **oku(ri)saki** destination, consignee
送行 **sōkō** sending (someone) off
送行会 **sōkōkai** going-away/farewell party
7 送状 **oku(ri)jō** invoice
送別 **sōbetsu** farewell, send-off
送別会 **sōbetsukai** going-away/farewell
party
送呈 **sōtei** send as a present
8 送受信機 **sōjushinki** transceiver
送油管 **sōyukan** oil pipeline
送届 **oku(ri)todo(keru)** see/escort (someone) to

送金 **sōkin** remittance
送金額 **sōkingaku** amount remitted
9 送信 **sōshin** transmission of a message
送信機 **sōshinki** transmitter
送風 **sōfū** forced air, ventilation
送風機 **sōfūki** blower, ventilator, fan
10 送倒 **oku(ri)tao(su)** push down from behind
(in sumo)
送狼 **oku(ri)ōkami** pursuing wolf; man who
keeps following a woman
送致 **sōchi** send
送料 **sōryō** shipping charges, postage
11 送達 **sōtatsu** convey, deliver, dispatch
送球 **sōkyū** throw a ball
12 送葬 **sōsō** funeral
送検 **sōken** send to the prosecutor's office
13 送話 **sōwa** transmission (of a telephone
message)
送話口 **sōwaguchi** (telephone) mouthpiece
送話料 **sōwaryō** telephone charges
送話器 **sōwaki** transmitter
送賃 **oku(ri)chin** shipping charges
送電 **sōden** transmission of electricity
送電線 **sōdensen** power lines
15 送還 **sōkan** send back, repatriate
20 送籍 **sōseki** transfer of domicile

—————— 2 ——————

5 申送 **mō(shi)oku(ru)** send word, write to;
transfer (a matter to someone else)
仕送 **shioku(ri)** allowance, remittance
目送 **mokusō** follow with one's eyes
6 伝送 **densō** transmit, relay
返送 **hensō** send back, return
宅送 **takusō** delivery
回送 **kaisō** forwarding, transportation; (bus)
returning to the barn, Out of Service
早送 **hayaoku(ri)** fast forward
虫送 **mushioku(ri)** torch procession to drive
away insects
7 別送 **bessō** by separate mail, under separate
cover
吹送 **fu(ki)oku(ru)** waft, blow over to
見送 **mioku(ru)** see (someone) off, watch till
out of sight
言送 **i(i)oku(ru)** send word
8 直送 **chokusō** direct delivery
追送 **tsuisō** send in addition
逆送 **gyakusō** send back
油送船 **yusōsen** oil tanker
油送管 **yusōkan** (oil) pipeline
放送 **hōsō** broadcast
放送局 **hōsōkyoku** broadcasting station
9 発送 **hassō** send, ship, forward
急送 **kyūsō** send by express, rush
持送 **mo(chi)oku(ri)** bracket, corbel
後送 **kōsō** send to the rear; send later

2

亻 冫

孑 阝

卩 刂

力

又 宀

亠 十

卜

疒

丷

厂 辶 6 ←

冂 几

匸

10 郵送 **yūsō** to mail
郵送料 **yūsōryō** postage
差送 **sa(shi)oku(ru)** send
荷送 **nioku(ri)** shipment, consignment
荷送人 **nioku(ri)nin** shipper
書送 **ka(ki)oku(ru)** write (to someone)
航送 **kōsō** ship (by ship/plane)
託送 **takusō** consignment
配送 **haisō** delivery, forwarding
11 運送 **unsō** transport, conveyance, shipping
運送会社 **unsō-gaisha** transport/express
　　company
運送店 **unsōten** forwarding agent, express
　　company
運送屋 **unsōya** forwarding agent, express
　　company
運送船 **unsōsen** cargo vessel, freighter
運送費 **unsōhi** transport/shipping expenses
運送業 **unsōgyō** transport business
運送業者 **unsōgyōsha** carrier, forwarding
　　agent
密送 **missō** send secretly
現送 **gensō** sending cash, shipping gold
移送 **isō** transfer, transport, remove
転送 **tensō** transmit, forward (mail)
12 葬送 **sōsō** attendance at a funeral
葬送行進曲 **sōsō kōshinkyoku** funeral march
順送 **jun'oku(ri)** send/pass on from person
　　to person
13 搬送 **hansō** convey, carry
電送 **densō** electrical transmission
電送写真 **densō shashin** telephoto
15 歓送 **kansō** a send-off
歓送会 **kansōkai** farewell party, send-off
16 積送 **sekisō, tsu(mi)oku(ri)** consignment,
　　shipment
輸送 **yusō** transport
輸送船 **yusōsen** transport ship
輸送量 **yusōryō** (volume of freight) traffic
輸送費 **yusōhi** shipping costs
輸送機 **yusōki** transport plane
20 護送 **gosō** escort, convoy
護送車 **gosōsha** paddy wagon
護送船 **gosōsen** convoy

————————— 3 —————————
5 生放送 **namahōsō** live broadcast
6 再放送 **saihōsō** rebroadcast
11 野辺送 **nobeoku(ri)** bury one's remains

————————— 4 —————————
6 多重放送 **tajū hōsō** multiplex broadcasting
有線放送 **yūsen hōsō** broadcasting by wire/
　　cable
8 実況放送 **jikkyō hōsō** on-the-spot broadcast
9 軍事輸送 **gunji yusō** military transport
12 無電放送 **muden hōsō** radio broadcast

迺 → 廼　**2q6.10**

2q6.10

廼　迺　　DAI, sunawachi in other words
　　　　　nanji thou, you
　　　　　no (possessive particle)

2q6.11

逅　　KŌ meet

————————— 2 —————————
16 邂逅 **kaikō** meet by chance, happen to meet

2q6.12

迴　　KAI go around

2q6.13

廻　迴　KAI, mawa(su) (tr.) turn
　　　　around　KAI, mawa(ru) (intr.)
　　　　turn around　megu(ru) go
　　　　around　megu(ri) girth

————————— 2 —————————
8 金廻 **kanemawa(ri)** circulation of money;
　　financial condition
13 猿廻 **sarumawa(shi)** monkey trainer
15 輪廻 **rinne** transmigration of souls

————————— 7 —————————

2q7.1

這　這　　SHA, ha(u) crawl, creep

————————— 1 —————————
3 這上 **ha(i)a(garu)** crawl up
這下 **ha(i)o(riru)** crawl down
這々 **hōhō** confusedly, in consternation
這々体 **hōhō(no)tei** hurriedly, precipitously
4 這込 **ha(i)ko(mu)** crawl into
5 這出 **ha(i)de(ru), ha(i)da(su)** crawl out
6 這回 **ha(i)mawa(ru)** crawl about
8 這松 **haimatsu** creeping pine
12 這登 **ha(i)nobo(ru)** crawl/clamber up

————————— 2 —————————
8 夜這 **yobai** creep in to see a woman
10 這這 **ha(i)ha(i)** (baby's) crawling
　　hōhō confusedly, in consternation
13 腹這 **haraba(i)** lying belly-down
15 横這 **yokoba(i)** crawl sideways

2q7.2 / 440

連 REN group, accompaniment
tsu(reru) take (someone) along
tsu(re) companion (ni) tsu(rete) as, along with, in proportion to
tsura(naru) stand in a row tsura(neru) link, put in a row

─────── 1 ───────

0 ソ連 **Soren** Soviet Union
2 連子 **tsure(k)ko** child brought by a second wife/husband
連子窓 **renjimado** lattice window
3 連山 **renzan** mountain range
4 連中 **renchū, renjū** companions, party, company, crowd, clique
連込 **tsu(re)ko(mu)** take (a lover) into a hotel)
連込宿 **tsu(re)ko(mi)yado** hotel catering to lovers, love/rendezvous hotel
連木 **rengi** wooden pestle
連日 **renjitsu** day after day, every day
5 連出 **tsu(re)da(su)** lead out, entice, abduct
連用 **ren'yō** continuous use
連用形 **ren'yōkei** stem (of a verb)
連去 **tsu(re)sa(ru)** lead away
連打 **renda** hit/strike/knock repeatedly
連句 **renku** linked verse
連立 **tsu(re)da(tsu)** accompany
renritsu alliance, coalition
連立内閣 **renritsu naikaku** coalition cabinet
連立方程式 **renritsu hōteishiki** simultaneous equations
6 連年 **rennen** every year
連休 **renkyū** consecutive holidays
連合 **rengō** union, league, federation, alliance, combination
tsu(re)a(i) spouse, mate
連合国 **rengōkoku** allied nations, allies
連合軍 **rengōgun** allied armies
連邦 **renpō** federation; federal
連名 **renmei** joint signature
連行 **renkō** take (a suspect to the police)
tsu(re)yu(ku) take (someone) along
7 連体形 **rentaikei** a participial adjective
連作 **rensaku** plant (a field) with the same crop year after year; story written by several writers in turn
連判 **renpan, renban** joint signature/seal
連判状 **renpanjō, renbanjō** jointly sealed compact
連坐 **renza** complicity
連吟 **rengin** duet, singing by two or more
連声 **renjō** (form of liaison illustrated by *an* + *on* pronounced *annon*)
8 連夜 **ren'ya** night after night, nightly

連呼 **renko** call/shout repeatedly
連枝 **renshi** brother (of a nobleman)
9 連発 **renpatsu** fire/shoot in rapid succession
連発銃 **renpatsujū** repeating firearm
連奏 **rensō** performance by two or more musicians
連係 **renkei** connection, liaison, contact
10 連借 **renshaku** joint debt
連帰 **tsu(re)kae(ru)** bring (someone) back/home
連帯 **rentai** solidarity; joint (liability)
連帯感 **rentaikan** (feeling/sense of) solidarity
連峰 **renpō** series of peaks, mountain range
連座 **renza** complicity
連珠 **renju** five-in-a-row game
連破 **renpa** successive wins
連記 **renki** list
11 連隊 **rentai** regiment
連隊長 **rentaichō** regimental commander
連隊旗 **rentaiki** regimental standard/colors
連動 **rendō** gears, linkage, drive
連添 **tsu(re)so(u)** be married to
連接 **rensetsu** connect
連理 **renri** (trees) with entwined branches
連累 **renrui** complicity
連敗 **renpai** successive defeats, losing streak
12 連弾曲 **rendankyoku** piano piece for four hands
連勝 **renshō** series of victories, winning streak
連衆 **tsu(re)shu** one's companions/party
連結 **renketsu** coupling, connection; consolidated
連結器 **renketsuki** coupler
連絡 **renraku** contact, liaison, communication; get/be in touch
連絡船 **renrakusen** ferryboat
13 連携 **renkei** in cooperation/concert with
連想 **rensō** association (of ideas)
連戦 **rensen** series of battles; battle after battle
連戦連勝 **rensen-renshō** succession of victories
連署 **rensho** joint signature
連盟 **renmei** league, federation, union
連続 **renzoku** continuous, consecutive, in a row
連載 **rensai** serialization
14 連歌 **renga** linked haiku
連綿 **renmen** consecutive, uninterrupted
連語 **rengo** compound word, phrase
連関 **renkan** relation, association, linkage
16 連濁 **rendaku** change of an unvoiced to a voiced sound in forming a compound word
17 連環 **renkan** links (of a chain)
18 連鎖 **rensa** chain, series

連鎖反応 **rensa hannō** chain reaction
連鎖店 **rensaten** chain store
連類 **renrui** same kind; accomplice
19 連覇 **renpa** successive championships
連禱 **rentō** litany
連繋 **renkei** connection, liaison, contact

──────── 2 ────────

1 一連 **ichiren** a series; a ream (of paper)
2 二連式 **nirenshiki** double, duplex
二連発 **nirenpatsu** double-barreled gun
二連銃 **nirenjū** double-barreled gun
4 不連続 **furenzoku** discontinuity
六連発 **roku renpatsu** six-chambered (revolver)
引連 **hi(ki)tsu(reru)** take (someone) along, bring with
5 打連 **u(chi)tsu(reru)** take (someone) along
8 注連飾 **shimekaza(ri)** sacred Shinto rope
注連縄 **shimenawa** sacred Shinto rope
国連 **Kokuren** United Nations, UN (short for 国際連合)
国連軍 **Kokurengun** UN troops
国連旗 **Kokurenki** UN flag
国連総会 **Kokuren Sōkai** UN General Assembly
10 流連 **ryūren** stay on
11 道連 **michizu(re)** traveling companion
常連 **jōren** regular companions/customers
13 愚連隊 **gurentai** hooligans, street gang
14 関連 **kanren** connection, relation, association
19 蘇連 **Soren** Soviet Union

──────── 3 ────────

2 二人連 **futarizu(re)** a party of two, couple
6 合従連衡 **gasshō-renkō** multi-party alliance (against a powerful enemy)
自動連結機 **jidō renketsuki** automatic coupler
7 伴天連 **Bateren** Portuguese Jesuit missionaries; Christianity
8 国際連合 **Kokusai Rengō** United Nations
取巻連 **to(ri)ma(ki)ren** one's entourage
9 連戦連勝 **rensen-renshō** succession of victories
10 家族連 **kazokuzu(re)** taking the family along
11 経団連 **Keidanren** Federation of Economic Organizations (Keidanren) (short for 経済団体連合)

──────── 4 ────────

4 中立労連 **Chūritsu Rōren** Federation of Independent Unions of Japan (short for 中立労働組合連絡会議)

2q7.3

HO flee, evade

迺

2q7.4 / 502

速

SOKU, haya(i) fast
haya(meru) quicken, accelerate
sumi(yaka) speedy, prompt

──────── 1 ────────

2 速力 **sokuryoku** speed, velocity
5 速写 **sokusha** quick copying; take a snapshot
6 速成 **sokusei** intensive training, short course
7 速決 **sokketsu** quick decision
8 速効 **sokkō** quick effect
速歩 **sokuho** fast walking, trot
9 速度 **sokudo** speed, velocity
速度計 **sokudokei** speedometer
10 速射 **sokusha** rapid fire
速射砲 **sokushahō** rapid-fire gun/cannon
速記 **sokki** shorthand
速記者 **sokkisha** shorthand writer, stenographer
速記術 **sokkijutsu** shorthand, stenography
速記録 **sokkiroku** shorthand notes
11 速達 **sokutatsu** special/express delivery
速球 **sokkyū** fast ball
速断 **sokudan** hasty conclusion; prompt decision
12 速報 **sokuhō** bulletin, news flash
速答 **sokutō** prompt reply
13 速戦即決 **sokusen-sokketsu** all-out surprise offensive, blitzkrieg
14 速算 **sokusan** rapid calculation
速読 **sokudoku** speed reading

──────── 2 ────────

5 加速度 **kasokudo** acceleration
迅速 **jinsoku** quick, prompt, speedy
目速 **mebaya(i)** quick to notice, sharp-eyed
6 全速力 **zensokuryoku** full/top speed
光速 **kōsoku** the speed of light
早速 **sassoku** at once, getting right to the point
7 快速 **kaisoku** high-speed; express (train)
快速船 **kaisokusen** high-speed ship
快速調 **kaisokuchō** allegro
初速 **shosoku** initial/muzzle velocity
足速 **ashibaya** quick, swift-footed
8 拙速 **sessoku** not elaborate but fast, rough-and-ready
9 変速 **hensoku** change speeds, shift gears
急速 **kyūsoku** prompt, swift, fast, speedy
急速度 **kyūsokudo** high speed
風速 **fūsoku** wind speed
風速計 **fūsokukei** anemometer
神速 **shinsoku** speed, swiftness
音速 **onsoku** the speed of sound
秒速 **byōsoku** speed (in meters) per second
10 高速 **kōsoku** high-speed; expressway
高速度 **kōsokudo** high speed

逸速 **ichihaya(ku)** quickly, promptly
流速 **ryūsoku** speed of a current
時速 **jisoku** speed per hour
敏速 **binsoku** promptness, alacrity
11 遅速 **chisoku** speed, how slow or fast
12 減速 **gensoku** speed reduction, deceleration

——————— 3 ———————

7 亜音速 **aonsoku** subsonic (speed)
即日速達 **sokujitsu sokutatsu** same-day
　　special delivery
12 超音速 **chōonsoku** supersonic speed
超高速度 **chōkōsokudo** superhigh-speed

2q7.5 / 1937

逓 遞

TEI successive; relay, send

——————— 1 ———————

9 逓信 **teishin** communications
12 逓減 **teigen** successive diminution

——————— 2 ———————

14 駅逓 **ekitei** postal service

酋 → 逎 **2q9.15**

2q7.6 / 1134

逐

CHIKU drive away; one by one, one
after another
o(u) drive away, pursue, follow

——————— 1 ———————

1 逐一 **chikuichi** one by one, in detail
4 逐日 **chikujitsu** day after day, daily
5 逐字的 **chikujiteki** word for word, literal
逐字訳 **chikujiyaku** word-for-word/literal
　　translation
6 逐年 **chikunen** year by year, annually
逐次 **chikuji** one by one, in sequence
7 逐条 **chikujō** section by section, point by
　　point
14 逐語的 **chikugoteki** word for word, literal
逐語訳 **chikugoyaku** word-for-word/literal
　　translation

——————— 2 ———————

7 角逐 **kakuchiku** compete, contend, vie
8 放逐 **hōchiku** expel
14 駆逐 **kuchiku** drive away, expel, get rid of
駆逐艦 **kuchikukan** destroyer

2q7.7

逑

KYŪ pair; gather, meet

2q7.8 / 1396

逝 逝

SEI, yu(ku) die

——————— 1 ———————

5 逝去 **seikyo** death
6 逝年 **yu(ku) toshi** (ring out) the old year
9 逝春 **yu(ku) haru** the departing spring

——————— 2 ———————

4 夭逝 **yōsei** premature death
6 早逝 **sōsei** early death
8 長逝 **chōsei** die, pass away
9 急逝 **kyusei** sudden/untimely death

2q7.9

逖

TEKI far

2q7.10 / 1685

透

TŌ, su(keru) shine through
su(ku) be transparent; leave a gap
su(kasu) look through; leave a space
su(kashi) watermark; openwork;
transparent **su(kasazu)** without delay/hesitation
tō(ru) shine through, permeate, penetrate
tō(su) let (light) through

——————— 1 ———————

5 透写 **tōsha** trace (out)
透写紙 **tōshashi** tracing paper
7 透見 **su(ki)mi** steal a glance, peep
8 透析 **tōseki** dialysis
透明 **tōmei** transparent
透明体 **tōmeitai** transparent body/medium
9 透通 **su(ki)tō(ru)** be transparent/see-through
11 透視 **tōshi** see through; fluoroscopy;
　　clairvoyance
透視力 **tōshiryoku** penetration; clairvoyant
　　powers
透視画法 **tōshigahō** perspective (drawing)
12 透絵 **su(kashi)e** a transparency (picture)
透間 **su(ki)ma** crevice, gap, opening, space
14 透察 **tōsatsu** insight, discernment
15 透徹 **tōtetsu** penetrate, permeate; be
　　transparent/intelligible

——————— 2 ———————

4 不透明 **futōmei** opaque
手透 **tesu(ki)** leisure, spare/idle time
7 見透 **mi(e)su(ku)** be transparent
misu(kasu) see through
8 肩透 **katasuka(shi)** dodging
10 浸透 **shintō** permeation, infiltration, osmosis
素透 **sudō(shi)** transparent, plain-glass
　　(eyeglasses)
14 滲透 **shintō** permeation, infiltration, osmosis

2

亻 冫
孑 阝
阝 刂
力 又
一 亠
宀
广 辶
門 几
匸

2q7.11 / 691

造 **ZŌ, tsuku(ru)** make, produce, build

── 1 ──

3 造上 **tsuku(ri)a(geru)** make, build up, complete
4 造化 **zōka** creation, nature
5 造本 **zōhon** making books
造付 **tsuku(ri)tsu(keru)** fasten firmly, build into
造石高 **zōkokudaka** brew, brewage
造石税 **zōkokuzei** liquor-making tax
6 造合 **tsuku(ri)a(waseru)** make and join together; make a duplicate
造次顛沛 **zōji-tenpai** a moment
造血 **zōketsu** blood making
造血剤 **zōketsuzai** blood-making medicine
7 造作 **zōsaku** house fixtures; facial features
zōsa trouble, difficulty
zōsa(nai) easy, simple
造作付 **zōsakutsu(ki)** furnished (house)
造兵 **zōhei** ordnance, arms manufacture
造兵廠 **zōheishō** arms factory, arsenal, armory
造形 **zōkei** molding, modeling
造形美術 **zōkei bijutsu** the plastic arts
造花 **zōka** (making) artificial flowers
造言 **zōgen** lie, fabrication, false report
造言飛語 **zōgen-higo** false report, wild rumor
8 造直 **tsuku(ri)nao(su)** remake, rebuild
造林 **zōrin** (re)forestation
造林学 **zōringaku** forestry
造物主 **Zōbutsushu** the Creator
造物者 **Zōbutsusha** the Creator
9 造型 **zōkei** molding, modeling
10 造酒 **zōshu** saké brewing
造酒屋 **zōshuya** saké brewer
造酒業 **zōshugyō** saké brewing industry
11 造船 **zōsen** shipbuilding
造船所 **zōsenjo** shipyard
造船業 **zōsengyō** shipbuilding industry
12 造営 **zōei** building, construction
造営物 **zōeibutsu** a building, structure
造営費 **zōeihi** construction costs
造替 **tsuku(ri)ka(eru)** remake, adapt
13 造園 **zōen** landscape gardening
造園術 **zōenjutsu** landscape gardening
造詣 **zōkei** scholarship, attainments
14 造鼻 **zōbi** nasal plastic surgery
造語 **zōgo** coined word
15 造幣 **zōhei** minting, coinage
造幣局 **zōheikyoku** the mint
16 造機 **zōki** engine construction
21 造艦 **zōkan** naval construction

── 2 ──

2 人造 **jinzō** artificial, synthetic, imitation
人造米 **jinzōmai** artificial rice
4 手造 **tezuku(ri)** handmade, homemade
5 石造 **ishizuku(ri), sekizō** masonry, of stone
7 乱造 **ranzō** overproduction; careless manufacture
形造 **katachizuku(ru)** form, shape, make
改造 **kaizō** remodel, convert, revamp
8 建造 **kenzō** build, construct
建造物 **kenzōbutsu** a building, structure
若造 **wakazō** youngster, stripling
9 俄造 **niwakazuku(ri)** makeshift, improvised
変造 **henzō** alter, deface, falsify, forge
急造 **kyūzō** build in a hurry
10 酒造 **shuzō** brewing, distilling
酒造家 **shuzōka** brewer, distiller
酒造場 **shuzōjō** brewery, distillery
酒造業 **shuzōgyō** brewery business
捏造 **netsuzō** fabrication, falsehood
荷造 **nizuku(ri)** packing
11 偽造 **gizō** forgery
密造 **mitsuzō** illicit manufacture, moonshining
粗造 **arazuku(ri)** rough-wrought
12 創造 **sōzō** creation
創造力 **sōzōryoku** creative power
創造的 **sōzōteki** creative
営造 **eizō** building, construction
営造物 **eizōbutsu** building, structure
無造作 **muzōsa** with ease; simple, artless
13 塑造 **sozō** modeling, molding, plastic (arts)
新造 **shinzō** newly built/made; wife, Mrs.
新造語 **shinzōgo** newly coined word
14 構造 **kōzō** structure, construction
構造上 **kōzōjō** structurally
構造主義 **kōzō shugi** structuralism
模造 **mozō** imitation
模造者 **mozōsha** imitator
模造品 **mozōhin** imitation
模造紙 **mozōshi** vellum paper
製造 **seizō** manufacture
製造元 **seizōmoto** the manufacturer
製造者 **seizōsha** manufacturer
製造業 **seizōgyō** manufacturing industry
15 鋳造 **chūzō** casting; minting, coinage
鋳造所 **chūzōsho** mint; foundry
16 築造 **chikuzō** building, construction
17 鍛造 **tanzō** forging
18 濫造 **ranzō** overproduction, slipshod manufacture
19 贋造 **ganzō** counterfeiting, forgery, fabrication
贋造者 **ganzōsha** counterfeiter, forger
贋造紙幣 **ganzō shihei** counterfeit currency
20 醸造 **jōzō** brewing, distilling
醸造学 **jōzōgaku** science of brewing

醸造所 **jōzōsho** brewery, distillery
醸造酒 **jōzōshu** brewage, liquor
醸造家 **jōzōka** brewer, distiller
醸造業 **jōzōgyō** brewing industry

──────── 3 ────────
10 格子造 **kōshi-zuku(ri)** latticework
校倉造 **azekura-zuku(ri)** (ancient architectural style using triangular logs which interlace and protrude at the building's corners)
書院造 **shoinzuku(ri)** (a traditional architectural style)
12 御新造 **goshinzo, goshinzō** new wife of a prominent person; wife
13 寝殿造 **shindenzuku(ri)** (a palace-style architecture)

──────── 4 ────────
4 天地創造 **tenchi sōzō** the Creation

──────── 5 ────────
17 環太平洋造山帯 **kan-Taiheiyō zōzantai** circum-Pacific orogeny

2q7.12

逡

SHUN shrink back

──────── 1 ────────
5 逡巡 **shunjun** hesitate, be reluctant

逕 → 径 3i5.5

2q7.13

逞

TEI, takuma(shii) big and strong, brawny, stalwart

──────── 2 ────────
4 不逞 **futei** insubordinate, rebellious, lawless

2q7.14

逍

SHŌ saunter, mosey

──────── 1 ────────
13 逍遙 **shōyō** walk, amble

2q7.15

逢

HŌ, a(u) meet

──────── 1 ────────
4 逢引 **a(i)bi(ki)** rendezvous, assignation, tryst

12 逢着 **hōchaku** encounter, face
19 逢瀬 **ōse** lovers' secret meeting, tryst, assignation

──────── 2 ────────
7 忍逢 **shino(bi)a(i)** clandestine/secret meeting, rendezvous, tryst

2q7.16 / 1072

途　途

TO way, road

──────── 1 ────────
3 途上 **tojō** on the way/road
4 途中 **tochū** on the way, en route
途中下車 **tochū gesha** stopover, layover
途中計時 **tochū keiji** lap time (in races)
途切 **togi(reru)** be interrupted, break off
途切途切 **togi(re)togi(re)** disconnected, intermittent
途方 **tohō(mo nai)** exorbitant, extraordinary, absurd
途方暮 **tohō (ni) ku(reru)** be at a loss, not know what to do
6 途次 **toji** on the way, en route
12 途絶 **toda(eru)** come to a stop
tozetsu suspension, interruption
14 途端 **totan** the (very) moment/minute, just when
19 途轍 **totetsu(mo nai)** inordinate, absurd

──────── 2 ────────
1 一途 **ichizu** wholeheartedly　**itto** way, course; the only way
3 三途川 **Sanzu (no) Kawa** the River Styx
山途 **santo** mountain road
4 中途 **chūto** midway, halfway
中途半端 **chūto-hanpa** half finished, incomplete
方途 **hōto** means, way
5 半途 **hanto** halfway; unfinished
用途 **yōto** use, purpose
目途 **mokuto** aim, goal, end, object
6 先途 **sendo** fateful turning point (in battle); death
7 別途 **betto** special
8 長途 **chōto** a long way/distance
使途 **shito** purpose for which money is spent
征途 **seito** military expedition; journey
9 前途 **zento** the road ahead, one's future prospects
前途有望 **zento yūbō** having a promising future
10 帰途 **kito** homeward journey
冥途 **meido** hades, realm of the dead
12 費途 **hito** expense item

イ　　2
冫
孑
阝
卩
刂
力
又
宀
亠
十
卜
夂
丷
厂
辶　7←
冂
几
匚

─────── 3 ───────

9 発展途上国 **hattentojōkoku** developing country
途切途切 **togi(re)togi(re)** disconnected, intermittent

2q7.17

迯

sako, seko ravine, valley

2q7.18 / 150

通

TSŪ, TSU go through, pass; in common; (as suffix) thorough knowledge of, an expert; (counter for letters/copies) **tō(ru)** go through, pass **tō(ri)** street; way, manner **-dō(ri)** street; as per, as, in accordance with, according to **tō(su)** let through **kayo(u)** go to and from, commute

─────── 1 ───────

0 通じる/ずる **tsū(jiru/zuru)** pass, run, lead to; be well versed in; be understood, make oneself understood, get through
1 通一片 **tō(ri)-ippen** passing, casual, perfunctory
通一遍 **tō(ri)-ippen** passing, casual, perfunctory
2 通人 **tsūjin** man about town
通力 **tsūriki** supernatural power
4 通切符 **tō(shi)kippu** through ticket
通分 **tsūbun** reduction (of fractions) to a common denominator
5 通矢 **tō(shi)ya** long-distance archery
通弁 **tsūben** interpreter, interpreting
通史 **tsūshi** outline of history
通用 **tsūyō** be in common use, be honored/valid, pass
通用口 **tsūyōguchi** service entrance, side door
通用門 **tsūyōmon** side door, service entrance
通用期間 **tsūyō kikan** period of (a ticket's) validity
通好 **tsūkō** friendship, amity
6 通気 **tsūki** ventilation
通気孔 **tsūkikō** vent, air hole
通合 **tō(ri)a(waseru)** happen to come along **tsū(ji)a(u)** plot together
通交 **tsūkō** diplomatic relations
通名 **tō(ri)na** popular name, commonly known as
通行 **tsūkō** passing, passage, transit, traffic **tō(ri)yu(ku)** pass by
通行人 **tsūkōnin** passer-by, pedestrian
通行止 **tsūkōdo(me)** Road Closed, No Thoroughfare
通行税 **tsūkōzei** toll, transit duty

通有 **tsūyū** in common
通有性 **tsūyūsei** common trait/characteristic
7 通抜 **tō(ri)nu(keru)** pass through
通告 **tsūkoku** notification, notice
通狂言 **tō(shi)kyōgen** (presentation of) a whole play
通学 **tsūgaku** attending school
通学生 **tsūgakusei** day student
通言 **tsūgen** popular saying
通言葉 **tō(ri)kotoba** catchword, jargon, argot, common phrase
8 通事 **tsūji** interpreter
通例 **tsūrei** usual(ly)
通念 **tsūnen** common(ly accepted) idea
通夜 **tsuya** wake, vigil
通知 **tsūchi** notification, notice
通知表 **tsūchihyō** report card
通知書 **tsūchisho** notice
通者 **tō(ri)mono** well-known person; man about town
通性 **tsūsei** common characteristic/property
通雨 **tō(ri)ame** passing shower
9 通信 **tsūshin** (tele)communications, correspondence, message, news, dispatch, report
通信社 **tsūshinsha** news agency
通信制 **tsūshinsei** system of education by correspondence
通信員 **tsūshin'in** correspondent, reporter
通信教育 **tsūshin kyōiku** education by correspondence
通信販売 **tsūshin hanbai** mail order
通信費 **tsūshinhi** postage, communications expenses
通信網 **tsūshinmō** communications network
通信簿 **tsūshinbo** report card
通信欄 **tsūshinran** correspondence column
通俗 **tsūzoku** popular, conventional
通俗化 **tsūzokuka** popularization
通俗的 **tsūzokuteki** popular
通院 **tsūin** go to hospital regularly (as an outpatient)
通風 **tsūfū** ventilation
通風孔 **tsūfūkō** vent, air hole
通風器 **tsūfūki** ventilator, aerator
通草 **akebi** (a type of shrub having tendrils)
通相場 **tō(ri)sōba** market price; accepted custom
通計 **tsūkei** total
通則 **tsūsoku** general rule
10 通称 **tsūshō** popular name, commonly known as
通航 **tsūkō** navigate, sail, ply
11 通商 **tsūshō** commerce, trade
通商産業省 **Tsūshōsangyōshō** Ministry of International Trade and Industry

通達 **tsūtatsu** communication, a circular (notice); proficiency, skill

通運 **tsūun** transport, forwarding, express

通道 **tō(ri)michi** pasage, path, route, one's way to

通過 **tsūka, tō(ri)su(giru)** pass by/through

通過駅 **tsūka eki** station at which the train does not stop

通掛 **tō(ri)ka(karu)** happen to come along **tō(ri)ga(kari), tō(ri)ga(ke)** while passing by

通帳 **tsūchō, kayo(i)chō** bankbook; chit book

通常 **tsūjō** normal(ly), general(ly), ordinary, regular

通常国会 **tsūjō kokkai** ordinary Diet session

通常服 **tsūjōfuku** everyday clothes

通廊 **tsūrō** corridor, passageway

通患 **tsūkan** a common misgiving; a common evil

通産相 **tsūsanshō** Minister of International Trade and Industry

通産省 **Tsūsanshō** MITI, Ministry of International Trade and Industry (short for 通商産業省)

通訳 **tsūyaku** interpreting; interpreter

通訳官 **tsūyakukan** official interpreter

通販 **tsūhan** mail order (short for 通信販売)

通貨 **tsūka** currency

12 通勤 **tsūkin** commute to work

通報 **tsūhō** report, dispatch, bulletin, news

通暁 **tsūgyō** be well versed in, have a thorough knowledge of

通越 **tō(ri)ko(su)** go past/beyond, pass through

通番号 **tō(shi)bangō** serial number

通筋 **tō(ri)suji** route, course, road

13 通義 **tsūgi** universal principle; the usual interpretation

通牒 **tsūchō** notification

通解 **tsūkai** commentary

通詰 **kayo(i)tsu(meru)** visit frequently, frequent

通話 **tsūwa** telephone call/conversation

通話口 **tsūwaguchi** (telephone) mouthpiece

通話料 **tsūwaryō** telephone-call charge

通路 **tsūro** aisle, passageway, path **kayo(i)ji** path, route

通電 **tsūden** cause an electric current to flow; circular telegram

14 通語 **tsūgo** jargon, cant

通説 **tsūsetsu** common opinion, popular view

通関 **tsūkan** customs clearance

15 通弊 **tsūhei** a common evil

通論 **tsūron** outline, introduction

16 通薬 **tsū(ji)gusuri** a laxative

通謀 **tsūbō** conspire with, work in collusion

17 通覧 **tsūran** look over; read through

18 通観 **tsūkan** general view/survey

21 通魔 **tō(ri)ma** phantom (killer/slasher)

─────────── 2 ───────────

1 一通 **hitotō(ri)** in general, briefly **ittsū** one copy (of a document)

2 二通 **nitsū** two copies **futatō(ri)** two ways/kinds, duplicate

人通 **hitodō(ri)** pedestrian traffic

3 大通 **ōdō(ri)** a main street, thoroughfare

4 元通 **motodō(ri)** as before

内通 **naitsū** secret understanding, collusion

中通 **chūdō(ri)** medium quality **nakadō(ri)** intermediate street

文通 **buntsū** correspondence

木通 **akebi** (a type of shrub having tendrils)

5 本通 **hondō(ri)** main street, boulevard

立通 **ta(chi)dō(shi)** standing all the way/while

目通 **medō(ri)** audience with; eye level **me (o) tō(su)** glance through

6 全通 **zentsū** be opened to through traffic

交通 **kōtsū** traffic, transport, communication

交通公社 **Kōtsū Kōsha** Japan Travel Bureau

交通費 **kōtsūhi** transportation expenses

交通機関 **kōtsu kikan** transportation facilities

共通 **kyōtsū** in common, shared

共通点 **kyōtsūten** something in common

共通語 **kyōtsūgo** common language

光通信 **hikari tsūshin** optical communication

7 似通 **nikayo(u)** resemble closely

角通 **kakutsū** sumo expert

吹通 **fu(ki)tō(su)** blow through; keep blowing

見通 **mitō(shi)** prospects, outlook, forecast; unobstructed view

私通 **shitsū** illicit love affair

言通 **i(i)tō(su)** persist in saying

8 刺通 **sa(shi)tō(su)** stab through, pierce

夜通 **yodō(shi)** all night long

直通 **chokutsū** direct communication, nonstop service

押通 **o(shi)tō(su)** push through, accomplish

突通 **tsu(ki)tō(ru)** pierce, penetrate

9 便通 **bentsū** bowel movement

変通 **hentsū** versatility, flexibility

透通 **su(ki)tō(ru)** be transparent/see-through

風通 **kazetō(shi)** ventilation

姦通 **kantsū** adultery

姦通罪 **kantsūzai** (the crime of) adultery

面通 **mendō(shi)** (police/identify-the-culprit) lineup

神通力 **jintsūriki, jinzūriki** supernatural power

思通 **omo(i)dō(ri)** as one likes, to one's satisfaction

食通 **shokutsū** gourmet

2

亻
冫
子
阝
卩
刂
力
又
宀
亠
十
匕
夂
丷
厂
辶 7
冂
几
匸

10 射通 **itō(su)** shoot through
流通 **ryūtsū** distribution, circulation
11 疎通 **sotsū** mutual understanding
疏通 **sotsū** mutual understanding
密通 **mittsū** illicit connection/intercourse, adultery
望通 **nozo(mi)dō(ri)** as desired
貫通 **kantsū** pass through, pierce
tsuranu(ki)tō(su) carry out (one's will)
12 着通 **kidō(shi)** wearing (the same clothes) all the time
普通 **futsū** ordinary, common, usual
普通人 **futsūjin** average person
普通選挙 **futsū senkyo** universal suffrage
遣通 **ya(ri)tō(su)** carry/see through, complete, accomplish
湯通 **yudō(shi)** steaming (cloth)
勝通 **ka(chi)tō(su)** win successive victories
幾通 **ikutō(ri)** how many ways
ikutsū how many copies/letters
開通 **kaitsū** opening to traffic
13 裏通 **uradō(ri)** alley, side street
14 精通 **seitsū** be well versed in
読通 **yo(mi)tō(su)** read it through
15 劇通 **gekitsū** drama expert
潮通 **shiodō(shi)** flow of seawater (over a beach)
罷通 **maka(ri)tō(ru)** force/have one's way, go unchallenged
16 融通 **yūzū** accommodation, loan; versatility

——————— 3 ———————

1 一方通行 **ippō tsūkō** one-way traffic
3 千枚通 **senmaidō(shi)** awl
4 予想通 **yosōdō(ri)** as expected
天眼通 **tengantsū** clairvoyance
文字通 **mojidō(ri)** literal(ly)
片側通行 **katagawa tsūkō** One Way (Traffic)
5 左側通行 **hidarigawa tsūkō** Keep Left
目抜通 **menu(ki)dō(ri)** main thoroughfare
6 気脈通 **kimyaku (o) tsū(jiru)** have a secret understanding with, be in collusion with
9 軍事通 **gunjitsū** military expert
海岸通 **kaigandō(ri)** road along the coast
10 消息通 **shōsokutsū** well informed person
12 貯金通帳 **chokin tsūchō** bankbook
13 電車通 **denshadō(ri)** street with a tramway
15 諸車通行止 **Shosha Tsūkōdo(me)** No Thoroughfare

——————— 4 ———————

1 一方交通 **ippō kōtsū** one-way traffic
6 有無相通 **umu-aitsū(jiru)** help each other, be complementary
9 音信不通 **onshin-futsū, inshin-futsū** no news of, haven't heard from

2q7.19

逗 逗　**TŌ** stop

——————— 1 ———————

2 逗子 **Zushi** (city, Kanagawa-ken)
10 逗留 **tōryū** stay, sojourn
逗留客 **tōryūkyaku** guest, visitor, sojourner

——————— 8 ———————

2q8.1 / 437

進　**SHIN, susu(mu)** advance, progress
susu(meru) advance, promote

——————— 1 ———————

0 2 進法 **nishinhō** binary (notation)
1 0 進法 **jisshinhō** decimal (notation)
1 6 進法 **jūrokushinhō** hexadecimal (notation)
2 進入 **shinnyū** enter, penetrate, go/come in
3 進上 **shinjō** give, present
4 進化 **shinka** evolution
進化論 **shinkaron** theory of evolution
進化論者 **shinkaronsha** evolutionist
進水 **shinsui** launch (a ship)
進水式 **shinsuishiki** launching ceremony
5 進出 **shinshutsu** advance, march, inroads, push
susu(mi)de(ru) step forward
6 進行 **shinkō** advance, progress, proceed
進行係 **shinkōgakari** person to expedite the proceedings, steering committee
7 進呈 **shintei** give, present
進呈本 **shinteihon** complimentary copy
進呈者 **shinteisha** presenter
進学 **shingaku** entrance to a higher school
進攻 **shinkō** attack, drive, advance upon
進言 **shingen** advice, proposal
8 進退 **shintai** advance or retreat, movement; course of action, attitude; resigning or staying on
進歩 **shinpo** progress, advance
進歩主義 **shinpo shugi** progressivism
進歩的 **shinpoteki** progressive
進歩党 **shinpotō** progressive party
進物 **shinmotsu** present, gift
進取 **shinshu** enterprising
9 進発 **shinpatsu** march off, start
進軍 **shingun** a march, an advance
進軍中 **shingunchū** on the march
進度 **shindo** (extent of) progress
進級 **shinkyū** promotion (to a higher grade)
10 進捗 **shinchoku** progress, advance
進展 **shinten** development, progress
進航 **shinkō** proceed, sail on

進貢 **shinkō** pay tribute
11 進運 **shin'un** progress, advance
12 進塁 **shinrui** advance (to second base)
13 進路 **shinro** course, way, route
14 進境 **shinkyō** progress, improvement
15 進撃 **shingeki** attack, charge, advance, onslaught
進駐 **shinchū** stationing, occupation
進駐軍 **shinchūgun** army of occupation
17 進講 **shinkō** give a lecture in the presence of the emperor

––––––––––– 2 –––––––––––

1 一進一退 **isshin-ittai** advance and retreat, fluctuating
2 二進法 **nishinhō** binary notation/system
十進 **jisshin** decimal
十進法 **jisshinhō** decimal/base-10 notation
3 寸進 **sunshin** inch along
4 亢進 **kōshin** rise, become exacerbated
日進月歩 **nisshin-geppo** rapid/constant progress
5 北進 **hokushin** advance northward
6 先進 **senshin** advance; seniority
先進国 **senshinkoku** advanced/developed nation
行進 **kōshin** march
行進曲 **kōshinkyoku** a (musical) march
共進会 **kyōshinkai** competitive exhibition, prize show
7 改進 **kaishin** reform, progress
改進的 **kaishinteki** progressive
改進党 **kaishintō** progressive party
8 盲進 **mōshin** advance recklessly, plunge headlong
直進 **chokushin** advance/go straight ahead
逆進 **gyakushin** backward movement
注進 **chūshin** information, warning
押進 **o(shi)susu(mu)** press onward/ahead
突進 **tosshin** rush, onrush, dash, charge
昇進 **shōshin** promotion, advancement
9 発進 **hasshin** takeoff, blast-off
促進 **sokushin** promote, encourage
促進剤 **sokushinzai** accelerator, accelerant
陞進 **shōshin** promotion, advancement
勇進 **yūshin** march bravely onward
南進 **nanshin** advance south
急進 **kyūshin** rapid progress; radical, extreme
急進主義 **kyūshin shugi** radicalism
急進的 **kyūshinteki** radical, extreme
急進派 **kyūshinha** radicals
急進党 **kyūshintō** radical party, radicals
前進 **zenshin** advance, drive, progress
挺進 **teishin** go ahead of, dash forward
挺進隊 **teishintai** advance corps
後進 **kōshin** coming along behind; one's juniors/successors; back up

後進地域 **kōshin chiiki** underdeveloped region
後進国 **kōshinkoku** backward country
後進性 **kōshinsei** backward
栄進 **eishin** promotion, advancement
10 猛進 **mōshin** rush forward, plunge ahead
特進 **tokushin** special promotion
貢進 **kōshin** pay tribute
11 推進 **suishin** propulsion, drive
推進力 **suishinryoku** thrust, impulse
寄進 **kishin** contribution, donation
累進 **ruishin** successive promotions; progressive, graduated
累進税 **ruishinzei** progressive/graduated tax
転進 **tenshin** shift one's position
12 勝進 **ka(chi)susu(mu)** win and advance to the next rank/round
詠進 **eishin** presentation of a poem (to the Court)
13 勧進 **kanjin** soliciting religious contributions
勧進元 **kanjinmoto** promoter, sponsor
勧進帳 **kanjinchō** subscription book
新進 **shinshin** rising, up-and-coming
14 漸進 **zenshin** gradual progress, steady advance
漸進的 **zenshinteki** gradual, moderate
増進 **zōshin** increase, furtherance, improvement
精進 **shōjin** diligence, devotion; purification
精進日 **shōjinbi** day of abstinence (from flesh foods)
精進料理 **shōjin ryōri** vegetarian dishes
精進揚 **shōjin'a(ge)** vegetable tempura
精進落 **shōjin'o(chi)** first meat after abstinence
15 邁進 **maishin** push/press on, strive
調進 **chōshin** prepare, supply
16 奮進 **funshin** pushing vigorously forward
20 驀進 **bakushin** rush onward
21 躍進 **yakushin** advance by leaps and bounds

––––––––––– 4 –––––––––––

4 心悸亢進 **shinki kōshin** palpitations
心悸昂進 **shinki kōshin** palpitations
11 猪突猛進 **chototsu mōshin** headlong rush
販売促進 **hanbai sokushin** sales promotion
12 葬送行進曲 **sōsō kōshinkyoku** funeral march

2q8.2 / 891

TAI catch up with

逮

––––––––––– 1 –––––––––––

8 逮夜 **taiya** eve of a death anniversary
10 逮捕 **taiho** arrest, capture
逮捕状 **taihojō** arrest warrant

2

イ 彳 孑 阝 阝 刂 力 又 宀 亠 十 ㇛ ⺍ ⺌ 厂 辶 ⼋ 冂 匚

2q8.3 / 1003

遊

YŪ, YU play; be idle; wander
aso(bu) play, enjoy oneself; take a
holiday; be idle **aso(baseru/basu)** let
play; leave idle; deign to
susa(bi) pastime, amusement

───────── 1 ─────────

2 遊人 **aso(bi)nin** gambler; jobless person
遊子 **yūshi** wanderer, traveler
3 遊女 **yūjo, aso(bi)me** prostitute
遊女屋 **yūjoya** brothel
遊山 **yusan** excursion, outing
遊弋 **yūyoku** cruise
5 遊民 **yūmin** idlers; the unemployed
遊半分 **aso(bi)hanbun** half in fun
遊好 **aso(bi)zu(ki)** pleasure seeker
6 遊休 **yūkyū** idle, unused
遊休資本 **yūkyū shihon** idle capital
遊仲間 **aso(bi)nakama** playmate
遊行 **yūkō** tour, wander; movement (of a
heavenly body)
7 遊里 **yūri** red-light district
遊技 **yūgi** games, amusement
遊技場 **yūgijō** place of amusement
遊吟 **yūgin** itinerant singing and reciting
遊君 **yūkun** courtesan
遊芸 **yūgei** music and dancing
遊学 **yūgaku** study far from home
遊言葉 **aso(base)kotoba** word ending with
-asobase, characteristic of very polite
feminine speech
8 遊泳 **yūei** swimming
遊泳術 **yūeijutsu** how to get along in the world
遊歩 **yūho** walk, stroll, promenade
遊牧 **yūboku** nomadic
遊金 **yūkin** idle money/funds
9 遊俠 **yūkyō** chivalrous man
遊郭 **yūkaku** red-light district
遊軍 **yūgun** reserve corps, flying column
遊客 **yūkyaku, yūkaku** excursionist; brothel
frequenter
遊相手 **aso(bi)aite** playmate
遊星 **yūsei** planet
遊食 **yūshoku** live in idleness
10 遊時間 **aso(bi)jikan** playtime, recess
11 遊動 **yūdō** not stationary, movable, mobile
遊動円木 **yūdō enboku** suspended horizontal
log, swinging pole (playground equipment)
遊動隊 **yūdōtai** mobile corps
遊猟 **yūryō** hunting
遊猟家 **yūryōka** hunter
遊猟期 **yūryōki** hunting season
遊船 **yūsen** pleasure boat, yacht
遊船宿 **yūsen'yado** boathouse

12 遊場 **aso(bi)ba** playground
遊廓 **yūkaku** red-light district
遊惰 **yūda** indolent, idle
13 遊園地 **yūenchi** amusement/theme park
遊楽 **yūraku** amusement, pleasure, recreation
遊資 **yūshi** idle capital/funds
14 遊歴 **yūreki** tour, pleasure trip
遊暮 **aso(bi)ku(rasu)** spend one's days in
idleness
遊説 **yūzei** speaking tour, political campaigning
遊説員 **yūzeiin** stumping candidate, election
canvassers
15 遊撃 **yūgeki** hit-and-run attack; shortstop
遊撃手 **yūgekishu** shortstop
遊撃隊 **yūgekitai** flying column, commando
unit
遊撃戦 **yūgekisen** guerrilla warfare
遊蕩 **yūtō** debauchery, licentiousness
遊蕩児 **yūtōji** dissipated person, fast liver
遊戯 **yūgi** games, amusement, entertainment
aso(bi)tawamu(reru) play, frolic
遊戯的 **yūgiteki** playful, sportive
16 遊興 **yūkyō** pleasure seeking, merrymaking
遊興者 **yūkyōsha** carouser, reveler
遊興税 **yūkyōzei** entertainment tax
遊興費 **yūkyōhi** amusement expenses
17 遊覧 **yūran** excursion, sightseeing
遊覧地 **yūranchi** pleasure resort, tourist point
遊覧客 **yūrankyaku** sightseers,
holidaymakers
遊覧船 **yūransen** excursion boat
18 遊離 **yūri** isolate, separate
遊離酸 **yūrisan** free acid

───────── 2 ─────────

3 川遊 **kawaaso(bi)** go boating/swimming in a
river
口遊 **kuchizusa(mu), kuchizusa(bu)** hum,
sing to oneself
4 水遊 **mizuaso(bi)** playing with/in water
手遊 **teaso(bi)** playing; plaything; gambling
火遊 **hiaso(bi)** playing with fire
5 外遊 **gaiyū** foreign travel/trip
巡遊 **jun'yū** tour
6 西遊 **seiyū, saiyū** trip to the west/West
再遊 **saiyū** return visit, second trip
回遊 **kaiyū** excursion; migratory
糸遊 **itoyū** shimmering of heated air
舟遊 **funaaso(bi), shūyū** boating
7 来遊 **raiyū** visit
吟遊詩人 **gin'yū shijin** troubadour, minstrel
8 夜遊 **yoaso(bi)** nighttime amusements
周遊 **shūyū** tour, excursion, round trip
周遊券 **shūyūken** excursion ticket
9 浮遊 **fuyū** float, waft, be suspended

浮遊生物 **fuyū seibutsu** plankton
客遊 **kakuyū** traveling abroad
10 宴遊 **en'yū** feasting and carousing
11 野遊 **noaso(bi)** picnic, outing
曽遊 **sōyū** previous visit
清遊 **seiyū** excursion, pleasure trip
悪遊 **waruaso(bi)** prank; evil pleasures
船遊 **funaaso(bi)** boating
雪遊 **yukiaso(bi)** playing in the snow
13 隠遊 **kaku(re)aso(bi)** clandestine visit to a red-light district
夢遊病者 **muyūbyōsha** sleepwalker
園遊会 **en'yūkai** garden party
14 豪遊 **gōyū** extravagant merrymaking, spree
歴遊 **rekiyū** tour
漫遊 **man'yū** trip, tour, travel
漫遊客 **man'yūkyaku** tourist, sightseer
18 雛遊 **hinaaso(bi)** playing with dolls (arranged on tiers)

——————— 3 ———————

8 物見遊山 **monomi yusan** pleasure trip
9 室内遊戯 **shitsunai yūgi** indoor/parlor games
10 桃色遊戯 **momo-iro yūgi** sex play

2q8.4

I long; winding, oblique

2q8.5

KI highway

達 → 達 **2q9.8**

2q8.6 / 734

ITSU flee, escape, be a recluse; stray from, digress; excel; be spirited **so(reru)** miss the mark; stray from, digress
so(rasu) avert, divert, dodge **haya(ru)** be rash/impetuous/impatient

——————— 1 ———————

0 逸する **is(suru)** miss (a chance), let escape; deviate from
4 逸文 **itsubun** lost writings
5 逸矢 **so(re)ya** stray arrow
逸出 **isshutsu** escape; excel
逸民 **itsumin** retired person, recluse

逸早 **ichihaya(ku)** quickly, promptly
7 逸走 **issō** scamper away, escape
逸材 **itsuzai** person of exceptional talent
逸足 **issoku** swift horse; prodigy
8 逸事 **itsuji** anecdote
9 逸速 **ichihaya(ku)** quickly, promptly
逸品 **ippin** superb article, masterpiece
10 逸書 **issho** lost book
11 逸脱 **itsudatsu** deviation, departure
逸球 **ikkyū** muffed ball
12 逸弾 **so(re)dama** stray bullet
13 逸楽 **itsuraku** idle pursuit of pleasure
逸話 **itsuwa** anecdote
14 逸聞 **itsubun** something not generally known
16 逸興 **ikkyō** very interesting/amusing

——————— 2 ———————

6 安逸 **an'itsu** idleness
7 秀逸 **shūitsu** superb, masterly
8 放逸 **hōitsu** self-indulgence, debauchery
9 俊逸 **shun'itsu** excellence, genius
独逸 **Doitsu** Germany
11 淫逸 **in'itsu** debauchery
12 散逸 **san'itsu** be scattered and lost
20 飄逸 **hyōitsu** buoyant, airy, aloof

2q8.7 / 92

週

SHŪ week

——————— 1 ———————

4 週日 **shūjitsu** weekday
5 週末 **shūmatsu** weekend
週刊 **shūkan** (published) weekly
週刊誌 **shūkanshi** a weekly (magazine)
6 週休 **shūkyū** weekly day off
12 週報 **shūhō** weekly bulletin/newspaper
週番 **shūban** duty for the week
週給 **shūkyū** weekly pay
週評 **shūhyō** weekly review
週間 **shūkan** week

——————— 2 ———————

1 一週 **isshū** a week
一週間 **isshūkan** a week
2 二週間 **nishūkan** two weeks, fortnight
4 今週 **konshū** this week
6 毎週 **maishū** every week, weekly
先週 **senshū** last week
7 来週 **raishū** next week
9 前週 **zenshū** last week, the week before
12 隔週 **kakushū** every other week

——————— 3 ———————

6 再来週 **saraishū** the week after next
8 受難週 **junanshū** Passion Week

———————— 9 ————————

2q9.1 / 1641

遇 **GŪ, GU** treat, deal with; meet
a(u) meet, encounter

———————— 1 ————————

0 遇する **gū(suru)** treat, deal with; entertain, receive

———————— 2 ————————

4 不遇 **fugū** misfortune, adversity; obscurity
5 礼遇 **reigū** cordial reception; honors, privileges
　処遇 **shogū** treatment
7 冷遇 **reigū** cold reception/treatment
8 厚遇 **kōgū** warm welcome, hospitality
　知遇 **chigū** favor, friendship
　奇遇 **kigū** chance meeting
9 待遇 **taigū** treatment, reception, entertainment, (hotel) service; salary, remuneration
10 殊遇 **shugū** special favor, cordial treatment
　配遇 **haigū** combination; spouse
　配遇者 **haigūsha** spouse
13 遭遇 **sōgū** encounter
　遭遇戦 **sōgūsen** encounter, engagement
14 境遇 **kyōgū** circumstances, environment
　酷遇 **kokugū** maltreatment
16 薄遇 **hakugū** cold/inhospitable reception
17 優遇 **yūgū** warm welcome, hospitality, favorable treatment
19 寵遇 **chōgū** special favor, patronage

———————— 4 ————————

3 千載一遇 **senzai-ichigū** a rare experience, chance of a lifetime
20 轗軻不遇 **kanka-fugū** ill fortune and lack of public recognition, obscurity

2q9.2

遁 遁遯 **TON** flee, hide

———————— 1 ————————

5 遁世 **tonsei** seclusion
　遁世者 **tonseisha** recluse, hermit
7 遁走 **tonsō** flee, (on the) run
13 遁辞 **tonji** excuse, evasion

———————— 2 ————————

13 隠遁 **inton** retirement, seclusion

2q9.3

遐 **KA** far, distant

遯 → 遁 **2q9.2**

2q9.4

遜 遜 **SON** inferior; humble
herikuda(ru) be humble/modest

———————— 1 ————————

6 遜色 **sonshoku** inferior

———————— 2 ————————

4 不遜 **fuson** arrogant, presumptuous
17 謙遜 **kenson** modesty, humility

———————— 4 ————————

13 傲岸不遜 **gōgan-fuson** arrogant, insolent, presumptuous

2q9.5

遑 **KŌ** flurried; leisure time
itoma time (to spare)

———————— 1 ————————

12 遑無 **itoma (ga) na(i)** have no time (to enumerate/react)

———————— 3 ————————

8 枚挙遑無 **maikyo (ni) itoma (ga) na(i)** too numerous to mention

2q9.6

遏 **ATSU** stop; suppress

2q9.7

逼 逼 **HITSU, HYOKU, sema(ru)** be pressing

———————— 1 ————————

7 逼迫 **hippaku** (money) stringency, austerity

遥 → 遙 **2q10.3**

2q9.8 / 448

達 達 **TATSU** reach, attain
-tachi (plural ending)
tat(te) earnest, urgent, pressing

———————— 1 ————————

0 達する **tas(suru)** reach, attain; amount to; become expert in; notify
　達し **tas(shi)** government notice

2 達人 **tatsujin** expert, master
4 達文 **tatsubun** clearly written composition
5 達弁 **tatsuben** eloquent, glib, fluent
6 達成 **tassei** achieve, attain
7 達見 **takken** insight, farsightedness
8 達者 **tassha** healthy, strong; proficient
11 達眼 **tatsugan** insight, farsightedness
12 達筆 **tappitsu** good penmanship; speedy
　　　 writing, flowing style
13 達意 **tatsui** intelligible, clear, lucid
16 達磨 **Daruma** Dharma (Indian priest who
　　　 brought Zen Buddhism to China circa
　　　 520 A.D.); tumbler, legless figurine
達磨忌 **Darumaki** (religious service on)
　　　 anniversary of Dharma's death
　　　 (October 5)
18 達観 **takkan** farsighted/philosophic view
19 達識 **tasshiki** insight, farsightedness

――――――― 2 ―――――――

2 人達 **hitotachi** people
3 上達 **jōtatsu** make progress, become proficient
口達者 **kuchidassha** talkative
4 内達 **naitatsu** unofficial notice
友達 **tomodachi** friend
公達 **kindachi** young nobleman
火達磨 **hidaruma** mass of flames, human
　　　 torch
5 用達 **yōtatsu, yōta(shi)** transaction of
　　　 business; government contractor,
　　　 purveyor
示達 **shitatsu** directive, instructions
6 伊達 **date** foppish, ostentatious
伊達男 **dateotoko** a dandy, fop
伊達巻 **datema(ki)** under-sash; rolled omelet
伝達 **dentatsu** transmit, convey, propagate
先達 **sendatsu** pioneer; leader; guide
　　　 sendat(te) the other day, recently
血達磨 **chidaruma** covered with blood
7 利達 **ritatsu** advancement in life
私達 **watakushitachi** we, us, our
8 到達 **tōtatsu** reach, attain
到達点 **tōtatsuten** destination
送達 **sōtatsu** convey, deliver, dispatch
明達 **meitatsu** wisdom, discernment
9 発達 **hattatsu** development, progress
速達 **sokutatsu** special/express delivery
通達 **tsūtatsu** communication, a circular
　　　 (notice); proficiency, skill
栄達 **eitatsu** distinction, fame, advancement
10 敏達 **bintatsu** wise
　　　 Bindatsu (emperor, 572–585)
配達 **haitatsu** deliver
配達人 **haitatsunin** deliveryman

配達先 **haitatsusaki** destination, receiver
配達料 **haitatsuryō** delivery charge
11 曹達 **sōda** soda
雪達磨 **yuki daruma** snowman
12 腕達者 **udedassha** strong/brawny man
14 熟達 **jukutatsu** proficiency, mastery, skill
練達 **rentatsu** skill, dexterity
15 調達 **chōtatsu, chōdatsu** procure, supply
16 諭達 **yutatsu** official instructions
17 厳達 **gentatsu** give strict orders
闊達 **kattatsu** magnanimous, generous

――――――― 3 ―――――――

5 未発達 **mihattatsu** undeveloped
幼友達 **osana tomodachi** childhood friend
12 御用達 **goyōtashi** purveyor to the government

――――――― 4 ―――――――

3 上意下達 **jōi katatsu** conveying the will of
　　　 those in authority to those who are
　　　 governed
下意上達 **kai jōtatsu** conveying the will of
　　　 those who are governed to those in
　　　 authority
7 即日速達 **sokujitsu sokutatsu** same-day
　　　 special delivery
9 茶飲友達 **chano(mi) tomodachi** crony, pal

2q9.9

逾   **YU** pass, go beyond

2q9.10 / 439

運   **UN** fate, luck; transport; operate
　　　 hako(bu) carry, transport

――――――― 1 ―――――――

2 運入 **hako(bi)i(reru)** carry/bring in
3 運上 **hako(bi)a(geru)** carry/bring up
4 運込 **hako(bi)ko(mu)** carry/bring in
5 運出 **hako(bi)da(su)** carry out
運用 **un'yō** make use of, apply, invest, put
　　　 into practice
運去 **hako(bi)sa(ru)** carry away/off
6 運気 **unki** fate, fortune
運休 **unkyū** (train) cancelled, not running
運任 **unmaka(se)** trusting to luck
運行 **unkō** movement; operate, run (planes,
　　　 trains)
7 運良 **un'yo(ku)** fortunately, luckily
運否天賦 **unpu-tenpu** trusting to chance
8 運命 **unmei** fate, destiny
運命付 **unmeizu(keru)** destine, doom

運命的 **unmeiteki** fateful
運命論 **unmeiron** fatalism
運命論者 **unmeironsha** fatalist
運送 **unsō** transport, conveyance, shipping
運送会社 **unsō-gaisha** transport/express company
運送店 **unsōten** forwarding agent, express company
運送屋 **unsōya** forwarding agent, express company
運送船 **unsōsen** cargo vessel, freighter
運送費 **unsōhi** transport/shipping expenses
運送業 **unsōgyō** transport business
運送業者 **unsōgyōsha** carrier, forwarding agent
運河 **unga** canal
9 運指 **unshi** fingering (in music)
運指法 **unshihō** fingering (in music)
10 運座 **unza** meeting of poets
運航 **unkō** operate, run (planes, ships)
運針 **unshin** handling the needle
運針縫 **unshinnu(i)** ordinary stitching
11 運動 **undō** motion, movement; exercise, sports; a movement, campaign
運動不足 **undō-busoku** lack of exercise
運動用具 **undō yōgu** sporting goods
運動会 **undōkai** athletic meet
運動服 **undōfuku** sportswear, uniform
運動界 **undōkai** the sporting world, sports
運動員 **undōin** campaigner, canvasser
運動家 **undōka** athlete, sportsman
運動場 **undōjō** playing/athletic field
運動帽 **undōbō** sports cap
運動費 **undōhi** campaign expenses
運動靴 **undōgutsu** athletic shoes, sneakers
運動欄 **undōran** the sports page/columns
運転 **unten** operate, run (a machine), drive (a car)
運転士 **untenshi** (ship's) mate, officer
運転手 **untenshu** driver, chauffeur
運転台 **untendai** motorman's seat, driver's cab
運転資金 **unten shikin** working capital, operating funds
12 運営 **un'ei** operation, management, administration
運筆 **unpitsu** strokes of the brush/pen
13 運勢 **unsei** one's fate, fortune, luck
運搬 **unpan** transport
運搬人 **unpannin** porter, carrier
運搬費 **unpanhi** transport charges, haulage
運試 **undame(shi)** try one's luck, take a chance
運賃 **unchin** fare; shipping/freight charges
14 運算 **unzan** mathematical operation, calculation

16 運輸 **un'yu** transport(ation)
運輸省 **Un'yushō** Ministry of Transport

――――――――― 2 ―――――――――

4 不運 **fuun** misfortune, bad luck
文運 **bun'un** cultural progress, enlightenment
円運動 **en undō** circular motion
水運 **suiun** water transport
5 好運 **kōun** good fortune, luck
6 気運 **kiun** trend, tendency
舟運 **shūun** transport by ship
7 社運 **shaun** company fortunes
8 非運 **hiun** misfortune, bad luck
命運 **meiun** fate
逆運 **gyakuun** reversal of fortunes
幸運 **kōun** good fortune, luck
幸運児 **kōunji** child of good fortune, lucky fellow
国運 **kokuun** national fortunes/fate
武運 **buun** the fortunes of war
取運 **to(ri)hako(bu)** start right in on, proceed to
9 通運 **tsūun** transport, forwarding, express
海運 **kaiun** marine transport, shipping
海運業 **kaiungyō** shipping, maritime trade
持運 **mo(chi)hako(bu)** carry, transport
皇運 **kōun** prosperity of the imperial throne
10 陸運 **rikuun** land transport
衰運 **suiun** declining fortunes
進運 **shin'un** progress, advance
家運 **kaun** family fortunes
時運 **jiun** tide of fortune
11 商運 **shōun** business fortunes
宿運 **shukuun** fate, destiny
悪運 **aku'un** evildoer's good luck; bad luck
12 悲運 **hiun** misfortune, hard luck
開運 **kaiun** improving one's luck
13 福運 **fukuun** happiness and good fortune
試運転 **shiunten** trial run
16 薄運 **hakuun** misfortune, ill luck
機運 **kiun** opportunity, chance, time
23 籤運 **kujiun** one's luck in lottery

――――――――― 3 ―――――――――

20 懸垂運動 **kensui undō** chin-ups
蠕動運動 **zendō undō** vermicular motion, peristalsis

2q9.11

迶

appare bravo, admirable

2q9.12

遉

TEI seek
sasuga as may be expected

2q9.13 / 1133

遂

SUI, to(geru) accomplish, attain, carry through
tsui (ni) finally

──────── 1 ────────
6 遂行 suikō accomplish, execute, perform

──────── 2 ────────
6 成遂 na(shi)to(geru) accomplish, carry out
7 完遂 kansui complete, attain
10 既遂 kisui consummated
11 添遂 so(i)to(geru) be married together one's whole life long; succeed in marrying
12 遣遂 ya(ri)to(geru) accomplish

──────── 4 ────────
6 自殺未遂 jisatsu misui attempted suicide

2q9.14 / 149

道

DŌ, TŌ road; prefecture (Hokkaidō)
michi way, path, road, street

──────── 1 ────────
0 道ならぬ michi(naranu) improper, illicit
  道すがら michi(sugara) on the way
3 道々 michimichi on the way, while walking
  道士 dōshi a Taoist
4 道元 Dōgen (Zen priest, 1200–1253)
  道中 dōchū travel, journey
  道中記 dōchūki traveler's journal
  道化 dōke clowning
  道化方 dōkekata clown
  道化役 dōkeyaku clown
  道化者 dōkemono jester, joker, wag
  道化師 dōkeshi clown
  道心 dōshin moral sense; piety, faith
6 道行 michiyu(ki) traveling scene; poem about travel scenery; eloping; Japanese traveling coat
7 道学 dōgaku Confucianism, Taoism, moral philosophy
  道学者 dōgakusha moralist
  道床 dōshō roadbed
8 道念 dōnen moral sense; priest's wife
  道具 dōgu tool, implement
  道具方 dōgukata stage hand
  道具立 dōguda(te) tool setup, stage setting
  道具屋 dōguya dealer in secondhand goods
  道具部屋 dōgu-beya toolroom; prop room
  道具箱 dōgubako toolbox
9 道俗 dōzoku priests and laity
  道連 michizu(re) traveling companion
  道草食 michikusa (o) ku(u) dawdle/loiter along the way
  道祖神 dōsojin travelers' guardian deity
10 道家 dōka a Taoist

道案内 michi annai guidance; guide; road marker
道教 dōkyō Taoism
道破 dōha declaration
11 道道 michimichi on the way, while walking
道理 dōri, kotowari reason, right, truth
12 道普請 michi bushin road repair
道場 dōjō (martial-arts) gymnasium; Buddhist seminary
道程 dōtei, michinori distance; journey
道筋 michisuji route, itinerary; reason
道順 michijun route, itinerary
13 道義 dōgi moral principles
道義心 dōgishin moral sense, scruples
道楽 dōraku hobby; dissipation, debauchery
道楽者 dōrakumono libertine, playboy
道楽息子 dōraku musuko prodigal son
道話 dōwa moral tale, parable
道路 dōro road, street, highway
14 道徳 dōtoku morality, morals
道徳上 dōtoku-jō from a moral viewpoint
道徳心 dōtokushin sense of morality
道徳学 dōtokugaku moral philosophy
道徳的 dōtokuteki moral, ethical
道徳律 dōtokuritsu moral law
道徳家 dōtokuka man of virtue
道歌 dōka didactic poem
道端 michibata roadside, wayside
15 道標 dōhyō, michi shirube road marker, milestone

──────── 2 ────────
2 二道 futamichi forked road, crossroads, two ways (to go)
入道 nyūdō entering the priesthood; priest
入道雲 nyūdōgumo thunderhead, cumulonimbus cloud
人道 jindō humanity; sidewalk
人道主義 jindō shugi humanitarianism
3 大道 daidō highway, main street; great moral principle
大道具 ōdōgu stage setting, scenery
女道楽 onna dōraku carnal pleasures
弓道 kyūdō (Japanese) archery
小道 komichi path, lane
小道具 kodōgu (stage) props
山道 sandō, yamamichi mountain path/pass
士道 shidō samurai code, chivalry
4 不道理 fudōri unreasonable; immoral
不道徳 fudōtoku immoral
天道 tendō the way of heaven, destiny
  tentō heaven, providence; the sun
天道虫 tentōmushi ladybug, ladybird beetle
天道様 tentōsama the sun; heaven
中道 chūdō middle-of-the-road
中道派 chūdōha centrists, middle-of-the-roaders

仏道 **butsudō** Buddhism
片道 **katamichi** one way
公道 **kōdō** highway; justice
水道 **suidō** piped water, waterworks, city water, aqueduct; waterway, channel
水道局 **suidōkyoku** water bureau
水道栓 **suidōsen** hydrant, tap
水道料 **suidōryō** water charges
水道管 **suidōkan** water pipe/main
王道 **ōdō** royal road; the rule of right, just rule
5 古道 **kodō** ancient road; ancient ways/morality
古道具 **furudōgu** secondhand goods, used furniture
古道具屋 **furudōguya** secondhand store
外道 **gedō** heresy; heretic
正道 **seidō** the right(eous) path
6 伝道 **dendō** evangelism, proselytizing, missionary work
伝道師 **dendōshi** evangelist
孝道 **kōdō** filial piety
色道 **shikidō** sexual passion
近道 **chikamichi** short cut
地道 **jimichi** steady, honest, fair, sober-minded
回道 **mawa(ri)michi** roundabout way
早道 **hayamichi** shortcut
血道 **chi (no) michi** (women's) dizziness, congestion of the brain, hysterics
糸道 **itomichi** samisen playing
7 求道 **kyūdō** seeking after truth
邪道 **jadō** evil course; heresy
別道 **waka(re)michi** forked road, branch-off, crossroads, parting of the ways
臣道 **shindō** the way of a loyal subject
坑道 **kōdō** (mine) shaft, level, gallery, tunnel
坂道 **sakamichi** hill road
赤道 **sekidō** the equator
抜道 **nu(ke)michi** bypass; secret path; way of escape, loophole
花道 **kadō** (the art of) flower arrangement
hanamichi runway from the stage through the audience
尿道 **nyōdō** urethra
村道 **sondō** village road
攻道具 **se(me)dōgu** offensive weapons
戻道 **modo(ri)michi** the way back
私道 **shidō** private road/path
町道場 **machi dōjō** martial-arts school in a town
車道 **shadō** roadway
8 非道 **hidō** inhuman, unjust, cruel, tyrranical
使道 **tsuka(i)michi** use
夜道 **yomichi** night journey
其道 **so(no) michi** line of business, field
逃道 **ni(ge)michi** way of escape, way out

沿道 **endō** along the road, roadside
泥道 **doromichi** muddy road
参道 **sandō** path/approach to a shrine
歩道 **hodō** footpath, sidewalk
歩道橋 **hodōkyō** pedestrian overpass
国道 **kokudō** national highway
林道 **rindō** forest road/trail
枝道 **edamichi** branch road
武道 **budō** military/martial arts, bushido
9 飛道具 **to(bi)dōgu** projectile weapon, firearms
通道 **tō(ri)michi** pasage, path, route, one's way to
海道 **kaidō** coastal highway
茶道 **chadō, sadō** tea ceremony
茶道具 **chadōgu** tea-things
県道 **kendō** prefectural highway
峠道 **tōgemichi** road through a mountain pass
柔道 **jūdō** judo
柔道家 **jūdōka** judo expert
神道 **shintō** Shintoism
政道 **seidō** politics, government
軌道 **kidō** (railroad) track; orbit
食道 **shokudō** the esophagus
食道楽 **ku(i)dōraku** gourmandizing; epicure
10 修道 **shūdō** living a religious life
修道女 **shūdōjo** (Catholic) nun
修道士 **shūdōshi** monk, friar
修道院 **shūdōin** monastery, convent, cloister
倡道 **shōdō** herald, lead
都道府県 **to-dō-fu-ken** prefectures
剣道 **kendō** Japanese fencing, kendo
帰道 **kae(ri)michi** the way back/home
華道 **kadō** flower arranging
桟道 **sandō** plank bridge
脇道 **wakimichi** byway, side road; digression
書道 **shodō** calligraphy
悟道 **godō** spiritual enlightenment
11 野道 **nomichi** path across a field
道道 **michimichi** on the way, while walking
唱道 **shōdō** advocate
婦道 **fudō** (duties of) womanhood
得道 **tokudō** attainment of (Buddhist) salvation
黄道 **kōdō, ōdō** the ecliptic
黄道吉日 **kōdō kichinichi, ōdō kichinichi** lucky day
黄道帯 **kōdōtai** the zodiac
寄道 **yo(ri)michi** stop in on one's way
悪道 **akudō** evil/wrong course
畦道 **azemichi** path between rice fields
細道 **hosomichi** narrow lane, path
責道具 **se(me)dōgu** instruments of torture
釣道具 **tsu(ri) dōgu** fishing tackle
雪道 **yukimichi** snowy road
魚道 **gyodō** path regularly taken by a school of fish; fish ladder, fishway

12 着道楽　**kidōraku**　love of fine clothes
善道　**zendō**　path of virtue, righteousness
遠道　**tōmichi**　long walk; roundabout way
報道　**hōdō**　reporting, news coverage
報道陣　**hōdōjin**　the press corps
弾道　**dandō**　trajectory
街道　**kaidō**　highway
極道　**gokudō**　wicked, brutal, profligate
極道者　**gokudōmono**　scoundrel, rogue
無道　**mudō**　wicked; unreasonable
筋道　**sujimichi**　reason, logic, coherence
間道　**kandō**　secret path, side road, shortcut
13 隠道　**kaku(re)michi**　secret passage
裏道　**uramichi**　back lane, secret path
農道　**nōdō**　farm road
煙道　**endō**　flue
新道　**shindō**　new road
置道　**o(ki)michi**　raised road
鉄道　**tetsudō**　railroad
鉄道便　**tetsudōbin**　transport by rail
鉄道馬車　**tetsudō basha**　horse-drawn streetcar
鉄道網　**tetsudōmō**　railway network
14 隧道　**suidō, zuidō**　tunnel
獄道　**gokudō**　wicked, brutal, profligate
獄道者　**gokudōsha**　scoundrel, rogue, rake
歌道　**kadō**　poetry
複道　**fukudō**　double roadways one above the other
15 舗道　**hodō**　paved street, pavement
横道　**yokomichi**　side street, crossroad; wrong way; side issue, digression; path of evil
権道　**kendō**　expediency
諸道　**shodō**　accomplishments
鋪道　**hodō**　paved road, pavement
16 儒道　**judō**　Confucianism
18 糧道　**ryōdō**　supply of provisions
19 覇道　**hadō**　military rule
21 魔道　**madō**　evil ways

───────── 3 ─────────

1 一本道　**ipponmichi**　straight road; road with no turnoffs
一筋道　**hitosujimichi**　straight road, road with no turnoffs
2 二重道徳　**nijū dōtoku**　double standard of morality
二筋道　**futasujimichi**　forked road, crossroads
3 大入道　**ōnyūdō**　large bald-shaven monster/specter
上水道　**jōsuidō**　piped/city water
下水道　**gesuidō**　drainage/sewer system, drain
5 北海道　**Hokkaidō**　(prefecture)
田舎道　**inakamichi**　country road
6 地下道　**chikadō**　underground passage
7 車馬道　**shabadō**　road for vehicles and horses
8 非人道　**hijindō**　inhumanity

東海道　**Tōkaidō**　the Tōkaidō highway
空手道　**karatedō**　karate
武士道　**bushidō**　bushido, the samurai code of chivalry
9 砂利道　**jarimichi**　gravel road
10 随神道　**Kannagara (no) Michi**　Shintoism
畜生道　**chikushōdō**　incest
家財道具　**kazai dōgu**　household effects
11 商売道具　**shōbai dōgu**　tools of the trade
紳士道　**shinshidō**　the code of a gentleman
12 無軌道　**mukidō**　trackless; erratic, aberrant
惟神道　**kannagara (no) michi**　Shintoism
13 蛸入道　**takonyūdō**　octopus; bald-headed man
15 敷島道　**Shikishima (no) michi**　Japanese poetry
餓鬼道　**gakidō**　(Buddhist) hell of hungry demons
18 難行道　**nangyōdō**　salvation through austerities
騎士道　**kishidō**　knighthood, chivalry

───────── 4 ─────────

3 大逆無道　**daigyaku-mudō**　high treason
上下水道　**jōgesuidō**　water and sewer service
4 文武両道　**bunbu-ryōdō**　both soldierly and scholarly arts
8 国有鉄道　**kokuyū tetsudō**　national railway
12 軽便鉄道　**keiben tetsudō**　narrow-gauge railroad
15 横断歩道　**ōdan hodō**　pedestrian crossing

2q9.15

SHŪ　strong, powerful

遒　酒

2q9.16 / 1160

HEN　widespread; (number of) times　**amane(ku)**　widely, generally, everywhere

遍　遍

───────── 1 ─────────

6 遍在　**henzai**　ubiquitous, omnipresent
13 遍路　**henro**　pilgrim; pilgrimage
14 遍歴　**henreki**　travels, pilgrimage

───────── 2 ─────────

1 一遍　**ippen**　once
3 万遍　**manben(naku)**　equally, uniformly, without exception
7 何遍　**nanben**　how many times
12 普遍　**fuhen**　universal, general
普遍的　**fuhenteki**　universal, general

───────── 3 ─────────

6 百万遍　**hyakumanben**　(praying) a million times
9 通一遍　**tō(ri)-ippen**　passing, casual, perfunctory

2

亻
冫
孑
阝
卩
刂
力
又
宀
亠
十
卜
厂
⻌9←
冂
几
匸

2q9.17 / 702

遅 遅   CHI, oso(i) late; slow
       oku(reru) be late/slow
       oku(rasu) defer, set back (a
       clock)

──────────── 1 ────────────

3 遅々 **chichi** slow, lagging
4 遅日 **chijitsu** (long) spring days
5 遅生 **osouma(re)** born after April 1 (school entrance date)
6 遅早 **oso(kare)haya(kare)** sooner or later
7 遅延 **chien** delay
8 遅刻 **chikoku** be late/tardy
  遅刻届 **chikoku todo(ke)** tardiness report
  遅刻者 **chikokusha** latecomer
  遅知恵 **osojie** late-developing intelligence
  遅参 **chisan** come late
9 遅発 **chihatsu** delayed start/action
  遅速 **chisoku** speed, how slow or fast
  遅咲 **osoza(ki)** late-blooming
10 遅脈 **chimyaku** slow pulse
  遅配 **chihai** delay in apportioning/delivery
12 遅着 **chichaku** late arrival
  遅鈍 **chidon** slow-witted, dull, stupid
13 遅滞 **chitai** delay; arrearage
  遅蒔 **osoma(ki)** late sowing
14 遅疑 **chigi** hesitate, vacillate

──────────── 2 ────────────

4 手遅 **teoku(re)** too late, belated
  月遅 **tsukioku(re)** a month late/old; back numbers (of a monthly)
5 出遅 **deoku(re), da(shi)oku(re)** off to a late start, belated
  申遅 **mō(shi)oku(reru)** be late in saying
  立遅 **ta(chi)oku(re)** get off to a late start, lag behind
6 気遅 **kioku(re)** timidity, diffidence
9 乗遅 **no(ri)oku(reru)** miss (a train)
11 遅遅 **chichi** slow, lagging

2q9.18 / 413

過   KA excess, too much; error
     su(giru) pass, go past; elapse; be more than, exceed; (as adjective or verb suffix) too ..., over-, to excess su(gosu) spend (time) ayama(tsu) err ayama(chi) error yo(giru) pass by

──────────── 1 ────────────

3 過大 **kadai** excessive, too much, unreasonable
  過小 **kashō** too small
4 過不及 **kafukyū** excess or deficiency
  過不足 **kafusoku** excess or deficiency
  過分 **kabun** excessive, undeserved

過少 **kashō** too few
過日 **kajitsu** the other day, recently
5 過半 **kahan** the greater part
  過半数 **kahansū** majority, more than half
  過失 **kashitsu** error, mistake; accident; negligence
  過失致死 **kashitsu chishi** accidental homicide, manslaughter
  過失致死罪 **kashitsu chishizai** accidental homicide, manslaughter
  過去 **kako** the past **su(gi)sa(ru)** pass
  過去完了 **kako kanryō** past perfect tense
  過去帳 **kakochō** death register
6 過多 **kata** excess, overabundance
  過年度 **kanendo** past fiscal/business year
  過行 **su(gi)yu(ku)** pass, go past
  過当 **katō** excessive, exorbitant, undue
7 過労 **karō** overwork
  過言 **kagon, kagen** exaggeration
9 過重 **kajū** overweight
  過信 **kashin** put too much confidence in
  過客 **kakaku** travelers passing through
  過度 **kado** excessive, too much
  過怠 **katai** negligence, fault
  過怠金 **kataikin** fine for default
  過食 **kashoku** overeating
10 過振 **kabu(ri)** overdraft
  過敏 **kabin** oversensitive, nervous
  過敏症 **kabinshō** hypersensitivity
  過称 **kashō** undeserved praise
  過料 **karyō, ayamachiryō** non-penal fine (cf. 科料)
  過般 **kahan** some time ago, recently
  過般来 **kahanrai** for some time
11 過剰 **kajō** excess, surplus
12 過渡 **kato** crossover, transient, transition
  過渡的 **katoteki** transitional
  過渡期 **katoki** transition period
  過量 **karyō** too much
  過越節 **Sugikoshi Setsu, Sugikoshi no Iwai** Passover
  過硫酸 **karyūsan** persulfuric acid, (potassium) persulfate
  過程 **katei** process
13 過飽和 **kahōwa** supersaturation
14 過誤 **kago** error
  過酷 **kakoku** severe, harsh
  過酸化 **kasanka** (hydrogen) peroxide
15 過賞 **kashō** undeserved praise
  過熱 **kanetsu** overheat, superheat
16 過激 **kageki** radical, extreme
  過激主義 **kageki shugi** radicalism, extremism
  過激派 **kagekiha** radicals, extremists

──────────── 2 ────────────

1 一過性 **ikkasei** transient, temporary

3 大過 **taika** serious mistake/error
大過去 **daikako** past perfect tense, pluperfect
口過 **kuchisu(gi)** make a living
小過 **shōka** minor error
5 半過去 **hankako** imperfect tense
功過 **kōka** merits and demerits
払過 **hara(i)su(giru)** overpay
打過 **u(chi)su(giru)** pass by (time)
6 多過 **ōsu(giru)** be too many/much
行過 **i(ki)su(gi), yu(ki)su(gi)** going too far, overdoing it
7 良過 **yosu(giru)** be too good
身過 **misu(gi)** living, livelihood
走過 **hashi(ri)su(giru)** run past; run too much
売過 **u(ri)su(gi)** overselling
見過 **misu(gosu)** overlook
言過 **i(i)su(giru)** overstate, go too far
8 使過 **tsuka(i)su(giru)** use too much, work (someone) too hard
9 通過 **tsūka, tō(ri)su(giru)** pass by/through
通過駅 **tsūka eki** station at which the train does not stop
昼過 **hirusu(gi)** (early) afternoon
思過 **omo(i)su(gosu)** worry too much, be overanxious
食過 **ta(be)su(gi), ku(i)su(gi)** overeating
11 経過 **keika** lapse, passage of time; progress, course, developments
12 遣過 **ya(ri)su(giru)** overdo, carry to excess
　　 ya(ri)su(gosu) let (someone) go past
超過 **chōka** exceed
超過額 **chōgaku** surplus, excess
焼過 **ya(ki)su(giru)** overcook
無過失 **mukashitsu** no-fault (liability)
煮過 **nisu(giru), nisu(gosu)** overboil
買過 **ka(i)su(giru)** buy too much/many
飲過 **no(mi)su(giru)** drink too much
13 罪過 **zaika** offense, sin, fault
14 読過 **dokka** skim through; overlook
15 黙過 **mokka** overlook, connive at
16 積過 **tsu(mi)su(giru)** overload
17 擦過傷 **sakkashō** abrasion, scratch
18 濾過 **roka** filtration

――――――― 3 ―――――――
9 胃酸過多症 **isankatashō** gastric hyperacidity
12 滋養過多 **jiyōkata** hypertrophy

――――――― 10 ―――――――

遡 → 溯 **3a10.2**

遡 → 溯 **3a10.2**

2q10.1

遘 **KŌ** meet

2q10.2 / 1173

遣 **KEN, tsuka(wasu)** send, dispatch; give
tsuka(u) use
ya(ru) give

――――――― 1 ―――――――
0 遣りこなす **ya(rikonasu)** manage (to do)
3 遣口 **ya(ri)kuchi** way of doing, method
4 遣切 **ya(ri)ki(renai)** cannot stand, cannot go on
遣込 **ya(ri)ko(meru)** refute, argue down
遣水 **ya(ri)mizu** stream built through a garden; water (a bonsai)
遣手 **ya(ri)te** man of ability/resourcefulness
遣方 **ya(ri)kata** way of doing, method
遣戸 **ya(ri)do** sliding door
5 遣出 **ya(ri)da(su)** begin, set about, take up
遣付 **ya(ri)tsu(keru)** be accustomed/used to
遣外 **kengai** sent abroad
6 遣合 **ya(ri)a(u)** do to each other, argue, compete
遣返 **ya(ri)kae(su)** try again, do over; retort, refute
遣尽 **ya(ri)tsuku(su)** do everything in one's power
7 遣抜 **ya(ri)nu(ku)** carry through, do thoroughly, accomplish, complete
8 遣直 **ya(ri)nao(su)** do over again, redo, start over
遣放 **ya(rip)pana(shi)** leave as is, leave half done; careless, negligent
遣取 **ya(ri)to(ri)** give and take, exchange, reciprocate
9 遣通 **ya(ri)tō(su)** carry/see through, complete, accomplish
10 遣唐使 **kentōshi** Japanese envoy to Tang-dynasty China
11 遣遂 **ya(ri)to(geru)** accomplish
遣過 **ya(ri)su(giru)** overdo, carry to excess
　　 ya(ri)su(gosu) let (someone) go past
遣掛 **ya(ri)ka(keru)** begin to do, set about
　　 ya(ri)ka(ke) unfinished, half done
12 遣場 **ya(ri)ba** disposal, use; place/where to put
13 遣損 **ya(ri)soko(nau)** bungle, muff, fail, mismanage
19 遣瀬 **yaruse(nai)** dreary, cheerless, disconsolate
遣繰 **ya(ri)ku(ri)** makeshift, getting by
遣繰算段 **ya(ri)ku(ri) sandan** getting by, tiding over

——————— 2 ———————

3 小遣 **kozuka(i)** spending money
　小遣銭 **kozuka(i)sen** spending money
4 分遣 **bunken** detachment, detail
　木遣 **kiya(ri)** (workmen's chant while) pulling/carrying a heavy load together
　心遣 **kokorozuka(i)** solicitude, consideration
　　 kokoroya(ri) diversion, recreation; thoughtfulness
6 気遣 **kizuka(i)** anxiety, fear, worry
　先遣 **senken** send ahead
7 見遣 **miya(ru)** look/glance at
8 金遣 **kanezuka(i)** way of spending money
9 派遣 **haken** dispatch, send
　派遣軍 **hakengun** expeditionary army
　派遣隊 **hakentai** contingent, detachment
　思遣 **omo(i)ya(ri)** consideration, sympathy, compassion
10 差遣 **saken** dispatch
　息遣 **ikizuka(i)** breathing
　蚊遣 **kaya(ri)** smudge fire to repel mosquitoes
12 筆遣 **fudezuka(i)** manner of writing, brushwork

——————— 3 ———————

6 両刀遣 **ryōtōtsuka(i)** two-sword fencer; expert in two fields
　仮名遣 **kanazuka(i)** kana orthography
7 言葉遣 **kotobazuka(i)** wording, expression
12 無駄遣 **mudazuka(i)** waste, squander

2q10.3

遙 遥 **YŌ, haru(ka)** far off, distant; long ago; by far

——————— 1 ———————

3 遙々 **harubaru** from afar, at a great distance
8 遙拝 **yōhai** worshipping from afar

——————— 2 ———————

9 逍遙 **shōyō** walk, amble

2q10.4 / 446

遠 **EN, ON, tō(i)** far, distant

——————— 1 ———————

0 遠ざかる **tō(zakaru)** become more distant, drift apart
　遠ざける **tō(zakeru)** keep at a distance, shun, abstain from
3 遠大 **endai** far-reaching, grand
　遠山 **tōyama, enzan** distant mountain
　遠山里 **tōyamazato** remote mountain village
4 遠日点 **enjitsuten, ennichiten** aphelion
　遠火 **tōbi** distant fire, low heat

遠方 **enpō** great distance, long way, far-off
遠心 **enshin** centrifugal
遠心力 **enshinryoku** centrifugal force
5 遠矢 **tōya** long-distance arrow/archery
　遠出 **tōde** going far away
　遠去 **tōza(karu)** become more distant, recede into the distance
　遠目 **tōme** distant view; farsightedness
6 遠交近攻 **enkō-kinkō** befriending distant countries and antagonizing neighbors
　遠近 **enkin** far and/or near, distance
　遠近法 **enkinhō** (law of) perspective
　遠回 **tōmawa(ri)** roundabout way, detour
　　 tōmawa(shi) roundabout expression
　遠因 **en'in** remote/underlying cause
　遠耳 **tōmimi** keen ears
7 遠来 **enrai** from afar
　遠走 **tō(p)pashi(ri)** go a long way/distance
　遠吠 **tōbo(e)** howling
　遠見 **tōmi** distant view
　遠足 **ensoku** excursion, outing, picnic, hike
8 遠泳 **en'ei** long-distance swim
　遠征 **ensei** (military) expedition, campaign; tour (by a team)
　遠征隊 **enseitai** expeditionary forces, invaders; visiting team
　遠歩 **tōaru(ki)** long walk
　遠国 **engoku, ongoku** faraway country, distant land
9 遠巻 **tōma(ki)** surround at a distance, form a wide circle around
　遠乗 **tōno(ri)** long ride
　遠浅 **tōasa** shallow for some distance from the shore, a shoal
　遠洋 **en'yō** ocean, deep sea
　遠海 **enkai** ocean, deep sea
　遠海魚 **enkaigyo** deep-sea fish
　遠祖 **enso** remote ancestors, forefathers
　遠音 **tōne** distant sound
10 遠島 **entō, tōjima** distant island
11 遠道 **tōmichi** long walk; roundabout way
　遠視 **enshi** farsightedness
　遠視眼 **enshigan** farsightedness
　遠望 **enbō** distant view
　遠戚 **enseki** distant relative
　遠眼 **engan** farsightedness
　遠眼鏡 **engankyō** eyeglasses for farsightedness
12 遠隔 **enkaku** distant, remote (control)
　遠景 **enkei** distant view
　遠距離 **enkyori** long distance, long-range
13 遠路 **enro, tōmichi** long distance/journey, roundabout way
　遠雷 **enrai** distant thunder
14 遠鳴 **tōna(ri)** distant sound (of thunder, the sea)

遠駆 **tōga(ke)** long gallop/march
15 遠慮 **enryo** reserve, restraint, diffidence;
　　　refrain from **enryo(naku)** frankly
遠慮深 **enryobuka(i)** reserved, bashful
遠縁 **tōen** distantly related
16 遠謀 **enbō** forethought, foresight

───────── 2 ─────────

3 久遠 **kuon, kyūen** eternity
5 以遠 **ien** farther than, beyond
永遠 **eien** eternity
6 迂遠 **uen** roundabout; circumlocutory
耳遠 **mimidō(i)** hard of hearing; strange, uncommon
10 高遠 **kōen** lofty, exalted
11 疎遠 **soen** estrangement; long silence
深遠 **shin'en** profound, deep, abstruse
望遠鏡 **bōenkyō** telescope
悠遠 **yūen** remoteness; eternity; repose
12 無遠慮 **buenryo** unreserved, forward, impertinent
敬遠 **keien** keep (someone) at a respectful distance
程遠 **hodotō(i)** far from
15 僻遠 **hekien** remote, out-of-the-way, outlying
遼遠 **ryōen** distant, remote
縁遠 **endō(i)** having dim marriage prospects; far removed from

───────── 3 ─────────

11 深謀遠慮 **shinbō-enryo** farsighted planning
12 無限遠 **mugen'en** (focused) at infinity

2q10.5 / 814

違 **I, chiga(u)** be different; be mistaken; cross/pass (someone) **chiga(eru)** alter **taga(u)** differ from; violate **taga(eru)** violate, break (a promise)

───────── 1 ─────────

0 に違いない **(ni) chiga(i nai)** for sure, no doubt
4 違反 **ihan** violation
5 違犯 **ihan** volation, offense
6 違式 **ishiki** irregularity, breach of form/etiquette
8 違法 **ihō** illegal
違和感 **iwakan** feeling ill at ease, discomfort, malaise
9 違勅 **ichoku** disobeying an imperial decree
違背 **ihai** violation, disobedience
違約 **iyaku** breach of contract, default
違約金 **iyakukin** breach-of-contract penalty
12 違棚 **chiga(i)dana** staggered shelves
14 違算 **isan** miscalculation
16 違憲 **iken** unconstitutionality
19 違警罪 **ikeizai** offense against police regulations

───────── 2 ─────────

2 入違 **i(re)chiga(i)** passing each other
人違 **hitochiga(i)** mistaken identity
3 大違 **ōchiga(i)** big difference
4 互違 **taga(i)chiga(i)** alternating
手違 **techiga(i)** hitch, something gone wrong
6 気違 **kichiga(i)** insanity; mania, craze; lunatic; enthusiast, fan
仲違 **nakataga(i)** quarrel, discord
考違 **kanga(e)chiga(i)** mistaken idea, wrong impression
行違 **yu(ki)chiga(i), i(ki)chiga(i)** crossing each other; going amiss
7 見違 **michiga(eru)** mistake for, not recognize **michiga(i)** misperception, mistake
言違 **i(i)chiga(eru)** misstate, misspeak
8 非違 **hii** lawlessness, unlawfulness
取違 **to(ri)chiga(eru)** mistake for, misconstrue
門違 **kadochiga(i)** calling at the wrong house, barking up the wrong tree
9 飛違 **to(bi)chiga(u)** fly/dodge about
段違 **danchiga(i)** difference in level, uneven (parallel bars)
相違 **sōi** difference, discrepancy
畑違 **hatakechiga(i)** out of one's line
食違 **ku(i)chiga(u)** cross each other; run counter to, differ, clash; go awry
10 差違 **sa(shi)chiga(eru)** err in refereeing (in sumo); make a bad move (in chess) **sai** difference
桁違 **ketachiga(i)** off/differing by an order of magnitude
書違 **ka(ki)chiga(eru)** miswrite
11 勘違 **kanchiga(i)** misunderstanding, mistaken idea
掛違 **ka(ke)chiga(u)** cross/pass (each other)
12 場違 **bachiga(i)** the wrong place, out of place
筋違 **sujichiga(e)** a cramp **sujichiga(i)** illogical; diagonal **sujika(i)** diagonal; brace
間違 **machiga(u)** be mistaken/wrong **machiga(eru)** mistake
13 腹違 **harachiga(i)** born of a different mother but having the same father
置違 **o(ki)chiga(eru)** put in the wrong place
14 種違 **tanechiga(i)** half-brother/half-sister by a different father; new strain, hybrid variety
読違 **yo(mi)chiga(i)** misreading
聞違 **ki(ki)chiga(eru), ki(ki)chiga(u)** mishear, be misinformed
15 踏違 **fu(mi)chiga(eru)** sprain (one's ankle), misstep
16 積違 **tsu(mori)chiga(i)** incorrect estimate
17 擦違 **su(re)chiga(u)** pass by each other

——————— 3 ———————
1 一味違 **hitoaji chiga(u)** with a unique flavor
了簡違 **ryōkenchiga(i)** mistaken idea; an imprudence
3 大間違 **ōmachiga(i)** big mistake
4 心得違 **kokoroechiga(i)** mistaken idea; indiscretion
5 本気違 **hon kichiga(i)** bibliomania; bibliomaniac
6 色気違 **irokichiga(i)** sex mania
7 見込違 **miko(mi)chiga(i)** miscalculation
見当違 **kentōchiga(i)** wrong guess
9 思惑違 **omowakuchiga(i)** disappointment, miscalculation
11 勘定違 **kanjōchiga(i)** miscalculation
14 管轄違 **kankatsuchiga(i)** lack of jurisdiction
15 罷間違 **maka(ri)machiga(eba)** if worse comes to worst
16 憲法違反 **kenpō ihan** unconstitutionality

——————— 4 ———————
11 野球気違 **yakyū kichiga(i)** baseball fan

蓮→蓮 **3k10.31**

遞→逓 **2q7.5**

——————— 11 ———————
2q11.1
遨 **GŌ** play, enjoyment

�遯→遁 **2q9.2**

2q11.2 / 1643
遭 **SŌ, a(u)** meet, encounter

——————— 1 ———————
11 遭遇 **sōgū** encounter
遭遇戦 **sōgūsen** encounter, engagement
18 遭難 **sōnan** disaster, accident, mishap, distress
遭難者 **sōnansha** victim, sufferer

2q11.3 / 415
適 **TEKI** suitable **kana(u)** suit, serve the purpose, be consistent with **tama** occasional, rare

——————— 1 ———————
0 適する **teki(suru)** fit, suit, be qualified for
4 適不適 **teki-futeki** fitness, suitability
適切 **tekisetsu** appropriate, pertinent
5 適正 **tekisei** proper, appropriate, right
適用 **tekiyō** apply
6 適任 **tekinin** fit, suited, competent
適任者 **tekininsha** well-qualified person
適任証 **tekininshō** certificate of competence
適合 **tekigō** conform to, suit, fit
適地 **tekichi** suitable site/land
適当 **tekitō** suitable, adequate
7 適作 **tekisaku** suitable crop
適否 **tekihi** propriety, fitness, aptitude
適役 **tekiyaku** suitable post/role
適応 **tekiō** adaptation, accommodation, adjustment
適応性 **tekiōsei** adaptability, flexibility
適応症 **tekiōshō** diseases for which a medicine is efficacious/indicated
適材 **tekizai** the right person
適材適所 **tekizai-tekisho** the right man in the right place
8 適例 **tekirei** good example, case in point
適法 **tekihō** lawful, legal
適宜 **tekigi** suitable, proper, as one thinks best
適者 **tekisha** suitable person
適者生存 **tekisha seizon** survival of the fittest
適性 **tekisei** aptitude, suitability
適所 **tekisho** the right/proper place
9 適度 **tekido** proper degree/amount, moderation
10 適帰 **tekki** lead to, follow
適従 **tekijū** follow
適格 **tekikaku, tekkaku** competent, eligible
適格者 **tekikakusha** qualified/eligible person
適時 **tekiji** timely; whenever appropriate
11 適訳 **tekiyaku** exact translation
12 適温 **tekion** suitable temperature
適量 **tekiryō** proper quantity/dosage
適評 **tekihyō** pertinent criticism, apt comment
13 適業 **tekigyō** suitable occupation
16 適薬 **tekiyaku** specific remedy
17 適齢 **tekirei** the right age
適齢期 **tekireiki** marriageable age
18 適職 **tekishoku** suitable occupation

——————— 2 ———————
4 不適 **futeki** unsuited, unfit, inappropriate
不適切 **futekisetsu** unsuitable, inappropriate
不適任 **futekinin** unfit, incompetent
不適当 **futekitō** unsuited, unfit, inappropriate
不適格 **futekikaku** unqualified, unacceptable
5 好適 **kōteki** ideally suited
6 自適 **jiteki** ease and comfort
7 快適 **kaiteki** comfortable, pleasant, agreeable

11 清適 **seiteki** (your) health, prosperity
12 最適 **saiteki** optimum, best suited

———————— 3 ————————
13 適不適 **teki-futeki** fitness, suitability
適材適所 **tekizai-tekisho** the right man in the right place

2q11.4 / 1767

遮 遮　**SHA, saegi(ru)** interrupt, obstruct, block

———————— 1 ————————
6 遮光 **shakō** shade, darken, cut off the light
11 遮断 **shadan** interception, isolation, cutoff
遮断器 **shadanki** circuit breaker
遮断機 **shadanki** railroad-crossing gate
15 遮蔽 **shahei** cover, shelter, shield, screen
遮蔽物 **shaheibutsu** cover, shelter

———————— 12 ————————

2q12.1 / 921

遷　**SEN** move, change
utsu(ru) move, change, shift

———————— 1 ————————
4 遷化 **senge** death/demise (of a high priest)
7 遷延 **sen'en** delay
8 遷幸 **senkō** emperor's departing the capital
10 遷都 **sento** transfer of the capital
遷座 **senza** transfer of a shrine
11 遷移 **sen'i** transition, change

———————— 2 ————————
5 左遷 **sasen** demotion
9 変遷 **hensen** changes, vicissitudes, transition

2q12.2

遶　**NYŌ, JŌ** surround

2q12.3 / 800

選　**SEN, era(bu), e(ru), sugu(ru), yo(ru)** choose, select

———————— 1 ————————
3 選士 **senshi** selected person
4 選分 **yo(ri)wa(keru), e(ri)wa(keru)** sort/single/pick out, winnow, cull
選手 **senshu** (sports) player
選手団 **senshudan** team, squad
選手村 **senshumura** Olympic village
選手権 **senshuken** championship title

5 選出 **senshutsu, era(bi)da(su), e(ri)da(su)** select, pick out
選民 **senmin** chosen people, the elect
選外 **sengai** left out, not chosen
選外佳作 **sengai kasaku** honorable mention
選好 **senkō** preference **yo(ri)gono(mi), e(ri)gono(mi)** fastidiousness
6 選任 **sennin** select, appointment
選考 **senkō** selection, screening
7 選良 **senryō** an elite; member of parliament
選別 **senbetsu** sort, grade
選抜 **senbatsu, e(ri)nu(ku)** select, choose, single out
選択 **sentaku** selection, choice, option, alternative
選択肢 **sentakushi** multiple choice
選択権 **sentakuken** right of choice, option
選局 **senkyoku** (TV) channel selection
8 選定 **sentei** select, choose
選者 **senja** judge, selector
選取 **yo(ri)do(ri)** take one's choice, pick out
9 選炭 **sentan** coal dressing/sorting
選炭婦 **sentanfu** coal dresser/sorter
選科 **senka** elective course
選科生 **senkasei** nonregular student
10 選挙 **senkyo** election
選挙人 **senkyonin** voter, elector
選挙区 **senkyoku** election district
選挙日 **senkyobi** election day
選挙法 **senkyohō** election law
選挙場 **senkyojō** polling place, the polls
選挙費 **senkyohi** campaign expenses
選挙戦 **senkyosen** election campaign
選挙権 **senkyoken** right to vote, franchise, suffrage
選屑 **e(ri)kuzu, yo(ri)kuzu** trash, refuse, waste
11 選球 **senkyū** (batter's) discrimination between pitched balls inside and outside the strike zone
選球眼 **senkyūgan** batting eye
12 選集 **senshū** selection, anthology
13 選鉱 **senkō** ore dressing/sorting
14 選歌 **senka** selection of poems; selected poem
選管 **senkan** election administration (short for 選挙管理委員会)
16 選衡 **senkō** selection, screening

———————— 2 ————————
2 入選 **nyūsen** be chosen (in a competition)
入選者 **nyūsensha** winner, successful competitor
人選 **jinsen** personnel selection
4 予選 **yosen** preliminary selection/screening, elimination round
互選 **gosen** co-optation, mutual election

2

イ
冫
子
阝
卩
刂
力
又
宀
一
十
卜
夂
⺍
厂
辶 12←
冂
几
匚

文選 **bunsen** anthology; typesetting
文選工 **bunsenkō** typesetter
公選 **kōsen** public election
手選 **tesen** handpicking (in mining)
5 民選 **minsen** popular election
6 再選 **saisen** re-election
再選挙 **saisenkyo** re-election
当選 **tōsen** be elected/selected, win
当選者 **tōsensha** successful candidate
自選 **jisen** elect oneself; make a selection from one's own works
7 決選 **kessen** final/runoff election
改選 **kaisen** reelection
私選 **shisen** personal choice/appointment
8 抽選 **chūsen** drawing, lottery
抽選券 **chūsenken** lottery/raffle ticket
官選 **kansen** government-appointed
国選弁護人 **kokusen bengonin** court-appointed defense counsel
10 特選 **tokusen** specially selected
被選挙人 **hisenkyonin** person eligible for election
被選挙権 **hisenkyoken** eligibility for election
11 婦選 **fusen** women's suffrage
粒選 **tsubuyo(ri)** cull, select
12 普選 **fusen** universal suffrage
落選 **rakusen** fail to get elected
落選者 **rakusensha** unsuccessful candidate
13 新選 **shinsen** newly elected/compiled
詩選 **shisen** poetry anthology
14 総選挙 **sōsenkyo** general election
精選 **seisen** careful/choice selection
17 厳選 **gensen** careful selection
謹選 **kinsen** respectfully chosen (for you)

──────── 3 ────────
4 予備選挙 **yobi senkyo** preliminary election, a primary
12 普通選挙 **futsū senkyo** universal suffrage

2q12.4 / 1172

遺

I, YUI, noko(su) leave behind; bequeath

──────── 1 ────────
2 遺子 **ishi** posthumous child; orphan
4 遺文 **ibun** (deceased's) unpublished works
5 遺失 **ishitsu** loss
遺失物 **ishitsubutsu** lost article
遺失品 **ishitsuhin** lost article
6 遺伝 **iden** heredity
遺伝子 **idenshi** gene
遺伝子工学 **idenshi kōgaku** genetic engineering
遺伝子組替 **idenshi kumika(e)** recombinant gene splicing

遺伝学 **idengaku** genetics
遺伝法 **idenhō** laws of heredity
遺伝病 **idenbyō** hereditary disease
7 遺体 **itai** corpse, remains
遺作 **isaku** (deceased's) unpublished works
遺臣 **ishin** surviving retainer
遺志 **ishi** dying wish
遺尿 **inyō** bed-wetting
遺児 **iji** orphan; posthumous child
遺言 **yuigon** will, last wishes
遺言状 **yuigonjō** will, testament
遺言者 **yuigonsha** testator
遺言書 **yuigonsho** will, testament
8 遺例 **irei** surviving example
遺命 **imei** will, dying instructions
遺孤 **iko** orphan
遺制 **isei** institution originating in the past
遺物 **ibutsu** relic, remains
9 遺風 **ifū** tradition, old custom
遺品 **ihin** articles left by the deceased
遺恨 **ikon** grudge, enmity, rancor
10 遺家族 **ikazoku** surviving family
遺骨 **ikotsu** one's remains/ashes
遺書 **isho** suicide note; note left by the deceased; posthumous works
遺留 **iryū** bequeath
遺留分 **iryūbun** heir's legal portion
遺留品 **iryūhin** lost article, article left behind
遺訓 **ikun** dying injunction
11 遺著 **icho** (deceased's) unpublished work
遺族 **izoku** surviving family
遺産 **isan** inheritance, estate
12 遺詠 **iei** poem by the deceased
13 遺業 **igyō** unfinished work (of the deceased)
遺棄 **iki** abandon, leave unattended
遺腹 **ifuku** posthumous child
遺愛 **iai** bequest, prized possession of the deceased
遺跡 **iseki** remains, ruins, relics
14 遺漏 **irō** omission, negligence, oversight
遺墨 **iboku** autograph of the deceased
遺徳 **itoku** benefit derived from the virtue of one's ancestors
遺髪 **ihatsu** lock of the deceased's hair
遺精 **isei** involuntary emission of semen, wet dream
15 遺稿 **ikō** (deceased's) unpublished works
16 遺骸 **igai** one's remains, corpse
遺憾 **ikan** regrettable
遺賢 **iken** able men left out of office
18 遺贈 **izō** bequest, legacy
遺蹟 **iseki** ruins, remains

──────── 2 ────────
9 拾遺 **shūi** gleanings
12 補遺 **hoi** supplement, addendum, appendix
13 聖遺物 **seiibutsu** religious relic

2q12.5

遼 遼

RYŌ distant

———— 1 ————
12 遼遠 **ryōen** distant, remote

2q12.6

暹

SEN sunrise

———— 1 ————
19 暹羅 **Shamu** Siam

2q12.7

邁

MAI go; excel

———— 1 ————
10 邁進 **maishin** push/press on, strive

———— 2 ————
8 英邁 **eimai** wise and brave, great
10 高邁 **kōmai** lofty, exalted

2q12.8 / 1938

遵

JUN follow, obey

———— 1 ————
6 遵行 **junkō** obey
遵守 **junshu** obey, observe
8 遵奉 **junpō** observe, adhere to, abide by
遵法 **junpō** law-abiding, work-to-rule (tactics)

遲 → 遅 **2q9.17**

導 → **5c9.3**

———— 13 ————

2q13.1

邀

YŌ, muka(eru) go to meet

———— 1 ————
15 邀撃 **yōgeki** ambush, attack

2q13.2

邂

KAI meet unexpectedly

———— 1 ————
9 邂逅 **kaikō** meet by chance, happen to meet

2q13.3 / 1491

避

HI, sa(keru), yo(keru) avoid

———— 1 ————
7 避妊 **hinin** contraception
避妊法 **hininhō** method of contraception
避妊薬 **hinin'yaku** a contraceptive, birth control pill
10 避病院 **hibyōin** isolation/quarantine hospital
12 避寒 **hikan** (spend the) winter at
避寒地 **hikanchi** winter resort
避暑 **hisho** (spend the) summer at
避暑地 **hishochi** summer resort
避暑客 **hishokyaku** summer residents
13 避雷針 **hiraishin** lightning rod
18 避難 **hinan** refuge, evacuation
避難民 **hinanmin** refugees, evacuees
避難者 **hinansha** refugees, evacuees
避難所 **hinanjo** shelter, place of safety

———— 2 ————
6 回避 **kaihi** avoid
7 忌避 **kihi** evasion, shirking; (legal) challenge
8 退避 **taihi** taking refuge, evacuation
逃避 **tōhi** escape, flight, evasion
逃避行 **tōhikō** runaway trip, flight
逃避的 **tōhiteki** escapist, evasive
雨避 **amayo(ke)** taking shelter from the rain
9 待避 **taihi** shunting (in railroading)
待避線 **taihisen** siding, sidetrack

———— 3 ————
4 不可避 **fukahi** inescapable, unavoidable, inevitable

———— 4 ————
14 徴兵忌避 **chōhei kihi** draft evasion

邉 → 辺 **2q2.1**

2q13.4 / 866

還

KAN, GEN, kae(ru) return

———— 1 ————
4 還元 **kangen** restore; reduce, deoxidize
5 還付 **kanpu** return, restore, refund
8 還幸 **kankō** return of the emperor
9 還俗 **genzoku** return to secular life, quit the priesthood

13 ←

2

亻
冫
孑
阝
卩
刂
力
又
宀
亠
十
卜
勹
丷
厂
丶
冂
几
匚

→13辶

10 還流　**kanryū**　return current, flowing back, reflux
11 還啓　**kankei**　return (of the empress)
12 還御　**kangyo**　return (of the emperor)
14 還暦　**kanreki**　one's 60th birthday

------- 2 -------

5 生還　**seikan**　come back alive; cross home plate
生還者　**seikansha**　survivor
召還　**shōkan**　recall, order to return
6 返還　**henkan**　return; repayment
8 送還　**sōkan**　send back, repatriate
往還　**ōkan**　coming and going, traffic; road
10 帰還　**kikan**　return, repatriation; feedback
帰還兵　**kikanhei**　repatriated soldiers
帰還者　**kikansha**　a repatriate
14 奪還　**dakkan**　recapture, retake
17 償還　**shōkan**　repayment, redemption, amortization

------- 3 -------

5 未帰還者　**mikikansha**　person still not repatriated

------- 4 -------

3 大政奉還　**taisei hōkan**　restoration of imperial rule

2q13.5

遽

KYO　sudden; flurried, agitated

------- 2 -------

9 急遽　**kyūkyo**　hastily, hurriedly

------- 14 -------

2q14.1

邇　迩　迩

JI　near, close

2q14.2

邃

SUI　deep in the interior

------- 2 -------

9 幽邃　**yūsui**　secluded and quiet

------- 15 -------

2q15.1

邐

REI, **ne(ru)**　proceed, walk slowly

邊 → 辺　2q2.1

------- 19 -------

2q19.1

邏

RA　go around

------- 2 -------

5 巡邏　**junra**　patrol, one's beat/rounds
19 警邏　**keira**　patrol(man)

------- 冂 2r -------

冂	円	用	冊	冋	网	同	而	罔	甬	周	岡	罔
0.1	2.1	3.1	0a5.42	3s3.1	4.1	4.2	4.3	5.1	5.2	6.1	6.2	6.3

朋	靑	耐	胄	冕
4b4.1	4b4.10	7.1	7.2	4c7.9

------- 0 -------

2r0.1

冂

KEI　remote area

------- 2 -------

2r2.1 / 13

円　圓

EN　circle; yen
maru(i)　round (like a disk)
maro(yaka)　round; mellow
mado(ka)　round; tranquil

------- 1 -------

4 円心　**enshin**　center of a circle
5 円本　**enpon**　one-yen book
7 円形　**enkei**　round shape, circle
8 円価　**enka**　value of the yen
円卓会議　**entaku kaigi**　round-table conference
円周　**enshū**　circumference
円周率　**enshūritsu**　ratio of circumference to diameter, pi, π
9 円陣　**enjin**　(people standing in a) circle
円弧　**enko**　arc
円屋根　**maruyane**　dome, cupola
円柱　**enchū**　column; cylinder; shaft
marubashira　column, cylinder

円為替 **enkawase** yen exchange
10 円高 **endaka** strong yen (exchange rate)
円座 **enza** sitting in a circle; round straw mat
11 円運動 **en undō** circular motion
円寂 **enjaku** nirvana; death of a priest/Buddha
円窓 **marumado** round window
円貨 **enka** yen currency
円転 **enten(taru)** orotund, smoothly rolling
円転滑脱 **enten-katsudatsu** versatile, all-around, tactful
円頂 **enchō** round top; tonsured head
12 円満 **enman** harmonious, smooth; well rounded
円筒 **entō** cylinder
13 円滑 **enkatsu** smooth, harmonious
円蓋 **engai** cupola, dome, vault
14 円熟 **enjuku** maturity, ripeness, perfection
15 円舞 **enbu** waltz
円墳 **enpun** burial mound
円盤 **enban** disk; discus
円盤投 **enbanna(ge)** the discus throw
16 円融 **En'yū** (emperor, 960–984)
円錐形 **ensuikei** cone
19 円鏡 **enkyō** round mirror

──────── 2 ────────

1 一円 **ichien** the whole area; one yen
3 大円 **daien** large circle; great circle
4 方円 **hōen** square or circular
5 半円 **han'en** semicircle
半円形 **han'enkei** semicircular
7 花円 **hanamaru** a small flowering cucumber
8 長円 **chōen** ellipse, oval
長円形 **chōenkei** ellipse, oval
13 楕円 **daen** ellipse
楕円形 **daenkei** ellipse, oval

──────── 3 ────────

3 大団円 **daidan'en** end, denouement, finale
5 外接円 **gaisetsuen** circumscribed circle
6 同心円 **dōshin'en** concentric circles
9 拾万円 **jūman'en** 100,000 yen
10 遊動円木 **yūdō enboku** suspended horizontal log, swinging pole (playground equipment)

──────── 3 ────────

2r3.1 / 107

用 **YŌ** business, errand; (as suffix) use, for ...
mochi(iru) use

──────── 1 ────────

2 用人 **yōnin** steward, factotum
4 用水 **yōsui** city/irrigation water
用水池 **yōsuichi, yōsuiike** reservoir
用水路 **yōsuiro** irrigation channel

用心 **yōjin** care, caution
用心深 **yōjinbuka(i)** careful, cautious, wary
用心棒 **yōjinbō** door bolt; cudgel; bodyguard
5 用字 **yōji** use of characters
用立 **yōda(teru)** lend, advance (money)
6 用件 **yōken** business, things to be done
用地 **yōchi** land for some use, lot, site
用向 **yōmu(ki)** business, errand
7 用兵 **yōhei** tactics
用役 **yōeki** service
用材 **yōzai** materials; lumber
用言 **yōgen** declinable word
用足 **yō (o) ta(su)** do one's business; go to the toilet
8 用事 **yōji** business, errand, something to attend to
用例 **yōrei** example, illustration
用命 **yōmei** order, command
用法 **yōhō** how to use, directions
用明 **Yōmei** (emperor, 585–587)
用具 **yōgu** tool, implement, apparatus, (sporting) goods
用金 **yōkin** money for public use; extraordinary levy
9 用便 **yōben** going to the toilet
用便後 **yōbengo** after stool
用途 **yōto** use, purpose
用品 **yōhin** supplies
用度 **yōdo** supplies; expenses
10 用益権 **yōekiken** usufruct
用紙 **yōshi** form (to be filled out); stationery
11 用達 **yōtatsu, yōta(shi)** transaction of business; government contractor, purveyor
用済 **yōzu(mi)** business finished, affairs settled
用捨 **yōsha** choose, select (what to adopt and what to reject)
用務 **yōmu** business (to attend to)
用務員 **yōmuin** servant, janitor, custodian
用船 **yōsen** chartered ship; chartering a ship
12 用量 **yōryō** dosage, dose
用無 **yōna(shi)** idle; unneeded, unwanted
用筆 **yōhitsu** brushes used; use of a brush
13 用意 **yōi** preparations, arrangements
用意周到 **yōi-shūtō** very careful, thoroughly prepared
14 用箋 **yōsen** form, blank, stationery
用語 **yōgo** term, terminology, vocabulary
15 用器 **yōki** instrument, tool
用器画 **yōkiga** mechanical drawing
用談 **yōdan** a business talk
18 用箪笥 **yōdansu** chest of drawers

──────── 2 ────────

2 入用 **nyūyō, i(ri)yō** need, demand

2

イ冫子阝卩刂力又宀亠十ト勹勹丶厂廴冂几匸

→3

3 土用 **doyō** dog days, midsummer
土用干 **doyōbo(shi)** summer airing (of clothes)
小用 **shōyō, koyō** small matter; urination
4 不用 **fuyō** unused, useless, waste
不用心 **buyōjin, fuyōjin** unsafe, insecure; careless
不用品 **fuyōhin** useless article, castoff
不用意 **fuyōi** unprepared, unguarded, careless
内用 **naiyō** for internal use; private business
収用 **shūyō** expropriation
公用 **kōyō** official business; public use; public expense
公用文 **kōyōbun** writing in the officially prescribed way
引用 **in'yō** quotation, citation
引用文 **in'yōbun** quotation
引用句 **in'yōku** quotation
引用符 **in'yōfu** quotation marks
日用 **nichiyō** for daily/everyday use
日用品 **nichiyōhin** daily necessities
5 代用 **daiyō** substitute
代用品 **daiyōhin** a substitute
代用食 **daiyōshoku** substitute food
外用 **gaiyō** for external use/application
外用薬 **gaiyōyaku** medicine to be applied externally (rather than ingested or injected)
6 多用 **tayō** busyness
任用 **nin'yō** appoint
肉用種 **nikuyōshu** breed of animal raised for meat
共用 **kyōyō** common use, shared
当用 **tōyō** current use, immediate needs
当用漢字 **Tōyō Kanji** (official list of 1,850 kanji recommended for general use; superseded by the 1,945 Jōyō Kanji)
有用 **yūyō** useful, serviceable, available
灯用 **tōyō** for illumination
自用 **jiyō** for personal/private use
7 作用 **sayō** action, function, effect
乱用 **ran'yō** misuse, abuse, misappropriation
学用品 **gakuyōhin** school supplies
応用 **ōyō** (practical) application
応用科学 **ōyō kagaku** applied science
応用問題 **ōyō mondai** problem to test ability to apply theoretical knowledge
社用 **shayō** for company business
社用族 **shayōzoku** expense-account aristrocrats
利用 **riyō** use, make use of
利用者 **riyōsha** user
私用 **shiyō** private use
8 画用紙 **gayōshi** drawing paper
使用 **shiyō** use, employ, utilize
使用人 **shiyōnin** employee
使用法 **shiyōhō** use, directions
使用者 **shiyōsha** user, consumer; employer
使用料 **shiyōryō** rental fee
使用量 **shiyōryō** amount used
使用権 **shiyōken** right to use
併用 **heiyō** use together, use in combination
効用 **kōyō** use, utility, effect
逆用 **gyakuyō** reverse (of the intended) use
実用 **jitsuyō** practical use, utility
実用主義 **jitsuyō shugi** pragmatism
実用的 **jitsuyōteki** practical
実用品 **jitsuyōhin** utility article
官用 **kan'yō** government business, official use
服用 **fukuyō** take (medicine)
所用 **shoyō** use; business, need
9 専用 **sen'yō** private/personal use, exclusively for
専用車 **sen'yōsha** personal car
専用機 **sen'yōki** personal airplane
重用 **jūyō** appoint to an important post
乗用車 **jōyōsha** passenger car
信用 **shin'yō** trust, confidence; credit; reputation
信用状 **shin'yōjō** letter of credit
信用取引 **shin'yō torihiki** credit transaction
信用組合 **shin'yō kumiai** credit union
俗用 **zokuyō** worldly matters
軍用 **gun'yō** for military use
軍用犬 **gun'yōken** army/military dog
軍用金 **gun'yōkin** war funds; campaign funds
軍用品 **gun'yōhin** military supplies, munitions, materiel
軍用鳩 **gun'yōbato** carrier pigeon
軍用機 **gun'yōki** warplane
急用 **kyūyō** urgent business
連用 **ren'yō** continuous use
連用形 **ren'yōkei** stem (of a verb)
通用 **tsūyō** be in common use, be honored/valid, pass
通用口 **tsūyōguchi** service entrance, side door
通用門 **tsūyōmon** side door, service entrance
通用期間 **tsūyō kikan** period of (a ticket's) validity
耐用年数 **taiyō nensū** useful lifetime, life
活用 **katsuyō** practical use; conjugate, inflect
活用形 **katsuyōkei** inflected form
活用語 **katsuyōgo** inflected word
要用 **yōyō** important matter; need; use
客用 **kyakuyō** for guests
食用 **shokuyō** edible, used for food
食用油 **shokuyō abura** cooking/edible oil
食用品 **shokuyōhin** food(stuffs)
10 借用 **shakuyō** borrowing, loan
借用者 **shakuyōsha** borrower
借用証書 **shakuyō shōsho** bond of debt

兼用 **ken'yō** combined use, serving two purposes
流用 **ryūyō** divert, misappropriate
浴用 **yokuyō** for the bath
起用 **kiyō** appoint, employ
挙用 **kyoyō** appoint, promote
財用 **zaiyō** uses of property; funds
11 商用 **shōyō** business
商用文 **shōyōbun** business correspondence
商用語 **shōyōgo** commercial term
運用 **un'yō** make use of, apply, invest, put into practice
混用 **kon'yō** mix, use together
採用 **saiyō** adopt, employ
常用 **jōyō** common/everyday/habitual use
常用者 **jōyōsha** constant user; addict
常用漢字 **Jōyō Kanji** (official list of 1,945 kanji recommended for general use)
悪用 **akuyō** misuse, abuse, perversion
舶用 **hakuyō** for ships, marine
転用 **ten'yō** divert, convert
12 着用 **chakuyō** have on, wear
善用 **zen'yō** put to good use
援用 **en'yō** claim, quote, invoke
登用 **tōyō** appoint; promote
御用 **goyō** your order/business; official business
御用地 **goyōchi** imperial estate
御用邸 **goyōtei** imperial villa
御用始 **goyō-haji(me)** reopening of offices after New Year's
御用納 **goyō-osa(me)** year-end office closing
御用商人 **goyō shōnin** purveyor to the government
御用達 **goyōtashi** purveyor to the government
御用組合 **goyō kumiai** company union
御用新聞 **goyō shinbun** government newspaper
御用聞 **goyōki(ki)** taking orders
無用 **muyō** useless; needless; without business; prohibited
無用心 **buyōjin** unsafe; incautious
無用長物 **muyō (no) chōbutsu** useless obstruction
雇用 **koyō** employment
雇用主 **koyōnushi** employer
雇用者 **koyōsha** employer
費用 **hiyō** expenses, cost
飲用 **in'yō** drinking
飲用水 **in'yōsui** drinking water
13 準用 **jun'yō** apply (mutatis mutandis)
適用 **tekiyō** apply
愛用 **aiyō** habitual use; favorite
節用 **setsuyō** frugality; dictionary
節用集 **setsuyōshū** dictionary, manual
試用 **shiyō** trial, tryout

路用 **royō** traveling expenses
14 徴用 **chōyō** commandeer, requisition, expropriate
徳用 **tokuyō** economical
徳用品 **tokuyōhin** economy(-size) goods
慣用 **kan'yō** in common use, common
慣用上 **kan'yōjō** by usage
慣用句 **kan'yōku** idiom, common expression
慣用語 **kan'yōgo** idiom, colloquial word/ phrase
算用 **san'yō** computation, calculation
算用数字 **san'yō sūji** Hindu-Arabic numerals
誤用 **goyō** misuse
雑用 **zatsuyō** miscellaneous things to attend to
需用 **juyō** consumption
需用家 **juyōka** consumer, customer
15 器用 **kiyō** dextrous, adroit, skillful
器用貧乏 **kiyō-binbō** Jack of all trades but master of none
16 薬用 **yakuyō** medicinal
18 濫用 **ran'yō** abuse, misuse, misappropriation
22 襲用 **shūyō** follow, adopt

——————— 3 ———————

3 工業用 **kōgyōyō** for industrial use
4 不信用 **fushin'yō** discredit, distrust
不器用 **bukiyō** clumsy, unskillful
反作用 **hansayō** reaction
5 皮算用 **kawazan'yō, kawasan'yō** counting one's pelts before catching the raccoons
6 再使用 **saishiyō** reuse
防火用水 **bōka yōsui** water for putting out fires
自家用 **jikayō** for private use
7 投票用紙 **tōhyō yōshi** ballot
学術用語 **gakujutsu yōgo** technical term
男子用 **danshiyō** for men, men's
8 非実用品 **hijitsuyōhin** unessential items
逆作用 **gyakusayō** adverse effect, reaction
官庁用語 **kanchō yōgo** official jargon
9 専門用語 **senmon yōgo** technical term
食卓用 **shokutakuyō** for table use
10 原稿用紙 **genkō yōshi** manuscript paper
家庭用 **kateiyō** for home use
家庭用品 **kateiyōhin** household goods
胸算用 **munazan'yō** mental arithmetic; expectation
11 運動用具 **undō yōgu** sporting goods
接客用 **sekkyakuyō** for customers
婦人用 **fujin'yō** for ladies, women's
紳士用 **shinshiyō** men's, for men
12 無器用 **bukiyō** clumsy

——————— 4 ———————

2 人材登用 **jinzai tōyō** selection of people for higher positions

6 自浄作用 **jijō-sayō** self-purification
自壊作用 **jikai sayō** disintegration
9 相互作用 **sōgo sayō** interaction
12 廃物利用 **haibutsu riyō** recycling

冊 → 冊 **0a5.42**

叵 → 回 **3s3.1**

───────── 4 ─────────

2r4.1

网

MŌ net

2r4.2 / 198

同 仝

DŌ, ona(ji) the same

───────── 1 ─────────

1 同一 **dōitsu** the same, identical, equal
同一人 **dōitsunin** the same person
同一人物 **dōitsu jinbutsu** the same person
同一視 **dōitsushi** consider alike, put in the same category
2 同人 **dōjin, dōnin** the same person, said person; clique, fraternity, coterie
同人雑誌 **dōjin zasshi** literary coterie magazine, small magazine
3 同工異曲 **dōkō-ikyoku** superficially different but essentially the same
同上 **dōjō** same as above, ditto
同士 **dōshi** fellow, companion
同士打 **dōshiu(chi)** fight among themselves
同士討 **dōshiu(chi)** internecine strife
4 同氏 **dōshi** the same person, said person, he, she
同化 **dōka** assimilation, adaptation
同仁 **dōjin** impartial benevolence
同文同種 **dōbun-dōshu** same script and same race
同日 **dōjitsu** the same day
同心 **dōshin** like-mindedness; concentricity
同心円 **dōshin'en** concentric circles
5 同好 **dōkō** similar tastes
同好会 **dōkōkai** association of like-minded people
同好者 **dōkōsha** people of similar tastes
同穴 **dōketsu** being buried in the same grave
6 同気 **dōki** of like disposition/mind
同年 **dōnen** that (same) year; same age

同年輩 **dōnenpai** persons of the same age
同列 **dōretsu** same row; same rank; company, attendance
同色 **dōshoku** the same color
同地 **dōchi** the same place, that place
同名 **dōmei** the same name
同名異人 **dōmei-ijin** different person of the same name
同行 **dōkō** go together, accompany
dōgyō fellow pilgrim/esthete
同行者 **dōkōsha** traveling companion
同舟 **dōshū** in/on the same boat
7 同位 **dōi** the same rank/position, coordinate
同位元素 **dōi genso** isotope
同伴 **dōhan** accompany, go with
同伴者 **dōhansha** companion
同体 **dōtai (ni)** as one, together
同角 **dōkaku** equal angles
同役 **dōyaku** colleague
同形 **dōkei** the same shape
同学 **dōgaku** the same school
同志 **dōshi** (persons) of like sentiment
同志会 **dōshikai** association of like-minded people
同局 **dōkyoku** the (same/said) bureau
同系 **dōkei** affiliated, akin
同車 **dōsha** take the same car, ride together
8 同事 **dōji** the same thing; no change
同価 **dōka** equivalent
同姓 **dōsei** the same surname
同居 **dōkyo** live in the same house
同居人 **dōkyonin** person living with the family, lodger
同国 **dōkoku** the same country/province; the (said) country
同朋 **dōhō** companions, one's fellows
同性 **dōsei** of the same sex; homogeneous; homosexual
同性愛 **dōseiai** homosexuality
同房 **dōbō** the same cell
同所 **dōsho** the same place, that (same) address
同門 **dōmon** fellow student
9 同乗 **dōjō** ride together
同点 **dōten** a tie/draw
同派 **dōha** the same sect
同型 **dōkei** the same type
同封 **dōfū** enclose
同室 **dōshitsu** the same room
同県 **dōken** the same prefecture
同胞 **dōhō** brothers, brethren
同胞愛 **dōhōai** brotherly love, fraternity
同祖 **dōso** common ancestor
同音 **dōon** the same sound; one voice
同音異義 **dōon-igi** the same pronunciation but different meanings

同音語 **dōongo** homophone, homonym
同級 **dōkyū** the same class
同級生 **dōkyūsei** classmate
10 同衾 **dōkin** sleep together
同郷 **dōkyō** the same village/province
同家 **dōke** the (same) family
同党 **dōtō** the same political party
同座 **dōza** sit together; the same theater; be implicated
同席 **dōseki** sit together
同格 **dōkaku** the same rank; apposition
同時 **dōji** at the same time, simultaneous
同時代 **dōjidai** contemporaneous
同病 **dōbyō** the same illness
11 同宿 **dōshuku** lodge together, stay at the same hotel
同窓生 **dōsōsei** schoolmate, fellow student, alumnus
同窓会 **dōsōkai** alumni association/meeting
同視 **dōshi** treat alike, make no distinction between
同族 **dōzoku** the same family/tribe
同情 **dōjō** sympathy
同異 **dōi** similarities and differences
同断 **dōdan** the same as before, ditto
同船 **dōsen** (take) the same ship
12 同棲 **dōsei** live together, cohabit with
同期 **dōki** the same period; the same class; synchronous
同期生 **dōkisei** (former) classmate
同然 **dōzen** the same as, virtually
同筆 **dōhitsu** the same handwriting
同等 **dōtō** equal, on a par with
同軸 **dōjiku** coaxial
13 同業 **dōgyō** the same trade/business
同勢 **dōzei** party, company
同義 **dōgi** the same meaning
同義語 **dōgigo** synonym
同腹 **dōfuku** born of the same womb; kindred spirits
同数 **dōsū** the same number
同感 **dōkan** the same sentiment, sympathy, concurrence
同意 **dōi** the same meaning; the same opinion; consent, agreement
同意見 **dōiken** the same opinion, like views
同意義 **dōigi** the same meaning
同意語 **dōigo** synonym
同罪 **dōzai** the same crime
同盟 **dōmei** alliance, league, union
Dōmei Japanese Confederation of Labor (short for 全日本労働総同盟)
同盟国 **dōmeikoku** ally
同盟軍 **dōmeigun** allied armies
14 同僚 **dōryō** colleague, associate
同様 **dōyō** the same (kind/way), similar

同種 **dōshu** the same kind, homogeneous
同説 **dōsetsu** the same opinion
15 同慶 **dōkei** a matter for mutual congratulation
同権 **dōken** the same rights, equal rights
同調 **dōchō** alignment; tuning
同質 **dōshitsu** the same quality/nature, homogeneous
同輩 **dōhai** one's equal, comrade, colleague
18 同職 **dōshoku** the same occupation, said occupation
同類 **dōrui** the same kind; accomplice
同額 **dōgaku** the same amount

───── 2 ─────

1 一同 **ichidō** all concerned, all of us
3 大同 **Daidō** (era, 806–810)
大同小異 **daidō-shōi** substantially the same, not much different
大同団結 **daidō danketsu** merger, combination
4 不同 **fudō** not uniform, unequal, uneven, not in order
不同化 **fudōka** nonassimilation
不同意 **fudōi** disagreement, dissent, objection
6 合同 **gōdō** combined, joint
会同 **kaidō** assembly, meeting
共同 **kyōdō** cooperation, collaboration, joint, collective
共同体 **kyōdōtai** community
共同者 **kyōdōsha** collaborator
共同性 **kyōdōsei** cooperation
8 協同 **kyōdō** cooperation, collaboration, partnership
10 帯同 **taidō** be accompanied by
11 混同 **kondō** confuse (one thing with another)
異同 **idō** difference
13 雷同 **raidō** following blindly
14 総同盟罷業 **sōdōmei higyō** general strike
15 敵同士 **katakidōshi** mutual enemies
賛同 **sandō** approval, support
18 類同 **ruidō** similar

───── 3 ─────

1 一心同体 **isshin-dōtai** one flesh; one in body and spirit
一視同仁 **isshi-dōjin** impartiality, universal brotherhood
5 四海同胞 **shikai-dōhō** universal brotherhood
6 同文同種 **dōbun-dōshu** same script and same race
7 呉越同舟 **Go-Etsu dōshū** enemies in the same boat
8 非売同盟 **hibai dōmei** sellers' strike
非買同盟 **hibai dōmei** boycott
欧州同盟 **Ōshū Dōmei** the European Union
11 異口同音 **iku-dōon** with one voice, unanimous

異体同心 **itai-dōshin** of one mind, perfect accord
12 期成同盟 **kisei dōmei** uniting to carry out (a plan)
13 新品同様 **shinpin dōyō** like new

———————— 4 ————————

5 付和雷同 **fuwa-raidō** follow blindly, echo
8 欧州共同体 **Ōshū Kyōdōtai** the European Community

2r4.3

而

JI, shika(shite) and, also, then
shika(mo) moreover

———————— 2 ————————

7 似而非 **ese-** false, would-be, pseudo-
形而上 **keijijō** metaphysical
形而上学 **keijijōgaku** metaphysics
形而下 **keijika** physical, material
形而下学 **keijikagaku** the physical sciences

———————— 5 ————————

2r5.1

冏

KEI, KYŌ clear, bright

2r5.2

甬

YŌ road with walls on both sides

———————— 6 ————————

2r6.1 / 91

周 周

SHŪ circuit, lap, circumference

———————— 1 ————————

4 周辺 **shūhen** periphery, environs, outskirts
6 周年 **shūnen** whole year, anniversary
周防 **Suō** (ancient kuni, Yamaguchi-ken)
周回 **shūkai** circumference, perimeter; surroundings
7 周囲 **shūi** circumference, perimeter; surroundings
周忌 **shūki** anniversary of a death
8 周到 **shūtō** meticulous, careful, thorough
周波 **shūha** cycle, wave, frequency
周波数 **shūhasū** frequency
周知 **shūchi** common knowledge, widely known
10 周遊 **shūyū** tour, excursion, round trip
周遊券 **shūyūken** excursion ticket
周航 **shūkō** circumnavigation

11 周旋 **shūsen** good offices, recommendation, mediation
周旋屋 **shūsen'ya** broker, employment agency
周旋料 **shūsenryō** brokerage, commission
周旋業 **shūsengyō** brokerage, commission agency
周章狼狽 **shūshō-rōbai** consternation, bewilderment, dismay
12 周期 **shūki** period, cycle
周期性 **shūkisei** periodic, cyclical

———————— 2 ————————

1 一周 **isshū** once around, a revolution/tour/lap
一周年 **isshūnen** one full year, anniversary
一周忌 **isshūki** first anniversary of a death
一周期 **isshūki** a period (in astronomy)
4 円周 **enshū** circumference
円周率 **enshūritsu** ratio of circumference to diameter, pi, π
5 半周 **hanshū** go halfway around
7 低周波 **teishūha** low frequency
10 高周波 **kōshūha** high-frequency

———————— 3 ————————

5 用意周到 **yōi-shūtō** very careful, thoroughly prepared

———————— 4 ————————

5 世界一周 **sekai isshū** round-the-world trip, circumnavigation

2r6.2

岡 塇

oka hill

———————— 1 ————————

3 岡山 **Okayama** (city, Okayama-ken)
岡山県 **Okayama-ken** (prefecture)
11 岡崎 **Okazaki** (city, Aichi-ken)

———————— 2 ————————

7 延岡 **Nobeoka** (city, Miyazaki-ken)
8 長岡 **Nagaoka** (city, Niigata-ken)
10 高岡 **Takaoka** (city, Toyama-ken)
11 盛岡 **Morioka** (city, Iwate-ken)
13 福岡 **Fukuoka** (city, Fukuoka-ken)
福岡県 **Fukuoka-ken** (prefecture)
14 静岡 **Shizuoka** (city, Shizuoka-ken)
静岡県 **Shizuoka-ken** (prefecture)

2r6.3

岡

MŌ, ami net

朋 → 朋 4b4.1

青 → 青 **4b4.10**

—————— 7 ——————

2r7.1 / 1415

耐

TAI, ta(eru) endure, withstand

—————— 1 ——————

3 耐久 **taikyū** endurance, persistence, permanence, durability
  耐久力 **taikyūryoku** durability, endurance
  耐久性 **taikyūsei** durability
4 耐切 **ta(e)ki(reru)** be able to endure, can stand
  耐水 **taisui** waterproof, watertight
  耐水性 **taisuisei** water resistance
  耐火 **taika** fireproof, fire-resistant
  耐火力 **taikaryoku** fire resistance
  耐火性 **taikasei** fire resistant
  耐火煉瓦 **taika renga** firebrick
5 耐用年数 **taiyō nensū** useful lifetime, life
7 耐忍 **ta(e)shino(bu)** bear patiently, put up with

12 耐湿 **taishitsu** dampproof
  耐湿性 **taishitsusei** resistance to moisture
  耐寒 **taikan** coldproof
14 耐酸 **taisan** acidproof, acid-resistant
15 耐熱 **tainetsu** heat-resistant
  耐熱鋼 **tainetsukō** refractory steel
  耐震 **taishin** earthquake-proof
  耐震性 **taishinsei** earthquake resistance, quakeproof

—————— 2 ——————

7 忍耐 **nintai** perseverance, patience, endurance
  忍耐強 **nintaizuyo(i)** patient, persevering

2r7.2

冑

CHŪ, kabuto helmet

—————— 2 ——————

5 甲冑 **katchū** armor (and helmet)

—————— 9 ——————

冕 → 冕 **4c7.9**

—————— 几 **2s** ——————

几	凡	㕚	凨	処	凩	夙	凪	咒	凭	風	凫	段
0.1	1.1	2.1	3.1	4i2.2	4.1	4.2	4.3	3d5.11	6.1	7.1	11b2.3	7.2

殷	毇	鳳	梵	凱	鳳
8.1	2j8.9	9.1	4a7.27	10.1	12.1

—————— 0 ——————

2s0.1

几

KI armrest; table

—————— 1 ——————

11 几帳 **kichō** screen, partition
  几帳面 **kichōmen** methodical, precise, punctilious

—————— 2 ——————

7 床几 **shōgi** camp/folding stool

—————— 1 ——————

2s1.1 / 1102

凡

BON, HAN common, ordinary, mediocre
oyo(so) approximately; generally
sube(te) all

—————— 1 ——————

2 凡人 **bonjin** ordinary person, man of mediocre ability

3 凡才 **bonsai** run-of-the-mill ability, mediocre talent
4 凡夫 **bonpu** ordinary man
  凡手 **bonshu** mediocre skill, ordinary talent
5 凡失 **bonshitsu** common error, muff, flub
6 凡百 **bonpyaku, bonbyaku** many, many kinds
7 凡作 **bonsaku** mediocre writing
8 凡例 **hanrei** explanatory notes; legend (on a map/diagram)
  凡退 **bontai** (batter) be put out easily
9 凡俗 **bonzoku** mediocre, common, vulgar
10 凡骨 **bonkotsu** ordinary person
  凡書 **bonsho** ordinary book
11 凡庸 **bon'yō** mediocre, commonplace, banal
  凡眼 **bongan** a layman's eye
12 凡策 **bonsaku** commonplace policy
13 凡愚 **bongu** common person
15 凡慮 **bonryo** ordinary minds/men

—————— 2 ——————

3 大凡 **ōyoso** approximately
5 平凡 **heibon** common, ordinary

2

8 非凡 **hibon** extraordinary, unusual
12 超凡 **chōbon** uncommon, extraordinary

─────── 3 ───────

5 平々凡々 **heihei-bonbon** commonplace, ordinary

─────── 2 ───────

イ
冫
孑
阝
卩
刂
力
又
宀
一
十
亠
卜
ケ
丷
厂
辶
冂
八
匸

→2

2s2.1

殳 **SHU** wooden halberd

─────── 3 ───────

2s3.1

凧 **tako** kite

─────── 1 ───────

6 凧糸 **takoito** kite string

─────── 2 ───────

5 奴凧 **yakkodako** kite in the shape of an ancient footman
12 絵凧 **edako** kite with a picture on it

処→ **4i2.2**

─────── 4 ───────

2s4.1

凩 **kogarashi** wintry wind

2s4.2

夙 **SHUKU, haya(i)** early

─────── 1 ───────

6 夙成 **shukusei** precociousness
7 夙志 **shukushi** long-cherished desire
8 夙夜 **shukuya** from morning till night

2s4.3

凪 **nagi** lull, calm
na(gu) become calm, die down

─────── 2 ───────

3 夕凪 **yūnagi** evening calm
大凪 **ōnagi** dead calm
12 朝凪 **asanagi** morning calm (at sea)

─────── 6 ───────

咒→呪 **3d5.11**

2s6.1

凭 **HYŌ, mota(reru)** lean on; lie heavy on one's stomach
yo(ru) lean on, rest against

─────── 1 ───────

11 凭掛 **mota(re)ka(karu)** lean against; rely on

─────── 7 ───────

2s7.1 / 29

風 **FŪ, FU** wind; appearance; style; custom
kaze, kaza- wind; a cold
furi deportment, behavior; form, pretense

─────── 1 ───────

2 風入 **kazai(re)** airing, ventilation
風子 **kaze (no) ko** (children are) outdoor creatures
風力 **fūryoku** wind power/force
3 風上 **kazakami** windward
風下 **kazashimo** leeward
風土 **fūdo** natural features, climate
風土病 **fūdobyō** endemic disease
風土記 **fudoki** description of the natural features of a region, a topography
風口 **kazaguchi** air intake
4 風化 **fūka** weathering; efflorescence
風切羽 **kazaki(ri)ba** flight feathers
風水害 **fūsuigai** wind and flood damage
風月 **fūgetsu** wind and moon, beauties of nature
5 風圧 **fūatsu** wind pressure
風穴 **kazaana** air hole
6 風気 **kazeke, kazake, kaza(k)ke** a slight cold
風合 **fūai** the feel, texture
風向 **fūkō** wind direction **kazemu(ki), kazamu(ki)** wind direction; situation
風光 **fūkō** scenery, natural beauty
風当 **kazea(tari), kazaa(tari)** force of the wind; criticism, opposition
7 風来坊 **fūraibō** wanderer, vagabond, hobo
風位 **fūi** wind direction
風体 **fūtei, fūtai** appearance, looks, attitude
風伯 **fūhaku** god of the wind
風邪 **kaze, fūja** a cold
風邪気 **kazeke, kaza(k)ke** a slight cold
風邪声 **kazagoe** hoarseness from a cold
風邪薬 **kazegusuri, kazagusuri** medicine/ remedy for a cold
風折 **kazao(re)** broken by the wind
風呂 **furo** bath; bathtub

風呂屋 **furoya** bathhouse, public bath
風呂桶 **furooke** bathtub
風呂場 **furoba** bathroom
風呂銭 **furosen** bath charge
風呂敷 **furoshiki** (square of cloth used to wrap goods and presents in)
風狂 **fūkyō** fanatic; ultra-refined
風災 **fūsai** wind damage
風見 **kazami** weather vane
風車 **fūsha** windmill
　　　kazaguruma pinwheel; windmill
風足 **kazaashi** wind speed
8 風刺 **fūshi** satire, sarcasm
風波 **fūha** wind and waves, storm, rough seas; discord, strife
風味 **fūmi** flavor, taste
風采 **fūsai** appearance, mien, bearing
風物 **fūbutsu** natural features; scenes and manners
風雨 **fūu** wind and rain, rainstorm
9 風信子 **fūshinshi** hyacinth
風信器 **fūshinki** weather vane
風俗 **fūzoku** manners, customs, morals
風俗画 **fūzokuga** painting depicting customs
風除 **kazayo(ke)** windbreak
風変 **fūgawa(ri)** eccentric, peculiar
風前 **fūzen** exposed to the wind
風前灯 **fūzen (no) tomoshibi** (like a) candle in the wind, precarious situation
風速 **fūsoku** wind speed
風速計 **fūsokukei** anemometer
風通 **kazetō(shi)** ventilation
風洞 **fūdō** wind tunnel
風姿 **fūshi** appearance, demeanor
風待 **kazama(chi), kazema(chi)** wait for a favorable wind
風神 **fūshin, fūjin** god of the wind
風神雷神 **fūjin-raijin** the gods of wind and thunder
風紀 **fūki** discipline, public morals
風食 **fūshoku** weathering, wind erosion
10 風浪 **fūrō** wind and waves, heavy seas
風流 **fūryū** elegant, refined, aesthetic
風帯 **fūtai** tassel
風害 **fūgai** wind/storm damage
風格 **fūkaku** character, personality, style
風教 **fūkyō** public morals
風致 **fūchi** taste, elegance; scenic beauty
風致林 **fūchirin** forest planted for scenic beauty
風疹 **fūshin** rubella, German measles
風馬牛 **fūbagyū** indifferent, of no concern; widely disparate
11 風窓 **kazamado** air hole, vent
風脚 **kazaashi** wind speed
風習 **fūshū** manners, customs, ways

風情 **fuzei** taste, appearance, air; elegance; entertainment, hospitality
風眼 **fūgan** gonorrheal ophthalmia
風袋 **fūtai** tare, weight of the packaging; outward appearance
風船 **fūsen** balloon
風雪 **fūsetsu** snowstorm, blizzard
12 風媒花 **fūbaika** wind-pollinated flower
風景 **fūkei** scene(ry), landscape, view
風景画 **fūkeiga** landscape painting
風琴 **fūkin** organ; accordion
風評 **fūhyō** rumor
風雲 **fūun** wind and clouds; times of change
　　　kazagumo wind clouds
風雲児 **fūunji** adventurer, soldier of fortune
13 風鈴 **fūrin** wind chime
風雅 **fūga** elegant, refined, tasteful
14 風塵 **fūjin** dust; worldly affairs
風貌 **fūbō** looks, features, appearance
風説 **fūsetsu** rumor
風聞 **fūbun** report, rumor
15 風儀 **fūgi** manners; (sexual) morality
風潮 **fūchō** tide; trend of the times, the social climate
風趣 **fūshu** natural charm, elegance, grace
風蝕 **fūshoku** weathering, wind erosion
16 風薬 **kazegusuri, kazagusuri** medicine/ remedy for a cold
風諭 **fūyu** hint, indirect suggestion, allegory
17 風霜 **fūsō** wind and frost; hardships
18 風鎮 **fūchin** decorative hanging-scroll weight
19 風靡 **fūbi** overwhelm, take by storm
風韻 **fūin** grace, tastefulness

───────── 2 ─────────

1 一風変 **ippū kawa(tta)** eccentric, queer; unconventional, original
3 川風 **kawakaze** river breeze
夕風 **yūkaze** evening breeze
大風 **ōkaze** strong wind, gale
小風 **kokaze** light breeze
山風 **yamakaze, sanpū** mountain wind
4 不風流 **bufūryū** lacking refinement, prosaic
中風 **chūbū, chūbu** paralysis, palsy
今風 **imafū** present/modern style
水風呂 **mizuburo** cold bath
手風琴 **tefūkin** accordion, concertina
5 北風 **kitakaze, hokufū** north wind
古風 **kofū** old custom, old style
台風 **taifū** typhoon
6 気風 **kifū, kippu** character, disposition, temper; morale, spirit
西風 **nishikaze, seifū** west wind
羽風 **hakaze** breeze caused by flapping wings
防風 **bōfū** protection/shelter against the wind
防風林 **bōfūrin** windbreak (forest)

向風	mu(kai)kaze	headwind
7 良風	ryōfū	good custom
良風美俗	ryōfū-bizoku	good customs
作風	sakufū	literary style
余風	yofū	surviving custom, holdover
谷風	tanikaze	valley wind
没風流	botsufūryū	prosaic, unrefined
狂風	kyōfū	raging winds
芸風	geifū	(acting) style, (musical) technique
学風	gakufū	academic traditions, a school (of thought), method of study, school character
8 画風	gafū	style of painting/drawing
東風	tōfū, kochi	east wind; spring wind
夜風	yokaze	night wind
追風	o(i)kaze, o(i)te	tailwind
逆風	gyakufū	adverse wind, headwind
送風	sōfū	forced air, ventilation
送風機	sōfūki	blower, ventilator, fan
波風	namikaze	wind and waves; discord
昔風	mukashifū	old-fashioned
宗風	shūfū	customs of a school; style
空風	kara(k)kaze	dry wind
国風	kokufū, kuniburi	national customs/songs
松風	matsukaze, shōfū	wind through the pines
欧風	ōfū	European/Western style, occidental
和風	wafū	Japanese style
雨風	amekaze	rain and wind
	amakaze	rainy wind
9 陣風	jinpū	squall, gust
南風	nanpū, minamikaze	south wind
美風	bifū	beautiful/admirable custom
通風	tsūfū	ventilation
通風孔	tsūfūkō	vent, air hole
通風器	tsūfūki	ventilator, aerator
洋風	yōfū	Western-style
海風	kaifū, umikaze	sea breeze
屏風	byōbu	folding screen
屏風岩	byōbu iwa	sheer cliff
春風	harukaze, shunpū	spring wind
神風	kamikaze	divine wind; kamikaze
威風	ifū	majesty, imposing air
威風堂々	ifū dōdō	pomp and circumstance
砂風	safū	sandstorm
砂風呂	sunaburo	sand bath
秋風	akikaze, shūfū	autumn breeze
10 陸風	rikufū	land(-to-sea) breeze
恋風	koikaze	zephyr of love
高風	kōfū	noble mien/character
浦風	urakaze	sea breeze
浜風	hamakaze	beach wind/breeze
家風	kafū	family custom/ways
唐風	karafū	Chinese style
校風	kōfū	school spirit/traditions

殺風景	sappūkei	drab, dull, tasteless
朔風	sakufū	north wind
時風	jifū	the current fashion
書風	shofū	style of calligraphy
烈風	reppū	violent wind, gale
扇風機	senpūki	(electric) fan
破風	hafu	(ornamental) gable eaves
疾風	shippū, hayate	gale, strong wind
疾風迅雷	shippū-jinrai	lightning speed
11 清風	seifū	cool/refreshing breeze
涼風	ryōfū, suzukaze	cool breeze
据風呂	su(e)furo	bathtub with water heater
強風	kyōfū	strong/high winds
旋風	senpū, tsumuji kaze	whirlwind, tornado
悪風	akufū	bad custom, a vice
異風	ifū	unusual custom; unusual style
軟風	nanpū	gentle breeze
12 蛮風	banpū	barbarous customs
蒸風呂	mu(shi)buro	Turkish bath, sauna
葉風	hakaze	breeze passing through leaves
寒風	kanpū	cold wind
朝風	asakaze	morning breeze
朝風呂	asaburo	morning bath
無風	mufū	windless, dead calm
無風流	mufūryū	lack of refinement
無風帯	mufūtai	the doldrums
順風	junpū	favorable/tail wind
13 微風	bifū	gentle breeze
14 遺風	ifū	tradition, old custom
徳風	tokufū	nobility of character
歌風	kafū	poetic style
鼻風邪	hanakaze	head cold
緑風	ryokufū	early-summer breeze
颱風	taifū	typhoon
醇風美俗	junpū bizoku	good morals and manners
15 潮風	shiokaze	sea breeze, salt air
横風	yokokaze	crosswind
暴風	bōfū	high winds, windstorm
暴風雨	bōfūu	rainstorm
暴風雪	bōfūsetsu	snowstorm, blizzard
暴風圏	bōfūken	storm zone/area
熱風	neppū	hot wind/blast
弊風	heifū	bad habit, evil practice, abuse
16 薫風	kunpū	balmy breeze
17 矯風	kyōfū	moral reform
颶風	gufū	typhoon
19 爆風	bakufū	blast
21 魔風	makaze	devil-caused/fearsome storm

--------- 3 ---------

3 大尽風吹	daijinkaze (o) fu(kasu)	display one's wealth
4 日本風	nihonfū	Japanese style
5 外国風	gaikokufū	foreign style/manners
田舎風	inakafū	rustic, country-style

6 多福風邪 **(o)tafuku kaze** mumps
西洋風 **seiyōfū** Western-style
当世風 **tōseifū** latest fashion, up-to-date
7 役人風 **yakunin kaze** air of official dignity
役所風 **(o)yakushofū** red tape, officialism
花鳥風月 **kachō-fūgetsu** the beauties of nature; elegant pursuits
季節風 **kisetsufū** seasonal wind, monsoon
8 定期風 **teikifū** periodic wind
枕屏風 **makurabyōbu** bedside screen
金屏風 **kinbyōbu** gold-leafed folding screen
10 陸軟風 **rikunanpū** land(-to-sea) breeze
破傷風 **hashōfū** tetanus, lockjaw
11 異国風 **ikokufū** foreign customs
12 隙間風 **sukimakaze** a draft
貿易風 **bōekifū** trade winds
15 談論風発 **danron-fūhatsu** animated conversation
17 臆病風 **okubyōkaze** panic, loss of nerve

――― 4 ―――

10 純日本風 **jun-Nihon-fū** classical Japanese style
馬耳東風 **bajitōfū** utter indifference, turn a deaf ear

梟→梟 **11b2.3**

2s7.2 / 362

段 **DAN** step; stairs; rank; column; paragraph
TAN (unit of cloth, 10.6 m by 34 cm); (unit of land area, about 0.1 hectare)

――― 1 ―――

0 段ボール **danbōru** corrugated cardboard
3 段々 **dandan** steps, terrace; gradually, increasingly
段々畑 **dandanbatake** terraced fields
5 段丘 **dankyū** terrace, bench
段平 **danbira** broadsword, sword
7 段別 **tanbetsu** land area, acreage
8 段歩 **tanbu** (unit of land area, about 0.1 hectare)
段物 **danmono** multi-act musical drama
段取 **dando(ri)** program, plan, arrangements
9 段段畑 **dandanbatake** terraced fields
段畑 **danbata** terraced fields
10 段差 **dansa** difference in level/ranking
11 段階 **dankai** stage, phase, step; rank, grade
12 段違 **danchiga(i)** difference in level, uneven (parallel bars)
段落 **danraku** end of a paragraph, section, period; conclusion, settlement
14 段鼻 **danbana** aquiline/Roman nose

――― 2 ―――

1 一段 **ichidan** one stage/step, all the more
一段落 **ichidanraku** a pause
3 三段跳 **sandanto(bi)** hop, step, and jump
三段構 **sandangama(e)** thorough preparation with fall-back options should anything go wrong
上段 **jōdan** upper row; raised portion of a floor, dais; seats of honor
a(gari)dan stairs, doorstep
下段 **gedan, kadan** lowest step/tier, lower column/part
4 中段 **chūdan** halfway up a stairway/slope; center column (of print)
手段 **shudan** means, measures
5 石段 **ishidan** stone steps
6 多段式 **tadanshiki** multistage
全段 **zendan** the whole page
7 別段 **betsudan** special, particular
初段 **shodan** lowest grade/rank
8 昇段 **shōdan** be promoted
9 前段 **zendan** the preceding paragraph/portion
段段 **dandan** steps, terrace; gradually, increasingly
段段畑 **dandanbatake** terraced fields
後段 **kōdan** latter part
10 値段 **nedan** price
格段 **kakudan** marked, exceptional, appreciable
特段 **tokudan** special
11 階段 **kaidan** steps, stairs, stairway
12 普段 **fudan** usual, ordinary; constant, ceaseless
普段着 **fudangi** everyday clothes
減段 **gentan** acreage reduction
14 算段 **sandan** contrive, try, manage
15 踏段 **fu(mi)dan** step, stair

――― 3 ―――

3 大上段 **daijōdan** raising a sword (to kill)
11 梯子段 **hashigodan** step, stair

――― 4 ―――

11 常套手段 **jōtō shudan** well-worn device, old trick
12 遣繰算段 **ya(ri)ku(ri) sandan** getting by, tiding over
無理算段 **muri-sandan** scrape together (money)

――― 8 ―――

2s8.1

殷 **IN** flourishing; dark red

――― 1 ―――

3 殷々 **in'in(to)** roaring, booming, pealing, reverberating
14 殷賑 **inshin** prosperous, thriving

2

2

亻 冫 子 阝 阝 刂 力 又 一 二 十 ケ 勹 丷 厂 辶 冂 几 匚 →9

殺 → **2j8.9**

───────── 9 ─────────

2s9.1

凰 Ō female mythical bird

───────── 2 ─────────

14 鳳凰 **hōō** mythical peacock-like bird which appears when peace and holiness prevail

梵 → **4a7.27**

───────── 10 ─────────

2s10.1

凱 GAI victory song; victory

───────── 右カラム ─────────

11 凱旋 **gaisen** triumphal return
凱旋門 **gaisenmon** arch of triumph
14 凱歌 **gaika** victory song

───────── 12 ─────────

2s12.1

鳳 HŌ male mythical bird

───────── 1 ─────────

5 鳳仙花 **hōsenka** a balsam
11 鳳凰 **hōō** mythical peacock-like bird which appears when peace and holiness prevail

───────── 2 ─────────

5 白鳳 **Hakuhō** (era, 672–686)
8 金鳳花 **kinpōge** buttercup

───────── 匚 2t ─────────

匚	区	巨	匹	叵	匡	匠	臣	匣	医	殴	矩	甚
0.1	2.1	2.2	2.3	3.1	4.1	4.2	4.3	5.1	5.2	6.1	7.1	0a9.10

匪	匿	區	躯	匯	匵	匳	毆	豎	甌	臨	黧
8.1	8.2	2t2.1	3d15.5	11.1	12.1	13.1	2t6.1	5b9.5	3d13.12	15.1	15.2

───────── 0 ─────────

2t0.1

匚 HŌ square container

───────── 2 ─────────

2t2.1 / 183

区 區 KU ward, municipal administrative district

───────── 1 ─────────

3 区々 **kuku** various, diverse, mixed; petty
4 区内 **kunai** in the ward/borough
区切 **kugi(ru)** punctuate; partition
区分 **kubun, kuwa(ke)** division, partition; classification
6 区会 **kukai** ward assembly
7 区別 **kubetsu** distinguish between
区役所 **kuyakusho** ward office
8 区長 **kuchō** head of the ward
区画 **kukaku** division, section

───────── 右カラム ─────────

区画整理 **kukaku seiri** land readjustment, readjustment of town lots
11 区域 **kuiki** boundary; zone, territory
12 区裁判所 **kusaibansho** local court
区間 **kukan** section, interval
14 区劃 **kukaku** division, section

───────── 2 ─────────

1 一区 **ikku** a district/ward; a section/division
4 区区 **kuku** various, diverse, mixed; petty
5 市区 **shiku** municipal district; streets
6 地区 **chiku** district, area, zone
7 学区 **gakku** school district
10 教区 **kyōku** parish
教区民 **kyōkumin** parishoners
13 鉱区 **kōku** mining area/concession
14 漁区 **gyoku** fishing area
管区 **kanku** district, precinct

───────── 3 ─────────

5 司教区 **shikyōku** diocese
7 赤線区域 **akasen kuiki** red-light district
投票区 **tōhyōku** voting district
学校区 **gakkōku** school district
9 軍管区 **gunkanku** military district

13 禁猟区 **kinryōku** game preserve
禁漁区 **kinryōku** no-fishing area
解放区 **kaihōku** liberated areas
14 選挙区 **senkyoku** election district

2t2.2 / 1293

巨 **KYO** large, gigantic

─────────── 1 ───────────
2 巨人 **kyojin** giant
3 巨万 **kyoman** millions, immense amount
巨大 **kyodai** huge, gigantic, enormous
5 巨石 **kyoseki** megalith
6 巨匠 **kyoshō** master, maestro
7 巨体 **kyotai** large body/build
巨材 **kyozai** big timber; great man
巨利 **kyori** huge profits
8 巨歩 **kyoho** giant strides/step
巨岩 **kyogan** huge rock
9 巨星 **kyosei** giant star; great/prominent man
10 巨財 **kyozai** vast fortune
11 巨視的 **kyoshiteki** macroscopic, in broad perspective
巨細 **kyosai** large and small matters; details
巨船 **kyosen** huge ship
12 巨弾 **kyodan** huge projectile, bombshell
巨富 **kyofu** vast wealth
巨費 **kyohi** great cost
13 巨漢 **kyokan** very large man, big fellow
巨資 **kyoshi** enormous amount of capital
14 巨像 **kyozō** huge statue/image
巨魁 **kyokai** ringleader, chief, boss
16 巨頭 **kyotō** leading figure, magnate, big name
18 巨軀 **kyoku** massive figure, large build
巨額 **kyogaku** enormous amount, vast sum
21 巨艦 **kyokan** large warship

2t2.3 / 1500

匹 **HITSU** same kind, comparable; a man
hiki (counter for animals); (unit of cloth length, about 21.8 m)

─────────── 1 ───────────
4 匹夫 **hippu** a man; man of humble position
匹夫匹婦 **hippu-hippu** humble men and women, common people
15 匹敵 **hitteki** rival, compare with, be a match for

─────────── 2 ───────────
1 一匹 **ippiki** one animal; 20 m bolt of cloth
一匹狼 **ippiki ōkami** lone wolf
10 馬匹 **bahitsu** horses

─────────── 3 ───────────
4 匹夫匹婦 **hippu-hippu** humble men and

women, common people
7 男一匹 **otoko ippiki** full-grown man

─────────── 7 ───────────
3 大山鳴動鼠一匹 **taizan meidō (shite) nezumi ippiki** The mountains have brought forth a mouse. Much ado about nothing much.

─────────── 3 ───────────

2t3.1

帀 **SŌ** go around

─────────── 4 ───────────

2t4.1

匡 **KYŌ** correct; save; help

2t4.2 / 1359

匠 **SHŌ** artisan, workman; idea, design
takumi artisan, mechanic, carpenter

─────────── 2 ───────────
2 刀匠 **tōshō** swordsmith
3 工匠 **kōshō** artisan, craftsman
5 巨匠 **kyoshō** master, maestro
6 名匠 **meishō** master artisan
8 宗匠 **sōshō** master, teacher
10 師匠 **shishō** master, teacher
11 船匠 **senshō** shipwright
13 意匠 **ishō** design, idea
18 鵜匠 **ushō, ujō** cormorant fisherman
24 鷹匠 **takajō** falconer

2t4.3 / 835

臣 **SHIN, JIN, omi** retainer, vassal, subject

─────────── 1 ───────────
2 臣子 **shinshi** retainer or child, retainers and children
3 臣下 **shinka** subject, retainer, vassal
5 臣民 **shinmin** subject, national
8 臣事 **shinji** service as a retainer
臣服 **shinpuku** obey, follow
10 臣従 **shinjū** service as a retainer
11 臣道 **shindō** the way of a loyal subject
12 臣属 **shinzoku** vassalage, subjection
13 臣節 **shinsetsu** loyalty to one's liege
20 臣籍 **shinseki** status as a subject
臣籍降下 **shinseki kōka** (royalty) becoming subjects

亻
冫
孑
阝
卩
刂
力
又
一
二
十
卜
ク
ソ
厂
辶
冂
几
匚 4 ←

2

2

─────────── 2 ───────────

3 大臣 **daijin** cabinet member, minister
　下臣 **kashin** lowly retainer
　小臣 **shōshin** lower-ranking vassal
5 旧臣 **kyūshin** an old retainer
6 老臣 **rōshin** senior vassal
　廷臣 **teishin** court official, courtier
　近臣 **kinshin** trusted vassal, personal attendant
　奸臣 **kanshin** treacherous vassal
7 佞臣 **neishin** crafty courtier, treacherous retainer
　乱臣 **ranshin** traitorous vassal, traitor
　君臣 **kunshin** ruler and ruled
8 使臣 **shishin** envoy
　侍臣 **jishin** courtier, attendant
　逆臣 **gyakushin** rebellious retainer, traitor
　忠臣 **chūshin** loyal retainer/subject
　忠臣蔵 **Chūshingura** (the 47 Ronin story)
10 陪臣 **baishin** undervassal
　家臣 **kashin** retainer, vassal
12 朝臣 **chōshin** courtier; the court
　　　 ason court noble
13 群臣 **gunshin** the whole body of officials
　幕臣 **bakushin** shogun's vassal
　愚臣 **gushin** foolish retainer; this humble vassal
　賊臣 **zokushin** rebel, traitor
14 遺臣 **ishin** surviving retainer
19 寵臣 **chōshin** favorite retainer

─────────── 3 ───────────

4 内大臣 **naidaijin** Lord Keeper of the Privy Seal
5 左大臣 **sadaijin** Minister of the Left
　右大臣 **udaijin** Minister of the Right

─────────── 4 ───────────

3 大蔵大臣 **ōkura daijin** Minister of Finance
4 内務大臣 **naimu daijin** (prewar) Home Minister
　文部大臣 **monbu daijin** Minister of Education
5 外務大臣 **gaimu daijin** Minister of Foreign Affairs
　司法大臣 **shihō daijin** Minister of Justice
7 伴食大臣 **banshoku daijin** figurehead minister
8 厚生大臣 **kōsei daijin** Minister of Health and Welfare
　法務大臣 **hōmu daijin** Minister of Justice
9 海軍大臣 **kaigun daijin** Minister of the Navy
14 総理大臣 **sōri daijin** prime minister

─────────── 5 ───────────

12 無任所大臣 **muninsho daijin** minister without portfolio

─────────── 6 ───────────

13 農林水産大臣 **nōrinsuisan daijin** Minister of Agriculture, Forestry and Fisheries

─────────── 5 ───────────

2t5.1

匣　**KŌ** box

2t5.2 / 220

医　醫　**I** medicine, healing art; physician

─────────── 1 ───────────

3 医大 **idai** medical university (short for 医科大学)
7 医学 **igaku** medicine, medical science
　医学生 **igakusei** medical student
　医学界 **igakukai** the medical world, medicine
　医学部 **igakubu** medical department/school
　医局 **ikyoku** medical office
8 医長 **ichō** head doctor
　医官 **ikan** medical officer
　医者 **isha** doctor, physician
9 医院 **iin** doctor's office, clinic, hospital
　医科 **ika** medical science; medical department
　医科大学 **ika daigaku** medical university/school
10 医員 **iin** physician, medical staff
　医師 **ishi** physician, doctor
　医師会 **ishikai** medical association/society
　医書 **isho** medical book
11 医術 **ijutsu** medicine, medical science
　医務室 **imushitsu** medical office
13 医業 **igyō** medical practice
16 医薬 **iyaku** medicine
　医薬品 **iyakuhin** pharmaceuticals
17 医療 **iryō** medical treatment, health care; medical

─────────── 2 ───────────

3 大医 **taii** great physician
　女医 **joi** woman doctor
5 目医者 **meisha** ophthalmologist, optometrist
6 名医 **meii** famous doctor, skilled physician
7 良医 **ryōi** good doctor, skilled physician
　町医者 **machi isha** practicing physician
8 侍医 **jii** court physician
　法医学 **hōigaku** forensic medicine
9 軍医 **gun'i** military surgeon
10 校医 **kōi** school physician
　針医 **harii** acupuncturist
11 庸医 **yōi** mediocre physician, quack
　船医 **sen'i** ship's doctor

12 無医村 **muison** doctorless village
歯医者 **haisha** dentist
筍医者 **takenoko isha** inexperienced doctor
16 獣医 **jūi** veterinarian
獣医学 **jūigaku** veterinary medicine
獣医業 **jūigyō** veterinary practice/business
17 鍼医者 **hariisha** acupuncturist
18 藪医者 **yabuisha** a quack

——————— 3 ———————
4 内科医 **naikai** physician, internist
5 外科医 **gekai** surgeon
主治医 **shujii** physician in charge/attendance
9 専門医 **senmon'i** (medical) specialist
保健医 **hoken'i** public-health physician
11 接骨医 **sekkotsui** bonesetter
産科医 **sankai** obstetrician
眼科医 **gankai** ophthalmologist
12 歯科医 **shikai** dentist
開業医 **kaigyōi** doctor in private practice
13 漢方医 **kanpōi** herbal physician, herbalist
21 顧問医 **komon'i** medical adviser

——————— 4 ———————
3 小児科医 **shōnikai** pediatrician
7 肛門科医 **kōmonkai** proctologist
11 婦人科医 **fujinkai** gynecologist

——————— 6 ———————
2t6.1 / 1940

殴 毆
    Ō, **nagu(ru)** beat, hit, strike

——————— 1 ———————
0 ぶん殴る **(bun)nagu(ru)** beat up, give a
    thrashing
4 殴込 **nagu(ri)ko(mi)** attack, raid
5 殴付 **nagu(ri)tsu(keru)** strike, beat, thrash
殴打 **ōda** assault (and battery)
10 殴殺 **nagu(ri)koro(su), ōsatsu** beat to death,
    strike dead

——————— 7 ———————
2t7.1

矩
    KU, **kane, sashigane** carpenter's
    square

——————— 1 ———————
4 矩尺 **kanejaku** carpenter's square; (unit of
    length, about 30.3 cm)
7 矩形 **kukei** rectangle

甚 → **0a9.10**

——————— 8 ———————
2t8.1

匪
    HI evil person; not, non-

——————— 1 ———————
13 匪賊 **hizoku** bandit, rebel, outlaw
——————— 2 ———————
3 土匪 **dohi** rebellious natives
10 拳匪 **Kenpi** the Boxers

2t8.2 / 1771

匿
    TOKU hide
    kakuma(u) shelter, hide

——————— 1 ———————
6 匿名 **tokumei** anonymous
——————— 2 ———————
10 秘匿 **hitoku** conceal, keep hidden/secret
13 隠匿 **intoku** concealment
15 蔵匿 **zōtoku** conceal, shelter, harbor

——————— 9 ———————
區 → 区 **2t2.1**

躯 → 軀 **3d15.5**

——————— 11 ———————
2t11.1

滙
    KI whirl, swirl

——————— 12 ———————
2t12.1

匱
    KI chest, coffer; have a shortage of

——————— 13 ———————
2t13.1

奩 奩
    REN box for comb, mirror,
    perfume, cosmetics

毆 → 殴 **2t6.1**

2

亻
冫
子
阝
卩
刂
力
又
宀
亠
十
ヒ
ケ
ゝ
厂
辶
冂
几
匸 13←

豎 → 豎 **5b9.5**

───────── 14 ─────────

甌 → **3d13.12**

───────── 15 ─────────

2t15.1 / 836

臨
RIN look out over; go to, be present; copy; rule, subjugate **nozo(mu)** face, confront; attend, be present

───────── 1 ─────────

4 臨月 **ringetsu** last month of pregnancy
5 臨写 **rinsha** copying
6 臨休 **rinkyū** special holiday (short for 臨時休校 or 臨時休業)
　臨地 **rinchi** on-site, on-the-spot
7 臨床 **rinshō** clinical
　臨床家 **rinshōka** clinician
8 臨幸 **rinkō** visit by the emperor
9 臨海 **rinkai** seaside, coastal, marine
　臨界 **rinkai** critical (temperature)
10 臨席 **rinseki** attendance, presence
　臨時 **rinji** temporary, provisional, extraordinary
　臨時費 **rinjihi** contingent expenses
　臨書 **rinsho** copying (from a model)

11 臨終 **rinjū** one's last moments, deathbed
12 臨港線 **rinkōsen** harbor railway line
　臨場 **rinjō** attendance, presence, visit
　臨御 **ringyo** visit by the emperor
　臨検 **rinken** inspection visit; raid, search
13 臨戦 **rinsen** going into battle/action
16 臨機 **rinki** expedient, as the situation requires
　臨機応変 **rinki-ōhen** adaptation to circumstances

───────── 2 ─────────

6 再臨 **sairin** the Second Coming
7 来臨 **rairin** one's attendance, presence
　君臨 **kunrin** reign
9 降臨 **kōrin** advent, descent
12 登臨 **tōrin** climb a height; ascend the throne
13 照臨 **shōrin** shine/look down on; rule; come (polite)
16 親臨 **shinrin** emperor's presence/visit

2t15.2

翳
EI shade, block the light, dim
kaza(su) hold up (to the light); stick (a flower) in one's hair
kasu(mu) have dim eyesight

───────── 1 ─────────

5 翳目 **kasu(mi)me** dim eyesight, partial blindness

───────── 2 ─────────

10 陰翳 **in'ei** shadow; shading; gloom
　振翳 **fu(ri)kaza(su)** fling up, brandish

氵 3a

水	永	氷	汁	汀	氾	辻	汝	汕	池	汚	汗	汲
0.1	1.1	1.2	2.1	2.2	2.3	3.1	3.2	3.3	3.4	3.5	3.6	3.7
江	汐	泛	汎	汞	沐	汨	汪	沁	沪	沖	決	沌
3.8	3.9	3.10	3.11	3.12	4.1	4.2	4.3	4.4	3a15.8	4.5	4.6	4.7
汰	沈	沃	沍	沚	沂	沙	汾	沒	没	汽	返	沢
4.8	4.9	4.10	2b4.3	4.11	4.12	4.13	4.14	3a4.15	4.15	4.16	4.17	4.18
沓	泣	泪	油	沸	泄	沫	油	泔	決	波	泌	泝
4.19	5.1	3a7.21	5.2	5.3	5.4	5.5	5.6	5.7	5.8	5.9	5.10	5.11
泯	泙	泳	泊	注	沮	泡	泓	法	況	沱	注	沿
5.12	5.13	5.14	5.15	5.16	5.17	5.18	5.19	5.20	5.21	5.22	3a5.16	5.23
沼	沛	沽	沾	治	泥	河	泗	泗	泉	泰	昶	津
5.24	5.25	5.26	5.27	5.28	5.29	5.30	5.31	5.32	5.33	5.34	4c5.16	6.1
浹	洩	浅	洒	洙	洫	洌	泇	洲	浮	洗	洛	洪
6.2	6.3	6.4	6.5	6.6	6.7	6.8	6.9	6.10	6.11	6.12	6.13	6.14
洸	活	洽	浄	洋	海	派	涎	洵	洶	洞	洄	酒
6.15	6.16	6.17	6.18	6.19	6.20	6.21	6.22	6.23	6.24	6.25	6.26	7.1

浦 7.2	涛 3a14.8	浬 7.3	浹 7.4	浪 7.5	浙 7.6	浜 7.7	涅 7.8	浩 7.9	流 7.10	浚 7.11	涇 7.12	涉 3a8.20
涓 7.13	浤 7.14	浣 7.15	消 7.16	涚 3a15.7	浸 7.17	浴 7.18	淳 7.19	涕 7.20	海 3a6.20	涌 3a9.31	涙 7.21	涵 3a8.35
淦 8.1	淮 8.2	淯 8.3	渚 3a9.1	淵 3a9.3	渤 3a9.3	淑 8.4	淋 8.5	淅 8.6	淞 8.7	淤 8.8	游 8.9	游 8.10
淇 8.11	淒 2b8.4	淕 8.12	渇 8.13	混 8.14	淡 8.15	淺 3a6.4	溪 8.16	淫 8.17	淨 3a6.18	清 8.18	渋 8.19	涉 8.20
深 8.21	添 8.22	淀 8.23	淙 8.24	淌 8.25	渮 8.26	淹 8.27	淪 8.28	液 8.29	済 8.30	涼 8.31	淬 8.32	淚 3a7.21
涯 8.33	淘 8.34	涵 8.35	涸 8.36	淼 8.37	渚 9.1	湛 9.2	淵 9.3	測 9.4	渳 9.5	渺 9.6	湫 9.7	湖 9.8
湘 9.9	湃 9.10	湮 9.11	湊 9.12	港 9.13	渭 9.14	湾 9.15	渫 9.16	渹 3a12.17	渣 9.17	湶 3a5.33	湟 9.18	湑 9.19
湍 9.20	温 9.21	湿 9.22	湯 9.23	渇 3a8.13	湲 9.24	満 9.25	渝 9.26	滋 9.27	渾 9.28	渟 9.29	渙 9.30	湧 9.31
涵 9.32	渥 9.33	潺 9.34	渡 9.35	漣 3a10.27	渦 9.36	減 9.37	溺 10.1	溯 10.2	溲 10.3	溥 10.4	溽 10.5	滑 10.6
滔 10.7	滝 10.8	溝 10.9	溍 10.10	溜 10.11	滉 10.12	温 3a9.21	溢 10.13	滯 10.14	溢 3a10.19	溪 3a8.16	溶 10.15	滓 10.16
漢 10.17	漠 10.18	溂 3a4.16	溢 10.19	滄 10.20	溟 10.21	漓 10.22	滂 10.23	溏 10.24	濾 3a15.8	源 10.25	滅 10.26	漣 10.27
涸 10.28	黎 10.29	漁 11.1	漼 3a17.3	漸 11.2	滸 11.3	漱 11.4	漲 11.5	滌 11.6	漕 11.7	漾 11.8	漂 11.9	滯 3a10.14
漆 11.10	漫 11.11	漬 11.12	満 3a9.25	漢 3a10.17	演 11.13	滴 11.14	滾 11.15	滷 11.16	滲 11.17	漚 11.18	漏 11.19	漉 11.20
漿 11.21	潮 12.1	澈 12.2	潡 3a12.11	漑 12.3	澎 12.4	潴 3a16.5	澆 12.5	潜 12.6	潽 12.7	潘 12.8	潷 3a10.11	潟 12.9
潔 12.10	澄 12.11	潭 12.12	潼 12.13	潰 12.14	潰 12.15	潦 12.16	潑 12.17	澁 3a8.19	潯 12.18	澗 3a12.19	澗 12.19	潤 12.20
激 13.1	澱 13.2	澣 13.3	澳 13.4	澡 13.5	澪 13.6	濃 13.7	澤 3a4.18	濁 13.8	濛 13.9	澹 13.10	濂 13.11	韜 13.12
瀾 14.1	瀞 3a16.2	鴻 14.2	濮 14.3	潜 3a12.6	濟 3a8.30	濡 14.4	濯 14.5	澀 3a8.19	濕 3a9.22	濘 14.6	濬 14.7	濤 14.8
濠 14.9	潤 8e9.3	瀏 15.1	濺 15.2	豬 3a16.5	濫 15.3	瀑 15.4	潘 15.5	瀉 15.6	瀆 15.7	濾 15.8	瀁 15.9	瀧 3a10.8
瀚 16.1	瀞 16.2	瀬 3a16.3	瀨 16.3	瀕 16.4	豬 16.5	潛 3a12.6	瀟 16.6	瀛 16.7	瀘 16.8	瀝 16.9	瀲 17.1	瀨 3a16.4
瀰 17.2	灌 17.3	瀾 17.4	灘 3a19.1	灘 19.1	灑 19.2	灣 3a9.15						

─────── 0 ───────

3a0.1 / 21

水 SUI water; Wednesday
　 mizu water

─────── 1 ───────

2 水入 mizui(re) water jug, pitcher
　　 mizui(razu de) privately, among
　　 ourselves
水力 suiryoku water/hydro power
水力工学 suiryoku kōgaku hydraulic
　　 engineering
水力学 suirikigaku, suiryokugaku hydrau-
　　 lics
水力発電所 suiryoku hatsudensho hydro-
　　 electric plant
3 水上 suijō (on the) water, aquatic
　　 minakami headwaters, source
水上生活者 suijō seikatsusha seafarer
水上飛行機 suijō hikōki hydroplane,
　　 seaplane
水上警察 suijō keisatsu water/harbor police
水上競技 suijō kyōgi water sports
水口 mizuguchi, mizukuchi spout, water
　　 inlet/outlet
4 水天彷彿 suiten-hōfutsu sea and sky
　　 merging into each other
水夫 suifu sailor, seaman
水中 suichū underwater, in the water
水化物 suikabutsu a hydrate
水分 suibun moisture, water content
水辺 suihen water's edge, shore
水引 mizuhiki multi-color string for tying
　　 gifts
水火 suika water and fire
水牛 suigyū water buffalo
水心 mizugokoro swimming; doing as one is
　　 done to
水戸 Mito (city, Ibaraki-ken)
5 水生 suisei aquatic (plant)
水母 kurage jellyfish
水仙 suisen daffodil; narcissus
水仕事 mizu shigoto scrubbing and washing
水平 suihei horizontal
水平面 suiheimen horizontal plane/surface
水平線 suiheisen the horizon; horizontal line
水圧 suiatsu water/hydraulic pressure
水圧計 suiatsukei water-pressure gauge
水圧機 suiatsuki hydraulic press
水玉 mizutama drop of water/dew; polka
　　 dots
水田 suiden paddy
6 水死 suishi drowning
水気 mizuke moisture, juiciness
　　 suiki dropsy; moisture, humidity, vapor

水防 suibō flood prevention
水色 mizu-iro sky blue, turquoise
水争 mizu araso(i) irrigation/water-rights
　　 dispute
水汲 mizuku(mi) drawing water
水先 mizusaki direction of a current; ship's
　　 course
水先案内 mizusaki annai pilot; piloting
水先案内人 mizusaki annainin (harbor) pilot
水成岩 suiseigan sedimentary rock
水虫 mizumushi athlete's foot
7 水位 suii water level
水位標 suiihyō watermark
水冷式 suireishiki water-cooled
水兵 suihei (navy) sailor
水兵服 suiheifuku sailor's uniform;
　　 (schoolgirl's) sailor suit
水呑百姓 mizuno(mi)-byakushō poor farmer
水牢 mizurō water-filled dungeon
水災 suisai flood
水攻 mizuze(me) cutting off the water to or
　　 inundating (a castle)
水利 suiri water use/supply/transport,
　　 irrigation
水車 suisha water wheel, turbine
8 水油 mizu-abura hair oil; lamp oil
水泳 suiei swimming
水泳大会 suiei taikai swimming meet
水泳着 suieigi swimming suit
水泳場 suieijō swimming place/pool
水泳帽 suieibō swimming/bathing cap
水泡 suihō foam, bubble
水治療法 suichiryōhō water cure, hydro-
　　 therapy
水茎 mizuguki writing brush
水茎跡 mizuguki (no) ato brush writing,
　　 calligraphy
水苔 mizugoke bog moss; encrustation
水底 suitei, minasoko sea/river bottom
水枕 mizu-makura water-filled pillow
水杯 mizu-sakazuki farewell cups of water
水肥 suihi liquid manure
水明 suimei shimmering of (sun)light on
　　 water
水炊 mizuta(ki) boiling (chicken)
水物 mizumono liquid, drink, fruit; matter of
　　 chance, a gamble
水性 suisei aqueous, water
　　 mizushō flirtatious, wanton
水性塗料 suisei toryō water-based paint
水門 suimon watergate, floodgate, penstock,
　　 sluice
9 水風呂 mizuburo cold bath
水洟 mizu(p)pana, mizubana runny nose,
　　 snivel
水洩 mizumo(ri) leak

水洗 **suisen, mizuara(i)** wash without soap, rinse
水洗便所 **suisen benjo** flush toilet
水垢 **mizuaka** encrustation, slime
水垢離 **mizugori** cold-water ablutions
水草 **suisō, mizukusa** aquatic plant
水茶屋 **mizuchaya** (Edo-period) roadside teahouse
水屋 **mizuya** hand-washing font for worshippers; cupboard; drinking-water seller
水面 **suimen, minomo** surface of the water
水柱 **mizubashira** column of water, waterspout
水枯 **mizuga(re)** drought
水星 **suisei** Mercury
水神 **suijin** water god
水音 **mizuoto** the sound of water
水臭 **mizukusa(i)** watery; lacking in intimacy, distant
水盃 **mizu-sakazuki** farewell cups of water
水食 **suishoku** erosion
10 水耕 **suikō** hydroponics
水耕法 **suikōhō** hydroponics
水陸 **suiriku** water and land, amphibious
水都 **suito** city on the water's edge
水差 **mizusa(shi)** water jug, pitcher
水遊 **mizuaso(bi)** playing with/in water
水流 **suiryū** current, stream of water
水浸 **mizubita(shi)** submerged, flooded; waterlogged
水浴 **suiyoku** bathing, cold bath
    mizua(bi) bathing
水捌 **mizuha(ke)** drainage
水害 **suigai** flood damage, flooding
水害防止 **suigai bōshi** flood prevention
水害地 **suigaichi** flood-stricken area
水害対策 **suigai taisaku** flood control/relief measures
水脈 **suimyaku** vein of water; water main
水時計 **mizu-dokei** water clock
水疱 **suihō** blister
水疱瘡 **mizubōsō** chicken pox
水紋 **suimon** concentric wavelets, ripples
水素 **suiso** hydrogen
水素爆弾 **suiso bakudan** hydrogen bomb
11 水商売 **mizu shōbai** trades dependent on public patronage (bars, restaurants, entertainment)
水瓶 **mizugame** water jar/jug
水運 **suiun** water transport
水道 **suidō** piped water, waterworks, city water, aqueduct; waterway, channel
水道局 **suidōkyoku** water bureau
水道栓 **suidōsen** hydrant, tap
水道料 **suidōryō** water charges
水道管 **suidōkan** water pipe/main

水深 **suishin** (water) depth
水域 **suiiki** area of the ocean, waters
水掛論 **mizuka(ke)ron** futile argument
水彩画 **suisaiga** a watercolor
水彩画家 **suisai gaka** watercolor painter
水彩絵具 **suisai e(no)gu** watercolors
水菓子 **mizugashi** fruit
水萍 **suihyō** floating weed
水菜 **mizuna** potherb mustard (greens for pickling)
水密 **suimitsu** watertight
水桶 **mizuoke** pail, bucket; cistern
水理学 **suirigaku** hydrography, hydraulics
水球 **suikyū** water polo
水族館 **suizokukan** (public) aquarium
水悪戯 **mizu itazura** playing with/in water
水産 **suisan** marine products
水産大学 **suisan daigaku** fisheries college
水産技師 **suisan gishi** fisheries expert
水産学 **suisangaku** the science of fisheries
水産物 **suisanbutsu** marine products
水産業 **suisangyō** fisheries, marine products industry
水盛 **mizumo(ri)** (using a) carpenter's level
水船 **mizubune** cistern, water trough; water-supply boat; swamped boat
水責 **mizuze(me)** water torture
水魚交 **suigyo (no) maji(wari)** intimate friendship
12 水禽 **suikin** waterfowl
水割 **mizuwa(ri)** (whiskey) diluted with water
水着 **mizugi** bathing suit, swimwear
水温 **suion** water temperature
水揚 **mizua(ge)** landing, unloading; earnings; watering (cut flowers so they last longer); deflowering
水落 **mizuo(chi)** solar plexus, pit of the stomach
水葬 **suisō** burial at sea
水蒸気 **suijōki** water vapor; steam
水棲 **suisei** aquatic (animal)
水脹 **mizubuku(re)** blister
水晶 **suishō** quartz, crystal
水晶体 **suishōtai** lens (of the eye)
水量 **suiryō** water volume
水量計 **suiryōkei** water meter
水無月 **minazuki** sixth lunar month, June
水煮 **mizuni** boiled (in unsalted water)
水番 **mizuban** irrigation-water watchman
水痘 **suitō** chicken pox
水筒 **suitō** water flask, canteen
水飲 **mizuno(mi)** drinking glass/fountain
水飲百姓 **mizuno(mi)-byakushō** poor farmer
13 水際 **mizugiwa, migiwa** water's edge, shore
水際立 **mizugiwada(tta)** splendid, fine
水勢 **suisei** force of water, current

3

氵 0 ←
土
扌
口
女
巾
犭
弓
彳
彡
艹
宀
⺌
山
圭
广
尸
口

水準 **suijun** water level; level, standard
水準器 **suijunki** (carpenter's) level
水溜 **mizuta(mari)** puddle, pool
水溶性 **suiyōsei** water-soluble
水溶液 **suiyōeki** aqueous solution
水源 **suigen** headwaters, source, fountainhead
水源地 **suigenchi** headwaters, source
水搔 **mizuka(ki)** web(foot), paddle
水嵩 **mizukasa** volume of water
水楢 **mizunara** (a variety of) oak
水腫 **suishu** dropsy; edema
水煙 **mizukemuri, suien** spray
水鉄砲 **mizudeppō** squirt gun
水雷 **suirai** torpedo; mine
水雷艇 **suiraitei** torpedo boat
14 水滴 **suiteki** drop of water
水漏 **mizumo(ri)** leak
水漉 **mizuko(shi)** filter, strainer
水増 **mizuma(shi)** water down, dilute, pad
水墨画 **suibokuga** India-ink painting
水蜜桃 **suimitsutō** (a variety of) peach
水様液 **suiyōeki** aqueous humor
水稲 **suitō** paddy/wet-land rice
水練 **suiren** swimming practice; (art of) swimming
水精 **suishō** quartz, crystal
水管 **suikan** water pipe/tube
水酸化物 **suisankabutsu** a hydroxide
水銀 **suigin** mercury
水銀灯 **suigintō** mercury lamp
水銀柱 **suiginchū** column of mercury
水飴 **mizuame** starch syrup
15 水澄 **mizusu(mashi)** whirligig beetle
水撒 **mizuma(ki)** sprinkling
水槽 **suisō** water tank/trough
水盤 **suiban** flower basin
水線 **suisen** waterline, draft line
水蝕 **suishoku** erosion
16 水薬 **mizugusuri, suiyaku** liquid medicine
水樽 **mizudaru** water cask
18 水曜日 **suiyōbi** Wednesday
水翻 **mizukobo(shi)** slop basin
水難 **suinan** sea disaster, flood, drowning
水難除 **suinan'yo(ke)** charm against drowning
19 水爆 **suibaku** hydrogen bomb (short for 水素爆弾)
水鏡 **mizu-kagami** reflecting water surface
水鶏 **kuina** rail, mud hen
22 水嚢 **suinō** water bag; filter, percolator

——— 2 ———

2 入水 **nyūsui, jusui** suicide by drowning
3 大水 **ōmizu** flood, inundation
上水 **jōsui** water supply, tap water
上水道 **jōsuidō** piped/city water

下水 **gesui** sewer, drain, drainage
下水道 **gesuidō** drainage/sewer system, drain
下水管 **gesuikan** sewer/drain (pipe)
小水 **shōsui** urine, urination
山水 **sansui** landscape, natural scenery
　　yamamizu mountain spring water
山水画 **sansuiga** landscape painting; a landscape
4 井水 **seisui** well water
天水 **tensui** rainwater
天水桶 **tensui oke** rain barrel
止水 **shisui** still water
分水界 **bunsuikai** watershed, (continental) divide
分水線 **bunsuisen** watershed, (continental) divide
分水嶺 **bunsuirei** watershed, (continental) divide
手水 **temizu, chōzu** water for washing the hands
手水場 **chōzuba** lavatory, toilet
月水 **gessui** menstruation
月水金 **ges-sui-kin** Mondays, Wednesdays, and Fridays
火水 **himizu** fire and water; discord
王水 **ōsui** aqua regia
5 出水 **shussui, demizu** flood, inundation, freshet
生水 **namamizu** unboiled water
加水分解 **kasui bunkai** hydrolysis
用水 **yōsui** city/irrigation water
用水池 **yōsuichi, yōsuiike** reservoir
用水路 **yōsuiro** irrigation channel
氷水 **kōrimizu** ice water; shaved ice
打水 **u(chi)mizu** watering, sprinkling
白水 **shiromizu** white water left after washing rice **shiramizu** white water, whitecaps
6 死水 **shi(ni)mizu** water given to a dying person
防水 **bōsui** waterproof, watertight; flooding prevention
防水布 **bōsuifu** waterproof cloth, tarpaulin, oilskin
羊水 **yōsui** amniotic fluid
迎水 **muka(e)mizu** pump-priming
汚水 **osui** filthy water, sewage
汗水 **asemizu** profuse sweat
江水 **kōsui** (Yangtze/Yangzi) river water
吃水 **kissui** draft (of a ship)
吃水線 **kissuisen** waterline
行水 **gyōzui** bath
7 含水炭素 **gansuitanso** carbohydrate
冷水 **reisui, hi(ya)mizu** cold water
冷水浴 **reisuiyoku** cold bath/shower
冷水摩擦 **reisui masatsu** rubdown with a cold wet towel

決水 **kessui** water breaking through (a dike)
花水木 **hanamizuki** dogwood
利水 **risui** water utilization, irrigation
8 逃水 **ni(ge)mizu** mirage of water
注水 **chūsui** pour water into, flood, douche
治水 **chisui** riverbank improvement, flood control
治水工事 **chisui kōji** riverbank works
泥水 **deisui, doromizu** muddy water
泥水社会 **doromizu shakai** red-light districts
泥水稼業 **doromizu kagyō** shameful occupation
河水 **kasui** river water
呼水 **yo(bi)mizu** pump-priming water
若水 **wakamizu** first water drawn on New Year's Day
岩水 **iwamizu** water flowing from rocks
放水 **hōsui** drainage, discharge
放水路 **hōsuiro** drainage canal/channel
放水管 **hōsuikan** drainpipe
雨水 **amamizu, usui** rainwater
9 重水 **jūsui** heavy water
重水素 **jūsuiso** heavy hydrogen, deuterium
降水 **kōsui** precipitation
降水量 **kōsuiryō** (amount of) precipitation
冠水 **kansui** be submerged/flooded
耐水 **taisui** waterproof, watertight
耐水性 **taisuisei** water resistance
風水害 **fūsuigai** wind and flood damage
泉水 **sensui** garden pond, fountain
洪水 **kōzui** flood, inundation, deluge
浄水 **jōsui** clean water, water purification
浄水池 **jōsuichi** filtration bed, clean-water reservoir
海水 **kaisui** seawater
海水浴 **kaisuiyoku** swimming in the ocean
海水浴場 **kaisuiyokujō** bathing beach
海水着 **kaisuigi** bathing/swimming suit
海水帽 **kaisuibō** bathing/swimming cap
炭水化物 **tansuikabutsu** carbohydrates
背水陣 **haisui (no) jin** last stand
畑水練 **hatake suiren** (like) learning swimming on dry land, book learning
秋水 **shūsui** clear autumn stream
香水 **kōsui** perfume
10 差水 **sa(shi)mizu** (adding) water
原水爆 **gensuibaku** atomic and hydrogen bombs, nuclear bombs
進水 **shinsui** launch (a ship)
進水式 **shinsuishiki** launching ceremony
流水 **ryūsui** running water, stream
浸水 **shinsui** be inundated
胸水 **kyōsui** fluid in the thoracic cavity
恐水病 **kyōsuibyō** hydrophobia, rabies
純水 **junsui** pure water
配水 **haisui** water supply/distribution

11 疎水 **sosui** drainage; canal
疏水 **sosui** drainage; canal
渇水 **kassui** water shortage
渇水期 **kassuiki** dry season, drought period
淡水 **tansui** freshwater
淡水化 **tansuika** desalin(iz)ation
淡水魚 **tansuigyo** freshwater fish
淡水湖 **tansuiko** freshwater lake
渓水 **keisui** mountain stream
清水 **shimizu, seisui** pure/clear water
    Shimizu (city, Shizuoka-ken); (surname) **Kiyomizu** (temple in Kyōto)
添水 **sōzu** deer scare (Japanese-garden contrivance in which water flows into a pivoted bamboo tube which repeatedly fills up, tips over, empties, then rights itself again, its lower end clopping against a stone); (also called 鹿威 shishiodo(shi))
排水 **haisui** drainage; displacement (of a ship)
排水量 **haisuiryō** displacement (of a ship)
排水路 **haisuiro** culvert, sewer system
排水管 **haisuikan** drainpipe
排水トン数 **haisui tonsū** displacement tonnage
脱水 **dassui** dehydration, desiccation
脱水機 **dassuiki** dehydrator, dryer
黒水引 **kuromizuhiki** black-and-white string
経水 **keisui** menstruation
断水 **dansui** water supply cutoff
軟水 **nansui** soft water
12 着水 **chakusui** landing on water, splashdown
遣水 **ya(ri)mizu** stream built through a garden; water (a bonsai)
湖水 **kosui** lake
温水 **onsui** warm water
湯水 **yumizu** hot and cold water
満水 **mansui** full to the brim with water
湧水 **wa(ki)mizu** spring water
減水 **gensui** low/subsiding water
揚水 **yōsui** pumping water
揚水車 **yōsuisha** scoop wheel
揚水所 **yōsuijo** pumping-up station
短水路 **tansuiro** short course, 25–50 m pool length
復水器 **fukusuiki** condenser
寒水 **kansui** cold water
検水 **kensui** water testing/measuring
無水 **musui** anhydrous, waterless, dry (weight)
散水 **sansui** water sprinkling
散水車 **sansuisha** street sprinkler truck
硬水 **kōsui** hard water
畳水練 **tatami suiren** like practicing swimming on a tatami, useless book learning
給水 **kyūsui** water supply

3

氵 0 ←
土
扌
口
女
巾
犭
弓
彳
彡
艹
宀
丷
山
耂
广
尸
口

3

→1 氵
  土
  扌
  日
  女
  巾
  犭
  弓
  彳
  彡
  艹
  宀
  屮
  山
  吉
  广
  尸
  口

給水所 **kyūsuijo** water station
給水栓 **kyūsuisen** faucet, hydrant
給水管 **kyūsuikan** water pipe
紫水晶 **murasakizuishō** amethyst
貯水 **chosui** storage of water
貯水池 **chosuichi** reservoir
貯水塔 **chosuitō** water tower
貯水量 **chosuiryō** pondage
貫水 **mora(i)mizu** water from a neighbor
軽水 **keisui** light water (reactor)
飲水 **no(mi)mizu** drinking water
雲水 **unsui** itinerant priest, mendicant
13 溝水 **dobumizu** ditch water
溜水 **tama(ri)mizu** standing/stagnant water
溢水 **issui** inundation
塩水 **shiomizu, ensui** salt water, brine
豊水期 **hōsuiki** rainy season
腹水 **fukusui** abdominal dropsy
煙水晶 **kemuri-zuishō** smoky quartz
聖水 **seisui** holy water
節水 **sessui** use water sparingly
鉱水 **kōsui** mineral water
14 漏水 **rōsui** water leakage
増水 **zōsui** (river) rise, swell, flood
静水 **seisui** still/stagnant water
碧水 **hekisui** blue water
導水 **dōsui** conduct water (into)
鼻水 **hanamizu** nasal mucus, runny nose
誘水 **saso(i)mizu** pump priming
領水 **ryōsui** territorial waters
15 潮水 **chōsui, shiomizu** seawater
潜水 **sensui** dive, submerge
潜水夫 **sensuifu** diver
潜水母艦 **sensui bokan** submarine tender
潜水服 **sensuifuku** diving suit
潜水病 **sensuibyō** the bends
潜水帽 **sensuibō** diving helmet
潜水器 **sensuiki** diving bell/apparatus
潜水艦 **sensuikan** a submarine
撒水 **sansui, sassui** watering, sprinkling
撒水車 **sansuisha, sassuisha** street sprinkler
撥水性 **hassuisei** water repellent/repellence
噴水 **funsui** jet of water; fountain
霊水 **reisui** miracle-working water
16 濁水 **dakusui** muddy water
18 覆水盆返 **fukusui bon (ni) kae(razu)** No use crying over spilt milk.
離水 **risui** (seaplane's) takeoff from water
20 灌水 **kansui** sprinkling, irrigation
鹹水魚 **kansuigyo** saltwater fish

———————— 3 ————————
3 大洪水 **Daikōzui** the Flood/Deluge
上下水道 **jōgesuidō** water and sewer service
山紫水明 **sanshi-suimei** purple hills and crystal streams, scenic beauty

4 日向水 **hinatamizu** sun-warmed water
5 石灰水 **sekkaisui** limewater
立板水 **ta(te)ita (ni) mizu** fluency, glibness, volubility, rattling on, logorrhea
6 地下水 **chikasui** underground water
8 岩清水 **iwashimizu** spring flowing from rocks
9 美顔水 **bigansui** face lotion
草入水晶 **kusai(ri)zuishō** crystal with impurities forming grass-blade patterns
炭化水素 **tanka suiso** hydrocarbon
炭酸水 **tansansui** carbonated water
食塩水 **shokuensui** saline solution
10 烏行水 **karasu (no) gyōzui** a quick bath
11 魚心水心 **uogokoro (areba) mizugokoro** helping each other
12 蒸溜水 **jōryūsui** distilled water
飲用水 **in'yōsui** drinking water
飲料水 **inryōsui** drinking water
13 農林水産大臣 **nōrinsuisan daijin** Minister of Agriculture, Forestry and Fisheries
農林水産省 **Nōrinsuisanshō** Ministry of Agriculture, Forestry and Fisheries
寝耳水 **nemimi (ni) mizu** a complete surprise
触発水雷 **shokuhatsu suirai** contact (sea) mine

———————— 4 ————————
1 一衣帯水 **ichii taisui** narrow strait
6 防火用水 **bōka yōsui** water for putting out fires
行雲流水 **kōun-ryūsui** floating clouds and flowing water; taking life easy
7 我田引水 **gaden insui** drawing water for one's own field, promoting one's own interests
8 明鏡止水 **meikyō-shisui** serene state of mind

———————— 6 ————————
5 生理的食塩水 **seiriteki shokuensui** saline solution

———————— 1 ————————

3a1.1 / 1207

永

EI, naga(i) long (time)

———————— 1 ————————
3 永久 **eikyū** permanence, perpetuity, eternity
Eikyū (era, 1113–1118)
永久歯 **eikyūshi** permanent tooth
永万 **Eiman** (era, 1165–1166)
永小作 **eikosaku** perpetual (land) lease
永小作権 **eikosakuken** perpetual (land) lease
4 永仁 **Einin** (era, 1293–1299)
5 永生 **eisei** eternal life, immortality
永世 **eisei** permanence, eternity

永正 **Eishō** (era, 1504–1521)
6 永年 **einen, naganen** many years, a long time
7 永承 **Eijō** (era, 1046–1053)
永住 **eijū** permanent residence
永劫 **eigō** eternal, forever
永享 **Eikyō** (era, 1429–1441)
永延 **Eien** (era, 987–989)
8 永長 **Eichō** (era, 1096–1097)
永治 **Eiji** (era, 1141–1142)
9 永保 **Eihō** (era, 1081–1084)
10 永祚 **Eiso** (era, 989–990)
永眠 **eimin** eternal sleep, death
11 永訣 **eiketsu** farewell forever, death
12 永遠 **eien** eternity
永禄 **Eiroku** (era, 1558–1570)
13 永続 **eizoku, nagatsuzu(ki)** perpetuity
14 永暦 **Eiryaku** (era, 1160)
18 永観 **Eikan** (era, 983–985)

——————— 2 ———————

3 大永 **Daiei** (era, 1521–1528)
4 元永 **Gen'ei** (era, 1118–1120)
天永 **Ten'ei** (era, 1110–1113)
文永 **Bun'ei** (era, 1264–1275)
日永 **hinaga** long (spring) day
6 安永 **An'ei** (era, 1772–1781)
7 寿永 **Juei** (era, 1182–1184)
応永 **Ōei** (era, 1394–1428)
8 建永 **Ken'ei** (era, 1206–1207)
宝永 **Hōei** (era, 1704–1711)
9 貞永 **Jōei** (era, 1232–1233)
11 康永 **Kōei** (era, 1342–1345)
13 寛永 **Kan'ei** (era, 1624–1643)
14 嘉永 **Kaei** (era, 1848–1854)

3a1.2 / 1206

氷 冰

HYŌ, kōri, hi ice
kō(ru) freeze (up)

——————— 1 ———————

3 氷刃 **hyōjin** keenly honed sword
氷山 **hyōzan** iceberg
4 氷水 **kōrimizu** ice water; shaved ice
7 氷豆腐 **kōridōfu** frozen tofu
8 氷河 **hyōga** glacier
氷河期 **hyōgaki** glacial period, ice age
氷枕 **kōri-makura** ice-filled pillow
氷雨 **hisame** a cold rain; hail
9 氷削機 **hyōsakuki** ice-shaving machine
氷点 **hyōten** the freezing point
氷点下 **hyōtenka** below the freezing point, below zero (Celsius)
氷海 **hyōkai** frozen sea, icy waters
氷挟 **kōribasa(mi)** ice tongs
氷室 **himuro, hyōshitsu** icehouse, coldroom
氷炭 **hyōtan** ice and charcoal; irreconcilable

氷屋 **kōriya** ice shop, iceman
氷砂糖 **kōrizatō** rock candy, crystal sugar
10 氷原 **hyōgen** ice field/floe
11 氷菓子 **kōrigashi** a frozen sweet
氷袋 **kōribukuro** ice bag/pack
氷雪 **hyōsetsu** ice and snow
12 氷期 **hyōki** ice age
氷晶 **hyōshō** ice crystals
氷結 **hyōketsu** freeze (over)
氷酢酸 **hyōsakusan** glacial acetic acid
13 氷塊 **hyōkai** lump/block of ice, ice floe
氷解 **hyōkai** thaw, melt away, be dispelled
氷詰 **kōrizu(me)** packed in ice
14 氷漬 **kōrizu(ke)** packed in ice, iced
15 氷醋酸 **hyōsakusan** glacial acetic acid
22 氷嚢 **hyōnō** ice bag/pack

——————— 2 ———————

5 北氷洋 **Hoppyōyō, Hokuhyōyō** the Arctic Ocean
7 花氷 **hanagōri** flowers frozen in ice
初氷 **hatsugōri** first ice of the winter
8 雨氷 **uhyō** freezing rain
9 削氷機 **sakuhyōki** ice-shaving machine
南氷洋 **Nanpyōyō** the Antarctic Ocean
浮氷 **fuhyō** drift ice, ice floe
海氷 **kaihyō** sea ice
砕氷 **saihyō** icebreaking; rubble ice
砕氷船 **saihyōsen** icebreaker
10 流氷 **ryūhyō** drift ice, ice floe
12 着氷 **chakuhyō** ice up, icing
結氷 **keppyō** freeze over, form ice
13 解氷 **kaihyō** thaw
14 製氷 **seihyō** icemaking
製氷所 **seihyōsho** ice plant
製氷機 **seihyōki** ice machine
16 薄氷 **usugōri, hakuhyō** thin ice
樹氷 **juhyō** frost/ice on trees
19 霧氷 **muhyō** rime, hoarfrost

——————— 3 ———————

4 月下氷人 **gekka hyōjin** matchmaker, go-between, cupid

——————— 2 ———————

3a2.1 / 1794

汁

JŪ juice
shiru, tsuyu juice, sap; soup, broth, gravy

——————— 1 ———————

8 汁物 **shirumono** soups
10 汁粉 **shiruko** sweet adzuki-bean soup with rice cake
11 汁液 **jūeki** juice

——————— 2 ———————

1 一汁一菜 **ichijū-issai** a simple meal
5 出汁 **da(shi)jiru, dashi** broth, (soup) stock

6 肉汁 **nikujū** meat juice, gravy, broth
灰汁 **aku** lye; harsh taste
旨汁 **uma(i) shiru** the cream, rakeoff
8 果汁 **kajū** fruit juice
毒汁 **dokujū** poisonous juices
苦汁 **kujū** bitter experience　**nigari** brine
9 茹汁 **yu(de)jiru** broth
胆汁 **tanjū** bile, gall
胆汁質 **tanjūshitsu** bilious/choleric (temperament)
10 狸汁 **tanukijiru** tanuki-meat soup
11 液汁 **ekijū** juice; sap
14 墨汁 **bokujū** India ink
鼻汁 **hanashiru** nasal mucus, runny nose
15 澄汁 **su(mashi)jiru** clear soup/broth
17 膿汁 **nōjū** pus
闇汁 **yamijiru** pot-luck soup to which each participant contributes and which is eaten with the lights out

――――― 3 ―――――
8 味噌汁 **miso shiru** miso soup
12 煮出汁 **nida(shi)jiru** soup stock, broth

3a2.2
汀　**TEI, migiwa** water's edge, shore

3a2.3
氾　**HAN** spread out

――――― 1 ―――――
18 氾濫 **hanran** flooding, inundation

――――― 3 ―――――

3a3.1
沑　**nuta** wetland, marsh

3a3.2
汝　**JO, nanji** you, thou

3a3.3
汕　**SAN** fish swimming; fishing with a net

3a3.4 / 119
池　**CHI, ike** pond, reservoir

――――― 1 ―――――
4 池心 **chishin** center/middle of a pond

――――― 2 ―――――
5 古池 **furuike** old pond
6 肉池 **nikuchi** ink-pad case
10 酒池肉林 **shuchi-nikurin** sumptuous feast
11 掘池 **ho(ri)ike** artificial pond/pool
13 溜池 **ta(me)ike** reservoir, cistern
蓮池 **hasuike** lotus pond
電池 **denchi** battery, dry cell
14 墨池 **bokuchi** ink(stone) well

――――― 3 ―――――
5 用水池 **yōsuichi, yōsuiike** reservoir
6 光電池 **kōdenchi** photoelectric cell
7 沈澱池 **chindenchi** settling pond/reservoir
9 浄水池 **jōsuichi** filtration bed, clean-water reservoir
11 乾電池 **kandenchi** dry cell, battery
12 貯水池 **chosuichi** reservoir
13 蓄電池 **chikudenchi** storage battery
15 養魚池 **yōgyochi** fish/breeding pond

3a3.5 / 693
汚　**O, kitana(i), kega(rawashii)** dirty
yogo(reru), kega(reru) become dirty
yogo(su), kega(su) make dirty

――――― 1 ―――――
4 汚水 **osui** filthy water, sewage
6 汚名 **omei** blot on one's name, stigma, dishonor
汚行 **okō** disgraceful conduct, scandal
8 汚物 **obutsu** dirt, filth; sewage
yogo(re)mono soiled things, the wash/laundry
9 汚点 **oten** stain, smudge, blot, disgrace
汚垢 **okō** dirt
汚染 **osen** pollution, contamination
汚臭 **oshū** foul odor
10 汚辱 **ojoku** disgrace, dishonor, obloquy
13 汚損 **oson** stain, soiling, corruption
14 汚塵 **ojin** filth
16 汚濁 **odaku** corruption, decadence
18 汚穢 **owai, oai** night soil, muck
汚穢屋 **owaiya** night-soil man
汚職 **oshoku** corruption, graft
汚職罪 **oshokuzai** bribery

――――― 2 ―――――
3 口汚 **kuchiyogo(shi)** small morsel
kuchigitana(i) foul-mouthed, abusive
13 腹汚 **haragitana(i)** low-minded
16 薄汚 **usugitana(i)** filthy, dirty-looking
18 顔汚 **kaoyogo(shi)** disgrace, discredit

――――― 3 ―――――
13 意地汚 **ijikitana(i)** greedy, gluttonous

3a3.6 / 1188

汗

KAN, ase sweat

——————— 1 ———————

0 汗ばむ **ase(bamu)** become moist with sweat, be slightly sweaty

汗だく **ase(daku)** be dripping with sweat

汗みずく **ase(mizuku)** be dripping with sweat

4 汗不知 **aseshirazu** prickly-heat/baby powder

汗水 **asemizu** profuse sweat

6 汗衣 **kan'i** underwear; sweaty clothes

汗血 **kanketsu** sweat and blood

8 汗知 **aseshi(razu)** prickly-heat/baby powder

汗取 **aseto(ri)** underwear

9 汗染 **aseji(mi)** sweat-stained

汗臭 **asekusa(i)** smelling of sweat

汗疣 **asemo** prickly heat, heat rash

10 汗疹 **asemo** prickly heat, heat rash

汗馬 **kanba** sweating horse

13 汗搔 **ase(k)ka(ki), aseka(ki)** heavy perspirer

汗腺 **kansen** sweat gland

18 汗顔 **kangan** sweating from shame

——————— 2 ———————

3 大汗 **ōase** profuse sweating

5 生汗 **namaase** a tense sweat

玉汗 **tama (no) ase** beads of sweat

6 多汗症 **takanshō** excessive sweating

7 冷汗 **hi(ya)ase, reikan** a cold sweat

8 油汗 **aburaase** clammy sweat

9 発汗 **hakkan** sweating

10 流汗 **ryūkan** perspiration

脂汗 **aburaase** greasy sweat

11 盗汗 **tōkan, nease** night sweat

13 寝汗 **nease** night sweat

3a3.7

KYŪ draw (water); busy
ku(mu) draw (water), ladle, dip, pump; consider, empathize with

——————— 1 ———————

2 汲入 **ku(mi)i(reru)** fill up (with water)

3 汲干 **ku(mi)ho(su)** drain, pump/bail out

汲上 **ku(mi)a(geru)** pump/scoop/draw up

汲々 **kyūkyū (to shite)** diligently, industriously

4 汲込 **ku(mi)ko(mu)** fill up (with water)

5 汲出 **ku(mi)da(su)** bail/scoop/pump out

汲立 **ku(mi)ta(te)** freshly drawn (from the well)

8 汲取 **ku(mi)to(ru)** draw (water), dip up (night soil); take into consideration, make allowances for

汲取便所 **ku(mi)to(ri) benjo** hole-in-the-floor/non-flush toilet

——————— 2 ———————

4 水汲 **mizuku(mi)** drawing water

6 汲汲 **kyūkyū (to shite)** diligently, industriously

15 潮汲 **shioku(mi)** drawing seawater (for salt-making)

3a3.8 / 821

江

KŌ river; the Yangtze/Yangzi river
e inlet, bay

——————— 1 ———————

3 江口 **kōkō** estuary

4 江水 **kōsui** (Yangtze/Yangzi) river water

江戸 **Edo** (old name for Tōkyō, 1603–1867)

江戸子 **Edo(k)ko** true Tōkyōite

江戸川 **Edogawa** (river, Chiba-ken)

江戸前 **Edomae** Edo-style (cooking)

5 江北 **kōhoku** north of the (Yangtze/Yangzi) river

6 江西 **Kōsei** Jiangxi (province)

7 江村 **kōson** river village

9 江南 **kōnan** south of the (Yangtze/Yangzi) river

12 江湖 **kōko** the public

——————— 2 ———————

2 入江 **i(ri)e** inlet, cove

6 近江 **Ōmi** (ancient kuni, Shiga-ken)

8 松江 **Matsue** (city, Shimane-ken)

11 堀江 **horie** canal

16 濁江 **nigo(ri)e** muddy inlet/creek

——————— 3 ———————

12 揚子江 **Yōsukō** the Yangtze/Yangzi river

13 楊子江 **Yōsukō** the Yangzi/Yangtze river

3a3.9

汐

SEKI, shio (evening) tide

——————— 1 ———————

3 汐干狩 **shiohiga(ri)** shell gathering at low tide

——————— 2 ———————

6 血汐 **chishio** blood

15 潮汐 **chōseki** (morning and evening) tide

3a3.10

泛 HAN float; broad, general

3a3.11

汎 HAN pan-

──────── 1 ────────

4 汎太平洋 **han-Taiheiyō** Pan-Pacific
9 汎神論 **hanshinron** pantheism
13 汎愛 **han'ai** philanthropy
　汎愛主義 **han'ai shugi** philanthropism
15 汎論 **hanron** outline, summary

──────── 2 ────────

5 広汎 **kōhan** wide(-ranging), extensive

3a3.12

汞 KŌ mercury

──────── 1 ────────

8 汞和金 **kōwakin** amalgam

──────── 2 ────────

5 甘汞 **kankō** calomel, mercurous chloride

──────── 4 ────────

3a4.1

沐 MOKU wash

──────── 1 ────────

10 沐浴 **mokuyoku** bathe, wash oneself

3a4.2

汨 KOTSU flowing
BEKI (name of a river in China)

3a4.3

汪 Ō expanse of water; large; pond, pool

3a4.4

沁 SHIN soak/seep in

沪→濾 **3a15.8**

3a4.5 / 1346

沖 沖 CHŪ, oki open sea, offing

──────── 1 ────────

0 沖する **chū(suru)** rise high (into the sky)
4 沖天 **chūten** rising skyward
　沖辺 **okibe** the offing, offshore
6 沖仲仕 **okinakashi** stevedore, longshoreman
　沖合 **okia(i)** open sea, offshore
10 沖値 **okine** free-overside price
11 沖釣 **okizu(ri)** offshore fishing
14 沖漁 **okiryō** offshore fishing
15 沖縄県 **Okinawa-ken** (prefecture)
16 沖積土 **chūsekido** alluvial soil
　沖積期 **chūsekiki** the alluvial epoch
　沖積層 **chūsekisō** alluvial stratum

3a4.6 / 356

決 決 KETSU, ki(meru) decide
ki(maru) be decided

──────── 1 ────────

0 決する **kes(suru)** determine, decide on, resolve
　決して **kes(shite)** (with negative) never, by no means
4 決文句 **ki(mari)monku** set phrase, conventional expression
　決水 **kessui** water breaking through (a dike)
　決手 **ki(me)te** deciding factor, clincher
　決心 **kesshin** determination, resolution
5 決付 **ki(me)tsu(keru)** take to task, scold
6 決死 **kesshi** desperate, do-or-die
　決死隊 **kesshitai** suicide corps
　決行 **kekkō** decisive action; carry out
7 決択 **kettaku** decide between, choose
　決志 **kesshi** resolve
8 決河 **kekka** river breaking through (its dikes)
　決定 **kettei** decision, determination
　決定版 **ketteiban** definitive edition
　決定的 **ketteiteki** decisive, conclusive, definitive
　決定権 **ketteiken** (right of) decision
　決定論 **ketteiron** determinism
10 決起 **kekki** spring to one's feet (with renewed resolve)
11 決済 **kessai** settlement (of accounts); liquidation
　決断 **ketsudan** decision, resolve
　決断力 **ketsudanryoku** resolution, determination
12 決着 **ketchaku** conclusiveness, settlement
　決勝 **kesshō** decision (in a contest)
　決勝点 **kesshōten** goal, finish line

決勝戦 **kesshōsen** finals
決勝線 **kesshōsen** goal/finish line
決然 **ketsuzen** resolute, decisive, firm
決裂 **ketsuretsu** breakdown, rupture, collapse
決裁 **kessai** decide upon, approve
決答 **kettō** definite answer
13 決戦 **kessen** decisive battle; playoffs
決意 **ketsui** determination, resolution
14 決選 **kessen** final/runoff election
決算 **kessan** settlement (of accounts); liquidation
決算日 **kessanbi** settlement day
決算報告 **kessan hōkoku** closing-of-accounts report, financial statement
決算期 **kessanki** accounting period/term
15 決潰 **kekkai** rupture, break, collapse
16 決壊 **kekkai** rupture, break, collapse
18 決闘 **kettō** duel
20 決議 **ketsugi** resolution, decision, vote
決議文 **ketsugibun** (written) resolution
決議事項 **ketsugi jikō** agenda, resolutions
決議案 **ketsugian** resolution, proposal
決議権 **ketsugiken** voting right, vote
決議機関 **ketsugi kikan** voting body; party organization, caucus
決議録 **ketsugiroku** minutes (of a meeting)

————————— 2 —————————

1 一決 **ikketsu** be agreed/settled
4 不決断 **fuketsudan** indecisive, vacillating, irresolute
月決 **tsukigi(me)** monthly (contract)
5 本決 **hongima(ri)** final decision
未決 **miketsu** pending, unsettled
未決囚 **miketsushū** unconvicted prisoner
未決済 **mikessai** outstanding (accounts)
未決算 **mikessan** outstanding (accounts)
可決 **kaketsu** approval, adoption (of a resolution)
処決 **shoketsu** settle, decide
6 先決 **senketsu** previous decision
先決問題 **senketsu mondai** question to be settled first
自決 **jiketsu** self-determination; resignation (from a post); suicide
7 即決 **sokketsu** prompt decision
即決裁判 **sokketsu saiban** summary trial
判決 **hanketsu** judgment, (judicial) decision
対決 **taiketsu** confrontation, showdown
否決 **hiketsu** rejection, voting down
8 取決 **toriki(me)** arrangement, agreement
9 専決 **senketsu** decide/act on one's own
速決 **sokketsu** quick decision
独決 **hito(ri)gi(me)** decide by oneself, take it for granted
10 既決 **kiketsu** decided, settled

既決囚 **kiketsushū** a convict
准決勝 **junkesshō** semifinals
11 採決 **saiketsu** voting
票決 **hyōketsu** vote, voting
終決 **shūketsu** settlement, conclusion
12 裁決 **saiketsu** decision, ruling
評決 **hyōketsu** verdict
13 準決勝 **junkesshō** semifinals
解決 **kaiketsu** solution, settlement
14 総決算 **sōkessan** complete financial statement
15 論決 **ronketsu** discuss and decide
20 議決 **giketsu** decision, resolution
議決権 **giketsuken** voting rights

————————— 3 —————————

5 未解決 **mikaiketsu** unsolved, unsettled
6 多数決 **tasūketsu** decision by the majority
10 原判決 **genhanketsu** the original decision/judgment

————————— 4 —————————

9 速戦即決 **sokusen-sokketsu** all-out surprise offensive, blitzkrieg
12 無罪判決 **muzai hanketsu** acquittal
衆議一決 **shūgi-ikketsu** decided unanimously

沛 → 3a5.25

3a4.7

沌 **TON** chaos

————————— 2 —————————

11 混沌 **konton** chaos, confusion
12 渾沌 **konton** chaos, confusion

3a4.8

汰 **TA** wash away the bad; sort, select

————————— 2 —————————

7 沙汰 **sata** case, matter, affair; news, notice, information; instructions; rumor
11 淘汰 **tōta** (natural) selection, weeding out

————————— 3 —————————

4 公沙汰 **ōyakezata** public affair
8 表沙汰 **omotezata** making public; lawsuit
取沙汰 **to(ri)zata** rumor, gossip
9 音沙汰 **otosata** news, tidings
12 無沙汰 **busata** silence, neglect to write/call

————————— 4 —————————

3 刃傷沙汰 **ninjōzata** bloodshed

10 烏滸沙汰 **oko(no)sata** absurd; impertinent
12 御無沙汰 **gobusata** neglect to visit/write

3a4.9 / 936

沈 **CHIN, JIN, shizu(mu)** (intr.) sink
shizu(meru) (tr.) sink

――――――― 1 ―――――――

2 沈丁花 **jinchōge, chinchōge** (sweet-smelling) daphne
3 沈下 **chinka** sinking, subsidence, settling
7 沈没 **chinbotsu** sinking
沈没船 **chinbotsusen** sunken ship
沈吟 **chingin** hum; meditate, muse
8 沈泥 **chindei** silt
9 沈降 **chinkō** sedimentation, precipitation
沈勇 **chin'yū** calm courage
沈香 **chinkō** aloe (wood)
沈香樹 **chinkōju** aloe
沈思 **chinshi** meditation, contemplation
11 沈設 **chinsetsu** lay (an undersea cable)
12 沈着 **chinchaku** composed, calm
沈痛 **chintsū** sad, sorrowful, grave
13 沈溺 **chindeki** be drowned in, be addicted to
沈滞 **chintai** stagnation, inactivity
14 沈静 **chinsei** stillness; stagnation
15 沈潜 **chinsen** be engrossed in
沈黙 **chinmoku** silence
16 沈澱 **chinden** precipitation, sedimentation
沈澱池 **chindenchi** settling pond/reservoir
沈澱物 **chindenbutsu** deposit, precipitate
沈澱槽 **chindensō** settling tank
沈積 **chinseki** sedimentation, depositing
29 沈鬱 **chin'utsu** melancholy, gloomy, depressed

――――――― 2 ―――――――

5 打沈 **u(chi)shizu(mu)** be depressed/dejected
6 自沈 **jichin** scuttle one's own boat
血沈 **ketchin** precipitation of blood
7 赤沈 **sekichin** blood sedimentation
9 浮沈 **fuchin, u(ki)shizu(mi)** rise and fall, ups and downs
10 消沈 **shōchin** dejected, despondent
15 撃沈 **gekichin** (attack and) sink
銷沈 **shōchin** dejected, depressed
19 爆沈 **bakuchin** blow up and sink
21 轟沈 **gōchin** sink instantly

――――――― 4 ―――――――

13 意気消沈 **iki-shōchin** dejected, despondent

3a4.10

沃 **YOKU** fertile; pour
YŌ (used phonetically)

――――――― 1 ―――――――

3 沃土 **yokudo** fertile land/soil
6 沃地 **yokuchi** fertile land/soil
10 沃素 **yōso** iodine
11 沃野 **yokuya** fertile field/plain

――――――― 2 ―――――――

8 肥沃 **hiyoku** fertile

 洰 → 洰 **2b4.3**

3a4.11

沚 **SHI** shore, shoal

3a4.12

沂 **GI** (name of a river in China)

3a4.13

沙 **SA, SHA, suna, isago** sand

――――――― 1 ―――――――

7 沙汰 **sata** case, matter, affair; news, notice, information; instructions; rumor
8 沙弥 **shami** Buddhist acolyte, novice
沙門 **shamon** Buddhist priest
13 沙漠 **sabaku** desert

――――――― 2 ―――――――

4 公沙汰 **ōyakezata** public affair
8 表沙汰 **omotezata** making public; lawsuit
取沙汰 **to(ri)zata** rumor, gossip
9 音沙汰 **otosata** news, tidings
毘沙門天 **Bishamon-ten** Vaisravana, god of treasure
12 無沙汰 **busata** silence, neglect to write/call

――――――― 3 ―――――――

3 刃傷沙汰 **ninjōzata** bloodshed
10 烏滸沙汰 **oko(no)sata** absurd; impertinent
11 曼珠沙華 **manjushage** cluster-amaryllis (also known as *higanbana*)
12 御無沙汰 **gobusata** neglect to visit/write

3a4.14

汾 **FUN** (name of a river in China)

沒 → 没 **3a4.15**

3a4.15 / 935

没 沒

BOTSU, MOTSU sink down; die

──────── 1 ────────

0 没する **bos(suru)** sink, set, go down; hide, disappear
2 没入 **botsunyū** be immersed/absorbed in
4 没収 **bosshū** confiscate
6 没年 **botsunen** one's age at death; year of death
没交渉 **bokkōshō** unrelated, independent
7 没我 **botsuga** self-effacement, selflessness
没却 **bokkyaku** ignore, forget
9 没風流 **botsufūryū** prosaic, unrefined
没後 **botsugo** after one's death, posthumous
没食子 **mosshokushi, bosshokushi** gallnut
10 没書 **bossho** rejected (manuscript)
11 没常識 **botsujōshiki** lack of common sense
没理想 **botsurisō** lack of ideals; realism (in literature)
12 没落 **botsuraku** downfall, ruin
没落者 **botsurakusha** a bankrupt; ruined people
15 没趣味 **bosshumi** insipid, prosaic, dull
16 没頭 **bottō** be engrossed/absorbed in

──────── 2 ────────

4 日没 **nichibotsu** sunset
日没前 **nichibotsuzen** before sunset
日没後 **nichibotsugo** after sunset
5 出没 **shutsubotsu** frequently appear (then disappear)
生没 **seibotsu** (year of one's) birth and death
6 死没 **shibotsu** death
7 沈没 **chinbotsu** sinking
沈没船 **chinbotsusen** sunken ship
9 陣没 **jinbotsu** be killed in action
10 埋没 **maibotsu** be buried; fall into obscurity
病没 **byōbotsu** death from illness, natural death
13 戦没 **senbotsu** death in battle, killed in action
戦没者 **senbotsusha** fallen soldier
15 潜没 **senbotsu** submerge, dive
18 覆没 **fukubotsu** capsize and sink

──────── 4 ────────

9 神出鬼没 **shinshutsu-kibotsu** elusive, phantom

3a4.16 / 135

汽 滊

KI steam

──────── 1 ────────

5 汽圧 **kiatsu** steam pressure

---

6 汽缶 **kikan** boiler
汽缶室 **kikanshitsu** boiler room
7 汽車 **kisha** train (drawn by a steam locomotive)
汽車弁当 **kisha bentō** railway lunch
汽車便 **kishabin** (sent) by rail
汽車賃 **kishachin** train fare
11 汽船 **kisen** steamship, steamer
汽笛 **kiteki** (steam) whistle, siren
12 汽艇 **kitei** (steam) launch
14 汽管 **kikan** steam pipe
汽関 **kikan** boiler, steam generator
16 汽機室 **kikishitsu** boiler/engine room
23 汽罐 **kikan** boiler

──────── 2 ────────

8 夜汽車 **yogisha** night train

──────── 3 ────────

3 川蒸汽 **kawajōki** river steamboat
10 陸蒸汽 **okajōki** steam train

3a4.17

汳

HEN (proper name)

3a4.18 / 994

沢 澤

TAKU swamp; blessing
sawa swamp, marsh

──────── 1 ────────

3 沢山 **takusan** many, much, plenty
6 沢地 **sawachi** swampland, marshes, bog
11 沢庵 **takuan** pickled daikon
沢庵漬 **takuanzuke** pickled daikon

──────── 2 ────────

2 子沢山 **kodakusan** many children (in the family)
4 手沢 **shutaku** soiled/shiny from much handling
手沢本 **shutakubon** a favorite book
6 光沢 **kōtaku** luster, gloss, polish
7 余沢 **yotaku** blessings, benefits
8 沼沢 **shōtaku** marsh, swamp
金沢 **Kanazawa** (city, Ishikawa-ken)
10 恵沢 **keitaku** favor, benefit
恩沢 **ontaku** favors, benefits
11 盛沢山 **mo(ri)dakusan** many, plenty, varied
14 徳沢 **tokutaku** grace
15 潤沢 **juntaku** plentiful, abundant; profit, favor; gloss, luster
18 藤沢 **Fujisawa** (city, Kanagawa-ken)
贅沢 **zeitaku** luxury, extravagance
贅沢品 **zeitakuhin** luxury item

3

氵 4←
土
扌
口
女
巾
犭
弓
彳
彡
艹
宀
⺌
山
吉
广
尸
口

3a4.19

沓 TŌ fluently; intermixed
kutsu shoes, boots

————— 1 —————
11 沓脱 kutsunu(gi) place to take one's shoes off (before entering the house)

————— 2 —————
13 鉄沓 kanagutsu horseshoe
14 雑沓 zattō hustle and bustle, congestion

————— 5 —————

3a5.1 / 1236

泣 KYŪ, na(ku) cry, weep na(kasu), na(kaseru) let/make (someone) cry na(keru) be moved to tears

————— 1 —————
3 泣上戸 na(ki)jōgo maudlin drinker
4 泣止 na(ki)ya(mu) stop crying
5 泣出 na(ki)da(su) burst into tears, start crying
泣付 na(ki)tsu(ku) entreat, implore
6 泣伏 na(ki)fu(su) throw oneself down crying
泣叫 na(ki)sake(bu) scream, cry, shriek, wail
泣虫 na(ki)mushi crybaby
7 泣声 na(ki)goe crying, tearful voice, sob
泣言 na(ki)goto complaint, grievance
8 泣味噌 na(ki)miso crybaby
泣明 na(ki)a(kasu) cry all night
9 泣面 na(ki)tsura, na(kit)tsura crying/tearful face
10 泣真似 na(ki)mane crocodile tears
泣笑 na(ki)wara(i) smile through one's tears
11 泣崩 na(ki)kuzu(reru) break down and cry
12 泣場 na(kase)ba pathetic scene
泣落 na(ki)o(tosu) persuade (someone) by tears
泣訴 kyūso appeal, implore
13 泣寝入 na(ki)ne-i(ri) cry oneself to sleep
泣腫 na(ki)ha(rasu) get swollen eyes from crying
14 泣暮 na(ki)ku(rasu) live in sorrow
17 泣濡 na(ki)nu(reru) be tear-stained
18 泣顔 na(ki)gao crying/tearful face

————— 2 —————
2 人泣 hitona(kase) nuisance to others
5 号泣 gōkyū wailing, lamentation
7 忍泣 shino(bi)na(ki) subdued sobbing
男泣 otokona(ki) weeping in spite of being a man
8 空泣 sorana(ki) crocodile tears
9 咽泣 muse(bi)na(ku) sob
悔泣 ku(yashi)na(ki) crying out of remorse
11 啜泣 susu(ri)na(ku) sob, blubber
12 貰泣 mora(i)na(ki) weeping in sympathy
13 隠泣 kaku(shi)na(ki) crying in secret
感泣 kankyū weep with emotion
15 嬉泣 ure(shi)na(ki) crying for joy

泪 → 涙 3a7.21

3a5.2

沺 DEN vast surging waters

3a5.3 / 1792

沸 FUTSU, wa(ku) boil, seethe wa(kasu) (bring to a) boil, heat up (the bath)

————— 1 —————
5 沸立 wa(ki)ta(tsu) boil up, seethe
6 沸返 wa(ki)kae(ru) seethe, be in an uproar
9 沸点 futten boiling point
20 沸騰 futtō boiling; excitement, agitation
沸騰点 futtōten boiling point

————— 2 —————
12 湯沸器 yuwa(kashi)ki hot-water heater
煮沸 shafutsu boiling

3a5.4

泄 SETSU, EI leak

————— 2 —————
11 排泄 haisetsu excretion, evacuation, discharge
排泄物 haisetsubutsu excrement, excretion

3a5.5

沫 MATSU foam, spray
awa foam, bubbles

————— 2 —————
8 泡沫 hōmatsu, utakata bubble; short-lived
9 飛沫 himatsu splash, spray

3a5.6 / 364

油 YU, YŪ, abura oil

————— 1 —————
0 油ぎる abura(giru) be greasy/fat
サラダ油 saradayu salad/vegetable oil

4 油井 **yusei** oil well
油井戸 **aburaido** oil well/spring
5 油圧 **yuatsu** oil pressure; hydraulic
油田 **yuden** oil field
6 油気 **aburake** oiliness, greasiness
油汗 **aburaase** clammy sweat
油虫 **aburamushi** aphid; cockroach
7 油状 **yujō** oily
8 油送船 **yusōsen** oil tanker
油送管 **yusōkan** (oil) pipeline
油性 **yusei** oily, oleaginous
油性塗料 **yusei toryō** oil-based paint
9 油単 **yutan** oilcloth
油染 **aburaji(miru)** become oily/grease-stained
10 油差 **aburasa(shi)** oil can, oiler
油脂 **yushi** fat, fats and oils
油砥石 **aburatoishi** oilstone
油紙 **aburagami, yushi** oiled paper, oilskins
11 油断 **yudan** inattentiveness, lack of vigilance
12 油揚 **aburaa(ge)** fried tofu
油壺 **aburatsubo** oil can, oiler
油然 **yūzen** gushingly, copiously
油絵 **aburae** oil painting
13 油障子 **aburashōji** translucent oilpapered sliding doors
油搾 **aburashibo(ri)** oil press
油搾器 **aburashiboriki** oil press
油煙 **yuen** lampblack, lamp soot
油照 **aburade(ri)** sultry sun
14 油層 **yusō** oil stratum
油管 **yukan** oil pipe
15 油槽 **yusō** oil tank
油槽車 **yusōsha** tank car
油槽船 **yusōsen** oil tanker
16 油濃 **aburako(i), abura(k)ko(i)** greasy, fatty, oily
油薬 **aburagusuri** ointment, salve
17 油糟 **aburakasu** oil cake, the soybean waste after the oil is pressed out
18 油蟬 **aburazemi** (a large brown cicada)

────────── 2 ──────────

4 水油 **mizu-abura** hair oil; lamp oil
5 石油 **sekiyu** petroleum, oil, kerosene
石油坑 **sekiyukō** oil well
6 灯油 **tōyu** lamp oil, kerosene
米油 **komeabura** rice-bran oil
7 肝油 **kan'yu** (cod-)liver oil
8 送油管 **sōyukan** oil pipeline
注油 **chūyu** oiling, lubrication
9 重油 **jūyu** heavy/crude oil
香油 **kōyu** scented hair oil, pomade
10 差油 **sa(shi)abura** lubricating oil; oil (a machine)
原油 **gen'yu** crude oil

桐油 **tōyu** tung/nut/wood oil
11 採油 **saiyu** extract oil, drill for oil
採油権 **saiyuken** oil concession, drilling rights
魚油 **gyoyu** fish oil
12 揚油 **a(ge)abura** frying oil
給油 **kyūyu** supplying oil, fueling, oiling
給油所 **kyūyusho** filling/gas station
給油船 **kyūyusen** oil tanker
軽油 **keiyu** light oil, gasoline
13 塗油 **toyu** unction, anointing
搾油 **sakuyu** press oil (from seeds)
椿油 **tsubaki abura** camellia oil
聖油 **seiyu** holy oil
鉱油 **kōyu** mineral oil
14 髪油 **kamiabura** hair oil
種油 **taneabura** rapeseed oil
製油 **seiyu** oil refining
製油所 **seiyujo** oil refinery
綿油 **wataabura** cottonseed oil
精油 **seiyu** refining/refined oil
精油所 **seiyusho** oil refinery
17 糠油 **nukaabura** rice-bran oil
18 醤油 **shōyu** soy sauce
19 鯨油 **geiyu** whale oil

────────── 3 ──────────

4 片脳油 **hennōyu** camphor oil
5 生醤油 **kijōyu** raw/pure soy sauce
白灯油 **hakutōyu** kerosene
石脳油 **sekinōyu** petroleum
6 灯心油 **tōshin'yu** lamp oil, kerosene
9 胡麻油 **goma abura** sesame-seed oil
食用油 **shokuyō abura** cooking/edible oil
10 脂肪油 **shibōyu** fatty oil
11 菜種油 **natane abura** rapeseed oil
12 減摩油 **genmayu** lubricating oil
減磨油 **genmayu** lubricating oil
揮発油 **kihatsuyu** volatile oils, gasoline
硬化油 **kōkayu** hydrogenated oil
14 綿実油 **menjitsuyu** cottonseed oil
15 潤滑油 **junkatsuyu** lubricating oil
樟脳油 **shōnōyu** camphor oil
16 薄荷油 **hakkayu** peppermint oil
機械油 **kikai abura** machine/lubricating oil
橄欖油 **kanran'yu** olive oil

────────── 4 ──────────

7 亜麻仁油 **amaniyu** linseed oil
13 蓖麻子油 **himashiyu** castor oil

3a5.7

KAN water in which rice has been washed

3a5.8

決

Ō billowy clouds; deep and broad

3a5.9 / 666

波

HA, nami wave

———————— 1 ————————

0 マイクロ波 **maikuroha** microwave
3 波及 **hakyū** extend to, affect, have repercussions
4 波止場 **hatoba** wharf, pier
5 波打際 **namiu(chi)giwa** shore
　波布 **habu** (a poisonous snake of Okinawa)
　波布茶 **habucha** stinkweed-seed tea
　波立 **namida(tsu)** be choppy/wavy, billow, ripple
7 波状 **hajō** wave, undulation
　波形 **namigata** wave form, corrugation
8 波長 **hachō** wavelength
　波枕 **namimakura** sleeping on the ocean, sea voyage
9 波乗 **namino(ri)** surfing
　波除 **namiyo(ke)** breakwater, sea wall
　波風 **namikaze** wind and waves; discord
　波面 **hamen** wave surface/front
10 波高 **hakō** height of a wave
　波浪 **harō** waves, billows
　波紋 **hamon** ripples; repercussions
11 波動 **hadō** wave, undulatory motion
12 波斯 **Perusha** Persia
　波間 **namima** the waves
13 波路 **namiji** sea route/voyage; the sea
15 波線 **hasen** wavy line
16 波頭 **hatō, namigashira** wave crest, whitecaps
17 波濤 **hatō** large waves, high seas, billows
19 波蘭 **Pōrando** Poland
20 波瀾 **haran** waves; commotion; wide fluctuations
　波瀾万丈 **haran-banjō** full of ups and downs, stormy, checkered

———————— 2 ————————

1 一波 **ippa** a school/sect
2 人波 **hitonami** surging crowd
3 夕波 **yūnami** evening waves
　大波 **ōnami** big wave, billow, swell
4 丹波 **Tanba** (ancient kuni, Kyōto-fu and Hyōgo-ken)
　中波 **chūha** medium wave (100–1500 kHz)
　中波帯 **chūhatai** medium-wave band, AM radio

5 白波 **shiranami** whitecaps; thief
6 防波提 **bōhatei** breakwater
　光波 **kōha** light wave
7 余波 **yoha** aftereffects, secondary effects, aftermath, consequences
　阿波 **Awa** (ancient kuni, Tokushima-ken)
8 長波 **chōha** long wave
　長波長 **chōhachō** long wavelength
　逆波 **sakanami** head/choppy seas
　周波 **shūha** cycle, wave, frequency
　周波数 **shūhasū** frequency
　底波 **sokonami** groundswell
　金波 **kinpa** golden waves
9 風波 **fūha** wind and waves, storm, rough seas; discord, strife
　津波 **tsunami** tsunami, "tidal" wave
　荒波 **aranami** rough/stormy seas
　音波 **onpa** sound wave
　秋波 **shūha** amorous glance, ogle
10 高波 **takanami** high wave/seas
　浦波 **uranami** breakers
11 寄波 **yo(se)nami** surf
12 短波 **tanpa** shortwave
　短波長 **tanpachō** short wavelength
　寒波 **kanpa** cold wave
　筑波 **Tsukuba** (city and university, Ibaraki-ken)
13 煙波 **enpa** hazy sea, spray
　電波 **denpa** electromagnetic waves, radio
　電波計 **denpakei** wave meter
14 銀波 **ginpa** silvery waves
15 横波 **yokonami** side/transverse wave
　熱波 **neppa** heat wave
　穂波 **honami** waves of grain
18 難波 **nanpa** shipwreck
　難波船 **nanpasen** shipwreck

———————— 3 ————————

3 女白波 **onna shiranami** woman robber
　山津波 **yamatsunami** landslide
6 伊呂波 **i-ro-ha** the Japanese alphabet; ABC's, rudiments
7 低周波 **teishūha** low frequency
10 高周波 **kōshūha** high-frequency
12 超音波 **chōonpa** ultrasonic waves
　超短波 **chōtanpa** ultrashort-wave, very high frequency
13 電磁波 **denjiha** electromagnetic waves
15 潮津波 **shiotsunami** tidal bore

3a5.10 / 1870

HITSU, HI flow, secrete

———————— 1 ————————

3 泌々 **shimijimi** keenly, deeply, thoroughly

7 泌尿 **hinyō** urinary
泌尿科 **hinyōka** urology
泌尿器 **hinyōki** urinary organs

────────── 2 ──────────

4 分泌 **bunpitsu** secretion
分泌物 **bunpitsubutsu** a secretion

────────── 3 ──────────

4 内分泌 **naibunpitsu, naibunpi** internal
secretion, endocrine

3a5.11

泝

SO, **sakanobo(ru)** go upstream

3a5.12

泯

BIN die out; dim

3a5.13

泙

HŌ surging (water)

────────── 1 ──────────

12 泙湃 **hōhai** surging (water)

3a5.14 / 1208

泳

EI, **oyo(gu)** swim

────────── 1 ──────────

8 泳法 **eihō** swimming style/stroke
泳者 **eisha** swimmer

────────── 2 ──────────

2 力泳 **rikiei** powerful swimming
4 水泳 **suiei** swimming
水泳大会 **suiei taikai** swimming meet
水泳着 **suieigi** swimming suit
水泳場 **suieijō** swimming place/pool
水泳帽 **suieibō** swimming/bathing cap
犬泳 **inuoyo(gi)** dog paddle
5 平泳 **hiraoyo(gi)** breaststroke
立泳 **ta(chi)oyo(gi)** tread water
9 独泳 **dokuei** swimming alone
背泳 **haiei, seoyo(gi)** swim the backstroke
10 遊泳 **yūei** swimming
遊泳術 **yūeijutsu** how to get along in the
world
胸泳 **kyōei** breaststroke
11 側泳 **sokuei** sidestroke
12 遠泳 **en'ei** long-distance swim
蛙泳 **kaeruoyo(gi)** the breast stroke

13 継泳 **keiei** relay swimming
15 横泳 **yokooyogi** side stroke
20 競泳 **kyōei** swimming race

3a5.15 / 1177

泊

HAKU overnight stay
to(maru) stay at, put up at
to(meru) put (someone) up (for the
night)

────────── 1 ──────────

6 泊地 **hakuchi** anchorage, berth
9 泊客 **to(mari)kyaku** overnight guest
11 泊掛 **to(mari)ga(ke)** be staying with, visiting
overnight
泊船 **hakusen** anchoring, berthing
12 泊番 **to(mari)ban** night duty
13 泊賃 **to(mari)chin** hotel charges

────────── 2 ──────────

1 一泊 **ippaku** an overnight stay
一泊二食付 **ippaku nishoku-tsu(ki)** with
overnight lodging and two meals
5 外泊 **gaihaku** overnight stay
6 休泊所 **kyūhakujo** place for resting and
sleeping
仮泊 **kahaku** temporary anchoring
11 停泊 **teihaku** anchorage, mooring
淡泊 **tanpaku** light, plain, simple; candid;
indifferent to
宿泊 **shukuhaku** lodging
宿泊人 **shukuhakunin** lodger, boarder, guest
宿泊所 **shukuhakujo** lodgings
宿泊料 **shukuhakuryō** hotel charges
13 寝泊 **netoma(ri)** stay at, lodge
碇泊 **teihaku** lie at anchor, be berthed/
moored
碇泊地 **teihakuchi** anchorage, berth
14 漂泊 **hyōhaku** wander, drift
16 錨泊 **byōhaku** anchorage

3a5.16 / 357

注 注

CHŪ note, comment; pour
tsu(gu) pour in
soso(gu) pour, flow
sa(su) pour, apply (eyedrops)

────────── 1 ──────────

2 注入 **chūnyū** injection; pour into, infuse
4 注文 **chūmon** order, commission
注文先 **chūmonsaki** where one places an
order
注文取 **chūmonto(ri)** taking orders
注文品 **chūmonhin** goods ordered
注文書 **chūmonsho** order form
注文帳 **chūmonchō** order book

3

氵 5←
土
扌
口
女
巾
犭
弓
彳
彡
艹
宀
屮
山
ヰ
广
尸
口

注文聞 **chūmonki(ki)** taking orders; order taker
注水 **chūsui** pour water into, flood, douche
5 注目 **chūmoku** attention, notice
8 注油 **chūyu** oiling, lubrication
9 注連飾 **shimekaza(ri)** sacred Shinto rope
注連縄 **shimenawa** sacred Shinto rope
10 注射 **chūsha** injection, shot
注射針 **chūshabari** hypodermic needle
注射液 **chūshaeki** injection (the liquid)
注射器 **chūshaki** hypodermic syringe, injector
注進 **chūshin** information, warning
注記 **chūki** make entries, write down
11 注視 **chūshi** close observation, scrutiny
注釈 **chūshaku** commentary, annotation
13 注解 **chūkai** commentary, notes
注解者 **chūkaisha** commentator
注解書 **chūkaisho** commentary
注意 **chūi** attention, caution, warning
注意力 **chūiryoku** attentiveness
注意事項 **chūi jikō** matter requiring attention; N.B.
注意書 **chūiga(ki)** notes, instructions
注意深 **chūibuka(i)** careful
注意報 **chūihō** (storm) warning

――――― 2 ―――――
4 不注意 **fuchūi** carelessness
5 付注 **fuchū** annotation
外注 **gaichū** order from outside suppliers (cf. 内製)
6 再注 **saichū** reorder
再注文 **saichūmon** reorder
自注 **jichū** annotation of one's own work
8 受注 **juchū** receive an order for
雨注 **uchū** shower (arrows) upon
9 発注 **hatchū** order (goods)
降注 **fu(ri)soso(gu)** rain/pour onto
要注意 **yōchūi** requiring care/caution
10 原注 **genchū** the original annotations
特注 **tokuchū** specially ordered (goods)
11 脚注 **kyakuchū** footnote
訳注 **yakuchū** translation and annotation
転注 **tenchū** using a kanji in an extended meaning
12 傍注 **bōchū** marginal notes
補注 **hochū** supplementary note
評注 **hyōchū** commentary, annotation
集注 **shūchū** concentrating one's attention on
集注本 **shūchūbon** variorum edition
13 傾注 **keichū** devotion, concentration
14 増注 **zōchū** additional notes
16 頭注 **tōchū** notes at the top of the page

――――― 3 ―――――
5 皮下注射 **hika chūsha** hypodermic injection

3a5.17

沮

SO, haba(mu) obstruct, prevent, impede, block, hamper

――――― 1 ―――――
12 沮喪 **sosō** dejection

3a5.18 / 1765

泡 泡

HŌ, awa, abuku bubble, foam, froth, suds

――――― 1 ―――――
5 泡立 **awada(teru)** beat into a froth, whip
泡立器 **awada(te)ki** eggbeater
泡立機 **awada(te)ki** eggbeater
8 泡沫 **hōmatsu, utakata** bubble; short-lived
11 泡粒 **awatsubu** a bubble
14 泡銭 **abukuzeni** ill-gotten/easy money

――――― 2 ―――――
1 一泡吹 **hitoawa fu(kaseru)** confound, upset (someone's plans)
4 水泡 **suihō** foam, bubble
6 気泡 **kihō** (air) bubble
9 発泡 **happō** foaming

3a5.19

泓

Ō deep clear water

3a5.20 / 123

法

HŌ, HA', HO' law; method; religion
nori doctrine, law; slope

――――― 1 ―――――
2 法人 **hōjin** juridical person, legal entity, corporation
法人税 **hōjinzei** corporation tax
法力 **hōriki** the merits/power of Buddhism
4 法文 **hōbun** (text of) the law; law and literature
法文化 **hōbunka** enact into law
法王 **hōō** the pope
法王庁 **Hōōchō** the Vatican
法王権 **hōōken** the papacy
5 法令 **hōrei** laws and (cabinet or ministerial) orders
法外 **hōgai** exorbitant, preposterous
法号 **hōgō** (priest's or deceased's) Buddhist name
法主 **hossu, hosshu** high priest
6 法廷 **hōtei** (law) court, courtroom

法名 **hōmyō** (priest's or deceased's) Buddhist name
法灯 **hōtō** the light/teachings of Buddhism
法式 **hōshiki** rule, regulation, rite
法衣 **hōi** vestments, priestly robes
7 法身 **hosshin** highest form of existence, soul (in Buddhism)
法医学 **hōigaku** forensic medicine
法学 **hōgaku** law, jurisprudence
法学士 **hōgakushi** LL.B., Bachelor of Laws
8 法事 **hōji** (Buddhist) memorial service
法例 **hōrei** the conflict-of-laws law
法制 **hōsei** legislation, laws
法典 **hōten** law code
法治 **hōchi** constitutional government
法治国 **hōchikoku** constitutional state
法官 **hōkan** judicial officer, judge
法定 **hōtei** legal, prescribed by law
法服 **hōfuku** judge's/barrister's/priest's robes
法的 **hōteki** legal, legalistic
9 法要 **hōyō** (Buddhist) memorial service
法律 **hōritsu** law
法律上 **hōritsujō** legally
法律学 **hōritsugaku** jurisprudence
法律屋 **hōritsuya** lawmonger
法律家 **hōritsuka** lawyer, jurist
法律案 **hōritsuan** proposed law
法律書 **hōritsusho** law book
法律語 **hōritsugo** legal term
法度 **hatto, hotto** law; prohibition, ban
法相 **hōshō** Minister of Justice
　　 Hossō (a Buddhist sect)
法皇 **hōō** ex-emperor who has become a monk
法政 **hōsei** law and government
法科 **hōka** law course/department
法界 **hōkai** the universe (in Buddhism)
法則 **hōsoku** law, rule
10 法師 **hōshi** (Buddhist) priest
法華経 **Hokekyō** the Lotus Sutra
法案 **hōan** (legislative) bill, measure
法悦 **hōetsu** religious exultation; ecstasy
法被 **happi** (workman's) livery coat
11 法曹 **hōsō** the legal profession
法曹界 **hōsōkai** legal circles, the bench and bar
法理 **hōri** legal principle
法理学 **hōrigaku** jurisprudence
法務 **hōmu** legal/judicial affairs
法務大臣 **hōmu daijin** Minister of Justice
法務官 **hōmukan** law officer, judge advocate
法務省 **Hōmushō** Ministry of Justice
法眼 **hōgen** (a high priestly rank in Buddhism)
法規 **hōki** laws and regulations
法経 **hōkei** law and economics
法貨 **hōka** legal tender

13 法楽 **hōraku** pleasure of a pious life; entertainment for the gods
法話 **hōwa** (Buddhist) sermon
14 法網 **hōmō** the net/clutches of the law
法語 **hōgo** (Buddhist) sermon
15 法幣 **hōhei** (Chinese) legal tender
法権 **hōken** legal right
法談 **hōdan** (Buddhist) sermon
法論 **hōron** doctrinal discussion; jurisprudence
17 法螺 **hora** trumpet shell; boast, brag
法螺吹 **horafu(ki)** boaster, braggart
10 法難 **hōnan** religious persecution

────────── 2 ──────────

3 寸法 **sunpō** measurements, dimensions; plan, arrangement
大法 **taihō** fundamental law
4 不法 **fuhō** unlawful, illegal, wrongful
内法 **uchinori** interior dimensions
仏法 **buppō** Buddhism
仏法僧 **buppōsō** Buddha, doctrine, and priesthood; broad-billed roller, Japanese scops owl
六法 **roppō** the six directions; the six law codes
六法全書 **roppō zensho** the statute books
文法 **bunpō** grammar
文法上 **bunpōjō** grammatically
公法 **kōhō** public law
手法 **shuhō** technique, method
方法 **hōhō** method, way, means
方法論 **hōhōron** methodology
5 民法 **minpō** civil law/code
末法 **mappō** latter days (of Buddhism), age of decadence
末法思想 **mappō shisō** pessimism due to the decadent-age theory
加法 **kahō** addition (in math)
用法 **yōhō** how to use, directions
句法 **kuhō** wording, phrasing
司法 **shihō** administration of justice, judicial
司法大臣 **shihō daijin** Minister of Justice
司法官 **shihōkan** judicial official
司法権 **shihōken** judicial powers, jurisdiction
尼法師 **ama hōshi** (Buddhist) nun
礼法 **reihō** courtesy, etiquette, manners
立法 **rippō** legislation, lawmaking
立法上 **rippōjō** legislative
立法府 **rippōfu** legislature
立法者 **rippōsha** legislator, lawmaker
立法権 **rippōken** legislative power
6 死法 **shihō** a dead law
伝法 **denpō, denbō** affected bravado
合法 **gōhō** legality, lawfulness
合法的 **gōhōteki** legal, lawful

3

氵 5←
土
扌
口
女
巾
犭
弓
彳
彡
艹
宀
丷
山
士
广
尸
口

刑法 **keihō** criminal law, the Criminal Code
如法 **nyohō** observance of Buddha's teachings
式法 **shikihō** ceremony, form, manners
7 良法 **ryōhō** good method
作法 **sahō** manners, etiquette
邪法 **jahō** sorcery, witchcraft; heresy
別法 **beppō** different method
兵法 **heihō** tactics, strategy
走法 **sōhō** (form/style of) running
技法 **gihō** technique
妙法 **myōhō** excellent method; mysteries, secrets; marvelous law of Buddha (short for 妙法法華経)
図法 **zuhō** drawing, draftsmanship
私法 **shihō** private law
8 非法 **hihō** illegal, unlawful, lawless
画法 **gahō** art of drawing/painting
泳法 **eihō** swimming style/stroke
英法 **Eihō** British/English law
宗法 **shūhō** rules of a religion
定法 **jōhō** established rule, convention, formula
国法 **kokuhō** the laws of a country
9 乗法 **jōhō** multiplication
便法 **benpō** easier method, shortcut
除法 **johō** division (in math)
軍法 **gunpō** military law; martial law; tactics, strategy
軍法会議 **gunpō kaigi** court-martial
海法 **kaihō** maritime law
律法 **rippō** law, rule
10 2進法 **nishinhō** binary (notation)
１０進法 **jisshinhō** decimal (notation)
１６進法 **jūrokushinhō** hexadecimal (notation)
家法 **kahō** family rules/recipe
骨法 **koppō** knack
書法 **shohō** penmanship, calligraphy
教法 **kyōhō** teachings, doctrines
秘法 **hihō** secret method/formula
11 商法 **shōhō** way of doing business; commercial law/code
密法 **mippō** (Buddhist) mysteries
常法 **jōhō** usual method; unvarying rule
脱法 **dappō** evasion of the law
脱法行為 **dappō kōi** an evasion of the law
理法 **rihō** law
現法 **genpō** local legal entity, company incorporated abroad (short for 現地法人)
悪法 **akuhō** bad law
12 違法 **ihō** illegal
減法 **genpō** subtraction
御法度 **gohatto** law, ordinance; prohibition
無法 **muhō** unjust, unlawful, outrageous
無法者 **muhōmono** outrageous fellow, outlaw

税法 **zeihō** tax law; method of taxation
筆法 **hippō** calligraphy technique; manner
馭法 **gyohō** horsemanship
13 農法 **nōhō** farming methods
適法 **tekihō** lawful, legal
滅法 **meppō** extraordinary, absurd; awfully; very
戦法 **senpō** tactics, strategy
新法 **shinpō** new method/law
罨法 **anpō** poultice, compress, pack
話法 **wahō** speech, parlance
14 暦法 **rekihō** calendar making
遵法 **junpō** law-abiding, work-to-rule (tactics)
漁法 **gyohō** fishing method
製法 **seihō** manufacturing process, recipe
算法 **sanpō** arithmetic
語法 **gohō** phraseology, usage, diction
説法 **seppō** (Buddhist) sermon
駄法螺 **dabora** bragging
15 儀法 **gihō** rule, commandment
影法師 **kagebōshi** person's shadow
論法 **ronpō** argument, reasoning, logic
16 憲法 **kenpō** constitution
憲法違反 **kenpō ihan** unconstitutionality
17 療法 **ryōhō** treatment, therapy, remedy
20 護法 **gohō** defense of the law/religion
21 魔法 **mahō** magic, sorcery, witchcraft
魔法使 **mahōtsuka(i)** magician, wizard
魔法瓶 **mahōbin** thermos bottle

— 3 —

1 一寸法師 **issunbōshi** dwarf, midget, Tom Thumb
2 二進法 **nishinhō** binary notation/system
十進法 **jisshinhō** decimal/base-10 notation
3 三角法 **sankakuhō** trigonometry
4 不作法 **busahō** bad manners, discourtesy
不調法 **buchōhō** impoliteness; carelessness; misconduct; awkward, inexperienced
予防法 **yobōhō** precautionary measures
切分法 **setsubunhō** syncopation
分類法 **bunruihō** system of classification
辻説法 **tsujiseppō** street preaching
水耕法 **suikōhō** hydroponics
少年法 **shōnenhō** juvenile law
尺貫法 **shakkanhō** old Japanese system of weights and measures
戸籍法 **kosekihō** the Family Registration Law
5 生兵法 **namabyōhō** untried tactics; smattering of knowledge
弁証法 **benshōhō** dialectic, dialectics
外為法 **Gaitamehō** Foreign Exchange (and Foreign Trade) Control Law (short for 外国為替及び外国貿易管理法)

正字法 **seijihō** orthography
正攻法 **seikōhō** frontal assault/attack
可能法 **kanōhō** potential mood
6 仮定法 **kateihō** subjunctive mood
行政法 **gyōseihō** administrative law
成文法 **seibunhō** statute/written law
自然法 **shizenhō** natural law
7 冷罨法 **reianpō** cold compress/pack
対位法 **taiihō** counterpoint
社団法人 **shadan hōjin** corporate juridical
    person
8 非合法 **higōhō** illegal
使用法 **shiyōhō** use, directions
盲滅法 **mekura meppō** recklessly, at
    random
版権法 **hankenhō** copyright law
直接法 **chokusetsuhō** direct method;
    indicative mood
直説法 **chokusetsuhō** indicative mood
治外法権 **chigaihōken** extraterritoriality
治療法 **chiryōhō** method of treatment,
    remedy
国文法 **kokubunpō** Japanese grammar
国際法 **kokusaihō** international law
9 発声法 **hasseihō** vocalization, enunciation
独禁法 **dokkinhō** antitrust laws, the Anti-
    Monopoly Law (short for 独占禁止法)
狩猟法 **shuryōhō** game laws
度量法 **doryōhō** measurement
相続法 **sōzokuhō** inheritance law
10 倒置法 **tōchihō** inversion (of normal word
    order)
修辞法 **shūjihō** rhetoric
健康法 **kenkōhō** how to keep fit, hygiene
帰納法 **kinōhō** inductive method
家族法 **kazokuhō** family(-rights) law
根本法 **konponhō** fundamental law
特許法 **tokkyohō** patent law
教会法 **kyōkaihō** canon law
教育法 **kyōikuhō** teaching method
教授法 **kyōjuhō** teaching method
破防法 **Habōhō** the Subversive Activities
    Prevention Law (short for 破壊活動防止
    法)
記数法 **kisūhō** numerical notation
財団法人 **zaidan hōjin** (incorporated)
    foundation
11 運指法 **unshihō** fingering (in music)
習慣法 **shūkanhō** common law
現行法 **genkōhō** existing law, law now in
    force
救助法 **kyūjohō** lifesaving
救急法 **kyūkyūhō** first aid
略記法 **ryakkihō** abridged notation (e.g., 五三
    for 五十三)

経済法 **keizaihō** economic laws
船舶法 **senpakuhō** shipping law
12 遠近法 **enkinhō** (law of) perspective
測定法 **sokuteihō** method of measurement;
    mensuration
温罨法 **on'anpō** hot compress
無手法 **mute(p)pō** reckless, rash
無作法 **busahō** bad manners, rudeness
無調法 **buchōhō** impolite; clumsy, unaccus-
    tomed to
琵琶法師 **biwa hōshi** lute-playing minstrel
訴訟法 **soshōhō** code of (civil/criminal)
    procedure
13 禁酒法 **kinshuhō** Prohibition (law)
誇張法 **kochōhō** hyperbole
14 選挙法 **senkyohō** election law
遺伝法 **idenhō** laws of heredity
演奏法 **ensōhō** (musical) execution, interpre-
    tation
演説法 **enzetsuhō** elocution, oratory
演繹法 **en'ekihō** deductive reasoning
慣習法 **kanshūhō** common law
複利法 **fukurihō** the compound interest
    method
精製法 **seiseihō** refining process
15 養生法 **yōjōhō** hygiene, rules of health
避妊法 **hininhō** method of contraception
熱療法 **netsuryōhō** heat therapy
16 操縦法 **sōjūhō** manipulation, control
衛生法 **eiseihō** hygiene, hygienics
薬事法 **yakujihō** the Pharmaceutical Affairs
    Law
17 擬人法 **gijinhō** personification

──────── 4 ────────

3 口不調法 **kuchi-buchōhō** awkward in
    expressing oneself
4 水治療法 **suichiryōhō** water cure, hydro-
    therapy
5 礼儀作法 **reigisahō** etiquette, courtesy,
    propriety
8 直接話法 **chokusetsu wahō** direct quotation
物理療法 **butsuriryōhō** physiotherapy
9 南無妙法蓮華経 **Namu Myōhō Rengekyō**
    Hail Lotus Sutra
透視画法 **tōshigahō** perspective (drawing)
指圧療法 **shiatsu ryōhō** finger-pressure
    treatment, chiropractic
10 起上小法師 **o(ki)a(gari) koboshi** self-
    righting toy
12 循環論法 **junkan ronpō** a circular argument
欽定憲法 **kintei kenpō** constitution granted
    by the emperor

──────── 5 ────────

17 優生保護法 **Yūsei Hogo Hō** Eugenic
    Protection Law

3

氵 5←
土
扌
囗
女
巾
犭
弓
彳
彡
艹
宀
⺍
山
吉
广
尸
口

3a5.21 / 850

況 況 **KYŌ** circumstances, situation
ma(shite) all the more so
iwa(n'ya) all the more so,
(with affirmative) still more,
(with negative) much less

3

→5 氵
土
扌
日
女
巾
犭
弓
彳
彡
艹
宀
⺌
山
亠
广
尸
口

——————— 2 ———————

4 不況 **fukyō** recession, business slump
5 市況 **shikyō** market conditions
比況 **hikyō** comparison, likening
好況 **kōkyō** prosperity, boom
6 近況 **kinkyō** recent situation, present state
7 状況 **jōkyō** circumstances
8 実況 **jikkyō** actual conditions
実況放送 **jikkyō hōsō** on-the-spot broadcast
9 活況 **kakkyō** activity, briskness, vigor
政況 **seikyō** political situation
11 商況 **shōkyō** business conditions
現況 **genkyō** the present situation
情況 **jōkyō** circumstances, state of affairs
情況証拠 **jōkyō shōko** circumstantial evidence
盛況 **seikyō** prosperity, success, boom
12 景況 **keikyō** the situation
悲況 **hikyō** plight, lamentable state
13 戦況 **senkyō** war situation
14 概況 **gaikyō** general situation, outlook

3a5.22

沱 **DA** flowing of tears

注 → 注 **3a5.16**

3a5.23 / 1607

沿 **EN** follow along
so(u) stand/lie along, run parallel to

——————— 1 ———————

8 沿岸 **engan** coast, shore
沿岸漁業 **engan gyogyō** coastal fishing
9 沿海 **enkai** coastal waters, coast
沿海州 **enkaishū** maritime provinces
沿革 **enkaku** history, development
11 沿道 **endō** along the road, roadside
15 沿線 **ensen** along the (train) line

——————— 2 ———————

3 川沿 **kawazo(i)** along the river

——————— 3 ———————

9 海岸沿 **kaiganzo(i)** along the coast/shore

3a5.24 / 996

沼 **SHŌ, numa** swamp, marsh

——————— 1 ———————

5 沼田 **numata** marshy rice field
6 沼気 **shōki** marsh gas, methane
沼地 **numachi, shōchi** marshes, swampland
7 沼沢 **shōtaku** marsh, swamp
9 沼津 **Numazu** (city, Shizuoka-ken)
12 沼湖 **shōko** swamps and lakes

——————— 2 ———————

8 泥沼 **doronuma** bog, quagmire
12 湖沼 **koshō** lakes and marshes
湖沼学 **koshōgaku** limnology

3a5.25

沛 **HAI** pouring rain; fall over

——————— 1 ———————

12 沛然 **haizen** torrential, downpour, cloudburst

——————— 2 ———————

19 顚沛 **tenpai** stumbling and falling; moment, instant

——————— 4 ———————

9 造次顚沛 **zōji-tenpai** a moment

3a5.26

沽 **KO, u(ru)** sell
ka(u) buy

——————— 1 ———————

8 沽券 **koken** credit, dignity, reputation

3a5.27

沾 **SEN, TEN** get wet; increase, gain

3a5.28 / 493

治 **JI, CHI** peace; govern; healing
osa(meru) govern; suppress
osa(maru) be at peace, be quelled
nao(ru) (intr.) heal **nao(su)** (tr.) heal

——————— 1 ———————

3 治下 **chika** under the rule of
4 治水 **chisui** riverbank improvement, flood control
治水工事 **chisui kōji** riverbank works
5 治世 **chisei** reign, rule
治平 **chihei** peace and tranquility

治外法権 **chigaihōken** extraterritoriality
6 治安 **chian** public peace/order
　Jian (era, 1021–1024)
治安条例 **chian jōrei** public-order regula-
　tions
治安維持 **chian iji** maintenance of public
　order
7 治承 **Jijō** (era, 1177–1181)
治乱 **chiran** war and/or peace
8 治国 **chikoku** government
治者 **chisha** ruler, governor
治具 **jigu** jig
11 治産 **chisan** property management
治略 **chiryaku** governance, rulercraft
14 治暦 **Jiryaku** (era, 1065–1069)
17 治療 **chiryō** medical treatment
治療代 **chiryōdai** medical fees/bill
治療学 **chiryōgaku** therapeutics
治療法 **chiryōhō** method of treatment,
　remedy
治療所 **chiryōsho** infirmary, clinic
治療師 **chiryōshi** therapist
治績 **chiseki** (record of one's) administration
18 治癒 **chiyu** heal, cure, recover
治癒力 **chiyuryoku** healing/recuperative
　power

──────── 2 ────────

3 万治 **Manji** (era, 1658–1661)
大治 **Daiji** (era, 1126–1131)
4 不治 **fuji, fuchi** incurable
元治 **Genji** (era, 1864–1865)
天治 **Tenji** (era, 1124–1126)
内治 **naiji, naichi** domestic/internal affairs
仁治 **Ninji** (era, 1240–1243)
文治 **bunchi, bunji** civilian administration
　Bunji (era, 1185–1190)
水治療法 **suichiryōhō** water cure, hydro-
　therapy
5 平治 **Heiji** (era, 1159–1160)
正治 **Shōji** (era, 1199–1201)
永治 **Eiji** (era, 1141–1142)
弘治 **Kōji** (era, 1555–1558)
主治医 **shujii** physician in charge/attendance
主治効能 **shuji kōnō** chief efficacy (of a
　drug)
6 全治 **zenchi, zenji** fully recover, heal
　completely
自治 **jichi** self-government
自治体 **jichitai** self-governing body,
　municipality
自治制 **jichisei** self-governing system
自治相 **jichisō** Home Affairs Minister
自治省 **Jichishō** Ministry of Home Affairs
自治領 **jichiryō** self-governing dominion
自治権 **jichiken** autonomy

7 灸治 **kyūji** moxa cauterization/treatments
8 長治 **Chōji** (era, 1104–1106)
建治 **Kenji** (era, 1275–1278)
退治 **taiji** subjugation; extermination, (pest)
　control
法治 **hōchi** constitutional government
法治国 **hōchikoku** constitutional state
宝治 **Hōji** (era, 1247–1249)
明治 **Meiji** (emperor and era, 1868–1912)
明治神宮 **Meiji Jingū** Meiji Shrine
明治維新 **Meiji Ishin** the Meiji Restoration
9 貞治 **Jōji** (era, 1362–1368)
政治 **seiji** politics
政治力 **seijiryoku** political influence
政治上 **seijijō** political
政治史 **seijishi** political history
政治犯 **seijihan** political offense/offender
政治学 **seijigaku** political science
政治的 **seijiteki** political
政治局 **seijikyoku** Politburo
政治屋 **seijiya** politician
政治家 **seijika** politician
政治熱 **seijinetsu** political fever
10 根治 **konchi, konji** radical/complete cure
被治者 **hichisha** the governed
11 康治 **Kōji** (era, 1142–1143)
救治 **kyūji** cure, remedy
救治策 **kyūjisaku** a cure
12 湯治 **tōji** hot-springs cure
湯治場 **tōjiba** spa
統治 **tōchi, tōji** reign, rule
統治者 **tōchisha, tōjisha** ruler, sovereign
統治権 **tōchiken** sovereignty
13 寛治 **Kanji** (era, 1087–1093)
禁治産 **kinchisan** (legally) incompetent
禁治産者 **kinchisansha** person adjudged
　incompetent
14 徳治 **Tokuji** (era, 1306–1308)
17 療治 **ryōji** medical treatment, remedy
18 難治 **nanji, nanchi** intractable

──────── 3 ────────

4 手療治 **teryōji** home treatment, doctoring
　oneself
9 荒療治 **araryōji** drastic/kill-or-cure treatment
12 揉療治 **mo(mi)ryōji** massage
13 準禁治産 **junkinchisan** quasi-incompetence
　(in law)
準禁治産者 **junkinchisansha** a quasi-
　incompetent (person)

──────── 4 ────────

3 三頭政治 **santō seiji** triumvirate
8 委任統治 **inin tōchi** mandate
9 専制政治 **sensei seiji** despotic government,
　autocracy
信託統治 **shintaku tōchi** trusteeship

3

氵 5←
土
扌
口
女
巾
犭
弓
彳
彡
艹
宀
丷
山
耂
广
尸
口

独裁政治 **dokusai seiji** dictatorship, autocracy
神権政治 **shinken seiji** theocracy
14 寡頭政治 **katō seiji** oligarchy

3a5.29 / 1621

DEI, doro mud

泥

─────────── 1 ───────────

3 泥土 **deido** mud
4 泥中 **deichū** in the mud
泥水 **deisui, doromizu** muddy water
泥水社会 **doromizu shakai** red-light districts
泥水稼業 **doromizu kagyō** shameful occupation
泥火山 **deikazan** mud volcano
5 泥仕合 **dorojiai** mudslinging
泥田 **dorota** muddy rice field, paddy
6 泥地 **deichi** swamp, marsh, mire, morass
7 泥状 **deijō** muddy, pasty
泥坊 **dorobō** thief, burglar
泥足 **doroashi** muddy feet
8 泥沼 **doronuma** bog, quagmire
泥板岩 **deibangan** shale
泥金 **deikin** gold paint
9 泥除 **doroyo(ke)** mudguards, mudflaps
泥海 **doroumi** muddy sea
泥炭 **deitan** peat
泥炭地 **deitanchi** peat bog
泥臭 **dorokusa(i)** smelling of mud; uncouth
11 泥道 **doromichi** muddy road
泥酔 **deisui** dead drunk
12 泥棒 **dorobō** thief, burglar
泥絵具 **doro e(no)gu** distemper, color wash
13 泥靴 **dorogutsu** muddy shoes/boots
泥試合 **dorojiai** mudslinging
泥鉱 **deikō** slime ore
15 泥縄 **doronawa** starting to make a rope to catch a just-discovered burglar, hasty/too-late measures
泥縄式 **doronawashiki** last-minute, eleventh-hour
17 泥濘 **deinei, nukarumi** mud, mire

─────────── 2 ───────────

7 沈泥 **chindei** silt
8 拘泥 **kōdei** adhere to, be a stickler for
金泥 **kindei, kondei** gold paint/dust
11 軟泥 **nandei** mud, sludge, ooze
12 雲泥差 **undei (no) sa** a great difference
14 銀泥 **gindei** silver paint

─────────── 3 ───────────

4 火事泥 **kajidoro** thief at a fire
7 芥子泥 **karashidei** mustard plaster

3a5.30 / 389

KA river; the Yellow river
kawa river

河

─────────── 1 ───────────

3 河川 **kasen** rivers
河川工事 **kasen kōji** river improvement, riparian works
河口 **kakō** mouth of a river, estuary
河口港 **kakōkō** estuary harbor
4 河内 **Kawachi** (ancient kuni, Ōsaka-fu)
河水 **kasui** river water
河心 **kashin** middle of the river
5 河北 **kahoku** north of the (Yellow) river
7 河床 **kashō** river bed
河系 **kakei** river system
8 河東 **katō** east of the (Yellow) river
河岸 **kashi** riverside; (riverside) fish market; place, scene; one's field/trade
kagan riverside, bank/shore of a river
河岸端 **kashibata** riverside
河底 **kawazoko, katei** river bed/bottom
9 河南 **Kanan** Henan (province; south of the Yellow river)
河峡 **kakyō** river canyon, gorge
河神 **kashin** river god
10 河原 **kawara** dry river bed
河原乞食 **kawara kojiki** actors (and beggars; a term of opprobrium)
河原物 **kawaramono** actors (a term of opprobrium)
河流 **karyū** stream
河畔 **kahan** riverside
河馬 **kaba** hippopotamus
11 河鹿 **kajika** singing frog
河豚 **fugu** globefish, blowfish, puffer
12 河港 **kakō** river port
河童 **kappa** (water-dwelling elf)

─────────── 2 ───────────

3 三河 **Mikawa** (ancient kuni, Aichi-ken)
大河 **taiga** large river
山河 **sanga** mountains and rivers
4 天河 **Ama(no)gawa** the Milky Way
5 氷河 **hyōga** glacier
氷河期 **hyōgaki** glacial period, ice age
白河 **Shirakawa** (emperor, 1072–1086)
白河夜船 **Shirakawa yofune** fast asleep
7 決河 **kekka** river breaking through (its dikes)
11 運河 **unga** canal
堀河 **Horikawa** (emperor, 1086–1107)
魚河岸 **uogashi** riverside fish market
12 渡河 **toka** crossing a river
14 銀河 **ginga** the Milky Way
17 駿河 **Suruga** (ancient kuni, Shizuoka-ken)

3a5.31

SHŪ, oyo(gu) swim

3a5.32

泗

SHI (name of a river in China); snivel

3a5.33 / 1192

泉 湶

SEN, izumi spring, fountain(head)

——————— 1 ———————

3 泉下 **senka** hades; the next world
4 泉水 **sensui** garden pond, fountain
5 泉石 **senseki** springs and rocks (in a garden)
15 泉熱 **Izumi netsu** Izumi fever (resembles scarlet fever)

——————— 2 ———————

7 冷泉 **reisen** cold mineral springs
   Reizei (emperor, 967–969)
8 和泉 **Izumi** (ancient kuni, Ōsaka-fu)
9 飛泉 **hisen** waterfall
11 渓泉 **keisen** valley spring
   清泉 **seisen** clear(-water) spring
   黄泉 **kōsen, yomi** hades, realm of the dead
   黄泉国 **yomi (no) kuni** hades, realm of the dead
12 温泉 **onsen** hot springs
   温泉郷 **onsenkyō** hot-springs town
   温泉場 **onsenba, onsenjō** spa, hot-springs resort
13 源泉 **gensen** fountainhead, source, origin
   源泉徴収 **gensen chōshū** collecting (taxes) at the source, withholding
   源泉課税 **gensen kazei** taxation at the source, withholding tax
   鉱泉 **kōsen** mineral springs
15 噴泉 **funsen** spring, geyser
   熱泉 **nessen** hot springs
   霊泉 **reisen** wonder-working fountain/spring

——————— 3 ———————

9 後冷泉 **Goreizei** (emperor, 1045–1068)
12 硫黄泉 **iōsen** sulfur springs
13 鉄鉱泉 **tekkōsen** rusty-water springs

3a5.34 / 1545

TAI calm, peaceful; large, wide; proud; Thailand

——————— 1 ———————

3 泰山 **taizan** large mountain; Mt. Taishan (in China)
4 泰斗 **taito** an authority, leading figure
5 泰平 **taihei** peace, tranquility
   泰平期 **taiheiki** period of peace
6 泰西 **taisei** the occident/West
   泰西名画 **taisei meiga** famous Western painting
   泰安 **taian** peace, tranquility
12 泰然 **taizen** calm, composed; firm
   泰然自若 **taizen-jijaku** imperturbable

——————— 2 ———————

6 安泰 **antai** peace; security
8 昌泰 **Shōtai** (era, 898–901)

昶→ 4c5.16

——————— 6 ———————

3a6.1 / 668

津

SHIN, tsu harbor, ferry; overflowing

——————— 1 ———————

0 津 **Tsu** (city, Mie-ken)
3 津々 **shinshin** brimfull
   津々浦々 **tsutsu-uraura** throughout the land, the entire country
8 津波 **tsunami** tsunami, "tidal" wave
10 津浪 **tsunami** tsunami, "tidal" wave
12 津軽海峡 **Tsugaru-kaikyō** (strait between Honshū and Hokkaidō)

——————— 2 ———————

3 大津 **Ōtsu** (city, Shiga-ken)
   山津波 **yamatsunami** landslide
   山津浪 **yamatsunami** landslide
4 天津乙女 **amatsuotome** celestial maiden
8 沼津 **Numazu** (city, Shizuoka-ken)
9 津津 **shinshin** brimfull
   津津浦浦 **tsutsu-uraura** throughout the land, the entire country
   秋津島 **Akitsushima** (ancient) Japan, Yamato
10 唐津焼 **karatsuya(ki)** earthenware, china
13 摂津 **Settsu** (ancient kuni, Hyōgo-ken)
14 綿津見 **watatsumi** (god of) the sea
15 潮津波 **shiotsunami** tidal bore

——————— 3 ———————

11 常磐津 **tokiwazu** (a type of samisen-accompanied ballad)
16 興味津津 **kyōmi-shinshin(taru)** very interesting, absorbing

3

氵 6←
土
扌
口
女
巾
犭
弓
彳
彡
艹
宀
丷
山
耂
广
尸
口

3a6.2

涕

I, hana nasal mucus, snivel, snot

─────── 1 ───────

8 涕垂小僧 **hanata(re) kozō** drippy-nosed little boy, snot-nose kid

─────── 2 ───────

4 水涕 **mizu(p)pana, mizubana** runny nose, snivel

3a6.3

洩

EI, SETSU, mo(ru/reru) leak (out)
mo(rasu) let leak, divulge

─────── 2 ───────

4 水洩 **mizumo(ri)** leak
14 漏洩 **rōei** leak; be disclosed/divulged
聞洩 **ki(ki)mo(rasu)** miss hearing, not catch

3a6.4 / 649

浅 淺

SEN, asa(i) shallow

─────── 1 ───────

0 浅はか **asa(haka)** frivolous, shallow, rash
浅ましい **asa(mashii)** wretched, miserable; despicable, shameful
4 浅手 **asade** slight/flesh wound
5 浅田 **asada** shallow paddy
7 浅学 **sengaku** superficial knowledge
浅見 **senken** superficial view
8 浅知恵 **asajie** shallow-witted
9 浅海魚 **senkaigyo** shallow-sea fish
浅草海苔 **Asakusa nori** sheets of dried seaweed
浅紅 **senkō** light/pale red, pink
11 浅黄 **asagi** light/pale yellow
浅黒 **asaguro(i)** dark-colored, swarthy
12 浅葱 **asagi** light/pale blue
浅間山 **Asamayama** (mountain, Nagano-ken)
13 浅蜊 **asari** (type of short-necked clam)
14 浅緑 **asamidori** light/pale green
15 浅慮 **senryo** indiscreet, imprudent
16 浅薄 **senpaku** shallow, superficial, flimsy
19 浅瀬 **asase** shoal, shallows, ford

─────── 2 ───────

11 深浅 **shinsen** depth
12 遠浅 **tōasa** shallow for some distance from the shore, a shoal

3a6.5

洒

SHA, SAI wash, rinse, sprinkle; free and easy

─────── 1 ───────

11 洒脱 **shadatsu** free and easy, unconstrained
12 洒落 **share** play on words, pun, joke, witticism **(o)share** dress up/stylishly **share(ru)** pun, be witty; dress up/stylishly **sharaku** free and easy, unconventional
洒落気 **share(k)ke** a bent for witticism; vanity in dress
洒落者 **sharemono** smart dresser, fop
洒落臭 **sharakusa(i)** cheeky, "smart"

─────── 2 ───────

19 瀟洒 **shōsha** elegant, stylish

3a6.6

洙

SHU (name of a river in China)

3a6.7

洫

KYOKU ditch

3a6.8

洌

RETSU pure

─────── 2 ───────

11 清洌 **seiretsu** clear, limpid

3a6.9

洳

JU wet

3a6.10

洲

SHŪ country, continent
su sandbank, shoals
shima island

─────── 2 ───────

4 中洲 **nakasu** sandbank/shoal in the middle of a river
5 白洲 **shirasu** sand bar; (law) court
9 砂洲 **sasu** sandbar, sandbank
12 満洲 **Manshū** Manchuria

─────── 3 ───────

3 三角洲 **sankakusu** delta

3a6.11 / 938

浮 浮

FU, u(ku) float, rise to the surface; feel buoyant/light-hearted; (money) be left over
u(ita) cheerful, buoyant;

frivolous **u(kanu)** glum **u(ki)** a float
u(kabu) float, rise to the surface   **u(kaberu)** set
afloat; show   **u(kareru)** be in buoyant/high
spirits   **u(kasu)** set afloat; save (money)
u(kasareru) be carried off, be captivated, be
exhilarated

────────── 1 ──────────

2 浮力 **furyoku** buoyancy, lift
3 浮上 **fujō** flotation, (submarine) surfacing;
    rise (in rank); (magnetic) levitation
  浮女 **u(kare)me** prostitute
4 浮心 **fushin** center of buoyancy
5 浮世 **u(ki)yo** this transitory world
  浮世草子 **ukiyozōshi** realistic novel (Edo
    period)
  浮世絵 **ukiyoe** (type of Japanese woodblock
    print)
  浮世絵師 **ukiyoeshi** ukiyoe artist
  浮付 **uwatsu(ku)** be fickle/flippant
  浮氷 **fuhyō** drift ice, ice floe
  浮立 **u(ki)ta(tsu)** be buoyant/exhilarated, be
    cheered up
6 浮気 **uwaki** (marital) infidelity, cheating,
    fickle
  浮名 **u(ki)na** love affair, scandal, rumor
7 浮身 **u(ki)mi** floating on one's back
  浮体 **futai** floating body (in physics)
  浮沈 **fuchin, u(ki)shizu(mi)** rise and fall, ups
    and downs
  浮言 **fugen** unfounded rumor
  浮足 **u(ki)ashi** heels-off-the-ground stance,
    poised to flee
  浮足立 **u(ki)ashida(tsu)** be ready to run
    away, waver
8 浮具 **u(ki)gu** water wings, a float
9 浮浮 **u(ki)u(ki)** buoyantly, jauntily
  浮城 **fujō** floating fortress, warship
  浮草 **u(ki)kusa** floating weeds, duckweed;
    precarious
10 浮遊 **fuyū** float, waft, be suspended
  浮遊生物 **fuyū seibutsu** plankton
  浮浪 **furō** vagrant, wandering
  浮浪人 **furōnin** vagrant, street bum
  浮浪児 **furōji** juvenile vagrant, gamin
  浮浪者 **furōsha** street bum, tramp, hobo
  浮流 **furyū** float about, drift
  浮華 **fuka** ostentation, foppery, frivolity
  浮荷 **u(ki)ni** flotsam, floatage
  浮島 **u(ki)shima** floating island
  浮桟橋 **u(ki)sanbashi** floating pier
  浮根 **u(ki)ne** roots of water plants
11 浮動 **fudō** floating, fluctuating
  浮游 **fuyū** float, waft, be suspended
  浮彫 **u(ki)bo(ri)** relief, embossed carving
  浮袋 **u(ki)bukuro** air bladder; life preserver,
    float

浮魚 **u(ki)uo** surface fish
12 浮揚 **fuyō** float, be buoyant
  浮雲 **u(ki)gumo** drifting cloud
13 浮寝 **u(ki)ne** sleeping in a ship; uneasy sleep
  浮腫 **muku(mu)** swell, bloat
    fushu, mukumi swelling, edema, dropsy
  浮腰 **u(ki)goshi** wavering, unsteady
14 浮漂 **fuhyō** float about, drift
  浮塵子 **unka** leafhopper, rice insect
  浮説 **fusetsu** wild rumor, canard
15 浮標 **fuhyō** buoy
  浮輪 **u(ki)wa** buoyant ring, a float
16 浮薄 **fuhaku** frivolous, flippant
  浮橋 **u(ki)hashi** floating/pontoon bridge
18 浮織 **u(ki)ori** weaving with raised figures,
    brocade
19 浮瀬 **u(kabu)se** lucky breaks, a chance

────────── 2 ──────────

9 浮浮 **u(ki)u(ki)** buoyantly, jauntily
  思浮 **omo(i)u(kaberu)** recall, hit upon
    omo(i)u(kabu) occur to one, come to
    mind
10 高浮彫 **takau(ki)bo(ri)** high relief
12 軽浮 **keifu** frivolous, fickle

────────── 3 ──────────

12 軽佻浮薄 **keichō-fuhaku** frivolous, flippant

3a6.12 / 692

洗   SEN, ara(u) wash

────────── 1 ──────────

5 洗出 **ara(i)da(su)** (inquire into and) identify
  洗礼 **senrei** baptism
  洗礼名 **senreimei** baptismal/Christian name
  洗礼式 **senreishiki** baptism (ceremony)
  洗立 **ara(i)ta(teru)** inquire into, ferret out
6 洗米 **senmai** washed rice
7 洗車 **sensha** car wash
  洗車場 **senshajō** car wash
  洗足 **sensoku** washing the feet
8 洗物 **ara(i)mono** the wash, laundry, washing
    up
9 洗浄 **senjō** wash, rinse, clean out
  洗面 **senmen** washing the face
  洗面台 **senmendai** washstand
  洗面所 **senmenjo** washroom, lavatory
  洗面器 **senmenki** wash basin
10 洗剤 **senzai** detergent
  洗流 **ara(i)naga(su)** wash away
  洗浚 **ara(i)zara(i)** one and all, everything
  洗晒 **ara(i)zara(shi)** shabby, worn-out (from
    repeated washing)
  洗粉 **ara(i)ko** powdered soap

3

氵 6←
土
扌
口
女
巾
犭
弓
行
彡
艹
宀
⺌
⺺
广
尸
口

11 洗張 **ara(i)ha(ri)** fulling; washing and stretching
洗脳 **sennō** brainwashing
洗眼 **sengan** eye washing
洗眼薬 **sengan'yaku** eyewash
12 洗場 **ara(i)ba** washing place
13 洗煉 **senren** refine, polish
洗鉱 **senkō** ore washing
14 洗滌 **sendeki, senjō** wash, rinse, clean
洗髪 **senpatsu** washing the hair, shampoo
ara(i)gami washed hair
洗練 **senren** refine, polish
16 洗薬 **ara(i)gusuri** lotion, a wash
17 洗濯 **sentaku** laundering
ara(i)susu(gi) washing and rinsing
洗濯板 **sentakuita** washboard
洗濯物 **sentakumono** the wash/laundry
洗濯屋 **sentakuya** laundry; laundryman
洗濯機 **sentakki, sentakuki** washing machine

─────── 2 ───────
3 丸洗 **maruara(i)** washing (a kimono) without taking it apart
4 水洗 **suisen, mizuara(i)** wash without soap, rinse
水洗便所 **suisen benjo** flush toilet
手洗 **teara(i)** washing the hands; lavatory
手洗所 **tearaijo** lavatory
手洗鉢 **teara(i)bachi** washbasin
5 皿洗 **saraara(i)** dishwashing; dishwasher
8 受洗 **jusen** baptism
受洗者 **jusensha** person baptized
杯洗 **haisen** basin for winecups, sink
12 筆洗 **hissen** brush-writing receptacle
14 髪洗 **kamiara(i)** washing the hair
髪洗粉 **kamiara(i)ko** shampoo powder
15 褄洗 **tsuma(mi)ara(i)** washing only the soiled parts

─────── 3 ───────
12 御手洗 **oteara(i)** lavatory
mitarashi holy water font at a shrine

3a6.13
洛
RAKU Kyōto, the capital

─────── 1 ───────
4 洛中 **rakuchū** in Kyōto

─────── 2 ───────
2 入洛 **juraku, nyūraku** visit to Kyōto
3 上洛 **jōraku** go/come to the capital

3a6.14 / 1435
洪
KŌ flood; vast

─────── 1 ───────
3 洪大 **kōdai** immense, vast, huge
4 洪水 **kōzui** flood, inundation, deluge
9 洪荒 **kōkō** first in the world; vast, rambling

─────── 2 ───────
3 大洪水 **Daikōzui** the Flood/Deluge

3a6.15
洸
KŌ sparkling (water)

3a6.16 / 237
活
KATSU life, activity **i(kiru)** live, be alive **i(keru)** keep alive; arrange flowers **i(ki)** freshness; stet

─────── 1 ───────
2 活人 **katsujin** a living person
活人画 **katsujinga** costumed people posing in a tableau vivant
活力 **katsuryoku** vitality, vigor
4 活火山 **kakkazan** active volcano
5 活弁 **katsuben** silent-movie interpreter/explainer (short for 活動写真の弁士)
活用 **katsuyō** practical use; conjugate, inflect
活用形 **katsuyōkei** inflected form
活用語 **katsuyōgo** inflected word
活字 **katsuji** printing/movable type
活字本 **katsujibon** printed book
6 活気 **kakki** liveliness, activity, vigor
活気付 **kakkizu(keru)** enliven, invigorate
7 活花 **i(ke)bana** flower arranging
8 活例 **katsurei** living example
活版 **kappan** movable-type printing
活版本 **kappanbon** printed book
活版所 **kappanjo** print shop
活版屋 **kappan'ya** print ship; printer
活況 **kakkyō** activity, briskness, vigor
活物 **katsubutsu** living being
活性 **kassei** active, activated
9 活発 **kappatsu** active, lively
活計 **kakkei** livelihood, living
10 活殺 **kassatsu** life and/or death
活殺自在 **kassatsu-jizai** power of life and death
11 活動 **katsudō** activity
活動写真 **katsudō shashin** moving pictures, movie
活動的 **katsudōteki** active, dynamic
活動家 **katsudōka** energetic person; activist
活眼 **katsugan** keen eye; insight
活魚 **i(ke)uo** caught fish kept alive in a tank
13 活路 **katsuro** means of escape, way out
14 活歴 **katsureki** historical drama

活語 **katsugo** living words; inflected word
15 活劇 **katsugeki** action scene/movie
活線 **kassen** live wire
21 活躍 **katsuyaku** be active

――――――― 2 ―――――――

3 大活躍 **daikatsuyaku** great/energetic activity
4 不活発 **fukappatsu** inactive, sluggish
手活 **tei(ke)** arranging flowers oneself; making (a geisha) one's wife or mistress
5 民活 **minkatsu** private-sector vitality
生活 **seikatsu** life, livelihood
生活力 **seikatsuryoku** vitality; earning power
生活苦 **seikatsuku** economic distress, hard times
生活圏 **seikatsuken** Lebensraum
生活費 **seikatsuhi** living expenses
生活難 **seikatsunan** economic distress, hard times
6 死活 **shikatsu** life or death
死活問題 **shikatsu mondai** a matter of life and death
自活 **jikatsu** support oneself
7 快活 **kaikatsu** cheerful, lively, merry
8 物活論 **bukkatsuron** animism
9 独活 **udo** (a rhubarb-like plant)
独活大木 **udo (no) taiboku** large and useless
肺活量 **haikatsuryō** lung capacity
10 敏活 **binkatsu** quick, alert, active, agile
12 復活 **fukkatsu** revival
復活祭 **Fukkatsusai** Easter

――――――― 3 ―――――――

4 公生活 **kōseikatsu** public life
7 私生活 **shiseikatsu** one's private life
8 実生活 **jisseikatsu** real/practical life
性生活 **sei seikatsu** sex life
9 食生活 **shokuseikatsu** eating/dietary habits
12 筍生活 **takenoko seikatsu** living by selling off one's personal effects
13 新生活 **shinseikatsu** a new life
15 課外活動 **kagai katsudō** extracurricular activities

――――――― 4 ―――――――

4 水上生活者 **suijō seikatsusha** seafarer

3a6.17

洽

KŌ far and wide

3a6.18 / 664

浄　淨

JŌ pure
kiyo(meru) purify

――――――― 1 ―――――――

3 浄土 **jōdo** pure land, (Buddhist) paradise

浄土宗 **Jōdoshū** the Jodo sect (of Buddhism)
浄土真宗 **Jōdo Shinshū** (a Buddhist sect, offshoot of the Jodo sect)
浄土教 **jōdokyō** Buddhist teachings concerning the Pure Land
4 浄化 **jōka** purification
浄水 **jōsui** clean water, water purification
浄水池 **jōsuichi** filtration bed, clean-water reservoir
浄火 **jōka** sacred fire
5 浄写 **jōsha** clean copy
6 浄地 **jōchi** sacred grounds
浄衣 **jōi, jōe** pure white robe
7 浄戒 **jōkai** precepts, commandments
9 浄界 **jōkai** sacred precincts; (Buddhist) paradise
10 浄書 **jōsho** clean copy
浄財 **jōzai** money offering, contribution
11 浄域 **jōiki** sacred precincts
13 浄罪 **jōzai** purgation (from sins)
14 浄瑠璃 **jōruri** (type of ballad-drama)
18 浄穢 **jōe** the pure and the profane

――――――― 2 ―――――――

4 不浄 **fujō** unclean, filthy, tainted, defiled
6 自浄 **jijō** self-cleansing, autopurification
自浄作用 **jijō-sayō** self-purification
9 洗浄 **senjō** wash, rinse, clean out
11 清浄 **seijō, shōjō** pure, clean, spotless
清浄無垢 **shōjō-muku** immaculate, pure and innocent

――――――― 3 ―――――――

6 西方浄土 **Saihō Jōdo** (Buddhist) Western Paradise
11 寂光浄土 **jakkō-jōdo** (Buddhist) paradise
12 御不浄 **gofujō** lavatory
極楽浄土 **gokuraku jōdo** (Buddhist) paradise

3a6.19 / 289

洋

YŌ ocean; foreign, Western, occidental

――――――― 1 ―――――――

2 洋刀 **yōtō** saber
3 洋上 **yōjō** on the ocean, seagoing, floating
4 洋犬 **yōken** Western-breed dog
5 洋本 **yōhon** Western book
6 洋行 **yōkō** foreign travel; company, firm
洋灯 **yōtō** lamp
洋式 **yōshiki** Western-style
7 洋学 **yōgaku** Western learning
洋学者 **yōgakusha** scholar of Western learning
8 洋画 **yōga** Western painting/movie
洋画家 **yōgaka** painter of Western-type pictures

洋服 **yōfuku** (Western-type) clothes
洋服屋 **yōfukuya** clothing store; tailor (shop)
9 洋風 **yōfū** Western-style
洋洋 **yōyō(taru)** wide, broad, vast
洋品 **yōhin** haberdashery
洋品店 **yōhinten** haberdashery
洋品屋 **yōhin'ya** haberdasher(y)
洋室 **yōshitsu** Western-style room
洋盃 **koppu** drinking glass
洋紅 **yōkō** carmine, crimson
洋食 **yōshoku** Western food
10 洋酒 **yōshu** Western liquor
洋書 **yōsho** Western/foreign book
洋紙 **yōshi** Western paper
11 洋菓子 **yōgashi** Western candies
洋梨 **yōnashi** Western pear
12 洋傘 **yōgasa** Western umbrella
洋琴 **yōkin** piano
洋装 **yōsō** Western dress
洋裁 **yōsai** (Western) dressmaking
洋裁師 **yōsaishi** dressmaker
洋間 **yōma** Western-style room
13 洋楽 **yōgaku** Western music
洋楽器 **yōgakki** Western musical instruments
14 洋髪 **yōhatsu** Western hair style
洋種 **yōshu** Western breed
洋綴 **yōto(ji)** Western-style binding
洋銀 **yōgin** nickel/German silver
16 洋館 **yōkan** Western-style building
19 洋蘭 **yōran** orchid

──────────── 2 ────────────

3 大洋 **taiyō** ocean
大洋州 **Taiyōshū** Oceania
5 北洋 **hokuyō** northern sea
外洋 **gaiyō** ocean, open sea
巡洋 **jun'yō** cruise
巡洋艦 **jun'yōkan** cruiser
6 両洋 **ryōyō** orient and occident; two-ocean
西洋 **seiyō** the West, the occident
西洋人 **seiyōjin** a Westerner
西洋化 **seiyōka** Westernization
西洋式 **seiyōshiki** Western-style
西洋画 **seiyōga** Western painting, oil painting
西洋風 **seiyōfū** Western-style
西洋紙 **seiyōshi** Western-style (machine-made) paper
8 東洋 **tōyō** the Orient
東洋人 **tōyōjin** an Oriental
和洋 **wayō** Japanese and Western
和洋折衷 **wayō setchū** blending of Japanese and Western styles
9 南洋 **Nan'yō** the South Seas
南洋諸島 **Nan'yō-shotō** the South Sea Islands
洋洋 **yōyō(taru)** wide, broad, vast

海洋 **kaiyō** ocean
海洋学 **kaiyōgaku** oceanography
茫洋 **bōyō** vast, boundless
12 遠洋 **en'yō** ocean, deep sea
渡洋 **toyō** transoceanic
極洋 **kyokuyō** polar seas
13 滂洋 **bōyō** vast, boundless

──────────── 3 ────────────

3 大西洋 **Taiseiyō** Atlantic Ocean
4 太平洋 **Taiheiyō** the Pacific Ocean
太平洋戦争 **Taiheiyō Sensō** the Pacific War, World War II
5 北氷洋 **Hoppyōyō, Hokuhyōyō** the Arctic Ocean
9 南氷洋 **Nanpyōyō** the Antarctic Ocean

──────────── 4 ────────────

5 北大西洋 **Kita Taiseiyō** the North Atlantic
6 汎太平洋 **han-Taiheiyō** Pan-Pacific
9 南太平洋 **Minami Taiheiyō** the South Pacific
17 環太平洋 **kan-Taiheiyō** Pan-Pacific, circum-Pacific
環太平洋火山帯 **kan-Taiheiyō kazantai** circum-Pacific volcanic belt
環太平洋地震帯 **kan-Taiheiyō jishintai** circum-Pacific seismic zone
環太平洋造山帯 **kan-Taiheiyō zōzantai** circum-Pacific orogeny

3a6.20 / 117

KAI, umi sea, ocean

海 海

──────────── 1 ────────────

2 海人 **ama, kaijin** fisherman
3 海千山千 **umisen-yamasen** experienced and shrewd, wily veteran, sly old dog
海上 **kaijō** ocean, seagoing, marine
海上権 **kaijōken** sea power
海口 **kaikō** harbor entrance
海女 **ama** woman (pearl) diver
海山 **umiyama** sea and mountains; depth and height
4 海内 **kaidai** the whole country
海中 **kaichū** in the sea
海辺 **umibe** seashore, beach
海水 **kaisui** seawater
海水浴 **kaisuiyoku** swimming in the ocean
海水浴場 **kaisuiyokujō** bathing beach
海水着 **kaisuigi** bathing/swimming suit
海水帽 **kaisuibō** bathing/swimming cap
海月 **kurage** jellyfish
海王星 **kaiōsei** Neptune
海牛 **kaigyū, umiushi** sea cow, manatee
5 海外 **kaigai** overseas, abroad

海外事情 **kaigai jijō** foreign news
海外版 **kaigaiban** overseas edition
海外発展 **kaigai hatten** overseas expansion
海外渡航 **kaigai tokō** foreign travel
海氷 **kaihyō** sea ice
6 海気 **kaiki** sea air/breeze
海防 **kaibō** coastal defense
海老 **ebi** shrimp, prawn; lobster
海老色 **ebi-iro** reddish brown
海老茶 **ebicha** brownish red, maroon
海老腰 **ebigoshi** stooped over, bent with age
海老錠 **ebijō** padlock
7 海里 **kairi** nautical mile
海角 **kaikaku** promontory, cape
海兵 **kaihei** marines
海兵隊 **kaiheitai** the Marine Corps
海坊主 **umibōzu** sea monster
海抜 **kaibatsu** elevation above sea level
海図 **kaizu** (marine) chart
8 海事 **kaiji** maritime affairs
海法 **kaihō** maritime law
海苔 **nori** laver (an edible seaweed)
海苔巻 **norima(ki)** (vinegared) rice rolled in seaweed
海岸 **kaigan** seashore, coast
海岸沿 **kaiganzo(i)** along the coast/shore
海岸通 **kaigandō(ri)** road along the coast
海岸線 **kaigansen** coastline; coastal rail line
海底 **kaitei** ocean floor, undersea
海国 **kaikoku** maritime country
海松 **umimatsu** pine on the seacoast
　　 miru (an edible seaweed)
海門 **kaimon** strait, channel
9 海軍 **kaigun** navy
海軍力 **kaigunryoku** naval power
海軍大臣 **kaigun daijin** Minister of the Navy
海軍国 **kaigunkoku** a naval power
海軍省 **Kaigunshō** Admiralty, Navy Department
海軍旗 **kaigunki** navy flag
海軍機 **kaigunki** navy plane
海風 **kaifū, umikaze** sea breeze
海洋 **kaiyō** ocean
海洋学 **kaiyōgaku** oceanography
海草 **kaisō** seaweeds, sea plants
海峡 **kaikyō** strait(s), channel, sound
海面 **kaimen** surface of the sea, sea level
　　 umizura surface of the sea
海胆 **uni** sea urchin
海星 **hitode** starfish
海神 **kaijin, kaishin, watatsumi** sea god
海食 **kaishoku** erosion caused by the sea
10 海豹 **azarashi, kaihyō** seal
海陸 **kairiku** land and sea, amphibious
海原 **unabara** the (vast) ocean
海浜 **kaihin** seashore, beach

海流 **kairyū** ocean current
海員 **kaiin** seaman, sailor
海容 **kaiyō** mercy, forgiveness
海馬 **kaiba** sea horse
11 海商 **kaishō** maritime commerce
海亀 **umigame** sea turtle
海運 **kaiun** marine transport, shipping
海運業 **kaiungyō** shipping, maritime trade
海道 **kaidō** coastal highway
海深 **kaishin** ocean depth
海域 **kaiiki** area of the ocean, waters
海猫 **umineko** black-tailed gull
海豚 **iruka** porpoise, dolphin
海産 **kaisan** marine products
海産物 **kaisanbutsu** marine products
海蛇 **umihebi** sea serpent
海魚 **kaigyo** ocean/saltwater fish
海鳥 **kaichō, umidori** seabird
12 海象 **kaishō** ocean conditions
　　 seiuchi walrus
海港 **kaikō** seaport
海湾 **kaiwan** gulf, bay
海葬 **kaisō** burial at sea
海棠 **kaidō** aronia (flowering shrub)
13 海鼠 **namako** trepang, sea slug
海際 **umigiwa** seaside, beach
海溝 **kaikō** an ocean deep, sea trench
海塩 **kaien** salt made from seawater
海損 **kaison** sea damage, average (loss)
海戦 **kaisen** naval battle
海賊 **kaizoku** pirate
海賊版 **kaizokuban** pirate edition
海路 **kairo, umiji** ocean route, sealane
14 海鳴 **umina(ri)** roar of the ocean
海髪 **ogo** (a seaweed)
海綿 **kaimen** sponge
海酸漿 **umihōzuki** whelk egg capsule (used for child's noisemaker)
海関 **kaikan** maritime customs
海関税 **kaikanzei** import duties
15 海潮 **kaichō** tide
海潮音 **kaichōon** sound of the tide
海蝕 **kaishoku** erosion caused by the sea
16 海獣 **kaijū** sea animal
海燕 **umitsubame** stormy petrel
18 海難 **kainan** sea disaster, shipwreck
19 海藻 **kaisō** seaweeds, marine plants
海羅 **funori** (a seaweed, used for laundry starch)
海霧 **kaimu** sea fog
26 海驢 **ashika** sea lion

────────── 2 ──────────

2 入海 **i(ri)umi** bay, inlet
3 大海 **taikai** the ocean
　 大海原 **ōunabara** the ocean, the vast sea

3

氵6←
土
扌
口
女
巾
犭
弓
彳
彡
艹
宀
⺌
山
圭
广
尸
口

上海 **Shanhai** Shanghai
山海 **sankai** mountains and seas; land and sea
4 内海 **uchiumi, naikai** inland sea, inlet, bay
公海 **kōkai** international waters
5 北海 **hokkai** northern sea
Hokkai the North Sea
北海道 **Hokkaidō** (prefecture)
外海 **gaikai, sotoumi** open sea, the high seas
氷海 **hyōkai** frozen sea, icy waters
布海苔 **funori** (a type of seaweed, used for laundry starch)
四海 **shikai** the four/seven seas, the whole world
四海同胞 **shikai-dōhō** universal brotherhood
6 死海 **Shikai** the Dead Sea
気海 **kikai** the atmosphere
近海 **kinkai** coastal waters, adjoining seas
近海魚 **kinkaigyo** coastal/shore fish
光海鞘 **hikari-boya** luminous plankton
血海 **chi (no) umi** a sea of blood
8 東海 **tōkai** eastern sea
東海道 **Tōkaidō** the Tōkaidō highway
制海権 **seikaiken** control of the seas, naval superiority
沿海 **enkai** coastal waters, coast
沿海州 **enkaishū** maritime provinces
泥海 **doroumi** muddy sea
官海 **kankai** officialdom
青海苔 **aonori** green laver (edible seaweed)
青海原 **aounabara** blue expanse of water
9 南海 **nankai** southern sea
浅海魚 **senkaigyo** shallow-sea fish
荒海 **araumi** rough sea
紅海 **Kōkai** the Red Sea
10 陸海 **rikukai** land and sea
陸海軍 **rikukaigun, rikkaigun** army and navy
航海 **kōkai** voyage, ocean navigation
航海日誌 **kōkai nisshi** ship's log
航海者 **kōkaisha** mariner, seaman
航海術 **kōkaijutsu** seamanship, navigation
11 深海 **shinkai** sea depths (200 m plus)
深海魚 **shinkaigyo** deep-sea fish
探海灯 **tankaitō** searchlight
掃海 **sōkai** mine sweeping
掃海艇 **sōkaitei** minesweeper
黄海 **Kōkai** the Yellow Sea
黒海 **Kokkai** the Black Sea
12 遠海 **enkai** ocean, deep sea
遠海魚 **enkaigyo** deep-sea fish
渡海 **tokai** crossing the ocean, passage
焼海苔 **ya(ki)nori** toasted seaweed
硯海 **suzuri (no) umi** the well of an inkstone
絶海 **zekkai** distant seas
雲海 **unkai** a sea of clouds
13 滄海 **sōkai** the blue sea

14 領海 **ryōkai** territorial waters
15 潮海 **shioumi** the sea
16 樹海 **jukai** a sea of trees/foliage
17 環海 **kankai** surrounding seas
18 臨海 **rinkai** seaside, coastal, marine

――― 3 ―――

4 支那海 **Shinakai** the China Sea
日本海 **Nihonkai** the Sea of Japan
5 北極海 **Hokkyokukai** the Arctic Ocean
6 地中海 **Chichūkai** the Mediterranean Sea
7 対馬海峡 **Tsushima-kaikyō** Tsushima Strait (between Tsushima and Iki Island)
初航海 **hatsukōkai** maiden voyage
8 宗谷海峡 **Sōya-kaikyō** (strait between Hokkaidō and Sakhalin)
9 南極海 **Nankyokukai** the Antarctic Ocean
津軽海峡 **Tsugaru-kaikyō** (strait between Honshū and Hokkaidō)
浅草海苔 **Asakusa nori** sheets of dried seaweed
12 象牙海岸 **Zōge Kaigan** Ivory Coast
間宮海峡 **Mamiya-kaikyō** (strait between Hokkaidō and Sakhalin)
14 鳴門海峡 **Naruto-kaikyō** (strait between Shikoku and Awaji island)
関門海峡 **Kanmon-kaikyō** (strait between Shimonoseki and Moji)

――― 4 ―――

5 処女航海 **shojo kōkai** maiden voyage
8 東支那海 **Higashi Shinakai** East China Sea
9 南支那海 **Minami Shinakai** the South China Sea
19 瀬戸内海 **Setonaikai** the Inland Sea

3a6.21 / 912

派

HA group, faction, sect, school (of thought/art); send, dispatch

――― 1 ―――

0 派する **ha(suru)** send, dispatch
4 派手 **hade** showy, flashy, gaudy
派手好 **hadezu(ki)** fond of display
5 派出 **hashutsu** dispatch, send out
派出所 **hashutsujo** police box; branch office
派出婦 **hashutsufu** visiting maid
派生 **hasei** derive from, originate with
派生的 **haseiteki** derivative, secondary
派生語 **haseigo** a derivative
7 派別 **habetsu** division (into factions)
派兵 **hahei** dispatch/send troops
12 派遣 **haken** dispatch, send
派遣軍 **hakengun** expeditionary army
派遣隊 **hakentai** contingent, detachment
14 派閥 **habatsu** clique, faction

—————— 2 ——————
4 分派 **bunpa** branch, offshoot, sect, faction
5 左派 **saha** leftists
  末派 **mappa** sect; underling
  右派 **uha** rightists, the Right
  旧派 **kyūha** of the old school/style, conservative
  立派 **rippa** splendid, fine, magnificent
6 同派 **dōha** the same sect
  各派 **kakuha** each party/faction/sect
  自派 **jiha** one's own party/faction
7 別派 **beppa** different sect/party/school
  学派 **gakuha** a school (of thought)
8 宗派 **shūha** sect, denomination
9 急派 **kyūha** dispatch, rush, expedite
  政派 **seiha** party faction
10 流派 **ryūha** school (of thought/art)
  党派 **tōha** party, faction
  党派心 **tōhashin** partisanship, factionalism
  特派 **tokuha** dispatch
  特派員 **tokuhain** (news) correspondent; delegate
  教派 **kyōha** sect, denomination
11 軟派 **nanpa** moderates; a masher
12 無派 **muha** unaffiliated, nonpartisan
  硬派 **kōha** tough elements, hardliners, hardcore
13 新派 **shinpa** new school (of thought/art)
  鳩派 **hatoha** the doves, soft-liners
14 増派 **zōha** send reinforcements
15 諸派 **shoha** minor (political) parties
24 鷹派 **takaha** the hawks, hardliners

—————— 3 ——————
2 人生派 **jinseiha** humanists
4 中道派 **chūdōha** centrists, middle-of-the-roaders
5 未来派 **miraiha** futurist (artists)
  古典派 **kotenha** the classical school
  正統派 **seitōha** orthodox school, fundamentalists
  主流派 **shuryūha** the leading faction
  立体派 **rittaiha** cubists
6 印象派 **inshōha** impressionist school
8 非党派的 **hitōhateki** nonpartisan
  実力派 **jitsuryokuha** powerful group
9 急進派 **kyūshinha** radicals
  革新派 **kakushinha** reformists
10 高踏派 **kōtōha** the transcendentalists
  浪漫派 **rōmanha** romantic school, romanticists
  耽美派 **tanbiha** the esthetic school
11 野獣派 **yajūha** Fauvists
  過激派 **kagekiha** radicals, extremists
  強硬派 **kyōkōha** hard-liners, diehards
  現実派 **genjitsuha** realists

12 超党派 **chōtōha** non-partisan
13 戦前派 **senzenha** prewar generation
  戦後派 **sengoha** postwar generation
  新義派 **Shingi-ha** New Shingon religion
16 穏和派 **onwaha** the moderates
  穏健派 **onkenha** the moderates

—————— 4 ——————
4 犬儒学派 **kenjugakuha** the Cynics

3a6.22

涎

SEN, yodare drooling saliva, slobber

—————— 1 ——————
11 涎掛 **yodareka(ke)** bib

—————— 2 ——————
8 垂涎 **suizen** watering at the mouth
10 竜涎香 **ryūzenkō** ambergris

3a6.23

洵

JUN sincere

3a6.24

洶

KYŌ gush forth, surge

3a6.25 / 1301

洞

DŌ cave; penetrate
hora cave, den

—————— 1 ——————
5 洞穴 **horaana, dōketsu** cave, den
7 洞見 **dōken** insight, penetration
8 洞門 **dōmon** cave entrance
11 洞視 **dōshi** insight, discernment
13 洞窟 **dōkutsu** cave, cavern
14 洞察 **dōsatsu, tōsatsu** insight, discernment
  洞察力 **dōsatsuryoku** insight
18 洞観 **dōkan** insight, intuition

—————— 2 ——————
8 空洞 **kūdō** cave, cavern; hollow, cavity
  空洞化 **kūdōka** hollwing out, deindustrialization
9 風洞 **fūdō** wind tunnel
11 雪洞 **bonbori** hand lamp; lampstand

—————— 3 ——————
5 石灰洞 **sekkaidō** limestone cave
17 鍾乳洞 **shōnyūdō** stalactite cave
20 鍾乳洞 **shōnyūdō** stalactite cave

3

氵 6 ←
土
扌
口
女
巾
犭
弓
彳
彡
艹
宀
丷
凵
耂
广
尸
口

3a6.26

迴 **KAI** flow around; go upstream

3

→6 氵
土
扌
口
女
巾
犭
弓
彳
彡
艹
宀
丷
山
亠
广
尸
口

7

3a7.1 / 517

酒 **SHU, sake, saka-** saké, rice wine; alcoholic drink, liquor

---

1

---

4 酒手 **sakate** drink money, tip
5 酒母 **shubo** rice-malt-yeast culture (from which saké is made)
酒仙 **shusen** heavy drinker
酒代 **sakadai, sakashiro** drink money, tip
酒好 **sakezu(ki)** drinker
酒石酸 **shusekisan** tartaric acid
6 酒気 **sakake, shuki** the smell of liquor
酒肉 **shuniku** saké and meat
酒色 **shushoku** wine and women
酒池肉林 **shuchi-nikurin** sumptuous feast
7 酒呑 **sakeno(mi)** drinker
酒乱 **shuran** drunken frenzy/violence
8 酒毒 **shudoku** alcoholism, alcohol poisoning
酒店 **sakamise, saketen** liquor store
酒杯 **shuhai** wine cup/glass
酒肴 **shukō, sakesakana** food and drink
9 酒保 **shuho** canteen, military base exchange
酒造 **shuzō** brewing, distilling
酒造家 **shuzōka** brewer, distiller
酒造場 **shuzōjō** brewery, distillery
酒造業 **shuzōgyō** brewery business
酒客 **shukaku** drinker
酒屋 **sakaya** wine dealer, liquor store
10 酒浸 **sakabita(ri), sakebita(ri)** steeped in liquor, always drinking
酒振舞 **sakaburuma(i)** wining and dining
酒徒 **shuto** drinking companions
酒家 **shuka** wine shop, pub; drinker
酒宴 **shuen** banquet, feast
酒席 **shuseki** banquet, feast
11 酒淫 **shuin** wine and women
酒盛 **sakamo(ri)** drinking bout, carousal
酒粕 **sakekasu, sakakasu** saké lees
酒断 **sakada(chi), sakeda(chi)** swearing off from drinking
酒販 **shuhan** liquor sales
12 酒場 **sakaba** bar, saloon, tavern
酒落 **share** play on words, pun, joke, witticism
(o)share dress up/stylishly
share(ru) pun, be witty; dress up/stylishly **sharaku** free and easy, unconventional

酒落気 **share(k)ke** a bent for witticism; vanity in dress
酒落者 **sharemono** smart dresser, fop
酒落臭 **sharakusa(i)** cheeky, "smart"
酒壺 **sakatsubo** saké jar
酒量 **shuryō** one's drinking capacity
酒税 **shuzei** liquor tax
酒飲 **sakeno(mi)** drinker
13 酒戦 **shusen** drinking bout
14 酒豪 **shugō** heavy drinker
酒精 **shusei** spirits, alcohol, liquor
15 酒器 **shuki** saké cup/vat
酒蔵 **sakagura** wine cellar, wineshop
16 酒興 **shukyō** conviviality, merrymaking
酒樽 **sakadaru** wine cask
18 酒癖 **sakekuse, sakeguse, shuheki** drinking habits
酒類 **shurui** alcoholic beverages, liquor

2

---

3 大酒 **ōzake, taishu** heavy drinking
大酒飲 **ōzakeno(mi)** heavy drinker
4 斗酒 **toshu** kegs/gallons of saké
火酒 **kashu** liquor
5 生酒 **kizake** pure saké
甘酒 **amazake** sweet saké
古酒 **furuzake** old saké, last year's saké
koshu well-cured saké
白酒 **shirozake** white saké
6 老酒 **rōshu** old wine
迎酒 **muka(e)zake** a drink to cure a hangover
地酒 **jizake** locally brewed saké
安酒 **yasuzake** cheap saké/liquor
7 作酒屋 **tsuku(ri)zakaya** saké brewer(y)
冷酒 **hi(ya)zake** cold saké
乱酒 **ranshu** drunken frenzy, vicious when drunk
利酒 **ki(ki)zake** wine tasting
8 毒酒 **dokushu** poisoned saké
居酒屋 **izakaya** tavern, pub, saloon
9 美酒 **bishu** excellent saké
造酒 **zōshu** saké brewing
造酒屋 **zōshuya** saké brewer
造酒業 **zōshugyō** saké brewing industry
洋酒 **yōshu** Western liquor
神酒 **(o)miki, shinshu** sacred saké, libation
祝酒 **iwa(i)zake** a drink in celebration
10 梅酒 **umeshu** plum brandy
11 清酒 **seishu** refined saké
深酒 **fukazake** excessive drinking
悪酒 **akushu** cheap/rotgut liquor
悪酒落 **warujare** joke in bad taste
粗酒 **soshu** cheap saké
12 御酒 **miki** sacred saké, saké offering
葷酒 **kunshu** leeks and liquor
朝酒 **asazake** morning drink of saké

無酒精 **mushusei** nonalcoholic
飲酒 **inshu** drinking (alcohol)
飲酒家 **inshuka** drinker
13 寝酒 **nezake** a drink before going to bed
禁酒 **kinshu** abstinence from alcohol, Prohibition
禁酒会 **kinshukai** temperance society
禁酒法 **kinshuhō** Prohibition (law)
新酒 **shinshu** new saké/wine
節酒 **sesshu** drinking in moderation
14 緑酒 **ryokushu** green/sweet wine
銘酒 **meishu** special-brand saké
銘酒屋 **meishuya** brothel
聞酒 **ki(ki)zake** wine tasting
駄酒落 **dajare** lame pun, corny joke
16 濁酒 **dakushu, nigo(ri)zake, doburoku** unrefined/raw saké
薬酒 **yakushu** medicinal liquor
燗酒 **kanzake** warmed saké

————————— 3 —————————
4 日本酒 **nihonshu** saké
6 自棄酒 **yakezake** drowning one's cares in saké
7 花見酒 **hanamizake** viewing cherry blossoms and drinking saké
8 果実酒 **kajitsushu** fruit wine
林檎酒 **ringoshu** hard cider
9 茶屋酒 **chayazake** saké drunk at a teahouse
10 振舞酒 **furuma(i)zake** a saké treat
特級酒 **tokkyūshu** special-grade saké
11 混合酒 **kongōshu** mixed drink, blended liquor
梯子酒 **hashigozake** barhopping, pub-crawling
雪見酒 **yukimizake** drinking saké while viewing snowy scenery
12 御神酒 **omiki** sacred saké, saké offering
葡萄酒 **budōshu** wine
20 醸造酒 **jōzōshu** brewage, liquor

————————— 4 —————————
5 白葡萄酒 **shiro-budōshu** white wine

3a7.2 / 1442

浦

HO, ura shore; inlet, bay

————————— 1 —————————
2 浦人 **urabito** seaside dweller
4 浦辺 **urabe** seacoast
8 浦波 **uranami** breakers
浦和 **Urawa** (city, Saitama-ken)
9 浦風 **urakaze** sea breeze
13 浦路 **uraji** coastal road

————————— 3 —————————
9 津々浦々 **tsutsu-uraura** throughout the land, the entire country

涛 → 濤 **3a14.8**

3a7.3

浬

RI, kairi nautical mile (1852 m)

3a7.4

浹

SHŌ far and wide; cycle, period

3a7.5 / 1753

浪

RŌ wander; waves

————————— 1 —————————
2 浪人 **rōnin** lordless samurai; unaffiliated/ jobless person, high-school graduate studying to pass a university entrance exam
6 浪曲 **rōkyoku** samisen-accompanied recital of ancient tales
7 浪花 **Naniwa** (old name for Ōsaka and vicinity)
浪花節 **naniwabushi** samisen-accompanied recital of ancient tales
12 浪費 **rōhi** waste, squander
浪費癖 **rōhiheki** spendthrift habits
14 浪漫主義 **rōman shugi** romanticism
浪漫的 **rōmanteki** romantic (school)
浪漫派 **rōmanha** romantic school, romanticists

————————— 2 —————————
8 逆浪 **sakanami, gyakurō** head/choppy sea
波浪 **harō** waves, billows
放浪 **hōrō** wander, rove
放浪者 **hōrōsha** wanderer, vagabond, vagrant
放浪癖 **hōrōheki** wanderlust
9 風浪 **fūrō** wind and waves, heavy seas
津浪 **tsunami** tsunami, "tidal" wave
浮浪 **furō** vagrant, wandering
浮浪人 **furōnin** vagrant, street bum
浮浪児 **furōji** juvenile vagrant, gamin
浮浪者 **furōsha** street bum, tramp, hobo
10 流浪 **rurō** wander about, roam
素浪人 **surōnin** (mere) lordless retainer
14 漂浪 **hyōrō** wandering

3

氵7 ←
土
扌
口
女
巾
犭
弓
彳
彡
艹
宀
屮
山
幸
广
尸
口

16 激浪 **gekirō** high waves, raging sea

———————— 3 ————————

3 山津浪 **yamatsunami** landslide

3a7.6

浙

SETSU (name of a river in China)

3a7.7 / 785

浜 濱

HIN beach, seashore;
Yokohama
hama beach, seashore

———————— 1 ————————

4 浜辺 **hamabe** beach, seashore
8 浜松 **Hamamatsu** (city, Shizuoka-ken)
9 浜風 **hamakaze** beach wind/breeze
　浜面 **hamazura** beach, seashore
12 浜焼 **hamaya(ki)** (sea bream) broiled whole (at the beach)

———————— 2 ————————

5 白浜 **shirahama** white beach
8 京浜 **Kei-Hin** Tōkyō-Yokohama
9 海浜 **kaihin** seashore, beach
　砂浜 **sunahama, sahin** sand beach
15 横浜 **Yokohama** (city, Kanagawa-ken)

———————— 3 ————————

13 新居浜 **Niihama** (city, Ehime-ken)

3a7.8

涅 涅

NE, NETSU (used phonetically); black soil/mud

———————— 1 ————————

14 涅槃 **nehan** nirvana
　涅槃会 **nehan'e** anniversary of Buddha's death
　涅槃経 **Nehangyō** (a Buddhist sutra)

3a7.9

浩 浩

KŌ wide, vast; vigorous

———————— 1 ————————

12 浩然 **kōzen** expansive, free and easy, openly
　浩然気 **kōzen (no) ki** spirits, morale

3a7.10 / 247

流

RYŪ, RU flow, current; (as suffix) style, school (of thought/art); (as suffix) rank, class, grade **naga(reru)** flow **naga(su)** let flow

———————— 1 ————————

2 流入 **ryūnyū** influx, flow in
　流人 **runin** an exile
3 流亡 **ryūbō** wander about far from home
4 流込 **naga(re)ko(mu)** flow/drift into
　　　naga(shi)ko(mu) wash down, pour into
　流水 **ryūsui** running water, stream
　流木 **ryūboku** driftwood
5 流矢 **naga(re)ya** stray arrow
　流出 **ryūshutsu, naga(re)de(ru), naga(re)da(su)** flow out
　流民 **ryūmin** drifting people, displaced persons
　流失 **ryūshitsu** be washed away
　流用 **ryūyō** divert, misappropriate
　流氷 **ryūhyō** drift ice, ice floe
　流布 **rufu** circulate, spread, disseminate
　流布本 **rufubon** popular edition
　流石 **sasuga** as might be expected
　流目 **naga(shi)me** sidelong glance
6 流年 **ryūnen** the passing years
　流会 **ryūkai** adjourn, call off (for lack of a quorum)
　流刑 **ryūkei** deportation, exile, banishment
　流刑地 **ryūkeichi** penal colony
　流刑者 **ryūkeisha** an exile
　流汗 **ryūkan** perspiration
　流行 **ryūkō, haya(ru)** be popular, be in fashion; be prevalent/epidemic
　流行文句 **haya(ri)monku** popular phrase
　流行色 **ryūkōshoku** fashionable/prevailing color
　流行地 **ryūkōchi** infected district
　流行児 **ryūkōji, hayari(k)ko** popular person
　流行言葉 **haya(ri)kotoba** popular expression
　流行性感冒 **ryūkōsei kanbō** influenza
　流行後 **ryūkōoku(re)** out of fashion
　流行病 **ryūkōbyō** an epidemic
　流行歌 **ryūkōka, haya(ri)uta** popular song
　流行語 **ryūkōgo** popular phrase, catchword
　流血 **ryūketsu** bloodshed
7 流体 **ryūtai** a fluid (in physics)
　流体力学 **ryūtai rikigaku** fluid dynamics
　流作業 **naga(re)sagyō** (assembly-)line operation
　流図 **naga(re)zu** flowchart
　流言 **ryūgen** false rumor
　流言飛語 **ryūgen-higo** rumor, gossip
8 流歩 **naga(re)aru(ku)** wander about
　流者 **naga(re)mono** vagrant, drifter
9 流連 **ryūren** stay on
　流速 **ryūsoku** speed of a current
　流通 **ryūtsū** distribution, circulation
　流派 **ryūha** school (of thought/art)
　流星 **ryūsei, naga(re)boshi** meteor, shooting/falling star

流星雨 **ryūseiu** meteor shower
流砂 **ryūsha, ryūsa** river sand, silt; desert
10 流浪 **rurō** wander about, roam
11 流動 **ryūdō** flowing, liquid (assets), current (liabilities)
流動体 **ryūdōtai** a fluid
流動物 **ryūdōbutsu** fluid, liquid
流動食 **ryūdōshoku** liquid diet/food
流域 **ryūiki** (river) basin/valley
流産 **ryūzan** miscarriage
流転 **ruten** constant change; wandering, vagrancy; reincarnation
12 流着 **naga(re)tsu(ku)** drift to, be washed ashore
流弾 **ryūdan, naga(re)dama** stray bullet
流量 **ryūryō** volume of flow, flux
流量計 **ryūryōkei** flow/current meter
13 流感 **ryūkan** flu, influenza (short for 流行性感冒)
流罪 **ruzai** exile, banishment
14 流暢 **ryūchō** fluent
流網 **naga(shi)ami** drift net
流説 **ryūsetsu** rumor, baseless report
15 流儀 **ryūgi** school (of thought), style, system, method
流線形 **ryūsenkei** streamlined
流線型 **ryūsenkei** streamlined
18 流離 **ryūri, sasura(u)** wander, roam
19 流麗 **ryūrei** flowing, elegant
流鏑馬 **yabusame** horseback archery
21 流露 **ryūro** disclose, reveal, express

——————— 2 ———————

1 一流 **ichiryū** a school (of art); first-rate, top-notch; unique
2 二流 **niryū** second-rate, inferior
3 三流 **sanryū** third-rate
大流行 **dairyūkō, ōhayari** the fashion/rage
上流 **jōryū** upstream; upper-class
下流 **karyū** downstream; lower-class
女流 **joryū** woman (writer/singer)
4 中流 **chūryū** middle class; middle part of a river
片流 **katanaga(re)** (roof) sloping one way only
支流 **shiryū** tributary, branch
分流 **bunryū** tributary
水流 **suiryū** current, stream of water
5 本流 **honryū** mainstream
末流 **matsuryū** descendants
他流 **taryū** another style, another school (of thought)
古流 **koryū** old style; old school (of art)
主流 **shuryū** mainstream
主流派 **shuryūha** the leading faction

立流 **ta(chi)naga(shi)** (waist-high) sink, basin
6 気流 **kiryū** air current
合流 **gōryū** confluence; join
交流 **kōryū** alternating current, AC; (cultural) exchange
名流 **meiryū** notables, celebrities
7 我流 **garyū** self-taught, one's own way
亜流 **aryū** adherent, follower, imitator
対流 **tairyū** convection
吹流 **fu(ki)naga(su)** blow away, blow off course **fu(ki)naga(shi)** streamer, pennant
乱流 **ranryū** turbulence
私流 **watakushiryū** one's personal method
8 受流 **u(ke)naga(su)** parry, turn aside
直流 **chokuryū** direct current, DC
奔流 **honryū** rushing current, torrent
逆流 **gyakuryū** backward flow, reverse current, regurgitation
河流 **karyū** stream
押流 **o(shi)naga(su)** wash/sweep away
底流 **teiryū** bottom current, undercurrent
物流 **butsuryū** physical distribution, dispatch/routing (of goods)
放流 **hōryū** set adrift, discharge, stock (with fish)
9 俗流 **zokuryū** the common throng, the vulgar masses
変流器 **henryūki** current transformer
急流 **kyūryū** swift current; rapids
風流 **fūryū** elegant, refined, aesthetic
浮流 **furyū** float about, drift
洗流 **ara(i)naga(su)** wash away
海流 **kairyū** ocean current
後流 **kōryū** slipstream
10 島流 **shimanaga(shi)** exile, banishment
時流 **jiryū** trend of the times
書流 **ka(ki)naga(su)** write with ease, dash off
11 偏流 **henryū** drift
混流 **konryū** crosscurrents, mixed flow
渓流 **keiryū** mountain stream
清流 **seiryū** clear stream
庶流 **shoryū** illegitimate family branch
細流 **sairyū** small stream
貫流 **kanryū** flow through
12 着流 **kinaga(shi)** everyday clothes, dishabille
湾流 **Wanryū** the Gulf Stream
渦流 **karyū** eddy, whirlpool
寒流 **kanryū** cold current
極流 **kyokuryū** polar current
検流計 **kenryūkei** current gauge, ammeter
検流器 **kenryūki** current gauge, ammeter
13 源流 **genryū** source, origin
暗流 **anryū** undercurrent
暖流 **danryū** warm (ocean) current
電流 **denryū** electric current

3

氵7←
土
扌
口
女
巾
犭
弓
彳
彡
艹
宀
⺍
山
青
广
尸
口

電流計 **denryūkei** ammeter, galvanometer

14 漂流 **hyōryū** drift, be adrift; wandering

漂流木 **hyōryūboku** driftwood

漂流民 **hyōryūmin** persons adrift; castaways

漂流者 **hyōryūsha** person adrift; castaway

漂流物 **hyōryūbutsu** flotsam

漂流記 **hyōryūki** castaway's account of foreign lands

漂流船 **hyōryūsen** drifting ship, a derelict

嫡流 **chakuryū** lineage of the eldest son

読流 **yo(mi)naga(su)** read fluently; skim, glance through

銀流 **ginnaga(shi)** silvering, tinsel

聞流 **ki(ki)naga(su)** pay no attention to

15 還流 **kanryū** return current, flowing back, reflux

潮流 **chōryū** tidal current; trend of the times

潜流 **senryū** undercurrent

横流 **yokonaga(shi)** sell through illegal channels

緩流 **kanryū** gentle current

質流 **shichinaga(re)** unredeemed pawn

16 激流 **gekiryū** swift/raging current

濁流 **dakuryū** muddy river, turbid water

整流 **seiryū** rectification, commutation (in electricity)

整流子 **seiryūshi** commutator

整流器 **seiryūki** rectifier

——————— 3 ———————

4 不風流 **bufūryū** lacking refinement, prosaic

5 台所流 **daidokoro (no) naga(shi)** the kitchen sink

6 行文流麗 **kōbun-ryūrei** fluent style/writing

行雲流水 **kōun-ryūsui** floating clouds and flowing water; taking life easy

灯籠流 **tōrōnaga(shi)** setting votive lanterns afloat

7 没風流 **botsufūryū** prosaic, unrefined

8 抵当流 **teitōnaga(re)** foreclosure

金釘流 **kanakugiryū** a scrawl

11 勘亭流 **Kantei-ryū** (style of calligraphy used in kabuki and sumo programs)

第一流 **dai-ichiryū** first-rate

12 無風流 **mufūryū** lack of refinement

18 鎔岩流 **yōganryū** lava flow

——————— 4 ———————

3 上昇気流 **jōshō kiryū** rising air current, updraft

上層気流 **jōsō kiryū** upper-air currents

3a7.11

浚   **SHUN, sara(u)** dredge

——————— 1 ———————

12 浚渫 **shunsetsu** dredge

浚渫船 **shunsetsusen** dredger

浚渫機 **shunsetsuki** dredger

——————— 2 ———————

9 洗浚 **ara(i)zara(i)** one and all, everything

15 蔵浚 **kurazara(e)** clearance sale

3a7.12

涇   **KEI** flow

涉→涉 **3a8.20**

3a7.13

涓   **KEN** trickle, droplet

3a7.14

浤   **KŌ** rising/surging waters; clear deep water

3a7.15

浣   **KAN** wash

——————— 1 ———————

13 浣腸 **kanchō** enema

3a7.16 / 845

消 消   **SHŌ, ke(su)** extinguish, turn off (a light), erase, cancel out **ki(eru)** go/die out, disappear

——————— 1 ———————

0 消ゴム **ke(shi)gomu** eraser

2 消入 **ki(e)i(ru)** vanish, fade away

4 消化 **shōka** digest

消化不良 **shōka furyō** indigestion

消化剤 **shōkazai** aid to digestion

消化液 **shōkaeki** digestive fluid/juices

消化腺 **shōkasen** digestive glands

消化管 **shōkakan** alimentary canal, digestive tract

消化器 **shōkaki** digestive organs

消火 **shōka** fire fighting

消火栓 **shōkasen** fire hydrant

消火器 **shōkaki** fire extinguisher

5 消失 **shōshitsu, ki(e)u(seru)** disappear, vanish, die out/away
消去 **shōkyo** eliminate, cancel out
消石灰 **shōsekkai** slaked lime, calcium hydroxide
6 消防 **shōbō** fire fighting, firemen
消防士 **shōbōshi** fireman
消防隊 **shōbōtai** fire brigade
消防組 **shōbōgumi** fire brigade
消防署 **shōbōsho** fire station
消印 **keshiin** postmark, cancellation stamp
消光 **shōkō** passing time, getting along
消灯 **shōtō** putting out the lights (cf. 点灯)
7 消却 **shōkyaku** efface, erase, extinguish (a debt)
消沈 **shōchin** dejected, despondent
8 消長 **shōchō** rise and fall
消果 **ki(e)ha(teru)** disappear, vanish
消毒 **shōdoku** disinfect, sterilize
消毒液 **shōdokueki** antiseptic solution
消毒器 **shōdokuki** sterilizer
消毒薬 **shōdokuyaku** disinfectant, antiseptic
消炎剤 **shōenzai** an antiphlogistic, balm
9 消炭 **ke(shi)zumi** cinders
消音器 **shōonki** muffler, silencer
10 消耗 **shōmō** consumption, attrition, wear and tear
消耗品 **shōmōhin** supplies, expendables
消耗戦 **shōmōsen** war of attrition
消消 **ki(e)gi(e)** about to die out
消息 **shōsoku** news, hearing from (someone)
消息子 **shōsokushi** (surgical) probe
消息文 **shōsokubun** personal letter
消息通 **shōsokutsū** well informed person
消息筋 **shōsokusuji** well informed sources
12 消壺 **ke(shi)tsubo** charcoal-extinguishing jar
消極 **shōkyoku** negative pole; passive
消極的 **shōkyokuteki** passive, negative
消極性 **shōkyokusei** passive
消然 **shōzen** dejected, despondent
消散 **shōsan** disperse, disappear, dissipate
消費 **shōhi** consumption
消費力 **shōhiryoku** consumer buying power
消費者 **shōhisha** consumer
消費物資 **shōhi busshi** consumer goods
消費高 **shōhidaka** (amount of) consumption
消費財 **shōhizai** consumer goods
消費税 **shōhizei** consumption/excise tax
消閑 **shōkan** killing time
13 消滅 **shōmetsu** become extinct, disappear, become void, be extinguished
消煙機 **shōenki** smoke consumer
14 消磁 **shōji** demagnetization

——————— 2 ———————

4 不消化 **fushōka** indigestion

不消化物 **fushōkabutsu** indigestible food
火消 **hike(shi)** firefighter; fire extinguisher
火消壺 **hike(shi)tsubo** charcoal extinguisher
5 打消 **u(chi)ke(shi)** denial, negation, negative (in grammar)
立消 **ta(chi)gi(e)** go/die/flicker/fizzle out
6 色消 **iroke(shi)** achromatic; unromantic, prosaic
7 吹消 **fu(ki)ke(su)** blow out (a candle)
私消 **shishō** embezzlement
8 毒消 **dokuke(shi)** antidote
抹消 **masshō** erase, cross out
取消 **to(ri)ke(su)** cancel, revoke, rescind
9 拭消 **fu(ki)ke(su)** wipe out/off, erase
10 消消 **ki(e)gi(e)** about to die out
11 帳消 **chōke(shi)** cancellation, writing off (debts)
12 揉消 **mo(mi)ke(su)** crush out (a cigarette), hush up, suppress
斑消 **muragi(e)** (snow) remaining in spots
費消 **hishō** spending; embezzlement
13 塗消 **nu(ri)ke(su)** paint out
搔消 **ka(ki)ke(su)** scratch/rub out, efface
解消 **kaishō** dissolution, liquidation; annulment; be settled/solved
14 魂消 **tamage(ru)** be astonished/flabbergasted
15 踏消 **fu(mi)ke(su)** stamp out (a fire)
19 艶消 **tsuyake(shi)** non-glossy, frosted (glass)

——————— 3 ———————

13 意気消沈 **iki-shōchin** dejected, despondent
罪障消滅 **zaishō shōmetsu** expiation of one's sins

——————— 4 ———————

12 雲散霧消 **unsan-mushō** vanishing like mist

浣 → 澣 **3a15.7**

3a7.17 / 1078

浸 SHIN, **hita(ru)** be soaked/steeped in
hita(su) soak, immerse
tsu(karu) be soaked in; be submerged

——————— 1 ———————

0 お浸し **(o)hita(shi)** boiled greens with dressing
4 浸水 **shinsui** be inundated
5 浸出 **shinshutsu** exuding, oozing out, percolation
浸礼 **shinrei** baptism by immersion
9 浸透 **shintō** permeation, infiltration, osmosis
浸染 **shinsen** permeate, infiltrate; dye
浸食 **shinshoku** erosion, corrosion
14 浸漬 **shinseki, shinshi** immerse, dip, soak, steep

15 浸潤 **shinjun** permeate, infiltrate, seep
浸蝕 **shinshoku** erosion, corrosion

———————— 2 ————————

2 入浸 **i(ri)bita(ru)** be steeped in water; stay long
4 水浸 **mizubita(shi)** submerged, flooded; waterlogged
7 含浸 **ganshin** impregnation
9 肺浸潤 **haishinjun** pulmonary tuberculosis
10 酒浸 **sakabita(ri), sakebita(ri)** steeped in liquor, always drinking

3a7.18 / 1128

浴

YOKU bathe, bath **a(biru)** pour on oneself, bathe in, be showered with **a(biseru)** pour on, shower upon

———————— 1 ————————

0 浴する **yoku(suru)** bathe/bask in
5 浴用 **yokuyō** for the bath
6 浴衣 **yukata, yokui** light cotton kimono, bathrobe
浴衣掛 **yukataga(ke)** wearing a yukata
9 浴後 **yokugo** after the bath
浴客 **yokkyaku, yokkaku** bather, hot springs guest
浴室 **yokushitsu** bathroom (not toilet)
12 浴場 **yokujō** bathroom, bath(house)
15 浴槽 **yokusō** bathtub

———————— 2 ————————

2 入浴 **nyūyoku** take a bath
4 水浴 **suiyoku** bathing, cold bath
mizua(bi) bathing
7 沐浴 **mokuyoku** bathe, wash oneself
10 座浴 **zayoku** sitz bath
11 混浴 **kon'yoku** mixed bathing (in a public bath)
12 温浴 **on'yoku** warm/hot bath
湯浴 **yua(mi)** bath

———————— 3 ————————

4 日光浴 **nikkōyoku** sunbath
7 冷水浴 **reisuiyoku** cold bath/shower
9 海水浴 **kaisuiyoku** swimming in the ocean
海水浴場 **kaisuiyokujō** bathing beach
13 電気浴 **denkiyoku** electric bath

3a7.19

淳

JUN pure; kind, warm-hearted

———————— 1 ————————

4 淳仁 **Junnin** (emperor, 758–764)
6 淳朴 **junboku** simple and honest
8 淳和 **Junna** (emperor, 823–833)

3a7.20

涕

TEI tears, crying

海 → 海 3a6.20

涌 → 湧 3a9.31

3a7.21 / 1239

涙 涙 泪

RUI, namida tear; sympathy

———————— 1 ————————

7 涙声 **namidagoe** tearful voice
8 涙金 **namidakin** consolation money
涙雨 **namidaame** a light rain; rain falling at a time of sorrow
10 涙脆 **namidamoro(i)** given to weeping
13 涙腺 **ruisen** tear gland
14 涙管 **ruikan** tear duct
18 涙顔 **namidagao** tearful face
22 涙嚢 **ruinō** tear sac

———————— 2 ————————

6 血涙 **chi (no) namida, ketsurui** tears of blood
7 声涙 **seirui (tomo ni kudaru)** speak through one's tears
8 空涙 **soranamida** crocodile tears
9 悔涙 **ku(yashi)namida** tears of vexation/regret
紅涙 **kōrui** tears of blood; tears of a beautiful woman
12 落涙 **rakurui** shed tears
13 催涙弾 **sairuidan** tear-gas bomb/grenade
暗涙 **anrui** silent tears
感涙 **kanrui** tears of gratitude
15 嬉涙 **ure(shi)namida** tears of joy
熱涙 **netsurui** hot/burning tears

———————— 3 ————————

4 不覚涙 **fukaku (no) namida** crying in spite of oneself
6 有難涙 **a(ri)gata-namida** tears of gratitude

涎 → 3a6.22

涵 → 涵 3a8.35

—————— 8 ——————

3a8.1
淦
KAN, aka bilge water

3a8.2
淮
WAI, E (name of a river in China)

3a8.3
淆
KŌ mixed together, turbid

—————— 2 ——————
11 混淆 konkō mix up, confuse, jumble together

渚→渚 3a9.1

渊→淵 3a9.3

渕→淵 3a9.3

3a8.4
渤
BOTSU (place name)

3a8.5 / 1668
淑
SHUKU good, virtuous; graceful, refined; idolize
shito(yaka) graceful, gentle, polite

—————— 1 ——————
3 淑女 shukujo lady, gentlewoman
14 淑徳 shukutoku feminine virtues
—————— 2 ——————
7 私淑 shishuku greatly admire, look up to
9 貞淑 teishuku chastity, modesty

3a8.6
淋
RIN rain, drip; lonely
sabi(shii) lonely

—————— 1 ——————
4 淋巴液 rinpaeki lymph
淋巴腺 rinpasen lymph gland

10 淋病 rinbyō gonorrhea
淋疾 rinshitsu gonorrhea
13 淋漓 rinri dripping, profuse
—————— 2 ——————
4 心淋 kokorosabi(shii) lonely, lonesome
8 物淋 monosabi(shii) lonely, lonesome

3a8.7
淅
SEKI wash (rice)

3a8.8
淞
SHŌ (name of a river in China)

3a8.9
淤
O mud, silt; clog up, obstruct

3a8.10
游
YŪ float; swim; wander; play
oyo(gu) swim

—————— 2 ——————
9 浮游 fuyū float, waft, be suspended

3a8.11
淇
KI (name of a river in China)

凄→凄 2b8.4

3a8.12
淕
RIKU, ROKU sleet, slush; (name of a wetland)

3a8.13 / 1622
渇 渴
KATSU, kawa(ku) dry up; be thirsty

—————— 1 ——————
0 渇する kas(suru) dry up; be thirsty
4 渇水 kassui water shortage
渇水期 kassuiki dry season, drought period

6 渇仰 **katsugō, katsugyō** adore, admire, idolize
11 渇望 **katsubō** thirst/crave/long for

───────── 2 ─────────

9 枯渇 **kokatsu** run dry, become depleted
10 飢渇 **kikatsu** hunger and thirst, starvation
11 涸渇 **kokatsu** run dry, be drained, become depleted

3a8.14 / 799

混

KON, **ma(zeru)** mix; include
ma(zaru), ma(jiru) be mixed

───────── 1 ─────────

0 混じる/ずる **kon(jiru/zuru)** mix
2 混入 **konnyū** mix in, adulterate
5 混用 **kon'yō** mix, use together
6 混合 **kongō** mixture, mixed, compound
　　 ma(ze)a(waseru) mix, blend, compound
混合物 **kongōbutsu** mixture, compound
混合酒 **kongōshu** mixed drink, blended liquor
混合語 **kongōgo** word derived/combined from two other words
混合機 **kongōki** mixer
混交 **konkō** mix up, confuse, jumble together
混返 **ma(ze)kae(su), ma(zek)kae(su)** stir up; interrupt, butt in
混同 **kondō** confuse (one thing with another)
混在 **konzai** be present together, coexist
混成 **konsei** mixture, combination, hybrid
混血 **konketsu** racial mixture
混血児 **konketsuji** person of mixed race, half-breed
7 混作 **konsaku** mixed crops
混沌 **konton** chaos, confusion
混乱 **konran** confusion, disorder, chaos
混声 **konsei** mixed voices
混声合唱 **konsei gasshō** mixed chorus
8 混迷 **konmei** be stupefied/befuddled/confused
混物 **ma(ze)mono, ma(jiri)mono** mixture, adulteration
混和 **konwa** mixture, mingling
混和物 **konwabutsu** mixture
混和性 **konwasei** miscibility
混和剤 **konwazai** a compound/blend
9 混信 **konshin** jamming, interference, crosstalk
10 混流 **konryū** crosscurrents, mixed flow
混浴 **kon'yoku** mixed bathing (in a public bath)
混紡 **konbō** mixed spinning, blended (yarn)
11 混淆 **konkō** mix up, confuse, jumble together
12 混然 **konzen** whole, entire, harmonious
13 混戦 **konsen** melee, free-for-all fight
混載 **konsai** mixed loading/cargo

14 混雑 **konzatsu** confusion, disorder, congestion
15 混線 **konsen** getting wires/lines crossed; confusion
16 混濁 **kondaku** become turbid/muddy/thick

───────── 2 ─────────

2 入混 **i(ri)maji(ru)** be mixed together
13 搗混 **tsu(ki)ma(zeru)** pound/mix together
搔混 **ka(ki)ma(zeru)** mix up, stir

3a8.15 / 1337

淡

TAN, **awa(i)** light, faint, pale; a little

───────── 1 ─────────

3 淡々 **tantan(taru)** unconcerned, indifferent; plain, light
4 淡水 **tansui** freshwater
淡水化 **tansuika** desalin(iz)ation
淡水魚 **tansuigyo** freshwater fish
淡水湖 **tansuiko** freshwater lake
5 淡白 **tanpaku** light, plain, simple; candid; indifferent to
6 淡色 **tanshoku** light color
7 淡赤色 **tansekishoku** rose color
8 淡泊 **tanpaku** light, plain, simple; candid; indifferent to
9 淡紅色 **tankōshoku** rose/salmon pink
11 淡彩 **tansai** light/thin coloring
淡黄色 **tankōshoku** light yellow, straw color
淡雪 **awayuki** light snow(fall)
12 淡紫色 **tanshishoku** light purple
13 淡褐色 **tankasshoku** light brown
淡路 **Awaji** (ancient kuni, Hyōgo-ken)
淡路島 **Awajishima** (island, Hyōgo-ken)
14 淡緑色 **tanryokushoku** light green
15 淡影 **tan'ei** adumbration, hint

───────── 2 ─────────

5 平淡 **heitan** plain, simple, light
7 冷淡 **reitan** indifferent, apathetic; cold, coldhearted
9 枯淡 **kotan** refined simplicity
11 淡淡 **tantan(taru)** unconcerned, indifferent; plain, light
16 濃淡 **nōtan** light and shade, concentration, shading

淺 → 浅 3a6.4

3a8.16 / 1884

渓 溪 谿

KEI valley

———— 1 ————

4 渓水 **keisui** mountain stream
7 渓谷 **keikoku** ravine, gorge, valley
9 渓泉 **keisen** valley spring
10 渓流 **keiryū** mountain stream
12 渓間 **keikan** ravine, in the valley

———— 2 ————

11 雪渓 **sekkei** snowy valley

3a8.17

淫 婬

IN lewd, indecent; excessive
mida(ra) lewd, obscene, indecent

———— 1 ————

0 淫する **in(suru)** indulge in; go to excess
7 淫佚 **in'itsu** debauchery
淫乱 **inran** lascivious, lustful
淫売 **inbai** prostitution
淫売婦 **inbaifu** prostitute
淫売宿 **inbaiyado** brothel
8 淫奔 **inpon** wanton, loose, lewd
淫雨 **in'u** prolonged (crop-damaging) rain
10 淫逸 **in'itsu** debauchery
淫祠 **inshi** shrine to an evil god
11 淫婦 **inpu** lewd woman, harlot
淫欲 **in'yoku** lust
12 淫猥 **inwai** indecent, obscene
13 淫楽 **inraku** carnal pleasure
15 淫蕩 **intō** dissipation, debauchery
淫慾 **in'yoku** lust
19 淫靡 **inbi** obscene, immoral, salacious

———— 2 ————

4 手淫 **shuin** masturbation
6 多淫 **tain** lascivious, lustful
7 邪淫 **jain** lewdness, adultery, incest
売淫 **baiin** prostitution
9 姦淫 **kan'in** illicit intercourse
10 酒淫 **shuin** wine and women

淨 → 浄 3a6.18

3a8.18 / 660

清 清

SEI, SHŌ pure, clear
SHIN Manchu/Qing dynasty
(1644 – 1911), China
kiyo(i) pure, clean, clear
kiyo(raka) clear   kiyo(meru) purify, cleanse
kiyo(maru) be purified/cleansed   su(masu) make
clear; act nonchalant, put on airs

———— 1 ————

3 清々 **seisei** feel refreshed/relieved
4 清元 **kiyomoto** (type of ballad drama)

清友 **seiyū** refined friend
清水 **shimizu, seisui** pure/clear water
    Shimizu (city, Shizuoka-ken); (surname)
    Kiyomizu (temple in Kyōto)
8 清冽 **seiretsu** clear, limpid
清国 **Shinkoku** China under the Manchu/
    Qing dynasty
清明 **seimei** pure and clear; 15th day after the
    vernal equinox
清所 **kiyodokoro** kitchen (in a noble's home)
清和 **Seiwa** (emperor, 858–876)
9 清風 **seifū** cool/refreshing breeze
清泉 **seisen** clear(-water) spring
清冽 **seiretsu** clear, limpid
清浄 **seijō, shōjō** pure, clean, spotless
清浄無垢 **shōjō-muku** immaculate, pure and
    innocent
清栄 **seiei** (your) health and prosperity
清音 **seion** unvoiced sound
清秋 **seishū** clear autumn (weather)
清香 **seikō** fragrance, perfume
10 清遊 **seiyū** excursion, pleasure trip
清酒 **seishu** refined saké
清流 **seiryū** clear stream
清書 **seisho** fair/clean copy
清教徒 **seikyōto** Puritans
清純 **seijun** pure (and innocent)
11 清貧 **seihin** honorable poverty
清清 **seisei** feel refreshed/relieved
清涼 **seiryō** cool, refreshing
清涼剤 **seiryōzai** refrigerant
清涼飲料 **seiryō inryō** carbonated beverage
清掃 **seisō** cleaning
清掃夫 **seisōfu** garbage man/collector
12 清朝 **Shinchō** Manchu/Qing dynasty
清朝体 **seichōtai** (a type of printed kanji
    resembling brush writing)
清閑 **seikan** quiet, tranquil, leisurely
13 清適 **seiteki** (your) health, prosperity
清廉 **seiren** integrity, uprightness
清廉潔白 **seiren-keppaku** spotless integrity
清楚 **seiso** neat and clean, tidy, trim
清福 **seifuku** happiness
清新 **seishin** fresh, new
清節 **seisetsu** integrity
14 清寧 **Seinei** (emperor, 480–484)
清算 **seisan** liquidation, settlement
15 清潔 **seiketsu** clean, neat, pure
清澄 **seichō** clear, limpid, serene
16 清興 **seikyō** refined amusement
清濁 **seidaku** purity and impurity; good and
    evil
17 清聴 **seichō** your kind attention (to my talk)

———— 2 ————

4 日清 **Nis-Shin** Japan and (Manchu-dynasty)
    China, Sino-Japanese

5 北清事変 **Hokushin jihen** the North China incident, the Boxer uprising
6 血清 **kessei** (blood) serum
8 岩清水 **iwashimizu** spring flowing from rocks
9 郭清 **kakusei** purify, clean up
10 祓清 **hara(i)kiyo(meru)** purify, exorcise
11 粛清 **shukusei** purge, cleanup, liquidation
清清 **seisei** feel refreshed/relieved
12 廓清 **kakusei** purification, cleanup, purge
21 露清 **Ro-Shin** Russia and China

3a8.19 / 1693

渋 澁 澀

JŪ, SHŪ, shibu(i) astringent, puckery; glum; quiet and tasteful **shibu(ru)** hesitate, be reluctant; have diarrhea-like bowel pains
shibu astringent taste (of unripe persimmons)

———————— 1 ————————

3 渋々 **shibushibu** reluctantly, grudgingly
5 渋皮 **shibukawa** astringent skin (of a chestnut)
6 渋色 **shibuiro** tan color
7 渋抜 **shibunu(ki)** removing the puckery taste (from persimmons)
8 渋味 **shibumi** puckery taste; severe elgance
9 渋茶 **shibucha** coarse tea
渋面 **jūmen, shibuzura, shibutsura** sour face, scowl
渋柿 **shibugaki** puckery persimmon
10 渋紙 **shibukami, shibugami** paper treated with astringent persimmon juice and used for a floor covering
13 渋滞 **jūtai** impeded flow, congestion, delay
渋腹 **shibu(ri)bara** diarrhea-like bowel pains

———————— 2 ————————

7 売渋 **u(ri)shibu(ru)** be reluctant/unwilling to sell
言渋 **i(i)shibu(ru)** hesitate to say, falter
8 苦渋 **kujū** bitter and puckery; distress, agony
9 茶渋 **chashibu** tea incrustations/stains
11 渋渋 **shibushibu** reluctantly, grudgingly
晦渋 **kaijū** obscure, ambiguous
18 難渋 **nanjū** suffering, distress, hardship

3a8.20 / 432

渉 涉

SHŌ go across/through; have to do with

———————— 1 ————————

5 渉外 **shōgai** public relations, liaison
11 渉猟 **shōryō** read extensively, search for far and wide

12 渉禽類 **shōkinrui** wading birds

———————— 2 ————————

3 干渉 **kanshō** intervention; interference
6 交渉 **kōshō** negotiations
10 徒渉 **toshō** fording
12 跋渉 **basshō** traverse, rove, hike

———————— 3 ————————

4 不干渉 **fukanshō** nonintervention
7 没交渉 **bokkōshō** unrelated, independent
12 無干渉 **mukanshō** nonintervention

3a8.21 / 536

深

SHIN, fuka(i) deep **fuka(meru)** (tr.) deepen, intensify **fuka(maru)** (intr.) deepen, intensify

———————— 1 ————————

2 深入 **fukai(ri)** go/get deep into
3 深々 **fukabuka** deeply **shinshin** getting late, silently (falling show), piercingly (cold)
深山 **miyama, shinzan** mountain recesses
深山烏 **miyamagarasu** mountain crow
深山楼 **miyamazakura** mountain cherry tree
4 深爪 **fukazume** cutting to the quick (of a fingernail)
深化 **shinka** deepening
深手 **fukade** deep wound, severe injury
6 深交 **shinkō** close friendship
7 深更 **shinkō** the dead of night, late at night
8 深長 **shinchō** profound, deep, abstruse
深刻 **shinkoku** serious, grave, acute
深刻化 **shinkokuka** intensification, aggravation
深夜 **shin'ya** late at night, the dead of night
深厚 **shinkō** deep, heartfelt, sincere
深味 **fukami** depth; deep place
深呼吸 **shinkokyū** deep breath(ing)
9 深甚 **shinjin** profound, deep
深浅 **shinsen** depth
深海 **shinkai** sea depths (200 m plus)
深海魚 **shinkaigyo** deep-sea fish
深度 **shindo** depth
深思 **shinshi** deep thinking
深紅 **shinku** deep/ruby red, crimson
深紅色 **shinkōshoku** deep/ruby red
10 深耕 **shinkō** deep plowing
深酒 **fukazake** excessive drinking
11 深深 **fukabuka** deeply **shinshin** getting late, silently (falling snow), piercingly (cold)
深彫 **fukabo(ri)** deep carving
深窓 **shinsō** secluded inner room; (upper-class daughter) brought up knowing nothing of the world
深情 **fukanasa(ke)** inordinate show of affection

深酔 **fukayo(i)** get very drunk
深雪 **shinsetsu** deep snow
12 深遠 **shin'en** profound, deep, abstruse
深淵 **shin'en** abyss
深奥 **shin'ō** esoteric principles, mysteries, secrets
深閑 **shinkan** still, quiet, deserted
深間 **fukama** depth(s); intimacy
13 深靴 **fukagutsu** (long) boots
深意 **shin'i** profound/deep meaning
14 深緑 **shinryoku, fukamidori** dark green
15 深慮 **shinryo** thoughtfulness, deliberateness, prudence
深潭 **shintan** abyss
深憂 **shin'yū** grave apprehension
16 深謀 **shinbō** shrewd planning, deep design
深謀遠慮 **shinbō-enryo** farsighted planning
17 深謝 **shinsha** heartfelt gratitude, sincere apology

――――― 2 ―――――
4 毛深 **kebuka(i)** hairy
水深 **suishin** (water) depth
木深 **kobuka(i)** deep in the woods
5 目深 **mabuka (ni)** (hat pulled) down over one's eyes
9 海深 **kaishin** ocean depth
草深 **kusabuka(i)** grassy; backwoods, remote
10 根深 **nebuka(i)** deep-rooted, ingrained
11 深深 **fukabuka** deeply **shinshin** getting late, silently (falling snow), piercingly (cold)
欲深 **yokufuka** greed, avarice
情深 **nasa(ke)buka(i)** compassionate, kindhearted
12 測深 **sokushin** (depth) sounding
最深 **saishin** deepest
奥深 **okubuka(i)** deep, profound
13 慎深 **tsutsushi(mi)buka(i)** discreet, cautious
罪深 **tsumibuka(i)** sinful, guilty, godless
14 疑深 **utaga(i)buka(i)** doubting, distrustful
16 憐深 **awa(remi)buka(i)** compassionate

――――― 3 ―――――
5 用心深 **yōjinbuka(i)** careful, cautious, wary
8 注意深 **chūibuka(i)** careful
11 執念深 **shūnenbuka(i)** tenacious; vengeful, spiteful
12 遠慮深 **enryobuka(i)** reserved, bashful
13 意味深長 **imi-shinchō** full of meaning
意義深 **igibuka(i)** full of meaning
16 興味深 **kyōmibuka(i)** very interesting

3a8.22 / 1433

添   **TEN, so(eru)** add to, append **so(u)** accompany; marry; meet (expectations)

――――― 1 ―――――
4 添文 **so(e)bumi** accompanying letter
添水 **sōzu** deer scare (Japanese-garden contrivance in which water flows into a pivoted bamboo tube which repeatedly fills up, tips over, empties, then rights itself again, its lower end clopping against a stone); (also called 鹿威 shishiodo(shi))
添木 **so(e)gi** brace, splint
5 添付 **tenpu** attach, append
添加 **tenka** annex, append, affix, add
添加物 **tenkabutsu** additives
添字 **soeji** subscript, superscript, index
7 添状 **so(e)jō** accompanying letter
添役 **so(e)yaku** secondary role
添乳 **so(e)ji** suckle (a child) in bed
添言葉 **so(e)kotoba** advice, encouragement
8 添物 **so(e)mono** addition, supplement, an extra
9 添乗員 **tenjōin** tour conductor
添臥 **so(i)bushi** sleeping together
添削 **tensaku** correct (a composition)
10 添書 **tensho, so(e)ga(ki)** accompanying letter; letter of introduction; additional writing, postscript
11 添遂 **so(i)to(geru)** be married together one's whole life long; succeed in marrying
12 添景 **tenkei** human-interest items (in a picture)
13 添寝 **so(i)ne** sleeping together

――――― 2 ―――――
2 力添 **chikarazo(e)** assistance
3 口添 **kuchizo(e)** advice, support, recommendation
山添 **yamazo(i)** by/along/in the mountains
4 介添 **kaizo(e)** helper, assistant
心添 **kokorozo(e)** advice, counsel
5 申添 **mō(shi)so(eru)** add (to what has been said)
付添 **tsu(ki)so(u)** attend on, accompany, escort
9 巻添 **ma(ki)zo(e)** involvement, entanglement
連添 **tsu(re)so(u)** be married to
後添 **nochizo(i)** one's second wife
10 差添 **sa(shi)zo(e)** one's shorter sword **sa(shi)zo(i)** assistance
書添 **ka(ki)so(eru)** add (a postscript)

3a8.23

淀   **TEN, DEN, yodo** pool (in a river), backwater **yodo(mu)** stagnate, be sedimented; hesitate, stammer

――――― 1 ―――――
3 淀川 **Yodogawa** (river, Ōsaka-fu)

─────────── 2 ───────────

7 言淀 **i(i)yodo(mu)** falter in saying, stammer

3a8.24

淙 **SŌ** sound of flowing water

─────────── 1 ───────────

3 淙々 **sōsō** murmuring, babbling

3a8.25

淌 **TŌ** flow

3a8.26

㴞 **KA** (name of a river in China)

3a8.27

淹 **EN** dip, soak, immerse; stop, linger

3a8.28

淪 **RIN, shizu(mu)** sink

3a8.29 / 472

液 **EKI** liquid, fluid
tsuyu juice, soup, broth

─────────── 1 ───────────

4 液化 **ekika** liquefy
5 液汁 **ekijū** juice; sap
7 液体 **ekitai** liquid
液状 **ekijō** liquid state, liquefied
8 液肥 **ekihi** liquid fertilizer
10 液剤 **ekizai** liquid medicine
12 液晶 **ekishō** liquid crystal
液量 **ekiryō** liquid measure, fluid (ounce)

─────────── 2 ───────────

5 汁液 **jūeki** juice
6 血液 **ketsueki** blood
血液型 **ketsuekigata** blood type
血液像 **ketsuekizō** hemogram
7 体液 **taieki** body fluids
乳液 **nyūeki** latex; milky lotion
8 毒液 **dokueki** poisonous liquid
9 胃液 **ieki** gastric juices
11 排液 **haieki** drainage (in surgery)

唾液 **daeki** saliva
唾液腺 **daekisen** salivary glands
粘液 **nen'eki** mucus
粘液質 **nen'ekishitsu** phlegmatic; mucous
13 溶液 **yōeki** solution
14 精液 **seieki** semen, sperm
15 漿液 **shōeki** juice, sap; blood serum
16 薬液 **yakueki** liquid medicine
樹液 **jueki** sap
輸液 **yueki** transfusion

─────────── 3 ───────────

4 不凍液 **futōeki** antifreeze
水溶液 **suiyōeki** aqueous solution
水様液 **suiyōeki** aqueous humor
8 注射液 **chūshaeki** injection (the liquid)
定着液 **teichakueki** fixing solution
10 消化液 **shōkaeki** digestive fluid/juices
消毒液 **shōdokueki** antiseptic solution
11 淋巴液 **rinpaeki** lymph
培養液 **baiyōeki** culture fluid/solution
現像液 **genzōeki** developing solution
12 葡萄液 **budōeki** grape juice
13 電解液 **denkaieki** electrolyte
16 濃溶液 **nōyōeki** concentrated solution

3a8.30 / 549

済 濟 **SAI, SEI** come to an end; accomplish; save, rescue; many **su(mu)** come to an end; be paid; suffice **su(masu)** finish, settle; pay; make do, manage **su(manai)** unpardonable, (I'm) sorry **su(mimasen)** Excuse me, I'm sorry **su(mi)** settled, done **-zu(mi)** completed, done, already ...ed **na(su)** pay back

─────────── 1 ───────────

5 済民 **saimin** relieving people's suffering
済生 **saisei** life saving
済世 **saisei** social reform
済世事業 **saisei jigyō** public-welfare work
9 済度 **saido** salvation, redemption
11 済崩 **na(shi)kuzu(shi)** (payment) by installments

─────────── 2 ───────────

4 内済 **naisai** settlement out of court
5 未済 **misai** unpaid, unsettled, outstanding
弁済 **bensai** (re)payment, settlement
用済 **yōzu(mi)** business finished, affairs settled
払済 **hara(i)zu(mi)** paid up, settled
弘済会 **kōsaikai** benefit association
6 気済 **ki (ga) su(mu)** be satisfied
返済 **hensai** repayment
共済 **kyōsai** mutual aid
共済組合 **kyōsai kumiai** mutual aid society

百済 **Kudara** (Korean kingdom, about 300–660)

成済 **na(ri)su(masu)** (completely) become

7 決済 **kessai** settlement (of accounts); liquidation

完済 **kansai** full payment, liquidation

9 皆済 **kaisai** payment in full

10 既済 **kisai** paid-up, already settled

11 救済 **kyūsai** relief, aid; emancipation

救済者 **kyūsaisha** reliever, savior

救済金 **kyūsaikin** relief fund

救済策 **kyūsaisaku** relief measure

経済 **keizai** economy, economics, economical use

経済人 **keizaijin** economic man

経済力 **keizairyoku** economic strength

経済上 **keizaijō** economically, financially

経済学 **keizaigaku** economics

経済法 **keizaihō** economic laws

経済的 **keizaiteki** economic, financial; economical

経済界 **keizaikai** financial circles

経済家 **keizaika** economist; thrifty person

経済欄 **keizairan** financial section/columns

——————— 3 ———————

4 不経済 **fukeizai** poor economy, waste

支払済 **shiharaizu(mi)** paid

5 未決済 **mikessai** outstanding (accounts)

6 多士済々 **tashi-seisei** many able people

8 受取済 **uketorizu(mi)** (payment) received

9 約定済 **yakujōzu(mi)** promised; engaged; sold

12 登録済 **tōrokuzu(mi)** registered

検定済 **kenteizu(mi)** (government) inspected/authorized

検査済 **kensazu(mi)** examined, passed

3a8.31 / 1204

涼 涼

RYŌ cool **suzu(shii)** cool, refreshing **suzu(mu)** cool off, enjoy the evening cool

——————— 1 ———————

5 涼台 **suzu(mi)dai** bench (for enjoying the evening cool)

6 涼気 **ryōki** the cool (air)

8 涼味 **ryōmi** the cool, coolness

涼雨 **ryōu** cooling rain

9 涼風 **ryōfū, suzukaze** cool breeze

涼客 **suzu(mi)kyaku** people enjoying the evening cool

涼秋 **ryōshū** cool autumn; ninth lunar month

——————— 2 ———————

3 夕涼 **yūsuzu(mi)** enjoy the evening cool

9 荒涼 **kōryō** bleak, desolate

10 納涼 **nōryō** enjoying the evening cool

11 清涼 **seiryō** cool, refreshing

清涼剤 **seiryōzai** refrigerant

清涼飲料 **seiryō inryō** carbonated beverage

12 朝涼 **asasuzu(mi)** the morning cool

晚涼 **banryō** the evening cool

3a8.32

淬

SAI, nira(gu) anneal, quench, temper

涙 → 涙 3a7.21

3a8.33 / 1461

涯

GAI shore; end, limit

——————— 2 ———————

4 天涯 **tengai** horizon; distant land

5 生涯 **shōgai** life, lifetime, career; for life, lifelong

13 際涯 **saigai** extremity, limits

14 境涯 **kyōgai** circumstances, one's lot

——————— 3 ———————

1 一生涯 **isshōgai** a lifetime, one's (whole) life

6 全生涯 **zenshōgai** one's entire life

13 新生涯 **shinshōgai** a new life/career

3a8.34

淘

TŌ select, cull; wash (rice)

——————— 1 ———————

7 淘汰 **tōta** (natural) selection, weeding out

3a8.35

涵 涵

KAN immerse

——————— 1 ———————

15 涵養 **kan'yō** cultivate, foster, develop

3a8.36

涸 涸

KO, ka(reru) dry up, go dry, become depleted **ka(rasu)** dry up, exhaust, deplete

——————— 1 ———————

11 涸渇 **kokatsu** run dry, be drained, become depleted

————————— 2 —————————

5 出涸 degara(shi) thin (tea), insipid

3a8.37

淼 BYŌ vast (expanse of water)

————————— 1 —————————

9 淼茫 byōbō vast (expanse of water)

→8 氵

土 **3a9.1**
扌
口 渚 渚   SHO, nagisa beach, shore
女
巾 **3a9.2**
犭
弓 湛   TAN, tata(eru) be filled with
彳
彡 ————————— 1 —————————
艹
宀 3 湛々 tantan brimming, overflowing
⺌ 12 湛然 tanzen brimming, overflowing; calm,
耂   composed
广
尸 **3a9.3**
口
淵 渕 渊   EN edge
                     fuchi deep water, abyss,
                     depths

————————— 1 —————————

13 淵源 engen origin, source, inception
18 淵叢 ensō center, home, cradle of

————————— 2 —————————

11 深淵 shin'en abyss

3a9.4 / 610

測   SOKU, haka(ru) measure

————————— 1 —————————

6 測地 sokuchi land surveying, geodetic
   測地学 sokuchigaku geodesy
8 測知 haka(ri)shi(ru) understand, fathom,
         calculate
   測定 sokutei measure
   測定法 sokuteihō method of measurement;
         mensuration
9 測度 sokudo measurement, gauging
   測音器 sokuonki sonometer, phonometer
10 測候 sokkō meteorological observation
   測候所 sokkōjo weather station
11 測深 sokushin (depth) sounding

12 測量士 sokuryōshi surveyor
   測量術 sokuryōjutsu (the science of)
         surveying
   測量船 sokuryōsen surveying ship
   測程器 sokuteiki (ship's) log
   測距儀 sokkyogi range finder
13 測微計 sokubikei micrometer
   測鉛 sokuen plumb bob, sounding lead
15 測線 sokusen measuring line
18 測難 haka(ri)gata(i) unfathomable

————————— 2 —————————

4 不測 fusoku unexpected; immeasurable
   予測 yosoku forecast, estimate
   天測 tensoku astronomical observations
5 目測 mokusoku measure by eye
8 実測 jissoku actual survey/measurement
   歩測 hosoku pace off (a distance)
9 計測 keisoku measuring, instrumentation
11 推測 suisoku conjecture, supposition
16 憶測 okusoku speculation, conjecture
17 臆測 okusoku speculation, conjecture
18 観測 kansoku observation, survey; thinking,
         opinion
   観測所 kansokujo observatory, observation
         station

————————— 4 —————————

6 気象観測 kishō kansoku meteorological
         observations

3a9.5

溂   RATSU lively

3a9.6

渺   BYŌ vast; tiny, slight

————————— 1 —————————

9 渺茫 byōbō vast, boundless

————————— 2 —————————

17 縹渺 hyōbyō hazy; vast

————————— 4 —————————

9 神韻縹渺 shin'in-hyōbyō an undefinable
         artistic excellence

3a9.7

湫   SHŪ, kute wetlands, marsh

3a9.8 / 467

湖   KO, mizuumi lake

─────────────── 1 ───────────────

3 湖上 **kojō** on the lake
4 湖水 **kosui** lake
  湖心 **koshin** center of a lake
8 湖沼 **koshō** lakes and marshes
  湖沼学 **koshōgaku** limnology
  湖岸 **kogan** lakeshore, lakeside
10 湖畔 **kohan** lakeshore, lakeside
12 湖港 **kokō** lake harbor

─────────────── 2 ───────────────

6 江湖 **kōko** the public
8 沼湖 **shōko** swamps and lakes
15 潟湖 **sekiko** lagoon
20 鹹湖 **kanko** salt/brackish lake

─────────────── 3 ───────────────

3 山中湖 **Yamanaka-ko** Lake Yamanaka (near Mt. Fuji)
4 火口湖 **kakōko** crater lake
11 淡水湖 **tansuiko** freshwater lake
12 琵琶湖 **Biwa-ko** Lake Biwa

3a9.9

湘 SHŌ (name of a river in China); the Sagami river (in Kanagawa-ken)

3a9.10

湃 HAI seething/foaming waves

─────────────── 2 ───────────────

8 泙湃 **hōhai** surging (water)
15 澎湃 **hōhai** surging, raging

3a9.11

湮 IN sink

─────────────── 1 ───────────────

13 湮滅 **inmetsu** extinction, destruction
29 湮鬱 **in'utsu** gloomy, melancholy

3a9.12

湊 SŌ, **minato** harbor, port

─────────────── 2 ───────────────

16 輻湊 **fukusō** influx, rush, congestion

3a9.13 / 669

港 港 KŌ, **minato** harbor, port

─────────────── 1 ───────────────

3 港口 **kōkō** harbor entrance

4 港内 **kōnai** in the harbor
5 港外 **kōgai** outside the harbor
7 港図 **kōzu** harbor map/charts
  港町 **minatomachi** port town/city
8 港門 **kōmon** harbor entrance
10 港都 **kōto** port city
11 港務 **kōmu** harbor service
  港務部 **kōmubu** harbor department/office
12 港湾 **kōwan** harbor
  港税 **kōzei** harbor/port dues

─────────────── 2 ───────────────

2 入港 **nyūkō** entering port
4 内港 **naikō** inner harbor
5 出港 **shukkō** leave port, put out to sea
  母港 **bokō** home port
7 良港 **ryōkō** good harbor
8 河港 **kakō** river port
  空港 **kūkō** airport
9 軍港 **gunkō** naval port/station
  海港 **kaikō** seaport
  要港 **yōkō** important/strategic port
  香港 **Honkon** Hong Kong
10 帰港 **kikō** return to port
11 商港 **shōkō** trading port
  寄港 **kikō** call at (a port)
12 着港 **chakkō** arrival in port
  湖港 **kokō** lake harbor
  開港 **kaikō** opening the port; an open port
  開港場 **kaikōjō** open/treaty port
14 漁港 **gyokō** fishing port
16 築港 **chikkō** harbor construction
18 臨港線 **rinkōsen** harbor railway line
  鎮港 **sakō** closing the ports

─────────────── 3 ───────────────

4 不凍港 **futōkō** ice-free port
6 自由港 **jiyūkō** free port
8 到着港 **tōchakukō** port of arrival
  河口港 **kakōkō** estuary harbor
11 商業港 **shōgyōkō** trading port
  船籍港 **sensekikō** ship's port of registry
16 輸入港 **yunyūkō** port of entry
  輸出港 **yushutsukō** exporting port

3a9.14

渭 I (name of a river in China)

3a9.15 / 670

湾 灣 WAN bay, gulf

─────────────── 1 ───────────────

2 湾入 **wannyū** inlet, gulf, bight
3 湾口 **wankō** bay entrance

3

氵9←
土
扌
口
女
巾
犭
弓
彳
彡
艹
宀
⺌
凵
丰
广
尸
口

4 湾内 **wannai** inside the bay
6 湾曲 **wankyoku** curve, curvature, bend
10 湾流 **Wanryū** the Gulf Stream
16 湾頭 **wantō** shore of a bay

————— 2 —————

5 台湾 **Taiwan** (island country near China)
9 海湾 **kaiwan** gulf, bay
　 峡湾 **kyōwan** fjord
12 港湾 **kōwan** harbor

————— 3 —————

10 真珠湾 **Shinju-wan** Pearl Harbor

3a9.16

漈　　　**SETSU** dredge, clean out

————— 2 —————

10 浚渫 **shunsetsu** dredge
　 浚渫船 **shunsetsusen** dredger
　 浚渫機 **shunsetsuki** dredger

洸→潑 **3a12.17**

3a9.17

渣 渣　　**SA** dregs

————— 1 —————

13 渣滓 **sashi** dregs, grounds, deposit, lees

————— 2 —————

10 残渣 **zansa** residue, dregs

涼→泉 **3a5.33**

3a9.18

湟　　　**KŌ** (name of a river in China)

3a9.19

滑　　　**SHO, shitami** dregs, lees

3a9.20

湍　　　**TAN** rapids

3a9.21 / 634

温 溫　　**ON, atata(kai/ka)** warm
　　　　atata(maru) (intr.) warm up
　　　　atata(meru) (tr.) warm up
　　　　nuku(i) warm
nuku(maru) (intr.) warm up (slightly)
nuku(meru) (tr.) warm up (slightly)
nukumo(ri), nuku(mi) (slight) warmth

————— 1 —————

3 温々 **nukunuku** comfortably warm, snug; brazen
4 温水 **onsui** warm water
5 温存 **onzon** keep, preserve, retain
　 温石 **onjaku** heated warming stone, pocket warmer
6 温色 **onshoku** warm color; calm facial expression
　 温血 **onketsu** warm-blooded (animal)
7 温良 **onryō** gentle, amiable
　 温床 **onshō** hotbed
　 温灸 **onkyū** moxibustion, moxa cautery
　 温言 **ongen** kind/gentle words
8 温厚 **onkō** gentle, courteous
　 温突 **ondoru** (Korean) floor heater
　 温和 **onwa** mild, gentle
9 温泉 **onsen** hot springs
　 温泉郷 **onsenkyō** hot-springs town
　 温泉場 **onsenba, onsenjō** spa, hot-springs resort
　 温室 **onshitsu** hothouse, greenhouse
　 温度 **ondo** temperature
　 温度計 **ondokei** thermometer
　 温故知新 **onko-chishin** learning from the past
10 温浴 **on'yoku** warm/hot bath
　 温帯 **ontai** temperate zone
　 温容 **on'yō** kindly face
　 温座 **onza** sitting peacefully
11 温習 **onshū** review, rehearse
　 温情 **onjō** warm, cordial, kindly
　 温情主義 **onjō shugi** paternalism
12 温温 **nukunuku** comfortably warm, snug; brazen
　 温湿布 **onshippu** hot compress
　 温湯 **ontō** warm bath
　 温順 **onjun** gentle, submissive, docile
13 温暖 **ondan** warm, mild
　 温罨法 **on'anpō** hot compress
　 温雅 **onga** affable and refined, gracious
18 温顔 **ongan** kindly face

————— 2 —————

4 水温 **suion** water temperature
5 平温 **heion** the usual temperature
6 気温 **kion** the (air) temperature
　 地温 **chion** soil/ground temperature
7 体温 **taion** body temperature

体温計 **taionkei** (clinical) thermometer
低温 **teion** low temperature
8 定温 **teion** constant temperature
9 保温 **hoon** keeping warm
室温 **shitsuon** room temperature
10 高温 **kōon** high temperature
11 常温 **jōon** normal temperature
12 温温 **nukunuku** comfortably warm, snug; brazen
検温 **ken'on** temperature measurement
検温器 **ken'onki** (clinical) thermometer
等温 **tōon** isothermal
13 適温 **tekion** suitable temperature
微温 **bion** lukewarm, tepid
微温湯 **biontō** lukewarm water

——————— 3 ———————
6 光高温計 **hikari-kōonkei** optical pyrometer

——————— 4 ———————
3 三寒四温 **sankan shion** alternation of three cold then four warm days

3a9.22 / 1169

湿 濕
SHITSU dampness, moisture
shime(ru) get damp/moist/wet
shime(su) moisten
shime(ppoi) damp, humid
shime(yaka) quiet, gentle; gloomy

——————— 1 ———————
5 湿布 **shippu** wet compress, poultice
湿田 **shitsuden** poorly drained paddy wet all year
6 湿気 **shikke, shikki** moisture, humidity
湿地 **shitchi** damp ground, bog
7 湿声 **shime(ri)goe** tearful voice
8 湿板 **shitsuban** wet plate (in photography)
湿性 **shissei** wet (pleurisy)
9 湿度 **shitsudo** humidity
湿度計 **shitsudokei** hygrometer
10 湿疹 **shisshin** eczema, rash
15 湿潤 **shitsujun** damp, moist, humid

——————— 2 ———————
6 防湿 **bōshitsu** dampproof
7 冷湿布 **reishippu** cold compress
9 耐湿 **taishitsu** dampproof
耐湿性 **taishitsusei** resistance to moisture
11 乾湿計 **kanshitsukei** hygrometer, humidity meter
12 温湿布 **onshippu** hot compress
寒湿 **kanshitsu** cold and moisture
検湿器 **kenshitsuki** hygrometer

3a9.23 / 632

湯
TŌ, TAN, yu hot water

——————— 1 ———————
3 湯上 **yua(gari)** just after a bath
湯口 **yuguchi** source of a hot spring
湯女 **yuna** hot-springs prostitute
4 湯元 **yumoto** source of a hot spring
湯文字 **yumoji** loincloth
湯水 **yumizu** hot and cold water
湯引 **yubi(ku)** parboil
5 湯加減 **yukagen** temperature of the bath water
湯札 **yufuda** bath ticket
6 湯気 **yuge** steam, vapor
7 湯冷 **yuza(me)** after-bath chill
yuza(mashi) boiled water cooled for drinking
湯呑 **yuno(mi)** teacup
湯豆腐 **yudōfu** boiled tofu
湯花 **yubana, yu (no) hana** flowers of sulfur, hot-springs encrustation
8 湯沸器 **yuwa(kashi)ki** hot-water heater
湯治 **tōji** hot-springs cure
湯治場 **tōjiba** spa
9 湯巻 **yuma(ki)** loincloth
湯通 **yudō(shi)** steaming (cloth)
湯垢 **yuaka** boiler scale, fur, encrustation
湯屋 **yuya** public bathhouse
10 湯釜 **yugama** cauldron, kettle
湯浴 **yua(mi)** bath
11 湯桶 **yuoke** bathtub
湯船 **yubune** bathtub
湯責 **yuze(me)** boiling-water torture
12 湯湯婆 **yutanpo** hot-water bottle/bag
湯場 **yuba** hot springs
湯葉 **yuba** dried tofu
湯煮 **yuni** boil, boiled
13 湯煎 **yusen** boiling, decoction
湯滝 **yudaki** hot-water falls, hot shower
湯殿 **yudono** bathroom
14 湯銭 **yusen** bathhouse charge
15 湯槽 **yubune** bathtub
湯熨 **yunoshi** steam ironing
16 湯薬 **tōyaku** infusion
20 湯灌 **yukan** washing a body for burial
21 湯麺 **tanmen** (Chinese dish of noodles, pork and fried vegetables in a broth)

——————— 2 ———————
2 入湯 **nyūtō** take a bath
3 上湯 **a(gari)yu** hot bath water (for rinsing oneself)
女湯 **onnayu** ladies' bath
5 白湯 **sayu** (plain) hot water
7 麦湯 **mugiyu** wheat tea, barley water
初湯 **hatsuyu** first bath (of the new year)
足湯 **ashiyu** footbath
8 長湯 **nagayu** a long bath

若湯 **wakayu** first hot bath on New Year's Day
9 重湯 **omoyu** thin rice gruel
茶湯 **cha(no)yu** tea ceremony
柚湯 **yuzuyu** citron hot-bath
10 差湯 **sa(shi)yu** (adding) hot water
埋湯 **u(me)yu** hot water cooled by adding cold water
留湯 **to(me)yu** (reusing) yesterday's bath water; one's own bath; using a public bath on a pay-by-the-month basis
11 産湯 **ubuyu** newborn baby's first bath
12 温湯 **ontō** warm bath
湯湯婆 **yutanpo** hot-water bottle/bag
朝湯 **asayu** morning bath
煮湯 **ni(e)yu** boiling water
13 腰湯 **koshiyu** hip/sitz bath
14 銭湯 **sentō** public bath
16 薬湯 **kusuriyu, yakutō** medicated bath

――――― 3 ―――――
13 微温湯 **biontō** lukewarm water

渇 → 渇 **3a8.13**

滯 → **3a10.14**

3a9.24

渓 **EN, KAN** flowing water

――――― 2 ―――――
12 潺湲 **senkan** babbling (brook)

3a9.25 / 201

満 滿 **MAN** full; Manchuria
mi(chiru) become full
mi(tasu) fill, fulfill

――――― 1 ―――――
1 満了 **manryō** expiration
2 満人 **Manjin** a Manchurian
3 満干 **mankan, mi(chi)hi** ebb and flow
満々 **manman** full of, brimming with
満山 **manzan** the whole hill/mountain
4 満天 **manten** the whole sky
満天下 **mantenka** the whole world
満水 **mansui** full to the brim with water
満月 **mangetsu** full moon
5 満目 **manmoku** as far as the eye can see
6 満州 **Manshū** Manchuria
満州事変 **Manshū Jihen** the Manchurian Incident

満州国 **Manshūkoku** Manchukuo
7 満身 **manshin** the whole body
満更 **manzara** (not) wholly/altogether
満作 **mansaku** bumper crop
満足 **manzoku** satisfaction
mi(chi)ta(riru) be contented
8 満杯 **manpai** full to capacity
9 満点 **manten** perfect score
満洲 **Manshū** Manchuria
満面 **manmen** the whole face
10 満員 **man'in** full to capacity
満座 **manza** the whole assembly, everyone
満悦 **man'etsu** delight, rapture
11 満堂 **mandō** the whole assembly/audience
12 満満 **mi(chi)mi(chiru)** fill up
manman full of, brimming with
満場 **manjō** the whole assembly/hall
満場一致 **manjō-itchi** unanimous
満喫 **mankitsu** have one's fill of, fully enjoy
満幅 **manpuku** full (breadth)
満腔 **mankō** wholehearted
満期 **manki** expiration (date)
満塁 **manrui** bases loaded
満開 **mankai** in full bloom
13 満蒙 **Man-Mō** Manchuria and Mongolia
満腹 **manpuku** full stomach/belly
満載 **mansai** full load
満鉄 **Mantetsu** South Manchuria Railway (short for 南満州鉄道)
15 満潮 **manchō** high tide
19 満願 **mangan** fulfillment of a vow
21 満艦飾 **mankanshoku** full dress, all decked out

――――― 2 ―――――
3 干満 **kanman** ebb and flow, tide
4 不満 **fuman** dissatisfaction, displeasure, discontent
不満足 **fumanzoku** dissatisfaction, displeasure, discontent
円満 **enman** harmonious, smooth; well rounded
日満 **Nichi-Man** Japan and Manchuria
5 未満 **miman** less than, below
6 充満 **jūman, michimichi(te iru)** be full of, be replete/teeming with
8 肥満 **himan** corpulence, obesity
肥満体 **himantai** plump/roly-poly physique
金満家 **kinmanka** rich man
9 南満 **Nanman** South Manchuria
南満州 **Minami Manshū** South Manchuria
盈満 **eiman** be full/ample
12 満満 **mi(chi)mi(chiru)** fill up
manman full of, brimming with
超満員 **chōman'in** crowded beyond capacity
13 豊満 **hōman** plump, corpulent, full-figured
腸満 **chōman** abdominal dropsy

飽満 **hōman** satiety, satiation

────── 3 ──────
6 自信満々 **jishin-manman** full of confidence
11 野心満々 **yashin-manman** full of ambition
得意満面 **tokui-manmen** pride
18 闘志満々 **tōshi-manman** full of fighting spirit
────── 4 ──────
11 欲求不満 **yokkyū fuman** frustration

3a9.26

渝

YU change, be transformed

3a9.27 / 1549

滋

JI grow; more and more; blessing; tasty

────── 1 ──────
8 滋味 **jimi** delicious/nourishing (food)
11 滋強飲料 **jikyō inryō** tonic drink
12 滋賀県 **Shiga-ken** (prefecture)
15 滋養 **jiyō** nourishment
滋養分 **jiyōbun** nutrient
滋養物 **jiyōbutsu** nourishing food, sustenance
滋養過多 **jiyōkata** hypertrophy

3a9.28

渾

KON all, whole; turbid
sube(te) all

────── 1 ──────
6 渾名 **adana** nickname
7 渾身 **konshin** one's whole body
渾沌 **konton** chaos, confusion
12 渾然 **konzen** whole, entire; harmonious
────── 2 ──────
12 雄渾 **yūkon** vigorous, bold, grand

3a9.29

渟

TEI, todo(maru) be still, stagnate

3a9.30

渙

KAN scatter

────── 1 ──────
9 渙発 **kanpatsu** proclamation

3a9.31

湧 涌

YŪ, YŌ, wa(ku) boil, seethe, well up, gush forth

────── 1 ──────
4 湧水 **wa(ki)mizu** spring water
5 湧出 **wa(ki)de(ru), yūshutsu** gush forth/out, well/bubble up
湧立 **wa(ki)ta(tsu)** well up, seethe
10 湧起 **wa(ki)o(koru)** arise

3a9.32

湎

MEN, BEN sink, drown, be immersed in

3a9.33

渥

AKU kindness

3a9.34

潺

SEN flowing, babbling (brook)

────── 1 ──────
12 潺湲 **senkan** babbling (brook)

3a9.35 / 378

渡

TO, wata(ru) cross
wata(su) hand over

────── 1 ──────
4 渡仏 **to-Futsu** going to France
5 渡世 **tosei** livelihood; occupation, trade
渡世人 **toseinin** gambler, gangster
6 渡合 **wata(ri)a(u)** cross swords, argue
渡守 **wata(shi)mori** ferryman
渡米 **to-Bei** going to America
渡舟 **wata(shi)bune** ferryboat
7 渡来 **torai** introduction, influx; visit
渡初 **wata(ri)zo(me)** bridge-opening ceremony
8 渡奉公 **wata(ri)bōkō** working as a servant at one place after another
渡河 **toka** crossing a river
渡英 **to-Ei** going to Britain
渡歩 **wata(ri)aru(ku)** wander about
渡板 **wata(ri)ita** gangplank
渡者 **wata(ri)mono** migratory worker; hobo; stranger
渡欧 **to-Ō** going to Europe
9 渡洋 **toyō** transoceanic

渡海 **tokai** crossing the ocean, passage
10 渡唐 **to-Tō** going to (Tang-dynasty) China
渡航 **tokō** voyage, passage, sailing, flight
渡航者 **tokōsha** foreign visitor, passenger
11 渡廊下 **wata(ri)rōka** covered passageway
渡船 **wata(shi)bune, tosen** ferry
渡船場 **tosenba, tosenjō** ferrying place
渡船賃 **tosenchin** ferry charge
渡鳥 **wata(ri)dori** migratory bird
12 渡場 **wata(shi)ba** ferrying place
渡御 **togyo** (emperor) proceeding to
13 渡賃 **wata(shi)chin** ferry charge
14 渡銭 **wata(shi)sen** ferry charge
16 渡橋式 **tokyōshiki** bridge-opening ceremony
渡頭 **totō** ferrying place

———————— 2 ————————

3 刃渡 **hawata(ri)** length of a blade
下渡 **sa(ge)wata(su)** grant; release
4 不渡 **fuwata(ri)** nonpayment, dishonoring (a bill)
内渡 **uchiwata(shi)** partial delivery/payment
手渡 **tewata(shi)** personal/hand delivery
引渡 **hi(ki)wata(su)** deliver, transfer, hand over
火渡 **hiwata(ri)** walking over hot coals
5 世渡 **yowata(ri)** get on in the world, make one's living
申渡 **mō(shi)wata(su)** tell, declare
払渡 **hara(i)wata(su)** pay (out/over), cash (a check)
6 先渡 **sakiwata(shi)** forward/future delivery
行渡 **yu(ki)wata(ru), i(ki)wata(ru)** extend, prevail, permeate, reach
7 佐渡 **Sado** (ancient kuni, Niigata-ken)
佐渡島 **Sado(ga)shima** (island, Niigata-ken)
冴渡 **sa(e)wata(ru)** get cold; freeze over
吹渡 **fu(ki)wata(ru)** blow over
売渡 **u(ri)wata(su)** sell, transfer, sign over
    u(ri)wata(shi) sale (and delivery)
見渡 **miwata(su)** look out over
言渡 **i(i)wata(su)** pronounce sentence; order; announce
8 受渡 **u(ke)wata(shi)** delivery, transfer
直渡 **jikawata(shi)** direct delivery
押渡 **o(shi)wata(ru)** come/go over, cross
知渡 **shi(re)wata(ru)** become widely known
明渡 **a(ke)wata(su)** vacate and surrender (the premises)
9 前渡 **maewata(shi)** advance payment/delivery
染渡 **shi(mi)wata(ru)** penetrate, pervade
10 差渡 **sa(shi)wata(ru)** cross in a boat
    sa(shi)wata(shi) distance across, diameter
垰渡 **Gomiwatari** (place name, Aomori-ken)
荷渡 **niwata(shi)** delivery

11 過渡 **kato** crossover, transient, transition
過渡的 **katoteki** transitional
過渡期 **katoki** transition period
船渡 **funawata(shi)** ferry; F.O.B.
13 置渡 **o(ki)wata(su)** lay over
14 鳴渡 **na(ri)wata(ru)** resound far and wide
綱渡 **tsunawata(ri)** tightrope walking
15 澄渡 **su(mi)wata(ru)** be crystal clear
16 橋渡 **hashiwata(shi)** bridge building; mediation
19 響渡 **hibi(ki)wata(ru)** resound, reverberate
20 譲渡 **jōto** assign, transfer, convey
    yuzu(ri)wata(su) turn over to, transfer
譲渡人 **jōtonin** assignor, grantor

———————— 3 ————————

7 即時渡 **sokujiwata(shi)** spot delivery
9 海外渡航 **kaigai tokō** foreign travel
11 船側渡 **sensoku-wata(shi)** Free Alongside Ship, ex-ship

漣 → 漣 3a10.27

3a9.36 / 1810

渦 **KA, uzu** swirl, vortex, whirlpool, eddy

———————— 1 ————————

4 渦中 **kachū** maelstrom, vortex
7 渦状 **kajō** spiral, whirled
9 渦巻 **uzuma(ki)** eddy, vortex, whirlpool; spiral, coil
渦星雲 **kaseiun** spiral nebula
10 渦流 **karyū** eddy, whirlpool
11 渦動 **kadō** vortex
15 渦潮 **uzushio** swirling seawater
渦線 **uzusen** a spiral
渦輪 **uzuwa** whorl, swirl

———————— 2 ————————

13 戦渦 **senka** the turmoil of war

3a9.37 / 715

減 **GEN** decrease **he(ru), me(ru)** decrease, diminish, dwindle **he(rasu/su)** reduce, decrease, curtail

———————— 1 ————————

0 減じる **gen(jiru)** decrease, lessen, subtract
3 減口 **he(razu)guchi** continuing to talk back (even when one has been defeated)
4 減収 **genshū** decrease in income
減反 **gentan** acreage reduction
減込 **me(ri)ko(mu)** sink/cave in, stick into
減水 **gensui** low/subsiding water

減少 **genshō** decrease, reduction, decline
5 減圧 **gen'atsu** pressure reduction
　減号 **gengō** subtraction/minus sign
6 減刑 **genkei** reduction of penalty/sentence
　減光 **genkō** extinguish, dim
7 減作 **gensaku** short crop, lower yield
8 減価 **genka** price reduction, discount
　減免 **genmen** reduction of or exemption from (taxes), mitigation and remission (of punishment)
　減退 **gentai** decline, ebb
　減法 **genpō** subtraction
9 減点 **genten** demerit mark
　減速 **gensoku** speed reduction, deceleration
　減段 **gentan** acreage reduction
　減食 **genshoku** cutting down on food; reduced rations
10 減耗 **genmō, genkō** decrease, shrinkage
　減俸 **genpō** salary reduction
　減衰 **gensui** decrease, dampen, attenuate
　減員 **gen'in** staff reduction, personnel cutback
　減殺 **gensatsu, gensai** lessen, diminish
　減租 **genso** tax reduction/cut
　減配 **genpai** reduce dividends/rations
11 減張 **me(ri)ha(ri)** loosening or tightening (of violin strings)
　減産 **gensan** lower production
12 減量 **genryō** lose weight, reduce the quantity
　減税 **genzei** tax cut/reduction
　減給 **genkyū** salary reduction, pay cut
　減筆 **genpitsu** writing abbreviatedly
　減等 **gentō** lowering the class, reduction, mitigation
　減軽 **genkei** reduction, mitigation
13 減償 **gensai** partial payment of a debt
　減損 **genson** decrease; loss, wear, depreciation
　減資 **genshi** reduction of capital
14 減算 **genzan** subtraction (in math)
15 減摩 **genma** reduction of friction, lubrication
　減摩油 **genmayu** lubricating oil
16 減磨 **genma** reduction of friction, lubrication
　減磨油 **genmayu** lubricating oil
17 減縮 **genshuku** reduction, cutback
18 減額 **gengaku** reduction, cut

————— 2 —————

3 口減 **kuchibe(rashi)** reducing the number of mouths to feed
5 半減 **hangen** reduction by half
　半減期 **hangenki** halflife (in physics)
　加減 **kagen** addition and subtraction; degree, extent, condition; adjust, keep within bounds; state of health; seasoning, flavor; allow for
　加減乗除 **kagenjōjo** addition, subtraction, multiplication, and division

目減 **mebe(ri)** weight loss
7 低減 **teigen** decline, decrease, reduce
9 削減 **sakugen** reduction, cutback
　逓減 **teigen** successive diminution
　計減 **haka(ri)be(ri)** giving short measure/weight
11 累減 **ruigen** regressive (tax)
12 軽減 **keigen** reduce, lighten, relieve
13 腹減 **hara (ga) he(ru)** be hungry
　節減 **setsugen** curtailing
14 漸減 **zengen** gradual decrease
　増減 **zōgen** increase and/or decrease
16 激減 **gekigen** sharp decrease, plummet
　磨減 **su(ri)he(rasu)** wear away, rub down
17 擦減 **su(ri)he(rasu)** wear away/down, rub off
　縮減 **shukugen** reduce

————— 3 —————

4 手加減 **tekagen** use discretion, make allowances; knack, tact, skill
　火加減 **hikagen** condition of the fire
5 好加減 **i(i) kagen** moderate, temperate, suitable; haphazard, irresponsible, not thorough, halfhearted
11 匙加減 **saji kagen** dosage, prescription; consideration, discretion, making allowances for
12 湯加減 **yukagen** temperature of the bath water
　煮加減 **ni(e)kagen** amount of boiling
13 塩加減 **shiokagen** seasoning with salt

————— 10 —————

3a10.1

溺　溺　DEKI, **obo(reru)** drown, be drowned; indulge in **obo(rasu)** drown (a cat); cause to indulge in

————— 1 —————

6 溺死 **dekishi, obo(re)ji(ni)** drowning
　溺死体 **dekishitai** drowned body
　溺死者 **dekishisha** drowned person
13 溺愛 **dekiai** dote upon

————— 2 —————

7 沈溺 **chindeki** be drowned in, be addicted to
10 耽溺 **tandeki** addiction, dissipation
11 酖溺 **tandeki** addiction, dissipation
12 惑溺 **wakudeki** indulge in, be addicted to, be infatuated with

3a10.2

溯　遡　遡　SO, **sakanobo(ru)** go upstream; go back to, be retroactive to

————— 1 —————

3 溯及 **sokyū, sakkyū** be retroactive

溯及的 **sokyūteki** retroactive
6 溯行 **sokō** go upstream
10 溯航 **sokō** go upstream, sail upriver

3a10.3

溲 SHŪ wash; urine

─────── 1 ───────

11 溲瓶 **shibin** piss pot/bottle

3a10.4

溥 FU far and wide

─────── 1 ───────

4 溥天 **futen** the whole world

3a10.5

溽 JOKU humid

3a10.6 / 1267

滑 KATSU, KOTSU, **sube(ru)** slide, glide, ski; slip; flunk an exam
sube(kkoi) smooth, slick, slippery
name(raka) smooth

─────── 1 ───────

4 滑止 **sube(ri)do(me)** tire chains; nonskid heels
滑込 **sube(ri)ko(mu)** slide into (second base)
5 滑出 **sube(ri)da(su)** start sliding; get underway
滑弁 **katsuben** slide valve
滑台 **sube(ri)dai** (playground) slide; launching platform
滑石 **kasseki** talc
7 滑走 **kassō** glide, slide, taxi
滑走路 **kassōro** runway
滑走輪 **kassōrin** landing gear
滑車 **kassha** pulley
8 滑空 **kakkū** glide
9 滑降 **kakkō** slide/ski down
10 滑剤 **katsuzai** lubricant
11 滑脱 **katsudatsu** versatile, resourceful
12 滑落 **sube(ri)o(chiru)** slip off/down
16 滑稽 **kokkei** comic, funny; joke
滑稽本 **kokkeibon** comic book (Edo period)

─────── 2 ───────

3 上滑 **uwasube(ri)** superficial, shallow; inattentive
4 円滑 **enkatsu** smooth, harmonious
5 平滑 **heikatsu** smooth, level, flat, even

6 地滑 **jisube(ri)** landslide
11 動滑車 **dōkassha** movable pulley, running block
15 潤滑 **junkatsu** lubrication
潤滑油 **junkatsuyu** lubricating oil

─────── 3 ───────

4 円転滑脱 **enten-katsudatsu** versatile, all-around, tactful

3a10.7

滔 TŌ overflow; large, broad

─────── 1 ───────

3 滔々 **tōtō** flowing (swiftly) along; fluently, eloquently
4 滔天 **tōten** overwhelming, irresistible

3a10.8 / 1759

滝 瀧 **taki** waterfall

─────── 1 ───────

0 ナイアガラ滝 **Naiagara-taki** Niagara-Falls
3 滝川 **takigawa** rapids
滝口 **takiguchi** top/crest of a waterfall
12 滝登 **takinobo(ri)** (salmon) climbing a waterfall
滝壺 **takitsubo** pool/basin below a waterfall
滝飲 **takino(mi)** gulping down a drink

─────── 2 ───────

5 白滝 **shirataki** white waterfall; konnyaku in spaghetti form
12 湯滝 **yudaki** hot-water falls, hot shower
雄滝 **odaki** the larger waterfall (of two)

3a10.9 / 1012

溝 KŌ, **mizo** ditch, gutter; groove, slot
dobu ditch, gutter, sewer

─────── 1 ───────

3 溝川 **mizogawa** ditch/trench with running water
4 溝水 **dobumizu** ditch water
8 溝板 **dobuita** boards covering a ditch
12 溝渠 **kōkyo** ditch, sewer, canal

─────── 2 ───────

9 海溝 **kaikō** an ocean deep, sea trench

3a10.10

滔 SHIN water

3a10.11

溜 溜

RYŪ drip, condense; accumulate **tama(ru)** collect, form a mass, accumulate
ta(meru) accumulate, save up

tama(ri) waiting room, gathering place
ta(me) sinkhole, cesspool

—————— 1 ——————

4 溜込 **ta(me)ko(mu)** save up, amass
  溜水 **tama(ri)mizu** standing/stagnant water
6 溜池 **ta(me)ike** reservoir, cistern
9 溜食 **ta(me)gu(i)** eat enough to last a long time
10 溜息 **ta(me)iki** sigh
12 溜飲 **ryūin** sour stomach
  溜飲下 **ryūin (ga) sa(garu)** feel satisfaction
13 溜置 **ta(me)o(ku)** store, stock up on

—————— 2 ——————

4 水溜 **mizuta(mari)** puddle, pool
  日溜 **hidama(ri)** sunny place; exposure to the sun
5 凹溜 **kubotama(ri)** a hollow; a pond formed in a hollow
7 芥溜 **gomita(me)** garbage heap
  足溜 **ashida(mari)** stand, foothold; stopping place; center of activity
8 肥溜 **koeda(me)** night-soil vat/pot
9 食溜 **ku(i)da(me)** stuffing oneself in order to go without eating for some time
11 掃溜 **ha(ki)da(me)** sweepings, rubbish heap
  乾溜 **kanryū** dry distillation, carbonization
12 蒸溜 **jōryū** distill
  蒸溜水 **jōryūsui** distilled water
  蒸溜器 **jōryūki** a still
  買溜 **ka(i)da(me)** hoarding

3a10.12

滉

KŌ deep and broad

温 → 温 3a9.21

3a10.13

溘

KŌ sudden, unexpected

3a10.14 / 964

滞 滞

TAI stay, stopping over
todokō(ru) be left undone/unpaid, be overdue, fall into arrears

—————— 1 ——————

4 滞仏 **tai-Futsu** staying in France
  滞日 **tai-Nichi** staying in Japan
6 滞伊 **tai-I** staying in Italy
  滞在 **taizai** stay, sojourn
  滞在中 **taizaichū** during one's stay
  滞在地 **taizaichi** where one is living
  滞在者 **taizaisha** sojourner, visitor
  滞在客 **taizaikyaku** (hotel) guest
  滞在費 **taizaihi** living expenses during one's stay
  滞米 **tai-Bei** staying in America
8 滞京 **taikyō** staying in the capital
  滞英 **tai-Ei** staying in Britain
  滞空 **taikū** staying in the air
  滞欧 **tai-Ō** staying in Europe
9 滞陣 **taijin** encampment
  滞独 **tai-Doku** staying in Germany
10 滞郷 **taikyō** living in one's native place
  滞留 **tairyū** stay, sojourn
  滞納 **tainō** delinquency (in payment)
  滞納処分 **tainō shobun** disposition for failure to pay (taxes)
  滞納者 **tainōsha** defaulter, (tax) delinquent
11 滞貨 **taika** freight congestion, accumulation of stock
21 滞露 **tai-Ro** staying in Russia

—————— 2 ——————

7 延滞 **entai** arrears, overdue (payment)
  沈滞 **chintai** stagnation, inactivity
9 食滞 **shokutai** lie heavy/undigested in one's stomach
11 停滞 **teitai** be stagnant, accumulate; fall into arrears
  遅滞 **chitai** delay; arrearage
  渋滞 **jūtai** impeded flow, congestion, delay
12 結滞 **kettai** intermittent (pulse)
16 凝滞 **gyōtai** delay

溢 → 溢 3a10.19

渓 → 渓 3a8.16

3a10.15 / 1392

溶

YŌ, **to(keru)** (intr.) melt, dissolve
to(kasu), to(ku) (tr.) melt, dissolve

—————— 1 ——————

4 溶化 **yōka** melt
6 溶合 **to(ke)a(u)** melt together, fade into
8 溶岩 **yōgan** lava

3 / 10←

溶明 **yōmei** fade-in (in movies)
溶性 **yōsei** soluble
10 溶剤 **yōzai** a solvent
11 溶液 **yōeki** solution
溶接 **yōsetsu** welding
12 溶媒 **yōbai** a solvent
13 溶暗 **yōan** fade-out, dissolve (in movies)
溶解 **yōkai** (intr.) melt, dissolve
溶解力 **yōkairyoku** solubility
溶解性 **yōkaisei** solubility
溶解点 **yōkaiten** melting point
溶解度 **yōkaido** solubility
溶鉱炉 **yōkōro** blast furnace
16 溶融 **yōyū** fuse, melt, molten

───── 2 ─────

4 不溶性 **fuyōsei** insoluble
水溶性 **suiyōsei** water-soluble
水溶液 **suiyōeki** aqueous solution
可溶性 **kayōsei** solubility
16 濃溶液 **nōyōeki** concentrated solution

3a10.16

滓

SHI, SAI, **kasu** dregs, grounds, sediment

───── 2 ─────

9 食滓 **ta(be)kasu** table scraps, leftovers
10 残滓 **zanshi, zansai** remnants, residue, dregs
12 渣滓 **sashi** dregs, grounds, deposit, lees
13 鉱滓 **kōsai, kōshi** slag
16 燃滓 **mo(e)kasu** cinders
18 濾滓 **rosai** filter cake

3a10.17 / 556

漢 漢

KAN Han (dynasty); China; (as suffix) man, fellow

───── 1 ─────

2 漢人 **Kanjin** a Chinese
3 漢土 **Kando** China
4 漢文 **kanbun** Chinese writing/classics
漢文学 **kanbungaku** Chinese literature
漢方 **kanpō** Chinese herbal medicine
漢方医 **kanpōi** herbal physician, herbalist
漢方薬 **kanpōyaku** a herbal medicine
5 漢民族 **Kan minzoku** the Han/Chinese people
漢字 **kanji** Chinese character, kanji
6 漢名 **kanmei, kanmyō** Chinese name
漢竹 **kanchiku** solid bamboo
7 漢学 **kangaku** Chinese literature
漢学者 **kangakusha** scholar of Chinese classics
8 漢和 **Kan-Wa** China and Japan, Chinese and Japanese (languages)
漢和辞典 **Kan-Wa jiten** kanji dictionary
9 漢音 **kan'on** Han-dynasty pronunciation (of a kanji)
10 漢書 **kansho** Chinese book/classics
11 漢族 **Kanzoku** the Han/Chinese people
漢訳 **kan'yaku** translation into classical Chinese
12 漢朝 **kanchō** Han dynasty
13 漢詩 **kanshi** Chinese poetry/poem
14 漢語 **kango** Chinese word
16 漢儒 **kanju** Chinese/Han-dynasty Confucian scholar
20 漢籍 **kanseki** Chinese book/classics

───── 2 ─────

4 凶漢 **kyōkan** scoundrel, outlaw, assassin
5 巨漢 **kyokan** very large man, big fellow
好漢 **kōkan** fine fellow
6 兇漢 **kyōkan** scoundrel, assailant, assassin
7 快漢 **kaikan** a most pleasant chap
8 国漢 **kokkan** Japanese and Chinese literature
怪漢 **kaikan** suspicious-looking person
和漢 **Wa-Kan** Japanese and Chinese
9 皇漢薬 **kōkan'yaku** Chinese herbal medicines
11 悪漢 **akkan** scoundrel, crook, ruffian, knave
酔漢 **suikan** a drunk
13 痴漢 **chikan** molester of women, masher
15 暴漢 **bōkan** ruffian, goon, thug
19 羅漢 **rakan** arhat, attainer of Nirvana

───── 3 ─────

4 木石漢 **bokusekikan** insensible person
5 好色漢 **kōshokukan** sensualist, lecher
6 当用漢字 **Tōyō Kanji** (official list of 1,850 kanji recommended for general use; superseded by the 1,945 Jōyō Kanji)
7 冷血漢 **reiketsukan** coldhearted person
阿羅漢 **arakan** arhat
8 和魂漢才 **wakon-kansai** Japanese spirit and Chinese learning
門外漢 **mongaikan** outsider; layman
9 卑劣漢 **hiretsukan** mean bastard, low-down skunk
11 常用漢字 **Jōyō Kanji** (official list of 1,945 kanji recommended for general use)
12 無頼漢 **buraikan** villain, hooligan, outlaw
硬骨漢 **kōkotsukan** man of firm character
15 熱血漢 **nekketsukan** fervent/hot-blooded man

3a10.18 / 1427

漠

BAKU desert; vast; vague

───── 1 ─────

3 漠々 **bakubaku** vast, boundless; vague, obscure

12 漠然 **bakuzen** vague, obscure

――――――― 2 ―――――――

5 広漠 **kōbaku** vast
7 沙漠 **sabaku** desert
8 空漠 **kūbaku** vast; vague
9 茫漠 **bōbaku** vague; vast
　砂漠 **sabaku** desert

――――――― 3 ―――――――

8 空々漠々 **kūkū-bakubaku** vast and empty

澃→汽 **3a4.16**

3a10.19

溢 溢　ITSU, afu(reru) overflow
　　　kobo(reru) be spilled
　　　kobo(su) spill

――――――― 1 ―――――――

4 溢水 **issui** inundation
6 溢血 **ikketsu** effusion of blood

――――――― 2 ―――――――

6 充溢 **jūitsu** overflow, abundance
9 乗溢 **no(ri)kobo(reru)** be packed to
　　　　overflowing with passengers
　咲溢 **sa(ki)kobo(reru)** bloom in profusion
11 脳溢血 **nōikketsu** cerebral apoplexy
15 横溢 **ōitsu** be filled/overflowing with

3a10.20

滄　SŌ blue

――――――― 1 ―――――――

9 滄海 **sōkai** the blue sea

3a10.21

溟　MEI dim, dark

3a10.22

漓　RI trickle; soak in; flow

――――――― 2 ―――――――

11 淋漓 **rinri** dripping, profuse

3a10.23

滂　BŌ flowing; vast

――――――― 1 ―――――――

9 滂洋 **bōyō** vast, boundless

3a10.24

溏　TŌ mud

滤→濾 **3a15.8**

3a10.25 / 580

源　GEN, minamoto source, origin
　　Minamoto the Genji family, the
　　Minamotos

――――――― 1 ―――――――

4 源氏 **Genji** Genji, the Minamoto family
　源氏物語 **Genji Monogatari** The Tale of
　　　　Genji
5 源平 **Gen-Pei** Genji and Heike clans, the
　　　　Minamoto and Taira families
9 源泉 **gensen** fountainhead, source, origin
　源泉徴収 **gensen chōshū** collecting (taxes)
　　　　at the source, withholding
　源泉課税 **gensen kazei** taxation at the source,
　　　　withholding tax
10 源流 **genryū** source, origin

――――――― 2 ―――――――

4 水源 **suigen** headwaters, source, fountainhead
　水源地 **suigenchi** headwaters, source
5 本源 **hongen** origin, root, cause, principle
　字源 **jigen** origin/history of a character
6 光源 **kōgen** light source
9 音源 **ongen** sound source
10 起源 **kigen** origin, beginning
　根源 **kongen** root, origin, source, cause
　桃源 **tōgen** Shangri-La, paradise
　桃源郷 **tōgenkyō** Shangri-La, paradise
　桃源境 **tōgenkyō** Shangri-La, paradise
　病源 **byōgen** cause of a disease
　病源菌 **byōgenkin** pathogenic bacteria, germ
　財源 **zaigen** revenue source; resourcefulness
12 淵源 **engen** origin, source, inception
　富源 **fugen** source of wealth, national
　　　　resources
　税源 **zeigen** source of tax revenue
　給源 **kyūgen** source of supply
　策源地 **sakugenchi** base of operations
13 資源 **shigen** resources
　電源 **dengen** power source
14 語源 **gogen** derivation, etymology
15 熱源 **netsugen** heat source
　震源 **shingen** epicenter
　震源地 **shingenchi** epicenter

――――――― 3 ―――――――

4 収入源 **shūnyūgen** source of income

3

氵 10←
土
扌
口
女
巾
犭
弓
彳
彡
艹
宀
⺍
山
吉
广
尸
口

8 供給源 **kyōkyūgen** source of supply
11 動力源 **dōryokugen** power source
情報源 **jōhōgen** news/information sources

———————— 4 ————————

4 天然資源 **tennen shigen** natural resources

3a10.26 / 1338

滅 **METSU, horo(biru)** fall into ruin, perish, die out   **horo(bosu)** ruin, destroy, overthrow, annihilate

———————— 1 ————————

2 滅入 **mei(ru)** feel depressed
3 滅亡 **metsubō** downfall, destruction
6 滅多 **metta (ni)** (with negative) seldom, rarely
滅多切 **mettagi(ri)** hacking to pieces
滅多矢鱈 **mettayatara** indiscriminate, frantic
滅多打 **mettau(chi)** random shooting
7 滅却 **mekkyaku** extinguish, destroy, efface
滅私奉公 **messhi hōkō** selfless patriotic service
8 滅法 **meppō** extraordinary, absurd; awfully; very
滅金 **mekki** gilt, plating, galvanizing
9 滅茶苦茶 **mechakucha** incoherent; preposterous; mess, wreck, ruin
滅茶滅茶 **mechamecha** mess, wreck, ruin
滅度 **metsudo** nirvana
滅相 **messō** absurd, unreasonable
11 滅菌 **mekkin** sterilization
12 滅裂 **metsuretsu** in chaos, incoherent

———————— 2 ————————

2 入滅 **nyūmetsu** death of a saint, entering Nirvana
4 不滅 **fumetsu** immortal, indestructible
幻滅 **genmetsu** disillusionment
仏滅 **butsumetsu** Buddha's death; unlucky day
5 必滅 **hitsumetsu** doomed to perish, mortal
生滅 **shōmetsu** birth and death, appearance and disappearance
6 死滅 **shimetsu** extinction, destruction
全滅 **zenmetsu** annihilation
灰滅 **kaimetsu** burn up, be destroyed
自滅 **jimetsu** natural decay; self-destruction; suicide
8 盲滅法 **mekura meppō** recklessly, at random
明滅 **meimetsu** flicker, glimmer
明滅灯 **meimetsutō** occulting light
9 点滅 **tenmetsu** switch/flash on and off
点滅器 **tenmetsuki** a switch
10 衰滅 **suimetsu** decline, downfall, ruin
消滅 **shōmetsu** become extinct, disappear, become void, be extinguished
破滅 **hametsu** ruin, destruction, downfall
討滅 **u(chi)horo(bosu)** destroy

11 掃滅 **sōmetsu** mopping up, annihilation
寂滅 **jakumetsu** Nirvana, death, annihilation
敗滅 **haimetsu** crushing defeat
12 湮滅 **inmetsu** extinction, destruction
埋滅 **inmetsu** extinction, annihiliation
廃滅 **haimetsu** ruin, decay
絶滅 **zetsumetsu** eradicate; become extinct
13 剿滅 **sōmetsu** annihilate
勦滅 **sōmetsu** annihilate, eradicate
罪滅 **tsumihorobo(shi)** atonement, amends, expiation, penance, conscience money
14 漸滅 **zenmetsu** gradual destruction
15 潰滅 **kaimetsu** be destroyed/annihilated
撃滅 **gekimetsu** destruction, annihilation
撲滅 **bokumetsu** eradication, extermination
摩滅 **mametsu** wear, abrasion
16 壊滅 **kaimetsu** destruction, annihilation
磨滅 **mametsu** wear, abrasion
18 覆滅 **fukumetsu** overthrow, destruction
21 殲滅 **senmetsu** annihilation, extermination

———————— 3 ————————

4 支離滅裂 **shiri-metsuretsu** incoherent, inconsistent, chaotic
13 滅茶滅茶 **mechamecha** mess, wreck, ruin

———————— 4 ————————

13 罪障消滅 **zaishō shōmetsu** expiation of one's sins
15 霊魂不滅 **reikon fumetsu** immortality of the soul

3a10.27

漣 漣 **REN, sazanami** ripples

3a10.28

溷 **KON** disorder; dirtiness; turbidity

———————— 1 ————————

16 溷濁 **kondaku** become turbid/muddy/cloudy

3a10.29

黎 **REI** black; many; dawn

———————— 1 ————————

8 黎明 **reimei** dawn, morning twilight

———————— 11 ————————

3a11.1 / 699

漁 **GYO, RYŌ** fishing   **isa(ru)** to fish   **asa(ru)** fish; hunt for

──────── 1 ────────

4 漁夫 **gyofu** fisherman
漁夫利 **gyofu (no) ri** profiting while others fight over a prize
漁区 **gyoku** fishing area
漁火 **gyoka, isa(ri)bi** fire for luring fish at night
5 漁民 **gyomin** fishermen
6 漁色 **gyoshoku** debauchery
漁色家 **gyoshokuka** lecher
7 漁労 **gyorō** fishing
漁村 **gyoson** fishing village
漁利 **gyori** fishing interests/profit
8 漁法 **gyohō** fishing method
漁者 **gyosha** fisherman
漁具 **gyogu** fishing gear/tackle
10 漁翁 **gyoō** old fisherman
漁師 **ryōshi** fisherman
漁家 **gyoka** fisherman's house
漁書 **gyosho** book-hunting
11 漁猟 **gyoryō** fishing (and hunting)
漁船 **gyosen, ryōsen** fishing boat/vessel
12 漁港 **gyokō** fishing port
漁場 **gyojō, ryōba** fishing ground/banks
漁期 **gyoki, ryōki** fishing season
13 漁業 **gyogyō** fishery, fishing industry
漁業権 **gyogyōken** fishing rights
14 漁歌 **gyoka** fisherman's song
漁網 **gyomō** fishing net
15 漁撈 **gyorō** fishing
16 漁獲 **gyokaku** fishing; catch, haul
漁獲物 **gyokakubutsu** a catch (of fish)

──────── 2 ────────

3 大漁 **tairyō** a large catch (of fish)
4 不漁 **furyō** poor catch (of fish)
7 沖漁 **okiryō** offshore fishing
11 密漁 **mitsuryō, mitsugyo** fish poaching
12 買漁 **ka(i)asa(ru)** hunt/shop around for
13 豊漁 **hōryō, hōgyo** abundant catch
禁漁 **kinryō** No Fishing
禁漁区 **kinryōku** no-fishing area
禁漁期 **kinryōki** closed (fishing) season

──────── 3 ────────

8 沿岸漁業 **engan gyogyō** coastal fishing

潅 → 灌 **3a17.3**

3a11.2 / 1400

漸

ZEN gradually
yōya(ku) gradually; finally; barely

──────── 1 ────────

5 漸加 **zenka** gradual increase, cumulative

6 漸次 **zenji** gradually
漸近 **zenkin** approach asymptotically, asymptotic (line/value)
9 漸降 **zenkō** gradual decline
10 漸進 **zenshin** gradual progress, steady advance
漸進的 **zenshinteki** gradual, moderate
漸時 **zenji** gradually
12 漸減 **zengen** gradual decrease
漸落 **zenraku** gradual fall/decline
13 漸滅 **zenmetsu** gradual destruction

──────── 2 ────────

6 西漸 **seizen** westward advance
8 東漸 **tōzen** advance eastward

3a11.3

湖

KO vicinity, shore

──────── 2 ────────

10 烏滸 **oko(gamashii)** presumptuous; ridiculous
烏滸沙汰 **oko(no)sata** absurd; impertinent

3a11.4

漱

SŌ, susu(gu) rinse the mouth, gargle

3a11.5

漲

CHŌ, minagi(ru) overflow

3a11.6

滌

TEKI, DEKI, JŌ wash, rinse

──────── 2 ────────

9 洗滌 **sendeki, senjō** wash, rinse, clean

3a11.7

漕

SŌ, ko(gu) row (a boat)

──────── 1 ────────

4 漕手 **ko(gi)te, sōshu** rower, oarsman
5 漕出 **ko(gi)da(su)** row out; begin to row
11 漕船 **ko(gi)bune** rowboat
12 漕着 **ko(gi)tsu(keru)** row up to, reach
漕艇 **sōtei** rowing, boating

──────── 2 ────────

6 回漕 **kaisō** shipping, sea transport

回漕店 **kaisōten** shipping agent
7 阿漕 **akogi** insatiable; cruel, harsh
20 競漕 **kyōsō** rowing race, regatta

3a11.8

漾　**YŌ** drift, flow

3a11.9 / 924

漂　**HYŌ, tadayo(u)** drift about, float

――――――― 1 ―――――――
5 漂失 **hyōshitsu** drift away
漂白剤 **hyōhakuzai** bleach
8 漂泊 **hyōhaku** wander, drift
9 漂砂 **hyōsa** drift sand
10 漂浪 **hyōrō** wandering
漂流 **hyōryū** drift, be adrift; wandering
漂流木 **hyōryūboku** driftwood
漂流民 **hyōryūmin** persons adrift; castaways
漂流者 **hyōryūsha** person adrift; castaway
漂流物 **hyōryūbutsu** flotsam
漂流記 **hyōryūki** castaway's account of
　　　foreign lands
漂流船 **hyōryūsen** drifting ship, a derelict
12 漂着 **hyōchaku** drift ashore
――――――― 2 ―――――――
9 浮漂 **fuhyō** float about, drift

滯 → 滞 **3a10.14**

3a11.10 / 1546

漆　**SHITSU, urushi** lacquer

――――――― 1 ―――――――
3 漆工 **shikkō** lacquer work(er)
6 漆気触 **urushikabure** lacquer poisoning
9 漆負 **urushima(ke)** lacquer poisoning
漆屋 **urushiya** lacquer shop
11 漆黒 **shikkoku** jet-black, pitch-black
漆細工 **urushizaiku** lacquerware
12 漆喰 **shikkui** mortar, plaster, stucco
漆絵 **urushie** lacquer painting
13 漆塗 **urushinu(ri)** lacquered, japanned
15 漆器 **shikki** lacquerware
――――――― 2 ―――――――
11 黒漆 **kokushitsu** black lacquer

3a11.11 / 1411

漫　**MAN** rambling, aimless; involuntarily **sozo(ro)** involuntarily, in spite of oneself, somehow (or other)

――――――― 1 ―――――――
3 漫才 **manzai** comic dialog
漫々 **manman** vast, boundless
4 漫文 **manbun** rambling essay
7 漫言 **mangen, sozo(ro)goto** rambling talk
8 漫画 **manga** cartoon, comic book/strip
漫画家 **mangaka** cartoonist
漫歩 **manpo, sozo(ro)aru(ki)** stroll, ramble, walk
漫雨 **sozo(ro)ame** sudden shower
10 漫遊 **man'yū** trip, tour, travel
漫遊客 **man'yūkyaku** tourist, sightseer
12 漫然 **manzen** random, rambling
漫筆 **manpitsu** random comments/essay
漫評 **manpyō** rambling criticism
14 漫読 **mandoku** browse, read randomly
15 漫罵 **manba** revile, deride, criticize irresponsibly
漫談 **mandan** chat, idle talk
漫談家 **mandanka** humorist
16 漫録 **manroku** random comments
――――――― 2 ―――――――
4 冗漫 **jōman** verbose, rambling
8 放漫 **hōman** lax, loose, reckless
10 浪漫主義 **rōman shugi** romanticism
浪漫的 **rōmanteki** romantic (school)
浪漫派 **rōmanha** romantic school, romanticists
12 散漫 **sanman** vague, desultory, loose
14 漫漫 **manman** vast, boundless
20 瀰漫 **biman** pervade, permeate, diffuse
21 爛漫 **ranman** in full glory, dazzling
――――――― 4 ―――――――
4 天真爛漫 **tenshin-ranman** naive, simple and innocent, unaffected

3a11.12 / 1793

漬　**SHI, tsu(keru)** soak, immerse, pickle, preserve **tsu(karu)** soak, steep, be submersed; be well seasoned

――――――― 1 ―――――――
4 漬込 **tsu(ke)ko(mu)** pickle
8 漬物 **tsukemono** pickled vegetables
10 漬梅 **tsu(ke)ume** pickling/pickled plums
11 漬菜 **tsu(ke)na** pickling/pickled greens
――――――― 2 ―――――――
5 氷漬 **kōrizu(ke)** packed in ice, iced
9 茶漬 **chazu(ke)** rice and tea mixed; simple meal

10 浸漬 **shinseki, shinshi** immerse, dip, soak, steep
   桜漬 **sakurazu(ke)** pickled cherry blossoms
11 菜漬 **nazu(ke)** pickled vegetables
   粕漬 **kasuzu(ke)** vegetables pickled in saké lees
12 酢漬 **suzu(ke)** pickling in vinegar
13 塩漬 **shiozu(ke)** pickling in salt

――――――― 3 ―――――――

1 一夜漬 **ichiyazuke** pickled just overnight; hastily prepared
3 大根漬 **daikonzu(ke)** pickled daikon
   山葵漬 **wasabizu(ke)** pickled horseradish
7 沢庵漬 **takuanzuke** pickled daikon
   芥子漬 **karashizu(ke)** mustard pickles
8 奈良漬 **narazu(ke)** pickles seasoned in saké lees
13 福神漬 **fukujinzu(ke)** vegetables pickled in soy sauce

――――――― 4 ―――――――

17 糠味噌漬 **nukamisozu(ke)** vegetables pickled in rice-bran miso

滿 → 満 **3a9.25**

漢 → 漢 **3a10.17**

3a11.13 / 344

EN performance, presentation, play

演

――――――― 1 ―――――――

0 演じる/ずる **en(jiru/zuru)** perform, play, act, enact
5 演出 **enshutsu** production, performance
   演出者 **enshutsusha** producer, director
   演出家 **enshutsuka** producer, director
7 演技 **engi** acting, performance
   演芸 **engei** entertainment, performance
   演芸会 **engeikai** an entertainment, variety show
   演芸者 **engeisha** performer
8 演武 **enbu** military/martial-arts exercises
   演武場 **enbujō** drill hall
9 演奏 **ensō** (musical) performance
   演奏曲目 **ensō kyokumoku** musical program
   演奏会 **ensōkai** concert, recital
   演奏法 **ensōhō** (musical) execution, interpretation
11 演習 **enshū** practice, exercises; (military) maneuvers; seminar
   演習林 **enshūrin** experimental forest

13 演義 **engi** amplification, commentary, popular adaptation
14 演歌 **enka** (a style of singing)
   演算 **enzan** operation (in math)
   演説 **enzetsu** speech, address
   演説法 **enzetsuhō** elocution, oratory
   演説者 **enzetsusha** speaker, orator
   演説家 **enzetsuka** speaker, orator
15 演舞場 **enbujō** playhouse, theater
   演劇 **engeki** drama, play
   演劇的 **engekiteki** dramatic, theatrical
   演劇界 **engekikai** (the world of) the theater
   演劇術 **engekijutsu** dramatics
   演劇場 **engekijō** theater, stage
16 演壇 **endan** rostrum, platform
18 演題 **endai** subject of a speech
19 演繹 **en'eki** deduce
   演繹法 **en'ekihō** deductive reasoning

――――――― 2 ―――――――

3 大演習 **daienshū** large-scale maneuvers, war games
   上演 **jōen** play, stage, perform
   口演 **kōen** oral narration
4 公演 **kōen** public performance
5 出演 **shutsuen** appear on stage, play, perform
   代演 **daien** substitute for another actor
   好演 **kōen** good acting/show
   主演 **shuen** starring
   主演者 **shuensha** star, leading actor
6 再演 **saien** repeat performance
   休演 **kyūen** suspend performances
   共演 **kyōen** coacting, costarring
7 助演 **joen** play a supporting role, co-star
   初演 **shoen** first performance, premiere
8 実演 **jitsuen** stage show, performance
9 独演 **dokuen** solo performance
   独演会 **dokuenkai** solo recital/performance
11 終演 **shūen** end of a performance
12 軽演劇 **keiengeki** light comedy
   開演 **kaien** beginning the performance
13 続演 **zokuen** continued run (of a show)
   試演 **shien** rehearsal, preview
15 熱演 **netsuen** impassioned performance
17 講演 **kōen** lecture, address
   講演会 **kōenkai** lecture meeting
   講演者 **kōensha** lecturer, speaker
20 競演 **kyōen** competitive performance, recital contest

――――――― 3 ―――――――

5 立会演説 **ta(chi)a(i) enzetsu** campaign speech in a joint meeting of candidates, debate
12 街頭演説 **gaitō enzetsu** street/soapbox speech
16 機動演習 **kidō enshū** maneuvers

3

氵 11←
土
扌
口
女
巾
犭
弓
彳
彡
艹
宀
丷
山
广
尸
口

3a11.14 / 1446

滴 **TEKI, shizuku** a drop
shitata(ru) drip, trickle

—————— 1 ——————
3 滴下 **tekika** drip, trickle down
16 滴薬 **tekiyaku** (medicine) drops
—————— 2 ——————
1 一滴 **itteki** a drop
4 水滴 **suiteki** drop of water
8 雨滴 **uteki** raindrop
9 点滴 **tenteki** falling drops, raindrops; intravenous drip
21 露滴 **roteki** dewdrop

3a11.15

滾 **KON** flow
tagi(ru) boil, seethe

—————— 1 ——————
3 滾々 **konkon** gushingly, copiously
—————— 2 ——————
12 煮滾 **ni(e)tagi(ru)** boil up, seethe

3a11.16

滷 **RO** brine

3a11.17

滲 **SHIN, niji(mu)** blot, ooze, spread, run, blur **shi(miru)** soak into; be infected; smart, hurt

—————— 1 ——————
4 滲込 **shinnyū** permeate, infiltrate, sink in
5 滲出 **shinshutsu** exude, ooze/seep out
滲出性 **shinshutsusei** weeping/exudative (eczema)
9 滲透 **shintō** permeation, infiltration, osmosis

3a11.18

滬 **KO** (name of a river in China)

3a11.19 / 1806

漏 **RŌ, mo(reru), mo(ru)** leak; be disclosed **mo(rasu)** let leak; divulge

—————— 1 ——————
3 漏口 **rōkō** a leak, vent
4 漏斗 **rōto, jōgo** funnel

漏斗状 **rōtojō** funnel-shaped
漏水 **rōsui** water leakage
5 漏出 **rōshutsu** leak out, escape
8 漏刻 **rōkoku** water clock
9 漏洩 **rōei** leak; be disclosed/divulged
12 漏無 **mo(re)na(ku)** without exception
13 漏電 **rōden** leakage of electricity, short circuit
14 漏聞 **rōbun** overhear

—————— 2 ——————
4 水漏 **mizumo(ri)** leak
欠漏 **ketsurō** omission
6 耳漏 **jirō** ear discharge, earwax
7 杜漏 **zurō** careless, negligent
言漏 **i(i)mo(rasu)** forget to mention
8 雨漏 **amamo(ri)** leak in the roof
10 書漏 **ka(ki)mo(rasu)** omit, leave out
討漏 **u(chi)mo(rasu)** let escape, fail to kill
11 疎漏 **sorō** carelessness, oversight
脱漏 **datsurō** omission
粗漏 **sorō** carelessness, oversight
14 遺漏 **irō** omission, negligence, oversight
聞漏 **ki(ki)mo(rasu)** miss hearing, not catch
17 膿漏 **nōrō** purulent discharge, pyorrhea

—————— 4 ——————
12 歯槽膿漏 **shisō nōrō** pyorrhea

3a11.20

漉 **ROKU, ko(su)** strain, filter, percolate
su(ku) make paper

—————— 1 ——————
10 漉紙 **koshigami** filter paper
—————— 2 ——————
4 水漉 **mizuko(shi)** filter, strainer
9 茶漉 **chako(shi)** tea strainer
10 紙漉 **kamisu(ki)** papermaking

3a11.21

漿 **SHŌ** juice; a drink; pasty substance

—————— 1 ——————
8 漿果 **shōka** berry
11 漿液 **shōeki** juice, sap; blood serum
—————— 2 ——————
6 血漿 **kesshō** (blood) plasma
11 脳漿 **nōshō** (fluid in) the brain, gray matter
14 酸漿 **hōzuki** bladder/ground cherry
—————— 3 ——————
9 海酸漿 **umihōzuki** whelk egg capsule (used for child's noisemaker)

3

→11 氵
土
扌
口
女
巾
犭
弓
彳
彡
艹
宀
⺌
屮
吉
广
尸
口

────────── 12 ──────────

3a12.1 / 468

潮

CHŌ, shio tide; morning tide; seawater
ushio tide, seawater

────────── 1 ──────────

2 潮入 shioi(ri) coming in of the tide
3 潮干 shiohi low/ebb tide
 潮干狩 shiohiga(ri) shell gathering (at low tide)
4 潮水 chōsui, shiomizu seawater
0 潮気 shioke salt air
 潮合 shioa(i) (waiting for) the tide, opportunity
 潮汲 shioku(mi) drawing seawater (for salt-making)
 潮汐 chōseki (morning and evening) tide
 潮先 shiosaki rising of the tide, time to begin
7 潮吹 shiofu(ki) spouting of a whale; (a thin-shelled surf clam)
 潮足 shioashi speed of the tide
8 潮垂 shiota(reru) shed copious tears
 潮門 chōmon tide gate
9 潮通 shiodō(shi) flow of seawater (over a beach)
 潮風 shiokaze sea breeze, salt air
 潮津波 shiotsunami tidal bore
 潮海 shioumi the sea
 潮型 shiogata type of tide (flood, neap, etc.)
 潮待 shioma(chi) waiting for the tide
 潮音 chōon the sound of waves
 潮紅 chōkō flush, redden
10 潮候 chōkō tide period, time of the tide
 潮差 chōsa tide range
 潮流 chōryū tidal current; trend of the times
 潮害 chōgai tide-water damage
 潮時 shiodoki (waiting for) the tide, opportunity
12 潮焼 shioya(ke) tanned by salt air
 潮間 shioma ebb tide
13 潮煙 shiokemuri salt spray
 潮解 chōkai deliquescence
 潮路 shioji tideway, channel; the sea
14 潮境 shiozakai boundary (between two ocean currents)
15 潮影 shiokage ripply wave pattern
 潮標 chōhyō tide mark
18 潮騒 shiosai roar of the sea
19 潮瀬 shiose, shioze sea current, tidal flow

────────── 2 ──────────

3 大潮 ōshio flood tide, spring tide
 干潮 kanchō, hishio, hikishio ebb tide
 小潮 koshio neap tide

4 引潮 hi(ki)shio ebb tide
5 主潮 shuchō the main current
6 血潮 chishio blood
7 低潮 teichō low tide
 赤潮 akashio red tide
 初潮 shochō one's first menstruation
8 退潮 taichō ebb/low tide
 逆潮 sakashio, gyakuchō head tide, countertide, weather tide, crosstide, adverse current
9 風潮 fūchō tide; trend of the times, the social climate
 海潮 kaichō tide
 海潮音 kaichōon sound of the tide
 思潮 shichō trend of thought
 紅潮 kōchō redden, flush, blush; menstruate
10 高潮 takashio high tide
  kōchō high tide; climax, peak
 高潮時 kōchōji time of high tide
 差潮 sa(shi)shio rising tide
11 黒潮 Kuroshio the Japan Current
12 満潮 manchō high tide
 渦潮 uzushio swirling seawater
 落潮 o(chi)shio, rakuchō low tide, ebb
 検潮器 kenchōki tide gauge
 朝潮 asashio morning tide
13 暗潮 anchō undercurrent
16 親潮 Oyashio the Okhotsk/Kurile current

────────── 3 ──────────

12 最高潮 saikōchō highwater mark; climax, peak

3a12.2

澈

TETSU clear, limpid, pure

徵 → 澄 3a12.11

3a12.3

溉

GAI pour, draw water

────────── 2 ──────────

20 灌溉 kangai irrigation

3a12.4

澎

HŌ turbulent water

────────── 1 ──────────

12 澎湃 hōhai surging, raging

潴 → 潴 **3a16.5**

3a12.5

溿
GYŌ sprinkle; thin, shallow, frivolous

——————— 1 ———————

7 溿季 **gyōki** decadence, degeneration

3a12.6 / 937

潜 潛 潜
SEN dive; hide
mogu(ru) dive; crawl
into **kugu(ru)** pass
under **kugu(ri)** wicket
gate, side gate, small doorway (built into a larger door) **hiso(mu)** lurk, lie hidden **hiso(meru)** conceal, hide **hiso(maru)** be hushed

——————— 1 ———————

2 潜入 **sennyū** infiltrate
4 潜込 **mogu(ri)ko(mu)** get/crawl/slip in; hide
潜水 **sensui** dive, submerge
潜水夫 **sensuifu** diver
潜水母艦 **sensui bokan** submarine tender
潜水服 **sensuifuku** diving suit
潜水病 **sensuibyō** the bends
潜水帽 **sensuibō** diving helmet
潜水器 **sensuiki** diving bell/apparatus
潜水艦 **sensuikan** a submarine
潜心 **senshin** meditation, absorption
潜戸 **kugu(ri)do** side gate, small doorway (built into a larger door)
6 潜伏 **senpuku** hide, be hidden; be dormant/latent
潜伏性 **senpukusei** latent (disease)
潜伏期 **senpukuki** incubation period
潜在 **senzai** latent, hidden, potential (cf. 顕在)
潜在的 **senzaiteki** latent, potential, dormant
潜在意識 **senzai ishiki** subconscious
潜行 **senkō** traveling incognito; go underground
7 潜没 **senbotsu** submerge, dive
8 潜幸 **senkō** secret visit by the emperor
10 潜流 **senryū** undercurrent
潜航 **senkō** cruise underwater, be submerged
潜航艇 **senkōtei** a submarine
11 潜望鏡 **senbōkyō** periscope
13 潜勢力 **senseiryoku** latent power, potential

——————— 2 ———————

7 沈潜 **chinsen** be engrossed in
10 原潜 **gensen** nuclear(-powered) sub(marine) (short for 原子力潜水艦)
13 搔潜 **ka(i)kugu(ru)** dodge through
14 駆潜艇 **kusentei** submarine chaser

3a12.7

潸
SAN flowing of tears

——————— 1 ———————

12 潸然 **sanzen** tearfully

3a12.8

潘
HAN water in which rice has been washed

潘 → 溜 **3a10.11**

3a12.9 / 1626

潟
SEKI, **kata** beach, tideland; lagoon, inlet

——————— 1 ———————

12 潟湖 **sekiko** lagoon

——————— 2 ———————

3 干潟 **higata** dry beach (at ebb tide), tideland
13 新潟 **Niigata** (city, Niigata-ken)
新潟県 **Niigata-ken** (prefecture)

3a12.10 / 1241

潔 潔
KETSU pure, clean
isagiyo(i) pure-hearted, clean, righteous; manly

——————— 1 ———————

5 潔白 **keppaku** pure, upright, of integrity
11 潔斎 **kessai** abstinence, purification
18 潔癖 **keppeki** love of cleanliness, fastidiousness

——————— 2 ———————

4 不潔 **fuketsu** filthy, dirty
9 貞潔 **teiketsu** chaste and pure
10 高潔 **kōketsu** high-minded, noble, upright
純潔 **junketsu** pure, unsullied, chaste
11 清潔 **seiketsu** clean, neat, pure
皎潔 **kōketsu, kyōketsu** noble, pure, upright
13 廉潔 **renketsu** honest, upright
18 簡潔 **kanketsu** concise

——————— 3 ———————

11 清廉潔白 **seiren-keppaku** spotless integrity

3a12.11 / 1334

澄 澂
CHŌ, **su(mu)** become clear
su(masu) make clear; perk up (one's ears); look nonchalant, put on airs

─────────── 1 ───────────

4 澄切 **su(mi)ki(ru)** become perfectly clear
5 澄汁 **su(mashi)jiru** clear soup/broth
8 澄明 **chōmei** clear, bright
9 澄屋 **su(mashi)ya** smug-looking person, prim-looking girl
12 澄渡 **su(mi)wata(ru)** be crystal clear
15 澄徹 **chōtetsu** clear, transparent

─────────── 2 ───────────

3 上澄 **uwazu(mi)** (clear) supernatant (liquid)
4 水澄 **mizusu(mashi)** whirligig beetle
6 行澄 **okona(i)su(masu)** follow Buddhist teachings; act like a good boy/girl
7 見澄 **misu(masu)** observe carefully, make sure
8 狙澄 **nera(i)su(masu)** take careful aim
取澄 **to(ri)su(masu)** put on airs
9 研澄 **to(gi)su(masu)** sharpen/polish well
11 清澄 **seichō** clear, limpid, serene
14 聞澄 **ki(ki)su(masu)** listen attentively

3a12.12

潭 **TAN** deep water; deep

─────────── 2 ───────────

11 深潭 **shintan** abyss

3a12.13

潼 **DŌ** high

3a12.14

潰 **KAI, tsubu(reru)** be crushed/destroyed/ruined, collapse; go bankrupt; be worn down **tsubu(su)** crush, wreck; kill (time) **tsui(eru)** collapse, be utterly defeated

─────────── 1 ───────────

7 潰走 **kaisō** be routed, stampede
10 潰値 **tsubu(shi)ne** scrap value
13 潰滅 **kaimetsu** be destroyed/annihilated
14 潰瘍 **kaiyō** ulcer

─────────── 2 ───────────

5 叩潰 **tata(ki)tsubu(su)** smash, crush
目潰 **metsubu(shi)** powdery substance to throw in someone's eyes to blind him
6 全潰 **zenkai** complete collapse/destruction
7 決潰 **kekkai** rupture, break, collapse
8 押潰 **o(shi)tsubu(su)** crush, smash, squash
虱潰 **shiramitsubu(shi ni)** one by one, thoroughly, with a fine-tooth comb
9 胃潰瘍 **ikaiyō** stomach ulcer

食潰 **ku(i)tsubu(su)** eat away, sponge off (someone)
11 捻潰 **hine(ri)tsubu(su)** crush between one's thumb and finger
崩潰 **hōkai** collapse, disintegration
酔潰 **yo(i)tsubu(reru)** be dead drunk
12 握潰 **nigi(ri)tsubu(su)** crush, crumple; shelve, table
飲潰 **no(mi)tsubu(reru)** get dead drunk **no(mi)tsubu(su)** drink (someone) under the table
13 塗潰 **nu(ri)tsubu(su)** paint out
搗潰 **tsu(ki)tsubu(su)** pound to a jelly
腸潰瘍 **chōkaiyō** intestinal ulcer
暇潰 **himatsubu(shi)** wasting/killing time
14 穀潰 **gokutsubu(shi)** idler, a do-nothing
15 踏潰 **fu(mi)tsubu(su)** crush underfoot
鋳潰 **itsubu(su)** melt down
16 磨潰 **su(ri)tsubu(su)** grind down; mash; deface; dissipate (one's fortune)
18 嚙潰 **ka(mi)tsubu(su)** chew up

3a12.15

漬 **FUN, fu(ku)** spout, gush forth

3a12.16

潦 **RŌ** heavy rainfall, runoff

3a12.17

潑 溌 **HATSU** sprinkle; lively, vigorous

─────────── 1 ───────────

9 潑剌 **hatsuratsu** lively, animated

澁 → 渋 3a8.19

3a12.18

潯 **JIN** shore, banks

潺 → 3a9.34

澗 → 澗 3a12.19

3a12.19

澗 澗   KAN (river in a) valley

3a12.20 / 1203

潤 JUN, uruo(u) become wet; profit by
uruo(i) moisture; gain; favor; charm
uruo(su) moisten, wet, water; profit,
enrich uru(mu) become wet/blurred/
clouded

———————— 1 ————————

6 潤色 **junshoku** embellishment
7 潤沢 **juntaku** plentiful, abundant; profit,
favor; gloss, luster
12 潤筆 **junpitsu** painting and writing
潤筆料 **junpitsuryō** writing/painting fee
13 潤滑 **junkatsu** lubrication
潤滑油 **junkatsuyu** lubricating oil
潤飾 **junshoku** embellishment

———————— 2 ————————

7 利潤 **rijun** profit
10 浸潤 **shinjun** permeate, infiltrate, seep
12 湿潤 **shitsujun** damp, moist, humid
13 豊潤 **hōjun** rich, abundant

———————— 3 ————————

9 肺浸潤 **haishinjun** pulmonary tuberculosis

———————— 13 ————————

3a13.1 / 1017

激 GEKI, hage(shii) violent, fierce,
strong, intense

———————— 1 ————————

0 激する **geki(suru)** get excited, be agitated/
enraged/exasperated
4 激化 **gekka, gekika** intensification, aggravation
7 激励 **gekirei** urge on, encourage
激声 **gekisei** excited/agitated voice
8 激突 **gekitotsu** crash, collision
9 激発 **gekihatsu** outburst, fit (of anger),
explosion
激甚 **gekijin** intense, fierce
激変 **gekihen** sudden change, upheaval
激昂 **gekkō, gekikō** get excited, be enraged/
indignant
激怒 **gekido** rage, wrath, fury
激臭 **gekishū** strong odor
10 激浪 **gekirō** high waves, raging sea
激流 **gekiryū** swift/raging current
激烈 **gekiretsu** violent, vehement, intense
11 激動 **gekidō** violent shaking; excitement, stir

激務 **gekimu** busy job, arduous work
激情 **gekijō** violent emotion, passion
12 激減 **gekigen** sharp decrease, plummet
激暑 **gekisho** intense heat
激越 **gekietsu** violent, vehement, fiery
激痛 **gekitsū** sharp pain
13 激戦 **gekisen** fierce fighting, hard-fought
contest
14 激増 **gekizō** sudden/sharp increase
激語 **gekigo** harsh language
15 激賞 **gekishō** praise highly, rave about
激憤 **gekifun** indignation, resentment
激論 **gekiron** heated argument
激震 **gekishin** severe earthquake
18 激闘 **gekitō** intense fighting, fierce battle

———————— 2 ————————

8 刺激 **shigeki** stimulus, stimulation
刺激的 **shigekiteki** stimulating
刺激剤 **shigekizai** a stimulant, irritant
9 急激 **kyūgeki** sudden, abrupt, drastic
11 過激 **kageki** radical, extreme
過激主義 **kageki shugi** radicalism, extremism
過激派 **kagekiha** radicals, extremists
13 感激 **kangeki** be deeply impressed/grateful
15 憤激 **fungeki** become enraged/indignant
16 奮激 **fungeki** be roused/inspired
17 矯激 **kyōgeki** radical, extreme

3a13.2

澱 DEN, ori dregs, sediment, a precipitate
yodo(mu) be stagnant; settle out,
deposit

———————— 1 ————————

10 澱粉 **denpun** starch
澱粉質 **denpunshitsu** starchiness

———————— 2 ————————

7 沈澱 **chinden** precipitation, sedimentation
沈澱池 **chindenchi** settling pond/reservoir
沈澱物 **chindenbutsu** deposit, precipitate
沈澱槽 **chindensō** settling tank

3a13.3

澣 KAN wash

3a13.4

澳 Ō deep; Austria
kuma bend (in a river)

———————— 1 ————————

8 澳門 **Makao** Macao

3a13.5

澡　SŌ wash

3a13.6

澪　REI, mio water route, shipping channel

——————— 1 ———————

15 澪標 miotsukushi channel marker

3a13.7 / 957

濃　NŌ dark, thick, undiluted ko(i) dark, deep (color); dense, thick (liquid), strong (coffee); intimate koma(yaka) warm, tender; detailed; deep, dark

——————— 1 ———————

4 濃化 nōka thicken, concentrate
8 濃厚 nōkō thickness, richness, strength
　濃青色 nōseishoku deep/dark blue
9 濃度 nōdo (degree of) concentration
　濃紅色 nōkōshoku deep red, crimson
11 濃淡 nōtan light and shade, concentration, shading
　濃密 nōmitsu thick, dense
　濃紺 nōkon dark/navy blue
12 濃紫 komurasaki deep purple
　濃紫色 nōshishoku deep purple
13 濃溶液 nōyōeki concentrated solution
　濃褐色 nōkasshoku dark brown
14 濃緑 nōryoku dark green
17 濃縮 nōshuku concentrate, enrich
19 濃艶 nōen charming, bewitching
　濃霧 nōmu dense fog

——————— 2 ———————

8 油濃 aburako(i), abura(k)ko(i) greasy, fatty, oily
9 信濃 Shinano (ancient kuni, Nagano-ken)
　美濃 Mino (ancient kuni, Gifu-ken)
10 脂濃 abura(k)ko(i) greasy, rich (foods)

澤 → 沢 3a4.18

3a13.8 / 1625

濁　DAKU, nigo(ru) become muddy/turbid; be voiced; be vague nigo(ri) muddiness, impurity; voiced sound/consonant; unrefined saké nigo(su) make turbid

——————— 1 ———————

4 濁水 dakusui muddy water

5 濁世 dakuse (this) corrupt world
6 濁江 nigo(ri)e muddy inlet/creek
7 濁声 damigoe, nigo(ri)goe thick/hoarse voice
9 濁点 dakuten voiced-consonant mark
　濁音 dakuon voiced sound
10 濁酒 dakushu, nigo(ri)zake, doburoku unrefined/raw saké
　濁流 dakuryū muddy river, turbid water

——————— 2 ———————

5 半濁音 handakuon semivoiced sound, p-sound
6 汚濁 odaku corruption, decadence
7 乳濁 nyūdaku emulsion
9 連濁 rendaku change of an unvoiced to a voiced sound in forming a compound word
11 混濁 kondaku become turbid/muddy/thick
　清濁 seidaku purity and impurity; good and evil
13 溷濁 kondaku become turbid/muddy/cloudy
20 懸濁 kendaku suspension

3a13.9

濛　MŌ light rainfall, drizzle; darkness

——————— 1 ———————

3 濛々 mōmō thick (fog), dim
9 濛昧 mōmai ignorant, benighted

3a13.10

澹　TAN calm, quiet; simple, light

——————— 2 ———————

11 惨澹 santan(taru) piteous, wretched, horrible
13 暗澹 antan gloomy, somber

3a13.11

濂　REN (name of a river in China)

3a13.12

鞜　TŌ, kutsu shoes, boots

——————— 14 ———————

3a14.1

灞　BI much, many

瀞→瀞 **3a16.2**

3a14.2

鴻 **KŌ** large, great; large wild goose

——————— 1 ———————

4 鴻毛 **kōmō** goose feathers; a trifle
10 鴻恩 **kōon** great benevolence/blessings

3a14.3

濮 **BOKU** (name of a river in China)

潛→潜 **3a12.6**

濟→済 **3a8.30**

3a14.4

濡 **JU, nu(reru)** get/be wet; make love
nu(rasu) wet, moisten, dip

——————— 1 ———————

4 濡仏 **nu(re)botoke** Buddhist image exposed to the weather
濡手粟 **nu(re)te (de) awa** easy money
6 濡色 **nu(re)iro** wet/glossy color
濡衣 **nu(re)ginu** wet clothes; false charge
濡衣着 **nu(re)ginu (o) ki(serareru)** be falsely accused
8 濡事 **nu(re)goto** love affair
12 濡落葉 **nu(re)o(chi)ba** wet fallen leaves
13 濡鼠 **nu(re)nezumi** (like a) drowned rat
14 濡髪 **nu(re)gami** newly-washed/glossy hair
15 濡縁 **nu(re)en** open veranda

——————— 2 ———————

8 泣濡 **na(ki)nu(reru)** be tear-stained

3a14.5 / 1561

濯 濯 **TAKU, susu(gu), soso(gu), yusu(gu)** wash, pour on, rinse

——————— 2 ———————

9 洗濯 **sentaku** laundering
ara(i)susu(gi) washing and rinsing
洗濯板 **sentakuita** washboard

洗濯物 **sentakumono** the wash/laundry
洗濯屋 **sentakuya** laundry; laundryman
洗濯機 **sentakki, sentakuki** washing machine

澀→渋 **3a8.19**

濕→湿 **3a9.22**

3a14.6

濘 **NEI** muddy

——————— 2 ———————

8 泥濘 **deinei, nukarumi** mud, mire

3a14.7

濬 **SHUN** deep
sara(u) dredge

3a14.8

濤 涛 **TŌ** waves, billows

——————— 2 ———————

7 狂濤 **kyōtō** raging waves
8 波濤 **hatō** large waves, high seas, billows
9 怒濤 **dotō** raging billows, high seas

3a14.9

濠 **GŌ** moat; Australia
hori moat

——————— 1 ———————

4 濠太剌利 **Ōsutoraria** Australia
6 濠州 **Gōshū** Australia

——————— 2 ———————

4 内濠 **uchibori** inner moat, moat within the castle walls
日濠 **Nichi-Gō** Japan and Australia
5 外濠 **sotobori** outer moat

澗→闊 **8e9.3**

——————— 15 ———————

3a15.1

瀏 **RYŪ** clear

3a15.2

濺

SEN sprinkle, splash

潴 → 瀦 3a16.5

3a15.3 / 1944

濫

RAN overflow; excessive, indiscriminate **mida(ri ni)** without authorization; without good reason; recklessly

——————— 1 ———————

0 濫りがましい/りがわしい **mida(rigamashii/rigawashii)** disorderly, immoral
2 濫入 **rannyū** enter without permission
5 濫出 **ranshutsu** publish in great quantity, flood the market
濫用 **ran'yō** abuse, misuse, misappropriation
濫立 **ranritsu** standing in disorder; (both good and bad candidates) coming forward in great numbers
6 濫伐 **ranbatsu** reckless deforestation
7 濫作 **ransaku** overproduction
9 濫発 **ranpatsu** overissue (of money)
濫造 **ranzō** overproduction, slipshod manufacture
11 濫設 **ransetsu** establish too many (schools)
12 濫費 **ranpi** waste, extravagance
14 濫読 **randoku** indiscriminate/random reading
16 濫獲 **rankaku** overfishing, overhunting
18 濫觴 **ranshō** origin, source, beginning

——————— 2 ———————

5 氾濫 **hanran** flooding, inundation

3a15.4

瀑

BAKU waterfall

——————— 1 ———————

5 瀑布 **bakufu** waterfall

——————— 2 ———————

9 飛瀑 **hibaku** waterfall

3a15.5

瀋

SHIN juice, broth

3a15.6

瀉

SHA flow out; have diarrhea; vomit **kuda(shi)** purgation, evacuation

——————— 1 ———————

6 瀉血 **shaketsu** bloodletting

——————— 2 ———————

1 一瀉千里 **issha-senri** in a rush, at full gallop
6 吐瀉 **tosha** vomiting and diarrhea
吐瀉物 **toshabutsu** vomit and bowel discharge

3a15.7

瀆 涜

TOKU defile, blaspheme; ditch

——————— 1 ———————

9 瀆神 **tokushin** blasphemy, sacrilege, profanity
瀆神罪 **tokushinzai** blasphemy, sacrilege, profanity
18 瀆職 **tokushoku** corruption, graft, bribery
瀆職罪 **tokushokuzai** bribery, graft

——————— 2 ———————

6 自瀆 **jitoku** masturbation
9 冒瀆 **bōtoku** blasphemy, sacrilege, desecration

3a15.8

濾 滤 沪

RO, ko(su) filter

——————— 1 ———————

10 濾紙 **roshi, ko(shi)gami** filter paper
11 濾過 **roka** filtration
13 濾滓 **rosai** filter cake

3a15.9

瀁

YŌ drift, flow; overflowing, vast

——————— 16 ———————

瀧 → 滝 3a10.8

3a16.1

瀚

KAN broad, vast

3a16.2

瀞 瀞

SEI pure, clear (water)
toro pool (in a river)

3

氵 16←
士
扌
口
女
巾
犭
弓
彳
彡
艹
宀
⺌
山
⺜
广
尸
口

瀬 → 瀨 3a16.3

3a16.3 / 1513

瀬 瀨

se shallows, shoal, rapids

——————— 1 ———————
- 4 瀬戸 **seto** strait(s), channel; porcelain
  瀬戸内海 **Setonaikai** the Inland Sea
  瀬戸引 **setobi(ki)** enameled
  瀬戸物 **setomono** porcelain, china, earthenware
  瀬戸焼 **setoya(ki)** porcelain, china
  瀬戸際 **setogiwa** crucial moment, crisis,
  brink
  瀬戸鉢 **setobachi** earthenware pot
- 15 瀬踏 **sebu(mi)** wading to test the depth, trial
  balloon, sounding out

——————— 2 ———————
- 3 川瀬 **kawase** shallows, rapids
- 5 立瀬 **ta(tsu)se** position (before others),
  predicament
- 6 年瀬 **toshi(no)se** end of year
  早瀬 **hayase** swift current, rapids
- 9 逢瀬 **ōse** lovers' secret meeting, tryst,
  assignation
  浅瀬 **asase** shoal, shallows, ford
  浮瀬 **u(kabu)se** lucky breaks, a chance
- 10 高瀬 **takase** shallows
  高瀬舟 **takasebune** flatboat, riverboat
- 12 遣瀬 **yaruse(nai)** dreary, cheerless, disconsolate
- 13 歳瀬 **toshi(no)se** year's end
- 15 潮瀬 **shiose, shioze** sea current, tidal flow

3a16.4

瀕 瀕

HIN draw near; shore

——————— 1 ———————
- 0 瀕する **hin(suru)** be on the verge of
- 6 瀕死 **hinshi** on the verge of death

3a16.5

潴 潴潴

CHO pool, puddle

潜 → 潜 3a12.6

3a16.6

瀟

SHŌ pure, fresh; heavy rain and wind

——————— 1 ———————
- 9 瀟洒 **shōsha** elegant, stylish

3a16.7

瀛

EI ocean; swamp

3a16.8

瀘

RO (name of a river in China)

3a16.9

瀝

REKI drip, trickle; filter

——————— 1 ———————
- 8 瀝青 **rekisei** pitch, bitumen, asphalt
  瀝青炭 **rekiseitan** bituminous/soft coal

——————— 2 ———————
- 3 土瀝青 **dorekisei** asphalt
- 8 披瀝 **hireki** express (one's opinion)

——————— 17 ———————

3a17.1

瀲

REN brimming; rippling

瀨 → 瀨 3a16.4

3a17.2

瀰

BI copious flow; broad, extensive

——————— 1 ———————
- 14 瀰漫 **biman** pervade, permeate, diffuse

3a17.3

灌 漼

KAN, soso(gu) pour, let flow

——————— 1 ———————
- 4 灌仏会 **kanbutsue** Buddha's-birthday
  celebration (April 8)

灌水　**kansui**　sprinkling, irrigation
灌木　**kanboku**　shrub, bush
13 灌腸　**kanchō**　enema
15 灌漑　**kangai**　irrigation

—————— 2 ——————

12 湯灌　**yukan**　washing a body for burial

3a17.4

瀾

RAN waves

—————— 2 ——————

7 狂瀾　**kyōran**　raging waves
8 波瀾　**haran**　waves; commotion; wide
　　　fluctuations
　波瀾万丈　**haran-banjō**　full of ups and
　　　downs, stormy, checkered

—————— 18 ——————

灘 → 灘　3a19.1

—————— 19 ——————

3a19.1

灘　灘

TAN, DAN, nada　open sea

3a19.2

灑

SHA, SAI　sprinkle, wash; free and easy

—————— 1 ——————

12 灑落　**sharaku**　free and easy, unconstrained

—————— 22 ——————

灣 → 湾　3a9.15

3

氵 19←
扌
扌
口
女
巾
犭
弓
彳
彡
艹
⺌
山
宀
广
尸
口

—————————— 土 3b ——————————

土	圠	去	赱	地	圭	屾	圷	寺	吉	至	先	在
0.1	2.1	2.2	3b4.9	3.1	3.2	3.3	3.4	3.5	3p3.1	3.6	3.7	3.8
坊	坎	址	坏	圻	坑	坂	均	走	赤	坐	坤	坩
4.1	4.2	4.3	4.4	4.5	4.6	4.7	4.8	4.9	4.10	4.11	5.1	5.2
坡	坪	垉	坼	坿	坦	幸	坌	城	垠	垢	垳	垣
5.3	5.4	5.5	5.6	5.7	5.8	5.9	5.10	6.1	6.2	6.3	6.4	6.5
垰	垤	垓	垪	垬	型	奎	封	赴	埔	埋	垜	埒
6.6	6.7	6.8	6.9	6.10	6.11	6.12	6.13	6.14	7.1	7.2	7.3	3b7.4
埒	埆	埃	恚	袁	盍	赳	起	堆	埀	堵	域	堋
7.4	7.5	7.6	7.7	7.8	7.9	7.10	7.11	8.1	8.2	3b9.2	8.3	8.4
埠	培	埦	埼	崒	埴	堀	基	堊	埜	堕	執	堪
8.5	8.6	8.7	8.8	8.9	8.10	8.11	8.12	8.13	0a11.5	8.14	8.15	9.1
堵	堯	埴	堺	埋	壻	場	堤	堝	塔	塚	塀	堰
9.2	9.3	9.4	9.5	2r6.2	3e9.3	9.6	9.7	9.8	9.9	9.10	9.11	9.12
堅	堡	釐	報	赧	超	趁	越	喪	塢	塊	塙	塩
9.13	9.14	9.15	9.16	9.17	9.18	9.19	4n8.2	9.20	10.1	10.2	10.3	10.4
塚	塡	塘	塾	塑	塒	塗	漥	塋	嗇	越	毀	塲
3b9.10	10.5	10.6	10.7	10.8	10.9	10.10	10.11	10.12	10.13	4n8.2	10.14	3b9.6
境	墟	増	塀	墮	墨	塹	墅	墜	赫	臺	甄	増
11.1	11.2	11.3	3b9.11	3b8.14	11.4	11.5	11.6	11.7	11.8	3d2.11	11.9	3b11.3
墳	墫	墫	墟	堚	墨	舗	鞋	墺	墻	壞	壤	壇
12.1	12.2	4a12.19	3b11.2	12.3	3b11.4	12.4	3k12.18	13.1	13.2	13.3	13.4	13.5

墾	壁	壚	墻	壕	壑	壓	趨	牆	壙	翹	壜	壞
13.6	13.7	14.1	14.2	14.3	14.4	2p3.1	14.5	14.6	15.1	15.2	16.1	3b13.3

壟	壤	壩	釄
16.2	3b13.4	3q12.5	3r21.1

———— 0 ————

3b0.1 / 24

土 **DO** earth, soil, ground; Saturday
　 TO, tsuchi earth, soil, ground

———— 1 ————

2 土人 **dojin** native, aborigine
　土人形 **tsuchi ningyō** clay figure/doll
3 土工 **dokō** earthwork; construction laborer
　土下座 **dogeza** bow while kneeling
4 土不踏 **tsuchifumazu** the arch of the foot
　土手 **dote** embankment, dike, levee
　土木 **doboku** civil engineering, public works
　土方 **dokata** construction laborer
5 土左衛門 **dozaemon** drowned person
　土民 **domin** natives, aborigines
　土用 **doyō** dog days, midsummer
　土用干 **doyōbo(shi)** summer airing (of clothes)
　土台 **dodai** foundation, groundwork; utterly
　土石 **doseki** cement
6 土気色 **tsuchike-iro** earth color
　土色 **tsuchi-iro** earth-color, ashen
　土地 **tochi** land
　土地柄 **tochigara** (nature of) the land
　土団子 **tsuchidango** mud pie
　土百姓 **dobyakushō** dirt farmer, peasant
　土耳古 **Toruko** Turkey
7 土佐 **Tosa** (ancient kuni, Kōchi-ken)
　土牢 **tsuchirō** underground prison, dungeon
　土足 **dosoku** shoes, footwear; feet with shoes on
　土足厳禁 **dosoku genkin** Remove Shoes
8 土建屋 **doken'ya** contractor
　土建業 **dokengyō** civil engineering and construction
　土金属 **dokinzoku** earth/terrigenous metals
9 土俗 **dozoku** local customs
　土俗学 **dozokugaku** folklore, ethnography
　土星 **dosei** Saturn
　土砂 **dosha** earth and sand
　土砂降 **doshabu(ri)** downpour
　土砂崩 **doshakuzu(re)** landslide, washout
　土臭 **tsuchikusa(i)** smelling of dirt; peasantly, rustic
10 土俵 **dohyō** the sumo ring; sandbag
　土俵入 **dohyōi(ri)** display of sumo wrestlers in the ring

土俵際 **dohyōgiwa** at the brink, critical moment
　土倉 **tsuchigura** underground storehouse
　土匪 **dohi** rebellious natives
　土竜 **mogura** mole
　土被 **tsuchikaburi** (white mushroom, diameter 4–18 cm); overburden, earth cover
11 土偶 **dogū** clay figure
　土瓶 **dobin** earthen teapot
　土黒 **tsuchiguro(i)** dark dirt color
　土産 **miyage** souvenir, present
　土産話 **miyagebanashi** story of one's travels
12 土着 **dochaku** native, indigenous
　土着民 **dochakumin** natives, aborigines
　土塀 **dobei** mud wall
　土葬 **dosō** interment, burial
　土焼 **tsuchiya(ki)** unglazed earthenware
　土筆 **tsukushi** field horsetail
　土間 **doma** room with a dirt floor
13 土塊 **dokai, tsuchikure** lump of earth, clod
　土煙 **tsuchi kemuri** cloud of dust
14 土製 **dosei** earthen, terra cotta
　土管 **dokan** earthen pipe, drainage tiles
　土語 **dogo** native tongue, dialect
15 土器 **doki, kawarake** unglazed earthenware, crockery
　土蔵 **dozō** storehouse, godown
　土質 **doshitsu** nature of the soil
　土踏 **tsuchifu(mazu)** the arch of the foot
16 土壌 **dojō** soil
　土壇場 **dotanba** place of execution, eleventh hour
　土龍 **mogura** mole
17 土鍋 **donabe** earthen pot
18 土曜 **doyō** Saturday
　土曜日 **doyōbi** Saturday
19 土瀝青 **dorekisei** asphalt
20 土饅頭 **domanjū** grave mound
22 土嚢 **donō** sandbag

———— 2 ————

3 寸土 **sundo** an inch of land
4 辺土 **hendo** remote region
　手土産 **temiyage** visitor's present
　心土 **shindo** subsoil
5 本土 **hondo** mainland
　平土間 **hiradoma** pit, orchestra (in a theater)
　白土 **shiratsuchi** kaolin; mortar
6 西土 **seido** western lands

全土 **zendo** the whole country
邦土 **hōdo** country, territory
安土桃山 **Azuchi-Momoyama** Azuchi-Momoyama (era, 1568–ca. 1603)
7 沃土 **yokudo** fertile land/soil
赤土 **akatsuchi** red clay/loam
希土 **kido** rare earth (element)
8 泥土 **deido** mud
苦土 **kudo** magnesia
底土 **sokotsuchi** subsoil
肥土 **ko(e)tsuchi** rich/fertile soil
9 風土 **fūdo** natural features, climate
風土病 **fūdobyō** endemic disease
風土記 **fudoki** description of the natural features of a region, a topography
浄土 **jōdo** pure land, (Buddhist) paradise
浄土宗 **Jōdoshu** the Jodo sect (of Buddhism)
浄土真宗 **Jōdo Shinshū** (a Buddhist sect, offshoot of the Jodo sect)
浄土教 **jōdokyō** Buddhist teachings concerning the Pure Land
封土 **hōdo** fief
荒土 **kōdo** wasteland
客土 **kyakudo, kakudo** topsoil brought in from elsewhere
砂土 **sado, shado** sandy soil
10 耕土 **kōdo** arable soil
凍土 **tōdo** frozen soil, tundra
陶土 **tōdo** potter's clay, kaolin
郷土 **kyōdo** one's native place; local
郷土文学 **kyōdo bungaku** local literature
郷土史 **kyōdoshi** local history
郷土色 **kyōdoshoku** local color
郷土愛 **kyōdoai** love for one's home province
冥土 **meido** hades, realm of the dead
差土 **sa(shi)tsuchi** (adding) flowerbed soil
唐土 **Tōdo** China, Cathay
珪土 **keido** silica
11 捲土重来 **kendo-chōrai/jūrai** comeback (from a defeat with renewed vigor)
黄土 **ōdo, kōdo** yellow ocher, loess
黒土 **kokudo, kurotsuchi** black soil
産土神 **ubusunagami** tutelary deity, genius loci
盛土 **mo(ri)tsuchi** raising the ground level
粘土 **nendo, nebatsuchi** clay
12 稀土 **kido** rare earth
焦土 **shōdo** scorched earth
13 漢土 **Kando** China
楽土 **rakudo** a paradise
置土 **o(ki)tsuchi** earth (from elsewhere) put on top
置土産 **o(ki)miyage** parting gift, souvenir
14 磁土 **jido** kaolin
痩土 **ya(se)tsuchi** barren soil
緑土 **ryokudo** green earth

領土 **ryōdo** territory
16 壁土 **kabetsuchi** wall mud, plaster, stucco
赭土 **shado** red ocher
17 糞土 **fundo** black earth; dirt, filth
18 覆土 **fukudo** covering (seeds) with soil
20 礬土 **hando, bando** alumina

―――――― 3 ――――――

7 沖積土 **chūsekido** alluvial soil
10 珪藻土 **keisōdo** diatomaceous earth, kieselguhr
紙粘土 **kaminendo** clay made from newsprint
14 腐葉土 **fuyōdo** soil from decayed fallen leaves, leaf mold
腐植土 **fushokudo** humus

―――――― 4 ――――――

6 西方浄土 **Saihō Jōdo** (Buddhist) Western Paradise
9 荒木田土 **araki-datsuchi** (a reddish clayey soil)
11 寂光浄土 **jakkō-jōdo** (Buddhist) paradise
12 極楽浄土 **gokuraku jōdo** (Buddhist) paradise
14 酸性白土 **sansei hakudo** acid/Kambara clay

―――――― 2 ――――――

3b2.1

坝 **iri** sluice, spout, floodgate, penstock

3b2.2 / 414

去 **KYO, KO, sa(ru)** leave, move away; pass, elapse

―――――― 1 ――――――

6 去年 **kyonen, kozo** last year
12 去就 **kyoshū** course of action, attitude
13 去勢 **kyosei** castrate

―――――― 2 ――――――

5 立去 **ta(chi)sa(ru)** leave, go away
6 死去 **shikyo** die
7 走去 **hashi(ri)sa(ru)** run away
抜去 **nu(ki)sa(ru)** overtake, surpass
吹去 **fu(ki)sa(ru)** blow away (intr.)
8 退去 **taikyo** leave, withdraw, evacuate
逃去 **ni(ge)sa(ru)** flee, disappear
取去 **to(ri)sa(ru)** take away, remove
9 飛去 **to(bi)sa(ru)** fly away/off
除去 **jokyo** remove, eliminate
連去 **tsu(re)sa(ru)** lead away
逝去 **seikyo** death
持去 **mo(chi)sa(ru)** carry away, make off with
拭去 **nugu(i)sa(ru)** wipe off, clear away

3

氵
土 2←
扌
口
女
巾
犭
弓
彳
彡
艹
宀
⺌
山
耂
广
尸
口

10 消去 **shōkyo** eliminate, cancel out
11 運去 **hako(bi)sa(ru)** carry away/off
過去 **kako** the past   **su(gi)sa(ru)** pass
過去完了 **kako kanryō** past perfect tense
過去帳 **kakochō** death register
捨去 **su(te)sa(ru)** forsake
12 遠去 **tōza(karu)** become more distant, recede into the distance
廃去 **haikyo** abandon
13 辞去 **jikyo** take one's leave
置去 **o(ki)za(ri)** desert, leave in the lurch
15 撤去 **tekkyo** withdraw, evacuate, remove
16 薨去 **kōkyo** death, demise

——————— 3 ———————

3 大過去 **daikako** past perfect tense, pluperfect
5 半過去 **hankako** imperfect tense
9 則天去私 **sokuten-kyoshi** selfless devotion to justice

走 → 走 3b4.9

——————— 3 ———————

3b3.1 / 118

地   **CHI** earth, land   **JI** ground, land, earth; texture, fabric; field (of a flag), background; natural (voice); respectability; musical accompaniment; in actuality; narrative part

——————— 1 ———————

0 地べた **ji(beta)** the ground/earth
2 地力 **chiryoku** fertility
3 地上 **chijō** (on the) ground/surface; in this world
地上軍 **chijōgun** ground forces
地下 **chika** underground; basement
地下水 **chikasui** underground water
地下牢 **chikarō** underground dungeon
地下足袋 **jika tabi** split-toed heavy-cloth work shoes
地下茎 **chikakei** rhizome
地下室 **chikashitsu** basement, cellar
地下道 **chikadō** underground passage
地下街 **chikagai** underground shopping mall
地下鉄 **chikatetsu** subway
地下線 **chikasen** underground cable/wire
地口 **jiguchi** play on words, pun
地山 **jiyama** natural ground
4 地元 **jimoto** local
地中 **chichū** underground, subterranean
地中海 **Chichūkai** the Mediterranean Sea
地文学 **chimongaku, chibungaku** physical geography
地辷 **jisube(ri)** landslide

地区 **chiku** district, area, zone
地引 **jibi(ki)** seine fishing
地引網 **jibi(ki)ami** dragnet, seine
地方 **chihō** region, area   **jikata** rural locality
地方色 **chihōshoku** local color
地方版 **chihōban** local edition
地方税 **chihōzei** local taxes
地心 **chishin** center of the earth
5 地代 **jidai** land rent
地平面 **chiheimen** horizontal plane
地平線 **chiheisen** the horizon
地主 **jinushi** landlord
地目 **chimoku** land category
6 地曳 **jibi(ki)** seine fishing
地曳網 **jibi(ki)ami** dragnet, seine
地合 **jia(i)** texture, weave, fabric
地色 **ji-iro** ground-color
地名 **chimei** place name
地回 **jimawa(ri)** from the vicinity, local; a street tough
地団駄踏 **jidanda (o) fu(mu)** stamp one's feet
地肌 **jihada** texture; skin; surface of the ground
地衣 **chii** lichen
地虫 **jimushi** grub, ground beetle
7 地位 **chii** position, status
地役権 **chiekiken** easement, (real) servitude
地形 **chikei** topography, terrain   **jigyō** ground leveling, groundwork
地形学 **chikeigaku** topography
地形図 **chikeizu** topographical/relief map
地学 **chigaku** physical geography
地声 **jigoe** one's natural voice
地図 **chizu** map
8 地表 **chihyō** surface of the earth
地価 **chika** land value/prices
地坪 **jitsubo** land/ground area
地味 **jimi** plain, subdued, undemonstrative, conservative   **chimi** (fertility of) the soil
地歩 **chiho** one's footing/standing/position
地底 **chitei** bowels of the earth
地固 **jigata(me)** ground leveling/preparation
地所 **jisho** (tract/plot of) land, ground
地取 **jido(ri)** layout of (a town)
地金 **jigane** metal, bullion; one's true character
9 地変 **chihen** natural calamity
地点 **chiten** spot, point, position
地持 **jimo(chi)** landowner
地狭 **chikyō** isthmus
地面 **jimen** ground, surface, land
地相 **chisō** (divination by) the lay of the land
地祇 **chigi** earthly deities
地政学 **chiseigaku** geopolitics
地界 **chikai** boundary
10 地酒 **jizake** locally brewed saké

地唄 **jiuta** ballad, folk song
地唄舞 **jiutamai** a traditional Kyōto dance performed to the accompaniment of *jiuta*
地帯 **chitai** zone, area, region, belt
地核 **chikaku** the earth's core
地租 **chiso** land tax
11 地動説 **chidōsetsu** heliocentric/Copernican theory
地道 **jimichi** steady, honest, fair, sober-minded
地域 **chiiki** region, area, zone
地域的 **chiikiteki** local, regional
地域差 **chiikisa** regional differences
地殻 **chikaku** the earth's crust
地理 **chiri** geography
地理学 **chirigaku** geography
地理学者 **chirigakusha** geographer
地球 **chikyū** earth, globe
地球儀 **chikyūgi** a globe of the world
12 地割 **jiwa(re)** fissure, crack in the ground
　　 jiwa(ri) allotment of land
地温 **chion** soil/ground temperature
地場 **jiba** local(ly owned)
地裁 **chisai** district court (short for 地方裁判所)
地税 **chizei** land tax
地軸 **chijiku** the earth's axis
13 地勢 **chisei** geographical features
地滑 **jisube(ri)** landslide
地蜂 **jibachi** digger wasp
地雷 **jirai** land mine
14 地獄 **jigoku** hell
地層 **chisō** stratum, layer
地模様 **jimoyō** background pattern
地磁気 **chijiki** the earth's magnetism
地誌 **chishi** topographical description
15 地蔵 **Jizō** (a Buddhist guardian deity of children)
地蔵顔 **jizōgao** plump cheerful face
地熱 **chinetsu, jinetsu** geothermal
地盤 **jiban** the ground; footing, base, constituency
地質 **chishitsu** geology, geological features; nature of the soil
　　 jishitsu quality/texture (of cloth)
地質学 **chishitsugaku** geology
地質図 **chishitsuzu** geological map
地震 **jishin** earthquake
地震学 **jishingaku** seismology
地震国 **jishinkoku** earthquake-prone country
地震計 **jishinkei** seismometer
地震帯 **jishintai** earthquake belt/zone
16 地積 **chiseki** land area, acreage
地頭 **jitō** lord of a manor
18 地鎮祭 **jichinsai** ground-breaking ceremony
19 地響 **jihibi(ki)** rumbling of the ground, earth tremor
20 地籍 **chiseki** land register

─────── 2 ───────

3 寸地 **sunchi** an inch of land
大地 **daichi** the ground, the (solid) earth
大地主 **ōjinushi** large landowner
大地震 **ōjishin, daijishin** major earthquake
下地 **shitaji** groundwork; aptitude for; first coat(ing)
土地 **tochi** land
土地柄 **tochigara** (nature of) the land
山地 **sanchi, yamachi** mountainous area
4 天地 **tenchi, ametsuchi** heaven and earth, all nature; top and bottom; world, realm, sphere
天地人 **tenchijin** heaven, earth, and man
天地万物 **tenchi-banbutsu** the whole universe, all creation
天地神明 **tenchi-shinmei** the gods of heaven and earth
天地創造 **tenchi sōzō** the Creation
内地 **naichi** inland; homeland; mainland
内地人 **naichijin** homelanders; people on Honshū
内地米 **naichimai** homegrown rice
切地 **ki(re)ji** fabric, cloth, material
辺地 **henchi** remote/out-of-the-way place
心地 **kokochi(yoi)** pleasant, comfortable
5 凹地 **ōchi** hollow, basin, depression
失地 **shitchi** lost territory
生地 **seichi** birthplace **kiji** cloth, material; one's true colors; unadorned
生地獄 **i(ki)jigoku** a living hell
平地 **heichi, hirachi** flatland, level ground, plain
外地 **gaichi** overseas (territory)
用地 **yōchi** land for some use, lot, site
台地 **daichi** plateau, tableland, height
布地 **nunoji** cloth
白地 **shiroji** white cloth/ground, blank
白地図 **hakuchizu** outline/contour map
石地蔵 **ishi Jizō** stone image of Jizo
立地 **ritchi** location, site selection
田地 **denchi, denji** paddy field, farmland
6 死地 **shichi** the jaws of death, fatal situation
任地 **ninchi** one's post, place of appointment
全地方 **zenchihō** the whole region
危地 **kichi** dangerous position, peril
近地点 **kinchiten** perigee
同地 **dōchi** the same place, that place
宅地 **takuchi** residential land
当地 **tōchi** this place, this part of the country
団地 **danchi** (public) housing development, apartment complex
各地 **kakuchi** every area; various places
7 低地 **teichi** low-lying ground, lowlands
余地 **yochi** room, place, margin, scope
沃地 **yokuchi** fertile land/soil
沢地 **sawachi** swampland, marshes, bog

3

氵
土 3←
扌
口
女
巾
犭
弓
彳
彡
艹
宀
⺍
山
士
广
尸
口

3

赤地 **akaji** red fabric; red (back)ground
折地図 **o(ri)chizu** folding map
芯地 **shinji** padding
局地 **kyokuchi** locality
局地化 **kyokuchika** localization
局地戦争 **kyokuchi sensō** limited war
見地 **kenchi** viewpoint, standpoint
車地 **shachi** capstan, windlass
8 厚地 **atsuji** thick cloth/fabric
泊地 **hakuchi** anchorage, berth
沼地 **numachi, shōchi** marshes, swampland
泥地 **deichi** swamp, marsh, mire, morass
拓地 **takuchi** opening up land (to cultivation)
実地 **jitchi** practical, on-site, in the field
官地 **kanchi** government land
空地 **a(ki)chi** vacant lot/land
服地 **fukuji** cloth, fabric, material
青地 **aoji** blue cloth/material/fabric
牧地 **bokuchi** grazing land, pasture
金地金 **kin jigane** gold bullion
門地 **monchi** lineage, family status
9 飛地 **to(bi)chi** detached land/territory, enclave
陣地 **jinchi** position, encampment
陣地戦 **jinchisen** position/stationary warfare
盆地 **bonchi** basin, round valley
浄地 **jōchi** sacred grounds
封地 **hōchi** fief
要地 **yōchi** important/strategic place
草地 **kusachi, sōchi** grassland, meadow
荒地 **a(re)chi** wasteland
畑地 **hatachi** farmland
砂地 **sunaji** sandy place/soil
10 耕地 **kōchi** arable/cultivated land
借地 **shakuchi, ka(ri)chi** leased land
陸地 **rikuchi** land
高地 **kōchi** high ground, highlands, plateau
埋地 **u(me)chi** reclaimed land
帯地 **obiji** sash material, obi cloth
素地 **sochi** groundwork, the makings of
料地 **ryōchi** preserve, estate
11 培地 **baichi** (bacteria) culture ground/ medium
基地 **kichi** (military) base
接地 **setchi** (electrical) ground(ing), earth
黒地 **kuroji** black background/cloth
現地 **genchi** the actual place; on the scene, in the field, local
産地 **sanchi** producing area
裂地 **kireji** fabric, cloth, material
紺地 **konji** dark-blue ground (cloth)
転地 **tenchi** change of air/scene
転地療養 **tenchi ryōyō** getting away for a change of climate for one's health
12 蛮地 **banchi** barbaric region
着地 **chakuchi** landing (in gymnastics)
測地 **sokuchi** land surveying, geodetic

測地学 **sokuchigaku** geodesy
湿地 **shitchi** damp ground, bog
寒地 **kanchi** cold region
属地 **zokuchi** territory, possession
極地 **kyokuchi** polar (regions)
検地 **kenchi** land surveying
勝地 **shōchi** scenic spot
無地 **muji** solid color
番地 **banchi** lot/house number
奥地 **okuchi** the interior, hinterland
貴地 **kichi** your place, there
貸地 **ka(shi)chi** land/lot for rent
13 裏地 **uraji** lining (cloth)
農地 **nōchi** farmland
農地改革 **nōchi kaikaku** agrarian reform
適地 **tekichi** suitable site/land
墓地 **bochi** cemetery
聖地 **seichi** the Holy Land; sacred ground
戦地 **senchi** battlefield, the front
意地 **iji** temperament; will power; obstinacy
意地汚 **ijikitana(i)** greedy, gluttonous
意地張 **iji(p)pa(ri)** obstinate (person)
意地悪 **ijiwaru(i)** ill-tempered, crabby
新地 **shinchi** new/reclaimed land
絹地 **kinuji** silk cloth
路地 **roji** alley, lane, path
14 境地 **kyōchi** state, stage, field, environment
窪地 **kubochi** low ground, hollow, depression
瘦地 **ya(se)chi** barren soil, unproductive land
緑地 **ryokuchi** green tract of land
緑地帯 **ryokuchitai** greenbelt
銀地 **ginji** silvery background
領地 **ryōchi** territory
15 僻地 **hekichi** remote place
蕃地 **banchi** barbaric region
窮地 **kyūchi** predicament
敷地 **shikichi** site, lot
敵地 **tekichi** enemy territory
霊地 **reichi** hallowed ground
16 薄地 **usuji** thin (cloth/metal)
整地 **seichi** ground leveling; soil preparation
築地 **tsukiji** reclaimed land
tsuiji roofed mud wall
錨地 **byōchi** anchorage
18 臨地 **rinchi** on-site, on-the-spot
織地 **o(ri)ji** texture; fabric
19 蟻地獄 **arijigoku** antlion, doodlebug
20 驀地 **masshigura** headlong, at full tilt
21 露地 **roji** the bare ground

─────── 3 ───────

1 一頭地抜 **ittōchi (o) nu(ku)** stand head and shoulders above others
2 人文地理 **jinbun chiri, jinmon chiri** anthropogeography
人心地 **hitogokochi** consciousness

3 三業地 **sangyōchi** licensed red-light district
工業地 **kōgyōchi** industrial area
工業地帯 **kōgyō chitai** industrial area
干拓地 **kantakuchi** reclaimed land, innings
小天地 **shōtenchi** small world, microcosm
小作地 **kosakuchi** tenant farm land
4 天長地久 **tenchō-chikyū** coeval with heaven and earth
天変地異 **tenpen-chii** cataclysm
中心地 **chūshinchi** center, metropolis
中国地方 **Chūgoku chihō** the Chūgoku region (Hiroshima, Okayama, Shimane, Tottori, and Yamaguchi prefectures)
片意地 **kata-iji** stubborn, bigoted
分県地図 **bunken chizu** maps grouped by prefecture
分譲地 **bunjōchi** a subdivision
公有地 **kōyūchi** public land
水害地 **suigaichi** flood-stricken area
水源地 **suigenchi** headwaters, source
5 北陸地方 **Hokuriku chihō** the Hokuriku region (Fukui, Ishikawa, Toyama, Niigata prefectures)
出生地 **shusshōchi, shusseichi** birthplace
出身地 **shusshinchi** native place, birthplace
本籍地 **honsekichi** one's legal domicile
生産地 **seisanchi** producing region
市街地 **shigaichi** urban district
占領地 **senryōchi** occupied territory
主産地 **shusanchi** chief producing region
立脚地 **rikkyakuchi** position, standpoint
目的地 **mokutekichi** destination
6 休閑地 **kyūkanchi** land lying fallow
行楽地 **kōrakuchi** pleasure resort
共有地 **kyōyūchi** public land, a common
安全地帯 **anzen chitai** safety zone/island
有租地 **yūsochi** taxable land
有感地震 **yūkan jishin** earthquake strong enough to feel
7 住心地 **su(mi)gokochi** livability, comfort
住宅地 **jūtakuchi** residential area/land
別天地 **bettenchi** another world
対蹠地 **taisekichi** the antipodes
災害地 **saigaichi** disaster-stricken area
私有地 **shiyūchi** private land
8 依怙地 **ikoji, ekoji** obstinacy, stubbornness
泥炭地 **deitanchi** peat bog
官有地 **kan'yūchi** government land
定住地 **teijūchi** fixed/permanent abode
空閑地 **kūkanchi** vacant land
底意地悪 **sokoiji waru(i)** spiteful, malcontented, cranky
居心地 **igokochi** comfortableness, coziness
居住地 **kyojūchi** place of residence
居留地 **kyoryūchi** settlement, concession
国有地 **kokuyūchi** national land

牧羊地 **bokuyōchi** sheep meadow
牧草地 **bokusōchi** pasture, grazing land
放牧地 **hōbokuchi** grazing land, pasture
所在地 **shozaichi** seat, location
所有地 **shoyūchi** the land one owns
所番地 **tokorobanchi** address
9 発祥地 **hasshōchi** cradle, birthplace
乗心地 **no(ri)gokochi** riding comfort
保養地 **hoyōchi** health resort
前任地 **zenninchi** one's former post
赴任地 **funinchi** one's place of appointment
狩猟地 **shuryōchi** hunting grounds
後進地域 **kōshin chiiki** underdeveloped region
荒廃地 **kōhaichi** wasteland, devastated area
食意地 **ku(i)iji** gluttony
10 耕作地 **kōsakuchi** arable/cultivated land
候補地 **kōhochi** proposed site
原産地 **gensanchi** place of origin, home, habitat
遊園地 **yūenchi** amusement/theme park
遊覧地 **yūranchi** pleasure resort, tourist point
流刑地 **ryūkeichi** penal colony
流行地 **ryūkōchi** infected district
埋立地 **u(me)ta(te)chi** reclaimed land
根拠地 **konkyochi** base (of operations)
扇状地 **senjōchi** alluvial fan, delta
租借地 **soshakuchi** leased territory
被害地 **higaichi** the stricken area
11 野営地 **yaeichi** camping ground
商業地 **shōgyōchi** business district
寄留地 **kiryūchi** one's temporary residence
酔心地 **yo(i)gokochi** pleasant drunken feeling
12 着尺地 **kijakuji** standard-length kimono cloth
着心地 **kigokochi** fit and feel (of clothes)
着陸地 **chakurikuchi** landing zone
揺籃地 **yōran (no) chi** the cradle of, birthplace
御用地 **goyōchi** imperial estate
御料地 **goryōchi** imperial estate, crown land
棲息地 **seisokuchi** habitat
植民地 **shokuminchi** colony
植民地化 **shokuminchika** colonization
無人地帯 **mujin chitai** no man's land
無間地獄 **muken jigoku** (a Buddhist hell)
策源地 **sakugenchi** base of operations
集散地 **shūsanchi** trading center, entrepôt
焦熱地獄 **shōnetsu jigoku** an inferno
開墾地 **kaikonchi** cultivated land
13 農牧地 **nōbokuchi** crop and grazing land
滞在地 **taizaichi** where one is living
夢心地 **yumegokochi** trance, ecstasy
寝心地 **negokochi** sleeping comfort
楽天地 **rakutenchi** a paradise; amusement center
戦災地 **sensaichi** war-ravaged area
碇泊地 **teihakuchi** anchorage, berth

3

氵
土 3←
扌
口
女
巾
犭
弓
彳
彡
艹
宀
⺍
山
土
广
尸
口

意気地 **ikuji (no nai), ikiji (no nai)** weak, spineless, helpless
新境地 **shinkyōchi** new area, fresh ground
試験地獄 **shiken jigoku** the hell of (entrance) exams
鉱産地 **kōsanchi** mineral-rich area
15 養蚕地 **yōsanchi** silkworm-raising district
避寒地 **hikanchi** winter resort
避暑地 **hishochi** summer resort
横意地 **yoko-iji** perverseness, obstinacy
震災地 **shinsaichi** quake-stricken area
震源地 **shingenchi** epicenter
駐屯地 **chūtonchi** (army) post
19 爆心地 **bakushinchi** center of the explosion

——————— 4 ———————
3 山間僻地 **sankan-hekichi** secluded mountain recesses
9 軍事基地 **gunji kichi** military base
10 俯仰天地 **fugyōtenchi** (nothing to be ashamed of) before God or man
航空基地 **kōkū kichi** air base
15 震天動地 **shinten-dōchi** (heaven-and-)earth-shaking
22 驚天動地 **kyōten-dōchi** earth-shaking, astounding

——————— 5 ———————
17 環太平洋地震帯 **kan-Taiheiyō jishintai** circum-Pacific seismic zone

3b3.2

圭 **KEI** corner, angle; jewel

——————— 2 ———————
2 刀圭 **tōkei** medicine
刀圭家 **tōkeika** physician

3b3.3

址 **mama** steep slope

3b3.4

圫 **akutsu** low-lying land

3b3.5 / 41

寺 **JI, tera** temple

——————— 1 ———————
2 寺子屋 **terakoya** temple primary school
6 寺守 **teramori** temple sexton

7 寺社 **jisha** temples and shrines
寺男 **teraotoko** temple sexton
8 寺参 **teramai(ri)** go to a temple to worship
9 寺院 **jiin** temple

——————— 2 ———————
3 大寺院 **daijiin** large temple
山寺 **yamadera** mountain temple
4 氏寺 **ujidera** clan temple
仏寺 **butsuji** Buddhist temple
5 末寺 **matsuji** branch temple
古寺 **koji, furudera** old temple
尼寺 **amadera** convent
7 社寺 **shaji** shrines and temples
13 禅寺 **zendera** Zen temple

——————— 3 ———————
8 国分寺 **kokubunji** (ancient) state-established provincial temple
金閣寺 **Kinkakuji** Temple of the Golden Pavilion
11 菩提寺 **bodaiji** one's family's temple
14 銀閣寺 **Ginkakuji** (temple in Kyōto)
17 檀那寺 **dannadera** one's family's temple

——————— 4 ———————
6 西本願寺 **Nishi Honganji** (main temple, in Kyōto, of Jōdo sect)

吉 → 吉 3p3.1

3b3.6 / 902

至 **SHI** utmost; (as prefix) to, until (place/time) **ita(ru)** arrive, lead to, attain **ita(ranai)** not good enough, inexperienced, careless **ita(tte)** very

——————— 1 ———————
2 至人 **shijin** man of utmost spiritual/moral cultivation
3 至大 **shidai** greatest possible, enormous
至上 **shijō** supreme, highest
至上命令 **shijō meirei** supreme/inviolable command; categorical imperative
至上権 **shijōken** supremacy, sovereignty
4 至公 **shikō** utmost fairness
至公至平 **shikō-shihei** utterly just
至心 **shishin** sincerity
6 至孝 **shikō** utmost filial piety
至近 **shikin** very near
至近弾 **shikindan** near miss
至当 **shitō** proper, fair, reasonable
至尽 **ita(reri)-tsu(kuseri)** complete, thorough
7 至妙 **shimyō** extremely skillful
至芸 **shigei** consummate artistic skill
至言 **shigen** wise saying

8 至幸 **shikō** supreme/utter happiness
至宝 **shihō** most valuable treasure
至所 **ita(ru) tokoro** everywhere
9 至便 **shiben** very convenient
至点 **shiten** solstice/equinoctial point
至急 **shikyū** urgent
至急便 **shikyūbin** express mail
至急報 **shikyūhō** urgent telegram/call
至要 **shiyō** essential, of paramount importance
10 至高 **shikō** supreme, sublime, highest
至高善 **shikōzen** the highest good
至純 **shijun** of absolute purity
11 至情 **shijō** sincerity
12 至善 **shizen** the highest good
至尊 **shison** His Majesty the Emperor
至極 **shigoku** very, quite, most
13 至楽 **shiraku** utmost pleasure
至福 **shifuku** supreme bliss, beatitude
至誠 **shisei** sincerity, heart and soul
15 至論 **shiron** very convincing argument
18 至難 **shinan** extreme difficulty

───────── 2 ─────────

5 冬至 **tōji** winter solstice
冬至線 **tōjisen** the Tropic of Capricorn
立至 **ta(chi)ita(ru)** come to, be reduced to
6 自…至… **ji...shi...** from (place/date) to (place/date)
10 夏至 **geshi** summer solstice
夏至線 **geshisen** the Tropic of Cancer

───────── 3 ─────────

6 至公至平 **shikō-shihei** utterly just
7 芸術至上主義 **geijutsushijō shugi** art for art's sake
10 恋愛至上主義 **ren'ai-shijō shugi** love for love's sake

3b3.7 / 50

先 SEN the future; priority, precedence
saki tip, point, end; (in the) lead; first priority; ahead; the future; previous, recent; objective, destination; sequel, the rest; the other party **ma(zu)** first (of all); nearly; anyway, well

───────── 1 ─────────

0 先んじる/んずる **saki(njiru/nzuru)** precede; anticipate, forestall
2 先入主 **sennyūshu** preconception, preoccupation, prejudice
先入観 **sennyūkan** preconception, preoccupation, prejudice
先人 **senjin** predecessor
3 先々 **sakizaki** the distant future; places one goes to; beforehand
先々月 **sensengetsu** the month before last

先口 **senkuchi** previous engagement/application
4 先太 **sakibuto** thicker toward the end, club-shaped
先天的 **sententeki** inborn, congenital, hereditary
先天性 **sentensei** congenital, hereditary
先手 **sente** the first move; the initiative
sakite front lines, vanguard
先月 **sengetsu** last month
先日 **senjitsu** the other day
先日付 **sakihizu(ke)** postdating, dating forward
先方 **senpō** the other party; destination
sakikata the other party
5 先生 **sensei** teacher, master, doctor
先史学 **senshigaku** prehistory
先代 **sendai** predecessor (in the family line); previous age/generation
先払 **sakibara(i)** advance payment; payment on delivery; forerunner
先立 **sakida(tsu)** go before, precede; die before; take precedence
6 先年 **sennen** former years; a few years ago
先任 **sennin** seniority
先任者 **senninsha** predecessor
先考 **senkō** one's late father
先先 **ma(zu)ma(zu)** tolerably
sakizaki the distant future; places one goes to; beforehand
先先月 **sensengetsu** the month before last
先在性 **senzaisei** priority
先行 **senkō** precede, go first
sakiyu(ki), sakii(ki) the future
先安 **sakiyasu** lower quotations for future months
先回 **sakimawa(ri)** anticipate, forestall; arrive ahead of
7 先住民族 **senjū minzoku** aborigines
先住者 **senjūsha** former occupant
先決 **senketsu** previous decision
先決問題 **senketsu mondai** question to be settled first
先走 **sakibashi(ru)** be forward/impertinent
先売 **sakiu(ri)** advance sale
先見 **senken** foresight
先見明 **senken (no) mei** farseeing intelligence
8 先非 **senpi** past error/sins
先例 **senrei** precedent
先刻 **senkoku** already, a while ago
先夜 **sen'ya** the other night
先知 **senchi** foreknowledge; speedy comprehension
先妻 **sensai** one's ex-/late wife
先物 **sakimono** futures

先物買 **sakimonoga(i)** forward buying; speculation

先取 **senshu** take/score first, preoccupy **sakido(ri)** receive in advance; anticipate

先金 **sakigane** advance payment

9 先発 **senpatsu** start in advance, go ahead of

先発隊 **senpatsutai** advance party

先便 **senbin** previous letter

先陣 **senjin** vanguard, advance guard

先帝 **sentei** the late emperor

先途 **sendo** fateful turning point (in battle); death

先客 **senkyaku** previous visitor/customer

先祖 **senzo** ancestor

先約 **sen'yaku** previous engagement; prior contract

10 先高 **sakidaka** higher quotations for future months

先進 **senshin** advance; seniority

先進国 **senshinkoku** advanced/developed nation

先週 **senshū** last week

先哲 **sentetsu** ancient sage

先師 **senshi** one's late teacher

先般 **senpan** the other day; some time ago

11 先達 **sendatsu** pioneer; leader; guide **sendat(te)** the other day, recently

先務 **senmu** priority task

先細 **sakiboso** tapering

先頃 **sakigoro** recently, the other day

12 先着 **senchaku** first arrival, first-come(-first-served)

先着順 **senchakujun** by order of arrival, in the order of receipt, (on a) first-come-first-served basis

先遣 **senken** send ahead

先渡 **sakiwata(shi)** forward/future delivery

先覚 **senkaku** learned man, pioneer

先覚者 **senkakusha** pioneer, leading spirit

先棒 **sakibō** front palanquin bearer; (someone's) cat's-paw

先勝 **senshō** win the first game/point

先程 **sakihodo** a while ago

13 先触 **sakibu(re)** preliminary/previous announcement

14 先端 **sentan** tip, point, end; the latest, advanced (technology)

先導 **sendō** guidance, leadership

先駆 **sakiga(ke)** the lead/initiative

先駆者 **senkusha** forerunner, pioneer

15 先隣 **sakidonari** next door but one

先輩 **senpai** senior, superior, elder, older graduate

先鋭 **sen'ei** radical

16 先賢 **senken** ancient sage

先頭 **sentō** (in the) lead, (at the) head

18 先鞭 **senben** the initiative, being first

先験的 **senkenteki** transcendental, a priori

19 先識 **senshiki** prior knowledge

20 先議権 **sengiken** right to prior consideration

———————— 2 ————————

1 一先 **hitoma(zu)** for the present

3 刃先 **hasaki** edge of a blade

口先 **kuchisaki** lips, mouth, snout; words, lip service

4 爪先 **tsumasaki** tip of the toe, tiptoe

切先 **ki(s)saki** the point of a sword

水先 **mizusaki** direction of a current; ship's course

水先案内 **mizusaki annai** pilot; piloting

水先案内人 **mizusaki annainin** (harbor) pilot

手先 **tesaki** fingers, dexterity; tool, agent

火先 **hisaki** flames; direction in which a fire is spreading **hosaki** flame tips

5 矛先 **hokosaki** point of a spear; aim of an attack

矢先 **yasaki** arrowhead; moment, point

出先 **desaki** destination

生先 **o(i)saki** one's future career, remaining years

目先 **mesaki** before one's eyes; immediate future; foresight; appearance

6 老先 **o(i)saki** one's remaining years

先先 **ma(zu)ma(zu)** tolerably **sakizaki** the distant future; places one goes to; beforehand

先先月 **sensengetsu** the month before last

舌先 **shitasaki** tip of the tongue

舌先三寸 **shitasaki-sanzun** eloquence

行先 **yu(ki)saki** destination **yu(ku)saki** where one goes; the future

行先々 **yu(ku) sakisaki (de)** wherever one goes

7 売先 **u(ri)saki** market, outlet, demand, buyers

8 使先 **tsuka(i)saki** the place one is sent to on an errand

送先 **oku(ri)saki** destination, consignee

宛先 **atesaki** address

突先 **tossaki** tip, end

店先 **misesaki** storefront

届先 **todo(ke)saki** where to report, receiver's address

明先 **a(kari)saki** (stand in someone's) light

肩先 **katasaki** (top of) the shoulder

門先 **kadosaki** front of a house, entrance

9 指先 **yubisaki** fingertip

後先 **atosaki** front and rear; both ends; sequence; context; circumstances, consequences

庭先 **niwasaki** in the garden

春先 **harusaki** early spring

祖先 **sosen** ancestor, forefathers
10 剣先 **kensaki** point of a sword/bayonet
胸先 **munasaki** the solar plexus; breast
旅先 **tabisaki** destination
軒先 **nokisaki** edge of the eaves; front of the house
11 率先 **sossén** take the initiative, be the first
舳先 **hesaki** bow, prow
12 勤先 **tsuto(me)saki** place of work, employer
最先端 **saisentan** the lead, forefront
筆先 **fudesaki** brush tip; writings
筒先 **tsutsusaki** pipe end, (gun) muzzle, (fireman holding the hose) nozzle
14 槍先 **yarisaki** spearhead, lance point
鼻先 **hanasaki** tip of the nose
15 潮先 **shiosaki** rising of the tide, time to begin
穂先 **hosaki** tip of an ear/spear/knife/brush
縁先 **ensaki** edge of the veranda
16 機先制 **kisen (o) sei(suru)** forestall, beat (someone) to it
17 優先 **yūsen** preference, priority
優先的 **yūsenteki** preferential
優先株 **yūsenkabu** preferred shares
優先権 **yūsenken** (right of) priority
鍬先 **kuwasaki** hoe blade

──────── 3 ────────

1 一寸先 **issun saki** an inch ahead; the immediate future
3 小手先 **kotesaki** (a good) hand (at)
4 太刀先 **tachisaki** tip of a sword; force of tongue
引越先 **hi(k)ko(shi)saki** where one moves to
5 玄関先 **genkansaki** entrance, front door
立回先 **ta(chi)mawa(ri)saki** (criminal's) hangout
6 行先先 **yu(ku) sakisaki (de)** wherever one goes
8 奉公先 **hōkōsaki** employer
注文先 **chūmonsaki** where one places an order
9 赴任先 **funinsaki** one's place of appointment
10 烏有先生 **Uyū-sensei** fictitious person
旅行先 **ryokōsaki** destination
配達先 **haitatsusaki** destination, receiver
11 得意先 **tokuisaki** customer
12 勤務先 **kinmusaki** place of employment, employer
就職先 **shūshokusaki** place of employment
15 養子先 **yōshisaki** one's adopted home

3b3.8 / 268

在

ZAI be, exist, be located/residing in; country(side), rural
a(ru) be, exist, be located in

──────── 1 ────────

4 在天 **zaiten** in heaven, heavenly

在中 **zaichū** within
在中物 **zaichūbutsu** contents
在日 **zai-Nichi** in Japan   **a(rishi)hi** bygone days; during one's lifetime
在日中 **zai-Nichichū** while in Japan
在方 **a(ri)kata** the way (it) should be
    zaikata rural district
5 在外 **zaigai** overseas, abroad
在外邦人 **zaigai hōjin** Japanese living abroad
6 在任 **zainin** hold office, be in office
在任中 **zaininchū** while in office
在宅 **zaitaku** be in, be at home
在米 **zai-Bei** in America
7 在来 **zairai, a(ri)ki(tari)** usual, customary
在位 **zaii** be on the throne, reign
在住 **zaijū** reside, dwell, live
在住者 **zaijūsha** resident
在役 **zaieki** in (military) service, serving a prison term
在学 **zaigaku** (enrolled) in school
在学生 **zaigakusei** student
8 在京 **zaikyō** residing in the capital, in Tōkyō
在京中 **zaikyōchū** while in the capital
在英 **zai-Ei** in Britain
在官 **zaikan** tenure of office
在官中 **zaikanchū** while in office
在官者 **zaikansha** officeholder
在所 **zaisho** the country; one's native place
9 在室 **zaishitsu** in one's room
10 在郷 **zaikyō, zaigō** (in the) country(side)
在荷 **zaika, a(ri)ni** goods in stock, inventory
在家 **zaike** layman (Buddhist)
在庫 **zaiko** (in) stock, inventory
在庫品 **zaikohin** goods on hand, stock
在校 **zaikō** be in school
在校生 **zaikōsei** present students
在留 **zairyū** reside, stay
在留民 **zairyūmin** residents
在留外人 **zairyū gaijin** foreign residents
在留邦人 **zairyū hōjin** Japanese residing abroad
11 在野 **zaiya** out of office/power
12 在勤 **zaikin** serve, hold office
14 在獄中 **zaigokuchū** while in prison
15 在監者 **zaikansha** prisoner, inmate
18 在韓 **zai-Kan** in South Korea
在職 **zaishoku** hold office, remain in office
20 在籍 **zaiseki** be enrolled

──────── 2 ────────

4 不在 **fuzai** absence
内在 **naizai** immanence, inherence, indwelling
内在的 **naizaiteki** immanent, inherent, intrinsic
介在 **kaizai** lie between

3

氵
→4 土
扌
口
女
巾
犭
弓
彡
彳
艹
宀
⺌
山
士
广
尸
口

5 存在 **sonzai** exist
存在論 **sonzairon** ontology
6 伏在 **fukuzai** lie hidden
近在 **kinzai** neighboring villages, suburbs
先在性 **senzaisei** priority
行在 **anzai** emperor's temporary residence
行在所 **anzaisho** emperor's temporary residence
自在 **jizai** freely movable, adjustable
自在画 **jizaiga** freehand drawing
自在鉤 **jizai kagi** height-adjustable hook for hanging a pot over a fire
8 実在 **jitsuzai** real existence, reality
実在論 **jitsuzairon** realism
所在 **shozai** whereabouts, location, site
所在地 **shozaichi** seat, location
9 点在 **tenzai** be dotted with
10 健在 **kenzai** in good health
11 偏在 **henzai** uneven distribution, maldistribution
遍在 **henzai** ubiquitous, omnipresent
混在 **konzai** be present together, coexist
現在 **genzai** now, present, current; present tense; actually
現在高 **genzaidaka** amount on hand
12 散在 **sanzai** be scattered here and there
13 滞在 **taizai** stay, sojourn
滞在中 **taizaichū** during one's stay
滞在地 **taizaichi** where one is living
滞在者 **taizaisha** sojourner, visitor
滞在客 **taizaikyaku** (hotel) guest
滞在費 **taizaihi** living expenses during one's stay
15 潜在 **senzai** latent, hidden, potential (cf. 顕在)
潜在的 **senzaiteki** latent, potential, dormant
潜在意識 **senzai ishiki** subconscious
駐在 **chūzai** stay, residence
駐在所 **chūzaisho** police substation
18 顕在 **kenzai** revealed, actual (cf. 潜在)

―――― 3 ――――
5 主権在民 **shuken-zaimin** sovereignty resides with the people

―――― 4 ――――
6 自由自在 **jiyū-jizai** free, unrestricted
7 伸縮自在 **shinshuku-jizai** elastic, flexible, telescoping
9 変幻自在 **hengen-jizai** ever-changing
活殺自在 **kassatsu-jizai** power of life and death

―――― 4 ――――

3b4.1 / 1858

坊 **BŌ, BO'** priest's residence; Buddhist priest; boy

―――― 1 ――――
0 坊や **bō(ya)** little boy, sonny
坊ちゃん **bot(chan)** (your) boy, young master
5 坊主 **bōzu** Buddhist priest, bonze; shaven head; boy, rascal
坊主刈 **bōzuga(ri)** close-cropped haircut
坊主頭 **bōzuatama** shaven/close-cropped head
6 坊守 **bōmori** sexton; low-ranking priest; priest's wife
8 坊舎 **bōsha** priests' quarters
12 坊間 **bōkan** on the market/streets, town (gossip)

―――― 2 ――――
3 丸坊主 **marubōzu** close-cropped, shaven (head)
小坊主 **kobōzu** young priest; sonny
5 立坊 **ta(chin)bō** stand around waiting; day laborer
7 赤坊 **aka(n)bō** baby
見坊 **mi(e)bō** vain person, fop
8 泥坊 **dorobō** thief, burglar
9 海坊主 **umibōzu** sea monster
茶坊主 **chabōzu** (shogun's) tea-serving attendant; sycophant
怒坊 **oko(rin)bō** quick-tempered/testy person
食坊 **ku(ishin)bō** glutton, gourmand
11 宿坊 **shukubō** temple lodgings for pilgrims
黒坊 **kuro(n)bō** nigger, darkie; black-clad stagehand
12 葱坊主 **negibōzu** flowering onion head
13 僧坊 **sōbō** priests' living quarters
隠坊 **kaku(ren)bō** hide-and-seek
onbō crematory worker
寝坊 **nebō** oversleeping; late riser
裸坊 **hadaka(n)bō** naked person

―――― 3 ――――
3 三日坊主 **mikka bōzu** one who can stick to nothing, "three-day monk"
4 木偶坊 **deku(no)bō** wooden doll, dummy
5 生臭坊主 **namagusa bōzu** worldly priest, corrupt monk
正覚坊 **shōgakubō** large sea turtle; heavy drinker
6 次男坊 **jinanbō** second son
7 見栄坊 **miebō** vain person, fop
9 風来坊 **fūraibō** wanderer, vagabond, hobo
12 朝寝坊 **asanebō** late riser
13 照照坊主 **te(ru)te(ru)bōzu** paper doll used in praying for good weather

―――― 4 ――――
8 味噌擂坊主 **misosu(ri) bōzu** petty priest

3b4.2

坎   **KAN, ana** pitfall

3b4.3

址 阯   **SHI, ato** traces, remnants

――――――― 2 ―――――――
9 城址 **jōshi** castle ruins

3b4.4

坏   **HAI, tsuki** bowl

――――――― 2 ―――――――
10 高坏 **takatsuki** serving table

3b4.5

圻   **KI** region surrounding the capital

3b4.6 / 1613

坑   **KŌ** pit, hole, mine

――――――― 1 ―――――――
3 坑口 **kōkō** mine entrance, pithead
4 坑内 **kōnai** in the mine
坑夫 **kōfu** miner
坑木 **kōboku** mine pillars/timbers
11 坑道 **kōdō** (mine) shaft, level, gallery, tunnel

――――――― 2 ―――――――
5 立坑 **ta(te)kō** (vertical) shaft, pit
8 金坑 **kinkō** gold mine
9 炭坑 **tankō** coal mine
炭坑夫 **tankōfu** coal miner
12 廃坑 **haikō** abandoned mine
13 鉄坑 **tekkō** iron mine
14 竪坑 **tatekō** (mine) shaft, pit
銀坑 **ginkō** silver mine
銅坑 **dōkō** copper mine
16 縦坑 **tatekō** (mine) shaft, pit

――――――― 3 ―――――――
5 石油坑 **sekiyukō** oil well

3b4.7 / 443

坂   **HAN, saka** slope, hill

――――――― 1 ―――――――
11 坂道 **sakamichi** hill road

――――――― 2 ―――――――
3 上坂 **nobo(ri)zaka** upward slope, uphill
下坂 **kuda(ri)zaka** downward slope, downhill
7 男坂 **otokozaka** the steeper slope
9 急坂 **kyūhan** steep hill
12 登坂 **nobo(ri)zaka** uphill slope, ascent

3b4.8 / 805

均   **KIN** equal, even
nara(su) to level/average
hito(shii) equal, equivalent

――――――― 1 ―――――――
1 均一 **kin'itsu** uniform
4 均分 **kinbun** divide equally
5 均圧 **kin'atsu** equal pressure
8 均斉 **kinsei** symmetry, balance
12 均等 **kintō** equality, uniformity, parity
15 均質 **kinshitsu** homogeneous
16 均衡 **kinkō** balance, equilibrium
均整 **kinsei** symmetry, balance
均霑 **kinten** have an equal share in

――――――― 2 ―――――――
4 不均斉 **fukinsei** asymmetrical, lop-sided
不均衡 **fukinkō** imbalance, disequilibrium
5 平均 **heikin** average, mean; balance, equilibrium
平均点 **heikinten** average mark/grade
13 掻均 **ka(ki)nara(su)** rake smooth, level out
15 踏均 **fu(mi)nara(su)** level by treading, beat (a path)

――――――― 3 ―――――――
16 機会均等 **kikai kintō** equal opportunity

3b4.9 / 429

走 走   **SŌ, hashi(ru)** run
hashi(ri) first (produce) of the season

――――――― 1 ―――――――
3 走上 **hashi(ri)a(garu)** run up
走下 **hashi(ri)kuda(ru), hashi(ri)o(riru)** run down
4 走込 **hashi(ri)ko(mu)** run into (a house)
5 走出 **hashi(ri)de(ru)** run out of (a house), pull out (from a station)
hashi(ri)da(su) start running
走去 **hashi(ri)sa(ru)** run away
6 走行 **sōkō** travel, cover distance
走行時間 **sōkō jikan** travel time
走行距離 **sōkō kyori** distance covered (in a given time)
走回 **hashi(ri)mawa(ru)** run around
7 走抜 **hashi(ri)nu(keru)** run through
hashi(ri)nu(ku) outrun
8 走使 **hashi(ri)zuka(i)** errand boy, messenger

3

走法 **sōhō** (form/style of) running
走狗 **sōku** hunting/running dog, (someone's) tool
走者 **sōsha** runner
9 走炭 **hashi(ri)zumi** sputtering charcoal
走査 **sōsa** scanning (in electronics)
10 走高跳 **hashi(ri)takato(bi)** running high jump
走書 **hashi(ri)ga(ki)** flowing/hasty handwriting
走破 **sōha** run the whole distance
走馬灯 **sōmatō** (like a) revolving lantern, kaleidoscopic
11 走過 **hashi(ri)su(giru)** run past; run too much
走寄 **hashi(ri)yo(ru)** come running, run up to
12 走幅跳 **hashi(ri)habato(bi)** running broad jump
走程 **sōtei** distance covered
走塁 **sōrui** base running
13 走路 **sōro** (race) track, course
14 走読 **hashi(ri)yo(mi)** read hurriedly, skim through

——————— 2 ———————

1 一走 **hitohashi(ri), hito(p)pashi(ri)** a run/spin
2 力走 **rikisō** run as fast as one can, sprint
3 才走 **saibashi(ru)** be sharp-witted, be a smart aleck
口走 **kuchibashi(ru)** blurt out, say
6 先走 **sakibashi(ru)** be forward/impertinent
帆走 **hansō** sail, be under sail
血走 **chibashi(ru)** become bloodshot
7 快走 **kaisō** fast running/sailing
8 奔走 **honsō** running about, efforts
逃走 **tōsō** flight, escape, desertion ni(ge)hashi(ru) run away
突走 **tsu(p)pashi(ru)** run at full speed
9 発走 **hassō** start; first race
独走 **dokusō** running alone
10 逸走 **issō** scamper away, escape
師走 **shiwasu** 12th lunar month
徒走 **kachibashi(ri)** running along on foot
疾走 **shissō** scamper, run at full speed
11 脱走 **dassō** escape, flee
脱走兵 **dassōhei** deserter
敗走 **haisō** rout, flight
12 遁走 **tonsō** flee, (on the) run
遠走 **tō(p)pashi(ri)** go a long way/distance
13 滑走 **kassō** glide, slide, taxi
滑走路 **kassōro** runway
滑走輪 **kassōrin** landing gear
継走 **keisō** relay race
馳走 **(go)chisō** feast, treat, entertainment, hospitality
15 潰走 **kaisō** be routed, stampede
暴走 **bōsō** run wild, run out of control
16 縦走 **jūsō** traverse the length of (a mountain range)

20 競走 **kyōsō** race

——————— 3 ———————

8 苦味走 **nigamibashi(tta)** sternly handsome
12 御馳走 **gochisō** feast, banquet, treat, hospitality

——————— 4 ———————

8 東奔西走 **tōhon-seisō** busy oneself, take an active interest in
10 徒歩競走 **toho kyōsō** walking race
11 断郊競走 **dankō kyōsō** cross-country race
14 駅伝競走 **ekiden kyōsō** long-distance relay race

3b4.10 / 207

赤

SEKI, SHAKU, aka(i), aka red
aka(ramu) become red, blush
aka(rameru/meru) make red, blush

——————— 1 ———————

0 赤ちゃん **aka(chan)** baby
2 赤子 **akago** baby **sekishi** baby; subjects
赤十字 **sekijūji** Red Cross
赤十字社 **Sekijūjisha** Red Cross Society
3 赤々 **aka-aka** brightly
赤土 **akatsuchi** red clay/loam
4 赤毛 **akage** red hair, red-headed
赤毛布 **akagetto** red blanket; country bumpkin
赤化 **sekka** communization
赤切符 **akagippu** third-class ticket
赤手 **sekishu** bare hand/fists
赤心 **sekishin** true heart, sincerity
5 赤本 **akahon** cheap storybook/novel
赤他人 **aka (no) tanin** a perfect/total stranger
赤外線 **sekigaisen** infrared rays
赤字 **akaji** deficit, in the red
赤札 **akafuda** clearance goods; sold goods
赤目 **akame** bloodshot/red eyes
6 赤色 **aka-iro, sekishoku** red
赤地 **akaji** red fabric; red (back)ground
赤肌 **akahada** plucked/abraded skin; naked
赤血球 **sekkekkyū** red corpuscles
7 赤身 **akami** lean meat; heartwood
赤沈 **sekichin** blood sedimentation
赤坊 **aka(n)bō** baby
赤赤 **aka-aka** brightly
赤貝 **akagai** ark shell
8 赤茄子 **akanasu** tomato
赤松 **akamatsu** red pine
赤門 **akamon** red gate; Tōkyō University
9 赤信号 **akashingō** red (traffic) light
赤軍 **Sekigun** Red Army
赤茶 **akacha** reddish brown
赤茶色 **akacha-iro** reddish brown
赤面 **sekimen** a blush **akatsura** red face; villain's role
赤砂糖 **akazatō** brown sugar

10 赤剥 **akamu(ke)** red skin, rubbed raw
赤恥 **akahaji** public disgrace
11 赤貧 **sekihin** abject poverty
赤道 **sekidō** the equator
赤黒 **akaguro(i)** dark red
12 赤帽 **akabō** redcap, luggage porter
赤痢 **sekiri** dysentery
赤紫 **aka-murasaki** purplish red
赤紫色 **aka-murasaki-iro** purplish red
赤飯 **sekihan, akameshi** (festive) rice with red beans
13 赤靴 **akagutsu** brown shoes
赤禍 **sekka** the Red Peril
赤新聞 **akashinbun** yellow journal
赤裸 **akahadaka** stark naked
赤裸々 **sekirara** stark naked; frank, outspoken
赤褐色 **sekkasshoku** reddish brown
赤誠 **sekisei** sincerity
赤電車 **akadensha** red-lamp car, last streetcar
赤電話 **akadenwa** public telephone
14 赤熊 **akaguma** brown bear
赤旗 **akahata** red flag; the Red Flag
sekki red/danger flag
赤銅 **shakudō** gold-copper alloy
赤銅色 **shakudō-iro** brown, bronze, tanned
15 赤潮 **akashio** red tide
赤蕪 **akakabu** red turnip
赤線区域 **akasen kuiki** red-light district
16 赤衛軍 **Sekieigun** the Red Guards
赤樫 **akagashi** red/evergreen oak
赤頭巾 **Akazukin(chan)** Little Red Riding Hood
17 赤燐 **sekirin** red phosphorus
18 赤顔 **aka(ra)gao** ruddy/florid face
19 赤鯛 **akadai** red sea bream
21 赤鰯 **aka iwashi** dried/salted sardines

──────── 2 ────────
4 日赤 **Nisseki** Japan Red Cross (short for 日本赤十字社)
7 赤赤 **aka-aka** brightly
10 真赤 **ma(k)ka** deep red, crimson
11 淡赤色 **tansekishoku** rose color
13 暗赤色 **ansekishoku** dark red
16 薄赤 **usuaka(i)** pale/light red

3b4.11
坐 **ZA** sit; somehow
suwa(ru) sit (For compounds, see 座 3q7.2)
──────── 2 ────────
7 対坐 **taiza** sit facing each other
9 連坐 **renza** complicity
独坐 **dokuza** sitting alone
13 鼎坐 **teiza** sit in a triangle
跪坐 **kiza** kneel down

14 端坐 **tanza** sit erect
15 黙坐 **mokuza** sit in silence
──────── 3 ────────
6 行住坐臥 **gyōjū-zaga** walking, stopping, sitting, and lying down; daily life

──────── 5 ────────
3b5.1
坤 **KON** (one of the eight divination signs); earth, land; womanly, feminine
──────── 2 ────────
11 乾坤 **kenkon** heaven and earth, yin and yang
乾坤一擲 **kenkon-itteki** risking everything, all or nothing

3b5.2
坩 **KAN** earthenware pot/jar
──────── 1 ────────
12 坩堝 **kanka, rutsubo** crucible, melting pot

3b5.3
坡 **HA, tsutsumi** embankment, dike

3b5.4 / 1896
坪 坪 **HEI, tsubo** (unit of area, exactly 400/121 square meters, or about 3.3 square meters)
──────── 1 ────────
13 坪数 **tsubosū** number of *tsubo*, area
──────── 2 ────────
5 立坪 **ta(te)tsubo** cubic *ken* (about 6 cubic meters)
6 地坪 **jitsubo** land/ground area
7 延坪 **no(be)tsubo** total floor space
8 建坪 **tatetsubo** floor space

3b5.5
坮 **HŌ** ground exposed by a landslide

3b5.6
坼 **TAKU** break, split open

3b5.7
坿 **FU** slope, hill

3b5.8

坦 **TAN** level, even

――――――― 1 ―――――――
3 坦々 **tantan** level, even; uneventful, peaceful

――――――― 2 ―――――――
5 平坦 **heitan** even, flat, level

――――――― 3 ―――――――
11 虚心坦懐 **kyoshin-tankai** frank, open-minded

3b5.9 / 684

幸 **KŌ, saiwa(i), shiawa(se), sachi** happiness, good fortune

――――――― 1 ―――――――
4 幸不幸 **kōfukō** good or ill fortune, happiness or misery
9 幸甚 **kōjin** very happy, much obliged
幸便 **kōbin** favorable opportunity
11 幸運 **kōun** good fortune, luck
幸運児 **kōunji** child of good fortune, lucky fellow
13 幸福 **kōfuku** happiness

――――――― 2 ―――――――
3 山幸 **yama (no) sachi** mountain food products
4 不幸 **fukō** unhappiness, misfortune
5 巡幸 **junkō** imperial tour
6 多幸 **takō** great happiness, good fortune
至幸 **shikō** supreme/utter happiness
行幸 **gyōkō, miyuki** visit/attendance by the emperor
10 射幸 **shakō** speculation
射幸心 **shakōshin** speculative spirit
12 御幸 **miyuki** visit/attendance by royalty
14 遷幸 **senkō** emperor's departing the capital
15 還幸 **kankō** return of the emperor
潜幸 **senkō** secret visit by the emperor
16 薄幸 **hakkō** misfortune, bad luck
18 臨幸 **rinkō** visit by the emperor

――――――― 3 ―――――――
4 勿怪幸 **mokke (no) saiwa(i)** stroke of good luck
8 幸不幸 **kōfukō** good or ill fortune, happiness or misery

3b5.10

垈 **nuta** swamp, wetlands

――――――― 6 ―――――――

3b6.1 / 720

城 **JŌ, shiro** castle

――――――― 1 ―――――――
3 城下 **jōka** castle town; seat of a daimyo's government
城下町 **jōkamachi** castle town
4 城内 **jōnai** inside the castle
5 城代 **jōdai** castle warden
城市 **jōshi** castle/walled town
城外 **jōgai** outside the castle
城主 **jōshu** lord of a castle
7 城兵 **jōhei** castle garrison
城址 **jōshi** castle ruins
8 城門 **jōmon** castle gate
9 城郭 **jōkaku** castle; castle walls
11 城砦 **jōsai** fort, citadel
12 城塁 **jōrui** fort
13 城塞 **jōsai** fort, citadel, stronghold
城跡 **shiroato** castle ruins/site
16 城壁 **jōheki** castle walls, ramparts

――――――― 2 ―――――――
2 入城 **nyūjō** entry into the fortress of the enemy
3 干城 **kanjō** bulwark, defender
山城 **yamajiro** mountain castle
Yamashiro (ancient kuni, Kyōto-fu)
4 牙城 **gajō** stronghold, inner citadel
王城 **ōjō** royal castle
5 出城 **dejiro** branch castle
古城 **kojō** old castle
平城 **Heizei** (emperor, 806–809)
平城京 **Heijōkyō** ancient Nara
6 名城 **meijō** famous/excellent castle
7 攻城 **kōjō** siege
8 孤城 **kojō** isolated/besieged castle
京城 **Keijō** Seoul
居城 **kyojō** daimyo's residential castle
金城 **kinjō** impregnable castle
金城鉄壁 **kinjō-teppeki** impregnable castle
9 浮城 **fujō** floating fortress, warship
茨城県 **Ibaraki-ken** (prefecture)
10 宮城 **kyūjō** imperial palace
宮城県 **Miyagi-ken** (prefecture)
根城 **nejiro** stronghold; base of operations
12 堅城 **kenjō** strong/impregnable castle
登城 **tojō** go to the castle
落城 **rakujō** fall of a castle
開城 **kaijō** capitulation (of a fortress)
13 傾城 **keisei** courtesan, prostitute; an infatuating beauty
15 敵城 **tekijō** enemy castle
磐城 **Iwaki** (ancient kuni, Fukushima-ken)

16 築城 **chikujō** castle construction; fortification
22 籠城 **rōjō** be under siege, hole up, be confined

——————————— 3 ———————————

4 不夜城 **fuyajō** nightless city, city that never sleeps

——————————— 4 ———————————

3 万里長城 **Banri (no) Chōjō** Great Wall of China

3b6.2

埌 **GIN** limit, boundary

3b6.3

垢 **KŌ, KU, aka** dirt, grime, scale, (ear)wax

——————————— 1 ———————————

7 垢抜 **akanu(ke)** refined, polished, urbane
9 垢染 **akaji(miru)** become grimy/dirty
17 垢擦 **akasu(ri)** cloth/pumice/loofah for rubbing the body clean when taking a bath
18 垢離 **kori** purification by ablution

——————————— 2 ———————————

4 水垢 **mizuaka** encrustation, slime
水垢離 **mizugori** cold-water ablutions
手垢 **teaka** soiling from handling
5 目垢 **meaka** eye wax/discharge/mucus
6 汚垢 **okō** dirt
耳垢 **mimiaka** earwax
12 湯垢 **yuaka** boiler scale, fur, encrustation
無垢 **muku** pure
16 頭垢 **fuke** dandruff

——————————— 3 ———————————

5 白無垢 **shiromuku** (dressed) all in white

——————————— 4 ———————————

11 清浄無垢 **shōjō-muku** immaculate, pure and innocent

3b6.4

垳 **gake** cliff
Gake (place name, Saitama-ken)
ike (used in proper names)

3b6.5 / 1276

垣 **EN, kaki** fence, hedge

——————————— 1 ———————————

10 垣根 **kakine** fence, hedge
12 垣越 **kakigo(shi)** over/through the fence

垣間見 **kaimami(ru)** peek in, get a glimpse

——————————— 2 ———————————

2 人垣 **hitogaki** human wall, crowd, throng
4 友垣 **tomogaki** friend
5 生垣 **i(ke)gaki** hedge
玉垣 **tamagaki** fence (of a shrine)
石垣 **ishigaki** stone wall
6 竹垣 **takegaki** bamboo fence/hedge
8 板垣 **itagaki** wooden fence
10 姫垣 **himegaki** low fence
袖垣 **sodegaki** low fence (flanking a gate)
11 斎垣 **igaki** shrine fence
13 腰垣 **koshigaki** hip-high fence

——————————— 3 ———————————

5 四目垣 **yo(tsu)megaki** lattice fence, trellis

3b6.6

垰 **tawa, tōge** mountain pass
Tao (ancient kuni)
akutsu low ground

3b6.7

垤 **TETSU** anthill; hill

3b6.8

垓 **GAI** boundary, border; staircase; hundred quintillion

3b6.9

垪 **ha** (used in proper names)

——————————— 1 ———————————

8 垪和 **Haga** (ancient kuni)　**Hagai** (surname)

3b6.10

垜 **DA** archery target mound

3b6.11 / 888

型 **KEI, kata, -gata** model, form, type

——————————— 1 ———————————

0 A型 **ēgata** Model A; (blood) type A
8 型板 **kataita** template
10 型破 **katayabu(ri)** unconventional, novel
型紙 **katagami** (dressmaking) pattern

3
氵
土 6←
扌
口
女
巾
犭
弓
彳
彡
宀
⺍
山
寺
广
尸
口

3

氵
→6 土
扌
口
女
巾
犭
弓
彳
彡
艹
宀
⺌
曲
毒
广
尸
口

────── 2 ──────

3 大型 **ōgata** large size
小型 **kogata** small-size
4 中型 **chūgata** medium size
5 母型 **bokei** matrix (in printing)
6 １９９６年型 **1996nen-gata** the 1996 model
同型 **dōkei** the same type
成型 **seikei** form, press, stamp out
7 足型 **ashigata** shoe last
8 並型 **namigata** ordinary/standard size
典型 **tenkei** type, pattern, model
典型的 **tenkeiteki** typical
押型 **o(shi)gata** impression taken by pressing
定型 **teikei** definite form, type
定型化 **teikeika** standardization
定型的 **teikeiteki** typical
定型詩 **teikeishi** poetry in a fixed form
金型 **kanagata** (metal) mold, die
9 造型 **zōkei** molding, modeling
10 原型 **genkei** prototype, model
紙型 **shikei** papier-mâché mold
11 船型 **senkei** type of vessel; model of a ship
13 靴型 **kutsugata** shoe last/tree
煩型 **urusagata** fastidious/faultfinding type
新型 **shingata** new model/style
14 像型 **zōkei** mold for cast images
髪型 **kamigata** hairdo
模型 **mokei** (scale) model; a mold
15 儀型 **gikei** model, pattern
潮型 **shiogata** type of tide (flood, neap, etc.)
熱型 **nekkei** type of fever
鋳型 **igata** a mold, cast
18 雛型 **hinagata** model, miniature, sample
類型 **ruikei** type, pattern

────── 3 ──────

4 手札型 **tefudagata** 11 cm high by 8 cm wide (photo)
5 外向型 **gaikōgata** outgoing type, extrovert
6 自由型 **jiyūgata** freestyle (wrestling)
血液型 **ketsuekigata** blood type
10 流線型 **ryūsenkei** streamlined
紋切型 **monki(ri)gata** conventional
11 理想型 **risōgata** ideal type
15 標準型 **hyōjungata** standard type
18 闘士型 **tōshigata** the athletic type

3b6.12

奎
KEI star/god ruling over literature

3b6.13 / 1463

封
FŪ seal, sealing
HŌ fief

────── 1 ──────

0 封じる/ずる **fū(jiru/zuru)** seal, enclose, blockade
封ずる **hō(zuru)** invest with a fief
2 封入 **fūnyū** enclose , seal in
3 封土 **hōdo** fief
4 封切 **fūki(ri)** new release, first run (of a movie)
封込 **fū(ji)ko(meru)** confine, contain, seal up
5 封目 **fū(ji)me** the seal (of an envelope)
6 封印 **fūin** (stamped) seal
封地 **hōchi** fief
8 封建 **hōken** feudalism
封建主義 **hōken shugi** feudalism
封建制 **hōkensei** feudalism
封建的 **hōkenteki** feudal(istic)
10 封殺 **fūsatsu** forced out (in baseball)
封書 **fūsho** sealed letter/document
12 封筒 **fūtō** envelope
15 封緘 **fūkan** seal
封緘葉書 **fūkan hagaki** lettercard
18 封鎖 **fūsa** blockade; freeze (assets)
21 封蠟 **fūrō** sealing wax

────── 2 ──────

1 一封 **ippū** a sealed letter/document; an enclosure
6 同封 **dōfū** enclose
虫封 **mushifū(ji)** incantation to prevent intestinal worms in a child
7 別封 **beppū** under separate cover
完封 **kanpū** complete blockade; shutout
10 帯封 **obifū** half-wrapper (in which magazines are mailed)
素封家 **sohōka** wealthy person/family
11 密封 **mippū** seal tight/up/hermetically
12 無封書状 **mufū shojō** unsealed letter
開封 **hira(ki)fū, kaifū** unsealed letter
17 厳封 **genpū** seal tight/hermetically

────── 3 ──────

8 金一封 **kin'ippū** gift of money (in an envelope)

赴 → **3b7.10**

3b6.14 / 1465

赴
FU, omomu(ku) go, proceed to; become

────── 1 ──────

6 赴任 **funin** proceed to one's new post
赴任地 **funinchi** one's place of appointment
赴任先 **funinsaki** one's place of appointment

── 7 ──

3b7.1

埔 **HO** (used in Chinese place names)

3b7.2 / 1826

埋 **MAI, u(meru), uzu(meru)** bury, fill up **u(maru), uzu(maru)** be buried (under), be filled up **u(moreru), uzu(moreru)** be buried; sink into obscurity **i(keru)** bury, bank (a fire)

── 1 ──
4 埋木 **u(me)ki** wood inlay, wooden plug
　　u(more)gi lignite; living in obscurity
　埋火 **uzu(mi)bi** banked fire
5 埋立 **u(me)ta(teru)** reclaim (land), fill in/up
　埋立地 **u(me)ta(te)chi** reclaimed land
6 埋伏 **maifuku** lie hidden; bury (to hide); impacted (tooth)
　埋合 **u(me)a(waseru)** make up for, compensate for
　埋地 **u(me)chi** reclaimed land
7 埋没 **maibotsu** be buried; fall into obscurity
9 埋草 **u(me)kusa** (page) filler
11 埋設 **maisetsu** lay (underground cables)
12 埋湯 **u(me)yu** hot water cooled by adding cold water
　埋葬 **maisō** burial, interment
　埋替 **u(me)ka(eru)** rebury, reinter
15 埋蔵 **maizō** buried stores, underground reserves
　埋蔵物 **maizōbutsu** buried property/ore
　埋蔵量 **maizōryō** (oil) reserves
　埋線 **maisen** underground cable

── 2 ──
5 生埋 **i(ki)u(me)** burying alive
　穴埋 **anau(me)** fill a gap; cover a deficit

3b7.3

堆 **gomi** garbage, refuse

── 1 ──
12 堆渡 **Gomiwatari** (place name, Aomori-ken)

埖 → 埒 **3b7.4**

3b7.4

埒 埓 **RACHI** enclosure, pale

── 1 ──
5 埒外 **rachigai** beyond the pale, beyond bounds
12 埒開 **rachi (ga) a(ku)** be settled/concluded

── 2 ──
4 不埒 **furachi** rude, insolent, outrageous, reprehensible
8 放埒 **hōratsu** profligate, loose, dissipated

3b7.5

埆 **KAKU** barren land

3b7.6

埃 **AI, hokori** dust

── 1 ──
3 埃及 **Ejiputo** Egypt

── 2 ──
9 砂埃 **sunabokori** dust, dust storm
14 塵埃 **jin'ai, chiri-hokori** dust and dirt; the drab world

3b7.7

恚 **I** anger

── 2 ──
15 瞋恚 **shin'i** wrath, indignation

3b7.8

袁 **EN** long robes

3b7.9

盍 **KŌ** come together, congregate, meet; cover

3b7.10

赳 **KYŪ** strong and brave

3b7.11 / 373

起 **KI** awakening, rise, beginning **o(kiru)** get/wake/be up; occur **o(koru)** occur, happen **o(kosu)** wake (someone) up; begin, start, create, cause **ta(tsu)** begin, start, rise up

── 1 ──
3 起工 **kikō** start construction

3

起工式 **kikōshiki** ground-breaking ceremony
起上 **o(ki)a(garu)** get up, rise
起上小法師 **o(ki)a(gari) koboshi** self-righting toy
4 起毛 **kimō** nap raising
5 起用 **kiyō** appoint, employ
起句 **kiku** opening line of a poem
起立 **kiritsu** stand up
6 起死 **kishi** saving from the jaws of death
起死回生 **kishi kaisei** resuscitation, revival
起伏 **kifuku** ups and downs, relief (map)
o(ki)fu(shi) getting up and lying down; morning and evening, daily life
起因 **kiin** originate in, be caused by
7 起承転結 **ki-shō-ten-ketsu** introduction, development, turn, and conclusion (rules for composing a Chinese poem)
起抜 **o(ki)nu(ke)** upon getting up
起床 **kishō** wake up, rise
8 起直 **o(ki)nao(ru)** sit up
起居 **kikyo** daily life **ta(chi)i** standing up and sitting down
起居振舞 **ta(chi)i furuma(i)** deportment, manners
9 起重機 **kijūki** crane, derrick
起臥 **kiga** daily life
起点 **kiten** starting point
起首 **kishu** beginning
起草 **kisō** draft, draw up
起草者 **kisōsha** drafter
10 起原 **kigen** origin, beginning
起案 **kian** draft, draw up
11 起動 **kidō** starting
起動機 **kidōki** starter, starting motor
起掛 **o(ki)ga(ke)** upon getting up
12 起結 **kiketsu** beginning and end
起筆 **kihitsu** begin to write
起訴 **kiso** prosecute, indict; sue, bring action against
起訴状 **kisojō** (written) indictment
13 起業 **kigyō** start a business, organize an undertaking
起債 **kisai** issue bonds, float a loan
起源 **kigen** origin, beginning
起電 **kiden** generation of electricity
起電力 **kidenryoku** electromotive force
起電機 **kidenki** electric motor
14 起算 **kisan** starting/computed from (a given date)
15 起稿 **kikō** begin writing, draft
起請 **kishō** vow, pledge
起請文 **kishōmon** written pledge, personal contract
19 起爆 **kibaku** priming (in explosives)
起爆剤 **kibakuzai** priming/triggering explosive

起爆薬 **kibakuyaku** priming/triggering explosive

――――――― 2 ―――――――

4 不起訴 **fukiso** nonprosecution, nonindictment
引起 **hi(ki)o(kosu)** lift/help up, raise; give rise to, cause
5 生起 **seiki** occur, arise
叩起 **tata(ki)o(kosu)** awaken, rouse
6 再起 **saiki** comeback; recovery
光起電力 **hikari-kidenryoku** photoelectromotive force
早起 **hayao(ki)** get up early
7 助起 **tasu(ke)oko(su)** help (someone) up
励起 **reiki** excitation
決起 **kekki** spring to one's feet (with renewed resolve)
吹起 **fu(ki)oko(su)** blow up (a wind), fan (flames)
8 併起 **heiki** occur simultaneously
勃起 **bokki** an erection
抱起 **da(ki)o(kosu)** lift/help (someone) up
呼起 **yo(bi)o(kosu)** wake, rouse; remind
突起 **tokki** protuberance, projection, protrusion
9 飛起 **to(bi)o(kiru)** jump out of bed; leap to one's feet
発起 **hokki** propose, promote, initiate
発起人 **hokkinin** promoter, originator
巻起 **ma(ki)o(kosu)** stir up, create
思起 **omo(i)o(kosu)** remember, recall
10 隆起 **ryūki** protuberance, bulge, rise, elevation
振起 **fu(rui)oko(su)** rouse/stir up, awaken, stimulate
書起 **ka(ki)oko(shi)** opening paragraph/words
11 捲起 **ma(ki)o(kosu)** stir up, create (a sensation)
掘起 **ho(ri)o(kosu)** dig/turn up
崛起 **kukki** rise, be towering
12 湧起 **wa(ki)o(koru)** arise
提起 **teiki** submit, raise (a question), bring (suit)
揺起 **yu(ri)o(kosu)** awaken by shaking
喚起 **kanki** evoke, awaken, call forth
惹起 **jakki, hi(ki)o(kosu)** bring about, cause, provoke
朝起 **asao(ki)** get up early
13 群起 **gunki** occur together
寝起 **neo(ki)** (one's disposition upon) awaking; sleeping and waking, daily living
想起 **sōki** recollection, remembrance
蜂起 **hōki** revolt, uprising
跳起 **ha(ne)o(kiru)** jump up, spring to one's feet
14 種起原 **shu (no) kigen** (Darwin's) The Origin of Species
誘起 **yūki** give rise to, lead to, cause

説起 **to(ki)o(kosu)** begin one's argument/story

15 縁起 **engi** history, origin; omen, luck

縁起直 **enginao(shi)** a change of luck

縁起物 **engimono** a lucky charm

鋤起 **su(ki)o(kosu)** plow up, turn over

16 興起 **kōki** rise, ascendancy

奮起 **funki** rouse oneself (to action), be inspired

19 蹶起 **kekki** rise up

21 躍起 **yakki** excitement, franticness, enthusiasm

————— 4 —————

2 七転八起 **nanakoro(bi)ya(oki)** ups and downs of life, Fall seven times and get up eight.

6 虫様突起 **chūyō tokki** the (vermiform) appendix

虫様突起炎 **chūyō tokkien** appendicitis

————— 8 —————

3b8.1

堆

TAI, uzutaka(i) piled high

————— 1 —————

5 堆石 **taiseki** moraine

8 堆肥 **taihi, tsumigoe** compost, barnyard manure

16 堆積 **taiseki** accumulation, pile, heap

3b8.2

埵

TA hard soil; (used phonetically)

堵 → 堵 3b9.2

3b8.3 / 970

域

IKI region, area

————— 1 —————

5 域外 **ikigai** outside the area

————— 2 —————

4 区域 **kuiki** boundary; zone, territory

水域 **suiiki** area of the ocean, waters

5 広域 **kōiki** wide area

6 西域 **seiiki** lands to the west of China

全域 **zen'iki** the whole area

邦域 **hōiki** country's borders/territory

地域 **chiiki** region, area, zone

地域的 **chiikiteki** local, regional

地域差 **chiikisa** regional differences

8 空域 **kūiki** airspace

9 浄域 **jōiki** sacred precincts

海域 **kaiiki** area of the ocean, waters

神域 **shin'iki** shrine precincts

音域 **on'iki** singing range, register

10 流域 **ryūiki** (river) basin/valley

11 異域 **iiki** a foreign land

13 聖域 **seiiki** holy ground, sacred precincts

戦域 **sen'iki** war zone, theater of war

14 境域 **kyōiki** boundary; grounds

領域 **ryōiki** territory; domain, field

15 霊域 **reiiki** sacred precincts/ground

18 職域 **shokuiki** occupation, one's post

————— 4 —————

7 赤線区域 **akasen kuiki** red-light district

9 後進地域 **kōshin chiiki** underdeveloped region

3b8.4

堋

HŌ bury; archery target mound

3b8.5

埠

FU wharf

————— 1 —————

16 埠頭 **futō** wharf, pier

3b8.6 / 1828

培

BAI, tsuchika(u) cultivate, foster

————— 1 —————

6 培地 **baichi** (bacteria) culture ground/medium

15 培養 **baiyō** cultivation, culture

培養液 **baiyōeki** culture fluid/solution

培養基 **baiyōki** culture medium

————— 2 —————

10 栽培 **saibai** cultivate, grow

————— 4 —————

9 促成栽培 **sokusei saibai** forcing culture, hothouse cultivation

3b8.7

埦

Ō, WAN bowl

3

氵
土 8←
扌
口
女
巾
犭
弓
彳
彡
艹
宀
⺌
山
畫
广
尸
口

3b8.8

埼

KI, saki cape, promontory

——————— 1 ———————

5 埼玉県 **Saitama-ken** (prefecture)

3b8.9

崒

SOTSU barren land

3b8.10

埴

SHOKU, hani clay

——————— 1 ———————

15 埴輪 **haniwa** (4th–7th century clay figurines buried with the dead)

3b8.11 / 1804

堀

hori moat, ditch, canal

——————— 1 ———————

3 堀川 **horikawa** canal
6 堀江 **horie** canal
8 堀河 **Horikawa** (emperor, 1086–1107)
12 堀割 **horiwari** canal, waterway
14 堀端 **horibata** edge of the moat/canal

——————— 2 ———————

5 外堀 **sotobori** outer moat
8 空堀 **karabori** dry moat/ditch
11 釣堀 **tsu(ri)bori** fishpond

3b8.12 / 450

基

KI basis, foundation; radical (in chemistry); (counter for heavy machines, etc.) **moto, motoi** basis, foundation, origin

——————— 1 ———————

0 基づく **moto(zuku)** be based/founded on
5 基本 **kihon** basic, fundamental, standard
基本的 **kihonteki** basic, fundamental
基本金 **kihonkin** endowment fund
基本給 **kihonkyū** basic salary, base pay
6 基色 **kishoku** (back)ground color
基地 **kichi** (military) base
7 基形 **kikei** basic form, type
8 基底 **kitei** base, basis, foundation
基板 **kiban** substrate
基金 **kikin** fund, endowment
9 基点 **kiten** cardinal point

基音 **kion** fundamental tone
10 基部 **kibu** base, foundation
13 基準 **kijun** standard, criterion, basis
基幹 **kikan** basic, key (industries)
基数 **kisū** cardinal number; the digits 1–9
基督 **Kirisuto** Christ
基督教 **Kirisutokyō** Christianity
15 基盤 **kiban** base, basis, foundation
基線 **kisen** base line, base (of a triangle)
基調 **kichō** keynote
18 基礎 **kiso** foundation, fundamentals
基礎的 **kisoteki** fundamental, basic

——————— 2 ———————

10 根基 **konki** root, origin
12 開基 **kaiki** founding; founder
13 塩基 **enki** base, alkali

——————— 3 ———————

9 軍事基地 **gunji kichi** military base
10 航空基地 **kōkū kichi** air base
11 培養基 **baiyōki** culture medium

3b8.13

堊

A, AKU white earth; paint; wall

——————— 2 ———————

5 白堊 **hakua** chalk(stone); white wall
白堊館 **Hakuakan** the White House

埜 → 野 **0a11.5**

3b8.14 / 1742

堕 墮

DA fall

——————— 1 ———————

0 堕する **da(suru)** descend to, degenerate
2 堕力 **daryoku** inertia, force of habit
9 堕胎 **datai** abortion
12 堕落 **daraku** depravity, corruption
堕落的 **darakuteki** depraved, corrupt
13 堕罪 **dazai** fall into sin

——————— 2 ———————

6 自堕落 **jidaraku** slovenly, loose, debauched

3b8.15 / 686

執

SHITSU, SHŪ, to(ru) take, grasp; carry out, execute

——————— 1 ———————

2 執刀 **shittō** performance of a surgical operation

4 執心 **shūshin** devotion, attachment, infatuation
6 執行 **shikkō** performance, execution
執行吏 **shikkōri** bailiff, court officer
執行猶予 **shikkō yūyo** stay of execution, suspended sentence
執行権 **shikkōken** executive authority
8 執事 **shitsuji** steward; deacon
執念 **shūnen** tenacity of purpose, vindictiveness
執念深 **shūnenbuka(i)** tenacious; vengeful, spiteful
執拗 **shitsuyō** obstinate, persistent
9 執政 **shissei** government; administrator, consul
11 執務 **shitsumu** discharging one's duties, business (hours)
12 執着 **shūchaku** attachment to, tenacity
執筆 **shippitsu** write (for a magazine)
執筆者 **shippitsusha** writer, contributor
15 執権 **shikken** regent

———————— 2 ————————

6 妄執 **mōshū** deep-seated delusion/obsession
7 我執 **gashū** egoistic attachment; obstinacy
8 固執 **koshitsu** hold fast to, persist in, insist on
11 偏執 **henshū** bigotry, obstinacy
13 愛執 **aishū** attachment to, fondness
15 確執 **kakushitsu** discord, strife

———————— 3 ————————

6 死刑執行 **shikei shikkō** execution

———————— 9 ————————

3b9.1 / 1913

堪

KAN, TAN, tae(ru) endure, withstand
kora(eru) bear, endure; control, stifle; pardon **kota(eru)** endure **tama(ru)** bear, put up with **tama(ranai)** can't stand it

———————— 1 ————————

5 堪弁 **kanben** pardon, forgive
7 堪忍 **kannin** patience, forbearance; forgiveness
堪忍袋 **kanninbukuro** patience, forbearance
8 堪性 **kora(e)shō** patience
10 堪能 **tannō** skill; be satisfied
18 堪難 **ta(e)gata(i), kora(e)gata(i)** unbearable, intolerable

———————— 2 ————————

9 持堪 **mo(chi)kota(eru)** hold out/up, last, stand, endure
15 踏堪 **fu(mi)kota(eru)** hold one's own, hold out

3b9.2

堵 堵

TO fence, enclosure; dwelling place

———————— 2 ————————

6 安堵 **ando** feel relieved, breathe easy

3b9.3

堯 尭

GYŌ high; far

3b9.4

堙

IN block, stop up; be buried; be destroyed

———————— 1 ————————

13 堙滅 **inmetsu** extinction, annihilation

3b9.5

堺

KAI, sakai boundary

———————— 1 ————————

0 堺 **Sakai** (city, Ōsaka-fu)

堁 → 岡 2r6.2

壻 → 婿 3e9.3

3b9.6 / 154

場 塲

JŌ, ba place

———————— 1 ————————

4 場内 **jōnai** within the premises/grounds/hall
5 場末 **basue** outskirts, suburbs
場代 **badai** admission fee
場外 **jōgai** outside the premises/grounds/hall
6 場合 **baai** case, occasion, circumstances
場当 **baa(tari)** grandstanding, applause-seeking
8 場所 **basho** place, location
場所柄 **bashogara** character of a place, location, situation, occasion
場所塞 **bashofusa(gi)** obstacle
9 場後 **baoku(re)** stage fright; nervousness
場面 **bamen** scene
10 場席 **baseki** room, space; seat, place

3

氵
土 9←
扌
口
女
巾
犭
弓
彳
彡
艹
宀
丷
山
士
广
尸
口

3

氵
→9 土
扌
口
女
巾
犭
弓
彳
彡
艹
宀
丷
山
圭
广
尸
口

12 場違 **bachiga(i)** the wrong place, out of place
13 場塞 **bafusa(gi)** something that takes up space
   場数踏 **bakazu (o) fu(mu)** gain experience
   場馴 **bana(re)** used to (the stage), experience

———————— 2 ————————

1 一場 **ichijō** one time, one place
2 入場 **nyūjō** entrance, admission
   入場券 **nyūjōken** admission/platform ticket
   入場者 **nyūjōsha** visitors, attendance
   入場門 **nyūjōmon** admission gate
   入場料 **nyūjōryō** admission fee
3 工場 **kōjō, kōba** factory, workshop, mill
   干場 **ho(shi)ba** a drying-ground
   下場 **o(ri)ba** place to get off, disembarking point
   弓場 **yumiba** archery ground
4 欠場 **ketsujō** fail to show up
5 矢場 **yaba** archery ground/range
   出場 **shutsujō** appear on stage, perform; participate in, enter (a competition)
   本場 **honba** home, habitat, the best place for
   市場 **shijō** market   **ichiba** marketplace
   台場 **daiba** fort, battery
   穴場 **anaba** good place known to few
   広場 **hiroba** plaza, public square
   冬場 **fuyuba** the winter season
   立場 **tachiba** standpoint, position, viewpoint
6 死場 **shi(ni)ba** place to die, place of death
   会場 **kaijō** meeting place; grounds
   刑場 **keijō** place of execution
   地場 **jiba** local(ly owned)
   行場 **yu(ki)ba** place to go/resort to, destination
   早場米 **hayabamai** early rice
   式場 **shikijō** ceremonial hall
7 来場 **raijō** attendance
   役場 **yakuba** town hall, public office
   売場 **u(ri)ba** sales counter, place where (tickcts) are sold
   売場係 **u(ri)bagakari** sales clerk
   見場 **mi(se)ba** highlight scene
        miba look, appearance
   初場所 **hatsubasho** New Year's grand sumo tournament
   足場 **ashiba** scaffold; foothold; convenience of location
8 其場 **so(no) ba** the place, on the spot, the occasion/situation
   其場限 **so(no)ba-kagi(ri)** makeshift, rough-and-ready
   其場逃 **so(no)ba-noga(re)** temporizing, stopgap
   其場凌 **so(no)ba-shino(gi)** makeshift, muddling through
   退場 **taijō** leave, exit, walk out

逃場 **ni(ge)ba** place of refuge; means of escape
泣場 **na(kase)ba** pathetic scene
茅場 **kayaba** field of grass/reeds
居場所 **ibasho** one's whereabouts, address
牧場 **bokujō, makiba** pasture, meadow, ranch
9 乗場 **no(ri)ba** (taxi) stand, bus stop, platform
急場 **kyūba** emergency, crisis
前場 **zenba** the morning (trading) session
洗場 **ara(i)ba** washing place
持場 **mo(chi)ba** one's post/rounds/jurisdiction
狩場 **ka(ri)ba** hunting grounds
後場 **goba** the afternoon (trading) session
相場 **sōba** market price; speculation; estimation
相場師 **sōbashi** speculator
春場所 **harubasho** the spring sumo tournament
砂場 **sunaba** sandbox; sand pit
音場 **onjō, onba** sound field
秋場所 **akibasho** autumn sumo tournament
10 射場 **shajō** shooting/rifle range; archery ground
遊場 **aso(bi)ba** playground
酒場 **sakaba** bar, saloon, tavern
浴場 **yokujō** bathroom, bath(house)
教場 **kyōjō** classroom
夏場 **natsuba** summertime, the summer season
夏場所 **natsubasho** the summer sumo tournament
馬場 **baba** riding ground
11 斎場 **saijō** site of a religious/funeral service
道場 **dōjō** (martial-arts) gymnasium; Buddhist seminary
捨場 **su(te)ba** dumping ground, dump
帳場 **chōba** counter, counting room, front office
猟場 **ryōba** game preserve, hunting ground
宿場 **shukuba** post town, relay station
宿場町 **shukuba machi** post/hotel town
寄場 **yo(ri)ba** place to meet/call at
祭場 **saijō** site of a ceremony
球場 **kyūjō** baseball grounds/stadium
現場 **genba, genjō** the actual spot; on the scene, at the site, in the field
盛場 **saka(ri)ba** bustling place, popular resort, amusement center
釣場 **tsu(ri)ba** fishing spot
閉場 **heijō** closing (the place)
12 遣場 **ya(ri)ba** disposal, use; place/where to put
湯場 **yuba** hot springs
満場 **manjō** the whole assembly/hall
満場一致 **manjō-itchi** unanimous
渡場 **wata(shi)ba** ferrying place
登場 **tōjō** come on stage; appear on the scene

焼場 **ya(ki)ba** crematory
飯場 **hanba** construction camp/bunkhouse
開場 **kaijō** opening
13 隠場 **kaku(re)ba** refuge, hiding place
　隠場所 **kaku(re)basho** refuge, hiding place
　農場 **nōjō** farm, ranch, plantation
　墓場 **hakaba** cemetery, graveyard
　戦場 **senjō** battlefield, the front
　置場 **o(ki)ba** place to put something
　電場 **denba, denjō** electric field
14 漁場 **gyojō, ryōba** fishing ground/banks
　磁場 **jiba, jijō** magnetic field
　踊場 **odo(ri)ba** dance hall/floor; (stairway)
　　landing
15 劇場 **gekijō** theater
　霊場 **reijō** sacred place, hallowed ground
16 壇場 **danjō** stage, platform, rostrum
18 臨場 **rinjō** attendance, presence, visit
　職場 **shokuba** workplace, job site
　難場 **nanba** difficult situation/stage
20 議場 **gijō** the floor (of the legislature)
21 露場 **rojō** weather measurement site
22 鱈場蟹 **tarabagani** king crab

———————— 3 ————————

3 工事場 **kōjiba** construction site
　土壇場 **dotanba** place of execution, eleventh
　　hour
　小劇場 **shōgekijō** little theater
4 分工場 **bunkōjō** branch plant/factory
　分教場 **bunkyōjō** detached classroom
　水泳場 **suieijō** swimming place/pool
　手水場 **chōzuba** lavatory, toilet
　火事場 **kajiba** scene of a fire
　火葬場 **kasōba** crematory
5 古戦場 **kosenjō** ancient battlefield
　正念場 **shōnenba** the crucial/now-or-never
　　moment
　石切場 **ishiki(ri)ba** quarry, stone pit
6 死刑場 **shikeijō** place of execution
　会議場 **kaigijō** meeting hall, place of
　　assembly
7 体操場 **taisōjō** gymnasium, exercise grounds
　芥捨場 **gomisu(te)ba** garbage dump
　町道場 **machi dōjō** martial-arts school in a
　　town
8 長丁場 **nagachōba** long stretch/scene
　波止場 **hatoba** wharf, pier
　実験場 **jikkenjō** proving/testing ground
　空相場 **karasōba** fictitious transaction
　昇降場 **shōkōjō** (station) platform
　炊事場 **suijiba** kitchen, cookhouse
　物干場 **monoho(shi)ba** place for drying
9 飛行場 **hikōjō** airport, airfield
　通相場 **tō(ri)sōba** market price; accepted
　　custom

風呂場 **furoba** bathroom
洗車場 **senshajō** car wash
独壇場 **dokudanjō** one's unrivaled field
独擅場 **dokusenjō** one's unrivaled field
狩猟場 **shuryōjō** game preserve
10 射的場 **shatekijō** rifle/shooting range
　射撃場 **shagekijō** shooting/rifle range
　修羅場 **shurajō, shuraba** scene of carnage
　遊技場 **yūgijō** place of amusement
　酒造場 **shuzōjō** brewery, distillery
　娯楽場 **gorakujō** place of amusement
　荷揚場 **nia(ge)ba** landing place
　宴会場 **enkaijō** banquet hall
　特売場 **tokubaijō** bargain counter/basement
　留置場 **ryūchijō** detention room, police cell
11 野球場 **yakyūjō** baseball park/stadium
　停車場 **teishajō, teishaba** railway station;
　　taxi stand
　運動場 **undōjō** playing/athletic field
　船着場 **funatsu(ki)ba** harbor, wharf
　魚市場 **uoichiba** fish market
12 普請場 **fushinba** construction site
　温泉場 **onsenba, onsenjō** spa, hot-springs
　　resort
　湯治場 **tōjiba** spa
　渡船場 **tosenba, tosenjō** ferrying place
　御猟場 **goryōba** imperial forest
　葬儀場 **sōgijō** funeral home
　屠殺場 **tosatsujō** slaughterhouse
　貿易場 **bōekijō** foreign market
　開港場 **kaikōjō** open/treaty port
13 愁嘆場 **shūtanba** pathetic/tragic scene
　試験場 **shikenjō** examination hall; laboratory,
　　proving grounds
　酪農場 **rakunōjō** dairy farm
　鉄工場 **tekkōjō** ironworks
　鉄火場 **tekkaba** gambling room
　電磁場 **denjiba** electromagnetic field
14 選挙場 **senkyojō** polling place, the polls
　演武場 **enbujō** drill hall
　演舞場 **enbujō** playhouse, theater
　演劇場 **engekijō** theater, stage
　練兵場 **renpeijō** parade ground
15 舞踏場 **butōjō** dance hall
　養豚場 **yōtonjō** hog/pig farm
　養魚場 **yōgyojō** fish farm/hatchery
　養鶏場 **yōkeijō** poultry farm
　調馬場 **chōbajō** riding ground
　駐車場 **chūshajō** parking lot
　駐輪場 **chūrinjō** bicycle parking lot
16 操車場 **sōshajō** switchyard
　積置場 **tsu(mi)o(ki)ba** storage/freight yard
17 闇相場 **yamisōba** black-market price
18 闘牛場 **tōgyūjō** bullring
19 蹴球場 **shūkyūjō** football/soccer/rugby field
20 競技場 **kyōgijō** stadium, sports arena

3

氵
土 9←
扌
口
女
巾
犭
弓
彳
彡
艹
宀
⺍
山
青
广
尸
口

競馬場 **keibajō** race track

―――――― 4 ――――――
1 一時預場 **ichiji azukarijō** baggage safe-keeping area
6 死体置場 **shitai o(ki)ba** morgue
8 青空市場 **aozora ichiba** open-air market
9 軍事工場 **gunji kōjō** war plant
海水浴場 **kaisuiyokujō** bathing beach
為替相場 **kawase sōba** exchange rate
10 株式市場 **kabushiki shijō** stock market
11 組立工場 **kumita(te) kōjō** assembly/knockdown plant
14 製缶工場 **seikan kōjō** cannery

3b9.7 / 1592
TEI, tsutsumi bank, embankment, dike

堤

―――――― 1 ――――――
6 堤防 **teibō** embankment, dike, levee
―――――― 2 ――――――
8 突堤 **tottei** jetty, pier, breakwater
12 堰堤 **entei** dam, weir
14 墨堤 **Bokutei** banks of the Sumida river
16 築堤 **chikutei** embankment, banking

3b9.8
KA crucible, melting pot

堝

―――――― 2 ――――――
8 坩堝 **kanka, rutsubo** crucible, melting pot

3b9.9 / 1840
TŌ tower

塔

―――――― 2 ――――――
5 石塔 **sekitō** tombstone, stone monument
6 尖塔 **sentō** pinnacle, spire, steeple
8 卒塔婆 **sotoba** wooden grave tablet, stupa
10 砲塔 **hōtō** gun turret
11 斜塔 **shatō** leaning tower (of Pisa)
13 鉄塔 **tettō** steel tower
19 蟻塔 **ari(no)tō** anthill
―――――― 3 ――――――
4 五重塔 **gojū (no) tō** five-storied pagoda
司令塔 **shireitō** control/conning tower
8 忠霊塔 **chūreitō** monument to the war dead
金字塔 **kinjitō** a pyramid; a monumental work
9 信号塔 **shingōtō** signal tower
12 象牙塔 **zōge (no) tō** ivory tower
貯水塔 **chosuitō** water tower
14 管制塔 **kanseitō** control tower
15 慰霊塔 **ireitō** cenotaph, memorial tower

3b9.10 / 1751
CHŌ, tsuka mound, hillock

塚 塚

―――――― 2 ――――――
5 石塚 **ishizuka** pile of stones, cairn
7 貝塚 **kaizuka** heap of shells
12 筆塚 **fudezuka** mound made over used writing brushes buried with a memorial service
19 蟻塚 **arizuka** anthill
―――――― 3 ――――――
1 一里塚 **ichirizuka** milestone
5 比翼塚 **hiyokuzuka** lovers' double grave

3b9.11 / 1805
HEI wall, fence

塀 塀

―――――― 2 ――――――
3 土塀 **dobei** mud wall
5 外塀 **sotobei** outer wall
石塀 **ishibei** stone wall
8 板塀 **itabei** board fence
―――――― 3 ――――――
11 船板塀 **funaitabei** fence made of old ship timbers

3b9.12
EN, seki dam
se(ku) dam up; check, stem, prevent

堰

―――――― 1 ――――――
4 堰止 **se(ki)to(meru)** dam up; check, stem
12 堰堤 **entei** dam, weir

3b9.13 / 1289
KEN, kata(i) hard, firm, solid

堅

―――――― 1 ――――――
2 堅人 **katajin** honest/serious person
4 堅太 **katabuto(ri)** solidly built (person)
堅木 **katagi** hardwood, oak
6 堅気 **katagi** honest, decent, straight
7 堅牢 **kenrō** strong, solid, (color)fast
堅忍 **kennin** perseverance, fortitude
8 堅果 **kenka** nut
堅苦 **katakuru(shii)** stiff-mannered, formal; punctilious
堅実 **kenjitsu** solid, sound, reliable
堅固 **kengo** strong, solid, steadfast
9 堅信礼 **kenshinrei** (Christian) confirmation
堅陣 **kenjin** stronghold

堅城　**kenjō**　strong/impregnable castle
堅持　**kenji**　hold fast to, adhere to
堅炭　**katazumi**　hard charcoal
12 堅塁　**kenrui**　stronghold
13 堅塩　**katashio**　rock salt
15 堅調　**kenchō**　firmness, bullish tone, rising trend (cf. 軟調)

──────── 2 ────────

3 口堅　**kuchigata(i)**　close-mouthed, discreet
4 中堅　**chūken**　main body (of troops), center, backbone, mainstay, main-line
　中堅企業　**chūken kigyō**　medium-size business/company
　手堅　**tegata(i)**　steady, firm; solid, reliable
8 底堅　**sokogata(i)**　(prices) holding firm, having bottomed out
　物堅　**monogata(i)**　honest, faithful, reliable

──────── 3 ────────

13 義理堅　**girigata(i)**　having a strong sense of duty

3b9.14

堡　**HO, HŌ**　fort

──────── 1 ────────
12 堡塁　**hōrui**　fort, stronghold
──────── 3 ────────
16 橋頭堡　**kyōtōhō**　bridgehead, beachhead

3b9.15

鐵　**TETSU**　old, elderly

3b9.16 / 685

報　**HŌ**　news, report; reward, retribution
　　muku(iru)　reward, retaliate

──────── 1 ────────
0 報じる/ずる　**hō(jiru/zuru)**　repay, requite; report, inform
7 報告　**hōkoku**　report
　報告者　**hōkokusha**　reporter, informer
　報告書　**hōkokusho**　(written) report/statement
8 報知　**hōchi**　information, news, intelligence
　報国　**hōkoku**　service to one's country, patriotism
10 報恩　**hōon**　repaying a kindness, gratitude
11 報道　**hōdō**　reporting, news coverage
　報道陣　**hōdōjin**　the press corps
13 報奨　**hōshō**　bonus, reward
　報酬　**hōshū**　remuneration
14 報徳　**hōtoku**　repaying a kindness, gratitude

17 報償　**hōshō**　compensation, reward, remuneration
　報謝　**hōsha**　requital of a favor, recompense

──────── 2 ────────
1 一報　**ippō**　a report, information
4 予報　**yohō**　forecast, preannouncement
　凶報　**kyōhō**　bad news
　内報　**naihō**　advance/confidential information
　公報　**kōhō**　official bulletin, communiqué
　月報　**geppō**　monthly report
　日報　**nippō**　daly report/newspaper
5 弘報　**kōhō**　publicity
　弘報部　**kōhōbu**　public relations department
　広報　**kōhō**　publicity
　広報部　**kōhōbu**　public relations department
6 年報　**nenpō**　annual report
　会報　**kaihō**　bulletin, report, transactions (of a society)
　返報　**henpō**　in return/retaliation for
　吉報　**kippō**　good news, glad tidings
　旬報　**junpō**　report issued every ten days
7 別報　**beppō**　another report
　応報　**ōhō**　retribution
　局報　**kyokuhō**　official bulletin; service telegram
　快報　**kaihō**　good news
　私報　**shihō**　private report/message
8 画報　**gahō**　illustrated magazine, news in pictures
　果報　**kahō**　good fortune, luck
　果報者　**kahōmono**　lucky person
　官報　**kanpō**　official gazette/telegram
9 飛報　**hihō**　urgent message
　急報　**kyūhō**　urgent message, alarm
　速報　**sokuhō**　bulletin, news flash
　通報　**tsūhō**　report, dispatch, bulletin, news
　後報　**kōhō**　later report, further information
　訃報　**fuhō**　news of someone's death
10 既報　**kihō**　previous report
　週報　**shūhō**　weekly bulletin/newspaper
　朗報　**rōhō**　good news, glad tidings
　時報　**jihō**　review; time signal
　特報　**tokuhō**　news bulletin
11 偽報　**gihō**　false report, canard
　陽報　**yōhō**　open reward (for a secret act of charity)
　虚報　**kyohō**　flase report, groundless rumor
　捷報　**shōhō**　news of victory
　情報　**jōhō**　information
　情報化社会　**jōhōka shakai**　information-oriented society
　情報屋　**jōhōya**　(horserace) tipster
　情報部　**jōhōbu**　information bureau
　情報源　**jōhōgen**　news/information sources
　情報網　**jōhōmō**　intelligence network

略報 **ryakuhō** brief report
敗報 **haihō** news of defeat
12 勝報 **shōhō** news of victory
無報酬 **muhōshū** without pay, for free
悲報 **hihō** sad news
13 彙報 **ihō** collection of reports, bulletin
続報 **zokuhō** follow-up report
詳報 **shōhō** full/detailed report
電報 **denpō** telegram
電報料 **denpōryō** telegram charges
14 誤報 **gohō** erroneous report/information
雑報 **zappō** miscellaneous news
15 確報 **kakuhō** definite news, confirmed report
16 諜報 **chōhō** intelligence, espionage
19 警報 **keihō** warning, alarm
警報機 **keihōki** warning device, alarm

————————— 3 —————————

1 一矢報 **isshi (o) muku(iru)** shoot back, retort
5 半官報 **hankanpō** semiofficial paper
6 至急報 **shikyūhō** urgent telegram/call
尽忠報国 **jinchū-hōkoku** loyalty and patriotism
7 決算報告 **kessan hōkoku** closing-of-accounts report, financial statement
8 注意報 **chūihō** (storm) warning

————————— 4 —————————

4 火災警報 **kasai keihō** fire alarm
6 因果応報 **inga-ōhō** reward according to deeds, retribution
19 警戒警報 **keikai keihō** an (air-raid) alert

3b9.17

赧 **TAN** redden, blush

3b9.18 / 1000

超 **CHŌ** super-, ultra-
ko(eru) go beyond, exceed
ko(su) go beyond, exceed

————————— 1 —————————

0 超 L S I **chōeruesuai** very large scale integrated circuits
2 超人 **chōjin** superman
超人的 **chōjinteki** superhuman
3 超凡 **chōbon** uncommon, extraordinary
6 超伝導 **chōdendō** superconductivity
超自然 **chōshizen** supernatural
超自然的 **chōshizenteki** supernatural
7 超克 **chōkoku** overcome, surmount
8 超弩級 **chōdokyū** superdreadnought-class
超国家主義 **chōkokka shugi** ultranationalism
超国家的 **chōkokkateki** ultranationalistic

9 超俗 **chōzoku** unworldly, aloof from the world
超音 **chōon** supersonic, ultrasonic
超音波 **chōonpa** ultrasonic waves
超音速 **chōonsoku** supersonic speed
10 超高速度 **chōkōsokudo** superhigh-speed
超党派 **chōtōha** non-partisan
超特作 **chōtokusaku** super production, feature film
超特急 **chōtokkyū** superexpress (train)
11 超過 **chōka** exceed
超過額 **chōkagaku** surplus, excess
超脱 **chōdatsu** transcend, stand aloof, rise above
超現実主義 **chōgenjitsu shugi** surrealism
12 超満員 **chōman'in** crowded beyond capacity
超短波 **chōtanpa** ultrashort-wave, very high frequency
超然(taru) **chōzen(taru)** transcendental, aloof
超然内閣 **chōzen naikaku** non-party government
超越 **chōetsu** transcend, rise above
超絶 **chōzetsu** transcend; excel, surpass
13 超感覚的 **chōkankakuteki** extrasensory
超電導 **chōdendō** superconductivity
18 超顕微鏡 **chōkenbikyō** ultramicroscope

————————— 2 —————————

2 入超 **nyūchō** excess of imports over exports, unfavorable balance of trade (short for 輸入超過)
5 出超 **shutchō** excess of exports over imports, favorable balance of trade (short for 輸出超過)

3b9.19

趁 **CHIN** go to; follow

越 → **4n8.2**

3b9.20 / 1678

喪 **SŌ, mo** mourning; loss

————————— 1 —————————

4 喪中 **mochū** period of mourning
喪心 **sōshin** be stunned/dazed/stupefied
5 喪失 **sōshitsu** loss
喪主 **moshu** chief mourner
8 喪服 **mofuku** mourning clothes
11 喪章 **moshō** mourning badge/band

—————————— 2 ——————————

8 沮喪 **sosō** dejection
国喪 **kokusō** national mourning
服喪 **fukumo** mourning
9 発喪 **hatsumo** death announcement

—————————— 3 ——————————

4 心神喪失 **shinshin sōshitsu** not of sound mind

—————————— 10 ——————————

3b10.1

塢

O fortress embankment; village

3b10.2 / 1524

塊

KAI, katamari lump, clod, clump

—————————— 1 ——————————

7 塊状 **kaijō** massive
8 塊茎 **kaikei** tuber
10 塊根 **kaikon** tuberous root

—————————— 2 ——————————

1 一塊 **hitokatama(ri)** a lump, a group
ikkai a lump
3 大塊 **taikai** large chunk, great mass
土塊 **dokai, tsuchikure** lump of earth, clod
5 氷塊 **hyōkai** lump/block of ice, ice floe
石塊 **sekkai, ishikoro, ishikure** pebble, stones
6 肉塊 **nikkai** piece of meat; the body
団塊 **dankai** lump, nodule; baby-boom (generation)
血塊 **kekkai** blood clot, clotted blood
8 金塊 **kinkai** gold nugget/bar/bullion
12 集塊 **shūkai** mass, cluster
13 鉛塊 **enkai** lead ingot
14 銀塊 **ginkai** silver ingot/bullion
15 鋳塊 **chūkai** ingot
16 凝塊 **gyōkai** a clot

3b10.3

墧

KAKU, KŌ hard/high/rocky ground
hanawa projecting part of a mountain, crag

3b10.4 / 1101

塩 鹽

EN, shio salt

—————————— 1 ——————————

2 塩入 **shioi(re)** salt shaker
4 塩化ビニル **enka biniru** vinyl chloride

塩分 **enbun** salt content, salinity
塩水 **shiomizu, ensui** salt water, brine
塩引 **shiobi(ki)** salt-cured; salted fish
5 塩出 **shioda(shi)** steep out the salt
塩加減 **shiokagen** seasoning with salt
塩田 **enden** salt field/farm
6 塩気 **shioke** saltiness
7 塩豆 **shiomame** salted beans
塩辛 **shiokara** salted fish (guts)
8 塩味 **shioaji** salty taste
塩物 **shiomono** salted food
10 塩梅 **anbai** seasoning; circumstances, condition, manner
塩素 **enso** chlorine
11 塩基 **enki** base, alkali
塩乾 **shiobo(shi)** salted and dried
塩魚 **shiozakana** salted fish
12 塩焼 **shioya(ki)** broiled with salt
塩税 **enzei** salt tax
14 塩漬 **shiozu(ke)** pickling in salt
塩酸 **ensan** hydrochloric acid
15 塩蔵 **enzō** preserve in salt
17 塩鮭 **shiozake, shiojake** salted salmon
18 塩類 **enrui** salts

—————————— 2 ——————————

1 一塩 **hitoshio** slightly salted
4 手塩 **teshio** table salt; small dish, saucer
手塩皿 **teshiozara** small dish, saucer
手塩掛 **teshio (ni) ka(kete)** (bring up) by hand
5 甘塩 **amajio** slightly salted
6 米塩 **beien** rice and salt; livelihood
8 苦塩 **nigashio, nigari** brine
岩塩 **gan'en** rock salt
9 海塩 **kaien** salt made from seawater
食塩 **shokuen** table salt
食塩水 **shokuensui** saline solution
12 堅塩 **katashio** rock salt
焼塩 **ya(ki)shio** baked/table salt
14 製塩 **seien** salt making
製塩業 **seiengyō** the salt industry
16 薄塩 **usujio** lightly salted
19 藻塩 **moshio** salt from burning seaweed
藻塩草 **moshiogusa** seaweed used in making salt; anthology

—————————— 3 ——————————

9 胡麻塩 **gomashio** salted toasted sesame seeds; gray-flecked hair
12 硝酸塩 **shosan'en** a nitrate

—————————— 5 ——————————

5 生理的食塩水 **seiriteki shokuensui** saline solution

塚 → 塚   **3b9.10**

3

氵
土 10←
扌
口
女
巾
犭
弓
彳
彡
艹
宀
屮
山
耂
广
尸
口

3b10.5

塡 填

TEN fill in

1

6 塡充 **tenjū** fill (up), plug
12 塡隙 **tengeki** caulking, filling
塡補 **tenpo** fill up; compensate for, make good; replenish, complete

2

6 充塡 **jūten** filling
12 装塡 **sōten** a charge (of gunpowder)
補塡 **hoten** fill, supply (a deficiency), compensate for

3b10.6

塘

TŌ embankment, dike

3b10.7 / 1674

塾

JUKU private/cram school

1

5 塾生 **jukusei** cram-school student
8 塾長 **jukuchō** cram-school principal

2

7 私塾 **shijuku** private school
10 家塾 **kajuku** private school
13 義塾 **gijuku** private school

3b10.8 / 1838

塑

SO (clay) molding, plastic

1

9 塑造 **sozō** modeling, molding, plastic (arts)
14 塑像 **sozō** clay figure, plastic image

2

5 可塑 **kaso** plastic
可塑物質 **kaso busshitsu** plastics
11 彫塑 **chōso** carving and (clay) modeling, the plastic arts

3b10.9

塒

SHI, negura nest, roost

3b10.10 / 1073

塗

TO, nu(ru) paint, apply (a coating), smear onto **mabu(su)** smear/sprinkle/cover with **mami(reru)** be smeared/spattered/covered with

1

3 塗工 **tokō** painter; painting
5 塗付 **nu(ri)tsu(keru)** smear, daub
塗布 **tofu** apply (a coating)
塗立 **nu(ri)ta(teru)** put on thick makeup
nu(ri)ta(te) freshly painted/plastered, Wet Paint
8 塗油 **toyu** unction, anointing
塗抹 **tomatsu** paint over/out, smear
塗物 **nu(ri)mono** lacquerware
9 塗盆 **nu(ri)bon** lacquered tray
塗炭 **totan** misery, distress
10 塗消 **nu(ri)ke(su)** paint out
塗料 **toryō** paint, paint and varnish
12 塗椀 **nu(ri)wan** lacquered bowl
塗替 **nu(ri)ka(eru)** repaint
塗散 **nu(ri)chi(rasu)** besmear, daub all over
塗装 **tosō** painting, coating
塗絵 **nu(ri)e** line drawing for coloring in
15 塗潰 **nu(ri)tsubu(su)** paint out
塗箸 **nu(ri)bashi** lacquered chopsticks
16 塗薬 **nu(ri)gusuri** ointment, liniment
17 塗擦 **tosatsu** smearing and rubbing, embrocation
塗擦剤 **tosatsuzai** liniment

2

3 上塗 **uwanu(ri)** final coat(ing)
下塗 **shitanu(ri)** undercoat(ing)
4 中塗 **nakanu(ri)** second/next-to-last coating (of lacquer)
5 白塗 **shironu(ri)** painted white
目塗 **menu(ri)** sealing, plastering up
6 朱塗 **shunu(ri)** red-lacquered
血塗 **chimami(re)** bloodstained
chinu(ru) smear with blood
11 黒塗 **kuronu(ri)** black-lacquered, painted black
粗塗 **aranu(ri)** rough/first coating (of plaster)
14 漆塗 **urushinu(ri)** lacquered, japanned
15 糊塗 **koto** patch up, temporize

3

4 水性塗料 **suisei toryō** water-based paint
8 夜光塗料 **yakō toryō** luminous paint
油性塗料 **yusei toryō** oil-based paint

3b10.11

漟

Ama (title of a Noh play)

3b10.12

塋

EI grave, burial mound

3b10.13

齰 **SHOKU, yabusa(ka)** grudgingly, reluctant

— 2 —

7 吝齰 **rinshoku** miserly, stingy
吝齰家 **rinshokuka** miser, niggard
10 悋齰家 **rinshokuka** miser, skinflint

越→ **4n8.2**

3b10.14

毀 **KI** break, destroy; censure
kobo(tsu), kowa(su) break, destroy
kobo(reru) be nicked/chipped/broken
kowa(reru) break, get broken, be ruined

— 1 —

8 毀物 **kowa(re)mono** fragile article
13 毀傷 **kishō** injury, damage
毀棄 **kiki** (willful) destruction
毀損 **kison** damage, injure
毀誉 **kiyo** criticism and/or praise
毀誉褒貶 **kiyo-hōhen** praise and/or criticism

— 2 —

8 取毀 **to(ri)kowa(su)** tear down, demolish

— 11 —

場→場 **3b9.6**

3b11.1 / 864

境 **KYŌ, KEI, sakai** boundary

— 1 —

4 境内 **keidai** precincts, grounds
5 境目 **sakaime** borderline; crisis
6 境地 **kyōchi** state, stage, field, environment
9 境界 **kyōkai** boundary, border
境界標 **kyōkaihyō** landmark, boundary stone
境界線 **kyōkaisen** border/boundary line
11 境遇 **kyōgū** circumstances, environment
境涯 **kyōgai** circumstances, one's lot
境域 **kyōiki** boundary; grounds

— 2 —

4 辺境 **henkyō** frontier, outlying region
心境 **shinkyō** state of mind
5 北境 **hokkyō** northern boundary/frontier
仙境 **senkyō** fairyland, enchanted land
6 老境 **rōkyō** old age

7 村境 **murazakai** edge of the village
見境 **misakai** distinction, discrimination
8 佳境 **kakyō** interesting part, climax (of a story)
逆境 **gyakkyō** adversity
苦境 **kukyō** distress, predicament, crisis
国境 **kokkyō, kunizakai** border, national boundary
国境線 **kokkyōsen** boundary line, border
9 俗境 **zokkyō** the lay world
幽境 **yūkyō** secluded place
10 進境 **shinkyō** progress, improvement
12 蛮境 **bankyō** land of barbarians
悲境 **hikyō** sad plight, distress
越境 **ekkyō** (illegally) crossing the border
順境 **junkyō** favorable circumstances, prosperity
13 新境地 **shinkyōchi** new area, fresh ground
詩境 **shikyō** the locale of a poem
14 端境 **hazakai** between harvests, lean period
端境期 **hazakaiki** off/between-crops season
15 潮境 **shiozakai** boundary (between two ocean currents)
窮境 **kyūkyō** predicament
霊境 **reikyō** sacred precincts/grounds
17 環境 **kankyō** environment
環境庁 **Kankyōchō** Environment Agency
21 魔境 **makyō** haunts of wickedness

— 3 —

10 桃源境 **tōgenkyō** Shangri-La, paradise
18 観楽境 **kanrakukyō** pleasure resort

3b11.2

墟 墟 **KYO, KO** ruins

— 2 —

12 廃墟 **haikyo** ruins

3b11.3 / 712

増 増 **ZŌ** increase **fu(eru), ma(su), ma(saru)** (intr.) increase, rise **fu(yasu), ma(su)** (tr.) increase, raise **ma(shi)** increase, extra; every (day); better, preferable

— 1 —

3 増大 **zōdai** increase
増大号 **zōdaigō** enlarged number/issue
4 増収 **zōshū** increased income/yield
増水 **zōsui** (river) rise, swell, flood
5 増刊 **zōkan** special edition, extra number
増加 **zōka** increase, addition, rise, growth
7 増兵 **zōhei** reinforcements
8 増長 **zōchō** grow presumptuous, get too big for one's britches

3

氵
土
扌 11←
口
女
巾
犭
弓
彳
彡
艹
宀
⺍
山
吉
广
尸
口

增刷 **zōsatsu** additional printing, reprints
增注 **zōchū** additional notes
9 增発 **zōhatsu** put on an extra train; increased issue (of bonds)
增発列車 **zōhatsu ressha** extra train
增派 **zōha** send reinforcements
增音器 **zōonki** amplifier
10 增俸 **zōhō** salary increase
增進 **zōshin** increase, furtherance, improvement
增員 **zōin** personnel increase
增配 **zōhai** increased dividends/rations
11 增強 **zōkyō** reinforce, augment, beef up
增産 **zōsan** increase in production
增設 **zōsetsu** build on, extend, establish/install more
12 增減 **zōgen** increase and/or decrease
增援 **zōen** reinforcement(s)
增幅 **zōfuku** amplification
增幅器 **zōfukuki** amplifier
增量 **zōryō** increase in quantity
增殖 **zōshoku** increase, multiply, propagate
增殖炉 **zōshokuro** breeder reactor
增税 **zōzei** tax increase
增補 **zōho** enlarge, supplement
增給 **zōkyū** salary increase, pay raise
13 增資 **zōshi** capital increase
14 增徴 **zōchō** levy extra taxes
16 增築 **zōchiku** build on, extend, enlarge
18 增額 **zōgaku** increase (the amount)

───────── 2 ─────────

4 水增 **mizuma(shi)** water down, dilute, pad
日增 **hima(shi ni)** (getting ...er) day by day
6 年增 **toshima** mature/older woman
8 建增 **tatema(shi)** extension, annex
弥增 **iyama(su)** go on increasing
9 急增 **kyūzō** sudden increase
10 倍增 **baizō, baima(shi)** to double
純增 **junzō** net increase
11 累增 **ruizō** successive increases
12 割增 **warima(shi)** extra (charge/payment)
焼增 **ya(ki)ma(shi)** an extra print (of a photo)
16 激增 **gekizō** sudden/sharp increase

───────── 3 ─────────

3 大年增 **ōtoshima** woman in her 40's
7 改訂增補 **kaitei-zōho** revised and enlarged

塀→塀 **3b9.11**

墮→堕 **3b8.14**

3b11.4 / 1705

墨　墨　**BOKU** India ink, ink stick; Mexico; Sumida river
sumi India ink, ink stick

───────── 1 ─────────

5 墨付 **sumitsu(ki)** handwriting, signed certificate
墨汁 **bokujū** India ink
6 墨西哥 **Mekishiko** Mexico
墨色 **sumi-iro** shade of India ink
墨池 **bokuchi** ink(stone) well
墨守 **bokushu** strict adherence (to tradition)
墨糸 **sumiito** inked marking string
8 墨画 **bokuga** India-ink drawing
9 墨客 **bokkaku** artist
墨染 **sumizo(me)** dyeing/dyed black
10 墨書 **sumiga(ki)** draw a picture with India ink only
11 墨痕 **bokkon** ink marks; handwriting
12 墨堤 **Bokutei** banks of the Sumida river
墨壺 **sumitsubo** inkpot; carpenter's inking device
墨絵 **sumie** India-ink drawing
15 墨縄 **suminawa** inked marking string

───────── 2 ─────────

2 入墨 **i(re)zumi** tattooing; tattoo
4 水墨画 **suibokuga** India-ink painting
5 白墨 **hakuboku** chalk
石墨 **sekiboku** graphite
7 芳墨 **hōboku** scented ink; your esteemed letter
芳墨帳 **hōbokuchō** autograph album
9 眉墨 **mayuzumi** eyebrow pencil
10 唐墨 **karasumi, tōboku** Chinese ink stick
12 筆墨 **hitsuboku** pen and ink
13 靴墨 **kutsuzumi** shoe polish, bootblack
14 遺墨 **iboku** autograph of the deceased
16 薄墨 **usuzumi** thin India ink
翰墨 **kanboku** brush and ink; writing, drawing
17 鍋墨 **nabezumi** kettle soot

3b11.5

塹　**ZAN** ditch, moat

───────── 1 ─────────

17 塹壕 **zangō** trench, dugout

3b11.6

墅　**SHO** shed; country house
YA countryside

3b11.7 / 1132

墜　TSUI fall

——— 1 ———
6 墜死 **tsuishi** fall to one's death
12 墜落 **tsuiraku** fall, (airplane) crash

——— 2 ———
5 失墜 **shittsui** lose, fall
15 撃墜 **gekitsui** shoot down

3b11.8

赫　**KAKU** red; glowing red hot; brilliant, gleaming

——— 1 ———
3 赫々 **kakkaku, kakukaku** brilliant, glorious, distinguished

臺 → 台 **3d2.11**

3b11.9

甄　**KEN** porcelain, china; make clear; distinguish between

——— 12 ———
增 → 増 **3b11.3**

3b12.1 / 1662

墳　**FUN** (burial) mound, tomb

——— 1 ———
13 墳墓 **funbo** grave, tomb

——— 2 ———
4 円墳 **enpun** burial mound
5 古墳 **kofun** ancient burial mound

3b12.2

墫　**CHO** ground, cliff, embankment

墫 → 樽 **4a12.19**

墟 → 墟 **3b11.2**

3b12.3

壀　**mama** steep slope

墨 → 墨 **3b11.4**

3b12.4 / 1443

舗 舗　**HO** shop, store

——— 1 ———
11 舗道 **hodō** paved street, pavement
12 舗装 **hosō** pavement, paving

——— 2 ———
6 老舗 **rōho, shinise** long-established shop/store
8 店舗 **tenpo** shop, store
9 茶舗 **chaho** tea store
11 商舗 **shōho** store, shop
15 弊舗 **heiho** our store, we
　質舗 **shichiho** pawnshop
16 薬舗 **yakuho** drugstore

鞋 → **3k12.18**

——— 13 ———

3b13.1

墺　**Ō** land, shore; Austria

——— 1 ———
4 墺太利 **Ōsutoria** Austria

3b13.2

墻　**SHŌ, kaki** fence, hedge

——— 1 ———
16 墻壁 **shōheki** fence and wall

3b13.3 / 1407

壊 壊　**KAI, E** break **kowa(su)** break, tear down, destroy, damage **kowa(reru)** break, get broken, be destroyed

——— 1 ———
6 壊血病 **kaiketsubyō** scurvy
7 壊乱 **kairan** corrupt, subvert

10 壊疽 **eso** gangrene
12 壊廃 **kaihai** ruin, decay
13 壊滅 **kaimetsu** destruction, annihilation

──────── 2 ────────

5 打壊 **bu(chi)kowa(su)** break, smash; ruin, upset (plans)
叩壊 **tata(ki)kowa(su)** knock apart, wreck
6 全壊 **zenkai** complete destruction
朽壊 **kyūkai** rot and crumble
自壊 **jikai** disintegration
自壊作用 **jikai sayō** disintegration
7 決壊 **kekkai** rupture, break, collapse
8 取壊 **to(ri)kowa(su)** tear down, demolish
10 倒壊 **tōkai** collapse, be destroyed
破壊 **hakai** destroy, demolish, collapse
破壊力 **hakairyoku** destructive power
破壊主義 **hakai shugi** vandalism
破壊的 **hakaiteki** destructive
破壊者 **hakaisha** destroyer, wrecker
11 崩壊 **hōkai** collapse, disintegration

3b13.4 / 1912

壌 壌 **JŌ** soil

──────── 2 ────────

3 土壌 **dojō** soil
4 天壌無窮 **tenjō mukyū** eternal as heaven and earth
5 平壌 **Heijō** Pyongyang
12 雲壌 **unjō** clouds and earth; great difference
15 霄壌 **shōjō** (different as) heaven and earth

3b13.5 / 1839

壇 **DAN** stage, rostrum, podium; altar; world (of art)

──────── 1 ────────

3 壇上 **danjō** on the platform/stage/altar
10 壇家 **danka** supporter/parishoner of a temple
12 壇場 **danjō** stage, platform, rostrum

──────── 2 ────────

3 土壇場 **dotanba** place of execution, eleventh hour
4 仏壇 **butsudan** household Buddhist altar
文壇 **bundan** the literary world; literary column
7 花壇 **kadan** flower bed/garden
戒壇 **kaidan** ordination platform in a temple
8 画壇 **gadan** the artists' world
9 降壇 **kōdan** leave the rostrum
独壇場 **dokudanjō** one's unrivaled field
10 俳壇 **haidan** the haiku world
教壇 **kyōdan** platform, rostrum, lecturn

11 祭壇 **saidan** altar
12 登壇 **tōdan** ascend the platform, take the rostrum
13 楽壇 **gakudan** the musical world
聖壇 **seidan** altar; pulpit
詩壇 **shidan** poetry circles
14 演壇 **endan** rostrum, platform
歌壇 **kadan** the world of poetry
15 劇壇 **gekidan** the stage/theater
論壇 **rondan** world of criticism; rostrum
17 講壇 **kōdan** rostrum
18 雛壇 **hinadan** tiered stand for displaying dolls

──────── 3 ────────

14 説教壇 **sekkyōdan** pulpit

3b13.6 / 1136

墾 **KON** open up farmland, bring under cultivation

──────── 2 ────────

12 開墾 **kaikon** clear (land), bring under cultivation
開墾地 **kaikonchi** cultivated land

──────── 3 ────────

5 未開墾 **mikaikon** uncultivated

3b13.7 / 1489

壁 **HEKI, kabe** wall

──────── 1 ────────

1 壁一重 **kabe hitoe** (separated by) just a wall
3 壁土 **kabetsuchi** wall mud, plaster, stucco
8 壁画 **hekiga** fresco, mural
壁板 **kabeita** wainscoting
10 壁紙 **kabegami** wallpaper
11 壁掛 **kabeka(ke)** tapestry; wall (phone)
12 壁訴訟 **kabesoshō** grumbling to oneself
13 壁際 **kabegiwa** by/near the wall
壁新聞 **kabe shinbun** wall newspaper/poster
15 壁蝨 **dani** tick, mite

──────── 2 ────────

4 内壁 **naiheki** inside wall
5 生壁 **namakabe** undried wall
外壁 **gaiheki** outer wall
白壁 **hakuheki, shirakabe** white(washed) wall
6 合壁 **kappeki, gappeki** next-door house just a wall away
防壁 **bōheki** barrier, bulwark
8 板壁 **itakabe** wooden wall
9 城壁 **jōheki** castle walls, ramparts
面壁 **menpeki** meditation facing a wall
胃壁 **iheki** stomach lining

10 胸壁 **kyōheki** wall of the chest; breastwork, parapet
11 側壁 **sokuheki** side wall
粗壁 **arakabe** rough-coated wall
12 隔壁 **kakuheki** partition, bulkhead, septum
塁壁 **ruiheki** ramparts, walls
絶壁 **zeppeki** precipice, cliff
13 障壁 **shōheki** barrier
腹壁 **fukuheki** the abdominal wall
腸壁 **chōheki** intestinal wall
鉄壁 **teppeki** iron wall; impregnable fortress
16 墻壁 **shōheki** fence and wall

——————— 3 ———————
4 火口壁 **kakōheki** crater wall
6 防火壁 **bōkaheki** fire wall

——————— 4 ———————
6 近所合壁 **kinjo gappeki** immediate neighborhood
8 金城鉄壁 **kinjō-teppeki** impregnable castle

——————— 14 ———————

3b14.1

壚 **mama** steep slope

3b14.2

壔 **TŌ** fort; hill; drum; cylinder

3b14.3

壕 **GŌ, KŌ, hori** moat, ditch, trench, dugout

——————— 2 ———————
14 塹壕 **zangō** trench, dugout
——————— 3 ———————
6 防空壕 **bōkūgō** air-raid/bomb shelter

3b14.4

壑 **KAKU** valley; ditch

壓 → 圧 **2p3.1**

3b14.5

趨 **SŪ, SHU** run; go; tend toward

——————— 1 ———————
6 趨向 **sūkō** trend, tendency
13 趨勢 **sūsei** trend, tendency
——————— 2 ———————
10 帰趨 **kisū** trend, tendency; consequence

3b14.6

牆 **SHŌ, kaki** fence, wall

——————— 15 ———————

3b15.1

壙 **KŌ** (grave) hole, cave

3b15.2

翹 **GYŌ** raise (one's head in expectation); excel

——————— 16 ———————

3b16.1

壜 罎 **TAN, DON, bin** bottle

壞 → 壊 **3b13.3**

3b16.2

壟 **RŌ** mound, hillock

——————— 1 ———————
11 壟断 **rōdan** monopolize

——————— 17 ———————

壤 → 壌 **3b13.4**

壚 → 塵 **3q12.5**

——————— 21 ———————

齺 → **3r21.1**

3

氵
土 16←
扌
口
女
巾
犭
弓
彳
彡
艹
宀
⺍
山
吉
广
尸
口

扌 3c

Left margin radical list (top to bottom): 氵 土 扌→ 口 女 巾 犭 弓 彳 彡 艹 宀 ⺌ 山 士 吉 广 尸 口 — section **3**

手 0.1	扎 1.1	扑 2.1	払 2.2	打 2.3	扣 3.1	托 3.2	扠 3.3	扱 3.4	叉 3.5	扛 3.6	扜 3.7	狂 4.1
找 4.2	抉 4.3	扱 3c3.5	扶 4.4	把 4.5	抔 4.6	折 4.7	抓 4.8	抖 4.9	拔 4.10	抄 4.11	抑 4.12	批 4.13
扑 4.14	抗 4.15	技 4.16	扮 4.17	投 4.18	抒 4.19	扼 4.20	择 4.21	抛 3c5.27	拓 5.1	拉 5.2	拜 5.3	拇 5.4
押 5.5	抻 5.6	抽 5.7	拑 5.8	抹 5.9	拌 5.10	拙 5.11	拂 3c2.2	拆 5.12	披 5.13	拍 5.14	抱 5.15	拗 5.16
拊 5.17	抵 5.18	拯 5.19	担 5.20	拐 5.21	拐 3c5.21	招 5.22	拈 5.23	抬 3c14.7	拵 5.24	拡 5.25	拠 5.26	抛 5.27
拘 5.28	拒 5.29	拏 5.30	挟 6.1	拷 6.2	捞 6.3	挒 6.4	挑 6.5	挌 6.6	挂 6.7	持 6.8	拱 6.9	按 6.10
拮 6.11	括 6.12	挼 6.13	拾 6.14	指 6.15	拍 3c5.14	挺 6.16	拭 6.17	拳 6.18	挈 6.19	捉 7.1	挿 7.2	捕 7.3
挾 3c6.1	捌 7.4	搜 7.5	捏 7.6	捍 7.7	挤 7.8	捋 7.9	捐 7.10	挨 7.11	挽 7.12	捩 7.13	振 3c8.31	振 7.14
挫 7.15	推 8.1	捫 8.2	捶 8.3	捷 8.4	揶 8.5	掀 8.6	排 8.7	捲 8.8	接 8.9	控 8.10	捧 8.11	捧 8.12
揭 8.13	採 8.14	授 8.15	探 8.16	捗 3c7.10	捺 8.17	掟 8.18	捥 8.19	措 8.20	描 8.21	掃 8.22	掩 8.23	掎 8.24
捻 8.25	捨 8.26	捨 3c8.26	掄 8.27	掠 8.28	掖 8.29	掉 8.30	挽 3c7.13	搔 3c10.11	掘 8.31	据 8.32	掇 8.33	掫 8.34
掬 8.35	掏 8.36	捆 3c11.6	掣 8.37	揀 9.1	插 3c7.2	搜 3c7.5	捲 3c8.9	揉 9.2	揆 9.3	提 9.4	揚 9.5	揭 3c8.13
揩 9.6	援 9.7	搖 9.8	揖 9.9	搭 9.10	揣 9.11	搽 9.12	揮 9.13	換 9.14	揃 9.15	握 9.16	揠 9.17	搻 9.18
搗 10.1	搬 10.2	搦 10.3	携 10.4	搏 10.5	摂 10.6	搆 10.7	搾 10.8	搨 10.9	搔 10.10	搖 10.11	搖 3c9.8	損 10.12
摸 10.13	搶 10.14	搚 10.15	搓 10.16	搏 11.1	摎 11.2	摺 11.3	摧 11.4	摘 11.5	摑 11.6	撃 11.7	摯 11.8	撲 12.1
撒 12.2	撤 12.3	撕 12.4	撈 12.5	撚 12.6	撫 12.7	播 12.8	撰 12.9	撞 12.10	撹 3c20.1	撥 12.11	撩 12.12	撮 12.13
撓 12.14	擒 12.15	撻 12.16	撼 13.1	播 13.2	擇 3c4.21	操 13.3	撿 13.4	擁 13.5	擅 13.6	據 3c5.26	擔 3c5.20	擊 3c11.7
擧 3n7.1	擘 13.7	擲 14.1	擬 14.2	擢 14.3	擤 14.4	擦 14.5	擯 14.6	擡 14.7	擠 14.8	擿 14.9	摘 14.10	擱 14.11
擾 15.1	擽 15.2	攅 3c19.2	揖 15.3	擺 15.4	擴 3c5.25	攀 15.5	攘 17.1	攝 3c10.6	攜 3c10.4	攤 19.1	攢 19.2	攣 19.3
攪 20.1	攫 20.2	攬 22.1										

3c0.1 / 57

SHU, te, ta- hand

手

1

0 手ぶらで **te(bura de)** empty-handed
手ずから **te(zukara)** with one's own hands, personally
1 手一杯 **te-ippai** hands full; barely making ends meet
2 手入 **tei(re)** repairs; care, tending
0 手工 **shukō** manual arts, handicraft
手工芸 **shukōgei** handicraft(s)
手工業 **shukōgyō** manual industry, handicrafts
手下 **teshita** subordinate, follower
手土産 **temiyage** visitor's present
手口 **teguchi** modus operandi, way, trick
4 手不足 **tebusoku** shorthanded, understaffed
手元 **temoto** at hand; in one's care; ready cash
手内 **te(no)uchi** palm; skill, capacity; (secret) intentions
手内職 **tenaishoku** manual piecework at home
手切 **tegi(re)** sever connections with, break up with
手切金 **tegi(re)kin** solatium for severing relations
手切話 **tegi(re)banashi** talk of separation
手文庫 **tebunko** small bookcase
手分 **tewa(ke)** dividing up the work
手込 **te (no) kon(da)** elaborate
tego(me) rape
手水 **temizu, chōzu** water for washing the hands
手水場 **chōzuba** lavatory, toilet
手引 **tebi(ki)** guidance; introduction, primer; good offices, introduction
手引書 **tebi(ki)sho** handbook, manual
手心 **tegokoro** making allowances, discretion, what to do
5 手出 **teda(shi)** interfere, have a hand in; strike the first blow
手本 **tehon** model, example, pattern
手弁当 **tebentō** bringing/buying one's own lunch
手甲 **te(no)kō** the back of the hand
tekkō covering for the back of the hand
手仕事 **teshigoto** hand work, manual labor
手仕舞 **tejima(i)** clearing of accounts, clearance (sale)
手代 **tedai** (sales) clerk
手付 **tetsu(ke)** earnest money, deposit
tetsu(ki) way of using one's hands

手付金 **tetsu(ke)kin** earnest money, deposit
手加減 **tekagen** use discretion, make allowances; knack, tact, skill
手写 **shusha** copy/transcribe by hand
手平 **te (no) hira** palm
手打 **teu(chi)** handmade; striking a bargain; killing by one's own hand
手広 **tebiro(i)** extensive; spacious
手札 **tefuda** name card; a hand (in card playing)
手札型 **tefudagata** 11 cm high by 8 cm wide (photo)
手玉 **tedama** beanbag
手玉取 **tedama (ni) to(ru)** lead by the nose, wrap around one's little finger
手立 **teda(te)** means, method
6 手休 **teyasu(mi)** rest, pause, break
手合 **tea(i)** fellow, chap **tea(wase)** game, contest; sale, transaction
手交 **shukō** hand over, deliver
手近 **tejika** close by, handy, familiar
手先 **tesaki** fingers, dexterity; tool, agent
手向 **temu(kau)** raise one's hand against, resist, oppose **tamu(ke)** offering (to gods and Buddha); parting/farewell gift **tamu(keru)** offer, pay tribute (to the dead)
手当 **tea(te)** (medical) treatment, care; allowance, (fringe) benefit
手当次第 **tea(tari) shidai** (whatever is) within reach, haphazardly
手回 **temawa(ri)** personal effects, one's things **temawa(shi)** prepare, get ready
手回品 **temawa(ri)hin** personal effects
手早 **tebaya(i)** quick, nimble, agile
7 手作 **tezuku(ri)** handmade, homemade
手余 **teama(su)** have/be too much to handle
手余者 **teama(shi)mono** someone hard to handle
手助 **tedasu(ke)** help
手兵 **shuhei** troops under one's command
手沢 **shutaku** soiled/shiny from much handling
手沢本 **shutakubon** a favorite book
手折 **tao(ru)** break off, pluck
手抜 **tenu(ki)** (intentional) omission **tenu(kari)** (unintentional) omission, oversight, error
手技 **shugi** skill, technique
手投弾 **tena(ge)dan** hand grenade
手形 **tegata** bill, (promissory) note
手芸 **shugei** handicrafts
手芸品 **shugeihin** handicrafts
手応 **tegota(e)** response, effect, resistance
手利 **teki(ki)** one clever with his hands; expert, master

3

氵
土
扌 0←
口
女
巾
犭
弓
彳
彡
艹
宀
⺌
山
吉
广
尸
口

3

手車 **teguruma** handcart
手足 **teashi** hands and feet
8 手長 **tenaga** long-armed person; kleptomaniac
手長猿 **tenagazaru** long-armed ape, gibbon
手刷 **tezu(ri)** hand-printing
手直 **tenao(shi)** adjust afterwards, readjust
手並 **tena(mi)** skill, performance
手斧 **chōna, teono** adz, hatchet
手厚 **teatsu(i)** warm, cordial, hospitable; generous
手法 **shuhō** technique, method
手押車 **teo(shi)guruma** pushcart, wheelbarrow
手拍子 **tebyōshi** beating time; carelessly
手招 **temane(ki)** beckoning
手拵 **tegoshira(e)** handmade, homemade
手始 **tehaji(me)** beginning, to start with
手妻 **tezuma** fingertips; sleight of hand
手空 **tea(ki)** leisure, spare/idle time
手枕 **temakura** using one's arm for a pillow
手明 **tea(ki)** leisure, spare/idle time
手者 **te(no)mono** one's men
手物 **te(no)mono** something in one's hand; specialty, strong point
手放 **tebana(su)** let go of, part with; leave unattended **tebana(shi)** without holding on to, left unattended; unreservedly
手性 **teshō** skill (with one's hands)
手取 **teto(ri)** skillful sumo wrestler; good manager **tedo(ri)** net (profit)
手取早 **te(t)to(ri)baya(i)** quick, rough-and-ready
手取足取 **teto(ri)-ashito(ri)** by the hands and feet, bodily, by main force
手取金 **tedo(ri)kin** take-home pay
手金 **tekin** earnest money, deposit
9 手巻 **tema(ki)** hand-rolled (cigarettes), wind-up (clock)
手負 **teo(i)** wounded
手首 **tekubi** wrist
手前 **temae** you; this side of, toward oneself; out of consideration for; tea-ceremony procedures; oneself
手前勝手 **temae-gatte** selfish
手透 **tesu(ki)** leisure, spare/idle time
手造 **tezuku(ri)** handmade, homemade
手風琴 **tefūkin** accordion, concertina
手段 **shudan** means, measures
手洗 **teara(i)** washing the hands; lavatory
手洗所 **tearaijo** lavatory
手洗鉢 **teara(i)bachi** washbasin
手活 **tei(ke)** arranging flowers oneself; making (a geisha) one's wife or mistress
手垢 **teaka** soiling from handling
手持 **temo(chi)** goods on hand, goods in stock

手持品 **temo(chi)hin** supplies, goods on hand
手拭 **tenugu(i), tefu(ki)** towel
手品 **tejina** sleight of hand, magic tricks, juggling
手品師 **tejinashi** magician, juggler
手狭 **tezema** narrow, cramped, small
手後 **teoku(re)** too late, belated
手荒 **teara** rough, rude, harsh; violent; outrageous
手相 **tesō** lines of the palm
手相学 **tesōgaku** palmistry
手相見 **tesōmi** palm reader
手相術 **tesōjutsu** palmistry
手柄 **tegara** meritorious deed(s), achievement
手柄者 **tegaramono** meritorious person
手柄話 **tegarabanashi** bragging of one's exploits
手柄顔 **tegaragao** triumphant look
手枷 **tekase, tegase** handcuffs, manacles
手柔 **teyawa(raka)** gently, kindly, leniently
手染 **tezo(me)** hand-dyed
10 手真似 **temane** gesture, hand signals
手遊 **teaso(bi)** playing; plaything; gambling
手捕 **tedo(ri)** capture, catch with one's hands
手捌 **tesaba(ki)** maneuvering, manipulation
手振 **tebu(ri)** hand waving, gesture
手荷物 **tenimotsu** luggage, (hand) baggage
手書 **shusho** write in one's own hand
手書 **tega(ki)** handwritten
手紙 **tegami** letter
手料理 **teryōri** home cooking
手討 **teu(chi)** killing with one's own hand/ sword
手記 **shuki** note, memo
手配 **tehai, tekuba(ri)** arrangements, preparations; disposition (of troops)
手酌 **tejaku** helping oneself to a drink
11 手毬 **temari** (traditional cloth) handball
手毬歌 **temari uta** handball song
手動 **shudō** manual, hand-operated
手動式 **shudōshiki** manual, hand-operated
手動車 **shudōsha** handcar
手遅 **teoku(re)** too late, belated
手淫 **shuin** masturbation
手掛 **tega(kari)** handhold; clue, lead **tega(keru)** handle, deal with; have experience in; rear, look after
手控 **tebika(e)** note, memo; holding back
手探 **tesagu(ri)** groping, fumbling
手帳 **techō** (pocket) notebook
手張 **teba(ri)** hand-glued; speculation
手強 **tezuyo(i), tegowa(i)** strong, firm, severe, formidable
手術 **shujutsu** (surgical) operation
手術台 **shujutsudai** operating table
手術衣 **shujutsui** operating gown

手術室 **shujutsushitsu** operating room
手術料 **shujutsuryō** operating fee
手彫 **tebo(ri)** hand-carved
手桶 **teoke** (wooden) bucket
手械 **tekase, tegase** handcuffs, manacles
手習 **tenara(i)** practice penmanship; learning
手袋 **tebukuro** gloves, mittens
手盛 **temo(ri)** helping oneself (to food); managing for one's own convience; trap, trick
手細工 **tezaiku** handicraft, handmade
手許 **temoto** at hand; in one's care; ready cash
手頃 **tegoro** handy; suitable; moderate
12 手隙 **tesuki** leisure, spare/idle time
手違 **techiga(i)** hitch, something gone wrong
手渡 **tewata(shi)** personal/hand delivery
手堅 **tegata(i)** steady, firm; solid, reliable
手提 **tesa(ge)** handbag
手提金庫 **tesa(ge)kinko** cash box, portable safe
手提袋 **tesa(ge)bukuro** handbag
手提鞄 **tesa(ge)kaban** briefcase, grip
手提籠 **tesa(ge)kago** handbasket
手短 **temiji(ka)** short, brief
手幅 **tehaba** handbreadth
手落 **teo(chi)** omission, slip, oversight, neglect
手植 **teu(e)** planted personally
手勝手 **tegatte** handling, skill
手腕 **shuwan** ability, skill
手腕家 **shuwanka** man of ability
手焙 **teabu(ri)** hand-warmer, small hibachi
手焼 **teya(ki)** home-baked
te (o) ya(ku) burn one's fingers, have a bitter experience with
手痛 **teita(i)** severe, serious, hard, heavy
手筋 **tesuji** lines of the palm; aptitude; means, method
手筈 **tehazu** program, plan, arrangements
手答 **tegota(e)** response, effect, resistance
手軽 **tegaru** easy, readily, simple, informal, without ado
手間 **tema** time, labor, trouble; wages
手間仕事 **tema shigoto** tedious work; piecework
手間取 **temado(ru)** take time, be delayed
手間隙 **temahima** labor and time, trouble
手間賃 **temachin** wages
手順 **tejun** procedure, routine, process
13 手業 **tewaza** hand work, skill
手傷 **tekizu** wound, injury
手際 **tegiwa** performance, execution; skill, deftness, workmanship
手勢 **tezei** troops under one's command
手裏 **te (no) ura, shuri** palm of the hand
手裏剣 **shuriken** throwing-knife
手塩 **teshio** table salt; small dish, saucer

手塩皿 **teshiozara** small dish, saucer
手塩掛 **teshio (ni) ka(kete)** (bring up) by hand
手数 **tesū** trouble, pains, care　**tekazu** trouble; number of moves (in a game)
手数料 **tesūryō** handling charge, fee
手続 **tetsuzu(ki)** procedure, formalities
手触 **tezawa(ri)** the feel, touch
手詰 **tezu(me)** pressing, final
tezu(mari) hard up, in a fix
手話 **shuwa** sign language
手跡 **shuseki** handwriting (specimen)
手鈎 **tekagi** hook
手飼 **tega(i)** rear, keep (a pet)
手馴 **tena(reru)** get used to, become practiced in
14 手選 **tesen** handpicking (in mining)
手摺 **tesu(ri)** handrail, railing
手攫 **tezuka(mi)** take/grasp with the fingers
手蔓 **tezuru** influence, connections, good offices, go-between
手窪 **te (no) kubo** the hollow of the hand
手榴弾 **shuryūdan, teryūdan** hand grenade
手旗 **tebata** hand flag
手旗信号 **tebata shingō** flag signaling, semaphore
手慣 **tena(reru)** get used to, become practiced in
手製 **tesei** handmade, homemade
手鼻 **tebana** blowing one's nose with one's fingers
手練 **shuren** dexterity, manual skill
teren coaxing, wiles
手練手管 **teren-tekuda** coaxing, wiles, beguiling
手綱 **tazuna** reins, bridle
手管 **tekuda** beguiling trick, art, wiles
手箒 **tebōki** hand/whisk broom
手踊 **teodo(ri)** posture dancing
15 手慰 **tenagusa(mi)** fingering; gambling
手緩 **tenuru(i)** slack, lax, lenient; slow, dilatory
手編 **tea(mi)** knit(ting) by hand
手縫 **tenu(i)** hand-sewn, hand-stitched
手箱 **tebako** case, box
手駒 **tegoma** captured shōgi piece (kept in reserve)
16 手薄 **teusu** weakness, shortage
手薬煉引 **tegusune hi(ite)** prepared, all set for
手懐 **tenazu(keru)** tame, domesticate; win over
手錠 **tejō** handcuffs
手頸 **tekubi** wrist
17 手厳 **tekibi(shii)** severe, scathing, harsh
手燭 **teshoku** (portable) candlestick
手療治 **teryōji** home treatment, doctoring oneself

氵
土
扌
口
女
巾
犭
弓
彳
彡
艹
宀
⺌
山
吉
广
尸
口

3

手鞠 **temari** (traditional cloth) handball
手鍋 **tenabe** pan
18 手癖 **tekuse** habit of pilfering, sticky fingers
手織 **teo(ri)** handweaving
手職 **teshoku** handicraft
手蹟 **shuseki** handwriting (specimen)
手離 **tebana(re) suru** no longer need constant care; be finished and ready to hand over
19 手繰 **tegu(ri)** spinning by hand; dragnet; procedure, management **tagu(ru)** reel in (pulling hand over hand)
手繰込 **tagu(ri)ko(mu)** haul in
手繰出 **tagu(ri)da(su)** pay out (a line); trace (a clue)
手鏡 **tekagami** hand mirror; model, example
20 手懸 **tega(kari)** handhold; clue, lead **teka(ke)** handhold; concubine
22 手籠 **tekago** handbasket **tegome** rape

─────────── 2 ───────────

1 一手 **itte** a move (in a game); sole, exclusive (agent) **hitote** by one's own effort
一手販売 **itte hanbai** sole agency
2 二手 **futate** two groups/bands
入手 **nyūshu** obtain, get
人手 **hitode** worker, hand, help
3 工手 **kōshu** workman
大手 **ōte** large, major (companies); front castle gate **ōde** both arms
大手門 **ōtemon** front gate of a castle
大手柄 **ōtegara** great exploit
大手筋 **ōtesuji** big traders, major companies
上手 **jōzu** skillful, good at **uwate** better at, superior to; upper part, upstream **kamite** upper part; upstream; right side of the stage (as seen from the audience)
下手 **heta** unskillful, poor at **shimote** lower part; left side of the stage (as seen from the audience) **shitate, shitade** humble position; alee
下手人 **geshunin** perpetrator, culprit, criminal
下手物 **getemono** low-quality article; strange things
凡手 **bonshu** mediocre skill, ordinary talent
土手 **dote** embankment, dike, levee
女手 **onnade** woman's handwriting; hiragana; a woman to do the work
弓手 **yunde** the bow/left hand
小手 **kote** forearm; gauntlet
小手先 **kotesaki** (a good) hand (at)
小手調 **koteshira(be)** tryout, rehearsal
山手 **yamate, yama(no)te** hilly residential section, bluff, uptown
4 不手際 **futegiwa** clumsy, unskilled, inept
元手 **motode** capital, funds
凶手 **kyōshu** (the work of an) evil person

天手古舞 **tentekoma(i)** hectic activity
中手 **nakate** mid-season rice/vegetables
刈手 **ka(ri)te** reaper, mower
切手 **kitte** (postage) stamp
双手 **sōshu** both hands
片手 **katate** one hand, one-handed
片手桶 **katate oke** bucket with handle on one side
片手落 **katateo(chi)** partial, one-sided
片手間 **katatema** in one's spare time, on the side
片手業 **katate waza** side job
引手 **hi(ki)te** handle, knob; patron, admirer **hi(ku)te** inviter, wooer, suitor
火手 **hi(no)te** flames, fire
王手 **ōte** check, checkmate (in shōgi)
5 巧手 **kōshu** a skill; skilled worker
左手 **hidarite** left hand
仕手 **shite** protagonist; speculator
古手 **furute** used/secondhand article; ex-, retired
平手 **hirate** palm; (play) equally, with no handicap
払手 **hara(i)te** payer
打手 **dashu** (cricket) batsman **u(chi)te** hitter, shooter
右手 **migite** right hand
好手 **kōshu** good move (in a game)
玉手箱 **tamatebako** treasure chest; Pandora's box
6 両手 **ryōte** both hands
両手花 **ryōte (ni) hana** have a double advantage; sit between two pretty women
兇手 **kyōshu** (work of an) evil person
合手 **a(ino)te** interlude; musical accompaniment; sideshow
老手 **rōshu** old hand, past master, veteran, expert
先手 **sente** the first move; the initiative **sakite** front lines, vanguard
名手 **meishu** expert
行手 **yu(ku)te** route, path, destination
安手 **yasude** cheap kind
当手 **tōte** we; our side
早手回 **hayatemawa(shi)** early preparations
衣手 **koromode** sleeve
7 作手 **tsuku(ri)te** maker, builder; tiller, cultivator
助手 **joshu** helper, assistant
決手 **ki(me)te** deciding factor, clincher
赤手 **sekishu** bare hand/fists
把手 **totte** handle, grip, knob
抜手 **nu(ki)te** overarm/overhand stroke
技手 **gishu** assistant engineer
投手 **tōshu** pitcher (in baseball)
吹手 **fu(ki)te** braggart

妙手 **myōshu** expert, master, virtuoso
売手 **u(ri)te** seller
攻手 **se(me)te** attacker, the offensive
見手 **mite** onlooker
初手 **shote** beginning
男手 **otokode** man's strength; man's hand-writing, kanji
足手纒 **ashitemato(i), ashidemato(i)** hindrance, encumbrance
8 長手 **nagate** long(ish), longitudinal; a stretcher (in bricklaying)
毒手 **dokushu** the clutches of
使手 **tsuka(i)te** user, consumer; employer; spendthrift; (fencing) master
受手 **u(ke)te** receiver (of a message)
其手 **so(no) te** that trick/move/way
厚手 **atsude** thick (paper)
追手 **otte, o(i)te** pursuer
逆手 **gyakute** foul/dirty trick
    sakate underhand/backhand (grip)
送手 **oku(ri)te** sender
拍手 **hakushu** handclapping, applause
    kashiwade handclapping (at a shrine)
担手 **nina(i)te** bearer, carrier
若手 **wakate** young person/man; younger member
苦手 **nigate** one's weak point; someone hard to deal with
空手 **karate** empty-handed; karate
空手形 **karategata** bad check; empty promise
空手道 **karatedō** karate
岩手県 **Iwate-ken** (prefecture)
国手 **kokushu** skilled physician; master go player
取手 **to(t)te** handle, knob   **to(ri)te** recipient
9 乗手 **no(ri)te** (horse) rider; passenger
孫手 **mago(no)te** back scratcher
軍手 **gunte** (thick white cotton) work gloves
浅手 **asade** slight/flesh wound
派手 **hade** showy, flashy, gaudy
派手好 **hadezu(ki)** fond of display
拱手 **kyōshu** fold one's arms
拱手傍観 **kyōshu bōkan** stand idly by
按手礼 **anshurei** laying on of hands, ordination
指手 **sa(shi)te** a move (in chess)
後手 **ushi(ro)de** with one's hands (tied) behind one's back   **gote** second player (in go); outmaneuvered, passive
相手 **aite** the other party, partner, opponent
相手方 **aitekata** the other party, opponent
相手役 **aiteyaku** a role opposite (someone), (dance) partner
柏手 **kashiwade** clap one's hands (in worship at a shrine)
為手 **na(ri)te** suitable person, candidate

約手 **yakute** promissory note (short for 約束手形)
食手 **ku(i)te** eater; glutton
10 射手 **ite, shashu** archer, bowman
借手 **ka(ri)te** borrower, lessee, tenant
高手小手 **takate-kote** (bound) hand and foot
差手 **sa(shi)te** (not) very
酒手 **sakate** drink money, tip
捕手 **hoshu** catcher   **to(ri)te** constable
徒手 **toshu** empty-handed; penniless
徒手体操 **toshu taisō** calisthenics without apparatus
挙手 **kyoshu** raising the hand, show of hands, salute
唐手 **karate** karate
脂手 **aburade** greasy/oily hand
書手 **ka(ki)te** writer; calligrapher, painter
砲手 **hōshu** gunner, artilleryman
袖手 **shūshu** putting one's hands in one's sleeves; shunning effort
袖手傍観 **shūshu-bōkan** look on with arms folded
討手 **u(t)te** punitive expedition, pursuers
隻手 **sekishu** one-armed
11 深手 **fukade** deep wound, severe injury
得手 **ete** strong point, forte, specialty
得手物 **etemono** one's specialty
得手勝手 **etekatte** self-centered, selfish
望手 **nozo(mi)te** aspirant, applicant; buyer
組手 **ku(mi)te** joints; karate kata performed with partner
舵手 **dashu** helmsman, coxswain
釣手 **tsu(ri)te** angler
12 着手 **chakushu** start, commence, proceed with
遣手 **ya(ri)te** man of ability/resourcefulness
揉手 **mo(mi)de** rub one's hands together
握手 **akushu** shake hands
弾手 **hi(ki)te** (guitar/piano) player
御手洗 **oteara(i)** lavatory
    mitarashi holy water font at a shrine
落手 **rakushu** receive; make a bad move
極手 **ki(me)te** winning move, decisive factor
勝手 **katte** as one pleases, arbitrary; kitchen; the situation
勝手口 **katteguchi** kitchen/back door
勝手不如意 **katte-funyoi** hard up (for money), bad off
勝手元 **kattemoto** one's financial circumstances
勝手次第 **katte-shidai** having one's own way
勝手向 **kattemu(ki)** one's financial circumstances
無手 **mute** empty-handed; unarmed; without funds
無手法 **mute(p)pō** reckless, rash
塁手 **ruishu** baseman

番手 **bante** (yarn) count, (sandpaper) number/grade

買手 **ka(i)te** buyer

痛手 **itade** serious wound; hard blow

貰手 **mora(i)te** receiver, recipient

貸手 **ka(shi)te** lender, lessor

飲手 **no(mi)te** heavy drinker

13 働手 **hatara(ki)te** worker, breadwinner; able man

裏手 **urate** at the back, rear

義手 **gishu** artificial arm/hand

搗手 **tsu(ki)te** pounder

搦手 **kara(me)te** (attack a castle from) the rear gate

鼓手 **koshu** drummer

楽手 **gakushu** musician, bandsman

新手 **arate** reinforcements; newcomer; new method/trick

置手紙 **o(ki)tegami** letter left behind

継手 **tsu(gi)te** joint, coupling, splice

触手 **shokushu** feeler, tentacle

話手 **hana(shi)te** speaker

鉤手 **kagi(no)te** right-angle bend

14 選手 **senshu** (sports) player

選手団 **senshudan** team, squad

選手村 **senshumura** Olympic village

選手権 **senshuken** championship title

漕手 **ko(gi)te, sōshu** rower, oarsman

構手 **kama(i)te** one who looks after another; companion

熊手 **kumade** rake

旗手 **kishu** standardbearer

歌手 **kashu** singer

網手 **tsunade** mooring/towing rope

語手 **kata(ri)te** narrator, storyteller

読手 **yo(mi)te** reader

聞手 **ki(ki)te** listener

駅手 **ekishu** station hand

15 舞手 **ma(i)te** dancer

養手 **yashina(i)te** supporter, provider

横手 **yokote** at one side, at one's side

敵手 **tekishu** adversary, the enemy

稼手 **kase(gi)te** breadwinner; hard worker

16 薄手 **usude** slight wound; thin (china)

懐手 **futokorode** hands in pockets, idly

17 濡手粟 **nu(re)te (de) awa** easy money

繊手 **senshu** slender hand

18 騎手 **kishu** rider, jockey

21 魔手 **mashu** one's evil hands, clutches

22 籠手 **kote** bracer, gauntlet; forearm

——— 3 ———

1 一挙手一投足 **ikkyoshu-ittōsoku** a slight effort, the least trouble

3 三塁手 **sanruishu** third baseman

口上手 **kuchijōzu** fair-spoken, glib

口下手 **kuchibeta** awkward tongue, poor talker

小切手 **kogitte** check, cheque

4 不得手 **fuete** unskillful, poor at, weak in

内野手 **naiyashu** infielder, baseman

手勝手 **tegatte** handling, skill

手練手管 **teren-tekuda** coaxing, wiles, beguiling

5 外野手 **gaiyashu** outfielder

好敵手 **kōtekishu** worthy opponent

6 交換手 **kōkanshu** switchboard operator

7 身勝手 **migatte** selfishness, having one's own way

応急手当 **ōkyū tea(te)** first aid

8 空下手 **karaheta, kara(p)peta** utterly inept

9 為替手形 **kawase tegata** bill (of exchange), draft

約束手形 **yakusoku tegata** promissory note

10 残業手当 **zangyō teate** overtime pay

遊相手 **aso(bi)aite** playmate

遊撃手 **yūgekishu** shortstop

11 運転手 **untenshu** driver, chauffeur

常套手段 **jōtō shudan** well-worn device, old trick

転轍手 **tentetsushu** switchman, pointsman

13 話相手 **hanashi aite** someone to talk to; companion

14 聞上手 **ki(ki)jōzu** a good listener

聞下手 **ki(ki)beta** a poor listener

16 操舵手 **sōdashu** helmsman

機関手 **kikanshu** (locomotive) engineer

整形手術 **seikei shujutsu** orthopedic operation

19 爆撃手 **bakugekishu** bombardier

——— 4 ———

4 手前勝手 **temae-gatte** selfish

6 自分勝手 **jibun-katte** having one's own way, selfish

9 飛入勝手 **tobii(ri) katte** open to all comers

10 高手小手 **takate-kote** (bound) hand and foot

記念切手 **kinen kitte** commemorative stamp

11 得手勝手 **etekatte** self-centered, selfish

——————— 1 ———————

3c1.1

扎

SATSU pull; bundle, tie up; prick, stab

——————— 2 ———————

3c2.1

扑

BOKU hit, beat; a whip

3c2.2 / 582

払 拂   **FUTSU, hara(u)** pay; sweep/ drive away

──────── 1 ────────

3 払下 **hara(i)sa(geru)** sell, dispose of
払下品 **hara(i)sa(ge)hin** articles sold off by the government
4 払込 **hara(i)ko(mu)** pay in/up, pay an installment
払手 **hara(i)te** payer
5 払出 **hara(i)da(su)** pay out, disburse; drive away
7 払戻 **hara(i)modo(su)** refund, reimburse
8 払底 **futtei** shortage, scarcity
払物 **hara(i)mono** article to be disposed of
9 払拭 **fusshoku** sweep away, wipe out
10 払残 **hara(i)noko(ri)** arrears, balance due
11 払過 **hara(i)su(giru)** overpay
払済 **hara(i)zu(mi)** paid up, settled
12 払渡 **hara(i)wata(su)** pay (out/over), cash (a check)
払落 **hara(i)o(tosu)** shake/brush off
払暁 **futsugyō** dawn
15 払箱 **(o)hara(i)bako** dismissal, firing

──────── 2 ────────

2 人払 **hitobara(i)** clear (the room) of people
4 不払 **fubara(i), fuhara(i)** nonpayment, default
内払 **uchibara(i)** partial payment
切払 **ki(ri)hara(u)** clear/chop away, lop off
支払 **shihara(u)** pay
支払人 **shiharainin** payer
支払日 **shiharaibi** pay day
支払済 **shiharaizu(mi)** paid
支払期日 **shiharaikijitsu** due date, maturity
厄払 **yakubara(i)** exorcism
引払 **hi(ki)hara(u)** clear out, leave, vacate
月払 **tsukibara(i)** monthly installments
5 出払 **dehara(u)** be all out of, have none left
未払 **mihara(i)** unpaid
打払 **u(chi)hara(u)** beat/shake/sweep off, drive away
6 先払 **sakibara(i)** advance payment; payment on delivery; forerunner
7 延払 **no(be)bara(i)** deferred payment
吹払 **fu(ki)hara(u)** blow away (tr.)
売払 **u(ri)hara(u)** sell off, dispose of
床払 **tokobara(i)** recovery from illness
利払 **ribara(i)** interest payment
8 受払 **u(ke)hara(i)** receipts and disbursements
直払 **jikibara(i)** cash payment
追払 **o(p)para(u), o(i)hara(u)** drive away
o(i)bara(i) later payment

所払 **tokorobara(i)** banishment from one's residence
取払 **to(ri)hara(u)** remove, clear away
9 前払 **maebara(i)** advance payment
咳払 **sekibara(i)** clearing one's throat
後払 **atobara(i)** deferred payment
10 振払 **fu(ri)hara(u)** shake off
11 掛払 **ka(ke)bara(i)** settlement of accounts
酔払 **yo(p)para(i)** a drunk
12 着払 **chakubara(i)** payment upon delivery, COD
焼払 **ya(ki)hara(u)** burn up/away
13 搔払 **ka(p)para(u)** walk off with, steal
15 蔵払 **kurabara(i)** clearance sale
賦払 **fubara(i), fuhara(i)** payment by installments
21 露払 **tsuyuhara(i)** herald, forerunner

──────── 3 ────────

1 一時払 **ichijibara(i)** lump-sum payment
4 分割払 **bunkatsubara(i)** payment in installments
厄介払 **yakkaibara(i)** good riddance
5 玄関払 **genkanbara(i)** refusal to see a visitor
7 即時払 **sokujibara(i)** immediate payment, at sight
8 参着払 **sanchakubara(i)** payment on demand/sight
定期払 **teikibara(i)** time/installment payments
門前払 **monzenbara(i)** turning (someone) away at the gate, refusing to see (someone)
11 現金払 **genkinbara(i)** cash payment
悪魔払 **akumabara(i)** exorcism
12 落着払 **o(chi)tsu(ki)hara(u)** be quite unperturbed
14 誓文払 **seimonbara(i)** bargain sale

3c2.3 / 1020

打   **DA, CHŌ** hit, strike
u(tsu) hit, strike, beat, shoot
bu(tsu) beat, strike   **dāsu** dozen

──────── 1 ────────

2 打力 **daryoku** batting power
3 打上 **u(chi)a(geru)** shoot up, launch (a rocket), cast up on shore, wash ashore; finish, close (a performance)
打上花火 **u(chi)a(ge) hanabi** skyrocket, fireworks
打下 **u(chi)o(rosu)** bring (a club) down on, strike a blow
4 打切 **u(chi)ki(ru)** end, close
打止 **u(chi)to(meru)** kill, shoot/bring down **u(chi)do(me)** end (of an entertainment/ match) **u(chi)ya(mu)** stop

3

打込 **u(chi)ko(mu)** drive/pound in, shoot into; fall madly in love, put (one's heart) into

打水 **u(chi)mizu** watering, sprinkling

打手 **dashu** (cricket) batsman
u(chi)te hitter, shooter

打方 **u(chi)kata** how to shoot; batting, stroking (in tennis)

5 打出 **u(chi)da(su)** begin to beat; open fire; hammer out; end, be over **u(tte)de(ru)**, **u(chi)de(ru)** sally forth, come forward **u(chi)da(shi)** close (of a show); embossing; delivery (of a ball)

打付 **u(chi)tsu(keru)** stroke, knock, dash against, nail to **u(chi)tsu(ke ni)** bluntly, flatly **u(tte)tsu(ke)** just right

打払 **u(chi)hara(u)** beat/shake/sweep off, drive away

6 打合 **u(chi)a(u)** hit each other, exchange blows **u(chi)a(waseru)** strike (one thing) against (another); prearrange **u(chi)a(wase)** previous arrangement, appointed (hour)

打返 **u(chi)kae(su)** hit back

打向 **u(chi)mu(kau)** face, confront; proceed to

打当 **u(chi)a(teru)** hit/dash against

7 打身 **u(chi)mi** bruise

打延 **u(chi)no(basu)** hammer out

打沈 **u(chi)shizu(mu)** be depressed/dejected

打抜 **u(chi)nu(ku)** punch/shoot through, perforate; stamp out (coins)

8 打建 **u(chi)ta(teru)** erect, build

打固 **u(chi)kata(meru)** harden by tamping

打明 **u(chi)a(keru)** confide in, reveal

打明話 **u(chi)a(ke)banashi** confidential talk, confession, revealing a secret

打者 **dasha** batter, hitter

打物 **u(chi)mono** wrought/forged work; sword; molded cake

打物師 **u(chi)monoshi** swordsmith

打取 **u(chi)to(ru)** catch, arrest; kill

打金 **u(chi)gane** (gun) hammer, cock

9 打変 **u(tte)kawa(ru)** change completely

打点 **daten** runs batted in, RBI

打負 **u(chi)ma(kasu)** beat, defeat

打首 **u(chi)kubi** beheading, decapitation

打連 **u(chi)tsu(reru)** take (someone) along

打砕 **u(chi)kuda(ku), bu(chi)kuda(ku)** break to pieces, smash, crush

10 打倒 **datō** overthrow **u(chi)tao(su)** knock down; overthrow

打消 **u(chi)ke(shi)** denial, negation, negative (in grammar)

打振 **u(chi)fu(ru)** wave, shake, brandish

打荷 **u(chi)ni** jetsam, jettisoned cargo

打殺 **u(chi)koro(su)** beat/shoot to death, strike/

shoot dead **bu(chi)koro(su)** beat to death

打破 **daha** break, destroy, overthrow **u(chi)yabu(ru)** break, knock down

打留 **u(chi)to(meru)** kill, shoot/bring down **u(chi)do(me)** end (of an entertainment/match)

11 打率 **daritsu** batting average

打過 **u(chi)su(giru)** pass by (time)

打掛 **u(chi)ka(karu), u(tte)ka(karu)** strike/hit at, assail **u(chi)ka(ke)** long outer garment

打捨 **u(chi)su(teru)** throw out, discard

打据 **u(chi)su(eru)** whip (a horse)

打菓子 **u(chi)gashi** molded confections

打萎 **u(chi)shio(reru)** droop; be downcast

打寄 **u(chi)yo(seru)** break upon (the shore), come (attacking)

打球 **dakyū** batting; batted ball

打貫 **u(chi)nu(ku)** pierce, shoot through

12 打割 **u(chi)wa(ru)** divide, split

打落 **u(chi)o(tosu)** knock/shoot down, lop off (branches)

打勝 **u(chi)ka(tsu)** defeat, conquer

打診 **dashin** percussion, tapping (in medicine); sound/feel out

打開 **dakai** a break, development, new turn

打順 **dajun** batting order

13 打傷 **u(chi)kizu** bruise

打損 **u(chi)soko(nau)** miss, fail to hit

打寛 **u(chi)kutsuro(gu)** make oneself comfortable, relax

打楽器 **dagakki** percussion instrument

打解 **u(chi)to(keru)** open one's heart, be frank

打解話 **u(chi)to(ke)banashi** friendly chat, heart-to-heart talk

打数 **dasū** times at bat

打続 **u(chi)tsuzu(ku)** long, long-continuing **u(chi)tsuzu(keru)** keep hitting/shooting

打電 **daden** send a telegram

14 打鳴 **u(chi)na(rasu)** make a sound, jingle, clap, ring

打網 **u(chi)ami** casting net

打算 **dasan** calculation, self-interest

打算的 **dasanteki** calculating, mercenary

15 打撃 **dageki** blow, shock; batting, hitting

打撃王 **dagekiō** leading/top batter

打撃率 **dagekiritsu** batting average

打撲 **daboku** bruise, contusion

打線 **dasen** batting lineup

16 打壊 **bu(chi)kowa(su)** break, smash; ruin, upset (plans)

17 打擲 **chōchaku** give a beating/thrashing

——————— 2 ———————

1 一打 **hitou(chi), ichida** a blow

4 中打 **nakau(chi)** middle third of a fish sliced lengthwise into three

手打 **teu(chi)** handmade; striking a bargain; killing by one's own hand

火打石 **hiu(chi)ishi** a flint

5 仕打 **shiu(chi)** treatment; behavior, conduct

代打 **daida** pinch-hitting

好打 **kōda** good hit

好打者 **kōdasha** (baseball) slugger

目打 **meu(chi)** perforation

田打 **tau(chi)** tilling a paddy field

6 舌打 **shitau(chi)** clicking one's tongue, tsk, tch

耳打 **mimiu(chi)** whisper in (someone's) ear

7 抜打 **nu(ki)u(chi)** whip out (a sword) and slash in one movement; surprise (inspection/exam)

抜打的 **nu(ki)u(chi)teki** without advance warning

乱打 **randa** pommeling, battering

麦打 **mugiu(chi)** wheat flailing/threshing

快打 **kaida** good hit (in baseball/golf)

8 盲打 **mekura-u(chi)** hitting blindly

殴打 **ōda** assault (and battery)

波打際 **namiu(chi)giwa** shore

狙打 **nera(i)u(chi)** take aim and shoot

杭打 **kuiu(chi)** pile driving

杭打機 **kuiu(chi)ki** pile driver

9 連打 **renda** hit/strike/knock repeatedly

畑打 **hatau(chi)** plowing up ground

10 値打 **neu(chi)** value, worth; dignity

真打 **shin'u(chi)** star performer

猛打 **mōda** hard hit, heavy blow

猛打者 **mōdasha** slugger (in baseball)

峰打 **mineu(chi)** strike (someone) with the back of one's sword

脈打 **myakuu(tsu)** pulsate, beat

11 強打 **kyōda** hit hard, slug

強打者 **kyōdasha** hard hitter, slugger

組打 **ku(mi)u(chi)** grapple/wrestle with

鳥打 **toriu(chi)** shooting birds; cap

鳥打帽 **toriu(chi)bō** cap

12 博打 **bakuchi** gambling

博打打 **bakuchiu(chi)** gambler

焼打 **ya(ki)u(chi)** attack by burning, set afire

塁打 **ruida** base hit, single

痛打 **tsūda** crushing blow, smash

13 裏打 **urau(chi)** lining; backing

碁打 **gou(chi)** go player

14 綿打 **watau(chi)** cotton willowing

網打 **amiu(chi)** net fishing

15 鋲打 **byōu(chi)** riveting

16 頭打 **atamau(chi), zuu(chi)** reach its peak/ceiling

17 犠打 **gida** sacrifice hit (in baseball)

闇打 **yamiu(chi)** an attack in the darkness; assassination, foul murder

18 鞭打 **muchiu(tsu)** whip, flog; urge on

鞭打症 **muchiu(chi)shō** whiplash

19 蠅打 **haeu(tsu)** fly swatter

――――――― 3 ―――――――

1 一網打尽 **ichimō dajin** a large catch, roundup; wholesale arrest

一騎打 **ikkiu(chi)** man-to-man combat

3 三塁打 **sanruida** three-base hit, triple

4 不意打 **fuiu(chi)** surprise attack

太刀打 **tachiu(chi)** cross swords with; contend, vie

5 本塁打 **honruida** home run

6 同士打 **dōshiu(chi)** fight among themselves

舌鼓打 **shitatsuzumi (o) u(tsu)** smack one's lips

11 釣瓶打 **tsurubeu(chi)** firing in rapid succession

12 博打打 **bakuchiu(chi)** gambler

博奕打 **bakuchiu(chi)** gambler

13 滅多打 **mettau(chi)** random shooting

――――――― 3 ―――――――

3c3.1

扣   **KŌ, hika(eru)** restrain, hold back
tata(ku) hit strike

――――――― 1 ―――――――

9 扣除 **kōjo** deduction, subtraction

16 扣頭 **kōtō** kowtow

3c3.2

扞   **KAN** defend against; cover

――――――― 1 ―――――――

10 扞格 **kankaku** opposing/resisting each other

3c3.3

托   **TAKU** entrust to, request; place onto

――――――― 1 ―――――――

13 托鉢 **takuhatsu** religious mendicancy; begging priest

――――――― 2 ―――――――

9 茶托 **chataku** teacup holder, saucer

――――――― 3 ―――――――

1 一蓮托生 **ichiren-takushō** sharing fate with another

3c3.4

扱   **sate** well, now

3c3.5 / 1258

扱 扱
KYŪ, SŌ, atsuka(u) handle, treat, deal with
shigo(ku) draw through the hand **shigo(ki)** squeezing through; rigorous training, hazing; woman's waistband **ko(ku)** thresh, strip off

——————— 1 ———————
2 扱人 **atsuka(i)nin** person in charge
3 扱下 **ko(ki)oro(su)** excoriate, criticize severely
8 扱使 **ko(ki)tsuka(u)** work (someone) hard
12 扱落 **ko(ki)o(tosu)** thresh, strip off

——————— 2 ———————
6 宅扱 **takuatsuka(i)** delivery to the house
8 取扱 **to(ri)atsuka(u)** treat, handle, deal with/ in, carry
取扱人 **toriatsukainin** agent, person in charge
9 客扱 **kyakuatsuka(i)** hospitality
10 荷扱 **niatsuka(i)** freight handling
根扱 **neko(gi)** uprooting
14 稲扱 **ineko(ki)** threshing (machine)

——————— 3 ———————
2 子供扱 **kodomoatsuka(i)** treating (someone) like a child

——————— 4 ———————
8 事務取扱 **jimu toriatsuka(i)** acting director

3c3.6

扠
SA fish spear, gaff
sate well, now

3c3.7

扛
KŌ lift, carry

——————— 4 ———————

3c4.1

抂
KYŌ, GŌ disorder

3c4.2

找
SŌ look for, seek; make change

3c4.3

抉 刔
KETSU gouge, dig out
egu(ru) gouge, scoop/scrape out, bore **koji(ru)** gouge; wrench, pry **kuji(ru)** scoop, pick (one's nose)

——————— 2 ———————
10 剔抉 **tekketsu** gouge out

扱→扱 3c3.5

3c4.4 / 1721

扶
FU, tasu(keru) help

——————— 1 ———————
7 扶助 **fujo** aid, support, relief
扶助料 **fujoryō** pension
8 扶育 **fuiku** bring up, tutor
9 扶持 **fuchi** aid, stipend
扶持米 **fuchimai** rice allowance
10 扶桑 **Fusō** Japan
12 扶植 **fushoku** plant, establish
15 扶養 **fuyō** support (a family)
扶養者 **fuyōsha** supporter, breadwinner
扶養家族 **fuyō kazoku** family dependents
17 扶翼 **fuyoku** aid, support

——————— 2 ———————
7 里扶持 **satobuchi** child-fostering expenses
9 食扶持 **ku(i)buchi** food/board expenses
10 家扶 **kafu** steward

——————— 3 ———————
8 宛行扶持 **ategaibuchi** discretionary allowance

3c4.5 / 1724

把
HA take, grasp; (counter for bundles/ sheaves)

——————— 1 ———————
4 把手 **totte** handle, grip, knob
9 把持 **haji** grasp, clasp
10 把捉 **hasoku** grasp, comprehend
12 把握 **haaku** grasp, comprehend

——————— 2 ———————
14 銃把 **jūha** (pistol's) grip

——————— 3 ———————
3 大雑把 **ōzappa** rough (guess); generous

3c4.6

抔
HŌ, HAI, suku(u) scoop up (in one's hand) **-nado** etc., and so forth

3c4.7 / 1394

折
SETSU, o(reru) (intr.) break, be folded, bend; turn (left/right); yield, compromise **o(ru)** (tr.) break, fold,

bend　**ori** occasion, opportunity

───────── 1 ─────────

0 折しも **ori(shimo)** just then
2 折入 **o(ri)i(tte)** earnestly
3 折々 **oriori** from time to time
折口 **o(re)kuchi** a split/break
4 折込 **o(ri)ko(mu)** tuck in, insert
　　 o(ri)ko(mi) an insert
折尺 **o(ri)jaku** (carpenter's) folding ruler
折方 **o(ri)kata** how to fold
折戸 **o(ri)do** folding doors
5 折半 **seppan** dividing into halves
折本 **o(ri)hon** folding book; folder
折句 **o(ri)ku** acrostic verse
折目 **o(ri)me** fold, crease
折目正 **o(ri)metada(shii)** good-mannered;
　　 ceremonious
6 折曲 **o(ri)ma(geru)** bend, turn up/down
折合 **o(ri)a(u)** come to an agreement
折返 **o(ri)kae(su)** fold back; double back
　　 o(ri)kae(shi) immediate (reply)
折返点 **o(ri)kae(shi)ten** (marathon) turn-
　　 back point
折地図 **o(ri)chizu** folding map
7 折角 **sekkaku** going to (much) trouble, on
　　 purpose, expressly; kindly
折折 **oriori** from time to time
8 折取 **o(ri)to(ru)** break off, pick (flowers)
9 折衷 **setchū** compromise, cross, blending
折衷主義 **setchū shugi** eclecticism
折重 **o(ri)kasa(naru)** overlap; telescope
10 折紙 **o(ri)gami** the art of paper folding;
　　 colored origami paper; authentication,
　　 testimonial
折紙付 **o(ri)gamitsu(ki)** certified, genuine
折釘 **o(re)kugi** broken/hooked nail, screw
　　 hook
12 折畳 **o(ri)tata(mu)** fold up
折畳式 **o(ri)tata(mi)shiki** folding, collaps-
　　 ible
折畳機 **o(ri)tata(mi)ki** (page-)folding
　　 machine
13 折節 **o(ri)fushi** occasionally
折詰 **o(ri)zu(me)** (food/lunch) packed in a
　　 cardboard/thin-wood box
14 折鞄 **o(ri)kaban** folding briefcase, portfolio
15 折衝 **sesshō** negotiation
折敷 **o(ri)shi(ku)** kneel
　　 o(ri)shi(ki) kneeling (position)
折箱 **o(ri)bako** small box made of cardboard
　　 or thin wood
18 折襟 **o(ri)eri** turned-down collar; lapel;
　　 lounge suit

19 折檻 **sekkan** chastise, punish; whipping,
　　 spanking

───────── 2 ─────────

3 三折 **mi(tsu)o(ri)** folded in three
4 夭折 **yōsetsu** premature death
中折 **nakao(ri)** folded in the middle
中折帽 **nakao(re)bō** felt hat, fedora
手折 **tao(ru)** break off, pluck
5 左折 **sasetsu** left turn
右折 **usetsu** turn right
6 気折 **kio(re)** depression, dejection
曲折 **kyokusetsu** winding, twists and turns;
　　 vicissitudes, complications
回折 **kaisetsu** diffraction
7 折折 **oriori** from time to time
8 屈折 **kussetsu** bending; refraction; inflection
枝折戸 **shio(ri)do** garden gate made of
　　 branches
9 風折 **kazao(re)** broken by the wind
指折 **yubio(ri)** leading, eminent
指折数 **yubio(ri) kazo(eru)** count on one's
　　 fingers
10 挫折 **zasetsu** setback, frustration, reverses
骨折 **kossetsu** broken bone, fracture
　　 honeo(ru) take pains, exert oneself
骨折損 **honeo(ri)zon** wasted effort
時折 **tokio(ri)** at times, occasionally
11 捩折 **ne(ji)o(ru)** twist off
雪折 **yukio(re)** broken/bent by snow
12 葛折 **tsuzurao(ri)** winding, meandering,
　　 zigzag
13 腰折 **koshio(re)** poorly written poem
14 端折 **hasho(ru)** tuck up; cut short, abridge

───────── 3 ─────────

6 気骨折 **kibone (ga) o(reru)** nerve-wracking
8 和洋折衷 **wayō setchū** blending of Japanese
　　 and Western styles

───────── 4 ─────────

2 九十九折 **tsuzurao(ri)** winding, meandering,
　　 zigzag
9 紆余曲折 **uyo-kyokusetsu** meandering,
　　 twists and turns, complications
12 無駄骨折 **mudaboneo(ri)** wasted/vain effort

3c4.8

抓　**SŌ** scratch, grasp, pinch
　　tsuma(mu) hold/take between fingers
　　and thumb　**tsune(ru)** pinch

3c4.9

抖　**TO, TŌ** shake, jiggle

3

氵
土
扌
口
女
巾
犭
弓
彳
彡
艹
宀
⺌
山
�
广
尸
口

4 ◀

3c4.10 / 1713

抜 抜 BATSU, nu(ku) pull out, remove, leave out; outdistance, surpass -nu(ki) without, leaving out; defeating
nu(keru) come/fall out; be omitted; be missing; escape nu(kasu) omit, skip over
nu(karu) make a blunder

――――――― 1 ―――――――

0 抜きんでる **nu(kinderu)** be outstanding, excel
　抜からぬ **nu(karanu)** shrewd, on one's guard
2 抜刀 **battō** draw one's sword; drawn sword
3 抜上 **nu(ke)a(garu)** be bald in front
4 抜毛 **nu(ke)ge** hair falling out, molting
　抜切 **nu(ke)ki(ru)** get rid of, be free from
　抜手 **nu(ki)te** overarm/overhand stroke
5 抜出 **nu(ki)da(su)** select, extract, pull out
　　nu(ke)da(su) slip out, sneak away; excel; choose the best　**nu(kin)de(ru), nu(ki)de(ru)** be outstanding, excel
　抜本 **bappon** eradication; radical
　抜写 **nu(ki)utsu(shi)** excerpt, extract
　抜去 **nu(ki)sa(ru)** overtake, surpass
　抜打 **nu(ki)u(chi)** whip out (a sword) and slash in one movement; surprise (inspection/exam)
　抜打的 **nu(ki)u(chi)teki** without advance warning
　抜穴 **nu(ke)ana** secret passage/exit; loophole
　抜目 **nu(ke)me** oversight　**nu(ke)me(nai)** alert, shrewd, cunning, clever
6 抜合 **nu(ki)a(waseru)** unsheathe (swords) at the same time
　抜糸 **basshi** take out the stitches
　　nu(ki)ito drawn thread
7 抜身 **nu(ki)mi** drawn sword
　抜作 **nu(ke)saku** dunce, nincompoop
　抜足 **nu(ki)ashi (de)** stealthily
　抜足差足 **nu(ki)ashi-sa(shi)ashi (de)** stealthily
8 抜刷 **nu(ki)zu(ri)** offprint
　抜参 **nu(ke)mai(ri)** secret pilgrimage
　抜放 **nu(ki)hana(su/tsu)** unsheathe, draw (a sword)
　抜取 **nu(ki)to(ru)** pull/take out, extract; pilfer, steal
10 抜剣 **bakken** draw one's sword
　抜差 **nu(ki)sa(shi)** insertions and deletions
　　nu(ki)sa(shinaranu) impossible, sticky (dilemma)
　抜荷 **nu(ki)ni** pilfer(ed) goods
　抜書 **nu(ki)ga(ki)** excerpt, clipping
　抜粋 **bassui** excerpt, extract, selection
11 抜道 **nu(ke)michi** bypass; secret path; way of escape, loophole

　抜萃 **bassui** extract, excerpt, selection, abstract, summary
　抜萃帳 **bassuichō** scrapbook
　抜殻 **nu(ke)gara** cast-off skin (of a cicada/snake)
12 抜落 **nu(ke)o(chiru)** fall out
　抜替 **nu(ke)ka(waru)** shed, molt, slought off
　抜歯 **basshi** extraction of a tooth
13 抜裏 **nu(ke)ura** bypass
　抜群 **batsugun** pre-eminent, outstanding
14 抜読 **nu(ki)yo(mi)** read from, read part of
　抜駆 **nu(ke)ga(ke)** steal a march on, forestall, scoop
16 抜錨 **batsubyō** weigh anchor, set sail
17 抜擢 **batteki** select, choose, pick out
18 抜顔 **nu(karanu) kao** a knowing look

――――――― 2 ―――――――

4 不抜 **fubatsu** firm, steadfast
　毛抜 **kenu(ki)** tweezers
　切抜 **ki(ri)nu(ku)** cut/clip out
　　kirinu(ki) a (newspaper) clipping
　切抜帳 **kirinu(ki)chō** scrapbook
　手抜 **tenu(ki)** (intentional) omission
　　tenu(kari) (unintentional) omission, oversight, error
　引抜 **hi(ki)nu(ku)** pull out, select
5 出抜 **da(shi)nu(ku)** forestall, anticipate, get the jump on, circumvent　**da(shi)nu(ke ni)** all of a sudden, unexpectedly
　生抜 **ha(e)nu(ki)** native-born
　打抜 **u(chi)nu(ku)** punch/shoot through, perforate; stamp out (coins)
　尻抜 **shirinu(ke)** forgetful
　目抜 **menu(ki)** main, principal
　目抜通 **menu(ki)dō(ri)** main thoroughfare
6 気抜 **kinu(ke)** lackadaisical; dispirited
　羽抜 **hanu(ke)** molting
　色抜 **ironu(ki)** decolor
7 身抜 **minu(ke)** get away from, get out of (one's circumstances)
　走抜 **hashi(ri)nu(keru)** run through
　　hashi(ri)nu(ku) outrun
　吹抜 **fu(ki)nu(ku)** blow through/over
　　fu(ki)nu(ki) ventilation, draft; streamer, pennant
　図抜 **zunu(keru)** tower above, be outstanding
　見抜 **minu(ku)** see through
　秀抜 **shūbatsu** excellent, pre-eminent
　言抜 **i(i)nu(ke)** excuse, evasion
8 刺抜 **togenu(ki)** tweezers
　刳抜 **ku(ri)nu(ku)** gouge out, bore a hole
　卓抜 **takubatsu** excellence, (pre)eminence
　追抜 **o(i)nu(ku)** overtake
　知抜 **shi(ri)nu(ku)** know thoroughly
　奇抜 **kibatsu** novel, original, unconventional

突抜 **tsu(ki)nu(keru)** pierce, go through
底抜 **sokonu(ke)** bottomless, unbounded
底抜騒 **sokonu(ke) sawa(gi)** boisterous merrymaking
9 俊抜 **shunbatsu** uncommon, above average
通抜 **tō(ri)nu(keru)** pass through
海抜 **kaibatsu** elevation above sea level
垢抜 **akanu(ke)** refined, polished, urbane
染抜 **so(me)nu(ku)** dye fast; leave undyed
shi(mi)nu(ki) removing stains
10 起抜 **o(ki)nu(ke)** upon getting up
栓抜 **sennu(ki)** corkscrew; bottle opener
骨抜 **honenu(ki)** boned; emasculated, watered down
書抜 **ka(ki)nu(ku)** copy out, excerpt, abstract
息抜 **ikinu(ki)** vent; rest, break, breather
釘抜 **kuginu(ki)** nail-puller, claw hammer
11 渋抜 **shibunu(ki)** removing the puckery taste (from persimmons)
掘抜 **ho(ri)nu(ku)** dig through, bore
掘抜井戸 **ho(ri)nu(ki) ido** a well
張抜 **ha(ri)nu(ki)** papier-mâché
12 遣抜 **ya(ri)nu(ku)** carry through, do thoroughly, accomplish, complete
勝抜 **ka(chi)nu(ku)** fight to victory
腑抜 **funu(ke)** lily-livered person, coward
歯抜 **hanu(ke)** toothless
筒抜 **tsutsunu(ke)** directly, clearly
間抜 **manu(ke)** stupid **ma (ga) nu(keru)** be stupid; be out of place/harmony
間抜面 **manu(ke)zura** stupid look
13 腰抜 **koshinu(ke)** coward(ice), weak-kneed milksop
戦抜 **tataka(i)nu(ku)** fight to the end
14 選抜 **senbatsu, e(ri)nu(ku)** select, choose, single out
綿抜 **watanu(ki)** unpadded kimono
駆抜 **ka(ke)nu(keru)** run through (a gate)
15 輪抜 **wanu(ke)** jumping through a hoop
踏抜 **fu(mi)nu(ku)** step through (the flooring); step on (a nail) and prick one's foot
18 簡抜 **kanbatsu** pick out, select
19 警抜 **keibatsu** extraordinary
22 籠抜 **kagonu(ke)** swindling (by slipping out the back door)

——————— 3 ———————

6 色気抜 **irokenu(ki)** without female companionship
8 拍子抜 **hyōshinu(ke)** disappointment
空気抜 **kūkinu(ki)** vent(ilator)
居合抜 **ia(i)nu(ki)** swordplay exhibition
9 度胆抜 **dogimo (o) nu(ku)** dumbfound, shock
10 素破抜 **suppanu(ku)** expose, unmask

——————— 4 ———————

1 一頭地抜 **ittōchi (o) nu(ku)** stand head and shoulders above others

3c4.11 / 1153

抑

SHŌ excerpt; make paper

——————— 1 ———————

5 抄出 **shōshutsu** take excerpts
抄本 **shōhon** excerpt, abridged transcript
抄写 **shōsha** excerpt, quotation
8 抄物 **shōmotsu, shōmono** notes, commentary (on a Chinese classic)
10 抄紙 **shōshi** papermaking
11 抄訳 **shōyaku** abridged translation
16 抄録 **shōroku** excerpt, abstract, summary

——————— 2 ———————

13 詩抄 **shishō** selection of poems

——————— 3 ———————

4 戸籍抄本 **koseki shōhon** extract from a family register

3c4.12 / 1057

抑

YOKU, osa(eru) hold down, hold in check, suppress, control
somosomo in the first place; well, now

——————— 1 ———————

3 抑々 **somosomo** in the first place; well, now
4 抑止 **yokushi** deter stave off
5 抑付 **osa(e)tsu(keru)** hold down, curb, control
抑圧 **yokuatsu** suppress, restrain
8 抑制 **yokusei** control, restrain, suppress, inhibit
抑制力 **yokuseiryoku** restraint, control
10 抑留 **yokuryū** detention, internment
抑留国 **yokuryūkoku** detaining country
抑留者 **yokuryūsha** detainee, internee
抑留所 **yokuryūjo** detention/internment camp
抑留船 **yokuryūsen** detained/interned ship
12 抑揚 **yokuyō** rising and falling of tones, modulation, intonation
18 抑難 **osa(e)gata(i)** irrepressible, uncontrollable

——————— 2 ———————

8 取抑 **to(ri)osa(eru)** catch, capture
17 謙抑 **ken'yoku** humbling oneself

3c4.13 / 1029

批

HI critique

——————— 1 ———————

7 批判 **hihan** criticism, critique, comment
批判的 **hihanteki** critical

9 批点 **hiten** correction marks (in a manuscript); emphasis marks; points to be criticized
10 批准 **hijun** ratification
批准書 **hijunsho** instrument of ratification
12 批評 **hihyō** criticism, critique, review
批評家 **hihyōka** critic, reviewer
批評眼 **hihyōgan** critical eye
18 批難 **hinan** criticize, denounce, condemn
20 批議 **higi** criticize, censure, blame

————————— 2 —————————

10 高批 **kōhi** your valued criticism
12 無批判 **muhihan** uncritical

————————— 3 —————————

5 本文批評 **honmon hihyō** textual criticism

3c4.14

扑

BEN, u(tsu) clap (one's hands)

3c4.15 / 824

抗

KŌ resist, anti-

————————— 1 —————————

0 抗する **kō(suru)** resist, defy, oppose
4 抗日 **kō-Nichi** anti-Japanese
5 抗生 **kōsei** antibiotic
抗生物質 **kōsei busshitsu** an antibiotic
抗弁 **kōben** plea, defense, protest, demurral
6 抗争 **kōsō** dispute; resistance
7 抗体 **kōtai** antibody
抗告 **kōkoku** appeal, protest, complaint
抗言 **kōgen** retort, contradiction
8 抗毒素 **kōdokuso** antitoxin, antidote
10 抗原 **kōgen** antigen
13 抗戦 **kōsen** resistance
20 抗議 **kōgi** protest, objection
抗議文 **kōgibun** (written) protest

————————— 2 —————————

4 反抗 **hankō** resistance, opposition, rebellion
反抗的 **hankōteki** rebellious, defiant, antagonistic
7 対抗 **taikō** oppose, counter
対抗馬 **taikōba** rival horse; rival candidate
対抗策 **taikōsaku** (counter)measures
8 抵抗 **teikō** resistance
抵抗力 **teikōryoku** (power of) resistance
抵抗器 **teikōki** resistor, rheostat
9 拮抗 **kikkō** competition, rivalry, antagonism

————————— 3 —————————

4 不可抗力 **fukakōryoku** force majeure, beyond one's control, unavoidable

12 無抵抗 **muteikō** nonresistance, passive obedience

3c4.16 / 871

技

GI skill, art, technique
waza technique; ability, feat

————————— 1 —————————

3 技工 **gikō** artisan, craftsman, technician
4 技手 **gishu** assistant engineer
5 技巧 **gikō** art, craftsmanship, technique
技巧的 **gikōteki** skillful
7 技芸 **gigei** arts, crafts, accomplishments
8 技法 **gihō** technique
技官 **gikan** technical official
10 技倆 **giryō** skill, ability
技倒 **gitō** technical knockout, TKO
技師 **gishi** engineer, technician
技師長 **gishichō** chief engineer
技能 **ginō** skill, technical ability
11 技術 **gijutsu** technology, technique, skill, art
技術上 **gijutsujō** technically
技術士 **gijutsushi** engineer, technician
技術者 **gijutsusha** technical expert
技術家 **gijutsuka** technician, specialist, expert
12 技量 **giryō** skill, ability

————————— 2 —————————

4 手技 **shugi** skill, technique
5 巧技 **kōgi** skilled workmanship
好技 **kōgi** fine play/game/acting
6 早技 **hayawaza** quick work; sleight of hand
7 体技 **taigi** competitive physical sports; strength and skill
余技 **yogi** avocation, hobby
妙技 **myōgi** extraordinary skill
快技 **kaigi** consummate skill
8 拙技 **setsugi** (my) clumsy efforts
国技 **kokugi** national skill/sport
放技 **hana(re)waza** feat, stunt
武技 **bugi** marital arts
9 神技 **shingi** consummate skill
10 遊技 **yūgi** games, amusement
遊技場 **yūgijō** place of amusement
特技 **tokugi** special skill, specialty
11 球技 **kyūgi** game in which a ball is used
12 無技巧 **mugikō** artless
無技能 **muginō** unskilled
14 演技 **engi** acting, performance
18 闘技 **tōgi** competition, contest, match
20 競技 **kyōgi** competition, match
競技会 **kyōgikai** athletic meet, contest
競技場 **kyōgijō** stadium, sports arena

————————— 3 —————————

4 水産技師 **suisan gishi** fisheries expert

——————— 4 ———————

2 十種競技 **jisshu kyōgi** decathlon
4 五種競技 **goshu kyōgi** pentathlon
水上競技 **suijō kyōgi** water sports

3c4.17

扮

FUN dress, attire

——————— 1 ———————

0 扮する **fun(suru)** dress up as, impersonate, play the role of
12 扮装 **funsō** impersonate

3c4.18 / 1021

投

TŌ, na(geru) throw

——————— 1 ———————

0 投じる **tō(jiru)** throw; invest in
2 投入 **tōnyū** throw into, commit (resources); invest **na(ge)i(reru)** throw into **na(ge)i(re)** free-style flower arrangement
3 投与 **tōyo** give (medicine), dose **na(ge)ata(eru)** throw (a bone) to (a dog)
  投上 **na(ge)a(geru)** toss/throw up
  投下 **tōka** throw down, drop; invest
4 投込 **na(ge)ko(mu)** throw/dump into
  投手 **tōshu** pitcher (in baseball)
5 投出 **na(ge)da(su)** throw/fling out; give up, renounce
  投付 **na(ge)tsu(keru)** throw at/against/down
  投石 **tōseki** throw stones
6 投合 **tōgō** coincide, agree with, meet
  投返 **na(ge)kae(su)** throw back
  投光器 **tōkōki** floodlight
7 投身 **tōshin** suicide by throwing oneself (into a river, from a building, in front of a train)
  投売 **na(ge)u(ri)** sell at a loss/sacrifice
  投売品 **na(ge)u(ri)hin** distress-sale merchandise
8 投函 **tōkan** mail (a letter)
  投物 **na(ge)mono** goods to be sold at a sacrifice
9 投飛 **na(ge)to(basu)** fling away
  投降 **tōkō** surrender
  投首 **na(ge)kubi** dropping one's head
  投映 **tōei** project (an image), cast
10 投射 **tōsha** projection (in math); incidence (in physics); throwing (spears)
  投射角 **tōshakaku** angle of incidence
  投射物 **tōshabutsu** projectile
  投射機 **tōshaki** projector
  投倒 **na(ge)tao(su)** throw (someone) down
  投荷 **na(ge)ni** jetsam, cargo cast overboard

投書 **tōsho** letter to the editor, contribution
投書家 **tōshoka** contributor, correspondent
投書欄 **tōshoran** readers' column
11 投掛 **na(ge)ka(keru)** throw at
  投捨 **na(ge)su(teru)** throw away
  投宿 **tōshuku** put up at (a hotel)
  投宿者 **tōshukusha** hotel guest
  投票 **tōhyō** vote
  投票区 **tōhyōku** voting district
  投票日 **tōhyōbi** voting day
  投票用紙 **tōhyō yōshi** ballot
  投票者 **tōhyōsha** voter
  投票所 **tōhyōjo** polling place, the polls
  投票率 **tōhyōritsu** (rate of) voter turnout
  投票数 **tōhyōsū** number of votes
  投票権 **tōhyōken** right to vote, suffrage
  投票箱 **tōhyōbako** ballot box
  投球 **tōkyū** throw a ball, pitch
12 投落 **na(ge)o(tosu)** throw down, drop
13 投業 **na(ge)waza** throwing trick/technique
  投棄 **tōki** abandon, give up
  投資 **tōshi** investment
14 投獄 **tōgoku** imprisonment
  投網 **toami** casting net
15 投影 **tōei** projection
  投影面 **tōeimen** plane of projection
  投影機 **tōeiki** projector
  投稿 **tōkō** contribution (to a magazine)
  投稿者 **tōkōsha** contributor (to a magazine)
  投稿欄 **tōkōran** readers' column
  投縄 **na(ge)nawa** lasso, lariat
16 投薬 **tōyaku** medication, prescription, dosage
  投機 **tōki** speculation
  投機心 **tōkishin** spirit of speculation
  投機的 **tōkiteki** speculative, risky
  投機家 **tōkika** speculator
  投機熱 **tōkinetsu** speculation fever
  投錨 **tōbyō** drop anchor, lie at anchor

——————— 2 ———————

2 力投 **rikitō** powerful pitching
4 手投弾 **tena(ge)dan** hand grenade
7 身投 **mina(ge)** drown oneself
  完投 **kantō** pitch a whole (baseball) game
11 毬投 **marina(ge)** play ball/catch
  掬投 **suku(i)na(ge)** tripping (in sumo)
  球投 **tamana(ge)** playing catch
  悪投 **akutō** bad/wild throw
  雪投 **yukina(ge)** throwing snowballs
12 無投票 **mutōhyō** dispensing with voting
  間投詞 **kantōshi** an interjection
13 続投 **zokutō** continue to pitch/rule, remain in office
14 槍投 **yarina(ge)** javelin throwing
15 輪投 **wana(ge)** quoits, ringtoss

——————— 3 ———————

2 人民投票 **jinmin tōhyō** plebiscite, referendum

4 円盤投 **enbanna(ge)** the discus throw
9 単記投票 **tanki tōhyō** voting for one person only
背負投 **shio(i)na(ge), seo(i)na(ge)** throw over one's shoulder; betrayal
10 砲丸投 **hōganna(ge)** the shot put
11 情意投合 **jōi-tōgō** mutual sentiment/ understanding
13 意気投合 **iki-tōgō** sympathy, mutual understanding

———————— 5 ————————

1 一挙手一投足 **ikkyoshu-ittōsoku** a slight effort, the least trouble

3c4.19

抒 **JO** tell

———————— 1 ————————

11 抒情 **jojō** expression of one's feelings, lyricism
抒情的 **jojōteki** lyrical
抒情詩 **jojōshi** lyric poem/poetry

3c4.20

扼 **YAKU** hold down; yoke

———————— 1 ————————

0 扼する **yaku(suru)** grip; have command of
10 扼殺 **yakusatsu** choke to death
12 扼腕 **yakuwan** clench one's arms (in anger/ vexation)

———————— 3 ————————

4 切歯扼腕 **sesshi-yakuwan** gnash one's teeth and clench one's arms on the chest (in vexation)

3c4.21 / 993

択 擇 **TAKU, era(bu)** choose, select

———————— 1 ————————

1 択一 **takuitsu** choosing an alternative
10 択捉島 **Etorofu-tō** (island, Russian Hokkaidō)

———————— 2 ————————

7 決択 **kettaku** decide between, choose
11 採択 **saitaku** adopt, select
14 選択 **sentaku** selection, choice, option, alternative
選択肢 **sentakushi** multiple choice
選択権 **sentakuken** right of choice, option

———————— 3 ————————

2 二者択一 **nisha-takuitsu** an alternative

抛 → 拋 **3c5.27**

拒 → **3c5.29**

———————— 5 ————————

3c5.1 / 1833

拓 **TAKU, hira(ku)** open, clear, bring (land) under cultivation

———————— 1 ————————

5 拓本 **takuhon** a rubbing (of an inscription)
6 拓地 **takuchi** opening up land (to cultivation)
12 拓殖 **takushoku** colonization, exploitation
拓殖者 **takushokusha** colonist

———————— 2 ————————

3 干拓 **kantaku** reclaim (land) by drainage
干拓地 **kantakuchi** reclaimed land, innings
12 開拓 **kaitaku** opening up land, development
開拓者 **kaitakusha** settler, pioneer

———————— 3 ————————

5 未開拓 **mikaitaku** undeveloped, unexploited

3c5.2

拉 **RATSU** crush; drag along **RA** Latin
hishi(geru) be crushed; be discouraged
hishi(gu) crush

———————— 1 ————————

0 拉する **ras(suru)** drag along, abduct
2 拉丁 **Raten** Latin
拉丁語 **Ratengo** Latin
10 拉致 **rachi, ratchi** take (someone) away

———————— 2 ————————

15 踏拉 **fu(mi)shida(ku)** trample, step on and break

3c5.3 / 1201

拝 拜 **HAI** worship; (prefix expressing respect) **oga(mu)** pray to, worship, venerate

———————— 1 ————————

0 拝する **hai(suru)** worship, pay respects to; receive (an imperial command); see (the emperor)
4 拝火教 **haikakyō** fire worship
5 拝礼 **hairei** worship
7 拝承 **haishō** I am informed that ...
拝呈 **haitei** presentation
拝見 **haiken** see, have a look at
8 拝命 **haimei** receive an official appointment
拝受 **haiju** receive, accept

拝物教 **haibutsukyō** fetishism
拝具 **haigu** Sincerely yours
拝金 **haikin** worship of money
拝金主義 **haikin shugi** mammonism
拝金宗 **haikinshū** mammonism
9 拝屋 **oga(mi)ya** medicine man, faith healer
拝眉 **haibi** personal meeting
10 拝倒 **oga(mi)tao(su)** entreat into consenting
拝借 **haishaku** borrow
11 拝啓 **haikei** Dear Sir/Madam
12 拝復 **haifuku** In reply to your letter
拝賀 **haiga** greetings, congratulations
13 拝殿 **haiden** outer shrine, hall of worship
拝辞 **haiji** resign, decline
14 拝察 **haisatsu** infer, guess, gather
拝読 **haidoku** read, note
拝聞 **haibun** listen to, hear
拝領 **hairyō** receive (from a superior)
拝領物 **hairyōbutsu** gift (from a superior)
15 拝謁 **haietsu** an audience (with the emperor)
17 拝聴 **haichō** listen to
拝謝 **haisha** thank
18 拝観 **haikan** see, inspect, visit
拝観料 **haikanryō** (museum) admission fee
拝顔 **haigan** personal meeting

─────── 2 ───────

3 三拝 **sanpai** worshiping three times
三拝九拝 **sanpai kyūhai** three kneelings and
  nine prostrations, kowtowing, bowing
  repeatedly
5 巡拝 **junpai** circuit pilgrimage
礼拝 **reihai, raihai** worship, services
礼拝堂 **reihaidō** chapel
6 再拝 **saihai** bowing twice
伏拝 **fu(shi)oga(mu)** kneel down and worship
8 参拝 **sanpai** worship, visit (a shrine/tomb)
11 崇拝 **sūhai** worship, adoration
崇拝者 **sūhaisha** worshiper
13 遥拝 **yōhai** worshipping from afar
跪拝 **kihai** kneel and pray
16 親拝 **shinpai** worship (by the emperor)

─────── 4 ───────

3 三拝九拝 **sanpai kyūhai** three kneelings and
  nine prostrations, kowtowing, bowing
  repeatedly
8 呪物崇拝 **jubutsu sūhai** fetishism
11 偶像崇拝 **gūzō sūhai** idol worship, idolatry

3c5.4

拇 **BO** thumb

─────── 1 ───────

6 拇印 **boin** thumbprint
9 拇指 **boshi** thumb

3c5.5 / 986

押 **Ō, o(su)** push **o(saeru)** restrain, hold
in check, suppress **o(sae)** (paper)weight;
rear guard, defense; control
o(shi) weight; authority, self-confidence;
a fall (in the stock market) **o(shite)** forcibly,
importunately

─────── 1 ───────

2 押入 **o(shi)i(re)** closet, wall cupboard
o(shi)i(ru) break into
o(shi)i(ri) burglar
3 押上 **o(shi)a(geru)** push/force up, raise
押下 **o(shi)sa(geru)** push/force down, depress
  ōka press (a key)
4 押切 **o(shi)ki(ru)** have one's own way, push
  through
押収 **ōshū** confiscation
押止 **o(shi)to(meru)** stop, check, prevent
押分 **o(shi)wa(keru)** push apart, work one's
  way through
押込 **o(shi)ko(mu)** push in, crowd into
o(shi)ko(mi) closet; burglar
o(shi)ko(meru) shut up, imprison
押込強盗 **o(shi)ko(mi) gōtō** burglar(y)
5 押出 **o(shi)da(shi)** presence, appearance;
  pushing out, extrusion
o(shi)da(su) push/squeeze out; crowd
  out; set out all together
押付 **o(shi)tsu(keru)** press against; force upon
o(shi)tsu(kegamashii) importunate
押広 **o(shi)hiro(geru)** extend, expand
押立 **o(shi)ta(teru)** raise, erect, set up
6 押合 **o(shi)a(u)** jostle one another
押印 **ōin** affixing a seal
押返 **o(shi)kae(su)** push back
押当 **o(shi)a(teru)** press/hold against
7 押迫 **o(shi)sema(ru)** press hard
押花 **o(shi)bana** pressed flowers
押売 **o(shi)u(ri)** high-pressure/importunate
  selling
押戻 **o(shi)modo(su)** push back; reject
8 押並 **o(shi)na(bete)** generally
押固 **o(shi)kata(meru)** press together
押板 **o(shi)ita** pressing board
9 押通 **o(shi)tō(su)** push through, accomplish
押型 **o(shi)gata** impression taken by pressing
10 押倒 **o(shi)tao(su)** push down
押借 **o(shi)ga(ri)** having to borrow
押進 **o(shi)susu(mu)** press onward/ahead
押流 **o(shi)naga(su)** wash/sweep away
押破 **o(shi)yabu(ru)** break through
11 押掛 **o(shi)ka(keru)** drop in on uninvited
押掛女房 **o(shi)ka(ke) nyōbō** a woman who
  pressured her husband into marrying her
押掛客 **o(shi)ka(ke)kyaku** uninvited guest

3

氵
土
扌 5←
口
女
巾
犭
弓
彳
彡
艹
宀
⺍
山
耂
广
尸
口

押捺 **ōnatsu** affix a seal
押寄 **o(shi)yo(seru)** push aside; advance on, besiege
押鈕 **o(shi)botan** pushbutton
押問答 **o(shi)mondō** heated questioning and answering, dispute
押頂 **o(shi)itada(ku)** raise reverently to one's head
12 押割麦 **o(shi)wa(ri) mugi** rolled barley/oats
押渡 **o(shi)wata(ru)** come/go over, cross
押葉 **o(shi)ba** pressed leaf
押絵 **o(shi)e** pasted-cloth picture
押開 **o(shi)hira(ku), o(shi)a(keru)** push/ force open
13 押詰 **o(shi)tsu(meru)** pack in
15 押潰 **o(shi)tsubu(su)** crush, smash, squash
押黙 **o(shi)dama(ru)** keep silent
17 押戴 **o(shi)itada(ku)** raise reverently to one's head
19 押韻 **ōin** rhyme
押韻詩 **ōinshi** rhyming poem, verse

——————— 2 ———————

3 下押 **shitao(su)** decline, sag, drop
4 手押車 **teo(shi)guruma** pushcart, wheelbarrow
5 尻押 **shirio(shi)** push from behind, boost, back, abet; instigator, wirepuller
6 虫押 **mushiosa(e)** medicine for children's irritability
7 花押 **kaō** signature, handwritten seal
8 空押 **karao(shi)** blind/inkless stamping
取押 **to(ri)osa(eru)** catch, capture
9 後押 **atoo(shi)** pushing from behind; backing, support
10 差押 **sa(shi)osa(eru)** attach, seize, impound
差押品 **sa(shi)osa(e)hin** attached/seized goods
12 棒押 **bōo(shi)** pole-pushing

——————— 3 ———————

5 目白押 **mejiroo(shi)** jostling, milling
12 無理押 **murio(shi)** pushing things too far
15 横車押 **yokoguruma (o) o(su)** be perverse, stubbornly persist (like trying to push a cart at right angles to its wheels)

3c5.6

押 **SHIN, CHIN** stretch, extend

3c5.7 / 987

抽 **CHŪ** pull, extract
nu(ku) pull out; surpass
hi(ku) pull

——————— 1 ———————

0 抽んでる **nuki(nderu)** be outstanding, excel
4 抽斗 **hikidashi** drawer

5 抽出 **chūshutsu** extraction, sampling
12 抽象 **chūshō** abstraction
抽象画 **chūshōga** abstract painting
抽象的 **chūshōteki** abstract
抽象論 **chūshōron** abstract argument/ discussion
14 抽選 **chūsen** drawing, lottery
抽選券 **chūsenken** lottery/raffle ticket
23 抽籤 **chūsen** drawing, lottery
抽籤券 **chūsenken** lottery/raffle ticket

3c5.8

拑 **KAN, tsugu(mu)** shut (one's mouth)

3c5.9 / 1914

抹 **MATSU** erase, expunge; rub, paint

——————— 1 ———————

9 抹茶 **matcha** powdered tea
抹香 **makkō** incense powder; incense
抹香臭 **makkōkusa(i)** smelling of religion
抹香鯨 **makkō kujira** sperm whale
10 抹消 **masshō** erase, cross out
抹殺 **massatsu** expunge; deny; ignore

——————— 2 ———————

1 一抹 **ichimatsu** a touch/tinge of
2 丁抹 **Denmāku** Denmark
13 塗抹 **tomatsu** paint over/out, smear

3c5.10

拌 **HAN** stir, mix

——————— 2 ———————

23 攪拌 **kakuhan** agitate, stir, churn
攪拌器 **kakuhanki** agitator, shaker, beater

3c5.11 / 1801

拙 **SETSU** unskillful, clumsy
mazu(i) poor(ly done), clumsy, bungling, unskillful

——————— 1 ———————

3 拙工 **sekkō** poor workman
4 拙文 **setsubun** (my) poor writing
6 拙宅 **settaku** my humble home
拙劣 **setsuretsu** clumsy, bungling, unskillful
7 拙作 **sessaku** (my) poor/clumsy work
拙技 **setsugi** (my) clumsy efforts
8 拙者 **sessha** I (humble)
9 拙速 **sessoku** not elaborate but fast, rough-and-ready

11 拙著 **setcho** my humble work
拙悪 **setsuaku** clumsy, fumbling
12 拙筆 **seppitsu** poor handwriting
拙策 **sessaku** poor policy, imprudent measure
15 拙稿 **sekkō** (my) poor manuscript

——————— 2 ———————
5 巧拙 **kōsetsu** skill, proficiency
13 稚拙 **chisetsu** artless, naive, childlike

拂→払 3c2.2

3c5.12
拆
TAKU split open/apart

3c5.13 / 1712
披
HI open

——————— 1 ———————
7 披見 **hiken** open and read (a letter)
14 披歴 **hireki** express (one's opinion)
19 披瀝 **hireki** express (one's opinion)
21 披露 **hirō** announcement
披露会 **hirōkai** (wedding) reception
披露宴 **hirōen** (wedding) reception

3c5.14 / 1178
拍 拍
HAKU, HYŌ beat (in music)
u(tsu) clap, slap

——————— 1 ———————
2 拍子 **hyōshi** time, tempo, beat; chance, moment
拍子木 **hyōshigi** wooden clappers
拍子抜 **hyōshinu(ke)** disappointment
4 拍手 **hakushu** handclapping, applause
kashiwade handclapping (at a shrine)
7 拍車 **hakusha** a spur

——————— 2 ———————
2 二拍子 **nibyōshi** double/two-part time
3 三拍子 **sanbyōshi** triple time (in music); three important requisites, triple-threat
4 手拍子 **tebyōshi** beating time; carelessly
5 白拍子 **shirabyōshi** female dancer (historical); prostitute
7 足拍子 **ashibyōshi** beating time with one's foot
8 突拍子 **toppyōshi (mo nai)** out of tune, exorbitant, very
10 脈拍 **myakuhaku** pulse (rate)
15 膝拍子 **hizabyōshi** beating time on one's knee

3c5.15 / 1285
抱 抱
HŌ, da(ku) hold in one's arms, embrace, hug
ida(ku) embrace, harbor (feelings); hold, have
kaka(eru) carry in one's arms; have (dependents); hire **kaka(e)** armful; employee

——————— 1 ———————
0 抱っこ **da(kko)** hug, hold in one's arms
3 抱上 **da(ki)a(geru)** take up in one's arms
4 抱止 **da(ki)to(meru)** hold (someone) back
抱込 **da(ki)ko(mu)** win (someone) over
kaka(e)ko(mu) hold/carry in one's arms
5 抱付 **da(ki)tsu(ku)** embrace, cling to
6 抱合 **da(ki)a(u)** embrace each other
da(ki)a(waseru) cause to embrace
hōgō combination; embrace
抱合売 **da(ki)a(wase) u(ri)** selling poorly selling articles in a tie-up with articles which sell well
7 抱卵 **hōran** brooding over eggs, incubation
抱卵期 **hōranki** incubation period
8 抱抱 **da(ki)kaka(eru)** hold/carry (in one's arms)
9 抱負 **hōfu** aspiration, ambition
抱括 **hōkatsu** inclusive, comprehensive
10 抱起 **da(ki)o(kosu)** lift/help (someone) up
11 抱寄 **da(ki)yo(seru)** hug/snuggle to one's breast
12 抱竦 **da(ki)suku(meru)** hug tight
13 抱腹 **hōfuku** holding one's sides in laughter
抱腹絶倒 **hōfuku-zettō** convulsed with laughter
15 抱締 **da(ki)shi(meru), ida(ki)shi(meru)** embrace closely, cuddle, hug
16 抱擁 **hōyō** embrace, hug
抱懐 **hōkai** harbor, cherish, entertain

——————— 2 ———————
1 一抱 **hitokaka(e)** an armful
4 介抱 **kaihō** nurse, care for
5 召抱 **me(shi)kaka(eru)** employ
7 辛抱 **shinbō** perseverance, patience
8 抱抱 **da(ki)kaka(eru)** hold/carry (in one's arms)

3c5.16
拗
YŌ, Ō, neji(ru) twist **neji(keru/kureru)** be twisted/warped; be perverse/cranky **koji(reru)** be twisted; go wrong, get out of order; become complicated; be peevish; get worse **koji(rasu)** make worse
su(neru) pout, sulk

——————— 1 ———————
8 拗者 **su(ne)mono** cross-grained person
9 拗音 **yōon** diphthong (written with a small や, ゆ, or よ, as in きゅ)

3

氵 土 扌 口 女 巾 犭 弓 彳 彡 艹 宀 丷 艹 卢 广 尸 口

5←

─────── 2 ───────

11 執拗 **shitsuyō** obstinate, persistent

3c5.17

拊

FU stroke, pat, tap

3c5.18 / 560

抵

TEI touch; reach; resist

─────── 1 ───────

6 抵当 **teitō** mortgage, hypothec
抵当物 **teitōbutsu** security, pawn, collateral
抵当流 **teitōnaga(re)** foreclosure
抵当権 **teitōken** mortgage, hypothec
7 抵抗 **teikō** resistance
抵抗力 **teikōryoku** (power of) resistance
抵抗器 **teikōki** resistor, rheostat
13 抵触 **teishoku** conflict with, be contrary to

─────── 2 ───────

3 大抵 **taitei** generally, usually; probably
12 無抵抗 **muteikō** nonresistance, passive obedience

─────── 3 ───────

8 並大抵 **namitaitei** ordinary

3c5.19

拯

JŌ rescue

3c5.20 / 1274

担 擔

TAN carry, bear **katsu(gu)** carry on the shoulder; play a trick on **nina(u)** carry on the shoulder; bear, take on

─────── 1 ───────

2 担子 **tanshi** sedan-chair (carried on shoulders); load, cargo, baggage
担子菌類 **tanshi kinrui** basidiomycetes
担子胞子 **tanshi hōshi** basidiospore
4 担手 **nina(i)te** bearer, carrier
6 担任 **tannin** charge, responsibility
担当 **tantō** being in charge, overseeing
担当者 **tantōsha** the one in charge
9 担保 **tanpo** a security, guarantee
担屋 **katsu(gi)ya** superstitious person; practical joker; peddler
担架 **tanka** stretcher

─────── 2 ───────

4 分担 **buntan** apportionment, sharing
5 加担 **katan** assistance, support; conspiracy, complicity

9 負担 **futan** burden, load, responsibility, liability
10 差担 **sa(shi)nina(i)** carry on the shoulders between two persons
荷担 **katan** support, side with, be a party to
荷担者 **katansha** participant, supporter, accomplice
12 無担保 **mutanpo** unsecured, without collateral

─────── 3 ───────

12 御幣担 **gohei-katsu(gi)** superstitious person

3c5.21 / 1916

拐 拐

KAI swindle; kidnap

─────── 1 ───────

10 拐帯 **kaitai** absconding with money

─────── 2 ───────

14 誘拐 **yūkai** kidnapping, abduction

拐 → 拐 3c5.21

3c5.22 / 455

招

SHŌ, mane(ku) beckon to, invite, summon; cause

─────── 1 ───────

7 招来 **shōrai** bring about, invite, incur
9 招待 **shōtai** invite
招待日 **shōtaibi** preview/invitation date
招待状 **shōtaijō** (written) invitation
招待券 **shōtaiken** complimentary ticket
招待客 **shōtaikyaku** invited guest
招待席 **shōtaiseki** reserved seats for guests
招客 **shokyaku** invitation; invited guest
10 招宴 **shōen** invitation to a banquet
招致 **shōchi** summons, invitation
11 招猫 **mane(ki)neko** beckoning (porcelain) cat
12 招集 **shōshū** call together, convene
13 招聘 **shōhei** invite
14 招魂 **shōkon** invocation of the spirits of the dead
招魂社 **shōkonsha** shrine to the war dead
招魂祭 **shōkonsai** memorial service; Memorial Day
15 招請 **shōsei** invite
招請国 **shōseikoku** inviting/host nation

─────── 2 ───────

4 手招 **temane(ki)** beckoning
10 差招 **sa(shi)mane(ku)** beckon to; take command of

3c5.23

拈 NEN pinch

拈 → 攤 3c14.7

3c5.24

拵 SON, koshira(eru) make, prepare

——————— 1 ———————

8 拵事 **koshira(e)goto** fabrication, made-up story
拵直 **koshira(e)nao(su)** remake, remodel
拵物 **koshira(e)mono** imitation, fake

——————— 2 ———————

3 下拵 **shitagoshira(e)** preliminary arrangements
4 手拵 **tegoshira(e)** handmade, homemade
6 仮拵 **karigoshira(e)** makeshift
7 身拵 **migoshira(e)** dress/outfit oneself; makeup
足拵 **ashigoshira(e)** footgear
10 荷拵 **nigoshira(e)** packing

3c5.25 / 1113

拡 擴 KAKU, hiro(geru) extend, enlarge
hiro(garu) spread, expand

——————— 1 ———————

3 拡大 **kakudai** magnification, expansion
拡大率 **kakudairitsu** magnifying power
拡大鏡 **kakudaikyō** magnifying glass
6 拡充 **kakujū** expansion, amplification
7 拡声器 **kakuseiki** loudspeaker
拡声機 **kakuseiki** loudspeaker
11 拡張 **kakuchō** extension, expansion
12 拡散 **kakusan** diffusion, scattering, proliferation

——————— 2 ———————

4 不拡大 **fukakudai** nonexpansion, nonaggravation, localization
9 軍拡 **gunkaku** military buildup
軍拡競争 **gunkaku kyōsō** arms race

3c5.26 / 1138

拠 據 KYO, KO, yo(ru) be based on, be due to

——————— 1 ———————

5 拠出 **kyoshutsu** contribute, donate
8 拠所 **yo(ri)dokoro** foundation, grounds, authority
9 拠点 **kyoten** (military) base, position

——————— 2 ———————

5 本拠 **honkyo** base, headquarters
占拠 **senkyo** occupation
8 依拠 **ikyo** dependence
典拠 **tenkyo** authority
10 根拠 **konkyo** basis, grounds, foundation
根拠地 **konkyochi** base (of operations)
12 割拠 **kakkyo** each a leader in his own sphere
証拠 **shōko** evidence, proof
証拠人 **shōkonin** witness
証拠立 **shōkoda(teru)** substantiate, corroborate
13 準拠 **junkyo** conform to, be pursuant to, be based on
15 論拠 **ronkyo** grounds, basis

——————— 4 ———————

11 情況証拠 **jōkyō shōko** circumstantial evidence
13 群雄割拠 **gun'yū kakkyo** rivalry of local barons

3c5.27

抛 抛 HŌ, nageu(tsu) fling/throw away

——————— 1 ———————

8 抛物線 **hōbutsusen** parabola
13 抛棄 **hōki** waive, abandon

3c5.28 / 1800

拘 KŌ seize, arrest; adhere to
kakawa(ru) have to do with
kakawa(razu) in spite of, regardless of

——————— 1 ———————

4 拘引 **kōin** arrest, custody
拘引状 **kōinjō** arrest warrant, summons
7 拘束 **kōsoku** restriction, constraint
拘束力 **kōsokuryoku** binding force (of a rule)
拘束者 **kōsokusha** person who restrains, captor
8 拘泥 **kōdei** adhere to, be a stickler for
10 拘留 **kōryū** detention, custody
拘留状 **kōryūjō** warrant for detention
拘留所 **kōryūjo** detention room, lockup
13 拘禁 **kōkin** confine, detain, imprison
拘置 **kōchi** keep in detention, confine, hold
拘置所 **kōchisho** house of detention, prison

3

氵 5←
土
扌
口
女
巾
犭
弓
彳
彡
艹
宀
⺌
山
⼟
广
尸
口

3c5.29 / 1295

拒

KYO, koba(mu) refuse, reject, decline

———————— 1 ————————

7 拒否 **kyohi** refusal, rejection, denial
拒否権 **kyohiken** (right of) veto
12 拒絶 **kyozetsu** refusal, rejection, repudiation

3c5.30

拏 拿

DA, NA catch, apprehend

———————— 6 ————————

3c6.1 / 1354

挾 挟

KYŌ, hasa(mu), sashihasa(mu) put between, interpose
hasa(maru) get between, be caught/hemmed/sandwiched between

———————— 1 ————————

4 挟切 **hasa(mi)ki(ru)** snip/clip (off)
挟込 **hasa(mi)ko(mu)** put between, insert
5 挟出 **hasa(mi)da(su)** clamp onto and take out
6 挟虫 **hasa(mi)mushi** earwig
10 挟将棋 **hasa(mi) shōgi** (a piece-capturing board game)
15 挟撃 **kyōgeki, hasa(mi)u(chi)** pincer attack

———————— 2 ————————

5 氷挟 **kōribasa(mi)** ice tongs
7 状挟 **jōbasa(mi)** letter clip/file
8 板挟 **itabasa(mi)** predicament, dilemma
10 差挟 **sa(shi)hasa(mu)** insert, put between, put in (a word); harbor, entertain
紙挟 **kamibasa(mi)** folder; clip

3c6.2 / 1720

拷

GŌ beat, torture

———————— 1 ————————

11 拷問 **gōmon** torture
拷問台 **gōmondai** the rack

3c6.3

拐

mushi(ru) pluck, tear off

3c6.4

挧

U, KU horse chestnut tree; (used in proper names)

3c6.5 / 1564

挑

CHŌ, ido(mu) challenge

———————— 1 ————————

9 挑発 **chōhatsu** arouse, excite, provoke
挑発的 **chōhatsuteki** provocative, suggestive
13 挑戦 **chōsen** challenge
挑戦状 **chōsenjō** written challenge
挑戦的 **chōsenteki** challenging, defiant, provocative
挑戦者 **chōsensha** challenger
15 挑撥 **chōhatsu** arouse, excite, provoke

3c6.6

挌

KAKU strike, hit, beat

3c6.7

挂

KEI, ka(keru) hang

3c6.8 / 451

持

JI, mo(tsu) have, possess; hold, maintain; wear, last **mo(chi)** wear, durability; charge, expenses; (ladies') wear **mo(teru)** be popular with; can hold/carry; propertied, the haves **mo(taseru)** let (someone) have, give; have (someone) hold/carry/bear; preserve, make last

———————— 1 ————————

3 持久 **jikyū** hold out, endure, persist
持久力 **jikyūryoku** endurance, stamina
持久策 **jikyūsaku** dilatory tactics
持久戦 **jikyūsen** war of attrition, endurance contest
持上 **mo(chi)a(geru)** raise, lift up; extol
mo(chi)a(garu) be lifted; arise, happen
4 持切 **mo(chi)ki(ru)** continue to hold, keep; hold all; maintain; talk of nothing else
持分 **mo(chi)bun** share, quota; holdings, interest in
持込 **mo(chi)ko(mu)** bring in; propose, lodge (a complaint)
5 持出 **mo(chi)da(su)** take out; run off with; propose, bring up
持去 **mo(chi)sa(ru)** carry away, make off with
持主 **mo(chi)nushi** owner, possessor
6 持行 **mo(tte) i(ku)/yu(ku)** take (along)
持回 **mo(chi)mawa(ru)** carry around
mo(chi)mawa(ri) decision-making by circular **mo(tte)mawa(tta)** roundabout

持成 **mo(te)na(shi)** treatment, reception, welcome, hospitality, entertainment

7 持来 **mo(tte) ku(ru)** bring (along)
mo(tte)ko(i) ideal, excellent, just right

持余 **mo(te)ama(su)** have more than one can manage

持余者 **mo(te)ama(shi)mono** nuisance, black sheep

持役 **mo(chi)yaku** one's role

持戒 **jikai** observance of the (Buddhist) commandments

8 持直 **mo(chi)nao(su)** improve, rally, recover; change one's grip/hold

持逃 **mo(chi)ni(ge)** make off with, abscond with

持送 **mo(chi)oku(ri)** bracket, corbel

持味 **mo(chi)aji** natural flavor, distinctive quality

持参 **jisan** bring, take, bear

持参人 **jisannin** bearer (of a check)

持参金 **jisankin** dowry

持歩 **mo(chi)aru(ku)** carry about

持物 **mo(chi)mono** one's property/belongings

9 持前 **mo(chi)mae** nature, property, characteristic

持持 **mo(chitsu)mo(taretsu)** helping one another

10 持帰 **mo(tte) kae(ru), mo(chi)kae(ru)** bring back, take home   **mo(chi)kae(ri)** (two burgers) to go

持荷 **mo(chi)ni** stock of goods, holdings; load

持家 **mo(chi)ie** one's (own) house

持株 **mo(chi)kabu** one's holdings/interest

持株会社 **mo(chi)kabu-gaisha** holding company

持病 **jibyō** chronic illness

11 持運 **mo(chi)hako(bu)** carry, transport

持掛 **mo(chi)ka(keru)** propose, offer

持寄 **mo(chi)yo(ru)** pool, bring a contribution to share

持崩 **mo(chi)kuzu(su)** ruin (oneself)

12 持堪 **mo(chi)kota(eru)** hold out/up, last, stand, endure

持場 **mo(chi)ba** one's post/rounds/jurisdiction

持替 **mo(chi)ka(eru)** shift from one hand to the other, change off

持越 **mo(chi)ko(su)** carry forward; defer; hold over

持統 **Jitō** (empress, 690–697)

13 持続 **jizoku** continuation, maintenance

持続的 **jizokuteki** continuous, lasting

14 持腐 **mo(chi)gusa(re)** useless possession

持説 **jisetsu** pet theory, one's cherished view

15 持論 **jiron** one's view, pet opinion

16 持薬 **jiyaku** medicine one takes regularly

――――――― 2 ―――――――

2 子持 **komo(chi)** a mother, maternity; pregnancy

力持 **chikaramo(chi)** strong man

3 女持 **onnamo(chi)** for women, ladies'

4 支持 **shiji** support

手持 **temo(chi)** goods on hand, goods in stock

手持品 **temo(chi)hin** supplies, goods on hand

心持 **kokoromo(chi)** feeling, mood; a little

5 加持 **kaji** incantation, faith-healing

6 気持 **kimo(chi)** feeling, mood

地持 **jimo(chi)** landowner

7 身持 **mimo(chi)** one's personal conduct; pregnant

住持 **jūji** chief priest of a temple

扶持 **fuchi** aid, stipend

扶持米 **fuchimai** rice allowance

把持 **haji** grasp, clasp

花持 **hanamo(chi)** how well cut flowers will remain unwilted

男持 **otokomo(chi)** men's, for men

8 長持 **nagamo(chi)** oblong chest; be durable, last

受持 **u(ke)mo(tsu)** have/take charge of

固持 **koji** adhere to, persist in

物持 **monomo(chi)** wealthy person

所持 **shoji** possess, have on one's person, carry

所持人 **shojinin** holder, bearer

所持者 **shojisha** holder, bearer

所持金 **shojikin** money on hand

所持品 **shojihin** one's personal effects

取持 **to(ri)mo(tsu)** treat, entertain; act as go-between

金持 **kanemo(chi)** rich person

9 保持 **hoji** maintain, preserve

保持者 **hojisha** holder (of a record)

矜持 **kyōji, kinji** dignity, pride

持持 **mo(chitsu)mo(taretsu)** helping one another

面持 **omomo(chi)** look, face

相持 **aimo(chi)** mutual help, give and take, sharing

10 家持 **iemo(chi)** house owner; householder

11 掛持 **ka(ke)mo(chi)** hold (part-time) positions concurrently

12 堅持 **kenji** hold fast to, adhere to

13 腹持 **haramo(chi)** slow digestion, feeling of fullness

14 鞄持 **kabanmo(chi)** private secretary, man Friday

槍持 **yarimo(chi)** spear bearer

旗持 **hatamo(chi)** standardbearer

維持 **iji** maintenance, support

20 護持 **goji** defend, protect, uphold

3

氵
土
扌 6←
口
女
巾
犭
弓
彳
彡
艹
宀
⺍
山
�
广
尸
口

─────────── 3 ───────────

3 大金持 **ōganemochi** very rich man
女房持 **nyōbōmo(chi)** married man
4 不身持 **fumimo(chi)** profligate, dissolute, licentious, loose
太鼓持 **taikomo(chi)** professional jester; flatterer
6 兇状持 **kyōjōmo(chi)** criminal at large
衣裳持 **ishōmo(chi)** one who has a large wardrobe
7 身上持 **shinshōmo(chi)** rich man; housekeeping
里扶持 **satobuchi** child-fostering expenses
8 所帯持 **shotaimo(chi)** housekeeping; married (wo)man
9 食扶持 **ku(i)buchi** food/board expenses
12 提灯持 **chōchinmo(chi)** lantern bearer; booster; hype
17 癇癪持 **kanshakumo(chi)** person with an explosive temper
24 癲癇持 **tenkanmo(chi)** an epileptic

─────────── 4 ───────────

8 治安維持 **chian iji** maintenance of public order
宛行扶持 **ategaibuchi** discretionary allowance

3c6.9

拱 **KYŌ, komanu(ku)** fold (one's arms)

─────────── 1 ───────────

4 拱手 **kyōshu** fold one's arms
拱手傍観 **kyōshu bōkan** stand idly by

3c6.10

按 **AN** hold; consider; investigate

─────────── 1 ───────────

4 按分 **anbun** proportional division
按分比例 **anbun hirei** proportionately, prorated
按手礼 **anshurei** laying on of hands, ordination
11 按排 **anbai** distribute, assign; adjust
15 按摩 **anma** massage; masseur, masseuse

3c6.11

拮 **KITSU** attack; work

─────────── 1 ───────────

7 拮抗 **kikkō** competition, rivalry, antagonism

11 拮据 **kikkyo** hard work, assiduousness

3c6.12 / 1260

括 **KATSU** tie together **kuku(ru)** tie up/together, bundle; fasten; hang (oneself) **kuru(mu)** wrap up, tuck in **kuru(meru)** wrap up; include all **kubi(reru)** be constricted, compressed

─────────── 1 ───────────

5 括付 **kuku(ri)tsu(keru)** tie up/together, tie down to
8 括枕 **kuku(ri) makura** stuffed pillow
9 括弧 **kakko** parentheses, brackets
括約筋 **katsuyakukin** sphincter (muscle)

─────────── 2 ───────────

1 一括 **ikkatsu** one lump/bundle; summing up
3 丸括弧 **marugakko** parentheses
5 包括 **hōkatsu** include, comprehend
包括的 **hōkatsuteki** inclusive, comprehensive
8 抱括的 **hōkatsuteki** inclusive, comprehensive
12 統括 **tōkatsu** generalize
14 概括 **gaikatsu** summary, generalization
総括 **sōkatsu** summarize, generalize
総括的 **sōkatsuteki** all-inclusive, overall
15 締括 **shi(me)kuku(ru)** tie fast; supervise; round out

3c6.13

拶 **SATSU** be imminent

─────────── 2 ───────────

10 挨拶 **aisatsu** greeting, salutation, courtesy call; address, message

─────────── 3 ───────────

12 無挨拶 **buaisatsu** impoliteness, incivility

3c6.14 / 1445

拾 **SHŪ, hiro(u)** pick up, find **JŪ** ten (in documents)

─────────── 1 ───────────

3 拾万円 **jūman'en** 100,000 yen
拾上 **hiro(i)a(geru)** pick up, pick out
5 拾出 **hiro(i)da(su)** pick/single out, select
拾主 **hiro(i)nushi** finder
8 拾物 **hiro(i)mono** something picked up, a find; a bargain
11 拾得 **shūtoku** pick up, find
拾得者 **shūtokusha** finder
拾得物 **shūtokubutsu** found article
12 拾集 **shūshū, hiro(i)atsu(meru)** collect, gather up

14 拾遺 **shūi** gleanings
   拾読 **hiro(i)yo(mi)** browse through (a book)

――――――― 2 ―――――――

4 収拾 **shūshū** control, cope with
8 命拾 **inochibiro(i)** narrow escape from death
10 屑拾 **kuzuhiro(i)** ragpicking; ragpicker
   骨拾 **kotsuhiro(i)** gathering (the deceased's) ashes
11 球拾 **tamahiro(i)** fetching balls; caddy

――――――― 3 ―――――――

10 紙屑拾 **kamikuzuhiro(i)** ragpicker
12 落穂拾 **o(chi)bohiro(i)** gleaning; gleaner

3c6.15 / 1041

指   **SHI, yubi** finger
      sa(su) point to

――――――― 1 ―――――――

2 指人形 **yubi ningyō** finger/glove puppet
4 指切 **yubiki(ri)** hooking each other's little finger (as a sign of a pledge)
   指手 **sa(shi)te** a move (in chess)
5 指令 **shirei** order, instructions
   指圧 **shiatsu** finger pressure
   指圧療法 **shiatsu ryōhō** finger-pressure treatment, chiropractic
   指示 **shiji** indication, instructions, directions **sa(shi)shime(su)** indicate, point out
   指示灯 **shijitō** pilot lamp, indicator light
   指示板 **shijiban** notice board
   指示器 **shijiki** indicator
6 指先 **yubisaki** fingertip
   指向 **shikō** directional (antenna)
   指向性 **shikōsei** directional (antenna)
   指名 **shimei** nominate, designate
   指名者 **shimeisha** nominator, designator
7 指折 **yubio(ri)** leading, eminent
   指折数 **yubio(ri) kazo(eru)** count on one's fingers
   指図 **sa(shi)zu** instructions, orders
   指図書 **sa(shi)zusho** (written) order, directions
8 指呼 **shiko** beckon
   指呼間 **shiko (no) aida/kan** within hailing distance
   指定 **shitei** appoint, designate
   指定席 **shiteiseki** reserved seats
   指板 **yubiita** fingerboard (on a guitar); (door) fingerplate
   指物 **sa(shi)mono** cabinetmaking, joinery
   指物屋 **sa(shi)monoya** cabinetmaker
   指物師 **sa(shi)monoshi** cabinetmaker
9 指南 **shinan** instruction, guidance
   指南役 **shinan'yaku** instructor, teacher
   指南車 **shinansha** (ancient Chinese) compass vehicle

指南番 **shinanban** instructor, teacher
10 指値 **sa(shi)ne** (buying/selling-)price limits
   指差 **yubisa(su)** point to
   指紋 **shimon** fingerprints, thumbprint
   指針 **shishin** compass/indicator needle; guide(line)
11 指貫 **yubinu(ki)** thimble
   sashinuki (type of formal garment)
12 指揮 **shiki** command, lead, direct
   指揮刀 **shikitō** saber, parade sword
   指揮下 **shikika** under one's command
   指揮官 **shikikan** commander
   指揮者 **shikisha** (orchestra) conductor, leader; commander, director
   指揮棒 **shikibō** baton
   指弾 **shidan** fillip, flicking/snapping one's fingers (at); rejection, disdain
13 指数 **shisū** index (number); exponent
   指話 **shiwa** finger language, dactylology
14 指摘 **shiteki** point out, indicate
   指導 **shidō** guidance, leadership
   指導者 **shidōsha** leader
   指導権 **shidōken** leadership
15 指標 **shihyō** index, indicator
   指輪 **yubiwa** (finger) ring
16 指頭 **shitō** fingertip

――――――― 2 ―――――――

1 一指 **isshi** a finger
2 十指 **jisshi** the ten fingers
3 小指 **koyubi** little finger
4 五指 **goshi** the five fingers
   中目指 **nakayubi, chūshi** middle finger
5 目指 **meza(su)** aim at
6 名指 **naza(shi)** calling/specifying by name
8 拇指 **boshi** thumb
   突指 **tsu(ki)yubi** sprained finger
   屈指 **kusshi** leading, one of the ...est
   物指 **monosa(shi)** ruler, measure, yardstick
9 後指 **ushi(ro) yubi** bird's hind toe; finger of scorn
   食指 **shokushi** the index finger
   食指動 **shokushi (ga) ugo(ku)** feel a craving for, want
11 運指 **unshi** fingering (in music)
   運指法 **unshihō** fingering (in music)
14 総指揮 **sōshiki** supreme command
   総指揮官 **sōshikikan** supreme commander
16 薬指 **kusuriyubi** third/ring finger
   親指 **oyayubi** thumb

――――――― 3 ―――――――

2 人差指 **hitosa(shi) yubi** index finger
   十二指腸 **jūnishichō** the duodenum
   十二指腸虫 **jūnishichōchū** hookworm
8 物価指数 **bukka shisū** price index
9 紅差指 **benisa(shi)yubi** the ring finger

3

氵
土
扌 6←
口
女
巾
犭
弓
彳
彡
艹
宀
屮
山
吉
广
尸
口

10 高々指 **takatakayubi** the middle finger
12 無名指 **mumeishi** the ring finger

拍→拍 **3c5.14**

3c6.16

挺
TEI pull out; excel, come to the fore
CHŌ (counter for guns, inksticks, candles, oars, palanquins, rickshaws)
teko lever

———————— 1 ————————
0 挺する **tei(suru)** take the lead, volunteer
2 挺入 **tekoi(re)** shore/prop up, bolster
挺子 **teko** lever
7 挺身 **teishin** come forward, volunteer
10 挺進 **teishin** go ahead of, dash forward
挺進隊 **teishintai** advance corps

———————— 2 ————————
1 一挺 **itchō** (counter for guns, ink sticks, oars, candles, palanquins, rickshaws)
8 空挺部隊 **kūtei butai** airborne troops, paratroops
金挺 **kanateko** crowbar
13 鉄挺 **kanateko** crowbar

3c6.17

拭
SHOKU, fu(ku), nugu(u) wipe

———————— 1 ————————
4 拭込 **fu(ki)ko(mu)** shine up, polish, wipe thoroughly
5 拭去 **nugu(i)sa(ru)** wipe off, clear away
8 拭取 **fu(ki)to(ru)** wipe off/away, mop up
10 拭消 **fu(ki)ke(su)** wipe out/off, erase
11 拭掃除 **fu(ki)sōji** cleaning (a house)
12 拭落 **nugu(i)oto(su), fu(ki)oto(su)** wipe off, rub out, scrub away

———————— 2 ————————
3 口拭 **kuchifu(ki)** napkin
4 手拭 **tenugu(i), tefu(ki)** towel
5 払拭 **fusshoku** sweep away, wipe out
尻拭 **shirinugu(i)** taking the blame/loss for someone else
11 乾拭 **karabu(ki)** wiping with a dry cloth
13 靴拭 **kutsufu(ki)** doormat
19 艶拭 **tsuyabu(ki)** rub and polish

3c6.18

拳 拳
KEN, GEN fist; respectful
kobushi fist

———————— 1 ————————
8 拳固 **genko** fist, knuckles
10 拳匪 **Kenpi** the Boxers
拳骨 **genkotsu** fist, knuckles
14 拳銃 **kenjū** pistol, handgun
18 拳闘 **kentō** boxing

———————— 2 ————————
8 空拳 **kūken** empty-handed, with one's bare hands
12 握拳 **nigi(ri)kobushi** clenched fist
13 鉄拳 **tekken** clenched fist
鉄拳制裁 **tekken seisai** the law of the fist

3c6.19

挈
KEI carry by hand

———————— 7 ————————

3c7.1

捉
SOKU, tora(eru) catch, capture

———————— 2 ————————
7 把捉 **hasoku** grasp, comprehend
択捉島 **Etorofu-tō** (island, Russian Hokkaidō)
10 捕捉 **hosoku** catch, capture, seize

3c7.2 / 1651

挿 插
SŌ, sa(su) insert
hasa(mu) put between, insert, interpose

———————— 1 ————————
2 挿入 **sōnyū** insert
4 挿木 **sa(shi)ki** (plant a) cutting
5 挿句 **sōku** parenthetical remark
7 挿花 **sa(shi)bana** flowers in a vase/lapel
挿図 **sōzu** figure, illustration
8 挿画 **sa(shi)e, sōga** illustration (in a book)
12 挿絵 **sa(shi)e** illustration (in a book)
13 挿話 **sōwa** episode, anecdote

———————— 2 ————————
4 内挿 **naisō** interpolation
5 外挿 **gaisō** extrapolation

———————— 3 ————————
1 一輪挿 **ichirinza(shi)** a vase for one flower

3c7.3 / 890

捕
HO, to(raeru/ru), tsuka(maeru) catch, grasp **to(rawareru), tsuka(maru)** be caught; hold on to

——————— 1 ———————
2 捕人 **to(raware)bito** captives
4 捕手 **hoshu** catcher **to(ri)te** constable
7 捕身 **to(raware no) mi** a captive, taken
　prisoner
8 捕物 **to(ri)mono** a capture, an arrest
　捕所 **to(rae)dokoro** the point, meaning
9 捕食 **hoshoku** prey upon
10 捕捉 **hosoku** catch, capture, seize
　捕殺 **hosatsu** catch and kill
11 捕球 **hokyū** catch (in baseball)
13 捕虜 **horyo** prisoner of war, captive
15 捕縄 **to(ri)nawa** rope for binding criminals
16 捕獲 **hokaku** capture, seizure
　捕縛 **hobaku** arrest, capture
19 捕鯨 **hogei** whaling
　捕鯨船 **hogeisen** whaling ship

——————— 2 ———————
4 分捕 **bundo(ru)** capture, seize, plunder
　分捕品 **bundo(ri)hin** botty, loot, spoils
　手捕 **tedo(ri)** capture, catch with one's hands
　引捕 **hi(t)tora(eru)** seize, capture, arrest
5 生捕 **i(ke)do(ru)** capture alive
　召捕 **me(shi)to(ru)** arrest, apprehend
10 逮捕 **taiho** arrest, capture
　逮捕状 **taihojō** arrest warrant
13 搦捕 **kara(me)to(ru)** apprehend, arrest

挟→挟 3c6.1

3c7.4
捌 **HATSU, HACHI, BETSU, saba(ku)** handle, deal with, dispose of; sell
saba(keru) sell, be in demand; be worldly-wise; be frank/sensible/sociable
ha(ke) drainage; sale, demand for

——————— 1 ———————
3 捌口 **ha(ke)guchi** outlet; market

——————— 2 ———————
4 水捌 **mizuha(ke)** drainage
　手捌 **tesaba(ki)** maneuvering, manipulation
7 売捌 **u(ri)saba(ki)** sale, selling
　足捌 **ashisaba(ki)** footwork
8 取捌 **to(ri)saba(ku)** manage, settle; judge, try

3c7.5 / 989
捜 捜 **SŌ, saga(su)** look/search for

——————— 1 ———————
5 捜出 **saga(shi)da(su)** find out, discover,
　locate

6 捜当 **saga(shi)a(teru)** find out, discover,
　locate
　捜回 **saga(shi)mawa(ru)** search/hunt around
7 捜求 **saga(shi)moto(meru)** seek
8 捜物 **saga(shi)mono** looking for something;
　something one is looking for
9 捜査 **sōsa** investigation
10 捜索 **sōsaku** search
　捜索隊 **sōsakutai** search party
12 捜絵 **saga(shi)e** picture puzzle

——————— 2 ———————
12 絵捜 **esaga(shi)** picture puzzle

——————— 3 ———————
10 家宅捜索 **kataku sōsaku** domiciliary search

3c7.6
捏 **NETSU** falsify
ko(neru) knead, mix

——————— 1 ———————
3 捏上 **de(tchi)a(geru)** fabricate, trump/frame up
6 捏返 **ko(ne)kae(su)** knead, mix; be muddy
　捏回 **ko(ne)mawa(su)** knead, mix; be muddy
9 捏造 **netsuzō** fabrication, falsehood
10 捏粉 **ko(ne)ko** dough
13 捏鉢 **ko(ne)bachi** kneading trough

3c7.7
捍 **KAN** defend, protect

3c7.8
挼 **RŌ, moteaso(bu)** play/twiddle with

3c7.9
捋 **RATSU** grab

3c7.10
捗 捗 **CHOKU, HO, hakado(ru)** make progress/headway, be coming along

——————— 1 ———————
3 捗々 **hakabaka(shii)** rapid, expeditious, active; satisfactory

——————— 2 ———————
10 進捗 **shinchoku** progress, advance

3

氵土扌口女巾犭弓彳彡艹宀丷山幸广尸口 7←

3c7.11

捐

EN throw away; donate

――――― 2 ―――――

5 出捐 **shutsuen** donate, contribute, bestow
13 義捐 **gien** donation, contribution
　義捐金 **gienkin** donation, contribution

3c7.12

挨

AI push open

――――― 1 ―――――

9 挨拶 **aisatsu** greeting, salutation, courtesy call; address, message

――――― 2 ―――――

12 無挨拶 **buaisatsu** impoliteness, incivility

3c7.13

挽 挽

BAN, hi(ku) saw (wood), grind (meat, coffee beans); pull (a cart)

――――― 1 ―――――

4 挽切 **hi(ki)ki(ru)** saw off
6 挽肉 **hi(ki)niku** ground meat
　挽回 **bankai** retrieve, recover, restore
9 挽茶 **hi(ki)cha** powdered tea
14 挽歌 **banka** dirge, funeral song

――――― 2 ―――――

4 木挽 **kobi(ki)** sawyer

捩 → 捩 3c8.31

3c7.14 / 954

振

SHIN, fu(ru) wave, shake; jilt
fu(rareru) be jilted/rebuffed
fu(ri) appearance, dress; feigning, pretense; swing, wave, shake; (dance) postures; leaning, slant **-bu(ri)** after a lapse of, for the first time in (two years); for (three days); manner, style **fu(reru)** lean toward; shake, swing, wag **fu(ruu)** shake, wield; flourish, be invigorated

――――― 1 ―――――

0 振った **fu(rutta)** splendid, brilliant, extraordinary
2 振子 **fu(ri)ko** pendulum
3 振上 **fu(ri)a(geru)** swing/lift up
4 振切 **fu(ri)ki(ru)** shake off, break free of

振分 **fu(ri)wa(keru)** divide in two, distribute
振分髪 **fu(ri)wa(ke)gami** hair parted and hanging down
振込 **fu(ri)ko(mu)** pay in, transfer (funds into an account)
振方 **fu(ri)kata** what to do (with oneself)
5 振出 **fu(ri)da(su)** shake out; draw (a bill); issue (a check); infuse, decoct
　fu(ri)da(shi) start; draft, issuing
振出人 **furidashinin** remitter, issuer
振出局 **furidashikyoku** the issuing (post) office (for a money order)
振付 **fu(ri)tsu(ke)** choreography
振払 **fu(ri)hara(u)** shake off
振立 **fu(ri)ta(teru)** shake/perk up, raise (one's voice)
6 振仮名 **fu(ri)gana** (small kana written above or beside a kanji to show its pronunciation)
振合 **fu(ri)a(i)** balancing, comparison, consideration, relationship
振返 **fu(ri)kae(ru)** turn one's head, look back
振向 **fu(ri)mu(ku)** turn toward, look back
振当 **fu(ri)a(teru)** assign (roles)
振回 **fu(ri)mawa(su)** wave about, brandish
7 振作 **shinsaku** encouragement
振乱 **fu(ri)mida(su)** shake (one's hair) loose, dishevel
8 振放 **fu(ri)hana(su)** shake off, break free of
9 振飛 **fu(ri)to(basu)** fling away
10 振起 **fu(rui)oko(su)** rouse/stir up, awaken, stimulate
11 振粛 **shinshuku** strict enforcement
振動 **shindō** vibration, oscillation
　fu(ri)ugo(ku) swing, shake, oscillate
振掛 **fu(ri)ka(keru)** sprinkle on, dust, splash
　fu(ri)ka(ke) condiment mix to be sprinkled over rice
振捨 **fu(ri)su(teru)** shake/cast off; desert, jilt
12 振幅 **shinpuku** amplitude
振落 **fu(ri)o(tosu)** shake/throw off
振替 **fu(ri)ka(eru)** change to, transfer (funds)
　furika(e) transfer
振替休日 **furikae kyūjitsu** substitute holiday (for one falling on a Sunday)
13 振鈴 **shinrei** ringing a (hand) bell
15 振舞 **furuma(u)** behave, conduct oneself; entertain, treat
振舞酒 **furuma(i)zake** a saké treat
振撒 **fu(ri)ma(ku)** strew about, scatter
16 振興 **shinkō** promotion, encouragement
17 振翳 **fu(ri)kaza(su)** fling up, brandish
18 振離 **fu(ri)hana(su)** shake off, break free of

――――― 2 ―――――

3 三振 **sanshin** strikeout (in baseball)

久振 hisa(shi)bu(ri) (for the first time in) a
　　　　 long time
大振 ōbu(ri) big swing; large size
口振 kuchibu(ri) way of talking; intimation
女振 onnabu(ri) a woman's looks/charms
小振 kobu(ri) small-size
4 不振 fushin dullness, slump, stagnation
手振 tebu(ri) hand waving, gesture
木振 kibu(ri) shape of a tree
5 打振 u(chi)fu(ru) wave, shake, brandish
立振舞 ta(chi)buruma(i) farewell dinner
　　　　 ta(chi)furuma(i) demeanor
6 気振 kebu(ri) look, air, bearing; indications
羽振 habu(ri) influence, power
共振 kyōshin resonance
7 身振 mibu(ri) gesture, gesticulation
形振 narifu(ri) one's appearance
見振 mi(nu) fu(ri) pretend not to see
男振 otokobu(ri), otoko(p)pu(ri) a man's
　　　　 bearing
言振 i(i)bu(ri), i(ip)pu(ri) way of speaking
8 知振 shi(ran)pu(ri), shi(ran) fu(ri) pretend-
　　　　 ing not to know, nonchalant
　　　　 shi(tta) fu(ri) pretending to know
空振 karabu(ri) swing and miss (in baseball)
歩振 aru(ki)bu(ri) way of walking, pace, gait
枝振 edabu(ri) shape of a tree
9 発振器 hasshinki oscillator
思振 omo(wase)bu(ri) coquetry; mystification
10 酒振舞 sakaburuma(i) wining and dining
書振 ka(ki)bu(ri) style of writing
素振 sobu(ri) manner, bearing, behavior
11 過振 kabu(ri) overdraft
強振 kyōshin swing (the bat) hard
脳振盪 nōshintō cerebral concussion
12 割振 wa(ri)fu(ru) allocate, allot, divide/
　　　　 distribute among
勤振 tsuto(me)bu(ri) how well one works,
　　　　 one's conduct
葉振 habu(ri) leaf arrangement, foliage
13 働振 hatara(ki)bu(ri) how one works,
　　　　 discharge of one's duty
話振 hana(shi)bu(ri) manner of speaking
14 旗振 hatafu(ri) flagman; flag-wagging
読振 yo(mi)bu(ri) way of reading

──────── 3 ────────
3 久方振 hisakatabu(ri) (for the first time in)
　　　　 a long time
4 勿体振 mottaibu(ru) put on airs, act self-
　　　　 important
7 体裁振 teisaibu(ru) put on airs, pose
8 武者振 mushabu(ri) valor, gallantry
武者振付 mushabu(ri)tsu(ku) pounce upon,
　　　　 devour
10 起居振舞 ta(chi)i furuma(i) deportment,
　　　　 manners

──────── 4 ────────
9 食思不振 shokushi fushin loss of appetite

3c7.15

挫 ZA, kuji(ku) sprain, dislocate; frustrate
(plans); crush, daunt　kuji(keru) be
broken/crushed/sprained, be disheartened

──────── 1 ────────
7 挫折 zasetsu setback, frustration, reverses
12 挫創 zasō contusion, fracture
13 挫傷 zashō sprain, fracture, bruise

──────── 2 ────────
11 捻挫 nenza sprain, wrench
13 頓挫 tonza setback, hitch, impasse

──────── 8 ────────

3c8.1 / 1233

推 SUI inference, conjecture; push ahead
o(su) infer, deduce; recommend,
propose

──────── 1 ────────
2 推力 suiryoku thrust
5 推古 Suiko (empress, 592–628)
6 推考 suikō infer, conjecture, deliberate
推当 o(shi)a(teru) guess
7 推究 suikyū inference
8 推知 suichi inference, conjecture
推参 suisan visiting (unannounced); rude
推定 suitei presumption, estimate
推服 suifuku admire, esteem
9 推計 suikei estimate
10 推進 suishin propulsion, drive
推進力 suishinryoku thrust, impulse
推挙 suikyo recommend (for a post)
推称 suishō praise, admiration
11 推理 suiri reasoning, inference
推理小説 suiri shōsetsu detective story,
　　　　 whodunit
推移 suii changes, transition, progress
推断 suidan infer, deduce, conclude
12 推測 suisoku conjecture, supposition
推量 suiryō inference, surmise
　　　　 o(shi)haka(ru) infer, guess
13 推奨 suishō recommend, commend
14 推敲 suikō polish, elaborate on, work over
推察 suisatsu guess, conjecture, surmise
推算 suisan calculate, reckon, estimate
15 推賞 suishō recommend, commend
推論 suiron reasoning, inference
16 推薦 suisen recommendation, nomination
推薦状 suisenjō letter of recommendation
推薦者 suisensha recommender
17 推戴 suitai have as president of

——— 2 ———
6 当推量 **a(te)zuiryō** guesswork
7 邪推 **jasui** unjust suspicion, mistrust
18 類推 **ruisui** (reasoning by) analogy

3c8.2

押

MON rub, grasp, pinch

——— 1 ———
12 押着 **monchaku** trouble, dispute

3c8.3

捶

SUI strike with a cane/whip

3c8.4

捷

SHŌ victory; fast

——— 1 ———
8 捷径 **shōkei** short cut, shorter way
12 捷報 **shōhō** news of victory
13 捷戦 **kachiikusa** a victory

——— 2 ———
9 敏捷 **binshō** nimble, agile; sharp, shrewd
12 軽捷 **keishō** agile, nimble

3c8.5

揶

YA banter, raillery

——— 1 ———
12 揶揄 **yayu** banter, raillery, poking fun

3c8.6 / 1464

掛

ka(karu) hang (intr.); cost (money), take (time) **ka(kari), kakari** expenses, tax; relation, connection **-ga(karu)** be tinged with **-ga(kari)** taking, requiring (3 days) **ka(keru)** hang (tr.); put on top of; turn on, start; spend; multiply; (as suffix) begin to, start ...ing **(ni) ka(kete wa)** in the matter of, as regards **ka(ke)** buckwheat noodles in broth; credit, account; (hat) rack, hook; (as suffix) half-(finished) **-ga(ke)** wearing, with … on; upon …ing; ten percent; times (as large)

——— 1 ———
4 掛引 **ka(ke)hi(ki)** bargaining, maneuvering
5 掛矢 **ka(ke)ya** large mallet
掛外 **ka(ke)hazu(shi)** hanging up and taking down, engaging and disengaging (gears)

掛払 **ka(ke)bara(i)** settlement of accounts
掛布団 **ka(ke)buton** quilt, coverlet
掛字 **ka(ke)ji** hanging scroll
掛札 **ka(ke)fuda** hanging notice plaque, nameplate
掛目 **ka(ke)me** weight
6 掛合 **ka(ke)a(u)** negotiate/bargain with **ka(ke)a(wasu)** multiply together; cross, interbreed **ka(kari)a(i)** involvement, implication in
7 掛売 **ka(ke)u(ri)** selling on credit
掛声 **ka(ke)goe** shout (of encouragement)
掛図 **ka(ke)zu** wall chart/map
8 掛物 **ka(ke)mono** hanging scroll; coverlet
掛取 **ka(ke)to(ri)** bill collection/collector
掛取引 **ka(ke)torihiki** credit transaction
掛金 **ka(ke)kin** installment (payment) **ka(ke)gane** latch, hasp
9 掛持 **ka(ke)mo(chi)** hold (part-time) positions concurrently
10 掛倒 **ka(ke)dao(re)** bad debt; earnings not covering expenses
掛値 **ka(ke)ne** overcharge
掛時計 **ka(ke)dokei** wall clock
掛紙 **ka(ke)gami** wrapper
11 掛商 **ka(ke)akina(i)** selling on credit
掛捨 **ka(ke)zu(te)** abandoning an installment contract
12 掛帳 **ka(ke)chō** charge-account book
掛違 **ka(ke)chiga(u)** cross/pass (each other)
掛替 **ka(ke)ka(eru)** replace, rebuild, substitute **ka(ke)ga(e)** substitute
掛買 **ka(ke)ga(i)** credit purchase
掛詞 **ka(ke)kotoba** play on words
掛軸 **ka(ke)jiku** hanging scroll
13 掛蒲団 **ka(ke)buton** quilt, coverlet
掛鉤 **ka(ke)kagi** hook
14 掛算 **ka(ke)zan** multiplication (in math)
15 掛蕎麦 **ka(ke)soba** buckwheat noodles in broth
16 掛橋 **ka(ke)hashi** (suspension) bridge

——— 2 ———
3 大掛 **ōgaka(ri)** large-scale
4 水掛論 **mizuka(ke)ron** futile argument
手掛 **tega(kari)** handhold; clue, lead **tega(keru)** handle, deal with; have experience in; rear, look after
引掛 **hi(k)ka(karu)** get caught/hooked/entangled **hi(k)ka(keru)** hang/hook/throw on; ensnare; cheat; have a quick drink
月掛 **tsukiga(ke)** monthly installments
日掛 **higa(ke)** daily installments
心掛 **kokoroga(ke)** intention; attention, care
5 出掛 **deka(keru)** go out, set out **de(gake)** about to go out

仕掛 **shikaka(ri)** beginning
    shika(ke) contrivance, device; scale, size; half finished
仕掛人 **shika(ke)nin** intriguer, schemer, plotter
打掛 **u(chi)ka(karu), u(tte)ka(karu)** strike/ hit at, assail   **u(chi)ka(ke)** long outer garment
立掛 **ta(chi)ka(keru)** begin to rise
目掛 **mega(keru)** aim at
6 気掛 **kiga(kari)** anxiety
帆掛船 **hoka(ke)bune** sailboat
行掛 **yu(ki)ga(ke), i(ki)ga(ke)** on the way   **yu(ki)ga(kari)** circumstances
7 投掛 **na(ge)ka(keru)** throw at
吹掛 **fu(ki)ka(keru)** blow/spray on   **fu(k)ka(keru)** blow/spray on; provoke, pick (a fight); ask too much, overcharge
売掛 **u(ri)ka(ke)** credit sales
声掛 **(o)koega(kari)** (influential person's) recommendation
肘掛 **hijika(ke)** arm (of a chair)
見掛 **mika(keru)** (happen to) see, notice
見掛倒 **mika(ke)dao(shi)** mere show
言掛 **i(i)ka(keru)** speak to; start talking   **i(i)ga(kari)** false accusation
足掛 **ashiga(kari)** foothold   **ashika(ke)** foothold, pedal, step; counting the first and last fractional (years of a time span) as a whole
8 追掛 **o(i)ka(keru)** chase, run after
凭掛 **mota(re)ka(karu)** lean against; rely on
泊掛 **to(mari)ga(ke)** be staying with, visiting overnight
押掛 **o(shi)ka(keru)** drop in on uninvited
押掛女房 **o(shi)ka(ke) nyōbō** a woman who pressured her husband into marrying her
押掛客 **o(shi)ka(ke)kyaku** uninvited guest
呼掛 **yo(bi)ka(keru)** call out to; call/appeal for
突掛 **tsu(ki)ka(karu)** lunge at
突掛草履 **tsu(k)ka(ke) zōri** slip-on straw sandles
肱掛 **hijika(ke)** arm (of a chair)
肩掛 **kataka(ke)** shawl
取掛 **to(ri)kaka(ru)** get started on, set about
9 飛掛 **to(bi)ka(karu)** pounce on, lunge for
乗掛 **no(ri)ka(keru)** be about to board; be riding on; get on top of, lean over; set about; collide with
降掛 **fu(ri)ka(karu)** fall on; befall, happen to; hang over; impend
前掛 **maeka(ke)** apron
通掛 **tō(ri)ka(karu)** happen to come along   **tō(ri)ga(kari/ke)** while passing by
涎掛 **yodareka(ke)** bib

持掛 **mo(chi)ka(keru)** propose, offer
神掛 **kamika(kete)** swearing by a god; for sure, absolutely
思掛 **omo(i)ga(kenai)** unexpected
食掛 **ta(be)ka(keru), ku(i)ka(keru)** begin to eat **ta(be)ka(ke), ku(i)ka(ke)** half-eaten **ku(tte)ka(karu)** lash out at, defy
10 射掛 **ika(keru)** attack with arrows
帰掛 **kae(ri)ga(ke)** upon leaving, on one's way back
差掛 **sa(shi)ka(karu)** hang over, overhang; be urgent; be imminent; approach, come near **sa(shi)ka(keru)** hold (an umbrella) over (someone)
差掛小屋 **sa(shi)ka(ke)goya** penthouse, lean-to
起掛 **o(ki)ga(ke)** upon getting up
振掛 **fu(ri)ka(keru)** sprinkle on, dust, splash **fu(ri)ka(ke)** condiment mix to be sprinkled over rice
11 窓掛 **madoka(ke)** curtain, blinds
寄掛 **yo(ri)ka(karu)** lean against **yo(se)ka(keru)** prop against
問掛 **to(i)ka(keru)** (begin to) ask, inquire
12 遣掛 **ya(ri)ka(keru)** begin to do, set about **ya(ri)ka(ke)** unfinished, half done
飲掛 **no(mi)ka(ke)** half-drunk (cup), half-smoked (cigarette)
13 働掛 **hatara(ki)ka(keru)** work on (someone), influence, appeal to; begin to work
腰掛 **koshika(keru)** sit down **koshika(ke)** seat; steppingstone (to something else)
腰掛仕事 **koshika(ke) shigoto** temporary work
腹掛 **haraga(ke)** cloth chest-and-belly cover
詰掛 **tsu(me)ka(keru)** throng to, besiege, crowd
話掛 **hana(shi)ka(keru)** speak to, accost
14 摑掛 **tsuka(mi)ka(karu)** grab at
総掛 **sōga(kari)** concerted effort, all together
15 撥掛 **ha(ne)ka(keru)** splash, bespatter
膝掛 **hizaka(ke)** lap robe/blanket
諸掛 **shoka(kari)** expenses
鋳掛 **ika(keru)** recast, mend
鋳掛屋 **ika(ke)ya** tinkerer, tinsmith
16 壁掛 **kabeka(ke)** tapestry; wall (phone)
親掛 **oyaga(kari)** dependence on one's parents
19 願掛 **ganga(ke)** say a prayer
22 襲掛 **oso(i)ka(karu)** pounce upon, attack

_____ 3 _____

2 之繞掛 **shinnyū (o) ka(keru)** emphasize, exaggerate
3 大仕掛 **ōjika(ke)** on a grand scale
千鳥掛 **chidoriga(ke)** catch/cross stitch; crossing

小屋掛 **koyaga(ke)** pitch camp; temporary hut/shack
4 手塩掛 **teshio (ni) ka(kete)** (bring up) by hand
6 色仕掛 **irojika(ke)** feigned affection
衣紋掛 **emonka(ke)** hanger/rack (for kimono)
10 浴衣掛 **yukataga(ke)** wearing a yukata
11 袈裟掛 **kesaga(ke)** hanging/slashed diagonally from the shoulder

───────── 4 ─────────

10 時計仕掛 **tokei-jika(ke)** clockwork
16 機械仕掛 **kikai-jika(ke)** mechanism

3c8.7

掀

KIN raise, hoist

3c8.8 / 1036

排

HAI exclude, reject, expel, anti-; push aside; push open; line up

───────── 1 ─────────

0 排する **hai(suru)** exclude, reject, expel; push aside; push open
4 排水 **haisui** drainage; displacement (of a ship)
排水トン数 **haisui tonsū** displacement tonnage
排水量 **haisuiryō** displacement (of a ship)
排水路 **haisuiro** culvert, sewer system
排水管 **haisuikan** drainpipe
排日 **hai-Nichi** anti-Japanese
5 排斥 **haiseki** exclude, expel, ostracize, boycott
排出 **haishutsu** discharge, exhaust; excretion
排出物 **haishutsubutsu** excreta
排他 **haita** exclusion
排他的 **haitateki** exclusive
排外 **haigai** anti-foreign
6 排気 **haiki** exhaust (fumes)
排気量 **haikiryō** (piston) displacement
排気管 **haikikan** exhaust pipe
排列 **hairetsu** arrangement, configuration
排米 **hai-Bei** anti-American
7 排卵 **hairan** ovulation
排尿 **hainyō** urination
8 排泄 **haisetsu** excretion, evacuation, discharge
排泄物 **haisetsubutsu** excrement, excretion
排英 **hai-Ei** anti-British
9 排便 **haiben** evacuation, defecation
排除 **haijo** exclude, remove, eliminate
11 排液 **haieki** drainage (in surgery)
排球 **haikyū** volleyball
排雪 **haisetsu** snow removal
15 排撃 **haigeki** reject, denounce

───────── 2 ─────────

9 按排 **anbai** distribute, assign; adjust

3c8.9

捲 捲

KEN, ma(ku) roll, wind, coil **maku(ru), meku(ru)** turn over (pages), roll up (one's sleeves); strip off **maku(reru)** be turned/rolled up

───────── 1 ─────────

3 捲上 **maku(ri)a(geru)** roll up; drive up (the enemy onto the hill) **maku(shi)a(geru)** roll up **ma(ki)a(geru)** wind up, roll up; weigh (anchor); fling up (dust); cheat (money) out of (a person)
捲土重来 **kendo-chōrai/-jūrai** comeback (from a defeat with renewed vigor)
5 捲立 **maku(shi)ta(teru)** talk volubly, rattle on
10 捲起 **ma(ki)o(kosu)** stir up, create (a sensation)

───────── 2 ─────────

4 日捲 **himeku(ri)** calendar pad
7 吹捲 **fu(ki)maku(ru)** sweep along, blow about
言捲 **i(i)maku(ru)** argue down, confute
10 席捲 **sekken** sweeping conquest
14 総捲 **sōmaku(ri)** general survey/review

3c8.10 / 486

接

SETSU touch, join **tsu(gu)** join to, piece together, splice **ha(gu)** patch

───────── 1 ─────────

0 接する **ses(suru)** touch, come in contact with; receive (guests), attend on
4 接収 **sesshū** requisition, take over
接木 **tsu(gi)ki** grafting; grafted tree
5 接目 **tsu(gi)me, ha(gi)me** joint, seam
6 接合 **setsugō** joining, union **ha(gi)a(waseru)** join/patch together
接合剤 **setsugōzai** glue, adhesive
接近 **sekkin** approach, draw near
接地 **setchi** (electrical) ground(ing), earth
7 接伴 **seppan** receive, entertain
接角 **sekkaku** adjacent angles
接吻 **seppun** kiss
接尾辞 **setsubiji** suffix
接尾語 **setsubigo** suffix
接見 **sekken** receive (visitors)
8 接受 **setsuju** receive, intercept
9 接待 **settai** reception, welcome; serving, offering
接待室 **settaishitsu** reception room
接客 **sekkyaku** receiving visitors/customers
接客用 **sekkyakuyō** for customers
接客係 **sekkyakugakari** receptionist
接客婦 **sekkyakufu** hostess, waitress
接客業 **sekkyakugyō** hotel and restaurant trade

10 接骨 **sekkotsu** bonesetting
接骨木 **niwatoko** elder (tree)
接骨医 **sekkotsui** bonesetter
接骨術 **sekkotsujutsu** bonesetting
11 接眼鏡 **setsugankyō** eyepiece
12 接着 **setchaku** adhesion
接着剤 **setchakuzai** adhesive, glue
13 接戦 **sessen** close combat/contest
接辞 **setsuji** an affix, prefixes and suffixes
接続 **setsuzoku** connection, joining
接続詞 **setsuzokushi** a conjunction
接触 **sesshoku** touch, contact; catalytic
接触点 **sesshokuten** point of contact/tangency
接触面 **sesshokumen** contact surface
14 接種 **sesshu** inoculation, vaccination
15 接穂 **tsu(gi)ho** grafting, slip, scion
接線 **sessen** a tangent
16 接頭辞 **settōji** prefix
接頭語 **settōgo** prefix

──────── 2 ────────
4 内接 **naisetsu** inscribed (circle)
5 外接 **gaisetsu** be circumscribed (in geometry)
外接円 **gaisetsuen** circumscribed circle
6 交接 **kōsetsu** copulation
近接 **kinsetsu** neighboring, contiguous, close-by
迎接 **geisetsu** meeting and entertaining
7 応接 **ōsetsu** reception (of visitors)
応接室 **ōsetsushitsu** reception room
応接間 **ōsetsuma** reception room, parlor
8 直接 **chokusetsu** direct
直接法 **chokusetsuhō** direct method; indicative mood
直接税 **chokusetsuzei** direct tax
直接話法 **chokusetsu wahō** direct quotation
逆接 **gyakusetsu** contrary conjunction, "but" relationship
芽接 **metsu(gi)** bud grafting, inlay graft
枝接 **edatsu(gi)** grafting
9 連接 **rensetsu** connect
面接 **mensetsu** interview
面接試問 **mensetsu shimon** oral examination
10 根接 **netsu(gi)** root grafting
骨接 **honetsu(gi)** bonesetting; bonesetter
11 密接 **missetsu** close, intimate
12 焼接 **ya(ki)tsu(gi)** cement (broken china) together by baking
間接 **kansetsu** indirect
間接税 **kansetsuzei** indirect tax
13 溶接 **yōsetsu** welding
15 隣接 **rinsetsu** border on, be contiguous, adjoin
17 鍛接 **tansetsu** forge welding
18 鎔接 **yōsetsu** welding
鎔接工 **yōsetsukō** welder
鎔接剤 **yōsetsuzai** welding flux
鎔接機 **yōsetsuki** welding machine

──────── 3 ────────
4 予防接種 **yobō sesshu** inoculation
18 謦咳接 **keigai (ni) ses(suru)** have the pleasure of meeting personally

3c8.11 / 1718

控 **KŌ, hika(eru)** hold back, refrain from; note down; wait **hika(e)** note, memo; duplicate, copy; waiting; brace, strut; a reserve

──────── 1 ────────
5 控目 **hika(e)me** moderate, reserved
8 控制 **kōsei** checking, controlling
控所 **hika(e)jo** waiting room
9 控除 **kōjo** deduct, subtract
控室 **hika(e)shitsu** waiting room
控屋敷 **hika(e) yashiki** villa, retreat
10 控書 **hika(e)ga(ki)** note, memo
11 控帳 **hika(e)chō** notebook
12 控訴 **kōso** appeal (to a higher court)
控訴状 **kōsojō** petition of appeal
控訴院 **kōsoin** court of appeal
控訴審 **kōsoshin** appeal trial
控訴権 **kōsoken** right of appeal

──────── 2 ────────
4 手控 **tebika(e)** note, memo; holding back
7 売控 **u(ri)hika(eru)** refrain from selling
10 差控 **sa(shi)hika(eru)** be moderate in; withhold, refrain from
12 買控 **ka(i)hika(eru)** refrain from buying

3c8.12

捧 **HŌ** hold in both hands; offer up **sasa(geru)** lift up; give, offer, dedicate

──────── 1 ────────
7 捧呈 **hōtei** present, offer, submit
8 捧物 **sasa(ge)mono** offering, sacrifice
13 捧腹 **hōfuku** holding one's sides in laughter
捧腹絶倒 **hōfuku-zettō** convulsed with laughter
14 捧読 **hōdoku** read reverently
捧銃 **sasa(ge)tsutsu** Present arms!

──────── 3 ────────
5 用心捧 **yōjinbō** door bolt; cudgel; bodyguard
9 指揮捧 **shikibō** baton

3c8.13 / 1624

揭 揭 **KEI, kaka(geru)** put up (a sign), hoist (a flag), display, publish, carry/run (an ad)

──────── 1 ────────
5 揭示 **keiji** notice, bulletin
揭示板 **keijiban** bulletin board

12 掲揚 **keiyō** hoist, fly, display (a flag)
13 掲載 **keisai** publish, print, carry/run (an ad)

——————— 2 ———————

9 前掲 **zenkei** the above-mentioned

3c8.14 / 933

採 採   **SAI, to(ru)** take (on), accept, employ; collect, gather

——————— 1 ———————

5 採用 **saiyō** adopt, employ
採石 **saiseki** quarrying
6 採伐 **saibatsu** timbering, felling
採光 **saikō** lighting
採血 **saiketsu** collect blood
7 採卵 **sairan** egg raising
採決 **saiketsu** voting
採択 **saitaku** adopt, select
採否 **saihi** adoption or rejection
8 採油 **saiyu** extract oil, drill for oil
採油権 **saiyuken** oil concession, drilling rights
採取 **saishu** gather, pick, harvest, extract
9 採点 **saiten** marking, grading, scoring
採点者 **saitensha** marker, grader, scorer
採炭 **saitan** coal mining
採炭所 **saitanjo** coal mine
10 採残 **to(ri)noko(su)** leave behind
11 採掘 **saikutsu** mining
12 採集 **saishū** collecting (butterflies)
13 採鉱 **saikō** mining
14 採種 **saishu** collecting seeds
採算 **saisan** profit
採算割 **saisanwa(re)** below cost
16 採録 **sairoku** record, transcribe

——————— 2 ———————

6 伐採 **bassai** felling, deforestation, cutting

——————— 3 ———————

12 植物採集 **shokubutsu saishū** plant collecting

3c8.15 / 602

授   **JU, sazu(keru)** give, grant; impart, teach
sazu(karu) be granted/taught

——————— 1 ———————

3 授与 **juyo** conferring, awarding
授与式 **juyoshiki** presentation ceremony
7 授乳 **junyū** breast-feeding, nursing
授乳期 **junyūki** period of lactation
授戒 **jukai** Buddhist initiation ceremony
8 授受 **juju** giving and receiving, transfer
授物 **sazu(kari)mono** gift, blessing, boon
10 授粉 **jufun** pollination
11 授産 **jusan** providing employment, placement

授産所 **jusanjo** vocational center (for the unemployed)
13 授業 **jugyō** teaching, instruction
授業料 **jugyōryō** tuition
14 授精 **jusei** fertilization
15 授賞 **jushō** awarding a prize
授権 **juken** authorize
17 授爵 **jushaku** confer nobility/peerage

——————— 2 ———————

3 口授 **kuju, kōju** oral teaching; dictation
4 天授 **tenju** natural gifts
    Tenju (era, 1375–1381)
6 伝授 **denju** instruct, initiate into
9 神授 **shinju** divine gift
10 教授 **kyōju** professor; teaching
教授団 **kyōjudan** faculty
教授法 **kyōjuhō** teaching method

——————— 3 ———————

7 助教授 **jokyōju** assistant professor

——————— 4 ———————

6 名誉教授 **meiyo kyōju** professor emeritus
10 個人教授 **kojin kyōju** private lessons

3c8.16 / 535

探   **TAN, sagu(ru)** search for
saga(su) look for

——————— 1 ———————

5 探出 **sagu(ri)da(su)** spy/sniff out (a secret)
6 探合 **sagu(ri)a(i)** probing each other's feelings
探当 **sagu(ri)a(teru)** grope for and find
探回 **sagu(ri)mawa(ru)** grope about
7 探求 **tankyū** quest, pursuit
探究 **tankyū** research, inquiry, study
探究心 **tankyūshin** spirit of inquiry
探究者 **tankyūsha** investigator
探足 **sagu(ri)ashi** groping one's way along
8 探知 **tanchi** detection
探知器 **tanchiki** detector
9 探海灯 **tankaitō** searchlight
探査 **tansa** inquiry, investigation
10 探険 **tanken** exploration, expedition
探索 **tansaku** search; inquiry, investigation
11 探偵 **tantei** (private) detective, investigator, spy
探偵小説 **tantei shōsetsu** detective story
探訪 **tanbō** inquire into, probe
12 探検 **tanken** exploration, expedition
探検家 **tankenka** explorer
探検記 **tankenki** account of an expedition
探検隊 **tankentai** exploration party
探勝 **tanshō** sightseeing
13 探照灯 **tanshōtō** searchlight

探鉱 **tankō** prospecting
14 探聞 **tanbun** sounding out indirectly
18 探題 **tandai** picking poem themes by lottery; commissioner (historical)

─────────── 2 ───────────

2 人探 **hitosaga(shi)** searching for someone
4 内探 **naitan** private inquiry, secret investigation
手探 **tesagu(ri)** groping, fumbling
5 字探 **jisaga(shi)** word puzzle
穴探 **anasaga(shi)** faultfinding
10 家探 **iesaga(shi)** house hunting
12 婿探 **mukosaga(shi)** looking for a husband for one's daughter
絵探 **esaga(shi)** picture puzzle
13 電探 **dentan** radar
21 露探 **rotan** Russian spy (in the Russo-Japanese War)

掾 → 掾 3c7.10

3c8.17

捺 **NATSU, o(su)** press down, stamp, affix a seal

─────────── 1 ───────────

6 捺印 **natsuin** seal (a document)
9 捺染 **nassen** (textile) printing

─────────── 2 ───────────

8 押捺 **ōnatsu** affix a seal

─────────── 3 ───────────

13 署名捺印 **shomei-natsuin** signature and seal

3c8.18

掟 **TŌ, okite** law, commandment, rule

3c8.19

捥 **WAN** arm **mo(gu)** pick (fruit from the tree/vine) **mogi(ru)** pluck/tear off, wrest away **mo(geru)** be torn off, come off

─────────── 1 ───────────

8 捥取 **mo(gi)to(ru)** break/tear off, wrest from

3c8.20 / 1200

措 **SO, o(ku)** put aside, leave as is, desist from; except

─────────── 1 ───────────

13 措辞 **soji** choice of words, phraseology

措置 **sochi** measure, steps

─────────── 2 ───────────

10 挙措 **kyoso** behavior, bearing

3c8.21 / 1469

描 **BYŌ, ega(ku)** draw, paint, sketch, depict, portray **ka(ku)** draw, paint; write, compose

─────────── 1 ───────────

5 描出 **ega(ki)da(su)** portray, depict
描写 **byōsha** depiction, portrayal, description
8 描画 **byōga** drawing, painting

─────────── 2 ───────────

3 寸描 **sunbyō** brief/thumbnail description
5 白描 **hakubyō** plain sketch
10 素描 **sobyō** rough sketch
12 絵描 **eka(ki)** painter, artist

3c8.22 / 1080

掃 掃 **SŌ, ha(ku)** sweep

─────────── 1 ───────────

5 掃出 **ha(ki)da(su)** sweep out
掃立 **ha(ki)ta(te)** newly/just swept
8 掃取 **ha(ki)to(ru)** sweep away/off
9 掃除 **sōji** cleaning, clean-up
掃除人 **sōjinin** cleaner, janitor
掃除夫 **sōjifu** cleaner, janitor
掃除婦 **sōjifu** cleaning lady/woman
掃除機 **sōjiki** vacuum cleaner
掃海 **sōkai** mine sweeping
掃海艇 **sōkaitei** minesweeper
10 掃射 **sōsha** sweeping fire, strafing
掃討 **sōtō** sweeping, clearing, mopping up
11 掃掃除 **ha(ki)sōji** sweeping and cleaning
掃捨 **ha(ki)su(teru)** sweep away/out
掃寄 **ha(ki)yo(seru)** sweep into a pile, sweep up
12 掃集 **ha(ki)atsu(meru)** sweep up/together
13 掃溜 **ha(ki)da(me)** sweepings, rubbish heap
掃滅 **sōmetsu** mopping up, annihilation
15 掃蕩 **sōtō** sweep, clear, mop up

─────────── 2 ───────────

1 一掃 **issō** a clean sweep
3 大掃除 **ōsōji** general house-cleaning, spring/fall cleaning
9 拭掃除 **fu(ki)sōji** cleaning (a house)
11 清掃 **seisō** cleaning
清掃夫 **seisōfu** garbage man/collector
掃掃除 **ha(ki)sōji** sweeping and cleaning
13 煤掃 **susuha(ki)** house cleaning

3

氵
土
扌
日
女
巾
犭
弓
彳
彡
艹
宀
⺍
山
吉
广
尸
口

8 ←

3

氵
土
扌
口
女
巾
犭
弓
彳
彡
艹
宀
灬
耂
广
尸
口

→ 8

------- 3 -------
10 真空掃除機 **shinkū sōjiki** vacuum cleaner
16 機銃掃射 **kijū sōsha** machine-gunning

3c8.23

掩

EN cover up; capture

------- 1 -------
13 掩蓋 **engai** covering; gun apron
15 掩撃 **engeki** surprise attack
掩蔽 **enpei** covering up; occultation
20 掩護 **engo** covering, protection

3c8.24

揖

KI pull, hold back

3c8.25

捻

NEN, hine(ru) twist; pinch **hine(ri)** a twist; a pinch **hine(kuru)** twirl, twist; tinker at **neji(ru)** twist **neji(reru)** be twisted

------- 1 -------
2 捻子 **neji** screw; (wind-up toy) spring
5 捻出 **nenshutsu** contrive, work out, raise (money) **hine(ri)da(su)** squeeze out; work/crank out, devise
10 捻挫 **nenza** sprain, wrench
11 捻転 **nenten** twisting, torsion
15 捻潰 **hine(ri)tsubu(su)** crush between one's thumb and finger

------- 2 -------
12 御捻 **ohine(ri)** gratuity wrapped in paper
13 腸捻転 **chōnenten** twist in the intestines, volvulus

3c8.26 / 1444

捨 捨

SHA, su(teru) throw away; abandon, forsake

------- 1 -------
2 捨子 **su(te)go** abandoned child, foundling
4 捨犬 **su(te)inu** stray dog
5 捨去 **su(te)sa(ru)** forsake
捨台詞 **su(te)zerifu** sharp parting remark
捨石 **su(te)ishi** ornamental garden rocks; rubble for river control; sacrifice stone/play (in go)
7 捨身 **su(te)mi** desperation
shashin renounce the flesh; die
捨売 **su(te)u(ri)** sacrifice sale
8 捨所 **su(te)dokoro** the place/time to throw away (one's life)

捨金 **su(te)gane** wasted money
10 捨値 **su(te)ne** giveaway price
捨書 **su(te)ga(ki)** rambling writing
11 捨猫 **su(te)neko** stray cat
12 捨象 **shashō** abstraction; disregard, ignore
捨場 **su(te)ba** dumping ground, dump
13 捨置 **su(te)o(ku)** leave as is, overlook
捨鉢 **su(te)bachi** despair, desperation

------- 2 -------
4 切捨 **ki(ri)su(teru)** cut down, slay; discard, cast away
5 世捨人 **yosu(te)bito** recluse, hermit
用捨 **yōsha** choose, select (what to adopt and what to reject)
打捨 **u(chi)su(teru)** throw out, discard
四捨五入 **shisha-gonyū** rounding off
7 投捨 **na(ge)su(teru)** throw away
芥捨場 **gomisu(te)ba** garbage dump
見捨 **misu(teru)** desert, abandon, forsake
言捨 **i(i)su(teru)** make a parting remark
8 呼捨 **yo(bi)su(te)** addressing someone by last name only, without affixing -san
取捨 **shusha** adoption or rejection
to(ri)su(teru) reject, discard
9 乗捨 **no(ri)su(teru)** get off; abandon (a ship), leave (a rented car) at the destination (of a one-way trip)
10 振捨 **fu(ri)su(teru)** shake/cast off; desert, jilt
書捨 **ka(ki)su(teru)** write and throw away
11 掛捨 **ka(ke)zu(te)** abandoning an installment contract
掃捨 **ha(ki)su(teru)** sweep away/out
脱捨 **nu(gi)su(teru)** throw off (clothes), kick off (shoes)
12 喜捨 **kisha** charity, donation
焼捨 **ya(ki)su(teru)** burn up, incinerate
14 聞捨 **ki(ki)su(teru)** ignore, overlook

捨→捨 3c8.26

3c8.27

掵

haba alluvial terraced land

3c8.28

掠

RYAKU, kasu(meru) rob, cheat; graze/brush/whiz/scud past **kasu(ru)** graze, glance off; squeeze, exploit **kasu(reru)** be blurred/indistinct

------- 1 -------
13 掠傷 **kasu(ri)kizu** scratch, bruise

14 掠奪 **ryakudatsu** plunder, loot, despoil

———————— 2 ————————

9 侵掠 **shinryaku** aggression, invasion
10 殺掠 **satsuryaku** killing and robbing

3c8.29

掖 **EKI** palace; aid, guide; (hold) under one's arm

3c8.30

掉 **TŌ, CHŌ** shake, wave, wag

———————— 1 ————————

7 掉尾 **tōbi** final (flurry), last

挽→挽 3c7.13

搔→搔 3c10.11

3c8.31

捩 捩 **REI, RETSU, neji(ru)** twist **yoji(ru)** twist **neji(reru)** be twisted **moji(ru)** twist; parody

———————— 1 ————————

2 捩子 **neji** screw; (wind-up toy) spring
3 捩上 **ne(ji)a(geru)** screw up, twist
4 捩切 **ne(ji)ki(ru)** twist/wrench off
 捩込 **ne(ji)ko(mu)** screw in; thrust into; protest to
6 捩曲 **ne(ji)ma(geru)** bend by twisting
 捩伏 **ne(ji)fu(seru)** throw/hold (someone) down
 捩向 **ne(ji)mu(keru)** twist toward
7 捩折 **ne(ji)o(ru)** twist off
8 捩取 **neji(ri)to(ru)** wrench off, wrest from
12 捩開 **ne(ji)a(keru)** wrench/pry open
13 捩鉢巻 **neji(ri)hachima(ki), ne(ji)hachima(ki)** twisted towel tied around one's head

———————— 2 ————————

8 逆捩食 **sakane(ji o) ku(waseru)** retort, criticize in return

3c8.32 / 1803

掘 **KUTSU, ho(ru)** dig

———————— 1 ————————

3 掘下 **ho(ri)sa(geru)** dig down, delve into

4 掘井戸 **ho(ri)ido** a well
 掘込 **ho(ri)ko(mu)** dig in(to)
5 掘出 **ho(ri)da(su)** dig out, unearth
 掘出物 **ho(ri)da(shi)mono** treasure trove; lucky find, bargain
6 掘返 **ho(ri)kae(su)** dig up
 掘池 **ho(ri)ike** artificial pond/pool
 掘当 **ho(ri)a(teru)** find, dig up, strike (oil)
7 掘抜 **ho(ri)nu(ku)** dig through, bore
 掘抜井戸 **ho(ri)nu(ki) ido** a well
9 掘削 **kussaku** excavation
10 掘起 **ho(ri)o(kosu)** dig/turn up
11 掘崩 **ho(ri)kuzu(su)** demolish
12 掘割 **ho(ri)wa(ri)** canal, ditch
 掘開 **ho(ri)hira(ku)** dig open
28 掘鑿 **kussaku** excavation

———————— 2 ————————

4 内掘 **uchibori** inner moat, moat within the castle walls
5 穴掘 **anaho(ri)** digging a hole, excavation; novice, bungler
8 金掘 **kaneho(ri)** miner
9 発掘 **hakkutsu** excavation; disinterment
10 根掘葉掘 **neho(ri)-haho(ri)** inquisitive about every detail
11 採掘 **saikutsu** mining
13 墓掘 **hakaho(ri)** grave digging/digger
 試掘 **shikutsu** prospecting
 試掘者 **shikutsusha** prospector
 試掘権 **shikutsuken** mining claim

———————— 3 ————————

21 露天掘 **rotenbo(ri)** strip mining

———————— 4 ————————

10 根掘葉掘 **neho(ri)-haho(ri)** inquisitive about every detail

3c8.33 / 1832

据 **KYO, su(eru)** set, place, install, put into position **su(waru)** sit, be set

———————— 1 ————————

5 据付 **su(e)tsu(keru)** set into position, install
9 据風呂 **su(e)furo** bathtub with water heater
13 据置 **su(e)o(ku)** leave as is, let stand
16 据膳 **su(e)zen** a meal set before one

———————— 2 ————————

5 打据 **u(chi)su(eru)** whip (a horse)
7 見据 **misu(eru)** fix one's eyes on, stare at
9 据据 **kikkyo** hard work, assiduousness
13 睨据 **nira(mi)su(eru)** glare at

3c8.34

撒 **SHU, SŌ** night watch

3

氵 土 扌 口 女 巾 犭 弓 彳 彡 艹 宀 ⺍ 山 耂 广 尸 口

8←

3c8.35

掬 **KIKU, suku(u)** scoop, dip up, ladle
musu(bu) scoop up (water) in one's hands

— 1 —

3 掬上 **suku(i)a(geru)** scoop/dip up
5 掬出 **suku(i)da(su)** bail/ladle out
7 掬投 **suku(i)na(ge)** tripping (in sumo)
8 掬取 **suku(i)to(ru)** scoop up, ladle out
14 掬網 **suku(i)ami** scoop/dip net

— 2 —

1 一掬 **ikkiku** one scoop (of water)

3c8.36

掏 **TŌ** scoop up, take out
su(ru) pick (someone's) pocket

— 1 —

7 掏児 **suri** pickpocket
13 掏摸 **suri** picking pockets; pickpocket

捆 → 擱 3c11.6

3c8.37

掣 **SEI** hold back, restrain

— 1 —

7 掣肘 **seichū** restraint, restrictions

— 9 —

3c9.1

揀 **KAN** select

插 → 挿 3c7.2

搜 → 捜 3c7.5

捲 → 捲 3c8.9

3c9.2

揉 **JŪ, mo(mu)** rub, massage; push and shove; debate vigorously; train, coach; worry **mo(mareru)** be buffeted about **mo(meru)** get into trouble/discord; be crumpled; be worried **mo(me)** trouble, discord

— 1 —

3 揉上 **mo(mi)a(ge)** sideburns
4 揉手 **mo(mi)de** rub one's hands together
5 揉出 **mo(mi)da(su)** squeeze out
8 揉事 **mo(me)goto** trouble, discord
10 揉消 **mo(mi)ke(su)** crush out (a cigarette), hush up, suppress
17 揉療治 **mo(mi)ryōji** massage

— 2 —

6 気揉 **ki (o) mo(mu)** worry, be anxious

— 3 —

4 内輪揉 **uchiwamo(me)** internal dissension, family trouble

3c9.3

揆 **KI** plan; path; uprising

— 2 —

1 一揆 **ikki** riot, insurrection

— 4 —

6 百姓一揆 **hyakushō ikki** peasants' uprising

3c9.4 / 628

提 **TEI** present, submit
CHŌ, sa(geru) carry (in the hand)

— 1 —

5 提出 **teishutsu** presentation, filing
提出者 **teishutsusha** proposer, mover
提示 **teiji** present, exhibit; bring up, suggest
6 提灯 **chōchin** (paper) lantern
提灯持 **chōchinmo(chi)** lantern bearer; booster; hype
7 提言 **teigen** proposal, suggestion
8 提供 **teikyō** offer, present
9 提要 **teiyō** summary, compendium
10 提起 **teiki** submit, raise (a question), bring (suit)
提案 **teian** proposition, proposal
提案者 **teiansha** proposer, proponent
11 提唱 **teishō** discourse, lecture; advocate
12 提琴 **teikin** violin
提琴家 **teikinka** violinist
提訴 **teiso** sue, bring action
13 提携 **teikei** cooperation, tie-up
提督 **teitoku** admiral, commodore
20 提議 **teigi** proposal, motion

— 2 —

4 手提 **tesa(ge)** handbag
手提金庫 **tesa(ge)kinko** cash box, portable safe
手提袋 **tesa(ge)bukuro** handbag
手提鞄 **tesa(ge)kaban** briefcase, grip

手提籠 **tesa(ge)kago** handbasket
9 前提 **zentei** premise, prerequisite
盆提灯 **bonjōchin** Bon Festival lantern
11 菩提 **bodai** Buddhahood, supreme enlightenment, salvation
菩提心 **bodaishin** aspiration for Buddhahood
菩提寺 **bodaiji** one's family's temple
菩提樹 **bodaiju** bo tree; linden tree; lime tree

———————— 3 ————————

3 大前提 **daizentei** major premise
弓張提灯 **yumiha(ri)jōchin** paper lantern
with bow-shaped handle
小前提 **shōzentei** minor premise
6 防波提 **bōhatei** breakwater
防砂提 **bōsatei** barricade to arrest shifting
sand

———————— 4 ————————

3 小田原提灯 **odawara-jōchin** collapsible
cylindrical paper lantern

3c9.5 / 631

揚   **YŌ** raise, elevate; praise
a(garu) rise   **a(geru)** raise; fry
a(ge) fried tofu, fried food; a tuck

———————— 1 ————————

2 揚子江 **Yōsukō** the Yangtze/Yangzi river
揚力 **yōryoku** (dynamic) lift
4 揚水 **yōsui** pumping water
揚水車 **yōsuisha** scoop wheel
揚水所 **yōsuijo** pumping-up station
揚戸 **a(ge)do** push-up door, shutter
5 揚句 **a(ge)ku** in the end, ultimately
7 揚言 **yōgen** profess, declare, assert
揚足取 **a(ge)ashi (o) to(ru)** find fault, carp at
8 揚油 **a(ge)abura** frying oil
揚板 **a(ge)ita** removable floorboards, trap
door
揚物 **a(ge)mono** fried food
9 揚屋 **a(ge)ya** brothel
10 揚陸 **yōriku** landing, unloading
揚荷 **a(ge)ni** cargo to be unloaded
12 揚程 **yōtei** lift (of a valve); head (height a
pump can lift water)
揚雲雀 **a(ge)hibari** (soaring) skylark
13 揚幕 **a(ge)maku** entrance curtain
17 揚鍋 **a(ge)nabe** frying pan

———————— 2 ————————

4 水揚 **mizua(ge)** landing, unloading; earnings; watering (cut flowers so they last
longer); deflowering
引揚者 **hi(ki)a(ge)sha** returnee
5 生揚 **namaa(ge)** fried tofu
6 色揚 **iroa(ge)** redye, restore the original color
7 抑揚 **yokuyō** rising and falling of tones,
modulation, intonation

8 油揚 **aburaa(ge)** fried tofu
空揚 **karaa(ge)** food fried without coating in
a batter
肩揚 **kataa(ge)** shoulder tuck (in clothes)
9 飛揚 **hiyō** flying, flight
発揚 **hatsuyō** exalt, enhance, promote
巻揚 **ma(ki)a(geru)** roll/wind up, hoist
巻揚機 **ma(ki)a(ge)ki** hoist, winch, windlass
浮揚 **fuyō** float, be buoyant
宜揚 **sen'yō** enhance, raise, exalt
昂揚 **kōyō** raise, heighten, uplift
10 陸揚 **rikua(ge)** land, unloading
高揚 **kōyō** heighten, enhance, exalt, promote
帯揚 **obia(ge)** sash to hold an obi in place
荷揚 **nia(ge)** unloading, discharge, landing
荷揚料 **nia(ge)ryō** landing charges
荷揚場 **nia(ge)ba** landing place
胴揚 **dōa(ge)** hoist (someone) shoulder-high
骨揚 **kotsua(ge)** gathering (the deceased's)
ashes
称揚 **shōyō** praise
11 揚揚 **keiyō** hoist, fly, display (a flag)
悠揚 **yūyō** composed, calm, serene
13 搔揚 **ka(ki)a(ge)** fritters
腰揚 **koshia(ge)** tuck at the waist
14 旗揚 **hataa(ge)** raising an army; launching a
business
総揚 **sōa(ge)** hire all (the geisha)
15 賞揚 **shōyō** praise, admiration
縫揚 **nu(i)a(ge)** a tuck (in a dress)
18 顕揚 **ken'yō** extol, exalt

———————— 3 ————————

13 意気揚々 **iki-yōyō** exultant, triumphant
14 精進揚 **shōjin'a(ge)** vegetable tempura

揭→掲 **3c8.13**

3c9.6

揩   **KAI** rub

3c9.7 / 1088

援 援   **EN, tasu(keru)** help, aid

———————— 1 ————————

5 援用 **en'yō** claim, quote, invoke
7 援助 **enjo** assistance, aid
援兵 **enpei** reinforcements
9 援軍 **engun** reinforcements
20 援護 **engo** protection, support, relief

2

4 支援 **shien** support, backing, aid
7 声援 **seien** (shouts of) encouragement, cheering
応援 **ōen** aid, support
応援団 **ōendan** rooting section, cheerleaders
9 後援 **kōen** assistance, aid, support
後援会 **kōenkai** supporters' association
後援者 **kōensha** supporter, backer
11 救援 **kyūen** relief, rescue
救援米 **kyūenmai** dole rice
救援軍 **kyūengun** reinforcements
13 義援 **gien** donation, contribution
義援金 **gienkin** donation, contribution
14 増援 **zōen** reinforcement(s)

3c9.8 / 1648

揺 搖 **YŌ, yu(reru)** (intr.) shake, sway, vibrate, roll, pitch, joggle **yu(rameku)** (intr.) shake, sway, vibrate, roll, pitch, joggle
yu(rugu/ragu) (intr.) shake, sway, vibrate, roll, pitch, joggle **yu(rasu)** (tr.) shake, rock, joggle
yu(ru) (tr.) shake, rock, joggle **yu(suru)** (tr.) shake, rock, joggle **yu(rugasu/suburu/saburu)** (tr.) shake, rock, joggle

1

5 揺出 **yu(rugi)de(ru)** wiggle out
6 揺曳 **yōei** flutter, tremble; drag; linger
揺返 **yu(ri)kae(shi)** aftershock
10 揺起 **yu(ri)o(kosu)** awaken by shaking
11 揺動 **yu(ri)ugo(kasu)** (tr.) shake **yu(re)ugo(ku)** (intr.) shake
12 揺揺 **yu(ra)yu(ra)** swaying, flickering
揺落 **yu(ri)o(tosu)** shake down/off
揺無 **yu(rugi)na(i)** firm, solid, steady
21 揺籃 **yōran** cradle
揺籃地 **yōran (no) chi** the cradle of, birthplace
揺籃期 **yōranki** infancy
22 揺籠 **yu(ri)kago** cradle

2

3 大揺 **ōyu(re)** upheaval
11 動揺 **dōyō** shaking, pitching, rolling; excitement, commotion, unrest
12 揺揺 **yu(ra)yu(ra)** swaying, flickering
15 横揺 **yokoyu(re)** rolling (from side to side)
16 縦揺 **tateyu(re)** (angle of) pitch

3

11 貧乏揺 **binbōyu(suri)** absent-minded shaking of knee or foot

3c9.9

揖 **ITSU, YU** bow with arms folded
SHŪ come together, assemble

3c9.10 / 1915

搭 **TŌ** board/load (a vehicle)

1

9 搭乗 **tōjō** board, get on
搭乗券 **tōjōken** boarding pass
13 搭載 **tōsai** load; embark; mounting (of electronic components)

3c9.11

揣 **SHI** consider

1

15 揣摩 **shima** conjecture, surmise, speculation

搔 → **3c10.11**

3c9.12

掾 **EN** help; subordinate official
jō (obsolete government-service rank)

3c9.13

揄 **YU** pull out

2

11 揶揄 **yayu** banter, raillery, poking fun

3c9.14 / 1652

揮 **KI** shake, brandish; scatter; direct, command

1

9 揮発 **kihatsu** volatile, vaporize
揮発油 **kihatsuyu** volatile oils, gasoline
揮発性 **kihatsusei** volatility
11 揮毫 **kigō** writing, painting, drawing

2

9 発揮 **hakki** exhibit, demonstrate, make manifest
指揮 **shiki** command, lead, direct
指揮刀 **shikitō** saber, parade sword
指揮下 **shikika** under one's command
指揮官 **shikikan** commander
指揮者 **shikisha** (orchestra) conductor, leader; commander, director
指揮棒 **shikibō** baton

3

14 総指揮 **sōshiki** supreme command
総指揮官 **sōshikikan** supreme commander

3c9.15 / 1586

換 換
KAN, ka(eru) substitute
ka(waru) be replaced, change over

1

6 換気 **kanki** ventilation
換気扇 **kankisen** ventilation fan
7 換言 **kangen (sureba)** in other words
8 換価 **kanka** realize, convert into money
換金 **kankin** realize, convert into money
10 換骨奪胎 **kankotsu-dattai** adapt, modify, recast
12 換着 **ka(e)gi** change of clothes
換喩 **kan'yu** metonymy
14 換算 **kansan** conversion, exchange
換算表 **kansanhyō** conversion table

2

4 不換 **fukan** inconvertible
互換性 **gokansei** compatibility, interchangeability
切換 **ki(ri)ka(eru)** change, exchange, convert; renew; replace; switch over
引換 **hi(ki)ka(eru)** exchange, change, convert
5 付換 **tsu(ke)ka(eru)** replace (with a new one)
召換 **me(shi)ka(e)** change of clothes
6 交換 **kōkan** exchange
交換手 **kōkanshu** switchboard operator
7 兌換 **dakan** convert(ible), non-fiat (paper money)
言換 **i(i)ka(eru)** say in other words
9 乗換 **no(ri)ka(e)** change conveyances, transfer
乗換券 **norikaeken** ticket for transfer
変換 **henkan** change, conversion, transformation (in math)
10 借換 **ka(ri)ka(e)** conversion, refunding, renewal
差換 **sa(shi)ka(eru)** replace, change
書換 **ka(ki)kae(ru)** rewrite; renew (a loan); transfer (ownership)
11 組換 **ku(mi)ka(eru)** rearrange, recombine
転換 **tenkan** conversion, changeover; diversion
転換期 **tenkanki** transition period, turning point
転換器 **tenkanki** commutator, switch
13 置換 **o(ki)kae(ru)** replace, transpose, rearrange **chikan** substitute, replace
15 踏換 **fu(mi)ka(eru)** shift one's footing
16 積換 **tsu(mi)ka(e)** reloading, transshipment

3

9 急転換 **kyūtenkan** sudden change, rapid switchover

4

6 気分転換 **kibun tenkan** a (refreshing) change, diversion
8 物々交換 **butsubutsu kōkan** barter

3c9.16

揃
SEN, soro(u) be complete, be all present; be uniform, be all alike
soro(i) a set, suit, suite
soro(eru) arrange (all together), complete; make even/uniform

---

2

1 一揃 **hitosoro(i)** a set, a suit
3 三揃 **mi(tsu)zoro(i)** three-piece suit
4 不揃 **fuzoro(i), fusoro(i)** not uniform, uneven, odd, unsorted
5 出揃 **desoro(u)** appear all together, be all present
8 取揃 **to(ri)soro(eru)** put/have all together
9 咲揃 **sa(ki)soro(u)** be in full bloom
11 粒揃 **tsubuzoro(i)** uniformly excellent
13 勢揃 **seizoro(i)** array, full lineup

3c9.17 / 1714

握
AKU, nigi(ru) grasp, grip, take/get hold of **nigi(ri)** grasp, grip; handful; rice/sushi ball

---

1

2 握力 **akuryoku** grasping power, grip
4 握手 **akushu** shake hands
9 握屋 **nigi(ri)ya** tightfisted, miser
10 握拳 **nigi(ri)kobushi** clenched fist
12 握飯 **nigi(ri)meshi** rice/sushi ball
15 握潰 **nigi(ri)tsubu(su)** crush, crumple; shelve, table
握締 **nigi(ri)shi(meru)** grasp tight
17 握鮨 **nigi(ri)zushi** sushi ball

2.

1 一握 **hitonigi(ri), ichiaku** a handful
7 把握 **haaku** grasp, comprehend
12 掌握 **shōaku** grasp, seize, have in hand

3c9.18

EN, ATSU pull out

10

3c10.1

TŌ, tsu(ku), ka(tsu) pound (rice to make mochi), hull, husk

1

4 搗手 **tsu(ki)te** pounder

3
氵
土
扌
口
女
巾
犭 10←
弓
彳
彡
艹
宀
⺌
山
耂
广
尸
口

3

氵 土 扌 口 女 巾 犭 弓 彳 彡 艹 宀 ⺍ 凵 耂 广 尸 口

→10

5 搗加 **ka(tete) kuwa(ete)** besides, to make matters worse
搗立 **tsu(ki)ta(te)** freshly pounded (mochi)
6 搗臼 **tsu(ki)usu** mortar (for pounding rice)
搗合 **ka(chi)a(u)** clash
11 搗混 **tsu(ki)ma(zeru)** pound/mix together
15 搗潰 **tsu(ki)tsubu(su)** pound to a jelly

———————— 2 ————————

5 半搗米 **hantsu(ki)mai** half-polished rice
6 米搗 **kometsu(ki)** rice polishing
7 麦搗 **mugitsu(ki)** polishing wheat
15 餅搗 **mochitsu(ki)** pounding rice to make mochi

3c10.2 / 1722

搬

HAN carry, transport

———————— 1 ————————

2 搬入 **hannyū** carry/send in
5 搬出 **hanshutsu** carry/take out
8 搬送 **hansō** convey, carry

———————— 2 ————————

11 運搬 **unpan** transport
運搬人 **unpannin** porter, carrier
運搬費 **unpanhi** transport charges, haulage

3c10.3

搦

JAKU, DAKU hold down; take; capture
kara(meru) bind, tie up, arrest

———————— 1 ————————

4 搦手 **kara(me)te** (attack a castle from) the rear gate
10 搦捕 **kara(me)to(ru)** apprehend, arrest

———————— 3 ————————

12 雁字搦 **ganjigarame** (bind) firmly, (bound) hand and foot

3c10.4 / 1686

携 攜

KEI, tazusa(eru) carry (in one's hand), have with/on one
tazusa(waru) participate in

———————— 1 ————————

6 携行 **keikō** carry with/along
10 携帯 **keitai** carry with; portable
携帯品 **keitaihin** personal effects, luggage

———————— 2 ————————

5 必携 **hikkei** indispensable; handbook, manual
9 連携 **renkei** in cooperation/concert with
相携 **aitazusa(ete)** together with, in couples
12 提携 **teikei** cooperation, tie-up

3c10.5

搏

HAKU, u(tsu) beat, strike

———————— 2 ————————

6 羽搏 **habata(ki)** flapping of wings, flutter

3c10.6 / 1692

摂 攝

SETSU act in place of; take

———————— 1 ————————

4 摂氏 **sesshi** Celsius, centigrade
5 摂生 **sessei** taking care of one's health
6 摂行 **sekkō** acting for another
8 摂取 **sesshu** ingest, take in
9 摂津 **Settsu** (ancient kuni, Hyōgo-ken)
摂政 **sesshō** regency; regent
10 摂家 **sekke** the line of regents and advisers
11 摂理 **setsuri** providence
摂理的 **setsuriteki** providential
14 摂関 **sekkan** regents and chief advisers
摂関家 **sekkanke** the line of regents and advisers
15 摂養 **setsuyō** taking care of one's health
20 摂護腺 **setsugosen** prostate gland

———————— 2 ————————

4 不摂生 **fusessei** neglect of one's health
5 包摂 **hōsetsu** connotation

3c10.7

搢

SHIN insert

———————— 1 ————————

11 搢紳 **shinshin** high-ranking person

3c10.8

搆

KŌ pull; cause

3c10.9 / 1497

搾

SAKU, shibo(ru) squeeze, press, extract, milk

———————— 1 ————————

5 搾出 **shibo(ri)da(su)** press/squeeze out
7 搾乳 **sakunyū** milk (a cow)
8 搾油 **sakuyu** press oil (from seeds)
搾取 **sakushu** exploitation

──────── 2 ────────

5 圧搾 **assaku** pressure, compression, compressed (air)
圧搾機 **assakuki** a press, compressor
8 油搾 **aburashibo(ri)** oil press
油搾器 **aburashiboriki** oil press

3c10.10

搨 **TŌ** trace, rub a copy (of a stone inscription)

3c10.11

搔 搔 **SŌ, ka(ku)** scratch; rake; paddle; cut off
ka(ki)- (emphatic prefix)

──────── 1 ────────

3 搔口説 **ka(ki)kudo(ku)** complain of, plead
4 搔切 **ka(ki)ki(ru)** cut (off)
搔分 **ka(ki)wa(keru)** push aside
搔込 **ka(ki)ko(mu)** rake/shovel in
5 搔出 **ka(i)da(su)** bail/ladle out
搔払 **ka(p)para(u)** walk off with, steal
搔玉 **ka(ki)tama** egg soup
搔立 **ka(ki)ta(teru)** stir/rake up, arouse
6 搔合 **ka(ki)a(waseru)** adjust, arrange
搔回 **ka(ki)mawa(su)** stir, churn; ransack, rummage around
7 搔均 **ka(ki)nara(su)** rake smooth, level out
搔乱 **ka(ki)mida(su)** disturb, upset
8 搔爬 **sōha** curettage, scraping out
搔退 **ka(ki)no(keru)** push aside, scratch away
搔毟 **ka(ki)mushi(ru)** tear, rend, rip up
9 搔巻 **ka(i)ma(ki)** sleeved quilt
10 搔消 **ka(ki)ke(su)** scratch/rub out, efface
11 搔混 **ka(ki)ma(zeru)** mix up, stir
搔寄 **ka(ki)yo(seru)** scrape/rake up
搔疵 **ka(ki)kizu** a scratch
搔痒 **sōyō** itching
12 搔揚 **ka(ki)a(ge)** fritters
搔落 **ka(ki)o(tosu)** scrape off/away; cut off
搔集 **ka(ki)atsu(meru)** rake together, gather up
14 搔摘 **ka(i)tsu(mamu)** summarize
搔鳴 **ka(ki)na(rasu)** strum, thrum
15 搔潜 **ka(i)kugu(ru)** dodge through
16 搔曇 **ka(ki)kumo(ru)** be overcast

──────── 2 ────────

4 水搔 **mizuka(ki)** web(foot), paddle
引搔 **hi(k)ka(ku)** scratch, claw
引搔回 **hi(k)ka(ki)mawa(su)** ransack, rummage through; carry on highhandedly
火搔 **hika(ki)** poker, fire rake
6 汗搔 **ase(k)ka(ki), aseka(ki)** heavy perspirer
耳搔 **mimika(ki)** earpick

7 足搔 **aga(ku)** paw (the ground/air), wriggle, struggle
11 雪搔 **yukika(ki)** snow shovel(ing)/plow(ing)

──────── 3 ────────

11 悪足搔 **waruaga(ki)** useless struggling/resistance
12 隔靴搔痒 **kakka-sōyō** irritation, impatience (like trying to scratch an itchy foot through the shoe)
13 寝首搔 **nekubi (o) ka(ku)** chop off someone's head while he is asleep

搖 → 揺 3c9.8

3c10.12 / 350

損 **SON** loss, damage; disadvantageous
soko(nau) harm, hurt, mar
soko(neru) harm, hurt, mar
-soko(nau) fail to, err in, mis-

──────── 1 ────────

0 損する **son(suru)** lose (money), incur a loss
損ずる/じる **son(zuru/jiru)** damage, harm, hurt
3 損亡 **sonmō** loss
5 損失 **sonshitsu** loss
8 損所 **sonsho** damaged part/spot
損金 **sonkin** financial loss
9 損保 **sonpo** casualty/nonlife insurance (short for 損害保険)
10 損耗 **sonmō** wear and tear, loss
損益分岐点 **son'eki bunkiten** break-even point
損益計算書 **son'eki keisansho** income/profit-and-loss statement
損害 **songai** damage, injury, loss
損害保険 **songai hoken** casualty/nonlife insurance
損害高 **songaidaka** (amount of) damage
損害賠償 **songai baishō** restitution, indemnification, (pay) damages
損料 **sonryō** rental charge
11 損得 **sontoku** advantages and disadvantages
13 損傷 **sonshō** damage, injury

──────── 2 ────────

3 大損 **ōzon** heavy loss
丸損 **maruzon** total loss
4 欠損 **kesson** deficit, loss
5 出損 **desoko(nau)** fail to go/come
生損 **u(mi)soko(nau)** miscarry
仕損 **shisoko(nau), shison(jiru)** make a mistake, fail, blunder
打損 **u(chi)soko(nau)** miss, fail to hit

6 死損 **shi(ni)soko(nau)** fail to die

shi(ni)zoko(nai) would-be suicide; one who has outlived his time

両損 **ryōzon** loss for both sides

全損 **zenson** total loss

汚損 **oson** stain, soiling, corruption

成損 **na(ri)sokona(u)** fail to become

7 見損 **misoko(nau)** fail to see, misjudge

言損 **i(i)soko(nau)** misspeak; fail to mention

8 受損 **u(ke)soko(nau)** fail to catch/parry

逃損 **ni(ge)sokona(u)** fail to escape

取損 **to(ri)soko(nau)** fail to take/get, miss

9 乗損 **no(ri)soko(nau)** miss (a train)

海損 **kaison** sea damage, average (loss)

10 射損 **isoko(nau), ison(jiru)** miss (the target)

書損 **ka(ki)soko(nau), ka(ki)son(jiru)** miswrite

破損 **hason** damage, breakage, breach

12 遣損 **ya(ri)soko(nau)** bungle, muff, fail, mismanage

減損 **genson** decrease; loss, wear, depreciation

13 毀損 **kison** damage, injure

数損 **kazo(e)soko(nau)** miscount

14 聞損 **ki(ki)sokona(u)** mishear, not catch

16 磨損 **mason** wear, friction loss

———— 3 ————

10 骨折損 **honeo(ri)zon** wasted effort

3c10.13

摸

MO search for; copy

———— 1 ————

10 摸索 **mosaku** groping

———— 2 ————

11 搯摸 **suri** picking pockets; pickpocket

———— 3 ————

13 暗中摸索 **anchū mosaku** groping in the dark

3c10.14

搶

SŌ, SHŌ thrust, poke; come together, assemble

3c10.15

搤

YAKU squeeze, strangle, clench

3c10.16

搓

SA braid; cut

———— 11 ————

3c11.1

搏

TAN roll into a ball; slap

3c11.2

摎

KYŪ tie into a bundle, coil around

3c11.3

摺 摺

SHŌ, SHŪ fold; rub; print; slide

su(ru) rub; print

———— 1 ————

5 摺本 **surihon** printed (but unbound) book

7 摺足 **su(ri)ashi** shuffling/sliding one's feet

11 摺動 **shūdō, shōdō** sliding

———— 2 ————

4 手摺 **tesu(ri)** handrail, railing

引摺 **hi(ki)zu(ru)** drag along

(o)**hi(ki)zu(ri)** slut

引摺込 **hi(ki)zu(ri)ko(mu)** drag in

引摺出 **hi(ki)zu(ri)da(su)** drag out

引摺回 **hi(ki)zu(ri)mawa(su)** drag around

木摺 **kizu(ri)** lath

5 石摺 **ishizu(ri)** rubbed copy of an inscription in stone

7 足摺 **ashizu(ri)** stamping/scraping one's feet

8 版摺 **hansu(ri)** printing from woodcuts

9 籾摺 **momisu(ri)** hulling rice

———— 3 ————

9 胡麻摺 **gomasu(ri)** flatterer, sycophant

3c11.4

摧

SAI, kuda(ku), kuda(keru) break up, crush

3c11.5 / 1447

摘

TEKI, tsu(mu) pick, pluck, nip; gather

tsuma(mu) pick up or hold between the thumb and fingers

———— 1 ————

4 摘切 **tsu(mi)ki(ru)** pick/nip/pluck off

5 摘出 **tekishutsu** pluck out, extract; expose

8 摘果 **tekika** thinning out fruit

摘芽 **tekiga** thinning out buds

摘取 **tsu(mi)to(ru)** pick, pluck

9 摘発 **tekihatsu** expose, unmask, uncover

摘発者 **tekihatsusha** exposer, informer

摘要 **tekiyō** summary, synopsis

摘草　**tsu(mi)kusa**　gathering wild greens
10 摘記　**tekki**　summarize
13 摘載　**tekisai**　summarize, give an excerpt
16 摘録　**tekiroku**　summary, précis

———————— 2 ————————

7 花摘　**hanatsu(mi)**　flower picking
9 指摘　**shiteki**　point out, indicate
茶摘　**chatsu(mi)**　tea picking/picker
茶摘歌　**chatsu(mi)uta**　tea-pickers' song
10 桑摘　**kuwatsu(mi)**　picking mulberry leaves
13 搔摘　**ka(i)tsu(mamu)**　summarize
14 鼻摘　**hanatsuma(mi)**　disgusting person, outcast

撻→　**3c12.16**

3c11.6

撾 捆　**KAKU**　grab; hit
tsuka(mu)　grab, grasp, grip
tsuka(mi)　handful; grip
tsuka(maru)　hold/hang on to
tsuka(maeru)　grab, catch, nab　**tsuka(maseru)**
make (someone) catch hold of; bribe; palm off, foist upon

———————— 1 ————————

5 撾出　**tsuka(mi)da(su)**　take out by handfuls
6 撾合　**tsuka(mi)a(u)**　grapple, tussle
8 撾所　**tsuka(mi)dokoro**　hold, grip
撾所無　**tsuka(mi)dokoro (no) na(i)**　slippery, evasive
撾取　**tsuka(mi)to(ru)**　snatch off, grasp
10 撾殺　**tsuka(mi)koro(su)**　squeeze to death
11 撾掛　**tsuka(mi)ka(karu)**　grab at

———————— 2 ————————

1 一撾　**hitotsuka(mi)**　a handful; a grasp
3 大撾　**ōzuka(mi)**　big handful; summary
4 手撾　**tezuka(mi)**　take/grasp with the fingers
引撾　**hi(t)tsuka(mu)**　grab, snatch
23 鷲撾　**washizuka(mi)**　clutch, grab

3c11.7 / 1016

擊 撃　**GEKI, u(tsu)**　attack; fire, shoot

———————— 1 ————————

4 撃止　**u(chi)to(meru)**　kill, bring down
撃方　**u(chi)kata**　how to fire (a gun)
7 撃沈　**gekichin**　(attack and) sink
8 撃退　**gekitai**　repulse, drive back, dislodge
9 撃発　**gekihatsu**　percussion (fuse)
撃砕　**gekisai**　shoot to pieces; defeat
10 撃剣　**gekken**　fencing, kendō

撃殺　**gekisatsu**　shoot dead
撃破　**gekiha**　defeat, rout, crush
13 撃滅　**gekimetsu**　destruction, annihilation
撃鉄　**gekitetsu**　rifle/gun hammer
14 撃墜　**gekitsui**　shoot down

———————— 2 ————————

1 一撃　**ichigeki**　a blow/hit
4 反撃　**hangeki**　counterattack
5 出撃　**shutsugeki**　sortie, sally
打撃　**dageki**　blow, shock; batting, hitting
打撃王　**dagekiō**　leading/top batter
打撃率　**dagekiritsu**　batting average
立撃　**ta(chi)u(chi)**　firing from a standing position
目撃　**mokugeki**　observe, witness
目撃者　**mokugekisha**　(eye)witness
6 羽撃　**habata(ki)**　flapping of wings
迎撃　**geigeki, muka(e)u(tsu)**　intercept (and attack)
7 迫撃　**hakugeki**　attack at close quarters
迫撃砲　**hakugekihō**　mortar
乱撃　**rangeki**　random shooting
攻撃　**kōgeki**　attack
攻撃的　**kōgekiteki**　aggresive, offensive
攻撃軍　**kōgekigun**　attacking army/force
攻撃戦　**kōgekisen**　aggressive war
8 盲撃　**mekura-u(chi)**　random shooting
直撃　**chokugeki**　direct hit
直撃弾　**chokugekidan**　direct hit
追撃　**tsuigeki, o(i)u(chi)**　pursuit, follow-up attack
追撃戦　**tsuigekisen**　pursuit battle, running fight
追撃機　**tsuigekiki**　pursuit/chase plane
狙撃　**sogeki, nera(i)u(chi)**　shooting, sniping
狙撃兵　**sogekihei**　sniper, sharpshooter
突撃　**totsugeki**　charge, assault
突撃隊　**totsugekitai**　shock troops
9 侵撃　**shingeki**　invade and attack
急撃　**kyūgeki**　surprise attack, raid
挟撃　**kyōgeki, hasa(mi)u(chi)**　pincer attack
要撃　**yōgeki**　ambush
10 射撃　**shageki**　shooting, firing
射撃場　**shagekijō**　shooting/rifle range
進撃　**shingeki**　attack, charge, advance, onslaught
遊撃　**yūgeki**　hit-and-run attack; shortstop
遊撃手　**yūgekishu**　shortstop
遊撃隊　**yūgekitai**　flying column, commando unit
遊撃戦　**yūgekisen**　guerrilla warfare
猛撃　**mōgeki**　severe blow, fierce attack
砲撃　**hōgeki**　shelling, bombardment
11 排撃　**haigeki**　reject, denounce
掩撃　**engeki**　surprise attack
12 痛撃　**tsūgeki**　severe blow, hard attack

13 雷撃 **raigeki** torpedo attack
雷撃機 **raigekiki** torpedo-carrying plane
電撃 **dengeki** electric shock; blitzkrieg
14 銃撃 **jūgeki** shooting
駁撃 **bakugeki** argue against, attack, refute
15 衝撃 **shōgeki** shock
16 邀撃 **yōgeki** ambush, attack
19 爆撃 **bakugeki** bombing
爆撃手 **bakugekishu** bombardier
爆撃機 **bakugekiki** bomber
22 襲撃 **shūgeki** attack, assault, raid, charge

——————— 3 ———————

8 逆攻撃 **gyakukōgeki** counterattack
9 重爆撃機 **jūbakugekiki** heavy bomber
10 猛反撃 **mōhangeki** fierce counterattack
猛攻撃 **mōkōgeki** fierce attack
14 総攻撃 **sōkōgeki** general/all-out offensive

——————— 4 ———————

1 一斉射撃 **issei shageki** volley, fusillade
2 人身攻撃 **jinshin kōgeki** personal attack
7 乱射乱撃 **ransha-rangeki** random shooting
21 艦砲射撃 **kanpō shageki** shelling from a
naval vessel

3c11.8

摯

SHI take, grab; sincere, serious; reach,
extend to; rough

——————— 2 ———————

10 真摯 **shinshi** earnest, sincere

——————— 12 ———————

3c12.1 / 1889

撲

BOKU, u(tsu) hit, strike

——————— 1 ———————

10 撲殺 **bokusatsu** clubbing to death
13 撲滅 **bokumetsu** eradication, extermination

——————— 2 ———————

5 打撲 **daboku** bruise, contusion
9 相撲 **sumō** sumo wrestling
相撲取 **sumōto(ri)** sumo wrestler

——————— 3 ———————

7 花相撲 **hanazumō** off-season sumo tournament
9 独相撲 **hito(ri)zumō** like wrestling with no
opponent
草相撲 **kusazumō** amateur/sandlot sumo
12 腕相撲 **udezumō** arm wrestling

3c12.2

撒

SAN, SATSU, ma(ku) scatter, strew;
sprinkle; give (someone) the slip

——————— 1 ———————

4 撒水 **sansui, sassui** watering, sprinkling
撒水車 **sansuisha, sassuisha** street sprinkler
5 撒布 **sanpu, sappu** scatter, sprinkle, spray;
dispersion
撒布剤 **sanpuzai, sappuzai** dusting powder
12 撒散 **ma(ki)chi(rasu)** scatter about; squander
15 撒餌 **ma(ki)e** scattered food; ground bait

——————— 2 ———————

4 水撒 **mizuma(ki)** sprinkling
7 豆撒 **mamema(ki)** bean-scattering ceremony
10 振撒 **fu(ri)ma(ku)** strew about, scatter

3c12.3 / 1423

撤

TETSU withdraw, remove

——————— 1 ———————

0 撤する **tes(suru)** withdraw, remove
4 撤収 **tesshū** withdraw, remove
5 撤去 **tekkyo** withdraw, evacuate, remove
6 撤回 **tekkai** withdraw, retract, rescind
7 撤兵 **teppei** withdraw troops, disengage
8 撤退 **tettai** withdraw, pull out, retreat
12 撤廃 **teppai** abolition, do away with, repeal

3c12.4

撕

SEI warn against
SHI break, rend, tear

3c12.5

撈

RŌ catch (fish)

——————— 2 ———————

14 漁撈 **gyorō** fishing

3c12.6

撚

NEN, yo(ru) twist, twine
yori twist, strand, ply
yo(reru) get twisted, be kinky

——————— 1 ———————

6 撚糸 **nenshi, yoriito** twisted thread/yarn,
twine

——————— 2 ———————

10 紙撚 **koyo(ri)** twisted-paper string

3c12.7

撫

BU, na(deru) stroke, pat, smooth down,
soothe, caress

——————— 1 ———————

2 撫子 **nadeshiko** a pink, a baby's breath

3 撫上 **na(de)a(geru)** comb back, stroke upward
撫下 **na(de)o(rosu)** stroke down
5 撫付 **na(de)tsu(keru)** comb/smooth down
　　na(de)tsu(ke) smoothed-down hair
8 撫育 **buiku** care, tending
撫肩 **na(de)gata** sloping/drooping shoulders
11 撫斬 **na(de)gi(ri)** clean sweep, wholesale slaughter

――――――― 2 ―――――――

8 逆撫 **sakana(de)** rub against the grain
9 宣撫 **senbu** placation, pacification
11 猫撫声 **nekona(de)goe** coaxing voice
13 愛撫 **aibu** caress, pet, fondle
15 慰撫 **ibu** pacify, soothe, humor
18 鎮撫 **chinbu** placate, quell, calm

――――――― 3 ―――――――

3 大和撫子 **Yamato nadeshiko** daughter/ woman of Japan

3c12.8

播

HA, BAN, ma(ku) sow, plant

――――――― 1 ―――――――

14 播種 **hashu** seeding, sowing, planting
16 播磨 **Harima** (ancient kuni, Hyōgo-ken)

――――――― 2 ―――――――

6 伝播 **denpa** propagation, dissemination

3c12.9

撰 撰

SEN select; compose, compile
era(bu) select

――――――― 1 ―――――――

7 撰述 **senjutsu** write, author, compile
8 撰者 **senja** author; selector
10 撰修 **senshū** writing, editing
12 撰集 **senshū** anthology

7 杜撰 **zusan** slipshod, careless(ly done)
9 勅撰 **chokusen** compilation for the emperor
勅撰集 **chokusenshū** emperor-commissioned anthology of poems

3c12.10

撞

DŌ, TŌ, SHU, tsu(ku) strike, hit

――――――― 1 ―――――――

4 撞木 **shumoku** T-shaped wooden bell hammer
12 撞着 **dōchaku** inconsistency

――――――― 2 ―――――――

20 鐘撞 **kanetsu(ki)** bell ringer/ringing

鐘撞堂 **kanetsu(ki)dō** bell tower, belfry

攪 → 攪 3c20.1

3c12.11

撥

HATSU, ha(neru) reject, eliminate; splash, splatter; hit, run over (a pedestrian); put an upward flip on the end of (a brush stroke in calligraphy); pronounce the kana "ん"; take a percentage/commission
ha(nekasu) splash, splatter　**bachi** plectrum, (samisen) pick; drumstick, gong stick

――――――― 1 ―――――――

4 撥水性 **hassuisei** water repellent/repellence
5 撥出 **ha(ne)da(su)** eliminate, reject
撥付 **ha(ne)tsu(keru)** refuse, turn down
6 撥返 **ha(ne)kae(su)** repulse, repel
7 撥乱 **hatsuran** quelling of upheaval
撥乱反正 **hatsuran hansei** restoration of public order
8 撥物 **ha(ne)mono** rejected goods
9 撥飛 **ha(ne)to(basu)** send (something) flying; spatter, splash
撥除 **ha(ne)no(keru)** push/brush aside
撥音 **hatsuon** the sound of the kana "ん"
11 撥掛 **ha(ne)ka(keru)** splash, bespatter
撥釣瓶 **ha(ne)tsurube** a well sweep

――――――― 2 ―――――――

4 反撥 **hanpatsu** repel; rebound, recover; oppose
9 挑撥 **chōhatsu** arouse, excite, provoke

3c12.12

撩

RYŌ disorder

――――――― 1 ―――――――

7 撩乱 **ryōran** (blooming) in profusion

3c12.13 / 1520

撮

SATSU, tsuma(mu) grasp between thumb and fingers, pick up
tsuma(mi) knob; pinch (of salt); snack food (e.g., peanuts) to be eaten while drinking　**to(ru)** take (a photo)

――――――― 1 ―――――――

4 撮方 **to(ri)kata** way of taking (a photo)
5 撮出 **tsuma(mi)da(su)** pick out, drag/throw out
8 撮直 **to(ri)nao(su)** retake (a photo)
撮物 **tsuma(mi)mono** snack food (e.g., peanuts) to be eaten while drinking

3

氵 土 扌 口 女 巾 犭 弓 彳 彡 宀 丷 山 圭 广 尸 口

12←

9 撮洗 **tsuma(mi)ara(i)** washing only the soiled parts
撮要 **satsuyō** compendium, summary, manual
撮食 **tsuma(mi)gu(i)** eating with the fingers; eating stealthily; corruption, graft
15 撮影 **satsuei** photography, filming
撮影所 **satsueijo** movie studio

——————— 2 ———————
10 特撮 **tokusatsu** specially photographed

3c12.14

撓

DŌ, TŌ, **tawa(mu)** (intr.) bend
tawa(meru) (tr.) bend
shina(u) bend, be pliant/flexible/supple

——————— 2 ———————
4 不撓不屈 **futō-fukutsu** inflexible, unyielding, indefatigable
5 可撓性 **katōsei** flexible, flexibility

3c12.15

擒

KIN capture; a captive

3c12.16

撻

TATSU whip, flog, strike

——————— 2 ———————
18 鞭撻 **bentatsu** whip, lash; urge/spur on, goad

——————— 13 ———————

3c13.1

撼

KAN move

——————— 2 ———————
15 震撼 **shinkan** shake, tremble

3c13.2

擂

su(ru) grind, mash

——————— 1 ———————
9 擂砕 **su(ri)kuda(ku)** grind down/fine, pulverize
10 擂粉木 **su(ri)kogi** wooden pestle
13 擂鉢 **su(ri)bachi** mortar (and pestle)
15 擂餌 **su(ri)e** ground food

——————— 3 ———————
8 味噌擂 **misosu(ri)** grinding miso; flattery
味噌擂坊主 **misosu(ri) bōzu** petty priest

擇→択 3c4.21

3c13.3 / 1655

操

SŌ, **ayatsu(ru)** manipulate, operate
misao chastity, virginity, constancy, fidelity, honor

——————— 1 ———————
2 操人形 **ayatsu(ri)ningyō** puppet, marionette
6 操行 **sōkō** conduct, deportment
操守 **sōshu** constancy, fidelity
7 操作 **sōsa** operation, handling, control
操車 **sōsha** operation (of trains)
操車係 **sōshagakari** train dispatcher
操車場 **sōshajō** switchyard
8 操典 **sōten** drill book/manual
11 操舵 **sōda** steering (of a ship)
操舵手 **sōdashu** helmsman
操舵室 **sōdashitsu** pilothouse
12 操短 **sōtan** curtailed operations (short for 操業短縮)
13 操業 **sōgyō** operation, work
操業率 **sōgyōritsu** percentage of capacity in operation
操業短縮 **sōgyō tanshuku** curtailed operations
操業費 **sōgyōhi** operating expenses
14 操練 **sōren** military exercises, drill
16 操縦 **sōjū** control, operate, manipulate
操縦士 **sōjūshi** pilot
操縦法 **sōjūhō** manipulation, control
操縦者 **sōjūsha** operator, manipulator; driver, pilot
操縦席 **sōjūseki** cockpit
操縦桿 **sōjūkan** joystick

——————— 2 ———————
6 糸操 **itoayatsu(ri)** manipulating a marionette
7 体操 **taisō** calisthenics, gymnastics
体操場 **taisōjō** gymnasium, exercise grounds
志操 **shisō** one's principles, integrity
11 情操 **jōsō** sentiment
13 節操 **sessō** fidelity, integrity; chastity
14 徳操 **tokusō** morality, virtue, chastity

——————— 3 ———————
12 無節操 **musessō** inconstant; unchaste

——————— 4 ———————
9 美容体操 **biyō taisō** calisthenics
10 徒手体操 **toshu taisō** calisthenics without apparatus
16 機械体操 **kikai taisō** gymnastics using equipment

3c13.4

撿

KEN inspect, check, control

3c13.5 / 1715

擁　YŌ　embrace

——————— 1 ———————
0 擁する　yō(suru)　embrace, hold in one's arms; have, possess; protect; lead
5 擁立　yōritsu　support, back
20 擁護　yōgo　protect, defend
　擁護者　yōgosha　defender, supporter, advocate

——————— 2 ———————
8 抱擁　hōyō　embrace, hug

3c13.6

擅　SEN, hoshiimama　self-indulgent, selfish, arbitrary, as one pleases

——————— 1 ———————
11 擅断　sendan　arbitrary decision

——————— 2 ———————
9 独擅場　dokusenjō　one's unrivaled field

據→拠　3c5.26

擔→担　3c5.20

擊→撃　3c11.7

擧→挙　3n7.1

3c13.7

擘　HAKU　break, crush; thumb

——————— 14 ———————

3c14.1

擲　TEKI, JAKU, nage(tsu)　throw away, abandon; relinquish, renounce
nagu(ru)　hit, beat, thrash

——————— 1 ———————
10 擲書　nagu(ri)ga(ki)　scribble, scrawl
12 擲弾　tekidan　grenade
　擲弾筒　tekidantō　grenade launcher

——————— 2 ———————
5 打擲　chōchaku　give a beating/thrashing

8 放擲　hōteki　abandon, lay aside, neglect

——————— 4 ———————
11 乾坤一擲　kenkon-itteki　risking everything, all or nothing

3c14.2 / 1517

擬　GI　imitate
maga(i)　imitation

——————— 1 ———————
0 擬する　gi(suru)　imitate; liken to, be considered as; aim (a gun) at
2 擬人　gijin　personification
　擬人化　gijinka　personification
　擬人法　gijinhō　personification
5 擬古　giko　imitating classical style
　擬古文　gikobun　(pseudo)classical style
　擬古主義　giko shugi　classicism
　擬古的　gikoteki　classical, pseudoarchaic
6 擬死　gishi　feigning death, playing possum
　擬羊皮紙　giyōhishi　parchment paper
7 擬声　gisei　onomatopoeia
　擬声語　giseigo　onomatopoetic word
8 擬制　gisei　(legal) fiction, fictitious
　擬宝珠　gibōshu, gibōshi　leek flower
　　　　　　gibōshu, giboshi　ornamental railing knob
　擬物　maga(i)mono　imitation
9 擬革紙　gikakushi　imitation leather
　擬音　gion　an imitated sound, sound effects
13 擬勢　gisei　sham display of forces, bluff
　擬戦　gisen　mock battle
14 擬態　gitai　mimesis, simulation
　擬製　gisei　imitation, forgery, copy

——————— 2 ———————
14 模擬　mogi　imitation, mock, dry-run, dummy, simulated
　模擬店　mogiten　refreshment booth, snack bar
　模擬戦　mogisen　war games, mock fight
　模擬試験　mogi shiken　trial examination

3c14.3

擢　擢　TEKI, TAKU　select; excel
nuki(nderu)　excel in, surpass

——————— 2 ———————
7 抜擢　batteki　select, choose, pick out

3c14.4

擤　SEI, ka(mu)　blow (one's nose)

3c14.5 / 1519

擦

SATSU, su(ru) rub, file, strike (a match)
su(reru) rub, chafe; become worn; lose one's simplicity   **kosu(ru)** rub, scrub
nasu(ru) rub on, smear; attribute to, blame on   **kasu(ru)** graze past; squeeze; exploit

――――――――― 1 ―――――――――

4 擦切 **su(ri)ki(reru)** wear out, be frayed
擦込 **su(ri)ko(mu)** rub/mix in
5 擦付 **su(ri)tsu(keru)** rub on/against, strike (a match)   **nasu(ri)tsu(keru)** attribute to, blame on; rub on, smear
6 擦合 **su(re)a(u)** rub/chafe against each other, be at variance with
10 擦剥 **su(ri)mu(ku)** abrade, chafe
11 擦過傷 **sakkashō** abrasion, scratch
12 擦違 **su(re)chiga(u)** pass by each other
擦減 **su(ri)he(rasu)** wear away/down, rub off
擦落 **su(ri)o(tosu)** run/file off
13 擦傷 **su(ri)kizu** abrasion, scratch
17 擦擦 **su(re)su(re)** passing/grazing close by; barely

――――――――― 2 ―――――――――

2 人擦 **hitozu(re)** sophistication
3 上擦 **uwazu(ru)** sound nervous/tense
6 当擦 **a(te)kosu(ri)** insinuating remark, innuendo
衣擦 **kinuzu(re)** rustling of clothes
耳擦 **mimikosu(ri)** whispering
7 床擦 **tokozu(re)** bedsore
8 股擦 **matazu(re)** thigh/saddle sore
9 垢擦 **akasu(ri)** cloth/pumice/loofah for rubbing the body clean when taking a bath
11 悪擦 **waruzu(re)** oversophistication
13 塗擦 **tosatsu** smearing and rubbing, embrocation
塗擦剤 **tosatsuzai** liniment
靴擦 **kutsuzu(re)** shoe sore
15 鞍擦 **kurazu(re)** saddle sores
摩擦 **masatsu** friction
摩擦音 **masatsuon** a fricative (sound)
17 擦擦 **su(re)su(re)** passing/grazing close by; barely

――――――――― 3 ―――――――――

7 阿婆擦 **abazu(re)** wicked woman, hussy

――――――――― 4 ―――――――――

7 冷水摩擦 **reisui masatsu** rubdown with a cold wet towel

3c14.6

擯

HIN push aside

―――――――――――― 1 ――――――――――――

5 擯斥 **hinseki** reject, disdain, ostracize

3c14.7

擡 姚

TAI, mota(geru) lift, raise

―――――――――――― 1 ――――――――――――

16 擡頭 **taitō** raise its head, come to the fore, be on the rise

3c14.8

擣

TŌ, tsu(ku) pound, beat
TŌ, u(tsu) pound, beat

―――――――――――― 1 ――――――――――――

6 擣衣 **tōi** pounding cloth to make it glossy

3c14.9

擠

SEI push aside

3c14.10

擿

TEKI expose, reveal; throw

3c14.11

擱

KAKU, o(ku) put/set down

―――――――――――― 1 ――――――――――――

10 擱座 **kakuza** run aground, be stranded
12 擱筆 **kakuhitsu** put down one's pen, finish writing

―――――――――― 15 ――――――――――

3c15.1

擾

JŌ disturb, throw into confusion

―――――――――――― 1 ――――――――――――

7 擾乱 **jōran** disturbance, riot

―――――――――――― 2 ――――――――――――

10 紛擾 **funjō** disorder, trouble, dispute
18 騒擾罪 **sōjōzai** sedition, rioting

3c15.2

RYAKU, kusugu(ru) tickle
kusugu(ttai) ticklish

攢→攅 **3c19.2**

3c15.3

擶　**SEN, tada(su)** straighten (an arrow)

3c15.4

擺　**HAI** open; shake

擴→拡 **3c5.25**

3c15.5

攀　**HAN** climb; pull; depend on
yo(jiru) climb, scale

――― 1 ―――

12 攀登 **yo(ji)nobo(ru)** climb, scale

――― 2 ―――

12 登攀 **tōhan** climb up, ascend

――――― 17 ―――――

3c17.1

攘　**JŌ** chase away; steal

――― 1 ―――

6 攘夷 **jōi** exclusion/expulsion of foreigners
攘夷論 **jōiron** anti-alien policy

――― 2 ―――

12 尊攘 **sonjō** Revere the emperor and expel the
barbarians. (short for 尊王攘夷)

――― 3 ―――

12 尊王攘夷 **sonnō-jōi** Revere the emperor and
expel the barbarians.

――――― 18 ―――――

攝→摂 **3c10.6**

攜→携 **3c10.4**

――――― 19 ―――――

3c19.1

攤　**TAN** open, broaden; apportion

3c19.2

攢 攅　**SAN** gather, come together

3c19.3

攣　**REN** crooked, bent; pine for

――― 2 ―――

4 引攣 **hi(ki)tsu(ru)** have a cramp/crick/tic/
spasm/twitch/convulsion
12 痙攣 **keiren** cramp, spasm, convulsions

――― 3 ―――

9 胃痙攣 **ikeiren** stomach convulsions/cramps

――――― 20 ―――――

3c20.1

攪 撹　**KAKU, KŌ** stir up, roil,
disturb, throw into confusion

――― 1 ―――

7 攪乱 **kakuran** disturb, disrupt, agitate
8 攪拌 **kakuhan** agitate, stir, churn
攪拌器 **kakuhanki** agitator, shaker, beater

3c20.2

攫　**KAKU, tsuka(mu)** grasp, hold on to
sara(u) carry off, snatch away, abduct

――― 2 ―――

1 一攫 **ikkaku** one grab
一攫千金 **ikkaku senkin** getting rich quick

――――― 22 ―――――

3c22.1

攬　**RAN** take, hold (in one's hand)

――― 2 ―――

4 収攬 **shūran** grasp; win over

口 3d

口 0.1	叶 2.1	叱 2.2	叩 2.3	叨 2.4	叺 2.5	叹 2.6	叫 3d3.4	叮 2.7	只 2.8	兄 2.9	号 2.10	台 2.11
可 2.12	句 2.13	司 2.14	右 2.15	吐 3.1	吁 3.2	吋 3.3	吒 3.4	吸 3.5	吼 3.6	吃 3.7	吊 3.8	舌 3.9
向 3.10	向 8e3.1	后 3.11	名 3.12	吠 4.1	吽 4.2	吹 4.3	呀 4.4	呐 4.5	叫 3d3.4	吻 4.6	听 4.7	吟 4.8
吭 4.9	吩 4.10	吮 4.11	呎 4.12	呆 4.13	呈 4.14	邑 4.15	品 3d6.15	吴 2o5.7	足 7d0.1	呉 2o5.7	呂 4.16	吾 4.17
告 4.18	吞 4.19	否 4.20	谷 2o5.3	乱 4.21	吴 2o5.7	豆 4.22	何 2a5.21	伺 2a5.23	君 4.23	呷 5.1	呻 5.2	味 5.3
呼 5.4	咄 5.5	咀 5.6	咋 5.7	咆 5.8	呶 5.9	呬 5.10	咒 5.11	咜 3d6.6	呟 5.12	咏 7a5.14	呵 5.13	知 5.14
咎 5.15	巫 5.16	奇 5.17	函 2b6.3	哂 6.1	哘 6.2	哮 6.3	咾 6.4	哇 6.5	咤 6.6	哄 6.7	咯 3d9.13	哐 6.8
哈 6.9	咳 6.10	咬 6.11	咲 6.12	呱 6.13	咽 6.14	品 6.15	毗 6.16	咨 6.17	咢 6.18	咼 6.19	剐 6.20	哉 4n5.4
面 3s6.1	咫 3r6.6	殆 6.21	唄 7.1	唖 3d8.3	哦 7.2	哽 7.3	哺 7.4	哩 7.5	啄 3d8.4	唪 7.6	唔 7.7	唆 7.8
哨 7.9	唳 3d8.15	員 7.10	唏 7.11	唇 7.12	哲 7.13	哭 3g6.7	勉 2n8.1	執 7.14	尌 3d6.20	氤 3s7.4	舐 7.15	哥 7.16
鬲 7.17	韋 7.18	唯 8.1	唾 8.2	啞 8.3	啄 8.4	唧 8.5	唪 8.6	唹 8.7	喝 8.8	唱 8.9	啖 8.10	啜 8.11
唸 8.12	啅 8.13	啗 8.14	唳 8.15	唯 8.16	啓 8.17	甜 8.18	超 3b9.18	喰 9.1	喊 9.2	唧 3i11.1	喇 9.3	喞 9.4
啾 9.5	喉 9.6	喫 9.7	喑 9.8	喟 9.9	喋 9.10	喝 3d8.8	喘 9.11	喧 9.12	喀 9.13	喙 9.14	喩 9.15	啼 9.16
嘵 9.17	喃 9.18	喚 9.19	嵒 9.20	啻 2j10.2	就 9.21	單 3n6.2	敔 9.22	舒 9.23	谼 9.24	喪 3b9.20	喬 9.25	登 9.26
短 9.27	殛 9.28	尋 9.29	貂 9.30	嗚 10.1	嗛 10.2	嗅 10.3	嗜 10.4	嗄 10.5	嗪 10.6	嘩 10.7	嘆 10.8	嗤 10.9
嗟 10.10	嗔 10.11	嚏 10.12	嗇 3b10.13	嗣 10.13	號 3d2.10	辞 5b8.4	群 10.14	羣 3d10.14	豊 10.15	鳴 11.1	嗷 11.2	嗽 11.3
嗹 11.4	嘈 11.5	噌 3d12.9	嘖 11.6	嘆 3d10.8	嘘 11.7	嘛 11.8	嘔 11.9	號 3d2.10	兢 11.10	砲 3s11.1	敲 11.11	奞 2t13.1
嘶 12.1	嘲 12.2	噉 12.3	嘸 12.4	噗 12.5	噛 3d15.2	噎 12.6	噂 12.7	噓 12.8	噴 3d11.7	噌 3d12.10	嶒 12.9	噂 12.10
嘱 12.11	髻 12.12	器 12.13	嚚 3d12.13	豌 12.14	舗 3b12.4	毆 2t6.1	靠 4g11.1	嘯 13.1	嘶 13.2	顛 13.3	嚘 13.4	嚛 13.5
噬 13.6	嘴 13.7	憶 13.8	噪 13.9	嚆 13.10	鬐 13.11	器 3d12.13	劒 2f8.5	舘 8b8.3	甌 13.12	豎 5b9.5	殫 13.13	豫 0a4.12

嚇	嚊	嘁	嚔	嚀	營	氈	貌	牆	矯	嘲	嚙	嚌
14.1	14.2	14.3	3d15.3	14.4	3n9.2	3s14.1	0a11.1	3b14.6	14.5	15.1	15.2	15.3
臨	豐	嚮	軀	顑	嚟	艷	嚶	礜	嚴	韜	獻	韶
2t15.1	3d10.15	15.4	15.5	16.1	16.2	16.3	17.1	17.2	3n14.1	17.3	3g9.6	17.4
飴	齣	體	囉	囀	嚼	囈	囁	囂	囐	孌	囊	囓
17.5	17.6	2a5.6	18.1	18.2	18.3	18.4	18.5	9a12.3	19.1	19.2	19.3	19.4
醫	囑	囑	艷	齶	齱							
4c19.1	2a19.4	3d12.11	3d16.3	21.1	3s21.1							

3

——— 0 ———

3d0.1 / 54

[口]

KŌ, KU, kuchi mouth

——— 1 ———

0 口まめ **kuchi(mame)** talkative, voluble
口さがない **kuchi(saganai)** gossipy, scandal-mongering
口コミ **kuchikomi** communication by word of mouth
2 口入 **kuchii(re)** act as go-between
口入屋 **kuchii(re)ya** employment agency
口八丁 **kuchihatchō** eloquent, talkative
3 口三味線 **kuchijamisen, kuchizamisen** humming a samisen tune; cajolery
口上 **kōjō** oral (statement)
口上手 **kuchijōzu** fair-spoken, glib
口上書 **kōjōsho** verbal note
口下手 **kuchibeta** awkward tongue, poor talker
口々 **kuchiguchi** each entrance/mouth
4 口不調法 **kuchi-buchōhō** awkward in expressing oneself
口元 **kuchimoto** (shape of the) mouth; near the entrance
口内炎 **kōnaien** stomatitis
口中 **kōchū** (interior of) the mouth
口切 **kuchiki(ri)** broach, break the silence
口止 **kuchido(me)** forbid to speak of
口止料 **kuchido(me)ryō** hush money
口分 **kuchiwa(ke)** assort, itemize
口火 **kuchibi** fuse
5 口出 **kuchida(shi)** meddling, butting in
口付 **kuchizu(ke)** kiss **kuchitsu(ki)** (shape of one's) mouth; manner of speech; mouthpiece (of a cigarette)
口外 **kōgai** divulge, reveal, tell
6 口気 **kōki** bad breath; way of talking
口任 **kuchimaka(se)** random talk
口伝 **kuchizute, kuchizuta(e)** word of mouth, oral tradition
口汚 **kuchiyogo(shi)** small morsel **kuchigitana(i)** foul-mouthed, abusive

口先 **kuchisaki** lips, mouth, snout; words, lip service
口舌 **kōzetsu** words, verbal (quarrel)
口当 **kuchia(tari)** taste; reception, hospitality
7 口承 **kōshō** word of mouth, oral tradition
口角 **kōkaku** corners of the mouth
口述 **kōjutsu** oral statement, dictation
口走 **kuchibashi(ru)** blurt out, say
口吻 **kōfun** way of speaking
口利 **kuchiki(ki)** eloquent person; spokesman; go-between, middleman
口言葉 **kuchi kotoba** spoken/colloquial word(s)
口車 **kuchiguruma** cajolery
8 口供 **kōkyō** affidavit, deposition
口供書 **kōkyōsho** affidavit, deposition
口直 **kuchinao(shi)** kill the aftertaste
口径 **kōkei** caliber, bore, aperture
口実 **kōjitsu** excuse, pretext
口明 **kuchia(ke)** beginning, opening
口取 **kuchito(ri)** groom, horseboy; side dish
口金 **kuchigane** spinneret, (cake-decorating) tip; (handbag) clasp; bottlecap; (light bulb) base; ferrule
9 口重 **kuchiomo** slow of speech; prudent
口拭 **kuchifu(ki)** napkin
口臭 **kōshū** bad breath, halitosis
口約 **kōyaku** oral agreement/promise
口約束 **kuchi yakusoku** oral agreement/promise
10 口凌 **kuchishino(gi)** hand-to-mouth living
口真似 **kuchimane** mimicry
口遊 **kuchizusa(mu), kuchizusa(bu)** hum, sing to oneself
口振 **kuchibu(ri)** way of talking; intimation
口唇 **kōshin** the lips
口座 **kōza** (bank) account
11 口達者 **kuchidassha** talkative
口過 **kuchisu(gi)** make a living
口添 **kuchizo(e)** advice, support, recommendation
口授 **kuju, kōju** oral teaching; dictation
口寄 **kuchiyo(se)** spiritism, necromancy; a medium

氵 土 扌 口 0← 女 巾 犭 弓 彳 彡 艹 宀 丷 山 吉 广 尸 口

3

氵 土 扌 口 女 巾 犭 弓 彳 彡 艹 宀 ⺌ 山 士 广 尸 口

→0

口悪 **kuchi (no) waru(i)** evil-mouthed, scurrilous
口惜 **kuchio(shii)** regrettable, mortifying
口移 **kuchiutsu(shi)** mouth-to-mouth feeding; word of mouth
口笛 **kuchibue** whistling
12 口割 **kuchi (o) wa(ru)** (break down and) confess
口減 **kuchibe(rashi)** reducing the number of mouths to feed
口堅 **kuchigata(i)** close-mouthed, discreet
口喧 **kuchiyakama(shii)** nagging, carping; talkative, gossipy
口幅 **kuchihaba(ttai)** talking big, bragging
口腔 **kōkō** the oral cavity
口腔外科 **kōkō geka** oral surgery
口絵 **kuchie** frontispiece
口答 **kuchigota(e)** backtalk, retort
 kōtō oral reply
口答試問 **kōtō shimon** oral examination/quiz
口証 **kōshō** oral testimony
口軽 **kuchigaru** glib, (too) talkative
口飲 **kuchino(mi)** drink from the bottle
13 口蓋 **kōgai** the palate, roof of the mouth
口蓋垂 **kōgaisui** the uvula
口塞 **kuchifusa(gi)** keeping someone from talking; food (served to guests)
口煩 **kuchiuru(sai)** nagging, too talkative
口数 **kuchikazu** number of mouths to feed; number of words, speech; number of shares/lots/items **kōsū** number of accounts/lots/items
口触 **kuchizawa(ri)** taste
口馴 **kuchina(rashi)** oral drill
14 口演 **kōen** oral narration
口慣 **kuchina(rashi)** oral drill
口碑 **kōhi** legend, tradition, folklore
口語 **kōgo** colloquial language
口語文 **kōgobun** colloquial language
口語体 **kōgotai** colloquial style, colloquialism
口語訳 **kōgoyaku** colloquial translation
口語詩 **kōgoshi** poem in colloquial style
口説 **kudo(ku)** persuade, entreat, woo, court **kuzetsu** quarrel; curtain lecture
口説落 **kudo(ki)o(tosu)** persuade, talk (someone) into, win over
口誦 **kōshō** humming; reading aloud
口銭 **kōsen** commission; net profit
15 口慰 **kuchinagusa(mi)** relieving boredom by talking, humming, or eating
口論 **kōron** argument, dispute
口調 **kuchō** tone, expression
口輪 **kuchiwa** muzzle
16 口頭 **kōtō** oral
口頭試問 **kōtō shimon** oral examination

18 口癖 **kuchiguse** habit of saying, favorite saying
口糧 **kōryō** rations
22 口籠 **kuchigomo(ru)** stammer; mumble

──────── 2 ────────

1 一口 **hitokuchi** a mouthful; a unit; a word
2 入口 **iriguchi** entrance
人口 **jinkō** population; common talk
3 三口 **mi(tsu)kuchi** harelip
川口 **kawaguchi** mouth of a river
 Kawaguchi (city, Saitama-ken)
大口 **ōguchi, ōkuchi** large mouth; bragging, exaggeration; large amount
大口径 **daikōkei** large-caliber
口口 **kuchiguchi** each entrance/mouth
小口 **koguchi** in small lots, small sum; end, edge; clue; beginning
山口県 **Yamaguchi-ken** (prefecture)
4 切口 **ki(ri)kuchi** cut end, opening
切口上 **ki(ri)kōjō** stiff and formal language
片口 **katakuchi** lipped bowl; one side of a story
水口 **mizuguchi, mizukuchi** spout, water inlet/outlet
手口 **teguchi** modus operandi, way, trick
火口 **kakō** (volcano) crater **higuchi** burner; muzzle (of a gun); origin of a fire
火口湖 **kakōko** crater lake
火口壁 **kakōheki** crater wall
戸口 **toguchi** doorway
5 出口 **deguchi** exit; outlet
半口 **hankuchi** half-share
甘口 **amakuchi** mild, light (flavor); sweet tooth; flattery
広口 **hirokuchi** wide-mouthed (bottle)
6 江口 **kōkō** estuary
地口 **jiguchi** play on words, pun
先口 **senkuchi** previous engagement/application
吸口 **su(i)kuchi** cigarette holder, mouthpiece (of a pipe)
早口 **hayakuchi, hayaguchi** fast talking
早口言葉 **hayakuchi kotoba** tongue twister
糸口 **itoguchi** thread end; beginning; clue
7 別口 **betsukuchi** different kind/item/lot
坑口 **kōkō** mine entrance, pithead
折口 **o(re)kuchi** a split/break
告口 **tsu(ge)guchi** tell on, snitch, tattle
呑口 **no(mi)guchi** bung hole, tap, spigot
売口 **u(re)kuchi** a market/demand for
辛口 **karakuchi** salty, spicy, dry (saké); preference for sharp taste
利口 **rikō** smart, clever, bright
利口者 **rikōmono** clever person
初口 **shokuchi** beginning

8 表口 **omoteguchi** front entrance/door
東口 **higashiguchi** east exit/entrance
毒口 **dokuguchi** venomous tongue, abusive remarks
受口 **u(ke)guchi** receiving window; notch, socket **u(ke)kuchi, u(ke)guchi** mouth with a protruding lower jaw
虎口 **kokō** tiger's mouth; dangerous situation
逃口 **ni(ge)guchi** way of escape, loophole
逃口上 **ni(ge)kōjō** excuse, evasion
河口 **kakō** mouth of a river, estuary
河口港 **kakōkō** estuary harbor
取口 **to(ri)guchi** sumo technique
金口 **kinguchi, kinkuchi, kinkō** gold-tipped
門口 **kadoguchi** front door, entrance
9 便口 **benkō** fair-spoken, smooth-tongued
降口 **o(ri)guchi, o(ri)kuchi** exit (from a station)
南口 **minamiguchi** south exit/entrance
前口上 **maekōjō** introductory remarks, prolog
風口 **kazaguchi** air intake
海口 **kaikō** harbor entrance
後口 **atokuchi** aftertaste; remainder; a later turn/appointment
秋口 **akiguchi** the beginning of autumn
10 陰口 **kageguchi** malicious gossip
捌口 **ha(ke)guchi** outlet; market
徒口 **adakuchi** empty words, lip service
宵口 **yoi (no) kuchi** early evening
烏口 **karasuguchi** drafting/ruling pen
砲口 **hōkō** muzzle (of a gun); caliber
竜口 **tatsu(no)kuchi** dragon-head gargoyle; spout (of a gutter)
袖口 **sodeguchi** edge of a sleeve, cuff
11 猪口 **choko** saké cup
窓口 **madoguchi** (ticket) window
悪口 **warukuchi, aku(tare)guchi, akkō** verbal abuse, speaking ill/evil of
悪口雑言 **akkō-zōgon** vituperation
異口同音 **iku-dōon** with one voice, unanimous
経口 **keikō** via the mouth, oral (medication)
蛇口 **jaguchi** faucet, tap
軟口蓋 **nankōgai** the soft palate
閉口 **heikō** be dumbfounded
12 勤口 **tsuto(me)guchi** position, place of employment
遣口 **ya(ri)kuchi** way of doing, method
港口 **kōkō** harbor entrance
湾口 **wankō** bay entrance
湯口 **yuguchi** source of a hot spring
減口 **he(razu)guchi** continuing to talk back (even when one has been defeated)
登口 **nobo(ri)guchi** starting point (for ascending a mountain)
落口 **o(chi)guchi** mouth of a river); spout;

beginning of the fall of leaves
焚口 **ta(ki)guchi** fuel-feed hole, furnace hatch
無口 **mukuchi** taciturn, reticent, laconic
雇口 **yato(i)guchi** employment, job
硬口蓋 **kōkōgai** the hard palate
衆口一致 **shūkō-itchi** unanimous
軽口 **karuguchi, karukuchi** witty remark; talkative
飲口 **no(mi)guchi** spigot, tap
no(mi)kuchi taste, flavor
間口 **maguchi** frontage, width
開口 **kaikō** opening, aperture; beginning one's speech
13 働口 **hatara(ki)guchi** job opening, employment
傷口 **kizuguchi** wound
裏口 **uraguchi** back door, rear entrance
滝口 **takiguchi** top/crest of a waterfall
搔口説 **ka(ki)kudo(ku)** complain of, plead
14 漏口 **rōkō** a leak, vent
歌口 **utaguchi** mouthpiece (of a flute); skill in reciting poetry
憎口 **niku(mare)guchi** offensive/malicious remarks
箝口 **kankō** keep silent about, gag, hush up
箝口令 **kankōrei** gag law/order
語口 **kata(ri)kuchi** way of talking/narrating
銃口 **jūkō** (gun) muzzle
鳶口 **tobiguchi** fireman's ax/hook
15 糊口 **kokō** (eke out a) livelihood
16 薄口 **usukuchi** thin(-cut), mild (flavor)
艙口 **sōkō** hatch, hatchway
17 藉口 **shakō** pretense, pretext
18 儲口 **mō(ke)guchi** profitable job
餬口 **kokō** a living, livelihood
鯉口 **koiguchi** mouth of a sword sheath
20 鰐口 **waniguchi** wide/large mouth; alligator (clip); (temple) gong

─────── 3 ───────

2 子宮口 **shikyūkō** the cervix
3 小利口 **korikō** clever, smart
4 冗談口 **jōdanguchi** a joke
5 出入口 **deiriguchi** entrance/exit
出札口 **shussatsuguchi** ticket window
7 改札口 **kaisatsuguchi** ticket gate, wicket
8 非常口 **hijōguchi** emergency exit
送話口 **sōwaguchi** (telephone) mouthpiece
昇降口 **shōkōguchi** (ship) entrance, hatchway
9 降車口 **kōshaguchi** gateway for arriving passengers, exit
通用口 **tsūyōguchi** service entrance, side door
通話口 **tsūwaguchi** (telephone) mouthpiece
背戸口 **sedoguchi** back door/gate/entrance
10 差出口 **sa(shi)deguchi** uncalled-for remark
12 就職口 **shūshokuguchi** job opening, employment

勝手口　**katteguchi** kitchen/back door
無駄口　**mudaguchi** idle talk, prattle
13 電話口　**denwaguchi** telephone (mouthpiece)
15 噴火口　**funkakō** crater
蝦蟇口　**gamaguchi** purse

─────────── 2 ───────────

3

氵
土
扌
→2 口
女
巾
犭
弓
彳
彡
艹
宀
丷
山
十
广
尸
囗

3d2.1

叶　**KYŌ, kana(eru)** grant, answer, hear (a prayer) **kana(u)** be fulfilled/granted

─────────── 2 ───────────

19 願叶　**nega(ttari)-kana(ttari)** just what one has been wanting

3d2.2

叱　**SHITSU, shika(ru)** scold, reprimand

─────────── 1 ───────────

5 叱付　**shika(ri)tsu(keru)** scold/rebuke severely
叱正　**shissei** correction
9 叱飛　**shika(ri)to(basu)** blow up at, bawl out
叱咤　**shitta** scold; spur on
11 叱責　**shisseki** reproach, reprimand

3d2.3

叩　**KŌ, tata(ku)** strike, hit, knock, slap, clap, rap, pat; sound out; criticize

─────────── 1 ───────────

3 叩大工　**tata(ki)daiku** clumsy carpenter
叩上　**tata(ki)a(geru)** work one's way up
4 叩切　**tata(ki)ki(ru)** hack down, chop off
叩込　**tata(ki)ko(mu)** drive/throw into; hammer in, inculcate
5 叩出　**tata(ki)da(su)** begin to beat; drive out; dismiss
叩付　**tata(ki)tsu(keru)** beat, thrash; throw at
叩台　**tata(ki)dai** (chopping) block
6 叩伏　**tata(ki)fu(seru)** knock down; utterly defeat
叩合　**tata(ki)a(u)** fight, exchange blows
7 叩売　**tata(ki)u(ri)** sacrifice sale
10 叩起　**tata(ki)o(kosu)** awaken, rouse
叩殺　**tata(ki)koro(su)** beat to death
12 叩割　**tata(ki)wa(ru)** break to pieces, smash
叩落　**tata(ki)o(tosu)** knock down/off
15 叩潰　**tata(ki)tsubu(su)** smash, crush
16 叩壊　**tata(ki)kowa(su)** knock apart, wreck
叩頭　**kōtō** kowtow, bow deeply

─────────── 2 ───────────

7 売叩　**u(ri)tata(ku)** drive down the price, undersell

11 袋叩　**fukurodata(ki)** gang up on and beat up
19 蠅叩　**haetata(ki)** fly swatter

3d2.4

叨　**TŌ** truly; graciously; gratuitously; ravenously

3d2.5

呀　**HA** open mouth

─────────── 2 ───────────

12 喇叭　**rappa** trumpet, bugle

3d2.6

叺　**kamasu** straw bag

叫 → 叫　3d3.4

3d2.7

叮　**TEI** courtesy, kindness

─────────── 1 ───────────

17 叮嚀　**teinei** polite, courteous

3d2.8

只　**SHI, tada** only, just; free, gratis

─────────── 1 ───────────

4 只今　**tadaima** just now
8 只奉公　**tadabōkō** serving without pay
只事　**tadagoto** trivial/common matter
只者　**tadamono** ordinary person
只取　**tadato(ri)** get (something) for nothing
9 只乗　**tadano(ri)** free/stolen ride
13 只働　**tadabatara(ki)** working without pay

─────────── 2 ───────────

10 真只中　**ma(t)tadanaka** right in the middle of

3d2.9 / 406

兄　**KEI, KYŌ, ani, (o)nii(san)** elder brother

─────────── 1 ───────────

3 兄上　**aniue** elder brother

7 兄弟 **kyōdai, ani-otōto** brothers (and sisters)
兄弟子 **anideshi** senior fellow student/apprentice
兄弟分 **kyōdaibun** sworn brother, buddy, pal
兄弟愛 **kyōdaiai** brotherly love
8 兄事 **keiji** regard as one's senior
12 兄貴 **aniki** elder brother; one's senior
13 兄嫁 **aniyome** elder brother's wife

––––––––––– 2 –––––––––––

3 亡兄 **bōkei** one's deceased elder brother
4 仁兄 **jinkei** (term of address for a friend)
父兄 **fukei** parents and older brothers, guardians
父兄会 **fukeikai** parents' association
6 次兄 **jikei** one's second-oldest elder brother
7 伯兄 **hakkei** eldest brother
乳兄弟 **chikyōdai** foster brother(s and sisters)
8 長兄 **chōkei** eldest brother
実兄 **jikkei** one's biological elder brother
10 従兄 **jūkei** elder male cousin
従兄弟 **itoko, jūkeitei** male cousin
家兄 **kakei** my elder brother
12 貴兄 **kikei** you (masculine)
13 慈兄 **jikei** affectionate elder brother
義兄 **gikei** elder brother-in-law
義兄弟 **gikyōdai** brother-in-law; stepbrother; sworn brother
愚兄 **gukei** my (foolish) elder brother
15 諸兄 **shokei** dear friends, gentlemen
諸兄姉 **shokeishi** ladies and gentlemen
16 親兄弟 **oya-kyōdai** one's parents and brothers and sisters
賢兄 **kenkei** (wise) elder brother/friend

––––––––––– 3 –––––––––––

2 又従兄弟 **mataitoko** second cousin

3d2.10 / 266

号 號

GŌ number; name; signal, sign; cry out

––––––––––– 1 –––––––––––

5 号令 **gōrei** command, order
号外 **gōgai** an extra (edition of a newspaper)
6 号叫 **gōkyō** calling in a loud voice
8 号泣 **gōkyū** wailing, lamentation
9 号音 **gōon** audible signal, call
11 号笛 **gōteki** horn, siren, whistle

––––––––––– 2 –––––––––––

1 一号 **ichigō** number one
2 二号 **nigō** No. 2; mistress, concubine
3 三号雑誌 **sangō zasshi** short-lived magazine
4 元号 **gengō** era name
欠号 **ketsugō** missing number/issue
5 本号 **hongō** current number (of a publication)

加号 **kagō** addition/plus sign
正号 **seigō** plus sign (+)
6 年号 **nengō** era name
毎号 **maigō** every issue (of a magazine)
次号 **jigō** the next issue
名号 **myōgō** Buddha's name
7 改号 **kaigō** changing the title; new name
初号 **shogō** first number/issue (of a magazine)
8 追号 **tsuigō** posthumous title
法号 **hōgō** (priest's or deceased's) Buddhist name
呼号 **kogō** cry out, declare
国号 **kokugō** name of a country
9 信号 **shingō** signal
信号灯 **shingōtō** signal light, blinker
信号塔 **shingōtō** signal tower
信号旗 **shingōki** signal/code flag
信号機 **shingōki** signal
除号 **jogō** division sign
哀号 **aigō** moan, wailing
負号 **fugō** minus sign (–)
前号 **zengō** preceding issue
屋号 **yagō** store name; stage-family name
怒号 **dogō** angry roar
10 俳号 **haigō** haiku poet's pen name
称号 **shōgō** title, degree
記号 **kigō** mark, symbol
11 商号 **shōgō** corporate name
略号 **ryakugō** abbreviation
船号 **sengō** ship's name
符号 **fugō** mark, symbol, code
12 尊号 **songō** honorific title
減号 **gengō** subtraction/minus sign
番号 **bangō** number
番号付 **bangōtsu(ke)** numbering
番号札 **bangōfuda** numbered (license) plate
等号 **tōgō** equal sign (=)
13 僧号 **sōgō** Buddhist name
暗号 **angō** code, cipher
暗号文 **angōbun** coded message, cryptogram
雅号 **gagō** pen name
15 標号 **hyōgō** symbol, emblem, sign
調号 **chōgō** key signature (in music)
16 諡号 **shigō** posthumous name
18 贈号 **zōgō** posthumous name
題号 **daigō** title

––––––––––– 3 –––––––––––

5 四角号碼 **shikaku gōma** (an encoding scheme which assigns to each kanji a four-digit number based on its four corners)
7 赤信号 **akashingō** red (traffic) light
8 青信号 **aoshingō** green (traffic) light
9 通番号 **tō(shi)bangō** serial number
背番号 **sebangō** number on a player's back
10 既刊号 **kikangō** back numbers

3

氵
土
扌
口 2←
女
巾
犭
弓
彳
彡
艹
宀
凵
卄
广
尸
口

特別号 **tokubetsugō** special number
特集号 **tokushūgō** special issue
記念号 **kinengō** commemorative issue (of a magazine)
11 終刊号 **shūkangō** final issue
12 創刊号 **sōkangō** first issue/number
博士号 **hakasegō** doctor's degree, Ph.D.
14 増大号 **zōdaigō** enlarged number/issue
旗信号 **hatashingō** semaphore, flag signal

—————— 4 ——————

4 手旗信号 **tebata shingō** flag signaling, semaphore
9 音部記号 **onbu kigō** (G) clef
12 腕木信号 **udegi shingō** semaphore
19 霧中信号 **muchū shingō** fog signal

3d2.11 / 492

台 臺

DAI, TAI stand, platform, base; tableland, heights; level, mark, (price/age) range; (counter for vehicles or machines)

utena calyx, (lily) pad; stand, pedestal; tower, hall

—————— 1 ——————

5 台北 **Taipei, Taihoku** Taipei (capital of Taiwan)
台本 **daihon** script, screenplay, libretto
台尻 **daijiri** butt/stock (of a gun)
台石 **daiishi** pedestal stone
6 台地 **daichi** plateau, tableland, height
7 台形 **daikei** trapezoid
8 台所 **daidokoro** kitchen
台所流 **daidokoro (no) naga(shi)** the kitchen sink
9 台風 **taifū** typhoon
10 台座 **daiza** pedestal
台紙 **daishi** (photo) mounting paper, mat
11 台帳 **daichō** ledger, register; script
12 台湾 **Taiwan** (island country near China)
台場 **daiba** fort, battery
台無 **daina(shi)** ruined, come to nought
台詞 **serifu** (actor's) lines, what one says
14 台閣 **taikaku** tall building; the cabinet
16 台頭 **taitō** rise to prominence, gain strength

—————— 2 ——————

3 土台 **dodai** foundation, groundwork; utterly
4 天台 **Tendai** (a Buddhist sect)
5 仙台 **Sendai** (city, Miyagi-ken)
叩台 **tata(ki)dai** chopping block
6 灯台 **tōdai** lighthouse
灯台守 **tōdaimori** lighthouse keeper
式台 **shikidai** step (in an entrance hall)
7 花台 **kadai** stand for a vase
見台 **kendai** bookrest, reading board
車台 **shadai** chassis
8 店台 **misedai** counter (in a store)

9 屋台 **yatai** a float; a stall
屋台店 **yatai mise** street stall, stand, booth
屋台骨 **yataibone** framework, foundation; means, property
食台 **shokudai** dining table
10 高台 **takadai** high ground, elevation
晒台 **sara(shi)dai** pillory, stocks, gibbet
砲台 **hōdai** gun battery, fort
11 涼台 **suzu(mi)dai** bench (for enjoying the evening cool)
捨台詞 **su(te)zerifu** sharp parting remark
窓台 **madodai** windowsill
船台 **sendai** shipbuilding berth
釣台 **tsu(ri)dai** stretcher, litter
12 番台 **bandai** bathhouse attendant('s raised seat)
貴台 **kidai** you
飯台 **handai** dining table
13 滑台 **sube(ri)dai** (playground) slide; launching platform
寝台 **shindai** bed
寝台車 **shindaisha** sleeping car
寝台券 **shindaiken** sleeping-car ticket
継台 **tsu(gi)dai** stock (of a graft)
15 舞台 **butai** stage
舞台負 **butaima(ke)** stage fright
舞台姿 **butaisugata** in stage costume
舞台面 **butaimen** scene, scenery
舞台裏 **butaiura** backstage
舞台劇 **butaigeki** stage play
舞台稽古 **butai geiko** dress rehearsal
盤台 **bandai** oval basin/tray
縁台 **endai** bench
輦台 **rendai** litter for carrying a traveler across a river
踏台 **fu(mi)dai** step, footstool, steppingstone
16 橋台 **hashidai, kyōdai** bridge abutment
17 燭台 **shokudai** candlestick, candlestand
18 鎮台 **chindai** garrison
19 鏡台 **kyōdai** dressing table
21 露台 **rodai** balcony

—————— 3 ——————

4 天文台 **tenmondai** observatory
手術台 **shujutsudai** operating table
5 処刑台 **shokeidai** the gallows
6 気象台 **kishōdai** weather station
回舞台 **mawa(ri)butai** revolving stage
7 見張台 **miha(ri)dai** watchtower
初舞台 **hatsubutai** one's stage debut
8 青瓦台 **Seigadai** the Blue House (South Korean presidential palace)
9 飛込台 **tobikomidai** diving board
前舞台 **maebutai** apron stage, proscenium
洗面台 **senmendai** washstand
拷問台 **gōmondai** the rack

独舞台 **hito(ri)butai** having the stage to oneself
10 展望台 **tenbōdai** observation platform
時計台 **tokeidai** clock stand/tower
11 運転台 **untendai** motorman's seat, driver's cab
断頭台 **dantōdai** guillotine
転車台 **tenshadai** turntable
12 絞首台 **kōshudai** gallows
証人台 **shōnindai** the witness stand/box
15 縫物台 **nu(i)monodai** sewing table
16 稽古台 **keikodai** something/someone to practice on
17 檜舞台 **hinoki butai** cypress-floored stage; high-class stage, limelight

――――――― 4 ―――――――
1 一人舞台 **hitori butai** unrivaled

3d2.12 / 388

可

KA possible, can, -able; good, approval

――――――― 1 ―――――――
3 可及的 **kakyūteki** as ... as possible
4 可分 **kabun** divisible, separable
可分性 **kabunsei** divisibility
6 可成 **kana(ri)** considerably, rather, quite
7 可決 **kaketsu** approval, adoption (of a resolution)
可否 **kahi** right or wrong, pro and con
9 可変 **kahen** variable, changeable
可哀相 **kawaisō** poor, pitiable, pathetic
10 可能 **kanō** possible
可能法 **kanōhō** potential mood
可能性 **kanōsei** possibility
11 可動 **kadō** movable, mobile
可動性 **kadōsei** mobility
可動橋 **kadōkyō** movable bridge
13 可溶性 **kayōsei** solubility
可塑 **kaso** plastic
可塑物質 **kaso busshitsu** plastics
可愛 **kawai(i)** cute, dear, sweet
15 可撓性 **katōsei** flexible, flexibility
16 可燃物 **kanenbutsu** combustibles, flammable substances
可燃性 **kanensei** combustible, flammable
可憐 **karen** lovely, cute, sweet; poor, pitiable
17 可聴性 **kachōsei** audibility
可鍛性 **katansei** malleability
18 可鎔性 **kayōsei** fusibility

――――――― 2 ―――――――
4 不可 **fuka** wrong, bad, improper, disapproved
不可入性 **fukanyūsei** impenetrability
不可分 **fukabun** indivisible, inseparable
不可欠 **fukaketsu** indispensable, essential
不可抗力 **fukakōryoku** force majeure,

beyond one's control, unavoidable
不可知 **fukachi** unknowable
不可知論 **fukachiron** agnosticism
不可侵 **fukashin** nonaggression; inviolable
不可思議 **fukashigi** mystery, wonder, miracle
不可能 **fukanō** impossible
不可解 **fukakai** mysterious, baffling
不可避 **fukahi** inescapable, unavoidable, inevitable
11 許可 **kyoka** permission, approval, authorization
許可制 **kyokasei** license system
許可証 **kyokashō** a permit, license
12 裁可 **saika** approval, sanction
14 認可 **ninka** approval
認可証 **ninkashō** permit, license
15 摩訶不思議 **maka-fushigi** profound mystery

――――――― 3 ―――――――
4 不認可 **funinka** disapproval, rejection
5 生半可 **namahanka** superficial, half-baked
12 御裁可 **gosaika** imperial sanction/approval

3d2.13 / 337

句

KU phrase, sentence, verse

――――――― 1 ―――――――
4 句切 **kugi(ru)** punctuate; mark off, partition
6 句会 **kukai** a haiku meeting
8 句法 **kuhō** wording, phrasing
9 句点 **kuten** period (the punctuation mark)
12 句集 **kushū** collection of haiku poems
13 句意 **kui** meaning of a phrase
14 句読 **kutō** punctuation
句読点 **kutōten** punctuation mark

――――――― 2 ―――――――
1 一句 **ikku** a phrase/verse/verse; (counter for haiku)
2 二句 **ni (no) ku** another word, rejoinder
3 上句 **kami(no)ku** the first part of a poem
下句 **shimo(no)ku** the last part of a poem
4 冗句 **jōku** redundant phrase
文句 **monku** phrase, expression; complaint, objection; excuse
5 半句 **hanku** a brief word
字句 **jiku** words and phrases, wording
6 名句 **meiku** well-put/famous phrase; noted haiku
成句 **seiku** set phrase, idiomatic expression
7 対句 **tsuiku** couplet, distich; antithesis
折句 **o(ri)ku** acrostic verse
妙句 **myōku** clever turn of phrase
狂句 **kyōku** comic haiku
秀句 **shūku** excellent haiku; quip, wisecrack
初句 **shoku** first line (of a poem)
8 佳句 **kaku** beautiful passage, literary gem
9 発句 **hokku** first line (of a *renga*); haiku

3

氵 土 扌 口 2← 女 巾 犭 弓 彳 彡 艹 宀 ⺍ 山 吉 广 尸 口

連句 **renku** linked verse
10 倒句 **tōku** inversion (of normal word order)
俳句 **haiku** haiku
起句 **kiku** opening line of a poem
挿句 **sōku** parenthetical remark
挙句 **ageku** in the end, ultimately
11 章句 **shōku** passage, chapter and verse
12 揚句 **a(ge)ku** in the end, ultimately
短句 **tanku** short phrase
結句 **kekku** conclusion (of a poem); after all
絶句 **zekku** stop short, forget one's lines;
  (Chinese poetry form)
13 禁句 **kinku** tabooed word/phrase
節句 **sekku** seasonal festival
節句働 **sekkubatara(ki)** working on a
  holiday (to make up for lost time)
詩句 **shiku** verse, stanza
14 豪句 **gōku** grandiloquence
語句 **goku** words and phrases
駄句 **daku** poor poem, doggerel
18 難句 **nanku** difficult phrase/passage
類句 **ruiku** similar phrase/haiku
題句 **daiku** epigraph
19 麗句 **reiku** beautiful phrase
警句 **keiku** epigram, witticism

——————— 3 ———————
4 引用句 **in'yōku** quotation
6 名文句 **meimonku** fine expression, famous
  words
7 決文句 **ki(mari)monku** set phrase, conventional expression
初節句 **hatsuzekku** child's first festival
10 凄文句 **sugomonku** menacing language
脅文句 **odo(shi)monku** threating words,
  menacing language
桃節句 **momo (no) sekku** Doll Festival
  (March 3)
殺文句 **koro(shi) monku** "killing" words,
  cajolery, clincher
11 菊節句 **Kiku (no) Sekku** Chrysanthemum
  Festival
常套句 **jōtōku** stock phrase, cliché
14 慣用句 **kan'yōku** idiom, common expression
18 雛節句 **hina (no) sekku** Girls' Doll Festival
  (March 3)

——————— 4 ———————
4 片言隻句 **hengen-sekku** few words
9 美辞麗句 **biji-reiku** flowery language
10 流行文句 **haya(ri)monku** popular phrase

3d2.14 / 842

司 **SHI** an official; government office
tsukasado(ru) govern, manage, conduct
tsukasa government office; director,
official

——————— 1 ———————
5 司令 **shirei** command, control; commander
司令官 **shireikan** commanding officer
司令部 **shireibu** headquarters, the command
司令塔 **shireitō** control/conning tower
6 司会 **shikai** preside over, officiate
司会者 **shikaisha** emcee, chairman
8 司直 **shichoku** judicial authorities
司法 **shihō** administration of justice, judicial
司法大臣 **shihō daijin** Minister of Justice
司法官 **shihōkan** judicial official
司法権 **shihōken** judicial powers, jurisdiction
9 司政官 **shiseikan** civil administrator
10 司書 **shisho** librarian
司教 **shikyō** (Catholic) bishop
司教区 **shikyōku** diocese
11 司祭 **shisai** (Catholic) priest
司祭職 **shisaishoku** (Catholic) priesthood

——————— 2 ———————
3 大司教 **daishikyō** archbishop, cardinal
  (Catholic)
上司 **jōshi** one's superior(s)
4 公司 **kōshi, konsu** company, firm (in China)
6 行司 **gyōji** sumo referee
有司 **yūshi** the authorities, officials
7 寿司 **sushi** sushi (raw fish and other delicacies with vinegared rice)
社司 **shashi** Shinto priest
8 門司 **Moji** (city, Fukuoka-ken)
9 軍司令部 **gunshireibu** military headquarters
軍司令官 **gunshireikan** army commander
10 宮司 **gūji** chief priest of a Shinto shrine
11 祭司 **saishi** high priest
14 総司令 **sōshirei** general headquarters,
  supreme command

——————— 3 ———————
3 大宮司 **daigūji** high priest of a grand shrine
5 立行司 **ta(te)gyōji** head sumo referee
12 御曹司 **onzōshi** son of a distinguished family

——————— 4 ———————
14 稲荷寿司 **inarizushi** fried tofu stuffed with
  vinegared rice

3d2.15 / 76

右 **U, YŪ, migi** right

——————— 1 ———————
3 右大臣 **udaijin** Minister of the Right
右上 **migi ue** upper right
右下 **migi shita** lower right
4 右辺 **uhen** right side
右手 **migite** right hand
右方 **uhō** right side, the right
右心房 **ushinbō** the right auricle

右心室　**ushinshitsu** the right ventricle
5 右左　**migi-hidari** right and left
6 右回　**migimawa(ri)** clockwise
7 右折　**usetsu** turn right
右利　**migiki(ki)** righthanded; righthander
右足　**migiashi, usoku** right foot/leg
8 右表　**uhyō** the chart at the right
右往左往　**uō-saō** go hither and thither
右岸　**ugan** right bank/shore (as one faces
　　　　downstream)
9 右巻　**migima(ki)** clockwise
右派　**uha** rightists, the Right
10 右党　**utō** rightists, the Right
右書　**migiga(ki)** written from right to left
11 右側　**migigawa, usoku** right side
右寄　**migiyo(ri)** leaning to the right; rightist
右舷　**ugen** starboard
12 右腕　**uwan, migiude** right arm
13 右傾　**ukei** leaning to the right, rightist
14 右端　**utan** right edge/end
17 右翼　**uyoku** right wing, rightists; right flank
右翼団体　**uyoku dantai** right-wing group
21 右顧左眄　**uko-saben** look right and left;
　　　　vacillate, waver

——————— 2 ———————
5 左右　**sayū** left and right; control, dominate,
　　　　govern, influence
10 座右　**zayū** close at hand
座右銘　**zayū (no) mei** one's motto
12 極右　**kyokuu** ultraright
最右翼　**saiuyoku** ultraright

——————— 3 ———————
5 左顧右眄　**sako-uben** irresolution, vacillation
7 言左右託　**gen (o) sayū (ni) taku(suru)**
　　　　equivocate, be noncommittal

——————— 4 ———————
9 前後左右　**zengo-sayū** in all directions

——————— 3 ———————

3d3.1 / 1253

吐　**TO, ha(ku)** spew, spit out, vomit, throw
up, belch, emit; express, give vent to;
confess　**tsu(ku)** breathe; disgorge; tell
(a lie)

——————— 1 ———————
3 吐下　**ha(ki)kuda(shi)** vomiting and purging
5 吐出　**ha(ki)da(su)** vomit, disgorge, spew out
6 吐気　**ha(ki)ke** nausea
吐血　**toketsu** vomit blood
8 吐物　**tobutsu** vomit
10 吐剤　**tozai** an emetic
吐息　**toiki** sigh
18 吐瀉　**tosha** vomiting and diarrhea
吐瀉物　**toshabutsu** vomit and bowel discharge

21 吐露　**toro** express, voice, speak out

——————— 2 ———————
9 音吐　**onto** voice
音吐朗々　**onto-rōrō** in a clear/ringing voice
14 嘘吐　**usotsu(ki)** liar, fibber
嘔吐　**ōto** vomiting

——————— 3 ———————
8 青息吐息　**aoiki-toiki** in dire distress
10 弱音吐　**yowane (o) ha(ku)** complain, cry uncle

3d3.2

吁　**KU, U, ā** (exclamation)

3d3.3

吋　**TŌ, inchi** inch

3d3.4 / 1252

叫　叫叫　**KYŌ, sake(bu)** shout,
cry out

——————— 1 ———————
7 叫声　**sake(bi)goe** a shout, cry, scream
12 叫喚　**kyōkan** shout, shriek, scream

——————— 2 ———————
5 矢叫　**yasake(bi)** archers' shout (upon loosing
　　　　a volley of arrows)
号叫　**gōkyō** calling in a loud voice
8 泣叫　**na(ki)sake(bu)** scream, cry, shriek, wail
12 絶叫　**zekkyō** scream, cry out, shout
雄叫　**otake(bi), osake(bi)** courageous shout,
　　　　war cry, roar

——————— 3 ———————
7 阿鼻叫喚　**abikyōkan** (two of Buddhism's
　　　　eight hells)

3d3.5 / 1256

吸　**KYŪ, su(u)** suck; inhale; smoke
(cigarettes)

——————— 1 ———————
2 吸入　**kyūnyū** inhale
吸入器　**kyūnyūki** inhaler, respirator
3 吸上　**su(i)a(geru)** suck/pump up
吸口　**su(i)kuchi** cigarette holder, mouthpiece
　　　　(of a pipe)
4 吸収　**kyūshū** absorb
吸収性　**kyūshūsei** absorbency
吸収剤　**kyūshūzai** an absorbent
吸込　**su(i)ko(mu)** inhale; suck in; swallow up

3

氵
土
扌
口 3←
女
巾
犭
弓
彳
彡
艹
宀
⺍
山
⺌
广
尸
口

吸引 **kyūin** absorb; attract
5 吸出 **su(i)da(su)** suck/pump out
吸付 **su(i)tsu(keru)** attract; light (a cigarette) from (another); be used to smoking (a pipe) **su(i)tsu(ku)** cling/stick to
6 吸血 **kyūketsu** sucking blood
吸血鬼 **kyūketsuki** vampire
8 吸物 **su(i)mono** soup
吸取 **su(i)to(ru)** suck/blot up, absorb; extort
吸取紙 **su(i)to(ri)gami** blotting paper
11 吸殻 **su(i)gara** cigar(ette) butt
12 吸着 **kyūchaku** adsorb
吸飲 **kyūin** (opium) smoking
su(i)no(mi) feeding/spout cup
14 吸管 **kyūkan** suction pipe, siphon
15 吸盤 **kyūban** sucker (on an octopus)

————— 2 —————
7 肝吸 **kimosu(i)** eel liver soup
8 呼吸 **kokyū** breathing, respiration
呼吸音 **kokyūon** respiratory sound
呼吸器 **kokyūki** respiratory organs

————— 3 —————
11 深呼吸 **shinkokyū** deep breath(ing)

————— 4 —————
13 腹式呼吸 **fukushiki kokyū** abdominal breathing

3d3.6

吼

KU, KŌ, ho(eru) bark, bay, bellow, roar, howl, cry

————— 1 —————
7 吼声 **ho(e)goe** bark, yelp, howl, roar

————— 3 —————
13 獅子吼 **shishiku** lion's roar; impassioned speech

3d3.7

吃

KITSU stutter; eat, drink
domo(ru) stutter, stammer

————— 1 —————
4 吃水 **kissui** draft (of a ship)
吃水線 **kissuisen** waterline
8 吃逆 **kitsugyaku, shakkuri** hiccups
9 吃音 **kitsuon** stuttering, stammering
22 吃驚 **kikkyō, bikkuri** be surprised

3d3.8

吊

CHŌ, tsu(ru), tsuru(su) hang, suspend
tsuru(shi) ready-made/hand-me-down clothes

————— 1 —————
3 吊上 **tsu(ri)a(geru)** hang up, suspend, hoist
tsuru(shi)a(ge) kangaroo court
吊下 **tsu(ri)sa(garu)** hang, dangle, be suspended
4 吊天井 **tsu(ri)tenjō** suspended ceiling
5 吊出 **tsu(ri)da(su)** pull out (a fish); lure out
吊目 **tsu(ri)me** slant eyes
9 吊革 **tsu(ri)kawa** (hanging) strap
吊柿 **tsuru(shi)gaki** dried persimmons

————— 2 —————
9 首吊 **kubitsu(ri)** hang oneself

3d3.9 / 1259

舌

ZETSU, shita tongue

————— 1 —————
5 舌代 **zetsudai** notice, circular
舌打 **shitau(chi)** clicking one's tongue, tsk, tch
6 舌先 **shitasaki** tip of the tongue
舌先三寸 **shitasaki-sanzun** eloquence
7 舌状 **zetsujō** tongue-shaped
舌利 **shitaki(ki)** taster
舌足 **shitata(razu)** lisping, tongue-tied
8 舌長 **shitanaga** talkative
舌苔 **zettai** fur on the tongue
9 舌音 **zetsuon** lingual sound
10 舌舐 **shitana(mezuri)** licking one's lips
13 舌鼓打 **shitatsuzumi (o) u(tsu)** smack one's lips
舌禍 **zekka** unfortunate slip of the tongue
舌戦 **zessen** war of words
舌触 **shitazawa(ri)** texture (of food)
14 舌端 **zettan** tip of the tongue
15 舌鋒 **zeppō** tongue
16 舌縺 **shitamotsu(re)** lisp, speech impediment
舌頭 **zettō** tip of the tongue
17 舌癌 **zetsugan** cancer of the tongue

————— 2 —————
3 口舌 **kōzetsu** words, verbal (quarrel)
5 弁舌 **benzetsu** speech, eloquence
6 両舌 **ryōzetsu** sowing discord by saying different things to different people, double-dealing
百舌 **mozu** shrike, butcher-bird
8 毒舌 **dokuzetsu** stinging tongue, blistering remarks
9 巻舌 **ma(ki)jita** rolling one's tongue, trill
11 猫舌 **nekojita** aversion to hot foods
悪舌 **akuzetsu** evil tongue, gossip
12 筆舌 **hitsuzetsu** the pen and the tongue
15 鴃舌 **gekizetsu** barbarian jabbering/tongue
21 饒舌 **jōzetsu** garrulous, talkative

饒舌家 **jōzetsuka** chatterbox

─────── **3** ───────

2 二枚舌 **nimaijita** forked tongue, duplicity
3 三寸舌 **sanzun (no) shita** eloquent tongue
8 長広舌 **chōkōzetsu** loquacity, long(-winded) talk

3d3.10 / 199

向 **KŌ, mu(kau)** face toward; proceed to
mu(ku/keru) (intr./tr.) turn toward
mu(kō) opposite side; the next (three years)

─────── **1** ───────

3 向上 **kōjō** improvement, advancement
4 向日性 **kōjitsusei, kōnichisei** heliotropic
6 向合 **mu(kai)a(u)** face each other
7 向学心 **kōgakushin** love of learning
　向見 **mu(kō)mi(zu)** rash, reckless, headlong
9 向風 **mu(kai)kaze** headwind
11 向側 **mu(kō)gawa** the opposite side, across from
13 向鉢巻 **mu(kō) hachimaki** rolled towel tied around the head

─────── **2** ───────

1 一向 **ikkō** (not) at all
3 刃向 **hamu(kau)** strike at; turn on, rise against, oppose, defy
　上向 **uwamu(ku)** look/turn upward, rise
　下向 **shitamu(ki)** downward look; downturn, decline
4 不向 **fumu(ki)** unsuitable, unfit
　内向性 **naikōsei** introverted
　手向 **temu(kau)** raise one's hand against, resist, oppose　**tamu(ke)** offering (to gods and Buddha); parting/farewell gift　**tamu(keru)** offer, pay tribute (to the dead)
　日向 **hinata(bokko)** bask in the sun　**Hyūga** (ancient kuni, Miyazaki-ken)
　日向水 **hinatamizu** sun-warmed water
　方向 **hōkō** direction
　方向板 **hōkōban** (train's) destination sign
5 北向 **kitamu(ki)** facing north
　出向 **demu(ku)** go to, leave for, repair to　**shukkō** repair to; be on loan (to a subsidiary), be seconded (to another company), temporary transfer
　出向社員 **shukkō shain** employee on loan to a subsidiary/another company
　仕向 **shimu(keru)** treat, act toward; dispatch
　外向 **gaikō** extroverted, outgoing
　外向性 **gaikōsei** extroverted, outgoing
　外向型 **gaikōgata** outgoing type, extrovert
　用向 **yōmu(ki)** business, errand
　打向 **u(chi)mu(kau)** face, confront; proceed to

冬向 **fuyumu(ki)** for winter
立向 **ta(chi)mu(kau)** face, stand against; head for
6 西向 **nishimu(ki)** facing west
　仰向 **aomu(keru)** turn to face upward
　回向 **ekō** a memorial service
7 志向 **shikō** intention, inclination
　見向 **mimu(ku)** look around/toward
　男向 **otokomu(ki)** for men
8 東向 **higashimu(ki)** facing east
　若向 **wakamu(ki)** intended for the young
　性向 **seikō** inclination, propensity
9 発向 **hakkō** departure
　俗向 **zokumu(ki)** popular (literature)
　南向 **minamimu(ki)** facing south
　前向 **maemu(ki)** forward-looking
　風向 **fūkō** wind direction　**kazemu(ki), kazamu(ki)** wind direction; situation
　指向 **shikō** directional (antenna)
　指向性 **shikōsei** directional (antenna)
　後向 **ushi(ro)mu(ki)** facing backward
　面向不背 **menkō-fuhai** beautiful from every angle, flawless
　背向 **haikō** turn one's back; turning toward and turning away, obedience and disobedience　**se (o) mu(keru)** turn one's back on
10 俯向 **utsumu(keru)** turn upside down, turn downward　**utsumu(ku)** look downward
　帰向 **kikō** hearken back to
　真向 **mamuka(i)** just opposite, right across from, face to face　**ma(k)kō** forehead; front
　差向 **sa(shi)mu(keru)** send around; point (a light) toward　**sa(shi)muka(i)** face to face
　振向 **fu(ri)mu(ku)** turn toward, look back
　夏向 **natsumu(ki)** for summer
11 偏向 **henkō** leanings, deviation; deflection
　動向 **dōkō** trend, attitude
　捩向 **ne(ji)mu(keru)** twist toward
　転向 **tenkō** turn/switch to, convert
　転向点 **tenkōten** turning point
12 筋向 **sujimu(kai)** diagonally opposite
13 傾向 **keikō** tendency, trend; inclination, leanings
　意向 **ikō** intention, inclination
　誂向 **atsura(e)mu(ki)** suitable, made to order
14 暮向 **ku(rashi)mu(ki)** circumstances, livelihood
15 横向 **yokomu(ki)** facing sidewise
　趣向 **shukō** plan, idea
17 趨向 **sūkō** trend, tendency
18 顔向 **kaomu(ke)** show one's face

─────── **3** ───────

2 子供向 **kodomomu(ki)** for children

3 万人向 **banninmu(ki)** for everyone, suiting all tastes
　大衆向 **taishūmu(ki)** for the general public, popular
10 陰日向 **kage-hinata** light and shade
12 勝手向 **kattemu(ki)** one's financial circumstances
13 新趣向 **shinshukō** new idea/contrivance

向 → 問 8e3.1

3d3.11 / 1119

后
KŌ empress
GO after
kisaki empress, queen

——————— 1 ———————
6 后妃 **kōhi** empress, queen

——————— 2 ———————
4 太后 **taikō** empress dowager, queen mother
5 母后 **bokō** empress dowager
9 皇后 **kōgō** empress, queen
　皇后陛下 **Kōgō Heika** Her Majesty the Empress

——————— 3 ———————
9 皇太后 **kōtaikō, kōtaigō** empress dowager, queen mother

3d3.12 / 82

名
MEI, MYŌ, na name; reputation, fame

——————— 1 ———————
0 名づける **na(zukeru)** name, call
　名うて **na(ute)** notorious
2 名人 **meijin** master, expert, virtuoso
　名人肌 **meijinhada** artist's temperamentalness
　名人芸 **meijingei** virtuosity
　名刀 **meitō** famed sword, fine blade
3 名工 **meikō** master craftsman
　名山 **meizan** famous mountain
　名士 **meishi** prominent figure, celebrity
4 名文 **meibun** excellent composition, fine prose
　名文句 **meimonku** fine expression, famous words
　名文家 **meibunka** fine writer
　名分 **meibun** moral duty; justice
　名手 **meishu** expert
　名木 **meiboku** historic tree; fine (incense) wood
　名月 **meigetsu** bright/full moon; moon on the 15th day of the 8th lunar month or the 13th day of the 9th lunar month
5 名代 **myōdai** proxy, deputy, representative
　　　 nadai well-known
　名付 **nazu(ke)** naming; fiancé(e)
　　　 nazu(keru) name, call, entitle
　名付主 **nazu(ke)nushi** person who names the newborn, godparent
　名付祝 **nazu(ke) iwa(i)** naming ceremony, christening
　名付親 **nazu(ke) oya** godparent
　名古屋 **Nagoya** (city, Aichi-ken)
　名号 **myōgō** Buddha's name
　名句 **meiku** well-put/famous phrase; noted haiku
　名字 **myōji** surname
　名札 **nafuda** name plate/tag
　名主 **nanushi** (ancient) village headman
　　　 na(zuke)nushi person who names the newborn, godparent
　名目 **meimoku** name, pretext; nominal, ostensible
6 名曲 **meikyoku** famous music
　名匠 **meishō** master artisan
7 名作 **meisaku** literary masterpiece
　名状 **meijō** describe
　名医 **meii** famous doctor, skilled physician
　名吟 **meigin** exquisite poem
　名君 **meikun** wise ruler
　名妓 **meigi** famous geisha
　名花 **meika** famous flower
　名声 **meisei** fame, reputation
　名利 **meiri** fame and wealth
　名利心 **meirishin** worldly ambition
　名言 **meigen** wise saying, apt remark
　名言集 **meigenshū** analects
8 名画 **meiga** famous picture, masterpiece
　名刺 **meishi** business card
　名刺入 **meishii(re)** card case
　名刹 **meisatsu** famous temple
　名実 **meijitsu** name and reality
　名実共 **meijitsu tomo (ni)** in fact as well as in name
　名宛 **naate** address (on an envelope)
　名宛人 **naatenin** addressee
　名物 **meibutsu** noted product (of a locality)
　名所 **meisho** noted places/sights
　名所旧跡 **meisho-kyūseki** scenic and historic places
　名取 **nato(ri)** one who has been given a professional name (in the arts) by one's teacher
　名門 **meimon** prestigious family/school
9 名乗 **nano(ru)** call oneself, profess to be
　名前 **namae** name
　名城 **meijō** famous/excellent castle
　名指 **naza(shi)** calling/specifying by name

名品 **meihin** fine article, gem, masterpiece
名香 **meikō** fine incense
10 名残 **nago(ri)** farewell; remembrance, keepsake; relics, vestiges
名残惜 **nago(ri)o(shii)** reluctant to part
名将 **meishō** famous commander
名高 **nadaka(i)** famous, renowned
名流 **meiryū** notables, celebrities
名家 **meika** distinguished family; a celebrity
名案 **meian** splendid idea, good plan
名称 **meishō** name, title, term, appellation
名馬 **meiba** fine horse/steed
11 名著 **meicho** famous work, great book
名寄 **nayo(se)** compilation of names of similar things/places/persons; listing of all one's accounts
名望 **meibō** reputation, popularity
名望家 **meibōka** person who is highly esteemed
名産 **meisan** noted product, specialty
名訳 **meiyaku** excellent translation
12 名勝 **meishō** scenic spot
名無 **nana(shi)** nameless, anonymous, unknown
名筆 **meihitsu** excellent calligraphy
名答 **meitō** excellent/apt answer
名詞 **meishi** noun
13 名僧 **meisō** famous priest
名義 **meigi** name; moral duty
名義上 **meigijō** nominal, titular
名誉 **meiyo** honor, glory, fame, prestige
名誉心 **meiyoshin** desire for fame
名誉教授 **meiyo kyōju** professor emeritus
名誉欲 **meiyoyoku** desire for fame
名誉職 **meiyoshoku** honary post
名数 **meisū** number of persons; a compound which includes a number
名辞 **meiji** term, name
名跡 **myōseki, meiseki** family name
14 名歌 **meika** famous/excellent poem
名歌集 **meikashū** poetry anthology
名聞 **meibun** fame, honor
15 名器 **meiki** exquisite/famous article/instrument
名編 **meihen** literary masterpiece
名論 **meiron** excellent opinion, sound argument
名調子 **meichōshi** eloquence
16 名薬 **meiyaku** famous medicine
17 名優 **meiyū** great actor, star
18 名題 **nadai** chief actor, star; title of a play
19 名簿 **meibo** name list, roster, roll
23 名鑑 **meikan** directory

───────── 2 ─────────

1 一名 **ichimei** one person; another name
2 人名 **jinmei** person's name

人名録 **jinmeiroku** name list, directory
人名簿 **jinmeibo** name list, directory
3 大名 **daimyō** feudal lord, daimyo
taimyō renown
大名旅行 **daimyō ryokō** spendthrift tour, junket
大名領 **daimyōryō** fief
下名 **kamei** the undermentioned/undersigned
4 不名誉 **fumeiyo** dishonor, disgrace
氏名 **shimei** surname and given name, (full) name
仏名 **butsumyō** a Buddha's name
5 本名 **honmyō, honmei** one's real name
失名 **shitsumei** nameless, anonymous
失名氏 **shitsumeishi** unknown/anonymous person
代名詞 **daimeishi** pronoun
令名 **reimei** fame, reputation, renown
功名 **kōmyō, kōmei** great achievement
功名心 **kōmyōshin** ambition, love of fame
幼名 **yōmei, yōmyō** one's childhood/infant name
6 仮名 **kana** kana, Japanese syllabary character
kamei, kemyō, karina pseudonym, alias, pen name
仮名草紙 **kanazōshi** story book written in kana
仮名遣 **kanazuka(i)** kana orthography
合名会社 **gōmei-gaisha** unlimited partnership
同名 **dōmei** the same name
同名異人 **dōmei-ijin** different person of the same name
汚名 **omei** blot on one's name, stigma, dishonor
地名 **chimei** place name
有名 **yūmei** famous
有名人 **yūmeijin** celebrity
有名無実 **yūmei-mujitsu** in name only
有名税 **yūmeizei** a penalty of greatness, noblesse oblige
7 別名 **betsumei** another name, alias, pseudonym
豆名月 **mame meigetsu** moon on the 13th day of the 9th lunar month
役名 **yakumei** official title
芳名 **hōmei** good name/reputation, your name
芳名録 **hōmeiroku** visitor's book, name list
芸名 **geimei** stage/professional name
学名 **gakumei** scientific name
売名 **baimei** self-advertising, publicity seeking
局名 **kyokumei** name of a radio/TV station, call letters
社名 **shamei** company name
改名 **kaimei** changing one's/the name
戒名 **kaimyō** Buddhist initiation/posthumous name

3

氵 土 扌 日 女 巾 犭 弓 彳 彡 艹 宀 爫 山 土 广 尸 口

→3

町名 **chōmei** town/street name
8 命名 **meimei** name, christen, call
法名 **hōmyō** (priest's or deceased's) Buddhist name
呼名 **yo(bi)na** one's given/popular name
知名 **chimei** noted, well-known
姓名 **seimei** name (surname and given name)
英名 **eimei** fame, glory, renown
実名 **jitsumei** one's real name
官名 **kanmei** official title
宛名 **atena** address
空名 **kūmei** in name only; false reputation
国名 **kokumei** name of a country
武名 **bumei** military renown
和名 **wamyō** Japanese name (of a Chinese)
　　 wamei Japanese name (of a plant/animal)
9 俗名 **zokumei** common name; secular name
　　 zokumyō secular name
除名 **jomei** expel, drop from membership
変名 **henmei, henmyō** assumed name, alias
美名 **bimei** good/reputable name
連名 **renmei** joint signature
通名 **tō(ri)na** popular name, commonly known as
浮名 **u(ki)na** love affair, scandal, rumor
指名 **shimei** nominate, designate
指名者 **shimeisha** nominator, designator
威名 **imei** renown, prestige
音名 **onmei** name of a musical note
10 俳名 **haimei** haiku poet's pen name
高名 **kōmyō** fame, renown; your name
　　 kōmei fame, renown
匿名 **tokumei** anonymous
徒名 **adana** rumor about a romance
家名 **kamei, kamyō, iena** family name/honor
書名 **shomei** (book) title
称名 **shōmyō** chanting "Hail Amida"
病名 **byōmei** name of the disease
記名 **kimei** register/sign one's name
11 偽名 **gimei** assumed name, alias
動名詞 **dōmeishi** gerund
虚名 **kyomei** false reputation, publicity
唯名論 **yuimeiron** nominalism
唱名 **shōmyō** chanting Buddha's name
著名 **chomei** prominent, well-known
悪名 **akumei, akumyō** ill repute, notoriety
異名 **imyō, imei** another name, nickname, alias
盛名 **seimei** renown, fame
12 渾名 **adana** nickname
御名 **mina** (God's) name
　　 gyomei emperor's name/signature
御名御璽 **gyomei-gyoji** imperial/privy seal
属名 **zokumei** generic name
勝名乗 **ka(chi)nano(ri)** be declared winner
無名 **mumei** anonymous; an unknown

無名氏 **mumeishi** anonymous person
無名指 **mumeishi** the ring finger
無名戦士 **mumei senshi** unknown soldier
筆名 **hitsumei** pen name, pseudonym
13 漢名 **kanmei, kanmyō** Chinese name
数名 **sūmei** several persons
署名 **shomei** signature
署名国 **shomeikoku** signatory (country)
署名捺印 **shomei-natsuin** signature and seal
罪名 **zaimei** name of the crime, the charge
賊名 **zokumei** (branded as a) rebel/traitor
雅名 **gamei** pen name; refined name for
雷名 **raimei** illustrious name
14 種名 **shumei** species name
綽名 **adana** nickname
15 嬌名 **kyōmei** reputation for beauty
17 醜名 **shūmei** notoriety, scandal　**shikona** sumo wrestler's professional name
18 類名 **ruimei** generic name
題名 **daimei** title
22 襲名 **shūmei** succeed to another's (stage) name

──────── 3 ────────

3 大義名分 **taigi-meibun** proper relationship between sovereign and subjects; justification, just cause
4 片仮名 **katakana** katakana, the non-cursive syllabary
5 平仮名 **hiragana** (the cursive syllabary)
8 送仮名 **oku(ri)gana** suffixed kana showing inflection
固有名詞 **koyū meishi** proper noun
9 洗礼名 **senreimei** baptismal/Christian name
草仮名 **sōgana** hiragana
10 泰西名画 **taisei meiga** famous Western painting
振仮名 **fu(ri)gana** (small kana written above or beside a kanji to show its pronunciation)
12 無記名 **mukimei** uninscribed (shares), unregistered (bond), blank (endorsement)
集合名詞 **shūgō meishi** collective noun

──────── 4 ────────

3 万葉仮名 **man'yōgana** kanji used phonetically
5 外様大名 **tozama daimyō** non-Tokugawa daimyo
9 変体仮名 **hentai-gana** anomalous (obsolete) kana
14 疑問代名詞 **gimon daimeishi** interrogative pronoun
関係代名詞 **kankei daimeishi** relative pronoun
19 譜代大名 **fudai daimyō** hereditary daimyo

―――――― 4 ――――――

3d4.1

吠

BEI, HAI, ho(eru) bark, bay, bellow, roar, howl, cry

―――――― 1 ――――――

7 吠陀 **Bēda** the Vedas
　吠声 **ho(e)goe** bark, yelp, howl, roar
9 吠面 **ho(e)zura** tearful face

―――――― 2 ――――――

12 遠吠 **tōbo(e)** howling

3d4.2

吽

KŌ, GŌ bark, growl

3d4.3 / 1255

吹

SUI, fu(ku) blow (tr. or intr.); smelt, mint; brag

―――――― 1 ――――――

3 吹上 **fu(ki)a(geru)** blow up(ward); wash (ashore)
　吹下 **fu(ki)o(rosu)** blow down(ward)
4 吹込 **fu(ki)ko(mu)** blow in; record (a song); inspire
　吹手 **fu(ki)te** braggart
5 吹矢 **fu(ki)ya** blowgun, dart
　吹出 **fu(ki)da(su)** begin to blow; breathe out; burst out laughing
　吹出物 **fu(ki)demono** skin rash, pimple
　吹付 **fu(ki)tsu(keru)** blow against
　吹去 **fu(ki)sa(ru)** blow away (intr.)
　吹払 **fu(ki)hara(u)** blow away (tr.)
7 吹抜 **fu(ki)nu(ku)** blow through/over
　　　 fu(ki)nu(ki) ventilation, draft; streamer, pennant
8 吹直 **fu(ki)nao(shi)** smelting, recoinage
　吹送 **fu(ki)oku(ru)** waft, blow over to
9 吹飛 **fu(ki)to(basu)** blow away
　吹奏 **suisō** blow/play (a flute)
　吹奏者 **suisōsha** wind-instrument player
　吹奏楽 **suisōgaku** wind-instrument music, brass
　吹通 **fu(ki)tō(su)** blow through; keep blowing
　吹荒 **fu(ki)a(reru), fu(ki)susa(bu)** blow violently, rage
10 吹倒 **fu(ki)tao(su)** blow down
　吹流 **fu(ki)naga(su)** blow away, blow off course **fu(ki)naga(shi)** streamer, pennant
　吹消 **fu(ki)ke(su)** blow out (a candle)

吹起 **fu(ki)oko(su)** blow up (a wind), fan (flames)
吹晒 **fu(ki)sara(shi)** exposed to the wind, wind-swept
11 吹掛 **fu(ki)ka(keru)** blow/spray on
　　　 fu(k)ka(keru) blow/spray on; provoke, pick (a fight); ask too much, overcharge
　吹捲 **fu(ki)maku(ru)** sweep along, blow about
　吹寄 **fu(ki)yo(seru)** drift, blow together
　吹雪 **fubuki** snowstorm, blizzard
12 吹渡 **fu(ki)wata(ru)** blow over
　吹落 **fu(ki)o(tosu)** blow down/off
　吹募 **fu(ki)tsuno(ru)** blow harder
　吹替 **fu(ki)ka(e)** substitute actor, stand-in; dubbing; recasting, reminting
　吹散 **fu(ki)chi(rasu)** scatter, blow about
14 吹鳴 **fu(ki)na(rasu)** blow (a whistle)
17 吹聴 **fuichō** publicize, trumpet, herald
19 吹曝 **fu(ki)sara(shi)** exposed to the wind, wind-swept

―――――― 2 ――――――

3 山吹 **yamabuki** yellow rose
　山吹色 **yamabuki-iro** orangish/golden yellow
4 火吹竹 **hifu(ki)dake** bamboo blowpipe (for charcoal fires)
7 花吹雪 **hanafubuki** falling cherry blossoms
10 息吹 **ibu(ki)** breath
11 笛吹 **fuefu(ki)** flute/fife/clarinet player
13 鼓吹 **kosui** inspire, instill
　鼓吹者 **kosuisha** advocate, propagator
15 潮吹 **shiofu(ki)** spouting of a whale; (a thin-shelled surf clam)
19 霧吹 **kirifu(ki)** sprayer, atomizer, vaporizer

―――――― 3 ――――――

1 一泡吹 **hitoawa fu(kaseru)** confound, upset (someone's plans)
8 法螺吹 **horafu(ki)** boaster, braggart

―――――― 4 ――――――

3 大尽風吹 **daijinkaze (o) fu(kasu)** display one's wealth

3d4.4

呀

GA open one's mouth, bare one's teeth; empty

3d4.5

呐

TOTSU stutter, stammer; shout

―――――― 1 ――――――

3 呐々 **totsu-totsu** falteringly
12 呐喊 **tokkan** yell a battle cry

叴 → 叫 **3d3.4**

3d4.6

吻 **FUN** snout, lips

――――― 1 ―――――
6 吻合 **fungō** coincidence; inosculation

――――― 2 ―――――
3 口吻 **kōfun** way of speaking
11 接吻 **seppun** kiss

3d4.7

听 **KIN** open-mouthed (laughter); listen to
pondo pound (the British unit of weight)

3d4.8 / 1250

吟 **GIN** sing, chant, recite

――――― 1 ―――――
0 吟じる **gin(jiru)** sing, chant, recite
8 吟味 **ginmi** close inquiry, scrutiny
10 吟遊詩人 **gin'yū shijin** troubadour, minstrel
11 吟唱 **ginshō** recite, chant
12 吟詠 **gin'ei** sing, recite; (compose a) poem
14 吟誦 **ginshō** recite, chant

――――― 2 ―――――
6 再吟味 **saiginmi** re-examine, review
　名吟 **meigin** exquisite poem
7 低吟 **teigin** sing in a low voice, hum
　即吟 **sokugin** improvisation, impromptu poem
　沈吟 **chingin** hum; meditate, muse
　秀吟 **shūgin** excellent poem
8 呻吟 **shingin** groan, moan
　苦吟 **kugin** laboriously compose (a poem)
9 連吟 **rengin** duet, singing by two or more
　独吟 **dokugin** vocal solo
10 高吟 **kōgin** recite (a poem) aloud
　遊吟 **yūgin** itinerant singing and reciting
　朗吟 **rōgin** recite, sing
12 詠吟 **eigin** reciting poetry
13 愛吟 **aigin** favorite poem; love to recite
　感吟 **kangin** reciting with emotion
　詩吟 **shigin** reciting Chinese poems

――――― 4 ―――――
8 放歌高吟 **hōka-kōgin** loud singing

3d4.9

吭 **KŌ** throat, neck; pivot

3d4.10

吩 **FUN** give an order; spout forth

3d4.11

吮 **SEN, su(u)** suck

――――― 1 ―――――
23 吮癰舐痔 **sen'yō shiji** sucking the pus from
someone's carbuncles and licking his
hemorrhoids (to curry favor)

3d4.12

呎 **fīto** feet, foot (the British unit of length,
about 30.5 cm)

3d4.13

呆 **HŌ** stupid　**BŌ, aki(reru)** be amazed/
astonished/appalled/aghast/shocked

――――― 1 ―――――
6 呆気 **akke** blank amazement
　呆気無 **akkena(i)** unsatisfying, not enough
　呆返 **aki(re)ka(eru)** be flabbergasted
8 呆果 **aki(re)ha(teru)** be astonished
12 呆然 **bōzen (to)** in blank amazement
18 呆顔 **aki(re)gao** amazed/dazed look

7 阿呆 **ahō** fool, jackass
　阿呆臭 **ahōkusa(i)** foolish, dumb, stupid
13 痴呆 **chihō** dementia; imbecility

――――― 5 ―――――
6 早発性痴呆症 **sōhatsusei chihōshō** schizophrenia

3d4.14 / 1590

呈 **TEI** offer, present, exhibit

――――― 1 ―――――
0 呈する **tei(suru)** offer, present, exhibit
3 呈上 **teijō** present, offer
5 呈示 **teiji** present, bring up
6 呈色 **teishoku** coloration

――――― 2 ―――――
8 送呈 **sōtei** send as a present
　拝呈 **haitei** presentation
10 進呈 **shintei** give, present
　進呈本 **shinteihon** complimentary copy

(margin left column)
3

氵
扌
口 →4
女
巾
犭
弓
彳
彡
艹
宀
屵
屮
广
尸
口

進呈者 **shinteisha** presenter
11 捧呈 **hōtei** present, offer, submit
13 献呈 **kentei** presentation (copy)
17 謹呈 **kintei** Respectfully presented, With the compliments of the author
18 贈呈 **zōtei** presentation, gift
　贈呈本 **zōteihon** presentation copy
　贈呈式 **zōteishiki** presentation ceremony
　贈呈者 **zōteisha** giver, donor
　贈呈品 **zōteihin** present, gift
21 露呈 **rotei** exposure, disclosure

3d4.15

邑　**YŪ** village, town; territory, dominion

品 → 品　3d6.15

吳 → 呉　2o5.7

足 →　　7d0.1

呉 →　　2o5.7

3d4.16

呂　**RO, RYO** backbone; tone

——————— 1 ———————
9 呂律 **roretsu** articulation, pronunciation
——————— 2 ———————
6 伊呂波 **i-ro-ha** the Japanese alphabet; ABC's, rudiments
9 風呂 **furo** bath; bathtub
　風呂屋 **furoya** bathhouse, public bath
　風呂桶 **furooke** bathtub
　風呂場 **furoba** bathroom
　風呂敷 **furoshiki** (square of cloth used to wrap goods and presents in)
　風呂銭 **furosen** bath charge
　律呂 **ritsuryo** rhythm and pitch
14 語呂 **goro** the sound, euphony
　語呂合 **goroa(wase)** play on words, pun
——————— 3 ———————
4 水風呂 **mizuburo** cold bath
9 砂風呂 **sunaburo** sand bath

11 据風呂 **su(e)furo** bathtub with water heater
12 蒸風呂 **mu(shi)buro** Turkish bath, sauna
　朝風呂 **asaburo** morning bath

3d4.17

吾　**GO, waga** my, our, one's own
　　ware I, oneself

——————— 1 ———————
2 吾人 **gojin** we
4 吾木紅 **waremokō** burnet (a flowering herb)
6 吾亦紅 **waremokō** burnet (a flowering herb)
15 吾輩 **wagahai** I, me

3d4.18 / 690

告　**KOKU, tsu(geru)** tell, announce, inform

——————— 1 ———————
3 告口 **tsu(ge)guchi** tell on, snitch, tattle
4 告文 **kokubun** written appeal of a case
　　　kōmon imperial proclamation
5 告白 **kokuhaku** confession
　告示 **kokuji** notification
　告示板 **kokujiban** bulletin board
7 告別 **kokubetsu** leave-taking, farewell
　告別式 **kokubetsushiki** funeral service
8 告知 **kokuchi** notice, announcement
　告知板 **kokuchiban** bulletin board
9 告発 **kokuhatsu** prosecution, indictment, accusation
　告発状 **kokuhatsujō** bill of indictment
　告発者 **kokuhatsusha** prosecutor, accuser, informant
12 告訴 **kokuso** accuse, charge, bring suit
　告訴人 **kokusonin** complainant
13 告辞 **kokuji** (farewell) address
16 告諭 **kokuyu** official notice, proclamation
——————— 2 ———————
3 上告 **jōkoku** appeal (to a higher court)
4 予告 **yokoku** advance notice; (movie) preview
　公告 **kōkoku** public notice
5 申告 **shinkoku** report, declaration, notification, filing
　布告 **fukoku** proclaim, declare, promulgate
　広告 **kōkoku** advertisement
　広告灯 **kōkokutō** advertising lights
　広告社 **kōkokusha** advertising agency
　広告取 **kōkokuto(ri)** advertising canvasser
　広告屋 **kōkokuya** ad agency; publicity man
　広告部 **kōkokubu** publicity department
　広告料 **kōkokuryō** advertising rates
　広告業 **kōkokugyō** advertising business
　広告欄 **kōkokuran** advertising columns, want ads

7 抗告 **kōkoku** appeal, protest, complaint
社告 **shakoku** public announcement (by a company)
戒告 **kaikoku** warning, admonition
8 忠告 **chūkoku** advice, admonition
9 急告 **kyūkoku** urgent notice
通告 **tsūkoku** notification, notice
宣告 **senkoku** sentence, verdict, pronouncement
訃告 **fukoku** obituary, death notice
10 原告 **genkoku** plaintiff
被告 **hikoku** defendant
被告人 **hikokunin** defendant
被告席 **hikokuseki** defendant's chair, the dock
11 密告 **mikkoku** secret information
密告者 **mikkokusha** informer, betrayer
12 報告 **hōkoku** report
報告者 **hōkokusha** reporter, informer
報告書 **hōkokusho** (written) report/statement
御告 **mitsuge, otsuge** oracle, divine message
無告 **mukoku** with nowhere to turn to, helpless
13 催告 **saikoku** notification, admonition
勧告 **kankoku** recommendation, advice
稟告 **rinkoku** notice, notification
14 誣告 **bukoku, fukoku** false charge, libel
誡告 **kaikoku** warning, caution
15 論告 **ronkoku** prosecutor's summation
16 親告 **shinkoku** personal statement/accusation
親告罪 **shinkokuzai** offense subject to prosecution only upon complaint (e.g., defamation)
諭告 **yukoku** counsel, admonition
17 謹告 **kinkoku** respectfully inform
19 警告 **keikoku** warning, admonition

––––––– 3 –––––––
9 信仰告白 **shinkō kokuhaku** profession of faith
12 無警告 **mukeikoku** without warning

––––––– 4 –––––––
3 三行広告欄 **sangyō kōkokuran** classified ads
6 刑事被告 **keiji hikoku** the accused, defendant
7 求人広告 **kyūjin kōkoku** help-wanted ad
決算報告 **kessan hōkoku** closing-of-accounts report, financial statement
9 宣戦布告 **sensen fukoku** declaration of war

3d4.19
呑 **DON, no(mu)** drink

––––––– 1 –––––––
3 呑口 **no(mi)guchi** bung hole, tap, spigot
4 呑込 **no(mi)ko(mu)** swallow; understand
6 呑気 **nonki** easygoing, free and easy, optimistic
呑気者 **nonkimono** happy-go-lucky person
7 呑兵衛 **no(n)bē** heavy drinker

––––––– 2 –––––––
1 一呑 **hitono(mi)** drinking at one draft/gulp
3 丸呑 **maruno(mi)** swallowing whole
4 水呑百姓 **mizuno(mi)-byakushō** poor farmer
6 早呑込 **hayano(mi)ko(mi)** hasty conclusion
7 乳呑子 **chinomigo** suckling child, infant
乳呑児 **chinomigo** nursing baby, unweaned child
8 併呑 **heidon** annexation, absorption
10 剣呑 **kennon** dangerous, risky
酒呑 **sakeno(mi)** drinker
12 湯呑 **yuno(mi)** teacup
18 鵜呑 **uno(mi)** swallow whole

3d4.20 / 1248
否 **HI** no, negative **ina** no, nay
ina(mu) refuse, decline; deny
ina(ya) as soon as, no sooner than; yes or no; objection; if, whether
iya no, nay; yes, well

––––––– 1 –––––––
3 否々 **iya-iya** grudgingly; by no means
7 否決 **hiketsu** rejection, voting down
否応 **iyaō** agreement or disagreement
否応無 **iyaōna(shi)** whether one likes it or not
8 否定 **hitei** denial, negation
否定文 **hiteibun** negative sentence
否定的 **hiteiteki** negative, contradictory
14 否認 **hinin** deny, repudiate

––––––– 2 –––––––
5 存否 **sonpi** existence, whether alive or dead
正否 **seihi** right and wrong
可否 **kahi** right or wrong, pro and con
6 安否 **anpi** whether safe or not, well-being
当否 **tōhi** right or wrong; propriety, suitability
成否 **seihi** success or failure
7 良否 **ryōhi** (whether) good or bad
否否 **iya-iya** grudgingly; by no means
8 拒否 **kyohi** refusal, rejection, denial
拒否権 **kyohiken** (right of) veto
実否 **jippi** fact or falsehood, the truth/facts
10 真否 **shinpi** true or false
11 運否天賦 **unpu-tenpu** trusting to chance
採否 **saihi** adoption or rejection
許否 **kyohi** approval or disapproval
13 適否 **tekihi** propriety, fitness, aptitude
14 認否 **ninpi** approval or disapproval

15 諾否 **dakuhi** acceptance or refusal, definite reply

賛否 **sanpi** approval or disapproval

———————— 3 ————————

2 二重否定 **nijū hitei** double negative

 2o5.3

3d4.21 / 689

乱 亂

RAN disorder; riot, rebellion
mida(su) put in disorder
mida(reru) be in disorder, be confused/disorganized

———————— 1 ————————

2 乱入 **rannyū** intrusion

乱入者 **rannyūsha** intruder, trespasser

乱丁 **ranchō** mixed-up collation/pagination

4 乱反射 **ranhansha** diffused reflection

乱心 **ranshin** derangement, insanity

5 乱民 **ranmin** insurgents, rioters, mob

乱世 **ransei** tumultuous times

乱用 **ran'yō** misuse, abuse, misappropriation

乱打 **randa** pommeling, battering

乱立 **ranritsu** profusion/flood (of candidates)

6 乱伐 **ranbatsu** indiscriminate deforestation

乱交 **rankō** orgy

乱行 **rangyō** immoral conduct, debauchery

7 乱臣 **ranshin** traitorous vassal, traitor

乱売 **ranbai** selling at a loss, dumping

乱足 **mida(re)ashi** out of step

8 乱国 **rangoku** troubled/strife-torn country

乱杭 **rangui** palisade

乱杭歯 **ranguiba** irregular teeth

9 乱発 **ranpatsu** random/reckless shooting

乱軍 **rangun** melee, free-for-all fight

乱造 **ranzō** overproduction; careless manufacture

10 乱射 **ransha** random shooting

乱射乱撃 **ransha-rangeki** random shooting

乱倫 **ranrin** immorality

乱酒 **ranshu** drunken frenzy, vicious when drunk

乱流 **ranryū** turbulence

乱脈 **ranmyaku** chaotic

11 乱麻 **ranma** chaos, anarchy

乱視 **ranshi** astigmatism

乱酔 **ransui** dead drunk

12 乱筆 **ranpitsu** hasty writing, scrawl

乱費 **ranpi** waste, extravagance

乱雲 **ran'un** nimbus/rain clouds

13 乱戦 **ransen** melee, free-for-all fight

乱痴気騒 **ranchiki sawa(gi)** boisterous merrymaking, spree

14 乱髪 **ranpatsu, mida(re)gami** disheveled hair

乱読 **randoku** indiscriminate reading

乱雑 **ranzatsu** disorder, confusion

15 乱舞 **ranbu** boisterous dance

乱撃 **rangeki** random shooting

乱暴 **ranbō** violence; rough, reckless

乱暴者 **ranbōmono** rowdy, vandal

乱箱 **mida(re)bako** lidless box for clothes

乱調 **ranchō** discord, disorder, confusion; wild (market) fluctuations

乱調子 **ranchōshi** discord, disorder, confusion; wild (market) fluctuations

16 乱獲 **rankaku** indiscriminate fishing/hunting

18 乱闘 **rantō** melee, free-for-all fight

22 乱籠 **mida(re)kago** clothes basket

———————— 2 ————————

3 大乱 **tairan** serious disturbance, rebellion

4 内乱 **nairan** civil war, rebellion

反乱 **hanran** rebellion, revolt

反乱者 **hanransha** rebel, insurgents

6 争乱 **sōran** rioting, disturbance

7 狂乱 **kyōran** frenzy, madness

8 治乱 **chiran** war and/or peace

国乱 **kokuran** civil strife

取乱 **to(ri)mida(su)** disarrange, mess up; be agitated/perturbed

9 叛乱 **hanran** rebellion, revolt

咲乱 **sa(ki)mida(reru)** bloom in profusion

胡乱 **uron** suspicious, questionable

思乱 **omo(i)mida(reru)** be distracted with the thought of

10 紊乱 **binran, bunran** disturb, derange, put into disorder

酒乱 **shuran** drunken frenzy/violence

振乱 **fu(ri)mida(su)** shake (one's hair) loose, dishevel

胴乱 **dōran** satchel, wallet, collecting case

紛乱 **funran** disorder

11 動乱 **dōran** upheaval, disturbance, riot

混乱 **konran** confusion, disorder, chaos

淫乱 **inran** lascivious, lustful

脳乱 **nōran** worry, anguish

12 散乱 **sanran** dispersion, scattering

chi(ri)mida(reru) be scattered about; be routed

惑乱 **wakuran** bewilderment, confusion

13 搔乱 **ka(ki)mida(su)** disturb, upset

禍乱 **karan** disturbances, upheavals

戦乱 **senran** the upheavals of war

14 腐乱 **furan** ulcerate, decompose

算乱 **san (o) mida(su)** in utter disorder

15 撥乱 **hatsuran** quelling of upheaval

撥乱反正 **hatsuran hansei** restoration of public order

撩乱 **ryōran** (blooming) in profusion

3

氵
土
扌
口   4 ←
女
巾
犭
弓
彳
彡
艹
宀
⺌
山
青
广
尸
口

→4

16 壊乱 **kairan** corrupt, subvert
　　積乱雲 **sekiran'un** cumulonimbus clouds
　　錯乱 **sakuran** distraction, derangement
　　霍乱 **kakuran** sunstroke, heatstroke
18 撹乱 **jōran** disturbance, riot
　　騒乱 **sōran** riot, disturbance
21 癨乱 **kakuran** heatstroke, sunstroke
23 攪乱 **kakuran** disturb, disrupt, agitate

──────── 3 ────────

1 一糸乱 **isshi mida(renai)** not a thread out of place, airtight (argument)
5 半狂乱 **hankyōran** half-crazed
7 乱射乱撃 **ransha-rangeki** random shooting

吳→呉 2o5.7

3d4.22 / 958

豆　**TŌ, ZU** bean, pea
　　　mame bean, pea; (as prefix) miniature

──────── 1 ────────

2 豆人形 **mame-ningyō** miniature doll
5 豆本 **mame-hon** miniature book, pocket edition
6 豆名月 **mame meigetsu** moon on the 13th day of the 9th lunar month
7 豆乳 **tōnyū** soybean milk
8 豆板 **mameita** slab of candied beans
　　豆板銀 **mameitagin** (an Edo-era coin)
9 豆炭 **mametan** round charcoal briquettes
10 豆粉 **mame(no)ko** soybean flour
12 豆絞 **mameshibo(ri)** spotted pattern
13 豆鉄砲 **mamedeppō** bean/pea shooter, popgun
　　豆電球 **mame-denkyū** miniature light bulb
14 豆腐 **tōfu** tofu, bean curd
　　豆銀 **mamegin** (an Edo-era coin)
15 豆撒 **mamema(ki)** bean-scattering ceremony
　　豆蔵 **mamezō** chatterbox, babbling fool

──────── 2 ────────

3 大豆 **daizu** soybean
　　小豆 **azuki** adzuki beans
　　小豆島 **Shōdoshima** (island, Kagawa-ken)
5 氷豆腐 **kōridōfu** frozen tofu
　　奴豆腐 **yakkodōfu** tofu cut into cubes
6 伊豆 **Izu** (ancient kuni, Shizuoka-ken)
　　伊豆半島 **Izu-hantō** Izu Peninsula (Shizuoka-ken)
　　肉豆蔻 **nikuzuku** nutmeg
　　血豆 **chimame** blood blister
8 空豆 **soramame** broad/fava bean
　　底豆 **sokomame** blister (on one's sole)
　　枝豆 **edamame** green soybeans

青豆 **aomame** green beans
炒豆 **i(ri)mame** parched/popped beans
9 俎豆 **sotō** altar (for offerings)
10 納豆 **nattō** fermented soybeans
　　蚕豆 **soramame** broad/fava bean
11 黒豆 **kuromame** black soybean
12 湯豆腐 **yudōfu** boiled tofu
　　焼豆腐 **ya(ki)dōfu** broiled tofu
　　煮豆 **nimame** boiled beans
13 煎豆腐 **i(ri)dōfu** bean curd boiled dry and seasoned
　　塩豆 **shiomame** salted beans
14 蜜豆 **mitsumame** boiled beans with molasses
　　緑豆 **ryokutō** (a variety of green bean)
15 豌豆 **endō** peas
18 鶉豆 **uzuramame** mottled kidney beans

──────── 3 ────────

5 甘納豆 **amanattō** adzuki-bean candy
8 青豌豆 **aoendō** green peas
9 南京豆 **nankinmame** peanuts
10 高野豆腐 **kōyadōfu** frozen tofu
　　莢豌豆 **sayaendō** field/garden pea
13 隠元豆 **ingenmame** kidney bean

何→ 2a5.21

伺→ 2a5.23

3d4.23 / 793

君　**KUN** (suffix for male names); ruler
　　　kimi you (in masculine speech); ruler

──────── 1 ────────

2 君子 **kunshi** gentleman, wise man
5 君代 **Kimi(ga)yo** (Japan's national anthem)
　　君主 **kunshu** monarch, sovereign
　　君主国 **kunshukoku** a monarchy
7 君臣 **kunshin** ruler and ruled
18 君臨 **kunrin** reign

──────── 2 ────────

2 人君 **jinkun** sovereign, ruler
3 大君 **ōkimi, ōgimi** sovereign
　　亡君 **bōkun** one's deceased lord
　　士君子 **shikunshi** man of learning and virtue, gentleman
4 夫君 **fukun** (your) husband
　　仁君 **jinkun** benevolent ruler
　　父君 **chichigimi, fukun** father (polite)
　　　　fukei male line, patriarchal (family)
　　辻君 **tsujigimi** streetwalker, prostitute
5 母君 **hahagimi** mother (polite)

幼君　**yōkun**　young master
尼君　**amagimi**　nun (respectful term)
主君　**shukun**　lord, master
6　名君　**meikun**　wise ruler
8　姉君　**anegimi**　elder sister
　　妻君　**saikun**　wife
　　若君　**wakagimi**　young lord
　　国君　**kokkun**　ruler, sovereign
　　明君　**meikun**　wise ruler
　　忠君　**chūkun**　loyalty to the sovereign
　　忠君愛国　**chūkun-aikoku**　loyalty and
　　　　patriotism
10　遊君　**yūkun**　courtesan
　　姫君　**himegimi**　princess
　　家君　**kakun**　head of the house; my father
　　　　kakei　family lineage
11　偽君子　**gikunshi, nisekunshi**　hypocrite, snob
　　庸君　**yōkun**　foolish ruler
　　細君　**saikun**　wife
12　貴君　**kikun**　you (masculine)
15　暴君　**bōkun**　tyrant, despot
　　諸君　**shokun**　(ladies and) gentlemen, you all
17　厳君　**genkun**　your esteemed father

―――――― 3 ――――――

5　立憲君主政体　**rikken kunshu seitai**
　　　　constitutional monarchy
9　専制君主　**sensei kunshu**　absolute monarch,
　　　　despot

―――――― 5 ――――――

3d5.1

呷　**KŌ**　sip; noisy; duck's cry
　　ao(ru)　gulp down

3d5.2

呻　**SHIN, ume(ku)**　groan, moan

―――――― 1 ――――――

7　呻吟　**shingin**　groan, moan

3d5.3 / 307

味　**MI, aji**　taste, flavor
　　aji(wau)　taste; relish, appreciate
　　aji(na)　clever, witty, smart

―――――― 1 ――――――

4　味方　**mikata**　friend, ally, supporter
5　味付　**ajitsu(ke)**　seasoning
6　味気無　**ajikena(i)**　irksome, wearisome, dreary
7　味見　**ajimi**　sample, taste
　　味利　**ajiki(ki)**　taster
10　味素　**Aji(no)moto**　monosodium glutamate,
　　　　MSG

12　味覚　**mikaku**　sense of taste
15　味噌　**miso**　miso (fermented bean paste)
　　味噌汁　**miso shiru**　miso soup
　　味噌歯　**miso(p)pa**　decayed baby tooth
　　味噌擂　**misosu(ri)**　grinding miso; flattery
　　味噌擂坊主　**misosu(ri) bōzu**　petty priest
　　味醂　**mirin**　sweet saké (for seasoning)
16　味蕾　**mirai**　taste buds

―――――― 2 ――――――

1　一味　**ichimi**　an ingredient; a touch/tinge of;
　　　　conspirators, gang
　　一味違　**hitoaji chiga(u)**　with a unique flavor
3　三味線　**shamisen, samisen**　samisen (three-
　　　　stringed instrument)
　　三味線弾　**shamisenhi(ki), samisenhi(ki)**
　　　　samisen player
　　大味　**ōaji**　flat-tasting, flavorless
　　丸味　**marumi**　roundness
4　中味　**nakami**　contents
　　切味　**ki(re)aji**　sharpness
5　甘味　**kanmi, amami**　sweetness
　　甘味料　**kanmiryō**　sweetener
　　加味　**kami**　flavoring, seasoning
　　正味　**shōmi**　net (weight)
　　好味　**kōmi**　good flavor; tasty foods
　　白味　**shiromi**　whiteness; white meat; white
　　　　of an egg
6　気味　**kimi**　feeling, sensation; a touch, tinge
　　気味悪　**kimi (no) waru(i)**　eerie, ominous,
　　　　weird
　　地味　**jimi**　plain, subdued, undemonstrative,
　　　　conservative　**chimi**　(fertility of) the soil
　　旨味　**umami**　tastiness, flavor
7　含味　**ganmi**　taste, relish, appreciate
　　吟味　**ginmi**　close inquiry, scrutiny
　　妙味　**myōmi**　charm, exquisite beauty
　　快味　**kaimi**　pleasure, delight
　　辛味　**karami**　sharp/pungent taste
8　毒味　**dokumi**　tasting for poison
　　毒味役　**dokumiyaku**　taster for poison
　　泣味噌　**na(ki)miso**　crybaby
　　苦味　**nigami**　bitter taste
　　苦味走　**nigamibashi(tta)**　sternly handsome
　　玩味　**ganmi**　relish, appreciate, enjoy
9　重味　**omomi**　weight; importance; emphasis;
　　　　dignity
　　美味　**oi(shii)**　good-tasting, delicious
　　　　bimi　good flavor; delicacies
　　風味　**fūmi**　flavor, taste
　　持味　**mo(chi)aji**　natural flavor, distinctive
　　　　quality
　　後味　**atoaji**　aftertaste
　　珍味　**chinmi**　delicacies
　　香味　**kōmi**　flavor
　　香味料　**kōmiryō**　seasoning, condiments
10　俳味　**haimi**　subdued haiku-like taste

3

氵
土
扌
口　5←
女
巾
犭
弓
彳
彡
艹
宀
丷
山
吉
广
尸
口

凄味　**sugomi** dreadfulness, ghastliness, weirdness
真味　**shinmi** a real taste
弱味　**yowami** a weakness
弱味噌　**yowamiso** weakling, coward
書味　**ka(ki)aji** the feel of the pen against the paper as one writes
11 渋味　**shibumi** puckery taste; severe elgance
深味　**fukami** depth; deep place
涼味　**ryōmi** the cool, coolness
強味　**tsuyomi** strength, strong point
黄味　**kimi(gakatta)** yellowish, cream-colored
脳味噌　**nōmiso** brains, gray matter
情味　**jōmi** charm, attraction; warmheartedness
12 滋味　**jimi** delicious/nourishing (food)
勝味　**ka(chi)mi** chances of winning
無味　**mumi** tasteless, flat, dry
無味乾燥　**mumi-kansō** dry as dust, uninteresting
13 塩味　**shioaji** salty taste
嫌味　**iyami** disagreeable, offensive, sarcastic
禅味　**zenmi** Zen flavor, unworldliness
意味　**imi** meaning, significance
意味付　**imizu(keru)** give meaning to
意味合　**imia(i)** meaning, implications
意味深長　**imi-shinchō** full of meaning
意味論　**imiron** semantics
新味　**shinmi** fresh taste, novelty
詩味　**shimi** poetic sentiment
雅味　**gami** tastefulness, artistry
14 厭味　**iyami** offensiveness, disagreeableness
酸味　**sanmi, su(i)mi** acidity, sourness
15 賞味　**shōmi** relish, appreciate
敵味方　**teki-mikata** friend or/and foe
趣味　**shumi** interest, liking, tastes; hobby
調味　**chōmi** seasoning, flavoring
調味料　**chōmiryō** condiments, seasonings
16 興味　**kyōmi** interest
興味津津　**kyōmi-shinshin(taru)** very interesting, absorbing
興味深　**kyōmibuka(i)** very interesting
薬味　**yakumi** spices, seasoning
17 糠味噌　**nuka miso** rice-bran miso
糠味噌漬　**nukamisozu(ke)** vegetables pickled in rice-bran miso
糞味噌　**kuso-miso** (confusing) the valuable and the worthless; sweeping denunciation

——————— 3 ———————

2 人情味　**ninjōmi** human interest, kindness
人間味　**ningenmi** humanity, human touch
3 口三味線　**kuchijamisen, kuchizamisen** humming a samisen tune; cajolery
小気味　**kokimi** feeling, sentiment
4 不気味　**bukimi** uncanny, weird, eerie, ominous

6 多趣味　**tashumi** many-sided interests
再吟味　**saiginmi** re-examine, review
有意味　**yūimi** significant
有難味　**a(ri)gatami** value, worth
7 没趣味　**bosshumi** insipid, prosaic, dull
8 底気味悪　**sokokimi waru(i)** eerie, ominous
或意味　**a(ru) imi (de)** in one/a sense
9 面白味　**omoshiromi** interest, enjoyment
11 野性味　**yaseimi** wildness, roughness
12 無気味　**bukimi** ominous, eerie
無意味　**muimi** meaningless, pointless
無趣味　**mushumi** lack of taste, vulgarity
16 薄気味悪　**usukimiwaru(i)** weird, eerie
醍醐味　**daigomi** taste, zest, charm; Buddha's gracious teachings

——————— 4 ———————

7 低回趣味　**teikai shumi** dilettantism
低徊趣味　**teikai shumi** dilettantism
11 乾燥無味　**kansō-mumi** dry, dull

3d5.4 / 1254

呼　**KO, yo(bu)** call

——————— 1 ———————

2 呼入　**yo(bi)i(reru)** call in
呼子　**yo(bi)ko** (police) whistle
3 呼上　**yo(bi)a(geru)** call out, call the roll
4 呼込　**yo(bi)ko(mu)** call in
呼水　**yo(bi)mizu** pump-priming water
5 呼出　**yo(bi)da(su)** call out/up/forth, summon
呼出状　**yo(bi)da(shi)jō** summons, subpoena
呼付　**yo(bi)tsu(keru)** call, send for, summon
呼号　**kogō** cry out, declare
呼立　**yo(bi)ta(teru)** call out, ask to come, summon
6 呼気　**koki** exhalation
呼迎　**yo(bi)muka(eru)** send for
呼返　**yo(bi)kae(su)** call back, recall
呼吸　**kokyū** breathing, respiration
呼吸音　**kokyūon** respiratory sound
呼吸器　**kokyūki** respiratory organs
呼名　**yo(bi)na** one's given/popular name
7 呼売　**yo(bi)u(ri)** hawking, peddling
呼声　**yo(bi)goe** a call, cry, shout
呼応　**koō** hail each other; act in concert
呼戻　**yo(bi)modo(su)** call back, recall
8 呼物　**yo(bi)mono** attraction, feature, main event
10 呼値　**yo(bi)ne** nominal price, price asked
呼起　**yo(bi)o(kosu)** wake, rouse; remind
呼称　**koshō** call, name
呼留　**yo(bi)to(meru)** call (to someone) to stop, challenge
11 呼掛　**yo(bi)ka(keru)** call out to; call/appeal for

呼捨 **yo(bi)su(te)** addressing someone by last name only, without affixing *-san*

呼寄 **yo(bi)yo(seru)** send for, summon, call together

12 呼集 **yo(bi)atsu(meru)** call together, convene

13 呼鈴 **yo(bi)rin** door bell, call bell, buzzer

14 呼慣 **yo(bi)na(reru)** be used to calling (someone by a certain name)

——————— 2 ———————

3 大呼 **taiko** cry aloud, shout

9 点呼 **tenko** roll call

連呼 **renko** call/shout repeatedly

指呼 **shiko** beckon

指呼間 **shiko (no) aida/kan** within hailing distance

10 称呼 **shōko** appellation, designation, name

疾呼 **shikko** call out, shout

11 深呼吸 **shinkokyū** deep breath(ing)

12 着呼 **chakko** incoming (telephone) call

喚呼 **kanko** call/cry out

13 嗚呼 **ā** (sigh)

15 歓呼 **kanko** cheer, ovation

——————— 3 ———————

9 卑弥呼 **Himiko** female ruler of the early Japanese political federation known as Yamatai (about 3rd century)

13 腹式呼吸 **fukushiki kokyū** abdominal breathing

3d5.5

咄

TOTSU (exclamation of surprise)
hanashi talk

——————— 1 ———————

13 咄嗟 **tossa** moment, instant

——————— 2 ———————

3 小咄 **kobanashi** a little story

3d5.6

咀

SO chew

——————— 1 ———————

21 咀嚼 **soshaku** chew, masticate; digest, assimilate (what one has read)

3d5.7

咋

SAKU shout; chew, eat

3d5.8

咆

HŌ bark, roar, howl

——————— 1 ———————

9 咆哮 **hōkō** roar, howl, yell

3d5.9

呶

DO noisy, annoying

3d5.10

咐

FU blow; tell (someone to do something)

3d5.11

呪 兕

JU spell, curse, incantation
noro(u) curse
majina(i) charm, spell, magical incantation

——————— 1 ———————

4 呪文 **jumon** spell, curse, magic formula

8 呪物 **jubutsu** fetish

呪物崇拝 **jubutsu sūhai** fetishism

11 呪術 **jujutsu** incantation, sorcery, magic

呪符 **jufu** charm, amulet, talisman

12 呪詛 **juso** curse, imprecation, anathema

16 呪縛 **jubaku** a spell

咜 → 咤 **3d6.6**

3d5.12

呟

GEN, tsubuya(ku) mutter, grumble

咏 → 詠 **7a5.14**

3d5.13

呵

KA, shika(ru) scold, reprimand

——————— 1 ———————

3 呵々 **kaka** ha ha (sound of laughter)

11 呵責 **kashaku** reproach, torment

——————— 2 ———————

11 唉呵 **tanka** caustic words

——————— 3 ———————

1 一気呵成 **ikki kasei** in one breath/stroke/stretch

3

氵
土
扌
口 5 ←
女
巾
犭
弓
彳
彡
艹
宀
䒑
山
辶
广
尸
口

3d5.14 / 214

知

CHI, shi(ru) (come to) know
shi(rase) information, news; omen

──────────── 1 ────────────

2 知人 **chijin** an acquaintance
  知力 **chiryoku** mental capacity, intellect
3 知己 **chiki** acquaintance, friend
4 知切 **shi(re)ki(tta)** obvious
  知友 **chiyū** acquaintance, friend
  知辺 **shi(ru)be** acquaintance, friend
  知日 **chi-Nichi** pro-Japanese
  知日家 **chi-Nichika** Nippophile
6 知合 **shi(ri)a(i)** an acquaintance
    shi(ri)a(u) know each other
  知名 **chimei** noted, well-known
  知行 **chigyō** fief, stipend
  知行取 **chigyōto(ri)** vassal, daimyo
7 知抜 **shi(ri)nu(ku)** know thoroughly
  知見 **chiken** knowledge, information; opinion
8 知事 **chiji** governor
  知命 **chimei** age 50
  知育 **chiiku** mental training
  知知 **shi(razu)-shi(razu)** unwittingly
  知的 **chiteki** intellectual, mental
  知者 **chisha** wise man
  知性 **chisei** intelligence, intellect
9 知勇 **chiyū** wisdom and valor
10 知振 **shi(ran)pu(ri), shi(ran) fu(ri)** pretending not to know, nonchalant
    shi(tta) fu(ri) pretending to know
  知能 **chinō** intelligence
  知能犯 **chinōhan** a non-violent crime
  知能的 **chinōteki** intellectual
  知恵 **chie** knowledge, intelligence, wisdom
  知恵者 **chiesha** man of wisdom/ideas
  知恵袋 **chiebukuro** one's close advisers
  知恵歯 **chieba** wisdom tooth
  知恵熱 **chie-netsu** teething fever
  知恵輪 **chie (no) wa** puzzle ring
11 知遇 **chigū** favor, friendship
  知得 **chitoku** know, learn
  知悉 **chishitsu** have full knowledge of
  知略 **chiryaku** resourcefulness
12 知渡 **shi(re)wata(ru)** become widely known
  知覚 **chikaku** perception
  知歯 **chishi** wisdom tooth
14 知徳 **chitoku** knowledge and virtue
15 知慮 **chiryo** foresight
16 知謀 **chibō** resourcefulness
18 知顔 **shi(ran) kao, shi(ranu) kao** pretending not to know, nonchalant
    shi(ri)gao knowing look
19 知識 **chishiki** knowledge
  知識人 **chishikijin** an intellectual

知識欲 **chishikiyoku** love of learning

──────────── 2 ────────────

1 一知半解 **itchi hankai** superficial knowledge
  了知 **ryōchi** understand, appreciate
2 入知恵 **i(re)jie** suggestion, hint
  人知 **jinchi** human intellect/knowledge
    hitoshi(renu/rezu) unknown to others, hidden, secret
3 才知 **saichi** wit, intelligence
  小知 **shōchi** superficial knowledge
4 不知 **fuchi** ignorance
  不知火 **shiranui, shiranuhi** sea fire/luminescence
  予知 **yochi** foresee, foretell, predict
  公知 **kōchi** (well/widely) known
5 巧知 **kōchi** skilled and knowledgeable
  未知 **michi** unknown, strange
  旧知 **kyūchi** an old friend(ship)
  主知主義 **shuchi shugi** intellectualism
  主知的 **shuchiteki** intellectual
6 全知 **zenchi** onmiscience
  全知全能 **zenchi-zennō** all-knowing and all-powerful
  汗知 **aseshi(razu)** prickly-heat/baby powder
  先知 **senchi** foreknowledge; speedy comprehension
  奸知 **kanchi** cunning, guile
  自知 **jichi** knowing oneself
7 良知 **ryōchi** intuition
  身知 **mishi(razu)** not knowing one's place, self-conceit
  承知 **shōchi** consent to; know, be aware of
  邪知 **jachi** perverted talent, guile, cunning
  告知 **kokuchi** notice, announcement
  告知板 **kokuchiban** bulletin board
  見知 **mishi(ri)** an acquaintance
    mishi(ranu), mi(zu)shi(razu) unfamiliar
    kenchi find out by inspecting
  見知越 **mishi(ri)go(shi)** well acquainted with
  言知 **i(i)shi(renu)** indescribable
8 命知 **inochishi(razu)** recklessness; daredevil
  周知 **shūchi** common knowledge, widely known
  知知 **shi(razu)-shi(razu)** unwittingly
  奇知 **kichi** genius
  府知事 **fuchiji** urban-prefectural governor
  物知 **monoshi(ri)** knowledgeable, erudite
  物知顔 **monoshi(ri)gao** knowing look
  性知識 **sei chishiki** information on sex
9 前知 **zenchi** prescience
  通知 **tsūchi** notification, notice
  通知表 **tsūchihyō** report card
  通知書 **tsūchisho** notice
  浅知恵 **asajie** shallow-witted
  後知恵 **atojie** hindsight

県知事 **kenchiji** prefectural governor
故知 **kochi** an old acquaintance; the wisdom of our forefathers
思知 **omo(i)shi(ru)** come to know, realize; repent of
10 既知 **kichi** (already) known
既知数 **kichisū** known quantity
高知 **Kōchi** (city, Kōchi-ken)
高知県 **Kōchi-ken** (prefecture)
辱知 **jokuchi** an acquaintance
恩知 **onshi(razu)** ingratitude; ingrate
素知顔 **soshi(ranu) kao** innocent look
恥知 **hajishi(razu)** shameless person
11 遅知恵 **osojie** late-developing intelligence
推知 **suichi** inference, conjecture
探知 **tanchi** detection
探知器 **tanchiki** detector
理知 **richi** intellect, intelligence
理知的 **richiteki** intellectual
悪知恵 **warujie** cunning, guile
12 測知 **haka(ri)shi(ru)** understand, fathom, calculate
報知 **hōchi** information, news, intelligence
量知 **haka(ri)shi(renai)** immeasurable
無知 **muchi** ignorance
無知蒙昧 **muchi-mōmai** unenlightened
衆知 **shūchi** the wisdom of many
13 猿知恵 **sarujie** shallow cleverness
愛知県 **Aichi-ken** (prefecture)
感知 **kanchi** perception, sensing
新知識 **shinchishiki** up-to-date knowledge
触知 **shokuchi** feel, perceive by touch
頓知 **tonchi** ready/quick wit
14 察知 **satchi** infer, gather, sense
熟知 **jukuchi** thorough knowledge, familiarity
認知 **ninchi** cognition; acknowledge (as one's offspring)
聞知 **bunchi, ki(ki)shi(ru)** learn of
関知 **kanchi** have to do with
15 霊知 **reichi** mystic wisdom
16 窺知 **kichi** perceive, understand
機知 **kichi** quick wit, resourcefulness
親知 **oyashi(razu)** wisdom tooth; dangerous place
21 露知 **tsuyushi(razu)** utterly ignorant

—————— 3 ——————

2 人見知 **hitomishi(ri)** be bashful before strangers
4 不可知 **fukachi** unknowable
不可知論 **fukachiron** agnosticism
不承知 **fushōchi** dissent, disagreement, noncompliance
予備知識 **yobi chishiki** preliminary knowledge, background
5 世間知 **sekenshi(razu)** ignorant of the ways of the world

6 汗不知 **aseshirazu** prickly-heat/baby powder
7 身程知 **mi(no)hodo shi(razu)** not knowing one's place
12 温故知新 **onko-chishin** learning from the past
13 義理知 **girishi(razu)** ungrateful person
14 読人知 **yo(mi)bito shi(razu)** anonymous (poem)
18 顔見知 **kaomishi(ri)** knowing someone by sight, a nodding acquaintance

3d5.15

咎
KYŪ, toga(meru) find fault with, rebuke; blame, criticize; challenge; become inflamed **toga** fault, blame; charge, offense

—————— 2 ——————

7 見咎 **mitoga(meru)** find fault with; question, challenge
14 聞咎 **ki(ki)toga(meru)** find fault with

3d5.16

亟
KYOKU fast, quick, sudden

3d5.17 / 1360

奇 竒
KI strange, odd; odd number **ku(shiki)** strange, curious, mysterious **ku(shikumo)** strange to say, mysteriously

—————— 1 ——————

2 奇人 **kijin** an eccentric
3 奇才 **kisai** genius, wizard, prodigy
奇々怪々 **kiki-kaikai** very strange, fantastic
5 奇功 **kikō** singular/phenomenal success
6 奇行 **kikō** eccentric conduct
7 奇兵 **kihei** shock troops, commandos
奇抜 **kibatsu** novel, original, unconventional
奇妙 **kimyō** strange, curious, odd
奇形 **kikei** deformity, abnormality
奇声 **kisei** queer/peculiar voice
8 奇効 **kikō** remarkable effect
奇知 **kichi** genius
奇岩 **kigan** strange-shaped rock
奇怪 **kikai** strange, weird; outrageous
9 奇計 **kikei** ingenious plan
10 奇骨 **kikotsu** eccentric
奇特 **kitoku** commendable; benevolent
奇病 **kibyō** strange disease
11 奇偶 **kigū** odd or even
奇遇 **kigū** chance meeting
奇術 **kijutsu** conjuring, sleight of hand
奇習 **kishū** strange custom
奇異 **kii** strange, odd, singular

奇貨 **kika** a curiosity; an opportunity
12 奇勝 **kishō** surprise victory; place of scenic beauty
奇策縦横 **kisaku-jūō** clever planning
13 奇数 **kisū** odd number
奇想 **kisō** original/fantastic idea
奇想天外 **kisō-tengai** original concept
奇跡 **kiseki** miracle
14 奇態 **kitai** strange, curious, wondrous
奇聞 **kibun** strange news, anecdote
15 奇縁 **kien** strange fate, curious coincidence
奇談 **kidan** strange story, adventure
17 奇矯 **kikyō** eccentric, erratic
18 奇観 **kikan** wondrous sight, marvel
奇蹟 **kiseki** miracle
19 奇麗 **kirei** pretty, beautiful; clean, neat
奇麗好 **kireizu(ki)** fond of cleanliness
奇麗事 **kireigoto** glossing over, whitewashing
奇麗所 **kireidoko** good-looking woman
奇警 **kikei** original, witty
22 奇襲 **kishū** surprise attack

――――― 2 ―――――
5 好奇 **kōki** curiosity, inquisitiveness
好奇心 **kōkishin** curiosity, inquisitiveness
6 伝奇 **denki** romance (fiction)
8 奇奇怪怪 **kiki-kaikai** very strange, fantastic
怪奇 **kaiki** mysterious, grotesque, eerie
怪奇小説 **kaiki shōsetsu** mystery/spooky story
9 珍奇 **chinki** strange, singular; novel
11 猟奇 **ryōki** seeking the bizarre
13 数奇 **sūki** adverse/varied fortune
数奇屋 **sukiya** tea-ceremony room/cottage
新奇 **shinki** novel, original

函 → 函 2b6.3

――――― 6 ―――――

3d6.1

哂 **SHIN** laugh/smile (in derision)

3d6.2

哘 **saso(u)** invite, entice

3d6.3

哮 **KŌ, take(ru)** roar, howl, growl, bellow

――――― 2 ―――――
8 咆哮 **hōkō** roar, howl, yell

3d6.4

咾 **RŌ** voice

――――― 1 ―――――
7 咾別 **Ikanbetsu** (place name, Hokkaidō)

3d6.5

哇 **A** fawning/laughing/child's voice

3d6.6

咤 咜 **TA** clicking one's tongue, smacking one's lips

――――― 2 ―――――
5 叱咤 **shitta** scold; spur on

3d6.7

哄 **KŌ** loud

――――― 1 ―――――
10 哄笑 **kōshō** loud laughter

咯 → 喀 3d9.13

3d6.8

咥 **TETSU** laugh; chew, eat
kuwa(eru) hold (a cigarette) in one's teeth/lips

3d6.9

哈 **GŌ** school of fish; movement of a fish's mouth

3d6.10

咳 **GAI, seki** a cough
se(ku) cough
shiwabuki a cough; clearing the throat

――――― 1 ―――――
3 咳上 **se(ki)a(geru)** have a fit of coughing; sob convulsively
4 咳止 **sekido(me)** cough medicine/lozenge
咳込 **se(ki)ko(mu)** have a fit of coughing

5 咳払 **sekibara(i)** clearing one's throat
14 咳嗽 **gaisō** cough, coughing

──────── 2 ────────

8 空咳 **karazeki, karaseki** dry/hacking cough
11 乾咳 **karazeki** a dry/hacking cough
18 謦咳接 **keigai (ni) ses(suru)** have the
　　pleasure of meeting personally

──────── 3 ────────

6 百日咳 **hyakunichizeki** whooping cough

3d6.11

咬

　　KŌ, ka(mu) bite

──────── 1 ────────

13 咬傷 **kōshō** a bite (wound)

──────── 2 ────────

13 鼠咬症 **sokōshō** rat-bite fever

3d6.12 / 927

咲

　　SHŌ, sa(ku) bloom, blossom

──────── 1 ────────

4 咲分 **sa(ki)wa(keru)** bloom in various colors
　　sa(ki)wa(ke) variegated flowering
5 咲出 **sa(ki)da(su), sa(ki)de(ru)** begin to
　　bloom, come out
7 咲乱 **sa(ki)mida(reru)** bloom in profusion
　咲初 **sa(ki)so(meru)** begin to bloom
10 咲残 **sa(ki)noko(ru)** be still in bloom
12 咲揃 **sa(ki)soro(u)** be in full bloom
13 咲溢 **sa(ki)kobo(reru)** bloom in profusion
　咲誇 **sa(ki)hoko(ru)** bloom in full glory

──────── 2 ────────

6 返咲 **kae(ri)za(ki)** second blooming;
　　comeback
　早咲 **hayaza(ki)** early-blooming; precocious
7 狂咲 **kuru(i)za(ki)** blooming out of season
9 後咲 **oku(re)za(ki)** late blossoms
　室咲 **muroza(ki)** hothouse/forced (flowers)
11 遅咲 **osoza(ki)** late-blooming

──────── 3 ────────

2 八重咲 **yaeza(ki)** double-flowering
5 四季咲 **shikiza(ki)** blooming all seasons
6 死花咲 **shi(ni)bana (o) sa(kaseru)** do
　　something just before one's death to win
　　glory

3d6.13

呱

　　KO (child's) crying

3d6.14

咽

　　IN, EN, ETSU, muse(bu) be choked
　　up, be smothered/suffocated
　　nodo throat

──────── 1 ────────

8 咽泣 **muse(bi)na(ku)** sob
12 咽喉 **inkō** throat
16 咽頭 **intō** pharynx
　咽頭炎 **intōen** pharyngitis

──────── 2 ────────

13 嗚咽 **oetsu** sobbing, weeping

──────── 3 ────────

0 耳鼻咽喉科 **jibiinkōka** ear, nose, and throat
　　specialty

3d6.15 / 230

品　品

　　HIN refinement; article
　　shina goods; quality

──────── 1 ────────

3 品々 **shinajina** various articles
4 品切 **shinagi(re)** out of stock, sold out
　品分 **shinawa(ke)** assort
5 品目 **hinmoku** item
6 品行 **hinkō** conduct, behavior, deportment
　品行方正 **hinkō-hōsei** respectable, irre-
　　proachable
7 品位 **hin'i** grade, quality, fineness; dignity
8 品定 **shinasada(me)** take stock of, judge
　品物 **shinamono** goods, merchandise
　品性 **hinsei** character
9 品柄 **shinagara** quality
10 品格 **hinkaku** grace, dignity
　品書 **shinaga(ki)** catalog, inventory, itemiza-
　　tion
12 品等 **hintō** grade, rating, quality
　品評 **hinpyō** criticism, commentary
　品評会 **hinpyōkai** competitive exhibition
　品詞 **hinshi** part of speech
13 品数 **hinsū, shinakazu** number of articles
14 品種 **hinshu** kind, variety, grade, breed
15 品調 **shinashira(be)** stocktaking
　品質 **hinshitsu** quality
16 品薄 **shinausu** short supply

──────── 2 ────────

1 一品 **ippin** an article/item; a dish/course
　一品料理 **ippin ryōri** dishes 'a la carte
2 人品 **jinpin** personal bearing/appearance,
　　character
3 上品 **jōhin** refined, elegant, genteel; first-
　　class article
　下品 **gehin** vulgar, coarse, gross
　小品 **shōhin** something small, short piece/
　　sketch

3

氵 土 扌 口 女 巾 犭 弓 彳 彡 艹 宀 屮 圭 广 尸 口

6 ←

3

氵 土 扌 日 女 巾 犭 弓 彳 彡 艹 宀 业 由 肀 广 尸 口

→ 6

---

4 不品行 **fuhinkō** loose moral conduct, profligacy
手品 **tejina** sleight of hand, magic tricks, juggling
手品師 **tejinashi** magician, juggler
5 出品 **shuppin** exhibit, display
出品者 **shuppinsha** exhibitor
出品物 **shuppinbutsu** an exhibit
代品 **daihin** a substitute
用品 **yōhin** supplies
6 気品 **kihin** dignity
返品 **henpin** returned goods, returns
名品 **meihin** fine article, gem, masterpiece
7 良品 **ryōhin** article of superior quality
作品 **sakuhin** a work
別品 **beppin** beautiful woman (slang)
売品 **baihin** article for sale
8 佳品 **kahin** choice article
物品 **buppin** goods, article, commodity
物品税 **buppinzei** commodity/excise tax
金品 **kinpin** money or/and valuables
9 洋品 **yōhin** haberdashery
洋品店 **yōhinten** haberdashery
洋品屋 **yōhin'ya** haberdasher(y)
品品 **shinajina** various articles
神品 **shinpin** inspired work, masterpiece
珍品 **chinpin** rare article, curio
食品 **shokuhin** food(stuffs)
食品店 **shokuhinten** grocery store
10 残品 **zanpin** remaining stock, unsold merchandise
残品整理 **zanpin seiri** clearance sale
部品 **buhin** parts
高品位テレビ **kōhin'i terebi** high-definition television
原品 **genpin** the original article
逸品 **ippin** superb article, masterpiece
納品 **nōhin** delivery
11 商品 **shōhin** goods, merchandise
商品券 **shōhinken** gift certificate
現品 **genpin** the actual goods; goods in stock
盗品 **tōhin** stolen goods, loot
粗品 **soshina, sohin** small gift
12 備品 **bihin** fixtures, furnishings, equipment
廃品 **haihin** scrap, waste, discards, junk
景品 **keihin** premium, present, giveaway
絶品 **zeppin** superb article, masterpiece
13 新品 **shinpin** new article, brand new
新品同様 **shinpin dōyō** like new
14 遺品 **ihin** articles left by the deceased
製品 **seihin** product, manufactured goods
雑品 **zappin** sundries, odds and ends
15 賞品 **shōhin** (nonmonetary) prize
16 薬品 **yakuhin** drugs; chemicals
22 贓品 **zōhin, shōhin** stolen goods

— 3 —

3 工作品 **kōsakuhin** handicrafts
工芸品 **kōgeihin** industrial-art objects
上等品 **jōtōhin** top-quality goods
4 不用品 **fuyōhin** useless article, castoff
予備品 **yobihin** spares, reserve supply
毛製品 **mōseihin** woolen goods
中古品 **chūkohin** secondhand goods
化粧品 **keshōhin** cosmetics, makeup
分捕品 **bundo(ri)hin** booty, loot, spoils
手回品 **temawa(ri)hin** personal effects
手芸品 **shugeihin** handicrafts
手持品 **temo(chi)hin** supplies, goods on hand
木製品 **mokuseihin** wood products
日用品 **nichiyōhin** daily necessities
5 必要品 **hitsuyōhin** necessities
必需品 **hitsujuhin** necessities, essentials
半製品 **hanseihin** semiprocessed goods
未成品 **miseihin** unfinished goods
未製品 **miseihin** unfinished goods
代用品 **daiyōhin** a substitute
加工品 **kakōhin** processed goods
払下品 **hara(i)sa(ge)hin** articles sold off by the government
主製品 **shuseihin** main products
6 全製品 **zenseihin** manufactured product
肉製品 **niku seihin** meat products
在庫品 **zaikohin** goods on hand, stock
有税品 **yūzeihin** goods subject to duty
7 更生品 **kōseihin** reconditioned article
医薬品 **iyakuhin** pharmaceuticals
投売品 **na(ge)u(ri)hin** distress-sale merchandise
学用品 **gakuyōhin** school supplies
乳製品 **nyūseihin** dairy products
見切品 **miki(ri)hin** bargain goods
見舞品 **mima(i)hin** gift to a sick person
8 非売品 **hibaihin** article not for sale
免税品 **menzeihin** duty-free goods
退蔵品 **taizōhin** hoarded goods, cache
注文品 **chūmonhin** goods ordered
参考品 **sankōhin** reference materials
実用品 **jitsuyōhin** utility article
官給品 **kankyūhin** government issues
国産品 **kokusanhin** domestic products
所持品 **shojihin** one's personal effects
9 発明品 **hatsumeihin** an invention
専売品 **senbaihin** monopoly goods
軍用品 **gun'yōhin** military supplies, munitions, materiel
軍需品 **gunjuhin** military supplies, materiel
美術品 **bijutsuhin** work of art
相当品 **sōtōhin** article of similar value
食用品 **shokuyōhin** food(stuffs)
食料品 **shokuryōhin** food(stuffs)
食料品店 **shokuryōhinten** grocery store

食料品商 **shokuryōhinshō** grocer
10 既製品 **kiseihin** manufactured/ready-made goods, goods in stock
部分品 **bubunhin** parts, components
高級品 **kōkyūhin** high-grade goods
差押品 **sa(shi)osa(e)hin** attached/seized goods
消耗品 **shōmōhin** supplies, expendables
娯楽品 **gorakuhin** plaything
格外品 **kakugaihin** nonstandard goods
格安品 **kakuyasuhin** bargain goods
骨董品 **kottōhin** curios, bric-a-brac
特売品 **tokubaihin** articles on sale
特価品 **tokkahin** bargain goods
特産品 **tokusanhin** specialty, special products
特許品 **tokkyohin** patented article
記念品 **kinenhin** souvenir, memento
11 副葬品 **fukusōhin** articles buried with the dead
密輸品 **mitsuyuhin** contraband
寄贈品 **kizōhin** gift, donation
規格品 **kikakuhin** standardized goods
粗悪品 **soakuhin** inferior goods
粗製品 **soseihin** crude articles
舶来品 **hakuraihin** imported goods
12 装飾品 **sōshokuhin** ornaments, decorations, accessories
買上品 **ka(i)a(ge)hin** purchases
統制品 **tōseihin** controlled goods
貯蔵品 **chozōhin** stored goods, stock
貴重品 **kichōhin** valuables
貿易品 **bōekihin** articles of commerce
13 携帯品 **keitaihin** personal effects, luggage
嗜好品 **shikōhin** luxury items
献納品 **kennōhin** donation
廉価品 **renkahin** low-priced goods
禁制品 **kinseihin** contraband
禁輸品 **kin'yuhin** contraband
戦利品 **senrihin** war spoils, booty
新製品 **shinseihin** new product
14 遺失品 **ishitsuhin** lost article
遺留品 **iryūhin** lost article, article left behind
徳用品 **tokuyōhin** economy(-size) goods
模造品 **mozōhin** imitation
練製品 **ne(ri)seihin** a fish-paste food
綿製品 **menseihin** cotton goods
精製品 **seiseihin** finished goods
15 慰問品 **imonhin** comfort articles, amenities
縫製品 **hōseihin** sewn goods
課税品 **kazeihin** taxable/dutiable goods
調度品 **chōdohin** household effects, furnishings
16 輸入品 **yunyūhin** imports
輸出品 **yushutsuhin** exports
錫製品 **suzu seihin** tinware
18 贈呈品 **zōteihin** present, gift

贈答品 **zōtōhin** gift, present
贅沢品 **zeitakuhin** luxury item
類似品 **ruijihin** an imitation

———————— 4 ————————

4 天下一品 **tenka ippin** best article under heaven
5 半加工品 **hankakōhin** semiprocessed goods
古美術品 **kobijutsuhin** old/ancient art object
目玉商品 **medama shōhin** bargain item to attract customers, loss leader
7 冷凍食品 **reitō shokuhin** frozen foods
8 非実用品 **hijitsuyōhin** unessential items
10 家庭用品 **kateiyōhin** household goods
16 輸出入品 **yushutsunyūhin** exports and imports

3d6.16

咔   **SHI** blame, censure; damage; this

3d6.17

咨   **SHI** inquire into; sigh, lament

3d6.18

咢   **GAKU** outspokenly

3d6.19

咼   **KA, KAI** crooked mouth; evil, dishonest

3d6.20

剋 尅   **KOKU** be victorious

———————— 2 ————————

3 下剋上 **gekokujō** the lower dominating the upper
9 相剋 **sōkoku** vie/conflict with each other

哉 →   **4n5.4**

面 →   **3s6.1**

咫 →   **3r6.6**

3d6.21

殆 **TAI, DAI, hoton(do)** almost
hotohoto quite, really

—————— 2 ——————

6 危殆 **kitai** danger, peril, jeopardy

—————— 7 ——————

3d7.1

唄 **BAI, uta** song

—————— 2 ——————

3 小唄 **kouta** ditty, ballad
6 地唄 **jiuta** ballad, folk song
地唄舞 **jiutamai** a traditional Kyōto dance performed to the accompaniment of *jiuta*
8 長唄 **nagauta** song accompanied on the samisen

唖 → 啞 **3d8.3**

3d7.2

哦 **GA** sing

3d7.3

哽 **KŌ** sob, get choked up

3d7.4

哺 **HO** take/hold in the mouth

—————— 1 ——————

7 哺乳 **honyū** lactation, suckling, nursing
哺乳動物 **honyū dōbutsu** mammal
哺乳瓶 **honyūbin** baby bottle
哺乳類 **honyūrui** mammal
8 哺育 **hoiku** suckle, nurse

3d7.5

哩 **RI, mairu** mile (about 1.6 km)

啄 → 啄 **3d8.4**

3d7.6

嗽 **RŌ, saezu(ru)** chirp, twitter, warble

3d7.7

唔 **GO** reading voice

3d7.8 / 1846

唆 **SA, sosonoka(su)** tempt, seduce, incite

—————— 2 ——————

5 示唆 **shisa** suggestion
10 教唆 **kyōsa** instigate, abet
教唆者 **kyōsasha** instigator
教唆罪 **kyōsazai** (the crime of) incitement

3d7.9

哨 哨 **SHŌ** stand guard/watch

—————— 1 ——————

7 哨兵 **shōhei** sentry, sentinel
哨戒 **shōkai** patrol, guard

—————— 2 ——————

9 前哨 **zenshō** outpost
前哨戦 **zenshōsen** preliminary skirmish
前哨線 **zenshōsen** scouting line

唳 → 唳 **3d8.15**

3d7.10 / 163

員 **IN** member; number

—————— 1 ——————

5 員外 **ingai** nonmembership
13 員数 **inzū** number of members/items

—————— 2 ——————

1 一員 **ichiin** a person; a member
2 人員 **jin'in** personnel, staff, crew
人員整理 **jin'in seiri** personnel cutback
3 工員 **kōin** factory worker, machine operator
4 冗員 **jōin** superfluous personnel, overstaffing
欠員 **ketsuin** vacant position, opening
5 正員 **seiin** full/regular member
6 吏員 **riin** an official

全員 **zen'in** all the members, the whole staff/ crew
会員 **kaiin** member
会員証 **kaiinshō** membership certificate/card
行員 **kōin** bank clerk/employee
団員 **dan'in** member (of a group)
成員 **seiin** member
7 兵員 **heiin** military personnel/strength
医員 **iin** physician, medical staff
役員 **yakuin** (company) officer, director
役員会 **yakuinkai** board meeting
局員 **kyokuin** bureau/post-office staff
社員 **shain** employee, staff
8 実員 **jitsuin** effective strength/personnel
官員 **kan'in** an official
定員 **teiin** prescribed number of personnel; (seating) capacity; quorum
店員 **ten'in** store employee, clerk
所員 **shoin** (member of the) staff, personnel
委員 **iin** committee member
委員会 **iinkai** committee
委員長 **iinchō** chairman
金員 **kin'in** money
9 係員 **kakariin** clerk in charge
海員 **kaiin** seaman, sailor
要員 **yōin** necessary personnel
客員 **kakuin, kyakuin** guest, honorary member, associate (editor)
10 随員 **zuiin** attendants, retinue
部員 **buin** staff, staff member
党員 **tōin** party member
座員 **zain** member of a troupe
教員 **kyōin** teacher, instructor; teaching staff
11 隊員 **taiin** member of a brigade/team
剰員 **jōin** superfluous personnel, overstaffing
動員 **dōin** mobilization
動員令 **dōinrei** mobilization order
常員 **jōin** regular personnel/member
現員 **gen'in** the present members
船員 **sen'in** crewman, seaman
12 満員 **man'in** full to capacity
減員 **gen'in** staff reduction, personnel cutback
幅員 **fukuin** breadth, extent
復員 **fukuin** demobilization
復員兵 **fukuinhei** demobilized soldier
雇員 **koin** employee
艇員 **teiin** (boat's) crew
13 楽員 **gakuin** orchestra/band member
署員 **shoin** office/station staff member
14 増員 **zōin** personnel increase
総員 **sōin** all hands, in full force
閣員 **kakuin** member of the cabinet
駅員 **ekiin** station employee/staff
15 課員 **kain** (member of the) section staff
16 館員 **kan'in** staff, personnel

18 職員 **shokuin** personnel, staff (member)
職員室 **shokuinshitsu** staff/teachers' room
職員録 **shokuinroku** list of government officials
20 議員 **giin** M.P., dietman, congressman

――――――― 3 ―――――――

3 女店員 **joten'in** salesgirl
女教員 **jokyōin** female teacher
小委員会 **shōiinkai** subcommittee
4 予備員 **yobiin** reserve men
公務員 **kōmuin** government employee
5 出張員 **shutchōin** agent, representative, dispatched official
代議員 **daigiin** representative, delegate
外交員 **gaikōin** canvasser, door-to-door/ traveling salesman
正会員 **seikaiin** full/regular member
正社員 **seishain** regular employee, full member of the staff
正教員 **seikyōin** regular/licensed teacher
用務員 **yōmuin** servant, janitor, custodian
6 会社員 **kaishain** company employee
8 事務員 **jimuin** clerk, office staff
協議員 **kyōgiin** delegate, conferee
9 乗務員 **jōmuin** train/plane crew
乗組員 **norikumiin** crew
通信員 **tsūshin'in** correspondent, reporter
政党員 **seitōin** party member
10 随行員 **zuikōin** attendants, entourage, retinue
遊説員 **yūzeiin** stumping candidate, election canvassers
従業員 **jūgyōin** employee
特派員 **tokuhain** (news) correspondent; delegate
教会員 **kyōkaiin** church member
教職員 **kyōshokuin** faculty, teaching staff
11 運動員 **undōin** campaigner, canvasser
添乗員 **tenjōin** tour conductor
常議員 **jōgiin** permanent member; standing committee
現業員 **gengyōin** outdoor/field worker
12 超満員 **chōman'in** crowded beyond capacity
評議員 **hyōgiin** councilor, trustee
13 準会員 **junkaiin** associate member
準社員 **junshain** junior employee, associate member
準教員 **junkyōin** assistant teacher
戦闘員 **sentōin** combatant, combat soldier
14 構成員 **kōseiin** member
総動員 **sōdōin** general mobilization
銀行員 **ginkōin** bank clerk/employee
15 審査員 **shinsain** judges, examiners

――――――― 4 ―――――――

5 出向社員 **shukkō shain** employee on loan to a subsidiary/another company
民生委員 **minsei iin** district welfare officer

3

氵
土
扌
口 7←
女
巾
犭
弓
彳
彡
艹
宀
⺌
山
青
广
尸
口

3d7.11

6 全院委員会 **zen'in iikai** committee of the whole house
7 図書館員 **toshokan'in** library clerk, librarian
8 非現業員 **higengyōin** office/desk worker
　非戦闘員 **hisentōin** noncombatant
　府会議員 **fukai giin** urban-prefectural assemblyman
11 常任委員会 **jōnin iinkai** standing committee

3d7.11

唏　**KI** lament, grieve

3d7.12 / 1737

唇 脣　**SHIN, kuchibiru** lip

――――――― 1 ―――――――
9 唇音 **shin'on** a labial (sound)
――――――― 2 ―――――――
3 上唇 **uwakuchibiru, jōshin** upper lip
　下唇 **shitakuchibiru, kashin** lower lip
　口唇 **kōshin** the lips
4 欠唇 **kesshin, iguchi** harelip
8 兎唇 **toshin, mitsukuchi, iguchi** harelip
9 紅唇 **kōshin** red lips
10 陰唇 **inshin** the labia
14 読唇術 **dokushinjutsu** lip reading

3d7.13 / 1397

哲　**TETSU** wisdom

――――――― 1 ―――――――
2 哲人 **tetsujin** wise man, philosopher
7 哲学 **tetsugaku** philosophy
　哲学者 **tetsugakusha** philosopher
11 哲理 **tetsuri** philosophy, philosophical principles
――――――― 2 ―――――――
6 西哲 **seitetsu** Western philosopher
　先哲 **sentetsu** ancient sage
8 明哲 **meitetsu** wise man
9 変哲 **hentetsu(mo nai)** commonplace
13 聖哲 **seitetsu** sage, wise man
16 賢哲 **kentetsu** wise man, the wise
――――――― 3 ―――――――
8 宗教哲学 **shūkyō tetsugaku** philosophy of religion
　実証哲学 **jisshō tetsugaku** positivism

哭 → 3g6.7

勉 → 2n8.1

3d7.14

孰　**JUKU, izu(re)** which, how, who

尉 → 尅 3d6.20

氪 → 3s7.4

3d7.15

舐　**SHI, na(meru)** lick; make light of, underrate **nebu(ru)** lick **na(mezuru)** lick one's lips

――――――― 2 ―――――――
6 舌舐 **shitana(mezuri)** licking one's lips
――――――― 3 ―――――――
7 吮癰舐痔 **sen'yō shiji** sucking the pus from someone's carbuncles and licking his hemorrhoids (to curry favor)

3d7.16

哥　**KA** song; elder brother

――――――― 2 ―――――――
28 鸚哥 **inko** parakeet
――――――― 3 ―――――――
14 墨西哥 **Mekishiko** Mexico

3d7.17

鬲　**KAKU, REKI, kanae** three-legged kettle

3d7.18

韋　**I, nameshigawa** leather

――――――― 1 ―――――――
14 韋駄天 **Idaten** Skanda, the fleet-footed god

――――――― 8 ―――――――

3d8.1 / 1234

唯　**YUI, I, tada, tatta** solely, only, merely

1

1 唯一 **yuiitsu, tada hito(tsu)** the only, sole
3 唯々諾々 **ii-dakudaku** quite willing, readily, obediently
4 唯今 **tadaima** right/just now
　唯心論 **yuishinron** idealism, spiritualism
6 唯名論 **yuimeiron** nominalism
7 唯我独尊 **yuiga-dokuson** self-conceit, vainglory
　唯我論 **yuigaron** solipsism
8 唯物史観 **yuibutsu shikan** materialistic interpretation of history
　唯物主義 **yuibutsu shugi** materialism
　唯物論 **yuibutsuron** materialism
9 唯美主義 **yuibi shugi** estheticism
　唯美的 **yuibiteki** esthetic
11 唯理論 **yuiriron** rationalism
19 唯識 **yuishiki** (Buddhist) spiritualism

2

10 真唯中 **ma(t)tadanaka** right in the middle of
11 唯唯諾諾 **ii-dakudaku** quite willing, readily, obediently

3d8.2

唾

DA, tsuba, tsubaki saliva

1

11 唾液 **daeki** saliva
　唾液腺 **daekisen** salivary glands
13 唾棄 **daki** spit out; detest, abhor

2

8 固唾飲 **katazu (o) no(mu)** be intensely anxious
9 眉唾物 **mayutsubamono** fake, cock-and-bull story

3d8.3

啞 唖

A, oshi mute, unable to speak

1

12 啞然 **azen (to)** dumbfounded, agape
13 啞鈴 **arei** dumbbell

2

8 盲啞 **mōa** blind and mute
　盲啞学校 **mōa gakkō** school for the blind and mute
22 聾啞 **rōa** deaf and mute
　聾啞者 **rōasha** a deaf-mute

3d8.4

啄 啄

TAKU, tsuiba(mu) peck at, pick up

1

4 啄木鳥 **kitsutsuki** woodpecker

3d8.5

唎

WA follow; childless

3d8.6

唖

KŪ angry voice; gargle; throat

3d8.7

唀

O laugh, smile

2

22 囎唀 **Soo** (place name, Kagoshima-ken)

3d8.8 / 1919

喝 喝

KATSU scold; raise one's voice

1

8 喝采 **kassai** applause, cheers
10 喝破 **kappa** declare, proclaim

2

1 一喝 **ikkatsu** a thundering cry, a roar
3 大喝 **taikatsu, daikatsu** bellow, roar, thunder, yell
9 恫喝 **dōkatsu** threaten, intimidate
10 脅喝 **kyōkatsu** threaten, intimidate
　恐喝 **kyōkatsu** threat, intimidation, blackmail
　恐喝罪 **kyōkatsuzai** extortion, blackmail

3d8.9 / 1646

唱

SHŌ, tona(eru) advocate, espouse; chant; cry, yell

1

6 唱名 **shōmyō** chanting Buddha's name
8 唱和 **shōwa** sing/cheer in chorus
10 唱値 **tona(e)ne** asking price
11 唱道 **shōdō** advocate
14 唱歌 **shōka** singing
　唱導 **shōdō** advocate

2

3 三唱 **sanshō** three cheers; sing three times
5 主唱 **shushō** advocate, promote, suggest
6 伝唱 **denshō** advocate, espouse
　合唱 **gasshō** chorus
　合唱曲 **gasshōkyoku** chorus, choral, part-song

合唱団 **gasshōdan** chorus, choir
合唱隊 **gasshōtai** chorus, choir
7 低唱 **teishō** hum, sing softly
吟唱 **ginshō** recite, chant
8 斉唱 **seishō** sing in unison
9 首唱 **shushō** advocate, suggest
首唱者 **shushōsha** advocate, proponent
独唱 **dokushō** vocal solo
10 高唱 **kōshō** sing loudly; advocate; emphasize
12 提唱 **teishō** discourse, lecture; advocate
絶唱 **zesshō** excellent poem/song
詠唱 **eishō** aria
13 暗唱 **anshō** recite (from memory)
愛唱 **aishō** love to sing
14 歌唱 **kashō** singing; song
15 輪唱 **rinshō** round, canon (in music)

——————— 3 ———————

2 二重唱 **nijūshō** vocal duet
3 三重唱 **sanjūshō** vocal trio

——————— 4 ———————

5 四部合唱 **shibu gasshō** (vocal) quartet
11 混声合唱 **konsei gasshō** mixed chorus

3d8.10

啖

TAN, kura(u) eat

——————— 1 ———————

8 啖呵 **tanka** caustic words

——————— 2 ———————

10 健啖 **kentan** hearty appetite, voracity, gluttony
健啖家 **kentanka** hearty eater, trencherman, glutton

3d8.11

啜

SETSU, susu(ru) sip, suck, sniffle

——————— 1 ———————

8 啜泣 **susu(ri)na(ku)** sob, blubber

3d8.12

唸

TEN, una(ru) groan, moan; growl; hum, buzz

3d8.13

啅

TAKU noisy; peck/pick at
TŌ chirping, twittering

3d8.14

啗

TAN eat; entice; include

3d8.15

唳 唳

REI cry, honking (of cranes or wild geese), droning (of cicadas)

3d8.16

啀

GAI, iga(mu) snarl at

——————— 1 ———————

6 啀合 **iga(mi)a(u)** snarl at each other, bicker, feud

3d8.17 / 1398

啓

KEI open; say

——————— 1 ———————

5 啓示 **keiji** revelation
9 啓発 **keihatsu** enlightenment, edification
13 啓蒙 **keimō** enlightenment, instruction, public education, edification
17 啓蟄 **keichitsu** (about March 6)

——————— 2 ———————

6 行啓 **gyōkei** visit/attendance by the empress or crown prince
8 拝啓 **haikei** Dear Sir/Madam
15 還啓 **kankei** return (of the empress)
17 謹啓 **kinkei** Dear Sir:, Gentlemen:

3d8.18

甜

TEN sweet

——————— 1 ———————

11 甜菜 **tensai** sugar beet
甜菜糖 **tensaitō** beet sugar

超 → **3b9.18**

——————— 9 ———————

3d9.1

喰

ku(u), kura(u) eat, drink; receive (a blow)

——————— 2 ———————

2 人喰 **hitoku(i)** man-eating, cannibalism
人喰人種 **hitoku(i) jinshu** cannibals
6 虫喰 **mushiku(i)** damage from worms, moth-eaten spot
14 漆喰 **shikkui** mortar, plaster, stucco

哑 → **3d8.3**

3d9.2

喊 **KAN** shout (a battle cry); shut (one's mouth)

—— 2 ——
7 吶喊 **tokkan** yell a battle cry

唧 → 衛 **3i11.1**

3d9.3

喇 **RATSU, RA** (used phonetically); rapid speech, chattering

—— 1 ——
5 喇叭 **rappa** trumpet, bugle
14 喇嘛教 **Ramakyō** Lamaism

3d9.4

唧 **SHOKU, SOKU** cry (of insects, birds, mice), sigh, burble **kako(tsu)** bewail, whine about

—— 1 ——
12 唧筒 **shokutō** pump

3d9.5

啾 **SHŪ** cry, whimper, neigh

3d9.6

喉 **KŌ, nodo** throat

—— 1 ——
4 喉元 **nodomoto** throat
喉仏 **nodobotoke** Adam's apple
9 喉首 **nodokubi** neck, throat
喉彦 **nodobiko** the uvula
16 喉頸 **nodokubi** neck, throat
喉頭 **kōtō** larynx
喉頭炎 **kōtōen** laryngitis
喉頭癌 **kōtōgan** cancer of the larynx

—— 2 ——
9 咽喉 **inkō** throat

—— 4 ——
6 耳鼻咽喉科 **jibiinkōka** ear, nose, and throat specialty

3d9.7 / 1240

喫 **KITSU** eat, drink, smoke

—— 1 ——
0 喫する **kis(suru)** eat, drink, smoke
9 喫茶 **kissa** tea drinking, teahouse
喫茶店 **kissaten** teahouse, café
13 喫煙 **kitsuen** smoking
喫煙車 **kitsuensha** smoking car
喫煙室 **kitsuenshitsu** smoking room
15 喫緊 **kikkin** urgent, pressing, vital
—— 2 ——
12 満喫 **mankitsu** have one's fill of, fully enjoy

3d9.8

喑 **IN, oshi** mute

3d9.9

喟 **KI** sigh

3d9.10

喋 **CHŌ, shabe(ru)** talk, speak

—— 1 ——
3 喋々 **chōchō** chatter on, be long-winded

喝 → 喝 **3d8.8**

3d9.11

喘 **ZEN, ae(gu)** pant, gasp, breathe hard

—— 1 ——
10 喘息 **zensoku** asthma

3d9.12

喧 **KEN, kamabisu(shii)** noisy, clamorous **yakama(shii)** noisy, boisterous; faultfinding; troublesome; much-talked-about; choosy

—— 1 ——
3 喧々囂々 **kenken-gōgō** pandemonium
6 喧伝 **kenden** bruit about, circulate
13 喧嘩 **kenka** quarrel

喧嘩早 **kenkabaya(i)** quick to quarrel, pugnacious

喧嘩腰 **kenkagoshi** hostile attitude

16 喧噪 **kensō** noisy, tumultuous

18 喧騒 **kensō** noise, din, clamor

——————— 2 ———————

3 大喧嘩 **ōgenka** big quarrel

口喧 **kuchiyakama(shii)** nagging, carping; talkative, gossipy

小喧 **koyakama(shii)** falutfinding, fussy

12 喧喧囂囂 **kenken-gōgō** pandemonium

——————— 3 ———————

4 夫婦喧嘩 **fūfu-genka** domestic quarrel

13 痴話喧嘩 **chiwa-genka** lovers' quarrel

3d9.13

喀 咯

KAKU, ha(ku) vomit, spit up

——————— 1 ———————

6 喀血 **kakketsu** spitting blood

13 喀痰 **kakutan** expectoration; sputum

3d9.14

噦

KAI, kuchibashi beak

——————— 2 ———————

10 容喙 **yōkai** meddling, interference

3d9.15

喩

YU, tato(eru) compare, liken

——————— 2 ———————

5 比喩 **hiyu** simile, metaphor, allegory

比喩的 **hiyuteki** figurative

8 直喩 **chokuyu** simile

12 換喩 **kan'yu** metonymy

13 隠喩 **in'yu** metaphor

暗喩 **an'yu** metaphor

20 譬喩 **hiyu** metaphor, figure of speech

3d9.16

啼

TEI, na(ku) cry, weep; (animals) cry

3d9.17

嘵

RYŌ high-pitched cry

——————— 2 ———————

18 嘲嘵 **ryūryō** clear, sonorous

3d9.18

喃

NAN sound of talking **nō** (exclamation to get someone's attention); (end-of-sentence particle)

3d9.19 / 1587

喚

KAN call **wame(ku)** cry, shout, clamor

——————— 1 ———————

7 喚声 **kansei, wame(ki)goe** shout, yell, scream, outcry

8 喚呼 **kanko** call/cry out

10 喚起 **kanki** evoke, awaken, call forth

11 喚問 **kanmon** summons

——————— 2 ———————

5 召喚 **shōkan** summons

6 叫喚 **kyōkan** shout, shriek, scream

——————— 4 ———————

7 阿鼻叫喚 **abikyōkan** (two of Buddhism's eight hells)

3d9.20

品

GAN rock

嗇 → **2j10.2**

3d9.21 / 934

就

SHŪ, JU, tsu(ku) settle in; take (a seat/position); depart; study (under a teacher) **tsu(keru)** place, appoint **(ni) tsu(ite)** concerning, about

——————— 1 ———————

4 就中 **nakanzuku** especially

6 就任 **shūnin** assumption of office

就任式 **shūninshiki** inauguration, installation

7 就役 **shūeki** be commissioned (a ship)

就学 **shūgaku** attend school

就労 **shūrō** work

就床 **shūshō** go to bed, retire

10 就眠 **shūmin** go to bed/sleep

就航 **shūkō** be commissioned (a ship)

13 就業 **shūgyō** employment

就業日数 **shūgyō nissū** days worked

就業率 **shūgyōritsu** percentage of employment

就寝 **shūshin** go to bed, retire
16 就縛 **shūbaku** catch and tie up
18 就職 **shūshoku** find employment
就職口 **shūshokuguchi** job opening, employment
就職先 **shūshokusaki** place of employment
就職斡旋 **shūshoku assen** job placement
就職難 **shūshokunan** job shortage

——————— 2 ———————
5 去就 **kyoshū** course of action, attitude
6 成就 **jōju** accomplish, achieve, succeed

單 → 単 3n6.2

3d9.22

敧
KI lean toward, prick up (one's ears)

3d9.23

舒
JO stretch; loosen; open; relax; mention

3d9.24

谺
KA, **kodama** echo

喪 → 3b9.20

3d9.25

喬
KYŌ high; boast

——————— 1 ———————
4 喬木 **kyōboku** tall tree

3d9.26 / 960

登
TŌ, TO climb; attendance at one's place of duty; making an entry in an official document **nobo(ru)** climb, ascend

——————— 1 ———————
3 登口 **nobo(ri)guchi** starting point (for ascending a mountain)
登山 **tozan** mountain climbing
登山者 **tozansha** mountain climber
登山家 **tozanka** mountaineer
登山期 **tozanki** mountain-climbing season

5 登仙 **tōsen** die; become a saint
登用 **tōyō** appoint; promote
登庁 **tōchō** attendance at office
7 登坂 **nobo(ri)zaka** uphill slope, ascent
8 登板 **tōban** go to the pitcher's mound
9 登院 **tōin** attend the diet/parliament
登城 **tojō** go to the castle
10 登高 **tōkō** climbing a height
登校 **tōkō** attend school
登記 **tōki** registration, recording
登記所 **tōkisho** registry (office)
登記料 **tōkiryō** registration fee
11 登舷礼 **tōgenrei** full crew's salute from the deck
登第 **tōdai** pass an examination
登頂 **tōchō** reach the summit
12 登場 **tōjō** come on stage; appear on the scene
登極 **tōkyoku** accession, enthronement
13 登楼 **tōrō** going up a tower; visiting a brothel
登載 **tōsai** register, record, enter
16 登壇 **tōdan** ascend the platform, take the rostrum
登録 **tōroku** registration
登録済 **tōrokuzu(mi)** registered
登録簿 **tōrokubo** the register
18 登臨 **tōrin** climb a height; ascend the throne
19 登攀 **tōhan** climb up, ascend
登簿 **tōbo** registration

——————— 2 ———————
3 山登 **yamanobo(ri)** mountain climbing
4 木登 **kinobo(ri)** tree climbing
8 岩登 **iwanobo(ri)** rock climbing
10 這登 **ha(i)nobo(ru)** crawl/clamber up
能登 **Noto** (ancient kuni, Ishikawa-ken)
能登半島 **Noto-hantō** (peninsula, Ishikawa-ken)
13 滝登 **takinobo(ri)** (salmon) climbing a waterfall
19 攀登 **yo(ji)nobo(ru)** climb, scale

——————— 3 ———————
2 人材登用 **jinzai tōyō** selection of people for higher positions
7 住民登録 **jūmin tōroku** resident registration

3d9.27 / 215

短
TAN, **mijika(i)** short

——————— 1 ———————
2 短刀 **tantō** short sword, dagger
3 短大 **tandai** junior college (short for 短期大学)
短才 **tansai** lacking in talent
短小 **tanshō** small
4 短毛 **tanmō** short hair
短毛種 **tanmōshu** short-haired

短文 **tanbun** short sentence/composition
短水路 **tansuiro** short course, 25–50 m pool length
短日 **tanjitsu** a short time
短日月 **tanjitsugetsu** a short time
5 短冊 **tanzaku** strip of paper for writing a poem on
短句 **tanku** short phrase
6 短気 **tanki** short temper, touchiness, hastiness
7 短兵急 **tanpeikyū** impetuous, sudden
短見 **tanken** shortsightedness, narrow view
短足 **tansoku** short legs
8 短命 **tanmei** short-lived
短夜 **miji(ka)yo** short (summer) night
短波 **tanpa** shortwave
短波長 **tanpachō** short wavelength
短所 **tansho** shortcoming, defect, fault
9 短信 **tanshin** brief note/message
短音 **tan'on** short sound
短音階 **tan'onkai** minor scale
10 短剣 **tanken** dagger; hour hand
短時日 **tanjijitsu** a short time
短針 **tanshin** hour hand
12 短期 **tanki** short period, short-term
短期大学 **tanki daigaku** junior college
短絡 **tanraku** short circuit
短艇 **tantei** boat, lifeboat
短評 **tanpyō** short criticism, brief review
短軸 **tanjiku** minor axis
短距離 **tankyori** short distance, short-range
13 短靴 **tangutsu** (low) shoes
短詩 **tanshi** short poem
短資 **tanshi** short-term loan (short for 短資金)
短資金 **tanshikin** short-term loan
14 短髪 **tanpatsu** short hair
短歌 **tanka** 31-syllable poem, tanka
短銃 **tanjū** pistol, handgun
15 短慮 **tanryo** quick/hot temper
短編 **tanpen** short piece/story/film
短篇 **tanpen** short piece/story/film
短篇小説 **tanpen shōsetsu** short story/novel
短調 **tanchō** minor key
17 短縮 **tanshuku** shorten, curtail, abridge
18 短軀 **tanku** short stature

——————— 2 ———————
4 手短 **temiji(ka)** short, brief
日短 **himijika** days getting shorter
6 気短 **kimijika** short-tempered, impatient
8 長短 **chōtan** (relative) length; merits and demerits, advantages and disadvantages
12 超短波 **chōtanpa** ultrashort-wave, very high frequency
最短 **saitan** shortest
16 操短 **sōtan** curtailed operations (short for 操業短縮)

——————— 3 ———————
12 軽薄短小 **keihaku-tanshō** small and light, compact (cf. 重厚長大)
16 操業短縮 **sōgyō tanshuku** curtailed operations

——————— 4 ———————
1 一長一短 **itchō ittan** advantages and disadvantages

3d9.28
殛 **KYOKU** execute, put to death

3d9.29 / 1082
尋 尋 **JIN, tazu(neru)** ask (a question), inquire; seek **hiro** (unit of length, about 182 cm)

——————— 1 ———————
2 尋人 **tazu(ne)bito** person being sought, missing person
8 尋物 **tazu(ne)mono** thing being searched for, lost article
11 尋常 **jinjō** normal, ordinary
尋常一様 **jinjō-ichiyō** common, mediocre
尋問 **jinmon** questioning, interrogation

3d9.30
貂 **CHŌ, ten** marten, sable

——————— 10 ———————
3d10.1
嗚 **O** sigh, crying sound **ā** ah, alas

——————— 1 ———————
8 嗚呼 **ā** (sigh)
9 嗚咽 **oetsu** sobbing, weeping

3d10.2
嗛 **KEN** insufficient; stuff into one's cheeks; satisfied

3d10.3
嗅 **KYŪ, ka(gu)** smell, sniff

——————— 1 ———————
4 嗅分 **ka(gi)wa(keru)** tell/differentiate by scent

5 嗅出 **ka(gi)da(su)** sniff out, get wind of
嗅付 **ka(gi)tsu(keru)** scent, smell out, detect
6 嗅当 **ka(gi)a(teru)** sniff out
9 嗅神経 **kyūshinkei** olfactory nerve
12 嗅覚 **kyūkaku** sense of smell
13 嗅煙草 **ka(gi)tabako** snuff

3d10.4

嗜 **SHI, tashina(mu)** like, have a taste for; be prudent **tashina(mi)** taste; discretion, modesty; one's accomplishments

——————— 1 ———————
5 嗜好 **shikō** taste, liking, preference
嗜好品 **shikōhin** luxury items
10 嗜眠 **shimin** lethargy, torpor

——————— 2 ———————
7 身嗜 **midashina(mi)** personal grooming

3d10.5

嗄 **SA, shaga(reru), shiwaga(reru), ka(reru)** become hoarse **ka(rasu)** make hoarse

——————— 1 ———————
7 嗄声 **shaga(re)goe** hoarse voice

3d10.6

嗉 **SO** craw

——————— 1 ———————
22 嗉嚢 **sonō** (bird's) crop, craw

3d10.7

嘩 譁 **KA** noisy

——————— 2 ———————
12 喧嘩 **kenka** quarrel
喧嘩早 **kenkabaya(i)** quick to quarrel, pugnacious
喧嘩腰 **kenkagoshi** hostile attitude

——————— 3 ———————
3 大喧嘩 **ōgenka** big quarrel

——————— 4 ———————
4 夫婦喧嘩 **fūfu-genka** domestic quarrel
13 痴話喧嘩 **chiwa-genka** lovers' quarrel

3d10.8 / 1246

嘆 嘆 **TAN, nage(ku)** grieve, lament, bemoan; deplore, regret **nage(kawashii)** deplorable

——————— 1 ———————
0 嘆じる/ずる **tan(jiru/zuru)** lament, deplore
7 嘆声 **tansei** sigh; lamentation
9 嘆美 **tanbi** admire, extol
嘆美者 **tanbisha** admirer, adorer
10 嘆息 **tansoku** sigh; lament
15 嘆賞 **tanshō** praise, admire
嘆賞者 **tanshōsha** admirer
19 嘆願 **tangan** entreaty, petition

——————— 2 ———————
3 三嘆 **santan** admire, praise, extol
8 長嘆 **chōtan** a long sigh
12 悲嘆 **hitan** grief, sorrow
痛嘆 **tsūtan** bitter regret, grief
詠嘆 **eitan** exclamation; admiration
13 傷嘆 **shōtan** crying in pain
嗟嘆 **satan** lament, deplore; admire, praise
愁嘆 **shūtan** lamentation, sorrow
愁嘆場 **shūtanba** pathetic/tragic scene
感嘆 **kantan** admiration, wonder, exclamation
感嘆符 **kantanfu** exclamation point (!)
慨嘆 **gaitan** regret, lament, deplore
15 賞嘆 **shōtan** praise, admire
賛嘆 **santan** extol, admire
22 讃嘆 **santan** praise, admiration
驚嘆 **kyōtan** admiration, wonder

——————— 3 ———————
19 髀肉嘆 **hiniku (no) tan** lamenting the lack of opportunity to show one's skill

3d10.9

嘶 嘶 **SHI** laugh at

3d10.10

嗟 **SA** lament **ā** ah

——————— 1 ———————
13 嗟嘆 **satan** lament, deplore; admire, praise
——————— 2 ———————
8 咄嗟 **tossa** moment, instant

3d10.11

嗔 **SHIN, ika(ru)** be angry

3d10.12

嗹 **REN** voluble, garrulous

3

氵
土
扌
口 10←
女
巾
犭
弓
彳
彡
艹
宀
丷
山
吉
广
尸
口

畲 → **3b10.13**

3d10.13 / 1917

嗣

SHI heir

——————— 1 ———————
2 嗣子 **shishi** heir

——————— 2 ———————
9 係嗣 **keishi** successor, heir
後嗣 **kōshi** heir
14 嫡嗣 **chakushi** legitimate heir

號 → 号 **3d2.10**

辞 → **5b8.4**

3d10.14 / 794

群 羣

GUN, mu(re), mura group,
crowd, flock, cluster, clump
mu(reru), mura(garu) crowd,
flock, swarm

——————— 1 ———————
3 群千鳥 **mura chidori** flock of plovers
群小 **gunshō** small, minor, insignificant
群山 **gunzan** many mountains, mountain range
5 群生 **gunsei** grow gregariously, grow in crowds
群立 **murada(tsu)** gather and stand together; take wing in a flock
6 群羊 **gun'yō** flock of sheep
群竹 **muratake** stand of bamboo
7 群体 **guntai** colony (of coral)
群臣 **gunshin** the whole body of officials
8 群盲 **gunmō** blind populace, illiterates
群居 **murei(ru)** crowd together
群青 **gunjō** ultramarine, navy blue
10 群起 **gunki** occur together
群峰 **gunpō** many peaks
群島 **guntō** group of islands, archipelago
群書 **gunsho** various books
群馬県 **Gunma-ken** (prefecture)
11 群盗 **guntō** gang of robbers
12 群落 **gunraku** grow in clusters/crowds
群棲 **gunsei** live gregariously
群衆 **gunshū** crowd, multitude
群雄 **gun'yū** rival chiefs

群雄割拠 **gun'yū kakkyo** rivalry of local barons
群集 **gunshū** crowd, multitude, mob (psychology) **mu(re)atsu(maru)** gather in large groups
14 群像 **gunzō** group of people (in an artwork)
15 群舞 **gunbu** group dance
20 群議 **gungi** multitude of opinions

——————— 2 ———————
1 一群 **hitomu(re), ichigun** a group; a flock, a crowd
3 大群 **taigun** large crowd/herd
6 羊群 **yōgun** flock of sheep
7 抜群 **batsugun** pre-eminent, outstanding
9 星群 **seigun** star cluster
11 魚群 **gyogun** school of fish
19 鶏群 **keigun** flock of chickens

羣 → 群 **3d10.14**

3d10.15 / 959

豊 豐

HŌ, yuta(ka) abundant, rich
toyo- excellent, rich

——————— 1 ———————
4 豊凶 **hōkyō** rich or poor harvest
豊中 **Toyonaka** (city, Ōsaka-fu)
豊水期 **hōsuiki** rainy season
6 豊年 **hōnen** year of abundance
7 豊作 **hōsaku** abundant harvest
9 豊前 **Buzen** (ancient kuni, Fukuoka-ken)
豊後 **Bungo** (ancient kuni, Ōita-ken)
12 豊満 **hōman** plump, corpulent, full-figured
豊富 **hōfu** abundant, affluent
13 豊葦原 **Toyoashihara** (ancient) Japan
14 豊漁 **hōryō, hōgyo** abundant catch
豊熟 **hōjuku** abundant harvest; ripen
15 豊潤 **hōjun** rich, abundant
16 豊橋 **Toyohashi** (city, Aichi-ken)
18 豊穣 **hōjō** abundant harvest
19 豊艶 **hōen** voluptuous
21 豊饒 **hōjō** fertile, productive

——————— 2 ———————
8 実豊 **mino(ri)yuta(ka)** fruitful

——————— 11 ———————
3d11.1 / 925

鳴

MEI, na(ku) (animals) cry, sing, howl
na(ru) (intr.) sound, ring
na(rasu) (tr.) sound, ring

——————— 1 ———————
2 鳴子 **naruko** clapper
4 鳴戸 **naruto** whirlpool, maelstrom

7 鳴声 **na(ki)goe** cry, call, chirping (of animals)
8 鳴物 **na(ri)mono** music(al instruments)
  鳴門 **naruto** whirlpool, maelstrom
  鳴門海峡 **Naruto-kaikyō** (strait between
    Shikoku and Awaji island)
9 鳴飛 **na(kazu)-to(bazu)** inactive, lying low
11 鳴動 **meidō** rumbling
12 鳴禽 **meikin** songbird
  鳴渡 **na(ri)wata(ru)** resound far and wide
19 鳴響 **na(ri)hibi(ku)** resound, reverberate

——————— 2 ———————

3 山鳴 **yamana(ri)** rumbling of a mountain
5 打鳴 **u(chi)na(rasu)** make a sound, jingle,
    clap, ring
6 共鳴 **kyōmei** resonance; sympathy
  耳鳴 **mimina(ri)** ringing in the ears
7 吹鳴 **fu(ki)na(rasu)** blow (a whistle)
9 海鳴 **umina(ri)** roar of the ocean
  怒鳴 **dona(ru)** shout at
10 高鳴 **takana(ru)** ring loud, clang, throb/beat
    audibly
  家鳴 **yana(ri)** rattling of a house
  烏鳴 **karasuna(ki)** caw/cry of the crow
12 遠鳴 **tōna(ri)** distant sound (of thunder, the
    sea)
  悲鳴 **himei** shriek, scream
13 搔鳴 **ka(ki)na(rasu)** strum, thrum
  雷鳴 **raimei** thunder
15 踏鳴 **fu(mi)na(rasu)** stamp noisily
19 爆鳴 **bakumei** detonation
  鶏鳴 **keimei** cockcrow, rooster's crowing

——————— 3 ———————

3 大山鳴動鼠一匹 **taizan meidō (shite)**
    nezumi ippiki The mountains have
    brought forth a mouse. Much ado about
    nothing much.

3d11.2
嗷
GŌ noisy; lamentation

3d11.3
嗽
SŌ, susu(gu) rinse, wash
ugai gargling

——————— 2 ———————

9 咳嗽 **gaisō** cough, coughing

3d11.4
嗾
SŌ, keshika(keru) sic (a dog) on,
instigate, egg on

——————— 2 ———————

8 使嗾 **shisō** instigate

3d11.5
嘈
SŌ noisy

噌 → 噲 **3d12.9**

3d11.6
嘖
SAKU noisy, loud; many

嘆 → 嘆 **3d10.8**

3d11.7
嘘 嘘
KYO, uso lie, falsehood, fib

——————— 1 ———————

2 嘘八百 **usohappyaku** a pack of lies
5 嘘字 **usoji** miswritten kanji
6 嘘吐 **usotsu(ki)** liar, fibber
9 嘘発見器 **uso hakkenki** lie detector

——————— 2 ———————

3 大嘘 **ōuso** big lie

3d11.8
嘛
MA (used phonetically)

——————— 2 ———————

12 喇嘛教 **Ramakyō** Lamaism

3d11.9
嘔
Ō vomiting

——————— 1 ———————

6 嘔吐 **ōto** vomiting

號 → 号 **3d2.10**

3d11.10
兢
KYŌ fear, apprehension

——————— 1 ———————

3 兢々 **kyōkyō** with fear (and trembling)

3d11.11

飽→ 3s11.1

3d11.11

敲 KŌ, tata(ku) hit, strike, tap

──────── 2 ────────
11 推敲 suikō polish, elaborate on, work over

奩→奩 2t13.1

──────── 12 ────────

3d12.1

嘶 SEI, inana(ku) neigh, whinny, bray

3d12.2

嘲 CHŌ, azake(ru) ridicule

──────── 1 ────────
7 嘲弄 chōrō ridicule
15 嘲罵 chōba taunt, revile, insult
──────── 2 ────────
6 自嘲 jichō self-scorn

3d12.3

噉 TAN, kura(u) eat

3d12.4

嘸 BU unclear
sazo how, indeed, surely

3d12.5

噀 SON spout water

嚙→齧 3d15.2

3d12.6

噎 ETSU, muse(bu), mu(seru) choke, get choked up

3d12.7

噚 Ei-biro fathom

3d12.8 / 1660

噴 FUN, fu(ku) emit, spout, spew forth

──────── 1 ────────
4 噴水 funsui jet of water; fountain
噴火 funka (volcanic) eruption
噴火口 funkakō crater
噴火山 funkazan volcano
5 噴出 funshutsu eruption, gushing, spouting
fu(ki)da(su) spew/gush/spurt out, discharge
9 噴泉 funsen spring, geyser
10 噴射 funsha jet, spray, injection
13 噴煙 fun'en (volcanic) smoke, exhaust fumes
19 噴霧器 funmuki sprayer, vaporizer
──────── 2 ────────
8 逆噴射 gyakufunsha retro-firing

嘘→嘘 3d11.7

噂→噂 3d12.10

3d12.9

噌 噌 SŌ noisy

──────── 2 ────────
8 味噌 miso miso (fermented bean paste)
味噌汁 miso shiru miso soup
味噌歯 miso(p)pa decayed baby tooth
味噌擂 misosu(ri) grinding miso; flattery
味噌擂坊主 misosu(ri) bōzu petty priest
──────── 3 ────────
8 泣味噌 na(ki)miso crybaby
10 弱味噌 yowamiso weakling, coward
11 脳味噌 nōmiso brains, gray matter
17 糠味噌 nuka miso rice-bran miso
糠味噌漬 nukamisozu(ke) vegetables pickled in rice-bran miso
糞味噌 kuso-miso (confusing) the valuable and the worthless; sweeping denunciation

3d12.10

噂 噂 SON, uwasa rumor, gossip

───────── 1 ─────────

13 噂話 **uwasabanashi** rumor, gossip, hearsay
14 噂種 **uwasa (no) tane** source of rumors, subject of gossip

3d12.11 / 1638

嘱 囑　**SHOKU** request, entrust, commission

───────── 1 ─────────

5 嘱目 **shokumoku** pay attention to, watch
10 嘱託 **shokutaku** put in charge of, commission; part-time employee
11 嘱望 **shokubō** expect much of

───────── 2 ─────────

8 依嘱 **ishoku** entrust with, commission
委嘱 **ishoku** entrust with

3d12.12

髫　**CHŌ** ponytail, bangs; young child

3d12.13 / 527

器 器 噐　**KI, utsuwa** container; apparatus; capacity, ability

───────── 1 ─────────

5 器用 **kiyō** dextrous, adroit, skillful
器用貧乏 **kiyō-binbō** Jack of all trades but master of none
7 器材 **kizai** tools and materials, equipment
8 器官 **kikan** organ (of the body)
器物 **kibutsu** container, utensil, implement, fixture
器具 **kigu** utensil, appliance, tool, apparatus
10 器財 **kizai** tools
11 器械 **kikai** apparatus, appliance
12 器量 **kiryō** looks; ability; dignity
器量人 **kiryōjin** talented person
13 器楽 **kigaku** instrumental music

───────── 2 ─────────

3 大器 **taiki** large container; great talent
大器晩成 **taiki bansei** Great talent blooms late.
才器 **saiki** talent, ability
土器 **doki, kawarake** unglazed earthenware, crockery
小器 **shōki** small receptacle; man of small caliber
4 不器用 **bukiyō** clumsy, unskillful
不器量 **bukiryō** ugly, homely
凶器 **kyōki** lethal weapon
什器 **jūki** utensil, appliance, furniture

公器 **kōki** public institution
火器 **kaki** firearms
5 用器 **yōki** instrument, tool
用器画 **yōkiga** mechanical drawing
石器 **sekki** stonework; stone implements
石器時代 **sekki jidai** the Stone Age
6 兇器 **kyōki** lethal weapon
名器 **meiki** exquisite/famous article/instrument
7 兵器 **heiki** weapon, arms
花器 **kaki** flower vase
尿器 **nyōki** bedpan, urinal
利器 **riki** sharp-edged tool; a convenience (of civilization)
8 宝器 **hōki** treasured article
性器 **seiki** sexual/genital organ
武器 **buki** weapon, arms
武器倉 **bukigura** armory
武器庫 **bukiko** armory
9 便器 **benki** toilet, urinal, bedpan
茶器 **chaki** tea-things
神器 **jingi, shinki** the (three) sacred treasures (mirror, sword, jewels)
計器 **keiki** meter, gauge, instruments
食器 **shokki** eating utensils
10 陶器 **tōki** china, ceramics, pottery
陶器商 **tōkishō** crockery dealer, chinashop
酒器 **shuki** saké cup/vat
容器 **yōki** container
紙器 **shiki** papier-mâché articles
11 祭器 **saiki** ceremonial equipment
12 量器 **ryōki** a measure (for volume)
無器用 **bukiyō** clumsy
鈍器 **donki** blunt object (used as a weapon)
13 楽器 **gakki** musical instrument
楽器店 **gakkiten** music shop
楽器屋 **gakkiya** music shop
愛器 **aiki** favorite musical instrument
鉄器 **tekki** ironware, hardware
14 漆器 **shikki** lacquerware
徳器 **tokki** virtue and talent; noble character
磁器 **jiki** porcelain
銀器 **ginki** silver utensils
銃器 **jūki** firearm
銅器 **dōki** copper/bronze utensil
15 熱器具 **netsukigu** heating appliances
16 衡器 **kōki** a balance, scales
機器 **kiki** machinery (and tools), equipment
19 臓器 **zōki** internal organs, viscera

───────── 3 ─────────

4 止音器 **shionki** (piano) damper
分光器 **bunkōki** spectroscope
分度器 **bundoki** protractor
水準器 **suijunki** (carpenter's) level
5 生殖器 **seishokki, seishokuki** reproductive organs
打楽器 **dagakki** percussion instrument

穴開器 **anaa(ke)ki** punch, perforator
6 気化器 **kikaki** carburetor
充電器 **jūdenki** charger
吸入器 **kyūnyūki** inhaler, respirator
7 冷却器 **reikyakuki** refrigerator, freezer,
　　　　　　cooler, (car) radiator
冷凍器 **reitōki** freezer
投光器 **tōkōki** floodlight
8 受話器 **juwaki** (telephone) receiver
送話器 **sōwaki** transmitter
油搾器 **aburashiboriki** oil press
泌尿器 **hinyōki** urinary organs
注射器 **chūshaki** hypodermic syringe,
　　　　　　injector
泡立器 **awada(te)ki** eggbeater
抵抗器 **teikōki** resistor, rheostat
拡声器 **kakuseiki** loudspeaker
呼吸器 **kokyūki** respiratory organs
弦楽器 **gengakki** string instrument, the
　　　　　　strings
青銅器 **seidōki** bronze ware/tools
炊飯器 **suihanki** (electric) rice cooker
放熱器 **hōnetsuki** radiator
9 発生器 **hasseiki** generator
発声器 **hasseiki** vocal organs
発振器 **hasshinki** oscillator
重火器 **jūkaki** heavy weapons
除草器 **josōki** weeder
変圧器 **hen'atsuki** transformer
変流器 **henryūki** current transformer
点滅器 **tenmetsuki** a switch
連結器 **renketsuki** coupler
通風器 **tsūfūki** ventilator, aerator
風信器 **fūshinki** weather vane
洗面器 **senmenki** wash basin
洋楽器 **yōgakki** Western musical instruments
指示器 **shijiki** indicator
砕炭器 **saitanki** coal crusher
計量器 **keiryōki** meter, gauge, scale
計算器 **keisanki** calculator
10 陶磁器 **tōjiki** ceramics, china and porcelain
消化器 **shōkaki** digestive organs
消火器 **shōkaki** fire extinguisher
消毒器 **shōdokuki** sterilizer
消音器 **shōonki** muffler, silencer
弱音器 **jakuonki** a damper, mute
核兵器 **kakuheiki** nuclear weapons
11 探知器 **tanchiki** detector
菓子器 **kashiki** cake-serving bowl
痕跡器官 **konseki kikan** vestigial organ
絃楽器 **gengakki** stringed instrument
転換器 **tenkanki** commutator, switch
転路器 **tenroki** railroad switch
12 測音器 **sokuonki** sonometer, phonometer
測程器 **sokuteiki** (ship's) log
湯沸器 **yuwa(kashi)ki** hot-water heater

復水器 **fukusuiki** condenser
循環器 **junkanki** circulatory organ
蒸溜器 **jōryūki** a still
検圧器 **ken'atsuki** pressure gauge
検流器 **kenryūki** current gauge, ammeter
検温器 **ken'onki** (clinical) thermometer
検湿器 **kenshitsuki** hygrometer
検潮器 **kenchōki** tide gauge
補聴器 **hochōki** hearing aid
集塵器 **shūjinki** dust collector
開閉器 **kaiheiki** make-and-break switch
13 遮断器 **shadanki** circuit breaker
蓄音器 **chikuonki** gramophone
蓄電器 **chikudenki** condenser, capacitor
孵卵器 **furanki** incubator
継電器 **keidenki** (electrical) relay
電熱器 **dennetsuki** electric heater
14 増音器 **zōonki** amplifier
増幅器 **zōfukuki** amplifier
複写器 **fukushaki** copier
管楽器 **kangakki** wind instruments
15 潜水器 **sensuiki** diving bell/apparatus
噴霧器 **funmuki** sprayer, vaporizer
緩衝器 **kanshōki** bumper, shock absorber
16 整流器 **seiryūki** rectifier
17 聴音器 **chōonki** sound detector
聴診器 **chōshinki** stethoscope
23 攪拌器 **kakuhanki** agitator, shaker, beater

——————————— 4 ———————————

3 三種神器 **Sanshu (no) Jingi** the Three Sacred
　　　　　　Treasures (mirror, sword, and jewels)
6 有鍵楽器 **yūken gakki** keyed (musical)
　　　　　　instrument
14 嘘発見器 **uso hakkenki** lie detector

器 → 器 **3d12.13**

3d12.14

豌

EN pea

——————————— 1 ———————————
7 豌豆 **endō** peas

——————————— 2 ———————————
8 青豌豆 **aoendō** green peas
10 莢豌豆 **sayaendō** field/garden pea

舗 → 舗 **3b12.4**

毆 → 殴 **2t6.1**

靠 → 靠　4g11.1

───── 13 ─────

3d13.1

嘯　SHŌ, usobu(ku) roar, howl; recite poetry, sing; brag; act nonchalant

───── 2 ─────
8 空嘯 sorausobu(ku) feign unconcern

3d13.2

噺　hanashi talk, story, tale

3d13.3

噸　ton ton (1000 kg; 2240 lbs; 2000 lbs; 1000 cubic feet; 40 cubic feet)

3d13.4

噯　AI breath

───── 1 ─────
6 噯気 okubi belch, burp

3d13.5

噤　KIN shut, close

3d13.6

噬　ZEI bite

3d13.7

嘴　SHI, kuchibashi, hashi beak

───── 1 ─────
5 嘴広鴨 hashibirogamo spoonbill
───── 2 ─────
9 砂嘴 sashi sandbar, sandspit
21 鶴嘴 tsuruhashi pick(ax)

3d13.8

噫　I, ā (exclamation)
　AI, okubi burp, belch

3d13.9

噪　SŌ be noisy

───── 2 ─────
12 喧噪 kensō noisy, tumultuous

3d13.10

嚆　KŌ call, cry, make a sound

───── 1 ─────
5 嚆矢 kōshi arrow rigged to buzz as it flies (shot at start of battle); beginning, kickoff

3d13.11

髻　KEI, tabusa, motodori topknot, queue

器 → 器　3d12.13

劔 → 剣　2f8.5

舘 → 館　8b8.3

3d13.12

甌　Ō, hotogi small jar, jug

───── 2 ─────
8 金甌無欠 kin'ō-muketsu, kinnō-muketsu perfect, unblemished

豎 → 竪　5b9.5

3d13.13

殫　TAN become exhausted; all

豫 → 予　0a4.12

——— 14 ———

3d14.1 / 1918

嚇

KAKU, odo(kasu), odo(su) threaten

——— 1 ———

3 嚇々 **kakukaku(taru), kakkaku(taru)** brilliant, glorious
9 嚇怒 **kakudo** fury, rage

——— 2 ———

9 威嚇 **ikaku** menace, threat
威嚇的 **ikakuteki** menacing, threatening

3d14.2

齂

HI breathing through the nose, snorting
kakame wife, one's old lady

3d14.3

嗽

KAI, shaku(ru) scoop
shakkuri hiccups

嚔 → 嚔 **3d15.3**

3d14.4

嚀

NEI courtesy, kindness

——— 2 ———

5 叮嚀 **teinei** polite, courteous

營 → 営 **3n9.2**

氈 → **3s14.1**

貌 → 貔 **0a11.1**

牆 → **3b14.6**

3d14.5 / 1925

矯

KYŌ, ta(meru) straighten; correct

——— 1 ———

5 矯正 **kyōsei** correct, reform
8 矯直 **ta(me)nao(su)** set up again, correct, reform, cure
9 矯風 **kyōfū** moral reform
矯眇 **ta(metsu)-suga(metsu)** with a scrutinizing eye
16 矯激 **kyōgeki** radical, extreme

——— 2 ———

8 奇矯 **kikyō** eccentric, erratic

——— 15 ———

3d15.1

嚠

RYŪ clear sound

——— 1 ———

12 嚠喨 **ryūryō** clear, sonorous

3d15.2

噛 噛

GŌ, KŌ, ka(mu) bite, gnaw, chew

——— 1 ———

4 噛切 **ka(mi)ki(ru)** bite off, gnaw through
噛分 **ka(mi)wa(keru)** understand, appreciate
5 噛付 **ka(mi)tsu(ku)** bite/snap at
6 噛合 **ka(mi)a(u)** bite each other; (gears) engage, mesh with
ka(mi)a(waseru) clench (one's teeth); engage (gears), mesh with
9 噛砕 **ka(mi)kuda(ku)** crunch; simplify
10 噛殺 **ka(mi)koro(su)** bite to death; suppress (a yawn)
13 噛傷 **ka(mi)kizu** a bite (wound)
噛煙草 **ka(mi)tabako** chewing tobacco
15 噛潰 **ka(mi)tsubu(su)** chew up
噛締 **ka(mi)shi(meru)** chew well; ponder

——— 2 ———

9 食噛 **ku(i)kaji(ru)** gnaw at, nibble; have a smattering of knowledge
11 脛噛 **sunekaji(ri)** hanger-on, sponger
12 歯噛 **haga(mi)** grinding one's teeth
18 臑噛 **sunekaji(ri)** hanger-on, sponger
臍噛 **hozo (o) ka(mu)** bitterly rue/regret

3d15.3

嚔 嚔

TEI, kushami, kusame sneeze

臨 → **2t15.1**

豐 → 豊　3d10.15

3d15.4

嚮　KYŌ, muka(u) face toward
saki earlier, before

――――― 1 ―――――

14 嚮導 kyōdō guidance; leader

3d15.5

軀 躯　KU, mukuro, karada body

――――― 1 ―――――

13 軀幹 kukan body, build, physique

――――― 2 ―――――

5 巨軀 kyoku massive figure, large build
6 老軀 rōku one's old bones, old age
7 体軀 taiku body; height; physique
8 長軀 chōku tall stature
10 病軀 byōku sickly constitution, poor health
12 短軀 tanku short stature
14 痩軀 sōku lean figure

――――― 16 ―――――

3d16.1

嚬　HIN, hiso(meru) wrinkle up (one's
brow), scowl

3d16.2

嚥　EN swallow, gulp (cf. 燕 3k13.16)

――――― 1 ―――――

3 嚥下 enge, enka swallowing

3d16.3

 艶 艷　EN, tsuya gloss, luster, sheen;
charm, romance, love
tsuya(meku) be glossy;
be romantic/sexy
tsuya(ppoi) romantic, sexy, coquettish
namame(ku) be charming/voluptuous
namame(kashii) charming, captivating,
voluptuous, lucious　ade(yaka) charming,
fascinating

――――― 1 ―――――

5 艶出 tsuyada(shi) polishing, glazing,
burnishing, calendering, mercerizing

艶布巾 tsuyabukin polishing cloth
8 艶事 tsuyagoto love affair, romance
艶物 tsuyamono love story
9 艶美 enbi beauty, charm
艶拭 tsuyabu(ki) rub and polish
10 艶消 tsuyake(shi) non-glossy, frosted (glass)
艶容 en'yō fascinating figure, charming look
艶書 ensho love letter
艶紙 tsuyagami glossy paper
艶笑小説 enshō shōsetsu love-comedy story/
novel
11 艶陽 en'yō balmy late spring
13 艶福 enpuku success in love
艶福家 enpukuka ladies' man, a gallant
14 艶種 tsuyadane love affair/rumor
艶聞 enbun love affair/rumor
19 艶麗 enrei captivatingly beautiful

――――― 2 ―――――

6 色艶 irotsuya (facial) color, complexion;
luster
7 妖艶 yōen voluptuous charm, bewitching
beauty
10 凄艶 seien bewitchingly beautiful
13 豊艶 hōen voluptuous
15 嬌艶 kyōen captivating beauty
16 濃艶 nōen charming, bewitching
17 優艶 yūen beautiful and refined, charming

――――― 17 ―――――

3d17.1

嚶　Ō chirping, (birds) singing together

3d17.2

嚳　KOKU announce, inform

嚴 → 厳　3n14.1

3d17.3

韜　TŌ bag for keeping a bow; wrap, cover
up

――――― 1 ―――――

11 韜晦 tōkai conceal (one's talent/identity)

戯 → 献　3g9.6

3

氵
土
扌
口　17←
女
巾
犭
弓
彳
彡
艹
宀
⺌
⺹
广
尸
口

3d17.4

齠 CHŌ baby teeth; young child

3d17.5

齝 nire(gamu), nige(gamu) chew the cud, ruminate

3d17.6

齣 SEKI act, scene (of a play); chapter, section (of a novel) koma scene (of a story/movie), frame (of a film)

─────── 2 ───────

1 一齣 hitokoma a frame (of a film); a scene

體→体 2a5.6

─────── 18 ───────

3d18.1

囃 SŌ, haya(su) accompany (music), beat/ clap time; banter hayashi (percussion) accompaniment

─────── 1 ───────

2 囃子 hayashi (percussion) accompaniment

─────── 2 ───────

7 言囃 i(i)haya(su) praise; spread (a report)

─────── 3 ───────

4 五人囃子 goninbayashi five court-musician dolls

3d18.2

囀 TEN, saezu(ru) chirp, twitter

3d18.3

嚼 SHAKU, ka(mu) chew

─────── 2 ───────

8 咀嚼 soshaku chew, masticate; digest, assimilate (what one has read)

3d18.4

囈 GEI delirious talk

─────── 1 ───────

7 囈言 uwagoto talking deliriously

14 囈語 geigo, tawagoto nonsense
uwagoto talking deliriously

3d18.5

囁 SHŌ, sasaya(ku) whisper

嚻→ 9a12.3

─────── 19 ───────

3d19.1

囎 SO, SHŌ (used in proper names)

─────── 1 ───────

11 囎唹 Soo (place name, Kagoshima-ken)

3d19.2

轡 HI, kutsuwa (horse's) bit

─────── 2 ───────

8 金轡 kanagutsuwa horse's bit; hush money

13 猿轡 sarugutsuwa a gag (in one's mouth)

3d19.3

囊 嚢 NŌ bag, pouch, sac

─────── 1 ───────

4 囊中 nōchū in the bag; in one's purse
囊中錐 nōchū (no) kiri Talent will show.

─────── 2 ───────

2 子囊 shinō ascus, seed pod

3 土囊 donō sandbag

4 水囊 suinō water bag; filter, percolator

5 氷囊 hyōnō ice bag/pack

6 気囊 kinō air sac/bladder
行囊 kōnō mailbag

9 胆囊 tannō gallbladder
胆囊炎 tannōen gallbladder inflammation
背囊 hainō knapsack
砂囊 sanō, sunabukuro sandbag; gizzard

10 陰囊 innō the scrotum
涙囊 ruinō tear sac

12 智囊 chinō brains, wits, ingenuity

13 嗉囊 sonō (bird's) crop, craw

14 精囊 seinō seminal vesicle

3d19.4

齬 GO uneven bite, discrepancy

───── 2 ─────
20 齟齬 **sogo** inconsistency, discrepancy, contradiction, conflict; go awry, fail in

───── 20 ─────

靨 → 4c19.1

───── 21 ─────

齧 → 齧 2a19.4

嚻 → 嘱 3d12.11

艶 → 艷 3d16.3

3d21.1

齶 GAKU, **haguki** the gums

齩 → 3s21.1

───── 3

女 3e

女	好	奴	如	妃	奸	妁	妄	妨	姸	妊	妖	妙
0.1	2.1	2.2	3.1	3.2	3.3	3.4	2j4.6	4.1	4.2	4.3	4.4	4.5
妣	妓	妝	妥	妬	姆	姓	妹	姐	妲	姑	姉	始
4.6	4.7	4.8	4.9	5.1	5.2	5.3	5.4	5.5	5.6	5.7	5.8	5.9
妻	妾	姨	姥	娜	姚	妊	娃	姪	姶	姻	姦	姿
5.10	5b3.2	6.1	6.2	6.3	6.4	3e4.3	6.5	6.6	6.7	6.8	6.9	6.10
要	娥	娘	娯	婀	甥	娉	娟	娩	娣	娠	姫	娑
6.11	7.1	7.2	7.3	7.4	7.5	7.6	7.7	7.8	7.9	7.10	7.11	7.12
婢	娵	娼	婚	姪	婉	婦	娩	娶	婁	婆	婪	嫂
8.1	8.2	8.3	8.4	3a8.17	8.5	8.6	3e7.8	8.7	8.8	8.9	8.10	9.1
媒	婿	媛	嫌	媚	媽	嫌	嫐	嫋	媳	媾	媼	嫁
9.2	9.3	9.4	3e10.7	9.5	10.1	3e10.7	5f12.1	10.2	10.3	10.4	10.5	10.6
嫌	嫉	嫩	嫖	嫣	嫦	嫡	嫗	嬌	嬋	嬉	嫻	嫺
10.7	10.8	11.1	11.2	11.3	11.4	11.5	11.6	12.1	12.2	12.3	3e12.4	12.4
嬢	嬖	嬛	嬬	嬰	嬪	孋	孺	孃	孅			
13.1	13.2	14.1	14.2	14.3	14.4	16.1	17.1	3e13.1	17.2			

───── 0 ─────

3e0.1 / 102

女 **JO, NYO, NYŌ, onna, me-** woman, female

───── 1 ─────
0 女らしい **onna(rashii)** womanly, ladylike
女だてらに **onna(datera ni)** although a woman, unladylike
2 女人 **nyonin** woman
女人禁制 **nyonin kinsei** closed to women
女子 **joshi** woman; women's **onna(no)ko**
girl **onago** girl, woman, maid
女子大生 **joshi daisei** a coed
3 女工 **jokō** woman factory worker
女丈夫 **jojōfu** heroic woman
女々 **meme(shii)** effeminate, unmanly
4 女天下 **onnadenka** a woman who is boss
女中 **jochū** maid
女文字 **onna moji** woman's handwriting; hiragana
女手 **onnade** woman's handwriting; hiragana; a woman to do the work
女王 **joō** queen
女王蜂 **joōbachi** queen bee

女心　**onnagokoro**　a woman's heart
5 女生　**josei**　schoolgirl, coed
女生徒　**joseito**　schoolgirl, coed
女世帯　**onnajotai**　household of women
女史　**joshi**　Mrs., Miss, Madam
女好　**onnazu(ki)**　fond of women; liked by women
女囚　**joshū**　female prisoner
女白波　**onna shiranami**　woman robber
女主　**onna aruji**　mistress, landlady, hostess
6 女色　**joshoku**　feminine charms, sensuality
7 女体　**nyotai, jotai**　woman's body
女兵　**johei**　woman soldier
女医　**joi**　woman doctor
女狂　**onnaguru(i)**　chase women, philander
女形　**onnagata, oyama**　female role
女学生　**jogakusei**　girl student
女学院　**jogakuin**　girls' academy
女学校　**jogakkō**　girls' school
女声　**josei**　female voice
女旱　**onna hideri**　shortage of women
女児　**joji**　(baby) girl
女系　**jokei**　female line(age), on the mother's side
8 女郎　**jorō**　prostitute
女郎花　**ominaeshi**　(a yellow-flowered plant)
女郎屋　**jorōya**　brothel
女官　**jokan, nyokan**　minor court lady
女店員　**joten'in**　salesgirl
女性　**josei**　woman; feminine gender
女性化　**joseika**　feminization
女性的　**joseiteki**　feminine
女性美　**joseibi**　womanly beauty
女性解放論　**josei kaihōron**　feminism
女房　**nyōbō**　wife; court lady
女房役　**nyōbōyaku**　helpmate
女房持　**nyōbōmo(chi)**　married man
9 女帝　**jotei**　empress
女持　**onnamo(chi)**　for women, ladies'
女神　**megami, joshin, nyoshin**　goddess
女皇　**jokō**　empress, queen
10 女将　**joshō, okami**　landlady, proprietress
女流　**joryū**　woman (writer/singer)
女振　**onnabu(ri)**　a woman's looks/charms
女帯　**onna obi**　woman's obi
女殺　**onnagoro(shi)**　ladykiller
女教員　**jokyōin**　female teacher
女教師　**jokyōshi**　female teacher
11 女道楽　**onna dōraku**　carnal pleasures
女盛　**onnazaka(ri)**　the prime of womanhood
12 女尊　**joson**　respect for women
女尊男卑　**joson-danpi**　putting women above men
女湯　**onnayu**　ladies' bath
女婿　**josei**　son-in-law
女装　**josō**　female attire, drag

女給　**jokyū**　waitress
13 女傑　**joketsu**　outstanding woman
女僧　**nyosō**　Buddhist nun
女嫌　**onnagira(i)**　misogynist
15 女権　**joken**　women's rights
女権論者　**jokenronsha**　feminist
16 女親　**onna oya**　mother
17 女優　**joyū**　actress
18 女難　**jonan**　trouble with women
20 女護島　**nyogo(ga)shima**　isle of women

──────── 2 ────────

1 乙女　**otome**　virgin, maiden
2 子女　**shijo**　children
3 工女　**kōjo**　factory girl
才女　**saijo**　talented woman
下女　**gejo**　maidservant, (house)maid
下女下男　**gejo-genan**　servants
下女中　**shimojochū**　kitchen maid
女女　**meme(shii)**　effeminate, unmanly
山女　**yamame**　(a kind of trout)
　　　akebi　(a kind of shrub having tendrils)
士女　**shijo**　men and women
4 天女　**tennyo**　celestial nymph, goddess
少女　**shōjo**　girl
王女　**ōjo**　princess
5 仙女　**sennyo, senjo**　fairy, nymph
幼女　**yōjo**　little/baby girl
処女　**shojo**　virgin
処女作　**shojosaku**　one's first (published) work
処女性　**shojosei**　virginity
処女航海　**shojo kōkai**　maiden voyage
処女膜　**shojomaku**　the hymen
6 次女　**jijo**　second daughter
孝女　**kōjo**　dutiful/devoted daughter
老女　**rōjo**　old woman; senior lady-in-waiting
色女　**iroonna**　mistress
7 巫女　**miko, fujo**　medium, sorceress; shrine maiden
妖女　**yōjo**　enchantress, a bewitching beauty
狂女　**kyōjo**　madwoman
児女　**jijo**　little girl; children
男女　**danjo, nannyo**　men and women
8 長女　**chōjo**　eldest daughter
侍女　**jijo**　lady in waiting
妻女　**saijo**　wife; wife and daughter(s)
彼女　**kanojo**　she; girlfriend, lover
官女　**kanjo**　court lady
9 信女　**shinnyo**　(title affixed to woman's posthumous Buddhist name)
貞女　**teijo**　chaste woman, faithful wife
美女　**bijo**　beautiful woman
美女桜　**bijozakura**　verbena
浮女　**u(kare)me**　prostitute
海女　**ama**　woman (pearl) diver
皇女　**kōjo**　imperial princess

10 遊女 **yūjo, aso(bi)me** prostitute
　　遊女屋 **yūjoya** brothel
　　宮女 **kyūjo** court lady
　　烈女 **retsujo** heroic woman
　　息女 **sokujo** daughter
　　鬼女 **kijo** she-devil; cruel woman
　　針女 **harime** seamstress
11 淑女 **shukujo** lady, gentlewoman
　　婦女 **fujo** woman
　　婦女子 **fujoshi** woman; woman and child
　　悪女 **akujo** wicked/ugly woman
　　雪女 **yukionna** snow fairy
　　雪女郎 **yukijorō** snow fairy
12 善女 **zennyo** woman Buddhist
　　湯女 **yuna** hot-springs prostitute
　　童女 **dōjo** girl
　　貴女 **kijo, anata** lady, you (feminine)
13 隠女 **kaku(shi)onna** a mistress
　　裸女 **rajo** nude woman
14 歌女 **utame** singer, songstress
　　端女 **hashi(ta)me** maidservant
15 養女 **yōjo** adopted daughter; stepdaughter; daughter-in-law
　　賤女 **shizu(no)me** woman of humble birth
17 優女 **yasa-onna** gentle woman
　　醜女 **shūjo, shikome** ugly woman
18 織女 **shokujo** woman textile worker
21 魔女 **majo** witch, sorceress

———————— 3 ————————

6 早乙女 **saotome** rice-planting girl
　　早少女 **saotome** rice-planting girl
7 男尊女卑 **danson-johi** predominance of men over women
8 押掛け女房 **o(shi)ka(ke) nyōbō** a woman who pressured her husband into marrying her
10 修道女 **shūdōjo** (Catholic) nun

———————— 4 ————————

4 天津乙女 **amatsuotome** celestial maiden
12 善男善女 **zennan-zennyo** devout men and women

———————— 2 ————————

3e2.1 / 104

好　　**KŌ, kono(mu), su(ku), su(ki)** like, be fond of **-zu(ki)** lover/fan of **yo(shi)**, **i(i), yo(i)** good, favorable, alright

———————— 1 ————————

1 好一対 **kōittsui** well-matched (couple)
2 好人物 **kōjinbutsu** good-natured person
3 好下物 **kōkabutsu** favorite dish/snack
　　好々爺 **kōkōya** good-natured old man
4 好天気 **kōtenki** fine weather
　　好手 **kōshu** good move (in a game)
5 好加減 **i(i) kagen** moderate, temperate, suitable; haphazard, irresponsible, not thorough, halfhearted
好古 **kōko** love of antiquities
好古癖 **kōkoheki** antiquarianism
好打 **kōda** good hit
好打者 **kōdasha** (baseball) slugger
好好 **su(ki)zu(ki)** a matter of individual preferences
6 好気 **i(i) ki** easygoing, happy-go-lucky; conceited
好印象 **kōinshō** good impression
好色 **kōshoku** sensuality, eroticism, lust
好色本 **kōshokubon** erotic story
好色家 **kōshokuka** sensualist, lecher
好色漢 **kōshokukan** sensualist, lecher
好成績 **kōseiseki** good results/record
7 好角家 **kōkakuka** sumo fan
好技 **kōgi** fine play/game/acting
好学 **kōgaku** love of learning
好材料 **kōzairyō** good material/data
好男子 **kōdanshi** handsome man
8 好事 **kōji** happy event; good act
　　kōzu curiosity, dilettantism
好事家 **kōzuka** dilettante, amateur
好例 **kōrei** good example, case in point
好況 **kōkyō** prosperity, boom
好味 **kōmi** good flavor; tasty foods
好奇 **kōki** curiosity, inquisitiveness
好奇心 **kōkishin** curiosity, inquisitiveness
好尚 **kōshō** taste, fashion
好者 **su(ki)mono** dilettante; lecher
好物 **kōbutsu** a favorite food
好放題 **su(ki)hōdai** doing just as one pleases
好取組 **kōtorikumi** good game/match
10 好個 **kōko** fine, good, ideal
好都合 **kōtsugō** favorable, good
好時期 **kōjiki** good season for
好時機 **kōjiki** opportune moment, the right time
11 好運 **kōun** good fortune, luck
好望 **kōbō** promising future
好悪 **kōo** likes and dislikes
好転 **kōten** a turn for the better
12 好機 **kōki** the right time
好晴 **kōsei** fine weather
好景気 **kōkeiki** business prosperity, boom
好焼 **(o)kono(mi)ya(ki)** (unsweetened batter fried with vegetable bits into a thick griddlecake)
好結果 **kōkekka** good results, success
好評 **kōhyō** favorable reception, popularity
13 好適 **kōteki** ideally suited
好漢 **kōkan** fine fellow
好嫌 **su(ki)kira(i)** likes and dislikes, preferences
好楽家 **kōgakuka** music lover

3

氵
土
扌
口
女 2←
巾
犭
弓
彳
彡
艹
宀
丷
艹
亠
广
尸
口

好感 **kōkan** good feeling, favorable impression

好戦 **kōsen** pro-war, warlike

好戦国 **kōsenkoku** warlike nation

好戦的 **kōsenteki** bellicose, warlike

好意 **kōi** good will, kindness, favor, friendliness

好意的 **kōiteki** friendly, with good intentions

14 好演 **kōen** good acting/show

15 好敵 **kōteki** worthy opponent

好敵手 **kōtekishu** worthy opponent

好誼 **kōgi** (your) kindness, favor, friendship

好調 **kōchō** good, favorable, satisfactory

好餌 **kōji** good bait, tempting offer

16 好機 **kōki** good opportunity, the right moment

好機会 **kōkikai** good opportunity, the right moment

18 好題目 **kōdaimoku** good topic

─────────── 2 ───────────

2 人好 **hitozu(ki)** amiability, attractiveness

3 大好 **daisu(ki)** very fond of, love

大好物 **daikōbutsu** a favorite food

女好 **onnazu(ki)** fond of women; liked by women

4 友好 **yūkō** friendship, amity

友好的 **yūkōteki** friendly, amicable

5 好好 **su(ki)zu(ki)** a matter of individual preferences

好好爺 **kōkōya** good-natured old man

旧好 **kyūkō** an old friendship

6 仲好 **nakayo(shi)** good friends

色好 **irogono(mi)** sensuality, lust

争好 **araso(i)zu(ki)** quarrelsome, contentious

同好 **dōkō** similar tastes

同好会 **dōkōkai** association of like-minded people

同好者 **dōkōsha** people of similar tastes

耳好 **jikō** earhole

7 良好 **ryōkō** good, favorable, satisfactory

男好 **otokozu(ki)** liked by men; amorous woman

8 物好 **monozu(ki)** curious, whimsical, eccentric

9 通好 **tsūkō** friendship, amity

相好 **sōgō (o kuzusu)** break into a smile

恰好 **kakkō** shape, form, figure, appearance; reasonable; approximately

10 修好 **shūkō** amity, friendship

遊好 **aso(bi)zu(ki)** pleasure seeker

酒好 **sakezu(ki)** drinker

時好 **jikō** fashion, vogue, fad

12 最好調 **saikōchō** in perfect form

絶好 **zekkō** splendid, first-rate

13 嗜好 **shikō** taste, liking, preference

嗜好品 **shikōhin** luxury items

愛好 **aikō** love, have a liking/taste for

愛好者 **aikōsha** lover of, fan, fancier

愛好家 **aikōka** lover of, fan, fancier

話好 **hana(shi)zu(ki)** talkative, chatty

14 選好 **senkō** preference **yo(ri)gono(mi), e(ri)gono(mi)** fastidiousness

15 横好 **yokozu(ki)** enthusiastically/amateurishly fond of

─────────── 3 ───────────

2 子供好 **kodomozu(ki)** fond of children

4 不恰好 **bukakkō** unshapely, clumsy

5 外出好 **gaishutsuzu(ki)** gadabout

6 年恰好 **toshi kakkō** approximate age

8 奇麗好 **kireizu(ki)** fond of cleanliness

9 派手好 **hadezu(ki)** fond of display

冒険好 **bōkenzu(ki)** venturesome

20 議論好 **gironzu(ki)** argumentative

3e2.2 / 1933

奴 **DO, NU, yakko** manservant, slave, fellow **yatsu** guy, fellow

─────────── 1 ───────────

5 奴凧 **yakkodako** kite in the shape of an ancient footman

7 奴豆腐 **yakkodōfu** tofu cut into cubes

11 奴婢 **dohi, nuhi** servants

16 奴隷 **dorei** slave

─────────── 2 ───────────

6 匈奴 **Kyōdo** the Huns

此奴 **koitsu** this guy/fellow

7 何奴 **doitsu** who

冷奴 **hi(ya)yakko** iced tofu

8 彼奴 **aitsu** that guy/fellow

13 農奴 **nōdo** serf

─────────── 3 ───────────

6 守銭奴 **shusendo** miser, niggard

7 売国奴 **baikokudo** traitor

3e3.1 / 1747

如 **JO, NYO, goto(ki/ku/shi)** like, such as, as if **shi(ku)** be equal to, be like **shi(kazu)** be better/best

─────────── 1 ───────────

3 如才 **josai(nai)** sharp, shrewd, adroit, tactful

4 如月 **kisaragi** 2nd lunar month

7 如来 **nyorai** a Buddha

如何 **ikaga, ika (ni)** how

如何物 **ikamono** spurious article, a fake

如何許 **ikabaka(ri)** how much

如何程 **ikahodo** how much/many

如何様 **ikayō** how, what kind **ikasama** bogus, fraud, swindle; how; I see

如何様師 **ikasamashi** swindler, sharpie
8 如法 **nyohō** observance of Buddha's teachings
如実 **nyojitsu** true to life, realistic
如雨露 **jōro** sprinkling can
11 如菩薩 **nyobosatsu** compassionate (as a Buddha)
13 如意 **nyoi** priest's staff, mace
21 如露 **joro** sprinkling can

———————— 2 ————————

1 一如 **ichinyo** oneness
4 不如意 **funyoi** contrary to one's wishes, hard up (for money)
欠如 **ketsujo** lack
7 何如 **ikan** what, how
8 突如 **totsujo** suddenly, unexpectedly
10 真如 **shinnyo** the absolute, absolute reality
21 躍如 **yakujo** vivid, true to life

———————— 3 ————————

11 釈迦如来 **Shaka Nyorai** Sakyamuni
16 薬師如来 **yakushi nyorai** a buddha who can cure any ailment
17 鞠躬如 **kikkyūjo** (bowing) respectfully

———————— 4 ————————

12 勝手不如意 **katte-funyoi** hard up (for money), bad off

———————— 5 ————————

6 百聞一見如 **hyakubun (wa) ikken (ni) shi(kazu)** Seeing for oneself once is better than hearing 100 accounts.

3e3.2 / 1756

妃

HI (married) princess, queen

———————— 1 ————————

13 妃殿下 **hidenka** Her Highness

———————— 2 ————————

6 后妃 **kōhi** empress, queen
9 皇妃 **kōhi** empress, queen

———————— 3 ————————

13 楊貴妃 **Yōkihi** Yang Guifei (beautiful Chinese queen, 719–756)

3e3.3

奸

KAN wicked

———————— 1 ————————

7 奸臣 **kanshin** treacherous vassal
8 奸知 **kanchi** cunning, guile
奸物 **kanbutsu** crook, wily fellow
9 奸計 **kankei** evil design, trick
11 奸商 **kanshō** dishonest merchant

奸悪 **kan'aku** wicked, treacherous
12 奸智 **kanchi** cunning, guile
奸策 **kansaku** sinister scheme

———————— 2 ————————

7 佞奸 **neikan** wily, treacherous
11 斬奸 **zankan** slaying the wicked
斬奸状 **zankanjō** statement of reasons for slaying (a traitor)

3e3.4

妁

SHAKU go-between

———————— 2 ————————

12 媒妁 **baishaku** matchmaking
媒妁人 **baishakunin** matchmaker, go-between

妄 → **2j4.6**

———————— 4 ————————

3e4.1 / 1182

妨

BŌ, samata(geru) prevent, obstruct, hamper

———————— 1 ————————

10 妨害 **bōgai** obstruction, disturbance, interference
妨害物 **bōgaibutsu** obstacle
13 妨碍 **bōgai** obstruction, disturbance, interference

3e4.2

妍

KEN good-looking, attractive

姉 → **3e5.8**

3e4.3 / 955

妊 姙

NIN, hara(mu) be pregnant

———————— 1 ————————

10 妊娠 **ninshin** be pregnant
妊娠中 **ninshinchū** during pregnancy
妊娠中絶 **ninshin chūzetsu** abortion
11 妊婦 **ninpu** pregnant woman
妊婦服 **ninpufuku** maternity wear/dress
妊産婦 **ninsanpu** expectant and nursing mothers

──────── 2 ────────

4 不妊 **funin** sterile, barren
不妊症 **funinshō** sterility, barrenness
15 避妊 **hinin** contraception
避妊法 **hininhō** method of contraception
避妊薬 **hinin'yaku** a contraceptive, birth control pill
16 懐妊 **kainin** pregnancy

3

3e4.4

妖

YŌ bewitching, enchanting; calamity

──────── 1 ────────

3 妖女 **yōjo** enchantress, a bewitching beauty
6 妖気 **yōki** ghostly, weird
8 妖怪 **yōkai** ghost, apparition
11 妖婦 **yōfu** enchantress, siren
妖婆 **yōba** witch, hag
妖術 **yōjutsu** magic, witchcraft, sorcery
12 妖雲 **yōun** ominous cloud
14 妖精 **yōsei** fairy, sprite, elf
19 妖艶 **yōen** voluptuous charm, bewitching beauty
21 妖魔 **yōma** ghost, apparition

──────── 2 ────────

9 面妖 **men'yō** strange, mysterious

3e4.5 / 1154

妙

MYŌ strange, odd; a mystery
tae(naru) exquisite, superb; delicate; charming; melodious

──────── 1 ────────

0 妙ちきりん **myō(chikirin)** strange, odd
4 妙手 **myōshu** expert, master, virtuoso
5 妙句 **myōku** clever turn of phrase
6 妙曲 **myōkyoku** fine music
7 妙技 **myōgi** extraordinary skill
8 妙法 **myōhō** excellent method; mysteries, secrets; marvelous law of Buddha
妙味 **myōmi** charm, exquisite beauty
妙所 **myōsho** point of beauty, charm
9 妙計 **myōkei** wise plan, clever trick
10 妙案 **myōan** good idea, ingenious plan
12 妙策 **myōsaku** ingenious plan
15 妙趣 **myōshu** beauties, charms
16 妙薬 **myōyaku** wonder drug
17 妙齢 **myōrei** youth

──────── 2 ────────

5 巧妙 **kōmyō** skillful, clever, deft
玄妙 **genmyō** abstruse, recondite, profound
白妙 **shirotae** white cloth; white

6 至妙 **shimyō** extremely skillful
7 即妙 **sokumyō** ready wit
8 奇妙 **kimyō** strange, curious, odd
9 美妙 **bimyō** exquisite, elegant
神妙 **shinmyō** mysterious, marvelous; admirable; gentle
珍妙 **chinmyō** odd, queer, fantastic
12 絶妙 **zetsumyō** superb, exquisite
軽妙 **keimyō** light and easy, lambent
13 微妙 **bimyō** delicate, subtle
14 精妙 **seimyō** fine, detailed, subtle
15 霊妙 **reimyō** miraculous, mysterious, wonderful

──────── 3 ────────

9 南無妙法蓮華経 **Namu Myōhō Rengekyō** Hail Lotus Sutra

──────── 4 ────────

6 当意即妙 **tōi-sokumyō** ready wit, repartee

3e4.6

姙

HI (one's deceased) mother

3e4.7

妓

GI, KI singing girl, geisha, prostitute

──────── 1 ────────

13 妓楼 **girō** brothel

──────── 2 ────────

6 老妓 **rōgi** old geisha
名妓 **meigi** famous geisha
7 芸妓 **geigi** geisha
9 美妓 **bigi** beautiful geisha
11 娼妓 **shōgi** prostitute
15 舞妓 **maiko** dancing girl

3e4.8

妝

SŌ, SHŌ dress up, makeup

3e4.9 / 930

妥 妥

DA peaceful, tranquil

──────── 1 ────────

6 妥当 **datō** proper, appropriate
妥当性 **datōsei** propriety, pertinence, validity
8 妥協 **dakyō** compromise
12 妥結 **daketsu** reach agreement

5

3e5.1

妬

TO, neta(mu) be jealous/envious of

1
4 妬心 **toshin** jealousy

2
13 嫉妬 **shitto** jealousy, envy
嫉妬心 **shittoshin** jealousy, envy

3e5.2

姆

BO, MO nursemaid

3e5.3 / 1746

姓

SEI, SHŌ surname
kabane title conferred by the emperor

1
4 姓氏 **seishi** surname
6 姓名 **seimei** name (surname and given name)

2
3 小姓 **koshō** page (to a noble)
5 本姓 **honsei** real/original surname
他姓 **tasei** another surname
旧姓 **kyūsei** former/maiden name
6 同姓 **dōsei** the same surname
百姓 **hyakushō** farmer, peasant
百姓一揆 **hyakushō ikki** peasants' uprising
7 改姓 **kaisei** change one's surname
9 俗姓 **zokusei** (priest's) secular surname
10 素姓 **sujō** birth, lineage, identity
11 庶姓 **shosei** illegitimacy
異姓 **isei** different surname

3
3 土百姓 **dobyakushō** dirt farmer, peasant
小百姓 **kobyakushō** petty farmer, peasant
12 鈍百姓 **donbyakushō** dumb farmer

4
4 水呑百姓 **mizuno(mi)-byakushō** poor farmer
水飲百姓 **mizuno(mi)-byakushō** poor farmer

3e5.4 / 408

妹

MAI, imōto, imo younger sister

1
9 妹背 **imose** closely related man and woman; man and wife; brother and sister
10 妹娘 **imōto musume** younger daughter

12 妹御 **imōtogo** your (younger) sister

2
7 弟妹 **teimai** younger brothers and sisters
8 姉妹 **shimai** sister(s); sister (city), affiliated (company), companion (volume)
実妹 **jitsumai** one's biological younger sister
10 従妹 **jūmai** younger female cousin
13 義妹 **gimai** younger sister-in-law
愚妹 **gumai** my (foolish) younger sister

3
10 従姉妹 **itoko, jūshimai** female cousin
13 義姉妹 **gishimai** sister-in-law; stepsister

4
2 又従姉妹 **mataitoko** second cousin

3e5.5

姐

SHA, ane girl; elder sister

1
12 姐御 **anego** gang boss's wife; woman boss

3e5.6

姐

DATSU (woman's name)

3e5.7

姑

KO, shūtome, shūto mother-in-law

1
10 姑息 **kosoku** makeshift, stopgap

2
3 小姑 **kojūtome, kojūto** one's spouse's sister
13 慈姑 **kuwai** arrowhead (an edible tuber)

3e5.8 / 407

姉

SHI, ane elder sister (o)nē(san), nē(san) elder sister; young lady; waitress nē(ya) maid

1
3 姉上 **aneue** elder sister
7 姉君 **anegimi** elder sister
8 姉妹 **shimai** sister(s); sister (city), affiliated (company), companion (volume)
10 姉娘 **ane musume** elder daughter
12 姉婿 **ane muko** elder sister's husband
姉御 **anego** gang boss's wife; woman boss
姉貴 **aneki** elder sister
14 姉様 **(o)nēsama, nēsama** elder sister

2
8 実姉 **jisshi** one's biological elder sister

3
氵 土 扌 口 女 巾 犭 弓 彳 彡 艹 宀 ⺌ 山 耂 广 尸 口

10 従姉 **jūshi** elder female cousin
従姉妹 **itoko, jūshimai** female cousin
13 義姉 **gishi** elder sister-in-law
義姉妹 **gishimai** sister-in-law; stepsister
15 諸姉 **shoshi** dear friends, ladies

——————— 3 ———————

2 又従姉妹 **mataitoko** second cousin
15 諸兄姉 **shokeishi** ladies and gentlemen

3e5.9 / 494

始 **SHI, haji(maru), haji(meru)** (intr./tr.) start, begin

——————— 1 ———————

5 始末 **shimatsu** circumstances; manage, dispose of, take care of; economize
始末屋 **shimatsuya** frugal person
始末書 **shimatsusho** written explanation/apology
9 始発 **shihatsu** first (train) departure
始祖 **shiso** founder, originator, father
10 始原 **shigen** origin, inception
11 始動 **shidō** starting (a machine)
始球 **shikyū** throwing the first ball (in baseball)
始終 **shijū** from first to last, all the while
12 始期 **shiki** initial date/period
13 始業 **shigyō** begin work, open
始業式 **shigyōshiki** opening ceremony

——————— 2 ———————

4 不始末 **fushimatsu** mismanagement, carelessness; lavish, spendthrift
手始 **tehaji(me)** beginning, to start with
月始 **tsukihaji(me)** beginning of the month
5 仕始 **shihaji(meru)** begin, start
6 年始 **nenshi** beginning of the year, New Year's
9 後始末 **atoshimatsu** settle, wind/finish up
10 原始 **genshi** origin; primitive
原始人 **genshijin** primitive man
原始的 **genshiteki** primitive, primeval, original
11 終始 **shūshi** from beginning to end
終始一貫 **shūshi-ikkan** constant, consistent
12 隗始 **Kai (yori) haji(meyo)** He who suggests it should go first.
創始 **sōshi** originate, create, found
創始者 **sōshisha** originator, founder
無始 **mushi** without beginning, since the infinite past
開始 **kaishi** begin, commence, start
13 跡始末 **atoshimatsu** winding-up, settlement, straightening up (afterwards)
14 聞始 **ki(ki)haji(meru)** begin to hear

——————— 3 ———————

1 一部始終 **ichibu shijū** full particulars
12 御用始 **goyō-haji(me)** reopening of offices after New Year's

3e5.10 / 671

妻 **SAI, tsuma** wife

——————— 1 ———————

2 妻子 **saishi** wife and child(ren)
3 妻女 **saijo** wife; wife and daughter(s)
4 妻戸 **tsumado** pair of paneled doors
7 妻君 **saikun** wife
8 妻妾 **saishō** wife and mistress(es)
9 妻室 **saishitsu** wife
10 妻恋 **tsumagoi** love for one's wife
妻帯 **saitai** marry
妻帯者 **saitaisha** married man
妻格子 **tsumagōshi** latticework

——————— 2 ———————

1 一妻多夫 **issai-tafu** polyandry
2 人妻 **hitozuma** (someone else's) wife
3 亡妻 **bōsai** one's late wife
4 内妻 **naisai** common-law wife
夫妻 **fusai** husband and wife, Mr. and Mrs.
切妻 **ki(ri)zuma** gable
手妻 **tezuma** fingertips; sleight of hand
5 正妻 **seisai** one's legal wife
6 多妻 **tasai** many wives
老妻 **rōsai** one's old wife
先妻 **sensai** one's ex-/late wife
有妻 **yūsai** married (man)
7 良妻 **ryōsai** good wife
良妻賢母 **ryōsai-kenbo** good wife and wise mother
8 若妻 **wakazuma** young wife
9 荊妻 **keisai** my wife (deprecatory)
後妻 **gosai** second wife
10 恐妻家 **kyōsaika** henpecked husband
病妻 **byōsai** one's invalid wife
11 悪妻 **akusai** bad wife
12 無妻 **musai** without a wife, single
無妻主義 **musai shugi** celibacy
13 愛妻 **aisai** one's beloved wife
愛妻家 **aisaika** devoted/uxorious husband
愚妻 **gusai** my (foolish) wife
新妻 **niizuma** new/young wife
14 稲妻 **inazuma** lightning
16 賢妻 **kensai** intelligent (house)wife

——————— 3 ———————

17 糟糠妻 **sōkō (no) tsuma** wife married in poverty

——————— 4 ———————

1 一夫多妻 **ippu-tasai** polygamy

妾 →   5b3.2

—————— 6 ——————

3e6.1

姨   I mother's/wife's sister

3e6.2

姥   BO, MO, uba old woman

—————— 2 ——————
3 山姥 **yamauba** mountain witch

3e6.3

娜   DA beautiful, graceful, lithe

—————— 2 ——————
10 婀娜 **ada, ada(ppoi), ada(meku)** charming, coquettish, captivating

3e6.4

姚   YŌ beautiful

姃 → 妊 3e4.3

3e6.5

娃   AI beautiful

3e6.6

姪   TETSU, mei neice

3e6.7

姶   Ō good-looking; quiet

姫 →   3e7.11

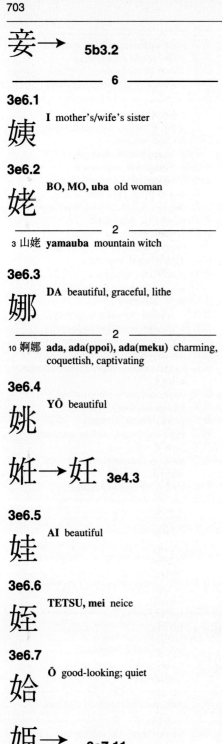

3e6.8 / 1748

姻   IN marriage

—————— 1 ——————
11 姻族 **inzoku** in-laws
   姻戚 **inseki** in-laws
—————— 2 ——————
11 婚姻 **kon'in** marriage
   婚姻届 **kon'in todoke** marriage registration

3e6.9

姦   KAN wicked, immoral
       kashima(shii) noisy, boisterous

—————— 1 ——————
0 姦する **kan(suru)** commit adultery/fornication; rape
4 姦夫 **kanpu** adulterer
8 姦物 **kanbutsu** crook, wily fellow
9 姦通 **kantsū** adultery
   姦通罪 **kantsūzai** (the crime of) adultery
   姦計 **kankei** evil design, trick
11 姦淫 **kan'in** illicit intercourse
   姦婦 **kanpu** adultress
   姦悪 **kan'aku** wicked, treacherous
—————— 2 ——————
11 強姦 **gōkan** rape
15 輪姦 **rinkan** gang rape
16 獣姦 **jūkan** bestiality
—————— 4 ——————
6 近親相姦 **kinshin sōkan** incest
16 親近相姦 **shinkin sōkan** incest

3e6.10 / 929

姿   SHI, sugata form, figure, shape, appearance, posture

—————— 1 ——————
7 姿見 **sugatami** full-length mirror
10 姿容 **shiyō** form, appearance
12 姿絵 **sugatae** portrait
13 姿勢 **shisei** posture, stance
14 姿態 **shitai** figure, pose
—————— 2 ——————
5 立姿 **ta(chi)sugata** standing position
7 忍姿 **shino(bi)sugata** disguise, incognito
   初姿 **hatsusugata** first dress-up (in New Year's kimono)
8 英姿 **eishi** impressive figure, noble mien
9 風姿 **fūshi** appearance, demeanor
   後姿 **ushi(ro) sugata** view (of someone) from the back

3

氵
土
扌
口
女 6 ←
巾
犭
弓
彳
彡
艹
宀
⺌
山
士
广
尸
口

→ 6

10 高姿勢 **kōshisei** high posture/profile, aggressive attitude
荷姿 **nisugata** type/style of packing
容姿 **yōshi** face and figure, appearance
旅姿 **tabisugata** traveling attire
12 絵姿 **esugata** portrait, likeness, picture
雄姿 **yūshi** gallant figure
13 寝姿 **nesugata** one's form while lying down/asleep
15 嬌姿 **kyōshi** lovely figure
17 優姿 **yasasugata** graceful figure
19 麗姿 **reishi** beautiful figure

─────── 3 ───────

15 舞台姿 **butaisugata** in stage costume

3e6.11 / 419

要要

YŌ main point, principal; necessary, essential
i(ru) need, be necessary
kaname pivot; main point

─────── 1 ───────

0 要する **yō(suru)** require, need
2 要人 **yōjin** important person, leading figure
5 要用 **yōyō** important matter; need; use
要目 **yōmoku** principal items
6 要件 **yōken** requisite, essentials
要地 **yōchi** important/strategic place
要因 **yōin** principal factor, chief cause
要旨 **yōshi** gist, purport, substance
要式 **yōshiki** formal
7 要求 **yōkyū** require, demand
要図 **yōzu** rough sketch
8 要注意 **yōchūi** requiring care/caution
要所 **yōsho** important/strategic place
要所要所 **yōsho-yōsho** every important place
要具 **yōgu** necessary tools
9 要点 **yōten** main point(s), gist
要約 **yōyaku** summary
10 要部 **yōbu** principal/essential part
要員 **yōin** necessary personnel
要害 **yōgai** stronghold, fortress
要素 **yōso** element, factor
11 要望 **yōbō** demand, cry for
要務 **yōmu** important business
要略 **yōryaku** summary, outline, synopsis
12 要港 **yōkō** important/strategic port
要項 **yōkō** the essential point(s)
13 要義 **yōgi** essence, digest, outline
要塞 **yōsai** fortress, stronghold
要路 **yōro** main road/artery; important post, responsible position
14 要綱 **yōkō** outline, general idea/plan
要領 **yōryō** gist, substance, synopsis
15 要撃 **yōgeki** ambush
要衝 **yōshō** important place

要談 **yōdan** important talks/discussion
要請 **yōsei** demand, call for, require
17 要償 **yōshō** claim for damages
要覧 **yōran** general survey, overview; catalog
18 要職 **yōshoku** important post/office

─────── 2 ───────

3 大要 **taiyō** summary, outline
4 不要 **fuyō** of no use, unneeded, waste
5 必要 **hitsuyō** necessary
必要物 **hitsuyōbutsu** necessities
必要品 **hitsuyōhin** necessities
必要悪 **hitsuyōaku** a necessary evil
主要 **shuyō** main, principal, essential, key
6 至要 **shiyō** essential, of paramount importance
7 体要 **taiyō** gist, main point
肝要 **kan'yō** important, vital
8 法要 **hōyō** (Buddhist) memorial service
枢要 **sūyō** pivotal, important
物要 **monoi(ri)** expenses
所要 **shoyō** (the time) needed/required
9 重要 **jūyō** important
重要性 **jūyōsei** importance, gravity
重要視 **jūyōshi** regard as important
紀要 **kiyō** bulletin, record, proceedings
11 猫要 **neko-i(razu)** rat poison
強要 **kyōyō** demand importunately, coerce, extort
12 提要 **teiyō** summary, compendium
14 摘要 **tekiyō** summary, synopsis
概要 **gaiyō** outline, synopsis
綱要 **kōyō** essentials, outline, summary
需要 **juyō** demand
15 撮要 **satsuyō** compendium, summary, manual
緊要 **kin'yō** of vital importance
18 顕要 **ken'yō** prominent, important

─────── 3 ───────

4 不必要 **fuhitsuyō** unnecessary
不得要領 **futoku-yōryō** vague, ambiguous
7 肝腎要 **kanjin-kaname** of crucial/vital importance
9 要所要所 **yōsho-yōsho** every important place

─────── 7 ───────

3e7.1

娥

GA beautiful (woman)

─────── 1 ───────

9 娥眉 **gabi** beautiful eyebrows/woman

─────── 2 ───────

14 嫦娥 **Kōga** (beautiful princess living on) the moon

3e7.2 / 1752

娘   **JŌ, musume** daughter; girl, young woman

— 1 —
- 4 娘心 **musumegokoro** girlish mind/innocence
- 6 娘気質 **musume katagi** the nature of a young woman
- 11 娘盛 **musumezaka(ri)** the prime of young womanhood
- 12 娘婿 **musumemuko** son-in-law

— 2 —
- 3 小娘 **komusume** (early-teenage) girl
- 5 生娘 **kimusume** virgin; innocent girl
- 8 妹娘 **imōto musume** younger daughter
- 姉娘 **ane musume** elder daughter
- 9 孫娘 **magomusume** granddaughter
- 13 愛娘 **manamusume** one's favorite daughter

— 3 —
- 1 一人娘 **hitori musume** an only daughter
- 3 小町娘 **komachi musume** beauty, belle, queen
- 5 田舎娘 **inakamusume** country girl
- 9 看板娘 **kanban musume** pretty girl who draws customers
- 12 婿取娘 **mukoto(ri) musume** daughter whose husband is adopted into her family
- 14 総領娘 **sōryō musume** eldest daughter
- 15 箱入娘 **hakoi(ri) musume** girl who has led a sheltered life

3e7.3 / 1437

娯 娯   **GO** pleasure, enjoyment

— 1 —
- 13 娯楽 **goraku** amusement, entertainment
- 娯楽品 **gorakuhin** plaything
- 娯楽室 **gorakushitsu** recreation room
- 娯楽場 **gorakujō** place of amusement
- 娯楽街 **gorakugai** amusement quarter
- 娯楽機関 **goraku kikan** recreational facilities

3e7.4

婀   **A** beautiful, graceful, lithe

— 1 —
- 9 婀娜 **ada, ada(ppoi), ada(meku)** charming, coquettish, captivating

3e7.5

娚   **NAN** loud talking

— 1 —
- 7 娚杉 **Meotosugi** (place name)

3e7.6

娉   **HEI** ask after (a woman's name); marry (a woman); good-looking

3e7.7

娟   **KEN, EN** beautiful

— 2 —
- 15 嬋娟 **senken** beautiful, captivating

3e7.8

娩 娩   **BEN** give birth to, bear

— 2 —
- 4 分娩 **bunben** childbirth, delivery
— 4 —
- 12 無痛分娩 **mutsū bunben** painless childbirth

3e7.9

娣   **TEI** younger sister; younger brother's wife

3e7.10 / 956

娠   **SHIN** pregnancy

— 2 —
- 7 妊娠 **ninshin** be pregnant
- 妊娠中 **ninshinchū** during pregnancy
- 妊娠中絶 **ninshin chūzetsu** abortion

3e7.11 / 1757

姫 姫   **KI, hime** princess

— 1 —
- 3 姫小松 **hime komatsu** a small pine
- 7 姫君 **himegimi** princess
- 9 姫垣 **himegaki** low fence
- 10 姫宮 **himemiya** princess
- 13 姫路 **Himeji** (city, Hyōgo-ken)
- 14 姫様 **himesama, hiisama** princess, nobleman's daughter
- 23 姫鑑 **hime kagami** a model young lady

2

1 一姫二太郎 **ichi-hime ni-Tarō** It's good to have a girl first and then a boy.
乙姫 **otohime** younger princess
3 山姫 **yamahime** mountain goddess
6 糸姫 **itohime** thread/weaving factory girl
13 椿姫 **Tsubakihime** (Verdi's) La Traviata
14 歌姫 **utahime** songstress
15 舞姫 **maihime** dancing girl
18 織姫 **o(ri)hime** woman textile worker

3

5 白雪姫 **Shirayuki-hime** Snow White (and the Seven Dwarfs)
7 佐保姫 **saohime** goddess of spring
10 竜田姫 **Tatsutahime** the goddess of autumn

3e7.12

娑 **SHA, SA** dance; (used phonetically)

1

11 娑婆 **shaba** this world, here below; the outside (of prison)
19 娑羅双樹 **shara sōju** sal tree

8

3e8.1

婢 **HI** maidservant

1

14 婢僕 **hiboku** servants, menials

2

5 奴婢 **dohi, nuhi** servants
10 従婢 **jūhi** female servant
14 僕婢 **bokuhi** male and female servants

3e8.2

娵 **SHU** (used in proper names)
SŌ beautiful woman

3e8.3

娼 **SHŌ** prostitute

1

7 娼妓 **shōgi** prostitute
10 娼家 **shōka** brothel
11 娼婦 **shōfu** prostitute

2

4 公娼 **kōshō** licensed prostitute

7 私娼 **shishō** unlicensed prostitute
私娼窟 **shishōkutsu** brothel
男娼 **danshō** male prostitute
12 廃娼 **haishō** abolition of prostitution

3e8.4 / 567

婚 **KON** marriage

1

5 婚礼 **konrei** wedding ceremony
9 婚姻 **kon'in** marriage
婚姻届 **kon'in todoke** marriage registration
婚約 **kon'yaku** engagement, betrothal
婚約者 **kon'yakusha** fiancé(e)
10 婚家 **konka** one's husband's family
12 婚期 **konki** marriageable age
15 婚儀 **kongi** wedding

2

3 大婚 **taikon** imperial wedding
5 未婚 **mikon** unmarried
未婚者 **mikonsha** unmarried person
6 再婚 **saikon** remarry
早婚 **sōkon** early marriage
成婚 **seikon** marriage
7 求婚 **kyūkon** proposal of marriage
求婚者 **kyūkonsha** suitor
初婚 **shokon** one's first marriage
8 金婚式 **kinkonshiki** golden wedding anniversary
9 重婚 **jūkon** bigamy
重婚者 **jūkonsha** bigamist
冠婚葬祭 **kankonsōsai** ceremonial occasions
10 既婚 **kikon** (already) married
既婚者 **kikonsha** married person
11 許婚 **iinazuke** one's betrothed
12 晩婚 **bankon** late marriage
結婚 **kekkon** marriage
結婚式 **kekkonshiki** wedding
13 新婚 **shinkon** newlywed
新婚旅行 **shinkon ryokō** honeymoon
14 銀婚式 **ginkonshiki** silver wedding anniversary
雑婚 **zakkon** intermarriage
18 離婚 **rikon** divorce

3

7 足入婚 **ashii(re)kon** tentative marriage
9 政略婚 **seiryakukon** marriage of convenience

4

2 二重結婚 **nijū kekkon** bigamy
5 写真結婚 **shashin kekkon** marriage arranged after seeing photos of each other
9 神前結婚 **shinzen kekkon** Shinto wedding
政略結婚 **seiryaku kekkon** marriage of convenience

婬 → 淫 **3a8.17**

3e8.5

婉
EN graceful

──────── 1 ────────
6 婉曲 **enkyoku** euphemistic, circumlocutory
9 婉美 **enbi** beauty, charm

──────── 2 ────────
17 優婉 **yūen** elegant, graceful

3e8.6 / 316

婦 婦
FU woman; wife

──────── 1 ────────
2 婦人 **fujin** lady, woman
　婦人用 **fujin'yō** for ladies, women's
　婦人会 **fujinkai** ladies' society
　婦人科 **fujinka** gynecology
　婦人科医 **fujinkai** gynecologist
　婦人病 **fujinbyō** women's diseases/disorders
　婦人警官 **fujin keikan** policewoman
3 婦女 **fujo** woman
　婦女子 **fujoshi** woman; woman and child
8 婦長 **fuchō** head nurse
11 婦道 **fudō** (duties of) womanhood
14 婦選 **fusen** women's suffrage
　婦徳 **futoku** womanly virtues
19 婦警 **fukei** policewoman

──────── 2 ────────
4 夫婦 **fūfu, meoto, myōto** husband and wife, couple
　夫婦喧嘩 **fūfu-genka** domestic quarrel
5 主婦 **shufu** housewife
6 老婦 **rōfu** old woman
7 妊婦 **ninpu** pregnant woman
　妊婦服 **ninpufuku** maternity wear/dress
　妖婦 **yōfu** enchantress, siren
8 毒婦 **dokufu** wicked woman
　命婦 **myōbu, meifu** woman official (historical)
　炊婦 **suifu** a (female) cook, kitchen maid
9 貞婦 **teifu** virtuous woman, faithful wife
　姦婦 **kanpu** adultress
10 家婦 **kafu** housewife
　烈婦 **reppu** heroic woman
　酌婦 **shakufu** waitress, barmaid
11 淫婦 **inpu** lewd woman, harlot
　娼婦 **shōfu** prostitute
　情婦 **jōfu** lover, mistress
　産婦 **sanpu** woman in/nearing childbirth

　産婦人科 **sanfujinka** obstetrics and gynecology
12 貴婦人 **kifujin** lady
13 農婦 **nōfu** farm woman
　新婦 **shinpu** bride
　裸婦 **rafu** nude woman
　節婦 **seppu** faithful wife
14 寡婦 **kafu, yamome** widow
16 賢婦 **kenpu** wise woman

──────── 3 ────────
7 助産婦 **josanpu** midwife
　妊産婦 **ninsanpu** expectant and nursing mothers
　売春婦 **baishunfu** prostitute
　初産婦 **shosanpu** woman having her first child
8 炊事婦 **suijifu** a (female) cook
9 保健婦 **hokenfu** public-health nurse
　派出婦 **hashutsufu** visiting maid
　看護婦 **kangofu** (female) nurse
　看護婦長 **kangofuchō** head nurse
10 家政婦 **kaseifu** housekeeper
11 淫売婦 **inbaifu** prostitute
　接客婦 **sekkyakufu** hostess, waitress
　掃除婦 **sōjifu** cleaning lady/woman
14 選炭婦 **sentanfu** coal dresser/sorter
　雑役婦 **zatsuekifu** maid
15 慰安婦 **ianfu** a comfort girl/woman, army prostitute
17 醜業婦 **shūgyōfu** prostitute

──────── 4 ────────
1 一夫一婦 **ippu-ippu** monogamy
4 匹夫匹婦 **hippu-hippu** humble men and women, common people
13 新郎新婦 **shinrō-shinpu** the bride and groom

婉 → 婉 **3e7.8**

3e8.7

娶
SHU, meto(ru) marry (a woman), take to wife

3e8.8

婁
RU tie, connect
RŌ (name of a constellation)

3e8.9 / 1931

婆
BA, babā, bā(san) old woman
bā(ya) wet nurse; elderly maid

──────── 1 ────────
19 婆羅門 **Baramon** Brahman

3

氵
土
扌
口
女 8 ←
巾
犭
弓
彳
彡
艹
宀
⺌
山
吉
广
尸
口

2

6 老婆 **rōba** old woman
老婆心 **rōbashin** old-womanish solicitude
7 阿婆擦 **abazu(re)** wicked woman, hussy
妖婆 **yōba** witch, hag
10 娑婆 **shaba** this world, here below; the outside (of prison)
狸婆 **tanuki baba** cunning old woman
鬼婆 **onibaba** witch, hag
11 産婆 **sanba** midwife
転婆 **(o)tenba** tomboy

3

8 卒塔婆 **sotoba** wooden grave tablet, stupa
12 湯湯婆 **yutanpo** hot-water bottle/bag
御転婆 **otenba** tomboy

3e8.10

婪

RAN be greedy/ravenous

2

11 貪婪 **donran, tanran** covetousness, greed

9

婢→ **3e8.1**

3e9.1

嫂

SŌ, aniyome elder brother's wife

3e9.2 / 1496

媒

BAI, nakadachi go-between

1

4 媒介 **baikai** mediation; matchmaking
媒介物 **baikaibutsu** medium, agency; carrier (of a disease)
6 媒酌 **baishaku** matchmaking
媒酌人 **baishakunin** matchmaker, go-between
7 媒体 **baitai** medium (in physics)
9 媒染 **baisen** color fixing
10 媒酌 **baishaku** matchmaking
媒酌人 **baishakunin** matchmaker, go-between
15 媒質 **baishitsu** medium (in physics)

2

6 虫媒花 **chūbaika** insect-pollinated flower
9 風媒花 **fūbaika** wind-pollinated flower
11 鳥媒花 **chōbaika** bird-pollinated flower
13 溶媒 **yōbai** a solvent

触媒 **shokubai** catalyst
15 霊媒 **reibai** a (spiritualistic) medium

3e9.3 / 1745

婿 壻 聟

SEI, muko son-in-law; bridegroom

1

2 婿入 **mukoi(ri)** marry into one's bride's family
8 婿取 **mukoto(ri)** get a husband for one's daughter
婿取娘 **mukoto(ri) musume** daughter whose husband is adopted into her family
11 婿探 **mukosaga(shi)** looking for a husband for one's daughter
15 婿養子 **muko-yōshi** son-in-law adopted as an heir

2

2 入婿 **i(ri)muko** man who takes his wife's name
3 女婿 **josei** son-in-law
7 花婿 **hanamuko** bridegroom
8 姉婿 **ane muko** elder sister's husband
10 娘婿 **musumemuko** son-in-law
13 愛婿 **aisei** one's (favorite) son-in-law

3e9.4

媛 媛

EN, hime princess

2

3 才媛 **saien** talented woman
13 愛媛県 **Ehime-ken** (prefecture)

嫌→嫌 3e10.7

3e9.5

媚

BI, ko(biru) flatter, humor, curry favor; flirt

1

14 媚態 **bitai** coquetry
16 媚薬 **biyaku** aphrodisiac, love potion

2

8 明媚 **meibi** beautiful, scenic

10

3e10.1

媽

BO, MO mother; mare

2

7 阿媽 **ama** amah, nurse

嫌→嫌 **3e10.7**

嫩→嬾 **5f12.1**

3e10.2

嫋 **JŌ, nayo(yaka), tao(yaka)** supple, slender, beautiful

3e10.3

媳 **SEKI** daughter-in-law

3e10.4

媾 **KŌ** association, meeting with

————————— 1 —————————
8 媾和 **kōwa** making peace, reconciliation

3e10.5

媼 **Ō** old woman; mother
ōna old woman

3e10.6 / 1749

嫁 **KA** marry (a man)
totsu(gu) get married
yome bride, young wife, daughter-in-law

————————— 1 —————————
0 嫁する/す **ka(suru/su)** marry (a man); lay (the blame) on
2 嫁入 **yomei(ri)** marriage, wedding
　嫁入支度 **yomei(ri)-jitaku** trousseau
8 嫁取 **yometo(ri)** taking a wife
11 嫁菜 **yomena** aster
12 嫁御 **yomego** bride
13 嫁資 **kashi** dowry

————————— 2 —————————
5 兄嫁 **aniyome** elder brother's wife
6 再嫁 **saika** remarriage
7 弟嫁 **otōtoyome** younger brother's wife
　花嫁 **hanayome** bride
　花嫁御寮 **hanayome goryō** bride
9 狐嫁入 **kitsune (no) yome-i(ri)** a line of foxfire; a light rain during sunshine
11 許嫁 **iinazuke** fiancée
　転嫁 **tenka** shift (the blame/responsibility)

嫌 嫌嬚 **KEN, GEN, kira(u/i)** dislike, hate
iya disagreeable
iya(garu) dislike, hate; be unwilling (to do something)

————————— 1 —————————
0 嫌がらせ **iya(garase)** harassment
　嫌らしい **iya(rashii)** unpleasant, offensive
6 嫌気 **iyake, iyaki** aversion, repugnance
7 嫌忌 **kenki** dislike, aversion
8 嫌味 **iyami** disagreeable, offensive, sarcastic
11 嫌悪 **ken'o** hatred, dislike, loathing
　嫌悪感 **ken'okan** hatred, dislike, loathing
13 嫌煙権 **ken'enken** non-smokers' rights
14 嫌疑 **kengi** suspicion
　嫌疑者 **kengisha** a suspect

————————— 2 —————————
2 人嫌 **hitogira(i)** avoiding others' company; misanthrope
3 大嫌 **daikira(i)** hate, abhor, detest
　女嫌 **onnagira(i)** misogynist
4 毛嫌 **kegira(i)** antipathy, aversion, prejudice
5 好嫌 **su(ki)kira(i)** likes and dislikes, preferences
7 忌嫌 **i(mi)kira(u)** detest, loathe, abhor
　男嫌 **otokogira(i)** man-hater
8 所嫌 **tokorokira(wazu)** everywhere, anywhere
9 負嫌 **ma(kezu)gira(i)** unyielding, determined to win
　食嫌 **ku(wazu)/ta(bezu)gira(i)** disliking without tasting; prejudice against
16 機嫌 **kigen** mood, humor, temper
　機嫌取 **kigento(ri)** pleasing another's humor; flatterer

————————— 3 —————————
2 人間嫌 **ningengira(i)** misanthropy; misanthrope
3 上機嫌 **jōkigen** good humor, high spirits
4 不機嫌 **fukigen** ill humor, sullenness
5 写真嫌 **shashingira(i)** camera shy
　外出嫌 **gaishutsugira(i)** a stay-at-home

————————— 4 —————————
1 一杯機嫌 **ippai kigen** slight intoxication
12 屠蘇機嫌 **toso kigen** drunk with New Year's saké

3e10.8

嫉 **SHITSU, sone(mu)** be jealous of, envy

————————— 1 —————————
8 嫉妬 **shitto** jealousy, envy
　嫉妬心 **shittoshin** jealousy, envy

3

氵 土 扌 口 女 巾 犭 弓 彳 彡 艹 宀 ⺍ 山 吉 广 尸 口

10←

—————— 11 ——————

3e11.1

嫩

DON, waka(i) young

—————— 1 ——————
8 嫩芽 **donga** bud, sprout
9 嫩草 **donsō, wakakusa** young grass
12 嫩葉 **don'yō, wakaba** young foliage

3e11.2

嫖

HYŌ wanton, pleasure seeking

—————— 1 ——————
9 嫖客 **hyōkaku** brothel customer/frequenter

3e11.3

嫣

EN smiling; bright and beautiful

—————— 1 ——————
12 嫣然 **enzen** smiling (coquettishly)

3e11.4

嫦

KŌ (proper name)

—————— 1 ——————
10 嫦娥 **Kōga** (beautiful princess living on) the moon

3e11.5 / 1932

嫡 嫡

CHAKU legitimate (child)

—————— 1 ——————
2 嫡子 **chakushi** legitimate child
5 嫡出子 **chakushutsushi** legitimate child
7 嫡男 **chakunan** eldest/legitimate son, heir
9 嫡孫 **chakuson** eldest son of one's son and heir
10 嫡流 **chakuryū** lineage of the eldest son
13 嫡嗣 **chakushi** legitimate heir

—————— 2 ——————
5 正嫡 **seichaku** legal wife; legitimate child
12 廃嫡 **haichaku** disinheritance

3e11.6

嫗

Ō, U old woman; mother

—————— 12 ——————

3e12.1

嬌

KYŌ attractive

—————— 1 ——————
6 嬌名 **kyōmei** reputation for beauty
7 嬌声 **kyōsei** lovely voice
9 嬌姿 **kyōshi** lovely figure
10 嬌笑 **kyōshō** attractive/charming smile
14 嬌態 **kyōtai** coquetry, coyness
19 嬌艶 **kyōen** captivating beauty

—————— 2 ——————
13 愛嬌 **aikyō** charm, winsomeness, attractiveness, courtesy
愛嬌者 **aikyōmono** charming fellow/girl

—————— 3 ——————
12 無愛嬌 **buaikyō** unamiable, unsociable

3e12.2

嬋

SEN beautiful, charming

—————— 1 ——————
10 嬋娟 **senken** beautiful, captivating

3e12.3

嬉

KI, ure(shii) happy, glad, delightful

—————— 1 ——————
8 嬉泣 **ure(shi)na(ki)** crying for joy
10 嬉涙 **ure(shi)namida** tears of joy
15 嬉戯 **kigi** frolic

嫺 → 嫻 3e12.4

3e12.4

嫻 嫺

KAN refined, elegant; skilled

—————— 1 ——————
13 嫻雅 **kanga** refined, elegant
14 嫻熟 **kanjuku** experienced, practiced

—————— 13 ——————

3e13.1 / 1836

嬢 孃

JŌ daughter; young lady

———————— 1 ————————

14 嬢様 **(o)jōsama** (your) daughter; young lady

———————— 2 ————————

5 令嬢 **reijō** your daughter, young lady
6 老嬢 **rōjō** old maid, spinster
12 御嬢様 **ojōsama** young lady, (your) daughter
13 愛嬢 **aijō** one's dear daughter

———————— 3 ————————

10 案内嬢 **annaijō** (girl) guide

3e13.2

婞
HEI well-liked, favorite (retainer/woman)

———————— 14 ————————

3e14.1

嫲
kakā one's wife (slang)

———————— 1 ————————

4 嫲天下 **kakādenka** the wife being boss

3e14.2

嬬
JU wife, mistress; weak

3e14.3

嬰
EI baby; sharp (in music)

———————— 1 ————————

7 嬰児 **eiji, midorigo** baby, infant

———————— 2 ————————

8 退嬰 **taiei** conservatism, retrogression
退嬰的 **taieiteki** conservative, retiring (disposition)

3e14.4

嬪
HIN wife

———————— 2 ————————

7 別嬪 **beppin** beautiful woman (slang)

———————— 16 ————————

3e16.1

嬾
RAN lazy, languid

———————— 17 ————————

3e17.1

孀
SŌ, **yamome** widow

孃 → 嬢 3e13.1

3e17.2

孅
SEN slender, delicate

———————— 1 ————————

10 孅弱 **senjaku** frail, delicate

巾 **3f**

巾	布	帆	帋	希	帙	帖	帛	帑	帝	帥	帝	帯
0.1	2.1	3.1	6a4.4	4.1	5.1	5.2	5.3	5.4	5.5	6.1	2j7.1	7.1

師	帰	帷	帳	帶	帽	幅	幀	幄	幇	幑	幌	幃
7.2	2f8.8	8.1	8.2	3f7.1	9.1	9.2	9.3	9.4	9.5	0a12.1	10.1	10.2

幎	幔	幗	爾	稀	幟	幡	幢	幣	幤	㡀	幪	歸
10.3	11.1	11.2	0a14.3	11.3	12.1	12.2	12.3	3f12.4	12.4	0a17.1	15.1	2f8.8

黼
0a19.1

———————— 0 ————————

3f0.1

巾
KIN a cloth, rag, towel
haba width, breadth

———————— 1 ————————

4 巾木 **habaki** baseboard, skirting board
12 巾着 **kinchaku** moneybag, purse
巾着切 **kinchakuki(ri)** cutpurse, pickpocket

氵 土 扌 口 女 巾 犭 弓 彳 彡 宀 艹 山 青 广 尸 囗

─────────── 2 ───────────

3 大巾 **ōhaba** by a large margin, substantial
小巾 **kohaba** narrow width/range
5 布巾 **fukin** dishcloth
9 茶巾 **chakin** tea cloth/napkin
10 値巾 **nehaba** price range/fluctuations
11 脛巾 **habaki** leggings, gaiters
13 腰巾着 **koshiginchaku** belt purse; one's shadow/follower-around
14 雑巾 **zōkin** wiping cloth, mopping rag
16 頭巾 **zukin** hood, kerchief

─────────── 3 ───────────

3 三角巾 **sankakukin** triangular bandage
7 赤頭巾 **Akazukin(chan)** Little Red Riding Hood
11 黒頭巾 **kurozukin** black hood
19 艶布巾 **tsuyabukin** polishing cloth

─────────── 2 ───────────

3f2.1 / 675

布

FU, HO cloth; spread
nuno cloth

─────────── 1 ───────────

2 布子 **nunoko** padded cotton clothes
3 布巾 **fukin** dishcloth
4 布引 **nunobi(ki)** cloth stretching
5 布令 **furei** official notice, proclamation
布石 **fuseki** strategically arrange stones (in go)
布目 **nunome** texture
6 布地 **nunoji** cloth
布団 **futon** bedding, sleeping mat, futon
7 布告 **fukoku** proclaim, declare, promulgate
8 布表紙 **nunobyōshi** cloth binding
布苔 **funori** (a type of seaweed, used for laundry starch)
9 布陣 **fujin** lineup, (troop) disposition
布海苔 **funori** (a type of seaweed, used for laundry starch)
布施 **fuse** alms, charity **Fuse** (city, Ōsaka-fu)
10 布教 **fukyō** proselyting, missionary work
11 布袋 **Hotei** (a potbellied god of fortune)
布袋腹 **hoteibara** potbelly, paunch
布設 **fusetsu** lay (cable/mines), build (a railway/road) (also spelled 敷設)
13 布置 **fuchi** arrangement, grouping, composition

─────────── 2 ───────────

4 毛布 **mōfu** blanket
分布 **bunpu** distribution
公布 **kōfu** promulgation
6 帆布 **hanpu, honuno** sailcloth, canvas
8 画布 **gafu** a canvas
波布 **habu** (a poisonous snake of Okinawa)
波布茶 **habucha** stinkweed-seed tea

若布 **wakame** (an edible seaweed)
昆布 **konbu, kobu** sea tangle, tang, kelp
昆布茶 **kobucha, konbucha** tang tea
9 発布 **happu** promulgation, proclamation
荒布 **arame** (an edible seaweed)
宣布 **senpu** proclaim, promulgate
客布団 **kyakubuton** bedding for guests
10 流布 **rufu** circulate, spread, disseminate
流布本 **rufubon** popular edition
財布 **saifu** purse, pocketbook, wallet
配布 **haifu** distribution, apportionment
11 掛布団 **ka(ke)buton** quilt, coverlet
麻布 **asanuno, mafu** hemp cloth, linen
粗布 **sofu** coarse cloth
12 湿布 **shippu** wet compress, poultice
葛布 **kuzufu** (waterproof) kudzu-fiber cloth
散布 **sanpu** dispersion, scattering, sprinkling
13 塗布 **tofu** apply (a coating)
腰布 **koshinuno** loincloth
腰布団 **koshibuton** cushion worn around the waist for warmth
絹布 **kenpu** silk (fabric)
頒布 **hanpu** distribute, circulate
14 綿布 **menpu** cotton (cloth)
15 撒布 **sanpu, sappu** scatter, sprinkle, spray; dispersion
撒布剤 **sanpuzai, sappuzai** dusting powder
敷布 **shikifu** (bed) sheet
敷布団 **shikibuton** floor mattress
18 瀑布 **bakufu** waterfall
19 艶布巾 **tsuyabukin** polishing cloth

─────────── 3 ───────────

6 防水布 **bōsuifu** waterproof cloth, tarpaulin, oilskin
7 亜麻布 **amanuno** linen
冷湿布 **reishippu** cold compress
赤毛布 **akagetto** red blanket; country bumpkin
9 宣戦布告 **sensen fukoku** declaration of war
12 温湿布 **onshippu** hot compress
13 煎餅布団 **senbei-buton** thinly stuffed futon/bedding
20 朧昆布 **oborokonbu, oborokobu** sliced tangle

─────────── 3 ───────────

3f3.1 / 1103

帆

HAN, ho sail

─────────── 1 ───────────

5 帆布 **hanpu, honuno** sailcloth, canvas
帆立貝 **hotategai** scallop (shell)
7 帆走 **hansō** sail, be under sail
9 帆前船 **homaesen** sailing vessel
帆柱 **hobashira** mast
10 帆桁 **hogeta** (sail) yard, boom

11 帆掛船 **hoka(ke)bune** sailboat
帆船 **hansen, hobune** sailing ship, sailboat
12 帆筵 **homushiro** sail mat
14 帆綱 **hozuna** halyard
15 帆影 **hokage** a sail (seen in the distance)
17 帆檣 **hanshō** mast

———————— 2 ————————

4 片帆 **kataho** reefed sail
5 出帆 **shuppan** set sail, depart
白帆 **shiraho** (boat with a) white sail
8 孤帆 **kohan** solitary sailboat
10 帰帆 **kihan** sail back
真帆 **maho** spread-out sail
16 機帆船 **kihansen** motor-powered sailing vessel

———————— 3 ————————

3 三角帆 **sankakuho** jib sail

———————— 4 ————————

帋 → 紙 **6a4.4**

3f4.1 / 676

希   **KI** desire, hope for; rare; Greece
     KE, mare rare
     koinega(u) entreat; desire, wish

———————— 1 ————————

3 希土 **kido** rare earth (element)
4 希少 **kishō** scarce
5 希世 **kisei** rare
希代 **kitai, kidai** uncommon, singular
6 希有 **keu** rare, unusual
7 希求 **kikyū** desire, seek, aspire to
11 希望 **kibō** wish, hope, desire
希望者 **kibōsha** applicant, candidate, aspirant
希釈 **kishaku** dilute
16 希薄 **kihaku** dilute, rarefied, thin, sparse
希臘 **Girishia** Greece

———————— 2 ————————

5 古希 **koki** age 70

———————— 5 ————————

3f5.1

帙   **CHITSU** Japanese-style book cover

———————— 1 ————————

2 帙入 **chitsui(ri)** book kept in a Japanese-style book cover

3f5.2

帖   **CHŌ** notebook   **JŌ** notebook; (counter for bundles of paper/seaweed); (counter for tatami mats: see 畳)

3f5.3

帛   **HAKU** silk cloth

———————— 2 ————————

15 幣帛 **heihaku** Shinto offerings of cloth, rope, or cut paper

3f5.4

帑   **DO** purse, treasury; wife and children

3f5.5

帚 菷   **SŌ, hōki** broom
     ha(ku) sweep

———————— 6 ————————

3f6.1 / 1935

帥   **SUI** leading troops

———————— 2 ————————

4 元帥 **gensui** field marshal, general of the army, admiral of the fleet
10 将帥 **shōsui** commander
12 統帥 **tōsui** the high command
統帥権 **tōsuiken** prerogative of supreme command
14 総帥 **sōsui** commander-in-chief

———————— 3 ————————

3 大元帥 **daigensui** generalissimo

帯 → **3f7.1**

帝 → 帝 **2j7.1**

———————— 7 ————————

3f7.1 / 963

帯 帶   **TAI** belt; zone   **obi** obi
     o(biru) wear/carry (a sword); have (the character of), be tinged with

———————— 1 ————————

0 帯する **tai(suru)** wear/carry (a sword); have (the character of), be tinged with; be entrusted withg
2 帯刀 **taitō** wear a sword
5 帯皮 **obikawa** leather belt
6 帯同 **taidō** be accompanied by

3

氵
士
扌
日
女
→ 7 巾
犭
弓
彳
彡
艹
宀
⺌
山
青
广
尸
口

帯地 **obiji** sash material, obi cloth
7 帯状 **obijō** (in the shape of a) narrow strip
帯芯 **obishin** sash padding
8 帯金 **obigane** iron band
9 帯封 **obifū** half-wrapper (in which magazines are mailed)
帯革 **obikawa** leather belt
10 帯剣 **taiken** sword at one's side; wear a sword
帯留 **obido(me)** sash clip
帯紙 **obigami** wrapper
12 帯揚 **obia(ge)** sash to hold an obi in place
13 帯鉄 **obitetsu** band iron
帯電 **taiden** having an electric charge
帯電体 **taidentai** charged body
14 帯緑 **tairyoku** greenish
15 帯勲 **taikun** wearing a decoration
16 帯鋸 **obinokogiri, obinoko** band saw

――――――― 2 ―――――――

1 一帯 **ittai** a region/zone; the whole place
3 丸帯 **maruobi** one-piece sash
上帯 **uwaobi** outer sash
下帯 **shitaobi** loincloth, waistcloth
女帯 **onna obi** woman's obi
5 包帯 **hōtai** bandage, dressing
世帯 **setai, shotai** household, home
世帯主 **setainushi** head of a household
付帯 **futai** incidental, accessory, ancillary, secondary
6 地帯 **chitai** zone, area, region, belt
7 束帯 **sokutai** full traditional court dress
角帯 **kakuobi** man's stiff obi/sash
声帯 **seitai** vocal cords
声帯模写 **seitai mosha** vocal mimicry
男帯 **otoko obi** man's obi
8 拐帯 **kaitai** absconding with money
妻帯 **saitai** marry
妻帯者 **saitaisha** married man
所帯 **shotai** household, home
所帯主 **shotainushi** head of the household
所帯持 **shotaimo(chi)** housekeeping; married (wo)man
所帯数 **shotaisū** number of households
9 連帯 **rentai** solidarity; joint (liability)
連帯感 **rentaikan** (feeling/sense of) solidarity
風帯 **fūtai** tassel
革帯 **kawaobi** leather belt
10 兼帯 **kentai** combined use, holding two posts
紐帯 **chūtai** band, bond, tie
11 眼帯 **gantai** eye bandage/patch
袋帯 **fukuroobi** double-woven obi
細帯 **hosoobi** undersash, girdle
12 靱帯 **jintai** ligament
着帯 **chakutai** wear a maternity belt
温帯 **ontai** temperate zone
寒帯 **kantai** frigid zone

13 携帯 **keitai** carry with; portable
携帯品 **keitaihin** personal effects, luggage
腰帯 **koshiobi** waistband (to hold a kimono in place)
腹帯 **haraobi, fukutai** (pregnant woman's) bellyband
暖帯 **dantai** the subtropics
15 熱帯 **nettai** torrid zone, the tropics
熱帯日 **nettaibi** midsummerday
熱帯夜 **nettaiya, nettaiyo** a night during which the temperature never falls below 25 degrees Celsius
熱帯林 **nettairin** tropical forest
熱帯性 **nettaisei** tropical
熱帯病 **netaibyō** tropical disease
熱帯魚 **nettaigyo** tropical fish
16 獣帯 **jūtai** the zodiac
17 繃帯 **hōtai** bandage
18 臍帯 **saitai, seitai** umbilical cord

――――――― 3 ―――――――

1 一衣帯水 **ichii taisui** narrow strait
3 女世帯 **onnajotai** household of women
4 中波帯 **chūhatai** medium-wave band, AM radio
月経帯 **gekkeitai** hygienic band, sanitary napkin
火山帯 **kazantai** volcanic zone
6 地震帯 **jishintai** earthquake belt/zone
7 亜寒帯 **akantai** subarctic zone
亜熱帯 **anettai** subtropics
季候帯 **kikōtai** climatic zone
男世帯 **otokojotai** all-male household
男所帯 **otokojotai** all-male household
9 昼夜帯 **chūyaobi** a two-faced obi
11 黄道帯 **kōdōtai** the zodiac
脱腸帯 **datchōtai** truss
救命帯 **kyūmeitai** life belt
12 森林帯 **shinrintai** forest zone
無風帯 **mufūtai** the doldrums
13 新世帯 **shinjotai** new home/household
14 痩世帯 **ya(se)jotai** poor household
緑地帯 **ryokuchitai** greenbelt

――――――― 4 ―――――――

3 工業地帯 **kōgyō chitai** industrial area
6 安全地帯 **anzen chitai** safety zone/island
衣冠束帯 **ikan-sokutai** full court dress; Shinto priest's vestments
12 無人地帯 **mujin chitai** no man's land

――――――― 7 ―――――――

17 環太平洋火山帯 **kan-Taiheiyō kazantai** circum-Pacific volcanic belt
環太平洋地震帯 **kan-Taiheiyō jishintai** circum-Pacific seismic zone
環太平洋造山帯 **kan-Taiheiyō zōzantai** circum-Pacific orogeny

3f7.2 / 409

師 SHI teacher, master; army

────────── 1 ──────────
6 師匠 **shishō** master, teacher
師団 **shidan** (army) division
師団長 **shidanchō** division commander
7 師弟 **shitei** master and pupil
師走 **shiwasu** 12th lunar month
15 師範 **shihan** teacher, instructor
師範学校 **shihan gakkō** normal school, teachers' college

────────── 2 ──────────
3 大師 **daishi** great (Buddhist) teacher, saint
弓師 **yumishi** bow maker
山師 **yamashi** speculator; charlatan; miner; timber dealer
5 矢師 **yashi** arrow maker, fletcher
占師 **uranaishi** fortuneteller
旧師 **kyūshi** one's former teacher
6 老師 **rōshi** aged teacher/priest
先師 **senshi** one's late teacher
7 良師 **ryōshi** good teacher
医師 **ishi** physician, doctor
医師会 **ishikai** medical association/society
技師 **gishi** engineer, technician
技師長 **gishichō** chief engineer
8 法師 **hōshi** (Buddhist) priest
牧師 **bokushi** pastor, minister
牧師館 **bokushikan** rectory, parsonage
9 軍師 **gunshi** tactician, strategist; schemer
律師 **risshi** exemplary Buddhist master
庭師 **niwashi** landscape gardener
祖師 **soshi** founder of a sect
研師 **to(gi)shi** polisher of swords
10 教師 **kyōshi** instructor, teacher
恩師 **onshi** one's honored teacher
針師 **harishi** needlemaker; acupuncturist
11 野師 **yashi** showman; charlatan, quack
猟師 **ryōshi** hunter
経師 **kyōji** scroll/screen mounter, picture framer
経師屋 **kyōjiya** scroll/screen mounter, picture framer; philan
釣師 **tsu(ri)shi** angler
12 絵師 **eshi** painter, artist
筏師 **ikadashi** raftsman
13 禅師 **zenji** Zen priest (a title)
14 漁師 **ryōshi** fisherman
導師 **dōshi** officiating priest; guru
15 箱師 **hakoshi** train thief
16 薬師 **Yakushi** the Buddha of healing
薬師如来 **yakushi nyorai** a buddha who can cure any ailment

17 厳師 **genshi** strict/esteemed teacher
講師 **kōshi** lecturer, instructor

────────── 3 ──────────
3 女教師 **jokyōshi** female teacher
4 手品師 **tejinashi** magician, juggler
5 打物師 **u(chi)monoshi** swordsmith
尼法師 **ama hōshi** (Buddhist) nun
6 曲芸師 **kyokugeishi** acrobat, tumbler
曲馬師 **kyokubashi** circus stunt rider
伝道師 **dendōshi** evangelist
印判師 **inbanshi** seal engraver
色事師 **irogotoshi** lady-killer, Don Juan
7 邯鄲師 **kantanshi** bedroom thief
8 表具師 **hyōgushi** picture mounter/framer
建築師 **kenchikushi** builder
治療師 **chiryōshi** therapist
具足師 **gusokushi** armorer
9 洋裁師 **yōsaishi** dressmaker
指物師 **sa(shi)monoshi** cabinetmaker
荒事師 **aragotoshi** actor who plays the part of a ruffian
宣教師 **senkyōshi** missionary
相場師 **sōbashi** speculator
研物師 **to(gi)monoshi** polisher of swords and mirrors
美容師 **biyōshi** beautician
思惑師 **omowakushi** speculator
10 俳諧師 **haikaishi** *haikai* poet
陰陽師 **on'yōji** fortuneteller, diviner
差物師 **sashimonoshi** cabinetmaker
家具師 **kagushi** cabinetmaker
時計師 **tokeishi** watchmaker, jeweler
教戒師 **kyōkaishi** prison chaplain
馬具師 **bagushi** harness maker, saddler
11 道化師 **dōkeshi** clown
彫刻師 **chōkokushi** engraver, carver, sculptor
理髪師 **rihatsushi** barber, hairdresser
12 勝負師 **shōbushi** gambler
裁断師 **saidanshi** cutter, tailor
詐欺師 **sagishi** swindler, con man
軽業師 **karuwazashi** acrobat, tumbler
14 説教師 **sekkyōshi** preacher
15 影法師 **kagebōshi** person's shadow
請負師 **ukeoishi** contractor
調律師 **chōritsushi** (piano) tuner
調剤師 **chōzaishi** pharmacist
調教師 **chōkyōshi** (animal) trainer
調馬師 **chōbashi** horse trainer
調理師 **chōrishi** a cook
調髪師 **chōhatsushi** barber
16 興行師 **kōgyōshi** impresario, show manager
薬剤師 **yakuzaishi** pharmacist
17 聴罪師 **chōzaishi** (Catholic) confessor
講釈師 **kōshakushi** (professional) storyteller
講談師 **kōdanshi** (professional) storyteller

21 魔術師 **majutsushi** magician, conjurer

――――――――― 4 ―――――――――

1 一寸法師 **issunbōshi** dwarf, midget, Tom Thumb
4 水産技師 **suisan gishi** fisheries expert
6 如何様師 **ikasamashi** swindler, sharpie
9 浮世絵師 **ukiyoeshi** ukiyoe artist
10 家庭教師 **katei kyōshi** (private) tutor
12 琵琶法師 **biwa hōshi** lute-playing minstrel
14 銀細工師 **ginzaikushi** silversmith

――――――――― 5 ―――――――――

10 起上小法師 **o(ki)a(gari) koboshi** self-righting toy

帰 → **2f8.8**

――――――――― 8 ―――――――――

3f8.1

帷 **I, tobari** curtain

――――――――― 1 ―――――――――

2 帷子 **katabira** light kimono
12 帷幄 **iaku** headquarters, general staff
13 帷幕 **ibaku** curtain; strategy-planning headquarters

3f8.2 / 1107

帳 **CHŌ** notebook, register, (telephone) directory, (bank)book
tobari curtain

――――――――― 1 ―――――――――

4 帳元 **chōmoto** manager, promoter; bookie
5 帳付 **chōtsu(ke)** bookkeeping; bookkeeper
帳尻 **chōjiri** balance of accounts
6 帳合 **chōa(i)** balancing/keeping accounts
9 帳面 **chōmen** notebook, account book
帳面面 **chōmenzura** accounts; appearance
10 帳消 **chōke(shi)** cancellation, writing off (debts)
12 帳場 **chōba** counter, counting room, front office
19 帳簿 **chōbo** (account) books, book (value)

――――――――― 2 ―――――――――

1 一帳羅 **itchōra** one's only good clothes
2 几帳 **kichō** screen, partition
几帳面 **kichōmen** methodical, precise, punctilious
4 手帳 **techō** (pocket) notebook
5 台帳 **daichō** ledger, register; script
9 通帳 **tsūchō, kayo(i)chō** bankbook; chit book
10 紙帳 **shichō** paper mosquito net

蚊帳 **kaya, kachō** mosquito net
記帳 **kichō** entry, registering, signature
11 掛帳 **ka(ke)chō** charge-account book
控帳 **hika(e)chō** notebook
宿帳 **yadochō** hotel register
12 開帳 **kaichō** put a Buddhist image on display; run a gambling house
15 緞帳 **donchō** drop curtain; second-rate (actor)

――――――――― 3 ―――――――――

4 切抜帳 **kirinu(ki)chō** scrapbook
日記帳 **nikkichō** diary
5 写真帳 **shashinchō** photo album
7 判取帳 **hanto(ri)chō** receipt/chit book
抜萃帳 **bassuichō** scrapbook
芳墨帳 **hōbokuchō** autograph album
8 奉加帳 **hōgachō** subscription/contributions list
受取帳 **uketorichō** receipt book
注文帳 **chūmonchō** order book
11 過去帳 **kakochō** death register
12 筆記帳 **hikkichō** notebook
13 勧進帳 **kanjinchō** subscription book
電話帳 **denwachō** telephone directory
14 練習帳 **renshūchō** exercise book, workbook
雑記帳 **zakkichō** notebook
16 閻魔帳 **enmachō** teacher's mark book

――――――――― 4 ―――――――――

12 貯金通帳 **chokin tsūchō** bankbook

帶 → 帯 **3f7.1**

――――――――― 9 ―――――――――

3f9.1 / 1105

帽 **BŌ** cap, hat, headgear

――――――――― 1 ―――――――――

2 帽子 **bōshi** hat, cap
帽子屋 **bōshiya** hat shop
11 帽章 **bōshō** badge on a cap

――――――――― 2 ―――――――――

5 正帽 **seibō** cap of a uniform
礼帽 **reibō** ceremonial/top hat
7 角帽 **kakubō** square college cap
赤帽 **akabō** redcap, luggage porter
学帽 **gakubō** school cap
8 制帽 **seibō** regulation/school cap
9 軍帽 **gunbō** military cap
10 烏帽子 **eboshi** noble's court headgear
夏帽子 **natsubōshi** summer/straw hat
11 脱帽 **datsubō** take off one's hat/cap
略帽 **ryakubō** ordinary cap
12 着帽 **chakubō** put on one's cap

無帽 **mubō** hatless
14 製帽 **seibō** hat/headgear making
綿帽子 **watabōshi** bride's silk-floss veil

───────── 3 ─────────

3 山高帽 **yamatakabō** derby hat, bowler
4 中折帽 **nakao(re)bō** felt hat, fedora
水泳帽 **suieibō** swimming/bathing cap
7 学生帽 **gakuseibō** school cap
9 飛行帽 **hikōbō** aviator's cap, flight helmet
海水帽 **kaisuibō** bathing/swimming cap
11 運動帽 **undōbō** sports cap
鳥打帽 **toriu(chi)bō** cap
13 戦闘帽 **sentōbō** field cap
15 潜水帽 **sensuibō** diving helmet

───────── 4 ─────────

8 制服制帽 **seifuku-seibō** cap and uniform

3f9.2 / 1380

幅　**FUKU** width; (counter for) hanging scrolls　**haba** width, breadth, range; influence

───────── 1 ─────────

5 幅広 **habahiro(i)** broad, extensive
　　habahiro wide
7 幅利 **habaki(ki)** man of influence
9 幅飛 **habato(bi)** longjump
10 幅員 **fukuin** breadth, extent
13 幅跳 **habato(bi)** longjump

───────── 2 ─────────

1 一幅 **ippuku** a scroll
3 川幅 **kawahaba** width of a river
大幅 **ōhaba** by a large margin, substantial
大幅物 **ōhabamono** full-width yard goods, broadcloth
口幅 **kuchihaba(ttai)** talking big, bragging
小幅 **kohaba** narrow width/range
4 中幅 **chūhaba** medium width
辺幅 **henpuku** one's personal appearance
手幅 **tehaba** handbreadth
5 広幅 **hirohaba** double width, broad(cloth)
立幅跳 **ta(chi)habato(bi)** standing long jump
6 全幅 **zenpuku** overall width; utmost
7 身幅 **mihaba** width (of a garment)
走幅跳 **hashi(ri)habato(bi)** running broad jump
8 並幅 **namihaba** standard-width cloth (about 36 cm)
肩幅 **katahaba** breadth of one's shoulders
9 恰幅 **kappuku** build, physique
10 値幅 **nehaba** price range, change in price
振幅 **shinpuku** amplitude
胸幅 **munehaba, munahaba** chest breadth
紙幅 **shifuku** paper width, space
11 船幅 **senpuku** (ship's) beam

12 満幅 **manpuku** full (breadth)
14 増幅 **zōfuku** amplification
増幅器 **zōfukuki** amplifier
15 横幅 **yokohaba** width, breadth
震幅 **shinpuku** seismic amplitude

3f9.3

幀　**TEI** (counter for) hanging scrolls

───────── 2 ─────────

12 装幀 **sōtei** binding

3f9.4

幄　**AKU** curtain; curtained-off area

───────── 2 ─────────

11 帷幄 **iaku** headquarters, general staff

3f9.5

幫　**HŌ** help

───────── 1 ─────────

7 幫助 **hōjo** aid and abet, support
12 幫間 **hōkan** jester; sycophant

帯 → 　**0a12.1**

───────── 10 ─────────

3f10.1

幌　**KŌ, horo** awning, hood, (folding) top

───────── 1 ─────────

10 幌馬車 **horobasha** covered wagon/carriage

───────── 2 ─────────

5 札幌 **Sapporo** (city, Hokkaidō)

3f10.2

幃　**I** scent pouch; curtain

3f10.3

幎　**BEKI** (cloth) covering

3

氵
土
扌
口
女
巾　10←
犭
弓
彳
彡
宀
屮
青
广
尸
口

11

3f11.1

幔 **MAN, BAN** curtain

3f11.2

幗 **KAKU** woman's head covering, veil

爾 → **0a14.3**

3f11.3

豨 **KI** wild boar

12

3f12.1

幟 **SHI, nobori** banner, streamer

---- 2 ----

14 旗幟 **kishi** flag, banner; one's stand/position
18 鯉幟 **koinobori** carp streamer (Boys' Festival decoration)

3f12.2

幡 **HAN, hata** flag

---- 2 ----

2 八幡 **Hachiman** the god of war
Yahata (city, Fukuoka-ken)
八幡宮 **Hachimangū** shrine of the god of war
6 因幡 **Inaba** (ancient kuni, Tottori-ken)

---- 4 ----

3 弓矢八幡 **yumiya hachiman** god of war

3f12.3

幢 **TŌ** flag, banner

幤 → 幣 **3f12.4**

3f12.4 / 1781

幣 幤 幣 **HEI** Shinto zigzag paper offerings; money **nusa** Shinto offerings of cloth, rope, or cut paper

---- 1 ----

7 幣束 **heisoku** Shinto offerings of cloth, rope, or cut paper
8 幣制 **heisei** monetary system
幣帛 **heihaku** Shinto offerings of cloth, rope, or cut paper
幣物 **heimotsu, heibutsu** Shinto offerings of cloth, rope, or cut paper
13 幣殿 **heiden** room between the hall of worship and inner sanctuary of a shrine

---- 2 ----

8 法幣 **hōhei** (Chinese) legal tender
国幣社 **kokuheisha** national shrine
9 造幣 **zōhei** minting, coinage
造幣局 **zōheikyoku** the mint
10 紙幣 **shihei** paper money
11 貨幣 **kahei** money, currency, coin
貨幣学 **kaheigaku** numismatics
12 御幣 **gohei** (sacred staff with) cut paper strips (Shinto)
御幣担 **gohei-katsu(gi)** superstitious person

---- 4 ----

19 贋造紙幣 **ganzō shihei** counterfeit currency

14

黻 → **0a17.1**

15

3f15.1

幬 **CHŪ, tobari** curtain

歸 → 帰 **2f8.8**

16

繍 → **0a19.1**

犭 3g

犬	尤	犯	犲	状	犹	狄	狂	狃	狆	犹	狀	狒
0.1	0a4.20	2.1	0a10.4	2b5.1	3j4.2	4.1	4.2	4.3	4.4	3g9.5	2b5.1	5.1

狎	狙	狛	狗	独	狭	狠	狐	狩	狢	狡	哭	狽
5.2	5.3	5.4	5.5	6.1	6.2	6.3	6.4	6.5	4i10.2	6.6	6.7	7.1
狸	狹	狼	猛	猖	猪	猊	猖	猜	猫	猟	猗	猝
7.2	3g6.2	7.3	7.4	7.5	8.1	8.2	8.3	8.4	8.5	8.6	8.7	8.8
就	猪	猴	猥	猩	猯	猶	献	猷	獅	猾	猿	漠
3d9.21	3g8.1	9.1	9.2	9.3	9.4	9.5	9.6	9.7	10.1	10.2	10.3	4c13.4
獄	奬	獠	獗	默	獣	獨	獲	獪	獰	獵	獸	獺
11.1	3n10.4	12.1	12.2	4d11.5	12.3	3g6.1	13.1	13.2	14.1	3g8.6	3g12.3	16.1
獻												
3g9.6												

─────────── 0 ───────────

3g0.1 / 280

犬　**KEN, inu** dog

─────────── 1 ───────────

3 犬小屋 **inugoya** doghouse, kennel
6 犬死 **inuji(ni)** die in vain
8 犬侍 **inuzamurai** shameless/cowardly samurai
　犬舎 **kensha** kennel, doghouse
　犬追物 **inuoumono** (noisy martial arts event of Kamakura period in which 36 mounted archers pursue and shoot at 150 dogs)
　犬泳 **inuoyo(gi)** dog paddle
9 犬狩 **inuga(ri)** mad-dog/wild-dog hunt
10 犬殺 **inukoro(shi)** dog catcher
　犬釘 **inukugi** spike
　犬馬 **kenba** my humble self
11 犬商 **inushō** dog fancier, kennelman
　犬猫 **inu-neko** dogs and cats
　犬張子 **inuha(ri)ko** papier-mâché dog
12 犬歯 **kenshi** canine tooth, eyetooth, cuspid
13 犬猿仲 **ken'en (no) naka** hating each other
16 犬儒学派 **kenjugakuha** the Cynics
23 犬鷲 **inuwashi** golden eagle

─────────── 2 ───────────

3 小犬 **koinu** puppy
　山犬 **yamainu** wild dog, coyote, wolf
4 仔犬 **koinu** puppy
6 牝犬 **mesu inu, meinu** female dog, bitch
7 狂犬 **kyōken** mad/rabid dog
　狂犬病 **kyōkenbyō** rabies
8 狛犬 **komainu** Korean dog (statue guarding shrine)
　忠犬 **chūken** faithful dog
9 軍犬 **gunken** army/military dog
　負犬 **ma(ke)inu** loser
　洋犬 **yōken** Western-breed dog
10 畜犬 **chikken, chikuken** keeping a dog; domestic dog

　畜犬税 **chikkenzei** dog tax
　猛犬 **mōken** vicious dog
　柴犬 **Shiba-inu** (a breed of small dog)
　病犬 **byōken** diseased dog
11 野犬 **yaken** stray dog
　捨犬 **su(te)inu** stray dog
　猟犬 **ryōken** hunting dog
12 斑犬 **madara inu, buchi inu** spotted dog
　番犬 **banken** watchdog
　雄犬 **osuinu** male dog
13 愛犬 **aiken** pet dog
　愛犬家 **aikenka** dog lover
　飼犬 **ka(i)inu** pet dog
14 雌犬 **mesuinu** female dog, bitch
16 橇犬 **soriinu** sled dog
18 闘犬 **tōken** dogfight(ing); fighting dog

─────────── 3 ───────────

4 日本犬 **nihonken** Japanese dog
8 盲導犬 **mōdōken** seeing-eye dog
9 軍用犬 **gun'yōken** army/military dog
　秋田犬 **Akita-ken, Akita inu** an Akita (husky-like) dog
11 野良犬 **norainu** stray dog
19 警察犬 **keisatsuken** police dog

尤 →　　　**0a4.20**

─────────── 2 ───────────

3g2.1 / 882

犯　**HAN** crime; (counter for criminal offenses) **oka(su)** commit (a crime), violate

─────────── 1 ───────────

2 犯人 **hannin** criminal, culprit, offender
6 犯行 **hankō** crime
9 犯則 **hansoku** violation, infraction
13 犯罪 **hanzai** crime
　犯罪人 **hanzainin** criminal, offender, convict

犯罪学 **hanzaigaku** criminology
犯罪者 **hanzaisha** criminal, offender, convict
犯跡 **hanseki** evidences of a crime

─────── 2 ───────

5 正犯 **seihan** principal offense/offender
正犯者 **seihansha** principal offender
主犯 **shuhan** principal offense/offender
主犯者 **shuhansha** principal offender
6 再犯 **saihan** second offense
再犯者 **saihansha** second offender
防犯 **bōhan** crime prevention
共犯 **kyōhan** complicity
共犯者 **kyōhansha** accomplice
7 初犯 **shohan** first offense/offender
8 性犯罪 **sei hanzai** sex crime
9 侵犯 **shinpan** invasion, violation
10 従犯 **jūhan** complicity; accomplice
11 累犯 **ruihan** repeated offense
累犯者 **ruihansha** repeat offender
盗犯 **tōhan** theft, burglary, robbery
12 違犯 **ihan** volation, offense
軽犯罪 **keihanzai** minor offense
13 戦犯 **senpan** war crime/criminal

─────── 3 ───────

6 刑事犯 **keijihan** criminal offense
8 知能犯 **chinōhan** a non-violent crime
国事犯 **kokujihan** political offense, treason
放火犯 **hōkahan** arson(ist)
9 軍事犯 **gunjihan** military offense
窃盗犯 **settōhan** thief
政治犯 **seijihan** political offense/offender
思想犯 **shisōhan** dangerous-thought offense
10 殺人犯 **satsujinhan** (the crime of) murder
11 強力犯 **gōrikihan** crime of violence
常習犯 **jōshūhan** habitual crime/criminal
現行犯 **genkōhan** crime/criminal witnessed
　　　 in the act, flagrante delicto
14 慣行犯 **kankōhan** habitual criminal
19 警察犯 **keisatsuhan** police offense

─────── 4 ───────

9 前科…犯 **zenka ...-han/...-pan** (a criminal
　 record of three) previous convictions

─────── 3 ───────

犲→豺 **0a10.4**

状→ **2b5.1**

尨→ **3j4.2**

3g4.1

狄 **TEKI** barbarian

─────── 2 ───────

6 夷狄 **iteki** barbarians, aliens

3g4.2 / 883

狂 **KYŌ** go mad/crazy; (as suffix) craze,
mania; enthusiast **kuru(u)** go crazy;
run amuck; get out of order
kuru(waseru/wasu) drive mad; upset
(plans) **kuru(i)** madness; out of order; going
wide of the mark **kuru(oshii)** mad (with grief)
kuru(washii) appearing to be crazy
fu(reru) go mad/crazy

─────── 1 ───────

0 狂する **kyō(suru)** go insane; be beside
　　　 oneself with
2 狂人 **kyōjin** insane person, lunatic
3 狂女 **kyōjo** madwoman
4 狂文 **kyōbun** humorous composition
狂犬 **kyōken** mad/rabid dog
狂犬病 **kyōkenbyō** rabies
5 狂句 **kyōku** comic haiku
6 狂死 **kyōshi, kuru(i)ji(ni)** death from madness
狂気 **kyōki** madness, insanity
狂妄 **kyōbō, kyōmō** mad, crazy
7 狂乱 **kyōran** frenzy, madness
狂言 **kyōgen** play, drama; program; Noh
　　　 farce; trick, sham
狂言自殺 **kyōgen jisatsu** faked suicide
8 狂奔 **kyōhon** rush madly about
狂的 **kyōteki** insane, frantic, fanatic
狂者 **kyōsha** insane person, lunatic
狂炎 **kyōen** fierce flames
9 狂信 **kyōshin** fanaticism
狂信的 **kyōshinteki** fanatical
狂信者 **kyōshinsha** fanatic, faddist
狂信性 **kyoshinsei** fanaticism
狂風 **kyōfū** raging winds
狂咲 **kuru(i)za(ki)** blooming out of season
12 狂喜 **kyōki** wild joy, rapture of delight
13 狂想曲 **kyōsōkyoku** rhapsody
狂詩 **kyōshi** comic poem
14 狂歌 **kyōka** comic tanka, satirical poem
狂態 **kyōtai** scandalous behavior
15 狂暴 **kyōbō** berserk, frenzied, furious
17 狂濤 **kyōtō** raging waves
18 狂騒 **kyōsō** mad uproar, frenzy, clamor
20 狂瀾 **kyōran** raging waves
狂騰 **kyōtō** sudden jump in prices
狂躁 **kyōsō** mad uproar, frenzy, clamor

—————— 2 ——————

3 女狂 **onnaguru(i)** chase women, philander
4 切狂言 **ki(ri)kyōgen** last act
5 半狂乱 **hankyōran** half-crazed
6 気狂 **ki (ga) kuru(u)** go mad/crazy
　色狂 **iroguru(i)** sex mania
　当狂言 **a(tari) kyōgen** a hit (play)
7 男狂 **otokoguru(i)** be man-crazy/wanton
8 佯狂 **yōkyō** feigned madness
　物狂 **monoguru(i)** insanity; madman
9 発狂 **hakkyō** madness, insanity
　俄狂言 **niwakakyōgen** mime, farce
　通狂言 **tō(shi)kyōgen** (presentation of) a whole play
　風狂 **fūkyō** fanatic; ultra-refined
　荒狂 **a(re)kuru(u)** rage, run amuck
10 能狂言 **nōkyōgen** Noh farce; Noh drama and kyōgen farce
　粋狂 **suikyō** caprice, whim
11 偏狂 **henkyō** monomania; monomaniac
　酔狂 **suikyō** whimsical, eccentric
　　yo(i)kuru(u) be raving drunk
12 替狂言 **ka(wari) kyōgen** next week's/month's program
　番狂 **bankuru(wase)** an upset (of plans)
13 頓狂 **tonkyō** flurried, hysteric, wild
14 踊狂 **odo(ri)kuru(u)** dance ecstatically
15 舞狂 **ma(i)kuru(u)** dance wildly, dance in a frenzy
　暴狂 **aba(re)kuru(u)** run amuck
　熱狂 **nekkyō** wild enthusiasm, frenzy, mania

—————— 3 ——————

6 死物狂 **shi(ni)monoguru(i)** struggle to the death; desperation, frantic efforts
　色情狂 **shikijōkyō** sex mania
8 放火狂 **hōkakyō** pyromania(c)
11 野球狂 **yakyūkyō** baseball fan
13 照葉狂言 **Teriha kyōgen** (a type of Noh entertainment)
14 読書狂 **dokushokyō** bibliophile
15 蔵書狂 **zōshokyō** bibliomania(c)

3g4.3

狃 **JŪ, na(reru)** get used to, learn

3g4.4

狆 **CHŪ, chin** Pekinese dog

—————— 1 ——————

0 狆ころ **chin(koro)** puppy

犹 → 猶 **3g9.5**

狀 → 状 **2b5.1**

—————— 5 ——————

3g5.1

狒 **HI** baboon

—————— 1 ——————

3 狒々 **hihi** baboon

3g5.2

狎 **KŌ, na(reru)** get used to, be familiar with

3g5.3

狙 **SO, nera(u)** aim at

—————— 1 ——————

5 狙打 **nera(i)u(chi)** take aim and shoot
8 狙所 **nera(i)dokoro** aim, objective
15 狙澄 **nera(i)su(masu)** take careful aim
　狙撃 **sogeki, nera(i)u(chi)** shooting, sniping
　狙撃兵 **sogekihei** sniper, sharpshooter

—————— 2 ——————

5 付狙 **tsu(ke)nera(u)** prowl after, keep watch on

—————— 3 ——————

8 空巣狙 **a(ki)sunera(i)** sneak thief, prowler

3g5.4

狛 **HAKU, koma** Korean dog

—————— 1 ——————

4 狛犬 **komainu** Korean dog (statue guarding shrine)

3g5.5

狗 **KU** dog, puppy

—————— 2 ——————

4 天狗 **tengu** long-nosed goblin; braggart
7 走狗 **sōku** hunting/running dog, (someone's) tool

3

氵
扌
口
女
巾
犭 5←
弓
彳
彡
艹
宀
凵
士
广
尸
口

---------- 3 ----------

6 羊頭狗肉 **yōtō-kuniku** advertising mutton but selling dog meat

10 烏天狗 **karasu tengu** crow-billed goblin

狐 → **3g6.4**

3

氵土扌口女巾 →6 犭弓彳彡艹宀丷山亠广尸口

---------- 6 ----------

3g6.1 / 219

独 獨

DOKU alone, on one's own; Germany **hito(ri)** alone **hito(rideni)** by itself, of its own accord

---------- 1 ----------

0 独りぼっち/りぼっち **hito(ribotchi/ripotchi)** all alone

2 独子 **hito(rik)ko, hito(ri)go** an only child

独力 **dokuryoku** one's own efforts, single-handed

4 独天下 **hito(ri)tenka, hito(ri)denka** sole figure, unchallenged master

独仏 **Doku-Futsu** Germany and France

5 独占 **dokusen** exclusive possession; monopoly

独占的 **dokusenteki** monopolistic

独芝居 **hito(ri)shibai** one-man show

独白 **dokuhaku** monolog, soliloquy

独立 **dokuritsu** independence **hito(ri)da(chi)** stand alone, be on one's own

独立心 **dokuritsushin** independent spirit

独立自尊 **dokuritsu-jison** independence and self-respect

独立国 **dokuritsukoku** independent country

独立独行 **dokuritsu-dokkō** independence, self-reliance

独立独歩 **dokuritsu-doppo** independence, self-reliance

独立権 **dokuritsuken** autonomy

6 独合点 **hito(ri)gaten** hasty conclusion

独行 **dokkō** self-reliance; traveling alone

独自 **dokuji** original, characteristic, indivudual, personal

7 独身 **dokushin, hito(ri)mi** unmarried

独身者 **dokushinsha** unmarried/single person

独住居 **hito(ri)zumai** living alone

独決 **hito(ri)gi(me)** decide by oneself, take it for granted

独走 **dokusō** running alone

独坐 **dokuza** sitting alone

独吟 **dokugin** vocal solo

独学 **dokugaku** self-study

独言 **hito(ri)goto** talking to oneself; soliloquy; monolog

8 独泳 **dokuei** swimming alone

独往 **dokuō** going one's own way

独英 **Doku-Ei** Germany and Britain, German-English (dictionary)

独歩 **hito(ri)aru(ki)** walking without assistance **doppo** ambulatory; peerless

独居 **dokkyo** solitude, solitary life

独者 **hito(ri)mono** single/unmarried person

独房 **dokubō** solitary cell

独和 **Doku-Wa** German-Japanese (dictionary)

9 独奏 **dokusō** instrumental solo

独奏会 **dokusōkai** instrumental recital

独活 **udo** (a rhubarb-like plant)

独活大木 **udo (no) taiboku** large and useless

独相撲 **hito(ri)zumō** like wrestling with no opponent

10 独修 **dokushū** self-study

独逸 **Doitsu** Germany

独案内 **hito(ri)annai** teach-yourself book

独座 **dokuza** sitting alone

独特 **dokutoku** unique, peculiar to

独酌 **dokushaku** drinking alone

11 独唱 **dokushō** vocal solo

独習 **dokushū** self-study

独習書 **dokushūsho** teach-yourself book

独眼 **dokugan** one-eyed, single-lens

独眼竜 **dokuganryū** one-eyed hero

独眼龍 **dokuganryū** one-eyed hero

独断 **dokudan** arbitrary decision; dogmatism

独断専行 **dokudan-senkō** arbitrary action

12 独創 **dokusō** originality, creativity

独創力 **dokusōryoku** creative talent, originality

独創的 **dokusōteki** original, creative

独創性 **dokusōsei** originality, inventiveness

独善 **hito(ri)yo(gari), dokuzen** self-righteous, complacent, smug

独善的 **dokuzenteki** self-righteous, complacent, smug

独裁 **dokusai** autocracy, dictatorship

独裁制 **dokusaisei** dictatorship

独裁的 **dokusaiteki** dictatorial

独裁者 **dokusaisha** dictator

独裁政治 **dokusai seiji** dictatorship, autocracy

13 独寝 **hito(ri)ne** sleeping alone

独楽 **koma** (spinning) top

独禁法 **dokkinhō** antitrust laws, the Anti-Monopoly Law (short for 独占禁止法)

独話 **dokuwa** talking to oneself; monolog

14 独演 **dokuen** solo performance

独演会 **dokuenkai** solo recital/performance

独暮 **hito(ri)gu(rashi)** living alone

独語 **dokugo** talking to oneself, soliloquy, monolog **Dokugo** German language

独領 **Dokuryō** German territory

15 独舞台 **hito(ri)butai** having the stage to
   oneself
16 独壇場 **dokudanjō** one's unrivaled field
   独擅場 **dokusenjō** one's unrivaled field

———————— 2 ————————

4 反独 **han-Doku** anti-German
  日独 **Nichi-Doku** Japan and Germany
6 西独 **Seidoku** West Germany
  米独 **Bei-Doku** the U.S. and Germany
7 対独 **tai-Doku** toward/with Germany
8 東独 **Tōdoku** East Germany
  孤独 **kodoku** solitary, isolated, lonely
  和独 **Wa-Doku** Japanese-German (dictionary),
      Japan and Germany
9 単独 **tandoku** independent, single-handed
  単独行為 **tandoku kōi** acting on one's own
  単独行動 **tandoku kōdō** acting on one's own
  単独講和 **tandoku kōwa** acting on one's own
13 滞独 **tai-Doku** staying in Germany
15 駐独 **chū-Doku** resident/stationed in
   Germany
16 親独 **shin-Doku** pro-German

———————— 3 ————————

9 独立独行 **dokuritsu-dokkō** independence,
   self-reliance
  独立独歩 **dokuritsu-doppo** independence,
   self-reliance
11 唯我独尊 **yuiga-dokuson** self-conceit,
   vainglory

3g6.2 / 1353

狭　狹 **KYŌ, sema(i)** narrow, small
   (in area)　**seba(maru/meru)**
   (intr./tr.) become/make narrow,
   contract　**sa-** (prefix used for
   euphony)

———————— 1 ————————

3 狭小 **kyōshō** narrow, cramped
  狭山 **sayama** mountain, hill
4 狭心症 **kyōshinshō** stricture of the heart,
   angina pectoris
8 狭苦 **semakuru(shii)** cramped
9 狭軌 **kyōki** narrow gauge
10 狭窄 **kyōsaku** constriction, stenosis
12 狭隘 **kyōai** narrow, cramped, too small
   狭間 **hazama** interstice; ravine; battlements
13 狭義 **kyōgi** narrow sense
19 狭霧 **sagiri** fog, mist

———————— 2 ————————

4 手狭 **tezema** narrow, cramped, small
5 広狭 **kōkyō** width, area
6 地狭 **chikyō** isthmus
8 若狭 **Wakasa** (ancient kuni, Fukui-ken)
  所狭 **tokorosema(i)** crowded

11 偏狭 **henkyō** narrow-minded, intolerant,
   parochial

3g6.3

狠 **KON** oppose, be contrary-minded

3g6.4

狐 **KO, kitsune** fox

———————— 1 ————————

4 狐火 **kitsunebi** foxfire, ignis fatuus
5 狐付 **kitsunetsu(ki)** possessed by a fox/spirit
10 狐狸 **kori** foxes and raccoon dogs; sly
   deceiver
13 狐嫁入 **kitsune (no) yome-i(ri)** a line of
   foxfire; a light rain during sunshine
14 狐疑 **kogi** doubt, indecision

———————— 2 ————————

5 古狐 **furugitsune** sly old fox
  白狐 **byakko** white fox
6 牝狐 **megitsune** female fox
8 青狐 **aogitsune** blue/arctic fox

3g6.5 / 1581

狩 **SHU, ka(ru)** hunt
   ka(ri), -ga(ri) hunting

———————— 1 ————————

2 狩人 **karyūdo, kariudo** hunter
3 狩小屋 **ka(ri)goya** hunting cabin, a blind
4 狩込 **ka(ri)ko(mi)** roundup, mass arrest
5 狩出 **ka(ri)da(su)** hunt/round up
  狩立 **ka(ri)ta(teru)** hunt up, chase (foxes)
6 狩衣 **ka(ri)ginu** (nobleman's silk garment)
11 狩猟 **shuryō** hunting
  狩猟会 **shuryōkai** hunting party
  狩猟地 **shuryōchi** hunting grounds
  狩猟法 **shuryōhō** game laws
  狩猟場 **shuryōjō** game preserve
  狩猟期 **shuryōki** open season
12 狩場 **ka(ri)ba** hunting grounds

———————— 2 ————————

3 山狩 **yamaga(ri)** hunt in the mountains
4 犬狩 **inuga(ri)** mad-dog/wild-dog hunt
5 石狩川 **Ishikari-gawa** (river, Hokkaidō)
8 兎狩 **usagiga(ri)** rabbit hunting
  虎狩 **toraga(ri)** tiger hunt
9 首狩 **kubiga(ri)** headhunting
  茸狩 **takega(ri)** mushroom gathering
10 桜狩 **sakuraga(ri)** looking for cherry
   blossoms

3

氵
土
扌
口
女
巾
犭 6←
弓
彳
彡
艹
宀
山
吉
广
尸
口

11 蛍狩 **hotaruga(ri)** firefly catching
14 熊狩 **kumaga(ri)** bear hunting
24 鷹狩 **takaga(ri)** falconry

──────── 3 ────────

6 汐干狩 **shiohiga(ri)** shell gathering at low tide
9 紅葉狩 **momijiga(ri)** outing for viewing autumn leaves
10 猛獣狩 **mōjūga(ri)** big-game hunting
11 野獣狩 **yajūga(ri)** wild animal hunt
15 潮干狩 **shiohiga(ri)** shell gathering (at low tide)

狢 → 貉 4i10.2

3g6.6

狡

KŌ, zuru(i), kosu(i) sly, cunning, crafty, tricky, dishonest

──────── 1 ────────

12 狡智 **kōchi** cunning, guile
13 狡猾 **kōkatsu** cunning, wily

3g6.7

哭

KOKU cry, keen

──────── 7 ────────

3g7.1

狽

BAI wolf

──────── 2 ────────

10 狼狽 **rōbai** consternation, confusion, panic

──────── 4 ────────

8 周章狼狽 **shūshō-rōbai** consternation, bewilderment, dismay

3g7.2

狸 貍

RI, tanuki raccoon dog; cunning person

──────── 1 ────────

5 狸汁 **tanukijiru** tanuki-meat soup
11 狸婆 **tanuki baba** cunning old woman
13 狸寝入 **tanuki ne-i(ri)** pretending to be an old woman

──────── 2 ────────

5 古狸 **furudanuki** old raccoon dog, veteran, old-timer
9 狐狸 **kori** foxes and raccoon dogs; sly deceiver

狹 → 狭 3g6.2

3g7.3

狼

RŌ wolf; confusion
ōkami wolf

──────── 1 ────────

7 狼男 **ōkami otoko** wolfman, werewolf
9 狼星 **Rōsei** Sirius, the Dog Star
10 狼狽 **rōbai** consternation, confusion, panic
17 狼藉 **rōzeki** disorder; violence, havoc
狼藉者 **rōzekimono** rioter, ruffian

──────── 2 ────────

4 天狼星 **Tenrōsei** Sirius, the Dog Star
8 虎狼 **korō** tigers and wolves; wild beasts; cruel man, brute
送狼 **oku(ri)ōkami** pursuing wolf; man who keeps following a woman
10 豺狼 **sairō** jackals and wolves; cruel/rapacious person

──────── 3 ────────

1 一匹狼 **ippiki ōkami** lone wolf
8 周章狼狽 **shūshō-rōbai** consternation, bewilderment, dismay
12 落花狼藉 **rakka-rōzeki** outrage, assault, rape

3g7.4 / 1579

猛

MŌ fierce, strong, intense
ta(keru) rush forth, rage, rave

──────── 1 ────────

3 猛々 **takedake(shii)** fierce, ferocious; audacious
4 猛反撃 **mōhangeki** fierce counterattack
猛犬 **mōken** vicious dog
猛火 **mōka** raging flames; heavy gunfire
5 猛打 **mōda** hard hit, heavy blow
猛打者 **mōdasha** slugger (in baseball)
7 猛攻撃 **mōkōgeki** fierce attack
8 猛毒 **mōdoku** virulent poison
猛虎 **mōko** ferocious tiger
猛者 **mosa** man of courage, stalwart, veteran
猛雨 **mōu** heavy rain, downpour
9 猛勇 **mōyū** dauntless courage
猛威 **mōi** ferocity, vehemence
猛省 **mōsei** serious reflection
10 猛射 **mōsha** heavy gunfire
猛将 **mōshō** brave general, strong contender
猛進 **mōshin** rush forward, plunge ahead
猛猛 **takedake(shii)** fierce, ferocious; audacious
猛烈 **mōretsu** fierce, violent, intense

猛訓練 **mōkunren** hard training
11 猛悪 **mōaku** savage, ferocious
猛鳥 **mōchō** bird of prey
12 猛禽 **mōkin** bird of prey
猛暑 **mōsho** intense heat
猛然 **mōzen** fiercely, savagely, resolutely
14 猛練習 **mōrenshū** intensive training
15 猛撃 **mōgeki** severe blow, fierce attack
16 猛獣 **mōjū** ferocious animal
猛獣使 **mōjūzuka(i)** wild-animal tamer
猛獣狩 **mōjūga(ri)** big-game hunting
19 猛爆 **mōbaku** heavy bombing
22 猛襲 **mōshū** furious attack, violent assault

——————— 2 ———————

4 凶猛 **kyōmō** fierce
6 兇猛 **kyōmō** fierce
8 弥猛心 **yatakegokoro** ardent spirit
9 勇猛 **yūmō** dauntless, intrepid, fearless
勇猛心 **yūmōshin** intrepid spirit
10 猛猛 **takedake(shii)** fierce, ferocious; audacious
12 雄猛 **yūmō** intrepid, dauntless, brave
17 獰猛 **dōmō** fierce

——————— 3 ———————

11 猪突猛進 **chototsu mōshin** headlong rush

3g7.5

猏

KEN short-tempered, dogmatic

——————— 1 ———————

4 猏介 **kenkai** obstinate, unyielding

——————— 8 ———————

3g8.1

猪　猪猪

CHO, inoshishi wild boar

——————— 1 ———————

3 猪口 **choko** saké cup
8 猪突 **chototsu** reckless, foolhardy
猪突猛進 **chototsu mōshin** headlong rush
猪武者 **inoshishi musha** daredevil
9 猪首 **ikubi** short and thick neck, bull neck
16 猪頸 **ikubi** short and thick neck, bull neck

3g8.2

猊　貌

GEI lion; high priest's throne

——————— 1 ———————

3 猊下 **geika** Your/His Holiness, Right Reverend

3g8.3

猖

SHŌ rage about, go berserk/wild

——————— 1 ———————

15 猖獗 **shōketsu** rage about, be rampant

3g8.4

猜

SAI envy, jealousy; doubt

——————— 1 ———————

7 猜忌 **saiki** envy, jealousy
14 猜疑 **saigi** suspicion, jealousy
猜疑心 **saigishin** suspicion, jealousy

3g8.5 / 1470

猫

BYŌ, neko cat

——————— 1 ———————

5 猫目石 **nekome-ishi** cat's-eye (of quartz)
6 猫舌 **nekojita** aversion to hot foods
猫耳 **nekomimi** ear with soft smelly wax
7 猫車 **nekoguruma** wheelbarrow
猫足 **nekoashi** carved table-leg
8 猫板 **nekoita** board at the side of a long brazier
9 猫要 **neko-i(razu)** rat poison
猫柳 **nekoyanagi** pussy willow
猫背 **nekoze** a bent back, stoop
10 猫被 **nekokabu(ri)** feigned innocence
11 猫脚 **nekoashi** carved table-leg
15 猫撫声 **nekona(de)goe** coaxing voice
17 猫糞 **nekobaba** appropriate/pocket (a found article) as one's own
18 猫額 **neko (no) hitai, nekobitai, byōgaku** (small as a) cat's forehead

——————— 2 ———————

3 小猫 **koneko** kitten
山猫 **yamaneko** wildcat
山猫争議 **yamaneko sōgi** wildcat strike
4 犬猫 **inu-neko** dogs and cats
7 牡猫 **oneko** tomcat
8 招猫 **mane(ki)neko** beckoning (porcelain) cat
9 海猫 **umineko** black-tailed gull
11 捨猫 **su(te)neko** stray cat
12 斑猫 **buchi neko** tabby cat
13 愛猫 **aibyō** pet cat
飼猫 **ka(i)neko** pet cat

——————— 3 ———————

3 三毛猫 **mikeneko** white-black-and-brown cat
11 野良猫 **noraneko** stray cat
21 麝香猫 **jakōneko** musk cat, civet

3g8.6 / 1580

猟　獵 RYŌ, ka(ri) hunting

― 1 ―

- 2 猟人 **kariudo, karyūdo, ryōjin** hunter
- 猟刀 **ryōtō** hunting knife
- 4 猟犬 **ryōken** hunting dog
- 6 猟色 **ryōshoku** lechery, debauchery
- 猟色家 **ryōshokuka** lecher, libertine
- 8 猟虎 **rakko** sea otter
- 猟奇 **ryōki** seeking the bizarre
- 猟官 **ryōkan** office-seeking
- 猟具 **ryōgu** hunting gear
- 10 猟師 **ryōshi** hunter
- 12 猟場 **ryōba** game preserve, hunting ground
- 猟期 **ryōki** hunting season
- 14 猟銃 **ryōjū** hunting gun, shotgun

― 2 ―

- 3 大猟 **tairyō** a large catch
- 4 不猟 **furyō** poor catch
- 5 出猟 **shutsuryō** going hunting
- 9 狩猟 **shuryō** hunting
- 狩猟会 **shuryōkai** hunting party
- 狩猟地 **shuryōchi** hunting grounds
- 狩猟法 **shuryōhō** game laws
- 狩猟場 **shuryōjō** game preserve
- 狩猟期 **shuryōki** open season
- 10 遊猟 **yūryō** hunting
- 遊猟家 **yūryōka** hunter
- 遊猟期 **yūryōki** hunting season
- 11 渉猟 **shōryō** read extensively, search for far and wide
- 密猟 **mitsuryō** poaching
- 12 御猟場 **goryōba** imperial forest
- 13 禁猟 **kinryō** No Hunting
- 禁猟区 **kinryōku** game preserve
- 禁猟期 **kinryōki** closed (hunting) season
- 14 漁猟 **gyoryō** fishing (and hunting)
- 銃猟 **jūryō** hunting

3g8.7

猗 I luxuriant growth; gentle, docile

3g8.8

猝 SOTSU sudden

就 → 3d9.21

― 9 ―

猪 → 猪 3g8.1

3g9.1

猴 KŌ monkey

― 2 ―

- 13 猿猴 **enkō** long-armed monkey

3g9.2

猥 WAI obscene
mida(ra) indecent, lewd
mida(rigamashii) indecent, immoral

― 1 ―

- 5 猥本 **waihon** pornographic book
- 14 猥雑 **waizatsu** vulgar, disorderly
- 15 猥談 **waidan** indecent talk, dirty story
- 17 猥褻 **waisetsu** obscene, lewd

― 2 ―

- 9 卑猥 **hiwai** indecent, obscene
- 11 淫猥 **inwai** indecent, obscene
- 13 鄙猥 **hiwai** indecent, obscene

3g9.3

猩 SHŌ orangutan

― 1 ―

- 3 猩々 **shōjō** orangutan; heavy drinker
- 猩々緋 **shōjōhi** scarlet
- 9 猩紅熱 **shōkōnetsu** scarlet fever

― 2 ―

- 11 黒猩々 **kuroshōjō** chimpanzee

3g9.4

猯 TAN, inoshishi wild boar

3g9.5 / 1583

猶 YŪ delay; still, still more
nao also, moreover; still; still more

― 1 ―

- 4 猶予 **yūyo** postponement, deferment
- 猶予期間 **yūyo kikan** grace period

― 3 ―

- 11 執行猶予 **shikkō yūyo** stay of execution, suspended sentence

3g9.6 / 1355

献 齍   **KEN, sasa(geru)** offer, present, dedicate
KON (counter for drinks)

——————— 1 ———————

0 献じる/ずる **ken(jiru/zuru)** offer, present, dedicate
3 献上 **kenjō** presentation
5 献本 **kenpon** presentation (copy)
  献立 **kondate** menu; arrangements, plan, program
  献立表 **kondatehyō** menu
6 献灯 **kentō** votive lantern
  献血 **kenketsu** blood donation
7 献身 **kenshin** self-sacrifice, dedication
  献身的 **kenshinteki** self-sacrificing, devoted
  献呈 **kentei** presentation (copy)
  献言 **kengen** petition, proposal, memorial
8 献杯 **kenpai** offer a drink/toast
  献物 **kenmotsu** offering, present
  献金 **kenkin** gift of money, contribution
  献金箱 **kenkinbako** contributions/offertory box
9 献茶 **kencha** powdered-tea offering
  献盃 **kenpai** offer a drink/toast
10 献納 **kennō** present, donate, dedicate
  献納者 **kennōsha** donor
  献納品 **kennōhin** donation
12 献策 **kensaku** suggest, propose, advise
  献詠 **ken'ei** dedicate a poem
13 献酬 **kenshū** exchange of saké cups
21 献饌 **kensen** offering (to a god)

——————— 2 ———————

1 一献 **ikkon** a cup (of saké)
4 文献 **bunken** literature (on a subject), bibliography
  文献学 **bunkengaku** bibliography, philology
8 奉献 **hōken** dedicate, offer, consecrate
10 貢献 **kōken** contribution, services

3g9.7

猷 猶   **YŪ** consult, deliberate, plan

——————— 10 ———————

3g10.1

獅   **SHI, shishi** lion

——————— 1 ———————

2 獅子 **shishi** lion
  獅子王 **shishiō** the king of beasts
  獅子吼 **shishiku** lion's roar; impassioned speech

獅子身中虫 **shishi-shinchū (no) mushi** treacherous friend
獅子鼻 **shishibana, shishi(p)pana** pug nose
獅子舞 **shishimai** lion-mask dance
獅子奮迅 **shishi funjin** great power and speed
獅子頭 **shishigashira** lion-head mask

——————— 2 ———————

6 牝獅子 **mejishi** lioness
10 唐獅子 **kara shishi** lion

3g10.2

猾   **KATSU** wily, cunning, crafty

——————— 2 ———————

9 狡猾 **kōkatsu** cunning, wily

3g10.3 / 1584

猿   **EN, saru, mashira** monkey

——————— 1 ———————

2 猿人 **enjin** ape-man
4 猿引 **saruhi(ki)** monkey trainer
5 猿芝居 **saru shibai** tricks performed by a monkey
6 猿回 **sarumawa(shi)** monkey trainer
7 猿似 **saruni** a chance resemblance
8 猿廻 **sarumawa(shi)** monkey trainer
  猿知恵 **sarujie** shallow cleverness
  猿股 **sarumata** drawers, undershorts
9 猿面 **sarumen** a face like a monkey's
10 猿真似 **sarumane** monkey-see monkey-do
12 猿猴 **enkō** long-armed monkey
13 猿楽 **sarugaku** (type of medieval farce)
16 猿賢 **sarugashiko(i)** cunning
22 猿轡 **sarugutsuwa** a gag (in one's mouth)

——————— 2 ———————

3 三猿 **mizaru, san'en** the three see-not, hear-not, speak-not monkeys
  山猿 **yamazaru** wild monkey; hillbilly
4 犬猿仲 **ken'en (no) naka** hating each other
11 野猿 **yaen** wild monkey

——————— 3 ———————

2 人類猿 **jinruien** anthropoid ape
4 手長猿 **tenagazaru** long-armed ape, gibbon
7 尾長猿 **onagazaru** long-tailed monkey
11 虚仮猿 **kokezaru** idiotic monkey
18 類人猿 **ruijin'en** anthropoid ape

——————— 4 ———————

13 意馬心猿 **iba-shin'en** (uncontrollable) passions

獏 → 獏 4c13.4

───── 11 ─────

3g11.1 / 884

GOKU prison

獄

───── 1 ─────

4 獄内 **gokunai** in prison
　獄中 **gokuchū** in prison
5 獄囚 **gokushū** prisoner
6 獄死 **gokushi** die in prison
　獄吏 **gokuri** jailer
　獄衣 **gokui** prison uniform
8 獄舎 **gokusha** prison, jail
　獄卒 **gokusotsu** prison guards; hell's tormenting devils
　獄門 **gokumon** prison gates; display of an executed criminal's decapitated head
9 獄屋 **gokuya** prison, jail
　獄則 **gokusoku** prison regulations
11 獄道 **gokudō** wicked, brutal, profligate
　獄道者 **gokudōsha** scoundrel, rogue, rake
　獄窓 **gokusō** prison window; prison

───── 2 ─────

2 入獄 **nyūgoku** imprisonment
3 下獄 **gegoku** be sent to prison
5 出獄 **shutsugoku** release from prison
6 地獄 **jigoku** hell
　在獄中 **zaigokuchū** while in prison
7 投獄 **tōgoku** imprisonment
　牢獄 **rōgoku** prison, jail
8 典獄 **tengoku** prison warden
10 破獄 **hagoku** jailbreak
11 脱獄 **datsugoku** escape from prison, jailbreak
　脱獄囚 **datsugokushū** escaped prisoner
13 煉獄 **rengoku** purgatory
　禁獄 **kingoku** imprisonment
14 疑獄 **gigoku** scandal
15 監獄 **kangoku** prison

───── 3 ─────

5 生地獄 **i(ki)jigoku** a living hell
6 仮出獄 **karishutsugoku** release on parole, out on bail
19 蟻地獄 **arijigoku** antlion, doodlebug

───── 4 ─────

12 無間地獄 **muken jigoku** (a Buddhist hell)
　焦熱地獄 **shōnetsu jigoku** an inferno
13 試験地獄 **shiken jigoku** the hell of (entrance) exams

奬 → 奨 3n10.4

───── 12 ─────

3g12.1

RYŌ hunting (at night)

獠

3g12.2

KETSU rage wildly, run amuck

獗

───── 2 ─────

11 猖獗 **shōketsu** rage about, be rampant

默 → 黙 4d11.5

3g12.3 / 1582

獣 獸

JŪ, kemono, kedamono animal, beast

───── 1 ─────

4 獣毛 **jūmō** animal hair, fur
　獣心 **jūshin** brutal heart
5 獣皮 **jūhi** animal skin, hide, pelt
6 獣肉 **jūniku** flesh of animals, meat
　獣行 **jūkō** brutal act, rape
7 獣医 **jūi** veterinarian
　獣医学 **jūigaku** veterinary medicine
　獣医業 **jūigyō** veterinary practice/business
8 獣的 **jūteki** bestial, animal, brutal
　獣性 **jūsei** animal nature, bestiality
9 獣姦 **jūkan** bestiality
　獣炭 **jūtan** incensed charcoal in animal shapes; charcoal made from animal blood or bones and used for medicine or bleaching
　獣疫 **jūeki** cattle disease
10 獣帯 **jūtai** the zodiac
　獣脂 **jūshi** animal fat, tallow
11 獣欲 **jūyoku** carnal desire, lust
15 獣慾 **jūyoku** carnal desire, lust
18 獣類 **jūrui** beasts, animals, brutes

───── 2 ─────

6 百獣 **hyakujū** all kinds of animals
8 怪獣 **kaijū** monster
9 海獣 **kaijū** sea animal
10 猛獣 **mōjū** ferocious animal
　猛獣使 **mōjūzuka(i)** wild-animal tamer
　猛獣狩 **mōjūga(ri)** big-game hunting
11 野獣 **yajū** wild animal/beast
　野獣主義 **yajū shugi** Fauvism
　野獣派 **yajūha** Fauvists
　野獣狩 **yajūga(ri)** wild animal hunt

鳥獣 **chōjū** birds and animals, wildlife
12 禽獣 **kinjū** birds and beasts, animals

——————— 3 ———————
1 一角獣 **ikkakujū** unicorn
2 人面獣心 **jinmen-jūshin** human face but brutal heart
5 四足獣 **shisokujū** quadruped
9 食肉獣 **shokunikujū** a carnivore
食蟻獣 **arikui** anteater

——————— 13 ———————

獨 → 独 3g6.1

3g13.1 / 1313

獲 **KAKU, e(ru)** obtain, acquire, gain

——————— 1 ———————
8 獲物 **emono** game, a catch, spoils
11 獲得 **kakutoku** acquire, gain, win
——————— 2 ———————
1 一獲 **ikkaku** one grab
7 乱獲 **rankaku** indiscriminate fishing/hunting
10 捕獲 **hokaku** capture, seizure
11 鹵獲 **rokaku** capture, plunder
鹵獲物 **rokakubutsu** booty, spoils, trophy
14 漁獲 **gyokaku** fishing; catch, haul
漁獲物 **gyokakubutsu** a catch (of fish)
18 濫獲 **rankaku** overfishing, overhunting

3g13.2

獪 **KAI** cunning, crafty, wily

——————— 2 ———————
6 老獪 **rōkai** crafty, astute, wily

——————— 14 ———————

3g14.1

獰 **DŌ** vicious

——————— 1 ———————
10 獰猛 **dōmō** fierce

——————— 15 ———————

獵 → 猟 3g8.6
獸 → 獣 3g12.3

——————— 16 ———————

3g16.1

獺 **DATSU, uso, kawauso** otter

——————— 2 ———————
3 川獺 **kawauso** otter

戲 → 献 3g9.6

——————————— 弓 3h ———————————

弓	引	弖	弘	弛	弦	弥	弩	弭	弧	弯	矧	躬
0.1	1.1	1.2	2.1	3.1	5.1	5.2	5.3	6.1	6.2	3h19.1	6.3	7.1

弱	張	弸	強	粥	弼	弾	發	彁	彈	彊	彌	彎
7.2	8.1	8.2	8.3	9.1	9.2	9.3	0a9.5	10.1	3h9.3	13.1	3h5.2	19.1

——————— 0 ———————

3h0.1 / 212

弓 **KYŪ, yumi** bow (for archery/violin)

——————— 1 ———————
4 弓手 **yunde** the bow/left hand
5 弓矢 **yumiya** bow and arrow

弓矢八幡 **yumiya hachiman** god of war
7 弓状 **kyūjō** bow-shaped, arched
弓形 **kyūkei** bow-shaped; circle segment
yumigata arch, arc, curve
8 弓弦 **yumizuru** bowstring
10 弓師 **yumishi** bow maker
弓馬 **kyūba** bow and horse; archery and horsemanship
11 弓道 **kyūdō** (Japanese) archery

弓張 **yumiha(ri)** paper lantern with bow-shaped handle
弓張月 **yumiha(ri)zuki** crescent moon
弓張提灯 **yumiha(ri)jōchin** paper lantern with bow-shaped handle
弓術 **kyūjutsu** (Japanese) archery
12 弓場 **yumiba** archery ground
13 弓勢 **yunzei** strength put forth in drawing a bow
15 弓箭 **kyūsen** bows and arrows; arms; war

————————— 2 —————————

3 大弓 **daikyū** bow; archery
5 半弓 **hankyū** small bow
石弓 **ishiyumi** crossbow, catapult
8 弩弓 **dokyū** catapult
弩弓艦 **dokyūkan** dreadnaught
14 綿弓 **watayumi** bow-shaped tool for willowing ginned cotton

————————— 3 —————————

10 破魔弓 **hamayumi** exorcising bow (used in roof-raising ceremonies); toy bow and arrow

————————— 1 —————————

3h1.1 / 216

引

IN, **hi(ku)** pull; attract; retreat, recede, withdraw; reduce, discount **-biki** (30%) discount **hi(keru)** close, be over

————————— 1 —————————

2 引力 **inryoku** gravitation, attraction
3 引上 **hi(ki)a(geru)** raise, increase; withdraw, leave
引下 **hi(ki)sa(garu)** withdraw, leave
hi(ki)o(rosu) pull down
4 引切無 **hi(k)ki(ri)na(shi ni)** incessantly
引分 **hi(ki)wa(ke)** tie, draw, standoff
引込 **hi(ki)ko(mu)** bring around, win over
hi(k)ko(mu) draw back, retire; sink, cave in; stand back; disappear
引込思案 **hi(k)ko(mi)jian** conservative, retiring
引手 **hi(ki)te** handle, knob; patron, admirer
hi(ku)te inviter, wooer, suitor
引火 **inka** ignite, catch fire
引火性 **inkasei** flammability
引火点 **inkaten** flash point
引戸 **hi(ki)do** sliding door
5 引出 **hi(ki)da(shi)** (desk) drawer
引写 **hi(ki)utsu(shi)** tracing, copy
引用 **in'yō** quotation, citation
引用文 **in'yōbun** quotation
引用句 **in'yōku** quotation
引用符 **in'yōfu** quotation marks
引払 **hi(ki)hara(u)** clear out, leave, vacate

引札 **hi(ki)fuda** handbill; lottery ticket
引立役 **hi(ki)ta(te)yaku** one who seeks to enhance another's position, foil, front/advance man, supporter
引目 **hi(ke)me** (feeling of) inferiority, reticence
6 引返 **hi(ki)kae(su)** turn back
引当金 **hi(ki)a(te)kin** reserve fund, appropriation
引回 **hi(ki)mawa(su)** pull around; lead about
7 引伸 **hi(ki)noba(su)** stretch/pad out, enlarge
引延 **hi(ki)noba(su)** stretch out; enlarge; defer
引抜 **hi(ki)nu(ku)** pull out, select
引見 **inken** interview, audience with
8 引例 **inrei** quotation, citation
引受 **hi(ki)u(keru)** undertake, consent to, accept responsibility for, guarantee
引受人 **hikiukenin** guarantor, acceptor (of a bill), underwriter
引直 **hi(ki)nao(su)** restore to, bring back to
引退 **intai** retire
引物 **hi(ki)mono** gift
引取 **hi(ki)to(ru)** take charge of; take back, claim; leave, retire; die
引取人 **hikitorinin** claimant; caretaker
引金 **hi(ki)gane** trigger
9 引連 **hi(ki)tsu(reru)** take (someone) along, bring with
引眉 **hi(ki)mayu** painted eyebrows
10 引倒 **hi(ki)tao(su)** pull/drag down
引剥 **hi(ki)ha(gu)** pull/strip off
引起 **hi(ki)o(kosu)** lift/help up, raise; give rise to, cause
引捕 **hi(t)tora(eru)** seize, capture, arrest
引時 **hi(ke)doki** closing time
引致 **inchi** take into custody
引被 **hi(k)kabu(ru)** pull over one's head
引留 **hi(ki)to(meru)** detain, keep/hold back, stop
11 引率 **insotsu** lead, head up
引率者 **insotsusha** leader
引掛 **hi(k)ka(karu)** get caught/hooked/entangled **hi(k)ka(keru)** hang/hook/throw on; ensnare; cheat; have a quick drink
引張 **hi(p)pa(ru)** pull, drag, tug at; take (someone) to
引菓子 **hi(ki)gashi** ornamental gift cakes
引窓 **hi(ki)mado** skylight, trap door
引寄 **hi(ki)yo(seru)** draw near/toward; attract
引船 **hi(ki)bune** tugboat
引責 **inseki** assume responsibility for
12 引渡 **hi(ki)wata(su)** deliver, transfer, hand over
引揚者 **hi(ki)a(ge)sha** returnee

引換 **hi(ki)ka(eru)** exchange, change, convert
引替 **hikika(e)** exchange, conversion
引替券 **hikika(e)ken** exchange ticket
引越 **hi(k)ko(su)** move (to a new residence)
引越先 **hi(k)ko(shi)saki** where one moves to
引裂 **hi(ki)sa(ku)** tear up/off, rip up/open, rend, separate
引絞 **hi(ki)shibo(ru)** draw back (a bow/curtains) as far as it/they will go; strain (one's voice)
引証 **inshō** quote, cite, adduce
13 引搔 **hi(k)ka(ku)** scratch, claw
引搔回 **hi(k)ka(ki)mawa(su)** ransack, rummage through; carry on highhandedly
引幕 **hi(ki)maku** (stage) curtain
引照 **inshō** reference
引数 **hikisū** argument (of a function)
引置 **inchi** take into custody
引続 **hi(ki)tsuzu(ki)** continuing
引継 **hi(ki)tsu(gu)** take/hand over; inherit
14 引摺 **hi(ki)zu(ru)** drag along
     (o)hi(ki)zu(ri) slut
引摺込 **hi(ki)zu(ri)ko(mu)** drag in
引摺出 **hi(ki)zu(ri)da(su)** drag out
引摺回 **hi(ki)zu(ri)mawa(su)** drag around
引摑 **hi(t)tsuka(mu)** grab, snatch
引算 **hi(ki)zan** subtraction (in math)
15 引潮 **hi(ki)shio** ebb tide
引締 **hi(ki)shi(meru)** tighten, stiffen, brace
18 引離 **hi(ki)hana(su)** pull apart; outdistance
19 引繰返 **hi(k)ku(ri)kae(ru)** be overturned, capsize, collapse; be reversed
     hi(k)ku(ri)kae(su) overturn, turn upside down, turn inside out
22 引籠 **hi(ki)komo(ru)** stay indoors, be confined indoors
23 引攣 **hi(ki)tsu(ru)** have a cramp/crick/tic/spasm/twitch/convulsion

———————— 2 ————————

3 万引 **manbi(ki)** shoplifting; shoplifter
小引 **shōin** short introduction/preface
4 勾引 **kōin** arrest, take into custody
勾引状 **kōinjō** arrest warrant, summons
天引 **tenbi(ki)** deduction (of interest) in advance
水引 **mizuhiki** multi-color string for tying gifts
手引 **tebi(ki)** guidance; introduction, primer; good offices, introduction
手引書 **tebi(ki)sho** handbook, manual
5 布引 **nunobi(ki)** cloth stretching
字引 **jibiki** dictionary
目引 **mehi(ki), mebi(ki)** attract the eye; dye colorfully; perforation for binding pages
目引袖引 **mehi(ki)-sodehi(ki)** (belittle by) winking and tugging at (someone's) sleeve

6 地引 **jibi(ki)** seine fishing
地引網 **jibi(ki)ami** dragnet, seine
吸引 **kyūin** absorb; attract
早引 **hayabi(ki)** leave early
7 延引 **en'in, ennin** delay
図引 **zuhi(ki)** drafting, drawing; draftsman
忌引 **kibi(ki)** absence due to a death in the family
車引 **kurumahi(ki)** rickshaw puller
8 長引 **nagabi(ku)** be prolonged, drag on
受引 **u(ke)hi(ku)** accept, consent
退引 **no(p)piki(naranu)** unavoidable, inescapable
拘引 **kōin** arrest, custody
拘引状 **kōinjō** arrest warrant, summons
歩引 **bubi(ki)** discount
底引網 **sokobi(ki)ami** dragnet, trawlnet
股引 **momohi(ki)** drawers, underpants; close-fitting workpants
取引 **torihiki** transaction, deal, business
取引所 **torihikijo, torihikisho** (stock) exchange
取引高 **torihikidaka** volume of business, turnover
9 孫引 **magobi(ki)** quoting secondhand, reference to secondary sources
首引 **kubi(p)pi(ki)** tug of war using necks; constantly referring to (a dictionary)
逢引 **a(i)bi(ki)** rendezvous, assignation, tryst
客引 **kyakuhi(ki)** soliciting customers; a tout
音引 **onbi(ki)** (dictionary) arranged by pronunciation (rather than stroke count)
10 値引 **nebi(ki)** discount
索引 **sakuin** index
差引 **sa(shi)hi(ku)** deduct
差引勘定 **sashihiki kanjō** account balance
根引 **nebi(ki)** uproot; redeem
馬引 **umahi(ki)** pack-horse tender
11 牽引 **ken'in** drag, tow, haul, pull
牽引力 **ken'inryoku** pulling power, traction
牽引車 **ken'insha** tractor
掛引 **ka(ke)hi(ki)** bargaining, maneuvering
強引 **gōin** by force, forcibly
宿引 **yadohi(ki)** hotel tout/runner
12 割引 **waribiki** discount
     wa(ri)bi(ku) give a discount
割引券 **waribikiken** discount coupon
湯引 **yubi(ku)** parboil
棚引 **tanabi(ku)** trail, hang over (fog/smoke)
棒引 **bōbi(ki)** cancellation, writing off
税引 **zeibi(ki)** after taxes, take-home (pay)
間引 **mabi(ki)** thinning out (plants)
13 塩引 **shiobi(ki)** salt-cured; salted fish
猿引 **saruhi(ki)** monkey trainer
福引 **fukubi(ki)** lottery, raffle
福引券 **fukubi(ki)ken** lottery ticket

野引 | **keibi(ki)** ruling; ruler
置引 | **o(ki)bi(ki)** baggage theft
14 綱引 | **tsunahi(ki)** tug-of-war
誘引 | **yūin** entice, induce, attract, allure
駆引 | **ka(ke)hi(ki)** bargaining, haggling, maneuvering
15 縁引 | **enbi(ki)** connection, relation
21 蠟引 | **rōbi(ki)** waxing
23 籤引 | **kujibi(ki)** drawing lots

——————— 3 ———————

5 生字引 | **i(ki)jibiki** walking dictionary
6 再割引 | **saiwaribiki** rediscount
7 我田引水 **gaden insui** drawing water for one's own field, promoting one's own interests
亜鉛引 | **aenbi(ki)** galvanized
8 直取引 | **jikitorihiki** spot/cash transaction
空取引 | **karatorihiki, kūtorihiki** fictitious transaction
金棒引 | **kanabōhi(ki)** night watchman; a gossip
10 差詰引詰 **sa(shi)tsu(me)-hi(ki)tsu(me)** shooting a flurry of arrows
11 商取引 | **shōtorihiki** business transaction
掛取引 | **ka(ke)torihiki** credit transaction
黒水引 | **kuromizuhiki** black-and-white string
13 鉄棒引 | **kanabōhi(ki)** night watchman; a gossip
14 総索引 | **sōsakuin** general index
17 闇取引 | **yamitorihiki** black-market dealings, illegal transaction
19 瀬戸引 | **setobi(ki)** enameled

——————— 4 ———————

4 手薬煉引 | **tegusune hi(ite)** prepared, all set for
5 目引袖引 | **mehi(ki)-sodehi(ki)** (belittle by) winking and tugging at (someone's) sleeve
9 信用取引 **shin'yō torihiki** credit transaction

3h1.2

弓 **te** (used phonetically)

——————— 2 ———————

3h2.1

弘 **KŌ, KŪ, hiro(i)** broad, wide

——————— 1 ———————

4 弘化 **Kōka** (era, 1844–1848)
弘仁 **Kōnin** (era, 810–824)
弘文 **Kōbun** (emperor, 671–672)
6 弘安 **Kōan** (era, 1278–1288)
8 弘長 **Kōchō** (era, 1261–1264)

弘治 **Kōji** (era, 1555–1558)
弘和 **Kōwa** (era, 1381–1384)
9 弘前 **Hirosaki** (city, Aomori-ken)
11 弘済会 **kōsaikai** benefit association
12 弘報 **kōhō** publicity
弘報部 **kōhōbu** public relations department

——————— 2 ———————

4 元弘 **Genkō** (era, 1331–1334)
13 寛弘 **Kankō** (era, 1004–1011)

——————— 3 ———————

3h3.1

弛 **SHI, CHI, taru(mu), yuru(mu)** (intr.) slacken, loosen, relax
tayu(mu) slacken one's efforts
yuru(meru) (tr.) loosen, slacken, relax

——————— 1 ———————

15 弛緩 **chikan, shikan** relaxation, slackening

——————— 2 ———————

4 中弛 **nakadaru(mi)** a slump

——————— 5 ———————

3h5.1 / 1226

弦 **GEN** bowstring; (violin) string; chord (in geometry); hypotenuse; quarter (phase of the moon) **tsuru** bowstring

——————— 1 ———————

4 弦月 **gengetsu** crescent moon
7 弦声 **gensei** sound of the strings
9 弦音 **tsuruoto** sound of a vibrating bowstring
13 弦楽 **gengaku** string (ensemble)
弦楽器 **gengakki** string instrument, the strings
14 弦歌 **genka** singing accompanied by string instruments
弦管 **genkan** wind and string instruments
15 弦線 **gensen** (violin) string, catgut

——————— 2 ———————

3 三弦 **sangen** three-stringed instrument; samisen
上弦 **jōgen** first quarter (phase of the moon)
下弦 **kagen** last quarter (phase of the moon)
弓弦 **yumizuru** bowstring
5 正弦 **seigen** sine
7 余弦 **yogen** cosine
14 管弦 **kangen** wind and string instruments; music
管弦楽団 **kangen gakudan** orchestra

3h5.2

弥 彌 **BI, MI, iya** all the more, increasingly

1

3 弥上 **iya(ga)ue (ni mo)** all the more
5 弥生 **yayoi** third lunar month; spring
   Yayoi (archaelogical period, 200 B.C.–
   250 A.D.)
6 弥次 **yaji** cheering; jeering; hecklers, spectators
   弥次馬 **yajiuma** bystanders, spectators,
   crowd of onlookers
7 弥陀 **Mida** Amitabha
10 弥猛心 **yatakegokoro** ardent spirit
11 弥勒 **Miroku** Maitreya
14 弥増 **iyama(su)** go on increasing
15 弥縫 **bihō** makeshift, stopgap, temporizing
   弥縫策 **bihōsaku** makeshift, stopgap measure

2

7 阿弥陀 **Amida** Amida Buddha; lottery;
   wearing a hat on the back of the head
   阿弥陀経 **Amidakyō** the Sukhavati sutra
   沙弥 **shami** Buddhist acolyte, novice
9 卑弥呼 **Himiko** female ruler of the early
   Japanese political federation known as
   Yamatai (about 3rd century)

3

19 曠日弥久 **kōjitsu bikyū** idle away one's
   time/years

4

4 元木阿弥 **moto (no) mokuami** losing what
   was gained, no better off
9 南無阿弥陀仏 **Namu Amida Butsu** Hail
   Amida Buddha

3h5.3

弩   **DO** crossbow

1

3 弩弓 **dokyū** catapult
   弩弓艦 **dokyūkan** dreadnaught

2

11 強弩 **kyōdo** strong crossbow
   強弩末 **kyōdo (no) sue** a once strong but
   now spent force
12 超弩級 **chōdokyū** superdreadnought-class

6

3h6.1

弭   **BI, ya(meru), ya(mu)** stop, cease
   yubazu the notches where the bowstring is attached to the bow

3h6.2 / 1481

弧   **KO** arc

1

6 弧光 **kokō** electric arc, arc lamp
   弧灯 **kotō** arc lamp
7 弧状 **kojō** arc-shaped
   弧形 **kokei** arc
15 弧線 **kosen** arc

2

4 円弧 **enko** arc
9 括弧 **kakko** parentheses, brackets
13 電弧 **denko** electric arc

3

3 丸括弧 **marugakko** parentheses

弯 → 彎 **3h19.1**

3h6.3

矧   **SHI** all the more, to say nothing of; the
   gums   **ha(gu)** fledge/feather (arrows)

7

3h7.1

躬   **KYŪ** body; self

1

6 躬行 **kyūkō** carry out oneself, practice

2

17 鞠躬如 **kikkyūjo** (bowing) respectfully

3h7.2 / 218

弱 弱   **JAKU** weak; (as suffix) a little
   less than   **yowa(i)** weak
   yowa(maru) grow weak
   yowa(meru) make weak,
weaken   **yowa(ru)** grow weak; be nonplussed/
floored

1

3 弱々 **yowayowa(shii)** weak-looking, frail,
   delicate
   弱小 **jakushō** puniness; youth
4 弱少 **jakushō** puniness; youth
6 弱気 **yowaki** faintheartedness; bearishness
   弱年 **jakunen** youth, young
   弱肉強食 **jakuniku-kyōshoku** survival of
   the fittest
   弱行 **jakkō** weakness in execution, irresoluteness
   弱虫 **yowamushi** weakling, coward, sissy
7 弱体 **jakutai** weak, effete
   弱体化 **jakutaika** weakening
8 弱卒 **jakusotsu** cowardly soldier

3

氵 土
扌 口
女 巾
犭 弓 7←
彳 彡
艹 宀
⺌ 山
幺 寺
广 戸
尸 口

弱味 **yowami** a weakness
弱味噌 **yowamiso** weakling, coward
弱国 **jakkoku** weak country
弱者 **jakusha, yowa(i) mono** the weak
9 弱冠 **jakkan** age 20; youth
弱点 **jakuten** weak point, a weakness
弱音吐 **yowane (o) ha(ku)** complain, cry uncle
弱音器 **jakuonki** a damper, mute
10 弱弱 **yowayowa(shii)** weak-looking, frail, delicate
11 弱視 **jakushi** poor eyesight
13 弱腰 **yowagoshi** weak attitude, timidity
15 弱敵 **jakuteki** weak enemy
弱輩 **jakuhai** young/inexperienced person
弱震 **jakushin** weak earthquake tremor
17 弱齢 **jakurei** youth

――――――― 2 ―――――――

4 文弱 **bunjaku** effeminate
5 幼弱 **yōjaku** young and weak
6 気弱 **kiyowa** timid, fainthearted
年弱 **toshiyowa** child born in the last half of the year
老弱 **rōjaku** infirmity/feebleness of old age
色弱 **shikijaku** slight color blindness
7 足弱 **ashiyowa** slow of foot, weak-legged
9 柔弱 **nyūjaku** weakness, enervation
胃弱 **ijaku** indigestion
10 衰弱 **suijaku** grow weak, become feeble
弱弱 **yowayowa(shii)** weak-looking, frail, delicate
脆弱 **zeijaku** fragile, frail, flimsy, brittle
病弱 **byōjaku** delicate constitution
11 虚弱 **kyojaku** weak, feeble, frail
貧弱 **hinjaku** poor, meager, scanty
強弱 **kyōjaku** (relative) strength
軟弱 **nanjaku** weak(-kneed)
12 惰弱 **dajaku** effect, soft
13 微弱 **bijaku** feeble
腰弱 **koshiyowa** weak-willed, unpersevering
暗弱 **anjaku** feeble-minded
16 薄弱 **hakujaku** feeble, flimsy
17 懦弱 **dajaku** effete, soft
繊弱 **senjaku** frail, delicate
19 羸弱 **ruijaku** delicate, frail
20 孅弱 **senjaku** frail, delicate

――――――― 3 ―――――――

16 薄志弱行 **hakushi-jakkō** indecisive and unenterprising

――――――― 8 ―――――――

3h8.1 / 1106

張

CHŌ stretch, spread; assert, boast; (counter for bows, string instruments, curtains) **ha(ru)** stretch, spread

――――――― 1 ―――――――

2 張子 **ha(ri)ko** papier-mâché
張力 **chōryoku** tension, tensile strength
3 張上 **ha(ri)a(geru)** raise/strain (one's voice)
4 張切 **ha(ri)ki(ru)** stretch tight; be tense/eager
張込 **ha(ri)ko(mu)** be on the lookout for, stake out; splurge
5 張本人 **chōhonnin** ringleader
張目 **ha(ri)me** edge of a piece of paper pasted onto another
6 張合 **ha(ri)a(u)** vie/compete with
7 張抜 **ha(ri)nu(ki)** papier-mâché
10 張倒 **ha(ri)tao(su)** knock down
張紙 **ha(ri)gami** sticker, (advertising) poster
張紙禁止 **ha(ri)gami kinshi** Post No Bills
12 張替 **ha(ri)ka(eru)** repaper, re-cover, reupholster
張裂 **ha(ri)sa(keru)** split open, burst
張番 **ha(ri)ban** stand watch/lookout; sentinel
13 張詰 **ha(ri)tsu(meru)** strain, make tense

――――――― 2 ―――――――

1 一張羅 **itchōra** one's only good clothes
3 夕張 **Yūbari** (city, Hokkaidō)
上張 **uwaba(ri)** face, coat, veneer
uwa(p)pa(ri) overalls, duster, smock
弓張 **yumiha(ri)** paper lantern with bow-shaped handle
弓張月 **yumiha(ri)zuki** crescent moon
弓張提灯 **yumiha(ri)jōchin** paper lantern with bow-shaped handle
4 切張 **ki(ri)ba(ri)** patching (a paper screen)
手張 **teba(ri)** hand-glued; speculation
犬張子 **inuha(ri)ko** papier-mâché dog
引張 **hi(p)pa(ru)** pull, drag, tug at; take (someone) to
5 出張 **shutchō** business trip
deba(ri) projection, ledge
出張店 **shutchōten** branch store
出張所 **shutchōjo** branch office
出張員 **shutchōin** agent, representative, dispatched official
主張 **shuchō** assertion, claim, contention
目張 **meba(ri)** paper over, weather-strip
6 気張 **kiba(ru)** exert oneself, make an effort; be extravagant, treat oneself to
7 我張 **ga (o) ha(ru)** be self-willed, insist on having one's own way
伸張 **shinchō** extension, expansion
角張 **kakuba(ru), kado(baru)** be angular; be stiff and formal
床張 **tokoba(ri)** flooring
尾張 **Owari** (ancient kuni, Aichi-ken)
見張 **miha(ru)** watch, be on the lookout for, stake out; open (one's eyes) wide
見張台 **miha(ri)dai** watchtower

見張所 **miha(ri)sho** lookout, crow's nest
見張番 **miha(ri)ban** watch, lookout, guard
言張 **i(i)ha(ru)** insist on, maintain
8 拡張 **kakuchō** extension, expansion
　突張 **tsu(p)pa(ru)** stretch (an arm) against,
　　plant (one's foot) on; insist on
　　tsu(p)pa(ri) prop, brace
　板張 **itaba(ri)** boarding, planking, wainscoting
　武張 **buba(ru)** be warrior-like
　金張 **kinba(ri)** gold-plated
9 洗張 **ara(i)ha(ri)** fulling; washing and
　　stretching
　威張 **iba(ru)** be proud, swagger
10 宵張 **yoi(p)pa(ri)** staying up till late; nightowl
　骨張 **honeba(ru)** get thin; persist in
　　honeba(tta) bony, thin
　息張 **ikiba(ru)** strain, bear down (in defecat-
　　ing or giving birth)
11 強張 **kowaba(ru)** become stiff
　欲張 **yokuba(ri)** greed, covetousness
12 減張 **me(ri)ha(ri)** loosening or tightening (of
　　violin strings)
　筋張 **sujiba(ru)** become stiff/sinewy;
　　be formal
13 嵩張 **kasaba(ru)** be bulky/unwieldly
　腰張 **koshiba(ri)** papering (on) the lower
　　part of a wall or sliding door
　絹張 **kinuba(ri)** silk covered
　誇張 **kochō** exaggeration
　誇張法 **kochōhō** hyperbole
　誇張的 **kochōteki** exaggerated, grandiloquent
　頑張 **ganba(ru)** persist in, stick to it, hang in
　　there
15 縄張 **nawaba(ri)** rope off; one's domain,
　　bailiwick
　縄張争 **nawaba(ri) araso(i)** jurisdictional
　　dispute, turf battle
　緊張 **kinchō** tension
　緊張緩和 **kinchō kanwa** détente
　踏張 **fu(n)ba(ru)** brace one's legs, stand firm,
　　hold out, persist in
16 膨張 **bōchō** swelling, expansion
　頬張 **hōba(ru)** stuff one's mouth with food
19 鯱張 **shachikoba(ru), shachihokoba(ru)** be
　　stiff and formal

────────── 3 ──────────

1 一点張 **ittenba(ri)** persistence
　一閑張 **ikkanba(ri)** lacquered papier-mâché
3 大威張 **ōiba(ri)** bragging
5 四角張 **shikakuba(ru)** be formal/stiff
7 見識張 **kenshikiba(ru)** assume an air of
　　importance
8 表面張力 **hyōmen chōryoku** surface tension
　空威張 **kara-iba(ri)** bluster, bravado; mock
　　dignity

10 格式張 **kakushikiba(ru)** stick to formalities
11 強突張 **gōtsukuba(ri)** headstrong
13 意地張 **iji(p)pa(ri)** obstinate (person)

────────── 4 ──────────

4 予防線張 **yobōsen (o) ha(ru)** guard against

3h8.2

弸　**HŌ** strong (bow); full

3h8.3 / 217

強

KYŌ, GŌ, tsuyo(i) strong
tsuyo(maru) become strong(er)
tsuyo(meru) make strong(er),
　　strengthen　**shi(iru)** force, compel
anaga(chi) (not) necessarily　**kowa(i)** tough,
hard, stiff

────────── 1 ──────────

2 強力 **kyōryoku** strength, power
　gōriki great physical strength; moun-
　　tain carrier-guide
　強力犯 **gōrikihan** crime of violence
3 強大 **kyōdai** powerful, mighty
4 強化 **kyōka** strengthen, fortify
　強引 **gōin** by force, forcibly
　強火 **tsuyobi** strong (cooking) fire, high heat
　強心剤 **kyōshinzai** heart stimulant
5 強弁 **kyōben** quibble, chop logic
　強圧 **kyōatsu** pressure, coercion
　強打 **kyōda** hit hard, slug
　強打者 **kyōdasha** hard hitter, slugger
6 強気 **tsuyoki** bullish (market)
　gōgi great, powerful, grand
　強壮 **kyōsō** strong, robust, sturdy
　強壮剤 **kyōsōzai** a tonic
　強行 **kyōkō** (en)force, ram through
　強行軍 **kyōkōgun** forced march
7 強兵 **kyōhei** powerful army, military buildup
　強迫 **kyōhaku** compel, coerce
　強迫観念 **kyōhaku kannen** obsession
　強言 **shiigoto** talking even though no one
　　wants to listed
8 強制 **kyōsei** compulsory, forced
　強制力 **kyōseiryoku** compelling/legal force
　強制処分 **kyōsei shobun** disposition by legal
　　compulsion
　強制労働 **kyōsei rōdō** forced labor
　強制的 **kyōseiteki** compulsory, forced
　強制疎開 **kyōsei sokai** forced evacuation/
　　removal, eviction
　強直 **kyōchoku, gōchoku** rigidity, stiffness;
　　honesty, integrity
　強味 **tsuyomi** strength, strong point
　強弩 **kyōdo** strong crossbow

3

氵
土
扌
口
女
巾
犭
弓 8←
彳
彡
艹
宀
⺮
凵
吉
广
尸
口

強弩末 **kyōdo (no) sue** a once strong but now spent force

強突張 **gōtsukuba(ri)** headstrong

強歩 **kyōho** walking race

強国 **kyōkoku** strong country, great power

強固 **kyōko** firm, solid, secure

強者 **kyōsha** strong person
　　gō(no)mono brave warrior; past master

強肩 **kyōken** strong-armed (baseball player)

9 強風 **kyōfū** strong/high winds

強姦 **gōkan** rape

強要 **kyōyō** demand importunately, coerce, extort

強度 **kyōdo** intensity, strength

強音 **kyōon** beat, accent, stess

10 強健 **kyōken** robust health

強将 **kyōshō** strong/brave general

強剛 **kyōgō** strong, robust, forceful

強振 **kyōshin** swing (the bat) hard

強弱 **kyōjaku** (relative) strength

強烈 **kyōretsu** strong, intense, powerful

強記 **kyōki** a good/retentive memory

11 強張 **kowaba(ru)** become stiff

強欲 **gōyoku** greedy, avaricious

強悪 **gōaku** great wickedness, villany

強情 **gōjō** stubbornness, obstinacy

強盗 **gōtō** burglar(y), robber(y)

12 強靱 **kyōjin** tough, tenacious

強硬 **kyōkō** firm, resolute, vigorous

強硬派 **kyōkōha** hard-liners, diehards

強訴 **gōso** direct petition

強飲 **gōin** heavy drinking

強飯 **kowameshi** rice with red beans, *sekihan*

13 強腰 **tsuyogoshi** firm attitude

14 強豪 **kyōgō** strong (contender), champion

強奪 **gōdatsu** rob, plunder, hijack, hold up

強奪者 **gōdatsusha** plunderer, robber

強奪物 **gōdatsubutsu** plunder, loot

15 強権 **kyōken** state power

強暴 **kyōbō** strong and rough, violent

強敵 **kyōteki, gōteki** formidable enemy

強慾 **gōyoku** greedy, avaricious

強談 **gōdan** importunate demands, vigorous negotiations

強請 **kyōsei, gōsei** importune; extort, blackmail

強調 **kyōchō** emphasis, stress

強震 **kyōshin** violent earthquake

22 強襲 **kyōshū** attack, storm

─────── 2 ───────

2 力強 **chikarazuyo(i)** forceful, vigorous, emboldened

4 辻強盗 **tsujigōtō** highway robbery/holdup

手強 **tezuyo(i), tegowa(i)** strong, firm, severe, formidableg

心強 **kokorozuyo(i)** reassuring, heartening

6 気強 **kizuyo(i)** reassuring; stout-hearted, resolute

年強 **toshizuyo** child born in the first half of the year

列強 **rekkyō** the great/world powers

8 屈強 **kukkyō** strong, robust

10 倔強 **kukkyō** stubborn

勉強 **benkyō** studying; diligence; sell cheap

勉強家 **benkyōka** diligent student, hard worker

根強 **nezuyo(i)** firmly rooted/established

11 牽強付会 **kenkyō-fukai** farfetched, distorted

粘強 **neba(ri)zuyo(i)** tenacious, persistent

12 滋強飲料 **jikyō inryō** tonic drink

富強 **fukyō** wealth and power

最強 **saikyō** strongest

補強 **hokyō** reinforce, shore up

13 頑強 **gankyō** stubborn, obstinate, unyielding

14 増強 **zōkyō** reinforce, augment, beef up

─────── 3 ───────

4 不勉強 **fubenkyō** idleness, failure to study

6 死後強直 **shigo kyōchoku** rigor mortis

7 忍耐強 **nintaizuyo(i)** patient, persevering

8 押込強盗 **o(shi)ko(mi) gōtō** burglar(y)

9 俄勉強 **niwakabenkyō** cramming

10 弱肉強食 **jakuniku-kyōshoku** survival of the fittest

12 博覧強記 **hakuran-kyōki** extensive reading and retentive memory

富国強兵 **fukoku-kyōhei** national wealth and military strength

無理強 **muriji(i)** coercion

17 糞勉強 **kusobenkyō** cramming

─────────── 9 ───────────

3h9.1

粥 鬻　**SHUKU, JUKU, kayu** rice gruel

─────── 1 ───────

13 粥腹 **kayubara** living on rice gruel

3h9.2

粥　**HITSU** help, assist; bend into shape
suke assistant official

─────── 2 ───────

14 輔弼 **hohitsu** advise, counsel

3h9.3 / 1539

弾 彈　**DAN** bullet, shell; bounce, rebound; pluck, play (a string instrument); censure, denounce
tama bullet　**hi(ku)** play

(guitar/piano) **hazu(mu)** bounce, become lively; fork out, splurge on **haji(keru)** split open; spring off **haji(ku)** snap, pluck; repel (water); work (a soroban) **haji(ki)** (metal) spring; marbles; (slang) pistol

─────────── 1 ───────────

0 弾じる/ずる **dan(jiru/zuru)** play (a string instrument)
お弾き **(o)haji(ki)** marbles
2 弾力 **danryoku** elasticity
弾力性 **danryokusei** elasticity, resilience, flexibility
3 弾丸 **dangan** projectile, bullet, shell
4 弾片 **danpen** shell splinter, shrapnel
弾込 **tamago(me)** loading (a gun)
弾手 **hi(ki)te** (guitar/piano) player
5 弾出 **haji(ki)da(su)** snap out; expel; calculate; squeeze out (the money needed)
弾圧 **dan'atsu** pressure, oppression, suppression
弾玉 **haji(ki)dama** marbles
7 弾初 **hi(ki)zome** the New Year's first playing of an instrument
8 弾劾 **dangai** impeachment, censure, denunciation
弾性 **dansei** elasticity
弾雨 **dan'u** a hail of bullets
9 弾奏 **dansō** play (guitar/piano)
弾奏者 **dansōsha** (guitar/piano) player
弾除 **tamayo(ke)** protection against bullets, bulletproof
11 弾道 **dandō** trajectory
弾痕 **dankon** bullet hole/mark
12 弾着点 **danchakuten** point of impact
弾着距離 **danchaku kyori** range (of a gun)
13 弾幕 **danmaku** barrage
14 弾語 **hi(ki)gata(ri)** reciting while playing (the samisen)
16 弾薬 **dan'yaku** ammunition
弾薬庫 **dan'yakuko** powder magazine
弾薬筒 **dan'yakutō** cartridge, round
弾頭 **dantō** warhead

─────────── 2 ───────────

4 凶弾 **kyōdan** assassin's bullet
5 巨弾 **kyodan** huge projectile, bombshell
6 兇弾 **kyōdan** assassin's bullet
肉弾 **nikudan** human bullet
肉弾戦 **nikudansen** human-wave warfare
防弾 **bōdan** bulletproof; bombproof
8 実弾 **jitsudan** live ammunition; money
空弾 **kūdan** a blank (cartridge)
9 飛弾 **hidan** flying bullet
連弾曲 **rendankyoku** piano piece for four hands
指弾 **shidan** fillip, flicking/snapping one's fingers (at); rejection, disdain

糾弾 **kyūdan** impeach, censure
10 逸弾 **so(re)dama** stray bullet
流弾 **ryūdan, naga(re)dama** stray bullet
核弾頭 **kakudantō** nuclear warhead
砲弾 **hōdan** shell, cannonball
12 着弾距離 **chakudan kyori** range (of a gun)
装弾 **sōdan** load (a gun)
13 煙弾 **endan** smoke bomb
14 榴弾 **ryūdan** shell
銃弾 **jūdan** bullet
15 敵弾 **tekidan** enemy bullets/shells/fire
17 擲弾 **tekidan** grenade
擲弾筒 **tekidantō** grenade launcher
19 爆弾 **bakudan** bomb
20 霰弾 **sandan** buckshot

─────────── 3 ───────────

4 不発弾 **fuhatsudan** unexploded shell/bomb, dud
手投弾 **tena(ge)dan** hand grenade
手榴弾 **shuryūdan, teryūdan** hand grenade
火山弾 **kazandan** volcanic boulders
6 曳光弾 **eikōdan** tracer bullet, illumination round
至近弾 **shikindan** near miss
8 直撃弾 **chokugekidan** direct hit
9 炸裂弾 **sakuretsudan** explosive shell
10 破甲弾 **hakōdan** armor-piercing shell
砲煙弾雨 **hōen-dan'u** smoke of guns and a hail of shells/bullets
12 焼夷弾 **shōidan** incendiary shell, firebomb
13 催涙弾 **sairuidan** tear-gas bomb/grenade
照明弾 **shōmeidan** flare, illumination round/shell
14 榴散弾 **ryūsandan** shrapnel shell
誘導弾 **yūdōdan** guided missile
19 爆裂弾 **bakuretsudan** explosive shell

─────────── 4 ───────────

3 三味線弾 **shamisenhi(ki), samisenhi(ki)** samisen player
4 水素爆弾 **suiso bakudan** hydrogen bomb
10 原子爆弾 **genshi bakudan** atom bomb

發 → 発 **0a9.5**

─────────── 10 ───────────

3h10.1
彃 **KA, SEI** galumph

─────────── 12 ───────────

彈 → 弾 **3h9.3**

3

氵 土 扌 口 女 巾 犭 弓 10←
彳 彡 艹 宀 屮 士 广 尸 口

3

3h13.1

疆   **KYŌ, GŌ** strong

彌 → 弥 **3h5.2**

3h19.1

彎 弯   **WAN** curve; stretching a bow

─────── 1 ───────

2 彎入 **wannyū** bay, gulf, bight
6 彎曲 **wankyoku** curve, bend, curvature

─────────────── 彳 **3i** ───────────────

彳	行	彷	役	彿	徃	彼	征	徂	低	徑	往	律
0.1	3.1	4.1	4.2	5.1	3i5.6	5.2	5.3	5.4	2a5.15	5.5	5.6	6.1

很	衍	待	後	徉	徇	徊	徑	徒	徐	從	徠	街
6.2	6.3	6.4	6.5	6.6	6.7	6.8	3i5.5	7.1	7.2	7.3	0a7.6	8.1

術	徘	得	徙	徛	從	徜	御	街	徨	復	徧	循
8.2	8.3	8.4	8.5	8.6	3i7.3	8.7	9.1	9.2	9.3	9.4	9.5	9.6

微	徭	徭	衙	徵	微	德	衝	徹	徵	德	衡	徼
10.1	10.2	10.3	11.1	11.2	3i10.1	11.3	12.1	12.2	3i11.2	3i11.3	13.1	13.2

衛	衞	衢	徽	徽	衢
13.3	3i13.3	14.1	14.2	20.1	21.1

─────── 0 ───────

3i0.1

彳   **TEKI** walk a short distance; stop, linger

─────── 3 ───────

3i3.1 / 68

行   **KŌ** go, proceed; do, carry out; bank **GYŌ** line (of text), row; walk along; do, carry out **AN** go, travel; carry with **i(ku), yu(ku)** go **i(keru)** can go; be good **okona(u)** do, carry out, conduct **kudari** (vertical) line of text)

─────── 1 ───────

0 行きずり **yu(kizuri)** passing, casual
2 行人 **kōjin** passerby
4 行文 **kōbun** writing, style, diction
行文流麗 **kōbun-ryūrei** fluent style/writing
行止 **yu(ki)do(mari), i(ki)do(mari)** dead end, impasse
行水 **gyōzui** bath
行手 **yu(ku)te** route, path, destination
行火 **anka** bed/foot warmer
行方 **yukue, yu(ki)gata** one's whereabouts **yu(ki)kata** how to go
行方不明 **yukue-fumei** missing

行方定 **yukue-sada(menu)** aimless, wandering
5 行末 **yu(ku)sue** the future
行平 **yukihira** earthenware casserole
行平鍋 **yukihiranabe** earthenware casserole
行司 **gyōji** sumo referee
行立 **yu(ki)ta(tsu)** set out; be effected, be set up
6 行年 **gyōnen, kōnen** one's age at death
行会 **yu(ki)a(u), i(ki)a(u)** meet, come upon
行列 **gyōretsu** queue, procession, parade; matrix (in math)
行交 **yu(ki)ka(u)** come and go
行返 **yu(ki)kae(ru)** go and return
行先 **yu(ki)saki** destination **yu(ku)saki** where one goes; the future
行先々 **yu(ku) sakisaki (de)** wherever one goes
行在 **anzai** emperor's temporary residence
行在所 **anzaisho** emperor's temporary residence
行行 **yu(ku)yu(ku)** on the way; in due time, some day
行当 **yu(ki)a(taru)** come upon, bump into **yu(ki)a(tari-battari)** haphazard, hit-or-miss
行李 **kōri** wicker trunk; baggage
行灯 **andon** paper-enclosed oil lamp
行成 **i(ki)na(ri)** all of a sudden
7 行来 **yu(ki)ki** come and go, associate with
行体 **gyōtai** semicursive form (of kanji)

行住坐臥 **gyōjū-zaga** walking, stopping, sitting, and lying down; daily life
行状 **gyōjō** behavior, conduct, deportment
行戻 **yu(ki)modo(ri)** round trip; divorced woman
8 行事 **gyōji** event, function, observance
行使 **kōshi** use, exercise (rights), put (money) into circulation
行幸 **gyōkō, miyuki** visit/attendance by the emperor
行届 **yu(ki)todo(ku)** be meticulous/thoughtful/thorough
行者 **gyōja** an ascetic
行所 **yu(ki)dokoro** one's destination/whereabouts
行金 **kōkin** bank funds
9 行軍 **kōgun** march, marching
行革 **gyōkaku** administrative reform (short for 行政改革)
行草 **gyōsō** semicursive and cursive (kanji)
行草体 **gyōsōtai** semicursive and cursive forms/styles
行春 **yu(ku) haru** departing spring
行為 **kōi** act, deed, conduct
行政 **gyōsei** administration
行政法 **gyōseihō** administrative law
行政官 **gyōseikan** administrative/executive official
行政権 **gyōseiken** administrative/executive authority
10 行倒 **i(ki)dao(re), yu(ki)dao(re)** lying dead on the road
行進 **kōshin** march
行進曲 **kōshinkyoku** a (musical) march
行員 **kōin** bank clerk/employee
行宮 **angū** (emperor's) temporary palace
行書 **gyōsho** semicursive calligraphy
行旅 **kōryo** travel; traveler
行悩 **yu(ki)naya(mu)** be deadlocked, be at a standstill
11 行動 **kōdō** action, conduct, behavior, operations
行動半径 **kōdō hankei** radius of action, range
行動主義 **kōdō shugi** behaviorism
行商 **gyōshō** itinerant trade, peddling
行商人 **gyōshōnin** peddler, traveling salesman
行過 **i(ki)su(gi), yu(ki)su(gi)** going too far, overdoing it
行掛 **yu(ki)ga(ke), i(ki)ga(ke)** on the way **yu(ki)ga(kari)** circumstances
行啓 **gyōkei** visit/attendance by the empress or crown prince
行脚 **angya** pilgrimage; travel on foot
行脚僧 **angyasō** itinerant priest
12 行着 **i(ki)tsu(ku), yu(ki)tsu(ku)** arrive at, reach

行違 **yu(ki)chiga(i), i(ki)chiga(i)** crossing each other; going amiss
行渡 **yu(ki)wata(ru), i(ki)wata(ru)** extend, prevail, permeate, reach
行場 **yu(ki)ba** place to go/resort to, destination
行程 **kōtei** distance; journey; march; itinerary; stroke (of a piston)
行雲流水 **kōun-ryūsui** floating clouds and flowing water; taking life easy
行間 **gyōkan** (reading) between the lines
13 行楽 **kōraku** excursion, outing
行楽地 **kōrakuchi** pleasure resort
行詰 **yu(ki)zu(mari), i(ki)zu(mari)** dead end, deadlock, standstill
行路 **kōro** path, road, course
行路病者 **kōro byōsha** person fallen ill on the road
行跡 **gyōseki** behavior, conduct
14 行暮 **yu(ki)ku(reru)** be still on the way as night falls
15 行儀 **gyōgi** manners, deportment, behavior
行澄 **okona(i)su(masu)** follow Buddhist teachings; act like a good boy/girl
行賞 **kōshō** conferring of awards
22 行嚢 **kōnō** mailbag

————————— 2 —————————

1 一行 **ichigyō** a line (of text) **ikkō** party, group; troupe
2 力行 **rikkō** strenuous efforts, exertion
3 三行 **sangyō** three lines (of text)
三行広告欄 **sangyō kōkokuran** classified ads
三行半 **mikudarihan** letter of divorce **sangyōhan** three and a half lines (of text)
大行 **taikō** great undertaking
大行天皇 **taikō tennō** the late emperor
4 不行状 **fugyōjō** misconduct, immorality
不行届 **fuyu(ki)todo(ki)** negligent, remiss, careless, incompetent
不行跡 **fugyōseki** misconduct, immorality
不行儀 **fugyōgi** bad manners, rudeness
予行 **yokō** rehearsal
凶行 **kyōkō** violence, murder
五行 **gogyō** the five elements (fire, wood, earth, metal, water)
心行 **kokoro yu(ku)** (as much) as one likes
5 代行 **daikō** acting for another
代行者 **daikōsha** agent, proxy
他行 **tagyō, takō** going out
刊行 **kankō** publish
刊行物 **kankōbutsu** a publication
平行 **heikō** parallel
平行四辺形 **heikōshihenkei** parallelogram
平行棒 **heikōbō** parallel bars
平行線 **heikōsen** parallel line
巡行 **junkō** patrol, tour, one's beat/rounds
犯行 **hankō** crime

3

氵 土 扌 口 女 巾 犭 弓 彳 彡 艹 宀 ⺌ 山 耂 广 尸 口

3←

立行 **ta(chi)yu(ku)** can keep going, can make a living

立行司 **ta(te)gyōji** head sumo referee

6 兇行 **kyōkō** violence, murder

壮行 **sōkō** rousing send-off

壮行会 **sōkōkai** farewell party

孝行 **kōkō** filial piety

同行 **dōkō** go together, accompany
dōgyō fellow pilgrim/esthete

同行者 **dōkōsha** traveling companion

汚行 **okō** disgraceful conduct, scandal

先行 **senkō** precede, go first
sakiyu(ki), sakii(ki) the future

行行 **yu(ku)yu(ku)** on the way; in due time, some day

光行差 **kōkōsa** aberration (in astronomy)

成行 **na(ri)yu(ki)** course (of events), developments

血行 **kekkō** circulation of the blood

舟行 **shūkō** sailing

7 邪行 **jakō** wickedness; go diagonally

即行 **sokkō** carry out immediately

励行 **reikō** strict enforcement

角行 **kakkō** (one of the "chessmen" in shōgi

決行 **kekkō** decisive action; carry out

走行 **sōkō** travel, cover distance

走行時間 **sōkō jikan** travel time

走行距離 **sōkō kyori** distance covered (in a given time)

乱行 **rangyō** immoral conduct, debauchery

売行 **u(re)yu(ki)** sale, demand for

尾行 **bikō** shadow, tail (someone)

改行 **kaigyō** start a new line/paragraph

私行 **shikō** one's private conduct/affairs

言行 **genkō** words and deeds

8 非行 **hikō** misdeed, misconduct, delinquency

爬行 **hakō** crawl, creep

奉行 **bugyō** magistrate, prefect

併行 **heikō** go by twos, go together

夜行 **yakō** night travel; night train

版行 **hankō** publication; one's seal

直行 **chokkō** going straight, direct, nonstop

並行 **heikō** parallel

退行 **taikō** regression, degeneration

逆行 **gyakkō** go back, move backward, run counter to

送行 **sōkō** sending (someone) off

送行会 **sōkōkai** going-away/farewell party

知行 **chigyō** fief, stipend

知行取 **chigyōto(ri)** vassal, daimyo

奇行 **kikō** eccentric conduct

径行 **keikō** go right ahead

苦行 **kugyō** penance, asceticism, mortification

苦行者 **kugyōsha** an ascetic

実行 **jikkō** put into practice, carry out, realize

実行力 **jikkōryoku** executive ability, action

宛行 **atega(u)** apply/hold/fasten to; allot; provide; choose for

宛行扶持 **ategaibuchi** discretionary allowance

歩行 **hokō** walking, ambulatory

歩行者 **hokōsha** pedestrian

歩行者天国 **hokōsha tengoku** street temporarily closed to vehicles, mall

性行 **seikō** character and conduct

性行為 **sei kōi** sex act, intercourse

所行 **shogyō** deed, act, work

9 飛行 **hikō** flight, flying, aviation

飛行士 **hikōshi** aviator

飛行服 **hikōfuku** flying suit, flight uniform

飛行便 **hikōbin** airmail

飛行家 **hikōka** aviator

飛行隊 **hikōtai** flying/air corps

飛行船 **hikōsen** airship, dirigible, blimp

飛行場 **hikōjō** airport, airfield

飛行帽 **hikōbō** aviator's cap, flight helmet

飛行艇 **hikōtei** flying boat, seaplane

飛行機 **hikōki** airplane

飛行機雲 **hikōkigumo** vapor trail, contrail

発行 **hakkō** publish, issue

発行日 **hakkōbi** date of issue

発行者 **hakkōsha** publisher

発行所 **hakkōsho** publishing house

専行 **senkō** acting on one's own authority/discretion

急行 **kyūkō** an express (train)

急行券 **kyūkōken** express ticket

急行便 **kyūkōbin** express mail

前行 **zenkō** one's former conduct; preceding

連行 **renkō** take (a suspect to the police)
tsu(re)yu(ku) take (someone) along

通行 **tsūkō** passing, passage, transit, traffic
tō(ri)yu(ku) pass by

通行人 **tsūkōnin** passer-by, pedestrian

通行止 **tsūkōdo(me)** Road Closed, No Thoroughfare

通行税 **tsūkōzei** toll, transit duty

洋行 **yōkō** foreign travel; company, firm

持行 **mo(tte) i/yu(ku)** take (along)

品行 **hinkō** conduct, behavior, deportment

品行方正 **hinkō-hōsei** respectable, irreproachable

独行 **dokkō** self-reliance; traveling alone

荒行 **aragyō** religious austerities, asceticism

単行本 **tankōbon** separate volume, in book form

昼行灯 **hiru andon** (useless as) a lantern in broad daylight

施行 **shikō** enforce; put into operation

紀行 **kikō** account of a journey

紀行文 **kikōbun** account of a journey

10 修行 **shūgyō, shugyō, shūkō** training, study, ascetic practices

修行者 **shugyōsha** practitioner of (Buddhist) austerities
陸行 **rikkō** go by land, travel overland
随行 **zuikō** attend on, accompany
随行員 **zuikōin** attendants, entourage, retinue
兼行 **kenkō** doing both
進行 **shinkō** advance, progress, proceed
進行係 **shinkōgakari** person to expedite the proceedings, steering committee
遊行 **yūkō** tour, wander; movement (of a heavenly body)
流行 **ryūkō, haya(ru)** be popular, be in fashion; be prevalent/epidemic
流行文句 **haya(ri)monku** popular phrase
流行色 **ryūkōshoku** fashionable/prevailing color
流行地 **ryūkōchi** infected district
流行児 **ryūkōji, hayari(k)ko** popular person
流行言葉 **haya(ri)kotoba** popular expression
流行性感冒 **ryūkōsei kanbō** influenza
流行後 **ryūkōku(re)** out of fashion
流行病 **ryūkōbyō** an epidemic
流行歌 **ryūkōka, haya(ri)uta** popular song
流行語 **ryūkōgo** popular phrase, catchword
躬行 **kyūkō** carry out oneself, practice
弱行 **jakkō** weakness in execution, irresoluteness
徒行 **tokō** go on foot, walk
徐行 **jokō** go/drive slowly
挙行 **kyokō** conduct, hold, celebrate, observe
烏行水 **karasu (no) gyōzui** a quick bath
旅行 **ryokō** trip, travel
旅行先 **ryokōsaki** destination
旅行者 **ryokōsha** traveler, tourist
旅行家 **ryokōka** traveler, tourist
旅行記 **ryokōki** record of one's trip
素行 **sokō** one's conduct, behavior
航行 **kōkō** navigation, sailing
11 商行為 **shōkōi** business transaction
運行 **unkō** movement; operate, run (planes, trains)
遂行 **suikō** accomplish, execute, perform
道行 **michiyu(ki)** traveling scene; poem about travel scenery; eloping; Japanese traveling coat
過行 **su(gi)yu(ku)** pass, go past
執行 **shikkō** performance, execution
執行吏 **shikkōri** bailiff, court officer
執行猶予 **shikkō yūyo** stay of execution, suspended sentence
執行権 **shikkōken** executive authority
強行 **kyōkō** (en)force, ram through
強行軍 **kyōkōgun** forced march
密行 **mikkō** prowl about, go secretly
現行 **genkō** present, current, existing
現行犯 **genkōhan** crime/criminal witnessed in the act, flagrante delicto

現行法 **genkōhō** existing law, law now in force
悪行 **akugyō, akkō** evildoing, wickedness
移行 **ikō** move, shift to
断行 **dankō** carry out (resolutely)
蛇行 **dakō** meander, zigzag
12 勤行 **gongyō** Buddhist religious services
蛮行 **bankō** barbarity, savagery
善行 **zenkō** good conduct/deed
雁行 **gankō** go/fly in echelon formation (like geese); keeping abreast (of each other)
落行 **o(chi)yu(ku)** flee
寒行 **kangyō** midwinter religious austerities
暑行 **Keikō** (emperor, 71–130)
敢行 **kankō** take decisive action, dare; carry out
奥行 **okuyu(ki)** depth (vs. height and width)
跛行 **hakō** limp
跛行景気 **hakō keiki** spotty boom/prosperity
鈍行 **donkō** slow (not express) train
雲行 **kumoyu(ki)** cloud movements; situation
13 溯行 **sokō** go upstream
携行 **keikō** carry with/along
摂行 **sekkō** acting for another
微行 **bikō** traveling incognito
愚行 **gukō** folly, foolish move
置行 **o(ki)yu(ku)** leave behind
続行 **zokkō** continuation
試行錯誤 **shikō-sakugo** trial and error
頒行 **hankō** distribution, dissemination
14 遵行 **junkō** obey
徳行 **tokkō** virtuous conduct
旗行列 **hata gyōretsu** flag procession
慣行 **kankō** usual practice, custom
慣行犯 **kankōhan** habitual criminal
銀行 **ginkō** bank
銀行券 **ginkōken** bank note
銀行界 **ginkōkai** the banking community
銀行員 **ginkōin** bank clerk/employee
銀行家 **ginkōka** banker
15 潜行 **senkō** traveling incognito; go underground
履行 **rikō** perform, fulfill, implement
横行 **ōkō** walk sideways; swagger; be rampant
横行闊歩 **ōkō-kappo** swagger around
膝行 **shikkō** go on one's knees
暴行 **bōkō** act of violence, assault, outrage
緩行 **kankō** go slow
緩行車 **kankōsha** local train
諸行 **shogyō** all worldly things
諸行無常 **shogyō-mujō** All things change. Nothing lasts.
16 興行 **kōgyō** entertainment industry
興行主 **kōgyōnushi, kōgyōshu** promoter, showman, producer

興行師 **kōgyōshi** impresario, show manager
操行 **sōkō** conduct, deportment
獣行 **jūkō** brutal act, rape
篤行 **tokkō** good deed, kind act
17 醜行 **shūkō** disgraceful conduct
18 蹠行動物 **shokō dōbutsu** a plantigrade (animal that walks on the whole sole of its foot, as man or bear)
難行 **nangyō** penance, self-mortification
難行苦行 **nangyō-kugyō** penance, self-mortification
難行道 **nangyōdō** salvation through austerities
騎行 **kikō** go on horseback
19 蟹行文字 **kaikō moji, kaikō monji** horizontal/Western writing

——————— 3 ———————

3 大流行 **dairyūkō, ōhayari** the fashion/rage
4 不正行為 **fusei kōi** an unfair practice, wrongdoing, malpractice, cheating, foul play
不品行 **fuhinkō** loose moral conduct, profligacy
不履行 **furikō** nonperformance, default
5 未発行 **mihakkō** unissued
6 年中行事 **nenjū gyōji** an annual event
7 余所行 **yosoyu(ki), yosoi(ki)** going out, formal (manners), one's best (attire)
初興行 **hatsukōgyō** first performance, premiere
8 逃避行 **tōhikō** runaway trip, flight
町奉行 **machi-bugyō** town magistrate
9 単独行為 **tandoku kōi** acting on one's own
単独行動 **tandoku kōdō** acting on one's own
昼興行 **hirukōgyō** matinée
10 旅興行 **tabikōgyō** road show
11 寄附行為 **kifu kōi** act of endowment, donation
脱法行為 **dappō kōi** an evasion of the law
12 葬送行進曲 **sōsō kōshinkyoku** funeral march
無言行 **mugon (no) gyō** ascetic silence
無償行為 **mushō kōi** gratuitous act, volunteer service
15 諸国行脚 **shokoku angya** walking tour of the country
論功行賞 **ronkō kōshō** conferring of honors
16 親孝行 **oyakōkō** filial piety
親銀行 **oyaginkō** parent bank

——————— 4 ———————

1 一方通行 **ippō tsūkō** one-way traffic
3 大名旅行 **daimyō ryokō** spendthrift tour, junket
4 片側通行 **katagawa tsūkō** One Way (Traffic)
水上飛行機 **suijō hikōki** hydroplane, seaplane
5 左側通行 **hidarigawa tsūkō** Keep Left

6 死刑執行 **shikei shikkō** execution
宇宙飛行士 **uchū hikōshi** astronaut
百鬼夜行 **hyakki-yakō, hyakki-yagyō** all sorts of demons roaming about at night; rampant evil, scandal, pandemonium
7 低空飛行 **teikū hikō** low-level flying
8 直情径行 **chokujō keikō** straightforward, impulsive
9 独立独行 **dokuritsu-dokkō** independence, self-reliance
独断専行 **dokudan-senkō** arbitrary action
昼夜兼行 **chūya-kenkō** 24 hours a day, around the clock
10 修学旅行 **shūgaku ryokō** school excursion, field trip
11 軟式飛行船 **nanshiki hikōsen** dirigible, balloon
12 無銭旅行 **musen ryokō** penniless travel, hitchhiking
13 新婚旅行 **shinkon ryokō** honeymoon
14 熟慮断行 **jukuryo-dankō** deliberate and decisive
15 諸車通行止 **Shosha Tsūkōdo(me)** No Thoroughfare
16 薄志弱行 **hakushi-jakkō** indecisive and unenterprising
18 難行苦行 **nangyō-kugyō** penance, self-mortification

——————— 4 ———————

3i4.1

彷 **HŌ** closely resemble; wander about, loiter; dim, indistinct

——————— 1 ———————

8 彷彿 **hōfutsu** closely resemble; dim, indistinct
12 彷徨 **hōkō** wander about; fluctuate
samayo(u) wander about

——————— 3 ———————

4 水天彷彿 **suiten-hōfutsu** sea and sky merging into each other

3i4.2 / 375

役 **YAKU** service, use; office, post
EKI service; battle

——————— 1 ———————

2 役人 **yakunin** public official
役人風 **yakunin kaze** air of official dignity
役人根性 **yakunin konjō** bureaucratism
4 役不足 **yakubusoku** dissatisfaction with one's role
役夫 **ekifu** laborer, coolie
5 役付 **yakuzu(ke)** allotment of roles, casting

役立 **yakuda(tsu), yaku (ni) ta(tsu)** be useful, serve the purpose
役目 **yakume** one's duty, role
役目柄 **yakumegara** by virtue of one's office
6 役名 **yakumei** official title
役回 **yakumawa(ri)** part, role, burden
8 役者 **yakusha** player, actor
役所 **yakusho** government office
役所風 **(o)yakushofū** red tape, officialism
9 役柄 **yakugara** nature of one's office/position
10 役員 **yakuin** (company) officer, director
役員会 **yakuinkai** board meeting
11 役得 **yakutoku** perquisite
役務 **ekimu** labor, service
12 役割 **yakuwa(ri)** role
役場 **yakuba** town hall, public office
役替 **yakuga(e)** change of post
13 役僧 **yakusō** sexton; assistant priest
15 役儀 **yakugi** one's duty, role

——————— 2 ———————

1 一役 **ichiyaku** an (important) office
    hitoyaku a role
一役買 **hitoyaku ka(u)** take on a role/task
2 二役 **futayaku** double role
子役 **koyaku** child's role; child actor/actress
3 三役 **san'yaku** the three highest sumo ranks under "yokozuna"; the three top-ranking officials
大役 **taiyaku** important task/role
上役 **uwayaku** senior official, one's superior
下役 **shitayaku** subordinate official, underling
小役人 **koyakunin** petty/minor official
4 止役 **to(me)yaku** role of stopping a quarrel, peacemaker
公役 **kōeki** public service, conscription
区役所 **kuyakusho** ward office
5 代役 **daiyaku** substitute, stand-in, understudy
市役所 **shiyakusho** city hall
用役 **yōeki** service
囚役 **shūeki** prison work
主役 **shuyaku** major role; star
立役 **ta(chi)yaku** leading role
立役者 **ta(te)yakusha** leading actor
6 老役 **fu(ke)yaku** role of an old person
同役 **dōyaku** colleague
地役権 **chiekiken** easement, (real) servitude
在役 **zaieki** in (military) service, serving a prison term
守役 **moriyaku** guardian
7 助役 **joyaku** assistant official
兵役 **heieki** military service
牢役人 **rōyakunin** jailer
労役 **rōeki** labor, work, toil
初役 **hatsuyaku** (actor's) first role
8 使役 **shieki** employ, use, set to work

免役 **men'eki** exemption from military service; release from prison
退役 **taieki** retirement from military service
苦役 **kueki** hard toil, drudgery; penal servitude
服役 **fukueki** penal servitude; military service
9 重役 **jūyaku** (company) director
郡役所 **gun'yakusho** county office
軍役 **gun'eki** military service
持役 **mo(chi)yaku** one's role
相役 **aiyaku** colleague
10 荷役 **niyaku** loading and unloading, cargo handling
脇役 **wakiyaku** supporting role
書役 **ka(ki)yaku** copyist, scribe
旅役者 **tabiyakusha** actor/troupe on the road
留役 **to(me)yaku** stopping a quarrel; peacemaker
配役 **haiyaku** cast(ing of roles)
11 側役 **sobayaku** personal attendant
添役 **so(e)yaku** secondary role
現役 **gen'eki** active service; commissioned
現役兵 **gen'ekihei** soldier on active duty
悪役 **akuyaku** the villain('s role)
12 就役 **shūeki** be commissioned (a ship)
嵌役 **hama(ri)yaku** well-suited role
13 適役 **tekiyaku** suitable post/role
徭役 **yōeki** statute labor, corvée
戦役 **sen'eki** war, campaign
14 憎役 **niku(mare)yaku** unpopular role, thankless task
端役 **hayaku** minor role/post
雑役 **zatsueki** odd jobs, chores
雑役夫 **zatsuekifu** handyman
雑役婦 **zatsuekifu** maid
聞役 **ki(ki)yaku** one who hears people's complaints
15 敵役 **katakiyaku, tekiyaku** villain's role
賦役 **fueki** compulsory labor, corvée
18 儲役 **mō(ke)yaku** lucrative position
懲役 **chōeki** penal servitude, imprisonment
難役 **nan'yaku** difficult role
顔役 **kaoyaku** influential man, boss
22 纒役 **mato(me)yaku** mediator

——————— 3 ———————

3 大根役者 **daikon yakusha** ham actor
千両役者 **senryō yakusha** great actor, star
女房役 **nyōbōyaku** helpmate
4 収入役 **shūnyūyaku** treasurer
引立役 **hi(ki)ta(te)yaku** one who seeks to enhance another's position, foil, front/advance man, supporter
5 世話役 **sewayaku** go-between, intermediary; sponsor; caretaker
主人役 **shujin'yaku** host(ess)
8 毒味役 **dokumiyaku** taster for poison

取締役 **torishimariyaku** (company) director
9 指南役 **shinan'yaku** instructor, teacher
相手役 **aiteyaku** a role opposite (someone), (dance) partner
相談役 **sōdan'yaku** adviser, consultant
11 道化役 **dōkeyaku** clown
12 検査役 **kensayaku** inspector, examiner
15 監査役 **kansayaku** auditor, inspector

────── 4 ──────
12 無期懲役 **muki chōeki** life imprisonment

────── 5 ──────

3i5.1

佛 髴

FUTSU resemble, seem; unclear, indistinct

────── 2 ──────
7 彷彿 **hōfutsu** closely resemble; dim, indistinct

────── 4 ──────
4 水天彷彿 **suiten-hōfutsu** sea and sky merging into each other

㣻→往 3i5.6

3i5.2 / 977

彼

HI he; that
kare he **ka(no), a(no)** that, the
are that

────── 1 ──────
3 彼女 **kanojo** she; girlfriend, lover
4 彼氏 **kareshi** he; boyfriend, lover
彼方 **kanata, anata** there, yonder; the other side
5 彼奴 **aitsu** that guy/fellow
彼処 **asoko, asuko, kashiko** that place, over there, yonder
7 彼我 **higa** oneself and others, each other
8 彼岸 **higan** equinoctal week; Buddhist services during equinoctal week; the other shore; goal
彼岸桜 **higanzakura** early-flowering cherry tree
9 彼是 **are-kore** this or/and that
12 彼等 **karera** they

────── 2 ──────
15 誰彼 **darekare, tarekare** this or that person; (many) people

3i5.3 / 1114

征

SEI go afar; conquer, vanquish

────── 1 ──────
6 征夷 **seii** pacifying the barbarians
征夷大将軍 **seii taishōgun** general in command of expeditionary forces to subjugate the barbarians
征伐 **seibatsu** subjugate, conquer, punish, exterminate
征衣 **seii** military uniform; traveling clothes
8 征服 **seifuku** conquer, subjugate; master
征服者 **seifukusha** conqueror
征服欲 **seifukuyoku** desire for conquest
9 征途 **seito** military expedition; journey
10 征討 **seitō** subjugation, pacification
13 征戦 **seisen** military expedition

────── 2 ──────
5 出征 **shussei** depart for the front, go to war
外征 **gaisei** foreign expedition/campaign
8 長征 **chōsei** long march
12 遠征 **ensei** (military) expedition, campaign; tour (by a team)
遠征隊 **enseitai** expeditionary forces, invaders; visiting team
16 親征 **shinsei** military expedition led by the emperor

3i5.4

徂

SO go

低→低 2a5.15

3i5.5 / 1475

径 徑逕

KEI path; diameter

────── 1 ──────
6 径行 **keikō** go right ahead
9 径庭 **keitei** great difference
13 径路 **keiro** course, route, process

────── 2 ──────
3 口径 **kōkei** caliber, bore, aperture
小径 **shōkei** lane, path
山径 **sankei** mountain path
4 内径 **naikei** inside diameter
5 半径 **hankei** radius
外径 **gaikei** outside diameter
8 直径 **chokkei** diameter
11 捷径 **shōkei** short cut, shorter way

────── 3 ──────
3 大口径 **daikōkei** large-caliber

8 直情径行 **chokujō keikō** straightforward,
impulsive

——————— 4 ———————

6 行動半径 **kōdō hankei** radius of action, range

3i5.6 / 918

往 往   Ō go; the first
yu(ku) go **i(nasu)** let go;
parry (an attack in sumo)

——————— 1 ———————

3 往々 **ōō** sometimes, occasionally, often
4 往日 **ōjitsu** ancient times
5 往生 **ōjō** die (and be reborn in paradise); give
in; be at one's wit's end
往生際悪 **ōjōgiwa (ga) waru(i)** accept defeat
with bad grace
往古 **ōko** ancient times
6 往年 **ōnen** in years gone by
7 往来 **ōrai** coming and going, traffic; road,
street; fluc
往来止 **ōraido(me)** Road Closed
8 往事 **ōji** the past
往往 **ōō** sometimes, occasionally, often
9 往信 **ōshin** letter/message requesting a reply
10 往時 **ōji** ancient times
往航 **ōkō** outward voyage
11 往訪 **ōhō** visit, call on
12 往復 **ōfuku** going and returning, round trip;
correspondence; association
往復切符 **ōfuku kippu** round trip ticket
往復葉書 **ōfuku hagaki** return postcard
往診 **ōshin** doctor's visit, house call
13 往路 **ōro** outward journey
15 往還 **ōkan** coming and going, traffic; road

——————— 2 ———————

3 大往生 **daiōjō** a peaceful death
5 古往今来 **koō-konrai** in all ages, since
antiquity
右往左往 **uō-saō** go hither and thither
立往生 **ta(chi)ōjō** be at a standstill, be stalled/
stranded; stand speechless (without a
rejoinder)
8 往往 **ōō** sometimes, occasionally, often
9 独往 **dokuō** going one's own way
10 既往 **kiō** the past
既往症 **kiōshō** previous illness, medical
history
既往歴 **kiōreki** patient's medical history

——————— 3 ———————

12 極楽往生 **gokuraku ōjō** a peaceful death
無理往生 **muri-ōjō** forced compliance

——————— 4 ———————

5 右往左往 **uō-saō** go hither and thither

——————— 6 ———————

3i6.1 / 667

律   **RITSU, RICHI** law, regulation;
rhythm

——————— 1 ———————

0 律する **ris(suru)** judge, measure
4 律文 **ritsubun** legal provisions; verse
5 律令 **ritsuryō, ritsurei** laws and orders (of
Nara and Heian period)
7 律呂 **ritsuryo** rhythm and pitch
8 律法 **rippō** law, rule
10 律師 **risshi** exemplary Buddhist master
律家 **rikke** (priest of) the Ritsu Buddhist sect
律格 **ritsukaku** rule; versification, metrical
scheme
11 律動 **ritsudō** rhythm, rhythmic movement
律旋 **rissen** (a mode in *gagaku* music)
13 律義 **richigi** honesty, integrity, loyalty
律義者 **richigimono** honest hardworking man
律詩 **risshi** (a Chinese verse form)
14 律語 **ritsugo** verse
15 律儀 **richigi** honesty, integrity, loyalty
律儀者 **richigimono** honest hardworking man

——————— 2 ———————

1 一律 **ichiritsu** uniform, even, equal
5 他律 **taritsu** heteronomy; non-autonomous
6 自律 **jiritsu** autonomy, self-control
自律神経 **jiritsu shinkei** autonomic nerve
7 呂律 **roretsu** articulation, pronunciation
戒律 **kairitsu** (Buddhist) precepts
8 法律 **hōritsu** law
法律上 **hōritsujō** legally
法律学 **hōritsugaku** jurisprudence
法律屋 **hōritsuya** lawmonger
法律家 **hōritsuka** lawyer, jurist
法律案 **hōritsuan** proposed law
法律書 **hōritsusho** law book
法律語 **hōritsugo** legal term
定律 **teiritsu** fixed law/rhythm
9 軍律 **gunritsu** martial law; articles of war;
military discipline
音律 **onritsu** melody, pitch, rhythm
紀律 **kiritsu** order, discipline
11 旋律 **senritsu** melody
規律 **kiritsu** regulations; order, discipline
15 調律 **chōritsu** tuning
調律師 **chōritsushi** (piano) tuner
19 韻律 **inritsu** rhythm, meter

——————— 3 ———————

4 不文律 **fubunritsu** unwritten law/rule
不規律 **fukiritsu** irregular, disorganized
6 因果律 **ingaritsu** principle of causality
成文律 **seibunritsu** statute/written law

3

氵
土
扌
口
女
巾
犭
弓
彳 6←
彡
艹
宀
⺍
山
吉
广
尸
口

11 道徳律 **dōtokuritsu** moral law
黄金律 **ōgonritsu** the golden rule
12 無規律 **mukiritsu** disorderly, undisciplined

3i6.2

很 **KON** disobey; dispute; very
moto(ru) go against, be contrary to

3i6.3

衍 **EN** overflow

—————————— 1 ——————————

4 衍文 **enbun** a redundancy

—————————— 2 ——————————

15 敷衍 **fuen** amplify, extend, develop

3i6.4 / 452

待 **TAI, ma(tsu)** wait, wait for

—————————— 1 ——————————

0 待った **ma(tta)** wait!, hold on
待ちぼうけ **ma(chibōke)** getting stood up
待ちくたびれる **ma(chikutabireru)** get fed up with waiting
6 待伏 **ma(chi)bu(se)** ambush, lying in wait
待合 **ma(chi)a(waseru)** wait for (as previously arranged) **ma(chi)a(i)** waiting room; geisha entertainment place
待合室 **machiaishitsu** waiting room
8 待佗 **ma(chi)wa(biru)** get anxious from long waiting
待命 **taimei** awaiting orders
待受 **ma(chi)u(keru)** await, expect
待明 **ma(chi)a(kasu)** wait all night
9 待待 **ma(chi ni) ma(tta)** long awaited
10 待倦 **ma(chi)agu(mu)** be tired of waiting
待兼 **ma(chi)ka(neru)** can't stand the wait
待針 **ma(chi)bari** marking pin
11 待遇 **taigū** treatment, reception, entertainment, (hotel) service; salary, remuneration
待望 **taibō** wait for expectantly, hope for, look forward to
待惚 **ma(chi)bō(ke)** getting stood up
12 待無 **ma(tta)na(shi)** without waiting
待焦 **ma(chi)ko(gareru)** wait impatiently for
14 待暮 **ma(chi)ku(rasu)** wait all day long
待構 **ma(chi)kama(eru)** be ready and waiting
15 待避 **taihi** shunting (in railroading)
待避線 **taihisen** siding, sidetrack
16 待機 **taiki** wait for an opportunity, watch and wait, stand by

—————————— 2 ——————————

2 人待顔 **hitoma(chi)gao** look of expectation
4 辻待 **tsujima(chi)** (rickshaw) waiting to be hired
心待 **kokoroma(chi)** expectation, anticipation
5 立待月 **ta(chi)ma(chi)zuki** 17-day-old moon
7 応待 **ōtai** receive (visitors), wait on (customers)
8 招待 **shōtai** invite
招待日 **shōtaibi** preview/invitation date
招待状 **shōtaijō** (written) invitation
招待券 **shōtaiken** complimentary ticket
招待客 **shōtaikyaku** invited guest
招待席 **shōtaiseki** reserved seats for guests
居待 **ima(chi)** sit and wait; 18-day-old moon
9 虐待 **gyakutai** treat cruelly, mistreat
風待 **kazama(chi), kazema(chi)** wait for a favorable wind
待待 **ma(chi ni) ma(tta)** long awaited
10 特待 **tokutai** special treatment, distinction
特待生 **tokutaisei** scholarship student
特待券 **tokutaiken** complimentary ticket
11 接待 **settai** reception, welcome; serving, offering
接待室 **settaishitsu** reception room
船待 **funama(chi)** waiting for a ship
12 期待 **kitai** expect, anticipate, place one's hopes on
款待 **kantai** warm welcome, hospitality
15 潮待 **shioma(chi)** waiting for the tide
歓待 **kantai** hospitality
17 優待 **yūtai** treat with consideration, receive hospitably
優待券 **yūtaiken** complimentary ticket

3i6.5 / 48

後 **GO, nochi** after, later
KŌ, ushi(ro) behind
ato afterward, subsequent; back, retro-
oku(reru) be late, lag behind

—————————— 1 ——————————

0 その後 **(sono)go** thereafter, later
後ろめたい **ushi(rometai)** underhanded, suspicious
1 後一条 **Goichijō** (emperor, 1016–1036)
2 後人 **kōjin** those coming later, posterity
3 後々 **atoato, nochinochi** the future
後口 **atokuchi** aftertaste; remainder; a later turn/appointment
後山条 **Gosanjō** (emperor, 1068–1072)
4 後天 **kōten** not inborn, a posteriori
後天的 **kōtenteki** acquired, cultivated
後天性 **kōtensei** acquired trait
後毛 **oku(re)ge** loose strands of hair, stray lock
後片付 **atokatazu(ke)** straightening up afterwards, putting things in order

後厄 **atoyaku** the year following one's critial year
後手 **ushi(ro)de** with one's hands (tied) behind one's back **gote** second player (in go); outmaneuvered, passive
後日 **gojitsu, gonichi** the future, another day
後日談 **gojitsudan** reminiscences
後方 **kōhō** the rear, back
5 後半 **kōhan** latter half
後半生 **kōhansei** the latter half of one's life
後半戦 **kōhansen** the latter half of a game
後生 **kōsei** born later, younger, junior **goshō** the next world
後生大事 **goshō daiji** religiously, earnestly
後世 **kōsei** later ages, posterity **gose** the next world
後仕舞 **atojimai** straightening up afterwards, winding up
後代 **kōdai** future generations, posterity
後払 **atobara(i)** deferred payment
6 後朱省 **Gosuzaku** (emperor, 1036–1045)
後年 **kōnen** in later/future years, afterward
後任 **kōnin** successor
後列 **kōretsu** the back row, rear rank
後先 **atosaki** front and rear; both ends; sequence; context; circumstances, consequences
後向 **ushi(ro)mu(ki)** facing backward
後光 **gokō** halo, corona
後光厳 **Gokōgon** (emperor, 1353–1371)
後回 **atomawa(shi)** deferring, postponing
7 後作 **atosaku** second crop
後冷泉 **Goreizei** (emperor, 1045–1068)
後述 **kōjutsu** discussed below
後学 **kōgaku** younger scholars; information for future reference
後序 **kōjo** postscript to a book, afterword
後尾 **kōbi** rear, tail
後図 **kōto** future plans
後戻 **atomodo(ri)** going backward, retrogression
後見 **kōken** guardianship; assistance
後見人 **kōkennin** (legal) guardian; assistant
後車 **kōsha** rear car
後足 **atoashi** hind leg/foot
8 後事 **kōji** future affairs; affairs after one's death
後刻 **gokoku** afterwards, later
後退 **kōtai** retreat, back up **atozusa(ri)** move/shrink/hold back
後送 **kōsō** send to the rear; send later
後押 **atoo(shi)** pushing from behind; backing, support
後味 **atoaji** aftertaste
後知恵 **atojie** hindsight
後始末 **atoshimatsu** settle, wind/finish up

後妻 **gosai** second wife
後肢 **kōshi** hind legs
後者 **kōsha** the latter
後金 **atokin, atogane** the remaining amount due
後門 **kōmon** back gate/door
9 後発 **kōhatsu** start out late, lag behind
後奏 **kōsō** postlude
後奏曲 **kōsōkyoku** postlude
後便 **kōbin** next letter, later mail
後陣 **kōjin** rear guard
後軍 **kōgun** rear guard, reserves
後前 **ushi(ro)-mae** with front and back reversed
後段 **kōdan** latter part
後指 **ushi(ro) yubi** bird's hind toe; finger of scorn
後咲 **oku(re)za(ki)** late blossoms
後姿 **ushi(ro) sugata** view (of someone) from the back
後後 **atoato, nochinochi** the future
後室 **kōshitsu** widow, dowager
後庭 **kōtei** back yard/garden
後面 **kōmen** back side/surface
後架 **kōka** toilet
後胤 **kōin** descendant
後悔 **kōkai** regret
後思案 **atojian** afterthought
10 後部 **kōbu** back part, rear, stern
後部灯 **kōbutō** taillight
後釜 **atogama** successor
後進 **kōshin** coming along behind; one's juniors/successors; back up
後進地域 **kōshin chiiki** underdeveloped region
後進国 **kōshinkoku** backward country
後進性 **kōshinsei** backward
後流 **kōryū** slipstream
後家 **goke** widow
後宮 **kōkyū** inner palace; harem; consort
後書 **atoga(ki)** postscript
後記 **kōki** postscript
11 後添 **nochizo(i)** one's second wife
後脚 **atoashi** hind legs
後祭 **ato (no) matsu(ri)** too late (for the fair)
後患 **kōkan** future trouble
後産 **atozan, nochizan** afterbirth, placenta
後略 **kōryaku** last part omitted
12 後場 **goba** the afternoon (trading) session
後報 **kōhō** later report, further information
後援 **kōen** assistance, aid, support
後援会 **kōenkai** supporters' association
後援者 **kōensha** supporter, backer
後葉 **kōyō** future generations, posterity; the pituitary gland
後棒 **atobō** rear palanquin bearer

3

氵 土 扌 口 女 巾 犭 弓 彳 彡 艹 宀 丷 屮 士 广 尸 口

6 ←

後期 **kōki** latter period/term, late (Nara); latter half (of the year)
後景 **kōkei** background, setting
後程 **nochihodo** later on
後項 **kōkō** the following paragraph/clause
13 後嗣 **kōshi** heir
後幕 **atomaku** the next scene/job
後楯 **ushi(ro)date** backing, support
後腹 **atobara** afterpains; child by one's second wife
後暗 **ushi(ro)gura(i)** shady, underhanded
後裔 **kōei** descendant
後置詞 **kōchishi** postposition
後続 **kōzoku** succeeding, following
後継 **kōkei** succession; successor
後継者 **kōkeisha** successor
後詰 **gozu(me)** rear guard
後鉢巻 **ushi(ro) hachimaki** twisted towel tied around one's head and knotted behind
後馳 **oku(re)ba(se)** belated, last-minute
14 後塵 **kōjin** dust raised in someone's wake; second best
後聞 **kōbun** later information
15 後編 **kōhen** concluding part/volume
後篇 **kōhen** last part, later volume, sequel
後輪 **kōrin, atowa** rear wheel
後輩 **kōhai** one's junior, younger generation
16 後衛 **kōei** rear guard
後賢 **kōken** wise men of the future
後頭 **kōtō** the back of the head
後頭部 **kōtōbu** the back of the head
18 後難 **kōnan, gōnan** future trouble, the consequences
21 後顧憂 **kōko (no) ure(i)** anxiety about those left behind after one is gone

———— 2 ————
2 人後 **jingo** not as good as others
3 亡後 **na(ki)ato** after one's death
4 予後 **yogo** recuperation, convalescence
丹後 **Tango** (ancient kuni, Kyōto-fu)
今後 **kongo** after this, henceforth
午後 **gogo** afternoon, p.m.
手後 **teoku(re)** too late, belated
月後 **tsukioku(re)** a month late/old; back numbers (of a monthly)
心後 **kokorookure** timidity
5 以後 **igo** from now/then on, (t)henceforth
生後 **seigo** after birth
立後 **ta(chi)oku(reru)** get off to a late start, lag behind
6 死後 **shigo** after death, posthumous
shi(ni)oku(reru) outlive, survive
死後強直 **shigo kyōchoku** rigor mortis
死後硬直 **shigo kōchoku** rigor mortis
気後 **kioku(re)** diffidence, timidity

羽後 **Ugo** (ancient kuni, Akita-ken)
老後 **rōgo** one's old age
7 別後 **betsugo** since parting, since we last saw each other
没後 **botsugo** after one's death, posthumous
8 事後 **jigo** after the fact, ex post facto, post-
事後承諾 **jigo shōdaku** approval after the fact
直後 **chokugo** immediately after
其後 **so(no)go** thereafter, later, since then
逃後 **ni(ge)oku(reru)** fail to escape
若後家 **wakagoke** young widow
国後島 **Kunashiri-tō** (island, Russian Hokkaidō)
肥後 **Higo** (ancient kuni, Kumamoto-ken)
明後日 **myōgonichi** the day after tomorrow
雨後 **ugo** after a rainfall
9 前後 **zengo** about, approximately; front and back, longitudinal; order, sequence
maeushi(ro) front and back
前後不覚 **zengo-fukaku** unconscious
前後左右 **zengo-sayū** in all directions
後後 **atoato, nochinochi** the future
背後 **haigo** back, rear, behind
食後 **shokugo** after a meal
10 真後 **maushi(ro)** right behind
浴後 **yokugo** after the bath
被後見者 **hikōkensha** ward
病後 **byōgo** after an illness, convalescence
11 産後 **sango** after childbirth
12 備後 **Bingo** (ancient kuni, Hiroshima-ken)
善後策 **zengosaku** remedial measures
場後 **baoku(re)** stage fright; nervousness
最後 **saigo** the last; the end
越後 **Echigo** (ancient kuni, Niigata-ken)
絶後 **zetsugo** never to be repeated/equaled
筑後 **Chikugo** (ancient kuni, Saga-ken)
13 豊後 **Bungo** (ancient kuni, Ōita-ken)
戦後 **sengo** after the war, postwar
戦後派 **sengoha** postwar generation
14 爾後 **jigo** thereafter
読後 **dokugo** after reading
読後感 **dokugokan** one's impressions (of a book)
銃後 **jūgo** the home front

———— 3 ————
4 日没後 **nichibotsugo** after sunset
5 用便後 **yōbengo** after stool
8 放課後 **hōkago** after school
9 紀元後 **kigengo** A.D.
10 流行後 **ryūkōoku(re)** out of fashion
11 終戦後 **shūsengo** after the war
13 数日後 **sūjitsugo** after several days

———— 4 ————
8 空前絶後 **kūzen-zetsugo** the first ever and probably last ever

3i6.6

徉 YŌ wander

——————— 2 ———————

11 徜徉 **shōyō** wander

3i6.7

徇 JUN herald, announce; follow, obey; seek; lay down one's life

3i6.8

徊 KAI wander

——————— 2 ———————

7 低徊 **teikai** loiter, linger
　低徊趣味 **teikai shumi** dilettantism
11 徘徊 **haikai** loiter, hang around, wander, prowl

——————— 7 ———————

徑→径 3i5.5

3i7.1 / 430

徒 TO on foot; companions; vain, useless　**ada** empty, vain　**itazu(ra)** in vain, to no purpose　**tada** in vain, only, merely　**muda** in vain, wasted, futile　**kachi** walking

——————— 1 ———————

2 徒人 **adabito** fickle person
3 徒口 **adakuchi** empty words, lip service
4 徒手 **toshu** empty-handed; penniless
　徒手体操 **toshu taisō** calisthenics without apparatus
　徒心 **adagokoro** fickleness
5 徒矢 **adaya** arrow which misses the target
　徒広 **dada(p)piro(i)** needlessly spacious
6 徒死 **toshi** die in vain
　徒刑 **tokei** penal servitude
　徒名 **adana** rumor about a romance
　徒行 **tokō** go on foot, walk
7 徒弟 **totei** apprentice
　徒走 **kachibashi(ri)** running along on foot
　徒花 **adabana** blossom yielding no seeds
　徒労 **torō** wasted effort
　徒言 **mudagoto** idle talk
　徒足 **mudaashi** a fruitless errand/trip
8 徒事 **tadagoto** trivial matter
　徒歩 **toho** walking
　徒歩競走 **toho kyōsō** walking race

徒物 **adamono** empty/ephemeral thing
徒武者 **kachimusha** foot soldier
9 徒食 **toshoku** life of idleness
10 徒荷 **kachini** foot traveler's baggage
　徒党 **totō** faction, clique, conspirators
　徒桜 **adazakura** ephemeral cherry blossoms
　徒骨 **mudabone** fruitless effort
11 徒渉 **toshō** fording
12 徒然 **tozen, tsurezure** tedium, idle hours
　徒費 **tohi** waste
13 徒業 **adawaza** useless thing
　徒夢 **adayume** idle dream
15 徒論 **toron** useless argument
　徒輩 **tohai** group, set, companions

——————— 2 ———————

4 凶徒 **kyōto** murderer, rioter, rebel, outlaw
　仏徒 **butto** a Buddhist
　反徒 **hanto** rebels, insurgents
5 生徒 **seito** student, pupil
　付徒 **tsu(ki)shitaga(u)** follow, accompany
　囚徒 **shūto** prisoner, convict
6 兇徒 **kyōto** murder, rioter, rebel, outlaw
7 学徒 **gakuto** scholar, student, disciple, follower
8 使徒 **shito** apostle
　逆徒 **gyakuto** rebel, traitor, insurgent
　宗徒 **shūto** adherent, believer
　　　 muneto principal vassals
　門徒 **monto** believer, adherent
9 信徒 **shinto** believer, follower, the faithful
　叛徒 **hanto** rebels, insurgents
10 酒徒 **shuto** drinking companions
　教徒 **kyōto** believer, adherent
12 博徒 **bakuto** gambler
　衆徒 **shūto** many priests
13 僧徒 **sōto** priests, monks
　聖徒 **seito** saint; disciple
　賊徒 **zokuto** rebels, traitors
15 暴徒 **bōto** rioters, mob
17 檀徒 **danto** temple supporter

——————— 3 ———————

3 女生徒 **joseito** schoolgirl, coed
6 回教徒 **kaikyōto** a Moslem
11 清教徒 **seikyōto** Puritans
　異教徒 **ikyōto** heathen, heretic, infidel
12 景教徒 **keikyōto** a Nestorian
13 新教徒 **shinkyōto** a Protestant

——————— 4 ———————

2 十二使徒 **jūni shito** the Twelve Apostles

3i7.2 / 1066

徐 JO, omomu(ro) slowly, gradually

——————— 1 ———————

3 徐々 **jojo** slowly, gradually

3

氵 土 扌 口 女 巾 犭 弓 彳 7← 彡 艹 宀 ⺣ 山 耂 广 尸 口

6 徐行 **jokō** go/drive slowly
8 徐歩 **joho** walk slowly, saunter, mosey

3i7.3 / 1482

従 從 从 **JŪ, JU, SHŌ** follow, obey; junior, subordinate **shitaga(u)** obey, comply with, follow **shitaga(tte)** consequently, therefore; in accordance with, in proportion to, as **shitaga(eru)** be attended by; conquer

—————— 1 ——————

3 従士 **jūshi** attendant, retainer
5 従兄 **jūkei** elder male cousin
　従兄弟 **itoko, jūkeitei** male cousin
　従犯 **jūhan** complicity; accomplice
6 従因 **jūin** secondary cause
7 従来 **jūrai** up to now, usual, conventional
　従弟 **jūtei** younger male cousin
8 従事 **jūji** engage in, carry on
　従卒 **jūsotsu** soldier-servant, orderly
　従妹 **jūmai** younger female cousin
　従姉 **jūshi** elder female cousin
　従姉妹 **itoko, jūshimai** female cousin
　従者 **jūsha** follower, attendant, valet
　従物 **jūbutsu** accessory (in law)
9 従軍 **jūgun** serve in a war
　従軍記者 **jūgun kisha** war correspondent
　従前 **jūzen** previous, former, hitherto
10 従容 **shōyō** calm, composed, serene
11 従婢 **jūhi** female servant
12 従属文 **jūzokubun** subordinate clause
　従属的 **jūzokuteki** subordinate, dependent
　従属節 **jūzokusetsu** subordinate clause
　従量税 **jūryōzei** tax/duty computed on the quantity rather than the value of a good
　従順 **jūjun** submissive, docile, gentle
13 従業 **jūgyō** be employed
　従業員 **jūgyōin** employee
14 従僕 **jūboku** male servant, attendant
18 従騎 **jūki** mounted attendants/retinue

—————— 2 ——————

2 又従兄弟 **mataitoko** second cousin
　又従姉妹 **mataitoko** second cousin
4 不従順 **fujūjun** disobedience
5 主従 **shujū** master and servant, lord and vassal
6 合従連衡 **gasshō-renkō** multi-party alliance (against a powerful enemy)
7 臣従 **shinjū** service as a retainer
　忍従 **ninjū** submission, resignation, meekness
8 侍従 **jijū** chamberlain
　盲従 **mōjū** blind obedience
　追従 **tsuijū** follow, imitate; be servile to **tsuishō** flattery, boot-licking
　屈従 **kutsujū** submit meekly to, yield

服従 **fukujū** obey, submit to
服従的 **fukujūteki** obedient, submissive
9 専従 **senjū** full-time (work)
面従 **menjū** outward obedience
面従腹背 **menjū-fukuhai** outward obedience but inward opposition, false obedience, passive resistance
10 陪従 **baijū** wait upon, accompany
随従 **zuijū** follow the lead of, play second fiddle to
随従者 **zuijūsha** henchman, follower, satellite
帰従 **kijū** surrender
家従 **kajū** steward, butler, attendant
13 適従 **tekijū** follow
14 僕従 **bokujū** servant
16 隷従 **reijū** slavery
17 聴従 **chōjū** follow (advice)

—————— 3 ——————

4 不服従 **fufukujū** insubordination

—————— 8 ——————

徠→来 **0a7.6**

御→ **3i9.1**

3i8.1

衒 **GEN** show off; peddle **tera(u)** show off, display

—————— 1 ——————

6 衒気 **genki** affectation, ostentation, vanity
7 衒学的 **gengakuteki** pedantic

3i8.2 / 187

術 術 **JUTSU** art, technique, means; conjury **sube** way, means, what to do

—————— 1 ——————

4 術中 **jutchū** trick, strategem, ruse
8 術者 **jussha** one skilled in a technique
9 術計 **jukkei** stratagem, ruse, trick
12 術無 **subena(shi)** nothing can be done
術策 **jussaku** stratagem, artifice, tricks
13 術数 **jussū** artifice, stratagem, wiles
14 術語 **jutsugo** technical term, terminology

—————— 2 ——————

3 弓術 **kyūjutsu** (Japanese) archery
4 幻術 **genjutsu** magic, sorcery, witchcraft
仁術 **jinjutsu** benevolent act; healing art
手術 **shujutsu** (surgical) operation

手術台 **shujutsudai** operating table
手術衣 **shujutsui** operating gown
手術室 **shujutsushitsu** operating room
手術料 **shujutsuryō** operating fee
方術 **hōjutsu** art; method; magic
5 仙術 **senjutsu** wizardry
7 巫術 **fujutsu** divination, sorcery, witchcraft
医術 **ijutsu** medicine, medical science
技術 **gijutsu** technology, technique, skill, art
技術上 **gijutsujō** technically
技術士 **gijutsushi** engineer, technician
技術者 **gijutsusha** technical expert
技術家 **gijutsuka** technician, specialist, expert
妖術 **yōjutsu** magic, witchcraft, sorcery
芸術 **geijutsu** art
芸術至上主義 **geijutsushijō shugi** art for
   art's sake
芸術的 **geijutsuteki** artistic
芸術院 **Geijutsuin** Academy of Art
芸術家 **geijutsuka** artist
芸術祭 **geijutsusai** art festival
学術 **gakujutsu** science, learning
学術用語 **gakujutsu yōgo** technical term
忍術 **ninjutsu** the art of remaining unseen
8 呪術 **jujutsu** incantation, sorcery, magic
奇術 **kijutsu** conjuring, sleight of hand
武術 **bujutsu** military/martial arts
9 美術 **bijutsu** art, fine arts
美術工芸 **bijutsu kōgei** artistic handicrafts,
   arts and crafts
美術史 **bijutsushi** art history
美術的 **bijutsuteki** artistic
美術院 **bijutsuin** academy of art
美術品 **bijutsuhin** work of art
美術界 **bijutsukai** the art world
美術家 **bijutsuka** artist
美術商 **bijutsushō** art dealer
美術館 **bijutsukan** art gallery
柔術 **jūjutsu** jujitsu
施術 **shijutsu** surgical operation
10 剣術 **kenjutsu** fencing
砲術 **hōjutsu** gunnery, artillery
秘術 **hijutsu** secret, the mysteries
針術 **shinjutsu** acupuncture
馬術 **bajutsu** horseback riding, dressage
12 棒術 **bōjutsu** pole fighting
詐術 **sajutsu** swindling
13 戦術 **senjutsu** tactics
戦術家 **senjutsuka** tactician
話術 **wajutsu** storytelling
14 槍術 **sōjutsu** spearsmanship
槍術家 **sōjutsuka** spearsman
算術 **sanjutsu** arithmetic
17 鍼術 **shinjutsu** acupuncture
21 魔術 **majutsu** magic, sorcery, witchcraft
魔術師 **majutsushi** magician, conjurer

───── 3 ─────
2 九星術 **kyūseijutsu** astrology
4 手相術 **tesōjutsu** palmistry
心霊術 **shinreijutsu** spiritualism
5 写真術 **shashinjutsu** photography
古美術品 **kobijutsuhin** old/ancient art object
外交術 **gaikōjutsu** diplomacy, diplomatic
   skill
占星術 **senseijutsu** astrology
処世術 **shoseijutsu** how to get on in life
6 気合術 **kia(i)jutsu** hypnotism
安死術 **anshijutsu** euthanasia
8 非芸術的 **higeijutsuteki** inartistic
建築術 **kenchikujutsu** architecture
9 保身術 **hoshinjutsu** the art of self-protection
降神術 **kōshinjutsu** spiritualism
美容術 **biyōjutsu** beauty treatment, cosmetology
美顔術 **biganjutsu** facial treatment
速記術 **sokkijutsu** shorthand, stenography
造園術 **zōenjutsu** landscape gardening
庭園術 **teienjutsu** landscape gardening
10 隆鼻術 **ryūbijutsu** nasal plastic surgery
遊泳術 **yūeijutsu** how to get along in the
   world
航空術 **kōkūjutsu** aeronautics, aviation
航海術 **kōkaijutsu** seamanship, navigation
11 接骨術 **sekkotsujutsu** bonesetting
12 測量術 **sokuryōjutsu** (the science of)
   surveying
13 催眠術 **saiminjutsu** hypnotism
腹話術 **fukuwajutsu** ventriloquism
電信術 **denshinjutsu** telegraphy
14 演劇術 **engekijutsu** dramatics
読心術 **dokushinjutsu** mind reading
読唇術 **dokushinjutsu** lip reading
銃剣術 **jūkenjutsu** bayonet fencing
15 霊交術 **reikōjutsu** spiritualism
16 錬金術 **renkinjutsu** alchemy
18 観掌術 **kanshōjutsu** palm-reading, palmistry
20 護身術 **goshinjutsu** art of self-defense

───── 4 ─────
3 工芸美術 **kōgei bijutsu** applied fine arts
9 造形美術 **zōkei bijutsu** the plastic arts
16 整形手術 **seikei shujutsu** orthopedic
   operation

3i8.3

徘 **HAI** wander

───── 1 ─────
9 徘徊 **haikai** loiter, hang around, wander,
   prow

3i8.4 / 374

得 TOKU profit, advantage   **e/u(ru)** gain, acquire, earn, win; (as suffix) can, be able to **e(tari)** fine, excellent   **e(te)** apt to

──────── 1 ────────

0 得する **toku(suru)** gain, come out ahead
得べかりし **u(bekarishi)** which one would have gained/earned, forgone (income)
3 得々 **tokutoku** proudly, triumphantly
4 得分 **tokubun** profits, winnings, one's share
得手 **ete** strong point, forte, specialty
得手物 **etemono** one's specialty
得手勝手 **etekatte** self-centered, selfish
得心 **tokushin** consent to, be persuaded of
5 得失 **tokushitsu** advantages and disadvantages
6 得安 **eyasu(i)** easily obtainable
7 得体 **etai** nature, character
得言 **e(mo)i(warenu)** indescribable
8 得物 **emono** weapon
9 得点 **tokuten** one's score, points made
得度 **tokudo** enter the (Buddhist) priesthood
11 得道 **tokudō** attainment of (Buddhist) salvation
得得 **tokutoku** proudly, triumphantly
得票 **tokuhyō** votes obtained
12 得策 **tokusaku** advantageous policy, wise plan
13 得業士 **tokugyōshi** special-school graduate
得意 **tokui** pride, triumph; one's strong point; customer; prosperity
得意気 **tokuige** proud, elated
得意先 **tokuisaki** customer
得意満面 **tokui-manmen** pride
得意顔 **tokuigao** triumphant look
18 得難 **egata(i)** hard to obtain, rare
得顔 **e(tari)gao** look of triumph

──────── 2 ────────

1 一得 **ittoku** one advantage, a merit
一得一失 **ittoku isshitsu** advantages and disadvantages
3 已得 **ya(mu o) e(nai)** unavoidable
4 不得手 **fuete** unskillful, poor at, weak in
不得要領 **futoku-yōryō** vague, ambiguous
不得策 **futokusaku** unwise, bad policy, ill-advised
不得意 **futokui** one's weak point
収得 **shūtoku** keep for one's own
心得 **kokoroe** knowledge, understanding
kokoroe(ru) know, understand
心得違 **kokoroechiga(i)** mistaken idea; indiscretion
心得難 **kokoroegata(i)** strange, inexplicable
心得顔 **kokoroegao** a knowing look

5 生得 **seitoku, shōtoku** by nature, innate
6 両得 **ryōtoku** double advantage
会得 **etoku** understanding, comprehension, appreciation
有得 **a(ri)u(ru)** could be, possible
自得 **jitoku** be self-content; acquire on one's own; understand, grasp
7 体得 **taitoku** realization, experience; comprehension, mastery
余得 **yotoku** additional gain, extra benefit
役得 **yakutoku** perquisite
見得 **mie** pose, posture
利得 **ritoku** profit, benefit, gain
8 知得 **chitoku** know, learn
所得 **shotoku** income, earnings
所得者 **shotokusha** income earner
所得税 **shotokuzei** income tax
所得層 **shotokusō** income level/bracket
所得顔 **tokoroegao** triumph, elation
所得額 **shotokugaku** (amount of) income
取得 **shutoku** acquire **to(ri)doku** gain, profit
9 拾得 **shūtoku** pick up, find
拾得者 **shūtokusha** finder
拾得物 **shūtokubutsu** found article
10 既得 **kitoku** already acquired
既得権 **kitokuken** vested rights/interests
修得 **shūtoku** learning, acquirement
納得 **nattoku** assent to, be convinced of
11 得得 **tokutoku** proudly, triumphantly
常得意 **jōtokui** regular customer
習得 **shūtoku** learn, master
欲得 **yokutoku** selfishness, self-interest
12 勝得 **ka(chi)e(ru)** win, achieve, earn, gain
無得点 **mutokuten** scoreless (game)
買得 **kaidoku** a good bargain/buy
13 損得 **sontoku** advantages and disadvantages
感得 **kantoku** realize, become aware of
14 説得 **settoku** persuasion
説得力 **settokuryoku** persuasiveness
16 獲得 **kakutoku** acquire, gain, win

──────── 3 ────────

3 大見得 **ōmie** ostentatious display, grand posture
4 不心得 **fukokoroe** imprudent, indiscreet
7 利害得失 **rigai-tokushitsu** pros and cons
10 純所得 **junshotoku** net income
12 無所得 **mushotoku** without any income

──────── 4 ────────

1 一挙両得 **ikkyo ryōtoku** killing two birds with one stone
4 不労所得 **furō shotoku** unearned/investment income
6 自業自得 **jigō-jitoku** reaping what one sows
12 勤労所得 **kinrō shotoku** earned income

3i8.5

徙

SHI, utsu(ru/su) (intr./tr.) move

3i8.6

徛

KI cross, traverse

從 → 従 3i7.3

3i8.7

徜

SHŌ wander

———————— 1 ————————

9 徜徉 **shōyō** wander

———————— 9 ————————

3i9.1 / 708

御

GYO control; (imperial honorific prefix) **GO-, o-, on-, mi-** (honorific prefix)

———————— 1 ————————

0 御する **gyo(suru)** control, manage
1 御一新 **goisshin** the Meiji restoration
2 御子 **miko** child of the king/emperor
　御八 **oyatsu** afternoon snack
3 御三家 **Gosanke** the three branch families of the Tokugawas
　御大 **ontai** the boss/chief
　御大葬 **gotaisō** imperial funeral
　御上 **okami** the emperor; the government/authorities; one's lord; madam, the Mrs.
　御下問 **gokamon** emperor's question
4 御不浄 **gofujō** lavatory
　御中 **onchū** To: (name of addressee organization), Dear Sirs:
　御手洗 **oteara(i)** lavatory
　　mitarashi holy water font at a shrine
5 御世 **miyo** reign, period
　御代 **miyo** reign, period
　御存 **gozon(ji)** (as) you know
　御用 **goyō** your order/business; official business
　御用地 **goyōchi** imperial estate
　御用邸 **goyōtei** imperial villa
　御用始 **goyō-haji(me)** reopening of offices after New Year's
　御用納 **goyō-osa(me)** year-end office closing

御用商人 **goyō shōnin** purveyor to the government
御用達 **goyōtashi** purveyor to the government
御用組合 **goyō kumiai** company union
御用新聞 **goyō shinbun** gov't newspaper
御用聞 **goyōki(ki)** taking orders
御字 **on(no)ji** quite satisfactory, excellent
6 御多忙中 **gotabōchū** while you are so busy
御朱印 **goshuin** sealed letter issued by a shogun
御朱印船 **goshuinsen** shogunate-licensed trading ship
御名 **mina** (God's) name
　　gyomei emperor's name/signature
御名御璽 **gyomei-gyoji** imperial/privy seal
御宇 **gyou** imperial reign
御衣 **gyoi** imperial clothes
7 御身 **onmi, omi** you
御来光 **goraikō** sunrise viewed from a mountaintop
御位 **mikurai** the throne
御伽 **otogi** keep company, entertain (guests); attend on, nurse
御伽国 **otogi (no) kuni** fairyland
御伽話 **otogibanashi** fairy tale
御陀仏 **odabutsu** dead man
御告 **mitsuge, otsuge** oracle, divine message
御言 **mikoto** what (your excellency) says
8 御免 **gomen** (I beg) your pardon; no thankyou, not me; permission
御法度 **gohatto** law, ordinance; prohibition
御幸 **miyuki** visit/attendance by royalty
御苑 **gyoen** imperial garden
御国 **okuni** your (native) country; your home (town); a daimyō's territory (Edo period)
御国入 **okunii(ri)** daimyō's return (from Edo); celebrity's homecoming
御国自慢 **okuni jiman** pride in one's native home province; boast of one's native place
御国言葉 **okuni kotoba** dialect, vernacular
御者 **gyosha** driver, cabman
御所 **gosho** imperial palace
御所車 **goshoguruma** canopied ox-drawn carriage
御門 **mikado** palace gate; emperor
9 御前 **omae** you　**mimae** before (God)
　　gozen before an exalted person; your excellency
御前会議 **gozen kaigi** council held in the presence of the emperor
御神火 **goshinka** volcanic fires
御神酒 **omiki** sacred saké, saké offering
10 御陵 **goryō** imperial tomb
御都合 **gotsugō** your convenience
御都合主義 **gotsugō shugi** opportunism

御真影 **goshin'ei** emperor's portrait
御酒 **miki** sacred saké, saké offering
御家人 **gokenin** a lower-grade vassal
御家芸 **oiegei** one's specialty
御家騒動 **oie sōdō** family quarrel
御宴 **gyoen** court banquet
御座所 **gozasho** the throne
御破算 **gohasan** clearing a soroban; starting afresh
御料 **goryō** imperial/crown property
御料地 **goryōchi** imperial estate, crown land
御託 **gotaku** tedious/impertinent talk
11 御捻 **ohine(ri)** gratuity wrapped in paper
御猟場 **goryōba** imperial forest
御曹司 **onzōshi** son of a distinguished family
御袋 **ofukuro** one's mom, mama
御転婆 **otenba** tomboy
12 御無沙汰 **gobusata** neglect to visit/write
御裁可 **gosaika** imperial sanction/approval
御詠 **gyoei** imperial poem
御詠歌 **goeika** Buddhist hymn/chant
御飯 **gohan** boiled rice; a meal
御飯時 **gohandoki** mealtime
御飯蒸 **gohanmu(shi)** rice steamer
13 御蔭 **okage** indebtedness, favor, thanks to
御殿 **goten** palace
御意 **gyoi** your will/pleasure
御新造 **goshinzo, goshinzō** new wife of a prominent person; wife
御辞儀 **ojigi** bow, greeting
御馳走 **gochisō** feast, banquet, treat, hospitality
14 御製 **gyosei** emperor's poem/composition
15 御幣 **gohei** (sacred staff with) cut paper strips (Shinto)
御幣担 **gohei-katsu(gi)** superstitious person
御影 **gyoei** portrait of a noble
御影石 **mikage ishi** granite
御慶 **gyokei** greetings, felicitations
御霊 **mitama** spirit of a dead person
御霊屋 **mitamaya** mausoleum, tomb
16 御嬢様 **ojōsama** young lady, (your) daughter
17 御輿 **mikoshi** portable/palanquin shrine
御覧 **goran** see, look at; give it a try
18 御難 **gonan** calamity, misfortune
御題 **gyodai** theme of the New Year's imperial poetry contest
御題目 **odaimoku** Nichiren prayer
19 御簾 **misu** bamboo blind/screen

————————— 2 —————————

3 大御所 **ōgosho** retired shōgun; influential figure, doyen
4 父御 **chichigo, tetego** your father
5 母御 **hahago** mother (polite)
母御前 **hahagoze, hahagozen** mother (polite)

6 防御 **bōgyo** defense
防御率 **bōgyoritsu** earned run average
7 弟御 **otōtogo** your younger brother
8 制御 **seigyo** control
妹御 **imōtogo** your (younger) sister
姐御 **anego** gang boss's wife; woman boss
姉御 **anego** gang boss's wife; woman boss
11 崩御 **hōgyo** death of the emperor
12 渡御 **togyo** (emperor) proceeding to
統御 **tōgyo** rule, control, administer
奥御殿 **okugoten** inner palace
13 嫁御 **yomego** bride
15 還御 **kangyo** return (of the emperor)
16 親御 **oyago** (your) parents
錦御旗 **nishiki (no) mihata** the imperial standard
18 臨御 **ringyo** visit by the emperor

————————— 3 —————————

2 人身御供 **hitomi gokū** human sacrifice, victim
3 大宮御所 **Ōmiya gosho** Empress Dowager's Palace
7 花嫁御寮 **hanayome goryō** bride
8 東宮御所 **Tōgū gosho** the Crown Prince's Palace
12 御名御璽 **gyomei-gyoji** imperial/privy seal

————————— 4 —————————

6 自動制御 **jidō seigyo** servocontrol

3i9.2 / 186

街 **GAI, KAI** street
machi town; streets, neighborhood

————————— 1 —————————

3 街上 **gaijō** on the street(s)
6 街灯 **gaitō** street lamp
7 街角 **machikado** street corner
11 街道 **kaidō** highway
13 街路 **gairo** street
街路樹 **gairoju** trees along a street
16 街録 **gairoku** recorded man-on-the-street interview (short for 街頭録音)
街頭 **gaitō** street
街頭募金 **gaitō bokin** street solicitation
街頭演説 **gaitō enzetsu** street/soapbox speech
街頭録音 **gaitō rokuon** recorded man-on-the-street interview

————————— 2 —————————

5 市街 **shigai** the streets; city, town
市街地 **shigaichi** urban district
市街戦 **shigaisen** street-to-street fighting
7 花街 **kagai** red-light district

————————— 3 —————————

6 地下街 **chikagai** underground shopping mall

10 娯楽街 **gorakugai** amusement quarter
11 商店街 **shōtengai** shopping area
商業街 **shōgyōgai** shopping street/area
貧民街 **hinmingai** slums
13 暗黒街 **ankokugai** the underworld
15 歓楽街 **kanrakugai** amusement center
16 繁華街 **hankagai** busy (shopping/entertainment) area
18 観楽街 **kanrakugai** amusement district
21 露店街 **rotengai** street of open-air stalls

3i9.3

徨
KŌ wander

——————— 2 ———————

7 彷徨 **hōkō** wander about; fluctuate
samayo(u) wander about

3i9.4 / 917

復
FUKU return to, be restored
mata again

——————— 1 ———————

0 復する **fuku(suru)** return to, be restored
4 復元 **fukugen** restoration (to the original state)
復仇 **fukkyū, fukukyū** revenge
復水器 **fukusuiki** condenser
5 復申 **fukushin** reply; report
復刊 **fukkan** republication, reissue
復古 **fukko** restoration (of the old regime)
復古調 **fukkochō** reactionary/revival mood
復旧 **fukkyū, fukukyū** restoration, recovery
6 復任 **fukunin** reappointment, reinstatement
復交 **fukkō** restoration of diplomatic relations
7 復位 **fukui** restoration, reinstatement
8 復命 **fukumei** report
復刻 **fukkoku** republication, reissue
9 復活 **fukkatsu** revival
復活祭 **Fukkatsusai** Easter
10 復帰 **fukki** return, comeback, reinstatement
復原 **fukugen** restoration (to the original state)
復員 **fukuin** demobilization
復員兵 **fukuinhei** demobilized soldier
復党 **fukutō** be reinstated in the party
復校 **fukkō, fukukō** return/readmission to school
復航 **fukkō** return voyage/flight
復配 **fukuhai** resumption of dividends
11 復習 **fukushū** review
13 復業 **fukugyō** return to work
14 復読 **fukudoku** reread, review

復誦 **fukushō** repeat back (to confirm than an order has been understood)
15 復権 **fukken, fukuken** restoration of rights, reinstatement, rehabilitation
復縁 **fukuen** reconciliation
16 復興 **fukkō** reconstruction, revival
18 復職 **fukushoku** reinstatement, reappointment
20 復籍 **fukuseki** reinstatement as a member; reregistering to one's original domicile
23 復讐 **fukushū** revenge
復讎 **fukushū** revenge

——————— 2 ———————

4 反復 **hanpuku** repetition
6 回復 **kaifuku** recovery
回復期 **kaifukuki** convalescence
7 克復 **kokufuku** be restored, return
8 拝復 **haifuku** In reply to your letter
往復 **ōfuku** going and returning, round trip; correspondence; association
往復切符 **ōfuku kippu** round trip ticket
往復葉書 **ōfuku hagaki** return postcard
9 重復 **chōfuku, jūfuku** duplication, repetition, overlapping, redundancy
恢復 **kaifuku** recovery
10 修復 **shūfuku** repair

——————— 4 ———————

1 一陽来復 **ichiyō-raifuku** return of spring

3i9.5

編
HEN everywhere

3i9.6 / 1479

循
JUN follow; circulate

——————— 1 ———————

17 循環 **junkan** circulation, cycle
循環系 **junkankei** the circulatory system
循環器 **junkanki** circulatory organ
循環論法 **junkan ronpō** a circular argument

——————— 2 ———————

6 因循 **injun** vacillating, conservative
11 悪循環 **akujunkan** vicious cycle/spiral

——————— 10 ———————

3i10.1 / 1419

微 微
BI, MI minute, slight
kasu(ka) faint, dim

——————— 1 ———————

2 微力 **biryoku** (my) poor ability, what little (I) can do

3

氵
土
扌
口
女
巾
犭
弓
彳
彡
艹
宀
⺌
山
幸
广
尸
口

10 ←

3 微才 **bisai** (my) meager talent
微々 **bibi(taru)** slight, tiny, insignificant
微小 **bishō** minute, microscopic
4 微分 **bibun** differential (calculus)
微分子 **bibunshi** particle, atom, molecule
微分学 **bibungaku** differential calculus
微分積分 **bibun-sekibun** differential and integral calculus
微少 **bishō** minute quantity
5 微生物 **biseibutsu** microorganism, microbe
微生物学 **biseibutsugaku** microbiology
微功 **bikō** minor achievement
6 微行 **bikō** traveling incognito
微光 **bikō** faint light, glimmer
7 微妙 **bimyō** delicate, subtle
8 微苦笑 **bikushō** wry/bittersweet smile
微服 **bifuku** incognito
微雨 **biu** light rain
9 微衷 **bichū** one's true feelings
微風 **bifū** gentle breeze
微音 **bion** a faint sound
10 微弱 **bijaku** feeble
微笑 **bishō, hohoe(mi)** smile
11 微動 **bidō** slight tremor, quiver
微視的 **bishiteki** microscopic
微細 **bisai** minute, fine, detailed
微粒子 **biryūshi** tiny particle, fine-grained
12 微温 **bion** lukewarm, tepid
微温湯 **biontō** lukewarm water
微量 **biryō** minute amount
微禄 **biroku** small stipend, pittance
13 微傷 **bishō** slight wound, minor injury, scratch
微微 **bibi(taru)** slight, tiny, insignificant
微意 **bii** small token (of gratitude)
微罪 **bizai** minor offense
14 微塵 **mijin** particle, bit, iota
15 微熱 **binetsu** a slight fever
微賤 **bisen** low rank, humble station, obscurity
微震 **bishin** slight earthquake/tremor
16 微積分 **bisekibun** differential and integral calculus

———————— 2 ————————

6 式微 **shikibi** decline, wane
10 衰微 **suibi** decline, fall into decay, wane
粉微塵 **konamijin** tiny fragments
11 細微 **saibi** minute, fine, detailed
12 測微計 **sokubikei** micrometer
極微 **kyokubi** infinitesimal, microscopic
軽微 **keibi** slight, insignificant
13 隠微 **inbi** hidden, escoteric, abstruse
微微 **bibi(taru)** slight, tiny, insignificant
16 機微 **kibi** inner workings, secrets, subtleties
18 顕微鏡 **kenbikyō** microscope

———————— 3 ————————

4 木端微塵 **koppa-mijin** splinters, smithereens
12 超顕微鏡 **chōkenbikyō** ultramicroscope

3i10.2

衙 **GA** government office

———————— 2 ————————

8 官衙 **kango** government office/authorities

3i10.3

徭 **YŌ, edachi** compulsory service to the state, corvée

———————— 1 ————————

7 徭役 **yōeki** statute labor, corvée

———————— 11 ————————

3i11.1

衘 啣 **KAN, kutsuwa** horse's bit **fuku(mu), kuwa(eru)** hold (a cigarette) in one's teeth/lips

———————— 2 ————————

10 馬銜 **hami** horse's bit

3i11.2 / 1420

徴 徵 **CHŌ** collect, demand; sign, indication **shirushi** sign, indication

———————— 1 ————————

0 徴する **chō(suru)** collect, charge (a fee), solicit, seek, demand
4 徴収 **chōshū** collect, levy, charge
5 徴用 **chōyō** commandeer, requisition, expropriate
7 徴兵 **chōhei** conscription; draftee
徴兵忌避 **chōhei kihi** draft evasion
徴兵制 **chōheisei** conscription system
徴兵免除 **chōhei menjo** draft exemption
徴兵検査 **chōhei kensa** examination for conscription
9 徴発 **chōhatsu** commandeer, requisition, press into service
徴発令 **chōhatsurei** requisition orders
10 徴候 **chōkō** sign, indication, symptom
12 徴募 **chōbo** enlistment, recruitment
徴税 **chōzei** tax collection, taxation
徴集 **chōshū** levy, recruit, conscript
徴集令 **chōshūrei** order calling up draftees

———————— 2 ————————

6 吉徴 **kitchō** good/lucky omen
8 追徴 **tsuichō** additional collection, supplementary charge
追徴金 **tsuichōkin** additional collection, supplementary charge

追徴税 **tsuichōzei** supplementary/penalty tax
明徴 **meichō** clarification
10 特徴 **tokuchō** distinctive feature, characteristic
12 象徴 **shōchō** symbol
象徴主義 **shōchō shugi** symbolism
象徴的 **shōchōteki** symbolic
象徴詩 **shōchōshi** symbolical/symbolist poetry
14 増徴 **zōchō** levy extra taxes

───────── 3 ─────────

13 源泉徴収 **gensen chōshū** collecting (taxes) at the source, withholding

微→微 3i10.1

3i11.3 / 1038

TOKU virtue

徳 德 悳

───────── 1 ─────────

3 徳川 **Tokugawa** (shogun family during Edo period)
4 徳化 **tokka** moral influence/reform
5 徳用 **tokuyō** economical
徳用品 **tokuyōhin** economy(-size) goods
徳目 **tokumoku** (classification of) virtues
6 徳行 **tokkō** virtuous conduct
7 徳沢 **tokutaku** grace
徳利 **tokuri, tokkuri** (pinch-necked) saké bottle
8 徳育 **tokuiku** moral education
徳治 **Tokuji** (era, 1306-1308)
徳性 **tokusei** moral character
9 徳風 **tokufū** nobility of character
徳政 **tokusei** benevolent government; debt moratorium
10 徳島 **Tokushima** (city, Tokushima-ken)
徳島県 **Tokushima-ken** (prefecture)
徳教 **tokkyō** moral teachings
11 徳望 **tokubō** moral influence
徳望家 **tokubōka** man of high moral repute
13 徳義 **tokugi** morality, integrity
徳義上 **tokugijō** morally, ethically
徳義心 **tokugishin** sense of morality/honor
15 徳器 **tokki** virtue and talent; noble character
16 徳操 **tokusō** morality, virtue, chastity

───────── 2 ─────────

2 人徳 **jintoku, nintoku** natural/personal virtue
3 三徳 **santoku** the three primary virtues (wisdom, benevolence, and valor)
才徳 **saitoku** talent and virtue
4 不徳 **futoku** lack of virtue, immorality, depravity

元徳 **Gentoku** (era, 1329–1331)
天徳 **Tentoku** (era, 957–961)
五徳 **gotoku** the five cardinal virtues (of Confucianism)
仁徳 **jintoku** benevolence, graciousness
Nintoku (emperor, 313–399)
文徳 **Montoku** (emperor, 850–858)
公徳 **kōtoku** public morality
公徳心 **kōtokushin** public-spiritedness
5 功徳 **kudoku, kōtoku** charity, virtuous acts, merit
正徳 **Shōtoku** (era, 1711–1716)
6 孝徳 **Kōtoku** (emperor, 645–654)
有徳 **yūtoku** virtuous
7 承徳 **Jōtoku** (era, 1097–1099)
享徳 **Kyōtoku** (era, 1452–1454)
延徳 **Entoku** (era, 1489–1492)
学徳 **gakutoku** learning and virtue
応徳 **Ōtoku** (era, 1084–1087)
8 長徳 **Chōtoku** (era, 995–999)
建徳 **Kentoku** (era, 1370–1372)
知徳 **chitoku** knowledge and virtue
宝徳 **Hōtoku** (era, 1449–1452)
明徳 **meitoku** illustrious virtue
武徳 **butoku** martial virtues
9 俊徳 **shuntoku** great virtue
美徳 **bitoku** virtue, noble attribute
背徳 **haitoku** immorality, corruption
神徳 **shintoku** divine power/virtue
悖徳 **haitoku** immorality
威徳 **itoku** virtue and influence
10 陰徳 **intoku** secret act of charity
高徳 **kōtoku** eminent virtue
恩徳 **ontoku** favor, mercy, grace
称徳 **Shōtoku** (empress, 764–770)
11 道徳 **dōtoku** morality, morals
道徳上 **dōtoku-jō** from a moral viewpoint
道徳心 **dōtokushin** sense of morality
道徳学 **dōtokugaku** moral philosophy
道徳的 **dōtokuteki** moral, ethical
道徳律 **dōtokuritsu** moral law
道徳家 **dōtokuka** man of virtue
淑徳 **shukutoku** feminine virtues
婦徳 **futoku** womanly virtues
崇徳 **Sutoku** (emperor, 1123–1141)
悪徳 **akutoku** vice, corruption, immorality
悪徳新聞 **akutoku shinbun** irresponsible/sensationalist newspaper
盛徳 **seitoku** illustrious virtues
12 報徳 **hōtoku** repaying a kindness, gratitude
13 寛徳 **Kantoku** (era, 1044–1045)
福徳 **fukutoku** good fortune
聖徳 **seitoku** imperial virtues
頌徳 **shōtoku** eulogizing someone's virtues
頌徳碑 **shōtokuhi** monument in honor of (someone)

3

氵 土 扌 口 女 巾 犭 弓 彳 彡 艹 宀 丷 彐 广 尸 口

11←

14 遺徳 **itoku** benefit derived from the virtue of
one's ancestors
聞(き)徳 **ki(ki)doku** worth hearing
16 燗徳利 **kandokuri** bottle for heating saké

――――――― 3 ―――――――
4 不道徳 **fudōtoku** immoral
――――――― 4 ―――――――
2 二重道徳 **nijū dōtoku** double standard of
morality

――――――― 12 ―――――――

3i12.1 / 1772

衝

SHŌ collide; highway; important point;
(planets in) opposition

――――――― 1 ―――――――
4 衝天 **shōten** in high spirits
衝心 **shōshin** heart failure (from beriberi)
8 衝突 **shōtotsu** collision; clash
11 衝動 **shōdō** impulse, urge, drive
衝動的 **shōdōteki** impulsive
15 衝撃 **shōgeki** shock
――――――― 2 ―――――――
7 折衝 **sesshō** negotiation
9 要衝 **yōshō** important place
12 雲衝 **kumotsu(ku)** towering
15 緩衝 **kanshō** buffer
緩衝国 **kanshōkoku** buffer state
緩衝器 **kanshōki** bumper, shock absorber
――――――― 3 ―――――――
5 正面衝突 **shōmen shōtotsu** head-on collision

3i12.2 / 1422

徹

TETSU go through

――――――― 1 ―――――――
0 徹する **tes(suru)** pierce, penetrate; go all-out;
stay up (all night)
8 徹夜 **tetsuya** stay up all night
徹底 **tettei** thorough, complete
徹底的 **tetteiteki** thorough, exhaustive
16 徹頭徹尾 **tettō-tetsubi** thoroughly, through
and through
――――――― 2 ―――――――
1 一徹 **ittetsu** obstinate, stubborn
一徹者 **ittetsumono** stubborn person
4 不徹底 **futettei** not thorough, halfway,
unconvincing, inconclusive
9 透徹 **tōtetsu** penetrate, permeate; be
transparent/intelligible
11 貫徹 **kantetsu** carry through, attain, realize
15 澄徹 **chōtetsu** clear, transparent

――――――― 3 ―――――――
15 徹頭徹尾 **tettō-tetsubi** thoroughly, through
and through

徴 → 徴 **3i11.2**

德 → 徳 **3i11.3**

――――――― 13 ―――――――

3i13.1 / 1585

衡

KŌ scales, weigh

――――――― 1 ―――――――
5 衡平 **kōhei** equitable
15 衡器 **kōki** a balance, scales
――――――― 2 ―――――――
5 平衡 **heikō** equilibrium, balance
7 均衡 **kinkō** balance, equilibrium
8 斉衡 **Saikō** (era, 854–857)
14 選衡 **senkō** selection, screening
銓衡 **senkō** selection, screening
15 権衡 **kenkō** balance, equilibrium
――――――― 3 ―――――――
4 不均衡 **fukinkō** imbalance, disequilibrium
9 度量衡 **doryōkō** weights and measures
――――――― 4 ―――――――
6 合従連衡 **gasshō-renkō** multi-party alliance
(against a powerful enemy)

3i13.2

徼

KYŌ, GYŌ seek; inquire; go around;
border

3i13.3 / 815

衛 衞

EI defend, protect

――――――― 1 ―――――――
5 衛生 **eisei** hygiene, sanitation
衛生上 **eiseijō** hygienic, sanitary
衛生兵 **eiseihei** (military) medic
衛生学 **eiseigaku** hygiene, hygienics
衛生法 **eiseihō** hygiene, hygienics
衛生的 **eiseiteki** hygienic, sanitary
衛生係 **eiseigakari** health officer
衛生班 **eiseihan** a sanitation detail
衛生隊 **eiseitai** medical corps
7 衛兵 **eihei** guards, sentinel

9 衛星 **eisei** satellite
衛星国 **eiseikoku** satellite (country)
衛星都市 **eisei toshi** satellite towns

—————— 2 ——————

4 不衛生 **fueisei** unsanitary, unhygienic
中衛 **chūei** middle guard (in volleyball);
    halfback (in soccer)
6 防衛 **bōei** defense
防衛庁 **Bōeichō** Defense Agency
近衛 **konoe** imperial guards; bodyguards
近衛兵 **konoehei** imperial guards; bodyguards
守衛 **shuei** (security) guard
自衛 **jiei** self-defense; bodyguard
自衛官 **jieikan** Self Defense Forces member
自衛隊 **Jieitai** Self Defense Forces
自衛権 **jieiken** right of self-defense
7 赤衛軍 **Sekieigun** the Red Guards
8 非衛生的 **hieiseiteki** unsanitary, unhygienic
性衛生 **sei eisei** sexual hygiene
門衛 **mon'ei** guard, gatekeeper
9 前衛 **zen'ei** advance guard, vanguard
後衛 **kōei** rear guard
紅衛兵 **Kōeihei** the Red Guards (in China)
13 禁衛 **kin'ei** the imperial guards
禁衛隊 **kin'eitai** the imperial guards
16 親衛 **shin'ei** leader's personal security
親衛兵 **shin'eihei** bodyguard
親衛隊 **shin'eitai** bodyguard troops
19 警衛 **keiei** guard, escort, patrol
20 護衛 **goei** guard, escort
護衛兵 **goeihei** guard, military escort

—————— 3 ——————

3 土左衛門 **dozaemon** drowned person
7 呑兵衛 **no(n)bē** heavy drinker
12 飲兵衛 **no(n)bē** heavy drinker
14 静止衛星 **seishi eisei** stationary satellite

—————— 4 ——————

5 正当防衛 **seitō bōei** legitimate self-defense

衞 → 衛 **3i13.3**

—————— 14 ——————

3i14.1

鵆 **chidori** plover

3i14.2

徽 **KI** good, fine; mark, badge, signal;
koto fret

—————— 1 ——————

11 徽章 **kishō** badge, insignia

—————— 20 ——————

3i20.1

黴 **BAI, kabi** mold, mildew, fungus
ka(biru), kabi(ru) get moldy/musty

—————— 1 ——————

4 黴止 **kabido(me)** anti-mildew preparation,
    fungicide
8 黴毒 **baidoku** syphilis
9 黴臭 **kabikusa(i)** moldy, musty
11 黴菌 **baikin** bacteria, germs

—————— 2 ——————

8 青黴 **aokabi** green mold; penicillium
11 黒黴 **kurokabi** bread mold

—————— 21 ——————

3i21.1

衢 **KU** crossroads

—————————— 彡 **3j** ——————————

彡	川	巛	形	尨	参	殄	髟	彩	彫	參	彪	須
0.1	0a3.2	0a3.2	4.1	4.2	5.1	6.1	7.1	8.1	8.2	3j5.1	8.3	9.1

彭	趁	髢	彰	髦	髪	影	髴	髻	髮	髭	鬐	髭
9.2	3b9.19	10.1	11.1	11.2	11.3	12.1	3i5.1	12.2	3j11.3	12.3	13.1	13.2

鬘
3s22.1

—————————— 0 ——————————

3j0.1

彡 **SAN** hair ornament

川 → **0a3.2**

巛 → 川 **0a3.2**

3

氵 扌 日 女 巾 犭 弓 彳 彡
→4 艹 宀 丷 屮 吉 广 尸 口

─────── 4 ───────

3j4.1 / 395

形 KEI, GYŌ, katachi, kata, -gata form, shape　nari form, figure, appearance

─────── 1 ───────

0 ハート形 **hātogata** heart-shaped
4 形木 **katagi** wooden model (of a dyeing pattern); wooden printing block
5 形代 **katashiro** paper image (used in purification ceremony)
6 形而上 **keijijō** metaphysical
　形而上学 **keijijōgaku** metaphysics
　形而下 **keijika** physical, material
　形而下学 **keijikagaku** the physical sciences
　形成 **keisei** formation, makeup
　形式 **keishiki** form; formality
　形式化 **keishikika** formalization
　形式主義 **keishiki shugi** formalism; red-tapism
　形式的 **keishikiteki** formal
　形式美 **keishikibi** beauty of form
　形式論 **keishikiron** formalism
7 形体 **keitai** form, shape, configuration
　narikatachi one's appearance
　形作 **katachizuku(ru)** form, shape, make
　形状 **keijō** form, shape
　形声 **keisei** type of kanji in which one part suggests the meaning and one the pronunciation (e.g., 河)
　形見 **katami** keepsake, memento
　形見分 **katamiwa(ke)** distribution of mementos (of the deceased)
9 形造 **katachizuku(ru)** form, shape, make
　形相 **gyōsō** features, looks, expression
　keisō phase, form, idea
10 形振 **narifu(ri)** one's appearance
　形容 **keiyō** form, appearance; describe, qualify, modify; figure of speech
　形容動詞 **keiyōdōshi** quasi-adjective used with -na (e.g., *shizuka*, *kirei*)
　形容詞 **keiyōshi** adjective
12 形象 **keishō** shape, figure, phenomenon
　形勝 **keishō** scenic beauty; good location
13 形勢 **keisei** situation, conditions, prospects
　形跡 **keiseki** traces, signs, evidence
14 形貌 **keibō** form, appearance
　形態 **keitai** form, shape, configuration
　形態学 **keitaigaku** morphology
15 形影 **keiei** a form and its shadow
16 形骸 **keigai** ruins, a mere skeleton

─────── 2 ───────

2 人形 **ningyō** doll, puppet
　人形芝居 **ningyō shibai** puppet show
3 大形 **ōgata** large size　**ōgyō** exaggeration

丸形 **marugata** round shape, circle
女形 **onnagata, oyama** female role
弓形 **kyūkei** bow-shaped; circle segment
　yumigata arch, arc, curve
小形 **kogata** small-size
山形 **yamagata** chevron, caret
　Yamagata (city, Yamagata-ken)
山形県 **Yamagata-ken** (prefecture)
4 中形 **chūgata** medium size
円形 **enkei** round shape, circle
手形 **tegata** bill, (promissory) note
月形 **tsukigata** crescent shape
方形 **hōkei** square
5 凹形 **ōkei** concavity; intaglio
外形 **gaikei** external form, outward appearance
外形的 **gaikeiteki** external, outward
台形 **daikei** trapezoid
字形 **jikei** type, print　**-jigata** -shaped
T字形 **tījigata** T-shaped
6 多形 **takei** multiform, polymorphous
全形 **zenkei** the whole shape
同形 **dōkei** the same shape
地形 **chikei** topography, terrain
　jigyō ground leveling, groundwork
地形学 **chikeigaku** topography
地形図 **chikeizu** topographical/relief map
有形 **yūkei** material, tangible
有形無形 **yūkei-mukei** tangible and intangible, material and spiritual
7 身形 **minari** one's personal appearance
体形 **taikei** form, figure
卵形 **tamagogata, rankei** egg-shaped, oval
忘形見 **wasu(re)gatami** memento, keepsake; posthumous child
角形 **kakugata** squared-off, angular
花形 **hanagata** floral pattern; flourish, ornament; star, popular person
図形 **zukei** diagram, figure, pattern
足形 **ashigata** footprint
8 刳形 **ku(ri)kata** molding
波形 **namigata** wave form, corrugation
奇形 **kikei** deformity, abnormality
実形 **jikkei** actual size
定形 **teikei** fixed/regular form
固形 **kokei** solid, solidified
固形体 **kokeitai** a solid
固形物 **kokeibutsu** a solid; solid food
固形便 **kokeiben** (normal) firm feces
9 陣形 **jinkei** battle array/formation
変形 **henkei** transformation, metamorphosis, modification, deformation
美形 **bikei** beautiful form/woman
造形 **zōkei** molding, modeling
造形美術 **zōkei bijutsu** the plastic arts
弧形 **kokei** arc
屋形 **yakata** house, mansion, boat cabin

屋形船 **yakatabune** houseboat, barge, pleasure boat
染形 **so(me)gata** dyeing stencil
星形 **hoshigata** star-shaped
10 原形 **genkei** original form
原形質 **genkeishitsu** protoplasm
矩形 **kukei** rectangle
扇形 **ōgigata, senkei** fan shape, sector, segment
11 隊形 **taikei** (troop) formation, order
基形 **kikei** basic form, type
菱形 **hishigata** diamond shape, rhombus
球形 **kyūkei** spherical, globular
異形 **ikei** heteromorphous
　　 igyō grotesque, fantastic
魚形 **gyokei** fish-like, fish-shaped
12 象形 **shōkei** hieroglyphic; type of kanji resembling what it represents
象形文字 **shōkei moji** hieroglyphics
無形 **mukei** intangible
無形文化財 **mukei-bunkazai** intangible cultural asset
歯形 **hagata** teeth marks/impression
筒形 **tsutsugata** cylindrical, barrel-shaped
雲形 **kumogata, unkei** cloud form
雲形定規 **kumogata jōgi** French curve
13 楔形文字 **kusabigata moji, sekkei moji** cuneiform writing
新形 **shingata** new model/style
畸形 **kikei** deformity, abnormality
畸形児 **kikeiji** deformed child
詩形 **shikei** verse form
跡形 **atokata** traces, evidence
14 模形 **mokei** (scale) model; a mold
痩形 **ya(se)gata** slender build, skinny
網形 **amigata** netlike, reticular
語形 **gokei** word form
15 線形 **senkei** linear; alignment
賦形剤 **fukeizai** excipient, vehicle
輪形 **rinkei, wagata** circle, ring shape
16 整形 **seikei** orthopedics
整形手術 **seikei shujutsu** orthopedic operation
整形外科 **seikei geka** plastic surgery
蹄形 **teikei** horseshoe/U shape
蹄形磁石 **teikei jishaku** horseshoe magnet
錐形 **suikei** pyramidal
17 優形 **yasagata** slender figure
鍬形 **kuwagata** the horns on a traditional Japanese helmet
19 櫛形 **kushigata** comb-like; round-top, arched (window)
20 蠕形動物 **zenkei dōbutsu** legless animal
24 鱗形 **urokogata** imbricate, scale-like

———————— 3 ————————
2 丁字形 **teijikei** T-shaped

十字形 **jūjikei** cross, cross-shaped
八辺形 **hachihenkei** octagon
3 三角形 **sankakkei, sankakukei** triangle
土人形 **tsuchi ningyō** clay figure/doll
小判形 **kobangata** oval, elliptical
4 五辺形 **gohenkei** pentagon
五角形 **gokakkei, gokakukei** pentagon
六角形 **rokkakukei, rokkakkei** hexagon
円錐形 **ensuikei** cone
方錐形 **hōsuikei** square pyramid
心臓形 **shinzōgata** heart-shaped
5 半円形 **han'enkei** semicircular
半月形 **hangetsugata** semicircular
生人形 **i(ki)ningyō** lifelike doll; living doll
平方形 **heihōkei** a square
正方形 **seihōkei** square
四角形 **shikakukei** quadrilateral, square
6 多辺形 **tahenkei** polygon
自由形 **jiyūgata** freestyle (swimming)
7 豆人形 **mame-ningyō** miniature doll
完了形 **kanryōkei** perfect tense
見目形 **mimekatachi** features, looks
8 長円形 **chōenkei** ellipse, oval
長方形 **chōhōkei** rectangle
命令形 **meireikei** imperative form
空手形 **karategata** bad check; empty promise
9 連用形 **ren'yōkei** stem (of a verb)
連体形 **rentaikei** participial adjective
活用形 **katsuyōkei** inflected form
指人形 **yubi ningyō** finger/glove puppet
相似形 **sōjikei** similar figures (in geometry)
10 流線形 **ryūsenkei** streamlined
紋切形 **monki(ri)gata** conventional
馬蹄形 **bateikei** horseshoe shape
11 斜方形 **shahōkei** rhombus
菊人形 **kiku ningyō** chrysanthemum-decorated doll
12 無定形 **muteikei** amorphous
13 楕円形 **daenkei** ellipse, oval
16 操人形 **ayatsu(ri)ningyō** puppet, marionette
17 藁人形 **wara ningyō** straw effigy
　　 螺旋形 **rasenkei** spiral, helical
18 雛人形 **hina ningyō** (Girls' Festival) doll
21 蠟人形 **rōningyō** wax figure

———————— 4 ————————
4 五月人形 **gogatsu ningyō** Boys' Festival dolls
5 正三角形 **seisankakkei, seisankakukei** equilateral triangle
6 有形無形 **yūkei-mukei** tangible and intangible, material and spiritual
9 為替手形 **kawase tegata** bill (of exchange), draft
　　 約束手形 **yakusoku tegata** promissory note

———————— 5 ————————
5 平行四辺形 **heikōshihenkei** parallelogram

3

氵
土
扌
口
女
巾
犭
弓
彳
彡 4←
艹
宀
⺍
山
士
广
尸
囗

〔氵 汁 扌 扪 女 巾 犭 弓 彳 彡 艹 宀 ⺌ 山 亠 广 尸 口 〕

→4

12 等辺三角形 **tōhen sankakkei, tōhen sankakukei** equilateral triangle
等脚三角形 **tōkyaku sankakkei, tōkyaku sankakukei** isosceles triangle

―――――――― 6 ――――――――

2 二等辺三角形 **nitōhen sankakkei, nitōhen sankakukei** isosceles triangle

3j4.2

厖

BŌ, muku shaggy dog

―――――――― 1 ――――――――

3 厖大 **bōdai** enormous, extensive, bulky

―――――――― 5 ――――――――

3j5.1 / 710

参 參

SAN go, come, visit; three (in documents); participate
mai(ru) go, come, visit; visit a temple/shrine; be nonplussed
(o)mai(ri) visit to a temple/shrine

―――――――― 1 ――――――――

0 参じる/ずる **san(jiru/zuru)** go, come, visit
2 参入 **sannyū** enter (a market), participate in
3 参与 **san'yo** participate; councilor
参与者 **san'yosha** participant
参上 **sanjō** visit, call on
4 参内 **sandai** palace visit
5 参加 **sanka** participate, take part
参加者 **sankasha** participant
6 参会 **sankai** attendance (at a meeting)
参会者 **sankaisha** those present
参列 **sanretsu** attendance, presence
参列者 **sanretsusha** those present
参考 **sankō** reference, consultation
参考人 **sankōnin** person to consult
参考品 **sankōhin** reference materials
参考書 **sankōsho** reference book/work
8 参画 **sankaku** participate (in the planning)
参画者 **sankakusha** person participating in the planning
参事 **sanji** councilor
参事会 **sanjikai** council
参事官 **sanjikan** councilor
参拝 **sanpai** worship, visit (a shrine/tomb)
9 参院 **San'in** House of Councilors (short for 参議院)
参政 **sansei** participation in government
参政権 **sanseiken** suffrage, franchise
10 参宮 **sangū** visit to the Ise Shrine
11 参道 **sandō** path/approach to a shrine
参堂 **sandō** visit (a temple/home)
12 参勤交代 **sankin kōtai** daimyo's alternate-year residence in Edo

参着 **sanchaku** arrival; payable on sight
参着払 **sanchakubara(i)** payment on demand/sight
参賀 **sanga** congratulatory palace visit
参集 **sanshū** assembling people together
13 参照 **sanshō** refer to, see, compare
参禅 **sanzen** Zen meditation
参戦 **sansen** enter a war
参詣 **sankei** temple/shrine visit, pilgrimage
16 参謀 **sanbō** staff officer; adviser
参謀長 **sanbōchō** chief of staff
18 参観 **sankan** visit, inspect
参観人 **sankannin** visitor
20 参議 **sangi** participation in government; councilor
参議院 **Sangiin** House of Councilors
22 参籠 **sanrō** sequester oneself in a temple/shrine for prayer

―――――――― 2 ――――――――

2 人参 **ninjin** carrot
4 不参加 **fusanka** nonparticipation
日参 **nissan** visit (a temple) daily
5 古参 **kosan** seniority
古参者 **kosansha** senior, old hand
礼参 **reimai(ri)** thanksgiving visit to a shrine
6 寺参 **teramai(ri)** go to a temple to worship
7 抜参 **nu(ke)mai(ri)** secret pilgrimage
見参 **kenzan** see, meet
8 直参 **jikisan** immediate vassal/retainer
9 降参 **kōsan** surrender; be nonplussed
持参 **jisan** bring, take, bear
持参人 **jisannin** bearer (of a check)
持参金 **jisankin** dowry
10 帰参 **kisan** return to one's former service/master
宮参 **miyamai(ri)** visit to a shrine
11 遅参 **chisan** come late
推参 **suisan** visiting (unannounced); rude
12 寒参 **kanmai(ri)** midwinter visit to a shrine
朝参 **asamai(ri)** morning visit to a shrine/temple
衆参両院 **shū-san ryōin** both Houses of the Diet
13 墓参 **hakamai(ri), bosan** visit to a grave
新参 **shinzan** newcomer, novice
裸参 **hadakamai(ri)** visiting a shrine naked (in winter)
馳参 **ha(se)san(jiru)** hurry to

―――――――― 3 ――――――――

6 伊勢参 **Ise-mai(ri)** Ise pilgrimage
8 毒人参 **doku ninjin** poison hemlock
10 恵方参 **ehōmai(ri)** New Year's visit to a shrine/temple which lies in a lucky directiong

―――――――― 4 ――――――――

12 朝鮮人参 **Chōsen ninjin** ginseng

───── 6 ─────

3j6.1

殄

TEN all, completely

───── 7 ─────

3j7.1

髟

HYŌ long hair

───── 8 ─────

3j8.1 / 932

彩

SAI, irodo(ru) color

───── 1 ─────

6 彩色 **saishiki** coloring, coloration
彩色画 **saishikiga** colored painting/picture
8 彩画 **saiga** colored painting/picture
12 彩雲 **saiun** glowing clouds
14 彩層 **saisō** (the sun's) chromosphere
彩管 **saikan** artist's brush

───── 2 ─────

4 水彩画 **suisaiga** a watercolor
水彩画家 **suisai gaka** watercolor painter
水彩絵具 **suisai e(no)gu** watercolors
5 生彩 **seisai** luster, brilliance, vividness
6 多彩 **tasai** colorful, multicolored
色彩 **shikisai** color, coloration
光彩 **kōsai** brilliance, splendor
8 迷彩 **meisai** camouflage
9 虹彩 **kōsai** iris (of the eye)
11 淡彩 **tansai** light/thin coloring
異彩 **isai** conspicuous (color), standing out
12 極彩色 **gokusaishiki** brilliant coloring, full color (illustrations)
14 精彩 **seisai** luster; vitality

3j8.2 / 1149

彫

CHŌ, ho(ru) carve, engrave, chisel, sculpt

───── 1 ─────

8 彫刻 **chōkoku** sculpture, carving, engraving
ho(ri)kiza(mu) engrave, carve
彫刻刀 **chōkokutō** chisel, graver
彫刻師 **chōkokushi** engraver, carver, sculptor
彫刻家 **chōkokuka** engraver, carver, sculptor
彫物 **ho(ri)mono** carving, engraving, sculpture
彫金 **chōkin** chasing, metal carving
13 彫塑 **chōso** carving and (clay) modeling, the plastic arts

14 彫像 **chōzō** carved statue, sculpture

───── 2 ─────

3 丸彫 **marubo(ri)** carving in the round
4 手彫 **tebo(ri)** hand-carved
木彫 **kibo(ri), mokuchō** wood carving
9 浮彫 **u(ki)bo(ri)** relief, embossed carving
11 深彫 **fukabo(ri)** deep carving
粗彫 **arabo(ri)** rough carving

───── 3 ─────

10 高浮彫 **takau(ki)bo(ri)** high relief
16 薄肉彫 **usunikubo(ri)** low relief, bas-relief

参 → 参 **3j5.1**

3j8.3

彪

HYŌ spotted, mottled, patterned; small tiger

───── 9 ─────

3j9.1

須

SU, SHU, subeka(raku) should, ought, necessary

───── 1 ─────

9 須臾 **shuyu** instant, moment

───── 2 ─────

5 必須 **hissu** indispensable, essential, compulsory
必須科目 **hissu kamoku** required subject
8 長須鯨 **nagasu kujira** razorback whale
9 急須 **kyūsu** teapot
15 横須賀 **Yokosuka** (city, Kanagawa-ken)

───── 3 ─────

10 恵比須 **Ebisu** (a god of wealth)
恵比須顔 **ebisugao** smiling/beaming face

3j9.2

彭

HŌ flourishing, vigorous; sound of a drum

趁 → **3b9.19**

───── 10 ─────

3j10.1

髢

TEI, kamoji tress of false hair

3

氵
土
扌
口
女
巾
犭
弓
彳
彡 10←
艹
宀
罒
山
青
广
尸
口

───────── 11 ─────────

3j11.1 / 1827

彰

SHŌ clear

───────── 2 ─────────

8 表彰 **hyōshō** commendation
18 顕彰 **kenshō** manifest, exhibit, display

3j11.2

髦

BŌ bangs; long hair; excellence

3j11.3 / 1148

髪 髮

HATSU, kami hair (on the head)

───────── 1 ─────────

4 髪毛 **kami (no) ke** hair (on the head)
髪切虫 **kamiki(ri) mushi** long-horned beetle
7 髪床 **kamidoko** barbershop
8 髪油 **kamiabura** hair oil
9 髪洗 **kamiara(i)** washing the hair
髪洗粉 **kamiara(i)ko** shampoo powder
髪型 **kamigata** hairdo
12 髪結 **kamiyu(i)** hairdressing; hairdresser
髪結床 **kamiyu(i)doko** (Edo) barbershop
13 髪際 **kamigiwa** the hairline
髪飾 **kamikaza(ri)** hair ornament
14 髪綱 **kamizuna** rope made of hair
18 髪癖 **kamikuse** kinkiness, curliness

───────── 2 ─────────

1 一髪 **ippatsu** a hair, a hair's-breadth
3 下髪 **sa(ge)gami** hair hanging down the back
4 毛髪 **mōhatsu** hair
切髪 **ki(ri)gami** cut hair; widow's hair style (historical)
5 弁髪 **benpatsu** pigtail, queue
白髪 **hakuhatsu, shiraga** white/gray hair
白髪染 **shiragazo(me)** hair dye
白髪頭 **shiraga atama** gray(-haired) head
6 有髪 **uhatsu** unshorn (nun)
7 束髪 **sokuhatsu** bun hairdo
乱髪 **ranpatsu, mida(re)gami** disheveled hair
8 長髪 **chōhatsu** long hair
垂髪 **suberakashi** hair tied at the back and hanging down   **ta(re)gami** long flowing hair
金髪 **kinpatsu** blond hair
9 剃髪 **teihatsu** tonsure, shaving the head
前髪 **maegami** forelock, bangs
美髪 **bihatsu** beautiful hairg
洗髪 **senpatsu** washing the hair, shampoo
ara(i)gami washed hair

洋髪 **yōhatsu** Western hair style
海髪 **ogo** (a seaweed)
染髪剤 **senpatsuzai** hair dye
怒髪天突 **dohatsu ten (o) tsu(ku)** be infuriated
11 黒髪 **kurokami, kokuhatsu** black hair
理髪 **rihatsu** haircutting, barbering
理髪店 **rihatsuten** barbershop
理髪師 **rihatsushi** barber, hairdresser
断髪 **danpatsu** cutting one's hair short
12 短髪 **tanpatsu** short hair
落髪 **rakuhatsu** tonsure
散髪 **sanpatsu** get/give a haircut; disheveled hair
散髪屋 **sanpatsuya** barber
結髪 **keppatsu** hairdressing, hairdo
間髪入 **kanhatsu (o) i(rezu)** imminently; immediately
14 遺髪 **ihatsu** lock of the deceased's hair
総髪 **sōhatsu** hair swept back and tied at the back of the head
銀髪 **ginpatsu** silvery hair
15 調髪 **chōhatsu** barbering
調髪師 **chōhatsushi** barber
16 頭髪 **tōhatsu** hair (on the head)
17 濡髪 **nu(re)gami** newly-washed/glossy hair
18 襟髪 **erigami** hair at the back of the head/neck
20 辮髪 **benpatsu** pigtail, queue

───────── 3 ─────────

4 日本髪 **nihongami** Japanese hairdo
8 若白髪 **wakashiraga** prematurely gray hair
10 振分髪 **fu(ri)wa(ke)gami** hair parted and hanging down
12 間一髪 **kan ippatsu** a hair's breadth

───────── 4 ─────────

2 九十九髪 **tsukumogami** old woman's hair
6 危機一髪 **kiki-ippatsu** imminent/hairbreadth danger

───────── 12 ─────────

3j12.1 / 854

影

EI, kage light; shadow, silhouette, image, reflection, figure, trace

───────── 1 ─────────

7 影身 **kagemi** person's shadow
8 影法師 **kagebōshi** person's shadow
影武者 **kagemusha** general's double; man behind the scenes, wirepuller
12 影絵 **kagee** shadow picture, silhouette
14 影像 **eizō** image
19 影響 **eikyō** effect, influence
影響力 **eikyōryoku** effect, influence
影響下 **eikyōka** under the influence of

———————— 2 ————————

2 人影 **hitokage, jin'ei** person's shadow, human form
4 幻影 **gen'ei** illusion, phantom
  片影 **hen'ei** shadow, sign, glimpse
  月影 **getsuei, tsukikage** moonlight
  日影 **hika(ge)** sunlight; shadow
  火影 **hokage** (forms moving in the) firelight
5 半影 **han'ei** penumbra
6 近影 **kin'ei** recent portrait/photograph
  帆影 **hokage** a sail (seen in the distance)
  灯影 **tōei** flicker of light
7 投影 **tōei** projection
  投影面 **tōeimen** plane of projection
  投影機 **tōeiki** projector
  形影 **keiei** a form and its shadow
  見影 **mi(ru) kage (mo nai)** dilapidated (beyond recognition)
8 孤影 **koei** a lone figure
  物影 **monokage** a form, shape
9 面影 **omokage** face, looks; trace, vestiges
10 射影 **shaei** projection (in math)
  残影 **zan'ei** traces, relics
  倒影 **tōei** reflection
  陰影 **in'ei** shadow; shading; gloom
  真影 **shin'ei** portrait, photograph
  隻影 **sekiei** a glimpse/sign/shadow
11 斜影 **shaei** obliquely cast shadow
  淡影 **tan'ei** adumbration, hint
  黒影 **kokuei** dark shadow
  船影 **sen'ei** signs/sight of a ship
12 御影 **gyoei** portrait of a noble
  御影石 **mikage ishi** granite
  雲影 **un'ei** a cloud
13 暗影 **an'ei** shadow, gloom
  照影 **shōei** portrait
15 潮影 **shiokage** ripply wave pattern
  撮影 **satsuei** photography, filming
  撮影所 **satsueijo** movie studio
  敵影 **tekiei** signs of the enemy

———————— 3 ————————

12 御真影 **goshin'ei** emperor's portrait
  朝日影 **asahikage** morning sunshine

髴 → 彿 3i5.1

3j12.2

髯

ZEN, hige beard (on the cheeks)

髪 → 髪 3j11.3

3j12.3

髱

HŌ heavy beard **tabo, tsuto** knot of hair at the back of the head; young woman

———————— 13 ————————

3j13.1

髷

KYOKU, mage topknot

———————— 2 ————————

3 丸髷 **marumage** married woman's hairdo

3j13.2

髭

SHI, hige mustache

———————— 2 ————————

5 付髭 **tsu(ke)hige** false mustache/beard
14 鼻髭 **hanahige** mustache

———————— 3 ————————

4 不精髭 **bushōhige** stubbly beard
12 無精髭 **bushōhige** stubbly beard

———————— 22 ————————

鬣 → 3s22.1

3

氵土扌口女巾犭弓彳彡艹宀丷山幸广尸口

13→

———————— 艹 3k ————————

芝	艾	甘	芋	芒	共	芍	芳	芯	芦	芙	芹	芭
2.1	2.2	0a5.32	3.1	3.2	3.3	3.4	4.1	4.2	4.3	4.4	4.5	4.6
芽	花	苅	芬	芥	芰	芸	芫	首	苗	苒	苺	英
3k5.9	4.7	4.8	4.9	4.10	4.11	4.12	4.13	5.1	5.2	5.3	5.4	5.5
茉	茂	苹	芽	苙	苴	若	苞	范	茄	苡	苑	苻
5.6	5.7	5.8	5.9	5.10	5.11	5.12	5.13	5.14	5.15	5.16	5.17	5.18
茄	苧	苓	荅	茎	苦	苫	茅	苔	昔	荐	苟	苟
5.19	5.20	5.21	5.22	5.23	5.24	5.25	5.26	5.27	5.28	5.29	5.30	5.31

3

氵
土
扌
口
女
巾
彳
犭
弓
彳
彡
→
宀
⺌
山
圭
广
尸
口

苣 5.32	尭 3b9.3	茸 6.1	革 6.2	茜 6.3	茉 6.4	茗 6.5	荊 2f7.3	茫 6.6	茹 6.7	茲 6.8	茯 6.9	荏 6.10
茨 6.11	荘 6.12	草 6.13	荸 6.14	茖 6.15	荞 6.16	巷 3k6.17	巷 6.17	荒 6.18	茶 6.19	荅 6.20	荔 6.21	莚 6f6.13
荀 6.22	茴 6.23	茵 6.24	華 7.1	莪 7.2	莢 7.3	莱 3k8.3	菟 0a8.5	莨 7.4	莉 7.5	莇 7.6	莊 3k6.12	莎 7.7
涺 3k13.11	荻 7.8	莅 7.9	荷 7.10	莠 7.11	莫 7.12	莫 7.13	莖 3k5.23	莞 7.14	荵 7.15	恭 7.16	荼 7.17	莟 7.18
莓 3k5.4	荳 7.19	菫 8.1	菓 8.2	莱 8.3	著 8.4	莨 8.5	菽 8.6	菽 8.7	菻 8.8	菘 8.9	菲 8.10	萠 3k8.11
萌 8.11	萍 8.12	菠 8.13	范 8.14	菰 8.15	黄 8.16	萁 8.17	萎 8.18	萋 8.19	菱 8.20	菩 8.21	菖 8.22	菎 8.23
葛 3k9.22	菁 8.24	菜 8.25	萱 8.26	菅 8.27	萆 3f5.5	萚 3q8.6	菟 8.28	萃 8.29	菊 8.30	萄 8.31	菌 8.32	菫 9.1
萬 0a3.8	著 3k8.4	韭 9.2	萸 9.3	葯 9.4	萩 9.5	萪 9.6	葫 9.7	葭 9.8	葭 9.9	葩 9.10	葹 9.11	葆 9.12
落 9.13	葎 9.14	葬 9.15	萼 9.16	葵 9.17	葱 9.18	葱 9.19	葉 9.20	葛 9.21	募 9.22	葢 9.23	3k10.15	萵 9.24
葺 9.25	萱 9.26	蚕 9.27	葷 9.28	蔻 9.29	蒂 3k11.8	菟 3k8.28	蓮 3k10.31	蓬 3k10.32	葡 9.30	黄 3k8.16	靭 2f10.4	靫 2f10.4
靫 2f10.4	蒹 10.1	蒴 10.2	蒟 10.3	蔀 10.4	蒜 10.5	蒻 10.6	蒲 10.7	蒋 10.8	蓚 3k11.5	蓍 10.9	蓐 10.10	曹 4c7.10
蓍 10.11	蒐 10.12	蓆 10.13	夢 10.14	蓋 10.15	蓄 10.16	蒭 0a10.6	蓁 10.17	墓 10.18	幕 10.19	蓉 10.20	蓽 10.21	蒼 10.22
蒙 10.23	蓑 10.24	蒿 10.25	蒡 10.26	蓊 10.27	蓙 10.28	蓆 10.29	蓮 10.30	蓬 10.31	靹 3k11.24	靴 10.34	蔦 11.1	
蔚 11.2	蔟 11.3	蔬 11.4	蒋 11.5	蔆 11.6	蕈 11.7	蔕 11.8	蔡 11.9	蓼 11.10	蔑 11.11	慕 11.12	摹 11.13	暮 11.14
蔓 11.15	蓿 11.16	蔲 11.17	蔲 3k11.17	蔘 11.18	蔗 11.19	蔔 11.20	鞁 11.21	鞍 11.22	鞅 11.23	鞆 11.24	鞄 11.25	蔽 12.1
蕀 12.2	蕐 12.3	蕩 12.4	蕕 12.5	蕉 12.6	蕪 12.7	蕎 12.8	蕃 12.9	蕈 12.10	蕘 12.11	蕋 3k12.14	蕋 12.12	蕁 12.13
蕊 12.14	蕁 3k9.16	蕨 12.15	蒲 12.16	藏 12.17	鞋 12.18	鞍 12.19	鞐 12.20	鞏 12.21	蕭 13.1	薊 13.2	薮 3k15.1	薪 13.3
蕗 13.4	薐 13.5	薜 13.6	薛 13.7	薙 13.8	蕷 13.9	薤 13.10	薄 13.11	薀 13.12	薇 13.13	薩 13.14	薬 13.15	燕 13.16
薯 3k14.3	薫 13.17	蕾 13.18	薑 13.19	薔 13.20	薜 13.21	薨 13.22	薗 3s10.1	蟇 13.23	薈 13.24	薦 13.25	貌 14.1	藉 14.2
薰 3k13.17	舊 4c1.1	薯 14.3	薑 14.4	薺 14.5	藁 14.6	艱 14.7	藪 15.1	藷 3k16.3	藕 15.2	藤 15.3	藩 15.4	藥 3k13.15
藝 3k4.12	藍 15.5	藜 15.6	繭 15.7	藏 3k12.17	鞭 15.8	鞳 15.9	蘇 16.1	龍 16.2	藷 16.3	藹 16.4	藕 16.5	蘋 16.6

蘊	蘸	藻	藥	蘆	蘭	蘭	轉	斂	蘚	蘽	蘖	蘗
16.7	3k16.1	16.8	3k12.14	3k4.3	16.9	16.10	16.11	17.1	17.2	17.3	4a13.10	17.4

蘯	驀	蘭	鞳	韃	蘿	韆
5h12.1	17.5	3k16.9	17.6	18.1	19.1	20.1

3

̣ 氵
土
扌
口
女
巾
犭
弓
彳
彡
艹 3 ←
宀
⺌
⺤
耂
广
尸
口

3k2.1 / 250

芝 **SHI, shiba** lawn, turf

――― 1 ―――
4 芝刈 **shibaka(ri)** lawn mowing
  芝刈機 **shibaka(ri)ki** lawn mower
5 芝生 **shibafu** lawn
6 芝地 **shibachi** grass plot, lawn
8 芝居 **shibai** stage play, theater
  芝居小屋 **shibaigoya** playhouse, theater
  芝居気 **shibaigi** striving for dramatic effect
9 芝草 **shibakusa** lawn

――― 2 ―――
6 安芝居 **yasushibai** cheap theater
7 伽芝居 **(o)togi shibai** fairy play, play for children
8 東芝 **Tōshiba** (company name)
9 独芝居 **hito(ri)shibai** one-man show
10 紙芝居 **kamishibai** picture-card show
13 猿芝居 **saru shibai** tricks performed by a monkey

――― 3 ―――
1 一人芝居 **hitori shibai** one-man show
2 人形芝居 **ningyō shibai** puppet show

3k2.2

艾 **GAI, mogusa** moxa
  yomogi mugwort

――― 2 ―――
8 苦艾 **nigayomogi** wormwood

甘→ **0a5.32**

――― 3 ―――

3k3.1 / 1909

芋 **U, imo** potato

――― 1 ―――
0 じゃが芋 **jagaimo** (white/Irish) potato

――― 2 ―――
7 里芋 **satoimo** taro
8 長芋 **nagaimo** yam

11 菊芋 **kikuimo** (Jerusalem) artichoke
12 焼芋 **ya(ki)imo** baked/roasted sweet potato

――― 3 ―――
16 薩摩芋 **satsumaimo** sweet potato

3k3.2

芒 **BŌ, nogi** beard (of grains)
  susuki eulalia (a long grass associated with autumn)

――― 1 ―――
12 芒硝 **bōshō** Glauber's salt, mirabilite

――― 2 ―――
6 光芒 **kōbō** shaft/flash of light

3k3.3 / 196

共 **KYŌ, tomo** both, all, as well as, including, together with

――― 1 ―――
3 共々 **tomodomo** together with
4 共切 **tomogi(re)** the same cloth
5 共存 **kyōson, kyōzon** coexistence
  共用 **kyōyō** common use, shared
  共犯 **kyōhan** complicity
  共犯者 **kyōhansha** accomplice
  共立 **kyōritsu** joint, common
6 共同 **kyōdō** cooperation, collaboration, joint, collective
  共同体 **kyōdōtai** community
  共同者 **kyōdōsha** collaborator
  共同性 **kyōdōsei** cooperation
  共有 **kyōyū** joint ownership
  共有地 **kyōyūchi** public land, a common
  共有者 **kyōyūsha** part owner, co-owner
  共有物 **kyōyūbutsu** joint property
  共有財産 **kyōyū zaisan** community property
7 共学 **kyōgaku** coeducation
8 共和制 **kyōwasei** republican form of government
  共和国 **kyōwakoku** republic
  共和党 **kyōwatō** republican party
9 共通 **kyōtsū** in common, shared
  共通点 **kyōtsūten** something in common
  共通語 **kyōtsūgo** common language
  共栄 **kyōei** mutual prosperity
  共栄圏 **kyōeiken** coprosperity sphere
  共食 **tomogu(i)** devouring each other

10 共倒 **tomodao(re)** mutual ruin
共益 **kyōeki** common benefit
共進会 **kyōshinkai** competitive exhibition, prize show
共振 **kyōshin** resonance
11 共済 **kyōsai** mutual aid
共済組合 **kyōsai kumiai** mutual aid society
共著 **kyōcho** coauthorship
共産 **kyōsan** communist
共産主義 **kyōsan shugi** communism
共産国家 **kyōsan kokka** communist state
共産党 **kyōsantō** communist party
共産圏 **kyōsanken** communist bloc
共訳 **kyōyaku** joint translation
12 共営 **kyōei** joint management
13 共働 **tomobatara(ki)** (husband and wife) both working, dual income
共催 **kyōsai** joint sponsorship
共寝 **tomone** sleeping together
共感 **kyōkan** sympathy, response
14 共演 **kyōen** coacting, costarring
共鳴 **kyōmei** resonance; sympathy
15 共稼 **tomokase(gi)** (husband and wife) both working, dual income
共編 **kyōhen** joint editorship
16 共謀 **kyōbō** conspiracy

───── 2 ─────
2 二共 **futa(tsu) tomo** both
4 中共 **Chūkyō** Chinese Communists, Communist China (short for 中国共産党)
公共 **kōkyō** public society, community
公共心 **kōkyōshin** public spirit, community-mindedness
公共団体 **kōkyō dantai** public body/organization
公共事業 **kōkyō jigyō** public works, utilities
反共 **hankyō** anticommunist
日共 **Nikkyō** Japan Communist Party (short for 日本共産党)
6 防共 **bōkyō** anticommunist
共共 **tomodomo** together with
7 身共 **midomo** I, we
10 容共 **yōkyō** pro-communist
15 諸共 **morotomo** all together

───── 3 ─────
2 二人共 **futaritomo** both (persons)
6 名実共 **meijitsu tomo (ni)** in fact as well as in name
8 欧州共同体 **Ōshū Kyōdōtai** the European Community

───── 5 ─────
4 中華人民共和国 **Chūka Jinmin Kyōwakoku** People's Republic of China

3k3.4
芍 **SHAKU** peony
───── 1 ─────
16 芍薬 **shakuyaku** peony

───── 4 ─────
3k4.1 / 1775
芳 **HŌ** fragrance; (honorific prefix) **kanba(shii), kō(bashii)** fragrant; favorable
───── 1 ─────
4 芳心 **hōshin** your good wishes, your kindness
6 芳名 **hōmei** good name/reputation, your name
芳名録 **hōmeiroku** visitor's book, name list
7 芳志 **hōshi** your good wishes, your kindness
9 芳信 **hōshin** your kind/esteemed letter
芳香 **hōkō** fragrance, perfume, aroma(tic)
芳紀 **hōki** age (of a young lady)
10 芳書 **hōsho** your kind/esteemed letter
芳烈 **hōretsu** rich aroma; fine achievement
11 芳情 **hōjō** your kindness
14 芳墨 **hōboku** scented ink; your esteemed letter
芳墨帳 **hōbokuchō** autograph album
芳醇 **hōjun** mellow, rich

3k4.2
芯 **SHIN** pith of a rush; wick; inner part (pencil lead, apple core, collar stay)
───── 1 ─────
5 芯出 **shinda(shi)** centering, aligning
6 芯地 **shinji** padding
───── 2 ─────
6 灯芯 **tōshin** wick
10 帯芯 **obishin** sash padding

3k4.3
芦 蘆 **RO, ashi, yoshi** reed, rush

3k4.4
芙 **FU** lotus; Mt. Fuji
───── 1 ─────
13 芙蓉 **fuyō** lotus; cotton rose

3k4.5
芹 **KIN, seri** parsley

3

3k4.6

芭　BA plantain, banana plant

——————— 1 ———————

15 芭蕉 **bashō** plantain, banana plant
Bashō (haiku poet, 1644–1694)

芽 → 芽 **3k5.9**

3k4.7 / 255

花 花　KA, KE, hana flower
hana(yaka) showy, gaudy, gay
hana(yagu) become showy/
brilliant

——————— 1 ———————

2 花入 **hanai(re)** vase
3 花山 **Kazan** (emperor, 984–986)
4 花文字 **hanamoji** capital letter; flowers
planted to form characters
花円 **hanamaru** a small flowering cucumber
花水木 **hanamizuki** dogwood
花火 **hanabi** fireworks
花火線香 **hanabi senkō** joss-stick fireworks,
sparklers; flash-in-the-pan
5 花生 **hanai(ke)** vase
花弁 **hanabira, kaben** petal
花代 **hanadai** price for flowers; geisha fee
花市 **hanaichi** flower market
花卉 **kaki** flowering plants
花氷 **hanagōri** flowers frozen in ice
花台 **kadai** stand for a vase
花札 **hanafuda** floral playing cards
花立 **hanata(te)** vase
6 花合 **hanaa(wase)** floral playing cards
花色 **hana-iro** light blue
花守 **hanamori** one who guards flowers or
cherry blossoms against theft
花尽 **hanazu(kushi)** listing many types of
flowers; many-flowered design
花自動車 **hana jidōsha** flower-bedecked
automobile
7 花束 **hanataba** bouquet
花作 **hanazuku(ri)** floriculture; florist
花吹雪 **hanafubuki** falling cherry blossoms
花形 **hanagata** floral pattern; flourish,
ornament; star, popular person
花売 **hanau(ri)** flower seller
花見 **hanami** viewing cherry blossoms
花見酒 **hanamizake** viewing cherry
blossoms and drinking saké
花季 **kaki** the flowering season
花町 **hanamachi** section of town where
geishas live

花言葉 **hana kotoba** the language of flowers
8 花供養 **hanakuyō** Buddha's-birthday
commemoration
花押 **kaō** signature, handwritten seal
花実 **kajitsu** flowers and fruit; form and
content
花明 **hanaa(kari)** soft brightness even at
evening due to an abundance of white
cherry blossoms
9 花信 **kashin** news of how the flowers are
blooming
花便 **hanadayo(ri)** news of how the flowers
are blooming
花冠 **kakan** corolla (of a flower)
花首 **hanakubi** the part where the flower
joins the stem
花持 **hanamo(chi)** how well cut flowers will
remain unwilted
花屋 **hanaya** flower shop, florist
花屋敷 **hana yashiki** flower garden
花相撲 **hanazumō** off-season sumo tournament
花柳 **karyū** blossoms and willows; demi-
monde; red-light district
花柳界 **karyūkai** geisha quarter, red-light
district
花柳病 **karyūbyō** venereal disease
花畑 **hanabatake** flower bed/garden
花神 **kashin** flower goddess; spirit of a flower
10 花茣蓙 **hana goza** floral-pattern mat
花時 **hanadoki** the cherry-blossom season
花時計 **hanadokei** flower-bed clock
花粉 **kafun** pollen
花恥 **hanaha(zukashii)** so beautiful as to put
a flower to shame
11 花野 **hanano** field of flowers
花野菜 **hanayasai** cauliflower
花瓶 **kabin, hanagame** vase
花道 **kadō** (the art of) flower arrangement
hanamichi runway from the stage
through the audience
花菖蒲 **hanashōbu** iris, blue flag
花崗岩 **kakōgan** granite
花梨 **karin** Chinese quince
花祭 **hanamatsu(ri)** Buddha's-birthday
festival
花盛 **hanazaka(ri)** in full bloom
花盗人 **hananusubito** one who steals flowers
or cherry-blossom branches
花紺青 **hana konjō** royal blue
花鳥 **kachō** flowers and birds
花鳥風月 **kachō-fūgetsu** the beauties of
nature; elegant pursuits
12 花婿 **hanamuko** bridegroom
花街 **kagai** red-light district

3

氵
辶
扌
口
女
巾
犭
弓
彳
彡
艹 4 ←
宀
⺌
山
土
广
尸
口

花落 **hanao(chi)** the part where the flower has fallen off
花葵 **hanaaoi** hollyhock
花椰菜 **hanayasai** cauliflower
花期 **kaki** the flowering season
花結 **hanamusu(bi)** rosette
花筵 **hana mushiro** floral-pattern mat
花筒 **hanazutsu** flower tube/vase
花軸 **kajiku** flower stalk
13 花嫁 **hanayome** bride
花嫁御寮 **hanayome goryō** bride
花園 **hanazono** flower garden
花電車 **hanadensha** decorated streetcar, (parade) float
14 花暦 **hanagoyomi** calendar with information about flower blooming seasons
花摘 **hanatsu(mi)** flower picking
花模様 **hanamoyō** floral pattern/design
花魁 **oiran** courtesan, prostitute
15 花器 **kaki** flower vase
花輪 **hanawa** wreath, garland
花鋏 **hanabasami** pruning shears
16 花壇 **kadan** flower bed/garden
花樹 **kaju** flowering tree
花曇 **hanagumo(ri)** cloudy weather in spring
17 花環 **hanawa** wreath, garland
19 花譜 **kafu** flower album
22 花籠 **hanakago** flower basket
23 花鰹 **hanagatsuo** dried bonito shavings

───────── 2 ─────────

1 一花 **hitohana** a flower; success
4 天花粉 **tenkafun** talcum powder
切花 **ki(ri)bana** cut flowers
火花 **hibana** sparks
5 出花 **debana** the first brew (of tea), fresh-brewed tea
生花 **i(ke)bana** flower arrangement
seika flower arrangement; natural flower
卯花 **u(no)hana** dcutzia (a flower); tofu lees/dregs
6 死花咲 **shi(ni)bana (o) sa(kaseru)** do something just before one's death to win glory
返花 **kae(ri)bana** flower blooming out of season, flower blooming for a second time
名花 **meika** famous flower
自花受粉 **jika jufun** self-pollination
7 尾花 **obana** (ears of) eulalia grass
初花 **hatsuhana** first flowers of the season
8 押花 **o(shi)bana** pressed flowers
国花 **kokka** national flower
9 造花 **zōka** (making) artificial flowers
活花 **i(ke)bana** flower arranging
草花 **kusabana, sōka** flowering plant, flower
香花 **kōge** incense and flowers

紅花 **benibana** safflower, saffron
10 残花 **zanka** a flower still in bloom
浪花 **Naniwa** (old name for Ōsaka and vicinity)
浪花節 **naniwabushi** samisen-accompanied recital of ancient tales
挿花 **sa(shi)bana** flowers in a vase/lapel
徒花 **adabana** blossom yielding no seeds
桜花 **ōka, sakurabana** cherry blossoms
梅花 **baika** plum blossoms
紙花 **kamibana** paper flowers
11 菊花 **kikka** chrysanthemum
異花受精 **ika jusei** cross-pollination
盛花 **mo(ri)bana** heaped-up flower arrangement
釣花 **tsu(ri)bana** flowers in a hanging vase
雪花 **sekka** snowflakes
12 湯花 **yubana, yu (no) hana** flowers of sulfur, hot-springs encrustation
落花 **rakka** falling/scattered petals
落花生 **rakkasei** peanuts
落花狼藉 **rakka-rōzeki** outrage, assault, rape
棉花 **menka** cotton boils, raw cotton
無花果 **ichijiku** fig
雄花 **obana** male flower
開花 **kaika** bloom, flower, blossom
14 綿花 **menka** (raw) cotton
総花 **sōbana** gratuities to everyone
総花式 **sōbanashiki** across-the-board (pay raise)
雌花 **mebana** female flower
18 顕花植物 **kenka shokubutsu** flowering plant

───────── 3 ─────────

3 女郎花 **ominaeshi** (a yellow-flowered plant)
5 打上花火 **u(chi)a(ge) hanabi** skyrocket, fireworks
石南花 **shakunage** rhododendron
石楠花 **shakunage** rhododendron
6 両手花 **ryōte (ni) hana** have a double advantage; sit between two pretty women
両性花 **ryōseika** bisexual flower
迎春花 **geishunka** flowers which bloom around New Year's time
虫媒花 **chūbaika** insect-pollinated flower
7 沈丁花 **jinchōge, chinchōge** (sweet-smelling) daphne
8 茉莉花 **matsurika** jasmine
金盞花 **kinsenka** marigold
金鳳花 **kinpōge** buttercup
9 風媒花 **fūbaika** wind-pollinated flower
10 高嶺花 **takane (no) hana** flower on an inaccessible height; the unattainable
11 雪月花 **setsugekka** snow, moon, and flowers
鳥媒花 **chōbaika** bird-pollinated flower

12 無駄花 **mudabana** flower which bears no
　　　 seed/fruit
　　紫陽花 **ajisai** hydrangea
14 鳳仙花 **hōsenka** a balsam

3k4.8

苅

　　ka(ru) cut (grass), mow

3k4.9

芬

　　FUN fragrance

———————— 1 ————————

3 芬々 **funpun** fragrant

3k4.10

芥

　　KAI mustard; tiny; trash
　　karashi mustard
　　akuta, gomi trash, rubbish

———————— 1 ————————

2 芥子 **karashi** mustard　**keshi** poppy
　芥子泥 **karashidei** mustard plaster
　芥子菜 **karashina** mustard plant, rape
　芥子粒 **keshitsubu** poppy seed; something
　　　tiny
　芥子漬 **karashizu(ke)** mustard pickles
8 芥取 **gomito(ri)** dustpan; garbage collector
9 芥屋 **gomiya** garbage man
11 芥捨場 **gomisu(te)ba** garbage dump
13 芥溜 **gomita(me)** garbage heap
15 芥箱 **gomibako** garbage box/bin, waste basket

———————— 2 ————————

12 厨芥 **chūkai** (kitchen) garbage
14 塵芥 **chiriakuta, jinkai** dust and garbage,
　　　trash

3k4.11

芟

　　SEN, SAN, ka(ru) cut, mow

3k4.12 / 435

芸　藝

　　　GEI art, craft; accomplish-
　　　ment, (dog's) trick

———————— 1 ————————

2 芸人 **geinin** artiste, performer
　芸子 **geiko** geisha
4 芸文 **geibun** art and literature
6 芸名 **geimei** stage/professional name
　芸当 **geitō** performance, feat, trick, stunt

7 芸妓 **geigi** geisha
8 芸事 **geigoto** accomplishments
　芸苑 **geien** art and literary circles
　芸林 **geirin** art and literary circles
　芸者 **geisha** geisha
9 芸風 **geifū** (acting) style, (musical) technique
10 芸能 **geinō** (public) entertainment; accom-
　　　plishments, attainments
　芸能人 **geinōjin** an entertainment personal-
　　　ity, star
　芸能界 **geinōkai** the entertainment world,
　　　show business
11 芸術 **geijutsu** art
　芸術至上主義 **geijutsushijō shugi** art for
　　　art's sake
　芸術的 **geijutsuteki** artistic
　芸術院 **Geijutsuin** Academy of Art
　芸術家 **geijutsuka** artist
　芸術祭 **geijutsusai** art festival
12 芸無 **geina(shi)** unaccomplished
15 芸談 **geidan** talk about one's art

———————— 2 ————————

1 一芸 **ichigei** an art
3 工芸 **kōgei** technical arts
　工芸学 **kōgeigaku** technology, polytechnics
　工芸美術 **kōgei bijutsu** applied fine arts
　工芸品 **kōgeihin** industrial-art objects
　才芸 **saigei** talent and accomplishment
4 文芸 **bungei** literary arts
　文芸学 **bungeigaku** the science of literature
　文芸欄 **bungeiran** literary column
　手芸 **shugei** handicrafts
　手芸品 **shugeihin** handicrafts
5 民芸 **mingei** folkcraft, folk art
6 多芸 **tagei** versatility, varied accomplishments
　曲芸 **kyokugei** acrobatics
　曲芸師 **kyokugeishi** acrobat, tumbler
　至芸 **shigei** consummate artistic skill
　安芸 **Aki** (ancient kuni, Hiroshima-ken)
　百芸 **hyakugei** jack-of-all-trades
7 技芸 **gigei** arts, crafts, accomplishments
　学芸 **gakugei** art and science, culture
　学芸会 **gakugeikai** (school) literary program
　足芸 **ashigei** foot tricks
8 非芸術的 **higeijutsuteki** inartistic
　表芸 **omotegei** one's principal accomplish-
　　　ment
　武芸 **bugei** marital arts
10 陶芸 **tōgei** ceramic art
　遊芸 **yūgei** music and dancing
　家芸 **(o)iegei** one's speciality
　旅芸人 **tabigeinin** itinerant performer
12 無芸 **mugei** having no accomplishments
13 隠芸 **kaku(shi)gei** parlor trick, hidden talent
　農芸 **nōgei** (the art of) agriculture, husbandry
　園芸 **engei** gardening

3

氵 土 扌 口 女 巾 犭 弓 彳 彡 艹 ← 4
宀 ⺌ 山 寺 广 尸 口

園芸家 **engeika** gardener, horticulturist
腹芸 **haragei** communicating by other than
    words and gestures, force of personality
14 演芸 **engei** entertainment, performance
演芸会 **engeikai** an entertainment, variety
    show
演芸者 **engeisha** performer
15 諸芸 **shogei** arts, accomplishments

────── 3 ──────

4 手工芸 **shukōgei** handicraft(s)
5 旦那芸 **dannagei** amateurism
6 名人芸 **meijingei** virtuosity
10 素人芸 **shirōtogei** amateur's skill
12 御家芸 **oiegei** one's specialty
13 殿様芸 **tonosamagei** dilettantism, amateurism

────── 4 ──────

9 美術工芸 **bijutsu kōgei** artistic handicrafts,
    arts and crafts

3k4.13

芫

GEN, GAN (a type of vetch)

苣 → 3k5.32

────── 5 ──────

3k5.1

苜

MOKU clover, medic

────── 1 ──────

14 苜蓿 **mokushuku, umagoyashi** clover, medic,
    alfalfa

3k5.2 / 1468

苗

BYŌ, MYŌ, **nae, nawa** seedling,
sapling, shoot

────── 1 ──────

4 苗木 **naegi** sapling, seedling
5 苗半作 **naehansaku** The seedlings determine
    the harvest.
苗代 **nawashiro, naeshiro** bed for rice
    seedlings
苗字 **myōji** surname
7 苗床 **naedoko** seedbed, nursery
10 苗圃 **byōho** seedbed, nursery

────── 2 ──────

6 早苗 **sanae** rice seedlings/sprouts
12 痘苗 **tōbyō** vaccine
14 種苗 **shubyō** seeds and seedlings

3k5.3

苒

ZEN dense growth

3k5.4

苺 莓

BAI, MAI, **ichigo** strawberry

────── 2 ──────

4 木苺 **kiichigo** raspberry

3k5.5 / 353

英

EI Britain, England, English; brilliant,
talented, gifted

────── 1 ──────

2 英人 **eijin** Briton, Englishman
3 英才 **eisai** gifted, talented
4 英文 **eibun** English, English composition
英文学 **eibungaku** English literature
5 英字 **eiji** English/roman letters
英字新聞 **eiji shinbun** English-language
    newspaper
英主 **eishu** wise ruler
6 英気 **eiki** energetic spirit, enthusiasm
英会話 **eikaiwa** English conversation
英名 **eimei** fame, glory, renown
英吉利 **Igirisu** England
英米 **Ei-Bei** Britain and the U.S.
7 英学 **eigaku** study of English
英学者 **eigakusha** English scholar
8 英京 **Eikyō** London, the British capital
英法 **Eihō** British/English law
英国 **Eikoku** Britain, the U.K.
英国人 **Eikokujin** Briton, Englishman
英明 **eimei** intelligent, clear-sighted
英和 **ei-wa** English-Japanese (dictionary)
9 英俊 **eishun** genius, prodigy, gifted person
英姿 **eishi** impressive figure, noble mien
11 英断 **eidan** decisive judgment, resolute step
英訳 **eiyaku** English translation
英貨 **Eika** British currency; British-made
    goods
12 英雄 **eiyū** hero
英雄主義 **eiyū shugi** heroism
英雄的 **eiyūteki** heroic
13 英傑 **eiketsu** great man, hero
英詩 **eishi** English poem/poetry
英資 **eishi** brilliant qualities, fine character
    Eishi British (investment) capital
14 英魂 **eikon** departed spirit
英語 **eigo** the English language
英語版 **eigoban** English-language edition

英領 **Eiryō** British territory
15 英邁 **eimai** wise and brave, great
英霊 **eirei** spirits of the war dead

——————— 2 ———————

3 大英帝国 **Dai-Ei Teikoku** the British
    Empire
大英断 **daieidan** bold decision
4 反英 **han-Ei** anti-British
日英 **Nichi-Ei** Japan and Britain/England
5 石英 **sekiei** quartz
石英灯 **sekieitō** quartz lamp
石英岩 **sekieigan** quartzite
6 在英 **zai-Ei** in Britain
米英 **Bei-Ei** the U.S. and Britain
7 対英 **tai-Ei** toward/with Britain
8 育英 **ikuei** education
和英 **Wa-Ei** Japanese-English (dictionary),
    Japan and England
9 俊英 **shun'ei** talent, genius, gifted person
独英 **Doku-Ei** Germany and Britain,
    German-English (dictionary)
11 排英 **hai-Ei** anti-British
12 渡英 **to-Ei** going to Britain
13 滞英 **tai-Ei** staying in Britain
15 駐英 **chū-Ei** resident/stationed in Britain
16 親英 **shin-Ei** pro-British, pro-English

——————— 3 ———————

12 紫雲英 **genge** Chinese milk vetch
13 蒲公英 **tanpopo** dandelion

3k5.6

茉   **MATSU** jasmine

——————— 1 ———————

10 茉莉花 **matsurika** jasmine

3k5.7 / 1467

茂 楙   **MO, shige(ru)** grow thick/
         rank/luxuriantly

——————— 1 ———————

6 茂合 **shige(ri)a(u)** grow luxuriantly

——————— 2 ———————

5 生茂 **o(i)shige(ru)** grow luxuriantly
8 逆茂木 **sakamogi** abatis
16 繁茂 **hanmo** luxuriant/dense growth

3k5.8

苹   **HEI** duckweed, mugwort

3k5.9 / 1455

芽 芽   **GA, me** a sprout, bud, germ
          me(gumu) bud, sprout

——————— 1 ———————

0 芽キャベツ **mekyabetsu** Brussels sprouts
5 芽出度 **medeta(i)** happy, congratulatory
芽生 **meba(e)** bud, sprout
9 芽胞 **gahō** spore
11 芽接 **metsu(gi)** bud grafting, inlay graft

——————— 2 ———————

4 木芽 **ki(no)me, ko(no)me** leaf bud; Japanese-
    pepper bud
5 出芽 **shutsuga** germinate, sprout
幼芽 **yōga** germ (in grains)
6 肉芽 **nikuga** granulation, proud flesh
7 麦芽 **bakuga** malt
麦芽糖 **bakugatō** malt sugar, maltose
8 若芽 **wakame** young buds, sprouts, shoots
9 発芽 **hatsuga** germination, sprouting
胚芽 **haiga** embryo bud, germ
胚芽米 **haigamai** whole rice (with the germ)
胎芽 **taiga** propagule, brood bud
11 萌芽 **hōga** germination; germ, sprout
12 葉芽 **yōga** leaf bud
13 新芽 **shinme** sprout, bud, shoot
14 摘芽 **tekiga** thinning out buds
嫩芽 **donga** bud, sprout

3k5.10

苙   **RYŪ** (a kind of herb); pigsty

3k5.11

苴   **SHO** hemp

3k5.12 / 544

若   **JAKU, NYAKU, waka(i)** young
    mo(shi) if, supposing **mo(shikuwa)** or
    shi(ku) be equal to, compare with

——————— 1 ———————

0 若やぐ **waka(yagu)** be rejuvenated
2 若人 **wakōdo** young person, a youth
3 若干 **jakkan** some, a number of
若々 **wakawaka(shii)** youthful
4 若水 **wakamizu** first water drawn on New
    Year's Day
若手 **wakate** young person/man; younger
    member
若木 **wakagi** young tree, sapling

<table>
<tr><td>

5 若布 **wakame** (an edible seaweed)
若旦那 **wakadanna** young master/gentleman
若白髪 **wakashiraga** prematurely gray hair
6 若死 **wakaji(ni)** die young
若気 **wakage** youthful vigor
若年 **jakunen** youth
若年寄 **waka-doshiyo(ri)** young person who looks/acts old
若返 **wakagae(ru)** be rejuvenated
若向 **wakamu(ki)** intended for the young
7 若作 **wakazuku(ri)** made up to look young
若君 **wakagimi** young lord
若禿 **wakaha(ge)** premature baldness
8 若妻 **wakazuma** young wife
若芽 **wakame** young buds, sprouts, shoots
若若 **wakawaka(shii)** youthful
若松 **wakamatsu** young pine tree; New Year's pine-tree decorations
若枝 **wakaeda** young branch, shoot
若者 **wakamono** young person/people
若武者 **wakamusha** young warrior
9 若造 **wakazō** youngster, stripling
若狭 **Wakasa** (ancient kuni, Fukui-ken)
若後家 **wakagoke** young widow
若草 **wakakusa, wakagusa** young grass
10 若宮 **wakamiya** young prince; shrine dedicated to the son of the god of the main shrine; newly built shrine
若党 **wakatō** young attendant/samurai
11 若菜 **wakana** young greens/herbs
若盛 **wakazaka(ri)** the prime/bloom of youth
12 若湯 **wakayu** first hot bath on New Year's Day
若葉 **wakaba** new leaves, fresh verdure
若衆 **wakashu** young man
若紫 **wakamurasaki** light purple
13 若隠居 **waka-inkyo** early retirement
若殿 **wakatono** young lord
若殿原 **wakatonobara** young samurais
14 若様 **wakasama** young master
若緑 **wakamidori** fresh verture
15 若輩 **jakuhai** young fellow/people; novice
19 若鶏 **wakadori** (spring) chicken, pullet

————————— 2 —————————

6 老若 **rōjaku, rōnyaku** young and old
自若 **jijaku** composure, calmness
7 杜若 **kakitsubata** iris, flag
8 若若 **wakawaka(shii)** youthful
12 傍若無人 **bōjaku-bujin** arrogant, insolent
16 瞠若 **dōjaku** be astonished

————————— 4 —————————

9 神色自若 **shinshoku-jijaku** calm and composed, unruffled
10 泰然自若 **taizen-jijaku** imperturbable

</td><td>

3k5.13

苞 **HŌ** wrapping
tsuto (straw) wrapper; souvenir gift

————————— 2 —————————

3 山苞 **yamazuto** mountain souvenirs

3k5.14

范 **HAN** bee; law; mold (for casting)

3k5.15

茆 **BŌ, kaya** thatch
nunawa water shield

3k5.16

苡 **I** adlay; plantain

3k5.17

苑 **EN** garden, farm

————————— 2 —————————

4 内苑 **naien** inner garden/park
5 外苑 **gaien** outer garden/park
7 芸苑 **geien** art and literary circles
12 御苑 **gyoen** imperial garden
15 蕀苑 **kyokuen** milkwort

3k5.18

苻 **FU** (a kudzu-like plant)

3k5.19

茄 **KA** eggplant

————————— 1 —————————

2 茄子 **nasu, nasubi** eggplant

————————— 2 —————————

7 赤茄子 **akanasu** tomato

3k5.20

苧 **CHO, karamushi** Chinese silk plant, ramie
o hemp thread

————————— 1 —————————

11 苧麻 **choma, karamushi** ramie

</td></tr>
</table>

3k5.21

芰 TŌ, fuki butterbur, bog rhubarb

3k5.22

苓 REI, RYŌ plant, herb, mushroom

―――――― 2 ――――――

9 茯苓 bukuryō (a type of herbal mushroom)

3k5.23 / 1474

茎 莖 KEI, kuki stem, stalk

―――――― 2 ――――――

4 水茎 mizuguki writing brush
水茎跡 mizuguki (no) ato brush writing, calligraphy
5 包茎 hōkei phimosis
10 陰茎 inkei penis
根茎 konkei root stalk, rhizome
11 球茎 kyūkei (plant) bulb
12 歯茎 haguki the gums
13 塊茎 kaikei tuber

―――――― 3 ――――――

6 地下茎 chikakei rhizome

3k5.24 / 545

苦 KU, kuru(shimu/shigaru) suffer
kuru(shimeru) torment
kuru(shii) painful niga(i) bitter
niga(ru) scowl

―――――― 1 ――――――

3 苦々 niganiga(shii) unpleasant, disgusting, scandalous
苦土 kudo magnesia
4 苦切 niga(ri)ki(ru) look sour, scowl
苦手 nigate one's weak point; someone hard to deal with
苦心 kushin pains, efforts
5 苦汁 kujū bitter experience nigari brine
苦艾 nigayomogi wormwood
6 苦肉 kuniku (desperate measure) at personal sacrifice
苦行 kugyō penance, asceticism, mortification
苦行者 kugyōsha an ascetic
苦虫 nigamushi (looking as if having bit into) a bitter-tasting bug
7 苦吟 kugin laboriously compose (a poem)
苦役 kueki hard toil, drudgery; penal servitude
苦学 kugaku study under adversity

苦学生 kugakusei self-supporting student
苦労 kurō trouble, hardships, adversity
苦労人 kurōnin worldly-wise man
苦労性 kurōshō given to worrying
苦言 kugen frank advice, exhortation
8 苦使 kushi overwork, exploit
苦味 nigami bitter taste
苦味走 nigamibashi(tta) sternly handsome
苦苦 niganiga(shii) unpleasant, disgusting, scandalous
苦杯 kuhai bitter cup, ordeal, defeat
9 苦衷 kuchū anguish, distress
苦界 kukai, kugai the world of suffering; life of prostitution
10 苦悩 kunō suffering, agony, distress
苦紛 kuru(shi)magi(re) driven by distress, in desperation
苦笑 kushō, nigawara(i) bitter/wry smile
11 苦渋 kujū bitter and puckery; distress, agony
苦情 kujō complaint, grievance
12 苦寒 kukan coldest season of the year; 12th lunar month
苦痛 kutsū pain
苦悶 kumon agony, anguish
13 苦塩 nigashio, nigari brine
苦楽 kuraku joys and sorrows
苦戦 kusen hard fighting; hard-fought
苦節 kusetsu loyalty under adversity
14 苦境 kukyō distress, predicament, crisis
15 苦慮 kuryo worry over
苦熱 kunetsu oppressive heat
18 苦難 kunan hardships, adversity
苦闘 kutō bitter struggle, uphill battle

―――――― 2 ――――――

2 八苦 hakku the eight pains (Buddhism)
4 心苦 kokoroguru(shii) painful to think of, against one's conscience
5 四苦八苦 shiku-hakku agony, dire distress
6 死苦 shiku agony of death
気苦労 kigurō worry, cares, anxiety
7 労苦 rōku labor, pains, toil
困苦 konku hardships, adversity
忍苦 ninku endurance, stoicism
辛苦 shinku hardship, privation, trouble
見苦 miguru(shii) unsightly; disgraceful
8 刻苦 kokku hard work
苦苦 niganiga(shii) unpleasant, disgusting, scandalous
固苦 katakuru(shii) stiff, formal, strict
9 重苦 omokuru(shii) heavy, ponderous, oppressive, awkward (expression)
狭苦 semakuru(shii) cramped
10 胸苦 munaguru(shii) feeling oppressed in the chest
息苦 ikiguru(shii) stifling, suffocating, stuffy
病苦 byōku suffering from illness

3

氵
土
扌
口
女
巾
犭
弓
彳
彡
艹 ← 5 ←
宀
⺌
山
吉
广
尸
口

3

氵 汢 扌 口 女 巾 犭 弓 彳 彡
→5 艹 宀 ⺶ 言 广 尸 口

11 貧苦 **hinku** hardships of poverty
　　責苦 **se(me)ku** torture
12 堅苦 **katakuru(shii)** stiff-mannered, formal; punctilious
　　暑苦 **atsukuru(shii), atsuguru(shii)** oppressively hot, sultry, sweltering
　　痛苦 **tsūku** pain, anguish
　　　　ita(mi)kuru(shimu) suffer
　　悶苦 **moda(e)kuru(shimu)** writhe in pain
13 微苦笑 **bikushō** wry/bittersweet smile
　　寝苦 **neguru(shii)** unable to sleep well
14 聞苦 **ki(ki)guru(shii)** offensive to the ear
15 熱苦 **atsukuru(shii)** sultry, sweltering, stifling
　　憂苦 **yūku** sorrow, distress
17 艱苦 **kanku** hardships, privation

――――――― 3 ―――――――
5 生活苦 **seikatsuku** economic distress, hard times
8 取越苦労 **to(ri)ko(shi)gurō** needless worry
11 悪戦苦闘 **akusen-kutō** fight desperately
12 無茶苦茶 **muchakucha** mixed up, confused; nonsensical; reckless, like mad
13 滅茶苦茶 **mechakucha** incoherent; preposterous; mess, wreck, ruin
18 難行苦行 **nangyō-kugyō** penance, self-mortification

――――――― 4 ―――――――
3 千辛万苦 **senshin-banku** countless hardships
5 四苦八苦 **shiku-hakku** agony, dire distress
11 粒粒辛苦 **ryūryū-shinku** assiduous effort
13 愛別離苦 **aibetsuriku** parting from loved ones

3k5.25

苫

SEN, toma rush matting

――――――― 1 ―――――――
9 苫屋 **tomaya** rush-thatched cottage

3k5.26

茅

BŌ, kaya any of various grasses or rushes suitable for thatching

――――――― 1 ―――――――
9 茅屋 **bōoku** thatched cottage; my humble abode
12 茅場 **kayaba** field of grass/reeds
　　茅葺 **kaya(bu)(ki)** thatched

3k5.27

苔

TAI, koke moss, lichen

――――――― 1 ―――――――
0 苔むした **koke(mushita)** moss-covered
20 苔蘚 **taisen** moss, lichen

――――――― 2 ―――――――
4 水苔 **mizugoke** bog moss; encrustation
5 布苔 **funori** (a type of seaweed, used for laundry starch)
6 舌苔 **zettai** fur on the tongue
　　光苔 **hika(ri)-goke** a luminous moss, Schistostega osmundacea
8 岩苔 **iwagoke** rock moss
9 海苔 **nori** laver (an edible seaweed)
　　海苔巻 **norima(ki)** (vinegared) rice rolled in seaweed
20 蘚苔 **sentai** mosses
　　蘚苔学 **sentaigaku** bryology

――――――― 3 ―――――――
5 布海苔 **funori** (a type of seaweed, used for laundry starch)
8 青海苔 **aonori** green laver (edible seaweed)
12 焼海苔 **ya(ki)nori** toasted seaweed

――――――― 4 ―――――――
9 浅草海苔 **Asakusa nori** sheets of dried seaweed

3k5.28 / 764

昔

SEKI, SHAKU, mukashi antiquity, long ago

――――――― 1 ―――――――
3 昔々 **mukashi mukashi** Once upon a time ...
4 昔日 **sekijitsu** old/former times
6 昔気質 **mukashi-katagi** old-time spirit, old-fashioned
　　昔年 **sekinen** (many) years ago
8 昔者 **mukashimono** old folks
9 昔風 **mukashifū** old-fashioned
10 昔時 **sekiji** old/former times
13 昔話 **mukashibanashi** old tale, legend
　　昔馴染 **mukashinaji(mi)** old friend
14 昔語 **mukashigata(ri)** old story

――――――― 2 ―――――――
1 一昔 **hitomukashi** about ten years ago
3 大昔 **ōmukashi** remote antiquity, long long ago
4 今昔 **konjaku** past and present
8 昔昔 **mukashi mukashi** Once upon a time ...
12 幾昔 **ikumukashi** how ancient

3k5.29

荐

SEN mat; repeatedly

3k5.30

苛 **KA** harsh
iji(meru) torment, bully, pick on
saina(mu) torment, harass; chastise

——————— 1 ———————

5 苛立 **irada(tsu)** get irritated/exasperated
irada(teru) irritate, exasperate
8 苛性 **kasei** caustic
10 苛烈 **karetsu** severe, relentless
14 苛酷 **kakoku** harsh, rigorous, cruel

3k5.31

苟 **KŌ, iyashiku(mo)** any, at all, in the least

3k5.32

苣 **KYO** torch; lettuce

——————— 2 ———————

12 萵苣 **chisha, chisa** lettuce

堯 → 堯 3b9.3

——————— 6 ———————

3k6.1

茸 **JŌ** grow thick
take, kinoko mushroom

——————— 1 ———————

9 茸狩 **takega(ri)** mushroom gathering

——————— 2 ———————

8 松茸 **matsutake, matsudake** (a kind of edible mushroom)
12 椎茸 **shiitake** (a variety of edible mushroom)
14 鼻茸 **hanatake, biji** nasal polyp

3k6.2 / 1075

革 **KAKU** reform; leather
kawa leather

——————— 1 ———————

8 革表紙 **kawabyōshi** leather cover/binding
革命 **kakumei** revolution
革命的 **kakumeiteki** revolutionary, radical
革命家 **kakumeika** a revolutionary
革命歌 **kakumeika** revolutionary song
革具 **kawagu** leather goods
9 革草履 **kawazōri** leather sandals
10 革帯 **kawaobi** leather belt

革砥 **kawato** razor strop
革紐 **kawahimo** (leather) strap, leash
11 革袋 **kawabukuro** leather bag; wineskin
革細工 **kawazaiku** leathercraft
13 革靴 **kawagutsu** leather shoes/boots
革新 **kakushin** reform, innovation
革新派 **kakushinha** reformists
14 革製 **kawasei** made of leather
革緒 **kawao** sword strap; clog thong
革綴 **kawato(ji)** leather binding
15 革質 **kakushitsu** leathery

——————— 2 ———————

4 爪革 **tsumakawa** toe cover, mud guard (on a clog)
反革命 **hankakumei** counterrevolution
5 皮革 **hikaku** hides, leather
6 吊革 **tsu(ri)kawa** (hanging) strap
行革 **gyōkaku** administrative reform (short for 行政改革)
7 改革 **kaikaku** reform, reorganization
改革者 **kaikakusha** reformer
改革案 **kaikakuan** reform bill/measure
8 沿革 **enkaku** history, development
底革 **sokogawa** sole leather, sole of a shoe
9 変革 **henkaku** change, reform, revolution
負革 **o(i)kawa** sling, carrying strap (on a rifle)
背革 **segawa** leatherback (book)
研革 **to(gi)kawa** strop
10 帯革 **obikawa** leather belt
紐革 **himokawa** strap, thong
馬革 **bakaku** horsehide
14 製革 **seikaku** leather making, tanning
製革所 **seikakujo** tannery
製革業 **seikakugyō** the tanning industry
総革 **sōgawa** full-leather binding
15 敷革 **shi(ki)gawa** inner sole
調革 **shira(be)gawa** belt (on machinery)
17 擬革紙 **gikakushi** imitation leather

——————— 4 ———————

8 宗教改革 **shūkyō kaikaku** the Reformation
13 農地改革 **nōchi kaikaku** agrarian reform

3k6.3

茜 **SEN, akane** madder; madder red

——————— 1 ———————

6 茜色 **akane-iro** madder red, crimson

3k6.4

茱 **SHU** river ginger tree; oleaster

——————— 1 ———————

12 茱萸 **gumi** oleaster

3k6.5

茗 **MYŌ, MEI** tea

―――――― 1 ――――――

10 茗荷 **myōga** ginger

荊→荆 **2f7.3**

3k6.6

茫 **BŌ** far and wide; vague

―――――― 1 ――――――

3 茫々 **bōbō** vague; vast
9 茫洋 **bōyō** vast, boundless
12 茫然 **bōzen** vacantly, in a daze
　茫然自失 **bōzen-jishitsu** abstraction,
　　stupefaction, entrancement
13 茫漠 **bōbaku** vague; vast

―――――― 2 ――――――

9 茫茫 **bōbō** vague; vast
12 淼茫 **byōbō** vast (expanse of water)
　渺茫 **byōbō** vast, boundless
13 蒼茫 **sōbō** blue expanse; dusky

3k6.7

茹 **JO, yu(deru), u(deru)** (tr.) boil
yu(daru), u(daru) (intr.) boil

―――――― 1 ――――――

5 茹汁 **yu(de)jiru** broth
　茹玉子 **yu/u(de)tamago** boiled egg
7 茹卵 **yu/u(de)tamago** boiled egg

―――――― 2 ――――――

5 生茹 **namayu(de)** half-boiled
10 釜茹 **kamayu(de)** boiling in a kettle

3k6.8

茲 **JI** grow; increase; here; year

3k6.9

茯 **BUKU** (a type of mushroom)

―――――― 1 ――――――

8 茯苓 **bukuryō** (a type of herbal mushroom)

3k6.10

荏 **JIN, e** perilla

3k6.11

茨 **SHI** thatch; brier
ibara brier

―――――― 1 ――――――

4 茨木 **Ibaraki** (city, Ōsaka-fu)
9 茨城県 **Ibaraki-ken** (prefecture)

3k6.12 / 1327

荘 莊 **SŌ** solemn; villa, inn; village
SHŌ manor

―――――― 1 ――――――

9 荘重 **sōchō** solemn, sublime, impressive
13 荘園 **shōen** manor
17 荘厳 **sōgon** sublime, grand, majestic

―――――― 2 ――――――

3 山荘 **sansō** mountain villa/chalet
6 老荘 **Rō-Sō** Laozi and Zhongzi, Lao-tzu and
　　Chung-tzu; Taoism
7 別荘 **bessō** villa, country place

3k6.13 / 249

草 **SŌ** grass, small plants; original; first
draft; cursive handwriting
kusa grass, small plants

―――――― 1 ――――――

0 草する **sō(suru)** write, draft
　草むしり **kusa(mushiri)** weeding
2 草入水晶 **kusai(ri)zuishō** crystal with
　　impurities forming grass-blade patterns
3 草丈 **kusatake** height of a (rice) plant
　草々 **sōsō** in haste; (closing words of a letter)
　草山 **kusayama** grass-covered hill
4 草刈 **kusaka(ri)** grass cutting, mowing
　草双紙 **kusazōshi** storybook with pictures
　草分 **kusawa(ke)** pioneer
　草木 **sōmoku, kusaki** plants and trees,
　　vegetation
5 草本 **sōhon** herbs; draft, manuscript
　草市 **kusa ichi** market selling flowers for the
　　Obon festival
6 草仮名 **sōgana** hiragana
　草色 **kusa-iro** dark/emerald green
　草地 **kusachi, sōchi** grassland, meadow
7 草花 **kusabana, sōka** flowering plant, flower
8 草枕 **kusamakura** make an overnight stay
　　while traveling

草肥 **kusagoe** compost
草物 **kusamono** short plants (used in flower arranging)
草取 **kusato(ri)** weeding
9 草臥 **kutabi(reru)** be tired/exhausted
草草 **sōsō** in haste; (closing words of a letter)
草屋 **kusaya, sōoku** thatched hut
草屋根 **kusayane** thatched roof
草相撲 **kusazumō** amateur/sandlot sumo
草枯 **kusaga(re)** withering of the grass; autumn
草紅葉 **kusamomiji** colored grasses of autumn
草食 **sōshoku** herbivorous
10 草原 **sōgen** grassy plain, grasslands
　　kusahara meadow, a green
草案 **sōan** (rough) draft
草根木皮 **sōkon-mokuhi** medicinal herb roots and tree barks
草書 **sōsho** cursive form of kanji, "grass hand"
草紙 **sōshi** storybook
11 草野球 **kusa-yakyū** sandlot baseball
草深 **kusabuka(i)** grassy; backwoods, remote
草堂 **sōdō** thatched hut; my humble abode
草笛 **kusabue** reed whistle
12 草創 **sōsō** inauguration, inception
草創期 **sōsōki** initial/early period
草葉 **kusaba** blade of grass
草葺 **kusabu(ki)** thatch
15 草鞋 **waraji** straw sandals
草鞋虫 **warajimushi** sow bug, wood louse
草鞋銭 **warajisen** traveling money
草履 **zōri** sandals, zori
草履取 **zōrito(ri)** sandal-carrier (servant)
草稿 **sōkō** (rough) draft, notes, manuscript
18 草叢 **kusamura** in the grass
20 草競馬 **kusakeiba** local horse race

――――――― 2 ―――――――

2 七草 **nanakusa** the seven plants (of spring/autumn)
3 干草 **ho(shi)gusa, ho(shi)kusa** dry grass, hay
千草 **chigusa** great variety of flowering plants
上草履 **uwazōri** indoor sandals
下草 **shitakusa, shitagusa** grass/weeds growing in the shade of a tree
小草 **ogusa** small grasses
4 天草 **tengusa** agar-agar
水草 **suisō, mizukusa** aquatic plant
5 民草 **tamikusa, tamigusa** the people, populace
本草 **honzō** plants, (medicinal) herbs
甘草 **kanzō** licorice
仕草 **shigusa** treatment, behavior, mannerisms
芝草 **shibakusa** lawn
6 行草 **gyōsō** semicursive and cursive (kanji)

行草体 **gyōsōtai** semicursive and cursive forms/styles
7 伽草子 **(o)togizōshi** fairy-tale book
言草 **i(i)gusa** one's words, remarks
8 毒草 **dokusō** poisonous plant
若草 **wakakusa, wakagusa** young grass
青草 **aokusa** green grass
牧草 **bokusō** grass, pasturage, meadow
牧草地 **bokusōchi** pasture, grazing land
9 除草 **josō** weeding
除草器 **josōki** weeder
勁草 **keisō** (strong and constant as a) plant that resists the changing winds
通草 **akebi** (a type of shrub having tendrils)
浅草海苔 **Asakusa nori** sheets of dried seaweed
浮草 **u(ki)kusa** floating weeds, duckweed; precarious
海草 **kaisō** seaweeds, sea plants
革草履 **kawazōri** leather sandals
草草 **sōsō** in haste; (closing words of a letter)
枯草 **ka(re)kusa** dried grass, hay
香草 **kōsō** aromatic herbs
10 埋草 **u(me)kusa** (page) filler
起草 **kisō** draft, draw up
起草者 **kisōsha** drafter
莎草 **hamasuge** coco grass
唐草 **karakusa** arabesque
唐草模様 **karakusa moyō** arabesque design
桜草 **sakurasō** primrose
夏草 **natsugusa** grass in summer
眠草 **nemu(ri)gusa** mimosa
笑草 **wara(i)gusa** topic of amusement
11 野草 **yasō** wild grass/plants
　　nogusa grass in a field
偲草 **shino(bu)gusa** hare's-foot fern
道草食 **michikusa (o) ku(u)** dawdle/loiter along the way
萱草 **wasuregusa** day lily
12 着草臥 **kikutabi(re)** worn out
萱草 **wasuregusa** day lily
絵草紙 **ezōshi** picture book
詠草 **eisō** draft of a poem
13 煙草 **tabako** tobacco
煙草入 **tabako-i(re)** tobacco pouch, cigarette case
煙草盆 **tabakobon** tobacco tray
煙草飲 **tabakono(mi)** smoker
詩草 **shisō** draft of a poem
詰草 **tsumekusa** white Dutch clover
飼草 **ka(i)gusa** hay
14 摘草 **tsu(mi)kusa** gathering wild greens
嫩草 **donsō, wakakusa** young grass
蔓草 **tsurukusa** vine, creeper
緑草 **ryokusō** green grass
語草 **kata(ri)gusa** topic (of conversation)
雑草 **zassō** weeds

15 質草 **shichigusa** article for pawning
霊草 **reisō** sacred herb
16 薬草 **yakusō** medicinal herbs
諠草 **wasuregusa** day lily
17 霞草 **kasumisō** baby's-breath (the flower)
19 藻草 **mogusa** water plant
藺草 **igusa** rush, reed
21 露草 **tsuyukusa** dayflower, spiderwort

——————— 3 ———————

2 八千草 **yachigusa** many plants
4 勿忘草 **wasurenagusa** forget-me-nots
月見草 **tsukimisō** evening primrose
5 母子草 **hahakogusa** cottonweed
6 仮名草紙 **kanazōshi** story book written in kana
百日草 **hyakunichisō** zinnia
8 刻煙草 **kiza(mi) tabako** shredded tobacco
突掛草履 **tsu(k)ka(ke) zōri** slip-on straw sandles
金魚草 **kingyosō** snapdragon
9 巻煙草 **ma(ki)tabako** cigarette
浮世草子 **ukiyozōshi** realistic novel (Edo period)
春七草 **haru (no) nanakusa** the seven herbs of spring
秋七草 **aki (no) nanakusa** the seven flowers of autumn
10 根無草 **nena(shi)gusa** duckweed; something unsettled, rootless person
11 菠薐草 **hōrensō** spinach
宿根草 **shukkonsō** perennial plant
13 嗅煙草 **ka(gi)tabako** snuff
蓮華草 **rengesō** purple vetch
福寿草 **fukujusō** Amur adonis
16 薄雪草 **usuyukisō** (a flowering alpine grass)
18 嚙煙草 **ka(mi)tabako** chewing tobacco
19 藻塩草 **moshiogusa** seaweed used in making salt; anthology
蠅取草 **haeto(ri)gusa** Venus flytrap

——————— 4 ———————

13 虞美人草 **gubijinsō** field poppy

3k6.14

莩 **HYŌ** starve
FU thin skin, film

3k6.15

茖 **KAKU** mountain leek, garlic

3k6.16

莽 **MŌ** grass, thicket

巷 → 巷 **3k6.17**

3k6.17

巷 巷 **KŌ, chimata** forked road; street; place, scene, quarter, arena

——————— 1 ———————

12 巷間 **kōkan** the town, people
14 巷説 **kōsetsu** rumor, town talk, gossip
15 巷談 **kōdan** town talk, gossip

3k6.18 / 1377

荒 **KŌ, ara(i/ppoi)** rough, wild, violent **a(reru)** become rough/stormy, run wild; go to ruin **a(re)** stormy weather; roughness, chapping **a(rasu)** devastate, lay waste **a(rageru)** raise (one's voice) **susa(bu), susa(mu)** grow wild; become rough

——————— 1 ———————

3 荒川 **Arakawa** (river in Tōkyō)
荒々 **araara(shii)** rough, rude, harsh, wild, violent
荒土 **kōdo** wasteland
4 荒天 **kōten** stormy weather
荒木 **araki** unbarked logs, rough timber
荒木田土 **araki-datsuchi** (a reddish clayey soil)
5 荒仕事 **arashigoto** heavy work, hard labor
荒布 **arame** (an edible seaweed)
荒立 **arada(tsu)** be agitated/aggravated **arada(teru)** exacerbate, exasperate
6 荒地 **a(re)chi** wasteland
荒行 **aragyō** religious austerities, asceticism
荒回 **a(re)mawa(ru)** rampage
荒肌 **a(re)hada** rough skin
7 荒狂 **a(re)kuru(u)** rage, run amuck
8 荒果 **a(re)ha(teru)** be dilapidated/desolate
荒事 **aragoto** bravado posturing
荒事師 **aragotoshi** actor who plays the part of a ruffian
荒波 **aranami** rough/stormy seas
荒者 **ara(kure)mono** rough fellow, rowdy
荒物 **aramono** kitchenware, sundries
荒物屋 **aramonoya** household goods store
荒放題 **a(re)hōdai** left to go to ruin
荒性 **a(re)shō** chapped skin
荒武者 **aramusha** rowdy, a tough, daredevil
9 荒巻 **aramaki** leaf-wrapped fish; salted salmon (New Year's gift)
荒削 **arakezu(ri)** rough planing/hewing
荒海 **araumi** rough sea
荒荒 **araara(shii)** rough, rude, harsh, wild, violent

荒神 **kōjin** kitchen god
　　 aragami fierce deity
10 荒涼 **kōryō** bleak, desolate
荒原 **kōgen** wilderness, wasteland
荒唐無稽 **kōtō-mukei** absurdity, nonsense
荒馬 **arauma** untamed horse
11 荒野 **a(re)no, arano, kōya** wilderness,
　　 wasteland
荒涼 **kōryō** bleak, desolate
12 荒廃 **kōhai** desolation, ruin, devastation
荒廃地 **kōhaichi** wasteland, devastated area
13 荒跡 **a(re)ato** ruins
14 荒寥 **kōryō** bleak, desolate
荒模様 **a(re)moyō** storm-threatening sky
荒誕 **kōtan** nonsense
15 荒稼 **arakase(gi)** a killing (in the stock
　　 market), a big haul; robbery
荒縄 **aranawa** straw rope
17 荒磯 **araiso** windswept seashore
荒療治 **araryōji** drastic/kill-or-cure treatment

────────── 2 ──────────

1 一荒 **hitoa(re)** a squall; a burst of anger
4 凶荒 **kyōkō** crop failure; famine
手荒 **teara** rough, rude, harsh; violent;
　　 outrageous
6 気荒 **kiara** violent-tempered
7 吹荒 **fu(ki)a(reru), fu(ki)susa(bu)** blow
　　 violently, rage
9 洪荒 **kōkō** first in the world; vast, rambling
荒荒 **araara(shii)** rough, rude, harsh, wild,
　　 violent
食荒 **ku(i)a(rasu)** devour; spoil by eating
　　 from; eat a bit of everything
12 備荒 **bikō** provision against famine
15 踏荒 **fu(mi)ara(su)** trample, ravage

────────── 3 ──────────

7 車上荒 **shajōara(shi)** theft from a parked car
10 破天荒 **hatenkō** unprecedented

3k6.19 / 251

茶

CHA, SA tea; light brown

────────── 1 ──────────

0 茶がかった **cha(gakatta)** brownish
2 茶人 **chajin, sajin** tea-ceremony expert; an
　　 eccentric
3 茶々 **chacha** interruption
茶巾 **chakin** tea cloth/napkin
4 茶化 **chaka(su)** make fun of
5 茶代 **chadai** charge for tea; tip
茶目 **chame(ru)** play pranks
茶目気 **chame(k)ke** waggish, playful
6 茶会 **chakai** tea party/ceremony
茶色 **cha-iro** (light) brown

茶托 **chataku** teacup holder, saucer
7 茶坊主 **chabōzu** (shogun's) tea-serving
　　 attendant; sycophant
茶杓 **chashaku** tea ladle
茶利 **chaki(ki)** tea tasting/taster
8 茶店 **chamise** teahouse
茶所 **chadokoro** tea-growing region
9 茶盆 **chabon** tea tray
茶茶 **chacha** interruption
茶室 **chashitsu** tea-ceremony room
茶屋 **chaya** teahouse; tea dealer
茶屋酒 **chayazake** saké drunk at a teahouse
茶柱 **chabashira** tea stalk floating upright in
　　 one's tea (a sign of good luck)
茶畑 **chabatake** tea plantation
10 茶釜 **chagama** teakettle
茶席 **chaseki** tea-ceremony seat
11 茶瓶 **chabin** teapot, tea urn
茶瓶頭 **chabin atama** bald head
茶道 **chadō, sadō** tea ceremony
茶道具 **chadōgu** tea-things
茶渋 **chashibu** tea incrustations/stains
茶菓 **chaka, saka** tea and cakes, light
　　 refreshments
茶菓子 **chagashi** teacakes
茶殻 **chagara** tea grounds
茶匙 **chasaji** teaspoon
茶断 **chada(chi)** abstinence from tea
12 茶湯 **cha(no)yu** tea ceremony
茶壺 **chatsubo** tea jar/canister
茶棚 **chadana** shelf for tea-things
茶番 **chaban** tea-ceremony assistant; farce,
　　 low comedy
茶番劇 **chabangeki** farce, low comedy
茶筅 **chasen** bamboo tea-ceremony whisk
茶筌 **chasen** bamboo tea-ceremony whisk
茶筒 **chazutsu** tea canister
茶飲 **chano(mi)** teacup; tea lover; tea drinking
茶飲友達 **chano(mi) tomodachi** crony, pal
茶飲茶碗 **chano(mi)jawan** teacup
茶飲話 **chano(mi)banashi** a chat over tea,
　　 gossip
茶飯 **chameshi** rice boiled in tea or mixed
　　 with soy sauce and saké
茶飯事 **sahanji** everyday occurrence
茶間 **cha(no)ma** living room
13 茶業 **chagyō** the tea industry/business
茶園 **chaen, saen** tea plantation
茶碗 **chawan** teacup; (rice) bowl
茶碗蒸 **chawanmu(shi)** steamed non-sweet
　　 custard of vegetables, egg, and meat
茶褐色 **chakasshoku** brown
茶話 **chabanashi** a chat over tea, gossip
茶話会 **sawakai, chawakai** tea party
14 茶漬 **chazu(ke)** rice and tea mixed; simple
　　 meal

3

氵土扌口女巾犭弓彳彡艹宀山土广尸口

茶漉 **chako(shi)** tea strainer
茶摘 **chatsu(mi)** tea picking/picker
茶摘歌 **chatsu(mi)uta** tea-pickers' song
15 茶舗 **chaho** tea store
茶器 **chaki** tea-things
茶寮 **charyō** tea-ceremony cottage
茶箱 **chabako** tea chest
茶請 **chau(ke)** teacakes
18 茶簞笥 **chadansu** tea cupboard/cabinet

──────── 2 ────────

4 水茶屋 **mizuchaya** (Edo-period) roadside teahouse
5 末茶 **matcha** powdered tea
甘茶 **amacha** hydrangea tea
古茶 **kocha** tea picked last year
白茶 **shiracha** straw-colored, faded
7 赤茶 **akacha** reddish brown
赤茶色 **akacha-iro** reddish brown
麦茶 **mugicha** wheat tea, barley water
8 抹茶 **matcha** powdered tea
空茶 **karacha** tea without cakes
9 点茶 **tencha** preparing tea (in tea ceremony)
茶茶 **chacha** interruption
紅茶 **kōcha** black tea
10 挽茶 **hi(ki)cha** powdered tea
粉茶 **konacha** powdered tea
11 渋茶 **shibucha** coarse tea
曼茶羅 **mandara** mandala, picture of Buddha
粗茶 **socha** (coarse) tea
12 喫茶 **kissa** tea drinking, teahouse
喫茶店 **kissaten** teahouse, café
葉茶 **haja, hacha** leaf tea
焙茶 **hō(ji)cha** toasted/roasted tea
無茶 **mucha** absurd; rash; excessive
無茶苦茶 **muchakucha** mixed up, confused; nonsensical; reckless, like mad
番茶 **bancha** coarse tea
焦茶 **ko(ge)cha** dark brown, umber
焦茶色 **ko(ge)cha-iro** dark brown, umber
13 煎茶 **sencha** green tea
滅茶苦茶 **mechakucha** incoherent; preposterous; mess, wreck, ruin
滅茶滅茶 **mechamecha** mess, wreck, ruin
献茶 **kencha** powdered-tea offering
新茶 **shincha** first tea of the season
14 製茶 **seicha** tea manufacturing
製茶業 **seichagyō** the tea manufacturing industry
緑茶 **ryokucha** green tea
銘茶 **meicha** quality-brand tea
16 薄茶 **usucha** weak tea
薄茶色 **usucha-iro** light brown, buff
磚茶 **dancha** brick tea

──────── 3 ────────

4 日常茶飯事 **nichijō sahanji** an everyday occurrence

8 波布茶 **habucha** stinkweed-seed tea
昆布茶 **kobucha, konbucha** tang tea
9 海老茶 **ebicha** brownish red, maroon
茶飲茶碗 **chano(mi)jawan** teacup

──────── 4 ────────

12 無茶苦茶 **muchakucha** mixed up, confused; nonsensical; reckless, like mad
13 滅茶苦茶 **mechakucha** incoherent; preposterous; mess, wreck, ruin
滅茶滅茶 **mechamecha** mess, wreck, ruin

3k6.20

苔 **TŌ** adzuki beans; thick

3k6.21

荔 **REI** scallion, leek

──────── 1 ────────

8 荔枝 **reishi** litchi (nut)

莚 → 筵 **6f6.13**

3k6.22

荀 **JUN** (type of plant); (proper name)

3k6.23

茴 **UI, KAI** fennel

──────── 1 ────────

9 茴香 **uikyō** fennel

3k6.24

茵 **IN, shitone** cushion

──────── 7 ────────

3k7.1 / 1074

華 **KA** flowery, brilliant; China
KE, hana flower, florid, showy, brilliant
hana(yaka) showy, gaudy, gay
hana(yagu) become showy/brilliant

──────── 1 ────────

3 華々 **hanabana(shii)** glorious, brilliant, resplendent

4 華氏 **kashi** Fahrenheitg
華中 **Kachū** central China
5 華北 **Kahoku** north China
華甲 **kakō** age 60
8 華実 **kajitsu** flowers and fruit; form and content
9 華美 **kabi** splendor, pomp, gorgeousness
11 華商 **kashō** overseas-Chinese merchant
華道 **kadō** flower arranging
華族 **kazoku** nobleman, peer
14 華僑 **Kakyō** overseas Chinese
17 華厳 **Kegon** (a Buddhist sect)
華厳宗 **Kegonshū** (a Buddhist sect)
華厳経 **Kegonkyō** the Avatamska sutra
華燭典 **kashoku (no) ten** wedding ceremony
19 華麗 **karei** splendid, magnificent

──── 2 ────

3 万華鏡 **mangekyō, bankakyō** kaleidoscope
4 中華 **Chūka** China
中華人民共和国 **Chūka Jinmin Kyōwakoku** People's Republic of China
中華民国 **Chūka Minkoku** Republic of China (Taiwan)
中華料理 **chūka ryōri** Chinese cooking/food
日華 **Nik-Ka** Japan and China
7 対華 **tai-Ka** toward/with China
8 法華経 **Hokekyō** the Lotus Sutra
国華 **kokka** national glory/pride
昇華 **shōka** sublimation
9 浮華 **fuka** ostentation, foppery, frivolity
栄華 **eiga** opulence, splendor, luxury
香華 **kōge** incense and flowers
10 華華 **hanabana(shii)** glorious, brilliant, resplendent
12 散華 **sange** Buddhist flower-scattering ceremony; heroic death (in battle)
13 蓮華 **renge** lotus, lotus flower
蓮華草 **rengesō** purple vetch
14 豪華 **gōka** luxurious, splendid, gorgeous
豪華版 **gōkaban** deluxe edition
精華 **seika** (quint)essence
16 繁華 **hanka** flourishing, bustling
繁華街 **hankagai** busy (shopping/entertainment) area

──── 3 ────

7 亜鉛華 **aenka** flowers of zinc, zinc oxide
12 硫黄華 **iōka** flowers of sulfur
17 優曇華 **udonge** udumbara plant (said to blossom once in 3,000 years); insect eggs (laid by a lacewing in a flower-like pattern whose shape portends good or ill fortune)

──── 4 ────

11 曼珠沙華 **manjushage** cluster-amaryllis (also known as *higanbana*)

──── 6 ────

9 南無妙法蓮華経 **Namu Myōhō Rengekyō** Hail Lotus Sutra

3k7.2
莪 **GA** (a kind of thistle)

──── 1 ────
13 莪蒿 **gakō** (a kind of thistle)

3k7.3
莢 **KYŌ, saya** pod, hull, husk, shell

──── 1 ────
15 莢豌豆 **sayaendō** field/garden pea
──── 2 ────
16 薬莢 **yakkyō** cartridge (case)

莱→萊 **3k8.3**
菟→兎 **0a8.5**

3k7.4
莨 **RŌ, tabako** tobacco

3k7.5
莉 **RI** jasmine
──── 2 ────
8 茉莉花 **matsurika** jasmine

3k7.6
莇 **JO** Chinese matrimony vine; tilling public fields, corvée **Asagara** (surname)

莊→荘 **3k6.12**

3k7.7
莎 **SA** sedge
──── 1 ────
9 莎草 **hamasuge** coco grass

3

芿 → 薄 **3k13.11**

3k7.8

荻

TEKI, ogi reed, rush

3k7.9

莅

RI proceed to, assume (a post)

3k7.10 / 391

荷

KA, ni load, cargo, baggage

———————— 1 ————————

3 荷下 **nio(roshi)** unloading, discharge
4 荷厄介 **niyakkai** burden, encumbrance
5 荷札 **nifuda** tag, label
荷主 **ninushi** owner, shipper, consignor
6 荷扱 **niatsuka(i)** freight handling
7 荷作 **nizuku(ri)** packing
荷役 **niyaku** loading and unloading, cargo
handling
荷車 **niguruma** cart, wagon
荷足 **niashi** ballast
荷足船 **nita(ri)bune** barge, lighter
8 荷受 **niu(ke)** receipt of goods
荷受入 **niu(ke)nin** consignee
荷送 **nioku(ri)** shipment, consignment
荷送人 **nioku(ri)nin** shipper
荷担 **katan** support, side with, be a party to
荷担者 **katansha** participant, supporter,
accomplice
荷拵 **nigoshira(e)** packing
荷物 **nimotsu** baggage; load
9 荷重 **kajū** load
荷卸 **nioro(shi)** unloading, discharge
荷負 **nio(i)** shouldering a load
荷造 **nizuku(ri)** packing
荷姿 **nisugata** type/style of packing
10 荷馬 **niuma** pack/draft horse
荷馬車 **nibasha** dray, wagon, cart
11 荷動 **niugo(ki)** movement of goods
荷船 **nibune** freighter; lighter, barge
12 荷渡 **niwata(shi)** delivery
荷揚 **nia(ge)** unloading, discharge, landing
荷揚料 **nia(ge)ryō** landing charges
荷揚場 **nia(ge)ba** landing place
荷葉 **kayō** lotus leaf
13 荷電 **kaden** electric charge
14 荷駄 **nida** horseload, pack
15 荷鞍 **nigura** pack saddle

16 荷薄 **niusu** scarcity of goods, short supply
荷積 **nizu(mi)** loading

———————— 2 ————————

2 入荷 **nyūka** fresh supply of goods
3 小荷物 **konimotsu** parcel, package
4 片荷 **katani** one-sided/lop-sided load
手荷物 **tenimotsu** luggage, (hand) baggage
5 出荷 **shukka** shipment, consignment
打荷 **u(chi)ni** jetsam, jettisoned cargo
6 在荷 **zaika, a(ri)ni** goods in stock, inventory
7 抜荷 **nu(ki)ni** pilfer(ed) goods
投荷 **na(ge)ni** jetsam, cargo cast overboard
初荷 **hatsuni** first cargo/shipment of the new
year
8 空荷 **karani** without a load/cargo
底荷 **sokoni** ballast
9 重荷 **omoni** heavy burden
jūka heavy load; heavy responsibility
負荷 **fuka** burden, load (electricity)
浮荷 **u(ki)ni** flotsam, floatage
持荷 **mo(chi)ni** stock of goods, holdings; load
茗荷 **myōga** ginger
10 倉荷 **kurani** warehouse goods
帰荷 **kae(ri)ni** return cargo
徒荷 **kachini** foot traveler's baggage
11 脚荷 **ashini** ballast
船荷 **funani** (ship's) cargo
船荷証券 **funani shōken** bill of lading
12 着荷 **chakuni, chakka** goods arrived
揚荷 **a(ge)ni** cargo to be unloaded
集荷 **shūka** collection of cargo/freight
13 新荷 **shinni** newly arrived goods
電荷 **denka** electrical charge
14 稲荷 **Inari** god of harvests, fox deity
稲荷寿司 **inarizushi** fried tofu stuffed with
vinegared rice
16 薄荷 **hakka** (pepper)mint, menthol
薄荷油 **hakkayu** peppermint oil
薄荷脳 **hakkanō** menthol
薄荷糖 **hakkatō** peppermint
積荷 **tsu(mi)ni** load, freight, cargo, shipment

———————— 3 ————————

10 陰電荷 **indenka** negative charge
11 陽電荷 **yōdenka** positive charge
13 新着荷 **shinchakuni** newly arrived goods

3k7.11

莠

YŪ (looking good but) bad
hagusa (a weed which looks like rice)

3k7.12

莫 莫

GO mat, matting

1
13 茣蓙 **goza** mat, matting

2
7 花茣蓙 **hana goza** floral-pattern mat

3k7.13
莫
BAKU empty; vast
BO, naka(re) must not, do not, be not

1
3 莫大 **bakudai** vast, immense, enormous
莫大小 **meriyasu** knitted goods
8 莫逆 **bakugyaku** firm friendship
莫逆友 **bakugyaku (no) tomo** steadfast friend

2
10 索莫 **sakubaku** bleak, desolate
12 落莫 **rakubaku** desolate, lonesome

莖 → 茎 3k5.23

3k7.14
莞
KAN reed, rush

1
14 莞爾 **kanji (to shite)** with a smile

3k7.15
荵
NIN, JIN, shinobu hare's-foot fern

3k7.16 / 1434
恭
KYŌ, uyauya(shii) respectful, reverent, deferential

1
10 恭倹 **kyōken** deference, respectfulness
12 恭敬 **kyōkei** reverence, respect
恭賀 **kyōga** respectful congratulations
恭賀新年 **kyōga shinnen** Happy New Year
恭順 **kyōjun** fealty, allegiance

3k7.17
荼
TO, DA (type of lettuce); reed ear; suffering

1
9 荼毘 **dabi** cremation

3k7.18
莟
GAN, tsubomi bud

莓 → 苺 3k5.4

3k7.19
荳
TŌ bean; nutmeg

1
14 荳蔲 **tōkō** nutmeg

8

3k8.1
菫
KIN, sumire a violet

3
3 三色菫 **sanshoku sumire** pansy

3k8.2 / 1535
菓
KA cake; fruit

1
2 菓子 **(o)kashi** candy, confection, pastry
菓子皿 **kashizara** cake plate
菓子屋 **kashiya** candy store, confectionery shop
菓子器 **kashiki** cake-serving bowl

2
3 干菓子 **higashi** dry candies
4 水菓子 **mizugashi** fruit
引菓子 **hi(ki)gashi** ornamental gift cakes
5 生菓子 **namagashi** unbaked cake
氷菓子 **kōrigashi** a frozen sweet
打菓子 **u(chi)gashi** molded confections
6 米菓 **beika** rice crackers
8 和菓子 **wagashi** Japanese-style confections
9 洋菓子 **yōgashi** Western candies
茶菓 **chaka, saka** tea and cakes, light refreshments
茶菓子 **chagashi** teacakes
11 盛菓子 **mo(ri)gashi** cakes heaped in a basket
粗菓 **soka** cakes, refreshments
12 蒸菓子 **mu(shi)gashi** steamed cake
14 製菓 **seika** candymaking
製菓業 **seikagyō** the confectionery industry
銘菓 **meika** quality-brand cakes

駄菓子 **dagashi** cheap candy
16 糖菓 **tōka** candy, sweets

3k8.3

萊 菜 **RAI** goosefoot, pigweed; weed (growing thickly); weed-overgrown field; remove/eliminate (weeds)

3k8.4 / 859

著 著 **CHO** literary work; clearly apparent **CHAKU** arrival; (counter for suits) **arawa(su)** write, publish **ichijiru(shii)** marked, striking, remarkable, conspicuous **ki(ru)** put on, wear, don

———————— 1 ————————

6 著名 **chomei** prominent, well-known
7 著作 **chosaku** writing, authorship
　著作者 **chosakusha** author, writer
　著作物 **chosakubutsu** a (literary) work, book
　著作家 **chosakka, chosakuka** author, writer
　著作権 **chosakuken** copyright
　著述 **chojutsu** write (books)
　著述家 **chojutsuka** writer, author
　著述業 **chojutsugyō** the literary profession
8 著明 **chomei** clear, plain
　著者 **chosha** author
10 著書 **chosho** a (literary) work

———————— 2 ————————

3 大著 **taicho** voluminous work; great work
6 合著 **gōcho** joint authorship
　近著 **kincho** a recent work
　名著 **meicho** famous work, great book
　共著 **kyōcho** coauthorship
　自著 **jicho** one's own (literary) work
8 拙著 **setcho** my humble work
9 前著 **zencho** the above-cited publication, ibid.
10 高著 **kōcho** your (literary) work
　原著 **gencho** the original work (not a translation)
　原著者 **genchosha** the author
13 新著 **shincho** new book/work
14 遺著 **icho** (deceased's) unpublished work
18 顕著 **kencho** notable, striking, marked

3k8.5

蓑 **CHŌ** (a type of plant)

3k8.6

蒴 **SHŪ, SHU** hemp; matting; good arrow **SU** growing in clumps; nest

3k8.7

菽 **SHUKU, mame** beans

3k8.8

菻 **RIN** (a kind of thistle)

3k8.9

菘 **SŪ** (a kind of rape)

3k8.10

菲 **HI** thin; inferior

———————— 1 ————————

3 菲才 **hisai** lack of ability

萠 → 萌 3k8.11

3k8.11

萌 萠 **HŌ, BŌ, mo(eru)** sprout, bud, put forth shoots **mo(yashi)** bean sprouts; malt **kiza(su)** show signs of **kiza(shi)** sprouting, germination; signs

———————— 1 ————————

5 萌出 **mo(e)de(ru)** sprout, bud
　萌立 **mo(e)ta(tsu)** sprout, bud
8 萌芽 **hōga** germination; germ, sprout
11 萌黄色 **moegi-iro** yellowish/light green

3k8.12

萍 **HEI, ukikusa** duckweed, mugwort

———————— 2 ————————

3 水萍 **suihyō** floating weed

3k8.13

菠 **HA** spinach

———————— 1 ————————

16 菠薐草 **hōrensō** spinach

3k8.14

范

yachi bog, wetlands
yara (used in proper names)

3k8.15

菰

KO, komo water oat, wild rice; rush/reed mat

3k8.16 / 780

黄 黃

KŌ, Ō, ki, ko yellow
ki(bamu) turn yellowish

——————— 1 ———————

3 黄土 **ōdo, kōdo** yellow ocher, loess
5 黄白 **kōhaku** yellow and white; gold and silver; money, bribery
    黄玉 **ōgyoku, kōgyoku** topaz
6 黄色 **ki-iro** yellow
    黄色人種 **ōshoku jinshu** the yellow race
7 黄身 **kimi** (egg) yolk
8 黄表紙 **kibyōshi** Edo-period comic book
    黄味 **kimi(gakatta)** yellowish, cream-colored
    黄昏 **kōkon, tasogare** dusk, evening twilight
    黄金 **ōgon, kogane** gold
    黄金色 **ōgonshoku, kogane-iro** gold color
    黄金律 **ōgonritsu** the golden rule
9 黄変米 **ōhenmai** discolored/spoiled rice
    黄泉 **kōsen, yomi** hades, realm of the dead
    黄泉国 **yomi (no) kuni** hades, realm of the dead
    黄海 **Kōkai** the Yellow Sea
10 黄疸 **ōdan** jaundice
    黄粉 **ki(na)ko** soybean flour
11 黄道 **kōdō, ōdō** the ecliptic
    黄道吉日 **kōdō kichinichi, ōdō kichinichi** lucky day
    黄道帯 **kōdōtai** the zodiac
    黄菖蒲 **kishōbu** yellow iris (the flower)
    黄菊 **kigiku** yellow chrysanthemum
    黄麻 **kōma, ōma** jute
12 黄葉 **kōyō** yellow (autumn) leaves
13 黄楊 **tsuge** box tree, boxwood
    黄禍 **kōka** the Yellow Peril
    黄鉄鉱 **ōtekkō** iron pyrite, fool's gold
14 黄塵 **kōjin** dust (in the air); this weary world
    黄熟 **kōjuku** turning yellow and ripening
    黄緑色 **ōryokushoku** yellowish green, olive
    黄銅 **ōdō, kōdō** brass
    黄銅色 **kōdōshoku** brass yellow
    黄銅鉱 **ōdōkō, kōdōkō** copper pyrite, fool's gold
15 黄熱 **ōnetsu, kōnetsu** yellow fever
    黄熱病 **ōnetsubyō, kōnetsubyō** yellow fever

17 黄燐 **ōrin** yellow/white phosphorus
20 黄櫨 **haze** sumac, wax tree

——————— 2 ———————

7 卵黄 **ran'ō** yolk
9 浅黄 **asagi** light/pale yellow
11 淡黄色 **tankōshoku** light yellow, straw color
    萌黄色 **moegi-iro** yellowish/light green
12 硫黄 **iō** sulfur
    硫黄泉 **iōsen** sulfur springs
    硫黄華 **iōka** flowers of sulfur
14 緑黄色 **ryokuōshoku** greenish yellow

3k8.17

其

KI, mamegara bean stalks and pods

3k8.18

I, na(eru) wither, droop, weaken; go numb, be paralyzed **shibo(mu), shio(reru), shina(biru)** wither, droop, shrivel

——————— 1 ———————

17 萎縮 **ishuku** wither, atrophy; be dispirited
19 萎靡 **ibi** decline, wane

——————— 2 ———————

5 打萎 **u(chi)shio(reru)** droop; be downcast

3k8.19

SEI luxuriant growth; beautiful

3k8.20

菱

RYŌ, hishi water chestnut; diamond shape, rhombus

——————— 1 ———————

7 菱形 **hishigata** diamond shape, rhombus
15 菱餅 **hishimochi** colored diamond-shaped rice cakes (for the March 3 Hina-matsuri doll festival)

——————— 2 ———————

3 三菱 **Mitsubishi** (company name)

3k8.21

菩

BO (used phonetically)

——————— 1 ———————

12 菩提 **bodai** Buddhahood, supreme enlightenment, salvation

3

氵
土
扌
口
女
巾
犭
弓
彳
彡
‡ 8 ←
宀
⺌
山
毒
广
尸
口

菩提心 **bodaishin** aspiration for Buddhahood
菩提寺 **bodaiji** one's family's temple
菩提樹 **bodaiju** bo tree; linden tree; lime tree
16 菩薩 **bosatsu** bodhisattva, Buddhist saint

────── 2 ──────
6 如菩薩 **nyobosatsu** compassionate (as a
Buddha)

────── 4 ──────
18 観世音菩薩 **Kanzeon Bosatsu** the Goddess
of Mercy

3k8.22
菖
SHŌ iris, flag (the flower)

────── 1 ──────
13 菖蒲 **ayame, shōbu** iris, flag

────── 2 ──────
7 花菖蒲 **hanashōbu** iris, blue flag
11 黄菖蒲 **kishōbu** yellow iris (the flower)

3k8.23
菎
KON (a type of fragrant herb); devil's-
tongue

葛 → 葛 **3k9.22**

3k8.24
菁
SEI leek flower; daikon

3k8.25 / 931
菜 菜
SAI vegetables
na vegetables; rape, mustard
plant

────── 1 ──────
0 サラダ菜 **saradana** romaine lettuce
9 菜食 **saishoku** vegetarian/herbivorous diet
菜食主義 **saishoku shugi** vegetarianism
12 菜葉 **na(p)pa** greens
菜葉服 **na(p)pafuku** overalls
13 菜園 **saien** vegetable garden
14 菜漬 **nazu(ke)** pickled vegetables
菜種 **natane** rapeseed, coleseed, colza
菜種油 **natane abura** rapeseed oil
15 菜箸 **saibashi** long/serving chopsticks

────── 2 ──────
4 水菜 **mizuna** potherb mustard (greens for
pickling)

5 白菜 **hakusai** Chinese/celery cabbage
玉菜 **tamana** cabbage
7 杉菜 **sugina** a field horsetail
8 若菜 **wakana** young greens/herbs
青菜 **aona** greens
9 前菜 **zensai** hors d'oeuvres
10 高菜 **takana** (a leaf mustard)
根菜類 **konsairui** root crops
11 野菜 **yasai** vegetables
野菜畑 **yasaibatake** vegetable garden
甜菜 **tensai** sugar beet
甜菜糖 **tensaitō** beet sugar
12 惣菜 **sōzai** side dish
13 嫁菜 **yomena** aster
14 漬菜 **tsu(ke)na** pickling/pickled greens
総菜 **sōzai** everyday food/side-dish

────── 3 ──────
7 花野菜 **hanayasai** cauliflower
花椰菜 **hanayasai** cauliflower
芥子菜 **karashina** mustard plant, rape

────── 4 ──────
1 一汁一菜 **ichijū-issai** a simple meal

3k8.26
萱
GI day lily

────── 1 ──────
9 萱草 **wasuregusa** day lily

3k8.27
菅
KAN, suge sedge

────── 1 ──────
10 菅原 **Sugawara** (surname)
11 菅笠 **sugegasa** hat woven from sedge

蒂 → 帚 **3f5.5**

菴 → 庵 **3q8.6**

3k8.28
菟 菟
TO dodder (the plant)

────── 2 ──────
4 木菟 **mimizuku** horned owl

3k8.29

萃

SUI gather together

───────── 2 ─────────

7 抜萃 **bassui** extract, excerpt, selection, abstract, summary
　　抜萃帳 **bassuichō** scrapbook

3k8.30 / 475

菊

KIKU chrysanthemum

───────── 1 ─────────

2 菊人形 **kiku ningyō** chrysanthemum-decorated doll
4 菊月 **kikuzuki** the ninth lunar month
6 菊芋 **kikuimo** (Jerusalem) artichoke
7 菊作 **kikuzuku(ri)** chrysanthemum growing/grower
　　菊判 **kikuban** 22-by-15 cm size
　　菊花 **kikka** chrysanthemum
13 菊節句 **Kiku (no) Sekku** Chrysanthemum Festival

───────── 2 ─────────

5 白菊 **shiragiku** white chrysanthemum
10 夏菊 **natsugiku** early crysanthemum
11 野菊 **nogiku** wild chrysanthemum; aster
　　黄菊 **kigiku** yellow chrysanthemum
12 寒菊 **kangiku** winter chrysanthemum
18 観菊 **kangiku** chrysanthemum-viewing
　　雛菊 **hinagiku** daisy

───────── 3 ─────────

9 除虫菊 **jochūgiku** Dalmatian pyrethrum
15 蝦夷菊 **Ezo-giku** China aster

3k8.31

萄

TŌ, DŌ grape

───────── 2 ─────────

12 葡萄 **budō** grape
　　葡萄色 **budō-iro** dark purple
　　葡萄状鬼胎 **budōjō kitai** vesicular/hydatid(iform) mole
　　葡萄状菌 **budōjōkin** staphylococcus
　　葡萄状球菌 **budōjōkyūkin** staphylococcus
　　葡萄畑 **budōbatake** vineyard
　　葡萄酒 **budōshu** wine
　　葡萄液 **budōeki** grape juice
　　葡萄棚 **budōdana** grapevine trellis
　　葡萄園 **budōzono, budōen** vineyard
　　葡萄糖 **budōtō** grape sugar, dextrose, glucose

───────── 3 ─────────

3 干葡萄 **ho(shi)budō** raisins
5 白葡萄酒 **shiro-budōshu** white wine
11 野葡萄 **nobudō** wild grapes

3k8.32 / 1222

菌

KIN bacteria, germ, fungus

───────── 1 ─────────

6 菌糸 **kinshi** mycelium
18 菌類 **kinrui** fungi
　　菌類学 **kinruigaku** mycology

───────── 2 ─────────

9 保菌者 **hokinsha** carrier (of a disease)
10 殺菌 **sakkin** sterilize, disinfect, pasteurize
　　殺菌力 **sakkinryoku** germicidal effect
　　殺菌剤 **sakkinzai** germicide, disinfectant
　　病菌 **byōkin** bacteria
11 桿菌 **kankin** bacillus
　　細菌 **saikin** bacteria, germ, microbe
　　細菌学 **saikingaku** bacteriology, microbiology
12 無菌 **mukin** germ-free, sterile, aseptic
13 滅菌 **mekkin** sterilization
23 黴菌 **baikin** bacteria, germs

───────── 3 ─────────

4 化膿菌 **kanōkin** suppurative germ
7 乳酸菌 **nyūsankin** lactic-acid bacteria
8 担子菌類 **tanshi kinrui** basidiomycetes
10 病原菌 **byōgenkin** pathogenic bacteria, germ
　　病源菌 **byōgenkin** pathogenic bacteria, germ
12 結核菌 **kekkakukin** tuberculosis germ
13 酵母菌 **kōbokin** yeast fungus

───────── 4 ─────────

12 葡萄状菌 **budōjōkin** staphylococcus

───────── 5 ─────────

12 葡萄状球菌 **budōjōkyūkin** staphylococcus

───────── 9 ─────────

3k9.1

董

TŌ correct, set right

───────── 2 ─────────

10 骨董 **kottō** curios, bric-a-brac
　　骨董品 **kottōhin** curios, bric-a-brac

萬 → 万　**0a3.8**

著 → 著　**3k8.4**

3k9.2

韮 韭　**KYŪ, nira** leek

3k9.3

萸　**YU** oleaster; river ginger tree

───── 2 ─────

9 茱萸 **gumi** oleaster

3k9.4

葯　**YAKU** anther (pollen pod at tip of stamen); (a type of tall grass)

3k9.5

萩　**SHŪ, hagi** bush clover

3k9.6

葂　**KA** (a type of wisteria)

3k9.7

葫　**KO** garlic

───── 1 ─────

19 葫蘆 **koro** gourd

3k9.8

葮　**DAN, mukuge** rose of Sharon, althea

3k9.9

葭　**KA, ashi, yoshi** reed

───── 1 ─────

17 葭簀 **yoshizu** reed screen/blind

3k9.10

葩　**HA** flower, petal

3k9.11

葹　**SHI, onamomi** cocklebur

3k9.12

葆　**HŌ** dense growth; keep, adhere to; conceal

3k9.13 / 839

落　**RAKU, o(chiru)** fall　**o(chi)** omission, error; point (of a joke); outcome　**o(tosu)** drop, let fall; lose　**o(toshi)** trap; false bottom; sluice

───── 1 ─────

0 落ちぶれる **o(chibureru)** be ruined, be reduced to poverty
　落ちこぼれる **o(chikoboreru)** (cart-loaded grain) fallen off and left behind, fallen/left behind (academically)
2 落丁 **rakuchō** missing pages
　落人 **ochibito, ochiudo, ochūdo** refugee; fugitive; deserter
　落子 **o(toshi)go** illegitimate child
3 落下 **rakka** fall, descend, drop
　落下傘 **rakkasan** parachute
　落下傘兵 **rakkasanhei** paratrooper
　落口 **o(chi)guchi** mouth (of a river); spout; beginning of the fall of leaves
4 落文 **o(toshi)bumi** letter purposely left behind
　落込 **o(chi)ko(mu)** fall/sink/cave in, (prices) decline
　落手 **rakushu** receive; make a bad move
　落日 **rakujitsu** setting sun
　落戸 **o(toshi)do** trap door
5 落字 **rakuji** omitted character
　落穴 **o(toshi)ana** pitfall, trap
　落札 **rakusatsu** successful bid
　落札人 **rakusatsunin** successful bidder
　落札値 **rakusatsune** contract/highest-bid price
　落主 **o(toshi)nushi** owner of a lost/found article
　落石 **rakuseki** falling/fallen rock, rockslide
　落目 **o(chi)me** declining fortunes, on the wane
6 落伍 **rakugo** fall out, straggle, drop behind
　落合 **o(chi)a(u)** come together, meet
　落行 **o(chi)yu(ku)** flee
　落成 **rakusei** completion of construction
　落成式 **rakuseishiki** building-completion ceremony
7 落体 **rakutai** falling body
　落卵 **o(toshi)tamago** poached egg
　落延 **o(chi)no(biru)** make good one's escape
　落花 **rakka** falling/scattered petals
　落花生 **rakkasei** peanuts
　落花狼藉 **rakka-rōzeki** outrage, assault, rape
8 落命 **rakumei** die
　落物 **o(toshi)mono** lost article

落武者 **o(chi)musha** fugitive warrior, straggler
9 落重 **o(chi)kasa(naru)** fall one upon another
落首 **rakushu** lampoon, satirical poem
落前 **o(toshi)mae** money which changes hands (in settlement of a fight)
落城 **rakujō** fall of a castle
落度 **o(chi)do** fault, error, blame, guilt
落胆 **rakutan** be discouraged/disheartened
落胤 **rakuin, o(toshi)dane** illegitimate child
10 落差 **rakusa** water level, head
落涙 **rakurui** shed tears
落莫 **rakubaku** desolate, lonesome
落栗 **o(chi)guri** fallen chestnut
落書 **rakuga(ki)** graffiti, scribblings
落紙 **o(toshi)gami** toilet paper
落馬 **rakuba** fall from one's horse
11 落陽 **rakuyō** setting sun
落球 **rakkyū** fail to catch a ball, muff
落第 **rakudai** failure in an exam
落第生 **rakudaisei** student who failed
落第点 **rakudaiten** failing mark
落魚 **o(chi)uo** sweetfish going downstream to spawn; deep-swimming fish; dead fish
12 落着 **o(chi)tsu(ku)** calm down
      rakuchaku be settled
落着払 **o(chi)tsu(ki)hara(u)** be quite unperturbed
落落 **o(chi)o(chi)** quietly, peacefully
落葉 **o(chi)ba** fallen leaves
      rakuyō shed leaves
落葉松 **karamatsu** larch
落葉樹 **rakuyōju** deciduous tree
落掌 **rakushō** receive
落無 **o(chi)na(ku)** without exception
落款 **rakkan** (painter's) signature
13 落話 **o(toshi)banashi** story with a comic ending
落飾 **rakushoku** tonsure
落雷 **rakurai** be struck by lightning
落零 **o(chi)kobo(re)** (cart-loaded grain) fallen off and left behind, fallen/left behind (academically)
14 落選 **rakusen** fail to get elected
落選者 **rakusensha** unsuccessful candidate
落髪 **rakuhatsu** tonsure
落語 **rakugo** comic storytelling
落語家 **rakugoka** comic storyteller
15 落潮 **o(chi)shio, rakuchō** low tide, ebb
落穂 **o(chi)bo** fallen (grain) ears, gleanings
落穂拾 **o(chi)bohiro(i)** gleaning; gleaner
落魄 **rakuhaku** straitened circumstances
      o(chi)bu(reru) be ruined, be reduced to poverty
落盤 **rakuban** cave-in
落縁 **o(chi)en** low veranda

16 落鮎 **o(chi)ayu** sweetfish going downstream to spawn
20 落籍 **rakuseki** no registration (in the census register); buying a geisha her contractual freedom

────────── 2 ──────────

2 力落 **chikarao(toshi)** discouragement, disappointment
3 及落 **kyūraku** passing or failure (in an exam)
下落 **geraku** fall, decline, deteriorate
4 切落 **ki(ri)oto(su)** cut down, lop off
反落 **hanraku** reactionary fall (in stock prices)
厄落 **yakuo(toshi)** escape from evil, exorcism
水落 **mizuo(chi)** solar plexus, pit of the stomach
手落 **teo(chi)** omission, slip, oversight, neglect
欠落 **ketsuraku** be missing/lacking
5 生落 **u(mare)o(chiru)** be born
      u(mi)o(tosu) give birth to
払落 **hara(i)o(tosu)** shake/brush off
打落 **u(chi)o(tosu)** knock/shoot down, lop off (branches)
叩落 **tata(ki)o(tosu)** knock down/off
6 気落 **kio(chi)** discouragement, despondency
灰落 **haio(toshi)** ashpan, ashtray
扱落 **ko(ki)o(tosu)** thresh, strip off
当落 **tōraku** election result
7 低落 **teiraku** fall, decline, slump
没落 **botsuraku** downfall, ruin
没落者 **botsurakusha** a bankrupt; ruined people
抜落 **nu(ke)o(chiru)** fall out
投落 **na(ge)o(tosu)** throw down, drop
吹落 **fu(ki)o(tosu)** blow down/off
花落 **hanao(chi)** the part where the flower has fallen off
村落 **sonraku** village, hamlet
見落 **mio(tosu)** overlook
言落 **i(i)o(tosu)** leave unsaid, neglect to mention
8 虎落 **mogari** bamboo palisade/drying-rack; extortion
虎落笛 **mogaribue** sound of the winter wind whistling through a fence
追落 **o(i)o(tosu)** capture (a fort)
逆落 **sakao(toshi)** headlong fall; downhill rush
泣落 **na(ki)o(tosu)** persuade (someone) by tears
突落 **tsu(ki)o(tosu)** push off/down
奈落 **naraku** hell, hades; theater basement
取落 **to(ri)o(tosu)** let fall; omit
雨落 **amao(chi)** the place that rainwater strikes in falling from the eaves
9 陥落 **kanraku** fall, surrender (of a city); sinking, a cave-in

3

氵 土 扌 口 女 巾 犭 弓 彳 彡
⼘⼘ 9 ←
宀 ⺌ 山 寺 广 尸 口

急落 **kyūraku** sudden/sharp decline
段落 **danraku** end of a paragraph, section, period; conclusion, settlement
洒落 **share** play on words, pun, joke, witticism
(o)**share** dress up/stylishly
share(ru) pun, be witty; dress up/stylishly
sharaku free and easy, unconventional
洒落気 **share(k)ke** a bent for witticism; vanity in dress
洒落者 **sharemono** smart dresser, fop
洒落臭 **sharakusa(i)** cheeky, "smart"
拭落 **nugu(i)oto(su), fu(ki)oto(su)** wipe off, rub out, scrub away
秋落 **akio(chi)** poor fall harvest; lower rice price at harvest time
10 射落 **io(tosu)** shoot down
凋落 **chōraku** wither, decline, wane
都落 **miyakoo(chi)** leave the capital, rusticate
部落 **buraku** community, settlement, village
部落民 **burakumin** (lowly class of people historically engaged in butchery and tanning)
剥落 **hakuraku** peel/fall off
洒落 **share** play on words, pun, joke, witticism
(o)**share** dress up/stylishly
share(ru) pun, be witty; dress up/stylishly
sharaku free and easy, unconventional
洒落気 **share(k)ke** a bent for witticism; vanity in dress
洒落者 **sharemono** smart dresser, fop
洒落臭 **sharakusa(i)** cheeky, "smart"
振落 **fu(ri)o(tosu)** shake/throw off
書落 **ka(ki)o(tosu)** omit, forget to write
竜落子 **tatsu (no) o(toshi)go** sea horse
11 堕落 **daraku** depravity, corruption
堕落的 **darakuteki** depraved, corrupt
脱落 **datsuraku** fall off, molt; be omitted; defect, desert, drop out
惨落 **sanraku** slump, sudden fall
産落 **u(mi)o(tosu)** give birth to; drop (a foal)
転落 **tenraku, koro(ge)o(chiru)** fall, slip down
12 揺落 **yu(ri)o(tosu)** shake down/off
落落 **o(chi)o(chi)** quietly, peacefully
腑落 **fu (ni) o(chinai)** cannot fathom/understand
焼落 **ya(ke)o(chiru)** burn and collapse
集落 **shūraku** settlement, community, town
13 滑落 **sube(ri)o(chiru)** slip off/down
搔落 **ka(ki)o(tosu)** scrape off/away; cut off
群落 **gunraku** grow in clusters/crowds
零落 **reiraku** be ruined, go broke
14 漸落 **zenraku** gradual fall/decline
墜落 **tsuiraku** fall, (airplane) crash
聚落 **shūraku** community, colony
読落 **yo(mi)o(tosu)** overlook in reading
説落 **to(ki)o(tosu)** win over, talk into

聞落 **ki(ki)o(tosu)** miss hearing, not catch
駆落 **ka(ke)o(chi)** elope
15 暴落 **bōraku** sudden drop, (stock-market) crash
磊落 **rairaku** unaffected, free and easy
17 濡落葉 **nu(re)o(chi)ba** wet fallen leaves
擦落 **su(ri)o(tosu)** run/file off
糞落着 **kusoo(chi)tsu(ki)** provokingly calm
19 蹴落 **keo(tosu)** kick down
20 騰落 **tōraku** fluctuations
競落 **se(ri)o(tosu)** bid for successfully
22 灑落 **sharaku** free and easy, unconstrained

——————— 3 ———————
1 一段落 **ichidanraku** a pause
3 口説落 **kudo(ki)o(tosu)** persuade, talk (someone) into, win over
4 片手落 **katateo(chi)** partial, one-sided
6 自堕落 **jidaraku** slovenly, loose, debauched
11 悪洒落 **warujare** joke in bad taste
13 楽屋落 **gakuyao(chi)** a matter not understood by outsiders, shoptalk, inside joke
14 精進落 **shōjin'o(chi)** first meat after abstinence
駄洒落 **dajare** lame pun, corny joke

——————— 4 ———————
18 難攻不落 **nankō-furaku** impregnable

3k9.14

RITSU, mugura creepers, trailing plants, vines

律

3k9.15 / 812

SŌ, hōmu(ru) bury, inter

葬

——————— 1 ———————
5 葬礼 **sōrei** funeral
6 葬式 **sōshiki** funeral
8 葬送 **sōsō** attendance at a funeral
葬送行進曲 **sōsō kōshinkyoku** funeral march
葬具 **sōgu** funeral accessories
11 葬祭 **sōsai** funerals and festivals
15 葬儀 **sōgi** funeral
葬儀社 **sōgisha** funeral home, undertaker's
葬儀屋 **sōgiya** undertaker, funeral home
葬儀場 **sōgijō** funeral home

——————— 2 ———————
3 大葬 **taisō** imperial funeral
土葬 **dosō** interment, burial
4 仏葬 **bussō** Buddhist funeral
公葬 **kōsō** public funeral
水葬 **suisō** burial at sea

火葬 **kasō** cremation
火葬場 **kasōba** crematory
6 会葬 **kaisō** attend a funeral
7 社葬 **shasō** company funeral
改葬 **kaisō** reburial, reinterment
8 送葬 **sōsō** funeral
国葬 **kokusō** state funeral
9 海葬 **kaisō** burial at sea
神葬 **shinsō** Shinto funeral
10 埋葬 **maisō** burial, interment
校葬 **kōsō** school funeral
11 副葬品 **fukusōhin** articles buried with the dead
密葬 **missō** private funeral
鳥葬 **chōsō** platform burial (exposing the body to carnivorous birds)

――――― 3 ―――――
9 冠婚葬祭 **kankonsōsai** ceremonial occasions
12 御大葬 **gotaisō** imperial funeral

3k9.16
萼 蕚 **GAKU** calyx, corolla

3k9.17
葵 **KI, aoi** mallow, hollyhock

――――― 2 ―――――
3 山葵 **wasabi** Japanese horseradish
山葵漬 **wasabizu(ke)** pickled horseradish
5 立葵 **ta(chi)aoi** hollyhock
7 花葵 **hanaaoi** hollyhock
13 蜀葵 **tachiaoi** hollyhock

3k9.18
惹 **JAKU, hi(ku)** attract; bring about

――――― 1 ―――――
10 惹起 **jakki, hi(ki)o(kosu)** bring about, cause, provoke

3k9.19 / 943
蒸 **JŌ, mu(su)** steam; be sultry
mu(reru) be steamed; get hot and stuffy
mu(rasu) steam **fu(kasu)** steam
fu(keru) be steamed/boiled

――――― 1 ―――――
6 蒸気 **jōki** vapor, steam; steamship
蒸気力 **jōkiryoku** steam power
蒸気船 **jōkisen** steamship, steamer

蒸返 **mu(shi)kae(su)** reheat; repeat, rehash
8 蒸物 **mu(shi)mono** steamed food
9 蒸発 **jōhatsu** evaporate; disappear
蒸発熱 **jōhatsunetsu** heat of evaporation
蒸風呂 **mu(shi)buro** Turkish bath, sauna
10 蒸釜 **mu(shi)gama** steaming kettle
蒸留 **jōryū** distill
11 蒸菓子 **mu(shi)gashi** steamed cake
12 蒸蒸 **mu(shi)mu(shi)** be sultry/sweltering
蒸暑 **mu(shi)atsu(i)** hot and humid, sultry
蒸焼 **mu(shi)ya(ki)** baking in a covered casserole
蒸散 **jōsan** transpiration, evaporation
13 蒸溜 **jōryū** distill
蒸溜水 **jōryūsui** distilled water
蒸溜器 **jōryūki** a still
14 蒸腐 **mu(re)gusa(re)** dry rot
17 蒸鍋 **mu(shi)nabe** steamer, casserole
22 蒸籠 **seirō, seiro** steaming basket

――――― 2 ―――――
3 川蒸気 **kawajōki** river steamboat
川蒸汽 **kawajōki** river steamboat
4 水蒸気 **suijōki** water vapor; steam
8 空蒸 **karamu(shi)** steaming
10 陸蒸汽 **okajōki** steam train
12 蒸蒸 **mu(shi)mu(shi)** be sultry/sweltering
18 燻蒸 **kunjō** fumigation
燻蒸剤 **kunjōzai** fumigant

――――― 3 ―――――
9 茶碗蒸 **chawanmu(shi)** steamed non-sweet custard of vegetables, egg, and meat
12 御飯蒸 **gohanmu(shi)** rice steamer
13 蒲団蒸 **futonmu(shi)** confining (someone) under several futons (for fun)

3k9.20
葱 **SŌ, negi** stone leek, Welsh/long onion

――――― 1 ―――――
7 葱坊主 **negibōzu** flowering onion head
――――― 2 ―――――
5 玉葱 **tamanegi** onion
9 浅葱 **asagi** light/pale blue

3k9.21 / 253
葉 **YŌ** leaf; (counter for thin flat objects)
ha, ha(ppa) leaf

――――― 1 ―――――
4 葉月 **hazuki** eighth lunar month
5 葉末 **hazue** leaf tip
7 葉牡丹 **habotan** ornamental kale
8 葉芽 **yōga** leaf bud

3

氵
土
扌
口
女
巾
犭
弓
彳
彡
→9 艹
宀
⺍
山
圭
广
尸
囗

葉物 **hamono** foliage plant
9 葉巻 **hamaki** cigar
葉風 **hakaze** breeze passing through leaves
葉茶 **haja, hacha** leaf tea
葉柄 **yōhei** leaf stem
10 葉陰 **hakage** under the leaves
葉振 **habu(ri)** leaf arrangement, foliage
葉桜 **hazakura** cherry tree in leaf
葉書 **hagaki** postcard
12 葉越 **hago(shi)** (seen) through the leaves
13 葉隠 **hagaku(re)** hide in the leaves
葉裏 **haura** underside of a leaf
14 葉緑素 **yōryokuso** chlorophyll
葉酸 **yōsan** folic acid

——————— 2 ———————

1 一葉 **ichiyō** a leaf; a page; a copy (of a photo)
2 二葉 **niyō** two leaves **futaba** bud, sprout
子葉 **shiyō** the first leaves of a sprouting seed, cotyledon
3 万葉仮名 **man'yōgana** kanji used phonetically
万葉集 **Man'yōshū** (Japan's oldest anthology of poems)
干葉 **hiba** dried daikon leaves
千葉 **Chiba** (city, Chiba-ken)
千葉県 **Chiba-ken** (prefecture)
下葉 **shitaba** lower leaves
4 中葉 **chūyō** about the middle (of an era)
双葉 **futaba** bud, sprout
木葉 **ki(no)ha, ko(no)ha** tree leaves, foliage
5 末葉 **matsuyō** end, close
広葉樹 **kōyōju** broadleaf tree
6 朽葉 **ku(chi)ba** decayed/dead leaves
百葉箱 **hyakuyōsō, hyakuyōbako** louver-sided box for housing meteorological gauges outdoors
7 言葉 **kotoba** words, expression, language
koto(no)ha words; tanka poem
言葉付 **kotobatsu(ki)** way of speaking
言葉尻 **kotobajiri** end of a word; slip of the tongue
言葉遣 **kotobazuka(i)** wording, expression
言葉質 **kotobajichi** pledge, promise
8 京葉 **Kei-Yō** Tōkyō-Chiba
押葉 **o(shi)ba** pressed leaf
若葉 **wakaba** new leaves, fresh verdure
松葉 **matsuba** pine needle
松葉杖 **matsubazue** crutches
枝葉 **shiyō, edaha** branches and leaves; ramifications; unimportant details
枝葉末節 **shiyō-massetsu** branches and leaves; unimportant details
青葉 **aoba** green leaves/foliage, greenery
9 前葉 **zen'yō** the preceding page
後葉 **kōyō** future generations, posterity; the pituitary gland

草葉 **kusaba** blade of grass
単葉 **tan'yō** simple leaf; monoplane
枯葉 **ka(re)ha** dead leaf
肺葉 **haiyō** lobe of a lung
紅葉 **kōyō** red (autumn) leaves
momiji maple tree; red (autumn) leaves
紅葉狩 **momijiga(ri)** outing for viewing autumn leaves
10 荷葉 **kayō** lotus leaf
針葉 **shin'yō** evergreen needles
針葉樹 **shin'yōju** needle-leaf tree, conifer
11 黄葉 **kōyō** yellow (autumn) leaves
菜葉 **na(p)pa** greens
菜葉服 **na(p)pafuku** overalls
麻葉 **asa(no)ha** hemp-leaf
12 湯葉 **yuba** dried tofu
落葉 **o(chi)ba** fallen leaves
rakuyō shed leaves
落葉松 **karamatsu** larch
落葉樹 **rakuyōju** deciduous tree
腊葉 **sakuyō** dried/pressed leaves
絵葉書 **ehagaki** picture postcard
13 蓮葉 **hasuha** lotus leaf
hasu(p)pa wanton, flighty, coquettish
照葉狂言 **Teriha kyōgen** (a type of Noh entertainment)
飼葉 **ka(i)ba** fodder
飼葉桶 **ka(i)baoke** manger
14 嫩葉 **don'yō, wakaba** young foliage
腐葉土 **fuyōdo** soil from decayed fallen leaves, leaf mold
複葉 **fukuyō** compound leaf; biplane
緑葉 **ryokuyō** green leaves
17 檜葉 **hiba** white-cedar leaf; hiba arborvitae (a shrub)
18 観葉植物 **kan'yō shokubutsu** foliage plant

——————— 3 ———————

3 口言葉 **kuchi kotoba** spoken/colloquial word(s)
4 双子葉 **sōshiyō** dicotyledonous
6 合言葉 **a(i)kotoba** password, watchword
7 里言葉 **sato kotoba** rural dialect; courtesans' language
花言葉 **hana kotoba** the language of flowers
売言葉買言葉 **u(ri)kotoba (ni) ka(i)kotoba** (an exchange of) fighting words
忌言葉 **i(mi)kotoba** tabooed word
8 逆言葉 **sakakotoba** word of opposite meaning; word pronounced backwards
往復葉書 **ōfuku hagaki** return postcard
国言葉 **(o)kunikotoba** dialect, vernacular
9 通言葉 **tō(ri)kotoba** catchword, jargon, argot, common phrase
封緘葉書 **fūkan hagaki** lettercard
草紅葉 **kusamomiji** colored grasses of autumn

単子葉 **tanshiyō** monocotyledonous
10 遊言葉 **aso(base)kotoba** word ending with *-asobase*, characteristic of very polite feminine speech
根掘葉掘 **neho(ri)-haho(ri)** inquisitive about every detail
桐一葉 **kiri hitoha** falling paulownia leaf (a sign of the arrival of autumn or of the beginning of the end)
書言葉 **ka(ki)kotoba** written language
11 添言葉 **so(e)kotoba** advice, encouragement
12 買言葉 **ka(i)kotoba** harsh retort to harsh words
13 隠言葉 **kaku(shi)kotoba** secret language, argot
話言葉 **hana(shi)kotoba** spoken language
14 歌言葉 **uta kotoba** poetic language/wording
15 褒言葉 **ho(me)kotoba** words of praise, laudatory remarks
17 濡落葉 **nu(re)o(chi)ba** wet fallen leaves

— 4 —

6 早口言葉 **hayakuchi kotoba** tongue twister
10 流行言葉 **haya(ri)kotoba** popular expression
12 御国言葉 **okuni kotoba** dialect, vernacular

— 6 —

7 売言葉買言葉 **u(ri)kotoba (ni) ka(i)kotoba** (an exchange of) fighting words

3k9.22

葛 葛 **KATSU** kudzu, arrowroot; vines
kuzu, tsuzura kudzu, arrowroot

— 1 —

5 葛布 **kuzufu** (waterproof) kudzu-fiber cloth
7 葛折 **tsuzurao(ri)** winding, meandering, zigzag
10 葛粉 **kuzuko** arrowroot starch/flour
15 葛餅 **kuzumochi** arrowroot-flour cake
18 葛藤 **kattō** entanglements, discord, trouble
22 葛籠 **tsuzura** wicker basket

3k9.23 / 1430

募 **BO, tsuno(ru)** appeal for, invite, raise; grow intense

— 1 —

7 募兵 **bohei** recruiting, enlistment, drafting
8 募金 **bokin** fund raising
12 募集 **boshū** recruiting; solicitation
13 募債 **bosai** floating a loan

— 2 —

3 大募集 **daiboshū** wholesale hiring/solicitation
4 公募 **kōbo** public appeal/solicitation
7 吹募 **fu(ki)tsuno(ru)** blow harder
応募 **ōbo** answer (an ad), apply for, enroll, enlist, subscribe for (shares)
応募者 **ōbosha** applicant, entrant, volunteer, subscriber (to bonds)
言募 **i(i)tsuno(ru)** argue with increasing vehemence
9 急募 **kyūbo** urgent recruiting, immediate hiring
思募 **omo(i)tsuno(ru)** think more and more of
14 徴募 **chōbo** enlistment, recruitment

— 3 —

12 街頭募金 **gaitō bokin** street solicitation
20 懸賞募集 **kenshō boshū** prize competition

葢→蓋 3k10.15

3k9.24

萵 **WA** lettuce

— 1 —

8 萵苣 **chisha, chisa** lettuce

3k9.25

葺 **SHŪ** reed, rush
fu(ku) to thatch, shingle, tile, install roofing

— 1 —

8 葺板 **fu(ki)ita** shingles
12 葺替 **fu(ki)ka(eru)** rethatch, retile, reroof

— 2 —

8 茅葺 **kayabu(ki)** thatched
板葺 **itabu(ki)** shingle/board roofing
9 草葺 **kusabu(ki)** thatch
12 萱葺 **kayabu(ki)** thatched
17 藁葺 **warabu(ki)** straw thatching

— 3 —

17 檜皮葺 **hiwadabu(ki)** cypess-bark roofing

3k9.26

萱 **KEN, kaya** day lily; reed, rush

— 1 —

9 萱草 **wasuregusa** day lily
12 萱葺 **kayabu(ki)** thatched

3k9.27

蛬 **KYŌ, kōrogi** cricket

3 氵 土 扌 口 女 巾 犭 弓 彳 彡 艹 9← 宀 ⺍ 山 士 广 尸 囗

3k9.28

葷 **KUN** plant with a strong taste/smell (ginger, leeks, garlic, etc.)

——— 1 ———

10 葷酒 **kunshu** leeks and liquor

3k9.29

蒚 **KAN** (a type of plant)

蒂→蔕 3k11.8

菟→菟 3k8.28

蓮→蓮 3k10.31

蓬→蓬 3k10.32

3k9.30

葡 **BU, HO** grape

——— 1 ———

11 葡萄 **budō** grape
葡萄色 **budō-iro** dark purple
葡萄状鬼胎 **budōjō kitai** vesicular/ hydatid(iform) mole
葡萄状菌 **budōjōkin** staphylococcus
葡萄状球菌 **budōjōkyūkin** staphylococcus
葡萄畑 **budōbatake** vineyard
葡萄酒 **budōshu** wine
葡萄液 **budōeki** grape juice
葡萄棚 **budōdana** grapevine trellis
葡萄園 **budōzono, budōen** vineyard
葡萄糖 **budōtō** grape sugar, dextrose, glucose

——— 2 ———

3 干葡萄 **ho(shi)budō** raisins
5 白葡萄酒 **shiro-budōshu** white wine
11 野葡萄 **nobudō** wild grapes

黃→黄 3k8.16

靭→靱 2f10.4

靫→靱 2f10.4

靫→靱 2f10.4

——— 10 ———

3k10.1

蒹 **KEN, ogi** (a kind of reed)

3k10.2

蒴 **SAKU** seed pod

——— 1 ———

8 蒴果 **sakuka** seed pod

3k10.3

蒟 **KON** konjak, devil's-tongue

——— 1 ———

13 蒟蒻 **konnyaku** konjak, devil's-tongue

3k10.4

蔀 **HŌ, shitomi** latticed shutters

3k10.5

蒜 **SAN** garlic

——— 2 ———

3 大蒜 **ninniku** garlic

3k10.6

蒻 **NYAKU, JAKU** cattail reed; konjak

——— 2 ———

13 蒟蒻 **konnyaku** konjak, devil's-tongue

3k10.7

蒔 **JI, SHI, ma(ku)** sow (seeds)

——— 1 ———

5 蒔付 **ma(ki)tsu(ke)** sowing, seeding

12 蒔絵 **makie** (gold) lacquerwork

───────── 2 ─────────
7 麦蒔 **mugima(ki)** sowing wheat/barley
8 金蒔絵 **kinmakie** gold lacquerwork
9 春蒔 **haruma(ki)** spring sowing
秋蒔 **akima(ki)** autumn sowing
10 高蒔絵 **takamakie** embossed gilt lacquerwork
11 遅蒔 **osoma(ki)** late sowing

蓏 → **3k12.3**

3k10.8

蒲 **HO, FU, BU, gama** cattail, bulrush, purple willow

───────── 1 ─────────
4 蒲公英 **tanpopo** dandelion
6 蒲団 **futon** futon, mattress, bedding
蒲団蒸 **futonmu(shi)** confining (someone) under several futons (for fun)
9 蒲柳質 **horyū (no) shitsu** delicate health
14 蒲鉾 **kamaboko** boiled fish paste
蒲鉾兵舎 **kamaboko heisha** Quonset hut

───────── 2 ─────────
6 羽蒲団 **hanebuton** feather-filled futon, down quilt
10 座蒲団 **zabuton** cushion
11 掛蒲団 **ka(ke)buton** quilt, coverlet
菖蒲 **ayame, shōbu** iris, flag
15 敷蒲団 **shikibuton** floor mattress
17 藁蒲団 **warabuton** straw mattress/pallet

───────── 3 ─────────
7 花菖蒲 **hanashōbu** iris, blue flag
11 黄菖蒲 **kishōbu** yellow iris (the flower)

蒋 → 蔣 **3k11.5**

3k10.9

蓚 **SHŪ** oxalic, oxalate

───────── 1 ─────────
14 蓚酸 **shūsan** oxalic acid

3k10.10

蔭 **IN, kage** shade; assistance

───────── 1 ─────────
0 蔭ながら **kage(nagara)** secretly

───────── 2 ─────────
4 日蔭 **hikage** the shade
日蔭者 **hikagemono** one who keeps out of the public eye
12 御蔭 **okage** indebtedness, favor, thanks to

───────── 3 ─────────
1 一樹蔭 **ichiju (no) kage** preordained fate

3k10.11

蓍 **SHI, medogi** sericea (stalks used for fortune-telling); yarrow

曹 → **4c7.10**

3k10.12

蒐 **SHŪ** gather

───────── 1 ─────────
12 蒐集 **shūshū** collect, gather, accumulate
蒐集家 **shūshūka** collector
蒐集癖 **shūshūheki** collecting habit/mania

3k10.13

蓖 **HI** castor-oil plant

───────── 1 ─────────
11 蓖麻 **hima** castor-oil plant
蓖麻子油 **himashiyu** castor oil

3k10.14 / 811

夢 梦 **MU, yume** dream

───────── 1 ─────────
4 夢幻 **mugen** dreams and fantasies
夢中 **muchū** rapture; absorption, intentness; frantic
夢心地 **yumegokochi** trance, ecstasy
5 夢占 **yume urana(i)** fortunetelling by dreams
6 夢合 **yumea(wase)** interpretation of dreams
7 夢判断 **yume handan** interpretation of dreams
夢見 **yumemi** dreaming, dream
8 夢枕 **yumemakura** in a dream
夢物語 **yume monogatari** account of a dream; fantastic story
10 夢遊病者 **muyūbyōsha** sleepwalker
11 夢現 **yumeutsutsu** dream and reality; half-dreaming

3

氵 氵 扌 口 女 巾 犭 弓 彳 彡
⺾ 10
宀 ⺌ 山 士 广 尸 口

12 夢寐 **mubi** (even while) asleep
13 夢解 **yumeto(ki)** interpretation of dreams
夢想 **musō** dream, vision, fancy
夢想家 **musōka** dreamer, visionary
夢路 **yumeji** dreamland
14 夢語 **yumegata(ri)** account of a dream; fantastic story
21 夢魔 **muma** disturbing dream, nightmare

——————— 2 ———————

4 幻夢 **genmu** dreams, visions
5 正夢 **masayume** dream which later comes true
7 初夢 **hatsuyume** first dream of the new year
8 迷夢 **meimu** illusion, delusion
逆夢 **sakayume** dream which is the opposite of what comes true
空夢 **sorayume** fabricated dream
10 徒夢 **adayume** idle dream
11 悪夢 **akumu** nightmare, disturbing dream
13 瑞夢 **zuimu** auspicious dream
15 霊夢 **reimu** inspired dream, vision, revelation

——————— 3 ———————

5 白日夢 **hakujitsumu** daydream
7 邯鄲夢 **Kantan (no) yume** vain dream of splendor and wealth
11 酔生夢死 **suisei-mushi** idle one's life away
12 無我夢中 **muga-muchū** total absorption, ecstasy

3k10.15

蓋 盖蓋屳

GAI, futa cover, lid **keda(shi)** probably

——————— 1 ———————

8 蓋明 **futaa(ke)** opening, commencement
蓋物 **futamono** covered container/dish
12 蓋然性 **gaizensei** probability

——————— 2 ———————

3 口蓋 **kōgai** the palate, roof of the mouth
口蓋垂 **kōgaisui** the uvula
4 天蓋 **tengai** canopy, baldachin
円蓋 **engai** cupola, dome, vault
火蓋 **hibuta** cover for a gun barrel
火蓋切 **hibuta (o) ki(ru)** open fire; commence
6 有蓋 **yūgai** covered, lidded
有蓋貨車 **yūgai kasha** boxcar
11 掩蓋 **engai** covering; gun apron
12 無蓋 **mugai** open, uncovered
無蓋貨車 **mugai kasha** open freight car
15 膝蓋骨 **shitsugaikotsu** kneecap, patella
膝蓋腱反射 **shitsugaiken hansha** knee-jerk reaction
16 頭蓋骨 **zugaikotsu** cranium, skull
17 鍋蓋 **nabebuta** pot lid

——————— 3 ———————

11 軟口蓋 **nankōgai** the soft palate
12 硬口蓋 **kōkōgai** the hard palate

3k10.16 / 1224

蓄

CHIKU, takuwa(eru) store, save, put aside

——————— 1 ———————

9 蓄音器 **chikuonki** gramophone
蓄音機 **chikuonki** gramophone
10 蓄財 **chikuzai** amassing of wealth
13 蓄電 **chikuden** charging with electricity
蓄電池 **chikudenchi** storage battery
蓄電器 **chikudenki** condenser, capacitor
16 蓄積 **chikuseki** accumulation, amassing
17 蓄膿症 **chikunōshō** sinusitis

——————— 2 ———————

7 含蓄 **ganchiku** implication, significance
12 備蓄 **bichiku** store (for emergencies), reserve
貯蓄 **chochiku** savings
貯蓄心 **chochikushin** thriftiness
13 電蓄 **denchiku** gramophone (short for 電気畜音機/器)

蒭 → 芻 0a10.6

3k10.17

蓁

SHIN dense growth, thicket

3k10.18 / 1429

墓

BO, haka a grave

——————— 1 ———————

5 墓穴 **boketsu** grave (pit)
墓石 **hakaishi, boseki** gravestone
6 墓地 **bochi** cemetery
墓守 **hakamori** gravekeeper
8 墓表 **bohyō** grave marker/post
墓参 **hakamai(ri), bosan** visit to a grave
墓所 **bosho, hakasho, hakadokoro** cemetery
9 墓前 **bozen** before the grave
11 墓掘 **hakaho(ri)** grave digging/digger
12 墓場 **hakaba** cemetery, graveyard
14 墓碑 **bohi** tombstone
墓碑銘 **bohimei** epitaph
墓誌 **boshi** epitaph
墓誌銘 **boshimei** epitaph
墓銘 **bomei** epitaph

15 墓標 **bohyō** grave marker/post

───────── 2 ─────────

10 陵墓 **ryōbo** imperial tomb
15 墳墓 **funbo** grave, tomb

3k10.19 / 1432

幕 **MAKU** (stage) curtain; act (of a play)
BAKU shogunate

───────── 1 ─────────

3 幕下 **makushita** junior-rank sumo wrestler
   bakka vassal; staff; follower
4 幕内 **makuuchi** senior-rank sumo wrestler
   maku(no)uchi rice-ball lunch; senior-rank sumo wrestler
  幕切 **makugi(re)** fall of the curtain (in a play)
5 幕末 **bakumatsu** latter days of the Tokugawa government
6 幕吏 **bakuri** shogunate official
  幕合 **makua(i)** intermission (between acts)
7 幕兵 **bakuhei** shogunate soldiers
  幕臣 **bakushin** shogun's vassal
8 幕舎 **bakusha** barracks, camp
  幕命 **bakumei** shogunate orders
  幕府 **bakufu** shogunate
9 幕軍 **bakugun** shogunate army
  幕屋 **makuya** tent, curtain-enclosed room
  幕政 **bakusei** shogunate government
  幕威 **bakui** authority/power of the shogunate
12 幕営 **bakuei** (military) camp
  幕開 **makua(ki), makua(ke)** opening of a play; beginning
14 幕僚 **bakuryō** staff, aide, adviser
20 幕議 **bakugi** shogunate council

───────── 2 ─────────

1 一幕 **hitomaku** one act
  一幕物 **hitomakumono** one-act play
3 三幕物 **sanmakumono** three-act play
  下幕 **sa(ge)maku** drop curtain
4 天幕 **tenmaku** curtain; tent
  内幕 **uchimaku** inside information
  中幕 **nakamaku** middle performance (of a three-item kabuki program)
  引幕 **hi(ki)maku** (stage) curtain
5 字幕 **jimaku** captions, superimposed dialog
  旧幕 **kyūbaku** the old feudal government, the shogunate
  旧幕府 **kyūbakufu** the old feudal government, the shogunate
7 佐幕 **sabaku** adherence to the shogunate
  序幕 **jomaku** curtain raiser, prelude
8 垂幕 **ta(re)maku** hanging screen, curtain
9 陣幕 **jinmaku** camp enclosure
  除幕式 **jomakushiki** unveiling (ceremony)

后幕 **atomaku** the next scene/job
10 倒幕 **tōbaku** overthrowing the shogunate
  剣幕 **kenmaku** angry/menacing look, glare
11 帷幕 **ibaku** curtain; strategy-planning headquarters
  黒幕 **kuromaku** black curtain; behind-the-scenes mastermind, wirepuller
  終幕 **shūmaku** curtainfall, end, close
12 揚幕 **a(ge)maku** entrance curtain
  弾幕 **danmaku** barrage
  開幕 **kaimaku** opening/raising the curtain
13 煙幕 **enmaku** smoke screen
14 銀幕 **ginmaku** silver screen
19 鯨幕 **kujiramaku** black-and-white curtain/bunting

───────── 3 ─────────

9 映写幕 **eishamaku** (projection) screen

3k10.20

蓉 **YŌ** lotus

───────── 2 ─────────

7 芙蓉 **fuyō** lotus; cotton rose

3k10.21

葦 **I, ashi, yoshi** reed, bulrush

───────── 1 ─────────

4 葦毛 **ashige** gray(-dappled) horse
11 葦笛 **ashibue** reed whistle/flute
17 葦簀 **yoshizu** reed screen/blind
19 葦簾 **yoshizu** reed screen/blind

───────── 2 ─────────

13 豊葦原 **Toyoashihara** (ancient) Japan

3k10.22

蒼 **SŌ, ao** blue; pale

───────── 1 ─────────

5 蒼白 **sōhaku** pale, pallid, wan
9 蒼茫 **sōbō** blue expanse; dusky
12 蒼然 **sōzen** blue; dim, dark
  蒼惶 **sōkō** bustling about, flurry
13 蒼鉛 **sōen** bismuth

───────── 2 ─────────

29 鬱蒼 **ussō** dense, thick, luxuriant

───────── 3 ─────────

5 古色蒼然 **koshoku-sōzen** antique-looking, hoary

3

氵
土
扌
口
女
巾
犭
弓
彳
彡
艹 ←10←
宀
⺍
山
寸
广
尸
口

3k10.23

蒙 **MŌ** Spanish moss; ignorance, darkness
kōmu(ru) receive, be subjected to

――――― 1 ―――――
5 蒙古 **Mōko** Mongolia
蒙古人 **Mōkojin** a Mongol(ian)
蒙古斑 **mōkohan** Mongolian spot
9 蒙昧 **mōmai** ignorant, benighted

――――― 2 ―――――
4 内蒙古 **Uchi Mōko** Inner Mongolia
5 外蒙 **Gaimō** Outer Mongolia
外蒙古 **Gaimōko, Soto Mōko** Outer
Mongolia
11 啓蒙 **keimō** enlightenment, instruction,
public education, edification
12 満蒙 **Man-Mō** Manchuria and Mongolia

――――― 3 ―――――
12 無知蒙昧 **muchi-mōmai** unenlightened

3k10.24

蓑 簑 簑 **SA, mino** (straw)
raincoat

――――― 2 ―――――
13 隠蓑 **kaku(re)mino** cloak that makes the
wearer invisible

3k10.25

蒿 **KŌ, yomogi** mugwort

――――― 2 ―――――
10 莪蒿 **gakō** (a kind of thistle)

3k10.26

蒡 **BŌ** burdock

――――― 2 ―――――
4 牛蒡 **gobō** burdock

3k10.27

薹 **Ō** flower stalk; vigorous growth

3k10.28

蓙 **ZA** mat, matting

――――― 2 ―――――
10 茣蓙 **goza** mat, matting

――――― 3 ―――――
7 花茣蓙 **hana goza** floral-pattern mat

3k10.29

蓆 **SEKI, mushiro** (straw) mat, matting

――――― 1 ―――――
14 蓆旗 **mushirobata** straw mat used as a flag

3k10.30

蓐 **JOKU, shitone** cushion, bed

3k10.31

蓮 蓮 蓮 **REN, hasu** lotus

――――― 1 ―――――
6 蓮池 **hasuike** lotus pond
10 蓮華 **renge** lotus, lotus flower
蓮華草 **rengesō** purple vetch
蓮根 **renkon** lotus root
12 蓮葉 **hasuha** lotus leaf
hasu(p)pa wanton, flighty, coquettish

――――― 2 ―――――
1 一蓮托生 **ichiren-takushō** sharing fate with
another
4 木蓮 **mokuren** magnolia
日蓮 **Nichiren** Buddhist priest (1222–1282)
who founded the Nichiren sect
5 白蓮 **byakuren** white lotus
9 紅蓮 **guren** red lotus blossom; blazing red

――――― 5 ―――――
9 南無妙法蓮華経 **Namu Myōhō Rengekyō**
Hail Lotus Sutra

3k10.32

蓬 蓬 **HŌ, yomogi** mugwort

鞄 → 鞄 **3k11.24**

3k10.34 / 1076

靴 **KA, kutsu** shoe, boot

———————— 1 ————————

3 靴下 **kutsushita** socks, stockings
靴下止 **kutsushitado(me)** garters
靴下留 **kutsushitado(me)** garters
8 靴直 **kutsunao(shi)** shoe repairing; shoemaker
靴底 **kutsuzoko** sole (of a shoe/boot)
9 靴型 **kutsugata** shoe last/tree
靴拭 **kutsufu(ki)** doormat
靴屋 **kutsuya** shoe store, shoemaker
靴音 **kutsuoto** sound of someone walking
10 靴紐 **kutsuhimo** shoelaces
11 靴脱 **kutsunu(gi)** (entranceway) place to
remove one's shoes
14 靴墨 **kutsuzumi** shoe polish, bootblack
靴篦 **kutsubera** shoehorn
16 靴磨 **kutsumiga(ki)** shoe polish; bootblack
17 靴擦 **kutsuzu(re)** shoe sore

———————— 2 ————————

3 上靴 **uwagutsu** house shoes, slippers,
overshoes
4 木靴 **kigutsu** wooden shoes
7 赤靴 **akagutsu** brown shoes
8 長靴 **nagagutsu** boots
泥靴 **dorogutsu** muddy shoes/boots
雨靴 **amagutsu** rubbers, overshoes
9 軍靴 **gunka** military shoes, combat boots
革靴 **kawagutsu** leather shoes/boots
11 深靴 **fukagutsu** (long) boots
雪靴 **yukigutsu** snowshoes, snow boots
12 隔靴掻痒 **kakka-sōyō** irritation, impatience
(like trying to scratch an itchy foot
through the shoe)
短靴 **tangutsu** (low) shoes
14 製靴 **seika** shoemaking
製靴業 **seikagyō** the shoemaking industry
17 藁靴 **waragutsu** straw shoes/boots
鞠靴 **marigutsu** football shoes

———————— 3 ————————

6 防寒靴 **bōkangutsu** arctic boots
9 乗馬靴 **jōbagutsu** riding boots
11 運動靴 **undōgutsu** athletic shoes, sneakers
13 戦闘靴 **sentōgutsu** combat boots
15 編上靴 **a(mi)a(ge)gutsu** lace-up boots

———————— 11 ————————

3k11.1

蔦
CHŌ, **tsuta** ivy

3k11.2

蔚
UTSU dense growth

3k11.3

蔟
ZOKU, SOKU, **mabushi** silkworm-
cocoon holders

3k11.4

蔬
SO vegetables; coarse, plain

3k11.5

蔣 蒋
SHŌ water oat, wild rice

———————— 1 ————————

4 蔣介石 **Shō Kaiseki** Chiang Kai-shek

3k11.6

菱
RYŌ, **hishi** water chestnut

3k11.7

蓴
SHUN (type of water plant)

3k11.8

蔕 蒂
TEI, TAI, **heta** calyx, stem

3k11.9

蔡
SAI (type of tortoise used for divination)

3k11.10

蓼
RIKU, RYŌ, **tade** polygonum,
smartweed, water pepper

3k11.11

蔑
BETSU, **sagesu(mu)** despise, scorn
naigashi(ro ni suru) despise, look
down on, set at naught

———————— 1 ————————

11 蔑視 **besshi** look down on, regard with
contempt

———————— 2 ————————

8 侮蔑 **bubetsu** contempt, scorn, slight
12 軽蔑 **keibetsu** contempt, scorn, disdain

3

氵 土 扌 口 女 巾 犭 弓 彳 彡 艹 ←11← 宀 丷 山 ま 广 尸 口

3k11.12 / 1431

慕

BO, shita(u) yearn for, dearly love; idolize
shita(washii) dear, beloved

──────── 1 ────────
11 慕情 **bojō** longing, love, affection

──────── 2 ────────
8 追慕 **tsuibo** cherish the memory of
9 思慕 **shibo** yearning, deep affection
10 恋慕 **renbo** fall in love with
ko(i)shita(u) yearn for, miss
12 敬慕 **keibo** love and respect
13 愛慕 **aibo** love, attachment, yearning

──────── 3 ────────
15 横恋慕 **yokorenbo** illicit love

3k11.13

摹

MO, BO copy, imitate

3k11.14 / 1428

暮

BO, ku(reru) (the day/year) come to an end **ku(re)** nightfall; year-end; end **ku(rasu)** live **ku(rashi)** (daily) living, life

──────── 1 ────────
4 暮六 **ku(re)mu(tsu)** 6 p.m. (bell)
暮方 **ku(re)gata** dusk, evening
ku(rashi)kata manner of living
6 暮色 **boshoku** evening twilight
暮向 **ku(rashi)mu(ki)** circumstances, livelihood
8 暮果 **ku(re)ha(teru)** get completely dark
暮夜 **boya** evening, night
9 暮春 **boshun** late spring
暮秋 **boshū** late fall

──────── 2 ────────
3 夕暮 **yūgu(re)** evening
4 日暮 **higu(re)** dusk, nightfall, sunset
6 行暮 **yu(ki)ku(reru)** be still on the way as night falls
7 言暮 **i(i)ku(rasu)** pass the time talking
8 泣暮 **na(ki)ku(rasu)** live in sorrow
明暮 **a(ke)ku(re)** morning and evening; all the time
9 盆暮 **Bon-kure** Bon and year-end seasons
独暮 **hito(ri)gu(rashi)** living alone
待暮 **ma(chi)ku(rasu)** wait all day long
10 遊暮 **aso(bi)ku(rasu)** spend one's days in idleness
11 野暮 **yabo** unrefined, rustic; stupid, senseless; stale, trite
野暮天 **yaboten** unrefined, rustic; stupid,

senseless; stale, trite
12 朝暮 **chōbo** morning and evening
13 歳暮 **seibo** year's end; year-end present
16 薄暮 **hakubo** nightfall, twilight

──────── 3 ────────
8 其日暮 **so(no)hi-gura(shi)** living from day to day, hand-to-mouth existence
9 途方暮 **tohō (ni) ku(reru)** be at a loss, not know what to do
11 貧乏暮 **binbōgu(rashi)** living in poverty
12 朝三暮四 **chōsan-boshi** being deceived by immediate gain (like the monkey who did not realize that being given four chestnuts in the morning and three in the evening amounts to the same as three in the morning and four in the evening)
朝令暮改 **chōrei-bokai** issuing an order in the morning and changing it in the evening, lack of constancy/principle

3k11.15

蔓

MAN, tsuru vine, tendril, runner

──────── 1 ────────
7 蔓延 **man'en** spread, be widespread
9 蔓草 **tsurukusa** vine, creeper

──────── 2 ────────
4 手蔓 **tezuru** influence, connections, good offices, go-between
8 金蔓 **kanezuru** money vine, source of money
18 藤蔓 **fujizura** wisteria vine

3k11.16

蓿

SHUKU clover, medic

──────── 2 ────────
8 苜蓿 **mokushuku, umagoyashi** clover, medic, alfalfa

3k11.17

蔻　蔲

KŌ, KU nutmeg

──────── 2 ────────
10 荳蔻 **tōkō** nutmeg

──────── 3 ────────
6 肉豆蔻 **nikuzuku** nutmeg

蔲 → 蔻 **3k11.17**

3k11.18
蔘　SHIN ginseng

3k11.19
蔗　SHO, SHA sugar cane

──── 2 ────
5 甘蔗 kansho sugar cane
　甘蔗糖 kanshotō cane sugar, sucrose

3k11.20
蔔　FUKU daikon

3k11.21
靺　MATSU (proper name)

──── 1 ────
18 靺鞨 Makkatsu (a barbarian Tungus tribe)

3k11.22
鞁　HI reins; saddle cover

3k11.23
鞅　Ō carry on one's shoulder
munagai martingale, breast harness

──── 1 ────
12 鞅掌 ōshō be busy with; attend to

3k11.24
鞆 鞆　tomo archer's leather arm guard

3k11.25
鞄 鞄　HŌ, kaban suitcase, briefcase, bag

──── 1 ────
9 鞄持 kabanmo(chi) private secretary, man Friday
──── 2 ────
7 折鞄 o(ri)kaban folding briefcase, portfolio
──── 3 ────
4 手提鞄 tesa(ge)kaban briefcase, grip

──── 12 ────

3k12.1
蔽 蔽　HEI, ō(u) cover, conceal

──── 2 ────
10 陰蔽 inpei conceal, cover up
11 掩蔽 enpei covering up; occultation
13 隠蔽 inpei conceal, suppress, cover up
　遮蔽 shahei cover, shelter, shield, screen
　遮蔽物 shaheibutsu cover, shelter

3k12.2
蕀　KYOKU milkwort

──── 1 ────
8 蕀苑 kyokuen milkwort

3k12.3
蓏　RA melon, berry

3k12.4
蕩　TŌ move; loose, licentious; enchant
toro(kasu) charm, captivate
toro(keru) be enraptured

──── 1 ────
6 蕩尽 tōjin squander
7 蕩児 tōji debauchee, libertine, prodigal son
──── 2 ────
7 見蕩 mito(reru) gaze on in rapture, be fascinated/charmed by
8 放蕩 hōtō dissipation, fast living
　放蕩息子 hōtō musuko prodigal son
10 遊蕩 yūtō debauchery, licentiousness
　遊蕩児 yūtōji dissipated person, fast liver
11 淫蕩 intō dissipation, debauchery
　掃蕩 sōtō sweep, clear, mop up
15 駘蕩 taitō mild, genial, balmy (spring breezes)

3k12.5
蕕　YŪ (a foul-smelling grass)

3k12.6
蕉　SHŌ banana

──── 2 ────
7 芭蕉 bashō plantain, banana plant
　Bashō (haiku poet, 1644–1694)

3k12.7

蕪
BU grow wild/rank; turnip
kabu, kabura turnip

——————— 1 ———————
14 蕪雑 **buzatsu** unpolished, crude
——————— 2 ———————
3 小蕪 **kokabu** small turnip
7 赤蕪 **akakabu** red turnip

3k12.8

蕎
KYŌ buckwheat

——————— 1 ———————
7 蕎麦 **soba** buckwheat; buckwheat noodles
蕎麦屋 **sobaya** soba shop
蕎麦粉 **sobako** buckwheat flour
蕎麦殻 **sobagara** buckwheat chaff
——————— 2 ———————
5 生蕎麦 **kisoba** buckwheat noodles
11 掛蕎麦 **ka(ke)soba** buckwheat noodles in broth

3k12.9

蕃
BAN barbarian; grow luxuriantly
HAN grow luxuriantly

——————— 1 ———————
6 蕃地 **banchi** barbaric region
——————— 2 ———————
5 生蕃 **seiban** wild tribesmen

3k12.10

蕈
JIN, kinoko, take mushroom

3k12.11

甍
BŌ, iraka roof tile; tiled roof

蕊 → 蕊 3k12.14

3k12.12

蕘
JŌ firewood

3k12.13

蕁
JIN nettle

——————— 1 ———————
11 蕁麻 **jinma, irakusa** nettle
蕁麻疹 **jinmashin** hives

3k12.14

蕊 蘂 蕋 橤
ZUI, shibe
stamen, pistil

——————— 2 ———————
12 雄蕊 **oshibe, yūzui** stamen
14 雌蕊 **meshibe, shizui** pistil

蕚 → 蕚 3k9.16

3k12.15

蕨
KETSU, warabi bracken, fernbrake

——————— 2 ———————
6 早蕨 **sawarabi** bracken/fern sprouts

3k12.16

蕑
KAN, GEN, fujibakama thoroughwort

3k12.17 / 1286

蔵 藏
ZŌ, kura storehouse,
warehouse, repository

——————— 1 ———————
0 蔵する **zō(suru)** own, have, keep; harbor, cherish
2 蔵入 **kurai(re)** warehousing
蔵人 **kurōdo, kurando** imperial-archives keeper
4 蔵元 **kuramoto** warehouse superintendent; saké brewer
5 蔵出 **kurada(shi)** delivery from a warehouse
蔵本 **zōhon** one's library
蔵払 **kurabara(i)** clearance sale
6 蔵米 **kuramai** stored rice
8 蔵版 **zōhan** copyrighted by
9 蔵屋敷 **kurayashiki** daimyo's city storehouse
蔵相 **zōshō** Finance Minister
10 蔵匿 **zōtoku** conceal, shelter, harbor
蔵浚 **kurazara(e)** clearance sale

蔵書 **zōsho** book collection, one's library
蔵書狂 **zōshokyō** bibliomania(c)
蔵書家 **zōshoka** book collector
12 蔵番 **kuraban** warehouse keeper
蔵開 **kurabira(ki)** first opening of a storehouse in the new year

――――――――― 2 ―――――――――

3 大蔵大臣 **ōkura daijin** Minister of Finance
大蔵省 **Ōkurashō** Ministry of Finance
大蔵経 **Daizōkyō** The collection of Classic
Buddhist Scriptures
土蔵 **dozō** storehouse, godown
4 収蔵 **shūzō** to store
5 包蔵 **hozo** contain, comprehend; imply;
entertain (an idea)
穴蔵 **anagura** cellar
6 死蔵 **shizō** hoard
西蔵 **Chibetto** Tibet
地蔵 **Jizō** (a Buddhist guardian deity of
children)
地蔵顔 **jizōgao** plump cheerful face
7 冷蔵 **reizō** cold storage, refrigeration
冷蔵室 **reizōshitsu** cold-room, cold-storage
locker
冷蔵庫 **reizōko** refrigerator
豆蔵 **mamezō** chatterbox, babbling fool
私蔵 **shizō** possess, own (personally)
8 退蔵 **taizō** hoard
退蔵品 **taizōhin** hoarded goods, cache
宝蔵 **hōzō** treasure house, treasury
所蔵 **shozō** in one's possession
武蔵 **Musashi** (ancient kuni, Saitama-ken
and Tōkyō-to)
金蔵 **kanegura** treasury; rich patron
9 珍蔵 **chinzō** treasured, prized
10 酒蔵 **sakagura** wine cellar, wineshop
埋蔵 **maizō** buried stores, underground
reserves
埋蔵物 **maizōbutsu** buried property/ore
埋蔵量 **maizōryō** (oil) reserves
家蔵 **kazō** household possessions
秘蔵 **hizō** treasure, prize, cherish
12 貯蔵 **chozō** storage, preservation
貯蔵所 **chozōsho** storage place
貯蔵品 **chozōhin** stored goods, stock
貯蔵室 **chozōshitsu** storeroom, stockroom
13 塩蔵 **enzō** preserve in salt
腹蔵 **fukuzō** being reserved, holding back
愛蔵 **aizō** treasure, cherish
15 熱蔵庫 **netsuzōko** heating cabinet, warmer
輪蔵 **rinzō** prayer wheel

――――――――― 3 ―――――――――

5 石地蔵 **ishi Jizō** stone image of Jizo
8 忠臣蔵 **Chūshingura** (the 47 Ronin story)
12 無尽蔵 **mujinzō** inexhaustible supply

3k12.18

鞋

AI straw sandals

――――――――― 2 ―――――――――

9 草鞋 **waraji** straw sandals
草鞋虫 **warajimushi** sow bug, wood louse
草鞋銭 **warajisen** traveling money

3k12.19

鞍

AN, kura saddle

――――――――― 1 ―――――――――

9 鞍屋 **kuraya** saddler
10 鞍部 **anbu** col, saddle (between mountains)
鞍馬 **anba** pommel/side horse (gymnastics
apparatus)
12 鞍替 **kuraga(e)** change one's quarters/job
17 鞍擦 **kurazu(re)** saddle sores

――――――――― 2 ―――――――――

10 荷鞍 **nigura** pack saddle

3k12.20

鞐

kohaze clasp, fastener

3k12.21

鞏

KYŌ hard, firm

――――――――― 1 ―――――――――

8 鞏固 **kyōko** firm, solid (also spelled 強固)

――――――――― 13 ―――――――――

3k13.1

蕭

SHŌ mugwort; lonely; silent, calm

――――――――― 1 ―――――――――

12 蕭然 **shōzen** bleak, desolate, lonely

3k13.2

薊

KEI, azami thistle

薮 → 藪 3k15.1

3

氵
土
扌
口
女
巾
犭
弓
彳
彡
←13←
宀
⺌
⺲
耂
广
尸
口

3k13.3 / 1910

薪

SHIN, takigi, maki firewood

――――――― 1 ―――――――
9 薪炭 **shintan** firewood and charcoal, fuel

――――――― 2 ―――――――
9 臥薪嘗胆 **gashin-shōtan** perseverance and determination

3k13.4

蕗

RO, fuki butterbur, bog rhubarb

――――――― 1 ―――――――
17 蕗薹 **fuki (no) tō** butterbur flower/stalk

3k13.5

薐

RŌ spinach

――――――― 2 ―――――――
11 菠薐草 **hōrensō** spinach

3k13.6

薜

HEI (a kind of vine)

3k13.7

薛

SETSU (a kind of mugwort)

3k13.8

薙

TEI, na(gu) mow down

3k13.9

蕷

YO yam

3k13.10

薤

KAI, nira scallion, shallot

3k13.11 / 1449

薄 荵

HAKU, usu(i) thin (paper), weak (tea), light (color)
usu(meru) dilute **usu(maru/**

ragu/reru) thin out, fade **usu(ppera)** thin; shallow, superficial, frivolous **susuki** eulalia (a grass associated with autumn)

――――――― 1 ―――――――
3 薄刃 **usuba** thin blade(d kitchen knife)
薄々 **usuusu** thinly, dimly, vaguely, hazily
薄口 **usukuchi** thin(-cut), mild (flavor)
4 薄化粧 **usugeshō** light makeup
薄切 **usugi(ri)** sliced thin
薄片 **hakuhen** thin leaf/layer, flake
薄手 **usude** slight wound; thin (china)
薄日 **usubi** soft beams of sunlight
5 薄皮 **usukawa** thin skin/layer, film
薄氷 **usugōri, hakuhyō** thin ice
薄白 **usujiro(i)** off-white
薄目 **usume** relatively light/thin; half-closed eyes
6 薄気味悪 **usukimiwaru(i)** weird, eerie
薄肉 **usuniku** light red, pinkish
薄肉彫 **usunikubo(ri)** low relief, bas-relief
薄色 **usuiro** light/pale color
薄汚 **usugitana(i)** filthy, dirty-looking
薄地 **usuji** thin (cloth/metal)
薄光 **hakkō** pale/faint light
7 薄赤 **usuaka(i)** pale/light red
薄志 **hakushi** weakness of will; small token of gratitude
薄志弱行 **hakushi-jakkō** indecisive and unenterprising
薄利 **hakuri** narrow profit margin
薄利多売 **hakuri-tabai** large-volume sales at low profit margin
8 薄命 **hakumei** ill-fated, unfortunate
薄幸 **hakkō** misfortune, bad luck
薄板 **usuita** thin board, sheet, veneer
薄明 **hakumei, usua(kari)** twilight, dim
薄物 **usumono** thin silk, light dress
9 薄茶 **usucha** weak tea
薄茶色 **usucha-iro** light brown, buff
薄紅 **usubeni, usukurenai** pinkish
10 薄倖 **hakkō** misfortune, bad luck
薄弱 **hakujaku** feeble, flimsy
薄荷 **hakka** (pepper)mint, menthol
薄荷油 **hakkayu** peppermint oil
薄荷脳 **hakkanō** menthol
薄荷糖 **hakkatō** peppermint
薄紙 **usugami** thin paper
薄紗 **hakusa** delicate gauze, gossamer
薄馬鹿 **usubaka** fool, simpleton, half-wit
11 薄遇 **hakugū** cold/inhospitable reception
薄運 **hakuun** misfortune, ill luck
薄黒 **usuguro(i)** dark, dusky, umber
薄情 **hakujō** unfeeling, heartless, coldhearted
薄雪 **usuyuki** light snow; sugar-coated cookie
薄雪草 **usuyukisō** (a flowering alpine grass)
12 薄着 **usugi** lightly/thinly dressed

薄寒 **usu(ra)samu(i)** chilly
薄焼 **usuya(ki)** lightly baked/fried
薄給 **hakkyū** meager salary
薄紫 **usumurasaki** light purple, orchid
薄雲 **usugumo** thin/feathery clouds
13 薄塩 **usujio** lightly salted
薄暗 **usugura(i), usukura(gari)** dimly lit, semi-dark, twilight
薄絹 **usuginu** thin/sheer silk
14 薄墨 **usuzumi** thin India ink
薄暮 **hakubo** nightfall, twilight
薄模様 **usumoyō** pattern dyed light purple; short supply
薄様 **usuyō** tracing paper
薄膜 **hakumaku, usumaku** thin film
薄端 **usubata** flat-top bronze vase
薄緑 **usumidori** light green
15 薄縁 **usuberi** bordered/thin matting
16 薄薄 **usuusu** thinly, dimly, vaguely, hazily
薄曇 **usugumo(ri)** slightly cloudy weather
17 薄謝 **hakusha** small token of gratitude
19 薄霧 **usugiri** thin mist

———————— 2 ————————
4 手薄 **teusu** weakness, shortage
6 肉薄 **nikuhaku** press hard, close in on
7 希薄 **kihaku** dilute, rarefied, thin, sparse
8 厚薄 **kōhaku** (relative) thickness; partiality
9 浅薄 **senpaku** shallow, superficial, flimsy
浮薄 **fuhaku** frivolous, flippant
品薄 **shinausu** short supply
10 原薄 **genbo** ledger, original register
荷薄 **niusu** scarcity of goods, short supply
12 稀薄 **kihaku** thin, weak, dilute, sparse
軽薄 **keihaku** insincere, frivolous, fickle
軽薄短小 **keihaku-tanshō** small and light, compact (cf. 重厚長大)
14 酷薄 **kokuhaku** brutality, inhumanity
16 薄薄 **usuusu** thinly, dimly, vaguely, hazily

———————— 4 ————————
12 軽佻浮薄 **keichō-fuhaku** frivolous, flippant

3k13.12

蘊

UN pile up, store
ON hornwort

3k13.13

薇

BI, zenmai osmund (a coiling edible fern)

———————— 2 ————————
16 薔薇 **bara, shōbi** rose, rosebush
———————— 3 ————————
11 野薔薇 **nobara** wild rose

3k13.14

薩 薩

SATSU salvation; Buddha

———————— 1 ————————
15 薩摩 **Satsuma** (ancient kuni, Kagoshima-ken)
薩摩芋 **satsumaimo** sweet potato
薩摩守 **satsuma (no) kami** one who steals a ride
———————— 2 ————————
11 菩薩 **bosatsu** bodhisattva, Buddhist saint
———————— 3 ————————
6 如菩薩 **nyobosatsu** compassionate (as a Buddha)
———————— 5 ————————
18 観世音菩薩 **Kanzeon Bosatsu** the Goddess of Mercy

3k13.15 / 359

薬 藥

YAKU, kusuri medicine; chemical

———————— 1 ————————
2 薬九層倍 **kusuri-kusōbai** the high markup on drug prices
4 薬方 **yakuhō** prescription
5 薬包 **yakuhō** gun cartridge
薬包紙 **yakuhōshi** a paper wrapping for a dose of medicine
薬代 **kusuridai, yakudai** charge for medicine
薬用 **yakuyō** medicinal
薬礼 **yakurei** medical charge
薬石効無 **yakusekikō na(ku)** all remedies having proved unavailing
7 薬学 **yakugaku** pharmacology
薬学士 **yakugakushi** Bachelor of Pharmacology
薬学者 **yakugakusha** pharmacologist
薬局 **yakkyoku** pharmacy
薬局方 **yakkyokuhō** pharmacopoeia
8 薬事法 **yakujihō** the Pharmaceutical Affairs Law
薬価 **yakuka, yakka** drug charge/prices
薬効 **yakkō** efficacy of a drug
薬味 **yakumi** spices, seasoning
薬店 **yakuten** drugstore
薬物 **yakubutsu** medicines, drugs
薬物学 **yakubutsugaku** pharmacology
9 薬指 **kusuriyubi** third/ring finger
薬品 **yakuhin** drugs; chemicals
薬草 **yakusō** medicinal herbs
薬室 **yakushitsu** dispensary, pharmacy; powder chamber
薬屋 **kusuriya** drugstore

3

氵
土
扌
口
女
巾
犭
弓
彳
彡
—— 13 ←
宀
⺌
山
圭
广
尸
口

薬食 **kusurigu(i)** eating (normally forbidden meat) for nutrition
10 薬剤 **yakuzai** medicine, drugs
薬剤学 **yakuzaigaku** pharmacology
薬剤師 **yakuzaishi** pharmacist
薬酒 **yakushu** medicinal liquor
薬師 **Yakushi** the Buddha of healing
薬師如来 **yakushi nyorai** a buddha who can cure any ailment
薬莢 **yakkyō** cartridge (case)
11 薬瓶 **kusuribin** medicine bottle, vial
薬液 **yakueki** liquid medicine
薬理 **yakuri** intended and side effects of drugs
薬理学 **yakurigaku** pharmacology
薬袋 **yakutai** small paper container for dispensing medicine
12 薬湯 **kusuriyu, yakutō** medicated bath
13 薬園 **yakuen** medicinal-herb garden
薬禍 **yakka** harmful side effects
14 薬種 **yakushu** drugs, pharmacopoeia
薬種店 **yakushuten** drugstore, apothecary
15 薬舗 **yakuho** drugstore
薬箱 **kusuribako** medicine chest
薬餌 **yakuji** medicine; medicine and food
22 薬籠 **yakurō** medicine chest
薬籠中物 **yakurōchū (no) mono** at one's beck and call
23 薬罐 **yakan** teakettle
薬罐頭 **yakan atama** bald head

――――――― 2 ―――――――

2 十薬 **jūyaku** (a foul-smelling herb; also known as *dokudami*)
3 丸薬 **gan'yaku** pill
下薬 **geyaku, kuda(shi)gusuri** laxative o(roshi)gusuri an abortifacient
4 水薬 **mizugusuri, suiyaku** liquid medicine
手薬煉引 **tegusune hi(ite)** prepared, all set for
火薬 **kayaku** gunpowder, explosives
火薬庫 **kayakuko** powder magazine
5 生薬 **kigusuri** herb medicine
生薬屋 **kigusuriya** drugstore, apothecary
仙薬 **sen'yaku** panacea, elixir
付薬 **tsu(ke)gusuri** medicine for external application, ointment
目薬 **megusuri** eye medicine/drops
6 名薬 **meiyaku** famous medicine
芍薬 **shakuyaku** peony
百薬 **hyakuyaku** all sorts of remedies
百薬長 **hyakuyaku (no) chō** (saké is) the best medicine
虫薬 **mushigusuri** medicine for intestinal worms
7 良薬 **ryōyaku** effective medicine
医薬 **iyaku** medicine
医薬品 **iyakuhin** pharmaceuticals
投薬 **tōyaku** medication, prescription, dosage

妙薬 **myōyaku** wonder drug
売薬 **baiyaku** patent medicine, drugs
8 毒薬 **dokuyaku** a poison
油薬 **aburagusuri** ointment, salve
服薬 **fukuyaku** take medicine
9 通薬 **tsū(ji)gusuri** a laxative
風薬 **kazegusuri, kazagusuri** medicine/remedy for a cold
洗薬 **ara(i)gusuri** lotion, a wash
持薬 **jiyaku** medicine one takes regularly
炸薬 **sakuyaku** explosives
神薬 **shin'yaku** wonder drug
施薬 **seyaku** (dispense) free medicine
10 差薬 **sa(shi)gusuri** eye drops; injection
座薬 **zayaku** suppository
眠薬 **nemu(ri)gusuri** sleeping drug/pills
秘薬 **hiyaku** secret medicine
粉薬 **konagusuri** medicine powder
11 麻薬 **mayaku** narcotics, drugs
惚薬 **ho(re)gusuri** love potion
12 湯薬 **tōyaku** infusion
媚薬 **biyaku** aphrodisiac, love potion
弾薬 **dan'yaku** ammunition
弾薬庫 **dan'yakuko** powder magazine
弾薬筒 **dan'yakutō** cartridge, round
散薬 **san'yaku** powdered medicine
硝薬 **shōyaku** gunpowder
装薬 **sōyaku** charging with gunpowder
釉薬 **uwagusuri** glaze, enamel
飲薬 **no(mi)gusuri** medicine meant to be ingested
13 傷薬 **kizugusuri** salve, ointment
煎薬 **sen(ji)gusuri, sen'yaku** medical decoction, herb tea
農薬 **nōyaku** agricultural chemicals
適薬 **tekiyaku** specific remedy
塗薬 **nu(ri)gusuri** ointment, liniment
新薬 **shin'yaku** new drug
置薬 **o(ki)gusuri** household medicines left by a door-to-door salesman who later collects money for the used portion
痲薬 **mayaku** narcotics
痺薬 **shibi(re)gusuri** anesthetic
試薬 **shiyaku** reagent
14 膏薬 **kōyaku** salve, ointment, plaster
滴薬 **tekiyaku** (medicine) drops
製薬 **seiyaku** manufacturing drugs; manufactured medicine
製薬会社 **seiyaku-gaisha** pharmaceutical company
鼻薬 **hanagusuri** bribe, hush money
痩薬 **ya(se)gusuri** reducing drug
練薬 **ne(ri)gusuri** ointment
15 劇薬 **gekiyaku** powerful medicine; deadly poison
霊薬 **reiyaku** wonder-working drug, elixir

19 爆薬 **bakuyaku** explosives

———————— 3 ————————
3 万能薬 **bannōyaku** cure-all, panacea
4 予防薬 **yobōyaku** a preventive/prophylactic medicine
内服薬 **naifukuyaku** medicine to be taken internally
毛生薬 **keha(e)gusuri** hair restorer
毛染薬 **kezo(me)gusuri** hair dye
5 外用薬 **gaiyōyaku** medicine to be applied externally (rather than ingested or injected)
7 即効薬 **sokkōyaku** quick remedy
対症薬 **taishōyaku** specific medicine
9 風邪薬 **kazegusuri, kazagusuri** medicine/remedy for a cold
洗眼薬 **sengan'yaku** eyewash
皇漢薬 **kōkan'yaku** Chinese herbal medicines
胃腸薬 **ichōyaku** stomach and bowel medicine
10 消毒薬 **shōdokuyaku** disinfectant, antiseptic
起爆薬 **kibakuyaku** priming/triggering explosive
特効薬 **tokkōyaku** specific remedy
11 常備薬 **jōbiyaku** household remedy
麻酔薬 **masuiyaku** an anesthetic/narcotic
救急薬 **kyūkyūyaku** first-aid medicine
13 催眠薬 **saimin'yaku** sleep-inducing drug
漢方薬 **kanpōyaku** a herbal medicine
睡眠薬 **suimin'yaku** sleeping drug/pills
頓服薬 **tonpukuyaku** drug to be taken once
14 綿火薬 **menkayaku** guncotton
駆虫薬 **kuchūyaku** vermicide, insect repellent
15 避妊薬 **hinin'yaku** a contraceptive, birth control pill

———————— 4 ————————
4 内股膏薬 **uchimata-kōyaku** duplicity, double-dealing; double-dealer, fence-sitter

3k13.16
EN, tsubame swallow (the bird) (cf. 嚥 3d16.2)

———————— 1 ————————
7 燕尾服 **enbifuku** swallow-tailed coat
燕麦 **enbaku** oats
11 燕雀 **enjaku** small birds

———————— 2 ————————
9 飛燕 **hien** flying swallow, swallow on the wing
海燕 **umitsubame** stormy petrel

薯 → 薯 **3k14.3**

3k13.17 / 1774
KUN, kao(ru) be fragrant, smell good

———————— 1 ————————
0 薫ずる **kun(zuru)** be/make fragrant
9 薫風 **kunpū** balmy breeze
薫染 **kunsen** good influence
薫香 **kunkō** incense; fragrance
10 薫陶 **kuntō** discipline, training, education

3k13.18
RAI, tsubomi bud

———————— 2 ————————
8 味蕾 **mirai** taste buds

3k13.19
KYŌ, hajikami ginger

———————— 2 ————————
5 生薑 **shōga** ginger

3k13.20
SHŌ water pepper (a kind of grass)

———————— 1 ————————
16 薔薇 **bara, shōbi** rose, rosebush

———————— 2 ————————
11 野薔薇 **nobara** wild rose

3k13.21
SHUN, mukuge rose of Sharon, althea

3k13.22
KŌ, mimaka(ru) die (said of a high-ranking person)

———————— 1 ————————
0 薨じる/ずる **kō(jiru/zuru)** die
5 薨去 **kōkyo** death, demise

薗 → 園 **3s10.1**

3k13.23

蟇 蟆　　**MA, hiki** toad

――――― 1 ―――――
12 蟇蛙 **hikigaeru** toad

――――― 2 ―――――
15 蝦蟇 **gama** toad
　　蝦蟇口 **gamaguchi** purse

3k13.24

薈　　**WAI** lush growth; clouds

3k13.25 / 1631

薦　　**SEN, susu(meru)** recommend; encourage, offer
　　komo straw mat

――――― 1 ―――――
5 薦包 **komozutsu(mi)** wrapped in straw matting
10 薦骨 **senkotsu** the sacrum
　　薦被 **komokabu(ri)** saké cask wrapped in straw matting

――――― 2 ―――――
6 自薦 **jisen** recommending oneself
10 特薦 **tokusen** specially recommended
11 推薦 **suisen** recommendation, nomination
　　推薦状 **suisenjō** letter of recommendation
　　推薦者 **suisensha** recommender

――――― 14 ―――――

3k14.1

蓽　　**BYŌ** make light of
　　BAKU far away; beautiful

3k14.2

藉　　**SHA, SEKI** rug; borrow, lend; make excuses; spread out; step on

――――― 1 ―――――
3 藉口 **shakō** pretense, pretext

――――― 2 ―――――
10 狼藉 **rōzeki** disorder; violence, havoc
　　狼藉者 **rōzekimono** rioter, ruffian
15 慰藉 **isha** consolation, solace
　　慰藉料 **isharyō** consolation money, solatium

――――― 4 ―――――
12 落花狼藉 **rakka-rōzeki** outrage, assault, rape

薰 → 薫 3k13.17

舊 → 旧 4c1.1

3k14.3

薯 薯　　**SHO, imo** potato

――――― 2 ―――――
5 甘薯 **kansho** sweet potato
10 唐薯 **karaimo** sweet potato

――――― 3 ―――――
10 馬鈴薯 **bareisho** (white/Irish) potato

3k14.4

薹　　**TAI, tō** flower stalk (gone to seed)

――――― 1 ―――――
5 薹立 **tō (ga) ta(tsu)** go to seed, be past one's prime

――――― 2 ―――――
16 蕗薹 **fuki (no) tō** butterbur flower/stalk

3k14.5

薺　　**SEI, SAI, nazuna** shepherd's-purse, mother's-heart

3k14.6

藁　　**KŌ, wara** straw

――――― 1 ―――――
2 藁人形 **wara ningyō** straw effigy
5 藁半紙 **warabanshi** (a low-grade paper)
6 藁灰 **warabai** straw ash
9 藁屋根 **warayane** straw-thatched roof
12 藁葺 **warabu(ki)** straw thatching
13 藁蒲団 **warabuton** straw mattress/pallet
　　藁靴 **waragutsu** straw shoes/boots

――――― 2 ―――――
7 麦藁 **mugiwara** (wheat) straw
13 寝藁 **newara** (stable) litter, straw
15 敷藁 **shi(ki)wara** litter, (horse bedding) straw

3k14.7

艱　　**KAN** difficulty, distress

— 1 —
8 艱苦 **kanku** hardships, privation
18 艱難 **kannan** adversity, trials

— 15 —

3k15.1

藪 薮 籔   **SŌ, yabu** thicket, grove

— 1 —
7 藪医者 **yabuisha** a quack
9 藪柑子 **yabukōji** spearflower
11 藪蛇 **yabuhebi** stirring up unnecessary trouble
13 藪睨 **yabunira(mi)** cross-eyed; wrong view

— 2 —
6 竹藪 **takeyabu** bamboo grove/thicket
11 笹藪 **sasayabu** bamboo-grass thicket

諸 → 諸 **3k16.3**

3k15.2

藕   **GŪ** lotus

3k15.3

藤 藤   **TŌ, fuji** wisteria

— 1 —
6 藤色 **fuji-iro** light purple, lilac, lavender
7 藤沢 **Fujisawa** (city, Kanagawa-ken)
12 藤棚 **fujidana** wisteria trellis
藤紫 **fujimurasaki** dark lilac, powder blue
14 藤蔓 **fujizura** wisteria vine

— 2 —
6 近藤 **Kondō** (surname)
11 斎藤 **Saitō** (surname)
12 葛藤 **kattō** entanglements, discord, trouble

3k15.4 / 1382

藩   **HAN** feudal clan/lord; enclosure

— 1 —
3 藩士 **hanshi** clansman, retainer
4 藩王 **han'ō** rajah
5 藩札 **hansatsu** paper money issued by a feudal clan
藩主 **hanshu** lord of a feudal clan
6 藩老 **hanrō** clan elder

7 藩邸 **hantei** daimyo's estate
藩学 **hangaku** samurai school for clan children
9 藩侯 **hankō** feudal lord, daimyo
藩政 **hansei** clan government
10 藩校 **hankō** clan school
14 藩閥 **hanbatsu** clanship, clannishness
16 藩儒 **hanju** scholar retained by a daimyo

— 2 —
5 旧藩 **kyūhan** former clan
旧藩主 **kyūhanshu** former feudal lord
6 列藩 **reppan** the various clans
11 脱藩 **dappan** leaving one's lord and becoming a lordless samurai
12 廃藩 **haihan** abolition of clans
廃藩置県 **haihan-chiken** the abolition of clans and establishment of prefectures
16 親藩 **shinpan** vassals related to the Tokugawa shoguns

藥 → 薬 **3k13.15**

藝 → 芸 **3k4.12**

3k15.5

藍   **RAN, ai** indigo plant; indigo (the color)

— 1 —
14 藍綬褒章 **ranju hōshō** blue ribbon medal

— 2 —
5 出藍 **shutsuran** excelling one's teacher
7 伽藍 **garan** Buddhist temple, monastery

3k15.6

藜   **REI, akaza** goosefoot, wild spinach

3k15.7 / 1911

繭   **KEN, mayu** cocoon

— 1 —
5 繭玉 **mayudama** (type of New Year's decoration)
6 繭糸 **kenshi** (cocoon and) silk thread

藏 → 蔵 **3k12.17**

3k15.8

鞭 **BEN, muchi** whip, rod

————— 1 —————
5 鞭打 **muchiu(tsu)** whip, flog; urge on
鞭打症 **muchiu(chi)shō** whiplash
15 鞭撻 **bentatsu** whip, lash; urge/spur on, goad

————— 2 —————
6 先鞭 **senben** the initiative, being first
10 教鞭 **kyōben** teacher's whip/rod
14 飴鞭 **ame (to) muchi** incentives and disincentives, carrot-and-stick

3k15.9

鞳 **TŌ** rumbling

————— 2 —————
20 鞳鞳 **tōtō** drumming; rumbling

————— 16 —————

3k16.1

蘇 蘓 **SO, SU, yomigae(ru)** come back to life, be revived/resuscitated

————— 1 —————
5 蘇生 **sosei** revival, resuscitation; resurrection
9 蘇連 **Soren** Soviet Union

————— 2 —————
7 阿蘇山 **Asosan** (mountain, Kumamoto-ken)
8 耶蘇 **Yaso** Jesus
耶蘇教 **yasokyō** Christianity
12 屠蘇 **toso** spiced (New Year's) saké
屠蘇機嫌 **toso kigen** drunk with New Year's saké
紫蘇 **shiso** beefsteak plant

3k16.2

蘢 **RŌ** prince's-feather; dense growth

3k16.3

藷 藷 **SHO, imo** potato

————— 2 —————
5 甘藷 **kansho** sweet potato

3k16.4

藹 **AI** many; luxuriant growth

3k16.5

蘱 **RAI** (a type of mugwort); cover, hide

3k16.6

蘋 **HIN** duckweed

3k16.7

蘊 **UN** pile up

蘓 → 蘇 **3k16.1**

3k16.8 / 1657

藻 **SŌ, mo** water plant

————— 1 —————
9 藻草 **mogusa** water plant
10 藻屑 **mokuzu** seaweeds
13 藻塩 **moshio** salt from burning seaweed
藻塩草 **moshiogusa** seaweed used in making salt; anthology
18 藻類 **sōrui** water plants, seaweeds

————— 2 —————
3 川藻 **kawamo** river/freshwater plants
才藻 **saisō** talent as a poet
4 文藻 **bunsō** literary talent
5 玉藻 **tamamo** seaweed
6 光藻 **hikari-mo** luminous algae
9 海藻 **kaisō** seaweeds, marine plants
10 珪藻土 **keisōdo** diatomaceous earth, kieselguhr
11 毬藻 **marimo** aegagropila
12 詞藻 **shisō** rhetorical embellishments; prose and poetry
13 詩藻 **shisō** rhetorical flourishes; prose and poetry
14 緑藻 **ryokusō** green algae

蘂 → 蕊 **3k12.14**

蘆 → 芦 **3k4.3**

3k16.9

蘭 蘭 **RAN** orchid; Dutch

─────── 1 ───────

7 蘭学 **Rangaku** study of the Dutch language and Western learning

─────── 2 ───────

4 仏蘭西 **Furansu** France
7 阿蘭陀 **Oranda** Holland
8 波蘭 **Pōrando** Poland
　盂蘭盆 **Urabon** o-Bon festival
　盂蘭盆会 **Urabon'e** o-Bon festival
　金蘭 **kinran** close friendship
9 洋蘭 **yōran** orchid
　室蘭 **Muroran** (city, Hokkaidō)
13 鈴蘭 **suzuran** lily-of-the-valley

─────── 3 ───────

10 竜絶蘭 **ryūzetsuran** century plant

3k16.10

蕑

RIN, i rush, reed

─────── 1 ───────

9 蕑草 **igusa** rush, reed

3k16.11

韛

HI, fuigo, fuigō bellows

─────── 17 ───────

3k17.1

薟

REN (a type of bitter vetch)

─────── 1 ───────

7 薟辛 **egara(i), egara(ppoi)** acrid, pungent

3k17.2

蘚

SEN moss

─────── 1 ───────

8 蘚苔 **sentai** mosses
　蘚苔学 **sentaigaku** bryology
18 蘚類 **senrui** moss, lichen

─────── 2 ───────

8 苔蘚 **taisen** moss, lichen

3k17.3

蘰

Katsura (surname)

蘖 → 檗 4a13.10

3k17.4

蘖

GETSU, hikobae shoots (sprouting from a stump)

─────── 2 ───────

4 分蘖 **bunketsu, bungetsu** offshoot

蘯 → 湯 5h12.1

3k17.5

驀

BAKU dashing forward

─────── 1 ───────

6 驀地 **masshigura** headlong, at full tilt
10 驀進 **bakushin** rush onward
12 驀然 **bakuzen** precipitately

蘭 → 蘭 3k16.9

3k17.6

鼞

TŌ drumming; rumbling

─────── 1 ───────

18 鼞鞳 **tōtō** drumming; rumbling

─────── 18 ───────

3k18.1

韃

DATSU (proper name)

─────── 1 ───────

14 韃靼 **Dattan** (a barbarian tribe)

─────── 19 ───────

3k19.1

蘿

RA, tsuta ivy, vines

─────── 20 ───────

3k20.1

韆

SEN swing, trapeze

─────── 2 ───────

18 鞦韆 **buranko** swing, trapeze

宀 3m

宀	字	穴	宄	它	宁	安	守	宇	宅	宋	牢	宏
0.1	2.1	2.2	2i2.1	2.3	2.4	3.1	3.2	3.3	3.4	4.1	4.2	4.3
宍	究	完	宗	宝	宕	実	宙	官	宜	定	宛	穹
4.4	4.5	4.6	5.1	5.2	5.3	5.4	5.5	5.6	5.7	5.8	5.9	5.10
突	空	宥	宣	客	室	窃	突	穿	家	宰	宴	害
5.11	5.12	6.1	6.2	6.3	6.4	6.5	3m5.11	6.6	7.1	7.2	7.3	7.4
宮	案	宵	寃	容	宦	穿	窄	竕	宸	宧	崔	寂
7.5	7.6	7.7	2i8.3	7.8	7.9	7.10	7.11	7.12	7.13	7.14	8.1	8.2
宿	寅	密	窕	窓	寄	窒	寇	寓	寐	寒	寔	富
8.3	8.4	8.5	8.6	8.7	8.8	8.9	8.10	9.1	9.2	9.3	9.4	9.5
窗	窖	窘	寝	塞	寛	寞	窠	窟	寤	寡	寨	搴
3m8.7	9.6	9.7	10.1	10.2	10.3	10.4	10.5	10.6	11.1	11.2	11.3	11.4
寥	察	蜜	寧	賓	實	寢	窪	寬	窩	籏	審	寮
11.5	11.6	11.7	11.8	3m12.3	3m5.4	3m10.1	11.9	3m10.3	11.10	11.11	12.1	12.2
賓	窮	寫	窯	窰	鞍	寰	憲	窺	窿	寠	靛	睿
12.3	12.4	2i3.1	12.5	3m12.5	3k12.19	13.1	13.2	13.3	13.4	13.5	13.6	14.1
賽	寨	竈	豁	竄	竅	寵	寶	寶	騫	竇	竈	竊
14.2	14.3	3m18.1	14.4	15.1	15.2	16.1	3m5.2	3m5.2	17.1	17.2	18.1	3m6.5

0

3m0.1

宀

BEN, MEN roof

2

3m2.1 / 110

字

JI character, letter   **aza** section of a village
azana nickname, one's popular name

--- 1 ---

4 字引 **jibiki** dictionary
5 字母 **jibo** letter; printing type
字句 **jiku** words and phrases, wording
7 字体 **jitai** form of a character, typeface
字余 **jiama(ri)** hypermetric
字形 **jikei** type, print **-jigata** -shaped
T字形 **tījigata** T-shaped
8 字画 **jikaku** strokes (of a kanji)
字典 **jiten** character dictionary
9 字面 **jimen, jizura** the appearance of written characters
字音 **jion** Chinese/on reading of a kanji
10 字訓 **jikun** Japanese/kun reading of a kanji
11 字探 **jisaga(shi)** word puzzle
13 字義 **jigi** meaning of a word

字源 **jigen** origin/history of a character
字幕 **jimaku** captions, superimposed dialog
字解 **jikai** interpretation of a kanji
字数 **jisū** number of characters

--- 2 ---

1 一字 **ichiji** a character/letter
一字千金 **ichiji senkin** great words
2 二字 **niji** two characters; name
丁字形 **teijikei** T-shaped
丁字路 **teijiro** T-junction of roads/streets
十字 **jūji** cross
十字火 **jūjika** crossfire
十字形 **jūjikei** cross, cross-shaped
十字軍 **Jūjigun** the Crusades, Crusaders
十字架 **jūjika** cross, crucifix
十字路 **jūjiro** crossroads, intersection
八字 **hachi (no) ji** figure eight
3 大字 **ōaza** major section of a village
dai(no)ji the character 大
小字 **shōji** small characters/type
koaza village subsection
4 太字 **futoji** bold-face lettering
文字 **moji, monji** character, letter
文字通 **mojidō(ri)** literal(ly)
文字盤 **mojiban** (clock) dial, (typewriter) keyboard
欠字 **ketsuji** omitted word, blank
5 生字引 **i(ki)jibiki** walking dictionary

写字 **shaji** copying, transcription
外字 **gaiji** kanji not officially recognized for everyday use; foreign letters/language
外字紙 **gaijishi** foreign-language newspaper
外字新聞 **gaiji shinbun** foreign-language newspaper
正字 **seiji** correct form of a kanji
正字法 **seijihō** orthography
用字 **yōji** use of characters
6 伏字 **fu(se)ji** characters (like ○ or ×) to indicate an unprintable word
邦字 **hōji** Japanese characters
邦字新聞 **hōji shinbun** Japanese-language newspaper
印字 **inji** printing, typing
名字 **myōji** surname
当字 **a(te)ji** kanji used phonetically; kanji used purely ideographically, disregarding usual readings
7 赤字 **akaji** deficit, in the red
8 苗字 **myōji** surname
英字 **eiji** English/roman letters
英字新聞 **eiji shinbun** English-language newspaper
宛字 **ateji** kanji used phonetically; kanji used purely ideographically, disregarding usual readings
国字 **kokuji** native script; made-in-Japan kanji not found in Chinese
和字 **waji** kana
金字 **kinji** gold/gilt letters
金字塔 **kinjitō** a pyramid; a monumental work
9 俗字 **zokuji** popular form of a kanji
点字 **tenji** Braille
逐字的 **chikujiteki** word for word, literal
逐字訳 **chikujiyaku** word-for-word/literal translation
活字 **katsuji** printing/movable type
活字本 **katsujibon** printed book
音字 **onji** phonogram, phonetic symbol
10 書字 **shoji** kanji writing (test)
11 虚字 **kyoji** kanji representing a verb or adjective
添字 **soeji** subscript, superscript, index
掛字 **ka(ke)ji** hanging scroll
梵字 **bonji** Sanskrit characters
脱字 **datsuji** omitted character/word
習字 **shūji** penmanship, calligraphy
黒字 **kuroji** in the black
略字 **ryakuji** simplified character; abbreviation
細字 **saiji** small characters/type
12 雁字搦 **ganjigarame** (bind) firmly, (bound) hand and foot
御字 **on(no)ji** quite satisfactory, excellent
落字 **rakuji** omitted character

検字 **kenji** stroke-count index
植字 **shokuji** typesetting
植字機 **shokujiki** typesetting machine
13 漢字 **kanji** Chinese character, kanji
数字 **sūji** digit, numeral, figures
数字上 **sūjijō** numerically, in figures
新字 **shinji** made-in-Japan kanji
新字体 **shinjitai** new form of a character
置字 **o(ki)ji** character skipped over when reading Chinese
14 嘘字 **usoji** miswritten kanji
誤字 **goji** incorrect character, misprint
踊字 **odo(ri)ji** character-repetition symbol (e.g., ヽ or ゝ)
15 篆字 **tenji** seal characters
16 親字 **oyaji** first character (of a dictionary entry)
頭字 **kashiraji** initials, acronym
18 難字 **nanji** hard-to-learn kanji
類字 **ruiji** similar kanji
題字 **daiji** prefatory phrase
19 識字 **shikiji** literacy
韻字 **inji** rhyming words

───────── 3 ─────────

1 一丁字 **itteiji** (can't read) a single letter
一文字 **ichimonji** a straight line
2 十文字 **jūmonji** cross
八文字 **hachimonji** the shape of the kanji 八 hachi (eight)
3 大文字 **ōmoji** capital letter　**daimonji** large character; the character 大
女文字 **onna moji** woman's handwriting; hiragana
小文字 **komoji** small/lowercase letters
5 白十字 **hakujūji** white cross
7 赤十字 **sekijūji** Red Cross
赤十字社 **Sekijūjisha** Red Cross Society
花文字 **hanamoji** capital letter; flowers planted to form characters
杓文字 **shamoji** dipper, ladle, scoop
8 金文字 **kinmoji** gold/gilt letters
9 南十字星 **minami jūjisei** the Southern Cross
11 康熙字典 **Kōki Jiten** the Kangxi zidian (a 42-volume 47,216-entry character dictionary published in China in 1716)
黒文字 **kuromoji** spicebush; toothpick
12 湯文字 **yumoji** loincloth
絵文字 **emoji** pictograph
14 複十字 **fukujūji** double-crosspiece cross (tuberculosis prevention symbol)
15 横文字 **yokomoji** European/horizontal writing
16 親文字 **oyamoji** capital letter
頭文字 **kashiramoji** initials; capital letter

───────── 4 ─────────

4 天平宝字 **Tenpyō Hōji** (era, 757–765)

3

氵
土
扌
口
女
巾
犭
弓
彳
彡
艹
宀 2←
丷
屮
士
广
尸
口

3

氵
土
扌
口
女
巾
犭
弓
彡
艹
→2宀
⺍
山
士
广
尸
口

5 写真植字 **shashin shokuji** photocomposition, phototypesetting
6 当用漢字 **Tōyō Kanji** (official list of 1,850 kanji recommended for general use; superseded by the 1,945 Jōyō Kanji)
8 表音文字 **hyōon moji** phonetic symbol/script
表意文字 **hyōi moji** ideograph
9 神代文字 **jindai moji** ancient Japanese characters
音標文字 **onpyō moji** phonetic characters
10 真一文字 **ma-ichimonji** in a straight line
11 常用漢字 **Jōyō Kanji** (official list of 1,945 kanji recommended for general use)
12 象形文字 **shōkei moji** hieroglyphics
13 楔形文字 **kusabigata moji, sekkei moji** cuneiform writing
14 算用数字 **san'yō sūji** Hindu-Arabic numerals
説文解字 **Setsumon Kaiji** (oldest Chinese character dictionary)
19 蟹行文字 **kaikō moji, kaikō monji** horizontal/Western writing

3m2.2 / 899

穴 穴

KETSU, ana hole; cave, den

――――― 1 ―――――
2 穴子 **anago** conger eel
8 穴居 **kekkyo** cave dwelling
穴居人 **kekkyojin** caveman
10 穴埋 **anau(me)** fill a gap; cover a deficit
穴馬 **anauma** darkhorse, longshot
11 穴探 **anasaga(shi)** faultfinding
穴掘 **anaho(ri)** digging a hole, excavation; novice, bungler
穴痔 **anaji** anal fistula
穴釣 **anazu(ri)** ice fishing
12 穴場 **anaba** good place known to few
穴植 **anau(e)** dibbling
穴開器 **anaa(ke)ki** punch, perforator
13 穴塞 **anafusa(gi)** plugging a hole; stopgap
15 穴蔵 **anagura** cellar

――――― 2 ―――――
1 一穴 **hito(tsu)ana** the same hole/den; one gang
3 大穴 **ōana** gaping hole; huge deficit; (make) a killing; (bet on) a long shot
孔穴 **kōketsu** hole
4 毛穴 **keana** pores
6 同穴 **dōketsu** being buried in the same grave
7 抜穴 **nu(ke)ana** secret passage/exit; loophole
8 長穴 **nagaana** slot
虎穴 **koketsu** tiger's den; dangerous situation
岩穴 **iwaana** rocky cave
金穴 **kinketsu** gold mine; source of money
9 風穴 **kazaana** air hole

洞穴 **horaana, dōketsu** cave, den
11 経穴 **keiketsu** spot for acupuncture/moxybustion
12 落穴 **o(toshi)ana** pitfall, trap
焼穴 **ya(ke)ana** a burn hole
覗穴 **nozo(ki)ana** peephole
13 鼠穴 **nezumiana** rathole, mousehole
墓穴 **boketsu** grave (pit)
節穴 **fushiana** knothole
14 竪穴 **tateana** pit
15 横穴 **yokoana** cave, tunnel
16 縦穴 **tateana** pit, vertically dug hole
鍵穴 **kagiana** keyhole

穴 → 冗 **2i2.1**

3m2.3

它

TA other

3m2.4

宁

CHO save, store; stop, linger

――――――――― 3 ―――――――――

3m3.1 / 105

安

AN peacefulness
yasu(i) cheap, inexpensive
yasu(raka) peaceful, tranquil

――――― 1 ―――――
0 安んじる **yasu(njiru)** be contented, be at ease
安っぽい **yasu(ppoi)** cheap-looking, tawdry, chintzy
安ぴか **yasu(pika)** bauble, cheap finery
ドル安 **doruyasu** weak dollar (relative to other currencies)
3 安上 **yasua(gari)** cheap, economical
安々 **yasuyasu** very peaceful; easily
安土桃山 **Azuchi-Momoyama** Azuchi-Momoyama (era, 1568–1603)
4 安元 **Angen** (era, 1175–1177)
安手 **yasude** cheap kind
安月給 **yasugekkyū** meager salary
安心 **anshin** feel relieved/reassured
安心立命 **anshin-ritsumei** spiritual peace and enlightenment
安心感 **anshinkan** sense of security
5 安永 **An'ei** (era, 1772–1781)
安芝居 **yasushibai** cheap theater
6 安死術 **anshijutsu** euthanasia
安気 **anki** ease of mind, at ease

安全 **anzen** safety
安全弁 **anzenben** safety valve
安全地帯 **anzen chitai** safety zone/island
安全保障 **anzen hoshō** (national) security
安全率 **anzenritsu** safety factor
安全第一 **anzen dai-ichi** Safety First
安全装置 **anzen sōchi** safety device
安全感 **anzenkan** sense of security
安危 **anki** safety (or danger), fate, welfare
安安 **yasuyasu** very peaceful; easily
7 安住 **anjū** live in peace
安否 **anpi** whether safe or not, well-being
安芸 **Aki** (ancient kuni, Hiroshima-ken)
安売 **yasuu(ri)** sell cheap
安利 **yasuri** low interest/profit
8 安価 **anka** low price
安直 **anchoku** cheap, inexpensive
安定 **antei** stability
安定板 **anteiban** stabilizing fin, stabilizer
安定性 **anteisei** stability
安定度 **anteido** (degree of) stability
安定感 **anteikan** sense of stability/security
安国 **yasukuni, ankoku** peacefully ruled
　　country
安固 **anko** secure, solid, stable
安易 **an'i** easy, easygoing
安物 **yasumono** cheap goods
安房 **Awa** (ancient kuni, Chiba-ken)
安和 **Anna** (era, 968–970)
9 安保 **anpo** (national) security (short for 安全
　　保障)
安保条約 **anpo jōyaku** security treaty
安臥 **anga** lie quiet in bed
安貞 **Antei** (era, 1227–1229)
安神立命 **anshin-ritsumei** spiritual peace
　　and enlightenment
安政 **Ansei** (era, 1854–1860)
10 安値 **yasune** low price
安逸 **an'itsu** idleness
安泰 **antai** peace; security
安酒 **yasuzake** cheap saké/liquor
安座 **anza** sitting on the floor with legs folded
安息 **ansoku** rest, repose
安息日 **ansokubi** sabbath
　　　ansokunichi the (Jewish) sabbath
　　　ansokujitsu the (Christian) sabbath
安息所 **ansokujo** resting place, haven
安息香 **ansokukō** benzoin
安息酸 **ansokusan** benzoic acid
安眠 **anmin** quiet sleep
安料理屋 **yasuryōriya** cheap restaurant
11 安宿 **yasuyado** cheap hotel
安康 **Ankō** (emperor, 453–456)
安産 **anzan** easy delivery/childbirth
12 安着 **anchaku** arrive safely
安普請 **yasubushin** flimsy building, jerry-built

安堵 **ando** feel relieved, breathe easy
安閑 **ankan** idly
　　　Ankan (emperor, 531–535)
13 安楽 **anraku** ease, comfort
安楽死 **anrakushi** euthanasia
安楽椅子 **anraku isu** easy chair
安置 **anchi** enshrine
14 安寧 **annei** public peace
　　　Annei (emperor, 549–511)
安寧秩序 **annei-chitsujo** peace and order
安静 **ansei** rest, quiet
15 安請合 **yasu(ke)a(i)** be too ready to make a
　　promise/commitment
16 安穏 **annon** peaceful, quiet, tranquil

──────────── 2 ────────────

1 一安心 **hitoanshin** feeling relieved for a while
3 久安 **Kyūan** (era, 1145–1151)
大安 **taian** lucky day
大安日 **taiannichi** lucky day
大安売 **ōyasuu(ri)** big (bargain) sale
小安 **shōan** somewhat at ease; content with
　　minor achievements, unambitious
4 不安 **fuan** uneasiness, apprehension; un-
　　settled, precarious; suspenseful, fearful
不安心 **fuanshin** uneasiness, apprehension
不安気 **fuange** uneasy, apprehensive
不安定 **fuantei** unstable, shaky
天安 **Tennan** (era, 857–859)
天安門 **Ten'anmon** Tiananmon, Gate of
　　Heavenly Peace (in Beijing)
仁安 **Nin'an** (era, 1166–1169)
文安 **Bunnan** (era, 1444–1449)
公安 **kōan** public order/safety
公安官 **kōankan** (railway) police
心安 **kokoroyasu(i)** feeling at ease, intimate,
　　friendly
心安立 **kokoroyasuda(te)** out of familiarity,
　　frank
5 平安 **heian** peace, tranquility; the Heian
　　period (794–1185)
平安京 **Heiankyō** ancient Kyōto
平安朝 **Heianchō** the Heian period (794–1185)
正安 **Shōan** (era, 1299–1302)
弘安 **Kōan** (era, 1278–1288)
目安 **meyasu** standard, yardstick
6 孝安 **Kōan** (emperor, 392–291 B.C.)
先安 **sakiyasu** lower quotations for future
　　months
安安 **yasuyasu** very peaceful; easily
7 承安 **Jōan** (era, 1171–1175)
応安 **Ōan** (era, 1368–1375)
8 治安 **chian** public peace/order
　　　Jian (era, 1021–1024)
治安条例 **chian jōrei** public-order regulations
治安維持 **chian iji** maintenance of public
　　order

3

氵
土
扌
口
女
巾
犭
弓
彳
彡
艹
宀 3←
⺍
山
士
广
尸
口

9 保安 **hoan** preservation of public peace,
security **Hōan** (era, 1120–1124)
保安官 **hoankan** sheriff
10 値安 **neyasu** low-priced
泰安 **taian** peace, tranquility
格安 **kakuyasu** inexpensive
格安品 **kakuyasuhin** bargain goods
11 偸安 **tōan** steal a moment of pleasure/rest;
stall for time
得安 **eyasu(i)** easily obtainable
康安 **Kōan** (era, 1361–1362)
12 割安 **wariyasu** comparatively cheap, a good
buy
硫安 **ryūan** ammonium sulfate
硝安 **shōan** ammonium nitrate
15 慰安 **ian** comfort, recreation, amusement
慰安会 **iankai** recreational get-together
慰安婦 **ianfu** comfort girl/woman, army
prostitute
霊安室 **reianshitsu** morgue
18 職安 **shokuan** (public) employment security
office (short for 公共職業安定所)

——————————— 3 ———————————

18 職業安定所 **shokugyō anteisho/jo** (public)
employment security office

3m3.2 / 490

守

SHU, SU, **mamo(ru)** protect; obey,
abide by **mori** babysitter; (lighthouse)
keeper **kami** feudal lord

——————————— 1 ———————————

0 お守り **(o)mamo(ri)** charm, amulet
2 守刀 **mamo(ri)gatana** sword for self-defense
5 守本尊 **mamo(ri)honzon** guardian deity
守札 **mamo(ri)fuda** paper charm
守旧 **shukyū** conservative
守立 **mo(ri)ta(teru)** bring up; support
6 守成 **shusei** preservation, maintenance
7 守兵 **shuhei** guards, garrison
守役 **moriyaku** guardian
9 守神 **mamo(ri)gami** guardian deity
10 守宮 **yamori** gecko, wall lizard
12 守備 **shubi** defense
守備兵 **shubihei** guards, garrison
守備隊 **shubitai** garrison, guards
13 守勢 **shusei** (on the) defensive
守戦 **shusen** defensive war/fight
14 守銭奴 **shusendo** miser, niggard
16 守衛 **shuei** (security) guard
20 守護 **shugo** protection, defense
守護神 **shugojin** guardian/tutelary deity,
mascot

——————————— 2 ———————————

2 子守 **komori** baby tending/sitting; nursemaid, baby sitter

子守歌 **komoriuta** lullaby
3 山守 **yamamori** forest ranger
4 太守 **taishu** governor-general, viceroy
天守閣 **tenshukaku** castle tower
6 死守 **shishu** desperately fought defense
防守 **bōshu** defense, the defensive
寺守 **teramori** temple sexton
7 坊守 **bōmori** sexton; low-ranking priest;
priest's wife
花守 **hanamori** one who guards flowers or
cherry blossoms against theft
攻守 **kōshu** offense and defense
見守 **mimamo(ru)** watch over
8 国守 **kokushu** (ancient) governor
固守 **koshu** adhere to, persevere in
門守 **kadomori** gatekeeper
9 保守 **hoshu** conservative
保守主義 **hoshu shugi** conservatism
保守的 **hoshuteki** conservative
保守党 **hoshutō** conservative party
看守 **kanshu** (prison) guard
10 家守 **yamori, iemori** caretaker, house agent
宮守 **miyamori** guarding a shrine; watchman
島守 **shimamori** island guard/caretaker
留守 **rusu** absence, being away from home;
looking after the house (while someone
is away); neglecting
留守中 **rusuchū** during one's absence
留守宅 **rusutaku** home whose master is
away
留守居 **rusui** looking after the house (while
someone is away); caretaker
留守番 **rusuban** looking after the house
(while someone is away); caretaker
留守番電話 **rusuban denwa** answering
machine
11 堂守 **dōmori** building guard
船守 **funamori** boat watchman
12 渡守 **wata(shi)mori** ferryman
13 墓守 **hakamori** gravekeeper
14 遵守 **junshu** obey, observe
墨守 **bokushu** strict adherence (to tradition)
関守 **sekimori** barrier keeper
15 確守 **kakushu** adhere to, be loyal to
監守 **kanshu** keeping watch over, custody
監守人 **kanshunin** custodian, (forest) ranger
16 操守 **sōshu** constancy, fidelity
17 厳守 **genshu** strict observance/adherence
18 鎮守 **chinju** local/tutelary deity
鎮守府 **chinjufu** naval station

——————————— 3 ———————————

6 灯台守 **tōdaimori** lighthouse keeper
8 居留守 **irusu** pretend not to be in (to avoid
callers)
16 薩摩守 **satsuma (no) kami** one who steals a
ride

3m3.3 / 990

宇

U sky, heavens; eaves, roof, house; country's border

——————— 1 ———————
4 宇内 **udai** the whole world
6 宇多 **Uda** (emperor, 887–897)
8 宇宙 **uchū** space, the universe
　宇宙学 **uchūgaku** cosmology
　宇宙服 **uchūfuku** space suit
　宇宙飛行士 **uchū hikōshi** astronaut
　宇宙船 **uchūsen** spaceship
　宇宙塵 **uchūjin** cosmic dust
　宇宙線 **uchūsen** cosmic rays
　宇宙論 **uchūron** cosmology
10 宇都宮 **Utsunomiya** (city, Tochigi-ken)
　宇部 **Ube** (city, Yamaguchi-ken)

——————— 2 ———————
3 大宇宙 **daiuchū** the great universe
6 気宇広大 **kiu-kōdai** magnanimous, big-hearted
9 眉宇 **biu** one's brow, eyebrows, face
10 胸宇 **kyōu** in one's heart
12 御宇 **gyou** imperial reign
19 羅宇 **rao** bamboo pipestem; Laos

——————— 4 ———————
2 八紘一宇 **hakkō-ichiu** universal brotherhood

3m3.4 / 178

宅

TAKU house, home, residence

——————— 1 ———————
0 お宅 **(o)taku** your house/company; you
6 宅地 **takuchi** residential land
　宅扱 **takuatsuka(i)** delivery to the house
8 宅送 **takusō** delivery
10 宅配便 **takuhaibin** parcel delivery business
12 宅診 **takushin** consultation at a clinic (rather than a house call)

——————— 2 ———————
4 火宅 **kataku** house on fire; this world of suffering
5 本宅 **hontaku** principal residence
6 在宅 **zaitaku** be in, be at home
　自宅 **jitaku** at one's home
7 住宅 **jūtaku** dwelling, residence, house, housing
　住宅地 **jūtakuchi** residential area/land
　住宅難 **jūtakunan** housing shortage
　邸宅 **teitaku** mansion, residence
　別宅 **bettaku** second residence
　社宅 **shataku** company house/apartment
　私宅 **shitaku** private home

8 舎宅 **shataku** house
　拙宅 **settaku** my humble home
　妾宅 **shōtaku** concubine's/mistress's house
10 帰宅 **kitaku** return/come home
　家宅 **kataku** house, premises
　家宅侵入 **kataku shinnyū** trespassing
　家宅捜索 **kataku sōsaku** domiciliary search
11 転宅 **tentaku** move (to a new address)
13 新宅 **shintaku** new residence; new branch family
15 弊宅 **heitaku** tumbledown shack; my humble home

——————— 3 ———————
10 留守宅 **rusutaku** home whose master is away

——————— 4 ———————
11 組立住宅 **kumita(te) jūtaku** prefab housing

——————— 5 ———————
3 下駄履住宅 **getaba(ki) jūtaku** apartment building whose first floor is occupied by stores and businesses

——————— 4 ———————

3m4.1

宋

SŌ Song/Sung (dynasty); dwell

——————— 1 ———————
5 宋代 **Sōdai** Sung dynasty/era
7 宋学 **Sōgaku** the learning of the Songs
9 宋音 **sōon** Song-dynasty reading (of a kanji)
12 宋朝 **Sōchō** Song dynasty

——————— 2 ———————
5 北宋 **Hokusō** early Sung dynasty (960–1127)
9 南宋 **Nansō** the Southern Songs (1127–1279)

3m4.2

牢

RŌ prison, jail; hardness

——————— 1 ———————
5 牢乎 **rōko** firm, solid, inflexible
6 牢死 **rōshi** die in prison
7 牢役人 **rōyakunin** jailer
8 牢固 **rōko** firm, solid, inflexible
9 牢屋 **rōya** prison, jail
10 牢破 **rōyabu(ri)** jailbreak
12 牢番 **rōban** prison guard, jailer
14 牢獄 **rōgoku** prison, jail

——————— 2 ———————
2 入牢 **nyūrō** imprisonment
3 土牢 **tsuchirō** underground prison, dungeon
4 水牢 **mizurō** water-filled dungeon
10 破牢 **harō** jailbreak

3

氵 丬 扌 口 女 巾 犭 弓 彳 彡 艹 宀 4 ← 龸 屮 土 广 尸 口

12 堅牢 **kenrō** strong, solid, (color)fast

—————— 3 ——————

6 地下牢 **chikarō** underground dungeon
10 座敷牢 **zashikirō** room for confining someone

3m4.3

宏 **KŌ** vast, large

—————— 1 ——————

3 宏大 **kōdai** vast, extensive, grand
6 宏壮 **kōsō** grand, imposing, magnificent

3m4.4

宍 **JIKU, shishi** meat, flesh

3m4.5 / 895

究 **KYŪ, kiwa(meru)** investigate thoroughly/exhaustively

—————— 1 ——————

8 究明 **kyūmei** study, investigation, inquiry
11 究理 **kyūri** philosophical thinking
12 究極 **kyūkyoku** final, ultimate

—————— 2 ——————

6 考究 **kōkyū** investigation, inquiry, research
7 学究 **gakkyū** scholar, student
学究的 **gakkyūteki** scholastic, academic
攻究 **kōkyū** study, research
8 追究 **tsuikyū** pursuit, inquiry
9 研究 **kenkyū** research
研究所 **kenkyūjo** (research) institute, laboratory
研究室 **kenkyūshitsu** laboratory, study room
研究家 **kenkyūka** researcher, student of
11 推究 **suikyū** inference
探究 **tankyū** research, inquiry, study
探究心 **tankyūshin** spirit of inquiry
探究者 **tankyūsha** investigator
15 論究 **ronkyū** discuss thoroughly
17 講究 **kōkyū** (specialized) study, research

—————— 3 ——————

10 核研究 **kakukenkyū** nuclear research

3m4.6 / 613

完 **KAN** completion

—————— 1 ——————

1 完了 **kanryō** complete, finish, conclude

完了形 **kanryōkei** perfect tense
3 完工 **kankō** completion (of construction)
5 完本 **kanpon** complete works/set
6 完全 **kanzen** complete, perfect
完全性 **kanzensei** completeness, perfection
完全無欠 **kanzen-muketsu** flawlessly perfect
完全雇傭 **kanzen koyō** full employment
完全数 **kanzensū** whole number, integer
完成 **kansei** completion, accomplishment
7 完投 **kantō** pitch a whole (baseball) game
9 完封 **kanpū** complete blockade; shutout
10 完納 **kannō** payment/delivery in full
11 完遂 **kansui** complete, attain
完済 **kansai** full payment, liquidation
完訳 **kan'yaku** complete translation
完敗 **kanpai** complete defeat
12 完備 **kanbi** fully equipped/furnished
完勝 **kanshō** complete victory
完結 **kanketsu** completion
18 完璧 **kanpeki** perfect, flawless

—————— 2 ——————

4 不完全 **fukanzen** incomplete, imperfect, faulty, defective
5 未完 **mikan** incomplete, unfinished
未完成 **mikansei** incomplete, unfinished
12 補完 **hokan** complement, supplement
補完税 **hokanzei** surtax

—————— 3 ——————

5 未来完了 **mirai kanryō** future perfect tense
11 過去完了 **kako kanryō** past perfect tense

—————— 5 ——————

3m5.1 / 616

宗 **SHŪ** religion, sect, denomination
SŌ head, leader
mune main/important point

—————— 1 ——————

5 宗主 **sōshu** suzerain
6 宗匠 **sōshō** master, teacher
宗旨 **shūshi** tenets, doctrine; sect, religion; one's principles
7 宗谷海峡 **Sōya-kaikyō** (strait between Hokkaidō and Sakhalin)
8 宗制 **shūsei** religious institutions
宗法 **shūhō** rules of a religion
宗国 **sōkoku** the home country
宗門 **shūmon** sect, religion
宗門改 **shūmon-arata(me)** religious census (Edo era)
9 宗風 **shūfū** customs of a school; style
宗派 **shūha** sect, denomination
宗祖 **shūso** founder of a sect
10 宗徒 **shūto** adherent, believer
muneto principal vassals

宗家 **sōke, sōka** head family; originator
宗教 **shūkyō** religion
宗教上 **shūkyōjō** from the standpoint of
　　religion
宗教心 **shūkyōshin** religiousness, piety
宗教史 **shūkyōshi** history of religion
宗教改革 **shūkyō kaikaku** the Reformation
宗教画 **shūkyōga** religious picture
宗教的 **shūkyōteki** religious
宗教性 **shūkyōsei** religious character
宗教哲学 **shūkyō tetsugaku** philosophy of
　　religion
宗教家 **shūkyōka** man of religion
宗教裁判 **shūkyō saiban** the Inquisition
宗教劇 **shūkyōgeki** religious drama
宗教観 **shūkyōkan** religious view
11 宗族 **sōzoku** one's family/relatives
宗務 **shūmu** religious affairs
宗規 **shūki** ruler of a religion
15 宗廟 **sōbyō** ancestral mausoleum

――――――― 2 ―――――――
3 大宗 **taisō** originator; leading figure; main
　　items
4 太宗 **taisō** imperial ancestor ranking highest
　　in achievement after the founder of the
　　dynasty
7 邪宗 **jashū** heretical sect; evil (foreign)
　　religion
邪宗門 **jashūmon** heretical religion
改宗 **kaishū** conversion (to another religion)
改宗者 **kaishūsha** a convert
9 祖宗 **sosō** ancestors, forefathers
皇宗 **kōsō** emperor's ancestors
10 時宗 **Jishū** (a Buddhist sect)
12 詞宗 **shisō** literary master
13 禅宗 **zenshū** the Zen sect
詩宗 **shisō** great poet
18 顕宗 **Kenzō** (emperor, 485–487)

――――――― 3 ―――――――
8 拝金宗 **haikinshū** mammonism
9 浄土宗 **Jōdoshū** the Jodo sect (of Buddhism)
10 華厳宗 **Kegonshū** (a Buddhist sect)

――――――― 4 ―――――――
9 浄土真宗 **Jōdo Shinshū** (a Buddhist sect,
　　offshoot of the Jodo sect)

――――――― 5 ―――――――
5 古義真言宗 **Kogi Shingon shū** the "old
　　meaning" sect of Esoteric Buddhism
13 新義真言宗 **Shingi Shingon shū** New
　　Shingon religion

3m5.2 / 296

宝　寶　寶

HŌ, takara treasure

――――――― 1 ―――――――
2 宝刀 **hōtō** treasured sword
5 宝永 **Hōei** (era, 1704–1711)
宝玉 **hōgyoku** precious stone, gem, jewel
宝石 **hōseki** precious stone, gem, jewel
6 宝舟 **takarabune** (picture of a) treasure ship
7 宝貝 **takaragai** cowrie, porcelain shell
8 宝典 **hōten** valued book; handbook
宝治 **Hōji** (era, 1247–1249)
宝物 **takaramono, hōmotsu** treasure
宝物殿 **hōmotsuden** treasury, museum
9 宝冠 **hōkan** crown, diadem
10 宝剣 **hōken** sacred/treasured sword
宝島 **takarajima** treasure island
宝庫 **hōko** treasure house
宝珠 **hōshu** precious jewel
11 宝亀 **Hōki** (era, 770–781)
宝船 **takarabune** (picture of a) treasure ship
14 宝暦 **Hōreki** (era, 1751–1764)
宝徳 **Hōtoku** (era, 1449–1452)
15 宝器 **hōki** treasured article
宝蔵 **hōzō** treasure house, treasury
宝箱 **takarabako** treasure chest, strongbox
23 宝籤 **takarakuji** lottery, raffle
宝鑑 **hōkan** valued book, handbook

――――――― 2 ―――――――
2 七宝 **shippō** the seven treasures (gold, silver,
　　lapis lazuli, pearls, crystal, agate, and
　　coral); cloisonné
七宝焼 **shippōyaki** cloisonné
子宝 **kodakara** the treasure that is children
3 三宝 **sanbō** the three treasures of Buddhism
　　(Buddha, the sutras, and the priesthood)
大宝 **Taihō** (era, 701–704)
4 什宝 **jūhō** treasured article
6 至宝 **shihō** most valuable treasure
7 延宝 **Enpō** (era, 1673–1681)
8 国宝 **kokuhō** national treasure
9 重宝 **chōhō** convenient, handy, useful
神宝 **shinpō** sacred/shrine treasures
珍宝 **chinpō** treasured article, valuables
10 家宝 **kahō** heirloom
秘宝 **hihō** (hidden) treasure
財宝 **zaihō** wealth, treasure, valuables
15 霊宝 **reihō** most precious treasure
17 擬宝珠 **gibōshu, gibōshi** leek flower
擬宝珠 **gibōshu, giboshi** ornamental railing
　　knob

――――――― 3 ―――――――
4 天平宝字 **Tenpyō Hōji** (era, 757–765)

――――――― 4 ―――――――
4 天平勝宝 **Tenpyō Shōhō** (era, 749–756)
天平感宝 **Tenpyō Kanpō** (era, 749)

3

氵
土
扌
口
女
巾
犭
弓
彳
彡
艹
宀 5←
灬
山
亠
广
尸
口

3m5.3

宥

TŌ excessive; broad, generous; cave

3m5.4 / 203

実

JITSU actual, real, true; sincerity
mi fruit, nut **mino(ru)** bear fruit
makoto sincerity **sane** seed inside a
(peach) stone; clitoris

──────── 1 ────────

2 実入 **mii(ri)** crop; earnings, gains
実子 **jisshi** one's biological child
実力 **jitsuryoku** actual ability, competence;
  arms, force
実力者 **jitsuryokusha** powerful person
実力派 **jitsuryokuha** powerful group
4 実収 **jisshū** actual income, take-home pay
実父 **jippu** one's biological father
5 実生 **mishō, miba(e)** seedling
実生活 **jisseikatsu** real/practical life
実母 **jitsubo** one's biological mother
実世界 **jissekai** the real/outside world
実世間 **jisseken** the real/everyday world
実存 **jitsuzon** existence
実存主義 **jitsuzon shugi** existentialism
実写 **jissha** on-the-spot pictures
実用 **jitsuyō** practical use, utility
実用主義 **jitsuyō shugi** pragmatism
実用的 **jitsuyōteki** practical
実用品 **jitsuyōhin** utility article
実兄 **jikkei** one's biological elder brother
6 実印 **jitsuin** one's registered seal
実刑 **jikkei** (prison) sentence with no stay of
  execution
実地 **jitchi** practical, on-site, in the field
実在 **jitsuzai** real existence, reality
実在論 **jitsuzairon** realism
実名 **jitsumei** one's real name
実行 **jikkō** put into practice, carry out, realize
実行力 **jikkōryoku** executive ability, action
7 実体 **jittai** substance, entity; three-dimensional
実体化 **jittaika** substantiate
実体論 **jittairon** substantialism, noumenalism
実状 **jitsujō** actual state of affairs
実弟 **jittei** one's biological younger brother
実否 **jippi** fact or falsehood, the truth/facts
実形 **jikkei** actual size
実学 **jitsugaku** practical science, realism
実労働 **jitsurōdō** actual labor
実社会 **jisshakai** the real world, actual
  society
実見 **jikken** actually see, witness

実利 **jitsuri** utility, practical advantage
実利主義 **jitsuri shugi** utilitarianism,
  materialism
8 実価 **jikka** real/intrinsic value; actual/cost
  price
実例 **jitsurei** example, illustration
実念論 **jitsunenron** realism
実効 **jikkō** practical effect
実直 **jitchoku** honest, steadfast
実況 **jikkyō** actual conditions
実況放送 **jikkyō hōsō** on-the-spot broadcast
実妹 **jitsumai** one's biological younger sister
実姉 **jisshi** one's biological elder sister
実物 **jitsubutsu** the real thing, the original
実物大 **jitsubutsudai** actual size
9 実相 **jissō** actual facts; (spiritual) reality
実施 **jisshi** put into effect, enforce
実科 **jikka** practical course
10 実益 **jitsueki** net profit, practical benefit
実員 **jitsuin** effective strength/personnel
実家 **jikka** one's parent's home
実株 **jitsukabu** shares actually traded
実証 **jikki** authentic account, true record
11 実動 **jitsudō** actual work
実習 **jisshū** practice, drill
実習生 **jisshūsei** trainee, apprentice
実理 **jitsuri** practical principles
実現 **jitsugen** come true, realize, materialize
実務 **jitsumu** business affairs/practice
実務家 **jitsumuka** businessman
実情 **jitsujō** actual state of affairs
12 実測 **jissoku** actual survey/measurement
実弾 **jitsudan** live ammunition; money
実検 **jikken** inspect (personally)
実景 **jikkei** actual view/scene
実量 **jitsuryō** real quantity
実装 **jissō** mounting, packaging
実証 **jisshō** actual proof
実証主義 **jisshō shugi** positivism
実証哲学 **jisshō tetsugaku** positivism
実証論 **jisshōron** positivism
実費 **jippi** actual expense; cost price
13 実業 **jitsugyō** industry, business
実業学校 **jitsugyō gakkō** vocational school
実業家 **jitsugyōka** industrialist, businessman
実際 **jissai** actual(ly), real(ly)
実際的 **jissaiteki** practical
実際家 **jissaika** practical man; expert
実豊 **mino(ri)yuta(ka)** fruitful
実数 **jissū** real number
実感 **jikkan** actual sensation, realization
実戦 **jissen** actual fighting, combat
実意 **jitsui** sincerity
実話 **jitsuwa** true story
実践 **jissen** in practice

実践的 **jissenteki** practical
実跡 **jisseki** actual traces, evidence
14 実像 **jitsuzō** real image
実歴 **jitsureki** actual experience
実演 **jitsuen** stage show, performance
実態 **jittai** actual conditions
実説 **jissetsu** true account
実聞 **jitsubun** hear with one's own ears
15 実権 **jikken** real power
実線 **jissen** solid line
実質 **jisshitsu** substance, essence, quality, content
実質的 **jisshitsuteki** substantial, essential, material, real
16 実録 **jitsuroku** authentic record, true account
17 実績 **jisseki** actual results, record of performance
18 実験 **jikken** experiment
実験的 **jikkenteki** experimental, empirical
実験者 **jikkensha** experimenter
実験所 **jikkenjo** experiment station
実験室 **jikkenshitsu** laboratory
実験場 **jikkenjō** proving/testing ground

———————— 2 ————————

3 口実 **kōjitsu** excuse, pretext
4 不実 **fujitsu** unfaithful, inconstant; false, untrue
内実 **naijitsu** the facts
中実 **chūjitsu** solid, not hollow
切実 **setsujitsu** acute, keen, urgent; earnest
木実 **ki(no)mi, ko(no)mi** fruit, nut, berry
5 史実 **shijitsu** historical fact
写実 **shajitsu** objective portrayal; realism
写実主義 **shajitsu shugi** realism, literalism
写実的 **shajitsuteki** realistic, true to life, graphic
6 瓜実顔 **urizanegao** oval/classic face
充実 **jūjitsu** repletion, completion, beefing up, making substantial
老実 **rōjitsu** loyal, faithful
名実 **meijitsu** name and reality
名実共 **meijitsu tomo (ni)** in fact as well as in name
如実 **nyojitsu** true to life, realistic
有実 **a(ri no) mi** pear
7 花実 **kajitsu** flowers and fruit; form and content
8 非実用品 **hijitsuyōhin** unessential items
非実際的 **hijissaiteki** impractical
果実 **kajitsu** fruit
果実酒 **kajitsushu** fruit wine
事実 **jijitsu** fact
事実上 **jijitsujō** in fact, actually
事実無根 **jijitsu mukon** contrary to fact, unfounded

其実 **so(no)jitsu** in reality
忠実 **chūjitsu** faithful, devoted, loyal
9 信実 **shinjitsu** sincerity, honesty
貞実 **teijitsu** faithful, devoted
首実検 **kubi jikken** inspection of a severed head; identification of a suspect
故実 **kojitsu** ancient customs
10 真実 **shinjitsu** truth, reality, the facts
真実性 **shinjitsusei** truth, authenticity, credibility
華実 **kajitsu** flowers and fruit; form and content
核実験 **kakujikken** nuclear testing
11 虚実 **kyojitsu** truth or falsehood; clever fighting, trying every strategy
現実 **genjitsu** actuality, reality
現実化 **genjitsuka** realize, turn (dreams) into reality
現実主義 **genjitsu shugi** realism
現実的 **genjitsuteki** realistic
現実性 **genjitsusei** actuality, reality
現実派 **genjitsuha** realists
現実感 **genjitsukan** sense of reality
現実暴露 **genjitsu bakuro** disillusionment
情実 **jōjitsu** personal circumstances/considerations
12 着実 **chakujitsu** steady, solid, trustworthy
堅実 **kenjitsu** solid, sound, reliable
無実 **mujitsu** false, unfounded; innocent
無実罪 **mujitsu (no) tsumi** false accusation
結実 **ketsujitsu** bear fruit
13 誠実 **seijitsu** sincere, faithful, truthful
14 綿実油 **menjitsuyu** cottonseed oil
15 確実 **kakujitsu** certain, reliable
質実 **shitsujitsu** plain and simple
質実剛健 **shitsujitsu-gōken** rough-hewn and robust
16 篤実 **tokujitsu** sincerity, faithfulness

———————— 3 ————————

4 不忠実 **fuchūjitsu** disloyal, unfaithful
不誠実 **fuseijitsu** insincere, unfaithful, dishonest
不確実 **fukakujitsu** uncertain, unreliable
6 自我実現 **jiga jitsugen** self-realization
8 非現実的 **higenjitsuteki** unrealistic
11 虚々実々 **kyokyo-jitsujitsu** clever fighting, trying every strategy
12 超現実主義 **chōgenjitsu shugi** surrealism

———————— 4 ————————

6 有名無実 **yūmei-mujitsu** in name only
10 既成事実 **kisei jijitsu** fait accompli
11 虚虚実実 **kyokyo-jitsujitsu** clever fighting, trying every strategy
13 禁断木実 **kindan (no) ko(no)mi** forbidden fruit

3

氵
土
扌
口
女
巾
犭
弓
彳
彡
艹
宀 5
⺌
山
士
广
尸
口

3m5.5 / 991

宙

CHŪ midair, space, heaven

——————— 1 ———————

6 宙返 **chūgae(ri)** somersault
9 宙乗 **chūno(ri)** suspended above the stage

——————— 2 ———————

6 宇宙 **uchū** space, the universe
宇宙学 **uchūgaku** cosmology
宇宙服 **uchūfuku** space suit
宇宙飛行士 **uchū hikōshi** astronaut
宇宙船 **uchūsen** spaceship
宇宙塵 **uchūjin** cosmic dust
宇宙線 **uchūsen** cosmic rays
宇宙論 **uchūron** cosmology

——————— 3 ———————

3 大宇宙 **daiuchū** the great universe

3m5.6 / 326

官

KAN government, the authorities; the (imperial) court; (as suffix) an official, officer

——————— 1 ———————

2 官人 **kanjin** an official
3 官女 **kanjo** court lady
4 官公庁 **kankōchō** government and municipal agencies
官公吏 **kankōri** public officials
官公署 **kankōsho** government and municipal offices
官辺 **kanpen** government, official
官辺筋 **kanpensuji** government/official sources
5 官民 **kanmin** government and people, public and private
官本 **kanpon** government publication
官用 **kan'yō** government business, official use
官庁 **kanchō** government office/authorities
官庁用語 **kanchō yōgo** official jargon
官立 **kanritsu** government(-established/-run)
6 官吏 **kanri** government official
官印 **kan'in** official seal
官地 **kanchi** government land
官名 **kanmei** official title
官有 **kan'yū** government-owned
官有地 **kan'yūchi** government land
官有林 **kan'yūrin** national forest
7 官位 **kan'i** office and rank; official rank
官邸 **kantei** official residence
官兵 **kanpei** government troops
官学 **kangaku** government school; official teachings
官私 **kanshi** public and private

8 官事 **kanji** government business
官舎 **kansha** official residence
官命 **kanmei** official orders/mission
官制 **kansei** government organization
官林 **kanrin** national forest
官服 **kanpuku** official uniform
官物 **kanbutsu** government property
官房 **kanbō** secretariat
官房長官 **kanbō chōkan** Chief Cabinet Secretary
官金 **kankin** government funds
9 官軍 **kangun** government/imperial troops
官海 **kankai** officialdom
官威 **kan'i** authority of the office/government
官省 **kanshō** government office/department
官界 **kankai** officialdom
官紀 **kanki** discipline among government officials
10 官修 **kanshū** government editing
官員 **kan'in** an official
官庫 **kanko** government storehouse
官能 **kannō** bodily functions; sensual, carnal
官能主義 **kannō shugi** sensualism
官能的 **kannōteki** sensuous, sensual, carnal
官記 **kanki** written appointment (to an office)
11 官務 **kanmu** official business
官船 **kansen** government ship
官許 **kankyo** government license
官設 **kansetsu** government(-established/-run)
12 官尊民卑 **kanson-minpi** exalting the government at the expense of the people
官報 **kanpō** official gazette/telegram
官営 **kan'ei** government-run
官給 **kankyū** government-supplied
官給品 **kankyūhin** government issues
官等 **kantō** official rank, civil-service grade
官費 **kanpi** government expense
官費生 **kanpisei** government-supported student
13 官業 **kangyō** government/state enterprise
官衙 **kanga** government office/authorities
官話 **Kanwa** the Mandarin language/dialect
14 官僚 **kanryō** bureaucracy, officialdom
官僚化 **kanryōka** bureaucratization
官僚主義 **kanryō shugi** bureaucracy
官僚制 **kanryōsei** bureaucracy
官僚的 **kanryōteki** bureaucratic
官歴 **kanreki** one's official career
官選 **kansen** government-appointed
官製 **kansei** government-made (postcard)
15 官権 **kanken** government authority
16 官憲 **kanken** the authorities
18 官職 **kanshoku** government post/service

——————— 2 ———————

3 大官 **taikan** high-ranking official
上官 **jōkan** senior official, one's superior

女官 **jokan, nyokan** minor court lady
小官 **shōkan** petty official
士官 **shikan** (military) officer
4 五官 **gokan** the five sense organs (eye, ear, nose, tongue, skin)
冗官 **jōkan** superfluous official, overstaffing
文官 **bunkan** civil official
5 左官 **sakan** plasterer
半官半民 **hankan-hanmin** semigovernmental
半官的 **hankanteki** semiofficial
半官報 **hankanpō** semiofficial paper
本官 **honkan** one's permanent post, principal assignment; I, the present official
仕官 **shikan** enter government/samurai's service
代官 **daikan** local governor, chief magistrate
6 任官 **ninkan** appointment, installation
次官 **jikan** vice-minister, undersecretary
在官 **zaikan** tenure of office
在官中 **zaikanchū** while in office
在官者 **zaikansha** officeholder
百官 **hyakkan** all government officials
7 位官 **ikan** rank and official position
佐官 **sakan** field officer
判官 **hangan** judge, magistrate
医官 **ikan** medical officer
技官 **gikan** technical official
8 長官 **chōkan** director, head, chief, secretary, administrator
免官 **menkan** dismissal
退官 **taikan** retire from office
法官 **hōkan** judicial officer, judge
武官 **bukan** military officer
9 係官 **kakarikan** official in charge
前官 **zenkan** one's former post
神官 **shinkan** Shinto priest
10 将官 **shōkan** general, admiral
高官 **kōkan** high official/office
兼官 **kenkan** additional post
宦官 **kangan** eunuch
教官 **kyōkan** instructor
11 副官 **fukukan, fukkan** adjutant, aide
猟官 **ryōkan** office-seeking
尉官 **ikan** officer below the rank of major
視官 **shikan** organ of sight
現官 **genkan** present post
12 廃官 **haikan** abolition of a post
属官 **zokkan** subordinate official
無官 **mukan** holding no office
13 感官 **kankan** sense organ
触官 **shokkan** tactile organ
14 僚官 **ryōkan** a (fellow) official
15 器官 **kikan** organ (of the body)
権官 **kenkan** powerful post/official
16 儒官 **jukan** official Confucian teacher

17 聴官 **chōkan** auditory organ
18 顕官 **kenkan** high official, dignitary
19 警官 **keikan** policeman
警官隊 **keikantai** police force/squad

─────── 3 ───────

3 下士官 **kashikan** noncommissioned officer
山林官 **sanrinkan** forester
4 公安官 **kōankan** (railway) police
5 弁務官 **benmukan** commissioner
外交官 **gaikōkan** diplomat
司令官 **shireikan** commanding officer
司法官 **shihōkan** judicial official
司政官 **shiseikan** civil administrator
6 行政官 **gyōseikan** administrative/executive official
式部官 **shikibukan** master of court ceremony
自衛官 **jieikan** Self Defense Forces member
8 事務官 **jimukan** administrative official, secretary, commissioner
法務官 **hōmukan** law officer, judge advocate
参事官 **sanjikan** councilor
林務官 **rinmukan** forestry officer, ranger
9 保安官 **hoankan** sheriff
通訳官 **tsūyakukan** official interpreter
指揮官 **shikikan** commander
神祇官 **jingikan** Shinto commissioner
政務官 **seimukan** parliamentary official
10 准士官 **junshikan** warrant officer
高等官 **kōtōkan** senior official
書記官 **shokikan** secretary
書記官長 **shokikanchō** chief secretary
秘書官 **hishokan** (private) secretary
財務官 **zaimukan** finance secretary
11 商務官 **shōmukan** commercial attaché
視学官 **shigakkan** school inspector
産学官 **sangakkan, sangakukan** industry, universities/academia, and government/officials
終身官 **shūshinkan** official appointed for life
12 検査官 **kensakan** inspector, examiner
検疫官 **ken'ekikan** quarantine officer
検察官 **kensatsukan** public prosecutor
検閲官 **ken'etsukan** censor, inspector
裁判官 **saibankan** the judge
13 試験官 **shikenkan** examiner
15 審判官 **shinpankan** judge, umpire, referee
監督官 **kantokukan** inspector, superintendent
監察官 **kansatsukan** inspector, police supervisor
16 親任官 **shinninkan** official personally appointed by the emperor
19 警察官 **keisatsukan** police officer
21 顧問官 **komonkan** councilor

3

氵
土
扌
口
女
巾
犭
弓
彳
彡
艹
宀 5
⺍
山
士
广
尸
口

─────────── 4 ───────────

4 文武百官 **bunbu hyakkan** civil and military officials

8 事務長官 **jimuchōkan** chief secretary

依願免官 **igan menkan** retirement at one's own request

官房長官 **kanbō chōkan** Chief Cabinet Secretary

国務長官 **kokumu chōkan** (U.S.) Secretary of State

9 軍司令官 **gunshireikan** army commander

政務次官 **seimu jikan** parliamentary vice-minister

11 婦人警官 **fujin keikan** policewoman

痕跡器官 **konseki kikan** vestigial organ

14 総指揮官 **sōshikikan** supreme commander

総務長官 **sōmu chōkan** director-general

18 観戦武官 **kansenbukan** military observer

3m5.7 / 1086

宜

GI, **yoro(shii)** good, alright **yoro(shiku)** regards, greetings; well, suitably **mube** true, well said

─────────── 2 ───────────

4 友宜 **yūgi** friendship, friendly relations

9 便宜 **bengi** convenience, expediency

便宜上 **bengijō** for convenience

10 時宜 **jigi** the right time for

13 適宜 **tekigi** suitable, proper, as one thinks best

16 機宜 **kigi** opportunity, occasion

19 禰宜 **negi** (lower rank of Shinto priest)

3m5.8 / 355

定

TEI, JŌ definite, fixed, constant, regular **sada(meru)** determine, decide **sada(me)** rule, provision; decision; arrangements; karma **sada(maru)** be determined/decided **sada(ka)** definite, certain

─────────── 1 ───────────

4 定収入 **teishūnyū** fixed income

定木 **jōgi** ruler, (T-)square; standard

定日 **teijitsu** fixed/appointed date

5 定本 **teihon** the authentic/standard text

定石 **jōseki** book moves (in go); formula, rule

定立 **teiritsu** thesis

6 定年 **teinen** age limit, retirement age

定休日 **teikyūbi** regular holiday, Closed (Tuesday)s

定式 **jōshiki, teishiki** prescribed/established form, formula, formality

7 定位 **teii** orientation; normal position

定住 **teijū** settle down/permanently

定住地 **teijūchi** fixed/permanent abode

定住者 **teijūsha** permanent resident

定形 **teikei** fixed/regular form

定見 **teiken** definite/settled opinion

定言 **teigen** categorical proposition

定足数 **teisokusū** quorum

8 定価 **teika** (fixed/set) price

定価表 **teikahyō** price list

定例 **teirei, jōrei** established usage, precedent; regular (meeting)

定命 **teimei** fate; (predetermined) lifespan **jōmyō** normal/alloted lifespan

定限 **teigen** limit, restrict

定刻 **teikoku** the scheduled/appointed time

定法 **jōhō** established rule, convention, formula

定性分析 **teisei bunseki** qualitative analysis

9 定冠詞 **teikanshi** definite article

定点 **teiten** fixed point

定型 **teikei** definite form, type

定型化 **teikeika** standardization

定型的 **teikeiteki** typical

定型詩 **teikeishi** poetry in a fixed form

定律 **teiritsu** fixed law/rhythm

定則 **teisoku** established rule, law

定食 **teishoku** regular meal, table d'hôte

10 定員 **teiin** prescribed number of personnel; (seating) capacity; quorum

定席 **jōseki** one's usual seat; variety hall

定格 **teikaku** rating, rated (voltage)

定時 **teiji** regular time/intervals, fixed period

定時制 **teijisei** part-time (school) system

定紋 **jōmon** family crest

11 定率 **teiritsu** fixed/flat rate

定宿 **jōyado** one's usual hotel

定常 **teijō** steady, stationary, regular, routine

定理 **teiri** theorem

定規 **teiki** prescribed **jōgi** ruler, (T-)square; standard

12 定着 **teichaku** fix, fasten, anchor

定着物 **teichakubutsu** fixtures

定着剤 **teichakuzai** fixing agent

定着液 **teichakueki** fixing solution

定温 **teion** constant temperature

定植 **teishoku** plant (seedlings) permanently

定期 **teiki** fixed period/term/intervals, regular (meeting); (train) pass, commuting ticket (short for 定期券)

定期払 **teikibara(i)** time/installment payments

定期券 **teikiken** (train) pass, commuting ticket

定期的 **teikiteki** periodic

定期風 **teikifū** periodic wind

定期船 **teikisen** regular(ly scheduled) ship

定量 **teiryō** fixed quantity; to measure; dose

定量分析 **teiryō bunseki** quantitative analysis

定款 **teikan** articles of incorporation, charter

定給 **teikyu** fixed salary/allowance

定評 **teihyō** acknowledged, recognized
13 定業 **teigyō** regular occupation
定義 **teigi** definition
定数 **teisū** a constant; fixed number; fate
定置 **teichi** stationary, fixed
14 定説 **teisetsu** established/accepted opinion
15 定盤 **jōban** surface plate/table, level block, molding board
定論 **teiron** generally accepted theory/view
16 定積 **teiseki** fixed area; constant volume
18 定礎式 **teisoshiki** cornerstone-laying ceremony
定職 **teishoku** regular occupation, steady job
定額 **teigaku** fixed amount, flat sum

――――――― 2 ―――――――

1 一定 **ittei** fixed, prescribed, regular, definite; fix, settle; standardize
ichijō definitely settled
一定不変 **ittei fuhen** invariable, permanent
4 不定 **futei, fujō** uncertain, indefinite, change-able
不定期 **futeiki** at irregular intervals, for an indefinite term
不定詞 **futeishi** an infinitive
予定 **yotei** plan, prearrangement, expectation
予定日 **yoteibi** scheduled date, expected date (of birth)
予定案 **yoteian** program, schedule
内定 **naitei** informal/tentative decision
公定 **kōtei** official(ly set)
公定歩合 **kōtei buai** official bank rate, rediscount rate
5 未定 **mitei** undecided, pending
平定 **heitei** suppress, subdue
6 仮定 **katei** supposition, assumption, hypoth-esis
仮定法 **kateihō** subjunctive mood
安定 **antei** stability
安定板 **anteiban** stabilizing fin, stabilizer
安定性 **anteisei** stability
安定度 **anteido** (degree of) stability
安定感 **anteikan** sense of stability/security
7 判定 **hantei** judgment, decision, verdict
判定勝 **hanteiga(chi)** win by a decision
決定 **kettei** decision, determination
決定版 **ketteiban** definitive edition
決定的 **ketteiteki** decisive, conclusive, definitive
決定権 **ketteiken** (right of) decision
決定論 **ketteiron** determinism
否定 **hitei** denial, negation
否定文 **hiteibun** negative sentence
否定的 **hiteiteki** negative, contradictory
改定 **kaitei** reform, revision
見定 **misada(meru)** make sure of, ascertain

8 限定 **gentei** limit, qualify, modify; define, determine
限定版 **genteiban** limited edition
制定 **seitei** enact, establish
協定 **kyōtei** agreement, accord
法定 **hōtei** legal, prescribed by law
国定 **kokutei** quasi-national, state-prescribed
固定 **kotei** fixed
固定給 **koteikyū** fixed salary
肯定 **kōtei** affirm
肯定文 **kōteibun** affirmative sentence
肯定的 **kōteiteki** affirmative
所定 **shotei** fixed, prescribed, stated
9 指定 **shitei** appoint, designate
指定席 **shiteiseki** reserved seats
品定 **shinasada(me)** take stock of, judge
査定 **satei** assessment
約定 **yakujō** promise, agreement
約定書 **yakujōsho** (written) contract/agreement
約定済 **yakujōzu(mi)** promised; engaged; sold
10 既定 **kitei** predetermined, prearranged, fixed
案定 **an(no)jō** as feared/expected, sure enough
特定 **tokutei** specify
11 勘定 **kanjō** calculation; account; settling an account
勘定日 **kanjōbi** settlement day
勘定高 **kanjōdaka(i)** calculating, mercenary
勘定書 **kanjōsho** bill, one's account
勘定違 **kanjōchiga(i)** miscalculation
剪定 **sentei** pruning
剪定鋏 **sentei-basami** pruning shears
推定 **suitei** presumption, estimate
規定 **kitei** stipulations, provisions, regulations
断定 **dantei** conclusion, decision
設定 **settei** establishment, creation
12 測定 **sokutei** measure
測定法 **sokuteihō** method of measurement; mensuration
検定 **kentei** official approval, inspection
検定料 **kenteiryō** examination fee
検定済 **kenteizu(mi)** (government) inspected/authorized
検定試験 **kentei shiken** (teacher) certifica-tion examination
無定形 **muteikei** amorphous
無定見 **muteiken** lack of principle, inconstant
裁定 **saitei** decision, ruling, arbitration
策定 **sakutei** devise, formulate (a plan/policy)
評定 **hyōtei** rating, evaluation
hyōjō conference, council
欽定 **kintei** authorized (by the emperor)
欽定訳聖書 **kinteiyaku seisho** the King James Bible

3

氵
土
扌
口
女
巾
犭
弓
彳
彡
艹
宀 5←
⺌
山
�
广
尸
口

欽定憲法 **kintei kenpō** constitution granted by the emperor

13 禅定 **zenjō** meditative concentration

想定 **sōtei** hypothesis, supposition

戡定 **kantei** (military) mopping-up

14 選定 **sentei** select, choose

算定 **santei** calculate, estimate

認定 **nintei** approval, acknowledgment

15 標定 **hyōtei** orient, range (a gun)

暫定 **zantei** tentative, provisional

暫定的 **zanteiteki** tentative, provisional

暫定案 **zanteian** tentative plan

確定 **kakutei** decision, definite

縁定 **ensada(me)** marriage (contract)

論定 **rontei** discuss and determine

18 鎮定 **chintei** suppress, subdue, pacify

20 議定 **gitei, gijō** agreement

議定書 **giteisho, gijōsho** a protocol

23 鑑定 **kantei** appraisal, expert opinion

鑑定人 **kanteinin** appraiser, expert (witness)

鑑定家 **kanteika** appraiser, expert (witness)

鑑定書 **kanteisho** expert's report

鑑定料 **kanteiryō** expert's/legal fee

─────── 3 ───────

4 不安定 **fuantei** unstable, shaky

5 未確定 **mikakutei** unsettled, pending

井勘定 **donburi kanjō** paying money into and out of a pot, keeping no records of revenues and expenditures, slipshod accounting, rough estimate

6 仮勘定 **karikanjō** suspense account

行方定 **yukue-sada(menu)** aimless, wandering

7 別勘定 **betsukanjō** separate account

杓子定規 **shakushi-jōgi** hard-and-fast rule

9 前勘定 **maekanjō** paying in advance

12 雲形定規 **kumogata jōgi** French curve

14 総勘定 **sōkanjō** final settlement

16 懐勘定 **futokoro kanjō** counting one's pocket money; one's financial situation

─────── 4 ───────

2 二重否定 **nijū hitei** double negative

5 目子勘定 **me(no)ko kanjō** measuring by eye; mental arithmetic

6 老少不定 **rōshō-fujō** Death comes to old and young alike.

9 軍事協定 **gunji kyōtei** military pact

10 差引勘定 **sashihiki kanjō** account balance

11 紳士協定 **shinshi kyōtei** gentleman's agreement

12 勤務評定 **kinmu hyōtei** job performance appraisal

18 職業安定所 **shokugyō anteisho/jo** (public) employment security office

─────── 5 ───────

3 小田原評定 **odawara hyōjō** endless debate, fruitless conference

3m5.9

EN just like, as if **a(teru)** address (a letter) **-ate** addressed to **sanaga(ra)** just like **-zutsu** apiece, each

─────── 1 ───────

0 宛てがう **a(tegau)** apply/hold/fasten to; allot; provide; choose for

5 宛字 **ateji** kanji used phonetically; kanji used purely ideographically, disregarding usual readings

6 宛先 **atesaki** address

宛名 **atena** address

宛行 **atega(u)** apply/hold/fasten to; allot; provide; choose for

宛行扶持 **ategaibuchi** discretionary allowance

─────── 2 ───────

6 名宛 **naate** address (on an envelope)

名宛人 **naatenin** addressee

3m5.10

穹

KYŪ sky

─────── 1 ───────

16 穹窿 **kyūryū** vault (of heaven)

3m5.11 / 898

突 突

TOTSU, tsu(ku) thrust, poke, strike

tsutsu(ku) poke, peck, pick at

─────── 1 ───────

2 突入 **totsunyū** rush/plunge into

3 突上 **tsu(ki)a(geru)** push/toss up; press/urge from below

4 突支 **tsukkai** prop, strut, support

突支棒 **tsukkaibō** prop, strut, support

突止 **tsu(ki)to(meru)** ascertain

突込 **tsu(ki)ko(mu), tsu(k)ko(mu)** thrust/poke/plunge into

5 突出 **tsu(ki)da(su)** thrust/push/stick out

tsu(ki)de(ru) jut/stick out, protrude

tosshutsu projection, protrusion

突付 **tsu(ki)tsu(keru)** thrust before, point (a gun) at

突立 **tsu(t)ta(tsu)** stand up (straight)

tsu(ki)ta(teru) stab, thrust violently, plant (one's feet)

突立上 **tsu(t)ta(chi)a(garu)** jump to one's feet

突目 **tsu(ki)me** getting poked in the eye

6 突合 tsu(ki)a(u) poke/jab each other
       tsu(ki)a(waseru) bring face to face;
       compare with
  突返 tsu(ki)kae(su) thrust back; refuse to
       accept
  突先 tossaki tip, end
  突如 totsujo suddenly, unexpectedly
  突当 tsu(ki)a(taru) run/bump into; reach the
       end tsu(ki)a(tari) collision; end (of a
       street/corridor)
7 突角 tokkaku convex angle
  突走 tsu(p)pashi(ru) run at full speed
  突抜 tsu(ki)nu(keru) pierce, go through
  突戻 tsu(ki)modo(su) thrust back; refuse to
       accept
8 突刺 tsu(ki)sa(su) stab, pierce
  突拍子 toppyōshi (mo nai) out of tune,
       exorbitant, very
  突突 tsu(t)tsu(ku) poke, prod, nudge
  突放 tsu(p)pana(su), tsu(ki)hana(su) cast
       off, forsake
9 突飛 toppi wild, fantastic, reckless, eccentric
       tsu(ki)to(basu) knock down, send flying
  突発 toppatsu occur suddenly, break out
  突除 tsu(ki)no(keru) push aside, elbow out
  突通 tsu(ki)tō(ru) pierce, penetrate
  突指 tsu(ki)yubi sprained finger
10 突倒 tsu(ki)tao(su) knock down
  突進 tosshin rush, onrush, dash, charge
  突起 tokki protuberance, projection
  突殺 tsu(ki)koro(su) stab to death
  突破 toppa break through, overcome
       tsu(ki)yabu(ru) break/crash through
11 突掛 tsu(ki)ka(karu) lunge at
  突掛草履 tsu(k)ka(ke) zōri slip-on straw
       sandles
  突張 tsu(p)pa(ru) stretch (an arm) against,
       plant (one's foot) on; insist on
       tsu(p)pa(ri) prop, brace
  突崩 tsu(ki)kuzu(su) knock down, raze, level
  突貫 tokkan charge, rush ahead
12 突堤 tottei jetty, pier, breakwater
  突落 tsu(ki)o(tosu) push off/down
  突棒 tsu(ki)bō cattle prod, goad
  突然 totsuzen suddenly, unexpectedly
  突然変異 totsuzen hen'i mutation
13 突傷 tsu(ki)kizu stab wound
  突詰 tsu(ki)tsu(meru) investigate, get to the
       bottom of; brood over
14 突端 toppana, tottan tip, point
15 突撃 totsugeki charge, assault
  突撃隊 totsugekitai shock troops
——————— 2 ———————
3 小突 kozu(ku) poke, prod, nudge
5 玉突 tamatsu(ki) billiards
  石突 ishizu(ki) hard tip (of an umbrella)

6 羽突 hanetsu(ki) battledore and shuttlecock
       (badminton-like game)
7 角突合 tsunotsu(ki)a(i) bickering, wrangling
  肘突 hijitsu(ki) elbow rest
8 追突 tsuitotsu rear-end collision
  突突 tsu(t)tsu(ku) poke, prod, nudge
10 唐突 tōtotsu abrupt
  胸突八丁 munatsu(ki) hatchō steepest part
       of the path up the mountain
11 猪突 chototsu reckless, foolhardy
  猪突猛進 chototsu mōshin headlong rush
  強突張 gōtsukuba(ri) headstrong
12 温突 ondoru (Korean) floor heater
  霊突 kumotsu(ku) towering
13 楯突 tatetsu(ku) oppose, defy
  煙突 entotsu chimney
15 衝突 shōtotsu collision; clash
16 激突 gekitotsu crash, collision
17 篠突雨 shinotsu(ku) ame driving/torrential
       rain
18 額突 nukazu(ku) bow low, kowtow
——————— 3 ———————
6 虫様突起 chūyō tokki the (vermiform)
       appendix
  虫様突起炎 chūyō tokkien appendicitis
——————— 4 ———————
5 正面衝突 shōmen shōtotsu head-on
       collision
9 怒髪天突 dohatsu ten (o) tsu(ku) be
       infuriated

3m5.12 / 140

空 KŪ sky; empty sora sky su/a(ku)
    be empty/unoccupied a(keru), empty,
    leave blank kara, kara(ppo) empty
    muna(shii) empty, vain, futile
utsu(ro) hollow, blank utsuke empty(-headed)

——————— 1 ———————
0 空オケ karaoke prerecorded orchestral
       accompaniment (tape and amplification
       system for amateur singers)
3 空下手 karaheta, kara(p)peta utterly inept
  空々 sorazora(shii) feigned, false, empty,
       transparent (lie) kūkū emptiness,
       nothing; absence of fleshly passions
  空々漠々 kūkū-bakubaku vast and empty
4 空元気 karagenki mere bravado
  空中 kūchū in the air/sky, aerial
  空中戦 kūchūsen air battle, aerial warfare
  空中線 kūchūsen antenna
  空文 kūbun dead letter, mere scrap of paper
  空手 karate empty-handed; karate
  空手形 karategata bad check; empty promise
  空手道 karatedō karate
5 空包 kūhō a blank (cartridge)

空母 **kūbo** aircraft carrier (short for 航空母艦)

空世辞 **karaseji** flattery, empty compliments

空写 **karautsu(shi)** clicking the camera shutter without taking a photo (because the film is improperly loaded or to advance the film)

空尻 **kara(k)ketsu** flat broke

空白 **kūhaku** blank, empty space, vacuum

空目 **sorame** misperception; upward look; pretending not to see

6 空死 **soraji(ni)** feign death

空気 **kūki** air, atmosphere; pneumatic

空気弁 **kūkiben** air valve

空気抜 **kūkinu(ki)** vent(ilator)

空気室 **kūkishitsu** air chamber

空気銃 **kūkijū** air gun/rifle

空合 **soraa(i)** weather

空缶 **a(ki)kan** empty can

空色 **sora-iro** sky blue; weather

空地 **a(ki)chi** vacant lot/land

空名 **kūmei** in name only; false reputation

空回 **karamawa(ri)** racing/idling (of an engine), skidding (of a car); fruitless effort

空耳 **soramimi** mishearing; feigned deafness

7 空身 **karami** without luggage, (traveling) light

空位 **kūi** vacant post, interregnum

空似 **sorani** chance resemblance

空冷式 **kūreishiki** air-cooled

空即是色 **kūsoku-zeshiki** void matter as tangible

空谷 **kūkoku** lonely valley

空豆 **soramame** broad/fava bean

空言 **soragoto, kūgen** falsehood, idle talk

空車 **kūsha, karaguruma** empty car, (taxi) For Hire

8 空念仏 **karanenbutsu** perfunctory praying, empty/fruitless talk

空泣 **sorana(ki)** crocodile tears

空押 **karao(shi)** blind/inkless stamping

空空 **sorazora(shii)** feigned, false, empty, transparent (lie) **kūkū** emptiness, nothing; absence of fleshly passions

空空漠漠 **kūkū-bakubaku** vast and empty

空所 **kūsho** a space/blank

空取引 **karatorihiki, kūtorihiki** fictitious transaction

9 空飛 **sorato(bu)** flying (saucer/carpet)

空発 **kūhatsu** random shooting; detonation which does not achieve the purpose

空便 **karabin, a(ki)bin** flight with no passengers

空軍 **kūgun** air force

空前 **kūzen** unprecedented

空前絶後 **kūzen-zetsugo** the first ever and probably last ever

空風 **kara(k)kaze** dry wind

空洞 **kūdō** cave, cavern; hollow, cavity

空洞化 **kūdōka** hollowing out, deindustrialization

空挺部隊 **kūtei butai** airborne troops, paratroops

空咳 **karazeki, karaseki** dry/hacking cough

空茶 **karacha** tea without cakes

空室 **kūshitsu** vacant room

空屋 **a(ki)ya** vacant house

空相場 **karasōba** fictitious transaction

空威張 **kara-iba(ri)** bluster, bravado; mock dignity

空音 **sorane** hearing a nonexistent sound; false/untimely (rooster) cry; a lie

10 空陸 **kūriku** land and air (forces)

空部屋 **a(ki)beya** vacant room

空涙 **soranamida** crocodile tears

空拳 **kūken** empty-handed, with one's bare hands

空振 **karabu(ri)** swing and miss (in baseball)

空荷 **karani** without a load/cargo

空家 **a(ki)ya** vacant house

空席 **kūseki** vacant seat, vacancy

空株 **karakabu** shares which one does not own

空梅雨 **karatsuyu** a dry rainy season

空時間 **a(ki)jikan** open period, spare time

空恐 **soraoso(roshii)** having vague fears

空砲 **kūhō** unloaded cannon; a blank (cartridge)

空眠 **soranemu(ri)** feigned sleep

空恥 **soraha(zukashii)** feeling ashamed/shy without knowing why

空笑 **sorawara(i)** forced laugh, feigned smile

11 空疎 **kūso** empty, without substance

空虚 **kūkyo** empty, hollow; inane

空瓶 **a(ki)bin** empty bottle

空域 **kūiki** airspace

空堀 **karabori** dry moat/ditch

空巣 **a(ki)su** sneak thief, prowler

空巣狙 **a(ki)sunera(i)** sneak thief, prowler

空殻 **a(ki)gara** empty shell/container

空理 **kūri** empty/impractical theory

空惚 **soratobo(keru)** pretend not to know

空転 **kūten** (engine) idling, getting nowhere

空釣 **karazu(ri)** fishing without bait

12 空隙 **kūgeki** gap, opening

空港 **kūkō** airport

空揚 **karaa(ge)** food fried without coating in a batter

空弾 **kūdan** a blank (cartridge)

空蒸 **karamu(shi)** steaming

空覚 **soraobo(e)** memorization

空喜 **karayoroko(bi)** premature/unjustified rejoicing

空景気 **karageiki** false economic prosperity

空費 **kūhi** waste

空閑地 **kūkanchi** vacant land

空間 **kūkan** space　**a(ki)ma** vacant room

13 空際 **kūsai** edge of the sky, horizon

空漠 **kūbaku** vast; vague

空夢 **sorayume** fabricated dream

空寝入 **sorane-i(ri)** pretend to be asleep

空腹 **kūfuku, su(ki)hara** empty stomach, hunger

空解 **sorado(ke)** come untied

空想 **kūsō** idle fancy, fiction, daydream

空想的 **kūsōteki** fanciful, visionary

空想家 **kūsōka** dreamer, idealist, utopian

空路 **kūro** air route; by air/plane

空鉄砲 **karadeppō** unloaded gun; a blank (cartridge)

空雷 **kūrai** aerial torpedo

空電 **kūden** (radio) static

14 空模様 **soramoyō** looks of the sky, weather

空説 **kūsetsu** baseless rumor

空閨 **kūkei** spouseless bedroom

15 空談 **kūdan** idle talk, gossip

空論 **kūron** empty/impractical theory

空調 **kūchō** air conditioning (short for 空気調節)

16 空嘯 **sorausobu(ku)** feign unconcern

空輸 **kūyu** air transport

空頼 **soradano(mi)** hoping against hope

18 空騒 **karasawa(gi)** much ado about nothing

19 空爆 **kūbaku** bombing, air raid (short for 空中爆撃)

20 空欄 **kūran** blank column

22 空襲 **kūshū** air raid/strike

23 空籤 **karakuji** a blank (in a lottery)

—————— 2 ——————

3 大空 **ōzora, taikū** the sky

上空 **jōkū** the sky/air, high-altitude **uwa(no)sora** inattentive, absent-minded

4 天空 **tenkū** the sky/air

中空 **chūkū** midair; hollow **nakazora** midair

手空 **tea(ki)** leisure, spare/idle time

5 冬空 **fuyuzora** winter sky

6 防空 **bōkū** air defense

防空壕 **bōkūgō** air-raid/bomb shelter

7 身空 **misora** one's lot/circumstaces

低空 **teikū** low altitude

低空飛行 **teikū hikō** low-level flying

対空 **taikū** antiaircraft

初空 **hatsuzora, hatsusora** the morning sky on New Year's Day

8 制空権 **seikūken** mastery of the air, air superiority

夜空 **yozora** night sky

空空 **sorazora(shii)** feigned, false, empty, transparent (lie)　**kūkū** emptiness, nothing; absence of fleshly passions

空空漠漠 **kūkū-bakubaku** vast and empty

青空 **aozora** the blue sky

青空市場 **aozora ichiba** open-air market

雨空 **amazora** rainy sky

9 架空 **kakū** overhead, aerial; fanciful, fictitious

星空 **hoshizora** starry sky

秋空 **akizora** autumn sky

10 高空 **kōkū, takazora** high altitude

真空 **shinkū** vacuum

真空掃除機 **shinkū sōjiki** vacuum cleaner

真空管 **shinkūkan** vacuum tube

旅空 **tabi (no) sora** away from home

航空 **kōkū** aviation, flight, aero-

航空士 **kōkūshi** aviator

航空母艦 **kōku bokan** aircraft carrier

航空写真 **kōkū shashin** aerial photo

航空会社 **kōkū-gaisha** airline (company)

航空学 **kōkūgaku** aeronautics

航空券 **kōkūken** flight/airplane ticket

航空便 **kōkūbin** airmail

航空家 **kōkūka** aviator

航空病 **kōkūbyō** airsickness

航空隊 **kōkūtai** air force

航空基地 **kōkū kichi** air base

航空術 **kōkūjutsu** aeronautics, aviation

航空船 **kōkūsen** airship, dirigible, blimp

航空路 **kōkūro** air route

航空機 **kōkūki** aircraft, airplane

11 虚空 **kokū** empty space, the air

雪空 **yukizora** snowy sky

12 寒空 **samuzora** wintry sky, cold weather

絵空言 **esoragoto** a fabrication, fantasy

13 滑空 **kakkū** glide

滞空 **taikū** staying in the air

14 領空 **ryōkū** territorial airspace

—————— 3 ——————

6 全日空 **Zennikkū** ANA, All Nippon Airways (short for 全日本空輸)

—————— 4 ——————

6 全日本空輸 **Zen Nippon Kūyu** All Nippon Airways

色即是空 **shikisoku-zekū** Matter is void. All is vanity.

—————— 6 ——————

宦 → **3m7.14**

3m6.1

宥　**YŪ, nada(meru)** soothe, placate

—————— 1 ——————

0 宥めすかす **nada(mesukasu)** soothe and humor, coax

3

8 宥和 **yūwa** appease, placate
宥和政策 **yūwa seisaku** appeasement policy
17 宥賺 **nada(me)suka(su)** soothe and humor, coax

――――――― 2 ―――――――

22 贖宥 **shokuyū** (Catholic) indulgence

3m6.2 / 625

宣

SEN announce
no(beru) state, declare

――――――― 1 ―――――――

0 宣する **sen(suru)** declare, proclaim, announce
3 宣下 **senge** imperial proclamation
4 宣化 **Senka** (emperor, 535–539)
5 宣布 **senpu** proclaim, promulgate
6 宣伝 **senden** propaganda; advertising, publicity
宣伝係 **sendengakari** public relations man
宣伝屋 **senden'ya** propagandist, publicist
宣伝部 **sendenbu** publicity department
宣伝隊 **sendentai** propaganda squad
宣伝費 **sendenhi** publicity/advertising expenses
宣伝業 **sendengyō** publicity/advertising business
宣伝業者 **senden gyōsha** publicist
宣伝戦 **sendensen** propaganda/advertising campaign
宣伝機関 **senden kikan** propaganda organ
宣旨 **senji** imperial command
7 宣告 **senkoku** sentence, verdict, pronouncement
宣言 **sengen** declaration, statement
宣言書 **sengensho** declaration, manifesto
8 宣命 **senmyō** imperial edict
宣明 **senmei** proclaim, declare
10 宣教 **senkyō** missionary work, evangelism
宣教師 **senkyōshi** missionary
12 宣揚 **sen'yō** enhance, raise, exalt
13 宣戦 **sensen** declaration of war
宣戦布告 **sensen fukoku** declaration of war
14 宣誓 **sensei** oath, vow, pledge
宣誓式 **senseishiki** administering an oath
宣誓書 **senseisho** written oath, deposition
15 宣撫 **senbu** placation, pacification

――――――― 2 ―――――――

8 逆宣伝 **gyakusenden** counterpropaganda
10 託宣 **takusen** oracle

3m6.3 / 641

客

KYAKU guest, customer, passenger
KAKU guest, customer, passenger; (as prefix) last (year)

――――――― 1 ―――――――

2 客人 **kyakujin, marōdo** visitor, guest
3 客土 **kyakudo, kakudo** topsoil brought in from elsewhere
4 客止 **kyakudo(me)** turning away customers, full house
客分 **kyakubun** guest, honorary member
客引 **kyakuhi(ki)** soliciting customers; a tout
客月 **kakugetsu** last month
5 客用 **kyakuyō** for guests
客布団 **kyakubuton** bedding for guests
6 客死 **kakushi, kyakushi** die abroad
客気 **kakki** youthful ardor, rashness
客年 **kakunen** last year
客扱 **kyakuatsuka(i)** hospitality
7 客来 **kyakurai** arrival of visitors
客体 **kyakutai, kakutai** object
客車 **kyakusha** passenger coach/train
客足 **kyakuashi** customers, clientele
8 客舎 **kakusha, kyakusha** hotel, inn
9 客室 **kyakushitsu** guest room, stateroom
10 客遊 **kakuyū** traveling abroad
客員 **kakuin, kyakuin** guest, honorary member, associate (editor)
客座 **kyakuza** seats for guests
客席 **kyakuseki** seats for guests
11 客商売 **kyakushōbai** a service/public-patronage trade
客船 **kyakusen** passenger ship/boat
12 客寓 **kakugū** sojourn, reside temporarily
客筋 **kyakusuji** quality of the clientele
客間 **kyakuma** guest room, parlor
13 客僧 **kyakusō** traveling priest
客殿 **kyakuden** reception hall
14 客種 **kyakudane** quality of the clientele
客語 **kyakugo, kakugo** object (in grammar)
16 客膳 **kyakuzen** guest's dinner tray
18 客観 **kyakkan, kakkan** object
客観主義 **kyakkan shugi, kakkan shugi** objectivism
客観的 **kyakkanteki, kakkanteki** objective
客観性 **kyakkansei, kakkansei** objectivity
客観視 **kyakkanshi** view objectively

――――――― 2 ―――――――

3 千客万来 **senkaku-banrai, senkyaku-banrai** thronged with customers/visitors
上客 **jōkyaku** guest of honor; good customer
5 外客 **gaikyaku** foreign visitor, tourist
正客 **shōkyaku** guest of honor
主客 **shukaku, shukyaku** host and guest, principal and auxiliary, subject and object
主客顛倒 **shukaku-tentō** reverse order, putting the cart before the horse
6 先客 **senkyaku** previous visitor/customer
7 来客 **raikyaku** visitor, caller

8 佳客 **kakyaku, kakaku** welcome guest; valued customer
孤客 **kokaku, kokyaku** a lone traveler
刺客 **shikaku** assassin
泊客 **to(mari)kyaku** overnight guest
招客 **shōkyaku** invitation; invited guest
9 乗客 **jōkyaku** passenger
俠客 **kyōkaku** chivalrous man, a gallant
相客 **aikyaku** fellow guest/passenger
珍客 **chinkyaku** welcome visitor
政客 **seikyaku** politician
食客 **shokkaku, shokkyaku** a (live-in) dependent
10 剣客 **kenkaku** swordsman, fencer
遊客 **yūkyaku, yūkaku** excursionist; brothel frequenter
酒客 **shukaku** drinker
浴客 **yokkyaku, yokkaku** bather, hot springs guest
旅客機 **ryokakki** passenger plane
11 過客 **kakaku** travelers passing through
涼客 **suzu(mi)kyaku** people enjoying the evening cool
接客 **sekkyaku** receiving visitors/customers
接客用 **sekkyakuyō** for customers
接客係 **sekkyakugakari** receptionist
接客婦 **sekkyakufu** hostess, waitress
接客業 **sekkyakugyō** hotel and restaurant trade
常客 **jōkyaku** regular customer/visitor
船客 **senkyaku** (ship) passenger
訪客 **hōkyaku, hōkaku** visitor, guest
貨客船 **kakyakusen, kakakusen** cargo-and-passenger ship
12 棋客 **kikyaku, kikaku** go/shogi player
13 碁客 **gokaku** go player
新客 **shinkyaku** new visitor/customer
雅客 **gakaku** man of taste, writer
14 墨客 **bokkaku** artist
嫖客 **hyōkaku** brothel customer/frequenter
15 賓客 **hinkaku, hinkyaku** honored guest, visitor
論客 **ronkyaku, ronkaku** polemicist
18 観客 **kankyaku** audience, spectators
観客層 **kankyakusō** stratum of the audience
21 顧客 **kokaku, kokyaku** customer

——————— 3 ———————
5 立見客 **ta(chi)mikyaku** standee, gallery
7 見物客 **kenbutsukyaku** spectator, audience, sightseer
見舞客 **mima(i)kyaku** hospital visitor
8 押掛客 **o(shi)ka(ke)kyaku** uninvited guest
招待客 **shōtaikyaku** invited guest
10 逗留客 **tōryūkyaku** guest, visitor, sojourner
遊覧客 **yūrankyaku** sightseers, holidaymakers

13 滞在客 **taizaikyaku** (hotel) guest
14 漫遊客 **man'yūkyaku** tourist, sightseer
15 避暑客 **hishokyaku** summer residents
18 観光客 **kankōkyaku** tourist, sightseer

3m6.4 / 166

室 **SHITSU** room, chamber
muro greenhouse; cellar

3

——————— 1 ———————
4 室内 **shitsunai** indoor(s), interior
室内音楽 **shitsunai ongaku** chamber music
室内遊戯 **shitsunai yūgi** indoor/parlor games
室内装飾 **shitsunai sōshoku** interior decorating
室内楽 **shitsunaigaku** chamber music
5 室外 **shitsugai** outdoor(s)
7 室町 **Muromachi** (era, 1338–1573)
8 室長 **shitsuchō** senior roommate; section chief
9 室咲 **muroza(ki)** hothouse/forced (flowers)
12 室温 **shitsuon** room temperature
19 室蘭 **Muroran** (city, Hokkaidō)

——————— 2 ———————
2 入室 **nyūshitsu** enter a room; become a member
4 内室 **naishitsu** one's wife
分室 **bunshitsu** isolated room, detached office
火室 **kashitsu** fire box/chamber
王室 **ōshitsu** royal family
心室 **shinshitsu** ventricle (of the heart)
5 令室 **reishitsu** your wife
正室 **seishitsu** one's legal wife
氷室 **himuro, hyōshitsu** icehouse, coldroom
石室 **ishimuro** stone hut
6 気室 **kishitsu** air chamber
同室 **dōshitsu** the same room
在室 **zaishitsu** be in one's room
7 別室 **besshitsu** separate/special room
私室 **shishitsu** private room
車室 **shashitsu** (train) compartment
8 画室 **gashitsu** artist's studio, atelier
妻室 **saishitsu** wife
空室 **kūshitsu** vacant room
岩室 **iwamuro** (small) stone cave
居室 **kyoshitsu** living room; one's own room
和室 **washitsu** Japanese-style room
9 帝室 **teishitsu** the imperial household
洋室 **yōshitsu** Western-style room
後室 **kōshitsu** widow, dowager
茶室 **chashitsu** tea-ceremony room
客室 **kyakushitsu** guest room, stateroom
皇室 **Kōshitsu** the Imperial Household, the reigning line
10 浴室 **yokushitsu** bathroom (not toilet)
宮室 **kyūshitsu** palace; royal family

氵 土 扌 口 女 巾 犭 弓 彳 彡 艹 宀 6← ⺍ 山 圭 广 尸 口

教室　**kyōshitsu**　classroom
病室　**byōshitsu**　sickroom, ward, infirmary
蚕室　**sanshitsu**　silkworm-raising room
11 側室　**sokushitsu**　noble's concubine
控室　**hika(e)shitsu**　waiting room
密室　**misshitsu**　secret/locked room
庵室　**anshitsu**　hermit's retreat
産室　**sanshitsu**　delivery room
船室　**senshitsu**　cabin, stateroom
12 温室　**onshitsu**　hothouse, greenhouse
寒室　**kanshitsu**　coldhouse (for raising frigid-zone plants)
貸室　**ka(shi)shitsu**　room for rent
13 寝室　**shinshitsu**　bedroom
鼓室　**koshitsu**　the atrium (of the ear)
暗室　**anshitsu**　darkroom
暖室　**danshitsu**　heated room; hothouse
継室　**keishitsu**　second wife
15 隣室　**rinshitsu**　the next/adjoining room
16 薬室　**yakushitsu**　dispensary, pharmacy; powder chamber

――――― 3 ―――――

4 手術室　**shujutsushitsu**　operating room
5 左心室　**sashinshitsu**　the left ventricle
右心室　**ushinshitsu**　the right ventricle
6 気密室　**kimitsushitsu**　airtight chamber
休憩室　**kyūkeishitsu**　resting room, lounge, lobby
会議室　**kaigishitsu**　meeting/conference room
地下室　**chikashitsu**　basement, cellar
7 更衣室　**kōishitsu**　clothes-changing room
冷蔵室　**reizōshitsu**　cold-room, cold-storage locker
医務室　**imushitsu**　medical office
汽缶室　**kikanshitsu**　boiler room
汽機室　**kikishitsu**　boiler/engine room
応接室　**ōsetsushitsu**　reception room
図書室　**toshoshitsu**　library (room)
8 事務室　**jimushitsu**　office
実験室　**jikkenshitsu**　laboratory
空気室　**kūkishitsu**　air chamber
9 美容室　**biyōshitsu**　beauty parlor, hairdresser's
待合室　**machiaishitsu**　waiting room
研究室　**kenkyūshitsu**　laboratory, study room
10 陳列室　**chinretsushitsu**　showroom
娯楽室　**gorakushitsu**　recreation room
展覧室　**tenranshitsu**　showroom
配膳室　**haizenshitsu**　service room, pantry
11 接待室　**settaishitsu**　reception room
12 喫煙室　**kitsuenshitsu**　smoking room
診察室　**shinsatsushitsu**　room where patients are examined
貯蔵室　**chozōshitsu**　storeroom, stockroom
貴賓室　**kihinshitsu**　room reserved for VIP guests

集会室　**shūkaishitsu**　meeting room/hall
13 解剖室　**kaibōshitsu**　dissecting room
電話室　**denwashitsu**　telephone booth
14 読書室　**dokushoshitsu**　reading room
15 謁見室　**ekkenshitsu**　audience chamber
談話室　**danwashitsu**　parlor, lounge
霊安室　**reianshitsu**　morgue
閲覧室　**etsuranshitsu**　reading room
16 操舵室　**sōdashitsu**　pilothouse
機関室　**kikanshitsu**　machine/engine room
18 職員室　**shokuinshitsu**　staff/teachers' room

3m6.5 / 1717

窃　竊　**SETSU, nusu(mu)** steal
hiso(ka) secret, stealthy

――――― 1 ―――――
8 窃取　**sesshu**　steal
11 窃盗　**settō**　theft, larceny; thief
窃盗犯　**settōhan**　thief
窃盗罪　**settōzai**　theft, larceny

――――― 2 ―――――
13 剽窃　**hyōsetsu**　plagiarism, pirating

突 → 突　3m5.11

3m6.6

窋　**SEI** pitfall

――――― 2 ―――――
9 陥穽　**kansei**　pitfall, trap

――――― 7 ―――――

3m7.1 / 165

家　**KA** house, family; (as suffix) -er, person, profession　**KE** house, family; (as suffix) the ... family, the house of ...　**ie** house　**-ya, ya-** house; shop

――――― 1 ―――――
2 家人　**kajin** the family　**kenin** retainer
家子郎党　**ie(no)ko rōtō**　one's followers
4 家元　**iemoto**　(head of a) school (of an art)
家内　**kanai**　my wife; family, home
家内工業　**kanai kōgyō**　home/cottage industry
家中　**iejū** the whole family; all over the house　**kachū** the whole family; retainer
家父　**kafu**　my father
5 家出　**iede**　leave home; run away from home
家付　**ietsu(ki)**　attached to the house; daughter who brings in a husband as joint heir

家令 **karei** steward, butler
家兄 **kakei** my elder brother
家主 **yanushi, ienushi** houseowner, landlord
6 家毎 **iegoto** at every house/door
家伝 **kaden** family tradition, handed down
   within the family
家老 **karō** chief retainer
家名 **kamei, kamyō, iena** family name/honor
家守 **yamori, iemori** caretaker, house agent
家宅 **kataku** house, premises
家宅侵入 **kataku shinnyū** trespassing
家宅捜索 **kataku sōsaku** domiciliary search
7 家来 **kerai** vassal, retainer, retinue
家作 **kasaku** house for rent
家臣 **kashin** retainer, vassal
家扶 **kafu** steward
家君 **kakun** head of the house; my father
家芸 **(o)iegei** one's speciality
家系 **kakei** family lineage
家系図 **kakeizu** family tree
8 家長 **kachō** family head, patriarch, matriarch
家事 **kaji** housework; domestic affairs
家並 **iena(mi)** row of houses; every house
家法 **kahō** family rules/recipe
家宝 **kahō** heirloom
家具 **kagu** furniture, furnishings
家具屋 **kaguya** furniture store
家具師 **kagushi** cabinetmaker
家門 **kamon** one's family/clan
9 家信 **kashin** news from home
家風 **kafū** family custom/ways
家持 **iemo(chi)** house owner; householder
家庭 **katei** home; family
家庭用 **kateiyō** for home use
家庭用品 **kateiyōhin** household goods
家庭的 **kateiteki** domestic/family (affairs)
家庭教師 **katei kyōshi** (private) tutor
家庭裁判所 **katei saibansho** Family Court
家庭欄 **kateiran** homemaker's column
家屋 **kaoku** house; building
家屋税 **kaokuzei** house tax
家屋敷 **ieyashiki** house and lot, estate
家相 **kasō** (lucky/unlucky) aspect of a house
家柄 **iegara** lineage, parentage; (of) good
   family
家政 **kasei** homemaking
家政学 **kaseigaku** home economics
家政科 **kaseika** home-economics course
家政婦 **kaseifu** housekeeper
家計 **kakei** family finances; livelihood
家計費 **kakeihi** household expenses/budget
家計簿 **kakeibo** household account-book
10 家借 **kashaku** renting a house
家郷 **kakyō** one's old home, one's birthplace
家畜 **kachiku** domestic animals, livestock
家従 **kajū** steward, butler, attendant
家格 **kakaku** family status

家紋 **kamon** family crest
家訓 **kakun** family precepts
家財 **kazai** household effects, belongings
家財道具 **kazai dōgu** household effects
11 家運 **kaun** family fortunes
家探 **iesaga(shi)** house hunting
家婦 **kafu** housewife
家族 **kazoku** family
家族法 **kazokuhō** family(-rights) law
家族的 **kazokuteki** like a member of the
   family
家族連 **kazokuzu(re)** taking the family along
家産 **kasan** family property, one's fortune
家移 **yautsu(ri)** moving
12 家禽 **kakin** domestic fowl, poultry
家禄 **karoku** hereditary stipend
家筋 **iesuji** lineage, family pedigree
家集 **kashū** poetry collection
13 家業 **kagyō** one's trade
家塾 **kajuku** private school
家数 **iekazu** number of houses
家督 **katoku** headship of a family
家督相続 **katoku sōzoku** succession as head
   of family
家督権 **katoku (no) ken** birthright, inheritance
家続 **ietsuzu(ki)** row of houses
家賃 **yachin** (house) rent
家資 **kashi** family property/estate
家路 **ieji** one's way home
家跡 **ieato** remains of a house; family name
家電 **kaden** household electrical products/
   appliances, consumer electronics (short
   for 家庭用電気製品)
14 家僕 **kaboku** manservant, houseboy
家鳴 **yana(ri)** rattling of a house
家構 **iegama(e)** structure/appearance of a
   house
15 家蔵 **kazō** household possessions
16 家憲 **kaken** family rules
家親 **kashin** one's parents
家鴨 **ahiru** (domestic) duck
18 家難 **kanan** family misfortune
19 家蠅 **iebae** housefly
家譜 **kafu** a genealogy, family tree
                    ──── 2 ────
1 一家 **ikka, ikke** a house/family/household;
   one's family; a style
一家団欒 **ikka danran** happy family circle,
   happy home
一家言 **ikkagen** one's own opinion, a
   personal view
2 人家 **jinka** a human habitation, dwelling
3 大家 **taika** mansion; illustrious/wealthy
   family; past master, authority
taike illustrious/wealthy family
ōya landlord; main building

大家族 **daikazoku** large family
山家 **yamaga, sanka** mountain home, chalet
4 仏家 **bukke** Buddhist temple/priest
分家 **bunke** branch family
公家 **kuge** imperial court; court noble
王家 **ōke** royal family
5 瓦家 **kawaraya** tile-roofed house
出家 **shukke** become a priest/monk; priest, monk
民家 **minka** private house
本家 **honke** main family; originator
生家 **seika** house of one's birth
史家 **shika** historian
他家 **take** another family
古家 **furuie** old house
平家 **hiraya** one-story house
　　　Heike the Taira family/clan
旧家 **kyūka** an old family
主家 **shuka** one's master's house
6 両家 **ryōke** both families
伝家 **denka** heirloom; trump card, last resort
全家 **zenka** the whole family
邦家 **hōka** one's country
同家 **dōke** the (same) family
在家 **zaike** layman (Buddhist)
名家 **meika** distinguished family; a celebrity
当家 **tōke** this house/family
自家 **jika** one's own (home)
自家中毒 **jika chūdoku** autotoxemia
自家用 **jikayō** for private use
自家受精 **jika jusei** self-fertilization
自家製 **jikasei** homemade, home-brewed
7 良家 **ryōka** good family
我家 **wa(ga)ya** our home/house
作家 **sakka** writer, novelist
住家 **sumika** where one lives, residence
別家 **bekke** branch family
兵家 **heika** soldier; tactician, strategist
売家 **u(ri)ya, u(ri)ie** house for sale
社家 **shake** hereditary family of Shinto priests
私家 **shika** personal, private
私家集 **shikashū** private/personal collection
町家 **chōka** tradesman's/town house
8 画家 **gaka** painter, artist
宗家 **sōke, sōka** head family; originator
実家 **jikka** one's parent's home
空家 **a(ki)ya** vacant house
国家 **kokka** state, nation, country
国家主義 **kokka shugi** nationalism
国家的 **kokkateki** national, state
武家 **buke** samurai
武家物 **bukemono** a samurai romance
9 持家 **mo(chi)ie** one's (own) house
律家 **rikke** (priest of) the Ritsu Buddhist sect
後家 **goke** widow
10 借家 **shakuya, shakka, ka(ri)ie, ka(ri)ya** rented house, house for rent

酒家 **shuka** wine shop, pub; drinker
宮家 **miyake** prince's residence/family
書家 **shoka** good penman, calligrapher
病家 **byōka** patient's home
11 商家 **shōka** store; merchant family
貧家 **hinka** poor home
道家 **dōka** a Taoist
娼家 **shōka** brothel
婚家 **konka** one's husband's family
12 御家人 **gokenin** a lower-grade vassal
御家芸 **oiegei** one's specialty
御家騒動 **oie sōdō** family quarrel
富家 **fuka** wealthy family
廃家 **haika** extinct family; abandoned house
　　　haike extinct family
朝家 **chōka** imperial household/family
絶家 **zekke** extinct family
貴家 **kika** your home
貸家 **ka(shi)ie, kashiya** house for rent
13 僧家 **sōka** Buddhist temple; Buddhist priest
隠家 **kaku(re)ga** retreat, refuge, hideout
農家 **nōka** farmhouse; farm household; farmer
摂家 **sekke** the line of regents and advisers
禅家 **zenka, zenke** Zen sect/temple/priest
話家 **hana(shi)ka** storyteller
14 豪家 **gōka** wealthy and powerful family
遺家族 **ikazoku** surviving family
漁家 **gyoka** fisherman's house
15 隣家 **rinka** neighboring house, next door
養家 **yōka** adoptive family
権家 **kenka** powerful/influential family
縁家 **enka** related family
諸家 **shoka** houses; schools of thought
賤家 **shizu(ga)ya** humble cottage, hovel
16 儒家 **juka** a Confucianist
壇家 **danka** supporter/parishoner of a temple
17 檀家 **danka** family supporting a temple
18 離家 **hana(re)ya** detached building

——— 3 ———

1 一軒家 **ikken'ya** isolated/freestanding/detached house
2 刀圭家 **tōkeika** physician
3 工業家 **kōgyōka** industrialist, manufacturer
小食家 **shōshokuka** light eater
小説家 **shōsetsuka** novelist, (fiction) writer
4 天皇家 **tennōke** the imperial family
文筆家 **bunpitsuka** literary man, writer
反動家 **handōka** a reactionary
手腕家 **shuwanka** man of ability
少食家 **shōshokuka** light eater
5 母子家庭 **boshi katei** fatherless home
母系家族 **bokei kazoku** matriarchal family
好色家 **kōshokuka** sensualist, lecher
好角家 **kōkakuka** sumo fan
好事家 **kōzuka** dilettante, amateur

好楽家 **kōgakuka** music lover
田舎家 **inakaya** country house
6 多作家 **tasakuka** prolific writer
多読家 **tadokuka** voracious reader, well-read person
企業家 **kigyōka** industrialist, entrepreneur
老大家 **rōtaika** veteran authority
老練家 **rōrenka** expert, veteran
名文家 **meibunka** fine writer
名望家 **meibōka** person who is highly esteemed
7 作曲家 **sakkyokuka** composer
努力家 **doryokuka** hard worker
吝嗇家 **rinshokuka** miser, niggard
扶養家族 **fuyō kazoku** family dependents
批評家 **hihyōka** critic, reviewer
技術家 **gijutsuka** technician, specialist, expert
投書家 **tōshoka** contributor, correspondent
投機家 **tōkika** speculator
芸術家 **geijutsuka** artist
声楽家 **seigakuka** vocalist
図案家 **zuanka** designer, patternmaker
社交家 **shakōka** sociable person
8 事務家 **jimuka** man of business, practical man
事業家 **jigyōka** entrepreneur; businessman, industrialist
迷信家 **meishinka** superstitious person
建築家 **kenchikuka** architect, building contractor
法律家 **hōritsuka** lawyer, jurist
知日家 **chi-Nichika** a Japan hand
若後家 **wakagoke** young widow
宗教家 **shūkyōka** man of religion
実務家 **jitsumuka** businessman
実業家 **jitsugyōka** industrialist, businessman
実際家 **jissaika** practical man; expert
空想家 **kūsōka** dreamer, idealist, utopian
金満家 **kinmanka** rich man
9 飛行家 **hikōka** aviator
発明家 **hatsumeika** inventor
発展家 **hattenka** man about town, playboy
専門家 **senmonka** specialist, expert
美食家 **bishokuka** epicure, gourmet
美術家 **bijutsuka** artist
活動家 **katsudōka** energetic person; activist
洋画家 **yōgaka** painter of Western-type pictures
革命家 **kakumeika** a revolutionary
柔道家 **jūdōka** judo expert
神秘家 **shinpika** a mystic
政治家 **seijika** politician
政略家 **seiryakuka** political tactician
研究家 **kenkyūka** researcher, student of
音楽家 **ongakka, ongakuka** musician
思想家 **shisōka** thinker

10 倹約家 **ken'yakuka** thrifty person, economizer
健啖家 **kentanka** hearty eater, trencherman, glutton
健脚家 **kenkyakuka** good walker
将軍家 **shōgunke** family to inherit the shogunate
陰謀家 **inbōka** schemer
勉強家 **benkyōka** diligent student, hard worker
遊猟家 **yūryōka** hunter
酒造家 **shuzōka** brewer, distiller
能文家 **nōbunka** skilled writer
能弁家 **nōbenka** good speaker, orator
特志家 **tokushika** volunteer, supporter
旅行家 **ryokōka** traveler, tourist
教育家 **kyōikuka** educator
敏腕家 **binwanka** able person, go-getter
恐妻家 **kyōsaika** henpecked husband
悋嗇家 **rinshokuka** miser, skinflint
素封家 **sohōka** wealthy person/family
航空家 **kōkūka** aviator
財政家 **zaiseika** financier
財産家 **zaisanka** wealthy person
11 野心家 **yashinka** ambitious person
運動家 **undōka** athlete, sportsman
道徳家 **dōtokuka** man of virtue
探検家 **tankenka** explorer
猟色家 **ryōshokuka** lecher, libertine
彫刻家 **chōkokuka** engraver, carver, sculptor
著作家 **chosakka, chosakuka** author, writer
著述家 **chojutsuka** writer, author
理財家 **rizaika** economist, financier
理想家 **risōka** idealist
理論家 **rironka** theorist
経世家 **keiseika** statesman, administrator
経済家 **keizaika** economist; thrifty person
12 創作家 **sōsakuka** writer, novelist
勤王家 **kinnōka** loyalist, royalist
勤皇家 **kinnōka** loyalist
博愛家 **hakuaika** philanthropist
超国家主義 **chōkokka shugi** ultranationalism
超国家的 **chōkokkateki** ultranationalistic
提琴家 **teikinka** violinist
登山家 **tozanka** mountaineer
御三家 **Gosanke** the three branch families of the Tokugawas
落語家 **rakugoka** comic storyteller
策動家 **sakudōka** schemer
評論家 **hyōronka** critic, commentator
飲酒家 **inshuka** drinker
13 慈善家 **jizenka** charitable person, philanthropist
摂関家 **sekkanke** the line of regents and advisers
蒐集家 **shūshūka** collector
夢想家 **musōka** dreamer, visionary

3

氵土扌口女巾犭弓彳彡艹宀7←⺌山耂广尸口

園芸家 **engeika** gardener, horticulturist
楽天家 **rakutenka** optimist
愛犬家 **aikenka** dog lover
愛好家 **aikōka** lover of, fan, fancier
愛妻家 **aisaika** devoted/uxorious husband
愛書家 **aishoka** book lover
愛鳥家 **aichōka** bird lover
愛禽家 **aikinka** bird lover
愛煙家 **aienka** (habitual) smoker
戦術家 **senjutsuka** tactician
戦略家 **senryakuka** strategist
詭弁家 **kibenka** sophist, quibbler
資本家 **shihonka** capitalist, financier
資産家 **shisanka** man of means
酪農家 **rakunōka** dairy farmer
14 厭世家 **enseika** pessimist
漁色家 **gyoshokuka** lecher
漫画家 **mangaka** cartoonist
漫談家 **mandanka** humorist
演出家 **enshutsuka** producer, director
演説家 **enzetsuka** speaker, orator
徳望家 **tokubōka** man of high moral repute
槍術家 **sōjutsuka** spearsman
総本家 **sōhonke** head family
精力家 **seiryokuka** energetic person
読書家 **dokushoka** (avid) book reader
銀行家 **ginkōka** banker
需用家 **juyōka** consumer, customer
15 劇作家 **gekisakka** playwright, dramatist
養鶏家 **yōkeika** poultry farmer
蔵書家 **zōshoka** book collector
権力家 **kenryokuka** powerful person
権謀家 **kenbōka** schemer, maneuverer
熱心家 **nesshinka** enthusiast, devotee
16 機業家 **kigyōka** textile manufacturer, weaver
親日家 **shin-Nichika** Nippophile
篤志家 **tokushika** benefactor, volunteer
18 臨床家 **rinshōka** clinician
翻訳家 **hon'yakuka** translator
19 艶福家 **enpukuka** ladies' man, a gallant
警世家 **keiseika** prophet, seer
20 議論家 **gironka** avid/good debater
醸造家 **jōzōka** brewer, distiller
21 饒舌家 **jōzetsuka** chatterbox
23 鑑定家 **kanteika** appraiser, expert (witness)
鑑識家 **kanshikika** a judge/connoisseur of, appraiser

─────── 4 ───────

4 水彩画家 **suisai gaka** watercolor painter
6 共産国家 **kyōsan kokka** communist state
14 閨秀作家 **keishū sakka** woman writer

3m7.2 / 1488

宰 SAI manage, rule

─────── 1 ───────

9 宰相 **saishō** prime minister, premier
14 宰領 **sairyō** management, supervision; manager, supervisor

─────── 2 ───────

4 太宰府 **Dazaifu** (ancient) Kyūshū government headquarters
5 主宰 **shusai** preside over, run, supervise
主宰者 **shusaisha** president, chairman

3m7.3 / 640

宴 EN feast, banquet
utage party, banquet

─────── 1 ───────

6 宴会 **enkai** banquet, dinner party
宴会場 **enkaijō** banquet hall
10 宴遊 **en'yū** feasting and carousing
宴席 **enseki** (one's seat in a) banquet hall
13 宴楽 **enraku** merrymaking, conviviality

─────── 2 ───────

3 小宴 **shōen** small dinner party
4 内宴 **naien** private dinner/banquet
7 別宴 **betsuen** farewell dinner
8 招宴 **shōen** invitation to a banquet
9 祝宴 **shukuen** congratulatory banquet, feast
10 酒宴 **shuen** banquet, feast
11 盛宴 **seien** grand banquet
12 御宴 **gyoen** court banquet
賀宴 **gaen** banquet
15 賜宴 **shien** court banquet
19 饗宴 **kyōen** banquet, feast, dinner

─────── 3 ───────

8 披露宴 **hirōen** (wedding) reception

3m7.4 / 518

害 GAI damage, harm, injury

─────── 1 ───────

4 害心 **gaishin** evil intent, malice, ill will
6 害虫 **gaichū** harmful insect, pest
8 害毒 **gaidoku** an evil (influence), harm
11 害悪 **gaiaku** an evil (influence), harm
害鳥 **gaichō** harmful bird
13 害意 **gaii** malice, ill will

─────── 2 ───────

3 干害 **kangai** drought damage
4 公害 **kōgai** pollution
水害 **suigai** flood damage, flooding
水害防止 **suigai bōshi** flood prevention
水害地 **suigaichi** flood-stricken area
水害対策 **suigai taisaku** flood control/relief measures

5 生害 **shōgai** be killed; commit suicide
加害 **kagai** do harm to, assault
加害者 **kagaisha** assailant, perpetrator
6 危害 **kigai** injury, harm
有害 **yūgai** harmful, noxious, injurious
有害無益 **yūgai-mueki** harmful, more harm than good
百害 **hyakugai** great harm/damage
自害 **jigai** suicide
虫害 **chūgai** damage from insects
7 冷害 **reigai** cold-weather damage
阻害 **sogai** impede, check, hinder, retard
迫害 **hakugai** persecution
迫害者 **hakugaisha** persecutor, oppressor
妨害 **bōgai** obstruction, disturbance, interference
妨害物 **bōgaibutsu** obstacle
旱害 **kangai** drought damage
災害 **saigai** disaster, accident
災害地 **saigaichi** disaster-stricken area
災害保険 **saigai hoken** accident insurance
利害 **rigai** advantages and disadvantages, interests
利害得失 **rigai-tokushitsu** pros and cons
利害関係 **rigai kankei** interests
8 毒害 **dokugai** poisoning
9 侵害 **shingai** infringement, violation
風害 **fūgai** wind/storm damage
要害 **yōgai** stronghold, fortress
10 凍害 **tōgai** frost damage
殺害 **satsugai** murder
殺害者 **satsugaisha** murderer, slayer
被害 **higai** damage, harm, injury
被害地 **higaichi** the stricken area
被害者 **higaisha** victim
病害 **byōgai** damage from blight
11 惨害 **sangai** heavy damage, devastation
雪害 **setsugai** damage from snow
12 寒害 **kangai** damage from cold/frost
無害 **mugai** harmless
13 傷害 **shōgai** injury, bodily harm
障害 **shōgai** obstacle, hindrance, impediment, handicap
障害物 **shōgaibutsu** obstacle, obstruction
損害 **songai** damage, injury, loss
損害保険 **songai hoken** casualty/nonlife insurance
損害高 **songaidaka** (amount of) damage
損害賠償 **songai baishō** restitution, indemnification, (pay) damages
煙害 **engai** smoke pollution
禍害 **kagai** disaster, harm
賊害 **zokugai** harm, kill; destruction caused by bandits
雹害 **hyōgai** hail damage
15 潮害 **chōgai** tide-water damage

弊害 **heigai** an evil, ill effects
震害 **shingai** earthquake damage
17 霜害 **sōgai** frost damage

――――― 3 ―――――
9 風水害 **fūsuigai** wind and flood damage
10 高障害 **kōshōgai** high hurdles
病虫害 **byōchūgai** damage from blight and insects
――――― 4 ―――――
1 一利一害 **ichiri ichigai** advantages and disadvantages
7 身体障害者 **shintai shōgaisha** physically handicapped person

3m7.5 / 721

宮 **KYŪ, GŪ, KU, miya** palace; prince, princess

――――― 1 ―――――
2 宮人 **miyabito** courtier
3 宮女 **kyūjo** court lady
4 宮内庁 **Kunaichō** Imperial Household Agency
宮内省 **Kunaishō** Imperial Household Department
宮中 **kyūchū** imperial court
5 宮仕 **miyazuka(e)** court/temple service
宮司 **gūji** chief priest of a Shinto shrine
6 宮刑 **kyūkei** castration
宮廷 **kyūtei** the court/place
宮守 **miyamori** guarding a shrine; watchman
8 宮参 **miyamai(ri)** visit to a shrine
宮居 **miyai** shrine compound; imperial palace
宮門 **kyūmon** palace gate
9 宮城 **kyūjō** imperial palace
宮城県 **Miyagi-ken** (prefecture)
宮室 **kyūshitsu** palace; royal family
10 宮家 **miyake** prince's residence/family
11 宮崎 **Miyazaki** (city, Miyazaki-ken)
宮崎県 **Miyazaki-ken** (prefecture)
13 宮殿 **kyūden** palace
14 宮様 **miyasama** prince, princess

――――― 2 ―――――
1 一宮 **Ichinomiya** (city, Aichi-ken)
2 子宮 **shikyū** the uterus, womb
子宮口 **shikyūkō** the cervix
子宮炎 **shikyūen** uteritis
子宮癌 **shikyūgan** cancer of the uterus
3 大宮 **Ōmiya** (city, Saitama-ken)
大宮司 **daigūji** high priest of a grand shrine
大宮御所 **Ōmiya gosho** Empress Dowager's Palace
大宮様 **ōmiya-sama** the empress dowager
4 天宮図 **tenkyūzu** horoscope
内宮 **Naigū, Naikū** Inner Shrine of Ise

中宮 **chūgū** palace of the empress; empress; emperor's second consort
王宮 **ōkyū** royal palace
5 幼宮 **itomiya** infant prince
外宮 **Gekū, Gegū** Outer Shrine of Ise
6 西宮 **Nishinomiya** (city, Hyōgo-ken)
行宮 **angū** (emperor's) temporary palace
守宮 **yamori** gecko, wall lizard
8 東宮 **tōgū** crown prince
東宮御所 **Tōgū gosho** the Crown Prince's Palace
迷宮 **meikyū** maze, labyrinth
参宮 **sangū** visit to the Ise Shrine
若宮 **wakamiya** young prince; shrine dedicated to the son of the god of the main shrine; newly built shrine
9 後宮 **kōkyū** inner palace; harem; consort
神宮 **jingū** Shinto shrine; the Ise Shrines
皇宮 **kōgū** imperial palace
10 姫宮 **himemiya** princess
竜宮 **ryūgū** Palace of the Dragon King
12 間宮海峡 **Mamiya-kaikyō** (strait between Hokkaidō and Sakhalin)
15 箱宮 **hakomiya** miniature temple
18 殯宮 **hinkyū** temporary imperial mortuary
離宮 **rikyū** detached palace

─────── 3 ───────
2 八幡宮 **Hachimangū** shrine of the god of war
3 大神宮 **Daijingū** the Grand Shrine (at Ise)
6 宇都宮 **Utsunomiya** (city, Tochigi-ken)

─────── 4 ───────
8 明治神宮 **Meiji Jingū** Meiji Shrine
9 皇太神宮 **Kōtai Jingū** the Ise Shrine

─────── 5 ───────
6 伊勢大神宮 **Ise Daijingū** the Grand Shrines of Ise

3m7.6 / 106

案 **AN** plan, proposal

─────── 1 ───────
0 案じる/ずる **an(jiru/zuru)** worry, be anxious; ponder
3 案山子 **kakashi** scarecrow; figurehead
4 案内 **annai** guidance, information
案内状 **annaijō** letter of invitation
案内図 **annaizu** information map
案内者 **annaisha** guide
案内所 **annaijo** information office/booth
案内書 **annaisho** guidebook
案内嬢 **annaijō** (girl) guide
案文 **anbun** draft
5 案出 **anshutsu** contrive, devise
案外 **angai** unexpectedly

6 案件 **anken** matter, case, item
8 案定 **an(no)jō** as feared/expected, sure enough
18 案顔 **an(ji)gao** worried look

─────── 2 ───────
1 一案 **ichian** a plan, idea
4 不案内 **fuannai** ignorant of, unfamiliar with
文案 **bun'an** draft
方案 **hōan** plan
5 本案 **hon'an** this proposal/plan
代案 **daian** alternate plan/proposal
立案 **ritsuan** plan, devise, draft
立案者 **ritsuansha** drafter, planner, designer
6 再案 **saian** revised plan/draft
考案 **kōan** idea, conception; plan, project; design, contrivance
名案 **meian** splendid idea, good plan
成案 **seian** definite plan
7 良案 **ryōan** good idea
対案 **taian** counterproposal
妙案 **myōan** good idea, ingenious plan
図案 **zuan** (ornamental) design, device
図案家 **zuanka** designer, patternmaker
私案 **shian** one's own plan
8 法案 **hōan** (legislative) bill, measure
物案 **monoan(ji)** worry, anxiety
具案 **guan** drafting a plan; specific plan
9 発案 **hatsuan** proposal
独案内 **hito(ri)annai** teach-yourself book
草案 **sōan** (rough) draft
思案 **shian** thought, consideration, mulling over; plan
10 原案 **gen'an** original proposal, draft
起案 **kian** draft, draw up
教案 **kyōan** teaching/lesson plan
11 勘案 **kan'an** take into consideration
道案内 **michi annai** guidance; guide; road marker
断案 **dan'an** conclusion, decision
12 創案 **sōan** original idea
創案者 **sōansha** originator, inventor
提案 **teian** proposition, proposal
提案者 **teiansha** proposer, proponent
廃案 **haian** rejected proposal, withdrawn draft
検案 **ken'an** (post-mortem) examination
答案 **tōan** examination paper
13 腹案 **fukuan** plan, forethought
愚案 **guan** foolish/my plan, my humble opinion
新案 **shin'an** new idea/design, novelty
試案 **shian** draft, tentative plan
鉄案 **tetsuan** irrevocable decision
18 翻案 **hon'an** an adaptation
20 懸案 **ken'an** unsettled/pending question
議案 **gian** bill, measure

─────── 3 ───────
4 予定案 **yoteian** program, schedule

予算案 **yosan'an** proposed budget
水先案内 **mizusaki annai** pilot; piloting
水先案内人 **mizusaki annainin** (harbor) pilot
7 決議案 **ketsugian** resolution, proposal
改革案 **kaikakuan** reform bill/measure
8 建議案 **kengian** proposition
法律案 **hōritsuan** proposed law
9 後思案 **atojian** afterthought
政府案 **seifuan** government bill/measure
10 修正案 **shūseian** proposed amendment
14 斡旋案 **assen'an** conciliation/arbitration proposal
15 暫定案 **zanteian** tentative plan

——————— 4 ———————

4 不信任案 **fushinnin'an** nonconfidence motion
引込思案 **hi(k)ko(mi)jian** conservative, retiring
14 鼻元思案 **hanamoto-jian** superficial view

3m7.7 / 1854

宵 宵　**SHŌ, yoi** evening, early night hours

——————— 1 ———————

3 宵口 **yoi (no) kuchi** early evening
4 宵月 **yoizuki** evening moon
8 宵明星 **yoi (no) myōjō** the evening star, Venus
11 宵張 **yoi(p)pa(ri)** staying up till late; nightowl
宵祭 **yoimatsu(ri)** eve (of a festival), vigil
12 宵越 **yoigo(shi)** (left over) from the previous evening
13 宵寝 **yoine** early to bed
17 宵闇 **yoiyami** evening twilight, dusk

——————— 2 ———————

4 今宵 **koyoi** this evening
9 春宵 **shunshō** spring evening
11 終宵 **shūshō** all night long

寃 → 冤 **2i8.3**

3m7.8 / 654

容　**YŌ** form, appearance; content; put/let in **i(reru)** put/let in, admit, accept; permit

——————— 1 ———————

6 容色 **yōshoku** looks, personal appearance
容共 **yōkyō** pro-communist
7 容体 **yōdai** (patient's) condition
yōdai(buru) put on airs, act important
8 容易 **yōi** easy, simple

9 容姿 **yōshi** face and figure, appearance
11 容赦 **yōsha** mercy, pardon, forgiveness
12 容喙 **yōkai** meddling, interference
容量 **yōryō** capacity, volume; capacitance
14 容疑 **yōgi** suspicion
容疑者 **yōgisha** a suspect
容貌 **yōbō** looks, personal appearance
容態 **yōdai** (patient's) condition
容認 **yōnin** admit, approve, accept
15 容儀 **yōgi** deportment, demeanor
容器 **yōki** container
16 容積 **yōseki** capacity, volume

——————— 2 ———————

0 山容 **san'yō** the shape/figure of a mountain
4 内容 **naiyō** content(s), substance
収容 **shūyō** accommodate, admit, receive
収容力 **shūyōryoku** (seating) capacity
収容所 **shūyōjo** home, asylum, camp
5 包容 **hōyō** comprehend, embrace, imply; tolerate
6 全容 **zen'yō** the full picture/story
7 形容 **keiyō** form, appearance; describe, qualify, modify; figure of speech
形容動詞 **keiyōdōshi** quasi-adjective used with -na (e.g., shizuka, kirei)
形容詞 **keiyōshi** adjective
8 受容 **juyō** receive, accept
9 陣容 **jin'yō** battle array, lineup
軍容 **gun'yō** military equipment; troop formation
変容 **hen'yō** changed appearance
変容期 **hen'yōki** period of changing appearance
美容 **biyō** beauty culture
美容体操 **biyō taisō** calisthenics
美容室 **biyōshitsu** beauty parlor, hairdresser's
美容院 **biyōin** beauty parlor, hairdresser's
美容師 **biyōshi** beautician
美容術 **biyōjutsu** beauty treatment, cosmetology
海容 **kaiyō** mercy, forgiveness
姿容 **shiyō** form, appearance
面容 **men'yō** countenance, looks, features
相容 **aii(renai)** incompatible
威容 **iyō** commanding presence, dignity
10 従容 **shōyō** calm, composed, serene
11 理容 **riyō** barbering, hairdressing
許容 **kyoyō** permission, tolerance
12 偉容 **iyō** magnificent appearance
温容 **on'yō** kindly face
13 寛容 **kan'yō** magnanimity, generosity, forbearance
14 認容 **nin'yō** admit, accept
15 儀容 **giyō** mien, bearing, manners
19 艶容 **en'yō** fascinating figure, charming look
麗容 **reiyō** beautiful form

3m7.9

宵 **YŌ** deep in; far

3m7.10

穿 **SEN, uga(tsu)** dig, drill, bore, pierce, penetrate; be incisive/apt/astute
hojiku(ru), hoji(ru) dig up; pick (one's nose); examine closely
ha(ku) wear, put on (shoes/pants)

———————— 1 ————————

3 穿孔 **senkō** perforation; punching, boring
穿孔機 **senkōki** perforator, drill, (key)punch
5 穿古 **ha(ki)furu(shi)** worn-out (shoes)
8 穿刺 **senshi** puncture (with a hypodermic needle), paracentesis, (spinal) tap
28 穿鑿 **sensaku** delve into, probe, scrutinize

3m7.11

窄 **SAKU** narrow **subo(mu/maru), tsubo(maru)** become narrow(er) **subo(meru), tsubo(meru)** make narrow(er), shrug (one's shoulders), purse (one's lips)

———————— 2 ————————

5 尻窄 **shirisubo(mari)** narrow toward the end; anticlimax, peter out
7 乳窄 **chichishibo(ri)** milking; milker
9 狭窄 **kyōsaku** constriction, stenosis

3m7.12

窈 **YŌ** elegant, refined

———————— 1 ————————

11 窈窕 **yōchō** graceful, elegant

3m7.13

宸 **SHIN** palace; emperor's

———————— 1 ————————

12 宸筆 **shinpitsu** emperor's autograph
16 宸翰 **shinkan** imperial letter

———————— 2 ————————

12 紫宸殿 **Shishinden** Hall for State Ceremonies

3m7.14

宦 **KAN** an official

———————— 1 ————————

8 宦官 **kangan** eunuch

———————— 8 ————————

3m8.1

雀 **tsuru** crane (the bird)

3m8.2 / 1669

寂 **JAKU, SEKI, sabi(shii)** lonely
sabi(reru) decline in prosperity
sabi elegant simplicity

———————— 1 ————————

0 寂として **seki (to shite)** silently, hushed, still
6 寂光浄土 **jakkō-jōdo** (Buddhist) paradise
12 寂然 **sekizen, jakunen** lonesome, desolate
13 寂滅 **jakumetsu** Nirvana, death, annihilation
寂寞 **sekibaku** lonesome, desolate
14 寂寥 **sekiryō** loneliness, desolation

———————— 2 ————————

2 入寂 **nyūjaku** death of a saint, entering Nirvana
4 円寂 **enjaku** nirvana; death of a priest/Buddha
心寂 **kokorosabi(shii)** lonely, lonesome
9 幽寂 **yūjaku** quiet, sequestered
12 閑寂 **kanjaku** quiet, tranquillity
14 静寂 **seijaku** silent, still, quiet

3m8.3 / 179

宿 **SHUKU, yado** lodging, inn
yado(ru) take shelter; be pregnant
yado(ri) (taking) shelter
yado(su) give shelter; conceive (a child)

———————— 1 ————————

4 宿六 **yadoroku** my hubby, my old man
宿引 **yadohi(ki)** hotel tout/runner
5 宿主 **yadonushi** landlord, host
shukushu (parasite's) host
6 宿老 **shukurō** elders, seniors
7 宿坊 **shukubō** temple lodgings for pilgrims
宿志 **shukushi** long-cherished desire
8 宿舎 **shukusha** lodgings, quarters, billet
宿命 **shukumei** fate, destiny
宿命的 **shukumeiteki** fatal
宿命論 **shukumeiron** fatalism
宿命論者 **shukumeironsha** fatalist
宿直 **shukuchoku** night duty/watch
宿泊 **shukuhaku** lodging
宿泊人 **shukuhakunin** lodger, boarder, guest
宿泊所 **shukuhakujo** lodgings
宿泊料 **shukuhakuryō** hotel charges
宿所 **shukusho** address, lodgings, quarters
9 宿便 **shukuben** long-retained feces, coprostasis
宿屋 **yadoya** inn
宿屋業 **yadoyagyō** the hotel business

宿怨 **shukuen** long-standing resentment/grudge
10 宿借 **yadoka(ri)** hermit crab
宿将 **shukushō** veteran general
宿根 **shukukon** root/bulb which remains alive after stem and leaves have withered
宿根草 **shukkonsō** perennial plant
宿料 **shukuryō** hotel charges
11 宿運 **shukuun** fate, destiny
宿帳 **yadochō** hotel register
宿望 **shukubō** long-cherished desire
宿悪 **shukuaku** old evils/crimes
宿患 **shukukan, shukkan** chronic illness; long-standing grief
12 宿場 **shukuba** post town, relay station
宿場町 **shukuba machi** post/hotel town
宿営 **shukuei** be billeted
宿替 **yadoga(e)** change of quarters
宿無 **yadona(shi)** homeless person, vagrant
宿痾 **shukua** chronic illness
13 宿業 **shukugō** karma, fate
宿意 **shukui** long-held opinion/grudge
宿罪 **shukuzai** sins of one's previous life
宿賃 **yadochin** hotel charges
14 宿銭 **yadosen** hotel charges
宿駅 **shukueki** post town, relay station
15 宿敵 **shukuteki** old enemy
宿弊 **shukuhei** a deep-rooted evil
宿縁 **shukuen** karma, fate
16 宿謀 **shukubō** premeditated plot
18 宿題 **shukudai** homework
19 宿願 **shukugan** long-cherished desire

──────────── 2 ────────────

3 下宿 **geshuku** lodging, room and board; boarding house
下宿人 **geshukunin** lodger, boarder
下宿屋 **geshukuya** boardinghouse
下宿料 **geshukuryō** room-and-board charge
4 止宿 **shishuku** lodging
止宿人 **shishukunin** lodger
分宿 **bunshuku** billeting, lodging separately
6 仮 (no) 宿 **kari (no) yado** temporary dwelling; this transient world
合宿 **gasshuku** lodging together
同宿 **dōshuku** lodge together, stay at the same hotel
安宿 **yasuyado** cheap hotel
7 投宿 **tōshuku** put up at (a hotel)
投宿者 **tōshukusha** hotel guest
8 定宿 **jōyado** one's usual hotel
雨宿 **amayado(ri)** taking shelter from the rain
9 相宿 **aiyado** stay at the same inn, share a room
星宿 **seishuku** constellation
11 野宿 **nojuku** camping out
寄宿 **kishuku** lodging, board
寄宿生 **kishukusei** dormitory student

寄宿舎 **kishukusha** dormitory
寄宿料 **kishukuryō** boarding expenses
常宿 **jōyado** regular hotel
船宿 **funayado** shipping agent; boathouse keeper
転宿 **tenshuku** change lodgings
12 無宿 **mushuku** homeless
無宿者 **mushukusha** vagrant, homeless wanderer
15 請宿 **u(ke)yado** servants' agency

──────────── 3 ────────────

4 木賃宿 **kichin'yado** cheap lodging house
9 連込宿 **tsu(re)ko(mi)yado** hotel catering to lovers, love/rendezvous hotel
10 遊船宿 **yūsen'yado** boathouse
11 隊商宿 **taishōjuku** caravansary
淫売宿 **inbaiyado** brothel

──────────── 4 ────────────

10 素人下宿 **shirōto geshuku** boarding house

3m8.4

寅 **IN, tora** third horary sign (tiger)

3m8.5 / 806

密 **MITSU** close, dense, crowded; minute, fine; secret; (as suffix) (water)-tight
hiso(ka) secret, private, stealthy

──────────── 1 ────────────

2 密入国 **mitsunyūkoku** smuggle oneself into a country
3 密々 **mitsumitsu** secretly, privately
5 密生 **missei** grow thick/luxuriantly
6 密会 **mikkai** clandestine meeting
密行 **mikkō** prowl about, go secretly
密旨 **misshi** secret orders
7 密告 **mikkoku** secret information
密告者 **mikkokusha** informer, betrayer
密売 **mitsubai** illicit sale, smuggling, bootlegging
8 密画 **mitsuga** detailed drawing
密事 **mitsuji** secret
密使 **misshi** secret messenger/agent
密送 **missō** send secretly
密法 **mippō** (Buddhist) mysteries
密林 **mitsurin** jungle, dense forest
9 密勅 **mitchoku** secret decree
密造 **mitsuzō** illicit manufacture, moonshining
密通 **mittsū** illicit connection/intercourse, adultery
密封 **mippū** seal tight/up/hermetically
密室 **misshitsu** secret/locked roomg
密度 **mitsudo** density
密約 **mitsuyaku** secret agreement

3

氵
土
扌
口
女
巾
犭
弓
彳
彡
艹
宀 8←
⺍
山
圭
广
尸
口

密計 **mikkei** secret plan, plot
10 密書 **missho** secret message
密教 **mikkyō** esoteric Buddhism; religious mysteries
密航 **mikkō** steal passage, stow away
密航者 **mikkōsha** stowaway
11 密偵 **mittei** spy, undercover agent
密接 **missetsu** close, intimate
密猟 **mitsuryō** poaching
密密 **mitsumitsu** secretly, privately
密閉 **mippei** shut tight, seal airtight
12 密着 **mitchaku** adhere to, stick fast
密葬 **missō** private funeral
密貿易 **mitsubōeki** smuggling
密集 **misshū** crowd/mass together
密雲 **mitsuun** thick/dense clouds
14 密漁 **mitsuryō, mitsugyo** fish poaching
密語 **mitsugo** whispers, confidential talk
15 密儀 **mitsugi** secret rites, mysteries
密談 **mitsudan** secret/confidential talk
16 密謀 **mitsubō** plot, intrigue
密輸 **mitsuyu** smuggling; contraband
密輸入 **mitsuyunyū** smuggling
密輸出 **mitsuyushutsu** smuggle out/abroad
密輸団 **mitsuyudan** smuggling ring
密輸品 **mitsuyuhin** contraband
密輸船 **mitsuyusen** smuggling vessel
20 密議 **mitsugi** secret conference/consultation

——————— 2 ———————
4 内密 **naimitsu** private, secret, confidential
水密 **suimitsu** watertight
心密 **kokorohiso(ka)** inwardly, secretly
6 気密 **kimitsu** airtight
気密室 **kimitsushitsu** airtight chamber
8 枢密院 **Sūmitsuin** Privy Council
10 秘密 **himitsu** a secret, confidential
11 疎密 **somitsu** sparseness or denseness, density
密密 **mitsumitsu** secretly, privately
細密 **saimitsu** minute, close, miniature
粗密 **somitsu** coarseness and fineness
13 隠密 **onmitsu** privacy, secrecy; detective, spy, secret agent
稠密 **chūmitsu** dense, crowded
詳密 **shōmitsu** detailed
14 綿密 **menmitsu** minute, close, meticulous
精密 **seimitsu** precision
15 緊密 **kinmitsu** close, tight
16 濃密 **nōmitsu** thick, dense
機密 **kimitsu** secret, secrecy
親密 **shinmitsu** friendly, close, intimate
緻密 **chimitsu** fine, close, minute, exact
17 厳密 **genmitsu** strict, precise

3m8.6

窕 **CHŌ** graceful, refined

——————— 2 ———————
10 窈窕 **yōchō** graceful, elegant

3m8.7 / 698

窓 窗 **SŌ, mado** window

——————— 1 ———————
3 窓口 **madoguchi** (ticket) window
5 窓外 **sōgai** out(side) the window
窓台 **madodai** windowsill
8 窓枠 **madowaku** window frame/sash
窓明 **madoa(kari)** light from a window
11 窓掛 **madoka(ke)** curtain, blinds
13 窓飾 **madokaza(ri)** window display

——————— 2 ———————
3 丸窓 **marumado** circular window
小窓 **komado** small window
4 天窓 **tenmado** skylight
円窓 **marumado** round window
引窓 **hi(ki)mado** skylight, trap door
5 出窓 **demado** bay window
6 同窓生 **dōsōsei** schoolmate, fellow student, alumnus
同窓会 **dōsōkai** alumni association/meeting
7 学窓 **gakusō** school
車窓 **shasō** car/train window
9 風窓 **kazamado** air hole, vent
11 深窓 **shinsō** secluded inner room; (upper-class daughter) brought up knowing nothing of the world
船窓 **sensō, funamado** porthole
舷窓 **gensō** porthole
12 開窓 **hira(ki)mado** casement window
13 鉄窓 **tessō** steel-barred (prison) window
飾窓 **kaza(ri)mado** show window
14 獄窓 **gokusō** prison window; prison
18 鎧窓 **yoroimado** louver window

——————— 3 ———————
2 二重窓 **nijū mado** double/storm window
9 連子窓 **renjimado** lattice window
10 格子窓 **kōshi mado** latticed window
12 嵌殺窓 **ha(me)goro(shi)mado** fixed sash window
無双窓 **musōmado** openable panel in a door

3m8.8 / 1361

寄 **KI** depend on; give; call at
yo(ru) approach, draw near; meet; drop in
yo(seru) bring near; push aside; gather together; send

——————— 1 ———————
3 寄与 **kiyo** contribute to, be conducive to
4 寄辺 **yo(ru)be** friend, protector, helper
寄木 **yo(se)gi** parquet, wood mosaic
yo(ri)ki driftwood

5 寄生　**kisei** parasitic
　寄生木　**yadorigi** mistletoe; parasitic plant
　寄生虫　**kiseichū** parasitic insects, parasite
　寄生物　**kiseibutsu** parasite
　寄付　**kifu** contribution, donation
　　　yo(se)tsu(keru) let come near
　　　yo(ri)tsu(ku) come near; open (the
　　　day's trading)
　寄付金　**kifukin** contributions
6 寄合　**yo(ri)a(i)** meeting, get-together
7 寄附　**kifu** contribution, donation
　寄附行為　**kifu kōi** act of endowment,
　　　donation
8 寄波　**yo(se)nami** surf
　寄居　**kikyo** temporary dwelling; staying with
　　　someone else
9 寄食　**kishoku** be parasitic, sponge off
10 寄値　**yo(ri)ne** opening price
　寄進　**kishin** contribution, donation
　寄席　**yose** variety-show hall
　寄書　**yo(se)ga(ki)** write/draw jointly
　　　kisho send a letter/article
　寄留　**kiryū** temporary residence, sojourn
　寄留地　**kiryūchi** one's temporary residence
　寄留届　**kiryū todo(ke)** notice of temporary
　　　domicile
　寄留者　**kiryūsha** temporary resident
　寄託　**kitaku** deposit with, entrust to
11 寄道　**yo(ri)michi** stop in on one's way
　寄掛　**yo(ri)ka(karu)** lean against
　　　yo(se)ka(keru) prop against
　寄宿　**kishuku** lodging, board
　寄宿生　**kishukusei** dormitory student
　寄宿舎　**kishukusha** dormitory
　寄宿料　**kishukuryō** boarding expenses
　寄寄　**yo(ri)yo(ri)** occasionally
12 寄港　**kikō** call at (a port)
　寄場　**yo(ri)ba** place to meet/call at
　寄寓　**kigū** lodge, live/stay with
　寄集　**yo(se)atsu(me)** miscellany, motley
　　　yo(ri)atsu(maru) assemble, meet
14 寄算　**yo(se)zan** addition (in math)
15 寄稿　**kikō** contribute to, write for
　寄稿者　**kikōsha** contributor (of articles)
　寄縋　**yo(ri)suga(ru)** cling to, rely on
17 寄鍋　**yo(se)nabe** chowder
18 寄贈　**kizō** donate, present
　寄贈者　**kizōsha** donor, contributor
　寄贈品　**kizōhin** gift, donation

──────────── 2 ────────────

2 人寄　**hitoyo(se)** an attraction, a draw
3 口寄　**kuchiyo(se)** spiritism, necromancy;
　　　a mediumg
4 片寄　**k4 kyo(ru)** lean to one side; be biased
　引寄　**hi(ki)yo(seru)** draw near/toward; attract
5 左寄　**hidariyo(ri)** leaning toward the left

打寄　**u(chi)yo(seru)** break upon (the shore),
　　　come (attacking)
右寄　**migiyo(ri)** leaning to the right; rightist
立寄　**ta(chi)yo(ru)** drop in on, stop at
6 年寄　**toshiyo(ri)** old person
　近寄　**chikayo(ru)** go/come near, approach
　名寄　**nayo(se)** compilation of names of similar
　　　things/places/persons; listing of all one's
　　　accounts
　耳寄　**mimiyo(ri)** welcome (news)
7 走寄　**hashi(ri)yo(ru)** come running, run up to
　吹寄　**fu(ki)yo(seru)** drift, blow together
　忍寄　**shino(bi)yo(ru)** steal near, sneak up
　言寄　**i(i)yo(ru)** court, woo
　車寄　**kurumayo(se)** carriage porch, porte-
　　　cochère
8 事寄　**kotoyo(sete)** under the pretext of
　逆寄　**sakayo(se)** counterattack
　押寄　**o(shi)yo(seru)** push aside; advance on,
　　　besiege
　抱寄　**da(ki)yo(seru)** hug/snuggle to one's
　　　breast
　呼寄　**yo(bi)yo(seru)** send for, summon, call
　　　together
　歩寄　**ayu(mi)yo(ri)** compromise
　取寄　**to(ri)yo(seru)** send for, order
9 南寄　**minamiyo(ri)** southerly (wind)
　持寄　**mo(chi)yo(ru)** pool, bring a contribu-
　　　tion to share
　思寄　**omo(i)yo(ru)** think of, recall
11 掃寄　**ha(ki)yo(seru)** sweep into a pile, sweep
　　　up
　寄寄　**yo(ri)yo(ri)** occasionally
　鳥寄　**toriyo(se)** birdcall
12 最寄　**moyo(ri)** nearest, nearby
13 掻寄　**ka(ki)yo(seru)** scrape/rake up
　数寄　**suki** refined taste; elegant pursuits
　数寄屋　**sukiya** tea-ceremony room/cottage
　詰寄　**tsu(me)yo(ru)** draw near, press upon
14 駆寄　**ka(ke)yo(ru)** rush up to
15 皺寄　**shiwayo(se)** shifting (the burden) to
19 繰寄　**ku(ri)yo(seru)** draw toward one
23 躙寄　**niji(ri)yo(ru)** edge/crawl/sidle up to

──────────── 3 ────────────

8 若年寄　**waka-doshiyo(ri)** young person who
　　　looks/acts old

3m8.9 / 1716

CHITSU plug up, obstruct; nitrogen

──────────── 1 ────────────

6 窒死　**chisshi** death from suffocation/
　　　asphyxiation
10 窒息　**chissoku** suffocation, asphyxiation

──── (margin, right) ────
3
氵
土
扌
口
女
巾
犭
弓
彳
彡
艹 ─ 8 ─
宀
⺌
山
亠
广
尸
口

窒息死 **chissokushi** death from suffocation/asphyxiation
窒素 **chisso** nitrogen

3m8.10

寇 寇

KŌ enemy; revenge

——— 2 ———

2 入寇 **nyūkō** invasion, encroachment
4 元寇 **Genkō** the Mongol invasions 1274 and 1281
10 倭寇 **wakō** Japanese pirates

——— 9 ———

3m9.1

寓

GŪ temporary abode; imply

——— 1 ———

8 寓居 **gūkyo** reside temporarily
13 寓意 **gūi** allegory, moral
寓話 **gūwa** fable, parable, allegory

——— 2 ———

6 仮寓 **kagū** temporary residence
9 客寓 **kakugū** sojourn, reside temporarily
11 寄寓 **kigū** lodge, live/stay with

3m9.2

寐

BI sleep

——— 2 ———

13 夢寐 **mubi** (even while) asleep
14 寤寐 **gobi (ni mo)** awake or asleep

3m9.3 / 457

寒 寒

KAN cold; midwinter
samu(i) cold, chilly

——— 1 ———

4 寒天 **kanten** agar-agar, gelatin; cold weather, wintry sky
寒中 **kanchū** the cold season
寒水 **kansui** cold water
寒月 **kangetsu** wintry moon
寒心 **kanshin** shudder at, be alarmed
6 寒気 **kanki, samuke** the cold
寒色 **kanshoku** a cold color
寒地 **kanchi** cold region
寒行 **kangyō** midwinter religious austerities
寒竹 **kanchiku** solid bamboo
7 寒冷 **kanrei** cold, chilly

寒冷前線 **kanrei zensen** cold front
寒卵 **kantamago** winter eggs
寒村 **kanson** poor/lonely village
8 寒波 **kanpa** cold wave
寒参 **kanmai(ri)** midwinter visit to a shrine
寒空 **samuzora** wintry sky, cold weather
寒国 **kankoku** cold country
寒肥 **kangoe** winter manuring
寒雨 **kan'u** cold/lonely rain
9 寒点 **kanten** points on the skin sensitive to the cold
寒風 **kanpū** cold wind
寒室 **kanshitsu** coldhouse (for raising frigid-zone plants)
寒威 **kan'i** intense/severe cold
寒紅梅 **kankōbai** winter red-blossom plum tree
10 寒剤 **kanzai** (ice-salt) mixture for cooling
寒流 **kanryū** cold current
寒帯 **kantai** frigid zone
寒害 **kangai** damage from cold/frost
寒梅 **kanbai** early plum blossoms
寒晒 **kanzara(shi)** exposure to cold weather
11 寒貧 **kanpin** very poor
寒菊 **kangiku** winter chrysanthemum
12 寒湿 **kanshitsu** cold and moisture
寒暑 **kansho** hot and cold; summer and winter
13 寒椿 **kantsubaki** winter camellia
寒暖 **kandan** hot and cold, temperature
寒暖計 **kandankei** thermometer
15 寒餅 **kanmochi** winter rice cake
16 寒稽古 **kangeiko** winter (judo) exercises

——— 2 ———

3 三寒四温 **sankan shion** alternation of three cold then four warm days
大寒 **daikan** coldest season, midwinter
小寒 **shōkan** winter's second-coldest period (around January 6)
4 心寒 **kokorosamu(i)** chilling
6 防寒 **bōkan** protection against the cold
防寒服 **bōkanfuku** winter/arctic clothes
防寒具 **bōkangu** cold-protection/arctic outfit
防寒靴 **bōkangutsu** arctic boots
肌寒 **hadazamu(i), hadasamu(i)** chilly
7 亜寒帯 **akantai** subarctic zone
余寒 **yokan** the lingering cold
8 夜寒 **yosamu, yozamu** the night cold
苦寒 **kukan** coldest season of the year; 12th lunar month
9 耐寒 **taikan** coldproof
春寒 **shunkan** the (early-)spring cold
10 素寒貧 **sukanpin** poverty; pauper
飢寒 **kikan** hunger and cold
11 悪寒 **okan** a chill with a fever
12 極寒 **gokkan** intense cold

朝寒 **asasamu** the morning cool/cold
暑寒 **shokan** heat and cold
14 酷寒 **kokkan** intense/bitter cold
15 膚寒 **hadasamu(i), hadazamu(i)** chilly
避寒 **hikan** (spend the) winter at
避寒地 **hikanchi** winter resort
16 薄寒 **usu(ra)samu(i)** chilly
頭寒足熱 **zukan-sokunetsu** keeping the head cool and the feet warm
17 厳寒 **genkan** intense cold

3m9.4

是

SHOKU real, true, actual

3m9.5 / 713

富 富

FU, FŪ, to(mu) be/become rich, abound in
tomi wealth

———————— 1 ————————
2 富力 **furyoku** wealth, resources
3 富山 **Toyama** (city, Toyama-ken)
富山県 **Toyama-ken** (prefecture)
富士川 **Fuji-kawa** (river, Shizuoka-ken)
富士山 **Fuji-san** Mt. Fuji
富士絹 **fujiginu** fuji silk
富士額 **fujibitai** hairline resembling the outline of Mt. Fuji
5 富札 **tomifuda** lottery ticket
6 富有 **fuyū** wealthy, affluent
8 富岳 **Fugaku** Mt. Fuji
富国 **fukoku** rich country, national enrichment
富国強兵 **fukoku-kyōhei** national wealth and military strength
富者 **fusha** rich person, the wealthy
10 富家 **fuka** wealthy family
11 富商 **fushō** wealthy merchant
富強 **fukyō** wealth and power
12 富裕 **fuyū** wealthy, affluent
富貴 **fūki, fukki** wealth and rank
13 富農 **funō** prosperous farmer
富源 **fugen** source of wealth, national resources
14 富豪 **fugō** wealthy man, millionaire
23 富籤 **tomikuji** lottery, lottery ticket

———————— 2 ————————
5 巨富 **kyofu** vast wealth
8 逆富士 **saka(sa) Fuji** inverted reflection of Mt. Fuji
国富 **kokufu** national wealth
11 貧富 **hinpu** rich and poor, wealth and poverty
13 豊富 **hōfu** abundant, affluent

窗 → 窓 **3m8.7**

3m9.6

窘

KIN be in distress
tashina(meru) reprove, berate, rebuke

3m9.7

窖

KŌ, anagura cellar

———————— 10 ————————
3m10.1 / 1079

寝 寢

SHIN, ne(ru) go to bed, sleep
ne sleep
ne(kasu) put to bed

———————— 1 ————————
0 寝しなに **ne(shina ni)** when going to bed
寝そべる **ne(soberu)** lie sprawled out
2 寝入 **nei(ri)** fall asleep
3 寝小便 **neshōben** bedwetting
4 寝不足 **nebusoku** lack of sleep
寝化粧 **negeshō** makeup/toilet before retiring
寝込 **neko(mu)** fall asleep; oversleep; be sick in bed
寝心地 **negokochi** sleeping comfort
5 寝台 **shindai** bed
寝台車 **shindaisha** sleeping car
寝台券 **shindaiken** sleeping-car ticket
6 寝返 **negae(ri)** tossing about while sleeping; switching sides
寝汗 **nease** night sweat
寝耳水 **nemimi (ni) mizu** a complete surprise
7 寝冷 **nebi(e)** catching cold while sleeping
寝忘 **newasu(re)** oversleep
寝坊 **nebō** oversleeping; late riser
寝床 **nedoko** bed
寝言 **negoto** talking in one's sleep
8 寝泊 **netoma(ri)** stay at, lodge
寝苦 **neguru(shii)** unable to sleep well
寝物語 **nemonogatari** talk while lying in bed
寝所 **shinjo, nedoko** bedroom
寝具 **shingu** bedding
9 寝巻 **nema(ki)** nightclothes
寝首搔 **nekubi (o) ka(ku)** chop off someone's head while he is asleep
寝姿 **nesugata** one's form while lying down/asleep
寝室 **shinshitsu** bedroom
寝相 **nezō** one's sleeping posture
寝食 **shinshoku** food and sleep
10 寝酒 **nezake** a drink before going to bed

3

氵 土
扌 口
女 巾
犭 弓
彳 彡
艹
宀 10←
⺌ 山
韋
广
尸
口

寝起 **neo(ki)** (one's disposition upon) awaking; sleeping and waking, daily living

寝息 **neiki** breathing of a sleeping person

11 寝惚 **nebo(keru)** be half asleep

寝袋 **nebukuro** sleeping bag

寝転 **nekoro(bu)** lie down, throw oneself down

12 寝覚 **neza(me)** waking from sleep

寝棺 **negan, nekan** coffin

寝椅子 **neisu** sofa, lounge chair

寝間 **nema** bedroom

寝間着 **nemaki** nightclothes

13 寝際 **negiwa** just before going to bed

寝殿 **shinden** (noble's) main residence

寝殿造 **shindenzuku(ri)** (a palace-style architecture)

14 寝様 **nezama** one's sleeping posture

寝静 **neshizu(maru)** fall asleep

17 寝藁 **newara** (stable) litter, straw

18 寝顔 **negao** one's sleeping face

――――――― 2 ―――――――

4 不寝番 **fushinban** night watch

片寝 **katane** sleep on one's side

6 仮寝 **karine** nap; stay at an inn

共寝 **tomone** sleeping together

早寝 **hayane** retiring early

8 泣寝入 **na(ki)ne-i(ri)** cry oneself to sleep

空寝入 **sorane-i(ri)** pretend to be asleep

9 浮寝 **u(ki)ne** sleeping in a ship; uneasy sleep

独寝 **hito(ri)ne** sleeping alone

昼寝 **hirune** nap, siesta

10 狸寝入 **tanuki ne-i(ri)** pretending to be an old woman

宵寝 **yoine** early to bed

旅寝 **tabine** put up at an inn

11 添寝 **so(i)ne** sleeping together

転寝 **koro(bi)ne, utatane** nap, doze

gorone sleep with one's clothes on

12 就寝 **shūshin** go to bed, retire

朝寝 **asane** morning sleep, late rising

朝寝坊 **asanebō** late riser

13 楽寝 **rakune** nap, rest

――――――― 3 ―――――――

4 不貞寝 **futene** stay in bed out of spite

14 雑魚寝 **zakone** sleep together in a group

3m10.2

塞

SOKU, SAI, fusa(gu) stop/plug up, close off, block, obstruct, fill **fusa(garu)** be closed/blocked/clogged/filled **se(ku)** dam up; check, stop, stem

――――――― 1 ―――――――

10 塞栓 **sokusen** an embolism

――――――― 2 ―――――――

3 口塞 **kuchifusa(gi)** keeping someone from talking; food (served to guests)

5 穴塞 **anafusa(gi)** plugging a hole; stopgap

立塞 **ta(chi)fusa(garu)** stand in the way, block

6 防塞 **bōsai** roadblock, barricade

充塞 **jūsoku** plug, fill up; be stopped/clogged up

7 阻塞気球 **sosai kikyū** barrage balloon

9 城塞 **jōsai** fort, citadel, stronghold

要塞 **yōsai** fortress, stronghold

11 梗塞 **kōsoku** stoppage; (monetary) stringency; infarction

閉塞 **heisoku** blockade; obstruction

to(ji)fusa(geru) close up, cover over

12 場塞 **bafusa(gi)** something that takes up space

――――――― 3 ―――――――

2 八方塞 **happō fusa(gari)** blocked in every direction, stymied

12 場所塞 **bashofusa(gi)** obstacle

13 腸閉塞 **chōheisoku** intestinal obstruction, ileus

――――――― 4 ―――――――

4 心筋梗塞 **shinkin kōsoku** myocardial infarction

3m10.3 / 1050

寛　寛

KAN magnanimity, leniency, generosity **kutsuro(gu)** relax, feel at home **kutsuro(geru)** loosen, relax

――――――― 1 ―――――――

3 寛大 **kandai** magnanimous, tolerant, lenient

4 寛元 **Kangen** (era, 1243–1246)

寛仁 **kanjin** magnanimous

Kannin (era, 1017–1020)

寛文 **Kanbun** (era, 1661–1672)

5 寛平 **Kanpyō** (era, 889–897)

寛正 **Kanshō** (era, 1460–1465)

寛永 **Kan'ei** (era, 1624–1643)

寛弘 **Kankō** (era, 1004–1011)

6 寛仮 **kanka** be tolerant toward

7 寛延 **Kan'en** (era, 1748–1750)

8 寛典 **kanten** leniency, clemency

寛厚 **kankō** generous, largehearted

寛治 **Kanji** (era, 1087–1093)

寛和 **Kanna** (era, 985–986)

9 寛保 **Kanpō** (era, 1741–1743)

寛政 **Kansei** (era, 1789–1800)

10 寛容 **kan'yō** magnanimity, generosity, forbearance

寛恕 **kanjo** magnanimity; forgiveness, pardon

12 寛喜 **Kangi** (era, 1229–1231)

寛裕 **kan'yū** magnanimity

14 寛徳 **Kantoku** (era, 1044–1045)

17 寛厳 **kangen** lenience or/and severity

寛闊 **kankatsu** ample, generous

—————— 2 ——————

5 打寛 **u(chi)kutsuro(gu)** make oneself comfortable, relax

8 長寛 **Chōkan** (era, 1163–1165)

3m10.4

寞 **BAKU** quiet, lonely

—————— 2 ——————

11 寂寞 **sekibaku** lonesome, desolate

3m10.5

窠 **KA** nest, hole

3m10.6

窟 **KUTSU, iwaya** cave, den

—————— 2 ——————

8 岩窟 **gankutsu** cave, cavern
9 洞窟 **dōkutsu** cave, cavern
11 巣窟 **sōkutsu** den, hangout, home
20 巌窟 **gankutsu** cave, cavern
21 魔窟 **makutsu** den (of thieves); brothel, red-light district

—————— 3 ——————

7 阿片窟 **ahenkutsu** opium den
屁理窟 **herikutsu** quibbling, sophistry
私娼窟 **shishōkutsu** brothel
11 貧民窟 **hinminkutsu** slums

—————— 11 ——————

3m11.1

寤 **GO** awaken

—————— 1 ——————

12 寤寐 **gobi (ni mo)** awake or asleep

3m11.2 / 1851

寡 **KA** few, small; alone, widowed

—————— 1 ——————

2 寡人 **kajin** I (used by royalty)
4 寡少 **kashō** little, few, scanty
5 寡占 **kasen** oligopoly
7 寡作 **kasaku** low production

寡兵 **kahei** small army/force
寡言 **kagen** taciturnity, reticence
11 寡婦 **kafu, yamome** widow
寡欲 **kayoku** unselfish, of few wants
13 寡勢 **kazei** small force
14 寡聞 **kabun** little knowledge, ill-informed
15 寡黙 **kamoku** taciturn, reticent
寡慾 **kayoku** unselfish, of few wants
16 寡頭政治 **katō seiji** oligarchy

—————— 2 ——————

6 多寡 **taka** quantity, number, amount
12 衆寡 **shūka** many vs. few, outnumbered

3m11.3

寨 **SAI** fort

3m11.4

搴 **KEN** take; hoist; pull out; shrink

3m11.5

寥 **RYŌ** lonely

—————— 1 ——————

3 寥々 **ryōryō** lonesome, quiet; few, rare

—————— 2 ——————

9 荒寥 **kōryō** bleak, desolate
11 寂寥 **sekiryō** loneliness, desolation

3m11.6 / 619

察 **SATSU** infer, see

—————— 1 ——————

0 察する **sas(suru)** surmise, judge; understand; sympathize with
察し **sas(shi)** conjecture, judgment, understanding; considerateness
8 察知 **satchi** infer, gather, sense

—————— 2 ——————

5 巡察 **junsatsu** patrol, one's rounds
6 考察 **kōsatsu** consideration, examination, study
8 拝察 **haisatsu** infer, guess, gather
明察 **meisatsu** discernment, insight
9 透察 **tōsatsu** insight, discernment
洞察 **dōsatsu, tōsatsu** insight, discernment
洞察力 **dōsatsuryoku** insight
査察 **sasatsu** inspection, observation

3

氵 汀 扌 口 女 巾 犭 弓 彳 彡 艹 宀 11←
丷 山 圭 广 尸 口

省察 **seisatsu** reflect on, consider, introspect
10 高察 **kōsatsu** your idea
11 偵察 **teisatsu** reconnaissance
偵察隊 **teisatsutai** reconnoitering party, patrol, scouts
偵察機 **teisatsuki** reconnaissance/spotter plane
推察 **suisatsu** guess, conjecture, surmise
視察 **shisatsu** inspection, observance
12 検察 **kensatsu** investigation and prosecution
検察庁 **kensatsuchō** public prosecutor's office
検察官 **kensatsukan** public prosecutor
診察 **shinsatsu** medical examination
診察日 **shinsatsubi** consultation day
診察券 **shinsatsuken** consultation ticket
診察室 **shinsatsushitsu** room where patients are examined
診察料 **shinsatsuryō** medical consultation fee
閲察 **binsatsu** compassion, sympathy
15 監察 **kansatsu** inspection; inspector, supervisor
監察官 **kansatsukan** inspector, police supervisor
16 賢察 **kensatsu** your discernment/understanding
18 観察 **kansatsu** observe, view
観察力 **kansatsuryoku** power of observation
観察者 **kansatsusha** observer
観察眼 **kansatsugan** an observing eye
19 警察 **keisatsu** police
警察力 **keisatsuryoku** police force
警察犬 **keisatsuken** police dog
警察犯 **keisatsuhan** police offense
警察庁 **Keisatsuchō** National Police Agency
警察官 **keisatsukan** police officer
警察署 **keisatsusho** police station
警察権 **keisatsuken** police power

———————— 3 ————————
12 無警察 **mukeisatsu** lawlessness, anarchy

———————— 4 ————————
4 水上警察 **suijō keisatsu** water/harbor police
9 軍事警察 **gunji keisatsu** military police
19 警乗警察 **keijō keisatsu** railway police

3m11.7

蜜 MITSU honey; nectar, molasses

———————— 1 ————————
4 蜜月 **mitsugetsu** honeymoon
7 蜜豆 **mitsumame** boiled beans with molasses
9 蜜柑 **mikan** mandarin orange, tangerine
13 蜜蜂 **mitsubachi** honeybee
21 蜜蠟 **mitsurō** beeswax

———————— 2 ————————
4 水蜜桃 **suimitsutō** (a variety of) peach
10 夏蜜柑 **natsumikan** Chinese citron
13 蜂蜜 **hachimitsu** honey
16 糖蜜 **tōmitsu** molasses, syrup

3m11.8 / 1412

寧 寧 NEI peaceful, quiet
mushi(ro) rather, preferably

———————— 1 ————————
4 寧日 **neijitsu** peaceful/quiet day

———————— 2 ————————
2 丁寧 **teinei** polite, courteous; careful, meticulous
6 安寧 **annei** public peace
Annei (emperor, 549–511)
安寧秩序 **annei-chitsujo** peace and order
11 清寧 **Seinei** (emperor, 480–484)
康寧 **kōnei** peaceful

賓 → 賓 **3m12.3**

實 → 実 **3m5.4**

寢 → 寝 **3m10.1**

3m11.9

窪 WA, A, **kubo(mu)** cave in, sink, become hollow **kubo(mi)** hollow, dent **kubo** depression, hollow

———————— 1 ————————
6 窪地 **kubochi** low ground, hollow, depression

———————— 2 ————————
4 手窪 **te (no) kubo** the hollow of the hand

寬 → 寛 **3m10.3**

3m11.10

窩 KA cave; cavity, hollow; hideaway

———————— 2 ————————
3 山窩 **sanka** nomadic mountain tribes
11 眼窩 **ganka** eye socket
13 蜂窩 **hōka** honeycomb

3m11.11

YU small door; pass through

─────── 12 ───────

3m12.1 / 1383

SHIN hearing, investigation, trial
tsumabi(raka) fully known, in detail

─────── 1 ───────

7 審判 **shinpan, shinban** decision, judgment, refereeing
審判官 **shinpankan** judge, umpire, referee
9 審美 **shinbi** esthetic appreciation
審美的 **shinbiteki** esthetic
審査 **shinsa** examination, investigation
審査員 **shinsain** judges, examiners
11 審理 **shinri** trial, inquiry, hearing
審問 **shinmon** trial, hearing, inquiry
20 審議 **shingi** deliberation, consideration
審議会 **shingikai** deliberative assembly, commission, council

─────── 2 ───────

1 一審 **isshin** first instance/trial
4 不審 **fushin** dubious, suspicious; strange
不審訊問 **fushin jinmon** questioning (by a policeman)
予審 **yoshin** preliminary examination, pretrial hearing
5 主審 **shushin** head umpire
6 再審 **saishin** re-examination, review, retrial
再審査 **saishinsa** re-examination
7 初審 **shoshin** first trial/instance
10 陪審 **baishin** jury
11 副審 **fukushin** sub-umpire, assistant referee
終審 **shūshin** final trial, last instance
12 塁審 **ruishin** base umpire
結審 **kesshin** conclusion of a trial/hearing
14 誤審 **goshin** error in refereeing
15 線審 **senshin** linesman (in tennis, etc.)
18 覆審 **fukushin** retrial, judicial review

─────── 3 ───────

3 下級審 **kakyūshin** lower court
11 控訴審 **kōsoshin** appeal trial

3m12.2 / 1323

RYŌ dormitory, hostel

─────── 1 ───────

5 寮生 **ryōsei** dormitory student
寮母 **ryōbo** dormitory matron
8 寮長 **ryōchō** dormitory director

14 寮歌 **ryōka** dormitory song

─────── 2 ───────

7 学寮 **gakuryō** dormitory
9 茶寮 **charyō** tea-ceremony cottage

─────── 3 ───────

5 母子寮 **boshiryō** home for mothers and children

─────── 4 ───────

7 花嫁御寮 **hanayome goryō** bride

3m12.3 / 1852

HIN guest

─────── 1 ───────

9 賓客 **hinkaku, hinkyaku** honored guest, visitor
10 賓格 **hinkaku** objective case (in grammar)
13 賓辞 **hinji** object (in grammar)

─────── 2 ───────

5 正賓 **seihin** guest of honor
主賓 **shuhin** guest of honor
6 迎賓 **geihin** welcoming guests
迎賓館 **geihinkan** reception hall, residence for guests
7 来賓 **raihin** guest, visitor
来賓席 **raihinseki** visitors' seats/gallery
8 国賓 **kokuhin** state guest
12 貴賓 **kihin** distinguished guest
貴賓室 **kihinshitsu** room reserved for VIP guests
貴賓席 **kihinseki** seats for the honored guests

3m12.4 / 897

窮

KYŪ distress **kiwa(maru)** reach an extreme; come to an end **kiwa(meru)** carry to extremes; bring to an end

─────── 1 ───────

0 窮する **kyū(suru)** be in need, be destitute, be in a dilemma
3 窮乏 **kyūbō** poverty
5 窮民 **kyūmin** the needy
6 窮死 **kyūshi** a miserable death
窮地 **kyūchi** predicament
7 窮余 **kyūyo** desperate
窮余一策 **kyūyo (no) issaku** last resort
窮状 **kyūjō** distress, dire straits
窮迫 **kyūhaku** financial distress, poverty
8 窮追 **kyūtsui** drive into a corner
窮屈 **kyūkutsu** narrow, cramped; formal, stiff, straitlaced; ill at ease
11 窮理 **kyūri** truthseeking
窮鳥 **kyūchō** a cornered bird

窮鳥懐入 **kyūchō futokoro (ni) hai(ru)**
(like a) bird in distress seeking refuge
12 窮極 **kyūkyoku** ultimate, eventual
窮無 **kiwama(ri)na(i)** endless
窮策 **kyūsaku** desperate measure, last resort
13 窮鼠 **kyūso** a cornered mouse/rat
14 窮境 **kyūkyō** predicament

─── 2 ───
7 困窮 **konkyū** poverty, distress
困窮者 **konkyūsha** the needy/destitute
11 貧窮 **hinkyū** dire poverty
12 無窮 **mukyū** endless, perpetual, eternal

─── 4 ───
4 天壌無窮 **tenjō mukyū** eternal as heaven and earth

寫→写 **2i3.1**

3m12.5 / 1789
窯窰 **YŌ, kama** kiln

─── 1 ───
4 窯元 **kamamoto** place where pottery is made
13 窯業 **yōgyō** ceramics (industry)
─── 2 ───
9 炭窯 **sumigama** charcoal kiln
─── 3 ───
5 石灰窯 **ishibaigama** limekiln

窰→窯 **3m12.5**

鞍→ **3k12.19**

─── 13 ───

3m13.1
寰 **KAN** capital region ruled directly by the emperor; the world
─── 2 ───
2 人寰 **jinkan** the world, people
14 塵寰 **jinkan** the dusty/mundane world

3m13.2 / 521
憲憲 **KEN** law
─── 1 ───
7 憲兵 **kenpei** military police, MP's

8 憲法 **kenpō** constitution
憲法違反 **kenpō ihan** unconstitutionality
9 憲政 **kensei** constitutional government
11 憲章 **kenshō** constitution, charter
─── 2 ───
3 大憲章 **Daikenshō** Magna Carta
5 立憲 **rikken** adopting a constitution
立憲君主政体 **rikken kunshu seitai** constitutional monarchy
立憲国 **rikkenkoku** constitutional country
立憲的 **rikkenteki** constitutional
6 合憲性 **gōkensei** constitutionality
8 官憲 **kanken** the authorities
国憲 **kokken** national constitution
10 家憲 **kaken** family rules
12 違憲 **iken** unconstitutionality
朝憲 **chōken** constitution
─── 3 ───
8 非立憲的 **hirikkenteki** unconstitutional
12 欽定憲法 **kintei kenpō** constitution granted by the emperor

3m13.3
窺 **KI, ukaga(u)** infer; peep into, watch for
─── 1 ───
8 窺知 **kichi** perceive, understand

3m13.4
窿 **RYŪ** arch, vault, dome
─── 2 ───
8 穹窿 **kyūryū** vault (of heaven)

3m13.5
癯 **yatsu(reru)** become emaciated/worn-out/haggard/gaunt
─── 2 ───
9 面癯 **omoyatsu(re)** haggard/worn-out look
10 旅癯 **tabiyatsu(re)** travel weariness

3m13.6
靛 **TEN, DEN** indigo, deep blue

─── 14 ───

3m14.1
謇 **KEN** stutter; speak frankly

3m14.2

賽 **SAI** temple visit; decide a contest; dice

———— 1 ————
0 賽ころ **sai(koro)** dice
14 賽銭 **saisen** money offering
賽銭箱 **saisenbako** offertory chest

3m14.3

蹇 **KEN, ashinae** limp, lameness; a cripple

竈 → 竈 3m18.1

3m14.4

豁 **KATSU** open up; wide

———— 1 ————
12 豁然 **katsuzen** in a flash; broad, vast
———— 2 ————
12 開豁 **kaikatsu** open (land); broad(-minded)

———— 15 ————

3m15.1

竄 **ZAN, SAN** flee; hide; renew; get into

———— 2 ————
7 改竄 **kaizan** alter, falsify, doctor

3m15.2

竅 **KYŌ** hole, cave

———— 16 ————

3m16.1

寵 **CHŌ** favor, patronage, affection

———— 1 ————
7 寵臣 **chōshin** favorite retainer
寵児 **chōji** favorite child, pet
11 寵遇 **chōgū** special favor, patronage
13 寵愛 **chōai** favor, affection

寶 → 宝 3m5.2

———— 17 ————

寶 → 宝 3m5.2

3m17.1

鶱 **KEN** lift up; err; hopping

3m17.2

竇 **TŌ** hole; doorway; ditch

———— 18 ————

3m18.1

竈 竈 **SŌ, kamado** kitchen stove, oven; household **hettsui** hearth, kitchen stove

———— 19 ————

竊 → 窃 3m6.5

———— ⌄ 3n ————

小	少	尔	尖	光	当	劣	肖	学	労	乳	毛	尚
0.1	1.1	0a14.3	3.1	3.2	3.3	3.4	4.1	4.2	4.3	4.4	5.1	0a13.1

尚	甾	争	歩	忝	栄	単	県	省	爰	挙	党	奚
5.2	5f5.4	2n4.2	5.3	5.4	6.1	6.2	6.3	5c4.7	6.4	7.1	7.2	7.3

孱	将	雀	巣	蛍	常	堂	雀	棠	営	覚	掌	就
7.4	2b8.3	8c3.2	8.1	8.2	8.3	8.4	8c3.2	9.1	9.2	9.3	9.4	3d9.21

嘗	誉	當	亂	舜	尠	奨	孵	嘗	裳	賞	輝	鴬
3n11.1	10.1	3n3.3	3d4.21	10.2	10.3	10.4	10.5	11.1	11.2	12.1	7c8.8	11b10.9

静　厳　谿　黨
4b10.9　14.1　3a8.16　3n7.2

─────── 0 ───────

3n0.1 / 27

3 小

SHŌ, chii(sai), ko-, o- little, small

─────── 1 ───────

2 小人 **kobito** dwarf, midget　**shōnin** child
　　shōjin insignificant/small-minded person
　小人物 **shōjinbutsu** stingy/base person
　小人数 **koninzū** small number of people
　小刀 **shōtō** shorter sword
　　kogatana (pocket)knife
3 小川 **ogawa** brook, creek
　　Ogawa (surname)
　小才 **kosai, shōsai** clever, smart
　小口 **koguchi** in small lots, small sum; end,
　　edge; clue; beginning
　小巾 **kohaba** narrow width/range
　小山 **koyama** hill, knoll
4 小爪 **kozume** root of a fingernail
　小天地 **shōtenchi** small world, microcosm
　小仏 **kobotoke** small image of Buddha
　小切手 **kogitte** check, cheque
　小文字 **komoji** small/lowercase letters
　小片 **shōhen** fragment, piece
　小分 **kowa(ke)** subdivide, classify
　小水 **shōsui** urine, urination
　小手 **kote** forearm; gauntlet
　小手先 **kotesaki** (a good) hand (at)
　小手調 **koteshira(be)** tryout, rehearsal
　小犬 **koinu** puppy
　小引 **shōin** short introduction/preface
　小火 **shōka, boya** small fire
　小牛 **koushi** calf
　小心 **shōshin** timid, faint-hearted; prudent
　小心者 **shōshinmono** timid person, coward
　小心翼々 **shōshin-yokuyoku** very timid/
　　cautious
5 小包 **kozutsumi** parcel, package
　小出 **koda(shi)** (take/dole out) in small
　　quantities, bit by bit
　小半日 **kohannichi** about half a day
　小半年 **kohannen** about six months
　小半時 **kohantoki** about half an hour
　小生 **shōsei** I, me
　小生意気 **konamaiki** conceit, impudence
　小史 **shōshi** a brief history
　小冊 **shōsatsu** booklet, pamphlet
　小冊子 **shōsasshi** booklet, pamphlet
　小市民 **shōshimin** petty bourgeois, lower
　　middle class

小正月 **koshōgatsu** Little New Year's, 14th-
　　16th of first lunar month
小用 **shōyō, koyō** small matter; urination
小字 **shōji** small characters/type
　　koaza village subsection
小石 **koishi** pebble, gravel
小田 **oda** rice field/paddy
小田原 **Odawara** (city, Kanagawa-ken)
小田原提灯 **odawara-jōchin** collapsible
　　cylindrical paper lantern
小田原評定 **odawara hyōjō** endless debate,
　　fruitless conference
小皿 **kozara** small plate, saucer
6 小気味 **kokimi** feeling, sentiment
小吏 **shōri** petty official
小曲 **shōkyoku** short musical piece
小休止 **shōkyūshi** brief recess, short break
小伝 **shōden** brief biography/account
小企業 **shōkigyō** small enterprises/business
小会 **shōkai** small gathering
小羊 **kohitsuji** lamb
小安 **shōan** somewhat at ease; content with
　　minor achievements, unambitious
小回 **komawa(ri)** sharp turn
小百合 **sayuri** lily
小百姓 **kobyakushō** petty farmer, peasant
小成 **shōsei** small success
小耳 **komimi (ni hasamu)** happen to overhear
7 小身 **shōshin** humble position/rank
小我 **shōga** the self/ego
小亜細亜 **Shō-Ajia** Asia Minor
小作 **kosaku** tenant farming
　　kozuku(ri) of small build, small size
小作人 **kosakunin** tenant farmer
小作地 **kosakuchi** tenant farm land
小作米 **kosakumai** rent paid in rice
小作料 **kosakuryō** farm rent
小作農 **kosakunō** tenant farming
小判 **koban** small size (paper); (obsolete
　　oval gold coin)
小判形 **kobangata** oval, elliptical
小兵 **kohyō** short (stature)
小臣 **shōshin** lower-ranking vassal
小坊主 **kobōzu** young priest; sonny
小豆 **azuki** adzuki beans
小豆島 **Shōdoshima** (island, Kagawa-ken)
小役人 **koyakunin** petty/minor official
小形 **kogata** small-size
小学生 **shōgakusei** elementary-school student
小学校 **shōgakkō** elementary school
小売 **kou(ri)** retail
小売店 **kou(ri)ten** retail store/outlet, retailer

小売商 **kou(ri)shō** retail trade
小声 **kogoe** low voice, whisper, murmur
小村 **shōson** hamlet, small village
小児 **shōni** little child, infant
小児科 **shōnika** pediatrics
小児科医 **shōnikai** pediatrician
小児麻痺 **shōni mahi** infantile paralysis, polio
小社 **shōsha** minor shrine; our company
小麦 **komugi** wheat
小麦色 **komugi-iro** cocoa brown
小麦粉 **komugiko** (wheat) flour
小見出 **komida(shi)** subheading, subtitle
小利 **shōri** small profit
小利口 **korikō** clever, smart
小利巧 **korikō** clever, smart
小町 **komachi** beauty, belle, queen
小町娘 **komachi musume** beauty, belle, queen
小男 **kootoko** short man
小言 **kogoto** scolding, faultfinding
小足 **koashi** mincing steps
8 小事 **shōji** small matter, trifle
小使 **kozukai(i)** handyman, errand boy
小刻 **kokiza(mi)** mincing, in small bits
小夜 **sayo** night
小夜中 **sayonaka** midnight
小夜曲 **sayokyoku** serenade
小夜更 **sayofu(kete)** late a night
小咄 **kobanashi** a little story
小知 **shōchi** superficial knowledge
小姓 **koshō** page (to a noble)
小姑 **kojūtome, kojūto** one's spouse's sister
小径 **shōkei** lane, path
小官 **shōkan** petty official
小突 **kozu(ku)** poke, prod, nudge
小国 **shōkoku** small country
小国民 **shōkokumin** rising generation
小枝 **koeda** twig, sprig
小肥 **kobuto(ri)** plump
小股 **komata** short steps
小者 **komono** menial, servant; small fry
小物 **komono** small articles, little thing
小委員会 **shōiinkai** subcommittee
小金 **kogane** small sum of money; small fortune
小雨 **kosame** light rain, drizzle
9 小乗仏教 **Shōjō bukkyō** Hinayana/Lesser-vehicle Buddhism
小乗的 **shōjōteki** narrow-minded
小便 **shōben** urine, urination
小便所 **shōbenjo** urinal
小勇 **shōyū** mere brute courage
小変 **shōhen** a slight change; minor incident
小首 **kokubi** neck; head
小前提 **shōzentei** minor premise
小風 **kokaze** light breeze
小型 **kogata** small-size

小指 **koyubi** little finger
小品 **shōhin** something small, short piece/sketch
小草 **ogusa** small grasses
小屋 **koya** hut, cabin, cottage, shed
小屋掛 **koyaga(ke)** pitch camp; temporary hut/shack
小柄 **kogara** short height, small build
kozuka knife attached to a sword sheath
小胆 **shōtan** timid, lily-livered; prudent
小春 **koharu** tenth lunar month, Indian summer
小春日和 **koharubiyori** balmy autumn day, Indian-summer day
小昼 **kohiru** a little before noon; mid-morning snack
小為替 **kogawase** money order
小盾 **kodate** small shield; screen, cover
小計 **shōkei** subtotal
小食 **shōshoku** eating little/sparingly
小食家 **shōshokuka** light eater
10 小倉 **kokura** duck cloth
Kokura (city, Fukuoka-ken)
小都市 **shōtoshi** small city/town
小都会 **shōtokai** small city/town
小高 **kodaka(i)** slightly elevated
小差 **shōsa** slight difference, narrow margin
小逕 **shōkei** lane, path
小振 **kobu(ri)** small-size
小唄 **kouta** ditty, ballad
小娘 **komusume** (early-teenage) girl
小荷物 **konimotsu** parcel, package
小宴 **shōen** small dinner party
小党 **shōtō** small political party
小島 **kojima** small island, islet
小脇 **kowaki** side (of the body)
小骨 **kobone** small bones
小袖 **kosode** quilted silk garment
小鬼 **kooni** little devil, imp, elf
小紋 **komon** fine pattern
小粋 **koiki** stylish, tasteful
小馬 **kouma** pony, colt
小馬鹿 **kobaka** a fool
11 小野 **ono** field   **Ono** (proper name)
小隊 **shōtai** platoon
小商 **koakina(i)** small trade, retail business
小瓶 **kobin** small bottle
小道 **komichi** path, lane
小道具 **kodōgu** (stage) props
小過 **shōka** minor error
小猫 **koneko** kitten
小窓 **komado** small window
小康 **shōkō** lull, respite
小脳 **shōnō** the cerebellum
小球 **shōkyū** small ball, globule
小欲 **shōyoku** not very covetous

3

氵
土
扌
口
女
巾
犭
弓
彳
彡
艹
宀
⺌ 0←
山
耂
广
尸
口

3

氵
土
扌
口
女
巾
犭
弓
彳
彡
艹
宀
→0 ⺍
⻖
⺧
广
尸
口

小悪 **shōaku** minor offense; venial sin
小規模 **shōkibo** small-scale
小異 **shōi** minor difference
小細工 **kozaiku** handiwork; tricks, wiles
小粒 **kotsubu** small grain, granule
小船 **kobune** boat, small craft
小笠原諸島 **Ogasawara-shotō** the Bonin Islands
小雪 **koyuki** a light snowfall
小魚 **kozakana** small fish, fry, fingerlings
小鳥 **kotori** (small) bird
12 小禽 **shōkin** small birds
小善 **shōzen** a small kindness
小遣 **kozuka(i)** spending money
小遣銭 **kozuka(i)sen** spending money
小喧 **koyakama(shii)** falutfinding, fussy
小幅 **kohaba** narrow width/range
小寒 **shōkan** winter's second-coldest period (around January 6)
小景 **shōkei** beautiful view/scenery
小量 **shōryō** small quantity
小禄 **shōroku** small stipend
小童 **kowappa, kowarawa, kowarabe** youngster, kid
小買 **koga(i)** buy in small quantities
小艇 **shōtei** small boat
小策 **shōsaku** pretty trick/artifice
小筒 **kozutsu** rifle, small arms; bamboo saké flask
小閑 **shōkan** short break/rest, lull
小間使 **komazuka(i)** chambermaid
小間物 **komamono** sundry wares, knick-knacks
小間物屋 **komamonoya** haberdashery
小順 **chii(sai) jun** increasing order, smallest first
13 小僧 **kozō** young Buddhist priest; errand boy; youngster, kid
小勢 **kozei** small force, small number of people
小舅 **kojūto** one's spouse's brother
小農 **shōnō** small farmer, peasant
小楯 **kodate** small shield; screen, cover
小楊子 **koyōji** toothpick
小槌 **kozuchi** small mallet, gavel
小腹 **kobara** belly, abdomen
小腸 **shōchō** the small intestines
小暗 **ogura(i), kogura(i)** dusky, shady
小数 **shōsū** (decimal) fraction
小数点 **shōsūten** decimal point
小意気 **koiki** stylish, tasteful
小節 **shōsetsu** minor principles; bar (in music)
小話 **shōwa, kobanashi** little story, anecdote
小路 **kōji** path, lane, narrow street
小鉢 **kobachi** small bowl
14 小像 **shōzō** small statue, figurine

小熊座 **kogumaza** Little Bear, Ursa Minor
小旗 **kobata** small flag
小歌 **kouta** ditty, ballad
小憎 **koniku(rashii)** hateful, provoking
小鼻 **kobana** sides of the nose, nostrils
小説 **shōsetsu** novel, story, fiction
小説家 **shōsetsuka** novelist, (fiction) writer
小踊 **koodo(ri)** dancing/jumping for joy
小銭 **kozeni** small change, coins
小銃 **shōjū** rifle, small arms
15 小劇場 **shōgekijō** little theater
小皺 **kojiwa** little wrinkles, crow's feet
小潮 **koshio** neap tide
小器 **shōki** small receptacle; man of small caliber
小蕪 **kokabu** small turnip
小膝 **kohiza** the knee
小敵 **shōteki** weak adversary
小編 **shōhen** short article/story
小箱 **kobako** small box/case
小篇 **shōhen** short article/story
16 小機転 **kogiten** quick-witted
小樽 **kodaru** keg **Otaru** (city, Hokkaidō)
小憩 **shōkei** short break/rest, recess
小賢 **kozaka(shii)** smart(-alecky), crafty, shrewd
小頭 **kogashira** subforeman, straw boss
小鴨 **kogamo** duckling; teal
17 小糠雨 **konukaame** fine/drizzling rain
18 小難 **shōnan** small misfortune, mishap
komuzuka(shii) troublesome, finicky
小額 **shōgaku** small amount
20 小競合 **kozeria(i)** skirmish; bickering, quarrel
21 小癪 **koshaku** impudent, cheeky
小躍 **koodo(ri)** dancing/jumping for joy
24 小鬢 **kobin** side lock (of hair)

_____ 2 _____

3 大小 **daishō** large and/or small size; (relative) size; long sword and short sword
dai(nari) shō(nari) more or less
大小便 **daishōben** defecation and urination
山小屋 **yamagoya** mountain hut
4 中小企業 **chūshō kigyō** small business(es)
犬小屋 **inugoya** doghouse, kennel
牛小屋 **ushigoya** cowshed, barn
5 永小作 **eikosaku** perpetual (land) lease
永小作権 **eikosakuken** perpetual (land) lease
広小路 **hirokōji** wide/main street
立小便 **ta(chi)shōben** urinate outdoors
6 仮小屋 **karigoya** temporary shed, booth
羊小屋 **hitsujigoya** sheep pen, sheepfold
7 私小説 **watakushi shōsetsu** novel narrated in the first person; autobiographical novel
shishōsetsu autobiographical novel
9 狭小 **kyōshō** narrow, cramped
狩小屋 **ka(ri)goya** hunting cabin, a blind

10 姫小松 **hime komatsu** a small pine
弱小 **jakushō** puniness; youth
針小棒大 **shinshō-bōdai** exaggeration
馬小屋 **umagoya** a stable
11 過小 **kashō** too small
袋小路 **fukurokōji** blind alley, cul-de-sac
細小 **saishō** small and fine, minute
船小屋 **funagoya** boathouse
鳥小屋 **torigoya** aviary; chicken coop
12 短小 **tanshō** small
極小 **kyokushō** minimum
最小 **saishō** smallest, minimum
最小限 **saishōgen** minimum
最小限度 **saishō gendo** minimum
番小屋 **bangoya** sentry box
13 群小 **gunshō** small, minor, insignificant
微小 **bishō** minute, microscopic
寝小便 **neshōben** bedwetting
矮小 **waishō** undersized
鳩小屋 **hatogoya** dovecote
15 膝小僧 **hizakozō** one's knees, kneecap
17 縮小 **shukushō** reduction, cut

——————— 3 ———————
3 三文小説 **sanmon shōsetsu** cheap novel
大同小異 **daidō-shōi** substantially the same, not much different
丸太小屋 **marutagoya** log cabin
5 芝居小屋 **shibaigoya** playhouse, theater
8 怪奇小説 **kaiki shōsetsu** mystery/spooky story
9 洟垂小僧 **hanata(re) kozō** drippy-nosed little boy, snot-nose kid
10 高手小手 **takate-kote** (bound) hand and foot
差掛小屋 **sa(shi)ka(ke)goya** penthouse, lean-to
起上小法師 **o(ki)a(gari) koboshi** self-righting toy
莫大小 **meriyasu** knitted goods
11 推理小説 **suiri shōsetsu** detective story, whodunit
探偵小説 **tantei shōsetsu** detective story
12 短篇小説 **tanpen shōsetsu** short story/novel
無限小 **mugenshō** infinitesimal
19 艶笑小説 **enshō shōsetsu** love-comedy story/novel

——————— 4 ———————
12 軽薄短小 **keihaku-tanshō** small and light, compact (cf. 重厚長大)

——————— 1 ———————
3n1.1 / 144
少 **SHŌ, suko(shi)** a little, a few
suku(nai) little, few

——————— 1 ———————
3 少々 **shōshō** a little, a few, slightly

少女 **shōjo** girl
6 少年 **shōnen** boy
少年法 **shōnenhō** juvenile law
少年院 **shōnen'in** reform school
少年感化院 **shōnen kankain** reform school
7 少佐 **shōsa** major, lieutenant commander
9 少食 **shōshoku** eating little/sparingly
少食家 **shōshokuka** light eater
10 少将 **shōshō** major general, rear admiral
11 少尉 **shōi** second lieutenant, ensign
12 少量 **shōryō** small quantity/dose
少閑 **shōkan** short break/rest, lull
13 少数 **shōsū** few; minority
少数民族 **shōsū minzoku** minority nationalities, ethnic minorities
16 少憩 **shōkei** short break/rest, recess
18 少額 **shōgaku** small amount

——————— 2 ———————
4 少少 **shōshō** a little, a few, slightly
5 幼少 **yōshō** infancy, childhood
6 年少 **nenshō** young
老少 **rōshō** young and old
老少不定 **rōshō-fujō** Death comes to old and young alike.
早少女 **saotome** rice-planting girl
7 希少 **kishō** scarce
8 些少 **sashō** slight, trifling, little, few
青少年 **seishōnen** young people, the young
9 美少年 **bishōnen** a handsome youth
弱少 **jakushō** puniness; youth
11 過少 **kashō** too few
12 減少 **genshō** decrease, reduction, decline
最少 **saishō** fewest; youngest
稀少 **kishō** scarce
軽少 **keishō** trifling, little
13 僅少 **kinshō** few, little
微少 **bishō** minute quantity
14 寡少 **kashō** little, few, scanty
16 頼少 **tano(mi)suku(nai)** hopeless, helpless, forlorn
17 鮮少 **senshō** (a) few/little

——————— 2 ———————
尔 → 爾 **0a14.3**

——————— 3 ———————
3n3.1
尖 **SEN, toga(ru), tonga(ru)** be pointed/sharp; be displeased
toga(rasu) make pointed, sharpen

——————— 1 ———————
7 尖兵 **senpei** point man, advance guard
尖声 **toga(ri)goe** shrill voice

3

氵土扌日女巾犭弓彳彡艹宀⺌山耂广尸口

12 尖塔 **sentō** pinnacle, spire, steeple
14 尖端 **sentan** pointed tip; spearhead, leading edge, latest (technology)
15 尖鋭 **sen'ei** acute; radical
尖鋭化 **sen'eika** become acute/radicalized
尖鋭分子 **sen'ei bunshi** radical elements
16 尖頭 **sentō** peak; cusp; spire
18 尖顔 **toga(ri)gao** pout

――――― 2 ―――――

9 肺尖 **haisen** apex of a lung
12 最尖端 **saisentan** the lead, forefront

3n3.2 / 138

光

KŌ, hikari light
hika(ru) shine

――――― 1 ―――――

0 光コンピュータ **hikari konpyūta** optical computer
光センサー **hikari sensā** optical sensor
光ダイオード **hikari daiōdo** photo-diode
光ディスク **hikari disuku** optical disk
光ファイバー **hikari faibā** optical fiber
2 光子 **kōshi** photon
光力 **kōryoku** intensity of light
4 光化学 **kōkagaku** photochemistry
光化学スモッグ **kōkagaku sumoggu** photochemical smog
光化学反応 **kōkagaku hannō, hikari kagaku hannō** photochemical reaction
光仁 **Kōnin** (emperor, 770–781)
6 光年 **kōnen** light-year
光合成 **kōgōsei** photosynthesis
光孝 **Kōkō** (emperor, 884–887)
光行差 **kōkōsa** aberration (in astronomy)
光芒 **kōbō** shaft/flash of light
7 光束 **kōsoku** beam/flux of light
光体 **kōtai** luminous body
光沢 **kōtaku** luster, gloss, polish
光学 **kōgaku** optics
8 光波 **kōha** light wave
光苔 **hika(ri)goke** a luminous moss, *Schistostega osmundacea*
光明 **kōmyō** light, hope
Kōmyō (emperor, 1337–1348)
光炎 **kōen** (light and) flame
光物 **hika(ri)mono** luminous phenomenon (shooting star, lightning, *ignis fatuus*), shiny object (metal, coin)
9 光冠 **kōkan** corona
光変調 **hikari henchō** optical modulation
光点 **kōten** luminous point
光速 **kōsoku** the speed of light
光通信 **hikari tsūshin** optical communication
光海鞘 **hikariboya** luminous plankton

光栄 **kōei** honor, glory, privilege
光度 **kōdo** brightness, luminosity
光度計 **kōdokei** photometer
光背 **kōhai** halo
10 光陰 **kōin** time
光高温計 **hikari-kōonkei** optical pyrometer
光起電力 **hikari-kidenryoku** photoelectromotive force
光梃子 **hikari teko** optical lever
11 光彩 **kōsai** brilliance, splendor
光産業 **hikari sangyō** optronics industry
12 光覚 **kōkaku** optic sense, sensation of light
光景 **kōkei** scene, sight
光量 **kōryō** radiation intensity
光焔 **kōen** (light and) flame
光集積回路 **hikari shūseki kairo** optical integrated circuit
13 光源 **kōgen** light source
光路 **kōro** optical path
光飽和 **kōhōwa, hikari hōwa** light saturation
光飽和点 **kōhōwaten** light saturation point
光電池 **kōdenchi** photoelectric cell
光電管 **kōdenkan** photocell, light sensor
14 光磁気ディスク **hikari-jiki disuku** magnetic-optical disk (MOD)
15 光熱 **kōnetsu** light and heat
光熱費 **kōnetsuhi** heating and electricity expenses
光線 **kōsen** light (rays/beam)
光輪 **kōrin** halo
光輝 **kōki** brightness, splendor
hika(ri)kagaya(ku) shine, sparkle
16 光頭 **kōtō** bald head
17 光厳 **Kōgon** (emperor, 1332–1333)
光環 **kōkan** corona
19 光藻 **hikari-mo** luminous algae

――――― 2 ―――――

2 七光 **nanahikari** enjoying advantages because of one's parent's/lord's fame or authority
4 分光 **bunkō** diffraction of light into a spectrum
分光学 **bunkōgaku** spectroscopy
分光器 **bunkōki** spectroscope
月光 **gekkō** moonlight
日光 **nikkō** sunshine, sunlight
Nikkō (town in Tochigi-ken)
日光浴 **nikkōyoku** sunbath
5 北光 **hokkō** the northern lights, aurora borealis
出光 **Idemitsu** (surname; company name)
白光 **hakkō** white light; corona
6 曳光弾 **eikōdan** tracer bullet, illumination round
旭光 **kyokkō** rays of the rising sun
灯光 **tōkō** light, lamplight, flashlight
竹光 **takemitsu** bamboo sword
7 余光 **yokō** afterglow, remaining light

冷光　**reikō**　cold light, luminescence
投光器　**tōkōki**　floodlight
8 夜光　**yakō**　glowing in the dark
夜光虫　**yakōchū**　night-glowing insect
夜光時計　**yakō-dokei**　luminous-dial watch
夜光塗料　**yakō toryō**　luminous paint
逆光　**gyakkō**　backlighting
逆光線　**gyakkōsen**　backlighting
底光　**sokobika(ri)**　subdued gloss
国光　**kokkō**　national glory/prestige
青光　**aobikari**　blue/green/phosphorescent light
怪光　**kaikō**　weird light, foxfire
金光　**kinpika**　glittering
9 発光　**hakkō**　luminous
発光体　**hakkōtai**　luminous body, corona
点光　**tenkō**　spotlight
風光　**fūkō**　scenery, natural beauty
弧光　**kokō**　electric arc, arc lamp
後光　**gokō**　halo, corona
後光厳　**Gokōgon**　(emperor, 1353–1371)
栄光　**eikō**　glory
背光　**haikō**　glory
春光　**shunkō**　spring scenery
威光　**ikō**　authority, power, influence
10 残光　**zankō**　afterglow
消光　**shōkō**　passing time, getting along
閃光　**senkō**　flash
11 偏光　**henkō**　polarized light, polarization
陽光　**yōkō**　sunshine, sunlight
採光　**saikō**　lighting
寂光浄土　**jakkō-jōdo**　(Buddhist) paradise
蛍光　**keikō**　fluorescent
蛍光灯　**keikōtō**　fluorescent lamp
蛍光体　**keikōtai**　fluorescent body
蛍光板　**keikōban**　fluorescent plate/screen
崇光　**Sūkō**　(emperor, 1349–1351)
脚光　**kyakkō**　footlights, limelight, spotlight
黒光　**kurobika(ri)**　black luster
眼光　**gankō**　glint of one's eye; insight
12 減光　**genkō**　extinguish, dim
極光　**kyokkō**　the northern/southern lights, aurora borealis/australis
暁光　**gyōkō**　the light of dawn
散光　**sankō**　scattered/diffused light
13 遮光　**shakō**　shade, darken, cut off the light
微光　**bikō**　faint light, glimmer
感光　**kankō**　exposure to light; photosensitive
感光板　**kankōban**　sensitized plate
感光度　**kankōdo**　(degree of) photosensitivity
電光　**denkō**　electric light; lightning
電光石火　**denkō-sekka**　a flash, an instant
14 稲光　**inabikari**　lightning
15 霊光　**reikō**　mysterious light
16 薄光　**hakkō**　pale/faint light
17 燐光　**rinkō**　phosphorescence

燭光　**shokkō**　a candlepower; candlelight
18 曙光　**shokō**　the light of dawn; good prospects
観光　**kankō**　sightseeing
観光団　**kankōdan**　tour group
観光客　**kankōkyaku**　tourist, sightseer
観光船　**kankōsen**　excursion ship
21 露光　**rokō**　exposure (in photography)
露光計　**rokōkei**　light meter

——————— 3 ———————

5 北極光　**hokkyokukō**　the northern lights, aurora borealis
9 南極光　**nankyokukō**　the aurora australis, the southern lights
12 御来光　**goraikō**　sunrise viewed from a mountaintop

3n3.3 / 77

当　當　**TŌ** (as prefix) this, the said, that **a(taru)** hit, be on target; correspond to **a(tari)** a hit/success; (as suffix) per **a(teru)** hit the mark; guess at; apply, put, place; allocate **a(te)** aim, goal; expectations; reliance, trustworthiness **masa (ni)** properly, just; indeed, truly; just about to, on the verge of

——————— 1 ———————

0 当てっこ　**a(tekko)**　guessing game
当てずっぽう　**a(tezuppō)**　guesswork
2 当人　**tōnin**　the one concerned, the said person, the person himself
4 当今　**tōkon**　at present, nowadays
当分　**tōbun**　for now, for a while
当手　**tōte**　we; our side
当月　**tōgetsu**　this month
当日　**tōjitsu**　the (appointed) day
当方　**tōhō**　I, we, on our part/side
5 当世　**tōsei**　modern times, nowadays
当世風　**tōseifū**　latest fashion, up-to-date
当代　**tōdai**　the present generation/day; those days; the present head of the family
当外　**a(tari)hazu(re)**　hit or miss, risk **a(te)hazu(re)**　a disappointment
当用　**tōyō**　current use, immediate needs
当用漢字　**Tōyō Kanji**　(official list of 1,850 kanji recommended for general use; superseded by the 1,945 Jōyō Kanji)
当字　**a(te)ji**　kanji used phonetically; kanji used purely ideographically, disregarding usual readings
当札　**a(tari)fuda**　winning lottery ticket
当主　**tōshu**　the present head of the family
6 当年　**tōnen**　the current year; that year **a(tari)doshi**　a good/abundant year
当地　**tōchi**　this place, this part of the country
7 当身　**a(te)mi**　a knockdown blow

3

氵 土 扌 口 女 巾 犭 弓 彳 彡 艹
→3 宀 ⺶ ⺍ 耂 广 尸 囗

当否 **tōhi** right or wrong; propriety, suitability
当狂言 **a(tari) kyōgen** a hit (play)
当局 **tōkyoku** the authorities
当局者 **tōkyokusha** the authorities
当社 **tōsha** this/our company; this shrine
当季 **tōki** this period/season
当初 **tōsho** initial, original; at the beginning
8 当事 **tōji** related matters
当事者 **tōjisha** the parties (concerned)
当夜 **tōya** that night; tonight
当直 **tōchoku** on duty
当店 **tōten** this shop/store, we
当国 **tōkoku** this/our country
当物 **a(te)mono** riddle, guessing; a covering
当所 **tōsho** this place　**a(te)do** aim, purpose
当金 **tōkin** (paying in) cash
9 当前 **a(tari)mae** a matter of course, natural, usual
当度 **tōdo** this time, now
当面 **tōmen** face, confront; immediate, urgent
当為 **tōi** what should be (done)
10 当家 **tōke** this house/family
当座 **tōza** for the time being, for some time; current (account)
当時 **tōji** at present; at that time
当馬 **a(te)uma** stallion brought near a mare to test readiness to mat, talking horse (for another candidate); spoiler (candidate)
11 当推量 **a(te)zuiryō** guesswork
12 当落 **tōraku** election result
当嵌 **a(te)ha(meru)** apply to, adapt
当期 **tōki** this period, the current term
当朝 **tōchō** the present court/dynasty
当然 **tōzen** of course, naturally
当惑 **tōwaku** be perplexed/nonplussed, be at a loss
当番 **tōban** being on duty
13 当障 **a(tari)sawa(ri ga nai)** inoffensive, harmless, noncommittal
当歳 **tōsai** this year; yearling
当歳児 **tōsaiji** a yearling
当意即妙 **tōi-sokumyō** ready wit, repartee
当節 **tōsetsu** these days, nowadays
当該 **tōgai** the said, relevant
当路 **tōro** the authorities
14 当選 **tōsen** be elected/selected, win
当選者 **tōsensha** successful candidate
17 当擦 **a(te)kosu(ri)** insinuating remark, innuendo
18 当職 **tōshoku** this occupation; one's present duties
23 当籤 **tōsen** win (a lottery)
当籤者 **tōsensha** prizewinner

─────────── 2 ───────────

2 人当 **hitoa(tari)** manners, demeanor
3 大当 **ōa(tari)** big hit, great success; (make) a

killing; bumper crop
口当 **kuchia(tari)** taste; reception, hospitality
4 不当 **futō** improper, unfair, wrongful
　　fua(tari) unpopularity, failure
手当 **tea(te)** (medical) treatment, care; allowance, (fringe) benefit
手当次第 **tea(tari) shidai** (whatever is) within reach, haphazardly
引当金 **hi(ki)a(te)kin** reserve fund, appropriation
日当 **hia(tari)** exposure to the sun; sunny place
　　nittō per-diem allowance, daily wages
心当 **kokoroa(tari)** knowledge, idea, clue
　　kokoroa(te) hope, anticipation; guess
5 本当 **hontō** true, real
失当 **shittō** improper, unfair, wrongful
弁当 **bentō** (box) lunch
弁当屋 **bentōya** lunch vendor
弁当箱 **bentōbako** lunch box
正当 **seitō** proper, just, justifiable, right, fair, reasonable, legitimate
正当防衛 **seitō bōei** legitimate self-defense
打当 **u(chi)a(teru)** hit/dash against
尻当 **shiria(te)** pants seat
目当 **mea(te)** guide(post); aim
　　ma(no)a(tari) before one's eyes
6 充当 **jūtō** allot, allocate, appropriate
至当 **shitō** proper, fair, reasonable
行当 **yu(ki)a(taru)** come upon, bump into
　　yu(ki)a(tari-battari) haphazard, hit-or-miss
7 体当 **taia(tari)** hurl oneself against
作当 **sakua(tari)** good crop
別当 **bettō** groom, footman, horsekeeper; steward, attendant
対当 **taitō** corresponding, equivalent
妥当 **datō** proper, appropriate
妥当性 **datōsei** propriety, pertinence, validity
芸当 **geitō** performance, feat, trick, stunt
肘当 **hijia(te)** (armor) elbowpiece
見当 **miata(ru)** be found, turn up
　　kentō aim, mark, guess, estimate, hunch; direction; approximately
見当違 **kentōchiga(i)** wrong guess
言当 **i(i)a(teru)** guess right
8 押当 **o(shi)a(teru)** press/hold against
抵当 **teitō** mortgage, hypothec
抵当物 **teitōbutsu** security, pawn, collateral
抵当流 **teitōnaga(re)** foreclosure
抵当権 **teitōken** mortgage, hypothec
担当 **tantō** being in charge, overseeing
担当者 **tantōsha** the one in charge
突当 **tsu(ki)a(taru)** run/bump into; reach the end　**tsu(ki)a(tari)** collision; end (of a street/corridor)
肩当 **kataa(te)** shoulder pad

9 風当 **kazea(tari), kazaa(tari)** force of the wind; criticism, opposition
面当 **tsuraa(te)** innuendo, spiteful remark
相当 **sōtō** suitable, appropriate; considerable; be equivalent to, correspond to
相当品 **sōtōhin** article of similar value
相当数 **sōtōsū** quite a number of
思当 **omo(i)a(taru)** occur to one, think of
10 射当 **ia(teru)** hit the target
差当 **sa(shi)a(tari)** for the time being
捜当 **saga(shi)a(teru)** find out, discover, locate
振当 **fu(ri)a(teru)** assign (roles)
胸当 **muna(te)** breastplate, chest protector
配当 **haitō** allotment, share, dividend
配当金 **haitōkin** dividend
11 陽当 **hia(tari)** exposure to the sun
勘当 **kandō** disinheritance
過当 **katō** excessive, exorbitant, undue
推当 **o(shi)a(teru)** guess
探当 **sagu(ri)a(teru)** grope for and find
掘当 **ho(ri)a(teru)** find, dig up, strike (oil)
脛当 **sunea(te)** shin guards
12 割当 **wa(ri)a(teru)** allocate, allot, divide/ distribute among
割当額 **wariategaku** allotment
場当 **baa(tari)** grandstanding, applause-seeking
順当 **juntō** right, regular, normal
13 適当 **tekitō** suitable, adequate
嗅当 **ka(gi)a(teru)** sniff out
腰当 **koshia(te)** a bustle
腹当 **haraa(te)** chest-and-stomach armor; bellyband
継当 **tsu(gi)a(te)** patchwork
該当 **gaitō** pertain to, come/fall under
該当者 **gaitōsha** the said person
14 罰当 **bachia(tari)** damned, cursed
総当 **sōa(tari)** round-robin (tournament)
16 鞘当 **sayaa(te)** rivalry (in love)
穏当 **ontō** proper, reasonable, moderate
18 臑当 **sunea(te)** shin guards

──────── 3 ────────

1 一人当 **hitoria(tari)** per person/capita
一騎当千 **ikki-tōsen** matchless, mighty
4 不適当 **futekitō** unsuited, unfit, inappropriate
不穏当 **fuontō** improper
手弁当 **tebentō** bringing/buying one's own lunch
8 事務当局 **jimu tōkyoku** the authorities in charge
居敷当 **ishikia(te)** kimono seat lining
12 無配当 **muhaitō** non-dividend-paying
13 腰弁当 **koshibentō** lunch tied to one's belt; lunch-carrying worker

蛸配当 **takohaitō** bogus dividends

──────── 4 ────────

7 汽車弁当 **kisha bentō** railway lunch
応急手当 **ōkyū tea(te)** first aid
10 残業手当 **zangyō teate** overtime pay

3n3.4 / 1150

劣

RETSU, **oto(ru)** be inferior to

──────── 1 ────────

4 劣化 **rekka** deterioration, degradation
8 劣者 **ressha** an inferior
劣性 **ressei** inferior; recessive (gene)
11 劣悪 **retsuaku** inferior, coarse
劣情 **retsujō** low passions, lust
12 劣等 **rettō** inferiority
劣等感 **rettōkan** inferiority complex
13 劣勢 **ressei** numerical inferiority

──────── 2 ────────

3 下劣 **geretsu** base, sordid, vulgar
7 低劣 **teiretsu** low grade; base, vulgar
見劣 **mioto(ri)** compare unfavorably with
8 陋劣 **rōretsu** mean, base, low, nasty, sneaky
拙劣 **setsuretsu** clumsy, bungling, unskillful
9 負劣 **ma(kezu)-oto(razu)** keeping up with (each other)
卑劣 **hiretsu** mean, contemptible, sneaking
卑劣漢 **hiretsukan** mean bastard, low-down skunk
11 庸劣 **yōretsu** mediocre; foolish
13 鄙劣 **hiretsu** base, sordid, dirty
愚劣 **guretsu** stupid, foolish
17 優劣 **yūretsu** superiority or inferiority, relative merits
masa(ru tomo) oto(ranai) in no way inferior to, at least as good as

──────── 3 ────────

17 優勝劣敗 **yūshō-reppai** survival of the fittest

──────── 4 ────────

3n4.1 / 844

肖

SHŌ resemble
ayaka(ru) be similarly lucky

──────── 1 ────────

8 肖者 **ayaka(ri)mono** lucky fellow
14 肖像 **shōzō** portrait
肖像画 **shōzōga** portrait

──────── 2 ────────

4 不肖 **fushō** unlike one's father; I (humble)

3

氵
土
扌
口
女
巾
犭
弓
彳
彡
艹
宀
⺌ 4←
山
寺
广
尸
口

3n4.2 / 109

学 學 斈

GAKU learning, study, science; (as suffix) -ology
mana(bu) learn, study

─────────── 1 ───────────

2 学力 **gakuryoku** scholastic ability, scholarship
3 学才 **sakusai** academic ability
学士 **gakushi** Bachelor of Arts, university graduate
学士院 **gakushiin** academy
4 学内 **gakunai** intramural, on-campus, school (newspaper)
学友 **gakuyū** schoolmate, alumnus
学友会 **gakuyūkai** alumni association
学区 **gakku** school district
5 学生 **gakusei** student
学生服 **gakuseifuku** school uniform
学生帽 **gakuseibō** school cap
学生証 **gakuseishō** student I.D.
学外 **gakugai** outside the school, off-campus
学用品 **gakuyōhin** school supplies
6 学年 **gakunen** school year, grade in school
学会 **gakkai** academic society
学名 **gakumei** scientific name
7 学位 **gakui** academic degree
学芸 **gakugei** art and science, culture
学芸会 **gakugeikai** (school) literary program
学究 **gakkyū** scholar, student
学究的 **gakkyūteki** scholastic, academic
8 学長 **gakuchō** dean, rector
学事 **gakuji** educational affairs; studies
学舎 **gakusha** school (building)
学制 **gakusei** educational system
学府 **gakufu** educational institution
学者 **gakusha** scholar
9 学院 **gakuin** academy
学風 **gakufū** academic traditions, a school (of thought), method of study, school character
学派 **gakuha** a school (of thought)
学科 **gakka** school subjects, curriculum, course
学界 **gakkai** academic/scientific world
学級 **gakkyū** school class, grade
学則 **gakusoku** school regulations
10 学修 **gakushū** learning, study
学部 **gakubu** academic department, faculty
学部長 **gakubuchō** dean of a university department
学徒 **gakuto** scholar, student, disciple, follower
学校 **gakkō** school
学校区 **gakkōku** school district

学校出 **gakkōde** school graduate, educated person
学校長 **gakkōchō** school principal
学校差 **gakkōsa** scholastic disparity among schools
11 学術 **gakujutsu** science, learning
学術用語 **gakujutsu yōgo** technical term
学窓 **gakusō** school
学堂 **gakudō** academy
学習 **gakushū** learning, study
学理 **gakuri** theory, scientific principle
学務 **gakumu** educational affairs
学問 **gakumon** learning, scholarship, education, science
12 学帽 **gakubō** school cap
学期 **gakki** school term, semester
学期末 **gakkimatsu** end of the term/semester
学童 **gakudō** schoolboy, schoolgirl, pupil
学殖 **gakushoku** learning, accomplishments
学費 **gakuhi** school expenses
13 学業 **gakugyō** schoolwork, scholastic achievement
学僧 **gakusō** learned priest
学際的 **gakusaiteki** interdisciplinary
学園 **gakuen** academy; campus
学資 **gakushi** school expenses, educational fund/endowment
14 学僕 **gakuboku** servant-student
学歴 **gakureki** one's academic background
学徳 **gakutoku** learning and virtue
学説 **gakusetsu** a theory
学閥 **gakubatsu** clique of graduates from the same school, old boy network
15 学寮 **gakuryō** dormitory
学監 **gakkan** dean, school superintendent
学課 **gakka** lessons, schoolwork
16 学館 **gakkan** academy, school
17 学績 **gakuseki** student's record
学齢 **gakurei** school age
19 学識 **gakushiki** learning, scholarly attainments
20 学籍 **gakuseki** school register
学籍簿 **gakusekibo** school register

─────────── 2 ───────────

2 入学 **nyūgaku** admission into school, matriculation
入学生 **nyūgakusei** new student
入学式 **nyūgakushiki** entrance ceremony
入学金 **nyūgakukin** entrance/matriculation fee
入学試験 **nyūgaku shiken** entrance exams
入学難 **nyūgakunan** difficulty of getting into a school
入学願書 **nyūgaku gansho** application for admission

力学 **rikigaku** dynamics, mechanics
3 工学 **kōgaku** engineering
工学士 **kōgakushi** Bachelor of Engineering
工学者 **kōgakusha** engineer
大学 **daigaku** university, college
大学生 **daigakusei** university/college student
大学院 **daigakuin** graduate school
才学 **saigaku** ability and learning
女学生 **jogakusei** girl student
女学院 **jogakuin** girls' academy
女学校 **jogakkō** girls' school
小学生 **shōgakusei** elementary-school student
小学校 **shōgakkō** elementary school
4 中学 **chūgaku** junior high school
中学生 **chūgakusei** junior-high-school student
中学校 **chūgakkō** junior high school
化学 **kagaku** chemistry (sometimes pronounced *bakegaku* to avoid confusion with 科学, science)
化学式 **kagaku shiki** chemical formula
化学者 **kagakusha** chemist
文学 **bungaku** literature
文学上 **bungakujō** literary
文学士 **bungakushi** Bachelor of Arts
文学史 **bungakushi** history of literature
文学会 **bungakukai** literary society
文学的 **bungakuteki** literary
文学者 **bungakusha** literary man, man of letters
文学界 **bungakukai** the literary world
文学部 **bungakubu** literature department/faculty
文学書 **bungakusho** a literary work
文学賞 **bungakushō** literary award
心学 **shingaku** practical/popularized ethics
5 生学者 **namagakusha** dilettante, dabbler
生学門 **namagakumon** superficial knowledge
史学 **shigaku** (study of) history
好学 **kōgaku** love of learning
6 休学 **kyūgaku** absence from school
同学 **dōgaku** the same school
地学 **chigaku** physical geography
在学 **zaigaku** (enrolled) in school
在学生 **zaigakusei** student
向学心 **kōgakushin** love of learning
共学 **kyōgaku** coeducation
光学 **kōgaku** optics
耳学問 **mimigakumon** learning acquired by listening
7 低学年 **teigakunen** elementary school grades 1 and 2
兵学 **heigaku** military science, tactics, strategy
医学 **igaku** medicine, medical science
医学生 **igakusei** medical student
医学界 **igakukai** the medical world, medicine
医学部 **igakubu** medical department/school

宋学 **Sōgaku** the learning of the Songs
見学 **kengaku** study by observation, tour (a factory)
私学 **shigaku** private school
初学者 **shogakusha** beginner, new student
8 夜学 **yagaku** evening classes, night school
夜学校 **yagakkō** night school
盲学校 **mōgakkō** school for the blind
退学 **taigaku** leave school, drop out
法学 **hōgaku** law, jurisprudence
法学士 **hōgakushi** LL.B., Bachelor of Laws
英学 **eigaku** study of English
英学者 **eigakusha** English scholar
苦学 **kugaku** study under adversity
苦学生 **kugakusei** self-supporting student
実学 **jitsugaku** practical science, realism
官学 **kangaku** government school; official teachings
国学 **kokugaku** study of Japanese literature
国学者 **kokugakusha** Japanese-classics scholar
林学 **ringaku** forestry
和学 **wagaku** Japanese literature
9 俗学 **zokugaku** shallow learning
軍学 **gungaku** military science, tactics, strategy
美学 **bigaku** esthetics
美学的 **bigakuteki** esthetic
通学 **tsūgaku** attending school
通学生 **tsūgakusei** day student
浅学 **sengaku** superficial knowledge
洋学 **yōgaku** Western learning
洋学者 **yōgakusha** scholar of Western learning
独学 **dokugaku** self-study
後学 **kōgaku** younger scholars; information for future reference
星学 **seigaku** astronomy
神学 **shingaku** theology
神学士 **shingakushi** Doctor of Divinity
神学校 **shingakkō** theological seminary
研学 **kengaku** study
科学 **kagaku** science
科学的 **kagakuteki** scientific
科学者 **kagakusha** scientist
疫学 **ekigaku** epidemiology
10 修学 **shūgaku** learning
修学旅行 **shūgaku ryokō** school excursion, field trip
高学年 **kōgakunen** upper (5th and 6th) grades in elementary school
勉学 **bengaku** study
進学 **shingaku** entrance to a higher school
遊学 **yūgaku** study far from home
哲学 **tetsugaku** philosophy
哲学者 **tetsugakusha** philosopher

3

氵土扌口女巾犭弓彳彡艹宀䒑山壴广尸口 4←

3

氵 扌 扌 日 女 巾 犭 弓 彳 彡 艹 宀 → 4 丷 凵 亠 广 尸 口

教学 **kyōgaku** education, educational affairs
留学 **ryūgaku** studying abroad
留学生 **ryūgakusei** student studying abroad
留学者 **ryūgakusha** person studying abroad
馬学 **bagaku** hippology
11 停学 **teigaku** suspension from school
道学 **dōgaku** Confucianism, Taoism, moral philosophy
道学者 **dōgakusha** moralist
衒学的 **gengakuteki** pedantic
視学 **shigaku** school inspection/inspector
視学官 **shigakkan** school inspector
理学 **rigaku** physical sciences, science
理学者 **rigakusha** scientist
理学界 **rigakukai, rigakkai** scientific world
産学官 **sangakkan, sangakukan** industry, universities/academia, and government/officials
経学 **keigaku** Confucianism
転学 **tengaku** change schools
12 博学 **hakugaku** broad knowledge, erudition
就学 **shūgaku** attend school
廃学 **haigaku** discontinue one's studies, leave school
晩学 **bangaku** education late in life
無学 **mugaku** unlettered, ignorant
13 農学 **nōgaku** (the science of) agriculture
農学士 **nōgakushi** agricultural expert, agronomist
漢学 **kangaku** Chinese literature
漢学者 **kangakusha** scholar of Chinese classics
奨学生 **shōgakusei** student on a scholarship
奨学金 **shōgakukin** a scholarship
禅学 **zengaku** Zen doctrines
数学 **sūgaku** mathematics
数学的 **sūgakuteki** mathematical
数学者 **sūgakusha** mathematician
新学期 **shingakki** new school term
詩学 **shigaku** study of poetry
14 歌学 **kagaku** poetry
碩学 **sekigaku** erudition; great scholar
語学 **gogaku** language learning; linguistics
語学者 **gogakusha** linguist
雑学 **zatsugaku** knowledge of various subjects
16 儒学 **jugaku** Confucianism
儒学者 **jugakusha** Confucianist, Confucian scholar
儒学界 **jugakkai** Confucianists
薬学 **yakugaku** pharmacology
薬学士 **yakugakushi** Bachelor of Pharmacology
薬学者 **yakugakusha** pharmacologist
篤学 **tokugaku** love of learning
18 藩学 **hangaku** samurai school for clan children

19 蘭学 **Rangaku** study of the Dutch language and Western learning
22 聾学校 **rōgakkō** school for the deaf

——— 3 ———

2 人相学 **ninsōgaku** physiognomy
人間学 **ningengaku** anthropology
人類学 **jinruigaku** anthropology
3 工芸学 **kōgeigaku** technology, polytechnics
土俗学 **dozokugaku** folklore, ethnography
山林学 **sanringaku** forestry
4 天文学 **tenmongaku** astronomy
天体学 **tentaigaku** uranology
文芸学 **bungeigaku** the science of literature
文理学 **bunrigaku** humanities and sciences
文献学 **bunkengaku** bibliography, philology
分光学 **bunkōgaku** spectroscopy
分類学 **bunruigaku** taxonomy
水力学 **suirikigaku, suiryokugaku** hydraulics
水理学 **suirigaku** hydrography, hydraulics
水産学 **suisangaku** the science of fisheries
手相学 **tesōgaku** palmistry
犬儒学派 **kenjugakuha** the Cynics
日本学 **nihongaku** Japanology
心理学 **shinrigaku** psychology
心霊学 **shinreigaku** psychics, spiritism
5 民俗学 **minzokugaku** folklore
民族学 **minzokugaku** ethnology
生化学 **seikagaku** biochemistry
生物学 **seibutsugaku** biology
生理学 **seirigaku** physiology
生態学 **seitaigaku** ecology
古銭学 **kosengaku** numismatics
犯罪学 **hanzaigaku** criminology
6 気候学 **kikōgaku** climatology
気象学 **kishōgaku** meteorology
朱子学 **Shushigaku** teachings of the Confucian philosopher Zhuzi (1130–1200), Neo-Confucianism
再入学 **sainyūgaku** readmission (to a school)
仮入学 **karinyūgaku** provisional enrollment, admission on probation
考古学 **kōkogaku** archeology (cf. 考現学)
考現学 **kōgengaku** study of modern phenomena (cf. 考古学)
地文学 **chimongaku, chibungaku** physical geography
地形学 **chikeigaku** topography
地政学 **chiseigaku** geopolitics
地理学 **chirigaku** geography
地理学者 **chirigakusha** geographer
地質学 **chishitsugaku** geology
地震学 **jishingaku** seismology
先史学 **senshigaku** prehistory
宇宙学 **uchūgaku** cosmology
光化学 **kōkagaku** photochemistry

光化学スモッグ **kōkagaku sumoggu** photochemical smog
光化学反応 **kōkagaku hannō, hikari kagaku hannō** photochemical reaction
7 冶金学 **yakingaku** metallurgy
形態学 **keitaigaku** morphology
社会学 **shakaigaku** sociology
系図学 **keizugaku** genealogy
言語学 **gengogaku** linguistics, philology
8 非科学的 **hikagakuteki** unscientific
毒物学 **dokubutsugaku** toxicology
盲啞学校 **mōa gakkō** school for the blind and mute
建築学 **kenchikugaku** architecture
法医学 **hōigaku** forensic medicine
法律学 **hōritsugaku** jurisprudence
法理学 **hōrigaku** jurisprudence
治療学 **chiryōgaku** therapeutics
英文学 **eibungaku** English literature
実業学校 **jitsugyō gakkō** vocational school
国文学 **kokubungaku** Japanese literature
国文学史 **kokubungakushi** history of Japanese literature
林間学校 **rinkan gakkō** outdoor school, camp
昆虫学 **konchūgaku** entomology
物理学 **butsurigaku** physics
放射学 **hōshagaku** radiology
金石学 **kinsekigaku** study of ancient stone monument inscriptions
金相学 **kinsōgaku** metallography
9 発生学 **hasseigaku** embryology
発音学 **hatsuongaku** phonetics
専門学校 **senmon gakkō** professional school
俗文学 **zokubungaku** popular literature
造林学 **zōringaku** forestry
海洋学 **kaiyōgaku** oceanography
栄養学 **eiyōgaku** (science of) nutrition, dietetics
胎生学 **taiseigaku** embryology
神経学 **shinkeigaku** neurology
神話学 **shinwagaku** mythology
政治学 **seijigaku** political science
政経学 **seikeigaku** politics and economics
音声学 **onseigaku** phonetics
音響学 **onkyōgaku** acoustics
音韻学 **on'ingaku** phonology
10 修辞学 **shūjigaku** rhetoric
倫理学 **rinrigaku** ethics, moral philosophy
高等学校 **kōtō gakkō** senior high school
師範学校 **shihan gakkō** normal school, teachers' college
家政学 **kaseigaku** home economics
骨相学 **kossōgaku** phrenology
書誌学 **shoshigaku** bibliography
教育学 **kyōikugaku** pedagogy, education
教義学 **kyōgigaku** dogmatics

病理学 **byōrigaku** pathology
純文学 **junbungaku** pure literature, belles lettres
紋章学 **monshōgaku** heraldry
航空学 **kōkūgaku** aeronautics
訓詁学 **kunkogaku** exegetics
財政学 **zaiseigaku** (the study of) finance
11 動力学 **dōrikigaku** kinetics, dynamics
動物学 **dōbutsugaku** zoology
道徳学 **dōtokugaku** moral philosophy
菌類学 **kinruigaku** mycology
理化学 **rikagaku** physics and chemistry
理財学 **rizaigaku** political economy
産科学 **sankagaku** obstetrics
細胞学 **saibōgaku** cytology
細菌学 **saikingaku** bacteriology, microbiology
経済学 **keizaigaku** economics
経営学 **keieigaku** (business) management
釈義学 **shakugigaku** exegesis
貨幣学 **kaheigaku** numismatics
軟文学 **nanbungaku** light literature
魚類学 **gyoruigaku** ichthyology
鳥類学 **chōruigaku** ornithology
12 博物学 **hakubutsugaku** natural history
測地学 **sokuchigaku** geodesy
湖沼学 **koshōgaku** limnology
植物学 **shokubutsugaku** botany
森林学 **shinringaku** forestry
幾何学 **kikagaku** geometry
幾何学的 **kikagakuteki** geometrical
結晶学 **kesshōgaku** crystallography
統計学 **tōkeigaku** statistics
軽文学 **keibungaku** light literature
13 漢文学 **kanbungaku** Chinese literature
微分学 **bibungaku** differential calculus
解剖学 **kaibōgaku** anatomy
鉱物学 **kōbutsugaku** mineralogy
14 歴史学 **rekishigaku** (the study of) history
遺伝学 **idengaku** genetics
層位学 **sōigaku** stratigraphy
静力学 **seirikigaku** statics
静電学 **seidengaku** electrostatics
磁気学 **jikigaku** magnetics
複式学級 **fukushiki gakkyū** combined class (of more than one grade)
語原学 **gogengaku** etymology
15 劇文学 **gekibungaku** dramatic literature
養護学級 **yōgo gakkyū** class for the handicapped
養護学校 **yōgo gakkō** school for the handicapped
熱力学 **netsurikigaku** thermodynamics
線虫学 **senchūgaku** nematology
論理学 **ronrigaku** logic
16 獣医学 **jūigaku** veterinary medicine

衛生学 **eiseigaku** hygiene, hygienics
薬物学 **yakubutsugaku** pharmacology
薬剤学 **yakuzaigaku** pharmacology
薬理学 **yakurigaku** pharmacology
機械学 **kikaigaku** mechanics
積分学 **sekibungaku** integral calculus
17 優生学 **yūseigaku** eugenics
20 蘚苔学 **sentaigaku** bryology
醸造学 **jōzōgaku** science of brewing

———————— 4 ————————

2 人文科学 **jinbun kagaku** cultural sciences
人間工学 **ningen kōgaku** ergonomics
3 工科大学 **kōka daigaku** engineering college
工業大学 **kōgyō daigaku** technical college
4 水力工学 **suiryoku kōgaku** hydraulic engineering
水産大学 **suisan daigaku** fisheries college
5 古生物学 **koseibutsugaku** paleontology
6 気体力学 **kitai rikigaku** aerodynamics
有機化学 **yūki kagaku** organic chemistry
自然科学 **shizen kagaku** the natural sciences
7 医科大学 **ika daigaku** medical university/school
形而上学 **keijijōgaku** metaphysics
形而下学 **keijikagaku** the physical sciences
応用科学 **ōyō kagaku** applied science
図書館学 **toshokangaku** library science
8 宗教哲学 **shūkyō tetsugaku** philosophy of religion
実証哲学 **jisshō tetsugaku** positivism
10 郷土文学 **kyōdo bungaku** local literature
流体力学 **ryūtai rikigaku** fluid dynamics
核物理学 **kakubutsurigaku** nuclear physics
純正科学 **junsei kagaku** pure science
12 短期大学 **tanki daigaku** junior college
13 微生物学 **biseibutsugaku** microbiology
電子工学 **denshi kōgaku** electronics
14 静電気学 **seidenkigaku** electrostatics
総合大学 **sōgō daigaku** university
16 機械工学 **kikai kōgaku** mechanical engineering

———————— 5 ————————

14 遺伝子工学 **idenshi kōgaku** genetic engineering

3n4.3 / 233

労 勞

RŌ labor, toil
itawa(ru) sympathize with, be kind to, take good care of
negira(u) thank for, show appreciation, reward

———————— 1 ————————

0 労する **rō(suru)** labor, exert oneself
2 労力 **rōryoku** trouble, effort; labor
7 労作 **rōsaku** toil, labor; laborious task

労役 **rōeki** labor, work, toil
労災保険 **rōsai hoken** workman's accident compensation insurance
8 労使 **rōshi** labor and management
労苦 **rōku** labor, pains, toil
11 労務 **rōmu** labor, work
労務者 **rōmusha** worker, laborer
労組 **rōso, rōkumi** labor union (short for 労働組合)
13 労働 **rōdō** labor, work, toil
労働力 **rōdōryoku** labor, manpower, workforce
労働者 **rōdōsha** worker, laborer
労働省 **Rōdōshō** Ministry of Labor
労働党 **rōdōtō** labor/Labour party
労働祭 **rōdōsai** Labor Day; May Day
労働組合 **rōdō kumiai** labor union
労農 **rōnō** workers and farmers
労農党 **rōnōtō** labor-farmer party
労賃 **rōchin** wages
労資 **rōshi** labor(ers) and capital(ists)

———————— 2 ————————

4 不労所得 **furō shotoku** unearned/investment income
心労 **shinrō** worry, anxiety
5 功労 **kōrō** meritorious service
功労者 **kōrōsha** man of distinguished service
7 辛労 **shinrō** hardship, struggle
足労 **sokurō** trouble of going somewhere
8 苦労 **kurō** trouble, hardships, adversity
苦労人 **kurōnin** worldly-wise man
苦労性 **kurōshō** given to worrying
実労働 **jitsurōdō** actual labor
所労 **shorō** indisposition, illness
9 重労働 **jūrōdō** heavy/hard labor
重労働者 **jūrōdōsha** heavy laborer
10 徒労 **torō** wasted effort
疲労 **hirō** fatigue
11 過労 **karō** overwork
12 勤労 **kinrō** labor, work
勤労奉仕 **kinrō hōshi** labor service
勤労者 **kinrōsha** worker, laborer
勤労所得 **kinrō shotoku** earned income
博労 **bakurō** horse trader
就労 **shūrō** work
軽労働 **keirōdō** light work
13 煩労 **hanrō** trouble, pains
14 漁労 **gyorō** fishing
15 勲労 **kunrō** meritorious/distinguished service
慰労 **irō** recognize (someone's) services
慰労会 **irōkai** dinner/party given in appreciation of someone's services
慰労金 **irōkin** bonus, gratuity

———————— 3 ————————

4 中立労連 **Chūritsu Rōren** Federation of

Independent Unions of Japan
6 気苦労 **kigurō** worry, cares, anxiety
　自由労働者 **jiyū rōdōsha** casual laborer
11 強制労動 **kyōsei rōdō** forced labor

—————— 4 ——————
8 取越苦労 **to(ri)ko(shi)gurō** needless worry
11 眼精疲労 **gansei hirō** eyestrain

3n4.4 / 939

乳

NYŪ, chi, chichi mother's milk; the breasts

—————— 1 ——————
4 乳化 **nyūka** emulsification
　乳牛 **nyūgyū, chichiushi** milk cow, dairy cattle
5 乳母 **uba** wet nurse
　乳母車 **ubaguruma** baby carriage/buggy
　乳幼児 **nyūyōji** infant
　乳兄弟 **chikyōdai** foster brother(s) and sisters)
　乳白色 **nyūhakushoku** milky white
7 乳状 **nyūjō** milky
　乳呑子 **chinomigo** suckling child, infant
　乳呑児 **chinomigo** nursing baby, unweaned child
　乳児 **nyūji** suckling baby, infant
8 乳房 **chibusa** breast
9 乳首 **chikubi** nipple
　乳臭 **chichikusa(i)** smelling of milk; babyish, callow **nyūshū** callowness, inexperience
10 乳剤 **nyūzai** an emulsion
　乳窄 **chichishibo(ri)** milking; milker
11 乳液 **nyūeki** latex; milky lotion
12 乳棒 **nyūbō** pestle
　乳歯 **nyūshi** milk tooth, baby teeth
　乳飲子 **chino(mi)go** suckling infant, babe in arms
　乳飲児 **chinomigo** (nursing) infant, baby
13 乳腺 **nyūsen** mammary gland
　乳鉢 **nyūbachi** mortar
14 乳製品 **nyūseihin** dairy products
　乳酸 **nyūsan** lactic acid
　乳酸菌 **nyūsankin** lactic-acid bacteria
16 乳濁 **nyūdaku** emulsion
　乳糖 **nyūtō** milk sugar, lactose
　乳頭 **nyūtō** nipple
17 乳癌 **nyūgan** breast cancer
18 乳離 **chibana(re), chichibana(re)** weaning
19 乳繰 **chichiku(ru)** have a secret love affair

—————— 2 ——————
4 牛乳 **gyūnyū** (cow's) milk
　牛乳屋 **gyūnyūya** milkman, milk dealer
5 母乳 **bonyū** mother's milk
6 全乳 **zennyū** whole milk
7 豆乳 **tōnyū** soybean milk

10 差乳 **sa(shi)jichi** breast full of milk; breast with protruding nipple
　哺乳 **honyū** lactation, suckling, nursing
　哺乳動物 **honyū dōbutsu** mammal
　哺乳瓶 **honyūbin** baby bottle
　哺乳類 **honyūrui** mammal
　粉乳 **funnyū** powdered milk
11 羝乳 **teinyū** impossible
　添乳 **so(e)ji** suckle (a child) in bed
　授乳 **junyū** breast-feeding, nursing
　授乳期 **junyūki** period of lactation
12 検乳 **kennyū** milk examination/testing
13 搾乳 **sakunyū** milk (a cow)
　煉乳 **rennyū** condensed milk
14 練乳 **rennyū** condensed milk
16 凝乳 **gyōnyū** curdled milk, curds
17 鍾乳石 **shōnyūseki** stalactite (also spelled 鐘乳石) (cf. 石筍)
　鍾乳洞 **shōnyūdō** stalactite cave
18 離乳 **rinyū** weaning
　離乳食 **rinyūshoku** baby food
　離乳期 **rinyūki** the weaning period
20 鍾乳石 **shōnyūseki** stalactite (also spelled 鐘乳石)
　鐘乳洞 **shōnyūdō** stalactite cave

—————— 3 ——————
5 生牛乳 **namagyūnyū** unprocessed milk (not powdered or condensed)
　石灰乳 **sekkainyū** milk of lime
11 脱脂乳 **dasshinyū** skim milk
14 酸敗乳 **sanpainyū** sour milk

—————— 5 ——————

3n5.1

毟

mushi(ru) pluck, pull out

—————— 2 ——————
13 掻毟 **ka(ki)mushi(ru)** tear, rend, rip up

甪 → 鼠 0a13.1

3n5.2 / 1853

尚　尙

SHŌ value, respect; further, still
nao further(more), still (more)

—————— 1 ——————
4 尚友 **shōyū** become close to ancient authors (by reading their works)
5 尚以 **naomo(tte)** still more, all the more
　尚且 **naoka(tsu)** furthermore; and yet
　尚古 **shōko** esteem for olden days

3

氵
土
扌
口
女
巾
犭
弓
彳
彡
艹
宀
⺌ 5←
山
耂
广
尸
口

6 尚早 **shōsō** premature, too early
7 尚更 **naosara** still more, all the more
8 尚武 **shōbu** militaristic, martial

——————— 2 ———————
5 好尚 **kōshō** taste, fashion
8 和尚 **oshō** chief priest of a temple
10 高尚 **kōshō** lofty, refined, advanced

畄 → 留 **5f5.4**

爭 → 争 **2n4.2**

3n5.3 / 431

步 歩

HO step, pace BU rate; 1 percent; (unit of area, same as *tsubo*) FU pawn (in Japanese chess) **aru(ku), ayu(mu)** walk

——————— 1 ———————
1 歩一歩 **ho-ippo** step by step
4 歩引 **bubi(ki)** discount
6 歩合 **buai** rate, percentage; commission **ayu(mi)a(u)** compromise
　歩合算 **buaizan** calculation of percentage
　歩行 **hokō** walking, ambulatory
　歩行者 **hokōsha** pedestrian
　歩行者天国 **hokōsha tengoku** street temporarily closed to vehicles, mall
7 歩兵 **hohei** foot soldier, infantry
8 歩卒 **hosotsu** infantryman
　歩武 **hobu** short distance; step, pace
9 歩度 **hodo** pace, cadence
　歩度計 **hodokei** pedometer
10 歩振 **aru(ki)bu(ri)** way of walking, pace, gait
　歩留 **budo(mari)** yield
11 歩道 **hodō** footpath, sidewalk
　歩道橋 **hodōkyō** pedestrian overpass
　歩寄 **ayu(mi)yo(ri)** compromise
　歩廊 **horō** corridor, arcade
12 歩割 **buwa(ri)** proportion; commission
　歩測 **hosoku** pace off (a distance)
13 歩数 **hosū** number of steps
　歩数計 **hosūkei** pedometer
15 歩調 **hochō** pace, step

——————— 2 ———————
1 一歩 **ippo** a step
4 日歩 **hibu** interest per 100 yen per day
　牛歩 **gyūho** snail's pace
5 巡歩 **megu(ri)aru(ku)** walk around
　巨歩 **kyoho** giant strides/step
　立歩 **ta(chi)aru(ki)** walking, toddling
6 地歩 **chiho** one's footing/standing/position
7 売歩 **u(ri)aru(ku)** peddle

初歩 **shoho** rudiments, ABCs
町歩 **chōbu** *chō* (0.992 hectare)
8 夜歩 **yoaru(ki)** walk about at night
退歩 **taiho** retrogress, backward step; degeneration
9 飛歩 **to(bi)aru(ku)** run around, gad about
急歩 **kyūho** fast walking
速歩 **sokuho** fast walking, trot
段歩 **tanbu** (unit of land area, about 0.1 hectare)
持歩 **mo(chi)aru(ku)** carry about
独歩 **hito(ri)aru(ki)** walking without assistance **doppo** ambulatory; peerless
10 進歩 **shinpo** progress, advance
進歩主義 **shinpo shugi** progressivism
進歩的 **shinpoteki** progressive
進歩党 **shinpotō** progressive party
遊歩 **yūho** walk, stroll, promenade
流歩 **naga(re)aru(ku)** wander about
徒歩 **toho** walking
徒歩競走 **toho kyōsō** walking race
徐歩 **joho** walk slowly, saunter, mosey
11 強歩 **kyōho** walking race
酔歩 **suiho** tipsy/staggering gait
12 遠歩 **tōaru(ki)** long walk
渡歩 **wata(ri)aru(ku)** wander about
散歩 **sanpo** walk, stroll
14 漫歩 **manpo, sozo(ro)aru(ki)** stroll, ramble, walk
練歩 **ne(ri)aru(ku)** parade, march
15 緩歩 **kanpo** slow walk
20 競歩 **kyōho** walking race
譲歩 **jōho** concession, compromise

——————— 3 ———————
1 一人歩 **hitoriaru(ki)** walking alone; walking/existing on one's own
4 五十歩百歩 **gojippo-hyappo** not much different
公定歩合 **kōtei buai** official bank rate, rediscount rate
7 邯鄲歩 **Kantan (no) ayu(mi)** like the young man who tried to learn how to walk stylishly like the people in Kantan, gave up his study before mastering it, and forgot how to walk at all
8 歩一歩 **ho-ippo** step by step
15 横断歩道 **ōdan hodō** pedestrian crossing

——————— 4 ———————
4 日進月歩 **nisshin-geppo** rapid/constant progress
9 独立独歩 **dokuritsu-doppo** independence, self-reliance
15 横行闊歩 **ōkō-kappo** swagger around

——————— 5 ———————
4 五十歩百歩 **gojippo-hyappo** not much different

3n5.4

TEN, katajike(nai) kind, gracious, more than one deserves
hazukashi(meru) put to shame

——— 1 ———

0 呑なくも **katajike(nakumo)** graciously
呑のうする **katajike(nō suru)** be favored/honored with

——— 6 ———

3n6.1 / 723

EI prosperity, glory
saka(eru) thrive, flourish, prosper
ha(eru) shine, be brilliant
ha(e) glory, honor, splendor

——— 1 ———

6 栄光 **eikō** glory
7 栄位 **eii** exalted position, high rank
9 栄冠 **eikan** laurels, crown, garland
栄枯 **eiko** flourishing and withering
栄枯盛衰 **eiko-seisui** prosperity and decline, rise and fall
10 栄辱 **eijoku** honor or/and disgrace
栄進 **eishin** promotion, advancement
栄華 **eiga** opulence, splendor, luxury
11 栄達 **eitatsu** distinction, fame, advancement
栄転 **eiten** be promoted
13 栄誉 **eiyo** honor, glory, fame
15 栄養 **eiyō** nutrition, nourishment
栄養分 **eiyōbun** a nutrient
栄養学 **eiyōgaku** (science of) nutrition, dietetics
栄養価 **eiyōka** food value
栄養剤 **eiyōzai** nutritional supplement, tonic
栄養素 **eiyōso** a nutrient

——— 2 ———

5 代栄 **ka(wari)ba(e)** change for the better
6 共栄 **kyōei** mutual prosperity
共栄圏 **kyōeiken** coprosperity sphere
光栄 **kōei** honor, glory, privilege
7 余栄 **yoei** posthumous honors
見栄 **mie** (for sake of) appearance, show
見栄坊 **miebō** vain person, fop
11 虚栄 **kyoei** vanity, vainglory
虚栄心 **kyoeishin** vanity, vainglory
清栄 **seiei** (your) health and prosperity
14 聞栄 **ki(ki)ba(e)** worth listening to
16 繁栄 **han'ei** prosperity

3n6.2 / 300

TAN single, simple, mere; (as prefix) mono-, uni-

——— 1 ———

1 単一 **tan'itsu** single, simple, individual

2 単子葉 **tanshiyō** monocotyledonous
単刀直入 **tantō-chokunyū** getting straight to the point
4 単元 **tangen** unit (of academic credit)
単文 **tanbun** simple sentence
6 単色 **tanshoku** single color, monochrome
単行本 **tankōbon** separate volume, in book form
単式 **tanshiki** simple system; single-entry (bookkeeping)
単衣 **tan'i, hitoe** (summer) kimono with no lining
7 単身 **tanshin** alone, unaided, away from home
単身銃 **tanshinjū** single-barreled gun
単位 **tan'i** unit, denomination
単作 **tansaku** single crop
単利 **tanri** simple interest
単利回 **tanrimawa(ri)** yield by a simple interest method
8 単価 **tanka** unit cost/price; univalent
単性 **tansei** unisexual
9 単発 **tanpatsu** single-engine (plane), single-shot (rifle)
単独 **tandoku** independent, single-handed
単独行為 **tandoku kōi** acting on one's own
単独行動 **tandoku kōdō** acting on one's own
単独講和 **tandoku kōwa** acting on one's own
単音 **tan'on** monosyllable; monotone
10 単純 **tanjun** simple
単純化 **tanjunka** simplification
単記投票 **tanki tōhyō** voting for one person only
11 単眼鏡 **tangankyō** monocle
単細胞 **tansaibō** single cell
12 単葉 **tan'yō** simple leaf; monoplane
単量体 **tanryōtai** monomer
13 単数 **tansū** singular (not plural)
単3アルカリ電池 **tan san arukari denchi** size AA alkali battery
14 単語 **tango** word
15 単線 **tansen** single line/track
単調 **tanchō** monotonous
18 単離 **tanri** isolation (in chemistry)

——— 2 ———

8 油単 **yutan** oilcloth
15 熱単位 **netsutan'i** heat/thermal unit
18 簡単 **kantan** simple, brief
簡単服 **kantanfuku** simple/light clothing

3n6.3 / 194

KEN prefecture
agata (ancient administrative district)

——— 1 ———

2 県人 **kenjin** native/resident of a prefecture

3

氵
土
扌
口
女
巾
犭
弓
彳
彡
艹
宀
⺌   6←
山
耂
广
尸
口

県人会 **kenjinkai** an association of people from the same prefecture
3 県下 **kenka** in the prefecture
5 県令 **kenrei** prefectural ordinance
県外 **kengai** outside the prefecture
県庁 **kenchō** prefectural office
県立 **kenritsu** prefectural
6 県会 **kenkai** prefectural assembly
県有 **ken'yū** owned by the prefecture
8 県知事 **kenchiji** prefectural governor
11 県道 **kendō** prefectural highway
12 県営 **ken'ei** run by the prefecture
20 県議 **kengi** prefectural assemblyman
県議会 **kengikai** prefectural assembly

───────── 2 ─────────
4 分県地図 **bunken chizu** maps grouped by prefecture
6 近県 **kinken** neighboring prefectures
同県 **dōken** the same prefecture
8 府県 **fuken** prefectures
9 郡県 **gunken** counties and prefectures

───────── 3 ─────────
3 三重県 **Mie-ken** (prefecture)
大分県 **Ōita-ken** (prefecture)
千葉県 **Chiba-ken** (prefecture)
山口県 **Yamaguchi-ken** (prefecture)
山形県 **Yamagata-ken** (prefecture)
山梨県 **Yamanashi-ken** (prefecture)
5 広島県 **Hiroshima-ken** (prefecture)
石川県 **Ishikawa-ken** (prefecture)
7 佐賀県 **Saga-ken** (prefecture)
兵庫県 **Hyōgo-ken** (prefecture)
沖縄県 **Okinawa-ken** (prefecture)
岐阜県 **Gifu-ken** (prefecture)
8 長野県 **Nagano-ken** (prefecture)
長崎県 **Nagasaki-ken** (prefecture)
岡山県 **Okayama-ken** (prefecture)
岩手県 **Iwate-ken** (prefecture)
青森県 **Aomori-ken** (prefecture)
奈良県 **Nara-ken** (prefecture)
9 茨城県 **Ibaraki-ken** (prefecture)
栃木県 **Tochigi-ken** (prefecture)
秋田県 **Akita-ken** (prefecture)
香川県 **Kagawa-ken** (prefecture)
10 高知県 **Kōchi-ken** (prefecture)
宮城県 **Miyagi-ken** (prefecture)
宮崎県 **Miyazaki-ken** (prefecture)
島根県 **Shimane-ken** (prefecture)
11 埼玉県 **Saitama-ken** (prefecture)
鳥取県 **Tottori-ken** (prefecture)
12 滋賀県 **Shiga-ken** (prefecture)
富山県 **Toyama-ken** (prefecture)
13 群馬県 **Gunma-ken** (prefecture)
福井県 **Fukui-ken** (prefecture)
福岡県 **Fukuoka-ken** (prefecture)

福島県 **Fukushima-ken** (prefecture)
愛知県 **Aichi-ken** (prefecture)
愛媛県 **Ehime-ken** (prefecture)
新潟県 **Niigata-ken** (prefecture)
14 徳島県 **Tokushima-ken** (prefecture)
静岡県 **Shizuoka-ken** (prefecture)
熊本県 **Kumamoto-ken** (prefecture)

───────── 4 ─────────
8 和歌山県 **Wakayama-ken** (prefecture)
9 神奈川県 **Kanagawa-ken** (prefecture)
10 都道府県 **to-dō-fu-ken** prefectures
11 鹿児島県 **Kagoshima-ken** (prefectue)
12 廃藩置県 **haihan-chiken** the abolition of clans and establishment of prefectures

省 → 5c4.7

3n6.4

爰

EN, koko here

───────── 1 ─────────
11 爰許 **kokomoto** here; I, me

───────── 7 ─────────

3n7.1 / 801

挙 擧 舉

KYO arrest, capture; name, give, cite **a(geru)** name, give, enumerate; arrest, apprehend **a(gete)** all, whole, in a body **a(garu)** be apprehended, be found/recovered **kozo(tte)** all, all together

───────── 1 ─────────
4 挙止 **kyoshi** bearing, carriage, demeanor
挙手 **kyoshu** raising the hand, show of hands, salute
5 挙用 **kyoyō** appoint, promote
挙句 **ageku** in the end, ultimately
6 挙行 **kyokō** conduct, hold, celebrate, observe
挙式 **kyoshiki** (wedding) ceremony
7 挙兵 **kyohei** raise an army
挙足取 **ageashi (o) to(ru)** find fault, carp at
8 挙国 **kyokoku** the whole nation
挙国一致 **kyokoku-itchi** national unity
11 挙動 **kyodō** behavior, movements
挙措 **kyoso** behavior, bearing
12 挙証 **kyoshō** establishing a fact, proof

───────── 2 ─────────
1 一挙 **ikkyo** one effort, a single action
一挙一動 **ikkyo-ichidō** one's every action
一挙手一投足 **ikkyoshu-ittōsoku** a slight effort, the least trouble

一挙両得 **ikkyo ryōtoku** killing two birds with one stone
3 大挙 **taikyo** en masse, in full force
6 再挙 **saikyo** second attempt
壮挙 **sōkyo** daring undertaking, heroic attempt
列挙 **rekkyo** enumerate, list
7 快挙 **kaikyo** splendid deed
言挙 **kotoa(ge)** verbal expression; dispute
8 枚挙 **maikyo** enumerate, count, list
枚挙遑無 **maikyo (ni) itoma (ga) na(i)** too numerous to mention
9 美挙 **bikyo** commendable act
科挙 **kakyo** (ancient) Chinese civil-service exams
11 推挙 **suikyo** recommend (for a post)
盛挙 **seikyo** grand undertaking
12 偉挙 **ikyo** great deeds
検挙 **kenkyo** arrest, apprehend
軽挙 **keikyo** rash act, imprudence
軽挙妄動 **keikyo-mōdō** act rashly
13 義挙 **gikyo** worthy undertaking; heroic deed
愚挙 **gukyo** foolish undertaking
14 選挙 **senkyo** election
選挙人 **senkyonin** voter, elector
選挙区 **senkyoku** election district
選挙日 **senkyobi** election day
選挙法 **senkyohō** election law
選挙場 **senkyojō** polling place, the polls
選挙費 **senkyohi** campaign expenses
選挙戦 **senkyosen** election campaign
選挙権 **senkyoken** right to vote, franchise, suffrage
15 暴挙 **bōkyo** violence; recklessness

——————— 3 ———————
6 再選挙 **saisenkyo** re-election
10 被選挙人 **hisenkyonin** person eligible for election
被選挙権 **hisenkyoken** eligibility for election
14 総選挙 **sōsenkyo** general election

——————— 4 ———————
4 予備選挙 **yobi senkyo** preliminary election, a primary
12 普通選挙 **futsū senkyo** universal suffrage

3n7.2 / 495

党　黨

TŌ party, faction

——————— 1 ———————
2 党人 **tōjin** party member, partisan
3 党大会 **tōtaikai** (political) convention
党与 **tōyo** companions, confederates
4 党内 **tōnai** intra-party
6 党色 **tōshoku** partisan coloring
党争 **tōsō** party rivalry, factionalism

7 党利 **tōri** party interests
9 党首 **tōshu** party leader
党派 **tōha** party, faction
党派心 **tōhashin** partisanship, factionalism
党是 **tōze** party policies/platform
党紀 **tōki** party discipline
党則 **tōsoku** party rules
10 党員 **tōin** party member
11 党務 **tōmu** party affairs
党情 **tōjō** the party's situation
党規 **tōki** party rules
党略 **tōryaku** party policies/platform
12 党費 **tōhi** party expenses/dues
13 党勢 **tōsei** strength of a party
14 党閥 **tōbatsu** faction, clique
15 党弊 **tōhei** party evils
党論 **tōron** party's view/platform
党輩 **tōhai** companions, associates
18 党類 **tōrui** faction, partisans, gang
20 党籍 **tōseki** registration/membership (in a party)
党議 **tōgi** party policy/conference

——————— 2 ———————
2 入党 **nyūtō** join a political party
3 与党 **yotō** party in power, ruling party
小党 **shōtō** small political party
4 友党 **yūtō** allied (political) party
分党 **buntō** secession from a party
王党 **ōtō** royalist party, Tories
5 左党 **satō** leftists, opposition party; drinker
甘党 **amatō** person with a sweet tooth
右党 **utō** rightists, the Right
立党 **rittō** founding of a party
6 両党 **ryōtō** both (political) parties, bipartisan
同党 **dōtō** the same political party
自党 **jitō** one's own party
7 余党 **yotō** remnants of a political party
改党 **kaitō** switching parties
辛党 **karatō** drinker
私党 **shitō** faction
8 非党派的 **hitōhateki** nonpartisan
郎党 **rōtō, rōdō** vassals, retainers
若党 **wakatō** young attendant/samurai
9 政党 **seitō** political party
政党員 **seitōin** party member
10 残党 **zantō** the remnants (of a defeated party)
郷党 **kyōtō** people of/from one's home town
徒党 **totō** faction, clique, conspirators
11 野党 **yatō** opposition party
粛党 **shukutō** purge (of a political party)
脱党 **dattō** leave/bolt the party
悪党 **akutō** scoundrel, blackguard
12 超党派 **chōtōha** non-partisan
復党 **fukutō** be reinstated in the party
結党 **kettō** formation of a party
13 解党 **kaitō** dissolution of a party

3

氵 土 扌 口 女 巾 犭 弓 彳 彡 艹 宀 丷 7←
山 耂 广 尸 口

愛党心 **aitōshin** party loyalty/spirit
18 離党 **ritō** secede from a party

———————— 3 ————————
3 与野党 **yoyatō** governing and opposition parties
4 公明党 **Kōmeitō** (a political party)
反対党 **hantaitō** opposition party
5 民主党 **Minshutō** Democratic Party
6 多数党 **tasūtō** majority party
共和党 **kyōwatō** republican party
共産党 **kyōsantō** communist party
自民党 **Jimintō** LDP, Liberal Democratic Party (short for 自由民主党)
自由党 **jiyūtō** liberal party
7 労働党 **rōdōtō** labor/Labour party
労農党 **rōnōtō** labor-farmer party
社会党 **shakaitō** socialist party
改進党 **kaishintō** progressive party
9 保守党 **hoshutō** conservative party
急進党 **kyūshintō** radical party, radicals
政府党 **seifutō** government party
10 進歩党 **shinpotō** progressive party
11 虚無党 **kyomutō** nihilists
12 尊王党 **Sonnōtō** Imperialists
無産党 **musantō** proletarian party

———————— 4 ————————
1 一国一党主義 **ikkoku-ittō shugi** one-party system
2 二大政党主義 **nidaiseitō shugi** the two-party system
4 不偏不党 **fuhen-futō** nonpartisan
10 家子郎党 **ie(no)ko rōtō** one's followers

3n7.3
奚
KEI servant
nanzo what, why

3n7.4
殍
HYŌ dying of starvation

将 → **2b8.3**

———————— 8 ————————
雀 → **8c3.2**

3n8.1 / 1538
巣 巢
SŌ, su nest, (spider) web, (bee)hive
su(kuu) build a nest

———————— 1 ————————
5 巣立 **suda(chi)** leave the nest, become independent
13 巣窟 **sōkutsu** den, hangout, home
15 巣箱 **subako** nesting box, birdhouse, hive
22 巣籠 **sugomo(ru)** to nest

———————— 2 ————————
5 古巣 **furusu** old nest, one's former haunt
7 卵巣 **ransō** ovary
8 空巣 **a(ki)su** sneak thief, prowler
空巣狙 **a(ki)sunera(i)** sneak thief, prowler
10 帰巣本能 **kisō honnō** homing instinct
13 蜂巣 **hachi (no) su** beehive, honeycomb
14 精巣 **seisō** spermary, testicle

———————— 3 ————————
14 蜘蛛巣 **kumo(no)su** spiderweb

3n8.2 / 1878
蛍 螢
KEI, hotaru firefly

———————— 1 ————————
4 蛍火 **keika** light of a firefly **hotarubi** light of a firefly; glowing embers
5 蛍石 **keiseki, hotaruishi** fluorite, fluorspar
6 蛍光 **keikō** fluorescent
蛍光灯 **keikōtō** fluorescent lamp
蛍光体 **keikōtai** fluorescent body
蛍光板 **keikōban** fluorescent plate/screen
9 蛍狩 **hotaruga(ri)** firefly catching
11 蛍袋 **hotarubukuro** bellflower
蛍雪 **keisetsu** diligent study (by the light of fireflies and reflection from snow)
蛍雪功 **keisetsu (no) kō** the fruits of diligent study

3n8.3 / 497
常
JŌ, tsune normal, usual, continual; always, continually
toko- ever-, everlasting

———————— 1 ————————
2 常人 **jōjin** ordinary person
3 常々 **tsunezune** always, constantly
4 常日頃 **tsunehigoro** always, usually
5 常世国 **tokoyo (no) kuni** far-off land; heaven; hades
常平倉 **jōheisō** granary
常用 **jōyō** common/everyday/habitual use
常用者 **jōyōsha** constant user; addict
常用漢字 **Jōyō Kanji** (official list of 1,945 kanji recommended for general use)
6 常任委員会 **jōnin iinkai** standing committee
常会 **jōkai** regular meeting/session
7 常住 **jōjū** everlasting; always; permanently residin

8 常事 **jōji** everyday affair/occurrence
常例 **jōrei** custom, conventional practice
常夜 **tokoyo** endless night
常法 **jōhō** usual method; unvarying rule
9 常連 **jōren** regular companions/customers
常客 **jōkyaku** regular customer/visitor
常軌 **jōki** usual/proper course
常食 **jōshoku** daily diet, staple food
10 常套 **jōtō** commonplace, conventional
常套手段 **jōtō shudan** well-worn device, old trick
常套句 **jōtōku** stock phrase, cliché
常套語 **jōtōgo** hackneyed expression, trite saying
常陸 **Hitachi** (ancient kuni, Ibaraki-ken)
常員 **jōin** regular personnel/member
常時 **jōji** usually, habitually, ordinarily
常夏 **tokonatsu** endless summer; a China pink (flower)
11 常得意 **jōtokui** regular customer
常宿 **jōyado** regular hotel
常常 **tsunezune** always, constantly
常習 **jōshū** custom, common practice, habit
常習犯 **jōshūhan** habitual crime/criminal
常習的 **jōshūteki** habitual, confirmed
常習者 **jōshūsha** habitual offender
常務 **jōmu** regular business, routine duties, executive (director)
常規 **jōki** established usage; common standard
常設 **jōsetsu** permanent, standing (committee)
12 常備 **jōbi** standing, permanent, regular
常備兵 **jōbihei** regular/standing army
常備金 **jōbikin** reserve fund
常備軍 **jōbigun** regular/standing army
常備薬 **jōbiyaku** household remedy
常勤 **jōkin** full-time (employment)
常温 **jōon** normal temperature
常勝 **jōshō** ever-victorious, invincible
常雇 **jōyato(i)** regular employee
13 常数 **jōsū** a constant (in math); fate
常置 **jōchi** permanent, standing (committee)
常節 **tokobushi** abalone, ear shell
14 常態 **jōtai** normal condition
常緑 **jōryoku** evergreen
常緑樹 **jōryokuju** an evergreen (tree)
15 常磐 **tokiwa** eternity
常磐木 **tokiwagi** an evergreen (tree)
常磐津 **tokiwazu** (a type of samisen-accompanied ballad)
常駐 **jōchū** permanently stationed
17 常闇 **tokoyami** perpetual darkness
19 常識 **jōshiki** common sense/knowledge
常識的 **jōshikiteki** matter-of-fact, practical
20 常議員 **jōgiin** permanent member; standing committee
——————— 2 ———————
4 五常 **gojō** the five cardinal virtues of

Confucianism (benevolence, justice, politeness, wisdom, fidelity)
日常 **nichijō** everyday, routine
日常茶飯事 **nichijō sahanji** an everyday occurrence
5 平常 **heijō** normal; normally, usually
正常 **seijō** normal
正常化 **seijōka** normalization
7 没常識 **botsujōshiki** lack of common sense
8 非常 **hijō** emergency; extraordinary; very, exceedingly, extremely
非常口 **hijōguchi** emergency exit
非常時 **hijōji** emergency, crisis
非常勤 **hijōkin** part-time work
非常線 **hijōsen** cordon
非常識 **hijōshiki** lacking common sense, absurd
定常 **teijō** steady, stationary, regular, routine
9 通常 **tsūjō** normal(ly), general(ly), ordinary, regular
通常国会 **tsūjō kokkai** ordinary Diet session
通常服 **tsūjōfuku** everyday clothes
恒常 **kōjō** constancy
恒常的 **kōjōteki** constant
11 常常 **tsunezune** always, constantly
異常 **ijō** anything unusual, abnormality
経常 **keijō** ordinary, current, working
経常費 **keijōhi** operating costs
12 尋常 **jinjō** normal, ordinary
尋常一様 **jinjō-ichiyō** common, mediocre
無常 **mujō** mutable, transitory, uncertain
14 綱常 **kōjō** morality, morals
——————— 4 ———————
15 諸行無常 **shogyō-mujō** All things change. Nothing lasts.

3n8.4 / 496

堂 **DŌ** temple; hall

——————— 1 ———————
3 堂上 **dōjō** on the roof; court nobles
堂々巡 **dōdōmegu(ri)** circle a temple in worship; going round and round (without getting anywhere); roll-call vote
6 堂守 **dōmori** building guard
11 堂堂 **dōdō(taru)** with pomp and glory, majestic, grand, magnificent
——————— 2 ———————
1 一堂 **ichidō** a building/hall; a temple/shrine; a room
4 天堂 **tendō** heaven, paradise
仏堂 **butsudō** Buddhist temple
辻堂 **tsujidō** wayside shrine
5 本堂 **hondō** main temple buildin

母堂 **bodō** mother (polite)
6 会堂 **kaidō** church, chapel; assembly hall
7 学堂 **gakudō** academy
8 参堂 **sandō** visit (a temple/home)
金堂 **kondō** (temple's) golden pavilion
9 草堂 **sōdō** thatched hut; my humble abode
食堂 **shokudō** dining hall, cafeteria
食堂車 **shokudōsha** dining car
11 堂堂 **dōdō(taru)** with pomp and glory, majestic, grand, magnificent
堂堂巡 **dōdōmegu(ri)** circle a temple in worship; going round and round (without getting anywhere); roll-call vote
経堂 **kyōdō** sutra library
12 満堂 **mandō** the whole assembly/audience
13 殿堂 **dendō** palatial building
禅堂 **zendō** temple for Zen study
聖堂 **seidō** Confucian temple; sanctuary, church
17 講堂 **kōdō** lecture hall

――――――― 3 ―――――――

3 大会堂 **daikaidō** cathedral
大聖堂 **daiseidō** cathedral
4 公会堂 **kōkaidō** public hall, civic center
5 正々堂々 **seisei-dōdō** fair and square, open and aboveboard
礼拝堂 **reihaidō** chapel
9 神楽堂 **kaguradō** Shinto dance pavilion
威風堂々 **ifū dōdō** pomp and circumstance
音楽堂 **ongakudō** concert hall
10 能楽堂 **nōgakudō** a Noh theater
教会堂 **kyōkaidō** church, place of worship
納骨堂 **nōkotsudō** ossuary, crypt
20 議事堂 **gijidō** assembly hall, parliament/diet building
鐘撞堂 **kanetsu(ki)dō** bell tower, belfry

――――――― 4 ―――――――

5 正正堂堂 **seisei-dōdō** fair and square, open and aboveboard
18 簡易食堂 **kan'i shokudō** fast-food diner

雀 → 8c3.2

――――――― 9 ―――――――

3n9.1

棠 **TŌ** wild pear/crabapple tree

――――――― 2 ―――――――

9 海棠 **kaidō** aronia (flowering shrub)
12 棣棠 **teitō** Japanese globeflower/kerria

3n9.2 / 722

営 **EI** run (a business); build; camp, barracks
itona(mu) conduct (business), operate, perform; build

――――――― 1 ―――――――

3 営々 **eiei (to)** strenuously, eagerly, busily
7 営利 **eiri** profit(-making)
8 営舎 **eisha** barracks
営林 **eirin** forest management
営所 **eisho** barracks, camp
9 営造 **eizō** building, construction
営造物 **eizōbutsu** building, structure
営庭 **eitei** barracks' parade ground
10 営倉 **eisō** guardhouse, brig
13 営業 **eigyō** (running a) business
営業費 **eigyōhi** operating expenses
18 営繕 **eizen** building and repair, maintenance

――――――― 2 ―――――――

2 入営 **nyūei** enlist (in the army)
4 屯営 **ton'ei** military camp, barracks, garrison
公営 **kōei** public, government-run
5 民営 **min'ei** private management, privately run
民営化 **min'eika** privatization, denationalization
本営 **hon'ei** headquarters
市営 **shiei** run by the city, municipal
冬営 **tōei** wintering; winter quarters
6 共営 **kyōei** joint management
自営 **jiei** self-management, independently run
7 兵営 **heiei** barracks
私営 **shiei** privately run/managed
8 非営利 **hieiriteki** nonprofit
舎営 **shaei** billeting, quarters
夜営 **yaei** camp(ing), bivouac
直営 **chokuei** direct management
官営 **kan'ei** government-run
府営 **fuei** run by an urban prefecture
国営 **kokuei** government-run, state-managed
国営化 **kokueika** nationalization
9 陣営 **jin'ei** camp
軍営 **gun'ei** military camp
造営 **zōei** building, construction
造営物 **zōeibutsu** a building, structure
造営費 **zōeihi** construction costs
県営 **ken'ei** run by the prefecture
省営 **shōei** operated by a ministry
10 都営 **toei** city-run, metropolitan
帰営 **kiei** return to barracks
兼営 **ken'ei** manage both, run two businesses
11 野営 **yaei** camp, bivouac
野営地 **yaeichi** camping ground
運営 **un'ei** operation, management, administration
宿営 **shukuei** be billeted
脱営 **datsuei** desertion from barracks

経営 **keiei** manage, operate, run
経営学 **keieigaku** (business) management
経営者 **keieisha** manager, operator
経営費 **keieihi** operating expenses
経営権 **keieiken** right of management
経営難 **keieinan** financial distress
設営 **setsuei** construction; preparations
12 営営 **eiei (to)** strenuously, eagerly, busily
13 幕営 **bakuei** (military) camp
15 敵営 **tekiei** the enemy's camp
21 露営 **roei** bivouac, camping out

——————— 3 ———————
3 大本営 **daihon'ei** imperial headquarters
6 自由営業 **jiyū eigyō** nonrestricted trade

——————— 4 ———————
6 多角経営 **takaku keiei** diversified management

3n9.3 / 605

覚 覺
KAKU, obo(eru) remember, bear in mind, learn; feel, experience **obo(ezu)** involuntarily, unwittingly, inspite of oneself **obo(shii)** looking like, apparently **sa(meru/masu)** (intr./tr.) awake, wake up **sato(ru)** realize

——————— 1 ———————
4 覚込 **obo(e)ko(mu)** learn, master
7 覚束 **obotsuka(nai)** uncertain, dubious, well-nigh hopeless, precarious
10 覚書 **obo(e)ga(ki)** memorandum
覚悟 **kakugo** be prepared/resolved/resigned to
13 覚際 **sa(me)giwa** on the verge of awaking
16 覚醒 **kakusei** awakening
覚醒剤 **kakuseizai** stimulant drugs

——————— 2 ———————
3 才覚 **saikaku** ready wit; raise (money); a plan
4 不覚 **fukaku** imprudence, failure, mistake
不覚涙 **fukaku (no) namida** crying in spite of oneself
幻覚 **genkaku** hallucination
予覚 **yokaku** premonition, hunch
心覚 **kokoroobo(e)** recollection; reminder
5 他覚的 **takakuteki** objective (symptoms)
正覚坊 **shōgakubō** large sea turtle; heavy drinker
圧覚 **akkaku** sensation of pressure
目覚 **meza(meru)** wake up, come awake
meza(mashii) striking, remarkable, spectacular
目覚時計 **meza(mashi)dokei** alarm clock
6 色覚 **shikikaku** color sense/vision
先覚 **senkaku** learned man, pioneer
先覚者 **senkakusha** pioneer, leading spirit
光覚 **kōkaku** optic sense, sensation of light

自覚 **jikaku** consciousness, awareness, realization
自覚症状 **jikaku shōjō** subjective symptoms, patient's complaints
7 見覚 **miobo(e)** recognition, familiarity
8 直覚 **chokkaku** intuition
直覚的 **chokkakuteki** intuitive
味覚 **mikaku** sense of taste
知覚 **chikaku** perception
空覚 **soraobo(e)** memorization
物覚 **monoobo(e)** memory
9 発覚 **hakkaku** be detected, come to light
11 習覚 **nara(i)obo(eru)** learn
視覚 **shikaku** sense of sight, vision
酔覚 **yo(i)za(me)** sobering up
12 痛覚 **tsūkaku** sense of pain
統覚 **tōkaku** apperception
13 嗅覚 **kyūkaku** sense of smell
寝覚 **neza(me)** waking from sleep
感覚 **kankaku** sense, the senses
感覚論 **kankakuron** sensualism; esthetics
触覚 **shokkaku** sense of touch
14 聞覚 **ki(ki)obo(eru)** learn by ear
16 錯覚 **sakkaku** illusion
17 聴覚 **chōkaku** sense of hearing

——————— 3 ———————
10 眠気覚 **nemukeza(mashi)** something to wake one up
11 視聴覚 **shichōkaku** audiovisual
12 超感覚的 **chōkankakuteki** extrasensory
無自覚 **mujikaku** unconscious of, blind to
無感覚 **mukankaku** insensible, numb, callous
17 聴視覚 **chōshikaku** audio-visual

——————— 4 ———————
9 前後不覚 **zengo-fukaku** unconscious

3n9.4 / 499

掌
SHŌ palm of the hand; administer **tsukasado(ru)** administer, preside over **tanagokoro** palm of the hand

——————— 1 ———————
3 掌大 **shōdai** palm-size
4 掌中 **shōchū** in the hand; pocket (edition)
掌中玉 **shōchū (no) tama** apple of one's eye
7 掌状 **shōjō** hand-shaped, palmate
8 掌典 **shōten** ritualist
12 掌握 **shōaku** grasp, seize, have in hand
14 掌管 **shōkan** manage, handle

——————— 2 ———————
6 合掌 **gasshō** join one's hands (in prayer)
7 車掌 **shashō** (train) conductor
12 落掌 **rakushō** receive
14 鞅掌 **ōshō** be busy with; attend to
管掌 **kanshō** take/have charge of, manage

18 観掌術 **kanshōjutsu** palm-reading, palmistry
職掌 **shokushō** office, duties

——————— 3 ———————

5 仙人掌 **saboten** cactus

就 → **3d9.21**

——————— 10 ———————

嘗 → 嘗 **3n11.1**

3n10.1 / 802

誉 譽
YO, **home(ru)** praise
homa(re) honor, glory

——————— 1 ———————

11 誉望 **yobō** glory, honor, fame

——————— 2 ———————

6 名誉 **meiyo** honor, glory, fame, prestige
名誉心 **meiyoshin** desire for fame
名誉教授 **meiyo kyōju** professor emeritus
名誉欲 **meiyoyoku** desire for fame
名誉職 **meiyoshoku** honary post
9 栄誉 **eiyo** honor, glory, fame
13 毀誉 **kiyo** criticism and/or praise
毀誉褒貶 **kiyo-hōhen** praise and/or criticism

——————— 3 ———————

4 不名誉 **fumeiyo** dishonor, disgrace

當 → 当 **3n3.3**

亂 → 乱 **3d4.21**

3n10.2

舜
SHUN type of morning glory; rose of
Sharon, althea

3n10.3

尠
SEN, **suku(nai)** few, little

3n10.4 / 1332

奨 奬 獎
SHŌ, **susu(meru)**
urge, encourage

——————— 1 ———————

7 奨励 **shōrei** encourage, promote, give
incentive
奨学生 **shōgakusei** student on a scholarship
奨学金 **shōgakukin** a scholarship

——————— 2 ———————

11 推奨 **suishō** recommend, commend
12 報奨 **hōshō** bonus, reward
13 勧奨 **kanshō** encouragement, promotion

3n10.5

孵
FU, **kae(su)** hatch, incubate

——————— 1 ———————

4 孵化 **fuka** incubation, hatching
7 孵卵 **furan** incubation, hatching
孵卵器 **furanki** incubator

——————— 11 ———————

3n11.1

嘗 嘗
SHŌ lick; once; try
na(meru) lick; underrate
katsu(te) once, formerly, ever

3 大嘗祭 **Daijōsai, Ōname-matsuri** first
Harvest Festival after an emperor's
enthronement
9 神嘗祭 **Kannamesai** Shinto Festival of New
Rice (October 17)
13 新嘗祭 **niinamesai** Harvest Festival
14 総嘗 **sōna(me)** sweeping victory

——————— 3 ———————

9 臥薪嘗胆 **gashin-shōtan** perseverance and
determination

3n11.2

裳
SHŌ, mo (traditional type) skirt

——————— 1 ———————

13 裳裾 **mosuso** skirt, train

——————— 2 ———————

6 衣裳 **ishō** clothes, wardrobe, dress
衣裳方 **ishōkata** (theater) wardrobe assistant
衣裳持 **ishōmo(chi)** one who has a large
wardrobe

——————— 12 ———————

3n12.1 / 500

賞
SHŌ prize; praise

——————— 1 ———————

0 賞する **shō(suru)** praise, admire
3 賞与 **shōyo** bonus, reward
　賞与金 **shōyokin** bonus
7 賞状 **shōjō** certificate of merit
8 賞味 **shōmi** relish, appreciate
　賞杯 **shōhai** trophy, prize cup
　賞玩 **shōgan** appreciate
　賞金 **shōkin** (cash) prize, monetary reward
9 賞美 **shōbi** admire, appreciate, prize
　賞品 **shōhin** (nonmonetary) prize
　賞盃 **shōhai** trophy, prize cup
12 賞牌 **shōhai** medal, medallion
　賞揚 **shōyō** praise, admiration
　賞詞 **shōshi** commendation
13 賞嘆 **shōtan** praise, admire
14 賞罰 **shōbatsu** reward and punishment, praise and censure
15 賞賜 **shōshi** reward
　賞賛 **shōsan** praise, admire
22 賞讃 **shōsan** praise, admire
23 賞鑑 **shōkan** appreciate, admire

——————— 2 ———————

2 入賞 **nyūshō** win a prize
　入賞者 **nyūshōsha** prizewinner
6 行賞 **kōshō** conferring of awards
8 受賞 **jushō** receive a prize
　受賞者 **jushōsha** prizewinner
9 信賞必罰 **shinshō-hitsubatsu** sure punishment and sure reward
10 特賞 **tokushō** special commendation/reward
　恩賞 **onshō** a reward
11 副賞 **fukushō** extra prize
　過賞 **kashō** undeserved praise
　推賞 **suishō** recommend, commend
　授賞 **jushō** awarding a prize
13 嘆賞 **tanshō** praise, admire
　嘆賞者 **tanshōsha** admirer
14 歎賞 **tanshō** admiration, praise
15 褒賞 **hōshō** prize, reward
16 激賞 **gekishō** praise highly, rave about
18 観賞 **kanshō** admiration, enjoyment
20 懸賞 **kenshō** offering prizes
　懸賞金 **kenshōkin** prize money, reward
　懸賞募集 **kenshō boshū** prize competition
　懸賞論文 **kenshō ronbun** prize essay
23 鑑賞 **kanshō** appreciation, enjoyment
　鑑賞力 **kanshōryoku** ability to appreciate
　鑑賞眼 **kanshōgan** an eye for

——————— 3 ———————

1 一等賞 **ittōshō** first prize
2 二等賞 **nitōshō** second prize
4 文学賞 **bungakushō** literary award
7 初受賞 **hatsujushō** winning a prize for the first time

10 残念賞 **zannenshō** consolation prize
17 優等賞 **yūtōshō** honor prize

——————— 4 ———————

15 論功行賞 **ronkō kōshō** conferring of honors

輝 → **7c8.8**

——————— 13 ———————

鴬 → 鶯 **11b10.9**

靜 → 静 **4b10.9**

——————— 14 ———————

3n14.1 / 822

厳　嚴　　GEN, GON, **kibi(shii)** severe, strict, rigorous, intense
ogoso(ka) solemn, grave, stately
ikame(shii) solemn, august

——————— 1 ———————

4 厳父 **genpu** strict father; your esteemed father
5 厳存 **genson** exist; be in full force
　厳正 **gensei** exact, strict, impartial
　厳冬 **gentō** severe winter
6 厳刑 **genkei** severe punishment
　厳守 **genshu** strict observance/adherence
7 厳君 **genkun** your esteemed father
　厳戒 **genkai** strict guard/watch
8 厳命 **genmei** strict orders
9 厳重 **genjū** strict, stringent, rigid
　厳封 **genpū** seal tight/hermetically
　厳科 **genka** severe punishment
10 厳師 **genshi** strict/esteemed teacher
　厳格 **genkaku** strict, stern, severe
11 厳粛 **genshuku** grave, serious, solemn
　厳達 **gentatsu** give strict orders
　厳密 **genmitsu** strict, precise
12 厳寒 **genkan** intense cold
　厳然 **genzen** solemn, grave, majestic
13 厳禁 **genkin** strictly prohibited
14 厳選 **gensen** careful selection
　厳罰 **genbatsu** severe punishment
15 厳談 **gendan** demand an explanation, protest strongly

——————— 2 ———————

4 手厳 **tekibi(shii)** severe, scathing, harsh
6 光厳 **Kōgon** (emperor, 1332–1333)
7 冷厳 **reigen** grim, stark, stern
　戒厳 **kaigen** being on guard
　戒厳令 **kaigenrei** martial law

3

氵
土
扌
口
女
巾
犭
弓
彳
彡
艹
宀 14→
屮
吉
广
尸
口

9 荘厳 **sōgon** sublime, grand, majestic
　威厳 **igen** dignity, majesty, stateliness
10 華厳 **Kegon** (a Buddhist sect)
　華厳宗 **Kegonshū** (a Buddhist sect)
　華厳経 **Kegonkyō** the Avatamska sutra
　峻厳 **shungen** strict, stern, harsh
12 尊厳 **songen** dignity
　森厳 **shingen** solemn, awe-inspiring
13 寛厳 **kangen** lenience or/and severity
14 端厳 **tangen** solemn and serene
17 謹厳 **kingen** stern, austere, solemn

————— 3 —————

3 土足厳禁 **dosoku genkin** Remove Shoes
　(sign)

4 火気厳禁 **kaki genkin** Danger: Flammable
9 後光厳 **Gokōgon** (emperor, 1353–1371)

谿 → 渓 **3a8.16**

————— 17 —————

黨 → 党 **3n7.2**

————— 山 3o —————

山	屵	屶	屹	出	岐	岌	岑	岌	岫	岬	岷	岬
0.1	3k10.15	2.1	3.1	0a5.22	4.1	4.2	4.3	4.4	5.1	5.2	5.3	5.4

岫	岨	帕	岾	岻	岩	岸	岳	岱	峡	峙	峠	峇
5.5	5.6	5.7	5.8	5.9	5.10	5.11	5.12	5.13	6.1	6.2	6.3	6.4

炭	幽	峯	峨	峺	峡	峻	峭	峰	峪	峩	峯	蚩
6.5	6.6	7.1	7.2	7.3	3o6.1	7.4	7.5	7.6	7.7	3o7.2	3o7.6	6d4.9

豈	島	努	峻	峥	崎	崙	崛	崕	崟	崔	崩	崑
7.8	7.9	0a10.6	8.1	8.2	8.3	3o8.10	8.4	3o8.11	8.5	8.6	8.7	8.8

崇	崗	崖	崗	嵎	嵌	嵜	嵋	嵐	邑	嵶	嵯	嵬
8.9	8.10	8.11	8.12	9.1	9.2	3o8.3	9.3	9.4	3d9.20	10.1	10.2	10.3

嵳	嵩	嶋	嶂	嶇	蒿	嶄	隆	嶝	嶢	皴	嶼	嶮
3o10.2	10.4	3o7.9	11.1	11.2	3o7.9	11.3	11.4	12.1	12.2	2h13.1	13.1	13.2

巇	嶷	嶺	嶽	豐	巇	巌	巍	巍	巒	巓		
13.3	14.1	14.2	3o5.12	3d10.15	17.1	17.2	18.1	18.2	19.1	20.1		

————— 0 —————

3o0.1 / 34

SAN, yama mountain

山

————— 1 —————

2 山人 **yamabito** mountain folk; hermit
　山刀 **yamagatana** woodsman's hatchet
3 山上 **sanjō** mountaintop
　山々 **yamayama** mountains; very much
　山口県 **Yamaguchi-ken** (prefecture)
　山女 **yamame** (a kind of trout)
　　akebi (a kind of shrub having tendrils)
　山小屋 **yamagoya** mountain hut
4 山中 **yamanaka, sanchū** in the mountains
　山中湖 **Yamanaka-ko** Lake Yamanaka (near
　　Mt. Fuji)
　山分 **yamawa(ke)** dividing equally
　山辺 **yamabe** the vicinity of a mountain

山水 **sansui** landscape, natural scenery
　yamamizu mountain spring water
山水画 **sansuiga** landscape painting;
　a landscape
山手 **yamate, yama(no)te** hilly residential
　section, bluff, uptown
山犬 **yamainu** wild dog, coyote, wolf
山火事 **yamakaji** forest fire
5 山出 **yamada(shi)** bumpkin, from the country
山主 **yamanushi** owner of a mountain; mine
　operator
6 山気 **sanki** mountain air　**yamagi, yamake**
　speculative spirit, venturesomeness
山伏 **yamabushi** mountain/itinerant priest
山羊 **yagi** goat
山羊鬚 **yagihige** goatee
山地 **sanchi, yamachi** mountainous area
山寺 **yamadera** mountain temple
山守 **yamamori** forest ranger

山肌 **yamahada** mountain's surface
7 山里 **yamazato** mountain village, hilly district
山吹 **yamabuki** yellow rose
山吹色 **yamabuki-iro** orangish/golden yellow
山形 **yamagata** chevron, caret
Yamagata (city, Yamagata-ken)
山形県 **Yamagata-ken** (prefecture)
山村 **sanson** mountain village
山男 **yamaotoko** (back)woodsman, hillbilly; alpinist
山系 **sankei** mountain system/range
8 山育 **yamasoda(chi)** mountain-bred
山河 **sanga** mountains and rivers
山幸 **yama (no) sachi** mountain food products
山径 **sankei** mountain path
山苞 **yamazuto** mountain souvenirs
山岳 **sangaku** mountains
山岳病 **sangakubyō** altitude sickness
山国 **yamaguni** mountainous district, hill country
山林 **sanrin** mountains and forests; mountain forest
山林学 **sanringaku** forestry
山林官 **sanrinkan** forester
山門 **sanmon** (two-story) temple gate
9 山途 **santo** mountain road
山風 **yamakaze, sanpū** mountain wind
山津波 **yamatsunami** landslide
山津浪 **yamatsunami** landslide
山海 **sankai** mountains and seas; land and sea
山城 **yamajiro** mountain castle
Yamashiro (ancient kuni, Kyōto-fu)
山姥 **yamauba** mountain witch
山狩 **yamaga(ri)** hunt in the mountains
山荘 **sansō** mountain villa/chalet
山峡 **sankyō, yamakai** gorge, ravine, valley, pass
山面 **yamazura** mountain's surface
山背 **yamase** a foehn-like wind; a cold early-summer wind in Tōhoku
sanpai the other side of a mountain
山神 **yama (no) kami** god of a mountain; one's wife
山彦 **yamabiko** echo
10 山陵 **sanryō** mountains and hills; imperial tomb
山陰 **san'in, yamakage** mountain recesses; northern slopes
山高帽 **yamatakabō** derby hat, bowler
山姫 **yamahime** mountain goddess
山師 **yamashi** speculator; charlatan; miner; timber dealer
山家 **yamaga, sanka** mountain home, chalet
山容 **san'yō** the shape/figure of a mountain
山桜 **yamazakura** wild cherry tree
山脈 **sanmyaku** mountain range

11 山野 **san'ya** fields and mountains
山勘 **yamakan** speculation, guesswork
山道 **sandō, yamamichi** mountain path/pass
山添 **yamazo(i)** by/along/in the mountains
山猫 **yamaneko** wildcat
山猫争議 **yamaneko sōgi** wildcat strike
山崩 **yamakuzu(re)** landslide
山梔子 **kuchinashi** Cape jasmine, gardenia
山梨県 **Yamanashi-ken** (prefecture)
山盛 **yamamo(ri)** heap(ing full)
山頂 **sanchō** summit
山鳥 **yamadori** pheasant; mountain bird
12 山登 **yamanobo(ri)** mountain climbing
山葵 **wasabi** Japanese horseradish
山葵漬 **wasabizu(ke)** pickled horseradish
山嵐 **yamaarashi** mountain storm
山椒 **sanshō** Japanese pepper (tree)
山椒魚 **sanshōuo** salamander
山焼 **yamaya(ki)** burning of dead grass
山番 **yamaban** forest ranger
山紫水明 **sanshi-suimei** purple hills and crystal streams, scenic beauty
山奥 **yamaoku** deep/back in the mountains
山颪 **yamaoroshi** wind blowing down a mountain
山間 **sankan** in the mountains
yamaai ravine, gorge
山間僻地 **sankan-hekichi** secluded mountain recesses
山開 **yamabira(ki)** opening a mountain for the climbing season
13 山際 **yamagiwa** by the mountains; skyline
山猿 **yamazaru** wild monkey; hillbilly
山腹 **sanpuku** hillside, mountainside
山稜 **sanryō** mountain ridge
山裾 **yamasuso** foot of a mountain
山蜂 **yamabachi** hornet
山賊 **sanzoku** mountain robber, bandit
山路 **yamaji** mountain road/trail
山鳩 **yamabato** turtledove
14 山鳴 **yamana(ri)** rumbling of a mountain
山窩 **sanka** nomadic mountain tribes
15 山膚 **yamahada** mountain's surface
山稼 **yamakase(gi)** work in the mountains
山霊 **sanrei** genius loci of a mountain
山駕籠 **yamakago** mountain palanquin
16 山積 **yamazu(mi)** big pile
17 山嶽 **sangaku** mountains
19 山麓 **sanroku** the foot of a mountain
山霧 **yamagiri** mountain fog
山鯨 **yamakujira** wild-boar meat
21 山躑躅 **yamatsutsuji** rhododendron
22 山籠 **yamagomo(ri)** seclude oneself in the mountains; retire to a mountain temple
23 山巓 **santen** summit

3

氵
土
扌
口
女
巾
犭
弓
彳
彡
艹
宀
丷
山 0←
耂
广
尸
口

──────── 2 ────────

1 一山 **hitoyama** a pile (of bananas); the whole mountain
2 人山 **hitoyama** crowd of people
3 大山 **taizan** large mountain
   Daisen (mountain, Tottori-ken)
   大山鳴動鼠一匹 **taizan meidō (shite) nezumi ippiki** The mountains have brought forth a mouse. Much ado about nothing much.
   下山 **gezan** come/go down a mountain; leave a temple
   小山 **koyama** hill, knoll
4 片山里 **katayamazato** remote mountain village
   火山 **kazan** volcano
   火山灰 **kazanbai** volcanic ash
   火山岩 **kazangan** igneous rock, lava
   火山帯 **kazantai** volcanic zone
   火山脈 **kazanmyaku** volcanic range
   火山弾 **kazandan** volcanic boulders
   火山礫 **kazanreki** volcanic pebbles
5 本山 **honzan** head temple; this temple
   他山 **tazan** another mountain/temple
   他山石 **tazan (no) ishi** object lesson
   氷山 **hyōzan** iceberg
   白山 **Hakusan** (mountain, Gifu-ken)
   石山 **ishiyama** quarry; stony mountain
   立山 **Tateyama** (mountain, Toyama-ken)
6 仰山 **gyōsan** many, much; grandiose
   地山 **jiyama** natural ground
   名山 **meizan** famous mountain
7 巫山戯 **fuzake(ru)** frolic, be playful, jest; flirt
   沢山 **takusan** many, much, plenty
   花山 **Kazan** (emperor, 984–986)
   床山 **tokoyama** (sumo wrestlers' or actors') hairdresser
   杣山 **somayama** timber forest
   禿山 **hageyama** bare/bald mountain
8 孤山 **kozan** lone mountain
   岡山 **Okayama** (city, Okayama-ken)
   岡山県 **Okayama-ken** (prefecture)
   岩山 **iwayama** rocky mountain
   松山 **Matsuyama** (city, Ehime-ken)
   青山 **seizan** blue mountain, green hills
   金山 **kinzan** gold mine   **kanayama** mine
9 連山 **renzan** mountain range
   海山 **umiyama** sea and mountains; depth and height
   狭山 **sayama** mountain, hill
   後山条 **Gosanjō** (emperor, 1068–1072)
   草山 **kusayama** grass-covered hill
   炭山 **tanzan** coal mine
   故山 **kozan** birthplace, home town
   砂山 **sunayama** dune
   秋山 **akiyama** mountains in autumn
10 剣山 **kenzan** frog (in ikebana)

高山 **kōzan** high mountain, alpine
高山病 **kōzanbyō** mountain/altitude sickness
釜山 **Fuzan, Pusan** Pusan
遊山 **yusan** excursion, outing
泰山 **taizan** large mountain; Mt. Taishan (in China)
案山子 **kakashi** scarecrow; figurehead
崋山 **Kazan** (name of a mountain in China)
桃山 **Momoyama** (era, 1576–1598)
夏山 **natsuyama** mountains in summer
留山 **to(me)yama** mountain where logging is prohibited
針山 **hariyama** pincushion
11 野山 **noyama** hills and fields
   深山 **miyama, shinzan** mountain recesses
   深山烏 **miyamagarasu** mountain crow
   深山楼 **miyamazakura** mountain cherry tree
   黒山 **kuroyama** large crowd
   雪山 **yukiyama** snow-covered mountain
12 遠山 **tōyama, enzan** distant mountain
   遠山里 **tōyamazato** remote mountain village
   満山 **manzan** the whole hill/mountain
   登山 **tozan** mountain climbing
   登山者 **tozansha** mountain climber
   登山家 **tozanka** mountaineer
   登山期 **tozanki** mountain-climbing season
   富山 **Toyama** (city, Toyama-ken)
   富山県 **Toyama-ken** (prefecture)
   焼山 **ya(ke)yama** mountain whose vegetation has burned; dormant volcano
   奥山 **okuyama** mountain recesses
   開山 **kaisan** (sect's) founder, originator
13 裏山 **urayama** hill at the back
   農山村 **nōsanson** agricultural and mountain villages
   群山 **gunzan** many mountains, mountain range
   福山 **Fukuyama** (city, Hiroshima-ken)
   裸山 **hadakayama** bare mountain/hills
   鉄山 **tetsuzan** iron mine
   鉱山 **kōzan** a mine
   鉱山業 **kōzangyō** mining
14 端山 **hayama** foothill
   銀山 **ginzan** silver mine
   銅山 **dōzan** copper mine
   関山 **seki (no) yama** the best one can do
15 霊山 **reizan** sacred mountain
16 築山 **tsukiyama** mound, artificial hill
18 離山 **rizan** lone mountain; leaving a temple

──────── 3 ────────

2 子沢山 **kodakusan** many children (in the family)
3 大本山 **daihonzan** headquarters temple (of a sect)
   大雪山 **Daisetsuzan** (mountain, Hokkaidō)

5 外輪山 **gairinzan** the outer crater, somma
 比叡山 **Hieizan** (mountain, Kyōto-fu)
6 死火山 **shikazan** extinct volcano
 休火山 **kyūkazan** dormant volcano
7 阿蘇山 **Asosan** (mountain, Kumamoto-ken)
8 泥火山 **deikazan** mud volcano
 和歌山 **Wakayama** (city, Wakayama-ken)
 和歌山県 **Wakayama-ken** (prefecture)
9 浅間山 **Asamayama** (mountain, Nagano-ken, Gunma-ken)
 活火山 **kakkazan** active volcano
 海千山千 **umisen-yamasen** experienced and shrewd, wily veteran, sly old dog
10 高野山 **Kōyasan** (mountain, Wakayama-ken)
11 崑崙山脈 **Konron-sanmyaku** the Kunlun mountains
 悪巫山戯 **warufuzake** prank, practical joke
 盛沢山 **mo(ri)dakusan** many, plenty, varied
12 富士山 **Fuji-san** Mt. Fuji
14 複火山 **fukukazan** compound volcano
 総本山 **sōhonzan** (sect's) head temple
15 噴火山 **funkazan** volcano
 磐梯山 **Bandai-san** (mountain, Fukushima-ken)
 箱根山 **Hakone-yama** (mountain, Kanagawa-ken)

———————— 4 ————————

6 安土桃山 **Azuchi-Momoyama** Azuchi-Momoyama (era, 1568–1603)
8 物見遊山 **monomi yusan** pleasure trip

———————— 6 ————————

17 環太平洋火山帯 **kan-Taiheiyō kazantai** circum-Pacific volcanic belt
 環太平洋造山帯 **kan-Taiheiyō zōzantai** circum-Pacific orogeny

———————— 1 ————————

屵 → 蓋 **3k10.15**

———————— 2 ————————

3o2.1

屴 **nata, tana** (used in proper names)

———————— 3 ————————

3o3.1

屹 **KITSU** be high, rise, tower

———————— 1 ————————

5 屹立 **kitsuritsu** rise, tower, soar

出 → **0a5.22**

———————— 4 ————————

3o4.1 / 872

岐 **KI** forked road

———————— 1 ————————

5 岐出 **waka(re)de(ru)** branch off, diverge
8 岐阜 **Gifu** (city, Gifu-ken)
 岐阜県 **Gifu-ken** (prefecture)
13 岐路 **kiro** fork in the road, crossroads

———————— 2 ————————

4 分岐 **bunki** branch off, fork, ramify, diverge
 分岐点 **bunkiten** branch/ramification/turning point, fork, junction
6 多岐 **taki** many branches/digressions/ramifications
7 壱岐 **Iki** (island and ancient kuni, Nagasaki-ken)
13 隠岐 **Oki** (ancient kuni, Shimane-ken)
 隠岐諸島 **Oki shotō** (group of islands, Shimane-ken)
22 讃岐 **Sanuki** (ancient kuni, Kagawa-kuni)

———————— 4 ————————

13 損益分岐点 **son'eki bunkiten** break-even point

3o4.2

岌 **KYŪ** high; dangerous

3o4.3

岑 **SHIN, mine** peak, mountaintop

3o4.4

岐 **SHI** disdain; foolish; ugly

———————— 5 ————————

3o5.1

峅 **kura** rocky place in the mountains (where a god is enshrined)

3o5.2

峠 **yuri** level spot part-way up a mountain

3o5.3

峧 **BIN, MIN** (name of mountain and river in China)

3o5.4 / 1363

岬 **misaki** promontory, headland, cape, point (of land)

3o5.5

岫 **KŌ** gorge, ravine; in the mountains
misaki cape, promontory

3o5.6

岨 **SO** rocky mountain

3o5.7

岶 **HAKU, HYAKU** dense mountain vegetation

3o5.8

岾 **yama** (used in proper names)

3o5.9

岻 **KO, JI, CHI** (name of a mountain)

3o5.10 / 1345

岩 **GAN, iwa** rock

——————— 1 ———————

3 岩山 **iwayama** rocky mountain
4 岩水 **iwamizu** water flowing from rocks
岩手県 **Iwate-ken** (prefecture)
岩戸 **iwato** cave door
5 岩代 **Iwashiro** (ancient kuni, Fukushima-ken)
岩穴 **iwaana** rocky cave
岩石 **ganseki** rock
7 岩床 **ganshō** bedrock
8 岩苔 **iwagoke** rock moss
9 岩乗 **ganjō** robust, solid, firm
岩室 **iwamuro** (small) stone cave
岩屋 **iwaya** cave, cavern
10 岩根 **iwane** base of a rock; rock, crag

11 岩清水 **iwashimizu** spring flowing from rocks
12 岩登 **iwanobo(ri)** rock climbing
岩棚 **iwadana** ledge
13 岩塩 **gan'en** rock salt
岩窟 **gankutsu** cave, cavern
17 岩礁 **ganshō** reef

——————— 2 ———————

4 天岩戸 **Ama(no)iwato** Gate of the Celestial Rock Cave
5 巨岩 **kyogan** huge rock
8 奇岩 **kigan** strange-shaped rock
9 砂岩 **sagan** sandstone
砕岩機 **saiganki** rock crusher
頁岩 **ketsugan** shale
10 珪岩 **keigan** quartzite
13 隠岩 **kaku(re)iwa** sunken rock, reef
溶岩 **yōgan** lava
18 鎔岩 **yōgan** lava
鎔岩流 **yōganryū** lava flow
20 礫岩 **rekigàn** conglomerate (rock)
28 鑿岩機 **sakuganki** rock drill

——————— 3 ———————

4 水成岩 **suiseigan** sedimentary rock
火山岩 **kazangan** igneous rock, lava
火成岩 **kaseigan** igneous rock
5 石灰岩 **sekkaigan** limestone
石英岩 **sekieigan** quartzite
6 成層岩 **seisōgan** stratified/sedimentary rock
7 花崗岩 **kakōgan** granite
8 泥板岩 **deibangan** shale
9 屏風岩 **byōbu iwa** sheer cliff
10 原成岩 **genseigan** primary rocks
12 斑糠岩 **hanreigan** gabbro

3o5.11 / 586

岸 **GAN, kishi** bank, shore, coast

——————— 1 ———————

8 岸和田 **Kishiwada** (city, Ōsaka-fu)

——————— 2 ———————

3 川岸 **kawagishi** riverbank
5 北岸 **hokugan** north coast, north bank
左岸 **sagan** left bank
右岸 **ugan** right bank/shore (as one faces downstream)
6 両岸 **ryōgan** both banks (of a river)
西岸 **seigan** west coast; west bank
7 対岸 **taigan** opposite shore
8 東岸 **tōgan** eastern coast; east bank
沿岸 **engan** coast, shore
沿岸漁業 **engan gyogyō** coastal fishing
河岸 **kashi** riverside; (riverside) fish market;

place, scene; one's field/trade
    kagan riverside, bank/shore of a river
河岸端 **kashibata** riverside
彼岸 **higan** equinoctal week; Buddhist services during equinoctal week; the other shore; goal
彼岸桜 **higanzakura** early-flowering cherry tree
9 海岸 **kaigan** seashore, coast
海岸沿 **kaiganzo(i)** along the coast/shore
海岸通 **kaigandō(ri)** road along the coast
海岸線 **kaigansen** coastline; coastal rail line
12 着岸 **chakugan** reach the shore
湖岸 **kogan** lakeshore, lakeside
13 傲岸 **gōgan** arrogant, haughty
傲岸不遜 **gōgan-fuson** arrogant, insolent, presumptuous
20 護岸 **gogan** shore/bank protection
護岸工事 **gogan kōji** riparian works

――――――― 3 ―――――――

11 魚河岸 **uogashi** riverside fish market

――――――― 4 ―――――――

12 象牙海岸 **Zōge Kaigan** Ivory Coast

3o5.12 / 1358

岳 嶽

    GAKU, take mountain, peak

――――――― 1 ―――――――

4 岳父 **gakufu** father of one's wife

――――――― 2 ―――――――

3 山岳 **sangaku** mountains
山岳病 **sangakubyō** altitude sickness
12 富岳 **Fugaku** Mt. Fuji
14 槍岳 **Yari(ga)take** (mountain, Nagano-ken)

――――――― 3 ―――――――

12 雲仙岳 **Unzendake** (mountain, Nagasaki-ken)

3o5.13

岱

    TAI (old name for Taishan, a mountain in China)

――――――― 6 ―――――――

3o6.1 / 1352

峡 峡

    KYŌ gorge, ravine

――――――― 1 ―――――――

7 峡谷 **kyōkoku** gorge, ravine, canyon
12 峡湾 **kyōwan** fjord
峡間 **kyōkan** between the mountains; ravine, defile

――――――― 2 ―――――――

3 山峡 **sankyō, yamakai** gorge, ravine, valley, pass
8 河峡 **kakyō** river canyon, gorge
9 海峡 **kaikyō** strait(s), channel, sound

――――――― 4 ―――――――

7 対馬海峡 **Tsushima-kaikyō** Tsushima Strait (between Tsushima and Iki Island)
8 宗谷海峡 **Sōya-kaikyō** (strait between Hokkaidō and Sakhalin)
9 津軽海峡 **Tsugaru-kaikyō** (strait between Honshū and Hokkaidō)
12 間宮海峡 **Mamiya-kaikyō** (strait between Hokkaidō and Sakhalin)
14 鳴門海峡 **Naruto-kaikyō** (strait between Shikoku and Awaji island)
    関門海峡 **Kanmon-kaikyō** (strait between Shimonoseki and Moji)

3o6.2

峙

    JI, sobada(tsu) tower, soar

――――――― 2 ―――――――

7 対峙 **taiji** confront each other, hold one's own against

3o6.3 / 1351

峠

    tōge mountain pass

――――――― 1 ―――――――

11 峠道 **tōgemichi** road through a mountain pass

3o6.4

峇

    KŌ mountain cave

3o6.5 / 1344

炭 炭

    TAN coal, charcoal, carbon
    sumi charcoal

――――――― 1 ―――――――

3 炭山 **tanzan** coal mine
4 炭化 **tanka** carbonization
炭化水素 **tanka suiso** hydrocarbon
炭化物 **tankabutsu** carbide
炭水化物 **tansuikabutsu** carbohydrates
炭火 **sumibi** charcoal fire
5 炭田 **tanden** coalfield
6 炭団 **tadon** charcoal ball/briquette
7 炭坑 **tankō** coal mine
炭坑夫 **tankōfu** coal miner

3

氵 土 扌 口 女 巾 犭 弓 彳 彡 艹 宀 氺 山 6← 耂 广 尸 口

9 炭屋 **sumiya** charcoal dealer
10 炭俵 **sumidawara** charcoal sack
炭庫 **tanko** coal bin
炭素 **tanso** carbon
炭素棒 **tansobō** carbon rod/points
12 炭焼 **sumiya(ki)** charcoal making/maker
13 炭鉱 **tankō** coal mine
14 炭塵 **tanjin** coal dust
炭層 **tansō** coal bed/seam
炭酸 **tansan** carbonic acid
炭酸水 **tansansui** carbonated water
炭酸紙 **tansanshi** carbon paper
15 炭窯 **sumigama** charcoal kiln
炭質 **tanshitsu** coal quality

———————— 2 ————————

4 木炭 **mokutan** charcoal
木炭画 **mokutanga** charcoal drawing
5 氷炭 **hyōtan** ice and charcoal; irreconcilable
石炭 **sekitan** coal
石炭殻 **sekitangara** (coal) cinders
石炭船 **sekitansen** coal ship
石炭層 **sekitansō** coal seam/bed
石炭酸 **sekitansan** carbolic acid, phenol
7 亜炭 **atan** lignite, brown coal
走炭 **hashi(ri)zumi** sputtering charcoal
豆炭 **mametan** round charcoal briquettes
8 泥炭 **deitan** peat
泥炭地 **deitanchi** peat bog
9 砕炭器 **saitanki** coal crusher
10 消炭 **ke(shi)zumi** cinders
骨炭 **kottan** bone charcoal
粉炭 **funtan** powdered coal
konazumi ground charcoal
配炭 **haitan** coal distribution
11 採炭 **saitan** coal mining
採炭所 **saitanjo** coal mine
黒炭 **kokutan** bituminous coal
12 堅炭 **katazumi** hard charcoal
給炭 **kyūtan** supplying coal, coaling
貯炭 **chotan** coal storage
貯炭所 **chotanjo** coal yard, coaling station
13 塗炭 **totan** misery, distress
煉炭 **rentan** briquette
褐炭 **kattan** brown coal, lignite
14 選炭 **sentan** coal dressing/sorting
選炭婦 **sentanfu** coal dresser/sorter
製炭 **seitan** charcoal making
製炭業 **seitangyō** the charcoal industry
16 獣炭 **jūtan** incensed charcoal in animal
shapes; charcoal made from animal
blood or bones and used for medicine or
bleaching
薪炭 **shintan** firewood and charcoal, fuel

———————— 3 ————————

6 有煙炭 **yūentan** soft/bituminous coal
7 含水炭素 **gansuitanso** carbohydrate

12 無煙炭 **muentan** anthracite coal
19 瀝青炭 **rekiseitan** bituminous/soft coal

———————— 4 ————————

1 一酸化炭素 **issanka tanso** carbon monoxide

3o6.6 / 1228

幽
YŪ quiet, deep
kasu(ka) faint, dim, indistinct

———————— 1 ————————

5 幽玄 **yūgen** the profound, occult
7 幽谷 **yūkoku** (deep) ravine, narrow valley
8 幽居 **yūkyo** live in seclusion
幽明 **yūmei** darkness and light; this world
and the next
幽門 **yūmon** pylorus
9 幽界 **yūkai** realm of the dead
10 幽冥 **yūmei** semidarkness; realm of the dead
11 幽寂 **yūjaku** quiet, sequestered
幽閉 **yūhei** confinement, imprisonment
12 幽閑 **yūkan** quiet, leisurely
14 幽境 **yūkyō** secluded place
15 幽霊 **yūrei** ghost
幽霊屋敷 **yūrei yashiki** haunted house
幽霊船 **yūreisen** phantom ship
幽霊話 **yūreibanashi** ghost story
17 幽邃 **yūsui** secluded and quiet
29 幽鬱 **yūutsu** melancholy, depression

———————— 2 ————————

11 船幽霊 **funayūrei** a sea spirit

———————— 7 ————————

3o7.1

崋
KA (proper name)

———————— 1 ————————

3 崋山 **Kazan** (name of a mountain in China)

3o7.2

峨 峩
GA high/steep mountain

———————— 1 ————————

3 峨々 **gaga(taru)** rugged, craggy
———————— 2 ————————
13 嵯峨 **Saga** (emperor, 809–823)

3o7.3

峺
KŌ block, obstruct

→ 6

峽 → 峡 3o6.1

3o7.4

峻 SHUN high, steep; severe, strict

――――― 1 ―――――
3 峻下剤 **shungezai** powerful laxative
7 峻別 **shunbetsu** sharp distinction
10 峻峰 **shunpō** steep peak
   峻烈 **shunretsu** severe, scathing, sharp
17 峻厳 **shungen** strict, stern, harsh

――――― 2 ―――――
9 急峻 **kyūshun** steep
10 険峻 **kenshun** steep
11 崇峻 **Sushun** (emperor, 587–592)

3o7.5

峭 SHŌ steep

3o7.6 / 1350

峰 峯 HŌ, mine peak, summit; back (of a sword)

――――― 1 ―――――
5 峰打 **mineu(chi)** strike (someone) with the back of one's sword

――――― 2 ―――――
9 連峰 **renpō** series of peaks, mountain range
10 高峰 **kōhō** lofty peak
   峻峰 **shunpō** steep peak
13 群峰 **gunpō** many peaks
15 霊峰 **reihō** sacred mountain

3o7.7

峪 YOKU valley, ravine

峨 → 峨 3o7.2

峯 → 峰 3o7.6

蚩 → 6d4.9

3o7.8

豈 GAI, KI, ani (exclamation of surprise)

3o7.9 / 286

島 嶋 嶌 TŌ, shima island

――――― 1 ―――――
2 島人 **tōjin** islander
3 島々 **shimajima** (many) islands
5 島民 **tōmin** islanders
  島巡 **shimamegu(ri)** tour of the island(s)
6 島守 **shimamori** island guard/caretaker
8 島育 **shimasoda(chi)** island-bred
  島国 **shimaguni** island country
  島国根性 **shimaguni konjō** insularity
10 島流 **shimanaga(shi)** exile, banishment
   島根県 **Shimane-ken** (prefecture)
   島破 **shimayabu(ri)** escaping from an island exile
16 島嶼 **tōsho** islands

――――― 2 ―――――
3 大島 **Ōshima** (frequent name for an island)
  千島列島 **Chishima-rettō** the Kurile Islands
  小島 **kojima** small island, islet
4 中島 **nakajima** island in a river or lake
5 半島 **hantō** peninsula
  本島 **hontō** main island; this island
  広島 **Hiroshima** (city, Hiroshima-ken)
  広島県 **Hiroshima-ken** (prefecture)
6 全島 **zentō** the whole island, all the islands
  列島 **rettō** archipelago
8 孤島 **kotō** solitary/desert island
  宝島 **takarajima** treasure island
9 浮島 **u(ki)shima** floating island
10 高島田 **takashimada** (a traditional hairdo)
   島島 **shimajima** (many) islands
   鬼島 **Oni(ga)shima** the island of ogres
11 鹿島立 **kashimada(chi)** set out on a journey
12 遠島 **entō, tōjima** distant island
   絶島 **zettō** isolated/desert island
13 群島 **guntō** group of islands, archipelago
   福島 **Fukushima** (city, Fukushima-ken)
   福島県 **Fukushima-ken** (prefecture)
14 徳島 **Tokushima** (city, Tokushima-ken)
   徳島県 **Tokushima-ken** (prefecture)
15 敷島 **Shikishima** (ancient) Japan
   敷島道 **Shikishima (no) michi** Japanese poetry
   諸島 **shotō** islands
18 離島 **ritō, hana(re)jima** outlying island

――――― 3 ―――――
2 八丈島 **Hachijōjima** (island, Tōkyō-to)

3 女護島 **nyogo(ga)shima** isle of women
小豆島 **Shōdoshima** (island, Kagawa-ken)
7 佐渡島 **Sado(ga)shima** (island, Niigata-ken)
択捉島 **Etorofu-tō** (island, Russian Hokkaidō)
8 国後島 **Kunashiri-tō** (island, Russian Hokkaidō)
9 珊瑚島 **sangotō** coral island
秋津島 **Akitsushima** (ancient) Japan, Yamato
11 淡路島 **Awajishima** (island, Hyōgo-ken)
鹿児島 **Kagoshima** (city, Kagoshima-ken)
鹿児島県 **Kagoshima-ken** (prefectue)
12 無人島 **mujintō** uninhabited island
14 種子島 **tane(ga)shima** matchlock gun, harquebus **Tanegashima** (island, Kagoshima-ken)

――――――― 4 ―――――――
3 千島列島 **Chishima-rettō** the Kurile Islands
6 伊豆半島 **Izu-hantō** Izu Peninsula (Shizuoka-ken)
8 奄美大島 **Amami Ōshima** (island, Kagoshima-ken)
9 南洋諸島 **Nan'yō-shotō** the South Sea Islands
10 能登半島 **Noto-hantō** (peninsula, Ishikawa-ken)
13 隠岐諸島 **Oki shotō** (group of islands, Shimane-ken)

――――――― 5 ―――――――
3 小笠原諸島 **Ogasawara-shotō** the Bonin Islands

窅 → **0a10.6**

――――――― 8 ―――――――
3o8.1

崚

RYŌ towering in a row

3o8.2

峭

SŌ high, steep

3o8.3 / 1362

崎 嵜

saki, misaki cape, promontory, headland, point (of land)

――――――― 2 ―――――――
3 川崎 **Kawasaki** (city, Kanagawa-ken)
5 尼崎 **Amagasaki** (city, Hyōgo-ken)
8 長崎 **Nagasaki** (city, Nagasaki-ken)
長崎県 **Nagasaki-ken** (prefecture)

岡崎 **Okazaki** (city, Aichi-ken)
10 高崎 **Takasaki** (city, Gunma-ken)
宮崎 **Miyazaki** (city, Miyazaki-ken)
宮崎県 **Miyazaki-ken** (prefecture)

崙 → 崘 **3o8.10**

3o8.4

崛

KUTSU rising high, towering above

――――――― 1 ―――――――
10 崛起 **kukki** rise, be towering

崕 → 崖 **3o8.11**

3o8.5

崟

GIN peak, mountaintop; steep, lofty

3o8.6

崔

SAI high (mountain)

3o8.7 / 1122

崩 崩

HŌ, kuzu(reru) crumble, fall to pieces, collapse
kuzu(su) demolish; change, break (a large bill); simplify
kuzu(shi) simplified form (of a kanji)

――――――― 1 ―――――――
0 崩じる/ずる **hō(jiru/zuru)** die
10 崩書 **kuzu(shi)ga(ki)** "grass-hand" calligraphy
12 崩御 **hōgyo** death of the emperor
15 崩潰 **hōkai** collapse, disintegration
16 崩壊 **hōkai** collapse, disintegration

――――――― 2 ―――――――
3 山崩 **yamakuzu(re)** landslide
4 切崩 **ki(ri)kuzu(su)** level (a hill), cut through (a mountain); break (a strike), split (the opposition)
8 泣崩 **na(ki)kuzu(reru)** break down and cry
突崩 **tsu(ki)kuzu(su)** knock down, raze, level
取崩 **to(ri)kuzu(su)** tear down, demolish; draw down (savings)
9 持崩 **mo(chi)kuzu(su)** ruin (oneself)
11 済崩 **na(shi)kuzu(shi)** (payment) by installments

掘崩 **ho(ri)kuzu(su)** demolish
崖崩 **gakekuzu(re)** landslide
12 着崩 **kikuzu(re)** worn out of shape
14 総崩 **sōkuzu(re)** general rout, collapse

——— 3 ———
3 土砂崩 **doshakuzu(re)** landslide, washout

3o8.8
崑
KON (place name)

——— 1 ———
11 崑崙山脈 **Konron-sanmyaku** the Kunlun mountains

3o8.9 / 1424
崇
SŪ respect, revere; lofty, sublime
aga(meru) respect, revere

——— 1 ———
6 崇光 **Sūkō** (emperor, 1349–1351)
8 崇拝 **sūhai** worship, adoration
崇拝者 **sūhaisha** worshiper
9 崇神 **Sujin** (emperor, 97–30 B.C.)
10 崇高 **sūkō** lofty, sublime, noble
崇峻 **Sushun** (emperor, 587–592)
12 崇敬 **sūkei** veneration, reverence
14 崇徳 **Sutoku** (emperor, 1123–1141)

——— 2 ———
12 尊崇 **sonsū** reverence, veneration

——— 3 ———
8 呪物崇拝 **jubutsu sūhai** fetishism
11 偶像崇拝 **gūzō sūhai** idol worship, idolatry

3o8.10
崙 崘
RON (place name)

3o8.11
崖 崕
GAI, gake cliff

——— 1 ———
11 崖崩 **gakekuzu(re)** landslide

——— 2 ———
11 断崖 **dangai** cliff, precipice
20 懸崖 **kengai** overhanging (a) cliff, precipice

3o8.12
崗
KŌ hill

——— 2 ———
7 花崗岩 **kakōgan** granite

——— 9 ———
3o9.1
嵎
GŪ mountain recesses

3o9.2
嵌 筬
KAN, ha(meru) inlay, set in, fit into, put on (gloves/ring); throw into; take in, cheat
ha(maru) fit/go/fall into; be deceived

——— 1 ———
4 嵌込 **ha(me)ko(mu)** fit into, insert, inlay
嵌木細工 **ha(me)kizaiku** inlaid woodwork
6 嵌合 **kangō, hamea(i)** fit into, engage
7 嵌役 **hama(ri)yaku** well-suited role
10 嵌殺 **ha(me)goro(shi)** fixed fitting
嵌殺窓 **ha(me)goro(shi) mado** fixed-sash window

——— 2 ———
6 当嵌 **a(te)ha(meru)** apply to, adapt
12 象嵌 **zōgan** inlay, damascene
25 鑲嵌 **jōkan** dental inlay

——— 3 ———
8 金象嵌 **kinzōgan** inlaying with gold

嵜 → 崎 3o8.3

3o9.3
嵋
BI (place name)

3o9.4
嵐
RAN, arashi storm, tempest

——— 2 ———
3 大嵐 **ōarashi** big storm
山嵐 **yamaarashi** mountain storm
8 夜嵐 **yoarashi** night storm
青嵐 **aoarashi, seiran** wind blowing through verdure
11 雪嵐 **yukiarashi** snowstorm

——— 3 ———
4 五十嵐 **Igarashi** (surname)
14 磁気嵐 **jikiarashi** magnetic storm

品→ **3d9.20**

嶌→島 **3o7.9**

────── 10 ──────

3o10.1

嶋

tao, tawa mountain pass

3o10.2

嵯　嵳

SA steep, rugged, craggy

────── 1 ──────

10 嵯峨 **Saga** (emperor, 809–823)

3o10.3

嵬

KAI high and flat; rock mountain topped with soil

嵳→嵯 **3o10.2**

3o10.4

嵩

SŪ, kasa bulk, volume, size, quantity
kasa(mu) grow bulky, increase in volume; mount up

────── 1 ──────

10 嵩高 **kasadaka** bulky, voluminous; high-handed
11 嵩張 **kasaba(ru)** be bulky/unwieldly

────── 2 ──────

4 水嵩 **mizukasa** volume of water
6 年嵩 **toshikasa** senior, older

────── 11 ──────

嶋→島 **3o7.9**

3o11.1

嶂

SHŌ steep, lofty

3o11.2

嶇

KU steep; danger, apprehension

3o11.3

嶄

ZAN, SAN high, steep, towering above

3o11.4

嶐

RYŪ shape of a mountain

────── 12 ──────

3o12.1

嶝

TŌ hill; uphill path

3o12.2

嶢

GYŌ high, towering

皺→ **2h13.1**

────── 13 ──────

3o13.1

嶼

SHO (small) island

────── 2 ──────

10 島嶼 **tōsho** islands

3o13.2

嶮

KEN, kewa(shii) steep

3o13.3

嶬

GI high, steep

────── 14 ──────

3o14.1

嶷

GYOKU towering above; clever, bright
GI (place name)

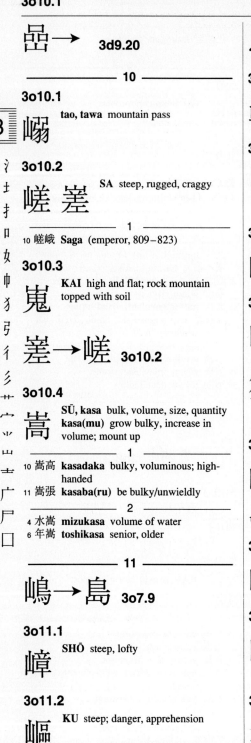
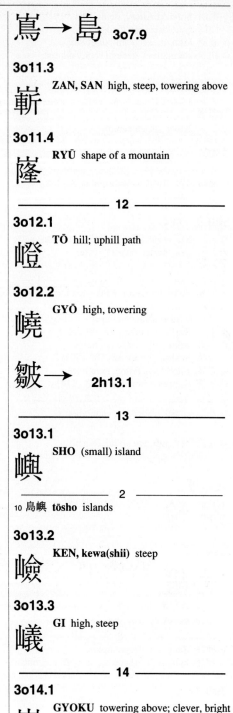

3o14.2

嶺

REI, mine, ne peak, summit

— 2 —
10 高嶺 **takane** lofty peak
高嶺花 **takane (no) hana** flower on an
inaccessible height; the unattainable

— 3 —
4 分水嶺 **bunsuirei** watershed, (continental)
divide

嶽 → 岳 **3o5.12**

豐 → 豊 **3d10.15**

— 17 —

3o17.1

巇

KI, GI steep

3o17.2

巖 巖

GAN rock, crag
iwao (massive) rock

— 1 —
13 巖窟 **gankutsu** cave, cavern
16 巖頭 **gantō** top of a rock

— 18 —

3o18.1

巉

ZAN rising precipitously/steeply

3o18.2

巍

GI high, large (mountain)

— 1 —
3 巍々 **gigi** lofty, towering
12 巍然 **gizen** lofty, towering

— 19 —

3o19.1

巒

RAN round peak; small mountains

— 20 —

3o20.1

巓

TEN summit

— 1 —
5 巓末 **tenmatsu** details, full particulars
— 2 —
3 山巓 **santen** summit

巖 → 巖 **3o17.2**

3p

士	壬	吉	壯	壮	志	壱	売	声	缶	表	夆	奘
0.1	1.1	3.1	2b4.2	2b4.2	4.1	4.2	4.3	4.4	2k4.6	0a8.6	3p7.1	7.1

壺	殻	喜	壷	壹	尌	殼	壼	聖	鼓	嘉	壽	皷
3p9.2	8.1	9.1	9.2	3p4.2	9.3	3p8.1	10.1	4f9.9	10.2	11.1	0a7.15	3p10.2

賣	殯	藝	蠱
3p4.3	13.1	15.1	19.1

— 0 —

3p0.1 / 572

士

SHI samurai; man; scholar

— 1 —
3 士女 **shijo** men and women
6 士気 **shiki** morale

7 士君子 **shikunshi** man of learning and
virtue, gentleman
8 士卒 **shisotsu** a private, soldier
士官 **shikan** (military) officer
11 士道 **shidō** samurai code, chivalry
士族 **shizoku** descendants of samurai
13 士農工商 **shinōkōshō** samurai-farmers-
artisans-merchants, the military, agricultural, industrial, and mercantile classes

14 士魂商才 **shikon-shōsai** samurai in spirit and merchant in business acumen

──────── 2 ────────

2 力士 **rikishi** sumo wrestler
3 下士 **kashi** noncommissioned officer
下士官 **kashikan** noncommissioned officer
4 文士 **bunshi** literary man
5 弁士 **benshi** speaker, orator; movie "explainer"
6 多士済々 **tashi-seisei** many able people
壮士 **sōshi** swashbuckler; ruffian
同士 **dōshi** fellow, companion
同士打 **dōshiu(chi)** fight among themselves
同士討 **dōshiu(chi)** internecine strife
名士 **meishi** prominent figure, celebrity
7 兵士 **heishi** soldier
学士 **gakushi** Bachelor of Arts, university graduate
学士院 **gakushiin** academy
8 居士 **koji** Buddhist layman
国士 **kokushi** distinguished citizen, patriot
武士 **bushi, mononofu** samurai, warrior
武士道 **bushidō** bushido, the samurai code of chivalry
9 信士 **shinshi** (title affixed to man's posthumous Buddhist name)
勇士 **yūshi** brave warrior
10 修士 **shūshi** master's degree, M.A., M.S.
准士官 **junshikan** warrant officer
将士 **shōshi** officers and men
郷士 **gōshi** country samurai
剣士 **kenshi** swordsman, fencer
高士 **kōshi** man of noble character
従士 **jūshi** attendant, retainer
烈士 **resshi** patriot, hero
11 道士 **dōshi** a Taoist
紳士 **shinshi** gentleman
紳士用 **shinshiyō** men's, for men
紳士協定 **shinshi kyōtei** gentleman's agreement
紳士服 **shinshifuku** men's clothing
紳士的 **shinshiteki** gentlemanly
紳士道 **shinshidō** the code of a gentleman
紳士録 **shinshiroku** a who's-who, directory
12 博士 **hakase, hakushi** Ph.D.
博士号 **hakasegō** doctor's degree, Ph.D.
富士川 **Fuji-kawa** (river, Shizuoka-ken)
富士山 **Fuji-san** Mt. Fuji
富士絹 **fujiginu** fuji silk
富士額 **fujibitai** hairline resembling the outline of Mt. Fuji
棋士 **kishi** (professional) go/shogi player
策士 **sakushi** tactician, schemer
13 隠士 **inshi** hermit, recluse
義士 **gishi** loyal retainer; righteous person; martyr

廉士 **renshi** pure uncovetous person
楽士 **gakushi** bandsman, musician
戦士 **senshi** warrior, soldier
14 豪士 **gōshi** samurai-farmer
選士 **senshi** selected person
銃士 **jūshi** musketeer
18 藩士 **hanshi** clansman, retainer
闘士 **tōshi** fighter for
闘士型 **tōshigata** the athletic type
騎士 **kishi** rider, horseman
騎士道 **kishidō** knighthood, chivalry

──────── 3 ────────

3 工学士 **kōgakushi** Bachelor of Engineering
4 文学士 **bungakushi** Bachelor of Arts
5 弁理士 **benrishi** patent attorney
弁護士 **bengoshi** lawyer, attorney
弁護士会 **bengoshikai** bar association
代議士 **daigishi** member of parliament/congress/diet
6 会計士 **kaikeishi** accountant
7 技術士 **gijutsushi** engineer, technician
8 非紳士的 **hishinshiteki** ungentlemanly
逆富士 **saka(sa) Fuji** inverted reflection of Mt. Fuji
法学士 **hōgakushi** LL.B., Bachelor of Laws
具眼士 **gugan(no)shi** man of discernment
9 飛行士 **hikōshi** aviator
神学士 **shingakushi** Doctor of Divinity
計理士 **keirishi** public accountant
10 修道士 **shūdōshi** monk, friar
都人士 **tojinshi** people of the capital
消防士 **shōbōshi** fireman
航空士 **kōkūshi** aviator
11 野武士 **nobushi** wandering samurai, free lance
運転士 **untenshi** (ship's) mate, officer
得業士 **tokugyōshi** special-school graduate
経理士 **keirishi** public accountant
12 測量士 **sokuryōshi** surveyor
税理士 **zeirishi** tax accountant
13 農学士 **nōgakushi** agricultural expert, agronomist
節博士 **fushi hakase** chanting intonation marks
15 敵同士 **katakidōshi** mutual enemies
16 操縦士 **sōjūshi** pilot
薬学士 **yakugakushi** Bachelor of Pharmacology
機関士 **kikanshi** (locomotive) engineer
18 闘牛士 **tōgyūshi** matador, bullfighter

──────── 4 ────────

3 三文文士 **sanmon bunshi** hack writer
12 無名戦士 **mumei senshi** unknown soldier

──────── 5 ────────

6 宇宙飛行士 **uchū hikōshi** astronaut

———— 1 ————

3p1.1

壬 **JIN, NIN** ninth in a series, "I" **mizunoe** ninth calendar sign

———— 3 ————

3p3.1 / 1141

吉 吉 **KICHI, KITSU, yoshi** good luck

———— 1 ————

4 吉凶 **kikkyō** (good or ill) fortune
吉日 **kichinichi, kichijitsu** lucky day
6 吉兆 **kitchō** good/lucky omen
8 吉事 **kichiji, kitsuji** auspicious event
吉例 **kichirei, kitsurei** (annual festive) custom
9 吉相 **kissō** good/lucky omen
10 吉原 **Yoshiwara** (proper name); (a former red-light district in Tōkyō)
吉祥 **kisshō** good/lucky omen
吉祥天 **Kichijōten** Sri-mahadevi, goddess of fortune
11 吉野 **Yoshino** (proper name); common cherry tree; (a type of thin high-quality paper)
12 吉報 **kippō** good news, glad tidings
14 吉徴 **kitchō** good/lucky omen
15 吉慶 **kikkei** congratulatory event, rejoicing

———— 2 ————

3 大吉 **daikichi** splendid luck
4 不吉 **fukitsu** inauspicious, unlucky
8 英吉利 **Igirisu** England
14 嘉吉 **Kakitsu** (era, 1441–1444)

———— 3 ————

11 黄道吉日 **kōdō kichinichi, ōdō kichinichi** lucky day

———— 4 ————

5 石部金吉 **Ishibe Kinkichi** man of strict morals

壮 → **2b4.2**

———— 4 ————

壯 → 壮 **2b4.2**

3p4.1 / 573

志 **SHI** will, intention; record; shilling **kokoroza(su)** intend, aim at, have in mind **kokorozashi** will, intention, aim

———— 1 ————

6 志気 **shiki** will, enthusiasm
志向 **shikō** intention, inclination
11 志望 **shibō** desire, ambition, choice
志望者 **shibōsha** aspirant
16 志操 **shisō** one's principles, integrity
19 志願者 **shigansha** applicant, candidate, volunteer, aspirant
志願書 **shigansho** (written) application

———— 2 ————

3 寸志 **sunshi** a little token (of one's appreciation)
大志 **taishi** ambition, aspiration
5 立志 **risshi** setting one's life goal
立志伝 **risshiden** success story
6 壮志 **sōshi** ambition
同志 **dōshi** (persons) of like sentiment
同志会 **dōshikai** association of like-minded people
夙志 **shukushi** long-cherished desire
有志 **yūshi** interest in; volunteer
有志者 **yūshisha** supporter, volunteer
7 決志 **kesshi** resolve
芳志 **hōshi** your good wishes, your kindness
初志 **shoshi** original intention
8 厚志 **kōshi** kindness, good wishes
10 特志家 **tokushika** volunteer, supporter
素志 **soshi** original purpose, longstanding aim
11 宿志 **shukushi** long-cherished desire
12 雄志 **yūshi** lofty ambition
13 意志 **ishi** will, volition
意志力 **ishiryoku** will power
意志的 **ishiteki** strong-willed, forceful
14 遺志 **ishi** dying wish
16 薄志 **hakushi** weakness of will; small token of gratitude
薄志弱行 **hakushi-jakkō** indecisive and unenterprising
篤志 **tokushi** benevolence, charity, zeal
篤志家 **tokushika** benefactor, volunteer
18 闘志 **tōshi** fighting spirit
闘志満々 **tōshi-manman** full of fighting spirit

———— 3 ————

8 青雲志 **seiun (no) kokorozashi** ambition for greatness, lofty aspirations

———— 4 ————

6 自由意志 **jiyū ishi** free will

3p4.2 / 1730

壱 壹 **ICHI, ITSU** one (in documents)

———— 1 ————

7 壱岐 **Iki** (island and ancient kuni, Nagasaki-ken)

3

氵
土
扌
口
女
巾
犭
弓
彳
彡
艹
宀
丷
山
吉 4 ←
广
尸
口

売 賣

BAI, u(ru) sell
u(reru) sell, be in demand

――――――― 1 ―――――――

2 売子 **u(rek)ko** popular person
　　u(ri)ko salesclerk
3 売上 **u(ri)a(ge)** sales
　売上高 **uria(ge)daka** amount sold, sales
　売口 **u(re)kuchi** a market/demand for
4 売切 **u(ri)ki(re)** sold out
　売文 **baibun** hack writing
　売文業 **baibungyō** hack writing
　売止 **u(ri)do(me)** suspension of sales
　売込 **u(ri)ko(mu)** sell (aggressively), push
　売手 **u(ri)te** seller
　売方 **u(ri)kata** salesmanship; seller
5 売出 **u(ri)da(shi)** sale
　売代 **u(ri)shiro** sales
　売付 **u(ri)tsu(keru)** sell to; foist, palm off
　売払 **u(ri)hara(u)** sell off, dispose of
　売叩 **u(ri)tata(ku)** drive down the price, undersell
　売広 **u(ri)hiro(meru)** extend sales of, find a market for
　売主 **u(ri)nushi** seller, vendor
　売立 **u(ri)ta(te)** selling off, auction
6 売先 **u(ri)saki** market, outlet, demand, buyers
　売名 **baimei** self-advertising, publicity seeking
　売行 **u(re)yu(ki)** sale, demand for
　売尽 **u(ri)tsuku(su)** sell off, clear out
　売血 **baiketsu** selling one's blood
7 売却 **baikyaku** sell off, dispose of
　売戻 **u(ri)modo(shi)** resale
　売初 **u(ri)zo(me)** placing on sale for the first time; first New Year's sale
　売言葉買言葉 **u(ri)kotoba (ni) ka(i)kotoba** (an exchange of) fighting words
　売足 **u(re)ashi** selling, a sale
8 売価 **baika** selling price
　売歩 **u(ri)aru(ku)** peddle
　売店 **baiten** (news)stand, kiosk
　売国 **baikoku** betrayal of one's country
　売国奴 **baikokudo** traitor
　売物 **u(ri)mono** (article) for sale, offerings
9 売飛 **u(ri)to(basu)** sell off
　売急 **u(ri)iso(gu)** be eager to sell, sell in haste
　売品 **baihin** article for sale
　売春 **baishun** prostitution
　売春婦 **baishunfu** prostitute
　売約 **baiyaku** sales contract
　売食 **u(ri)gu(i)** live by selling one's possessions
10 売残 **u(re)noko(ri)** goods left unsold; unmarried woman

売値 **u(ri)ne** selling price
売高 **u(re)daka** (amount of) sales
売捌 **u(ri)saba(ki)** sale, selling
売家 **u(ri)ya, u(ri)ie** house for sale
11 売過 **u(ri)su(gi)** overselling
　売淫 **baiin** prostitution
　売渋 **u(ri)shibu(ru)** be reluctant/unwilling to sell
　売掛 **u(ri)ka(ke)** credit sales
　売控 **u(ri)hika(eru)** refrain from selling
　売惜 **u(ri)o(shimu)** be indisposed to sell, hold back, restrict sales
12 売渡 **u(ri)wata(su)** sell, transfer, sign over
　　u(ri)wata(shi) sale (and delivery)
　売場 **u(ri)ba** sales counter, place where (tickets) are sold
　売場係 **u(ri)bagakari** sales clerk
　売買 **baibai** buying and selling, trade, sale
16 売薬 **baiyaku** patent medicine, drugs

――――――― 2 ―――――――

3 大売出 **ōu(ri)da(shi)** big sale
　小売 **kou(ri)** retail
　小売店 **kou(ri)ten** retail store/outlet, retailer
　小売商 **kou(ri)shō** retail trade
4 中売 **nakau(ri)** walking around selling snacks and drinks to the audience in a theater or spectators in a stadium; walk-around vendor
　切売 **ki(ri)u(ri)** sell by the piece
　公売 **kōbai** public auction
5 叩売 **tata(ki)u(ri)** sacrifice sale
　立売 **ta(chi)u(ri)** street peddling/peddler
6 多売 **tabai** large sales volume
　先売 **sakiu(ri)** advance sale
　安売 **yasuu(ri)** sell cheap
　虫売 **mushiu(ri)** insect peddler
7 身売 **miu(ri)** selling oneself (into bondage)
　即売 **sokubai** sale on the spot
　即売会 **sokubaikai** exhibition and spot sale
　別売 **betsuuri** sold separately, optional
　投売 **na(ge)u(ri)** sell at a loss/sacrifice
　投売品 **na(ge)u(ri)hin** distress-sale merchandise
　乱売 **ranbai** selling at a loss, dumping
　花売 **hanau(ri)** flower seller
　初売 **hatsuu(ri)** first sale of the new year
8 非売同盟 **hibai dōmei** sellers' strike
　非売品 **hibaihin** article not for sale
　受売 **u(ke)u(ri)** retailing; second-hand (knowledge)
　直売 **chokubai** direct sales
　建売 **ta(te)u(ri)** build (houses) to sell; ready-built (house)
　押売 **o(shi)u(ri)** high-pressure/importunate sellin

呼売 **yo(bi)u(ri)** hawking, peddling
店売 **miseu(ri)** sell in stores
物売 **monou(ri)** peddler
9 発売 **hatsubai** sale
専売 **senbai** monopoly
専売品 **senbaihin** monopoly goods
専売特許 **senbai tokkyo** patent
専売権 **senbaiken** monopoly
卸売 **oroshiu(ri)** wholesale
前売 **maeu(ri)** advance sale
前売券 **maeu(ri)ken** ticket sold in advance
計売 **haka(ri)u(ri)** sell by measure/weight
10 特売 **tokubai** special sale
特売品 **tokubaihin** articles on sale
特売場 **tokubaijō** bargain counter/basement
11 商売 **shōbai** business, trade, transaction;
occupation
商売人 **shōbainin** merchant; professional
商売気 **shōbaigi** business-mindedness, profit
motive
商売気質 **shōbai katagi** mercenary spirit
商売柄 **shōbaigara** in one's line of business
商売道具 **shōbai dōgu** tools of the trade
商売替 **shōbaiga(e)** change one's occupation
商売筋 **shōbaisuji** business connections
商売敵 **shōbaigataki** business competitor
淫売 **inbai** prostitution
淫売婦 **inbaifu** prostitute
淫売宿 **inbaiyado** brothel
掛売 **ka(ke)u(ri)** selling on credit
捨売 **su(te)u(ri)** sacrifice sale
密売 **mitsubai** illicit sale, smuggling,
bootlegging
販売 **hanbai** sales, selling
販売人 **hanbainin** seller, agent
販売元 **hanbaimoto** selling agency
販売店 **hanbaiten** shop, store
販売所 **hanbaisho** shop, store
販売促進 **hanbai sokushin** sales promotion
転売 **tenbai** resale
12 量売 **haka(ri)u(ri)** sell by measure/weight
焼売 **shūmai** (Chinese-style steamed meat-
and-vegetable dumpling)
煮売屋 **niu(ri)ya** eatery, cheap restaurant
貸売 **ka(shi)u(ri)** sale on credit
13 廉売 **renbai** bargain sale
試売 **shibai** trial sale, test marketing
14 駅売 **ekiu(ri)** sold/vendor at a station
15 請売 **u(ke)u(ri)** retailing
20 競売 **kyōbai, se(ri)u(ri)** auction
競売人 **kyōbainin** auctioneer

———————— 3 ————————

2 人身売買 **jinshin baibai** slave trade
3 大安売 **ōyasuu(ri)** big (bargain) sale
4 水商売 **mizu shōbai** trades dependent on
public patronage (bars, restaurants,
entertainment)
8 抱合売 **da(ki)a(wase) u(ri)** selling poorly
selling articles in a tie-up with articles
which sell well
9 客商売 **kyakushōbai** a service/public-
patronage trade
13 新発売 **shinhatsubai** new(ly marketed)
product
新聞売 **shinbun'u(ri)** news dealer

———————— 4 ————————

1 一手販売 **itte hanbai** sole agency
2 人気商売 **ninki shōbai** occupation dependent on public favor
6 自動販売機 **jidō hanbaiki** vending machine
8 委託販売 **itaku hanbai** selling on consign-
ment/commission
9 通信販売 **tsūshin hanbai** mail order
11 訪問販売 **hōmon hanbai** door-to-door sales
16 薄利多売 **hakuri-tabai** large-volume sales at
low profit margin

3p4.4 / 746

声 聲   SEI, SHŌ, koe, kowa- voice

———————— 1 ————————

6 声色 **seishoku** voice and countenance; songs
and women
    kowairo tone of voice; vocal mimicry
声自慢 **koejiman** proud of one's singing voice
8 声価 **seika** reputation, fame, popularity
声明 **seimei** declaration, (public) statement,
proclamation
9 声変 **koega(wari)** change/cracking of voice
声音 **kowane** tone of voice, timbre
    seion vocal sound
10 声高 **kowadaka** (in a) loud voice
声涙 **seirui (tomo ni kudaru)** speak through
one's tears
声帯 **seitai** vocal cords
声帯模写 **seitai mosha** vocal mimicry
11 声掛 **(o)koega(kari)** (influential person's)
recommendation
12 声援 **seien** (shouts of) encouragement,
cheering
声量 **seiryō** volume of one's voice
13 声楽 **seigaku** vocal music, (study) voice
声楽家 **seigakuka** vocalist
15 声調 **seichō** tone of voice
17 声優 **seiyū** radio actor/actress, dubber

———————— 2 ————————

1 一声 **issei, hitokoe** a voice/cry
2 人声 **hitogoe** voice
3 大声 **ōgoe** loud voice
    taisei loud voice; sonorous voice

3

氵
土
扌
口
女
巾
犭
弓
彳
彡
艹
宀
丷
山
士 4←
广
尸
口

女声 **josei** female voice
小声 **kogoe** low voice, whisper, murmur
5 四声 **shisei** the four tones (of Chinese)
6 肉声 **nikusei** natural voice (not via microphone)
地声 **jigoe** one's natural voice
叫声 **sake(bi)goe** a shout, cry, scream
吼声 **ho(e)goe** bark, yelp, howl, roar
名声 **meisei** fame, reputation
尖声 **toga(ri)goe** shrill voice
有声 **yūsei** voiced (sound)
有声音化 **yūseionka** vocalization, voicing
7 作声 **tsuku(ri)goe** disguised voice
低声 **teisei** low voice, whisper
含声 **fuku(mi)goe** muffled voice
吠声 **ho(e)goe** bark, yelp, howl, roar
形声 **keisei** type of kanji in which one part suggests the meaning and one the pronunciation (e.g., 河)
忍声 **shino(bi)goe** in a whisper
男声 **dansei** male voice
8 泣声 **na(ki)goe** crying, tearful voice, sob
拡声器 **kakuseiki** loudspeaker
拡声機 **kakuseiki** loudspeaker
呼声 **yo(bi)goe** a call, cry, shout
奇声 **kisei** queer/peculiar voice
弦声 **gensei** sound of the strings
和声 **wasei** harmony (in music)
雨声 **usei** the sound of rain
9 発声 **hassei** utterance, speaking
発声法 **hasseihō** vocalization, enunciation
発声器 **hasseiki** vocal organs
変声期 **henseiki** age of puberty/voice-cracking
美声 **bisei** beautiful voice
連声 **renjō** (form of liaison illustrated by *an + on* pronounced *annon*)
怒声 **dosei** angry/excited voice
音声 **onsei, onjō** voice, audio
音声学 **onseigaku** phonetics
秋声 **shūsei** (sound of) the autumn wind
10 高声 **kōsei** loud voice
涙声 **namidagoe** tearful voice
砲声 **hōsei** sound of firing/shelling
笑声 **wara(i)goe, shōsei** laughter
11 混声 **konsei** mixed voices
混声合唱 **konsei gasshō** mixed chorus
掛声 **ka(ke)goe** shout (of encouragement)
悪声 **akusei** bad voice/reputation
産声 **ubugoe** newborn baby's first cry
笛声 **tekisei** sound of a flute/whistle
訛声 **damigoe** thick voice
12 蛮声 **bansei** raucous voice
湿声 **shime(ri)goe** tearful voice

喚声 **kansei, wame(ki)goe** shout, yell, scream, outcry
無声 **musei** silent, noiseless, voiceless
無声映画 **musei eiga** silent movie
無声音 **museion** unvoiced sound
13 裏声 **uragoe** falsetto
嗄声 **shaga(re)goe** hoarse voice
嘆声 **tansei** sigh; lamentation
話声 **hana(shi)goe** a voice
14 鳴声 **na(ki)goe** cry, call, chirping (of animals)
歌声 **utagoe** singing voice
歓声 **tansei** sigh (of lament/admiration)
鼻声 **hanagoe, bisei** nasal voice
銃声 **jūsei** sound of a gunshot
鬨声 **toki (no) koe** battle/war cry
15 嬌声 **kyōsei** lovely voice
歓声 **kansei** shout of joy, cheer
罵声 **basei** jeers, boos, hisses
震声 **furu(e)goe** tremulous/quavering voice
16 激声 **gekisei** excited/agitated voice
濁声 **damigoe, nigo(ri)goe** thick/hoarse voice
17 擬声 **gisei** onomatopoeia
擬声語 **giseigo** onomatopoetic word
20 鐘声 **shōsei** sound/ringing of a bell

———— 3 ————

3 大音声 **daionjō** loud/stentorian voice
8 金切声 **kanaki(ri)goe** shrill voice, shriek
9 風邪声 **kazagoe** hoarseness from a cold
10 胴間声 **dōmagoe** thick/dissonant voice
11 猫撫声 **nekona(de)goe** coaxing voice
21 鶴一声 **tsuru (no) hitokoe** the voice of authority

缶→ **2k4.6**

———— 6 ————

表→ **0a8.6**

———— 7 ————

羘→奘 **3p7.1**

3p7.1

奘 羘   **JŌ, SŌ, ZŌ** large, great

———— 8 ————

壷→壺 **3p9.2**

3p8.1 / 1728

殻 殻
KAKU, kara husk, hull, shell

————————— 1 —————————
9 殻竿 **karazao** a flail

————————— 2 —————————
4 双殻類 **sōkakurui** bivalves
5 出殻 **da(shi)gara** used tea leaves, (coffee) grounds
甲殻 **kōkaku** shell, carapace
甲殻類 **kōkakurui** crustaceans
外殻 **gaikaku** shell, crust
6 灰殻 **haigara** ashes
地殻 **chikaku** the earth's crust
吸殻 **su(i)gara** cigar(ette) butt
耳殻 **jikaku** auricle, external ear
7 卵殻 **rankaku** eggshell
抜殻 **nu(ke)gara** cast-off skin (of a cicada/snake)
貝殻 **kaigara** (sea) shell
貝殻虫 **kaigaramushi** scale (insect/louse)
貝殻追放 **kaigara tsuihō** ostracism
貝殻骨 **kaigarabone** the shoulder blade
8 空殻 **a(ki)gara** empty shell/container
9 茶殻 **chagara** tea grounds
枳殻 **karatachi** trifoliate orange tree
紅殻 **benigara** red-ocher rouge
籾殻 **momigara** rice hulls, chaff
16 燃殻 **mo(e)gara** cinders, embers

————————— 3 —————————
5 石炭殻 **sekitangara** (coal) cinders
15 蕎麦殻 **sobagara** buckwheat chaff

————————— 9 —————————

3p9.1 / 1143

喜 㐂
KI, yoroko(bu) be glad, rejoice
yoroko(bashii) joyful, glad

————————— 1 —————————
6 喜色 **kishoku** joyful look, all smiles
7 喜寿 **kiju** one's 77th birthday
8 喜事 **yoroko(bi)goto** happy event
9 喜勇 **yoroko(bi)isa(mu)** be in high spirits
喜怒 **kido** joy and anger
喜怒哀楽 **kidoairaku** joy-anger-sorrow-pleasure, emotions
10 喜悦 **kietsu** joy, delight
11 喜捨 **kisha** charity, donation
14 喜歌劇 **kikageki** comic opera
15 喜劇 **kigeki** a comedy
喜憂 **kiyū** joy and sorrow

————————— 2 —————————
1 一喜一憂 **ikki ichiyū** alternation of joy and sorrow, hope and fear
3 大喜 **ōyoroko(bi)** great joy
4 天喜 **Tengi** (era, 1053–1058)
7 延喜 **Engi** (era, 901–923)
狂喜 **kyōki** wild joy, rapture of delight
8 空喜 **karayoroko(bi)** premature/unjustified rejoicing
欣喜 **kinki** joy, delight
欣喜雀踊 **kinki-jakuyaku** jump for joy
12 悲喜 **hiki** joy and sorrow
悲喜劇 **hikigeki** tragicomedy
13 寛喜 **Kangi** (era, 1229–1231)
15 歓喜 **kanki** joy, delight
17 糠喜 **nukayoroko(bi)** premature rejoicing
22 驚喜 **kyōki** pleasant surprise

3p9.2

壺 壷
KO, tsubo jar, pot; spot for applying moxa; one's aim

————————— 1 —————————
12 壺焼 **tsuboya(ki)** shellfish cooked in its shell

————————— 2 —————————
7 肘壺 **hijitsubo** eye (of a hook-and-eye fastener)
8 油壺 **aburatsubo** oil can, oiler
金壺眼 **kanatsubo manako** large sunken eyes (showing anxiety/mistrust)
9 茶壺 **chatsubo** tea jar/canister
10 酒壺 **sakatsubo** saké jar
消壺 **ke(shi)tsubo** charcoal-extinguishing jar
骨壺 **kotsutsubo** mortuary urn
13 滝壺 **takitsubo** pool/basin below a waterfall
痰壺 **tantsubo** spittoon, cuspidor
蛸壺 **takotsubo** octopus trap; foxhole
14 墨壺 **sumitsubo** inkpot; carpenter's inking device

————————— 3 —————————
4 火消壺 **hike(shi)tsubo** charcoal extinguisher

壹 → 壱 3p4.2

3p9.3

尌
JU set up

殻 → 殻 3p8.1

─────── 10 ───────

3p10.1

壺

KON courtyard path; lady

─────── 1 ───────

10 壺訓 **konkun** training in ladylike manners

聖 → 聖 **4f9.9**

3p10.2 / 1147

鼓 皷

KO, tsuzumi hand drum

─────── 1 ───────

0 鼓す/する **ko(su/suru)** beat; rouse, muster (courage)
4 鼓手 **koshu** drummer
7 鼓吹 **kosui** inspire, instill
  鼓吹者 **kosuisha** advocate, propagator
9 鼓室 **koshitsu** the atrium (of the ear)
11 鼓動 **kodō** (heart) beat
  鼓笛隊 **kotekitai** drum-and-bugle corps, fife-and-drum band
13 鼓腸 **kochō** flatulence, bloating
14 鼓膜 **komaku** the eardrum
15 鼓舞 **kobu** encouragement, inspiration

─────── 2 ───────

4 太鼓 **taiko** drum
  太鼓判 **taikoban** large seal
  太鼓持 **taikomo(chi)** professional jester; flatterer
  太鼓腹 **taikobara** paunch, potbelly
6 舌鼓打 **shitatsuzumi (o) u(tsu)** smack one's lips
9 勇鼓 **yū (o) ko(su)** muster one's courage
13 腹鼓 **haratsuzumi** drumming on one's belly; eating one's fill
  鉦鼓 **shōko** bells and drums
14 旗鼓 **kiko** colors and drums; army

─────── 3 ───────

3 大太鼓 **ōdaiko** large drum, bass drum
9 陣太鼓 **jindaiko** war drum
13 触太鼓 **fu(re)daiko** drum beating (to herald the start of sumo wrestling)

─────── 11 ───────

3p11.1

嘉

KA good, happy, auspicious
yomi(suru) praise, applaud

─────── 1 ───────

4 嘉元 **Kagen** (era, 1303–1306)
  嘉日 **kajitsu** auspicious day
5 嘉永 **Kaei** (era, 1848–1854)
6 嘉吉 **Kakitsu** (era, 1441–1444)
7 嘉承 **Kajō** (era, 1106–1108)
  嘉応 **Kaō** (era, 1169–1171)
9 嘉保 **Kahō** (era, 1094–1096)
10 嘉祥 **kashō** good omen
  Kashō (era, 848–851)
  嘉納 **kanō** approve, appreciate; accept with pleasure
12 嘉禄 **Karoku** (era, 1225–1227)
13 嘉禎 **Katei** (era, 1235–1238)
14 嘉暦 **Karyaku** (era, 1326–1329)

─────── 2 ───────

5 正嘉 **Shōka** (era, 1257–1259)

壽 → 寿 **0a7.15**

皷 → 鼓 **3p10.2**

─────── 12 ───────

賣 → 売 **3p4.3**

─────── 13 ───────

3p13.1

殪

EI die; bury

─────── 15 ───────

3p15.1

鼕

TŌ drum-beating

─────── 19 ───────

3p19.1

蠹 蠧

TO worm-eaten; damage

─────── 1 ───────

8 蠹毒 **todoku** worm damage, being eaten away from within
11 蠹魚 **togyo, shimi** clothes moth, bookworm

广 3q

广	広	庁	疒	疒	庄	床	応	庇	序	庚	府	底
0.1	2.1	2.2	3q12.6	3q13.3	3.1	4.1	4.2	4.3	4.4	5.1	5.2	5.3

店	庖	庖	度	庠	庭	庫	座	唐	席	康	庸	麻
5.4	3q5.5	5.5	6.1	6.2	6.3	7.1	7.2	7.3	7.4	8.1	8.2	8.3

廊	鹿	庵	庶	厠	廓	廊	廂	廃	厨	廉	廈	殷
8.4	8.5	8.6	8.7	2p9.1	9.1	3q8.4	9.2	9.3	2p10.1	10.1	10.2	2p12.2

麾	廖	腐	塵	厨	廠	厮	廟	廐	廡	塵	摩	庵
11.1	11.2	11.3	11.4	2p10.1	12.1	12.2	12.3	2p12.2	12.4	12.5	12.6	12.7

廢	廣	慶	廨	塵	磨	廩	縻	糜	麋	臂	應	夔
3q9.3	3q2.1	12.8	13.1	13.2	13.3	13.4	14.1	14.2	6b11.4	14.3	3q4.2	15.1

磨	糜	蠱	麕	靡	廬	麒	麗	廳	麟	魔	麝	鷹
15.2	6b11.4	8a11.10	16.1	16.2	16.3	16.4	16.5	3q2.2	18.1	18.2	18.3	21.1

廳	麤
3q2.2	30.1

3 氵土扌口女巾犭弓彳彡艹宀丷凵士广尸口

0

3q0.1

広

GEN cave (dwelling); ridgepole

2

3q2.1 / 694

広 廣

KŌ, hiro(i), hiro(yaka) broad, wide, spacious, extensive
hiro(geru) extend, enlarge
hiro(garu) spread, expand
hiro(meru) broaden, propagate
hiro(maru) spread, be propagated

1

3 広大 **kōdai** vast, extensive, huge
広大無辺 **kōdai-muhen** boundless, immeasurable, vast
広口 **hirokuchi** wide-mouthed (bottle)
広小路 **hirokōji** wide/main street
5 広広 **hirobiro** extensive, vast, spacious
6 広壮 **kōsō** grand, magnificent, imposing
広汎 **kōhan** wide(-ranging), extensive
7 広角 **kōkaku** wide-angle (lens)
広告 **kōkoku** advertisement
広告灯 **kōkokutō** advertising lights
広告社 **kōkokusha** advertising agency
広告取 **kōkokuto(ri)** advertising canvasser
広告屋 **kōkokuya** ad agency; publicity man
広告部 **kōkokubu** publicity department
広告料 **kōkokuryō** advertising rates
広告業 **kōkokugyō** advertising business
広告欄 **kōkokuran** advertising columns, want ads
広言 **kōgen** bragging, boastful speech
9 広狭 **kōkyō** width, area
広軌 **kōki** broad-gauge (railway)
10 広原 **kōgen** wide plain, open country
広島 **Hiroshima** (city, Hiroshima-ken)
広島県 **Hiroshima-ken** (prefecture)
11 広野 **kōya** open field/country
広表 **kōbō** area, expanse
広域 **kōiki** wide area
12 広場 **hiroba** plaza, public square
広報 **kōhō** publicity
広報部 **kōhōbu** public relations department
広幅 **hirohaba** double width, broad(cloth)
広葉樹 **kōyōju** broadleaf tree
広量 **kōryō** largehearted, generous
広間 **hiroma** hall; spacious room
13 広義 **kōgi** broad sense
広漠 **kōbaku** vast
15 広縁 **hiroen** broad veranda; eaves
広範 **kōhan** wide(-ranging), extensive
広範囲 **kōhan'i** wide range/scope
17 広闊 **kōkatsu** spacious, extensive, wide

2

3 大広間 **ōhiroma** grand hall
4 手広 **tebiro(i)** extensive; spacious
5 末広 **suehiro** folding fan **suehiro(gari)** spreading/widening out toward the end; prospering as time goes on
広広 **hirobiro** extensive, vast, spacious
7 売広 **u(ri)hiro(meru)** extend sales of, find a market for

3

氵
土
扌
口
女
巾
犭
弓
彳
彡
艹
宀
⺌
⺽
耂
→2 广
尸
口

8 長広舌 **chōkōzetsu** loquacity, long(-winded) talk
押広 **o(shi)hiro(geru)** extend, expand
取広 **to(ri)hiro(geru)** enlarge, expand, spread out
9 背広 **sebiro** business suit
10 徒広 **dada(p)piro(i)** needlessly spacious
12 幅広 **habahiro(i)** broad, extensive
habahiro wide
開広 **a(ke)hiro(geru)** open up/wide
16 嘴広鴨 **hashibirogamo** spoonbill
燃広 **mo(e)hiro(garu)** (flames) spread
19 繰広 **ku(ri)hiro(geru)** unfold

───────── 3 ─────────

3 三行広告欄 **sangyō kōkokuran** classified ads
6 気宇広大 **kiu-kōdai** magnanimous, big-hearted
7 求人広告 **kyūjin kōkoku** help-wanted ad

3q2.2 / 763

庁 廳 廰

CHŌ government office, agency

───────── 1 ─────────

8 庁舎 **chōsha** government-office building

───────── 2 ─────────

4 支庁 **shichō** (government) branch office
公庁 **kōchō** government office
5 市庁 **shichō** municipal office
8 退庁 **taichō** leaving the office
官庁 **kanchō** government office/authorities
官庁用語 **kanchō yōgo** official jargon
府庁 **fuchō** urban-prefectural office
9 院庁 **inchō** retired emperor's office
県庁 **kenchō** prefectural office
政庁 **seichō** government office
10 都庁 **Tochō** Tōkyō Government Office
12 登庁 **tōchō** attendance at office
開庁 **kaichō** opening (of a government office)

───────── 3 ─────────

6 気象庁 **Kishōchō** Meteorological Agency
防衛庁 **Bōeichō** Defense Agency
8 法王庁 **Hōōchō** the Vatican
官公庁 **kankōchō** government and municipal agencies
林野庁 **Rin'yachō** Forestry Agency
10 宮内庁 **Kunaichō** Imperial Household Agency
特許庁 **Tokkyochō** Patent Office
教皇庁 **Kyōkōchō** the Vatican
12 検察庁 **kensatsuchō** public prosecutor's office
17 環境庁 **Kankyōchō** Environment Agency
19 警視庁 **Keishichō** Metropolitan Police Agency

警察庁 **Keisatsuchō** National Police Agency

───────── 3 ─────────

3q3.1

庄

SHŌ in the country; level

───────── 1 ─────────

9 庄屋 **shōya** village headman
13 庄園 **shōen** manor

───────── 4 ─────────

3q4.1 / 826

床 牀

SHŌ, toko bed; floor
yuka floor   **yuka(shii)** admirable; charming; tasteful

───────── 1 ─────────

2 床入 **tokoi(ri)** consummation of marriage
床几 **shōgi** camp/folding stool
3 床上 **yukaue** on the floor, (flooded) above floor level
tokoa(ge) recovery from illness
床下 **yukashita** below the floor
床山 **tokoyama** (sumo wrestlers' or actors') hairdresser
5 床払 **tokobara(i)** recovery from illness
6 床机 **shōgi** camp/folding stool
8 床店 **tokomise** booth, stall
床板 **tokoita** alcove floorboard
yukaita floorboards
床虱 **tokojirami** bedbug
9 床屋 **tokoya** barber, barbershop
床柱 **tokobashira** ornamental alcove post
11 床張 **tokoba(ri)** flooring
12 床間 **toko(no)ma** alcove (in a Japanese-style room)
13 床置 **tokoo(ki)** alcove ornament
17 床擦 **tokozu(re)** bedsore
18 床離 **tokobana(re)** get out of bed

───────── 2 ─────────

3 川床 **kawadoko** riverbed
4 火床 **kashō, hidoko** fire bed/grate
心床 **kokoroyuka(shii)** tasteful, admirable, charming
8 河床 **kashō** river bed
苗床 **naedoko** seedbed, nursery
岩床 **ganshō** bedrock
9 臥床 **gashō** be confined to bed
胡床 **agura (o kaku)** sit cross-legged
10 起床 **kishō** wake up, rise
砲床 **hōshō** gun platform/emplacement
病床 **byōshō** sickbed
11 道床 **dōshō** roadbed
船床 **funadoko** boat's floorboards

釣床 **tsu(ri)doko** hammock
12 着床 **chakushō** become implanted
温床 **onshō** hotbed
就床 **shūshō** go to bed, retire
13 寝床 **nedoko** bed
置床 **o(ki)doko** movable tokonoma alcove
路床 **roshō** roadbed
鉄床 **kanatoko** anvil
鉱床 **kōshō** ore/mineral deposits
14 髪床 **kamidoko** barbershop
銃床 **jūshō** stock (of a gun)
18 臨床 **rinshō** clinical
臨床家 **rinshōka** clinician
離床 **rishō** get up; leave one's sickbed

────── 3 ──────

3 万年床 **mannendoko** bedding/futon left
   spread out on the floor during the daytime
14 髪結床 **kamiyu(i)doko** (Edo) barbershop

3q4.2 / 827

応 應
Ō reply, respond; comply with, fulfill, satisfy **kota(eru)** answer, respond; be felt keenly, be telling **ira(e)** reply

────── 1 ──────

0 応じる **ō(jiru)** respond; consent to; satisfy, meet (a need)
2 応力 **ōryoku** stress
4 応仁 **Ōnin** (era, 1467–1469)
応分 **ōbun** appropriate, fitting
5 応召 **ōshō** be drafted
応召兵 **ōshōhei** draftee
応用 **ōyō** (practical) application
応用科学 **ōyō kagaku** applied science
応用問題 **ōyō mondai** problem to test ability to apply theoretical knowledge
応永 **Ōei** (era, 1394–1428)
6 応安 **Ōan** (era, 1368–1375)
7 応対 **ōtai** receive (visitors), wait on (customers)
8 応長 **Ōchō** (era, 1311–1312)
応和 **Ōwa** (era, 961–964)
9 応信 **ōshin** answer signal, countersignal
応保 **Ōhō** (era, 1161–1163)
応変 **ōhen** expediency
応急 **ōkyū** emergency, temporary, stopgap
応急手当 **ōkyū tea(te)** first aid
応急策 **ōkyūsaku** emergency/stopgap measure
応待 **ōtai** receive (visitors), wait on (customers)
応神 **Ōjin** (emperor, 270–310)
10 応射 **ōsha** return fire
応砲 **ōhō** return fire
11 応接 **ōsetsu** reception (of visitors)
応接室 **ōsetsushitsu** reception room

応接間 **ōsetsuma** reception room, parlor
12 応報 **ōhō** retribution
応援 **ōen** aid, support
応援団 **ōendan** rooting section, cheerleaders
応募 **ōbo** answer (an ad), apply for, enroll, enlist, subscribe for (shares)
応募者 **ōbosha** applicant, entrant, volunteer, subscriber (to bonds)
応答 **ōtō** answer, reply, response
応訴 **ōso** countersuit
13 応戦 **ōsen** accept a challenge, fight back
応酬 **ōshū** reply
14 応徳 **Ōtoku** (era, 1084–1087)
15 応諾 **ōdaku** consent, accept

────── 2 ──────

1 一応 **ichiō** once; tentatively; in outline
4 元応 **Gen'ō** (era, 1319–1321)
天応 **Ten'ō** (era, 781–782)
内応 **naiō** secret understanding, collusion
文応 **Bun'ō** (era, 1260–1261)
反応 **hannō** reaction, response
手応 **tegota(e)** response, effect, resistance
5 正応 **Shōō** (era, 1288–1293)
7 承応 **Jōō** (era, 1652–1655)
即応 **sokuō** conform/adapt to, meet
対応 **taiō** correspond to, be equivalent to; cope with
対応策 **taiōsaku** (counter)measures
延応 **En'ō** (era, 1239–1240)
否応 **iyaō** agreement or disagreement
否応無 **iyaōna(shi)** whether one likes it or not
8 供応 **kyōō** treat, banquet, dinner
呼応 **koō** hail each other; act in concert
明応 **Meiō** (era, 1492–1501)
9 貞応 **Jōō** (era, 1222–1224)
相応 **sōō** suitable, fitting
12 歯応 **hagota(e)** crispiness felt when sinking one's teeth into
策応 **sakuō** in concert/collusion with
順応 **junnō** adapt/conform to
順応力 **junnōryoku** adaptability
順応性 **junnōsei** adaptability
13 適応 **tekiō** adaptation, accommodation, adjustment
適応性 **tekiōsei** adaptability, flexibility
適応症 **tekiōshō** diseases for which a medicine is efficacious/indicated
照応 **shōō** correspond to, agree/coincide with
感応 **kannō** response; inspiration; sympathy; induce, influence
14 暦応 **Ryakuō** (era, 1338–1342)
嘉応 **Kaō** (era, 1169–1171)
15 慶応 **Keiō** (a university); (era, 1865–1868)
18 観応 **Kan'ō** (era, 1350–1352)
19 饗応 **kyōō** hold a banquet, wine and dine

3

氵 土 扌 口 女 犭 弓 彳 彡 艹 宀 ⺌ 凵 广
→4 尸 口

──────── 3 ────────

4 不相応 **fusōō** out of proportion to, unsuited, inappropriate, undue

6 因果応報 **inga-ōhō** reward according to deeds, retribution

8 其相応 **sore sōō** in its own way

10 核反応 **kakuhannō** nuclear reaction
核反応炉 **kakuhannōro** nuclear reactor

15 質疑応答 **shitsugi-ōtō** question-and-answer (session)

18 臨機応変 **rinki-ōhen** adaptation to circumstances

──────── 4 ────────

9 連鎖反応 **rensa hannō** chain reaction

──────── 5 ────────

6 光化学反応 **kōkagaku hannō, hikari kagaku hannō** photochemical reaction

3q4.3

庇

HI, kaba(u) protect, shield
hisashi eaves; canopy; visor

──────── 1 ────────

20 庇護 **higo** protection, patronage

──────── 2 ────────

5 目庇 **mabisashi** eyeshade; visor

11 雪庇 **seppi, yukibisashi** overhanging snow

3q4.4 / 770

序

JO beginning; preface; order, sequence
tsuide order; occasion, chance

──────── 1 ────────

4 序文 **jobun** preface, foreword, introduction

6 序曲 **jokyoku** overture, prelude
序次 **joji** order, sequence
序列 **joretsu** order, sequence, rank

7 序言 **jogen** preface, foreword, introduction

9 序奏 **josō** introduction (in music)

12 序詞 **joshi** preface, prolog
序開 **jobira(ki)** beginning, opening

13 序幕 **jomaku** curtain raiser, prelude
序数 **josū** ordinal number

14 序説 **josetsu** introdution, preface

15 序盤 **joban** opening moves (in go)
序盤戦 **jobansen** beginning of a campaign
序論 **joron** introduction, preface

──────── 2 ────────

6 次序 **jijo** order, system, arrangement
自序 **jijo** author's preface

9 後序 **kōjo** postscript to a book, afterword

10 秩序 **chitsujo** order, system, regularity
秩序正 **chitsujo-tada(shii)** in good order

12 順序 **junjo** order, sequence; procedure

16 機序 **kijo** mechanism (in biology)

──────── 3 ────────

8 長幼序 **chōyō (no) jo** Elders first.

12 無秩序 **muchitsujo** disorder, chaos; anomie

13 新秩序 **shinchitsujo** new order

──────── 4 ────────

6 安寧秩序 **annei-chitsujo** peace and order

──────── 5 ────────

3q5.1

庚

KŌ seventh in a series, "G"
kanoe seventh calendar sign

3q5.2 / 504

府

FU urban prefecture; government office; storehouse

──────── 1 ────────

3 府下 **fuka** suburban districts

5 府令 **furei** urban-prefectural ordinance
府庁 **fuchō** urban-prefectural office
府立 **furitsu** run by an urban prefecture

6 府会 **fukai** urban-prefectural assembly
府会議員 **fukai giin** urban-prefectural assemblyman

8 府知事 **fuchiji** urban-prefectural governor

9 府県 **fuken** prefectures

12 府営 **fuei** run by an urban prefecture
府税 **fuzei** urban-prefectural tax

20 府議会 **fugikai** urban-prefectural assembly

──────── 2 ────────

5 甲府 **Kōfu** (city, Yamanashi-ken)

7 別府 **Beppu** (city, Ōita-ken)
学府 **gakufu** educational institution

8 国府 **kokufu, kokubu** (ancient) provincial office/capital
枢府 **Sūfu** Privy Council

9 首府 **shufu** capital
政府 **seifu** the government
政府案 **seifuan** government bill/measure
政府党 **seifutō** government party
政府側 **seifugawa** the government (side)
政府筋 **seifusuji** government sources
政府間 **seifukan** government-to-government

10 冥府 **meifu** hades, realm of the dead

13 幕府 **bakufu** shogunate

19 覇府 **hafu** shogunate

──────── 3 ────────

3 大阪府 **Ōsaka-fu** (prefecture)

4 太宰府 **Dazaifu** (ancient) Kyūshū government headquarters
反政府 **hanseifu** antigovernment

5 旧幕府 **kyūbakufu** the old feudal government, the shogunate

5 旧幕府 **kyūbakufu** the old feudal government, the shogunate
　立法府 **rippōfu** legislature
6 仮政府 **kariseifu** provisional government
8 京都府 **Kyōto-fu** (prefecture)
9 軍政府 **gunseifu** military government
10 都道府県 **to-dō-fu-ken** prefectures
11 現政府 **genseifu** the present government
12 無政府 **museifu** anarchy
　無政府主義 **museifu shugi** anarchism
　無政府主義者 **museifushugisha** anarchist
14 総理府 **sōrifu** Prime Minister's Office
　総督府 **sōtokufu** government-general
18 鎮守府 **chinjufu** naval station

3q5.3 / 562

底

TEI, soko bottom

─────────── 1 ───────────

2 底入 **sokoi(re)** (prices) bottoming out
　底力 **sokojikara** latent energy/strength
3 底土 **sokotsuchi** subsoil
4 底止 **teishi** come to an end
　底辺 **teihen** base (in geometry)
　底引網 **sokobi(ki)ami** dragnet, trawlnet
5 底本 **teihon** the original text
　底石 **sokoishi** broken-rock base, hardcore
6 底気味悪 **sokokimi waru(i)** eerie, ominous
　底曳網 **sokobi(ki)ami** dragnet, trawlnet
　底光 **sokobika(ri)** subdued gloss
7 底冷 **sokobi(e)** chilled to the bone
　底角 **teikaku** base angle
　底抜 **sokonu(ke)** bottomless, unbounded
　底抜騒 **sokonu(ke) sawa(gi)** boisterous merrymaking
　底豆 **sokomame** blister (on one's sole)
8 底波 **sokonami** groundswell
　底固 **sokogata(i)** (prices) holding firm, having bottomed out
9 底革 **sokogawa** sole leather, sole of a shoe
10 底値 **sokone** rock-bottom price
　底流 **teiryū** bottom current, undercurrent
　底荷 **sokoni** ballast
12 底割 **sokowa(re)** (prices) falling through the floor, the bottom dropping out
　soko (o) wa(tte) (speaking) frankly, holding nothing back
　底堅 **sokogata(i)** (prices) holding firm, having bottomed out
　底無 **sokona(shi)** bottomless
13 底意 **sokoi** inmost thoughts, underlying motive
　底意地悪 **sokoiji waru(i)** spiteful, malcontented, cranky
16 底積 **sokozu(mi)** goods stowed at the bottom

─────────── 2 ───────────

3 上底 **a(ge)zoko** raised/false bottom
4 水底 **suitei, minasoko** sea/river bottom
　心底 **shinsoko, shintei** the bottom of one's heart
5 平底 **hirazoko** flat bottom
　平底船 **hirazokobune** flat-bottomed boat
　払底 **futtei** shortage, scarcity
6 地底 **chitei** bowels of the earth
　糸底 **itozoko** bottom rim (of an earthenware cup)
　耳底 **jitei** ears
7 谷底 **tanizoko, tanisoko** bottom of a valley/ravine
8 到底 **tōtei** (cannot) possibly, (not) at all, utterly, absolutely
　河底 **kawazoko, katei** river bed/bottom
9 海底 **kaitei** ocean floor, undersea
10 根底 **kontei** root, basis, foundation
　胸底 **kyōtei** one's inmost heart
11 基底 **kitei** base, basis, foundation
　眼底出血 **gantei shukketsu** hemorrhage in the fundus of the eye
　船底 **funazoko, sentei** ship's bottom
12 奥底 **okusoko, okuzoko** depths, bottom
13 靴底 **kutsuzoko** sole (of a shoe/boot)
15 徹底 **tettei** thorough, complete
　徹底的 **tetteiteki** thorough, exhaustive
17 鍋底景気 **nabezoko keiki** prolonged recession

─────────── 3 ───────────

2 二重底 **nijūzoko** double bottom/sole
4 不徹底 **futettei** not thorough, halfway, unconvincing, inconclusive

3q5.4 / 168

店

TEN, mise, tana- shop, store

─────────── 1 ───────────

2 店子 **tanako** tenant
5 店仕舞 **misejima(i)** close shop (for the day); go out of business
　店台 **misedai** counter (in a store)
　店主 **tenshu** shopkeeper, proprietor
6 店先 **misesaki** storefront
7 店売 **miseu(ri)** sell in stores
8 店長 **tenchō** store/shop manager
9 店卸 **tanaoroshi** taking inventory; fault-finding
　店屋 **ten'ya** store; cooked-food store
　店屋物 **ten'yamono** take-out food
10 店借 **tanaga(ri)** renting a house, tenancy
　店員 **ten'in** store employee, clerk
　店晒 **tanazara(shi)** shopworn goods

3

氵
土
扌
口
女
巾
犭
弓
彳
彡
艹
宀
丷
屮
耂
广 5 ←
尸
口

12 店番 **miseban** tending store; salesman
店貸 **tanaga(shi)** renting out a house
店開 **misebira(ki)** open shop (for the day);
go into business
13 店賃 **tanachin** house rent
店飾 **misekaza(ri)** window dressing
15 店舗 **tenpo** shop, store
店請 **tanau(ke)** surety for a tenant
16 店頭 **tentō** storefront, shop window, store,
over-the-counter

———————— 2 ————————

3 女店員 **joten'in** salesgirl
4 支店 **shiten** a branch (store/office)
分店 **bunten** branch store
5 出店 **demise** branch store
shutten open a new store
本店 **honten** head office; main store; this store
6 全店 **zenten** the whole store, all the stores
当店 **tōten** this shop/store, we
7 角店 **kadomise** corner store
売店 **baiten** (news)stand, kiosk
床店 **tokomise** booth, stall
8 夜店 **yomise** night stall; night fair
9 茶店 **chamise** teahouse
10 借店 **ka(ri)dana** rented shop
酒店 **sakamise, saketen** liquor store
書店 **shoten** bookstore; publisher
軒店 **nokimise** small shop under another
building's eaves
11 商店 **shōten** store, shop
商店街 **shōtengai** shopping area
閉店 **heiten** store closing
12 貸店 **ka(shi)mise** store for rent
開店 **kaiten** opening a new store; opening
the store for the day
13 裏店 **uradana** house in an alley
新店 **shinmise** new store
15 弊店 **heiten** our shop, we
質店 **shichiten** pawnshop
16 薬店 **yakuten** drugstore
21 露店 **roten** street stall, vending booth
露店商 **rotenshō** stall keeper/vendor
露店街 **rotengai** street of open-air stalls

———————— 3 ————————

3 工務店 **kōmuten** engineering firm
大商店 **daishōten** emporium
小売店 **kou(ri)ten** retail store/outlet, retailer
5 出張店 **shutchōten** branch store
代理店 **dairiten** agent, agency
6 回漕店 **kaisōten** shipping agent
百貨店 **hyakkaten** department store
8 板門店 **Hanmonten** Panmunjom
取次店 **toritsugiten** agency, distributor
9 専門店 **senmonten** specialty store
連鎖店 **rensaten** chain store

洋品店 **yōhinten** haberdashery
屋台店 **yatai mise** street stall, stand, booth
食品店 **shokuhinten** grocery store
10 特約店 **tokuyakuten** special agent, chain store
11 運送店 **unsōten** forwarding agent, express
company
理髪店 **rihatsuten** barbershop
販売店 **hanbaiten** shop, store
12 割烹店 **kappōten** restaurant
喫茶店 **kissaten** teahouse, café
飲食店 **inshokuten** restaurant
13 楽器店 **gakkiten** music shop
14 模擬店 **mogiten** refreshment booth, snack bar
総本店 **sōhonten** head office
16 薬種店 **yakushuten** drugstore, apothecary

———————— 4 ————————

9 食料品店 **shokuryōhinten** grocery store

庖 → 庖 3q5.5

3q5.5

庖 庖

HŌ kitchen, cooking, cook

———————— 1 ————————

2 庖丁 **hōchō** kitchen knife

———————— 3 ————————

5 出刃庖丁 **debabōchō** pointed kitchen knife
6 肉切庖丁 **nikuki(ri)bōchō** butcher knife
8 刺身庖丁 **sashimi-bōchō** fish-slicing knife

———————— 6 ————————

3q6.1 / 377

度

DO, TAKU, TO degree; extent,
measure, limit; (how many) times
tabi time, occasion
-ta(i) (verb suffix) want to …

———————— 1 ————————

3 度々 **tabitabi** often, frequently
5 度外 **dohazu(re)** extraordinary, excessive
度外視 **dogaishi** disregard, ignore
6 度合 **doa(i)** degree, extent, rate
7 度忘 **dowasu(re)** forget for the moment, slip
one's mind
9 度重 **tabikasa(naru)** repeatedly
度度 **tabitabi** often, frequently
度胆抜 **dogimo (o) nu(ku)** dumbfound, shock
10 度胸 **dokyō** courage, pluck, mettle
11 度盛 **domo(ri)** gradation, scale
12 度量 **doryō** magnanimity, generosity
度量法 **doryōhō** measurement
度量衡 **doryōkō** weights and measures

13 度数 **dosū** number of times/degrees
18 度難 **do(shi)gata(i)** beyond saving, incorrigible

──────────── 2 ────────────

1 一度 **ichido, hitotabi** once, one time
2 二度 **nido** two times
二度目 **nidome** for the second time, again
丁度 **chōdo** exactly
3 大度 **taido** magnanimous
4 今度 **kondo** this time; next time
支度 **shitaku** preparation, arrangements
分度器 **bundoki** protractor
尺度 **shakudo** (linear) measure, scale, yardstick, standard
5 用度 **yōdo** supplies; expenses
6 年度 **nendo** fiscal/business year
毎度 **maido** each time; frequently; always
再度 **saido** twice, a second time, again
印度 **Indo** India
此度 **ko(no) tabi** at this time
光度 **kōdo** brightness, luminosity
光度計 **kōdokei** photometer
当度 **tōdo** this time, now
忖度 **sontaku** conjecture, surmise, judge
7 伸度 **shindo** elasticity, ductility
低度 **teido** low degree
何度 **nando** how many times; how many degrees
角度 **kakudo** angle
8 限度 **gendo** limit
制度 **seido** system
法度 **hatto, hotto** law; prohibition, ban
歩度 **hodo** pace, cadence
歩度計 **hodokei** pedometer
明度 **meido** brightness, luminosity
9 速度 **sokudo** speed, velocity
速度計 **sokudokei** speedometer
度度 **tabitabi** often, frequently
10 都度 **tsudo** each time, whenever
高度 **kōdo** high(ly developed), advanced, sophisticated; altitude
高度計 **kōdokei** altimeter
進度 **shindo** (extent of) progress
純度 **jundo** purity
11 過度 **kado** excessive, too much
深度 **shindo** depth
済度 **saido** salvation, redemption
強度 **kyōdo** intensity, strength
得度 **tokudo** enter the (Buddhist) priesthood
密度 **mitsudo** density
視度 **shido** visibility
経度 **keido** longitude
粘度 **nendo** viscosity
頂度 **chōdo** exactly
12 測度 **sokudo** measurement, gauging
温度 **ondo** temperature

温度計 **ondokei** thermometer
湿度 **shitsudo** humidity
湿度計 **shitsudokei** hygrometer
落度 **o(chi)do** fault, error, blame, guilt
極度 **kyokudo** to the highest degree, extreme
幾度 **ikudo** how many times, how often
硬度 **kōdo** (degree of) hardness
程度 **teido** extent, degree, level
軽度 **keido** to a slight degree
13 傾度 **keido** inclination, gradient
適度 **tekido** proper degree/amount, moderation
滅度 **metsudo** nirvana
照度 **shōdo** (intensity of) illumination
数度 **sūdo** several times
感度 **kando** (degree of) sensitivity
節度 **setsudo** rule, standard; moderation
零度 **reido** zero (degrees), the freezing point
14 態度 **taido** attitude, stance, posture
精度 **seido** precision, accuracy
酸度 **sando** acidity
15 熱度 **netsudo** degree of heat/enthusiasm
調度 **chōdo** household effects, furnishings
調度品 **chōdohin** household effects, furnishings
輝度 **kido** (degree of) brightness
震度 **shindo** earthquake intensity
16 濃度 **nōdo** (degree of) concentration
緯度 **ido** latitude
17 糞度胸 **kusodokyō** reckless bravery
聴度 **chōdo** audibility
頻度 **hindo** frequency, rate of occurrence
頻度数 **hindosū** frequency
鮮度 **sendo** (degree of) freshness
18 襟度 **kindo** magnanimity, generosity

──────────── 3 ────────────

4 心支度 **kokorojitaku** mental readiness/attitude
5 本年度 **honnendo** this fiscal/business year
生鮮度 **seisendo** freshness
加速度 **kasokudo** acceleration
冬支度 **fuyujitaku** preparations for winter; winter clothing
6 安定度 **anteido** (degree of) stability
7 身支度 **mijitaku** grooming, outfit, preparations
8 東印度会社 **Higashi Indo Gaisha** East India Company
逃支度 **ni(ge)jitaku** make ready to flee
芽出度 **medeta(i)** happy, congratulatory
明暗度 **meiando** brightness, light intensity
雨支度 **amajitaku** preparing for rain
9 急速度 **kyūsokudo** high speed
前年度 **zennendo** the preceding business/fiscal year
10 帰支度 **kae(ri)jitaku** preparations to return

3

氵
土
扌
口
女
巾
犭
弓
彳
彡
艹
宀
⺌
山
吉
广 6←
尸
口

高々度 **kōkōdo** high-altitude
高速度 **kōsokudo** high speed
高緯度 **kōido** high/cold latitudes
旅支度 **tabijitaku** travel preparations/outfit
純分度 **junbundo** fineness (of gold)
11 過年度 **kanendo** past fiscal/business year
12 御法度 **gohatto** law, ordinance; prohibition
13 傾斜度 **keishado** gradient
溶解度 **yōkaido** solubility
感光度 **kankōdo** (degree of) photosensitivity

─────────── 4 ───────────

3 三々九度 **sansankudo** exchange of nuptial cups
4 氏族制度 **shizoku seido** the family/clan system
5 母系制度 **bokei seido** matriarchal system
12 超高速度 **chōkōsokudo** superhigh-speed
最大限度 **saidai gendo** maximum
最小限度 **saishō gendo** minimum
13 嫁入支度 **yomei(ri)-jitaku** trousseau

3q6.2

庠

SHŌ school

3q6.3 / 1112

庭

TEI, niwa garden, yard

─────────── 1 ───────────

3 庭下駄 **niwageta** garden clogs
4 庭木 **niwaki** garden tree, shrubbery
庭木戸 **niwakido** garden gate
5 庭石 **niwaishi** garden stones
6 庭先 **niwasaki** in the garden
10 庭師 **niwashi** landscape gardener
11 庭球 **teikyū** tennis
12 庭番 **niwaban** garden watchman; shogun's secret agent
13 庭園 **teien** garden
庭園術 **teienjutsu** landscape gardening

─────────── 2 ───────────

4 内庭 **uchiniwa, naitei** inner court, courtyard
中庭 **nakaniwa** courtyard
5 矢庭 **yaniwa (ni)** suddenly, immediately
平庭 **hiraniwa** garden with no hills
石庭 **ishiniwa** rock garden
8 径庭 **keitei** great difference
9 前庭 **zentei, maeniwa** front yard/garden
後庭 **kōtei** back yard/garden
10 家庭 **katei** home; family
家庭用 **kateiyō** for home use
家庭用品 **kateiyōhin** household goods
家庭的 **kateiteki** domestic/family (affairs)

家庭教師 **katei kyōshi** (private) tutor
家庭裁判所 **katei saibansho** Family Court
家庭欄 **kateiran** homemaker's column
校庭 **kōtei** schoolyard, campus
12 営庭 **eitei** barracks' parade ground
奥庭 **okuniwa** inner garden, back yard
13 裏庭 **uraniwa** back garden/yard
15 箱庭 **hakoniwa** miniature garden

─────────── 3 ───────────

11 軟式庭球 **nanshiki teikyū** softball tennis

─────────── 4 ───────────

5 母子家庭 **boshi katei** fatherless home

─────────── 7 ───────────

3q7.1 / 825

庫

KO, KU, kura storehouse

─────────── 1 ───────────

13 庫裏 **kuri** priests' quarters; temple kitchen

─────────── 2 ───────────

2 入庫 **nyūko** warehousing, storage; entering the car barn
4 文庫 **bunko** stationery box; bookcase; library
文庫本 **bunkobon** small paperback book (page size 14.8 x 10.5 cm)
公庫 **kōko** municipal treasury; finance corporation
6 在庫 **zaiko** (in) stock, inventory
在庫品 **zaikohin** goods on hand, stock
7 兵庫県 **Hyōgo-ken** (prefecture)
車庫 **shako** garage, carbarn
8 宝庫 **hōko** treasure house
官庫 **kanko** government storehouse
国庫 **kokko** national treasury
武庫 **buko** armory
金庫 **kinko, kanegura** safe, vault; cashbox; depository, treasury; rich patron
金庫破 **kinkoyabu(ri)** safe-cracking
9 炭庫 **tanko** coal bin
10 倉庫 **sōko** warehouse
書庫 **shoko** library, book stacks

─────────── 3 ───────────

4 手文庫 **tebunko** small bookcase
火薬庫 **kayakuko** powder magazine
7 冷蔵庫 **reizōko** refrigerator
8 武器庫 **bukiko** armory
10 格納庫 **kakunōko** hangar
12 弾薬庫 **dan'yakuko** powder magazine
15 熱蔵庫 **netsuzōko** heating cabinet, warmer
16 機関庫 **kikanko** locomotive shed, round-house

─────────── 4 ───────────

4 手提金庫 **tesa(ge)kinko** cash box, portable safe

3q7.2 / 786

ZA seat; theater, troupe; constellation
suwa(ru) sit down

───────── 1 ─────────

0 座する **za(suru)** sit; be implicated in
4 座元 **zamoto** theater manager, producer
座中 **zachū** in the room; member of the troupe
座込 **suwa(ri)ko(mu)** sit down, stage a sit-in
5 座付 **zatsu(ki)** (actor) attached to a theater
座右 **zayū** close at hand
座右銘 **zayū (no) mei** one's motto
座礼 **zarei** bow while sitting
座主 **zasu, zashu** head priest of a temple
6 座州 **zasu** run aground, be beached
7 座位 **zai** seating order, precedence
8 座長 **zachō** chairman, moderator; troupe leader
座所 **zasho** one's seat
座金 **zagane** (metal) washer
9 座乗 **zajō** be aboard
座臥 **zaga** sitting and lying down
座食 **zashoku** live in idleness
10 座高 **zakō** one's height when seated
座浴 **zayoku** sitz bath
座員 **zain** member of a troupe
座席 **zaseki** seat
座骨 **zakotsu** hip bone
座骨神経 **zakotsu shinkei** sciatic nerve
座骨神経痛 **zakotsu shinkeitsū** sciatic
   neuralgia
11 座視 **zashi** merely sit and watch (without
   helping)
13 座業 **zagyō** sedentary work
座蒲団 **zabuton** cushion
座禅 **zazen** (Zen) meditation
14 座像 **zazō** seated image
15 座標 **zahyō** (Cartesian) coordinates
座敷 **zashiki** room, drawing room
座敷牢 **zashikirō** room for confining someone
座談 **zadan** conversation
座談会 **zadankai** round-table discussion,
   symposium
16 座興 **zakyō** for the amusement/entertainment
   of those present
座薬 **zayaku** suppository
座頭 **zagashira** troupe leader
   zatō blind man/musician
17 座礁 **zashō** run aground (on a reef)
18 座職 **zashoku** sedentary work

───────── 2 ─────────

1 一座 **ichiza** all present, the company; a troupe
3 上座 **kamiza, jōza** top seat, place of honor
下座 **geza** squat, kneel **shimoza** lower seat
口座 **kōza** (bank) account
4 中座 **chūza** leave before (a meeting) is over

仏座 **butsuza** seat of a Buddhist idol
円座 **enza** sitting in a circle; round straw mat
王座 **ōza** the throne, the crown
5 正座 **seiza** sit straight (on one's heels)
   shōza seat of honor
台座 **daiza** pedestal
玉座 **gyokuza** the throne
6 多座機 **tazaki** multi-seated airplane
列座 **retsuza** presence, attendance
同座 **dōza** sit together; the same theater;
   be implicated
安座 **anza** sitting on the floor with legs folded
当座 **tōza** for the time being, for some time;
   current (account)
7 即座 **sokuza** prompt, on the spot
対座 **taiza** sit facing each other
車座 **kurumaza** sitting in a circle
8 長座 **chōza** stay long
股座 **matagura** crotch
9 前座 **zenza** opening performance; minor
   performer
連座 **renza** complicity
独座 **dokuza** sitting alone
客座 **kyakuza** seats for guests
胡座 **agura (o kaku)** sit cross-legged
星座 **seiza** constellation
10 高座 **kōza** platform, dais, stage; upper seat
11 運座 **unza** meeting of poets
12 着座 **chakuza** take a seat
温座 **onza** sitting peacefully
満座 **manza** the whole assembly, everyone
御座所 **gozasho** the throne
奥座敷 **okuzashiki** inner/back room
貸座敷 **ka(shi)zashiki** brothel
13 鼎座 **teiza** sit in a triangle
14 遷座 **senza** transfer of a shrine
静座 **seiza** sit quietly
端座 **tanza** sit erect
複座 **fukuza** two-seater
複座機 **fukuzaki** two-seater airplane
銀座 **ginza** silver mint; the Ginza
15 横座標 **ōzahyō** abscissa, x-coordinate
黙座 **mokuza** sit in silence
縁座 **enza** complicity through kinship
蠍座 **sasori-za** Scorpio
16 縦座標 **tatezahyō** ordinate, y-coordinate
17 擱座 **kakuza** run aground, be stranded
講座 **kōza** course (of lectures); professorship,
   chair
18 鎮座 **chinza** be enshrined
離座敷 **hana(re) zashiki** detached room
21 露座 **roza** sitting out in the open

───────── 3 ─────────

3 土下座 **dogeza** bow while kneeling
小熊座 **kogumaza** Little Bear, Ursa Minor
7 牡牛座 **Oushiza** (the constellation) Taurus

3

氵
土
扌
日
女
巾
犭
弓
彳
彡
艹
宀
丷
屮
耂
广 7←
尸
口

3

氵
土
扌
口
女
巾
犭
弓
彳
彡
艹
宀
⺍
山
寺
→ 7 广
尸
口

4

12 結跏趺座 **kekkafuza** sitting in lotus position/posture

3q7.3 / 1697

唐

TŌ Tang (dynasty); China; foreign
Kara China, Cathay; foreign

1

2 唐人 **Tōjin, karabito** a Chinese/foreigner
3 唐土 **Tōdo** China, Cathay
4 唐天 **tōten** velveteen
唐天竺 **Kara-Tenjiku** China and India
唐手 **karate** karate
唐木 **karaki** rare foreign wood
唐戸 **karado** Chinese-style gate
5 唐本 **tōhon** books from China
6 唐衣 **karakoromo, karagoromo** ancient Chinese clothes; strange clothes
唐糸 **karaito, tōito** foreign thread/yarn
7 唐辛子 **tōgarashi** cayenne/red pepper
8 唐画 **tōga** Chinese(-style) painting
唐突 **tōtotsu** abrupt
唐国 **Karakuni** China
唐松 **karamatsu** larch
唐物 **karamono** imported goods
唐物屋 **karamonoya** foreign-goods dealer/store
唐物商 **tōbutsushō** foreign-goods store
唐金 **karakane** bronze
唐門 **karamon** Chinese-style gate
9 唐変木 **tōhenboku** blockhead, oaf
唐風 **karafū** Chinese style
唐津焼 **karatsuya(ki)** earthenware, china
唐草 **karakusa** arabesque
唐草模様 **karakusa moyō** arabesque design
唐胡麻 **tōgoma** castor-oil bean
唐音 **tōon** Tang-dynasty reading (of a kanji)
唐紅 **karakurenai** crimson, scarlet
10 唐紙 **karakami** bamboo paper(-covered sliding door)
唐馬 **karauma** (ancient) foreign horse
11 唐船 **karafune, tōsen** Chinese/foreign ship
12 唐傘 **karakasa** paper umbrella
唐朝 **Tōchō** the Tang dynasty
唐硯 **tōken** Chinese ink slab
13 唐獅子 **kara shishi** lion
唐詩 **tōshi** Tang-dynasty poem
14 唐墨 **karasumi, tōboku** Chinese ink stick
唐様 **karayō** Chinese style
唐歌 **karauta** Chinese poem
唐語 **kara kotoba** Chinese/foreign language
16 唐錦 **karanishiki** Chinese brocade
17 唐薯 **karaimo** sweet potato
18 唐櫃 **karabitsu** six-legged Chinese-style chest

2

4 毛唐 **ketō** hairy barbarian, foreigner (short for 毛唐人)
毛唐人 **ketōjin** hairy barbarian, foreigner
9 荒唐無稽 **kōtō-mukei** absurdity, nonsense
12 遣唐使 **kentōshi** Japanese envoy to Tang-dynasty China
渡唐 **to-Tō** going to (Tang-dynasty) China

3q7.4 / 379

席

SEKI seat, place

1

3 席上 **sekijō** at the meeting, on the occasion
6 席次 **sekiji** seating order, precedence
8 席画 **sekiga** impromptu drawing
9 席巻 **sekken** sweeping conquest
10 席料 **sekiryō** room/cover charge, admission fee
11 席捲 **sekken** sweeping conquest
12 席順 **sekijun** seating order, precedence

2

1 一席 **isseki** a speech/story/feast
3 上席 **jōseki** seniority, precedence; place of honor
4 中席 **nakaseki** the entertainment (scheduled by a music hall) for the second ten days of the month
欠席 **kesseki** absence, nonattendance
欠席届 **kesseki todo(ke)** report of absence
欠席者 **kessekisha** absentee
5 出席 **shusseki** attendance
出席者 **shussekisha** those present, the attendance
出席率 **shussekiritsu** percentage of attendance
出席簿 **shussekibo** roll book, attendance record
末席 **masseki, basseki** lowest-ranking seat
主席 **shuseki** top place, first, head, chairman
立席 **ta(chi)seki** standing room (only)
6 会席 **kaiseki** meeting place; poetry meeting; group dinner
会席料理 **kaiseki ryōri** banquet food served on individual trays
会席膳 **kaisekizen** dinner tray
次席 **jiseki** associate, junior, assistant; runner-up
列席 **resseki** attend, be present
列席者 **ressekisha** those present
同席 **dōseki** sit together
7 即席 **sokuseki** extemporaneous, impromptu, instant (foods)
即席料理 **sokuseki ryōri** quick meal

別席 **besseki** different/special seat, separate room
初席 **hatsuseki** first variety-show performance of the new year
8 退席 **taiseki** leave one's seat; withdraw, retire
定席 **jōseki** one's usual seat; variety hall
空席 **kūseki** vacant seat, vacancy
枕席 **chinseki** pillow and mat, bed
9 首席 **shuseki** head, chief, chairman
茶席 **chaseki** tea-ceremony seat
客席 **kyakuseki** seats for guests
10 陪席 **baiseki** sitting as an associate (judge)
酒席 **shuseki** banquet, feast
宴席 **enseki** (one's seat in a) banquet hall
座席 **zaseki** seat
11 寄席 **yose** variety-show hall
12 着席 **chakuseki** take a seat
場席 **baseki** room, space; seat, place
貸席 **ka(shi)seki** hall/rooms for rent; brothel
15 隣席 **rinseki** the seat next to one
18 臨席 **rinseki** attendance, presence
20 議席 **giseki** seat in parliament/congress

—————————— 3 ——————————

5 外野席 **gaiyaseki** bleachers
立見席 **ta(chi)miseki** standing room, gallery
7 来賓席 **raihinseki** visitors' seats/gallery
見物席 **kenbutsuseki** seats (at a game/theater)
8 招待席 **shōtaiseki** reserved seats for guests
9 指定席 **shiteiseki** reserved seats
10 被告席 **hikokuseki** defendant's chair, the dock
記者席 **kishaseki** seats for the press
12 傍聴席 **bōchōseki** seats for the public, visitors' gallery
無欠席 **mukesseki** perfect attendance
証人席 **shōninseki** the witness stand/box
貴賓席 **kihinseki** seats for the honored guests
16 操縦席 **sōjūseki** cockpit
18 観覧席 **kanranseki** seats, grandstand

—————————— 8 ——————————

3q8.1 / 894

康

KŌ peaceful

—————————— 1 ——————————

4 康元 **Kōgen** (era, 1256–1257)
5 康平 **Kōhei** (era, 1058–1065)
康正 **Kōshō** (era, 1455–1457)
康永 **Kōei** (era, 1342–1345)
6 康安 **Kōan** (era, 1361–1362)
8 康治 **Kōji** (era, 1142–1143)
康和 **Kōwa** (era, 1099–1104)
9 康保 **Kōhō** (era, 964–968)
13 康熙字典 **Kōki Jiten** the Kangxi zidian (a 42-volume 47,216-entry character dictionary published in China in 1716)
14 康寧 **kōnei** peaceful

—————————— 2 ——————————

3 小康 **shōkō** lull, respite
6 安康 **Ankō** (emperor, 453–456)
10 健康 **kenkō** health; healthy, sound
健康体 **kenkōtai** healthy body
健康児 **kenkōji** healthy child
健康法 **kenkōhō** how to keep fit, hygiene
健康的 **kenkōteki** healthful
健康保険 **kenkō hoken** health insurance
健康美 **kenkōbi** healthy beauty
健康診断 **kenkō shindan** medical examination, physical checkup

—————————— 3 ——————————

4 不健康 **fukenkō** unhealthy, unhealthful

3q8.2 / 1696

庸

YŌ employ; ordinary; tax paid in cloth in lieu of in labor

—————————— 1 ——————————

3 庸才 **yōsai** mediocre talent
6 庸劣 **yōretsu** mediocre; foolish
7 庸医 **yōi** mediocre physician, quack
庸君 **yōkun** foolish ruler
13 庸愚 **yōgu** mediocrity; dim-wittedness

—————————— 2 ——————————

3 凡庸 **bon'yō** mediocre, commonplace, banal
4 中庸 **chūyō** the golden mean, middle path, moderation
12 雇庸 **koyō** employment, hiring

3q8.3 / 1529

麻

MA, asa flax, hemp

—————————— 1 ——————————

5 麻布 **asanuno, mafu** hemp cloth, linen
6 麻糸 **asaito** linen thread, hemp yarn
10 麻疹 **hashika, mashin** measles
11 麻酔 **masui** anesthesia
麻酔薬 **masuiyaku** an anesthetic/narcotic
麻雀 **mājan** mahjong
12 麻葉 **asa(no)ha** hemp-leaf
13 麻裏 **asaura** hemp-soled straw sandals
麻睡 **masui** anesthesia
麻痺 **mahi** paralysis
15 麻縄 **asanawa** hemp rope
16 麻薬 **mayaku** narcotics, drugs

—————————— 2 ——————————

3 大麻 **taima** marijuana; Shinto paper amulet
ōasa hemp
7 亜麻 **ama** flax, linen

3

氵 土 扌 口 女 巾 犭 弓 彳 彡 艹 宀 ⺌ 山 ⻖ 广 8←
尸 囗

亜麻仁 **amani** linseed, flaxseed
亜麻仁油 **amaniyu** linseed oil
亜麻布 **amanuno** linen
亜麻製 **amasei** flaxen, linen
亜麻織物 **ama orimono** flax fabrics, linen
乱麻 **ranma** chaos, anarchy
8 苧麻 **choma, karamushi** ramie
9 胡麻 **goma** sesame (seeds)
胡麻油 **goma abura** sesame-seed oil
胡麻和 **gomaa(e)** salad with vinegar dressing
胡麻塩 **gomashio** salted toasted sesame seeds; gray-flecked hair
胡麻摺 **gomasu(ri)** flatterer, sycophant
11 黄麻 **kōma, ōma** jute
12 鈍麻 **donma** dullness
13 蓖麻 **hima** castor-oil plant
蓖麻子油 **himashiyu** castor oil
14 製麻 **seima** hemp/jute dressing, flax spinning
15 蕁麻 **jinma, irakusa** nettle
蕁麻疹 **jinmashin** hives

——————— 3 ———————
3 小児麻痺 **shōni mahi** infantile paralysis, polio
4 心臓麻痺 **shinzō mahi** heart failure/attack
5 白胡麻 **shirogoma** white sesame seeds
6 全身麻酔 **zenshin masui** general anasthesia
7 局部麻酔 **kyokubu masui** local anesthetic
10 唐胡麻 **tōgoma** castor-oil bean

3q8.4 / 981

廊 廊

RŌ corridor, hall

——————— 1 ———————
3 廊下 **rōka** corridor, hall

——————— 2 ———————
6 回廊 **kairō** corridor
8 画廊 **garō** picture gallery
歩廊 **horō** corridor, arcade
9 通廊 **tsūrō** corridor, passageway
12 渡廊下 **wata(ri) rōka** covered passageway

3q8.5

鹿

ROKU, shika deer

——————— 1 ———————
4 鹿爪 **shikatsume(rashii)** formal, solemn
5 鹿皮 **shikagawa** deerskin
6 鹿肉 **shikaniku** venison
7 鹿児島 **Kagoshima** (city, Kagoshima-ken)
鹿児島県 **Kagoshima-ken** (prefecture)
9 鹿威 **shishiodo(shi)** deer scare (Japanese-garden contrivance in which water flows

into a pivoted bamboo tube which repeatedly fills up, tips over, empties, then rights itself again, its lower end clopping against a stone); (also called 添水 **sōzu**)
10 鹿島立 **kashimada(chi)** set out on a journey

——————— 2 ———————
6 牝鹿 **mejika** doe, hind
7 牡鹿 **ojika** stag, buck
8 河鹿 **kajika** singing frog
10 馬鹿 **baka** fool, idiot, stupid; to a ridiculous degree
13 馴鹿 **tonakai** reindeer

——————— 3 ———————
3 大馬鹿 **ōbaka** big fool
小馬鹿 **kobaka** a fool
16 薄馬鹿 **usubaka** fool, simpleton, half-wit
親馬鹿 **oyabaka** overfond parent
21 麝香鹿 **jakōjika** musk deer

——————— 4 ———————
5 四月馬鹿 **shigatsu baka** April fool

3q8.6

庵 菴

AN, iori hermit's cottage, retreat

——————— 1 ———————
5 庵主 **anshu** hermitage master; tea-ceremony host; cloistered Buddhist nun
9 庵室 **anshitsu** hermit's retreat

——————— 2 ———————
6 仮庵 **kariio** booth, tabernacle, temporary dwelling
7 沢庵 **takuan** pickled daikon
沢庵漬 **takuanzuke** pickled daikon
13 僧庵 **sōan** monk's cell, hermitage

3q8.7 / 1766

庶

SHO all; illegitimate child

——————— 1 ———————
2 庶子 **shoshi** illegitimate child
5 庶出 **shoshutsu** illegitimate birth
庶民 **shomin** the (common) people
庶生 **shosei** illegitimate birth
7 庶系 **shokei** illegitimate lineage
8 庶姓 **shosei** illegitimacy
9 庶政 **shosei** all phases of government
10 庶流 **shoryū** illegitimate family branch
11 庶務 **shomu** general affairs
12 庶幾 **shoki** desire, hope

——— 9 ———

廁→厠 2p9.1

3q9.1

廓 KAKU enclosure; quarter; large; empty
kuruwa enclosure; quarter; red-light district

——— 1 ———

11 廓清 kakusei purification, cleanup, purge

——— 2 ———

10 遊廓 yūkaku red-light district
15 輪廓 rinkaku outline, contours

廊→廊 3q8.4

3q9.2

廂 SHŌ, SŌ, hisashi hallway; eaves

3q9.3 / 961

廃 廢
HAI obsolete; discontinue, do away with; crippled
suta(reru/ru) become outmoded, go out of fashion

——— 1 ———

0 廃する hai(suru) abolish, abandon; repeal, annul; decompose; discontinue
2 廃人 haijin a cripple/invalid
廃刀 haitō abolish the wearing of swords
4 廃止 haishi abolition, abrogation
5 廃刊 haikan discontinue publication
廃去 haikyo abandon
6 廃合 haigō abolition and amalgamation, reorganization
7 廃位 haii depose, dethrone
廃兵 haihei disabled soldier
廃坑 haikō abandoned mine
廃学 haigaku discontinue one's studies, leave school
8 廃官 haikan abolition of a post
廃物 haibutsu waste, refuse, scrap
廃物利用 haibutsu riyō recycling
9 廃除 haijo remove, exclude
廃帝 haitei deposed emperor, ex-king
廃品 haihin scrap, waste, discards, junk
廃屋 haioku abandoned house
10 廃家 haika extinct family; abandoned house
haike extinct family
廃案 haian rejected proposal, withdrawn draft
廃校 haikō (permanent) school closing

廃疾 haishitsu disabled, crippled
廃馬 haiba worn-out horse, jade
11 廃娼 haishō abolition of prostitution
廃船 haisen scrapped vessel
12 廃税 haizei abolition of a tax
廃絶 haizetsu become extinct
13 廃業 haigyō going out of business
廃棄 haiki do away with, scrap, rescind
廃棄物 haikibutsu waste matter, wastes
廃滅 haimetsu ruin, decay
廃園 haien abandoned garden
廃置 haichi abolition and establishment
14 廃墟 haikyo ruins
廃嫡 haichaku disinheritance
廃語 haigo obsolete word
16 廃頽 haitai decay, deterioration, decadence
18 廃藩 haihan abolition of clans
廃藩置県 haihan-chiken the abolition of clans and establishment of prefectures
23 廃鑑 haikan decommissioned warship

——— 2 ———

5 存廃 sonpai continuation or abolition, existence
6 全廃 zenpai total abolition
老廃 rōhai old, superannuated
老廃物 rōhaibutsu waste matter/products
7 改廃 kaihai alterations and abolitions, reorganization
8 退廃 taihai corruption, decadence
退廃的 taihaiteki corrupt, decadent
9 荒廃 kōhai desolation, ruin, devastation
荒廃地 kōhaichi wasteland, devastated area
15 撤廃 teppai abolition, do away with, repeal
16 興廃 kōhai rise and fall, destiny
壊廃 kaihai ruin, decay
頽廃 taihai decadence, corruption
頽廃的 taihaiteki decadent, corrupt

——— 10 ———

厨→厨 2p10.1

3q10.1 / 1689

廉 REN purity; honest; low price
kado grounds, charge, suspicion; point
yasu(i) cheap, inexpensive

——— 1 ———

3 廉士 renshi pure uncovetous person
5 廉正 rensei pure-hearted
6 廉吏 renri an honest official
7 廉売 renbai bargain sale
8 廉価 renka low price
廉価版 renkaban cheap/popular edition
廉価品 renkahin low-priced goods

氵 土 扌 口 女 巾 犭 弓 彳 彡 宀 爫 山 青 广 10← 尸 口

廉直 **renchoku** integrity, honesty
10 廉恥心 **renchishin** sense of shame/honor
15 廉潔 **renketsu** honest, upright

──────── 2 ────────

1 一廉 **hitokado, ikkado** superior, uncommon, full-fledged, respectable
7 低廉 **teiren** low-priced
10 破廉恥 **harenchi** shameless, disgraceful
11 清廉 **seiren** integrity, uprightness
清廉潔白 **seiren-keppaku** spotless integrity

3q10.2

厦 厦　　KA large house

──────── 11 ────────

廄 → 厩 2p12.2

3q11.1

麼　　BA, MA small, fine; what, how

3q11.2

廖　　RYŌ empty; name

3q11.3 / 1245

腐　　FU, kusa(ru), kusa(reru) rot, decay
kusa(rasu) let rot/spoil, corrode
kusa(su) disparage

──────── 1 ────────

4 腐心 **fushin** take pains, be intent on
6 腐肉 **funiku** tainted meat; carrion; gangrene
腐朽 **fukyū** decay, molder, rot, decompose
7 腐卵 **furan** bad egg
腐乱 **furan** ulcerate, decompose
8 腐刻 **fukoku** etching
9 腐食 **fushoku** corrosion
11 腐敗 **fuhai** decomposition, decay; corrpution
12 腐葉土 **fuyōdo** soil from decayed fallen leaves, leaf mold
腐植土 **fushokudo** humus
15 腐縁 **kusa(re)en** unpleasant but unseverable relationship
腐蝕 **fushoku** corrosion
16 腐儒 **fuju** worthless scholar, pedant
21 腐爛 **furan** ulcerate, decompose

──────── 2 ────────

5 立腐 **ta(chi)gusa(re)** rotting on the vine; dilapidation

目腐 **mekusa(re)** bleary-eyed person
目腐金 **mekusa(re)gane** pittance
6 防腐 **bōfu** preservation against decay
防腐剤 **bōfuzai** a preservative, antiseptic
7 豆腐 **tōfu** tofu, bean curd
9 持腐 **mo(chi)gusa(re)** useless possession
10 陳腐 **chinpu** out-of-date, commonplace, trite, worn out, threadbare
12 蒸腐 **mu(re)gusa(re)** dry rot

──────── 3 ────────

4 不貞腐 **futekusa(reru)** become sulky/spiteful
5 氷豆腐 **kōridōfu** frozen tofu
奴豆腐 **yakkodōfu** tofu cut into cubes
12 湯豆腐 **yudōfu** boiled tofu
焼豆腐 **ya(ki)dōfu** broiled tofu
13 煎豆腐 **i(ri)dōfu** bean curd boiled dry and seasoned

──────── 4 ────────

10 高野豆腐 **kōyadōfu** frozen tofu

3q11.4

塵　　JIN dust; the mundane world
chiri dust; trash, rubbish
gomi garbage, trash

──────── 1 ────────

7 塵芥 **chiriakuta, jinkai** dust and garbage, trash
8 塵取 **chirito(ri)** dustpan
9 塵除 **chiriyo(ke)** dust cloth/cover
塵界 **jinkai** this mundane life
10 塵埃 **jin'ai, chiri-hokori** dust and dirt; the drab world
塵紙 **chirigami** coarse (toilet) paper
16 塵寰 **jinkan** the dusty/mundane world

──────── 2 ────────

6 防塵 **bōjin** dustproof
灰塵 **kaijin** ashes and dust
汚塵 **ojin** filth
7 余塵 **yojin** trailing dust; aftereffects
9 俗塵 **zokujin** the world, earthly affairs
風塵 **fūjin** dust; worldly affairs
浮塵子 **unka** leafhopper, rice insect
後塵 **kōjin** dust raised in someone's wake; second best
炭塵 **tanjin** coal dust
砂塵 **sajin** cloud of sand, sandstorm
11 黄塵 **kōjin** dust (in the air); this weary world
12 集塵器 **shūjinki** dust collector
13 微塵 **mijin** particle, bit, iota
煙塵 **enjin** dust; particulate matter in smokestack smoke; battle scene
戦塵 **senjin** the dust of battle

──────── 3 ────────

6 宇宙塵 **uchūjin** cosmic dust

10 粉微塵 **konamijin** tiny fragments
———————— 4 ————————
4 木端微塵 **koppa-mijin** splinters, smithereens

———————— 12 ————————

廚 → 厨 **2p10.1**

3q12.1
廠 廠 廠
SHŌ workshop; shed
———————— 2 ————————
3 工廠 **kōshō** arsenal
———————— 3 ————————
9 造兵廠 **zōheishō** arms factory, arsenal, armory

3q12.2
廝 厮
SHI servant

3q12.3
廟
BYŌ mausoleum; shrine; palace
———————— 2 ————————
8 宗廟 **sōbyō** ancestral mausoleum
9 祖廟 **sobyō** ancestral mausoleum/tomb
13 聖廟 **seibyō** Confucian temple
15 霊廟 **reibyō** mausoleum, shrine

厩 → 厩 **2p12.2**

塵 → **3q13.2**

3q12.4
廡
BU (walking under the) eaves

3q12.5
廛 壥
TEN shop, store; residence, mansion

3q12.6 / 1530
摩 庅
MA rub, scrape
sasu(ru) pat, stroke, rub

———————— 1 ————————
0 摩する **ma(suru)** graze, scrape; nearly touch
4 摩天楼 **matenrō** skyscraper
5 摩可不思議 **maka-fushigi** profound mystery
7 摩利支天 **Marishiten** Marici, Buddhist god of war
12 摩訶不思議 **maka-fushigi** profound mystery
13 摩滅 **mametsu** wear, abrasion
17 摩擦 **masatsu** friction
摩擦音 **masatsuon** a fricative (sound)
19 摩羅 **mara** penis
———————— 2 ————————
6 多摩川 **Tamagawa** (river, Tōkyō-to/Kanagawa-ken)
9 按摩 **anma** massage; masseur, masseuse
研摩 **kenma** grinding, polishing; studying
12 減摩 **genma** reduction of friction, lubrication
減摩油 **genmayu** lubricating oil
揣摩 **shima** conjecture, surmise, speculation
16 薩摩 **Satsuma** (ancient kuni, Kagoshima-ken)
薩摩芋 **satsumaimo** sweet potato
薩摩守 **satsuma (no) kami** one who steals a ride
20 護摩 **goma** sacred fire
護摩灰 **goma(no)hai** thief posing as a fellow traveler
———————— 3 ————————
7 冷水摩擦 **reisui masatsu** rubdown with a cold wet towel

3q12.7
麾
KI, **sashimane(ku)** beckon to; command
———————— 1 ————————
3 麾下 **kika** under one's command

廢 → 廃 **3q9.3**

廣 → 広 **3q2.1**

3q12.8 / 1632
慶
KEI rejoice; congratulate
yoroko(bu) rejoice, be happy over
———————— 1 ————————
4 慶弔 **keichō** congratulations and condolences
6 慶兆 **keichō** good omen
7 慶応 **Keiō** (a university); (era, 1865–1868)
8 慶長 **Keichō** (era, 1596–1615)
慶事 **keiji** happy event, matter for congratualtions

3

氵
土
扌
口
女
巾
犭
弓
彳
彡
艹
宀
⺍
山
青
广 12←
尸
口

9 慶祝 **keishuku** congratulation; celebration
12 慶賀 **keiga** congratulation
慶雲 **Keiun** (era, 704–708)
13 慶福 **keifuku** happiness, blessings, welfare

———————— 2 ————————

3 大慶 **taikei** great happiness
4 元慶 **Gangyō** (era, 877–885)
天慶 **Tengyō** (era, 938–947)
5 弁慶 **Benkei** (legendary warrior-monk, ?–1189)
正慶 **Shōkei** (era, 1332–1338)
6 同慶 **dōkei** a matter for mutual congratulation
吉慶 **kikkei** congratulatory event, rejoicing
7 延慶 **Enkei** (era, 1308–1311)
12 御慶 **gyokei** greetings, felicitations

———————— 3 ————————

4 内弁慶 **uchi-Benkei** tough-acting at home (but meek before outsiders)
10 陰弁慶 **kage-Benkei** a lion at home but meek before outsiders

———————— 13 ————————

3q13.1

廨

GE, KAI government office

3q13.2

麈

SHU moose; priest's horsehair flapper
ōjika moose, elk

3q13.3 / 1531

磨 庋

MA, miga(ku) polish, brush
su(ru) rub, chafe, file; lose

———————— 1 ————————

3 磨上 **miga(ki)a(geru)** polish up
9 磨研紙 **makenshi** emery paper, sandpaper
磨砂 **miga(ki)zuna** polishing sand
10 磨耗 **mamō** wear and tear, abrasion
磨紙 **miga(ki)gami** sandpaper, emery paper
磨粉 **miga(ki)ko** polishing powder
12 磨減 **su(ri)he(rasu)** wear away, rub down
13 磨滅 **mametsu** wear, abrasion
磨損 **mason** wear, friction loss
15 磨潰 **su(ri)tsubu(su)** grind down; mash; deface; dissipate (one's fortune)

———————— 2 ————————

9 研磨 **kenma** grinding, polishing; studying
11 達磨 **Daruma** Dharma (Indian priest who brought Zen Buddhism to China circa 520 A.D.); tumbler, legless figurine

達磨忌 **Darumaki** (religious service on) anniversary of Dharma's death (October 5)
球磨川 **Kumagawa** (river, Kumamoto-ken)
12 減磨 **genma** reduction of friction, lubrication
減磨油 **genmayu** lubricating oil
琢磨 **takuma** diligent application
歯磨 **hamiga(ki)** toothpaste
歯磨粉 **hamiga(ki)ko** tooth powder
13 靴磨 **kutsumiga(ki)** shoe polish; bootblack
14 練磨 **renma** train, practice, drill
15 播磨 **Harima** (ancient kuni, Hyōgo-ken)

———————— 3 ————————

4 火達磨 **hidaruma** mass of flames, human torch
6 血達磨 **chidaruma** covered with blood
11 雪達磨 **yuki daruma** snowman
14 練歯磨 **ne(ri)hamiga(ki)** toothpaste

———————— 4 ————————

4 切磋琢磨 **sessa-takuma** work hard/assiduously
6 百戦錬磨 **hyakusen-renma** battle-seasoned, veteran

3q13.4

廩

RIN (rice) storage shed; stipend
kura (rice) storage shed

———————— 14 ————————

3q14.1

縻

BI rope through a bull's nose; tie up

3q14.2

糜

BI rice gruel; ulceration

———————— 1 ————————

21 糜爛 **biran** be inflamed, fester; decompose

麛 → 6b11.4

3q14.3

膺

YŌ breast, chest; hit, strike

———————— 1 ————————

18 膺懲 **yōchō** punish, chastise

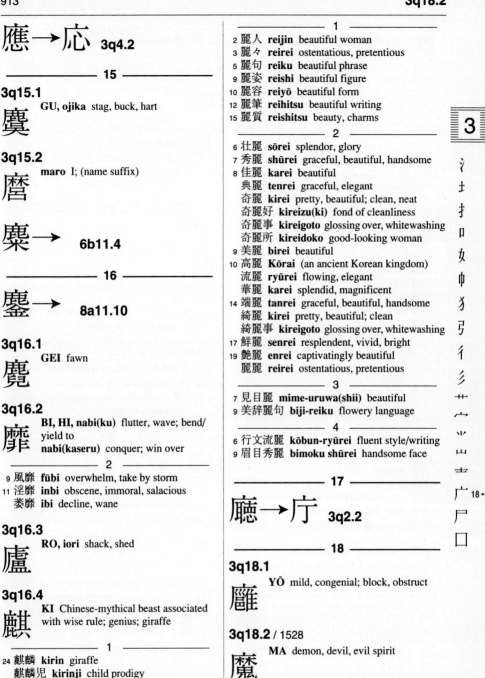

應→応 3q4.2

—————————— 15 ——————————

3q15.1
麌 GU, ojika stag, buck, hart

3q15.2
麿 maro I; (name suffix)

麋→ 6b11.4

—————————— 16 ——————————

鏖→ 8a11.10

3q16.1
麑 GEI fawn

3q16.2
靡 BI, HI, nabi(ku) flutter, wave; bend/
yield to
nabi(kaseru) conquer; win over
—————————— 2 ——————————
9 風靡 fūbi overwhelm, take by storm
11 淫靡 inbi obscene, immoral, salacious
萎靡 ibi decline, wane

3q16.3
廬 RO, iori shack, shed

3q16.4
麒 KI Chinese-mythical beast associated
with wise rule; genius; giraffe
—————————— 1 ——————————
24 麒麟 kirin giraffe
麒麟児 kirinji child prodigy

3q16.5 / 1630
麗 REI, RAI, uruwa(shii) beautiful,
pretty, lovely urara(ka) beautiful
(weather), bright, serene

—————————— 1 ——————————
2 麗人 reijin beautiful woman
3 麗々 reirei ostentatious, pretentious
5 麗句 reiku beautiful phrase
9 麗姿 reishi beautiful figure
10 麗容 reiyō beautiful form
12 麗筆 reihitsu beautiful writing
15 麗質 reishitsu beauty, charms
—————————— 2 ——————————
6 壮麗 sōrei splendor, glory
7 秀麗 shūrei graceful, beautiful, handsome
8 佳麗 karei beautiful
典麗 tenrei graceful, elegant
奇麗 kirei pretty, beautiful; clean, neat
奇麗好 kireizu(ki) fond of cleanliness
奇麗事 kireigoto glossing over, whitewashing
奇麗所 kireidoko good-looking woman
9 美麗 birei beautiful
10 高麗 Kōrai (an ancient Korean kingdom)
流麗 ryūrei flowing, elegant
華麗 karei splendid, magnificent
14 端麗 tanrei graceful, beautiful, handsome
綺麗 kirei pretty, beautiful; clean
綺麗事 kireigoto glossing over, whitewashing
17 鮮麗 senrei resplendent, vivid, bright
19 艶麗 enrei captivatingly beautiful
麗麗 reirei ostentatious, pretentious
—————————— 3 ——————————
7 見目麗 mime-uruwa(shii) beautiful
9 美辞麗句 biji-reiku flowery language
—————————— 4 ——————————
6 行文流麗 kōbun-ryūrei fluent style/writing
9 眉目秀麗 bimoku shūrei handsome face

—————————— 17 ——————————

廳→庁 3q2.2

—————————— 18 ——————————

3q18.1
靨 YŌ mild, congenial; block, obstruct

3q18.2 / 1528
魔 MA demon, devil, evil spirit

—————————— 1 ——————————
2 魔力 maryoku magical power, charm
3 魔女 majo witch, sorceress
4 魔手 mashu one's evil hands, clutches
魔王 maō the devil, Satan

3

氵 土
扌 口
女 巾
犭 弓
彳 彡
艹 宀
⺌ 山
辶 耂
广 18←
尸 口

8 魔法 **mahō** magic, sorcery, witchcraft
魔法使 **mahōtsuka(i)** magician, wizard
魔法瓶 **mahōbin** thermos bottle
魔物 **mamono** demon, devil
魔性 **mashō** diabolical
9 魔除 **mayo(ke)** charm against evil, talisman
魔風 **makaze** devil-caused/fearsome storm
魔神 **majin** evil deity, devil
魔界 **makai** world of devils/evil
11 魔道 **madō** evil ways
魔術 **majutsu** magic, sorcery, witchcraft
魔術師 **majutsushi** magician, conjurer
13 魔窟 **makutsu** den (of thieves); brothel, red-light district
14 魔境 **makyō** haunts of wickedness
15 魔魅 **mami** a deceiving/tempting spirit
19 魔羅 **mara** penis

——————— 2 ———————

4 天魔 **tenma** evil spirit, demon
5 白魔 **hakuma** snow, the white devil
6 伏魔殿 **fukumaden** abode of demons
色魔 **shikima** lady-killer, libertine
7 邪魔 **jama** hinder, obstruct, get in the way, interfere, bother, disturb
邪魔者 **jamamono** person who gets in the way
邪魔物 **jamamono** obstacle, impediment, nuisance
妖魔 **yōma** ghost, apparition
9 通魔 **tō(ri)ma** phantom (killer/slasher)
10 破魔弓 **hamayumi** exorcising bow (used in roof-raising ceremonies); toy bow and arrow
病魔 **byōma** demon of ill health, disease
11 悪魔 **akuma** devil
悪魔払 **akumabara(i)** exorcism
13 夢魔 **muma** disturbing dream, nightmare
睡魔 **suima** sleepiness, the sandman
14 誤魔化 **gomaka(su)** cheat, deceive; gloss over; tamper with, doctor
16 閻魔 **Enma** the King of Hades
閻魔帳 **enmachō** teacher's mark book

——————— 3 ———————

11 断末魔 **danmatsuma** one's dying moments

3q18.3

麝

JA musk deer

——————— 1 ———————

9 麝香 **jakō** musk
麝香猫 **jakōneko** musk cat, civet
麝香鹿 **jakōjika** musk deer
麝香鼠 **jakōnezumi** muskrat

——————— 21 ———————

3q21.1

鷹

YŌ, Ō, taka hawk

——————— 1 ———————

6 鷹匠 **takajō** falconer
9 鷹派 **takaha** the hawks, hardliners
鷹狩 **takaga(ri)** falconry

——————— 2 ———————

3 大鷹 **ōtaka** goshawk
8 夜鷹 **yotaka** nighthawk; prostitute

——————— 3 ———————

18 鵜目鷹目 **u(no)me-taka(no)me (de)** with a sharp/keen eye

——————— 22 ———————

廳 → 庁 **3q2.2**

——————— 30 ———————

3q30.1

麁
鹿鹿

SO rough, crude, coarse

—————————— 尸 **3r** ——————————

尸	尺	尻	尼	尽	尿	尾	屁	局	届	屇	屈	居
0.1	1.1	2.1	2.2	3.1	4.1	4.2	4.3	4.4	5.1	3r5.1	5.2	5.3

屎	眉	屍	屋	孱	屏	昼	恐	屓	展	屐	屑	屠
6.1	5c4.9	6.2	6.3	6.4	6.5	4c5.15	6.6	7.1	7.2	7.3	7.4	3r9.2

屏	属	屠	屢	犀	殿	厦	層	履	層	甓	屬	屓
3r6.5	9.1	9.2	3r11.1	9.3	10.1	11.1	11.2	12.1	3r11.2	5b13.1	3r9.1	3r7.1

釃												
21.1												

—————— 0 ——————

3r0.1

尸 **SHI, shikabane** corpse

—————— 1 ——————

3r1.1 / 1895

尺 **SHAKU, SEKI** (unit of length, about 30 cm); measure, length

—————— 1 ——————

2 尺八 **shakuhachi** bamboo flute/recorder
3 尺寸 **sekisun, shakusun** a bit/little
7 尺余 **shakuyo** more than a foot (long/high)
8 尺取虫 **shakuto(ri)mushi** inchworm
9 尺度 **shakudo** (linear) measure, scale, yardstick, standard
10 尺骨 **shakkotsu** the ulna
11 尺貫法 **shakkanhō** old Japanese system of weights and measures

—————— 2 ——————

3 三尺 **sanjaku** three (Japanese) feet; waistband, obi; loincloth
4 六尺 **rokushaku** six feet (tall); palanquin bearer
7 折尺 **o(ri)jaku** (carpenter's) folding ruler
8 長尺物 **chōjakumono, chōshakumono** long/lengthy item (film)
9 巻尺 **ma(ki)jaku** (roll-up) tape measure
10 矩尺 **kanejaku** carpenter's square; (unit of length, about 30.3 cm)
12 着尺 **kijaku** standard length of cloth for a kimono
着尺地 **kijakuji** standard-length kimono cloth
間尺合 **mashaku (ni) a(wanai)** not be worth it
13 照尺 **shōshaku** gunsights
17 縮尺 **shukushaku** reduced scale
19 鯨尺 **kujirajaku** (unit of length, about 37.8 cm)

—————— 3 ——————

5 生半尺 **namahanjaku** half-done, unfinished
9 計算尺 **keisanjaku** slide rule

—————— 2 ——————

3r2.1

尻 **KŌ, shiri** buttocks, fanny, backside, rear end; tail end

—————— 1 ——————

3 尻上 **shiria(gari)** rising (intonation)
尻下 **shirisa(gari)** falling off toward the end
4 尻切 **shiriki(re)** left unfinished
尻込 **shirigo(mi)** flinch, shrink back, hesitate
5 尻目 **shirime** looking askance
6 尻当 **shiria(te)** pants seat

7 尻抜 **shirinu(ke)** forgetful
尻尾 **shippo** tail; end
8 尻押 **shirio(shi)** push from behind, boost, back, abet; instigator, wirepuller
9 尻重 **shiriomo** slow-moving person
尻拭 **shirinugu(i)** taking the blame/loss for someone else
10 尻窄 **shirisubo(mari)** narrow toward the end; anticlimax, peter out
尻馬乗 **shiriuma (ni) no(ru)** imitate/follow blindly
12 尻軽 **shirigaru** wanton, loose
15 尻餅 **shirimochi** falling on one's behind/fanny

—————— 2 ——————

3 川尻 **kawajiri** lower stream; mouth of a river
5 台尻 **daijiri** butt/stock (of a gun)
目尻 **mejiri** outside corner of the eye
8 長尻 **nagajiri** overstaying one's welcome
空尻 **kara(k)ketsu** flat broke
11 帳尻 **chōjiri** balance of accounts
17 鍋尻 **nabejiri** pot's outside bottom

—————— 3 ——————

7 言葉尻 **kotobajiri** end of a word; slip of the tongue

3r2.2 / 1620

尼 **NI, ama** nun

—————— 1 ——————

6 尼寺 **amadera** convent
7 尼君 **amagimi** nun (respectful term)
8 尼法師 **ama hōshi** (Buddhist) nun
10 尼将軍 **ama shōgun** woman general
11 尼崎 **Amagasaki** (city, Hyōgo-ken)
13 尼僧 **nisō** nun
尼僧院 **nisōin** convent

—————— 2 ——————

13 僧尼 **sōni** monks and nuns
禅尼 **zenni** Zen nun

—————— 3 ——————

5 比丘尼 **bikuni** Buddhist priestess

—————— 4 ——————

11 釈迦牟尼 **Shakamuni** Sakyamuni, Gautama, Buddha

—————— 3 ——————

3r3.1 / 1726

尽 盡 **JIN, tsu(kusu)** exhaust, use up; render (service), make efforts **tsu(kasu)** exhaust, use up, run out of
tsu(kiru) become exhausted/depleted, run out, end
kotogoto(ku) all, entirely, completely

—————— 1 ——————

2 尽力 **jinryoku** efforts, exertions; assistance

3
氵
土
扌
口
女
巾
犭
弓
彳
彡
艹
宀
丷
山
彐
广
尸 3←
口

4 尽日 **jinjitsu** all day; last day
5 尽未来 **jinmirai** forever
8 尽忠 **jinchū** loyalty
尽忠報国 **jinchū-hōkoku** loyalty and patriotism
13 尽瘁 **jinsui** devote all one's efforts to

─────── 2 ───────

3 大尽 **daijin** millionaire, magnate; lavish spender
大尽風吹 **daijinkaze (o) fu(kasu)** display one's wealth
4 心尽 **kokorozu(kushi)** kindness, solicitude, efforts
5 立尽 **ta(chi)tsu(kusu)** continue standing
6 至尽 **ita(reri)-tsu(kuseri)** complete, thorough
自尽 **jijin** suicide
7 花尽 **hanazu(kushi)** listing many types of flowers; many-flowered design
売尽 **u(ri)tsuku(su)** sell off, clear out
見尽 **mitsu(kusu)** see all
言尽 **i(i)tsu(kusu)** tell all, exhaust (a subject)
8 使尽 **tsuka(i)tsu(kusu)** use up, exhaust
物尽 **monozuku(shi)** exhaustive, comprehensive
取尽 **to(ri)tsu(kusu)** take all
金尽 **kanezu(ku de)** by force of money, at any cost
9 食尽 **ku(i)tsu(kusu)** eat up, consume
10 書尽 **ka(ki)tsu(kusu)** write out in full
12 遣尽 **ya(ri)tsu(kusu)** do everything in one's power
極尽 **kiwa(me)tsu(kusu)** investigate thoroughly
焼尽 **ya(ki)tsu(kusu)** burn up, consume, reduce to ashes
ya(ke)tsu(kiru) burn itself out
焚尽 **ta(ki)tsu(kusu)** burn up, run out of (fuel)
無尽 **mujin** inexhaustible, endless; mutual financing association
無尽蔵 **mujinzō** inexhaustible supply
14 読尽 **yo(mi)tsu(kusu)** read it all
聞尽 **ki(ki)tsu(kusu)** hear it all
15 蕩尽 **tōjin** squander
論尽 **ron(ji)tsu(kusu)** discuss exhaustively
16 燃尽 **mo(e)tsu(kusu)** burn completely

─────── 3 ───────

11 理不尽 **rifujin** unreasonable, unjust

─────── 4 ───────

1 一網打尽 **ichimō dajin** a large catch, roundup; wholesale arrest
16 縦横無尽 **jūō-mujin** all around, no end of

─────── 4 ───────

3r4.1 / 1869

NYŌ, yubari urine

尿

─────── 1 ───────

5 尿石 **nyōseki** urinary calculus
8 尿毒症 **nyōdokushō** uremia
10 尿素 **nyōso** urea
11 尿瓶 **shibin** pisspot, bedpan
尿道 **nyōdō** urethra
12 尿検査 **nyō kensa** urinalysis
尿量 **nyōryō** amount of urination
13 尿意 **nyōi** the urge to urinate
14 尿管 **nyōkan** ureter
尿酸 **nyōsan** uric acid
15 尿器 **nyōki** bedpan, urinal

─────── 2 ───────

6 血尿 **ketsunyō** bloody urine
7 利尿 **rinyō** urination
利尿剤 **rinyōzai** a diuretic
8 夜尿症 **yanyōshō** bed-wetting
泌尿 **hinyō** urinary
泌尿科 **hinyōka** urology
泌尿器 **hinyōki** urinary organs
放尿 **hōnyō** urination
9 屎尿 **shinyō** excreta
11 排尿 **hainyō** urination
12 検尿 **kennyō** urinalysis
14 遺尿 **inyō** bed-wetting
導尿 **dōnyō** withdraw urine, catheterize
16 糖尿病 **tōnyōbyō** diabetes
輸尿管 **yunyōkan** the ureter
17 糞尿 **funnyō** feces and urine, excreta

3r4.2 / 1868

BI, o tail

尾

─────── 1 ───────

3 尾上 **o(no)e** mountain ridge/top
6 尾羽 **oha** tail feathers
尾行 **bikō** shadow, tail (someone)
尾灯 **bitō** taillight
7 尾花 **obana** (ears of) eulalia grass
8 尾長鳥 **onagadori** blue magpie; long-tailed bird
尾長猿 **onagazaru** long-tailed monkey
10 尾根 **one** mountain ridge
尾骨 **bikotsu** the coccyx
11 尾張 **Owari** (ancient kuni, Aichi-ken)
14 尾端 **bitan** tip of a tail, tail end
15 尾骶骨 **biteikotsu** the coccyx, tailbone
16 尾錠金 **bijōgane** buckle, clasp
尾頭付 **okashiratsu(ki)** whole fish
17 尾翼 **biyoku** tail (of an airplane)
21 尾鰭 **ohire** tail and fin; embellishments, exaggeration **obire** caudal fin
22 尾籠 **birō** indelicate, indecent, risqué

─────────── 2 ───────────

3 大尾 **taibi** end, finale
5 末尾 **matsubi** end, last, final
尻尾 **shippo** tail; end
6 交尾 **kōbi** copulation, mating
8 追尾 **tsuibi** pursuit, tracking
9 巻尾 **kanbi** end of a book
首尾一貫 **shubi-ikkan** logically consistent, coherent
首尾良 **shubiyo(ku)** successfully
後尾 **kōbi** rear, tail
11 接尾辞 **setsubiji** suffix
接尾語 **setsubigo** suffix
掉尾 **tōbi** final (flurry), last
船尾 **senbi** the stern, aft
12 結尾 **ketsubi** end, conclusion
13 鳩尾 **kyūbi, mizoochi, mizuochi** solar plexus, pit of the stomach
14 語尾 **gobi** word ending
語尾変化 **gobi henka** inflection
銃尾 **jūbi** breech (of a gun)
16 燕尾服 **enbifuku** swallow-tailed coat
機尾 **kibi** tail of an airplane
鴟尾 **shibi** ornamental ridge-end tile
21 艦尾 **kanbi** stern, aft (of a warship)
26 驥尾付 **kibi (ni) fu(su)** follow (another's) lead

─────────── 3 ───────────

3 上首尾 **jōshubi** a (great) success, satisfactory result
4 不首尾 **fushubi** failure; disgrace, disfavor

─────────── 4 ───────────

10 竜頭蛇尾 **ryūtō-dabi** strong start but weak finish
15 徹頭徹尾 **tettō-tetsubi** thoroughly, through and through

3r4.3

屁

HI, he fart
onara (audible) fart

─────────── 1 ───────────

0 すかしっ屁 **(sukaship)pe** inaudible/silent fart
11 屁理窟 **herikutsu** quibbling, sophistry

─────────── 2 ───────────

8 放屁 **hōhi** break wind

─────────── 3 ───────────

7 言出屁 **i(i)da(ship)pe, i(i)da(shi)be** The one who brought up the subject must act first. The one who says "What's that smell?" is the one who farted.

3r4.4 / 170

局

KYOKU bureau, office; (radio/TV) station; situation; local
tsubone court lady('s apartment)

─────────── 1 ───────────

5 局外 **kyokugai** the outside
局外中立 **kyokugai chūritsu** neutrality
局外者 **kyokugaisha** outsider, onlooker
6 局地 **kyokuchi** locality
局地化 **kyokuchika** localization
局地戦争 **kyokuchi sensō** limited war
局名 **kyokumei** name of a radio/TV station, call letters
8 局長 **kyokuchō** bureau chief, director, postmaster
局限 **kyokugen** localize, limit
局所 **kyokusho** local
9 局面 **kyokumen** (chessboard) position; situation
10 局部 **kyokubu** part, section; local; the affected region; one's private parts
局部麻酔 **kyokubu masui** local anesthetic
局員 **kyokuin** bureau/post-office staff
局留 **kyokudo(me)** general delivery
11 局務 **kyokumu** bureau business
12 局報 **kyokuhō** official bulletin; service telegram
局番 **kyokuban** telephone-exchange number

─────────── 2 ───────────

3 大局 **taikyoku** the general/total situation
4 内局 **naikyoku** bureau (within a ministry)
支局 **shikyoku** a branch (office)
支局長 **shikyokuchō** branch manager
分局 **bunkyoku** branch office
5 本局 **honkyoku** main/central office
外局 **gaikyoku** bureau whose director has authority independent of the ministry
6 全局 **zenkyoku** the whole situation
同局 **dōkyoku** the (same/said) bureau
当局 **tōkyoku** the authorities
当局者 **tōkyokusha** the authorities
7 対局 **taikyoku** play a game (of go)
医局 **ikyoku** medical office
8 事局 **jikyoku** circumstances
9 政局 **seikyoku** political situation
10 部局 **bukyoku** department, bureau
時局 **jikyoku** the situation
破局 **hakyoku** catastrophe, ruin
11 終局 **shūkyoku** end, conclusion; endgame
12 結局 **kekkyoku** after all, in the end
開局 **kaikyoku** opening a new office/bureau
13 戦局 **senkyoku** the war situation
新局面 **shinkyokumen** new aspect
14 選局 **senkyoku** (TV) channel selection
16 薬局 **yakkyoku** pharmacy
薬局方 **yakkyokuhō** pharmacopoeia
親局 **oyakyoku** key (broadcast) station
18 難局 **nankyoku** difficult situation, crisis

3

氵
土
扌
口
女
巾
犭
弓
彳
彡
艹
宀
⺌
凵
士
广
尸 4←
口

3

氵 土 扌 口 女 巾 犭 弓 彳 彡 艹 宀 ⺌ 出 吉 广 →5 尸 口

---------------- **3** ----------------

4 水道局 **suidōkyoku** water bureau
8 事務局 **jimukyoku** secretariat, executive office
　放送局 **hōsōkyoku** broadcasting station
9 造幣局 **zōheikyoku** the mint
　政治局 **seijiyoku** Politburo
10 郵便局 **yūbinkyoku** post office
　振出局 **furidashikyoku** the issuing (post) office (for a money order)
　書記局 **shokikyoku** secretariat
12 着信局 **chakushinkyoku** destination post office
　検事局 **kenjikyoku** prosecutor's office
13 電信局 **denshinkyoku** telegraph office
　電話局 **denwakyoku** telephone office

---------------- **4** ----------------

8 事務当局 **jimu tōkyoku** the authorities in charge

---------------- **5** ----------------

3r5.1 / 992

届 届

todo(ku) reach, arrive
todo(keru) report, notify; send, deliver

---------------- **1** ----------------

5 届出 **todokeide, todokede** report, notification
6 届先 **todo(ke)saki** where to report, receiver's address
10 届書 **todo(ke)sho** (written) report, notification

---------------- **2** ----------------

4 不届 **futodo(ki)** insolent, rude
5 未届 **mitodo(ke)** failing to report
　付届 **tsu(ke)todo(ke)** tip, present; bribe
6 行届 **yu(ki)todo(ku)** be meticulous/thoughtful/thorough
7 見届 **mitodo(keru)** verify, make sure of
8 送届 **oku(ri)todo(keru)** see/escort (someone) to
12 無届 **mutodo(ke)** without advance notice
14 聞届 **ki(ki)todo(keru)** grant (a request), accede to

---------------- **3** ----------------

4 不行届 **fuyu(ki)todo(ki)** negligent, remiss, careless, incompetent
　欠席届 **kesseki todo(ke)** report of absence
　欠勤届 **kekkin todo(ke)** report of absence
5 出生届 **shusseitodoke** report of birth
6 死亡届 **shibō todo(ke)** report of a death
11 遅刻届 **chikoku todo(ke)** tardiness report
　婚姻届 **kon'in todoke** marriage registration
　寄留届 **kiryū todo(ke)** notice of temporary domicile

屈→届 **3r5.1**

3r5.2 / 1802

屈

KUTSU bend; yield **kaga(mu)** bend/lean over, stoop, crouch **kaga(meru)** bend (one's leg/body), incline

---------------- **1** ----------------

0 屈する **kus(suru)** bend, bend over; yield to, be daunted
6 屈曲 **kukkyoku** crookedness; refraction; curvature
　屈伏 **kuppuku** submit/yield/surrender to
7 屈伸 **kusshin** extension and contraction; bending and stretching
　屈折 **kussetsu** bending; refraction; inflection
8 屈服 **kuppuku** submit, yield, surrender
9 屈指 **kusshi** leading, one of the ...est
10 屈辱 **kutsujoku** humiliation, indignity
　屈辱的 **kutsujokuteki** humiliating, disgraceful
　屈従 **kutsujū** submit meekly to, yield
　屈託 **kuttaku** be worried/troubled; ennui, boredom
11 屈強 **kukkyō** strong, robust
12 屈筋 **kukkin** flexor muscle

---------------- **2** ----------------

4 不屈 **fukutsu** indomitable
8 退屈 **taikutsu** boring, dull
　退屈凌 **taikutsu-shino(gi)** killing time
9 前屈 **zenkutsu** bend forward
　maekaga(mi) slouch
　怠屈 **taikutsu** boredom, tedium
　卑屈 **hikutsu** mean-spirited, servile
11 偏屈 **henkutsu** eccentric, bigoted, narrow-minded
　理屈 **rikutsu** theory; reason, logic; argument; pretext
15 窮屈 **kyūkutsu** narrow, cramped; formal, stiff, straitlaced; ill at ease

---------------- **4** ----------------

4 不撓不屈 **futō-fukutsu** inflexible, unyielding, indefatigable

3r5.3 / 171

居

KYO, KO, i(ru) be (present), exist

---------------- **1** ----------------

3 居丈高 **itakedaka** overbearing, domineering
　居士 **koji** Buddhist layman
4 居中 **kyochū** standing in-between
　居中調停 **kyochū-chōtei** mediation, arbitration

居心地 **igokochi** comfortableness, coziness
5 居乍 **inaga(ra)** as one sits, without stirring
6 居合 **ia(waseru)** happen to be present
居合抜 **ia(i)nu(ki)** swordplay exhibition
7 居住 **kyojū** reside
　　　izuma(i) one's sitting posture
居住地 **kyojūchi** place of residence
居住者 **kyojūsha** resident, inhabitant
居住費 **kyojūhi** housing expenses
居住権 **kyojūken** right of residence
8 居直 **inao(ru)** sit up straight; change one's attitude, come on strong; turn violent, resort to threat
居並 **inara(bu)** sit in a row, be arrayed
居所 **idokoro, kyosho** one's whereabouts, address, residence
9 居城 **kyojō** daimyo's residential castle
居待 **ima(chi)** sit and wait; 18-day-old moon
居室 **kyoshitsu** living room; one's own room
居食 **igu(i)** live in idleness
10 居残 **inoko(ru)** remain behind, work overtime
居候 **isōrō** hanger-on, dependent, sponger
居酒屋 **izakaya** tavern, pub, saloon
居眠 **inemu(ri)** doze, drowse
居留 **kyoryū** reside
居留民 **kyoryūmin** residents
居留地 **kyoryūchi** settlement, concession
居留守 **irusu** pretend not to be in (to avoid callers)
12 居着 **itsu(ku)** settle down
居場所 **ibasho** one's whereabouts, address
居然 **kyozen** calm, unruffled
居間 **ima** living room
13 居催促 **izaisoku** not leave till (a debt is) paid
15 居敷当 **ishikia(te)** kimono seat lining

――――――――― 2 ―――――――――

5 芝居 **shibai** stage play, theater
芝居小屋 **shibaigoya** playhouse, theater
芝居気 **shibaigi** striving for dramatic effect
穴居 **kekkyo** cave dwelling
穴居人 **kekkyojin** caveman
立居 **ta(chi)i** standing and sitting; daily getting about
6 仲居 **nakai** waitress
同居 **dōkyo** live in the same house
同居人 **dōkyonin** person living with the family, lodger
7 住居 **jūkyo, sumai** residence, dwelling
別居 **bekkyo** (legal) separation, living apart
8 長居 **nagai** stay too long
9 独居 **dokkyo** solitude, solitary life
幽居 **yūkyo** live in seclusion
10 起居 **kikyo** daily life　**ta(chi)i** standing up and sitting down
起居振舞 **ta(chi)i furuma(i)** deportment, manners

宮居 **miyai** shrine compound; imperial palace
11 寄居 **kikyo** temporary dwelling; staying with someone else
転居 **tenkyo** moving, change of address
閉居 **heikyo** stay indoors
鳥居 **torii** Shinto shrine archway
12 寓居 **gūkyo** reside temporarily
雲居 **kumoi** the sky; palace; the imperial court
閑居 **kankyo** live in seclusion/leisure
13 隠居 **inkyo** retirement; retired person; old person
群居 **murei(ru)** crowd together
新居 **shinkyo** one's new residence/home
新居浜 **Niihama** (city, Ehime-ken)
14 端居 **hashii** at the perimeter of the house, on the veranda
雑居 **zakkyo** dwell together
雑居ビル **zakkyobiru** building housing various businesses
15 敷居 **shikii** threshold, doorsill
16 鴨居 **kamoi** lintel
17 蟄居 **chikkyo** staying indoors; house arrest
18 謫居 **takkyo** exile
22 籠居 **rōkyo** stay indoors

――――――――― 3 ―――――――――

6 安芝居 **yasushibai** cheap theater
7 伽芝居 **(o)togi shibai** fairy play, play for children
8 若隠居 **waka-inkyo** early retirement
9 独芝居 **hito(ri)shibai** one-man show
独住居 **hito(ri)zumai** living alone
10 都住居 **miyakozumai** city life
留守居 **rusui** looking after the house (while someone is away); caretaker
紙芝居 **kamishibai** picture-card show
13 猿芝居 **saru shibai** tricks performed by a monkey
楽隠居 **rakuinkyo** comfortable retirement

――――――――― 4 ―――――――――

1 一人芝居 **hitori shibai** one-man show
2 人形芝居 **ningyō shibai** puppet show

――――――――― 6 ―――――――――

3r6.1

屎　　　　　　　SHI, **kuso** shit

――――――――― 1 ―――――――――

7 屎尿 **shinyō** excreta

――――――――― 2 ―――――――――

5 目屎 **mekuso** eye wax/discharge/mucus
14 鼻屎 **hanakuso** snot, booger

眉 →　　**5c4.9**

3r6.2

屍

SHI, shikabane corpse

――――― 1 ―――――

7 屍体 **shitai** corpse

――――― 2 ―――――

6 死屍 **shishi** corpse
12 検屍 **kenshi** coroner's inquest, autopsy

3r6.3 / 167

屋

OKU, ya roof, house; shop, dealer

――――― 1 ―――――

3 屋上 **okujō** roof, rooftop
4 屋内 **okunai** indoor(s)
5 屋外 **okugai** outdoor(s)
屋号 **yagō** store name; stage-family name
屋台 **yatai** a float; a stall
屋台店 **yatai mise** street stall, stand, booth
屋台骨 **yataibone** framework, foundation; means, property
7 屋形 **yakata** house, mansion, boat cabin
屋形船 **yakatabune** houseboat, barge, pleasure boat
10 屋根 **yane** roof
屋根伝 **yanezuta(i)** from roof to roof
屋根屋 **yaneya** roofer, thatcher
15 屋敷 **yashiki** mansion
屋敷町 **yashiki machi** exclusive residential section

――――― 2 ―――――

3 万屋 **yorozuya** general merchant/store
大屋 **ōya** landlord
上屋 **uwaya** a shed
上屋敷 **kamiyashiki** (daimyo's) main residence
下屋敷 **shimoyashiki** (daimyo's) villa
小屋 **koya** hut, cabin, cottage, shed
小屋掛 **koyaga(ke)** pitch camp; temporary hut/shack
4 円屋根 **maruyane** dome, cupola
水屋 **mizuya** hand-washing font for worshippers; cupboard; drinking-water seller
火屋 **hoya** lamp chimney
牛屋 **gyūya** butcher shop, beef restaurant
5 瓦屋 **kawaraya** tilemaker; tiler; tile-roofed house
瓦屋根 **kawara yane** tiled roof
本屋 **hon'ya** bookstore
母屋 **omoya** main building
平屋 **hiraya** one-story house
平屋根 **hirayane** flat roof

氷屋 **kōriya** ice shop, iceman
玉屋 **tamaya** jeweler
石屋 **ishiya** stone cutter/dealer
6 伏屋 **fu(se)ya** humble cottage, hovel
仮屋 **kariya** temporary shelter
肉屋 **nikuya** butcher (shop)
庄屋 **shōya** village headman
米屋 **komeya** rice dealer
7 何屋 **nan(demo)ya** jack-of-all-trades, handyman
角屋敷 **kadoyashiki** corner house
花屋 **hanaya** flower shop, florist
花屋敷 **hana yashiki** flower garden
芥屋 **gomiya** garbage man
牢屋 **rōya** prison, jail
床屋 **tokoya** barber, barbershop
社屋 **shaoku** office/company building
車屋 **kurumaya** rickshaw puller/station; cartwright
8 長屋 **nagaya** tenement building
東屋 **azumaya** arbor, bower, summerhouse
陋屋 **rōoku** squalid hut, hovel; my humble abode
拝屋 **oga(mi)ya** medicine man, faith healer
担屋 **katsu(gi)ya** superstitious person; practical joker; peddler
苫屋 **tomaya** rush-thatched cottage
茅屋 **bōoku** thatched cottage; my humble abode
空屋 **a(ki)ya** vacant house
岩屋 **iwaya** cave, cavern
店屋 **ten'ya** store; cooked-food store
店屋物 **ten'yamono** take-out food
板屋 **itaya** shingle/board roof(ed house)
板屋根 **itayane** shingle/wooden roof
的屋 **tekiya** charlatan; stall-keeper
9 陣屋 **jin'ya** encampment
草屋 **kusaya, sōoku** thatched hut
草屋根 **kusayane** thatched roof
茶屋 **chaya** teahouse; tea dealer
茶屋酒 **chayazake** saké drunk at a teahouse
炭屋 **sumiya** charcoal dealer
研屋 **to(gi)ya** grinder, sharpener, polisher
10 陸屋根 **rokuyane** flat roof
部屋 **heya** room, apartment
部屋代 **heyadai** room rent
部屋住 **heyazu(mi)** dependent, hanger-on; heir who has not yet taken over
部屋割 **heyawa(ri)** assignment of rooms
部屋着 **heyagi** house dress, dressing gown
酒屋 **sakaya** wine dealer, liquor store
家屋 **kaoku** house; building
家屋税 **kaokuzei** house tax
家屋敷 **ieyashiki** house and lot, estate
屑屋 **kuzuya** junkman
株屋 **kabuya** stockbroker

殺屋 **koro(shi)ya** hired killer
破屋 **haoku** dilapidated house, hovel
紙屋 **kamiya** paper store/dealer
納屋 **naya** (storage) shed
粉屋 **konaya** flour dealer, miller
蚊屋 **kaya** mosquito net
馬屋 **umaya** a stable
馬屋肥 **umayago(e)** horse manure
11 控屋敷 **hika(e) yashiki** villa, retreat
宿屋 **yadoya** inn
宿屋業 **yadoyagyō** the hotel business
桶屋 **okeya** cooper
産屋 **ubuya** maternity room
紺屋 **kon'ya, kōya** dyer, dyer's shop
問屋 **ton'ya** wholesaler
魚屋 **sakanaya** fish shop/seller
鳥屋 **toya** coop, roost; molting; kabuki actors' greenroom
12 傘屋 **kasaya** umbrella shop
湯屋 **yuya** public bathhouse
揚屋 **a(ge)ya** brothel
握屋 **nigi(ri)ya** tightfisted, miser
廃屋 **haioku** abandoned house
畳屋 **tatamiya** tatami maker/dealer/store
飲屋 **no(mi)ya** bar, saloon, tavern
飯屋 **meshiya** eating house
13 裏屋 **uraya** back-street house, slum
幕屋 **makuya** tent, curtain-enclosed room
靴屋 **kutsuya** shoe store, shoemaker
楽屋 **gakuya** dressing room, greenroom, backstage, behind the scenes
楽屋落 **gakuyao(chi)** a matter not understood by outsiders, shoptalk, inside joke
楽屋話 **gakuyabanashi** backstage talk
照屋 **te(re)ya** one who is easily embarrassed
置屋 **o(ki)ya** geisha house
飾屋 **kaza(ri)ya** jewelry maker
14 漆屋 **urushiya** lacquer shop
獄屋 **gokuya** prison, jail
綿屋 **wataya** cotton dealer
15 澄屋 **su(mashi)ya** smug-looking person, prim-looking girl
蔵屋敷 **kurayashiki** daimyo's city storehouse
鞍屋 **kuraya** saddler
熱屋 **atsu(gari)ya** person sensitive to the heat
黙屋 **dama(ri)ya** silent/taciturn person
締屋 **shi(mari)ya** thrifty person
箱屋 **hakoya** boxmaker
質屋 **shichiya** pawnshop
霊屋 **tamaya** mausoleum, ancestral shrine
16 薬屋 **kusuriya** drugstore
機屋 **hataya** weaver
17 藁屋根 **warayane** straw-thatched roof
闇屋 **yamiya** black marketeer

鮨屋 **sushiya** sushi shop
18 鞣屋 **name(shi)ya** tanner(y)
22 鰻屋 **unagiya** eel shop

─────── 3 ───────

2 入母屋 **irimoya** roof with eaves below the gables
八百屋 **yaoya** vegetable store; jack-of-all-trades
3 大部屋 **ōbeya** large room; actors' common room
下宿屋 **geshukuya** boardinghouse
土建屋 **doken'ya** contractor
口入屋 **kuchii(re)ya** employment agency
女郎屋 **jorōya** brothel
山小屋 **yamagoya** mountain hut
4 反物屋 **tanmonoya** dry-goods store
水茶屋 **mizuchaya** (Edo-period) roadside teahouse
犬小屋 **inugoya** doghouse, kennel
牛小屋 **ushigoya** cowshed, barn
牛乳屋 **gyūnyūya** milkman, milk dealer
5 生薬屋 **kigusuriya** drugstore, apothecary
弁当屋 **bentōya** lunch vendor
写真屋 **shashin'ya** photographer, photo studio
古本屋 **furuhon'ya** used/secondhand book store
広告屋 **kōkokuya** ad agency; publicity man
6 気取屋 **kido(ri)ya** affected person, poseur
両替屋 **ryōgaeya** money-exchange shop
仮小屋 **karigoya** temporary shed, booth
羊小屋 **hitsujigoya** sheep pen, sheepfold
汚穢屋 **owaiya** night-soil man
寺子屋 **terakoya** temple primary school
名古屋 **Nagoya** (city, Aichi-ken)
米問屋 **komedon'ya** rice wholesaler
7 作酒屋 **tsuku(ri)zakaya** saké brewer(y)
阿古屋貝 **akoyagai** pearl oyster
呉服屋 **gofukuya** dry-goods store
材木屋 **zaimokuya** lumberyard, lumber dealer
利権屋 **riken'ya** concession hunter, grafter
足袋屋 **tabiya** tabi seller/shop
8 表具屋 **hyōguya** picture mounter/framer
建具屋 **tateguya** cabinetmaker
周旋屋 **shūsen'ya** broker, employment agency
法律屋 **hōritsuya** lawmonger
始末屋 **shimatsuya** frugal person
空部屋 **a(ki)beya** vacant room
居酒屋 **izakaya** tavern, pub, saloon
青物屋 **aomonoya** vegetable store, greengrocer
玩具屋 **omochaya** toy shop
金物屋 **kanamonoya** hardware store
金魚屋 **kingyoya** goldfish seller
9 便利屋 **benriya** handyman

3

氵 土 扌 口 女 姉 巾 犭 弓 彳 彡 艹 宀 ⺌ 山 耂 广 →6 尸 口

卸問屋 **oroshiton'ya** wholesaler
造酒屋 **zōshuya** saké brewer
風呂屋 **furoya** bathhouse, public bath
洗濯屋 **sentakuya** laundry; laundryman
活版屋 **kappan'ya** print ship; printer
洋服屋 **yōfukuya** clothing store; tailor (shop)
洋品屋 **yōhin'ya** haberdasher(y)
指物屋 **sa(shi)monoya** cabinetmaker
狩小屋 **ka(ri)goya** hunting cabin, a blind
荒物屋 **aramonoya** household goods store
宣伝屋 **senden'ya** propagandist, publicist
幽霊屋敷 **yūrei yashiki** haunted house
屋根屋 **yaneya** roofer, thatcher
染物屋 **so(me)monoya** dyer
政治屋 **seijiya** politician
10 差物屋 **sashimonoya** cabinetmaker
遊女屋 **yūjoya** brothel
家具屋 **kaguya** furniture store
唐物屋 **karamonoya** foreign-goods dealer/
store
時計屋 **tokeiya** watch store, jeweler
旅籠屋 **hatagoya** inn
料理屋 **ryōriya** restaurant
馬小屋 **umagoya** a stable
11 運送屋 **unsōya** forwarding agent, express
company
道具屋 **dōguya** dealer in secondhand goods
菓子屋 **kashiya** candy store, confectionery
shop
乾物屋 **kanbutsuya** grocer, grocery store
情報屋 **jōhōya** (horserace) tipster
眼鏡屋 **meganeya** optician
経師屋 **kyōjiya** scroll/screen mounter, picture
framer; philan
船小屋 **funagoya** boathouse
船問屋 **funadon'ya** shipping agent
鳥小屋 **torigoya** aviary; chicken coop
12 帽子屋 **bōshiya** hat shop
御霊屋 **mitamaya** mausoleum, tomb
葬儀屋 **sōgiya** undertaker, funeral home
植木屋 **uekiya** gardener, nurseryman
煮売屋 **niu(ri)ya** eatery, cheap restaurant
散髪屋 **sanpatsuya** barber
番小屋 **bangoya** sentry box
貸本屋 **ka(shi)hon'ya** lending library
貸部屋 **ka(shi)beya** room for rent
13 裏長屋 **uranagaya** back-street tenement
楽器屋 **gakkiya** music shop
数奇屋 **sukiya** tea-ceremony room/cottage
数寄屋 **sukiya** tea-ceremony room/cottage
電気屋 **denkiya** electrical appliance store/
dealer
鳩小屋 **hatogoya** dovecote
14 銘酒屋 **meishuya** brothel
15 蕎麦屋 **sobaya** soba shop
鋳掛屋 **ika(ke)ya** tinkerer, tinsmith

16 機械屋 **kikaiya** machinist
錠前屋 **jōmaeya** locksmith
17 鍛冶屋 **kajiya** blacksmith

——— 4 ———

1 一膳飯屋 **ichizen meshiya** eatery, diner
2 子供部屋 **kodomo-beya** children's room,
nursery
3 丸太小屋 **marutagoya** log cabin
小間物屋 **komamonoya** haberdashery
4 不動産屋 **fudōsan'ya** real estate agent
文房具屋 **bunbōguya** stationery store
5 古道具屋 **furudōguya** secondhand store
芝居小屋 **shibaigoya** playhouse, theater
6 安料理屋 **yasuryōriya** cheap restaurant
10 差掛小屋 **sa(shi)ka(ke)goya** penthouse,
lean-to
11 道具部屋 **dōgu-beya** toolroom; prop room
12 棟割長屋 **munewa(ri) nagaya** long tenement/
partitioned building

3r6.4

屏

SEN weak; steep

3r6.5

屏 屛

BYŌ folding screen
HEI wall, fence

——— 1 ———

9 屏風 **byōbu** folding screen
屏風岩 **byōbu iwa** sheer cliff

——— 2 ———

8 枕屏風 **makurabyōbu** bedside screen
金屏風 **kinbyōbu** gold-leafed folding screen

昼→ **4c5.15**

3r6.6

咫

SHI short; hand-span

——— 7 ———

3r7.1

屓 屭

KI exert great strength

——— 2 ———

21 贔屓 **hiiki** favor, partiality, pro-(Japanese)
贔屓目 **hiikime** viewing favorably

———————— 3 ————————
7 身贔屓 **mibiiki** nepotism

———————— 4 ————————
8 依怙贔屓 **ekohiiki** favoritism, bias

3r7.2 / 1129

展

TEN expand

———————— 1 ————————
5 展示 **tenji** exhibition, display
展示会 **tenjikai** show, exhibition
8 展性 **tensei** malleability
10 展翅板 **tenshiban** setting board (for spreading butterfly-specimen wings)
11 展望 **tenbō** view, outlook, prospects
展望台 **tenbōdai** observation platform
12 展開 **tenkai** unfold, develop, evolve; deploy,
fan out; expand (a math expression),
develop (into a two-dimensional surface)
17 展覧 **tenran** exhibition
展覧会 **tenrankai** exhibition
展覧会絵 **Tenrankai (no) e** Pictures at an
Exhibition (Mussorgsky, 1874)
展覧物 **tenranbutsu** exhibit
展覧室 **tenranshitsu** showroom
18 展観 **tenkan** exhibition

———————— 2 ————————
7 伸展 **shinten** extension, stretching
9 発展 **hatten** expansion, growth, development
発展性 **hattensei** growth potential
発展途上国 **hattentojōkoku** developing
country
発展家 **hattenka** man about town, playboy
10 個展 **koten** one-man exhibition
進展 **shinten** development, progress
16 親展 **shinten** confidential, personal (letter)
親展書 **shintensho** confidential/personal letter

———————— 4 ————————
9 海外発展 **kaigai hatten** overseas expansion

3r7.3

展

GEKI clogs, footwear

3r7.4

屑

SETSU, kuzu trash, waste, scrap;
scum, dregs (of society)

———————— 1 ————————
2 屑入 **kuzui(re)** trash can/receptacle
6 屑糸 **kuzuito** waste threads
屑米 **kuzumai** broken rice

9 屑拾 **kuzuhiro(i)** ragpicking; ragpicker
屑屋 **kuzuya** junkman
13 屑鉄 **kuzutetsu** scrap iron
22 屑籠 **kuzukago** wastebasket

———————— 2 ————————
4 切屑 **ki(ri)kuzu** scraps, chips, shavings
木屑 **kikuzu** shavings, chips
6 糸屑 **itokuzu** waste thread, ravelings
8 金屑 **kanakuzu** scrap metal, filings
9 削屑 **kezu(ri)kuzu** shavings
10 紙屑 **kamikuzu** waste paper
紙屑拾 **kamikuzuhiro(i)** ragpicker
紙屑籠 **kamikuzukago** wastebasket
13 鉄屑 **tetsukuzu** scrap iron
鉋屑 **kannakuzu** wood shavings
14 選屑 **e(ri)kuzu, yo(ri)kuzu** trash, refuse, waste
16 鋸屑 **nokokuzu** sawdust
19 藻屑 **mokuzu** seaweeds

———————— 3 ————————
3 大鋸屑 **ogakuzu** sawdust

———————— 8 ————————

屠 → 屠   **3r9.2**

屏 → 屏   **3r6.5**

———————— 9 ————————

3r9.1 / 1637

属 屬

ZOKU belong to, be attached
to; genus; subordinate official
SHOKU belong to, be attached
to

———————— 1 ————————
0 属する **zoku(suru)** belong to, fall under, be
affiliated with
5 属目 **shokumoku** attention, observation
6 属吏 **zokuri** subordinate official
属地 **zokuchi** territory, possession
属名 **zokumei** generic name
8 属官 **zokkan** subordinate official
属国 **zokkoku** a dependency, vassal state
属性 **zokusei** attribute
11 属望 **shokubō** pin one's hopes on, expect
much of
14 属僚 **zokuryō** subordinates
属領 **zokuryō** territory, possession, dependency

———————— 2 ————————
5 付属 **fuzoku** attached, associated, auxiliary
7 亜属 **azoku** subgenus
附属 **fuzoku** attached, affiliated, ancillary

3

氵 土 扌 口 女 巾 犭 弓 彳 彡 艹 宀 丷 曲 耂 广 尸 ← 9 口

3

氵 土 扌 口 女 巾 犭 弓 彳 彡 艹 宀 ⺌ 山 青 广 →9 尸 口

臣属 **shinzoku** vassalage, subjection
8 直属 **chokuzoku** under the direct control of
服属 **fukuzoku** become a retainer, yield allegience to
所属 **shozoku** be attached/assigned to
金属 **kinzoku** metal
金属工業 **kinzoku kōgyō** metalworking industry
金属性 **kinzokusei** metallic
金属製 **kinzokusei** made of metal
9 専属 **senzoku** belong exclusively to, be attached to
軍属 **gunzoku** civilian employee of the military
10 部属 **buzoku** section, division
帰属 **kizoku** revert to, belong to, be ascribed to
従属文 **jūzokubun** subordinate clause
従属的 **jūzokuteki** subordinate, dependent
従属節 **jūzokusetsu** subordinate clause
11 眷属 **kenzoku** family, household, kith and kin
転属 **tenzoku** be transferred
12 尊属 **sonzoku** ancestor
14 種属 **shuzoku** kind, genus, species
16 隷属 **reizoku** be subordinate to

———————— 3 ————————

3 土金属 **dokinzoku** earth/terrigenous metals
8 非金属 **hikinzoku** nonmetallic
9 重金属 **jūkinzoku** heavy metals
12 無所属 **mushozoku** unaffiliated, independent
貴金属 **kikinzoku** precious metals
軽金属 **keikinzoku** light metals

———————— 4 ————————

8 非鉄金属 **hitetsu kinzoku** nonferrous metals

3r9.2

屠 屠

TO, hofu(ru) slaughter, butcher

———————— 1 ————————

8 屠所 **tosho** slaughterhouse
10 屠畜 **tochiku** butchering, slaughter
屠殺 **tosatsu** butchering, slaughter
屠殺場 **tosatsujō** slaughterhouse
19 屠蘇 **toso** spiced (New Year's) saké
屠蘇機嫌 **toso kigen** drunk with New Year's saké

屢 → 屡 **3r11.1**

3r9.3

犀

SAI rhinoceros

———————— 1 ————————

7 犀利 **sairi** keen, acute, penetrating

屛 → **3r6.4**

———————— 10 ————————

3r10.1 / 1130

殿

DEN, TEN hall, palace; mister
tono lord; mansion   **-dono** Mr.
shingari rear

———————— 1 ————————

3 殿上人 **tenjōbito, denjōbito** court noble
殿下 **Denka** His/Your Highness
4 殿方 **tonogata** gentlemen, men's
11 殿堂 **dendō** palatial building
14 殿様 **tonosama** lord, prince
殿様芸 **tonosamagei** dilettantism, amateurism

———————— 2 ————————

4 内殿 **naiden** inner shrine
仏殿 **butsuden** Buddhist temple
5 本殿 **honden** main/inner shrine
6 妃殿下 **hidenka** Her Highness
7 別殿 **betsuden** palace/shrine annex
社殿 **shaden** main shrine building
8 拝殿 **haiden** outer shrine, hall of worship
若殿 **wakatono** young lord
若殿原 **wakatonobara** young samurais
昇殿 **shōden** entry into the inner sanctum; access to the imperial court
金殿 **kinden** golden palace
金殿玉楼 **kinden gyokurō** palatial residence
9 便殿 **binden, benden** imperial resting room
客殿 **kyakuden** reception hall
神殿 **shinden** temple, shrine
10 高殿 **takadono** stately mansion
宮殿 **kyūden** palace
12 湯殿 **yudono** bathroom
御殿 **goten** palace
貴殿 **kiden** you (masculine)
13 寝殿 **shinden** (noble's) main residence
寝殿造 **shindenzuku(ri)** (a palace-style architecture)
15 幣殿 **heiden** room between the hall of worship and inner sanctuary of a shrine
霊殿 **reiden** shrine, mausoleum

———————— 3 ————————

3 大仏殿 **daibutsuden** temple with a huge image of Buddha
6 伏魔殿 **fukumaden** abode of demons
8 宝物殿 **hōmotsuden** treasury, museum
9 神楽殿 **kaguraden** Shinto dance pavilion
皇霊殿 **Kōreiden** the Imperial Ancestors' Shrine

12 紫宸殿 **Shishinden** Hall for State Ceremonies
奥御殿 **okugoten** inner palace

─────────── 11 ───────────

3r11.1

屢 屡

RU, shibashiba often, all the time

3r11.2 / 1367

層 層

SŌ layer, level, stratum, (social) class

─────────── 1 ───────────

7 層位学 **sōigaku** stratigraphy
層状 **sōjō** in layers, stratified
12 層雲 **sōun** stratus clouds
13 層楼 **sōrō** tall building
16 層積雲 **sōsekiun** stratocumulus clouds

─────────── 2 ───────────

1 一層 **issō** still more, all the more
3 上層 **jōsō** upper layer/stratum
上層気流 **jōsō kiryū** upper-air currents
上層雲 **jōsōun** upper clouds
下層 **kasō** lower layer, substratum; lower classes
5 皮層 **hisō** the cortex
外層 **gaisō** outer layer
6 地層 **chisō** stratum, layer
各層 **kakusō** every stratum/class
成層岩 **seisōgan** stratified/sedimentary rock
成層圏 **seisōken** the stratosphere
8 油層 **yusō** oil stratum
9 巻層雲 **kensōun** cirrostratus clouds
炭層 **tansō** coal bed/seam
10 高層 **kōsō** high-altitude, high-rise (building)
高層雲 **kōsōun** altostratus clouds
11 階層 **kaisō** tier; social stratum, class
彩層 **saisō** (the sun's) chromosphere
断層 **dansō** (geological) fault; gap
13 鉱層 **kōsō** ore bed
16 積層 **sekisō** lamination, building up layers

─────────── 3 ───────────

4 中間層 **chūkansō** middle stratum/class
支配層 **shihaisō** the ruling class
5 白亜層 **hakuasō** chalk bed/stratum
石炭層 **sekitansō** coal seam/bed
7 亜成層圏 **asei sōken** substratosphere
沖積層 **chūsekisō** alluvial stratum
8 所得層 **shotokusō** income level/bracket
10 真珠層 **shinjusō** mother-of-pearl
12 最下層 **saikasō** lowest class (of people)
14 読者層 **dokushasō** class of readers
16 薬九層倍 **kusuri-kusōbai** the high markup on drug prices
18 観客層 **kankyakusō** stratum of the audience

─────────── 12 ───────────

3r12.1 / 1635

履

RI footwear; take steps, do
ha(ku) put on, wear (shoes/pants)

─────────── 1 ───────────

4 履中 **Richū** (emperor, 400–405)
6 履行 **rikō** perform, fulfill, implement
8 履物 **ha(ki)mono** footwear
10 履修 **rishū** study, complete (a course)
14 履歴 **rireki** one's background, career; hysteresis
履歴書 **rirekisho** personal history, vita

─────────── 2 ───────────

3 上履 **uwabaki** slippers
下履 **shitaba(ki)** footwear; underpants
4 不履行 **furikō** nonperformance, default
木履 **pokkuri, bokuri** girls' wooden shoes
9 草履 **zōri** sandals, zori
草履取 **zōrito(ri)** sandal-carrier (servant)

─────────── 3 ───────────

3 上草履 **uwazōri** indoor sandals
下駄履住宅 **getaba(ki) jūtaku** apartment building whose first floor is occupied by stores and businesses
9 革草履 **kawazōri** leather sandals

─────────── 4 ───────────

8 突掛草履 **tsu(k)ka(ke) zōri** slip-on straw sandles

層 → 層   **3r11.2**

─────────── 15 ───────────

甓 →   **5b13.1**

─────────── 18 ───────────

屬 → 属   **3r9.1**

─────────── 21 ───────────

屭 → 屓   **3r7.1**

3r21.1

齷

AKU fretful

─────────── 1 ───────────

22 齷齪 **akuseku, akusaku** fussily, busily

3

氵
土
扌
口
女
巾
犭
弓
彳
彡
艹
宀
⺌
山
青
广
尸 21←
口

口 3s

口	口	口	日	囚	四	回	因	団	困	囲	囲	図
3d0.1	3s5.1	3s4.2	1.1	2.1	2.2	3.1	3.2	3.3	4.1	4.2	3s3.1	4.3

㕥	国	固	囹	面	囿	囵	圃	㝹	圄	恩	勉	氤
4.4	5.1	5.2	5.3	6.1	6.2	3s5.1	7.1	7.2	7.3	4k6.23	2n8.1	7.4

國	圏	圕	圉	圏	園	圍	圓	啬	團	圖	砲	圜
3s5.1	3s9.1	8.1	8.2	9.1	10.1	3s4.2	2r2.1	3b10.13	3s3.3	3s4.3	11.1	13.1

豫	氈	貔	牆	鹼	飴	麵	醫	鹹	鬮
0a4.12	14.1	0a11.1	3b14.6	3s21.1	3d17.5	4i17.1	4c19.1	21.1	22.1

氵
土
扌
口
女
巾
犭
弓
彳
彡
艹
宀
⺍
山
言
广
尸
→1 口

--- 0 ---

口 → **3d0.1**

口 → 国 **3s5.1**

口 → 囲 **3s4.2**

--- 1 ---

3s1.1

日

ETSU, iwa(ku) say; reason, pretext; a history/past

--- 1 ---

5 日付 **iwa(ku)tsu(ki)** (someone) with a past

3s2.1 / 1195

囚

SHŪ arrest, imprison; prisoner **torawa(reru)** be captured/apprehended; be in thrall to, be seized with

--- 1 ---

2 囚人 **shūjin** prisoner, convict
6 囚衣 **shūi** prisoner's clothes
7 囚役 **shūeki** prison work
10 囚徒 **shūto** prisoner, convict

--- 2 ---

3 女囚 **joshū** female prisoner
7 男囚 **danshū** male prisoner
13 虜囚 **ryoshū** captive, prisoner (of war)
14 獄囚 **gokushū** prisoner

--- 3 ---

5 未決囚 **miketsushū** unconvicted prisoner
6 死刑囚 **shikeishū** criminal sentenced to die
10 既決囚 **kiketsushū** a convict
11 脱獄囚 **datsugokushū** escaped prisoner

3s2.2 / 6

四

SHI, yot(tsu), yo(tsu), yon, yo- four

--- 1 ---

2 四人 **yonin** four people
四人乗 **yoninno(ri)** four-seater
四人組 **yoningumi** group/gang of four, foursome
四子 **yo(tsu)go** quadruplets
四十 **yonjū, shijū** forty
3 四千 **yonsen** four thousand
4 四天王 **shitennō** the four Deva kings; the big four
四切 **yo(tsu)gi(ri)** cut into four pieces, quarter; 30.5 by 25.5 cm (photo size)
四六判 **shirokuban** duodecimo, 12mo
四六時中 **shirokujichū** 24 hours a day, constantly
四分五裂 **shibun-goretsu** disruption, disintegration
四分六 **shiburoku** six-to-four (ratio/chance)
四分音符 **shibu/shibun onpu** quarter note
四月 **shigatsu** April
yon(ka)getsu four months
四月馬鹿 **shigatsu baka** April fool
四日 **yokka** four days; the fourth (day of the month)
四日市 **Yokkaichi** (city, Mie-ken)
四方 **shihō, yomo** all (four) directions/sides
四方八方 **shihō-happō** in every direction, far and wide
5 四民 **shimin** the four classes (samurai, farmers, artisans, merchants)
四半分 **shihanbun** quarter, fourth
四半期 **shihanki** quarter (of a year)
四目垣 **yo(tsu)megaki** lattice fence, trellis
6 四次元 **yojigen, shijigen, yonjigen** fourth dimension, four dimensions
四百 **yonhyaku** four hundred
四百四病 **shihyakushibyō** every kind of disease

四百余州 **shihyakuyoshū** all China
四旬節 **Shijunsetsu** Lent
7 四阿 **azumaya** arbor, bower, gazebo
四角 **shikaku** square; quadrilateral
    yo(tsu)kado four corners; intersection
四角号碼 **shikaku gōma** (an encoding
    scheme which assigns to each kanji a
    four-digit number based on its four
    corners)
四角四面 **shikaku-shimen** methodical, prim
四角形 **shikakukei** quadrilateral, square
四角張 **shikakuba(ru)** be formal/stiff
四声 **shisei** the four tones (of Chinese)
四囲 **shii** circumference, girth; surroundings
四児 **yo(tsu)go** quadruplets
四季 **shiki** the four seasons
四季咲 **shikiza(ki)** blooming all seasons
四足獣 **shisokujū** quadruped
8 四苦八苦 **shiku-hakku** agony, dire distress
四国 **Shikoku** (island)
四肢 **shishi** the limbs
9 四重奏 **shijūsō** (instrumental) quartet
四海 **shikai** the four/seven seas, the whole
    world
四海同胞 **shikai-dōhō** universal brotherhood
四面 **shimen** all (four) sides
四面楚歌 **shimen-soka** surrounded by
    enemies, without allies
四則 **shisoku** the four basic arithmetic
    operations (+, −, *, /)
10 四部合奏 **shibu gassō** (instrumental) quartet
四部合唱 **shibu gasshō** (vocal) quartet
四桁 **yoketa, yonketa** four-digit
四時 **yoji** four o'clock
    shiji the/all four seasons
四書 **Shisho** the Four Chinese Classics
11 四隅 **yosumi** four corners
四捨五入 **shisha-gonyū** rounding off
12 四割 **yonwari, shiwari** forty percent
    yo(tsu)wa(ri) divide into four, quarter
四散 **shisan** disperse, scatter
13 四聖 **shisei** the four great sages (Buddha,
    Christ, Confucius, Socrates)
15 四隣 **shirin** the whole neighborhood, the
    surrounding countries
四輪車 **yonrinsha** four-wheeled vehicle
21 四顧 **shiko** look all around

─────────── 2 ───────────
10 真四角 **mashikaku** square
11 第四階級 **dai-shi kaikyū** the fourth estate,
    the proletariat

─────────── 3 ───────────
3 三寒四温 **sankan shion** alternation of three
    cold then four warm days
5 平行四辺形 **heikōshihenkei** parallelogram

四百四病 **shihyakushibyō** every kind of
    disease
四角四面 **shikaku-shimen** methodical, prim

─────────── 4 ───────────
6 再三再四 **saisan-saishi** over and over again
12 朝三暮四 **chōsan-boshi** being deceived by
    immediate gain (like the monkey who
    did not realize that being given four
    chestnuts in the morning and three in the
    evening amounts to the same as three in
    the morning and four in the evening)

─────────── 3 ───────────

3s3.1 / 90

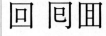

KAI, E (how many)
times, (which) round/
inning; go around
mawa(ru) go/turn
around **mawa(ri)** turning around; circumference; surroundings, vicinity **mawa(su)** (tr.) turn;
send around **mawa(shi)** loincloth **megu(ru)**
make a cycle; make one's rounds; surround,
concern **megu(rasu)** surround; ponder

─────────── 1 ───────────
0 回りくどい **mawa(rikudoi)** roundabout,
    circuitous
4 回天 **kaiten** herculean task, moving heaven
    and earth
回収 **kaishū** recover, reclaim, collect,
    withdraw from circulation
回文 **kaibun** palindrome; a circular
5 回付 **kaifu** transmit, pass on to, refer to
回礼 **kairei** round of courtesy calls
6 回合 **megu(ri)a(wase), mawa(ri)a(wase)**
    turn of fate, chance
回向 **ekō** a memorial service
回虫 **kaichū** intestinal worm, roundworm
7 回折 **kaisetsu** diffraction
回忌 **kaiki** anniversary of one's death
8 回送 **kaisō** forwarding, transportation; (bus)
    returning to the barn, Out of Service
回国 **kaikoku** traveling about the country,
    pilgrimage
回者 **mawa(shi)mono** spy, secret agent
9 回春 **kaishun** rejuvenation
10 回帰 **kaiki** recurrent; regression (coefficient)
回帰熱 **kaikinetsu** recurrent fever
回帰線 **kaikisen** the tropics (of Cancer and
    Capricorn); regression line
回遊 **kaiyū** excursion; migratory
回教 **kaikyō** Islam, Mohammedanism
回教国 **kaikyōkoku** Moslem country
回教徒 **kaikyōto** a Moslem
回航 **kaikō** navigation, cruise
回訓 **kaikun** the requested instructions

3

氵
土
扌
口
女
巾
犭
弓
彳
彡
艹
宀
⺌
山
土
广
尸
口 3←

3

氵
土
扌
口
女
巾
犭
弓
彳
彡
艹
宀
丷
山
吉
广
尸
→3 口

11 回動 **kaidō** rotate
回道 **mawa(ri)michi** roundabout way
回廊 **kairō** corridor
回旋 **kaisen** rotation, revolution, convolution, coiling, spiraling
回船 **kaisen** barge, cargo vessel
回転 **kaiten** revolve, rotate, swivel
回転木馬 **kaiten mokuba** carrousel
回転儀 **kaitengi** gyroscope
12 回復 **kaifuku** recovery
回復期 **kaifukuki** convalescence
回番 **mawa(ri)ban** taking turns
回答 **kaitō** reply
回診 **kaishin** doctor's hospital rounds
13 回数 **kaisū** number of times, frequency
回数券 **kaisūken** (train) coupon tickets
回想 **kaisō** retrospection, reminiscence
回想録 **kaisōroku** memoirs
回路 **kairo** (electrical) circuit
14 回漕 **kaisō** shipping, sea transport
回漕店 **kaisōten** shipping agent
回読 **kaidoku** read (a book) in turn
15 回舞台 **mawa(ri)butai** revolving stage
回避 **kaihi** avoid
回線 **kaisen** (electrical) circuit
回縁 **mawa(ri)en** veranda extending around two or more sides of the building
17 回覧 **kairan** read and pass on, circulate
21 回顧 **kaiko** recollect, look back on
回顧的 **kaikoteki** retrospective
回顧録 **kaikoroku** memoirs, reminiscences

───────── 2 ─────────

1 一回 **ikkai** once, one time; a game; an inning
hitomawa(ri) a turn/round
一回分 **ikkaibun** a dose; an installment
一回忌 **ikkaiki** first anniversary of a death
一回転 **ikkaiten, ichikaiten** one revolution/rotation
一回戦 **ikkaisen** first game/round (of tennis)
2 七回忌 **shichikaiki** seventh anniversary of a death
3 大回 **ōmawa(ri)** the long way around, circuitous route
上回 **uwamawa(ru)** be more than, exceed
下回 **shitamawa(ru)** be less than, fall short of
shitamawa(ri) subordinate work; underling; utility actor
小回 **komawa(ri)** sharp turn
4 今回 **konkai** this time, lately
切回 **ki(ri)mawa(su)** run around killing; manage, run, control
手回 **temawa(ri)** personal effects, one's things
temawa(shi) prepare, get ready
手回品 **temawa(ri)hin** personal effects
引回 **hi(ki)mawa(su)** pull around; lead about

5 北回帰線 **Kita Kaikisen** the Tropic of Cancer
左回 **hidarimawa(ri)** counterclockwise
出回 **demawa(ru)** appear on the market
付回 **tsu(ke)mawa(ru)** follow around, tag after
巡回 **junkai** tour, patrol, one's rounds
右回 **migimawa(ri)** clockwise
礼回 **reimawa(ri)** round of thank-you visits
立回先 **ta(chi)mawa(ri)saki** (criminal's) hangout
皿回 **saramawa(shi)** dish-spinning trick
6 年回 **toshimawa(ri)** luck associated with one's age
毎回 **maikai** every time
次回 **jikai** next time
迂回 **ukai** detour
近回 **chikamawa(ri)** neighborhood, vicinity; short cut
地回 **jimawa(ri)** from the vicinity, local; a street tough
先回 **sakimawa(ri)** anticipate, forestall; arrive ahead of
早回 **hayamawa(ri)** a dash around (the world)
7 低回 **teikai** loiter, linger
低回趣味 **teikai shumi** dilettantism
何回 **nankai** how many times
走回 **hashi(ri)mawa(ru)** run around
役回 **yakumawa(ri)** part, role, burden
見回 **mimawa(ru)** make an inspection tour, look around, patrol
利回 **rimawa(ri)** yield (on investments)
初回 **shokai** the first time
言回 **i(i)mawa(shi)** expression, phrasing
足回 **ashimawa(ri)** chassis
8 追回 **o(i)mawa(su)** chase/follow around; order about
逃回 **ni(ge)mawa(ru)** run around trying to escape, dodge
周回 **shūkai** circumference, perimeter; surroundings
空回 **karamawa(ri)** racing/idling (of an engine), skidding (of a car); fruitless effort
取回 **to(ri)mawa(su)** manage, treat
金回 **kanemawa(ri)** circulation of money; financial condition
9 飛回 **to(bi)mawa(ru)** fly/jump/rush around
乗回 **no(ri)ma(wasu), no(ri)ma(waru)** drive/ride around
南回帰線 **Minami Kaikisen** the Tropic of Capricorn
前回 **zenkai** last time
持回 **mo(chi)mawa(ru)** carry around
mo(chi)mawa(ri) decision-making by circular **mo(tte)mawa(tta)** roundabout
後回 **atomawa(shi)** deferring, postponing

荒回 **a(re)mawa(ru)** rampage
星回 **hoshimawa(ri)** one's star/fortune
思回 **omo(i)mawa(su)** recall, ponder
10 差回 **sa(shi)mawa(su)** send (a car) around
這回 **ha(i)mawa(ru)** crawl about
捜回 **saga(shi)mawa(ru)** search/hunt around
捏回 **ko(ne)mawa(su)** knead, mix; be muddy
挽回 **bankai** retrieve, recover, restore
振回 **fu(ri)mawa(su)** wave about, brandish
根回 **nemawa(shi)** doing the groundwork, pre-selling (a proposal), consensus-building
胴回 **dōmawa(ri)** one's girth
旅回 **tabimawa(ri)** touring
馬回 **umamawa(ri)** daimyo's mounted guards
11 探回 **sagu(ri)mawa(ru)** grope about
旋回 **senkai** turning, revolving, circling
転回 **tenkai** rotate, revolve
12 遠回 **tōmawa(ri)** roundabout way, detour
    tōmawa(shi) roundabout expression
補回 **hokai** extra innings (in baseball)
補回戦 **hokaisen** game extended into overtime
飲回 **no(mi)mawa(su)** pass (the bottle) around
13 搔回 **ka(ki)mawa(su)** stir, churn; ransack, rummage around
猿回 **sarumawa(shi)** monkey trainer
腰回 **koshimawa(ri)** one's hip measurement
数回 **sūkai** several times
睨回 **ne(me)mawa(su)** glare around
裾回 **susomawa(shi)** hemline (of a kimono)
触回 **fu(re)mawa(ru)** spread (a rumor), bruit about
節回 **fushimawa(shi)** melody
跳回 **ha(ne)mawa(ru), to(bi)mawa(ru), odo(ri)mawa(ru)** jump about, cavort, gambol
14 奪回 **dakkai** recapture, retake
駆回 **ka(ke)mawa(ru), ka(kezuri)mawa(ru)** run around
15 撤回 **tekkai** withdraw, retract, rescind
暴回 **aba(re)mawa(ru)** run riot/amuck, rampage
輪回 **wamawa(shi)** hoop rolling
16 盥回 **taraimawa(shi)** feat of spinning a washtub on one's feet; (officeholding) in rotation; detention at one police station after another
19 繰回 **ku(ri)mawa(su)** make shift, roll over (a debt)

───────── 3 ─────────
4 引搔回 **hi(k)ka(ki)mawa(su)** ransack, rummage through; carry on highhandedly
引摺回 **hi(ki)zu(ri)mawa(su)** drag around

5 田舎回 **inakamawa(ri)** tour of the country, provincial tour
6 早手回 **hayatemawa(shi)** early preparations
9 単利回 **tanrimawa(ri)** yield by a simple interest method
10 起死回生 **kishi kaisei** resuscitation, revival
時計回 **tokeimawa(ri)** clockwise
12 最終回 **saishūkai** the last time/inning
集積回路 **shūseki kairo** integrated circuit

───────── 4 ─────────
6 光集積回路 **hikari shūseki kairo** optical integrated circuit

3s3.2 / 554

因 **IN** cause, factor **china(mu)** be associated with **china(mi ni)** in this connection, by the way **yo(ru)** be due to, be based on **yo(tte)** therefore, consequently

───────── 1 ─────────
2 因子 **inshi** factor (in math); gene
5 因由 **in'yu** cause
8 因果 **inga** cause and effect; fate; misfortune
因果応報 **inga-ōhō** reward according to deeds, retribution
因果者 **ingamono** unlucky/ill-fated person
因果律 **ingaritsu** principle of causality
9 因盾 **injun** vacillating, conservative
11 因習 **inshū** custom, convention
12 因循 **injun** vacillating, conservative
13 因業 **ingō** heartless, cruel
因数 **insū** factor (in math)
因数分解 **insū bunkai** factorization
15 因幡 **Inaba** (ancient kuni, Tottori-ken)
因縁 **innen** fate; connection; origin; pretext
22 因襲 **inshū** custom, convention

───────── 2 ─────────
1 一因 **ichiin** a cause
4 内因 **naiin** internal cause
5 外因 **gaiin** external cause, exogenous
主因 **shuin** main cause, primary factor
6 死因 **shiin** cause of death
近因 **kin'in** proximate cause
成因 **seiin** cause, origin
9 要因 **yōin** principal factor, chief cause
10 真因 **shin'in** true cause/reason
原因 **gen'in** cause
原因不明 **gen'in fumei** of unknown cause/origin
起因 **kiin** originate in, be caused by
従因 **jūin** secondary cause
病因 **byōin** cause of the disease, etiology
素因 **soin** contributing factor, cause
11 偶因 **gūin** contingent cause
副因 **fukuin** secondary cause

3

氵
土
扌
口
女
巾
犭
弓
彳
彡
艹
宀
丷
凵
土
广
尸
口 3←

悪因悪果 **akuin-akka** Evil breeds evil.
敗因 **haiin** a cause of defeat
12 善因善果 **zen'in-zenka** Good actions lead to good results.
遠因 **en'in** remote/underlying cause
勝因 **shōin** cause of victory
訴因 **soin** cause of action, charge, count
13 禍因 **kain** cause of trouble, seeds of evil
14 導因 **dōin** incentive, motive, cause
誘因 **yūin** enticement, inducement

————————— 3 —————————

14 遺伝因子組替 **iden'inshi kumika(e)** recombinant gene splicing

3s3.3 / 491

DAN, TON, DON group

団 團

————————— 1 —————————

2 団子 **dango** dumpling
団子鼻 **dangobana** flat/pug nose
6 団交 **dankō** collective bargaining (short for 団体交渉)
団地 **danchi** (public) housing development, apartment complex
7 団体 **dantai** group, organization
8 団長 **danchō** leader (of a group)
10 団員 **dan'in** member (of a group)
団栗 **donguri** acorn
団栗眼 **donguri manako** goggle-eyed
団扇 **uchiwa** round fan
12 団結 **danketsu** unity, solidarity
団結心 **danketsushin** spirit of solidarity
13 団塊 **dankai** lump, nodule; baby-boom (generation)
14 団旗 **danki** association's flag
23 団欒 **danran** happy/family circle

————————— 2 —————————

1 一団 **ichidan** a group
2 入団 **nyūdan** join, enlist
3 大団円 **daidan'en** end, denouement, finale
土団子 **tsuchidango** mud pie
4 分団 **bundan** branch, (local) chapter
公団 **kōdan** public (housing) corporation
5 左団扇 **hidari uchiwa** (living in) ease and luxury
布団 **futon** bedding, sleeping mat, futon
6 気団 **kidan** air mass
地団駄踏 **jidanda (o) fu(mu)** stamp one's feet
7 兵団 **heidan** army corps
社団 **shadan** corporation, association
社団法人 **shadan hōjin** corporate juridical person
9 軍団 **gundan** army corps
炭団 **tadon** charcoal ball/briquette

星団 **seidan** star cluster
10 師団 **shidan** (army) division
師団長 **shidanchō** division commander
旅団 **ryodan** brigade
教団 **kyōdan** religious society/order
財団 **zaidan** foundation, financial group
財団法人 **zaidan hōjin** (incorporated) foundation
11 経団連 **Keidanren** Federation of Economic Organizations (Keidanren) (short for 経済団体連合会)
船団 **sendan** fleet, convoy
12 焼団子 **ya(ki)dango** toasted dumpling
黍団子 **kibidango** millet-flour dumpling
集団 **shūdan** group, mass, crowd
集団的 **shūdanteki** collectively
13 蒲団 **futon** futon, mattress, bedding
蒲団蒸 **futonmu(shi)** confining (someone) under several futons (for fun)
楽団 **gakudan** orchestra, band
解団 **kaidan** disband
15 劇団 **gekidan** troupe, theatrical company
16 親団体 **oyadantai** parent organization

————————— 3 —————————

1 一家団欒 **ikka danran** happy family circle, happy home
3 大同団結 **daidō danketsu** merger, combination
4 公共団体 **kōkyō dantai** public body/organization
5 代表団 **daihyōdan** delegation, mission
外交団 **gaikōdan** diplomatic corps
外郭団体 **gaikaku dantai** auxiliary organization
右翼団体 **uyoku dantai** right-wing group
6 曲馬団 **kyokubadan** circus troupe
合唱団 **gasshōdan** chorus, choir
羽蒲団 **hanebuton** feather-filled futon, down quilt
自警団 **jikeidan** vigilance committee, vigilantes
7 応援団 **ōendan** rooting section, cheerleaders
8 使節団 **shisetsudan** mission, delegation
青年団 **seinendan** young men's association
9 院外団 **ingaidan** lobbying group
客布団 **kyakubuton** bedding for guests
10 座蒲団 **zabuton** cushion
教授団 **kyōjudan** faculty
11 掛布団 **ka(ke)buton** quilt, coverlet
掛蒲団 **ka(ke)buton** quilt, coverlet
密輸団 **mitsuyudan** smuggling ring
13 義和団 **Giwadan** the Boxers
腰布団 **koshibuton** cushion worn around the waist for warmth
14 選手団 **senshudan** team, squad

15 暴力団 **bōryokudan** gangster organization
敷布団 **shikibuton** floor mattress
敷蒲団 **shikibuton** floor mattress
17 藁蒲団 **warabuton** straw mattress/pallet
18 観光団 **kankōdan** tour group
19 警防団 **keibōdan** civil defense corps

───────── 4 ─────────

6 交響楽団 **kōkyō gakudan** symphony orchestra
13 煎餅布団 **senbei-buton** thinly stuffed futon/bedding
14 管弦楽団 **kangen gakudan** orchestra
管絃楽団 **kangen gakudan** orchestra

──────────── 4 ────────────

3s4.1 / 558

木

KON, koma(ru) be distressed

───────── 1 ─────────

4 困切 **koma(ri)ki(ru)** be in a fix, be at a loss
7 困却 **konkyaku** embarrassment, dilemma
8 困果 **koma(ri)ha(teru)** be greatly troubled/nonplussed
困苦 **konku** hardships, adversity
困者 **koma(ri)mono** good-for-nothing, nuisance, pest
12 困惑 **konwaku** perplexity, dilemma
15 困窮 **konkyū** poverty, distress
困窮者 **konkyūsha** the needy/destitute
16 困憊 **konpai** exhaustion, fatigue
18 困難 **konnan** difficulty, trouble

───────── 2 ─────────

11 貧困 **hinkon** poverty; lack

3s4.2 / 1194

囲 圍

I, kako(mu/u) surround, enclose, encircle

───────── 1 ─────────

8 囲者 **kako(i)mono** kept woman, mistress
囲炉裏 **irori** sunken hearth
13 囲碁 **igo** go (the board game)
18 囲繞 **ijō, inyō** surround

───────── 2 ─────────

5 包囲 **hōi** surround, encircle, besiege
外囲 **sotogako(i)** outer fence
四囲 **shii** circumference, girth; surroundings
7 攻囲 **kōi** siege
8 周囲 **shūi** circumference, perimeter; surroundings
板囲 **itagako(i)** board/plank fence
取囲 **to(ri)kako(mu)** surround, encircle

9 重囲 **jūi, chōi** close siege
10 胸囲 **kyōi** girth/circumference of the chest
11 雪囲 **yukigako(i)** shelter against snow
12 雰囲気 **fun'iki** atmosphere, ambience
13 腰囲 **yōi** one's hip measurement
腹囲 **fukui** girth of the abdomen
15 範囲 **han'i** extent, scope, range
範囲内 **han'inai** within the limits of
16 頭囲 **tōi** girth of the head
17 霜囲 **shimogako(i)** (straw) covering to protect against frost

───────── 3 ─────────

5 広範囲 **kōhan'i** wide range/scope

囲 → 回 3s3.1

3s4.3 / 339

図 圖

ZU drawing, diagram, plan
TO, haka(ru) plan, seek (to effect), strive/work for, (try to) bring about

───────── 1 ─────────

3 図工 **zukō** draftsman
図々 **zūzū(shii)** impudent, brazen, cheeky
4 図太 **zubuto(i)** impudent, audacious
図引 **zuhi(ki)** drafting, drawing; draftsman
5 図示 **zushi** explanatory diagram, illustration
6 図式 **zushiki** diagram, graph
7 図体 **zūtai** one's body/frame
図抜 **zunu(keru)** tower above, be outstanding
図形 **zukei** diagram, figure, pattern
8 図表 **zuhyō** chart, table, graph
図画 **zuga** drawing
図版 **zuhan** plate, figure, illustration
図法 **zuhō** drawing, draftsmanship
図取 **zudo(ri)** sketching; sketch, plan
9 図面 **zumen** drawing, sketch, plan, blueprints
図柄 **zugara** pattern, design
図星 **zuboshi** the bull's-eye
10 図案 **zuan** (ornamental) design, device
図案家 **zuanka** designer, patternmaker
図書 **tosho** books
図書室 **toshoshitsu** library (room)
図書館 **toshokan** library
図書館学 **toshokangaku** library science
図書館長 **toshokanchō** head librarian
図書館員 **toshokan'in** library clerk, librarian
13 図解 **zukai** explanatory diagram, illustration
14 図説 **zusetsu** explanatory diagram, illustration
23 図鑑 **zukan** picture book

───────── 2 ─────────

3 上図 **jōzu** the upper diagram/illustration
下図 **shitazu** rough sketch
kazu the lower illustration

3

氵
土
扌
口
女
巾
犭
弓
彳
彡
艹
宀
丷
屮
圭
广
尸
口 4←

3

氵 土 扌 口 女 巾 犭 弓 彳 彡 艹 宀 ⺍ 山 士 广 尸
→4 囗

4 不図 **futo** suddenly, unexpectedly, by chance
方図 **hōzu** end, limit
5 付図 **fuzu** attached diagram
6 全図 **zenzu** complete map; whole view
企図 **kito** plan, project, undertaking
合図 **aizu** signal, sign
壮図 **sōto** grand undertaking
地図 **chizu** map
7 作図 **sakuzu** drawing figures, construction (in geometry)
図図 **zūzū(shii)** impudent, brazen, cheeky
系図 **keizu** genealogy, family tree
系図学 **keizugaku** genealogy
8 版図 **hanto** territory, dominion
9 海図 **kaizu** (marine) chart
指図 **sa(shi)zu** instructions, orders
指図書 **sa(shi)zusho** (written) order, directions
要図 **yōzu** rough sketch
後図 **kōto** future plans
星図 **seizu** star chart, celestial map
10 原図 **genzu** the original drawing
流図 **naga(re)zu** flowchart
挿図 **sōzu** figure, illustration
11 掛図 **ka(ke)zu** wall chart/map
略図 **ryakuzu** rough sketch, outline map
異図 **ito** ulterior motive
12 港図 **kōzu** harbor map/charts
絵図 **ezu** drawing, illustration, diagram, plan
絵図面 **ezumen** plan, design
雄図 **yūto** ambitious undertaking
13 愚図 **guzu** dullard, irresolute person
愚図付 **guzutsu(ku)** dawdle, be irresolute
愚図愚図 **guzuguzu** dawdle, hesitate
意図 **ito** intention, aim
14 構図 **kōzu** compose, plan out, design
製図 **seizu** drafting, drawing, cartography
17 縮図 **shukuzu** reduced/scaled-down drawing

───────── 3 ─────────

4 天気図 **tenkizu** weather map
天体図 **tentaizu** celestial map, star chart
天宮図 **tenkyūzu** horoscope
心電図 **shindenzu** electrocardiogram
5 平面図 **heimenzu** plane view, floor plan
正面図 **shōmenzu** front view
白地図 **hakuchizu** outline/contour map
6 気象図 **kishōzu** weather map
地形図 **chikeizu** topographical/relief map
地質図 **chishitsuzu** geological map
7 折地図 **o(ri)chizu** folding map
見取図 **mito(ri)zu** sketch (map)
10 俯瞰図 **fukanzu** bird's-eye/overhead view
家系図 **kakeizu** family tree
案内図 **annaizu** information map
11 野放図 **nohōzu** wild, unbridled
側面図 **sokumenzu** side view

斜視図 **shashizu** perspective view
断面図 **danmenzu** cross-sectional view
設計図 **sekkeizu** plan, blueprint
鳥瞰図 **chōkanzu** bird's-eye view

───────── 4 ─────────

4 五十音図 **gojūonzu** the kana syllabary table
分県地図 **bunken chizu** maps grouped by prefecture
13 愚図愚図 **guzuguzu** dawdle, hesitate

3s4.4

化 **KA, otori** decoy

───────── 5 ─────────

3s5.1 / 40

国 國 圀 **KOKU** country **kuni** country; (ancient) province; one's native province/country

───────── 1 ─────────

0 お国 **(o)kuni** your (native) country; your home (town); a daimyō's territory (Edo period)
お国ことば **(o)kuni (kotoba)** dialect, vernacular
2 国入 **(o)kunii(ri)** daimyō's return (from Edo); celebrity's homecoming
国力 **kokuryoku** national strength/resources
3 国々 **kuniguni** countries, nations
国士 **kokushi** distinguished citizen, patriot
4 国内 **kokunai** domestic
国中 **kokuchū, kunijū** the whole country
国文 **kokubun** Japanese-language; Japanese literature
国文学 **kokubungaku** Japanese literature
国文学史 **kokubungakushi** history of Japanese literature
国文法 **kokubunpō** Japanese grammar
国文科 **kokubunka** Japanese literature course
国分寺 **kokubunji** (ancient) state-established provincial temple
国手 **kokushu** skilled physician; master go player
国王 **kokuō** king
5 国民 **kokumin** the/a people, a national; national
国民化 **kokuminka** nationalization
国民服 **kokuminfuku** national uniform (for civilians)
国民的 **kokuminteki** national
国民性 **kokuminsei** national character
国民軍 **kokumingun** national army
国本 **kokuhon** foundations of the nation

国母 **kokubo** empress, empress dowager
国史 **kokushi** national/Japanese history
国外 **kokugai** outside the country, abroad
国号 **kokugō** name of a country
国字 **kokuji** native script; made-in-Japan kanji not found in Chinese
国主 **kokushu** lord, governor, daimyo
国立 **kokuritsu** national (park/library) **Kunitachi** (city, Tōkyō-to)
6 国会 **kokkai** national assembly, parliament, diet, congress
国防 **kokubō** national defense
国防色 **kokubōshoku** khaki
国防軍 **kokubōgun** national defense forces
国防費 **kokubōhi** defense expenditures
国交 **kokkō** diplomatic relations
国名 **kokumei** name of a country
国守 **kokushu** (ancient) governor
国光 **kokkō** national glory/prestige
国有 **kokuyū** national ownership
国有化 **kokuyūka** nationalization
国有地 **kokuyūchi** national land
国有鉄道 **kokuyū tetsudō** national railway
国自慢 **(o)kuni jiman** pride in one's native home province; boast of one's native place
7 国体 **kokutai** national structure/essence **Kokutai** (short for 国民体育大会) National Athletic Meet
国別 **kunibetsu** classified by countries
国技 **kokugi** national skill/sport
国乱 **kokuran** civil strife
国君 **kokkun** ruler, sovereign
国花 **kokka** national flower
国学 **kokugaku** study of Japanese literature
国学者 **kokugakusha** Japanese-classics scholar
国利 **kokuri** national interests
国利民福 **kokuri-minpuku** the national interest and the welfare of the people
国言葉 **(o)kuni kotoba** dialect, vernacular
8 国事 **kokuji** affairs of state
国事犯 **kokujihan** political offense, treason
国使 **kokushi** envoy
国典 **kokuten** national lawcode; state ceremony; national literary classic
国法 **kokuhō** the laws of a country
国宝 **kokuhō** national treasure
国定 **kokutei** quasi-national, state-prescribed
国府 **kokufu, kokubu** (ancient) provincial office/capital
国国 **kuniguni** countries, nations
9 国連 **Kokuren** United Nations, UN (short for 国際連合)
国連軍 **Kokurengun** UN troops
国連旗 **Kokurenki** UN flag
国連総会 **Kokuren Sōkai** UN General Assembly
国風 **kokufū, kuniburi** national customs/songs
国後島 **Kunashiri-tō** (island, Russian Hokkaidō)
国柄 **kunigara** national character
国是 **kokuze** national policy
国政 **kokusei** government, national administration
国威 **kokui** national prestige
10 国都 **kokuto** national capital
国益 **kokueki** national interests/benefit
国辱 **kokujoku** national disgrace
国華 **kokka** national glory/pride
国家 **kokka** state, nation, country
国家主義 **kokka shugi** nationalism
国家的 **kokkateki** national, state
国庫 **kokko** national treasury
国書 **kokusho** (ambassador's) credentials; sovereign's message; national literature
国教 **kokkyō** state religion/church
国恩 **kokuon** one's debt to one's country
国粋 **kokusui** national characteristics
国粋主義 **kokusui shugi** ultranationalism
国恥 **kokuchi** national humiliation
11 国運 **kokuun** national fortunes/fate
国道 **kokudō** national highway
国祭日 **kokusaibi** national holiday
国務 **kokumu** affairs of state
国務長官 **kokumu chōkan** (U.S.) Secretary of State
国患 **kokkan** national disaster
国情 **kokujō** the conditions in a country
国産 **kokusan** domestic-made
国産品 **kokusanhin** domestic products
12 国喪 **kokusō** national mourning
国葬 **kokusō** state funeral
国富 **kokufu** national wealth
国営 **kokuei** government-run, state-managed
国営化 **kokueika** nationalization
国税 **kokuzei** national tax
国策 **kokusaku** national policy
国費 **kokuhi** national expenditures, government spending
13 国債 **kokusai** national debt/bonds
国際 **kokusai** international
国際化 **kokusaika** internationalization
国際主義 **kokusai shugi** internationalism
国際法 **kokusaihō** international law
国際的 **kokusaiteki** international
国際連合 **Kokusai Rengō** United Nations
国際間 **kokusaikan** international
国際語 **kokusaigo** international language
国勢 **kokusei** strength/condition of a country
国勢調査 **kokusei chōsa** (national) census
国漢 **kokkan** Japanese and Chinese literature

国禁 **kokkin** national prohibition
国賊 **kokuzoku** traitor, rebel
国鉄 **Kokutetsu** national railway, JNR (short for 日本国有鉄道)
国電 **kokuden** national railway electric train, JNR trains (short for 国鉄電車)
14 国選弁護人 **kokusen bengonin** court-appointed defense counsel
国境 **kokkyō, kunizakai** border, national boundary
国境線 **kokkyōsen** boundary line, border
国旗 **kokki** national flag
国歌 **kokka** national anthem
国語 **kokugo** national/Japanese language
15 国幣社 **kokuheisha** national shrine
国賓 **kokuhin** state guest
国権 **kokken** sovereign right; national prestige
国論 **kokuron** public opinion/discussion
16 国憲 **kokken** national constitution
18 国難 **kokunan** national crisis/disaster
19 国璽 **kokuji** the seal of state
20 国籍 **kokuseki** nationality, citizenship

———————— 2 ————————

1 一国 **ikkoku** stubborn, hotheaded; the whole country
一国一党主義 **ikkoku-ittō shugi** one-party system
2 入国 **nyūkoku** entering a country, immigration
3 三国 **sangoku** three countries
三国一 **sangoku-ichi** unparalleled in Japan, China, and India
万国 **bankoku** all nations
万国博覧会 **bankoku hakurankai** world's fair
万国旗 **bankokuki** flags of all nations
大国 **taikoku** large country; major nation
亡国 **bōkoku** ruined country, national ruin
小国 **shōkoku** small country
小国民 **shōkokumin** rising generation
山国 **yamaguni** mountainous district, hill country
4 天国 **tengoku** paradise, heaven
内国 **naikoku** home country, domestic
内国産 **naikokusan** domestically produced
中国 **Chūgoku** China; Western tip of Honshū, comprising Hiroshima, Okayama, Shimane, Tottori, and Yamaguchi prefectures
中国人 **chūgokujin** a Chinese
中国地方 **Chūgoku chihō** the Chūgoku region (Hiroshima, Okayama, Shimane, Tottori, and Yamaguchi prefectures)
公国 **kōkoku** duchy, principality
王国 **ōkoku** kingdom, monarchy
5 北国 **hokkoku, kitaguni** northern provinces, northern countries

出国 **shukkoku** departure from a country
本国 **hongoku** one's own country
生国 **shōkoku** one's native country/place
母国 **bokoku** one's mother/native country
母国語 **bokokugo** one's mother/native tongue
他国 **takoku** foreign country; another province
他国人 **takokujin** foreigner, stranger
他国民 **takokumin** other nations/peoples
他国者 **takokumono** stranger, person from another place
外国 **gaikoku** foreign country; foreign
外国人 **gaikokujin** foreigner
外国風 **gaikokufū** foreign style/manners
外国船 **gaikokusen** foreign ship
外国債 **gaikokusai** foreign loan
外国語 **gaikokugo** foreign language
四国 **Shikoku** (island)
立国 **rikkoku** nation building, founding of a state
6 西国 **saigoku** the western countries; western Japan
全国 **zenkoku, zengoku** the whole country, nationwide, national
全国人民代表体会 **Zenkoku jinmin daihyō taikai** (Chinese) National People's Congress
全国民 **zenkokumin** the entire nation
全国的 **zenkokuteki** nationwide
邦国 **hōkoku** country, nations
列国 **rekkoku** the powers, all nations
近国 **kingoku** neighboring country/province
同国 **dōkoku** the same country/province; the (said) country
安国 **yasukuni, ankoku** peacefully ruled country
当国 **tōkoku** this/our country
回国 **kaikoku** traveling about the country, pilgrimage
各国 **kakkoku** all/various countries
自国 **jikoku** one's own country
自国語 **jikokugo** one's own language
米国 **Beikoku** the United States
7 我国 **wa(ga)kuni** our country
伽国 **(o)togi (no) kuni** fairyland, never-never land
乱国 **rangoku** troubled/strife-torn country
売国 **baikoku** betrayal of one's country
売国奴 **baikokudo** traitor
8 非国民 **hikokumin** unpatriotic person
建国 **kenkoku** founding of a country
治国 **chikoku** government
英国 **Eikoku** Britain, the U.K.
英国人 **Eikokujin** Briton, Englishman
宗国 **sōkoku** the home country
国国 **kuniguni** countries, nations

9 軍国 **gunkoku** militaristic nation, a belligerent
軍国主義 **gunkoku shugi** militarism
帝国 **teikoku** empire
帝国主義 **teikoku shugi** imperialism
海国 **kaikoku** maritime country
胡国 **kokoku** (ancient northern-China)
barbarian nations
神国 **shinkoku** land of the gods
祖国 **sokoku** one's homeland/fatherland
祖国愛 **sokokuai** love for one's country
皇国 **kōkoku** the (Japanese) Empire
故国 **kokoku** one's homeland, native country
10 郷国 **kyōkoku** one's native land
帰国 **kikoku** return to one's country
弱国 **jakkoku** weak country
挙国 **kyokoku** the whole nation
挙国一致 **kyokoku-itchi** national unity
島国 **shimaguni** island country
島国根性 **shimaguni konjō** insularity
唐国 **Karakuni** China
殉国 **junkoku** dying for one's country
純国産 **junkokusan** all-domestic (product)
11 清国 **Shinkoku** China under the Manchu/
Qing dynasty
強国 **kyōkoku** strong country, great power
救国 **kyūkoku** national salvation
異国 **ikoku, kotokuni** foreign country
異国風 **ikokufū** foreign customs
経国 **keikoku** administration, statecraft
雪国 **yukiguni** snow country
12 遠国 **engoku, ongoku** faraway country,
distant land
報国 **hōkoku** service to one's country,
patriotism
超国家主義 **chōkokka shugi** ultranationalism
超国家的 **chōkokkateki** ultranationalistic
御国 **okuni** your (native) country; your home
(town); a daimyō's territory (Edo period)
御国入 **okunii(ri)** victor's return (home)
御国自慢 **okuni jiman** pride in one's native
home province; boast of one's native
place
御国言葉 **okuni kotoba** dialect, vernacular
寒国 **kankoku** cold country
富国 **fukoku** rich country, national enrichment
富国強兵 **fukoku-kyōhei** national wealth
and military strength
属国 **zokkoku** a dependency, vassal state
開国 **kaikoku** founding/opening of a country
13 傾国 **keikoku** a beauty, siren; courtesan,
prostitute
暖国 **dankoku, dangoku** warm country
愛国 **aikoku** patriotism
愛国心 **aikokushin** patriotism

愛国主義 **aikoku shugi** patriotism
愛国者 **aikokusha** patriot
戦国時代 **sengoku jidai** era of civil wars
靖国神社 **Yasukuni-jinja** (shrine in Tōkyō
dedicated to fallen Japanese soldiers)
14 領国 **ryōgoku** daimyo's domain
15 隣国 **ringoku** neighboring country
敵国 **tekikoku** enemy country
敵国語 **tekikokugo** the enemy's language
憂国 **yūkoku** patriotism
諸国 **shokoku** all/various countries
諸国行脚 **shokoku angya** walking tour of
the country
10 興国 **kōkoku** making a country prosperous;
prosperous country
Kōkoku (era, 1340–1346)
18 韓国 **Kankoku** South Korea
鎖国 **sakoku** national isolation
闔国 **kōkoku** the whole country
20 護国 **gokoku** defense of the country
21 露国 **Rokoku** Russia

——————— 3 ———————

1 一等国 **ittōkoku** a first-class power
2 二重国籍 **nijū kokuseki** dual nationality
3 工業国 **kōgyōkoku** industrial nation
4 内陸国 **nairikukoku** landlocked country
中立国 **chūritsukoku** neutral country
文明国 **bunmeikoku** civilized country
反帝国主義 **han-teikoku shugi** anti-
imperialism
5 出入国 **shutsunyūkoku** emigration and
immigration
民主国 **minshukoku** democratic country, a
democracy
加盟国 **kameikoku** member nation, signatory
好戦国 **kōsenkoku** warlike nation
立憲国 **rikkenkoku** constitutional country
6 再入国 **sainyūkoku** re-entry (into a country)
合衆国 **Gasshūkoku** United States
同盟国 **dōmeikoku** ally
地震国 **jishinkoku** earthquake-prone country
先進国 **senshinkoku** advanced/developed
nation
共和国 **kyōwakoku** republic
共産国家 **kyōsan kokka** communist state
回教国 **kaikyōkoku** Moslem country
自由国 **jiyūkoku** free/independent nation
7 抑留国 **yokuryūkoku** detaining country
君主国 **kunshukoku** a monarchy
条約国 **jōyakukoku** signatory
8 非愛国的 **hiaikokuteki** unpatriotic, disloyal
夜見国 **yomi (no) kuni** hades, abode of the
dead
協商国 **kyōshōkoku** allies
法治国 **hōchikoku** constitutional state

招請国 **shōseikoku** inviting/host nation
枢軸国 **sūjikukoku** the Axis powers
9 保護国 **hogokoku** protectorate
連合国 **rengōkoku** allied nations, allies
通常国会 **tsūjō kokkai** ordinary Diet session
海軍国 **kaigunkoku** a naval power
独立国 **dokuritsukoku** independent country
後進国 **kōshinkoku** backward country
11 野蛮国 **yabankoku** uncivilized country
商業国 **shōgyōkoku** mercantile nation
黄泉国 **yomi (no) kuni** hades, realm of the dead
密入国 **mitsunyūkoku** smuggle oneself into a country
常世国 **tokoyo (no) kuni** far-off land; heaven; hades
第三国 **dai-sangoku** third country/power
第三国人 **dai-sangokujin** third-country national
12 満州国 **Manshūkoku** Manchukuo
御伽国 **otogi (no) kuni** fairyland
最恵国 **saikeikoku** most-favored nation
13 農業国 **nōgyōkoku** agricultural country
瑞穂国 **Mizuho(no)kuni** Japan, Land of Vigorous Rice Plants
戦敗国 **senpaikoku** defeated nation
戦勝国 **senshōkoku** victorious nation
新教国 **shinkyōkoku** Protestant country
新興国 **shinkōkoku** emerging nation
署名国 **shomeikoku** signatory (country)
15 敵性国 **tekiseikoku** hostile country
緩衝国 **kanshōkoku** buffer state
締約国 **teiyakukoku** treaty signatories
締盟国 **teimeikoku** treaty signatories
諸外国 **shogaikoku** foreign countries
調印国 **chōinkoku** a signatory
16 衛星国 **eiseikoku** satellite (country)

───────── 4 ─────────

3 大英帝国 **Dai-Ei Teikoku** the British Empire
4 中華民国 **Chūka Minkoku** Republic of China (Taiwan)
6 尽忠報国 **jinchū-hōkoku** loyalty and patriotism
7 低開発国 **teikaihatsukoku** less-developed countries
8 東亜諸国 **Tōa shokoku** the countries of East Asia
忠君愛国 **chūkun-aikoku** loyalty and patriotism
10 被保護国 **hihogokoku** protectorate, dependency

───────── 5 ─────────

8 歩行者天国 **hokōsha tengoku** street temporarily closed to vehicles, mall
9 発展途上国 **hattentojōkoku** developing country

───────── 7 ─────────

4 中華人民共和国 **Chūka Jinmin Kyōwakoku** People's Republic of China

3s5.2 / 972

固   **KO, kata(i)** hard, firm, solid
kata(maru/meru) (intr./tr.) harden, solidify   **moto(yori)** from the beginning; of course

───────── 1 ─────────

6 固守 **koshu** adhere to, persevere in
固有 **koyū** its own, peculiar, characteristic
固有名詞 **koyū meishi** proper noun
固有値 **koyūchi** eigenvalue
7 固体 **kotai** a solid
固形 **kokei** solid, solidified
固形体 **kokeitai** a solid
固形物 **kokeibutsu** a solid; solid food
固形便 **kokeiben** (normal) firm feces
8 固陋 **korō** narrow-minded, hidebound, extremely conservative
固苦 **katakuru(shii)** stiff, formal, strict
固定 **kotei** fixed
固定給 **koteikyū** fixed salary
9 固持 **koji** adhere to, persist in
10 固疾 **koshitsu** chronic illness
11 固執 **koshitsu** hold fast to, persist in, insist on
固唾飲 **katazu (o) no(mu)** be intensely anxious
12 固着 **kochaku** adhere/stick to
13 固辞 **koji** firmly decline/refuse

───────── 2 ─────────

5 打固 **u(chi)kata(meru)** harden by tamping
6 地固 **jigata(me)** ground leveling/preparation
安固 **anko** secure, solid, stable
7 牢固 **rōko** firm, solid, inflexible
足固 **ashigata(me)** walking practice
8 押固 **o(shi)kata(meru)** press together
底固 **sokogata(i)** (prices) holding firm, having bottomed out
10 差固 **sa(shi)kata(meru)** shut tight; warn sternly
拳固 **genko** fist, knuckles
11 強固 **kyōko** firm, solid, secure
断固 **danko** firm, resolute
12 堅固 **kengo** strong, solid, steadfast
13 禁固 **kinko** imprisonment
頑固 **ganko** stubborn, obstinate
14 練固 **ne(ri)kata(meru)** harden by kneading
15 鞏固 **kyōko** firm, solid (also spelled 強固)
踏固 **fu(mi)kata(meru)** tramp/pack down
16 凝固 **gyōko** solidify, congeal, coagulate
ko(ri)kata(maru) coagulate; be fanatical
凝固点 **gyōkoten** freezing point
18 臍固 **hozo (o) kata(meru)** resolve to, make up one's mind

3s5.3

令

REI prison

──────── 1 ────────

10 囹圄 **reigo** prison
11 囹圉 **reigyo** prison

──────── 6 ────────

3s6.1 / 274

面

MEN face; mask; surface; aspect, facet; page
omote, omo, tsura face

──────── 1 ────────

0 面する **men(suru)** face, border, front on
2 面子 **mentsu** face, honor
　　menko cardboard game doll
3 面上 **menjō** (expressed) on one's face
　面々 **menmen** every one, all
5 面付 **tsuratsu(ki)** expression, look
　面皮 **menpi** countenance
　面皮厚 **tsura (no) kawa (no) atsu(i)** brazen-faced, impudent, nervy
　面白 **omoshiro(i)** interesting; amusing
　面白半分 **omoshiro-hanbun** half in fun, jokingly
　面白味 **omoshiromi** interest, enjoyment
　面立 **omoda(chi)** looks, features
　面目 **menmoku, menboku** face, honor, dignity
　面目一新 **menboku isshin** take on a completely new aspect
　面目無 **menbokuna(i)** ashamed
6 面伏 **omobu(se)** shame-faced
　面会 **menkai** interview, meeting
　面会人 **menkainin** visitor, caller
　面会日 **menkaibi** one's at-home day
　面色 **menshoku** complexion, expression
　面向不背 **menkō-fuhai** beautiful from every angle, flawless
　面当 **tsuraa(te)** innuendo, spiteful remark
7 面体 **mentei** face, looks
　面忘 **omowasu(re)** fail to recognize
　面妖 **men'yō** strange, mysterious
　面疔 **menchō** facial cabuncle/boil
8 面長 **omonaga** elongated/oval face
　面取 **mento(ri)** rounding off the corners/edges, beveling, chamfering
9 面変 **omoga(wari)** change in one's looks
　面前 **menzen** in the presence of, before
　面通 **mendō(shi)** (police/identify-the-culprit) lineup
　面持 **omomo(chi)** look, face
　面面 **menmen** every one, all

面相 **mensō** face, looks
面映 **omoha(yui)** embarrassing, awkward
面食 **menku(i)** emphasizing good looks (in choosing a mate)
　　menku(rau) be flurried/disconcerted
10 面倒 **mendō** trouble, difficulty; taking care of, tending to
　面倒臭 **mendōkusa(i)** troublesome, a big bother
　面部 **menbu** face, facial region
　面皰 **nikibi** pimple
　面差 **omoza(shi)** looks, features
　面従 **menjū** outward obedience
　面従腹背 **menjū-fukuhai** outward obedience but inward opposition, false obedience, passive resistance
　面容 **men'yō** countenance, looks, features
11 面接 **mensetsu** interview
　面接試問 **mensetsu shimon** oral examination
　面舵 **omokaji** turning to starboard
　面責 **menseki** reprove (someone) to his face
13 面詰 **menkitsu** reprove (someone) to his face
14 面構 **tsuragama(e)** expression, look
　面憎 **tsuraniku(i)** disgusting, offensive
　面魂 **tsuradamashii** (determined) expression
15 面影 **omokage** face, looks; trace, vestiges
　面罵 **menba** revile (someone) to his face
　面談 **mendan** meet and talk with
　面輪 **omowa** features, looks
16 面壁 **menpeki** meditation facing a wall
　面窶 **omoyatsu(re)** haggard/worn-out look
　面積 **menseki** area
19 面識 **menshiki** acquaintance

──────── 2 ────────

1 一面 **ichimen** one side/phase; the whole surface; first page (of a newspaper)
　一面観 **ichimenkan** one-sided view
　一面識 **ichimenshiki** knowing someone by sight, a passing acquaintance
2 七面倒 **shichimendō** great trouble, difficulty
　七面鳥 **shichimenchō** turkey
　人面獣心 **jinmen-jūshin** human face but brutal heart
　八面 **hachimen** eight faces; all sides
　八面六臂 **hachimen roppi** eight faces and six arms; versatile talent
　八面玲瓏 **hachimen-reirō** beautiful from all sides; perfect serenity, affability
3 三面 **sanmen** three sides/faces; page 3 (of a newspaper)
　三面六臂 **sanmen roppi** as if having three faces and six arms, versatile, all-around, doing the work of many
　三面記事 **sanmen kiji** page-3 news, police news, human-interest stories

工面 **kumen** contrive, manage, make do; raise (funds); (pecuniary) circumstances

上面 **jōmen** surface, top, exterior **uwatsura, uwa(t)tsura** surface, appearances

山面 **yamazura** mountain's surface

4 不面目 **fumenboku** shame, disgrace

内面 **naimen** inside, interior, inner

内面的 **naimenteki** internal, inside, inner

文面 **bunmen** text, wording, purport

片面 **katamen, katatsura, kataomote** one side

反面 **hanmen** the other side, on the other hand

水面 **suimen, minomo** surface of the water

月面 **getsumen** the moon's/lunar surface

方面 **hōmen** direction; district; standpoint; aspect, phase

5 凸面 **totsumen** convex (surface)

凸面鏡 **totsumenkyō** convex mirror/lens

凹面 **ōmen** concave (surface)

凹面鏡 **ōmenkyō** concave mirror/lens

矢面 **yaomote** facing incoming arrows, brunt

半面 **hanmen** half the face; one side, half; the other side

生面 **seimen** new field; first meeting

他面 **tamen** the other side, on the other hand

平面 **heimen** plane, level surface

平面図 **heimenzu** plane view, floor plan

平面鏡 **heimenkyō** plane mirror

外面 **gaimen** exterior, outward appearance, surface

正面 **shōmen** front, head-on **matomo** front, head-on; honest

正面図 **shōmenzu** front view

正面衝突 **shōmen shōtotsu** head-on collision

字面 **jimen, jizura** the appearance of written characters

四面 **shimen** all (four) sides

四面楚歌 **shimen-soka** surrounded by enemies, without allies

白面 **hakumen** white/pale face; inexperience **shirafu** sober

6 多面 **tamen** many sides/facets

多面体 **tamentai** polyhedron

死面 **shimen** death mask

両面 **ryōmen** both faces/sides

両面刷 **ryōmenzu(ri)** printing on both sides

仮面 **kamen** mask, disguise

全面 **zenmen** the whole surface; full-scale, all-out

全面的 **zenmenteki** all-out, full, general

地面 **jimen** ground, surface, land

当面 **tōmen** face, confront; immediate, urgent

百面相 **hyakumensō** many phases/faces

7 体面 **taimen** honor, prestige, appearances

対面 **taimen** interview, meeting; facing each other

赤面 **sekimen** a blush **akatsura** red face; villain's role

吹面 **ho(e)zura** tearful face

局面 **kyokumen** (chessboard) position; situation

図面 **zumen** drawing, sketch, plan, blueprints

8 表面 **hyōmen** surface

表面化 **hyōmenka** come to the surface/fore, become an issue

表面的 **hyōmenteki** on the surface, outwardly

表面張力 **hyōmen chōryoku** surface tension

画面 **gamen** scene, picture, (TV etc.) screen

券面 **kenmen** the face of a banknote/cetificate

直面 **chokumen** be faced with, confront

泣面 **na(ki)tsura, na(kit)tsura** crying/tearful face

波面 **hamen** wave surface/front

9 前面 **zenmen** front, front side

洗面 **senmen** washing the face

洗面台 **senmendai** washstand

洗面所 **senmenjo** washroom, lavatory

洗面器 **senmenki** wash basin

海面 **kaimen** surface of the sea, sea level **umizura** surface of the sea

後面 **kōmen** back side/surface

面面 **menmen** every one, all

背面 **haimen** rear, back, reverse

界面 **kaimen** interface, boundary, surface

10 部面 **bumen** phase, aspect, field, side

真面目 **majime** serious-minded, earnest, honest **shinmenmoku** one's true self/character; seriousness, earnestness

浜面 **hamazura** beach, seashore

能面 **nōmen** Noh mask

書面 **shomen** letter, document; in writing

鬼面 **kimen** devil's face/mask; bluff

紙面 **shimen** (newspaper) space

素面 **sumen** sober face **shirafu** soberness

馬面 **umazura** horse face

11 側面 **sokumen** side, flank

側面図 **sokumenzu** side view

側面観 **sokumenkan** side view

斜面 **shamen** slope, inclined plane

渋面 **jūmen, shibuzura, shibutsura** sour face, scowl

帳面 **chōmen** notebook, account book

帳面面 **chōmenzura** accounts; appearance

球面 **kyūmen** spherical surface

細面 **hosoomote** slender face

断面 **danmen** (cross) section

断面図 **danmenzu** cross-sectional view

12 満面 **manmen** the whole face

場面 **bamen** scene

膨面 **fuku(ret)tsura** sulky/sullen look, pout

13 裏面 **rimen** back, reverse side; background, behind the scenes

猿面 **sarumen** a face like a monkey's
新面目 **shinmenmoku** new aspect/phase
路面 **romen** road surface
路面電車 **romen densha** streetcar
鉄面皮 **tetsumenpi** brazen, impudent
14 鼻面 **hanazura** muzzle, snout
瘦面 **ya(se)omote** thin face
誌面 **shimen** page of a magazine
15 横面 **yokotsura, yoko(t)tsura** side of the face
盤面 **banmen** surface of a board/record
17 臆面 **okumen** shy face
18 覆面 **fukumen** mask
覆面子 **fukumenshi** anonymous writer
顔面 **ganmen** the face
額面 **gakumen** face value, par
22 覿面 **tekimen** immediate, prompt
24 顰面 **shika(met)tsura, shika(me)zura** frown, scowl

———————— 3 ————————
2 几帳面 **kichōmen** methodical, precise, punctilious
4 不真面目 **fumajime** not serious-minded, insincere
仏頂面 **butchōzura** sour face, pout, scowl
切断面 **setsudanmen** section, cutting plane
水平面 **suiheimen** horizontal plane/surface
6 多方面 **tahōmen** various, different, many-sided, versatile
防毒面 **bōdokumen** gas mask
地平面 **chiheimen** horizontal plane
各方面 **kaku hōmen** every direction, all quarters
7 投影面 **tōeimen** plane of projection
社会面 **shakaimen** local-news page
初対面 **shotaimen** first meeting
9 軍事面 **gunjimen** military aspects
急斜面 **kyūshamen** steep slope/incline
10 真正面 **ma(s)shōmen** directly opposite, right in front
11 接触面 **sesshokumen** contact surface
帳面面 **chōmenzura** accounts; appearance
12 結像面 **ketsuzōmen** focal plane
絵図面 **ezumen** plan, design
間抜面 **manu(ke)zura** stupid look
13 傾斜面 **keishamen** inclined plane
暗黒面 **ankokumen** the dark/seamy side
新生面 **shinseimen** new aspect/field
新局面 **shinkyokumen** new aspect
15 舞台面 **butaimen** scene, scenery
横断面 **ōdanmen** cross section
17 糞真面目 **kusomajime** humorless earnestness

———————— 4 ————————
5 四角四面 **shikaku-shimen** methodical, prim
11 得意満面 **tokui-manmen** pride

3s6.2
甬 **YŪ, sono** game preserve, pasture, garden

畧 → 国 **3s5.1**

———————— 7 ————————
3s7.1
圃 **HO** field (for crops), garden, orchard

———————— 2 ————————
5 田圃 **tanbo** rice field
8 苗圃 **byōho** seedbed, nursery

3s7.2
圂 **KON** pigsty; toilet, privy
kawaya toilet, privy

3s7.3
圄 **GO, GYO** prison; capture, apprehend

———————— 2 ————————
8 囹圄 **reigo** prison

恩 → **4k6.23**

勉 → **2n8.1**

3s7.4
氤 **IN** spirited

———————— 8 ————————
國 → 国 **3s5.1**

圈 → 圏 **3s9.1**

3s8.1
圊 **SEI** toilet, privy

3s8.2

圉 GYO prison; horse tender, ostler

―――――― 2 ――――――

8 圄圉 **reigyo** prison

―――――― 9 ――――――

3s9.1 / 508

圏 圈 KEN circle, range, sphere

―――――― 1 ――――――

4 圏内 **kennai** within the range/orbit of
5 圏外 **kengai** outside the range/orbit of

―――――― 2 ――――――

3 大圏 **taiken** great circle
　大圏航路 **taiken kōro** great-circle route
6 気圏 **kiken** the atmosphere
12 極圏 **kyokken** the Arctic/Antarctic Circle

―――――― 3 ――――――

3 大気圏 **taikiken** the atmosphere
5 北極圏 **hokkyokuken** the Arctic Circle, the Arctic
　生活圏 **seikatsuken** Lebensraum
6 共栄圏 **kyōeiken** coprosperity sphere
　共産圏 **kyōsanken** communist bloc
　成層圏 **seisōken** the stratosphere
9 南極圏 **Nankyokuken** the Antarctic Circle, the Antarctic
13 電離圏 **denriken** ionosphere
14 磁気圏 **jikiken** magnetosphere
15 暴風圏 **bōfūken** storm zone/area

―――――― 4 ――――――

7 亜成層圏 **asei sōken** substratosphere

―――――― 10 ――――――

3s10.1 / 447

園 薗 EN, sono garden

―――――― 1 ――――――

2 園丁 **entei** gardener
7 園芸 **engei** gardening
　園芸家 **engeika** gardener, horticulturist
　園児 **enji** kindergarten child/pupil
8 園長 **enchō** head of a kindergarten/zoo
9 園亭 **entei** arbor, bower, gazebo
10 園遊会 **en'yūkai** garden party

―――――― 2 ――――――

4 公園 **kōen** park
5 田園 **den'en** fields and gardens; the country, rural areas
　田園詩 **den'enshi** pastoral poem

6 庄園 **shōen** manor
　竹園生 **take (no) sonoo** bamboo garden; the imperial family
7 花園 **hanazono** flower garden
　学園 **gakuen** academy; campus
9 造園 **zōen** landscape gardening
　造園術 **zōenjutsu** landscape gardening
　荘園 **shōen** manor
　茶園 **chaen, saen** tea plantation
　庭園 **teien** garden
　庭園術 **teienjutsu** landscape gardening
　祇園 **Gion** (name of a shrine, festival, and red-light district in Kyōto)
10 桑園 **sōen** mulberry farm/orchard
　遊園地 **yūenchi** amusement/theme park
　桃園 **momozono** peach orchard
　梅園 **baien** plum orchard
11 菜園 **saien** vegetable garden
　梨園 **rien** pear orchard; the theatrical world
12 廃園 **haien** abandoned garden
13 農園 **nōen** farm, plantation
　楽園 **rakuen** a paradise
15 霊園 **reien** cemetery park
16 薬園 **yakuen** medicinal-herb garden

―――――― 3 ――――――

5 幼稚園 **yōchien** kindergarten
8 果樹園 **kajuen** orchard
9 保育園 **hoikuen** nursery school
11 動物園 **dōbutsuen** zoo
12 葡萄園 **budōzono, budōen** vineyard
　植物園 **shokubutsuen** botanical garden
15 養樹園 **yōjuen** tree nursery, arboretum

圍 → 囲 3s4.2

圓 → 円 2r2.1

嗇 → 3b10.13

―――――― 11 ――――――

團 → 団 3s3.3

圖 → 図 3s4.3

3s11.1

皰 HŌ pockmarks

—————— 13 ——————

3s13.1

圜   **KAN** surround
       EN round; go around

豫→予   **0a4.12**

—————— 14 ——————

3s14.1

氈   **SEN** woolen cloth, rug

—————— 2 ——————

4 毛氈 **mōsen** rug, carpet

貌→狐   **0a11.1**

牆→   **3b14.6**

—————— 16 ——————

鹻→鹼   **3s21.1**

—————— 17 ——————

齝→   **3d17.5**

麵→麺   **4i17.1**

—————— 20 ——————

靨→   **4c19.1**

—————— 21 ——————

3s21.1

鹼 鹼   **KEN** saltiness, brine; lye; soap

—————— 2 ——————

5 石鹼 **sekken** soap

—————— 4 ——————

8 逆性石鹼 **gyakusei sekken** antiseptic soap

—————— 22 ——————

3s22.1

鬣   **RYŌ, tategami** mane

———————— 木 **4a** ————————

木	札	初	朸	权	朴	机	杁	朽	李	朶	杜	杉
0.1	1.1	2.1	2.2	4a11.18	2.3	2.4	2.5	2.6	2.7	2.8	3.1	3.2
杣	杙	杖	杆	杆	材	杠	杞	枥	机	村	杓	杏
3.3	3.4	3.5	3.6	4a7.7	3.7	3.8	3.9	4a5.28	3.10	3.11	3.12	3.13
杢	条	林	柱	枋	枚	枦	栈	枅	枡	杮	柄	枕
3.14	4i4.1	4.1	4.2	4.3	4.4	4a16.2	4a3.7	4.5	4.6	4a5.25	4.7	4.8
杵	杷	杯	析	枇	杪	枌	松	杭	枝	枠	杼	板
4.9	4.10	4.11	4.12	4.13	4.14	4.15	4.16	4.17	4.18	4.19	4.20	4.21
枢	㭟	杳	杰	枩	采	枀	柘	柆	相	栅	柚	柑
4.22	3q4.1	4.23	2a11.6	4a4.16	4.24	4a6.34	5.1	5.2	5.3	5.4	5.5	5.6
栂	柵	柄	析	柤	柱	柞	柏	柾	枹	柳	柎	枷
5.7	5.8	5.9	5.10	5.11	5.12	5.13	5.14	5.15	5.16	5.17	5.18	5.19
柢	枵	枳	柁	柊	柿	枯	栫	枥	柯	枸	枢	查
5.20	5.21	5.22	5.23	5.24	5.25	5.26	5.27	5.28	5.29	5.30	5.31	5.32
果	某	柔	染	架	栈	栖	株	栲	根	柧	椰	桁
0a8.8	5.33	5.34	5.35	5.36	6.1	6.2	6.3	6.4	6.5	6.6	6.7	6.8

3

氵 汒
扌 扎
口 女
巾 犭
弓 彳
彡 艹
宀 䒑
产 青
广 尸
口 22←

4

→ 木 月 日 火 礻 王 牛 方 攵 心 戸 戈

栩 6.9	桃 6.10	桓 6.11	桴 6.12	桂 6.13	档 6.14	桜 6.15	桔 6.16	格 6.17	桙 6.18	栫 6.19	桎 6.20	桧 4a13.8
栲 6.21	核 6.22	桅 6.23	校 6.24	桙 6.25	栓 6.26	梅 6.27	栂 6.28	栢 4a5.14	梃 6.29	桐 6.30	框 6.31	栗 6.32
柴 6.33	栞 6.34	桑 2h8.1	殺 6.35	栽 4n6.1	梼 4a14.4	梗 7.1	梠 7.2	彬 7.3	桝 4a4.6	梛 7.4	梓 7.5	梙 4a14.3
棺 7.6	桿 7.7	桔 7.8	梧 7.9	梳 7.10	梭 7.11	梠 7.12	梢 7.13	桃 7.14	淳 7.15	梋 7.16	梯 7.17	桶 7.18
梅 4a6.27	梶 7.19	桐 7.20	梔 7.21	械 7.22	梱 7.23	梨 7.24	梁 7.25	桀 7.26	梦 3k10.14	梵 2m9.3	梵 7.27	梟 7.28
梲 7.29	殺 4a6.35	耕 0a10.13	耗 0a10.12	椎 8.1	椚 8.2	棟 8.3	棣 8.4	椏 8.5	椰 8.6	椰 4a9.5	椒 8.7	椡 8.8
椥 8.9	棚 8.10	極 8.11	椊 8.12	椪 8.13	棋 8.14	椄 8.15	棲 8.16	棱 8.17	棉 8.18	椌 8.19	棒 8.20	椙 8.21
棍 8.22	棧 4a6.1	椿 8.23	棕 8.24	棺 8.25	椀 8.26	椅 8.27	検 8.28	棯 8.29	棆 8.30	椋 8.31	植 8.32	椪 8.33
椨 8.34	椥 8.35	椆 8.36	椢 8.37	棹 8.38	槌 4a9.27	巣 3n8.1	森 8.39	棊 4a8.14	渠 8.40	弑 8.41	棟 9.1	楮 9.2
楯 9.3	椹 9.4	榔 4a7.15	椰 9.5	楸 9.6	棯 3k5.7	椴 9.7	楜 9.8	榊 4a10.3	猢 9.9	楼 9.10	楔 9.11	椶 4a8.24
楳 4a6.27	楞 9.12	楕 9.13	楪 9.14	楾 9.15	椿 9.16	楊 9.17	楷 9.18	楹 9.19	楫 9.20	椌 9.21	椽 9.22	楢 4a9.23
楢 9.23	楴 9.24	楠 9.25	楡 9.26	樋 4a10.28	槌 9.27	楓 9.28	楽 9.29	楚 9.30	楪 9.31	躱 9.32	鳩 10.1	概 10.2
榊 10.3	榎 10.4	榑 10.5	榾 10.6	梗 10.7	榱 10.8	槐 10.9	構 10.10	榛 10.11	榴 10.12	榻 10.13	榲 10.14	樺 10.15
模 10.16	榕 10.17	橙 10.18	槙 10.19	槍 10.20	槇 10.21	槁 10.22	槙 10.23	榜 10.24	様 10.25	槎 10.26	槙 4a10.27	槇 10.27
樋 10.28	榧 10.29	槃 10.30	槊 10.31	榮 3n6.1	業 0a13.3	鴇 11.1	槲 11.2	樅 11.3	槻 11.4	楕 4a9.13	楼 4a9.10	樗 11.5
槫 11.6	槽 11.7	標 11.8	樛 11.9	様 4a10.25	樟 11.10	標 11.11	榑 11.12	横 11.13	槵 11.14	槿 11.15	樒 11.16	樏 11.17
権 11.18	槭 11.19	樞 4a4.22	槧 11.20	樊 11.21	樂 4a9.29	機 12.1	樸 12.2	樹 12.3	橄 12.4	概 4a10.2	樫 12.5	樵 12.6
橅 12.7	橋 12.8	橦 12.9	橙 12.10	橘 12.11	橃 12.12	楢 12.13	橇 12.14	横 4a11.13	橈 12.15	橲 12.16	橆 12.17	橡 12.18
樽 4a12.19	橰 12.19	橤 12.20	榮 3k12.14	橄 13.1	檞 13.2	橿 13.3	橾 4a15.3	檀 13.4	檜 13.5	檍 4a15.5	檑 13.6	檬 13.7
檜 13.8	検 4a8.28	檐 13.9	檗 13.10	檀 13.11	檴 14.1	櫂 4a11.16	檸 14.2	檳 14.3	檮 14.4	檻 14.5	鬆 14.6	鞣 14.7
橼 15.1	櫓 15.2	櫟 15.3	檻 15.4	櫛 15.5	櫑 15.6	櫝 15.7	櫚 15.8	籠 15.9	攀 3c15.5	櫧 16.1	櫨 16.2	櫪 16.3

欄	礬	櫻	欅	檽	權	欄	欒	欐	譟	櫨	欖	欟
16.4	5a15.2	4a6.15	17.1	17.2	4a11.18	4a16.4	19.1	4a21.1	19.2	21.1	22.1	24.1

鬱	欝
25.1	4d26.1

─────────── 0 ───────────

4a0.1 / 22

BOKU, MOKU, ki, ko- tree, wood

木

─────────── 1 ───────────

2 木乃伊 **miira** mummy
　木刀 **bokutō** wooden sword
3 木工 **mokkō** woodworking; carpenter
　木下 **Kinoshita** (surname)
4 木太刀 **kidachi** wooden sword
　木毛 **mokumō, mokuge** wood wool (for packing)
　木仏 **kibotoke, kibutsu** wooden Buddha
　木切 **kigi(re)** piece/chip of wood
　木片 **mokuhen** block/chip/splinter of wood
　木戸 **kido** gate, wicket, entrance; castle gate
　木戸札 **kidofuda** wooden admission ticket
　木戸番 **kidoban** gatekeeper
　木戸銭 **kidosen** admission fee
5 木末 **konure** twigs, treetops
　木皮 **mokuhi** bark
　木札 **kifuda** wooden ticket/tag
　木石 **bokuseki** trees and stones, inanimate objects
　木石漢 **bokusekikan** insensible person
　木立 **kodachi** grove, thicket
　木目 **mokume** (wood's) grain
　　　　kime grain, texture
　木皿 **kizara** wooden dish
6 木瓜 **boke** Japanese/flowering quince
　木羽 **koba** shingles
　木灰 **kibai** wood ashes
　木肌 **kihada** bark
　木耳 **kikurage** Jew's-ear (mushroom used in Chinese cooking)
7 木材 **mokuzai** wood, lumber
8 木版 **mokuhan** wood-block print(ing)
　木版本 **mokuhanbon** xylographic book
　木版画 **mokuhanga** wood-block print
　木版刷 **mokuhanzu(ri)** wood engraving
　木苺 **kiichigo** raspberry
　木芽 **ki(no)me, ko(no)me** leaf bud; Japanese-pepper bud
　木実 **ki(no)mi, ko(no)mi** fruit, nut, berry
　木杯 **mokuhai** wooden cup
9 木通 **akebi** (a type of shrub having tendrils)
　木炭 **mokutan** charcoal
　木炭画 **mokutanga** charcoal drawing

　木枯 **koga(rashi)** wintry wind
　木星 **mokusei** Jupiter
　木食 **mokujiki** fruit diet
　木食虫 **kiku(i)mushi** wood borer
10 木陰 **kokage** tree shade
　木剣 **bokken** wooden sword
　木挽 **kobi(ki)** sawyer
　木振 **kibu(ri)** shape of a tree
　木屑 **kikuzu** shavings, chips
　木栓 **mokusen** wooden cork/plug, bung
　木骨 **mokkotsu** wooden frame, half-timbered
　木釘 **kikugi** wooden peg
　木馬 **mokuba** wooden/rocking/carrousel/gymnastics horse
11 木偶坊 **deku(no)bō** wooden doll, dummy
　木深 **kobuka(i)** deep in the woods
　木彫 **kibo(ri), mokuchō** wood carving
　木菟 **mimizuku** horned owl
　木理 **mokuri** (wood's) grain
　木船 **mokusen** wooden ship
　木訥 **bokutotsu** rugged honesty
　木魚 **mokugyo** wooden temple drum
12 木曾川 **Kisogawa** (river, Gifu-ken)
　木遣 **kiya(ri)** (workmen's chant while) pulling/carrying a heavy load together
　木登 **kinobo(ri)** tree climbing
　木葉 **ki(no)ha, ko(no)ha** tree leaves, foliage
　木琴 **mokkin** xylophone
　木間 **ko(no)ma** in the trees
13 木隠 **kogaku(re)** hidden behind trees
　木蓮 **mokuren** magnolia
　木靴 **kigutsu** wooden shoes
　木煉瓦 **mokurenga** wooden blocks/bricks
　木賊 **tokusa** shave grass, scouring rushes
　木賃宿 **kichin'yado** cheap lodging house
14 木像 **mokuzō** wooden image
　木摺 **kizu(ri)** lath
　木端 **ki(no)hashi, koppa** chip of wood; worthless thing/person
　木端微塵 **koppa-mijin** splinters, smithereens
　木製 **mokusei** wooden, made of wood
　木製品 **mokuseihin** wood products
　木綿 **momen** cotton (cloth)
　　　　kiwata cotton (plant)
　木綿糸 **momen'ito** cotton thread
　木綿物 **momenmono** cotton goods/clothing
　木精 **mokusei** wood/methyl alcohol; echo
　木管 **mokkan** wooden pipe/bobbin
15 木舞 **komai** lath

4

木 ⊍←
月
日
火
ネ
王
牛
方
攵
心
戸
戈

木履 **pokkuri, bokuri** girls' wooden shoes
木槿 **mukuge** rose of Sharon
木箱 **kibako** wooden box
木質 **mokushitsu** woody, ligneous
木鋏 **kibasami** pruning shears
木霊 **kodama** spirit of a tree; echo
17 木螺旋 **mokuneji** wood screw
18 木曜 **mokuyō** Thursday
木曜日 **mokuyōbi** Thursday
木叢 **komura** thicket
21 木鐸 **bokutaku** bell with a wooden clapper; leader

――――――― 2 ―――――――

1 一木 **ichiboku** one tree
3 大木 **taiboku** large tree
丸木 **maruki** log
丸木舟 **marukibune** dugout canoe
丸木船 **marukibune** dugout canoe
丸木橋 **marukibashi** log bridge
叉木 **matagi** forked tree/branch
千木 **chigi** ornamental upward-projecting rafters on a shrine roof
土木 **doboku** civil engineering, public works
巾木 **habaki** baseboard, skirting board
4 元木阿弥 **moto (no) mokuami** losing what was gained, no better off
止木 **to(mari)gi** perch, roost
5 生木 **namaki** living tree; unseasoned wood
古木 **koboku** old tree
白木 **shiraki** plain/unpainted/unvarnished wood
冬木立 **fuyukodachi** leafless trees in winter
立木 **ta(chi)ki** standing tree/timber
6 伐木 **batsuboku** felling, cutting, logging
老木 **rōboku, o(i)ki** old tree
名木 **meiboku** historic tree; fine (incense) wood
朽木 **ku(chi)ki, kyūboku** decayed tree/wood
肋木 **rokuboku** wall bars (for calisthenics)
7 低木 **teiboku** shrub
坑木 **kōboku** mine pillars/timbers
吾木紅 **waremokō** burnet (a flowering herb)
形木 **katagi** wooden model (of a dyeing pattern); wooden printing block
杣木 **somagi** lumber, timber
材木 **zaimoku** wood, lumber
材木屋 **zaimokuya** lumberyard, lumber dealer
材木商 **zaimokushō** lumber business/dealer
肘木 **hijiki** ancon, bracket, corbel
8 受木 **u(ke)gi** a support
版木 **hangi** printing/engraving block, woodcut
並木 **namiki** row of trees; roadside tree
並木路 **namiki michi** tree-lined street
苗木 **naegi** sapling, seedling
若木 **wakagi** young tree, sapling
定木 **jōgi** ruler, (T-)square; standard

林木 **rinboku** forest tree
枕木 **makuragi** railroad tie
松木 **matsu(no)ki** pine tree
青木 **aoki** Japanese laurel
取木 **to(ri)ki** layer(ing) (in gardening)
9 冠木門 **kabukimon** gate with overhead crossbar
連木 **rengi** wooden pestle
茨木 **Ibaraki** (city, Ōsaka-fu)
草木 **sōmoku, kusaki** plants and trees, vegetation
荒木 **araki** unbarked logs, rough timber
荒木田土 **araki-datsuchi** (a reddish clayey soil)
庭木 **niwaki** garden tree, shrubbery
庭木戸 **niwakido** garden gate
枯木 **ka(re)ki** dead tree
栃木県 **Tochigi-ken** (prefecture)
神木 **shinboku** sacred tree
香木 **kōboku** aromatic tree, fragrant wood
10 高木 **kōboku** tall tree   **Takagi** (surname)
流木 **ryūboku** driftwood
埋木 **u(me)ki** wood inlay, wooden plug
　　 u(more)gi lignite; living in obscurity
挿木 **sa(shi)ki** (plant a) cutting
唐木 **karaki** rare foreign wood
晒木綿 **sara(shi)momen** bleached cotton cloth
11 添木 **so(e)gi** brace, splint
接木 **tsu(gi)ki** grafting; grafted tree
啄木鳥 **kitsutsuki** woodpecker
寄木 **yo(se)gi** parquet, wood mosaic
　　 yo(ri)ki driftwood
梶木 **kaji(no)ki** mulberry tree (used for paper)
梟木 **kyōboku** post for displaying a severed head; gibbet
黒木 **kuroki** unbarked logs; ebony, blackwood
経木 **kyōgi** wood shavings, chips
粗木 **araki** unbarked logs
12 雁木 **gangi** steps on a pier; toothing gear, escapement; zigzag; covered alley
堅木 **katagi** hardwood, oak
喬木 **kyōboku** tall tree
嵌木細工 **ha(me)kizaiku** inlaid woodwork
棟木 **munagi** ridgepole, ridge beam
椋木 **muku(no)ki** (type of deciduous tree)
植木 **ueki** garden/potted plant
植木屋 **uekiya** gardener, nurseryman
植木鉢 **uekibachi** flowerpot
腕木 **udegi** arm, crosspiece, bracket
腕木信号 **udegi shingō** semaphore
軸木 **jikugi** scroll rod; matchstick; splint
13 裏木戸 **urakido** back door
鈴木 **Suzuki** (surname)
14 榾木 **hodagi, hotagi** firewood; wood for growing mushrooms on

榛木 **han(no)ki** black alder
鼻木 **hanagi** (bull's) wooden nose ring
算木 **sangi** divination/calculation blocks
雑木 **zōki, zatsuboku** miscellaneous trees
雑木林 **zōkibayashi, zōbokurin** grove of
　　　trees of various species
15 撞木 **shumoku** T-shaped wooden bell hammer
標木 **hyōboku** signpost, grave post
横木 **yokogi** crosspiece, (cross)bar, (fence) rail
霊木 **reiboku** sacred tree
16 樹木 **jumoku** trees
親木 **oyagi** the host plant (of a graft)
積木 **tsu(mi)ki** toy blocks; piled timber
錦木 **nishikigi** winged spindle tree
頸木 **kubiki** yoke
20 灌木 **kanboku** shrub, bush
23 鰹木 **katsuogi** log on the ridge of a shrine roof

———————— 3 ————————
6 合歓木 **nemunoki** silk tree
回転木馬 **kaiten mokuba** carrousel
7 花水木 **hanamizuki** dogwood
杉並木 **suginamiki** avenue of sugi trees
8 逆茂木 **sakamogi** abatis
拍子木 **hyōshigi** wooden clappers
松並木 **matsunamiki** avenue/row of pines
9 草根木皮 **sōkon-mokuhi** medicinal herb
　　　roots and tree barks
10 唐変木 **tōhenboku** blockhead, oaf
11 接骨木 **niwatoko** elder (tree)
寄生木 **yadorigi** mistletoe; parasitic plant
常磐木 **tokiwagi** an evergreen (tree)
13 禁断木実 **kindan (no) ko(no)mi** forbidden
　　　fruit
14 漂流木 **hyōryūboku** driftwood
16 擂粉木 **su(ri)kogi** wooden pestle

———————— 4 ————————
9 独活大木 **udo (no) taiboku** large and useless
10 遊動円木 **yūdō enboku** suspended horizontal
　　　log, swinging pole (playground equip-
　　　ment)

———————— 1 ————————

4a1.1 / 1157

札 SATSU paper money, slip of paper;
　　a bid, tender
　　fuda label, tag, sign; chit, ticket; amulet

———————— 1 ————————
0 お札 **(o)satsu** paper money, bank note
4 札止 **fudado(me)** Sold Out
5 札付 **fudatsu(ki)** tagged (with a brand name),
　　　marked; notorious
7 札束 **satsutaba** wad of money, bundle/roll of
　　　bills
8 札所 **fudasho** amulet-issuing office
13 札幌 **Sapporo** (city, Hokkaidō)

———————— 2 ————————
1 一札 **issatsu** a document/bond
一札入 **issatsu i(reru)** give a signed statement/
　　　I.O.U.
2 入札 **nyūsatsu** tender, bid, bidding
入札者 **nyūsatsusha** bidder
3 下札 **sa(ge)fuda** tag, label
4 切札 **ki(ri)fuda** trump card
辻札 **tsujifuda** street-corner bulletin board
手札 **tefuda** name card; a hand (in card
　　　playing)
手札型 **tefudagata** 11 cm high by 8 cm wide
　　　(photo)
引札 **hi(ki)fuda** handbill; lottery ticket
木札 **kifuda** wooden ticket/tag
5 出札 **shussatsu** issuing tickets
出札口 **shussatsuguchi** ticket window
付札 **tsu(ke)fuda** tag, label
正札 **shōfuda** price tag, label
立札 **ta(te)fuda** bulletin/notice board
6 合札 **a(i)fuda** check, tally
名札 **nafuda** name plate/tag
守札 **mamo(ri)fuda** paper charm
当札 **a(tari)fuda** winning lottery ticket
7 赤札 **akafuda** clearance goods; sold goods
花札 **hanafuda** floral playing cards
改札 **kaisatsu** check/clip/collect tickets
改札口 **kaisatsuguchi** ticket gate, wicket
利札 **risatsu, rifuda** (interest) coupon
8 表札 **hyōsatsu** nameplate, doorplate
取札 **to(ri)fuda** cards to be picked up (in the
　　　New Year's card game)
門札 **monsatsu, kadofuda** nameplate
9 飛札 **hisatsu** urgent letter
10 高札 **kōsatsu** bulletin board; highest bid
荷札 **nifuda** tag, label
書札 **shosatsu** letter
紙札 **kamifuda** label, tag
納札 **nōsatsu** votive tablet (left at a temple)
11 偽札 **nisesatsu** counterfeit paper money
掛札 **ka(ke)fuda** hanging notice plaque,
　　　nameplate
12 湯札 **yufuda** bath ticket
落札 **rakusatsu** successful bid
落札人 **rakusatsunin** successful bidder
落札値 **rakusatsune** contract/highest-bid
　　　price
葬札 **sōrei** funeral
富札 **tomifuda** lottery ticket
検札 **kensatsu** examine/check tickets
無札 **musatsu** (passenger) without a ticket
絵札 **efuda** picture card
貼札 **ha(ri)fuda** placard, poster, label
貴札 **kisatsu** your letter
集札係 **shūsatsugakari** ticket collector
開札 **kaisatsu** opening of bids

4

木 1←
月
日
火
礻
王
牛
方
攵
欠
心
戸
戈

13 禁札 **kinsatsu** prohibition-notice board
新札 **shinsatsu** new paper money
15 標札 **hyōsatsu** nameplate, doorplate
質札 **shichifuda** pawn ticket
18 藩札 **hansatsu** paper money issued by a feudal clan
19 贋札 **nisesatsu, gansatsu** counterfeit currency
23 鑑札 **kansatsu** a license

3

4 木戸札 **kidofuda** wooden admission ticket
12 無鑑札 **mukansatsu** without a license
番号札 **bangōfuda** numbered (license) plate

4

→2 木 月 日 火 ネ 王 牛 方 文 欠 心 戸 戈

2

4a2.1

杤

TŌ (type of tree)

4a2.2

朸

RYOKU, ōgo carrying pole

权→権 4a11.18

4a2.3 / 1466

朴

BOKU simple, plain

1

8 朴念仁 **bokunenjin** unsociable close-mouthed person
朴直 **bokuchoku** simple and honest, ingenuous
11 朴訥 **bokutotsu** rugged honesty

2

10 淳朴 **junboku** simple and honest
純朴 **junboku** simple and honest
素朴 **soboku** simple, artless, ingenuous
14 醇朴 **junboku** simple and honest
15 質朴 **shitsuboku** simple, unsophisticated

4a2.4 / 1305

机

KI, tsukue desk

1

3 机上 **kijō** desk-top, academic, theoretical, armchair
4 机辺 **kihen** near the desk

2

7 床机 **shōgi** camp/folding stool

4a2.5

杁

iri sluice, spout, floodgate, penstock
Eburi (place name, Fukuoka-ken)

4a2.6 / 1628

朽

KYŪ, ku(chiru) rot, decay

1

4 朽木 **ku(chi)ki, kyūboku** decayed tree/wood
8 朽果 **ku(chi)ha(teru)** rot away
12 朽葉 **ku(chi)ba** decayed/dead leaves
16 朽壊 **kyūkai** rot and crumble

2

4 不朽 **fukyū** immortal, everlasting
6 老朽 **rōkyū** age, decrepitude
14 腐朽 **fukyū** decay, molder, rot, decompose

4a2.7

李

RI, sumomo plum

2

6 行李 **kōri** wicker trunk; baggage

4a2.8

朶

DA branch; hang down

2

3 万朶 **banda** many branches
6 耳朶 **mimitabu** earlobe **jida** earlobe, ears
11 粗朶 **soda** twigs, brushwood
12 歯朶 **shida** fern

3

4a3.1

杜

TO, ZU crab apple, wild pear; stop, block, close
mori woods, grove (with a shrine)

1

8 杜若 **kakitsubata** iris, flag
杜松 **toshō** juniper tree
12 杜絶 **tozetsu** be blocked/obstructed
14 杜漏 **zurō** careless, negligent
15 杜撰 **zusan** slipshod, careless(ly done)
18 杜鵑 **hototogisu** cuckoo

4a3.2 / 1872

杉   sugi Japan(ese) cedar, cryptomeria, sugi

—————— 1 ——————

4 杉戸 **sugido** door made of sugi wood
5 杉皮 **sugikawa** sugi bark
7 杉材 **sugizai** sugi wood
8 杉並木 **suginamiki** avenue of sugi trees
11 杉菜 **sugina** a field horsetail
15 杉箸 **sugibashi** chopsticks made of sugi wood

—————— 2 ——————

6 糸杉 **itosugi** cypress
10 姪杉 **Meotosugi** (place name)

—————— 3 ——————

1 一本杉 **ipponsugi** a solitary cedar tree
9 神代杉 **jindaisugi** lignitized cedar

4a3.3

杣   soma timber forest; lumber; woodcutter

—————— 1 ——————

2 杣人 **somabito** woodcutter, woodsman
3 杣山 **somayama** timber forest
4 杣木 **somagi** lumber, timber

4a3.4

杙   YOKU, kui stake, tethering post

—————— 2 ——————

12 棒杙 **bōgui** stake, pile
16 橋杙 **hashigui** bridge pile/pillar

4a3.5

杖   JŌ, tsue staff, cane

—————— 1 ——————

9 杖柱 **tsue-hashira** staff and pillar, person one depends on

—————— 2 ——————

11 側杖 **sobazue** blow received by a bystander
12 傍杖 **sobazue** blow received by a bystander
13 禅杖 **zenjō** beating-stick to keep Zen meditators from dozing
16 錫杖 **shakujō** priest's staff

—————— 3 ——————

8 松葉杖 **matsubazue** crutches

4a3.6

杆   KAN, tate shield
     teko lever

—————— 2 ——————

14 槓杆 **kōkan** lever

杆 → 桿 **4a7.7**

4a3.7 / 552

材 柭   ZAI wood, lumber; material; talent

—————— 1 ——————

4 材木 **zaimoku** wood, lumber
   材木屋 **zaimokuya** lumberyard, lumber dealer
   材木商 **zaimokushō** lumber business/dealer
10 材料 **zairyō** materials, ingredients; data; factors
13 材幹 **zaikan** ability
15 材質 **zaishitsu** quality (of the material/lumber)

—————— 2 ——————

2 人材 **jinzai** man of talent, personnel
   人材登用 **jinzai tōyō** selection of people for higher positions
4 木材 **mokuzai** wood, lumber
   心材 **shinzai** heartwood
5 用材 **yōzai** materials; lumber
   巨材 **kyozai** big timber; great man
   好材料 **kōzairyō** good material/data
   石材 **sekizai** (building) stone
   石材商 **sekizaishō** stone dealer
6 防材 **bōzai** boom, fender (to block a harbor entrance)
   米材 **beizai** American timber
7 良材 **ryōzai** good timber; people of ability
   角材 **kakuzai** rectangular timber/lumber
   杉材 **sugizai** sugi wood
8 建材 **kenzai** construction materials
   取材 **shuzai** news gathering, coverage
10 部材 **buzai** (structural) member
   原材料 **genzairyō** raw materials
   逸材 **itsuzai** person of exceptional talent
   教材 **kyōzai** teaching materials
   素材 **sozai** a material; subject matter
13 適材 **tekizai** the right person
   適材適所 **tekizai-tekisho** the right man in the right place
   資材 **shizai** materials, supplies
   鉄材 **tetsuzai** iron/steel material
14 構材 **kōzai** construction materials
   製材 **seizai** sawing; lumber
   製材工 **seizaikō** sawyer
   製材所 **seizaisho** sawmill
15 器材 **kizai** tools and materials, equipment
   線材 **senzai** wire rod
16 鋼材 **kōzai** steel (as a material)

4

木 3 →
月
日
火
礻
王
牛
方
攵
欠
心
戸
戈

18 礎材 **sozai** foundation materials
題材 **daizai** subject matter, theme

4a3.8

杠

KŌ flagpole; large beam
chigi large beam

─────── 1 ───────
10 杠秤 **kōshō, chigibakari** large beam balance

4a3.9

杞

KI, KO river willow

─────── 1 ───────
15 杞憂 **kiyū** imaginary/groundless fears

─────── 2 ───────
9 枸杞 **kuko** Chinese matrimony vine

栃 → 栃 **4a5.28**

4a3.10

杌

GOTSU tree stump; stool

4a3.11 / 191

村 邨

SON, mura village

─────── 1 ───────
2 村人 **murabito** villager
村八分 **murahachibu** ostracism
3 村上 **Murakami** (surname); (emperor, 946–967)
4 村夫子 **sonpūshi** educated person in the country
5 村民 **sonmin** villagers
村立 **sonritsu** established by the village
6 村会 **sonkai** village assembly
村有 **son'yū** village-owned
8 村長 **sonchō** village mayor
村雨 **murasame** passing shower
11 村道 **sondō** village road
村祭 **muramatsu(ri)** village festival
12 村落 **sonraku** village, hamlet
村童 **sondō** village boy/child
村税 **sonzei** village tax
村費 **sonpi** village expenses
14 村境 **murazakai** edge of the village

─────── 2 ───────
3 小村 **shōson** hamlet, small village

山村 **sanson** mountain village
6 近村 **kinson** neighboring villages
江村 **kōson** river village
7 町村 **chōson** towns and villages, municipality
10 帰村 **kison** return to one's village
12 寒村 **kanson** poor/lonely village
13 農村 **nōson** farm village, rural community
14 漁村 **gyoson** fishing village
15 僻村 **hekison** remote village
隣村 **tonarimura, rinson** neighboring village
弊村 **heison** impoverished village; our humble village
18 離村 **rison** rural exodus

─────── 3 ───────
5 市町村 **shichōson** cities, towns, and villages; municipalities
12 無医村 **muison** doctorless village
13 農山村 **nōsanson** agricultural and mountain villages
14 選手村 **senshumura** Olympic village

4a3.12

杓

SHAKU ladle, dipper; handle

─────── 1 ───────
2 杓子 **shakushi** dipper, ladle, scoop
杓子定規 **shakushi-jōgi** hard-and-fast rule
4 杓文字 **shamoji** dipper, ladle, scoop

─────── 2 ───────
8 金杓子 **kanajakushi** metal ladle, dipper
9 茶杓 **chashaku** tea ladle
柄杓 **hishaku** ladle, dipper, scoop

4a3.13

杏

KYŌ, anzu apricot

─────── 2 ───────
14 銀杏 **ginnan** gingko nut **ichō** gingko tree

─────── 3 ───────
4 巴旦杏 **hatankyō, hadankyō** almond tree; plum
7 牡丹杏 **botankyō** plum

4a3.14

杢

moku carpenter

条 → **4i4.1**

─────────── 4 ───────────

4a4.1 / 127

林 **RIN, hayashi** woods, forest

─────────── 1 ───────────

4 林木 **rinboku** forest tree
5 林立 **rinritsu** stand close together in large numbers
7 林学 **ringaku** forestry
9 林政 **rinsei** forest management
11 林野 **rin'ya** forests and fields, woodlands
　林野庁 **Rin'yachō** Forestry Agency
　林道 **rindō** forest road/trail
　林務官 **rinmukan** forestry officer, ranger
　林産 **rinsan** forest products
　林産物 **rinsanbutsu** forest products
12 林間学校 **rinkan gakkō** outdoor school, camp
13 林業 **ringyō** forestry
16 林檎 **ringo** apple
　林檎酒 **ringoshu** hard cider

─────────── 2 ───────────

3 山林 **sanrin** mountains and forests; mountain forest
　山林学 **sanringaku** forestry
　山林官 **sanrinkan** forester
6 竹林 **takebayashi, chikurin** bamboo grove
7 伯林 **Berurin** Berlin
　芸林 **geirin** art and literary circles
8 官林 **kanrin** national forest
　松林 **matsubayashi** pine woods
9 造林 **zōrin** (re)forestation
　造林学 **zōringaku** forestry
10 梅林 **bairin** plum orchard/grove
　書林 **shorin** bookstore
11 密林 **mitsurin** jungle, dense forest
12 営林 **eirin** forest management
　植林 **shokurin** tree planting, afforestation
　森林 **shinrin** woods, forest
　森林学 **shinringaku** forestry
　森林帯 **shinrintai** forest zone
　焼林檎 **ya(ki)ringo** baked apple
13 農林 **nōrin** agriculture and forestry
　農林水産大臣 **nōrinsuisan daijin** Minister of Agriculture, Forestry and Fisheries
　農林水産省 **Nōrinsuisanshō** Ministry of Agriculture, Forestry and Fisheries
　禅林 **zenrin** Zen temple
　辞林 **jirin** dictionary
14 緑林 **ryokurin** (mounted) bandits
16 樹林 **jurin** forest
　翰林 **kanrin** literary circles
　翰林院 **kanrin'in** academy, institute

─────────── 3 ───────────

2 人工林 **jinkōrin** planted forest

4 公有林 **kōyūrin** public forest
6 防風林 **bōfūrin** windbreak (forest)
　防砂林 **bōsarin** trees planted to arrest shifting sand
　防雪林 **bōsetsurin** snowbreak (forest)
8 官有林 **kan'yūrin** national forest
9 風致林 **fūchirin** forest planted for scenic beauty
　砂防林 **sabōrin** erosion-control forest
10 原生林 **genseirin** primeval/virgin forest
14 演習林 **enshūrin** experimental forest
　雑木林 **zōkibayashi, zōbokurin** grove of trees of various species
16 熱帯林 **nettairin** tropical forest

─────────── 4 ───────────

10 酒池肉林 **shuchi-nikurin** sumptuous feast

4a4.2

枉 **Ō** bend, distort; against one's will; unjust **ma(geru)** bend, distort; force (someone)

4a4.3

枋 **HŌ** raft, boat

4a4.4 / 1156

枚 **MAI** (counter for thin, flat objects)

─────────── 1 ───────────

10 枚挙 **maikyo** enumerate, count, list
　枚挙違無 **maikyo (ni) itoma (ga) na(i)** too numerous to mention
13 枚数 **maisū** number of sheets

─────────── 2 ───────────

1 一枚 **ichimai** one sheet
　一枚看板 **ichimai kanban** one's only suit; leading actor; sole issue, slogan
2 二枚目 **nimaime** (role of a) handsome man/beau
　二枚舌 **nimaijita** forked tongue, duplicity
3 三枚 **sanmai** three sheets
　三枚目 **sanmaime** comedian
　大枚 **taimai** large amount of money
　千枚通 **senmaidō(shi)** awl

枦→櫨 **4a16.2**

桟→材 **4a3.7**

4a4.5

枅 KEI rafter   Hijiki (place name)

4a4.6

枡 桝 masu square wooden measuring cup

4 → 4 木 月 日 火 衤 王 牛 方 攵 欠 心 戸 戈

柿 → 柿   4a5.25

4a4.7

柄 ZEI, hozo tenon

4a4.8

枕 CHIN, makura pillow

—————— 1 ——————
0 枕カバー **makura kabā** pillowcase
4 枕元 **makuramoto** bedside
　枕辺 **makurabe, chinpen** bedside
　枕木 **makuragi** railroad tie
9 枕屏風 **makurabyōbu** bedside screen
10 枕席 **chinseki** pillow and mat, bed
11 枕許 **makuramoto** bedside
12 枕詞 **makurakotoba** prefatory word, set epithet
16 枕頭 **chintō** bedside

—————— 2 ——————
4 水枕 **mizu-makura** water-filled pillow
　手枕 **temakura** using one's arm for a pillow
5 北枕 **kitamakura** sleeping with one's head toward the north
　氷枕 **kōri-makura** ice-filled pillow
6 仮枕 **karimakura** nap
7 肘枕 **hijimakura** one's elbow used for a pillow
8 長枕 **nagamakura** bed bolster
　波枕 **namimakura** sleeping on the ocean, sea voyage
9 括枕 **kuku(ri) makura** stuffed pillow
　草枕 **kusamakura** make an overnight stay while traveling
10 旅枕 **tabi makura** sleeping away from home; journey
13 夢枕 **yumemakura** in a dream
14 歌枕 **utamakura** place famed in poetry
15 膝枕 **hizamakura** using someone's lap for a pillow

4a4.9

杵 SHO, kine long-handled wooden pestle, (rice/grain) pounder

—————— 1 ——————
9 杵柄 **kinezuka** grain-pounder handle; experience, skill

4a4.10

杷 HA rake

—————— 2 ——————
8 枇杷 **biwa** loquat

4a4.11 / 1155

杯 盃 HAI cup; (counter for cupfuls)   sakazuki winecup (for saké)

—————— 1 ——————
8 杯事 **sakazukigoto** drinking feast; exchange of nuptial cups; pledging over cups of wine
9 杯洗 **haisen** basin for winecups, sink

—————— 2 ——————
1 一杯 **ippai** a cup of; a drink; full; to the utmost
　一杯機嫌 **ippai kigen** slight intoxication
3 大杯 **taihai** large cup, goblet
4 水杯 **mizu-sakazuki** farewell cups of water
　木杯 **mokuhai** wooden cup
5 玉杯 **gyokuhai** jade cup
6 返杯 **henpai** offer the cup in return
7 別杯 **beppai** farewell cup/dinner
8 苦杯 **kuhai** bitter cup, ordeal, defeat
　金杯 **kinpai** gold cup/goblet
9 祝杯 **shukuhai** a toast
10 酒杯 **shuhai** wine cup/glass
　納杯 **nōhai** the last cup
11 乾杯 **kanpai** a toast; Cheers!
12 満杯 **manpai** full to capacity
13 献杯 **kenpai** offer a drink/toast
14 罰杯 **bappai** penalty cup (the loser must drink)
　銀杯 **ginpai** silver cup
15 賞杯 **shōhai** trophy, prize cup
　賜杯 **shihai** trophy (from the emperor)

—————— 3 ——————
2 力一杯 **chikara-ippai** with all one's might
4 天皇杯 **Tennōhai** the Emperor's Trophy
　手一杯 **te-ippai** hands full; barely making ends meet
13 腹一杯 **hara ippai** full stomach; to one's heart's content

14 精一杯 **sei-ippai** with all one's might
17 優勝杯 **yūshōhai** championship cup

4a4.12 / 1393

析

SEKI divide, take apart, analyze

───────── 1 ─────────
5 析出 **sekishutsu** be deposited, precipitate; educe, extract

───────── 2 ─────────
4 分析 **bunseki** analysis
9 透析 **tōseki** dialysis
13 解析 **kaiseki** analysis (branch of math)

───────── 4 ─────────
8 定性分析 **teisei bunseki** qualitative analysis
定量分析 **teiryō bunseki** quantitative analysis
14 精神分析 **seishin bunseki** psychoanalysis

4a4.13

枇

BI loquat

───────── 1 ─────────
8 枇杷 **biwa** loquat

4a4.14

杪

BYŌ, kozue twig; treetop

4a4.15

枌

FUN, sogi shingle

4a4.16 / 696

松 枩

SHŌ, matsu pine

───────── 1 ─────────
3 松山 **Matsuyama** (city, Ehime-ken)
4 松内 **matsu(no)uchi** New Year's Week
松木 **matsu(no)ki** pine tree
5 松本 **Matsumoto** (city, Nagano-ken)
6 松阪 **Matsuzaka** (city, Mie-ken)
松江 **Matsue** (city, Shimane-ken)
松虫 **matsumushi** (a kind of cricket)
松竹 **matsutake** New Year's pine-and-bamboo decorations
松竹梅 **shō-chiku-bai** pine-bamboo-plum (as sign of congratulations or to designate three things of equal rank)

8 松並木 **matsunamiki** avenue/row of pines
松林 **matsubayashi** pine woods
松明 **taimatsu** (pine) torch
9 松風 **matsukaze, shōfū** wind through the pines
松茸 **matsutake, matsudake** (a kind of edible mushroom)
松柏 **shōhaku** pines and oaks, conifer, evergreen
10 松原 **matsubara** pine grove
11 松毬 **matsukasa** pinecone
松笠 **matsukasa** pinecone
12 松葉 **matsuba** pine needle
松葉杖 **matsubazue** crutches
21 松露 **shōro** (a kind of edible mushroom)
22 松籟 **shōrai** soughing of the wind through the pines

───────── 2 ─────────
5 市松 **ichimatsu** checkered (pattern)
6 老松 **o(i)matsu, rōshō** old pine tree
米松 **beimatsu** Douglas/Oregon fir
7 赤松 **akamatsu** red pine
杜松 **toshō** juniper tree
8 若松 **wakamatsu** young pine tree; New Year's pine-tree decorations
門松 **kadomatsu** New Year's pine-and-bamboo decorations
9 海松 **umimatsu** pine on the seacoast
miru (an edible seaweed)
10 高松 **Takamatsu** (city, Kagawa-ken)
這松 **haimatsu** creeping pine
浜松 **Hamamatsu** (city, Shizuoka-ken)
唐松 **karamatsu** larch
11 黒松 **kuromatsu** black pine
12 雄松 **omatsu** black pine
13 椴松 **todomatsu** fir

───────── 3 ─────────
10 姫小松 **hime komatsu** a small pine
12 落葉松 **karamatsu** larch
15 蝦夷松 **Ezo-matsu** silver fir, spruce
17 磯馴松 **sonarematsu** seashore pine (wind-blown to the contours of the terrain)

───────── 4 ─────────
5 白砂青松 **hakusha-seishō** white sand and green pines, beautiful seashore scene

4a4.17

杭

KŌ, kui stake, post, piling

───────── 1 ─────────
5 杭打 **kuiu(chi)** pile driving
杭打機 **kuiu(chi)ki** pile driver

───────── 2 ─────────
7 乱杭 **rangui** palisade

乱杭歯 **ranguiba** irregular teeth
12 棒杭 **bōgui** stake, pile
16 橋杭 **hashigui** bridge pile/pillar

4a4.18 / 870

枝

SHI, eda branch

──────── 1 ────────

7 枝折戸 **shio(ri)do** garden gate made of branches
　枝豆 **edamame** green soybeans
8 枝垂柳 **shida(re)yanagi** weeping willow
　枝垂桜 **shida(re)zakura** droopy-branch cherry tree
9 枝枯病 **edaga(re)byō** twig blight
10 枝振 **edabu(ri)** shape of a tree
11 枝隊 **shitai** detachment (of troops)
　枝道 **edamichi** branch road
　枝接 **edatsu(gi)** grafting
12 枝葉 **shiyō, edaha** branches and leaves; ramifications; unimportant details
　枝葉末節 **shiyō-massetsu** branches and leaves; unimportant details
13 枝幹 **shikan** trunk and branches

──────── 2 ────────

3 小枝 **koeda** twig, sprig
8 若枝 **wakaeda** young branch, shoot
9 連枝 **renshi** brother (of a nobleman)
　荔枝 **reishi** litchi (nut)
　枯枝 **ka(re)eda** dead branch
13 楊枝 **yōji** toothpick; toothbrush
16 整枝 **seishi** pruning

──────── 3 ────────

4 爪楊枝 **tsumayōji** toothpick
8 金雀枝 **enishida** broom, genista (a shrub)

4a4.19 / 1907

枠

waku frame, framework; limit, confines

──────── 1 ────────

4 枠内 **wakunai** within the limits
5 枠外 **wakugai** beyond the limits
11 枠組 **wakugumi** frame, framework; framing

──────── 2 ────────

4 戸枠 **towaku** door frame
11 窓枠 **madowaku** window frame/sash
　黒枠 **kurowaku** black border/edges

4a4.20

杼

CHO, hi shuttle (on a loom)

──────── 1 ────────

16 杼機 **choki** shuttle and reed

4a4.21 / 1047

板

HAN, BAN, ita board, plank

──────── 1 ────────

2 板子 **itago** floor planks (in a small boat)
4 板戸 **itado** wooden door
5 板石 **itaishi** flagstone, slab, a slate
　板目 **itame** grain (in wood)
7 板囲 **itagako(i)** board/plank fence
8 板金 **itagane, bankin** sheet metal, metal plate
　板門店 **Hanmonten** Panmunjom
9 板前 **itamae** a cook
　板垣 **itagaki** wooden fence
　板挟 **itabasa(mi)** predicament, dilemma
　板屋 **itaya** shingle/board roof(ed house)
　板屋根 **itayane** shingle/wooden roof
10 板紙 **itagami** cardboard, pasteboard
11 板張 **itaba(ri)** boarding, planking, wainscoting
12 板塀 **itabei** board fence
　板葺 **itabu(ki)** shingle/board roofing
　板硝子 **itagarasu** plate glass
　板間 **ita(no)ma** wooden floor
　板間稼 **ita(no)ma kase(gi)** bathhouse thief
15 板敷 **itaji(ki)** wooden/plank floor
16 板壁 **itakabe** wooden wall
　板橋 **itabashi** wooden bridge; gangplank

──────── 2 ────────

3 上板 **a(ge)ita** movable floorboards; trap door
4 戸板 **toita** door, door-board
5 甲板 **kanpan, kōhan** deck
　平板 **heiban** flat board, slat; monotonous
　立板水 **ta(te)ita (ni) mizu** fluency, glibness, volubility, rattling on, logorrhea
　目板 **meita** batten plate, panel strip, eyeboard
6 合板 **gōhan, gōban** plywood
7 延板 **no(be)ita** board for making udon, etc.; hammered-out metal
　豆板 **mameita** slab of candied beans
　豆板銀 **mameitagin** (an Edo-era coin)
　床板 **tokoita** alcove floorboard
　　yukaita floorboards
8 画板 **gaban** drawing/drafting board
　厚板 **atsuita** thick board, plank, plate (glass), heavy (metal) sheet; heavy brocaded obi
　泥板岩 **deibangan** shale
　押板 **o(shi)ita** pressing board
9 型板 **kataita** template
　指板 **yubiita** fingerboard (on a guitar); (door) fingerplate
　柿板 **kokeraita** shingle

看板 **kanban** sign(board)
看板娘 **kanban musume** pretty girl who draws customers
10 胸板 **munaita** the chest
11 基板 **kiban** substrate
猫板 **nekoita** board at the side of a long brazier
黒板 **kokuban** blackboard
船板 **funaita** ship plank/timber
船板塀 **funaitabei** fence made of old ship timbers
魚板 **gyoban** temple's fish-shaped wooden time-gong
12 湿板 **shitsuban** wet plate (in photography)
渡板 **wata(ri)ita** gangplank
揚板 **a(ge)ita** removable floorboards, trap door
登板 **tōban** go to the pitcher's mound
葺板 **fu(ki)ita** shingles
棚板 **tanaita** shelf (board), tray
裁板 **ta(chi)ita** tailor's cutting board
13 溝板 **dobuita** boards covering a ditch
腰板 **koshiita** baseboard, wainscoting
跳板 **ha(ne)ita, to(bi)ita** springboard
鉄板 **teppan** steel plate; griddle
14 種板 **taneita** (photographic) negative; (projection) slide
銅板 **dōban** sheet copper
15 敷板 **shi(ki)ita** planking, floor boards
踏板 **fu(mi)ita** treadle, pedal, running board
16 壁板 **kabeita** wainscoting
薄板 **usuita** thin board, sheet, veneer
鋼板 **kōhan, kōban** steel plate
18 鎧板 **yoroiita** louver board, slat
19 鏡板 **kagamiita** panel (board)

────── 3 ──────
3 上甲板 **jōkanpan** upper deck
4 天井板 **tenjō ita** ceiling boards
中甲板 **chūkōhan, chūkanpan** main deck
方向板 **hōkōban** (train's) destination sign
5 正甲板 **seikanpan** main deck
立看板 **ta(te)kanban** standing signboard
6 伝言板 **dengonban** message/bulletin board
羽子板 **hagoita** battledore, pingpong-like paddle
羽目板 **hameita** paneling, wainscoting
安定板 **anteiban** stabilizing fin, stabilizer
7 亜鉛板 **aenban** zinc plate
告示板 **kokujiban** bulletin board
告知板 **kokuchiban** bulletin board
8 表看板 **omote-kanban** sign out in front; figurehead, mask
金看板 **kinkanban** gold-lettered sign; slogan
9 飛込板 **tobikomiita** diving board
洗濯板 **sentakuita** washboard

指示板 **shijiban** notice board
10 展翅板 **tenshiban** setting board (for spreading butterfly-specimen wings)
11 掲示板 **keijiban** bulletin board
蛍光板 **keikōban** fluorescent plate/screen
13 感光板 **kankōban** sensitized plate
跳躍板 **chōyakuban** springboard
15 調色板 **chōshokuban** palette
16 鋼鉄板 **kōtetsuban** steel plate

────── 4 ──────
1 一枚看板 **ichimai kanban** one's only suit; leading actor; sole issue, slogan

4a4.22 / 1023

枢 樞   **SŪ, toboso** pivot

────── 1 ──────
8 枢府 **Sūfu** Privy Council
9 枢要 **sūyō** pivotal, important
11 枢密院 **Sūmitsuin** Privy Council
12 枢軸 **sūjiku** pivot, axis, center
枢軸国 **sūjikukoku** the Axis powers
16 枢機 **sūki** important state affairs
枢機卿 **sūkikei** (Catholic) cardinal

────── 2 ──────
4 中枢 **chūsū** center, pivot, nucleus

牀→床 3q4.1

4a4.23

杳   **YŌ** dim, indistinct

杰→傑 2a11.6

枩→松 4a4.16

4a4.24

采 采   **SAI** general's baton; dice; take; coloring; appearance; territory

────── 1 ──────
10 采配 **saihai** flywhisk-like baton of command

────── 2 ──────
9 風采 **fūsai** appearance, mien, bearing
10 納采 **nōsai** betrothal gift
11 喝采 **kassai** applause, cheers

木 4 ←
月
日
火
礻
王
牛
方
攵
欠
心
戸
戈

栞 → 栞 **4a6.34**

─────── 5 ───────

4a5.1

柘

SHA wild mulberry tree

─────── 1 ───────

14 柘榴 **zakuro** pomegranate
柘榴石 **zakuroishi** garnet
柘榴鼻 **zakuro-bana** swollen red nose, strawberry nose

4a5.2

粒

RŌ bent/broken tree

4a5.3 / 146

相

SŌ each other, reciprocal; aspect, phase, physiognomy
SHŌ (government) minister
ai- together, fellow-, each other

─────── 1 ───────

3 相々傘 **aiaigasa (de)** under the same umbrella
4 相互 **sōgo** mutual, reciprocal
相互作用 **sōgo sayō** interaction
相手 **aite** the other party, partner, opponent
相手方 **aitekata** the other party, opponent
相手役 **aiteyaku** a role opposite (someone), (dance) partner
5 相生 **aio(i)** growing from the same root
相好 **sōgō (o kuzusu)** break into a smile
6 相伝 **sōden** inheritance, handed down
相合傘 **aia(i)gasa (de)** under the same umbrella
相次 **aitsu(gu)** follow in succession
相当 **sōtō** suitable, appropriate; considerable; be equivalent to, correspond to
相当品 **sōtōhin** article of similar value
相当数 **sōtōsū** quite a number of
7 相身互 **aimitaga(i)** mutual sympathy/help
相似 **sōji** resemblance, similarity, analogy
相似形 **sōjikei** similar figures (in geometry)
相対 **sōtai** relativity
　　　 aitai facing each other, directly
相対主義 **sōtai shugi** relativism
相対的 **sōtaiteki** relative
相対性 **sōtaisei** relativity
相弟子 **aideshi** fellow pupil/apprentice
相役 **aiyaku** colleague
相応 **sōō** suitable, fitting
8 相性 **aishō** affinity, compatibility

9 相乗 **aino(ri)** riding together
　　　 sōjō multiply together
相俟 **aima(tte)** coupled with, in cooperation with
相変 **aikawa(razu)** as usual
相持 **aimo(chi)** mutual help, give and take, sharing
相剋 **sōkoku** vie/conflict with each other
相客 **aikyaku** fellow guest/passenger
相相傘 **aiaigasa (de)** under the same umbrella
相思 **sōshi** mutual affection
相思相愛 **sōshi-sōai** mutual love
10 相容 **aii(renai)** incompatible
相殺 **sōsai** offset, countervail
相討 **aiu(chi)** striking each other simultaneously
11 相宿 **aiyado** stay at the same inn, share a room
12 相違 **sōi** difference, discrepancy
相場 **sōba** market price; speculation; estimation
相場師 **sōbashi** speculator
相棒 **aibō** pal, partner, accomplice
相等 **sōtō** equality, equivalence
13 相携 **aitazusa(ete)** together with, in couples
相槌 **aizuchi** (anvil) hammering in alternation; giving responses to make the conversation go smoothly
相愛 **sōai** mutual love
相続 **sōzoku** inheritance, succession
相続人 **sōzokunin** heir
相続争 **sōzoku araso(i)** inheritance dispute
相続法 **sōzokuhō** inheritance law
相続者 **sōzokusha** heir
相続税 **sōzokuzei** inheritance tax
相続権 **sōzokuken** (right of) inheritance
14 相模 **Sagami** (ancient kuni, Kanagawa-ken)
相模川 **Sagami-gawa** (river, Kanagawa-ken)
相貌 **sōbō** features, looks, physiognomy
相関 **sōkan** correlation
相関的 **sōkanteki** interrelated
15 相撲 **sumō** sumo wrestling
相撲取 **sumōto(ri)** sumo wrestler
相談 **sōdan** consult, confer; proposal; arrangements
相談役 **sōdan'yaku** adviser, consultant
相談所 **sōdanjo** consultation office
19 相識 **sōshiki** acquaintance

─────── 2 ───────

2 入相 **i(ri)ai** sunset
人相 **ninsō** facial features, physiognomy
人相占 **ninsō urana(i)** divination by facial features
人相学 **ninsōgaku** physiognomy
人相見 **ninsōmi** physiognomist
人相書 **ninsōga(ki)** description of one's looks
3 三相 **sansō** three-phase (current)

大相撲 **ōzumō** grand sumo tournament; exciting match

下相談 **shitasōdan** preliminary talks/ arrangements

4 不相応 **fusōō** out of proportion to, unsuited, inappropriate, undue

内相 **naishō** (prewar) Home Minister

文相 **bunshō** Education Minister

手相 **tesō** lines of the palm

手相学 **tesōgaku** palmistry

手相見 **tesōmi** palm reader

手相術 **tesōjutsu** palmistry

5 世相 **sesō** phase of life, the times, world conditions

皮相 **hisō** superficial, outward

外相 **gaishō** the Foreign Minister

6 死相 **shisō** shadow of death

仮相 **kasō** appearance, phenomenon

地相 **chisō** (divination by) the lay of the land

吉相 **kissō** good/lucky omen

血相 **kessō** a look, expression

7 位相 **isō** phase

形相 **gyōsō** features, looks, expression

keisō phase, form, idea

花相撲 **hanazumō** off-season sumo tournament

8 事相 **jisō** aspect, phase, phenomenon

其相応 **sore sōō** in its own way

厚相 **kōshō** Welfare Minister

法相 **hōshō** Minister of Justice

Hossō (a Buddhist sect)

実相 **jissō** actual facts; (spiritual) reality

空相場 **karasōba** fictitious transaction

物相飯 **mossōmeshi** prison food

金相学 **kinsōgaku** metallography

9 首相 **shushō** prime minister

通相場 **tō(ri)sōba** market price; accepted custom

独相撲 **hito(ri)zumō** like wrestling with no opponent

草相撲 **kusazumō** amateur/sandlot sumo

面相 **mensō** face, looks

相相傘 **aiaigasa (de)** under the same umbrella

10 陸相 **rikushō** War Minister

険相 **kensō** forbidding/sinister look

真相 **shinsō** the truth/facts, the real situation

遊相手 **aso(bi)aite** playmate

家相 **kasō** (lucky/unlucky) aspect of a house

宰相 **saishō** prime minister, premier

骨相 **kossō** physique, (cranial) physiognomy

骨相学 **kossōgaku** phrenology

時相 **jisō** tense (in grammar)

11 貧相 **hinsō** poor-looking, seedy

悪相 **akusō** evil face/look

粗相 **sosō** carelessness, blunder

12 卿相 **keishō** court nobles and state ministers

腕相撲 **udezumō** arm wrestling

13 農相 **nōshō** Agriculture (, Forestry and Fisheries) Minister

滅相 **messō** absurd, unreasonable

寝相 **nezō** one's sleeping posture

福相 **fukusō** (plump) happy face

瑞相 **zuisō** good omen

話相手 **hanashi aite** someone to talk to; companion

14 様相 **yōsō** aspect, phase, condition

15 蔵相 **zōshō** Finance Minister

諸相 **shosō** various phases/aspects

17 闇相場 **yamisōba** black-market price

18 観相 **kansō** reading character or fortunes by physiognomy, palmistry, phrenology, etc.

——————— 3 ———————

1 一子相伝 **isshi sōden** (secret) handed down from father to son

5 可哀相 **kawaisō** poor, pitiable, pathetic

6 近親相姦 **kinshin sōkan** incest

有無相通 **umu-aitsū(jiru)** help each other, be complementary

百面相 **hyakumensō** many phases/faces

自治相 **jichisō** Home Affairs Minister

7 肝胆相照 **kantan-aite(rasu)** be intimate friends

9 通産相 **tsūsanshō** Minister of International Trade and Industry

相思相愛 **sōshi-sōai** mutual love

為替相場 **kawase sōba** exchange rate

10 家督相続 **katoku sōzoku** succession as head of family

時代相 **jidaisō** trend of the times

11 動物相 **dōbutsusō** fauna

12 琴瑟相和 **kinshitsu aiwa(su)** be happily married

13 跡目相続 **atome sōzoku** heirship

14 種々相 **shujusō** various phases/aspects

種種相 **shujusō** various aspects/phases

16 親近相姦 **shinkin sōkan** incest

4a5.4

柵 柵　　**SAKU** fence, palisade, stockade
shigarami weir, small dam

——————— 2 ———————

13 鉄柵 **tessaku** iron railing/fence

4a5.5

柚　　**YŪ, YU, JIKU, yuzu** citron

——————— 1 ———————

2 柚子 **yuzu** citron

6 柚色 **yuzu-iro** lemon yellow

12 柚湯 **yuzuyu** citron hot-bath

4

木 5←
月
日
火
礻
王
牛
方
攵
欠
心
戸
戈

4a5.6

柑 **KAN** citrus fruit

——————— 1 ———————
16 柑橘類 **kankitsurui** citrus fruits
——————— 2 ———————
12 椪柑 **ponkan** (a fruit native to India)
14 蜜柑 **mikan** mandarin orange, tangerine
18 藪柑子 **yabukōji** spearflower
——————— 3 ———————
10 夏蜜柑 **natsumikan** Chinese citron

4a5.7

栂 **toga, tsuga** Japanese hemlock

4a5.8

柮 **TOTSU** cut branches

——————— 2 ———————
14 榾柮 **kottotsu** chip/piece of (fire)wood

4a5.9 / 985

柄 **HEI, e, tsuka** handle, grip, hilt
gara pattern, design; build, physique; character

——————— 1 ———————
7 柄杓 **hishaku** ladle, dipper, scoop
9 柄染 **garazo(me)** pattern (not solid-color) dyeing
——————— 2 ———————
2 人柄 **hitogara** character, personality; personal appearance
3 大柄 **ōgara** large build; large pattern (on a kimono)
小柄 **kogara** short height, small build
kozuka knife attached to a sword sheath
4 中柄 **chūgara** medium size, medium pattern, medium stature
手柄 **tegara** meritorious deed(s), achievement
手柄者 **tegaramono** meritorious person
手柄話 **tegarabanashi** bragging of one's exploits
手柄顔 **tegaragao** triumphant look
日柄 **higara** what kind of day (lucky or unlucky)
心柄 **kokorogara** mood, frame of mind
5 矢柄 **yagara** arrow shaft
6 色柄 **irogara** colored pattern
7 身柄 **migara** one's person
作柄 **sakugara** crop conditions; quality (of art)
役柄 **yakugara** nature of one's office/position

図柄 **zugara** pattern, design
8 長柄 **nagae** long handle; spear
事柄 **kotogara** matters, affairs, circumstances
国柄 **kunigara** national character
杵柄 **kinezuka** grain-pounder handle; experience, skill
所柄 **tokorogara** locality, the occasion
取柄 **to(ri)e** worth, mention
9 品柄 **shinagara** quality
10 家柄 **iegara** lineage, parentage; (of) good family
骨柄 **kotsugara** build, physique, personal appearance
11 訳柄 **wakegara** reason, circumstances
12 葉柄 **yōhei** leaf stem
絵柄 **egara** pattern, design
間柄 **aidagara** relationship
13 新柄 **shingara** new pattern
辞柄 **jihei** pretext
続柄 **tsuzu(ki)gara** family relationship
話柄 **wahei** topic
14 総柄 **sōgara** all-patterned (clothes)
銘柄 **meigara** name, brand, issue (of shares)
15 横柄 **ōhei** arrogant, haughty
権柄 **kenpei** authority, power, imperiousness
16 縞柄 **shimagara** striped pattern

——————— 3 ———————
3 大手柄 **ōtegara** great exploit
土地柄 **tochigara** (nature of) the land
7 役目柄 **yakumegara** by virtue of one's office
10 時節柄 **jisetsugara** in these times
11 商売柄 **shōbaigara** in one's line of business
12 場所柄 **bashogara** character of a place, location, situation, occasion

4a5.10

柝 **TAKU** wooden clappers

4a5.11

柤 **SA** railing

4a5.12 / 598

柱 **CHŪ, hashira** pillar, column, pole

——————— 1 ———————
5 柱石 **chūseki** pillar, mainstay, cornerstone
7 柱状 **chūjō** pillar-shaped, columnar
10 柱時計 **hashiradokei** wall clock
14 柱暦 **hashiragoyomi** wall calendar
16 柱頭 **chūtō** capital (of a column)

_____ 2 _____

2 人柱 **hitobashira** human sacrifice
4 中柱 **nakabashira** pillar in the middle of a
room
支柱 **shichū** prop, support, fulcrum, under-
pinnings
円柱 **marubashira** column
enchū column; cylinder; shaft
水柱 **mizubashira** column of water, waterspout
火柱 **hibashira** pillar of flames
5 石柱 **sekichū** stone pillar
6 帆柱 **hobashira** mast
7 束柱 **tsuka-bashira** supporting post between
beam and roof ridge
角柱 **kakuchū** square pillar; prism (in
geometry)
床柱 **tokobashira** ornamental alcove post
杖柱 **tsue-hashira** staff and pillar, person
one depends on
男柱 **otokobashira** large pillars on either
side of a bridge
貝柱 **kaibashira** (boiled scallop) adductor
muscle
8 門柱 **monchū, monbashira** gatepost
9 茶柱 **chabashira** tea stalk floating upright in
one's tea (a sign of good luck)
10 脊柱 **sekichū** spinal column, spine, backbone
蚊柱 **kabashira** column of swarming
mosquitoes
13 電柱 **denchū** telephone/utility pole
14 鼻柱 **hana(p)pashira, hanabashira** the
septum; the bridge of the nose
緑柱石 **ryokuchūseki** beryl
15 標柱 **hyōchū** pylon, marker post
16 親柱 **oyabashira** main pillar
17 霜柱 **shimobashira** ice/frost columns

_____ 3 _____

3 大黒柱 **daikokubashira** central pillar; pillar,
mainstay
4 水銀柱 **suiginchū** column of mercury
13 電信柱 **denshinbashira** telegraph pole

4a5.13

柞 **SAKU, hahaso** (various kinds of oaks)

4a5.14

柏 栢 **HAKU, BYAKU, kashiwa**
oak

_____ 1 _____

4 柏手 **kashiwade** clap one's hands (in worship
at a shrine)

14 柏槇 **byakushin** juniper tree
15 柏餅 **kashiwa mochi** rice cake wrapped in an
oak leaf

_____ 2 _____

8 松柏 **shōhaku** pines and oaks, conifer,
evergreen

4a5.15

柾 **masa** straight grain
masaki spindle tree

_____ 1 _____

5 柾目 **masame** straight grain

4a5.16

枹 **FU, bachi** drumstick, gong stick
HŌ (type of tree)

4a5.17 / 1871

柳 **RYŪ, yanagi** willow tree

_____ 1 _____

9 柳眉 **ryūbi** beautiful eyebrows
13 柳腰 **yanagigoshi** slender graceful hips

_____ 2 _____

3 川柳 **kawayanagi** purple willow
6 糸柳 **itoyanagi** weeping willow
7 花柳 **karyū** blossoms and willows; demi-
monde; red-light district
花柳界 **karyūkai** geisha quarter, red-light
district
花柳病 **karyūbyō** venereal disease
11 猫柳 **nekoyanagi** pussy willow
13 蒲柳質 **horyū (no) shitsu** delicate health
楊柳 **kawayanagi** purple willow **yōryū**
purple willows and weeping willows
15 箱柳 **hakoyanagi** aspen
17 檉柳 **teiryū, gyoryū** tamarisk

_____ 3 _____

8 枝垂柳 **shida(re)yanagi** weeping willow

4a5.18

柎 **FU** raft; calyx

4a5.19

枷 **KA, kase** shackles

_____ 2 _____

4 手枷 **tekase, tegase** handcuffs, manacles

4

木 5←
月
日
火
礻
王
牛
方
攵
欠
心
戸
戈

7 足枷 **ashikase** fetters, shackles
9 首枷 **kubikase** pillory; encumbrance

4a5.20

枳 **TEI** root; be based on

──── 2 ────
10 根柢 **kontei** root, basis, foundation

4a5.21

㭎 **KAI, tsue** cane, walking stick

4a5.22

枳 **KI, karatachi** trifoliate orange tree (thorny tree used for hedges)

──── 1 ────
11 枳殻 **karatachi** trifoliate orange tree

4a5.23

柁 **DA, kaji** rudder

4a5.24

柊 **SHŪ, hiiragi** holly tree

4a5.25

柿 枾 **SHI, kaki** persimmon (tree/fruit)
kokera shingle

──── 1 ────
8 柿板 **kokeraita** shingle

──── 2 ────
6 吊柿 **tsuru(shi)gaki** dried persimmons
7 串柿 **kushigaki** persimmons dried on skewers
11 渋柿 **shibugaki** puckery persimmon
14 熟柿 **jukushi** ripe persimmon
熟柿主義 **jukushi shugi** wait-and-see policy
熟柿臭 **jukushikusa(i)** smelling of liquor
16 樽柿 **tarugaki** persimmons sweetened in a saké cask

4a5.26 / 974

枯 **KO, ka(reru)** wither, die (vegetation)
ka(rasu) cause to wither, kill (vegetation), let dry

──── 1 ────
0 枯ばむ **kare(bamu)** begin to wither
4 枯木 **ka(re)ki** dead tree
6 枯死 **koshi** wither, die
8 枯枝 **ka(re)eda** dead branch
9 枯草 **ka(re)kusa** dried grass, hay
11 枯野 **ka(re)no** desolate fields
枯渇 **kokatsu** run dry, become depleted
枯淡 **kotan** refined simplicity
12 枯葉 **ka(re)ha** dead leaf

──── 2 ────
4 水枯 **mizuga(re)** drought
木枯 **koga(rashi)** wintry wind
5 末枯 **uraga(reru)** (leaves) wither (as winter approaches)
冬枯 **fuyuga(re)** withering in winter; slack business in winter
立枯 **ta(chi)ga(re)** blight, withering
8 枝枯病 **edaga(re)byō** twig blight
9 草枯 **kusaga(re)** withering of the grass; autumn
栄枯 **eiko** flourishing and withering
栄枯盛衰 **eiko-seisui** prosperity and decline, rise and fall
10 夏枯 **natsuga(re)** summer slack season
17 霜枯 **shimoga(re)** frost-withered, wintry, bleak
霜枯時 **shimoga(re)doki** winter

4a5.27

栫 **SEN** weir

4a5.28

栃 杤 **tochi** horse chestnut tree

──── 1 ────
4 栃木県 **Tochigi-ken** (prefecture)

4a5.29

柯 **KA** ax handle; branch

4a5.30

枸 **KU** trifoliate orange tree, quince
KŌ crooked; Chinese matrimony vine

──── 1 ────
7 枸杞 **kuko** Chinese matrimony vine
19 枸櫞 **kuen** (a type of citron)
枸櫞酸 **kuensan** citric acid

4a5.31

枢 KYŪ, hitsugi coffin

——————— 1 ———————
7 枢車 **kyūsha** hearse

——————— 2 ———————
15 霊枢 **reikyū** coffin, casket
霊枢車 **reikyūsha** hearse

4a5.32 / 624

査 SA investigate

——————— 1 ———————
8 査定 **satei** assessment
11 査問 **samon** inquiry, hearing
査問会 **samonkai** (court of) inquiry, hearing
12 査証 **sashō** visa; investigation and attestation
14 査察 **sasatsu** inspection, observation

——————— 2 ———————
5 巡査 **junsa** patrolman, cop
主査 **shusa** chairman of an investigation committee, president of a board of examiners
6 考査 **kōsa** consideration; test, exam
7 走査 **sōsa** scanning (in electronics)
10 捜査 **sōsa** investigation
11 探査 **tansa** inquiry, investigation
12 検査 **kensa** inspection, examination
検査役 **kensayaku** inspector, examiner
検査官 **kensakan** inspector, examiner
検査所 **kensajo** inspection station
検査済 **kensazu(mi)** examined, passed
13 照査 **shōsa** irradiation
14 精査 **seisa** close investigation
15 審査 **shinsa** examination, investigation
審査員 **shinsain** judges, examiners
監査 **kansa** inspection; auditing
監査役 **kansayaku** auditor, inspector
調査 **chōsa** investigation, inquiry, survey, research
踏査 **tōsa** survey, field investigation
23 鑑査 **kansa** inspect, evaluate

——————— 2 ———————
3 下検査 **shitakensa** preliminary inspection
6 再検査 **saikensa** re-examination
再審査 **saishinsa** re-examination
再調査 **saichōsa** reinvestigation
7 尿検査 **nyō kensa** urinalysis

——————— 4 ———————
5 世論調査 **seron chōsa, yoron chōsa** (public-opinion) poll
8 国勢調査 **kokusei chōsa** (national) census
14 徴兵検査 **chōhei kensa** examination for conscription
17 輿論調査 **yoron chōsa** public-opinion survey, poll

果 →  0a8.8

4a5.33 / 1494

某 BŌ a certain, one
nanigashi a certain person/amount
soregashi a certain person; I

——————— 1 ———————
4 某氏 **bōshi** a certain person
某月 **bōgetsu** a certain month
5 某市 **bōshi** a certain city
6 某年 **bōnen** a certain year
8 某所 **bōsho** a certain place
14 某誌 **bōshi** a certain magazine

——————— 2 ———————
7 何某 **nanigashi** a certain person; a certain amount
15 誰某 **taresore** Mr. So-and-so

4a5.34 / 774

柔 JŪ, NYŪ, yawa(rakai/raka/i) soft
yawa(ra) jujitsu

——————— 1 ———————
3 柔々 **yawayawa** softly, gently; gradually
6 柔肌 **yawahada** soft skin
8 柔物 **yawa(raka)mono** silks
柔和 **nyūwa** gentle, mild(-mannered)
10 柔弱 **nyūjaku** weakness, enervation
11 柔道 **jūdō** judo
柔道家 **jūdōka** judo expert
柔術 **jūjutsu** jujitsu
柔軟 **jūnan** soft, supple, flexible
柔軟性 **jūnansei** pliability, suppleness
12 柔順 **jūjun** docile, submissive, gentle

——————— 2 ———————
4 手柔 **teyawa(raka)** gently, kindly, leniently
8 物柔 **monoyawa(raka)** mild, gentle, suave
9 柔柔 **yawayawa** softly, gently; gradually
16 懐柔 **kaijū** be conciliatory, win over
17 優柔 **yūjū** indecisiveness
優柔不断 **yūjū-fudan** indecisiveness

4a5.35 / 779

染 SEN, so(meru) dye, color
so(me) dyeing **so(maru)** be dyed/imbued with **shi(miru)** soak in; be infected; smart, hurt **shi(mi)** stain, blot, smudge

——————— 1 ———————
4 染毛剤 **senmōzai** hair dye

木 5←
月
日
火
ネ
王
牛
方
攵
欠
心
戸
戈

4

染分 **so(me)wa(ke)** dyed in various colors
染込 **shi(mi)ko(mu)** soak into, permeate; be instilled with　**so(me)ko(mu)** dye in
染方 **so(me)kata** dyeing process
5 染出 **so(me)da(su)** dye
染付 **so(me)tsu(keru)** dye in
　　shi(mi)tsu(ku) be dyed in deeply, be stained
6 染色 **senshoku** dyeing, staining
染色体 **senshokutai** chromosome
染返 **so(me)kae(su)** redye
7 染抜 **so(me)nu(ku)** dye fast; leave undyed
　　shi(mi)nu(ki) removing stains
染形 **so(me)gata** dyeing stencil
8 染直 **so(me)nao(su)** redye
染物 **so(me)mono** dyeing; dyed goods
染物屋 **so(me)monoya** dyer
10 染料 **senryō** dye, dyestuffs
染粉 **so(me)ko** dye, dyestuffs
12 染渡 **shi(mi)wata(ru)** penetrate, pervade
染筆料 **senpitsuryō** writing fee
14 染髪剤 **senpatsuzai** hair dye
染模様 **so(me)moyō** printed/dyed pattern
18 染織 **senshoku** dyeing and weaving

――――――― 2 ―――――――

4 毛染 **kezo(me)** hair coloring/dyeing
毛染薬 **kezo(me)gusuri** hair dye
手染 **tezo(me)** hand-dyed
6 伝染 **densen** contagion, infection
伝染病 **densenbyō** contagious/communicable disease
色染 **irozo(me)** dyeing
汚染 **osen** pollution, contamination
汗染 **aseji(mi)** sweat-stained
血染 **chizo(me)** bloodstained
8 油染 **aburaji(miru)** become oily/grease-stained
9 垢染 **akaji(miru)** become grimy/dirty
柄染 **garazo(me)** pattern (not solid-color) dyeing
紅染 **benizo(me)** red-dyed cloth
10 浸染 **shinsen** permeate, infiltrate; dye
脂染 **aburaji(miru)** become oily, be grease-stained
11 捺染 **nassen** (textile) printing
12 媒染 **baisen** color fixing
煮染 **nishi(meru)** boil hard with soy sauce
絞染 **shibo(ri)zo(me)** tie-dyeing
13 愛染明王 **Aizenmyōō** Ragaraja, six-armed god of love
感染 **kansen** infection, contagion
馴染 **naji(mi)** familiar
14 墨染 **sumizo(me)** dyeing/dyed black
16 薫染 **kunsen** good influence

――――――― 3 ―――――――

5 幼馴染 **osana najimi** childhood playmate
白髪染 **shiragazo(me)** hair dye
田舎染 **inakajimi(ru)** be countrified
8 昔馴染 **mukashinaji(mi)** old friend

4a5.36 / 755

架　**KA** hang up, mount, build; rack, shelf, stand　**ka(keru)** build (a bridge)　**ka(karu)** hang, be built

――――――― 1 ―――――――

0 架する **ka(suru)** build (a bridge), lay (cable)
8 架空 **kakū** overhead, aerial; fanciful, fictitious
11 架設 **kasetsu** construction, laying
13 架電 **kaden** send by wire/fax
15 架線 **kasen** aerial wiring
16 架橋 **kakyō** bridge building

――――――― 2 ―――――――

8 画架 **gaka** easel
担架 **tanka** stretcher
9 後架 **kōka** toilet
10 高架 **kōka** elevated, overhead
書架 **shoka** bookshelf
12 筆架 **hikka** pen rack
14 銃架 **jūka** gun rest/mount
16 橋架 **kyōka** bridge girder

――――――― 3 ―――――――

2 十字架 **jūjika** cross, crucifix
3 三脚架 **sankyakuka** tripod

――――――― 6 ―――――――

4a6.1 / 1906

桟　棧　**SAN** suspension bridge; jetty; shelf; crosspiece, frame, bolt (of a door)

――――――― 1 ―――――――

10 桟俵 **sandawara** round straw lid (on the ends of a rice bag)
11 桟道 **sandō** plank bridge
15 桟敷 **sajiki** reviewing stand, box, gallery
16 桟橋 **sanbashi** wharf, jetty
　　sankyō wharf; bridge

――――――― 2 ―――――――

9 浮桟橋 **u(ki)sanbashi** floating pier
22 聾桟敷 **tsunbo sajiki** the upper gallery

――――――― 3 ―――――――

4 天井桟敷 **tenjō sajiki** the upper gallery

4a6.2

栖　**SEI** live in, inhabit; nest; rest

4a6.3 / 741

株 **kabu** share (of stock); (tree) stump, (tulip) bulb

——————— 1 ———————
4 株分 **kabuwa(ke)** spread of a plant by sending out branching roots
5 株主 **kabunushi** shareholder, stockholder
6 株式 **kabushiki** shares, stocks
株式市場 **kabushiki shijō** stock market
株式会社 **kabushiki-gaisha, kabushiki kaisha** corporation, Co., Ltd.
8 株価 **kabuka** share price, stock prices
株券 **kabuken** share/stock certificate
株金 **kabukin** money/investment for a share
9 株屋 **kabuya** stockbroker

——————— 2 ———————
2 子株 **kokabu** new shares of stock
3 大株主 **ōkabunushi** large shareholder
4 刈株 **ka(ri)kabu** stubble
切株 **ki(ri)kabu** stump, stubble
5 古株 **furukabu** old-timer
8 実株 **jitsukabu** shares actually traded
空株 **karakabu** shares which one does not own
9 持株 **mo(chi)kabu** one's holdings/interest
持株会社 **mo(chi)kabu-gaisha** holding company
故株 **furukabu** old-timer, veteran
13 新株 **shinkabu** new shares
14 雑株 **zatsukabu, zakkabu** miscellaneous stocks
16 親株 **oyakabu** old share (before a stock split)
頭株 **atamakabu** leader, top men

——————— 3 ———————
17 優先株 **yūsenkabu** preferred shares

4a6.4

栲 **GŌ, KŌ** sumac
tae cloth (woven from tree fibers)

4a6.5 / 314

根 **KON** root; perseverance
ne root; base, origin

——————— 1 ———————
0 根っから **ne(kkara)** (not) at all, (not) in the least; by nature, a born (merchant)
根こそぎ **ne(kosogi)** root and all, completely
2 根子 **nekko** root; stump
4 根元 **kongen** root, origin, cause
nemoto part near the root, base
根太 **neda** joist   **nebuto** a boil

根切 **negi(ri)** pit excavation
根分 **newa(ke)** divide the roots (and transplant)
根引 **nebi(ki)** uproot; redeem
根方 **nekata** root, lower part
5 根本 **konpon** root, cause; basis
nemoto part near the root, base
根本主義 **konpon shugi** fundamentalism
根本法 **konponhō** fundamental law
根本的 **konponteki** fundamental, radical
根付 **netsu(ke)** ornamental button for suspending a pouch from a belt
根比 **konkura(be)** endurance contest
6 根気 **konki** patience, perseverance
根気負 **konkima(ke)** be outpersevered
根扱 **neko(gi)** uprooting
根回 **nemawa(shi)** doing the groundwork, pre-selling (a proposal), consensus-building
8 根治 **konchi, konji** radical/complete cure
根拠 **konkyo** basis, grounds, foundation
根拠地 **konkyochi** base (of operations)
根茎 **konkei** root stalk, rhizome
根底 **kontei** root, basis, foundation
根性 **konjō** disposition, spirit, nature
根性骨 **konjōbone** spirit, disposition
9 根負 **konma(ke)** be outpersevered
根城 **nejiro** stronghold; base of operations
根柢 **kontei** root, basis, foundation
10 根差 **neza(su)** take root; stem from
11 根深 **nebuka(i)** deep-rooted, ingrained
根基 **konki** root, origin
根接 **netsu(gi)** root grafting
根掘葉掘 **neho(ri)-haho(ri)** inquisitive about every detail
根強 **nezuyo(i)** firmly rooted/established
根菜類 **konsairui** root crops
根雪 **neyuki** lingering snow
12 根無 **nena(shi)** rootless; groundless
根無草 **nena(shi)gusa** duckweed; something unsettled, rootless person
根絶 **konzetsu, nedaya(shi)** eradication
13 根際 **negiwa** area around the root
根源 **kongen** root, origin, source, cause
根幹 **konkan** root and trunk; basis, keynote
15 根瘤 **konryū** root nodules

——————— 2 ———————
3 大根 **daikon** daikon, Japanese radish
大根役者 **daikon yakusha** ham actor
大根卸 **daikon oro(shi)** grated daikon; daikon grater
大根漬 **daikonzu(ke)** pickled daikon
4 毛根 **mōkon** hair root
心根 **kokorone** inner feelings; disposition
5 矢根 **ya(no)ne** arrowhead

4

木
月
日
火 6 ←
礻
王
牛
方
攵
欠
心
戸
戈

付根 **tsu(ke)ne** root, joint, base, crotch
6 気根 **kikon** energy, perseverance; aerial root
7 尾根 **one** mountain ridge
利根 **rikon** bright, clever
利根川 **Tone-gawa** (river, Chiba-ken)
男根 **dankon** penis, phallus
8 岩根 **iwane** base of a rock; rock, crag
性根 **shōkon** perseverance
shōne one's disposition
9 浮根 **u(ki)ne** roots of water plants
垣根 **kakine** fence, hedge
草根木皮 **sōkon-mokuhi** medicinal herb roots and tree barks
屋根 **yane** roof
屋根伝 **yanezuta(i)** from roof to roof
屋根屋 **yaneya** roofer, thatcher
10 島根県 **Shimane-ken** (prefecture)
息根 **iki(no)ne** life
病根 **byōkon** cause of a disease; root of an evil
11 宿根 **shukukon** root/bulb which remains alive after stem and leaves have withered
宿根草 **shukkonsō** perennial plant
球根 **kyūkon** (plant) bulb
12 善根 **zenkon** good deed, act of charity
無根 **mukon** groundless, unfounded
歯根 **shikon** root of a tooth
鈍根 **donkon** slow-witted, inept
13 塊根 **kaikon** tuberous root
蓮根 **renkon** lotus root
禍根 **kakon** root of evil, source of calamity
14 精根 **seikon** energy, vitality
語根 **gokon** stem, root of a word
15 盤根 **bankon** coiled root
盤根錯節 **bankon-sakusetsu** knotty/thorny/complex situation
箱根 **Hakone** (resort area near Mt. Fuji)
箱根山 **Hakone-yama** (mountain, Kanagawa-ken)
16 機根 **kikon** talent, gift

────────── 3 ──────────

2 二乗根 **nijōkon** square root
3 三乗根 **sanjōkon** cube root
干大根 **ho(shi) daikon** dried daikon
下大根 **o(roshi) daikon** grated daikon
下種根性 **gesu konjō** mean feelings
4 円屋根 **maruyane** dome, cupola
5 瓦屋根 **kawara yane** tiled roof
平方根 **heihōkon** square root
平屋根 **hirayane** flat roof
立方根 **rippōkon** cube root
6 百合根 **yurine** lily bulb
自乗根 **jijōkon** square root
7 役人根性 **yakunin konjō** bureaucratism
8 追羽根 **o(i)bane** battledore and shuttlecock

板屋根 **itayane** shingle/wooden roof
9 草屋根 **kusayane** thatched roof
10 陸屋根 **rokuyane** flat roof
島国根性 **shimaguni konjō** insularity
14 精限根限 **seikagi(ri)-konkagi(ri)** with all one's might
17 藁屋根 **warayane** straw-thatched roof

────────── 4 ──────────

8 事実無根 **jijitsu mukon** contrary to fact, unfounded
9 砂糖大根 **satō daikon** sugar beet
14 練馬大根 **Nerima daikon** daikon (grown in Nerima, Tōkyō); woman's fat legs

────────── 5 ──────────

2 二十日大根 **hatsuka daikon** radish

4a6.6

柧 **KO, KA** corner, spire; goblet, winecup

4a6.7

梛 **DA, nagi** (type of tall evergreen tree)

4a6.8

桁 **KŌ, keta** beam, girder; digit, place (in numbers)

────────── 1 ──────────

5 桁外 **ketahazu(re)** extraordinary
12 桁違 **ketachiga(i)** off/differing by an order of magnitude

────────── 2 ──────────

1 一桁 **hitoketa** single digit
2 二桁 **futaketa** two digits, double-digit
3 三桁 **miketa** three digits
4 五桁 **goketa** five digits
5 四桁 **yoketa, yonketa** four-digit
6 帆桁 **hogeta** (sail) yard, boom
衣桁 **ikō** clothes rack
16 橋桁 **hashigeta** bridge girder

4a6.9

栩 **KU** (a kind of oak)

4a6.10 / 1567

桃 **TŌ, momo** peach

——————————— 1 ———————————

3 桃山 **Momoyama** (era, 1576–1598)
6 桃色 **momo-iro** pink
　桃色遊戯 **momo-iro yūgi** sex play
13 桃源 **tōgen** Shangri-La, paradise
　桃源郷 **tōgenkyō** Shangri-La, paradise
　桃源境 **tōgenkyō** Shangri-La, paradise
　桃園 **momozono** peach orchard
　桃節句 **momo (no) sekku** Doll Festival
　　(March 3)

——————————— 2 ———————————

9 胡桃 **kurumi** walnut
　胡桃割 **kurumiwa(ri)** nutcracker
　扁桃 **hentō** almond
　扁桃腺 **hentōsen** the tonsils
　扁桃腺炎 **hentōsen'en** tonsillitis
10 桜桃 **ōtō** cherry; cherry and peach

——————————— 3 ———————————

4 水蜜桃 **suimitsutō** (a variety of) peach
6 安土桃山 **Azuchi-Momoyama** Azuchi-
　　Momoyama (era, 1568–1603)
7 夾竹桃 **kyōchikutō** oleander, phlox

4a6.11

桓
　KAN marking post

——————————— 1 ———————————

8 桓武 **Kanmu** (emperor, 781–806)

4a6.12

桴
　FU, bachi drumstick
　ikada raft

4a6.13

桂
　KEI cinnamon/cassia tree; bay-leaf
　tree; the moon
　katsura katsura tree

——————————— 1 ———————————

5 桂皮 **keihi** cassia bark, cinnamon
9 桂冠 **keikan** crown of laurel
　桂冠詩人 **keikan shijin** poet laureate

——————————— 2 ———————————

4 月桂 **gekkei** laurel; the moon
　月桂冠 **gekkeikan** crown of laurel, laurels
　月桂樹 **gekkeiju** laurel/bay tree
6 肉桂 **nikkei** cinnamon

4a6.14

档
　TŌ bookshelf, archives

4a6.15 / 928

桜 櫻
　Ō, sakura cherry tree

——————————— 1 ———————————

0 桜んぼ **sakura(nbo)** cherry
6 桜肉 **sakuraniku** horsemeat
　桜色 **sakura-iro** pink, cerise
7 桜花 **ōka, sakurabana** cherry blossoms
9 桜狩 **sakuraga(ri)** looking for cherry
　　blossoms
　桜草 **sakurasō** primrose
10 桜桃 **ōtō** cherry; cherry and peach
　桜時 **sakuradoki** cherry-blossom season
14 桜漬 **sakurazu(ke)** pickled cherry blossoms

——————————— 2 ———————————

3 山桜 **yamazakura** wild cherry tree
6 糸桜 **itozakura** droopy-branch cherry tree
8 夜桜 **yozakura** cherry trees at night
10 徒桜 **adazakura** ephemeral cherry blossoms
12 葉桜 **hazakura** cherry tree in leaf
18 観桜 **kan'ō** viewing the cherry blossoms
　観桜会 **kan'ōkai** cherry-blossom viewing
　　party

——————————— 3 ———————————

8 彼岸桜 **higanzakura** early-flowering cherry
　　tree
　枝垂桜 **shida(re)zakura** droopy-branch
　　cherry tree
9 美女桜 **bijozakura** verbena

4a6.16

桔
　KITSU, KETSU (used in plant names)

——————————— 1 ———————————

11 桔梗 **kikyō, kikkō** Chinese bellflower,
　balloonflower

4a6.17 / 643

格
　KAKU, KŌ status, rank; standard, rule;
　case (in grammar)

——————————— 1 ———————————

2 格子 **kōshi** lattice, bars, grating, grille
　格子戸 **kōshido** lattice door
　格子造 **kōshi-zuku(ri)** latticework
　格子窓 **kōshi mado** latticed window
　格子縞 **kōshijima** checkered pattern
3 格上 **kakua(ge)** promotion, upgrading
　格下 **kakusa(ge)** demotion, downgrading
4 格天井 **gōtenjō** coffered ceiling
5 格付 **kakuzu(ke)** grading, rating
　格外 **kakuhazu(re)** ungraded, irregular

4

木 6←
月
日
火
礻
王
牛
方
攵
欠
心
戸
戈

格外品 **kakugaihin** nonstandard goods
6 格安 **kakuyasu** inexpensive
格安品 **kakuyasuhin** bargain goods
格式 **kakushiki** status, social standing;
    formalities
格式張 **kakushikiba(ru)** stick to formalities
7 格別 **kakubetsu** particularly, exceptionally
格言 **kakugen** saying, proverb, maxim
9 格段 **kakudan** marked, exceptional, appreciable
10 格差 **kakusa** gap, differential
格納 **kakunō** to store, house
格納庫 **kakunōko** hangar
15 格調 **kakuchō** tone, style
18 格闘 **kakutō** fist fight, scuffle

———————— 2 ————————

2 人格 **jinkaku** character, personality
人格化 **jinkakuka** personification
人格者 **jinkakusha** man of character
4 欠格 **kekkaku** lack of qualifications
5 出格子 **degōshi** projecting lattice, latticed
    bay window
本格的 **honkakuteki** full-scale, genuine, in
    earnest
失格 **shikkaku** disqualification
正格 **seikaku** orthodox
主格 **shukaku** nominative case
6 気格 **kikaku** dignity
合格 **gōkaku** pass (an exam/inspection)
同格 **dōkaku** the same rank; apposition
扞格 **kankaku** opposing/resisting each other
7 体格 **taikaku** physique, constitution
別格 **bekkaku** special, exceptional
社格 **shakaku** status of a shrine/company
8 価格 **kakaku** price, cost, value
価格表 **kakakuhyō** price list
妻格子 **tsumagōshi** latticework
定格 **teikaku** rating, rated (voltage)
昇格 **shōkaku** promotion to a higher status,
    upgrading
炉格子 **rogōshi** (furnace) grate
性格 **seikaku** character, personality
9 変格 **henkaku** irregular (inflection)
風格 **fūkaku** character, personality, style
品格 **hinkaku** grace, dignity
律格 **ritsukaku** rule; versification, metrical
    scheme
神格 **shinkaku** godhood, divinity
神格化 **shinkakuka** deification
10 家格 **kakaku** family status
骨格 **kokkaku** skeleton, frame, one's build
破格 **hakaku** exceptional, unusual
11 規格 **kikaku** standard, norm
規格化 **kikakuka** standardization
規格品 **kikakuhin** standardized goods

13 適格 **tekikaku, tekkaku** competent, eligible
適格者 **tekikakusha** qualified/eligible
    person
資格 **shikaku** qualifications, competence
鉄格子 **tetsugōshi** iron bars, grating
14 歌格 **kakaku** poetry rules/style
語格 **gokaku** grammar
15 賓格 **hinkaku** objective case (in grammar)
17 厳格 **genkaku** strict, stern, severe

———————— 3 ————————

4 不合格 **fugōkaku** failure (in an exam),
    rejection, disqualification
不適格 **futekikaku** unqualified, unacceptable
5 目的格 **mokutekikaku** the objective case
6 全人格 **zenjinkaku** one's whole personality
有資格者 **yūshikakusha** qualified person
8 所有格 **shoyūkaku** the possessive case
12 無資格 **mushikaku** unqualified
無資格者 **mushikakusha** unqualified/
    incompetent person

———————— 4 ————————

2 二重人格 **nijū jinkaku** double/split personality
5 末端価格 **mattan kakaku** end-user price,
    street value

4a6.18

榜

KO (type of tree); empty

4a6.19

桛

kase reel, skein

4a6.20

桎

SHITSU, ashikase fetters

———————— 1 ————————

11 桎梏 **shikkoku** fetters and manacles, shackles

桧 → 檜 **4a13.8**

4a6.21

桲

BOTSU quince

———————— 2 ————————

14 榲桲 **otsubotsu** quince

4a6.22 / 1212

核 核   **KAKU** core, nucleus; (as prefix) nuclear
sane fruit stone, kernel, seed

──────── 1 ────────

4 核分裂 **kakubunretsu** nuclear fission
核反応 **kakuhannō** nuclear reaction
核反応炉 **kakuhannōro** nuclear reactor
核心 **kakushin** core, kernel
7 核兵器 **kakuheiki** nuclear weapons
8 核実験 **kakujikken** nuclear testing
核物理学 **kakubutsurigaku** nuclear physics
核武装 **kakubusō** nuclear arms
9 核研究 **kakukenkyū** nuclear research
12 核弾頭 **kakudantō** nuclear warhead
16 核燃料 **kakunenryō** nuclear fuel
核融合 **kakuyūgō** nuclear fusion

──────── 2 ────────

4 中核 **chūkaku** kernel, core, nucleus
6 地核 **chikaku** the earth's core
10 陰核 **inkaku** the clitoris
12 結核 **kekkaku** tuberculosis
結核菌 **kekkakukin** tuberculosis germ
15 熱核 **netsukaku** thermonuclear

──────── 3 ────────

9 肺結核 **haikekkaku** pulmonary tuberculosis
10 原子核 **genshikaku** atomic nucleus
12 結晶核 **kesshōkaku** nucleus of a crystal

4a6.23

栴   **SEI, momiji** maple tree; colorful autumn foliage

4a6.24 / 115

校   **KŌ, KYŌ** school; (printing) proof

──────── 1 ────────

1 校了 **kōryō** proofreading completed
4 校内 **kōnai** in the school (grounds), intramural
校友 **kōyū** schoolmate, alumnus
校友会 **kōyūkai** alumni association
5 校本 **kōhon** complete/annotated text
校外 **kōgai** outside the school, off-campus, extra-curricular
校外生 **kōgaisei** extension/correspondence course student
校正 **kōsei** proofreading
校正刷 **kōseizu(ri)** (galley) proofs
校正係 **kōseigakari** proofreader
校主 **kōshu** private-school owner
7 校医 **kōi** school physician
8 校長 **kōchō** principal, headmaster

校舎 **kōsha** school building
校服 **kōfuku** school uniform
校具 **kōgu** school equipment
校門 **kōmon** school gate
9 校風 **kōfū** school spirit/traditions
校庭 **kōtei** schoolyard, campus
校紀 **kōki** school discipline/standards
校訂 **kōtei** revision
校訂版 **kōteiban** revised edition
校則 **kōsoku** school regulations
10 校倉 **azekura** ancient log storehouse
校倉造 **azekura-zuku(ri)** (ancient architectural style using triangular logs which interlace and protrude at the building's corners)
校訓 **kōkun** school precepts/motto
11 校務 **kōmu** school affairs
校章 **kōshō** school badge/pin
校規 **kōki** school regulations
12 校葬 **kōsō** school funeral
校註 **kōchū** proofreading and annotation
14 校僕 **kōboku** school servant; student-servant
校旗 **kōki** school flag
校歌 **kōka** school song
15 校閲 **kōetsu** revise, supervise

──────── 2 ────────

2 入校 **nyūkō** entering school, matriculation
3 三校 **sankō** third proof
4 分校 **bunkō** branch school
5 母校 **bokō** one's alma mater
6 再校 **saikō** second proof
休校 **kyūkō** school closing
全校 **zenkō** the whole school, all the schools
在校 **zaikō** be in school
在校生 **zaikōsei** present students
7 対校 **taikō** interschool, intercollegiate
対校試合 **taikō-jiai** interschool match
学校 **gakkō** school
学校区 **gakkōku** school district
学校出 **gakkōde** school graduate, educated person
学校長 **gakkōchō** school principal
学校差 **gakkōsa** scholastic disparity among schools
初校 **shokō** first proofs
8 退校 **taikō** leaving school
放校 **hōkō** expulsion from school
10 将校 **shōkō** (commissioned) officer
帰校 **kikō** return to school
高校 **kōkō** senior high school (short for 高等学校)
高校生 **kōkōsei** senior-high-school student
11 転校 **tenkō** changing schools
閉校 **heikō** closing the school
12 登校 **tōkō** attend school

4

木
月 6 ←
日
火
礻
王
牛
方
攵
欠
心
戸
戈

復校 **fukkō, fukukō** return/readmission to school
廃校 **haikō** (permanent) school closing
検校 **kengyō** blind court musician
開校 **kaikō** opening a new school
開校式 **kaikōshiki** school opening ceremony
13 愛校心 **aikōshin** love for one's school
18 藩校 **hankō** clan school

——————— 3 ———————

3 女学校 **jogakkō** girls' school
小学校 **shōgakkō** elementary school
4 予備校 **yobikō** preparatory school
中学校 **chūgakkō** junior high school
8 夜学校 **yagakkō** night school
盲学校 **mōgakkō** school for the blind
9 神学校 **shingakkō** theological seminary
22 聾学校 **rōgakkō** school for the deaf

——————— 4 ———————

8 盲唖学校 **mōa gakkō** school for the blind and mute
実業学校 **jitsugyō gakkō** vocational school
林間学校 **rinkan gakkō** outdoor school, camp
9 専門学校 **senmon gakkō** professional school
10 高等学校 **kōtō gakkō** senior high school
師範学校 **shihan gakkō** normal school, teachers' college
15 養護学校 **yōgo gakkō** school for the handicapped

4a6.25

梓   **U, hoko** halberd

4a6.26 / 1842

栓   **SEN** stopper, cork, plug, spigot, tap, hydrant

——————— 1 ———————

7 栓抜 **sennu(ki)** corkscrew; bottle opener

——————— 2 ———————

4 木栓 **mokusen** wooden cork/plug, bung
6 血栓 **kessen** thrombus
血栓症 **kessenshō** thrombosis
9 音栓 **onsen** (organ) stop
13 塞栓 **sokusen** an embolism

——————— 3 ———————

4 水道栓 **suidōsen** hydrant, tap
6 防火栓 **bōkasen** fire hydrant
10 消火栓 **shōkasen** fire hydrant
11 脳血栓 **nōkessen** cerebral thrombosis
12 給水栓 **kyūsuisen** faucet, hydrant

4a6.27 / 1734

梅 梅 楳   **BAI, ume** Japanese plum/apricot (tree)

——————— 1 ———————

3 梅干 **umebo(shi)** pickled plums
7 梅花 **baika** plum blossoms
梅見 **umemi** plum-blossom viewing
8 梅毒 **baidoku** syphilis
梅毒性 **baidokusei** syphilitic
梅林 **bairin** plum orchard/grove
梅雨 **baiu, tsuyu** the rainy season
9 梅畑 **umebatake** plum orchard
10 梅酒 **umeshu** plum brandy
12 梅酢 **umezu** plum juice/vinegar
13 梅園 **baien** plum orchard
14 梅暦 **umegoyomi** plum blossoms as a harbinger of spring

——————— 2 ———————

2 入梅 **nyūbai** beginning of the rainy season
5 生梅 **namaume** fresh-picked plum
白梅 **shiraume** white-blossom plum tree; white plum blossoms
8 空梅雨 **karatsuyu** a dry rainy season
青梅 **aoume** unripe plum
9 紅梅 **kōbai** red plum blossoms
12 寒梅 **kanbai** early plum blossoms
13 塩梅 **anbai** seasoning; circumstances, condition, manner
14 漬梅 **tsu(ke)ume** pickling/pickled plums
18 観梅 **kanbai** viewing the plum blossoms

——————— 3 ———————

8 松竹梅 **shō-chiku-bai** pine-bamboo-plum (as sign of congratulations or to designate three things of equal rank)
12 寒紅梅 **kankōbai** winter red-blossom plum tree

4a6.28

栴   **SEN** (used in plant names)

——————— 1 ———————

17 栴檀 **sendan** Japanese bead tree

栢 → 柏   **4a5.14**

4a6.29

梃   **TEI, CHŌ, teko** lever

——————— 1 ———————

2 梃子 **teko** lever

─────── 2 ───────

6 光梃子 **hikari teko** optical lever

4a6.30

桐　**TŌ, kiri** paulownia tree

─────── 1 ───────

1 桐一葉 **kiri hitoha** falling paulownia leaf (a sign of the arrival of autumn or of the beginning of the end)
5 桐生 **Kiryū** (city, Gunma-ken)
8 桐油 **tōyu** tung/nut/wood oil

4a6.31

框　**KYŌ, kamachi** (door)frame

4a6.32

栗　**RITSU, kuri** chestnut

─────── 1 ───────

4 栗毛 **kurige** chestnut-color/bay/sorrel (horse)
5 栗石 **kuriishi** cobblestones
13 栗鼠 **risu** squirrel

─────── 2 ───────

4 片栗粉 **katakuriko** dogtooth-violet starch
5 甘栗 **amaguri** roasted sweet chestnuts
6 団栗 **donguri** acorn
　団栗眼 **donguri manako** goggle-eyed
10 柴栗 **shibaguri** (a variety of small chestnut)
11 毬栗 **igaguri** chestnuts in burrs
　毬栗頭 **igaguri atama** close-cropped head, burr haircut
12 割栗石 **wa(ri)guriishi** broken stones, macadam
　落栗 **o(chi)guri** fallen chestnut
　勝栗 **ka(chi)guri** dried chestnut
　焼栗 **ya(ki)guri** roasted chestnuts
15 膝栗毛 **hizakurige** go on foot, hike it

4a6.33

柴　**SAI, shiba** brushwood, firewood

─────── 1 ───────

4 柴犬 **Shiba-inu** (a breed of small dog)
10 柴栗 **shibaguri** (a variety of small chestnut)

4a6.34

栞 栞　**KAN, shiori** bent branch to mark a trail; bookmark; guidebook

桑→　**2h8.1**

4a6.35 / 576

殺 殺　**SATSU, SETSU** kill **SAI** lessen **koro(su)** kill **so(gu)** cut/slash off; diminish, dampen, spoil **so(geru)** split, splinter; be sunken in

─────── 1 ───────

2 殺人 **satsujin** murder
　殺人犯 **satsujinhan** (the crime of) murder
　殺人的 **satsujinteki** murderous, deadly, terrific, hectic, cutthroat
　殺人鬼 **satsujinki** bloodthirsty killer
　殺人罪 **satsujinzai** murder
4 殺文句 **koro(shi) monku** "killing" words, cajolery, clincher
5 殺生 **sesshō** destroy life, kill (animals)
　殺生戒 **sesshōkai** Buddhist precept against killing
　殺生禁断 **sesshō kindan** hunting and fishing prohibited
6 殺気 **sakki** bloodthirstiness
　殺気立 **sakkida(tsu)** grow excited/menacing
　殺伐 **satsubatsu** bloodthirsty, brutal, savage
　殺虫剤 **satchūzai** insecticide
8 殺到 **sattō** rush, stampede
9 殺陣 **tate** swordplay
　殺風景 **sappūkei** drab, dull, tasteless
　殺屋 **koro(shi)ya** hired killer
10 殺害 **satsugai** murder
　殺害者 **satsugaisha** murderer, slayer
11 殺掠 **satsuryaku** killing and robbing
　殺菌 **sakkin** sterilize, disinfect, pasteurize
　殺菌力 **sakkinryoku** germicidal effect
　殺菌剤 **sakkinzai** germicide, disinfectant
　殺略 **satsuryaku** killing and robbing
13 殺傷 **sasshō** killing or wounding, casualties
　殺意 **satsui** intent to murder
15 殺戮 **satsuriku** massacre, bloodbath

─────── 2 ───────

2 人殺 **hitogoro(shi)** murder; murderer
　子殺 **kogoro(shi)** infanticide
3 女殺 **onnagoro(shi)** ladykiller
4 切殺 **ki(ri)koro(su)** slay, put to the sword
　犬殺 **inukoro(shi)** dog catcher
5 半殺 **hangoro(shi)** half killed
　生殺 **seisatsu** life and death
　　namagoro(shi) half-kill; keep in suspense
　生殺与奪 **seisatsu-yodatsu** (the power to) kill or let live
　他殺 **tasatsu** murder

木 6←
月
日
火
礻
王
牛
方
攵
欠
心
戸
戈

4

打殺 **u(chi)koro(su)** beat/shoot to death, strike/shoot dead
bu(chi)koro(su) beat to death
叩殺 **tata(ki)koro(su)** beat to death
6 忙殺 **bōsatsu** keep (someone) busily occupied
自殺 **jisatsu** suicide
自殺未遂 **jisatsu misui** attempted suicide
自殺的 **jisatsuteki** suicidal
自殺者 **jisatsusha** a suicide (the person)
7 扼殺 **yakusatsu** choke to death
見殺 **migoro(shi)** watch (someone) die
8 毒殺 **dokusatsu** a poisoning
併殺 **heisatsu** double play (in baseball)
刺殺 **sa(shi)koro(su)** stab to death
shisatsu stab to death; put out (a runner)
殴殺 **nagu(ri)koro(su), ōsatsu** beat to death, strike dead
抹殺 **massatsu** expunge; deny; ignore
突殺 **tsu(ki)koro(su)** stab to death
取殺 **to(ri)koro(su)** curse/haunt to death
9 虐殺 **gyakusatsu** massacre
活殺 **kassatsu** life and/or death
活殺自在 **kassatsu-jizai** power of life and death
封殺 **fūsatsu** forced out (in baseball)
相殺 **sōsai** offset, countervail
皆殺 **minagoro(shi)** massacre, mass murder
故殺 **kosatsu** intentional murder
10 射殺 **shasatsu, ikoro(su)** shoot to death
捕殺 **hosatsu** catch and kill
悩殺 **nōsatsu** enchant, captivate
笑殺 **shōsatsu** laugh off
11 惨殺 **zansatsu** murder, massacre, slaughter
惨殺者 **zansatsusha** murderer, slayer
盛殺 **mo(ri)koro(su)** kill by poisoning
12 減殺 **gensatsu, gensai** lessen, diminish
嵌殺 **ha(me)goro(shi)** fixed fittings
嵌殺窓 **ha(me)goro(shi) mado** fixed sash window
屠殺 **tosatsu** butchering, slaughter
屠殺場 **tosatsujō** slaughterhouse
焼殺 **ya(ki)koro(su)** burn (someone) to death
補殺 **hosatsu** an assist (in baseball)
絞殺 **kōsatsu** strangle to death; hang
13 暗殺 **ansatsu** assassination
暗殺者 **ansatsusha** assassin
飼殺 **ka(i)goro(shi)** keep (a pet) till he dies
14 擱殺 **tsuka(mi)koro(su)** squeeze to death
銃殺 **jūsatsu** shoot dead
15 撃殺 **gekisatsu** shoot dead
撲殺 **bokusatsu** clubbing to death
黙殺 **mokusatsu** take no notice of, ignore
締殺 **shi(me)koro(su)** strangle to death
踏殺 **fu(mi)koro(su)** trample to death
16 磔殺 **takusatsu** crucifixion (and stoning)
謀殺 **bōsatsu** premeditated murder

17 嬲殺 **nabu(ri)goro(shi)** torture to death
18 噛殺 **ka(mi)koro(su)** bite to death; suppress (a yawn)
19 蹴殺 **kekoro(su)** kick to death
鏖殺 **ōsatsu** massacre
22 轢殺 **rekisatsu, hi(ki)koro(su)** run over and kill

─── 3 ───
2 二人殺 **futarigoro(shi)** double murder

─── 4 ───
7 狂言自殺 **kyōgen jisatsu** faked suicide
9 飛込自殺 **tobiko(mi) jisatsu** suicide by jumping in front of an oncoming train

栽 → **4n6.1**

─── 7 ───
梼 → 檮 **4a14.4**

4a7.1
梗 **KŌ** in general; block, close off

─── 1 ───
13 梗塞 **kōsoku** stoppage; (monetary) stringency; infarction
14 梗概 **kōgai** outline, summary

─── 2 ───
10 桔梗 **kikyō, kikkō** Chinese bellflower, balloonflower

─── 3 ───
4 心筋梗塞 **shinkin kōsoku** myocardial infarction

4a7.2
桾 **KUN** (type of fruit tree)

椒 → **4a8.7**

4a7.3
彬 **HIN** splendid in both form and content **akiraka** clear

桝 → 枡 **4a4.6**

4a7.4

榊 shikimi Japanese star anise

4a7.5

梓 SHI catalpa tree; (wood-block) printing; publishing
azusa catalpa tree

——————— 2 ———————
3 上梓 **jōshi** publishing; wood-block printing

梽→檳 **4a14.3**

4a7.6

槞 YŪ sickle handle; (type of tree)

4a7.7

桿 杆 KAN rod, pole, stick

——————— 1 ———————
7 桿状 **kanjō** rod-shaped
11 桿菌 **kankin** bacillus
——————— 2 ———————
14 槓桿 **kōkan** lever
——————— 3 ———————
16 操縦桿 **sōjūkan** joystick

4a7.8

梏 KOKU, tekase manacles

——————— 2 ———————
10 桎梏 **shikkoku** fetters and manacles, shackles

4a7.9

梧 GO, aogiri Chinese parasol tree, Phoenix tree

——————— 1 ———————
3 梧下 **goka** To: (addressee)

4a7.10

梳 SO, kushi comb
kushikezu(ru) comb

4a7.11

梭 SA, hi shuttle (on a loom)

——————— 1 ———————
11 梭魚 **kamasu** barracuda

4a7.12

梠 RYO, hisashi eaves

4a7.13

梢 梢 SHI, kozue twig; treetop

——————— 2 ———————
5 末梢 **masshō** tip of a twig; periphery; nonessentials, trifles
末梢神経 **masshō shinkei** peripheral nerves

4a7.14

椛 kaba birch
momiji maple

4a7.15

椁 槨 KAKU outer box for a coffin

4a7.16

桷 KAKU, taruki rafter
zumi (type of tall tree in the apple family)

4a7.17

梯 TEI, hashigo ladder; barhopping, pub-crawling

——————— 1 ———————
2 梯子 **hashigo** ladder; barhopping, pub-crawling
梯子車 **hashigosha** (firefighting) ladder truck
梯子乗 **hashigono(ri)** acrobatic ladder-top stunts
梯子段 **hashigodan** step, stair
梯子酒 **hashigozake** barhopping, pub-crawling
7 梯状 **teijō** trapezoid; echelon formation
——————— 2 ———————
11 階梯 **kaitei** step, stairs, ladder; threshold, steppingstone; guide, primer, manual

船梯子 **funabashigo** gangway
舷梯 **gentei** gangway (ladder)
釣梯子 **tsu(ri)bashigo** rope ladder
魚梯 **gyotei** fish ladder, fishway
14 綱梯子 **tsunabashigo** rope ladder
15 磐梯山 **Bandai-san** (mountain, Fukushima-ken)
縄梯子 **nawabashigo** rope ladder

———————— 3 ————————

19 繰出梯子 **ku(ri)da(shi)bashigo** extension ladder

4a7.18

桶

TŌ, oke tub, bucket

———————— 1 ————————

9 桶屋 **okeya** cooper

———————— 2 ————————

4 水桶 **mizuoke** pail, bucket; cistern
手桶 **teoke** (wooden) bucket
火桶 **hioke** round wooden brazier
6 早桶 **hayaoke** coffin
8 肥桶 **koeoke** night-soil bucket
10 秣桶 **magusaoke** manger
12 湯桶 **yuoke** bathtub
棺桶 **kan'oke** coffin
13 飼桶 **ka(i)oke** manger

———————— 3 ————————

4 天水桶 **tensui oke** rain barrel
片手桶 **katate oke** bucket with handle on one side
9 風呂桶 **furooke** bathtub
13 飼葉桶 **ka(i)baoke** manger

梅 → 梅 **4a6.27**

4a7.19

梶

BI, kaji mulberry tree; oar

———————— 1 ————————

4 梶木 **kaji(no)ki** mulberry tree (used for paper)
12 梶棒 **kajibō** (rickshaw) shafts, thills

4a7.20

桐

KYOKU, kanjiki snowshoes

4a7.21

梔

SHI, kuchinashi Cape jasmine, gardenia

———————— 1 ————————

2 梔子 **kuchinashi** Cape jasmine, gardenia

———————— 2 ————————

3 山梔子 **kuchinashi** Cape jasmine, gardenia

4a7.22 / 529

械

KAI fetters; machine

———————— 2 ————————

4 手械 **tekase, tegase** handcuffs, manacles
15 器械 **kikai** apparatus, appliance
16 機械 **kikai** machine
機械工 **kikaikō** mechanic, machinist
機械工学 **kikai kōgaku** mechanical engineering
機械工業 **kikai kōgyō** the machine industry
機械化 **kikaika** mechanization, mechanized
機械文明 **kikai bunmei** machine civilization
機械仕掛 **kikai-jika(ke)** mechanism
機械体操 **kikai taisō** gymnastics using equipment
機械学 **kikaigaku** mechanics
機械油 **kikai abura** machine/lubricating oil
機械的 **kikaiteki** mechanical
機械屋 **kikaiya** machinist
機械製 **kikaisei** machine-made
機械編 **kikaia(mi)** machine-knit

———————— 4 ————————

3 工作機械 **kōsaku kikai** machine tools

4a7.23

梱

KON, shikimi threshold, doorsill
kori bundle, bale

———————— 1 ————————

5 梱包 **konpō** packing, packaging

4a7.24

梨

RI, nashi pear, pear tree

———————— 1 ————————

13 梨園 **rien** pear orchard; the theatrical world

———————— 2 ————————

3 山梨県 **Yamanashi-ken** (prefecture)
7 花梨 **karin** Chinese quince
9 洋梨 **yōnashi** Western pear

4a7.25

梁

RYŌ bridge beams
hari, utsubari beam, girder
yana weir, fish trap

2

12 棟梁 **tōryō** pillar, mainstay; chief, leader, foreman
13 跳梁 **chōryō** be rampant, dominate
14 鼻梁 **biryō** bridge of the nose
16 橋梁 **kyōryō** bridge

4a7.26

桀

KETSU, togura chicken roost

梦 → 夢 3k10.14

棥 → 2m9.3

4a7.27

梵

BON Sanskrit; purity; Buddhist believer; Brahman

1

4 梵天 **Bonten** Brahma, the Creator
5 梵字 **bonji** Sanskrit characters
8 梵刹 **bonsetsu** (Buddhist) temple
14 梵語 **bongo** Sanskrit
20 梵鐘 **bonshō** temple bell

4a7.28

梟

KYŌ owl; strong; expose (a severed head) **fukurō** owl

1

4 梟木 **kyōboku** post for displaying a severed head; gibbet

4a7.29

桗 桗

SETSU, udatsu short ridgepole support used in roof-raising

1

3 桗上 **udatsu (ga) a(garanai)** have no hope of being a success in the world

殺 → 殺 4a6.35

耕 → 0a10.13

耗 → 0a10.12

8

4a8.1

椎

TSUI hit; backbone
tsuchi hammer
shii (a species of oak)

1

9 椎茸 **shiitake** (a variety of edible mushroom)
10 椎骨 **tsuikotsu** vertebra

2

10 胸椎 **kyōtsui** the thoracic vertebrae
脊椎 **sekitsui** vertebra; spinal column, spine
脊椎動物 **sekitsui dōbutsu** vertebrates
13 腰椎 **yōtsui** lumbar vertebra
16 頸椎 **keitsui** the cervical vertebrae

4a8.2

椚

kunugi (a species of oak)

4a8.3 / 1406

棟

TŌ, mune, muna- ridge of a roof; ridgepole, ridge beam; (counter for buildings)

1

3 棟上 **munea(ge)** ridgepole raising
棟上式 **munea(ge)shiki** roof-raising ceremony
4 棟木 **munagi** ridgepole, ridge beam
5 棟瓦 **munagawara** ridge tile
11 棟梁 **tōryō** pillar, mainstay; chief, leader, foreman
12 棟割長屋 **munewa(ri) nagaya** long tenement/partitioned building

2

3 上棟式 **jōtōshiki** ridgepole-raising/roof-laying ceremony
7 別棟 **betsumune** another building, annex
10 病棟 **byōtō** ward

4a8.4

棣

TEI flowering almond

1

12 棣棠 **teitō** Japanese globeflower/kerria

4a8.5

椏

mata crotch (in a tree)

4

木 8 ←
月
日
火
衤
王
牛
方
攵
欠
心
戸
戈

4a8.6

椰

YA palm/coconut tree

――――――― 1 ―――――――
2 椰子 **yashi** palm/coconut tree

――――――― 2 ―――――――
7 花椰菜 **hanayasai** cauliflower

---

4 槨→槨 **4a9.5**

→8 木月日火ネ王牛方攵欠心戸戈

4a8.7

椒

SHŌ Japanese pepper tree

――――――― 2 ―――――――
3 山椒 **sanshō** Japanese pepper (tree)
　山椒魚 **sanshōuo** salamander
9 胡椒 **koshō** pepper
　胡椒入 **koshōi(re)** pepper skaker
13 榴椒 **koshō** pepper

4a8.8

椡

TŌ (a species of oak)

4a8.9

椥

nagi (type of evergreen tree)

4a8.10 / 1908

棚

tana shelf

――――――― 1 ―――――――
3 棚上 **tanaa(ge)** put on the shelf, shelve
4 棚引 **tanabi(ku)** trail, hang over (fog/smoke)
8 棚板 **tanaita** shelf (board), tray
9 棚卸 **tanaoroshi** inventory, stock-taking

――――――― 2 ―――――――
4 戸棚 **todana** cupboard, cabinet, closet
5 本棚 **hondana** bookshelf
8 岩棚 **iwadana** ledge
　炉棚 **rodana** mantelpiece
9 茶棚 **chadana** shelf for tea-things
　神棚 **kamidana** household altar-shelf
10 陸棚 **rikudana** continental shelf
　書棚 **shodana** bookshelf
11 釣棚 **tsu(ri)dana** hanging shelf

12 違棚 **chiga(i)dana** staggered shelves
13 飾棚 **kaza(ri)dana** display shelves/case
18 藤棚 **fujidana** wisteria trellis

――――――― 3 ―――――――
3 大陸棚 **tairikudana** continental shelf
10 陳列棚 **chinretsudana** display rack/case
12 葡萄棚 **budōdana** grapevine trellis

4a8.11 / 336

極

KYOKU end, pole　GOKU very, extremely　kiwa(meru) go to the end, study thoroughly; carry to extremes　kiwa(mete) extremely　kiwa(maru) come to an end, reach an extreme　kiwa(mi) height, end　ki(me) arrangement, agreement　ki(mari) settlement, conclusion; rule, convention

――――――― 1 ―――――――
2 極力 **kyokuryoku** to the utmost, to the best of one's ability, as much as possible
3 極大 **kyokudai** maximum
　極上 **gokujō** finest, top-quality
　極小 **kyokushō** minimum
4 極内 **gokunai** top-secret, confidential
　極切 **kima(ri)ki(tta)** fixed, definite; stereo-typed; self-evident
　極手 **ki(me)te** winning move, decisive factor
　極月 **gokugetsu** the last month of the year, December
5 極北 **kyokuhoku** the far north, North Pole
　極左 **kyokusa** ultraleft
　極付 **ki(me)tsu(keru)** take to task, reprimand
　極右 **kyokuu** ultraright
6 極印 **gokuin** hallmark, stamp, impress
　極刑 **kyokkei** capital punishment; maximum penalty
　極地 **kyokuchi** polar (regions)
　極光 **kyokkō** the northern/southern lights, aurora borealis/australis
　極尽 **kiwa(me)tsuku(su)** investigate thoroughly
7 極言 **kyokugen** go so far as to say
8 極東 **kyokutō** the Far East
　極限 **kyokugen** limit, extremity
　極所 **kyokusho** end, extremity
9 極点 **kyokuten** highest/lowest point
　極前線 **kyokuzensen** polar front
　極洋 **kyokuyō** polar seas
　極度 **kyokudo** to the highest degree, extreme
10 極流 **kyokuryū** polar current
　極致 **kyokuchi** culmination, acme
　極秘 **gokuhi** top-secret, confidential
11 極貧 **gokuhin** dire poverty
　極道 **gokudō** wicked, brutal, profligate
　極道者 **gokudōmono** scoundrel, rogue

極彩色 **gokusaishiki** brilliant coloring, full color (illustrations)
極悪 **gokuaku** heinous
　　 ki(mari)waru(i) awkward, embarrassed
極悪人 **gokuakunin** utter scoundrel
12 極寒 **gokkan** intense cold
極圏 **kyokken** the Arctic/Antarctic Circle
極暑 **gokusho** intense heat
極量 **kyokuryō** maximum dose
13 極微 **kyokubi** infinitesimal, microscopic
極楽 **gokuraku** paradise
極楽往生 **gokuraku ōjō** a peaceful death
極楽浄土 **gokuraku jōdo** (Buddhist) paradise
極楽鳥 **gokurakuchō** bird of paradise
極意 **gokui** mystery, secrets, quintessence
14 極端 **kyokutan** extreme
極製 **gokusei** the best made
15 極熱 **gokunetsu** intense heat
極論 **kyokuron** extreme argument; go so far as to say

─────── 2 ───────

4 天極 **tenkyoku** the celestial poles
分極 **bunkyoku** polarization
月極 **tsukigi(me)** monthly (contract)
5 北極 **hokkyoku** the North Pole
北極光 **hokkyokukō** the northern lights, aurora borealis
北極海 **Hokkyokukai** the Arctic Ocean
北極星 **hokkyokusei** the North Star, Polaris
北極圏 **hokkyokuken** the Arctic Circle, the Arctic
北極熊 **hokkyokuguma** polar bear
6 両極 **ryōkyoku** both extremities; both poles
両極端 **ryōkyokutan** both extremes
至極 **shigoku** very, quite, most
7 究極 **kyūkyoku** final, ultimate
見極 **mikiwa(meru)** see through, discern, ascertain, grasp
8 取極 **to(ri)ki(meru)** arrange, agree upon
9 南極 **Nankyoku** the South Pole
南極光 **nankyokukō** the aurora australis, the southern lights
南極海 **Nankyokukai** the Antarctic Ocean
南極圏 **Nankyokuken** the Antarctic Circle, the Antarctic
皇極 **Kōgyoku** (empress, 642–645)
10 陰極 **inkyoku** negative pole, cathode
陰極線 **inkyokusen** cathode rays
消極 **shōkyoku** negative pole; passive
消極的 **shōkyokuteki** passive, negative
消極性 **shōkyokusei** passive
11 陽極 **yōkyoku** positive pole, anode
終極 **shūkyoku** ultimate, final
12 登極 **tōkyoku** accession, enthronement
13 電極 **denkyoku** electrode, pole, terminal
14 磁極 **jikyoku** magnetic pole

15 窮極 **kyūkyoku** ultimate, eventual
16 積極 **sekkyoku** positive
積極的 **sekkyokuteki** positive, active
積極性 **sekkyokusei** positiveness

4a8.12

榜　KEN, **magemono** wickerwork

4a8.13

梻　**shide** (a deciduous tree in the birch family)

4a8.14 / 1835

棋 棊　KI go; shogi, Japanese chess

─────── 1 ───────

3 棋士 **kishi** (professional) go/shogi player
9 棋客 **kikyaku, kikaku** go/shogi player
15 棋敵 **kiteki** one's opponent in go/shogi
19 棋譜 **kifu** record of a go/shogi game

─────── 2 ───────

10 将棋 **shōgi** *shōgi*, Japanese chess
将棋倒 **shōgidao(shi)** falling like a row of dominoes
将棋盤 **shōgiban** *shōgi* board, chessboard

─────── 3 ───────

9 飛将棋 **to(bi)shōgi** halma
挟将棋 **hasa(mi) shōgi** (a piece-capturing board game)

4a8.15

椄　SETSU, **tsu(gu)** graft

4a8.16

棲　SEI, **su(mu)** live, dwell

─────── 1 ───────

10 棲息 **seisoku** live in, inhabit
棲息地 **seisokuchi** habitat

─────── 2 ───────

4 水棲 **suisei** aquatic (animal)
6 両棲 **ryōsei** amphibious (animal)
同棲 **dōsei** live together, cohabit with
10 陸棲 **rikusei** (living on) land
13 隠棲 **insei** live in seclusion
群棲 **gunsei** live gregariously

4

木
月
日
火
礻
王
牛
方
攵
欠
心
戸
戈

8 ←

4a8.17

棱 **RYŌ** corner, edge, ruggedness

4a8.18

棉 **MEN, wata** cotton

——— 1 ———
7 棉花 **menka** cotton bolls, raw cotton

4a8.19

椌 **KŌ** (type of ancient musical instrument); unadorned tool

4a8.20 / 1543

棒 **BŌ** stick, pole

——— 1 ———
4 棒引 **bōbi(ki)** cancellation, writing off
5 棒立 **bōda(chi)** standing bolt upright
7 棒状 **bōjō** cylindrical
棒杙 **bōgui** stake, pile
8 棒使 **bōtsuka(i)** pole fighting/fighter
棒押 **bōo(shi)** pole-pushing
棒杭 **bōgui** stake, pile
9 棒紅 **bōbeni** lipstick
10 棒倒 **bōtao(shi)** topple-the-other-team's-pole game
棒高飛 **bōtakato(bi)** pole vault
棒高跳 **bōtakato(bi)** pole vault
11 棒術 **bōjutsu** pole fighting
棒組 **bōgu(mi)** typesetting
13 棒暗記 **bōanki** indiscriminate memorization
14 棒磁石 **bōjishaku** bar magnet
棒読 **bōyo(mi)** reading aloud in a monotone; reading Chinese in Chinese word order
16 棒縞 **bōjima** stripes
棒鋼 **bōkō** bar steel
22 棒鱈 **bōdara** dried cod

——— 2 ———
4 片棒 **katabō (o katsugu)** take part, have a hand in
心棒 **shinbō** axle, shaft, mandrel, stem
6 先棒 **sakibō** front palanquin bearer; (someone's) cat's-paw
7 延棒 **no(be)bō** (metal) bar
乳棒 **nyūbō** pestle
8 泥棒 **dorobō** thief, burglar
突棒 **tsu(ki)bō** cattle prod, goad

金棒 **kanabō** iron rod
金棒引 **kanabōhi(ki)** night watchman; a gossip
9 後棒 **atobō** rear palanquin bearer
相棒 **aibō** pal, partner, accomplice
11 梶棒 **kajibō** (rickshaw) shafts, thills
12 棍棒 **konbō** club, stick
痛棒 **tsūbō** harsh criticism
13 鉄棒 **tetsubō, kanabō** iron bar/rod; (gymnastics) horizontal bar
鉄棒引 **kanabōhi(ki)** night watchman; a gossip
14 綿棒 **menbō** cotton swab
箆棒 **berabō** absurd; awful, darn
飴棒 **ame(n)bō** lollipop, sucker
15 横棒 **yokobō** (horizontal) bar
編棒 **a(mi)bō** knitting needle/pin
19 警棒 **keibō** policeman's club/nightstick
20 麺棒 **menbō** rolling pin

——— 3 ———
5 平行棒 **heikōbō** parallel bars
8 突支棒 **tsukkaibō** prop, strut, support
9 炭素棒 **tansobō** carbon rod/points
10 針小棒大 **shinshō-bōdai** exaggeration

4a8.21

椙 **sugi** Japanese cedar, cryptomeria

4a8.22

棍 **KON** cane, stick

——— 1 ———
12 棍棒 **konbō** club, stick

棧 → 桟 **4a6.1**

4a8.23

楛 **KON, nemunoki** silk tree

4a8.24

棕 椶 **SHU** hemp plant

——— 1 ———
19 棕櫚 **shuro** hemp plant

4a8.25 / 1825

棺　**KAN, hitsugi** coffin

——————— 1 ———————
11 棺桶 **kan'oke** coffin

——————— 2 ———————
2 入棺 **nyūkan** placing into the coffin
5 出棺 **shukkan** carry a coffin out
　石棺 **sekkan, sekikan** sarcophagus, stone coffin
10 陶棺 **tōkan** earthenware coffin
　納棺 **nōkan** placing in the coffin
13 寝棺 **negan, nekan** coffin

4a8.26

椀　**WAN** bowl

——————— 2 ———————
13 塗椀 **nu(ri)wan** lacquered bowl

4a8.27

椅　**I** chair

——————— 1 ———————
2 椅子 **isu** chair, seat, couch

——————— 2 ———————
7 車椅子 **kurumaisu** wheelchair
8 長椅子 **nagaisu** sofa, couch
13 寝椅子 **neisu** sofa, lounge chair
21 藤椅子 **tōisu** rattan/wickerwork chair

——————— 3 ———————
6 安楽椅子 **anraku isu** easy chair

4a8.28 / 531

検 檢　**KEN** investigation, inspection

——————— 1 ———————
4 検分 **kenbun** inspect, examine
　検水 **kensui** water testing/measuring
5 検出 **kenshutsu** detect
　検収 **kenshū** (inspection and) acceptance
　検圧 **ken'atsu** measuring pressure
　検圧器 **ken'atsuki** pressure gauge
　検字 **kenji** stroke-count index
　検札 **kensatsu** examine/check tickets
6 検死 **kenshi** coroner's inquest, autopsy
　検印 **ken'in** stamp of approval
　検地 **kenchi** land surveying
7 検束 **kensoku** detention, custody, arrest

　検乳 **kennyū** milk examination/testing
　検尿 **kennyō** urinalysis
　検車 **kensha** vehicle inspection
8 検事 **kenji** public procurator/prosecutor
　検事局 **kenjikyoku** prosecutor's office
　検定 **kentei** official approval, inspection
　検定料 **kenteiryō** examination fee
　検定済 **kenteizu(mi)** (government) inspected/authorized
　検定試験 **kentei shiken** (teacher) certification examination
9 検便 **kenben** examination of stools
　検屍 **kenshi** coroner's inquest, autopsy
　検査 **kensa** inspection, examination
　検査役 **kensayaku** inspector, examiner
　検査官 **kensakan** inspector, examiner
　検査所 **kensajo** inspection station
　検査済 **kensazu(mi)** examined, passed
　検疫 **ken'eki** quarantine
　検疫官 **ken'ekikan** quarantine officer
　検疫所 **ken'ekisho** quarantine station
10 検索 **kensaku** retrieval, lookup, reference
　検流計 **kenryūkei** current gauge, ammeter
　検流器 **kenryūki** current gauge, ammeter
　検案 **ken'an** (post-mortem) examination
　検挙 **kenkyo** arrest, apprehend
　検校 **kengyō** blind court musician
　検討 **kentō** examine, study, look into
　検針 **kenshin** checking a meter/gauge
11 検視 **kenshi** investigation into the facts
　検眼 **kengan** eye examination, optometry
　検眼鏡 **kengankyō** ophthalmoscope
　検問 **kenmon** inspect, examine, check
　検問所 **kenmonjo** checkpoint
12 検温 **ken'on** temperature measurement
　検温器 **ken'onki** (clinical) thermometer
　検湿器 **kenshitsuki** hygrometer
　検番 **kenban** geisha call-office
　検証 **kenshō** verification, inspection
　検診 **kenshin** medical examination
　検診日 **kenshinbi** medical-examination day
14 検察 **kensatsu** investigation and prosecution
　検察庁 **kensatsuchō** public prosecutor's office
　検察官 **kensatsukan** public prosecutor
　検算 **kenzan** check the figures, verify the accounts
15 検潮器 **kenchōki** tide gauge
　検閲 **ken'etsu** censorship; inspection (of troops)
　検閲官 **ken'etsukan** censor, inspector
16 検糖計 **kentōkei** saccarimeter
19 検鏡 **kenkyō** microscopic examination

——————— 2 ———————
3 下検分 **shitakenbun** preliminary examination

下検査 **shitakensa** preliminary inspection
4 不検束 **fukensoku** unrestrained
5 巡検 **junken** inspection tour
6 再検査 **saikensa** re-examination
　再検討 **saikentō** re-examination, reappraisal, review
7 判検事 **hankenji** judges and prosecutors/procurators
　尿検査 **nyō kensa** urinalysis
　車検 **shaken** auto inspection (certificate)
8 受検 **juken** undergo investigation
　送検 **sōken** send to the prosecutor's office
　実検 **jikken** inspect (personally)
9 点検 **tenken** inspection
11 探検 **tanken** exploration, expedition
　探検家 **tankenka** explorer
　探検記 **tankenki** account of an expedition
　探検隊 **tankentai** exploration party
18 臨検 **rinken** inspection visit; raid, search

——————— 3 ———————

9 首実検 **kubi jikken** inspection of a severed head; identification of a suspect
14 徴兵検査 **chōhei kensa** examination for conscription

4a8.29

梣

NEN (type of fruit tree)

4a8.30

楡

RIN camphor tree

4a8.31

椋

RYŌ, muku (type of deciduous tree); gray starling

——————— 1 ———————

4 椋木 **muku(no)ki** (type of deciduous tree)
11 椋鳥 **mukudori** gray starling; bumpkin, easily duped person

4a8.32 / 424

植

SHOKU, u(eru) plant
u(waru) be planted

——————— 1 ———————

4 植込 **u(e)ko(mi)** thick growth of plants, shrubbery
　植木 **ueki** garden/potted plant
　植木屋 **uekiya** gardener, nurseryman
　植木鉢 **uekibachi** flowerpot

5 植民 **shokumin** colonization, settlement; colonist, settler
　植民地 **shokuminchi** colony
　植民地化 **shokuminchika** colonization
　植付 **u(e)tsu(keru)** plant, implant
　植皮 **shokuhi** skin grafting
　植字 **shokuji** typesetting
　植字機 **shokujiki** typesetting machine
8 植林 **shokurin** tree planting, afforestation
　植物 **shokubutsu** plant
　植物学 **shokubutsugaku** botany
　植物性 **shokubutsusei** vegetable (oil)
　植物界 **shokubutsukai** the plant kingdom
　植物病 **shokubutsubyō** plant disease
　植物採集 **shokubutsu saishū** plant collecting
　植物園 **shokubutsuen** botanical garden
　植物誌 **shokubutsushi** a flora/herbal
　植物質 **shokubutsushitsu** vegetable matter
12 植替 **u(e)ka(eru)** transplant, replant
16 植樹 **shokuju** tree planting
　植樹祭 **shokujusai** Arbor Day

——————— 2 ———————

2 入植 **nyūshoku** settlement, immigration
4 手植 **teu(e)** planted personally
5 写植 **shashoku** photocomposition, phototypesetting (short for 写真植字)
　穴植 **anau(e)** dibbling
　田植 **tau(e)** rice-planting
　田植歌 **tau(e) uta** rice-planting song
7 扶植 **fushoku** plant, establish
8 定植 **teishoku** plant (seedlings) permanently
9 秋植 **akiu(e)** autumn planting
11 動植物 **dōshokubutsu** plants and animals, flora and fauna
　移植 **ishoku** transplant
13 試植 **shishoku** experimental planting
　鉢植 **hachiu(e)** potted plant
14 腐植土 **fushokudo** humus
　誤植 **goshoku** misprint

——————— 3 ———————

5 写真植字 **shashin shokuji** photocomposition, phototypesetting
13 裸子植物 **rashi shokubutsu** gymnospermous plant
15 養蜂植物 **yōhō shokubutsu** plants for bees
18 観葉植物 **kan'yō shokubutsu** foliage plant
　顕花植物 **kenka shokubutsu** flowering plant

4a8.33

椪

PON (derived from the Indian place name Poona)

——————— 1 ———————

9 椪柑 **ponkan** (a fruit native to India)

4a8.34

榑 **tabu, tafu** (an evergreen in the camphor-tree family)

4a8.35

梈 **KIKU** oak

4a8.36

椌 **KŌ** mast crossbeam

4a8.37

椢 **KAI, soko** bottom
hako box
kunugi (a type of oak)

4a8.38

棹 **TŌ, sao** pole

——————— 1 ———————
0 棹さす **sao(sasu)** pole (a boat)

槌 → 槌 **4a9.27**

巢 → 巣 **3n8.1**

4a8.39 / 128

森 **SHIN, mori** woods, forest

——————— 1 ———————
8 森林 **shinrin** woods, forest
森林学 **shinringaku** forestry
森林帯 **shinrintai** forest zone
12 森閑 **shinkan (to shita)** still, hushed, silent
17 森厳 **shingen** solemn, awe-inspiring
19 森羅万象 **shinra-banshō** all creation, the universe
——————— 2 ———————
8 青森 **Aomori** (city, Aomori-ken)
青森県 **Aomori-ken** (prefecture)

棊 → 棋 **4a8.14**

4a8.40

渠 **KYO** ditch; ringleader; he

——————— 1 ———————
14 渠魁 **kyokai** ringleader, chief, boss
——————— 2 ———————
11 船渠 **senkyo** dock
12 開渠 **kaikyo** open channel
13 溝渠 **kōkyo** ditch, sewer, canal
暗渠 **ankyo** closed/covered conduit, underground drain, culvert

4a8.41

弒 **SHII, SHI, koro(su)** kill (one's lord)

——————— 1 ———————
0 弒する **shii(suru)** assassinate, murder (one's lord)
8 弒逆 **shiigyaku** murder (of one's lord/parent), regicide

——————— 9 ———————

4a9.1

楝 **REN, ōchi** Japanese bead tree

4a9.2

楮 **CHO, kōzo** paper mulberry

4a9.3

楯 **JUN, tate** shield

——————— 1 ———————
8 楯突 **tatetsu(ku)** oppose, defy
——————— 2 ———————
3 小楯 **kodate** small shield; screen, cover
9 後楯 **ushi(ro)date** backing, support

4a9.4

椹 **JIN, sawara** (a type of cypress)

榔 → 桹 **4a7.15**

木 9←
月
日
火
礻
王
牛
方
攵
欠
心
戸
戈

4

4a9.5

榔 榔

RŌ betel palm tree

——— 2 ———

18 檳榔 **binrō** betel palm tree
檳榔子 **binrōji** betel palm tree

4a9.6

楸

SHŪ, kisasage, hisagi Japanese catalpa

楙→茂 **3k5.7**

4a9.7

椴

TAN, todomatsu fir

——— 1 ———

8 椴松 **todomatsu** fir

4a9.8

楜

KO pepper

——— 1 ———

12 楜椒 **koshō** pepper

榊→榊 **4a10.3**

4a9.9

貅

KYŪ ferocious leopard-like animal, fierce beast; brave warrior

——— 2 ———

11 豼貅 **hikyū** ferocious beast; brave warrior

4a9.10 / 1841

楼 樓

RŌ tower, turret, lookout

——— 1 ———

3 楼上 **rōjō** upper story, balcony
8 楼門 **rōmon** two-story gate
14 楼閣 **rōkaku** many-story building, castle

——— 2 ———

7 妓楼 **girō** brothel

8 青楼 **seirō** brothel
10 高楼 **kōrō** tall building, skyscraper
11 望楼 **bōrō** watchtower
12 登楼 **tōrō** going up a tower; visiting a brothel
14 層楼 **sōrō** tall building
20 鐘楼 **shōrō** bell tower, belfry

——— 3 ———

2 八重楼 **yaezakura** double-flowering cherry tree
5 白玉楼 **hakugyokurō** (among) the dead, deceased
11 深山楼 **miyamazakura** mountain cherry tree
13 蜃気楼 **shinkirō** mirage
15 摩天楼 **matenrō** skyscraper

——— 4 ———

8 金殿玉楼 **kinden gyokurō** palatial residence

4a9.11

楔

SETSU, kusabi wedge

——— 1 ———

7 楔形文字 **kusabigata moji, sekkei moji** cuneiform writing

椶→棕 **4a8.24**

楳→梅 **4a6.27**

4a9.12

楞

RYŌ, kado corner, protrusion

4a9.13

楕 橢

DA ellipse

——— 1 ———

4 楕円 **daen** ellipse
楕円形 **daenkei** ellipse, oval

4a9.14

楪

CHA lacquered dish

4a9.15

椋

hanzō container for pouring water

4a9.16

椿

CHIN, tsubaki camellia

――――――1――――――
8 椿事 **chinji** accident; sudden occurrence
　椿油 **tsubaki abura** camellia oil
10 椿姫 **Tsubakihime** (Verdi's) La Traviata
――――――2――――――
12 寒椿 **kantsubaki** winter camellia
――――――3――――――
5 白玉椿 **shiratama tsubaki** white camellia

4a9.17

楊

YŌ purple willow

――――――1――――――
2 楊子江 **Yōsukō** the Yangzi/Yangtze river
8 楊枝 **yōji** toothpick; toothbrush
9 楊柳 **kawayanagi** purple willow
　　　yōryū purple willows and weeping
　　　willows
12 楊貴妃 **Yōkihi** Yang Guifei (beautiful
　　　Chinese queen, 719–756)
――――――2――――――
3 小楊子 **koyōji** toothpick
4 爪楊枝 **tsumayōji** toothpick
11 黄楊 **tsuge** box tree, boxwood

4a9.18

楷

KAI block/noncursive style; rule,
model

――――――1――――――
10 楷書 **kaisho** noncursive (kanji), printed style

4a9.19

楹

EI, hashira pillar

4a9.20

楫

SHŪ, kaji rudder

4a9.21

榁

muro needle juniper

4a9.22

椽

TEN rafter

楢→楢 **4a9.23**

4a9.23

楢 楢

YŪ, SHŪ, nara oak

――――――2――――――
4 水楢 **mizunara** (a variety of) oak

4a9.24

楴

TEI ornamental hairpin

4a9.25

楠

NAN, kusunoki camphor tree

――――――2――――――
5 石楠花 **shakunage** rhododendron

4a9.26

楡

YU, nire elm

樋→樋 **4a10.28**

4a9.27

槌 槌

TSUI, tsuchi hammer, mallet

――――――2――――――
3 才槌 **saizuchi** small wooden mallet
　才槌頭 **saizuchi atama** head with protruding
　　　forehead and occiput, hammerhead
　小槌 **kozuchi** small mallet, gavel
8 金槌 **kanazuchi** hammer
　金槌頭 **kanazuchi-atama** hard-headed;
　　　stubborn
9 相槌 **aizuchi** (anvil) hammering in alterna-
　　　tion; giving responses to make the
　　　conversation go smoothly
13 鉄槌 **tettsui** hammer

4

木 月 日 火 ネ 王 牛 方 攵 欠 心 戸 戈 9←

4a9.28

楓 **FŪ, kaede** maple tree

4a9.29 / 358

楽 樂
GAKU music
RAKU pleasure; comfort, ease, relief **tanoshi(mu)** enjoy; look forward to
tano(shii) fun, enjoyable, pleasant

─────────── 1 ───────────

2 楽人 **gakujin** musician, minstrel
　　　rakujin person living at ease
3 楽才 **gakusai** musical talent
　楽々 **rakuraku** comfortably, with great ease
　楽土 **rakudo** a paradise
　楽士 **gakushi** bandsman, musician
4 楽天 **rakuten** optimism
　楽天主義 **rakuten shugi** optimism
　楽天地 **rakutenchi** a paradise; amusement center
　楽天的 **rakutenteki** optimistic, cheerful
　楽天家 **rakutenka** optimist
　楽手 **gakushu** musician, bandsman
6 楽曲 **gakkyoku** musical composition/piece
　楽団 **gakudan** orchestra, band
8 楽長 **gakuchō** band leader, conductor
　楽典 **gakuten** rules of musical composition
9 楽屋 **gakuya** dressing room, greenroom, backstage, behind the scenes
　楽屋落 **gakuyao(chi)** a matter not understood by outsiders, shoptalk, inside joke
　楽屋話 **gakuyabanashi** backstage talk
　楽音 **gakuon** musical tone
　楽界 **gakkai** the world of music
10 楽員 **gakuin** orchestra/band member
　楽書 **rakuga(ki)** graffiti
11 楽隊 **gakutai** band, orchestra
　楽章 **gakushō** a movement (of a symphony)
12 楽勝 **rakushō** easy victory
　楽焼 **rakuya(ki)** hand-molded pottery
13 楽隠居 **rakuinkyo** comfortable retirement
　楽寝 **rakune** nap, rest
　楽園 **rakuen** a paradise
　楽楽 **rakuraku** comfortably, with great ease
　楽聖 **gakusei** musical master
15 楽劇 **gakugeki** opera, musical drama
　楽器 **gakki** musical instrument
　楽器店 **gakkiten** music shop
　楽器屋 **gakkiya** music shop
　楽調 **gakuchō** musical tone
16 楽壇 **gakudan** the musical world
18 楽観 **rakkan** optimism
　楽観主義 **rakkan shugi** optimism

　楽観的 **rakkanteki** optimistic, hopeful
19 楽譜 **gakufu** musical notation, sheet music, the score

─────────── 2 ───────────

4 文楽 **bunraku** puppet theater
5 打楽器 **dagakki** percussion instrument
　好楽家 **kōgakuka** music lover
　礼楽 **reigaku** etiquette and music
　田楽 **dengaku** ritual music and dancing; tofu baked with miso
6 気楽 **kiraku** feeling at ease, easygoing, comfortable
　伎楽 **gigaku** (an ancient mask show)
　邦楽 **hōgaku** (traditional) Japanese music
　至楽 **shiraku** utmost pleasure
　行楽 **kōraku** excursion, outing
　行楽地 **kōrakuchi** pleasure resort
　安楽 **anraku** ease, comfort
　安楽死 **anrakushi** euthanasia
　安楽椅子 **anraku isu** easy chair
7 佚楽 **itsuraku** idle pleasure
　伯楽 **hakuraku, hakurō, bakurō** horse expert/dealer
　享楽 **kyōraku** enjoyment
　享楽主義 **kyōraku shugi** epicureanism
　声楽 **seigaku** vocal music, (study) voice
　声楽家 **seigakuka** vocalist
　快楽 **kairaku, keraku** pleasure
　快楽主義 **kairaku shugi** hedonism, epicureanism
8 法楽 **hōraku** pleasure of a pious life; entertainment for the gods
　弦楽 **gengaku** string (ensemble)
　弦楽器 **gengakki** string instrument, the strings
　苦楽 **kuraku** joys and sorrows
　和楽 **wagaku** Japanese-style music
9 奏楽 **sōgaku** instrumental music
　俗楽 **zokugaku** popular/vulgar music
　軍楽 **gungaku** military/martial music
　軍楽隊 **gungakutai** military band
　哀楽 **airaku** grief and pleasure
　洋楽 **yōgaku** Western music
　洋楽器 **yōgakki** Western musical instruments
　独楽 **koma** (spinning) top
　神楽 **kagura** Shinto music and dancing
　神楽堂 **kaguradō** Shinto dance pavilion
　神楽殿 **kaguraden** Shinto dance pavilion
　音楽 **ongaku** music
　音楽会 **ongakkai, ongakukai** concert
　音楽家 **ongakka, ongakuka** musician
　音楽隊 **ongakutai** band, orchestra
　音楽堂 **ongakudō** concert hall
10 俱楽部 **kurabu** club
　遊楽 **yūraku** amusement, pleasure, recreation
　逸楽 **itsuraku** idle pursuit of pleasure
　娯楽 **goraku** amusement, entertainment

娯楽品 **gorakuhin** plaything
娯楽室 **gorakushitsu** recreation room
娯楽場 **gorakujō** place of amusement
娯楽街 **gorakugai** amusement quarter
娯楽機関 **goraku kikan** recreational facilities
宴楽 **enraku** merrymaking, conviviality
能楽 **nōgaku** Noh drama
能楽堂 **nōgakudō** a Noh theater
悦楽 **etsuraku** joy, pleasure, gaiety
11 道楽 **dōraku** hobby; dissipation, debauchery
道楽者 **dōrakumono** libertine, playboy
道楽息子 **dōraku musuko** prodigal son
淫楽 **inraku** carnal pleasure
絃楽 **gengaku** string music
絃楽器 **gengakki** stringed instrument
12 極楽 **gokuraku** paradise
極楽往生 **gokuraku ōjō** a peaceful death
極楽浄土 **gokuraku jōdo** (Buddhist) paradise
極楽鳥 **gokurakuchō** bird of paradise
愉楽 **yuraku** pleasure, joy
13 猿楽 **sarugaku** (type of medieval farce)
楽楽 **rakuraku** comfortably, with great ease
聖楽 **seigaku** sacred music
雅楽 **gagaku** ancient Japanese court music
14 管楽 **kangaku** wind-instrument music
管楽器 **kangakki** wind instruments
15 舞楽 **bugaku** old Japanese court-dance music
器楽 **kigaku** instrumental music
歓楽 **kanraku** pleasure, enjoyment
歓楽街 **kanrakugai** amusement center
18 観楽街 **kanrakugai** amusement district
観楽境 **kanrakukyō** pleasure resort

――――――――― 3 ―――――――――

3 千秋楽 **senshūraku** the last day (of a play's run)
女道楽 **onna dōraku** carnal pleasures
4 太平楽 **taiheiraku** idle/irresponsible talk
6 交響楽団 **kōkyō gakudan** symphony orchestra
有鍵楽器 **yūken gakki** keyed (musical) instrument
7 里神楽 **sato kagura** sacred dance performance in a Shinto shrine
吹奏楽 **suisōgaku** wind-instrument music, brass
9 室内楽 **shitsunaigaku** chamber music
食道楽 **ku(i)dōraku** gourmandizing; epicure
12 着道楽 **kidōraku** love of fine clothes
軽音楽 **keiongaku** light music
13 催馬楽 **saibara** (type of *gagaku* song)
14 管弦楽団 **kangen gakudan** orchestra
管絃楽団 **kangen gakudan** orchestra

――――――――― 4 ―――――――――

9 室内音楽 **shitsunai ongaku** chamber music
12 喜怒哀楽 **kidoairaku** joy-anger-sorrow-pleasure, emotions

4a9.30

楚 **SO** bramble; whip, cane

――――――― 1 ―――――――
3 楚々 **soso(taru)** tasteful, graceful
――――――― 2 ―――――――
11 清楚 **seiso** neat and clean, tidy, trim
――――――― 3 ―――――――
5 四面楚歌 **shimen-soka** surrounded by enemies, without allies

4a9.31

牒 **CHŌ** label; a circular

――――――― 2 ―――――――
9 通牒 **tsūchō** notification
11 符牒 **fuchō** mark, symbol, code

4a9.32

躱 **TA, kawa(su)** dodge, parry, avoid

――――――――― 10 ―――――――――

4a10.1

樫 **kashi** oak; (used in proper names)

4a10.2 / 1459

概 概 **GAI** general, approximate
ōmu(ne) generally

――――――― 1 ―――――――
0 概して **gai(shite)** generally, on the whole
7 概見 **gaiken** overview, outline
概言 **gaigen** general remarks, summary
8 概念 **gainen** general idea, concept
概念化 **gainenka** generalization
概念的 **gainenteki** general, conceptual
概況 **gaikyō** general situation, outlook
9 概括 **gaikatsu** summary, generalization
概要 **gaiyō** outline, synopsis
概計 **gaikei** rough estimate
概則 **gaisoku** general rules/principles
11 概略 **gairyaku** outline, summary
13 概数 **gaisū** round/approximate numbers
14 概貌 **gaibō** general appearance, outline
概算 **gaisan** rough estimate
概説 **gaisetsu** general statement, outline
15 概論 **gairon** general remarks, outline, introduction

4

木 月 日 火 礻 王 牛 方 攵 欠 心 戸 戈   10←

18 概観 **gaikan** overview, outline, survey

───────── 2 ─────────

1 一概 **ichigai** unconditionally, sweepingly
3 大概 **taigai** in general; mostly; probably; moderate, reasonable
11 梗概 **kōgai** outline, summary
18 類概念 **ruigainen** genus, generic concept

4a10.3

榊 榊　**sakaki** (a species of tree)

4a10.4

榎　**KA, enoki** nettle tree, hackberry

4a10.5

槫　**FU, kure** unbarked lumber

4a10.6

榾　**KOTSU, hoda, hota** chip/piece of wood, firewood

───────── 1 ─────────

4 榾木 **hodagi, hotagi** firewood; wood for growing mushrooms on
9 榾柮 **kottotsu** chip/piece of (fire)wood

4a10.7

榠　**hokuso** (type of tree)

4a10.8

榴　**RŌ** cage

4a10.9

槐　**KAI, enju** Japanese pagoda tree

4a10.10 / 1010

構 構　**KŌ, kama(eru)** build, set up; assume a stance/position
kama(e) posture, stance; structure, appearance; enclosure
kama(u) mind, care about; meddle in; look after

───────── 1 ─────────

0 お構いなしに **(o)kama(i nashi ni)** regardless of
4 構内 **kōnai** premises, grounds, precincts
構文 **kōbun** sentence construction, syntax
構手 **kama(i)te** one who looks after another; companion
5 構外 **kōgai** outside the premises
6 構成 **kōsei** composition, makeup
構成分子 **kōsei bunshi** components
構成員 **kōseiin** member
7 構図 **kōzu** compose, plan out, design
構材 **kōzai** construction materials
9 構造 **kōzō** structure, construction
構造上 **kōzōjō** structurally
構造主義 **kōzō shugi** structuralism
13 構想 **kōsō** conception, plan
16 構築 **kōchiku** construction

───────── 2 ─────────

4 心構 **kokorogama(e)** mental attitude/readiness
5 外構 **sotogama(e)** exterior, outward appearance
6 気構 **kigama(e)** readiness, anticipation
7 身構 **migama(e)** stand ready, be on guard
8 表構 **omotegama(e)** facade
門構 **mongama(e), kadogama(e)** style of a gate
9 待構 **ma(chi)kama(eru)** be ready and waiting
面構 **tsuragama(e)** expression, look
10 家構 **iegama(e)** structure/appearance of a house
11 虚構 **kyokō** fabricated, false, unfounded
12 結構 **kekkō** fine, good, alright; quite
16 機構 **kikō** mechanism, organization

───────── 3 ─────────

3 三段構 **sandangama(e)** thorough preparation with fall-back options should anything go wrong

4a10.11

榛　**SHIN, hashibami** hazel tree
han black alder

───────── 1 ─────────

4 榛木 **han(no)ki** black alder

4a10.12

榴　**RYŪ** pomegranate

───────── 1 ─────────

12 榴弾 **ryūdan** shell
榴散弾 **ryūsandan** shrapnel shell

──────── 2 ────────
4 手榴弾 **shuryūdan, teryūdan** hand grenade
5 石榴 **zakuro** pomegranate
9 柘榴 **zakuro** pomegranate
  柘榴石 **zakuroishi** garnet
  柘榴鼻 **zakuro-bana** swollen red nose,
     strawberry nose

4a10.13
榻
TŌ chair, sofa

4a10.14
榲
OTSU quince

──────── 1 ────────
10 榲桲 **otsubotsu** quince

4a10.15
樺
KA, kaba, kanba birch

──────── 1 ────────
4 樺太 **Karafuto** Sakhalin

──────── 2 ────────
5 白樺 **shirakaba, shirakanba** white birch

4a10.16 / 1425
模 橅
MO, BO copy, imitate

──────── 1 ────────
0 模する **mo(suru)** copy, imitate, model after
5 模写 **mosha** copy, replica
7 模形 **mokei** (scale) model; a mold
9 模造 **mozō** imitation
  模造者 **mozōsha** imitator
  模造品 **mozōhin** imitation
  模造紙 **mozōshi** vellum paper
  模型 **mokei** (scale) model; a mold
10 模倣 **mohō** copy, imitation
  模索 **mosaku** groping, trial and error
14 模様 **moyō** pattern, design; appearance;
     situation
  模様替 **moyōga(e)** remodeling, alterations
15 模糊 **moko** dim, faint, indistinct
  模範 **mohan** model, exemplar
  模範生 **mohansei** model student
  模範的 **mohanteki** exemplary
17 模擬 **mogi** imitation, mock, dry-run, dummy,
     simulated
  模擬店 **mogiten** refreshment booth, snack bar

模擬戦 **mogisen** war games, mock fight
模擬試験 **mogi shiken** trial examination

──────── 2 ────────
6 色模様 **iromoyō** color pattern; love scene
  地模様 **jimoyō** background pattern
7 花模様 **hanamoyō** floral pattern/design
8 空模様 **soramoyō** looks of the sky, weather
  雨模様 **amamoyō, amemoyō** signs of rain
9 荒模様 **a(re)moyō** storm-threatening sky
  相模 **Sagami** (ancient kuni, Kanagawa-ken)
  相模川 **Sagami-gawa** (river, Kanagawa-ken)
  染模様 **so(me)moyō** printed/dyed pattern
11 規模 **kibo** scale, scope
  雪模様 **yukimoyō** threatening to snow
13 裾模様 **suso moyō** skirt design
14 総模様 **sōmoyō** all-patterned (clothes)
15 縫模様 **nu(i)moyō** embroidered figures
16 薄模様 **usumoyō** pattern dyed light purple;
     short supply
  縞模様 **shimamoyō** striped pattern
18 織模様 **o(ri)moyō** woven design

──────── 3 ────────
3 大規模 **daikibo** large-scale
  小規模 **shōkibo** small-scale
4 天気模様 **tenki moyō** weather conditions
7 声帯模写 **seitai mosha** vocal mimicry
10 唐草模様 **karakusa moyō** arabesque design

4a10.17
榕
YŌ banyan tree

──────── 1 ────────
16 榕樹 **akō** banyan tree

4a10.18
橲
GAI, KAI alder

4a10.19
槓
KŌ, teko lever

──────── 1 ────────
7 槓杆 **kōkan** lever
11 槓桿 **kōkan** lever

4a10.20
槍
SŌ, yari spear, lance, javelin

──────── 1 ────────
5 槍玉 **yaridama (ni ageru)** make a victim of

4

木
月 10←
日
火
礻
王
牛
方
攵
欠
心
戸
戈

6 槍先 **yarisaki** spearhead, lance point
7 槍投 **yarina(ge)** javelin throwing
8 槍岳 **Yari(ga)take** (mountain, Nagano-ken)
9 槍持 **yarimo(chi)** spear bearer
10 槍衾 **yaribusuma** line of spears held ready to attack
11 槍術 **sōjutsu** spearsmanship
槍術家 **sōjutsuka** spearsman
18 槍騎兵 **sōkihei** lancer

―――― 2 ――――

6 竹槍 **takeyari** bamboo spear
15 横槍 **yokoyari** interruption

4
→10 木 月 日 火 ネ 王 牛 方 攵 心 戸 戈

4a10.21
槙
BEI (type of tree)

4a10.22
槁
KŌ wither, dry out

4a10.23
槥
SUI, **taruki** rafter

4a10.24
榜
BŌ oar; whip; nameplate

―――― 2 ――――

15 標榜 **hyōbō** profess, advocate

4a10.25 / 403
様 樣
YŌ way, manner; similar, like; condition -sama Mr., Mrs., Miss **sama** condition **zama** state, predicament, spectacle

―――― 1 ――――

2 様子 **yōsu** situation, aspect, appearance
3 様々 **samazama** various, varied
5 様付 **samazu(ke)** address (someone) with "-sama"
6 様式 **yōshiki** style, form
7 様体 **yōtai** situation, condition
9 様変 **samaga(wari)** change in the situation
様相 **yōsō** aspect, phase, condition
14 様態 **yōtai** form; situation, condition

―――― 2 ――――

1 一様 **ichiyō** uniformity, evenness; equality, impartiality

2 二様 **niyō** two ways
人様 **hitosama** other people
3 大様 **ōyō** magnanimous; lordly
上様 **uesama** (title of respect)
4 不様 **buzama** unshapely, unsightly, awkward, clumsy, uncouth
仏様 **hotoke-sama** a Buddha; deceased person
今様 **imayō** present/modern style
文様 **mon'yō** pattern
水様液 **suiyōeki** aqueous humor
王様 **ōsama** king
5 左様 **sayō** such, like that; yes, indeed; well, let me see
母様 **(o)kāsama** mother, mama
仕様 **shiyō** specifications; way, method
外様 **tozama** outside the group; non-Tokugawa daimyo
外様大名 **tozama daimyō** non-Tokugawa daimyo
6 多様 **tayō** diverse, varied
多様性 **tayōsei** diversity, variety
死様 **shi(ni)zama** manner of death
両様 **ryōyō** both ways, two ways
考様 **kanga(e)yō** way of thinking, viewpoint
此様 **ko(no) yō** such, this kind of, in this way
同様 **dōyō** the same (kind/way), similar
有様 **a(ri)sama, a(ri)yō** situation, circumstances, spectacle; the truth
虫様突起 **chūyō tokki** the (vermiform) appendix
虫様突起炎 **chūyō tokkien** appendicitis
7 佐様 **sayō** such; yes, indeed; well...
何様 **nanisama** who (polite); indeed, truly
見様 **miyō** way of looking, viewpoint
言様 **i(i)yō** way of saying
8 使様 **tsuka(i)yō** how to use
其様 **so(no) yō** that kind of, (in) that way
逆様 **sakasama** upside-down, reverse, backwards
姉様 **(o)nēsama, nēsama** elder sister
若様 **wakasama** young master
取様 **to(ri)yō** way of taking, interpretation
9 皆様 **minasama** all (of you), Ladies and Gentlemen!
神様 **kamisama** God; god
食様 **ta(be)yō** manner of eating
10 姫様 **himesama, hiisama** princess, nobleman's daughter
宮様 **miyasama** prince, princess
唐様 **karayō** Chinese style
紋様 **mon'yō** (textile) pattern
11 異様 **iyō** strange, outlandish
12 斯様 **kayō** such
無様 **buzama** misshapen, clumsy, awkward

然様 **sayō** so, thus, such
奥様 **okusama** (your) wife, married lady, ma'am
貴様 **kisama** you (deprecatory)
13 寝様 **nezama** one's sleeping posture
殿様 **tonosama** lord, prince
殿様芸 **tonosamagei** dilettantism, amateurism
続様 **tsuzu(ke)zama** consecutively, in a row
14 模様 **moyō** pattern, design; appearance; situation
模様替 **moyōga(e)** remodeling, alterations
様様 **samazama** various, varied
15 横様 **yokosama** sideways, laterally
憚様 **habaka(ri)sama** Thanks for your trouble.
16 嬢様 **(o)jōsama** (your) daughter; young lady
薄様 **usuyō** tracing paper

——————— 3 ———————
3 大宮様 **ōmiya-sama** the empress dowager
4 天道様 **tentōsama** the sun; heaven
内裏様 **(o)dairi-sama** emperor and empress dolls
5 生神様 **i(ki)gamisama** a living god
旦那様 **danna-sama** master; husband; gentleman
6 色模様 **iromoyō** color pattern; love scene
地模様 **jimoyō** background pattern
如何様 **ikayō** how, what kind   **ikasama** bogus, fraud, swindle; how; I see
如何様師 **ikasamashi** swindler, sharpie
7 花模様 **hanamoyō** floral pattern/design
8 空模様 **soramoyō** looks of the sky, weather
雨模様 **amamoyō, amemoyō** signs of rain
9 荒模様 **a(re)moyō** storm-threatening sky
染模様 **so(me)moyō** printed/dyed pattern
皆々様 **minaminasama** everyone, all of you
11 雪模様 **yukimoyō** threatening to snow
12 御嬢様 **ojōsama** young lady, (your) daughter
13 禁裏様 **kinrisama** the emperor
愁傷様 **(go)shūshō-sama** My heartfelt sympathy.
裾模様 **suso moyō** skirt design
14 種々様々 **shuju-samazama** all kinds of, diverse
総模様 **sōmoyō** all-patterned (clothes)
15 縫模様 **nu(i)moyō** embroidered figures
16 薄模様 **usumoyō** pattern dyed light purple; short supply
縞模様 **shimamoyō** striped pattern
18 織模様 **o(ri)moyō** woven design

——————— 4 ———————
4 天気模様 **tenki moyō** weather conditions
6 多種多様 **tashu-tayō** various, diversified
10 唐草模様 **karakusa moyō** arabesque design

12 尋常一様 **jinjō-ichiyō** common, mediocre
13 新品同様 **shinpin dōyō** like new
14 種種様様 **shuju-samazama** all kinds of, diverse

4a10.26

槎

SA, ikada raft
ki(ru) cut (slantwise)

槙 → 槇   **4a10.27**

4a10.27

槇 槇

TEN, SHIN twig
maki Chinese black pine

——————— 2 ———————
9 柏槙 **byakushin** juniper tree

4a10.28

樋 樋

TŌ, toi (wooden) pipe, gutter

——————— 2 ———————
10 軒樋 **nokidoi** gutter along the eaves

4a10.29

榧

HI, kaya Japanese nutmeg/plum-yew

4a10.30

槃

HAN tub

——————— 2 ———————
10 涅槃 **nehan** nirvana
涅槃会 **nehan'e** anniversary of Buddha's death
涅槃経 **Nehangyō** (a Buddhist sutra)

4a10.31

槊

SAKU, hoko halberd

榮 → 栄   **3n6.1**

業 →   **0a13.3**

4

10←
木
月
日
火
礻
王
牛
方
攵
欠
心
戸
戈

——— 11 ———

4a11.1

槝

TŌ (type of bird); vine

4a11.2

槲

KOKU, kashiwa oak

4a11.3

樅

SHŌ, momi fir

4a11.4

槻

KI, tsuki zelkova/keyaki tree

榮→椿 **4a9.13**

樓→楼 **4a9.10**

4a11.5

樗

CHO, ōchi Japanese bead tree

4a11.6

槫

TAN, SEN hearse

4a11.7 / 1644

槽

SŌ tub, tank, vat

——— 2 ———

4 水槽 **suisō** water tank/trough
8 油槽 **yusō** oil tank
  油槽車 **yusōsha** tank car
  油槽船 **yusōsen** oil tanker
10 浴槽 **yokusō** bathtub
12 湯槽 **yubune** bathtub
  歯槽 **shisō** tooth socket
  歯槽膿漏 **shisō nōrō** pyorrhea

——— 3 ———

7 沈澱槽 **chindensō** settling tank

4a11.8 / 923

標

HYŌ sign, mark
shirube guide, handbook
shirushi mark, sign, indication

——— 1 ———

4 標木 **hyōboku** signpost, grave post
5 標本 **hyōhon** specimen, sample
  標号 **hyōgō** symbol, emblem, sign
  標札 **hyōsatsu** nameplate, doorplate
  標示 **hyōji** indicate, mark
  標石 **hyōseki** boundary stone; milestone
6 標灯 **hyōtō** signal light, pilot lamp
8 標定 **hyōtei** orient, range (a gun)
  標的 **hyōteki** target, mark
9 標柱 **hyōchū** pylon, marker post
10 標高 **hyōkō** height above sea level
  標記 **hyōki** a mark, marking
11 標章 **hyōshō** ensign, emblem, badge, mark
12 標註 **hyōchū** annotations (in the top margin)
13 標準 **hyōjun** standard, norm, criterion
  標準化 **hyōjunka** standardization
  標準型 **hyōjungata** standard type
  標準時 **hyōjunji** standard/universal time
  標準語 **hyōjungo** the standard language
14 標榜 **hyōbō** profess, advocate
  標旗 **hyōki** marker flag
  標語 **hyōgo** slogan, motto
15 標縄 **shimenawa** paper-festooned sacred rope
18 標題 **hyōdai** title, heading, caption
19 標識 **hyōshiki** (land)mark, marking, sign, signal, tag

——— 2 ———

5 目標 **mokuhyō** target, goal, objective
6 灯標 **tōhyō** light buoy
7 里標 **rihyō** milestone
9 浮標 **fuhyō** buoy
  指標 **shihyō** index, indicator
  星標 **seihyō** asterisk
  音標文字 **onpyō moji** phonetic characters
  界標 **kaihyō** boundary mark
10 座標 **zahyō** (Cartesian) coordinates
11 商標 **shōhyō** trademark
  商標権 **shōhyōken** trademark rights
  道標 **dōhyō, michi shirube** road marker, milestone
13 墓標 **bohyō** grave marker/post
  路標 **rohyō** road sign
14 旗標 **hatajirushi** the design on a flag; banner, slogan
15 潮標 **chōhyō** tide mark
16 澪標 **miotsukushi** channel marker
19 警標 **keihyō** warning sign

——— 3 ———

4 水位標 **suiihyō** watermark
7 里程標 **riteihyō** milepost

10 航路標識 **kōro hyōshiki** navigation marker/
   beacon
14 境界標 **kyōkaihyō** landmark, boundary stone
15 横座標 **ōzahyō** abscissa, x-coordinate
16 縦座標 **tatezahyō** ordinate, y-coordinate

4a11.9

穋 **KYŪ** bend, droop, undulate

様 → 様 4a10.25

4a11.10

樟 **SHŌ, kusu, kusunoki** camphor tree

───── 1 ─────

11 樟脳 **shōnō** camphor
   樟脳油 **shōnōyu** camphor oil

4a11.11

樏 **RUI, kanjiki** snowshoes

4a11.12

橰 **KŌ** well sweep

4a11.13 / 781

横 横 **Ō** horizontal
        yoko side; horizontal direction

───── 1 ─────

0 横たえる **yoko(taeru)** lay (oneself) down,
   lie down; place across
   横たわる **yoko(tawaru)** lie down;
   be horizontal
4 横太 **yokobuto(ri)** pudgy, stocky
   横切 **yokogi(ru)** cross, traverse, intersect
   横文字 **yokomoji** European/horizontal writing
   横手 **yokote** at one side, at one's side
   横木 **yokogi** crosspiece, (cross)bar, (fence) rail
5 横付 **yokozu(ke)** bring alongside
   横好 **yokozu(ki)** enthusiastically/amateurishly
   fond of
   横穴 **yokoana** cave, tunnel
   横目 **yokome** side glance; crosscut (saw)
6 横死 **ōshi** violent death
   横合 **yokoa(i)** (from the) side

横向 **yokomu(ki)** facing sidewise
横行 **ōkō** walk sideways; swagger; be rampant
横行闊歩 **ōkō-kappo** swagger around
横糸 **yokoito** woof
7 横位 **ōi** transverse presentation (of a fetus)
横見 **yokomi** side glance
横町 **yokochō** side street, lane, alley
横車押 **yokoguruma (o) o(su)** be perverse,
   stubbornly persist (like trying to push a
   cart at right angles to its wheels)
8 横長 **yokonaga** oblong
横逆 **ōgyaku** perverse, obstinate, unreasonable
横波 **yokonami** side/transverse wave
横泳 **yokooyogi** side stroke
横取 **yokodo(ri)** usurp, steal away
横雨 **yokoame** a driving rain
9 横臥 **ōga** lie on one's side
横降 **yokobu(ri)** a driving rain
横風 **yokokaze** crosswind
横面 **yokotsura, yoko(t)tsura** side of the face
横柄 **ōhei** arrogant, haughty
10 横倒 **yokodao(shi)** topple sideways
横恋慕 **yokorenbo** illicit love
横這 **yokoba(i)** crawl sideways
横浜 **Yokohama** (city, Kanagawa-ken)
横流 **yokonaga(shi)** sell through illegal
   channels
横座標 **ōzahyō** abscissa, x-coordinate
横書 **yokoga(ki)** writing horizontally
横痃 **ōgen, yokone** chancre, bubo
11 横隊 **ōtai** rank, line
横道 **yokomichi** side street, crossroad; wrong
   way; side issue, digression; path of evil
横断 **ōdan** cross, traverse
横断歩道 **ōdan hodō** pedestrian crossing
横断者 **ōdansha** street-crossing pedestrians
横断面 **ōdanmen** cross section
横笛 **yokobue** flute, fife
横転 **ōten** lateral turn; barrel roll
12 横隔膜 **ōkakumaku** the diaphragm
横着 **ōchaku** dishonest; cunning; impudent;
   lazy; selfish
横揺 **yokoyu(re)** rolling (from side to side)
横幅 **yokohaba** width, breadth
横須賀 **Yokosuka** (city, Kanagawa-ken)
横棒 **yokobō** (horizontal) bar
横筋 **yokosuji** transversal; horizontal stripes
横軸 **yokojiku** horizontal shaft; x-axis
横雲 **yokogumo** bank of clouds
13 横溢 **ōitsu** be filled/overflowing with
横腹 **yokohara, yokobara, yoko(p)para** side,
   flank
横意地 **yoko-iji** perverseness, obstinacy
横睨 **yokonira(mi)** sharp sidelong glance/
   glare
横罫 **yokokei** horizontal lines

4

木 11←
月
日
火
礻
王
牛
方
攵
欠
心
戸
戈

14 横槍 **yokoyari** interruption
横様 **yokosama** sideways, laterally
横綴 **yokoto(ji)** oblong binding
横綱 **yokozuna** sumo champion
横奪 **ōdatsu** usurp, seize, steal
横領 **ōryō** misappropriate, embezzle, usurp
15 横隣 **yokodonari** nextdoor, to one's side
横暴 **ōbō** high-handed, tyrannical
横線 **ōsen** horizontal line
横震 **ōshin** horizontal (earthquake) shock
16 横縞 **yokojima** horizontal stripes
18 横顔 **yokogao** profile, side view, silhouette
20 横議 **ōgi** arguing persistently

─────── 2 ───────

9 専横 **sen'ō** arbitrary, high-handed, tyrannical
16 縦横 **jūō, tate-yoko** length and breadth, vertical and horizontal
縦横無尽 **jūō-mujin** all around, no end of

─────── 4 ───────

8 奇策縦横 **kisaku-jūō** clever planning

4a11.14

槻 **KAN** grove

4a11.15

槿 **KIN** rose of Sharon, althea; morning glory

─────── 2 ───────

4 木槿 **mukuge** rose of Sharon

4a11.16

樒 樒 **MITSU, shikimi** Japanese star anise

4a11.17

槫 **SŌ, su** nest
suku(u) dip, scoop up
ta(eru) come to an end

4a11.18 / 335

権 权 權 **KEN, GON** authority, power; a right

─────── 1 ───────

0 スト権 **sutoken** right to strike
2 権力 **kenryoku** power, authority, influence
権力主義 **kenryoku shugi** authoritarianism
権力争 **kenryoku araso(i)** struggle for supremacy/power

権力者 **kenryokusha** powerful person
権力家 **kenryokuka** powerful person
権力側 **kenryokugawa** the more powerful side
4 権化 **gonge** incarnation, embodiment
7 権助 **gonsuke** manservant
権利 **kenri** a right
権利金 **kenrikin** key money
8 権限 **kengen** authority, power, jurisdiction
権官 **kenkan** powerful post/official
権門 **kenmon** powerful person
9 権変 **kenpen** meeting the situation as it arises; trickery
権柄 **kenpei** authority, power, imperiousness
権威 **ken'i** authority; an authority
権威主義 **ken'i shugi** authoritarianism
権威的 **ken'iteki** authoritative
権威者 **ken'isha** an authority
権威筋 **ken'i suji** authoritative sources
10 権益 **ken'eki** (rights and) interests
権原 **kengen** title (to territory)
権家 **kenka** powerful/influential family
権能 **kennō** authority, power
11 権道 **kendō** expediency
権現 **gongen** incarnation (of Buddha), avatar (of Tokugawa Ieyasu)
12 権貴 **kenki** (person of) rank and influence
13 権勢 **kensei** power, influence
16 権衡 **kenkō** balance, equilibrium
権謀 **kenbō** strategem, scheme, ruse
権謀家 **kenbōka** schemer, maneuverer

─────── 2 ───────

2 人権 **jinken** human rights
人権蹂躙 **jinken jūrin** infringement of human rights
3 三権分立 **sanken bunritsu** separation of powers (legislative, executive, and judicial)
大権 **taiken** supreme power/authority
女権 **joken** women's rights
女権論者 **jokenronsha** feminist
4 夫権 **fuken** husband's rights
分権 **bunken** decentralization of authority
父権 **fuken** paternal rights
王権 **ōken** royal authority
5 民権 **minken** civil rights
失権 **shikken** forfeiture of rights, disenfranchisement
母権 **boken** maternal authority
主権 **shuken** sovereignty
主権在民 **shuken-zaimin** sovereignty resides with the people
主権者 **shukensha** sovereign, supreme ruler
6 全権 **zenken** full authority
全権大使 **zenken taishi** ambassador plenipotentiary

同権 **dōken** the same rights, equal rights
有権者 **yūkensha** qualified person, eligible voter
7 利権 **riken** rights, (vested) interests, (mining) concession
利権屋 **riken'ya** concession hunter, grafter
私権 **shiken** private rights
8 版権 **hanken** copyright
版権法 **hankenhō** copyright law
法権 **hōken** legal right
実権 **jikken** real power
官権 **kanken** government authority
国権 **kokken** sovereign right; national prestige
金権 **kinken** the power of money, plutocracy
9 専権 **senken** exclusive right; arbitrary power
神権 **shinken** divine right (of kings)
神権政治 **shinken seiji** theocracy
政権 **seiken** political power, administration
政権欲 **seiken'yoku** ambition for political power
威権 **iken** authority, power
10 特権 **tokken** privilege, prerogative; option (to buy)
特権者 **tokkensha** privileged person
教権 **kyōken** educational/ecclesiastical authority
11 商権 **shōken** commercial rights
執権 **shikken** regent
授権 **juken** authorize
強権 **kyōken** state power
12 復権 **fukken, fukuken** restoration of rights, reinstatement, rehabilitation
越権 **ekken** overstepping one's authority
訴権 **soken** standing/right to sue
集権 **shūken** centralization of power
13 債権 **saiken** credit, claims
債権者 **saikensha** creditor
棄権 **kiken** abstain from voting; renounce one's rights, withdraw
棄権者 **kikensha** nonvoter
15 質権 **shichiken** pledge
16 親権 **shinken** parental authority
親権者 **shinkensha** person in parental authority
18 職権 **shokken** one's official authority
19 覇権 **haken** hegemony, domination

————————— 3 —————————

4 支配権 **shihaiken** control, supremacy
公民権 **kōminken** civil rights, citizenship
戸主権 **koshuken** status/authority as family head
5 生存権 **seizonken** right to live
代理権 **dairiken** right of representation, power of attorney
市民権 **shiminken** citizenship, civil rights

用益権 **yōekiken** usufruct
司法権 **shihōken** judicial powers, jurisdiction
主導権 **shudōken** leadership
立法権 **rippōken** legislative power
6 至上権 **shijōken** supremacy, sovereignty
先議権 **sengiken** right to prior consideration
地役権 **chiekiken** easement, (real) servitude
行政権 **gyōseiken** administrative/executive authority
自主権 **jishuken** autonomy
自治権 **jichiken** autonomy
自衛権 **jieiken** right of self-defense
7 決定権 **ketteiken** (right of) decision
決議権 **ketsugiken** voting right, vote
投票権 **tōhyōken** right to vote, suffrage
8 使用権 **shiyōken** right to use
制空権 **seikūken** mastery of the air, air superiority
制海権 **seikaiken** control of the seas, naval superiority
法王権 **hōōken** the papacy
抵当権 **teitōken** mortgage, hypothec
拒否権 **kyohiken** (right of) veto
参政権 **sanseiken** suffrage, franchise
居住権 **kyojūken** right of residence
所有権 **shoyūken** ownership
9 発言権 **hatsugenken** right to speak, a voice
専有権 **sen'yūken** exclusive right, monopoly
専売権 **senbaiken** monopoly
海上権 **kaijōken** sea power
指導権 **shidōken** leadership
独立権 **dokuritsuken** autonomy
相続権 **sōzokuken** (right of) inheritance
10 既得権 **kitokuken** vested rights/interests
家督権 **katoku (no) ken** birthright, inheritance
特許権 **tokkyoken** patent
租借権 **soshakuken** lease, leasehold
11 商標権 **shōhyōken** trademark rights
執行権 **shikkōken** executive authority
控訴権 **kōsoken** right of appeal
採油権 **saiyuken** oil concession, drilling rights
著作権 **chosakuken** copyright
経営権 **keieiken** right of management
12 裁判権 **saibanken** jurisdiction
統治権 **tōchiken** sovereignty
統帥権 **tōsuiken** prerogative of supreme command
13 嫌煙権 **ken'enken** non-smokers' rights
試掘権 **shikutsuken** mining claim
14 選手権 **senshuken** championship title
選択権 **sentakuken** right of choice, option
選挙権 **senkyoken** right to vote, franchise, suffrage
漁業権 **gyogyōken** fishing rights
15 黙秘権 **mokuhiken** the right to remain silent

17 優先権 **yūsenken** (right of) priority
18 翻訳権 **hon'yakuken** translation rights
19 警察権 **keisatsuken** police power
20 議決権 **giketsuken** voting rights

―――――― 4 ――――――

4 中央集権 **chūō shūken** centralization of
government
5 永小作権 **eikosakuken** perpetual (land) lease
8 治外法権 **chigaihōken** extraterritoriality
10 被選挙権 **hisenkyoken** eligibility for election

4a11.19

榿

SEKI (a type of maple)

樞→枢 **4a4.22**

4a11.20

槧

ZAN, SEN printed book

4a11.21

樊

HAN cage; fence, pen, enclosure

樂→楽 **4a9.29**

―――――― 12 ――――――

4a12.1 / 528

機

KI machine; airplane; opportunity,
occasion
hata loom

―――――― 1 ――――――

3 機才 **kisai** quick-wittedness
機上 **kijō** aboard the airplane
4 機内 **kinai** inside the airplane
5 機巧 **kikō** contrivance; cleverness
機甲 **kikō** armored
6 機会 **kikai** opportunity, occasion, chance
機会均等 **kikai kintō** equal opportunity
機先制 **kisen (o) sei(suru)** forestall, beat
(someone) to it
機帆船 **kihansen** motor-powered sailing
vessel
7 機体 **kitai** fuselage
機序 **kijo** mechanism (in biology)

機尾 **kibi** tail of an airplane
8 機長 **kichō** (airplane) captain
機知 **kichi** quick wit, resourcefulness
機宜 **kigi** opportunity, occasion
9 機変 **kihen** adaptation to circumstances
機首 **kishu** nose of an airplane
機屋 **hataya** weaver
10 機根 **kikon** talent, gift
機能 **kinō** a function
機能的 **kinōteki** functional
機敏 **kibin** astute, shrewd, quick
11 機動 **kidō** mechanized, mobile
機動力 **kidōryoku** mobility, maneuverability
機動化 **kidōka** mechanization
機動隊 **kidōtai** riot squad
機動演習 **kidō enshū** maneuvers
機運 **kiun** opportunity, chance, time
機密 **kimitsu** secret, secrecy
機械 **kikai** machine
機械工 **kikaikō** mechanic, machinist
機械工学 **kikai kōgaku** mechanical engineering
機械工業 **kikai kōgyō** the machine industry
機械化 **kikaika** mechanization, mechanized
機械文明 **kikai bunmei** machine civilization
機械仕掛 **kikai-jika(ke)** mechanism
機械体操 **kikai taisō** gymnastics using
equipment
機械学 **kikaigaku** mechanics
機械油 **kikai abura** machine/lubricating oil
機械的 **kikaiteki** mechanical
機械屋 **kikaiya** machinist
機械製 **kikaisei** machine-made
機械編 **kikaia(mi)** machine-knit
機略 **kiryaku** resourcefulness, expedients
機転 **kiten** quick wit
12 機智 **kichi** quick wit, resourcefulness
機軸 **kijiku** axis, axle; plan, contrivance
13 機業 **kigyō** the textile industry
機業界 **kigyōkai** the textile world
機業家 **kigyōka** textile manufacturer, weaver
機嫌 **kigen** mood, humor, temper
機嫌取 **kigento(ri)** pleasing another's humor;
flatterer
機微 **kibi** inner workings, secrets, subtleties
機雷 **kirai** (land/sea) mine
機雷原 **kiraigen** minefield
14 機構 **kikō** mechanism, organization
機種 **kishu** model, type of machine
機銃 **kijū** machine gun
機銃掃射 **kijū sōsha** machine-gunning
機関 **kikan** engine; machinery, organ(ization)
機関士 **kikanshi** (locomotive) engineer
機関手 **kikanshu** (locomotive) engineer
機関車 **kikansha** locomotive
機関室 **kikanshitsu** machine/engine room

機関庫 **kikanko** locomotive shed, roundhouse
機関紙 **kikanshi** organization's newspaper
機関誌 **kikanshi** organization's publication
機関銃 **kikanjū** machine gun
機関雑誌 **kikan zasshi** organization's
　　publication
15 機器 **kiki** machinery (and tools), equipment
機縁 **kien** opportunity
機鋒 **kihō** point, brunt (of an attack)
17 機翼 **kiyoku** airplane wing
18 機織 **hatao(ri)** weaving, weaver, grasshopper
機織虫 **hatao(ri)mushi** grasshopper

───────── 2 ─────────

3 万機 **bankl** state affairs
上機嫌 **jōkigen** good humor, high spirits
小機転 **kogiten** quick-witted
4 不機嫌 **fukigen** ill humor, sullenness
天機 **tenki** profound secret; the emperor's
　　health
心機 **shinki** mind, mental attitude
心機一転 **shinki-itten** change of attitude
5 好機 **kōki** good opportunity, the right moment
好機会 **kōkikai** good opportunity, the right
　　moment
6 危機 **kiki** crisis
危機一髪 **kiki-ippatsu** imminent/hairbreadth
　　danger
有機 **yūki** organic
有機化学 **yūki kagaku** organic chemistry
有機体 **yūkitai** organism
有機的 **yūkiteki** organic
有機物 **yūkibutsu** organic matter, organism
7 汽機室 **kikishitsu** boiler/engine room
投機 **tōki** speculation
投機心 **tōkishin** spirit of speculation
投機的 **tōkiteki** speculative, risky
投機家 **tōkika** speculator
投機熱 **tōkinetsu** speculation fever
8 杼機 **choki** shuttle and reed
枢機 **sūki** important state affairs
枢機卿 **sūkikei** (Catholic) cardinal
9 重機関銃 **jūkikanjū** heavy machine gun
降機 **kōki** deplane
契機 **keiki** opportunity, chance
軍機 **gunki** military secret
造機 **zōki** engine construction
待機 **taiki** wait for an opportunity, watch and
　　wait, stand by
春機発動期 **shunki hatsudōki** puberty
10 時機 **jiki** opportunity, time, occasion
11 動機 **dōki** motive
商機 **shōki** business opportunity
舵機 **daki** steering gear, rudder
転機 **tenki** turning point
12 無機 **muki** inorganic

無機物 **mukibutsu** inorganic substance,
　　minerals
軽機 **keiki** light machine gun
軽機関銃 **keikikanjū** light machine gun
13 農機具 **nōkigu** farm equipment
愛機 **aiki** one's own airplane/camera/machine
戦機 **senki** the time to strike; military secret
新機軸 **shinkijiku** new departure; novel idea
電機 **denki** electrical machinery
電機子 **denkishi** armature
14 僚機 **ryōki** consort plane
15 熱機関 **netsukikan** heat engine
敵機 **tekki** enemy plane
18 臨機 **rinki** expedient, as the situation requires
臨機応変 **rinki-ōhen** adaptation to circum-
　　stances
織機 **shokki** loom

───────── 3 ─────────

1 一杯機嫌 **ippai kigen** slight intoxication
3 工作機械 **kōsaku kikai** machine tools
4 内燃機関 **nainen kikan** internal-combustion
　　engine
刈取機 **ka(ri)to(ri)ki** reaper, harvester
切断機 **setsudanki** cutter, cutting machine
双発機 **sōhatsuki** twin-engine airplane
双胴機 **sōdōki** twin-fuselage airplane
水圧機 **suiatsuki** hydraulic press
日航機 **Nikkōki** JAL (Japan Air Lines) plane
5 写真機 **shashinki** camera
圧延機 **atsuenki** rolling machine/mill
圧搾機 **assakuki** a press, compressor
圧縮機 **asshukuki** compressor
氷削機 **hyōsakuki** ice-shaving machine
好時機 **kōjiki** opportune moment, the right
　　time
芝刈機 **shibaka(ri)ki** lawn mower
6 多発機 **tahatsuki** multi-engine airplane
多座機 **tazaki** multi-seated airplane
印刷機 **insatsuki** printing press
交通機関 **kōtsū kikan** transportation
　　facilities
自販機 **jihanki** vending machine (short for
　　自動販売機)
7 決議機関 **ketsugi kikan** voting body; party
　　organization, caucus
折畳機 **o(ri)tata(mi)ki** (page-)folding
　　machine
投射機 **tōshaki** projector
投影機 **tōeiki** projector
8 制動機 **seidōki** brake
受信機 **jushinki** (radio) receiver
受像機 **juzōki** television set
追撃機 **tsuigekiki** pursuit/chase plane
送信機 **sōshinki** transmitter
送風機 **sōfūki** blower, ventilator, fan

4

木 12←
月
日
火
礻
王
牛
方
攵
欠
心
戸
戈

泡立機 **awada(te)ki** eggbeater
拡声機 **kakuseiki** loudspeaker
杭打機 **kuiu(chi)ki** pile driver
昇降機 **shōkōki** elevator
金融機関 **kin'yū kikan** financial institutions
9 飛行機 **hikōki** airplane
飛行機雲 **hikōkigumo** vapor trail, contrail
発電機 **hatsudenki** generator, dynamo
巻揚機 **ma(ki)a(ge)ki** hoist, winch, windlass
専用機 **sen'yōki** personal airplane
信号機 **shingōki** signal
削氷機 **sakuhyōki** ice-shaving machine
軍用機 **gun'yōki** warplane
洗濯機 **sentakki, sentakuki** washing machine
海軍機 **kaigunki** navy plane
宣伝機関 **senden kikan** propaganda organ
映写機 **eishaki** projector
砕岩機 **saiganki** rock crusher
砕鉱機 **saikōki** ore crusher
計算機 **keisanki** computer
10 耕耘機 **kōunki** cultivator, tiller
陸上機 **rikujōki** land-based airplane
浚渫機 **shunsetsuki** dredger
消煙機 **shōenki** smoke consumer
起重機 **kijūki** crane, derrick
起動機 **kidōki** starter, starting motor
起電機 **kidenki** electric motor
娯楽機関 **goraku kikan** recreational facilities
穿孔機 **senkōki** perforator, drill, (key)punch
特別機 **tokubetsuki** special airplane
特務機関 **tokumu kikan** military intelligence organization
旅客機 **ryokakki** passenger plane
扇風機 **senpūki** (electric) fan
航空機 **kōkūki** aircraft, airplane
11 偵察機 **teisatsuki** reconnaissance/spotter plane
剪裁機 **sensaiki** shearing machine
混合機 **kongōki** mixer
掃除機 **sōjiki** vacuum cleaner
脱水機 **dassuiki** dehydrator, dryer
脱穀機 **dakkokuki** threshing machine
乾燥機 **kansōki** dryer; desiccator
船外機 **sengaiki** outboard motor
転轍機 **tentetsuki** railroad switch
12 屠蘇機嫌 **toso kigen** drunk with New Year's saké
植字機 **shokujiki** typesetting machine
焼玉機関 **ya(ki)dama kikan** hot-bulb/semidiesel engine
開閉機 **kaiheiki** circuit breaker
13 遮断機 **shadanki** railroad-crossing gate
蓄音機 **chikuonki** gramophone
戦闘機 **sentōki** fighter (plane)
雷撃機 **raigekiki** torpedo-carrying plane
電信機 **denshinki** a telegraph
電動機 **dendōki** electric motor
電算機 **densanki** computer
14 端末機 **tanmatsuki** (computer) terminal
製氷機 **seihyōki** ice machine
製粉機 **seifunki** flour mill/grinder
複座機 **fukuzaki** two-seater airplane
15 輪転機 **rintenki** rotary press
16 輸送機 **yusōki** transport plane
録音機 **rokuonki** recorder
17 謄写機 **tōshaki** mimeograph machine, copier
聴音機 **chōonki** sound detector
18 鎔接機 **yōsetsuki** welding machine
19 爆撃機 **bakugekiki** bomber
警報機 **keihōki** warning device, alarm
21 艦載機 **kansaiki** carrier-based plane
23 鑽孔機 **sankōki** boring machine
28 鑿岩機 **sakuganki** rock drill

─── 4 ───
8 送受信機 **sōjushinki** transceiver
9 重爆撃機 **jūbakugekiki** heavy bomber

─── 5 ───
4 水上飛行機 **suijō hikōki** hydroplane, seaplane
6 自動連結機 **jidō renketsuki** automatic coupler
自動販売機 **jidō hanbaiki** vending machine
10 真空掃除機 **shinkū sōjiki** vacuum cleaner

4a12.2
樸
BOKU unprocessed (lumber), as is

─── 1 ───
8 樸直 **bokuchoku** simple and honest

─── 2 ───
10 素樸 **soboku** simple, artless, ingenuous
15 質樸 **shitsuboku** simple, unsophisticated

─── 3 ───
3 大相樸 **ōzumō** grand sumo tournament; exciting match

4a12.3 / 1144
樹
JU, ki tree, bush
ta(teru) set up, establish

─── 1 ───
4 樹木 **jumoku** trees
5 樹皮 **juhi** (tree) bark
樹氷 **juhyō** frost/ice on trees
樹立 **juritsu** establish, found
7 樹身 **jushin** (tree) trunk
8 樹林 **jurin** forest
9 樹海 **jukai** a sea of trees/foliage
10 樹陰 **juin, kokage** shade of a tree

樹脂 **jushi** resin
11 樹液 **jueki** sap
12 樹間 **jukan** in the trees
13 樹幹 **jukan** (tree) trunk
17 樹齢 **jurei** age of a tree

——————— 2 ———————
1 一樹 **ichiju** one tree, the same tree
一樹蔭 **ichiju (no) kage** preordained fate
3 大樹 **taiju** large tree
5 幼樹 **yōju** young tree
6 老樹 **rōju** old tree
7 花樹 **kaju** flowering tree
8 果樹 **kaju** fruit tree
果樹園 **kajuen** orchard
12 植樹 **shokuju** tree planting
植樹祭 **shokujusai** Arbor Day
13 矮樹 **waiju** dwarf tree
14 榕樹 **akō** banyan tree
緑樹 **ryokuju** green-leaved tree, greenery
15 養樹園 **yōjuen** tree nursery, arboretum

——————— 3 ———————
4 月桂樹 **gekkeiju** laurel/bay tree
5 広葉樹 **kōyōju** broadleaf tree
6 合成樹脂 **gōsei jushi** synthetic resin, plastic
7 沈香樹 **chinkōju** aloe
系統樹 **keitōju** tree diagram showing
evolutionary descent
10 針葉樹 **shin'yōju** needle-leaf tree, conifer
11 菩提樹 **bodaiju** bo tree; linden tree; lime tree
常緑樹 **jōryokuju** an evergreen (tree)
12 街路樹 **gairoju** trees along a street
落葉樹 **rakuyōju** deciduous tree

——————— 4 ———————
10 娑羅双樹 **shara sōju** sal tree

4a12.4

橄
KAN, kanari Java almond tree; olive
tree

——————— 1 ———————
26 橄欖 **kanran** Java almond tree; olive tree
橄欖油 **kanran'yu** olive oil

概 → 概 4a10.2

4a12.5

樫
kashi oak

——————— 2 ———————
7 赤樫 **akagashi** red/evergreen oak

4a12.6

樵
SHŌ, kikori woodcutting; woodcutter

——————— 1 ———————
4 樵夫 **shōfu** woodcutter

4a12.7

橅
BO, MO, buna beech

4a12.8 / 597

橋
KYŌ, hashi bridge

——————— 1 ———————
5 橋台 **hashidai, kyōdai** bridge abutment
7 橋杙 **hashigui** bridge pile/pillar
8 橋杭 **hashigui** bridge pile/pillar
9 橋架 **kyōka** bridge girder
10 橋桁 **hashigeta** bridge girder
11 橋梁 **kyōryō** bridge
橋脚 **kyōkyaku** bridge pier
12 橋普請 **hashi-bushin** bridge construction
橋渡 **hashiwata(shi)** bridge building;
mediation
14 橋銭 **hashisen** bridge toll
16 橋頭 **kyōtō** vicinity of a bridge
橋頭堡 **kyōtōhō** bridgehead, beachhead

——————— 2 ———————
2 八橋 **ya(tsu)hashi** zigzag bridge
4 反橋 **so(ri)hashi, so(ri)bashi** arched bridge
5 石橋 **ishibashi, sekkyō** stone bridge
6 仮橋 **karibashi** temporary bridge
8 板橋 **itabashi** wooden bridge; gangplank
9 前橋 **Maebashi** (city, Gunma-ken)
浮橋 **u(ki)hashi** floating/pontoon bridge
架橋 **kakyō** bridge building
神橋 **shinkyō** sacred bridge
10 陸橋 **rikkyō** bridge over land, overpass,
viaduct
桟橋 **sanbashi** wharf, jetty
sankyō wharf; bridge
11 掛橋 **ka(ke)hashi** (suspension) bridge
船橋 **funabashi, senkyō** pontoon bridge
Funabashi (city, Chiba-ken)
釣橋 **tsu(ri)bashi** suspension bridge
12 渡橋式 **tokyōshiki** bridge-opening ceremony
開橋 **kaikyō** opening a new bridge
13 豊橋 **Toyohashi** (city, Aichi-ken)
跳橋 **ha(ne)bashi** drawbridge
鉄橋 **tekkyō** steel/railroad bridge
20 懸橋 **ka(ke)hashi** suspension bridge; viaduct

21 艦橋 **kankyō** the bridge (of a warship)

――――――― 3 ―――――――

1 一本橋 **ipponbashi** log bridge
2 二重橋 **Nijūbashi** the Double Bridge (at the Imperial Palace)
3 丸木橋 **marukibashi** log bridge
5 可動橋 **kadōkyō** movable bridge
8 歩道橋 **hodōkyō** pedestrian overpass
9 浮桟橋 **u(ki)sanbashi** floating pier
11 眼鏡橋 **meganebashi** arch bridge
12 開閉橋 **kaiheikyō** drawbridge
13 跳開橋 **chōkaikyō** drawbridge
　 跨線橋 **kosenkyō** bridge over railroad tracks

4a12.9

橦 **TŌ** (type of tree)
SHŌ poke, hit

4a12.10

橙 **TŌ, daidai** bitter orange

――――――― 1 ―――――――

6 橙色 **daidai-iro** orange (color)

4a12.11

橘 **KITSU** citrus fruits
tachibana mandarin orange

――――――― 2 ―――――――

9 柑橘類 **kankitsurui** citrus fruits

4a12.12

橲 **SAI, fushi** knot (in wood)

4a12.13

楢 **masa** straight grain

4a12.14

橇 **KYŌ, ZEI, sori** sled, sleigh, sledge, skid

――――――― 1 ―――――――

4 橇犬 **soriinu** sled dog

――――――― 2 ―――――――

10 馬橇 **basori** horse-drawn sleigh

横→横 4a11.13

4a12.15

橈 **DŌ** bend
JŌ, kai oar

4a12.16

櫁 **tsusa** (used in proper names)

――――――― 1 ―――――――

10 櫁原 **Tsusahara** (place name, Fukushima-ken)

4a12.17

檎 **KIN, GO** apple

――――――― 2 ―――――――

8 林檎 **ringo** apple
　 林檎酒 **ringoshu** hard cider

――――――― 3 ―――――――

12 焼林檎 **ya(ki)ringo** baked apple

4a12.18

橡 **SHŌ, tochi** horse chestnut tree

樽→樽 4a12.19

4a12.19

樽 樽 墫 **SON, taru** barrel, cask, keg, tub

――――――― 1 ―――――――

9 樽柿 **tarugaki** persimmons sweetened in a saké cask
13 樽詰 **taruzu(me)** barreled, in casks

――――――― 2 ―――――――

3 小樽 **kodaru** keg　**Otaru** (city, Hokkaidō)
4 水樽 **mizudaru** water cask
10 酒樽 **sakadaru** wine cask

4a12.20

檠 **KEI** straighten (a bow); lamp (stand)

榮 → 蕊 **3k12.14**

4a13.1

橄
    GEKI official circular; manifesto

──────── 1 ────────
4 橄文 **gekibun** manifesto

4a13.2

橂
    KAI, **kashiwa** oak

4a13.3

檉
    TEI tamarisk

──────── 1 ────────
9 檉柳 **teiryū, gyoryū** tamarisk

櫟 → 櫟 **4a15.3**

4a13.4

檣 艢
    SHŌ, **hobashira** mast

──────── 1 ────────
16 檣頭 **shōtō** masthead
──────── 2 ────────
6 帆檣 **hanshō** mast

4a13.5

橿
    KYŌ, **kashi** oak

櫛 → 櫛 **4a15.5**

4a13.6

檍
    OKU ilex, holm oak, birdlime tree

4a13.7

檬
    MŌ lemon tree

──────── 2 ────────
18 檸檬 **neimō** lemon tree

4a13.8

檜 桧
    KAI, **hinoki, hi** Japanese cypress, white cedar

──────── 1 ────────
5 檜皮 **hiwada** cypress bark
  檜皮葺 **hiwadabu(ki)** cypess-bark roofing
12 檜葉 **hiba** white-cedar leaf; hiba arborvitae (a shrub)
15 檜舞台 **hinoki butai** cypress-floored stage; high-class stage, limelight

檢 → 検 **4a8.28**

4a13.9

檐
    EN, **noki** eaves

4a13.10

檗 蘗
    HAKU, **kihada** Amur/Chinese cork tree

4a13.11

檀 檀
    DAN, TAN sandalwood, rosewood, chinaberry tree **mayumi** spindle tree

──────── 1 ────────
6 檀那寺 **dannadera** one's family's temple
10 檀徒 **danto** temple supporter
  檀家 **danka** family supporting a temple
──────── 2 ────────
5 白檀 **byakudan** sandalwood
10 栴檀 **sendan** Japanese bead tree
11 黒檀 **kokutan** ebony, blackwood

──────── 14 ────────

4a14.1

櫂
    TŌ, **kai** oar

檻 → 檻 **4a11.16**

4a14.2

檸　**NEI, DŌ** lemon tree

――― 1 ―――
17 檸檬 **neimō** lemon tree

4a14.3

檳 梹　**BIN, HIN** betel palm tree

――― 1 ―――
13 檳榔 **binrō** betel palm tree
　　檳榔子 **binrōji** betel palm tree

4a14.4

檮 梼　**TŌ** stump; foolish, ignorant

4a14.5

櫃　**KI, hitsu** chest, coffer

――― 2 ―――
6 米櫃 **komebitsu** rice bin; breadwinner; means of livelihood
10 唐櫃 **karabitsu** six-legged Chinese-style chest
12 飯櫃 **meshibitsu** (wooden) container for boiled rice

4a14.6

鬆　**SHŌ** loose, disheveled
　　su pore, cavity (in overboiled diakon)

4a14.7

鞣　**JŪ, name(su)** tan (hides)
　　nameshi, nameshigawa leather

――― 1 ―――
5 鞣皮 **jūhi, name(shi)gawa** leather
　　鞣皮業 **jūhigyō** tannery
9 鞣屋 **name(shi)ya** tanner(y)

――― 15 ―――

4a15.1

櫞　**EN** (a type of citron)

――― 2 ―――
9 枸櫞 **kuen** (a type of citron)
　　枸櫞酸 **kuensan** citric acid

4a15.2

櫓　**RO** oar; tower
　　yagura tower, turret; scaffolding

――― 3 ―――
4 火見櫓 **hi(no)mi yagura** fire-lookout tower
8 物見櫓 **monomi yagura** watchtower

4a15.3

櫟 檪　**REKI, kunugi** (a type of oak)

4a15.4

檻　**KAN, ori** cage, pen; cell, jail

――― 2 ―――
7 折檻 **sekkan** chastise, punish; whipping, spanking

4a15.5

櫛 櫛　**SHITSU, kushi** comb

――― 1 ―――
5 櫛比 **shippi** stand close together in a long row
7 櫛形 **kushigata** comb-like; round-top, arched (window)

4a15.6

櫑　**RAI** decorated wine cask; decorated sword hilt

4a15.7

櫝　**TOKU** chest, coffer; coffin

4a15.8

櫚　**RO** Chinese quince

――― 2 ―――
12 棕櫚 **shuro** hemp plant

4a15.9

麓　**ROKU, fumoto** foot of a mountain

――― 2 ―――
3 山麓 **sanroku** the foot of a mountain

攀 → 3c15.5

譽 → 5a15.2

―――――― 16 ――――――

4a16.1

橁   SHO oak

4a16.2

櫨 枦 枦   **haze** sumac, wax tree
masugata square wooden capital (at the top of a pillar)

―――― 1 ――――

7 櫨谷 **Kataragai** (place name, Shimane-ken)

―――― 2 ――――

11 黄櫨 **haze** sumac, wax tree

4a16.3

櫪   REKI manger, fodder trough; horse barn

4a16.4 / 1202

欄 欄   **RAN** (newspaper) column, blank, space (on a form); railing **obashima** handrail

―――― 1 ――――

3 欄干 **rankan** railing, banister
5 欄外 **rangai** margin (of a page)
12 欄間 **ranma** transom

―――― 2 ――――

3 上欄 **jōran** top/preceding column
8 空欄 **kūran** blank column
10 高欄 **kōran** balustrade, bannister, handrail

―――― 3 ――――

4 文芸欄 **bungeiran** literary column
5 広告欄 **kōkokuran** advertising columns, want ads
7 投書欄 **tōshoran** readers' column
投稿欄 **tōkōran** readers' column
9 通信欄 **tsūshinran** correspondence column
10 家庭欄 **kateiran** homemaker's column
書評欄 **shohyōran** book review column/ section
11 運動欄 **undōran** the sports page/columns
経済欄 **keizairan** financial section/columns

―――― 4 ――――

6 死亡者欄 **shibōsharan** obituary column

―――― 5 ――――

3 三行広告欄 **sangyō kōkokuran** classified ads

―――――― 17 ――――――

櫻 → 桜 4a6.15

4a17.1

欅   KYO, keyaki zelkova/keyaki tree

4a17.2

櫺   REI, renji latticework

―――― 1 ――――

2 櫺子 **renji** latticework

權 → 権 4a11.18

欄 → 欄 4a16.4

―――――― 19 ――――――

4a19.1

欒   **RAN** soapberry tree; shaddock; ancon, corbel; pleasant gathering

―――― 2 ――――

6 団欒 **danran** happy/family circle

―――― 4 ――――

1 一家団欒 **ikka danran** happy family circle, happy home

欄 → 欗 4a21.1

4a19.2

譟   SŌ hurry; high

―――――― 21 ――――――

4a21.1

欛 欄   HA, tsuka hilt, handle

4   木 月 日 火 礻 王 牛 方 欠 心 戸 戈 21←

---------- 22 ----------

4a22.1

櫃

RAN Java almond tree

---------- 2 ----------

16 橄欖 **kanran** Java almond tree; olive tree
橄欖油 **kanran'yu** olive oil

---------- 24 ----------

4a24.1

櫸

tsuki keyaki, zelkova tree

---------- 25 ----------

4a25.1

鬱 欝 欎

UTSU melancholy, gloom, depression; accumulate, become congested, be pent up; dense growth **fusa(gu)** feel depressed, mope

---------- 1 ----------

3 鬱々 **utsuutsu** gloomily, cheerlessly
4 鬱込 **fusa(gi)ko(mu)** be depressed, feel low, mope

6 鬱気 **ukki** gloom, melancholy
鬱血 **ukketsu** blood congestion, engorgement
8 鬱金色 **ukon-iro** saffron color
10 鬱陶 **uttō(shii)** gloomy, depressing
13 鬱蒼 **ussō** dense, thick, luxuriant
15 鬱憤 **uppun** resentment, rancor, grudge
16 鬱積 **usseki** be pent up, be congested

---------- 2 ----------

6 気鬱 **kiutsu** gloom, melancholy, depression
気鬱症 **kiutsushō** melancholia, depression
7 沈鬱 **chin'utsu** melancholy, gloomy, depressed
9 幽鬱 **yūutsu** melancholy, depression
10 陰鬱 **in'utsu** gloomy, dismal, melancholy
12 湮鬱 **in'utsu** gloomy, melancholy
13 暗鬱 **an'utsu** gloomy, melancholy
15 憂鬱 **yūutsu** melancholy, dejection, gloom
憂鬱症 **yūutsushō** melancholia, hypochondria
憂鬱質 **yūutsushitsu** prone to depression
20 躁鬱病 **sōutsubyō** manic-depressive psychosis
29 鬱鬱 **utsuutsu** gloomily, cheerlessly

---------- 26 ----------

爨 → 4d26.1

---------- 月 4b ----------

月	肉	肋	肌	有	肚	肝	肘	肛	肓	朋	肪	肶
0.1	2a4.20	2.1	2.2	2.3	3.1	3.2	3.3	3.4	2j5.3	4.1	4.2	4.3
胁	肬	肥	服	肢	股	肱	青	肯	宥	肴	胃	胛
4.4	5i4.1	4.5	4.6	4.7	4.8	4.9	4.10	4.11	3m6.1	4.12	4c5.6	5.1
胖	胐	胙	胞	胆	胝	胚	肺	胎	俞	脉	胡	胄
5.2	5.3	5.4	5.5	5.6	5.7	5.8	5.9	5.10	5.11	4b6.8	5.12	2r7.2
胥	胥	背	胤	胱	胯	脇	脆	胼	朕	脂	脈	胸
5.13	5.14	5.15	5.16	6.1	6.2	6.3	6.4	6.5	6.6	6.7	6.8	6.9
胴	朗	朔	脊	骨	能	脯	豚	脮	脚	腆	脛	脛
6.10	6.11	6.12	6.13	6.14	6.15	7.1	7.2	4b6.11	7.3	7.4	7.5	7.6
脳	脱	脈	朗	脣	脹	脾	腓	勝	腊	腕	腔	臍
7.7	7.8	4b6.8	4b6.11	3d7.12	8.1	8.2	8.3	8.4	8.5	8.6	8.7	4b14.2
腋	腑	腱	腿	期	朝	萁	殼	腫	腴	腰	腹	腮
8.8	8.9	8.10	4b9.10	8.11	8.12	4b8.11	8.13	9.1	9.2	9.3	9.4	9.5
腺	腥	腸	腟	腦	腿	腎	骭	腠	膊	脐	膃	膈
9.6	9.7	9.8	9.9	4b7.7	9.10	9.11	9.12	10.1	10.2	10.3	10.4	10.5
膜	膀	膂	静	骰	趙	膚	滕	膠	膝	腸	膵	膕
10.6	10.7	10.8	10.9	10.10	10.11	11.1	11.2	11.3	11.4	4b9.8	11.5	11.6
骶	膣	膨	膳	膰	膝	膸	膟	膩	骼	骸	鞘	膽
11.7	4b9.9	12.1	12.2	12.3	12.4	4b15.3	4b14.3	12.5	12.6	12.7	12.8	13.1

（左余白・縦組み）
4
→22 木 月 月 日 火 衤 王 牛 方 攵 攵 心 尸 戈

膿	臆	膽	朦	臉	膾	臀	臂	臑	臍	髓	髀	鵬
13.2	13.3	4b5.6	13.4	13.5	13.6	13.7	13.8	14.1	14.2	14.3	5f14.3	15.1

臓	臘	覇	朧	臕	騰	臚	髏	臟	髓	臠	體	髑
15.2	15.3	15.4	16.1	16.2	16.3	16.4	17.1	4b15.2	4b14.3	7a18.1	2a5.6	6d17.2

醫
4c19.1

--- 0 ---

4b0.1 / 17

月

GETSU moon; month; Monday
GATSU month
tsuki moon; month

--- 1 ---

3 月下 **gekka** in the moonlight
月下氷人 **gekka hyōjin** matchmaker, go-between, cupid
月々 **tsukizuki** every month
4 月水 **gessui** menstruation
月水金 **ges-sui-kin** Mondays, Wednesdays, and Fridays
月日 **gappi** date
tsukihi months and days, time
5 月末 **getsumatsu, tsukizue** end of the month
月世界 **gessekai** the lunar world, the moon
月刊 **gekkan** monthly publication
月払 **tsukibara(i)** monthly installments
月旦 **gettan** first day of the month; commentary
6 月毎 **tsukigoto (ni)** every month
月次 **getsuji** monthly **tsukinami** every month; commonplace, trite
月光 **gekkō** moonlight
7 月決 **tsukigi(me)** monthly (contract)
月形 **tsukigata** crescent shape
月見 **tsukimi** viewing the moon
月見草 **tsukimisō** evening primrose
月足 **tsukita(razu)** premature birth
8 月長石 **getchōseki** moonstone
月例 **getsurei** monthly
月夜 **tsukiyo** moonlit night
月並 **tsukina(mi)** every month; commonplace, trite
月始 **tsukihaji(me)** beginning of the month
月明 **getsumei, tsukiaka(ri)** moonlight
9 月後 **tsukioku(re)** a month late/old; back numbers (of a monthly)
月面 **getsumen** the moon's/lunar surface
月食 **gesshoku** eclipse of the moon
10 月俸 **geppō** monthly salary
月桂 **gekkei** laurel; the moon
月桂冠 **gekkeikan** crown of laurel, laurels
月桂樹 **gekkeiju** laurel/bay tree
11 月遅 **tsukioku(re)** a month late/old; back

numbers (of a monthly)
月掛 **tsukiga(ke)** monthly installments
月産 **gessan** monthly production/output
月経 **gekkei** menstruation
月経帯 **gekkeitai** hygienic band, sanitary napkin
12 月割 **tsukiwa(ri)** per month, monthly installments
月報 **geppō** monthly report
月極 **tsukigi(me)** monthly (contract)
月雇 **tsukiyato(i)** hiring by the month
月越 **tsukigo(shi)** left (unpaid) from last month
月番 **tsukiban** monthly duty/shift
月給 **gekkyū** (monthly) salary
月給日 **gekkyūbi** payday
月給取 **gekkyūto(ri)** salaried worker
月評 **geppyō** monthly review
15 月影 **getsuei, tsukikage** moonlight
月賦 **geppu** monthly installments
月輪 **tsuki (no) wa** halo around the moon
getsurin the moon
月蝕 **gesshoku** eclipse of the moon
17 月齢 **getsurei** number of days since the new moon; (infant's) age in months
月謝 **gessha** monthly tuition
18 月曜 **getsuyō** Monday
月曜日 **getsuyōbi** Monday
月額 **getsugaku** monthly amount

--- 2 ---

1 一月 **ichigatsu** January **ik(ka)getsu, hitotsuki, ichigetsu** one month
2 二月 **nigatsu** February
futatsuki two months
七月 **shichigatsu** July
九月 **kugatsu** September **kyū(ka)getsu, ku(ka)getsu** nine months
十月 **jūgatsu** October
八月 **hachigatsu** August
3 三月 **sangatsu** March
san(ka)getsu, mitsuki three months
夕月 **yūzuki** evening moon
夕月夜 **yūzukiyo** moonlit evening
4 五月 **gogatsu** May **satsuki** fifth month of the lunar calendar
五月人形 **gogatsu ningyō** Boys' Festival dolls

五月雨 **samidare, satsuki ame** early-summer rain

五月晴 **satsukiba(re)** fine weather during the rainy season

今月 **kongetsu** this month

六月 **rokugatsu** June

文月 **fuzuki, fumizuki** July (of lunar calendar)

月月 **tsukizuki** every month

日月 **jitsugetsu, nichigetsu** sun and moon; time

5 半月 **hantsuki** half a month

hangetsu half moon, semicircle

半月刊 **hangekkan** a semimonthly

半月形 **hangetsugata** semicircular

本月 **hongetsu** this month

卯月 **uzuki** fourth lunar month

正月 **shōgatsu** the New Year; January

四月 **shigatsu** April **yon(ka)getsu** four months

四月馬鹿 **shigatsu baka** April fool

6 年月 **nengetsu, toshitsuki** months and years, time

年月日 **nengappi** date

毎月 **maigetsu, maitsuki** every month, monthly

先月 **sengetsu** last month

名月 **meigetsu** bright/full moon; moon on the 15th day of the 8th lunar month or the 13th day of the 9th lunar month

如月 **kisaragi** 2nd lunar month

安月給 **yasugekkyū** meager salary

当月 **tōgetsu** this month

7 来月 **raigetsu** next month

何月 **nangatsu** what month

nan(ka)getsu how many months

8 長月 **nagatsuki** ninth lunar month

例月 **reigetsu** every month

弦月 **gengetsu** crescent moon

明月 **meigetsu** bright/full moon

9 風月 **fūgetsu** wind and moon, beauties of nature

海月 **kurage** jellyfish

客月 **kakugetsu** last month

某月 **bōgetsu** a certain month

星月夜 **hoshizukiyo** starlit night

10 残月 **zangetsu** the moon in the morning sky

宵月 **yoizuki** evening moon

祥月 **shōtsuki** the month of one's death

祥月命日 **shōtsuki meinichi** anniversary of one's death

11 偃月刀 **engetsutō** scimitar

菊月 **kikuzuki** the ninth lunar month

皐月 **kōgetsu, satsuki** fifth lunar month

産月 **u(mi)zuki** last month of pregnancy

翌月 **yokugetsu** the following month

累月 **ruigetsu** for months

雪月花 **setsugekka** snow, moon, and flowers

12 隔月 **kakugetsu** every other month

満月 **mangetsu** full moon

葉月 **hazuki** eighth lunar month

寒月 **kangetsu** wintry moon

極月 **gokugetsu** the last month of the year, December

無月 **mugetsu** moonless (sky)

無月謝 **mugessha** free tuition

幾月 **ikutsuki** how many months

13 歳月 **saigetsu** time, years

新月 **shingetsu** new/crescent moon

睦月 **mutsuki** first lunar month, January

14 蜜月 **mitsugetsu** honeymoon

17 虧月 **kigetsu** waning moon

霜月 **shimotsuki** eleventh lunar month

18 臨月 **ringetsu** last month of pregnancy

観月 **kangetsu** viewing the moon

——————— 3 ———————

2 十一月 **jūichigatsu** November

十二月 **jūnigatsu** December

3 三日月 **mikazuki** crescent moon

弓張月 **yumiha(ri)zuki** crescent moon

小正月 **koshōgatsu** Little New Year's, 14th-16th of first lunar month

4 水無月 **minazuki** sixth lunar month, June

日進月歩 **nisshin-geppo** rapid/constant progress

5 生年月日 **seinengappi** date of birth

旧正月 **kyūshōgatsu** the lunar New Year

立待月 **ta(chi)ma(chi)zuki** 17-day-old moon

6 再来月 **saraigetsu** the month after next

先々月 **sensengetsu** the month before last

7 何箇月 **nankagetsu** how many months

豆名月 **mame meigetsu** moon on the 13th day of the 9th lunar month

9 神無月 **kannazuki** tenth lunar month, October

12 短日月 **tanjitsugetsu** a short time

閑日月 **kanjitsugetsu** leisure

——————— 4 ———————

5 出生年月日 **shusshō nengappi, shussei nengappi** date of birth

7 花鳥風月 **kachō-fūgetsu** the beauties of nature; elegant pursuits

肉 → **2a4.20**

——————— 2 ———————

4b2.1

肋 **ROKU, abara** rib

——————— 1 ———————
4 肋木 **rokuboku** wall bars (for calisthenics)
10 肋骨 **rokkotsu, abarabone** ribs
12 肋間 **rokkan** between the ribs
14 肋膜 **rokumaku** the pleura
肋膜炎 **rokumakuen** pleurisy

4b2.2 / 1306

肌

KI, hada skin; disposition

——————— 1 ———————
6 肌合 **hadaa(i)** disposition, temperament
肌色 **hada-iro** flesh-colored
7 肌身 **hadami** the body, one's person
11 肌脱 **hadanu(gi)** bare to the waist
肌理 **kime** grain, texture
12 肌着 **hadagi** underwear
肌寒 **hadazamu(i), hadasamu(i)** chilly
13 肌触 **hadazawa(ri)** the touch/feel
19 肌襦袢 **hadajuban** underwear

——————— 2 ———————
1 一肌脱 **hitohada nu(gu)** pitch in and help
2 人肌 **hitohada** (warmth of) the skin
3 山肌 **yamahada** mountain's surface
4 片肌脱 **katahada nu(gu)** bare one shoulder;
   help out
   木肌 **kihada** bark
5 石肌 **ishihada** (cut) stone's surface
6 地肌 **jihada** texture; skin; surface of the
   ground
7 赤肌 **akahada** plucked/abraded skin; naked
9 荒肌 **a(re)hada** rough skin
   柔肌 **yawahada** soft skin
10 素肌 **suhada** bare skin
11 鳥肌 **torihada** goose flesh/pimples
15 諸肌 **morohada** stripped to the waist
   餅肌 **mochihada** smooth white skin
17 鮫肌 **samehada** fishskin, dry/scaly skin
20 競肌 **kio(i)hada** gallantry

——————— 3 ———————
6 名人肌 **meijinhada** artist's
   temperamentalness

4b2.3 / 265

有

YŪ, U, a(ru) be, exist; have

——————— 1 ———————
0 有する **yū(suru)** have, possess, own
   有りもしない **a(ri mo shinai)** nonexistent
2 有人 **yūjin** manned
   有力 **yūryoku** influential, powerful
   有力者 **yūryokusha** influential/powerful
   person

3 有丈 **a(rit)take** all there is
   有孔質 **yūkōshitsu** porous
4 有夫 **yūfu** married (woman)
   有切 **a(ri)ki(re)** remnants (of cloth), unsold
   leftovers
   有心 **yūshin** thoughtful consideration
      ushin orthodox style (poem)
5 有史 **yūshi** historical, in recorded history
   有史以来 **yūshi irai** since the dawn of
   history
   有功 **yūkō** merit(orious)
   有功章 **yūkōshō** medal for merit
   有用 **yūyō** useful, serviceable, available
   有司 **yūshi** the authorities, officials
   有田焼 **Aritaya(ki)** Arita porcelainware
6 有気音 **yūkion** an aspirate
   有合 **a(ri)a(u)** happen to be on hand
      a(ri)a(wase) what is on hand
   有色 **yūshoku** colored (race)
   有名 **yūmei** famous
   有名人 **yūmeijin** celebrity
   有名無実 **yūmei-mujitsu** in name only
   有名税 **yūmeizei** a penalty of greatness,
   noblesse oblige
   有米 **a(ri)mai** rice on hand
7 有体 **a(ri)tei** the plain truth, like it is
   有体物 **yūtaibutsu** something tangible
   有余 **a(ri)ama(ru)** be superfluous, be more
   than enough **yūyo** more than
   有形 **yūkei** material, tangible
   有形無形 **yūkei-mukei** tangible and intangible, material and spiritual
   有志 **yūshi** interest in; volunteer
   有志者 **yūshisha** supporter, volunteer
   有声 **yūsei** voiced (sound)
   有声音化 **yūseionka** vocalization, voicing
   有利 **yūri** advantageous, profitable, favorable
8 有毒 **yūdoku** poisonous
   有事 **yūji** emergency
   有価 **yūka** valuable, negotiable
   有価物 **yūkabutsu** valuables
   有価証券 **yūka shōken** (negotiable) securities
   有限 **yūgen** limited, finite
      a(ru) kagi(ri) as long as there is/are any
   有限会社 **yūgen-gaisha** limited liability
   company, Ltd.
   有刺 **yūshi** thorny, barbed
   有刺鉄線 **yūshi tessen** barbed wire
   有効 **yūkō** effective, valid
   有卦 **uke** lucky period
   有妻 **yūsai** married (man)
   有実 **a(ri no) mi** pear
   有明 **aria(ke)** dawn (with the moon visible)
   有性 **yūsei** sexual (reproduction)
   有耶無耶 **uyamuya** noncommittal
   有金 **a(ri)gane** ready cash

4

木 月 2←
日 火 衤
王 牛
方 攵
欠 心
戸
戈

4

木
→2 月
日
火
ネ
王
牛
方
攵
欠
心
戸
戈

9 有為 **yūi** capable, effective, promising
ui vicissitudes of life
有為転変 **ui-tenpen** vicissitudes of life
有神論 **yūshinron** theism
10 有高 **a(ri)daka** amount/goods on hand
有畜 **yūchiku** with livestock
有畜農業 **yūchiku nōgyō** diversified farming
有兼 **a(ri)ka(nenai)** not impossible, possible
有益 **yūeki** beneficial, profitable
有害 **yūgai** harmful, noxious, injurious
有害無益 **yūgai-mueki** harmful, more harm
than good
有能 **yūnō** capable, competent
有租地 **yūsochi** taxable land
有料 **yūryō** fee-charging, toll (road), pay
(toilet)
11 有得 **a(ri)u(ru)** could be, possible
有理 **yūri** rational (number)
有望 **yūbō** promising, hopeful
有情 **ujō** sentient being/life
有産 **yūsan** having property/wealth
有産階級 **yūsan kaikyū** the propertied class
有袋動物 **yūtai dōbutsu** a marsupial
有終美 **yūshū (no) bi** crowning glory,
splendid finish
有頂天 **uchōten** ecstasy, rapture
12 有象無象 **uzō-muzō** all things tangible and
intangible; the rabble, riffraff
有勝 **a(ri)ga(chi)** apt to happen, common
有期 **yūki** for a definite period
有期刑 **yūkikei** penal servitude for a stated
term
有無 **umu** existence of, whether there is or
isn't; yes or no
有無相通 **umu-aitsū(jiru)** help each other,
be complementary
有税 **yūzei** subject to tax, dutiable
有税品 **yūzeihin** goods subject to duty
有衆 **yūshū** the people/multitude
有給 **yūkyū** salaried
有給休暇 **yūkyū kyūka** paid vacation
有閑 **yūkan** having leisure
有閑階級 **yūkan kaikyū** the leisure class
13 有蓋 **yūgai** covered, lidded
有蓋貨車 **yūgai kasha** boxcar
有煙炭 **yūentan** soft/bituminous coal
有数 **yūsū** prominent, leading, top
有感地震 **yūkan jishin** earthquake strong
enough to feel
有意 **yūi** intentional; (statistically) significant
有意味 **yūimi** significant
有意的 **yūiteki** intentional; (statistically)
significant
有意義 **yūigi** significant
有罪 **yūzai** guilty
有罪人 **yūzaijin** guilty person

有触 **a(ri)fu(reta)** commonplace, frequent
有資格者 **yūshikakusha** qualified person
14 有徳 **yūtoku** virtuous
有髪 **uhatsu** unshorn (nun)
有様 **a(ri)sama, a(ri)yō** situation, circumstances, spectacle; the truth
15 有権者 **yūkensha** qualified person, eligible
voter
有勲者 **yūkunsha** holder of a decoration
有線 **yūsen** by wire
有線放送 **yūsen hōsō** broadcasting by wire/
cable
16 有機 **yūki** organic
有機化学 **yūki kagaku** organic chemistry
有機体 **yūkitai** organism
有機的 **yūkiteki** organic
有機物 **yūkibutsu** organic matter, organism
有鍵楽器 **yūken gakki** keyed (musical)
instrument
17 有償 **yūshō** for a consideration/compensation
有爵 **yūshaku** titled, of the peerage
18 有職 **yūshoku** employed
yūsoku, yūshoku person versed in
court and military practices, scholar
有職者 **yūshokusha** employed person
有難 **a(ri)gata(i)** welcome, thankful
a(ri)ga(tō) thank you
有難迷惑 **a(ri)gata-meiwaku** unwelcome
favor
有難味 **a(ri)gatami** value, worth
有難涙 **a(ri)gata-namida** tears of gratitude
19 有識 **yūshiki** learned, intellectual
有識者 **yūshikisha** learned person, an
intellectual

───── 2 ─────

3 万有 **ban'yū** all things, all creation; universal
万有神教 **ban'yū shinkyō** pantheism
4 公有 **kōyū** publicly owned
公有地 **kōyūchi** public land
公有林 **kōyūrin** public forest
5 民有 **min'yū** privately owned
市有 **shiyū** city-owned
占有 **sen'yū** exclusive possession, occupancy
6 共有 **kyōyū** joint ownership
共有地 **kyōyūchi** public land, a common
共有者 **kyōyūsha** part owner, co-owner
共有物 **kyōyūbutsu** joint property
共有財産 **kyōyū zaisan** community property
7 含有 **gan'yū** contain
含有量 **gan'yūryō** quantity of a constituent
substance, content
享有 **kyōyū** enjoy, possess
希有 **keu** rare, unusual
村有 **son'yū** village-owned
私有 **shiyū** privately owned
私有地 **shiyūchi** private land

私有物 **shiyūbutsu** private property
8 併有 **heiyū** own together, combine
官有 **kan'yū** government-owned
官有地 **kan'yūchi** government land
官有林 **kan'yūrin** national forest
国有 **kokuyū** national ownership
国有化 **kokuyūka** nationalization
国有地 **kokuyūchi** national land
国有鉄道 **kokuyū tetsudō** national railway
固有 **koyū** its own, peculiar, characteristic
固有名詞 **koyū meishi** proper noun
固有値 **koyūchi** eigenvalue
所有 **shoyū** ownership, possession
所有主 **shoyūnushi** owner
所有地 **shoyūchi** the land one owns
所有者 **shoyūsha** owner
所有格 **shoyūkaku** the possessive case
所有権 **shoyūken** ownership
具有 **guyū** have, possess
9 専有 **sen'yū** exclusive possession
専有権 **sen'yūken** exclusive right, monopoly
保有 **hoyū** possess, hold, maintain
保有者 **hoyūsha** possessor, holder, owner
通有 **tsūyū** in common
通有性 **tsūyūsei** common trait/characteristic
県有 **ken'yū** owned by the prefecture
10 兼有 **ken'yū** having both
烏有先生 **Uyū-sensei** fictitious person
烏有帰 **uyū (ni) ki(suru)** be reduced to ashes
特有 **tokuyū** characteristic of, peculiar to
特有性 **tokuyūsei** peculiarity
11 現有 **gen'yū** existing, present, actually possessed
12 富有 **fuyū** wealthy, affluent
稀有 **keu** rare, uncommon, extraordinary
14 領有 **ryōyū** possession

——————— 3 ———————
9 前途有望 **zento yūbō** having a promising future
12 無何有郷 **mukau (no) sato** an unspoiled paradise, utopia

——————— 3 ———————

4b3.1
肚 **TO, hara** belly, abdomen

4b3.2 / 1272
肝 **KAN** liver
kimo liver; pluck, courage

——————— 1 ———————
2 肝入 **kimoi(ri)** sponsorship, good offices

4 肝太 **kimo (ga) futo(i)** bold, courageous
肝心 **kanjin** main, vital, essential
5 肝玉 **kimo(t)tama** pluck, courage, grit
6 肝吸 **kimosu(i)** eel liver soup
7 肝冷 **kimo (o) hiya(su)** be startled/frightened
8 肝油 **kan'yu** (cod-)liver oil
肝炎 **kan'en** hepatitis
9 肝要 **kan'yō** important, vital
肝胆 **kantan** liver and gall; one's inmost heart
肝胆相照 **kantan-aite(rasu)** be intimate friends
12 肝硬変 **kankōhen** cirrhosis of the liver
13 肝煎 **kimoi(ri)** sponsorship, good offices
肝腎 **kanjin** main, vital, essential
肝腎要 **kanjin-kaname** of crucial/vital importance
肝試 **kimodame(shi)** test of courage
14 肝魂 **kimo(t)tama** pluck, courage, grit
19 肝臓 **kanzō** liver
肝臓炎 **kanzōen** hepatitis

——————— 2 ———————
4 心肝 **shinkan, kokorogimo** heart
9 肺肝 **haikan** lungs and liver; one's inmost heart

4b3.3
肘 **CHŪ, hiji** elbow

——————— 1 ———————
4 肘木 **hijiki** ancon, bracket, corbel
6 肘当 **hijia(te)** (armor) elbowpiece
8 肘突 **hijitsu(ki)** elbow rest
肘枕 **hijimakura** one's elbow used for a pillow
肘金 **hijigane** hook (of a hook-and-eye fastener)
11 肘掛 **hijika(ke)** arm (of a chair)
12 肘壺 **hijitsubo** eye (of a hook-and-eye fastener)
13 肘鉄 **hijitetsu** rebuff, rejection
肘鉄砲 **hijideppō** rebuff, rejection
14 肘関節 **hiji kansetsu** elbow joint

——————— 2 ———————
4 片肘 **katahiji** one elbow
12 掣肘 **seichū** restraint, restrictions

4b3.4
肛 **KŌ** the anus

——————— 1 ———————
8 肛門 **kōmon** the anus
肛門科医 **kōmonkai** proctologist

4
木
月 3←
日
火
礻
王
牛
方
攵
欠
心
戸
戈

─────────────── 2 ───────────────
11 脱肛 **dakkō** prolapse of the rectum

肓 → **2j5.3**

─────────────── 4 ───────────────

4b4.1

朋 朋　**HŌ** (class)mate, comrade, companion

─────────────── 1 ───────────────
4 朋友 **hōyū** friend, companion
15 朋輩 **hōbai** comrade, friend, fellow, mate

─────────────── 2 ───────────────
6 同朋 **dōhō** companions, one's fellows

4b4.2 / 1857

肪　**BŌ** (animal) fat

─────────────── 2 ───────────────
10 脂肪 **shibō** fat, grease
脂肪油 **shibōyu** fatty oil
脂肪酸 **shibōsan** fatty acid
脂肪質 **shibōshitsu** fats, lipids

4b4.3

肫　**JUN** dried meat

4b4.4

肭　**DOTSU** fur seal

─────────────── 2 ───────────────
14 膃肭臍 **ottosei** seal (the animal)

胱 → 疣 **5i4.1**

4b4.5 / 1723

肥　**HI, ko(eru)** get fat; grow fertile **koe** manure, night soil **ko(yasu)** fertilize; fatten **ko(yashi)** manure, night soil **futo(ru)** get fat

─────────────── 1 ───────────────
3 肥大 **hidai** fleshiness, corpulence
肥土 **ko(e)tsuchi** rich/fertile soil

5 肥立 **hida(tsu)** grow up; recover (after childbirth)
7 肥沃 **hiyoku** fertile
肥車 **ko(yashi)guruma, koeguruma** night-soil cart
8 肥育 **hiiku** fattening (livestock)
肥厚 **hikō** thickening (of the skin)
肥厚性鼻炎 **hikōsei bien** hypertrophic rhinitis
9 肥前 **Hizen** (ancient kuni, Nagasaki-ken)
肥後 **Higo** (ancient kuni, Kumamoto-ken)
10 肥料 **hiryō** manure, fertilizer
11 肥桶 **koeoke** night-soil bucket
12 肥満 **himan** corpulence, obesity
肥満体 **himantai** plump/roly-poly physique
13 肥溜 **koeda(me)** night-soil vat/pot

─────────────── 2 ───────────────
3 下肥 **shimogoe** night soil, manure
小肥 **kobuto(ri)** plump
4 水肥 **suihi** liquid manure
8 追肥 **tsuihi, o(i)goe** supplementary fertilizer/manuring
金肥 **kinpi** store-bought/chemical fertilizer
9 草肥 **kusagoe** compost
施肥 **sehi** apply manure/fertilizer
10 差肥 **sa(shi)goe** (spreading) fertilizer
馬肥 **umago(yashi)** burr clover, medic
11 液肥 **ekihi** liquid fertilizer
堆肥 **taihi, tsumigoe** compost, barnyard manure
魚肥 **gyohi** fertilizer made from fish
12 寒肥 **kangoe** winter manuring
補肥 **hohi** supplementary fertilizer
14 緑肥 **ryokuhi** green manure
16 積肥 **tsu(mi)goe** compost, manure heap

─────────────── 3 ───────────────
10 馬屋肥 **umayago(e)** horse manure

4b4.6 / 683

服　**FUKU** clothes, dress; dose; obey, serve; admit to

─────────────── 1 ───────────────
0 服する **fuku(suru)** yield/submit to, obey; admit; serve (in the army), discharge (duties)
5 服用 **fukuyō** take (medicine)
6 服地 **fukuji** cloth, fabric, material
7 服役 **fukueki** penal servitude; military service
8 服毒 **fukudoku** take poison
服制 **fukusei** dress regulations, uniform
10 服部 **Hattori** (surname)
服従 **fukujū** obey, submit to
服従的 **fukujūteki** obedient, submissive
11 服務 **fukumu** (public) service, duties
服務年限 **fukumu nengen** tenure of office

12 服喪 **fukumo** mourning
服属 **fukuzoku** become a retainer, yield allegience to
服量 **fukuryō** dosage, dose
服装 **fukusō** dress, attire
服装随意 **fukusō zuii** informal attire
13 服罪 **fukuzai** plead guilty, confess
服飾 **fukushoku** clothing and accessories, attire
16 服薬 **fukuyaku** take medicine

──────── 2 ────────

1 一服 **ippuku** a dose; a smoke; a rest/break; a lull, calm market
4 不服 **fufuku** dissatisfaction, protest
不服従 **fufukujū** insubordination
元服 **genpuku** ceremony of attaining manhood
内服 **naifuku** take (medicine) internally
内服薬 **naifukuyaku** medicine to be taken internally
心服 **shinpuku** admiration and devotion
5 古服 **furufuku** old clothes
平服 **heifuku** ordinary clothes, out of uniform
正服 **seifuku** a uniform
圧服 **appuku** overpower, keep down
礼服 **reifuku** formal dress
冬服 **fuyufuku** winter clothing
6 合服 **a(i)fuku** between-season clothing, spring or fall wear
式服 **shikifuku** ceremonial dress
衣服 **ifuku** clothes, clothing
7 承服 **shōfuku** compliance, consent, submission
克服 **kokufuku** conquest, subjugation
呉服 **gofuku** cloth/dry goods, draperies
呉服屋 **gofukuya** dry-goods store
臣服 **shinpuku** obey, follow
私服 **shifuku** plainclothes, civilian clothes
8 制服 **seifuku** uniform
制服制帽 **seifuku-seibō** cap and uniform
法服 **hōfuku** judge's/barrister's/priest's robes
征服 **seifuku** conquer, subjugate; master
征服者 **seifukusha** conqueror
征服欲 **seifukuyoku** desire for conquest
官服 **kanpuku** official uniform
屈服 **kuppuku** submit, yield, surrender
和服 **wafuku** Japanese clothes, kimono
9 信服 **shinpuku** be convinced
便服 **benpuku** civilian clothes
降服 **kōfuku** surrender
軍服 **gunpuku** military uniform
美服 **bifuku** fine clothes
洋服 **yōfuku** (Western-type) clothes
洋服屋 **yōfukuya** clothing store; tailor (shop)
威服 **ifuku** awe into submission
10 帰服 **kifuku** surrender, submission
校服 **kōfuku** school uniform

夏服 **natsufuku** summer clothes/wear
悦服 **eppuku** willing submission
被服 **hifuku** clothing
紋服 **monpuku** clothing bearing one's family crest
11 斎服 **saifuku** vestments
推服 **suifuku** admire, esteem
黒服 **kurofuku** black clothes
祭服 **saifuku** vestments
略服 **ryakufuku** everyday clothes, informal dress
粗服 **sofuku** coarse/poor clothing
12 着服 **chakufuku** put on clothes; embezzle
喪服 **mofuku** mourning clothes
敬服 **keifuku** admire, think highly of
間服 **aifuku** between-season wear
13 微服 **bifuku** incognito
感服 **kanpuku** admiration
頓服 **tonpuku** (medicine to) take in one dose
頓服薬 **tonpukuyaku** drug to be taken once
14 慴服 **shōfuku** fear and obey
綿服 **menpuku** cotton clothes

──────── 3 ────────

2 子供服 **kodomofuku** children's wear
3 大礼服 **taireifuku** court dress, full-dress uniform
4 水兵服 **suiheifuku** sailor's uniform; (schoolgirl's) sailor suit
6 防寒服 **bōkanfuku** winter/arctic clothes
宇宙服 **uchūfuku** space suit
7 作業服 **sagyōfuku** work clothes
妊婦服 **ninpufuku** maternity wear/dress
学生服 **gakuseifuku** school uniform
社交服 **shakōfuku** party clothes, evening dress
8 事務服 **jimufuku** office clothes
夜会服 **yakaifuku** evening dress
国民服 **kokuminfuku** national uniform (for civilians)
9 飛行服 **hikōfuku** flying suit, flight uniform
通常服 **tsūjōfuku** everyday clothes
10 既製服 **kiseifuku** ready-made clothing
11 運動服 **undōfuku** sportswear, uniform
菜葉服 **na(p)pafuku** overalls
紳士服 **shinshifuku** men's clothing
13 戦闘服 **sentōfuku** battle dress
15 潜水服 **sensuifuku** diving suit
16 燕尾服 **enbifuku** swallow-tailed coat
18 簡単服 **kantanfuku** simple/light clothing

4b4.7 / 1146

SHI limbs

肢

──────── 1 ────────

7 肢体 **shitai** limbs; body and limbs

4

木 月 日 火 礻 王 牛 方 攵 欠 心 戸 戈

4←

```
                    2
 3 上肢 jōshi upper limbs, arms
   下肢 kashi lower limbs, legs
 5 四肢 shishi the limbs
 9 前肢 zenshi forelimbs, front leg
   後肢 kōshi hind legs
13 義肢 gishi artificial limb
                    3
14 選択肢 sentakushi multiple choice
```

4b4.8

股
KO thigh; crotch   mata crotch
momo upper leg, thigh, femur

```
                    1
 4 股引 momohi(ki) drawers, underpants;
          close-fitting workpants
 6 股肉 momoniku (ground) round, ham
 8 股肱 kokō right-hand man
10 股座 matagura crotch
   股旅 matatabi gambler's wandering life
12 股間 kokan in the crotch
14 股関節 kokansetsu hip joint
17 股擦 matazu(re) thigh/saddle sore
                    2
 2 二股 futamata bifurcation, fork, parting of
          the ways
 3 小股 komata short steps
 4 太股 futomomo thigh
   内股 uchimomo, uchimata inner thigh
          uchimata (ni) (walking) pigeon-toed
   内股膏薬 uchimata-kōyaku duplicity, double-
          dealing; double-dealer, fence-sitter
 8 刺股 sasumata two-pronged weapon for
          catching criminals (historical)
13 猿股 sarumata drawers, undershorts
19 蟹股 ganimata bowlegged
```

4b4.9

肱
KŌ arm; ability
hiji elbow

```
                    1
11 肱掛 hijika(ke) arm (of a chair)
                    2
 8 股肱 kokō right-hand man
```

4b4.10 / 208

青 青
SEI, SHŌ, ao(i), ao blue,
green; unripe

```
                    1
 0 青ざめる ao(zameru) turn pale
```

```
   青そこひ ao(sokohi) glaucoma
 2 青二才 aonisai callow youth, stripling
 3 青大将 aodaishō (a nonpoisonous green
          snake)
   青々 aoao(shita) fresh and green, verdant
   青山 seizan blue mountain, green hills
 4 青天 seiten the blue sky
   青天井 aotenjō the blue sky
   青天白日 seiten-hakujitsu clear weather;
          cleared of suspicion, proved innocent
   青天霹靂 seiten (no) hekireki a bolt from
          the blue
   青内障 aosokohi glaucoma
   青化物 seikabutsu a cyanide
   青少年 seishōnen young people, the young
   青木 aoki Japanese laurel
 5 青瓦台 Seigadai the Blue House (South
          Korean presidential palace)
   青史 seishi history, annals
   青写真 aojashin, aoshashin blueprints
   青白 aojiro(i) pale, pallid, wan
   青玉 seigyoku sapphire
   青田 aota, aoda green rice field
   青田買 aotaga(i) buying yet unharvested rice;
          signing up prospective graduates as
          employees
 6 青年 seinen young man/people, a youth
   青年会 seinenkai young (wo)men's associa-
          tion
   青年団 seinendan young men's association
   青色 seishoku blue
   青地 aoji blue cloth/material/fabric
   青光 aobikari blue/green/phosphorescent
          light
   青虫 aomushi green caterpillar, grub
   青竹 aodake green bamboo
 7 青豆 aomame green beans
   青貝 aogai limpet; mother-of-pearl
 8 青果 seika vegetables and fruits
   青果物 seikabutsu vegetables and fruits
   青空 aozora the blue sky
   青空市場 aozora ichiba open-air market
   青青 aoao(shita) fresh and green, verdant
   青物 aomono green vegetables
   青物屋 aomonoya vegetable store,
          greengrocer
 9 青信号 aoshingō green (traffic) light
   青海苔 aonori green laver (edible seaweed)
   青海原 aounabara blue expanse of water
   青狐 aogitsune blue/arctic fox
   青草 aokusa green grass
   青春 seishun youth
   青春期 seishunki youth, adolescence
   青臭 aokusa(i) smelling grassy/unripe;
          inexperienced
10 青梅 aoume unripe plum
```

青書 **seisho** bluebook, government report
青息 **aoiki** an anxious sigh
青息吐息 **aoiki-toiki** in dire distress
青馬 **aouma** dark horse with a lustrous coat
11 青菜 **aona** greens
青票 **aohyō** blue ballot, opposing vote
12 青葉 **aoba** green leaves/foliage, greenery
青嵐 **aoarashi, seiran** wind blowing through verdure
青森 **Aomori** (city, Aomori-ken)
青森県 **Aomori-ken** (prefecture)
青畳 **aodatami** new/green straw mat
青筋 **aosuji** blue vein
青雲 **seiun** blue sky; high rank
青雲志 **seiun (no) kokorozashi** ambition for greatness, lofty aspirations
13 青楼 **seirō** brothel
青電話 **aodenwa** public telephone
14 青磁 **seiji, aoji** celadon porcelain
青緑 **aomidori** dark green
青酸 **seisan** hydrogen cyanide, prussic acid
青酸カリ **seisan kari** potassium cyanide
青銅 **seidō, karakane** bronze
青銅色 **seidōshoku** bronze-color
青銅器 **seidōki** bronze ware/tools
15 青豌豆 **aoendō** green peas
16 青膨 **aobuku(re)** dropsical swelling
17 青瓢箪 **aobyōtan** green calabash/gourd; pale-faced weakling
19 青蠅 **aobae** bluebottle fly, blowfly
23 青黴 **aokabi** green mold; penicillium
24 青鷺 **aosagi** blue heron

――――――― 2 ―――――――

4 丹青 **tansei** red and blue; a painting
8 刺青 **shisei, irezumi** tattooing
青青 **aoao(shita)** fresh and green, verdant
10 真青 **ma(s)sao** deep blue; ghastly pale
11 紺青 **konjō** Prussian blue, ultramarine
13 群青 **gunjō** ultramarine, navy blue
14 緑青 **rokushō** verdigris, green/copper rust
16 濃青色 **nōseishoku** deep/dark blue
19 瀝青 **rekisei** pitch, bitumen, asphalt
瀝青炭 **rekiseitan** bituminous/soft coal

――――――― 3 ―――――――

3 万年青 **omoto** (a plant in the lily family)
土瀝青 **dorekisei** asphalt
5 白砂青松 **hakusha-seishō** white sand and green pines, beautiful seashore scene
7 花紺青 **hana konjō** royal blue

4b4.11 / 1262

肯　　**KŌ, gae(njiru/nzuru)** agree to, consent

――――――― 1 ―――――――

8 肯定 **kōtei** affirm

肯定文 **kōteibun** affirmative sentence
肯定的 **kōteiteki** affirmative
14 肯綮 **kōkei** (to the) point, (on the) mark

――――――― 2 ―――――――

9 首肯 **shukō** assent/agree to

宥 → **3m6.1**

4b4.12

肴　　**KŌ, sakana** cooking, delicacies; snack food to munch on while drinking; fish

――――――― 2 ―――――――

10 酒肴 **shukō, sakesakana** food and drink

冒 → 冒 **4c5.6**

――――――― 5 ―――――――

4b5.1

胛　　**KŌ** shoulder blade

――――――― 2 ―――――――

8 肩胛骨 **kenkōkotsu** shoulder blade

4b5.2

胖　　**HAN** fat; abundant

4b5.3

朏　　**HI** new/crescent moon

4b5.4

胙　　**SO, himorogi** meat offerings

4b5.5 / 1284

胞 胞　　**HŌ** sac, sheath; placenta, afterbirth

――――――― 1 ―――――――

2 胞子 **hōshi** spore
6 胞衣 **hōi, ena** placenta, afterbirth

――――――― 2 ―――――――

6 同胞 **dōhō** brothers, brethren

同胞愛 **dōhōai** brotherly love, fraternity
8 芽胞 **gahō** spore
11 細胞 **saibō** cell (in biology)
細胞学 **saibōgaku** cytology

────────── 3 ──────────

7 卵細胞 **ransaibō** egg cell, ovum
8 担子胞子 **tanshi hōshi** basidiospore
9 単細胞 **tansaibō** single cell

────────── 4 ──────────

5 四海同胞 **shikai-dōhō** universal brotherhood

4 木 月 日 火 礻 王 牛 方 攵 欠 心 戸 戈
→5

4b5.6 / 1273

胆 膽

TAN, kimo, i gallbladder;
pluck, courage

────────── 1 ──────────

2 胆力 **tanryoku** courage, mettle
5 胆汁 **tanjū** bile, gall
胆汁質 **tanjūshitsu** bilious/choleric (temperament)
胆石 **tanseki** gallstone
胆石病 **tansekibyō** cholelithiasis, gallstones
胆石症 **tansekishō** cholelithiasis, gallstones
9 胆勇 **tan'yū** courage, pluck, dauntlessness
11 胆略 **tanryaku** courage and resourcefulness
20 胆礬 **tanban** copper sulfate, blue vitriol
22 胆囊 **tannō** gallbladder
胆囊炎 **tannōen** gallbladder inflammation

────────── 2 ──────────

3 大胆 **daitan** bold, daring
大胆不敵 **daitan-futeki** audacious, daredevil
小胆 **shōtan** timid, lily-livered; prudent
4 心胆 **shintan** one's heart
7 肝胆 **kantan** liver and gall; one's inmost heart
肝胆相照 **kantan-aite(rasu)** be intimate friends
8 放胆 **hōtan** bold, fearless, daring
9 海胆 **uni** sea urchin
度胆抜 **dogimo (o) nu(ku)** dumbfound, shock
10 竜胆 **rindō** bellflower, gentian
12 落胆 **rakutan** be discouraged/disheartened
14 豪胆 **gōtan** stouthearted, dauntless
魂胆 **kontan** soul; ulterior motive

────────── 4 ──────────

9 臥薪嘗胆 **gashin-shōtan** perseverance and determination

4b5.7

胝

CHI, tako callus, corn

────────── 2 ──────────

10 胼胝 **tako** callus, corn

4b5.8

胚

HAI embryo; pregnancy

────────── 1 ──────────

8 胚芽 **haiga** embryo bud, germ
胚芽米 **haigamai** whole rice (with the germ)
9 胚胎 **haitai** become pregnant; originate in

4b5.9 / 1277

肺

HAI lung

────────── 1 ──────────

5 肺出血 **haishukketsu** discharge of blood from the lungs
6 肺尖 **haisen** apex of a lung
7 肺肝 **haikan** lungs and liver; one's inmost heart
8 肺炎 **haien** pneumonia
肺門 **haimon** hilum of a lung
9 肺活量 **haikatsuryō** lung capacity
10 肺浸潤 **haishinjun** pulmonary tuberculosis
肺病 **haibyō** lung/pulmonary disease
11 肺患 **haikan** lung ailment
肺魚 **haigyo** lungfish
12 肺葉 **haiyō** lobe of a lung
肺腑 **haifu** the lungs; one's inmost heart
肺結核 **haikekkaku** pulmonary tuberculosis
17 肺癌 **haigan** lung cancer
19 肺臓 **haizō** the lungs

────────── 2 ──────────

10 珪肺症 **keihaishō** silicosis
13 鉄肺 **tetsu (no) hai** iron lung

4b5.10 / 1296

胎

TAI womb, uterus

────────── 1 ──────────

4 胎内 **tainai** in the womb
胎中 **taichū** in the womb
5 胎生 **taisei** viviparous
胎生学 **taiseigaku** embryology
7 胎児 **taiji** fetus
8 胎毒 **taidoku** congenital eczema
胎芽 **taiga** propagule, brood bud
10 胎教 **taikyō** prenatal care
11 胎動 **taidō** fetal movement, quickening
胎動期 **taidōki** the quickening period
15 胎盤 **taiban** placenta, afterbirth

────────── 2 ──────────

5 母胎 **botai** womb, uterus
6 死胎 **shitai** dead fetus

8 受胎 **jutai** conception, fertilization
9 胚胎 **haitai** become pregnant; originate in
11 堕胎 **datai** abortion
16 懐胎 **kaitai** pregnancy, gestation

———————— 4 ————————

12 換骨奪胎 **kankotsu-dattai** adapt, modify, recast

———————— 5 ————————

12 葡萄状鬼胎 **budōjō kitai** vesicular/hydatid(iform) mole

4b5.11

YU relaxed, at ease

脉 → 脈   **4b6.8**

4b5.12

胡

KO, GO, U barbarian, foreign

———————— 1 ————————

6 胡瓜 **kyūri** cucumber
7 胡乱 **uron** suspicious, questionable
　胡床 **agura (o kaku)** sit cross-legged
8 胡国 **kokoku** (ancient northern-China) barbarian nations
10 胡座 **agura (o kaku)** sit cross-legged
　胡桃 **kurumi** walnut
　胡桃割 **kurumiwa(ri)** nutcracker
11 胡麻 **goma** sesame (seeds)
　胡麻油 **goma abura** sesame-seed oil
　胡麻和 **gomaa(e)** salad with vinegar dressing
　胡麻塩 **gomashio** salted toasted sesame seeds; gray-flecked hair
　胡麻摺 **gomasu(ri)** flatterer, sycophant
12 胡椒 **koshō** pepper
　胡椒入 **koshōi(re)** pepper skaker
　胡散臭 **usankusa(i)** suspicious, questionable
15 胡蝶 **kochō** butterfly
19 胡籙 **yanagui** quiver (for arrows)

———————— 2 ————————

5 白胡麻 **shirogoma** white sesame seeds
10 唐胡麻 **tōgoma** castor-oil bean

胄 →   **2r7.2**

4b5.13

胄

CHŪ lineage, descent

4b5.14

胥

SHO together, mutual; subordinate official

4b5.15 / 1265

背

HAI, se back; one's height   sei one's height   somu(ku) turn one's back on, act contrary to, defy   somu(keru) avert, turn away

———————— 1 ————————

3 背丈 **setake** one's height
4 背中 **senaka** one's back
　背中合 **senakaa(wase)** back to back
　背反 **haihan** revolt, rebel
　背水陣 **haisui (no) jin** last stand
　背戸 **sedo** back door/gate/entrance
　背戸口 **sedoguchi** back door/gate/entrance
5 背比 **seikura(be)** comparing heights
　背広 **sebiro** business suit
6 背任 **hainin** breach of trust
　背任罪 **haininzai** breach of trust
　背向 **haikō** turn one's back; turning toward and turning away, obedience and disobedience
　背 **se (o) mu(keru)** turn one's back on
　背光 **haikō** glory
7 背伸 **seno(bi)** stretch oneself, stand on tiptoes
8 背泳 **haiei, seoyo(gi)** swim the backstroke
9 背信 **haishin** breach of faith, betrayal, infidelity
　背負 **seo(u), sho(u)** carry on one's back, shoulder, be burdened with
　背負投 **shio(i)na(ge), seo(i)na(ge)** throw over one's shoulder; betrayal
　背後 **haigo** back, rear, behind
　背革 **segawa** leatherback (book)
　背面 **haimen** rear, back, reverse
　背約 **haiyaku** breach of promise
10 背部 **haibu** the back, posterior
　背高 **seitaka** tall
　背骨 **sebone** backbone, spine
　背教 **haikyō** apostasy
　背教者 **haikyōsha** apostate
11 背理 **hairi** irrational, absurd
12 背景 **haikei** background
　背番号 **sebangō** number on a player's back
　背筋 **sesuji** line of the backbone; seam down the back   **haikin** the muscles of the back
　背筋力 **haikinryoku** back-muscle strength
　背開 **sebira(ki)** slice a fish down its back
13 背馳 **haichi** be contrary to
14 背徳 **haitoku** immorality, corruption
18 背離 **hairi** estrangement, alienation
21 背鰭 **sebire** dorsal fin
22 背嚢 **hainō** knapsack

木
月 5←
日
火
礻
王
牛
方
攵
欠
心
戸
戈

左 column:

──────── 2 ────────
3 上背 **uwazei** height, stature
山背 **yamase** a foehn-like wind; a cold early-summer wind in Tōhoku
sanpai the other side of a mountain
4 中背 **chūzei** average height
6 光背 **kōhai** halo
8 妹背 **imose** closely related man and woman; man and wife; brother and sister
10 紙背 **shihai** reverse side of the paper
11 猫背 **nekoze** a bent back, stoop
12 違背 **ihai** violation, disobedience
13 腹背 **fukuhai** front and back

──────── 4 ────────
4 中肉中背 **chūniku-chūzei** medium height and build
9 面向不背 **menkō-fuhai** beautiful from every angle, flawless
面従腹背 **menjū-fukuhai** outward obedience but inward opposition, false obedience, passive resistance

4b5.16

胤

IN, tane descendant, issue, offspring

──────── 2 ────────
9 後胤 **kōin** descendant
12 落胤 **rakuin, o(toshi)dane** illegitimate child

──────── 6 ────────

4b6.1

胱

KŌ bladder

──────── 2 ────────
14 膀胱 **bōkō** urinary bladder
膀胱結石 **bōkō kesseki** bladder stones

4b6.2

胯

KO, mata crotch

4b6.3

脇

KYŌ, waki side, armpit, flank; supporting role

──────── 1 ────────
3 脇下 **waki (no) shita** armpit; armhole
5 脇目 **wakime** onlooker's eyes; looking aside
7 脇役 **wakiyaku** supporting role
脇見 **wakimi** look aside/away

右 column:

10 脇差 **wakiza(shi)** short sword
脇息 **kyōsoku** armrest
11 脇道 **wakimichi** byway, side road; digression
13 脇腹 **wakibara** one's side

──────── 2 ────────
3 小脇 **kowaki** side (of the body)
4 片脇 **katawaki** one's side, under one's arm; one side, aside

4b6.4

脆

ZEI, moro(i) fragile, brittle

──────── 1 ────────
8 脆性 **zeisei** brittleness
10 脆弱 **zeijaku** fragile, frail, flimsy, brittle
──────── 2 ────────
10 涙脆 **namidamoro(i)** given to weeping

4b6.5

胼

HEN callus, corn

──────── 1 ────────
9 胼胝 **tako** callus, corn

4b6.6 / 1921

朕 朕

CHIN (imperial) we

4b6.7 / 1042

脂

SHI, abura (animal) fat
yani resin, gum; tar, nicotine; earwax, eye discharge

──────── 1 ────────
0 脂ぎった **abura(gitta)** greasy, oily
3 脂下 **yanisa(garu)** put on airs, be self-complacent
4 脂太 **aburabuto(ri)** obese, fat
脂手 **aburade** greasy/oily hand
6 脂気 **aburake** oily, greasy
脂汗 **aburaase** greasy sweat
7 脂身 **aburami** fat (on meat)
8 脂肪 **shibō** fat, grease
脂肪油 **shibōyu** fatty oil
脂肪酸 **shibōsan** fatty acid
脂肪質 **shibōshitsu** fats, lipids
脂性 **aburashō** fatty
9 脂染 **aburaji(miru)** become oily, be grease-stained
10 脂粉 **shifun** rouge and powder, cosmetics
15 脂質 **shishitsu** fats, lipids
16 脂濃 **abura(k)ko(i)** greasy, rich (foods)

——————— 2 ———————

4 牛脂 **gyūshi** beef tallow
8 油脂 **yushi** fat, fats and oils
11 豚脂 **tonshi** lard
脱脂 **dasshi** fat removal; nonfat, skim (milk)
脱脂乳 **dasshinyū** skim milk
脱脂綿 **dasshimen** absorbent cotton
16 凝脂 **gyōshi** solidified fat; beautiful white skin
獣脂 **jūshi** animal fat, tallow
樹脂 **jushi** resin
19 鯨脂 **geishi** blubber
20 臙脂 **enji** rouge
臙脂色 **enji-iro** deep red

——————— 4 ———————

6 合成樹脂 **gōsei jushi** synthetic resin, plastic

4b6.8 / 913

脈 脈 脉   **MYAKU** pulse, vein, blood vessel

——————— 1 ———————

3 脈々 **myakumyaku** continuous, unbroken
5 脈打 **myakuu(tsu)** pulsate, beat
7 脈状 **myakujō** veinlike
8 脈拍 **myakuhaku** pulse (rate)
脈所 **myakudokoro** spot on the body where the pulse can be felt; vital point
11 脈動 **myakudō** pulsation
12 脈搏 **myakuhaku** pulse (rate)
脈絡 **myakuraku** logical connection, coherence
14 脈管 **myakkan** blood vessel, duct

——————— 2 ———————

1 一脈 **ichimyaku** vein, thread, connection
2 人脈 **jinmyaku** (network of) personal connections
3 山脈 **sanmyaku** mountain range
4 文脈 **bunmyaku** context
支脈 **shimyaku** spur, feeder, branch
水脈 **suimyaku** vein of water; water main
5 平脈 **heimyaku** normal pulse
主脈 **shumyaku** the main mountain range
6 死脈 **shimyaku** fatal pulse; exhausted ore vein
気脈通 **kimyaku (o) tsū(jiru)** have a secret understanding with, be in collusion with
血脈 **ketsumyaku** blood vessel/relationship
7 乱脈 **ranmyaku** chaotic
8 命脈 **meimyaku** life
金脈 **kinmyaku** gold vein
10 脈脈 **myakumyaku** continuous, unbroken
11 動脈 **dōmyaku** artery
動脈硬化 **dōmyaku kōka** hardening of the arteries
動脈硬化症 **dōmyaku kōkashō** arteriosclerosis

遅脈 **chimyaku** slow pulse
13 鉱脈 **kōmyaku** vein of ore
14 静脈 **jōmyaku** vein
静脈血 **jōmyakuketsu** venous blood
静脈炎 **jōmyakuen** phlebitis
語脈 **gomyaku** interrelationship of words, context

——————— 3 ———————

3 大動脈 **daidōmyaku** aorta
大静脈 **daijōmyaku** the vena cava
4 不整脈 **fuseimyaku** irregular pulse
火山脈 **kazanmyaku** volcanic range
8 金鉱脈 **kinkōmyaku** gold vein
16 頸動脈 **keidōmyaku** the carotid artery
頸静脈 **keijōmyaku** the jugular vein

——————— 4 ———————

11 崑崙山脈 **Konron-sanmyaku** the Kunlun mountains

4b6.9 / 1283

胸   **KYŌ, mune, muna-** chest, breast; heart, feelings

——————— 1 ———————

3 胸三寸 **munesanzun** heart, mind, feelings
4 胸元 **munamoto** the solar plexus; breast
胸毛 **munage** chest hair; breast down
胸中 **kyōchū** one's bosom, heart, feelings
胸水 **kyōsui** fluid in the thoracic cavity
6 胸先 **munasaki** the solar plexus; breast
胸宇 **kyōu** in one's heart
胸当 **munea(te)** breastplate, chest protector
7 胸囲 **kyōi** girth/circumference of the chest
8 胸泳 **kyōei** breaststroke
胸苦 **munaguru(shii)** feeling oppressed in the chest
胸突八丁 **munatsu(ki) hatchō** steepest part of the path up the mountain
胸底 **kyōtei** one's inmost heart
胸板 **munaita** the chest
9 胸郭 **kyōkaku** the chest, thorax
10 胸倉 **munagura** the lapels
胸部 **kyōbu** the chest
胸高 **munadaka** (wearing an obi) high
胸骨 **kyōkotsu** breastbone, sternum
12 胸幅 **munehaba, munahaba** chest breadth
胸椎 **kyōtsui** the thoracic vertebrae
胸焼 **muneya(ke)** heartburn
胸痛 **kyōtsū** chest pain
胸奥 **kyōō** one's inmost heart
胸間 **kyōkan** breast, chest
13 胸裏 **kyōri** one's inmost heart
胸飾 **munekaza(ri)** brooch
14 胸像 **kyōzō** (sculptured) bust
胸膜 **kyōmaku** the pleura

4 ← 6

木 月 日 火 礻 王 牛 方 攵 欠 心 戸 戈

胸膜炎 **kyōmakuen** pleurisy
胸算 **munazan** mental arithmetic; expectation
胸算用 **munazan'yō** mental arithmetic; expectation
16 胸壁 **kyōheki** wall of the chest; breastwork, parapet
胸懐 **kyōkai** one's heart/thoughts
胸積 **munazu(mori)** mental arithmetic; expectation
18 胸襟 **kyōkin** heart, bosom
胸騒 **munasawa(gi)** uneasiness; apprehension

——————— 2 ———————
6 気胸 **kikyō** pneumothorax
9 度胸 **dokyō** courage, pluck, mettle
13 鳩胸 **hatomune** pigeon-breasted

——————— 3 ———————
17 糞度胸 **kusodokyō** reckless bravery

4b6.10 / 1300

胴

DŌ torso, trunk

——————— 1 ———————
3 胴上 **dōa(ge)** hoist (someone) shoulder-high
4 胴中 **dōnaka** torso
6 胴回 **dōmawa(ri)** one's girth
7 胴体 **dōtai** the body, torso; fuselage
胴忘 **dōwasu(re)** have a lapse of memory, forget for the moment
胴乱 **dōran** satchel, wallet, collecting case
8 胴長 **dōnaga** long-torsoed
胴金 **dōgane** metal clasp
9 胴巻 **dōma(ki)** money belt
11 胴欲 **dōyoku** avarice, greed; cruelty
12 胴着 **dōgi** undergarment; chest protector (worn in kendo)
胴揚 **dōa(ge)** hoist (someone) shoulder-high
胴間声 **dōmagoe** thick/dissonant voice
15 胴慾 **dōyoku** avarice, greed; cruelty
胴締 **dōji(me)** belt, waistband
胴震 **dōburu(i)** shivering, trembling

——————— 2 ———————
4 双胴機 **sōdōki** twin-fuselage airplane

4b6.11 / 1754

朗 朗 脼

RŌ, hoga(raka) clear, bright, cheerful

——————— 1 ———————
3 朗々 **rōrō** clear, sonorous
7 朗吟 **rōgin** recite, sing
12 朗報 **rōhō** good news, glad tidings
朗詠 **rōei** recite
14 朗読 **rōdoku** read aloud

——————— 2 ———————
8 明朗 **meirō** clear, open, cheerful
12 晴朗 **seirō** clear, fair, fine

——————— 3 ———————
4 不明朗 **fumeirō** gloomy; dubious; dishonest
9 音吐朗々 **onto-rōrō** in a clear/ringing voice

4b6.12

朔

SAKU beginning; north
tsuitachi first day of the month

——————— 1 ———————
5 朔北 **sakuhoku** north
9 朔風 **sakufū** north wind

——————— 2 ———————
11 晦朔 **kaisaku** last and first days of successive months

4b6.13

脊

SEKI back, spine
se one's height

——————— 1 ———————
9 脊柱 **sekichū** spinal column, spine, backbone
12 脊椎 **sekitsui** vertebra; spinal column, spine
脊椎動物 **sekitsui dōbutsu** vertebrates
18 脊髄 **sekizui** spinal cord

——————— 2 ———————
11 脳脊髄膜炎 **nōsekizuimakuen** cerebrospinal meningitis

4b6.14 / 1266

骨

KOTSU, hone bone

——————— 1 ———————
2 骨子 **kosshi** bones; essentials, gist
3 骨上 **kotsua(ge)** gathering (the deceased's) ashes
4 骨太 **honebuto** large-boned, stoutly built
骨化 **kokka** ossification
骨片 **koppen** pieces of bone
6 骨休 **honeyasu(me)** relaxation, recreation
骨肉 **kotsuniku** one's flesh and blood, kin
骨灰 **kotsubai** bone ashes
7 骨身 **honemi** flesh and bones; marrow
骨折 **kossetsu** broken bone, fracture
honeo(ru) take pains, exert oneself
骨折損 **honeo(ri)zon** wasted effort
骨抜 **honenu(ki)** boned; emasculated, watered down
8 骨法 **koppō** knack
9 骨拾 **kotsuhiro(i)** gathering (the deceased's) ashes

4

→6

木
月
日
火
ネ
王
牛
方
攵
欠
心
戸
戈

骨炭 **kottan** bone charcoal
骨相 **kossō** physique, (cranial) physiognomy
骨相学 **kossōgaku** phrenology
骨柄 **kotsugara** build, physique, personal appearance
10 骨格 **kokkaku** skeleton, frame, one's build
骨粉 **koppun** bone meal, powdered bone
11 骨接 **honetsu(gi)** bonesetting; bonesetter
骨張 **honeba(ru)** get thin; persist in
honeba(tta) bony, thin
骨惜 **honeo(shimi)** avoid effort, spare oneself
骨組 **honegu(mi)** skeleton; framework
骨軟化症 **kotsunankashō** osteomalacia
骨頂 **kotchō** height (of folly)
12 骨牌 **koppai, karuta** (Japanese-style) playing cards
骨揚 **kotsua(ge)** gathering the (deceased's) ashes
骨董 **kottō** curios, bric-a-brac
骨董品 **kottōhin** curios, bric-a-brac
骨壺 **kotsutsubo** mortuary urn
骨無 **honena(shi)** rickets; spineless/weak-willed person
13 骨幹 **kokkan** one's frame, build
骨節 **kossetsu, honebushi** joint
hone(p)pushi joint; spirit, strong character
14 骨膜 **kotsumaku** the periosteum
骨膜炎 **kotsumakuen** periostitis
15 骨盤 **kotsuban** the pelvis
骨箱 **kotsubako** box for the deceased's ashes
骨質 **kosshitsu** bony tissue
18 骨髄 **kotsuzui** marrow
骨髄炎 **kotsuzuien** osteomyelitis

───── 2 ─────

2 人骨 **jinkotsu** human bones
3 万骨 **bankotsu** thousands of lives
凡骨 **bonkotsu** ordinary person
小骨 **kobone** small bones
4 分骨 **bunkotsu** bury parts of a person's ashes in separate places
尺骨 **shakkotsu** the ulna
木骨 **mokkotsu** wooden frame, half-timbered
5 仙骨 **senkotsu** philosophical turn of mind
白骨 **hakkotsu** bleached bones, skeleton
6 気骨 **kikotsu** spirit, mettle, backbone
kibone mental effort
気骨折 **kibone (ga) o(reru)** nerve-wracking
老骨 **rōkotsu** one's old bones
肋骨 **rokkotsu, abarabone** ribs
7 尾骨 **bikotsu** the coccyx
8 奇骨 **kikotsu** eccentric
性骨 **shōkotsu, seikotsu** one's unique touch/talent
武骨 **bukotsu** boorish, uncouth
9 侠骨 **kyōkotsu** chivalrous spirit

俗骨 **zokkotsu** vulgar temperament; lowly person
背骨 **sebone** backbone, spine
10 拳骨 **genkotsu** fist, knuckles
徒骨 **mudabone** fruitless effort
座骨 **zakotsu** hip bone
座骨神経 **zakotsu shinkei** sciatic nerve
座骨神経痛 **zakotsu shinkeitsū** sciatic neuralgia
胸骨 **kyōkotsu** breastbone, sternum
竜骨 **ryūkotsu** keel
納骨 **nōkotsu** depositing the (deceased's) ashes
納骨堂 **nōkotsudō** ossuary, crypt
粉骨 **funkotsu** assiduousness
粉骨砕身 **funkotsu-saishin** do one's utmost
恥骨 **chikotsu** the pubic bone
馬骨 **uma (no) hone** person of unknown origin, stranger, Joe Blow
11 接骨 **sekkotsu** bonesetting
接骨木 **niwatoko** elder (tree)
接骨医 **sekkotsui** bonesetter
接骨術 **sekkotsujutsu** bonesetting
脛骨 **keikotsu** shinbone, tibia
船骨 **senkotsu** ribs of a ship
軟骨 **nankotsu** cartilage
12 蛮骨 **bankotsu** brute courage, recklessness
換骨奪胎 **kankotsu-dattai** adapt, modify, recast
椎骨 **tsuikotsu** vertebra
無骨 **bukotsu** boorish, uncouth
無骨者 **bukotsumono** boor, lout, churl
硬骨 **kōkotsu** hard bone; stalwart, unyielding
硬骨漢 **kōkotsukan** man of firm character
筋骨 **kinkotsu, sujibone** sinews and bones
距骨 **kyokotsu** the anklebone
13 腰骨 **koshibone** hipbone; perseverence
鉄骨 **tekkotsu** steel frame
14 遺骨 **ikotsu** one's remains/ashes
鼻骨 **bikotsu** the nasal bone/cartilage
15 踝骨 **kakotsu** anklebone
16 薦骨 **senkotsu** the sacrum
骸骨 **gaikotsu** skeleton
整骨 **seikotsu** bone-setting, osteopathy
親骨 **oyabone** outer ribs of a folding fan
頬骨 **hōbone** cheekbone
頸骨 **keikotsu** neckbones
頭骨 **tōkotsu** cranial bones, skull
18 鎖骨 **sakotsu** the clavicle, collarbone
顎骨 **gakkotsu** jawbone
19 鏤骨 **rukotsu** painstaking
21 露骨 **rokotsu** open, undisguised, frank; conspicuous; lewd
26 顴骨 **kankotsu, kenkotsu** cheekbone

───── 3 ─────

7 尾骶骨 **biteikotsu** the coccyx, tailbone

貝殻骨 **kaigarabone** the shoulder blade
8 肩甲骨 **kenkōkotsu** shoulder blade
肩胛骨 **kenkōkotsu** shoulder blade
9 屋台骨 **yataibone** framework, foundation; means, property
10 根性骨 **konjōbone** spirit, disposition
12 無駄骨 **mudabone** wasted/vain effort
無駄骨折 **mudaboneo(ri)** wasted/vain effort
15 膝蓋骨 **shitsugaikotsu** kneecap, patella
16 頭蓋骨 **zugaikotsu** cranium, skull
25 顱頂骨 **rochōkotsu** parietal bone

4b6.15 / 386

能 **NŌ** ability, function; Noh drama
yo(ku) skillfully

─────── 1 ───────
0 能くする **yo(ku) suru** be skilled in
2 能力 **nōryoku** ability, capacity, talent
4 能文 **nōbun** skilled in writing
能文家 **nōbunka** skilled writer
5 能弁 **nōben** eloquence, oratory
能弁家 **nōbenka** good speaker, orator
6 能吏 **nōri** capable official
7 能狂言 **nōkyōgen** Noh farce; Noh drama and kyōgen farce
8 能事 **nōji** one's work
9 能面 **nōmen** Noh mask
10 能書 **nōsho** calligraphy **nōga(ki)** advertising one's wares, boasting
11 能動 **nōdō** activity
能動的 **nōdōteki** active
能動態 **nōdōtai** active voice (in grammar)
能率 **nōritsu** efficiency
能率的 **nōritsuteki** efficient
12 能登 **Noto** (ancient kuni, Ishikawa-ken)
能登半島 **Noto-hantō** (peninsula, Ishikawa-ken)
能筆 **nōhitsu** calligraphy, skilled penmanship
13 能楽 **nōgaku** Noh drama
能楽堂 **nōgakudō** a Noh theater

─────── 2 ───────
3 万能 **bannō** omnipotent, all-around, all-purpose **mannō** all-purpose
万能薬 **bannōyaku** cure-all, panacea
才能 **sainō** talent, ability
4 不能 **funō** impossible; impotent
5 本能 **honnō** instinct
可能 **kanō** possible
可能法 **kanōhō** potential mood
可能性 **kanōsei** possibility
6 多能 **tanō** versatile
全能 **zennō** omnipotence
有能 **yūnō** capable, competent
7 良能 **ryōnō** natural ability

低能 **teinō** low intelligence, mentally deficient
低能児 **teinōji** retarded child; backward pupil
技能 **ginō** skill, technical ability
芸能 **geinō** (public) entertainment; accomplishments, attainments
芸能人 **geinōjin** an entertainment personality, star
芸能界 **geinōkai** the entertainment world, show business
8 非能率的 **hinōritsuteki** inefficient
効能 **kōnō** efficacy, effect
知能 **chinō** intelligence
知能犯 **chinōhan** a non-violent crime
知能的 **chinōteki** intellectual
官能 **kannō** bodily functions; sensual, carnal
官能主義 **kannō shugi** sensualism
官能的 **kannōteki** sensuous, sensual, carnal
性能 **seinō** performance, efficiency
12 堪能 **tannō** skill; be satisfied
智能 **chinō** intelligence
無能 **munō** incompetent, ineffective
無能力 **munōryoku** incompetent; impotent
無能力者 **munōryokusha** an incompetent
15 権能 **kennō** authority, power
16 機能 **kinō** a function
機能的 **kinōteki** functional
18 職能 **shokunō** function; job performance
職能給 **shokunōkyū** merit pay

─────── 3 ───────
4 不可能 **fukanō** impossible
7 低性能 **teiseinō** low efficiency
8 放射能 **hōshanō** radioactivity, radiation
10 高性能 **kōseinō** high-performance
12 無技能 **muginō** unskilled

─────── 4 ───────
5 主治効能 **shuji kōnō** chief efficacy (of a drug)
6 全知全能 **zenchi-zennō** all-knowing and all-powerful
10 帰巣本能 **kisō honnō** homing instinct

─────── 7 ───────

4b7.1

脯 **HO, hojishi** dried meat

4b7.2 / 796

豚 **TON, buta** pig

─────── 1 ───────
0 豚カツ **tonkatsu** pork cutlet
6 豚肉 **butaniku** pork

7 豚児 **tonji** my son (humble)
8 豚舎 **tonsha** pigsty, pigpen
10 豚脂 **tonshi** lard
15 豚箱 **butabako** police lockup, jail

————— 2 —————

8 河豚 **fugu** globefish, blowfish, puffer
9 海豚 **iruka** porpoise, dolphin
12 焼豚 **ya(ki)buta, ya(ki)ton** roast pork
14 雌豚 **mebuta** sow
15 養豚 **yōton** hog raising
　養豚者 **yōtonsha** hog raiser, pig farmer
　養豚場 **yōtonjō** hog/pig farm

腺→朗 **4b6.11**

4b7.3 / 1784

脚 **KYAKU, KYA, ashi** leg

————— 1 —————

2 脚力 **kyakuryoku** walking ability
3 脚下 **kyakka** at one's feet
5 脚半 **kyahan** leggings, gaiters
　脚本 **kyakuhon** script, play
　脚付 **ashitsu(ki)** with legs; gait
　脚立 **kyatatsu** stepladder
6 脚気 **kakke** beriberi
　脚色 **kyakushoku** dramatization, stage/film adaptation
　脚色者 **kyakushokusha** dramatizer, adapter
　脚光 **kyakkō** footlights, limelight, spotlight
8 脚注 **kyakuchū** footnote
10 脚部 **kyakubu** leg
　脚荷 **ashini** ballast
11 脚絆 **kyahan** leggings, gaiters
12 脚註 **kyakuchū** footnote
15 脚線美 **kyakusenbi** leg beauty/shapeliness
19 脚韻 **kyakuin** rhyme

————— 2 —————

3 三脚 **sankyaku** tripod; three legs
　三脚架 **sankyakuka** tripod
4 日脚 **hiashi** daytime; sun's position
　火脚 **hiashi** spreading of a fire
5 失脚 **shikkyaku** lose one's standing, be overthrown, fall
　立脚 **rikkyaku** be based on
　立脚地 **rikkyakuchi** position, standpoint
　立脚点 **rikkyakuten** position, standpoint
6 両脚規 **ryōkyakuki** compass (for drawing circles)
　行脚 **angya** pilgrimage; travel on foot
　行脚僧 **angyasō** itinerant priest
8 雨脚 **amaashi, ameashi** speed of a moving

rain front; streaks of falling rain
9 飛脚 **hikyaku** express messenger, courier
　前脚 **zenkyaku, maeashi** forelegs, front leg
　風脚 **kazaashi** wind speed
　後脚 **atoashi** hind legs
10 健脚 **kenkyaku** strong legs
　健脚家 **kenkyakuka** good walker
　馬脚 **bakyaku** horse's legs; one's true character
11 猫脚 **nekoashi** carved table-leg
12 等脚三角形 **tōkyaku sankakkei, tōkyaku sankakukei** isosceles triangle
　雲脚 **kumoashi** movement of clouds
13 鉄脚 **tekkyaku** iron legs
16 橋脚 **kyōkyaku** bridge pier
19 韻脚 **inkyaku** (metrical) foot

————— 4 —————

2 二人三脚 **ninin-sankyaku** three-legged race
15 諸国行脚 **shokoku angya** walking tour of the country

4b7.4

腆 **TEN** much, abundant; kind, considerate

4b7.5

脰 **TŌ** nape; throat; shin

4b7.6

脛 **KEI, sune, hagi** shin, (lower) leg

————— 1 —————

3 脛巾 **habaki** leggings, gaiters
6 脛当 **sunea(te)** shin guards
10 脛骨 **keikotsu** shinbone, tibia
18 脛噛 **sunekaji(ri)** hanger-on, sponger

————— 2 —————

4 毛脛 **kezune** hairy legs
14 痩脛 **ya(se)zune** skinny legs

4b7.7 / 1278

脳 腦 **NŌ** brain

————— 1 —————

3 脳下垂体 **nōkasuitai** pituitary gland
4 脳天 **nōten** crown of the head
　脳中 **nōchū** in one's head
5 脳出血 **nōshukketsu** cerebral hemorrhage

6 脳死 **nōshi** brain death

脳充血 **nōjūketsu** brain congestion

脳血栓 **nōkessen** cerebral thrombosis

7 脳乱 **nōran** worry, anguish

8 脳卒中 **nōsotchū** cerebral apoplexy

脳味噌 **nōmiso** brains, gray matter

脳炎 **nōen** encephalitis

10 脳振盪 **nōshintō** cerebral concussion

脳脊髄膜炎 **nōsekizuimakuen** cerebrospinal
meningitis

脳病 **nōbyō** brain disorder

脳病院 **nōbyōin** hospital for brain diseases

脳症 **nōshō** brain fever

11 脳貧血 **nōhinketsu** cerebral anemia

脳軟化症 **nōnankashō** encephalomalacia

12 脳裡 **nōri** the brain, one's mind

13 脳裏 **nōri** the brain, one's mind

脳溢血 **nōikketsu** cerebral apoplexy

14 脳膜 **nōmaku** (cerebral) meninges

脳膜炎 **nōmakuen** meningitis

15 脳漿 **nōshō** (fluid in) the brain, gray matter

脳震盪 **nōshintō** cerebral concussion

18 脳髄 **nōzui** the brain

───────── 2 ─────────

3 大脳 **dainō** the cerebrum

小脳 **shōnō** the cerebellum

4 中脳 **chūnō** the midbrain

片脳 **hennō** (refined) camphor

片脳油 **hennōyu** camphor oil

5 主脳 **shunō** leader

主脳会談 **shunō kaidan** summit conference

主脳会議 **shunō kaigi** summit conference

石脳油 **sekinōyu** petroleum

9 首脳 **shunō** leader

首脳会談 **shunō kaidan** summit conference

首脳部 **shunōbu** leaders, top management

前脳 **zennō** the forebrain

洗脳 **sennō** brainwashing

12 間脳 **kannō** the interbrain

15 樟脳 **shōnō** camphor

樟脳油 **shōnōyu** camphor oil

16 頭脳 **zunō** brains, head

───────── 3 ─────────

4 日本脳炎 **Nihon nōen** Japanese encephalitis

16 薄荷脳 **hakkanō** menthol

4b7.8 / 1370

脱 脱

DATSU omit; escape **nu(gu)**
take off (clothes) **nu(gasu)**
strip off clothes, undress
(someone)
nu(geru) come/slip off

───────── 1 ─────────

0 脱する **das(suru)** escape from; be omitted;
take off (clothes); omit

脱サラ **datsusara** quit one's salaried office
job (and become self-employed)

2 脱力 **datsuryoku** be drained of strength

脱力感 **datsuryokukan** feeling of exhaustion

4 脱毛 **datsumō, nu(ke)ge** falling-out/removal
of hair

脱毛剤 **datsumōzai** a depilatory

脱毛症 **datsumōshō** alopecia, baldness

脱文 **datsubun** missing passage, lacuna

脱水 **dassui** dehydration, desiccation

脱水機 **dassuiki** dehydrator, dryer

5 脱出 **dasshutsu** escape from; prolapse

nu(ke)da(su) slip away

脱皮 **dappi** shedding, molting, emergence

脱字 **datsuji** omitted character/word

6 脱臼 **dakkyū** become dislocated

脱会 **dakkai** withdrawal (from an organization)

脱色 **dasshoku** decoloration, bleaching

脱衣 **datsui** take off one's clothes, undress

脱衣所 **datsuisho, datsuijo** changing/
dressing room

7 脱却 **dakkyaku** free oneself from, slough off

脱走 **dassō** escape, flee

脱走兵 **dassōhei** deserter

脱肛 **dakkō** prolapse of the rectum

8 脱兎 **datto** dashing away, fast as a rabbit

脱退 **dattai** secede, withdraw

脱法 **dappō** evasion of the law

脱法行為 **dappō kōi** an evasion of the law

9 脱俗 **datsuzoku** withdraw from the world,
become a hermit

脱俗的 **datsuzokuteki** unworldly, saintly

脱臭 **dasshū** deodorize

脱臭剤 **dasshūzai** deodorant, deodorizer

10 脱党 **dattō** leave/bolt the party

脱脂 **dasshi** fat removal; nonfat, skim (milk)

脱脂乳 **dasshinyū** skim milk

脱脂綿 **dasshimen** absorbent cotton

脱疽 **dasso** gangrene

11 脱捨 **nu(gi)su(teru)** throw off (clothes), kick
off (shoes)

脱船 **dassen** desert/jump ship

12 脱帽 **datsubō** take off one's hat/cap

脱落 **datsuraku** fall off, molt; be omitted;
defect, desert, drop out

脱営 **datsuei** desertion from barracks

脱税 **datsuzei** tax evasion

13 脱腸 **datchō** hernia, rupture

脱腸帯 **datchōtai** truss

14 脱漏 **datsurō** omission

脱獄 **datsugoku** escape from prison, jailbreak

脱獄囚 **datsugokushū** escaped prisoner

脱穀 **dakkoku** threshing

脱穀機 **dakkokuki** threshing machine

15 脱稿 **dakkō** finish writing, complete

脱監 **dakkan** escape from prison, jailbreak
脱線 **dassen** derailment; digression
18 脱藩 **dappan** leaving one's lord and becoming a lordless samurai
脱離 **datsuri** disconnect (oneself) from
21 脱艦 **dakkan** desertion from a warship

—————— 2 ——————

6 肌脱 **hadanu(gi)** bare to the waist
8 沓脱 **kutsunu(gi)** place to take one's shoes off (before entering the house)
9 洒脱 **shadatsu** free and easy, unconstrained
10 剥脱 **hakudatsu** come/peel off
逸脱 **itsudatsu** deviation, departure
11 虚脱 **kyodatsu** prostration, collapse
12 超脱 **chōdatsu** transcend, stand aloof, rise above
13 滑脱 **katsudatsu** versatile, resourceful
靴脱 **kutsunu(gi)** (entranceway) place to remove one's shoes
解脱 **gedatsu** (Buddhist) deliverance, salvation
14 誤脱 **godatsu** errors and omissions
15 膚脱 **hadanu(gi)** bare to the waist
16 潁脱 **eidatsu** outstanding ability
18 離脱 **ridatsu** secession, separation, abolition, renunciation

—————— 3 ——————

1 一肌脱 **hitohada nu(gu)** pitch in and help
4 片肌脱 **katahada nu(gu)** bare one shoulder; help out
片膚脱 **katahada nu(gu)** bare one shoulder; help out

—————— 4 ——————

4 円転滑脱 **enten-katsudatsu** versatile, all-around, tactful

脈→脈 **4b6.8**

朗→朗 **4b6.11**

脣→唇 **3d7.12**

—————— 8 ——————

4b8.1 / 1922

脹
CHŌ, fuku(reru), fuku(ramu) swell, get big, expand
fuku(ramasu) cause to swell, expand

—————— 1 ——————

9 脹面 **fuku(ret)tsura** sulky/sullen look, pout

10 脹粉 **fuku(rashi)ko** baking powder

—————— 2 ——————

3 下脹 **shimobuku(re)** swelling on the lower part of the face/body
4 水脹 **mizubuku(re)** blister
火脹 **hibuku(re)** burn blister
13 腫脹 **shuchō** swelling, boil
16 膨脹 **bōchō** swelling, expansion

4b8.2

脾
HI the spleen

—————— 1 ——————

19 脾臓 **hizō** the spleen

4b8.3

腓
HI, fukurahagi, komura calf (of the leg)

4b8.4 / 509

勝 勝
SHŌ, ka(tsu) win
ka(chi) victory, win
-gachi be apt to, tend to
masa(ru) excel, be superior to
sugu(reru) excel, be excellent

—————— 1 ——————

4 勝手 **katte** as one pleases, arbitrary; kitchen; the situation
勝手口 **katteguchi** kitchen/back door
勝手不如意 **katte-funyoi** hard up (for money), bad off
勝手元 **kattemoto** one's financial circumstances
勝手次第 **katte-shidai** having one's own way
勝手向 **kattemu(ki)** one's financial circumstances
5 勝目 **ka(chi)me** chances of winning
6 勝気 **ka(chi)ki** determined to succeed
勝地 **shōchi** scenic spot
勝名乗 **ka(chi)nano(ri)** be declared winner
勝因 **shōin** cause of victory
7 勝抜 **ka(chi)nu(ku)** fight to victory
勝利 **shōri** victory
勝利者 **shōrisha** victor, winner
8 勝逃 **ka(chi)ni(ge)** quit while one is ahead
勝味 **ka(chi)mi** chances of winning
勝者 **shōsha** winner, victor
勝放 **ka(chi)hana(su)** win by a wide margin
9 勝負 **shōbu** victory or defeat; match, showdown
勝負事 **shōbugoto** game of skill/chance
勝負師 **shōbushi** gambler

木 月 日 火 ネ 王 牛 方 攵 欠 心 戸 戈

4

8←

4

→ 8

木 月 日 火 礻 王 牛 方 攵 欠 心 戸 戈

勝通 **ka(chi)tō(su)** win successive victories
勝星 **ka(chi)boshi** (mark indicating) a win
10 勝残 **ka(chi)noko(ru)** make the finals
勝進 **ka(chi)susu(mu)** win and advance to the next rank/round
勝栗 **ka(chi)guri** dried chestnut
11 勝率 **shōritsu** percentage of wins
勝得 **ka(chi)e(ru)** win, achieve, earn, gain
勝敗 **shōhai** victory or defeat
12 勝報 **shōhō** news of victory
勝景 **shōkei** beautiful scenery, fine view
勝越 **ka(chi)ko(shi)** ahead by (so many) wins
勝訴 **shōso** winning a lawsuit
13 勝戦 **ka(chi)ikusa** victorious battle
勝続 **ka(chi)tsuzu(ke)** victories in a row
勝誇 **ka(chi)hoko(ru)** triumph, exult in victory
14 勝算 **shōsan** chances of success
勝鬨 **ka(chi)doki** shout of victory

───────── 2 ─────────

3 大勝 **taishō** decisive victory
大勝利 **daishōri** decisive victory
丸勝 **maruga(chi)** complete/overwhelming victory
4 手勝手 **tegatte** handling, skill
5 必勝 **hisshō** sure victory
圧勝 **asshō** overwhelming victory
打勝 **u(chi)ka(tsu)** defeat, conquer
立勝 **ta(chi)masa(ru)** surpass, excel
6 再勝 **saishō** another win
全勝 **zenshō** complete victory
先勝 **senshō** win the first game/point
名勝 **meishō** scenic spot
有勝 **a(ri)ga(chi)** apt to happen, common
7 身勝手 **migatte** selfishness, having one's own way
我勝 **warega(chi ni)** everyone for himself
決勝 **kesshō** decision (in a contest)
決勝点 **kesshōten** goal, finish line
決勝戦 **kesshōsen** finals
決勝線 **kesshōsen** goal/finish line
形勝 **keishō** scenic beauty; good location
完勝 **kanshō** complete victory
快勝 **kaishō** a sweeping victory
辛勝 **shinshō** narrow victory
男勝 **otokomasa(ri)** strong-minded, spirited
8 奇勝 **kishō** surprise victory; place of scenic beauty
9 連勝 **renshō** series of victories, winning streak
10 殊勝 **shushō** admirable, praiseworthy, commendable
健勝 **kenshō** healthy, robust, hale and hearty
11 探勝 **tanshō** sightseeing
常勝 **jōshō** ever-victorious, invincible
12 景勝 **keishō** picturesque scenery

無勝負 **mushōbu** a tie/draw, undecided
絶勝 **zesshō** breathtaking view
13 楽勝 **rakushō** easy victory
戦勝 **senshō** victory
戦勝国 **senshōkoku** victorious nation
戦勝者 **senshōsha** victor
16 曇勝 **kumo(ri)ga(chi)** broken clouds, mostly cloudy
親勝 **oyamasa(ri)** a child surpassing his parents
17 優勝 **yūshō** victory, championship
優勝劣敗 **yūshō-reppai** survival of the fittest
優勝杯 **yūshōhai** championship cup
優勝者 **yūshōsha** winner, champion, title-holder
優勝旗 **yūshōki** championship pennant

───────── 3 ─────────

1 一六勝負 **ichiroku shōbu** gambling; a gamble
4 天平勝宝 **Tenpyō Shōhō** (era, 749–756)
手前勝手 **temae-gatte** selfish
6 自分勝手 **jibun-katte** having one's own way, selfish
7 判定勝 **hanteiga(chi)** win by a decision
9 飛入勝手 **tobii(ri) katte** open to all comers
10 准決勝 **junkesshō** semifinals
真剣勝負 **shinken-shōbu** fighting with real swords; game played in earnest
11 得手勝手 **etekatte** self-centered, selfish
13 準決勝 **junkesshō** semifinals

───────── 4 ─────────

6 百戦百勝 **hyakusen-hyakushō** ever-victorious
9 連戦連勝 **rensen-renshō** succession of victories

4b8.5

腊

SEKI, hojishi dried meat

───────── 1 ─────────

12 腊葉 **sakuyō** dried/pressed leaves

4b8.6 / 1299

腕

WAN, ude arm; skill
kaina arm

───────── 1 ─────────

2 腕力 **wanryoku** physical strength
4 腕木 **udegi** arm, crosspiece, bracket
腕木信号 **udegi shingō** semaphore
5 腕比 **udekura(be)** contest of strength/skill
腕白 **wanpaku** naughty, mischievous
腕立 **udeda(te)** fight, resort to force
腕立伏 **udeta(te)fu(se)** push-ups
6 腕次第 **ude-shidai** according to one's ability

腕自慢 **udejiman** proud of one's skill
7 腕利 **udeki(ki)** skilled, able
9 腕首 **udekubi** the wrist
腕前 **udemae** ability, skill
腕相撲 **udezumō** arm wrestling
10 腕時計 **udedokei** wristwatch
11 腕達者 **udedassha** strong/brawny man
腕章 **wanshō** armband, arm badge, chevron
腕組 **udegu(mi)** fold one's arms
13 腕節 **ude(p)pushi** muscular strength
腕試 **udedame(shi)** test of strength/skill
14 腕関節 **wankansetsu** the wrist joint
15 腕輪 **udewa** bracelet

———— 2 ————
3 才腕 **saiwan** ability, skill
上腕 **jōwan** the upper arm
4 片腕 **kataude** one arm; right-hand man
手腕 **shuwan** ability, skill
手腕家 **shuwanka** man of ability
5 左腕 **hidariude** left arm
  sawan left-handed pitcher
右腕 **uwan, migiude** right arm
6 両腕 **ryōude** both arms
7 扼腕 **yakuwan** clench one's arms (in anger/vexation)
快腕 **kaiwan** remarkable ability
利腕 **ki(ki)ude** one's more dexterous arm
8 怪腕 **kaiwan** remarkable ability
10 敏腕 **binwan** able, capable
敏腕家 **binwanka** able person, go-getter
11 細腕 **hosoude** thin arm; poor ability, slender means
13 鉄腕 **tetsuwan** strong untiring arm
14 辣腕 **ratsuwan** astute, sharp
痩腕 **ya(se)ude** thin arm; meager income

———— 4 ————
4 切歯扼腕 **sesshi-yakuwan** gnash one's teeth and clench one's arms on the chest (in vexation)

4b8.7

腔 **KŌ, KŪ** body cavity

———— 2 ————
3 口腔 **kōkō** the oral cavity
口腔外科 **kōkō geka** oral surgery
7 体腔 **taikō, taikū** body cavity
12 満腔 **mankō** wholehearted
13 腹腔 **fukkō, fukukō, fukukū** the abdominal/peritoneal cavity
14 鼻腔 **bikō** the nasal cavity

臍 → 臍 4b14.2

4b8.8

腋 **EKI, waki** armpit, side

———— 1 ————
3 腋下 **ekika, waki(no)shita** armpit
4 腋毛 **wakige** underarm hair
8 腋明 **wakia(ki)** placket (in a skirt)
9 腋臭 **wakiga** underarm odor

4b8.9

腑 **FU** viscera, bowels; mind; reason, understanding

———— 1 ————
5 腑甲斐無 **fugaina(i)** faint-hearted, feckless
7 腑抜 **funu(ke)** lily-livered person, coward
12 腑落 **fu (ni) o(chinai)** cannot fathom/understand

———— 2 ————
4 六腑 **roppu** the six entrails (large intestine; small intestine; gallbladder; stomach; organs of ingestion, digestion, and excretion; urinary bladder)
9 肺腑 **haifu** the lungs; one's inmost heart
19 臓腑 **zōfu** entrails, viscera

———— 4 ————
4 五臓六腑 **gozō-roppu** the five viscera and six entrails

4b8.10

腱 **KEN** tendon

———— 1 ————
0 アキレス腱 **Akiresuken** Achille's tendon/heel

———— 3 ————
15 膝蓋腱反射 **shitsugaiken hansha** knee-jerk reaction

腿 → 腿 4b9.10

4b8.11 / 449

期 期碁 **KI, GO** time, period, term

———— 1 ————
0 期する **ki(suru)** expect, anticipate, hope for, count on
期せずして **ki(sezu shite)** unexpectedly, accidentally

4

木 相
→ 8 月
日
火
ネ
王
牛
方
攵
欠
心
戸
戈

4 期日 **kijitsu** (appointed) day/date, term, due date
5 期末 **kimatsu** end of the term/period
6 期成 **kisei** realization (of a plan)
期成同盟 **kisei dōmei** uniting to carry out (a plan)
期米 **kimai** rice for future delivery
8 期限 **kigen** term, period, due date, deadline
9 期首 **kishu** beginning of the term/period
期待 **kitai** expect, anticipate, place one's hopes on
12 期間 **kikan** term, period

─────── 2 ───────

1 一期 **ichigo** one's lifespan
ikki a term, a half year, a quarter
2 二期 **niki** two terms; twice a year
3 上期 **kamiki** the first half (of the year)
下期 **shimoki** the latter/second half (of the year)
4 予期 **yoki** expect, anticipate
中期 **chūki** middle period
今期 **konki** the present/current term
5 半期 **hanki** half term, half year
末期 **makki** closing years, last stage
matsugo hour of death, deathbed
氷期 **hyōki** ice age
好期 **kōki** the right time
冬期 **tōki** winter season, wintertime
6 死期 **shiki** time of death, one's last hour
年期 **nenki** term of service, apprenticeship; experience
年期奉公 **nenki bōkō** apprenticeship
毎期 **maiki** every term
任期 **ninki** term of office, tenure
会期 **kaiki** term, session (of a legislature)
次期 **jiki** next term
刑期 **keiki** prison term
同期 **dōki** the same period; the same class; synchronous
同期生 **dōkisei** (former) classmate
当期 **tōki** this period, the current term
有期 **yūki** for a definite period
有期刑 **yūkikei** penal servitude for a stated term
早期 **sōki** early stage/phase
早期診断 **sōki shindan** early diagnosis
7 何期 **nanki** how many periods; what period
延期 **enki** postpone, defer, prolong
花期 **kaki** the flowering season
学期 **gakki** school term, semester
学期末 **gakkimatsu** end of the term/semester
初期 **shoki** early period/stage, beginning
初期化 **shokika** initialization
8 長期 **chōki** long-term, long-range
長期戦 **chōkisen** prolonged/protracted war

画期的 **kakkiteki** epoch-making, revolutionary
周期 **shūki** period, cycle
周期性 **shūkisei** periodic, cyclical
始期 **shiki** initial date/period
定期 **teiki** fixed period/term/intervals, regular (meeting) (short for 定期券)
定期払 **teikibara(i)** time/installment payments
定期券 **teikiken** (train) pass, commuting ticket
定期的 **teikiteki** periodic
定期風 **teikifū** periodic wind
定期船 **teikisen** regular(ly scheduled) ship
所期 **shoki** expectation, anticipation
雨期 **uki** the rainy season
9 前期 **zenki** the first/preceding term
後期 **kōki** latter period/term, late (Nara); latter half (of the year)
秋期 **shūki** autumn, fall
10 残期 **zanki** remaining period, unexpired term
時期 **jiki** time, season
夏期 **kaki** the summer period
納期 **nōki** payment date, delivery deadline
11 婚期 **konki** marriageable age
猟期 **ryōki** hunting season
終期 **shūki** expiration, close, end
転期 **tenki** crisis (of an illness)
12 満期 **manki** expiration (date)
短期 **tanki** short period, short-term
短期大学 **tanki daigaku** junior college
最期 **saigo** one's last moments, death
無期 **muki** indefinite
無期刑 **mukikei** life imprisonment
無期延期 **muki enki** indefinite postponement
無期限 **mukigen** indefinite, without time limit
無期懲役 **muki chōeki** life imprisonment
13 農期 **nōki** farming season
14 漁期 **gyoki, ryōki** fishing season

─────── 3 ───────

1 一周期 **isshūki** a period (in astronomy)
3 上半期 **kamihanki** the first half (of the year)
下半期 **kahanki, shimohanki** the latter half (of the year)
4 不定期 **futeiki** at irregular intervals, for an indefinite term
収縮期血圧 **shūshukuki ketsuatsu** systolic blood pressure
収穫期 **shūkakuki** harvest time
支払期日 **shiharaikijitsu** due date, maturity
5 半減期 **hangenki** halflife (in physics)
幼年期 **yōnenki** childhood
幼児期 **yōjiki** young childhood, infancy
氷河期 **hyōgaki** glacial period, ice age
好時期 **kōjiki** good season for
四半期 **shihanki** quarter (of a year)
6 全盛期 **zenseiki** golden age, heyday

回復期 **kaifukuki** convalescence
成熟期 **seijukuki** puberty, adolescence
7 更年期 **kōnenki** menopause
沖積期 **chūsekiki** the alluvial epoch
決算期 **kessanki** accounting period/term
8 抱卵期 **hōranki** incubation period
青春期 **seishunki** youth, adolescence
9 発情期 **hatsujōki** puberty; mating season
変声期 **henseiki** age of puberty/voice-cracking
変容期 **hen'yōki** period of changing appearance
通用期間 **tsūyō kikan** period of (a ticket's) validity
狩猟期 **shuryōki** open season
草創期 **sōsōki** initial/early period
胎動期 **taidōki** the quickening period
思春期 **shishunki** puberty
10 倦怠期 **kentaiki** period of weariness
遊猟期 **yūryōki** hunting season
泰平期 **taiheiki** period of peace
11 過渡期 **katoki** transition period
渇水期 **kassuiki** dry season, drought period
授乳期 **junyūki** period of lactation
産卵期 **sanranki** breeding/spawning season
転換期 **tenkanki** transition period, turning point
12 揺籃期 **yōranki** infancy
登山期 **tozanki** mountain-climbing season
猶予期間 **yūyo kikan** grace period
最盛期 **saiseiki** golden age, heyday; the best season for
13 農閑期 **nōkanki** farmers' slack season
農繁期 **nōhanki** farmers' busy season
適齢期 **tekireiki** marriageable age
豊水期 **hōsuiki** rainy season
禁猟期 **kinryōki** closed (hunting) season
禁漁期 **kinryōki** closed (fishing) season
新学期 **shingakki** new school term
14 端境期 **hazakaiki** off/between-crops season
15 潜伏期 **senpukuki** incubation period
18 離乳期 **rinyūki** the weaning period

———————— 4 ————————
12 無期延期 **muki enki** indefinite postponement

———————— 5 ————————
9 春機発動期 **shunki hatsudōki** puberty

4b8.12 / 469

朝 朝   **CHŌ** morning; dynasty
   asa, ashita morning

———————— 1 ————————
0 朝っぱらから **asa(ppara kara)** so early in the morning
3 朝三暮四 **chōsan-boshi** being deceived by immediate gain (like the monkey who did not realize that being given four chestnuts in the morning and three in the evening amounts to the same as three in the morning and four in the evening)
朝夕 **chōseki, asayū** morning and/till evening, day and night, constantly
4 朝日 **asahi** morning/rising sun
朝日影 **asahikage** morning sunshine
朝方 **asagata** (toward) morning
5 朝令暮改 **chōrei-bokai** issuing an order in the morning and changing it in the evening, lack of constancy/principle
朝刊 **chōkan** morning paper/edition
朝市 **asaichi** morning market/fair
朝礼 **chōrei** morning meeting/exercises
朝立 **asada(chi)** early-morning departure; morning erection
6 朝廷 **chōtei** imperial court
朝凪 **asanagi** morning calm (at sea)
朝早 **asa haya(ku)** early in the morning
7 朝来 **chōrai** since morning
朝臣 **chōshin** courtier; the court
   ason court noble
朝見 **chōken** imperial audience
8 朝参 **asamai(ri)** morning visit to a shrine/temple
朝明 **asaa(ke)** daybreak, dawn
9 朝風 **asakaze** morning breeze
朝風呂 **asaburo** morning bath
朝政 **chōsei** imperial government
朝威 **chōi** imperial prestige/authority
朝食 **chōshoku** breakfast
10 朝帰 **asagae(ri)** returning home in the morning after an all-night stay
朝酒 **asazake** morning drink of saké
朝起 **asao(ki)** get up early
朝家 **chōka** imperial household/family
朝恩 **chōon** the sovereign's favor
朝貢 **chōkō** bring tribute
11 朝野 **chōya** government and people, the whole nation
朝涼 **asasuzu(mi)** the morning cool
12 朝湯 **asayu** morning bath
朝寒 **asasamu** the morning cool/cold
朝朝 **asa(na)asa(na)** morning after morning
朝晩 **asaban** morning and evening; always
朝焼 **asaya(ke)** red sunrise
朝賀 **chōga** retainers' New Year's greeting to the emperor
朝飯 **asahan, asameshi** breakfast
朝飯前 **asameshimae** (easy enough to do) before breakfast
朝間 **asama** during the morning
13 朝寝 **asane** morning sleep, late rising
朝寝坊 **asanebō** late riser

朝腹 **asa(p)para (kara)** before breaking the night's fast, early in the morning
14 朝暮 **chōbo** morning and evening
朝駆 **asaga(ke)** attack at dawn
15 朝潮 **asashio** morning tide
朝敵 **chōteki** enemy of the court, rebel
朝餉 **asage** breakfast
16 朝憲 **chōken** constitution
朝曇 **asagumo(ri)** cloudy morning
17 朝霞 **asagasumi** morning mist
朝鮮 **Chōsen** Korea
朝鮮人 **Chōsenjin** a Korean
朝鮮人参 **Chōsen ninjin** ginseng
18 朝顔 **asagao** morning glory
19 朝霧 **asagiri** morning fog
20 朝議 **chōgi** court council
21 朝露 **chōro, asatsuyu** morning dew
24 朝靄 **asamoya** morning haze/mist

―――――――― 2 ――――――――
1 一朝 **itchō** a time, a short period
一朝一夕 **itchō-isseki** in a day, in a short time
2 入朝 **nyūchō** visit Japan, arrive in Japan
4 今朝 **kesa, konchō** this morning
今朝方 **kesagata** this morning
王朝 **ōchō** dynasty
5 北朝 **Hokuchō** the Northern Dynasty
北朝鮮 **Kita Chōsen** North Korea
6 毎朝 **maiasa** every morning
当朝 **tōchō** the present court/dynasty
早朝 **sōchō** early morning
7 来朝 **raichō** visit to Japan, arrival in Japan
宋朝 **Sōchō** Song dynasty
8 明朝 **myōchō** tomorrow morning
Minchō Ming dynasty; Ming style (of printed kanji; the most widely used typeface, with a thickening at the right end of protruding horizontal strokes)
9 昨朝 **sakuchō** yesterday morning
10 帰朝 **kichō** return from abroad
唐朝 **Tōchō** the Tang dynasty
11 清朝 **Shinchō** Manchu/Qing dynasty
清朝体 **seichōtai** (a type of printed kanji resembling brush writing)
翌朝 **yokuchō, yokuasa** the next morning
異朝 **ichō** foreign court; foreign country
12 朝朝 **asa(na)asa(na)** morning after morning
13 漢朝 **kanchō** Han dynasty
14 歴朝 **rekichō** successive reigns/dynasties

―――――――― 3 ――――――――
5 平安朝 **Heianchō** the Heian period (794 – 1185)
9 南北朝 **Nanbokuchō** the Northern and Southern Dynasties (439 – 589 in China, 1336 – 1392 in Japan)

碁 → 期 **4b8.11**

4b8.13

敊 **KŌ** mixing, confusion

―――――――― 9 ――――――――
4b9.1

腫 **SHU** tumor, swelling
ha(reru) swell, become swollen
ha(rasu) cause to swell, inflame

―――――――― 1 ――――――――
3 腫上 **ha(re)a(garu)** swell up
8 腫物 **ha(re)mono, shumotsu** swelling, boil, tumor, abscess
12 腫脹 **shuchō** swelling, boil
14 腫瘍 **shuyō** tumor

―――――――― 2 ――――――――
4 水腫 **suishu** dropsy; edema
6 肉腫 **nikushu** sarcoma
8 泣腫 **na(ki)ha(rasu)** get swollen eyes from crying
9 浮腫 **muku(mu)** swell, bloat
fushu, mukumi swelling, edema, dropsy
17 膿腫 **nōshu** abscess
癌腫 **ganshu** cancer tumor, carcinoma

―――――――― 3 ――――――――
11 蚯蚓腫 **mimizuba(re)** welt

4b9.2

腴 **YU** grow fat; fat, grease

4b9.3 / 1298

腰 **YŌ, koshi** the pelvic region, loins, hips, the small of the back

―――――――― 1 ――――――――
2 腰刀 **koshigatana** short sword
3 腰上 **koshia(ge)** tuck at the waist
腰巾着 **koshiginchaku** belt purse; one's shadow/follower-around
4 腰元 **koshimoto** lady's maid
5 腰弁 **koshiben** petty official, low-salaried worker
腰弁当 **koshibentō** lunch tied to one's belt; lunch-carrying worker
腰付 **koshitsu(ki)** gait, carriage, posture
腰布 **koshinuno** loincloth

腰布団 **koshibuton** cushion worn around the waist for warmth
6 腰気 **koshike** leucorrhea, vaginal discharge
腰肉 **koshiniku** loin, sirloin
腰羽目 **koshibame** hip-high wainscoting
腰当 **koshia(te)** a bustle
腰回 **koshimawa(ri)** one's hip measurement
7 腰折 **koshio(re)** poorly written poem
腰抜 **koshinu(ke)** coward(ice), weak-kneed milksop
腰囲 **yōi** one's hip measurement
8 腰板 **koshiita** baseboard, wainscoting
腰物 **koshi (no) mono** sword worn at one's side
9 腰巻 **koshima(ki)** underskirt, waistband; book wrapper
腰垣 **koshigaki** hip-high fence
腰砕 **koshikuda(ke)** becoming weak-kneed
10 腰部 **yōbu** the pelvic region, waist, hips, loins
腰高 **koshidaka** hip-high; high-hipped (unstable sumo stance), haughty
腰高障子 **koshidaka shōji** sliding door with hip-high paneling
腰帯 **koshiobi** waistband (to hold a kimono in place)
腰弱 **koshiyowa** weak-willed, unpersevering
腰骨 **koshibone** hipbone; perseverence
11 腰掛 **koshika(keru)** sit down **koshika(ke)** seat; steppingstone (to something else)
腰掛仕事 **koshika(ke) shigoto** temporary work
腰張 **koshiba(ri)** papering (on) the lower part of a wall or sliding door
12 腰湯 **koshiyu** hip/sitz bath
腰揚 **koshia(ge)** tuck at the waist
腰椎 **yōtsui** lumbar vertebra
腰痛 **yōtsū** lumbago
15 腰縄 **koshinawa** waist cord (for tying prisoners)
————— 2 —————
3 及腰 **oyo(bi)goshi** a bent back
丸腰 **marugoshi** swordless, unarmed
4 中腰 **chūgoshi** half-sitting/half-standing posture
5 本腰入 **hongoshi (o) i(reru)** make an earnest effort, get down to business
7 足腰 **ashikoshi** legs and loins
8 受腰 **u(ke)goshi** stance for catching
逃腰 **ni(ge)goshi** preparation to flee; evasive attitude
物腰 **monogoshi** manner, demeanor
9 浮腰 **u(ki)goshi** wavering, unsteady
柳腰 **yanagigoshi** slender graceful hips
10 弱腰 **yowagoshi** weak attitude, timidity
11 強腰 **tsuyogoshi** firm attitude
細腰 **saiyō, hosogoshi** slender hips

12 無腰 **mugoshi** unarmed
15 蝦腰 **ebigoshi** bent with age
18 襟腰 **erikoshi** height of the neck
————— 3 —————
9 海老腰 **ebigoshi** stooped over, bent with age
12 喧嘩腰 **kenkagoshi** hostile attitude

4b9.4 / 1271

腹 **FUKU, hara** belly, stomach; heart, mind
(o)naka belly, stomach

————— 1 —————
1 腹一杯 **hara ippai** full stomach; to one's heart's content
2 腹子 **harako** fish eggs
腹八分 **hara hachibu** eating to only 80 percent of stomach capacity
3 腹下 **harakuda(shi)** diarrhea; laxative
4 腹中 **fukuchū** in one's heart
腹切 **haraki(ri)** suicide by disembowelment
腹水 **fukusui** abdominal dropsy
腹心 **fukushin** confidant, trusted associate
5 腹皮 **harakawa** skin of a fish's abdomen
腹立 **harada(tsu)** get angry
腹立紛 **harada(chi)magi(re)** a fit of rage
6 腹合 **haraa(wase)** facing each other
腹汚 **haragitana(i)** low-minded
腹当 **haraa(te)** chest-and-stomach armor; bellyband
腹式呼吸 **fukushiki kokyū** abdominal breathing
腹虫 **hara (no) mushi** intestinal worms; one's heart, anger
7 腹芸 **haragei** communicating by other than words and gestures, force of personality
腹囲 **fukui** girth of the abdomen
8 腹具合 **haraguai** condition of one's bowels
9 腹巻 **harama(ki)** waistband, bellyband
腹変 **haraga(wari)** born of a different mother but having the same father; changing one's mind, going back on one's word
腹持 **haramo(chi)** slow digestion, feeling of fullness
腹背 **fukuhai** front and back
10 腹部 **fukubu** abdomen, belly
腹這 **haraba(i)** lying belly-down
腹帯 **haraobi, fukutai** (pregnant woman's) bellyband
腹案 **fukuan** plan, forethought
腹時計 **haradokei** one's sense of time
11 腹掛 **haraga(ke)** cloth chest-and-belly cover
腹黒 **haraguro(i)** black-hearted, scheming
12 腹違 **harachiga(i)** born of a different mother but having the same father
腹減 **hara (ga) he(ru)** be hungry

4

木
月
日 9←
火
礻
王
牛
方
攵
欠
心
戸
戈

4

木
月
日
火
礻
王
牛
方
攵
欠
心
戸
戈

→9

腹腔 **fukkō, fukukō, fukukū** the abdominal/peritoneal cavity

腹痛 **fukutsū, haraita** stomachache, abdominal pain

腹筋 **fukkin, fukukin, harasuji** abdominal muscles

13 腹鼓 **haratsuzumi** drumming on one's belly; eating one's fill

腹話術 **fukuwajutsu** ventriloquism

14 腹膜 **fukumaku** the peritoneum

腹膜炎 **fukumakuen** peritonitis

15 腹蔵 **fukuzō** being reserved, holding back

16 腹壁 **fukuheki** the abdominal wall

腹積 **harazu(mori)** anticipating what someone will do; resolve, determination

18 腹癒 **harai(se)** revenge, retaliation

———— 2 ————

3 下腹 **shitabara, shitahara, shita(p)para** abdomen, belly

下腹部 **kafukubu** abdomen

小腹 **kobara** belly, abdomen

山腹 **sanpuku** hillside, mountainside

4 太腹 **futo(p)para** generous; bold

中腹 **chūfuku** mountain side, halfway up

chū(p)para offended, in a huff

切腹 **seppuku** disembowelment, harakiri

片腹 **katahara** one side (of the body)

片腹痛 **katahara-ita(i)** ridiculous, absurd

心腹 **shinpuku** sincerity; one's confidant

5 正腹 **seifuku** legitimate (child)

立腹 **rippuku** get angry, lose one's temper

6 同腹 **dōfuku** born of the same womb; kindred spirits

虫腹 **mushibara** pain from roundworms

7 私腹 **shifuku** one's own pocket/purse

8 追腹 **tsuifuku, o(i)bara** committing harakiri to follow one's dead master

抱腹 **hōfuku** holding one's sides in laughter

抱腹絶倒 **hōfuku-zettō** convulsed with laughter

空腹 **kūfuku, su(ki)hara** empty stomach, hunger

妾腹 **shōfuku, mekakebara** born of a concubine/mistress

9 負腹立 **ma(ke)bara (o) ta(teru)** get angry upon losing

後腹 **atobara** afterpains; child by one's second wife

10 剛腹 **gōfuku** magnanimous; obstinate

脇腹 **wakibara** one's side

11 渋腹 **shibu(ri)bara** diarrhea-like bowel pains

捧腹 **hōfuku** holding one's sides in laughter

捧腹絶倒 **hōfuku-zettō** convulsed with laughter

異腹 **ifuku** born of a different womb/mother

船腹 **senpuku** bottoms, cargo space

蛇腹 **jabara** accordion-like folds, bellows; cornice

魚腹 **gyofuku** fishes' bellies/entrails

12 割腹 **kappuku** disembowelment, harakiri

満腹 **manpuku** full stomach/belly

粥腹 **kayubara** living on rice gruel

朝腹 **asa(p)para (kara)** before breaking the night's fast, early in the morning

13 業腹 **gōhara** resentment, spite, vexation

裏腹 **urahara** the contrary, opposite

詰腹 **tsu(me)bara** forced harakiri

14 遺腹 **ifuku** posthumous child

15 皺腹 **shiwabara** wrinkled abdomen, old belly

横腹 **yokohara, yokobara, yoko(p)para** side, flank

22 鱈腹 **tarafuku** (eat) to one's heart's content

———— 3 ————

4 太鼓腹 **taikobara** paunch, potbelly

5 布袋腹 **hoteibara** potbelly, paunch

9 面従腹背 **menjū-fukuhai** outward obedience but inward opposition, false obedience, passive resistance

4b9.5

腮

SAI, ago jaw

4b9.6

腺

SEN gland

———— 1 ————

10 腺病質 **senbyōshitsu** weak constitution

15 腺熱 **sennetsu** glandular fever

———— 2 ————

6 汗腺 **kansen** sweat gland

7 乳腺 **nyūsen** mammary gland

10 涙腺 **ruisen** tear gland

———— 3 ————

5 甲状腺 **kōjōsen** thyroid gland

9 前立腺 **zenritsusen** prostate gland

扁桃腺 **hentōsen** the tonsils

扁桃腺炎 **hentōsen'en** tonsillitis

10 消化腺 **shōkasen** digestive glands

11 淋巴腺 **rinpasen** lymph gland

唾液腺 **daekisen** salivary glands

13 摂護腺 **setsugosen** prostate gland

4b9.7

腥

SEI, namagusa(i) smelling of fish/blood, smelling raw

───────── 1 ─────────

8 腥物 **namagusamono** raw things (like fish and meat)

───────── 2 ─────────

6 血腥 **chinamagusa(i)** smelling of blood, bloody

4b9.8 / 1270

腸　腸　 **CHŌ, harawata, wata** intestines, entrails

───────── 1 ─────────

8 腸炎 **chōen** enteritis
11 腸捻転 **chōnenten** twist in the intestines, volvulus
  腸閉塞 **chōheisoku** intestinal obstruction, ileus
12 腸満 **chōman** abdominal dropsy
13 腸詰 **chōzu(me)** sausage
15 腸潰瘍 **chōkaiyō** intestinal ulcer
  腸線 **chōsen** catgut
16 腸壁 **chōheki** intestinal wall

───────── 2 ─────────

3 大腸 **daichō** large intestine, colon
  大腸炎 **daichōen** colitis
  小腸 **shōchō** the small intestines
6 羊腸 **yōchō(taru)** winding, zigzag, meandering
8 盲腸 **mōchō** appendix
  盲腸炎 **mōchōen** appendicitis
  直腸 **chokuchō** the rectum
9 胃腸 **ichō** stomach and intestines
  胃腸病 **ichōbyō** gastrointestinal disorder
  胃腸薬 **ichōyaku** stomach and bowel medicine
10 浣腸 **kanchō** enema
11 脱腸 **datchō** hernia, rupture
  脱腸帯 **datchōtai** truss
  断腸 **danchō** heartbreak
12 結腸 **ketchō** the colon
13 鼓腸 **kochō** flatulence, bloating
20 灌腸 **kanchō** enema

───────── 4 ─────────

2 十二指腸 **jūnishichō** the duodenum
  十二指腸虫 **jūnishichōchū** hookworm

4b9.9

膣　膣　 **CHITSU** vagina

腦 → 脳   4b7.7

4b9.10

腿　腿　 **TAI, momo** (upper) leg

───────── 2 ─────────

3 大腿 **daitai** thigh, femur
  上腿 **jōtai** thigh

4b9.11

腎　 **JIN** kidney

───────── 1 ─────────

5 腎石 **jinseki** kidney stone
8 腎炎 **jin'en** nephritis
  腎盂 **jin'u** the renal pelvis
  腎盂炎 **jin'uen** pyelitis
19 腎臓 **jinzō** kidney
  腎臓炎 **jinzōen** nephritis
  腎臓病 **jinzōbyō** kidney disease
  腎臓結石 **jinzō kesseki** kidney stones

───────── 2 ─────────

7 肝腎 **kanjin** main, vital, essential
  肝腎要 **kanjin-kaname** of crucial/vital importance
11 副腎 **fukujin** adrenal gland

4b9.12

骭　 **KAN, hagi** leg, shin

───────── 10 ─────────

膝 →   **4b11.2**

4b10.1

膄　 **SHŪ, SHU** become emaciated/thin

4b10.2

膊　 **HAKU** arm

───────── 2 ─────────

3 上膊 **jōhaku** the upper arm

4b10.3

膌　 **SEKI** become emaciated/thin

4

木 月 日 火 礻 王 牛 方 攵 欠 心 戸 戈   10←

4b10.4

膃 OTSU fur seal

——————— 1 ———————

8 膃肭臍 ottosei seal (the animal)

4b10.5

膈 KAKU the diaphragm

——————— 1 ———————

14 膈膜 kakumaku the diaphragm

4b10.6 / 1426

膜 MAKU membrane

——————— 2 ———————

4 内膜 naimaku lining membrane
5 弁膜 benmaku valve (in internal organs)
皮膜 himaku membrane, integument, skin
6 肋膜 rokumaku the pleura
肋膜炎 rokumakuen pleurisy
7 角膜 kakumaku cornea
角膜炎 kakumakuen inflammation of the cornea
10 胸膜 kyōmaku the pleura
胸膜炎 kyōmakuen pleurisy
骨膜 kotsumaku the periosteum
骨膜炎 kotsumakuen periostitis
11 脳膜 nōmaku (cerebral) meninges
脳膜炎 nōmakuen meningitis
粘膜 nenmaku mucous membrane
12 結膜 ketsumaku conjunctiva, inner eyelid
結膜炎 ketsumakuen conjunctivitis
13 鼓膜 komaku the eardrum
腹膜 fukumaku the peritoneum
腹膜炎 fukumakuen peritonitis
14 膈膜 kakumaku the diaphragm
網膜 mōmaku the retina
16 薄膜 hakumaku, usumaku thin film

——————— 3 ———————

5 処女膜 shojomaku the hymen
15 横隔膜 ōkakumaku the diaphragm

——————— 4 ———————

11 脳脊髄膜炎 nōsekizuimakuen cerebrospinal meningitis

4b10.7

膀 BŌ bladder

——————— 1 ———————

10 膀胱 bōkō urinary bladder
膀胱結石 bōkō kesseki bladder stones

4b10.8

膂 RYO backbone

——————— 1 ———————

2 膂力 ryoryoku strength, brawn

4b10.9 / 663

静 靜 SEI, JŌ, shizu, shizu(ka) quiet, peaceful, still
shizu(meru) calm, soothe, quell
shizu(maru) grow quiet/calm, subside, die down

——————— 1 ———————

2 静力学 seirikigaku statics
3 静々 shizushizu quietly, calmly, gently
4 静止 seishi still, standstill, at rest, stationary, static state
静止画 seishiga still life
静止衛星 seishieisei (geo)stationary satellite
静水 seisui still/stagnant water
静心 shizugokoro calm spirit
6 静返 shizu(mari)kae(ru) become perfectly quiet
8 静夜 seiya quiet night
静岡 Shizuoka (city, Shizuoka-ken)
静岡県 Shizuoka-ken (prefecture)
静的 seiteki static
静物 seibutsu still life
静物画 seibutsuga still-life picture, still life
9 静思 seishi meditation, comtemplation
10 静座 seiza sit quietly
静脈 jōmyaku vein
静脈血 jōmyakuketsu venous blood
静脈炎 jōmyakuen phlebitis
11 静粛 seishuku silent, still, quiet
静寂 seijaku silent, still, quiet
13 静電気 seidenki static electricity
静電気学 seidenkigaku electrostatics
静電学 seidengaku electrostatics
14 静静 shizushizu quietly, calmly, gently
静態 seitai static, stationary
15 静養 seiyō rest, recuperate
16 静穏 seion calm, tranquil
17 静謐 seihitsu peace, tranquility
18 静観 seikan calmly wait and see

——————— 2 ———————

3 大静脈 daijōmyaku the vena cava
4 心静 kokoroshizu(ka) calm, serene, at peace
5 平静 heisei calm, serene, tranquil

6 安静 **ansei** rest, quiet
7 冷静 **reisei** calm, cool, unruffled
　沈静 **chinsei** stillness; stagnation
8 物静 **monoshizu(ka)** quiet, still, calm
11 動静 **dōsei** movements, conditions
12 閑静 **kansei** quiet, peaceful
13 寝静 **neshizu(maru)** fall asleep
14 静静 **shizushizu** quietly, calmly, gently
16 頸静脈 **keijōmyaku** the jugular vein
18 鎮静 **chinsei** calm, quiet, soothed
　鎮静剤 **chinseizai** tranquilizer, sedative

4b10.10

骰

TŌ, sai dice

――――――― 1 ―――――――
2 骰子 **sai** dice

4b10.11

趙

CHŌ (proper name); stab; walk slowly

――――――― 11 ―――――――

4b11.1

膟

SETSU, sori (used in proper names)

4b11.2

滕

TŌ rising water

4b11.3

膠

KŌ, nikawa glue

――――――― 1 ―――――――
4 膠化 **kōka** gelatinize, change into a colloid
12 膠着 **kōchaku** agglutination; stalemate
　膠着剤 **kōchakuzai** glue, binder
　膠着語 **kōchakugo** an agglutinative language
15 膠質 **kōshitsu** colloid, gelatinous, gluey

4b11.4

膝

SHITSU, hiza knee; lap

――――――― 1 ―――――――
3 膝下 **shikka** at the knees (of one's parents)
　膝小僧 **hizakozō** one's knees, kneecap

4 膝元 **hizamoto** at the knees (of one's parents)
　膝反射 **shitsuhansha** knee-jerk reaction
6 膝行 **shikkō** go on one's knees
8 膝拍子 **hizabyōshi** beating time on one's knee
　膝枕 **hizamakura** using someone's lap for a
　　pillow
10 膝栗毛 **hizakurige** go on foot, hike it
11 膝掛 **hizaka(ke)** lap robe/blanket
13 膝蓋骨 **shitsugaikotsu** kneecap, patella
　膝蓋腱反射 **shitsugaiken hansha** knee-jerk
　　reaction
14 膝関節 **shitsukansetsu** the knee joint
16 膝頭 **hizagashira** kneecap

――――――― 2 ―――――――
3 小膝 **kohiza** the knee
4 片膝 **katahiza** one knee
5 立膝 **ta(te)hiza** (sit with) one knee drawn up
15 諸膝 **morohiza** both knees

腸→腸 **4b9.8**

4b11.5

膵

SUI the pancreas

――――――― 1 ―――――――
19 膵臓 **suizō** the pancreas

4b11.6

膕

KAKU, KYAKU, hikagami the back/
hollow of the knee, the ham

4b11.7

骶

TEI backside, buttocks, bottom

――――――― 2 ―――――――
7 尾骶骨 **biteikotsu** the coccyx, tailbone

膣→膣 **4b9.9**

――――――― 12 ―――――――

4b12.1 / 1145

膨

BŌ swell, expand
fuku(reru/ramu) swell, expand; sulk

――――――― 1 ―――――――
3 膨大 **bōdai** swelling; large, enormous

10 膨粉 **fuku(rashi)ko** baking powder
11 膨張 **bōchō** swelling, expansion
12 膨脹 **bōchō** swelling, expansion

———— 2 ————

3 下膨 **shimobuku(re)** swelling of the lower part of the face/body
8 青膨 **aobuku(re)** dropsical swelling
12 着膨 **kibuku(re)** wear thick clothes, bundle up

4b12.2

膳 **ZEN** food offering; serving tray; (counter for pairs of chopsticks)

———— 2 ————

1 一膳 **ichizen** a bowl (of rice); a pair (of chopsticks)
一膳飯屋 **ichizen meshiya** eatery, diner
2 二膳 **ni (no) zen** (tray with) side-dishes
9 客膳 **kyakuzen** guest's dinner tray
食膳 **shokuzen** dining table
10 配膳 **haizen** set the table
配膳室 **haizenshitsu** service room, pantry
11 据膳 **su(e)zen** a meal set before one

———— 3 ————

6 会席膳 **kaisekizen** dinner tray

4b12.3

膰 **HAN, himorogi** meat offerings

4b12.4

縢 **TŌ** leggings; tie up; close, shut

臙→臘 **4b15.3**

䯒→髄 **4b14.3**

4b12.5

膩 **JI** smooth; oily

4b12.6

骼 **KAKU** bone

4b12.7

骸 **GAI** bone, body
mukuro body; corpse

———— 1 ————

10 骸骨 **gaikotsu** skeleton

———— 2 ————

3 亡骸 **na(ki)gara** one's remains, corpse
6 死骸 **shigai** corpse
7 形骸 **keigai** ruins, a mere skeleton
10 残骸 **zangai** remains, corpse, wreckage
14 遺骸 **igai** one's remains, corpse

4b12.8

鞘 鞘 **SHŌ, saya** scabbard, sheath, cap; markup, margin, spread; (bean) shells

———— 1 ————

6 鞘当 **sayaa(te)** rivalry (in love)
8 鞘取 **sayato(ri)** brokerage

———— 2 ————

7 利鞘 **rizaya** profit margin
10 値鞘 **nezaya** margin, spread (in prices)

———— 3 ————

6 光海鞘 **hikari-boya** luminous plankton

———————— 13 ————————

4b13.1 / 1779

謄 謄 **TŌ** copy

———— 1 ————

5 謄本 **tōhon** transcript, copy
謄写 **tōsha** copy, duplication
謄写版 **tōshaban** mimeograph
謄写料 **tōsharyō** copying charge
謄写機 **tōshaki** mimeograph machine, copier

———— 3 ————

4 戸籍謄本 **koseki tōhon** copy of a family register

4b13.2

膿 **NŌ** pus
u(mu) form pus, fester, suppurate
umi pus

———— 1 ————

5 膿汁 **nōjū** pus
10 膿疱 **nōhō** pustule
13 膿腫 **nōshu** abscess
14 膿漏 **nōrō** purulent discharge, pyorrhea

———— 2 ————

4 化膿 **kanō** suppurate, fester

4
木
月
日
火
礻
王
牛
方
攵
欠
心
戸
戈
→12

化膿菌 **kanōkin** suppurative germ
6 血膿 **chiumi** bloody pus
13 蓄膿症 **chikunōshō** sinusitis

───── 3 ─────

12 歯槽膿漏 **shisō nōrō** pyorrhea

4b13.3

臆　　**OKU** breast, heart, mind; timidity

───── 1 ─────

0 臆する **oku(suru)** fear, hesitate, be timid
9 臆面 **okumen** shy face
10 臆病 **okubyō** cowardly, timid
　臆病者 **okubyōmono** coward
　臆病風 **okubyōkaze** panic, loss of nerve
11 臆断 **okudan** conjecture, supposition, surmise
12 臆測 **okusoku** speculation, conjecture
14 臆説 **okusetsu** hypothesis, conjecture

───── 2 ─────

8 怖臆 **o(mezu)-oku(sezu)** fearlessly, undaunted

膽 → 胆　**4b5.6**

4b13.4

朦　　**MŌ** dim, obscure

───── 1 ─────

3 朦々 **mōmō** dimly lit, gloomy
20 朦朧 **mōrō** dim, hazy

4b13.5

臉　　**KEN** area between eye and cheek; face

4b13.6

膾　　**KAI, namasu** mincemeat; vinegared vegetable-and-fish salad

───── 1 ─────

8 膾炙 **kaisha** (food) in everyone's mouth, (topic) on everyone's lips

4b13.7

臀　　**DEN, shiri** rump, buttocks

───── 1 ─────

10 臀部 **denbu** the buttocks, posterior

4b13.8

臂　　**HI, hiji** elbow; arm

───── 2 ─────

1 一臂 **ippi** a (helping) hand, one's bit
4 片臂 **katahiji** one elbow

───── 4 ─────

2 八面六臂 **hachimen roppi** eight faces and six arms; versatile talent
3 三面六臂 **sanmen roppi** as if having three faces and six arms, versatile, all-around, doing the work of many

───── 14 ─────

4b14.1

臑　　**DŌ** arm, elbow
　　　sune shin, leg

───── 1 ─────

6 臑当 **sunea(te)** shin guards
18 臑嚙 **sunekaji(ri)** hanger-on, sponger

4b14.2

臍 臍　　**SEI, SAI, heso, hozo** navel, belly button

───── 1 ─────

3 臍下丹田 **seika-tanden** center of the abdomen
6 臍曲 **hesoma(gari)** cranky person, grouch
8 臍固 **hozo (o) kata(meru)** resolve to, make up one's mind
10 臍帯 **saitai, seitai** umbilical cord
14 臍緒 **heso(no)o** umbilical cord
18 臍嚙 **hozo (o) ka(mu)** bitterly rue/regret
19 臍繰 **hesoku(ri)** secret savings
　臍繰金 **hesoku(ri)gane** secret savings

───── 3 ─────

14 膃肭臍 **ottosei** seal (the animal)

4b14.3 / 1740

髄 髄 膸　　**ZUI** marrow, pith

───── 2 ─────

4 心髄 **shinzui** the soul/essence of
5 玉髄 **gyokuzui** chalcedony
7 延髄 **enzui** the hindbrain
9 神髄 **shinzui** (quint)essence, soul
10 真髄 **shinzui** essence, spirit, soul
　脊髄 **sekizui** spinal cord
　骨髄 **kotsuzui** marrow

4

14 ←

木 月 日 火 礻 王 牛 方 攵 欠 心 戸 戈

骨髄炎 **kotsuzuien** osteomyelitis
11 脳髄 **nōzui** the brain
12 歯髄 **shizui** pulp of a tooth
14 精髄 **seizui** (quint)essence

――――――― 3 ―――――――

11 脳脊髄膜炎 **nōsekizuimakuen** cerebrospinal
meningitis

髀 → 髀 5f14.3

――――――― 15 ―――――――

4b15.1

鵬

HŌ, ōtori huge mythical bird

4b15.2 / 1287

臓 臓

ZŌ internal organs

――――――― 1 ―――――――

8 臓物 **zōmotsu** entrails, giblets
12 臓腑 **zōfu** entrails, viscera
15 臓器 **zōki** internal organs, viscera

――――――― 2 ―――――――

4 内臓 **naizō** internal organs
五臓 **gozō** the five viscera (lungs, heart,
spleen, liver, kidneys)
五臓六腑 **gozō-roppu** the five viscera and
six entrails
心臓 **shinzō** the heart; nerve, cheek
心臓形 **shinzōgata** heart-shaped
心臓炎 **shinzōen** inflammation of the heart
心臓部 **shinzōbu** the heart of
心臓病 **shinzōbyō** heart disease
心臓麻痺 **shinzō mahi** heart failure/attack
7 肝臓 **kanzō** liver
肝臓炎 **kanzōen** hepatitis
9 肺臓 **haizō** the lungs
12 脾臓 **hizō** the spleen
13 腎臓 **jinzō** kidney
腎臓炎 **jinzōen** nephritis
腎臓病 **jinzōbyō** kidney disease
腎臓結石 **jinzō kesseki** kidney stones
15 膵臓 **suizō** the pancreas

4b15.3

臘 臈

RŌ twelfth lunar month

――――――― 2 ―――――――

5 旧臘 **kyūrō** last December, end of last year
7 希臘 **Girishia** Greece

4b15.4 / 1633

覇

HA supremacy, domination, hegemony

――――――― 1 ―――――――

6 覇気 **haki** ambition, aspirations
8 覇府 **hafu** shogunate
覇者 **hasha** supreme ruler; champion
11 覇道 **hadō** military rule
13 覇業 **hagyō** domination, hegemony
15 覇権 **haken** hegemony, domination

――――――― 2 ―――――――

6 那覇 **Naha** (city, Okinawa-ken)
争覇 **sōha** contend for supremacy
8 制覇 **seiha** mastery, supremacy; championship
9 連覇 **renpa** successive championships

――――――― 16 ―――――――

4b16.1

朧

RŌ, oboro dim, faint, hazy

――――――― 1 ―――――――

6 朧気 **oboroge** hazy, vague, faint
8 朧昆布 **oborokonbu, oborokobu** sliced tangle

――――――― 2 ―――――――

17 朦朧 **mōrō** dim, hazy

4b16.2

臙

EN throat; rouge

――――――― 1 ―――――――

10 臙脂 **enji** rouge
臙脂色 **enji-iro** deep red

4b16.3 / 1780

騰 騰

TŌ rise (in prices)

――――――― 1 ―――――――

12 騰落 **tōraku** fluctuations
騰貴 **tōki** rise (in prices)
13 騰勢 **tōsei** rising/upward trend

――――――― 2 ―――――――

3 上騰 **jōtō** rise, jump, advance
4 反騰 **hantō** reactionary rise (in stock prices),
rally
7 狂騰 **kyōtō** sudden jump in prices
8 沸騰 **futtō** boiling; excitement, agitation
沸騰点 **futtōten** boiling point

昇騰 **shōtō** rise, go up, soar
9 急騰 **kyūtō** sudden rise (in prices)
  昂騰 **kōtō** sudden rise (in prices)
10 高騰 **kōtō** steep rise (in prices)
13 続騰 **zokutō** continued rise (in prices)
15 暴騰 **bōtō** sudden rise (in prices)

———————— 3 ————————
8 物価騰貴 **bukka tōki** rise in prices

4b16.4
臚
RO skin; tell, report

———————— 17 ————————
4b17.1
髏
RO skull

———————— 2 ————————
23 髑髏 **dokuro, sarekōbe, sharekōbe** skull

———————— 18 ————————
臓 → 臟   **4b15.2**
髄 → 髓   **4b14.3**

———————— 19 ————————
爨 →   **7a18.1**
體 → 体   **2a5.6**
髑 →   **6d17.2**

4   17←
木 月 日 火 礻 王 牛 方 攵 心 尸 戈

———————————— 日 **4c** ————————————

日	曰	旧	旦	白	早	旨	百	亘	旬	旭	旱	皀
0.1	3s1.1	1.1	1.2	1.3	2.1	2.2	2.3	2.4	2.5	2.6	3.1	3.2
兌	児	向	明	旺	呆	昌	昇	昊	旻	晨	易	昂
4c10.6	3.3	8e4.3	4.1	4.2	4.3	4.4	4.5	4.6	4.7	4.8	4.9	4c5.11
昆	昏	昔	冐	的	者	旺	映	昧	昨	昭	眈	昵
4.10	4.11	3k5.28	4c5.6	4.12	4.13	4c14.1	5.1	5.2	5.3	5.4	4c15.2	5.5
冒	星	曷	是	昜	昂	昂	阪	春	皆	泉	昼	者
5.6	5.7	5.8	5.9	5.10	5.11	5.12	2f8.8	5.13	5.14	3a5.33	5.15	4c4.13
昶	晒	時	晄	晦	晃	晏	晃	書	耆	晋	晉	殉
5.16	6.1	6.2	4c6.5	4c7.3	6.3	6.4	6.5	6.6	6.7	6.8	4c6.8	6.9
晤	晧	晩	晦	晞	晟	曻	晨	曼	冕	曹	晢	習
7.1	7.2	4c8.3	7.3	7.4	7.5	7.6	7.7	7.8	7.9	7.10	4c8.4	7.11
皐	匙	乾	皎	晝	皕	曉	晴	暎	晚	晰	暑	晶
7.12	7.13	7.14	7.15	4c5.15	7.16	8.1	8.2	4c5.1	8.3	8.4	8.5	8.6
晁	景	量	最	曾	智	替	皓	皖	殼	朝	兜	奢
8.7	8.8	8.9	8.10	2o9.3	8.11	8.12	8.13	8.14	8.15	4b8.12	8.16	8.17
暇	暗	暘	暖	暄	暉	暑	暈	既	幹	晳	貊	曄
9.1	9.2	9.3	9.4	9.5	9.6	4c8.5	9.7	0a10.5	9.8	9.9	9.10	10.1
暝	幹	暢	鉏	貌	暾	暴	暫	皚	羯	甗	鬻	殤
10.2	10.3	10.4	10.5	10.6	11.1	11.2	11.3	11.4	11.5	11.6	11.7	11.8
暸	曉	曇	瞥	暨	翰	豬	赭	曙	曖	曚	甌	貘
5c12.4	4c8.1	12.1	12.2	12.3	12.4	3g8.1	12.5	4c14.2	13.1	13.2	13.3	13.4
鞳	曜	曙	韓	鞞	觴	覆	曝	曠	響	覈	氈	曦
3a13.12	14.1	14.2	14.3	14.4	14.5	14.6	15.1	15.2	15.3	4h15.1	15.4	16.1

馨 曩 響 曬 靃 鼺
16.2　17.1　4c15.3　4c6.1　19.1　19.2

─────────── 0 ───────────

4c0.1 / 5

日　NICHI day; sun; Sunday; (as prefix or suffix) Japan　JITSU, hi sun; day -ka day (of the month), (number of) days

─────── 1 ───────

4

木
月
→ 0 日
火
礻
王
牛
方
攵
欠
心
戸
戈

0 日ソ **Nis-So** Japan and the Soviet Union
2 日入 **hi(no)i(ri)** sunset
　日子 **nisshi** (number of) days, time
3 日夕 **nisseki** day and night
　日丸 **hi(no)maru** the Japanese/red-sun flag
　日干 **hibo(shi)** sun-dried
　日々 **hibi** daily; days
　　　 nichi-nichi daily, every day
4 日中 **Nit-Chū** Japan and China
　　　 nitchū during the day
　　　 hinaka broad daylight, daytime
　日仏 **Nichi-Futsu** Japan and France
　日切 **higi(ri)** fixed date; setting the date
　日支 **Nis-Shi** Japan and China
　日月 **jitsugetsu, nichigetsu** sun and moon; time
5 日出 **hi(no)de** sunrise
　日本 **Nihon, Nippon** Japan
　日本一 **Nihon-ichi, Nippon-ichi** Japan's best
　日本人 **Nihonjin, Nipponjin** a Japanese
　日本刀 **nihontō** Japanese sword
　日本三景 **Nihon sankei** Japan's three noted scenic sights (Matsushima, Miyajima, Amanohashidate)
　日本中 **Nihonjū, Nipponjū** all over Japan
　日本化 **nihonka** Japanization, Nipponization
　日本犬 **nihonken** Japanese dog
　日本史 **Nihonshi** Japanese history
　日本主義 **Nihon shugi** Japanism
　日本学 **nihongaku** Japanology
　日本画 **nihonga** Japanese-style painting/ drawing
　日本的 **nihonteki** (very) Japanese
　日本風 **nihonfū** Japanese style
　日本海 **Nihonkai** the Sea of Japan
　日本酒 **nihonshu** saké
　日本紙 **nohonshi** Japanese paper
　日本脳炎 **Nihon nōen** Japanese encephalitis
　日本訳 **nihon'yaku** Japanese translation
　日本晴 **nihonba(re)** clear cloudless sky, beautiful weather
　日本間 **nihonma** Japanese-style room
　日本髪 **nihongami** Japanese hairdo
　日本製 **nihonsei** made in Japan
　日本語 **nihongo** the Japanese language
　日付 **hizuke** day, dating

日付変更線 **hizuke henkōsen** the international date line
日刊 **nikkan** a daily (newspaper)
日加 **Nik-Ka** Japan and Canada
日比 **Nip-Pi** Japan and the Philippines
日用 **nichiyō** for daily/everyday use
日用品 **nichiyōhin** daily necessities
日永 **hinaga** long (spring) day
日立 **hida(tsu)** grow up; recover (after childbirth)　**Hitachi** (city, Ibaraki-ken); (electronics company)
日目 **hi(no)me** sun, sunlight
6 日毎 **higoto (ni)** every day, daily
　日伊 **Nichi-I** Japan and Italy
　日次 **nichiji** day, date
　日印 **Nichi-In** Japan and India
　日向 **hinata(bokko)** bask in the sun　**Hyūga** (ancient kuni, Miyazaki-ken)
　日向水 **hinatamizu** sun-warmed water
　日共 **Nikkyō** Japan Communist Party (short for 日本共産党)
　日光 **nikkō** sunshine, sunlight　**Nikkō** (town in Tochigi-ken)
　日光浴 **nikkōyoku** sunbath
　日当 **hia(tari)** exposure to the sun; sunny place　**nittō** per-diem allowance, daily wages
　日米 **Nichi-Bei** Japan and America, Japan-U.S.
7 日延 **hino(be)** postponement
　日没 **nichibotsu** sunset
　日没前 **nichibotsuzen** before sunset
　日没後 **nichibotsugo** after sunset
　日赤 **Nisseki** Japan Red Cross (short for 日本赤十字社)
　日系 **nikkei** of Japanese descent
8 日限 **nichigen** time limit, date, term
　日夜 **nichiya** day and night, constantly
　日参 **nissan** visit (a temple) daily
　日英 **Nichi-Ei** Japan and Britain/England
　日歩 **hibu** interest per 100 yen per day
　日欧 **Nichi-Ō** Japan and Europe
　日和 **hiyori** the weather; fair weather; the situation
　日和見 **hiyorimi** weather forecasting; weathervane; wait and see
　日取 **hido(ri)** (set) the date, schedule
9 日除 **hiyo(ke)** sunshade, awning, blind
　日独 **Nichi-Doku** Japan and Germany
　日柄 **higara** what kind of day (lucky or unlucky)
　日計 **nikkei** daily account/expenses; the day's total

日食 **nisshoku** solar eclipse
10 日射病 **nisshabyō** sunstroke
日陰 **hikage** the shade
日陰者 **hikagemono** one who keeps out of
the public eye
日帰 **higae(ri)** a one-day (trip)
日差 **hiza(shi)** sunlight
日進月歩 **nisshin-geppo** rapid/constant
progress
日華 **Nik-Ka** Japan and China
日時 **nichiji** date and hour, time
日時計 **hidokei** sundial
日航機 **Nikkōki** JAL (Japan Air Lines) plane
日記 **nikki** diary, journal
日記帳 **nikkichō** diary
11 日清 **Nis-Shin** Japan and (Manchu-dynasty)
China, Sino-Japanese
日掛 **higa(ke)** daily installments
日捲 **himeku(ri)** calendar pad
日常 **nichijō** everyday, routine
日常茶飯事 **nichijō sahanji** an everyday
occurrence
日脚 **hiashi** daytime; sun's position
日章旗 **nisshōki** the Japanese/Rising-Sun flag
日産 **nissan** daily production/output
Nissan (automobile company)
日盛 **hizaka(ri)** midday
日貨 **nikka** Japanese goods/currency
日頃 **higoro** usually, always; for a long time
12 日傘 **higasa** parasol
日割 **hiwa(ri)** daily/per-diem rate
日勤 **nikkin** daily work
日満 **Nichi-Man** Japan and Manchuria
日報 **nippō** daily report/newspaper
日短 **himijika** days getting shorter
日焼 **hiya(ke)** sunburn; suntan
日雇 **hiyato(i)** hiring by the day
日程 **nittei** the day's schedule/agenda
日給 **nikkyū** daily wages
日貸 **higa(shi)** lending by the day
13 日溜 **hidama(ri)** sunny place; exposure to
the sun
日蔭 **hikage** the shade
日蔭者 **hikagemono** one who keeps out of
the public eye
日蓮 **Nichiren** Buddhist priest (1222–1282)
who founded the Nichiren sect
日照 **nisshō, hide(ri)** sunshine, drought, dry
weather
日照計 **nisshōkei** heliograph
日数 **nissū, hikazu** number of days
日電 **Nichiden** (short for 日本電気) NEC
(Corporation)
14 日豪 **Nichi-Gō** Japan and Australia
日増 **hima(shi ni)** (getting ...er) day by day
日暮 **higu(re)** dusk, nightfall, sunset

日銀 **Nichigin** Bank of Japan (short for 日本
銀行)
15 日影 **hika(ge)** sunlight; shadow
日稼 **hikase(gi)** day labor
日課 **nikka** daily lessons/work
日輪 **nichirin** the sun
日蝕 **nisshoku** solar eclipse
16 日録 **nichiroku** journal, daily record
17 日濠 **Nichi-Gō** Japan and Australia
日鮮 **Nis-Sen** Japan and Korea
18 日曜 **nichiyō** Sunday
日曜日 **nichiyōbi** Sunday
日曜版 **nichiyōban** Sunday edition
日韓 **Nik-Kan** Japan and South Korea
日覆 **hio(i), hiō(i)** sunshade, awning, blind
21 日露 **Nichi-Ro** Japan and Russia

──────── 2 ────────

1 一日 **ichinichi, ichijitsu** one/a day
tsuitachi the first (day of the month)
一日千秋 **ichinichi-senshū, ichijitsu-senshū**
days seeming like years
一日中 **ichinichi-jū** all day long
一日長 **ichijitsu (no) chō** superior, a little
better
2 二日 **futsuka** two days; the 2nd (day of the
month)
二日酔 **futsukayo(i)** a hangover
入日 **i(ri)hi** the setting sun
七日 **nanoka, nanuka** the seventh (day of
the month); seven days
九日 **kokonoka** the ninth (day of the month);
nine days
十日 **tōka** the tenth (day of the month); ten
days
八日 **yōka** eight days; the eighth (of the
month)
3 三日三晩 **mikka miban** three days and three
nights
三日天下 **mikka tenka** short-lived reign
三日月 **mikazuki** crescent moon
三日坊主 **mikka bōzu** one who can stick to
nothing, "three-day monk"
夕日 **yūhi** the setting sun
大日本 **Dai-Nippon, Dai-Nihon** (Great) Japan
4 不日 **fujitsu** at an early date, before long
元日 **ganjitsu** New Year's Day
凶日 **kyōjitsu** unlucky day
天日 **tenpi, tenjitsu** the sun
五日 **itsuka** five days; the 5th (day of the
month)
中日 **Chū-Nichi** China and Japan **chūnichi**
day of the equinox **nakabi, chūnichi**
the middle day (of a sumo tournament)
今日 **kyō, konnichi** today
六日 **muika** the sixth (day of the month); six
days

4

木
月
日 0 ←
火
衤
王
牛
方
文
欠
心
戸
戈

4

木 月 日 火 礻 王 牛 方 攵 欠 心 戸 戈

→0

父日 **Chichi (no) Hi** Father's Day
反日 **han-Nichi** anti-Japanese
厄日 **yakubi** unlucky/critical day
月日 **gappi** date **tsukihi** months and days, time
日日 **hibi** daily; days
nichi-nichi daily, every day
5 半日 **hannichi** half day
本日 **honjitsu** today
末日 **matsujitsu** last day (of a month)
他日 **tajitsu** some (other) day
平日 **heijitsu** weekday; everyday
四日 **yokka** four days; the fourth (day of the month)
四日市 **Yokkaichi** (city, Mie-ken)
白日 **hakujitsu** daytime, broad daylight
白日夢 **hakujitsumu** daydream
6 両日 **ryōjitsu** both days; two days
西日 **nishibi** the afternoon sun
西日本 **Nishi Nihon** western Japan
毎日 **mainichi** every day, daily
休日 **kyūjitsu** holiday, day off
全日本 **zen-Nihon, zen-Nippon** all Japan
全日本空輸 **Zen Nihon Kūyu** All Nippon Airways
全日制 **zennichisei** full-time (school) system
全日空 **Zennikkū** ANA, All Nippon Airways (short for 全日本空輸)
近日 **kinjitsu** soon, in a few days
近日点 **kinjitsuten** perihelion
同日 **dōjitsu** the same day
先日 **senjitsu** the other day
先日付 **sakihizu(ke)** postdating, dating forward
在日 **zai-Nichi** in Japan **a(rishi)hi** bygone days; during one's lifetime
在日中 **zai-Nichichū** while in Japan
向日性 **kōjitsusei, kōnichisei** heliotropic
当日 **tōjitsu** the (appointed) day
吉日 **kichinichi, kichijitsu** lucky day
尽日 **jinjitsu** all day; last day
百日咳 **hyakunichizeki** whooping cough
百日草 **hyakunichisō** zinnia
百日紅 **sarusuberi** crape myrtle, Indian lilac
旬日 **junjitsu** ten-day period
旭日 **kyokujitsu** the rising sun
旭日昇天 **kyokujitsu-shōten** the rising sun
旭日章 **Kyokujitsushō** the Order of the Rising Sun
旭日旗 **kyokujitsuki** the Rising Sun flag
式日 **shikijitsu** ceremonial occasion
7 来日 **rainichi** come to Japan
何日 **nannichi** how many days; what day of the month
余日 **yojitsu** days left, remaining time
即日 **sokujitsu** on the same day

即日速達 **sokujitsu sokutatsu** same-day special delivery
対日 **tai-Nichi** toward/with Japan
延日数 **no(be)nissū** total number of days
抗日 **kō-Nichi** anti-Japanese
忌日 **kijitsu, kinichi** death anniversary
i(mi)bi purification-and-fast day; unlucky day
初日 **hatsuhi** New Year's Day sunrise
shonichi first/opening day
初日出 **hatsuhi(no)de** New Year's Day sunrise
8 非日 **hi-Nichi** un-Japanese
表日本 **Omote Nihon** Pacific side of Japan
例日 **reijitsu** weekday
命日 **meinichi** anniversary of a death
其日 **so(no) hi** that (very) day
其日暮 **so(no)hi-gura(shi)** living from day to day, hand-to-mouth existence
其日稼 **so(no)hi-kase(gi)** day labor
知日 **chi-Nichi** familiarity with Japan
知日家 **chi-Nichika** a Japan hand
往日 **ōjitsu** ancient times
昔日 **sekijitsu** old/former times
定日 **teijitsu** fixed/appointed date
明日 **myōnichi, asu** tomorrow
a(kuru) hi the next/following day
或日 **a(ru) hi** one day
9 前日 **zenjitsu** the day before
連日 **renjitsu** day after day, every day
逐日 **chikujitsu** day after day, daily
後日 **gojitsu, gonichi** the future, another day
後日談 **gojitsudan** reminiscences
昨日 **sakujitsu, kinō** yesterday
昼日中 **hiruhinaka** daytime, broad daylight
祝日 **shukujitsu, iwa(i)bi** festival day, holiday
秋日 **shūjitsu** autumn day
秋日和 **akibiyori** clear fall weather
10 陰日向 **kage-hinata** light and shade
週日 **shūjitsu** weekday
時日 **jijitsu** the date/time; time, days
烈日 **retsujitsu** blazing sun
旅日記 **tabinikki** travel diary
純日本風 **jun-Nihon-fū** classical Japanese style
紋日 **monbi** holiday
11 偶日 **gūjitsu** even-numbered day of the month
斎日 **saijitsu** fast day
遅日 **chijitsu** (long) spring days
過日 **kajitsu** the other day, recently
排日 **hai-Nichi** anti-Japanese
常日頃 **tsunehigoro** always, usually
晦日 **misoka, kaijitsu** the last day of the month
祭日 **saijitsu** holiday; festival day

悪日 **akunichi, akubi** unlucky day
翌日 **yokujitsu** the next/following day
累日 **ruijitsu** many days, day after day
終日 **shūjitsu, hinemosu** all day long
訪日 **hō-Nichi** visiting Japan
頃日 **keijitsu** recently, these days
12 隔日 **kakujitsu** every other day, alternate days
遠日点 **enjitsuten, ennichiten** aphelion
短日 **tanjitsu** a short time
短日月 **tanjitsugetsu** a short time
落日 **rakujitsu** setting sun
期日 **kijitsu** (appointed) day/date, term, due date
朝日 **asahi** morning/rising sun
朝日影 **asahikage** morning sunshine
幾日 **ikunichi** how many days; what day of the month
閑日月 **kanjitsugetsu** leisure
13 裏日本 **ura-Nihon, ura-Nippon** Sea-of-Japan side of Japan
滞日 **tai-Nichi** staying in Japan
聖日 **seijitsu** holy day; the Sabbath
数日 **sūjitsu** a few days, several days
数日中 **sūjitsuchū** within a few days
数日来 **sūjitsurai** for the last few days
数日後 **sūjitsugo** after several days
数日間 **sūnichikan** for several days
14 暦日 **rekijitsu** calendar, time
寧日 **neijitsu** peaceful/quiet day
嘉日 **kajitsu** auspicious day
旗日 **hatabi** national holiday
15 縁日 **ennichi** festival day, fair
駐日 **chū-Nichi** resident/stationed in Japan
16 薄日 **usubi** soft beams of sunlight
親日 **shin-Nichi** pro-Japanese
親日家 **shin-Nichika** Nippophile
18 曜日 **yōbi** day of the week
離日 **rinichi** leave Japan
19 曠日弥久 **kōjitsu bikyū** idle away one's time/years

───────── 3 ─────────

1 一両日 **ichiryōjitsu** a day or two
一昨日 **issakujitsu, ototoi, ototsui** the day before yesterday
2 二十日 **hatsuka** the 20th (day of the month); 20 days
二十日大根 **hatsuka daikon** radish
二十日鼠 **hatsuka nezumi** mouse
3 三七日 **minanoka, minanuka, sanshichinichi** 21st day after a death
三十日 **sanjūnichi** the 30th (day of the month); 30 days **misoka** the last day of the month
三箇日 **sanganichi** the first three days of the new year
大安日 **taiannichi** lucky day

大晦日 **Ōmisoka** last day of the year; New Year's Eve
土曜日 **doyōbi** Saturday
小半日 **kohannichi** about half a day
小春日和 **koharubiyori** balmy autumn day, Indian-summer day
4 予定日 **yoteibi** scheduled date, expected date (of birth)
文化日 **Bunka (no) Hi** Culture Day (November 3)
支払日 **shiharaibi** pay day
公休日 **kōkyūbi** legal holiday
水曜日 **suiyōbi** Wednesday
木曜日 **mokuyōbi** Thursday
月給日 **gekkyūbi** payday
月曜日 **getsuyōbi** Monday
日曜日 **nichiyōbi** Sunday
火曜日 **kayōbi** Tuesday
5 出勤日 **shukkinbi** workday
6 両三日 **ryōsannichi** two or three days
年月日 **nengappi** date
休業日 **kyūgyōbi** business holiday
安息日 **ansokubi** sabbath
     ansokunichi the (Jewish) sabbath
     ansokujitsu the (Christian) sabbath
7 何曜日 **nan'yōbi, naniyōbi** what day of the week
決算日 **kessanbi** settlement day
投票日 **tōhyōbi** voting day
初七日 **shonanoka, shonanuka** (religious service on) the seventh day after someone's death
8 受難日 **junanbi** Good Friday
招待日 **shōtaibi** preview/invitation date
定休日 **teikyūbi** regular holiday, Closed (Tuesday)s
国祭日 **kokusaibi** national holiday
明後日 **myōgonichi** the day after tomorrow
金曜日 **kin'yōbi** Friday
9 発行日 **hakkōbi** date of issue
面会日 **menkaibi** one's at-home day
春分日 **shunbun (no) hi** the vernal equinox (a holiday, about March 21)
祝祭日 **shukusaijitsu** festival, holiday
10 俸給日 **hōkyūbi** payday
航海日誌 **kōkai nisshi** ship's log
記念日 **kinenbi** memorial day, anniversary
11 勘定日 **kanjōbi** settlement day
翌翌日 **yokuyokujitsu** two days later/after
12 就業日数 **shūgyō nissū** days worked
短時日 **tanjijitsu** a short time
検診日 **kenshinbi** medical-examination day
最終日 **saishūbi** the last day
給料日 **kyūryōbi** payday
診察日 **shinsatsubi** consultation day
開会日 **kaikaibi** opening day

4

木
月
日 0←
火
礻
王
牛
方
攵
欠
心
戸
戈

13 電休日 **denkyūbi** a no-electricity day
14 選挙日 **senkyobi** election day
精進日 **shōjinbi** day of abstinence (from flesh foods)
誕生日 **tanjōbi** birthday
15 熱帯日 **nettaibi** midsummerday
16 親方日丸 **oyakata hi(no)maru** "the government will foot the bill" attitude, budgetry irresponsibility

───────── 4 ─────────

1 一昨昨日 **issakusakujitsu, sakiototoi, sakiototsui** three days ago
2 二百十日 **nihyaku tōka** 210th day from the first day of spring, the "storm day"
4 支払期日 **shiharaikijitsu** due date, maturity
5 生年月日 **seinengappi** date of birth
8 青天白日 **seiten-hakujitsu** clear weather; cleared of suspicion, proved innocent
9 秋霜烈日 **shūsō-retsujitsu** withering frost and scorching sun; harsh, severe, exacting
10 振替休日 **furikae kyūjitsu** substitute holiday (for one falling on a Sunday)
祥月命日 **shōtsuki meinichi** anniversary of one's death
11 黄道吉日 **kōdō kichinichi, ōdō kichinichi** lucky day
12 晴天白日 **seiten-hakujitsu** clear weather; proved innocent
13 聖金曜日 **Seikin'yōbi** Good Friday

───────── 5 ─────────

2 二百二十日 **nihyaku hatsuka** 220th day from the first day of spring, about September 10 (a time of typhoons)
5 出生年月日 **shusshō nengappi, shussei nengappi** date of birth

日 → **3s1.1**

───────── 1 ─────────

4c1.1 / 1216

KYŪ old, former

旧 舊

───────── 1 ─────────

4 旧友 **kyūyū** an old friend
5 旧世界 **kyūsekai** the Old World
旧正月 **kyūshōgatsu** the lunar New Year
旧好 **kyūkō** an old friendship
旧冬 **kyūtō** last winter
6 旧年 **kyūnen** the old year, last year
旧交 **kyūkō** an old friendship
旧式 **kyūshiki** old-type, old-fashioned
7 旧来 **kyūrai** from old times, traditional

旧体制 **kyūtaisei** the old regime/establishment
旧臣 **kyūshin** an old retainer
8 旧例 **kyūrei** old custom, tradition
旧版 **kyūhan** old edition
旧知 **kyūchi** an old friend(ship)
旧姓 **kyūsei** former/maiden name
9 旧派 **kyūha** of the old school/style, conservative
旧怨 **kyūen** an old grudge
旧思想 **kyūshisō** old-fashioned/outmoded ideas
旧約 **kyūyaku** old promise/covenant; the Old Testament
旧約聖書 **Kyūyaku Seisho** the Old Testament
10 旧師 **kyūshi** one's former teacher
旧家 **kyūka** an old family
旧時 **kyūji** old/past times
旧恩 **kyūon** old favors, past kindness
旧称 **kyūshō** old name, former title
11 旧習 **kyūshū** an old custom
旧悪 **kyūaku** one's past misdeeds
13 旧債 **kyūsai** an old debt
旧幕 **kyūbaku** the old feudal government, the shogunate
旧幕府 **kyūbakufu** the old feudal government, the shogunate
旧跡 **kyūseki** historic ruins
14 旧暦 **kyūreki** the old (lunar) calendar
旧態 **kyūtai** the old/former state of affairs
旧慣 **kyūkan** old customs
15 旧劇 **kyūgeki** kabuki
旧弊 **kyūhei** an old evil; old-fashioned, behind the times
旧誼 **kyūgi** an old friendship
18 旧藩 **kyūhan** former clan
旧藩主 **kyūhanshu** former feudal lord
旧観 **kyūkan** former appearance/state
19 旧臘 **kyūrō** last December, end of last year

───────── 2 ─────────

6 守旧 **shukyū** conservative
9 故旧 **kokyū** an old acquaintance
10 倍旧 **baikyū** redoubled, increased
12 復旧 **fukkyū, fukukyū** restoration, recovery
13 新旧 **shinkyū** new and old
14 聞旧 **ki(ki)furu(shita)** hackneyed, trite
16 懐旧 **kaikyū** yearning for the old days
親旧 **shinkyū** relatives and old friends

───────── 3 ─────────

6 名所旧跡 **meisho-kyūseki** scenic and historic places

4c1.2

TAN morning, dawn

旦

━━━━━━━━ 1 ━━━━━━━━

3 旦夕 **tanseki** morning and evening, day and night
6 旦那 **danna** master; husband; gentleman
旦那芸 **dannagei** amateurism
旦那様 **danna-sama** master; husband; gentleman

━━━━━━━━ 2 ━━━━━━━━

1 一旦 **ittan** once
3 大旦那 **ōdanna** benefactor (of a temple); proprietor, man of the house
4 元旦 **gantan** New Year's Day
巴旦杏 **hatankyō, hadankyō** almond tree; plum
月旦 **gettan** first day of the month; commentary
8 若旦那 **wakadanna** young master/gentleman
13 歳旦 **saitan** New Year's Day; the New Year

4c1.3 / 205

白

HAKU white; Belgium
BYAKU, shiro, shiro(i), shira- white
shira(mu) grow light **shira** feigned ignorance

━━━━━━━━ 1 ━━━━━━━━

0 白バイ **shirobai** white motorcycle; motorcycle policeman
2 白人 **hakujin** a white, Caucasian
白人種 **hakujinshu** white race
白子 **shirako** milt, soft roe; albino
　　　 shiroko albino　**shirasu** young sardines
白子干 **shirasubo(shi)** dried young sardines
白子鳩 **shirakobato** collared dove
白十字 **hakujūji** white cross
3 白刃 **hakujin, shiraha** naked blade, drawn sword
白下 **shiroshita** treacle, molasses
白々 **shirojiro** pure white
　　　 shirajira dawning　**shirajira(shii)** feigning ignorance; barefaced (lie)
　　　 hakuhaku very clear
白土 **shiratsuchi** kaolin; mortar
白山 **Hakusan** (mountain, Gifu-ken)
4 白太 **shirata** sapwood
白文 **hakubun** unpunctuated Chinese text
白水 **shiromizu** white water left after washing rice
　　　 shiramizu white water, whitecaps
白木 **shiraki** plain/unpainted/unvarnished wood
白日 **hakujitsu** daytime, broad daylight
白日夢 **hakujitsumu** daydream
5 白玉 **shiratama** white gem, pearl; rice-flour dumpling
白玉粉 **shiratamako** rice flour

白玉楼 **hakugyokurō** (among) the dead, deceased
白玉椿 **shiratama tsubaki** white camellia
6 白羽 **shiraha** white feather
白羽矢立 **shiraha (no) ya (ga) ta(tsu)** be selected (for a task/post)
白色 **hakushoku** white
白地 **shiroji** white cloth/ground, blank
白地図 **hakuchizu** outline/contour map
白帆 **shiraho** (boat with a) white sail
白光 **hakkō** white light; corona
白百合 **shirayuri** Easter lily
白灯油 **hakutōyu** kerosene
白衣 **hakui, byakue, byakui** white robe, lab coat
白血病 **hakketsubyō** leukemia
白血球 **hakkekkyū** white corpuscles
白糸 **shiraito** white thread
白米 **hakumai** polished rice
白耳義 **Berugī** Belgium
7 白身 **shiromi** whiteness; white meat; white of an egg
白亜 **hakua** chalk
白亜層 **hakuasō** chalk bed/stratum
白亜館 **Hakuakan** the White House
白状 **hakujō** confess, admit
白兵戦 **hakuheisen** hand-to-hand fighting
白妙 **shirotae** white cloth; white
白系露人 **hakkei rojin** a White Russian, Byelorussian
8 白兎 **shirousagi** white rabbit
白夜 **hakuya, byakuya** bright (arctic) night
白波 **shiranami** whitecaps; thief
白河 **Shirakawa** (emperor, 1072–1086)
白河夜船 **Shirakawa yofune** fast asleep
白拍子 **shirabyōshi** female dancer (historical); prostitute
白味 **shiromi** whiteness; white meat; white of an egg
白金 **hakkin** platinum
白雨 **hakuu** shower
9 白洲 **shirasu** sand bar; (law) court
白狐 **byakko** white fox
白茶 **shiracha** straw-colored, faded
白面 **hakumen** white/pale face; inexperience
　　　 shirafu sober
白胡麻 **shirogoma** white sesame seeds
白星 **shiroboshi** white dot (sign of victory/success)
白昼 **hakuchū** daytime, broad daylight
白砂 **hakusha, hakusa** white sand
白砂青松 **hakusha-seishō** white sand and green pines, beautiful seashore scene
白砂糖 **shirozatō** white sugar
白眉 **hakubi** finest, best example, epitome
10 白酒 **shirozake** white saké

4

木 月 日 火 礻 王 牛 方 攵 欠 心 戸 戈

→ 1

白浜 **shirahama** white beach
白梅 **shiraume** white-blossom plum tree; white plum blossoms
白骨 **hakkotsu** bleached bones, skeleton
白書 **hakusho** whitepaper, report
白扇 **hakusen** white fan
白紙 **hakushi, shirakami** white paper; blank paper, carte blanche; flyleaf, clean slate
白粉 **oshiroi** face powder/paint
白馬 **hakuba, shirouma** white horse
11 白堊 **hakua** chalk(stone); white wall
白堊館 **Hakuakan** the White House
白描 **hakubyō** plain sketch
白菜 **hakusai** Chinese/celery cabbage
白菊 **shiragiku** white chrysanthemum
白黒 **shiro-kuro** black-and-white; right or wrong, guilty or innocent
白票 **hakuhyō** white/affirmative vote; blank ballot
白眼 **hakugan, shirome** the whites of the eyes
白眼視 **hakuganshi** look askance/coldly at
白雪 **shirayuki, hakusetsu** (white) snow
白雪姫 **Shirayuki-hime** Snow White (and the Seven Dwarfs)
白魚 **shirauo** whitebait, icefish
白鳥 **hakuchō** swan
12 白湯 **sayu** (plain) hot water
白葡萄酒 **shiro-budōshu** white wine
白焼 **shiraya(ki)** unseasoned broiled fish
白無垢 **shiromuku** (dressed) all in white
白装束 **shiroshōzoku** (clothed) all in white
白雲 **shirakumo, hakuun** white/fleecy clouds
13 白鼠 **shironezumi** white rat/mouse
白滝 **shirataki** white waterfall; konnyaku in spaghetti form
白塗 **shironu(ri)** painted white
白蓮 **byakuren** white lotus
白痴 **hakuchi** idiot
白話 **hakuwa** colloquial Chinese
白鉛 **hakuen** white lead
白雉 **Hakuchi** (era, 650–672)
14 白鳳 **Hakuhō** (era, 672–686)
白墨 **hakuboku** chalk
白髪 **hakuhatsu, shiraga** white/gray hair
白髪染 **shiragazo(me)** hair dye
白髪頭 **shiraga atama** gray(-haired) head
白樺 **shirakaba, shirakanba** white birch
白旗 **shirahata, hakki** white flag (of truce/surrender)
白磁 **hakuji** white china/porcelain
白銅 **hakudō** nickel
白銅貨 **hakudōka** a nickel (coin)
15 白熱 **hakunetsu** white heat, incandescence; heated, exciting
白熱化 **hakunetsuka** heat up, reach a climax

白熱灯 **hakunetsutō** incandescent lamp
白熱戦 **hakunetsusen** intense fighting, thrilling game
白線 **hakusen** white line
16 白壁 **hakuheki, shirakabe** white(washed) wall
17 白檀 **byakudan** sandalwood
19 白蟻 **shiroari** termite
21 白魔 **hakuma** snow, the white devil
白露 **Hakuro** White Russia, Byelorussia
22 白癬 **hakusen** ringworm
23 白鑞 **hakurō** solder; pewter

───────── 2 ─────────

3 大白 **taihaku** large cup, goblet
女白波 **onna shiranami** woman robber
4 太白 **taihaku** Venus; refined sugar; thick silk thread
片白 **katahaku** a liquor brewed from rice and malt
5 生白 **namajiro(i), namatchiro(i)** pale, pallid
白白 **shirojiro** pure white
     shirajira dawning   **shirajira(shii)** feigning ignorance; barefaced (lie)
     hakuhaku very clear
目白押 **mejiroo(shi)** jostling, milling
6 色白 **irojiro** light-complexioned, fair-skinned
灰白 **kaihaku** light gray, ashen
自白 **jihaku** confession
7 余白 **yohaku** blank space, margin
卵白 **ranpaku** white of an egg, albumin
告白 **kokuhaku** confession
乳白色 **nyūhakushoku** milky white
8 建白 **kenpaku** memorial, petition
建白書 **kenpakusho** memorial, petition
追白 **tsuihaku** postscript, P.S.
若白髪 **wakashiraga** prematurely gray hair
空白 **kūhaku** blank, empty space, vacuum
青白 **aojiro(i)** pale, pallid, wan
明白 **meihaku** clear, unmistakable
9 飛白 **kasuri** splashed pattern
独白 **dokuhaku** monolog, soliloquy
面白 **omoshiro(i)** interesting; amusing
面白半分 **omoshiro-hanbun** half in fun, jokingly
面白味 **omoshiromi** interest, enjoyment
紅白 **kōhaku** red and white
10 真白 **ma(s)shiro** pure white
純白 **junpaku** pure white
11 淡白 **tanpaku** light, plain, simple; candid; indifferent to
黄白 **kōhaku** yellow and white; gold and silver; money, bribery
黒白 **kuro-shiro, kokuhaku, kokubyaku** black and white; right and wrong
蛋白 **tanpaku** protein; albumen
蛋白質 **tanpakushitsu** protein; albumen

雪白 **seppaku** snow-white
12 腕白 **wanpaku** naughty, mischievous
斑白 **hanpaku** grizzled
敬白 **keihaku** Sincerely yours,
13 蒼白 **sōhaku** pale, pallid, wan
煉白粉 **ne(ri)oshiroi** face powder
鉛白 **enpaku** white lead
14 漂白剤 **hyōhakuzai** bleach
鼻白 **hanajiro(mu)** look disappointed/daunted
精白 **seihaku** refine, polish (rice)
精白米 **seihakumai** polished rice
精白糖 **seihakutō** refined sugar
関白 **kanpaku** emperor's chief advisor; domineering husband
15 潔白 **keppaku** pure, upright, of integrity
16 薄白 **usujiro(i)** off-white

——————— 3 ———————

5 矢飛白 **yagasuri** arrow-feather pattern
8 青天白日 **seiten-hakujitsu** clear weather; cleared of suspicion, proved innocent
明々白々 **meimei-hakuhaku** perfectly clear
12 晴天白日 **seiten-hakujitsu** clear weather; proved innocent
14 酸性白土 **sansei hakudo** acid/Kambara clay

——————— 4 ———————

9 信仰告白 **shinkō kokuhaku** profession of faith
亭主関白 **teishu kanpaku** autocratic husband
11 清廉潔白 **seiren-keppaku** spotless integrity

——————— 2 ———————

4c2.1 / 248

早 SŌ, SA', SA, **haya(i)** early; fast
haya(meru) hasten, accelerate
haya(maru) be hasty

——————— 1 ———————

0 早とちり **haya(tochiri)** hastily jumping to the wrong conclusion
1 早乙女 **saotome** rice-planting girl
3 早々 **sōsō** early, immediately; Hurriedly yours, **hayabaya** early, immediately
早口 **hayakuchi, hayaguchi** fast talking
早口言葉 **hayakuchi kotoba** tongue twister
4 早天 **sōten** dawn, early morning
早分 **hayawa(kari)** quick understanding; guide, handbook
早手回 **hayatemawa(shi)** early preparations
早引 **hayabi(ki)** leave early
早少女 **saotome** rice-planting girl
5 早出 **hayade** early arrival (at the office)
早生 **hayau(mare)** born between January 1 and April 1 **wase** early-ripening (rice); precocious
早生児 **sōseiji** prematurely born baby

早世 **sōsei** early death
早仕舞 **hayajimai** early closing
早目 **hayame (ni)** a little early (leaving leeway)
6 早死 **hayaji(ni)** die young/prematurely
早合点 **hayagaten** hasty conclusion
早老 **sōrō** premature old age
早回 **hayamawa(ri)** a dash around (the world)
早早 **sōsō** early, immediately; Hurriedly yours, **hayabaya** early, immediately
早耳 **hayamimi** quick-eared, in the know
7 早技 **hayawaza** quick work; sleight of hand
早呑込 **hayano(mi)ko(mi)** hasty conclusion
早見表 **hayamihyō** chart, table
早足 **hayaashi** quick pace, fast walking
8 早退 **sōtai** leave early
早送 **hayaoku(ri)** fast forward
早苗 **sanae** rice seedlings/sprouts
早取 **hayato(ri)** snapshot
早取写真 **hayato(ri) shashin** snapshot
9 早発性痴呆症 **sōhatsusei chihōshō** schizophrenia
早変 **hayaga(wari)** quick change (of costume)
早急 **sōkyū, sakkyū** urgently, without delay
早速 **sassoku** at once, getting right to the point
早逝 **sōsei** early death
早咲 **hayaza(ki)** early-blooming; precocious
早春 **sōshun** early spring
早計 **sōkei** premature, hasty, rash
10 早起 **hayao(ki)** get up early
早書 **hayaga(ki)** writing hurriedly
早教育 **sōkyōiku** early education
早馬 **hayauma** post horse, steed
11 早道 **hayamichi** shortcut
早婚 **sōkon** early marriage
早桶 **hayaoke** coffin
早産 **sōzan** premature birth
早産児 **sōzanji** premature baby
12 早場米 **hayabamai** early rice
早期 **sōki** early stage/phase
早期診断 **sōki shindan** early diagnosis
早朝 **sōchō** early morning
早晩 **sōban** sooner or later
早番 **hayaban** the first/early shift
早飯 **hayameshi** eating fast/early
13 早業 **hayawaza** quick work; sleight of hand
早寝 **hayane** retiring early
14 早熟 **sōjuku** maturing early, precocious
早稲 **wase** early-ripening (rice); precocious
15 早蕨 **sawarabi** bracken/fern sprouts
早駕籠 **hayakago** express palanquin
19 早瀬 **hayase** swift current, rapids
20 早鐘 **hayagane** fire bell/alarm

——————— 2 ———————

4 手早 **tebaya(i)** quick, nimble, agile
5 目早 **mebaya(i)** quick to notice, sharp-eyed

6 気早 **kibaya** quick-tempered
早早 **sōsō** early, immediately; Hurriedly yours,
hayabaya early, immediately
7 足早 **ashibaya** quick, swift-footed
8 尚早 **shōsō** premature, too early
10 逸早 **ichihaya(ku)** quickly, promptly
素早 **subaya(i)** quick, nimble
11 遅早 **oso(kare)haya(kare)** sooner or later
12 朝早 **asa haya(ku)** early in the morning
最早 **mohaya** already, by now; (not) any
longer

─────────── 3 ───────────

4 手取早 **te(t)to(ri)baya(i)** quick, rough-and-
ready
5 矢継早 **yatsu(gi)baya (ni)** rapid-fire, in
quick succession
12 喧嘩早 **kenkabaya(i)** quick to quarrel,
pugnacious

4c2.2 / 1040

旨 **SHI, mune** purport, content, gist, (to
the effect) that; instructions
uma(i) tasty, delicious; skillful, good
at; successful; wise

─────────── 1 ───────────

5 旨汁 **uma(i) shiru** the cream, rakeoff
8 旨味 **umami** tastiness, flavor

─────────── 2 ───────────

3 大旨 **ōmune** the main idea, gist
4 内旨 **naishi** secret orders
5 本旨 **honshi** the main purpose
主旨 **shushi** gist, purport, object
8 宗旨 **shūshi** tenets, doctrine; sect, religion;
one's principles
9 勅旨 **chokushi** imperial order/wishes
要旨 **yōshi** gist, purport, substance
宣旨 **senji** imperial command
10 特旨 **tokushi** special consideration
教旨 **kyōshi** doctrine, tenet
11 密旨 **misshi** secret orders
13 聖旨 **seishi** the imperial will
15 趣旨 **shushi** purport, meaning, aim, object
論旨 **ronshi** point of an argument
16 諭旨 **yushi** official suggestion (to a subordinate)

4c2.3 / 14

百 **HYAKU** hundred
momo hundred; many

─────────── 1 ───────────

2 百人一首 **hyakunin-isshu** 100 poems by
100 poets (a collection of 100 *tanka*;
basis for the popular card game *uta
karuta*)

3 百万 **hyakuman** million
百万長者 **hyakumanchōja** (multi-)million-
aire
百万遍 **hyakumanben** (praying) a million
times
4 百分比 **hyakubunhi** percentage
百分率 **hyakubunritsu** percentage
百日咳 **hyakunichizeki** whooping cough
百日草 **hyakunichisō** zinnia
百日紅 **sarusuberi** crape myrtle, Indian lilac
百方 **hyappō** in every way
5 百出 **hyakushutsu** arise in great numbers
6 百年祭 **hyakunensai** a centennial
百合 **yuri** lily
百合根 **yurine** lily bulb
百舌 **mozu** shrike, butcher-bird
7 百芸 **hyakugei** jack-of-all-trades
百足 **mukade** centipede
8 百姓 **hyakushō** farmer, peasant
百姓一揆 **hyakushō ikki** peasants' uprising
百官 **hyakkan** all government officials
9 百発百中 **hyappatsu-hyakuchū** on target
every time
百点 **hyakuten** 100 points, perfect score
百面相 **hyakumensō** many phases/faces
百科 **hyakka** many subjects/topics
百科全書 **hyakka zensho** encyclopedia
百科事典 **hyakka jiten** encyclopedia
百科辞典 **hyakka jiten** encyclopedia
百計 **hyakkei** every means
10 百倍 **hyakubai** a hundredfold
百害 **hyakugai** great harm/damage
百鬼夜行 **hyakki-yakō, hyakki-yagyō** all
sorts of demons roaming about at night;
rampant evil, scandal, pandemonium
百般 **hyappan** every kind of, all
11 百済 **Kudara** (Korean kingdom, about 300–
660)
百貨店 **hyakkaten** department store
12 百葉箱 **hyakuyōsō, hyakuyōbako** louver-
sided box for housing meteorological
gauges outdoors
13 百戦百勝 **hyakusen-hyakushō** ever-
victorious
百戦錬磨 **hyakusen-renma** battle-seasoned,
veteran
百雷 **hyakurai** a hundred thunderclaps
14 百態 **hyakutai** various phases
百聞一見如 **hyakubun (wa) ikken (ni)
shi(kazu)** Seeing for oneself once is
better than hearing 100 accounts.
16 百獣 **hyakujū** all kinds of animals
百薬 **hyakuyaku** all sorts of remedies
百薬長 **hyakuyaku (no) chō** (saké is) the
best medicine
百錬 **hyakuren** well tempered/trained

18 百難 **hyakunan** all obstacles, all sorts of trouble

——————— 2 ———————

2 二百二十日 **nihyaku hatsuka** 220th day from the first day of spring, about September 10 (a time of typhoons)
二百十日 **nihyaku tōka** 210th day from the first day of spring, the "storm day"
八百万 **yaoyorozu** myriads, countless
八百長 **yaochō** rigged affair, fixed game
八百屋 **yaoya** vegetable store; jack-of-all-trades
3 三百 **sanbyaku** 300; many
三百代言 **sanbyaku daigen** shyster lawyer, pettifogger
凡百 **bonpyaku, bonbyaku** many, many kinds
土百姓 **dobyakushō** dirt farmer, peasant
小百合 **sayuri** lily
小百姓 **kobyakushō** petty farmer, peasant
5 四百 **yonhyaku** four hundred
四百四病 **shihyakushibyō** every kind of disease
四百余州 **shihyakuyoshū** all China
白百合 **shirayuri** Easter lily
6 年百年中 **nenbyaku-nenjū** all year round
10 鬼百合 **oniyuri** tiger lily
11 黒百合 **kuroyuri** (a variety of dark-purple lily)
12 鈍百姓 **donbyakushō** dumb farmer
13 数百 **sūhyaku** several hundred

——————— 3 ———————

4 文武百官 **bunbu hyakkan** civil and military officials
水呑百姓 **mizuno(mi)-byakushō** poor farmer
水飲百姓 **mizuno(mi)-byakushō** poor farmer
6 百発百中 **hyappatsu-hyakuchū** on target every time
百戦百勝 **hyakusen-hyakushō** ever-victorious
14 嘘八百 **usohappyaku** a pack of lies

——————— 4 ———————

4 五十歩百歩 **gojippo-hyappo** not much different

4c2.4

亘 **SEN, KŌ, wata(ru)** range/extend over, span

——————— 1 ———————

8 亘長 **kōchō** span, interval, distance

4c2.5 / 338

旬 **JUN** ten-day period
shun the season for (oysters/vegetables)

4 旬日 **junjitsu** ten-day period
5 旬刊 **junkan** published every ten days
12 旬報 **junpō** report issued every ten days

——————— 2 ———————

3 上旬 **jōjun** the first ten days of a month
下旬 **gejun** 21st through last day of a month
4 中旬 **chūjun** middle ten days of a month, mid-(May)
5 四旬節 **Shijunsetsu** Lent
7 初旬 **shojun** first ten days of the month

4c2.6

旭 **KYOKU, asahi** the morning/rising sun

——————— 1 ———————

3 旭川 **Asahikawa** (city, Hokkaidō)
4 旭日 **kyokujitsu** the rising sun
旭日昇天 **kyokujitsu-shōten** the rising sun
旭日章 **Kyokujitsushō** the Order of the Rising Sun
旭日旗 **kyokujitsuki** the Rising Sun flag
6 旭光 **kyokkō** rays of the rising sun
13 旭暉 **kyokki** rays of the rising sun
14 旭旗 **kyokki** the Rising Sun flag

——————— 3 ———————

4c3.1

旱 **KAN, hideri** drought

——————— 1 ———————

4 旱天 **kanten** drought, dry weather
10 旱害 **kangai** drought damage
15 旱魃 **kanbatsu** drought

——————— 2 ———————

3 女旱 **onna hideri** shortage of women

4c3.2

皀 **KYŪ, HYOKU, KYŌ, KŌ** fragrant; grain

皃 → 貌 4c10.6

4c3.3 / 1217

児 兒 **JI, NI, ko** child

——————— 1 ———————

3 児女 **jijo** little girl; children

4
木 月 日 3←
火 ネ 王 牛 方 攵 欠 心 戸 戈

9 児孫 **jison** children and grandchildren, descendants
12 児童 **jidō** child, juvenile
15 児戯 **jigi** mere child's play

―――――― 2 ――――――

3 女児 **joji** (baby) girl
小児 **shōni** little child, infant
小児科 **shōnika** pediatrics
小児科医 **shōnikai** pediatrician
小児麻痺 **shōni mahi** infantile paralysis, polio
5 幼児 **yōji** small child, tot, baby
幼児食 **yōjishoku** baby food
幼児期 **yōjiki** young childhood, infancy
四児 **yo(tsu)go** quadruplets
6 死児 **shiji** dead child; stillborn child
7 乳児 **nyūji** suckling baby, infant
男児 **danji** boy, son
8 孤児 **koji, minashigo** orphan
孤児院 **kojiin** orphanage
育児 **ikuji** care/raising of children
逆児 **sakago** breech baby/presentation
9 胎児 **taiji** fetus
10 健児 **kenji** vigorous boy
病児 **byōji** sick child
蚕児 **sanji** silkworm
託児所 **takujisho** day nursery
11 掏児 **suri** pickpocket
鹿児島 **Kagoshima** (city, Kagoshima-ken)
鹿児島県 **Kagoshima-ken** (prefectue)
豚児 **tonji** my son (humble)
産児 **sanji** newborn baby; bearing children
12 童児 **dōji** child
13 園児 **enji** kindergarten child/pupil
愛児 **aiji** one's dear child
稚児 **chigo** child; child in a Buddhist procession
14 遺児 **iji** orphan; posthumous child
15 蕩児 **tōji** debauchee, libertine, prodigal son
17 嬰児 **eiji, midorigo** baby, infant
19 寵児 **chōji** favorite child, pet
22 驕児 **kyōji** spoiled child

―――――― 3 ――――――

4 天才児 **tensaiji** child prodigy
双生児 **sōseiji** twins
6 死産児 **shisanji** stillborn baby
当歳児 **tōsaiji** a yearling
早生児 **sōseiji** prematurely born baby
早産児 **sōzanji** premature baby
7 低能児 **teinōji** retarded child; backward pupil
乳幼児 **nyūyōji** infant
乳呑児 **chinomigo** nursing baby, unweaned child
乳飲児 **chinomigo** (nursing) infant, baby
快男児 **kaidanji** a fine fellow
私生児 **shiseiji** illegitimate child

初生児 **shoseiji** newborn baby
初産児 **shosanji** one's first(born) child
8 幸運児 **kōunji** child of good fortune, lucky fellow
金雀児 **enishida** broom, genista (a shrub)
9 風雲児 **fūunji** adventurer, soldier of fortune
浮浪児 **furōji** juvenile vagrant, gamin
10 健康児 **kenkōji** healthy child
遊蕩児 **yūtōji** dissipated person, fast liver
流行児 **ryūkōji, hayari(k)ko** popular person
11 混血児 **konketsuji** person of mixed race, half-breed
問題児 **mondaiji** problem child
13 新生児 **shinseiji** newborn baby
畸形児 **kikeiji** deformed child
19 麒麟児 **kirinji** child prodigy

―――――― 6 ――――――

1 一卵性双生児 **ichiransei sōseiji** identical twins

間 → 間 8e4.3

―――――― 4 ――――――

4c4.1 / 18

明 **MEI** light **MYŌ** light; next, following
MIN Ming (dynasty) **a(kari)** light, clearness **aka(rui)** bright **aki(raka)** clear **a(keru), aka(rumu), aka(ramu)** become light **a(ku)** be open/visible **a(kasu)** pass (the night); divulge **a(kuru)** next, following

―――――― 1 ――――――

3 明々白々 **meimei-hakuhaku** perfectly clear
4 明文 **meibun** express provision
明文化 **meibunka** state explicitly, stipulate
明月 **meigetsu** bright/full moon
明日 **myōnichi, asu** tomorrow
a(kuru) hi the next/following day
明方 **a(ke)gata** dawn
5 明白 **meihaku** clear, unmistakable
明示 **meiji** clearly state
明主 **meishu** wise ruler
明石 **Akashi** (city, Hyōgo-ken)
6 明色 **meishoku** bright color
明先 **a(kari)saki** (stand in someone's) light
7 明君 **meikun** wise ruler
明応 **Meiō** (era, 1492–1501)
明快 **meikai** clear, lucid
明言 **meigen** declare, assert
8 明盲 **a(ki)mekura** blind; illiterate
明治 **Meiji** (emperor and era, 1868–1912)
明治神宮 **Meiji Jingū** Meiji Shrine
明治維新 **Meiji Ishin** the Meiji Restoration
明明白白 **meimei-hakuhaku** perfectly clear

明和 **Meiwa** (era, 1764–1772)
9 明後日 **myōgonichi** the day after tomorrow
明度 **meido** brightness, luminosity
明星 **myōjō** Venus, the morning/evening star; (literary) star
10 明哲 **meitetsu** wise man
明朗 **meirō** clear, open, cheerful
明敏 **meibin** intelligent, discerning
明記 **meiki** clearly state, specify, stipulate
11 明達 **meitatsu** wisdom, discernment
明眸 **meibō** bright eyes
明細 **meisai** details, particulars
明細書 **meisaisho** detailed statement
明断 **meidan** clear/definite judgment
12 明渡 **a(ke)wata(su)** vacate and surrender (the premises)
明媚 **meibi** beautiful, scenic
明朝 **myōchō** tomorrow morning
      Minchō Ming dynasty; Ming style (of printed kanji; the most widely used typeface, with a thickening at the right end of protruding horizontal strokes)
明晰 **meiseki** clear, distinct, lucid
明答 **meitō** definite answer
13 明滅 **meimetsu** flicker, glimmer
明滅灯 **meimetsutō** occulting light
明暗 **meian** light and dark, shading
明暗度 **meiando** brightness, light intensity
明解 **meikai** clear (explanation)
14 明暦 **Meireki** (era, 1655–1657)
明徴 **meichō** clarification
明徳 **meitoku** illustrious virtue
明暮 **a(ke)ku(re)** morning and evening; all the time
明察 **meisatsu** discernment, insight
15 明確 **meikaku** clear, distinct, well-defined
17 明瞭 **meiryō** clear, distinct, obvious
18 明離 **a(ke)hana(reru)** become light, dawn
19 明鏡 **meikyō** clear mirror
明鏡止水 **meikyō-shisui** serene state of mind
20 明礬 **myōban** alum
明鐘 **a(ke no) kane** bell tolling daybreak

——————— 2 ———————

3 口明 **kuchia(ke)** beginning, opening
4 不明 **fumei** unclear, unknown; ignorance
不明朗 **fumeirō** gloomy; dubious; dishonest
不明瞭 **fumeiryō** unclear, indistinct
元明 **Genmei** (empress, 707–715)
天明 **tenmei** dawn, daybreak
      Tenmei (era, 1781–1789)
仁明 **Ninmyō** (emperor, 833–850)
文明 **bunmei** civilization, culture
      Bunmei (era, 1469–1487)
文明史 **bunmeishi** history of civilization
文明国 **bunmeikoku** civilized country

文明病 **bunmeibyō** a disease of civilization
文明開化 **bunmei kaika** civilization and enlightenment
分明 **bunmei, bunmyō** clear, distinct
公明 **kōmei** just, fair
公明正大 **kōmei-seidai** just, fair
公明党 **Kōmeitō** (a political party)
水明 **suimei** shimmering of (sun)light on water
手明 **tea(ki)** leisure, spare/idle time
月明 **getsumei, tsukiaka(ri)** moonlight
5 未明 **mimei** (pre-)dawn
失明 **shitsumei** lose one's eyesight, go blind
弁明 **benmei** explanation, justification
平明 **heimei** plain, clear, simple
用明 **Yōmei** (emperor, 585–587)
打明 **u(chi)a(keru)** confide in, reveal
打明話 **u(chi)a(ke)banashi** confidential talk, confession, revealing a secret
目明 **mea(ki)** sighted/educated person
      mea(kashi) police detective (Edo era)
6 西明 **nishi a(kari)** evening twilight, afterglow
光明 **kōmyō** light, hope
      Kōmyō (emperor, 1337–1348)
有明 **aria(ke)** dawn (with the moon visible)
灯明 **tōmyō** light offered to a god
自明 **jimei** self-evident, self-explanatory
7 判明 **hanmei** become clear, be ascertained
克明 **kokumei** faithful, conscientious
花明 **hanaa(kari)** soft moonlight even at evening due to an abundance of white cherry blossoms
究明 **kyūmei** study, investigation, inquiry
声明 **seimei** declaration, (public) statement, proclamation
忌明 **i(mi)a(ke), kia(ke)** end of mourning
言明 **genmei** declaration, (definite) statement
      i(i)a(kasu) talk all night
8 表明 **hyōmei** state, express, announce
夜明 **yoa(kashi)** stay up all night
      yoa(ke) dawn, daybreak
斉明 **Saimei** (empress, 655–661)
泣明 **na(ki)a(kasu)** cry all night
英明 **eimei** intelligent, clear-sighted
松明 **taimatsu** (pine) torch
明明白白 **meimei-hakuhaku** perfectly clear
9 発明 **hatsumei** invention
発明者 **hatsumeisha** inventor
発明品 **hatsumeihin** an invention
発明家 **hatsumeika** inventor
透明 **tōmei** transparent
透明体 **tōmeitai** transparent body/medium
待明 **ma(chi)a(kasu)** wait all night
宣明 **senmei** proclaim, declare
幽明 **yūmei** darkness and light; this world and the next

4

木
月
日 4←
火
礻
王
牛
方
攵
欠
心
戸
戈

星明 **hoshia(kari)** starlight
神明 **shinmei** deity, God
糾明 **kyūmei** study, inquiry; investigation
10 宵明星 **yoi (no) myōjō** the evening star, Venus
11 清明 **seimei** pure and clear; 15th day after the vernal equinox
著明 **chomei** clear, plain
窓明 **madoa(kari)** light from a window
釈明 **shakumei** explanation, vindication
雪明 **yukia(kari)** snow light
12 腋明 **wakia(ki)** placket (in a skirt)
朝明 **asaa(ke)** daybreak, dawn
無明 **mumyō** ignorance, darkness
証明 **shōmei** proof, corroboration
証明書 **shōmeisho** certificate
欽明 **Kinmei** (emperor, 539–571)
飲明 **no(mi)a(kasu)** drink all night
開明 **kaimei** civilization, enlightenment
13 溶明 **yōmei** fade-in (in movies)
蓋明 **futaa(ke)** opening, commencement
照明 **shōmei** illumination, lighting
照明弾 **shōmeidan** flare, illumination round/ shell
解明 **kaimei, to(ki)a(kasu)** explicate, elucidate
14 種明 **tanea(kashi)** revealing how a trick is done
聡明 **sōmei** wise, sagacious
語明 **kata(ri)a(kasu)** talk all night
説明 **setsumei, to(ki)a(kashi)** explanation
説明文 **setsumeibun** (written) explanation
説明的 **setsumeiteki** explanatory
説明者 **setsumeisha** explainer, exponent
説明書 **setsumeisho** (written) explanation, instructions, manual
15 黎明 **reimei** dawn, morning twilight
澄明 **chōmei** clear, bright
16 薄明 **hakumei, usua(kari)** twilight, dim
賢明 **kenmei** wise, intelligent
17 鮮明 **senmei** clear, distinct
18 簡明 **kanmei** terse, brief, clear
20 闡明 **senmei** clarify, explain

———————— 3 ————————
4 不透明 **futōmei** opaque
不鮮明 **fusenmei** indistinct, blurred
6 先見明 **senken (no) mei** farseeing intelligence
8 非文明 **hibunmei** uncivilized
13 愛染明王 **Aizenmyōō** Ragaraja, six-armed god of love
新発明 **shinhatsumei** new invention

———————— 4 ————————
3 山紫水明 **sanshi-suimei** purple hills and crystal streams, scenic beauty
4 天地神明 **tenchi-shinmei** the gods of heaven and earth
6 行方不明 **yukue-fumei** missing

10 原因不明 **gen'in fumei** of unknown cause/ origin
16 機械文明 **kikai bunmei** machine civilization

4c4.2

旺 **Ō** flourishing; beautiful

———————— 1 ————————
11 旺盛 **ōsei** flourishing, in prime condition

4c4.3

杲 **KŌ** clear; high

4c4.4

昌 **SHŌ** prosperous; bright, clear

———————— 1 ————————
10 昌泰 **Shōtai** (era, 898–901)

4c4.5 / 1777

昇 **SHŌ, nobo(ru)** rise, be promoted

———————— 1 ————————
6 昇任 **shōnin** be promoted, advance
9 昇降 **shōkō** rise and fall, ascend and descend
昇降口 **shōkōguchi** (ship) entrance, hatchway
昇降場 **shōkōjō** (station) platform
昇降機 **shōkōki** elevator
昇段 **shōdan** be promoted
昇級 **shōkyū** promotion to a higher grade
10 昇進 **shōshin** promotion, advancement
昇華 **shōka** sublimation
昇格 **shōkaku** promotion to a higher status, upgrading
12 昇給 **shōkyū** pay raise
13 昇殿 **shōden** entry into the inner sanctum; access to the imperial court
20 昇騰 **shōtō** rise, go up, soar

———————— 2 ————————
3 上昇 **jōshō** rise, ascend, climb
上昇気流 **jōshō kiryū** rising air current, updraft

———————— 3 ————————
6 旭日昇天 **kyokujitsu-shōten** the rising sun

4c4.6

昊 **KŌ** sky; big
sora the sky

4c4.7

旻

BIN the (autumn) sky

4c4.8

昃

SHOKU, katamu(ku) decline, go down, set (said of the sun)

4c4.9 / 759

易

EKI divination
I, yasa(shii), -yasu(i) easy

——————— 1 ———————
3 易々 **ii(taru), yasuyasu** easy, simple
8 易者 **ekisha** fortuneteller

——————— 2 ———————
4 不易 **fueki** immutable
5 生易 **namayasa(shii)** easy, simple
　平易 **heii** easy; plain, simple
6 曲易 **ma(ge)yasu(i)** easy to bend, supple, pliant, flexible
　安易 **an'i** easy, easygoing
7 改易 **kaieki** attainder
9 便易 **ben'i** easy, convenient
　変易 **ka(wari)yasu(i)** changeable, inconstant
10 容易 **yōi** easy, simple
12 割易 **wa(re)yasu(i)** fragile
　貿易 **bōeki** trade, commerce
　貿易会社 **bōeki-gaisha** trading firm
　貿易風 **bōekifū** trade winds
　貿易品 **bōekihin** articles of commerce
　貿易商 **bōekishō** trader
　貿易場 **bōekijō** foreign market
　貿易業 **bōekigyō** the trading business
　軽易 **keii** easy, light, simple
13 辟易 **hekieki** shrink from, be daunted
14 読易 **yo(mi)yasu(i)** easy to read
16 燃易 **mo(e)yasu(i)** flammable
18 簡易 **kan'i** simple, easy
　簡易保険 **kan'i hoken** post-office life insurance
　簡易食堂 **kan'i shokudō** fast-food diner
　簡易裁判所 **kan'i saibansho** summary court
　難易 **nan'i** (relative) difficulty

——————— 3 ———————
4 片貿易 **katabōeki** one-way/unbalanced trade
11 密貿易 **mitsubōeki** smuggling

——————— 4 ———————
3 万世不易 **bansei fueki** everlasting, eternal
9 保護貿易 **hogo bōeki** protectionistic trade
11 勘合貿易 **kangō bōeki** licensed trade

昂 → 昂 4c5.11

4c4.10 / 1874

昆

KON elder brother; later, descendants; insect

——————— 1 ———————
5 昆布 **konbu, kobu** sea tangle, tang, kelp
　昆布茶 **kobucha, konbucha** tang tea
6 昆虫 **konchū** insect
　昆虫学 **konchūgaku** entomology

——————— 2 ———————
20 朧昆布 **oborokonbu, oborokobu** sliced tangle

4c4.11

昏

KON dark; evening, dusk
kura(i) dark

——————— 1 ———————
3 昏々 **konkon (to)** dead to the world, fast (asleep)
8 昏迷 **konmei** be stupefied/bewildered
10 昏倒 **kontō** faint, swoon
13 昏睡 **konsui** coma; trance, deep sleep

——————— 2 ———————
11 黄昏 **kōkon, tasogare** dusk, evening twilight

昔 → 3k5.28

胃 → 冒 4c5.6

4c4.12 / 210

的 的

TEKI (attributive suffix), -istic; target, mark
mato target, mark

——————— 1 ———————
4 的中 **tekichū** hit the mark, come true, guess right
5 的外 **matohazu(re)** wide of the mark; out of focus
9 的屋 **tekiya** charlatan; stall-keeper
15 的確 **tekikaku, tekkaku** precise, accurate, unerring

——————— 2 ———————
2 人的 **jinteki** human, personal
4 内的 **naiteki** inner, intrinsic
　公的 **kōteki** public, official
　心的 **shinteki** mental

5 史的 **shiteki** historical
外的 **gaiteki** external, outward
目的 **mokuteki** purpose, object, aim
目的地 **mokutekichi** destination
目的格 **mokutekikaku** the objective case
目的語 **mokutekigo** object (in grammar)
目的論 **mokutekiron** teleology
6 肉的 **nikuteki** fleshly, physical
7 狂的 **kyōteki** insane, frantic, fanatic
私的 **shiteki** private, personal
8 法的 **hōteki** legal, legalistic
知的 **chiteki** intellectual, mental
物的 **butteki** material, physical
性的 **seiteki** sexual
取的 **to(ri)teki** minor-rank sumo wrestler
金的 **kinteki** the bull's-eye
9 美的 **biteki** esthetic
10 射的 **shateki** target shooting
射的場 **shatekijō** rifle/shooting range
病的 **byōteki** morbid, diseased, abnormal
11 動的 **dōteki** dynamic, kinetic
12 量的 **ryōteki** quantitative
13 詩的 **shiteki** poetic
詩的情緒 **shiteki jōcho** poetic mood
14 静的 **seiteki** static
端的 **tanteki** direct, frank, point-blank
15 劇的 **gekiteki** dramatic
標的 **hyōteki** target, mark
質的 **shitsuteki** qualitative
霊的 **reiteki** spiritual
16 獣的 **jūteki** bestial, animal, brutal

———————— 3 ————————

1 一方的 **ippōteki** one-sided, unilateral
一時的 **ichijiteki** temporary
一般的 **ippanteki** general
一義的 **ichigiteki** unambiguous
2 二元的 **nigenteki** dual(istic), two-element
二次的 **nijiteki** secondary
二義的 **nigiteki** secondary
人工的 **jinkōteki** artificial
人為的 **jin'iteki** artificial
力動的 **rikidōteki** dynamic
3 大々的 **daidaiteki** great, grand, on a large scale
大乗的 **daijōteki** broad-minded
女性的 **joseiteki** feminine
小乗的 **shōjōteki** narrow-minded
4 内在的 **naizaiteki** immanent, inherent, intrinsic
内面的 **naimenteki** internal, inside, inner
友好的 **yūkōteki** friendly, amicable
文化的 **bunkateki** cultural
文学的 **bungakuteki** literary
片務的 **henmuteki** unilateral, one-sided
支配的 **shihaiteki** dominant, overriding

反抗的 **hankōteki** rebellious, defiant, antagonistic
反射的 **hanshateki** reflecting, reflective(ly), reflexive(ly)
反動的 **handōteki** reactionary
日本的 **nihonteki** (very) Japanese
心理的 **shinriteki** psychological, mental
5 包括的 **hōkatsuteki** inclusive, comprehensive
民主的 **minshuteki** democratic
半官的 **hankanteki** semiofficial
本格的 **honkakuteki** full-scale, genuine, in earnest
本質的 **honshitsuteki** in substance, essential
生理的 **seiriteki** physiological
生理的食塩水 **seiriteki shokuensui** saline solution
世俗的 **sezokuteki** worldly
世間的 **sekenteki** worldly, earthly
代表的 **daihyōteki** representative, typical
他覚的 **takakuteki** objective (symptoms)
功利的 **kōriteki** utilitarian, businesslike
写実的 **shajitsuteki** realistic, true to life, graphic
古典的 **kotenteki** classical
外交的 **gaikōteki** diplomatic
外形的 **gaikeiteki** external, outward
比喩的 **hiyuteki** figurative
比較的 **hikakuteki** relative(ly), comparative(ly)
圧制的 **asseiteki** oppressive, repressive
圧倒的 **attōteki** overwhelming
巨視的 **kyoshiteki** macroscopic, in broad perspective
打算的 **dasanteki** calculating, mercenary
可及的 **kakyūteki** as ... as possible
好戦的 **kōsenteki** bellicose, warlike
好意的 **kōiteki** friendly, with good intentions
示威的 **jiiteki** demonstrative, threatening
主知的 **shuchiteki** intellectual
主動的 **shudōteki** autonomous
主情的 **shujōteki** emotional, emotive
主観的 **shukanteki** subjective
立体的 **rittaiteki** three-dimensional
立憲的 **rikkenteki** constitutional
6 多辺的 **tahenteki** multilateral
多角的 **takakuteki** many-sided, versatile, diversified, multilateral
両性的 **ryōseiteki** bisexual, androgynous
伝統的 **dentōteki** traditional
全国的 **zenkokuteki** nationwide
全面的 **zenmenteki** all-out, full, general
全般的 **zenpanteki** general, overall, across-the-board
合法的 **gōhōteki** legal, lawful
合理的 **gōriteki** rational, reasonable, logical
肉体的 **nikutaiteki** sensual, corporal

肉感的 **nikkanteki** suggestive, voluptuous
印象的 **inshōteki** impressive, graphic
近代的 **kindaiteki** modern
地域的 **chiikiteki** local, regional
先天的 **sententeki** inborn, congenital, hereditary
先験的 **senkenteki** transcendental, a priori
回顧的 **kaikoteki** retrospective
有意的 **yūiteki** intentional; (statistically) significant
有機的 **yūkiteki** organic
自主的 **jishuteki** independent, autonomous
自発的 **jihatsuteki** spontaneous, voluntary
自殺的 **jisatsuteki** suicidal
自動的 **jidōteki** automatic
自然的 **shizenteki** natural
7 良心的 **ryōshinteki** conscientious
体系的 **taikeiteki** systematic
即物的 **sokubutsuteki** matter-of-fact
対外的 **taigaiteki** external
対称的 **taishōteki** symmetrical
対象的 **taishōteki** objective
対照的 **taishōteki** (sharply) contrasting
決定的 **ketteiteki** decisive, conclusive, definitive
抜打的 **nu(ki)u(chi)teki** without advance warning
批判的 **hihanteki** critical
技巧的 **gikōteki** skillful
投機的 **tōkiteki** speculative, risky
抒情的 **jojōteki** lyrical
否定的 **hiteiteki** negative, contradictory
狂信的 **kyōshinteki** fanatical
形式的 **keishikiteki** formal
芸術的 **geijutsuteki** artistic
学究的 **gakkyūteki** scholastic, academic
学際的 **gakusaiteki** interdisciplinary
社会的 **shakaiteki** social
社交的 **shakōteki** social, sociable
改進的 **kaishinteki** progressive
攻撃的 **kōgekiteki** aggresive, offensive
利己的 **rikoteki** selfish
系統的 **keitōteki** systematic
8 表面的 **hyōmenteki** on the surface, outwardly
画一的 **kakuitsuteki** uniform, standard
画期的 **kakkiteki** epoch-making, revolution-ary
事務的 **jimuteki** businesslike, practical
刺激的 **shigekiteki** stimulating
刹那的 **setsunateki** momentary, ephemeral
効果的 **kōkateki** effective
受動的 **judōteki** passive
盲目的 **mōmokuteki** blind (devotion)
直覚的 **chokkakuteki** intuitive
直感的 **chokkanteki** intuitive
直観的 **chokkanteki** intuitive

典型的 **tenkeiteki** typical
建設的 **kensetsuteki** constructive
退廃的 **taihaiteki** corrupt, decadent
退嬰的 **taieiteki** conservative, retiring (disposition)
逃避的 **tōhiteki** escapist, evasive
逆説的 **gyakusetsuteki** paradoxical
抽象的 **chūshōteki** abstract
知能的 **chinōteki** intellectual
英雄的 **eiyūteki** heroic
宗教的 **shūkyōteki** religious
実用的 **jitsuyōteki** practical
実際的 **jissaiteki** practical
実践的 **jissenteki** practical
実質的 **jisshitsuteki** substantial, essential, material, real
実験的 **jikkenteki** experimental, empirical
官能的 **kannōteki** sensuous, sensual, carnal
官僚的 **kanryōteki** bureaucratic
定型的 **teikeiteki** typical
定期的 **teikiteki** periodic
空想的 **kūsōteki** fanciful, visionary
屈辱的 **kutsujokuteki** humiliating, disgraceful
国民的 **kokuminteki** national
国家的 **kokkateki** national, state
国際的 **kokusaiteki** international
服従的 **fukujūteki** obedient, submissive
肯定的 **kōteiteki** affirmative
物理的 **butsuriteki** physical (properties)
物質的 **busshitsuteki** material, physical
具体的 **gutaiteki** concrete, specific, definite
具象的 **gushōteki** concrete, not abstract
9 飛躍的 **hiyakuteki** rapid, by leaps and bounds
発作的 **hossateki** spasmodic, fitful
発動的 **hatsudōteki** active
専制的 **senseiteki** despotic, autocratic, arbitrary
専門的 **senmonteki** professional, technical
保守的 **hoshuteki** conservative
侵略的 **shinryakuteki** aggressive
軍事的 **gunjiteki** military
急進的 **kyūshinteki** radical, extreme
美学的 **bigakuteki** esthetic
美術的 **bijutsuteki** artistic
逐字的 **chikujiteki** word for word, literal
逐語的 **chikugoteki** word for word, literal
通俗的 **tsūzokuteki** popular
活動的 **katsudōteki** active, dynamic
派生的 **haseiteki** derivative, secondary
封建的 **hōkenteki** feudal(istic)
挑発的 **chōhatsuteki** provocative, suggestive
挑戦的 **chōsenteki** challenging, defiant, provocative
持続的 **jizokuteki** continuous, lasting
独占的 **dokusenteki** monopolistic
独創的 **dokusōteki** original, creative

4

木
月
日 4←
火
礻
王
牛
方
攵
欠
心
戸
戈

独善的 **dokuzenteki** self-righteous, complacent, smug
独裁的 **dokusaiteki** dictatorial
後天的 **kōtenteki** acquired, cultivated
革命的 **kakumeiteki** revolutionary, radical
客観的 **kyakkanteki, kakkanteki** objective
相対的 **sōtaiteki** relative
相関的 **sōkanteki** interrelated
冒険的 **bōkenteki** adventurous, risky
神秘的 **shinpiteki** mystic(al), mysterious
政治的 **seijiteki** political
恒久的 **kōkyūteki** permanent
恒常的 **kōjōteki** constant
威圧的 **iatsuteki** coercive, domineering
威嚇的 **ikakuteki** menacing, threatening
科学的 **kagakuteki** scientific
思索的 **shisakuteki** speculative, meditative
計画的 **keikakuteki** planned, systematic, intentional
軌範的 **kihanteki** model, exemplary
10 倫理的 **rinriteki** ethical
健康的 **kenkōteki** healthful
個人的 **kojinteki** individual, personal, self-centered
個性的 **koseiteki** personal, individual
部分的 **bubunteki** partial, here and there
帰納的 **kinōteki** inductive (reasoning)
脅迫的 **kyōhakuteki** threatening, menacing
高圧的 **kōatsuteki** high-handed, coercive
高踏的 **kōtōteki** transcendent
原始的 **genshiteki** primitive, primeval, original
原則的 **gensokuteki** in principle/general
進歩的 **shinpoteki** progressive
遊戯的 **yūgiteki** playful, sportive
浪漫的 **rōmanteki** romantic (school)
消極的 **shōkyokuteki** passive, negative
従属的 **jūzokuteki** subordinate, dependent
家庭的 **kateiteki** domestic/family (affairs)
家族的 **kazokuteki** like a member of the family
根本的 **konponteki** fundamental, radical
殺人的 **satsujinteki** murderous, deadly, terrific, hectic, cutthroat
能動的 **nōdōteki** active
能率的 **nōritsuteki** efficient
教育的 **kyōikuteki** educational, instructive
教訓的 **kyōkunteki** instructive, edifying
教義的 **kyōgiteki** doctrinal
致命的 **chimeiteki** fatal, lethal, deadly, mortal
恣意的 **shiiteki** arbitrary, selfish
扇情的 **senjōteki** sensational, suggestive, racy
破壊的 **hakaiteki** destructive
耽美的 **tanbiteki** esthetic
記録的 **kirokuteki** record(-breaking)
11 野心的 **yashinteki** ambitious

野性的 **yaseiteki** wild, rough
偶発的 **gūhatsuteki** accidental, incidental, occasional
副次的 **fukujiteki** secondary
虚無的 **kyomuteki** nihilistic
運命的 **unmeiteki** fateful
道徳的 **dōtokuteki** moral, ethical
過渡的 **katoteki** transitional
基本的 **kihonteki** basic, fundamental
基礎的 **kisoteki** fundamental, basic
堕落的 **darakuteki** depraved, corrupt
排他的 **haitateki** exclusive
唯美的 **yuibiteki** esthetic
強制的 **kyōseiteki** compulsory, forced
衒学的 **gengakuteki** pedantic
宿命的 **shukumeiteki** fatal
常習的 **jōshūteki** habitual, confirmed
常識的 **jōshikiteki** matter-of-fact, practical
脱俗的 **datsuzokuteki** unworldly, saintly
理知的 **richiteki** intellectual
理性的 **riseiteki** reasonable
理想的 **risōteki** ideal
理論的 **rironteki** theoretical
現世的 **genseteki, genseiteki** worldly, temporal
現実的 **genjitsuteki** realistic
規則的 **kisokuteki** regular, orderly, systematic
規範的 **kihanteki** normative
紳士的 **shinshiteki** gentlemanly
経済的 **keizaiteki** economic, financial; economical
経験的 **keikenteki** experiential, empirical
断片的 **danpenteki** fragmentary
断続的 **danzokuteki** intermittent, off-and-on
12 創作的 **sōsakuteki** creative
創造的 **sōzōteki** creative
象徴的 **shōchōteki** symbolic
普遍的 **fuhenteki** universal, general
超人的 **chōjinteki** superhuman
最終的 **saishūteki** final, ultimate
無意的 **muiteki** unwilling; meaningless
散文的 **sanbunteki** prosaic
散発的 **sanpatsuteki** sporadic
欺瞞的 **gimanteki** deceptive, fraudulent, false
悲劇的 **higekiteki** tragic
悲観的 **hikanteki** pessimistic
装飾的 **sōshokuteki** ornamental, decorative
統一的 **tōitsuteki** unified, uniform
統計的 **tōkeiteki** statistical
絶対的 **zettaiteki** absolute
絶望的 **zetsubōteki** hopeless, desperate
貴族的 **kizokuteki** aristocratic
集合的 **shūgōteki** collective
集団的 **shūdanteki** collectively
集約的 **shūyakuteki** intensive

13 義務的 **gimuteki** obligatory, compulsory
溯及的 **sokyūteki** retroactive
摂理的 **setsuriteki** providential
献身的 **kenshinteki** self-sacrificing, devoted
微視的 **bishiteki** microscopic
楽天的 **rakutenteki** optimistic, cheerful
楽観的 **rakkanteki** optimistic, hopeful
数学的 **sūgakuteki** mathematical
数理的 **sūriteki** mathematical
感情的 **kanjōteki** emotional, sentimental
感傷的 **kanshōteki** sentimental
戦闘的 **sentōteki** fighting, militant
意志的 **ishiteki** strong-willed, forceful
意識的 **ishikiteki** consciously
継続的 **keizokuteki** continuous
誇張的 **kochōteki** exaggerated, grandilo-
     quent
試験的 **shikenteki** experimental, tentative
14 厭世的 **enseiteki** world-weary, pessimistic
歴史的 **rekishiteki** historic(al)
漸進的 **zenshinteki** gradual, moderate
演劇的 **engekiteki** dramatic, theatrical
概念的 **gainenteki** general, conceptual
模範的 **mohanteki** exemplary
煽情的 **senjōteki** suggestive, sensational
綜合的 **sōgōteki** comprehensive, overall
総合的 **sōgōteki** comprehensive, overall
総括的 **sōkatsuteki** all-inclusive, overall
精神的 **seishinteki** mental, spiritual
説明的 **setsumeiteki** explanatory
説話的 **setsuwateki** narrative (style)
15 儀礼的 **gireiteki** formal, courtesy (call)
潜在的 **senzaiteki** latent, potential, dormant
衝動的 **shōdōteki** impulsive
徹底的 **tetteiteki** thorough, exhaustive
審美的 **shinbiteki** esthetic
権威的 **ken'iteki** authoritative
暫定的 **zanteiteki** tentative, provisional
敵対的 **tekitaiteki** hostile, antagonistic
魅力的 **miryokuteki** attractive, charming,
     captivating
論理的 **ronriteki** logical
16 衛生的 **eiseiteki** hygienic, sanitary
機能的 **kinōteki** functional
機械的 **kikaiteki** mechanical
積極的 **sekkyokuteki** positive, active
頽廃的 **taihaiteki** decadent, corrupt
17 優先的 **yūsenteki** preferential
擬古的 **gikoteki** classical, pseudoarchaic
犠牲的 **giseiteki** self-sacrificing
18 観念的 **kannenteki** ideal, ideological
職業的 **shokugyōteki** professional
離散的 **risanteki** discrete
19 爆発的 **bakuhatsuteki** explosive (popularity)
22 驚異的 **kyōiteki** amazing, phenomenal
23 蠱惑的 **kowakuteki** alluring

———————— 4 ————————

4 不生産的 **fuseisanteki** unproductive
6 多神教的 **tashinkyōteki** polytheistic
8 非人間的 **hiningenteki** inhuman, impersonal
非生産的 **hiseisanteki** nonproductive,
     unproductive
非立憲的 **hirikkenteki** unconstitutional
非合理的 **higōriteki** unreasonable, irrational
非芸術的 **higeijutsuteki** inartistic
非社会的 **hishakaiteki** antisocial
非社交的 **hishakōteki** unsociable, retiring
非実際的 **hijissaiteki** impractical
非科学的 **hikagakuteki** unscientific
非党派的 **hitōhateki** nonpartisan
非能率的 **hinōritsuteki** inefficient
非現実的 **higenjitsuteki** unrealistic
非紳士的 **hishinshiteki** ungentlemanly
非営利的 **hieiriteki** nonprofit
非愛国的 **hiaikokuteki** unpatriotic, disloyal
非論理的 **hironriteki** illogical, irrational
非衛生的 **hieiseiteki** unsanitary, unhygienic
11 第二次的 **dai-nijiteki** secondary
第二義的 **dai-nigiteki** of secondary impor-
     tance
12 超自然的 **chōshizenteki** supernatural
超国家的 **chōkokkateki** ultranationalistic
超感覚的 **chōkankakuteki** extrasensory
幾何学的 **kikagakuteki** geometrical

4c4.13 / 164

者 者   SHA, mono person

———————— 2 ————————

2 二者 **nisha** two things/persons
二者択一 **nisha-takuitsu** an alternative
3 三者会談 **sansha kaidan** three-party
     conference
亡者 **mōja** the dead; ghost
小者 **komono** menial, servant; small fry
4 仏者 **bussha** a Buddhist; Buddhist priest
仁者 **jinsha** man of virtue
手者 **te(no)mono** one's men
王者 **ōja, ōsha** king
5 巧者 **kōsha** skillful, adept, tactful
弁者 **bensha** speaker, orator
幼者 **yōsha** child, infant
占者 **uranaisha** fortuneteller
打者 **dasha** batter, hitter
只者 **tadamono** ordinary person
好者 **su(ki)mono** dilettante; lecher
6 死者 **shisha** dead person, the dead
両者 **ryōsha** both persons; both things
壮者 **sōsha** man in his prime
行者 **gyōja** an ascetic
劣者 **ressha** an inferior

回者 **mawa(shi)mono** spy, secret agent
7 作者 **sakusha** author
何者 **nanimono** who
医者 **isha** doctor, physician
走者 **sōsha** runner
狂者 **kyōsha** insane person, lunatic
役者 **yakusha** player, actor
芸者 **geisha** geisha
肖者 **ayaka(ri)mono** lucky fellow
学者 **gakusha** scholar
困者 **koma(ri)mono** good-for-nothing,
nuisance, pest
囲者 **kako(i)mono** kept woman, mistress
忍者 **ninja** ninja, spy-assassin (historical)
見者 **kensha** viewer, (Noh) audience
利者 **ki(ke)mono** influential person
8 長者 **chōja** millionaire, rich person
使者 **shisha** messenger, envoy
侍者 **jisha** attendant, valet; altar boy
其者 **so(no)mono** himself, herself
soresha professional; geisha, prostitute
其者上 **soreshaa(gari)** former geisha/
prostitute
泳者 **eisha** swimmer
治者 **chisha** ruler, governor
拙者 **sessha** I (humble)
拗者 **su(ne)mono** cross-grained person
知者 **chisha** wise man
若者 **wakamono** young person/people
昔者 **mukashimono** old folks
易者 **ekisha** fortuneteller
牧者 **bokusha** shepherd, herdsman
武者 **musha** warrior
武者修業 **musha shugyō** knight-errantry
武者振 **mushabu(ri)** valor, gallantry
武者振付 **mushabu(ri)tsu(ku)** pounce upon,
devour
武者絵 **mushae** picture of a warrior
武者震 **mushaburu(i)** tremble with excitement
9 信者 **shinja** believer, adherent, the faithful
除者 **no(ke)mono** outcast
勇者 **yūsha** brave/courageous man
冠者 **kanja, kaja** young man come of age
変者 **ka(wari)mono** an eccentric
前者 **zensha** the former
通者 **tō(ri)mono** well-known person; man
about town
独者 **hito(ri)mono** single/unmarried person
後者 **kōsha** the latter
荒者 **ara(kure)mono** rough fellow, rowdy
怠者 **nama(ke)mono** idler, lazybones
思者 **omo(i)mono** sweetheart
10 流者 **naga(re)mono** vagrant, drifter
猛者 **mosa** man of courage, stalwart, veteran
弱者 **jakusha, yowa(i) mono** the weak

従者 **jūsha** follower, attendant, valet
晒者 **sara(shi)mono** (pilloried) criminal on
public display
病者 **byōsha** sick person
笑者 **wara(ware)mono** laughingstock
記者 **kisha** newspaper reporter, journalist
記者会見 **kisha kaiken** news/press conference
記者席 **kishaseki** seats for the press
11 偽者 **itsuwa(ri)mono** imposter, liar
貧者 **hinja** poor man, pauper
達者 **tassha** healthy, strong; proficient
強者 **kyōsha** strong person
gō(no)mono brave warrior; past master
術者 **jussha** one skilled in a technique
著者 **chosha** author
悪者 **warumono** bad fellow, scoundrel
患者 **kanja** a patient
盛者 **shōja** prosperous person
訳者 **yakusha** translator
敗者 **haisha** the defeated, loser
12 尊者 **sonja** Buddhist saint; one's superior
渡者 **wata(ri)mono** migratory worker; hobo;
stranger
御者 **gyosha** driver, cabman
富者 **fusha** rich person, the wealthy
勝者 **shōsha** winner, victor
然者 **sa(ru)mono** a man of no common order
慌者 **awa(te)mono** absent-minded person,
scatterbrain
筆者 **hissha** the writer/author
評者 **hyōsha** critic, reviewer
間者 **kanja** spy
馭者 **gyosha** driver, coachman
13 働者 **hatara(ki)mono** hard worker
傷者 **shōsha** injured person
適者 **tekisha** suitable person
適者生存 **tekisha seizon** survival of the fittest
聖者 **seija** saint, holy man
愚者 **oro(ka)mono, gusha** fool, jackass
14 選者 **senja** judge, selector
漁者 **gyosha** fisherman
導者 **dōsha** guide
読者 **dokusha** reader
読者層 **dokushasō** class of readers
15 撰者 **senja** author; selector
暴者 **aba(re)mono** rowdy, ruffian
戯者 **tawa(ke)mono** fool
縁者 **enja** a relative
編者 **hensha** editor, compiler
論者 **ronsha** disputant; advocate; this writer, I
16 儒者 **jusha** a Confucianist
諜者 **chōja** spy
賢者 **kenja** wise man, the wise
17 優者 **yūsha** superior individual
聴者 **chōsha** listener

19 覇者 **hasha** supreme ruler; champion
識者 **shikisha** intelligent/informed people

———————— 3 ————————

1 一人者 **hitorimono** someone alone; unmarried/single person
一徹者 **ittetsumono** stubborn person
2 入札者 **nyūsatsusha** bidder
入会者 **nyūkaisha** new member
入場者 **nyūjōsha** visitors, attendance
入選者 **nyūsensha** winner, successful competitor
入賞者 **nyūshōsha** prizewinner
丁年者 **teinensha** adult
人気者 **ninkimono** popular person, a favorite
人格者 **jinkakusha** man of character
子福者 **kobukusha** person blessed with many children
3 工学者 **kōgakusha** engineer
与太者 **yotamono, yotamon** a good-for-nothing
亡命者 **bōmeisha** exile, emigré
口達者 **kuchidassha** talkative
小心者 **shōshinmono** timid person, coward
4 不具者 **fugusha** cripple, disabled person
不信者 **fushinja** unbeliever
予言者 **yogensha** prophet
予約者 **yoyakusha** subscriber
中年者 **chūnenmono** middle-aged person; late starter
化学者 **kagakusha** chemist
文学者 **bungakusha** literary man, man of letters
支配者 **shihaisha** ruler, administrator
分限者 **bugensha** wealthy man
反乱者 **hanransha** rebel, insurgents
厄介者 **yakkaimono** a dependent; nuisance
手余者 **teama(shi)mono** someone hard to handle
手柄者 **tegaramono** meritorious person
引率者 **insotsusha** leader
引揚者 **hi(ki)a(ge)sha** returnee
日陰者 **hikagemono** one who keeps out of the public eye
日蔭者 **hikagemono** one who keeps out of the public eye
欠席者 **kessekisha** absentee
欠勤者 **kekkinsha** absentee
心酔者 **shinsuisha** ardent admirer, devotee
5 出品者 **shuppinsha** exhibitor
出席者 **shussekisha** those present, the attendance
未婚者 **mikonsha** unmarried person
失業者 **shitsugyōsha** unemployed person
生存者 **seizonsha** survivor
生学者 **namagakusha** dilettante, dabbler

生残者 **seizansha** survivor
生還者 **seikansha** survivor
弁護者 **bengosha** defender, advocate
代行者 **daikōsha** agent, proxy
代表者 **daihyōsha** a representative
他国者 **takokumono** stranger, person from another place
加害者 **kagaisha** assailant, perpetrator
功労者 **kōrōsha** man of distinguished service
古参者 **kosansha** senior, old hand
外来者 **gairaisha** person from abroad
正犯者 **seihansha** principal offender
正直者 **shōjikimono** honest person, man of integrity
圧制者 **asseisha** oppressor, despot, tyrant
巡礼者 **junreisha** pilgrim
司会者 **shikaisha** emcee, chairman
好打者 **kōdasha** (baseball) slugger
犯罪者 **hanzaisha** criminal, offender, convict
主犯者 **shuhansha** principal offender
主宰者 **shusaisha** president, chairman
主催者 **shusaisha** sponsor, organizer
主義者 **shugisha** -ist, advocate (of a theory/doctrine)
主演者 **shuensha** star, leading actor
主権者 **shukensha** sovereign, supreme ruler
主謀者 **shubōsha** (ring)leader, mastermind
立役者 **ta(te)yakusha** leading actor
立法者 **rippōsha** legislator, lawmaker
立案者 **ritsuansha** drafter, planner, designer
目医者 **meisha** ophthalmologist, optometrist
目撃者 **mokugekisha** (eye)witness
田舎者 **inakamono** person from the country, rustic, rube
6 死亡者 **shibōsha** the deceased, fatalities
死亡者欄 **shibōsharan** obituary column
死傷者 **shishōsha** casualties, killed and wounded
気丈者 **kijōmono** stout-hearted fellow
年長者 **nenchōsha** a senior, older person
再犯者 **saihansha** second offender
仲介者 **chūkaisha** mediator, intermediary, middleman
仲裁者 **chūsaisha** arbitrator, mediator
印刷者 **insatsusha** printer
列席者 **ressekisha** those present
老年者 **rōnensha** old people, the aged
近眼者 **kingansha** nearsighted person
近親者 **kinshinsha, kinshinja** close relative
同好者 **dōkōsha** people of similar tastes
同行者 **dōkōsha** traveling companion
同伴者 **dōhansha** companion
先任者 **senninsha** predecessor
先住者 **senjūsha** former occupant
先覚者 **senkakusha** pioneer, leading spirit
先駆者 **senkusha** forerunner, pioneer

4

木 月 日 火 ネ 王 牛 方 文 欠 心 戸 戈

4←

在住者 **zaijūsha** resident
在官者 **zaikansha** officeholder
在監者 **zaikansha** prisoner, inmate
共犯者 **kyōhansha** accomplice
共同者 **kyōdōsha** collaborator
共有者 **kyōyūsha** part owner, co-owner
当局者 **tōkyokusha** the authorities
当事者 **tōjisha** the parties (concerned)
当選者 **tōsensha** successful candidate
当籤者 **tōsensha** prizewinner
因果者 **ingamono** unlucky/ill-fated person
有力者 **yūryokusha** influential/powerful
　　 person
有志者 **yūshisha** supporter, volunteer
有権者 **yūkensha** qualified person, eligible
　　 voter
有勲者 **yūkunsha** holder of a decoration
有職者 **yūshokusha** employed person
有識者 **yūshikisha** learned person, an
　　 intellectual
成上者 **na(ri)a(gari)mono** upstart, parvenu
自殺者 **jisatsusha** a suicide (the person)
7 来観者 **raikansha** visitor (to an exhibit)
我武者羅 **gamushara** reckless, daredevil
余所者 **yosomono** stranger
求婚者 **kyūkonsha** suitor
邪魔者 **jamamono** person who gets in the
　　 way
即死者 **sokushisha** persons killed instantly
助力者 **joryokusha** helper, supporter
助言者 **jogensha** adviser, counselor
迫害者 **hakugaisha** persecutor, oppressor
没落者 **botsurakusha** a bankrupt; ruined
　　 people
扶養者 **fuyōsha** supporter, breadwinner
抑留者 **yokuryūsha** detainee, internee
技術者 **gijutsusha** technical expert
投宿者 **tōshukusha** hotel guest
投票者 **tōhyōsha** voter
投稿者 **tōkōsha** contributor (to a magazine)
吹奏者 **suisōsha** wind-instrument player
告発者 **kokuhatsusha** prosecutor, accuser,
　　 informant
呑気者 **nonkimono** happy-go-lucky person
乱入者 **rannyūsha** intruder, trespasser
乱暴者 **ranbōmono** rowdy, vandal
希望者 **kibōsha** applicant, candidate, aspirant
狂信者 **kyōshinsha** fanatic, faddist
労務者 **rōmusha** worker, laborer
労働者 **rōdōsha** worker, laborer
志望者 **shibōsha** aspirant
志願者 **shigansha** applicant, candidate,
　　 volunteer, aspirant
応募者 **ōbosha** applicant, entrant, volunteer,
　　 subscriber (to bonds)
局外者 **kyokugaisha** outsider, onlooker

困窮者 **konkyūsha** the needy/destitute
改宗者 **kaishūsha** a convert
改革者 **kaikakusha** reformer
利口者 **rikōmono** clever person
利用者 **riyōsha** user
初心者 **shoshinsha** beginner
初学者 **shogakusha** beginner, new student
町医者 **machi isha** practicing physician
8 果報者 **kahōmono** lucky person
使用者 **shiyōsha** user, consumer; employer
供給者 **kyōkyūsha** supplier
受刑者 **jukeisha** a convict
受血者 **juketsusha** blood recipient
受洗者 **jusensha** person baptized
受益者 **juekisha** beneficiary
受配者 **juhaisha** recipient of an allotment
受給者 **jukyūsha** pensioner
受領者 **juryōsha** recipient
受賞者 **jushōsha** prizewinner
受贈者 **juzōsha** recipient (of a gift)
受難者 **junansha** sufferer
受験者 **jukensha** examinee
協力者 **kyōryokusha** collaborator, coworker
建設者 **kensetsusha** builder
建築者 **kenchikusha** builder
建議者 **kengisha** proposer
追放者 **tsuihōsha** purgee, deportee
追跡者 **tsuisekisha** pursuer
逃亡者 **tōbōsha** runaway, fugitive, deserter
注解者 **chūkaisha** commentator
拓殖者 **takushokusha** colonist
担当者 **tantōsha** the one in charge
拘束者 **kōsokusha** person who restrains,
　　 captor
知恵者 **chiesha** man of wisdom/ideas
妻帯者 **saitaisha** married man
征服者 **seifukusha** conqueror
参与者 **san'yosha** participant
参加者 **sankasha** participant
参会者 **sankaisha** those present
参列者 **sanretsusha** those present
参画者 **sankakusha** person participating in
　　 the planning
英学者 **eigakusha** English scholar
若武者 **wakamusha** young warrior
苦行者 **kugyōsha** an ascetic
実力者 **jitsuryokusha** powerful person
実験者 **jikkensha** experimenter
定住者 **teijūsha** permanent resident
歩行者 **hokōsha** pedestrian
歩行者天国 **hokōsha tengoku** street
　　 temporarily closed to vehicles, mall
居住者 **kyojūsha** resident, inhabitant
国学者 **kokugakusha** Japanese-classics
　　 scholar
放浪者 **hōrōsha** wanderer, vagabond, vagrant

所有者 **shoyūsha** owner
所持者 **shojisha** holder, bearer
所得者 **shotokusha** income earner
武辺者 **buhenmono** warrior
具眼者 **gugansha** discerning/observant person
委任者 **ininsha** mandator
9 発行者 **hakkōsha** publisher
発見者 **hakkensha** discoverer
発言者 **hatsugensha** speaker
発明者 **hatsumeisha** inventor
重婚者 **jūkonsha** bigamist
重傷者 **jūshōsha** seriously injured person
信奉者 **shinpōsha** adherent, believer, devotee
保有者 **hoyūsha** possessor, holder, owner
保持者 **hojisha** holder (of a record)
保菌者 **hokinsha** carrier (of a disease)
保護者 **hogosha** protector, guardian
侵入者 **shinnyūsha** invader, intruder
侵略者 **shinryakusha** aggressor, invader
院外者 **ingaisha** lobbyist; persons outside
congress/parliament
変質者 **henshitsusha** a pervert/deviant
負傷者 **fushōsha** injured person, the wounded
首唱者 **shushōsha** advocate, proponent
首謀者 **shubōsha** ringleader, mastermind
前任者 **zenninsha** one's predecessor
前科者 **zenkamono** person with a criminal
record
速記者 **sokkisha** shorthand writer, stenographer
造物者 **Zōbutsusha** the Creator
洒落者 **sharemono** smart dresser, fop
浮浪者 **furōsha** street bum, tramp, hobo
洋学者 **yōgakusha** scholar of Western
learning
挑戦者 **chōsensha** challenger
持余者 **mo(te)ama(shi)mono** nuisance,
black sheep
拾得者 **shūtokusha** finder
指名者 **shimeisha** nominator, designator
指揮者 **shikisha** (orchestra) conductor,
leader; commander, director
指導者 **shidōsha** leader
独身者 **dokushinsha** unmarried/single person
独裁者 **dokusaisha** dictator
律義者 **richigimono** honest hardworking man
律儀者 **richigimono** honest hardworking man
後援者 **kōensha** supporter, backer
後継者 **kōkeisha** successor
荒武者 **aramusha** rowdy, a tough, daredevil
相続者 **sōzokusha** heir
背教者 **haikyōsha** apostate
為政者 **iseisha** statesman, administrator
祖述者 **sojutsusha** exponent
科学者 **kagakusha** scientist
卑怯者 **hikyōmono** coward

計画者 **keikakusha** planner
食詰者 **ku(i)tsu(me)mono** a down-and-outer
10 既婚者 **kikonsha** married person
残存者 **zansonsha** survivor, holdover
耕作者 **kōsakusha** tiller, plowman, farmer
候補者 **kōhosha** candidate
修行者 **shugyōsha** practitioner of (Buddhist)
austerities
修験者 **shugenja** ascetic mountain-dwelling
monk
借用者 **shakuyōsha** borrower
凍死者 **tōshisha** person frozen to death
随伴者 **zuihansha** attendant, follower, retinue
随従者 **zuijūsha** henchman, follower, satellite
部外者 **bugaisha** outsider
帰還者 **kikansha** a repatriate
高年者 **kōnensha** elderly person
高齢者 **kōreisha** elderly person
差出者 **sa(shi)demono** intruder, meddler,
busybody
原作者 **gensakusha** the original author (of a
translated work)
原著者 **genchosha** the author
進呈者 **shinteisha** presenter
遊興者 **yūkyōsha** carouser, reveler
酒落者 **sharemono** smart dresser, fop
流刑者 **ryūkeisha** an exile
消費者 **shōhisha** consumer
起草者 **kisōsha** drafter
哲学者 **tetsugakusha** philosopher
狼藉者 **rōzekimono** rioter, ruffian
猛打者 **mōdasha** slugger (in baseball)
徒武者 **kachimusha** foot soldier
荷担者 **katansha** participant, supporter,
accomplice
案内者 **annaisha** guide
容疑者 **yōgisha** a suspect
殺害者 **satsugaisha** murderer, slayer
殉教者 **junkyōsha** martyr
殉難者 **junnansha** martyr, victim
特権者 **tokkensha** privileged person
旅行者 **ryokōsha** traveler, tourist
旅役者 **tabiyakusha** actor/troupe on the road
教育者 **kyōikusha** educator
教唆者 **kyōsasha** instigator
教職者 **kyōshokusha** teacher, clergyman
扇動者 **sendōsha** instigator, agitator
破産者 **hasansha** bankrupt person
破壊者 **hakaisha** destroyer, wrecker
被災者 **hisaisha** victim, sufferer
被治者 **hichisha** the governed
被害者 **higaisha** victim
被疑者 **higisha** a suspect
被爆者 **hibakusha** bombing victims
留学者 **ryūgakusha** person studying abroad
納税者 **nōzeisha** taxpayer

4

木
月
日
火 4←
ネ
王
牛
方
攵
欠
心
戸
戈

航海者 **kōkaisha** mariner, seaman
配遇者 **haigūsha** spouse
11 疎開者 **sokaisha** evacuee
偽善者 **gizensha** hypocrite
側近者 **sokkinsha** close associate
道化者 **dōkemono** jester, joker, wag
道学者 **dōgakusha** moralist
道楽者 **dōrakumono** libertine, playboy
遅刻者 **chikokusha** latecomer
執筆者 **shippitsusha** writer, contributor
推薦者 **suisensha** recommender
採点者 **saitensha** marker, grader, scorer
探究者 **tankyūsha** investigator
婚約者 **kon'yakusha** fiancé(e)
猪武者 **inoshishi musha** daredevil
強打者 **kyōdasha** hard hitter, slugger
強奪者 **gōdatsusha** plunderer, robber
著作者 **chosakusha** author, writer
密告者 **mikkokusha** informer, betrayer
密航者 **mikkōsha** stowaway
寄留者 **kiryūsha** temporary resident
寄稿者 **kikōsha** contributor (of articles)
寄贈者 **kizōsha** donor, contributor
常用者 **jōyōsha** constant user; addict
常習者 **jōshūsha** habitual offender
崇拝者 **sūhaisha** worshiper
脚色者 **kyakushokusha** dramatizer, adapter
理学者 **rigakusha** scientist
救助者 **kyūjosha** rescuer
救済者 **kyūsaisha** reliever, savior
惨死者 **zanshisha** mangled corpse
惨殺者 **zansatsusha** murderer, slayer
移住者 **ijūsha** emigrant, immigrant
累犯者 **ruihansha** repeat offender
異端者 **itansha** heretic
紹介者 **shōkaisha** introducer
経営者 **keieisha** manager, operator
経験者 **keikensha** experienced person
粗忽者 **sokotsumono** careless/absentminded person
第三者 **dai-sansha** third person/party
訪問者 **hōmonsha** visitor, caller
設立者 **setsuritsusha** founder, organizer
設計者 **sekkeisha** designer
責任者 **sekininsha** person in charge
12 傍観者 **bōkansha** onlooker, bystander
創立者 **sōritsusha** founder
創始者 **sōshisha** originator, founder
創案者 **sōansha** originator, inventor
創業者 **sōgyōsha** founder
勤労者 **kinrōsha** worker, laborer
勤続者 **kinzokusha** person of long service, senior worker
遁世者 **tonseisha** recluse, hermit
渡航者 **tokōsha** foreign visitor, passenger
報告者 **hōkokusha** reporter, informer

提出者 **teishutsusha** proposer, mover
提案者 **teiansha** proposer, proponent
登山者 **tozansha** mountain climber
弾奏者 **dansōsha** (guitar/piano) player
落武者 **o(chi)musha** fugitive warrior, straggler
落選者 **rakusensha** unsuccessful candidate
極道者 **gokudōmono** scoundrel, rogue
勝利者 **shōrisha** victor, winner
腕達者 **udedassha** strong/brawny man
晴眼者 **seigansha** sighted/non-blind person
焼死者 **shōshisha** person burned to death
無礼者 **bureimono, bureisha** insolent person
無法者 **muhōmono** outrageous fellow, outlaw
無骨者 **bukotsumono** boor, lout, churl
無宿者 **mushukusha** vagrant, homeless wanderer
無産者 **musansha** proletarian, have-nots
無職者 **mushokusha** the unemployed
無籍者 **musekimono** person without registered domicile; vagrant; outcast
欺瞞者 **gimansha** deceiver, swindler
雇用者 **koyōsha** employer
給血者 **kyūketsusha** blood donor
統治者 **tōchisha, tōjisha** ruler, sovereign
統率者 **tōsotsusha** commander, leader
統轄者 **tōkatsusha** the one in charge
絶対者 **zettaisha** the Absolute
歯医者 **haisha** dentist
筆記者 **hikkisha** copyist
筍医者 **takenoko isha** inexperienced doctor
註釈者 **chūshakusha** annotator, commentator
開拓者 **kaitakusha** settler, pioneer
13 債務者 **saimusha** debtor
債権者 **saikensha** creditor
剽軽者 **hyōkinmono** jokester, wag
裏切者 **uragi(ri)mono** betrayer, traitor
棄権者 **kikensha** nonvoter
義務者 **gimusha** debtor, obligor, responsible person
遭難者 **sōnansha** victim, sufferer
適任者 **tekininsha** well-qualified person
適格者 **tekikakusha** qualified/eligible person
溺死者 **dekishisha** drowned person
滞在者 **taizaisha** sojourner, visitor
滞納者 **tainōsha** defaulter, (tax) delinquent
漢学者 **kangakusha** scholar of Chinese classics
嘆美者 **tanbisha** admirer, adorer
嘆賞者 **tanshōsha** admirer
嫌疑者 **kengisha** a suspect
献納者 **kennōsha** donor
鼓吹者 **kosuisha** advocate, propagator
暗殺者 **ansatsusha** assassin
解説者 **kaisetsusha** commentator

数学者 **sūgakusha** mathematician
愛好者 **aikōsha** lover of, fan, fancier
愛国者 **aikokusha** patriot
愛玩者 **aigansha** lover, admirer, fancier
愛飲者 **aiinsha** habitual drinker
愛読者 **aidokusha** reader, subscriber
愛嬌者 **aikyōmono** charming fellow/girl
戦死者 **senshisha** fallen soldier
戦没者 **senbotsusha** fallen soldier
戦災者 **sensaisha** war victims
戦歿者 **senbotsusha** fallen soldier
戦勝者 **senshōsha** victor
新患者 **shinkanja** new patient
継承者 **keishōsha** successor
該当者 **gaitōsha** the said person
試掘者 **shikutsusha** prospector
飼育者 **shiikusha** raiser, breeder
預金者 **yokinsha** depositor
14 厭人者 **enjinsha** misanthrope
遺言者 **yuigonsha** testator
漂流者 **hyōryūsha** person adrift; castaway
演出者 **enshutsusha** producer, director
演芸者 **engeisha** performer
演説者 **enzetsusha** speaker, orator
摘発者 **tekihatsusha** exposer, informer
獄道者 **gokudōsha** scoundrel, rogue, rake
模造者 **mozōsha** imitator
斡旋者 **assensha** mediator, intermediary
端武者 **hamusha** common soldier, private
製作者 **seisakusha** manufacturer, producer
製造者 **seizōsha** manufacturer
誘惑者 **yūwakusha** tempter, seducer
語学者 **gogakusha** linguist
説明者 **setsumeisha** explainer, exponent
誓約者 **seiyakusha** party to a covenant
関係者 **kankeisha** interested party, those concerned
領収者 **ryōshūsha** receiver, recipient
15 養育者 **yōikusha** rearer, guardian
養豚者 **yōtonsha** hog raiser, pig farmer
避難者 **hinansha** refugees, evacuees
影武者 **kagemusha** general's double; man behind the scenes, wirepuller
横断者 **ōdansha** street-crossing pedestrians
権力者 **kenryokusha** powerful person
権威者 **ken'isha** an authority
暴動者 **bōdōsha** rioter, rebel, insurgent
敵性者 **tekiseisha** person of enemy character
監視者 **kanshisha** guard, caretaker, watchman
編集者 **henshūsha** editor
請願者 **seigansha** petitioner, applicant
調子者 **chōshimono** person easily elated
賛成者 **sanseisha** approver, supporter
質問者 **shitsumonsha** questioner
16 儒学者 **jugakusha** Confucianist, Confucian scholar

操縦者 **sōjūsha** operator, manipulator; driver, pilot
擁護者 **yōgosha** defender, supporter, advocate
薬学者 **yakugakusha** pharmacologist
親権者 **shinkensha** person in parental authority
17 優勝者 **yūshōsha** winner, champion, title-holder
臆病者 **okubyōmono** coward
犠牲者 **giseisha** victim
懇願者 **kongansha** supplicant, petitioner
聴取者 **chōshusha** (radio) listener
聴視者 **chōshisha** (TV) viewer(s)
講演者 **kōensha** lecturer, speaker
購入者 **kōnyūsha** purchaser, buyer
購買者 **kōbaisha** buyer
購読者 **kōdokusha** subscriber
鍼医者 **hariisha** acupuncturist
18 藪医者 **yabuisha** a quack
観察者 **kansatsusha** observer
観覧者 **kanransha** spectator, visitor
翻訳者 **hon'yakusha** translator
贈与者 **zōyosha** donor
贈呈者 **zōteisha** giver, donor
鎧武者 **yoroimusha** warrior in armor
離職者 **rishokusha** the unemployed
闖入者 **chinnyūsha** intruder, trespasser
19 贋造者 **ganzōsha** counterfeiter, forger
20 競争者 **kyōsōsha** competitor, rival
22 聾唖者 **rōasha** a deaf-mute

──────── 4 ────────

3 大根役者 **daikon yakusha** ham actor
千両役者 **senryō yakusha** great actor, star
下請業者 **shitauke gyōsha** subcontractor
女権論者 **jokenronsha** feminist
5 未成年者 **miseinensha** a minor
未帰還者 **mikikansha** person still not repatriated
未経験者 **mikeikensha** person having no experience
外来患者 **gairai kanja** outpatient
6 地理学者 **chirigakusha** geographer
行路病者 **kōro byōsha** person fallen ill on the road
有資格者 **yūshikakusha** qualified person
百万長者 **hyakumanchōja** (multi-)millionaire
8 建築業者 **kenchiku gyōsha** builder
9 重労働者 **jūrōdōsha** heavy laborer
宣伝業者 **senden gyōsha** publicist
10 進化論者 **shinkaronsha** evolutionist
従軍記者 **jūgun kisha** war correspondent
被保護者 **hihogosha** ward
被後見者 **hikōkensha** ward
11 運送業者 **unsōgyōsha** carrier, forwarding agent

4

木
月
日　4←
火
礻
王
牛
方
攵
欠
心
戸
戈

宿命論者 **shukumeironsha** fatalist
第一人者 **dai-ichininsha** foremost/leading person
12 最近親者 **saikinshinsha** nearest relative, next of kin
無能力者 **munōryokusha** an incompetent
無資格者 **mushikakusha** unqualified/incompetent person
悲観論者 **hikanronsha** pessimist
13 夢遊病者 **muyūbyōsha** sleepwalker
禁治産者 **kinchisansha** person adjudged incompetent
15 億万長者 **okumanchōja** multimillionaire, billionaire
16 穏和論者 **onwaronsha** a moderate

——————— 5 ———————
4 分離主義者 **bunri shugisha** separatist, secessionist
反動主義者 **handō shugisha** a reactionary
水上生活者 **suijō seikatsusha** seafarer
6 自由労働者 **jiyū rōdōsha** casual laborer
7 身体障害者 **shintai shōgaisha** physically handicapped person
13 準禁治産者 **junkinchisansha** a quasi-incompetent (person)

——————— 6 ———————
12 無政府主義者 **museifushugisha** anarchist

——————— 5 ———————

旺 → 曜 **4c14.1**

4c5.1 / 352

映 暎
EI, utsu(su) reflect; project; take (a photo)
utsu(ru) be reflected/projected
ha(eru) shine, be brilliant

——————— 1 ———————
0 映じる/ずる **ei(jiru/zuru)** be reflected in, shine on; impress, appear to
5 映写 **eisha** project (a picture onto a screen)
映写幕 **eishamaku** (projection) screen
映写機 **eishaki** projector
8 映画 **eiga** movie, film
映画化 **eigaka** make a movie version of
映画界 **eigakai** the cinema/screen world
映画劇 **eigageki** film drama
映画館 **eigakan** movie theater
14 映像 **eizō** image, reflection

——————— 2 ———————
3 夕映 **yūba(e)** evening/sunset glow
上映 **jōei** screen, show, play (a movie)
4 反映 **han'ei** reflect, mirror

5 代映 **ka(wari)ba(e)** change for the better
7 投映 **tōei** project (an image), cast
見映 **miba(e)** (attractive) appearance
9 面映 **omoha(yui)** embarrassing, awkward
13 照映 **te(ri)ha(eru)** be lit up, glow
続映 **zokuei** continued run (of a movie)
15 劇映画 **gekieiga** movie/film drama
20 競映 **kyōei** competitive film exhibition

——————— 3 ———————
5 出来映 **dekiba(e)** result, effect, workmanship, performance
6 再上映 **saijōei** reshowing (of a movie)
12 無声映画 **musei eiga** silent movie

4c5.2

昧
MAI dark; foolish; dawn

——————— 2 ———————
3 三昧 **sanmai** concentration, absorption
13 蒙昧 **mōmai** ignorant, benighted
愚昧 **gumai** stupid, ignorant, asinine
16 濛昧 **mōmai** ignorant, benighted
17 曖昧 **aimai** vague, ambiguous, equivocal
曚昧 **mōmai** unenlightened, benighted, ignorant

——————— 4 ———————
12 無知蒙昧 **muchi-mōmai** unenlightened

4c5.3 / 361
昨
SAKU past, yesterday, last (year)

——————— 1 ———————
3 昨夕 **sakuyū** last/yesterday evening
4 昨今 **sakkon** nowadays, recently
昨日 **sakujitsu, kinō** yesterday
6 昨年 **sakunen** last year
8 昨非今是 **sakuhi-konze** reversing one's way of thinking
昨夜 **sakuya, yūbe** last night/evening
12 昨朝 **sakuchō** yesterday morning
昨暁 **sakugyō** at dawn yesterday
昨晩 **sakuban** last evening/night

——————— 2 ———————
1 一昨日 **issakujitsu, ototoi, ototsui** the day before yesterday
一昨年 **issakunen, ototoshi** the year before last
一昨昨日 **issakusakujitsu, sakiototoi, sakiototsui** three days ago
一昨昨年 **issakusakunen, sakiototoshi** three years ago
一昨昨夜 **issakusakuya** three nights ago

4c5.4 / 997

昭

SHŌ bright, clear

――――――― 1 ―――――――
8 昭和 **Shōwa** (emperor and era, 1926–1989)
――――――― 2 ―――――――
6 孝昭 **Kōshō** (emperor, 475–393 B.C.)

昡 → 曠 4c15.2

4c5.5

昵

JITSU become familiar with

――――――― 1 ―――――――
6 昵近 **jikkin** intimate, familiar
17 昵懇 **jikkon** intimate, familiar

4c5.6 / 1104

冒 冒

BŌ, oka(su) risk, brave, defy, dare

――――――― 1 ―――――――
10 冒険 **bōken** adventure
　　冒険好 **bōkenzu(ki)** venturesome
　　冒険的 **bōkenteki** adventurous, risky
　　冒険談 **bōkendan** account of one's adventures
16 冒頭 **bōtō** beginning, opening (paragraph)
18 冒瀆 **bōtoku** blasphemy, sacrilege, desecration
――――――― 2 ―――――――
13 感冒 **kanbō** a cold, the flu
――――――― 5 ―――――――
10 流行性感冒 **ryūkōsei kanbō** influenza

4c5.7 / 730

星

SEI, hoshi star

――――――― 1 ―――――――
4 星斗 **seito** stars
　　星月夜 **hoshizukiyo** starlit night
5 星占 **hoshiurana(i)** astrology, horoscope
6 星回 **hoshimawa(ri)** one's star/fortune
　　星団 **seidan** star cluster
7 星形 **hoshigata** star-shaped
　　星学 **seigaku** astronomy
　　星図 **seizu** star chart, celestial map
　　星条旗 **seijōki** the Stars and Stripes flag
8 星空 **hoshizora** starry sky

　　星明 **hoshia(kari)** starlight
10 星座 **seiza** constellation
11 星宿 **seishuku** constellation
　　星章 **seishō** badge, star
12 星雲 **seiun** nebula
　　星雲説 **seiunsetsu** the nebular hypothesis
13 星群 **seigun** star cluster
15 星標 **seihyō** asterisk
17 星霜 **seisō** years, time
――――――― 2 ―――――――
2 九星術 **kyūseijutsu** astrology
3 土星 **dosei** Saturn
4 水星 **suisei** Mercury
　　木星 **mokusei** Jupiter
　　火星 **kasei** Mars
　　火星人 **kaseijin** a Martian
5 占星術 **senseijutsu** astrology
　　巨星 **kyosei** giant star; great/prominent man
　　白星 **shiroboshi** white dot (sign of victory/success)
　　目星 **meboshi** aim, object
7 図星 **zuboshi** the bull's-eye
　　初星 **hatsuboshi** first star-mark (indicating a win in sumo)
8 明星 **myōjō** Venus, the morning/evening star; (literary) star
　　金星 **kinsei** (the planet) Venus
　　　　　　kinboshi glorious victory
9 負星 **ma(ke)boshi** mark indicating a loss
　　海星 **hitode** starfish
　　恒星 **kōsei** fixed star
10 将星 **shōsei** general, commander
　　遊星 **yūsei** planet
　　流星 **ryūsei, naga(re)boshi** meteor, shooting/falling star
　　流星雨 **ryūseiu** meteor shower
　　狼星 **Rōsei** Sirius, the Dog Star
11 彗星 **suisei, hōkiboshi** comet
　　晨星 **shinsei** morning star
　　黒星 **kuroboshi** black spot/dot; bull's-eye; a defeat, failure
12 渦星雲 **kaseiun** spiral nebula
　　勝星 **ka(chi)boshi** (mark indicating) a win
　　暁星 **gyōsei** morning star, Venus
　　惑星 **wakusei** planet
　　惑星間 **wakuseikan** interplanetary
13 煌星 **kiraboshi** glittering stars
　　照星 **shōsei** gunbarrel bead, front sight
　　新星 **shinsei** nova; new (movie) star
　　矮星 **waisei** dwarf star
16 衛星 **eisei** satellite
　　衛星国 **eiseikoku** satellite (country)
　　衛星都市 **eisei toshi** satellite towns
――――――― 3 ―――――――
1 一等星 **ittōsei** first-magnitude star

4

木
月
日　5←
火
礻
王
牛
方
攵
欠
心
戸
戈

4 天王星 **Tennōsei** Uranus
　天狼星 **Tenrōsei** Sirius, the Dog Star
5 北斗星 **Hokutosei** the Big Dipper
　北極星 **hokkyokusei** the North Star, Polaris
9 海王星 **kaiōsei** Neptune
10 冥王星 **Meiōsei** Pluto
　宵明星 **yoi (no) myōjō** the evening star, Venus
14 綺羅星 **kiraboshi** glittering stars

────────── 4 ──────────

5 北斗七星 **Hokuto Shichisei** the Big Dipper
9 南十字星 **minami jūjisei** the Southern Cross
14 静止衛星 **seishi eisei** (geo)stationary satellite

4c5.8

葛 **KATSU, nanzo** why, how
itsu when

4c5.9 / 1591

是 **ZE** right, correct, just; policy
kore this

────────── 1 ──────────

3 是々非々 **zeze-hihi** fair and unbiased
5 是正 **zesei** correct, rectify
8 是非 **zehi** right and wrong; by all means
14 是認 **zenin** approval, sanction

────────── 2 ──────────

7 社是 **shaze** company policy
8 彼是 **are-kore** this or/and that
　国是 **kokuze** national policy
10 党是 **tōze** party policies/platform
13 頑是 **ganze(nai)** innocent, artless; helpless

────────── 3 ──────────

6 色即是空 **shikisoku-zekū** Matter is void. All is vanity.
8 空即是色 **kūsoku-zeshiki** void matter as tangible

────────── 4 ──────────

9 昨非今是 **sakuhi-konze** reversing one's way of thinking

4c5.10

易 **YŌ** open; sun

4c5.11

昂 昂 **KŌ** rise

────────── 1 ──────────

12 昂揚 **kōyō** raise, heighten, uplift
　昂然 **kōzen** elated, triumphant
16 昂奮 **kōfun** get excited

20 昂騰 **kōtō** sudden rise (in prices)

────────── 2 ──────────

10 軒昂 **kenkō** rising high; in high spirits
16 激昂 **gekkō, gekikō** get excited, be enraged/indignant

────────── 3 ──────────

4 心悸昂進 **shinki kōshin** palpitations

4c5.12

昴 **BŌ, Subaru** the Pleiades (constellation)

昆 → 4c4.10

皈 → 帰 2f8.8

4c5.13 / 460

春 **SHUN** spring; beginning of the year; sex
haru spring

────────── 1 ──────────

0 春めく **haru(meku)** become springlike
2 春七草 **haru (no) nanakusa** the seven herbs of spring
4 春分 **shunbun** the vernal equinox
　春分日 **shunbun (no) hi** the vernal equinox (a holiday, about March 21)
　春分点 **shunbunten** the vernal equinoctal point
5 春本 **shunpon** pornographic book
6 春色 **shunshoku** spring scenery
　春先 **harusaki** early spring
　春光 **shunkō** spring scenery
7 春季 **shunki** spring(time)
8 春画 **shunga** obscene picture, pornography
　春雨 **harusame, shun'u** spring rain; bean-jelly sticks
9 春巻 **haruma(ki)** egg roll
　春風 **harukaze, shunpū** spring breeze
　春秋 **shunjū** spring and autumn; years
10 春宵 **shunshō** spring evening
　春夏秋冬 **shun-ka-shū-tō** the four seasons, the year round
　春眠 **shunmin** (pleasant) springtime sleep
11 春陽 **shun'yō** (warm) spring sunshine
　春情 **shunjō** sexual passion
12 春着 **harugi** spring/New-Year's clothes
　春場所 **harubasho** the spring sumo tournament
　春寒 **shunkan** the (early-)spring cold
　春景 **shunkei** spring scene
　春景色 **haru-geshiki** spring scenery

13 春蒔 **haruma(ki)** spring sowing
　春暖 **shundan** warm spring weather
　春雷 **shunrai** spring thunder
14 春歌 **shunka** bawdy song
16 春機発動期 **shunki hatsudōki** puberty
17 春霞 **haru-gasumi** spring haze
18 春闘 **shuntō** spring labor offensive (short for 春季闘争)

———————— 2 ————————

3 小春 **koharu** tenth lunar month, Indian summer
　小春日和 **koharubiyori** balmy autumn day, Indian-summer day
5 立春 **risshun** the first day of spring
6 仲春 **chūshun** mid-spring, March
　迎春 **geishun** welcoming the new year
　迎春花 **geishunka** flowers which bloom around New Year's time
　行春 **yu(ku) haru** departing spring
　回春 **kaishun** rejuvenation
　早春 **sōshun** early spring
7 来春 **raishun** next spring
　売春 **baishun** prostitution
　売春婦 **baishunfu** prostitute
　季春 **kishun** late spring
　初春 **shoshun** early spring
8 青春 **seishun** youth
　青春期 **seishunki** youth, adolescence
9 逝春 **yu(ku) haru** the departing spring
　思春期 **shishunki** puberty
10 残春 **zanshun** the last days of spring
12 晩春 **banshun** the latter part of spring
13 新春 **shinshun** the New Year
14 暮春 **boshun** late spring

4c5.14 / 587

皆　　KAI, mina, minna all

———————— 1 ————————

3 皆々様 **minaminasama** everyone, all of you
5 皆目 **kaimoku** utterly; (not) at all
6 皆伝 **kaiden** initiation into all the mysteries (of an art)
10 皆既 **kaiki** total eclipse, totality
　皆既食 **kaikishoku** total eclipse, totality
　皆既蝕 **kaikishoku** total eclipse, totality
　皆殺 **minagoro(shi)** massacre, mass murder
　皆納 **kainō** (tax) payment in full
11 皆済 **kaisai** payment in full
12 皆勤 **kaikin** perfect attendance
　皆勤賞 **kaikinshō** reward for perfect attendance
　皆無 **kaimu** nothing/none at all
14 皆様 **minasama** all (of you), Ladies and Gentlemen!

———————— 2 ————————

9 皆皆様 **minaminasama** everyone, all of you

泉 → 3a5.33

4c5.15 / 470

昼 晝　　CHŪ, hiru daytime, noon

———————— 1 ————————

3 昼下 **hirusa(gari)** early afternoon
4 昼日中 **hiruhinaka** daytime, broad daylight
6 昼休 **hiruyasu(mi)** lunch/noontime break
　昼行灯 **hiru andon** (useless as) a lantern in broad daylight
8 昼夜 **chūya** day and night
　昼夜兼行 **chūya-kenkō** 24 hours a day, around the clock
　昼夜帯 **chūyaobi** a two-faced obi
9 昼前 **hirumae** forenoon; just before noon
　昼食 **chūshoku** lunch
11 昼過 **hirusu(gi)** (early) afternoon
　昼頃 **hirugoro** about noon
12 昼飯 **hirumeshi, chūhan** lunch
　昼間 **hiruma, chūkan** daytime, during the day
13 昼寝 **hirune** nap, siesta
15 昼餉 **hiruge** lunch
16 昼興行 **hirukōgyō** matinée
　昼餐 **chūsan** luncheon

———————— 2 ————————

3 小昼 **kohiru** a little before noon; mid-morning snack
5 白昼 **hakuchū** daytime, broad daylight
8 夜昼 **yoru-hiru** day and night
10 真昼 **mahiru** broad daylight, midday
　真昼間 **ma(p)piruma** broad daylight

者 → 者 4c4.13

4c5.16

昶　　CHŌ long day; clear

———————— 6 ————————

4c6.1

晒 曬　　SAI, sara(su) bleach; expose to sara(shi) bleaching; bleached cotton

———————— 1 ————————

4 晒木綿 **sara(shi)momen** bleached cotton cloth

4

木 月 日 火 ネ 王 牛 方 攵 欠 心 戸 戈

6 ←

5 晒台 **sara(shi)dai** pillory, stocks, gibbet
8 晒者 **sara(shi)mono** (pilloried) criminal on public display
9 晒首 **sara(shi)kubi** gibbeted severed head
10 晒粉 **sara(shi)ko** bleaching powder

——————— 2 ———————

7 吹晒 **fu(ki)sara(shi)** exposed to the wind, wind-swept
8 店晒 **tanazara(shi)** shopworn goods
9 洗晒 **ara(i)zara(shi)** shabby, worn-out (from repeated washing)
10 恥晒 **hajisara(shi)** a disgrace
11 野晒 **nozara(shi)** weather-beaten
12 寒晒 **kanzara(shi)** exposure to cold weather

4c6.2 / 42

時

JI, toki time; hour

——————— 1 ———————

0 時に **toki (ni)** now, by the way, in passing
  時ならぬ **toki(naranu)** untimely, inopportune; unexpected
  時めく **toki(meku)** prosper, flourish
2 時人 **jijin** contemporaries
3 時下 **jika** now, at present
  時々 **tokidoki** sometimes
  時々刻々 **jiji-kokukoku** hourly, minute by minute
4 時化 **shike(ru)** be stormy; be badly off; be gloomy
  時文 **jibun** contemporary/modern writing
  時分 **jibun** time, hour, season
  時日 **jijitsu** the date/time; time, days
5 時世 **jisei** the times
  時代 **jidai** era, period, age
  時代物 **jidaimono** an antique; a historical drama
  時代相 **jidaisō** trend of the times
  時代劇 **jidaigeki** period/costume drama
  時外 **tokihazu(re)** unseasonable, untimely, inopportune
  時好 **jikō** fashion, vogue, fad
7 時折 **tokio(ri)** at times, occasionally
  時局 **jikyoku** the situation
8 時事 **jiji** current events
  時価 **jika** current/market price
  時限 **jigen** time limit; time (bomb)
  時制 **jisei** tense (in grammar)
  時刻 **jikoku** time, hour
  時刻表 **jikokuhyō** timetable, schedule
  時効 **jikō** prescription, statute of limitations
  時宗 **Jishū** (a Buddhist sect)
  時宜 **jigi** the right time for
  時雨 **shigure** an off-and-on late-autumn/early-winter rain

9 時俗 **jizoku** customs/ways of the times
  時速 **jisoku** speed per hour
  時風 **jifū** the current fashion
  時相 **jisō** tense (in grammar)
  時計 **tokei** clock, watch, timepiece
  時計工 **tokeikō** watchmaker
  時計仕掛 **tokei-jika(ke)** clockwork
  時計台 **tokeidai** clock stand/tower
  時計回 **tokeimawa(ri)** clockwise
  時計屋 **tokeiya** watch store, jeweler
  時計師 **tokeishi** watchmaker, jeweler
10 時候 **jikō** season, time of year; weather
  時候外 **jikōhazu(re)** unseasonable
  時差 **jisa** time difference, staggered
  jisa(boke) jet lag
  時流 **jiryū** trend of the times
  時時 **tokidoki** sometimes
  時時刻刻 **jiji-kokukoku** hourly, minute by minute
11 時偶 **tokitama** once in a while, on rare occasions
  時運 **jiun** tide of fortune
  時務 **jimu** current affairs
12 時報 **jihō** review; time signal
  時期 **jiki** time, season
  時給 **jikyū** payment by the hour
  時評 **jihyō** (editorial) commentary
  時間 **jikan** an hour; time
  時間表 **jikanhyō** timetable, schedule
  時間給 **jikankyū** payment by the hour
13 時勢 **jisei** the times/Zeitgeist
  時節 **jisetsu** season; the times; opportunity
  時節柄 **jisetsugara** in these times
15 時弊 **jihei** evils of the times
  時論 **jiron** commentary on current events; current opinion
16 時機 **jiki** opportunity, time, occasion
20 時鐘 **jishō** (ship's) time bell

——————— 2 ———————

1 一時 **ichiji** a time; at one time; for a time
  ittoki twelfth part of a day
  hitotoki a little while, a short period
  ichidoki at a/one time
  一時払 **ichijibara(i)** lump-sum payment
  一時的 **ichijiteki** temporary
  一時金 **ichijikin** lump sum
  一時預場 **ichiji azukarijō** baggage safe-keeping area
3 夕時雨 **yūshigure** evening shower
  寸時 **sunji** moment, minute
4 不時 **fuji** unforeseen, emergency
  不時着 **fujichaku** emergency landing
  今時 **imadoki** today, nowadays; this time of day
  片時 **katatoki, henji** moment, instant

水時計 **mizu-dokei** water clock
引時 **hi(ke)doki** closing time
日時 **nichiji** date and hour, time
日時計 **hidokei** sundial
5 幼時 **yōji** childhood, infancy
平時 **heiji** normal times, peacetime
好時期 **kōjiki** good season for
好時機 **kōjiki** opportune moment, the right
    time
四時 **yoji** four o'clock **shiji** the/all four
    seasons
旧時 **kyūji** old/past times
6 死時 **shi(ni)doki** the time to die
毎時 **maiji** every hour, per hour
近時 **kinji** recent, modern
同時 **dōji** at the same time, simultaneous
同時代 **dōjidai** contemporaneous
当時 **tōji** at present; at that time
7 何時 **nanji** what time, when
何時迄 **itsu made** till when, how soon/long
何時間 **nanjikan** how many hours
即時 **sokuji** immediately, on the spot
即時払 **sokujibara(i)** immediate payment, at
    sight
即時渡 **sokujiwata(shi)** spot delivery
別時 **betsuji** another time; time of separation
花時 **hanadoki** the cherry-blossom season
花時計 **hanadokei** flower-bed clock
初時雨 **hatsushigure** first winter rain
8 長時間 **chōjikan** a long time
往時 **ōji** ancient times
昔時 **sekiji** old/former times
定時 **teiji** regular time/intervals, fixed period
定時制 **teijisei** part-time (school) system
空時間 **a(ki)jikan** open period, spare time
金時計 **kindokei** gold watch
9 柱時計 **hashiradokei** wall clock
砂時計 **sunadokei** hourglass
計時 **keiji** timing, clocking
計時係 **keijigaka(ri)** timekeeper
食時 **ta(be)doki** the season for (oysters)
10 随時 **zuiji** at any time, whenever required
遊時間 **aso(bi)jikan** playtime, recess
桜時 **sakuradoki** cherry-blossom season
時時 **tokidoki** sometimes
時時刻刻 **jiji-kokukoku** hourly, minute by
    minute
夏時間 **natsujikan** daylight-saving time
11 掛時計 **ka(ke)dokei** wall clock
常時 **jōji** usually, habitually, ordinarily
現時代 **genjidai** the present age
盛時 **seiji** prime of life; era of prosperity/glory
    saka(ri)doki prosperous/busy time;
    rutting season
経時変化 **keiji henka** change with the
    passage of time, aging
12 短時日 **tanjijitsu** a short time

腕時計 **udedokei** wristwatch
幾時 **ikuji** what time
買時 **ka(i)doki** the best time to buy
飯時 **meshidoki** mealtime
13 適時 **tekiji** timely; whenever appropriate
腹時計 **haradokei** one's sense of time
戦時 **senji** wartime, war period
戦時下 **senjika** during the war, wartime
戦時中 **senjichū** during the war, wartime
戦時色 **senjishoku** wartime look/aspect
戦時体制 **senji taisei** war footing
戦時産業 **senji sangyō** wartime industry
歳時記 **saijiki** almanac
新時代 **shinjidai** new era
置時計 **o(ki)dokei** table clock
零時 **reiji** 12:00 (noon or midnight)
鳩時計 **hatodokei** cuckoo clock
14 漸時 **zenji** gradually
15 潮時 **shiodoki** (waiting for) the tide, opportu-
    nity
暫時 **zanji** for a (short) time
18 臨時 **rinji** temporary, provisional, extraordi-
    nary
臨時費 **rinjihi** contingent expenses
瞬時 **shunji** moment, instant
蝉時雨 **semishigure** outburst of cicada
    droning

──────── 3 ────────

3 夕飯時 **yūhandoki** suppertime
4 小半時 **kohantoki** about half an hour
4 収穫時 **shūkakuji** time of harvest
5 幼年時代 **yōnen jidai** childhood
四六時中 **shirokujichū** 24 hours a day,
    constantly
石器時代 **sekki jidai** the Stone Age
目覚時計 **meza(mashi)dokei** alarm clock
7 走行時間 **sōkō jikan** travel time
8 非常時 **hijōji** emergency, crisis
夜光時計 **yakō-dokei** luminous-dial watch
9 食事時 **shokujidoki** mealtime
10 高潮時 **kōchōji** time of high tide
書入時 **ka(ki)i(re)doki** the busiest season
12 御飯時 **gohandoki** mealtime
13 戦国時代 **sengoku jidai** era of civil wars
15 標準時 **hyōjunji** standard/universal time
16 懐中時計 **kaichū-dokei** pocket watch
17 霜枯時 **shimoga(re)doki** winter

──────── 4 ────────

9 途中計時 **tochū keiji** lap time (in races)

晄 → 晃 **4c6.5**

晦 → 晦 **4c7.3**

4

木
月
日 6←
火
示
王
牛
方
文
欠
心
戸
戈

晟→ 4c7.5

4c6.3

晁 CHŌ (proper name)

4c6.4

晏 AN late; sunset; peaceful

4c6.5

晃 KŌ clear, bright

4c6.6 / 131

書 SHO, ka(ku) write; draw
fumi books; letter, note

─────── 1 ───────

2 書入 ka(ki)i(reru) write/fill in, enter
　書入時 ka(ki)i(re)doki the busiest season
3 書上 ka(ki)a(geru) finish writing; write out
　書下 ka(ki)kuda(su) write down
　　ka(ki)o(rosu) write a new novel/play
4 書中 shochū in the letter/document/book
　書分 ka(ki)wa(keru) distinguish in writing
　書込 ka(ki)ko(mu) write/fill in, enter
　書手 ka(ki)te writer; calligrapher, painter
　書方 ka(ki)kata how to write; penmanship
5 書出 ka(ki)da(su) begin to write; make an
　　excerpt; make out a bill
　　ka(ki)da(shi) opening paragraph/words
　書生 shosei student; student-houseboy
　書生論 shoseiron impractical argument
　書冊 shosatsu books
　書付 ka(ki)tsu(keru) note down
　　ka(ki)tsu(ke) note; bill
　書加 ka(ki)kuwa(eru) add (a postscript)
　書写 ka(ki)utsu(su) transcribe, trace
　　shosha transcribing; penmanship
　書字 shoji kanji writing (test)
　書札 shosatsu letter
　書立 ka(ki)ta(teru) write/play up, feature;
　　enumerate
　書目 shomoku catalog of books, bibliography
6 書伝 ka(ki)tsuta(eru) set forth in writing
　　(for posterity)
　書名 shomei (book) title
　書尽 ka(ki)tsu(kusu) write out in full

書式 shoshiki (blank) form
7 書体 shotai style of calligraphy/type
　書状 shojō letter
　書判 ka(ki)han written seal, signature
　書抜 ka(ki)nu(ku) copy out, excerpt, abstract
　書役 ka(ki)yaku copyist, scribe
　書改 ka(ki)arata(meru) rewrite
　書見 shoken reading
　書初 ka(ki)zo(me) first writing of the new
　　year
　書言葉 ka(ki)kotoba written language
　書足 ka(ki)ta(su) add (a postscript)
8 書表 ka(ki)ara(wasu) express/describe in
　　writing
　書画 shoga pictures and writings
　書直 ka(ki)nao(su) rewrite
　書送 ka(ki)oku(ru) write (to someone)
　書法 shohō penmanship, calligraphy
　書味 ka(ki)aji the feel of the pen against the
　　paper as one writes
　書店 shoten bookstore; publisher
　書林 shorin bookstore
　書物 shomotsu books
　書房 shobō library; bookstore
　書具合 ka(ki)guai the feel of the pen against
　　the paper as one writes
9 書信 shoshin letter, message
　書院 shoin writing alcove with a window;
　　a study; drawing room; publishing house
　書院造 shoinzuku(ri) (a traditional architec-
　　tural style)
　書風 shofū style of calligraphy
　書面 shomen letter, document; in writing
　書架 shoka bookshelf
10 書残 ka(ki)noko(su) leave (a will) behind;
　　omit, leave out; leave half-written
　書流 ka(ki)naga(su) write with ease, dash off
　書起 ka(ki)oko(shi) opening paragraph/words
　書振 ka(ki)bu(ri) style of writing
　書家 shoka good penman, calligrapher
　書庫 shoko library, book stacks
　書留 kakitome registered mail
　　ka(ki)to(meru) write down
　書留料 kakitomeryō registration fee
　書紋 ka(ki)mon hand-drawn family crest
　書記 shoki secretary, clerk
　　ka(ki)shiru(su) write down, record
　書記局 shokikyoku secretariat
　書記長 shokichō chief secretary
　書記官 shokikan secretary
　書記官長 shokikanchō chief secretary
11 書斎 shosai study, library, den
　書道 shodō calligraphy
　書添 ka(ki)so(eru) add (a postscript)
　書捨 ka(ki)su(teru) write and throw away
　書終 ka(ki)owa(ru) finish writing

書経 **Shokyō** the Shu Jing (a Confucianist classic)
12 書割 **ka(ki)wa(ri)** setting, background
書違 **ka(ki)chiga(eru)** miswrite
書換 **ka(ki)kae(ru)** rewrite; renew (a loan); transfer (ownership)
書落 **ka(ki)o(tosu)** omit, forget to write
書棚 **shodana** bookshelf
書替 **ka(ki)ka(eru)** rewrite; renew (a loan); transfer (ownership)
書散 **ka(ki)chi(rasu)** scribble, scrawl
書評 **shohyō** book review
書評欄 **shohyōran** book review column/ section
書証 **shoshō** documentary evidence
13 書肆 **shoshi** bookstore
書損 **ka(ki)soko(nau), ka(ki)son(jiru)** miswrite
書聖 **shosei** master calligrapher
書置 **ka(ki)o(ki)** note left behind; will
書続 **ka(ki)tsuzu(keru)** continue to write
書賃 **ka(ki)chin** writing/copying fee
14 書漏 **ka(ki)mo(rasu)** omit, leave out
書慣 **ka(ki)na(reru)** get used to writing
書誤 **ka(ki)ayama(ru)** miswrite
書誌 **shoshi** bibliography
書誌学 **shoshigaku** bibliography
16 書翰 **shokan** letter, note
18 書簡 **shokan** letter, note
書簡文 **shokanbun** epistolary style
書簡紙 **shokanshi** stationery
書類 **shorui** documents, papers
20 書籍 **shoseki** books
書籍商 **shosekishō** bookseller, bookstore
書籍業 **shosekigyō** bookselling and publishing business

───── 2 ─────

3 寸書 **sunsho** brief note, a line
上書 **uwaga(ki)** the writing on the outside, the address
下書 **shitaga(ki)** rough draft
凡書 **bonsho** ordinary book
4 仏書 **bussho** Buddhist literature/scriptures
六書 **rikusho** the six types of kanji
文書 **monjo, bunsho** document; correspondence; records
分書 **wa(kachi)ga(ki)** writing with a space between words
手書 **shusho** write in one's own hand
tega(ki) handwritten
5 本書 **honsho** the text/script; this book
史書 **shisho** history book, a history
代書 **daisho** scribe, amanuensis
古書 **kosho** old/rare book
司書 **shisho** librarian
右書 **migiga(ki)** written from right to left

四書 **Shisho** the Four Chinese Classics
白書 **hakusho** whitepaper, report
6 伝書鳩 **denshobato** carrier pigeon
全書 **zensho** complete book, compendium
返書 **hensho** reply
行書 **gyōsho** semicursive calligraphy
早書 **hayaga(ki)** writing hurriedly
自書 **jisho** one's own writing, autograph
血書 **kessho** writing in blood
7 良書 **ryōsho** good book
佚書 **issho** lost book
但書 **tada(shi)ga(ki)** proviso
伺書 **ukaga(i)sho** written request for instructions
別書 **waka(chi)ga(ki)** write leaving a space between words
角書 **tsunoga(ki)** two-line subtitle
兵書 **heisho** book on military science
医書 **isho** medical book
没書 **bossho** rejected (manuscript)
走書 **hashi(ri)ga(ki)** flowing/hasty handwriting
抜書 **nu(ki)ga(ki)** excerpt, clipping
投書 **tōsho** letter to the editor, contribution
投書家 **tōshoka** contributor, correspondent
投書欄 **tōshoran** readers' column
芳書 **hōsho** your kind/esteemed letter
図書 **tosho** books
図書室 **toshoshitsu** library (room)
図書館 **toshokan** library
図書館学 **toshokangaku** library science
図書館長 **toshokanchō** head librarian
図書館員 **toshokan'in** library clerk, librarian
私書 **shisho** private document/letter
私書箱 **shishobako** post-office box
8 奉書 **hōsho** thick high-quality paper
追書 **o(tte)ga(ki)** postscript, P.S.
届書 **todo(ke)sho** (written) report, notification
国書 **kokusho** (ambassador's) credentials; sovereign's message; national literature
青書 **seisho** bluebook, government report
肩書 **kataga(ki)** one's title, degree
所書 **tokoroga(ki)** address
和書 **washo** book bound in Japanese style
9 信書 **shinsho** letter, correspondence
俗書 **zokusho** cheap fiction; unrefined handwriting
勅書 **chokusho** imperial rescript
軍書 **gunsho** military book, war history
前書 **maega(ki)** preface, foreword
浄書 **jōsho** clean copy
洋書 **yōsho** Western/foreign book
封書 **fūsho** sealed letter/document
品書 **shinaga(ki)** catalog, inventory, itemization
後書 **atoga(ki)** postscript

草書 **sōsho** cursive form of kanji, "grass hand"
珍書 **chinsho** rare book
10 原書 **gensho** the original document
逸書 **issho** lost book
能書 **nōsho** calligraphy　**nōga(ki)** advertising one's wares, boasting
教書 **kyōsho** (presidential) message
秘書 **hisho** (private) secretary
秘書官 **hishokan** (private) secretary
秘書課 **hishoka** secretariat
11 清書 **seisho** fair/clean copy
添書 **tensho, so(e)ga(ki)** accompanying letter; letter of introduction; additional writing, postscript
控書 **hika(e)ga(ki)** note, memo
捨書 **su(te)ga(ki)** rambling writing
著書 **chosho** a (literary) work
密書 **missho** secret message
寄書 **yo(se)ga(ki)** write/draw jointly　**kisho** send a letter/article
崩書 **kuzu(shi)ga(ki)** "grass-hand"
略書 **ryakusho** abbreviation
細書 **hosoga(ki)** close/fine writing
経書 **keisho** Confucian classics
断書 **kotowa(ri)ga(ki)** explanatory note
訳書 **yakusho** a translation
12 落書 **rakuga(ki)** graffiti, scribblings
葉書 **hagaki** postcard
覚書 **obo(e)ga(ki)** memorandum
焚書 **funsho** book burning
散書 **chi(rashi)ga(ki)** write irregularly
稀書 **kisho** rare book
絵書 **eka(ki)** painter, artist
筆書 **(hito)fudega(ki)** writing without redipping the brush into the inkwell
筋書 **sujiga(ki)** synopsis, outline, plan
証書 **shōsho** deed, bond, in writing
詔書 **shōsho** imperial edict/rescript
詞書 **kotobaga(ki)** foreword; notes
貴書 **kisho** your letter
13 裏書 **uraga(ki)** endorsement; certificate of genuineness; proof
漢書 **kansho** Chinese book/classics
群書 **gunsho** various books
楷書 **kaisho** noncursive (kanji), printed style
楽書 **rakuga(ki)** graffiti
禁書 **kinsho** banned book
聖書 **Seisho** the Bible
愛書家 **aishoka** book lover
新書 **shinsho** new book; largish paperback size
辞書 **jisho** dictionary
14 遺書 **isho** suicide note; note left by the deceased; posthumous works
漁書 **gyosho** book-hunting
墨書 **sumiga(ki)** draw a picture with India ink only

歌書 **kasho** book of poems
端書 **hashiga(ki)** introduction, preface; postscript
読書 **dokusho** reading　**yo(mi)ka(ki)** reading and writing
読書人 **dokushojin** (avid) book reader
読書力 **dokushoryoku** reading ability
読書会 **dokushokai** reading club
読書狂 **dokushokyō** bibliophile
読書室 **dokushoshitsu** reading room
読書界 **dokushokai** the reading public
読書家 **dokushoka** (avid) book reader
雑書 **zassho** miscellaneous books; book on miscellaneous subjects
聞書 **ki(ki)ga(ki)** (taking) notes
15 蔵書 **zōsho** book collection, one's library
蔵書狂 **zōshokyō** bibliomania(c)
蔵書家 **zōshoka** book collector
横書 **yokoga(ki)** writing horizontally
箱書 **hakoga(ki)** painter's/calligrapher's autograph on the box
篆書 **tensho** seal characters
請書 **u(ke)sho** written acknowledgment
調書 **chōsho** protocol, record
16 儒書 **jusho** Confucianist writings
隷書 **reisho** (ancient squared style of kanji)
親書 **shinsho** handwritten letter
積書 **tsu(mori)ga(ki)** written estimate
縦書 **tatega(ki)** vertical writing
頭書 **tōsho** superscription, headnote; the above-mentioned　**kashiraga(ki)** heading
17 擲書 **nagu(ri)ga(ki)** scribble, scrawl
講書 **kōsho** interpretation of a book
謹書 **kinsho** respectfully written
購書 **kōsho** purchasing/purchased books
18 臨書 **rinsho** copying (from a model)
叢書 **sōsho** series, library
類書 **ruisho** books of the same kind
19 艶書 **ensho** love letter
曝書 **bakusho** airing of books
璽書 **jisho** document bearing imperial seal
願書 **gansho** written request, application

───── 3 ─────

2 人相書 **ninsōga(ki)** description of one's looks
3 上申書 **jōshinsho** written report/statement
口上書 **kōjōsho** verbal note
口供書 **kōkyōsho** affidavit, deposition
4 内申書 **naishinsho** student's school record
文学書 **bungakusho** a literary work
公文書 **kōbunsho** official document
手引書 **tebi(ki)sho** handbook, manual
5 由来書 **yuraisho** history, memoirs
申込書 **mōshikomisho** an application

申請書 **shinseisho** application, petition
古文書 **komonjo, kobunsho** ancient documents
6 自習書 **jishūsho** teach-yourself book
血統書 **kettōsho** pedigree
7 批准書 **hijunsho** instrument of ratification
志願書 **shigansho** (written) application
見積書 **mitsumorisho** written estimate
私文書 **shibunsho** private document
8 受領書 **juryōsho** receipt
建白書 **kenpakusho** memorial, petition
注文書 **chūmonsho** order form
注解書 **chūkaisho** commentary
注意書 **chūiga(ki)** notes, instructions
法律書 **hōritsusho** law book
始末書 **shimatsusho** written explanation/apology
参考書 **sankōsho** reference book/work
明細書 **meisaisho** detailed statement
祈禱書 **kitōsho** prayer book
怪文書 **kaibunsho** defamatory literature of unknown source
9 専門書 **senmonsho** technical books
契約書 **keiyakusho** contract
通知書 **tsūchisho** notice
指図書 **sa(shi)zusho** (written) order, directions
独習書 **dokushūsho** teach-yourself book
宣言書 **sengensho** declaration, manifesto
宣誓書 **senseisho** written oath, deposition
約定書 **yakujōsho** (written) contract/agreement
計算書 **keisansho** statement (of account)
10 陳述書 **chinjutsusho** statement, declaration
陳情書 **chinjōsho** petition, representation
案内書 **annaisho** guidebook
教科書 **kyōkasho** textbook
11 勘定書 **kanjōsho** bill, one's account
規則書 **kisokusho** prospectus; regulations
12 報告書 **hōkokusho** (written) report/statement
無封書状 **mufū shojō** unsealed letter
稀覯書 **kikōsho** rare book
絵葉書 **ehagaki** picture postcard
筆頭書 **hittōsha** head of the household (listed first on the family register)
答申書 **tōshinsho** report, findings
証明書 **shōmeisho** certificate
診断書 **shindansho** medical certificate
13 福音書 **Fukuinsho** the Gospels
愛読書 **aidokusho** favorite book
意見書 **ikensho** written opinion
新刊書 **shinkansho** a new publication
14 遺言書 **yuigonsho** will, testament
歎願書 **tangansho** written petition
箇条書 **kajōga(ki)** an itemization

説明書 **setsumeisho** (written) explanation, instructions, manual
誓約書 **seiyakusho** written pledge, covenant
領収書 **ryōshūsho** receipt
15 履歴書 **rirekisho** personal history, vita
趣意書 **shuisho** prospectus
請求書 **seikyūsho** application, claim, bill
請願書 **seigansho** (written) petition
質問書 **shitsumonsho** written inquiry, questionnaire
16 親展書 **shintensho** confidential/personal letter
親類書 **shinruigaki** list of one's relatives
18 翻訳書 **hon'yakusho** a translation
20 議定書 **giteisho, gijōsho** a protocol
23 鑑定書 **kanteisho** expert's report

─────── 4 ───────

2 入学願書 **nyūgaku gansho** application for admission
4 六法全書 **roppō zensho** the statute books
5 旧約聖書 **Kyūyaku Seisho** the Old Testament
6 百科全書 **hyakka zensho** encyclopedia
8 往復葉書 **ōfuku hagaki** return postcard
9 封緘葉書 **fūkan hagaki** lettercard
10 借用証書 **shakuyō shōsho** bond of debt
特筆大書 **tokuhitsu-taisho** write large, single out
13 新約聖書 **shin'yaku seisho** the New Testament

─────── 5 ───────

12 欽定訳聖書 **kinteiyaku seisho** the King James Bible
13 損益計算書 **son'eki keisansho** income/profit-and-loss statement

4c6.7

耆   **KI** old age

─────── 2 ───────

7 伯耆 **Hōki** (ancient kuni, Tottori-ken)

4c6.8

晉 晉   **SHIN** advance

皆 →   **4c5.14**

晉 → 晋   **4c6.8**

4c6.9 / 1799

殉 **JUN** follow (someone) into death; lay down one's life

─────── 1 ───────

0 殉じる/ずる **jun(jiru/zuru)** die a martyr; follow (someone) into death (by committing suicide)
6 殉死 **junshi** kill oneself on the death of one's lord
8 殉国 **junkoku** dying for one's country
10 殉教 **junkyō** martyrdom
殉教者 **junkyōsha** martyr
18 殉職 **junshoku** dying in the line of duty
殉難 **junnan** martyrdom
殉難者 **junnansha** martyr, victim

─────── 7 ───────

4c7.1

晤 **GO** meet with; clear

4c7.2

晧 **KŌ** bright; pure

─────── 1 ───────

12 晧礬 **kōban** zinc sulfate

晚→晚 **4c8.3**

4c7.3

晦 晦 **KAI** dark, night; last day of the month **kura(i)** dark **kura(masu)** hide, slip away **misoka, tsugomori** the last day of the month

─────── 1 ───────

4 晦日 **misoka, kaijitsu** the last day of the month
10 晦冥 **kaimei** darkness
晦朔 **kaisaku** last and first days of successive months
11 晦渋 **kaijū** obscure, ambiguous

─────── 2 ───────

3 大晦 **ōtsugomori** last day of the year
大晦日 **Ōmisoka** last day of the year; New Year's Eve
17 諂晦 **tōkai** conceal (one's talent/identity)
20 韜晦 **tōkai** conceal (one's talent/identity)

4c7.4

晞 **KI** dry out, expose to the sun

4c7.5

晟 **SEI, JŌ** clear

4c7.6

晛 勗 **KYOKU** be diligent

4c7.7

晨 **SHIN** morning, dawn

─────── 1 ───────

9 晨星 **shinsei** morning star
19 晨鶏 **shinkei** rooster crowing at dawn

4c7.8

曼 **MAN** wide; long; (used phonetically)

─────── 1 ───────

7 曼陀羅 **mandara** mandala, picture of Buddha
9 曼荼羅 **mandara** mandala, picture of Buddha
10 曼珠沙華 **manjushage** cluster-amaryllis (also known as *higanbana*)

4c7.9

冕 冕 **BEN** crown (having a brim draped with bead strings)

4c7.10 / 1929

曹 **SŌ, ZŌ** friend, comrade; officer

─────── 1 ───────

8 曹長 **sōchō** sergeant major, master sergeant
11 曹達 **sōda** soda

─────── 2 ───────

7 兵曹 **heisō** warrant officer
8 法曹 **hōsō** the legal profession
法曹界 **hōsōkai** legal circles, the bench and bar
9 重曹 **jūsō** sodium bicarbonate, baking soda
軍曹 **gunsō** sergeant
12 御曹司 **onzōshi** son of a distinguished family

晳 → 晰 4c8.4

4c7.11 / 591

習 習 **SHŪ, nara(u)** learn

—— 1 ——
4 習込 **nara(i)ko(mu)** learn thoroughly, master
5 習字 **shūji** penmanship, calligraphy
7 習作 **shūsaku** a study, étude
8 習事 **nara(i)goto** practice, training, drill
　習性 **shūsei** habit, way, peculiarity
9 習俗 **shūzoku** manners and customs, usages
11 習得 **shūtoku** learn, master
12 習覚 **nara(i)obo(eru)** learn
14 習熟 **shūjuku** mastery, proficiency
　習慣 **shūkan** custom, habit
　習慣法 **shūkanhō** common law
　習練 **shūren** practice, training, drill
18 習癖 **shūheki** habit, peculiarity

—— 2 ——
4 予習 **yoshū** lesson preparation
　手習 **tenara(i)** practice penmanship; learning
5 旧習 **kyūshū** an old custom
6 伝習 **denshū** learn, be instructed
　因習 **inshū** custom, convention
　自習 **jishū** studying by oneself
　自習書 **jishūsho** teach-yourself book
7 学習 **gakushū** learning, study
　見習 **minara(u)** learn (by observation), follow (someone's) example
　見習工 **minara(i)kō** apprentice
　見習中 **minara(i)chū** in training
　言習 **i(i)nara(washi)** tradition, legend; common saying
8 陋習 **rōshū** evil practice/custom, abuse
　奇習 **kishū** strange custom
　実習 **jisshū** practice, drill
　実習生 **jisshūsei** trainee, apprentice
9 俗習 **zokushū** (popular) custom
　風習 **fūshū** manners, customs, ways
　独習 **dokushū** self-study
　独習書 **dokushūsho** teach-yourself book
　食習慣 **shokushūkan** eating habits
10 既習 **kishū** already learned
　教習 **kyōshū** training, instruction
　教習所 **kyōshūjo** training institute
11 常習 **jōshū** custom, common practice, habit
　常習犯 **jōshūhan** habitual crime/criminal
　常習的 **jōshūteki** habitual, confirmed
　常習者 **jōshūsha** habitual offender
　悪習 **akushū** bad habit, vice
　悪習慣 **akushūkan** bad habit, evil practice

12 蛮習 **banshū** barbarous custom
　温習 **onshū** review, rehearse
　復習 **fukushū** review
　補習 **hoshū** supplementary/continuing (education)
14 演習 **enshū** practice, exercises; (military) maneuvers; seminar
　演習林 **enshūrin** experimental forest
　慣習 **kanshū** custom, practice
　慣習法 **kanshūhō** common law
　練習 **renshū** practice, exercise
　練習不足 **renshū-busoku** out/lack of training
　練習帳 **renshūchō** exercise book, workbook
16 弊習 **heishū** corrupt custom, bad habit
17 講習 **kōshū** short course, training
　講習会 **kōshūkai** short course, class, training conference

—— 3 ——
3 大演習 **daienshū** large-scale maneuvers, war games
10 猛練習 **mōrenshū** intensive training
11 商慣習 **shōkanshū** commercial practices

—— 4 ——
16 機動演習 **kidō enshū** maneuvers

4c7.12

皐 皋 **KŌ** swamp; shore

—— 1 ——
4 皐月 **kōgetsu, satsuki** fifth lunar month

4c7.13

匙 **SHI, saji** spoon

—— 1 ——
5 匙加減 **saji kagen** dosage, prescription; consideration, discretion, making allowances for

—— 2 ——
9 茶匙 **chasaji** teaspoon

4c7.14 / 1190

乾 **KAN** dry　**KEN** heaven; emperor　**kawa(ku)** become dry, dry up　**kawa(kasu)** dry (out), parch　**ho(su)** dry; drink (a cup) dry

—— 1 ——
3 乾干 **karabo(shi)** sun-dried fish/vegetables
4 乾元 **Kengen** (era, 1302–1303)
5 乾田 **kanden** dry rice field
7 乾季 **kanki** the dry season
8 乾坤 **kenkon** heaven and earth, yin and yang

乾坤一擲 **kenkon-itteki** risking everything, all or nothing
乾杯 **kanpai** a toast; Cheers!
乾物 **kanbutsu** dry provisions, groceries
乾物屋 **kanbutsuya** grocer, grocery store
乾性 **kansei** dry (pleurisy), xero-
9 乾拭 **karabu(ki)** wiping with a dry cloth
乾咳 **karazeki** a dry/hacking cough
10 乾留 **kanryū** dry distillation, carbonization
12 乾湿計 **kanshitsukei** hygrometer, humidity meter
乾飯 **kareii, hoshiii** dried boiled rice
13 乾溜 **kanryū** dry distillation, carbonization
乾酪 **kanraku** cheese
乾電池 **kandenchi** dry cell, battery
17 乾燥 **kansō** dry, drying, dehydrated
乾燥季 **kansōki** the dry season
乾燥剤 **kansōzai** desiccant
乾燥無味 **kansō-mumi** dry, dull
乾燥機 **kansōki** dryer; desiccator
乾瓢 **kanpyō** dried gourd strips
22 乾癬 **kansen** psoriasis

——————— 2 ———————
3 干乾 **hibo(shi)** starved to death
5 生乾 **namagawa(ki)** damp-dry
10 陰乾 **kagebo(shi)** drying in the shade
13 塩乾 **shiobo(shi)** salted and dried

——————— 3 ———————
12 無味乾燥 **mumi-kansō** dry as dust, uninteresting

4c7.15

皎

KŌ, KYŌ white; shining; pure

——————— 1 ———————
15 皎潔 **kōketsu, kyōketsu** noble, pure, upright

兜→ **4c8.16**

晝→昼 **4c5.15**

4c7.16

皕

hekutoguramu hectogram, hundred grams

——————— 8 ———————

4c8.1 / 1658

暁 曉

GYŌ, akatsuki dawn, daybreak; in the event of

——————— 1 ———————
4 暁天 **gyōten** dawn, daybreak
6 暁光 **gyōkō** the light of dawn
9 暁星 **gyōsei** morning star, Venus
17 暁闇 **akatsukiyami** a moonless dawn

——————— 2 ———————
5 払暁 **futsugyō** dawn
9 通暁 **tsūgyō** be well versed in, have a thorough knowledge of
昨暁 **sakugyō** at dawn yesterday
11 翌暁 **yokugyō** at dawn the next morning

4c8.2 / 662

晴 晴

SEI, ha(reru) clear up
ha(re) fair/cloudless weather
ha(rete) openly, publicly
ha(rasu) dispel, clear away/up

——————— 1 ———————
0 晴れやか **ha(reyaka)** clear, bright; beaming, cheerful
晴れがましい **ha(regamashii)** conspicuous (and feeling awkward)
3 晴上 **ha(re)a(garu)** clear up
4 晴天白日 **seiten-hakujitsu** clear weather; proved innocent
8 晴雨 **seiu** rain or shine
晴雨計 **seiukei** barometer
10 晴耕雨読 **seikō-udoku** tilling the fields when the sun shines and reading at home when it rains
晴朗 **seirō** clear, fair, fine
11 晴眼者 **seigansha** sighted/non-blind person
12 晴着 **ha(re)gi** one's best clothes
晴晴 **ha(re)ba(reshii)** clear, cloudless; cheerful; splendid
晴間 **ha(re)ma** interval of clear weather

——————— 2 ———————
3 夕晴 **yūba(re)** clearing up in the evening
4 天晴 **appa(re)** admirable, splendid, bravo!
5 好晴 **kōsei** fine weather
6 気晴 **kiba(rashi)** diversion, pastime, recreation
7 快晴 **kaisei** fine weather, clear skies
見晴 **miha(rasu)** command a view of
9 点晴 **tensei** adding the eyes and other finishing touches to a painting (of a dragon)
秋晴 **akiba(re)** clear autumn weather
10 素晴 **suba(rashii)** splendid, magnificent
11 雪晴 **yukiba(re)** clearing after a snowfall
12 晴晴 **ha(re)ba(reshii)** clear, cloudless; cheerful; splendid
15 憂晴 **u(sa)bara(shi)** diversion, distractiong

---------- 3 ----------

4 五月晴 **satsukiba(re)** fine weather during
the rainy season

日本晴 **nihonba(re)** clear cloudless sky,
beautiful weather

---------- 4 ----------

8 画竜点晴 **garyō-tensei** completing the eyes
of a painted dragon; the finishing
touches

画龍点晴 **garyō-tensei** completing the eyes
of a painted dragon; the finishing
touches

暎 → 映 4c5.1

4c8.3 / 736

晚 晚

BAN evening, night

---------- 1 ----------

5 晚生 **okute** late(-maturing) rice; late crops
晚冬 **bantō** the latter part of winter
6 晚年 **bannen** latter part of one's life
7 晚学 **bangaku** education late in life
9 晚春 **banshun** the latter part of spring
晚秋 **banshū** the latter part of autumn
10 晚夏 **banka** the latter part of summer
晚酌 **banshaku** an evening drink (of saké)
11 晚涼 **banryō** the evening cool
晚婚 **bankon** late marriage
12 晚景 **bankei** evening scene; evening
晚飯 **banmeshi** evening meal, supper
13 晚節 **bansetsu** one's final years
14 晚稲 **bantō, okute** late(-maturing) rice
16 晚餐 **bansan** dinner, supper
晚餐会 **bansankai** dinner party, banquet
20 晚鐘 **banshō** evening/curfew bell

---------- 2 ----------

1 一晚 **hitoban** a night, one evening; all night
4 今晚 **konban** this evening, tonight
6 毎晚 **maiban** every evening, nightly
早晚 **sōban** sooner or later
9 昨晚 **sakuban** last evening/night
11 翌晚 **yokuban** the next evening/night
12 隔晚 **kakuban** every other evening
朝晚 **asaban** morning and evening; always
13 歳晚 **saiban** year's end

---------- 3 ----------

3 大器晚成 **taiki bansei** Great talent blooms
late.

---------- 4 ----------

3 三日三晚 **mikka miban** three days and three
nights

4c8.4

晰 晢

SEKI clear

---------- 2 ----------

8 明晰 **meiseki** clear, distinct, lucid

4c8.5 / 638

暑 暑

SHO, atsu(i) hot (weather)

---------- 1 ----------

0 暑がる **atsu(garu)** feel the heat, swelter
4 暑中 **shochū** midsummer, hot season
暑中見舞 **shochū mima(i)** inquiry after
(someone's) health in the hot season
6 暑気 **atsuke, shoki** the heat; heatstroke
暑行 **Keikō** (emperor, 71–130)
8 暑苦 **atsukuru(shii), atsuguru(shii)** oppressively hot, sultry, sweltering
10 暑凌 **atsu(sa)shino(gi)** relief from the heat
12 暑寒 **shokan** heat and cold
15 暑熱 **shonetsu** the summer heat

---------- 2 ----------

3 大暑 **taisho** midsummer day (about July 24)
8 炎暑 **ensho** intense heat, hot weather
10 残暑 **zansho** the lingering summer heat
猛暑 **mōsho** intense heat
12 蒸暑 **mu(shi)atsu(i)** hot and humid, sultry
寒暑 **kansho** hot and cold; summer and winter
極暑 **gokusho** intense heat
14 酷暑 **kokusho** intense/sweltering heat
15 避暑 **hisho** (spend the) summer at
避暑地 **hishochi** summer resort
避暑客 **hishokyaku** summer residents
16 激暑 **gekisho** intense heat

4c8.6 / 1645

晶

SHŌ clear; crystal

---------- 2 ----------

4 水晶 **suishō** quartz, crystal
水晶体 **suishōtai** lens (of the eye)
5 氷晶 **hyōshō** ice crystals
11 液晶 **ekishō** liquid crystal
12 結晶 **kesshō** crystallization; crystal
結晶学 **kesshōgaku** crystallography
結晶核 **kesshōkaku** nucleus of a crystal

---------- 3 ----------

12 紫水晶 **murasakizuishō** amethyst
13 煙水晶 **kemuri-zuishō** smoky quartz

---------- 4 ----------

9 草入水晶 **kusai(ri)zuishō** crystal with
impurities forming grass-blade patterns

4

木
月
日 8←
火
礻
王
牛
方
攵
欠
心
戸
戈

4c8.7

罪
HI be separated

4c8.8 / 853

景
KEI view, scene

─────── 1 ───────

6 景気 **keiki** business conditions
景気付 **keikizu(ku)** become active, pick up
景仰 **keigyō** adoration, admiration; love of
virtue **keikō** love of virtue
景色 **keshiki** scenery
8 景況 **keikyō** the situation
景物 **keibutsu** (seasonal) scenery; gift,
premium
9 景品 **keihin** premium, present, giveaway
10 景教 **keikyō** Nestorianism
景教徒 **keikyōto** a Nestorian
12 景勝 **keishō** picturesque scenery
18 景観 **keikan** spectacular view, a sight

─────── 2 ───────

2 八景 **hakkei** the eight beautiful sights (of a
region)
3 三景 **sankei** three famous scenic spots
夕景色 **yūgeshiki** evening scene/view
上景気 **jōkeiki** boom, prosperity, a brisk
economy
小景 **shōkei** beautiful view/scenery
4 不景気 **fukeiki** business slump, recession;
cheerless, gloomy
5 好景気 **kōkeiki** business prosperity, boom
6 全景 **zenkei** complete view, panorama
光景 **kōkei** scene, sight
8 佳景 **kakei** beautiful view
夜景 **yakei** night view
実景 **jikkei** actual view/scene
空景気 **karageiki** false economic prosperity
9 俄景気 **niwakageiki** temporary boom
叙景 **jokei** description of scenery
点景 **tenkei** human-interest details in a picture
前景 **zenkei** foreground
前景気 **maegeiki** prospects, outlook
美景 **bikei** beautiful view
盆景 **bonkei** tray landscape
風景 **fūkei** scene(ry), landscape, view
風景画 **fūkeiga** landscape painting
後景 **kōkei** background, setting
背景 **haikei** background
春景 **shunkei** spring scene
春景色 **haru-geshiki** spring scenery
11 添景 **tenkei** human-interest items (in a picture)
情景 **jōkei** scene; nature and sentiment

雪景 **sekkei** snowy scene
雪景色 **yukigeshiki** snowy landscape
12 遠景 **enkei** distant view
勝景 **shōkei** beautiful scenery, fine view
晩景 **bankei** evening scene; evening
絶景 **zekkei** picturesque scenery

─────── 3 ───────

6 糸偏景気 **itohen keiki** textile boom
8 金偏景気 **kanehen keiki** metal-industry boom
9 軍需景気 **gunju keiki** war prosperity
神護景雲 **Jingo Keiun** (era, 767–769)
10 殺風景 **sappūkei** drab, dull, tasteless
12 跛行景気 **hakō keiki** spotty boom/prosperity
17 鍋底景気 **nabezoko keiki** prolonged
recession

─────── 4 ───────

4 日本三景 **Nihon sankei** Japan's three noted
scenic sights (Matsushima, Miyajima,
Amanohashidate)

4c8.9 / 411

量
RYŌ quantity
haka(ru) measure, weigh

─────── 1 ───────

2 量子 **ryōshi** quantum
量子論 **ryōshiron** quantum theory
4 量込 **haka(ri)ko(mu)** measure liberally, give
overweight
5 量目 **ryōme** weight
7 量売 **haka(ri)u(ri)** sell by measure/weight
8 量直 **haka(ri)nao(su)** measure again, reweigh
量知 **haka(ri)shi(renai)** immeasurable
量的 **ryōteki** quantitative
11 量産 **ryōsan** mass production (short for 大量
生産)
13 量感 **ryōkan** volume, bulk, massiveness
15 量器 **ryōki** a measure (for volume)

─────── 2 ───────

2 力量 **rikiryō** physical strength; ability,
capacity
3 大量 **tairyō** large quantity
大量生産 **tairyō seisan** mass production
小量 **shōryō** small quantity
4 不量見 **furyōken** indiscretion; evil intent
斤量 **kinryō** weight
分量 **bunryō** quantity, amount
水量 **suiryō** water volume
水量計 **suiryōkei** water meter
少量 **shōryō** small quantity/dose
欠量 **ketsuryō** amount of shortfall, ullage
5 用量 **yōryō** dosage, dose
広量 **kōryō** largehearted, generous
6 多量 **taryō** large quantity, a great deal
全量 **zenryō** the whole quantity

考量 **kōryō** consider, weigh
光量 **kōryō** radiation intensity
7 体量 **tairyō** one's weight
技量 **giryō** skill, ability
声量 **seiryō** volume of one's voice
尿量 **nyōryō** amount of urination
8 実量 **jitsuryō** real quantity
定量 **teiryō** fixed quantity; to measure; dose
定量分析 **teiryō bunseki** quantitative analysis
服量 **fukuryō** dosage, dose
物量 **butsuryō** amount of material resources
雨量 **uryō** (amount of) rainfall
雨量計 **uryōkei** rain gauge
0 重量 **jūryō** weight
重量感 **jūryōkan** massiveness, heft
負量 **furyō** negative/minus quantity
単量体 **tanryōtai** monomer
度量 **doryō** magnanimity, generosity
度量法 **doryōhō** measurement
度量衡 **doryōkō** weights and measures
音量 **onryō** (sound) volume
思量 **shiryō** thought, consideration
計量 **keiryō** measure, weigh
計量器 **keiryōki** meter, gauge, scale
10 酒量 **shuryō** one's drinking capacity
流量 **ryūryō** volume of flow, flux
流量計 **ryūryōkei** flow/current meter
従量税 **jūryōzei** tax/duty computed on the quantity rather than the value of a good
容量 **yōryō** capacity, volume; capacitance
純量 **junryō** net weight
酌量 **shakuryō** consideration, extenuation
11 商量 **shōryō** consideration, deliberation
過量 **karyō** too much
液量 **ekiryō** liquid measure, fluid (ounce)
推量 **suiryō** inference, surmise
　　　 o(shi)haka(ru) infer, guess
12 測量士 **sokuryōshi** surveyor
測量術 **sokuryōjutsu** (the science of) surveying
測量船 **sokuryōsen** surveying ship
減量 **genryō** lose weight, reduce the quantity
極量 **kyokuryō** maximum dose
無量 **muryō** beyond measure, immense
裁量 **sairyō** discretion
等量 **tōryō** equivalent
軽量 **keiryō** lightweight
雲量 **unryō** (degree of) cloudiness
13 適量 **tekiryō** proper quantity/dosage
微量 **biryō** minute amount
数量 **sūryō** quantity
雅量 **garyō** magnanimity
電量 **denryō** amount of electricity
14 増量 **zōryō** increase in quantity
総量 **sōryō** gross weight
15 器量 **kiryō** looks; ability; dignity

器量人 **kiryōjin** talented person
熱量 **netsuryō** (amount of) heat, calories
質量 **shitsuryō** mass (in physics); quantity and quality
16 積量 **sekiryō** loadage, carrying capacity

───────── 3 ─────────

4 不器量 **bukiryō** ugly, homely
分子量 **bunshiryō** molecular weight
5 生産量 **seisanryō** amount produced, output, production
目分量 **mebunryō** measuring by eye
6 当推量 **a(te)zuiryō** guesswork
7 含有量 **gan'yūryō** quantity of a constituent substance, content
8 使用量 **shiyōryō** amount used
9 降水量 **kōsuiryō** (amount of) precipitation
降雨量 **kōuryō** (amount of) rainfall
肺活量 **haikatsuryō** lung capacity
10 原子量 **genshiryō** atomic weight
埋蔵量 **maizōryō** (oil) reserves
致死量 **chishiryō** lethal dose
配給量 **haikyūryō** a ration
11 排水量 **haisuiryō** displacement (of a ship)
排気量 **haikiryō** (piston) displacement
12 無重量 **mujūryō** weightlessness
絶対量 **zettairyō** absolute amount
貯水量 **chosuiryō** pondage
13 睡眠量 **suiminryō** amount of sleep
電気量 **denkiryō** amount of electricity
14 総重量 **sōjūryō** gross weight
16 積載量 **sekisairyō** carrying capacity, load
輸送量 **yusōryō** (volume of freight) traffic

───────── 4 ─────────

3 千万無量 **senman-muryō** innumerable
13 感慨無量 **kangai-muryō** full of emotion

4c8.10 / 263

最　**SAI, motto(mo)** the most
　　 ito- very, extremely

───────── 1 ─────────

0 最も **ito(mo)** very, extremely
3 最大 **saidai** maximum, greatest, largest
最大限 **saidaigen** maximum
最大限度 **saidai gendo** maximum
最上 **saijō** best, highest
最上川 **Mogamigawa** (river, Yamagata-ken)
最下 **saika** lowest; worst
最下位 **saikai** lowest rank
最下層 **saikasō** lowest class (of people)
最小 **saishō** smallest, minimum
最小限 **saishōgen** minimum
最小限度 **saishō gendo** minimum
4 最中 **saichū, sanaka** the midst/height of
　　 monaka middle; bean-jam-filled wafers

────────

4

木
月
日　8←
火
ネ
王
牛
方
文
欠
心
戸
戈

最少 **saishō** fewest; youngest
5 最左翼 **saisayoku** ultraleft
最古 **saiko** oldest
最右翼 **saiuyoku** ultraright
最好調 **saikōchō** in perfect form
6 最多数 **saitasū** greatest number, plurality
最西 **saisei** westernmost
最近 **saikin** recently; latest, newest
最近親者 **saikinshinsha** nearest relative, next of kin
最先端 **saisentan** the lead, forefront
最尖端 **saisentan** the lead, forefront
最早 **mohaya** already, by now; (not) any longer
7 最良 **sairyō** best
最低 **saitei** lowest, minimum
最初 **saisho** the first/beginning
8 最長 **saichō** longest
最東 **saitō** easternmost
9 最南 **sainan** southernmost
最前 **saizen** forefront; a little while ago
最前列 **saizenretsu** the front lines
最前線 **saizensen** forefront, front lines
最後 **saigo** the last; the end
10 最高 **saikō** maximum, best; great
最高点 **saikōten** highest point/score
最高裁 **Saikōsai** Supreme Court
最高裁判所 **Saikō Saibansho** Supreme Court
最高潮 **saikōchō** highwater mark; climax, peak
最恵国 **saikeikoku** most-favored nation
11 最深 **saishin** deepest
最強 **saikyō** strongest
最寄 **moyo(ri)** nearest, nearby
最悪 **saiaku** worst
最盛期 **saiseiki** golden age, heyday; the best season for
最終 **saishū** the last, the end; final
最終日 **saishūbi** the last day
最終回 **saishūkai** the last time/inning
最終的 **saishūteki** final, ultimate
12 最善 **saizen** (do one's) best
最短 **saitan** shortest
最期 **saigo** one's last moments, death
最敬礼 **saikeirei** profound obeisance, most respectful bow
13 最適 **saiteki** optimum, best suited
最愛 **saiai** dearest, beloved
最新 **saishin** newest, latest
最新式 **saishinshiki** latest type/style

———————— 2 ————————
10 真最中 **ma(s)saichū** right in the midst/middle of, at the height of

曾 → 曽 **2o9.3**

智

CHI knowledge, wisdom, intellect

———————— 1 ————————
2 智力 **chiryoku** intelligence
10 智能 **chinō** intelligence
11 智略 **chiryaku** resourcefulness, ingenuity
12 智歯 **chishi** wisdom tooth
15 智慧 **chie** knowledge, wisdom
16 智謀 **chibō** resourcefulness, ingenuity
19 智識 **chishiki** knowledge, wisdom
22 智嚢 **chinō** brains, wits, ingenuity

———————— 2 ————————
2 人智 **jinchi** human intellect, knowledge
3 才智 **saichi** wit and intelligence
上智 **jōchi** supreme wisdom
　　 Jōchi Sophia (University)
4 天智 **Tenji** (emperor, 668–671)
5 世智辛 **sechigara(i)** hard (times), tough (life)
6 全智 **zenchi** onmiscience
奸智 **kanchi** cunning, guile
9 狡智 **kōchi** cunning, guile
神智 **shinchi** divine wisdom
13 頓智 **tonchi** quick/ready wit
16 叡智 **eichi** wisdom, intelligence; intellect
機智 **kichi** quick wit, resourcefulness

4c8.12 / 744

替

TAI, ka(eru) replace
ka(e)- spare, substitute, exchange
ka(waru) be replaced

———————— 1 ————————
5 替玉 **ka(e)dama** substitute, stand-in, ringer
7 替狂言 **ka(wari) kyōgen** next week's/month's program
10 替馬 **ka(e)uma** spare horse
12 替着 **ka(e)gi** a change of clothing
14 替歌 **ka(e)uta** a parody (of a song)

———————— 2 ————————
2 入替 **i(re)ka(eru)** replace, substitute
4 切替 **ki(ri)ka(eru)** change, exchange, convert; renew; replace; switch over
引替 **hikika(e)** exchange, conversion
引替券 **hikika(e)ken** exchange ticket
5 代替 **daitai, daiga(e)** substitute, alternative
代替物 **daitaibutsu** a substitute
立替 **ta(te)ka(eru)** pay in advance; pay for another
立替金 **ta(te)ka(e)kin** an advance
6 両替 **ryōgae** money exchange
両替人 **ryōgaenin** money changer
両替屋 **ryōgaeya** money-exchange shop

交替 **kōtai** take turns, alternate, relieve, work in shifts

衣替 **koromoga(e)** seasonal change of clothes

7 抜替 **nu(ke)ka(waru)** shed, molt, slought off

吹替 **fu(ki)ka(e)** substitute actor, stand-in; dubbing; recasting, reminting

役替 **yakuga(e)** change of post

言替 **i(i)ka(eru)** say in other words

8 表替 **omotega(e)** refacing tatami mats

建替 **ta(te)ka(e)** rebuilding, reconstruction

肩替 **kataga(wari)** change of palanquin bearers; takeover, transfer (of a business)

所替 **tokoroga(e)** moving (to a new address)

取替 **to(ri)ka(eru)** (ex)change, replace

9 造替 **tsuku(ri)ka(eru)** remake, adapt

持替 **mo(chi)ka(eru)** shift from one hand to the other, change off

為替 **kawase** (foreign) exchange; money order

為替手形 **kawase tegata** bill (of exchange), draft

為替相場 **kawase sōba** exchange rate

10 差替 **sa(shi)ka(eru)** replace, change

埋替 **u(me)ka(eru)** rebury, reinter

振替 **fu(ri)ka(eru)** change to, transfer (funds) **furika(e)** transfer

振替休日 **furikae kyūjitsu** substitute holiday (for one falling on a Sunday)

書替 **ka(ki)ka(eru)** rewrite; renew (a loan); transfer (ownership)

11 掛替 **ka(ke)ka(eru)** replace, rebuild, substitute   **ka(ke)ga(e)** substitute

張替 **ha(ri)ka(eru)** repaper, re-cover, reupholster

宿替 **yadoga(e)** change of quarters

12 着替 **kiga(e)** changing clothes; change of clothes

茸替 **fu(ki)ka(eru)** rethatch, retile, reroof

植替 **u(e)ka(eru)** transplant, replant

畳替 **tatamiga(e)** replace old tatami with new ones

13 塗替 **nu(ri)ka(eru)** repaint

詰替 **tsu(me)ka(eru)** repack, refill

14 読替 **yo(mi)ka(eru)** read (a kanji) with a different pronunciation; read (one term) for (another)

15 鞍替 **kuraga(e)** change one's quarters/job

16 積替 **tsu(mi)ka(e)** reloading, transshipment

19 繰替 **ku(ri)ka(eru)** exchange, swap; divert (money)

───── 3 ─────

3 小為替 **kogawase** money order

4 片為替 **katagawase** exchange imbalance

円為替 **enkawase** yen exchange

11 商売替 **shōbaiga(e)** change one's occupation

14 模様替 **moyōga(e)** remodeling, alterations

───── 5 ─────

14 遺伝子組替 **idenshi kumika(e)** recombinant gene splicing

4c8.13

皓   **KŌ** white; clear, gleaming

───── 1 ─────

12 皓歯 **kōshi** white/pearly teeth

20 皓礬 **kōban** zinc sulfate

4c8.14

皖   **KAN** Venus (the star); (place name)

4c8.15

骰   **KYŪ** surrender

朝 → 朝   **4b8.12**

4c8.16

兜   **TŌ, TO, kabuto** helmet, headpiece

───── 1 ─────

6 兜虫 **kabutomushi** beetle

7 兜町 **Kabuto-chō** (area of Tōkyō, site of Tōkyō Stock Exchange)

19 兜蟹 **kabutogani** horseshoe/king crab

───── 2 ─────

13 鉄兜 **tetsukabuto** steel helmet

4c8.17

奢   **SHA, ogo(ru)** be extravagant; treat (someone to)

───── 1 ─────

8 奢侈 **shashi** luxury, extravagance

───── 2 ─────

14 豪奢 **gōsha** luxurious, grand, sumptuous

22 驕奢 **kyōsha** luxury, extravagance

───── 9 ─────

4c9.1 / 1064

暇   **KA, hima** free time, leisure **itoma** leisure, spare time; leave-taking

───── 1 ─────

3 暇乞 **itomago(i)** leave-taking, farewell visit

4

木 月 日 火 礻 王 牛 方 攵 欠 心 戸 戈   9←

8 暇取 **himado(ru)** take a long time, be delayed
15 暇潰 **himatsubu(shi)** wasting/killing time

───── 2 ─────

3 寸暇 **sunka** a moment's leisure, spare moments
6 休暇 **kyūka** holiday, vacation, leave of absence
7 余暇 **yoka** spare time, leisure
12 閑暇 **kanka** leisure, spare time
15 請暇 **seika** requesting a vacation
　賜暇 **shika** leave of absence, furlough

───── 4 ─────

6 有給休暇 **yūkyū kyūka** paid vacation

4c9.2 / 348

暗   **AN, kura(i)** dark
kura(gari) darkness
kura(mu) grow dark; be dazzled/blinded
kura(masu) hide, slip away

───── 1 ─────

3 暗々 **an'an** darkness; covertly
　暗々裡 **an'anri** tacitly; covertly
4 暗中 **anchū** in the dark; in secret
　暗中飛躍 **anchū hiyaku** secret maneuvering
　暗中摸索 **anchū mosaku** groping in the dark
5 暗号 **angō** code, cipher
　暗号文 **angōbun** coded message, cryptogram
　暗示 **anji** suggestion, hint
6 暗合 **angō** coincidence
　暗色 **anshoku** dark color
7 暗赤色 **ansekishoku** dark red
8 暗夜 **an'ya** dark night
9 暗室 **anshitsu** darkroom
10 暗流 **anryū** undercurrent
　暗涙 **anrui** silent tears
　暗弱 **anjaku** feeble-minded
　暗殺 **ansatsu** assassination
　暗殺者 **ansatsusha** assassin
　暗記 **anki** memorization
　暗記物 **ankimono** something to be memorized
11 暗唱 **anshō** recite (from memory)
　暗黒 **ankoku** darkness
　暗黒面 **ankokumen** the dark/seamy side
　暗黒街 **ankokugai** the underworld
　暗転 **anten** scenery change while the stage is unlit
12 暗喩 **an'yu** metaphor
　暗渠 **ankyo** closed/covered conduit, underground drain, culvert
　暗然 **anzen** sad, doleful
　暗紫色 **anshishoku** dark purple
　暗雲 **an'un** dark clouds
13 暗暗 **an'an** darkness; covertly
　暗暗裡 **an'anri** tacitly; covertly

暗愚 **angu** feeble-minded, imbecile
　暗褐色 **ankasshoku** dark brown
14 暗緑色 **anryokushoku** dark green
　暗算 **anzan** mental arithmetic
　暗誦 **anshō** recite (from memory)
15 暗潮 **anchō** undercurrent
　暗影 **an'ei** shadow, gloom
　暗黙 **anmoku** silence
　暗黙了解 **anmoku (no) ryōkai** tacit understanding
16 暗澹 **antan** gloomy, somber
17 暗礁 **anshō** unseen reef/rock, snag
　暗闇 **kurayami** darkness
18 暗闘 **antō** secret enmity/feud
21 暗躍 **an'yaku** secret maneuvering
29 暗鬱 **an'utsu** gloomy, melancholy

───── 2 ─────

3 丸暗記 **maruanki** learn by heart/rote
　小暗 **ogura(i), kogura(i)** dusky, shady
4 仄暗 **honogura(i)** dim(ly lit)
8 明暗 **meian** light and dark, shading
　明暗度 **meiando** brightness, light intensity
　物暗 **monogura(i)** dark, dim
9 後暗 **ushi(ro)gura(i)** shady, underhanded
10 真暗 **makkura** pitch-dark
　真暗闇 **makkurayami** utter darkness
12 棒暗記 **bōanki** indiscriminate memorization
　無暗 **muyami** thoughtless, rash; excessive; unnecessary
13 溶暗 **yōan** fade-out, dissolve (in movies)
　暗暗 **an'an** darkness; covertly
　暗暗裡 **an'anri** tacitly; covertly
16 薄暗 **usugura(i), usukura(gari)** dimly lit, semi-dark, twilight

───── 3 ─────

14 疑心暗鬼 **gishin-anki** Suspicion creates monsters in the dark. Suspicion feeds on itself.

4c9.3

暘   **YŌ** sunrise

4c9.4 / 635

暖 暖   **DAN, atata(kai/ka)** warm
atata(maru/meru) (intr./tr.) warm up

───── 1 ─────

5 暖冬 **dantō** warm/mild winter
　暖冬異変 **dantō ihen** abnormally warm winter
6 暖気 **danki** warmth, warm weather
8 暖国 **dankoku, dangoku** warm country
　暖炉 **danro** fireplace, hearth, stove
　暖房 **danbō** heating

暖取 **dan (o) to(ru)** warm oneself (at the fire)
9 暖室 **danshitsu** heated room; hothouse
10 暖流 **danryū** warm (ocean) current
暖帯 **dantai** the subtropics
19 暖簾 **noren** shop-entrance curtain; reputation, goodwill

───────── 2 ─────────

5 生暖 **namaatataka(i)** lukewarm
9 春暖 **shundan** warm spring weather
12 温暖 **ondan** warm, mild
寒暖 **kandan** hot and cold, temperature
寒暖計 **kandankei** thermometer

4c9.5

暄

KEN warm (weather)

4c9.6

暉

KI light; shine

───────── 2 ─────────

6 旭暉 **kyokki** rays of the rising sun

暑 → 暑 **4c8.5**

4c9.7

暈

UN, kasa halo (around the moon)
boka(su) shade off; be blurry
bo(keru) fade, become dim

───────── 2 ─────────

10 眩暈 **gen'un, memai** vertigo, dizziness

既 → 既 **0a10.5**

4c9.8 / 1189

幹

KAN main part
miki (tree) trunk

───────── 1 ─────────

8 幹事 **kanji** manager, secretary
幹事長 **kanjichō** executive secretary, secretary-general
10 幹部 **kanbu** (top) executives, management
15 幹線 **kansen** main/trunk line

───────── 2 ─────────

3 才幹 **saikan** ability, talent
5 主幹 **shukan** editor in chief
7 材幹 **zaikan** ability

8 枝幹 **shikan** trunk and branches
10 根幹 **konkan** root and trunk; basis, keynote
骨幹 **kokkan** one's frame, build
11 基幹 **kikan** basic, key (industries)
13 新幹線 **Shinkansen** New Trunk Line, bullet train
14 語幹 **gokan** stem, root of a word
16 樹幹 **jukan** (tree) trunk
18 軀幹 **kukan** body, build, physique

4c9.9

晳

SEKI pale-skinned, white

4c9.10

貊

BAKU barbarians

───────── 10 ─────────

4c10.1

曄

YŌ shine; flourishing

4c10.2

暝

MEI dark, dim; nightfall

4c10.3

斡

ATSU go around; ladle handle; rule, administer

───────── 1 ─────────

11 斡旋 **assen** mediation, good offices, placement
斡旋者 **assensha** mediator, intermediary
斡旋案 **assen'an** conciliation/arbitration proposal

───────── 3 ─────────

12 就職斡旋 **shūshoku assen** job placement

4c10.4

暢

CHŌ stretch, be relaxed

───────── 1 ─────────

6 暢気 **nonki** easygoing, happy-go-lucky

───────── 2 ─────────

8 怪暢 **kaichō** carefree feeling
10 流暢 **ryūchō** fluent

4

木
月
日 10←
火
礻
王
牛
方
攵
欠
心
戸
戈

4c10.5

鞟

TAN tanned hide, leather

——————— 2 ———————

21 韃鞟 **Dattan** (a barbarian tribe)

4c10.6

貌 皃

BŌ form, appearance; countenance

——————— 2 ———————

5 外貌 **gaibō** external appearance, exterior, one's looks
6 全貌 **zenbō** the full picture/story
7 状貌 **jōbō** looks, appearance
   形貌 **keibō** form, appearance
9 変貌 **henbō** transformation
   美貌 **bibō** good looks
   風貌 **fūbō** looks, features, appearance
   相貌 **sōbō** features, looks, physiognomy
10 容貌 **yōbō** looks, personal appearance
14 概貌 **gaibō** general appearance, outline

——————— 11 ———————

4c11.1

暾

TON sunrise, sun's rays

4c11.2 / 1014

暴

BŌ violence BAKU expose, reveal **aba(reru)** act violently, rage, rampage, run amuck **aba(ku)** disclose, expose, bring to light

——————— 1 ———————

2 暴子 **aba(rek)ko** unruly child
   暴力 **bōryoku** violence, force
   暴力団 **bōryokudan** gangster organization
4 暴込 **aba(re)ko(mu)** storm/burst into
5 暴出 **aba(re)da(su)** get rowdy, go on a rampage
   暴民 **bōmin** mob, rioters
6 暴行 **bōkō** act of violence, assault, outrage
   暴回 **aba(re)mawa(ru)** run riot/amuck, rampage
7 暴状 **bōjō** outrage, atrocity, violence
   暴走 **bōsō** run wild, run out of control
   暴君 **bōkun** tyrant, despot
   暴狂 **aba(re)kuru(u)** run amuck
   暴戻 **bōrei** tyrannical, brutal
   暴利 **bōri** excessive profits, usury
8 暴逆 **bōgyaku** outrage, atrocity, violence
   暴者 **aba(re)mono** rowdy, ruffian

9 暴発 **bōhatsu** accidental/spontaneous firing
   暴虐 **bōgyaku** outrage, atrocity, violence
   暴風 **bōfū** high winds, windstorm
   暴風雨 **bōfūu** rainstorm
   暴風雪 **bōfūsetsu** snowstorm, blizzard
   暴風圏 **bōfūken** storm zone/area
   暴政 **bōsei** tyranny, oppressive rule
   暴威 **bōi** tyranny, great violence, havoc
   暴食 **bōshoku** gluttony, gorging oneself
10 暴徒 **bōto** rioters, mob
   暴挙 **bōkyo** violence; recklessness
   暴馬 **aba(re)uma** restive/runaway horse
11 暴動 **bōdō** riot, disturbance, uprising
   暴動者 **bōdōsha** rioter, rebel, insurgent
   暴悪 **bōaku** violence, tyranny, savagery
12 暴落 **bōraku** sudden drop, (stock-market) crash
   暴飲 **bōin** heavy/excessive drinking
13 暴漢 **bōkan** ruffian, goon, thug
14 暴慢 **bōman** insolent, arrogant, overbearing
15 暴論 **bōron** irrational/wild argument
20 暴騰 **bōtō** sudden rise (in prices)
21 暴露 **bakuro** expose, bring to light

——————— 2 ———————

4 凶暴 **kyōbō** ferocity, brutality, savagery
6 兇暴 **kyōbō** ferocity, brutality, savagery
   自暴自棄 **jibō-jiki** desperation, despair
7 乱暴 **ranbō** violence; rough, reckless
   乱暴者 **ranbōmono** rowdy, vandal
   狂暴 **kyōbō** berserk, frenzied, furious
11 強暴 **kyōbō** strong and rough, violent
   粗暴 **sobō** wild, rough, violent
15 横暴 **ōbō** high-handed, tyrannical

——————— 3 ———————

11 現実暴露 **genjitsu bakuro** disillusionment

4c11.3 / 1399

暫

ZAN, shibara(ku) for a while

——————— 1 ———————

8 暫定 **zantei** tentative, provisional
   暫定的 **zanteiteki** tentative, provisional
   暫定案 **zanteian** tentative plan
10 暫時 **zanji** for a (short) time

4c11.4

皚

GAI (snowy) white

4c11.5

羯

KATSU, KETSU barbarian; castrated ram

4c11.6

翫 翫　**GAN, moteaso(bu)** play with, enjoy, make sport of

4c11.7

翥　**SHO** fly up, take wing

4c11.8

殤　**SHŌ** dying at a young age

──────── 12 ────────

暸 → 暸　5c12.4

曉 → 暁　4c8.1

4c12.1 / 637

曇　**DON, kumo(ru)** cloud up, get cloudy

──────── 1 ────────

0 曇りガラス **kumo(ri)garasu** frosted glass
4 曇天 **donten** cloudy/overcast sky
12 曇勝 **kumo(ri)ga(chi)** broken clouds, mostly cloudy

──────── 2 ────────

5 本曇 **hongumo(ri)** rain-threatening overcast
7 花曇 **hanagumo(ri)** cloudy weather in spring
8 雨曇 **amagumo(ri)** overcast weather
10 高曇 **takagumo(ri)** overcast with wispy high-altitude clouds
11 雪曇 **yukigumo(ri)** threatening to snow
12 朝曇 **asagumo(ri)** cloudy morning
13 掻曇 **ka(ki)kumo(ru)** be overcast
16 薄曇 **usugumo(ri)** slightly cloudy weather
17 優曇華 **udonge** udumbara plant (said to blossom once in 3,000 years); insect eggs (laid by a lacewing in a flower-like pattern whose shape portends good or ill fortune)

4c12.2

暼　**HETSU, HECHI** setting sun

4c12.3

曁　**KI** and, along with; reach, extend to

4c12.4

翰 翰　**KAN** (a mountain bird); (feather) writing brush; letter

──────── 1 ────────

8 翰林 **kanrin** literary circles
　翰林院 **kanrin'in** academy, institute
14 翰墨 **kanboku** brush and ink; writing, drawing

──────── 2 ────────

10 宸翰 **shinkan** imperial letter
　書翰 **shokan** letter, note
12 貴翰 **kikan** your letter

猪 → 猪　3g8.1

4c12.5

赭　**SHA** red

──────── 1 ────────

3 赭土 **shado** red ocher
18 赭顔 **shagan** ruddy face

──────── 13 ────────

曙 → 曙　4c14.2

4c13.1

曖　**AI** dark; not clear

──────── 1 ────────

9 曖昧 **aimai** vague, ambiguous, equivocal

4c13.2

曚　**MŌ** darkness

──────── 1 ────────

9 曚昧 **mōmai** unenlightened, benighted, ignorant

4c13.3

甑 甑　**SŌ, koshiki** (rice-)steaming pot

4c13.4

貘 獏　**BAKU** tapir

鞜→ **3a13.12**

──────── 14 ────────

4c14.1 / 19

曜 旺 曜

YŌ day of the week; light; shine

──────── 1 ────────
4 曜日 **yōbi** day of the week
──────── 2 ────────
3 土曜 **doyō** Saturday
　土曜日 **doyōbi** Saturday
4 水曜日 **suiyōbi** Wednesday
　木曜 **mokuyō** Thursday
　木曜日 **mokuyōbi** Thursday
　月曜 **getsuyō** Monday
　月曜日 **getsuyōbi** Monday
　日曜 **nichiyō** Sunday
　日曜日 **nichiyōbi** Sunday
　日曜版 **nichiyōban** Sunday edition
　火曜日 **kayōbi** Tuesday
7 何曜日 **nan'yōbi, naniyōbi** what day of the week
8 金曜 **kin'yō** Friday
　金曜日 **kin'yōbi** Friday
11 黒曜石 **kokuyōseki** obsidian
──────── 3 ────────
13 聖金曜日 **Seikin'yōbi** Good Friday

4c14.2

曙 曙

SHO, akebono dawn, daybreak

──────── 1 ────────
6 曙光 **shokō** the light of dawn; good prospects

4c14.3

韓

KAN, Kara Korea

──────── 1 ────────
2 韓人 **Kanjin** a Korean (historical)
8 韓国 **Kankoku** South Korea
──────── 2 ────────
4 日韓 **Nik-Kan** Japan and South Korea
6 在韓 **zai-Kan** in South Korea

4c14.4

鞨

KATSU boots; drum

──────── 2 ────────
14 靺鞨 **Makkatsu** (a barbarian Tungus tribe)

4c14.5

觴

SHŌ (saké) cup

──────── 2 ────────
18 濫觴 **ranshō** origin, source, beginning

4c14.6 / 1634

覆 覆

FUKU cover; overturn
ō(u) cover; conceal
ō(i) cover, covering
kutsugae(ru) be overturned
kutsugae(su) overturn, overthrow

──────── 1 ────────
3 覆土 **fukudo** covering (seeds) with soil
4 覆水盆返 **fukusui bon (ni) kae(razu)** No use crying over spilt milk.
7 覆没 **fukubotsu** capsize and sink
8 覆刻 **fukkoku** reproduce, republish
　覆刻本 **fukkokubon** reissued book
9 覆奏 **fukusō** reinvestigate and report
　覆面 **fukumen** mask
　覆面子 **fukumenshi** anonymous writer
13 覆滅 **fukumetsu** overthrow, destruction
15 覆審 **fukushin** retrial, judicial review
　覆輪 **fukurin** ornamental border/fringe

──────── 2 ────────
4 反覆 **hanpuku** repeat; reverse oneself
　日覆 **hio(i), hiō(i)** sunshade, awning, blind
8 雨覆 **amaō(i)** waterproof covering, tarpaulin
10 被覆 **hifuku** covering, coating, insulation
11 転覆 **tenpuku** overturn, overthrow
19 顛覆 **tenpuku** overturn

──────── 15 ────────

4c15.1

曝

BAKU, sara(su) expose (to the sun/air/weather)

──────── 1 ────────
10 曝書 **bakusho** airing of books
21 曝露 **bakuro** expose, bring to light
──────── 2 ────────
7 吹曝 **fu(ki)sara(shi)** exposed to the wind, wind-swept
8 雨曝 **amazara(shi)** exposed to rain, weather-beaten
10 被曝 **hibaku** exposure (to radiation)

4c15.2

曠 眖

KŌ clear; broad, large; empty

──────── 1 ────────

4 曠日弥久 **kōjitsu bikyū** idle away one's time/years
5 曠世 **kōsei** unprecedented, unmatched
曠古 **kōko** unprecedented, historic
11 曠野 **kōya** broad plain, prairie
18 曠職 **kōshoku** neglecting one's duties

4c15.3 / 856

響 響 **KYŌ, hibi(ku)** sound, resound, be echoed; affect

──────── 1 ────────
12 響渡 **hibi(ki)wata(ru)** resound, reverberate
──────── 2 ────────
4 反響 **hankyō** echo, reverberation; repercussions, reaction
6 交響曲 **kōkyōkyoku** symphony
交響楽団 **kōkyō gakudan** symphony orchestra
地響 **jihibi(ki)** rumbling of the ground, earth tremor
9 音響 **onkyō** sound
音響学 **onkyōgaku** acoustics
10 差響 **sa(shi)hibi(ku)** affect, influence
14 鳴響 **na(ri)hibi(ku)** resound, reverberate
15 影響 **eikyō** effect, influence
影響力 **eikyōryoku** effect, influence
影響下 **eikyōka** under the influence of

覈 → 4h15.1

4c15.4

羶 **SEN, namagusa(i)** smelling like a sheep

──────── 16 ────────

4c16.1

曦 **GI** the sun

4c16.2

馨 **KEI, kao(ru)** be fragrant
kanba(shii), kōba(shii) fragrant; favorable

──────── 17 ────────

4c17.1

曩 **NŌ, saki** before, preceding

䜿 → 響 4c15.3

──────── 19 ────────

曬 → 晒 4c6.1

4c19.1

靨 **YŌ, ekubo** dimple

4c19.2

鼹 **EN** mole (the animal)

──────── 1 ────────
13 鼹鼠 **mogura** mole

4

木 月 日 火 礻 王 牛 方 攵 欠 心 戸 戈

19←

──────────── 火 4d ────────────

火	灯	灼	灸	災	炊	炉	炒	炎	炙	畑	炳	炸
0.1	2.1	3.1	3.2	3.3	4.1	4.2	4.3	4.4	4.5	5.1	5.2	5.3
炮	炬	炯	烝	為	烙	烘	烟	烈	烋	烏	烽	焏
5.4	5.5	5.6	5.7	5.8	6.1	6.2	4d9.3	6.3	6.4	6.5	7.1	4d5.6
焔	黒	焉	煉	焙	焜	焠	焼	焔	焱	焚	無	黒
4d8.5	7.2	7.3	4d9.2	8.1	8.2	8.3	8.4	8.5	8.6	8.7	8.8	4d7.2
煮	然	為	毯	煩	煉	煙	煨	煠	煤	煌	煬	煖
8.9	8.10	4d5.8	8.11	9.1	9.2	9.3	9.4	9.5	9.6	9.7	9.8	9.9
煥	熙	照	煦	煎	煢	熄	熅	熔	煩	煽	熏	熟
9.10	9.11	9.12	9.13	2o11.2	9.14	10.1	10.2	8a10.1	10.3	10.4	4d14.1	10.5

熙	熊	燉	熨	勲	熈	熱	默	熬	燋	燃	燔	燎
4d9.11	10.6	11.1	11.2	11.3	4d9.11	11.4	11.5	11.6	12.1	12.2	12.3	12.4

燈	燒	熾	燵	燧	燗	燜	燕	熹	黔	燊	燬	燠
4d2.1	4d8.4	12.5	12.6	12.7	4d12.8	12.8	3k13.16	12.9	12.10	4d8.5	13.1	13.2

燦	燐	燭	燥	黛	黜	點	燻	爐	燿	�	燹	點
13.3	13.4	13.5	13.6	13.7	13.8	2m7.2	14.1	14.2	14.3	14.4	14.5	14.6

爍	爆	爐	黥	爛	黶	爨
15.1	15.2	4d4.2	16.1	17.1	22.1	26.1

4

木
月
日
→0 火
礻
王
牛
方
攵
欠
心
戸
戈

────────── 0 ──────────

4d0.1 / 20

火

KA fire; Tuesday
hi, ho fire

────────── 1 ──────────

0 とろ火 **(toro)bi** low fire
2 火入 **hii(re)** first lighting (of a furnace); heating (to prevent spoilage); setting brush afire
　火力 **karyoku** caloric force, thermal/steam-generated power
3 火干 **hibo(shi)** drying by fire; fire-dried
　火口 **kakō** (volcano) crater
　　higuchi burner; muzzle (of a gun); origin of a fire
　火口湖 **kakōko** crater lake
　火口壁 **kakōheki** crater wall
　火山 **kazan** volcano
　火山灰 **kazanbai** volcanic ash
　火山岩 **kazangan** igneous rock, lava
　火山帯 **kazantai** volcanic zone
　火山脈 **kazanmyaku** volcanic range
　火山弾 **kazandan** volcanic boulders
　火山礫 **kazanreki** volcanic pebbles
4 火元 **himoto** origin of a fire
　火夫 **kafu** stoker, fireman
　火中 **kachū** in the fire, midst of the flames
　火片 **kahen** sparks
　火水 **himizu** fire and water; discord
　火手 **hi(no)te** flames, fire
5 火矢 **hiya** flaming/incendiary arrow
　火失 **kashitsu** accidental fire
　火付 **hitsu(ke)** arson; instigator, firebrand
　　hitsu(ki) kindling
　火加減 **hikagen** condition of the fire
　火打石 **hiu(chi)ishi** a flint
　火玉 **hidama** ball of fire
　火皿 **hizara** fire grate; chafing dish; bowl of a pipe
6 火気 **kaki** fire　**hi(no)ke** heat of fire
　火気厳禁 **kaki genkin** Danger: Flammable
　火刑 **kakei** execution by fire, burning at the stake

火色 **hi-iro** flame color
火先 **hisaki** flames; direction in which a fire is spreading　**hosaki** flame tips
火宅 **kataku** house on fire; this world of suffering
火成岩 **kaseigan** igneous rock
7 火吹竹 **hifu(ki)dake** bamboo blowpipe (for charcoal fires)
火花 **hibana** sparks
火床 **kashō, hidoko** fire bed/grate
火災 **kasai** fire, conflagration
火災保険 **kasai hoken** fire insurance
火災警報 **kasai keihō** fire alarm
火攻 **hize(me)** fire attack
火見 **hi(no)mi** fire-lookout tower
火見櫓 **hi(no)mi yagura** fire-lookout tower
火車 **hi (no) kuruma** fiery chariot of (Buddhist) hell; financial distress
8 火事 **kaji** fire, conflagration
火事見舞 **kaji mima(i)** sympathy visit after a fire
火事泥 **kajidoro** thief at a fire
火事場 **kajiba** scene of a fire
火炉 **karo** furnace
火炎 **kaen** flame
火炎瓶 **kaenbin** firebomb, Molotov cocktail
火炙 **hiabu(ri)** execution by fire, burning at the stake
火門 **kamon** cannon muzzle
9 火除 **hiyo(ke)** protection against fire
火急 **kakyū** urgent, emergency
火室 **kashitsu** fire box/chamber
火屋 **hoya** lamp chimney
火柱 **hibashira** pillar of flames
火星 **kasei** Mars
火星人 **kaseijin** a Martian
10 火遊 **hiaso(bi)** playing with fire
火酒 **kashu** liquor
火消 **hike(shi)** firefighter; fire extinguisher
火消壺 **hike(shi)tsubo** charcoal extinguisher
火砲 **kahō** gun, cannon
11 火達磨 **hidaruma** mass of flames, human torch
火桶 **hioke** round wooden brazier

火脚 **hiashi** spreading of a fire
火移 **hiutsu(ri)** catching fire, igniting
火責 **hize(me)** ordeal/torture by fire
12 火渡 **hiwata(ri)** walking over hot coals
火葬 **kasō** cremation
火葬場 **kasōba** crematory
火脹 **hibuku(re)** burn blister
火焙 **hiabu(ri)** execution by fire, burning at the stake
火焔 **kaen** flame
火焚 **hita(ki)** making a fire
火番 **hi(no)ban** fire/night watchman
火筒 **hozutsu** gun, firearms
13 火傷 **kashō, yakedo** a burn
火勢 **kasei** force of the flames
火掻 **hika(ki)** poker, fire rake
火蓋 **hibuta** cover for a gun barrel
火蓋切 **hibuta (o) ki(ru)** open fire; commence
火煙 **kaen** fire and smoke
火照 **hote(ri)** glow, heat; burning sensation
火鉢 **hibachi** charcoal brazier, hibachi
14 火種 **hidane** live coals (for kindling)
15 火器 **kaki** firearms
火影 **hokage** (forms moving in the) firelight
火熨斗 **hinoshi** an iron (for ironing clothes)
火熱 **kanetsu** heat
火縄 **hinawa** fuse (cord)
火縄銃 **hinawajū** matchlock, harquebus
火線 **kasen** firing line
火箸 **hibashi** tongs
火箭 **kasen, hiya** flaming/incendiary arrow
16 火薬 **kayaku** gunpowder, explosives
火薬庫 **kayakuko** powder magazine
火燵 **kotatsu** heated floor well, foot warmer
18 火曜日 **kayōbi** Tuesday
火難 **kanan** fire, conflagration
火難除 **kanan'yo(ke)** charm against fire

———————— 2 ————————

3 大火 **taika** large fire, conflagration
大火傷 **ōyakedo** severe burn
下火 **shitabi** burning low; waning
口火 **kuchibi** fuse
小火 **shōka, boya** small fire
山火事 **yamakaji** forest fire
4 天火 **tenpi** oven; (waffle) iron
　　　tenka fire caused by lightning
中火 **chūbi** medium heat (in cooking)
切火 **ki(ri)bi** flint sparks; purification by fire
水火 **suika** water and fire
引火 **inka** ignite, catch fire
引火性 **inkasei** flammability
引火点 **inkaten** flash point
5 出火 **shukka** (outbreak of) fire
失火 **shikka** an accidental fire

付火 **tsu(ke)bi** arson
石火 **sekka** flint fire; a flash
石火矢 **ishibiya** (ancient) cannon
6 死火山 **shikazan** extinct volcano
休火山 **kyūkazan** dormant volcano
防火 **bōka** fire prevention, fire fighting, fireproof
防火戸 **bōkado** fire door
防火用水 **bōka yōsui** water for putting out fires
防火栓 **bōkasen** fire hydrant
防火壁 **bōkaheki** fire wall
近火 **kinka, chikabi** a fire in one's neighborhood
迎火 **muka(e)bi** fire to welcome departed souls home
行火 **anka** bed/foot warmer
灯火 **tōka** a light, lamplight
灯火管制 **tōka kansei** lighting control, blackout, brownout
自火 **jika** a fire starting in one's own home
7 劫火 **gōka** world-destroying conflagration
花火 **hanabi** fireworks
花火線香 **hanabi senkō** joss-stick fireworks, sparklers; flash-in-the-pan
8 長火鉢 **nagahibachi** oblong brazier
送火 **oku(ri)bi** bonfire for speeding home the spirits of the dead
泥火山 **deikazan** mud volcano
拝火教 **haikakyō** fire worship
炉火 **roka** hearth fire
放火 **hōka** arson
放火犯 **hōkahan** arson(ist)
放火狂 **hōkakyō** pyromania(c)
怪火 **kaika** fire of mysterious origin; foxfire
門火 **kadobi** funeral/wedding/Obon bonfire (at the gate)
9 飛火 **to(bi)hi** flying sparks, leaping flames
発火 **hakka** ignition, combustion; discharge, firing
発火点 **hakkaten** ignition/flash point
重火器 **jūkaki** heavy weapons
点火 **tenka** ignite
急火 **kyūka** a sudden fire; a nearby fire
耐火 **taika** fireproof, fire-resistant
耐火力 **taikaryoku** fire resistance
耐火性 **taikasei** fire resistant
耐火煉瓦 **taika renga** firebrick
活火山 **kakkazan** active volcano
浄火 **jōka** sacred fire
狐火 **kitsunebi** foxfire, ignis fatuus
炭火 **sumibi** charcoal fire
神火 **shinka** sacred flame, divine fire
10 残火 **zanka** remaining fire, embers
消火 **shōka** fire fighting
消火栓 **shōkasen** fire hydrant

4

木
月
日
火 0←
礻
王
牛
方
攵
欠
心
戸
戈

消火器 **shōkaki** fire extinguisher
埋火 **uzu(mi)bi** banked fire
猛火 **mōka** raging flames; heavy gunfire
烈火 **rekka** raging fire
砲火 **hōka** gunfire, shellfire
鬼火 **onibi** will-o'-the-wisp, ignis fatuus
11 野火 **nobi** brush/prairie fire
強火 **tsuyobi** strong (cooking) fire, high heat
蛍火 **keika** light of a firefly　**hotarubi** light of a firefly; glowing embers
烽火 **noroshi** signal fire
情火 **jōka** the flame of love
船火事 **funakaji** a fire aboard ship
12 着火 **chakka** ignition, combustion
遠火 **tōbi** distant fire, low heat
焼火箸 **ya(ke)hibashi** red-hot tongs
焚火 **ta(ki)bi** open-air fire, bonfire
貰火 **mora(i)bi** catch fire (from a neighboring burning building)
13 業火 **gōka** hell fire
聖火 **seika** sacred flame/torch
戦火 **senka** (the flames of) war
置火燵 **o(ki)gotatsu** portable brazier
鉄火 **tekka** red-hot iron; gambling; swords and guns; fierce temperament
鉄火巻 **tekkama(ki)** seaweed-wrapped tuna sushi
鉄火場 **tekkaba** gambling room
雷火 **raika** fire caused by lightning
14 漁火 **gyoka, isa(ri)bi** fire for luring fish at night
導火線 **dōkasen** fuse; cause, occasion
種火 **tanebi** pilot light/flame
複火山 **fukukazan** compound volcano
綿火薬 **menkayaku** guncotton
銃火 **jūka** gunfire
15 噴火 **funka** (volcanic) eruption
噴火口 **funkakō** crater
噴火山 **funkazan** volcano
箱火鉢 **hako hibachi** box-enclosed brazier
16 燎火 **ryōka** bonfire
篝火 **kagaribi** bonfire
17 燐火 **rinka** phosphorescence, foxfire
18 鎮火 **chinka** be extinguished
類火 **ruika** a spreading fire

――――――― 3 ―――――――
2 十字火 **jūjika** crossfire
4 不知火 **shiranui, shiranuhi** sea fire/luminescence
11 第三火 **dai-san (no) hi** nuclear energy
12 御神火 **goshinka** volcanic fires

――――――― 4 ―――――――
4 五輪聖火 **Gorin seika** Olympic torch
5 打上花火 **u(chi)a(ge) hanabi** skyrocket, fireworks
13 電光石火 **denkō-sekka** a flash, an instant

――――――― 5 ―――――――
17 環太平洋火山帯 **kan-Taiheiyō kazantai** circum-Pacific volcanic belt

――――――― 2 ―――――――
4d2.1 / 1333

灯 燈　**TŌ, hi, tomoshibi, akashi** a light, lamp

――――――― 1 ―――――――
3 灯下 **tōka** beneath the lamp, (read) by lamplight
4 灯火 **tōka** a light, lamplight
灯火管制 **tōka kansei** lighting control, blackout, brownout
灯心 **tōshin** wick
灯心油 **tōshin'yu** lamp oil, kerosene
5 灯用 **tōyō** for illumination
灯台 **tōdai** lighthouse
灯台守 **tōdaimori** lighthouse keeper
6 灯光 **tōkō** light, lamplight, flashlight
7 灯芯 **tōshin** wick
8 灯油 **tōyu** lamp oil, kerosene
灯明 **tōmyō** light offered to a god
15 灯影 **tōei** flicker of light
灯標 **tōhyō** light buoy
22 灯籠 **tōrō** (hanging/garden) lantern
灯籠流 **tōrōnaga(shi)** setting votive lanterns afloat

――――――― 2 ―――――――
3 万灯 **mandō** votive lanterns hung in a row
万灯会 **mandōe** Buddhist lantern festival
4 幻灯 **gentō** magic lantern, slides
5 白灯油 **hakutōyu** kerosene
6 行灯 **andon** paper-enclosed oil lamp
7 尾灯 **bitō** taillight
8 孤灯 **kotō** a solitary light
法灯 **hōtō** the light/teachings of Buddhism
門灯 **montō** gate light
9 点灯 **tentō** light (a lamp) (cf. 消灯)
洋灯 **yōtō** lamp
弧灯 **kotō** arc lamp
神灯 **shintō** sacred/festival lantern
紅灯 **kōtō** red lantern; red-light (district)
10 消灯 **shōtō** putting out the lights (cf. 点灯)
鬼灯 **hōzuki** bladder/ground cherry
軒灯 **kentō** eaves lantern, door light
11 舷灯 **gentō** running lights
釣灯籠 **tsu(ri)dōrō** hanging lantern
魚灯 **gyotō** fish-luring lights
12 提灯 **chōchin** (paper) lantern
提灯持 **chōchinmo(chi)** lantern bearer; booster; hype
街灯 **gaitō** street lamp
無灯 **mutō** no lighting, lights out

13 献灯 **kentō** votive lantern
電灯 **dentō** electric light
電灯料 **dentōryō** electric-lighting charges
15 標灯 **hyōtō** signal light, pilot lamp
22 龕灯 **gandō** altar lamp; hand lantern
龕灯返 **gandōgae(shi)** apparatus for
changing stage scenery

——————— 3 ———————

4 天井灯 **tenjōtō** ceiling light
水銀灯 **suigintō** mercury lamp
5 広告灯 **kōkokutō** advertising lights
白熱灯 **hakunetsutō** incandescent lamp
石英灯 **sekieitō** quartz lamp
7 走馬灯 **sōmatō** (like a) revolving lantern,
kaleidoscopic
8 明滅灯 **meimetsutō** occulting light
9 信号灯 **shingōtō** signal light, blinker
前照灯 **zenshōtō** headlights
盆提灯 **bonjōchin** Bon Festival lantern
風前灯 **fūzen (no) tomoshibi** (like a) candle
in the wind, precarious situation
指示灯 **shijitō** pilot lamp, indicator light
後部灯 **kōbutō** taillight
昼行灯 **hiru andon** (useless as) a lantern in
broad daylight
11 探海灯 **tankaitō** searchlight
探照灯 **tanshōtō** searchlight
蛍光灯 **keikōtō** fluorescent lamp
終夜灯 **shūyatō** nightlight
雪見灯籠 **yukimidōrō** ornamental three-
legged stone lantern
12 集魚灯 **shūgyotō** fish-luring light

——————— 4 ———————

3 弓張提灯 **yumiha(ri)jōchin** paper lantern
with bow-shaped handle
16 懐中電灯 **kaichū dentō** flashlight

——————— 5 ———————

3 小田原提灯 **odawara-jōchin** collapsible
cylindrical paper lantern

——————— 3 ———————

4d3.1

灼

SHAKU burning red hot; bright

——————— 1 ———————

15 灼熱 **shakunetsu** red/scorching hot, incandescent

4d3.2

灸

KYŪ moxa cautery, moxibustion

——————— 1 ———————

8 灸治 **kyūji** moxa cauterization/treatments

9 灸点 **kyūten** moxa-treatment points

——————— 2 ———————

10 針灸 **shinkyū** acupuncture and moxibustion
12 温灸 **onkyū** moxibustion, moxa cautery
17 鍼灸 **shinkyū** acupuncture and moxibustion

4d3.3 / 1335

災

SAI, wazawa(i) misfortune, disaster

——————— 1 ———————

4 災厄 **saiyaku** misfortune, disaster, accident
10 災害 **saigai** disaster, accident
災害地 **saigaichi** disaster-stricken area
災害保険 **saigai hoken** accident insurance
13 災禍 **saika** disaster, accident, misfortune
18 災難 **sainan** mishap, accident, calamity

——————— 2 ———————

4 天災 **tensai** natural disaster
水災 **suisai** flood
火災 **kasai** fire, conflagration
火災保険 **kasai hoken** fire insurance
火災警報 **kasai keihō** fire alarm
7 労災保険 **rōsai hoken** workman's accident
compensation insurance
9 風災 **fūsai** wind damage
10 息災 **sokusai** safety, safe and sound
被災 **hisai** be stricken, suffer from
被災者 **hisaisha** victim, sufferer
13 戦災 **sensai** war devastation
戦災地 **sensaichi** war-ravaged area
戦災者 **sensaisha** war victims
15 震災 **shinsai** earthquake disaster
震災地 **shinsaichi** quake-stricken area

——————— 3 ———————

3 大震災 **daishinsai** great earthquake; the 1923
Tōkyō earthquake

——————— 4 ———————

1 一病息災 **ichibyō-sokusai** One who has an
illness is careful of his health and lives
long.
12 無病息災 **mubyō-sokusai** in perfect health

——————— 4 ———————

4d4.1 / 1791

炊

SUI, ta(ku) boil (rice), cook

——————— 1 ———————

4 炊夫 **suifu** a (male) cook
5 炊出 **ta(ki)da(shi)** emergency group cooking
8 炊事 **suiji** cooking
炊事婦 **suijifu** a (female) cook

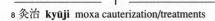

4

木
月
日
火 4←
礻
王
牛
方
攵
欠
心
戸
戈

炊事場 **suijiba** kitchen, cookhouse
炊具 **suigu** cooking utensils
11 炊婦 **suifu** a (female) cook, kitchen maid
12 炊飯器 **suihanki** (electric) rice cooker
30 炊爨 **suisan** cooking

───────── 2 ─────────

4 水炊 **mizuta(ki)** boiling (chicken)
6 自炊 **jisui** do one's own cooking
8 追炊 **o(i)da(ki)** boil some more (rice)
12 煮炊 **nita(ki)** cooking
飯炊 **meshita(ki)** rice cooking
14 雑炊 **zōsui** porridge of rice and vegetables

4d4.2 / 1790

炉 爐

RO furnace, hearth

───────── 1 ─────────

4 炉辺 **rohen, robata** fireside, hearth
炉火 **roka** hearth fire
10 炉格子 **rogōshi** (furnace) grate
12 炉棚 **rodana** mantelpiece
14 炉端 **robata** fireside, hearth
16 炉頭 **rotō** around the hearth

───────── 2 ─────────

4 火炉 **karo** furnace
7 囲炉裏 **irori** sunken hearth
9 香炉 **kōro** censer
10 高炉 **kōro** blast furnace
夏炉冬扇 **karo-tōsen** useless things (like a fireplace in summer or a fan in winter)
11 転炉 **tenro** revolving furnace, converter
12 焜炉 **konro** portable cooking stove
13 暖炉 **danro** fireplace, hearth, stove
煖炉 **danro** fireplace, hearth, stove
16 懐炉 **kairo** pocket heater
懐炉灰 **kairobai** pocket-heater fuel

───────── 3 ─────────

4 反射炉 **hansharo** reverberatory furnace
13 溶鉱炉 **yōkōro** blast furnace
電気炉 **denkiro** electric furnace
14 増殖炉 **zōshokuro** breeder reactor
18 鎔鉱炉 **yōkōro** blast furnace

───────── 4 ─────────

10 核反応炉 **kakuhannōro** nuclear reactor

4d4.3

炒

SHŌ, SŌ, i(ru) roast, toast, parch, pan fry ita(meru) fry (in a hot pan)

───────── 1 ─────────

5 炒玉子 **i(ri)tamago** scrambled eggs
7 炒豆 **i(ri)mame** parched/popped beans
12 炒飯 **chāhan** (Chinese fried-rice dish)

炬→ **4d5.5**

4d4.4 / 1336

炎

EN flame; (as suffix) inflammation of the ..., -itis
honō, homura flame

───────── 1 ─────────

3 炎上 **enjō** go up in flames, burst into flames
炎々 **en'en** blazing, fiery
4 炎天 **enten** hot weather, blazing sun
10 炎症 **enshō** inflammation
12 炎暑 **ensho** intense heat, hot weather
15 炎熱 **ennetsu** scorching/sweltering heat

───────── 2 ─────────

4 火炎 **kaen** flame
火炎瓶 **kaenbin** firebomb, Molotov cocktail
6 気炎 **kien** big talk; high spirits
気炎万丈 **kien-banjō** high spirits
光炎 **kōen** (light and) flame
7 狂炎 **kyōen** fierce flames
肝炎 **kan'en** hepatitis
8 毒炎 **dokuen** flame producing poisonous fumes
炎炎 **en'en** blazing, fiery
9 肺炎 **haien** pneumonia
胃炎 **ien** stomach inflammation, gastritis
10 消炎剤 **shōenzai** an antiphlogistic, balm
11 陽炎 **yōen, kagerō** heat shimmer
脳炎 **nōen** encephalitis
13 腸炎 **chōen** enteritis
腎炎 **jin'en** nephritis
14 鼻炎 **bien** nasal inflammation

───────── 3 ─────────

2 子宮炎 **shikyūen** uteritis
3 大腸炎 **daichōen** colitis
口内炎 **kōnaien** stomatitis
4 内耳炎 **naijien** inflammation of the inner ear
中耳炎 **chūjien** otitis media, tympanitis
心臓炎 **shinzōen** inflammation of the heart
5 外耳炎 **gaijien** inflammation of the outer ear, otitis externa
6 気管炎 **kikan'en** tracheitis
肋膜炎 **rokumakuen** pleurisy
虫垂炎 **chūsuien** appendicitis
7 角膜炎 **kakumakuen** inflammation of the cornea
肝臓炎 **kanzōen** hepatitis
8 盲腸炎 **mōchōen** appendicitis
9 咽頭炎 **intōen** pharyngitis
胆嚢炎 **tannōen** gallbladder inflammation
10 胸膜炎 **kyōmakuen** pleurisy
骨膜炎 **kotsumakuen** periostitis
骨髄炎 **kotsuzuien** osteomyelitis

4

木 月 日 火 衤 王 牛 方 欠 心 戸 戈

11 脳膜炎 **nōmakuen** meningitis
12 喉頭炎 **kōtōen** laryngitis
　結膜炎 **ketsumakuen** conjunctivitis
　歯齦炎 **shigin'en** gingivitis
13 腹膜炎 **fukumakuen** peritonitis
　腎盂炎 **jin'uen** pyelitis
　腎臓炎 **jinzōen** nephritis
14 静脈炎 **jōmyakuen** phlebitis
　関節炎 **kansetsuen** arthritis

———————— 4 ————————
4 日本脳炎 **Nihon nōen** Japanese encephalitis
6 気管支炎 **kikanshien** bronchitis
9 扁桃腺炎 **hentōsen'en** tonsillitis

———————— 5 ————————
6 虫様突起炎 **chūyō tokkien** appendicitis
8 肥厚性鼻炎 **hikōsei bien** hypertrophic rhinitis
11 脳脊髄膜炎 **nōsekizuimakuen** cerebrospinal
　　meningitis

4d4.5

炙

SHA, abu(ru) roast, broil, toast

———————— 2 ————————
4 火炙 **hiabu(ri)** execution by fire, burning at
　　the stake
17 膾炙 **kaisha** (food) in everyone's mouth,
　　(topic) on everyone's lips

———————— 5 ————————
4d5.1 / 36

畑

hata, hatake cultivated field

———————— 1 ————————
4 畑水練 **hatake suiren** (like) learning
　　swimming on dry land, book learning
5 畑打 **hatau(chi)** plowing up ground
6 畑地 **hatachi** farmland
7 畑作 **hatasaku** dry-field farming
8 畑物 **hatakemono** farm produce
12 畑違 **hatakechiga(i)** out of one's line
13 畑鼠 **hatanezumi** field mouse

———————— 2 ————————
5 田畑 **tahata** fields and rice paddies
7 花畑 **hanabatake** flower bed/garden
　麦畑 **mugibatake** wheat field
9 段畑 **danbata** terraced fields
　茶畑 **chabatake** tea plantation
10 桑畑 **kuwabatake** mulberry field
　梅畑 **umebatake** plum orchard
12 焼畑 **ya(ki)bata** burned-over fields
14 種畑 **tanebatake** seed garden

———————— 3 ————————
9 段々畑 **dandanbatake** terraced fields
11 野菜畑 **yasaibatake** vegetable garden
12 葡萄畑 **budōbatake** vineyard

4d5.2

炳

HEI clear

4d5.3

炸

SAKU explode; fry

———————— 1 ————————
12 炸裂 **sakuretsu** explode, burst
　炸裂弾 **sakuretsudan** explosive shell
16 炸薬 **sakuyaku** explosives

4d5.4

炮

HŌ roast, broil; light a bonfire

4d5.5

炬

KO, KYO torch, signal fire

———————— 1 ————————
16 炬燵 **kotatsu** heated floor well, foot warmer
———————— 2 ————————
13 置炬燵 **o(ki)gotatsu** portable brazier

4d5.6

炯　烱

KEI clear, bright

———————— 1 ————————
3 炯々 **keikei** glaring, penetrating
11 炯眼 **keigan** gleaming eyes; insightful,
　　discerning

4d5.7

烝

JŌ many; offer, dedicate; to steam

———————— 1 ————————
5 烝民 **jōmin** the common people, the masses

4d5.8 / 1484

為　爲

I, na(su), su(ru) do
na(ru) be, become
tame for sake of, in order to;
because of

———————— 1 ————————
4 為手 **na(ri)te** suitable person, candidate

9 為政者 **iseisha** statesman, administrator
12 為替 **kawase** (foreign) exchange; money order
為替手形 **kawase tegata** bill (of exchange), draft
為替相場 **kawase sōba** exchange rate

───────── 2 ─────────

2 人為 **jin'i** human agency, artifice
人為的 **jin'iteki** artificial
3 小為替 **kogawase** money order
4 天為 **ten'i** providential, natural
片為替 **katagawase** exchange imbalance
円為替 **enkawase** yen exchange
5 外為法 **Gaitamehō** Foreign Exchange (and Foreign Trade) Control Law (short for 外国為替及び外国貿易管理法)
6 行為 **kōi** act, deed, conduct
当為 **tōi** what should be (done)
有為 **yūi** capable, effective, promising
ui vicissitudes of life
有為転変 **ui-tenpen** vicissitudes of life
7 作為 **sakui** artificiality; commission (of a crime)
8 所為 **shoi** work, feat **sei** an effect of, due to
12 無為 **mui** idleness, inaction
敢為 **kan'i** daring, intrepid, brave

───────── 3 ─────────

8 性行為 **sei kōi** sex act, intercourse
11 商行為 **shōkōi** business transaction
12 無作為 **musakui** random (sample)

───────── 4 ─────────

4 不正行為 **fusei kōi** an unfair practice, wrongdoing, malpractice, cheating, foul play
9 単独行為 **tandoku kōi** acting on one's own
11 寄附行為 **kifu kōi** act of endowment, donation
脱法行為 **dappō kōi** an evasion of the law
12 無償行為 **mushō kōi** gratuitous act, volunteer service

───────── 6 ─────────

4d6.1

烙

RAKU to brand (cattle/criminals)

───────── 1 ─────────

6 烙印 **rakuin** branding iron; brand, mark, stigma

───────── 2 ─────────

12 焙烙 **hōraku** earthen parching/baking pan

4d6.2

烘

KŌ bonfire; burn

烟 → 煙 **4d9.3**

4d6.3 / 1331

烈

RETSU, hage(shii) violent, intense

───────── 1 ─────────

3 烈々 **retsuretsu** ardent, fierce, fervent
烈女 **retsujo** heroic woman
烈士 **resshi** patriot, hero
4 烈夫 **reppu** patriot, hero
烈日 **retsujitsu** blazing sun
烈火 **rekka** raging fire
9 烈風 **reppū** violent wind, gale
11 烈婦 **reppu** heroic woman
15 烈震 **resshin** violent earthquake

───────── 2 ─────────

6 壮烈 **sōretsu** heroic, brave
7 芳烈 **hōretsu** rich aroma; fine achievement
8 苛烈 **karetsu** severe, relentless
忠烈 **chūretsu** unswerving loyalty
武烈 **Buretsu** (emperor, 498–506)
9 勇烈 **yūretsu** brave, valiant, intrepid
貞烈 **teiretsu** very virtuous/chaste
10 猛烈 **mōretsu** fierce, violent, intense
峻烈 **shunretsu** severe, scathing, sharp
烈烈 **retsuretsu** ardent, fierce, fervent
11 強烈 **kyōretsu** strong, intense, powerful
12 痛烈 **tsūretsu** severe, bitter, scathing
13 義烈 **giretsu** nobility of soul, heroism
14 酷烈 **kokuretsu** intense, rigorous
15 熱烈 **netsuretsu** ardent, impassioned
16 激烈 **gekiretsu** violent, vehement, intense
熾烈 **shiretsu** keen, fierce, hot

───────── 3 ─────────

9 秋霜烈日 **shūsō-retsujitsu** withering frost and scorching sun; harsh, severe, exacting

4d6.4

休

KŌ boasting
KYŪ fortunate; beautiful

4d6.5

烏

U, O, karasu crow, raven

───────── 1 ─────────

3 烏口 **karasuguchi** drafting/ruling pen
4 烏天狗 **karasu tengu** crow-billed goblin
6 烏瓜 **karasuuri** snake gourd
烏合衆 **ugō(no)shū** disorderly crowd, mob

烏羽玉 **ubatama** jet/raven/pitch black
烏行水 **karasu (no) gyōzui** a quick bath
烏有先生 **Uyū-sensei** fictitious person
烏有帰 **uyū (ni) ki(suru)** be reduced to ashes
7 烏麦 **karasumugi** oats
烏貝 **karasugai** (a freshwater mussel)
8 烏金 **karasugane** money lent at daily interest
12 烏帽子 **eboshi** noble's court headgear
13 烏賊 **ika** squid, cuttlefish
14 烏滸 **oko(gamashii)** presumptuous; ridiculous
烏滸沙汰 **oko(no)sata** absurd; impertinent
烏鳴 **karasuna(ki)** caw/cry of the crow

───────── 3 ─────────

3 三羽烏 **sanbagarasu** triumvirate
11 深山烏 **miyamagarasu** mountain crow

───────── 7 ─────────

4d7.1

烽

HŌ, noroshi signal fire

───────── 1 ─────────

4 烽火 **noroshi** signal fire

焖→焖 **4d5.6**

焔→焔 **4d8.5**

4d7.2 / 206

黒 黑

KOKU, kuro, kuro(i) black
kuro(bamu/zumu/maru) become black/dark
kuro(meru) make black, blacken

───────── 1 ─────────

2 黒人 **kokujin** a black, Negro
黒子 **kuroko** black-clad stagehand
kokushi (facial) mole; miniscule thing
hokuro (facial) mole
黒八丈 **kurohachijō** (a type of thick black silk)
3 黒々 **kuroguro** dark black
黒土 **kokudo, kurotsuchi** black soil
黒山 **kuroyama** large crowd
4 黒内障 **kokunaishō** black cataract, amaurosis
黒文字 **kuromoji** spicebush; toothpick
黒水引 **kuromizuhiki** black-and-white string
黒木 **kuroki** unbarked logs; ebony, blackwood

5 黒字 **kuroji** in the black
黒白 **kuro-shiro, kokuhaku, kokubyaku** black and white; right and wrong
黒石 **kuroishi** black stone (in go)
黒目 **kurome** black eyes; the iris and pupil
6 黒死病 **kokushibyō** bubonic plague, black death
黒色 **kokushoku** black
黒地 **kuroji** black background/cloth
黒光 **kurobika(ri)** black luster
黒百合 **kuroyuri** (a variety of dark-purple lily)
黒衣 **kokui** black clothes
黒血 **kurochi** blackish/purulent blood
黒米 **kurogome** unpolished rice
黒竹 **kurochiku** black bamboo
7 黒作 **kurozuku(ri)** salted cuttlefish mixed with their ink
黒坊 **kuro(n)bō** nigger, darkie; black-clad stagehand
黒豆 **kuromame** black soybean
8 黒表 **kokuhyō** blacklist
黒松 **kuromatsu** black pine
黒枠 **kurowaku** black border/edges
黒板 **kokuban** blackboard
黒服 **kurofuku** black clothes
黒房 **kurobusa** black tassel hung over the northwest of a sumo ring
9 黒点 **kokuten** black/dark spot; sunspot
黒海 **Kokkai** the Black Sea
黒炭 **kokutan** bituminous coal
黒星 **kuroboshi** black spot/dot; bull's-eye; a defeat, failure
黒砂糖 **kurozatō** unrefined/brown sugar
11 黒黒 **kuroguro** dark black
黒船 **kurofune** the black ships (historical)
12 黒猩々 **kuroshōjō** chimpanzee
黒焼 **kuroya(ki)** charred
黒斑 **kurobuchi, kurofu** black spots/patches
黒装束 **kuroshōzoku** black clothes
黒痣 **kuroaza** (facial) mole
黒焦 **kuroko(ge)** charred, burned black
黒雲 **kurokumo, kokuun** dark clouds
13 黒塗 **kuronu(ri)** black-lacquered, painted black
黒幕 **kuromaku** black curtain; behind-the-scenes mastermind, wirepuller
黒煙 **kokuen, kurokemuri** black smoke
黒褐色 **kokkasshoku** blackish brown
黒鉛 **kokuen** black lead, graphite
14 黒漆 **kokushitsu** black lacquer
黒髪 **kurokami, kokuhatsu** black hair
黒熊 **kurokuma** black bear
15 黒潮 **Kuroshio** the Japan Current
黒影 **kokuei** dark shadow
黒穂病 **kurohobyō** smut, blight
黒縁 **kurobuchi** black-rimmed (eyeglasses)

4

木
月
日
火 7←
衤
王
牛
方
攵
欠
心
戸
戈

16 黒頭巾 **kurozukin** black hood
17 黒檀 **kokutan** ebony, blackwood
18 黒曜石 **kokuyōseki** obsidian
19 黒蟻 **kuroari** black ant
23 黒黴 **kurokabi** bread mold

——— 2 ———

3 大黒 **Daikoku** god of wealth
大黒柱 **daikokubashira** central pillar; pillar, mainstay
土黒 **tsuchiguro(i)** dark dirt color
4 中黒 **nakaguro** the centered-dot punctuation mark (·)
5 白黒 **shiro-kuro** black-and-white; right or wrong, guilty or innocent
6 色黒 **iroguro** dark-complexioned, dark-skinned
7 赤黒 **akaguro(i)** dark red
9 浅黒 **asaguro(i)** dark-colored, swarthy
10 真黒 **ma(k)kuro** jet-black, coal-black
11 黒黒 **kuroguro** dark black
12 歯黒 **(o)haguro** tooth blackening
13 腹黒 **haraguro(i)** black-hearted, scheming
暗黒 **ankoku** darkness
暗黒面 **ankokumen** the dark/seamy side
暗黒街 **ankokugai** the underworld
14 漆黒 **shikkoku** jet-black, pitch-black
16 薄黒 **usuguro(i)** dark, dusky, umber

4d7.3

焉
EN, izuku(nzo) how, why

——— 2 ———

11 終焉 **shūen** one's last moments, death
13 慊焉 **ken'en** be dissatisfied/displeased

——— 8 ———

煉 → 煉 **4d9.2**

4d8.1

焙
HŌ, abu(ru) roast, broil, toast, grill

——— 1 ———

0 焙じる **hō(jiru)** fire, heat, roast, toast
9 焙茶 **hō(ji)cha** toasted/roasted tea
10 焙烙 **hōraku** earthen parching/baking pan

——— 2 ———

4 手焙 **teabu(ri)** hand-warmer, small hibachi
火焙 **hiabu(ri)** execution by fire, burning at the stake

4d8.2

焜
KON shine

——— 1 ———

8 焜炉 **konro** portable cooking stove

4d8.3

焠
SAI, nama(su), nira(gu) quench, temper, anneal

4d8.4 / 920

焼 燒
SHŌ, ya(ku) (tr.) burn; roast, broil, bake **ya(keru)** (intr.) burn; be roasted/broiled/baked

——— 1 ———

2 焼入 **ya(ki)i(re)** hardening, tempering
3 焼刃 **ya(ki)ba** tempered blade
焼上 **ya(ki)a(geru)** burn up; bake
焼山 **ya(ke)yama** mountain whose vegetation has burned; dormant volcano
4 焼太 **ya(ke)buto(ri)** becoming richer after a fire
焼太刀 **ya(ki)tachi** tempered-bladed sword
焼切 **ya(ke)ki(ru)** burn itself out
ya(ki)ki(ru) burn out/off
焼火箸 **ya(ke)hibashi** red-hot tongs
5 焼出 **ya(ke)da(sareru)** be burned out/homeless
焼失 **shōshitsu** be destroyed by fire
焼付 **ya(ki)tsu(keru)** bake onto, bake (china), fuse
ya(ki)tsu(ku) be burned/seared onto
焼払 **ya(ki)hara(u)** burn up/away
焼打 **ya(ki)u(chi)** attack by burning, set afire
焼穴 **ya(ke)ana** a burn hole
焼玉機関 **ya(ki)dama kikan** hot-bulb/semidiesel engine
焼石 **ya(ke)ishi** heated stone
焼立 **ya(ki)ta(te)** fresh baked/roasted
6 焼死 **shōshi, ya(ke)ji(ni)** be burned to death
焼死体 **shōshitai** charred body/remains
焼死者 **shōshisha** person burned to death
焼夷弾 **shōidan** incendiary shell, firebomb
焼肉 **ya(ki)niku** roast/broiled meat
焼印 **ya(ki)in** branding iron; brand, mark, stigma
焼灰 **ya(ke)bai** ashes
焼芋 **ya(ki)imo** baked/roasted sweet potato
焼尽 **ya(ki)tsuku(su)** burn up, consume, reduce to ashes
ya(ke)tsu(kiru) burn itself out
焼団子 **ya(ki)dango** toasted dumpling
焼成 **shōsei** calcination
焼米 **ya(ki)gome** parched/roasted rice

7 焼串　**ya(ki)gushi**　skewer, spit
焼却　**shōkyaku**　destroy by fire, incinerate
焼判　**ya(ki)han, ya(ki)ban**　branding iron; brand, mark, stigma
焼売　**shūmai**　(Chinese-style steamed meat-and-vegetable dumpling)
焼豆腐　**ya(ki)dōfu**　broiled tofu
焼戻　**ya(ki)modo(su)**　anneal, temper
8 焼直　**ya(ki)nao(su)**　rebake; rehash, adapt
焼林檎　**ya(ki)ringo**　baked apple
焼物　**ya(ki)mono**　pottery, ceramics; roast food
焼金　**ya(ki)gane**　branding/marking iron
9 焼海苔　**ya(ki)nori**　toasted seaweed
焼畑　**ya(ki)bata**　burned-over fields
焼香　**shōkō**　burn incense
10 焼残　**ya(ke)noko(ru)**　remain unburned, escape the fire
焼栗　**ya(ki)guri**　roasted chestnuts
焼殺　**ya(ki)koro(su)**　burn (someone) to death
焼討　**ya(ki)u(chi)**　attack by burning, set afire
焼酎　**shōchū**　(a low-grade liquor)
11 焼野　**ya(ke)no**　burnt field
焼野原　**ya(ke)nohara**　burned-out area
焼過　**ya(ki)su(giru)**　overcook
焼接　**ya(ki)tsu(gi)**　cement (broken china) together by baking
焼捨　**ya(ki)su(teru)**　burn up, incinerate
焼豚　**ya(ki)buta, ya(ki)ton**　roast pork
焼痕　**shōkon**　scar from a burn
焼魚　**ya(ki)zakana**　broiled fish
焼鳥　**ya(ki)tori**　grilled chicken
12 焼場　**ya(ki)ba**　crematory
焼落　**ya(ke)o(chiru)**　burn and collapse
焼結　**shōketsu**　sintering
焼絵　**ya(ki)e**　pyrograph; pyrography
焼筆　**ya(ki)fude**　charcoal (sketching) pencil
焼鈍　**shōdon, ya(ki)nama(shi)**　annealing
焼飯　**ya(ki)meshi**　fried rice
焼焦　**ya(ke)ko(ge)**　burn hole, scorch
13 焼塩　**ya(ki)shio**　baked/table salt
焼跡　**ya(ke)ato**　fire ruins
14 焼増　**ya(ki)ma(shi)**　an extra print (of a photo)
焼網　**ya(ki)ami**　toasting/broiling grill
15 焼餅　**ya(ki)mochi**　toasted rice cake; jealousy

――――――― 2 ―――――――

3 夕焼　**yūya(ke)**　red/glowing sunset
丸焼　**maruya(ki)**　barbecue
　　　maruya(ke)　totally destroyed by fire
土焼　**tsuchiya(ki)**　unglazed earthenware
山焼　**yamaya(ki)**　burning of dead grass
4 毛焼　**keya(ki)**　singe
手焼　**teya(ki)**　home-baked
　　　te (o) ya(ku)　burn one's fingers, have a bitter experience with
日焼　**hiya(ke)**　sunburn; suntan
5 半焼　**han'ya(ke)**　half-burnt; half-done, rare

生焼　**namaya(ke)**　half-cooked, underdone, rare
付焼刃　**tsu(ke)yakiba**　affectation, pretension
好焼　**(o)kono(mi)ya(ki)**　(unsweetened batter fried with vegetable bits into a thick griddlecake)
白焼　**shiraya(ki)**　unseasoned broiled fish
6 全焼　**zenshō**　be totally destroyed by fire
7 串焼　**kushiya(ki)**　spit-roasted
卵焼　**tamagoyaki**　fried eggs; square frypan
延焼　**enshō**　spread of a fire
貝焼　**kaiya(ki)**　cooked in the shell
9 炭焼　**sumiya(ki)**　charcoal making/maker
10 浜焼　**hamaya(ki)**　(sea bream) broiled whole (at the beach)
胸焼　**muneya(ke)**　heartburn
素焼　**suya(ki)**　unglazed pottery, bisque
11 野焼　**noya(ki)**　winter burning of the fields
黒焼　**kuroya(ki)**　charred
雪焼　**yukiya(ke)**　tanned by snow-reflected sunlight
12 蒸焼　**mu(shi)ya(ki)**　baking in a covered casserole
壺焼　**tsuboya(ki)**　shellfish cooked in its
朝焼　**asaya(ke)**　red sunrise
筏焼　**ikadaya(ki)**　split-open fish speared on spits and broiled
軽焼　**karuya(ki)**　wafer, cracker
13 塩焼　**shioya(ki)**　broiled with salt
楽焼　**rakuya(ki)**　hand-molded pottery
照焼　**te(ri)ya(ki)**　fish broiled with soy sauce
14 網焼　**amiya(ki)**　grilled (steak)
15 潮焼　**shioya(ke)**　tanned by salt air
鋤焼　**sukiya(ki)**　sukiyaki
16 薄焼　**usuya(ki)**　lightly baked/fried
燃焼　**nenshō**　combustion
17 罅焼　**hibiya(ki)**　crackleware
鍋焼　**nabeya(ki)**　boiled in a pot, baked in a casserole
霜焼　**shimoya(ke)**　frostbite
18 類焼　**ruishō**　a spreading fire
19 鯛焼　**taiya(ki)**　fish-shaped griddle cake filled with bean jam

――――――― 3 ―――――――

2 七宝焼　**shippōyaki**　cloisonné
5 目玉焼　**medamaya(ki)**　sunny-side-up fried eggs
6 有田焼　**Aritaya(ki)**　Arita porcelainware
10 唐津焼　**karatsuya(ki)**　earthenware, china
19 瀬戸焼　**setoya(ki)**　porcelain, china

4d8.5

焔　焔燄　　　　EN, honō　flame

――――――― 1 ―――――――

3 焔々　**en'en**　blazing, fiery

12 焔硝 **enshō** gunpowder; niter

─────── 2 ───────

4 火焔 **kaen** flame
6 気焔 **kien** big talk; high spirits
気焔万丈 **kien-banjō** high spirits
光焔 **kōen** (light and) flame

4d8.6

焱

EN, honō flame, blaze

4d8.7

焚

FUN, ta(ku) burn, light a fire; cook

─────── 1 ───────

3 焚口 **ta(ki)guchi** fuel-feed hole, furnace hatch
4 焚火 **ta(ki)bi** open-air fire, bonfire
5 焚付 **ta(ki)tsu(keru)** light, kindle; instigate
6 焚尽 **ta(ki)tsu(kusu)** burn up, run out of (fuel)
8 焚物 **ta(ki)mono** firewood
10 焚書 **funsho** book burning

─────── 2 ───────

4 火焚 **hita(ki)** making a fire

4d8.8 / 93

無

MU, BU not; (as prefix) un-, without, -less, -free **na(shi)** not be; (as suffix) without **na(i)** not be **na(kusu)** lose; get rid of; run out of **na(ku naru)** be gone/lost/missing, run out of; die

─────── 1 ───────

1 無一文 **muichimon** penniless
無一物 **muichibutsu, muichimotsu** penniless
2 無二 **muni** peerless, unequaled
無二無三 **muni-musan** like mad, furiously; forcibly
無人 **mujin, munin** uninhabited; unmanned **bunin** shortage of help
無人地帯 **mujin chitai** no man's land
無人島 **mujintō** uninhabited island
無力 **muryoku** powerless, ineffectual, feeble; incompetent
3 無才 **musai** untalented, incompetent
無干渉 **mukanshō** nonintervention
無上 **mujō** supreme, greatest, highest
無下 **muge (ni)** (refuse) flatly, (denounce) roundly
無口 **mukuchi** taciturn, reticent, laconic
4 無毛 **mumō** hairless
無双 **musō** unequaled, unparalleled
無双窓 **musōmado** openable panel in a door

無分別 **mufunbetsu** imprudent, thoughtless, rash
無辺 **muhen** limitless, boundless, infinite
無辺際 **muhensai** limitless, boundless, infinite
無水 **musui** anhydrous, waterless, dry (weight)
無手 **mute** empty-handed; unarmed; without funds
無手法 **mute(p)pō** reckless, rash
無月 **mugetsu** moonless (sky)
無月謝 **mugessha** free tuition
無方針 **muhōshin** without a plan
無欠 **muketsu** flawless
無欠席 **mukesseki** perfect attendance
無心 **mushin** absorbed in (play); request, cadge
5 無生 **musei** lifeless, inanimate
無生物 **museibutsu** inanimate object
無代 **mudai** free, without charge
無比 **muhi** incomparable, matchless, unrivaled
無用 **muyō** useless; needless; without business; prohibited
無用心 **buyōjin** unsafe; incautious
無用長物 **muyō (no) chōbutsu** useless obstruction
無札 **musatsu** (passenger) without a ticket
無礼 **burei** discourtesy, rudeness
無礼者 **bureimono, bureisha** insolent person
無礼講 **bureikō** free-and-easy get-together
無主物 **mushubutsu** ownerless article/property
6 無死 **mushi** no outs (and bases loaded)
無気力 **mukiryoku** spiritless, flabby, gutless
無気味 **bukimi** ominous, eerie
無休 **mukyū** no holidays, always open (shop)
無任所大臣 **muninsho daijin** minister without portfolio
無防備 **mubōbi** defenseless, unfortified
無考 **mukanga(e)** thoughtless, rash
無色 **mushoku** colorless, achromatic
無地 **muji** solid color
無名 **mumei** anonymous; an unknown
無名氏 **mumeishi** anonymous person
無名指 **mumeishi** the ring finger
無名戦士 **mumei senshi** unknown soldier
無尽 **mujin** inexhaustible, endless; mutual financing association
無尽蔵 **mujinzō** inexhaustible supply
無灯 **mutō** no lighting, lights out
無自覚 **mujikaku** unconscious of, blind to
無血 **muketsu** bloodless, without bloodshed
7 無我 **muga** selflessness, self-forgetfulness
無我夢中 **muga-muchū** total absorption, ecstasy
無位 **mui** without rank, commoner
無体 **mutai** forcible; intangible (assets)

無作法 **busahō** bad manners, rudeness
無作為 **musakui** random (sample)
無住 **mujū** (temple) without a resident priest
無何有郷 **mukau (no) sato** an unspoiled paradise, utopia
無邪気 **mujaki** innocent, ingenuous
無医村 **muison** doctorless village
無沙汰 **busata** silence, neglect to write/call
無批判 **muhihan** uncritical
無技巧 **mugikō** artless
無技能 **muginō** unskilled
無投票 **mutōhyō** dispensing with voting
無告 **mukoku** with nowhere to turn to, helpless
無形 **mukei** intangible
無形文化財 **mukei-bunkazai** intangible cultural asset
無花果 **ichijiku** fig
無芸 **mugei** having no accomplishments
無学 **mugaku** unlettered, ignorant
無声 **musei** silent, noiseless, voiceless
無声映画 **musei eiga** silent movie
無声音 **museion** unvoiced sound
無条件 **mujōken** unconditional
無利子 **murishi** non-interest-bearing
無利息 **murisoku** non-interest-bearing
無私 **mushi** unselfish, disinterested
無季 **muki** (haiku) without reference to a season
無言 **mugon** silent, mute
無言行 **mugon (no) gyō** ascetic silence
無言劇 **mugongeki** pantomime
8 無表情 **muhyōjō** expressionless
無毒 **mudoku** nonpoisonous
無事 **buji** safe and sound
無事故 **mujiko** without accident/trouble
無価 **muka** priceless
無価値 **mukachi** worthless
無念 **munen** regret, resentment, vexation
無念無想 **munen-musō** blank state of mind
無限 **mugen** infinite
無限大 **mugendai** infinity
無限小 **mugenshō** infinitesimal
無限遠 **mugen'en** (focused) at infinity
無制限 **museigen** unlimited, unrestricted
無効 **mukō** null, void, invalid, ineffective
無免許 **mumenkyo** without a license
無法 **muhō** unjust, unlawful, outrageous
無法者 **muhōmono** outrageous fellow, outlaw
無抵抗 **muteikō** nonresistance, passive obedience
無担保 **mutanpo** unsecured, without collateral
無味 **mumi** tasteless, flat, dry
無味乾燥 **mumi-kansō** dry as dust, uninteresting

無知 **muchi** ignorance
無知蒙昧 **muchi-mōmai** unenlightened
無始 **mushi** without beginning, since the infinite past
無妻 **musai** without a wife, single
無妻主義 **musai shugi** celibacy
無実 **mujitsu** false, unfounded; innocent
無実罪 **mujitsu (no) tsumi** false accusation
無官 **mukan** holding no office
無定形 **muteikei** amorphous
無定見 **muteiken** lack of principle, inconstant
無届 **mutodo(ke)** without advance notice
無明 **mumyō** ignorance, darkness
無性 **musei** asexual **mushō** thoughtless; inordinate **bushō** lazy
無所得 **mushotoku** without any income
無所属 **mushozoku** unaffiliated, independent
9 無重力 **mujūryoku** weightlessness
無重量 **mujūryō** weightlessness
無信心 **mushinjin** impiety, unbelief, infidelity
無冠 **mukan** uncrowned
無造作 **muzōsa** with ease; simple, artless
無風 **mufū** windless, dead calm
無風流 **mufūryū** lack of refinement
無風帯 **mufūtai** the doldrums
無派 **muha** unaffiliated, nonpartisan
無垢 **muku** pure
無封書状 **mufū shojō** unsealed letter
無茶 **mucha** absurd; rash; excessive
無茶苦茶 **muchakucha** mixed up, confused; nonsensical; reckless, like mad
無為 **mui** idleness, inaction
無神経 **mushinkei** insensible to
無神論 **mushinron** atheism
無政府 **museifu** anarchy
無政府主義 **museifu shugi** anarchism
無政府主義者 **museifushugisha** anarchist
無音 **buin** long silence, neglect to write/call
muon silent
無臭 **mushū** odorless
無思慮 **mushiryo** thoughtless, imprudent
無計画 **mukeikaku** unplanned, haphazard
無軌道 **mukidō** trackless; erratic, aberrant
10 無残 **muzan** cruel, ruthless; pitiful
無畜 **muchiku** without livestock
無差別 **musabetsu** indiscriminate
無益 **mueki** useless, futile
無酒精 **mushusei** nonalcoholic
無挨拶 **buaisatsu** impoliteness, incivility
無害 **mugai** harmless
無根 **mukon** groundless, unfounded
無骨 **bukotsu** boorish, uncouth
無骨者 **bukotsumono** boor, lout, churl
無能 **munō** incompetent, ineffective
無能力 **munōryoku** incompetent; impotent
無能力者 **munōryokusha** an incompetent

無教会主義 **mukyōkai shugi** Nondenominationalism (a Japanese Christian sect)
無教育 **mukyōiku** uneducated
無秩序 **muchitsujo** disorder, chaos; anomie
無病 **mubyō** well, healthy
無病息災 **mubyō-sokusai** in perfect health
無症状 **mushōjō** without symptoms
無紋 **mumon** solid color; without a crest
無料 **muryō** without charge, free
無粋 **busui** lacking elegance, unromantic
無恥 **muchi** shameless, brazen
無記名 **mukimei** uninscribed (shares), unregistered (bond), blank (endorsement)
無配 **muhai** non-dividend-paying
無配当 **muhaitō** non-dividend-paying
11 無停車 **muteisha** nonstop
無偏 **muhen** unbiased, impartial
無道 **mudō** wicked; unreasonable
無過失 **mukashitsu** no-fault (liability)
無得点 **mutokuten** scoreless (game)
無菌 **mukin** germ-free, sterile, aseptic
無宿 **mushuku** homeless
無宿者 **mushukusha** vagrant, homeless wanderer
無常 **mujō** mutable, transitory, uncertain
無視 **mushi** ignore, disregard
無理 **muri** unreasonable; impossible, beyond one's power, too difficult; by force, against one's will; strain oneself
無理心中 **muri shinjū** murder-suicide
無理矢理 **muriyari** forcibly, under compulsion
無理押 **murio(shi)** pushing things too far
無理往生 **muri-ōjō** forced compliance
無理取 **murido(ri)** exaction, extortion
無理強 **muriji(i)** coercion
無理無体 **muri-mutai** forcible
無理解 **murikai** lack of understanding
無理数 **murisū** irrational number
無理算段 **muri-sandan** scrape together (money)
無理難題 **muri-nandai** unreasonable demand
無欲 **muyoku** free from avarice
無情 **mujō** unfeeling, callous, cruel
無産 **musan** without property
無産者 **musansha** proletarian, have-nots
無産党 **musantō** proletarian party
無産階級 **musan kaikyū** the proletariat
無規律 **mukiritsu** disorderly, undisciplined
無疵 **mukizu** undamaged, unblemished, unhurt
無経験 **mukeiken** inexperience
無断 **mudan** unannounced; unauthorized
無聊 **buryō** ennui, tedium, boredom
無責任 **musekinin** irresponsibility

12 無辜 **muko** innocent, harmless
無着陸 **muchakuriku** nonstop (flight)
無遠慮 **buenryo** unreserved, forward, impertinent
無報酬 **muhōshū** without pay, for free
無帽 **mubō** hatless
無勝負 **mushōbu** a tie/draw, undecided
無期 **muki** indefinite
無期刑 **mukikei** life imprisonment
無期延期 **muki enki** indefinite postponement
無期限 **mukigen** indefinite, without time limit
無期懲役 **muki chōeki** life imprisonment
無量 **muryō** beyond measure, immense
無税 **muzei** tax-free, duty-free
無痛 **mutsū** painless
無痛分娩 **mutsū bunben** painless childbirth
無給 **mukyū** unpaid, nonsalaried
無統制 **mutōsei** uncontrolled
無筆 **muhitsu** illiterate, unlettered
無策 **musaku** resourceless, at a loss
無答責 **mutōseki** not liable
無間地獄 **muken jigoku** (a Buddhist hell)
13 無傷 **mukizu** uninjured, undamaged, unblemished
無勢 **buzei** numerical inferiority
無慈悲 **mujihi** merciless, ruthless
無蓋 **mugai** open, uncovered
無蓋貨車 **mugai kasha** open freight car
無腰 **mugoshi** unarmed
無暗 **muyami** thoughtless, rash; excessive; unnecessary
無煙 **muen** smokeless
無煙炭 **muentan** anthracite coal
無数 **musū** innumerable, countless
無愛想 **buaisō** unsociable, curt
無愛嬌 **buaikyō** unamiable, unsociable
無想 **musō** making one's mind a blank
無感覚 **mukankaku** insensible, numb, callous
無碍 **muge** free of obstacles
無意 **mui** lack of will/meaning
無意味 **muimi** meaningless, pointless
無意義 **muiteki** unwilling; meaningless
無意義 **muigi** meaningless, not significant
無意識 **muishiki** unconscious, involuntary
無罪 **muzai** innocent, not guilty
無罪判決 **muzai hanketsu** acquittal
無節制 **musessei** intemperate
無節操 **musessō** inconstant; unchaste
無試験 **mushiken** without an examination
無賃 **muchin** free of charge
無賃乗車 **muchin jōsha** free/stolen ride
無資力 **mushiryoku** without funds
無資本 **mushihon** without capital/funds
無資格 **mushikaku** unqualified
無資格者 **mushikakusha** unqualified/incompetent person

無鉄砲　**muteppō** reckless, rash
無電　**muden** wireless, radio
無電放送　**muden hōsō** radio broadcast
無頓着　**mutonjaku, mutonchaku** indifferent/unattentive to
14 無様　**buzama** misshapen, clumsy, awkward
無精　**bushō** lazy
無精卵　**museiran** unfertilized egg
無精髭　**bushōhige** stubbly beard
無銭　**musen** without money
無銭旅行　**musen ryokō** penniless travel, hitchhiking
無銭飲食　**musen inshoku** jumping a restaurant bill
無銘　**mumei** unsigned, bearing no signature
無雑　**muzatsu** pure, unadulterated
無関心　**mukanshin** indifference, unconcern, apathy
無関係　**mukankei** unrelated, irrelevant
無駄　**muda** futile, useless, wasteful
無駄口　**mudaguchi** idle talk, prattle
無駄死　**mudaji(ni)** die in vain
無駄花　**mudabana** flower which bears no seed/fruit
無駄足　**mudaashi** make a fruitless trip/visit
無駄食　**mudagu(i)** eat between meals; eat but not work, live in idleness
無駄骨　**mudabone** wasted/vain effort
無駄骨折　**mudaboneo(ri)** wasted/vain effort
無駄遣　**mudazuka(i)** waste, squander
無駄飯　**mudameshi** eat but not work, live in idleness
無駄話　**mudabanashi** idle talk, gossip
15 無慮　**muryo** as many as, approximately
無器用　**bukiyō** clumsy
無窮　**mukyū** endless, perpetual, eternal
無熱　**munetsu** with no fever
無敵　**muteki** invincible, unrivaled
無線　**musen** wireless, radio
無線電信　**musen denshin** radiotelegraph
無線電話　**musen denwa** radiotelephone
無縁　**muen** unrelated; with no surviving relatives
無縁仏　**muenbotoke** a deceased having no one to tend his grave
無趣味　**mushumi** lack of taste, vulgarity
無論　**muron** of course, naturally
無調法　**buchōhō** impolite; clumsy, unaccustomed to
16 無機　**muki** inorganic
無機物　**mukibutsu** inorganic substance, minerals
無稽　**mukei** unfounded
無糖　**mutō** sugar-free, unsweetened
無謀　**mubō** incautious, reckless
無頼　**burai** villainous

無頼漢　**buraikan** villain, hooligan, outlaw
無頭　**mutō** headless
17 無償　**mushō** free, gratuitous
無償行為　**mushō kōi** gratuitous act, volunteer service
無闇　**muyami** thoughtless, rash; excessive; unnecessary
18 無職　**mushoku** unemployed; no occupation
無職者　**mushokusha** the unemployed
無難　**bunan** safe, acceptable
無類　**murui** finest, choicest
無題　**mudai** untitled
19 無警告　**mukeikoku** without warning
無警察　**mukeisatsu** lawlessness, anarchy
無韻詩　**muinshi** blank verse, unrhymed poem
20 無競争　**mukyōsō** without competition, unopposed
無籍者　**musekimono** person without registered domicile; vagrant; outcast
23 無鑑札　**mukansatsu** without a license

────────── 2 ──────────

2 力無　**chikarana(ge)** feebly, dejectedly
4 父無子　**chichina(shi)go, tetena(shi)go** fatherless/illegitimate child
水無月　**minazuki** sixth lunar month, June
心無　**kokorona(i)** heartless, cruel; thoughtless, ill-considered
5 用無　**yōna(shi)** idle; unneeded, unwanted
台無　**daina(shi)** ruined, come to nought
白無垢　**shiromuku** (dressed) all in white
6 気無精　**kibushō** laziness
名無　**nana(shi)** nameless, anonymous, unknown
有無　**umu** existence of, whether there is or isn't; yes or no
有無相通　**umu-aitsū(jiru)** help each other, be complementary
7 芸無　**geina(shi)** unaccomplished
8 事無　**koto(mo)na(ge)** careless, casual, nonchalant　**kotona(ku)** without incident, uneventfully
限無　**kagi(ri)na(i)** boundless, endless, unlimited
底無　**sokona(shi)** bottomless
9 南無阿弥陀仏　**Namu Amida Butsu** Hail Amida Buddha
南無妙法蓮華経　**Namu Myōhō Rengekyō** Hail Lotus Sutra
首無　**kubina(shi)** headless
待無　**ma(tta)na(shi)** without waiting
皆無　**kaimu** nothing/none at all
神無月　**kannazuki** tenth lunar month, October
珍無類　**chinmurui** singular, phenomenal, strange

4

木 月 日 火 礻 王 牛 方 攵 欠 心 戸 戈

8←

10 根無 **nena(shi)** rootless; groundless
根無草 **nena(shi)gusa** duckweed; something unsettled, rootless person
骨無 **honena(shi)** rickets; spineless/weak-willed person
袖無 **sodena(shi)** sleeveless
11 隈無 **kumana(ku)** in every nook and cranny, everywhere
虚無 **kyomu** nothingness
虚無主義 **kyomu shugi** nihilism
虚無的 **kyomuteki** nihilistic
虚無党 **kyomutō** nihilists
虚無僧 **komusō** mendicant flute-playing Zen priest
術無 **subena(shi)** nothing can be done
宿無 **yadona(shi)** homeless person, vagrant
情無 **nasa(ke)na(i)** unfeeling, cruel; pitiful, miserable
訳無 **wakena(i)** easy, simple
12 遑無 **itoma (ga) na(i)** have no time (to enumerate/react)
揺無 **yu(rugi)na(i)** firm, solid, steady
御無沙汰 **gobusata** neglect to visit/write
落無 **o(chi)na(ku)** without exception
程無 **hodona(ku)** soon (afterward), by and by
絶無 **zetsumu** nothing, naught, nil
間無 **ma(mo)na(ku)** presently, in a little while, soon
13 詮無 **senna(i)** useless, unavailing
14 漏無 **mo(re)na(ku)** without exception
端無 **hashina(ku mo)** suddenly, unexpectedly, by chance **hashi(ta)na(i)** vulgar
種無 **tanena(shi)** seedless
15 窮無 **kiwama(ri)na(i)** endless
16 親無 **oyana(shi)** parentless, orphaned
親無子 **oyana(shi)go** orphan
18 難無 **nanna(ku)** without difficulty

――――― 3 ―――――

1 一文無 **ichimonna(shi)** penniless
3 大逆無道 **daigyaku-mudō** high treason
千万無量 **senman-muryō** innumerable
4 勿体無 **mottaina(i)** more than one deserves, too good for; wasteful
天下無双 **tenka-musō** unique, unequaled
天下無比 **tenka-muhi** unique, incomparable
天衣無縫 **ten'i-muhō** flawless, perfect
天壌無窮 **tenjō mukyū** eternal as heaven and earth
公平無私 **kōhei-mushi** fair and disinterested
引切無 **hi(k)ki(ri)na(shi ni)** incessantly
5 広大無辺 **kōdai-muhen** boundless, immeasurable, vast
6 有名無実 **yūmei-mujitsu** in name only
有形無形 **yūkei-mukei** tangible and intangible, material and spiritual

有耶無耶 **uyamuya** noncommittal
有害無益 **yūgai-mueki** harmful, more harm than good
有象無象 **uzō-muzō** all things tangible and intangible; the rabble, riffraff
7 何気無 **nanigena(ku)** unintentionally; nonchalantly
呆気無 **akkena(i)** unsatisfying, not enough
否応無 **iyaōna(shi)** whether one likes it or not
完全無欠 **kanzen-muketsu** flawlessly perfect
8 事実無根 **jijitsu mukon** contrary to fact, unfounded
味気無 **ajikena(i)** irksome, wearisome, dreary
取留無 **to(ri)to(me)na(i)** rambling, fanciful, incoherent, pointless
金甌無欠 **kin'ō-muketsu, kinnō-muketsu** perfect, unblemished
9 荒唐無稽 **kōtō-mukei** absurdity, nonsense
面目無 **menbokuna(i)** ashamed
10 致方無 **ita(shi)kata (ga) na(i)** it can't be helped
11 清浄無垢 **shōjō-muku** immaculate, pure and innocent
乾燥無味 **kansō-mumi** dry, dull
12 傍若無人 **bōjaku-bujin** arrogant, insolent
無二無三 **muni-musan** like mad, furiously; forcibly
無念無想 **munen-musō** blank state of mind
無理無体 **muri-mutai** forcible
然気無 **sa(ri)gena(i)** nonchalant, casual
13 傲慢無礼 **gōman-burei** arrogant and insolent
感慨無量 **kangai-muryō** full of emotion
14 摑所無 **tsuka(mi)dokoro (no) na(i)** slippery, evasive
15 諸行無常 **shogyō-mujō** All things change. Nothing lasts.
16 縦横無尽 **jūō-mujin** all around, no end of

――――― 4 ―――――

8 枚挙遑無 **maikyo (ni) itoma (ga) na(i)** too numerous to mention
12 腑甲斐無 **fugaina(i)** faint-hearted, feckless
16 薬石効無 **yakusekikō na(ku)** all remedies having proved unavailing

黑 → 黒 **4d7.2**

4d8.9 / 1795

煮 煮 **SHA, ni(eru/ru)** (intr./tr.) boil, cook **ni** cooking **ni(yasu)** (tr.) boil

――――― 1 ―――――

3 煮干 **nibo(shi)** dried sardines
煮上 **ni(e)a(garu), nia(garu)** boil up, be thoroughly cooked

4 煮切 **ni(e)ki(ranai)** undercooked; indecisive
煮込 **niko(mu)** boil well, stew, cook together
煮方 **nikata** way of cooking; a cook
5 煮出 **nida(su)** boil down, decoct
煮出汁 **nida(shi)jiru** soup stock, broth
煮付 **nitsu(ke)** vegetables/fish boiled hard
　　　with soy sauce
煮加減 **ni(e)kagen** amount of boiling
煮立 **nita(tsu)** boil up, come to a boil
6 煮返 **ni(e)kae(su)** reboil, cook over again
7 煮豆 **nimame** boiled beans
煮売屋 **niu(ri)ya** eatery, cheap restaurant
8 煮沸 **shafutsu** boiling
煮炊 **nita(ki)** cooking
煮物 **nimono** cooking; cooked food
9 煮染 **nishi(meru)** boil hard with soy sauce
11 煮過 **nisu(giru), nisu(gosu)** overboil
煮魚 **nizakana** fish boiled with soy sauce
12 煮湯 **ni(e)yu** boiling water
13 煮詰 **nitsu(maru)** be boiled down
14 煮滾 **ni(e)tagi(ru)** boil up, seethe
16 煮凝 **nikogo(ri)** jellied/congealed fish (broth)
19 煮繰返 **ni(e)ku(ri)kae(ru)** boil, seethe

─────────── 2 ───────────

4 水煮 **mizuni** boiled (in unsalted water)
5 半煮 **hanni(e)** parboiled
生煮 **namani(e)** half-cooked, underdone
7 佃煮 **tsukudani** (boiled dish of small fish,
　　　shellfish, soy sauce, etc.)
12 湯煮 **yuni** boil, boiled
14 雑煮 **zōni** rice cakes boiled with vegetables

─────────── 3 ───────────

5 甘露煮 **kanroni** sweet dish of boiled fish or
　　　shellfish
9 砂糖煮 **satōni** preserved by boiling with
　　　sugar, candied

4d8.10 / 651

然 **ZEN, NEN** as, like　**sō, sa** such
sō(shite) and　**sa(ru)** a certain, such
sa(redo) but, however　**sa(ri to wa)** if
so, well　**shika** so, thus　**shika(shi)** but,
however　**shika(ru)** be so　**shika(ru ni)** but,
nevertheless　**shika(ri)** yes, quite so
shika(rubeki) as it should be, proper, right

─────────── 1 ───────────

0 然らしめる **shika(rashimeru)** make it so,
　　　decree
3 然々 **shikajika** such and such; and so on
5 然乍 **shika(shi)naga(ra)** however
6 然気無 **sa(ri)gena(i)** nonchalant, casual
然迄 **samade** to that extent, so much
8 然者 **sa(ru)mono** a man of no common order
12 然斯 **so(u)ko(u)** this and that; meanwhile
然程 **sahodo** so much, very

14 然様 **sayō** so, thus, such
15 然諾重 **zendaku (o) omo(njiru)** keep one's
　　　word

─────────── 2 ───────────

4 天然 **tennen** natural
天然色 **tennenshoku** natural color,
　　　technicolor
天然記念物 **tennen kinenbutsu** natural
　　　monument
天然痘 **tennentō** smallpox
天然資源 **tennen shigen** natural resources
公然 **kōzen** open, public
5 必然 **hitsuzen** inevitability, necessity
必然性 **hitsuzensei** inevitability, necessity
本然 **honzen, honnen** natural, inborn,
　　　inherent
未然 **mizen** before (it) happens, beforehand
平然 **heizen** calm, composed, unruffled
6 全然 **zenzen** entirely, utterly, (not) at all
同然 **dōzen** the same as, virtually
当然 **tōzen** of course, naturally
自然 **shizen** nature; natural
自然人 **shizenjin** natural (uncultured) person;
　　　natural (not juridical) person
自然力 **shizenryoku** forces of nature
自然主義 **shizen shugi** naturalism
自然石 **shizenseki** natural stone/gem
自然死 **shizenshi** natural death
自然色 **shizenshoku** natural color
自然法 **shizenhō** natural law
自然的 **shizenteki** natural
自然物 **shizenbutsu** natural object
自然美 **shizenbi** natural beauty
自然科学 **shizen kagaku** the natural
　　　sciences
自然界 **shizenkai** the realm of nature
自然数 **shizensū** natural number, positive
　　　integer
自然観 **shizenkan** one's outlook on nature
7 冷然 **reizen** cold, indifferent, coldhearted
判然 **hanzen** clear, distinct, definite
決然 **ketsuzen** resolute, decisive, firm
呆然 **bōzen (to)** in blank amazement
8 画然 **kakuzen (to)** distinctly, sharply
依然 **izen (to shite)** still, as ever
勃然 **botsuzen (to)** suddenly; in a fit of anger
油然 **yūzen** gushingly, copiously
沛然 **haizen** torrential, downpour, cloudburst
突然 **totsuzen** suddenly, unexpectedly
突然変異 **totsuzen hen'i** mutation
居然 **kyozen** calm, unruffled
欣然 **kinzen** joyful, glad, cheerful
忽然 **kotsuzen** suddenly
怫然 **futsuzen** indignant, sullen
9 俄然 **gazen** all of a sudden, all at once
茫然 **bōzen** vacantly, in a daze

4

木
月
日
火　8←
ネ
王
牛
方
攵
欠
心
戸
戈

茫然自失 **bōzen-jishitsu** abstraction, stupefaction, entrancement
昂然 **kōzen** elated, triumphant
恬然 **tenzen** coolly, nonchalantly
10 陶然 **tōzen** pleasantly drunk; enraptured
泰然 **taizen** calm, composed; firm
泰然自若 **taizen-jijaku** imperturbable
浩然 **kōzen** expansive, free and easy, openly
浩然気 **kōzen (no) ki** spirits, morale
消然 **shōzen** dejected, despondent
猛然 **mōzen** fiercely, savagely, resolutely
徒然 **tozen, tsurezure** tedium, idle hours
悚然 **shōzen** in horror, with a shudder
悄然 **shōzen** dejected, dispirited
純然 **junzen** pure, sheer, utter
紛然 **funzen** confused, in a jumble
11 粛然 **shukuzen** solemnly
偶然 **gūzen** by chance, happen to ...
率然 **sotsuzen** suddenly, unexpectedly
混然 **konzen** whole, entire, harmonious
啞然 **azen (to)** dumbfounded, agape
寂然 **sekizen, jakunen** lonesome, desolate
悠然 **yūzen** calm, with perfect composure
悵然 **chōzen** sad, sorrowful
釈然 **shakuzen** with sudden illumination, well satisfied with (an explanation)
断然 **danzen** resolutely, flatly, decidedly
12 翕然 **kyūzen** with one accord
湛然 **tanzen** brimming, overflowing; calm, composed
渾然 **konzen** whole, entire; harmonious
超然 **chōzen(taru)** transcendental, aloof
超然内閣 **chōzen naikaku** non-party government
然然 **shikajika** such and such; and so on
敢然 **kanzen** bold, fearless
愕然 **gakuzen** in surprise/terror, aghast, shocked
間然 **kanzen** open to criticism
悶然 **binzen** pitiful, sad
13 傲然 **gōzen(taru)** proud, arrogant, haughty
傑然 **ketsuzen** resolute, decisive, determined
隠然 **inzen** latent, hidden
漠然 **bakuzen** vague, obscure
蓋然性 **gaizensei** probability
蒼然 **sōzen** blue; dim, dark
暗然 **anzen** sad, doleful
愁然 **shūzen (to shite)** sorrowfully, mournfully
慨然 **gaizen** indignantly, deploringly
慄然 **ritsuzen** with horror, with a shudder
14 歴然 **rekizen** clear, unmistakable
漫然 **manzen** random, rambling
嫣然 **enzen** smiling (coquettishly)
端然 **tanzen** correct, proper
雑然 **zatsuzen** in disorder

截然 **setsuzen** distinct, clear, sharp
15 凛然 **rinzen(taru)** awe-inspiring, commanding
潸然 **sanzen** tearfully
黙然 **mokunen** silent, mute, tacit
憮然 **buzen** discouraged; surprised
憤然 **funzen** indignantly
確然 **kakuzen** distinct, clear-cut
毅然 **kizen** dauntless, resolute
16 蕭然 **shōzen** bleak, desolate, lonely
整然 **seizen** orderly, regular, systematic, neat and trim
瞠然 **dōzen** amazed
奮然 **funzen** resolutely, corageously
17 豁然 **katsuzen** in a flash; broad, vast
厳然 **genzen** solemn, grave, majestic
燦然 **sanzen** brilliant, radiant, resplendent
瞭然 **ryōzen** clear, obvious
18 翻然 **honzen** all of a sudden
顕然 **kenzen** obvious, manifest, clear, conspicuous, prominent
騒然 **sōzen** noisy, tumultuous
19 蹶然 **ketsuzen** springing to one's feet
20 驀然 **bakuzen** precipitately
飄然 **hyōzen** aimlessly, casually
21 巍然 **gizen** lofty, towering
黯然 **anzen** gloomy, doleful
轟然 **gōzen (to)** with a roar, deafeningly
22 儼然 **genzen** solemn, august

――――――― 3 ―――――――

3 大自然 **daishizen** Mother Nature
4 不自然 **fushizen** unnatural
12 超自然 **chōshizen** supernatural
超自然的 **chōshizenteki** supernatural
14 総天然色 **sōtennenshoku** in full (natural) color

――――――― 4 ―――――――

1 一目瞭然 **ichimoku ryōzen** clear at a glance, obvious
5 古色蒼然 **koshoku-sōzen** antique-looking, hoary
11 理路整然 **riro-seizen** well-argued, cogent, logical

爲 → 為 **4d5.8**

4d8.11

毯 **TAN** wool rug

――――――― 2 ―――――――

12 絨毯 **jūtan** rug, carpet

————— 9 —————

4d9.1 / 1849

煩 HAN, BON, wazura(u) worry about, be troubled by; be ill
wazura(wasu) trouble, bother, annoy
wazura(washii) troublesome, tangled
urusa(i) annoying, irksome, fastidious, noisy

————— 1 —————

6 煩多 **hanta** so many as to be a nuisance
 煩忙 **hanbō** busy, pressed with business
7 煩労 **hanrō** trouble, pains
9 煩型 **urusagata** fastidious/faultfinding type
10 煩悩 **bonnō** evil passions, carnal desires
11 煩務 **hanmu** troublesome/hectic work
 煩累 **hanrui** cares, annoyances
12 煩悶 **hanmon** worry, anguish
14 煩瑣 **hansa** troublesome, vexatious; complicated
 煩語 **hango** prolix/tedious language
 煩雑 **hanzatsu** complicated, troublesome

————— 2 —————

2 子煩悩 **kobonnō** fond of one's children
3 口煩 **kuchiuru(sai)** nagging, too talkative
8 長煩 **nagawazura(i)** a long/protracted illness
9 思煩 **omo(i)wazura(u)** worry about, feel anxious
10 恋煩 **koiwazura(i)** lovesickness

4d9.2

煉 煉 REN, ne(ru) refine (metals)
ne(ri) kneading over fire

————— 1 —————

0 煉りようかん **ne(ri)yōkan** bean jelly
5 煉瓦 **renga** brick
 煉白粉 **ne(ri)oshiroi** face powder
6 煉合 **ne(ri)a(waseru)** knead together, compound
 煉羊羹 **ne(ri)yōkan** bean jelly
7 煉乳 **rennyū** condensed milk
8 煉物 **ne(ri)mono** paste, pastries, bean jelly, paste jewelry; festival procession
9 煉炭 **rentan** briquette
14 煉獄 **rengoku** purgatory
15 煉餌 **ne(ri)e** paste bait/feed

————— 2 —————

4 木煉瓦 **mokurenga** wooden blocks/bricks
9 洗煉 **senren** refine, polish
15 敷煉瓦 **shi(ki)renga** paving bricks

————— 3 —————

4 手薬煉引 **tegusune hi(ite)** prepared, all set for
9 耐火煉瓦 **taika renga** firebrick

4d9.3 / 919

煙 烟 EN, kemuri, kemu smoke
kemu(ru), kebu(ru) smoke, smolder
kemu(i), kebu(i) smoky

————— 1 —————

4 煙水晶 **kemuri-zuishō** smoky quartz
5 煙出 **kemuda(shi)** chimney
8 煙毒 **endoku** smoke pollution
 煙波 **enpa** hazy sea, spray
 煙突 **entotsu** chimney
 煙雨 **en'u** fine/drizzling rain
9 煙草 **tabako** tobacco
 煙草入 **tabako-i(re)** tobacco pouch, cigarette case
 煙草盆 **tabakobon** tobacco tray
 煙草飲 **tabakono(mi)** smoker
10 煙害 **engai** smoke pollution
11 煙道 **endō** flue
12 煙弾 **endan** smoke bomb
 煙筒 **entō** chimney
13 煙幕 **enmaku** smoke screen
14 煙塵 **enjin** dust; particulate matter in smokestack smoke; battle scene
 煙管 **enkan** chimney, flue **kiseru** tobacco pipe with metal bowl and mouthpiece and bamboo stem
 煙管乗 **kiseruno(ri)** ride a train with tickets only for the first and last stretches of the route
17 煙霞 **enka** smoke and mist; scenic views
19 煙霧 **enmu** mist, fog, smog

————— 2 —————

3 土煙 **tsuchi kemuri** cloud of dust
4 水煙 **mizukemuri, suien** spray
 火煙 **kaen** fire and smoke
6 有煙炭 **yūentan** soft/bituminous coal
 血煙 **chikemuri** spray of blood
8 刻煙草 **kiza(mi) tabako** shredded tobacco
 油煙 **yuen** lampblack, lamp soot
9 発煙 **hatsuen** emitting smoke, fuming
 巻煙草 **ma(ki)tabako** cigarette
 砂煙 **sunakemuri** cloud of dust
10 消煙機 **shōenki** smoke consumer
 砲煙 **hōen** cannon smoke
 砲煙弾雨 **hōen-dan'u** smoke of guns and a hail of shells/bullets
11 黒煙 **kokuen, kurokemuri** black smoke
12 喫煙 **kitsuen** smoking
 喫煙車 **kitsuensha** smoking car
 喫煙室 **kitsuenshitsu** smoking room
 無煙 **muen** smokeless
 無煙炭 **muentan** anthracite coal
 硝煙 **shōen** gunpowder smoke
 紫煙 **shien** tobacco smoke

4

木
月
日
火 9←
礻
王
牛
方
攵
欠
心
戸
戈

雲煙 **un'en** clouds and smoke; a landscape
13 嗅煙草 **ka(gi)tabako** snuff
嫌煙権 **ken'enken** non-smokers' rights
煤煙 **baien** soot and smoke
禁煙 **kin'en** No Smoking
愛煙家 **aienka** (habitual) smoker
節煙 **setsuen** smoking in moderation
15 潮煙 **shiokemuri** salt spray
噴煙 **fun'en** (volcanic) smoke, exhaust fumes
18 嚙煙草 **ka(mi)tabako** chewing tobacco
19 爆煙 **bakuen** smoke of an explosion

4d9.4

煨 **WAI** banked fire

4d9.5

煠 **YŌ, SŌ** burn, boil, fry
ita(meru) fry, sauté

4d9.6

煤 **BAI, susu** soot

———————— 1 ————————
11 煤掃 **susuha(ki)** house cleaning
13 煤煙 **baien** soot and smoke

4d9.7

煌 **KŌ, kira(meku)** sparkle, gleam, twinkle
kira(biyaka) glittering, resplendent

———————— 1 ————————
3 煌々 **kōkō** bright, brilliant
9 煌星 **kiraboshi** glittering stars

4d9.8

煬 **YŌ** roast, burn

4d9.9

煖 **DAN** warm

———————— 1 ————————
8 煖炉 **danro** fireplace, hearth, stove
煖房 **danbō** heating

4d9.10

煥 **KAN** shine, gleam

———————— 1 ————————
9 煥発 **kanpatsu** blaze, glitter
———————— 3 ————————
3 才気煥発 **saiki-kanpatsu** brilliant, wise

4d9.11

熙 熈 凞 **KI** shine; wide; calm; enjoy

———————— 2 ————————
11 康熙字典 **Kōki Jiten** the Kangxi zidian (a 42-volume 47,216-entry character dictionary published in China in 1716)

4d9.12 / 998

照 **SHŌ, te(ru)** shine **te(ri)** sunshine; dry weather; gloss, luster **te(rasu)** shine on **te(reru)** feel embarrassed

———————— 1 ————————
3 照上 **te(ri)a(garu)** clear up after a rain
4 照込 **te(ri)ko(mi)** sunshine; drought
照尺 **shōshaku** gunsights
5 照付 **te(ri)tsu(keru)** shine down on
6 照合 **te(rashi)a(waseru)** check by comparison
shōgō check against, verify
照会 **shōkai** inquiry
照返 **te(ri)kae(su)** reflect
7 照応 **shōō** correspond to, agree/coincide with
8 照明 **shōmei** illumination, lighting
照明弾 **shōmeidan** flare, illumination round/shell
照性 **te(re)shō** bashful, easily embarrassed
照雨 **te(ri)ame** a rain during sunshine
9 照度 **shōdo** (intensity of) illumination
照屋 **te(re)ya** one who is easily embarrassed
照査 **shōsa** irradiation
照映 **te(ri)ha(eru)** be lit up, glow
照星 **shōsei** gunbarrel bead, front sight
照臭 **te(re)kusa(i)** embarrassed
10 照射 **shōsha** irradiation
12 照葉狂言 **Teriha kyōgen** (a type of Noh entertainment)
照焼 **te(ri)ya(ki)** fish broiled with soy sauce
13 照隠 **te(re)kaku(shi)** covering up one's embarrassment
照準 **shōjun** aiming, sights
照照坊主 **te(ru)te(ru)bōzu** paper doll used in praying for good weather
15 照影 **shōei** portrait
17 照覧 **shōran** see clearly; witness
18 照臨 **shōrin** shine/look down on; rule; come (polite)
———————— 2 ————————
4 天照大神 **Amaterasu Ōmikami** the Sun Goddess

引照 **inshō** reference
日照 **nisshō, hide(ri)** sunshine, drought, dry
  weather
日照計 **nisshōkei** heliograph
火照 **hote(ri)** glow, heat; burning sensation
6 返照 **henshō** evening glow; reflected light
7 対照 **taishō** contrast
  対照的 **taishōteki** (sharply) contrasting
8 油照 **aburade(ri)** sultry sun
  参照 **sanshō** refer to, see, compare
9 前照灯 **zenshōtō** headlights
10 残照 **zanshō** afterglow
11 探照灯 **tanshōtō** searchlight
13 照照坊主 **te(ru)te(ru)bōzu** paper doll used
  in praying for good weather
18 観照 **kanshō** contemplation, reflecting upon
——————— 4 ———————
7 肝胆相照 **kantan-aite(rasu)** be intimate
  friends
12 貸借対照表 **taishakutaishōhyō** balance sheet

4d9.13

煦

KU warm

4d9.14

煎 →   2o11.2

4d9.14

煢

KEI all alone, without any family;
worry

——————— 10 ———————
4d10.1

熄

SOKU come to an end; (flames) die out

——————— 2 ———————
11 終熄 **shūsoku** come to an end

4d10.2

熅

UN, iki(re) sultriness, stuffiness

熔 → 鎔   8a10.1

4d10.3

熕

KŌ cannon

4d10.4

煽 煽

SEN, ao(ru) fan (flames), blow;
incite   **ao(gu)** fan (a fire);
instigate   **oda(teru)** incite;
flatter

——————— 1 ———————
4 煽止 **ao(ri)do(me)** doorstop
5 煽立 **ao(gi)ta(teru)** instigate
11 煽動 **sendō** instigate, abet, agitate, incite
  煽情 **senjō** suggestive, lascivious
  煽情的 **senjōteki** suggestive, sensational
——————— 2 ———————
12 買煽 **ka(i)ao(ru)** bid up, rig (the market)

熏 → 燻   4d14.1

4d10.5 / 687

熟

JUKU, u(reru) ripen, come to maturity
u(mu) ripen; be overripe

——————— 1 ———————
0 熟す **juku(su)** be ripe, reach maturity; (of
  words) come into common use; acquire
  skill
6 熟考 **jukkō** mature reflection, due deliberation
  熟成 **jukusei** ripening, maturation, aging
8 熟知 **jukuchi** thorough knowledge, familiarity
9 熟柿 **jukushi** ripe persimmon
  熟柿主義 **jukushi shugi** wait-and-see policy
  熟柿臭 **jukushikusa(i)** smelling of liquor
  熟思 **jukushi** careful consideration
10 熟眠 **jukumin** sound sleep
11 熟達 **jukutatsu** proficiency, mastery, skill
  熟視 **jukushi** stare at, study, scrutinize
13 熟睡 **jukusui** sound sleep
14 熟練 **jukuren** practiced skill, mastery
  熟練工 **jukurenkō** skilled workman/
  craftsman
  熟語 **jukugo** word of two or more kanji,
  compound; phrase
  熟読 **jukudoku** read thoroughly/carefully
15 熟慮 **jukuryo** mature consideration
  熟慮断行 **jukuryo-dankō** deliberate and
  decisive
  熟談 **jukudan** careful discussion/consultation
17 熟覧 **jukuran** scrutiny
20 熟議 **jukugi** due deliberation/discussion

——————— 2 ———————
4 不熟練 **fujukuren** unskilled
  円熟 **enjuku** maturity, ripeness, perfection
5 半熟 **hanjuku** half-boiled, soft-boiled; half-
  ripe

4

木 月 日 火 礻 王 牛 方 攵 欠 心 戸 戈

10←

未熟 **mijuku** not yet ripe; premature; immature, inexperienced
6 老熟 **rōjuku** mature skill, maturity, mellowness
早熟 **sōjuku** maturing early, precocious
成熟 **seijuku** ripen; mature
成熟期 **seijukuki** puberty, adolescence
10 修熟 **shūjuku** developing skill
11 黄熟 **kōjuku** turning yellow and ripening
習熟 **shūjuku** mastery, proficiency
13 豊熟 **hōjuku** abundant harvest; ripen
15 嫻熟 **kanjuku** experienced, practiced
21 爛熟 **ranjuku** overripeness; full maturity

熙 → 熙 **4d9.11**

4d10.6

熊   **YŪ, kuma** bear

———————— 1 ————————
4 熊手 **kumade** rake
5 熊本 **Kumamoto** (city, Kumamoto-ken)
熊本県 **Kumamoto-ken** (prefecture)
9 熊狩 **kumaga(ri)** bear hunting
13 熊蜂 **kumabachi** hornet
22 熊襲 **Kumaso** (ancient tribe of southern Kyūshū)
———————— 2 ————————
3 小熊座 **kogumaza** Little Bear, Ursa Minor
7 赤熊 **akaguma** brown bear
11 黒熊 **kurokuma** black bear
14 雌熊 **meguma** female bear
———————— 3 ————————
5 北極熊 **hokkyokuguma** polar bear

———————— 11 ————————

4d11.1

燉   **TON** fiery

燨 →   **4d12.6**

4d11.2

熨   **I, UTSU, no(su)** iron (clothes), smooth out   **noshi** flatiron

———————— 1 ————————
4 熨斗 **noshi** decorative paper strip attached to a gift

熨斗目 **noshime** samurai's ceremonial robe
———————— 2 ————————
4 火熨斗 **hinoshi** an iron (for ironing clothes)
12 湯熨 **yunoshi** steam ironing

4d11.3 / 1773

勲 勳   **KUN** merit
           isao meritorious deed

———————— 1 ————————
5 勲功 **kunkō** distinguished service, merits
7 勲位 **kun'i** order of merit
勲労 **kunrō** meritorious/distinguished service
10 勲記 **kunki** commendation, diploma
11 勲章 **kunshō** order, decoration, medal
12 勲等 **kuntō** order of merit
17 勲爵 **kunshaku** order of merit and peerage
———————— 2 ————————
5 功勲 **kōkun** meritorious service
6 有勲者 **yūkunsha** holder of a decoration
7 位勲 **ikun** rank and order of merit
8 武勲 **bukun** military achievements
9 叙勲 **jokun** confer a decoration
10 殊勲 **shukun** distinguished service
帯勲 **taikun** wearing a decoration
12 偉勲 **ikun** great achievement, distinguished service

熙 → 熙 **4d9.11**

4d11.4 / 645

熱   **NETSU** heat; fever; mania, enthusiasm
       atsu(i) hot

———————— 1 ————————
0 熱する **nes(suru)** heat, make hot; become hot/excited
熱っぽい **netsu(ppoi)** enthusiastic, fervent
2 熱力学 **netsurikigaku** thermodynamics
4 熱中 **netchū** be enthusiastic/crazy about, be engrossed/absorbed in
熱心 **nesshin** enthusiasm, zeal
熱心家 **nesshinka** enthusiast, devotee
5 熱弁 **netsuben** fervent speech
熱処理 **netsushori** heat treatment
6 熱気 **nekki** hot air; heat; enthusiasm
熱気 **netsuke** feverishness
熱血 **nekketsu** hot blood, fiery zeal, ardor
熱血漢 **nekketsukan** fervent/hot-blooded man
7 熱低 **nettei** tropical depression, cyclone
熱冷 **netsusa(mashi)** an antipyretic
熱延 **netsuen** hot rolling

熱狂　**nekkyō** wild enthusiasm, frenzy, mania
8 熱波　**neppa** heat wave
熱苦　**atsukuru(shii)** sultry, sweltering, stifling
熱性　**nessei** enthusiastic, earnest
9 熱発　**neppatsu** have a fever
熱風　**neppū** hot wind/blast
熱泉　**nessen** hot springs
熱型　**nekkei** type of fever
熱単位　**netsutan'i** heat/thermal unit
熱度　**netsudo** degree of heat/enthusiasm
熱屋　**atsu(gari)ya** person sensitive to the heat
熱砂　**nessa** hot sand (bath)
10 熱射病　**nesshabyō** heatstroke, sunstroke
熱涙　**netsurui** hot/burning tears
熱帯　**nettai** torrid zone, the tropics
熱帯日　**nettaibi** midsummerday
熱帯夜　**nettaiya, nettaiyo** a night during which the temperature never falls below 25 degrees Celsius
熱帯林　**nettairin** tropical forest
熱帯性　**nettaisei** tropical
熱帯病　**nettaibyō** tropical disease
熱帯魚　**nettaigyo** tropical fish
熱核　**netsukaku** thermonuclear
熱烈　**netsuretsu** ardent, impassioned
熱病　**netsubyō** fever
11 熱球　**nekkyū** hot pitch (in baseball)
熱望　**netsubō** ardent wish, fervent hope
熱情　**netsujō** fervor, ardor, passion
12 熱量　**netsuryō** (amount of) heat, calories
13 熱源　**netsugen** heat source
熱愛　**netsuai** ardent love, devotion
熱感　**nekkan** feverish feeling
熱戦　**nessen** fierce fighting; close contest
熱意　**netsui** enthusiasm, zeal, ardor
熱誠　**nessei** earnestness, warmth, emthusiasm, sincerity
熱鉄　**nettetsu** hot/molten steel
熱雷　**netsurai** heat thunderstorm
熱電対　**netsudentsui** thermocouple
14 熱演　**netsuen** impassioned performance
15 熱器具　**netsukigu** heating appliances
熱蔵庫　**netsuzōko** heating cabinet, warmer
熱線　**nessen** heat rays; hot wire
熱論　**netsuron** heated argument/discussion
熱賛　**nessan** enthusiastic/wholehearted approval
16 熱機関　**netsukikan** heat engine
熱燗　**atsukan** hot saké
17 熱療法　**netsuryōhō** heat therapy
18 熱闘　**nettō** hard-fought contest
19 熱願　**netsugan** fervent plea, earnest entreaty

――――――― 2 ―――――――

4 不熱心　**funesshin** unenthusiastic, indifferent, halfhearted
火熱　**kanetsu** heat

5 加熱　**kanetsu** heating
平熱　**heinetsu** normal temperature
比熱　**hinetsu** specific heat
白熱　**hakunetsu** white heat, incandescence; heated, exciting
白熱化　**hakunetsuka** heat up, reach a climax
白熱灯　**hakunetsutō** incandescent lamp
白熱戦　**hakunetsusen** intense fighting, thrilling game
6 地熱　**chinetsu, jinetsu** geothermal
光熱　**kōnetsu** light and heat
光熱費　**kōnetsuhi** heating and electricity expenses
7 亜熱帯　**anettai** subtropics
体熱　**tainetsu** body heat
余熱　**yonetsu** remaining heat
灼熱　**shakunetsu** red/scorching hot, incandescent
8 苦熱　**kunetsu** oppressive heat
炎熱　**ennetsu** scorching/sweltering heat
放熱　**hōnetsu** radiate heat; radiant heat
放熱器　**hōnetsuki** radiator
9 発熱　**hatsunetsu** generation of heat; have a fever
耐熱　**tainetsu** heat-resistant
耐熱鋼　**tainetsukō** refractory steel
泉熱　**Izumi netsu** Izumi fever (resembles scarlet fever)
胃熱　**inetsu** gastric fever
10 残熱　**zannetsu** the lingering summer heat
高熱　**kōnetsu** high fever
11 過熱　**kanetsu** overheat, superheat
黄熱　**ōnetsu, kōnetsu** yellow fever
黄熱病　**ōnetsubyō, kōnetsubyō** yellow fever
悪熱　**onetsu** fever following a chill
情熱　**jōnetsu** passion, enthusiasm
12 極熱　**gokunetsu** intense heat
暑熱　**shonetsu** the summer heat
無熱　**munetsu** with no fever
焦熱　**shōnetsu** scorching heat
焦熱地獄　**shōnetsu jigoku** an inferno
13 微熱　**binetsu** a slight fever
腺熱　**sennetsu** glandular fever
解熱　**genetsu** alleviate fever
解熱剤　**genetsuzai** an antipyretic
電熱　**dennetsu** electric heat
電熱器　**dennetsuki** electric heater
14 稲熱病　**imochibyō** rice blight
酷熱　**kokunetsu** intense/scorching heat

――――――― 3 ―――――――

4 太陽熱　**taiyōnetsu** solar heat
6 再帰熱　**saikinetsu** recurrent fever
回帰熱　**kaikinetsu** recurrent fever
7 投機熱　**tōkinetsu** speculation fever
8 知恵熱　**chie-netsu** teething fever

4

木
月
日
火　11←
礻
王
牛
方
攵
欠
心
戸
戈

9 政治熱 **seijinetsu** political fever
11 野球熱 **yakyūnetsu** baseball fever/mania
産褥熱 **sanjokunetsu** puerperal fever
12 猩紅熱 **shōkōnetsu** scarlet fever
蒸発熱 **jōhatsunetsu** heat of evaporation
間欠熱 **kanketsunetsu** intermittent fever
間歇熱 **kanketsunetsu** intermittent fever
16 融解熱 **yūkainetsu** heat of fusion

———————— 4 ————————

16 頭寒足熱 **zukan-sokunetsu** keeping the head cool and the feet warm

4d11.5 / 1578

黙 黙

MOKU, dama(ru) become/be silent, say nothing
danma(ri) silence, reticence
moda(su) be silent, not say; leave as is

———————— 1 ————————

3 黙々 **mokumoku** silent, mute, tacit
4 黙止 **mokushi** remain silent, leave as is
黙込 **dama(ri)ko(mu)** fall silent, say no more
5 黙示 **mokushi** revelation; implied
黙示録 **Mokushiroku** Revelations, the Apocalypse
黙礼 **mokurei** bow silently
6 黙考 **mokkō** contemplation, meditation
7 黙坐 **mokuza** sit in silence
8 黙念 **mokunen** silent, mute, tacit
9 黙契 **mokkei** a tacit understanding
黙屋 **dama(ri)ya** silent/taciturn person
黙思 **mokushi** contemplation
黙約 **mokuyaku** a tacit agreement
10 黙座 **mokuza** sit in silence
黙殺 **mokusatsu** take no notice of, ignore
黙秘 **mokuhi** keep silent about, keep secret
黙秘権 **mokuhiken** the right to remain silent
11 黙過 **mokka** overlook, connive at
黙視 **mokushi** overlook, connive at
黙許 **mokkyo** tacit permission, connivance
12 黙然 **mokunen** silent, mute, tacit
13 黙想 **mokusō** meditation, contemplation
14 黙読 **mokudoku** read silently
黙認 **mokunin** tacit approval/admission
15 黙劇 **mokugeki** pantomime
黙黙 **mokumoku** silent, mute, tacit
黙諾 **mokudaku** tacit consent
18 黙難 **moda(shi)gata(i)** hard to overlook
19 黙禱 **mokutō** silent prayer/tribute

———————— 2 ————————

7 沈黙 **chinmoku** silence
8 押黙 **o(shi)dama(ru)** keep silent
13 暗黙 **anmoku** silence
暗黙了解 **anmoku (no) ryōkai** tacit understanding

14 寡黙 **kamoku** taciturn, reticent
15 黙黙 **mokumoku** silent, mute, tacit

4d11.6

熬

GŌ, i(ru) parch, roast

———————— 12 ————————

4d12.1

燋

SHŌ torch; scorch; worry

4d12.2 / 652

燃

NEN, mo(eru), mo(yuru) burn, blaze
mo(yasu), mo(su) (tr.) burn

———————— 1 ————————

3 燃上 **mo(e)a(garu)** blaze up, burst into flames
4 燃切 **mo(e)ki(ru)** burn (itself) out
5 燃出 **mo(e)da(su)** begin to burn, ignite
燃付 **mo(e)tsu(ku)** catch fire, ignite
燃広 **mo(e)hiro(garu)** (flames) spread
燃立 **mo(e)ta(tsu)** blaze up, be ablaze
6 燃尽 **mo(e)tsu(kusu)** burn completely
8 燃易 **mo(e)yasu(i)** flammable
9 燃思 **mo(eru) omo(i), mo(yuru) omo(i)** burning passion
10 燃残 **mo(e)noko(ri)** embers
燃差 **mo(e)sa(shi)** embers
燃料 **nenryō** fuel
11 燃殻 **mo(e)gara** cinders, embers
燃移 **mo(e)utsu(ru)** (flames) spread to
燃盛 **mo(e)saka(ru)** be ablaze, burn fiercely
12 燃焼 **nenshō** combustion
燃費 **nenpi** fuel cost; fuel economy (km/liter)
13 燃滓 **mo(e)kasu** cinders
15 燃質 **nenshitsu** combustibility

———————— 2 ————————

4 不燃性 **funensei** nonflammable, incombustible
内燃機関 **nainen kikan** internal-combustion engine
5 可燃物 **kanenbutsu** combustibles, flammable substances
可燃性 **kanensei** combustible, flammable
6 再燃 **sainen** reignite, revive
10 核燃料 **kakunenryō** nuclear fuel

4d12.3

燔

HAN burn

——————— 1 ———————
11 燔祭 **hansai** burn offerings

4d12.4

燎 **RYŌ** bonfire; burn

——————— 1 ———————
4 燎火 **ryōka** bonfire
10 燎原 **ryōgen (no) hi** prairie fire, wildfire

燈→灯 **4d2.1**

燒→焼 **4d8.4**

4d12.5

熾 **SHI** burning; flourishing
oko(su) start a fire, kindle

——————— 1 ———————
10 熾烈 **shiretsu** keen, fierce, hot

4d12.6

燵 **TATSU** heated floor well, foot-warmer

——————— 2 ———————
4 火燵 **kotatsu** heated floor well, foot warmer
9 炬燵 **kotatsu** heated floor well, foot warmer
——————— 3 ———————
13 置火燵 **o(ki)gotatsu** portable brazier
置炬燵 **o(ki)gotatsu** portable brazier

4d12.7

燧 **SUI, hiuchi** a flint

——————— 1 ———————
5 燧石 **hiuchiishi, suiseki** a flint

爛→爛 **4d12.8**

4d12.8

爛 爛 **KAN** warming saké
RAN boil

——————— 1 ———————
0 爛する **kan(suru)** heat saké

7 爛冷 **kanza(mashi)** leftover warmed saké
10 爛酒 **kanzake** warmed saké
14 爛徳利 **kandokuri** bottle for heating saké
——————— 2 ———————
15 熱爛 **atsukan** hot saké

燕→ **3k13.16**

4d12.9

熹 **KI** burn; faint light

4d12.10

黔 **KEN** black

餤→焔 **4d8.5**

——————— 13 ———————

4d13.1

燨 **KI** blaze

4d13.2

燠 **IKU** warm
U soothing voice
oki live coals, embers

4d13.3

燦 **SAN** bright, brilliant

——————— 1 ———————
3 燦々 **sansan** bright, brilliant, radiant
12 燦然 **sanzen** brilliant, radiant, resplendent
21 燦爛 **sanran** brilliant, shining, glittering

4d13.4

燐 **RIN** phosphorus

——————— 1 ———————
3 燐寸 **matchi** matches
4 燐火 **rinka** phosphorescence, foxfire
6 燐光 **rinkō** phosphorescence

4

木
月
日
火 13←
ネ
王
牛
方
攵
欠
心
戸
戈

14 燐酸 **rinsan** phosphoric acid; (as prefix) ... phosphate

——————— 2 ———————

7 赤燐 **sekirin** red phosphorus
11 黄燐 **ōrin** yellow/white phosphorus

4d13.5

燭

SHOKU (candle)light; a candlepower

——————— 1 ———————

5 燭台 **shokudai** candlestick, candlestand
6 燭光 **shokkō** a candlepower; candlelight

——————— 2 ———————

4 手燭 **teshoku** (portable) candlestick
10 華燭典 **kashoku (no) ten** wedding ceremony
21 蠟燭 **rōsoku** candle

4d13.6 / 1656

燥

SŌ dry

——————— 2 ———————

10 高燥 **kōsō** elevated, high and dry
11 乾燥 **kansō** dry, drying, dehydrated
　乾燥季 **kansōki** the dry season
　乾燥剤 **kansōzai** desiccant
　乾燥無味 **kansō-mumi** dry, dull
　乾燥機 **kansōki** dryer; desiccator
12 焦燥 **shōsō** impatience, fretfulness

——————— 4 ———————

12 無味乾燥 **mumi-kansō** dry as dust, uninteresting

4d13.7

黛

TAI, **mayuzumi** blue-black eyebrow coloring

4d13.8

黜

CHUTSU reject, dismiss

點 → 点 2m7.2

——————— 14 ———————

4d14.1

燻　熏

KUN, **ibu(ru)** smoke, smolder, fume **ibu(su), kusu(beru), fusu(beru)** smoke, fumigate **kusu(buru), fusu(buru/boru)**

smoke, smolder, become sooty; stay indoors; remain in obscurity　**kuyu(rasu)** smoke (a cigar)

——————— 1 ———————

12 燻蒸 **kunjō** fumigation
　燻蒸剤 **kunjōzai** fumigant
14 燻製 **kunsei** smoked (fish)
　燻銀 **ibu(shi)gin** oxidized silver; refined

——————— 2 ———————

10 蚊燻 **kaibu(shi)** smoking out mosquitoes

4d14.2

爐

JIN embers

——————— 2 ———————

6 灰爐 **kaijin** (reduced to) ashes
7 余爐 **yojin** embers, smoldering fire

4d14.3

燿

YŌ, **kagaya(ku)** shine, gleam

4d14.4

鞦

SHŪ, **shirigai** crupper

——————— 1 ———————

23 鞦韆 **buranko** swing, trapeze

4d14.5

燹

SEN grass/war-caused fire

4d14.6

黠

KATSU clever, bright; sly, crafty

——————— 15 ———————

4d15.1

爍

SHAKU shine; melt

4d15.2 / 1015

爆

BAKU explode
ha(zeru) burst/pop open, split

——————— 1 ———————

4 爆心 **bakushin** center of the explosion

爆心地 **bakushinchi** center of the explosion
6 爆死 **bakushi** death from bombing
爆竹 **bakuchiku** firecraker
7 爆沈 **bakuchin** blow up and sink
9 爆発 **bakuhatsu** explosion
爆発力 **bakuhatsuryoku** explosive force
爆発的 **bakuhatsuteki** explosive (popularity)
爆発物 **bakuhatsubutsu** explosives
爆発性 **bakuhatsusei** explosive (bullets)
爆風 **bakufū** blast
爆砕 **bakusai** blasting
爆音 **bakuon** (sound of an) explosion, roar (of an engine)
10 爆破 **bakuha** blast, blow up
爆笑 **bakushō** burst out laughing
12 爆弾 **bakudan** bomb
爆裂 **bakuretsu** explosion, blasting
爆裂弾 **bakuretsudan** explosive shell
13 爆傷 **bakushō** blast damage
爆煙 **bakuen** smoke of an explosion
爆雷 **bakurai** depth charge
14 爆鳴 **bakumei** detonation
15 爆撃 **bakugeki** bombing
爆撃手 **bakugekishu** bombardier
爆撃機 **bakugekiki** bomber
16 爆薬 **bakuyaku** explosives

─────── 2 ───────
4 水爆 **suibaku** hydrogen bomb (short for 水素爆弾)
6 自爆 **jibaku** suicide explosion
8 盲爆 **mōbaku** indiscriminate bombing
空爆 **kūbaku** bombing, air raid (short for 空中爆撃)
9 重爆撃機 **jūbakugekiki** heavy bomber
10 原爆 **genbaku** atomic bomb (short for 原子爆弾)
原爆症 **genbakushō** illnesses caused by atomic-bomb radiation
起爆 **kibaku** priming (in explosives)
起爆剤 **kibakuzai** priming/triggering explosive
起爆薬 **kibakuyaku** priming/triggering explosive
猛爆 **mōbaku** heavy bombing
被爆 **hibaku** being bombed
被爆者 **hibakusha** bombing victims

─────── 3 ───────
4 水素爆弾 **suiso bakudan** hydrogen bomb
10 原子爆弾 **genshi bakudan** atom bomb

原水爆 **gensuibaku** atomic and hydrogen bombs, nuclear bombs

─────── 16 ───────

爐 → 炉 **4d4.2**

4d16.1

黥   **GEI, irezumi** tattooing (as a punishment)

─────── 17 ───────
4d17.1

爛   **RAN** inflamed; colorful
tada(reru) be inflamed/sore

─────── 1 ───────
3 爛々 **ranran** glaring, fiery
5 爛目 **tada(re)me** bleary/sore eyes
14 爛漫 **ranman** in full glory, dazzling
爛熟 **ranjuku** overripeness; full maturity

─────── 2 ───────
12 絢爛 **kenran(taru)** gorgeous, dazzling, gaudy
14 腐爛 **furan** ulcerate, decompose
17 糜爛 **biran** be inflamed, fester; decompose
燦爛 **sanran** brilliant, shining, glittering

─────── 3 ───────
4 天真爛漫 **tenshin-ranman** naive, simple and innocent, unaffected

─────── 22 ───────
4d22.1

黶   **EN** birthmark, mole; black

─────── 26 ───────
4d26.1

爨   **SAN** cook, boil

─────── 2 ───────
8 炊爨 **suisan** cooking

─────── 礻 **4e** ───────

示	礼	祁	社	祀	奈	祉	祇	祈	神	祓	祕	祐
0.1	1.1	2.1	3.1	3.2	3.3	4.1	4.2	4.3	5.1	5.2	5d5.6	5.3

4

木
月
日
火
礻   26←
王
牛
方
攵
欠
心
戸
戈

祖	祝	祢	祚	祇	祠	崇	祥	票	祭	尉	祷	視
5.4	5.5	4e14.1	5.6	5.7	5.8	5.9	6.1	6.2	6.3	6.4	4e14.2	7.1

祺	禄	禁	福	禅	禎	禍	禊	褉	隷	禪	禧	禦
8.1	8.2	8.3	9.1	9.2	9.3	9.4	9.5	10.1	11.1	4e9.2	12.1	12.2

瓢	隸	禰	禱	禮	禳
12.3	4e11.1	14.1	14.2	4e1.1	17.1

4

木 月 日 火 礻 王 牛 方 攵 欠 心 戸 戈

→0

─────────── 0 ───────────

4e0.1 / 615

示

JI, SHI, shime(su) show
shime(shi) deportment, discipline (by example); revelation

─────────── 1 ───────────

6 示合 **shime(shi)a(u)** inform/show each other
9 示威 **jii** show of force, demonstration
示威的 **jiiteki** demonstrative, threatening
10 示唆 **shisa** suggestion
示教 **shikyō** instruction, guidance
11 示達 **shitatsu** directive, instructions
示現 **jigen** revelation, manifestation
15 示談 **jidan** out-of-court settlement

─────────── 2 ───────────

4 予示 **yoji** show signs of, foreshadow
内示 **naiji** unofficial announcement
公示 **kōji** public announcement
7 呈示 **teiji** present, bring up
告示 **kokuji** notification
告示板 **kokujiban** bulletin board
図示 **zushi** explanatory diagram, illustration
8 表示 **hyōji** indicate, express, display
例示 **reiji** give an example of
明示 **meiji** clearly state
9 指示 **shiji** indication, instructions, directions
sa(shi)shime(su) indicate, point out
指示灯 **shijitō** pilot lamp, indicator light
指示板 **shijiban** notice board
指示器 **shijiki** indicator
10 展示 **tenji** exhibition, display
展示会 **tenjikai** show, exhibition
教示 **kyōji** instruct, teach, enlighten
訓示 **kunji** instruction
11 掲示 **keiji** notice, bulletin
掲示板 **keijiban** bulletin board
啓示 **keiji** revelation
12 提示 **teiji** present, exhibit; bring up, suggest
開示 **kaiji** disclose, make public
13 暗示 **anji** suggestion, hint
誇示 **koji** display, flaunt
15 標示 **hyōji** indicate, mark
黙示 **mokushi** revelation; implied
黙示録 **Mokushiroku** Revelations, the Apocalypse

16 諭示 **yushi** admonition, instructions
18 顕示 **kenji** show, unveil, reveal

─────────── 1 ───────────

4e1.1 / 620

礼 禮

REI, RAI courtesy; salutation, salute, bow; gratitude; return present

─────────── 1 ───────────

6 礼回 **reimawa(ri)** round of thank-you visits
礼式 **reishiki** etiquette
7 礼状 **reijō** letter of thanks
8 礼典 **reiten** ceremony, ritual, rites
礼法 **reihō** courtesy, etiquette, manners
礼拝 **reihai, raihai** worship, services
礼拝堂 **reihaidō** chapel
礼参 **reimai(ri)** thanksgiving visit to a shrine
礼服 **reifuku** formal dress
礼物 **reimotsu** gift
礼金 **reikin** honorarium, fee
10 礼砲 **reihō** (21-gun) salute
11 礼遇 **reigū** cordial reception; honors, privileges
12 礼帽 **reibō** ceremonial/top hat
礼装 **reisō** ceremonial/full dress
13 礼楽 **reigaku** etiquette and music
礼節 **reisetsu** decorum, propriety, politeness
15 礼儀 **reigi** courtesy, politeness, propriety
礼儀正 **reigitada(shii)** polite, courteous
礼儀作法 **reigisahō** etiquette, courtesy, propriety
礼賛 **raisan** worship, adore, glorify
22 礼讃 **raisan** worship, adore, glorify

─────────── 2 ───────────

1 一礼 **ichirei** a bow/greeting
3 大礼 **tairei** state ceremony; enthronement
大礼服 **taireifuku** court dress, full-dress uniform
4 欠礼 **ketsurei** neglect of courtesies
5 失礼 **shitsurei** rudeness, discourtesy
巡礼 **junrei** pilgrimage; pilgrim
巡礼者 **junreisha** pilgrim
立礼 **ritsurei** stand and bow
目礼 **mokurei** nod, greet by eye
6 返礼 **henrei** return gift, in return for
回礼 **kairei** round of courtesy calls

8 非礼 **hirei** impolite
典礼 **tenrei** ceremony
拝礼 **hairei** worship
9 洗礼 **senrei** baptism
洗礼名 **senreimei** baptismal/Christian name
洗礼式 **senreishiki** baptism (ceremony)
10 浸礼 **shinrei** baptism by immersion
座礼 **zarei** bow while sitting
11 虚礼 **kyorei** empty formalities
婚礼 **konrei** wedding ceremony
祭礼 **sairei** festival, ritual
12 割礼 **katsurei** circumcision
朝礼 **chōrei** morning meeting/exercises
無礼 **burei** discourtesy, rudeness
無礼者 **bureimono, bureisha** insolent person
無礼講 **bureikō** free-and-easy get-together
敬礼 **keirei** salutation, salute, bow
答礼 **tōrei** return courtesy/salute
答礼使節 **tōrei shisetsu** envoy sent to return courtesies
答礼砲 **tōreihō** gun salute fired in return
15 儀礼 **girei** etiquette, courtesy
儀礼的 **gireiteki** formal, courtesy (call)
黙礼 **mokurei** bow silently
16 薬礼 **yakurei** medical charge
縟礼 **jokurei** tedious formalities, red tape
17 謝礼 **sharei** remuneration, honorarium

——————— 3 ———————

3 三顧礼 **sanko (no) rei** special confidence (in someone)
9 按手礼 **anshurei** laying on of hands, ordination
12 堅信礼 **kenshinrei** (Christian) confirmation
登舷礼 **tōgenrei** full crew's salute from the deck
最敬礼 **saikeirei** profound obeisance, most respectful bow

——————— 4 ———————

13 傲慢無礼 **gōman-burei** arrogant and insolent
16 繁文縟礼 **hanbun-jokurei** tedious formalities, red tape

——————— 2 ———————

4e2.1

祁 祁   **KI** intense; large

——————— 3 ———————

4e3.1 / 308

社 祉   **SHA** company; Shinto shrine
         yashiro Shinto shrine

——————— 1 ———————

4 社内 **shanai** in the company/shrine

社中 **shachū** office staff; troupe
社友 **shayū** friend of the firm; colleague
5 社外 **shagai** outside the company
社外船 **shagaisen** tramp steamer/vessel
社用 **shayō** for company business
社用族 **shayōzoku** expense-account aristrocrats
社司 **shashi** Shinto priest
社主 **shashu** head of a company
6 社会 **shakai** society, social
社会人 **shakaijin** full member of society
社会化 **shakaika** socialization
社会民主主義 **shakai minshu shugi** social democracy
社会主義 **shakai shugi** socialism
社会学 **shakaigaku** sociology
社会的 **shakaiteki** social
社会性 **shakaisei** social nature
社会面 **shakaimen** local-news page
社会科 **shakaika** social studies, civics
社会部 **shakaibu** local-news section, city desk
社会党 **shakaitō** socialist party
社会悪 **shakaiaku** social evils
社会福祉 **shakai fukushi** social welfare
社交 **shakō** society, social life
社交服 **shakōfuku** party clothes, evening dress
社交的 **shakōteki** social, sociable
社交性 **shakōsei** sociability
社交界 **shakōkai** (high) society
社交家 **shakōka** sociable person
社寺 **shaji** shrines and temples
社名 **shamei** company name
社宅 **shataku** company house/apartment
社団 **shadan** corporation, association
社団法人 **shadan hōjin** corporate juridical person
7 社告 **shakoku** public announcement (by a company)
8 社長 **shachō** company president
社命 **shamei** company orders
9 社屋 **shaoku** office/company building
社是 **shaze** company policy
社則 **shasoku** company regulations
10 社員 **shain** employee, staff
社家 **shake** hereditary family of Shinto priests
社格 **shakaku** status of a shrine/company
社訓 **shakun** precepts for employees
11 社運 **shaun** company fortunes
社務 **shamu** shrine/company affairs
社務所 **shamusho** shrine office
社章 **shashō** company logo/emblem
12 社葬 **shasō** company funeral
社費 **shahi** company expenses
13 社業 **shagyō** the company's business
社僧 **shasō** priest residing at a shrine
社債 **shasai** (company) bonds, debentures

4

木 月 日 火 礻 3← 王 牛 方 攵 欠 心 戸 戈

社殿 **shaden** main shrine building
14 社旗 **shaki** company flag
社歌 **shaka** company anthem/song
社説 **shasetsu** an editorial
社領 **sharyō** shrine land
15 社線 **shasen** private railway line
16 社頭 **shatō** front of a shrine

──────── 2 ────────

2 入社 **nyūsha** joining a company
3 大社 **taisha** grand shrine; Izumo Shrine
小社 **shōsha** minor shrine; our company
4 支社 **shisha** a branch (office)
分社 **bunsha** branch shrine
公社 **kōsha** public corporation
5 出社 **shussha** go/come to the office
本社 **honsha** head office; main shrine; this shrine
末社 **massha** subordinate shrine; professional jester
正社員 **seishain** regular employee, full member of the staff
6 会社 **kaisha** company, corporation
会社員 **kaishain** company employee
寺社 **jisha** temples and shrines
当社 **tōsha** this/our company; this shrine
8 非社会的 **hishakaiteki** antisocial
非社交的 **hishakōteki** unsociable, retiring
退社 **taisha** retirement from a company; leaving the office
実社会 **jisshakai** the real world, actual society
9 神社 **jinja** Shinto shrine
10 郷社 **gōsha** village shrine
11 商社 **shōsha** trading company, business firm
12 結社 **kessha** association, society
貴社 **kisha** your company
13 準社員 **junshain** junior employee, associate member
15 弊社 **heisha** our company, we
17 講社 **kōsha** religious association

──────── 3 ────────

2 子会社 **kogaisha** a subsidiary
5 出向社員 **shukkō shain** employee on loan to a subsididary/another company
出版社 **shuppansha** publishing house, publisher
広告社 **kōkokusha** advertising agency
8 泥水社会 **doromizu shakai** red-light districts
招魂社 **shōkonsha** shrine to the war dead
国幣社 **kokuheisha** national shrine
9 通信社 **tsūshinsha** news agency
12 葬儀社 **sōgisha** funeral home, undertaker's
13 新聞社 **shinbunsha** newspaper (company)
16 親会社 **oyagaisha** parent company

──────── 4 ────────

6 合弁会社 **gōben-gaisha** joint venture (company)

合名会社 **gōmei-gaisha** unlimited partnership
合資会社 **gōshi-gaisha** limited partnership
交通公社 **Kōtsū Kōsha** Japan Travel Bureau
有限会社 **yūgen-gaisha** limited liability company, Ltd.
7 赤十字社 **Sekijūjisha** Red Cross Society
9 保険会社 **hoken-gaisha** insurance company
持株会社 **mo(chi)kabu-gaisha** holding company
10 株式会社 **kabushiki-gaisha, kabushiki kaisha** corporation, Co., Ltd.
航空会社 **kōkū-gaisha** airline (company)
11 商事会社 **shōji-gaisha** business company
運送会社 **unsō-gaisha** transport/express company
情報化社会 **jōhōka shakai** information-oriented society
12 貿易会社 **bōeki-gaisha** trading firm
13 靖国神社 **Yasukuni-jinja** (shrine in Tōkyō dedicated to fallen Japanese soldiers)
14 製薬会社 **seiyaku-gaisha** pharmaceutical company

──────── 5 ────────

8 東印度会社 **Higashi Indo Gaisha** East India Company

4e3.2

祀

SHI, matsu(ru) deify, worship; year

──────── 2 ────────

6 合祀 **gōshi** enshrine together
11 祭祀 **saishi** rites, religious services
祭祀料 **saishiryō** grant for funeral expenses

4e3.3

奈

NA what?, how?

──────── 1 ────────

7 奈良 **Nara** (city, Nara-ken)
奈良県 **Nara-ken** (prefecture)
奈良漬 **narazu(ke)** pickles seasoned in saké lees
12 奈落 **naraku** hell, hades; theater basement

──────── 2 ────────

5 加奈陀 **Kanada** Canada
9 神奈川県 **Kanagawa-ken** (prefecture)

──────── 4 ────────

4e4.1 / 1390

祉 祉

SHI happiness

—————— 2 ——————

13 福祉 **fukushi** welfare, well-being

—————— 4 ——————

7 社会福祉 **shakai fukushi** social welfare

4e4.2

祇 祇   **GI** local god; the gods

—————— 1 ——————

13 祇園 **Gion** (name of a shrine, festival, and red-light district in Kyōto)

—————— 2 ——————

6 地祇 **chigi** earthly deities
9 神祇 **jingi** deities of heaven and earth
  神祇官 **jingikan** Shinto commissioner

4e4.3 / 621

祈 祈   **KI, ino(ru)** pray; wish
        ino(ri) prayer

—————— 1 ——————

8 祈念 **kinen** a prayer
11 祈祷 **kitō** prayer
14 祈誓 **kisei** vow, oath
15 祈請 **kisei** vow, oath
19 祈禱 **kitō** prayer
  祈禱書 **kitōsho** prayer book
  祈願 **kigan** a prayer

—————— 2 ——————

5 主祈 **Shu (no) Ino(ri)** the Lord's Prayer

—————— 5 ——————

4e5.1 / 310

神 神   **SHIN, JIN, kami, kan-, kō-** god, God

—————— 1 ——————

0 神さびる **kami(sabiru)** be hallowed/peaceful
2 神人 **shinjin** gods and men; demigod
  神力 **shinryoku, shinriki** divine power
3 神々 **kōgō(shii)** divine, sublime, awe-inspiring **kamigami** gods
4 神仏 **shinbutsu** gods and Buddha; Shinto and Buddhism
  神化 **shinka** deification, apotheosis
  神父 **shinpu** (Catholic) priest, Father
  神木 **shinboku** sacred tree
  神火 **shinka** sacred flame, divine fire
  神戸 **Kōbe** (city, Hyōgo-ken)
5 神出鬼没 **shinshutsu-kibotsu** elusive, phantom
  神仙 **shinsen** hermit-wizard

神代 **jindai** age/era of the gods
神代文字 **jindai moji** ancient Japanese characters
神代杉 **jindaisugi** lignitized cedar
神功 **Jingū** (empress, 201-269)
神主 **kannushi** Shinto priest
6 神気 **shinki** energy, spirits; mind
神曲 **Shinkyoku** (Dante's) Divine Comedy
神州 **shinshū** land of the gods, Japan
神色 **shinshoku** mind and countenance
神色自若 **shinshoku-jijaku** calm and composed, unruffled
神灯 **shintō** sacred/festival lantern
神式 **shinshiki** Shinto rites
7 神来 **shinrai** inspiration
神体 **shintai** relic in a Shinto shrine
神助 **shinjo** divine aid
神技 **shingi** consummate skill
神妙 **shinmyō** mysterious, marvelous; admirable; gentle
神学 **shingaku** theology
神学士 **shingakushi** Doctor of Divinity
神学校 **shingakkō** theological seminary
神社 **jinja** Shinto shrine
8 神事 **shinji** Shinto rituals
神宝 **shinpō** sacred/shrine treasures
神官 **shinkan** Shinto priest
神国 **shinkoku** land of the gods
神明 **shinmei** deity, God
神奈川県 **Kanagawa-ken** (prefecture)
神性 **shinsei** divine nature, godhood
神武 **Jinmu** (emperor, 660–585 B.C.)
9 神信心 **kami-shinjin** piety, devoutness
神降 **kamio(roshi)** spiritualism; séance
神変 **shinpen** immeasurable/mysterious change
神変不思儀 **shinpen-fushigi** miracle, marvel
神前 **shinzen** before God, at the shrine
神前結婚 **shinzen kekkon** Shinto wedding
神速 **shinsoku** speed, swiftness
神通力 **jintsūriki, jinzūriki** supernatural power
神風 **kamikaze** divine wind; kamikaze
神品 **shinpin** inspired work, masterpiece
神祇 **jingi** deities of heaven and earth
神祇官 **jingikan** Shinto commissioner
神神 **kōgō(shii)** divine, sublime, awe-inspiring **kamigami** gods
神政 **shinsei** theocracy
神威 **shin'i** God's/gods' majesty
10 神剣 **shinken** sacred/divine sword
神酒 **(o)miki, shinshu** sacred saké, libation
神宮 **jingū** Shinto shrine; the Ise Shrines
神格 **shinkaku** godhood, divinity
神格化 **shinkakuka** deification
神秘 **shinpi** mystery

4

木
月
日
火
礻 5←
王
牛
方
攵
欠
心
戸
戈

神秘主義 **shinpi shugi** mysticism
神秘的 **shinpiteki** mystic(al), mysterious
神秘家 **shinpika** a mystic
神秘説 **shinpisetsu** mysticism
神秘劇 **shinpigeki** mystery drama
神託 **shintaku** oracle, divine message
神馬 **shinme** sacred horse
11 神亀 **Jikki** (era, 724–728)
神道 **shintō** Shintoism
神域 **shin'iki** shrine precincts
神掛 **kamika(kete)** swearing by a god; for sure, absolutely
神授 **shinju** divine gift
神経 **shinkei** nerve
神経学 **shinkeigaku** neurology
神経系 **shinkeikei** nervous system
神経病 **shinkeibyō** nervous disorder
神経症 **shinkeishō** nervous disorder
神経痛 **shinkeitsū** neuralgia
神経戦 **shinkeisen** war of nerves
神経節 **shinkeisetsu** ganglion
神経質 **shinkeishitsu** nervous, high-strung
神符 **shinpu** charm, amulet, talisman
12 神葬 **shinsō** Shinto funeral
神棚 **kamidana** household altar-shelf
神智 **shinchi** divine wisdom
神無月 **kannazuki** tenth lunar month, October
神童 **shindō** child prodigy, wunderkind
13 神業 **kamiwaza** the work of God; superhuman feat
神隠 **kamikaku(shi)** be spirited away
kamigaku(re) (gods') hiding
神殿 **shinden** temple, shrine
神楽 **kagura** Shinto music and dancing
神楽堂 **kaguradō** Shinto dance pavilion
神楽殿 **kaguraden** Shinto dance pavilion
神聖 **shinsei** holy; sanctity, dignity
神聖視 **shinseishi** regard as sacred
神意 **shin'i** God's will, providence
神話 **shinwa** myth, mythology
神話学 **shinwagaku** mythology
神詣 **kamimō(de)** shrine visiting
14 神徳 **shintoku** divine power/virtue
神嘗祭 **Kannamesai** Shinto Festival of New Rice (October 17)
神様 **kamisama** God; god
神罰 **shinbatsu** divine punishment
15 神慮 **shinryo** divine will, decree of heaven
神器 **jingi, shinki** the (three) sacred treasures (mirror, sword, jewels)
神権 **shinken** divine right (of kings)
神権政治 **shinken seiji** theocracy
神霊 **shinrei** spirit
16 神薬 **shin'yaku** wonder drug
神橋 **shinkyō** sacred bridge
神憑 **kamigaka(ri)** divine/spirit possession

神頼 **kamidano(mi)** calling on God when in distress
17 神輿 **mikoshi** (Shinto) palanquin shrine
18 神髄 **shinzui** (quint)essence, soul
神職 **shinshoku** Shinto priest(hood)
神鎮 **kamishizu(maru)** (a god) be quietly present
19 神璽 **shinji** sacred jewels (one of the three sacred treasures); emperor's seal
神韻 **shin'in(-hyōbyō)** an undefinable artistic excellence
神韻縹渺 **shin'in-hyōbyō** an undefinable artistic excellence
神鏡 **shinkyō** sacred mirror (one of the three sacred treasures)
20 神懸 **kamiga(kari)** divine/spirit possession
神護景雲 **Jingo Keiun** (era, 767–769)
21 神饌 **shinsen** food-and-wine offering to the gods

——————— 2 ———————

1 一神教 **isshinkyō** monotheism
2 入神 **nyūshin** inspired, divine
3 大神宮 **Daijingū** the Grand Shrine (at Ise)
女神 **megami, joshin, nyoshin** goddess
山神 **yama (no) kami** god of a mountain; one's wife
4 天神 **tenjin** the heavenly gods; Michizane's spirit **amatsukami** the heavenly gods
氏神 **ujigami** patron deity
水神 **suijin** water god
心神 **shinshin** mind
心神喪失 **shinshin sōshitsu** not of sound mind
5 半神 **hanshin** demigod
失神 **shisshin** faint, lose consciousness
生神 **i(ki)gami** a living god
生神様 **i(ki)gamisama** a living god
石神 **ishigami, shakujin** a stone that is worshipped, a stone god
6 多神教 **tashinkyō** polytheism
多神教的 **tashinkyōteki** polytheistic
多神論 **tashinron** polytheism
死神 **shi(ni)gami** god of death; death
阪神 **Han-Shin** Ōsaka-Kōbe area
汎神論 **hanshinron** pantheism
安神立命 **anshin-ritsumei** spiritual peace and enlightenment
守神 **mamo(ri)gami** guardian deity
有神論 **yūshinron** theism
7 里神楽 **sato kagura** sacred dance performance in a Shinto shrine
邪神 **jashin** evil deity, demon, false god
花神 **kashin** flower goddess; spirit of a flower
応神 **Ōjin** (emperor, 270–310)
見神 **kenshin** beatific vision

8 河神 **kashin** river god
牧神 **bokushin** god of livestock raising, Pan
武神 **bushin** god of war
9 降神術 **kōshinjutsu** spiritualism
軍神 **gunshin** god of war; war hero
風神 **fūshin, fūjin** god of the wind
風神雷神 **fūjin-raijin** the gods of wind and
thunder
海神 **kaijin, kaishin, watatsumi** sea god
荒神 **kōjin** kitchen god
aragami fierce deity
神 **kōgō(shii)** divine, sublime, awe-inspiring
kamigami gods
祖神 **soshin** ancestral gods
10 随神道 **Kannagara (no) Michi** Shintoism
竜神 **ryūjin** dragon god/king
鬼神 **kijin, kishin, onigami** fierce god;
departed soul
11 崇神 **Sujin** (emperor, 97–30 B.C.)
祭神 **saishin** the enshrined deity
視神経 **shishinkei** optic nerve
理神論 **rishinron** deism
12 御神火 **goshinka** volcanic fires
御神酒 **omiki** sacred saké, saké offering
無神経 **mushinkei** insensible to
無神論 **mushinron** atheism
敬神 **keishin** reverence, piety, devoutness
惟神道 **kannagara (no) michi** Shintoism
結神 **musu(bi no) kami** Cupid
歯神経 **shishinkei** dental nerve
貴神 **kishin** (gentle)man of rank
13 傷神 **shōshin** heartbreak, sorrow
嗅神経 **kyūshinkei** olfactory nerve
福神 **fukujin** god of good fortune
福神漬 **fukujinzu(ke)** vegetables pickled in
soy sauce
雷神 **raijin** the god of thunder
14 歌神 **kashin** god(dess) of poetry, muse
精神 **seishin** mind, spirit
精神力 **seishinryoku** force of will
精神分析 **seishin bunseki** psychoanalysis
精神分裂症 **seishin bunretsushō** schizophrenia
精神的 **seishinteki** mental, spiritual
精神科 **seishinka** psychiatry
精神病 **seishinbyō** mental illness/disorder
17 聴神経 **chōshinkei** auditory nerve
18 瀆神 **tokushin** blasphemy, sacrilege, profanity
瀆神罪 **tokushinzai** blasphemy, sacrilege,
profanity
21 魔神 **majin** evil deity, devil

——————— 3 ———————
2 七福神 **Shichifukujin** the Seven Gods of
Good Fortune
3 三種神器 **Sanshu (no) Jingi** the Three Sacred

Treasures (mirror, sword, and jewels)
万有神教 **ban'yū shinkyō** pantheism
4 太陽神 **taiyōshin** sun god
天平神護 **Tenpyō Jingo** (era, 765–767)
天地神明 **tenchi-shinmei** the gods of heaven
and earth
5 末梢神経 **masshō shinkei** peripheral nerves
6 守護神 **shugojin** guardian/tutelary deity,
mascot
自律神経 **jiritsu shinkei** autonomic nerve
8 京阪神 **Kei-Han-Shin** Kyōto-Ōsaka-Kōbe
明治神宮 **Meiji Jingū** Meiji Shrine
9 皇太神宮 **Kōtai Jingū** the Ise Shrine
疫病神 **yakubyōgami** god of the plague
10 座骨神経 **zakotsu shinkei** sciatic nerve
座骨神経痛 **zakotsu shinkeitsū** sciatic
neuralgia
11 貧乏神 **binbōgami** god of poverty
道祖神 **dōsojin** travelers' guardian deity
産土神 **ubusunagami** tutelary deity, genius
loci
13 靖国神社 **Yasukuni-jinja** (shrine in Tōkyō
dedicated to fallen Japanese soldiers)

——————— 4 ———————
4 天照大神 **Amaterasu Ōmikami** the Sun
Goddess
6 伊勢大神宮 **Ise Daijingū** the Grand Shrines
of Ise
9 風神雷神 **fūjin-raijin** the gods of wind and
thunder
10 鬼子母神 **Kishibojin, Kishimojin** (goddess
of children)

4e5.2

祓 **FUTSU, hara(u)** exorcise
harai purification, exorcism

——————— 1 ———————
11 祓清 **hara(i)kiyo(meru)** purify, exorcise

——————— 2 ———————
3 大祓 **ōharai** exorcism; Shinto purification
ceremony

祕 → 秘 **5d5.6**

4e5.3

祐 祐 **YŪ** help

——————— 1 ———————
12 祐筆 **yūhitsu** amanuensis, secretary

4

木
月
日
火
礻   5←
王
牛
方
攵
欠
心
戸
戈

4e5.4 / 622

祖 祖
SO ancestor

─────────── 1 ───────────

4 祖父 **sofu** grandfather
祖父母 **sofubo** grandparents
5 祖母 **sobo** grandmother
6 祖先 **sosen** ancestor, forefathers
7 祖述 **sojutsu** expound/propagate one's master's doctrines
祖述者 **sojutsusha** exponent
8 祖宗 **sosō** ancestors, forefathers
祖国 **sokoku** one's homeland/fatherland
祖国愛 **sokokuai** love for one's country
9 祖神 **soshin** ancestral gods
10 祖師 **soshi** founder of a sect
13 祖業 **sogyō** family business of many generations
15 祖廟 **sobyō** ancestral mausoleum/tomb

─────────── 2 ───────────

4 元祖 **ganso** originator, founder, inventor, pioneer
太祖 **taiso** first emperor (of a dynasty), founder
父祖 **fuso** forefathers, ancestors
6 同祖 **dōso** common ancestor
先祖 **senzo** ancestor
8 始祖 **shiso** founder, originator, father
宗祖 **shūso** founder of a sect
9 皇祖 **kōso** Founder of the Empire
10 高祖 **kōso** founder of a dynasty/sect
高祖父 **kōsofu** great-great-grandfather
高祖母 **kōsobo** great-great-grandmother
教祖 **kyōso** founder of a sect
11 曽祖父 **sōsofu, hiijiji** great-grandfather
曽祖母 **sōsobo, hiibaba** great-grandmother
道祖神 **dōsojin** travelers' guardian deity
12 遠祖 **enso** remote ancestors, forefathers
開祖 **kaiso** (sect) founder, originator
14 鼻祖 **biso** founder, originator
15 養祖父 **yōsofu** foster grandfather
養祖母 **yōsobo** foster grandmother

4e5.5 / 851

祝 祝
SHUKU, SHŪ, iwa(u) celebrate, congratulate

─────────── 1 ───────────

0 祝する **shuku(suru)** celebrate, congratulate, bless
4 祝文 **shukubun** congratulatory message
祝日 **shukujitsu, iwa(i)bi** festival day, holiday
6 祝返 **iwa(i)gae(shi)** return gift
7 祝言 **shūgen** congratulations; celebration; wedding

8 祝事 **iwa(i)goto** auspicious/festive occasion
祝典 **shukuten** celebration, festival
祝杯 **shukuhai** a toast
祝物 **iwa(i)mono** congratulatory gift
10 祝酒 **iwa(i)zake** a drink in celebration
祝宴 **shukuen** congratulatory banquet, feast
祝砲 **shukuhō** (21-gun) salute
11 祝祭 **shukusai** festival, holiday
祝祭日 **shukusaijitsu** festival, holiday
12 祝詞 **norito** Shinto prayer
shukushi congratulatory message
祝賀 **shukuga** celebration; congratulations
祝賀会 **shukugakai** a celebration
13 祝福 **shukufuku** blessing, benediction
祝意 **shukui** congratulations
祝辞 **shukuji** (speech of) congratulations
祝電 **shukuden** telegram of congratulations
15 祝儀 **shūgi** (wedding) celebration
19 祝禱 **shukutō** benediction, blessing

─────────── 2 ───────────

3 万祝 **maiwai** fisherman's coat (given by shipowner to crew to congratulate them on a big catch)
4 内祝 **uchiiwa(i)** family celebration; small present on the occasion of a family celebration
内祝言 **naishūgen** private wedding
7 言祝 **kotoho(gu)** congratulate
9 前祝 **maeiwa(i)** advance celebration
12 間祝 **maiwa(i)** fisherman's coat (given by shipowner to crew to congratulate them on a big catch)
間祝着 **maiwa(i)gi** festive fisherman's kimono
15 慶祝 **keishuku** congratulation; celebration

─────────── 3 ───────────

6 名付祝 **nazu(ke) iwa(i)** naming ceremony, christening
14 誕生祝 **tanjō iwa(i)** birthday celebration

祢 → 禰 4e14.1

4e5.6

祚
SO happiness; imperial throne; year

─────────── 2 ───────────

5 永祚 **Eiso** (era, 989–990)

4e5.7

祇
SHI be respectful

4e5.8

祠

SHI worship, deify; festival; small shrine
hokora small shrine

———————— 2 ————————

11 淫祠 **inshi** shrine to an evil god

4e5.9

祟

SUI, tata(ru) bring evil upon, curse, haunt

———————— 6 ————————

4e6.1 / 1576

祥 祥

SHŌ, JŌ happiness; good omen

———————— 1 ————————

4 祥月 **shōtsuki** the month of one's death
祥月命日 **shōtsuki meinichi** anniversary of one's death

———————— 2 ————————

4 不祥 **fushō** inauspicious; disgraceful, deplorable
6 吉祥 **kisshō** good/lucky omen
吉祥天 **Kichijōten** Sri-mahadevi, goddess of fortune
9 発祥 **hasshō** origin, beginnings
発祥地 **hasshōchi** cradle, birthplace
13 瑞祥 **zuishō** good omen
14 嘉祥 **kashō** good omen
Kashō (era, 848–851)

4e6.2 / 922

票

HYŌ slip of paper, ballot, vote

———————— 1 ————————

7 票決 **hyōketsu** vote, voting
13 票数 **hyōsū** number of votes

———————— 2 ————————

1 一票 **ippyō** a vote
5 白票 **hakuhyō** white/affirmative vote; blank ballot
6 伝票 **denpyō** slip of paper
7 投票 **tōhyō** vote
投票区 **tōhyōku** voting district
投票日 **tōhyōbi** voting day
投票用紙 **tōhyō yōshi** ballot
投票者 **tōhyōsha** voter
投票所 **tōhyōjo** polling place, the polls
投票率 **tōhyōritsu** (rate of) voter turnout
投票数 **tōhyōsū** number of votes

投票権 **tōhyōken** right to vote, suffrage
投票箱 **tōhyōbako** ballot box
8 青票 **aohyō** blue ballot, opposing vote
11 得票 **tokuhyō** votes obtained
12 散票 **sanpyō** scattered votes
証票 **shōhyō** voucher
開票 **kaihyō** ballot counting
開票所 **kaihyōjo** ballot-counting place

———————— 3 ————————

8 受験票 **jukenhyō** examination admission ticket
12 無投票 **mutōhyō** dispensing with voting
14 認識票 **ninshikihyō** identification tag

———————— 4 ————————

2 人民投票 **jinmin tōhyō** plebiscite, referendum
9 単記投票 **tanki tōhyō** voting for one person only

4e6.3 / 617

祭

SAI, matsu(ru) deify; worship
matsu(ri) festival

———————— 1 ————————

3 祭上 **matsu(ri)a(geru)** exalt (someone)
4 祭文 **saimon, saibun** Shinto funeral prayer; address to the gods
祭込 **matsu(ri)ko(mu)** give (someone) a sinecure; recommend a fool for a post
祭日 **saijitsu** holiday; festival day
5 祭司 **saishi** high priest
祭礼 **sairei** festival, ritual
祭主 **saishu** officiating priest; chief priest of the Ise Shrines
6 祭式 **saishiki** ritual, rites, ceremony
8 祭事 **saiji** festival, ritual, rites
祭典 **saiten** festival, ritual
祭服 **saifuku** vestments
祭祀 **saishi** rites, religious services
祭祀料 **saishiryō** grant for funeral expenses
祭具 **saigu** ceremonial equipment
9 祭神 **saishin** the enshrined deity
祭政 **saisei** church and state
祭政一致 **saisei-itchi** theocracy
12 祭場 **saijō** site of a ceremony
15 祭儀 **saigi** festival
祭器 **saiki** ceremonial equipment
16 祭壇 **saidan** altar

———————— 2 ————————

3 大祭 **taisai, ōmatsu(ri)** grand festival
5 司祭 **shisai** (Catholic) priest
司祭職 **shisaishoku** (Catholic) priesthood
6 年祭 **nensai** anniversary
血祭 **chimatsu(ri)** blood offering (to the war god)

7 助祭 **josai** (Catholic) deacon
花祭 **hanamatsu(ri)** Buddha's-birthday festival
村祭 **muramatsu(ri)** village festival
8 例祭 **reisai** regular/annual festival
国祭日 **kokusaibi** national holiday
9 盆祭 **Bon-matsu(ri)** Bon Festival
後祭 **ato (no) matsu(ri)** too late (for the fair)
祝祭 **shukusai** festival, holiday
祝祭日 **shukusaijitsu** festival, holiday
秋祭 **akimatsu(ri)** autumn festival
10 宵祭 **yoimatsu(ri)** eve (of a festival), vigil
夏祭 **natsumatsu(ri)** summer festival
12 葬祭 **sōsai** funerals and festivals
16 燔祭 **hansai** burn offerings
親祭 **shinsai** Shinto rites conducted by the emperor
18 雛祭 **hinamatsu(ri)** Girls' Doll Festival (March 3)

_____ 3 _____

3 大嘗祭 **Daijōsai, Ōname-matsuri** first Harvest Festival after an emperor's enthronement
4 収穫祭 **shūkakusai** harvest festival
文化祭 **bunkasai** cultural festival
6 地鎮祭 **jichinsai** ground-breaking ceremony
百年祭 **hyakunensai** a centennial
7 芸術祭 **geijutsusai** art festival
労働祭 **rōdōsai** Labor Day; May Day
8 招魂祭 **shōkonsai** memorial service; Memorial Day
9 前夜祭 **zen'yasai** (Christmas) Eve
神嘗祭 **Kannamesai** Shinto Festival of New Rice (October 17)
10 記念祭 **kinensai** commoration, anniversary
12 復活祭 **Fukkatsusai** Easter
植樹祭 **shokujusai** Arbor Day
13 聖誕祭 **Seitansai** Christmas
感謝祭 **kanshasai** Thanksgiving
新嘗祭 **niinamesai** Harvest Festival
15 慰霊祭 **ireisai** memorial service
17 謝肉祭 **shanikusai** carnival
18 鎮魂祭 **chinkonsai** services for the deceased

_____ 4 _____

9 冠婚葬祭 **kankonsōsai** ceremonial occasions

4e6.4 / 1617

尉

I officer

_____ 1 _____

8 尉官 **ikan** officer below the rank of major

_____ 2 _____

3 大尉 **taii** captain; lieutenant

4 中尉 **chūi** first lieutenant; lieutenant junior grade
少尉 **shōi** second lieutenant, ensign
10 准尉 **jun'i** warrant officer

_____ 7 _____

祷 → 禱 **4e14.2**

4e7.1 / 606

視 視

SHI see, look at; (as suffix) regard as

_____ 1 _____

2 視力 **shiryoku** visual acuity, eyesight
7 視角 **shikaku** angle of vision; viewpoint
視学 **shigaku** school inspection/inspector
視学官 **shigakkan** school inspector
8 視官 **shikan** organ of sight
9 視点 **shiten** center of one's field of view; viewpoint
視度 **shido** visibility
視神経 **shishinkei** optic nerve
視界 **shikai** field/range of vision, visibility
10 視差 **shisa** parallax
11 視野 **shiya** field of vision/view
12 視覚 **shikaku** sense of sight, vision
視診 **shishin** (diagnosis by) visual inspection
14 視察 **shisatsu** inspection, observance
15 視線 **shisen** line of vision, one's eyes/gaze
17 視聴 **shichō** looking and listening, attention
視聴率 **shichōritsu** (TV show popularity) rating
視聴覚 **shichōkaku** audiovisual

_____ 2 _____

1 一視同仁 **isshi-dōjin** impartiality, universal brotherhood
4 幻視 **genshi** visual hallucination
内視鏡 **naishikyō** endoscope
5 巡視 **junshi** inspection tour, patrol
巡視艇 **junshitei** patrol boat
巨視的 **kyoshiteki** macroscopic, in broad perspective
6 仰視 **gyōshi** look up
近視 **kinshi** nearsightedness
近視眼 **kinshigan** myopia
同視 **dōshi** treat alike, make no distinction between
7 乱視 **ranshi** astigmatism
8 直視 **chokushi** look straight at, face squarely
虎視眈々 **koshi-tantan** with hostile vigilance, waiting one's chance (to pounce)

虎視耽々 **koshi-tantan** with hostile vigilance, waiting one's chance (to pounce)

注視 **chūshi** close observation, scrutiny

9 重視 **jūshi** attach great importance to

透視 **tōshi** see through; fluoroscopy; clairvoyance

透視力 **tōshiryoku** penetration; clairvoyant powers

透視画法 **tōshigahō** perspective (drawing)

洞視 **dōshi** insight, discernment

10 既視感 **kishikan** (feeling of) déjà vu

弱視 **jakushi** poor eyesight

座視 **zashi** merely sit and watch (without helping)

11 斜視 **shashi** strabismus (cross-eye or walleye), squint

斜視図 **shashizu** perspective view

12 傍視 **bōshi** look on from the side

遠視 **enshi** farsightedness

遠視眼 **enshigan** farsightedness

検視 **kenshi** investigation into the facts

無視 **mushi** ignore, disregard

覘視孔 **tenshikō** peephole

軽視 **keishi** belittle, neglect, scorn

13 微視的 **bishiteki** microscopic

14 蔑視 **besshi** look down on, regard with contempt

熟視 **jukushi** stare at, study, scrutinize

複視 **fukushi** double vision

15 黙視 **mokushi** overlook, connive at

敵視 **tekishi** regard with hostility

監視 **kanshi** monitor, keep watch over

監視者 **kanshisha** guard, caretaker, watchman

監視所 **kanshisho** lookout, guard/observation post

監視船 **kanshisen** guard boat, cutter

16 凝視 **gyōshi** stare, steady gaze, fixation

17 環視 **kanshi** concentrated attention (of others)

聴視 **chōshi** listening to and watching

聴視者 **chōshisha** (TV) viewer(s)

聴視料 **chōshiryō** television fee

聴視覚 **chōshikaku** audio-visual

19 警視 **keishi** police superintendent

警視庁 **Keishichō** Metropolitan Police Agency

━━━━━━━ 3 ━━━━━━━

5 白眼視 **hakuganshi** look askance/coldly at

6 同一視 **dōitsushi** consider alike, put in the same category

9 重大視 **jūdaishi** regard as important/serious

重要視 **jūyōshi** regard as important

客観視 **kyakkanshi** view objectively

度外視 **dogaishi** disregard, ignore

神聖視 **shinseishi** regard as sacred

11 偶像視 **gūzōshi** idolize

━━━━━━━ 8 ━━━━━━━

4e8.1

祺

KI fortunate; peace of mind

4e8.2

禄 祿

ROKU fief, stipend, allowance; happiness

━━━━━━━ 1 ━━━━━━━

10 禄高 **rokudaka** (amount of a samurai's) stipend/salary

━━━━━━━ 2 ━━━━━━━

3 小禄 **shōroku** small stipend

4 元禄 **Genroku** (era, 1688–1704)

天禄 **Tenroku** (era, 970–973)

文禄 **Bunroku** (era, 1592–1596)

5 永禄 **Eiroku** (era, 1558–1570)

7 享禄 **Kyōroku** (era, 1528–1532)

8 長禄 **Chōroku** (era, 1457–1460)

10 俸禄 **hōroku** stipend, pay, salary

俸禄米 **hōrokumai** rice given in payment for services

高禄 **kōroku** high salary

家禄 **karoku** hereditary stipend

11 貫禄 **kanroku** weight, dignity

13 微禄 **biroku** small stipend, pittance

福禄寿 **Fukurokuju** (tall-headed god of happiness, wealth, and longevity)

14 嘉禄 **Karoku** (era, 1225–1227)

4e8.3 / 482

禁

KIN prohibition

━━━━━━━ 1 ━━━━━━━

0 禁じる/ずる **kin(jiru/zuru)** prohibit, ban, forbid; abstain from

4 禁中 **kinchū** the court, the imperial household

禁止 **kinshi** prohibition

禁止令 **kinshirei** prohibition (decree), ban

5 禁令 **kinrei** prohibition, ban, interdict

禁圧 **kin'atsu** suppress, ban, prohibit

禁句 **kinku** tabooed word/phrase

禁札 **kinsatsu** prohibition-notice board

7 禁忌 **kinki** taboo; contraindication

禁戒 **kinkai** commandment

禁足 **kinsoku** confinement

8 禁制 **kinsei** prohibition, ban

禁制品 **kinseihin** contraband

禁治産 **kinchisan** (legally) incompetent

禁治産者 **kinchisansha** person adjudged incompetentg

4

木 月 日 火 ネ 王 牛 方 攵 欠 心 戸 戈

8←

禁固 **kinko** imprisonment
禁物 **kinmotsu** forbidden things, taboo
10 禁酒 **kinshu** abstinence from alcohol, Prohibition
禁酒会 **kinshukai** temperance society
禁酒法 **kinshuhō** Prohibition (law)
禁書 **kinsho** banned book
禁教 **kinkyō** prohibited religion
11 禁猟 **kinryō** No Hunting
禁猟区 **kinryōku** game preserve
禁猟期 **kinryōki** closed (hunting) season
禁欲 **kin'yoku** control of passions, self-denial, abstinence
禁欲主義 **kin'yoku shugi** asceticism, stoicism
禁断 **kindan** prohibition; withdrawal (symptoms)
禁断木実 **kindan (no) ko(no)mi** forbidden fruit
禁転載 **kintensai** Reproduction Prohibited, Copyright
禁鳥 **kinchō** protected bird
12 禁裡 **kinri** the imperial palace/court
禁絶 **kinzetsu** stamp out, ban
13 禁裏 **kinri** the imperial palace/court
禁裏様 **kinrisama** the emperor
禁煙 **kin'en** No Smoking
14 禁漁 **kinryō** No Fishing
禁漁区 **kinryōku** no-fishing area
禁漁期 **kinryōki** closed (fishing) season
禁獄 **kingoku** imprisonment
15 禁慾 **kin'yoku** control of passions, self-denial, abstinence
16 禁衛 **kin'ei** the imperial guards
禁衛隊 **kin'eitai** the imperial guards
禁輸 **kin'yu** embargo on export/import
禁輸品 **kin'yuhin** contraband
禁錮 **kinko** imprisonment

───────── 2 ─────────
5 失禁 **shikkin** incontinence (of urine/feces)
8 拘禁 **kōkin** confine, detain, imprison
国禁 **kokkin** national prohibition
9 独禁法 **dokkinhō** antitrust laws, the Anti-Monopoly Law (short for 独占禁止法)
11 軟禁 **nankin** house arrest
13 準禁治産 **junkinchisan** quasi-incompetence (in law)
準禁治産者 **junkinchisansha** a quasi-incompetent (person)
解禁 **kaikin** lifting a ban, open season
15 監禁 **kankin** imprison, confine
17 厳禁 **genkin** strictly prohibited

───────── 3 ─────────
3 女人禁制 **nyonin kinsei** closed to women
5 立入禁止 **tachiiri kinshi** Keep Out
8 金解禁 **kin kaikin** lifting the gold embargo

10 殺生禁断 **sesshō kindan** hunting and fishing prohibited
11 張紙禁止 **ha(ri)gami kinshi** Post No Bills

───────── 4 ─────────
3 土足厳禁 **dosoku genkin** Remove Shoes (sign)
4 火気厳禁 **kaki genkin** Danger: Flammable

───────── 9 ─────────

4e9.1 / 1379

福 福 **FUKU** fortune, blessing, happiness; wealth, welfare

───────── 1 ─────────
3 福々 **fukubuku(shii)** (fat and) happy-looking
福山 **Fukuyama** (city, Hiroshima-ken)
4 福井 **Fukui** (city, Fukui-ken)
福井県 **Fukui-ken** (prefecture)
福引 **fukubi(ki)** lottery, raffle
福引券 **fukubi(ki)ken** lottery ticket
7 福寿 **fukuju** happiness and longevity
福寿草 **fukujusō** Amur adonis
福助 **fukusuke** large-headed dwarf who brings good luck
福利 **fukuri** welfare, well-being
8 福岡 **Fukuoka** (city, Fukuoka-ken)
福岡県 **Fukuoka-ken** (prefecture)
福祉 **fukushi** welfare, well-being
9 福相 **fukusō** (plump) happy face
福神 **fukujin** god of good fortune
福神漬 **fukujinzu(ke)** vegetables pickled in soy sauce
福音 **fukuin** the Gospel; good news
福音書 **Fukuinsho** the Gospels
10 福島 **Fukushima** (city, Fukushima-ken)
福島県 **Fukushima-ken** (prefecture)
11 福運 **fukuun** happiness and good fortune
12 福禄寿 **Fukurokuju** (tall-headed god of happiness, wealth, and longevity)
13 福福 **fukubuku(shii)** (fat and) happy-looking
14 福徳 **fukutoku** good fortune

───────── 2 ─────────
2 七福神 **Shichifukujin** the Seven Gods of Good Fortune
子福 **kobuku** blessed with many children
子福者 **kobukusha** person blessed with many children
3 万福 **banpuku** all health and happiness
大福 **daifuku** great fortune, good luck
4 天福 **tenpuku** blessing of heaven
Tenpuku (era, 1233–1234)
5 民福 **minpuku** national welfare
6 多福 **(o)tafuku** ugly/homely woman
多福風邪 **(o)tafuku kaze** mumps

至福 **shifuku** supreme bliss, beatitude
7 利福 **rifuku** benefit and happiness
8 追福 **tsuifuku** memorial service
幸福 **kōfuku** happiness
9 祝福 **shukufuku** blessing, benediction
10 冥福 **meifuku** happiness in the next world, repose of someone's soul
11 清福 **seifuku** happiness
12 裕福 **yūfuku** wealth, affluence
13 福福 **fukubuku(shii)** (fat and) happy-looking
禍福 **kafuku** fortune and misfortune, weal or woe
15 慶福 **keifuku** happiness, blessings, welfare
19 艶福 **enpuku** success in love
艶福家 **enpukuka** ladies' man, a gallant

——————— 3 ———————
7 阿多福 **otafuku** ugly/homely woman
社会福祉 **shakai fukushi** social welfare

——————— 4 ———————
8 国利民福 **kokuri-minpuku** the national interest and the welfare of the people

4e9.2 / 1540
禅 禪   **ZEN** Zen Buddhism

——————— 1 ———————
5 禅尼 **zenni** Zen nun
6 禅寺 **zendera** Zen temple
7 禅学 **zengaku** Zen doctrines
禅杖 **zenjō** beating-stick to keep Zen meditators from dozing
8 禅味 **zenmi** Zen flavor, unworldliness
禅宗 **zenshū** the Zen sect
禅定 **zenjō** meditative concentration
禅林 **zenrin** Zen temple
禅門 **zenmon** entering the Zen priesthood
10 禅師 **zenji** Zen priest (a title)
禅家 **zenka, zenke** Zen sect/temple/priest
11 禅堂 **zendō** temple for Zen study
禅問答 **zen mondō** Zen/incomprehensible dialog
13 禅僧 **zensō** Zen priest
禅話 **zenwa** a talk on Zen philosophy
20 禅譲 **zenjō** abdication

——————— 2 ———————
8 参禅 **sanzen** Zen meditation
10 座禅 **zazen** (Zen) meditation

4e9.3
禎 禎   **TEI** happy; correct

——————— 2 ———————
14 嘉禎 **Katei** (era, 1235–1238)

4e9.4 / 1809
禍 禍   **KA, maga, wazawai** calamity, misfortune

——————— 1 ———————
6 禍因 **kain** cause of trouble, seeds of evil
7 禍乱 **karan** disturbances, upheavals
8 禍事 **magagoto** evil, disaster, mishap
10 禍害 **kagai** disaster, harm
禍根 **kakon** root of evil, source of calamity
11 禍患 **kakan** disaster, calamity; an evil
13 禍福 **kafuku** fortune and misfortune, weal or woe

——————— 2 ———————
3 大禍 **taika** great disaster
6 舌禍 **zekka** unfortunate slip of the tongue
7 赤禍 **sekka** the Red Peril
災禍 **saika** disaster, accident, misfortune
11 黄禍 **kōka** the Yellow Peril
惨禍 **sanka** terrible disaster, catastrophe
12 筆禍 **hikka** serious slip of the pen
13 戦禍 **senka** war damage, ravages of war
15 輪禍 **rinka** traffic accident
16 薬禍 **yakka** harmful side effects

4e9.5
禊   **KEI, misogi** Shinto purification ceremony

——————— 10 ———————
4e10.1
禑   **SHOKU** (proper name)

——————— 11 ———————
4e11.1 / 1934
隷 隸   **REI** servant; criminal; follow; (a style of kanji)

——————— 1 ———————
10 隷従 **reijū** slavery
隷書 **reisho** (ancient squared style of kanji)
12 隷属 **reizoku** be subordinate to

——————— 2 ———————
5 奴隷 **dorei** slave

——————— 12 ———————
禪 → 禅 4e9.2

4

木 月 日 火 礻 王 牛 方 攵 欠 心 戸 戈

11←

4e12.1

禧　**KI** fortunate, auspicious

4e12.2

禦　**GYO, fuse(gu)** defend against, prevent

———— 2 ————

6 防禦 **bōgyo** defense

4e12.3

瓢　**HYŌ, hisago** gourd

———— 1 ————

6 瓢虫 **tentōmushi** ladybug, ladybird beetle
18 瓢箪 **hyōtan** gourd, calabash
　瓢箪鯰 **hyōtan namazu** slippery fellow

———— 2 ————

3 干瓢 **kanpyō** dried gourd shavings
8 青瓢箪 **aobyōtan** green calabash/gourd;
　　pale-faced weakling
11 乾瓢 **kanpyō** dried gourd strips

隷 → 隷 4e11.1

———— 14 ————

4e14.1

禰 禰 祢 祢　**DEI, NE** ancestral shrine

———— 1 ————

8 禰宜 **negi** (lower rank of Shinto priest)

4e14.2

禱 祷　**TŌ, ino(ru)** pray

———— 2 ————

8 祈禱 **kitō** prayer
　祈禱書 **kitōsho** prayer book
9 連禱 **rentō** litany
　祝禱 **shukutō** benediction, blessing
15 黙禱 **mokutō** silent prayer/tribute

———— 16 ————

禮 → 礼 4e1.1

———— 17 ————

4e17.1

禳　**JŌ, hara(u)** exorcise, drive away (evil spirits)

———— 王 4f ————

王	壬	玉	主	全	玖	弄	玩	珊	玻	珀	珈	玳
0.1	3p1.1	0.2	1.1	2a4.16	3.1	3.2	4.1	5.1	5.2	5.3	5.4	5.5
珍	弥	玲	珂	皇	珥	珠	班	珪	琰	珞	珮	理
5.6	4f5.6	5.7	5.8	5.9	6.1	6.2	6.3	6.4	4f17.1	6.5	6.6	7.1
球	琅	琢	現	珸	琉	聖	望	琢	琳	斑	琲	琺
7.2	4f9.1	4f8.1	7.3	7.4	7.5	3b8.13	7.6	8.1	8.2	8.3	8.4	8.5
瑛	瑠	琥	琶	琵	琴	瑯	瑕	瑚	瑁	瑤	瑞	琿
8.6	8.7	8.8	8.9	8.10	8.11	9.1	9.2	9.3	9.4	9.5	9.6	9.7
瑜	聖	瑟	瑪	瑰	瑠	瑶	瑣	璃	瑳	瑩	瑱	對
9.8	9.9	9.10	10.1	10.2	10.3	4f9.5	10.4	10.5	10.6	10.7	10.8	2j5.5
業	璋	瑾	璞	璠	躾	環	璧	瓊	璽	瓏	瓔	
0a13.3	11.1	11.2	12.1	4f10.3	12.2	13.1	13.2	14.1	14.2	16.1	17.1	

———— 0 ————

4f0.1 / 294

王　**Ō** king

———— 1 ————

2 王子 **ōji** prince
3 王女 **ōjo** princess
4 王化 **ōka** emperor's benevolent influence
　王水 **ōsui** aqua regia

王手 **ōte** check, checkmate (in shōgi)
7 王位 **ōi** the throne, the crown
8 王事 **ōji** the emperor's/king's cause
王国 **ōkoku** kingdom, monarchy
王者 **ōja, ōsha** king
9 王侯 **ōkō** princes, royalty
王冠 **ōkan** crown; bottle cap
王城 **ōjō** royal castle
王室 **ōshitsu** royal family
王政 **ōsei** imperial rule, monarchy
10 王家 **ōke** royal family
王宮 **ōkyū** royal palace
王党 **ōtō** royalist party, Tories
王座 **ōza** the throne, the crown
11 王道 **ōdō** royal road; the rule of right, just rule
王族 **ōzoku** royal family, royalty
12 王朝 **ōchō** dynasty
14 王様 **ōsama** king
15 王権 **ōken** royal authority

——————— 2 ———————

2 二王 **Niō** fierce-looking temple-guarding Deva Kings
二王門 **Niōmon** temple gate guarded by Deva statues
八王子 **Hachiōji** (city, Tōkyō-to)
3 大王 **daiō** great king
女王 **joō** queen
女王蜂 **joōbachi** queen bee
4 天王星 **Tennōsei** Uranus
仁王 **Niō** Deva kings (guarding temple gate)
仁王門 **Niōmon** temple gate guarded by two fierce Deva king statues
6 列王 **retsuō** chronicles of the kings
8 法王 **hōō** the pope
法王庁 **Hōōchō** the Vatican
法王権 **hōōken** the papacy
国王 **kokuō** king
9 帝王 **teiō** monarch, emperor
帝王切開 **teiō sekkai** Caesarean section
海王星 **kaiōsei** Neptune
10 冥王星 **Meiōsei** Pluto
竜王 **ryūō** dragon god/king
12 勤王 **kinnō** loyalty to the emperor/king
勤王家 **kinnōka** loyalist, royalist
尊王 **sonnō** reverence for the emperor, advocacy of imperial rule
尊王党 **Sonnōtō** Imperialists
尊王攘夷 **sonnō-jōi** Revere the emperor and expel the barbarians.
15 諸王 **shoō** all/many kings
16 親王 **shinnō** imperial prince
18 藩王 **han'ō** rajah
21 魔王 **maō** the devil, Satan

——————— 3 ———————

4 内親王 **naishinnō** imperial/royal princess

5 打撃王 **dagekiō** leading/top batter
四天王 **shitennō** the four Deva kings; the big four
13 獅子王 **shishiō** the king of beasts

——————— 4 ———————

13 愛染明王 **Aizenmyōō** Ragaraja, six-armed god of love

壬 → 　**3p1.1**

4f0.2 / 295

玉　**GYOKU** gem, jewel
　　tama ball

——————— 1 ———————

0 玉ねぎ **tamanegi** onion
玉レタス **tamaretasu** iceberg lettuce
2 玉子 **tamago** egg
4 玉手箱 **tamatebako** treasure chest; Pandora's box
5 玉石 **gyokuseki** gems and stones; wheat and chaff　**tamaishi** round stone, boulder
6 玉汗 **tama (no) ase** beads of sweat
玉虫 **tamamushi** iridescent-winged insect
玉虫色 **tamamushi-iro** iridescent; ambiguous
7 玉体 **gyokutai** the emperor's person/presence
8 玉突 **tamatsu(ki)** billiards
玉杯 **gyokuhai** jade cup
9 玉乗 **tamano(ri)** balancing on a ball; dancer on a ball
玉垣 **tamagaki** fence (of a shrine)
玉屋 **tamaya** jeweler
玉砕 **gyokusai** death for honor
10 玉座 **gyokuza** the throne
11 玉菜 **tamana** cabbage
玉転 **tamakoro(gashi)** bowling, bowls
12 玉葱 **tamanegi** onion
玉軸受 **tamajikuu(ke)** ball bearing
13 玉蜀黍 **tōmorokoshi** corn, maize
14 玉緒 **tama(no)o** bead string; thread of life
18 玉髄 **gyokuzui** chalcedony
19 玉藻 **tamamo** seaweed
玉璽 **gyokuji** imperial seal
21 玉露 **gyokuro** refined green tea

——————— 2 ———————

3 上玉 **jōdama** fine jewel; best article
4 勾玉 **magatama** comma-shaped jewels
水玉 **mizutama** drop of water/dew; polka dots
手玉 **tedama** beanbag
手玉取 **tedama (ni) to(ru)** lead by the nose, wrap around one's little finger
火玉 **hidama** ball of fire

木 月 日 火 礻 王 牛 方 攵 欠 心 戸 戈

4

0 ←

5 矢玉 **yadama** arrows and bullets
半玉 **hangyoku** child geisha, apprentice entertainer
白玉 **shiratama** white gem, pearl; rice-flour dumpling
白玉粉 **shiratamako** rice flour
白玉楼 **hakugyokurō** (among) the dead, deceased
白玉椿 **shiratama tsubaki** white camellia
目玉 **medama, me (no) tama** eyeball
(o)medama a scolding
目玉商品 **medama shōhin** bargain item to attract customers, loss leader
目玉焼 **medamaya(ki)** sunny-side-up fried eggs
6 年玉 **toshidama** New Year's gift
7 肝玉 **kimo(t)tama** pluck, courage, grit
8 宝玉 **hōgyoku** precious stone, gem, jewel
青玉 **seigyoku** sapphire
炒玉子 **i(ri)tamago** scrambled eggs
金玉 **kintama** gold ball; testicles
kingyoku gold and jewels
9 首玉 **kubi(t)tama, kubitama** neck
茹玉子 **yu/u(de)tamago** boiled egg
紅玉 **kōgyoku** a ruby
10 剣玉 **kendama** ball-and-cup toy
珠玉 **shugyoku** gem, jewel, jewelry
11 埼玉県 **Saitama-ken** (prefecture)
黄玉 **ōgyoku, kōgyoku** topaz
悪玉 **akudama** bad guy, the villain
粗玉 **aratama** gem in the rough
雪玉 **yukidama** snowball
12 善玉 **zendama** good guy
弾玉 **haji(ki)dama** marbles
替玉 **ka(e)dama** substitute, stand-in, ringer
焼玉機関 **ya(ki)dama kikan** hot-bulb/ semidiesel engine
硬玉 **kōgyoku** jadeite
13 煎玉子 **i(ri)tamago** scrambled eggs
搔玉 **ka(ki)tama** egg soup
14 槍玉 **yaridama (ni ageru)** make a victim of
碧玉 **hekigyoku** jasper
緑玉 **ryokugyoku** emerald
緑玉石 **ryokugyokuseki** emerald
飴玉 **amedama** toffies, taffies, hard candies
16 親玉 **oyadama** boss, chief, leader
18 繭玉 **mayudama** (type of New Year's decoration)

———— 3 ————

3 大目玉 **ōmedama** big eyes; a scolding, dressing-down
8 金科玉条 **kinka-gyokujō** a golden rule
金殿玉楼 **kinden gyokurō** palatial residence
10 射干玉 **nubatama** pitch-black, darkness
烏羽玉 **ubatama** jet/raven/pitch black
12 掌中玉 **shōchū (no) tama** apple of one's eye

17 癇癪玉 **kanshakudama** fit of anger; firecracker

———— 1 ————

4f1.1 / 155

主 主 SHU, SU, SHŪ master; Lord; the main thing **nushi** owner; master **omo** main, principal **aruji** master

———— 1 ————

0 主として **shu (to shite)** mainly, chiefly
2 主人 **shujin** master; one's husband
主人公 **shujinkō** main character, hero (of a story)
主人役 **shujin'yaku** host(ess)
主力 **shuryoku** main force/strength
4 主文 **shubun** the text
5 主犯 **shuhan** principal offense/offender
主犯者 **shuhansha** principal offender
6 主任 **shunin** person in charge
主刑 **shukei** principal penalty
主色 **shushoku** predominant color
主因 **shuin** main cause, primary factor
主旨 **shushi** gist, purport, object
主成分 **shuseibun** main ingredient
7 主我 **shuga** ego, self
主我主義 **shuga shugi** egoism, love of self
主位 **shui** leading position, first place
主体 **shutai** the subject; main part
主体性 **shutaisei** subjectivity, independence
主君 **shukun** lord, master
主役 **shuyaku** major role; star
8 主事 **shuji** manager, director
主治医 **shujii** physician in charge/attendance
主治効能 **shuji kōnō** chief efficacy (of a drug)
主知主義 **shuchi shugi** intellectualism
主知的 **shuchiteki** intellectual
主祈 **Shu (no) Ino(ri)** the Lord's Prayer
9 主要 **shuyō** main, principal, essential, key
主客 **shukaku, shukyaku** host and guest, principal and auxiliary, subject and object
主客顛倒 **shukaku-tentō** reverse order, putting the cart before the horse
主査 **shusa** chairman of an investigation committee, president of a board of examiners
主計 **shukei** paymaster, accountant
主食 **shushoku** a staple food
主食物 **shushokumotsu** a staple food
10 主将 **shushō** commander-in-chief; captain (of a team)
主部 **shubu** main part; subject (in grammar)
主流 **shuryū** mainstream
主流派 **shuryūha** the leading faction
主従 **shujū** master and servant, lord and vassal

主家 **shuka** one's master's house
主宰 **shusai** preside over, run, supervise
主宰者 **shusaisha** president, chairman
主席 **shuseki** top place, first, head, chairman
主格 **shukaku** nominative case
主脈 **shumyaku** the main mountain range
主教 **shukyō** bishop, prelate
11 主動 **shudō** leadership
主動的 **shudōteki** autonomous
主唱 **shushō** advocate, promote, suggest
主婦 **shufu** housewife
主張 **shuchō** assertion, claim, contention
主脳 **shunō** leader
主脳会談 **shunō kaidan** summit conference
主脳会議 **shunō kaigi** summit conference
主務 **shumu** competent (authorities)
主情的 **shujōteki** emotional, emotive
主産地 **shusanchi** chief producing region
主産物 **shusanbutsu** main product
主眼 **shugan** main point/purpose
主眼点 **shuganten** main point/purpose
12 主筆 **shuhitsu** editor in chief
主訴 **shuso** main complaint/suit
主軸 **shujiku** main shaft/axis
13 主催 **shusai** sponsor, promote
主催者 **shusaisha** sponsor, organizer
主義 **shugi** -ism, principle
主義者 **shugisha** -ist, advocate (of a theory/
doctrine)
主幹 **shukan** editor in chief
主戦 **shusen** advocating going to war; top
(player)
主意 **shui** gist, purport, object
14 主演 **shuen** starring
主演者 **shuensha** star, leading actor
主導 **shudō** leadership
主導権 **shudōken** leadership
主製品 **shuseihin** main products
主管 **shukan** be in charge of, supervise,
manage(r)
主語 **shugo** subject (in grammar)
主領 **shuryō** leader, chief, boss
15 主潮 **shuchō** the main current
主審 **shushin** head umpire
主賓 **shuhin** guest of honor
主権 **shuken** sovereignty
主権在民 **shuken-zaimin** sovereignty
resides with the people
主権者 **shukensha** sovereign, supreme ruler
16 主謀者 **shubōsha** (ring)leader, mastermind
17 主翼 **shuyoku** main wing (of an airplane)
18 主観 **shukan** subjectivity; subject, ego
主観主義 **shukan shugi** subjectivism
主観的 **shukanteki** subjective
主観性 **shukansei** subjectivity
主観論 **shukanron** subjectivism

主題 **shudai** theme, subject matter
主題歌 **shudaika** theme song

────────── 2 ──────────

3 大主教 **daishukyō** archbishop (Protestant)
女主 **onna aruji** mistress, landlady, hostess
山主 **yamanushi** owner of a mountain; mine
operator
4 天主 **Tenshu** Lord of Heaven, God
天主教 **Tenshukyō** Roman Catholicism
戸主 **koshu** head of a family/household
戸主権 **koshuken** status/authority as family
head
5 民主 **minshu** democratic
民主化 **minshuka** democratization
民主主義 **minshu shugi** democracy
民主国 **minshukoku** democratic country, a
democracy
民主的 **minshuteki** democratic
民主党 **Minshutō** Democratic Party
6 地主 **jinushi** landlord
名主 **nanushi** (ancient) village headman
na(zuke)nushi person who names the
newborn, godparent
当主 **tōshu** the present head of the family
自主 **jishu** independent, autonomous
自主的 **jishuteki** independent, autonomous
自主権 **jishuken** autonomy
7 坊主 **bōzu** Buddhist priest, bonze; shaven
head; boy, rascal
坊主刈 **bōzuga(ri)** close-cropped haircut
坊主頭 **bōzuatama** shaven/close-cropped
head
君主 **kunshu** monarch, sovereign
君主国 **kunshukoku** a monarchy
売主 **u(ri)nushi** seller, vendor
社主 **shashu** head of a company
8 送主 **oku(ri)nushi** sender
法主 **hossu, hosshu** high priest
英主 **eishu** wise ruler
宗主 **sōshu** suzerain
店主 **tenshu** shopkeeper, proprietor
国主 **kokushu** lord, governor, daimyo
明主 **meishu** wise ruler
金主 **kinshu** financial backer
9 亭主 **teishu** husband; master, host
亭主関白 **teishu kanpaku** autocratic husband
城主 **jōshu** lord of a castle
持主 **mo(chi)nushi** owner, possessor
拾主 **hiro(i)nushi** finder
神主 **kannushi** Shinto priest
施主 **seshu** chief mourner; donor, benefactor;
builder
故主 **koshu** one's former master
10 借主 **ka(ri)nushi** borrower, renter
倉主 **kuranushi** warehouse owner

4

木
月
日
火
ネ
王
牛
方
攵
欠
心
戸
戈

1←

荷主 **ninushi** owner, shipper, consignor
家主 **yanushi, ienushi** houseowner, landlord
座主 **zasu, zashu** head priest of a temple
株主 **kabunushi** shareholder, stockholder
校主 **kōshu** private-school owner
教主 **kyōshu** founder of a sect
馬主 **bashu** horse owner
11 斎主 **saishu** presiding priest
宿主 **yadonushi** landlord, host
     shukushu (parasite's) host
庵主 **anshu** hermitage master; tea-ceremony
     host; cloistered Buddhist nun
祭主 **saishu** officiating priest; chief priest of
     the Ise Shrines
救主 **suku(i)nushi** rescuer; the Savior
船主 **senshu, funanushi** shipowner
12 喪主 **moshu** chief mourner
落主 **o(toshi)nushi** owner of a lost/found
     article
無主物 **mushubutsu** ownerless article/
     property
雇主 **yato(i)nushi** employer
買主 **ka(i)nushi** buyer
貸主 **ka(shi)nushi** lender; landlord
13 債主 **saishu** creditor
盟主 **meishu** the leader, leading power
飼主 **ka(i)nushi** (pet) owner, master
預主 **azu(kari)nushi** person with whom
     something is entrusted, possessor
14 領主 **ryōshu** feudal lord
16 賢主 **kenshu** wise lord
18 儲主義 **mō(ke)shugi** moneymaking
藩主 **hanshu** lord of a feudal clan

──────── 3 ────────

2 人文主義 **jinbun shugi** humanism
人本主義 **jinpon shugi** humanism
人道主義 **jindō shugi** humanitarianism
3 大地主 **ōjinushi** large landowner
大株主 **ōkabunushi** large shareholder
丸坊主 **marubōzu** close-cropped, shaven
     (head)
小坊主 **kobōzu** young priest; sonny
4 分離主義者 **bunri shugisha** separatist,
     secessionist
反動主義者 **handō shugisha** a reactionary
日本主義 **Nihon shugi** Japanism
5 民本主義 **minpon shugi** democracy
民主主義 **minshu shugi** democracy
世帯主 **setainushi** head of a household
功利主義 **kōri shugi** utilitarianism
写実主義 **shajitsu shugi** realism, literalism
古典主義 **koten shugi** classicism
平和主義 **heiwa shugi** pacifism
旧藩主 **kyūhanshu** former feudal lord
主我主義 **shuga shugi** egoism, love of self

主知主義 **shuchi shugi** intellectualism
主観主義 **shukan shugi** subjectivism
6 全体主義 **zentai shugi** totalitarianism
合理主義 **gōri shugi** rationalism
印象主義 **inshō shugi** impressionism
近代主義 **kindai shugi** modernism
汎愛主義 **han'ai shugi** philanthropism
先入主 **sennyūshu** preconception, preoccu-
     pation, prejudice
名付主 **nazu(ke)nushi** person who names
     the newborn, godparent
行動主義 **kōdō shugi** behaviorism
共産主義 **kyōsan shugi** communism
自己主義 **jiko shugi** egoism, selfishness
自由主義 **jiyū shugi** liberalism
自然主義 **shizen shugi** naturalism
7 享楽主義 **kyōraku shugi** epicureanism
折衷主義 **setchū shugi** eclecticism
形式主義 **keishiki shugi** formalism; red-
     tapism
社会主義 **shakai shugi** socialism
快楽主義 **kairaku shugi** hedonism, epicure-
     anism
利己主義 **riko shugi** selfishness
8 画一主義 **kakuitsu shugi** standardization
事大主義 **jidai shugi** worship of the powerful
事勿主義 **kotonaka(re) shugi** hoping that all
     turns out well
利那主義 **setsuna shugi** living only for (the
     pleasures of) the moment
拝金主義 **haikin shugi** mammonism
英雄主義 **eiyū shugi** heroism
実存主義 **jitsuzon shugi** existentialism
実用主義 **jitsuyō shugi** pragmatism
実利主義 **jitsuri shugi** utilitarianism,
     materialism
実証主義 **jisshō shugi** positivism
官能主義 **kannō shugi** sensualism
官僚主義 **kanryō shugi** bureaucracy
国家主義 **kokka shugi** nationalism
国粋主義 **kokusui shugi** ultranationalism
国際主義 **kokusai shugi** internationalism
所有主 **shoyūnushi** owner
所帯主 **shotainushi** head of the household
9 専制主義 **sensei shugi** absolutism, despotism
重商主義 **jūshō shugi** mercantilism
重農主義 **jūnō shugi** physiocracy
保守主義 **hoshu shugi** conservatism
軍国主義 **gunkoku shugi** militarism
帝国主義 **teikoku shugi** imperialism
急進主義 **kyūshin shugi** radicalism
造物主 **Zōbutsushu** the Creator
海坊主 **umibōzu** sea monster
封建主義 **hōken shugi** feudalism
茶坊主 **chabōzu** (shogun's) tea-serving
     attendant; sycophant

客観主義 **kyakkan shugi, kakkan shugi**
　objectivism
相対主義 **sōtai shugi** relativism
神秘主義 **shinpi shugi** mysticism
10 個人主義 **kojin shugi** individualism
進歩主義 **shinpo shugi** progressivism
浪漫主義 **rōman shugi** romanticism
根本主義 **konpon shugi** fundamentalism
破壊主義 **hakai shugi** vandalism
耽美主義 **tanbi shugi** estheticism
11 野獣主義 **yajū shugi** Fauvism
商業主義 **shōgyō shugi** commercialism
虚無主義 **kyomu shugi** nihilism
過激主義 **kageki shugi** radicalism, extremism
唯物主義 **yuibutsu shugi** materialism
唯美主義 **yuibi shugi** estheticism
菜食主義 **saishoku shugi** vegetarianism
理想主義 **risō shugi** idealism
現実主義 **genjitsu shugi** realism
救世主 **Kyūseishu** the Savior/Messiah
12 象徴主義 **shōchō shugi** symbolism
温情主義 **onjō shugi** paternalism
葱坊主 **negibōzu** flowering onion head
無妻主義 **musai shugi** celibacy
雇用主 **koyōnushi** employer
絶対主義 **zettai shugi** absolutism
13 農本主義 **nōhon shugi** agriculture-first
　policy, physiocracy
楽天主義 **rakuten shugi** optimism
楽観主義 **rakkan shugi** optimism
禁欲主義 **kin'yoku shugi** asceticism,
　stoicism
愛他主義 **aita shugi** altruism
愛国主義 **aikoku shugi** patriotism
裸体主義 **ratai shugi** nudism
詰込主義 **tsu(me)ko(mi) shugi** education
　emphasizing cramming and memoriza-
　tion rather than understanding
資本主義 **shihon shugi** capitalism
14 厭世主義 **ensei shugi** pessimism
構造主義 **kōzō shugi** structuralism
熟柿主義 **jukushi shugi** wait-and-see policy
15 権力主義 **kenryoku shugi** authoritarianism
権威主義 **ken'i shugi** authoritarianism
敵本主義 **tekihon shugi** feint, pretense,
　having ulterior motives
16 興行主 **kōgyōnushi, kōgyōshu** promoter,
　showman, producer
積読主義 **tsu(n)doku shugi** acquiring books
　without reading them
17 擬古主義 **giko shugi** classicism

――――――― 4 ―――――――
3 三日坊主 **mikka bōzu** one who can stick to
　nothing, "three-day monk"
4 反帝国主義 **han-teikoku shugi** anti-
　imperialism

5 生臭坊主 **namagusa bōzu** worldly priest,
　corrupt monk
立憲君主政体 **rikken kunshu seitai**
　constitutional monarchy
7 社会民主主義 **shakai minshu shugi** social
　democracy
9 専制君主 **sensei kunshu** absolute monarch,
　despot
12 超国家主義 **chōkokka shugi** ultranationalism
超現実主義 **chōgenjitsu shugi** surrealism
御都合主義 **gotsugō shugi** opportunism
無政府主義 **museifu shugi** anarchism
無政府主義者 **museifushugisha** anarchist
無教会主義 **mukyōkai shugi**
　Nondenominationalism (a Japanese
　Christian sect)
13 照照坊主 **te(ru)te(ru)bōzu** paper doll used
　in praying for good weather

――――――― 5 ―――――――
1 一国一党主義 **ikkoku-ittō shugi** one-party
　system
2 二大政党主義 **nidaiseitō shugi** the two-
　party system
7 芸術至上主義 **geijutsushijō shugi** art for
　art's sake
社会民主主義 **shakai minshu shugi** social
　democracy
8 味噌擂坊主 **misosu(ri) bōzu** petty priest
10 恋愛至上主義 **ren'ai-shijō shugi** love for
　love's sake

玉→　**4f0.2**

――――――― 2 ―――――――
全→全　**2a4.16**

――――――― 3 ―――――――
4f3.1
玖
　KYŪ beautiful black jewel; nine

4f3.2
弄
　RŌ, iji(ru), iji(kuru), moteaso(bu)
　play/trifle/tamper with

――――――― 1 ―――――――
0 弄する **rō(suru)** play/trifle/tamper with
――――――― 2 ―――――――
8 侮弄 **burō** ridicule

4

木 月 日 火 礻 王 牛 方 攵 欠 心 戸 戈

3←

玩弄 **ganrō** play with, toy with, make sport of
玩弄物 **ganrōbutsu** plaything
13 愚弄 **gurō** make a fool of, ridicule, mock
15 嘲弄 **chōrō** ridicule
18 翻弄 **honrō** trifle with, make sport of

—————— 4 ——————

4f4.1

玩

GAN, moteaso(bu) play/toy/trifle with

—————— 1 ——————

7 玩弄 **ganrō** play with, toy with, make sport of
玩弄物 **ganrōbutsu** plaything
8 玩味 **ganmi** relish, appreciate, enjoy
玩具 **gangu, omocha** toy
玩具屋 **omochaya** toy shop

—————— 2 ——————

13 愛玩 **aigan** cherish, treasure, prize
愛玩者 **aigansha** lover, admirer, fancier
愛玩物 **aiganbutsu** prized possession
15 賞玩 **shōgan** appreciate

—————— 5 ——————

4f5.1

珊

SAN coral; jingling, rustling

—————— 1 ——————

13 珊瑚 **sango** coral
珊瑚虫 **sangochū** coral insect/polyp
珊瑚島 **sangotō** coral island
珊瑚珠 **sangoju** coral beads
珊瑚礁 **sangoshō** coral reef

4f5.2

玻

HA glass, crystal

—————— 1 ——————

14 玻璃 **hari** glass, crystal

珪→ **4f6.4**

4f5.3

珀

HAKU amber

—————— 2 ——————

12 琥珀 **kohaku** amber

4f5.4

珈

KA ornamental hairpin

—————— 1 ——————

12 珈琲 **kōhī** coffee

4f5.5

玳

TAI sea turtle; tortoiseshell

—————— 1 ——————

13 玳瑁 **taimai** hawksbill/tortoiseshell turtle; tortoiseshell

4f5.6 / 1215

珍 珎

CHIN rare, strange, curious
mezura(shii) new, novel; rare, unusual

—————— 1 ——————

5 珍本 **chinpon** rare book
7 珍妙 **chinmyō** odd, queer, fantastic
8 珍事 **chinji** rare event, singular incident
珍味 **chinmi** delicacies
珍奇 **chinki** strange, singular; novel
珍宝 **chinpō** treasured article, valuables
珍物 **chinbutsu** a curiosity
9 珍重 **chinchō** value highly, prize
珍品 **chinpin** rare article, curio
珍客 **chinkyaku** welcome visitor
10 珍書 **chinsho** rare book
11 珍現象 **chingenshō** strange phenomenon
珍鳥 **chinchō** rare bird
12 珍無類 **chinmurui** singular, phenomenal, strange
珍貴 **chinki** rare, valuable
14 珍説 **chinsetsu** strange view, novel theory
珍聞 **chinbun** (piece of) news
15 珍蔵 **chinzō** treasured, prized
珍談 **chindan** news, anecdote, piece of gossip
22 珍襲 **chinshū** treasured, prized

—————— 2 ——————

7 別珍 **betchin** velveteen
8 物珍 **monomezura(shii)** curious
10 袖珍本 **shūchinbon** pocket-size book

珎→珍 **4f5.6**

4f5.7

玲

REI sound of jewels, tinkling; clear, brilliant

—————————— 3 ——————————

2 八面玲瓏 **hachimen-reirō** beautiful from all sides; perfect serenity, affability

4f5.8

珂

KA white agate; mother-of-pearl

4f5.9 / 297

皇

KŌ, Ō emperor

—————————— 1 ——————————

2 皇子 **kōshi, ōji** imperial prince
3 皇女 **kōjo** imperial princess
4 皇太子 **kōtaishi** crown prince
皇太后 **kōtaikō, kōtaigō** empress dowager, queen mother
皇太孫 **kōtaison** emperor's eldest direct-line grandson
皇太神宮 **Kōtai Jingū** the Ise Shrine
6 皇考 **kōkō** the late emperor
皇后 **kōgō** empress, queen
皇后陛下 **Kōgō Heika** Her Majesty the Empress
皇妃 **kōhi** empress, queen
7 皇位 **kōi** imperial throne
8 皇宗 **kōsō** emperor's ancestors
皇国 **kōkoku** the (Japanese) Empire
9 皇孫 **kōson** imperial grandchild/descendant
皇軍 **kōgun** imperial army
皇帝 **kōtei** emperor
皇室 **Kōshitsu** the Imperial Household, the reigning line
皇祖 **kōso** Founder of the Empire
皇威 **kōi** imperial prestige/power
皇紀 **kōki** (...th year of the) imperial era (since Emperor Jinmu's accession in 660 B.C.)
10 皇宮 **kōgū** imperial palace
皇恩 **kōon** imperial favor
11 皇運 **kōun** prosperity of the imperial throne
皇族 **kōzoku** (member of) the imperial family
12 皇極 **Kōgyoku** (empress, 642–645)
皇統 **kōtō** imperial line
13 皇漢薬 **kōkan'yaku** Chinese herbal medicines
14 皇旗 **kōki** imperial standard
15 皇霊 **kōrei** spirits of deceased royalty
皇霊殿 **Kōreiden** the Imperial Ancestors' Shrine

—————————— 2 ——————————

3 上皇 **jōkō** ex-emperor
女皇 **jokō** empress, queen

4 天皇 **tennō** Emperor of Japan
天皇制 **tennōsei** the emperor system
天皇杯 **Tennōhai** the Emperor's Trophy
天皇陛下 **Tennō Heika** His Majesty the Emperor
天皇家 **tennōke** the imperial family
天皇旗 **tennōki** the imperial standard
8 法皇 **hōō** ex-emperor who has become a monk
10 教皇 **kyōkō** the pope
教皇庁 **Kyōkōchō** the Vatican
12 勤皇 **kinnō** loyalty to the emperor
勤皇家 **kinnōka** loyalist

—————————— 4 ——————————

3 大行天皇 **taikō tennō** the late emperor

—————————— 6 ——————————

4f6.1

珥

JI ear bauble; hilt

4f6.2 / 1504

珠

SHU, JU, tama gem, jewel

—————————— 1 ——————————

5 珠玉 **shugyoku** gem, jewel, jewelry
14 珠算 **shuzan** calculation on the abacus

—————————— 2 ——————————

8 念珠 **nenju** rosary
宝珠 **hōshu** precious jewel
9 連珠 **renju** five-in-a-row game
10 真珠 **shinju** pearl
真珠色 **shinju-iro** pearl gray
真珠貝 **shinjugai** pearl oyster
真珠取 **shinjuto(ri)** pearl fishing; pearl diver
真珠湾 **Shinju-wan** Pearl Harbor
真珠層 **shinjusō** mother-of-pearl
11 曼珠沙華 **manjushage** cluster-amaryllis (also known as *higanbana*)
13 数珠 **juzu, zuzu** string of beads, rosary

—————————— 3 ——————————

9 珊瑚珠 **sangoju** coral beads
17 擬宝珠 **gibōshu, gibōshi** leek flower **gibōshu, gibōshi** ornamental railing knob

4f6.3 / 1381

班

HAN squad, corps, group

—————————— 1 ——————————

8 班長 **hanchō** group leader
9 班点 **hanten** spot, dot, fleck, speck

4

木
月
日
火
衤
王 6←
牛
方
攵
欠
心
戸
戈

━━━━━━━━ 2 ━━━━━━━━

6 西班牙 **Supein** Spain
9 首班 **shuhan** head, leader

━━━━━━━━ 3 ━━━━━━━━

11 救護班 **kyūgohan** relief squad, rescue party
16 衛生班 **eiseihan** a sanitation detail

4f6.4

珪 硅
KEI silicon

━━━━━━━━ 1 ━━━━━━━━

3 珪土 **keido** silica
5 珪石 **keiseki** silica
8 珪岩 **keigan** quartzite
9 珪肺症 **keihaishō** silicosis
珪砂 **keisha** silica sand, silica
10 珪素 **keiso** silicon
14 珪酸 **keisan** silicic acid
19 珪藻土 **keisōdo** diatomaceous earth, kieselguhr

瑛 → 瓔 **4f17.1**

4f6.5

珞
RAKU necklace of jewels

━━━━━━━━ 2 ━━━━━━━━

21 瓔珞 **yōraku** necklace of jewels

4f6.6

珮
HAI bauble, jewel

━━━━━━━━ 7 ━━━━━━━━

4f7.1 / 143

理
RI reason, justice, truth, principle
kotowari reason

━━━━━━━━ 1 ━━━━━━━━

4 理不尽 **rifujin** unreasonable, unjust
理化学 **rikagaku** physics and chemistry
5 理由 **riyū** reason, cause
理外 **rigai** transcendental, supernatural
7 理学 **rigaku** physical sciences, science
理学者 **rigakusha** scientist
理学界 **rigakukai, rigakkai** scientific world
8 理非 **rihi** the rights and wrongs, relative merits

理事 **riji** director, trustee
理事会 **rijikai** board of directors/trustees
理事長 **rijichō** chairman, president
理念 **rinen** idea, doctrine, ideology
理法 **rihō** law
理知 **richi** intellect, intelligence
理知的 **richiteki** intellectual
理屈 **rikutsu** theory; reason, logic; argument; pretext
理性 **risei** reason, reasoning power
理性的 **riseiteki** reasonable
9 理神論 **rishinron** deism
理科 **rika** science
10 理容 **riyō** barbering, hairdressing
理財 **rizai** economy, finance
理財学 **rizaigaku** political economy
理財家 **rizaika** economist, financier
13 理解 **rikai** understand, comprehend
理解力 **rikairyoku** comprehension
理想 **risō** ideal
理想化 **risōka** idealize
理想主義 **risō shugi** idealism
理想的 **risōteki** ideal
理想型 **risōgata** ideal type
理想郷 **risōkyō** ideal land, Shangri-La, utopia
理想家 **risōka** idealist
理詰 **rizu(me)** persuasion, reasoning
理路 **riro** reasoning, argument
理路整然 **riro-seizen** well-argued, cogent, logical
14 理髪 **rihatsu** haircutting, barbering
理髪店 **rihatsuten** barbershop
理髪師 **rihatsushi** barber, hairdresser
15 理論 **riron** theory
理論的 **rironteki** theoretical
理論家 **rironka** theorist

━━━━━━━━ 2 ━━━━━━━━

1 一理 **ichiri** a principle, a reason
3 大理石 **dairiseki** marble
4 天理 **tenri** the law of nature, rule of heaven
天理教 **Tenrikyō** the Tenriism sect (founded 1838)
文理 **bunri** context, line of thought; science and literature
文理学 **bunrigaku** humanities and sciences
公理 **kōri** axiom
水理学 **suirigaku** hydrography, hydraulics
木理 **mokuri** (wood's) grain
心理 **shinri** mental state, psychology
心理学 **shinrigaku** psychology
心理的 **shinriteki** psychological, mental
5 生理 **seiri** physiology; menstruation
生理学 **seirigaku** physiology
生理的 **seiriteki** physiological
生理的食塩水 **seiriteki shokuensui** saline solution

弁理 **benri** management
弁理士 **benrishi** patent attorney
代理 **dairi** representation, agency, proxy,
　　agent, alternate, acting (minister)
代理人 **dairinin** agent, proxy, substitute,
　　representative
代理店 **dairiten** agent, agency
代理業 **dairigyō** business of an agent, agency
代理権 **dairiken** right of representation,
　　power of attorney
玄理 **genri** abstruse theory, esoteric mystery
処理 **shori** treat, manage, deal with
6 合理 **gōri** rationality
合理化 **gōrika** rationalization, streamlining
合理主義 **gōri shugi** rationalism
合理的 **gōriteki** rational, reasonable, logical
合理性 **gōrisei** rationality, reasonableness
地理 **chiri** geography
地理学 **chirigaku** geography
地理学者 **chirigakusha** geographer
肌理 **kime** grain, texture
有理 **yūri** rational (number)
7 没理想 **botsurisō** lack of ideals; realism (in
　　literature)
究理 **kyūri** philosophical thinking
学理 **gakuri** theory, scientific principle
屁理窟 **herikutsu** quibbling, sophistry
条理 **jōri** logic, reason
8 非理 **hiri** unreasonable, absurd
事理 **jiri** reason, facts, sense
受理 **juri** accept
法理 **hōri** legal principle
法理学 **hōrigaku** jurisprudence
実理 **jitsuri** practical principles
定理 **teiri** theorem
空理 **kūri** empty/impractical theory
物理 **butsuri** law of nature; physics
物理学 **butsurigaku** physics
物理的 **butsuriteki** physical (properties)
物理療法 **butsuriryōhō** physiotherapy
9 連理 **renri** (trees) with entwined branches
背理 **hairi** irrational, absurd
計理士 **keirishi** public accountant
10 修理 **shūri** repair
修理工 **shūrikō** repairman
修理中 **shūrichū** under repair
倫理 **rinri** ethics, morals
倫理学 **rinrigaku** ethics, moral philosophy
倫理的 **rinriteki** ethical
真理 **shinri** truth
原理 **genri** principle, theory
哲理 **tetsuri** philosophy, philosophical
　　principles
教理 **kyōri** doctrine, tenet, creed, dogma
病理 **byōri** cause and course of a disease
病理学 **byōrigaku** pathology

純理 **junri** pure reason, scientific principle
純理論 **junriron** rationalism
料理 **ryōri** cooking, cuisine; dish, food
料理人 **ryōrinin** a cook
料理屋 **ryōriya** restaurant
11 道理 **dōri, kotowari** reason, right, truth
推理 **suiri** reasoning, inference
推理小説 **suiri shōsetsu** detective story,
　　whodunit
唯理論 **yuiriron** rationalism
情理 **jōri** heart and mind, emotion and reason
経理 **keiri** accounting
経理士 **keirishi** public accountant
12 無理 **muri** unreasonable; impossible, beyond
　　one's power, too difficult; by force,
　　against one's will; strain oneself
無理心中 **muri shinjū** murder-suicide
無理矢理 **muriyari** forcibly, under compul-
　　sion
無理押 **murio(shi)** pushing things too far
無理往生 **muri-ōjō** forced compliance
無理取 **murido(ri)** exaction, extortion
無理強 **muriji(i)** coercion
無理無体 **muri-mutai** forcible
無理解 **murikai** lack of understanding
無理数 **murisū** irrational number
無理算段 **muri-sandan** scrape together
　　(money)
無理難題 **muri-nandai** unreasonable demand
税理士 **zeirishi** tax accountant
13 義理 **giri** sense of duty/honor, decency,
　　courtesy, debt of gratitude
義理人情 **giri-ninjō** duty versus/and human
　　feelings
義理立 **girida(te)** do one's duty
義理合 **giria(i)** social relationship
義理知 **girishi(razu)** ungrateful person
義理堅 **girigata(i)** having a strong sense of
　　duty
摂理 **setsuri** providence
摂理的 **setsuriteki** providential
数理 **sūri** mathematical (principles)
数理上 **sūrijō** mathematically
数理的 **sūriteki** mathematical
14 総理 **sōri** prime minister
総理大臣 **sōri daijin** prime minister
総理府 **sōrifu** Prime Minister's Office
管理 **kanri** administration, supervision,
　　control, management
管理人 **kanrinin** manager, superintendent
管理職 **kanrishoku** administrative position;
　　the management
15 審理 **shinri** trial, inquiry, hearing
窮理 **kyūri** truthseeking
論理 **ronri** logic
論理上 **ronrijō** logically (speaking)

4

木
月
日
火
礻
王　7←
牛
方
攵
欠
心
戸
戈

論理学 **ronrigaku** logic
論理的 **ronriteki** logical
調理 **chōri** cooking
調理人 **chōrinin** a cook
調理師 **chōrishi** a cook
16 薬理 **yakuri** intended and side effects of drugs
薬理学 **yakurigaku** pharmacology
整理 **seiri** arrangement, adjustment; liquidation, reorganization; retrenchment, curtailment
整理部 **seiribu** (newspaper's) copy desk
整理箱 **seiribako** filing cabinet
整理箪笥 **seiridansu** chest of drawers

———————— 3 ————————

4 不合理 **fugōri** unreasonable, irrational
不条理 **fujōri** unreasonable, irrational
不道理 **fudōri** unreasonable; immoral
不義理 **fugiri** dishonesty, injustice; dishonor; ingratitude
手料理 **teryōri** home cooking
6 安料理屋 **yasuryōriya** cheap restaurant
8 非合理的 **higōriteki** unreasonable, irrational
非論理的 **hironriteki** illogical, irrational
10 核物理学 **kakubutsurigaku** nuclear physics
13 節料理 **(o)sechi ryōri** New Year's foods
15 熱処理 **netsushori** heat treatment

———————— 4 ————————

1 一品料理 **ippin ryōri** dishes 'a la carte
2 人文地理 **jinbun chiri, jinmon chiri** anthropogeography
人員整理 **jin'in seiri** personnel cutback
4 中華料理 **chūka ryōri** Chinese cooking/food
区画整理 **kukaku seiri** land readjustment, readjustment of town lots
6 会席料理 **kaiseki ryōri** banquet food served on individual trays
7 即席料理 **sokuseki ryōri** quick meal
10 残品整理 **zanpin seiri** clearance sale
12 無理矢理 **muriyari** forcibly, under compulsion
14 精進料理 **shōjin ryōri** vegetarian dishes

4f7.2 / 726

球   **KYŪ, tama** ball, sphere, globe, bulb

———————— 1 ————————

7 球体 **kyūtai** sphere
球技 **kyūgi** game in which a ball is used
球投 **tamana(ge)** playing catch
球形 **kyūkei** spherical, globular
8 球茎 **kyūkei** (plant) bulb
9 球乗 **tamano(ri)** balancing/dancer on a ball
球拾 **tamahiro(i)** fetching balls; caddy
球面 **kyūmen** spherical surface

10 球根 **kyūkon** (plant) bulb
12 球場 **kyūjō** baseball grounds/stadium
13 球電 **kyūden** ball lightning
14 球算 **tamazan** calculation on the abacus
15 球戯 **kyūgi** game in which a ball is used; billiards
16 球磨川 **Kumagawa** (river, Kumamoto-ken)

———————— 2 ————————

3 小球 **shōkyū** small ball, globule
4 天球 **tenkyū** the celestial sphere
天球儀 **tenkyūgi** a celestial globe
水球 **suikyū** water polo
5 半球 **hankyū** hemisphere
打球 **dakyū** batting; batted ball
6 死球 **shikyū** dead ball (in baseball)
気球 **kikyū** (hot-air/helium) balloon
地球 **chikyū** earth, globe
地球儀 **chikyūgi** a globe of the world
血球 **kekkyū** blood corpuscle
7 投球 **tōkyū** throw a ball, pitch
8 制球 **seikyū** (pitcher's) control
直球 **chokkyū** straight ball/pitch
卓球 **takkyū** table tennis, ping-pong
送球 **sōkyū** throw a ball
始球 **shikyū** throwing the first ball (in baseball)
9 飛球 **hikyū** fly ball
速球 **sokkyū** fast ball
庭球 **teikyū** tennis
10 逸球 **ikkyū** muffed ball
捕球 **hokyū** catch (in baseball)
11 野球 **yakyū** baseball
野球気違 **yakyū kichiga(i)** baseball fan
野球狂 **yakyūkyō** baseball fan
野球場 **yakyūjō** baseball park/stadium
野球熱 **yakyūnetsu** baseball fever/mania
排球 **haikyū** volleyball
琉球 **Ryūkyū** the Ryukyu islands; (ancient kuni, Okinawa-ken)
眼球 **gankyū** eyeball
軟球 **nankyū** softball
12 落球 **rakkyū** fail to catch a ball, muff
硬球 **kōkyū** hard/regulation ball
13 電球 **denkyū** light bulb
14 選球 **senkyū** (batter's) discrimination between pitched balls inside and outside the strike zone
選球眼 **senkyūgan** batting eye
誘球 **saso(i)dama** a pitch to get the batter to swing at the ball
15 熱球 **nekkyū** hot pitch (in baseball)
緩球 **kankyū** slow ball
18 難球 **nankyū** hard-to-catch batted ball
19 蹴球 **shūkyū** football
蹴球場 **shūkyūjō** football/soccer/rugby field
22 籠球 **rōkyū** basketball

─────────── 3 ───────────

5 北半球 **Kita Hankyū** Northern Hemisphere
  白血球 **hakkekkyū** white corpuscles
6 西半球 **nishi hankyū** Western Hemisphere
7 赤血球 **sekkekkyū** red corpuscles
  豆電球 **mame-denkyū** miniature light bulb
8 東半球 **higashi hankyū** Eastern Hemisphere
9 南半球 **minami hankyū** the Southern
  Hemisphere
  草野球 **kusa-yakyū** sandlot baseball
12 軽気球 **keikikyū** (hot-air/helium) balloon
13 裸電球 **hadaka denkyū** light bulb without a
  lampshade

─────────── 1 ───────────

7 阻塞気球 **sosai kikyū** barrage balloon
11 軟式庭球 **nanshiki teikyū** softball tennis
  軟式野球 **nanshiki yakyū** softball
12 葡萄状球菌 **budōjōkyūkin** staphylococcus

琅→瑯 **4f9.1**

琢→琢 **4f8.1**

4f7.3 / 298

現 GEN present, existing, actual
ara(wasu) show, indicate, express
ara(wareru) appear, emerge, be
expressed **utsutsu** reality;
consciousness; reverie, absent-mindedness

─────────── 1 ───────────

3 現下 **genka** the present time
4 現今 **genkon** now, today
5 現出 **genshutsu, ara(ware)de(ru)** appear,
  emerge
  現生 **gennama** hard cash
  現世 **gense, gensei, genze, utsu(shi)yo** this
  present world
  現世的 **genseteki, genseiteki** worldly,
  temporal
  現世紀 **genseiki** this century
  現代 **gendai** the present age, today, modern
  times
  現代人 **gendaijin** people today
  現代化 **gendaika** modernization
  現代版 **gendaiban** modern edition
  現代語 **gendaigo** modern language
  現存 **genson, genzon** living, existing, extant
6 現任 **gennin** present post, incumbent
  現地 **genchi** the actual place; on the scene, in
  the field, local
  現在 **genzai** now, present, current; present
  tense; actually

現在高 **genzaidaka** amount on hand
現行 **genkō** present, current, existing
現行犯 **genkōhan** crime/criminal witnessed
  in the act, flagrante delicto
現行法 **genkōhō** existing law, law now in
  force
現有 **gen'yū** existing, present, actually
  possessed
7 現住所 **genjūsho** present address
現状 **genjō** present situation, current state of
  affairs
現役 **gen'eki** active service; commissioned
現役兵 **gen'ekihei** soldier on active duty
8 現制 **gensei** present system
現送 **gensō** sending cash, shipping gold
現法 **genpō** local legal entity, company
  incorporated abroad (short for 現地法人)
現況 **genkyō** the present situation
現実 **genjitsu** actuality, reality
現実化 **genjitsuka** realize, turn (dreams) into
  reality
現実主義 **genjitsu shugi** realism
現実的 **genjitsuteki** realistic
現実性 **genjitsusei** actuality, reality
現実派 **genjitsuha** realists
現実感 **genjitsukan** sense of reality
現実暴露 **genjitsu bakuro** disillusionment
現官 **genkan** present post
現物 **genbutsu** the actual goods, in kind, spot
  (trading)
現金 **genkin** cash
現金化 **genkinka** convert to cash, cash (a
  check)
現金払 **genkinbara(i)** cash payment
9 現前 **genzen** before one's eyes
現品 **genpin** the actual goods; goods in stock
現政府 **genseifu** the present government
10 現俸 **genpō** present salary
現高 **gendaka** the present amount
現員 **gen'in** the present members
現時代 **genjidai** the present age
12 現象 **genshō** phenomenon
現象界 **genshōkai** the phenomenal world
現場 **genba, genjō** the actual spot; on the
  scene, at the site, in the field
13 現業 **gengyō** work-site operations
現業員 **gengyōin** outdoor/field worker
現勢 **gensei** present state; actual strength
現数 **gensū** actual number, effective strength
14 現像 **genzō** developing (film)
現像液 **genzōeki** developing solution
18 現職 **genshoku** present post, incumbent

─────────── 2 ───────────

5 出現 **shutsugen** appear, show up
示現 **jigen** revelation, manifestation
6 再現 **saigen** reappearance, return; revival

考現学 **kōgengaku** study of modern phenomena (cf. 考古学)
7 体現 **taigen** embody, personify
8 非現実的 **higenjitsuteki** unrealistic
非現業 **higengyō** clerical/non-field work
非現業員 **higengyōin** office/desk worker
表現 **hyōgen** expression
実現 **jitsugen** come true, realize, materialize
具現 **gugen** embodiment, incarnation
9 発現 **hatsugen** revelation, manifestation
珍現象 **chingenshō** strange phenomenon
12 超現実主義 **chōgenjitsu shugi** surrealism
13 夢現 **yumeutsutsu** dream and reality; half-dreaming
15 権現 **gongen** incarnation (of Buddha), avatar (of Tokugawa Ieyasu)
18 顕現 **kengen** manifestation

——————— 3 ———————
16 頭角現 **tōkaku (o) ara(wasu)** be preeminent

——————— 4 ———————
6 自我実現 **jiga jitsugen** self-realization

4f7.4

珸
GO jewel

4f7.5

琉
RYŪ, RU lapis lazuli

——————— 1 ———————
11 琉球 **Ryūkyū** the Ryukyu islands; (ancient kuni, Okinawa-ken)
14 琉璃 **ruru** lapis lazuli

堲 → 3b8.13

4f7.6 / 673

望
BŌ, MŌ hope, desire; look into the distance; full moon **nozo(mu)** desire, hope for; see, command a view of **nozo(mashii)** desirable, advisable **mochi** full

——————— 1 ———————
4 望手 **nozo(mi)te** aspirant, applicant; buyer
5 望外 **bōgai** unexpected
6 望次第 **nozo(mi) shidai** as desired, on demand
7 望見 **bōken** watch from afar
9 望通 **nozo(mi)dō(ri)** as desired
10 望郷 **bōkyō** homesickness, nostalgia
12 望遠鏡 **bōenkyō** telescope

13 望楼 **bōrō** watchtower
望蜀 **bōshoku** insatiable

——————— 2 ———————
1 一望千里 **ichibō-senri** vast, boundless
2 人望 **jinbō** popularity
3 大望 **taimō, taibō** ambition, aspirations
4 切望 **setsubō** earnest desire, yearning
5 本望 **honmō** long-cherished desire; satisfaction
失望 **shitsubō** disappointment, despair
好望 **kōbō** promising future
6 多望 **tabō** promising, with bright prospects
名望 **meibō** reputation, popularity
名望家 **meibōka** person who is highly esteemed
有望 **yūbō** promising, hopeful
7 希望 **kibō** wish, hope, desire
希望者 **kibōsha** applicant, candidate, aspirant
志望 **shibō** desire, ambition, choice
志望者 **shibōsha** aspirant
8 非望 **hibō** inordinate ambition
所望 **shomō** desire, request
9 信望 **shinbō** confidence and popularity, prestige
要望 **yōbō** demand, cry for
待望 **taibō** wait for expectantly, hope for, look forward to
威望 **ibō** influence and popularity
10 既望 **kibō** 16th night of a lunar month
高望 **takanozo(mi)** aim (too) high, be ambitious
展望 **tenbō** view, outlook, prospects
展望台 **tenbōdai** observation platform
11 渇望 **katsubō** thirst/crave/long for
宿望 **shukubō** long-cherished desire
欲望 **yokubō** desire, craving
眺望 **chōbō** a view (from a window)
12 遠望 **enbō** distant view
属望 **shokubō** pin one's hopes on, expect much of
衆望 **shūbō** public confidence, popularity
絶望 **zetsubō** despair
絶望的 **zetsubōteki** hopeless, desperate
13 羨望 **senbō** envy
誉望 **yobō** glory, honor, fame
14 徳望 **tokubō** moral influence
徳望家 **tokubōka** man of high moral repute
15 潜望鏡 **senbōkyō** periscope
嘱望 **shokubō** expect much of
熱望 **netsubō** ardent wish, fervent hope
17 輿望 **yobō** popularity, esteem; trust, confidence
懇望 **konbō** entreaty, earnest request
18 観望 **kanbō** observe, watch, wait and see
19 願望 **ganbō, ganmō** wish, desire
26 矚望 **shokubō** hope much from

────────── 3 ──────────

10 倚門望 **imon (no) bō** a mother's love
(leaning on the gate longing for her
child's return home)

────────── 4 ──────────

9 前途有望 **zento yūbō** having a promising
future

────────── 8 ──────────

4f8.1

琢 琢   **TAKU** polish

────────── 1 ──────────

16 琢磨 **takuma** diligent application

────────── 3 ──────────

4 切磋琢磨 **sessa-takuma** work hard/assidu-
ously

4f8.2

琳   **RIN** jewel; tinkling of jewelry

4f8.3

斑   **HAN** spot **buchi, madara, hadara,
fu** spots, patches, streaks, spotted,
speckled, mottled, dappled
mura unevenness, lack of uniformity;
blotches, blemishes; capriciousness

────────── 1 ──────────

2 斑入 **fui(ri)** spotted, mottled, variegated
4 斑犬 **madara inu, buchi inu** spotted dog
斑牛 **madara ushi** brindled cow
5 斑白 **hanpaku** grizzled
6 斑気 **muragi, muraki** capricious
9 斑点 **hanten** spot, speck
10 斑消 **muragi(e)** (snow) remaining in spots
斑紋 **hanmon** spot, speckle
斑馬 **madara uma** piebald horse; zebra
11 斑猫 **buchi neko** tabby cat
斑雪 **madara yuki, hadara yuki** snow
remaining in spots
13 斑鳩 **ikaru, ikaruga** grosbeak, Japanese
hawfinch
20 斑糲岩 **hanreigan** gabbro

────────── 2 ──────────

1 一斑 **ippan** a part, a glimpse, an outline
5 母斑 **bohan** birthmark
6 血斑 **keppan** blood spot
11 黒斑 **kurobuchi, kurofu** black spots/patches
雀斑 **sobakasu** freckles
12 紫斑病 **shihanbyō** purpura

────────── 3 ──────────

13 蒙古斑 **mōkohan** Mongolian spot

4f8.4

琲   **HAI** pierce; stringed pearls

────────── 2 ──────────

9 珈琲 **kōhī** coffee

4f8.5

琺   **HŌ** enamel

────────── 1 ──────────

13 琺瑯 **hōrō** enamel, enameled ware
琺瑯質 **hōrōshitsu** (tooth) enamel

4f8.6

瑛   **EI** sparkle of jewelry, crystal

4f8.7

瑙 碯   **NŌ** agate, onyx

────────── 2 ──────────

14 瑪瑙 **menō** agate, onyx

4f8.8

琥   **KO** jeweled utensil; amber

────────── 1 ──────────

9 琥珀 **kohaku** amber

4f8.9

琶   **HA** lute

────────── 2 ──────────

12 琵琶 **biwa** lute
琵琶法師 **biwa hōshi** lute-playing minstrel
琵琶湖 **Biwa-ko** Lake Biwa

4f8.10

琵   **BI, HI** lute

────────── 1 ──────────

12 琵琶 **biwa** lute

4

亻 月 日 火 礻 王 牛 方 攵 欠 心 戸 戈

8 ←

琵琶法師 **biwa hōshi** lute-playing minstrel
琵琶湖 **Biwa-ko** Lake Biwa

4f8.11 / 1251

琴 **KIN** harp
koto koto (the musical instrument)

──────── 1 ────────
4 琴爪 **kotozume** plectrum
13 琴瑟相和 **kinshitsu aiwa(su)** be happily married
15 琴線 **kinsen** heartstrings

──────── 2 ────────
4 木琴 **mokkin** xylophone
8 和琴 **wagon** Japanese harp, ancient koto
9 風琴 **fūkin** organ; accordion
　 洋琴 **yōkin** piano
12 提琴 **teikin** violin
　 提琴家 **teikinka** violinist
14 竪琴 **tategoto** harp, lyre

──────── 3 ────────
1 一絃琴 **ichigenkin** one-stringed instrument
4 手風琴 **tefūkin** accordion, concertina

──────── 9 ────────

4f9.1

瑯 琅 **RŌ** jewel

──────── 2 ────────
12 琺瑯 **hōrō** enamel, enameled ware
　 琺瑯質 **hōrōshitsu** (tooth) enamel

4f9.2

瑕 **KA, kizu** flaw, blemish

──────── 1 ────────
11 瑕疵 **kashi** defect, flaw
15 瑕瑾 **kakin** flaw, defect

4f9.3

瑚 **KO, GO** coral; ancestral-offering receptacle

──────── 2 ────────
9 珊瑚 **sango** coral
　 珊瑚虫 **sangochū** coral insect/polyp
　 珊瑚島 **sangotō** coral island
　 珊瑚珠 **sangoju** coral beads
　 珊瑚礁 **sangoshō** coral reef

4f9.4

瑁 **MAI** hawksbill/tortoiseshell turtle

──────── 2 ────────
9 玳瑁 **taimai** hawksbill/tortoiseshell turtle; tortoiseshell

4f9.5

瑶 瑤 **YŌ** (beautiful as a) jewel

4f9.6

瑞 **ZUI** good omen; Switzerland; Sweden
mizu good omen; young and fresh

──────── 1 ────────
3 瑞々 **mizumizu(shii)** young and vivacious
6 瑞気 **zuiki** good omen
　 瑞西 **Suisu** Switzerland
　 瑞兆 **zuichō** good omen
8 瑞典 **Suēden** Sweden
9 瑞相 **zuisō** good omen
10 瑞祥 **zuishō** good omen
11 瑞鳥 **zuichō** bird of good omen
12 瑞雲 **zuiun** auspicious clouds
13 瑞夢 **zuimu** auspicious dream
15 瑞穂国 **Mizuho(no)kuni** Japan, Land of Vigorous Rice Plants

──────── ────────
13 瑞瑞 **mizumizu(shii)** young and vivacious

4f9.7

琿 **KON** jewel

4f9.8

瑜 **YU** jewel

──────── 1 ────────
7 瑜伽 **yuga** yoga

4f9.9 / 674

聖 聖 **SEI, SHŌ** holy, sacred; saint, sage **hijiri** emperor; sage; saint; master

──────── 1 ────────
0 聖なる **sei(naru)** holy, sacred
2 聖人 **seijin** sage, saint, holy man

3 聖上 **seijō** the emperor
4 聖公会 **Seikōkai** Episcopal/Anglican Church
聖水 **seisui** holy water
聖日 **seijitsu** holy day; the Sabbath
聖火 **seika** sacred flame/torch
5 聖母 **Seibo** the Holy Mother
聖代 **seidai** glorious reign
6 聖地 **seichi** the Holy Land; sacred ground
聖旨 **seishi** the imperial will
7 聖寿 **seiju** the emperor's age
聖別 **seibetsu** consecrate, sanctify
8 聖画像 **seigazō** sacred image, icon
聖夜 **seiya** Christmas Eve
聖典 **seiten** sage's writings; holy book, scriptures
聖油 **seiyu** holy oil
聖者 **seija** saint, holy man
聖武 **Shōmu** (emperor, 724–749)
聖金曜日 **Seikin'yōbi** Good Friday
10 聖哲 **seitetsu** sage, wise man
聖徒 **seito** saint; disciple
聖書 **Seisho** the Bible
聖教 **seikyō** sacred teachings; Christianity
聖恩 **seion** imperial favor
聖訓 **seikun** sacred teachings
11 聖域 **seiiki** holy ground, sacred precincts
聖堂 **seidō** Confucian temple; sanctuary, church
聖断 **seidan** imperial decision
12 聖雄 **seiyū** holy man, hero saint
13 聖業 **seigyō** sacred work; imperial achievements
聖楽 **seigaku** sacred music
聖戦 **seisen** holy war, crusade
14 聖像 **seizō** sacred image, icon
聖遺物 **seiibutsu** religious relic
聖徳 **seitoku** imperial virtues
聖歌 **seika** sacred song, hymn
聖歌隊 **seikatai** choir
聖誕祭 **Seitansai** Christmas
15 聖慮 **seiryo** imperial wishes
聖廟 **seibyō** Confucian temple
聖霊 **Seirei** Holy Spirit
16 聖壇 **seidan** altar; pulpit
聖賢 **seiken** sages, saints
18 聖職 **seishoku** ministry, clergy, holy orders

──────── 2 ────────
3 大聖 **taisei** great sage
大聖堂 **daiseidō** cathedral
5 四聖 **shisei** the four great sages (Buddha, Christ, Confucius, Socrates)
6 列聖式 **resseishiki** canonization
9 神聖 **shinsei** holy; sanctity, dignity
神聖視 **shinseishi** regard as sacred
10 書聖 **shosei** master calligrapher

13 楽聖 **gakusei** musical master
詩聖 **shisei** great poet
14 歌聖 **kasei** great poet

──────── 3 ────────
4 五輪聖火 **Gorin seika** Olympic torch
5 旧約聖書 **Kyūyaku Seisho** the Old Testament
13 新約聖書 **shin'yaku seisho** the New Testament

──────── 4 ────────
12 欽定訳聖書 **kinteiyaku seisho** the King James Bible

4f9.10

瑟

SHITSU large koto

──────── 2 ────────
12 琴瑟相和 **kinshitsu aiwa(su)** be happily married

──────── 10 ────────

4f10.1

瑪

ME agate, onyx

──────── 1 ────────
12 瑪瑙 **menō** agate, onyx

4f10.2

瑰

KAI jewel; excellent, fine, rare

4f10.3

瑠 璢

RU lapis lazuli

──────── 1 ────────
14 瑠璃 **ruri** lapis lazuli
瑠璃色 **ruri-iro** sky blue, azure
──────── 2 ────────
9 浄瑠璃 **jōruri** (type of ballad-drama)

瑤 → 瑶 4f9.5

4f10.4

瑣

SA small; chain

──────── 1 ────────
3 瑣々 **sasa** trifling; tedious; tinkling

4

木月日火礻王牛方攵欠心戸戈   10←

8 瑣事 **saji** petty/trivial matter

─────── 2 ───────

13 煩瑣 **hansa** troublesome, vexatious; complicated

4f10.5

璃
RI lapis lazuli

─────── 2 ───────

9 玻璃 **hari** glass, crystal
11 琉璃 **ruru** lapis lazuli
14 瑠璃 **ruri** lapis lazuli
瑠璃色 **ruri-iro** sky blue, azure

─────── 3 ───────

9 浄瑠璃 **jōruri** (type of ballad-drama)

4f10.6

瑳
SA polish

4f10.7

瑩
EI clear

4f10.8

瑱
TEN earring

對 → 対 **2j5.5**

業 → **0a13.3**

─────── 11 ───────

4f11.1

璋
SHŌ ceremonial jeweled implement

瑠 → **4f10.3**

4f11.2

瑾
KIN beautiful/red jewel

─────── 2 ───────

13 瑕瑾 **kakin** flaw, defect

─────── 12 ───────

4f12.1

璞
HAKU unpolished/uncut gem

璢 → 瑠 **4f10.3**

4f12.2

躾
shitsuke teaching manners, upbringing, discipline
shitsu(keru) teach manners, rear, train

─────── 2 ───────

4 不躾 **bushitsuke** ill-breeding, bad manners

─────── 13 ───────

4f13.1 / 865

環 環
KAN, wa, tamaki ring, circle, loop

─────── 1 ───────

4 環太平洋 **kan-Taiheiyō** pan-Pacific, circum-Pacific
環太平洋火山帯 **kan-Taiheiyō kazantai** circum-Pacific volcanic belt
環太平洋地震帯 **kan-Taiheiyō jishintai** circum-Pacific seismic zone
環太平洋造山帯 **kan-Taiheiyō zōzantai** circum-Pacific orogeny
7 環状 **kanjō** ring, loop, annulation
環状線 **kanjōsen** loop/belt line
9 環海 **kankai** surrounding seas
11 環視 **kanshi** concentrated attention (of others)
13 環節 **kansetsu** segment (of a worm)
14 環境 **kankyō** environment
環境庁 **Kankyōchō** Environment Agency
17 環礁 **kanshō** atoll

─────── 2 ───────

1 一環 **ikkan** a link, a part
6 光環 **kōkan** corona
耳環 **mimiwa** earring
7 花環 **hanawa** wreath, garland
8 金環 **kinkan** gold ring; (sun's) corona
金環食 **kinkanshoku** total eclipse of the sun
9 連環 **renkan** links (of a chain)
12 循環 **junkan** circulation, cycle
循環系 **junkankei** the circulatory system

4

木 月 日 火 礻 王 牛 方 攵 欠 心 戸 戈

→10

循環器 **junkanki** circulatory organ
循環論法 **junkan ronpō** a circular argument

——————— 3 ———————
2 子午環 **shigokan** meridian circle
11 悪循環 **akujunkan** vicious cycle/spiral

4f13.2

璧

HEKI, tama pierced jewel-disk, jewel; splendid

——————— 2 ———————
7 完璧 **kanpeki** perfect, flawless

——————— 14 ———————
4f14.1

瓊

KEI red/beautiful jewel

4f14.2 / 1887

璽

JI imperial seal

——————— 1 ———————
10 璽書 **jisho** document bearing imperial seal

——————— 2 ———————
5 玉璽 **gyokuji** imperial seal
6 印璽 **inji** imperial/state seal
8 国璽 **kokuji** the seal of state
9 神璽 **shinji** sacred jewels (one of the three sacred treasures); emperor's seal

——————— 4 ———————
12 御名御璽 **gyomei-gyoji** imperial/privy seal

——————— 16 ———————
4f16.1

瓏

RŌ sound of jewels; clear

——————— 4 ———————
2 八面玲瓏 **hachimen-reirō** beautiful from all sides; perfect serenity, affability

——————— 17 ———————
4f17.1

瓔 瑛

YŌ, EI necklace of jewels

——————— 1 ———————
10 瓔珞 **yōraku** necklace of jewels

——————— 牛 4g ———————

牛	生	牝	牟	牡	告	牧	物	牲	牴	特	悟	犂
0.1	0a5.29	2.1	2.2	3.1	3d4.18	4.1	4.2	5.1	5.2	6.1	7.1	4g8.2

犇	犁	甦	解	犒	犖	犇	犛	犠	犢	犠
8.1	8.2	0a12.6	9.1	10.1	10.2	11.1	11.2	13.1	15.1	4g13.1

——————— 0 ———————
4g0.1 / 281

牛

GYŪ, GO, ushi cow, bull, ox, cattle

——————— 1 ———————
2 牛刀 **gyūtō** butcher knife
3 牛小屋 **ushigoya** cowshed, barn
4 牛方 **ushikata** oxcart driver, teamster
5 牛皮 **gyūhi** cowhide
6 牛肉 **gyūniku** beef
牛缶 **gyūkan** canned beef
牛耳 **gyūji(ru)** lead, head, control, command, direct
7 牛乳 **gyūnyū** (cow's) milk
牛乳屋 **gyūnyūya** milkman, milk dealer
牛車 **gyūsha, ushiguruma** oxcart
gissha (Heian-period) cow carriage

8 牛舎 **gyūsha** cowshed, barn
牛歩 **gyūho** snail's pace
9 牛屋 **gyūya** butcher shop, beef restaurant
牛疫 **gyūeki** cattle plague, rinderpest
10 牛脂 **gyūshi** beef tallow
牛馬 **gyūba** horses and cattle/oxen
12 牛痘 **gyūtō** cowpox, vaccine
牛飲馬食 **gyūin-bashoku** heavy eating and drinking
牛飯 **gyūmeshi** beef and rice
13 牛蒡 **gobō** burdock
牛酪 **gyūraku** butter
牛飼 **ushika(i)** cowherd, cowboy
17 牛鍋 **gyūnabe** sukiyaki
23 牛罐 **gyūkan** canned beef

——————— 2 ———————
3 小牛 **koushi** calf
4 水牛 **suigyū** water buffalo

5 生牛乳 **namagyūnyū** unprocessed milk (not powdered or condensed)
6 肉牛 **nikugyū** beef cattle
7 乳牛 **nyūgyū, chichiushi** milk cow, dairy cattle
牡牛 **oushi** bull, ox, steer
牡牛座 **Oushiza** (the constellation) Taurus
8 牧牛 **bokugyū** grazing/pasturing cattle
和牛 **wagyū** Japanese cow
9 海牛 **kaigyū, umiushi** sea cow, manatee
12 斑牛 **madara ushi** brindled cow
犂牛 **rigyū** brindled ox
雄牛 **oushi** bull, ox, steer
14 種牛 **taneushi** breeding bull
雌牛 **meushi** cow
15 蝸牛 **katatsumuri** snail
18 闘牛 **tōgyū** bullfight(ing); fighting bull
闘牛士 **tōgyūshi** matador, bullfighter
闘牛場 **tōgyūjō** bullring

——— 3 ———
9 風馬牛 **fūbagyū** indifferent, of no concern; widely disparate

——— 1 ———
生→ **0a5.29**

——— 2 ———
4g2.1
牝
HIN, mesu, men, me- female

——— 1 ———
4 牝犬 **mesu inu, meinu** female dog, bitch
6 牝羊 **mehitsuji** female sheep, ewe
7 牝牡 **mesu-osu** male and female
牝狐 **megitsune** female fox
11 牝鹿 **mejika** doe, hind
13 牝獅子 **mejishi** lioness
19 牝鶏 **hinkei** hen

4g2.2
牟
MU, BŌ mooing of a cow; greedy, gluttonous; barley

——— 2 ———
3 大牟田 **Ōmuta** (city, Fukuoka-ken)

——— 3 ———
11 釈迦牟尼 **Shakamuni** Sakyamuni, Gautama, Buddhag

——— 3 ———
4g3.1
牡
BO, osu, on-, o- male

——— 1 ———
4 牡丹 **botan** peony (shrub)
牡丹杏 **botankyō** plum
牡丹刷毛 **botanbake** (powder) puff, down pad
牡丹雪 **botan yuki** large snowflakes
牡丹餅 **botamochi** rice cake covered with bean jam
牡牛 **oushi** bull, ox, steer
牡牛座 **Oushiza** (the constellation) Taurus
10 牡馬 **ouma** male horse, stallion
11 牡猫 **oneko** tomcat
牡鹿 **ojika** stag, buck
20 牡蠣 **kaki** oyster

——— 2 ———
6 牝牡 **mesu-osu** male and female
12 葉牡丹 **habotan** ornamental kale

告→ **3d4.18**

——— 4 ———
4g4.1 / 731
牧
BOKU, maki pasture

——— 1 ———
2 牧人 **bokujin** herder, ranch hand
4 牧夫 **bokufu** herder, ranch hand
牧牛 **bokugyū** grazing/pasturing cattle
5 牧民 **bokumin** governing
6 牧羊 **bokuyō** sheep raising
牧羊地 **bokuyōchi** sheep meadow
牧地 **bokuchi** grazing land, pasture
8 牧者 **bokusha** shepherd, herdsman
9 牧草 **bokusō** grass, pasturage, meadow
牧草地 **bokusōchi** pasture, grazing land
牧神 **bokushin** god of livestock raising, Pan
10 牧畜 **bokuchiku** livestock/cattle raising
牧畜業 **bokuchikugyō** stock farming, ranching
牧師 **bokushi** pastor, minister
牧師館 **bokushikan** rectory, parsonage
11 牧野 **bokuya** pasture land, ranch
牧笛 **bokuteki** shepherd's flute
12 牧場 **bokujō, makiba** pasture, meadow, ranch
牧童 **bokudō** shepherd boy, cowboy
14 牧歌 **bokka** pastoral song

——— 2 ———
8 放牧 **hōboku** let graze, put to pasture
放牧地 **hōbokuchi** grazing land, pasture
10 遊牧 **yūboku** nomadic
13 農牧 **nōboku** raising crops and livestock, general farming
農牧地 **nōbokuchi** crop and grazing land

4g4.2 / 79

物

BUTSU, MOTSU, mono thing, object

——————— 1 ———————

2 物入 **monoi(ri)** expenses
3 物乞 **monogo(i)** begging
物干 **monoho(shi)** (frame for) drying clothes
物干竿 **monoho(shi)zao** washline pole
物干場 **monoho(shi)ba** place for drying
物々 **monomono(shii)** showy, imposing, elaborate
物々交換 **butsubutsu kōkan** barter
4 物分 **monowa(kari)** understanding
物心 **monogokoro** discretion, judgment
busshin matter and mind
5 物本 **mono (no) hon** (in some) book
物好 **monozu(ki)** curious, whimsical, eccentric
6 物件 **bukken** thing, article, physical object, a property
物交 **bukkō, butsukō** barter (short for 物々交換)
物色 **busshoku** look for; select
物尽 **monozuku(shi)** exhaustive, comprehensive
7 物体 **buttai** body, object, substance
物別 **monowaka(re)** rupture, failure (to reach agreement)
物忘 **monowasu(re)** forgetfulness
物狂 **monoguru(i)** insanity; madman
物売 **monou(ri)** peddler
物忌 **monoi(mi)** fast, abstinence
物見 **monomi** sightseeing; watchtower; scout, patrol
物見事 **mono(no)migoto (ni)** splendidly
物見高 **monomidaka(i)** burning with curiosity
物見遊山 **monomi yusan** pleasure trip
物見櫓 **monomi yagura** watchtower
物言 **monoi(u)** speak, talk
物足 **monota(rinai)** unsatisfying, something missing
8 物事 **monogoto** things, matters
物価 **bukka** (commodity) prices
物価指数 **bukka shisū** price index
物価高 **bukkadaka** high prices
物価騰貴 **bukka tōki** rise in prices
物知 **monoshi(ri)** knowledgeable, erudite
物知顔 **monoshi(ri)gao** knowing look
物的 **butteki** material, physical
物物 **monomono(shii)** showy, imposing, elaborate
物物交換 **butsubutsu kōkan** barter
物性 **bussei** physical properties

物怖 **monoo(ji)** timidity
物怪 **mono(no)ke** specter, evil spirit
物具 **mono(no)gu** weapons, armor
物取 **monoto(ri)** thief
9 物哀 **mono (no) awa(re)** pathos, esthetic sense
物活論 **bukkatsuron** animism
物持 **monomo(chi)** wealthy person
物指 **monosa(shi)** ruler, measure, yardstick
物品 **buppin** goods, article, commodity
物品税 **buppinzei** commodity/excise tax
物要 **monoi(ri)** expenses
物相飯 **mossōmeshi** prison food
物柔 **monoyawa(raka)** mild, gentle, suave
物珍 **monomezura(shii)** curious
物故 **bukko** die; be deceased
物音 **monooto** a noise/sound
物臭 **monogusa** lazy
物思 **monoomo(i)** pensiveness, reverie; anxiety
10 物凄 **monosugo(i)** awful, terrific, tremendous
物陰 **monokage** cover, hiding; a form, shape
物真似 **monomane** doing imitations, mimicry
物差 **monosa(shi)** ruler, measure, yardstick
物流 **butsuryū** physical distribution, dispatch/routing (of goods)
物案 **monoan(ji)** worry, anxiety
物恐 **monoosoro(shii)** frightening, horrible
物納 **butsunō** payment in kind
物納税 **butsunōzei** tax paid in kind
物恥 **monoha(zukashii)** shy, bashful
物笑 **monowara(i)** laughingstock, joke
11 物淋 **monosabi(shii)** lonely, lonesome
物理 **butsuri** law of nature; physics
物理学 **butsurigaku** physics
物理的 **butsuriteki** physical (properties)
物理療法 **butsuriryōhō** physiotherapy
物欲 **butsuyoku** worldly desires/ambition
物情 **butsujō** public feeling
物惜 **monoo(shimi)** be stingy
物産 **bussan** products, produce, commodities
物断 **monoda(chi)** abstinence
12 物象 **busshō** object; material phenomenon
物堅 **monogata(i)** honest, faithful, reliable
物覚 **monoobo(e)** memory
物量 **butsuryō** amount of material resources
物悲 **monogana(shii)** sad, melancholy
物越 **monogo(shi ni)** with something in between
物税 **butsuzei** tax on goods and possessions
物貰 **monomora(i)** beggar; sty (on the eyelid)
13 物腰 **monogoshi** manner, demeanor
物暗 **monogura(i)** dark, dim
物数 **mono (no) kazu** something of value
物置 **monoo(ki)** storeroom, shed
物資 **busshi** goods, resources
物馴 **monona(reru)** be used to, be experienced in, be at ease in

4

⺮
月
日
火
ネ
王
牛
方 4←
攵
欠
心
戸
戈

4

木
月
日
火
礻
王
→ 4 牛
方
攵
欠
心
戸
戈

14 物静 **monoshizu(ka)** quiet, still, calm
物慣 **monona(reru)** be used to, be experienced in, be at ease in
物種 **monodane** the fundamental thing
物語 **monogatari** tale, story
15 物影 **monokage** a form, shape
物憂 **monou(i)** languid, weary, dull
物慾 **butsuyoku** worldly desires/ambition
物質 **busshitsu** matter, substance
物質的 **busshitsuteki** material, physical
18 物騒 **busso** unsettled, troubled, dangerous
monosawa(gashii) noisy, boisterous
19 物識 **monoshi(ri)** knowledgeable, erudite
20 物議 **butsugi** public criticism/discussion

───────── 2 ─────────

1 一物 **ichimotsu** an article, a thing; ulterior motive, designs
2 入物 **i(re)mono** receptacle, container
人物 **jinbutsu** person; one's character; character (in a story); man of ability
人物画 **jinbutsuga** portrait
人物像 **jinbutsuzo** statue, picture
3 万物 **banbutsu, banmotsu** all things, all creation
万物霊長 **banbutsu (no) reicho** man, the lord of creation
大物 **omono** big thing; great man, big shot; big game
刃物 **hamono** edged tool, cutlery
干物 **himono** dried fish **ho(shi)mono** laundry (hung up) to be dried
上物 **jomono** high-quality article **uwamono** buildings on a plot of land
下物 **o(ri)mono** uterine discharge, menstruation; afterbirth
小物 **komono** small articles, little thing
4 太物 **futomono** dry/piece goods
什物 **jumotsu** utensil; furniture, fixtures; treasure
化物 **ba(ke)mono** ghost, spook
冗物 **jobutsu** redundancy
文物 **bunbutsu** civilization
反物 **tanmono** dry/piece goods, textiles
反物屋 **tanmonoya** dry-goods store
水物 **mizumono** liquid, drink, fruit; matter of chance, a gamble
手物 **te(no)mono** something in one's hand; specialty, strong point
引物 **hi(ki)mono** gift
5 出物 **demono** rash, boil; secondhand article **da(shi)mono** performance, program
本物 **honmono** genuine article, the real thing
失物 **u(se)mono** lost article
生物 **seibutsu, i(ki)mono** living creature, life **namamono** uncooked food, unbaked cake

生物学 **seibutsugaku** biology
生物界 **seibutsukai** plants and animals, life
他物 **tabutsu, ta(no)mono** the other thing; another's property
召物 **me(shi)mono** (polite) food, drink, clothing
古物 **furumono, kobutsu** old things, secondhand goods, curios, antiques
古物商 **kobutsusho** curio/secondhand dealer
外物 **gaibutsu** external object, foreign matter
比物 **kura(be)mono** comparison, match
汁物 **shirumono** soups
払物 **hara(i)mono** article to be disposed of
打物 **u(chi)mono** wrought/forged work; sword; molded cake
打物師 **u(chi)monoshi** swordsmith
好物 **kobutsu** a favorite food
礼物 **reimotsu** gift
冬物 **fuyumono** winter clothing
立物 **ta(te)mono** leading actor
6 死物 **shibutsu** lifeless thing, inanimate object
死物狂 **shi(ni)monoguru(i)** struggle to the death; desperation, frantic efforts
考物 **kanga(e)mono** puzzle, problem
色物 **iromono** colored fabrics
汚物 **obutsu** dirt, filth; sewage **yogo(re)mono** soiled things, the wash/laundry
先物 **sakimono** futures
先物買 **sakimonoga(i)** forward buying; speculation
吐物 **tobutsu** vomit
吸物 **su(i)mono** soup
名物 **meibutsu** noted product (of a locality)
奸物 **kanbutsu** crook, wily fellow
安物 **yasumono** cheap goods
光物 **hika(ri)mono** luminous phenomenon (shooting star, lightning, *ignis fatuus*), shiny object (metal, coin)
当物 **a(te)mono** riddle, guessing; a covering
7 我物 **wa(ga)mono** one's own (property)
我物顔 **wa(ga)monogao** as if one's own
作物 **sakumotsu** crops **tsuku(ri)mono** artificial product; decoration; fake; crop
低物価 **teibukka** low prices
何物 **nanimono** what
即物的 **sokubutsuteki** matter-of-fact
別物 **betsumono** something else, exception, special case
忘物 **wasu(re)mono** something forgotten
対物鏡 **taibutsukyo** objective lens
抄物 **shomotsu, shomono** notes, commentary (on a Chinese classic)
投物 **na(ge)mono** goods to be sold at a sacrifice
売物 **u(ri)mono** (article) for sale, offerings

見物 **kenbutsu** sightseeing
　　mimono a sight, spectacle, attraction
見物人 **kenbutsunin** spectator, sightseer
見物客 **kenbutsukyaku** spectator, audience, sightseer
見物席 **kenbutsuseki** seats (at a game/theater)
私物 **shibutsu** private property
初物 **hatsumono** first produce of the season
初物食 **hatsumonogu(i)** novelty seeker
8 長物 **chōbutsu** useless item, white elephant
長物語 **nagamonogatari** a tedious talk
果物 **kudamono** fruit
毒物 **dokubutsu** poisonous substance
毒物学 **dokubutsugaku** toxicology
事物 **jibutsu** things, affairs
供物 **kumotsu, sona(e)mono** votive offering
刷物 **su(ri)mono** printed matter
典物 **tenbutsu** article to pawn
其物 **so(no)mono** (in) itself
建物 **tatemono** a building
拝物教 **haibutsukyō** fetishism
拵物 **koshira(e)mono** imitation, fake
抛物線 **hōbutsusen** parabola
呼物 **yo(bi)mono** attraction, feature, main event
呪物 **jubutsu** fetish
呪物崇拝 **jubutsu sūhai** fetishism
宝物 **takaramono, hōmotsu** treasure
宝物殿 **hōmotsuden** treasury, museum
実物 **jitsubutsu** the real thing, the original
実物大 **jitsubutsudai** actual size
官物 **kanbutsu** government property
青物 **aomono** green vegetables
青物屋 **aomonoya** vegetable store, greengrocer
物物 **monomono(shii)** showy, imposing, elaborate
物物交換 **butsubutsu kōkan** barter
放物線 **hōbutsusen** parabola
怪物 **kaibutsu** monster, apparation; mystery man
和物 **a(e)mono** dishes dressed with vinegar, miso, sesame, seeds etc.
金物 **kanamono** hardware
金物屋 **kanamonoya** hardware store
9 巻物 **ma(ki)mono** scroll
乗物 **no(ri)mono** vehicle
俗物 **zokubutsu** worldly-minded person, person of vulgar tastes
造物主 **Zōbutsushu** the Creator
造物者 **Zōbutsusha** the Creator
風物 **fūbutsu** natural features; scenes and manners
段物 **danmono** multi-act musical drama
洗物 **ara(i)mono** the wash, laundry, washing up

活物 **katsubutsu** living being
持物 **mo(chi)mono** one's property/belongings
拾物 **hiro(i)mono** something picked up, a find; a bargain
指物 **sa(shi)mono** cabinetmaking, joinery
指物屋 **sa(shi)monoya** cabinetmaker
指物師 **sa(shi)monoshi** cabinetmaker
品物 **shinamono** goods, merchandise
姦物 **kanbutsu** crook, wily fellow
草物 **kusamono** short plants (used in flower arranging)
荒物 **aramono** kitchenware, sundries
荒物屋 **aramonoya** household goods store
柔物 **yawa(raka)mono** silks
染物 **so(me)mono** dyeing; dyed goods
染物屋 **so(me)monoya** dyer
畑物 **hatakemono** farm produce
祝物 **iwa(i)mono** congratulatory gift
珍物 **chinbutsu** a curiosity
施物 **hodoko(shi)mono** alms, charity
研物 **to(gi)mono** sharpening swords, polishing mirrors
研物師 **to(gi)monoshi** polisher of swords and mirrors
音物 **inmotsu** gift, present
香物 **kō(no)mono** pickled vegetables
食物 **ta(be)mono, shokumotsu, ku(i)mono** food　**ku(wase)mono** a fake; imposter
10 残物 **zanbutsu, noko(ri)mono** remnants, scraps, leftovers
俵物 **tawaramono, hyōmotsu** (marine) products in straw bags
借物 **ka(ri)mono** something borrowed
差物屋 **sashimonoya** cabinetmaker
差物師 **sashimonoshi** cabinetmaker
原物 **genbutsu** the original
進物 **shinmotsu** present, gift
捕物 **to(ri)mono** a capture, an arrest
捜物 **saga(shi)mono** looking for something; something one is looking for
徒物 **adamono** empty/ephemeral thing
従物 **jūbutsu** accessory (in law)
荷物 **nimotsu** baggage; load
唐物 **karamono** imported goods
唐物屋 **karamonoya** foreign-goods dealer/ store
唐物商 **tōbutsushō** foreign-goods store
核物理学 **kakubutsurigaku** nuclear physics
書物 **shomotsu** books
夏物 **natsumono** summer clothing
被物 **kabu(ri)mono** headgear, headdress
笑物 **wara(i)mono** laughingstock, butt of ridicule
財物 **zaibutsu** property
貢物 **mitsu(gi)mono, kōbutsu, kōmotsu** tribute

4

木
月
日
火
礻
王
牛　4 ←
方
攵
欠
心
戸
戈

4

木 月 日 火 礻 王 牛 方 攵 欠 心 戸 戈

→ 4

配物 **kuba(ri)mono** gifts
11 偽物 **gibutsu, nisemono** a counterfeit/fake
陽物 **yōbutsu** the phallus
動物 **dōbutsu** animal
動物学 **dōbutsugaku** zoology
動物性 **dōbutsusei** animal (protein)
動物相 **dōbutsusō** fauna
動物界 **dōbutsukai** animal kingdom
動物園 **dōbutsuen** zoo
動物愛 **dōbutsuai** love for animals
動物愛護 **dōbutsu aigo** being kind to animals, animal welfare
動物誌 **dōbutsushi** fauna, zoography
混物 **ma(ze)mono, ma(jiri)mono** mixture, adulteration
添物 **so(e)mono** addition, supplement, an extra
掛物 **ka(ke)mono** hanging scroll; coverlet
捧物 **sasa(ge)mono** offering, sacrifice
授物 **sazu(kari)mono** gift, blessing, boon
唯物史観 **yuibutsu shikan** materialistic interpretation of history
唯物主義 **yuibutsu shugi** materialism
唯物論 **yuibutsuron** materialism
得物 **emono** weapon
彫物 **ho(ri)mono** carving, engraving, sculpture
乾物 **kanbutsu** dry provisions, groceries
乾物屋 **kanbutsuya** grocer, grocery store
現物 **genbutsu** the actual goods; in kind, spot (trading)
産物 **sanbutsu** product
袋物 **fukuromono** bags and pouches
異物 **ibutsu** foreign substance/body
疵物 **kizumono** defective article; deflowered girl
組物 **kumimono** braid, braiding
断物 **ta(chi)mono** foods abstained from
貨物 **kamotsu** freight, cargo
貨物車 **kamotsusha** freight car
貨物船 **kamotsusen** freighter
貨物駅 **kamotsueki** freight depot
12 割物 **wa(re)mono** broken article; fragile article
博物学 **hakubutsugaku** natural history
博物館 **hakubutsukan** museum
着物 **kimono** clothes, kimono
揚物 **a(ge)mono** fried food
尋物 **tazu(ne)mono** thing being searched for, lost article
落物 **o(toshi)mono** lost article
蒸物 **mu(shi)mono** steamed food
葉物 **hamono** foliage plant
廃物 **haibutsu** waste, refuse, scrap
廃物利用 **haibutsu riyō** recycling
植物 **shokubutsu** plant
植物学 **shokubutsugaku** botany

植物性 **shokubutsusei** vegetable (oil)
植物界 **shokubutsukai** the plant kingdom
植物病 **shokubutsubyō** plant disease
植物採集 **shokubutsu saishū** plant collecting
植物園 **shokubutsuen** botanical garden
植物誌 **shokubutsushi** a flora/herbal
植物質 **shokubutsushitsu** vegetable matter
景物 **keibutsu** (seasonal) scenery; gift, premium
焼物 **ya(ki)mono** pottery, ceramics; roast food
焚物 **ta(ki)mono** firewood
煮物 **nimono** cooking; cooked food
買物 **ka(i)mono** shopping, purchase
詠物 **eibutsu** nature poem
詠物詩 **eibutsushi** nature poem
貰物 **mora(i)mono** present, gift
軸物 **jikumono** scroll (picture)
酢物 **su(no)mono** vinegared dish
鈍物 **donbutsu** blockhead, dunce
飲物 **no(mi)mono** (something to) drink, beverage
13 傑物 **ketsubutsu** great man, outstanding figure
傷物 **kizumono** damaged goods
催物 **moyō(shi)mono** public event, show
際物 **kiwamono** seasonal goods
塩物 **shiomono** salted food
塗物 **nu(ri)mono** lacquerware
毀物 **kowa(re)mono** fragile article
献物 **kenmotsu** offering, present
夢物語 **yume monogatari** account of a dream; fantastic story
蓋物 **futamono** covered container/dish
寝物語 **nemonogatari** talk while lying in bed
腫物 **ha(re)mono, shumotsu** swelling, boil, tumor, abscess
腰物 **koshi (no) mono** sword worn at one's side
腥物 **namagusamono** raw things (like fish and meat)
煉物 **ne(ri)mono** paste, pastries, bean jelly, paste jewelry; festival procession
禁物 **kinmotsu** forbidden things, taboo
解物 **to(ki)mono** old clothes to be unsewn
愚物 **gubutsu** fool, blockhead
裾物 **susomono** lower-grade goods
置物 **o(ki)mono** ornament; figurehead
絹物 **kinumono** silk goods
続物 **tsuzu(ki)mono** a serial (story)
継物 **tsu(gi)mono** patch
詰物 **tsu(me)mono** stuffing, packing, padding
鉢物 **hachimono** food served in bowls; potted plant
鉱物 **kōbutsu** mineral
鉱物学 **kōbutsugaku** mineralogy
鉱物質 **kōbutsushitsu** mineral matter

飾物 **kaza(ri)mono** ornament, decoration; figurehead

預物 **azu(ke)mono** article left in someone's charge

14 遺物 **ibutsu** relic, remains

漬物 **tsukemono** pickled vegetables

鳴物 **na(ri)mono** music(al instruments)

静物 **seibutsu** still life

静物画 **seibutsuga** still-life picture, still life

端物 **hamono** incomplete set, odds and ends

種物 **tanemono** seeds; flavored soba; shaved ice with fruit syrup

種物商 **tanemonoshō** seed seller/store

穀物 **kokumotsu** grain

練物 **ne(ri)mono** paste (cakes/gems); procession, (parade) float

語物 **kata(ri)mono** (theme of a) narrative

読物 **yo(mi)mono** reading matter

雑物 **zatsubutsu** miscellaneous things; impurities

聞物 **ki(ki)mono** something worth hearing, highlight

駄物 **damono** low-grade goods, trash

15 撥物 **ha(ne)mono** rejected goods

撮物 **tsuma(mi)mono** snack food (e.g., peanuts) to be eaten while drinking

器物 **kibutsu** container, utensil, implement, fixture

幣物 **heimotsu, heibutsu** Shinto offerings of cloth, rope, or cut paper

履物 **ha(ki)mono** footwear

敷物 **shikimono** carpet, rug, cushion

慰物 **nagusa(mi)mono** object of pleasure, plaything

編物 **a(mi)mono** knitting; knitted goods

縫物 **nu(i)mono** sewing, needlework

縫物台 **nu(i)monodai** sewing table

調物 **shira(be)mono** matter for inquiry

賜物 **tamamono** gift

質物 **shichimono** pawned article

鋳物 **imono** article of cast metal, a casting

16 獲物 **emono** game, a catch, spoils

薄物 **usumono** thin silk, light dress

薬物 **yakubutsu** medicines, drugs

薬物学 **yakubutsugaku** pharmacology

憑物 **tsu(ki)mono** possessing spirit, curse, obsession

縞物 **shimamono** striped cloth

謡物 **utaimono** Noh recitation piece

17 擬物 **maga(i)mono** imitation

嬲物 **nabu(ri)mono** laughingstock

戴物 **itada(ki)mono** gift

鍋物 **nabemono** food served in the pot

闇物資 **yamibusshi** black-market goods

18 儲物 **mō(ke)mono** good bargain, windfall

織物 **orimono** cloth, fabric, textiles

織物商 **orimonoshō** draper

織物業 **orimonogyō** the textile business

贈物 **oku(ri)mono** gift, present

難物 **nanbutsu** hard-to-handle person/problem

19 贋物 **ganbutsu, nisemono** imitation, counterfeit, forgery

艶物 **tsuyamono** love story

臓物 **zōmotsu** entrails, giblets

21 魔物 **mamono** demon, devil

22 贓物 **zōbutsu** stolen goods

贖物 **agamono, agana(i)mono** an indemnification; scapegoat, substitute

23 齏物 **aemono** (dishes dressed with vinegar, miso, sesame seeds, etc.)

───────── 3 ─────────

1 一人物 **ichijinbutsu** a person of consequence

一幕物 **hitomakumono** one-act play

3 三幕物 **sanmakumono** three-act play

工作物 **kōsakubutsu** a building; manufactured goods

大人物 **daijinbutsu** great man

大好物 **daikōbutsu** a favorite food

大幅物 **ōhabamono** full-width yard goods, broadcloth

下手物 **getemono** low-quality article; strange things

小人物 **shōjinbutsu** stingy/base person

小荷物 **konimotsu** parcel, package

小間物 **komamono** sundry wares, knickknacks

小間物屋 **komamonoya** haberdashery

4 不純物 **fujunbutsu** impurities, foreign matter

天産物 **tensanbutsu** natural products

毛織物 **keorimono** woolen goods

化合物 **kagōbutsu** chemical compound

収穫物 **shūkakubutsu** harvest, crop, yield

分泌物 **bunpitsubutsu** a secretion

厄介物 **yakkaimono** burden, nuisance

水化物 **suikabutsu** a hydrate

水産物 **suisanbutsu** marine products

手荷物 **tenimotsu** luggage, (hand) baggage

犬追物 **inuoumono** (noisy martial arts event of Kamakura period in which 36 mounted archers pursue and shoot at 150 dogs)

木綿物 **momenmono** cotton goods/clothing

5 必要物 **hitsuyōbutsu** necessities

出来物 **dekimono** skin eruption, rash, pimple, boil, a growth

出版物 **shuppanbutsu** a publication

出品物 **shuppinbutsu** an exhibit

生臭物 **namagusamono** raw foods (forbidden to monks)

生産物 **seisanbutsu** product, produce

代替物 **daitaibutsu** a substitute

4

木 月 日 火 礻 王 牛 方 攵 欠 忄 戸 戈

4←

4

木
月
日
火
礻
王
→ 4 牛
方
攵
欠
心
戸
戈

刊行物 **kankōbutsu** a publication
古生物 **koseibutsu** extinct plants and animals
古生物学 **koseibutsugaku** paleontology
可塑物質 **kaso busshitsu** plastics
可燃物 **kanenbutsu** combustibles, flammable substances
好人物 **kōjinbutsu** good-natured person
好下物 **kōkabutsu** favorite dish/snack
主食物 **shushokumotsu** a staple food
主産物 **shusanbutsu** main product
6 伝記物 **denkimono** biographical literature
合成物 **gōseibutsu** a compound/synthetic
印刷物 **insatsubutsu** printed matter
老廃物 **rōhaibutsu** waste matter/products
危険物 **kikenbutsu** hazardous articles, explosives and combustibles
在中物 **zaichūbutsu** contents
吐瀉物 **toshabutsu** vomit and bowel discharge
如何物 **ikamono** spurious article, a fake
共有物 **kyōyūbutsu** joint property
有体物 **yūtaibutsu** something tangible
有価物 **yūkabutsu** valuables
有機物 **yūkibutsu** organic matter, organism
自然物 **shizenbutsu** natural object
7 夾雑物 **kyōzatsubutsu** admixture, impurities
邪魔物 **jamamono** obstacle, impediment, nuisance
対象物 **taishōbutsu** object, subject, target
角質物 **kakushitsubutsu** horny/keratinous material
沈澱物 **chindenbutsu** deposit, precipitate
抗生物質 **kōsei busshitsu** an antibiotic
投射物 **tōshabutsu** projectile
吹出物 **fu(ki)demono** skin rash, pimple
妨害物 **bōgaibutsu** obstacle
見世物 **misemono** show, exhibition
見返物資 **mikae(ri) busshi** collateral goods
私有物 **shiyūbutsu** private property
季節物 **kisetsumono** things in season
8 長尺物 **chōjakumono, chōshakumono** long/lengthy item (film)
奉納物 **hōnōbutsu** votive offering
事々物々 **jiji-butsubutsu** everything
到来物 **tōraimono** something received as a gift
建造物 **kenzōbutsu** a building, structure
建築物 **kenchikubutsu** a building, structure
河原物 **kawaramono** actors (a term of opprobrium)
拝領物 **hairyōbutsu** gift (from a superior)
抵当物 **teitōbutsu** security, pawn, collateral
定着物 **teichakubutsu** fixtures
店屋物 **ten'yamono** take-out food
固形物 **kokeibutsu** a solid; solid food
林産物 **rinsanbutsu** forest products

青化物 **seikabutsu** a cyanide
青果物 **seikabutsu** vegetables and fruits
玩弄物 **ganrōbutsu** plaything
怪人物 **kaijinbutsu** mystery man
武家物 **bukemono** a samurai romance
9 軍記物語 **gunki monogatari** war chronicle
造営物 **zōeibutsu** a building, structure
洗濯物 **sentakumono** the wash/laundry
海産物 **kaisanbutsu** marine products
拾得物 **shūtokubutsu** found article
炭化物 **tankabutsu** carbide
眉唾物 **mayutsubamono** fake, cock-and-bull story
10 耕作物 **kōsakubutsu** farm products
陸産物 **rikusanbutsu** land products
郵便物 **yūbinbutsu** mail
差上物 **sa(shi)a(ge)mono** gift
原産物 **gensanbutsu** primary products
流動物 **ryūdōbutsu** fluid, liquid
消費物資 **shōhi busshi** consumer goods
埋蔵物 **maizōbutsu** buried property/ore
展覧物 **tenranbutsu** exhibit
時代物 **jidaimono** an antique; a historical drama
特産物 **tokusanbutsu** special product (of a locality), indigenous to
記念物 **kinenbutsu** souvenir, memento
11 副食物 **fukushokubutsu** side dish; supplementary food
副産物 **fukusanbutsu** by-product
動植物 **dōshokubutsu** plants and animals, flora and fauna
鹵獲物 **rokakubutsu** booty, spoils, trophy
混合物 **kongōbutsu** mixture, compound
混和物 **konwabutsu** mixture
添加物 **tenkabutsu** additives
排出物 **haishutsubutsu** excreta
排泄物 **haisetsubutsu** excrement, excretion
掘出物 **ho(ri)da(shi)mono** treasure trove; lucky find, bargain
強奪物 **gōdatsubutsu** plunder, loot
得手物 **etemono** one's specialty
著作物 **chosakubutsu** a (literary) work, book
寄生物 **kiseibutsu** parasite
産出物 **sanshutsubutsu** product
頂戴物 **chōdaimono** something received as a gift
12 滋養物 **jiyōbutsu** nourishing food, sustenance
媒介物 **baikaibutsu** medium, agency; carrier (of a disease)
営造物 **eizōbutsu** building, structure
廃棄物 **haikibutsu** waste matter, wastes
無一物 **muichibutsu, muichimotsu** penniless
無生物 **museibutsu** inanimate object
無主物 **mushubutsu** ownerless article/property

無機物　**mukibutsu**　inorganic substance, minerals
絵巻物　**emakimono**　picture scroll
証拠物　**shōkobutsu**　physical evidence
飲食物　**inshokubutsu**　food and drink
13 障害物　**shōgaibutsu**　obstacle, obstruction
農作物　**nōsakubutsu**　crops, farm produce
農産物　**nōsanbutsu**　agricultural products
遮蔽物　**shaheibutsu**　cover, shelter
源氏物語　**Genji Monogatari**　The Tale of Genji
微生物　**biseibutsu**　microorganism, microbe
微生物学　**biseibutsugaku**　microbiology
暗記物　**ankimono**　something to be memorized
聖遺物　**seiibutsu**　religious relic
愛玩物　**aiganbutsu**　prized possession
絹織物　**kinuorimono**　silk fabrics
14 遺失物　**ishitsubutsu**　lost article
漁獲物　**gyokakubutsu**　a catch (of fish)
漂流物　**hyōryūbutsu**　flotsam
綿織物　**men'orimono**　cotton goods
酸化物　**sankabutsu**　oxide
15 縁起物　**engimono**　a lucky charm
16 懐中物　**kaichūmono**　pocketbook, wallet
18 贈与物　**zōyobutsu**　gift, present
19 瀬戸物　**setomono**　porcelain, china, earthenware
爆発物　**bakuhatsubutsu**　explosives

—————— 4 ——————

4 不消化物　**fushōkabutsu**　indigestible food
天地万物　**tenchi-banbutsu**　the whole universe, all creation
中心人物　**chūshin jinbutsu**　central figure, key person
水酸化物　**suisankabutsu**　a hydroxide
6 同一人物　**dōitsu jinbutsu**　the same person
有袋動物　**yūtai dōbutsu**　a marsupial
7 亜麻織物　**ama orimono**　flax fabrics, linen
8 事事物物　**jiji-butsubutsu**　everything
9 浮遊生物　**fuyū seibutsu**　plankton
炭水化物　**tansuikabutsu**　carbohydrates
10 哺乳動物　**honyū dōbutsu**　mammal
脊椎動物　**sekitsui dōbutsu**　vertebrates
被保険物　**hihokenbutsu**　insured property
11 軟体動物　**nantai dōbutsu**　mollusk
12 無用長物　**muyō (no) chōbutsu**　useless obstruction
13 裸子植物　**rashi shokubutsu**　gymnospermous plant
15 養蜂植物　**yōhō shokubutsu**　plants for bees
16 薬籠中物　**yakurōchū (no) mono**　at one's beck and call
18 観葉植物　**kan'yō shokubutsu**　foliage plant
蹠行動物　**shokō dōbutsu**　a plantigrade

(animal that walks on the whole sole of its foot, as man or bear)
顕花植物　**kenka shokubutsu**　flowering plant
20 蠕形動物　**zenkei dōbutsu**　legless animal

—————— 5 ——————

4 天然記念物　**tennen kinenbutsu**　natural monument

—————— 5 ——————

4g5.1 / 729

性

SEI, nie　sacrifice, offering

—————— 2 ——————

17 犠牲　**gisei**　sacrifice
犠牲的　**giseiteki**　self-sacrificing
犠牲者　**giseisha**　victim

4g5.2

牴

TEI　touch, feel

—————— 1 ——————

13 牴触　**teishoku**　conflict

—————— 6 ——————

4g6.1 / 282

特

TOKU　special

—————— 1 ——————

3 特大　**tokudai**　extra large
特上　**tokujō**　finest, choicest
5 特出　**tokushutsu**　superior, excellent
特功　**tokkō**　special efficacy
特写　**tokusha**　special/exclusive photo
特立　**tokuritsu**　conspicuous; independent
6 特色　**tokushoku**　characteristic, distinguishing feature, peculiarity
特有　**tokuyū**　characteristic of, peculiar to
特有性　**tokuyūsei**　peculiarity
特旨　**tokushi**　special consideration
7 特別　**tokubetsu**　special, extraordinary
特別号　**tokubetsugō**　special number
特別機　**tokubetsuki**　special airplane
特技　**tokugi**　special skill, specialty
特志家　**tokushika**　volunteer, supporter
特売　**tokubai**　special sale
特売品　**tokubaihin**　articles on sale
特売場　**tokubaijō**　bargain counter/basement
特利　**tokuri**　extra-high interest (rate)
8 特長　**tokuchō**　distinctive feature, characteristic; strong point, forte, merit

4

木
月
日
火
礻
王
牛　6←
方
攵
欠
心
戸
戈

特使 **tokushi** special envoy/messenger
特価 **tokka** special/reduced price
特価品 **tokkahin** bargain goods
特例 **tokurei** special case, exception
特命 **tokumei** specially appointed
特効 **tokkō** special efficacy
特効薬 **tokkōyaku** specific remedy
特免 **tokumen** special license; dispensation
特典 **tokuten** special favor, privilege
特注 **tokuchū** specially ordered (goods)
特定 **tokutei** specify
特性 **tokusei** distinctive quality, characteristic, trait
9 特発 **tokuhatsu** special (train); idiopathic
特点 **tokuten** special favor, privilege
特急 **tokkyū** limited express (train)
特段 **tokudan** special
特派 **tokuha** dispatch
特派員 **tokuhain** (news) correspondent; delegate
特待 **tokutai** special treatment, distinction
特待生 **tokutaisei** scholarship student
特待券 **tokutaiken** complimentary ticket
特科兵 **tokkahei** technical soldier
特科隊 **tokkatai** technical corps
特級 **tokkyū** special grade
特級酒 **tokkyūshu** special-grade saké
特約 **tokuyaku** special contract
特約店 **tokuyakuten** special agent, chain store
10 特殊 **tokushu** special
特殊性 **tokushusei** peculiarity, characteristic
特殊鋼 **tokushukō** special steel
特高 **tokkō** political-control police (short for 特別高等警察)
特進 **tokushin** special promotion
特恵 **tokukei, tokkei** special favor, preferential
特称 **tokushō** the particular
特記 **tokki** special mention
特配 **tokuhai** special ration/dividend, bonus
11 特赦 **tokusha** amnesty
特務 **tokumu** special duty/service
特務機関 **tokumu kikan** military intelligence organization
特産 **tokusan** special product, (local) specialty; indigenous
特産物 **tokusanbutsu** special product (of a locality), indigenous to
特産品 **tokusanhin** specialty, special products
特異 **tokui** singular, peculiar, unique
特異性 **tokuisei** singularity, peculiar characteristics
特異質 **tokuishitsu** idiosyncrasy
特許 **tokkyo** patent; special permission
特許庁 **Tokkyochō** Patent Office
特許状 **tokkyojō** charter, special license

特許法 **tokkyohō** patent law
特許品 **tokkyohin** patented article
特許権 **tokkyoken** patent
特設 **tokusetsu** specially established/installed
12 特報 **tokuhō** news bulletin
特装 **tokusō** specially equipped
特装版 **tokusōban** specially bound edition
特筆 **tokuhitsu** make special mention of
特筆大書 **tokuhitsu-taisho** write large, single out
特等 **tokutō** special grade
特集 **tokushū** special edition/collection
特集号 **tokushūgō** special issue
13 特電 **tokuden** special telegram/dispatch
14 特選 **tokusen** specially selected
特徴 **tokuchō** distinctive feature, characteristic
特種 **tokudane** exclusive news, scoop
tokushu special kind/type
特製 **tokusei** special make, deluxe
特需 **tokuju** emergency/wartime demand
15 特撮 **tokusatsu** specially photographed
特賞 **tokushō** special commendation/reward
特権 **tokken** privilege, prerogative; option (to buy)
特権者 **tokkensha** privileged person
特質 **tokushitsu** characteristic, trait
16 特薦 **tokusen** specially recommended

——— 2 ———
8 奇特 **kitoku** commendable; benevolent
9 独特 **dokutoku** unique, peculiar to
12 超特作 **chōtokusaku** super production, feature film
超特急 **chōtokkyū** superexpress (train)

——— 3 ———
9 専売特許 **senbai tokkyo** patent

——— 7 ———
4g7.1

悟 **GO** go against, be contrary to

犁 → 犂 **4g8.2**

——— 8 ———
4g8.1

犇 **HON, hishime(ku)** mill about, jostle; squeak
hishi (to) firmly, tightly

——— 1 ———
3 犇々 **hishihishi** firmly, tightly; thronging

4g8.2

犁 犂
RI, REI, suki plow

――――― 1 ―――――
4 犁牛 **rigyū** brindled ox
14 犁箆 **sukibera** plow blade, plowshare

甦 → **0a12.6**

――――― 9 ―――――

4g9.1 / 474

解 觧
KAI, GE explanation, solution
to(ku) untie, loosen, unravel;
cancel, release **to(kasu)** comb
to(keru) come loose; be solved
hodo(ku) untie **hodo(keru)** come untied
waka(ru) understand

――――― 1 ―――――
0 解する **kai(suru)** understand, interpret, construe
　解せない **ge(senai)** pass understanding, be beyond one
5 解氷 **kaihyō** thaw
6 解任 **kainin** dismissal, release
　解団 **kaidan** disband
　解式 **kaishiki** solution (in math)
7 解体 **kaitai** dismantle
　解決 **kaiketsu** solution, settlement
8 解毒剤 **gedokuzai** antidote
　解版 **kaihan** distribute/unset type
　解析 **kaiseki** analysis (branch of math)
　解明 **kaimei, to(ki)a(kasu)** explicate, elucidate
　解物 **to(ki)mono** old clothes to be unsewn
　解放 **kaihō, to(ki)hana(tsu)** liberate, release, set free
　解放区 **kaihōku** liberated areas
9 解除 **kaijo** cancel, rescind; release from
　解約 **kaiyaku** cancellation of a contract
10 解剖 **kaibō** dissection, autopsy; analysis
　解剖学 **kaibōgaku** anatomy
　解剖室 **kaibōshitsu** dissecting room
　解消 **kaishō** dissolution, liquidation; annulment; be settled/solved
　解党 **kaitō** dissolution of a party
11 解隊 **kaitai** disband, demobilize
　解脱 **gedatsu** (Buddhist) deliverance, salvation
　解釈 **kaishaku** interpretation, elucidation
12 解散 **kaisan** disperse, break up, disband, dissolve

　解雇 **kaiko** discharge, dismissal
　解答 **kaitō** answer, solution
13 解禁 **kaikin** lifting a ban, open season
14 解像 **kaizō** (image) resolution, definition
　解語 **kaigo** understanding a word
　解読 **kaidoku** decipher, decrypt
　解説 **kaisetsu** explanation, commentary
　解説者 **kaisetsusha** commentator
15 解熱 **genetsu** alleviate fever
　解熱剤 **genetsuzai** an antipyretic
18 解職 **kaishoku** discharge, dismissal
　解題 **kaidai** bibliographical notes
28 解纜 **kairan** sailing, leaving

――――― 2 ―――――
1 了解 **ryōkai** understand, comprehend; Roger!
4 分解 **bunkai** analysis, breakdown, decomposition, disassembly, disintegration
5 瓦解 **gakai** collapse, fall to pieces
　未解決 **mikaiketsu** unsolved, unsettled
　弁解 **benkai** explanation, vindication, justification, defense, excuse, apology
　正解 **seikai** correct interpretation/solution, the right answer
　氷解 **hyōkai** thaw, melt away, be dispelled
　打解 **u(chi)to(keru)** open one's heart, be frank
　打解話 **u(chi)to(ke)banashi** friendly chat, heart-to-heart talk
　字解 **jikai** interpretation of a kanji
6 曲解 **kyokkai** strained interpretation, distortion
7 図解 **zukai** explanatory diagram, illustration
　見解 **kenkai** opinion, view
8 例解 **reikai** example, illustration
　注解 **chūkai** commentary, notes
　注解者 **chūkaisha** commentator
　注解書 **chūkaisho** commentary
　空解 **sorado(ke)** come untied
　明解 **meikai** clear (explanation)
　和解 **wakai** amicable settlement, compromise
　金解禁 **kin kaikin** lifting the gold embargo
9 俗解 **zokkai** popular interpretation
　通解 **tsūkai** commentary
11 理解 **rikai** understand, comprehend
　理解力 **rikairyoku** comprehension
　略解 **ryakkai** brief explanation
　訳解 **yakkai** annotated translation
　雪解 **yukige, yukido(ke)** thaw
12 絵解 **eto(ki)** explanation of/by a picture
　註解 **chūkai** notes, commentary
13 溶解 **yōkai** (intr.) melt, dissolve
　溶解力 **yōkairyoku** solubility
　溶解性 **yōkaisei** solubility
　溶解点 **yōkaiten** melting point
　溶解度 **yōkaido** solubility
　夢解 **yumeto(ki)** interpretation of dreams

詳解 **shōkai** detailed explanation
電解 **denkai** electrolysis
電解液 **denkaieki** electrolyte
電解質 **denkaishitsu** electrolyte
14 誤解 **gokai** misunderstanding
読解 **yo(mi)to(ku)** decipher
領解 **ryōkai** understanding, consent
15 潮解 **chōkai** deliquescence
16 融解 **yūkai** fuse, melt, dissolve
融解点 **yūkaiten** melting point
融解熱 **yūkainetsu** heat of fusion
17 霜解 **shimodo(ke)** thawing
18 鎔解 **yōkai** melt, fuse
鎔解性 **yōkaisei** fusibility
難解 **nankai** hard to understand

——————— 3 ———————
3 女性解放論 **josei kaihōron** feminism
4 不可解 **fukakai** mysterious, baffling
5 生分解性 **seibunkaisei** biodegradable
6 死体解剖 **shitai kaibō** autopsy
12 無理解 **murikai** lack of understanding
14 説文解字 **Setsumon Kaiji** (oldest Chinese character dictionary)

——————— 4 ———————
1 一知半解 **itchi hankai** superficial knowledge
5 加水分解 **kasui bunkai** hydrolysis
6 因数分解 **insū bunkai** factorization
13 暗黙了解 **anmoku (no) ryōkai** tacit understanding

——————— 10 ———————
4g10.1
犒 **KŌ, negira(u)** thank for, show appreciation

4g10.2
犖 **RAKU** brindled cow; bright; excel

——————— 11 ———————
4g11.1
靠 靠 **KŌ, mota(reru)** lean on/against

4g11.2
犛 **RI** yak

——————— 13 ———————
4g13.1 / 728
犧 犠 **GI** sacrifice

——————— 1 ———————
5 犧打 **gida** sacrifice hit (in baseball)
9 犧牲 **gisei** sacrifice
犧牲的 **giseiteki** self-sacrificing
犧牲者 **giseisha** victim

——————— 15 ———————
4g15.1
犢 **TOKU, koushi** calf

——————— 1 ———————
14 犢鼻褌 **tokubikon** loincloth

——————— 16 ———————
犠 → 犧 **4g13.1**

——————— 方 4h ———————

方	放	於	施	斾	旄	斿	旅	旌	旋	族	旒	旗
0.1	4.1	4.2	5.1	6.1	6.2	6.3	6.4	7.1	7.2	7.3	9.1	10.1

髣	旛	旙	覊	籠
10.2	4h14.1	14.1	15.1	22.1

——————— 0 ———————
4h0.1 / 70
方 **HŌ** direction, side; square
kata person (polite); direction; (as verb suffix) way/method of ...ing, how to ...
masa (ni) precisely, indeed

——————— 1 ———————
3 方寸 **hōsun** square *sun*; one's mind/intentions
方丈 **hōjō** ten feet square; chief priest('s quarters)
方々 **katagata** people, ladies and gentlemen
hōbō every direction
4 方今 **hōkon** at present, nowadays

方円 **hōen** square or circular
5 方正 **hōsei** correct behavior
6 方向 **hōkō** direction
方向板 **hōkōban** (train's) destination sign
方式 **hōshiki** formula; form; method, system;
　formalities, usage
方舟 **hakobune** (Noah's) ark
7 方里 **hōri** square *ri*
方位 **hōi** direction, bearing, azimuth
方角 **hōgaku** direction
方形 **hōkei** square
方図 **hōzu** end, limit
方言 **hōgen** dialect
8 方法 **hōhō** method, way, means
方法論 **hōhōron** methodology
9 方便 **hōben** expedient, means, instrument
方陣 **hōjin** square formation, phalanx; magic
　square
方途 **hōto** means, way
方面 **hōmen** direction; district; standpoint;
　aspect, phase
10 方案 **hōan** plan
方針 **hōshin** compass needle; course, policy
11 方術 **hōjutsu** art; method; magic
方眼紙 **hōganshi** graph paper
方略 **hōryaku** plan
12 方程式 **hōteishiki** equation
方策 **hōsaku** plan
16 方錐 **hōsui** square pyramid; square drill
方錐形 **hōsuikei** square pyramid

────── 2 ──────

1 一方 **ippō** one side; on one hand, on the other
　hand; one party, the other party; nothing
　but, only   **hitokata(narazu)** greatly,
　immensely
一方交通 **ippō kōtsū** one-way traffic
一方的 **ippōteki** one-sided, unilateral
一方通行 **ippō tsūkō** one-way traffic
2 二方 **futakata** both people
八方 **happō** all sides/directions
八方美人 **happō bijin** one who is affable to
　everybody
八方塞 **happō fusa(gari)** blocked in every
　direction, stymied
3 三方 **sanbō** three sides; small stand for
　placing an offering on
久方振 **hisakatabu(ri)** (for the first time in)
　a long time
夕方 **yūgata** evening
大方 **ōkata** probably; almost, mostly; people
　in general
上方 **jōhō** upper part, above, upward
　kamigata Kyōto-Ōsaka area
下方 **kahō** lower part, downward, below
土方 **dokata** construction laborer

4 今方 **imagata** a moment ago
双方 **sōhō** both parties/sides
片方 **katahō, katappō, katakata** one side/
　party, the other side/party
公方 **kubō** imperial court; shogun, warlord
父方 **chichikata** on the father's side, paternal
牛方 **ushikata** oxcart driver, teamster
方方 **katagata** people, ladies and gentlemen
　hōbō every direction
5 北方 **hoppō** north, northward, northern
左方 **sahō** the left
出方 **dekata** attitude; a move
母方 **hahakata** the mother's side (of the
　family)
仕方 **shikata** way, method, means, how to
他方 **tahō** another side/direction; on the other
　hand
平方 **heihō** square (of a number); square
　(meter)
平方形 **heihōkei** a square
平方根 **heihōkon** square root
外方 **gaihō** outward
　soppo (look) the other way
正方形 **seihōkei** square
打方 **u(chi)kata** how to shoot; batting,
　stroking (in tennis)
右方 **uhō** right side, the right
四方 **shihō, yomo** all (four) directions/sides
四方八方 **shihō-happō** in every direction,
　far and wide
処方 **shohō** prescription
立方 **rippō** cube (of a number), cubic (meter)
立方体 **rippōtai** a cube
立方根 **rippōkon** cube root
目方 **mekata** weight
6 多方面 **tahōmen** various, different, many-
　sided, versatile
死方 **shi(ni)kata** how to die, how one died
両方 **ryōhō** both
西方 **seihō** west, western, westward
西方浄土 **Saihō Jōdo** (Buddhist) Western
　Paradise
考方 **kanga(e)kata** way of thinking, viewpoint
此方 **ko(no)hō** this one; I, we
　ko(no) kata since; this person
　kochira, kotchi, konata here, this side
地方 **chihō** region, area   **jikata** rural locality
地方色 **chihōshoku** local color
地方版 **chihōban** local edition
地方税 **chihōzei** local taxes
先方 **senpō** the other party; destination
　sakikata the other party
在方 **a(ri)kata** the way (it) should be
　zaikata rural district
行方 **yukue, yu(ki)gata** one's whereabouts
　yu(ki)kata how to go

4

亻月日火礻王牛方攵欠心戸戈

0←

行方不明 **yukue-fumei** missing	船方 **funakata** boatman
行方定 **yukue-sada(menu)** aimless, wandering	12 遣方 **ya(ri)kata** way of doing, method
当方 **tōhō** I, we, on our part/side	遠方 **enpō** great distance, long way, far-off
百方 **hyappō** in every way	朝方 **asagata** (toward) morning
各方面 **kaku hōmen** every direction, all quarters	無方針 **muhōshin** without a plan
7 身方 **mikata** friend, ally, supporter	煮方 **nikata** way of cooking; a cook
里方 **satokata** one's wife's family	裁方 **ta(chi)kata** cutting, cut (of one's clothes)

4

木
月
日
火
礻
王
牛
→0 方
攵
欠
心
戸
戈

行方不明 **yukue-fumei** missing
行方定 **yukue-sada(menu)** aimless, wandering
当方 **tōhō** I, we, on our part/side
百方 **hyappō** in every way
各方面 **kaku hōmen** every direction, all quarters
7 身方 **mikata** friend, ally, supporter
里方 **satokata** one's wife's family
作方 **tsuku(ri)kata** how to make; style of building, construction, workmanship
何方 **donata** who
dochira where, what place; which
izukata which, whichever
折方 **o(ri)kata** how to fold
売方 **u(ri)kata** salesmanship; seller
快方 **kaihō** recovery, convalescence
見方 **mikata** viewpoint, way of looking at
言方 **i(i)kata** way of saying
8 長方形 **chōhōkei** rectangle
東方 **tōhō** east, eastward, eastern
使方 **tsuka(i)kata** how to use, management
直方体 **chokuhōtai** rectangular parallelepiped
建方 **ta(te)kata** architectural style; how to build
味方 **mikata** friend, ally, supporter
彼方 **kanata, anata** there, yonder; the other side
明方 **a(ke)gata** dawn
9 南方 **nanpō** south, southern, southward
前方 **zenpō** front **maekata** before; immature
途方 **tohō(mo nai)** exorbitant, extraordinary, absurd
途方暮 **tohō (ni) ku(reru)** be at a loss, not know what to do
後方 **kōhō** the rear, back
染方 **so(me)kata** dyeing process
食方 **ta(be)kata, ku(i)kata** manner of eating
10 借方 **ka(ri)kata** debit, debtor side; way of borrowing
振方 **fu(ri)kata** what to do (with oneself)
根方 **nekata** root, lower part
書方 **ka(ki)kata** how to write; penmanship
教方 **oshi(e)kata** teaching method
致方 **ita(shi)kata** way, method, means
致方無 **ita(shi)kata (ga) na(i)** it can't be helped
恵方 **ehō** lucky direction
恵方参 **ehōmai(ri)** New Year's visit to a shrine/temple which lies in a lucky direction
秘方 **hihō** secret method/formula
馬方 **umakata** pack-horse tender
11 斜方形 **shahōkei** rhombus
粗方 **arakata** mostly, roughly, nearly

船方 **funakata** boatman
12 遣方 **ya(ri)kata** way of doing, method
遠方 **enpō** great distance, long way, far-off
朝方 **asagata** (toward) morning
無方針 **muhōshin** without a plan
煮方 **nikata** way of cooking; a cook
裁方 **ta(chi)kata** cutting, cut (of one's clothes)
買方 **ka(i)kata** buyer; how to buy
結方 **yu(i)kata** hair style
貴方 **kihō, anata** you
貸方 **ka(shi)kata** creditor; credit side
開方 **kaihō** extraction of roots (in math)
13 裏方 **urakata** lady consort; stagehand
漢方 **kanpō** Chinese herbal medicine
漢方医 **kanpōi** herbal physician, herbalist
漢方薬 **kanpōyaku** a herbal medicine
殿方 **tonogata** gentlemen, men's
話方 **hana(shi)kata** way of speaking
詮方 **senkata(naku)** unavoidably, helplessly
14 暮方 **ku(re)gata** dusk, evening
ku(rashi)kata manner of living
複方 **fukuhō** compounded drug (prescription)
綴方 **tsuzu(ri)kata** spelling; composition, theme **to(ji)kata** binding
読方 **yo(mi)kata** reading, pronunciation (of a character)
聞方 **ki(ki)kata** way of hearing/listening
15 撃方 **u(chi)kata** how to fire (a gun)
撮方 **to(ri)kata** way of taking (a photo)
縫方 **nu(i)kata** way of sewing; sewer
諸方 **shohō** all directions
16 薬方 **yakuhō** prescription
親方 **oyakata** (gang) boss
親方日丸 **oyakata hi(no)maru** "the government will foot the bill"
積方 **tsu(mi)kata** way of piling/loading
18 織方 **o(ri)kata** type of weave; how to weave

──────── 3 ────────

2 二次方程式 **niji hōteishiki** quadratic equation
4 今朝方 **kesagata** this morning
片一方 **kata-ippō** one side/party, the other side/party
6 全地方 **zenchihō** the whole region
衣裳方 **ishōkata** (theater) wardrobe assistant
8 所々方々 **shosho-hōbō** everywhere
9 連立方程式 **renritsu hōteishiki** simultaneous equations
品行方正 **hinkō-hōsei** respectable, irreproachable
相手方 **aitekata** the other party, opponent
11 道化方 **dōkekata** clown
道具方 **dōgukata** stage hand
15 敵味方 **teki-mikata** friend or/and foe
16 薬局方 **yakkyokuhō** pharmacopoeia

親仁方 **oyajikata** role of an old man

—————————— 4 ——————————

4 中国地方 **Chūgoku chihō** the Chūgoku
  region (Hiroshima, Okayama, Shimane,
  Tottori, and Yamaguchi prefectures)
5 北陸地方 **Hokuriku chihō** the Hokuriku
  region (Fukui, Ishikawa, Toyama,
  Niigata prefectures)
  四方八方 **shihō-happō** in every direction,
  far and wide
8 所所方方 **shosho-hōbō** everywhere

—————————— 4 ——————————

4h4.1 / 512

放

HŌ, hana(tsu) set free, release; fire (a
gun); emit **hana(su)** set free, release,
let go **hana(reru)** get free of
hō(ru) throw; leave as is
ho(ttarakasu) neglect, lay aside, leave undone

—————————— 1 ——————————

4 放水 **hōsui** drainage, discharge
  放水路 **hōsuiro** drainage canal/channel
  放水管 **hōsuikan** drainpipe
  放火 **hōka** arson
  放火犯 **hōkahan** arson(ist)
  放火狂 **hōkakyō** pyromania(c)
  放心 **hōshin** be absentminded; feel reassured
5 放出 **hōshutsu** release, discharge, emit
  hō(ri)da(su) throw out; expel; abandon
6 放任 **hōnin** nonintervention
  放血 **hōketsu** bloodletting
7 放技 **hana(re)waza** feat, stunt
  放尿 **hōnyō** urination
  放屁 **hōhi** break wind
  放言 **hōgen** talk at random
8 放念 **hōnen** feel at ease, relax
  放免 **hōmen** release, acquittal
  放送 **hōsō** broadcast
  放送局 **hōsōkyoku** broadcasting station
  放牧 **hōboku** let graze, put to pasture
  放牧地 **hōbokuchi** grazing land, pasture
  放物線 **hōbutsusen** parabola
9 放逐 **hōchiku** expel
  放胆 **hōtan** bold, fearless, daring
10 放射 **hōsha** radiation, emission, discharge
  放射学 **hōshagaku** radiology
  放射性 **hōshasei** radioactive
  放射能 **hōshanō** radioactivity, radiation
  放射雲 **hōshaun** radioactive cloud
  放射線 **hōshasen** radiation
  放逸 **hōitsu** self-indulgence, debauchery
  放浪 **hōrō** wander, rove
  放浪者 **hōrōsha** wanderer, vagabond, vagrant
  放浪癖 **hōrōheki** wanderlust

放流 **hōryū** set adrift, discharge, stock (with
  fish)
放埓 **hōratsu** profligate, loose, dissipated
放校 **hōkō** expulsion from school
放恣 **hōshi** self-indulgent, licentious
11 放鳥 **hōchō** setting birds free; bird to be
  released
12 放散 **hōsan** radiate, diffuse, emanate;
  evaporate
13 放肆 **hōshi** self-indulgent, licentious
  放棄 **hōki** abandon, renounce, waive, forfeit
  放置 **hōchi** let alone, leave as is, leave to
  chance
  放資 **hōshi** investment
  放電 **hōden** electric discharge
14 放漫 **hōman** lax, loose, reckless
  放歌 **hōka** sing loudly
  放歌高吟 **hōka-kōgin** loud singing
15 放蕩 **hōtō** dissipation, fast living
  放蕩息子 **hōtō musuko** prodigal son
  放熱 **hōnetsu** radiate heat; radiant heat
  放熱器 **hōnetsuki** radiator
  放課後 **hōkago** after school
  放談 **hōdan** random/unreserved talk
  放論 **hōron** harangue, rant
16 放縦 **hōjū** self-indulgence, debauchery
17 放擲 **hōteki** abandon, lay aside, neglect
18 放題 **-hōdai** (as verb suffix) as much as one
  pleases, all you can (eat)

—————————— 2 ——————————

4 切放 **ki(ri)hana(su)** cut off/apart, sever,
  separate
  手放 **tebana(su)** let go of, part with; leave
  unattended **tebana(shi)** without
  holding on to, left unattended; unreservedly
5 出放題 **dehōdai** free flow; saying whatever
  comes to mind
  生放送 **namahōsō** live broadcast
  仕放題 **shihōdai** have one's own way
  好放題 **su(ki)hōdai** doing just as one pleases
6 再放送 **saihōsō** rebroadcast
7 抜放 **nu(ki)hana(su), nu(ki)hana(tsu)**
  unsheathe, draw (a sword)
  言放 **i(i)hana(tsu)** declare, assert
8 奔放 **honpō** wild, extravagant, uninhibited
  追放 **tsuihō** banishment; purge
  追放者 **tsuihōsha** purgee, deportee
  突放 **tsu(p)pana(su), tsu(ki)hana(su)** cast
  off, forsake
  取放題 **to(ri)hōdai** all-you-can-take
9 荒放題 **a(re)hōdai** left to go to ruin
  食放題 **ta(be)hōdai, ku(i)hōdai** eating as
  much as one pleases, all-you-can-eat
10 借放 **ka(rip)pana(shi)** borrowing without
  returning

振放 **fu(ri)hana(su)** shake off, break free of
11 野放 **nobana(shi)** putting to pasture; leaving things to themselves
野放図 **nohōzu** wild, unbridled
粗放 **sohō** careless; non-intensive (farming)
釈放 **shakuhō** release, discharge
12 遣放 **ya(rip)pana(shi)** leave as is, leave half done; careless, negligent
勝放 **ka(chi)hana(su)** win by a wide margin
開放 **kaihō, a(ke)hana(su)** (fling/leave) open
a(kep)pana(shi) left open; open, frank
13 解放 **kaihō, to(ki)hana(tsu)** liberate, release, set free
解放区 **kaihōku** liberated areas
14 豪放 **gōhō** manly and openhearted

─────── 3 ───────

6 多重放送 **tajū hōsō** multiplex broadcasting
仮釈放 **karishakuhō** release on parole
有線放送 **yūsen hōsō** broadcasting by wire/cable
自由放任 **jiyū hōnin** nonintervention, laissez-faire
7 言成放題 **i(i)na(ri) hōdai** submissive to (someone)
8 実況放送 **jikkyō hōsō** on-the-spot broadcast
12 無電放送 **muden hōsō** radio broadcast

─────── 4 ───────

3 女性解放論 **josei kaihōron** feminism
7 貝殻追放 **kaigara tsuihō** ostracism

4h4.2

於 **O, (ni) oi(te)** at, in, on, as for, as to
(ni) o(keru) at, in

─────── 5 ───────

4h5.1 / 1004

施 **SHI, SE, hodoko(su)** give, bestow; carry out, perform, conduct

─────── 1 ───────

3 施工 **sekō, shikō** construct, build, execute
5 施主 **seshu** chief mourner; donor, benefactor; builder
6 施行 **shikō** enforce; put into operation
施米 **semai** rice given as charity
8 施肥 **sehi** apply manure/fertilizer
施物 **hodoko(shi)mono** alms, charity
9 施政 **shisei** administration, governing
11 施術 **shijutsu** surgical operation
施設 **shisetsu** facilities, institution
12 施策 **shisaku** a measure/policy
15 施餓鬼 **segaki** service for the unmourned dead

16 施薬 **seyaku** (dispense) free medicine
施錠 **sejō** locking a lock
17 施療 **seryō** (give) free medical treatment

─────── 2 ───────

5 布施 **fuse** alms, charity
Fuse (city, Ōsaka-fu)
8 実施 **jisshi** put into effect, enforce

─────── 3 ───────

9 軍事施設 **gunji shisetsu** military installations

─────── 6 ───────

4h6.1

旆 **SEN** woolen cloth

─────── 1 ───────

6 旆那 **senna** senna

4h6.2

旄 **BŌ** tassel on a flag; long-haired cow; old man

4h6.3

旆 **HAI** flag

4h6.4 / 222

旅 **RYO, tabi** trip, travel, journey

─────── 1 ───────

2 旅人 **tabibito, tabinin, ryojin** traveler, wayfarer
4 旅支度 **tabijitaku** travel preparations/outfit
旅日記 **tabinikki** travel diary
旅心 **tabigokoro** one's mood while traveling; yen to travel
5 旅出 **tabide** departure
旅立 **tabida(tsu)** start on a journey
6 旅先 **tabisaki** destination
旅行 **ryokō** trip, travel
旅行先 **ryokōsaki** destination
旅行者 **ryokōsha** traveler, tourist
旅行家 **ryokōka** traveler, tourist
旅行記 **ryokōki** record of one's trip
旅回 **tabimawa(ri)** touring
旅団 **ryodan** brigade
7 旅住 **tabizuma(i)** one's stopping place on a trip
旅役者 **tabiyakusha** actor/troupe on the road
旅芸人 **tabigeinin** itinerant performer
8 旅舎 **ryosha** hotel, inn

→ 4

旅券 **ryoken** passport
旅空 **tabi (no) sora** away from home
旅枕 **tabi makura** sleeping away from home; journey
　旅所 **tabisho** resting place for a palanquin shrine
9 旅姿 **tabisugata** traveling attire
　旅客機 **ryokakki** passenger plane
10 旅疲 **tabizuka(re)** travel fatigue
11 旅商人 **tabishōnin, tabiakindo** peddler, traveling salesman
　旅情 **ryojō** one's mood while traveling
12 旅程 **ryotei** distance to be covered; itinerary
　旅装 **ryosō** traveling clothes
　旅費 **ryohi** traveling expenses
13 旅僧 **tabisō** traveling priest
　旅寝 **tabine** put up at an inn
　旅愁 **ryoshū** loneliness on a journey
　旅路 **tabiji** journey
15 旅稼 **tabikase(gi)** work away from home
16 旅興行 **tabikōgyō** road show
　旅疲 **tabiyatsu(re)** travel weariness
　旅館 **ryokan** inn, hotel
　旅館業 **ryokangyō** the hotel business
22 旅籠 **hatago** inn
　旅籠屋 **hatagoya** inn

―――――― 2 ――――――

6 行旅 **kōryo** travel; traveler
8 長旅 **nagatabi** long journey
　股旅 **matatabi** gambler's wandering life
11 船旅 **funatabi** voyage

―――――― 3 ――――――

1 一人旅 **hitoritabi** traveling alone
3 大名旅行 **daimyō ryokō** spendthrift tour, junket
6 死出旅 **shide (no) tabi** journey to the next world
10 修学旅行 **shūgaku ryokō** school excursion, field trip
12 無銭旅行 **musen ryokō** penniless travel, hitchhiking
13 新婚旅行 **shinkon ryokō** honeymoon

―――――― 7 ――――――

4h7.1
旌
SEI flag; praise

―――――― 1 ――――――

14 旌旗 **seiki** flag, banner

4h7.2 / 1005
旋
SEN go around, revolve, rotate

―――――― 1 ――――――

4 旋毛 **tsumuji** whorl of hair on the head
　旋毛曲 **tsumujima(gari)** cranky person
6 旋回 **senkai** turning, revolving, circling
9 旋風 **senpū, tsumuji kaze** whirlwind, tornado
　旋律 **senritsu** melody
11 旋転 **senten** turning, rotation, revolution
15 旋盤 **senban** lathe
　旋盤工 **senbankō** lathe operator, turner

―――――― 2 ――――――

6 回旋 **kaisen** rotation, revolution, convolution, coiling, spiraling
8 周旋 **shūsen** good offices, recommendation, mediation
　周旋屋 **shūsen'ya** broker, employment agency
　周旋料 **shūsenryō** brokerage, commission
　周旋業 **shūsengyō** brokerage, commission agency
9 律旋 **rissen** (a mode in *gagaku* music)
12 凱旋 **gaisen** triumphal return
　凱旋門 **gaisenmon** arch of triumph
14 斡旋 **assen** mediation, good offices, placement
　斡旋者 **assensha** mediator, intermediary
　斡旋案 **assen'an** conciliation/arbitration proposal
17 螺旋 **rasen** spiral, helix　**neji** screw; stopcock; (wind-up) spring
　螺旋形 **rasenkei** spiral, helical

―――――― 3 ――――――

4 木螺旋 **mokuneji** wood screw

―――――― 4 ――――――

12 就職斡旋 **shūshoku assen** job placement

施 → **4h6.3**

4h7.3 / 221
族
ZOKU family, tribe
yakara family, relatives; fellows, gang

―――――― 1 ――――――

0 ながら族 **nagarazoku** those who do two things at once (eat/study while watching TV)
8 族長 **zokuchō** patriarch
10 族称 **zokushō** one's class (nobility, samurai, or commoner)
15 族縁 **zokuen** family ties
20 族籍 **zokuseki** class and domicile

―――――― 2 ――――――

1 一族 **ichizoku** a family/household
3 士族 **shizoku** descendants of samurai

4 氏族 **shizoku** family, clan
  氏族制度 **shizoku seido** the family/clan system
  水族館 **suizokukan** (public) aquarium
  王族 **ōzoku** royal family, royalty
5 民族 **minzoku** race, a people
  民族学 **minzokugaku** ethnology
  民族性 **minzokusei** racial/national trait
6 同族 **dōzoku** the same family/tribe
  血族 **ketsuzoku** blood relative, kin
7 亜族 **azoku** subtribe
8 宗族 **sōzoku** one's family/relatives
9 姻族 **inzoku** in-laws
  皇族 **kōzoku** (member of) the imperial family
10 部族 **buzoku** tribe
  華族 **kazoku** nobleman, peer
  家族 **kazoku** family
  家族法 **kazokuhō** family(-rights) law
  家族的 **kazokuteki** like a member of the family
  家族連 **kazokuzu(re)** taking the family along
11 眷族 **kenzoku** family, household, kith and kin
  魚族 **gyozoku** fishes
12 蛮族 **banzoku** savage tribe
  貴族 **kizoku** the nobility
  貴族的 **kizokuteki** aristocratic
  貴族院 **Kizokuin** the House of Peers/Lords
13 漢族 **Kanzoku** the Han/Chinese people
14 豪族 **gōzoku** powerful family/clan
  遺族 **izoku** surviving family
  種族 **shuzoku** race, tribe
  語族 **gozoku** a family of languages
  閥族 **batsuzoku** clan, clique
16 親族 **shinzoku** relatives

————— 3 —————

3 大家族 **daikazoku** large family
7 社用族 **shayōzoku** expense-account aristrocrats
11 斜陽族 **shayōzoku** impoverished aristocracy
13 漢民族 **Kan minzoku** the Han/Chinese people
14 遺家族 **ikazoku** surviving family

————— 4 —————

4 少数民族 **shōsū minzoku** minority nationali-ties, ethnic minorities
5 母系家族 **bokei kazoku** matriarchal family
6 先住民族 **senjū minzoku** aborigines
7 扶養家族 **fuyō kazoku** family dependents

————— 9 —————

4h9.1

旒

  RYŪ (counter for flags)

————— 10 —————

4h10.1 / 1006

旗

  KI, hata flag, banner

————— 1 —————

3 旗下 **kika** under the banner of
4 旗手 **kishu** standardbearer
  旗日 **hatabi** national holiday
5 旗本 **hatamoto** direct vassal of the shogun
6 旗印 **hatajirushi** the design on a flag; banner, slogan
  旗色 **hatairo** the tide of war; things, the situation
  旗行列 **hata gyōretsu** flag procession
9 旗信号 **hatashingō** semaphore, flag signal
  旗亭 **kitei** inn; restaurant
  旗持 **hatamo(chi)** standardbearer
10 旗振 **hatafu(ri)** flagman; flag-wagging
12 旗揚 **hataa(ge)** raising an army; launching a business
13 旗鼓 **kiko** colors and drums; army
15 旗幟 **kishi** flag, banner; one's stand/position
  旗標 **hatajirushi** the design on a flag; banner, slogan
16 旗頭 **hatagashira** leader, boss
21 旗艦 **kikan** flagship

————— 2 —————

1 一旗 **hitohata** a flag; an undertaking
3 小旗 **kobata** small flag
4 弔旗 **chōki** flag draped in black, flag at half-staff
  反旗 **hanki** standard/banner of revolt
  手旗 **tebata** hand flag
  手旗信号 **tebata shingō** flag signaling, semaphore
5 半旗 **hanki** flag at half-staff
  白旗 **shirahata, hakki** white flag (of truce/surrender)
6 団旗 **danki** association's flag
  旭旗 **kyokki** the Rising Sun flag
7 赤旗 **akahata** red flag; the Red Flag
  sekki red/danger flag
  社旗 **shaki** company flag
8 国旗 **kokki** national flag
9 降旗 **kōki** white flag (of surrender)
  軍旗 **gunki** battle flag, colors, ensign
  叛旗 **hanki** standard/banner of revolt
  皇旗 **kōki** imperial standard
10 校旗 **kōki** school flag
11 隊旗 **taiki** flag of a unit
  旌旗 **seiki** flag, banner
13 義旗 **giki** flag/banner of righteousness
  蓆旗 **mushirobata** straw mat used as a flag

戦旗 **senki** battle flag
15 標旗 **hyōki** marker flag
敵旗 **tekki** enemy flag

————— 3 —————

3 三色旗 **sanshokuki** tricolor flag
三角旗 **sankakuki** pennant
万国旗 **bankokuki** flags of all nations
4 天皇旗 **tennōki** the imperial standard
五輪旗 **Gorinki** Olympic flag
日章旗 **nisshōki** the Japanese/Rising-Sun flag
6 旭日旗 **kyokujitsuki** the Rising Sun flag
8 国連旗 **Kokurenki** UN flag
9 信号旗 **shingōki** signal/code flag
連隊旗 **rentaiki** regimental standard/colors
海軍旗 **kaigunki** navy flag
星条旗 **seijōki** the Stars and Stripes flag
11 商船旗 **shōsenki** merchant flag
13 戦闘旗 **sentōki** battle flag
16 錦御旗 **nishiki (no) mihata** the imperial
    standard
17 優勝旗 **yūshōki** championship pennant

4h10.2

髣
　　HŌ resemble; dimly

————— 1 —————

15 髣髴 **hōfutsu** resemble closely; faintly

————————— 12 —————————

旙 → 旛 **4h14.1**

————————— 14 —————————

4h14.1

旛 旛
　　HAN banner, streamer

————————— 15 —————————

4h15.1

覈
　　KAKU investigate

————————— 22 —————————

4h22.1

鼇 鰲
　　GŌ great sea turtle

————————————— 攵 4i —————————————

攵	夂	孜	冬	处	改	攸	収	攻	各	条	灸	麦
0.1	0.2	2k4.4	2.1	2.2	3.1	2a5.13	2h2.2	3.2	3.3	4.1	4d3.2	4.2
政	故	教	致	效	敏	敕	救	敖	赦	敍	敦	夏
5.1	5.2	6.1	6.2	2g6.2	6.3	2g7.1	7.1	7.2	7.3	2h7.1	7.4	7.5
敏	務	散	敞	敝	敬	敢	麥	麸	数	皴	愛	貉
4i6.3	7.6	8.1	8.2	8.3	8.4	8.5	4i4.2	4i12.2	9.1	2h10.1	10.1	10.2
數	敷	敵	髪	弊	憂	麩	整	斂	麺	麭	蠡	鼇
4i9.1	11.1	11.2	3j11.3	11.3	12.1	12.2	12.3	13.1	4i17.1	13.2	14.1	14.2
斃	蓼	麵	變	鼇								
14.3	3p15.1	17.1	2j7.3	20.1								

————————— 0 —————————

4i0.1

攵
　　BOKU hit, tap

4i0.2

夂
　　CHI be/come late

————————— 2 —————————

攷 → 考 **2k4.4**

4i2.1 / 459

冬
　　TŌ, fuyu winter

————— 1 —————

0 冬めく **fuyu(meku)** become wintry

4 冬天 **tōten** wintry weather/sky
冬支度 **fuyujitaku** preparations for winter; winter clothing
冬木立 **fuyukodachi** leafless trees in winter
6 冬休 **fuyuyasu(mi)** winter vacation
冬至 **tōji** winter solstice
冬至線 **tōjisen** the Tropic of Capricorn
冬向 **fuyumu(ki)** for winter
7 冬季 **tōki** winter(time), the winter season
8 冬空 **fuyuzora** winter sky
冬服 **fuyufuku** winter clothing
冬物 **fuyumono** winter clothing
9 冬枯 **fuyuga(re)** withering in winter; slack business in winter
10 冬将軍 **Fuyu Shōgun** Gen. Winter, Jack Frost
冬眠 **tōmin** hibernation
12 冬着 **fuyugi** winter clothing
冬場 **fuyuba** the winter season
冬営 **tōei** wintering; winter quarters
冬期 **tōki** winter season, wintertime
冬越 **fuyugo(shi)** pass the winter
22 冬籠 **fuyugomo(ri)** stay indoors for the winter, hibernate

———————— 2 ————————

5 玄冬 **gentō** winter
旧冬 **kyūtō** last winter
立冬 **rittō** the first day of winter
6 仲冬 **chūtō** mid-winter, December
7 忍冬 **nindō, suikazura** honeysuckle
初冬 **shotō** beginning of winter; tenth lunar month
10 真冬 **mafuyu** dead of winter, midwinter
12 晩冬 **bantō** the latter part of winter
越冬 **ettō** pass the winter
13 暖冬 **dantō** warm/mild winter
暖冬異変 **dantō ihen** abnormally warm winter
17 厳冬 **gentō** severe winter

———————— 3 ————————

10 夏炉冬扇 **karo-tōsen** useless things (like a fireplace in summer or a fan in winter)

———————— 4 ————————

9 春夏秋冬 **shun-ka-shū-tō** the four seasons, the year round

4i2.2 / 1137

処 處
SHO manage, deal with; punish
tokoro place

———————— 1 ————————

0 処する **sho(suru)** deal with, treat; sentence, condemn; behave, act
3 処女 **shojo** virgin
処女作 **shojosaku** one's first (published) work
処女性 **shojosei** virginity
処女航海 **shojo kōkai** maiden voyage
処女膜 **shojomaku** the hymen
4 処分 **shobun** disposal, disposition; punishment
処方 **shohō** prescription
5 処世 **shosei** conduct of life, getting on
処世訓 **shoseikun** rules for living
処世術 **shoseijutsu** how to get on in life
6 処刑 **shokei** punish, execute
処刑台 **shokeidai** the gallows
7 処決 **shoketsu** settle, decide
11 処遇 **shogū** treatment
処理 **shori** treat, manage, deal with
処断 **shodan** judge, decide; deal with
13 処置 **shochi** disposition, measures, steps
14 処罰 **shobatsu** punishment, penalty

———————— 2 ————————

4 止処 **to(me)do** termination, end
5 出処 **shussho, dedokoro** source, origin
未処置 **mishochi** untreated
目処 **medo** prospect, outlook; goal
6 死処 **shisho** where to die, where one died
仮処分 **karishobun** provisional disposition
此処 **koko** here, this place
此処迄 **koko made** to this point, up to now
7 何処 **izuko, izuku, doko** where
何処迄 **doko made** how far
対処 **taisho** deal/cope with
8 其処 **soko** that place, there **soredokoro(ka)** on the contrary, far from it
其処許 **sokomoto** you
彼処 **asoko, asuko, kashiko** that place, over there, yonder
10 随処 **zuisho** everywhere, anywhere
11 偶処 **gūsho** be/live together
12 善処 **zensho** take appropriate action; (as an official's term of art) do nothing for the present
15 熱処理 **netsushori** heat treatment

———————— 3 ————————

6 刑事処分 **keiji shobun** criminal punishment
11 強制処分 **kyōsei shobun** disposition by legal compulsion
13 滞納処分 **tainō shobun** disposition for failure to pay (taxes)

———————— 3 ————————

4i3.1 / 514

改
KAI, arata(meru) alter, renew, reform
arata(mete) anew; again, on another occasion **arata(maru)** be altered/renewed/corrected

———————— 1 ————————

4 改元 **kaigen** change to a new era (name)

改心 **kaishin** reform (oneself)
5 改令 **kairei** countermand an order
改正 **kaisei** revision, amendment; improvement
改号 **kaigō** changing the title; new name
改札 **kaisatsu** check/clip/collect tickets
改札口 **kaisatsuguchi** ticket gate, wicket
6 改印 **kaiin** change one's seal
改名 **kaimei** changing one's/the name
改行 **kaigyō** start a new line/paragraph
7 改良 **kairyō** improvement, reform
改作 **kaisaku** adaptation (of a play)
8 改版 **kaihan** revised edition
改姓 **kaisei** change one's surname
改宗 **kaishū** conversion (to another religion)
改宗者 **kaishūsha** a convert
改定 **kaitei** reform, revision
改易 **kaieki** attainder
9 改変 **kaihen** change, alter, renovate
改造 **kaizō** remodel, convert, revamp
改革 **kaikaku** reform, reorganization
改革者 **kaikakusha** reformer
改革案 **kaikakuan** reform bill/measure
改訂 **kaitei** revision
改訂版 **kaiteiban** revised edition
改訂増補 **kaitei-zōho** revised and enlarged
10 改修 **kaishū** repair, improvement
改進 **kaishin** reform, progress
改進的 **kaishinteki** progressive
改進党 **kaishintō** progressive party
改党 **kaitō** switching parties
改悟 **kaigo** repentance, remorse, contrition
改悛 **kaishun** repentance, penitence
改称 **kaishō** rename, retitle
11 改悪 **kaiaku** change for the worse, deterioration
改組 **kaiso** reorganize, reshuffle
12 改善 **kaizen** improvement
改葬 **kaisō** reburial, reinterment
改廃 **kaihai** alterations and abolitions, reorganization
改装 **kaisō** remodel, refurbish
13 改新 **kaishin** renovation, reformation
14 改暦 **kaireki** new year; calendar reform
改選 **kaisen** reelection
15 改編 **kaihen** reorganize, redo
改鋳 **kaichū** recast, remint
16 改築 **kaichiku** rebuild, remodel, alter
18 改竄 **kaizan** alter, falsify, doctor
改題 **kaidai** retitle, rename

——————— 2 ———————

7 更改 **kōkai** renovate, renew, reform
言改 **i(i)arata(meru)** correct oneself, rephrase
9 悔改 **ku(i)arata(me)** repentance, penitence
10 書改 **ka(ki)arata(meru)** rewrite

14 暦改正 **koyomi kaisei** calendar reform

——————— 3 ———————

2 人種改良 **jinshu kairyō** eugenics
8 宗門改 **shūmon-arata(me)** religious census (Edo era)
宗教改革 **shūkyō kaikaku** the Reformation
13 農地改革 **nōchi kaikaku** agrarian reform

——————— 4 ———————

12 朝令暮改 **chōrei-bokai** issuing an order in the morning and changing it in the evening, lack of constancy/principle

收→ **2a5.13**

收→収 **2h2.2**

4i3.2 / 819

攻 **KŌ, se(meru)** attack

——————— 1 ———————

2 攻入 **se(me)i(ru)** invade, penetrate
4 攻手 **se(me)te** attacker, the offensive
6 攻伐 **kōbatsu** subjugation
攻防 **kōbō** offense and defense
攻守 **kōshu** offense and defense
7 攻究 **kōkyū** study, research
攻囲 **kōi** siege
9 攻城 **kōjō** siege
10 攻倦 **se(me)agu(mu)** become disheartened in conducting a siege
11 攻道具 **se(me)dōgu** offensive weapons
攻略 **kōryaku** capture, occupy, invade
13 攻勢 **kōsei** the offensive
15 攻撃 **kōgeki** attack
攻撃的 **kōgekiteki** aggressive, offensive
攻撃軍 **kōgekigun** attacking army/force
攻撃戦 **kōgekisen** aggressive war

——————— 2 ———————

4 内攻 **naikō** (disease) attacking internal organs
反攻 **hankō** counteroffensive, counterattack
水攻 **mizuze(me)** cutting off the water to or inundating (a castle)
火攻 **hize(me)** fire attack
5 正攻法 **seikōhō** frontal assault/attack
8 逆攻撃 **gyakukōgeki** counterattack
9 専攻 **senkō** academic specialty, one's major
侵攻 **shinkō** invasion
10 進攻 **shinkō** attack, drive, advance upon
猛攻撃 **mōkōgeki** fierce attack
14 総攻撃 **sōkōgeki** general/all-out offensive

4

亻月日火礻王牛方攵欠心戸戈

18 難攻不落 **nankō-furaku** impregnable

——————— 3 ———————
2 人身攻撃 **jinshin kōgeki** personal attack

——————— 4 ———————
12 遠交近攻 **enkō-kinkō** befriending distant countries and antagonizing neighbors

4i3.3 / 642

各

KAKU, onoono each, every; various

——————— 1 ———————
2 各人 **kakujin** each person, everyone
3 各々 **onoono** each, every, respectively
4 各方面 **kaku hōmen** every direction, all quarters
各戸 **kakko** every door, door-to-door
6 各地 **kakuchi** every area; various places
各自 **kakuji** each person, everyone
7 各位 **kakui** gentlemen, you all
8 各国 **kakkoku** all/various countries
各所 **kakusho** each place, various places
9 各派 **kakuha** each party/faction/sect
各省 **kakushō** each ministry
各界 **kakkai, kakukai** every field, various circles
10 各個 **kakko** each, individual, one by one
各部 **kakubu** every part/department, various parts
各般 **kakuhan** all, every, various
11 各階 **kakkai, kakukai** each/every floor
12 各項 **kakkō, kakukō** each item/clause
14 各層 **kakusō** every stratum/class
各種 **kakushu** every kind, various types
各駅 **kakueki** every station
各駅停車 **kakuekiteisha** local train
15 各論 **kakuron** detailed discussion

——————— 2 ———————
6 各各 **onoono** each, every, respectively

——————— 4 ———————

4i4.1 / 564

条 條

JŌ article, clause; line, stripe

——————— 1 ———————
4 条文 **jōbun** the text, provisions
5 条令 **jōrei** law, ordinance, rule, regulation
条目 **jōmoku** articles, provisions, terms
6 条件 **jōken** condition, stipulation
条件付 **jōkentsu(ki)** conditional
8 条例 **jōrei** regulation, law, ordinance, rule
9 条約 **jōyaku** treaty

条約国 **jōyakukoku** signatory
11 条理 **jōri** logic, reason
条章 **jōshō** provisions, articles, clauses
条規 **jōki** stipulations, provisions, rules
条痕 **jōkon** streak
12 条款 **jōkan** clause, provision
条項 **jōkō** articles and paragraphs, stipulations
13 条鉄 **jōtetsu** bar/rod iron

——————— 2 ———————
1 一条 **ichijō** a line/streak; a matter; a passage (from a book)
Ichijō (emperor, 986–1011)
3 三条 **Sanjō** (emperor, 1011–1016)
4 不条理 **fujōri** unreasonable, irrational
6 仮条約 **karijōyaku** provisional treaty
次条 **jijō** the following article
7 別条 **betsujō** anything wrong, mishap
言条 **i(i)jō** although
9 発条 **hatsujō** a spring
信条 **shinjō** article of faith, creed
前条 **zenjō** preceding article
逐条 **chikujō** section by section, point by point
星条旗 **seijōki** the Stars and Stripes flag
軌条 **kijō** rails
10 索条 **sakujō** cable, rope
11 悪条件 **akujōken** unfavorable conditions, handicap
12 無条件 **mujōken** unconditional
13 鉄条網 **tetsujōmō** barbed-wire entanglements
14 箇条 **kajō** article, provision, item
箇条書 **kajōga(ki)** an itemization
15 線条 **senjō** filament, streak, line
17 繊条 **senjō** filament
18 鎵条 **sakujō** cable

——————— 3 ———————
5 平和条約 **heiwa jōyaku** peace treaty
6 安保条約 **anpo jōyaku** security treaty
8 治安条例 **chian jōrei** public-order regulations
9 後一条 **Goichijō** (emperor, 1016–1036)
後山条 **Gosanjō** (emperor, 1068–1072)
17 講和条約 **kōwa jōyaku** peace treaty

——————— 4 ———————
8 金科玉条 **kinka-gyokujō** a golden rule

灸 → 4d3.2

4i4.2 / 270

麦 麥

BAKU, mugi wheat, barley, rye, oats

——————— 1 ———————
5 麦打 **mugiu(chi)** wheat flailing/threshing

7 麦作 **mugisaku** wheat cultivation
8 麦芽 **bakuga** malt
　麦芽糖 **bakugatō** malt sugar, maltose
9 麦茶 **mugicha** wheat tea, barley water
　麦畑 **mugibatake** wheat field
　麦秋 **bakushū** barley harvest time
10 麦粉 **mugiko** (wheat) flour
11 麦笛 **mugibue** wheat-straw whistle
12 麦湯 **mugiyu** wheat tea, barley water
　麦飯 **mugimeshi** boiled barley and rice
　麦焦 **mugiko(gashi)** parched-barley flour
13 麦搗 **mugitsu(ki)** polishing wheat
　麦蒔 **mugima(ki)** sowing wheat/barley
15 麦踏 **mugifu(mi)** treading barley/wheat plants
17 麦藁 **mugiwara** (wheat) straw

───────── 2 ─────────

3 大麦 **ōmugi** barley
　小麦 **komugi** wheat
　小麦色 **komugi-iro** cocoa brown
　小麦粉 **komugiko** (wheat) flour
6 米麦 **beibaku** rice and barley; grains
7 冷麦 **hi(ya)mugi** iced noodles
10 烏麦 **karasumugi** oats
13 裸麦 **hadakamugi** (a species of) rye
　鳩麦 **hatomugi** adlay, pearl barley
14 精麦 **seibaku** cleaning/cleaned wheat/barley
15 蕎麦 **soba** buckwheat; buckwheat noodles
　蕎麦屋 **sobaya** soba shop
　蕎麦粉 **sobako** buckwheat flour
　蕎麦殻 **sobagara** buckwheat chaff
16 燕麦 **enbaku** oats

───────── 3 ─────────

5 生蕎麦 **kisoba** buckwheat noodles
8 押割麦 **o(shi)wa(ri) mugi** rolled barley/oats
11 掛蕎麦 **ka(ke)soba** buckwheat noodles in broth

───────── 5 ─────────

4i5.1 / 483

政

SEI, SHŌ, matsurigoto government, rule

───────── 1 ─────────

4 政友 **seiyū** political ally
5 政令 **seirei** government ordinance, cabinet order
　政庁 **seichō** government office
6 政争 **seisō** political dispute
7 政体 **seitai** form/system of government
　政局 **seikyoku** political situation
　政見 **seiken** political views
8 政事 **seiji** political/administrative affairs
　政況 **seikyō** political situation
　政治 **seiji** politics
　政治力 **seijiryoku** political influence

政治上 **seijijō** political
政治史 **seijishi** political history
政治犯 **seijihan** political offense/offender
政治学 **seijigaku** political science
政治局 **seijikyoku** Politbüro
政治的 **seijiteki** political
政治屋 **seijiya** politician
政治家 **seijika** politician
政治熱 **seijinetsu** political fever
政府 **seifu** the government
政府案 **seifuan** government bill/measure
政府党 **seifutō** government party
政府側 **seifugawa** the government (side)
政府筋 **seifusuji** government sources
政府間 **seifukan** government-to-government
政所 **mandokoro** government office (historical)
9 政変 **seihen** change of government
政派 **seiha** party faction
政客 **seikyaku** politician
政界 **seikai** the political arena
10 政党 **seitō** political party
政党員 **seitōin** party member
政教 **seikyō** church and state; government and education
11 政商 **seishō** businessman with political ties
政道 **seidō** politics, government
政務 **seimu** political/government affairs
政務次官 **seimu jikan** parliamentary vice-minister
政務官 **seimukan** parliamentary official
政情 **seijō** political situation
12 政略 **seiryaku** political strategy; expedient
政略家 **seiryakuka** political tactician
政略婚 **seiryakukon** marriage of convenience
政略結婚 **seiryaku kekkon** marriage of convenience
政経学 **seikeigaku** politics and economics
12 政策 **seisaku** policy
13 政戦 **seisen** political campaign
14 政綱 **seikō** political principles/platform
15 政権 **seiken** political power, administration
政権欲 **seiken'yoku** ambition for political power
政敵 **seiteki** political opponent
政談 **seidan** political talk; discussion of law cases
政論 **seiron** political discussion

───────── 2 ─────────

3 大政 **taisei** administration of a country; imperial rule
大政奉還 **taisei hōkan** restoration of imperial rule
4 内政 **naisei** domestic/internal affairs
仁政 **jinsei** benevolent rule

4

木
月
日
火
礻
王
牛
方 5←
文
欠
心
戸
戈

文政 **bunsei** educational administration
  Bunsei (era, 1818–1830)
反政府 **hanseifu** antigovernment
王政 **ōsei** imperial rule, monarchy
5 民政 **minsei** civil/civilian government
失政 **shissei** misgovernment, misrule
市政 **shisei** city government, municipal
  administration
司政官 **shiseikan** civil administrator
6 仮政府 **kariseifu** provisional government
地政学 **chiseigaku** geopolitics
行政 **gyōsei** administration
行政法 **gyōseihō** administrative law
行政官 **gyōseikan** administrative/executive
  official
行政権 **gyōseiken** administrative/executive
  authority
安政 **Ansei** (era, 1854–1860)
7 町政 **chōsei** town government
8 法政 **hōsei** law and government
参政 **sansei** participation in government
参政権 **sanseiken** suffrage, franchise
国政 **kokusei** government, national administration
林政 **rinsei** forest management
9 専政 **sensei** absolutism, despotism
院政 **insei** government by an ex-emperor
軍政 **gunsei** military government/administra-
  tion
軍政府 **gunseifu** military government
帝政 **teisei** imperial government/rule
虐政 **gyakusei** oppressive government,
  tyranny
為政者 **iseisha** statesman, administrator
神政 **shinsei** theocracy
施政 **shisei** administration, governing
秕政 **hisei** misgovernment, misrule
10 郵政 **yūsei** postal system
郵政省 **Yūseishō** Ministry of Posts and
  Telecommunications
家政 **kasei** homemaking
家政学 **kaseigaku** home economics
家政科 **kaseika** home-economics course
家政婦 **kaseifu** housekeeper
秕政 **hisei** misgovernment, misrule
財政 **zaisei** (public) finances
財政上 **zaiseijō** fiscal
財政学 **zaiseigaku** (the study of) finance
財政家 **zaiseika** financier
11 執政 **shissei** government; administrator,
  consul
庶政 **shosei** all phases of government
祭政 **saisei** church and state
祭政一致 **saisei-itchi** theocracy
現政府 **genseifu** the present government
悪政 **akusei** misrule

12 善政 **zensei** good government
朝政 **chōsei** imperial government
無政府 **museifu** anarchy
無政府主義 **museifu shugi** anarchism
無政府主義者 **museifushugisha** anarchist
13 農政 **nōsei** agricultural administration
摂政 **sesshō** regency; regent
幕政 **bakusei** shogunate government
寛政 **Kansei** (era, 1789–1800)
新政 **shinsei** new government/regime
14 徳政 **tokusei** benevolent government; debt
  moratorium
15 暴政 **bōsei** tyranny, oppressive rule
弊政 **heisei** misrule, maladministration
16 憲政 **kensei** constitutional government
親政 **shinsei** direct imperial rule
18 藩政 **hansei** clan government

————— 3 —————
2 二大政党主義 **nidaiseitō shugi** the two-
  party system
3 三頭政治 **santō seiji** triumvirate
9 専制政治 **sensei seiji** despotic government,
  autocracy
独裁政治 **dokusai seiji** dictatorship,
  autocracy
宥和政策 **yūwa seisaku** appeasement policy
神権政治 **shinken seiji** theocracy
14 寡頭政治 **katō seiji** oligarchy

————— 5 —————
5 立憲君主政体 **rikken kunshu seitai**
  constitutional monarchy

4i5.2 / 173

故 **KO** old, former; deceased, (as prefix)
  the late ...; intentional; matter
  yue reason, cause; circumstances
  furu(i) old

————— 1 —————
0 それ故 **soreyue** therefore, hence, that is why
2 故人 **kojin** the deceased
3 故山 **kozan** birthplace, home town
5 故旧 **kokyū** an old acquaintance
故主 **koshu** one's former master
6 故老 **korō** an elder, old-timer
8 故事 **koji** historical event
故事来歴 **koji-raireki** origin and history
故知 **kochi** an old acquaintance; the wisdom
  of our forefathers
故実 **kojitsu** ancient customs
故国 **kokoku** one's homeland, native country
10 故郷 **kokyō, furusato** birthplace, home town
故株 **furukabu** old-timer, veteran
故殺 **kosatsu** intentional murder
故紙 **koshi** wastepaper
12 故買 **kobai** buy stolen goods, fence

13 故障 **koshō** out of order, breakdown, trouble, accident, hindrance, obstacle; objection
故障車 **koshōsha** disabled car
故意 **koi** intention, purpose

――――――― 2 ―――――――
4 反故 **hogo, hogu** wastepaper, mere scrap of paper
5 生故郷 **u(mare)kokyō** one's birthplace, native place
7 何故 **naze, naniyue** why
8 事故 **jiko** accident; unavoidable circumstances
其故 **soreyue** therefore
物故 **bukko** die; be deceased
12 温故知新 **onko-chishin** learning from the past
15 縁故 **enko** connection, relation

――――――― 3 ―――――――
12 無事故 **mujiko** without accident/trouble

――――――― 6 ―――――――

4i6.1 / 245

教 教

KYŌ teaching; religion
oshi(eru) teach
oshi(e) a teaching, precept
oso(waru) be taught

――――――― 1 ―――――――
2 教子 **oshi(e)go** one's (former) student, disciple
4 教化 **kyōka** culture, education, enlightenment
教父 **kyōfu** church father; godfather, sponsor
教込 **oshi(e)ko(mu)** inculcate
教区 **kyōku** parish
教区民 **kyōkumin** parishioners
教方 **oshi(e)kata** teaching method
5 教本 **kyōhon** textbook
教生 **kyōsei** student teacher
教母 **kyōbo** godmother, sponsor
教示 **kyōji** instruct, teach, enlighten
教主 **kyōshu** founder of a sect
6 教会 **kyōkai** church
教会史 **kyōkaishi** church history
教会法 **kyōkaihō** canon law
教会員 **kyōkaiin** church member
教会堂 **kyōkaidō** church, place of worship
教会暦 **kyōkaireki** church calendar
教団 **kyōdan** religious society/order
教旨 **kyōshi** doctrine, tenet
7 教学 **kyōgaku** education, educational affairs
教材 **kyōzai** teaching materials
教戒 **kyōkai** exhortation, preaching
教戒師 **kyōkaishi** prison chaplain
8 教育 **kyōiku** education
教育上 **kyōikujō** educationwise
教育会 **kyōikukai** educational association
教育学 **kyōikugaku** pedagogy, education

教育法 **kyōikuhō** teaching method
教育的 **kyōikuteki** educational, instructive
教育者 **kyōikusha** educator
教育界 **kyōikukai** (the world of) education
教育家 **kyōikuka** educator
教育費 **kyōikuhi** school/education expenses
教典 **kyōten** scriptures
教法 **kyōhō** teachings, doctrines
教官 **kyōkan** instructor
教具 **kyōgu** teaching tools/aids
9 教派 **kyōha** sect, denomination
教室 **kyōshitsu** classroom
教祖 **kyōso** founder of a sect
教皇 **kyōkō** the pope
教皇庁 **Kyōkōchō** the Vatican
教科 **kyōka** subject, curriculum
教科目 **kyōkamoku** school subjects
教科書 **kyōkasho** textbook
教則 **kyōsoku** teaching rules
教則本 **kyōsokubon** (music) practice book
10 教唆 **kyōsa** instigate, abet
教唆者 **kyōsasha** instigator
教唆罪 **kyōsazai** (the crime of) incitement
教員 **kyōin** teacher, instructor; teaching staff
教師 **kyōshi** instructor, teacher
教徒 **kyōto** believer, adherent
教案 **kyōan** teaching/lesson plan
教書 **kyōsho** (presidential) message
教訓 **kyōkun** lesson, precept, moral
教訓的 **kyōkunteki** instructive, edifying
11 教授 **kyōju** professor; teaching
教授団 **kyōjudan** faculty
教授法 **kyōjuhō** teaching method
教習 **kyōshū** training, instruction
教習所 **kyōshūjo** training institute
教理 **kyōri** doctrine, tenet, creed, dogma
教務 **kyōmu** school/educational affairs
12 教場 **kyōjō** classroom
教程 **kyōtei** teaching method, course; textbook
13 教義 **kyōgi** doctrine, dogma, tenet
教義学 **kyōgigaku** dogmatics
教義的 **kyōgiteki** doctrinal
14 教導 **kyōdō** instruction, training, coaching
教練 **kyōren** (military) drill
教誨 **kyōkai** exhortation, preaching
15 教養 **kyōyō** culture, education, refinement
教権 **kyōken** educational/ecclesiastical authority
16 教壇 **kyōdan** platform, rostrum, lecturn
教諭 **kyōyu** instructor, teacher
教頭 **kyōtō** head teacher
18 教鞭 **kyōben** teacher's whip/rod
教職 **kyōshoku** the teaching profession
教職者 **kyōshokusha** teacher, clergyman
教職員 **kyōshokuin** faculty, teaching staff

4
木 月 日 火 礻 王 牜 方 攵 6←
欠 心 戸 戈

──────── 2 ────────

3 女教員 **jokyōin** female teacher
女教師 **jokyōshi** female teacher
4 仏教 **bukkyō** Buddhism
文教 **bunkyō** education, culture
分教場 **bunkyōjō** detached classroom
公教 **kōkyō** Roman Catholicism
公教会 **Kōkyōkai** Catholic Church
5 正教 **seikyō** orthodoxy; Greek Orthodox Church
正教会 **Seikyōkai** Greek Orthodox Church
正教員 **seikyōin** regular/licensed teacher
司教 **shikyō** (Catholic) bishop
司教区 **shikyōku** diocese
布教 **fukyō** proselyting, missionary work
示教 **shikyō** instruction, guidance
主教 **shukyō** bishop, prelate
6 再教育 **saikyōiku** retraining
回教 **kaikyō** Islam, Mohammedanism
回教国 **kaikyōkoku** Moslem country
回教徒 **kaikyōto** a Moslem
早教育 **sōkyōiku** early education
7 邪教 **jakyō** heretical religion, heathenism
助教授 **jokyōju** assistant professor
8 宗教 **shūkyō** religion
宗教上 **shūkyōjō** from the standpoint of religion
宗教心 **shūkyōshin** religiousness, piety
宗教史 **shūkyōshi** history of religion
宗教改革 **shūkyō kaikaku** the Reformation
宗教画 **shūkyōga** religious picture
宗教的 **shūkyōteki** religious
宗教性 **shūkyōsei** religious character
宗教哲学 **shūkyō tetsugaku** philosophy of religion
宗教家 **shūkyōka** man of religion
宗教裁判 **shūkyō saiban** the Inquisition
宗教劇 **shūkyōgeki** religious drama
宗教観 **shūkyōkan** religious view
国教 **kokkyō** state religion/church
性教育 **sei kyōiku** sex education
9 信教 **shinkyō** religion, religious belief
風教 **fūkyō** public morals
宣教 **senkyō** missionary work, evangelism
宣教師 **senkyōshi** missionary
胎教 **taikyō** prenatal care
背教 **haikyō** apostasy
背教者 **haikyōsha** apostate
政教 **seikyō** church and state; government and education
10 高教 **kōkyō** your instructions/suggestions
殉教 **junkyō** martyrdom
殉教者 **junkyōsha** martyr
11 道教 **dōkyō** Taoism
清教徒 **seikyōto** Puritans
密教 **mikkyō** esoteric Buddhism; religious mysteries

異教 **ikyō** heathenism, paganism, heresy
異教徒 **ikyōto** heathen, heretic, infidel
12 景教 **keikyō** Nestorianism
景教徒 **keikyōto** a Nestorian
無教会主義 **mukyōkai shugi** Nondenominationalism (a Japanese Christian sect)
無教育 **mukyōiku** uneducated
13 準教員 **junkyōin** assistant teacher
禁教 **kinkyō** prohibited religion
聖教 **seikyō** sacred teachings; Christianity
新教 **shinkyō** Protestantism
新教国 **shinkyōkoku** Protestant country
新教徒 **shinkyōto** a Protestant
14 徳教 **tokkyō** moral teachings
説教 **sekkyō** sermon
説教師 **sekkyōshi** preacher
説教壇 **sekkyōdan** pulpit
15 調教 **chōkyō** break in, train (animals)
調教師 **chōkyōshi** (animal) trainer
16 儒教 **jukyō** Confucianism

──────── 3 ────────

1 一神教 **isshinkyō** monotheism
3 大司教 **daishikyō** archbishop, cardinal (Catholic)
大主教 **daishukyō** archbishop (Protestant)
4 天主教 **Tenshukyō** Roman Catholicism
天理教 **Tenrikyō** the Tenriism sect (founded 1838)
6 多神教 **tashinkyō** polytheism
多神教的 **tashinkyōteki** polytheistic
全人教育 **zenjin kyōiku** well-rounded education, education for the whole man
名誉教授 **meiyo kyōju** professor emeritus
8 長老教会 **Chōrō Kyōkai** Presbyterian Church
拝火教 **haikakyō** fire worship
拝物教 **haibutsukyō** fetishism
耶蘇教 **yasokyō** Christianity
9 軍事教練 **gunji kyōren** military training
通信教育 **tsūshin kyōiku** education by correspondence
浄土教 **jōdokyō** Buddhist teachings concerning the Pure Land
10 個人教授 **kojin kyōju** private lessons
家庭教師 **katei kyōshi** (private) tutor
11 基督教 **Kirisutokyō** Christianity
12 喇嘛教 **Ramakyō** Lamaism
13 義務教育 **gimu kyōiku** compulsory education

──────── 4 ────────

3 万有神教 **ban'yū shinkyō** pantheism
大乗仏教 **Daijō Bukkyō** Mahayana Buddhism, Great-Vehicle Buddhism
小乗仏教 **Shōjō bukkyō** Hinayana/Lesser-vehicle Buddhism

4i6.2 / 903

致 **CHI, ita(su)** do (deferential); bring about, cause

――――――― 1 ―――――――

4 致方 **ita(shi)kata** way, method, means
致方無 **ita(shi)kata (ga) na(i)** it can't be helped
6 致死 **chishi** fatal, lethal, deadly, mortal
致死量 **chishiryō** lethal dose
8 致命的 **chimeiteki** fatal, lethal, deadly, mortal
致命傷 **chimeishō** fatal wound/injury

――――――― 2 ―――――――

1 一致 **itchi** agree
一致点 **itchiten** point of agreement
4 引致 **inchi** take into custody
6 合致 **gatchi** agreement, concurrence, conforming to
8 送致 **sōchi** send
拉致 **rachi, ratchi** take (someone) away
招致 **shōchi** summons, invitation
9 風致 **fūchi** taste, elegance; scenic beauty
風致林 **fūchirin** forest planted for scenic beauty
12 極致 **kyokuchi** culmination, acme
筆致 **hitchi** brush stroke; (writing) style
13 雅致 **gachi** elegance, asthetic effect
14 誘致 **yūchi** attract, lure; bring about
19 韻致 **inchi** excellent taste, elegance

――――――― 3 ―――――――

4 不一致 **fuitchi** disagreement, incompatibility
11 過失致死 **kashitsu chishi** accidental homicide, manslaughter
過失致死罪 **kashitsu chishizai** accidental homicide, manslaughter

――――――― 4 ―――――――

6 全会一致 **zenkai-itchi** unanimous
7 言文一致 **genbun itchi** unification of the written and spoken language
10 挙国一致 **kyokoku-itchi** national unity
11 祭政一致 **saisei-itchi** theocracy
12 満場一致 **manjō-itchi** unanimous
衆口一致 **shūkō-itchi** unanimous
15 霊肉一致 **reiniku itchi** oneness of body and soul

効→効 **2g6.2**

4i6.3 / 1735

敏 敏 **BIN** agile, alert

――――――― 1 ―――――――

9 敏速 **binsoku** promptness, alacrity

敏活 **binkatsu** quick, alert, active, agile
11 敏達 **bintatsu** wise
Bindatsu (emperor, 572–585)
敏捷 **binshō** nimble, agile; sharp, shrewd
12 敏腕 **binwan** able, capable
敏腕家 **binwanka** able person, go-getter
13 敏感 **binkan** sensitive

――――――― 2 ―――――――

4 不敏 **fubin** not clever, untalented, inept
8 明敏 **meibin** intelligent, discerning
9 俊敏 **shunbin** keen, quick-witted
11 過敏 **kabin** oversensitive, nervous
過敏症 **kabinshō** hypersensitivity
15 鋭敏 **cibin** sharp, keen, acute
16 機敏 **kibin** astute, shrewd, quick

――――――― 7 ―――――――

敕→勅 **2g7.1**

4i7.1 / 725

救 **KYŪ, suku(u)** rescue, save, aid

――――――― 1 ―――――――

3 救上 **suku(i)a(geru)** rescue, pick up
5 救出 **kyūshutsu** rescue
suku(i)da(su) rescue from, help out of
救民 **kyūmin** aiding disaster victims
救世 **kyūsei** salvation of the world
救世主 **Kyūseishu** the Savior/Messiah
救世軍 **Kyūseigun** the Salvation Army
救主 **suku(i)nushi** rescuer; the Savior
6 救米 **suku(i)mai** rice given as charity
7 救助 **kyūjo** rescue, relief, aid
救助米 **kyūjomai** dole rice
救助法 **kyūjohō** lifesaving
救助者 **kyūjosha** rescuer
救助隊 **kyūjotai** rescue party
救助船 **kyūjosen** rescue ship, lifeboat
救助網 **kyūjoami** (streetcar) cowcatcher; safety net
8 救命 **kyūmei** lifesaving
救命具 **kyūmeigu** life preserver
救命索 **kyūmeisaku** lifeline
救命帯 **kyūmeitai** life belt
救命袋 **kyūmeibukuro** escape chute
救命艇 **kyūmeitei** lifeboat
救命網 **kyūmeimō** safety net
救治 **kyūji** cure, remedy
救治策 **kyūjisaku** a cure
救国 **kyūkoku** national salvation
9 救急 **kyūkyū** emergency (relief)

救急車 **kyūkyūsha** ambulance
救急法 **kyūkyūhō** first aid
救急策 **kyūkyūsaku** emergency measures
救急箱 **kyūkyūbako** first-aid kit
救急薬 **kyūkyūyaku** first-aid medicine
救恤 **kyūjutsu** relief, aid
11 救貧 **kyūhin** poverty assistance
救貧院 **kyūhin'in** poorhouse
救済 **kyūsai** relief, aid; emancipation
救済者 **kyūsaisha** reliever, savior
救済金 **kyūsaikin** relief fund
救済策 **kyūsaisaku** relief measure
救船 **suku(i)bune** rescue ship, lifeboat
12 救援 **kyūen** relief, rescue
救援米 **kyūenmai** dole rice
救援軍 **kyūengun** reinforcements
18 救難 **kyūnan** rescue, salvage
20 救護 **kyūgo** relief, aid, rescue
救護米 **kyūgomai** dole rice
救護所 **kyūgosho** first-aid station
救護班 **kyūgohan** relief squad, rescue party

4i7.2

敖 **GŌ** play; be proud

4i7.3 / 1570

赦 **SHA, yuru(su)** forgive, pardon

――――――― 1 ―――――――

8 赦免 **shamen** pardon, clemency
赦免状 **shamenjō** (letter of) pardon
13 赦罪 **shazai** pardon, absolution

――――――― 2 ―――――――

3 大赦 **taisha** amnesty; plenary indulgence
10 容赦 **yōsha** mercy, pardon, forgiveness
特赦 **tokusha** amnesty
恩赦 **onsha** amnesty, general pardon

敍 → 叙 **2h7.1**

4i7.4

敦 **TON** warm, kindly; work hard; big

――――――― 2 ―――――――

10 倫敦 **Rondon** London

4i7.5 / 461

夏 **KA, GE, natsu** summer

――――――― 1 ―――――――

0 夏ばて **natsu(bate)** listlessness during hot
summer weather
3 夏山 **natsuyama** mountains in summer
6 夏休 **natsuyasu(mi)** summer vacation
夏羽織 **natsubaori** summer haori coat
夏至 **geshi** summer solstice
夏至線 **geshisen** the Tropic of Cancer
夏向 **natsumu(ki)** for summer
夏衣 **natsugoromo** summer clothing
7 夏季 **kaki** summer(time), the summer season
8 夏服 **natsufuku** summer clothes/wear
夏炉冬扇 **karo-tōsen** useless things (like a
fireplace in summer or a fan in winter)
夏物 **natsumono** summer clothing
9 夏負 **natsuma(ke)** succumb to summer heat
夏草 **natsugusa** grass in summer
夏枯 **natsuga(re)** summer slack season
10 夏時間 **natsujikan** daylight-saving time
11 夏菊 **natsugiku** early crysanthemum
夏祭 **natsumatsu(ri)** summer festival
12 夏着 **natsugi** summer wear/clothes
夏場 **natsuba** summertime, the summer
season
夏場所 **natsubasho** the summer sumo
tournament
夏帽子 **natsubōshi** summer/straw hat
夏期 **kaki** the summer period
14 夏蜜柑 **natsumikan** Chinese citron
夏瘦 **natsuya(se)** loss of weight in summer

――――――― 2 ―――――――

5 半夏 **hange** eleventh day after the summer
solstice, final day for seed-sowing
立夏 **rikka** the first day of summer
6 仲夏 **chūka** mid-summer, June
7 初夏 **shoka** early summer
9 春夏秋冬 **shun-ka-shū-tō** the four seasons,
the year round
10 残夏 **zanka** the last days of summer
真夏 **manatsu** midsummer
11 常夏 **tokonatsu** endless summer; a China
pink (flower)
盛夏 **seika** the height of summer
12 晩夏 **banka** the latter part of summer
15 銷夏 **shōka** spending the summer

敏 → 敏 **4i6.3**

4i7.6 / 235

務 **MU, tsuto(meru)** work, serve

――――――― 2 ―――――――

3 工務 **kōmu** engineering

工務店 **kōmuten** engineering firm
工務所 **kōmusho** engineering office
4 内務 **naimu** internal/domestic affairs
内務大臣 **naimu daijin** (prewar) Home Minister
内務省 **Naimushō** (prewar) Ministry of Home Affairs
双務契約 **sōmu keiyaku** bilateral contract
片務的 **henmuteki** unilateral, one-sided
公務 **kōmu** public service, official business
公務員 **kōmuin** government employee
5 弁務官 **benmukan** commissioner
世務 **seimu** public/worldly affairs
代務 **daimu** management for another
外務 **gaimu** foreign affairs
外務大臣 **gaimu daijin** Minister of Foreign Affairs
外務省 **Gaimushō** Ministry of Foreign Affairs
用務 **yōmu** business (to attend to)
用務員 **yōmuin** servant, janitor, custodian
主務 **shumu** competent (authorities)
6 任務 **ninmu** duty, task, function
刑務所 **keimusho** prison
先務 **senmu** priority task
成務 **Seimu** (emperor, 131–190)
7 医務室 **imushitsu** medical office
役務 **ekimu** labor, service
学務 **gakumu** educational affairs
労務 **rōmu** labor, work
労務者 **rōmusha** worker, laborer
局務 **kyokumu** bureau business
社務 **shamu** shrine/company affairs
社務所 **shamusho** shrine office
8 事務 **jimu** business, clerical work
事務当局 **jimu tōkyoku** the authorities in charge
事務局 **jimukyoku** secretariat, executive office
事務長 **jimuchō** head official; manager
事務長官 **jimuchōkan** chief secretary
事務官 **jimukan** administrative official, secretary, commissioner
事務服 **jimufuku** office clothes
事務的 **jimuteki** businesslike, practical
事務所 **jimusho** office
事務取扱 **jimu toriatsuka(i)** acting director
事務室 **jimushitsu** office
事務員 **jimuin** clerk, office staff
事務家 **jimuka** man of business, practical man
法務 **hōmu** legal/judicial affairs
法務大臣 **hōmu daijin** Minister of Justice
法務官 **hōmukan** law officer, judge advocate
法務省 **Hōmushō** Ministry of Justice
宗務 **shūmu** religious affairs
実務 **jitsumu** business affairs/practice

実務家 **jitsumuka** businessman
官務 **kanmu** official business
国務 **kokumu** affairs of state
国務長官 **kokumu chōkan** (U.S.) Secretary of State
林務官 **rinmukan** forestry officer, ranger
服務 **fukumu** (public) service, duties
服務年限 **fukumu nengen** tenure of office
9 専務 **senmu** special duty; principal business; managing/executive (director)
乗務員 **jōmuin** train/plane crew
俗務 **zokumu** worldly concerns, daily routine
軍務 **gunmu** military affairs
急務 **kyūmu** urgent business, pressing need
要務 **yōmu** important business
政務 **seimu** political/government affairs
政務次官 **seimu jikan** parliamentary vice-minister
政務官 **seimukan** parliamentary official
10 残務 **zanmu** unfinished business
兼務 **kenmu** additional post
党務 **tōmu** party affairs
校務 **kōmu** school affairs
時務 **jimu** current affairs
特務 **tokumu** special duty/service
特務機関 **tokumu kikan** military intelligence organization
教務 **kyōmu** school/educational affairs
財務 **zaimu** financial affairs
財務官 **zaimukan** finance secretary
11 商務 **shōmu** commercial affairs
商務官 **shōmukan** commercial attaché
執務 **shitsumu** discharging one's duties, business (hours)
常務 **jōmu** regular business, routine duties, executive (director)
庶務 **shomu** general affairs
責務 **sekimu** duty, obligation
12 勤務 **kinmu** service, work, duty
勤務先 **kinmusaki** place of employment, employer
勤務評定 **kinmu hyōtei** job performance appraisal
港務 **kōmu** harbor service
港務部 **kōmubu** harbor department/office
税務 **zeimu** tax business
税務署 **zeimusho** tax office
13 業務 **gyōmu** business, work, operations, duties
債務 **saimu** debt, liabilities
債務者 **saimusha** debtor
義務 **gimu** obligation, duty
義務心 **gimushin** sense of duty
義務的 **gimuteki** obligatory, compulsory
義務者 **gimusha** debtor, obligor, responsible person

4

木
月
日
火
衤
王
牛
方
攵 7←
欠
心
戸
戈

義務教育 **gimu kyōiku** compulsory education
農務 **nōmu** agricultural affairs
煩務 **hanmu** troublesome/hectic work
14 総務 **sōmu** general affairs; manager
総務長官 **sōmu chōkan** director-general
総務部長 **sōmu buchō** head of the general affairs department
総務課 **sōmuka** general affairs section
雑務 **zatsumu** miscellaneous duties
16 激務 **gekimu** busy job, arduous work
18 職務 **shokumu** job, office, duties
19 警務 **keimu** police affairs

─────────── 8 ───────────

4i8.1 / 767

散

SAN, chi(ru) scatter, (leaves) fall, disperse **chi(rasu)** scatter, strew **chi(rashi)** handbill **chi(rakasu)** scatter, disarrange **chi(rakaru)** lie scattered, be in disorder **chi(rabaru)** be scattered about

─────────── 1 ───────────

0 散じる **san(jiru)** scatter, disperse, spread; dispel
3 散々 **sanzan** thoroughly, scathingly, to the full
4 散切 **zangi(ri)** regular haircut (no topknot)
散切頭 **zangi(ri) atama** cropped head
散文 **sanbun** prose
散文的 **sanbunteki** prosaic
散文詩 **sanbunshi** prose poem
散水 **sansui** water sprinkling
散水車 **sansuisha** street sprinkler truck
5 散失 **sanshitsu** be scattered and lost
散布 **sanpu** dispersion, scattering, sprinkling
6 散会 **sankai** adjourn, break up
散在 **sanzai** be scattered here and there
散光 **sankō** scattered/diffused light
7 散兵 **sanpei** skirmisher
散乱 **sanran** dispersion, scattering **chi(ri)mida(reru)** be scattered about; be routed
散見 **sanken** be found here and there
8 散歩 **sanpo** walk, stroll
9 散発 **sanpatsu** scattered shots/hits
散発的 **sanpatsuteki** sporadic
10 散逸 **san'itsu** be scattered and lost
散華 **sange** Buddhist flower-scattering ceremony; heroic death (in battle)
散書 **chi(rashi)ga(ki)** write irregularly
散財 **sanzai** incur expenses; squander
11 散票 **sanpyō** scattered votes
12 散散 **sanzan** thoroughly, scathingly, to the full **chi(ri)ji(ri)** scattered, separate
散策 **sansaku** walk, stroll

散開 **sankai** deploy, fan out
14 散漫 **sanman** vague, desultory, loose
散髪 **sanpatsu** get/give a haircut; disheveled hair
散髪屋 **sanpatsuya** barber
16 散薬 **san'yaku** powdered medicine

─────────── 2 ───────────

1 一散 **issan** at top speed
4 分散 **bunsan** breakup, dispersion, variance
5 四散 **shisan** disperse, scatter
6 気散 **kisan(ji)** diversion, recreation, amusement
7 吹散 **fu(ki)chi(rasu)** scatter, blow about
言散 **i(i)chi(rasu)** say all sorts of things
8 退散 **taisan** (intr.) disperse, break up
追散 **o(i)chi(rasu)** disperse, scatter, put to rout
逃散 **ni(ge)chi(ru)** flee in all directions, scatter, be routed **chōsan, tōsan** serfs' fleeing
拡散 **kakusan** diffusion, scattering, proliferation
放散 **hōsan** radiate, diffuse, emanate; evaporate
取散 **to(ri)chi(rasu)** strew/scatter about
9 飛散 **hisan, to(bi)chi(ru)** scatter, disperse
発散 **hassan** give forth, emit, exhale, radiate, evaporate; divergent
胡散臭 **usankusa(i)** suspicious, questionable
胃散 **isan** medicinal stomach powder
食散 **ku(i)chi(rasu)** eat untidily, eat a bit of everything
10 消散 **shōsan** disperse, disappear, dissipate
書散 **ka(ki)chi(rasu)** scribble, scrawl
12 蒸散 **jōsan** transpiration, evaporation
散散 **sanzan** thoroughly, scathingly, to the full **chi(ri)ji(ri)** scattered, separate
集散 **shūsan** collection and distribution
集散地 **shūsanchi** trading center, entrepôt
雲散 **unsan** dispersing like clouds
雲散霧消 **unsan-mushō** vanishing like mist
閑散 **kansan** leisure; (market) inactivity
13 塗散 **nu(ri)chi(rasu)** besmear, daub all over
解散 **kaisan** disperse, break up, disband, dissolve
14 榴散弾 **ryūsandan** shrapnel shell
15 撒散 **ma(ki)chi(rasu)** scatter about; squander
18 離散 **risan** scatter, disperse
離散的 **risanteki** discrete
19 蹴散 **kechi(rasu)** kick around, put to rout
霧散 **musan** dissipate, vanish

─────────── 3 ───────────

1 一目散 **ichimokusan** at top speed

4i8.2

做

SHŌ high and flat; broad, spacious

4i8.3

HEI, yabu(reru) be worn out, be dilapidated; be defeated

——————— 1 ———————

6 敝衣 **heii** shabby clothes

4i8.4 / 705

敬

KEI, KYŌ, uyama(u) respect, revere

——————— 1 ———————

5 敬白 **keihaku** Sincerely yours,
  敬礼 **keirei** salutation, salute, bow
6 敬老 **keirō** respect for the aged
8 敬服 **keifuku** admire, think highly of
  敬具 **keigu** Sincerely yours,
9 敬神 **keishin** reverence, piety, devoutness
10 敬虔 **keiken** piety, devotion, reverence
  敬称 **keishō** honorific title
12 敬遠 **keien** keep (someone) at a respectful distance
13 敬愛 **keiai** love and respect, veneration
  敬意 **keii** respect, homage
14 敬慕 **keibo** love and respect
  敬語 **keigo** an honorific, term of respect

——————— 2 ———————

4 不敬 **fukei** disrespect, irreverence, blasphemy, profanity
  不敬罪 **fukeizai** lese majesty
5 失敬 **shikkei** rudeness, disrespect
6 自敬 **jikei** self-respect
9 畏敬 **ikei** awe and respect, reverence
10 恭敬 **kyōkei** reverence, respect
11 崇敬 **sūkei** veneration, reverence
12 尊敬 **sonkei** respect, esteem, honor
  最敬礼 **saikeirei** profound obeisance, most respectful bow
13 愛敬 **aikei** love and respect

4i8.5 / 1691

KAN daring, bold **ae(te)** daringly, positively, venture to ... **ae(nai)** sad, tragic, pitiful; frail, feeble; transitory

——————— 1 ———————

6 敢行 **kankō** take decisive action, dare; carry out
9 敢為 **kan'i** daring, intrepid, brave
12 敢然 **kanzen** bold, fearless
18 敢闘 **kantō** fight courageously

——————— 2 ———————

8 果敢 **haka(nai)** fleeting, transitory; vain, hopeless **kakan** resolute, determined, bold

取敢 **to(ri)a(ezu)** for the present; first of all; immediately
9 勇敢 **yūkan** courageous, brave, heroic

麥 → 麦 **4i4.2**

麩 → 麩 **4i12.2**

——————— 9 ———————

4i9.1 / 225

数 數

SŪ number; (as prefix) several, a number of
SU, kazu number
kazo(eru) count

——————— 1 ———————

0 数ヶ所 **sūkasho** several places
2 数人 **sūnin** several persons
  数子 **kazu(no)ko** herring roe
  数十 **sūjū** dozens/scores of
3 数万 **sūman** tens of thousands
  数千 **sūsen** several thousand
  数上 **kazo(e)a(geru)** count up, enumerate
  数々 **kazukazu** many
4 数切 **kazo(e)kire(nai)** countless
  数分間 **sūfunkan** for a few minutes, several minutes
  数日 **sūjitsu** a few days, several days
  数日中 **sūjitsuchū** within a few days
  数日来 **sūjitsurai** for the last few days
  数日後 **sūjitsugo** after several days
  数日間 **sūnichikan** for several days
5 数字 **sūji** digit, numeral, figures
  数字上 **sūjijō** numerically, in figures
  数立 **kazo(e)ta(teru)** count up, enumerate
6 数多 **kazuō(ku), amata** many, great numbers of
  数年 **sūnen** several years
  kazo(e)doshi one's calendar-year age (reckoned racehorse-style)
  数次 **sūji** for a number of times
  数列 **sūretsu** series (in math)
  数名 **sūmei** several persons
  数回 **sūkai** several times
  数百 **sūhyaku** several hundred
7 数学 **sūgaku** mathematics
  数学的 **sūgakuteki** mathematical
  数学者 **sūgakusha** mathematician
8 数刻 **sūkoku** several hours
  数直 **kazo(e)nao(su)** do a recount, count over
  数奇 **sūki** adverse/varied fortune
  数奇屋 **sukiya** tea-ceremony room/cottage

数取 **kazuto(ri)** tally; scorer; counting game
9 数度 **sūdo** several times
数秒 **sūbyō** for several seconds
10 数倍 **sūbai** several times as (large), several-fold
数値 **sūchi** numerical value
数個 **sūko** several (objects)
数珠 **juzu, zuzu** string of beads, rosary
11 数寄 **suki** refined taste; elegant pursuits
数寄屋 **sukiya** tea-ceremony room/cottage
数理 **sūri** mathematical (principles)
数理上 **sūrijō** mathematically
数理的 **sūriteki** mathematical
12 数量 **sūryō** quantity
数詞 **sūshi** numeral, number word
13 数損 **kazo(e)soko(nau)** miscount
数数 **kazukazu** many
14 数歌 **kazo(e)uta** counting-out rhyme
数種 **sūshu** several kinds
数種類 **sūshurui** several kinds
数語 **sūgo** a few words
15 数億 **sūoku** hundreds of millions

———— 2 ————

2 丁数 **chōsū** number of pages; even numbers
人数 **ninzū, ninzu, hitokazu** number of people
十数 **jūsū** ten-odd, a dozen or so
3 大数 **taisū** large number; round numbers
口数 **kuchikazu** number of mouths to feed; number of words, speech; number of shares/lots/items **kōsū** number of accounts/lots/items
小数 **shōsū** (decimal) fraction
小数点 **shōsūten** decimal point
4 中数 **chūsū** arithmetic mean, average
分数 **bunsū** fraction
手数 **tesū** trouble, pains, care **tekazu** trouble; number of moves (in a game)
手数料 **tesūryō** handling charge, fee
引数 **hikisū** argument (of a function)
少数 **shōsū** few; minority
少数民族 **shōsū minzoku** minority nationalities, ethnic minorities
日数 **nissū, hikazu** number of days
戸数 **kosū** number of house/households
5 半数 **hansū** half the number
冊数 **sassū** number of books
代数 **daisū** algebra
正数 **seisū** positive number
打数 **dasū** times at bat
字数 **jisū** number of characters
6 多数 **tasū** a large number; majority
多数決 **tasūketsu** decision by the majority
多数党 **tasūtō** majority party

年数 **nensū** number of years
件数 **kensū** number of cases/items
全数 **zensū** the whole number, all
次数 **jisū** degree (in math)
同数 **dōsū** the same number
名数 **meisū** number of persons; a compound which includes a number
回数 **kaisū** number of times, frequency
回数券 **kaisūken** (train) coupon tickets
因数 **insū** factor (in math)
因数分解 **insū bunkai** factorization
有数 **yūsū** prominent, leading, top
7 里数 **risū** mileage, distance
対数 **taisū** logarithm
序数 **josū** ordinal number
8 画数 **kakusū** number of strokes (of a kanji)
命数 **meisū** one's natural lifespan; destiny
函数 **kansū** function (in math)
逆数 **gyakusū** a reciprocal
坪数 **tsubosū** number of *tsubo*, area
奇数 **kisū** odd number
実数 **jissū** real number
定数 **teisū** a constant; fixed number; fate
歩数 **hosū** number of steps
歩数計 **hosūkei** pedometer
枚数 **maisū** number of sheets
物数 **mono (no) kazu** something of value
9 係数 **keisū** coefficient
除数 **josū** divisor
変数 **hensū** a variable (in math)
点数 **tensū** points, marks, score
負数 **fusū** negative number
指数 **shisū** index (number); exponent
品数 **hinsū, shinakazu** number of articles
単数 **tansū** singular (not plural)
度数 **dosū** number of times/degrees
恒数 **kōsū** a constant
級数 **kyūsū** series/progression (in math)
計数 **keisū** counting, calculation
10 倍数 **baisū** a multiple
俵数 **hyōsū** number of straw bags
個数 **kosū** number of objects/articles
部数 **busū** number of copies, circulation
員数 **inzū** number of members/items
家数 **iekazu** number of houses
紙数 **shisū** number of pages, space
素数 **sosū** a prime (number)
記数法 **kisūhō** numerical notation
軒数 **kensū** number of houses
11 偶数 **gūsū** even number
虚数 **kyosū** imaginary number
基数 **kisū** cardinal number; the digits 1–9
術数 **jussū** artifice, stratagem, wiles
常数 **jōsū** a constant (in math); fate
票数 **hyōsū** number of votes
現数 **gensū** actual number, effective strength

異数 **isū** exceptional, unusual
12 場数踏 **bakazu (o) fu(mu)** gain experience
無数 **musū** innumerable, countless
間数 **kensū** number of *ken* in length
　　 makazu number of rooms
13 数数 **kazukazu** many
14 暦数 **rekisū** calendar; one's fate; number of
　　 years
概数 **gaisū** round/approximate numbers
端数 **hasū** fractional part, odd sum
複数 **fukusū** plural
総数 **sōsū** total (number)
総トン数 **sōtonsū** gross tonnage
算数 **sansū** arithmetic, math, calculation
語数 **gosū** number of words
16 整数 **seisū** integer
頭数 **tōsū, atamakazu** number of persons

————— 3 —————

3 大多数 **daitasū** the great majority
小人数 **koninzū** small number of people
4 公約数 **kōyakusū** common divisor
公倍数 **kōbaisū** common multiple
5 出生数 **shusseisū, shusshōsū** number of live
　　 births
6 多人数 **taninzū** a large number of people
死亡数 **shibōsū** number of deaths
仮分数 **kabunsū** improper fraction
自然数 **shizensū** natural number, positive
　　 integer
7 延日数 **no(be)nissū** total number of days
投票数 **tōhyōsū** number of votes
完全数 **kanzensū** whole number, integer
8 周波数 **shūhasū** frequency
定足数 **teisokusū** quorum
所帯数 **shotaisū** number of households
9 指折数 **yubio(ri) kazo(eru)** count on one's
　　 fingers
相当数 **sōtōsū** quite a number of
10 既知数 **kichisū** known quantity
11 過半数 **kahansū** majority, more than half
排水トン数 **haisui tonsū** displacement
　　 tonnage
12 最多数 **saitasū** greatest number, plurality
無理数 **murisū** irrational number
14 算用数字 **san'yō sūji** Hindu-Arabic
　　 numerals
17 頻度数 **hindosū** frequency

————— 4 —————

3 三角函数 **sankaku kansū** trigonometric
　　 function
8 物価指数 **bukka shisū** price index
9 耐用年数 **taiyō nensū** useful lifetime, life
12 就業日数 **shūgyō nissū** days worked
等比級数 **tōhi kyūsū** geometric progression
等差級数 **tōsa kyūsū** arithmetic progression

皴→ **2h10.1**

————— 10 —————

4i10.1 / 259

愛 　**AI** love; (as prefix) beloved, favorite
　　me(deru) love; admire, appreciate
　　ito(shii) dear, beloved
　　mana- beloved, favorite

————— 1 —————

2 愛人 **aijin** lover
4 愛犬 **aiken** pet dog
愛犬家 **aikenka** dog lover
5 愛他 **aita** altruism
愛他主義 **aita shugi** altruism
愛用 **aiyō** habitual use; favorite
愛好 **aikō** love, have a liking/taste for
愛好者 **aikōsha** lover of, fan, fancier
愛好家 **aikōka** lover of, fan, fancier
7 愛別離苦 **aibetsuriku** parting from loved
　　 ones
愛弟子 **manadeshi** favorite pupil
愛吟 **aigin** favorite poem; love to recite
愛児 **aiji** one's dear child
愛車 **aisha** one's (cherished) car
8 愛育 **aiiku** tender loving care
愛知県 **Aichi-ken** (prefecture)
愛妻 **aisai** one's beloved wife
愛妻家 **aisaika** devoted/uxorious husband
愛国 **aikoku** patriotism
愛国心 **aikokushin** patriotism
愛国主義 **aikoku shugi** patriotism
愛国者 **aikokusha** patriot
愛玩 **aigan** cherish, treasure, prize
愛玩者 **aigansha** lover, admirer, fancier
愛玩物 **aiganbutsu** prized possession
愛妾 **aishō** one's mistress
9 愛孫 **aison** beloved grandchild
愛染明王 **Aizenmyōō** Ragaraja, six-armed
　　 god of love
10 愛郷 **aikyō** love for one's home town
愛郷心 **aikyōshin** home-town pride
愛娘 **manamusume** one's favorite daughter
愛党心 **aitōshin** party loyalty/spirit
愛校心 **aikōshin** love for one's school
愛書家 **aishoka** book lover
愛息 **aisoku** beloved son
愛称 **aishō** term of endearment, pet name
愛馬 **aiba** one's favorite horse
11 愛執 **aishū** attachment to, fondness
愛唱 **aishō** love to sing
愛猫 **aibyō** pet cat
愛欲 **aiyoku** love and lust, passion
愛情 **aijō** love, affection

4

亻月日火礻王牛方攵欠心戸戈

10←

4

木 月 日 火 礻 王 牛 方 攵 欠 心 戸 戈

→10

愛惜 **aiseki** grieve for, miss
愛鳥 **aichō** pet bird
愛鳥家 **aichōka** bird lover
12 愛禽 **aikin** favorite bird
愛禽家 **aikinka** bird lover
愛着 **aichaku, aijaku** attachment, affection
愛婿 **aisei** one's (favorite) son-in-law
愛媛県 **Ehime-ken** (prefecture)
愛敬 **aikei** love and respect
愛飲 **aiin** like to drink
愛飲者 **aiinsha** habitual drinker
13 愛煙家 **aienka** (habitual) smoker
愛想 **aiso, aisō** amiability, sociability
14 愛慕 **aibo** love, attachment, yearning
愛憎 **aizō** love and/or hate
愛読 **aidoku** like to read
愛読者 **aidokusha** reader, subscriber
愛読書 **aidokusho** favorite book
愛誦 **aishō** love to read
15 愛撫 **aibu** caress, pet, fondle
愛器 **aiki** favorite musical instrument
愛嬌 **aikyō** charm, winsomeness, attractiveness, courtesy
愛嬌者 **aikyōmono** charming fellow/girl
愛蔵 **aizō** treasure, cherish
愛憫 **aibin** pity, compassion
愛戯 **aigi** love play
16 愛嬢 **aijō** one's dear daughter
愛機 **aiki** one's own airplane/camera/machine
20 愛護 **aigo** treat kindly, protect
21 愛顧 **aiko** patronage, favor

――――――― 2 ―――――――

4 仁愛 **jin'ai** benevolence, charity, love
切愛 **setsuai** deep love
友愛 **yūai** friendship, brotherly love
5 他愛 **taai** altruism
可愛 **kawai(i)** cute, dear, sweet
6 汎愛 **han'ai** philanthropy
汎愛主義 **han'ai shugi** philanthropism
自愛 **jiai** self-love, self-regard; selfishness
7 求愛 **kyūai** courting, courtship
8 非愛国的 **hiaikokuteki** unpatriotic, disloyal
盲愛 **mōai** blind love
忠愛 **chūai** devotion, loyalty
性愛 **seiai** sexual love
9 信愛 **shin'ai** love and believe in
相愛 **sōai** mutual love
10 恋愛 **ren'ai** love
恋愛至上主義 **ren'ai-shijō shugi** love for love's sake
恋愛観 **ren'aikan** philosophy of love
恩愛 **on'ai** kindness and love, affection
純愛 **jun'ai** pure/Platonic love
11 偏愛 **hen'ai** partiality, favoritism
情愛 **jōai** affection, love

12 割愛 **katsuai** part with (reluctantly), give up, spare, share
博愛 **hakuai** philanthropy
博愛家 **hakuaika** philanthropist
最愛 **saiai** dearest, beloved
無愛想 **buaisō** unsociable, curt
無愛嬌 **buaikyō** unamiable, unsociable
敬愛 **keiai** love and respect, veneration
13 慈愛 **jiai** affection, kindness, love
溺愛 **dekiai** dote upon
14 遺愛 **iai** bequest, prized possession of the deceased
15 熱愛 **netsuai** ardent love, devotion
16 親愛 **shin'ai** affection, love; dear
17 鍾愛 **shōai** love dearly
19 寵愛 **chōai** favor, affection

――――――― 3 ―――――――

2 人間愛 **ningen'ai** human love
人類愛 **jinruiai** love for mankind
5 母性愛 **boseiai** a mother's love, maternal affection
兄弟愛 **kyōdaiai** brotherly love
6 同性愛 **dōseiai** homosexuality
同胞愛 **dōhōai** brotherly love, fraternity
8 忠君愛国 **chūkun-aikoku** loyalty and patriotism
9 祖国愛 **sokokuai** love for one's country
10 郷土愛 **kyōdoai** love for one's home province
11 動物愛 **dōbutsuai** love for animals
動物愛護 **dōbutsu aigo** being kind to animals, animal welfare
15 隣人愛 **rinjin'ai** love of one's fellow man

――――――― 4 ―――――――

9 相思相愛 **sōshi-sōai** mutual love

4i10.2

貉 狢　　　**KAKU, mujina** badger

――――――― 11 ―――――――

數 → 数 **4i9.1**

4i11.1 / 1451

敷　　　**FU, shi(ku)** spread, lay, put down

――――――― 1 ―――――――

5 敷皮 **shi(ki)gawa** fur cushion, bearskin rug
敷写 **shi(ki)utsu(shi)** tracing
敷布 **shikifu** (bed) sheet
敷布団 **shikibuton** floor mattress

敷石 **shikiishi** paving stone, flagstone
6 敷地 **shikichi** site, lot
8 敷居 **shikii** threshold, doorsill
敷板 **shi(ki)ita** planking, floor boards
敷物 **shikimono** carpet, rug, cushion
敷金 **shikikin** (security) deposit
9 敷衍 **fuen** amplify, extend, develop
敷革 **shi(ki)gawa** inner sole
敷砂 **shi(ki)suna** sand for spreading (in a garden)
10 敷島 **Shikishima** (ancient) Japan
敷島道 **Shikishima (no) michi** Japanese poetry
11 敷設 **fusetsu** lay (cable/mines), build (a railway/road) (also spelled 布設)
13 敷蒲団 **shikibuton** floor mattress
敷煉瓦 **shi(ki)renga** paving bricks
敷詰 **shi(ki)tsu(meru)** spread all over, cover with
17 敷藁 **shi(ki)wara** litter, (horse bedding) straw

———————— 2 ————————

3 上敷 **uwaji(ki)** carpet
下敷 **shitaji(ki)** mat, desk pad; pinned under, crushed beneath; model, pattern
4 中敷 **nakaji(ki)** spread inside, lay in the middle
7 折敷 **o(ri)shi(ku)** kneel
o(ri)shi(ki) kneeling (position)
8 居敷当 **ishikia(te)** kimono seat lining
板敷 **itaji(ki)** wooden/plank floor
金敷 **kanashi(ki)** anvil
9 屋敷 **yashiki** mansion
屋敷町 **yashiki machi** exclusive residential section
10 倉敷 **kurashiki** storage place; storage charges **Kurashiki** (city, Okayama-ken)
倉敷料 **kurashikiryō** storage charges
釜敷 **kamashi(ki)** pad to set a kettle on
座敷 **zashiki** room, drawing room
座敷牢 **zashikirō** room for confining someone
桟敷 **sajiki** reviewing stand, box, gallery
13 跡敷 **atoshiki** head of family
鉄敷 **kanashi(ki)** anvil

———————— 3 ————————

3 上屋敷 **kamiyashiki** (daimyo's) main residence
下屋敷 **shimoyashiki** (daimyo's) villa
7 角屋敷 **kadoyashiki** corner house
花屋敷 **hana yashiki** flower garden
9 風呂敷 **furoshiki** a square of cloth used to wrap goods and presents in
10 家屋敷 **ieyashiki** house and lot, estate
11 控屋敷 **hika(e) yashiki** villa, retreat
12 奥座敷 **okuzashiki** inner/back room

貸座敷 **ka(shi)zashiki** brothel
15 蔵屋敷 **kurayashiki** daimyo's city storehouse
18 離座敷 **hana(re) zashiki** detached room
22 聾桟敷 **tsunbo sajiki** the upper gallery

———————— 4 ————————

4 天井桟敷 **tenjō sajiki** the upper gallery
9 幽霊屋敷 **yūrei yashiki** haunted house

4i11.2 / 416

敵

TEKI enemy, competitor, opponent
kataki enemy, rival; revenge

———————— 1 ————————

0 敵する **teki(suru)** fight against, face, be a match for
4 敵中 **tekichū** midst of the enemy
敵手 **tekishu** adversary, the enemy
5 敵本主義 **tekihon shugi** feint, pretense, having ulterior motives
6 敵同士 **katakidōshi** mutual enemies
敵地 **tekichi** enemy territory
7 敵対 **tekitai** hostility, antagonism
敵対心 **tekitaishin** enmity, animosity
敵対的 **tekitaiteki** hostile, antagonistic
敵兵 **tekihei** enemy soldier
敵役 **katakiyaku, tekiyaku** villain's role
8 敵味方 **teki-mikata** friend or/and foe
敵国 **tekikoku** enemy country
敵国語 **tekikokugo** the enemy's language
敵性 **tekisei** of enemy character, hostile
敵性国 **tekiseikoku** hostile country
敵性者 **tekiseisha** person of enemy character
9 敵陣 **tekijin** enemy camp/position/lines
敵軍 **tekigun** enemy army, hostile forces
敵前 **tekizen** before/facing the enemy
敵城 **tekijō** enemy castle
10 敵将 **tekishō** enemy general
敵討 **katakiu(chi)** revenge, vendetta
11 敵側 **tekigawa** the enemy's side
敵視 **tekishi** regard with hostility
敵情 **tekijō** the enemy's movements
敵船 **tekisen** enemy ship
12 敵弾 **tekidan** enemy bullets/shells/fire
敵営 **tekiei** the enemy's camp
13 敵勢 **tekizei** the enemy's strength/forces
敵愾心 **tekigaishin** hostility, animosity
敵意 **tekii** enmity, hostility, animosity
14 敵旗 **tekki** enemy flag
15 敵影 **tekiei** signs of the enemy
16 敵機 **tekki** enemy plane
21 敵艦 **tekikan** enemy ship
敵艦隊 **teki kantai** enemy fleet
22 敵襲 **tekishū** attack by the enemy

———————— 2 ————————

3 大敵 **taiteki** archenemy; formidable opponent

4

木
月
日
火
礻
王
牛
方
攵 11←
欠
心
戸
戈

小敵	**shōteki**	weak adversary
4 不敵	**futeki**	bold, daring, fearless
天敵	**tenteki**	natural enemy
仇敵	**kyūteki**	bitter enemy
公敵	**kōteki**	public enemy
匹敵	**hitteki**	rival, compare with, be a match for
5 外敵	**gaiteki**	foreign enemy
好敵	**kōteki**	worthy opponent
好敵手	**kōtekishu**	worthy opponent
目敵	**me (no) kataki**	enemy, object of hostility
7 対敵	**taiteki**	toward/with the enemy
9 政敵	**seiteki**	political opponent
10 残敵	**zanteki**	enemy survivors/stragglers
恋敵	**koigataki**	one's rival in love
索敵	**sakuteki**	searching for the enemy
弱敵	**jakuteki**	weak enemy
素敵	**suteki**	splendid, marvelous, great
11 強敵	**kyōteki, gōteki**	formidable enemy
宿敵	**shukuteki**	old enemy
12 棋敵	**kiteki**	one's opponent in go/shogi
朝敵	**chōteki**	enemy of the court, rebel
無敵	**muteki**	invincible, unrivaled
15 論敵	**ronteki**	opponent (in an argument)

——————— 3 ———————

11 商売敵	**shōbaigataki**	business competitor

——————— 4 ———————

3 大胆不敵	**daitan-futeki**	audacious, daredevil

髪→ **3j11.3**

4i11.3 / 1782

弊 弊 **HEI** evil, abuse, vice; (as prefix) our (humble)

——————— 1 ———————

6 弊宅	**heitaku**	tumbledown shack; my humble home
弊衣	**heii**	shabby clothes
7 弊村	**heison**	impoverished village; our humble village
弊社	**heisha**	our company, we
8 弊店	**heiten**	our shop, we
9 弊風	**heifū**	bad habit, evil practice, abuse
弊政	**heisei**	misrule, maladministration
10 弊害	**heigai**	an evil, ill effects
11 弊習	**heishū**	corrupt custom, bad habit
15 弊舗	**heiho**	our store, we

——————— 2 ———————

5 旧弊	**kyūhei**	an old evil; old-fashioned, behind the times
7 余弊	**yohei**	a lingering evil
9 通弊	**tsūhei**	a common evil
10 党弊	**tōhei**	party evils

時弊	**jihei**	evils of the times
疲弊	**hihei**	impoverishment, exhaustion
病弊	**byōhei**	an evil, ill effect
11 宿弊	**shukuhei**	a deep-rooted evil
悪弊	**akuhei**	an evil, vice, abuse
情弊	**jōhei**	favoritism
14 語弊	**gohei**	faulty/misleading expression
16 積弊	**sekihei**	deep-seated/longstanding evil

——————— 12 ———————

4i12.1 / 1032

憂 **YŪ, ure(eru), ure(u)** grieve, be distressed/anxious **ure(e/i)** grief, distress, anxiety **u(i)** sad, unhappy, gloomy

——————— 1 ———————

0 憂さ	**u(sa)**	sadness, gloom, melancholy
4 憂心	**yūshin**	grieving heart
5 憂目	**u(ki)me**	grief, misery, hardship
6 憂色	**yūshoku**	worried look, gloom
7 憂身	**u(ki)mi (o yatsusu)**	be utterly/slavishly devoted to
8 憂苦	**yūku**	sorrow, distress
憂国	**yūkoku**	patriotism
11 憂患	**yūkan**	sorrow, distress, cares
12 憂晴	**u(sa)bara(shi)**	diversion, distraction
憂悶	**yūmon**	anguish, mortification
13 憂愁	**yūshū**	melancholy, grief, gloom
15 憂慮	**yūryo**	anxiety, apprehension, cares
18 憂顔	**ure(i)gao**	sorrowful face, troubled look
29 憂鬱	**yūutsu**	melancholy, dejection, gloom
憂鬱症	**yūutsushō**	melancholia, hypochondria
憂鬱質	**yūutsushitsu**	prone to depression

——————— 2 ———————

4 内憂	**naiyū**	internal/domestic discord
7 杞憂	**kiyū**	imaginary/groundless fears
8 物憂	**monou(i)**	languid, weary, dull
11 深憂	**shin'yū**	grave apprehension
12 喜憂	**kiyū**	joy and sorrow

——————— 3 ———————

9 後顧憂	**kōko (no) ure(i)**	anxiety about those left behind after one is gone

——————— 4 ———————

1 一喜一憂	**ikki ichiyū**	alternation of joy and sorrow, hope and fear

4i12.2

麩 麩 麩 **FU, fusuma** wheat bran

——————— 2 ———————

4 天麩羅	**tenpura**	tempura, Japanese-style fried foods
5 生麩	**shōfu**	wheat starch

4

木 月 日 火 礻 王 牛 方 文 欠 心 戸 戈

→11

4i12.3 / 503

整 **SEI, totono(eru)** put in order, arrange, prepare **totono(u)** be put in order, be arranged/prepared

― 1 ―
6 整合 **seigō** adjust, coordinate
整列 **seiretsu** stand in a row, line up
整地 **seichi** ground leveling; soil preparation
7 整形 **seikei** orthopedics
整形手術 **seikei shujutsu** orthopedic operation
整形外科 **seikei geka** plastic surgery
8 整版 **seihan** block printing, plate making
整枝 **seishi** pruning
9 整除 **seijo** divide exactly
10 整流 **seiryū** rectification, commutation (in electricity)
整流子 **seiryūshi** commutator
整流器 **seiryūki** rectifier
整骨 **seikotsu** bone-setting, osteopathy
11 整理 **seiri** arrangement, adjustment; liquidation, reorganization; retrenchment, curtailment
整理部 **seiribu** (newspaper's) copy desk
整理箱 **seiribako** filing cabinet
整理箪笥 **seiridansu** chest of drawers
12 整備 **seibi** make/keep ready for use, maintain, equip
整然 **seizen** orderly, regular, systematic, neat and trim
13 整数 **seisū** integer
整頓 **seiton** in proper order, neat
15 整調 **seichō** head oarsman

― 2 ―
4 不整脈 **fuseimyaku** irregular pulse
7 均整 **kinsei** symmetry, balance
10 修整 **shūsei** retouching (in photography)
12 補整 **hosei** manipulation, adjustment
14 端整 **tansei** orderly, well formed
15 調整 **chōsei** adjust, regulate, coordinate

― 3 ―
2 人員整理 **jin'in seiri** personnel cutback
4 区画整理 **kukaku seiri** land readjustment, readjustment of town lots
10 残品整理 **zanpin seiri** clearance sale
11 理路整然 **riro-seizen** well-argued, cogent, logical

― 13 ―

4i13.1

斂 **REN** collect; converge

― 2 ―
4 収斂 **shūren** convergent; astringent

麺 → 麵 **4i17.1**

4i13.2

麭 **HŌ** wheat/barley cakes

― 14 ―

4i14.1

蟊 **SHŪ** grasshopper

― 1 ―
18 蟊螽 **kirigirisu** grasshopper, katydid, leaf cricket

4i14.2

釐 **RI** pay; few; (unit of currency/length)

4i14.3

斃 **HEI, tao(reru)** collapse and die, fall dead

― 1 ―
6 斃死 **heishi** fall dead, perish

― 15 ―

鼕 → **3p15.1**

― 17 ―

4i17.1

麺 麵 麵 麭 䴵 **MEN** noodles; wheat flour

― 1 ―
12 麵棒 **menbō** rolling pin
18 麵類 **menrui** noodles

― 2 ―
10 索麵 **sōmen** vermicelli, noodles
素麵 **sōmen** vermicelli, thin noodles
12 湯麵 **tanmen** (Chinese dish of noodles, pork and fried vegetable in a broth)
14 製麵所 **seimenjo** noodle factory

― 19 ―

變 → 変 **2j7.3**

─────────── 20 ───────────

4i20.1

鼈

BETSU, suppon snapping turtle, terrapin

─────────── 1 ───────────

5 鼈甲 **bekkō** tortoiseshell
鼈甲色 **bekkō-iro** amber color

─────────── 欠 4j ───────────

欠	欣	欧	欲	欵	歃	瓷	欺	款	欹	歃	歇	歉
0.1	4.1	4.2	7.1	7.2	7.3	7.4	8.1	8.2	8.3	9.1	9.2	10.1

歌	歎	歓	歐	歔	歟	歠	歛	歡	懿
10.2	10.3	11.1	4j4.2	12.1	12.2	13.1	13.2	4j11.1	4k18.2

─────────── 0 ───────────

4j0.1 / 383

欠 缺

KETSU, ka(ku) lack
ka(kasu) miss (a meeting)
ka(keru) be lacking
ka(ke/kera) broken piece,
fragment **akubi** yawn

─────────── 1 ───────────

3 欠乏 **ketsubō** lack, scarcity, shortage, deficiency
4 欠文 **ketsubun** missing part, lacuna, gap
欠片 **kakera** broken piece, fragment
5 欠本 **keppon** missing volume
欠号 **ketsugō** missing number/issue
欠字 **ketsuji** omitted word, blank
欠礼 **ketsurei** neglect of courtesies
欠目 **ka(ke)me** break, rupture; short weight
6 欠如 **ketsujo** lack
7 欠伸 **akubi** yawn
9 欠除 **ketsujo** remove, eliminate
欠陥 **kekkan** defect, deficiency, shortcoming
欠点 **ketten** defect, flaw, faults
欠食 **kesshoku** go without a meal
10 欠員 **ketsuin** vacant position, opening
欠唇 **kesshin, iguchi** harelip
欠席 **kesseki** absence, nonattendance
欠席届 **kesseki todo(ke)** report of absence
欠席者 **kessekisha** absentee
欠格 **kekkaku** lack of qualifications
欠航 **kekkō** suspension of (ferry) service
欠配 **keppai** suspension of rations/payments
12 欠勤 **kekkin** absence (from work)
欠勤届 **kekkin todo(ke)** report of absence
欠勤者 **kekkinsha** absentee
欠勤率 **kekkinritsu** rate of absenteeism
欠場 **ketsujō** fail to show up
欠落 **ketsuraku** be missing/lacking
欠量 **ketsuryō** amount of shortfall, ullage
欠番 **ketsuban** missing number
13 欠損 **kesson** deficit, loss
14 欠漏 **ketsurō** omission

─────────── 2 ───────────

3 大欠伸 **ōakubi** big yawn
切欠 **kirika(ki)** notch
5 出欠 **shukketsu** attendance or absence
生欠伸 **namaakubi** slight yawn
7 身欠鰊 **mika(ki) nishin** dried herring
8 事欠 **kotoka(ku)** lack, be in need of
金欠 **kinketsu** shortage of money
金欠病 **kinketsubyō** shortage of money
10 病欠 **byōketsu** absence due to illness
12 無欠 **muketsu** flawless
無欠席 **mukesseki** perfect attendance
補欠 **hoketsu** filling a vacancy
間欠 **kanketsu** intermittent
間欠熱 **kanketsunetsu** intermittent fever

─────────── 3 ───────────

4 不可欠 **fukaketsu** indispensable, essential

─────────── 4 ───────────

7 完全無欠 **kanzen-muketsu** flawlessly perfect
8 金甌無欠 **kin'ō-muketsu, kinnō-muketsu** perfect, unblemished

─────────── 6 ───────────

2 九仞功一簣欠 **kyūjin (no) kō (o) ikki (ni) ka(ku)** failure on the verge of success

─────────── 4 ───────────

4j4.1

欣

KIN rejoice

─────────── 1 ───────────

7 欣快 **kinkai** pleasant, happy, delightful
12 欣喜 **kinki** joy, delight
欣喜雀踊 **kinki-jakuyaku** jump for joy
欣然 **kinzen** joyful, glad, cheerful

4j4.2 / 1022

欧 歐

Ō Europe

——————— 1 ———————

4 欧化 **ōka** Europeanization, Westernization
欧文 **ōbun** European language, roman script
6 欧州 **Ōshū** Europe
欧州共同体 **Ōshū Kyōdōtai** the European Community
欧州同体 **Ōshū Dōmei** the European Union
欧米 **Ō-Bei** Europe and America, the West
7 欧亜 **Ō-A** Europe and Asia
9 欧風 **ōfū** European/Western style, occidental
19 欧羅巴 **Yōroppa** Europe

——————— 2 ———————

4 中欧 **Chūō** central Europe
日欧 **Nichi-Ō** Japan and Europe
5 北欧 **Hokuō** Northern Europe
北欧人 **Hokuōjin** a Northern European, a Scandinavian
6 西欧 **Seiō** Western Europe, the West
西欧人 **Seiōjin** Westerner, European
西欧化 **Seiōka** Westernization
全欧 **zen-Ō** all Europe
7 対欧 **tai-Ō** toward/with Europe
8 東欧 **Tōō** Eastern Europe
9 南欧 **Nan'ō** Southern Europe
12 渡欧 **to-Ō** going to Europe
13 滞欧 **tai-Ō** staying in Europe

——————— 7 ———————

4j7.1 / 1127

欲 慾

YOKU covetousness; desire
ho(shii) want
hos(suru) desire, want

——————— 1 ———————

4 欲心 **yokushin** avarice, selfishness
5 欲目 **yokume** partiality, favorable view
7 欲求 **yokkyū** wants, desires
欲求不満 **yokkyū fuman** frustration
8 欲念 **yokunen** desire, wishes, passions
11 欲深 **yokufuka** greed, avarice
欲張 **yokuba(ri)** greed, covetousness
欲得 **yokutoku** selfishness, self-interest
欲望 **yokubō** desire, craving
欲情 **yokujō** passions, desires

——————— 2 ———————

3 大欲 **taiyoku** greed, avarice, covetousness
小欲 **shōyoku** not very covetous
6 多欲 **tayoku** avarice, greed, covetousness
肉欲 **nikuyoku** carnal desires
色欲 **shikiyoku** sexual desire, lust
7 我欲 **gayoku** selfishness
邪欲 **jayoku** evil/carnal passion
利欲 **riyoku** greed, mercenariness
私欲 **shiyoku** self-interest
8 制欲 **seiyoku** control of one's passions

物欲 **butsuyoku** worldly desires/ambition
性欲 **seiyoku** sexual desire
9 食欲 **shokuyoku** appetite
10 胴欲 **dōyoku** avarice, greed; cruelty
11 貪欲 **don'yoku** avaricious, covetous
淫欲 **in'yoku** lust
強欲 **gōyoku** greedy, avaricious
情欲 **jōyoku** passions, sexual desire
12 無欲 **muyoku** free from avarice
13 禁欲 **kin'yoku** control of passions, self-denial, abstinence
禁欲主義 **kin'yoku shugi** asceticism, stoicism
愛欲 **aiyoku** love and lust, passion
意欲 **iyoku** will, desire, zest
14 寡欲 **kayoku** unselfish, of few wants
16 獣欲 **jūyoku** carnal desire, lust

——————— 3 ———————

6 名誉欲 **meiyoyoku** desire for fame
8 知識欲 **chishikiyoku** love of learning
征服欲 **seifukuyoku** desire for conquest
9 政権欲 **seiken'yoku** ambition for political power

4j7.2

歖   **AI** (exclamation)

4j7.3

歔   **KI** sob, grieve, lament

——————— 2 ———————

16 歔欷 **kyōki** sobbing

4j7.4

瓷   **JI, SHI** porcelain, china

——————— 8 ———————

4j8.1 / 1499

欺   **GI, azamu(ku)** deceive, cheat, dupe

——————— 1 ———————

16 欺瞞 **giman** deception, fraud, trickery
欺瞞的 **gimanteki** deceptive, fraudulent, false
欺瞞者 **gimansha** deceiver, swindler

——————— 2 ———————

12 詐欺 **sagi** fraud
詐欺師 **sagishi** swindler, con man
詐欺罪 **sagizai** fraud

4j8.2 / 1727

款

KAN article, section; goodwill, friendship

——————— 1 ———————

9 款待 **kantai** warm welcome, hospitality

——————— 2 ———————

7 条款 **jōkan** clause, provision
8 定款 **teikan** articles of incorporation, charter
9 約款 **yakkan** agreement, stipulation
10 借款 **shakkan** loan
12 落款 **rakkan** (painter's) signature

4j8.3

欹

KI, sobada(teru) prick up (one's ears)

——————— 9 ———————

4j9.1

歃

SŌ, susu(ru) sip, suck, slurp

4j9.2

歇

KETSU become depleted, run out of; rest, stop

——————— 2 ———————

12 間歇 **kanketsu** intermittent
間歇熱 **kanketsunetsu** intermittent fever

——————— 10 ———————

4j10.1

歉

KEN insufficiency, lack, shortage

4j10.2 / 392

歌 謌

KA, uta song; poem
uta(u) sing; recite

——————— 1 ———————

2 歌人 **kajin** poet
3 歌口 **utaguchi** mouthpiece (of a flute); skill in reciting poetry
歌女 **utame** singer, songstress
4 歌手 **kashu** singer
歌心 **utagokoro** poetic disposition
5 歌仙 **kasen** great poet
6 歌曲 **kakyoku** (art) song, lied

歌合 **utaawa(se)** poetry contest
歌会 **kakai, utakai** poetry party/competition
7 歌学 **kagaku** poetry
歌声 **utagoe** singing voice
歌言葉 **uta kotoba** poetic language/wording
8 歌枕 **utamakura** place famed in poetry
9 歌風 **kafū** poetic style
歌神 **kashin** god(dess) of poetry, muse
10 歌姫 **utahime** songstress
歌格 **kakaku** poetry rules/style
歌書 **kasho** book of poems
歌留多 **karuta** playing cards
11 歌道 **kadō** poetry
歌唱 **kashō** singing; song
12 歌詠 **utayo(mi)** poet
歌詞 **kashi** the lyrics/words (of a song)
歌集 **kashū** poetry anthology
13 歌聖 **kasei** great poet
14 歌碑 **kahi** monument inscribed with a poem
歌誦 **kashō** sing (loudly)
15 歌舞 **kabu** singing and dancing, entertainment
歌舞伎 **kabuki** kabuki
歌劇 **kageki** opera
歌稿 **kakō** manuscript of a poem
歌論 **karon** poetry review
歌調 **kachō** melody, tune
16 歌壇 **kadan** the world of poetry
歌謡 **kayō** song, ballad
歌謡曲 **kayōkyoku** popular song
18 歌題 **kadai** title of a poem

——————— 2 ———————

3 小歌 **kouta** ditty, ballad
4 弔歌 **chōka** dirge
反歌 **hanka** short poem appended to a long poem
5 古歌 **furuuta** old song/poem
6 返歌 **henka** poem in reply
名歌 **meika** famous/excellent poem
名歌集 **meikashū** poetry anthology
舟歌 **funauta** sailor's song, chantey
7 作歌 **sakka** writing songs/poems
狂歌 **kyōka** comic tanka, satirical poem
社歌 **shaka** company anthem/song
秀歌 **shūka** excellent tanka/poem
8 長歌 **chōka, nagauta** long epic poem
弦歌 **genka** singing accompanied by string instruments
国歌 **kokka** national anthem
牧歌 **bokka** pastoral song
放歌 **hōka** sing loudly
放歌高吟 **hōka-kōgin** loud singing
和歌 **waka** 31-syllable poem, tanka
和歌山 **Wakayama** (city, Wakayama-ken)
和歌山県 **Wakayama-ken** (prefecture)
9 俗歌 **zokka** popular/folk song, ditty
軍歌 **gunka** military song

哀歌 **aika** plaintive song, elegy, lament
連歌 **renga** linked haiku
春歌 **shunka** bawdy song
10 恋歌 **koiuta, koika, renka** love song/poem
高歌 **kōka** loud singing
挽歌 **banka** dirge, funeral song
唐歌 **karauta** Chinese poem
校歌 **kōka** school song
11 道歌 **dōka** didactic poem
唱歌 **shōka** singing
情歌 **jōka** love song
船歌 **funauta** sailor's song, chantey
12 凱歌 **gaika** victory song
短歌 **tanka** 31-syllable poem, tanka
喜歌劇 **kikageki** comic opera
替歌 **ka(e)uta** a parody (of a song)
悲歌 **hika** elegy, dirge
童歌 **warabeuta** traditional children's song
詠歌 **eika** composition of a poem; (Buddhist) chant
飲歌 **no(meya)uta(e)** carousing, revelry
13 聖歌 **seika** sacred song, hymn
聖歌隊 **seikatai** choir
数歌 **kazo(e)uta** counting-out rhyme
誄歌 **ruika** dirge
詩歌 **shiika, shika** poetry
雅歌 **Gaka** the Song of Solomon
頌歌 **shōka** hymn of praise, anthem
14 選歌 **senka** selection of poems; selected poem
漁歌 **gyoka** fisherman's song
演歌 **enka** (a style of singing)
鼻歌 **hanauta** humming, crooning
雑歌 **zōka** miscellaneous poems
15 寮歌 **ryōka** dormitory song
戯歌 **za(re)uta** comic song, limerick
賛歌 **sanka** paean, praise
18 謳歌 **ōka** glorify, sing the praises of
類歌 **ruika** similar song
22 讃歌 **sanka** paean, praise

—————— 3 ——————
2 子守歌 **komoriuta** lullaby
3 大和歌 **Yamato-uta** 31-syllable poem, tanka
4 手毬歌 **temari uta** handball song
5 主題歌 **shudaika** theme song
田植歌 **tau(e) uta** rice-planting song
8 追悼歌 **tsuitōka** dirge
9 革命歌 **kakumeika** revolutionary song
茶摘歌 **chatsu(mi)uta** tea-pickers' song
10 流行歌 **ryūkōka, haya(ri)uta** popular song
12 御詠歌 **goeika** Buddhist hymn/chant
15 賛美歌 **sanbika** hymn
22 讃美歌 **sanbika** hymn

—————— 4 ——————
5 古今和歌集 **Kokinwakashū** (poetry anthology, early tenth century)

四面楚歌 **shimen-soka** surrounded by enemies, without allies

4j10.3

歎 **TAN, nage(ku)** sigh, grieve over, lament, bemoan, deplore

—————— 1 ——————
7 歎声 **tansei** sigh (of lament/admiration)
10 歎息 **tansoku** sigh, lament
歎称 **tanshō** admiration, praise
11 歎異鈔 **Tannishō** (a collection of Buddhist teachings)
15 歎賞 **tanshō** admiration, praise
19 歎願 **tangan** petition, appeal
歎願書 **tangansho** written petition

—————— 2 ——————
12 詠歎 **eitan** exclamation; admiration
13 愁歎 **shūtan** lamentation, sorrow

—————— 11 ——————

4j11.1 / 1052

歓 歡 **KAN** joy, pleasure

—————— 1 ——————
4 歓心買 **kanshin (o) ka(u)** curry favor
6 歓迎 **kangei** welcome
歓迎会 **kangeikai** welcoming meeting, reception
7 歓声 **kansei** shout of joy, cheer
8 歓送 **kansō** a send-off
歓送会 **kansōkai** farewell party, send-off
歓呼 **kanko** cheer, ovation
9 歓待 **kantai** hospitality
12 歓喜 **kanki** joy, delight
13 歓楽 **kanraku** pleasure, enjoyment
歓楽街 **kanrakugai** amusement center
15 歓談 **kandan** pleasant chat

—————— 2 ——————
6 合歓 **gōkan** enjoy together
合歓木 **nemunoki** silk tree
9 哀歓 **aikan** joys and sorrows

歐 → 欧 4j4.2

—————— 12 ——————

4j12.1

歙 **KYŪ** come together, meet; put away, store

4
木 月 日 火 礻 王 牛 方 攵 欠 心 戸 戈
12←

4j12.2

歔 KYŌ sob

─────── 1 ───────

11 歔歔 **kyōki** sobbing

─────── 13 ───────

4j13.1

歟 YO (used for sentence particles)

4j13.2

歛 KAN hope for, wish; give

─────── 17 ───────

歡 → 歓 4j11.1

─────── 18 ───────

懿 → 4k18.2

───────── 心 **4k** ─────────

心	必	忖	忙	忍	忌	忘	忸	快	忱	忻	悴	忤
0.1	0a5.16	3.1	3.2	3.3	3.4	2j5.4	4.1	4.2	4.3	4.4	4k8.12	4.5
忠	忽	忝	怫	快	怦	性	怳	怖	怕	怛	怯	怜
4.6	4.7	3n5.4	5.1	5.2	5.3	5.4	5.5	5.6	5.7	5.8	5.9	5.10
怪	怙	泳	怡	怩	恂	忽	怎	怒	怨	恚	急	怠
5.11	5.12	5.13	5.14	5.15	5.16	5.17	5.18	5.19	5.20	3b7.7	2n7.2	5.21
恤	恨	恢	悖	恒	恃	恍	恪	恬	恰	恊	悔	恢
6.1	6.2	6.3	6.4	6.5	6.6	6.7	6.8	6.9	6.10	6.11	6.12	4k6.3
恂	恟	恫	惠	息	恕	恐	恷	恁	恣	恚	羞	恩
6.13	6.14	6.15	6.16	6.17	6.18	6.19	6.20	6.21	6.22	3b7.7	2o8.3	6.23
恭	悚	悧	悸	悍	悟	悋	悛	悁	悟	悄	悩	悼
3k7.16	7.1	7.2	7.3	7.4	7.5	7.6	7.7	7.8	7.9	7.10	7.11	7.12
悗	悌	悦	悔	悃	悪	患	悉	悠	惟	悵	惧	倦
7.13	7.14	7.15	4k6.12	7.16	7.17	7.18	7.19	7.20	8.1	8.2	8.3	8.4
惨	悽	悾	惕	情	惚	惜	悳	悴	悼	惆	惘	惠
8.5	8.6	8.7	8.8	8.9	8.10	8.11	3i11.3	8.12	8.13	8.14	8.15	4k6.16
惑	悪	惣	悲	瑟	惻	愀	愎	愕	惚	惰	惶	惺
8.16	4k7.17	8.17	8.18	4f9.10	9.1	9.2	9.3	9.4	9.5	9.6	9.7	9.8
愒	慌	愃	惴	惱	愉	偏	愚	愁	愍	想	愆	舂
9.9	9.10	9.11	9.12	4k7.11	9.13	9.14	9.15	9.16	9.17	9.18	9.19	9.20
愈	慈	感	惡	慊	愬	慨	博	慎	慄	愧	慍	愴
2a11.16	2o11.1	9.21	4k7.17	10.1	10.2	10.3	2k10.1	10.4	10.5	10.6	10.7	10.8
慥	愫	願	慇	愨	態	惡	慈	慂	慝	慽	慟	傲
10.9	10.10	10.11	10.12	10.13	10.14	4k7.17	2o11.1	10.15	10.16	4k11.12	11.1	11.2
博	慓	慴	慘	慯	憎	慢	慣	慚	慵	慷	感	慰
11.3	11.4	11.5	4k8.5	11.6	11.7	11.8	11.9	4k11.14	11.10	11.11	11.12	11.13
慙	憇	慾	慫	慧	慨	慳	憔	憮	憚	憧	憤	憬
11.14	4k12.10	4j7.1	11.15	11.16	4k10.3	12.1	12.2	12.3	12.4	12.5	12.6	12.7

憎	憫	榮	愁	憩	憊	憑	憙	懈	懊	憾	憐	憶
4k11.7	12.8	3k12.14	12.9	12.10	12.11	12.12	12.13	13.1	13.2	13.3	13.4	13.5

懌	懆	懍	懐	憺	懃	懇	懋	懦	懣	懲	應	懴
13.6	13.7	13.8	13.9	13.10	13.11	13.12	13.13	14.1	14.2	14.3	3q4.2	4k17.1

懲	懶	懷	懸	懺	懽	懼	懾	懿	戀	戆
4k14.3	16.1	4k13.9	16.2	17.1	17.2	4k8.3	18.1	18.2	2j8.2	8d17.1

--- 0 ---

4k0.1 / 97

SHIN, kokoro heart, mind; core

--- 1 ---

2 心力 **shinryoku** mental power, faculties
3 心丈夫 **kokorojōbu** secure, reassured
心土 **shindo** subsoil
4 心太 **tokoroten** gelidium jelly (pushed through a screen to make a spaghetti-like food)
心中 **shinjū** lovers' double suicide; murder-suicide **shinchū** in one's heart
心支度 **kokorojitaku** mental readiness/attitude
5 心付 **kokorozu(ke)** tip, gratuity
心外 **shingai** unexpected; regrettable
心立 **kokoroda(te)** disposition, temperament
6 心気 **shinki** mind, mood
心地 **kokochi(yoi)** pleasant, comfortable
心行 **kokoro yu(ku)** (as much) as one likes
心安 **kokoroyasu(i)** feeling at ease, intimate, friendly
心安立 **kokoroyasuda(te)** out of familiarity, frank
心当 **kokoroa(tari)** knowledge, idea, clue
kokoroa(te) hope, anticipation; guess
心尽 **kokorozu(kushi)** kindness, solicitude, efforts
心血 **shinketsu** one's heart's blood, heart and soul
7 心身 **shinshin** mind and body, psychosomatic
心学 **shingaku** practical/popularized ethics
心労 **shinrō** worry, anxiety
心床 **kokoroyuka(shii)** tasteful, admirable, charming
心材 **shinzai** heartwood
心肝 **shinkan, kokorogimo** heart
8 心長閑 **kokoronodoka** peaceful, at ease
心事 **shinji** one's mind/motives
心苦 **kokoroguru(shii)** painful to think of, against one's conscience
心底 **shinsoko, shintei** the bottom of one's heart
心服 **shinpuku** admiration and devotion

心的 **shinteki** mental
心性 **shinsei** mind; disposition
心房 **shinbō** auricle (of the heart)
心金 **shingane** core bar/grid, mandrel
9 心変 **kokoroga(wari)** change of mind, inconstancy
心持 **kokoromo(chi)** feeling, mood; a little
心待 **kokoroma(chi)** expectation, anticipation
心後 **kokorōkure** timidity
心室 **shinshitsu** ventricle (of the heart)
心柄 **kokorogara** mood, frame of mind
心胆 **shintan** one's heart
心神 **shinshin** mind
心神喪失 **shinshin sōshitsu** not of sound mind
心音 **shin'on** heart tone, phonocardio-
10 心残 **kokoronoko(ri)** regret, reluctance
心根 **kokorone** inner feelings; disposition
心悸亢進 **shinki kōshin** palpitations
心悸昂進 **shinki kōshin** palpitations
心配 **shinpai** worry, anxiety, concern
心配事 **shinpaigoto** cares, worries, troubles
心配性 **shinpaishō** worrying disposition
11 心淋 **kokorosabi(shii)** lonely, lonesome
心添 **kokorozo(e)** advice, counsel
心掛 **kokoroga(ke)** intention; attention, care
心強 **kokorozuyo(i)** reassuring, heartening
心得 **kokoroe** knowledge, understanding
kokoroe(ru) know, understand
心得違 **kokoroechiga(i)** mistaken idea; indiscretion
心得難 **kokoroegata(i)** strange, inexplicable
心得顔 **kokoroegao** a knowing look
心寂 **kokorosabi(shii)** lonely, lonesome
心密 **kokorohiso(ka)** inwardly, secretly
心理 **shinri** mental state, psychology
心理学 **shinrigaku** psychology
心理的 **shinriteki** psychological, mental
心情 **shinjō** one's heart/feelings
心眼 **shingan** one's mind's eye
心移 **kokoroutsu(ri)** fickleness, perfidy
心細 **kokoroboso(i)** forlorn, disheartened
心組 **kokorogu(mi)** intention
心許 **kokorobaka(ri)** trifling, mere token
kokoromoto(nai) uneasy, apprehensive; unreliable
心酔 **shinsui** be fascinated by, ardently admire

心酔者 **shinsuisha** ardent admirer, devotee
12 心隔 **kokoroheda(te)** unconfiding
心象 **shinshō** mental image
心遣 **kokorozuka(i)** solicitude, consideration
kokoroya(ri) diversion, recreation; thoughtfulness
心寒 **kokorosamu(i)** chilling
心覚 **kokoroobo(e)** recollection; reminder
心棒 **shinbō** axle, shaft, mandrel, stem
心無 **kokorona(i)** heartless, cruel; thoughtless, ill-considered
心痛 **shintsū** mental anguish, heartache
心筋 **shinkin** heart muscle, myocardium
心筋梗塞 **shinkin kōsoku** myocardial infarction
心証 **shinshō** one's impression of; judge's personal opinion of a case
心軽 **kokorogaru(i)** rash, giddy, light
13 心腹 **shinpuku** sincerity; one's confidant
心意 **shin'i** mind
心意気 **kokoroiki** disposition, spirit, sentiment
心置 **kokoroo(ki naku)** without reserve, frankly
心電図 **shindenzu** electrocardiogram
心電計 **shindenkei** electrocardiograph
14 心像 **shinzō** mental image
心境 **shinkyō** state of mind
心構 **kokorogama(e)** mental attitude/ readiness
心静 **kokoroshizu(ka)** calm, serene, at peace
心憎 **kokoroniku(i)** detestable; tasteful, admirable, excellent
心魂 **shinkon** one's heart
心緒 **shincho** mind, emotions
心算 **shinsan** intention
15 心霊 **shinrei** spirit, soul; psychic
心霊学 **shinreigaku** psychics, spiritism
心霊術 **shinreijutsu** spiritualism
16 心機 **shinki** mind, mental attitude
心機一転 **shinki-itten** change of attitude
心積 **kokorozu(mori)** readiness
心頼 **kokorodano(mi)** dependence, reliance, hope, expectation
心頭 **shintō** heart, mind
17 心優 **kokoroyasa(shii)** kind, considerate
18 心髄 **shinzui** the soul/essence of
心騒 **kokorosawa(gi)** uneasiness
19 心臓 **shinzō** the heart; nerve, cheek
心臓形 **shinzōgata** heart-shaped
心臓炎 **shinzōen** inflammation of the heart
心臓部 **shinzōbu** the heart of
心臓病 **shinzōbyō** heart disease
心臓麻痺 **shinzō mahi** heart failure/attack
心願 **shingan** heartfelt desire; prayer

——— 2 ———
1 一心 **isshin, hito(tsu)kokoro** one mind; the whole heart, wholehearted
一心同体 **isshin-dōtai** one flesh; one in body and spirit
2 二心 **futagokoro** duplicity, double-dealing
人心 **jinshin** people's hearts
人心地 **hitogokochi** consciousness
3 寸心 **sunshin** a little token (of one's gratitude)
下心 **shitagokoro** ulterior motive
女心 **onnagokoro** a woman's heart
小心 **shōshin** timid, faint-hearted; prudent
小心者 **shōshinmono** timid person, coward
小心翼々 **shōshin-yokuyoku** very timid/ cautious
4 不心得 **fukokoroe** imprudent, indiscreet
天心 **tenshin** zenith; divine will, providence
内心 **naishin** one's heart/mind, inward thoughts
丹心 **tanshin** sincerity
中心 **chūshin** center
中心人物 **chūshin jinbutsu** central figure, key person
中心地 **chūshinchi** center, metropolis
中心点 **chūshinten** center
仏心 **busshin, hotokegokoro** Buddha's heart
仁心 **jinshin** benevolence, humanity
円心 **enshin** center of a circle
水心 **mizugokoro** swimming; doing as one is done to
手心 **tegokoro** making allowances, discretion, what to do
5 以心伝心 **ishin-denshin** telepathy, tacit understanding
左心房 **sashinbō** the left auricle
左心室 **sashinshitsu** the left ventricle
民心 **minshin** popular sentiment
本心 **honshin** one's right mind, one's senses; real intention/motive, true sentiment; conscience
失心 **shisshin** faint, lose consciousness
甘心 **kanshin** contentment, satisfaction
幼心 **osanagokoro** child's mind/heart
外心 **gaishin** center of the circumscribed circle; double-mindedness
用心 **yōjin** care, caution
用心深 **yōjinbuka(i)** careful, cautious, wary
用心棒 **yōjinbō** door bolt; cudgel; bodyguard
右心房 **ushinbō** the right auricle
右心室 **ushinshitsu** the right ventricle
6 気心 **kigokoro** disposition, temperament
休心 **kyūshin** feel at ease, rest assured
会心 **kaishin** congeniality, satisfaction
孝心 **kōshin** filial devotion
同心 **dōshin** like-mindedness; concentricity
同心円 **dōshin'en** concentric circles

池心 **chishin** center/middle of a pond
地心 **chishin** center of the earth
至心 **shishin** sincerity
安心 **anshin** feel relieved/reassured
安心立命 **anshin-ritsumei** spiritual peace and enlightenment
安心感 **anshinkan** sense of security
有心 **yūshin** thoughtful consideration
ushin orthodox style (poem)
灯心 **tōshin** wick
灯心油 **tōshin'yu** lamp oil, kerosene
7 良心 **ryōshin** conscience
良心的 **ryōshinteki** conscientious
身心 **shinshin** body and mind
里心 **satogokoro** honesickness, nostalgia
住心地 **su(mi)gokochi** livability, comfort
求心力 **kyūshinryoku** centripetal force
邪心 **jashin** wicked heart, evil intent
決心 **kesshin** determination, resolution
赤心 **sekishin** true heart, sincerity
乱心 **ranshin** derangement, insanity
芳心 **hōshin** your good wishes, your kindness
肝心 **kanjin** main, vital, essential
改心 **kaishin** reform (oneself)
戒心 **kaishin** preparedness, vigilance, caution
私心 **shishin** selfish motive
初心 **shoshin** inexperience; original intention
初心者 **shoshinsha** beginner
8 毒心 **dokushin** malice, spite
逆心 **gyakushin** treachery
河心 **kashin** middle of the river
妬心 **toshin** jealousy
苦心 **kushin** pains, efforts
居心地 **igokochi** comfortableness, coziness
物心 **monogokoro** discretion, judgment
busshin matter and mind
放心 **hōshin** be absentminded; feel reassured
9 発心 **hosshin** religious awakening; resolution
衷心 **chūshin** one's inmost heart/feelings
専心 **senshin** concentration, undivided attention, singleness of purpose
重心 **jūshin** center of gravity
乗心地 **no(ri)gokochi** riding comfort
信心 **shinjin** faith, belief, piety
変心 **henshin** change of mind, fickleness
浮心 **fushin** center of buoyancy
狭心症 **kyōshinshō** stricture of the heart, angina pectoris
恒心 **kōshin** constancy, steadfastness
10 都心 **toshin** heart of the city, midtown
帰心 **kishin** longing for home
恋心 **koigokoro** (awakening of) love
娘心 **musumegokoro** girlish mind/innocence
徒心 **adagokoro** fickleness
害心 **gaishin** evil intent, malice, ill will
核心 **kakushin** core, kernel

旅心 **tabigokoro** one's mood while traveling; yen to travel
11 野心 **yashin** ambition
野心的 **yashinteki** ambitious
野心家 **yashinka** ambitious person
野心満々 **yashin-manman** full of ambition
虚心 **kyoshin** disinterested, unbiased
虚心坦懐 **kyoshin-tankai** frank, open-minded
道心 **dōshin** moral sense; piety, faith
執心 **shūshin** devotion, attachment, infatuation
唯心論 **yuishinron** idealism, spiritualism
強心剤 **kyōshinzai** heart stimulant
得心 **tokushin** consent to, be persuaded of
欲心 **yokushin** avarice, selfishness
悪心 **akushin** evil intent, sinister motive
情心 **nasa(ke)gokoro** sympathy, compassion
異心 **ishin** treachery, intrigue
盗心 **tōshin** propensity to steal, thievishness
細心 **saishin** careful, scrupulous
酔心地 **yo(i)gokochi** pleasant drunken feeling
魚心水心 **uogokoro (areba) mizugokoro** helping each other
12 着心地 **kigokochi** fit and feel (of clothes)
善心 **zenshin** virtue, conscience, moral sense
遠心 **enshin** centrifugal
遠心力 **enshinryoku** centrifugal force
湖心 **koshin** center of a lake
喪心 **sōshin** be stunned/dazed/stupefied
寒心 **kanshin** shudder at, be alarmed
無心 **mushin** absorbed in (play); request, cadge
童心 **dōshin** child's mind/feelings
痛心 **tsūshin** worry
絵心 **egokoro** artistic bent/eye
雄心 **yūshin** heroic spirit, aspiration, ambition
焦心 **shōshin** impatience, anxiousness
13 傷心 **shōshin** heartbreak, sorrow
義心 **gishin** chivalrous/public spirit
夢心地 **yumegokochi** trance, ecstasy
寝心地 **negokochi** sleeping comfort
腹心 **fukushin** confidant, trusted associate
感心 **kanshin** be impressed by, admire
誠心 **seishin** sincerity
誠心誠意 **seishin-seii** sincerely, wholeheartedly
詩心 **shishin** poetic sentiment
鉄心 **tesshin** iron core; iron/firm will
14 疑心 **gishin** suspicion, fear, apprehension
疑心暗鬼 **gishin-anki** Suspicion creates monsters in the dark. Suspicion feeds on itself.
腐心 **fushin** take pains, be intent on
静心 **shizugokoro** calm spirit
歌心 **utagokoro** poetic disposition
慢心 **manshin** be conceited

読心術 **dokushinjutsu** mind reading
関心 **kanshin** interest, concern
関心事 **kanshinji** matter of concern
15 潜心 **senshin** meditation, absorption
衝心 **shōshin** heart failure (from beriberi)
熱心 **nesshin** enthusiasm, zeal
熱心家 **nesshinka** enthusiast, devotee
憂心 **yūshin** grieving heart
歓心買 **kanshin (o) ka(u)** curry favor
16 獣心 **jūshin** brutal heart
親心 **oyagokoro** parental affection
19 爆心 **bakushin** center of the explosion
爆心地 **bakushinchi** center of the explosion

────────── 3 ──────────

1 一安心 **hitoanshin** feeling relieved for a while
2 子供心 **kodomogokoro** a child's mind/heart
4 不用心 **buyōjin, fuyōjin** unsafe, insecure; careless
不安心 **fuanshin** uneasiness, apprehension
不信心 **fushinjin** lack of faith, nonbelief
不熱心 **funesshin** unenthusiastic, indifferent, halfhearted
公共心 **kōkyōshin** public spirit, community-mindedness
公徳心 **kōtokushin** public-spiritedness
5 出来心 **dekigokoro** sudden impulse, whim
功名心 **kōmyōshin** ambition, love of fame
好奇心 **kōkishin** curiosity, inquisitiveness
6 老婆心 **rōbashin** old-womanish solicitude
向学心 **kōgakushin** love of learning
名利心 **meirishin** worldly ambition
名誉心 **meiyoshin** desire for fame
団結心 **danketsushin** spirit of solidarity
自制心 **jiseishin** self-control
自尊心 **jisonshin** self-esteem; conceit
7 克己心 **kokkishin** spirit of self-denial
投機心 **tōkishin** spirit of speculation
8 依頼心 **iraishin** spirit of dependence
弥猛心 **yatakegokoro** ardent spirit
宗教心 **shūkyōshin** religiousness, piety
忠誠心 **chūseishin** loyalty, devotion, sincerity
9 勇猛心 **yūmōshin** intrepid spirit
独立心 **dokuritsushin** independent spirit
神信心 **kami-shinjin** piety, devoutness
10 射利心 **sharishin** mercenary spirit
射幸心 **shakōshin** speculative spirit
射倖心 **shakōshin** mercenary spirit
党派心 **tōhashin** partisanship, factionalism
恐怖心 **kyōfushin** feeling of terror
11 虚栄心 **kyoeishin** vanity, vainglory
羞恥心 **shūchishin** sense of shame
道義心 **dōgishin** moral sense, scruples
道徳心 **dōtokushin** sense of morality
探究心 **tankyūshin** spirit of inquiry
猜疑心 **saigishin** suspicion, jealousy
菩提心 **bodaishin** aspiration for Buddhahood

12 無用心 **buyōjin** unsafe; incautious
無信心 **mushinjin** impiety, unbelief, infidelity
無理心中 **muri shinjū** murder-suicide
無関心 **mukanshin** indifference, unconcern, apathy
貯蓄心 **chochikushin** thriftiness
13 慈悲心 **jihishin** benevolence
義侠心 **gikyōshin** chivalrous spirit, public-spiritedness
義務心 **gimushin** sense of duty
嫉妬心 **shittoshin** jealousy, envy
廉恥心 **renchishin** sense of shame/honor
愛国心 **aikokushin** patriotism
愛郷心 **aikyōshin** home-town pride
愛党心 **aitōshin** party loyalty/spirit
愛校心 **aikōshin** love for one's school
意馬心猿 **iba-shin'en** (uncontrollable) passions
鉄石心 **tessekishin** iron/steadfast will
14 徳義心 **tokugishin** sense of morality/honor
憎悪心 **zōoshin** hatred, malice
15 敵対心 **tekitaishin** enmity, animosity
敵愾心 **tekigaishin** hostility, animosity
16 懐疑心 **kaigishin** doubt, skepticism

────────── 4 ──────────

1 一意専心 **ichii-senshin** wholeheartedly
2 人面獣心 **jinmen-jūshin** human face but brutal heart
5 以心伝心 **ishin-denshin** telepathy, tacit understanding
6 多情仏心 **tajō-busshin** tenderheartedness
11 異体同心 **itai-dōshin** of one mind, perfect accord
魚心水心 **uogokoro (areba) mizugokoro** helping each other

必 → **0a5.16**

────────── 3 ──────────

4k3.1

忖 **SON** conjecture

────────── 1 ──────────

9 忖度 **sontaku** conjecture, surmise, judge

4k3.2 / 1373

忙 **BŌ, isoga(shii), sewa(shii)** busy

────────── 1 ──────────

0 忙しない **sewa(shinai)** restless, in a hurry
4 忙中 **bōchū** during the busyness of work
10 忙殺 **bōsatsu** keep (someone) busily occupied

─────────── 2 ───────────

6 多忙 **tabō** busy
気忙 **kizewa(shii)** restless, fidgety
9 忽忙 **sōbō** busy, in a hurry
13 煩忙 **hanbō** busy, pressed with business
16 繁忙 **hanbō** busy, pressed

─────────── 3 ───────────

12 御多忙中 **gotabōchū** while you are so busy

4k3.3 / 1414

忍 忍

NIN, shino(bu) bear, endure; hide, lie hidden
shino(baseru) hide, conceal
shino(bi) stealing into; incognito/surreptitious visit; spy, scout; sneak thief

─────────── 1 ───────────

0 忍びやか **shino(biyaka)** stealthy, secret
2 忍入 **shino(bi)i(ru)** steal/sneak into, slip in
4 忍込 **shino(bi)ko(mu)** steal/sneak into, slip in
5 忍冬 **nindō, suikazura** honeysuckle
6 忍会 **shino(bi)a(i)** clandestine/secret meeting, rendezvous, tryst
7 忍声 **shino(bi)goe** in a whisper
忍足 **shino(bi)ashi** stealthy steps
8 忍泣 **shino(bi)na(ki)** subdued sobbing
忍苦 **ninku** endurance, stoicism
忍者 **ninja** ninja, spy-assassin (historical)
9 忍逢 **shino(bi)a(i)** clandestine/secret meeting, rendezvous, tryst
忍耐 **nintai** perseverance, patience, endurance
忍耐強 **nintaizuyo(i)** patient, persevering
忍姿 **shino(bi)sugata** disguise, incognito
忍音 **shino(bi)ne** subdued sobbing
10 忍従 **ninjū** submission, resignation, meekness
忍笑 **shino(bi)wara(i)** stifled laugh, giggle, chuckle, snickering
11 忍術 **ninjutsu** the art of remaining unseen
忍寄 **shino(bi)yo(ru)** steal near, sneak up
18 忍難 **shino(bi)gata(i)** unbearable

─────────── 2 ───────────

9 耐忍 **ta(e)shino(bu)** bear patiently, put up with
10 残忍 **zannin** cruel, brutal, ruthless
残忍性 **zanninsei** cruelty, brutality
陰忍 **innin** endure, be patient, put up with
12 堪忍 **kannin** patience, forbearance; forgiveness
堪忍袋 **kanninbukuro** patience, forbearance
堅忍 **kennin** perseverance, fortitude
13 隠忍 **innin** patience, endurance

4k3.4 / 1797

忌

KI mourning; death anniversary; avoid, shun **i(mu)** hate, loathe; avoid, shun
i(mi) mourning; abstinence, taboo
ima(washii) abominable, disgusting, scandalous; ominous

─────────── 1 ───────────

3 忌々 **imaima(shii)** vexing, provoking
4 忌中 **kichū** in mourning
忌引 **kibi(ki)** absence due to a death in the family
忌日 **kijitsu, kinichi** death anniversary
i(mi)bi purification-and-fast day; unlucky day
7 忌言葉 **i(mi)kotoba** tabooed word
8 忌明 **i(mi)a(ke), kia(ke)** end of mourning
13 忌嫌 **i(mi)kira(u)** detest, loathe, abhor
15 忌避 **kihi** evasion, shirking; (legal) challenge
忌憚 **kitan(nai)** without reserve, frank, outspoken
17 忌諱 **kii, kiki** displeasure, offense

─────────── 2 ───────────

6 年忌 **nenki** anniversary of a death
回忌 **kaiki** anniversary of one's death
7 忌忌 **i(ma)i(mashii)** vexing, provoking
8 周忌 **shūki** anniversary of a death
物忌 **monoi(mi)** fast, abstinence
11 猜忌 **saiki** envy, jealousy
13 嫌忌 **kenki** dislike, aversion
禁忌 **kinki** taboo; contraindication

─────────── 3 ───────────

1 一回忌 **ikkaiki** first anniversary of a death
一周忌 **isshūki** first anniversary of a death
2 七回忌 **shichikaiki** seventh anniversary of a death
11 達磨忌 **Darumaki** (religious service on) anniversary of Dharma's death (October 5)
14 徴兵忌避 **chōhei kihi** draft evasion

 忘 →   **2j5.4**

─────────── 4 ───────────

4k4.1

忸

JIKU shame

─────────── 1 ───────────

8 忸怩 **jikuji(taru)** embarrassed, put to shame

4k4.2 / 1409

快

KAI, kokoroyo(i) pleasant, delightful
kokoroyo(shi) be willing/pleased to
kokoroyo(ge) pleasant

─────────── 1 ───────────

4 快方 **kaihō** recovery, convalescence
5 快弁 **kaiben** eloquence
快打 **kaida** good hit (in baseball/golf)
7 快走 **kaisō** fast running/sailing

4

木
月
日
火
礻
王
牛
方
攵
欠
→ 4 心
戸
戈

快技 **kaigi** consummate skill
快男子 **kaidanshi** agreeable/straightforward chap
快男児 **kaidanji** a fine fellow
8 快事 **kaiji** gratifying matter, pleasure
快味 **kaimi** pleasure, delight
快雨 **kaiu** refreshing rain
9 快便 **kaiben** a refreshing defecation
快美 **kaibi** sweet, mellow, pleasant
快速 **kaisoku** high-speed; express (train)
快速船 **kaisokusen** high-speed ship
快速調 **kaisokuchō** allegro
快活 **kaikatsu** cheerful, lively, merry
快哉 **kaisai** shout of delight
10 快挙 **kaikyo** splendid deed
快眠 **kaimin** pleasant sleep
快記録 **kaikiroku** a fine record
12 快報 **kaihō** good news
快勝 **kaishō** a sweeping victory
快腕 **kaiwan** remarkable ability
快晴 **kaisei** fine weather, clear skies
快絶 **kaizetsu** delightful
13 快適 **kaiteki** comfortable, pleasant, agreeable
快漢 **kaikan** a most pleasant chap
快楽 **kairaku, keraku** pleasure
快楽主義 **kairaku shugi** hedonism, epicureanism
快感 **kaikan** pleasant/agreeable feeling
15 快談 **kaidan** pleasant chat
快諾 **kaidaku** ready consent
快調 **kaichō** harmony; excellent condition
17 快闊 **kaikatsu** cheerful, lively, merry
18 快癒 **kaiyu** recovery, convalescence

——————————— 2 ———————————
4 不快 **fukai** unpleasant, uncomfortable; displeased
6 全快 **zenkai** complete recovery, full cure
8 明快 **meikai** clear, lucid
欣快 **kinkai** pleasant, happy, delightful
11 爽快 **sōkai** thrilling, exhilarating
12 愉快 **yukai** pleasant, merry, cheerful
痛快 **tsūkai** keen pleasure, thrill, delight
軽快 **keikai** light, nimble, jaunty, lilting
14 豪快 **gōkai** exciting, stirring, heroic

——————————— 3 ———————————
4 不愉快 **fuyukai** unpleasant, disagreable

4k4.3

忱
SHIN sincere

4k4.4

忻
KIN rejoice; open (one's heart)

�→悴 **4k8.12**

4k4.5

忤
GO, sakara(u), moto(ru) go against, be contrary to

4k4.6 / 1348

忠
CHŪ loyalty, faithfulness

——————————— 1 ———————————
4 忠犬 **chūken** faithful dog
6 忠孝 **chūkō** loyalty and filial piety
7 忠良 **chūryō** loyal
忠臣 **chūshin** loyal retainer/subject
忠臣蔵 **Chūshingura** (the 47 Ronin story)
忠告 **chūkoku** advice, admonition
忠君 **chūkun** loyalty to the sovereign
忠君愛国 **chūkun-aikoku** loyalty and patriotism
忠言 **chūgen** good advice
8 忠実 **chūjitsu** faithful, devoted, loyal
9 忠信 **chūshin** loyalty, faithfulness, devotion
忠勇 **chūyū** loyalty and bravery
忠貞 **chūtei** fidelity
10 忠烈 **chūretsu** unswerving loyalty
忠純 **chūjun** unswerving loyalty
12 忠勤 **chūkin** faithful service
忠順 **chūjun** allegiance, loyalty, obedience
13 忠義 **chūgi** loyalty
忠義立 **chūgida(te)** act of loyalty
忠愛 **chūai** devotion, loyalty
忠節 **chūsetsu** loyalty, devotion
忠誠 **chūsei** loyalty, allegiance
忠誠心 **chūseishin** loyalty, devotion, sincerity
14 忠僕 **chūboku** faithful (man)servant
忠魂 **chūkon** the loyal dead, faithful spirit
忠魂碑 **chūkonhi** monument to the war dead
15 忠霊塔 **chūreitō** monument to the war dead

——————————— 2 ———————————
4 不忠 **fuchū** disloyalty, infidelity
不忠実 **fuchūjitsu** disloyal, unfaithful
6 返忠 **kae(ri)chū** switching loyalties, betrayal
尽忠 **jinchū** loyalty
尽忠報国 **jinchū-hōkoku** loyalty and patriotism
13 誠忠 **seichū** loyal

4k4.7

忽
KOTSU, tachima(chi) immediately, all of a sudden
yuruga(se) neglect, slight

────────── 1 ──────────
12 忽然 **kotsuzen** suddenly

────────── 2 ──────────
11 粗忽 **sokotsu** carelessness
粗忽者 **sokotsumono** careless/absentminded person

忝 → **3n5.4**

────────── 5 ──────────

4k5.1
佛 **FUTSU** angry, in ill humor

────────── 1 ──────────
12 佛然 **futsuzen** indignant, sullen

4k5.2
怏 **Ō** dissatisfied, discontent

────────── 1 ──────────
3 怏々 **ōō** despondent, in low spirits

4k5.3
怦 **HŌ** in a hurry, excited, agitated

4k5.4 / 98
性 **SEI** sex; nature, character; (as suffix) -ness, -ity
SHŌ temperament, propensity
saga one's nature; custom

────────── 1 ──────────
4 性分 **shōbun** nature, disposition
5 性生活 **sei seikatsu** sex life
性犯罪 **sei hanzai** sex crime
6 性交 **seikō** sexual intercourse
性向 **seikō** inclination, propensity
性行 **seikō** character and conduct
性行為 **sei kōi** sex act, intercourse
7 性状 **seijō** properties, characteristics
性別 **seibetsu** sex, whether male or female
8 性知識 **sei chishiki** information on sex
性的 **seiteki** sexual
9 性急 **seikyū** impetuous, impatient
10 性差別 **sei sabetsu** sex discrimination
性根 **shōkon** perseverance
shōne one's disposition
性格 **seikaku** character, personality

性骨 **shōkotsu, seikotsu** one's unique touch/ talent
性能 **seinō** performance, efficiency
性教育 **sei kyōiku** sex education
性病 **seibyō** sexually-transmitted/venereal disease
11 性欲 **seiyoku** sexual desire
性悪 **seiaku, shōwaru** evil nature
性悪説 **seiakusetsu** the view that human nature is basically evil
性情 **seijō** temperament, character, nature
性問題 **sei mondai** sex problem
12 性善説 **seizensetsu** the view that human nature is basically good
13 性愛 **seiai** sexual love
性感 **seikan** sexual feeling, erogenous (zone)
15 性器 **seiki** sexual/genital organ
性慾 **seiyoku** sexual desire
16 性衛生 **sei eisei** sexual hygiene
18 性懲 **shōko(ri)** learning from bitter experience
性癖 **seiheki** disposition, proclivity

────────── 2 ──────────
2 人性 **jinsei** human nature; humanity
3 女性 **josei** woman; feminine gender
女性化 **joseika** feminization
女性的 **joseiteki** feminine
女性美 **joseibi** womanly beauty
女性解放論 **josei kaihōron** feminism
4 天性 **tensei** natural, born (musician)
中性 **chūsei** neuter; (chemically) neutral; sterile
中性子 **chūseishi** neutron
水性 **suisei** aqueous, water
mizushō flirtatious, wanton
水性塗料 **suisei toryō** water-based paint
手性 **teshō** skill (with one's hands)
心性 **shinsei** mind; disposition
5 本性 **honshō, honsei** true nature/character
母性 **bosei** motherhood, maternal
母性愛 **boseiai** a mother's love, maternal affection
6 気性 **kishō** disposition, temperament, spirit
両性 **ryōsei** both sexes
両性花 **ryōseika** bisexual flower
両性的 **ryōseiteki** bisexual, androgynous
仮性 **kasei** false (symptoms)
合性 **a(i)shō** compatibility, affinity
同性 **dōsei** of the same sex; homogeneous; homosexual
同性愛 **dōseiai** homosexuality
劣性 **ressei** inferior; recessive (gene)
有性 **yūsei** sexual (reproduction)
7 良性 **ryōsei** benign (tumor)
身性 **mijō** one's background; one's personal conduct

4

扌 月 日 火 礻 王 牛 方 攵 欠 心 5←
戸 戈

低性能 **teiseinō** low efficiency
冷性 **hi(e)shō** oversensitivity to cold
延性 **ensei** ductility
男性 **dansei** man, male; masculinity
男性美 **danseibi** masculine beauty
8 毒性 **dokusei** virulence, toxicity
剛性 **gōsei** rigidity, stiffness
逆性石鹸 **gyakusei sekken** antiseptic soap
油性 **yusei** oily, oleaginous
油性塗料 **yusei toryō** oil-based paint
知性 **chisei** intelligence, intellect
苛性 **kasei** caustic
定性分析 **teisei bunseki** qualitative analysis
物性 **bussei** physical properties
9 変性 **hensei** degenerate, denature
急性 **kyūsei** acute (not chronic)
急性病 **kyūseibyō** acute illness
通性 **tsūsei** common characteristic/property
活性 **kassei** active, activated
品性 **hinsei** character
荒性 **a(re)shō** chapped skin
単性 **tansei** unisexual
相性 **aishō** affinity, compatibility
神性 **shinsei** divine nature, godhood
恒性 **kōsei** constant, permanent
10 個性 **kosei** individuality, idiosyncrasy
個性的 **koseiteki** personal, individual
陰性 **insei** negative; dormant
高性能 **kōseinō** high-performance
真性 **shinsei** inborn nature
展性 **tensei** malleability
根性 **konjō** disposition, spirit, nature
根性骨 **konjōbone** spirit, disposition
脆性 **zeisei** brittleness
脂性 **aburashō** fatty
特性 **tokusei** distinctive quality, characteristic, trait
悟性 **gosei** wisdom, understanding
素性 **sujō** birth, lineage, identity
11 野性 **yasei** wild nature, uncouthness
野性味 **yaseimi** wildness, roughness
野性的 **yaseiteki** wild, rough
陽性 **yōsei** positive
習性 **shūsei** habit, way, peculiarity
乾性 **kansei** dry (pleurisy), xero-
理性 **risei** reason, reasoning power
理性的 **riseiteki** reasonable
悪性 **akusei** malignant, vicious, pernicious
　　 akushō evil nature; licentiousness
異性 **isei** the opposite sex
粘性 **nensei** viscosity
軟性下疳 **nansei gekan** soft chancre
12 善性 **zensei** innate goodness of human nature
湿性 **shissei** wet (pleurisy)
堪性 **kora(e)shō** patience
弾性 **dansei** elasticity

属性 **zokusei** attribute
無性 **musei** asexual **mushō** thoughtless; inordinate **bushō** lazy
惰性 **dasei** inertia
硬性 **kōsei** hardness
雄性 **yūsei** male
13 稟性 **rinsei, hinsei** nature, character
適性 **tekisei** aptitude, suitability
溶性 **yōsei** soluble
照性 **te(re)shō** bashful, easily embarrassed
感性 **kansei** sensitivity; the senses
資性 **shisei** nature, disposition
飽性 **a(ki)shō** fickleness, flightiness
14 厭性 **a(ki)shō** fickleness, flighty temperament
徳性 **tokusei** moral character
慢性 **mansei** chronic
慢性化 **manseika** become chronic
慣性 **kansei** inertia
磁性 **jisei** magnetism
酸性 **sansei** acidity
酸性白土 **sansei hakudo** acid/Kambara clay
酸性雨 **sanseiu** acid rain
雌性 **shisei** female
15 熱性 **nessei** enthusiastic, earnest
敵性 **tekisei** of enemy character, hostile
敵性国 **tekiseikoku** hostile country
敵性者 **tekiseisha** person of enemy character
霊性 **reisei** divine nature, spirituality
16 凝性 **ko(ri)shō** single-minded enthusiasm, fastidiousness
獣性 **jūsei** animal nature, bestiality
17 優性 **yūsei** dominant (gene)
癇性 **kanshō** irritability, irascibility
21 魔性 **mashō** diabolical

───── 3 ─────
1 一卵性双生児 **ichiransei sōseiji** identical twins
一過性 **ikkasei** transient, temporary
一般性 **ippansei** generality
2 人間性 **ningensei** human nature, humanity
3 大衆性 **taishūsei** popularity
4 不溶性 **fuyōsei** insoluble
不燃性 **funensei** nonflammable, incombustible
互換性 **gokansei** compatibility, interchangeability
内向性 **naikōsei** introverted
水溶性 **suiyōsei** water-soluble
引火性 **inkasei** flammability
心配性 **shinpaishō** worrying disposition
5 必然性 **hitsuzensei** inevitability, necessity
民族性 **minzokusei** racial/national trait
生産性 **seisansei** productivity
甲斐性 **kaishō** resourcefulness, competence

外向性 **gaikōsei** extroverted, outgoing
可分性 **kabunsei** divisibility
可能性 **kanōsei** possibility
可動性 **kadōsei** mobility
可溶性 **kayōsei** solubility
可撓性 **katōsei** flexible, flexibility
可燃性 **kanensei** combustible, flammable
可聴性 **kachōsei** audibility
可鍛性 **katansei** malleability
可鎔性 **kayōsei** fusibility
主体性 **shutaisei** subjectivity, independence
主観性 **shukansei** subjectivity
処女性 **shojosei** virginity
6 多孔性 **takōsei** porosity
多発性 **tahatsusei** multiple (sclerosis)
多様性 **tayōsei** diversity, variety
合理性 **gōrisei** rationality, reasonableness
合憲性 **gōkensei** constitutionality
危険性 **kikensei** riskiness, danger
先天性 **sentensei** congenital, hereditary
先在性 **senzaisei** priority
吸収性 **kyūshūsei** absorbency
向日性 **kōjitsusei, kōnichisei** heliotropic
共同性 **kyōdōsei** cooperation
安定性 **anteisei** stability
早発性痴呆症 **sōhatsusei chihōshō** schizo-
     phrenia
自発性 **jihatsusei** spontaneousness
7 伸縮性 **shinshukusei** elasticity
迫真性 **hakushinsei** true to life, realistic
妥当性 **datōsei** propriety, pertinence, validity
狂信性 **kyoshinsei** fanaticism
完全性 **kanzensei** completeness, perfection
社会性 **shakaisei** social nature
社交性 **shakōsei** sociability
8 免疫性 **men'ekisei** immunity (from a disease)
周期性 **shūkisei** periodic, cyclical
苦労性 **kurōshō** given to worrying
宗教性 **shūkyōsei** religious character
国民性 **kokuminsei** national character
肥厚性鼻炎 **hikōsei bien** hypertrophic rhinitis
放射性 **hōshasei** radioactive
金属性 **kinzokusei** metallic
9 発展性 **hattensei** growth potential
重要性 **jūyōsei** importance, gravity
信憑性 **sinpyōsei** credibility, authenticity
信頼性 **shinraisei** reliability
通有性 **tsūyūsei** common trait/characteristic
耐久性 **taikyūsei** durability
耐水性 **taisuisei** water resistance
耐火性 **taikasei** fire resistant
耐湿性 **taishitsusei** resistance to moisture
耐震性 **taishinsei** earthquake resistance,
     quakeproof
指向性 **shikōsei** directional (antenna)
独創性 **dokusōsei** originality, inventiveness

後天性 **kōtensei** acquired trait
後進性 **kōshinsei** backward
客観性 **kyakkansei, kakkansei** objectivity
相対性 **sōtaisei** relativity
柔軟性 **jūnansei** pliability, suppleness
恒久性 **kōkyūsei** permanence
10 残忍性 **zanninsei** cruelty, brutality
将来性 **shōraisei** future, possibilities,
     prospects
真実性 **shinjitsusei** truth, authenticity,
     credibility
流行性感冒 **ryūkōsei kanbō** influenza
消極性 **shōkyokusei** passive
梅毒性 **baidokusei** syphilitic
特有性 **tokuyūsei** peculiarity
特殊性 **tokushusei** peculiarity, characteristic
特異性 **tokuisei** singularity, peculiar
     characteristics
11 動物性 **dōbutsusei** animal (protein)
貧乏性 **binbōshō** destined to poverty
混和性 **konwasei** miscibility
現実性 **genjitsusei** actuality, reality
12 揮発性 **kihatsusei** volatility
弾力性 **danryokusei** elasticity, resilience,
     flexibility
植物性 **shokubutsusei** vegetable (oil)
順応性 **junnōsei** adaptability
13 適応性 **tekiōsei** adaptability, flexibility
溶解性 **yōkaisei** solubility
蓋然性 **gaizensei** probability
感受性 **kanjusei** sensibility, sensitivity
14 滲出性 **shinshutsusei** weeping/exudative
     (eczema)
導電性 **dōdensei** conductivity
15 潜伏性 **senpukusei** latent (disease)
撥水性 **hassuisei** water repellent/repellence
熱帯性 **nettaisei** tropical
16 親近性 **shinkinsei** familiarity
積極性 **sekkyokusei** positiveness
18 鎔解性 **yōkaisei** fusibility
19 爆発性 **bakuhatsusei** explosive (bullets)

──────── 4 ────────

3 下種根性 **gesu konjō** mean feelings
4 不可入性 **fukanyūsei** impenetrability
5 生分解性 **seibunkaisei** biodegradable
7 役人根性 **yakunin konjō** bureaucratism
10 島国根性 **shimaguni konjō** insularity

4k5.5

忄亍 **JUTSU, oso(reru)** fear
     izana(u) invite, entice

──────── 1 ────────

11 怵惕 **jutteki** fear

4k5.6 / 1814

怖
FU, kowa(i) frightening, scary
kowa(garu) fear, be afraid
kowa(gari) timidity, cowardice
o(jiru/jikeru) fear, be afraid
oso(reru) fear, be apprehensive

———————— 1 ————————

6 怖気 **o(ji)ke, ozoke** fear, timidity, nervousness
8 怖怖 **o(zu)o(zu), o(ji)o(ji)** timorously, nervously
17 怖臆 **o(mezu)-oku(sezu)** fearlessly, undaunted

———————— 2 ————————

2 人怖 **hitooji** (child's) fear of strangers
8 物怖 **monoo(ji)** timidity
怖怖 **o(zu)o(zu), o(ji)o(ji)** timorously, nervously
9 畏怖 **ifu** awe, fear, dread
10 恐怖 **kyōfu** fear, terror
恐怖心 **kyōfushin** feeling of terror
恐怖症 **kyōfushō** phobia, morbid fear
恐怖感 **kyōfukan** sense of fear

4k5.7

怕
HA fear, worry; possibly

4k5.8

怛
DATSU, TAN be sad/dejected; fear

4k5.9

怯
KYŌ fear, cowardice
obi(eru) become frightened, be scared
hiru(mu) flinch, wince, be daunted

———————— 1 ————————

17 怯懦 **kyōda** cowardly, timid

———————— 2 ————————

9 卑怯 **hikyō** cowardly; mean, foul, unfair
卑怯者 **hikyōmono** coward

4k5.10

怜
REI wise

———————— 1 ————————

10 怜悧 **reiri** wise, clever

4k5.11 / 1476

怪 恠
KAI, KE mystery; apparition
aya(shimu) doubt, be skeptical; marvel at, be surprised
aya(shii/shige) dubious, suspicious-looking; strange, mysterious   **ke(shikaran/shikaranu)** disgraceful, outrageous, shameful, rude

———————— 1 ————————

2 怪人物 **kaijinbutsu** mystery man
怪力 **kairiki** superhuman strength
4 怪文書 **kaibunsho** defamatory literature of unknown source
怪火 **kaika** fire of mysterious origin; foxfire
6 怪死 **kaishi** mysterious death
怪気 **aya(shi)ge** suspicious, questionable, shady; faltering
怪光 **kaikō** weird light, foxfire
7 怪我 **kega** injury, wound; accident, chance
怪我人 **keganin** injured person, the wounded
8 怪事 **kaiji** mystery, wonder, scandal
怪事件 **kaijiken** strange/mystery case
怪奇 **kaiki** mysterious, grotesque, eerie
怪奇小説 **kaiki shōsetsu** mystery/spooky story
怪物 **kaibutsu** monster, apparition; mystery man
11 怪異 **kaii** mysterious, grotesque; monster
怪盗 **kaitō** phantom thief
怪魚 **kaigyo** strange/monstrous fish
怪鳥 **kaichō** strange/ominous bird
12 怪腕 **kaiwan** remarkable ability
怪童 **kaidō** unusually big/strong boy
怪訝 **kegen** suspicious, dubious
13 怪傑 **kaiketsu** extraordinary man
怪漢 **kaikan** suspicious-looking person
14 怪暢 **kaichō** carefree feeling
怪説 **kaisetsu** strange rumor/theory
怪聞 **kaibun** strange rumor; scandal
15 怪談 **kaidan** ghost story
16 怪獣 **kaijū** monster

———————— 2 ————————

4 幻怪 **genkai** strange, mysterious
勿怪幸 **mokke (no) saiwa(i)** stroke of good luck
7 妖怪 **yōkai** ghost, apparition
8 奇怪 **kikai** strange, weird; outrageous
物怪 **mono(no)ke** specter, evil spirit

———————— 3 ————————

8 奇々怪々 **kiki-kaikai** very strange, fantastic

4k5.12

怙
KO depend/rely on; father

———————— 1 ————————

9 怙恃 **koji** depend/rely on; father and mother

4k5.13

恢 **kora(eru)** bear, stand, endure, put up with

4k5.14

怡 **I** rejoice, enjoy

4k5.15

怩 **JI** shame

—————— 2 ——————
7 忸怩 **jikuji(taru)** embarrassed, put to shame

4k5.16

恂 **KU** foolish; fear

4k5.17

怱 **SŌ** busy, in a hurry

—————— 1 ——————
3 怱々 **sōsō** hurry, flurry, rush; Yours in haste
6 怱忙 **sōbō** busy, in a hurry
8 怱卒 **sōsotsu** hurried, hasty, sudden

4k5.18

怎 **SHIN, ikade, nanzo** why, how

4k5.19 / 1596

怒 **DO, oko(ru), ika(ru)** become angry
ika(ri) anger, wrath

—————— 1 ——————
0 怒りっぽい **oko(rippoi)** touchy, snappish, irascible
3 怒上戸 **oko(ri) jōgo** one who gets angry when drunk
5 怒号 **dogō** angry roar
6 怒気 **doki** (fit of) anger
7 怒坊 **oko(rin)bō** quick-tempered/testy person
   怒声 **dosei** angry/excited voice
8 怒肩 **ika(ri)gata** square shoulders
14 怒鳴 **dona(ru)** shout at

怒髪天突 **dohatsu ten (o) tsu(ku)** be infuriated
17 怒濤 **dotō** raging billows, high seas

—————— 2 ——————
12 喜怒 **kido** joy and anger
   喜怒哀楽 **kidoairaku** joy-anger-sorrow-pleasure, emotions
15 憤怒 **fundo, funnu** anger, wrath, indignation
16 激怒 **gekido** rage, wrath, fury
17 嚇怒 **kakudo** fury, rage

4k5.20

怨 **EN, ON, ura(mu)** bear a grudge, resent, reproach
ura(meshii) reproachful, resentful, rueful

—————— 1 ——————
7 怨言 **engen, ura(mi)goto** grudge, grievance, reproach
8 怨念 **onnen** grudge, malice, hatred
9 怨恨 **enkon** grudge, enmity

—————— 2 ——————
5 旧怨 **kyūen** an old grudge
7 私怨 **shien** personal grudge
11 宿怨 **shukuen** long-standing resentment/grudge

恚 → **3b7.7**

急 → **2n7.2**

4k5.21 / 1297

怠 **TAI** laziness, neglect
okota(ru) neglect, be remiss in, default on   **nama(keru)** be idle/lazy, neglect

—————— 1 ——————
8 怠屈 **taikutsu** boredom, tedium
   怠者 **nama(ke)mono** idler, lazybones
12 怠惰 **taida** idleness, laziness, sloth
13 怠業 **taigyō** work stoppage, slow-down strike
14 怠慢 **taiman** negligence, dereliction, inattention

—————— 2 ——————
10 倦怠 **kentai** fatigue, weariness
   倦怠期 **kentaiki** period of weariness
   倦怠感 **kentaikan** fatigue
11 過怠 **katai** negligence, fault
   過怠金 **kataikin** fine for default
15 緩怠 **kantai** laxity, neglect (of duty/courtesy)
16 懈怠 **kaitai, ketai** lazy, negligent

木
月
日
火
ネ
王
牛
方
攵
欠
心 5 ←
戸
戈

4

───────── 6 ─────────

4k6.1

恤　JUTSU take pity, sympathize
megu(mu) show mercy to, give in
charity

───────── 1 ─────────

7 恤兵 **juppei** soldiers' relief

───────── 2 ─────────

11 救恤 **kyūjutsu** relief, aid

4k6.2 / 1755

恨　KON, ura(mu) bear a grudge, resent,
reproach　ura(meshii) reproachful,
resentful, rueful

───────── 1 ─────────

7 恨言 **ura(mi)goto** grudge, grievance,
reproach
8 恨事 **konji** regrettable/deplorable matter

───────── 2 ─────────

4 片恨 **kataura(mi)** one-sided grudge
6 多恨 **takon** many regrets, great discontent
7 私恨 **shikon** secret grudge
8 逆恨 **sakaura(mi)** requited resentment;
resentment based on a misunderstanding
9 怨恨 **enkon** grudge, enmity
悔恨 **kaikon** remorse, regret, contrition
12 痛恨 **tsūkon** great sorrow, bitterness
痛恨事 **tsūkonji** matter for deep regret
14 遺恨 **ikon** grudge, enmity, rancor

───────── 4 ─────────

6 多情多恨 **tajō-takon** taking everything to
heart

4k6.3

恢　恢　KAI wide, large

───────── 1 ─────────

3 恢々 **kaikai** broad, extensive
12 恢復 **kaifuku** recovery

4k6.4

悖　HAI, moto(ru) go against, be contrary to

───────── 1 ─────────

4 悖反 **haihan** run counter to, violate
7 悖戻 **hairei** disobey, be contrary to
14 悖徳 **haitoku** immorality

4k6.5 / 1275

恒　恆　KŌ always, constant, fixed
tsune (ni) always

───────── 1 ─────────

3 恒久 **kōkyū** permanence, perpetuity
恒久化 **kōkyūka** perpetuation
恒久的 **kōkyūteki** permanent
恒久性 **kōkyūsei** permanence
4 恒心 **kōshin** constancy, steadfastness
5 恒存 **kōzon** conservation (of energy)
8 恒例 **kōrei** established practice, custom
恒性 **kōsei** constant, permanent
9 恒星 **kōsei** fixed star
11 恒常 **kōjō** constancy
恒常的 **kōjōteki** constant
恒産 **kōsan** fixed/real property
13 恒数 **kōsū** a constant

4k6.6

恃　JI depend/rely on; mother

───────── 2 ─────────

8 怙恃 **koji** depend/rely on; father and mother
9 矜恃 **kyōji, kinji** dignity, pride

4k6.7

恍　KŌ forgetting oneself; indistinct

───────── 1 ─────────

11 恍惚 **kōkotsu** rapture, ecstasy, trance

4k6.8

恪　KAKU careful, meticulous

───────── 1 ─────────

12 恪勤 **kakkin, kakugon** working earnestly

4k6.9

恬　TEN composure, indifference

───────── 1 ─────────

12 恬然 **tenzen** coolly, nonchalantly

4k6.10

恰　KŌ, KA', ataka(mo) as if, just like

───────── 1 ─────────

5 恰好 **kakkō** shape, form, figure, appearance;
reasonable; approximately
12 恰幅 **kappuku** build, physique

─────── 2 ───────
4 不恰好 **bukakkō** unshapely, clumsy
6 年恰好 **toshi kakkō** approximate age

4k6.11

恊 **KYŌ** threaten

4k6.12 / 1733

悔 悔 **KAI, KE, ku(iru)** regret
ku(yamu) regret; mourn for, offer condolences
kuya(shii) vexatious, vexing

─────── 1 ───────
7 悔状 **ku(yami)jō** letter of condolence
悔改 **ku(i)arata(me)** repentance, penitence
悔言 **ku(yami)goto** words of condolence
8 悔泣 **ku(yashi)na(ki)** crying out of remorse
9 悔恨 **kaikon** remorse, regret, contrition
10 悔涙 **ku(yashi)namida** tears of vexation/regret
悔悟 **kaigo** remorse, repentance, penitence
悔紛 **ku(yashi)magi(re)** out of spite/chagrin

─────── 2 ───────
9 後悔 **kōkai** regret
20 懺悔 **zange, sange** repentance, contrition

恢 → 恢 4k6.3

4k6.13

恂 **JUN** sincere; fear; sudden; blinking

4k6.14

恟 **KYŌ** fear

4k6.15

恫 **DŌ** feel distressed; fear; threaten

─────── 1 ───────
11 恫喝 **dōkatsu** threaten, intimidate

4k6.16 / 1219

恵 恵 **KEI, E, megu(mu)** bless, bestow a favor

─────── 1 ───────
3 恵与 **keiyo** give, present, bestow
4 恵方 **ehō** lucky direction
恵方参 **ehōmai(ri)** New Year's visit to a shrine/temple which lies in a lucky direction
5 恵比須 **Ebisu** (a god of wealth)
恵比須顔 **ebisugao** smiling/beaming face
7 恵沢 **keitaku** favor, benefit
18 恵贈 **keizō** receive a gift

─────── 2 ───────
4 互恵 **gokei** reciprocity, mutual benefit
天恵 **tenkei** gift of nature, natural advantages
仁恵 **jinkei** graciousness, benevolence, mercy
8 知恵 **chie** knowledge, intelligence, wisdom
知恵者 **chiesha** man of wisdom/ideas
知恵袋 **chiebukuro** one's close advisers
知恵歯 **chieba** wisdom tooth
知恵熱 **chie-netsu** teething fever
知恵輪 **chie (no) wa** puzzle ring
10 特恵 **tokukei, tokkei** special favor, preferential
恩恵 **onkei** benefit, favor, grace
12 最恵国 **saikeikoku** most-favored nation
13 慈恵 **jikei** charity

─────── 3 ───────
2 入知恵 **i(re)jie** suggestion, hint
9 浅知恵 **asajie** shallow-witted
後知恵 **atojie** hindsight
11 遅知恵 **osojie** late-developing intelligence
悪知恵 **warujie** cunning, guile
13 猿知恵 **sarujie** shallow cleverness

4k6.17 / 1242

息 **SOKU** son; breath **iki** breath
iki(mu) strain, bear down (in defecating or giving birth)

─────── 1 ───────
2 息子 **musuko** son
3 息女 **sokujo** daughter
4 息切 **ikigi(re)** shortness of breath
6 息休 **kyūsoku** a rest, breather
7 息抜 **ikinu(ki)** vent; rest, break, breather
息吹 **ibu(ki)** breath
息災 **sokusai** safety, safe and sound
8 息苦 **ikiguru(shii)** stifling, suffocating, stuffy
9 息巻 **ikima(ku)** be in a rage, fume
息急切 **ikise(ki)ki(ru)** pant, gasp
息臭 **ikikusa(i)** having a foul breath
10 息根 **iki(no)ne** life
11 息張 **ikiba(ru)** strain, bear down (in defecating or giving birth)
12 息遣 **ikizuka(i)** breathing
13 息継 **ikitsu(gi)** breathing spell, rest
息詰 **ikizu(maru)** be stifled, gasp

14 息緒 **iki(no)o** life

——————— 2 ———————

1 一息 **hitoiki** a breath; a pause/break; (a little more) effort
2 子息 **shisoku** son
3 大息 **taisoku** sigh
5 生息 **seisoku** live, multiply, inhabit
生息子 **kimusuko** unsophisticated young man
令息 **reisoku** your son
6 気息 **kisoku** breathing
気息奄々 **kisoku-en'en** gasping for breath, dying
休息 **kyūsoku** rest
休息所 **kyūsokujo** resting room, lounge
吐息 **toiki** sigh
安息 **ansoku** rest, repose
安息日 **ansokubi** sabbath
　　　 ansokunichi the (Jewish) sabbath
　　　 ansokujitsu the (Christian) sabbath
安息所 **ansokujo** resting place, haven
安息香 **ansokukō** benzoin
安息酸 **ansokusan** benzoic acid
虫息 **mushi (no) iki** faint breathing, almost dead
7 利息 **risoku** interest (on a loan)
8 姑息 **kosoku** makeshift, stopgap
青息 **aoiki** an anxious sigh
青息吐息 **aoiki-toiki** in dire distress
10 消息 **shōsoku** news, hearing from (someone)
消息子 **shōsokushi** (surgical) probe
消息文 **shōsokubun** personal letter
消息通 **shōsokutsū** well informed person
消息筋 **shōsokusuji** well informed sources
脇息 **kyōsoku** armrest
11 窒息 **chissoku** suffocation, asphyxiation
窒息死 **chissokushi** death from suffocation/asphyxiation
終息 **shūsoku** cessation, eradication
12 喘息 **zensoku** asthma
棲息 **seisoku** live in, inhabit
棲息地 **seisokuchi** habitat
絶息 **zessoku** breathe one's last, expire
13 溜息 **ta(me)iki** sigh
嘆息 **tansoku** sigh; lament
寝息 **neiki** breathing of a sleeping person
愛息 **aisoku** beloved son
愚息 **gusoku** my (foolish) son
14 歎息 **tansoku** sigh, lament
鼻息 **hanaiki, bisoku** breathing through the nose; one's pleasure

——————— 3 ———————

1 一人息子 **hitori musuko** an only son
一病息災 **ichibyō-sokusai** One who has an illness is careful of his health and lives long.

8 長大息 **chōtaisoku** a long sigh
放蕩息子 **hōtō musuko** prodigal son
11 道楽息子 **dōraku musuko** prodigal son
12 無利息 **murisoku** non-interest-bearing
無病息災 **mubyō-sokusai** in perfect health

——————— 4 ———————

8 青息吐息 **aoiki-toiki** in dire distress

4k6.18

恕 **JO** magnanimity, tolerance; considerateness, sympathy

——————— 2 ———————

13 寛恕 **kanjo** magnanimity; forgiveness, pardon

4k6.19 / 1602

恐 恐 **KYŌ, oso(reru)** fear, be afraid **oso(re)** fear, danger, risk of **oso(roshii)** terrible, frightful, awful **oso(raku)** perhaps **kowa(i)** frightening, scary

——————— 1 ———————

0 恐れながら **oso(renagara)** most humbly/respectfully
2 恐入 **oso(re)i(ru)** be overwhelmed (with gratitude/shame), be astonished, be sorry to trouble, beg pardon; be defeated, yield; plead guilty
3 恐々 **kyōkyō** respect (in letters)
　　　 kowagowa timidly
4 恐水病 **kyōsuibyō** hydrophobia, rabies
5 恐乍 **oso(re)naga(ra)** most humbly/respectfully
6 恐多 **oso(re)ō(i)** gracious, august
8 恐妻家 **kyōsaika** henpecked husband
恐怖 **kyōfu** fear, terror
恐怖心 **kyōfushin** feeling of terror
恐怖症 **kyōfushō** phobia, morbid fear
恐怖感 **kyōfukan** sense of fear
10 恐恐 **kyōkyō** respect (in letters)
　　　 oso(ru)oso(ru) fearfully, gingerly, respectfully **kowagowa** timidly
恐悦 **kyōetsu** delight, joy, pleasure
恐竜 **kyōryū** dinosaur
11 恐喝 **kyōkatsu** threat, intimidation, blackmail
恐喝罪 **kyōkatsuzai** extortion, blackmail
12 恐慌 **kyōkō** panic
16 恐龍 **kyōryū** dinosaur
17 恐縮 **kyōshuku** be very grateful/sorry

——————— 2 ———————

3 大恐慌 **daikyōkō** great panic
8 空恐 **soraoso(roshii)** having vague fears
物恐 **monoosoro(shii)** frightening, horrible

10 恐恐 **kyōkyō** respect (in letters)
oso(ru)oso(ru) fearfully, gingerly, respectfully   **kowagowa** timidly

———————— 3 ————————

13 戦々恐々 **sensen-kyōkyō** with fear and trembling; with trepidation

4k6.20

恍

KYŪ be contrary to

4k6.21

恁

IN, JIN like this, thus

4k6.22

恣

SHI, hoshiimama as one pleases, self-indulgent, arbitrary

———————— 1 ————————

13 恣意 **shii** arbitrariness, selfishness
恣意的 **shiiteki** arbitrary, selfish

———————— 2 ————————

8 放恣 **hōshi** self-indulgent, licentious

恚 → **3b7.7**

恙 → **2o8.3**

4k6.23 / 555

恩

ON kindness, goodness, favor

———————— 1 ————————

2 恩人 **onjin** benefactor, patron
6 恩返 **ongae(shi)** repayment of a favor
7 恩沢 **ontaku** favors, benefits
8 恩命 **onmei** gracious words/command
恩典 **onten** favor, privilege, grace
恩知 **onshi(razu)** ingratitude; ingrate
9 恩威 **on'i** stern but kindly
10 恩師 **onshi** one's honored teacher
恩恵 **onkei** benefit, favor, grace
11 恩赦 **onsha** amnesty, general pardon
恩情 **onjō** compassion, affection
12 恩給 **onkyū** pension
13 恩義 **ongi** favor, debt of gratitude
恩愛 **on'ai** kindness and love, affection

14 恩徳 **ontoku** favor, mercy, grace
15 恩賞 **onshō** a reward
恩賜 **onshi** gift from the emperor
18 恩顔 **ongan** kindly look, gentle face
21 恩顧 **onko** favors, patronage
23 恩讐 **onshū** love and hate

———————— 2 ————————

3 大恩 **daion, taion** great debt of gratitude
4 天恩 **ten'on** benevolence of the emperor; the grace of heaven
5 旧恩 **kyūon** old favors, past kindness
7 忘恩 **bōon** ingratitude
8 厚恩 **kōon** great kindness/favor
国恩 **kokuon** one's debt to one's country
9 皇恩 **kōon** imperial favor
10 殊恩 **shuon** special favor
高恩 **kōon** great benevolence/blessings
12 報恩 **hōon** repaying a kindness, gratitude
朝恩 **chōon** the sovereign's favor
13 聖恩 **seion** imperial favor
感恩 **kan'on** gratitude
17 鴻恩 **kōon** great benevolence/blessings
謝恩 **shaon** gratitude
謝恩会 **shaonkai** thank-you party, testimonial dinner

恭 → **3k7.16**

———————— 7 ————————

4k7.1

悚

SHŌ fear, horror

———————— 1 ————————

12 悚然 **shōzen** in horror, with a shudder

4k7.2

俐 俐

RI clever

———————— 2 ————————

8 怜俐 **reiri** wise, clever

4k7.3

悸

KI pulsate; tremble

———————— 2 ————————

4 心悸亢進 **shinki kōshin** palpitations
心悸昂進 **shinki kōshin** palpitations
11 動悸 **dōki** palpitation, throbbing (of the heart)

4k7.4

悍 **KAN** strong, violent, rough, spirited

─────── 1 ───────
10 悍馬 **kanba** unruly/mettlesome horse

─────── 2 ───────
13 剽悍 **hyōkan** fierce; daring
14 慓悍 **hyōkan** quick and strong, fierce
　精悍 **seikan** intrepid, dauntless

4k7.5 / 1438

悟 **GO, sato(ru)** perceive, understand, realize, be enlightened
sato(ri) comprehension, understanding; satori, spiritual awakening

─────── 1 ───────
2 悟入 **gonyū** attain (Buddhist) enlightenment
8 悟性 **gosei** wisdom, understanding
11 悟道 **godō** spiritual enlightenment

─────── 2 ───────
3 大悟 **taigo, daigo** great wisdom; (Buddhist) enlightenment
7 改悟 **kaigo** repentance, remorse, contrition
9 悔悟 **kaigo** remorse, repentance, penitence
12 覚悟 **kakugo** be prepared/resolved/resigned to
16 頴悟 **eigo** bright, intelligent

4k7.6

悋 **RIN, yabusa(ka)** stingy, stinting, begrudging
neta(mu) be jealous, envy

─────── 1 ───────
6 悋気 **rinki** jealousy, envy
11 悋惜 **rinseki** begrudging, a poor loser
13 悋嗇家 **rinshokuka** miser, skinflint

4k7.7

悛 **SHUN** amend, reform

─────── 2 ───────
7 改悛 **kaishun** repentance, penitence

4k7.8

悁 **EN** anger; worry　**KEN** impatience

4k7.9

悒 **YŪ** feel depressed

4k7.10

悄 **SHŌ** anxiety; quiet

─────── 1 ───────
3 悄々 **shōshō** anxious, worried; quiet
12 悄然 **shōzen** dejected, dispirited

4k7.11 / 1279

悩 悩 **NŌ, naya(mu)** be troubled/distressed, suffer
naya(masu) afflict, beset, worry

─────── 1 ───────
10 悩殺 **nōsatsu** enchant, captivate

─────── 2 ───────
5 立悩 **ta(chi)naya(mu)** hesitate, come to a standstill, be held up
6 行悩 **yu(ki)naya(mu)** be deadlocked, be at a standstill
7 伸悩 **no(bi)naya(mu)** be sluggish, stagnate, level off, mark time
8 苦悩 **kunō** suffering, agony, distress
9 思悩 **omo(i)naya(mu)** worry, agonize, be perplexed
13 煩悩 **bonnō** evil passions, carnal desires
16 懊悩 **ōnō** anguish, worry, trouble

─────── 3 ───────
2 子煩悩 **kobonnō** fond of one's children

4k7.12

惇 **SHUN, TON, atsu(i)** kind, considerate

4k7.13

悗 **BAN, MAN** be perplexed

4k7.14

悌 **TEI** deferring to one's elders

4k7.15 / 1368

悦 悦 **ETSU** joy
yoroko(bu) rejoice, be glad

─────── 1 ───────
8 悦服 **eppuku** willing submission
13 悦楽 **etsuraku** joy, pleasure, gaiety

─────── 2 ───────
8 法悦 **hōetsu** religious exultation; ecstasy

4

木
月
日
火
ネ
王
牛
方
攵
→7 心
戸
戈

10 恐悦 **kyōetsu** delight, joy, pleasure
12 満悦 **man'etsu** delight, rapture
　 喜悦 **kietsu** joy, delight
　 愉悦 **yuetsu** joy

悔 → 悔 **4k6.12**

4k7.16

悃 **KON** sincerity, honesty

4k7.17 / 304

悪　悪 **AKU** evil, vice　**waru(i)** bad　**a(shikarazu)** without taking offense　**-niku(i)** difficult, hard to …

──────── 1 ────────

0 悪たれ **aku(tare)** mischievous boy; verbal abuse
　 悪びれる **waru(bireru)** be timid/fazed
2 悪人 **akunin** evildoer, scoundrel, the wicked
3 悪口 **warukuchi, aku(tare)guchi, akkō** verbal abuse, speaking ill/evil of
　 悪口雑言 **akkō-zōgon** vituperation
　 悪女 **akujo** wicked/ugly woman
4 悪太郎 **akutarō** bad/naughty boy
　 悪天候 **akutenkō** bad weather
　 悪化 **akka** worsening, deterioration
　 悪友 **akuyū** bad companion(s)
　 悪文 **akubun** poor writing style
　 悪日 **akunichi, akubi** unlucky day
　 悪心 **akushin** evil intent, sinister motive
5 悪巧 **warudaku(mi)** wiles, scheme, plot, machinations
　 悪用 **akuyō** misuse, abuse, perversion
　 悪玉 **akudama** bad guy, the villain
6 悪気 **warugi** evil intent, malice, ill will
　 悪舌 **akuzetsu** evil tongue, gossip
　 悪名 **akumei, akumyō** ill repute, notoriety
　 悪行 **akugyō, akkō** evildoing, wickedness
　 悪因悪果 **akuin-akka** Evil breeds evil.
　 悪血 **akuchi, oketsu** impure blood
7 悪巫山戯 **warufuzake** prank, practical joke
　 悪阻 **tsuwari, oso** morning sickness
　 悪投 **akutō** bad/wild throw
　 悪役 **akuyaku** the villain('s role)
　 悪声 **akusei** bad voice/reputation
　 悪条件 **akujōken** unfavorable conditions, handicap
　 悪足搔 **waruaga(ki)** useless struggling/resistance
8 悪事 **akuji** evil deed

悪例 **akurei** bad example/precedent
悪念 **akunen** evil thought
悪逆 **akugyaku** heinous, treacherous
悪法 **akuhō** bad law
悪知恵 **warujie** cunning, guile
悪妻 **akusai** bad wife
悪者 **warumono** bad fellow, scoundrel
悪性 **akusei** malignant, vicious, pernicious
　　　 akushō evil nature; licentiousness
悪所 **akusho** dangerous place; brothel
9 悪風 **akufū** bad custom, a vice
　 悪相 **akusō** evil face/look
　 悪政 **akusei** misrule
　 悪臭 **akushū** offensive odor, stench
　 悪疫 **akueki** plague, pestilence, epidemic
　 悪計 **akkei, akukei** evil scheme, plot, trick
　 悪食 **akushoku, akujiki** eat repulsive things
10 悪遊 **waruaso(bi)** prank; evil pleasures
　 悪酒 **akushu** cheap/rotgut liquor
　 悪酒落 **warujare** joke in bad taste
　 悪党 **akutō** scoundrel, blackguard
　 悪鬼 **akki** demon, evil spirit
　 悪疾 **akushitsu** malignant/virulent disease
11 悪運 **aku'un** evildoer's good luck; bad luck
　 悪道 **akudō** evil/wrong course
　 悪習 **akushū** bad habit, vice
　 悪習慣 **akushūkan** bad habit, evil practice
　 悪貨 **akka** bad money
　 悪酔 **waruyo(i)** drink oneself sick; become unpleasant when drunk
12 悪循環 **akujunkan** vicious cycle/spiral
　 悪寒 **okan** a chill with a fever
　 悪童 **akudō** naughty boy
　 悪税 **akuzei** unreasonable tax
　 悪筆 **akuhitsu** poor handwriting
　 悪評 **akuhyō** bad reputation; unfavorable criticism
13 悪業 **akugyō** evil, wickedness
　　　 akugō evil karma
　 悪僧 **akusō** dissolute priest
　 悪漢 **akkan** scoundrel, crook, ruffian, knave
　 悪夢 **akumu** nightmare, disturbing dream
　 悪感 **akkan** unpleasant feeling
　　　 okan a chill with a fever
　 悪感情 **akukanjō, akkanjō** ill will, animosity, unfavorable impression
　 悪戦 **akusen** hard-fought battle
　 悪戦苦闘 **akusen-kutō** fight desperately
　 悪意 **akui** evil intent, malice, ill will
　 悪路 **akuro** bad/dirt road
14 悪徳 **akutoku** vice, corruption, immorality
　 悪徳新聞 **akutoku shinbun** irresponsible/sensationalist newspaper
　 悪態 **akutai** foul language, cusswords
　 悪辣 **akuratsu** unscrupulous, wily
　 悪銭 **akusen** ill-gotten money

4

木
月
日
火
礻
王
牛
方
攵
欠
心 7←
戸
戈

15 悪熱 **onetsu** fever following a chill
悪弊 **akuhei** an evil, vice, abuse
悪戯 **akugi, itazura** prank, mischief
悪罵 **akuba** vilification, abuse
悪縁 **akuen** evil fate; unfortunate love
悪質 **akushitsu** evil, vicious, unscrupulous;
of poor quality
悪霊 **akuryō, akurei** evil spirit
16 悪賢 **warugashiko(i)** cunning, sly, crafty, wily
17 悪擦 **waruzu(re)** oversophistication
18 悪癖 **akuheki, waruguse** bad habit, vice
21 悪魔 **akuma** devil
悪魔払 **akumabara(i)** exorcism

─────── 2 ───────

3 大悪人 **daiakunin** utter scoundrel
口悪 **kuchi (no) waru(i)** evil-mouthed,
scurrilous
小悪 **shōaku** minor offense; venial sin
4 凶悪 **kyōaku** heinous, brutal, fiendish
水悪戯 **mizu itazura** playing with/in water
5 好悪 **kōo** likes and dislikes
旧悪 **kyūaku** one's past misdeeds
6 色悪 **iroaku** handsome villain
奸悪 **kan'aku** wicked, treacherous
劣悪 **retsuaku** inferior, coarse
7 邪悪 **jaaku** wicked, malicious, sinister
改悪 **kaiaku** change for the worse, deterioration
8 毒悪 **dokuaku** great wickedness
拙悪 **setsuaku** clumsy, fumbling
性悪 **seiaku, shōwaru** evil nature
性悪説 **seiakusetsu** the view that human
nature is basically evil
9 俗悪 **zokuaku** vulgar, coarse
姦悪 **kan'aku** wicked, treacherous
10 険悪 **ken'aku** dangerous, threatening, serious
猛悪 **mōaku** savage, ferocious
害悪 **gaiaku** an evil (influence), harm
11 偽悪 **giaku** pretending to be evil
強悪 **gōaku** great wickedness, villany
宿悪 **shukuaku** old evils/crimes
粗悪 **soaku** coarse, crude, inferior
粗悪品 **soakuhin** inferior goods
12 善悪 **zen'aku** good and evil
yo(shi)waru(shi), yo(shi)a(shi) good
and bad, good or bad
yo(kare)a(shikare) right or wrong, for
better or worse
極悪 **gokuaku** heinous
ki(mari)waru(i) awkward, embarrassed
極悪人 **gokuakunin** utter scoundrel
最悪 **saiaku** worst
13 嫌悪 **ken'o** hatred, dislike, loathing
嫌悪感 **ken'okan** hatred, dislike, loathing
罪悪 **zaiaku** crime, sin, vice

罪悪感 **zaiakukan** guilty conscience
14 厭悪 **en'o** dislike, detest, abhor
憎悪 **zōo** hatred, abhorrence
憎悪心 **zōoshin** hatred, malice
聞悪 **ki(ki)niku(i)** hard to hear; awkward to
ask
15 暴悪 **bōaku** violence, tyranny, savagery
16 積悪 **sekiaku** accumulated sin, series of
crimes
17 醜悪 **shūaku** ugly, abominable, scandalous
18 懲悪 **chōaku** punishment of evil
21 露悪 **roaku** boasting of one's wickedness

─────── 3 ───────

5 必要悪 **hitsuyōaku** a necessary evil
6 気味悪 **kimi (no) waru(i)** eerie, ominous,
weird
7 社会悪 **shakaiaku** social evils
11 悪因悪果 **akuin-akka** Evil breeds evil.
13 意地悪 **ijiwaru(i)** ill-tempered, crabby

─────── 4 ───────

8 往生際悪 **ōjōgiwa (ga) waru(i)** accept
defeat with bad grace
底気味悪 **sokokimi waru(i)** eerie, ominous
底意地悪 **sokoiji waru(i)** spiteful,
malcontented, cranky
13 勧善懲悪 **kanzen-chōaku** rewarding good
and punishing evil, didactic/morality
(play)
16 薄気味悪 **usukimiwaru(i)** weird, eerie

4k7.18 / 1315

患

KAN, wazura(u) be ill, suffer from

─────── 1 ───────

8 患者 **kanja** a patient
10 患部 **kanbu** diseased part, the affected area

─────── 2 ───────

3 大患 **taikan** serious illness; great cares
4 内患 **naikan** internal/domestic trouble
5 外患 **gaikan** foreign/external troubles
8 長患 **nagawazura(i)** a long/protracted illness
国患 **kokkan** national disaster
9 重患 **jūkan** serious illness
急患 **kyūkan** emergency patient/case
通患 **tsūkan** a common misgiving; a common
evil
後患 **kōkan** future trouble
肺患 **haikan** lung ailment
10 病患 **byōkan, ya(mi)wazura(i)** sickness
疾患 **shikkan** disease, ailment
11 宿患 **shukukan, shukkan** chronic illness;
long-standing grief
13 禍患 **kakan** disaster, calamity; an evil

新患者 **shinkanja** new patient
15 憂患 **yūkan** sorrow, distress, cares

———— 3 ————

5 外来患者 **gairai kanja** outpatient

4k7.19

悉

SHITSU, tsu(kusu) exhaust, include everything
kotogoto(ku) all, completely

———— 2 ————

8 知悉 **chishitsu** have full knowledge of

4k7.20 / 1597

悠

YŪ distant; leisure

———— 1 ————

3 悠久 **yūkyū** eternity, perpetuity
悠々 **yūyū** calm, composed, leisurely
8 悠長 **yūchō** leisurely, slow, easygoing
12 悠遠 **yūen** remoteness; eternity; repose
悠揚 **yūyō** composed, calm, serene
悠然 **yūzen** calm, with perfect composure

———— 8 ————

4k8.1

惟

I, omonmi(ru) ponder, reflect on
omo(u) think over

———— 1 ————

9 惟神道 **kannagara (no) michi** Shintoism

4k8.2

悵

CHŌ be sad/disappointed

———— 1 ————

12 悵然 **chōzen** sad, sorrowful

4k8.3

惧 懼

KU fear, danger, risk
oso(reru) fear, be apprehensive

———— 2 ————

6 危惧 **kigu** fear, misgivings, apprehension

4k8.4

倦

KEN be respectful
u(mu) grow tired

4k8.5 / 1725

惨 慘

SAN, ZAN, miji(me) piteous, wretched, miserable
mugo(i) cruel, harsh

———— 1 ————

6 惨死 **zanshi** tragic/violent death
惨死体 **zanshitai** mangled corpse
惨死者 **zanshisha** mangled corpse
7 惨状 **sanjō** miserable state, disastrous scene
8 惨事 **sanji** disaster, tragic accident
10 惨害 **sangai** heavy damage, devastation
惨殺 **zansatsu** murder, massacre, slaughter
惨殺者 **zansatsusha** murderer, slayer
11 惨敗 **zanpai** crushing defeat
12 惨落 **sanraku** slump, sudden fall
惨絶 **sanzetsu** brutal
13 惨禍 **sanka** terrible disaster, catastrophe
15 惨劇 **sangeki** tragedy, tragic event
16 惨澹 **santan(taru)** piteous, wretched, horrible

———— 2 ————

10 凄惨 **seisan** ghastly, gruesome, lurid
陰惨 **insan** dreary, dismal, gloomy
12 悲惨 **hisan** tragic, wretched, pitiable

4k8.6

悽

SEI, ita(mu) be sad/sorrowful

———— 1 ————

13 悽愴 **seisō** desolate, dreary

4k8.7

悾

KŌ sincerity

4k8.8

惕

TEKI fear

———— 2 ————

8 怵惕 **jutteki** fear

4k8.9 / 209

情 情

JŌ, SEI feelings, emotion; circumstances
nasa(ke) sympathy, compassion

———— 1 ————

2 情人 **jōjin** lover, sweetheart
4 情夫 **jōfu** lover, paramour
情火 **jōka** the flame of love
情心 **nasa(ke)gokoro** sympathy, compassion
5 情史 **jōshi** love story

4

木
月
日
火
礻
王
牛
方
攵
欠
心 8←
戸
戈

4

木 月 日 火 礻 王 牛 方 攵 欠 心 戸 戈

→ 8

6 情死 **jōshi** lovers' double suicide
情交 **jōkō** intimacy
7 情状 **jōjō** circumstances, conditions
8 情事 **jōji** love affair
情念 **jōnen** sentiment, passions
情況 **jōkyō** circumstances, state of affairs
情況証拠 **jōkyō shōko** circumstantial
    evidence
情味 **jōmi** charm, attraction; warmheartedness
情実 **jōjitsu** personal circumstances/consider-
    ations
11 情深 **nasa(ke)buka(i)** compassionate,
    kindhearted
情婦 **jōfu** lover, mistress
情理 **jōri** heart and mind, emotion and reason
情欲 **jōyoku** passions, sexual desire
12 情報 **jōhō** information
情報化社会 **jōhōka shakai** information-
    oriented society
情報屋 **jōhōya** (horserace) tipster
情報部 **jōhōbu** information bureau
情報源 **jōhōgen** news/information sources
情報網 **jōhōmō** intelligence network
情景 **jōkei** scene; nature and sentiment
情無 **nasa(ke)na(i)** unfeeling, cruel; pitiful,
    miserable
13 情勢 **jōsei** situation, condition, circumstances
情愛 **jōai** affection, love
情感 **jōkan** emotion, sentiment
情意 **jōi** emotion and will; sentiment
情意投合 **jōi-tōgō** mutual sentiment/
    understanding
情痴 **jōchi** love foolery
情話 **jōwa** lover's talk; love story
14 情歌 **jōka** love song
情緒 **jōcho** emotion, feelings
15 情熱 **jōnetsu** passion, enthusiasm
情弊 **jōhei** favoritism
情趣 **jōshu** mood, sentiment; artistic effect
情誼 **jōgi** friendship, fellowship
情調 **jōchō** atmosphere, mood, tone, spirit
16 情操 **jōsō** sentiment

—————— 2 ——————

2 人情 **ninjō** human feelings, humanity,
    kindness
人情味 **ninjōmi** human interest, kindness
3 下情 **kajō** conditions of the common people
4 内情 **naijō** internal conditions; true state of
    affairs
友情 **yūjō** friendship, fellowship
心情 **shinjō** one's heart/feelings
5 民情 **minjō** the people's situation
世情 **sejō** world conditions; human nature
主情的 **shujōteki** emotional, emotive
6 多情 **tajō** inconstant, wanton, flirty; senti-
    mentalism

多情仏心 **tajō-busshin** tenderheartedness
多情多恨 **tajō-takon** taking everything to
    heart
多情多感 **tajō-takan** emotional, sentimental
肉情 **nikujō** carnal desire
色情 **shikijō** sexual desire, lust
色情狂 **shikijōkyō** sex mania
近情 **kinjō** recent conditions, present state
同情 **dōjō** sympathy
至情 **shijō** sincerity
劣情 **retsujō** low passions, lust
有情 **ujō** sentient being/life
7 余情 **yojō** suggestiveness, lingering charm
抒情 **jojō** expression of one's feelings,
    lyricism
抒情的 **jojōteki** lyrical
抒情詩 **jojōshi** lyric poem/poetry
芳情 **hōjō** your kindness
私情 **shijō** personal feelings, bias
8 非情 **hijō** inanimate; unfeeling
表情 **hyōjō** (facial) expression
事情 **jijō** circumstances, reasons
直情 **chokujō** straightforward, impulsive
直情径行 **chokujō keikō** straightforward,
    impulsive
厚情 **kōjō** kindness, good wishes, hospitality
苦情 **kujō** complaint, grievance
実情 **jitsujō** actual state of affairs
国情 **kokujō** the conditions in a country
物情 **butsujō** public feeling
性情 **seijō** temperament, character, nature
9 発情 **hatsujō** sexual arousal, (in) heat
発情期 **hatsujōki** puberty; mating season
衷情 **chūjō** one's inmost feelings
俗情 **zokujō** mundane affairs; worldly-
    mindedness
叙情 **jojō** description of feelings, lyricism
叙情詩 **jojōshi** lyric poem/poetry
哀情 **aijō** sadness
風情 **fuzei** taste, appearance, air; elegance;
    entertainment, hospitality
春情 **shunjō** sexual passion
政情 **seijō** political situation
10 陳情 **chinjō** petition, appeal, lobbying
陳情書 **chinjōsho** petition, representation
恋情 **renjō** love, affection
    koinasake lovesickness
真情 **shinjō** one's feelings/heart
党情 **tōjō** the party's situation
旅情 **ryojō** one's mood while traveling
恩情 **onjō** compassion, affection
扇情 **senjō** inflammatory
扇情的 **senjōteki** sensational, suggestive,
    racy
純情 **junjō** pure-minded emotion, naïveté,
    devotion

11 深情 **fukanasa(ke)** inordinate show of
affection
強情 **gōjō** stubbornness, obstinacy
欲情 **yokujō** passions, desires
12 温情 **onjō** warm, cordial, kindly
温情主義 **onjō shugi** paternalism
無情 **mujō** unfeeling, callous, cruel
13 愛情 **aijō** love, affection
感情 **kanjō** feelings, emotion
感情的 **kanjōteki** emotional, sentimental
痴情 **chijō** blind love, passion, infatuation
詩情 **shijō** poetic sentiment
14 慕情 **bojō** longing, love, affection
煽情 **senjō** suggestive, lascivious
煽情的 **senjōteki** suggestive, sensational
15 熱情 **netsujō** fervor, ardor, passion
敵情 **tekijō** the enemy's movements
16 激情 **gekijō** violent emotion, passion
薄情 **hakujō** unfeeling, heartless, coldhearted
17 懇情 **konjō** kindliness, warm friendship

——— 3 ———
4 不人情 **funinjō** unfeeling, callous
8 非人情 **hininjō** inhuman, unfeeling
11 悪感情 **akukanjō, akkanjō** ill will, animosity, unfavorable impression
12 無表情 **muhyōjō** expressionless
惻隠情 **sokuin (no) jō** pity, compassion
13 詩的情緒 **shiteki jōcho** poetic mood

——— 4 ———
9 海外事情 **kaigai jijō** foreign news
13 義理人情 **giri-ninjō** duty versus/and human feelings

4k8.10

惚 KOTSU, **ho(reru)** fall in love with
bo(keru) become dull-witted/senile; be out of focus, fade

——— 1 ———
4 惚込 **ho(re)ko(mu)** fall in love, be charmed
6 惚気 **noroke(ru)** speak fondly of one's beloved
11 惚惚 **ho(re)bo(re)** fondly, enchanted
16 惚薬 **ho(re)gusuri** love potion

——— 2 ———
6 自惚 **unubo(reru)** be conceited
7 見惚 **mito(reru), miho(reru)** gaze on in rapture, be fascinated/charmed by
8 空惚 **soratobo(keru)** pretend not to know
9 待惚 **ma(chi)bō(ke)** getting stood up
恍惚 **kōkotsu** rapture, ecstasy, trance
11 惚惚 **ho(re)bo(re)** fondly, enchanted
13 寝惚 **nebo(keru)** be half asleep
14 聞惚 **ki(ki)ho(reru)** listen to with rapt attention

——— 3 ———
1 一目惚 **hitomebo(re)** love at first sight

4k8.11 / 765

惜 SEKI, **o(shii)** regrettable; precious; wasteful **o(shimu)** regret; value; begrudge, be sparing of, be reluctant to part with

——— 1 ———
6 惜気 **o(shi)ge** regret
7 惜別 **sekibetsu** reluctant parting
11 惜敗 **sekihai** narrow defeat

——— 2 ———
3 口惜 **kuchio(shii)** regrettable, mortifying
7 売惜 **u(ri)o(shimu)** be indisposed to sell, hold back, restrict sales
8 物惜 **monoo(shimi)** be stingy
9 哀惜 **aiseki** grief, sorrow
負惜 **ma(ke)o(shimi)** unwillingness to admit defeat
10 残惜 **noko(ri)o(shii)** regrettable, reluctant
骨惜 **honeo(shimi)** avoid effort, spare oneself
悋惜 **rinseki** begrudging, a poor loser
12 痛惜 **tsūseki** great sorrow, deep regret
13 愛惜 **aiseki** grieve for, miss

——— 3 ———
1 一文惜 **ichimon'oshi(mi)** stinginess; miser
6 名残惜 **nago(ri)o(shii)** reluctant to part

悳 → 徳 3i11.3

4k8.12

悴 忰 SUI become emaciated
segare (my) son

——— 2 ———
15 憔悴 **shōsui** become emaciated/haggard

4k8.13 / 1680

悼 TŌ, **ita(mu)** grieve over, mourn

——— 1 ———
13 悼辞 **tōji** message of condolence, funeral address

——— 2 ———
8 追悼 **tsuitō** mourning; memorial (address)
追悼会 **tsuitōkai** memorial services
追悼歌 **tsuitōka** dirge
9 哀悼 **aitō** condolence, sympathy, mourning

4 | 木 月 日 火 礻 王 牛 方 攵 欠 心 戸 戈 | 8←

4k8.14

惆   CHŪ grieve over; be disappointed

4k8.15

惘   BŌ unclear
     aki(reru) be astonished, be taken aback

惠 → 恵 4k6.16

4k8.16 / 969

惑   WAKU, mado(u) go astray, be misguided/tempted

——————— 1 ———————
- 7 惑乱 **wakuran** bewilderment, confusion
- 9 惑星 **wakusei** planet
- 惑星間 **wakuseikan** interplanetary
- 13 惑溺 **wakudeki** indulge in, be addicted to, be infatuated with

——————— 2 ———————
- 4 不惑 **fuwaku** age 40
- 幻惑 **genwaku** fascination, bewitching
- 戸惑 **tomado(i)** become disoriented/confused
- 6 当惑 **tōwaku** be perplexed/nonplussed, be at a loss
- 7 困惑 **konwaku** perplexity, dilemma
- 8 迷惑 **meiwaku** trouble, annoyance, inconvenience
- 逃惑 **ni(ge)mado(u)** run about trying to escape
- 9 思惑 **omowaku** thought, intention
- **omo(i)mado(u)** be unable to make up one's mind
- 思惑師 **omowakushi** speculator
- 思惑違 **omowakuchiga(i)** disappointment, miscalculation
- 思惑買 **omowakuga(i)** speculative buying
- 10 眩惑 **genwaku** blind, dazzle, daze
- 14 疑惑 **giwaku** suspicion, distrust, misgivings
- 誘惑 **yūwaku** temptation, seduction
- 誘惑者 **yūwakusha** tempter, seducer
- 15 魅惑 **miwaku** fascination, charm, lure
- 23 蠱惑 **kowaku** enchant, fascinate, seduce
- 蠱惑的 **kowakuteki** alluring

——————— 4 ———————
- 6 有難迷惑 **a(ri)gata-meiwaku** unwelcome favor

惡 → 悪 4k7.17

4k8.17

惣   SŌ all

——————— 1 ———————
- 11 惣菜 **sōzai** side dish

4k8.18 / 1034

悲   HI, kana(shii) sad
     kana(shimu) be sad, mourn for, regret

——————— 1 ———————
- 6 悲曲 **hikyoku** plaintive melody
- 悲壮 **hisō** tragic heroism
- 8 悲況 **hikyō** plight, lamentable state
- 9 悲哀 **hiai** sorrow, grief, sadness
- 10 悲恋 **hiren** disappointed love
- 11 悲運 **hiun** misfortune, hard luck
- 悲惨 **hisan** tragic, wretched, pitiable
- 12 悲報 **hihō** sad news
- 悲喜 **hiki** joy and sorrow
- 悲喜劇 **hikigeki** tragicomedy
- 悲痛 **hitsū** bitter, grief, sorrow
- 13 悲業 **higō** misfortune, unnatural (death)
- 悲傷 **hishō** be sad/distressed
- 悲嘆 **hitan** grief, sorrow
- 悲愁 **hishū** sorrow, pathos
- 悲愴 **hisō** (overcome one's) grief, sadness
- 悲話 **hiwa** sad story
- 14 悲境 **hikyō** sad plight, distress
- 悲鳴 **himei** shriek, scream
- 悲歌 **hika** elegy, dirge
- 15 悲劇 **higeki** tragedy
- 悲劇的 **higekiteki** tragic
- 悲憤 **hifun** indignation, resentment
- 悲調 **hichō** plaintive air, touch of sadness
- 18 悲観 **hikan** pessimism
- 悲観的 **hikanteki** pessimistic
- 悲観説 **hikansetsu** pessimism
- 悲観論 **hikanron** pessimism
- 悲観論者 **hikanronsha** pessimist
- 19 悲願 **higan** Buddhist prayer for mankind; earnest wish

——————— 2 ———————
- 8 物悲 **monogana(shii)** sad, melancholy
- 13 慈悲 **jihi** compassion, mercy, charity
- 慈悲心 **jihishin** benevolence

——————— 3 ———————
- 12 無慈悲 **mujihi** merciless, ruthless

——————— 4 ———————
- 3 大慈大悲 **daiji-daihi** mercy and compassion

瑟 → 4f9.10

—————— 9 ——————

4k9.1

惻 SOKU pity; devote oneself to

—————— 1 ——————
13 惻隠情 **sokuin (no) jō** pity, compassion

4k9.2

愀 SHŪ, SHŌ suddenly change one's expression; be sorrowful

4k9.3

愎 FUKU go against, disobey

—————— 2 ——————
10 剛愎 **gōfuku** magnanimous; obstinate

4k9.4

愕 GAKU, odoro(ku) be surprised/frightened

—————— 1 ——————
12 愕然 **gakuzen** in surprise/terror, aghast, shocked
—————— 2 ——————
22 驚愕 **kyōgaku** astonishment; alarm, consternation

4k9.5

愡 SŌ meaningless; (foot) race

4k9.6 / 1743

惰 DA lazy, inactive
okota(ru) neglect

—————— 1 ——————
2 惰力 **daryoku** inertia
6 惰気 **daki** inactivity, dullness
8 惰性 **dasei** inertia
10 惰弱 **dajaku** effect, soft
惰眠 **damin** idle slumber, lethargy
—————— 2 ——————
9 怠惰 **taida** idleness, laziness, sloth
10 遊惰 **yūda** indolent, idle
12 勤惰 **kinda** (degree of) diligence or indolence
19 懶惰 **randa** indolence, laziness

4k9.7

惶 KŌ fear

—————— 2 ——————
13 蒼惶 **sōkō** bustling about, flurry

4k9.8

惺 SEI realize

4k9.9

愒 KATSU threaten
KAI be greedy
KEI rest

4k9.10 / 1378

慌 KŌ, awa(teru) get flustered, be in a flurry, panic awa(tadashii) bustling, flurried, confused

—————— 1 ——————
0 慌てふためく **awa(tefutameku)** be in a fluster, panic
8 慌者 **awa(te)mono** absent-minded person, scatterbrain
—————— 2 ——————
10 恐慌 **kyōkō** panic
—————— 3 ——————
3 大恐慌 **daikyōkō** great panic

4k9.11

愃 KEN, KAN abundant, generous; forget

4k9.12

惴 ZUI fear, be afraid

惱 → 悩 4k7.11

4k9.13 / 1598

愉 愉 YU joy, pleasure
tano(shii) pleasant, delightful, fun

—————— 1 ——————
7 愉快 **yukai** pleasant, merry, cheerful
10 愉悦 **yuetsu** joy

4

木
月
日
火
礻
王
牛
方
攵
欠
心 9 ←
戸
戈

13 愉楽 **yuraku** pleasure, joy

——————— 2 ———————
4 不愉快 **fuyukai** unpleasant, disagreeable

4k9.14

偏
HEN narrow-minded

4k9.15 / 1642

愚
GU foolish; (self-deprecatory prefix)
oro(ka), oro(kashii) foolish, stupid

——————— 1 ———————
2 愚人 **gujin** fool, idiot
5 愚民 **gumin** ignorant people, rabble
愚兄 **gukei** my (foolish) elder brother
6 愚考 **gukō** my humble opinion
愚行 **gukō** folly, foolish move
愚劣 **guretsu** stupid, foolish
7 愚作 **gusaku** a poor work, trash
愚弟 **gutei** my (foolish) younger brother
愚臣 **gushin** foolish retainer; this humble
    vassal
愚図 **guzu** dullard, irresolute person
愚図付 **guzutsu(ku)** dawdle, be irresolute
愚図愚図 **guzuguzu** dawdle, hesitate
愚弄 **gurō** make a fool of, ridicule, mock
愚見 **guken** my humble opinion
8 愚直 **guchoku** simple honesty, tactless
    frankness
愚妹 **gumai** my (foolish) younger sister
愚妻 **gusai** my (foolish) wife
愚者 **oro(ka)mono, gusha** fool, jackass
愚物 **gubutsu** fool, blockhead
9 愚連隊 **gurentai** hooligans, street gang
愚昧 **gumai** stupid, ignorant, asinine
愚計 **gukei** foolish/my plan
10 愚案 **guan** foolish/my plan, my humble
     opinion
愚挙 **gukyo** foolish undertaking
愚息 **gusoku** my (foolish) son
11 愚問 **gumon** stupid question
愚問愚答 **gumon-gutō** silly dialog
12 愚策 **gusaku** foolish/ill-advised plan
愚鈍 **gudon** stupid, half-witted, asinine
13 愚僧 **gusō** this foolish priest
愚意 **gui** my humble view
愚痴 **guchi** idle complaint, grumbling
14 愚説 **gusetsu** foolish/my opinion
15 愚論 **guron** foolish argument/opinion

——————— 2 ———————
3 凡愚 **bongu** common person
6 迂愚 **ugu** silly, stupid

11 庸愚 **yōgu** mediocrity; dim-wittedness
12 衆愚 **shūgu** the ignorant rabble
13 暗愚 **angu** feeble-minded, imbecile
痴愚 **chigu** stupidity, imbecility
頑愚 **gangu** stupid and obstinate
16 賢愚 **kengu** wise or foolish

——————— 3 ———————
13 愚図愚図 **guzuguzu** dawdle, hesitate
愚問愚答 **gumon-gutō** silly dialog

4k9.16 / 1601

愁
SHŪ, **ure(i)** grief, sorrow, distress;
anxiety, cares   **ure(eru)** grieve, be
distressed; fear, be apprehensive

——————— 1 ———————
6 愁色 **shūshoku** worried/sorrowful look
9 愁眉 **shūbi** worried brow/look
愁思 **shūshi** worry, distress, grief
12 愁然 **shūzen (to shite)** sorrowfully, mourn-
    fully
愁訴 **shūso** plea, supplication
愁雲 **shūun** cloud/atmosphere of gloom
13 愁傷 **shūshō** grief, sorrow
愁傷様 **(go)shūshō-sama** My heartfelt
    sympathy.
愁嘆 **shūtan** lamentation, sorrow
愁嘆場 **shūtanba** pathetic/tragic scene
14 愁歎 **shūtan** lamentation, sorrow

——————— 2 ———————
9 哀愁 **aishū** sadness, sorrow, grief
10 郷愁 **kyōshū** homesickness, nostalgia
旅愁 **ryoshū** loneliness on a journey
12 悲愁 **hishū** sorrow, pathos
15 憂愁 **yūshū** melancholy, grief, gloom
18 離愁 **rishū** the sorrow of parting

4k9.17

愍
BIN pity; grieve over

4k9.18 / 147

想
SŌ, SO idea, thought
omo(u) think of, call to mind

——————— 1 ———————
8 想念 **sōnen** idea, conception
想到 **sōtō** think of, consider, hit upon
想定 **sōtei** hypothesis, supposition
10 想起 **sōki** recollection, remembrance
14 想像 **sōzō** imagine
想像力 **sōzōryoku** (powers of) imagination
想像上 **sōzōjō** imaginary

─────────── 2 ───────────

4 幻想 **gensō** fantasy, illusion
  幻想曲 **gensōkyoku** fantasy, fantasia
  予想 **yosō** expect, anticipate, conjecture, imagine; estimate
  予想外 **yosōgai** unexpected, unforeseen
  予想通 **yosōdō(ri)** as expected
  予想高 **yosōdaka** estimated amount
6 仮想 **kasō** imaginary, supposed, virtual (mass), hypothetical
  妄想 **mōsō, bōsō** wild fantasy, delusion
  回想 **kaisō** retrospection, reminiscence
  回想録 **kaisōroku** memoirs
7 狂想曲 **kyōsōkyoku** rhapsody
8 夜想曲 **yasōkyoku** nocturne
  迷想 **meisō** illusion, fallacy
  追想 **tsuisō** recollection, reminiscences
  奇想 **kisō** original/fantastic idea
  奇想天外 **kisō-tengai** original concept
  空想 **kūsō** idle fancy, fiction, daydream
  空想的 **kūsōteki** fanciful, visionary
  空想家 **kūsōka** dreamer, idealist, utopian
9 発想 **hassō** conception; expression (in music)
  連想 **rensō** association (of ideas)
  思想 **shisō** thought, idea
  思想犯 **shisōhan** dangerous-thought offense
  思想界 **shisōkai** world of thought, realm of ideas
  思想家 **shisōka** thinker
10 随想 **zuisō** occasional thoughts
  随想録 **zuisōroku** occasional thoughts, essays
  冥想 **meisō** meditation, contemplation
11 理想 **risō** ideal
  理想化 **risōka** idealize
  理想主義 **risō shugi** idealism
  理想的 **risōteki** ideal
  理想型 **risōgata** ideal type
  理想郷 **risōkyō** ideal land, Shangri-La, utopia
  理想家 **risōka** idealist
12 着想 **chakusō** idea, conception
  無想 **musō** making one's mind a blank
13 夢想 **musō** dream, vision, fancy
  夢想家 **musōka** dreamer, visionary
  愛想 **aiso, aisō** amiability, sociability
  感想 **kansō** one's thoughts, impressions
  感想文 **kansōbun** (written) description of one's impressions
  意想外 **isōgai** unexpected, surprising
  詩想 **shisō** thought of a poem
14 構想 **kōsō** conception, plan
  綺想曲 **kisōkyoku** capriccio
15 黙想 **mokusō** meditation, contemplation
  瞑想 **meisō** meditation, contemplation
18 観想 **kansō** meditation, contemplation
20 懸想 **kesō** fall in love
  懸想文 **kesōbumi, kesōbun** love letter

─────────── 3 ───────────

5 旧思想 **kyūshisō** old-fashioned/outmoded ideas
7 没理想 **botsurisō** lack of ideals; realism (in literature)
12 無愛想 **buaisō** unsociable, curt

─────────── 4 ───────────

4 収穫予想 **shūkaku yosō** crop estimate
5 末法思想 **mappō shisō** pessimism due to the decadent-age theory
12 無念無想 **munen-musō** blank state of mind

4k9.19

憲   **KEN** make a mistake

4k9.20

惷   **SHUN** confusion; foolish

愈 → 愈 **2a11.16**

慈 → **2o11.1**

4k9.21 / 262

感 感   **KAN** feeling, sensation

─────────── 1 ───────────

0 感じる/ずる **kan(jiru/zuru)** feel
  感じ **kan(ji)** feeling, sensation
2 感入 **kan(ji)i(ru)** be deeply impressed
4 感化 **kanka** influence, inspiration, reform
  感化院 **kankain** reformatory
  感心 **kanshin** be impressed by, admire
5 感付 **kanzu(ku)** suspect, sense
6 感光 **kankō** exposure to light; photosensitive
  感光板 **kankōban** sensitized plate
  感光度 **kankōdo** (degree of) photosensitivity
7 感状 **kanjō** (letter of) commendation
  感吟 **kangin** reciting with emotion
  感応 **kannō** response; inspiration; sympathy; induce, influence
8 感受 **kanju** (radio) reception, susceptibility
  感受性 **kanjusei** sensibility, sensitivity
  感泣 **kankyū** weep with emotion
  感知 **kanchi** perception, sensing
  感官 **kankan** sense organ

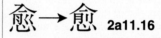

4

木 月 日 火 礻 王 牛 方 攵 欠 心 戸 戈 9←

感服 **kanpuku** admiration
感性 **kansei** sensitivity; the senses
9 感度 **kando** (degree of) sensitivity
感染 **kansen** infection, contagion
感冒 **kanbō** a cold, the flu
10 感涙 **kanrui** tears of gratitude
感恩 **kan'on** gratitude
11 感動 **kandō** impression, inspiration, emotion, excitement
感得 **kantoku** realize, become aware of
感情 **kanjō** feelings, emotion
感情的 **kanjōteki** emotional, sentimental
12 感覚 **kankaku** sense, the senses
感覚論 **kankakuron** sensualism; esthetics
13 感傷 **kanshō** sentimentality
感傷的 **kanshōteki** sentimental
感嘆 **kantan** admiration, wonder, exclamation
感嘆符 **kantanfu** exclamation point (!)
感想 **kansō** one's thoughts, impressions
感想文 **kansōbun** (written) description of one's impressions
感慨 **kangai** deep emotion
感慨無量 **kangai-muryō** full of emotion
感触 **kanshoku** the touch/feel, texture
感電 **kanden** electric shock
14 感銘 **kanmei** impression (on one's mind)
16 感興 **kankyō** interest, pleasure
感激 **kangeki** be deeply impressed/grateful
感懐 **kankai** deep impression
感奮 **kanpun** be inspired/moved to action
17 感謝 **kansha** gratitude, appreciation
感謝状 **kanshajō** letter of thanks
感謝祭 **kanshasai** Thanksgiving

───── 2 ─────

3 万感 **bankan** flood of emotions
4 不感症 **fukanshō** sexual frigidity
予感 **yokan** premonition, hunch
五感 **gokan** the five senses
六感 **rokkan** the six senses; sixth sense
反感 **hankan** antipathy, animosity
5 好感 **kōkan** good feeling, favorable impression
6 多感 **takan** sensitive, sentimental, emotional
肉感 **nikkan** sexual feeling, sensuality
肉感的 **nikkanteki** suggestive, voluptuous, sensual
色感 **shikikan** color sense/vision
同感 **dōkan** the same sentiment, sympathy, concurrence
共感 **kyōkan** sympathy, response
有感地震 **yūkan jishin** earthquake strong enough to feel
7 体感 **taikan** bodily sensation
快感 **kaikan** pleasant/agreeable feeling
8 直感 **chokkan** intuition

直感的 **chokkanteki** intuitive
実感 **jikkan** actual sensation, realization
性感 **seikan** sexual feeling, erogenous (zone)
所感 **shokan** one's impressions, opinion
9 哀感 **aikan** sadness, pathos
美感 **bikan** sense of beauty
音感 **onkan** sense of sound/pitch
10 随感 **zuikan** random thoughts/impressions
流感 **ryūkan** flu, influenza (short for 流行性感冒)
敏感 **binkan** sensitive
11 偶感 **gūkan** random thoughts
悪感 **akkan** unpleasant feeling
okan a chill with a fever
悪感情 **akukanjō, akkanjō** ill will, animosity, unfavorable impression
情感 **jōkan** emotion, sentiment
12 善感 **zenkan** successful vaccination, positive reaction
超感覚的 **chōkankakuteki** extrasensory
量感 **ryōkan** volume, bulk, massiveness
無感覚 **mukankaku** insensible, numb, callous
鈍感 **donkan** obtuse, thick, insensitive
13 触感 **shokkan** the feel; sense of touch
14 語感 **gokan** connotations of a word; linguistic sense
雑感 **zakkan** miscellaneous impressions
15 熱感 **nekkan** feverish feeling
霊感 **reikan** inspiration

───── 3 ─────

4 天平感宝 **Tenpyō Kanpō** (era, 749)
少年感化院 **shōnen kankain** reform school
5 正義感 **seigikan** sense of justice
立体感 **rittaikan** sense of depth
6 安心感 **anshinkan** sense of security
安全感 **anzenkan** sense of security
安定感 **anteikan** sense of stability/security
劣等感 **rettōkan** inferiority complex
9 重量感 **jūryōkan** massiveness, heft
信頼感 **shinraikan** feeling of trust
連帯感 **rentaikan** (feeling/sense of) solidarity
10 既視感 **kishikan** (feeling of) déjà vu
倦怠感 **kentaikan** fatigue
恐怖感 **kyōfukan** sense of fear
11 脱力感 **datsuryokukan** feeling of exhaustion, fatigue
現実感 **genjitsukan** sense of reality
第六感 **dai-rokkan** sixth sense
責任感 **sekininkan** sense of responsibility
12 違和感 **iwakan** feeling ill at ease, discomfort, malaise
13 嫌悪感 **ken'okan** hatred, dislike, loathing
罪悪感 **zaiakukan** guilty conscience
14 読後感 **dokugokan** one's impressions (of a book)

16 親近感 **shinkinkan** feeling of familiarity
17 優越感 **yūetsukan** superiority complex

――――――― 4 ―――――――

6 多情多感 **tajō-takan** emotional, sentimental
10 流行性感冒 **ryūkōsei kanbō** influenza

惡 → 悪 **4k7.17**

――――――― 10 ―――――――

4k10.1

慊

KEN, **akita(riru)** be satisfied with

――――――― 1 ―――――――

0 慊りない **akita(rinai)** be dissatisfied with
11 慊焉 **ken'en** be dissatisfied/displeased

4k10.2

愬

SO complain of

4k10.3 / 1460

慨 慨

GAI, **nage(ku)** regret, lament, bemoan

――――――― 1 ―――――――

5 慨世 **gaisei** concern for the public
12 慨然 **gaizen** indignantly, deploringly
13 慨嘆 **gaitan** regret, lament, deplore

――――――― 2 ―――――――

6 気概 **kigai** spirit, mettle, pluck
13 感慨 **kangai** deep emotion
   感慨無量 **kangai-muryō** full of emotion
14 慷慨 **kōgai** lament, deplore
15 憤慨 **fungai** indignation, resentment

博 → 博 **2k10.1**

4k10.4 / 1785

慎 愼

SHIN, **tsutsushi(mu)** be discreet/careful; restrain oneself, refrain from **tsutsu(mashii)** modest, reserved

――――――― 1 ―――――――

9 慎重 **shinchō** cautious
11 慎深 **tsutsushi(mi)buka(i)** discreet, cautious

――――――― 2 ―――――――

17 謹慎 **kinshin** be on one's best behavior; be confined to one's home

――――――― 3 ―――――――

4 不謹慎 **fukinshin** imprudent, rash

4k10.5

慄

RITSU fear; shudder, shiver
onono(ku) shudder, tremble

――――――― 1 ―――――――

12 慄然 **ritsuzen** with horror, with a shudder

――――――― 2 ―――――――

13 戦慄 **senritsu** shudder, tremble, shiver

4k10.6

愧

KI, **ha(jiru)** feel ashamed

――――――― 1 ―――――――

6 愧死 **kishi** die of shame/humiliation

――――――― 2 ―――――――

15 慙愧 **zanki** shame, humiliation; compunction

4k10.7

慍

UN, ON, **ika(ru)** be angry
ura(mu) be resentful

4k10.8

愴

SŌ, **ita(mu)** be sad, grieve

――――――― 2 ―――――――

10 凄愴 **seisō** desolate, dreary
11 悽愴 **seisō** desolate, dreary
12 悲愴 **hisō** (overcome one's) grief, sadness

4k10.9

慥

ZŌ serious-minded, sincere
tashika certain, for sure; probably

4k10.10

愾

GAI, KI anger; sigh

――――――― 2 ―――――――

15 敵愾心 **tekigaishin** hostility, animosity

4k10.11

愿 GEN respectful; honest

4k10.12

慇 IN courtesy

――――― 1 ―――――
17 慇懃 **ingin** polite, courteous; intimate

4k10.13

愨 KAKU respectful; sincerely

4k10.14 / 387

態 TAI condition, appearance
waza (to) intentionally

――――― 1 ―――――
3 態々 **wazawaza** on purpose, deliberately
9 態度 **taido** attitude, stance, posture
13 態勢 **taisei** preparedness, stance

――――― 2 ―――――
5 失態 **shittai** blunder, mismanagement; disgrace
　生態 **seitai** mode of life, ecology
　生態学 **seitaigaku** ecology
　世態 **setai** social conditions, the world
　旧態 **kyūtai** the old/former state of affairs
6 百態 **hyakutai** various phases
7 状態 **jōtai** state of affairs, situation
　狂態 **kyōtai** scandalous behavior
　形態 **keitai** form, shape, configuration
　形態学 **keitaigaku** morphology
8 事態 **jitai** situation, state of affairs
　奇態 **kitai** strange, curious, wondrous
　実態 **jittai** actual conditions
9 重態 **jūtai** in serious/critical condition
　変態 **hentai** metamorphosis; abnormal, perverted
　姿態 **shitai** figure, pose
10 容態 **yōdai** (patient's) condition
　病態 **byōtai** patient's condition
11 常態 **jōtai** normal condition
　悪態 **akutai** foul language, cusswords
　酔態 **suitai** drunkenness
12 媚態 **bitai** coquetry
13 痴態 **chitai** foolishness, silliness
14 様態 **yōtai** form; situation, condition
　静態 **seitai** static, stationary
　態態 **wazawaza** on purpose, deliberately

15 嬌態 **kyōtai** coquetry, coyness
17 擬態 **gitai** mimesis, simulation
　醜態 **shūtai** unseemly sight, disgraceful behavior

――――― 3 ―――――
8 受動態 **judōtai** passive voice
10 能動態 **nōdōtai** active voice (in grammar)

悪 → 悪 4k7.17

慈 → 慈 2o11.1

4k10.15

溿 YŌ, susu(meru) recommend

――――― 2 ―――――
15 慫溿 **shōyō** advise, suggest, recommend, persuade

4k10.16

慝 TOKU bad, evil; disaster

――――― 11 ―――――
慽 → 感 4k11.12

4k11.1

慟 DŌ cry in sadness, keen

4k11.2

慠 GŌ proud

――――― 1 ―――――
14 慠慢 **gōman** arrogant, haughty

4k11.3

慱 TAN grieving

4k11.4

慓 HYŌ fast, quick

——————— 1 ———————

10 慓悍 **hyōkan** quick and strong, fierce

4k11.5

憒 **SHŌ** fear

——————— 1 ———————

6 憒伏 **shōfuku** fear and prostrate oneself before; fear and obey
8 憒服 **shōfuku** fear and obey

慘 → 惨 4k8.5

4k11.6

傷 **SHŌ** be sad, grieve

4k11.7 / 1365

憎 憎 **ZŌ, niku(mu/garu)** hate **niku(i/rashii)** hateful, horrible, repulsive **niku(shimi)** hatred, animosity

——————— 1 ———————

2 憎子 **niku(marek)ko** bad/naughty boy
3 憎々 **nikuniku(shii)** hateful, loathsome, malicious
  憎口 **niku(mare)guchi** offensive/malicious remarks
6 憎気 **nikuge** hatred, ill will
  憎合 **niku(mi)a(u)** hate one another
7 憎役 **niku(mare)yaku** unpopular role, thankless task
11 憎悪 **zōo** hatred, abhorrence
  憎悪心 **zōoshin** hatred, malice

——————— 2 ———————

3 小憎 **koniku(rashii)** hateful, provoking
4 心憎 **kokoroniku(i)** detestable; tasteful, admirable, excellent
5 生憎 **ainiku** unfortunately
9 面憎 **tsuraniku(i)** disgusting, offensive
13 愛憎 **aizō** love and/or hate
14 憎憎 **nikuniku(shii)** hateful, loathsome, malicious

4k11.8 / 1410

慢 **MAN** lazy; scorn, deride; prolonged, chronic; boasting

——————— 1 ———————

4 慢心 **manshin** be conceited

8 慢性 **mansei** chronic
  慢性化 **manseika** become chronic

——————— 2 ———————

6 自慢 **jiman** be proud of
  自慢高慢 **jiman-kōman** with great pride
  自慢話 **jimanbanashi** boastful talk, bragging
  自慢顔 **jimangao** boastful look
7 我慢 **gaman** put up with, bear, endure, be patient
8 侮慢 **buman** insult, contempt
9 怠慢 **taiman** negligence, dereliction, inattention
10 高慢 **kōman** proud, haughty, supercilious
13 傲慢 **gōman** proud, arrogant, haughty
  傲慢無礼 **gōman-burei** arrogant and insolent
14 傲慢 **gōman** arrogant, haughty
15 暴慢 **bōman** insolent, arrogant, overbearing
  緩慢 **kanman** sluggish, slack

——————— 3 ———————

2 力自慢 **chikara jiman** boasting of one's strength
7 声自慢 **koejiman** proud of one's singing voice
8 国自慢 **(o)kuni jiman** pride in one's home province; boast of one's native place
12 腕自慢 **udejiman** proud of one's skill
14 痩我慢 **ya(se)gaman** endure for sake of pride

——————— 4 ———————

6 自慢高慢 **jiman-kōman** with great pride
12 御国自慢 **okuni jiman** pride in one's home province; boast of one's native place

4k11.9 / 915

慣 **KAN, na(reru)** get used to **na(rasu)** accustom to; tame

——————— 1 ———————

5 慣用 **kan'yō** in common use, common
  慣用上 **kan'yōjō** by usage
  慣用句 **kan'yōku** idiom, common expression
  慣用語 **kan'yōgo** idiom, colloquial word/phrase
6 慣行 **kankō** usual practice, custom
  慣行犯 **kankōhan** habitual criminal
8 慣例 **kanrei** custom, precedent
  慣例上 **kanreijō** conventionally, traditionally
  慣性 **kansei** inertia
11 慣習 **kanshū** custom, practice
  慣習法 **kanshūhō** common law

——————— 2 ———————

3 口慣 **kuchina(rashi)** oral drill
4 不慣 **funa(re)** inexperienced in, unfamiliar with
  手慣 **tena(reru)** get used to, become practiced in

4

木
月
日
火
礻
王
牛
方
攵
欠
心 11 ←
戸
戈

5 世慣 **yona(reru)** get used to the world, become worldly-wise
旧慣 **kyūkan** old customs
6 耳慣 **mimina(reru)** be used to hearing
7 見慣 **mina(reru)** get used to seeing, be familiar to
8 使慣 **tsuka(i)na(reru)** get accustomed to using, get used to
呼慣 **yo(bi)na(reru)** be used to calling (someone by a certain name)
物慣 **monona(reru)** be used to, be experienced in, be at ease in
肩慣 **katana(rashi)** (pitcher's) warming up
10 書慣 **ka(ki)na(reru)** get used to writing
11 商慣習 **shōkanshū** commercial practices
習慣 **shūkan** custom, habit
習慣法 **shūkanhō** common law
13 飼慣 **ka(i)na(rasu)** domesticate, tame
14 読慣 **yo(mi)na(reru)** be used to reading
聞慣 **ki(ki)na(reru)** get used to hearing

———————— 3 ————————

9 食習慣 **shokushūkan** eating habits
11 悪習慣 **akushūkan** bad habit, evil practice

慚 → 慙 **4k11.14**

4k11.10

慵

YŌ, monou(i) languid

4k11.11

慷

KŌ, nage(ku) lament, bemoan

———————— 1 ————————

13 慷慨 **kōgai** lament, deplore

4k11.12

感 慽

SEKI be sad, grieve

4k11.13 / 1618

慰

I, nagusa(meru) comfort, console; amuse, cheer up
nagusa(mu) be diverted/amused; banter; make a plaything of

———————— 1 ————————

5 慰半分 **nagusa(mi)hanbun** partly for pleasure

---

6 慰安 **ian** comfort, recreation, amusement
慰安会 **iankai** recreational get-together
慰安婦 **ianfu** a comfort girl/woman, army prostitute
7 慰労 **irō** recognize (someone's) services
慰労会 **irōkai** dinner/party given in appreciation of someone's services
慰労金 **irōkin** bonus, gratuity
8 慰物 **nagusa(mi)mono** object of pleasure, plaything
10 慰留 **iryū** dissuade from resigning
11 慰問 **imon** consolation, sympathy
慰問状 **imonjō** letter of condolence
慰問品 **imonhin** comfort articles, amenities
15 慰撫 **ibu** pacify, soothe, humor
慰霊 **irei** repose of the deceased's soul
慰霊祭 **ireisai** memorial service
慰霊塔 **ireitō** cenotaph, memorial tower
17 慰藉 **isha** consolation, solace
慰藉料 **isharyō** consolation money, solatium
慰謝 **isha** consolation, solace
慰謝料 **isharyō** consolation money, solatium

———————— 2 ————————

3 口慰 **kuchinagusa(mi)** relieving boredom by talking, humming, or eating
4 弔慰 **chōi** condolences, sympathy
弔慰金 **chōikin** condolence money
手慰 **tenagusa(mi)** fingering; gambling
6 自慰 **jii** self-consolation; masturbation
7 言慰 **i(i)nagusa(meru)** console

4k11.14

慙 慚

ZAN, ha(jiru) feel ashamed/humiliated

———————— 1 ————————

13 慙愧 **zanki** shame, humiliation; compunction

憩 → 憩 **4k12.10**

慾 → 欲 **4j7.1**

4k11.15

慫

SHŌ, susu(meru) recommend

———————— 1 ————————

14 慫慂 **shōyō** advise, suggest, recommend, persuade

4k11.16

慧 **KEI** wise, clever, astute

——————— 1 ———————
10 慧眼 **keigan** sharp eye, keen insight
——————— 2 ———————
12 智慧 **chie** knowledge, wisdom

——————— 12 ———————

慨 → 慨 4k10.3

4k12.1

慳 **KEN** reluctant to part with, stingy; hardhearted

——————— 2 ———————
7 邪慳 **jaken** harsh, cruel

4k12.2

憔 **SHŌ** become haggard/care-worn

——————— 1 ———————
11 憔悴 **shōsui** become emaciated/haggard

4k12.3

憮 **BU** be disappointed/surprised

——————— 1 ———————
12 憮然 **buzen** discouraged; surprised

4k12.4

憚 **TAN, habaka(ru)** be afraid of, shrink from; (clouds) spread

——————— 1 ———————
5 憚乍 **habaka(ri)naga(ra)** I dare say, Excuse me, but …
14 憚様 **habaka(ri)sama** Thanks for your trouble.
——————— 2 ———————
7 忌憚 **kitan(nai)** without reserve, frank, outspoken

4k12.5

憧 **DŌ, SHŌ, akoga(reru)** yearn for, aspire to, admire

——————— 1 ———————
15 憧憬 **dōkei, shōkei** longing, aspiration

4k12.6 / 1661

憤 **FUN, ikidō(ru)** resent, be indignant/enraged

——————— 1 ———————
6 憤死 **funshi** die in a fit of anger; be put out (with men on base)
9 憤怒 **fundo, funnu** anger, wrath, indignation
12 憤然 **funzen** indignantly
13 憤慨 **fungai** indignation, resentment
16 憤激 **fungeki** become enraged/indignant
18 憤懣 **funman** indignation, anger, resentment
——————— 2 ———————
4 公憤 **kōfun** public indignation
7 余憤 **yofun** pent-up anger, rage
私憤 **shifun** personal grudge
9 発憤 **happun** be roused to action
12 悲憤 **hifun** indignation, resentment
痛憤 **tsūfun** great indignation
13 義憤 **gifun** righteous indignation
16 激憤 **gekifun** indignation, resentment
29 鬱憤 **uppun** resentment, rancor, grudge

4k12.7

憬 **KEI, akoga(reru)** yearn for, aspire to, admire

——————— 2 ———————
15 憧憬 **dōkei, shōkei** longing, aspiration

憎 → 憎 4k11.7

4k12.8

憫 **BIN** take pity; grieve

——————— 2 ———————
4 不憫 **fubin** pitiful, poor
13 愛憫 **aibin** pity, compassion
16 憐憫 **renbin** compassion, pity, mercy

蕊 → 蕊 3k12.14

4k12.9

憖 **GIN, namaji, namaji(i), namaji(kka)** halfheartedly; rashly; at all

木 月 日 火 礻 王 珡 牛 方 攵 欠 心 12← 戸 戈

4

4k12.10 / 1243

憩 憇

KEI, iko(u) rest, relax
iko(i) rest, relaxation

———————— 2 ————————

3 小憩 **shōkei** short break/rest, recess
4 少憩 **shōkei** short break/rest, recess
6 休憩 **kyūkei** recess, break, intermission
休憩所 **kyūkeijo** resting room, lounge, lobby
休憩室 **kyūkeishitsu** resting room, lounge, lobby

4k12.11

憊

HAI fatigue

———————— 2 ————————

7 困憊 **konpai** exhaustion, fatigue

4k12.12

憑

HYŌ be based on, rely on; be demon-possessed **tsu(ku)** possess, haunt, obsess **tsu(kareru)** be spirit-possessed, be haunted by

———————— 1 ————————

8 憑物 **tsu(ki)mono** possessing spirit, curse, obsession

———————— 2 ————————

9 信憑性 **sinpyōsei** credibility, authenticity
神憑 **kamigaka(ri)** divine/spirit possession

4k12.13

憙

KI, yoroko(bu) rejoice
kono(mu) like, prefer
ā (exclamation)

———————— 13 ————————

4k13.1

懈

KAI, KE, okota(ru) be lazy/negligent

———————— 1 ————————

9 懈怠 **kaitai, ketai** lazy, negligent

4k13.2

懊

Ō sorrow, regret

———————— 1 ————————

10 懊悩 **ōnō** anguish, worry, trouble

4k13.3 / 1815

憾

KAN, ura(mu) regret, be sorry for

———————— 1 ————————

7 憾言 **ura(mi)goto** words of regret

———————— 2 ————————

14 遺憾 **ikan** regrettable

4k13.4

憐

REN, awa(remu) pity, feel compassion, sympathize with
awa(remi) pity, compassion

———————— 1 ————————

11 憐深 **awa(remi)buka(i)** compassionate
15 憐憫 **renbin** compassion, pity, mercy

———————— 2 ————————

5 可憐 **karen** lovely, cute, sweet; poor, pitiable
9 哀憐 **airen** pity, compassion

4k13.5 / 381

憶 憶

OKU remember, think
omo(u) think of, remember

———————— 1 ————————

8 憶念 **okunen** something always kept in mind
10 憶病 **okubyō** cowardice, timidity
11 憶断 **okudan** conjecture, surmise, guess
12 憶測 **okusoku** speculation, conjecture
14 憶説 **okusetsu** hypothesis, conjecture, surmise

———————— 2 ————————

8 追憶 **tsuioku** recollection, reminiscences
10 記憶 **kioku** memory
記憶力 **kiokuryoku** memory (ability)

4k13.6

懌

EKI rejoice

4k13.7

懆

SŌ unease

4k13.8

懍

RIN fear, tremble

4k13.9 / 1408

懐 懷

KAI pocket; nostalgia
natsu(kashii) dear, fond, longed-for
natsu(kashimu) yearn for
natsu(ku) take kindly to   **natsu(keru)** win over; tame   **futokoro** breast (pocket)

——————— 1 ———————

2 懐刀 **futokoro-gatana** dagger; confidant
4 懐中 **kaichū** one's pocket
懐中物 **kaichūmono** pocketbook, wallet
懐中時計 **kaichū-dokei** pocket watch
懐中電灯 **kaichū dentō** flashlight
懐中鏡 **kaichūkagami** pocket mirror
懐手 **futokorode** hands in pockets, idly
5 懐古 **kaiko** nostalgia
懐古談 **kaikodan** reminiscences
懐旧 **kaikyū** yearning for the old days
7 懐妊 **kainin** pregnancy
8 懐炉 **kairo** pocket heater
懐炉灰 **kairobai** pocket-heater fuel
懐具合 **futokoro guai** one's financial circumstances
9 懐柔 **kaijū** be conciliatory, win over
懐胎 **kaitai** pregnancy, gestation
10 懐郷 **kaikyō** nostalgic reminiscence
懐郷病 **kaikyōbyō** nostalgia, homesickness
懐剣 **kaiken** dagger
懐紙 **kaishi** pocket paper hankies; paper for writing poems on
11 懐勘定 **futokoro kanjō** counting one's pocket money; one's financial situation
14 懐疑 **kaigi** doubt, skepticism
懐疑心 **kaigishin** doubt, skepticism
懐疑説 **kaigisetsu** skepticism
懐疑論 **kaigiron** skepticism

——————— 2 ———————

2 人懐 **hitonatsu(koi)**, **hitonatsu(kkoi)** amiable, sociable, friendly
hitonatsu(kashii) lonesome (for)
4 内懐 **uchibutokoro** inside pocket; one's true intention
手懐 **tenazu(keru)** tame, domesticate; win over
7 述懐 **jukkai** reminiscences
8 追懐 **tsuikai** recollection, reminiscences
抱懐 **hōkai** harbor, cherish, entertain
所懐 **shokai** one's impressions, opinion
10 胸懐 **kyōkai** one's heart/thoughts
素懐 **sokai** long-held desire
13 感懐 **kankai** deep impression
雅懐 **gakai** esthetic sentiment
18 襟懐 **kinkai** one's heart, inner thoughts

——————— 3 ———————

15 窮鳥懐入 **kyūchō futokoro (ni) hai(ru)** (like a) bird in distress seeking refuge

——————— 4 ———————

11 虚心坦懐 **kyoshin-tankai** frank, open-minded

4k13.10

憺

TAN peace of mind

4k13.11

懃

KIN considerate, courteous

——————— 2 ———————

14 慇懃 **ingin** polite, courteous; intimate

4k13.12 / 1135

懇

KON, nengo(ro) friendly, cordial, intimate, kind

——————— 1 ———————

3 懇々 **konkon (to)** earnestly, repeatedly
4 懇切 **konsetsu** cordial, exhaustive, detailed
8 懇命 **konmei** kind words
11 懇望 **konbō** entreaty, earnest request
懇情 **konjō** kindliness, warm friendship
13 懇意 **kon'i** intimacy, friendship, kindness
懇話 **konwa** friendly talk, chat
懇話会 **konwakai** social get-together
15 懇談 **kondan** cordial conversation, chat
懇談会 **kondankai** get-together, friendly discussion
懇請 **konsei** entreaty, earnest request
16 懇親 **konshin** friendship, intimacy
懇親会 **konshinkai** social gathering
懇篤 **kontoku** kind, cordial
17 懇懇 **konkon (to)** earnestly, repeatedly
19 懇願 **kongan** entreaty, earnest appeal
懇願者 **kongansha** supplicant, petitioner

——————— 2 ———————

7 別懇 **bekkon** intimacy
9 昵懇 **jikkon** intimate, familiar
17 懇懇 **konkon (to)** earnestly, repeatedly

4k13.13

懋

BŌ strive; flourish

——————— 14 ———————

4k14.1

懦

DA timidity, cowardice

——————— 1 ———————

4 懦夫 **dafu** weakling, coward

10 懦弱 **dajaku** effete, soft

――――――― 2 ―――――――

8 怯懦 **kyōda** cowardly, timid

4k14.2

漫

MAN, MON be in agony

――――――― 2 ―――――――

16 憤懣 **funman** indignation, anger, resentment

4k14.3 / 1421

懲 懲

CHŌ, ko(riru) learn from experience, be taught a lesson, be sick of **ko(rasu)** chastise, punish, discipline

――――――― 1 ―――――――

0 懲らしめる **ko(rashimeru)** chastise, punish, discipline, teach a lesson

7 懲役 **chōeki** penal servitude, imprisonment

懲戒 **chōkai** disciplinary punishment, official reprimand

11 懲悪 **chōaku** punishment of evil

14 懲罰 **chōbatsu** disciplinary measure, punishment

18 懲懲 **ko(ri)go(ri)** learn from experience, have had enough of

――――――― 2 ―――――――

8 性懲 **shōko(ri)** learning from bitter experience

17 膺懲 **yōchō** punish, chastise

――――――― 3 ―――――――

12 無期懲役 **muki chōeki** life imprisonment

13 勧善懲悪 **kanzen-chōaku** rewarding good and punishing evil, didactic/morality (play)

應 → 応 3q4.2

――――――― 15 ―――――――

懺 → 懺 4k17.1

懲 → 懲 4k14.3

――――――― 16 ―――――――

4k16.1

懶

RAN, RAI, monou(i) languid **okota(ru)** be lazy/negligent

――――――― 1 ―――――――

12 懶惰 **randa** indolence, laziness

懷 → 懐 4k13.9

4k16.2 / 911

懸

KEN, KE, ka(karu) hang **ka(keru)** hang; offer, give

――――――― 1 ―――――――

8 懸垂 **kensui** suspension, dangling; chin-ups

懸垂運動 **kensui undō** chin-ups

懸念 **kenen** fear, apprehension

懸命 **kenmei** eager, going all-out; risking one's life

10 懸案 **ken'an** unsettled/pending question

11 懸崖 **kengai** overhanging (a) cliff, precipice

12 懸隔 **kenkaku** disparity, gap

ka(ke)heda(taru) be far apart, differ widely **ka(ke)heda(teru)** estrange

13 懸想 **kesō** fall in love

懸想文 **kesōbumi, kesōbun** love letter

15 懸賞 **kenshō** offering prizes

懸賞金 **kenshōkin** prize money, reward

懸賞募集 **kenshō boshū** prize competition

懸賞論文 **kenshō ronbun** prize essay

16 懸壅垂 **ken'yōsui** the uvula

懸濁 **kendaku** suspension

懸橋 **ka(ke)hashi** suspension bridge; viaduct

18 懸離 **ka(ke)hana(reru)** be far apart, differ widely

――――――― 2 ―――――――

4 手懸 **tega(kari)** handhold; clue, lead **teka(ke)** handhold; concubine

6 気懸 **kigaka(ri)** anxiety

8 命懸 **inochiga(ke)** life-or-death, risky, desperate

9 神懸 **kamiga(kari)** divine/spirit possession

14 踊懸 **odo(ri)ka(karu)** spring upon, jump at

21 躍懸 **odo(ri)ka(karu)** spring upon, jump at

――――――― 3 ―――――――

1 一生懸命 **isshōkenmei** with all one's might

一所懸命 **isshokenmei** with all one's might

――――――― 17 ―――――――

4k17.1

懺 懺

ZAN, SAN, ku(iru) feel remorse, regret

――――――― 1 ―――――――

9 懺悔 **zange, sange** repentance, contrition

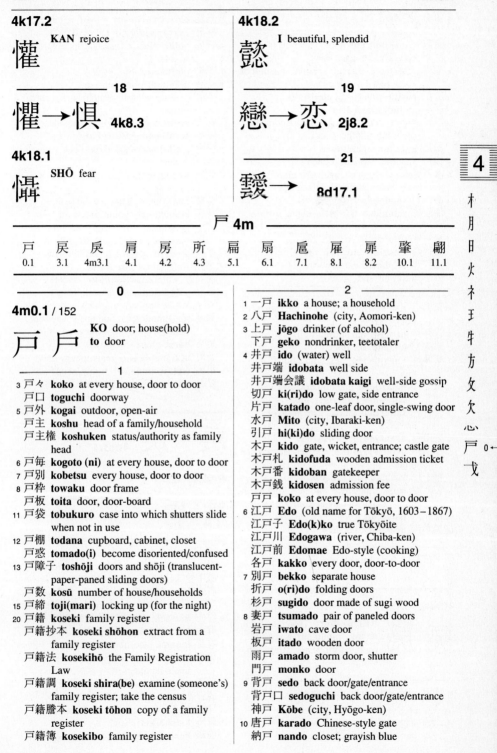

4k17.2

懽   **KAN** rejoice

——————— 18 ———————

懼 → 惧   **4k8.3**

4k18.1

懾   **SHŌ** fear

4k18.2

懿   **I** beautiful, splendid

——————— 19 ———————

戀 → 恋   **2j8.2**

——————— 21 ———————

戁 →   **8d17.1**

——————— 戸 **4m** ———————

戸	戻	戻	肩	房	所	扁	扇	扈	雇	扉	肇	翩
0.1	3.1	4m3.1	4.1	4.2	4.3	5.1	6.1	7.1	8.1	8.2	10.1	11.1

4 木 月 日 火 ネ 王 牛 方 攵 欠 心 戸 0 戈

——————— 0 ———————

4m0.1 / 152

戸 戸   **KO** door; house(hold)
         to door

——————— 1 ———————

3 戸々 **koko** at every house, door to door
戸口 **toguchi** doorway
5 戸外 **kogai** outdoor, open-air
戸主 **koshu** head of a family/household
戸主権 **koshuken** status/authority as family head
6 戸毎 **kogoto (ni)** at every house, door to door
7 戸別 **kobetsu** every house, door to door
8 戸枠 **towaku** door frame
戸板 **toita** door, door-board
11 戸袋 **tobukuro** case into which shutters slide when not in use
12 戸棚 **todana** cupboard, cabinet, closet
戸惑 **tomado(i)** become disoriented/confused
13 戸障子 **toshōji** doors and shōji (translucent-paper-paned sliding doors)
戸数 **kosū** number of house/households
15 戸締 **toji(mari)** locking up (for the night)
20 戸籍 **koseki** family register
戸籍抄本 **koseki shōhon** extract from a family register
戸籍法 **kosekihō** the Family Registration Law
戸籍調 **koseki shira(be)** examine (someone's) family register; take the census
戸籍謄本 **koseki tōhon** copy of a family register
戸籍簿 **kosekibo** family register

——————— 2 ———————

1 一戸 **ikko** a house; a household
2 八戸 **Hachinohe** (city, Aomori-ken)
3 上戸 **jōgo** drinker (of alcohol)
下戸 **geko** nondrinker, teetotaler
4 井戸 **ido** (water) well
井戸端 **idobata** well side
井戸端会議 **idobata kaigi** well-side gossip
切戸 **ki(ri)do** low gate, side entrance
片戸 **katado** one-leaf door, single-swing door
水戸 **Mito** (city, Ibaraki-ken)
引戸 **hi(ki)do** sliding door
木戸 **kido** gate, wicket, entrance; castle gate
木戸札 **kidofuda** wooden admission ticket
木戸番 **kidoban** gatekeeper
木戸銭 **kidosen** admission fee
戸戸 **koko** at every house, door to door
6 江戸 **Edo** (old name for Tōkyō, 1603–1867)
江戸子 **Edo(k)ko** true Tōkyōite
江戸川 **Edogawa** (river, Chiba-ken)
江戸前 **Edomae** Edo-style (cooking)
各戸 **kakko** every door, door-to-door
7 別戸 **bekko** separate house
折戸 **o(ri)do** folding doors
杉戸 **sugido** door made of sugi wood
8 妻戸 **tsumado** pair of paneled doors
岩戸 **iwato** cave door
板戸 **itado** wooden door
雨戸 **amado** storm door, shutter
門戸 **monko** door
9 背戸 **sedo** back door/gate/entrance
背戸口 **sedoguchi** back door/gate/entrance
神戸 **Kōbe** (city, Hyōgo-ken)
10 唐戸 **karado** Chinese-style gate
納戸 **nando** closet; grayish blue

4

→ 3

12 遣戸 **ya(ri)do** sliding door
揚戸 **a(ge)do** push-up door, shutter
落戸 **o(toshi)do** trap door
開戸 **hira(ki)do** hinged door
14 豪戸 **gōko** ancient administrative clan unit of about two dozen persons
鳴戸 **naruto** whirlpool, maelstrom
網戸 **amido** screen door
15 潜戸 **kugu(ri)do** side gate, small doorway (built into a larger door)
編戸 **a(mi)do** braided door
18 鎧戸 **yoroido** Venetian blinds
19 瀬戸 **seto** strait(s), channel; porcelain
瀬戸内海 **Setonaikai** the Inland Sea
瀬戸引 **setobi(ki)** enameled
瀬戸物 **setomono** porcelain, china, earthenware
瀬戸焼 **setoya(ki)** porcelain, china
瀬戸際 **setogiwa** crucial moment, crisis, brink
瀬戸鉢 **setobachi** earthenware pot
繰戸 **ku(ri)do** sliding door

─────── 3 ───────

4 天岩戸 **Ama(no)iwato** Gate of the Celestial Rock Cave
5 古井戸 **furuido** old unused well
6 防火戸 **bōkado** fire door
7 車井戸 **kuruma ido** well with a pulley and rope
8 泣上戸 **na(ki)jōgo** maudlin drinker
油井戸 **aburaido** oil well/spring
枝折戸 **shio(ri)do** garden gate made of branches
9 庭木戸 **niwakido** garden gate
怒上戸 **oko(ri)jōgo** one who gets angry when drunk
10 格子戸 **kōshido** lattice door
笑上戸 **wara(i)jōgo** one who gets jolly when drunk; one who laughs readily
11 掘井戸 **ho(ri)ido** a well
13 裏木戸 **urakido** back door

─────── 4 ───────

11 掘抜井戸 **ho(ri)nu(ki) ido** a well

─────── 3 ───────

4m3.1 / 1238

戻 戻 **REI, modo(ru)** go/come back, return **modo(su)** give/send back, return, restore; throw up, vomit

─────── 1 ───────

11 戻道 **modo(ri)michi** the way back

─────── 2 ───────

5 出戻 **demodo(ri)** divorced woman (back at her parents' home)

払戻 **hara(i)modo(su)** refund, reimburse
立戻 **ta(chi)modo(ru)** return to
6 行戻 **yu(ki)modo(ri)** round trip; divorced woman
7 売戻 **u(ri)modo(shi)** resale
8 受戻 **u(ke)modo(su)** redeem
逆戻 **gyakumodo(ri)** turn/go back, revert, relapse
押戻 **o(shi)modo(su)** push back; reject
呼戻 **yo(bi)modo(su)** call back, recall
突戻 **tsu(ki)modo(su)** thrust back; refuse to accept
取戻 **to(ri)modo(su)** take back, regain, recoup, catch up on
9 巻戻 **ma(ki)modo(shi)** rewind (a tape)
後戻 **atomodo(ri)** going backward, retrogression
悖戻 **hairei** disobey, be contrary to
10 差戻 **sa(shi)modo(su)** send/refer back
12 割戻 **wa(ri)modo(su)** rebate
割戻金 **wa(ri)modo(shi)kin** a rebate
焼戻 **ya(ki)modo(su)** anneal, temper
買戻 **ka(i)modo(su)** buy back, redeem
15 舞戻 **ma(i)modo(ru)** find one's way back, return
暴戻 **bōrei** tyrannical, brutal
請戻 **u(ke)modo(shi)** redemption
16 積戻 **tsu(mi)modo(su)** reship, send back
19 繰戻 **ku(ri)modo(su)** put back

─────── 4 ───────

戻 → 戻 **4m3.1**

4m4.1 / 1264

肩 肩 **KEN, kata** shoulder

─────── 1 ───────

2 肩入 **katai(re)** support, assistance
3 肩上 **kataa(ge)** shoulder tuck (in clothes)
5 肩甲骨 **kenkōkotsu** shoulder blade
肩代 **kataga(wari)** change of palanquin bearers; takeover, transfer (of a business)
6 肩先 **katasaki** (top of) the shoulder
肩当 **kataa(te)** shoulder pad
7 肩身 **katami** face, honor
肩車 **kataguruma** (give a child a ride) on one's shoulders
9 肩透 **katasuka(shi)** dodging
肩胛骨 **kenkōkotsu** shoulder blade
10 肩書 **kataga(ki)** one's title, degree
11 肩掛 **kataka(ke)** shawl
肩章 **kenshō** epaulette, shoulder pips

12 肩揚 **kataa(ge)** shoulder tuck (in clothes)
肩幅 **katahaba** breadth of one's shoulders
肩替 **kataga(wari)** change of palanquin bearers; takeover, transfer (of a business)
14 肩慣 **katana(rashi)** (pitcher's) warming up

——————— 2 ———————

4 双肩 **sōken** one's shoulders
5 比肩 **hiken** rank with, be comparable to
9 怒肩 **ika(ri)gata** square shoulders
11 強肩 **kyōken** strong-armed (baseball player)
15 撫肩 **na(de)gata** sloping/drooping shoulders

4m4.2 / 1237

房 房

BŌ a room; tassel
fusa tassel, tuft, cluster

——————— 1 ———————

3 房々 **fusafusa** tufty, bushy, profuse (hair)
4 房毛 **fusage** lock, tuft, tassel
房中 **bōchū** in the room/bedroom
8 房事 **bōji** sexual intercourse

——————— 2 ———————

3 工房 **kōbō** studio, atelier
女房 **nyōbō** wife; court lady
女房役 **nyōbōyaku** helpmate
女房持 **nyōbōmo(chi)** married man
4 文房具 **bunbōgu** writing materials, stationery
文房具屋 **bunbōguya** stationery store
心房 **shinbō** auricle (of the heart)
6 同房 **dōbō** the same cell
安房 **Awa** (ancient kuni, Chiba-ken)
7 冷房 **reibō** air conditioning
冷房車 **reibōsha** air-conditioned car
乳房 **chibusa** breast
8 官房 **kanbō** secretariat
官房長官 **kanbō chōkan** Chief Cabinet Secretary
房房 **fusafusa** tufty, bushy, profuse (hair)
9 独房 **dokubō** solitary cell
10 書房 **shobō** library; bookstore
11 黒房 **kurobusa** black tassel hung over the northwest of a sumo ring
船房 **senbō** cabin, stateroom
12 厨房 **chūbō** kitchen, galley
13 僧房 **sōbō** priests' living quarters
暖房 **danbō** heating
煖房 **danbō** heating
蜂房 **hōbō** beehive, apiary
14 閨房 **keibō** bedroom, bedchamber
15 監房 **kanbō** (prison) cell

——————— 3 ———————

5 左心房 **sashinbō** the left auricle
右心房 **ushinbō** the right auricle

——————— 4 ———————

8 押掛女房 **o(shi)ka(ke) nyōbō** a woman who pressured her husband into marrying her

4m4.3 / 153

所 所

SHO, tokoro, toko place

——————— 1 ———————

3 所々 **tokorodokoro, shosho** here and there
所々方々 **shosho-hōbō** everywhere
5 所以 **yuen** the reason, why
所存 **shozon** thought, opinion
所用 **shoyō** use; business, need
所払 **tokorobara(i)** banishment from one's residence
6 所在 **shozai** whereabouts, location, site
所在地 **shozaichi** seat, location
所行 **shogyō** deed, act, work
所有 **shoyū** ownership, possession
所有主 **shoyūnushi** owner
所有地 **shoyūchi** the land one owns
所有者 **shoyūsha** owner
所有格 **shoyūkaku** the possessive case
所有権 **shoyūken** ownership
7 所作 **shosa** conduct, bearing
所作事 **shosagoto** dance drama, posture dance
所労 **shorō** indisposition, illness
所見 **shoken** one's views, impressions
8 所長 **shochō** director, head, manager
所定 **shotei** fixed, prescribed, stated
所所 **tokorodokoro, shosho** here and there
所所方方 **shosho-hōbō** everywhere
9 所信 **shoshin** one's belief, conviction, opinion
所持 **shoji** possess, have on one's person, carry
所持人 **shojinin** holder, bearer
所持者 **shojisha** holder, bearer
所持金 **shojikin** money on hand
所持品 **shojihin** one's personal effects
所要 **shoyō** (the time) needed/required
所狭 **tokorosema(i)** crowded
所柄 **tokorogara** locality, the occasion
所為 **shoi** work, feat **sei** an effect of, due to
所思 **shoshi** one's thoughts, opinion
10 所員 **shoin** (member of the) staff, personnel
所帯 **shotai** household, home
所帯主 **shotainushi** head of the household
所帯持 **shotaimo(chi)** housekeeping; married (wo)man
所帯数 **shotaisū** number of households
所書 **tokoroga(ki)** address
11 所得 **shotoku** income, earnings
所得者 **shotokusha** income earner
所得税 **shotokuzei** income tax
所得層 **shotokusō** income level/bracket

4

木 月 日 火 礻 王 牛 方 攵 欠 心 戸 4← 戈

4

木 月 日 火 ネ 王 牛 方 攵 欠 心 戸 戈

→ 4

所得顔 **tokoroegao** triumph, elation
所得額 **shotokugaku** (amount of) income
所望 **shomō** desire, request
所産 **shosan** product, result
12 所属 **shozoku** be attached/assigned to
所期 **shoki** expectation, anticipation
所替 **tokoroga(e)** moving (to a new address)
所番地 **tokorobanchi** address
13 所業 **shogyō** deed, act, work
所嫌 **tokorokira(wazu)** everywhere, anywhere
所感 **shokan** one's impressions, opinion
所詮 **shosen** after all
所載 **shosai** printed, published
14 所管 **shokan** jurisdiction
所説 **shosetsu** one's statement, opinion
所領 **shoryō** territory
15 所蔵 **shozō** in one's possession
所論 **shoron** argument
16 所懐 **shokai** one's impressions, opinion
所謂 **iwayuru** what is called, so-called
17 所轄 **shokatsu** jurisdiction
19 所願 **shogan** desire, wish, request

───────── 2 ─────────

1 一所 **ik(ka)sho, issho, hitotokoro** one place; the same place
一所懸命 **isshokenmei** with all one's might
2 入所 **nyūsho** entrance, admission; imprisonment
3 大所 **ōdokoro** rich family; important person/company
4 不所存 **fushozon** imprudence, indiscretion
屯所 **tonsho** post, garrison; police station
支所 **shisho** branch office, substation
5 凹所 **ōsho** concavity, hollow, depression
出所 **shussho** source, origin; be released from prison **dedokoro** source, origin
他所 **tasho** another place
台所 **daidokoro** kitchen
台所流 **daidokoro (no) naga(shi)** the kitchen sink
札所 **fudasho** amulet-issuing office
立所 **ta(chi)dokoro (ni)** immediately, at once, on the spot
6 死所 **shisho** where to die, where one died
会所 **kaisho** meeting place; club
近所 **kinjo** neighborhood, vicinity
近所合壁 **kinjo gappeki** immediate neighborhood
同所 **dōsho** the same place, that (same) address
地所 **jisho** (tract/plot of) land, ground
至所 **ita(ru) tokoro** everywhere
在所 **zaisho** the country; one's native place
名所 **meisho** noted places/sights

名所旧跡 **meisho-kyūseki** scenic and historic places
行所 **yu(ki)dokoro** one's destination/whereabouts
当所 **tōsho** this place **a(te)do** aim, purpose
各所 **kakusho** each place, various places
米所 **komedokoro** rice-producing area
7 住所 **jūsho, su(mi)dokoro** address; residence, domicile
住所録 **jūshoroku** address book
余所 **yoso** another place; other, strange
余所目 **yosome** someone else's eye, casual observer
余所行 **yosoyu(ki), yosoi(ki)** going out, formal (manners), one's best (attire)
余所見 **yosomi** look away
余所者 **yosomono** stranger
妙所 **myōsho** point of beauty, charm
役所 **yakusho** government office
役所風 **(o)yakushofū** red tape, officialism
局所 **kyokusho** local
見所 **midokoro** the part most worth seeing; promise, merit **mi(ta) tokoro** judging from the appearance
利所 **ki(ki)dokoro** effective/important point
男所帯 **otokojotai** all-male household
8 長所 **chōsho** one's strong point, advantages
拠所 **yo(ri)dokoro** foundation, grounds, authority
狙所 **nera(i)dokoro** aim, objective
空所 **kūsho** a space/blank
居所 **idokoro, kyosho** one's whereabouts, address, residence
所所 **tokorodokoro, shosho** here and there
所所方方 **shosho-hōbō** everywhere
或所 **a(ru) tokoro (de)** in a certain place
取所 **to(ri)dokoro** worth, merit
9 便所 **benjo** toilet, lavatory
臥所 **fushido** place to sleep, bed
急所 **kyūsho** vital point, vulnerable spot; crux, key (to)
要所 **yōsho** important/strategic place
要所要所 **yōsho-yōsho** every important place
茶所 **chadokoro** tea-growing region
某所 **bōsho** a certain place
政所 **mandokoro** government office (historical)
10 随所 **zuisho** everywhere, anywhere
高所 **kōsho** elevation, height; altitude; broad view
捕所 **to(rae)dokoro** the point, meaning
座所 **zasho** one's seat
脈所 **myakudokoro** spot on the body where the pulse can be felt; vital point
旅所 **tabisho** resting place for a palanquin shrine

純所得 **junshotoku** net income
納所 **nassho** temple office
紋所 **mondokoro** (family) crest
配所 **haisho** place of exile
11 勘所 **kandokoro** the point (on a violin string)
to press to get the desired tone; vital
point, crux
清所 **kiyodokoro** kitchen (in a noble's home)
控所 **hika(e)jo** waiting room
捨所 **su(te)dokoro** the place/time to throw
away (one's life)
宿所 **shukusho** address, lodgings, quarters
悪所 **akusho** dangerous place; brothel
12 場所 **basho** place, location
場所柄 **bashogara** character of a place,
location, situation, occasion
場所塞 **bashofusa(gi)** obstacle
短所 **tansho** shortcoming, defect, fault
御所 **gosho** imperial palace
御所車 **goshoguruma** canopied ox-drawn
carriage
営所 **eisho** barracks, camp
屠所 **tosho** slaughterhouse
極所 **kyokusho** end, extremity
無所得 **mushotoku** without any income
無所属 **mushozoku** unaffiliated, independent
番所 **bansho** sentry box
貴所 **kisho** your place, you
13 適所 **tekisho** the right/proper place
損所 **sonsho** damaged part/spot
墓所 **bosho, hakasho, hakadokoro** cemetery
寝所 **shinjo, nedoko** bedroom
置所 **o(ki)dokoro** place to put something
詰所 **tsu(me)sho** office; guard room; crew's
room　**tsu(maru) tokoro** that is, after all
預所 **azu(kari)sho** depository, warehouse
14 攫所 **tsuka(mi)dokoro** hold, grip
攫所無 **tsuka(mi)dokoro (no) na(i)** slippery,
evasive
箇所 **kasho** place, part, passage (in a book)
聞所 **ki(ki)dokoro** the part/point to listen for
関所 **sekisho** border station, checkpoint
16 賢所 **Kashikodokoro** Palace Sanctuary
18 難所 **nansho** difficult pass/stage
闕所 **kessho** confiscation of an estate

────────── 3 ──────────

0 ３ヶ所 **sankasho** three places
3 工務所 **kōmusho** engineering office
大御所 **ōgosho** retired shōgun; influential
figure, doyen
小便所 **shōbenjo** urinal
4 不労所得 **furō shotoku** unearned/investment
income
収容所 **shūyōjo** home, asylum, camp
公文所 **kumonjo** government office
(historical)

区役所 **kuyakusho** ward office
手洗所 **tearaijo** lavatory
5 出張所 **shutchōjo** branch office
市役所 **shiyakusho** city hall
6 休泊所 **kyūhakujo** place for resting and
sleeping
休息所 **kyūsokujo** resting room, lounge
休憩所 **kyūkeijo** resting room, lounge, lobby
仮出所 **karishussho** release on parole, out
on bail
会議所 **kaigisho** meeting hall, site of a
conference
印刷所 **insatsujo** press, print shop
刑務所 **keimusho** prison
行在所 **anzaisho** emperor's temporary
residence
安息所 **ansokujo** resting place, haven
7 抑留所 **yokuryūjo** detention/internment
camp
投票所 **tōhyōjo** polling place, the polls
社務所 **shamusho** shrine office
見張所 **miha(ri)sho** lookout, crow's nest
初場所 **hatsubasho** New Year's grand sumo
tournament
8 事務所 **jimusho** office
協議所 **kyōgisho** conference site
治療所 **chiryōsho** infirmary, clinic
拘留所 **kōryūjo** detention room, lockup
拘置所 **kōchisho** house of detention, prison
奇麗所 **kireidoko** good-looking woman
実験所 **jikkenjo** experiment station
居場所 **ibasho** one's whereabouts, address
取引所 **torihikijo, torihikisho** (stock)
exchange
9 発行所 **hakkōsho** publishing house
発電所 **hatsudensho** power plant, generating
station
保育所 **hoikujo** nursery school
保健所 **hokenjo** health center
保養所 **hoyōsho, hoyōjo** sanitarium, rest
home
郡役所 **gun'yakusho** county office
変電所 **hendensho** transformer substation
造船所 **zōsenjo** shipyard
洗面所 **senmenjo** washroom, lavatory
活版所 **kappanjo** print shop
派出所 **hashutsujo** police box; branch office
相談所 **sōdanjo** consultation office
春場所 **harubasho** the spring sumo tournament
研究所 **kenkyūjo** (research) institute,
laboratory
研修所 **kenshūjo** training institute/center
秋場所 **akibasho** autumn sumo tournament
10 案内所 **annaijo** information office/booth
教習所 **kyōshūjo** training institute

4

忄
月
日
火
礻
王
牛
方
攵
欠
心
戸　4←
戈

夏場所 **natsubasho** the summer sumo tournament
託児所 **takujisho** day nursery
配給所 **haikyūjo** distribution point
配電所 **haidensho** power station
11 停留所 **teiryūjo** stopping place, (bus) stop
採炭所 **saitanjo** coal mine
授産所 **jusanjo** vocational center (for the unemployed)
宿泊所 **shukuhakujo** lodgings
脱衣所 **datsuisho, datsuijo** changing/dressing room
現住所 **genjūsho** present address
救護所 **kyūgosho** first-aid station
販売所 **hanbaisho** shop, store
12 勤労所得 **kinrō shotoku** earned income
測候所 **sokkōjo** weather station
揚水所 **yōsuijo** pumping-up station
登記所 **tōkisho** registry (office)
御座所 **gozasho** the throne
検査所 **kensajo** inspection station
検疫所 **ken'ekisho** quarantine station
検問所 **kenmonjo** checkpoint
無任所大臣 **muninsho daijin** minister without portfolio
裁判所 **saibansho** (law) court
給水所 **kyūsuijo** water station
給油所 **kyūyusho** filling/gas station
診療所 **shinryōjo** clinic
貯炭所 **chotanjo** coal yard, coaling station
貯蔵所 **chozōsho** storage place
集会所 **shūkaijo** meeting place, assembly hall
集結所 **shūketsusho** place of assembly
開票所 **kaihyōjo** ballot-counting place
13 隠場所 **kaku(re)basho** refuge, hiding place
数ヶ所 **sūkasho** several places
碁会所 **gokaisho, gokaijo** go club
14 製氷所 **seihyōsho** ice plant
製作所 **seisakujo** factory, works, workshop
製材所 **seizaisho** sawmill
製版所 **seihanjo** platemaking shop
製油所 **seiyujo** oil refinery
製革所 **seikakujo** tannery
製粉所 **seifunjo** flour mill
製鉄所 **seitetsujo** ironworks
製糖所 **seitōjo** sugar refinery
製錬所 **seirenjo** refinery, smelting works
製鋼所 **seikōjo** steel plant
製麺所 **seimenjo** noodle factory
精油所 **seiyusho** oil refinery
精錬所 **seirenjo** refinery, smelter
精練所 **seirenjo** refinery, smelter
15 隣近所 **tonarikinjo** neighborhood
避難所 **hinanjo** shelter, place of safety
撮影所 **satsueijo** movie studio

監視所 **kanshisho** lookout, guard/observation post
鋳造所 **chūzōsho** mint; foundry
駐在所 **chūzaisho** police substation
16 興信所 **kōshinjo** detective/investigative agency
17 療養所 **ryōyōjo** sanitarium
鍛工所 **tankōjo, tankōsho** foundry
18 観測所 **kansokujo** observatory, observation station
20 醸造所 **jōzōsho** brewery, distillery

──────── 4 ────────

3 大宮御所 **Ōmiya gosho** Empress Dowager's Palace
4 区裁判所 **kusaibansho** local court
水洗便所 **suisen benjo** flush toilet
6 汲取便所 **ku(mi)to(ri) benjo** hole-in-the-floor/non-flush toilet
8 東宮御所 **Tōgū gosho** the Crown Prince's Palace
9 要所要所 **yōsho-yōsho** every important place
13 適材適所 **tekizai-tekisho** the right man in the right place

──────── 5 ────────

4 水力発電所 **suiryoku hatsudensho** hydro-electric plant
10 家庭裁判所 **katei saibansho** Family Court
11 商工会議所 **Shōkō Kaigisho** Chamber of Commerce and Industry
12 最高裁判所 **Saikō Saibansho** Supreme Court
18 職業安定所 **shokugyō anteisho, shokugyō anteijo** (public) employment security office
簡易裁判所 **kan'i saibansho** summary court

──────── 6 ────────

10 原子力発電所 **genshiryoku hatsudensho** nuclear power plant

──────── 5 ────────

4m5.1

扁 扁　**HEN** doorplate, nameplate; flat; small

──────── 1 ────────

5 扁平 **henpei** flat
扁平足 **henpeisoku** flat feet
6 扁舟 **henshū** small boat, skiff
10 扁桃 **hentō** almond
扁桃腺 **hentōsen** the tonsils
扁桃腺炎 **hentōsen'en** tonsillitis
18 扁額 **hengaku** framed picture

——————— 6 ———————

4m6.1 / 1555

扇　　SEN, ōgi folding fan
　　　ao(gu) fan

——————— 1 ———————

2 扇子 **sensu** folding fan
7 扇状 **senjō** fan-shaped
　扇状地 **senjōchi** alluvial fan, delta
　扇形 **ōgigata, senkei** fan shape, sector, segment
9 扇風機 **senpūki** (electric) fan
11 扇動 **sendō** incitement, instigation, agitation
　扇動者 **sendōsha** instigator, agitator
　扇情 **senjō** inflammatory
　扇情的 **senjōteki** sensational, suggestive, racy

——————— 2 ———————

5 白扇 **hakusen** white fan
6 団扇 **uchiwa** round fan
8 金扇 **kinsen** gilt (folding) fan
13 鉄扇 **tessen** iron-ribbed folding fan
14 銀扇 **ginsen** silver-colored folding fan
15 舞扇 **maiōgi** dancer's fan

——————— 3 ———————

5 左団扇 **hidari uchiwa** (living in) ease and luxury
12 換気扇 **kankisen** ventilation fan

——————— 4 ———————

10 夏炉冬扇 **karo-tōsen** useless things (like a fireplace in summer or a fan in winter)

——————— 7 ———————

4m7.1

启　　KO follow

——————— 2 ———————

12 跋扈 **bakko** prevalence, rampancy, domination

——————— 8 ———————

4m8.1 / 1553

雇 雇　KO, yato(u) employ, hire; charter
　　　yato(i) employee

——————— 1 ———————

2 雇入 **yato(i)i(reru)** employ, hire; charter
　雇人 **yato(i)nin** employee; servant
3 雇口 **yato(i)guchi** employment, job
5 雇用 **koyō** employment
　雇用主 **koyōnushi** employer
　雇用者 **koyōsha** employer
　雇主 **yato(i)nushi** employer
10 雇員 **koin** employee
11 雇庸 **koyō** employment, hiring
13 雇傭 **koyō** employment, hiring
　雇賃 **yato(i)chin** wages

——————— 2 ———————

4 月雇 **tsukiyato(i)** hiring by the month
　日雇 **hiyato(i)** hiring by the day
11 常雇 **jōyato(i)** regular employee
13 解雇 **kaiko** discharge, dismissal

——————— 3 ———————

7 完全雇傭 **kanzen koyō** full employment

4m8.2 / 1556

扉 扉　HI, tobira door (hinged, not sliding)

——————— 2 ———————

8 門扉 **monpi** doors of a gate
12 開扉 **kaihi** open the door
13 鉄扉 **teppi** iron door

——————— 10 ———————

4m10.1

肇　　CHŌ begin, found; rectify

——————— 11 ———————

4m11.1

翩　　HEN, hirugae(ru) flap, flutter

——————— 1 ———————

18 翩翻 **henpon** fluttering

————————— 戈 4n —————————

戈	弋	式	戉	戊	成	戌	戍	戎	弎	戒	式	弐
0.1	0.2	1.1	1.2	1.3	2.1	2.2	2.3	2.4	2.5	3.1	3.2	3.3

弐	我	戔	或	咸	威	武	哉	栽	戛	戚	戟	憂
3.4	0a7.10	4.1	4.2	5.1	5.2	5.3	5.4	6.1	7.1	7.2	8.1	4n7.1

4 — 木 月 日 火 礻 王 牛 方 攵 欠 心 戸 戈 11←

越	牋	殘	幾	裁	哉	戦	盞	感	斌	歳	戳	截
8.2	8.3	0a10.11	8.4	5e6.9	9.1	9.2	9.3	4k9.21	9.4	9.5	10.1	8c6.3

鳶	戲	臧	戮	戰	戱	戴	戳	殯	巉	鹹	殲	戳
11b3.1	11.1	11.2	11.3	4n9.2	4n11.1	5f12.2	14.1	4n17.1	3o17.1	16.1	17.1	18.1

4

木 月 日 火 礻 王 牛 方 攵 欠 心 戸 戈
→0 戈

0

4n0.1

戈

KA, hoko halberd; arms

2

3 干戈 **kanka** shield and halberd; weapons; war

4n0.2

弋

YOKU stake; arrow with weighted cord (for entangling game); capture; black **igurumi** arrow to which a weighted cord is attached

---

2

10 遊弋 **yūyoku** cruise

1

4n1.1

式

ICHI one

4n1.2

戉

ETSU, masakari broadax, battle-ax

4n1.3

戊

BO fifth in a series, "E" **tsuchinoe** fifth calendar sign

2

4n2.1 / 261

成

SEI, JŌ, na(ru) become, consist of **na(su)** do; form

1

0 お成り **(o)na(ri)** visit/departure of a high personage
2 成人 **seijin** adult
　成人式 **seijinshiki** Coming-of-Age-Day (Jan. 15) ceremony
3 成上 **na(ri)a(garu)** rise to prominence
　成上者 **na(ri)a(gari)mono** upstart, parvenu

　成下 **na(ri)sa(garu)** come down in the world, be reduced to
4 成仏 **jōbutsu** attain Nirvana; die
　成文 **seibun** composition, writing
　成文化 **seibunka** put in writing, codify
　成文法 **seibunhō** statute/written law
　成文律 **seibunritsu** statute/written law
　成分 **seibun** composition, content, ingredient, component
5 成代 **na(ri)ka(waru)** take the place of (someone)
　成功 **seikō** success
　成句 **seiku** set phrase, idiomatic expression
　成立 **seiritsu** come into being, be formed/ effected **na(ri)ta(tsu)** consist of; be effected, come into being **na(ri)ta(chi)** origin, history, makeup
6 成年 **seinen** (age of) majority, adulthood
　成年式 **seinenshiki** coming-of-age ceremony
　成行 **na(ri)yu(ki)** course (of events), developments
　成因 **seiin** cause, origin
　成虫 **seichū** adult insect
7 成体 **seitai** (insect's) adult form **na(ri)katachi** appearance
　成否 **seihi** success or failure
8 成長 **seichō** growth
　成果 **seika** result, fruit **na(ri)ha(teru)** become, be reduced to **na(re) (no) ha(te)** the wreck of one's former self
　成育 **seiiku** growth, development
　成典 **seiten** law code; established rites
　成金 **narikin** new rich, parvenu
9 成型 **seikei** form, press, stamp out
　成約 **seiyaku** conclude a contract
10 成員 **seiin** member
　成案 **seian** definite plan
11 成遂 **na(shi)to(geru)** accomplish, carry out
　成済 **na(ri)su(masu)** (completely) become
　成婚 **seikon** marriage
　成務 **Seimu** (emperor, 131–190)
　成敗 **seibai** punish, bring to justice **seihai** success or failure
12 成就 **jōju** accomplish, achieve, succeed
13 成業 **seigyō** completion of one's work/ studies
　成損 **na(ri)sokona(u)** fail to become
14 成層岩 **seisōgan** stratified/sedimentary rock

成層圏 **seisōken** the stratosphere
成熟 **seijuku** ripen; mature
成熟期 **seijukuki** puberty, adolescence
成算 **seisan** prospects of success
成語 **seigo** set phrase, idiomatic expression
17 成績 **seiseki** results, (business) performance
成績表 **seisekihyō** report/score card

──────── 2 ────────
3 大成 **taisei** complete, accomplish; compile; attain greatness
小成 **shōsei** small success
4 不成功 **fuseikō** failure
不成立 **fuseiritsu** failure, rejection
小成績 **fuseiseki** poor results/performance
天成 **tensei** natural, born (musician)
天成美 **tensei (no) bi** natural beauty
化成 **kasei** transformation, chemical synthesis
双成 **futana(ri)** androgynous, hermaphrodite
水成岩 **suiseigan** sedimentary rock
火成岩 **kaseigan** igneous rock
5 未成年 **miseinen** minority, not of age
未成年者 **miseinensha** a minor
未成品 **miseihin** unfinished goods
生成 **seisei** creation, formation, generation
平成 **Heisei** (era, 1989–)
可成 **kana(ri)** considerably, rather, quite
好成績 **kōseiseki** good results/record
主成分 **shuseibun** main ingredient
6 両成敗 **ryōseibai** punishing both parties
合成 **gōsei** synthetic, composite, combined
合成物 **gōseibutsu** a compound/synthetic
合成語 **gōseigo** a compound (word)
合成樹脂 **gōsei jushi** synthetic resin, plastic
合成繊維 **gōsei sen'i** synthetic fiber
老成 **rōsei** mature
夙成 **shukusei** precociousness
行成 **i(ki)na(ri)** all of a sudden
守成 **shusei** preservation, maintenance
7 亜成層圏 **asei sōken** substratosphere
作成 **sakusei** draw up, prepare
助成 **josei** foster, promote, aid
助成金 **joseikin** subsidy, grant
形成 **keisei** formation, makeup
完成 **kansei** completion, accomplishment
言成 **i(i)na(ri)** (doing) whatever (someone) says
言成放題 **i(i)na(ri) hōdai** submissive to (someone)
8 京成 **Kei-Sei** Tōkyō-Narita
育成 **ikusei** rearing, training
取成 **to(ri)na(shi)** intercession
9 促成 **sokusei** growth promotion
促成栽培 **sokusei saibai** forcing culture, hothouse cultivation

俄成金 **niwakanarikin** overnight millionaire
変成 **hensei** metamorphosis
速成 **sokusei** intensive training, short course
持成 **mo(te)na(shi)** treatment, reception, welcome, hospitality, entertainment
10 既成 **kisei** existing, established
既成事実 **kisei jijitsu** fait accompli
原成岩 **genseigan** primary rocks
11 偶成 **gūsei** contingent, fortuitous
陽成 **Yōzei** (emperor, 876–884)
達成 **tassei** achieve, attain
混成 **konsei** mixture, combination, hybrid
組成 **sosei** composition, makeup
船成金 **funanarikin** shipping magnate
転成 **tensei** be transformed, change into
12 落成 **rakusei** completion of construction
落成式 **rakuseishiki** building-completion ceremony
期成 **kisei** realization (of a plan)
期成同盟 **kisei dōmei** uniting to carry out (a plan)
焼成 **shōsei** calcination
結成 **kessei** formation, organization
集成 **shūsei** collect, compile
14 構成 **kōsei** composition, makeup
構成分子 **kōsei bunshi** components
構成員 **kōseiin** member
熟成 **jukusei** ripening, maturation, aging
15 養成 **yōsei** train, educate, cultivate
編成 **hensei** organize, put together
賛成 **sansei** agreement, approbation
賛成者 **sanseisha** approver, supporter
16 錬成 **rensei** training
18 織成 **o(ri)na(su)** weave (a picture)
20 醸成 **jōsei** brew; cause, bring about

──────── 3 ────────
4 不賛成 **fusansei** disapproval, disagreement
5 未完成 **mikansei** incomplete, unfinished
6 再編成 **saihensei** reorganization, reshuffle
光合成 **kōgōsei** photosynthesis
7 即身成仏 **sokushin jōbutsu** attaining Buddhahood while still alive
12 集大成 **shūtaisei** compilation

──────── 4 ────────
1 一気呵成 **ikki kasei** in one breath/stroke/stretch
3 大器晩成 **taiki bansei** Great talent blooms late.

4n2.2

JUTSU, inu eleventh horary sign (dog)

4

木 月 日 火 礻 王 牛 方 攵 欠 心 戸 戈 2←

4n2.3

成

JU protect, defend (the country's borders)

————— 1 —————

8 成卒 **jusotsu** border guard

4n2.4

戎

JŪ warrior; battle
ebisu barbarian

————— 1 —————

6 戎衣 **jūi** armor; military uniform

4n2.5

弍

NI two

————— 3 —————

4n3.1 / 876

戒

KAI, imashi(meru) admonish, warn
imashi(me) instructions

————— 1 —————

4 戒心 **kaishin** preparedness, vigilance, caution
6 戒名 **kaimyō** Buddhist initiation/posthumous name
7 戒告 **kaikoku** warning, admonition
9 戒律 **kairitsu** (Buddhist) precepts
16 戒壇 **kaidan** ordination platform in a temple
17 戒厳 **kaigen** being on guard
戒厳令 **kaigenrei** martial law

————— 2 —————

2 十戒 **jikkai** the ten Buddhist precepts
6 自戒 **jikai** self-discipline; admonish oneself
8 受戒 **jukai** Buddhist confirmation
9 浄戒 **jōkai** precepts, commandments
持戒 **jikai** observance of the (Buddhist) commandments
10 哨戒 **shōkai** patrol, guard
教戒 **kyōkai** exhortation, preaching
教戒師 **kyōkaishi** prison chaplain
破戒 **hakai** breaking the (Buddhist) commandments
訓戒 **kunkai** admonition, warning
11 斎戒 **saikai** purification
授戒 **jukai** Buddhist initiation ceremony
13 禁戒 **kinkai** commandment
17 厳戒 **genkai** strict guard/watch
18 懲戒 **chōkai** disciplinary punishment, official reprimand
19 警戒 **keikai** warning, (pre)caution; vigilance

警戒色 **keikaishoku** warning color
警戒線 **keikaisen** police cordon
警戒警報 **keikai keihō** an (air-raid) alert

————— 3 —————

10 殺生戒 **sesshōkai** Buddhist precept against killing

4n3.2 / 525

式

SHIKI ceremony, rite; formula, expression (in math); (as suffix) type, style, system

————— 1 —————

4 式日 **shikijitsu** ceremonial occasion
5 式台 **shikidai** step (in an entrance hall)
式目 **shikimoku** law code (historical)
6 式次 **shikiji** the program of a ceremony
8 式事 **shikiji** ceremony, observance
式典 **shikiten** ceremonies
式法 **shikihō** ceremony, form, manners
式服 **shikifuku** ceremonial dress
10 式部 **shikibu** master of ceremony/protocol
式部官 **shikibukan** master of court ceremony
式部省 **Shikibushō** Ministry of Ceremony
12 式場 **shikijō** ceremonial hall
13 式微 **shikibi** decline, wane
式辞 **shikiji** address, message, oration

————— 2 —————

1 一式 **isshiki** a complete set; all, the whole
4 仏式 **busshiki** Buddhist rites
公式 **kōshiki** formula, formality
方式 **hōshiki** formula; form; method, system; formalities, usage
5 本式 **honshiki** regular, orthodox
古式 **koshiki** old style, ancient ritual
正式 **seishiki** formal, official
旧式 **kyūshiki** old-type, old-fashioned
礼式 **reishiki** etiquette
7 形式 **keishiki** form; formality
形式化 **keishikika** formalization
形式主義 **keishiki shugi** formalism; red-tapism
形式的 **keishikiteki** formal
形式美 **keishikibi** beauty of form
形式論 **keishikiron** formalism
図式 **zushiki** diagram, graph
8 例式 **reishiki** regular ceremony; established form
其式 **soreshiki** only that much
法式 **hōshiki** rule, regulation, rite
定式 **jōshiki, teishiki** prescribed/established form, formula, formality
9 洋式 **yōshiki** Western-style
要式 **yōshiki** formal
単式 **tanshiki** simple system; single-entry (bookkeeping)

神式 **shinshiki** Shinto rites
10 挙式 **kyoshiki** (wedding) ceremony
株式 **kabushiki** shares, stocks
株式市場 **kabushiki shijō** stock market
株式会社 **kabushiki-gaisha, kabushiki kaisha** corporation, Co., Ltd.
格式 **kakushiki** status, social standing; formalities
格式張 **kakushikiba(ru)** stick to formalities
書式 **shoshiki** (blank) form
11 祭式 **saishiki** ritual, rites, ceremony
略式 **ryakushiki** informal, summary
軟式飛行船 **nanshiki hikōsen** dirigible, balloon
軟式庭球 **nanshiki teikyū** softball tennis
軟式野球 **nanshiki yakyū** softball
12 違式 **ishiki** irregularity, breach of form/ etiquette
葬式 **sōshiki** funeral
硬式 **kōshiki** hard, rigid
等式 **tōshiki** an equality
13 腹式呼吸 **fukushiki kokyū** abdominal breathing
解式 **kaishiki** solution (in math)
新式 **shinshiki** new-type, new-style, modern
跡式 **atoshiki** head of family
14 様式 **yōshiki** style, form
複式 **fukushiki** double-entry (bookkeeping)
複式学級 **fukushiki gakkyū** combined class (of more than one grade)
15 儀式 **gishiki** ceremony
諸式 **shoshiki** prices

――――――― 3 ―――――――

2 二連式 **nirenshiki** double, duplex
入学式 **nyūgakushiki** entrance ceremony
3 上棟式 **jōtōshiki** ridgepole-raising/roof-laying ceremony
4 化学式 **kagaku shiki** chemical formula
分列式 **bunretsushiki** march-past, military review
水冷式 **suireishiki** water-cooled
手動式 **shudōshiki** manual, hand-operated
方程式 **hōteishiki** equation
5 出初式 **dezomeshiki** firemen's New Year's demonstrations
6 多発式 **tahatsushiki** multi-engined
多段式 **tadanshiki** multistage
多項式 **takōshiki** polynomial expression
西洋式 **seiyōshiki** Western-style
列聖式 **resseishiki** canonization
成人式 **seijinshiki** Coming-of-Age-Day (Jan. 15) ceremony
成年式 **seinenshiki** coming-of-age ceremony
自動式 **jidōshiki** automatic
7 即位式 **sokuishiki** enthronement ceremony, coronation

折畳式 **o(ri)tata(mi)shiki** folding, collapsible
告別式 **kokubetsushiki** funeral service
8 非公式 **hikōshiki** unofficial
泥縄式 **doronawashiki** last-minute, eleventh-hour
始業式 **shigyōshiki** opening ceremony
定礎式 **teisoshiki** cornerstone-laying ceremony
空冷式 **kūreishiki** air-cooled
金婚式 **kinkonshiki** golden wedding anniversary
9 発会式 **hakkaishiki** opening ceremony
除幕式 **jomakushiki** unveiling (ceremony)
洗礼式 **senreishiki** baptism (ceremony)
宣誓式 **senseishiki** administering an oath
10 進水式 **shinsuishiki** launching ceremony
起工式 **kikōshiki** ground-breaking ceremony
訓令式 **kunreishiki** (a system of romanization which differs from Hepburn romanization in such syllables as *shi/si, tsu/tu, cha/tya*)
11 授与式 **juyoshiki** presentation ceremony
組立式 **kumita(te)shiki** prefab, collapsible
終業式 **shūgyōshiki** closing ceremony
12 渡橋式 **tokyōshiki** bridge-opening ceremony
就任式 **shūninshiki** inauguration, installation
落成式 **rakuseishiki** building-completion ceremony
棟上式 **munea(ge)shiki** roof-raising ceremony
最新式 **saishinshiki** latest type/style
竣工式 **shunkōshiki** completion ceremony
結婚式 **kekkonshiki** wedding
開会式 **kaikaishiki** opening ceremony
開校式 **kaikōshiki** school opening ceremony
13 電子式 **denshishiki** electronic
電動式 **dendōshiki** electric (not manual)
14 総花式 **sōbanashiki** across-the-board (pay raise)
銀婚式 **ginkonshiki** silver wedding anniversary
16 親任式 **shinninshiki** ceremony of investitute by the emperor
17 戴冠式 **taikanshiki** coronation
18 観兵式 **kanpeishiki** military review, parade
観艦式 **kankanshiki** naval review
贈呈式 **zōteishiki** presentation ceremony

――――――― 4 ―――――――

5 立太子式 **rittaishi-shiki** investiture of the crown prince

――――――― 5 ―――――――

2 二次方程式 **niji hōteishiki** quadratic equation
9 連立方程式 **renritsu hōteishiki** simultaneous equations

4

木
月
日
火
礻
王
牛
方
攵
欠
心
戸
戈 3←

4n3.3 / 1030

NI two (in documents)

弍 貳貳

4n3.4

SAN three

弎

我 → **0a7.10**

4

4n4.1

戔

ZAN damage; remain
SEN slight

4n4.2

或

WAKU, a(ru) a certain, a, some, one
arui(wa) or; perhaps

——————— 1 ———————

2 或人 **a(ru) hito** somebody, a certain person
4 或日 **a(ru) hi** one day
8 或所 **a(ru) tokoro (de)** in a certain place
13 或意味 **a(ru) imi (de)** in one/a sense

——————— 5 ———————

4n5.1

咸

KAN all; same

4n5.2 / 1339

威

I authority, dignity, majesty; threat
odo(su) threaten

——————— 1 ———————

2 威力 **iryoku** power, might, authority, influence
3 威丈高 **itakedaka** domineering, overbearing
5 威令 **irei** authority
威圧 **iatsu** coercion
威圧的 **iatsuteki** coercive, domineering
6 威名 **imei** renown, prestige
威光 **ikō** authority, power, influence
8 威服 **ifuku** awe into submission
威武 **ibu** authority and force
9 威信 **ishin** prestige, dignity

威風 **ifū** majesty, imposing air
威風堂々 **ifū dōdō** pomp and circumstance
10 威容 **iyō** commanding presence, dignity
11 威張 **iba(ru)** be proud, swagger
威望 **ibō** influence and popularity
13 威勢 **isei** power, influence; high spirits
14 威徳 **itoku** virtue and influence
15 威儀 **igi** dignity, majesty, solemnity
威権 **iken** authority, power
17 威嚇 **ikaku** menace, threat
威嚇的 **ikakuteki** menacing, threatening
威厳 **igen** dignity, majesty, stateliness

——————— 2 ———————

3 大威張 **ōiba(ri)** bragging
5 示威 **jii** show of force, demonstration
示威的 **jiiteki** demonstrative, threatening
7 兵威 **heii** military power
8 官威 **kan'i** authority of the office/government
空威張 **kara-iba(ri)** bluster, bravado; mock dignity
国威 **kokui** national prestige
武威 **bui** military power/prestige
9 神威 **shin'i** God's/gods' majesty
皇威 **kōi** imperial prestige/power
10 脅威 **kyōi** threat, menace
猛威 **mōi** ferocity, vehemence
恩威 **on'i** stern but kindly
11 鹿威 **shishiodo(shi)** deer scare (Japanese-garden contrivance in which water flows into a pivoted bamboo tube which repeatedly fills up, tips over, empties, then rights itself again, its lower end clopping against a stone); (also called 添水 **sōzu**)
12 寒威 **kan'i** intense/severe cold
朝威 **chōi** imperial prestige/authority
13 幕威 **bakui** authority/power of the shogunate
15 権威 **ken'i** authority; an authority
権威主義 **ken'i shugi** authoritarianism
権威的 **ken'iteki** authoritative
権威者 **ken'isha** an authority
権威筋 **ken'i suji** authoritative sources
暴威 **bōi** tyranny, great violence, havoc

——————— 3 ———————

11 虚仮威 **kokeodo(shi)** empty threat, mere show, bluff

4n5.3 / 1031

武

BU, MU military

——————— 1 ———————

2 武人 **bujin** military man
武力 **buryoku** military force
3 武士 **bushi, mononofu** samurai, warrior

武士道 **bushidō** bushido, the samurai code of chivalry
4 武辺 **buhen** military affairs
武辺者 **buhenmono** warrior
5 武弁 **buben** soldier
武功 **bukō** military exploits
6 武名 **bumei** military renown
7 武技 **bugi** marital arts
武芸 **bugei** marital arts
8 武官 **bukan** military officer
武者 **musha** warrior
武者修業 **musha shugyō** knight-errantry
武者振 **mushabu(ri)** valor, gallantry
武者振付 **mushabu(ri)tsu(ku)** pounce upon, devour
武者絵 **mushae** picture of a warrior
武者震 **mushaburu(i)** tremble with excitement
武具 **bugu** arms, armor
武門 **bumon** military family/class
9 武勇 **buyū** bravery, valor
武勇伝 **buyūden** story of marital heroics
武神 **bushin** god of war
武威 **bui** military power/prestige
10 武将 **bushō** military commander
武家 **buke** samurai
武家物 **bukemono** a samurai romance
武庫 **buko** armory
武骨 **bukotsu** boorish, uncouth
武烈 **Buretsu** (emperor, 498–506)
11 武運 **buun** the fortunes of war
武道 **budō** military/martial arts, bushido
武張 **buba(ru)** be warrior-like
武術 **bujutsu** military/martial arts
武略 **buryaku** strategy, tactics
武断 **budan** militarism
12 武備 **bubi** armaments, defenses
武装 **busō** arms; armed (neutrality)
14 武徳 **butoku** martial virtues
15 武器 **buki** weapon, arms
武器倉 **bukigura** armory
武器庫 **bukiko** armory
武蔵 **Musashi** (ancient kuni, Saitama-ken and Tōkyō-to)
武勲 **bukun** military achievements
23 武鑑 **bukan** book of heraldry

——————— 2 ———————
4 天武 **Tenmu** (emperor, 673–686)
文武 **bunbu** literary and military arts, pen and sword **Monmu** (emperor, 697–707)
文武両道 **bunbu-ryōdō** both soldierly and scholarly arts
文武百官 **bunbu hyakkan** civil and military officials
公武 **kōbu** nobles and soldiers; imperial court and shogunate

公武合体 **kōbu gattai** union of imperial court and shogunate
6 西武 **Seibu** (company name)
再武装 **saibusō** rearmament
7 我武者羅 **gamushara** reckless, daredevil
8 非武装 **hibusō** demilitarized (zone), unarmed (neutrality)
建武 **Kenmu** (era, 1334–1336)
若武者 **wakamusha** young warrior
尚武 **shōbu** militaristic, martial
歩武 **hobu** short distance; step, pace
9 荒武者 **aramusha** rowdy, a tough, daredevil
神武 **Jinmu** (emperor, 660–585 B.C.)
威武 **ibu** authority and force
10 徒武者 **kachimusha** foot soldier
桓武 **Kanmu** (emperor, 781–806)
核武装 **kakubusō** nuclear arms
11 野武士 **nobushi** wandering samurai, free lance
偃武 **enbu** cease hostilities
猪武者 **inoshishi musha** daredevil
12 落武者 **o(chi)musha** fugitive warrior, straggler
13 聖武 **Shōmu** (emperor, 724–749)
14 演武 **enbu** military/martial-arts exercises
演武場 **enbujō** drill hall
端武者 **hamusha** common soldier, private
15 影武者 **kagemusha** general's double; man behind the scenes, wirepuller
18 鎧武者 **yoroimusha** warrior in armor

——————— 3 ———————
18 観戦武官 **kansenbukan** military observer

4n5.4

哉 **SAI** how, what, alas, (question particle)

——————— 2 ———————
7 快哉 **kaisai** shout of delight
12 善哉 **zenzai** Well done!; thick bean-jam soup

——————— 6 ———————
戚→ **4n7.2**

4n6.1 / 1125

栽 **SAI** planting

——————— 1 ———————
11 栽培 **saibai** cultivate, grow
——————— 2 ———————
9 盆栽 **bonsai** bonsai, potted dwarf tree

4

木 月 日 火 礻 王 牛 方 攵 欠 心 戸 戈 6←

——————— 3 ———————
9 促成栽培 **sokusei saibai** forcing culture, hothouse cultivation

——————— 7 ———————

4n7.1

戛 戞

KATSU halberd; strike, hit; clanging sound

4n7.2

戚

SEKI battleax; relatives, kin; sadness

——————— 2 ———————
9 姻戚 **inseki** in-laws
12 遠戚 **enseki** distant relative
16 親戚 **shinseki** a relative

——————— 8 ———————

4n8.1

戟

GEKI halberd; poke, prod

——————— 2 ———————
8 刺戟 **shigeki** stimulus, stimulation
10 剣戟 **kengeki** sword and halberd, arms, weapons

戞 → 戛 4n7.1

4n8.2 / 1001

越

ETSU cross, go beyond, exceed; Vietnam **ko(su/eru)** cross, go beyond, exceed **-go(shi)** across, over, through

——————— 1 ———————
0 ソ越 **So-Etsu** Soviet Union and Vietnam, Soviet-Vietnamese
4 越中 **Etchū** (ancient kuni, Toyama-ken)
5 越冬 **ettō** pass the winter
6 越年 **etsunen** tide over the year end; pass the winter, hibernate
9 越南 **Etsunan, Betonamu** Vietnam
　越前 **Echizen** (ancient kuni, Fukui-ken)
　越後 **Echigo** (ancient kuni, Niigata-ken)
14 越境 **ekkyō** (illegally) crossing the border
15 越権 **ekken** overstepping one's authority

——————— 2 ———————
3 川越 **kawago(e/shi)** crossing a river
　　Kawagoe (city, Saitama-ken)

4 中越 **Chū-Etsu** China and Vietnam
　引越 **hi(k)ko(su)** move (to a new residence)
　引越先 **hi(k)ko(shi)saki** where one moves to
　月越 **tsukigo(shi)** left (unpaid) from last month
5 冬越 **fuyugo(shi)** pass the winter
7 呉越同舟 **Go-Etsu dōshū** enemies in the same boat
　見越 **miko(su)** anticipate, foresee; look across
8 卓越 **takuetsu** be superior, excel, surpass
　追越 **o(i)ko(su)** overtake
　物越 **monogo(shi ni)** with something in between
　取越 **to(ri)ko(su)** anticipate, do ahead of time
　取越苦労 **to(ri)ko(shi)gurō** needless worry
9 飛越 **to(bi)ko(su)** jump over, fly across
　乗越 **no(ri)ko(su)** ride past, pass
　負越 **ma(ke)ko(shi)** more losses than wins
　通越 **tō(ri)ko(su)** go past/beyond, pass through
　垣越 **kakigo(shi)** over/through the fence
　持越 **mo(chi)ko(su)** carry forward; defer; hold over
10 借越 **ka(ri)ko(su)** overdraw
　借越金 **ka(ri)ko(shi)kin** overdraft, debt balance
　差越 **sa(shi)ko(eru)** go out of turn, jump the queue **sa(shi)ko(su)** go out of turn; cross; send, give
　宵越 **yoigo(shi)** (left over) from the previous evening
11 過越節 **Sugikoshi Setsu, Sugikoshi no Iwai** Passover
12 超越 **chōetsu** transcend, rise above
　葉越 **hago(shi)** (seen) through the leaves
　勝越 **ka(chi)ko(shi)** ahead by (so many) wins
　貸越 **ka(shi)ko(shi)** overdraft
14 僭越 **sen'etsu** insolent, presumptuous
15 罷越 **maka(ri)ko(su)** go to, visit, call on
　踏越 **fu(mi)ko(eru)** step across, overstep
16 激越 **gekietsu** violent, vehement, fiery
17 優越 **yūetsu** superiority, supremacy
　優越感 **yūetsukan** superiority complex
19 繰越 **ku(ri)ko(su)** transfer, carry forward
　繰越金 **kurikoshikin** balance brought forward
21 躍越 **odo(ri)ko(su)** jump over

——————— 3 ———————
7 見知越 **mishi(ri)go(shi)** well acquainted with

4n8.3

牋

SEN letter, writing

残 → 残   0a10.11

4n8.4 / 877

幾   **KI, iku-** how much/many; some, several

— 1 —

0 幾つ **iku(tsu)** how many/old
  幾ら **iku(ra)** how much
  幾らか **iku(raka)** some, something; somewhat
2 幾人 **ikunin** how many people
3 幾万 **ikuman** tens of thousands
  幾才 **ikusai** how old, what age
  幾千 **ikusen** thousands
4 幾分 **ikubun** some, a portion
  幾月 **ikutsuki** how many months
  幾日 **ikunichi** how many days; what day of the month
6 幾多 **ikuta** many, various
  幾年 **ikunen, ikutose** how many years
7 幾何 **kika** geometry
  幾何学 **kikagaku** geometry
  幾何学的 **kikagakuteki** geometrical
8 幾夜 **ikuyo** how many nights; many a night
  幾昔 **ikumukashi** how ancient
9 幾重 **ikue** how many folds/ply; repeatedly; earnestly
  幾通 **ikutō(ri)** how many ways
  ikutsū how many copies/letters
  幾度 **ikudo** how many times, how often
10 幾時 **ikuji** what time
11 幾許 **ikubaku** how much/many
12 幾程 **ikuhodo** how much/many

— 2 —

11 庶幾 **shoki** desire, hope

裁 →   5e6.9

— 9 —

4n9.1

戡   **KAN** victory

— 1 —

8 戡定 **kantei** (military) mopping-up

4n9.2 / 301

戦 戰   **SEN, ikusa** war, battle
     tataka(u) wage war; fight
     onono(ku) shudder, tremble

wanana(ku) tremble   **soyo(gu)** rustle, stir, sway, tremble, quiver

— 1 —

0 戦わす **tataka(wasu)** bring about a fight; match skills; argue
2 戦力 **senryoku** war-fighting capacity
3 戦々恐々 **sensen-kyōkyō** with fear and trembling; with trepidation
  戦々兢々 **sensen-kyōkyō** with fear and trembling; with trepidation
  戦士 **senshi** warrior, soldier
4 戦中 **senchū** during the war
  戦友 **sen'yū** comrade-in-arms, fellow soldier, (army) buddy
  戦火 **senka** (the flames of) war
5 戦史 **senshi** military/war history
  戦功 **senkō** military exploits, distinguished war service
  戦犯 **senpan** war crime/criminal
6 戦死 **senshi** death in battle, killed in action
  戦死者 **senshisha** fallen soldier
  戦列 **senretsu** line of battle
  戦争 **sensō** war
  戦争中 **sensōchū** during the war
  戦地 **senchi** battlefield, the front
7 戦没 **senbotsu** death in battle, killed in action
  戦没者 **senbotsusha** fallen soldier
  戦抜 **tataka(i)nu(ku)** fight to the end
  戦乱 **senran** the upheavals of war, war-torn (region)
  戦役 **sen'eki** war, campaign
  戦局 **senkyoku** the war situation
  戦災 **sensai** war devastation
  戦災地 **sensaichi** war-ravaged area
  戦災者 **sensaisha** war victims
  戦利品 **senrihin** war spoils, booty
  戦車 **sensha** tank
  戦車隊 **senshatai** tank corps
  戦車戦 **senshasen** tank battle/warfare
8 戦果 **senka** war results
  戦歿 **senbotsu** death in battle, killed in action
  戦歿者 **senbotsusha** fallen soldier
  戦法 **senpō** tactics, strategy
  戦況 **senkyō** war situation
  戦国時代 **sengoku jidai** era of civil wars
9 戦陣 **senjin** the front, battlefield
  戦前 **senzen** before the war, prewar
  戦前派 **senzenha** prewar generation
  戦後 **sengo** after the war, postwar
  戦後派 **sengoha** postwar generation
10 戦時 **senji** wartime, war period
  戦時下 **senjika** during the war, wartime
  戦時中 **senjichū** during the war, wartime
  戦時色 **senjishoku** wartime look/aspect
  戦時体制 **senji taisei** war footing
  戦時産業 **senji sangyō** wartime industry

4

木
月
日
火
衤
王
牛
方
攵
欠
心
戸
戈 9 ←

戦病死 **senbyōshi** death from disease contracted at the front

戦記 **senki** account of a war

11 戦隊 **sentai** corps, squadron

戦域 **sen'iki** war zone, theater of war

戦術 **senjutsu** tactics

戦術家 **senjutsuka** tactician

戦略 **senryaku** strategy

戦略上 **senryakujō** strategic

戦略家 **senryakuka** strategist

戦敗 **senpai** defeat (in war)

戦敗国 **senpaikoku** defeated nation

12 戦備 **senbi** military preparedness

戦渦 **senka** the turmoil of war

戦場 **senjō** battlefield, the front

戦勝 **senshō** victory

戦勝国 **senshōkoku** victorious nation

戦勝者 **senshōsha** victor

戦費 **senpi** war expenditures

戦雲 **sen'un** clouds of war

13 戦傷 **senshō** war wound

戦債 **sensai** war debts/bonds

戦禍 **senka** war damage, ravages of war

戦慄 **senritsu** shudder, tremble, shiver

戦戦恐恐 **sensen-kyōkyō** with fear and trembling, with trepidation

戦戦兢兢 **sensen-kyōkyō** with fear and trembling, with trepidation

戦意 **sen'i** intent to fight, fighting spirit

戦跡 **senseki** old battlefield

14 戦歴 **senreki** war experience, combat record

戦塵 **senjin** the dust of battle

戦旗 **senki** battle flag

戦端 **sentan** hostilities

15 戦線 **sensen** battle line, front

16 戦機 **senki** the time to strike; military secret

17 戦績 **senseki** war record; score

18 戦闘 **sentō** combat, battle, fighting

戦闘力 **sentōryoku** fighting strength

戦闘服 **sentōfuku** battle dress

戦闘的 **sentōteki** fighting, militant

戦闘員 **sentōin** combatant, combat soldier

戦闘帽 **sentōbō** field cap

戦闘靴 **sentōgutsu** combat boots

戦闘旗 **sentōki** battle flag

戦闘機 **sentōki** fighter (plane)

戦闘艦 **sentōkan** battleship

21 戦艦 **senkan** battleship

2

---

1 一戦 **issen** a battle, a game/bout

2 力戦 **rikisen** hard fighting

3 大戦 **taisen** great/world war

4 不戦 **fusen** renunciation of war

内戦 **naisen** civil war

反戦 **hansen** antiwar

5 古戦場 **kosenjō** ancient battlefield

好戦 **kōsen** pro-war, warlike

好戦国 **kōsenkoku** warlike nation

好戦的 **kōsenteki** bellicose, warlike

主戦 **shusen** advocating going to war; top (player)

6 死戦 **shisen** death struggle

休戦 **kyūsen** truce, cease-fire

合戦 **kassen** battle

会戦 **kaisen** battle

防戦 **bōsen** a defensive fight

交戦 **kōsen** war, hostilities, combat

舌戦 **zessen** war of words

守戦 **shusen** defensive war/fight

百戦百勝 **hyakusen-hyakushō** ever-victorious

百戦錬磨 **hyakusen-renma** battle-seasoned, veteran

血戦 **kessen** bloody battle

7 作戦 **sakusen** (military) operation, tactics

冷戦 **reisen** cold war

対戦 **taisen** wage war, compete

決戦 **kessen** decisive battle; playoffs

抗戦 **kōsen** resistance

乱戦 **ransen** melee, free-for-all fight

応戦 **ōsen** accept a challenge, fight back

8 非戦論 **hisenron** pacifism

非戦闘員 **hisentōin** noncombatant

征戦 **seisen** military expedition

参戦 **sansen** enter a war

苦戦 **kusen** hard fighting; hard-fought

実戦 **jissen** actual fighting, combat

和戦 **wasen** peace and war

9 勇戦 **yūsen** brave/desperate fight

連戦 **rensen** series of battles; battle after battle

連戦連勝 **rensen-renshō** succession of victories

速戦即決 **sokusen-sokketsu** all-out surprise offensive, blitzkrieg

海戦 **kaisen** naval battle

挑戦 **chōsen** challenge

挑戦状 **chōsenjō** written challenge

挑戦的 **chōsenteki** challenging, defiant, provocative

挑戦者 **chōsensha** challenger

宣戦 **sensen** declaration of war

宣戦布告 **sensen fukoku** declaration of war

政戦 **seisen** political campaign

10 陸戦 **rikusen** land combat/warfare

陸戦隊 **rikusentai** landing forces

酒戦 **shusen** drinking bout

砲戦 **hōsen** artillery battle/engagement

11 野戦 **yasen** open warfare, field operations

停戦 **teisen** cease-fire, armistice
商戦 **shōsen** commercial competition, sales battle
混戦 **konsen** melee, free-for-all fight
捷戦 **kachiikusa** a victory
接戦 **sessen** close combat/contest
悪戦 **akusen** hard-fought battle
悪戦苦闘 **akusen-kutō** fight desperately
終戦 **shūsen** end of the war
終戦後 **shūsengo** after the war
敗戦 **haisen** lost battle, defeat
転戦 **tensen** take part in various battles
12 善戦 **zensen** put up a good fight
勝戦 **ka(chi)ikusa** victorious battle
筆戦 **hissen** a war of the pen
策戦 **sakusen** (military) operation
開戦 **kaisen** outbreak of war
13 義戦 **gisen** holy war, crusade
聖戦 **seisen** holy war, crusade
戦戦恐恐 **sensen-kyōkyō** with fear and trembling, with trepidation
戦戦競競 **sensen-kyōkyō** with fear and trembling, with trepidation
督戦 **tokusen** urge on to fight bravely
督戦隊 **tokusentai** supervising unit
14 緒戦 **shosen, chosen** beginning of a war
15 熱戦 **nessen** fierce fighting; close contest
論戦 **ronsen** verbal battle, controversy
16 激戦 **gekisen** fierce fighting, hard-fought contest
奮戦 **funsen** hard fighting
17 擬戦 **gisen** mock battle
18 臨戦 **rinsen** going into battle/action
観戦 **kansen** watch a battle/game
観戦武官 **kansenbukan** military observer
難戦 **nansen** hard fighting

————————— 3 —————————

1 一回戦 **ikkaisen** first game/round (of tennis)
2 人民戦線 **jinmin sensen** popular front
4 中盤戦 **chūbansen** the middle game (in chess and other board games); the midst of an election campaign
弔合戦 **tomura(i) gassen** battle to avenge a death
5 市街戦 **shigaisen** street-to-street fighting
白兵戦 **hakuheisen** hand-to-hand fighting
白熱戦 **hakunetsusen** intense fighting, thrilling game
石合戦 **ishi gassen** stone-throwing fight
立体戦 **rittaisen** three-dimensional warfare
6 肉弾戦 **nikudansen** human-wave warfare
争奪戦 **sōdatsusen** contest/scramble/struggle for

7 決勝戦 **kesshōsen** finals
序盤戦 **jobansen** beginning of a campaign
局地戦争 **kyokuchi sensō** limited war
攻撃戦 **kōgekisen** aggressive war
8 長期戦 **chōkisen** prolonged/protracted war
追撃戦 **tsuigekisen** pursuit battle, running fight
空中戦 **kūchūsen** air battle, aerial warfare
9 陣地戦 **jinchisen** position/stationary warfare
南北戦争 **Nanboku Sensō** the War Between the States, the (U.S.) Civil War
前哨戦 **zenshōsen** preliminary skirmish
持久戦 **jikyūsen** war of attrition, endurance contest
後半戦 **kōhansen** the latter half of a game
宣伝戦 **sendensen** propaganda/advertising campaign
神経戦 **shinkeisen** war of nerves
10 遊撃戦 **yūgekisen** guerrilla warfare
消耗戦 **shōmōsen** war of attrition
11 終盤戦 **shūbansen** endgame, final battle
雪合戦 **yuki gassen** snowball fight
雪辱戦 **setsujokusen** return match, a fight for vindication
12 無名戦士 **mumei senshi** unknown soldier
補回戦 **hokaisen** game extended into overtime
13 遭遇戦 **sōgūsen** encounter, engagement
戦車戦 **senshasen** tank battle/warfare
14 選挙戦 **senkyosen** election campaign
模擬戦 **mogisen** war games, mock fight
総力戦 **sōryokusen** total war
18 騎馬戦 **kibasen** cavalry battle

————————— 4 —————————

4 太平洋戦争 **Taiheiyō Sensō** the Pacific War, World War II
5 世界大戦 **sekai taisen** World War

4n9.3

盞 SEN saké cup

————————— 2 —————————

8 金盞花 **kinsenka** marigold

感→感 **4k9.21**

4n9.4

斌 HIN beautiful harmony of appearance and content

4
木
月
日
火
ネ
王
牛
方
攵
欠
心
戸
戈 9←

4n9.5 / 479

歳

SAI year; harvest; (as suffix) … years old
SEI year **toshi** year, one's age

———————— 1 ————————

2 歳入 **sainyū** annual revenue
3 歳々 **saisai** annual, every year
4 歳月 **saigetsu** time, years
5 歳出 **saishutsu** annual expenditures
 歳末 **saimatsu** year's end
 歳市 **toshi (no) ichi** year-end market (cf. 節季市)
 歳旦 **saitan** New Year's Day; the New Year
6 歳次 **saiji** year
7 歳余 **saiyo** longer than a year
8 歳事 **saiji** the year's events
9 歳首 **saishu** beginning of the year
10 歳時記 **saijiki** almanac
12 歳晩 **saiban** year's end
 歳費 **saihi** annual expenditures
13 歳歳 **saisai** annual, every year
14 歳暮 **seibo** year's end; year-end present
19 歳瀬 **toshi(no)se** year's end

———————— 2 ————————

1 一歳 **issai** one year old
3 万歳 **banzai** hurrah
 千歳 **chitose** a thousand years
6 当歳 **tōsai** this year; yearling
 当歳児 **tōsaiji** a yearling
7 何歳 **nansai** how many years old
13 歳歳 **saisai** annual, every year

———————— 3 ————————

2 二十歳 **hatachi** 20 years old, age 20

越→ **4n8.2**

———————— 10 ————————

4n10.1

戬

SEN destroy; happiness

截→ **8c6.3**

———————— 11 ————————

鳶→ **11b3.1**

4n11.1 / 1573

戯 戲

GI, GE, tawamu(reru) play, sport; jest; flirt
tawa(keru) act foolish
ja/za(reru) be playful, gambol

———————— 1 ————————

6 戯曲 **gikyoku** drama, play
7 戯作 **gesaku** light literature, popular fiction
 戯言 **za(re)goto** joke
8 戯画 **giga** a caricature
 戯者 **tawa(ke)mono** fool
14 戯歌 **za(re)uta** comic song, limerick

———————— 2 ————————

7 児戯 **jigi** mere child's play
10 遊戯 **yūgi** games, amusement, entertainment
 aso(bi)tawamu(reru) play, frolic
 遊戯的 **yūgiteki** playful, sportive
11 球戯 **kyūgi** game in which a ball is used; billiards
 悪戯 **akugi, itazura** prank, mischief
13 愛戯 **aigi** love play
15 嬉戯 **kigi** frolic

———————— 3 ————————

4 水悪戯 **mizu itazura** playing with/in water
7 巫山戯 **fuzake(ru)** frolic, be playful, jest; flirt

———————— 4 ————————

9 室内遊戯 **shitsunai yūgi** indoor/parlor games
10 桃色遊戯 **momo-iro yūgi** sex play
11 悪巫山戯 **warufuzake** prank, practical joke

4n11.2

臧

ZŌ good; bribe; servant

4n11.3

戮

RIKU kill; shame; together

———————— 2 ————————

7 孥戮 **doriku** executing wife and children together with the criminal
10 殺戮 **satsuriku** massacre, bloodbath

———————— 12 ————————

戰→戦 **4n9.2**

———————— 13 ————————

戲→戯 **4n11.1**

戴 → **5f12.2**

─────────── 14 ───────────

4n14.1

戳 TAKU poke, prod

─────────── 15 ───────────

殲 → 殲 **4n17.1**

─────────── 16 ───────────

巉 → **3o17.1**

4n16.1

鹹 KAN, kara(i) salty

─────────── 1 ───────────

4 鹹水魚 **kansuigyo** saltwater fish
12 鹹湖 **kanko** salt/brackish lake

─────────── 17 ───────────

4n17.1

殲 殲 SEN massacre, destroy

─────────── 1 ───────────

13 殲滅 **senmetsu** annihilation, extermination

─────────── 18 ───────────

4n18.1

戳 KU halberd

─────────────── 石 **5a** ───────────────

石	矼	研	斫	砂	砌	砒	砕	破	砠	砲	砥	砧
0.1	3.1	4.1	4.2	4.3	4.4	4.5	4.6	5.1	5.2	5.3	5.4	5.5

砥	砺	研	硅	砦	硬	硯	硫	硜	硲	硝	硲	碓
8a5.15	5a14.1	5a4.1	4f6.4	6.1	7.1	7.2	7.3	7.4	7.5	7.6	7.7	8.1

碑	硼	碚	碍	碕	碇	碗	磁	碌	砕	碁	婆	碩
5a9.2	8.2	8.3	8.4	8.5	8.6	8.7	4f8.7	8.8	5a4.6	8.9	8.10	9.1

礁	碑	碬	碣	碩	磁	碧	碼	硝	碓	磅	磋	磴
5a5.5	9.2	9.3	9.4	5a9.1	9.6	9.7	10.1	10.2	10.3	10.4	10.5	10.6

碾	磊	磐	磚	磔	磧	磬	磯	礁	磽	磴	磧	礎
10.7	10.8	10.9	11.1	11.2	11.3	11.4	12.1	12.2	12.3	12.4	13.1	13.2

礑	礒	礙	礦	礪	礫	礬						
13.3	13.4	5a8.4	8a5.15	14.1	15.1	15.2						

─────────── 0 ───────────

5a0.1 / 78

石 SEKI, SHAKU, ishi stone
KOKU (unit of volume, about 180 liters)

─────────── 1 ───────────

2 石子詰 **ishikozu(me)** execution by burying alive under stones
3 石川県 **Ishikawa-ken** (prefecture)
　石工 **sekkō, ishiku** stone mason/cutter
　石弓 **ishiyumi** crossbow, catapult

　石山 **ishiyama** quarry; stony mountain
4 石仏 **ishibotoke, sekibutsu** stone image of Buddha
　石化 **sekka** petrify, fossilize
　石切 **ishiki(ri)** stonecutting, quarrying
　石切場 **ishiki(ri)ba** quarry, stone pit
　石文 **ishibumi** (inscribed) stone monument
　石片 **sekihen** piece of stone
　石火 **sekka** flint fire; a flash
　石火矢 **ishibiya** (ancient) cannon
6 石臼 **ishiusu** stone mill/mortar
　石合戦 **ishi gassen** stone-throwing fight

石灰 **sekkai, ishibai** lime
石灰水 **sekkaisui** limewater
石灰石 **sekkaiseki** limestone
石灰乳 **sekkainyū** milk of lime
石灰岩 **sekkaigan** limestone
石灰洞 **sekkaidō** limestone cave
石灰窯 **ishibaigama** limekiln
石地蔵 **ishi Jizō** stone image of Jizo
石肌 **ishihada** (cut) stone's surface
石竹 **sekichiku** a pink (the flower)
石竹色 **sekichiku-iro** pink (the color)
7 石材 **sekizai** (building) stone
石材商 **sekizaishō** stone dealer
石見 **Iwami** (ancient kuni, Shimane-ken)
8 石版 **sekiban** lithograph(y)
石版画 **sekibanga** lithograph
石版刷 **sekibanzu(ri)** lithography
石斧 **sekifu** stone ax
石油 **sekiyu** petroleum, oil, kerosene
石油坑 **sekiyukō** oil well
石英 **sekiei** quartz
石英灯 **sekieitō** quartz lamp
石英岩 **sekieigan** quartzite
石突 **ishizu(ki)** hard tip (of an umbrella)
石門 **sekimon** stone gate
9 石南花 **shakunage** rhododendron
石造 **ishizuku(ri), sekizō** masonry, of stone
石段 **ishidan** stone steps
石垣 **ishigaki** stone wall
石狩川 **Ishikari-gawa** (river, Hokkaidō)
石室 **ishimuro** stone hut
石炭 **sekitan** coal
石炭殻 **sekitangara** (coal) cinders
石炭船 **sekitansen** coal ship
石炭層 **sekitansō** coal seam/bed
石炭酸 **sekitansan** carbolic acid, phenol
石庭 **ishiniwa** rock garden
石屋 **ishiya** stone cutter/dealer
石柱 **sekichū** stone pillar
石神 **ishigami, shakujin** a stone that is worshipped, a stone god
石音 **ishioto** sound of a go stone slapped onto the board
10 石部金吉 **Ishibe Kinkichi** man of strict morals
石高 **kokudaka** crop, yield; stipend
石粉 **ishiko** stone dust
11 石脳油 **sekinōyu** petroleum
石細工 **ishizaiku** masonry
石組 **ishigu(mi)** arrangement of garden rocks
12 石塔 **sekitō** tombstone, stone monument
石塚 **ishizuka** pile of stones, cairn
石塀 **ishibei** stone wall
石棺 **sekkan, sekikan** sarcophagus, stone coffin
石畳 **ishidatami** stone pavement/flooring

石筆 **sekihitsu** slate pencil
石筍 **sekijun** stalagmite (cf. 鐘乳石)
13 石塊 **sekkai, ishikoro, ishikure** pebble, stones
石楠花 **shakunage** rhododendron
14 石像 **sekizō** stone image/statue
石膏 **sekkō** gypsum, plaster (of Paris)
石墨 **sekiboku** graphite
石摺 **ishizu(ri)** rubbed copy of an inscription in stone
石榴 **zakuro** pomegranate
石碑 **sekihi** tombstone, (stone) monument
石綿 **ishiwata, sekimen** asbestos
15 石器 **sekki** stonework; stone implements
石器時代 **sekki jidai** the Stone Age
石盤 **sekiban** a slate
16 石橋 **ishibashi, sekkyō** stone bridge
石頭 **ishiatama** hard head; stubborn
19 石鹼 **sekken** soap
石蹴 **ishike(ri)** hopscotch
21 石蠟 **sekirō** paraffin
24 石鹼 **sekken** soap

———————— 2 ————————

1 一石二鳥 **isseki nichō** killing two birds with one stone
3 千石船 **sengokubune** large junk (Edo period)
土石 **doseki** cement
小石 **koishi** pebble, gravel
4 化石 **kaseki** fossil
切石 **ki(ri)ishi** hewn/quarried stone
木石 **bokuseki** trees and stones, inanimate objects
木石漢 **bokusekikan** insensible person
5 生石灰 **seisekkai, kisekkai** quicklime
巨石 **kyoseki** megalith
台石 **daiishi** pedestal stone
布石 **fuseki** strategically arrange stones (in go)
玉石 **gyokuseki** gems and stones; wheat and chaff **tamaishi** round stone, boulder
立石 **ta(te)ishi** stone signpost, milestone, stone stood on end
7 角石 **kakuishi** square stone
投石 **tōseki** throw stones
尿石 **nyōseki** urinary calculus
8 長石 **chōseki** feldspar
宝石 **hōseki** precious stone, gem, jewel
定石 **jōseki** book moves (in go); formula, rule
岩石 **ganseki** rock
底石 **sokoishi** broken-rock base, hardcore
板石 **itaishi** flagstone, slab, a slate
明石 **Akashi** (city, Hyōgo-ken)
金石 **kinseki** metals and rocks; stone monument
金石文 **kinsekibun** inscription on a stone monument
金石学 **kinsekigaku** study of ancient stone monument inscriptions

9 飛石 **to(bi)ishi** stepping-stones
飛石伝 **to(bi)ishizuta(i)** following stepping-stones
盆石 **bonseki** miniature landscape on a tray
造石高 **zōkokudaka** brew, brewage
造石税 **zōkokuzei** liquor-making tax
泉石 **senseki** springs and rocks (in a garden)
庭石 **niwaishi** garden stones
柱石 **chūseki** pillar, mainstay, cornerstone
胆石 **tanseki** gallstone
胆石病 **tansekibyō** cholelithiasis, gallstones
胆石症 **tansekishō** cholelithiasis, gallstones
砕石 **saiseki** rubble, broken stone
10 酒石酸 **shusekisan** tartaric acid
流石 **sasuga** as might be expected
消石灰 **shōsekkai** slaked lime, calcium hydroxide
栗石 **kuriishi** cobblestones
珪石 **keiseki** silica
砥石 **toishi** whetstone
11 隅石 **sumiishi** cornerstone
堆石 **taiseki** moraine
採石 **saiseki** quarrying
捨石 **su(te)ishi** ornamental garden rocks; rubble for river control; sacrifice stone/play (in go)
蛍石 **keiseki, hotaruishi** fluorite, fluorspar
黒石 **kuroishi** black stone (in go)
12 隕石 **inseki** meteorite
温石 **onjaku** heated warming stone, pocket warmer
落石 **rakuseki** falling/fallen rock, rockslide
焼石 **ya(ke)ishi** heated stone
硝石 **shōseki** saltpeter
結石 **kesseki** (gall/kidney) stones
歯石 **shiseki** dental calculus, tartar
軽石 **karuishi** pumice stone
13 滑石 **kasseki** talc
墓石 **hakaishi, boseki** gravestone
腎石 **jinseki** kidney stone
碁石 **goishi** go stone
置石 **o(ki)ishi** decorative garden stone
詰石 **tsu(me)ishi** foundation stone
鉄石 **tesseki** iron and stone; adamant, firm
鉄石心 **tessekishin** iron/steadfast will
鉱石 **kōseki** ore, mineral, (radio) crystal
14 碑石 **hiseki** tombstone, (stone) monument
磁石 **jishaku, jiseki** magnet
磁石盤 **jishakuban** (mariner's) compass
殞石 **inseki** meteorite
15 標石 **hyōseki** boundary stone; milestone
敷石 **shikiishi** paving stone, flagstone
磐石 **banjaku** huge rock
盤石 **banjaku** huge rock
輝石 **kiseki** pyroxene, augite
踏石 **fu(mi)ishi** steppingstone

16 薬石効無 **yakusekikō na(ku)** all remedies having proved unavailing
燧石 **hiuchiishi, suiseki** a flint
18 礎石 **soseki** foundation (stone)
21 蠟石 **rōseki** pagodite, pencil stone

──────── 3 ────────

3 大理石 **dairiseki** marble
大盤石 **daibanjaku** large stone, huge rock
4 月長石 **getchōseki** moonstone
火打石 **hiu(chi)ishi** a flint
5 他山石 **tazan (no) ishi** object lesson
石灰石 **sekkaiseki** limestone
6 自然石 **shizenseki** natural stone/gem
8 逆性石鹼 **gyakusei sekken** antiseptic soap
油砥石 **aburatoishi** oilstone
金剛石 **kongōseki** diamond
雨垂石 **amada(re) ishi** dripstone (to catch roof runoff)
9 柘榴石 **zakuroishi** garnet
11 猫目石 **nekome-ishi** cat's-eye (of quartz)
黒曜石 **kokuyōseki** obsidian
蛇紋石 **jamonseki** serpentine, ophiolite
12 割栗石 **wa(ri)guriishi** broken stones, macadam
御影石 **mikage ishi** granite
棒磁石 **bōjishaku** bar magnet
13 試金石 **shikinseki** touchstone; test
電光石火 **denkō-sekka** a flash, an instant
電磁石 **denjishaku** electromagnet
14 蔣介石 **Shō Kaiseki** Chiang Kai-shek
緑玉石 **ryokugyokuseki** emerald
緑柱石 **ryokuchūseki** beryl
誕生石 **tanjōseki** birthstone
17 鍾乳石 **shōnyūseki** stalactite (also spelled 鐘乳石) (cf. 石筍)
20 鐘乳石 **shōnyūseki** stalactite (cf. 鍾乳石)

──────── 4 ────────

7 良二千石 **ryōnisenseki** good local official
13 腎臓結石 **jinzō kesseki** kidney stones
14 膀胱結石 **bōkō kesseki** bladder stones
16 蹄形磁石 **teikei jishaku** horseshoe magnet

──────────── 3 ────────────

5a3.1

矼   **KŌ** stepping-stone; hard; serious-minded

──────────── 4 ────────────

5a4.1 / 896

研 研   **KEN, to(gu)** whet, hone, sharpen; polish; wash (rice)

──────── 1 ────────

5 研立 **to(gi)ta(te)** freshly sharpened

7 研究 **kenkyū** research
  研究所 **kenkyūjo** (research) institute,
    laboratory
  研究室 **kenkyūshitsu** laboratory, study room
  研究家 **kenkyūka** researcher, student of
  研学 **kengaku** study
8 研物 **to(gi)mono** sharpening swords,
    polishing mirrors
  研物師 **to(gi)monoshi** polisher of swords
    and mirrors
9 研革 **to(gi)kawa** strop
  研屋 **to(gi)ya** grinder, sharpener, polisher
10 研修 **kenshū** study and training
  研修所 **kenshūjo** training institute/center
  研師 **to(gi)shi** polisher of swords
15 研澄 **to(gi)su(masu)** sharpen/polish well
  研摩 **kenma** grinding, polishing; studying
16 研磨 **kenma** grinding, polishing; studying
23 研鑽 **kensan** study

──────── 2 ────────

10 核研究 **kakukenkyū** nuclear research
11 粗研 **arato(gi)** rough grinding
16 磨研紙 **makenshi** emery paper, sandpaper

5a4.2

斫

SHAKU cut (with a sword)

5a4.3 / 1151

砂

SA, SHA, suna, isago sand

──────── 1 ────────

2 砂子 **sunago** sand; gold/silver dust
3 砂上 **sajō** (built) on the sand
  砂土 **sado, shado** sandy soil
  砂山 **sunayama** dune
5 砂丘 **sakyū** dune
6 砂防 **sabō** prevention of sand erosion
  砂防林 **sabōrin** erosion-control forest
  砂州 **sasu** sandbar, sandbank
  砂地 **sunaji** sandy place/soil
7 砂利 **jari** gravel
  砂利道 **jarimichi** gravel road
8 砂岩 **sagan** sandstone
  砂金 **sakin, shakin** gold dust, placer gold
9 砂風 **safū** sandstorm
  砂風呂 **sunaburo** sand bath
  砂洲 **sasu** sandbar, sandbank
10 砂原 **sunahara** sandy plain
  砂浜 **sunahama, sahin** sand beach
  砂埃 **sunabokori** dust, dust storm
  砂時計 **sunadokei** hourglass
11 砂袋 **sunabukuro** sandbag; gizzard
  砂粒 **sunatsubu** grain of sand

砂船 **sunabune** dredging boat
12 砂場 **sunaba** sandbox; sand pit
  砂絵 **sunae** sand picture
13 砂漠 **sabaku** desert
  砂煙 **sunakemuri** cloud of dust
  砂鉄 **satetsu, shatetsu** iron/magnetic sand
14 砂塵 **sajin** cloud of sand, sandstorm
16 砂嘴 **sashi** sandbar, sandspit
  砂糖 **satō** sugar
  砂糖大根 **satō daikon** sugar beet
  砂糖煮 **satōni** preserved by boiling with
    sugar, candied
  砂糖黍 **satō kibi** sugar cane
20 砂礫 **sareki, shareki** gravel, pebbles
22 砂嚢 **sanō, sunabukuro** sandbag; gizzard

──────── 2 ────────

3 土砂 **dosha** earth and sand
  土砂降 **doshabu(ri)** downpour
  土砂崩 **doshakuzu(re)** landslide, washout
5 氷砂糖 **kōrizatō** rock candy, crystal sugar
  白砂 **hakusha, hakusa** white sand
  白砂青松 **hakusha-seishō** white sand and
    green pines, beautiful seashore scene
  白砂糖 **shirozatō** white sugar
6 防砂林 **bōsarin** trees planted to arrest
    shifting sand
  防砂提 **bōsatei** barricade to arrest shifting
    sand
7 角砂糖 **kakuzatō** sugar cubes
  辰砂 **shinsha** cinnabar
  赤砂糖 **akazatō** brown sugar
8 金砂 **kinsha** gold dust
10 真砂 **masago** sand
  流砂 **ryūsha, ryūsa** river sand, silt; desert
  珪砂 **keisha** silica sand, silica
11 黒砂糖 **kurozatō** unrefined/brown sugar
  盛砂 **mo(ri)zuna** (ceremonial) piles of sand
13 硼砂 **hōsha** borax
14 漂砂 **hyōsa** drift sand
  銀砂子 **ginsunago** silver dust
15 熱砂 **nessa** hot sand (bath)
  敷砂 **shi(ki)suna** sand for spreading (in a
    garden)
16 磨砂 **miga(ki)zuna** polishing sand

──────── 3 ────────

8 金剛砂紙 **kongōshashi** emery paper

5a4.4

砌

SAI, SEI, migiri time, occasion

5a4.5

砒

HI arsenic

────────── 1 ──────────

10 砒素 **hiso** arsenic
14 砒酸 **hisan** arsenic acid, ... arsenate

────────── 2 ──────────

7 亜砒酸 **ahisan** arsenious acid, ... arsenite

5a4.6 / 1710

砕 碎

SAI, **kuda(ku)** break, smash,
pulverize **kuda(keru)** break,
be crushed; become familiar
kuda(keta) broken; plain,
familiar, friendly

────────── 1 ──────────

4 砕片 **saihen** fragment, splinter
5 砕氷 **saihyō** icebreaking; rubble ice
　砕氷船 **saihyōsen** icebreaker
　砕石 **saiseki** rubble, broken stone
6 砕米 **kuda(ke)mai** broken rice
8 砕岩機 **saiganki** rock crusher
9 砕炭器 **saitanki** coal crusher
13 砕鉱 **saikō** ore crushing
　砕鉱機 **saikōki** ore crusher

────────── 2 ──────────

5 打砕 **u(chi)kuda(ku), bu(chi)kuda(ku)**
　　break to pieces, smash, crush
　玉砕 **gyokusai** death for honor
10 破砕 **hasai** crushing, smashing, fragmentation
　粉砕 **funsai** pulverize, crush
13 腰砕 **koshikuda(ke)** becoming weak-kneed
15 撃砕 **gekisai** shoot to pieces; defeat
　踏砕 **fu(mi)kuda(ku)** crush underfoot
16 擂砕 **su(ri)kuda(ku)** grind down/fine,
　　pulverize
18 噛砕 **ka(mi)kuda(ku)** crunch; simplify
19 爆砕 **bakusai** blasting

────────── 3 ──────────

10 粉骨砕身 **funkotsu-saishin** do one's utmost

────────── 5 ──────────

5a5.1 / 665

破

HA, **yabu(ru/ku)** tear, rip, break
yabu(reru/keru) get torn/broken

────────── 1 ──────────

0 破れかぶれ **yabu(re-kabure)** desperation
4 破天荒 **hatenkō** unprecedented
　破片 **hahen** broken piece, fragment, splinter
5 破甲弾 **hakōdan** armor-piercing shell
　破目 **yabu(re)me** a tear, split
6 破瓜 **haka** age 16 (for girls); age 64 (for men);
　　deflowering
　破防法 **Habōhō** the Subversive Activities
　　Prevention Law (short for 破壊活動防止法)

破竹 **hachiku** splitting bamboo
7 破邪 **haja** defeating evil
　破邪顕正 **haja-kenshō** smiting evil and
　　spreading the truth
　破牢 **harō** jailbreak
　破局 **hakyoku** catastrophe, ruin
　破戒 **hakai** breaking the (Buddhist) com-
　　mandments
8 破門 **hamon** excommunication, expulsion
9 破風 **hafu** (ornamental) gable eaves
　破屋 **haoku** dilapidated house, hovel
　破砕 **hasai** crushing, smashing, fragmentation
　破約 **hayaku** breach of contract/promise
10 破倫 **harin** immorality
　破格 **hakaku** exceptional, unusual
11 破断 **hadan** rupture, break
　破産 **hasan** bankruptcy
　破産者 **hasansha** bankrupt person
　破船 **hasen** shipwreck
12 破裂 **haretsu** bursting, rupture, explosion
13 破傷風 **hashōfū** tetanus, lockjaw
　破棄 **haki** annulment, repudiation, abroga-
　　tion, reversal
　破滅 **hametsu** ruin, destruction, downfall
　破損 **hason** damage, breakage, breach
　破廉恥 **harenchi** shameless, disgraceful
14 破獄 **hagoku** jailbreak
　破綻 **hatan** failure, breakdown, bankruptcy
　破算 **hasan** clear the abacus, recalculate
15 破談 **hadan** cancellation, breaking off,
　　rejection
16 破壊 **hakai** destroy, demolish, collapse
　破壊力 **hakairyoku** destructive power
　破壊主義 **hakai shugi** vandalism
　破壊的 **hakaiteki** destructive
　破壊者 **hakaisha** destroyer, wrecker
17 破鍋 **wa(re)nabe** cracked pot
18 破顔 **hagan** broad smile
　破顔一笑 **hagan-isshō** break into a grin
19 破鏡 **hakyō** broken mirror; divorce
20 破鐘 **wa(re)gane** cracked bell
21 破魔弓 **hamayumi** exorcising bow (used in
　　roof-raising ceremonies); toy bow and
　　arrow

────────── 2 ──────────

3 大破 **taiha** serious damage, havoc, ruin
5 打破 **daha** break, destroy, overthrow
　　u(chi)yabu(ru) break, knock down
7 走破 **sōha** run the whole distance
　牢破 **rōyabu(ri)** jailbreak
　見破 **miyabu(ru)** see through
　言破 **i(i)yabu(ru)** confute, argue down
8 押破 **o(shi)yabu(ru)** break through
　突破 **toppa** break through, overcome
　　tsu(ki)yabu(ru) break/crash through
9 発破 **happa** blasting

5

石
立
目
禾
礻
田
皿
疒

5 ←

連破 **renpa** successive wins
型破 **katayabu(ri)** unconventional, novel
看破 **kanpa, miyabu(ru)** see through, detect
10 島破 **shimayabu(ri)** escaping from an island exile
素破抜 **suppanu(ku)** expose, unmask
11 道破 **dōha** declaration
喝破 **kappa** declare, proclaim
12 御破算 **gohasan** clearing a soroban; starting afresh
14 読破 **dokuha, yo(mi)yabu(ru)** read it through
15 撃破 **gekiha** defeat, rout, crush
論破 **ronpa** refute, argue down
18 難破 **nanpa** shipwreck
難破船 **nanpasen** shipwreck
19 爆破 **bakuha** blast, blow up
蹴破 **keyabu(ru)** kick open (a door)

———————— 3 ————————
8 金庫破 **kinkoyabu(ri)** safe-cracking

5a5.2

SO stony hill/mountain

岨

5a5.3 / 1764

砲 砲

HŌ gun, cannon
tsutsu gun

———————— 1 ————————
3 砲丸 **hōgan** cannonball
砲丸投 **hōganna(ge)** the shot put
砲口 **hōkō** muzzle (of a gun); caliber
4 砲手 **hōshu** gunner, artilleryman
砲火 **hōka** gunfire, shellfire
5 砲台 **hōdai** gun battery, fort
6 砲列 **hōretsu** gun battery, emplacement
7 砲身 **hōshin** gun barrel
砲兵 **hōhei** artillery; artilleryman, gunner
砲声 **hōsei** sound of firing/shelling
砲床 **hōshō** gun platform/emplacement
砲車 **hōsha** gun carriage
8 砲金 **hōkin** gun metal
砲門 **hōmon** muzzle of a gun; gunport, embrasure
11 砲術 **hōjutsu** gunnery, artillery
12 砲塔 **hōtō** gun turret
砲弾 **hōdan** shell, cannonball
13 砲煙 **hōen** cannon smoke
砲煙弾雨 **hōen-dan'u** smoke of guns and a hail of shells/bullets
砲戦 **hōsen** artillery battle/engagement
15 砲撃 **hōgeki** shelling, bombardment
21 砲艦 **hōkan** gunboat

———————— 2 ————————
3 大砲 **taihō** cannon, gun, artillery
4 弔砲 **chōhō** artillery funeral salute
火砲 **kahō** gun, cannon
5 礼砲 **reihō** (21-gun) salute
6 臼砲 **kyūhō** mortar
7 応砲 **ōhō** return fire
8 空砲 **kūhō** unloaded cannon; a blank (cartridge)
9 発砲 **happō** firing, discharge, shooting
重砲 **jūhō** heavy gun/artillery
祝砲 **shukuhō** (21-gun) salute
11 野砲 **yahō** field gun/artillery
野砲兵 **yahōhei** field artilleryman
12 答砲 **tōhō** gun salute fired in return
13 鉄砲 **teppō** gun
鉄砲傷 **teppō kizu** gunshot wound
14 銃砲 **jūhō** guns, firearms
19 警砲 **keihō** warning gun/shot
21 艦砲 **kanpō** ship's guns
艦砲射撃 **kanpō shageki** shelling from a naval vessel

———————— 3 ————————
4 水鉄砲 **mizudeppō** squirt gun
7 迫撃砲 **hakugekihō** mortar
豆鉄砲 **mamedeppō** bean/pea shooter, popgun
肘鉄砲 **hijideppō** rebuff, rejection
8 空鉄砲 **karadeppō** unloaded gun; a blank (cartridge)
9 速射砲 **sokushahō** rapid-fire gun/cannon
10 高角砲 **kōkakuhō** high-angle/antiaircraft gun
高射砲 **kōshahō** antiaircraft gun
紙鉄砲 **kamideppō** popgun
12 無鉄砲 **muteppō** reckless, rash
答礼砲 **tōreihō** gun salute fired in return

———————— 4 ————————
8 長射程砲 **chōshateihō** long-range gun/artillery

5a5.4

砥

SHI, to, toishi whetstone
to(gu) whet, hone, polish

———————— 1 ————————
5 砥石 **toishi** whetstone
10 砥粉 **to(no)ko** polishing powder

———————— 2 ————————
8 油砥石 **aburatoishi** oilstone
9 革砥 **kawato** razor strop
11 粗砥 **arato** coarse grindstone/whetstone

5a5.5

砧 碪

CHIN, kinuta fulling block

砿 → 鉱 **8a5.15**

砺 → 礪 **5a14.1**

─────────── 6 ───────────

研 → 研 **5a4.1**

硅 → 珪 **4f6.4**

5a6.1

砦 SAI, toride fort, fortifications

─────────── 2 ───────────
9 城砦 **jōsai** fort, citadel

─────────── 7 ───────────

5a7.1 / 1009

硬 KŌ, kata(i) hard, firm

─────────── 1 ───────────
3 硬口蓋 **kōkōgai** the hard palate
4 硬化 **kōka** hardening
硬化油 **kōkayu** hydrogenated oil
硬化症 **kōkashō** sclerosis
硬水 **kōsui** hard water
5 硬玉 **kōgyoku** jadeite
6 硬式 **kōshiki** hard, rigid
8 硬直 **kōchoku** rigid, firm, inflexible
硬性 **kōsei** hardness
9 硬派 **kōha** tough elements, hardliners, hardcore
硬度 **kōdo** (degree of) hardness
10 硬骨 **kōkotsu** hard bone; stalwart, unyielding
硬骨漢 **kōkotsukan** man of firm character
11 硬球 **kōkyū** hard/regulation ball
硬貨 **kōka** coin; hard currency
硬軟 **kōnan** (relative) hardness
12 硬筆 **kōhitsu** pen or pencil (rather than brush)
15 硬質 **kōshitsu** hard, rigid

─────────── 2 ───────────
5 生硬 **seikō** crude, immature, unrefined
7 肝硬変 **kankōhen** cirrhosis of the liver
11 強硬 **kyōkō** firm, resolute, vigorous
強硬派 **kyōkōha** hard-liners, diehards

─────────── 3 ───────────
6 死後硬直 **shigo kōchoku** rigor mortis
11 動脈硬化 **dōmyaku kōka** hardening of the arteries
動脈硬化症 **dōmyaku kōkashō** arteriosclerosis

5a7.2

硯 KEN, suzuri inkstone

─────────── 1 ───────────
9 硯海 **suzuri (no) umi** the well of an inkstone
13 硯箱 **suzuribako** inkstone case
─────────── 2 ───────────
10 唐硯 **tōken** Chinese ink slab

5a7.3 / 1856

硫 RYŪ sulfur

─────────── 1 ───────────
6 硫安 **ryūan** ammonium sulfate
11 硫黄 **iō** sulfur
硫黄泉 **iōsen** sulfur springs
硫黄華 **iōka** flowers of sulfur
14 硫酸 **ryūsan** sulfuric acid, ... sulfate
硫酸紙 **ryūsanshi** parchment paper
─────────── 2 ───────────
5 加硫 **karyū** vulcanization
7 亜硫酸 **aryūsan** sulfurous acid, ... sulfite
8 和硫 **waryū** vulcanization
11 過硫酸 **karyūsan** persulfuric acid, (potassium) persulfate

5a7.4

硜 KŌ sound of stones struck together; petty

5a7.5

硴 kaki oyster

5a7.6 / 1855

硝 SHŌ saltpeter

─────────── 1 ───────────
2 硝子 **garasu** glass
5 硝石 **shōseki** saltpeter
6 硝安 **shōan** ammonium nitrate

5a7.7

13 硝煙 **shōen** gunpowder smoke
14 硝酸 **shōsan** nitric acid, ... nitrate
　　硝酸塩 **shosan'en** a nitrate
　　硝酸銀 **shōsangin** silver nitrate
16 硝薬 **shōyaku** gunpowder

_____ 2 _____

8 板硝子 **itagarasu** plate glass
6 芒硝 **bōshō** Glauber's salt, mirabilite
12 熖硝 **enshō** gunpowder; niter

5a7.7

硲

hazama ravine, gorge, gap

_____ 8 _____

5

→ 7 石
　　立
　　目
　　禾
　　ネ
　　田
　　皿
　　疒

5a8.1

碓

TAI, usu (pedal-operated) mortar (for hulling grain)

碑 → 碑 5a9.2

5a8.2

硼

HŌ boron

_____ 1 _____

9 硼砂 **hōsha** borax
10 硼素 **hōso** boron
14 硼酸 **hōsan** boric acid

5a8.3

碚

HAI mound; bud

5a8.4

碍　礙

GAI obstacle

_____ 1 _____

2 碍子 **gaishi** insulator

_____ 2 _____

7 妨碍 **bōgai** obstruction, disturbance, interference
12 無碍 **muge** free of obstacles

5a8.5

碕

KI promontory, cape

5a8.6

碇

TEI, ikari anchor

_____ 1 _____

8 碇泊 **teihaku** lie at anchor, be berthed/moored
　　碇泊地 **teihakuchi** anchorage, berth

5a8.7

碗

WAN porcelain bowl, teacup

_____ 2 _____

9 茶碗 **chawan** teacup; (rice) bowl
　　茶碗蒸 **chawanmu(shi)** steamed non-sweet custard of vegetables, egg, and meat

_____ 4 _____

9 茶飲茶碗 **chano(mi)jawan** teacup

碯 → 瑙 4f8.7

5a8.8

碌

ROKU satisfactory, decent, worth mentioning

_____ 1 _____

3 碌々 **rokuroku** in idleness; sufficiently, decently

_____ 2 _____

10 耄碌 **mōroku** senility, dotage

砕 → 砕 5a4.6

5a8.9 / 1834

碁

GO (the board game) go

_____ 1 _____

5 碁打 **gou(chi)** go player
　　碁石 **goishi** go stone
6 碁会 **gokai** go club/meet
　　碁会所 **gokaisho, gokaijo** go club
9 碁客 **gokaku** go player
15 碁盤 **goban** go board
　　碁盤割 **gobanwa(ri)** partitioned like a checkerboard
　　碁盤縞 **gobanjima** checked/lattice pattern

—————— 2 ——————

7 囲碁 **igo** go (the board game)
16 賭碁 **kakego** go played for stakes

5a8.10

碆 **HA** stone weight at the end of a cord attached to an arrow (for entangling game); arrowhead

—————— 9 ——————

5a9.1

碩 碩 **SEKI** great

—————— 1 ——————

7 碩学 **sekigaku** erudition; great scholar

礎 → 砧 5a5.5

5a9.2 / 1522

碑 碑 **HI** tombstone, monument **ishibumi** (inscribed) stone monument

—————— 1 ——————

4 碑文 **hibun** epitaph, inscription
5 碑石 **hiseki** tombstone, (stone) monument
14 碑銘 **himei** inscription, epitaph

—————— 2 ——————

3 口碑 **kōhi** legend, tradition, folklore
5 石碑 **sekihi** tombstone, (stone) monument
8 建碑 **kenpi** erection of a monument
13 墓碑 **bohi** tombstone
    墓碑銘 **bohimei** epitaph
14 歌碑 **kahi** monument inscribed with a poem

—————— 3 ——————

8 忠魂碑 **chūkonhi** monument to the war dead
10 記念碑 **kinenhi** monument
13 頌徳碑 **shōtokuhi** monument in honor of (someone)

5a9.3

碬 **KA** grinder

5a9.4

碣 **KETSU** large rock

碩 → 碩 5a9.1

5a9.6 / 1548

磁 **JI** magnetism; porcelain

—————— 1 ——————

2 磁力 **jiryoku** magnetic force, magnetism
3 磁土 **jido** kaolin
4 磁化 **jika** magnetization
6 磁石 **jishaku, jiseki** magnet
    磁石盤 **jishakuban** (mariner's) compass
6 磁気 **jiki** magnetism, magnetic
    磁気学 **jikigaku** magnetics
    磁気圏 **jikiken** magnetosphere
    磁気嵐 **jikiarashi** magnetic storm
7 磁束 **jisoku** magnetic flux
8 磁性 **jisei** magnetism
9 磁界 **jikai** magnetic field
10 磁針 **jishin** magnetic needle
12 磁場 **jiba, jijō** magnetic field
    磁極 **jikyoku** magnetic pole
13 磁鉄 **jitetsu** magnetic iron
    磁鉄鉱 **jitekkō** magnetite, loadstone
15 磁器 **jiki** porcelain

—————— 2 ——————

5 白磁 **hakuji** white china/porcelain
6 地磁気 **chijiki** the earth's magnetism
    光磁気ディスク **hikari-jiki disuku** magnetic-optical disk (MOD)
9 青磁 **seiji, aoji** celadon porcelain
10 陶磁器 **tōjiki** ceramics, china and porcelain
    消磁 **shōji** demagnetization
12 棒磁石 **bōjishaku** bar magnet
13 電磁石 **denjishaku** electromagnet
    電磁気 **denjiki** electromagnetic
    電磁波 **denjiha** electromagnetic waves
    電磁場 **denjiba** electromagnetic field
    電磁鉄 **denjitetsu** electromagnet

—————— 3 ——————

16 蹄形磁石 **teikei jishaku** horseshoe magnet

5a9.7

碧 **HEKI** blue, green

—————— 1 ——————

4 碧水 **hekisui** blue water
5 碧玉 **hekigyoku** jasper
11 碧眼 **hekigan** blue eyes

—————— 2 ——————

11 紺碧 **konpeki** deep blue, azure

5

石 9 ←
立
目
禾
衤
田
皿
疒

─────── 10 ───────

5a10.1

磲 **BA, ME** number; wharf; agate
yādo, yāru yard (91.44 cm)

─────── 4 ───────

5 四角号碼 **shikaku gōma** (an encoding scheme which assigns to each kanji a four-digit number based on its four corners)

5a10.2

硈 **KATSU** stone implement

5a10.3 / 603

確 **KAKU, tashi(ka)** certain, sure
tashi(kameru) make sure of, verify
shika (to) certainly, definitely, exactly, clearly, fully, firmly

─────── 1 ───────

0 確たる **kaku(taru)** certain, firm, definite
5 確乎 **kakko** firm, determined
確立 **kakuritsu** establishment, settlement
6 確守 **kakushu** adhere to, be loyal to
7 確言 **kakugen** state definitely, affirm
8 確実 **kakujitsu** certain, reliable
確定 **kakutei** decision, definite
9 確信 **kakushin** firm belief, conviction
確保 **kakuho** secure, ensure
確約 **kakuyaku** definite promise
11 確率 **kakuritsu** probability
確執 **kakushitsu** discord, strife
12 確報 **kakuhō** definite news, confirmed report
確然 **kakuzen** distinct, clear-cut
確答 **kakutō** definite answer
確証 **kakushō** proof positive, corroboration
14 確認 **kakunin** confirm, verify
確説 **kakusetsu** established theory
確聞 **kakubun** learn from reliable sources
15 確論 **kakuron** incontrovertible argument, established theory

─────── 2 ───────

4 不確 **futashi(ka)** uncertain, unreliable, indefinite
不確実 **fukakujitsu** uncertain, unreliable
5 未確定 **mikakutei** unsettled, pending
正確 **seikaku** exact, precise, accurate
6 再確認 **saikakunin** reaffirmation
8 明確 **meikaku** clear, distinct, well-defined
的確 **tekikaku, tekkaku** precise, accurate, unerring
14 精確 **seikaku** accurate, precise, exact

─────── 3 ───────

4 不正確 **fuseikaku** inaccurate

5a10.4

磅 **BŌ, HŌ** become obstructed
pondo pound (British unit of currency or weight)

5a10.5

磋 **SA** polish

─────── 2 ───────

4 切磋琢磨 **sessa-takuma** work hard/assiduously

5a10.6

磑 **GAI** stone mortar, hand mill

5a10.7

碾 **TEN** mortar, hand mill
hi(ku) grind

5a10.8

磊 **RAI** many stones; easygoing

─────── 1 ───────

12 磊落 **rairaku** unaffected, free and easy

5a10.9

磐 **BAN, HAN, iwa** rock, crag

─────── 1 ───────

5 磐石 **banjaku** huge rock
9 磐城 **Iwaki** (ancient kuni, Fukushima-ken)
11 磐梯山 **Bandai-san** (mountain, Fukushima-ken)

─────── 2 ───────

11 常磐 **tokiwa** eternity
常磐木 **tokiwagi** an evergreen (tree)
常磐津 **tokiwazu** (a type of samisen-accompanied ballad)

─────── 11 ───────

5a11.1

磚 **SEN** tile

───────────── 1 ─────────────
9 磚茶 **dancha** brick tea

5a11.2

礫 **TAKU** crucifixion; pulling limb from limb; exposing a (criminal's) corpse
haritsuke crucifixion

───────────── 1 ─────────────
6 磔刑 **haritsuke, takkei** crucifixion
10 磔殺 **takusatsu** crucifixion (and stoning)

5a11.3

磧 **SEKI** expanse of sand
kawara pebbly beach/shore

───────────── 1 ─────────────
4 磧中 **sekichū** in the desert

5a11.4

磬 **KEI** lambda-shaped gong

───────────── 12 ─────────────

5a12.1

磯 **KI, iso** (rocky) beach, seashore

───────────── 1 ─────────────
4 磯辺 **isobe** (rocky) beach, seashore
11 磯釣 **isozu(ri)** fishing from seashore rocks
13 磯馴松 **sonarematsu** seashore pine (wind-blown to the countours of the terrain)

───────────── 2 ─────────────
9 荒磯 **araiso** windswept seashore

5a12.2 / 1768

礁 **SHŌ** sunken rock

───────────── 2 ─────────────
8 岩礁 **ganshō** reef
10 座礁 **zashō** run aground (on a reef)
13 暗礁 **anshō** unseen reef/rock, snag
17 環礁 **kanshō** atoll
18 離礁 **rishō** refloat (a reefbound ship)

───────────── 3 ─────────────
9 珊瑚礁 **sangoshō** coral reef

5a12.3

磽 **KŌ** rocky, barren

5a12.4

磴 **TŌ** stone steps/bridge

───────────── 13 ─────────────

5a13.1

礇 **IKU** jewel

5a13.2 / 1515

礎 **SO, ishizue** cornerstone, foundation (stone)

───────────── 1 ─────────────
5 礎石 **soseki** foundation (stone)
7 礎材 **sozai** foundation materials

───────────── 2 ─────────────
8 定礎式 **teisoshiki** cornerstone-laying ceremony
11 基礎 **kiso** foundation, fundamentals
基礎的 **kisoteki** fundamental, basic

5a13.3

礑 **TŌ** bottom, base
hata slap, bang; all of a sudden

5a13.4

礒 **GI** rock   **iso** beach, shore

───────────── 14 ─────────────

礙 → 碍 5a8.4

礦 → 鉱 8a5.15

5a14.1

礪 砺 **REI** rough grindstone/whetstone; polish

───────────── 15 ─────────────

5a15.1

礫 **REKI, tsubute** stone, pebble

───────────── 1 ─────────────
8 礫岩 **rekigan** conglomerate (rock)

5
石 15←
立
目
禾
衤
田
皿
疒

<hr>

─────── 2 ───────
5 瓦礫 **gareki** rubble; rubbish
9 飛礫 **tsubute** stone throwing; thrown stone
砂礫 **sareki, shareki** gravel, pebbles
─────── 3 ───────
4 火山礫 **kazanreki** volcanic pebbles

5a15.2

礬
BAN, HAN alum

─────── 1 ───────
3 礬土 **hando, bando** alumina
─────── 2 ───────
8 明礬 **myōban** alum
9 胆礬 **tanban** copper sulfate, blue vitriol
11 皓礬 **kōban** zinc sulfate
12 皓礬 **myōban** zinc sulfate

─────────── 立 **5b** ───────────

立	計	辛	幵	妾	竓	妢	音	彦	竒	竝	竚	站
0.1	2.1	2.2	3.1	3.2	4.1	4.2	4.3	4.4	3d5.17	2o6.1	5.1	5.2

竜	翊	竡	章	産	竟	翌	竦	竣	埈	童	殢	靖
5.3	6.1	6.2	6.3	6.4	6.5	6.6	7.1	7.2	2a7.19	7.3	7.4	8.1

意	新	韵	辞	辟	竭	端	遭	颯	竪	辣	韶	毅
8.2	8.3	7b12.2	8.4	8.5	9.1	9.2	9.3	9.4	9.5	9.6	9.7	10.1

龍	辧	親	辨	孹	辭	競	瓣	黯	競	龘	龘	龘
5b5.3	0a5.30	11.1	0a5.30	13.1	5b8.4	15.1	0a5.30	16.1	5b15.1	43.1	59.1	

─────── 0 ───────

5b0.1 / 121

立
RITSU, RYŪ, ta(tsu) stand, rise
ta(teru) set up, raise
rittoru liter

─────── 1 ───────
0 立ちはだかる **ta(chihadakaru)** stand with feet planted wide apart, block the way
2 立入 **ta(chi)i(ru)** enter, trespass, pry into
立入禁止 **tachiiri kinshi** Keep Out
3 立上 **ta(chi)a(garu)** stand up; start
ta(chi)nobo(ru) rise, ascend
立小便 **ta(chi)shōben** urinate outdoors
立山 **Tateyama** (mountain, Toyama-ken)
4 立太子 **rittaishi** investiture of the crown prince
立太子式 **rittaishi-shiki** investiture of the crown prince
立毛 **ta(chi)ge** crops yet to be harvested
立切 **ta(te)ki(ru)** close/shut up
立止 **ta(chi)do(maru)** stop, halt, stand still
立込 **ta(chi)ko(mu)** be crowded
ta(chi)ko(meru) hang over, envelop
立木 **ta(chi)ki** standing tree/timber
立方 **rippō** cube (of a number), cubic (meter)
立方体 **rippōtai** a cube
立方根 **rippōkon** cube root
5 立代 **ta(chi)ka(wari)** taking turns
立付 **ta(te)tsu(ke)** how smoothly (a sliding door) opens and shuts; continuously, at a stretch
立巡 **ta(chi)megu(ru)** stand/move about
立去 **ta(chi)sa(ru)** leave, go away
立札 **ta(te)fuda** bulletin/notice board
立礼 **ritsurei** stand and bow
立冬 **rittō** the first day of winter
立石 **ta(te)ishi** stone signpost, milestone, stone stood on end
6 立会 **ta(chi)a(i)** attendance, presence, witnessing; (trading) session
立会人 **tachiainin** observer, witness
立会演説 **ta(chi)a(i) enzetsu** campaign speech in a joint meeting of candidates, debate
立交 **ta(chi)ma(jiru)** join
立返 **ta(chi)kae(ru)** return to
立地 **ritchi** location, site selection
立至 **ta(chi)ita(ru)** come to, be reduced to
立向 **ta(chi)mu(kau)** face, stand against; head for
立行 **ta(chi)yu(ku)** can keep going, can make a living
立行司 **ta(te)gyōji** head sumo referee
立尽 **ta(chi)tsu(kusu)** continue standing
立回先 **ta(chi)mawa(ri)saki** (criminal's) hangout
7 立身 **risshin** success in life, getting ahead
立身出世 **risshin-shusse** success in life
立体 **rittai** a solid (body), three-dimensional

立体的 **rittaiteki** three-dimensional
立体美 **rittaibi** beauty of sculpture
立体派 **rittaiha** cubists
立体感 **rittaikan** sense of depth
立体戦 **rittaisen** three-dimensional warfare
立体鏡 **rittaikyō** stereoscope
立坊 **ta(chin)bō** stand around waiting; day laborer   **ta(te)kō** (vertical) shaft, pit
立坑 **ta(te)kō** (vertical) shaft, pit
立役 **ta(chi)yaku** leading role
立役者 **ta(te)yakusha** leading actor
立志 **risshi** setting one's life goal
立志伝 **risshiden** success story
立売 **ta(chi)u(ri)** street peddling/peddler
立戻 **ta(chi)modo(ru)** return to
立見 **ta(chi)mi** watch (a play) while standing
立見客 **ta(chi)mikyaku** standee, gallery
立見席 **ta(chi)miseki** standing room, gallery
立言 **ritsugen** expression of one's view, proposal
8 立命 **ritsumei** philosophical peace of mind
立直 **ta(te)nao(ru)** recover, rally, pick up
立並 **ta(chi)nara(bu)** stand in a row; be equal to
立迷 **ta(chi)mayo(u)** float along, drift
立退 **ta(chi)no(ku)** move out (of the premises)
立泳 **ta(chi)oyo(gi)** tread water
立法 **rippō** legislation, lawmaking
立法上 **rippōjō** legislative
立法府 **rippōfu** legislature
立法者 **rippōsha** legislator, lawmaker
立法権 **rippōken** legislative power
立坪 **ta(te)tsubo** cubic ken (about 6 cubic meters)
立往生 **ta(chi)ōjō** be at a standstill, be stalled/stranded; stand speechless (without a rejoinder)
立歩 **ta(chi)aru(ki)** walking, toddling
立居 **ta(chi)i** standing and sitting; daily getting about
立国 **rikkoku** nation building, founding of a state
立板水 **ta(te)ita (ni) mizu** fluency, glibness, volubility, rattling on, logorrhea
立物 **ta(te)mono** leading actor
立所 **ta(chi)dokoro (ni)** immediately, at once, on the spot
9 立飛 **ta(chi)to(bi)** standing plunge
立前 **ta(te)mae** principle, policy, official stance
立通 **ta(chi)dō(shi)** standing all the way/while
立派 **rippa** splendid, fine, magnificent
立姿 **ta(chi)sugata** standing position
立待月 **ta(chi)ma(chi)zuki** 17-day-old moon
立後 **ta(chi)oku(reru)** get off to a late start, lag behind

立枯 **ta(chi)ga(re)** blight, withering
立春 **risshun** the first day of spring
立看板 **ta(te)kanban** standing signboard
立秋 **risshū** the first day of autumn
立食 **ta(chi)gu(i), risshoku** eating while standing
10 立射 **rissha** firing from a standing position
立候補 **rikkōho** stand/run for office, announce one's candidacy
立流 **ta(chi)naga(shi)** (waist-high) sink, basin
立消 **ta(chi)gi(e)** go/die/flicker/fizzle out
立振舞 **ta(chi)buruma(i)** farewell dinner   **ta(chi)furuma(i)** demeanor
立案 **ritsuan** plan, devise, draft
立案者 **ritsuansha** drafter, planner, designer
立党 **rittō** founding of a party
立席 **ta(chi)seki** standing room (only)
立夏 **rikka** the first day of summer
立悩 **ta(chi)naya(mu)** hesitate, come to a standstill, be held up
11 立遅 **ta(chi)oku(re)** get off to a late start, lag behind
立掛 **ta(chi)ka(keru)** begin to rise
立寄 **ta(chi)yo(ru)** drop in on, stop at
立脚 **rikkyaku** be based on
立脚地 **rikkyakuchi** position, standpoint
立脚点 **rikkyakuten** position, standpoint
12 立場 **tachiba** standpoint, position, viewpoint
立幅跳 **ta(chi)habato(bi)** standing long jump
立葵 **ta(chi)aoi** hollyhock
立勝 **ta(chi)masa(ru)** surpass, excel
立替 **ta(te)ka(eru)** pay in advance; pay for another
立替金 **ta(te)ka(e)kin** an advance
立竦 **ta(chi)suku(mu)** be petrified
立番 **ta(chi)ban** stand guard; a guard
立証 **risshō** prove, establish
立飲 **ta(chi)no(mi)** drinking while standing
13 立業 **ta(chi)waza** (judo) standing techniques
立働 **ta(chi)hatara(ku)** work
立塞 **ta(chi)fusa(garu)** stand in the way, block
立腹 **rippuku** get angry, lose one's temper
立続 **ta(te)tsuzu(ke)** in succession
立詰 **ta(chi)zu(me)** keep on standing
立話 **ta(chi)banashi** standing and chatting
14 立像 **ritsuzō** (standing) statue
立腐 **ta(chi)gusa(re)** rotting on the vine; dilapidation
立網 **ta(te)ami** set net
立読 **ta(chi)yo(mi)** read while standing (at a magazine rack)
立聞 **ta(chi)gi(ki)** overhear, eavesdrop
15 立撃 **ta(chi)u(chi)** firing from a standing position
立膝 **ta(te)hiza** (sit with) one knee drawn up

5

石
立 0 ←
目
禾
衤
田
罒
皿
疒

立論 **ritsuron** put forth an argument
16 立憲 **rikken** adopting a constitution
立憲君主政体 **rikken kunshu seitai** constitutional monarchy
立憲国 **rikkenkoku** constitutional country
立憲的 **rikkenteki** constitutional
立稽古 **ta(chi)geiko** rehearsal
立錐 **rissui** (not enough room to) drive in an awl
18 立襟 **ta(chi)eri** stand-up collar
立騒 **ta(chi)sawa(gu)** raise a din/to-do
19 立瀬 **ta(tsu)se** position (before others), predicament
立願 **ritsugan** offer a prayer (to a god)
22 立籠 **ta(te)komo(ru)** hole up, remain in seclusion, entrench oneself

─────────── 2 ───────────

3 夕立 **yūdachi** sudden afternoon shower
4 中立 **chūritsu** neutrality
中立労連 **Chūritsu Rōren** Federation of Independent Unions of Japan (short for 中立労働組合連絡会議)
中立国 **chūritsukoku** neutral country
切立 **ki(ri)ta(tsu)** rise perpendicularly
ki(ri)ta(te) freshly cut
分立 **bunritsu** separation (of powers), independence
公立 **kōritsu** public (institution)
手立 **teda(te)** means, method
引立役 **hi(ki)ta(te)yaku** one who seeks to enhance another's position, foil, front/advance man, supporter
木立 **kodachi** grove, thicket
日立 **hida(tsu)** grow up; recover (after childbirth) **Hitachi** (city, Ibaraki-ken); (electronics company)
心立 **kokoroda(te)** disposition, temperament
5 矢立 **yata(te)** portable brush-and-ink case
生立 **u(mi)ta(te)** fresh-laid (eggs)
u(mare)ta(te) newborn
o(i)ta(chi) one's childhood, growing up
申立 **mō(shi)ta(teru)** state, declare
仕立 **shita(te)** sewing, tailoring; outfitting
存立 **sonritsu** existence, subsistence
市立 **shiritsu** municipal, city(-run)
用立 **yōda(teru)** lend, advance (money)
目立 **meda(tsu)** be conspicuous, stand out
6 気立 **kida(te)** disposition, temperament
両立 **ryōritsu** coexist, be compatible
仲立 **nakada(chi)** intermediation; agent, broker; go-between
色立 **iro(meki)ta(tsu)** become excited/enlivened
汲立 **ku(mi)ta(te)** freshly drawn (from the well)

先立 **sakida(tsu)** go before, precede; die before; take precedence
帆立貝 **hotategai** scallop (shell)
行立 **yu(ki)ta(tsu)** set out; be effected, be set up
共立 **kyōritsu** joint, common
守立 **mo(ri)ta(teru)** bring up; support
屹立 **kitsuritsu** rise, tower, soar
成立 **seiritsu** come into being, be formed/effected **na(ri)ta(tsu)** consist of; be effected, come into being
na(ri)ta(chi) origin, history, makeup
自立 **jiritsu** stand on one's own, be independent
7 佇立 **choritsu** stand still
対立 **tairitsu** confrontation, opposing
角立 **kadoda(tsu)** be pointed/sharp, be rough; sound harsh
乱立 **ranritsu** profusion/flood (of candidates)
役立 **yakuda(tsu), yaku (ni) ta(tsu)** be useful, serve the purpose
花立 **hanata(te)** vase
売立 **u(ri)ta(te)** selling off, auction
村立 **sonritsu** established by the village
見立 **mita(teru)** diagnose, judge; select
私立 **shiritsu** private (sometimes pronounced *watakushiritsu* to avoid confusion with 市立, municipal)
町立 **chōritsu** (established by the) town
言立 **i(i)ta(teru)** state, assert
足立 **Adachi** (surname)
8 非立憲的 **hirikkenteki** unconstitutional
表立 **omoteda(tsu)** become public/known
孤立 **koritsu** be isolated
刷立 **su(ri)ta(te)** fresh/hot off the presses
直立 **chokuritsu** stand erect/upright, rise perpendicularly
直立不動 **chokuritsu-fudō** standing at attention
建立 **konryū** erection, building
追立 **o(i)ta(teru)** send/drive away, pack off, evict
逆立 **sakada(chi)** handstand, standing on one's head **sakada(tsu)** stand on end
sakada(teru) set on end, bristle/ruffle up
沸立 **wa(ki)ta(tsu)** boil up, seethe
波立 **namida(tsu)** be choppy/wavy, billow, ripple
泡立 **awada(teru)** beat into a froth, whip
泡立器 **awada(te)ki** eggbeater
泡立機 **awada(te)ki** eggbeater
押立 **o(shi)ta(teru)** raise, erect, set up
呼立 **yo(bi)ta(teru)** call out, ask to come, summon
苛立 **irada(tsu)** get irritated/exasperated
irada(teru) irritate, exasperate

官立 **kanritsu** government(-established/-run)
定立 **teiritsu** thesis
突立 **tsu(t)ta(tsu)** stand up (straight)
　　　tsu(ki)ta(teru) stab, thrust violently, plant (one's feet)
突立上 **tsu(t)ta(chi)a(garu)** jump to one's feet
府立 **furitsu** run by an urban prefecture
国立 **kokuritsu** national (park/library)
　　　Kunitachi (city, Tōkyō-to)
林立 **rinritsu** stand close together in large numbers
肥立 **hida(tsu)** grow up; recover (after childbirth)
取立 **to(ri)ta(teru)** collect (a debt); appoint; patronize **to(ri)ta(te)** fresh-picked; collection **to(ri)ta(tete)** in particular
取立金 **toritatekin** money collected
9 飛立 **to(bi)ta(tsu)** take wing; jump up
重立 **omoda(tta)** principal, leading, prominent
陣立 **jinda(te)** battle array/formation
剃立 **so(ri)ta(te)** freshly shaven
前立腺 **zenritsusen** prostate gland
連立 **tsu(re)da(tsu)** accompany
　　　renritsu alliance, coalition
連立内閣 **renritsu naikaku** coalition cabinet
連立方程式 **renritsu hōteishiki** simultaneous equations
浮立 **u(ki)ta(tsu)** be buoyant/exhilarated, be cheered up
洗立 **ara(i)ta(teru)** inquire into, ferret out
独立 **dokuritsu** independence
　　　hito(ri)da(chi) stand alone, be on one's own
独立心 **dokuritsushin** independent spirit
独立自尊 **dokuritsu-jison** independence and self-respect
独立国 **dokuritsukoku** independent country
独立独行 **dokuritsu-dokkō** independence, self-reliance
独立独歩 **dokuritsu-doppo** independence, self-reliance
独立権 **dokuritsuken** autonomy
狩立 **ka(ri)ta(teru)** hunt up, chase (foxes)
荒立 **arada(tsu)** be agitated/aggravated **arada(teru)** exacerbate, exasperate
県立 **kenritsu** prefectural
面立 **omoda(chi)** looks, features
研立 **to(gi)ta(te)** freshly sharpened
思立 **omo(i)ta(tsu)** set one's mind on, plan
10 都立 **toritsu** metropolitan, municipal
差立 **sa(shi)ta(teru)** send, forward
埋立 **u(me)ta(teru)** reclaim (land), fill in/up
埋立地 **u(me)ta(te)chi** reclaimed land
起立 **kiritsu** stand up
振立 **fu(ri)ta(teru)** shake/perk up, raise (one's voice)

書立 **ka(ki)ta(teru)** write/play up, feature; enumerate
特立 **tokuritsu** conspicuous; independent
旅立 **tabida(tsu)** start on a journey
留立 **to(me)da(te)** dissuade, stop, prevent
献立 **uneda(te)** building ridges, furrowing
11 捲立 **maku(shi)ta(teru)** talk volubly, rattle on
掃立 **ha(ki)ta(te)** newly/just swept
萌立 **mo(e)ta(tsu)** sprout, bud
巣立 **suda(chi)** leave the nest, become independent
脚立 **kyatatsu** stepladder
組立 **ku(mi)ta(teru)** construct, assemble
組立工 **kumita(te)kō** assembler, fitter
組立工場 **kumita(te) kōjō** assembly/knockdown plant
組立式 **kumita(te)shiki** prefab, collapsible
組立住宅 **kumita(te) jūtaku** prefab housing
粒立 **tsubuda(tsu)** become grainy/foamy
設立 **setsuritsu** establishment, founding
設立者 **setsuritsusha** founder, organizer
責立 **se(me)ta(teru)** torture; urge
12 毳立 **kebada(tsu)** be fluffy/plush
傘立 **kasata(te)** umbrella stand
創立 **sōritsu** establishment, founding
創立者 **sōritsusha** founder
湧立 **wa(ki)ta(tsu)** well up, seethe
棒立 **bōda(chi)** standing bolt upright
腕立 **udeda(te)** fight, resort to force
腕立伏 **udeta(te)fu(se)** push-ups
朝立 **asada(chi)** early-morning departure; morning erection
焼立 **ya(ki)ta(te)** fresh baked/roasted
煮立 **nita(tsu)** boil up, come to a boil
粟立 **awada(tsu)** have gooseflesh
筆立 **fudeta(te)** writing-brush stand
開立 **kairyū** determining the cube root
13 際立 **kiwada(tsu)** be conspicuous/prominent
隠立 **kaku(shi)da(te)** keep secret
塗立 **nu(ri)ta(teru)** put on thick makeup **nu(ri)ta(te)** freshly painted/plastered, Wet Paint
搗立 **tsu(ki)ta(te)** freshly pounded (mochi)
搔立 **ka(ki)ta(teru)** stir/rake up, arouse
群立 **murada(tsu)** gather and stand together; take wing in a flock
献立 **kondate** menu; arrangements, plan, program
献立表 **kondatehyō** menu
腹立 **harada(tsu)** get angry
腹立紛 **harada(chi)magi(re)** a fit of rage
数立 **kazo(e)ta(teru)** count up, enumerate
鼎立 **teiritsu** three-cornered (contest)
継立 **tsu(gi)ta(te)** relay
節立 **fushi(kure)da(tsu)** be knotty/gnarled/bony

飾立 **kaza(ri)ta(teru)** adorn, deck out
14 煽立 **ao(gi)ta(teru)** instigate
総立 **sōda(chi)** everyone standing up together
駆立 **ka(ri)ta(teru)** round up; spur on
ka(ke)ta(tsu) gallop after, pursue
15 褒立 **ho(me)ta(teru)** praise, applaud
確立 **kakuritsu** establishment, settlement
16 凝立 **gyōritsu** stand absolutely still
擁立 **yōritsu** support, back
樹立 **juritsu** establish, found
燃立 **mo(e)ta(tsu)** blaze up, be ablaze
積立 **tsu(mi)ta(teru)** save up, amass
積立金 **tsumitatekin** a reserve (fund)
奮立 **furu(i)ta(tsu)** be stirred/roused
17 薹立 **tō (ga) ta(tsu)** go to seed, be past one's prime
18 濫立 **ranritsu** standing in disorder; (both good and bad candidates) coming forward in great numbers
顔立 **kaoda(chi)** features, looks
騒立 **sawa(gi)ta(teru)** raise a big fuss/furor
sawa(gi)ta(tsu) be agitated
19 蹴立 **keta(teru)** kick up
鯱立 **shachihokoda(chi)** standing on one's hands/head; exerting great effort

———————— 3 ————————

1 一本立 **ipponda(chi)** independence
2 二本立 **nihonda(te)** double feature (movie)
二頭立 **nitōda(te)** two-horse (cart)
4 不成立 **fuseiritsu** failure, rejection
水際立 **mizugiwada(tta)** splendid, fine
心安立 **kokoroyasuda(te)** out of familiarity, frank
5 冬木立 **fuyukodachi** leafless trees in winter
目鼻立 **mehanada(chi)** looks, features
6 気負立 **kio(i)ta(tsu)** rouse oneself, get psyched up
安心立命 **anshin-ritsumei** spiritual peace and enlightenment
安神立命 **anshin-ritsumei** spiritual peace and enlightenment
7 角目立 **tsunomeda(tsu)** be pointed/sharp, be rough; sound harsh
8 忠義立 **chūgida(te)** act of loyalty
9 俄仕立 **niwakajita(te)** improvised, extemporaneous
負腹立 **ma(ke)bara (o) ta(teru)** get angry upon losing
浮足立 **u(ki)ashida(tsu)** be ready to run away, waver
10 殺気立 **sakkida(tsu)** grow excited/menacing
11 道具立 **dōguda(te)** tool setup, stage setting
鹿島立 **kashimada(chi)** set out on a journey
12 証拠立 **shōkoda(teru)** substantiate, corroborate

13 義理立 **girida(te)** do one's duty
詮議立 **sengida(te)** thorough investigation
14 総毛立 **sōkeda(tsu)** hair stand on end, have goose flesh

———————— 4 ————————

3 三権分立 **sanken bunritsu** separation of powers (legislative, executive, and judicial)
5 白羽矢立 **shiraha (no) ya (ga) ta(tsu)** be selected (for a task/post)
7 局外中立 **kyokugai chūritsu** neutrality

———————— 2 ————————

5b2.1

卝 **dekarittoru** decaliter, ten liters

5b2.2 / 1487

辛 **SHIN** bitter, trying; eighth in a series, "H" **kanoto** eighth calendar sign **kara(i)** hot, spicy, salty; hard, trying **karo(ujite), kara(kumo)** barely **tsura(i)** painful, trying, tough

———————— 1 ————————

3 辛々 **karagara** barely
辛口 **karakuchi** salty, spicy, dry (saké); preference for sharp taste
5 辛目 **karame** salty
6 辛気 **shinki** fretfulness
辛気臭 **shinkikusa(i)** fretful
辛夷 **kobushi** cucumber tree (a magnolia-like tree whose large white blossoms resemble fists)
7 辛労 **shinrō** hardship, struggle
8 辛抱 **shinbō** perseverance, patience
辛味 **karami** sharp/pungent taste
辛苦 **shinku** hardship, privation, trouble
10 辛党 **karatō** drinker
12 辛勝 **shinshō** narrow victory
14 辛辣 **shinratsu** bitter, biting, harsh
辛酸 **shinsan** hardship, privation

———————— 2 ————————

3 千辛万苦 **senshin-banku** countless hardships
7 辛辛 **karagara** barely
9 香辛料 **kōshinryō** spices, seasoning
10 唐辛子 **tōgarashi** cayenne/red pepper
13 塩辛 **shiokara** salted fish (guts)
14 聞辛 **ki(ki)zura(i)** hard to hear/ask
20 薭辛 **egara(i), egara(ppoi)** acrid, pungent

———————— 3 ————————

5 世智辛 **sechigara(i)** hard (times), tough (life)
11 粒粒辛苦 **ryūryū-shinku** assiduous effort

3

5b3.1

圲

kirorittoru kiloliter, thousand liters

5b3.2

妾

SHŌ, mekake concubine, mistress
warawa I, me (in feminine speech)

1

6 妾宅 **shōtaku** concubine's/mistress's house
13 妾腹 **shofuku, mekakebara** born of a
concubine/mistress

2

7 男妾 **otoko mekake** male paramour
8 妻妾 **saishō** wife and mistress(es)
13 愛妾 **aishō** one's mistress

4

5b4.1

粍

miririttoru milliliter, cubic centimeter

5b4.2

竕

deshirittoru deciliter, tenth of a liter

5b4.3 / 347

音

ON, IN, oto, ne sound

1

3 音叉 **onsa** tuning fork
音上 **ne (o) a(geru)** give in, cry uncle
4 音引 **onbi(ki)** (dictionary) arranged by
pronunciation (rather than stroke count)
5 音字 **onji** phonogram, phonetic symbol
6 音曲 **ongyoku, onkyoku** song with samisen
accompaniment; musical performances
音色 **neiro, onshoku** tone quality, timbre
音吐 **onto** voice
音吐朗々 **onto-rōrō** in a clear/ringing voice
音名 **onmei** name of a musical note
7 音沙汰 **otosata** news, tidings
音声 **onsei, onjō** voice, audio
音声学 **onseigaku** phonetics
8 音波 **onpa** sound wave
音物 **inmotsu** gift, present
9 音信 **onshin, inshin, otozure** a communication, letter, news

音信不通 **onshin-futsū, inshin-futsū** no news
of, haven't heard from
音便 **onbin** (for sake of) euphony
音速 **onsoku** the speed of sound
音律 **onritsu** melody, pitch, rhythm
10 音部記号 **onbu kigō** (G) clef
音栓 **onsen** (organ) stop
音訓 **onkun** Chinese and Japanese pronunciations of a kanji
11 音階 **onkai** (musical) scale
音域 **on'iki** singing range, register
音符 **onpu** (musical) note; the part of a kanji
indicating its pronunciation
音訳 **on'yaku** transliteration
12 音場 **onjō, onba** sound field
音量 **onryō** (sound) volume
音程 **ontei** (musical) interval, step
13 音源 **ongen** sound source
音楽 **ongaku** music
音楽会 **ongakkai, ongakukai** concert
音楽家 **ongakka, ongakuka** musician
音楽隊 **ongakutai** band, orchestra
音楽堂 **ongakudō** concert hall
音感 **onkan** sense of sound/pitch
音痴 **onchi** tone deaf
音節 **onsetsu** syllable
14 音管 **onkan** organ pipe
音読 **ondoku** reading aloud
on'yo(mi) the Chinese reading of a kanji
15 音標文字 **onpyō moji** phonetic characters
音盤 **onban** phonograph record
音締 **neji(me)** tuning; tune, melody
音調 **onchō** tone, tune, rhythm, euphony
音質 **onshitsu** tone quality
16 音頭 **ondo** leading a song/refrain
19 音響 **onkyō** sound
音響学 **onkyōgaku** acoustics
音譜 **onpu** (written) notes, the score
音韻 **on'in** phoneme
音韻学 **on'ingaku** phonology
音韻論 **on'inron** phonemics, phonology

2

1 一音節 **ichionsetsu** one syllable
2 子音 **shiin** consonant
3 大音声 **daionjō** loud/stentorian voice
4 止音器 **shionki** (piano) damper
水音 **mizuoto** the sound of water
心音 **shin'on** heart tone, phonocardio-
5 半音 **han'on** half tone, half step (in music)
本音 **honne** real intention, underlying motive
母音 **boin** vowel
号音 **gōon** audible signal, call
字音 **jion** Chinese/on reading of a kanji
石音 **ishioto** sound of a go stone slapped onto
the board

6 多音節 **taonsetsu** polysyllable
気音 **kion** an aspirate
全音 **zen'on** whole tone (in music)
全音符 **zen'onpu** whole note
羽音 **haoto** flapping of wings
防音 **bōon** sound-deadening, soundproof(ing)
同音 **dōon** the same sound; one voice
同音異義 **dōon-igi** the same pronunciation but different meanings
同音語 **dōongo** homophone, homonym
吃音 **kitsuon** stuttering, stammering
舌音 **zetsuon** lingual sound
7 亜音速 **aonsoku** subsonic (speed)
低音 **teion** bass (in music); low voice, sotto voce
余音 **yoin** lingering tone, reverberation; aftertaste, suggestiveness
呉音 **goon** Wu-dynasty *on* reading of a kanji (e.g., 男 read as *nan*)
延音 **en'on** elongated (vowel) sound
宋音 **sōon** Song-dynasty reading (of a kanji)
声音 **kowane** tone of voice, timbre
   seion vocal sound
忍音 **shino(bi)ne** subdued sobbing
初音 **hatsune** (bird's) first song
足音 **ashioto** sound of footsteps
8 長音 **chōon** a long sound/vowel, long tone, dash
長音階 **chōonkai** major scale
長音符 **chōonpu** long-vowel mark, macron
表音文字 **hyōon moji** phonetic symbol/script
拗音 **yōon** diphthong (written with a small や, ゅ, or ょ, as in きゅ)
弦音 **tsuruoto** sound of a vibrating bowstring
空音 **sorane** hearing a nonexistent sound; false/untimely (rooster) cry; a lie
物音 **monooto** a noise/sound
和音 **waon** chord (in music)
9 発音 **hatsuon** pronunciation
発音学 **hatsuongaku** phonetics
促音 **sokuon** assimilated sound (represented by a small つ or, in romanization, a doubled letter)
美音 **bion** beautiful voice
単音 **tan'on** monosyllable; monotone
訃音 **fuin** news of someone's death
10 高音 **kōon, takane** high-pitched tone/key, loud sound
原音 **gen'on** the fundamental tone (in physics)
消音器 **shōonki** muffler, silencer
唇音 **shin'on** a labial (sound)
弱音吐 **yowane (o) ha(ku)** complain, cry uncle
弱音器 **jakuonki** a damper, mute
唐音 **tōon** Tang-dynasty reading (of a kanji)
11 疎音 **soin** long silence, neglecting to keep in touch

清音 **seion** unvoiced sound
基音 **kion** fundamental tone
強音 **kyōon** beat, accent, stess
転音 **ten'on** euphonic change, elision
12 雁音 **kari(ga)ne** (cry/honk of a) wild goose
遠音 **tōne** distant sound
測音器 **sokuonki** sonometer, phonometer
超音 **chōon** supersonic, ultrasonic
超音波 **chōonpa** ultrasonic waves
超音速 **chōonsoku** supersonic speed
短音 **tan'on** short sound
短音階 **tan'onkai** minor scale
無音 **buin** long silence, neglect to write/call
   muon silent
歯音 **shion** a dental sound (t, s, etc.)
筒音 **tsutsuoto** sound of a gun
軽音楽 **keiongaku** light music
13 漢音 **kan'on** Han-dynasty pronunciation (of a kanji)
微音 **bion** a faint sound
蓄音器 **chikuonki** gramophone
蓄音機 **chikuonki** gramophone
靴音 **kutsuoto** sound of someone walking
楽音 **gakuon** musical tone
福音 **fukuin** the Gospel; good news
福音書 **Fukuinsho** the Gospels
14 増音器 **zōonki** amplifier
複音 **fukuon** (harmonica) with a double row of blowholes
鼻音 **bion** nasal sound
雑音 **zatsuon** noise, static
15 潮音 **chōon** the sound of waves
撥音 **hatsuon** the sound of the kana "ん"
16 濁音 **dakuon** voiced sound
諧音 **kaion** melody, harmony
録音 **rokuon** (sound) recording
録音機 **rokuonki** recorder
17 擬音 **gion** an imitated sound, sound effects
聴音 **chōon** hearing, sound detection
聴音器 **chōonki** sound detector
聴音機 **chōonki** sound detector
18 観音 **Kannon** the Goddess of Mercy
観音開 **kannonbira(ki)** (hinged) double doors
類音 **ruion** similar sound/pronunciation
類音語 **ruiongo** words which sound similar
騒音 **sōon** noise
19 爆音 **bakuon** (sound of an) explosion, roar (of an engine)
21 轟音 **gōon** deafening roar/boom

――――――――― 3 ―――――――――

2 二分音符 **nibun onpu** half note
八分音符 **hachibu onpu** an eighth note (♪)
4 五十音図 **gojūonzu** the kana syllabary table
五十音順 **gojūonjun** in "aiueo" order of the kana alphabet

中高音部 **chūkōonbu** alto, mezzo-soprano
5 半母音 **hanboin** semivowel
　半濁音 **handakuon** semivoiced sound, p-
　　sound
　半諧音 **hankaion** assonance
　四分音符 **shibu onpu, shibun onpu** quarter
　　note
6 有気音 **yūkion** an aspirate
　有声音化 **yūseionka** vocalization, voicing
8 呼吸音 **kokyūon** respiratory sound
9 海潮音 **kaichōon** sound of the tide
　室内音楽 **shitsunai ongaku** chamber music
12 無声音 **museion** unvoiced sound
　装飾音 **sōshokuon** grace note
14 複母音 **fukuboin** diphthong
15 摩擦音 **masatsuon** a fricative (sound)
18 観世音 **Kanzeon** the Goddess of Mercy
　観世音菩薩 **Kanzeon Bosatsu** the Goddess
　　of Mercy

———————— 4 ————————
10 馬頭観音 **batōkannon** image of the god
　　Kannon with a horse's head
11 異口同音 **iku-dōon** with one voice, unani-
　　mous
12 街頭録音 **gaitō rokuon** recorded man-on-
　　the-street interview

5b4.4
彦 彦　　　　**GEN, hiko** fine young man

———————— 2 ————————
3 山彦 **yamabiko** echo
12 喉彦 **nodobiko** the uvula

奇 → 奇 **3d5.17**

———————— 5 ————————
竝 → 並 **2o6.1**

5b5.1
竚　　**CHO** stop, linger

5b5.2
站　　**TAN** stop, halt

———————— 2 ————————
7 兵站 **heitan** military supplies, logistics
　兵站部 **heitanbu** supply/logistical department

5b5.3 / 1758
竜 龍　　　**RYŪ, RYŌ, tatsu** dragon

———————— 1 ————————
3 竜口 **tatsu(no)kuchi** dragon-head gargoyle;
　　spout (of a gutter)
4 竜王 **ryūō** dragon god/king
5 竜田姫 **Tatsutahime** the goddess of autumn
8 竜券 **tatsuma(ki)** tornado
　竜虎 **ryūko** dragon and tiger, titans
9 竜涎香 **ryūzenkō** ambergris
　竜胆 **rindō** bellflower, gentian
　竜神 **ryūjin** dragon god/king
10 竜宮 **ryūgū** Palace of the Dragon King
　竜骨 **ryūkotsu** keel
　竜馬 **ryūme** splendid horse/steed
12 竜落子 **tatsu (no) o(toshi)go** sea horse
　竜絶蘭 **ryūzetsuran** century plant
16 竜頭 **ryūzu** watch stem
　竜頭蛇尾 **ryūtō-dabi** strong start but weak
　　finish
18 竜顔 **ryūgan** the emperor's countenance

———————— 2 ————————
3 土竜 **mogura** mole
8 画竜点晴 **garyō-tensei** completing the eyes
　　of a painted dragon; the finishing touches
9 臥竜 **garyō** reclining dragon; great man in
　　obscurity
10 恐竜 **kyōryū** dinosaur

———————— 3 ————————
9 独眼竜 **dokuganryū** one-eyed hero

———————— 6 ————————
5b6.1
翊　　**YOKU** flying; help, assist; the follow-
　　ing day

5b6.2
頧　　**hekutorittoru** hectoliter, hundred liters

5b6.3 / 857
章　　**SHŌ** chapter; badge, mark

———————— 1 ————————
5 章句 **shōku** passage, chapter and verse
11 章魚 **tako** octopus
13 章節 **shōsetsu** chapters and sections

--------------- 2 ---------------

4 文章 **bunshō** composition, writing; article, essay
　文章語 **bunshōgo** literary language
　文章論 **bunshōron** syntax, grammar
　日章旗 **nisshōki** the Japanese/Rising-Sun flag
7 社章 **shashō** company logo/emblem
　条章 **jōshō** provisions, articles, clauses
8 周章狼狽 **shūshō-rōbai** consternation, bewilderment, dismay
　肩章 **kenshō** epaulette, shoulder pips
9 前章 **zenshō** the preceding chapter
　星章 **seishō** badge, star
10 校章 **kōshō** school badge/pin
　紋章 **monshō** crest, coat of arms
　紋章学 **monshōgaku** heraldry
　記章 **kishō** medal, badge, insignia
11 略章 **ryakushō** miniature decoration, medal, ribbon
12 喪章 **moshō** mourning badge/band
　帽章 **bōshō** badge on a cap
　腕章 **wanshō** armband, arm badge, chevron
　詞章 **shishō** poetry and prose
13 楽章 **gakushō** a movement (of a symphony)
15 褒章 **hōshō** medal
　標章 **hyōshō** ensign, emblem, badge, mark
　勲章 **kunshō** order, decoration, medal
16 憲章 **kenshō** constitution, charter
17 徽章 **kishō** badge, insignia
18 襟章 **erishō** (collar/lapel) badge

--------------- 3 ---------------

3 大憲章 **Daikenshō** Magna Carta
6 有功章 **yūkōshō** medal for merit
　旭日章 **Kyokujitsushō** the Order of the Rising Sun

--------------- 4 ---------------

18 藍綬褒章 **ranju hōshō** blue ribbon medal

5b6.4 / 278

産 產

SAN give birth to; produce, (as suffix) product of; property
u(mu) give birth/rise to
u(mareru) be born
ubu birth; infant

--------------- 1 ---------------

0 お産 **(o)san** childbirth
　産する **san(suru)** produce, yield
3 産土神 **ubusunagami** tutelary deity, genius loci
4 産毛 **ubuge** downy hair, fluff, fuzz
　産月 **u(mi)zuki** last month of pregnancy
5 産出 **sanshutsu** production, yield, output
　産出物 **sanshutsubutsu** product
　産出高 **sanshutsudaka** output, yield, production

6 産気 **sanke** labor pains
　産気付 **sankezu(ki)** beginning of labor
　産地 **sanchi** producing area
7 産卵 **sanran** egg laying, spawning
　産卵期 **sanranki** breeding/spawning season
　産別 **sanbetsu** industry-by-industry (unions)
　産学官 **sangakkan, sangakukan** industry, universities/academia, and government/officials
　産声 **ubugoe** newborn baby's first cry
　産児 **sanji** newborn baby; bearing children
8 産物 **sanbutsu** product
　産具 **sangu** obstetrical supplies
　産金 **sankin** gold mining
9 産院 **san'in** maternity hospital
　産前 **sanzen** before childbirth/delivery
　産後 **sango** after childbirth
　産室 **sanshitsu** delivery room
　産屋 **ubuya** maternity room
　産科 **sanka** obstetrics
　産科医 **sankai** obstetrician
　産科学 **sankagaku** obstetrics
10 産馬 **sanba** horse breeding
11 産婦 **sanpu** woman in/nearing childbirth
　産婦人科 **sanfujinka** obstetrics and gynecology
　産婆 **sanba** midwife
12 産着 **ubugi** newborn baby's first clothes
　産湯 **ubuyu** newborn baby's first bath
13 産業 **sangyō** industry
　産業界 **sangyōkai** (the) industry
15 産褥 **sanjoku** childbed, confinement
　産褥熱 **sanjokunetsu** puerperal fever
16 産親 **u(mi no) oya** one's biological parent; originator, the father of
18 産額 **sangaku** output, yield, production

--------------- 2 ---------------

3 土産 **miyage** souvenir, present
　土産話 **miyagebanashi** story of one's travels
4 天産物 **tensanbutsu** natural products
　中産階級 **chūsan kaikyū** middle class
　水産 **suisan** marine products
　水産大学 **suisan daigaku** fisheries college
　水産技師 **suisan gishi** fisheries expert
　水産学 **suisangaku** the science of fisheries
　水産物 **suisanbutsu** marine products
　水産業 **suisangyō** fisheries, marine products industry
　月産 **gessan** monthly production/output
　日産 **nissan** daily production/output
　　Nissan (automobile company)
5 出産 **shussan** childbirth
　生産 **seisan** production
　生産力 **seisanryoku** (productive) capacity, productivity

生産地 **seisanchi** producing region
生産物 **seisanbutsu** product, produce
生産性 **seisansei** productivity
生産高 **seisandaka** output, production, yield
生産財 **seisanzai** producer's goods
生産量 **seisanryō** amount produced, output, production
生産費 **seisanhi** production costs
主産地 **shusanchi** chief producing region
主産物 **shusanbutsu** main product
6 多産 **tasan** multiparous; fecund, prolific
多産系 **tasankei** the type that bears many children
死産 **shizan** stillbirth
死産児 **shisanji** stillborn baby
年産 **nensan** annual production
名産 **meisan** noted product, specialty
共産 **kyōsan** communist
共産主義 **kyōsan shugi** communism
共産国家 **kyōsan kokka** communist state
共産党 **kyōsantō** communist party
共産圏 **kyōsanken** communist bloc
安産 **anzan** easy delivery/childbirth
光産業 **hikari sangyō** optronics industry
有産 **yūsan** having property/wealth
有産階級 **yūsan kaikyū** the propertied class
早産 **sōzan** premature birth
早産児 **sōzanji** premature baby
米産 **beisan** rice production
7 助産 **josan** midwifery
助産院 **josan'in** maternity hospital
助産婦 **josanpu** midwife
妊産婦 **ninsanpu** expectant and nursing mothers
初産 **shosan, shozan, uizan, hatsuzan** one's first childbirth
初産児 **shosanji** one's first(born) child
初産婦 **shosanpu** woman having her first child
8 逆産 **gyakuzan, gyakusan** foot presentation, breech birth
治産 **chisan** property management
国産 **kokusan** domestic-made
国産品 **kokusanhin** domestic products
林産 **rinsan** forest products
林産物 **rinsanbutsu** forest products
物産 **bussan** products, produce, commodities
所産 **shosan** product, result
9 通産相 **tsūsanshō** Minister of International Trade and Industry
通産省 **Tsūsanshō** MITI, Ministry of International Trade and Industry (short for 通商産業省)
海産 **kaisan** marine products
海産物 **kaisanbutsu** marine products
後産 **atozan, nochizan** afterbirth, placenta

恒産 **kōsan** fixed/real property
10 倒産 **tōsan** bankruptcy
陸産 **rikusan** land products
陸産物 **rikusanbutsu** land products
畜産 **chikusan** livestock raising
原産地 **gensanchi** place of origin, home, habitat
原産物 **gensanbutsu** primary products
流産 **ryūzan** miscarriage
家産 **kasan** family property, one's fortune
特産 **tokusan** special product, (local) specialty; indigenous
特産物 **tokusanbutsu** special product (of a locality), indigenous to
特産品 **tokusanhin** specialty, special products
破産 **hasan** bankruptcy
破産者 **hasansha** bankrupt person
財産 **zaisan** estate, assets, property
財産家 **zaisanka** wealthy person
財産税 **zaisanzei** property tax
11 副産物 **fukusanbutsu** by-product
動産 **dōsan** movable/personal property
授産 **jusan** providing employment, placement
授産所 **jusanjo** vocational center (for the unemployed)
12 減産 **gensan** lower production
量産 **ryōsan** mass production (short for 大量生産)
無産 **musan** without property
無産者 **musansha** proletarian, have-nots
無産党 **musantō** proletarian party
無産階級 **musan kaikyū** the proletariat
殖産 **shokusan** increase in production/assets
13 農産 **nōsan** agricultural products
農産物 **nōsanbutsu** agricultural products
資産 **shisan** assets, property
資産家 **shisanka** man of means
鉱産地 **kōsanchi** mineral-rich area
14 遺産 **isan** inheritance, estate
増産 **zōsan** increase in production
18 難産 **nanzan** a difficult delivery/childbirth

──────── 3 ────────

4 不生産的 **fuseisanteki** unproductive
不動産 **fudōsan** immovable property, real estate
不動産屋 **fudōsan'ya** real estate agent
内国産 **naikokusan** domestically produced
手土産 **temiyage** visitor's present
6 再生産 **saiseisan** reproduction
8 非生産的 **hiseisanteki** nonproductive, unproductive
9 通商産業省 **Tsūshōsangyōshō** Ministry of International Trade and Industry
10 純国産 **junkokusan** all-domestic (product)
13 禁治産 **kinchisan** (legally) incompetent

5

石
立 6←
目
禾
衤
田
皿
疒

禁治産者 **kinchisansha** person adjudged incompetent
戦時産業 **senji sangyō** wartime industry
置土産 **o(ki)miyage** parting gift, souvenir

———————— 4 ————————
3 大量生産 **tairyō seisan** mass production
6 共有財産 **kyōyū zaisan** community property
13 準禁治産 **junkinchisan** quasi-incompetence (in law)
準禁治産者 **junkinchisansha** a quasi-incompetent (person)
農林水産大臣 **nōrinsuisan daijin** Minister of Agriculture, Forestry and Fisheries
農林水産省 **Nōrinsuisanshō** Ministry of Agriculture, Forestry and Fisheries

5b6.5

竟 **KYŌ** come to an end; finally, after all

5b6.6 / 592

翌 翌 **YOKU** the next/following

———————— 1 ————————
4 翌月 **yokugetsu** the following month
翌日 **yokujitsu** the next/following day
6 翌年 **yokunen, yokutoshi** the following year
11 翌翌日 **yokuyokujitsu** two days later/after
翌翌年 **yokuyokunen** two years later/after
12 翌朝 **yokuchō, yokuasa** the next morning
翌暁 **yokugyō** at dawn the next morning
翌晩 **yokuban** the next evening/night

———————— 7 ————————

5b7.1

竦 **SHŌ** revere, fear **suku(mu)** crouch, cower **suku(meru)** duck (one's head), shrug (one's shoulders); make (someone) crouch/cringe

———————— 2 ————————
5 立竦 **ta(chi)suku(mu)** be petrified
8 抱竦 **da(ki)suku(meru)** hug tight
10 射竦 **isuku(meru)** shoot and make (the enemy) take cover, pin down

5b7.2

竣 **SHUN** end, be completed

———————— 1 ————————
3 竣工 **shunkō** completion (of construction)

竣工式 **shunkōshiki** completion ceremony
5 竣功 **shunkō** completion (of construction)

竢 → 俟 2a7.19

5b7.3 / 410

童 **DŌ, warabe** child

———————— 1 ————————
2 童子 **dōji** child, boy
3 童女 **dōjo** girl
4 童心 **dōshin** child's mind/feelings
7 童児 **dōji** child
8 童画 **dōga** pictures for children
9 童貞 **dōtei** (male) virgin
13 童話 **dōwa** children's story, fairy tale
童話劇 **dōwageki** a play for children
14 童歌 **warabeuta** traditional children's song
16 童謡 **dōyō** children's song, nursery rhyme
18 童顔 **dōgan** childlike/boyish face

———————— 2 ————————
3 大童 **ōwarawa** feverish activity, great effort
小童 **kowappa, kowarawa, kowarabe** youngster, kid
4 天童 **tendō** cherub; gods disguised as children
5 幼童 **yōdō** small child
7 学童 **gakudō** schoolboy, schoolgirl, pupil
村童 **sondō** village boy/child
児童 **jidō** child, juvenile
8 河童 **kappa** (water-dwelling elf)
牧童 **bokudō** shepherd boy, cowboy
怪童 **kaidō** unusually big/strong boy
9 神童 **shindō** child prodigy, wunderkind
11 悪童 **akudō** naughty boy

5b7.4

殕 **FU, ne(ru)** grow moldy

———————— 8 ————————

5b8.1

靖 靖 **SEI, yasu(i)** peaceful

———————— 1 ————————
8 靖国神社 **Yasukuni-jinja** (shrine in Tōkyō dedicated to fallen Japanese soldiers)
———————— 2 ————————
13 綏靖 **Suizei** (emperor, 581–549 B.C.)

5b8.2 / 132

意 **I** will, heart, mind, thought; meaning, sense

───── 1 ─────

2 意力 **iryoku** will power
4 意中 **ichū** one's mind/thoughts
意中人 **ichū (no) hito** the one in one's thoughts, one's beloved
5 意外 **igai** unexpected, surprising
6 意気 **iki** spirits, morale
意気込 **ikigo(mu)** be enthusiastic about
意気地 **ikuji (no nai), ikiji (no nai)** weak, spineless, helpless
意気投合 **iki-tōgō** sympathy, mutual understanding
意気消沈 **iki-shōchin** dejected, despondent
意気揚々 **iki-yōyō** exultant, triumphant
意匠 **ishō** design, idea
意地 **iji** temperament; will power; obstinacy
意地汚 **ijikitana(i)** greedy, gluttonous
意地張 **iji(p)pa(ri)** obstinate (person)
意地悪 **ijiwaru(i)** ill-tempered, crabby
意向 **ikō** intention, inclination
7 意志 **ishi** will, volition
意志力 **ishiryoku** will power
意志的 **ishiteki** strong-willed, forceful
意図 **ito** intention, aim
意見 **iken** opinion
意見書 **ikensho** written opinion
8 意表 **ihyō** surprise, something unexpected
意味 **imi** meaning, significance
意味付 **imizu(keru)** give meaning to
意味合 **imia(i)** meaning, implications
意味深長 **imi-shinchō** full of meaning
意味論 **imiron** semantics
9 意思 **ishi** intent, purpose, mind
10 意馬心猿 **iba-shin'en** (uncontrollable) passions
11 意欲 **iyoku** will, desire, zest
意訳 **iyaku** free translation
13 意義 **igi** meaning, significance
意義深 **igibuka(i)** full of meaning
意想外 **isōgai** unexpected, surprising
15 意趣 **ishu** malice, vindictiveness
意趣返 **ishugae(shi)** revenge
19 意識 **ishiki** consciousness, awareness
意識的 **ishikiteki** consciously

───── 2 ─────

1 一意 **ichii** unambiguous; single-minded
一意専心 **ichii-senshin** wholeheartedly
2 人意 **jin'i** public sentiment
3 大意 **taii** gist, outline, summary
上意 **jōi** the emperor's wishes
上意下達 **jōi katatsu** conveying the will of those in authority to those who are governed
下意上達 **kai jōtatsu** conveying the will of those who are governed to those in authority
小意気 **koiki** stylish, tasteful
4 不意 **fui** sudden, unexpected
不意打 **fuiu(chi)** surprise attack
天意 **ten'i** divine will, providence
内意 **naii** intention; personal opinion
弔意 **chōi** condolences, sympathy
介意 **kaii** care about, concern oneself with
文意 **bun'i** meaning (of a passage)
片意地 **kata-iji** stubborn, bigoted
反意語 **han'igo** antonym
心意 **shin'i** mind
心意気 **kokoroiki** disposition, spirit, sentiment
5 民意 **min'i** will of the people
本意 **hon'i** one's real intention
失意 **shitsui** despair, disappointment; adversity
生意気 **namaiki** conceited, impertinent, smart-alecky
他意 **tai** another intention, ulterior motive, malice
用意 **yōi** preparations, arrangements
用意周到 **yōi-shūtō** very careful, thoroughly prepared
句意 **kui** meaning of a phrase
好意 **kōi** good will, kindness, favor, friendliness
好意的 **kōiteki** friendly, with good intentions
主意 **shui** gist, purport, object
6 任意 **nin'i** optional, voluntary, discretionary, arbitrary
合意 **gōi** mutual consent, agreement
会意 **kaii** formation of a kanji from meaningful components (e.g., 人 + 言 = 信)
同意 **dōi** the same meaning; the same opinion; consent, agreement
同意見 **dōiken** the same opinion, like views
同意義 **dōigi** the same meaning
同意語 **dōigo** synonym
如意 **nyoi** priest's staff, mace
当意即妙 **tōi-sokumyō** ready wit, repartee
有意 **yūi** intentional; (statistically) significant
有意味 **yūimi** significant
有意的 **yūiteki** intentional; (statistically) significant
有意義 **yūigi** significant
自意識 **jiishiki** self-consciousness
7 来意 **raii** purpose of one's visit
我意 **gai** self-will, obstinacy
作意 **sakui** central theme, motif; intention
含意 **gan'i** implication

5
石
立 8←
日
禾
衤
田
罒
皿
疒

別意 **betsui** different opinion; malice; intention to part
決意 **ketsui** determination, resolution
尿意 **nyōi** the urge to urinate
私意 **shii** selfishness, bias
8 表意文字 **hyōi moji** ideograph
厚意 **kōi** kindness, favor, courtesy
注意 **chūi** attention, caution, warning
注意力 **chūiryoku** attentiveness
注意事項 **chūi jikō** matter requiring attention; N.B.
注意書 **chūiga(ki)** notes, instructions
注意深 **chūibuka(i)** careful
注意報 **chūihō** (storm) warning
実意 **jitsui** sincerity
底意 **sokoi** inmost thoughts, underlying motive
底意地悪 **sokoiji waru(i)** spiteful, malcontented, cranky
或意味 **a(ru) imi (de)** in one/a sense
9 発意 **hatsui** initiative, suggestion, original idea
便意 **ben'i** urge to go to the toilet, call of nature
美意識 **biishiki** esthetic awareness
神意 **shin'i** God's will, providence
祝意 **shukui** congratulations
故意 **koi** intention, purpose
食意地 **ku(i)iji** gluttony
10 随意 **zuii** voluntary, optional
　　manimani at the mercy of, with (the wind)
随意筋 **zuiikin** voluntary muscle
真意 **shin'i** real intention, true motive; true meaning
原意 **gen'i** original/primary meaning
害意 **gaii** malice, ill will
殺意 **satsui** intent to murder
恣意 **shii** arbitrariness, selfishness
恣意的 **shiiteki** arbitrary, selfish
留意 **ryūi** give heed to, be mindful of
配意 **haii** consideration, concern
11 達意 **tatsui** intelligible, clear, lucid
深意 **shin'i** profound/deep meaning
得意 **tokui** pride, triumph; one's strong point; customer; prosperity
得意気 **tokuige** proud, elated
得意先 **tokuisaki** customer
得意満面 **tokui-manmen** pride
得意顔 **tokuigao** triumphant look
宿意 **shukui** long-held opinion/grudge
悪意 **akui** evil intent, malice, ill will
情意 **jōi** emotion and will; sentiment
情意投合 **jōi-tōgō** mutual sentiment/ understanding
転意 **ten'i** figurative/extended meaning

12 隔意 **kakui** reserve, estrangement
創意 **sōi** original idea, inventiveness
着意 **chakui** conception; caution
善意 **zen'i** good faith; well-intentioned; favorable sense
御意 **gyoi** your will/pleasure
寓意 **gūi** allegory, moral
極意 **gokui** mystery, secrets, quintessence
無意 **mui** lack of will/meaning
無意味 **muimi** meaningless, pointless
無意的 **muiteki** unwilling; meaningless
無意義 **muigi** meaningless, not significant
無意識 **muishiki** unconscious, involuntary
敬意 **keii** respect, homage
衆意 **shūi** the ideas of the people
筆意 **hitsui** writing
貴意 **kii** your wishes/request
賀意 **gai** congratulatory feeling
13 微意 **bii** small token (of gratitude)
愚意 **gui** my humble view
戦意 **sen'i** intent to fight, fighting spirit
辞意 **jii** intention to resign
誠意 **seii** sincerity, good faith
14 総意 **sōi** consensus
語意 **goi** meaning of a word
15 横意地 **yoko-iji** perverseness, obstinacy
熱意 **netsui** enthusiasm, zeal, ardor
敵意 **tekii** enmity, hostility, animosity
趣意 **shui** purport, meaning, aim, object
趣意書 **shuisho** prospectus
賛意 **san'i** approval
鋭意 **eii** zealously, diligently
17 懇意 **kon'i** intimacy, friendship, kindness
謝意 **shai** gratitude; apology
18 翻意 **hon'i** change one's mind
題意 **daii** meaning of the subject

3
---

3 小生意気 **konamaiki** conceit, impudence
4 不本意 **fuhon'i** reluctant, unwilling, to one's regret
不用意 **fuyōi** unprepared, unguarded, careless
不同意 **fudōi** disagreement, dissent, objection
不如意 **funyoi** contrary to one's wishes, hard up (for money)
不注意 **fuchūi** carelessness
不随意 **fuzuii** involuntary
不随意筋 **fuzuiikin** involuntary muscle
不得意 **futokui** one's weak point
不誠意 **fuseii** insincere, unfaithful, dishonest
6 自由意志 **jiyū ishi** free will
9 要注意 **yōchūi** requiring care/caution
11 常得意 **jōtokui** regular customer
15 潜在意識 **senzai ishiki** subconscious

4
---

8 服装随意 **fukusō zuii** informal attire

13 誠心誠意 **seishin-seii** sincerely, wholeheartedly
———————— 5 ————————
12 勝手不如意 **katte-funyoi** hard up (for
money), bad off

5b8.3 / 174

新

SHIN, atara(shii), ara(ta), nii- new

———————— 1 ————————
2 新入 **shinnyū** new, incoming, entering
新入生 **shinnyūsei** new student, freshman
新人 **shinjin** newcomer, new face
新刀 **shintō** newly-forged/modern sword
3 新工夫 **shinkufū** new device/gadget
4 新手 **arate** reinforcements; newcomer; new
method/trick
新月 **shingetsu** new/crescent moon
5 新生 **shinsei** new life
新生児 **shinseiji** newborn baby
新生命 **shinseimei** new life
新生活 **shinseikatsu** a new life
新生面 **shinseimen** new aspect/field
新生涯 **shinshōgai** a new life/career
新世界 **shinsekai** new world; the New World
新世帯 **shinjotai** new home/household
新刊 **shinkan** new publication
新刊書 **shinkansho** a new publication
新字 **shinji** made-in-Japan kanji
新字体 **shinjitai** new form of a character
新札 **shinsatsu** new paper money
新旧 **shinkyū** new and old
新田 **shinden** new rice field
6 新年 **shinnen** the New Year
新曲 **shinkyoku** new tune/composition
新任 **shinnin** new appointment
新地 **shinchi** new/reclaimed land
新宅 **shintaku** new residence; new branch
family
新式 **shinshiki** new-type, new-style, modern
新米 **shinmai** new rice; beginner
7 新来 **shinrai** newcomer
新体 **shintai** new form/style
新体制 **shintaisei** new system/order
新体詩 **shintaishi** new-style poem/poetry
新作 **shinsaku** a new work/composition
新兵 **shinpei** new soldier, recruit
新形 **shingata** new model/style
新学期 **shingakki** new school term
新局面 **shinkyokumen** new aspect
新車 **shinsha** new car
8 新例 **shinrei** new example/precedent
新郎 **shinrō** bridegroom
新郎新婦 **shinrō-shinpu** the bride and groom

新制 **shinsei** new system
新版 **shinpan** new publication/edition
新法 **shinpō** new method/law
新味 **shinmi** fresh taste, novelty
新知識 **shinchishiki** up-to-date knowledge
新奇 **shinki** novel, original
新妻 **niizuma** new/young wife
新参 **shinzan** newcomer, novice
新芽 **shinme** sprout, bud, shoot
新店 **shinmise** new store
新居 **shinkyo** one's new residence/home
新居浜 **Niihama** (city, Ehime-ken)
9 新発売 **shinhatsubai** new(ly marketed)
product
新発見 **shinhakken** new discovery
新発足 **shinhossoku** a fresh start
新発明 **shinhatsumei** new invention
新盆 **niibon** first Obon festival after one's
death
新造 **shinzō** newly built/made; wife, Mrs.
新造語 **shinzōgo** newly coined word
新派 **shinpa** new school (of thought/art)
新型 **shingata** new model/style
新品 **shinpin** new article, brand new
新品同様 **shinpin dōyō** like new
新茶 **shincha** first tea of the season
新客 **shinkyaku** new visitor/customer
新面目 **shinmenmoku** new aspect/phase
新柄 **shingara** new pattern
新星 **shinsei** nova; new (movie) star
新春 **shinshun** the New Year
新政 **shinsei** new government/regime
新秋 **shinshū** early autumn
新香 **shinkō, shinko** pickled vegetables
新紀元 **shinkigen** new ear/epoch
新約 **shin'yaku** the New Testament
新約聖書 **shin'yaku seisho** the New
Testament
新訂 **shintei** new revision
新訂版 **shinteiban** newly revised edition
10 新修 **shinshū** new compilation
新値 **shinne** new price
新陳代謝 **shinchintaisha** metabolism
新進 **shinshin** rising, up-and-coming
新酒 **shinshu** new saké/wine
新荷 **shinni** newly arrived goods
新案 **shin'an** new idea/design, novelty
新株 **shinkabu** new shares
新時代 **shinjidai** new era
新書 **shinsho** new book; largish paperback
size
新教 **shinkyō** Protestantism
新教国 **shinkyōkoku** Protestant country
新教徒 **shinkyōto** a Protestant
新秩序 **shinchitsujo** new order
新記録 **shinkiroku** new record

5

石
立 8←
目
禾
衣
田
皿
广

新馬 **shinba** new/unbroken horse
11 新道 **shindō** new road
新婚 **shinkon** newlywed
新婚旅行 **shinkon ryokō** honeymoon
新婦 **shinpu** bride
新著 **shincho** new book/work
新患者 **shinkanja** new patient
新規 **shinki** new
新釈 **shinshaku** new interpretation
新設 **shinsetsu** newly established
新訳 **shin'yaku** new translation
新雪 **shinsetsu** new-fallen/fresh snow
12 新着 **shinchaku** newly arrived
新着荷 **shinchakuni** newly arrived goods
新装 **shinsō** new equipment, refurbishing, redecorated
新開 **shinkai** newly opened/developed
13 新義 **shingi** new meaning; **Shingi** New Shingon religion (short for 新義真言宗)
新義派 **Shingi-ha** New Shingon religion
新義真言宗 **Shingi Shingon shū** New Shingon religion
新幹線 **Shinkansen** New Trunk Line, bullet train
14 新暦 **shinreki** new/Gregorian calendar
新選 **shinsen** newly elected/compiled
新境地 **shinkyōchi** new area, fresh ground
新嘗祭 **niinamesai** Harvest Festival
新種 **shinshu** new type/species
新穀 **shinkoku** new rice
新製品 **shinseihin** new product
新緑 **shinryoku** fresh verdure
新語 **shingo** new word, neologism
新説 **shinsetsu** new theory
新聞 **shinbun** newspaper
新聞代 **shinbundai** newspaper subscription charge
新聞売 **shinbun'u(ri)** news dealer
新聞社 **shinbunsha** newspaper (company)
新聞界 **shinbunkai** the newspaper world
新聞紙 **shinbunshi** newspaper (paper)
新聞業 **shinbungyō** the newspaper business
15 新劇 **shingeki** new drama
新潟 **Niigata** (city, Niigata-ken)
新潟県 **Niigata-ken** (prefecture)
新趣向 **shinshukō** new idea/contrivance
新調 **shinchō** have (clothes) made
新鋳 **shinchū** newly cast/minted
新鋭 **shin'ei** new (and powerful)
16 新興 **shinkō** new, rising
新興国 **shinkōkoku** emerging nation
新薬 **shin'yaku** new drug
新機軸 **shinkijiku** new departure; novel idea
新築 **shinchiku** newly built
新館 **shinkan** new building, annex
17 新鮮 **shinsen** fresh

18 新顔 **shingao** new face, newcomer

———————— 2 ————————

1 一新 **isshin** complete change, reform, renovation
一新紀元 **isshin kigen** a new era
5 生新 **namaatara(shii)** brand new
目新 **meatara(shii)** novel, original
6 耳新 **mimiatara(shii)** new, novel
7 更新 **kōshin** renew, renovate
赤新聞 **akashinbun** yellow journal
改新 **kaishin** renovation, reformation
8 刷新 **sasshin** reform, renovation
9 革新 **kakushin** reform, innovation
革新派 **kakushinha** reformists
10 真新 **maatara(shii)** brand new
11 清新 **seishin** fresh, new
斬新 **zanshin** novel, original, latest
12 御新造 **goshinzo, goshinzō** new wife of a prominent person; wife
最新 **saishin** newest, latest
最新式 **saishinshiki** latest type/style
14 維新 **ishin** (the Meiji) restoration
16 壁新聞 **kabe shinbun** wall newspaper/poster

———————— 3 ————————

5 外字新聞 **gaiji shinbun** foreign-language newspaper
6 邦字新聞 **hōji shinbun** Japanese-language newspaper
8 英字新聞 **eiji shinbun** English-language newspaper
10 恭賀新年 **kyōga shinnen** Happy New Year
11 悪徳新聞 **akutoku shinbun** irresponsible/sensationalist newspaper
12 御一新 **goisshin** the Meiji restoration
御用新聞 **goyō shinbun** government newspaper
13 新郎新婦 **shinrō-shinpu** the bride and groom
17 謹賀新年 **kinga shinnen** Happy New Year

———————— 4 ————————

8 明治維新 **Meiji Ishin** the Meiji Restoration
9 面目一新 **menboku isshin** take on a completely new aspect
12 温故知新 **onko-chishin** learning from the past

韵 → 韻 7b12.2

5b8.4 / 688

辞 辭　**JI** word; resign, quit
ya(meru) quit, resign

———————— 1 ————————

0 辞する **ji(suru)** resign; decline; leave

5 辞世 **jisei** passing away; deathbed poem
辞令 **jirei** written appointment/order; wording, phraseology
辞去 **jikyo** take one's leave
6 辞任 **jinin** resign
辞色 **jishoku** words and looks
8 辞表 **jihyō** (letter of) resignation
辞典 **jiten** dictionary
辞退 **jitai** decline, refuse
辞林 **jirin** dictionary
9 辞柄 **jihei** pretext
10 辞書 **jisho** dictionary
13 辞彙 **jii** dictionary
辞意 **jii** intention to resign
15 辞儀 **jigi** bow, greeting; decline, refuse
18 辞職 **jishoku** resignation, quitting
辞職願 **jishoku nega(i)** letter of resignation
20 辞譲 **jijō** decline in favor of someone else

———————— 2 ————————

4 弔辞 **chōji** message of condolence, memorial address
5 世辞 **seji** flattery, compliment
6 返辞 **henji** reply
名辞 **meiji** term, name
式辞 **shikiji** address, message, oration
7 別辞 **betsuji** parting words, farewell address
告辞 **kokuji** (farewell) address
言辞 **genji** words, speech, language
8 拝辞 **haiji** resign, decline
固辞 **koji** firmly decline/refuse
9 美辞 **biji** flowery language
美辞麗句 **biji-reiku** flowery language
祝辞 **shukuji** (speech of) congratulations
10 修辞 **shūji** figure of speech, rhetoric
修辞学 **shūjigaku** rhetoric
修辞法 **shūjihō** rhetoric
訓辞 **kunji** an admonitory speech, instructions
11 虚辞 **kyoji** lie, falsehood
接辞 **setsuji** an affix, prefixes and suffixes
措辞 **soji** choice of words, phraseology
悼辞 **tōji** message of condolence, funeral address
12 遁辞 **tonji** excuse, evasion
御辞儀 **ojigi** bow, greeting
答辞 **tōji** formal reply
14 総辞職 **sōjishoku** mass resignation
15 褒辞 **hōji** words of praise
賓辞 **hinji** object (in grammar)
贅辞 **sanji** praise
17 謝辞 **shaji** a speech of thanks; apology
18 題辞 **daiji** prefatory phrase, epigraph
19 繋辞 **keiji** copula, link verb
22 讃辞 **sanji** praise

———————— 3 ————————

6 百科辞典 **hyakka jiten** encyclopedia

8 空世辞 **karaseji** flattery, empty compliments
11 接尾辞 **setsubiji** suffix
接頭辞 **settōji** prefix
13 漢和辞典 **Kan-Wa jiten** kanji dictionary

5b8.5

辟

HEKI avoid; ruler

———————— 1 ————————

8 辟易 **hekieki** shrink from, be daunted

———————— 9 ————————

5b9.1

竭

KETSU exhaust, use all up

5b9.2 / 1418

端

TAN end, tip; origin; correct
hashi end, edge   **hata** side, edge, nearby   **ha** edge   **hana** beginning, inception; end, tip

———————— 1 ————————

0 端た **hashi(ta)** fractional part, odd sum; fragment, scrap
端たない **hashi(tanai)** vulgar
端くれ/っくれ **hashi(kure/kkure)** scrap, bit, fag end
2 端子 **tanshi** (electrical) terminal
3 端々 **hashibashi** odds and ends, parts
端女 **hashi(ta)me** maidservant
端山 **hayama** foothill
4 端午 **tango** Boys' Day (May 5)
5 端本 **hahon** odd volume, incomplete set
端末機 **tanmatsuki** (computer) terminal
端正 **tansei** correct, right, proper
6 端近 **hashijika** near the edge/threshold
7 端坐 **tanza** sit erect
端折 **hasho(ru)** tuck up; cut short, abridge
端役 **hayaku** minor role/post
8 端居 **hashii** at the perimeter of the house, on the veranda
端的 **tanteki** direct, frank, point-blank
端物 **hamono** incomplete set, odds and ends
端武者 **hamusha** common soldier, private
端金 **hashi(ta)gane** small change
10 端座 **tanza** sit erect
端書 **hashiga(ki)** introduction, preface; postscript
12 端無 **hashina(ku mo)** suddenly, unexpectedly, by chance   **hashi(ta)na(i)** vulgar
端然 **tanzen** correct, proper

5

石
立 9←
目
禾
衤
田
罒
皿
广

端艇 **tantei** boat, lighter
13 端数 **hasū** fractional part, odd sum
14 端境 **hazakai** between harvests, lean period
端境期 **hazakaiki** off/between-crops season
端端 **hashibashi** odds and ends, parts
端緒 **tansho, tancho** beginning, first step, clue
端綱 **hazuna** (horse's) halter
端銭 **hasen** small change
16 端整 **tansei** orderly, well formed
17 端厳 **tangen** solemn and serene
19 端麗 **tanrei** graceful, beautiful, handsome

───────── 2 ─────────

1 一端 **ittan** a part; a general idea
3 川端 **kawabata** riverside
Kawabata (surname)
万端 **bantan** everything, all
上端 **jōtan** upper end, top, tip
下端 **katan** lower end
shita(p)pa lower position; underling
4 切端 **ki(re)hashi** cut-off piece/end, scraps
片端 **katahashi, kata(p)pashi** one end, one
side; small piece **katawa** deformed/
disabled person; deformed, unbalanced
kata(p)pashi (kara) one by one, one
after another
木端 **ki(no)hashi, koppa** chip of wood;
worthless thing/person
木端微塵 **koppa-mijin** splinters, smithereens
5 北端 **hokutan** northern extremity/tip
半端 **hanpa** fragment; incomplete set;
fraction; remnant; incomplete
末端 **mattan** end, tip, terminal
末端価格 **mattan kakaku** end-user price,
street value
右端 **utan** right edge/end
目端 **mehashi** quick wit, tact
6 多端 **tatan** many items; busyness
両端 **ryōtan, ryōhashi** both ends, both edges;
sitting on the fence
年端 **toshiha** age, years
争端 **sōtan** beginning of a dispute
先端 **sentan** tip, point, end; the latest,
advanced (technology)
舌端 **zettan** tip of the tongue
尖端 **sentan** pointed tip; spearhead, leading
edge, latest (technology)
7 兵端 **heitan** (commencement of) hostilities
尾端 **bitan** tip of a tail, tail end
8 突端 **toppana, tottan** tip, point
炉端 **robata** fireside, hearth
9 発端 **hottan** origin, beginning
南端 **nantan** southern extremity/tip
途端 **totan** the (very) moment/minute, just
when
10 軒端 **nokibata, nokiba** (edge of) the eaves

11 道端 **michibata** roadside, wayside
堀端 **horibata** edge of the moat/canal
異端 **itan** heresy
異端者 **itansha** heretic
終端 **shūtan** terminus, terminal
船端 **funabata** ship's side, gunwale
12 極端 **kyokutan** extreme
筆端 **hittan** brush/pen tip; writing/painting
style
13 戦端 **sentan** hostilities
継端 **tsu(gi)ha** topic to keep the conversation
going
14 端端 **hashibashi** odds and ends, parts
16 薄端 **usubata** flat-top bronze vase
26 釁端 **kintan** origin of a dispute

───────── 3 ─────────

3 大川端 **ōkawabata** banks of the Sumida
River (in Tōkyō)
4 井戸端 **idobata** well side
井戸端会議 **idobata kaigi** well-side gossip
5 圧着端子 **atchaku tanshi** crimp contact
6 両極端 **ryōkyokutan** both extremes
8 河岸端 **kashibata** riverside
12 最先端 **saisentan** the lead, forefront
最尖端 **saisentan** the lead, forefront

───────── 4 ─────────

4 中途半端 **chūto-hanpa** half finished,
incomplete
6 多事多端 **taji-tatan** eventful, busy
15 諸事万端 **shoji-bantan** everything

5b9.3

渥

senchirittoru centiliter, ten cubic
centimeters

5b9.4

颯

SATSU, sat(to) sudden, quick

───────── 1 ─────────

3 颯々 **sassatsu** rustling, soughing
11 颯爽 **sassō** dashing, smart, gallant

5b9.5

竪　豎

JU, tate vertical, upright

───────── 1 ─────────

5 竪穴 **tateana** pit
7 竪坑 **tatekō** (mine) shaft, pit
11 竪笛 **tatebue** recorder, upright flute
12 竪琴 **tategoto** harp, lyre

5b9.6

辣

RATSU bitter, severe

───────── 1 ─────────
12 辣腕 **ratsuwan** astute, sharp

───────── 2 ─────────
7 辛辣 **shinratsu** bitter, biting, harsh
11 悪辣 **akuratsu** unscrupulous, wily

5b9.7

韶

SHŌ music; spring

───────── 10 ─────────

5b10.1

毅

KI strong

───────── 1 ─────────
12 毅然 **kizen** dauntless, resolute

───────── 2 ─────────
10 剛毅 **gōki** hardy, stout-hearted

───────── 11 ─────────

龍 → 竜 5b5.3

瓣 → 弁 0a5.30

5b11.1 / 175

親

SHIN intimacy; parent; (as prefix) pro-
(American) **oya** parent
shita(shii) intimate, close (friend)
shita(shimu) get to know better,
become friendly with

───────── 1 ─────────
2 親子 **oyako, shinshi** parent and child
親子丼 **oyako donburi** bowl of rice topped
with chicken and egg
4 親不孝 **oyafukō** lack of filial piety
親元 **oyamoto** one's parents' home
親仁方 **oyajikata** role of an old man
親切 **shinsetsu** kind, friendly
親切気 **shinsetsugi** kindliness
親友 **shin'yū** close friend
親文字 **oyamoji** capital letter
親分 **oyabun** boss, chief
親分子分 **oyabun-kobun** boss and underlings

親父 **oyaji** one's father; the old man, the boss
親木 **oyagi** the host plant (of a graft)
親日 **shin-Nichi** pro-Japanese
親日家 **shin-Nichika** Nippophile
親王 **shinnō** imperial prince
親方 **oyakata** (gang) boss
親方日丸 **oyakata hi(no)maru** "the government will foot the bill" attitude, budgetary irresponsibility
親心 **oyagokoro** parental affection
5 親出 **oyada(shi)** first character (of a dictionary entry) protruding into the margin;
main entry
親代 **oyaga(wari)** (one who is) acting as a
parent, guardian
親兄弟 **oya-kyōdai** one's parents and
brothers and sisters
親字 **oyaji** first character (of a dictionary
entry)
親旧 **shinkyū** relatives and old friends
親玉 **oyadama** boss, chief, leader
6 親任 **shinnin** personal appointment by the
emperor
親任式 **shinninshiki** ceremony of investiture
by the emperor
親任官 **shinninkan** official personally
appointed by the emperor
親会社 **oyagaisha** parent company
親交 **shinkō** friendship, intimacy
親孝行 **oyakōkō** filial piety
親近 **shinkin** familiarity
親近性 **shinkinsei** familiarity
親近相姦 **shinkin sōkan** incest
親近感 **shinkinkan** feeling of familiarity
親団体 **oyadantai** parent organization
親米 **shin-Bei** pro-American
7 親身 **shinmi** blood relation; kind, cordial
親里 **oyazato** one's parents' home
親告 **shinkoku** personal statement/accusation
親告罪 **shinkokuzai** offense subject to
prosecution only upon complaint (e.g.,
defamation)
親局 **oyakyoku** key (broadcast) station
親見出 **oyamida(shi)** heading, main entry
8 親拝 **shinpai** worship (by the emperor)
親知 **oyashi(razu)** wisdom tooth; dangerous
place
親征 **shinsei** military expedition led by the
emperor
親英 **shin-Ei** pro-British, pro-English
親和 **shinwa** friendship, fellowship, fraternity
親和力 **shinwaryoku** (chemical) affinity
9 親指 **oyayubi** thumb
親独 **shin-Doku** pro-German
親柱 **oyabashira** main pillar
親政 **shinsei** direct imperial rule

親思 **oyaomo(i)** affection for one's parents
10 親展 **shinten** confidential, personal (letter)
親展書 **shintensho** confidential/personal letter
親株 **oyakabu** old share (before a stock split)
親骨 **oyabone** outer ribs of a folding fan
親書 **shinsho** handwritten letter
親馬鹿 **oyabaka** overfond parent
11 親疎 **shinso** degree of intimacy
親掛 **oyaga(kari)** dependence on one's parents
親密 **shinmitsu** friendly, close, intimate
親祭 **shinsai** Shinto rites conducted by the emperor
親族 **shinzoku** relatives
親戚 **shinseki** a relative
親船 **oyabune** mother ship
親許 **oyamoto** one's parents' home
親鳥 **oyadori** parent bird
12 親善 **shinzen** friendship, amity, goodwill
親御 **oyago** (your) parents
親勝 **oyamasa(ri)** a child surpassing his parents
親無 **oyana(shi)** parentless, orphaned
親無子 **oyana(shi)go** orphan
親裁 **shinsai** imperial decision
親筆 **shinpitsu** one's own handwriting
親等 **shintō** degree of consanguinity/kinship
13 親愛 **shin'ai** affection, love; dear
親睦 **shinboku** friendship
親睦会 **shinbokukai** social get-together
親署 **shinsho** (emperor's) personal signature
親電 **shinden** (emperor's) telegram
14 親銀行 **oyaginkō** parent bank
15 親潮 **Oyashio** the Okhotsk/Kurile current
親権 **shinken** parental authority
親権者 **shinkensha** person in parental authority
親閲 **shin'etsu** personal inspection
16 親衛 **shin'ei** leader's personal security
親衛兵 **shin'eihei** bodyguard
親衛隊 **shin'eitai** bodyguard troops
18 親臨 **shinrin** emperor's presence/visit
親藩 **shinpan** vassals related to the Tokugawa shoguns
親類 **shinrui** relatives
親類付合 **shinrui-zu(ki)a(i)** association among relatives; intimate association
親類書 **shinruigaki** list of one's relatives
20 親譲 **oyayuzu(ri)** inheritance, heredity
21 親露 **shin-Ro** pro-Russian
30 親鸞 **Shinran** (Buddhist priest, 1173–1262)

——————— 2 ———————

2 二親 **futaoya** (both) parents
3 女親 **onna oya** mother
4 不親切 **fushinsetsu** unkind, unfriendly

内親王 **naishinnō** imperial/royal princess
片親 **kataoya** one parent
父親 **chichioya, teteoya** father
5 生親 **u(mi no) oya** one's biological father; originator, creator
母親 **hahaoya** mother
6 両親 **ryōshin** (both) parents
肉親 **nikushin** blood relationship/relative
近親 **kinshin** close relative
近親者 **kinshinsha, kinshinja** close relative
近親相姦 **kinshin sōkan** incest
7 里親 **sato oya** foster parent
男親 **otoko oya** father
8 育親 **soda(te no) oya** foster parent
和親 **washin** friendship, amity, harmony
10 家親 **kashin** one's parents
11 産親 **u(mi no) oya** one's biological parent; originator, the father of
12 等親 **tōshin** degree of kinship
15 養親 **yōshin, yashina(i)oya** adoptive/foster parents
17 懇親 **konshin** friendship, intimacy
懇親会 **konshinkai** social gathering

——————— 3 ———————

1 一等親 **ittōshin** first-degree relative, immediate family
2 二等親 **nitōshin** a second-degree relative
6 名付親 **nazu(ke) oya** godparent
12 最近親者 **saikinshinsha** nearest relative, next of kin

辨 → 弁 **0a5.30**

——————— 13 ———————

5b13.1

甓

HEKI, BYAKU (flooring) tiles

——————— 14 ———————

辭 → 辞 **5b8.4**

——————— 15 ———————

5b15.1 / 852

競 競

KYŌ, KEI, kiso(u), kio(u) compete, vie for
se(ru) compete, vie; bid for
se(ri) auction **-kura** race, contest

——————— 1 ———————

3 競上 **se(ri)a(geru)** bid up (the price)

5
→ 13

競々 **kyōkyō** fear and trepidation
5 競市 **se(ri)ichi** an auction (house)
6 競合 **kyōgō** competition, rivalry
   se(ri)a(u) compete with, vie for
   競争 **kyōsō** competition
   競争者 **kyōsōsha** competitor, rival
   競肌 **kio(i)hada** gallantry
7 競走 **kyōsō** race
   競技 **kyōgi** competition, match
   競技会 **kyōgikai** athletic meet, contest
   競技場 **kyōgijō** stadium, sports arena
   競売 **kyōbai, se(ri)u(ri)** auction
   競売人 **kyōbainin** auctioneer
8 競泳 **kyōei** swimming race
   競歩 **kyōho** walking race
9 競映 **kyōei** competitive film exhibition
10 競馬 **keiba** horse race/racing
   競馬馬 **keiba uma** race horse
   競馬場 **keibajō** race track
12 競落 **se(ri)o(tosu)** bid for successfully
   競艇 **kyōtei** boat race/racing
14 競漕 **kyōsō** rowing race, regatta
   競演 **kyōen** competitive performance, recital
   contest
15 競輪 **keirin** bicycle race/racing
20 競競 **kyōkyō** fear and trepidation

————————— 2 —————————
3 小競合 **kozeria(i)** skirmish; bickering,
   quarrel
9 草競馬 **kusakeiba** local horse race
   食競 **ta(bek)kura** eating contest
12 無競争 **mukyōsō** without competition,
   unopposed
20 競競 **kyōkyō** fear and trepidation

————————— 3 —————————
2 二種競技 **nishu kyōgi** biathlon
   十種競技 **jisshu kyōgi** decathlon
3 三種競技 **sanshu kyōgi** triathlon

4 五種競技 **goshu kyōgi** pentathlon
   水上競技 **suijō kyōgi** water sports
9 軍拡競争 **gunkaku kyōsō** arms race
10 徒歩競走 **toho kyōsō** walking race
11 断郊競走 **dankō kyōsō** cross-country race
14 駅伝競走 **ekiden kyōsō** long-distance relay
   race

瓣 → 弁 **0a5.30**

————————— 16 —————————
5b16.1

黯   AN black, dark

————————— 1 —————————
12 黯然 **anzen** gloomy, doleful

————————— 17 —————————
競 → 競 **5b15.1**

————————— 43 —————————
5b43.1

龍龍   **DŌ, TŌ** dragons on the move
龍龍

————————— 59 —————————
5b59.1

龍龍   **TETSU** garrulous, verbose
龍龍

——————————————— 5c ———————————————

目	自	見	具	直	眄	眇	臭	看	眈	盼	省	盾
0.1	1.1	2.1	3.1	2k6.2	4.1	4.2	4.3	4.4	4.5	4.6	4.7	4.8

眉	眛	眠	眩	眤	臭	眼	眦	眺	眸	眴	眶	眷
4.9	5.1	5.2	5.3	5.4	5c4.3	6.1	5c6.7	6.2	6.3	6.4	6.5	6.6

皆	覓	規	䁖	睇	覘	覗	殖	睢	睡	睥	睫	睨
6.7	6.8	6.9	6.10	7.1	7.2	7.3	7.4	8.1	8.2	8.3	8.4	8.5

睦	睛	睚	督	鼎	睹	鼻	覡	導	瞎	瞋	瞑	瞟
8.6	8.7	8.8	8.9	8.10	9.1	5f9.3	9.2	9.3	10.1	10.2	10.3	11.1

瞞	瞠	観	覦	覷	瞰	瞳	瞶	瞭	瞥	譀	鼾	覧
11.2	11.3	5c9.1	11.4	11.5	12.1	12.2	12.3	12.4	12.5	5f12.3	12.6	12.7

5

石 立 目 禾 衤 田 皿 疒

59 ←

靚	覬	瞬	曖	曚	瞼	瞻	瞽	観	覲	覺	覽	矕
12.8	12.9	13.1	13.2	13.3	13.4	13.5	13.6	13.7	13.8	3n9.3	5c12.7	19.1

矚
21.1

─────── 0 ───────

5c0.1 / 55

目 **MOKU, BOKU** eye; classification, order (in taxonomy)　**me** eye; (suffix for ordinals), -th　**ma** eye

─────── 1 ───────

0 目する **moku(suru)** regard as
目まぐるしい **me(magurushii)** dizzy, giddy
2 目子勘定 **me(no)ko kanjō** measuring by eye; mental arithmetic
目子算 **me(no)kozan** measuring by eye; mental arithmetic
目八分 **mehachibu** (hold an offering) a little below eye level; most respectfully; about eight-tenths full
3 目上 **meue** one's superior/senior
目下 **meshita** one's subordinate/junior
mokka at present, now
4 目今 **mokkon** at present, now
目分量 **mebunryō** measuring by eye
目引 **mehi(ki), mebi(ki)** attract the eye; dye colorfully; perforation for binding pages
目引袖引 **mehi(ki)-sodehi(ki)** (belittle by) winking and tugging at (someone's) sleeve
目方 **mekata** weight
5 目付 **metsu(ki)** a look, expression of the eyes
目打 **meu(chi)** perforation
目尻 **mejiri** outside corner of the eye
目白押 **mejiroo(shi)** jostling, milling
目礼 **mokurei** nod, greet by eye
目玉 **medama, me (no) tama** eyeball
(o)medama a scolding
目玉商品 **medama shōhin** bargain item to attract customers, loss leader
目玉焼 **medamaya(ki)** sunny-side-up fried eggs
目処 **medo** prospect, outlook; goal
目立 **meda(tsu)** be conspicuous, stand out
6 目次 **mokuji** table of contents
目印 **mejirushi** mark, sign
目色 **me (no) iro** color of one's eyes; one's facial/eye expression
目先 **mesaki** before one's eyes; immediate future; foresight; appearance
目安 **meyasu** standard, yardstick
目当 **mea(te)** guide(post); aim
ma(no)a(tari) before one's eyes

目早 **mebaya(i)** quick to notice, sharp-eyed
7 目角 **mekado** corner of the eye; sharp look
目医者 **meisha** ophthalmologist, optometrist
目抜 **menu(ki)** main, principal
目抜通 **menu(ki)dō(ri)** main thoroughfare
目庇 **mabisashi** eyeshade; visor
目見 **memi(e)** audience, interview; (stage) debut; (servant's) service on approval
目利 **meki(ki)** judging; a judge/connoisseur of
8 目毒 **me(no)doku** something tempting
目刺 **meza(shi)** dried sardines (tied together with a string through their eyes)
目送 **mokusō** follow with one's eyes
目板 **meita** batten plate, panel strip, eyeboard
目明 **mea(ki)** sighted/educated person
mea(kashi) police detective (Edo era)
目的 **mokuteki** purpose, object, aim
目的地 **mokutekichi** destination
目的格 **mokutekikaku** the objective case
目的語 **mokutekigo** object (in grammar)
目的論 **mokutekiron** teleology
9 目前 **me (no) mae, mokuzen** before one's eyes; immediate (gain)
目速 **mebaya(i)** quick to notice, sharp-eyed
目途 **mokuto** aim, goal, end, object
目通 **medō(ri)** audience with; eye level
me (o) tō(su) glance through
目垢 **meaka** eye wax/discharge/mucus
目指 **meza(su)** aim at
目屎 **mekuso** eye wax/discharge/mucus
目星 **meboshi** aim, object
10 目差 **meza(su)** aim at
目眩 **mekurume(ku)** be dizzy, have blurred vision　**memai** dizziness
目配 **mekuba(se)** give a meaningful look
mekuba(ri) be watchful, look about
11 目深 **mabuka (ni)** (hat pulled) down over one's eyes
目掛 **mega(keru)** aim at
目張 **meba(ri)** paper over, weather-strip
目移 **meutsu(ri)** distraction, difficulty in choosing
目盛 **memo(ri)** scale, gradations
12 目測 **mokusoku** measure by eye
目減 **mebe(ri)** weight loss
目覚 **meza(meru)** wake up, come awake
meza(mashii) striking, remarkable, spectacular
目覚時計 **meza(mashi)dokei** alarm clock

13 目障 **mezawa(ri)** eyesore, offensive sight
目隠 **mekaku(shi)** blindfold; screen
目塗 **menu(ri)** sealing, plastering up
目新 **meatara(shii)** novel, original
目詰 **mezu(mari)** clogging (of a mesh/filter)
14 目腐 **mekusa(re)** bleary-eyed person
目腐金 **mekusa(re)gane** pittance
目端 **mehashi** quick wit, tact
目鼻 **mehana** eyes and nose; (take) shape
目鼻立 **mehanada(chi)** looks, features
目算 **mokusan** expectation, estimate
目語 **mokugo** signal with one's eye
15 目潰 **metsubu(shi)** powdery substance to throw in someone's eyes to blind him
目撃 **mokugeki** observe, witness
目撃者 **mokugekisha** (eye)witness
目標 **mokuhyō** target, goal, objective
目敵 **me (no) kataki** enemy, object of hostility
目縁 **mabuchi** eyelid
目論 **mokuro(mi)** plan, project, intention
16 目薬 **megusuri** eye medicine/drops
目録 **mokuroku** catalog, list, inventory
17 目糞 **mekuso** eye wax/discharge/mucus
18 目顔 **megao** a look, expression

————— 2 —————

1 一目 **hitome, ichimoku** a glance/look
hito(tsu)me one-eyed (goblin)
一目惚 **hitomebo(re)** love at first sight
一目散 **ichimokusan** at top speed
一目瞭然 **ichimoku ryōzen** clear at a glance, obvious
2 二目 **futame** for a/the second time
丁目 **chōme** city block-size area (used in addresses)
人目 **hitome** notice, attention
3 大目玉 **ōmedama** big eyes; a scolding, dressing-down
大目見 **ōme (ni) mi(ru)** overlook (faults), let go, view with tolerance
上目 **uwame** upward glance, upturned eyes
a(gari)me slanting eyes (temple side higher than nose side)
下目 **shitame** downward glance; look down on
saga(ri)me on the decline; drooping eyes (temple side lower than nose side)
4 斤目 **kinme** weight
五目 **gomoku** hodgepodge
五目並 **gomokunara(be)** five-in-a-row game
五目飯 **gomokumeshi** a rice, fish, and vegetable dish
切目 **ki(re)me** rift, gap, break; end, pause, interruption
ki(ri)me cut; end, conclusion
文目 **ayame** designs, patterns; distinction

片目 **katame** one eye, one-eyed
引目 **hi(ke)me** (feeling of) inferiority, reticence
木目 **mokume** (wood's) grain
kime grain, texture
日目 **hi(no)me** sun, sunlight
欠目 **ka(ke)me** break, rupture; short weight
5 出目 **deme** protruding eyes, goggle-eyed
付目 **tsu(ke)me** purpose; weak point to take advantage of
正目 **masame** straight grain (in wood)
布目 **nunome** texture
尻目 **shirime** looking askance
四目垣 **yo(tsu)megaki** lattice fence, trellis
6 死目 **shi(ni)me** the moment of death
合目 **a(wase)me** joint, seam
羽目 **hame** situation, predicament; panel, wainscoting
羽目板 **hameita** paneling, wainscoting
色目 **irome** amorous glance
近目 **chikame** nearsighted; shortsighted
地目 **chimoku** land category
吊目 **tsu(ri)me** slant eyes
名目 **meimoku** name, pretext; nominal, ostensible
早目 **hayame (ni)** a little early (leaving leeway)
式目 **shikimoku** law code (historical)
血目 **chime** bloodshot eye
糸目 **itome** a fine thread
耳目 **jimoku** eye and ear; attention, notice
7 低目 **hikume** on the low side
別目 **waka(re)me** turning point, junction, parting of the ways
角目立 **tsunomeda(tsu)** be pointed/sharp, be rough; sound harsh
赤目 **akame** bloodshot/red eyes
折目 **o(ri)me** fold, crease
折目正 **o(ri)metada(shii)** good-mannered; ceremonious
抜目 **nu(ke)me** oversight **nu(ke)me(nai)** alert, shrewd, cunning, clever
役目 **yakume** one's duty, role
役目柄 **yakumegara** by virtue of one's office
条目 **jōmoku** articles, provisions, terms
辛目 **karame** salty
見目 **mi(ru) me** the sight; power of observation **mi(ta) me** to look at
mime features, looks
見目形 **mimekatachi** features, looks
見目麗 **mime-uruwa(shii)** beautiful
利目 **ki(ki)me** effect, efficacy
8 刮目 **katsumoku** watch eagerly/closely
刻目 **kiza(mi)me** notch, nick
効目 **ki(ki)me** effect, efficacy
夜目 **yome** in the dark

盲目 **mōmoku** blindness
盲目的 **mōmokuteki** blind (devotion)
逆目 **sakame** against the grain
注目 **chūmoku** attention, notice
突目 **tsu(ki)me** getting poked in the eye
空目 **sorame** misperception; upward look; pretending not to see
板目 **itame** grain (in wood)
金目 **kaneme** (monetary) value
9 変目 **ka(wari)me** change, turning point, transition
負目 **o(i)me** debt
封目 **fū(ji)me** the seal (of an envelope)
品目 **hinmoku** item
要目 **yōmoku** principal items
茶目 **chame(ru)** play pranks
茶目気 **chame(k)ke** waggish, playful
面目 **menmoku, menboku** face, honor, dignity
面目一新 **menboku isshin** take on a completely new aspect
面目無 **menbokuna(i)** ashamed
柾目 **masame** straight grain
皆目 **kaimoku** utterly; (not) at all
眉目 **bimoku, mime** features, looks, face
眉目秀麗 **bimoku shūrei** handsome face
科目 **kamoku** subject, course (of study); item, classification
10 高目 **takame** high, on the high side
流目 **naga(shi)me** sidelong glance
脇目 **wakime** onlooker's eyes; looking aside
書目 **shomoku** catalog of books, bibliography
破目 **yabu(re)me** a tear, split
針目 **harime** seam, stitch
釘目 **kugime** location of the nail
11 側目 **sokumoku** watch for attentively
掛目 **ka(ke)me** weight
接目 **tsu(gi)me, ha(gi)me** joint, seam
控目 **hika(e)me** moderate, reserved
猫目石 **nekome-ishi** cat's-eye (of quartz)
張目 **ha(ri)me** edge of a piece of paper pasted onto another
黒目 **kurome** black eyes; the iris and pupil
欲目 **yokume** partiality, favorable view
眼目 **ganmoku** gist, main point
細目 **saimoku** details, particulars
　　 hosome narrow eyes/opening
粗目 **zarame** (brown) crystal sugar
蛇目 **ja(no)me** bull's-eye design (on an oilpaper umbrella)
蛇目傘 **ja(no)megasa** umbrella with a bull's-eye design
貫目 **kanme** (unit of weight, about 3.75 kg)
雪目 **yukime** snow blindness
魚目 **uo(no)me** corn (on the foot)

鳥目 **torime** night blindness
　　 chōmoku (an ancient coin); money
12 傍目 **okame, hatame** looking on by an outsider, kibitzing
傍目八目 **okame-hachimoku** Lookers-on see more than the players.
割目 **wa(re)me** crack, crevice
着目 **chakumoku** notice, observe
遠目 **tōme** distant view; farsightedness
満目 **manmoku** as far as the eye can see
落目 **o(chi)me** declining fortunes, on the wane
属目 **shokumoku** attention, observation
勝目 **ka(chi)me** chances of winning
量目 **ryōme** weight
税目 **zeimoku** tariff/tax items
裂目 **sa(ke)me** rip, split, crack, fissure
畳目 **tatamime** fold, crease; the mesh of a tatami
衆目 **shūmoku** public attention
痛目 **ita(i)me** a painful experience
結目 **musu(bi)me** knot
筋目 **sujime** fold, crease; lineage; logic
費目 **himoku** expense item
軽目 **karume** light weight
項目 **kōmoku** heading, item
13 隠目付 **kaku(shi)metsuke** spy, detective (historical)
裏目 **urame** the reverse (of the intended outcome)
継目 **tsu(gi)me** joint, seam
節目 **fushime** knot (in wood); turning point
跡目 **atome** successor (as head of family)
跡目相続 **atome sōzoku** heirship
鳩目 **hatome** eyelet, grommet
14 境目 **sakaime** borderline; crisis
徳目 **tokumoku** (classification of) virtues
種目 **shumoku** item
綴目 **to(ji)me, tsuzu(ri)me** seam
総目録 **sōmokuroku** complete catalog
網目 **kōmoku** gist, main points
網目 **amime** net mesh
酷目 **hido(i)me** a bitter experience, a hard time
駄目 **dame** no good
15 僻目 **higame** squint; error; bias; misjudgment
嘱目 **shokumoku** pay attention to, watch
横目 **yokome** side glance; crosscut (saw)
憂目 **u(ki)me** grief, misery, hardship
瞑目 **meimoku** close one's eyes; die
編目 **a(mi)me** knitting stitch/mesh
縫目 **nu(i)me** seam, stitch
課目 **kamoku** subject (in school), item
16 薄目 **usume** relatively light/thin; half-closed eyes

瞠目 **dōmoku** stare in wonder
頭目 **tōmoku** chief, head of, leader
17 翳目 **kasu(mi)me** dim eyesight, partial blindness
霞目 **kasumime** purblind/blurred eyes
18 織目 **o(ri)me** texture
題目 **daimoku** title; topic; the Nichiren prayer "*namumyōhōrengekyō*"
鵜目鷹目 **u(no)me-taka(no)me (de)** with a sharp/keen eye
19 繋目 **tsuna(gi)me** joint
21 爛目 **tada(re)me** bleary/sore eyes
22 籠目 **kagome** woven-bamboo pattern
26 嘱目 **shokumoku** pay attention to, note

──────── 3 ────────

1 一合目 **ichigōme** first station (of ten up a mountain)
2 二言目 **futakotome** second word; the topic one's talk constantly turns to
二枚目 **nimaime** (role of a) handsome man/beau
二度目 **nidome** for the second time, again
二番目 **nibanme** No. 2, second
八分目 **hachibunme, hachibume** eight-tenths; moderation
3 三枚目 **sanmaime** comedian
4 不面目 **fumenboku** shame, disgrace
5 好題目 **kōdaimoku** good topic
7 何代目 **nandaime** what ordinal number
余所目 **yosome** someone else's eye, casual observer
10 真面目 **majime** serious-minded, earnest, honest   **shinmenmoku** one's true self/character; seriousness, earnestness
教科目 **kyōkamoku** school subjects
素人目 **shirōtome** untrained eye
12 御題目 **odaimoku** Nichiren prayer
13 腰羽目 **koshibame** hip-high wainscoting
新面目 **shinmenmoku** new aspect/phase
15 熨斗目 **noshime** samurai's ceremonial robe
21 贔屓目 **hiikime** viewing favorably

──────── 4 ────────

4 不真面目 **fumajime** not serious-minded, insincere
天下分目 **tenka-wa(ke)me** decisive, fateful
5 必修科目 **hisshū kamoku** required subject
必須科目 **hissu kamoku** required subject
12 傍目八目 **okame-hachimoku** Lookers-on see more than the players.
14 演奏曲目 **ensō kyokumoku** musical program
17 糞真面目 **kusomajime** humorless earnest-ness
18 鵜目鷹目 **u(no)me-taka(no)me (de)** with a sharp/keen eye

──────── 1 ────────

5c1.1 / 62

自

JI self; (as prefix) from (date/place)
SHI self   **mizuka(ra)** oneself, personally, on one's own **ono(zukara), ono(zuto)** of itself, spontaneously, naturally

──────── 1 ────────

0 自…至… **ji…shi…** from (place/date) to (place/date)
2 自力 **jiryoku** one's own strength/efforts
jiriki one's own strength/efforts; (Buddhist) salvation by works
自力本願 **jiriki hongan** salvation by works
自力更生 **jiriki kōsei** be saved by one's own efforts
3 自己 **jiko** self-, oneself, one's own
自己主義 **jiko shugi** egoism, selfishness
自己紹介 **jiko shōkai** introduce oneself
自刃 **jijin** suicide by sword
4 自今 **jikon** henceforth
自分 **jibun** oneself, one's own
自分自身 **jibun-jishin** oneself
自分勝手 **jibun-katte** having one's own way, selfish
自火 **jika** a fire starting in one's own home
5 自民党 **Jimintō** LDP, Liberal Democratic Party (short for 自由民主党)
自失 **jishitsu** be dazed/absent-minded
自生 **jisei** spontaneous generation; grow in the wild
自弁 **jiben** paying one's own expenses
自由 **jiyū** freedom, liberty; free
自由化 **jiyūka** liberalization
自由主義 **jiyū shugi** liberalism
自由刑 **jiyūkei** punishment by confinement, imprisonment
自由自在 **jiyū-jizai** free, unrestricted
自由形 **jiyūgata** freestyle (swimming)
自由労働者 **jiyū rōdōsha** casual laborer
自由国 **jiyūkoku** free/independent nation
自由放任 **jiyū hōnin** nonintervention, laissez-faire
自由型 **jiyūgata** freestyle (wrestling)
自由党 **jiyūtō** liberal party
自由訳 **jiyūyaku** free translation
自由港 **jiyūkō** free port
自由営業 **jiyū eigyō** nonrestricted trade
自由業 **jiyūgyō** freelance occupation, self-employed
自由意志 **jiyū ishi** free will
自由詩 **jiyūshi** free verse
自他 **jita** self and others; transitive and intransitive
自存 **jison** exist of itself

5

石
立
目 1←
禾
禾
田
罒
皿
疒

自用 **jiyō** for personal/private use
自白 **jihaku** confession
自主 **jishu** independent, autonomous
自主的 **jishuteki** independent, autonomous
自主権 **jishuken** autonomy
自立 **jiritsu** stand on one's own, be independent
6 自任 **jinin** fancy/regard oneself as
自伝 **jiden** autobiography
自在 **jizai** freely movable, adjustable
自在画 **jizaiga** freehand drawing
自在鉤 **jizai kagi** height-adjustable hook for hanging a pot over a fire
自宅 **jitaku** at one's home
自尽 **jijin** suicide
7 自身 **jishin** oneself, itself
自身番 **jishinban** (Edo-era) guardhouses
自我 **jiga** self, ego
自我実現 **jiga jitsugen** self-realization
自体 **jitai** itself; one's own body
自作 **jisaku** made/grown/written by oneself
自作農 **jisakunō** (non-tenant) owner-farmer
自余 **jiyo** the others/rest
自助 **jijo** self-help, self-reliance
自決 **jiketsu** self-determination; resignation (from a post); suicide
自沈 **jichin** scuttle one's own boat
自花受粉 **jika jufun** self-pollination
自序 **jijo** author's preface
自戒 **jikai** self-discipline; admonish oneself
自利 **jiri** self-interest, personal gain
自足 **jisoku** self-sufficiency
8 自画 **jiga** picture painted by oneself
自画像 **jigazō** self-portrait
自画賛 **jigasan** praising one's own picture
自供 **jikyō** confession
自制 **jisei** self-control, self-restraint
自制心 **jiseishin** self-control
自注 **jichū** annotation of one's own work
自治 **jichi** self-government
自治体 **jichitai** self-governing body, municipality
自治制 **jichisei** self-governing system
自治相 **jichisō** Home Affairs Minister
自治省 **Jichishō** Ministry of Home Affairs
自治領 **jichiryō** self-governing dominion
自治権 **jichiken** autonomy
自知 **jichi** knowing oneself
自若 **jijaku** composure, calmness
自国 **jikoku** one's own country
自国語 **jikokugo** one's own language
自明 **jimei** self-evident, self-explanatory
自炊 **jisui** do one's own cooking
9 自発 **jihatsu** spontaneous
自発的 **jihatsuteki** spontaneous, voluntary
自発性 **jihatsusei** spontaneousness

自重 **jijū** (truck's) weight when empty
自重 **jichō** self-esteem; taking care of oneself; prudence, caution
自乗 **jijō** square (of a number)
自乗根 **jijōkon** square root
自信 **jishin** confidence (in oneself)
自信満々 **jishin-manman** full of confidence
自叙 **jijo** writing one's own story
自叙伝 **jijoden** autobiography
自負 **jifu** be proud of oneself, be conceited
自首 **jishu** surrender (to the police)
自前 **jimae** paying one's own expenses, independent (geisha)
自活 **jikatsu** support oneself
自浄 **jijō** self-cleansing, autopurification
自浄作用 **jijō-sayō** self-purification
自派 **jiha** one's own party/faction
自律 **jiritsu** autonomy, self-control
自律神経 **jiritsu shinkei** autonomic nerve
自省 **jisei** self-examination, reflection
10 自修 **jishū** teaching oneself, self-study
自差 **jisa** deviation (of a compass needle)
自家 **jika** one's own (home)
自家中毒 **jika chūdoku** autotoxemia
自家用 **jikayō** for private use
自家受精 **jika jusei** self-fertilization
自家製 **jikasei** homemade, home-brewed
自害 **jigai** suicide
自党 **jitō** one's own party
自殺 **jisatsu** suicide
自殺未遂 **jisatsu misui** attempted suicide
自殺的 **jisatsuteki** suicidal
自殺者 **jisatsusha** a suicide (the person)
自書 **jisho** one's own writing, autograph
自称 **jishō** self-styled; first person (in grammar)
自記 **jiki** written by oneself, recording (barometer)
11 自粛 **jishuku** self-restraint
自動 **jidō** automatic
自動式 **jidōshiki** automatic
自動車 **jidōsha** motor vehicle, automobile
自動制御 **jidō seigyo** servocontrol
自動的 **jidōteki** automatic
自動巻 **jidōma(ki)** self-winding (watch)
自動連結機 **jidō renketsuki** automatic coupler
自動販売機 **jidō hanbaiki** vending machine
自動詞 **jidōshi** intransitive verb
自堕落 **jidaraku** slovenly, loose, debauched
自得 **jitoku** be self-content; acquire on one's own; understand, grasp
自著 **jicho** one's own (literary) work
自習 **jishū** studying by oneself
自習書 **jishūsho** teach-yourself book
自惚 **unubo(reru)** be conceited

自販機 **jihanki** vending machine (short for 自動販売機)

自責 **jiseki** self-reproach

自責点 **jisekiten** earned run (in baseball)

自転 **jiten** rotation

自転車 **jitensha** bicycle

自問 **jimon** question oneself

自問自答 **jimon-jitō** answering one's own question, sololiquy, monolog

12 自尊 **jison** self-esteem; conceit

自尊心 **jisonshin** self-esteem; conceit

自営 **jiei** self-management, independently run

自覚 **jikaku** consciousness, awareness, realization

自覚症状 **jikaku shōjō** subjective symptoms, patient's complaints

自然 **shizen** nature; natural

自然人 **shizenjin** natural (uncultured) person; natural (not juridical) person

自然力 **shizenryoku** forces of nature

自然主義 **shizen shugi** naturalism

自然石 **shizenseki** natural stone/gem

自然死 **shizenshi** natural death

自然色 **shizenshoku** natural color

自然法 **shizenhō** natural law

自然的 **shizenteki** natural

自然物 **shizenbutsu** natural object

自然美 **shizenbi** natural beauty

自然科学 **shizen kagaku** the natural sciences

自然界 **shizenkai** the realm of nature

自然数 **shizensū** natural number, positive integer

自然観 **shizenkan** one's outlook on nature

自敬 **jikei** self-respect

自裁 **jisai** suicide

自給 **jikyū** self-support, self-supplying

自給自足 **jikyū-jisoku** self-sufficiency

自筆 **jihitsu** one's own handwriting

自評 **jihyō** self-criticism

自費 **jihi** at one's own expense

自費出版 **jihi shuppan** publishing at one's own expense, vanity press

13 自業自得 **jigō-jitoku** reaping what one sows

自棄 **yake, jiki** desperation, despair

自棄酒 **yakezake** drowning one's cares in saké

自適 **jiteki** ease and comfort

自滅 **jimetsu** natural decay; self-destruction; suicide

自愛 **jiai** self-love, self-regard; selfishness

自意識 **jiishiki** self-consciousness

自署 **jisho** signature, autograph

14 自選 **jisen** elect oneself; make a selection from one's own works

自慢 **jiman** be proud of

自慢高慢 **jiman-kōman** with great pride

自慢話 **jimanbanashi** boastful talk, bragging

自慢顔 **jimangao** boastful look

自製 **jisei** made by oneself, homemade

自認 **jinin** acknowledge, admit

自説 **jisetsu** one's own view

15 自嘲 **jichō** self-scorn

自暴自棄 **jibō-jiki** desperation, despair

自慰 **jii** self-consolation; masturbation

自縄自縛 **jijō-jibaku** tied up with one's own rope, caught in one's own trap

自賠責 **jibaiseki** auto liability (insurance) (short for 自動車損害賠償責任保険)

自賛 **jisan** self-praise

16 自壊 **jikai** disintegration

自壊作用 **jikai sayō** disintegration

自衛 **jiei** self-defense; bodyguard

自衛官 **jieikan** Self Defense Forces member

自衛隊 **Jieitai** Self Defense Forces

自衛権 **jieiken** right of self-defense

自薦 **jisen** recommending oneself

18 自涜 **jitoku** masturbation

19 自爆 **jibaku** suicide explosion

自警 **jikei** self-warning, vigilance; local police

自警団 **jikeidan** vigilance committee, vigilantes

22 自讃 **jisan** self-praise

─────────── 2 ───────────

2 刀自 **tōji** lady, matron, Madam

力自慢 **chikara jiman** boasting of one's strength

3 大自然 **daishizen** Mother Nature

4 不自由 **fujiyū** inconvenience, discomfort; privation; disability, handicap

不自然 **fushizen** unnatural

6 各自 **kakuji** each person, everyone

7 花自動車 **hana jidōsha** flower-bedecked automobile

声自慢 **koejiman** proud of one's singing voice

私自身 **watakushi jishin** personally, as for me

8 国自慢 **(o)kuni jiman** pride in one's home province; boast of one's native place

9 独自 **dokuji** original, characteristic, indivudual, personal

12 超自然 **chōshizen** supernatural

超自然的 **chōshizenteki** supernatural

腕自慢 **udejiman** proud of one's skill

無自覚 **mujikaku** unconscious of, blind to

貸自動車 **ka(shi)-jidōsha** rental car

軽自動車 **keijidōsha** light car

─────────── 3 ───────────

6 自分自身 **jibun-jishin** oneself

自由自在 **jiyū-jizai** free, unrestricted

自問自答 **jimon-jitō** answering one's own question, sololiquy, monolog

自給自足 **jikyū-jisoku** self-sufficiency

5

石
立
目
禾
示
田
皿
疒

1←

自業自得 **jigō-jitoku** reaping what one sows

自暴自棄 **jibō-jiki** desperation, despair

自縄自縛 **jijō-jibaku** tied up with one's own rope, caught in one's own trap

7 伸縮自在 **shinshuku-jizai** elastic, flexible, telescoping

狂言自殺 **kyōgen jisatsu** faked suicide

9 飛込自殺 **tobiko(mi) jisatsu** suicide by jumping in front of an oncoming train

変幻自在 **hengen-jizai** ever-changing

活殺自在 **kassatsu-jizai** power of life and death

独立自尊 **dokuritsu-jison** independence and self-respect

茫然自失 **bōzen-jishitsu** abstraction, stupefaction, entrancement

神色自若 **shinshoku-jijaku** calm and composed, unruffled

10 泰然自若 **taizen-jijaku** imperturbable

8 御国自慢 **okuni jiman** pride in one's home province; boast of one's native place

───── 2 ─────

5c2.1 / 63

見 **KEN, mi(ru)** see   **mi(eru)** be visible, can see   **mi(seru)** show
mami(eru) have an audience with, see

───── 1 ─────

0 見せびらかす **mi(sebirakasu)** show off, flaunt

見せしめ **mi(seshime)** object lesson, warning, example

見てくれ **mi(tekure)** appearance, for show

2 見入 **mii(ru)** gaze at, scrutinize; captivate

3 見上 **mia(geru)** look up at/to, admire

見下 **mio(rosu)** command a view of
mikuda(su) look down on, despise
misa(geru) look down on, despise

見下果 **misa(ge)ha(teru)** look down on, scorn
misa(ge)ha(teta) contemptible, low-down

4 見切 **miki(ru)** see all; abandon, sell at a sacrifice

見切品 **miki(ri)hin** bargain goods

見収 **miosa(me)** last/farewell look

見分 **miwa(keru)** tell apart, distinguish between, recognize; judge, identify

見込 **miko(mi)** prospects, promise, hope, possibility

見込違 **miko(mi)chiga(i)** miscalculation

見手 **mite** onlooker

見方 **mikata** viewpoint, way of looking at

5 見出 **miida(su)** find, discover, pick out
mida(shi) heading, caption, headline

見出語 **mida(shi)go** headword, entry word

見本 **mihon** sample, specimen

見本市 **mihon ichi** sample/trade fair

見本組 **mihongu(mi)** specimen page

見失 **miushina(u)** lose sight of, miss

見世物 **misemono** show, exhibition

見付 **mitsu(keru)** find
mitsu(karu) be found

見付門 **mitsukemon** castle lookout gate

見比 **mikura(beru)** compare (by eying)

見台 **kendai** bookrest, reading board

見立 **mita(teru)** diagnose, judge; select

見目 **mi(ru) me** the sight; power of observation   **mi(ta) me** to look at
mime features, looks

見目形 **mimekatachi** features, looks

見目麗 **mime-uruwa(shii)** beautiful

6 見合 **mia(u)** look at each other; offset
mia(i) arranged-marriage interview
mia(waseru) exchange glances; set off against; postpone, abandon

見交 **mika(wasu)** exchange glances

見返 **mikae(ru)** look back at
mikae(shi) inside the cover

見返物資 **mikae(ri) busshi** collateral goods

見地 **kenchi** viewpoint, standpoint

見向 **mimu(ku)** look around/toward

見守 **mimamo(ru)** watch over

見当 **miata(ru)** be found, turn up
kentō aim, mark, guess, estimate, hunch; direction; approximately

見当違 **kentōchiga(i)** wrong guess

見劣 **mioto(ri)** compare unfavorably with

見尽 **mitsu(kusu)** see all

見回 **mimawa(ru)** make an inspection tour, look around, patrol

7 見附 **mitsuke** the approach to a castle gate

見忘 **miwasu(reru)** forget, fail to recognize

見坊 **mi(e)bō** vain person, fop

見抜 **minu(ku)** see through

見学 **kengaku** study by observation, tour (a factory)

見見 **mi(ru)mi(ru)** in an instant
mi(su)mi(su) before one's very eyes

見初 **miso(meru)** see for the first time; fall in love at first sight

8 見果 **miha(teru)** see till the end

見事 **migoto** beautiful, splendid

見限 **mikagi(ru)** abandon, forsake

見受 **miu(keru)** see, come across; judge from the appearance

見直 **minao(su)** take another look at, reevaluate; think better of; get better

見逃 **minoga(su)** overlook

見送 **mioku(ru)** see (someone) off, watch till out of sight

見知 **mishi(ri)** an acquaintance
mishi(ranu), mi(zu)shi(razu) unfamiliar
kenchi find out by inspecting
見知越 **mishi(ri)go(shi)** well acquainted with
見咎 **mitoga(meru)** find fault with; question,
challenge
見参 **kenzan** see, meet
見苦 **miguru(shii)** unsightly; disgraceful
見定 **misada(meru)** make sure of, ascertain
見届 **mitodo(keru)** verify, make sure of
見者 **kensha** viewer, (Noh) audience
見物 **kenbutsu** sightseeing
mimono a sight, spectacle, attraction
見物人 **kenbutsunin** spectator, sightseer
見物客 **kenbutsukyaku** spectator, audience,
sightseer
見物席 **kenbutsuseki** seats (at a game/
theater)
見所 **midokoro** the part most worth seeing;
promise, merit **mi(ta) tokoro** judging
from the appearance
見取 **mito(ru), mi(te)to(ru)** see and understand
見取図 **mito(ri)zu** sketch (map)
見金 **mi(se)gane** money to show (that one
has money)
9 見変 **mika(eru)** prefer; forsake for another
見透 **mi(e)su(ku)** be transparent
misu(kasu) see through
見通 **mitō(shi)** prospects, outlook, forecast;
unobstructed view
見栄 **mie** (for sake of) appearance, show
見栄坊 **miebō** vain person, fop
見映 **miba(e)** (attractive) appearance
見神 **kenshin** beatific vision
見計 **mihaka(ru), mihaka(rau)** select at
one's discretion; time (one's visit)
10 見残 **minoko(su)** leave without seeing
見兼 **mika(neru)** be unable to just idly watch
見振 **mi(nu) fu(ri)** pretend not to see
見殺 **migoro(shi)** watch (someone) die
見破 **miyabu(ru)** see through
見納 **miosa(me)** last/farewell look
見料 **kenryō** (fortuneteller's/admission) fee
11 見做 **mina(su)** regard as, consider, deem
見過 **misu(gosu)** overlook
見掛 **mika(keru)** (happen to) see, notice
見掛倒 **mika(ke)dao(shi)** mere show
見捨 **misu(teru)** desert, abandon, forsake
見据 **misu(eru)** fix one's eyes on, stare at
見張 **miha(ru)** watch, be on the lookout for,
stake out; open (one's eyes) wide
見張台 **miha(ri)dai** watchtower
見張所 **miha(ri)sho** lookout, crow's nest
見張番 **miha(ri)ban** watch, lookout, guard
見得 **mie** pose, posture

見習 **minara(u)** learn (by observation), follow
(someone's) example
見習工 **minara(i)kō** apprentice
見習中 **minara(i)chū** in training
見惚 **mito(reru), miho(reru)** gaze on in
rapture, be fascinated/charmed by
見頃 **migoro** the best time to see
12 見遣 **miya(ru)** look/glance at
見違 **michiga(eru)** mistake for, not recognize
michiga(i) misperception, mistake
見渡 **miwata(su)** look out over
見場 **mi(se)ba** highlight scene
miba look, appearance
見落 **mio(tosu)** overlook
見覚 **miobo(e)** recognition, familiarity
見極 **mikiwa(meru)** see through, discern,
ascertain, grasp
見晴 **miha(rasu)** command a view of
見越 **miko(su)** anticipate, foresee; look across
見開 **mihira(ku)** open (one's eyes) wide
mihira(ki) double-page spread
13 見隠 **mi(e)gaku(re)** now in and now out of
view
見損 **misoko(nau)** fail to see, misjudge
見解 **kenkai** opinion, view
見詰 **mitsu(meru)** gaze/stare at
見飽 **mia(kiru)** get tired of looking at
見馴 **mina(reru)** get used to seeing, be
familiar to
14 見境 **misakai** distinction, discrimination
見様 **miyō** way of looking, viewpoint
見慣 **mina(reru)** get used to seeing, be
familiar to
見誤 **miaya(maru)** missee, mistake
見聞 **kenbun, kenmon, miki(ki)** information, knowledge, experience
15 見舞 **mima(u)** inquire after (someone's
health), visit (someone in hospital)
見舞人 **mima(i)nin** sympathizer, visitor
見舞状 **mima(i)jō** how-are-you/get-well card
見舞金 **mima(i)kin** money gift to a sick
person
見舞品 **mima(i)hin** gift to a sick person
見舞客 **mima(i)kyaku** hospital visitor
見澄 **misu(masu)** observe carefully, make sure
見影 **mi(ru) kage (mo nai)** dilapidated
(beyond recognition)
見蕩 **mito(reru)** gaze on in rapture, be
fascinated/charmed by
16 見積 **mitsu(moru)** estimate, assess
見積書 **mitsumorisho** written estimate
見縊 **mikubi(ru)** belittle, slight, disparage
18 見繕 **mitsukuro(u)** select at one's discretion
見離 **mihana(su)** desert, abandon, give up
19 見識 **kenshiki** opinion; discernment, insight;
pride, dignity

見識張 **kenshikiba(ru)** assume an air of importance

22 見霽 **miharu(kasu)** have a panoramic view

───────── 2 ─────────

1 一見 **ikken** take a look at, glance at

了見 **ryōken** idea; intention; decision, discretion; forgive

2 人見知 **hitomishi(ri)** be bashful before strangers

3 大見得 **ōmie** ostentatious display, grand posture

下見 **shitami** preliminary inspection, preview; clapboard, siding

小見出 **komida(shi)** subheading, subtitle

4 予見 **yoken** foresee, foreknow

内見 **naiken** private viewing, preview

引見 **inken** interview, audience with

月見 **tsukimi** viewing the moon

月見草 **tsukimisō** evening primrose

火見 **hi(no)mi** fire-lookout tower

火見櫓 **hi(no)mi yagura** fire-lookout tower

5 未見 **miken** unacquainted, unknown

他見 **taken** showing to others

外見 **gaiken** external/outward appearance

石見 **Iwami** (ancient kuni, Shimane-ken)

立見 **ta(chi)mi** watch (a play) while standing

立見客 **ta(chi)mikyaku** standee, gallery

立見席 **ta(chi)miseki** standing room, gallery

目見 **memi(e)** audience, interview; (stage) debut; (servant's) service on approval

6 会見 **kaiken** interview

此見 **ko(re)mi(yogashi ni)** ostentatiously, flauntingly, to attract attention

先見 **senken** foresight

先見明 **senken (no) mei** farseeing intelligence

向見 **mu(kō)mi(zu)** rash, reckless, headlong

早見表 **hayamihyō** chart, table

7 束見本 **tsuka-mihon** pattern volume, dummy (of a book to be printed)

邪見 **jaken** wrong view

形見 **katami** keepsake, memento

形見分 **katamiwa(ke)** distribution of mementos (of the deceased)

花見 **hanami** viewing cherry blossoms

花見酒 **hanamizake** viewing cherry blossoms and drinking saké

見見 **mi(ru)mi(ru)** in an instant

mi(su)mi(su) before one's very eyes

私見 **shiken** personal opinion

初見 **shoken** seeing for the first time

8 毒見 **dokumi** tasting for poison

夜見世 **yomise** night fair; night stall

夜見国 **yomi (no) kuni** hades, abode of the dead

卓見 **takken** farsighted, incisive, broad vision

拝見 **haiken** see, have a look at

披見 **hiken** open and read (a letter)

味見 **ajimi** sample, taste

知見 **chiken** knowledge, information; opinion

実見 **jikken** actually see, witness

定見 **teiken** definite/settled opinion

物見 **monomi** sightseeing; watchtower; scout, patrol

物見事 **mono(no)migoto (ni)** splendidly

物見高 **monomidaka(i)** burning with curiosity

物見遊山 **monomi yusan** pleasure trip

物見櫓 **monomi yagura** watchtower

所見 **shoken** one's views, impressions

9 発見 **hakken** discover

発見者 **hakkensha** discoverer

俗見 **zokken** layman's opinion, popular view

透見 **su(ki)mi** steal a glance, peep

風見 **kazami** weather vane

浅見 **senken** superficial view

洞見 **dōken** insight, penetration

姿見 **sugatami** full-length mirror

後見 **kōken** guardianship; assistance

後見人 **kōkennin** (legal) guardian; assistant

政見 **seiken** political views

10 高見 **kōken** your (esteemed) opinion/views

梅見 **umemi** plum-blossom viewing

脇見 **wakimi** look aside/away

書見 **shoken** reading

11 偏見 **henken** biased view, prejudice

達見 **takken** insight, farsightedness

接見 **sekken** receive (visitors)

望見 **bōken** watch from afar

異見 **iken** different opinion; objection

盗見 **nusu(mi)mi(ru)** steal a glance

細見 **saiken** close inspection

雪見 **yukimi** snowy scenery

雪見灯籠 **yukimidōrō** ornamental three-legged stone lantern

雪見酒 **yukimizake** drinking saké while viewing snowy scenery

12 創見 **sōken** original view, originality

遠見 **tōmi** distant view

短見 **tanken** shortsightedness, narrow view

朝見 **chōken** imperial audience

散見 **sanken** be found here and there

13 隠見 **inken** appear then disappear (repeatedly)

鄙見 **hiken** my humble opinion

夢見 **yumemi** dreaming, dream

愚見 **guken** my humble opinion

意見 **iken** opinion

意見書 **ikensho** written opinion

14 概見 **gaiken** overview, outline

総見 **sōken** go to see in a large group

管見 **kanken** narrow view; one's views

15 横見 **yokomi** side glance

謁見 **ekken** have an audience with
謁見室 **ekkenshitsu** audience chamber
16 親見出 **oyamida(shi)** heading, main entry
17 瞥見 **bekken** glance, glimpse
18 顔見 **kaomi(se)** show one's face (in public)
顔見知 **kaomishi(ri)** knowing someone by sight, a nodding acquaintance
19 識見 **shikiken, shikken** knowledge, discernment
21 露見 **roken** be found out, come to light

———————— 3 ————————

1 一寸見 **chottomi** a glance/glimpse
2 人相見 **ninsōmi** physiognomist
3 大目見 **ōme (ni) mi(ru)** overlook (faults), let go, view with tolerance
4 不量見 **furyōken** indiscretion; evil intent
手相見 **tesōmi** palm reader
日和見 **hiyorimi** weather forecasting; weathervane; wait and see
火事見舞 **kaji mima(i)** sympathy visit after a fire
5 未発見 **mihakken** undiscovered, unexplored
6 同意見 **dōiken** the same opinion, like views
7 余所見 **yosomi** look away
忘形見 **wasu(re)gatami** memento, keepsake; posthumous child
9 垣間見 **kaimami(ru)** peek in, get a glimpse
10 被後見者 **hikōkensha** ward
12 暑中見舞 **shochū mima(i)** inquiry after (someone's) health in the hot season
無定見 **muteiken** lack of principle, inconstant
13 新発見 **shinhakken** new discovery
14 嘘発見器 **uso hakkenki** lie detector
綿津見 **watatsumi** (god of) the sea

———————— 4 ————————

6 百聞一見如 **hyakubun (wa) ikken (ni) shi(kazu)** Seeing for oneself once is better than hearing 100 accounts.
10 記者会見 **kisha kaiken** news/press conference

———————— 3 ————————

5c3.1 / 420

具 具

GU tool, equipment, gear; (soup) ingredients, (pizza) topping **sona(eru)** equip, furnish, provide
sona(waru) be furnished/provided with
tsubusa (ni) minutely, in detail

———————— 1 ————————

5 具申 **gushin** (full) report (to a superior)
6 具有 **guyū** have, possess
7 具体 **gutai** concrete, specific, definite
具体化 **gutaika** embodiment, materialization
具体的 **gutaiteki** concrete, specific, definite

具体策 **gutaisaku** specific measures
具状 **gujō** (full) report (to a superior)
具足 **gusoku** completeness; armor
具足師 **gusokushi** armorer
10 具陳 **guchin** formal statement
具案 **guan** drafting a plan; specific plan
11 具現 **gugen** embodiment, incarnation
具眼 **gugan** discernment
具眼士 **gugan(no)shi** man of discernment
具眼者 **gugansha** discerning/observant person
12 具備 **gubi** have, possess, be endowed with
具象化 **gushōka** make concrete
具象画 **gushōga** representational painting
具象的 **gushoteki** concrete, not abstract

———————— 2 ————————

3 工具 **kōgu** tool, implement
4 不具 **fugu, katawa** physical deformity/disability
不具者 **fugusha** cripple, disabled person
仏具 **butsugu** Buddhist altar articles
5 用具 **yōgu** tool, implement, apparatus, (sporting) goods
8 表具屋 **hyōguya** picture mounter/framer
表具師 **hyōgushi** picture mounter/framer
夜具 **yagu** bedding
建具 **tategu** household fittings, fixtures
建具屋 **tateguya** cabinetmaker
治具 **jigu** jig
拝具 **haigu** Sincerely yours
炊具 **suigu** cooking utensils
玩具 **gangu, omocha** toy
玩具屋 **omochaya** toy shop
物具 **mono(no)gu** weapons, armor
武具 **bugu** arms, armor
金具 **kanagu** metal fittings, bracket
雨具 **amagu** rain gear, rainwear
9 浮具 **u(ki)gu** water wings, a float
要具 **yōgu** necessary tools
革具 **kawagu** leather goods
香具 **kōgu** incense set, perfumes
10 索具 **sakugu** rigging, gear, tackle
家具 **kagu** furniture, furnishings
家具屋 **kaguya** furniture store
家具師 **kagushi** cabinetmaker
校具 **kōgu** school equipment
書具合 **ka(ki)guai** the feel of the pen against the paper as one writes
教具 **kyōgu** teaching tools/aids
留具 **to(me)gu** clasp, latch, fastening
馬具 **bagu** harness, horse gear
馬具師 **bagushi** harness maker, saddler
11 道具 **dōgu** tool, implement
道具方 **dōgukata** stage hand
道具立 **dōguda(te)** tool setup, stage setting

5

石
立
目 3←
禾
衤
田
皿

疒

道具屋 **dōguya** dealer in secondhand goods
道具部屋 **dōgu-beya** toolroom; prop room
道具箱 **dōgubako** toolbox
猟具 **ryōgu** hunting gear
祭具 **saigu** ceremonial equipment
産具 **sangu** obstetrical supplies
船具 **funagu, sengu** ship's rigging
釣具 **tsu(ri)gu** fishing tackle
12 葬具 **sōgu** funeral accessories
敬具 **keigu** Sincerely yours,
装具 **sōgu** equipment, accouterments
13 絵具 **e(no)gu** paints, colors, pigments
農具 **nōgu** farm implements
寝具 **shingu** bedding
腹具合 **haraguai** condition of one's bowels
14 漁具 **gyogu** fishing gear/tackle
綱具 **tsunagu** rigging
15 器具 **kigu** utensil, appliance, tool, apparatus
締具 **shi(me)gu** (ski) bindings
16 懐具合 **futokoro guai** one's financial circumstances

──────── 3 ────────

3 大道具 **ōdōgu** stage setting, scenery
小道具 **kodōgu** (stage) props
4 文房具 **bunbōgu** writing materials, stationery
文房具屋 **bunbōguya** stationery store
5 出来具合 **dekiguai** workmanship, result, performance
古道具 **furudōgu** secondhand goods, used furniture
古道具屋 **furudōguya** secondhand store
6 防寒具 **bōkangu** cold-protection/arctic outfit
7 攻具 **se(me)dōgu** offensive weapons
8 泥絵具 **doro e(no)gu** distemper, color wash
9 飛道具 **to(bi)dōgu** projectile weapon, firearms
茶道具 **chadōgu** tea-things
11 救命具 **kyūmeigu** life preserver
責道具 **se(me)dōgu** instruments of torture
釣道具 **tsu(ri) dōgu** fishing tackle
12 装身具 **sōshingu** personal accessories
13 農機具 **nōkigu** farm equipment
15 熱器具 **netsukigu** heating appliances

──────── 4 ────────

4 水彩絵具 **suisai e(no)gu** watercolors
10 家財道具 **kazai dōgu** household effects
11 商売道具 **shōbai dōgu** tools of the trade
運動用具 **undō yōgu** sporting goods

直 → **2k6.2**

盾 → **5c4.8**

──────── 4 ────────

5c4.1

眄

BEN look at askance, glare at

──────── 4 ────────

5 左顧右眄 **sako-uben** irresolution, vacillation
右顧左眄 **uko-saben** look right and left; vacillate, waver

5c4.2

眇

BYŌ small; distant
sugame one eye smaller/injured/blind; squinting, cross-eyed, wall-eyed

──────── 2 ────────

17 矯眇 **ta(metsu)-suga(metsu)** with a scrutinizing eye

5c4.3 / 1244

臭   臭

SHŪ odor **kusa(i)** foul-smelling; (as suffix) smelling of **nio(i)** odor, smell

──────── 1 ────────

6 臭気 **shūki** offensive odor, stink, stench
10 臭素 **shūso** bromine
臭素酸 **shūsosan** bromic acid, … bromate
13 臭跡 **shūseki** scent, trail

──────── 2 ────────

3 土臭 **tsuchikusa(i)** smelling of dirt; peasantly, rustic
口臭 **kōshū** bad breath, halitosis
4 水臭 **mizukusa(i)** watery; lacking in intimacy, distant
5 生臭 **namagusa(i)** smelling of fish/blood
生臭坊主 **namagusa bōzu** worldly priest, corrupt monk
生臭物 **namagusamono** raw foods (forbidden to monks)
古臭 **furukusa(i)** old, musty, outdated, trite, stale
6 防臭 **bōshū** deodorization
防臭剤 **bōshūzai** deodorant, deodorizer
汚臭 **oshū** foul odor
汗臭 **asekusa(i)** smelling of sweat
7 体臭 **taishū** body odor; a characteristic
余臭 **yoshū** lingering smell
乳臭 **chichikusa(i)** smelling of milk; babyish, callow
nyūshū callowness, inexperience
男臭 **otokokusa(i)** smelling like a man, masculine
8 泥臭 **dorokusa(i)** smelling of mud; uncouth
青臭 **aokusa(i)** smelling grassy/unripe; inexperienced

物臭 **monogusa** lazy
和臭 **washū** Japanese tinge/flavor
9 俗臭 **zokushū** vulgarity, worldly-mindedness
10 息臭 **ikikusa(i)** having a foul breath
11 脱臭 **dasshū** deodorize
脱臭剤 **dasshūzai** deodorant, deodorizer
悪臭 **akushū** offensive odor, stench
異臭 **ishū** offensive smell
12 爺臭 **jijikusa(i)** old-mannish
腋臭 **wakiga** underarm odor
無臭 **mushū** odorless
鈍臭 **norokusa(i)** slow, sluggish
焦臭 **ko(ge)kusa(i), kinakusa(i)** smelling burnt
13 照臭 **te(re)kusa(i)** embarrassed
14 銅臭 **dōshū** mercenary spirit
16 激臭 **gekishū** strong odor
23 黴臭 **kabikusa(i)** moldy, musty

――――――― 3 ―――――――

7 阿呆臭 **ahōkusa(i)** foolish, dumb, stupid
辛気臭 **shinkikusa(i)** fretful
8 抹香臭 **makkōkusa(i)** smelling of religion
9 洒落臭 **sharakusa(i)** cheeky, "smart"
面倒臭 **mendōkusa(i)** troublesome, a big bother
胡散臭 **usankusa(i)** suspicious, questionable
10 陰気臭 **inkikusa(i)** gloomy-looking
洒落臭 **sharakusa(i)** cheeky, "smart"
素人臭 **shirōtokusa(i)** amateurish
14 熟柿臭 **jukushikusa(i)** smelling of liquor

5c4.4 / 1316
看
KAN, mi(ru) see, watch

――――――― 1 ―――――――

6 看守 **kanshu** (prison) guard
8 看板 **kanban** sign(board)
看板娘 **kanban musume** pretty girl who draws customers
看取 **kanshu** perceive, notice, detect
　　 mito(ru) tend the sick
10 看破 **kanpa, miyabu(ru)** see through, detect
看病 **kanbyō** tending the sick, nursing
11 看做 **mina(su)** regard as, consider, deem
20 看護 **kango** tend the sick, care for, nurse
看護人 **kangonin** male nurse
看護兵 **kangohei** military nurse, medic
看護婦 **kangofu** (female) nurse
看護婦長 **kangofuchō** head nurse

――――――― 2 ―――――――

5 立看板 **ta(te)kanban** standing signboard
8 表看板 **omote-kanban** sign out in front; figurehead, mask

金看板 **kinkanban** gold-lettered sign; slogan

――――――― 3 ―――――――

1 一枚看板 **ichimai kanban** one's only suit; leading actor; sole issue, slogan

5c4.5
眈
TAN watch intently

――――――― 3 ―――――――

8 虎視眈々 **koshi-tantan** with hostile vigilance, waiting one's chance (to pounce)

5c4.6
眄
KEI glare at; toil

5c4.7 / 145
省
SEI, kaeri(miru) reflect upon, give heed to SHŌ (government) ministry; province (in China); be sparing of, save (space) habu(ku) omit, eliminate; curtail, cut down on

――――――― 1 ―――――――

0 省エネ **shōene** energy saving
2 省力化 **shōryokuka** labor saving
5 省令 **shōrei** ministerial order
11 省略 **shōryaku** abbreviate, omit
12 省営 **shōei** operated by a ministry
14 省察 **seisatsu** reflect on, consider, introspect

――――――― 2 ―――――――

3 三省 **sansei** introspection, reflection (three times a day)
4 内省 **naisei** introspection, reflection
反省 **hansei** reflection, introspection; reconsideration
6 各省 **kakushō** each ministry
自省 **jisei** self-examination, reflection
8 官省 **kanshō** government office/department
10 帰省 **kisei** returning to one's home town (for the holidays)
猛省 **mōsei** serious reflection

――――――― 3 ―――――――

3 大蔵省 **Ōkurashō** Ministry of Finance
4 内務省 **Naimushō** (prewar) Ministry of Home Affairs
文部省 **Monbushō** Ministry of Education
5 外務省 **Gaimushō** Ministry of Foreign Affairs
6 式部省 **Shikibushō** Ministry of Ceremony
自治省 **Jichishō** Ministry of Home Affairs
7 労働省 **Rōdōshō** Ministry of Labor

8 厚生省 **Kōseishō** Ministry of Health and
Welfare
建設省 **Kensetsushō** Ministry of Construction
法務省 **Hōmushō** Ministry of Justice
9 通産省 **Tsūsanshō** MITI, Ministry of
International Trade and Industry (short
for 通商産業省)
海軍省 **Kaigunshō** Admiralty, Navy
Department
後朱省 **Gosuzaku** (emperor, 1036–1045)
10 陸軍省 **Rikugunshō** Ministry of War
郵政省 **Yūseishō** Ministry of Posts and
Telecommunications
宮内省 **Kunaishō** Imperial Household
Department
11 運輸省 **Un'yushō** Ministry of Transport

————————— 5 —————————

9 通商産業省 **Tsūshōsangyōshō** Ministry of
International Trade and Industry
13 農林水産省 **Nōrinsuisanshō** Ministry of
Agriculture, Forestry and Fisheries

5c4.8 / 772

盾

JUN, tate shield

————————— 2 —————————

3 小盾 **kodate** small shield; screen, cover
5 矛盾 **mujun** contradiction
6 因盾 **injun** vacillating, conservative

5c4.9

眉

BI, MI, mayu eyebrow

————————— 1 —————————

4 眉毛 **mayuge** eyebrows
5 眉目 **bimoku, mime** features, looks, face
眉目秀麗 **bimoku shūrei** handsome face
6 眉宇 **biu** one's brow, eyebrows, face
11 眉唾物 **mayutsubamono** fake, cock-and-bull
story
12 眉間 **miken** between the eyebrows
14 眉墨 **mayuzumi** eyebrow pencil

————————— 2 —————————

4 引眉 **hi(ki)mayu** painted eyebrows
5 白眉 **hakubi** finest, best example, epitome
8 拝眉 **haibi** personal meeting
9 柳眉 **ryūbi** beautiful eyebrows
10 娥眉 **gabi** beautiful eyebrows/woman
12 焦眉 **shōbi** urgent, pressing
13 愁眉 **shūbi** worried brow/look

————————— 5 —————————

5c5.1

眛

MAI dark

5c5.2 / 849

眠

MIN, nemu(ru) sleep
nemu(i), nemu(tai) sleepy, drowsy,
tired

————————— 1 —————————

6 眠気 **nemuke** sleepiness, drowsiness
眠気覚 **nemukeza(mashi)** something to wake
one up
9 眠草 **nemu(ri)gusa** mimosa
10 眠病 **nemu(ri)byō** sleeping sickness
16 眠薬 **nemu(ri)gusuri** sleeping drug/pills

————————— 2 —————————

1 一眠 **hitonemu(ri)** a short sleep, a nap
4 不眠 **fumin** sleeplessness
不眠不休 **fumin-fukyū** without sleep or rest,
day and night
不眠症 **fuminshō** insomnia
5 永眠 **eimin** eternal sleep, death
冬眠 **tōmin** hibernation
6 仮眠 **kamin** nap
安眠 **anmin** quiet sleep
7 快眠 **kaimin** pleasant sleep
8 空眠 **soranemu(ri)** feigned sleep
居眠 **inemu(ri)** doze, drowse
9 春眠 **shunmin** (pleasant) springtime sleep
12 就眠 **shūmin** go to bed/sleep
惰眠 **damin** idle slumber, lethargy
13 催眠 **saimin** hypnosis
催眠剤 **saiminzai** sleep-inducing drug
催眠術 **saiminjutsu** hypnotism
催眠薬 **saimin'yaku** sleep-inducing drug
嗜眠 **shimin** lethargy, torpor
睡眠 **suimin** sleep
睡眠剤 **suiminzai** sleeping drug/pills
睡眠量 **suiminryō** amount of sleep
睡眠薬 **suimin'yaku** sleeping drug/pills
14 熟眠 **jukumin** sound sleep

眄→ 5c4.1

5c5.3

眩

GEN, kurume(ku) get dizzy
mabu(shii), mabayu(i) glaring,
blinding, dazzling

————————— 1 —————————

12 眩惑 **genwaku** blind, dazzle, daze

13 眩暈 **gen'un, memai** vertigo, dizziness

─────────── 2 ───────────

5 目眩 **mekurume(ku)** be dizzy, have blurred vision **memai** dizziness

5c5.4

昵

TEI, DAI glance/gaze at

臭 → 臭 5c4.3

─────────── 6 ───────────

5c6.1 / 848

眼

GAN, GEN, me, manako eye

─────────── 1 ───────────

2 眼力 **ganriki** insight, discernment, observation
3 眼孔 **gankō** eyehole; eye socket
  眼下 **ganka** below one's eyes
4 眼中 **ganchū** in one's eyes/consideration
5 眼目 **ganmoku** gist, main point
6 眼気 **ganki** eye disease
  眼光 **gankō** glint of one's eye; insight
8 眼底出血 **gantei shukketsu** hemorrhage in the fundus of the eye
9 眼前 **ganzen** before one's eyes
  眼科 **ganka** ophthalmology
  眼科医 **gankai** ophthalmologist
  眼界 **gankai** field/range of vision
10 眼差 **manaza(shi)** a look, expression
  眼帯 **gantai** eye bandage/patch
  眼病 **ganbyō** eye disease
  眼疾 **ganshitsu** eye disease
11 眼球 **gankyū** eyeball
14 眼窩 **ganka** eye socket
  眼精疲労 **gansei hirō** eyestrain
18 眼瞼 **ganken** eyelid
19 眼識 **ganshiki** discernment, insight
  眼鏡 **megane, gankyō** (eye)glasses
  眼鏡屋 **meganeya** optician
  眼鏡蛇 **megane hebi** cobra
  眼鏡橋 **meganebashi** arch bridge

─────────── 2 ───────────

1 一眼 **ichigan** one eye; single lens
2 入眼 **i(re)me** artificial/glass eye
3 凡眼 **bongan** a layman's eye
4 天眼通 **tengantsū** clairvoyance
  双眼 **sōgan** both eyes; binocular
  双眼鏡 **sōgankyō** binoculars

片眼 **katame** one eye, one-eyed
方眼紙 **hōganshi** graph paper
心眼 **shingan** one's mind's eye
5 凹眼鏡 **ōgankyō** concave-lens eyeglasses
左眼 **sagan** left eye
史眼 **shigan** historical view, sense of history
白眼 **hakugan, shirome** the whites of the eyes
白眼視 **hakuganshi** look askance/coldly at
主眼 **shugan** main point/purpose
主眼点 **shuganten** main point/purpose
6 両眼 **ryōgan** both eyes
肉眼 **nikugan** the naked/unaided eye
老眼 **rōgan** farsightedness
老眼鏡 **rōgankyō** eyeglasses for farsightedness
色眼鏡 **iromegane** colored glasses; prejudiced view
近眼 **kingan, chikame** nearsighted; shortsighted
近眼者 **kingansha** nearsighted person
近眼鏡 **kingankyō** eyeglasses for nearsightedness
血眼 **chimanako** bloodshot eye; frantic
虫眼鏡 **mushimegane** magnifying glass
8 法眼 **hōgen** (a high priestly rank in Buddhism)
具眼 **gugan** discernment
具眼士 **gugan(no)shi** man of discernment
具眼者 **gugansha** discerning/observant person
9 俗眼 **zokugan** layman's eye, popular opinion
点眼 **tengan** apply eyedrops/eyewash
風眼 **fūgan** gonorrheal ophthalmia
洗眼 **sengan** eye washing
洗眼薬 **sengan'yaku** eyewash
活眼 **katsugan** keen eye; insight
独眼 **dokugan** one-eyed, single-lens
独眼竜 **dokuganryū** one-eyed hero
独眼龍 **dokuganryū** one-eyed hero
単眼鏡 **tangankyō** monocle
炯眼 **keigan** gleaming eyes; insightful, discerning
10 隻眼 **sekigan** one-eyed
11 達眼 **tatsugan** insight, farsightedness
接眼鏡 **setsugankyō** eyepiece
酔眼 **suigan** drunken/bleary eyes
雪眼鏡 **yuki megane** snow goggles
魚眼レンズ **gyogan renzu** fisheye lens
12 象眼 **zōgan** inlay, damascene
着眼 **chakugan** notice, observe
着眼点 **chakuganten** viewpoint
遠眼 **engan** farsightedness
遠眼鏡 **engankyō** eyeglasses for farsightedness
検眼 **kengan** eye examination, optometry
検眼鏡 **kengankyō** ophthalmoscope

5

石
立
目 6←
禾
礻
田
皿
疒

晴眼者 **seigansha** sighted/non-blind person
開眼 **kaigen, kaigan** spiritual awakening;
   consecrating a newly made image
13 義眼 **gigan** artificial eye
裸眼 **ragan** the naked eye
14 碧眼 **hekigan** blue eyes
複眼 **fukugan** compound eye (of an insect)
鼻眼鏡 **hanamegane** pince-nez
銃眼 **jūgan** gunport, crenel
15 慧眼 **keigan** sharp eye, keen insight

——————— 3 ———————

1 一隻眼 **issekigan** discerning eye
3 千里眼 **senrigan** clairvoyant
6 近視眼 **kinshigan** myopia
団栗眼 **donguri manako** goggle-eyed
7 批評眼 **hihyōgan** critical eye
8 金象眼 **kinzōgan** inlaying with gold
金壺眼 **kanatsubo manako** large sunken
   eyes (showing anxiety/mistrust)
12 遠視眼 **enshigan** farsightedness
14 選球眼 **senkyūgan** batting eye
18 観察眼 **kansatsugan** an observing eye
23 鑑賞眼 **kanshōgan** an eye for
鑑識眼 **kanshikigan** discerning eye

眦 → 眥 **5c6.7**

5c6.2 / 1565

眺

CHŌ, naga(meru) look/gaze at, watch

——————— 1 ———————

11 眺望 **chōbō** a view (from a window)

5c6.3

眸

BŌ pupil (of the eye)

——————— 2 ———————

4 双眸 **sōbō** (the pupils of) both eyes
8 明眸 **meibō** bright eyes

5c6.4

眴

SHUN wink; blink

5c6.5

眶

KYŌ eyelid

5c6.6

眷

KEN look around; regard with affection

——————— 1 ———————

10 眷恋 **kenren** strong attachment, deep affection
11 眷族 **kenzoku** family, household, kith and kin
12 眷属 **kenzoku** family, household, kith and kin
21 眷顧 **kenko** favor, patronage

5c6.7

眥 眦

SHI, SAI, manajiri glare,
angry look

5c6.8

覓

BEKI seek

5c6.9 / 607

規

KI standard, measure

——————— 1 ———————

5 規正 **kisei** regulate, control, readjust
8 規制 **kisei** regulation, control
規定 **kitei** stipulations, provisions, regulations
9 規律 **kiritsu** regulations; order, discipline
規約 **kiyaku** agreement, pact, rules
規則 **kisoku** regulation, rule
規則的 **kisokuteki** regular, orderly, systematic
規則書 **kisokusho** prospectus; regulations
10 規格 **kikaku** standard, norm
規格化 **kikakuka** standardization
規格品 **kikakuhin** standardized goods
12 規程 **kitei** regulations, bylaws
13 規準 **kijun** standard, criterion
14 規模 **kibo** scale, scope
15 規範 **kihan** standard, norm, criterion
規範的 **kihanteki** normative

——————— 2 ———————

3 大規模 **daikibo** large-scale
小規模 **shōkibo** small-scale
4 不規律 **fukiritsu** irregular, disorganized
不規則 **fukisoku** irregular, unsystematic
内規 **naiki** private rules, bylaws
5 正規 **seiki** regular, normal, formal, legal
正規軍 **seikigun** regular army
6 会規 **kaiki** rules of a society
7 条規 **jōki** stipulations, provisions, rules
8 例規 **reiki** established rule
法規 **hōki** laws and regulations

宗規 **shūki** ruler of a religion
定規 **teiki** prescribed
      jōgi ruler, (T-)square; standard
9 軍規 **gunki** military regulations
10 党規 **tōki** party rules
校規 **kōki** school regulations
11 常規 **jōki** established usage; common standard
12 無規律 **mukiritsu** disorderly, undisciplined
13 新規 **shinki** new

———————— 3 ————————
6 両脚規 **ryōkyakuki** compass (for drawing circles)

———————— 4 ————————
7 杓子定規 **shakushi-jōgi** hard-and-fast rule
12 雲形定規 **kumogata jōgi** French curve

5c6.10

逵   **KI** road

———————— 7 ————————

5c7.1

睇   **TEI** look askance at; peek at

5c7.2

覘   **TEN** inquire, peek

———————— 1 ————————
11 覘視孔 **tenshikō** peephole

5c7.3

覗   **SHI, nozo(ku)** peek, peep, peer

———————— 1 ————————
4 覗込 **nozo(ki)ko(mu)** look/peek/peer into
5 覗穴 **nozo(ki)ana** peephole

5c7.4 / 1506

殖   **SHOKU, fu(eru)** increase, grow in number
      fu(yasu) increase, add to

———————— 1 ————————
10 殖財 **shokuzai** increasing one's wealth/fortune, money-making
11 殖産 **shokusan** increase in production/assets

———————— 2 ————————
5 生殖 **seishoku** reproduction, procreation

生殖器 **seishokki, seishokuki** reproductive organs
7 学殖 **gakushoku** learning, accomplishments
利殖 **rishoku** moneymaking
8 拓殖 **takushoku** colonization, exploitation
拓殖者 **takushokusha** colonist
11 貨殖 **kashoku** money-making
14 増殖 **zōshoku** increase, multiply, propagate
増殖炉 **zōshokuro** breeder reactor
15 養殖 **yōshoku** raising, culture, cultivation
16 繁殖 **hanshoku** breed, multiply

———————— 8 ————————

5c8.1

睢   **KI, SUI** look at

5c8.2 / 1071

睡   **SUI** sleep

———————— 1 ————————
7 睡余 **suiyo** after awakening
10 睡眠 **suimin** sleep
睡眠剤 **suiminzai** sleeping drug/pills
睡眠量 **suiminryō** amount of sleep
睡眠薬 **suimin'yaku** sleeping drug/pills
21 睡魔 **suima** sleepiness, the sandman

———————— 2 ————————
1 一睡 **issui** a short sleep, a nap
4 午睡 **gosui** nap, siesta
6 仮睡 **kasui** nap
8 昏睡 **konsui** coma; trance, deep sleep
11 麻睡 **masui** anesthesia
14 熟睡 **jukusui** sound sleep

5c8.3

睥   **HEI** glare at

———————— 1 ————————
13 睥睨 **heigei** glare at, watch

5c8.4

睫   **SHŌ, matsuge** eyelashes

———————— 1 ————————
4 睫毛 **matsuge** eyelashes

———————— 2 ————————
8 逆睫 **saka(sa)matsuge, sakamatsuge** turned-in eyelashes

5

石
立
目   8 ←
禾
示
田
皿
疒

5c8.5

睨 **GEI, nira(mu)** glare/scowl at; watch with suspicion; estimate

——————— 1 ———————

5 睨付 **nira(mi)tsu(keru), ne(me)tsu(keru)** glare/scowl at
6 睨合 **nira(mi)a(u)** glare at each other
nira(mi)a(waseru) take (something) for comparison
睨返 **nira(mi)kae(su), ne(me)kae(su)** glare back
睨回 **ne(me)mawa(su)** glare around
10 睨倒 **nira(mi)tao(su)** stare (someone) down, outstare
11 睨据 **nira(mi)su(eru)** glare at

——————— 2 ———————

13 睥睨 **heigei** glare at, watch
15 横睨 **yokonira(mi)** sharp sidelong glance/glare
18 藪睨 **abunira(mi)** cross-eyed; wrong view

5c8.6

睦 **BOKU, mutsu(majii)** getting along well together, harmonious, friendly, intimate

——————— 1 ———————

4 睦月 **mutsuki** first lunar month, January
7 睦言 **mutsugoto** lovers' talk

——————— 2 ———————

8 和睦 **waboku** rapprochement, reconciliation, peace
16 親睦 **shinboku** friendship
親睦会 **shinbokukai** social get-together

5c8.7

睛 **SEI, hitomi** pupil (of the eye)

5c8.8

眥 **GAI, manajiri** glare, angry look

5c8.9 / 1670

督 **TOKU** lead, command; superintend, supervise

——————— 1 ———————

7 督励 **tokurei** encourage, urge
9 督促 **tokusoku** urge, press, dun
13 督戦 **tokusen** urge on to fight bravely

督戦隊 **tokusentai** supervising unit

——————— 2 ———————

10 家督 **katoku** headship of a family
家督相続 **katoku sōzoku** succession as head of family
家督権 **katoku (no) ken** birthright, inheritance
11 基督 **Kirisuto** Christ
基督教 **Kirisutokyō** Christianity
12 提督 **teitoku** admiral, commodore
14 総督 **sōtoku** governor-general
総督府 **sōtokufu** government-general
15 監督 **kantoku** supervision, direction; (movie) director, (team) manager
監督下 **kantokuka** under the jurisdiction of
監督官 **kantokukan** inspector, superintendent

——————— 3 ———————

3 大監督 **daikantoku** archbishop (Anglican)

5c8.10

鼎 **TEI, kanae** three-legged kettle

——————— 1 ———————

5 鼎立 **teiritsu** three-cornered (contest)
7 鼎坐 **teiza** sit in a triangle
10 鼎座 **teiza** sit in a triangle
15 鼎談 **teidan** three-person conversation, tripartite talks

——————— 9 ———————

5c9.1

睹 覩 **TO** look at, see

鼻→ 5f9.3

5c9.2

覡 **GEKI, kannagi** medium, oracle

5c9.3 / 703

導 **DŌ, michibi(ku)** lead, guide
shirube guide(post)

——————— 1 ———————

2 導入 **dōnyū** bring in, introduce
4 導水 **dōsui** conduct water (into)
導火線 **dōkasen** fuse; cause, occasion

6 導因 **dōin** incentive, motive, cause
7 導体 **dōtai** conductor (of electricity/heat)
　導尿 **dōnyō** withdraw urine, catheterize
8 導者 **dōsha** guide
10 導師 **dōshi** officiating priest; guru
13 導電体 **dōdentai** conductor (of electricity)
　導電性 **dōdensei** conductivity
　導電率 **dōdenritsu** conductivity
14 導管 **dōkan** conduit, pipe, duct, vessel
15 導線 **dōsen** a lead, conducting wire

─────── 2 ───────

4 不導体 **fudōtai** nonconductor
5 半導体 **handōtai** semiconductor
　主導 **shudō** leadership
　主導権 **shudōken** leadership
6 伝導 **dendō** conduction
　先導 **sendō** guidance, leadership
7 良導体 **ryōdōtai** good conductor
8 盲導犬 **mōdōken** seeing-eye dog
9 指導 **shidō** guidance, leadership
　指導者 **shidōsha** leader
　指導権 **shidōken** leadership
10 教導 **kyōdō** instruction, training, coaching
　訓導 **kundō** instruct, guide
11 唱導 **shōdō** advocate
12 善導 **zendō** proper guidance
　補導 **hodō** guidance
14 誘導 **yūdō** induction; incitement; guidance
　誘導体 **yūdōtai** (chemical) derivative
　誘導弾 **yūdōdan** guided missile
　輔導 **hodō** guidance
18 嚮導 **kyōdō** guidance; leader

─────── 3 ───────

4 不良導体 **furyō dōtai** nonconductor, poor
　　conductor
12 超伝導 **chōdendō** superconductivity
　超電導 **chōdendō** superconductivity

─────── 10 ───────

5c10.1

瞎

KATSU blind eye; one eye

5c10.2

瞋

SHIN, **ika(ru)** be angry

─────── 1 ───────

10 瞋恚 **shin'i** wrath, indignation

5c10.3

瞑

MEI, **tsubu(ru)** close (one's eyes)

─────── 1 ───────

0 瞑する/す **mei(suru/su)** close one's eyes;
　die/rest in peace
5 瞑目 **meimoku** close one's eyes; die
13 瞑想 **meisō** meditation, contemplation

─────── 11 ───────

5c11.1

瞟

HYŌ glance at

5c11.2

瞞

MAN deception; dim, obscure

─────── 1 ───────

12 瞞着 **manchaku** deceive, trick, dupe

─────── 2 ───────

12 欺瞞 **giman** deception, fraud, trickery
　欺瞞的 **gimanteki** deceptive, fraudulent, false
　欺瞞者 **gimansha** deceiver, swindler

5c11.3

瞠

DŌ stare at

─────── 1 ───────

5 瞠目 **dōmoku** stare in wonder
8 瞠若 **dōjaku** be astonished
12 瞠然 **dōzen** amazed

靚 → 睹 5c9.1

5c11.4

覷

YU aspire to rise above one's social
station

5c11.5

靦

TEN unashamed

─────── 12 ───────

5c12.1

瞰

KAN see (from above), overlook

─────── 2 ───────

10 俯瞰 **fukan** overlook, have a bird's-eye view

5

石
立
目 12←
禾
衤
罒
皿
疒

俯瞰図 **fukanzu** bird's-eye/overhead view
11 鳥瞰図 **chōkanzu** bird's-eye view

5c12.2

瞳 瞳

DŌ, hitomi pupil (of the eye)

──────── 1 ────────
3 瞳孔 **dōkō** pupil (of the eye)

5c12.3

瞶

KI see everything

5c12.4

瞭 瞭

RYŌ clear

──────── 1 ────────
12 瞭然 **ryōzen** clear, obvious

──────── 2 ────────
8 明瞭 **meiryō** clear, distinct, obvious

──────── 3 ────────
1 一目瞭然 **ichimoku ryōzen** clear at a glance, obvious
4 不明瞭 **fumeiryō** unclear, indistinct

5c12.5

瞥 瞥

BETSU glance, glimpse

──────── 1 ────────
7 瞥見 **bekken** glance, glimpse

──────── 2 ────────
1 一瞥 **ichibetsu** a glance/look

5c12.6

馘

KAKU sever an ear; behead

──────── 1 ────────
9 馘首 **kakushu** decapitate; dismissal

──────── 2 ────────
8 俘馘 **fukaku** sever a captive's left ear

馘→ 5f12.3

5c12.7 / 1291

覧 覽

RAN, mi(ru) see, look at

──────── 1 ────────
0 ご覧 **goran** see, look at (honorific)

──────── 2 ────────
1 一覧 **ichiran** a look/glance; a summary; catalog
一覧表 **ichiranhyō** table, list
3 上覧 **jōran** imperial inspection
4 天覧 **tenran** inspection by the emperor
内覧 **nairan** private viewing, preview
収覧 **shūran** grasp; win over
5 巡覧 **junran** tour, sightseeing
6 回覧 **kairan** read and pass on, circulate
8 供覧 **kyōran** display, show
9 便覧 **benran** manual, handbook
通覧 **tsūran** look over; read through
要覧 **yōran** general survey, overview; catalog
10 借覧 **shakuran** borrow and read
高覧 **kōran** your perusal
遊覧 **yūran** excursion, sightseeing
遊覧地 **yūranchi** pleasure resort, tourist point
遊覧客 **yūrankyaku** sightseers, holidaymakers
遊覧船 **yūransen** excursion boat
展覧 **tenran** exhibition
展覧会 **tenrankai** exhibition
展覧会絵 **Tenrankai (no) e** Pictures at an Exhibition (Mussorgsky, 1874)
展覧物 **tenranbutsu** exhibit
展覧室 **tenranshitsu** showroom
笑覧 **shōran** your inspection
12 博覧 **hakuran** extensive reading/knowledge; open to the public
博覧会 **hakurankai** exhibition, exposition, fair
博覧強記 **hakuran-kyōki** extensive reading and retentive memory
御覧 **goran** see, look at; give it a try
貴覧 **kiran** see, observe (honorific)
13 照覧 **shōran** see clearly; witness
14 熟覧 **jukuran** scrutiny
総覧 **sōran** preside over, control
15 閲覧 **etsuran** perusal, inspection, reading
閲覧室 **etsuranshitsu** reading room
16 縦覧 **jūran** inspection; reading
18 観覧 **kanran** view, see, inspect
観覧車 **kanransha** Ferris wheel
観覧券 **kanranken** admission ticket
観覧者 **kanransha** spectator, visitor
観覧席 **kanranseki** seats, grandstand
観覧料 **kanranryō** admission fee

──────── 4 ────────
3 万国博覧会 **bankoku hakurankai** world's fair

5c12.8

観

KŌ (happen to) meet

——————— 2 ———————
12 稀覯本 **kikōbon** rare book
　　稀覯書 **kikōsho** rare book

5c12.9

覬

KI covet high rank

——————— 13 ———————

5c13.1 / 1732

瞬　瞬

SHUN, matata(ku), mabata(ku), majiro(gu), shibatata(ku), shibata(ku) wink, blink, twinkle

——————— 1 ———————
8 瞬刻 **shunkoku** instant, moment
10 瞬時 **shunji** moment, instant
12 瞬間 **shunkan** instant, moment

——————— 2 ———————
1 一瞬 **isshun** a moment, an instant
　一瞬間 **isshunkan** a moment, an instant

5c13.2

曖

AI hidden, unclear

5c13.3

曚

MŌ blind; ignorant

5c13.4

瞼

KEN, mabuta eyelid

——————— 2 ———————
3 上瞼 **uwamabuta** upper eyelid
　下瞼 **shitamabuta** lower eyelid
11 眼瞼 **ganken** eyelid

5c13.5

瞻

SEN look at

5c13.6

瞽

KO blind

5c13.7 / 604

観　觀

KAN appearance; view, outlook
mi(ru) see, view

——————— 1 ———————
0 観ずる **kan(zuru)** view, contemplate
4 観月 **kangetsu** viewing the moon
5 観世音 **Kanzeon** the Goddess of Mercy
　観世音菩薩 **Kanzeon Bosatsu** the Goddess of Mercy
6 観光 **kankō** sightseeing
　観光団 **kankōdan** tour group
　観光客 **kankōkyaku** tourist, sightseer
　観光船 **kankōsen** excursion ship
7 観兵式 **kanpeishiki** military review, parade
　観応 **Kan'ō** (era, 1350–1352)
8 観念 **kannen** idea; sense (of duty)
　観念的 **kannenteki** ideal, ideological
　観念論 **kannenron** idealism (in philosophy)
9 観点 **kanten** viewpoint
　観客 **kankyaku** audience, spectators
　観客層 **kankyakusō** stratum of the audience
　観相 **kansō** reading character or fortunes by physiognomy, palmistry, phrenology, etc.
　観音 **Kannon** the Goddess of Mercy
　観音開 **kannonbira(ki)** (hinged) double doors
10 観桜 **kan'ō** viewing the cherry blossoms
　観桜会 **kan'ōkai** cherry-blossom viewing party
　観梅 **kanbai** viewing the plum blossoms
11 観菊 **kangiku** chrysanthemum-viewing
　観望 **kanbō** observe, watch, wait and see
12 観象 **kanshō** meterological observation
　観測 **kansoku** observation, survey; thinking, opinion
　観測所 **kansokujo** observatory, observation station
　観葉植物 **kan'yō shokubutsu** foliage plant
　観掌術 **kanshōjutsu** palm-reading, palmistry
　観衆 **kanshū** audience, spectators
13 観楽街 **kanrakugai** amusement district
　観楽境 **kanrakukyō** pleasure resort
　観照 **kanshō** contemplation, reflecting upon
　観想 **kansō** meditation, contemplation
　観戦 **kansen** watch a battle/game
　観戦武官 **kansenbukan** military observer
14 観察 **kansatsu** observe, view
　観察力 **kansatsuryoku** power of observation
　観察者 **kansatsusha** observer

5

石
立
目
禾
示
田
罒
皿
疒

13←

観察眼 **kansatsugan** an observing eye
15 観劇 **kangeki** theatergoing
観賞 **kanshō** admiration, enjoyment
17 観覧 **kanran** view, see, inspect
観覧車 **kanransha** Ferris wheel
観覧券 **kanranken** admission ticket
観覧者 **kanransha** spectator, visitor
観覧席 **kanranseki** seats, grandstand
観覧料 **kanranryō** admission fee
21 観艦式 **kankanshiki** naval review

———————— 2 ————————

3 大観 **taikan** comprehensive view, general survey; philosophical outlook
4 内観 **naikan** introspection
5 史観 **shikan** view of history
外観 **gaikan** external appearance
永観 **Eikan** (era, 983–985)
旧観 **kyūkan** former appearance/state
主観 **shukan** subjectivity; subject, ego
主観主義 **shukan shugi** subjectivism
主観的 **shukanteki** subjective
主観性 **shukansei** subjectivity
主観論 **shukanron** subjectivism
6 壮観 **sōkan** grand/awe-inspiring sight
7 来観 **raikan** inspection visit
来観者 **raikansha** visitor (to an exhibit)
8 直観 **chokkan** intuition
直観的 **chokkanteki** intuitive
拝観 **haikan** see, inspect, visit
拝観料 **haikanryō** (museum) admission fee
奇観 **kikan** wondrous sight, marvel
参観 **sankan** visit, inspect
参観人 **sankannin** visitor
9 貞観 **Jōgan** (era, 859–877)
美観 **bikan** fine view, beautiful sight
通観 **tsūkan** general view/survey
洞観 **dōkan** insight, intuition
客観 **kyakkan, kakkan** object
客観主義 **kyakkan shugi, kakkan shugi** objectivism
客観的 **kyakkanteki, kakkanteki** objective
客観性 **kyakkansei, kakkansei** objectivity
客観視 **kyakkanshi** view objectively
10 陪観 **baikan** view with one's superior
展観 **tenkan** exhibition
11 達観 **takkan** farsighted/philosophic view
盛観 **seikan** grand spectacle
12 偉観 **ikan** grand sight
傍観 **bōkan** look on, remain a spectator
傍観者 **bōkansha** onlooker, bystander
景観 **keikan** spectacular view, a sight
悲観 **hikan** pessimism
悲観的 **hikanteki** pessimistic
悲観説 **hikansetsu** pessimism
悲観論 **hikanron** pessimism

悲観論者 **hikanronsha** pessimist
13 楽観 **rakkan** optimism
楽観主義 **rakkan shugi** optimism
楽観的 **rakkanteki** optimistic, hopeful
14 概観 **gaikan** overview, outline, survey
静観 **seikan** calmly wait and see
16 諦観 **teikan** clear vision; resign oneself to

———————— 3 ————————

1 一面観 **ichimenkan** one-sided view
2 人生観 **jinseikan** one's philosophy of life
5 世界観 **sekaikan** world view
6 気象観測 **kishō kansoku** meteorological observations
先入観 **sennyūkan** preconception, preoccupation, prejudice
自然観 **shizenkan** one's outlook on nature
8 宗教観 **shūkyōkan** religious view
10 恋愛観 **ren'aikan** philosophy of love
馬頭観音 **batōkannon** image of the god Kannon with a horse's head
11 側面観 **sokumenkan** side view
強迫観念 **kyōhaku kannen** obsession
終末観 **shūmatsukan** eschatology
14 厭世観 **enseikan** pessimistic view of life, Weltschmerz
歴史観 **rekishikan** philosophy/view of history

———————— 4 ————————

9 拱手傍観 **kyōshu bōkan** stand idly by
10 袖手傍観 **shūshu-bōkan** look on with arms folded
11 唯物史観 **yuibutsu shikan** materialistic interpretation of history

5c13.8

觀 **KIN, mami(eru)** see, have an audience with

———————— 15 ————————

覺→覚 **3n9.3**

———————— 17 ————————

覽→覧 **5c12.7**

———————— 19 ————————

5c19.1

 矕 **RAN, misona(wasu)** see, view

5c21.1

SHOKU look intently at

矚

——————— 1 ———————

5 矚目 **shokumoku** pay attention to, note
11 矚望 **shokubō** hope much from

——————— 禾 **5d** ———————

禾	利	私	季	秀	禿	和	委	秋	秒	科	秕	香
0.1	2.1	2.2	2.3	2.4	2.5	3.1	3.2	4.1	4.2	4.3	4.4	4.5
秼	秩	秧	秤	秡	秘	租	称	秬	秦	移	稈	程
5.1	5.2	5.3	5.4	5.5	5.6	5.7	5.8	5.9	5.10	6.1	7.1	7.2
稍	税	稀	黍	稚	稗	棋	稜	稔	稙	稠	矮	種
7.3	7.4	7.5	7.6	8.1	8.2	8.3	8.4	8.5	8.6	8.7	8.8	9.1
稗	稱	稲	甃	穀	稷	穂	稻	稼	裕	稿	黎	穀
5d8.2	5d5.8	9.2	9.3	9.4	10.1	10.2	5d9.2	10.3	10.4	10.5	3a10.29	5d9.4
穆	穋	稽	穏	積	穐	臻	穗	糎	黏	稽	穰	穢
11.1	11.2	11.3	11.4	11.5	5d4.1	11.6	5d10.2	5d8.1	6b5.4	13.1	13.2	13.3
穫	馥	魏	穏	馫	馨	穰	黐	穐				
13.4	13.5	13.6	5d11.4	14.1	4c16.2	5d13.2	17.1	5d4.1				

——————— 0 ———————

5d0.1

KA grain, rice
nogi beard (of grain)

禾

——————— 1 ———————

5 禾本科 **kahonka** grasses

——————— 2 ———————

5d2.1 / 329

RI advantage; interest (on a loan)
ki(ku) take effect, work
ki(kasu) make effective, use, exercise

利

——————— 1 ———————

0 利する **ri(suru)** benefit, do good, profit, gain
2 利子 **rishi** interest (on a loan)
3 利己 **riko** self-interest
利己主義 **riko shugi** selfishness
利己的 **rikoteki** selfish
利刃 **rijin** sharp sword
利上 **ria(ge)** raising the interest rate
利下 **risa(ge)** lowering the interest rate
利口 **rikō** smart, clever, bright
利口者 **rikōmono** clever person
4 利水 **risui** water utilization, irrigation
5 利他 **rita** altruism
利付 **ritsu(ki)** interest-bearing
利用 **riyō** use, make use of
利用者 **riyōsha** user

利払 **ribara(i)** interest payment
利札 **risatsu, rifuda** (interest) coupon
利目 **ki(ki)me** effect, efficacy
6 利回 **rimawa(ri)** yield (on investments)
7 利尿 **rinyō** urination
利尿剤 **rinyōzai** a diuretic
8 利者 **ki(ke)mono** influential person
利所 **ki(ki)dokoro** effective/important point
利金 **rikin** interest, gains
9 利発 **rihatsu** cleverness, intelligence
利便 **riben** convenience
利点 **riten** advantage, point in favor
利食 **rigu(i)** profit taking
10 利益 **rieki** profit, gain; benefit, advantage
(go)riyaku divine favor
利益代表 **rieki daihyō** representing (another
country's) diplomatic interests
利酒 **ki(ki)zake** wine tasting
利害 **rigai** advantages and disadvantages,
interests
利害得失 **rigai-tokushitsu** pros and cons
利害関係 **rigai kankei** interests
利根 **rikon** bright, clever
利根川 **Tone-gawa** (river, Chiba-ken)
利息 **risoku** interest (on a loan)
11 利率 **riritsu** rate of interest
利達 **ritatsu** advancement in life
利得 **ritoku** profit, benefit, gain
利欲 **riyoku** greed, mercenariness
12 利腕 **ki(ki)ude** one's more dexterous arm
利殖 **rishoku** moneymaking

利鈍 **ridon** sharp or blunt, bright or dull
13 利福 **rifuku** benefit and happiness
15 利潤 **rijun** profit
利器 **riki** sharp-edged tool; a convenience (of civilization)
利権 **riken** rights, (vested) interests, (mining) concession
利権屋 **riken'ya** concession hunter, grafter
16 利鞘 **rizaya** profit margin

─────── 2 ───────

1 一利 **ichiri** one advantage
一利一害 **ichiri ichigai** advantages and disadvantages
3 口利 **kuchiki(ki)** eloquent person; spokesman; go-between, middleman
小利 **shōri** small profit
小利口 **korikō** clever, smart
小利巧 **korikō** clever, smart
4 不利 **furi** (to one's) disadvantage, handicap
不利益 **furieki** (to one's) disadvantage
元利 **ganri** principal and interest
分利 **bunri** crisis (of an illness), critical
水利 **suiri** water use/supply/transport, irrigation
手利 **teki(ki)** one clever with his hands; expert, master
5 左利 **hidariki(ki)** left-handed; left-hander; a drinker
功利 **kōri** utility; utilitarian
功利主義 **kōri shugi** utilitarianism
功利的 **kōriteki** utilitarian, businesslike
巨利 **kyori** huge profits
右利 **migiki(ki)** righthanded; righthander
目利 **meki(ki)** judging; a judge/connoisseur of
6 気利 **ki (ga) ki(ku)** be clever, be considerate; be stylish
年利 **nenri** annual interest
舌利 **shitaki(ki)** taster
名利 **meiri** fame and wealth
名利心 **meirishin** worldly ambition
安利 **yasuri** low interest/profit
有利 **yūri** advantageous, profitable, favorable
自利 **jiri** self-interest, personal gain
7 我利 **gari** one's own interests, self-interest
低利 **teiri** low interest
私利 **shiri** self-interest, personal profit
足利 **Ashikaga** (era, 1392–1573), the Muromachi period; (city, Tochigi-ken)
8 舎利 **shari** Buddha's bones; a saint's bones
味利 **ajiki(ki)** taster
実利 **jitsuri** utility, practical advantage
実利主義 **jitsuri shugi** utilitarianism, materialism
国利 **kokuri** national interests
国利民福 **kokuri-minpuku** the national interest and the welfare of the people

金利 **kinri** (rate of) interest
9 便利 **benri** convenient, handy
便利屋 **benriya** handyman
茶利 **chaki(ki)** tea tasting/taster
単利 **tanri** simple interest
単利回 **tanrimawa(ri)** yield by a simple interest method
砂利 **jari** gravel
砂利道 **jarimichi** gravel road
10 射利 **shari** love of money
射利心 **sharishin** mercenary spirit
冥利 **myōri** divine favor, providence, luck
高利 **kōri** high interest (rate)
高利貸 **kōriga(shi)** usury; usurer
党利 **tōri** party interests
特利 **tokuri** extra-high interest (rate)
純利 **junri** net profit
11 商利 **shōri** commercial profit
12 幅利 **habaki(ki)** man of influence
営利 **eiri** profit(-making)
犀利 **sairi** keen, acute, penetrating
勝利 **shōri** victory
勝利者 **shōrisha** victor, winner
腕利 **udeki(ki)** skilled, able
無利子 **murishi** non-interest-bearing
無利息 **murisoku** non-interest-bearing
13 福利 **fukuri** welfare, well-being
戦利品 **senrihin** war spoils, booty
14 漁利 **gyori** fishing interests/profit
徳利 **tokuri, tokkuri** (pinch-necked) saké bottle
複利 **fukuri** compound interest
複利法 **fukurihō** the compound interest method
15 摩利支天 **Marishiten** Marici, Buddhist god of war
権利 **kenri** a right
権利金 **kenrikin** key money
暴利 **bōri** excessive profits, usury
鋭利 **eiri** sharp, keen
16 薄利 **hakuri** narrow profit margin
薄利多売 **hakuri-tabai** large-volume sales at low profit margin

─────── 3 ───────

3 大勝利 **daishōri** decisive victory
4 仏舎利 **busshari** Buddha's ashes
6 伊太利 **Itaria, Itarii** Italy
7 亜米利加 **Amerika** America
低金利 **teikinri** low interest
8 非営利的 **hieiriteki** nonprofit
英吉利 **Igirisu** England
12 廃物利用 **haibutsu riyō** recycling
14 漁夫利 **gyofu (no) ri** profiting while others fight over a prize
16 墺太利 **Ōsutoria** Austria

5

石
立
目
禾
田
皿
广

→ 2

燗徳利 **kandokuri** bottle for heating saké

――――――― 4 ―――――――

17 濠太剌利 **Ōsutoraria** Australia

5d2.2 / 125

私 **SHI** private
watakushi I, me, my
hiso(ka) secret, private

――――――― 1 ―――――――

2 私人 **shijin** private individual
3 私大 **shidai** private college (short for 私立大学)
私小説 **watakushi shōsetsu** novel narrated in the first person; autobiographical novel
shishōsetsu autobiographical novel
4 私文書 **shibunsho** private document
私心 **shishin** selfish motive
5 私生子 **shiseishi** illegitimate child
私生児 **shiseiji** illegitimate child
私生活 **shiseikatsu** one's private life
私用 **shiyō** private use
私立 **shiritsu** private (sometimes pronounced *watakushiritsu* to avoid confusion with 市立, municipal)
6 私曲 **shikyoku** corrupt practices, graft
私印 **shiin** personal seal
私刑 **shikei** taking the law into one's own hand, lynch law
私考 **shikō** personal opinion
私行 **shikō** one's private conduct/affairs
私宅 **shitaku** private home
私有 **shiyū** privately owned
私有地 **shiyūchi** private land
私有物 **shiyūbutsu** private property
私自身 **watakushi jishin** personally, as for me
7 私邸 **shitei** private residence
私兵 **shihei** private army
私学 **shigaku** private school
私見 **shiken** personal opinion
私利 **shiri** self-interest, personal profit
8 私事 **shiji, watakushigoto** personal affairs
私版 **shihan** private publication
私法 **shihō** private law
私服 **shifuku** plainclothes, civilian clothes
私的 **shiteki** private, personal
私物 **shibutsu** private property
私金融 **shikin'yū** private financing/funds
9 私信 **shishin** private message
私通 **shitsū** illicit love affair
私室 **shishitsu** private room
私怨 **shien** personal grudge
私恨 **shikon** secret grudge
10 私益 **shieki** personal gain, self-interest
私流 **watakushiryū** one's personal method
私消 **shishō** embezzlement

私家 **shika** personal, private
私家集 **shikashū** private/personal collection
私案 **shian** one's own plan
私党 **shitō** faction
私書 **shisho** private document/letter
私書箱 **shishobako** post-office box
私記 **shiki** private record
私財 **shizai** private funds
11 私達 **watakushitachi** we, us, our
私道 **shidō** private road/path
私淑 **shishuku** greatly admire, look up to
私娼 **shishō** unlicensed prostitute
私娼窟 **shishōkutsu** brothel
私欲 **shiyoku** self-interest
私情 **shijō** personal feelings, bias
私設 **shisetsu** private, nongovernmental
12 私報 **shihō** private report/message
私営 **shiei** privately run/managed
私費 **shihi** private expense, one's own expense
13 私塾 **shijuku** private school
私腹 **shifuku** one's own pocket/purse
私意 **shii** selfishness, bias
私鉄 **shitetsu** private railway line
14 私選 **shisen** personal choice/appointment
私製 **shisei** homemade, private (postcard)
私語 **shigo** secret talk, whispering
私説 **shisetsu** one's own view
15 私蔵 **shizō** possess, own (personally)
私権 **shiken** private rights
私慾 **shiyoku** self-interest, selfish desires
私憤 **shifun** personal grudge
私線 **shisen** private railway line
私論 **shiron** one's personal view
18 私闘 **shitō** personal feud
20 私議 **shigi** private discussion; backbiting; personal view

――――――― 2 ―――――――

1 一私人 **isshijin, ichishijin** a private individual
4 公私 **kōshi** public and private
8 官私 **kanshi** public and private
12 無私 **mushi** unselfish, disinterested
13 滅私奉公 **messhi hōkō** selfless patriotic service

――――――― 4 ―――――――

4 公平無私 **kōhei-mushi** fair and disinterested
9 則天去私 **sokuten-kyoshi** selfless devotion to justice

5d2.3 / 465

季 **KI** season

――――――― 1 ―――――――

5 季末 **kimatsu** end of the term

5

石
立
目
禾 2←
衤
田
罒
皿
疒

季刊 **kikan** quarterly publication
季刊誌 **kikanshi** a quarterly (magazine)
9 季春 **kishun** late spring
10 季候 **kikō** climate
季候帯 **kikōtai** climatic zone
13 季節 **kisetsu** season, time of year
季節物 **kisetsumono** things in season
季節風 **kisetsufū** seasonal wind, monsoon
14 季語 **kigo** word indicating the season (in haiku)
18 季題 **kidai** seasonal theme (in haiku)

——————— 2 ———————

5 四季 **shiki** the four seasons
四季咲 **shikiza(ki)** blooming all seasons
冬季 **tōki** winter season
6 当季 **tōki** this period/season
7 花季 **kaki** the flowering season
8 雨季 **uki** the rainy season
9 春季 **shunki** spring(time)
秋季 **shūki** autumn, fall
11 乾季 **kanki** the dry season
12 無季 **muki** (haiku) without reference to a season
13 節季 **sekki** end of the year/season
節季仕舞 **sekki-jimai** year-end closeout
節季市 **sekki-ichi** a year-end fair
15 澆季 **gyōki** decadence, degeneration

——————— 3 ———————

11 乾燥季 **kansōki** the dry season

5d2.4 / 1683

秀

SHŪ, hii(deru) excel, surpass

——————— 1 ———————

3 秀才 **shūsai** talented man, bright boy/girl
5 秀句 **shūku** excellent haiku; quip, wisecrack
7 秀抜 **shūbatsu** excellent, pre-eminent
秀吟 **shūgin** excellent poem
10 秀逸 **shūitsu** superb, masterly
14 秀歌 **shūka** excellent tanka/poem
19 秀麗 **shūrei** graceful, beautiful, handsome

——————— 2 ———————

9 俊秀 **shunshū** genius, man of exceptional talent
14 閨秀 **keishū** accomplished woman
閨秀作家 **keishū sakka** woman writer
17 優秀 **yūshū** superior, excellent

——————— 3 ———————

9 眉目秀麗 **bimoku shūrei** handsome face

5d2.5

禿

TOKU, ha(geru) become bald
hage baldness
chibi(ru) wear away

——————— 1 ———————

3 禿上 **ha(ge)a(garu)** go bald, recede (hairline)
禿山 **hageyama** bare/bald mountain
16 禿頭 **hageatama, tokutō** bald head
禿頭病 **tokutōbyō** (pathological) baldness

——————— 2 ———————

8 若禿 **wakaha(ge)** premature baldness

——————— 3 ———————

5d3.1 / 124

和

WA, O peace, harmony; Japan(ese)
yawa(rageru) soften, make calm
yawa(ragu) soften, become calm
nago(mu) soften, become mild
nago(yaka) mild, gentle, congenial **a(eru)** dress (food with vinegar/miso, sesame seeds, etc.)

——————— 1 ———————

0 和する **wa(suru)** make peace, become reconciled; harmonize
4 和文 **wabun** Japanese (writing)
和牛 **wagyū** Japanese cow
5 和本 **wahon** book bound in Japanese style
和平 **wahei** peace
和字 **waji** kana
6 和気 **waki** harmony, peacefulness
和合 **wagō** harmony, concord
和名 **wamyō** Japanese name (of a Chinese)
wamei Japanese name (of a plant/animal)
7 和学 **wagaku** Japanese literature
和声 **wasei** harmony (in music)
8 和協 **wakyō** harmony and cooperation
和英 **Wa-Ei** Japanese-English (dictionary), Japan and England
和尚 **oshō** chief priest of a temple
和服 **wafuku** Japanese clothes, kimono
和物 **a(e)mono** dishes dressed with vinegar, miso, sesame seeds, etc.
9 和衷 **wachū** harmony, concord
和風 **wafū** Japanese style
和泉 **Izumi** (ancient kuni, Ōsaka-fu)
和洋 **wayō** Japanese and Western
和洋折衷 **wayō setchū** blending of Japanese and Western styles
和独 **Wa-Doku** Japanese-German (dictionary), Japan and Germany
和室 **washitsu** Japanese-style room
和音 **waon** chord (in music)
和臭 **washū** Japanese tinge/flavor
和食 **washoku** Japanese food
10 和書 **washo** book bound in Japanese style
和紙 **washi** Japanese paper
和訓 **wakun** Japanese reading (of a kanji)
11 和菓子 **wagashi** Japanese-style confections
和船 **wasen** Japanese-style (wooden) ship

和訳 **wayaku** translation into Japanese
12 和琴 **wagon** Japanese harp, ancient koto
和硫 **waryū** vulcanization
和裝 **wasō** Japanese clothing/binding
和裁 **wasai** sewing kimonos
13 和漢 **Wa-Kan** Japanese and Chinese
和楽 **wagaku** Japanese-style music
和解 **wakai** amicable settlement, compromise
和戦 **wasen** peace and war
和睦 **waboku** rapprochement, reconciliation, peace
14 和歌 **waka** 31-syllable poem, tanka
和歌山 **Wakayama** (city, Wakayama-ken)
和歌山県 **Wakayama-ken** (prefecture)
和製 **wasei** made in Japan
和魂漢才 **wakon-kansai** Japanese spirit and Chinese learning
和算 **wasan** Japanese mathematics
和語 **wago** (native) Japanese word
和銅 **Wadō** (era, 708–715)
15 和談 **wadan** a talk to settle differences
16 和親 **washin** friendship, amity, harmony
20 和議 **wagi** peace negotiations, reconciliation; composition (proceedings)
22 和讃 **wasan** (Buddhist) hymns of praise

––––––––––––– 2 –––––––––––––

3 大和 **Yamato** ancient Japan
大和絵 **Yamato-e** medieval picture in Japanese rather than Chinese style
大和歌 **Yamato-uta** 31-syllable poem, tanka
大和魂 **Yamato-damashii** the Japanese spirit
大和撫子 **Yamato nadeshiko** daughter/ woman of Japan
4 不和 **fuwa** discord, trouble, strife
元和 **Genna** (era, 1615–1624)
天和 **Tenna** (era, 1681–1684)
中和 **chūwa** neutralize
仁和 **Ninna** (era, 885–889)
文和 **Bunna** (era, 1352–1356)
日和 **hiyori** the weather; fair weather; the situation
日和見 **hiyorimi** weather forecasting; weathervane; wait and see
5 付和 **fuwa** blindly follow others
付和雷同 **fuwa-raidō** follow blindly, echo
平和 **heiwa** peace
平和主義 **heiwa shugi** pacificism
平和条約 **heiwa jōyaku** peace treaty
正和 **Shōwa** (era, 1312–1317)
弘和 **Kōwa** (era, 1381–1384)
6 共和制 **kyōwasei** republican form of government
共和国 **kyōwakoku** republic
共和党 **kyōwatō** republican party
安和 **Anna** (era, 968–970)

7 承和 **Shōwa** (era, 834–848)
享和 **Kyōwa** (era, 1801–1804)
承和金 **kōwakin** amalgam
応和 **Ōwa** (era, 961–964)
8 長和 **Chōwa** (era, 1012–1017)
協和 **kyōwa** harmony, concord, concert
英和 **ei-wa** English-Japanese (dictionary)
岸和田 **Kishiwada** (city, Ōsaka-fu)
明和 **Meiwa** (era, 1764–1772)
9 貞和 **Jōwa** (era, 1345–1350)
垪和 **Haga** (ancient kuni) **Hagai** (surname)
独和 **Doku-Wa** German-Japanese (dictionary)
宥和 **yūwa** appease, placate
宥和政策 **yūwa seisaku** appeasement policy
柔和 **nyūwa** gentle, mild(-mannered)
昭和 **Shōwa** (emperor and era, 1926–1989)
10 倡和 **shōwa** singing in harmony
浦和 **Urawa** (city, Saitama-ken)
淳和 **Junna** (emperor, 823–833)
11 混和 **konwa** mixture, mingling
混和物 **konwabutsu** mixture
混和性 **konwasei** miscibility
混和剤 **konwazai** a compound/blend
清和 **Seiwa** (emperor, 858–876)
唱和 **shōwa** sing/cheer in chorus
康和 **Kōwa** (era, 1099–1104)
12 違和感 **iwakan** feeling ill at ease, discomfort, malaise
温和 **onwa** mild, gentle
13 義和団 **Giwadan** the Boxers
漢和 **Kan-Wa** China and Japan, Chinese and Japanese (languages)
漢和辞典 **Kan-Wa jiten** kanji dictionary
媾和 **kōwa** making peace, reconciliation
寛和 **Kanna** (era, 985–986)
飽和 **hōwa** saturation
飽和点 **hōwaten** saturation point
14 総和 **sōwa** (sum) total
15 養和 **Yōwa** (era, 1181–1182)
緩和 **kanwa** relieve, ease, alleviate, relax
調和 **chōwa** harmony
16 親和 **shinwa** friendship, fellowship, fraternity
親和力 **shinwaryoku** (chemical) affinity
穏和 **onwa** mild, gentle, genial
穏和派 **onwaha** the moderates
穏和論者 **onwaronsha** a moderate
融和 **yūwa** harmony, reconciliation
17 講和 **kōwa** make peace with
講和条約 **kōwa jōyaku** peace treaty

––––––––––––– 3 –––––––––––––

4 不調和 **fuchōwa** disharmony, disagreement
5 古今和歌集 **Kokinwakashū** (poetry anthology, early tenth century)
6 光飽和 **kōhōwa** light saturation
光飽和点 **kōhōwaten** light saturation point

5

石
立
目
禾 3←
衤
田
罒
皿
疒

9 胡麻和 **gomaa(e)** salad with vinegar dressing
秋日和 **akibiyori** clear fall weather
11 過飽和 **kahōwa** supersaturation

──────── 4 ────────

3 小春日和 **koharubiyori** balmy autumn day, Indian-summer day
9 単独講和 **tandoku kōwa** acting on one's own
12 琴瑟相和 **kinshitsu aiwa(su)** be happily married
15 緊張緩和 **kinchō kanwa** détente

──────── 6 ────────

4 中華人民共和国 **Chūka Jinmin Kyōwakoku** People's Republic of China

5

石
立
目
禾
衤
田
皿
疒

→3

5d3.2 / 466

委

I, yuda(neru) entrust to
maka(seru/su) entrust/leave to
kuwa(shii) detailed, full

──────── 1 ────────

5 委付 **ifu** abandonment (of rights)
6 委曲 **ikyoku** details, full particulars
委任 **inin** trust, mandate, authorization
委任状 **ininjō** power of attorney
委任者 **ininsha** mandator
委任統治 **inin tōchi** mandate
10 委員 **iin** committee member
委員会 **iinkai** committee
委員長 **iinchō** chairman
委託 **itaku** entrust to, put in (someone's) charge
委託金 **itakukin** money in trust
委託販売 **itaku hanbai** selling on consignment/commission
11 委細 **isai** details, particular
13 委棄 **iki** abandonment, desertion
15 委嘱 **ishoku** entrust with
17 委縮 **ishuku** shriveling, contraction, atrophy
20 委譲 **ijō** transfer/assign to

──────── 2 ────────

3 小委員会 **shōiinkai** subcommittee

──────── 3 ────────

4 公取委 **Kōtorii** Fair Trade Commission (short for 公正取引委員会)
5 民生委員 **minsei iin** district welfare officer
6 全院委員会 **zen'in iinkai** committee of the whole house
11 常任委員会 **jōnin iinkai** standing committee

──────── 4 ────────

5d4.1 / 462

秋 穐 龝

SHŪ, aki autumn, fall

──────── 1 ────────

2 秋七草 **aki (no) nanakusa** the seven flowers of autumn
秋刀魚 **sanma** mackerel/saury pike
3 秋口 **akiguchi** the beginning of autumn
秋山 **akiyama** mountains in autumn
4 秋分 **shūbun** fall equinox
秋水 **shūsui** clear autumn stream
秋日 **shūjitsu** autumn day
秋日和 **akibiyori** clear fall weather
5 秋田 **Akita** (city, Akita-ken)
秋田犬 **Akita-ken, Akita inu** an Akita (husky-like) dog
秋田県 **Akita-ken** (prefecture)
6 秋気 **shūki** the autumn air
秋色 **shūshoku** autumn colors/scenery
秋虫 **akimushi** insects heard in autumn
7 秋作 **akisaku** crops sown/harvested in autumn
秋冷 **shūrei** the chill/cold of autumn
秋声 **shūsei** (sound of) the autumn wind
秋季 **shūki** autumn, fall
8 秋郊 **shūkō** fields in autumn
秋波 **shūha** amorous glance, ogle
秋空 **akizora** autumn sky
秋雨 **shūu, akisame** autumn rain
9 秋風 **akikaze, shūfū** autumn breeze
秋津島 **Akitsushima** (ancient) Japan, Yamato
秋思 **shūshi** the sentimental feeling of fall
10 秋高 **akidaka** large fall harvest; high rice price due to poor fall harvest
秋蚕 **shūsan** fall silkworms
11 秋祭 **akimatsu(ri)** autumn festival
12 秋場所 **akibasho** autumn sumo tournament
秋落 **akio(chi)** poor fall harvest; lower rice price at harvest time
秋植 **akiu(e)** autumn planting
秋期 **shūki** autumn, fall
秋晴 **akiba(re)** clear autumn weather
13 秋蒔 **akima(ki)** autumn sowing
16 秋霖 **shūrin** long rainy spell in autumn
17 秋霜 **shūsō** autumn frost
秋霜烈日 **shūsō-retsujitsu** withering frost and scorching sun; harsh, severe, exacting

──────── 2 ────────

3 千秋 **senshū** a thousand years, many years
千秋楽 **senshūraku** the last day (of a play's run)
4 中秋 **chūshū** 15th day of the eighth lunar month; mid-autumn
5 立秋 **risshū** the first day of autumn
6 仲秋 **chūshū** mid-autumn, September
7 麦秋 **bakushū** barley harvest time
初秋 **shoshū** early autumn
9 春秋 **shunjū** spring and autumn; years

10 残秋 **zanshū** the last days of autumn
11 清秋 **seishū** clear autumn (weather)
　涼秋 **ryōshū** cool autumn; ninth lunar month
12 晩秋 **banshū** the latter part of autumn
13 新秋 **shinshū** early autumn
14 暮秋 **boshū** late fall

───── 3 ─────

9 春夏秋冬 **shun-ka-shū-tō** the four seasons, the year round

───── 4 ─────

1 一日千秋 **ichinichi-senshū, ichijitsu-senshū** days seeming like years

5d4.2 / 1152

秒

BYŌ second (of time/arc)

───── 1 ─────

9 秒速 **byōsoku** speed (in meters) per second
10 秒針 **byōshin** second hand (of a clock)
14 秒読 **byōyo(mi)** countdown

───── 2 ─────

3 寸秒 **sunbyō** moment, second
4 分秒 **funbyō** a moment
13 数秒 **sūbyō** for several seconds

5d4.3 / 320

科

KA course (of study), branch, department, faculty, family (in taxonomy)
toga fault, blame
shina actions, deportment; coquetry

───── 1 ─────

0 科する **ka(suru)** inflict, impose
2 科人 **toganin** criminal, offender
5 科目 **kamoku** subject, course (of study); item, classification
7 科学 **kagaku** science
　科学的 **kagakuteki** scientific
　科学者 **kagakusha** scientist
8 科長 **kachō** department head
10 科挙 **kakyo** (ancient) Chinese civil-service exams
　科料 **karyō, togaryō** minor fine (cf. 過料)

───── 2 ─────

3 工科 **kōka** engineering course
　工科大学 **kōka daigaku** engineering college
4 予科 **yoka** preparatory course
　内科 **naika** internal medicine
　内科医 **naikai** physician, internist
　文科 **bunka** liberal arts
　分科 **bunka** department, section, branch, course
5 外科 **geka** surgery
　外科医 **gekai** surgeon

6 全科 **zenka** complete course/curriculum
　百科 **hyakka** many subjects/topics
　百科全書 **hyakka zensho** encyclopedia
　百科事典 **hyakka jiten** encyclopedia
　百科辞典 **hyakka jiten** encyclopedia
　耳科 **jika** otology
7 別科 **bekka** special course
　兵科 **heika** branch of the army
　医科 **ika** medical science; medical department
　医科大学 **ika daigaku** medical university/school
　学科 **gakka** school subjects, curriculum, course
8 非科学的 **hikagakuteki** unscientific
　法科 **hōka** law course/department
　実科 **jikka** practical course
　金科玉条 **kinka-gyokujō** a golden rule
9 専科 **senka** special course
　前科者 **zenkamono** person with a criminal record
　前科…犯 **zenka …-han/-pan** (a criminal record of three) previous convictions
10 特科兵 **tokkahei** technical soldier
　特科隊 **tokkatai** technical corps
　教科 **kyōka** subject, curriculum
　教科目 **kyōkamoku** school subjects
　教科書 **kyōkasho** textbook
11 商科 **shōka** business course
　理科 **rika** science
　産科 **sanka** obstetrics
　産科医 **sankai** obstetrician
　産科学 **sankagaku** obstetrics
　眼科 **ganka** ophthalmology
　眼科医 **gankai** ophthalmologist
　転科 **tenka** change one's course/major
12 歯科 **shika** dentistry
　歯科医 **shikai** dentist
13 農科 **nōka** agriculture department; agricultural course
　罪科 **zaika** offense, crime; punishment
14 選科 **senka** elective course
　選科生 **senkasei** nonregular student
17 厳科 **genka** severe punishment

───── 3 ─────

2 人文科学 **jinbun kagaku** cultural sciences
3 小児科 **shōnika** pediatrics
　小児科医 **shōnikai** pediatrician
5 必修科目 **hisshū kamoku** required subject
　必須科目 **hissu kamoku** required subject
　皮膚科 **hifuka** dermatology
　禾本科 **kahonka** grasses
6 自然科学 **shizen kagaku** the natural sciences
　耳鼻科 **jibika** otorhinology
7 応用科学 **ōyō kagaku** applied science
　肛門科医 **kōmonkai** proctologist

社会科 **shakaika** social studies, civics
初等科 **shotōka** elementary/beginners' course
8 受験科 **jukenka** exam-coaching course
泌尿科 **hinyōka** urology
国文科 **kokubunka** Japanese literature course
10 家政科 **kaseika** home-economics course
純正科学 **junsei kagaku** pure science
11 婦人科 **fujinka** gynecology
婦人科医 **fujinkai** gynecologist
14 精神科 **seishinka** psychiatry

───────── 4 ─────────

3 口腔外科 **kōkō geka** oral surgery
11 産婦人科 **sanfujinka** obstetrics and gynecology
16 整形外科 **seikei geka** plastic surgery

───────── 5 ─────────

6 耳鼻咽喉科 **jibiinkōka** ear, nose, and throat specialty

5d4.4

秕 **HI** bad **shiina** immature ear of grain

───────── 1 ─────────

9 秕政 **hisei** misgovernment, misrule

5d4.5 / 1682

香 **KŌ, KYŌ, kao(ri), ka** fragrance, aroma **kao(ru)** smell good/sweet

───────── 1 ─────────

3 香川県 **Kagawa-ken** (prefecture)
香々 **kōkō** pickled vegetables
4 香水 **kōsui** perfume
香木 **kōboku** aromatic tree, fragrant wood
6 香気 **kōki** fragrance, aroma
香合 **kōgō** incense container
7 香花 **kōge** incense and flowers
香辛料 **kōshinryō** spices, seasoning
香車 **kyōsha** spear (a piece in the game shogi)
8 香典 **kōden** condolence gift
香典返 **kōdengae(shi)** return present for a condolence gift
香油 **kōyu** scented hair oil, pomade
香味 **kōmi** flavor
香味料 **kōmiryō** seasoning, condiments
香炉 **kōro** censer
香物 **kō(no)mono** pickled vegetables
香具 **kōgu** incense set, perfumes
9 香草 **kōsō** aromatic herbs
10 香華 **kōge** incense and flowers
香料 **kōryō** spice; perfume; condolence gift
12 香奠 **kōden** condolence gift

香奠返 **kōdengae(shi)** return present for a condolence gift
香港 **Honkon** Hong Kong

───────── 2 ─────────

6 色香 **iroka** color and scent; beauty, loveliness
名香 **meikō** fine incense
7 余香 **yokō** lingering fragrance
沈香 **chinkō** aloe (wood)
沈香樹 **chinkōju** aloe
芳香 **hōkō** fragrance, perfume, aroma(tic)
8 抹香 **makkō** incense powder; incense
抹香臭 **makkōkusa(i)** smelling of religion
抹香鯨 **makkō kujira** sperm whale
9 茴香 **uikyō** fennel
香香 **kōkō** pickled vegetables
10 残香 **zankō** lingering scent
11 清香 **seikō** fragrance, perfume
移香 **utsu(ri)ga** lingering scent
12 焼香 **shōkō** burn incense
13 新香 **shinkō, shinko** pickled vegetables
14 練香 **ne(ri)kō** pastille
15 線香 **senkō** incense/joss stick
線香代 **senkōdai** (geisha's) time charge
16 薫香 **kunkō** incense; fragrance
21 麝香 **jakō** musk
麝香猫 **jakōneko** musk cat, civet
麝香鹿 **jakōjika** musk deer
麝香鼠 **jakōnezumi** muskrat

───────── 3 ─────────

6 安息香 **ansokukō** benzoin
10 竜涎香 **ryūzenkō** ambergris

───────── 4 ─────────

7 花火線香 **hanabi senkō** joss-stick fireworks, sparklers; flash-in-the-pan
10 蚊取線香 **katori senkō** mosquito-repellent incense

───────── 5 ─────────

5d5.1

秣 **MATSU, magusa** fodder, forage, hay, feed

───────── 1 ─────────

11 秣桶 **magusaoke** manger

───────── 2 ─────────

18 糧秣 **ryōmatsu** provisions and fodder

5d5.2 / 1508

秩 **CHITSU** order, sequence; salary

───────── 1 ─────────

7 秩序 **chitsujo** order, system, regularity

秩序正 **chitsujo-tada(shii)** in good order

――――――― 2 ―――――――
12 無秩序 **muchitsujo** disorder, chaos; anomie
13 新秩序 **shinchitsujo** new order

――――――― 3 ―――――――
6 安寧秩序 **annei-chitsujo** peace and order

5d5.3
秧
Ō (rice) seedling

5d5.4
秤
SHŌ, BIN, hakari (weighing) scales, balance

――――――― 2 ―――――――
4 天秤 **tenbin** a balance, pair of scales; carrying pole, yoke
7 杠秤 **kōshō, chigibakari** large beam balance

――――――― 3 ―――――――
6 両天秤 **ryōtenbin** two alternatives

5d5.5
秡
HATSU, BACHI damaged grain

5d5.6 / 807
秘 祕
HI secret
hi(meru) conceal, keep secret
hiso(ka) secret

――――――― 1 ―――――――
0 秘する **hi(suru)** conceal, keep secret
4 秘仏 **hibutsu** Buddhist image kept hidden
秘文 **himon** magic formula, incantation
秘方 **hihō** secret method/formula
5 秘本 **hihon** treasured/secret book
秘史 **hishi** secret history
6 秘曲 **hikyoku** secret/esoteric music
秘伝 **hiden** secret, esoteric mysteries
8 秘事 **hiji** secret; mystery **hi(me)goto** secret
秘法 **hihō** secret method/formula
秘宝 **hihō** (hidden) treasure
9 秘計 **hikei** secret plan
10 秘匿 **hitoku** conceal, keep hidden/secret
秘書 **hisho** (private) secretary
秘書官 **hishokan** (private) secretary
秘書課 **hishoka** secretariat
11 秘術 **hijutsu** secret, the mysteries
秘密 **himitsu** a secret, confidential
秘訣 **hiketsu** secret, the key to

12 秘結 **hiketsu** constipation
秘奥 **hiō** secrets, mysteries
秘策 **hisaku** secret plan
13 秘話 **hiwa** secret story, unknown episode
15 秘蔵 **hizō** treasure, prize, cherish
16 秘薬 **hiyaku** secret medicine
秘録 **hiroku** secret record/document

――――――― 2 ―――――――
9 便秘 **benpi** constipation
神秘 **shinpi** mystery
神秘主義 **shinpi shugi** mysticism
神秘的 **shinpiteki** mystic(al), mysterious
神秘家 **shinpika** a mystic
神秘説 **shinpisetsu** mysticism
神秘劇 **shinpigeki** mystery drama
12 極秘 **gokuhi** top-secret, confidential
15 黙秘 **mokuhi** keep silent about, keep secret
黙秘権 **mokuhiken** the right to remain silent

――――――― 3 ―――――――
10 部外秘 **bugaihi** to be kept secret from outsiders, Restricted

5d5.7 / 1083
租
SO crop tax, tribute

――――――― 1 ―――――――
9 租界 **sokai** (foreign) settlement, concession
10 租借 **soshaku** lease (land)
租借地 **soshakuchi** leased territory
租借権 **soshakuken** lease, leasehold
12 租税 **sozei** taxes

――――――― 2 ―――――――
4 公租 **kōso** tax
6 地租 **chiso** land tax
有租地 **yūsochi** taxable land
8 免租 **menso** tax exemption
12 減租 **genso** tax reduction/cut

5d5.8 / 978
称 稱
SHŌ name, title
tona(eru) name, call, entitle
tata(eru) praise, admire

――――――― 1 ―――――――
0 称する **shō(suru)** name, call, entitle; claim, purport
5 称号 **shōgō** title, degree
6 称名 **shōmyō** chanting "Hail Amida"
8 称呼 **shōko** appellation, designation, name
9 称美 **shōbi** praise, admiration
12 称揚 **shōyō** praise
14 称徳 **Shōtoku** (empress, 764–770)
15 称賛 **shōsan** praise

2

2 人称 **ninshō** person, personal (in grammar)
4 公称 **kōshō** nominal
5 旧称 **kyūshō** old name, former title
6 仮称 **kashō** tentative/provisional/working name
近称 **kinshō** (in grammar) denoting nearness to the speaker
名称 **meishō** name, title, term, appellation
自称 **jishō** self-styled; first person (in grammar)
7 別称 **besshō** another name, alias, pseudonym
対称 **taishō** symmetry; second person (in grammar)
対称的 **taishōteki** symmetrical
対称軸 **taishōjiku** axis of symmetry
改称 **kaishō** rename, retitle
8 併称 **heishō** rank with, classify together
呼称 **koshō** call, name
9 俗称 **zokushō** popular/vernacular name
美称 **bishō** euphemism
通称 **tsūshō** popular name, commonly known as
10 特称 **tokushō** the particular
11 偽称 **gishō** misrepresentation
過称 **kashō** undeserved praise
推称 **suishō** praise, admiration
族称 **zokushō** one's class (nobility, samurai, or commoner)
略称 **ryakushō** abbreviation
異称 **ishō** another name, alias, pseudonym
12 尊称 **sonshō** honorific title
敬称 **keishō** honorific title
詐称 **sashō** misrepresent oneself
13 愛称 **aishō** term of endearment, pet name
誇称 **koshō** exaggeration
雅称 **gashō** pen name; elegant/poetical name for
14 僭称 **senshō** pretend to, assume a title
歎称 **tanshō** admiration, praise
総称 **sōshō** general/generic term
誤称 **goshō** misnomer
15 襃称 **ho(me)tata(eru)** laud, praise, admire
17 謙称 **kenshō** humble expression

3

1 一人称 **ichininshō** first person (in grammar)
2 二人称 **nininshō** second person (in grammar)
3 三人称 **sanninshō** third person (in grammar)

4

11 第一人称 **dai-ichininshō** first person (in grammar)
第二人称 **dai-nininshō** second person (in grammar)
第三人称 **dai-sanninshō** third person (in grammar)

5d5.9

租

KYO (a type of millet)

5d5.10

秦

SHIN Manchu dynasty

6

5d6.1 / 1121

移

I, utsu(ru) move (to a new residence), change, pass to, (of a disease) be catching
utsu(su) move (one's residence/office), transfer, pass on (one's cold to someone)
utsu(rou) change, shift, fade

1

2 移入 **inyū** bring in, import
5 移出 **ishutsu** ship out, export
移民 **imin** immigration, emigration; immigrant, emigrant, settler
6 移気 **utsu(ri)gi** fickle, capricious
移行 **ikō** move, shift to
7 移身 **utsu(ri)mi** nimble, quick, adroit
移住 **ijū** migration, moving
移住者 **ijūsha** emigrant, immigrant
8 移送 **isō** transfer, transport, remove
9 移乗 **ijō** change vehicles, transfer
移変 **utsu(ri)kawa(ri)** changes, transition
移香 **utsu(ri)ga** lingering scent
11 移動 **idō** moving, migration
移転 **iten** move, change of address
12 移植 **ishoku** transplant
14 移管 **ikan** transfer of control/jurisdiction
15 移調 **ichō** transpose (musical keys)
移駐 **ichū** move, transfer
20 移籍 **iseki** transfer of one's domiciliary registration

2

3 口移 **kuchiutsu(shi)** mouth-to-mouth feeding; word of mouth
4 火移 **hiutsu(ri)** catching fire, igniting
心移 **kokoroutsu(ri)** fickleness, perfidy
5 目移 **meutsu(ri)** distraction, difficulty in choosing
9 気移 **kiutsu(ri)** fickleness
飛移 **to(bi)utsu(ru)** jump from one thing to another
乗移 **no(ri)utsu(ru)** change (vehicles), transfer; possess, inspirit
変移 **hen'i** change, alteration, mutation
10 家移 **yautsu(ri)** moving
11 推移 **suii** changes, transition, progress

転移 **ten'i** change, spread, metastasis
14 遷移 **sen'i** transition, change
16 燃移 **mo(e)utsu(ru)** (flames) spread to

───────── 7 ─────────

5d7.1

程

    KAN, wara grain stems, straw

5d7.2 / 417

程

    TEI, hodo extent, degree

───────── 1 ─────────

3 程々 **hodohodo** moderately, not overdoing it
6 程合 **hodoa(i)** extent, limit
  程近 **hodochika(i)** nearby
7 程良 **hodoyo(i)** good, favorable, proper;
    moderate; vague, noncommittal
9 程度 **teido** extent, degree, level
11 程経 **hodohe(te)** after a while
12 程遠 **hodotō(i)** far from
  程無 **hodona(ku)** soon (afterward), by and by

───────── 2 ─────────

3 工程 **kōtei** process; progress of the work
  上程 **jōtei** introduce (a bill), put on the agenda
4 毛程 **kehodo(mo)** (not) a bit
  中程 **nakahodo** middle, halfway
  今程 **imahodo** recently
  日程 **nittei** the day's schedule/agenda
  方程式 **hōteishiki** equation
6 此程 **ko(no)hodo** the other day, recently
  先程 **sakihodo** a while ago
  行程 **kōtei** distance; journey; march;
    itinerary; stroke (of a piston)
7 身程 **mi(no)hodo** one's place, social standing
  身程知 **mi(no)hodo shi(razu)** not knowing
    one's place
  里程 **ritei** mileage, distance
  里程標 **riteihyō** milepost
  何程 **nanihodo** to what extent, how much
  余程 **yohodo, yo(p)podo** very, much, to a
    great degree
  走程 **sōtei** distance covered
8 其程 **sorehodo** so, so much, to that extent
9 後程 **nochihodo** later on
  音程 **ontei** (musical) interval, step
10 射程 **shatei** range (of a gun/missile)
  旅程 **ryotei** distance to be covered; itinerary
  教程 **kyōtei** teaching method, course;
    textbook
  航程 **kōtei** distance covered, flight
11 道程 **dōtei, michinori** distance; journey

過程 **katei** process
規程 **kitei** regulations, bylaws
12 測程器 **sokuteiki** (ship's) log
  揚程 **yōtei** lift (of a valve); head (height a
    pump can lift water)
  然程 **sahodo** so much, very
  幾程 **ikuhodo** how much/many
  程程 **hodohodo** moderately, not overdoing it
13 路程 **rotei** distance, mileage
15 課程 **katei** course, curriculum

───────── 3 ─────────

6 如何程 **ikahodo** how much/many
8 長射程砲 **chōshateihō** long-range gun/
    artillery

───────── 4 ─────────

2 二次方程式 **niji hōteishiki** quadratic equation
9 連立方程式 **renritsu hōteishiki** simulta-
    neous equations

5d7.3

稍

    SHŌ, yaya somewhat, a little

5d7.4 / 399

税

    ZEI tax

───────── 1 ─────────

4 税収 **zeishū** tax revenues
  税込 **zeiko(mi)** including tax
  税引 **zeibi(ki)** after taxes, take-home (pay)
5 税目 **zeimoku** tariff/tax items
6 税吏 **zeiri** customs collector/officer
8 税表 **zeihyō** tariff (schedule)
  税制 **zeisei** tax system
  税法 **zeihō** tax law; method of taxation
  税金 **zeikin** tax
11 税率 **zeiritsu** tax rate, tariff
  税理士 **zeirishi** tax accountant
  税務 **zeimu** tax business
  税務署 **zeimusho** tax office
13 税源 **zeigen** source of tax revenue
14 税関 **zeikan** customs; customshouse
  税関吏 **zeikanri** customs officer/inspector
  税関長 **zeikanchō** director of customs

───────── 2 ─────────

4 収税 **shūzei** tax collection
  収税吏 **shūzeiri** tax collector
5 市税 **shizei** city tax
6 年税 **nenzei** annual tax
  印税 **inzei** royalties
  地税 **chizei** land tax
  有税 **yūzei** subject to tax, dutiable

5

石
立
目
禾
田
皿
疒

7 ←

有税品 **yūzeihin** goods subject to duty
血税 **ketsuzei** conscription; heavy taxation
7 村税 **sonzei** village tax
町税 **chōzei** town tax
8 免税 **menzei** tax exemption
免税品 **menzeihin** duty-free goods
府税 **fuzei** urban-prefectural tax
国税 **kokuzei** national tax
物税 **butsuzei** tax on goods and possessions
9 重税 **jūzei** heavy tax
10 郵税 **yūzei** postage
都税 **tozei** metropolitan tax
酒税 **shuzei** liquor tax
租税 **sozei** taxes
納税 **nōzei** payment of taxes
納税者 **nōzeisha** taxpayer
納税額 **nōzeigaku** amount of tax (to be) paid
11 脱税 **datsuzei** tax evasion
悪税 **akuzei** unreasonable tax
12 港税 **kōzei** harbor/port dues
減税 **genzei** tax cut/reduction
廃税 **haizei** abolition of a tax
無税 **muzei** tax-free, duty-free
間税 **kanzei** indirect tax
13 塩税 **enzei** salt tax
14 増税 **zōzei** tax increase
徴税 **chōzei** tax collection, taxation
雑税 **zatsuzei** miscellaneous taxes
関税 **kanzei** customs, tariff, duty
関税率 **kanzeiritsu** customs rates/tariff
15 課税 **kazei** taxtion
課税品 **kazeihin** taxable/dutiable goods
課税率 **kazeiritsu** tax rate
賦税 **fuzei** taxation

─────── 3 ───────

2 人頭税 **jintōzei** poll tax
5 付加税 **fukazei** surtax
6 地方税 **chihōzei** local taxes
有名税 **yūmeizei** a penalty of greatness,
  noblesse oblige
7 住民税 **jūminzei** inhabitants tax
8 非課税 **hikazei** tax exemption
事業税 **jigyōzei** business tax
直接税 **chokusetsuzei** direct tax
追徴税 **tsuichōzei** supplementary/penalty tax
法人税 **hōjinzei** corporation tax
物品税 **buppinzei** commodity/excise tax
物納税 **butsunōzei** tax paid in kind
所得税 **shotokuzei** income tax
9 造石税 **zōkokuzei** liquor-making tax
通行税 **tsūkōzei** toll, transit duty
海関税 **kaikanzei** import duties
相続税 **sōzokuzei** inheritance tax
10 畜犬税 **chikkenzei** dog tax
遊興税 **yūkyōzei** entertainment tax

消費税 **shōhizei** consumption/excise tax
従量税 **jūryōzei** tax/duty computed on the
  quantity rather than the value of a good
家屋税 **kaokuzei** house tax
財産税 **zaisanzei** property tax
11 累進税 **ruishinzei** progressive/graduated tax
12 補完税 **hokanzei** surtax
間接税 **kansetsuzei** indirect tax
16 輸入税 **yunyūzei** import duties/tariff
輸出税 **yushutsuzei** export duties/tax

─────── 4 ───────

13 源泉課税 **gensen kazei** taxation at the
  source, withholding tax

─────── 5 ───────

5 付加価値税 **fuka-kachi zei** value-added tax

5d7.5

稀
    KI, KE, mare rare

─────── 1 ───────

3 稀土 **kido** rare earth
4 稀少 **kishō** scarce
5 稀代 **kidai, kitai** uncommon, rare
6 稀有 **keu** rare, uncommon, extraordinary
10 稀書 **kisho** rare book
11 稀釈 **kishaku** dilution
16 稀薄 **kihaku** thin, weak, dilute, sparse
17 稀覯本 **kikōbon** rare book
稀覯書 **kikōsho** rare book

─────── 2 ───────

5 古稀 **koki** age 70

5d7.6

黍
    SHO, kibi millet

─────── 1 ───────

6 黍団子 **kibidango** millet-flour dumpling

─────── 2 ───────

13 蜀黍 **morokoshi** millet, sorghum

─────── 3 ───────

5 玉蜀黍 **tōmorokoshi** corn, maize
9 砂糖黍 **satō kibi** sugar cane

─────── 8 ───────

5d8.1 / 1230

稚 稺
    CHI, itokena(i) young (child)

─────── 1 ───────

6 稚気 **chiki** childlike state of mind

7 稚児 **chigo** child; child in a Buddhist
     procession
8 稚拙 **chisetsu** artless, naive, childlike
11 稚魚 **chigyo** young fish, fry, fingerling

——————— 2 ———————
2 丁稚 **detchi** apprentice
  丁稚奉公 **detchi bōkō** apprenticeship
5 幼稚 **yōchi** infantile, immature
  幼稚園 **yōchien** kindergarten

5d8.2

稗 稗   **HAI** small
         hic (a barnyard grass)

5d8.3

稘   **KI** one year; straw

5d8.4

稜   **RYŌ** corner; majesty

——————— 1 ———————
15 稜線 **ryōsen** ridgeline
——————— 2 ———————
3 山稜 **sanryō** mountain ridge

5d8.5

稔   **JIN, NEN** ripen, harvest; year

5d8.6

稙   **CHOKU, SHOKU** early(-maturing
        rice)

5d8.7

稠   **CHŪ, CHŌ** many; dense growth

——————— 1 ———————
11 稠密 **chūmitsu** dense, crowded
——————— 2 ———————
11 粘稠 **nenchū, nenchō** thick and viscous

5d8.8

矮   **WAI** low; short, dwarf

——————— 1 ———————
2 矮人 **waijin** dwarf, midget
3 矮小 **waishō** undersized
9 矮星 **waisei** dwarf star
16 矮樹 **waiju** dwarf tree

——————— 9 ———————

5d9.1 / 228

種   **SHU** kind, type, species; seed
      tane seed; kind, species; cause, source
      kusa, -gusa cause, source (of ridicule/
        conversation)

——————— 1 ———————
2 種子 **shushi** seed, pit
  種子島 **tane(ga)shima** matchlock gun,
        harquebus
        Tanegashima (island, Kagoshima-ken)
3 種下 **taneo(roshi)** sowing, seeding, planting
  種々 **shuju, kusagusa** various
  種々相 **shujusō** various phases/aspects
  種々様々 **shuju-samazama** all kinds of,
        diverse
  種々雑多 **shuju-zatta** various, every sort of
4 種切 **tanegi(re)** running out of seeds/
        materials
  種火 **tanebi** pilot light/flame
  種牛 **taneushi** breeding bull
5 種本 **tanehon** source book, manual
  種付 **tanetsu(ke)** mating, stud service
  種皮 **shuhi** seed coat
  種目 **shumoku** item
6 種名 **shumei** species name
7 種別 **shubetsu** classification, assortment
8 種油 **taneabura** rapeseed oil
  種苗 **shubyō** seeds and seedlings
  種板 **taneita** (photographic) negative;
        (projection) slide
  種明 **tanea(kashi)** revealing how a trick is
        done
  種物 **tanemono** seeds; flavored soba; shaved
        ice with fruit syrup
  種物商 **tanemonoshō** seed seller/store
  種取 **taneto(ri)** growing plants for seeds,
        raising livestock for breeding; news
        gathering
9 種変 **tanegawa(ri)** half-brother/half-sister by
        a different father; new strain, hybrid
        variety
  種畑 **tanebatake** seed garden
10 種畜 **shuchiku** breeding stock
  種起原 **shu (no) kigen** (Darwin's) The Origin
        of Species
  種紙 **tanegami** (silkworm) egg card
  種馬 **taneuma** stud horse, sire

5

石
立
目
禾 9←
衤
田
皿
疒

11 種族 **shuzoku** race, tribe
12 種違 **tanechiga(i)** half-brother/half-sister by a different father; new strain, hybrid variety
種属 **shuzoku** kind, genus, species
種無 **tanena(shi)** seedless
種痘 **shutō** vaccination, inoculation
14 種種 **shuju, kusagusa** various
種種相 **shujusō** various aspects/phases
種種様様 **shuju-samazama** all kinds of, diverse
種種雑多 **shuju-zatta** various, every sort of
18 種類 **shurui** kind, type, sort
種類別 **shuruibetsu** classification, assortment

─────── 2 ───────

1 一種 **isshu** a kind, a species; one kind
2 人種 **jinshu** race (of people)
人種改良 **jinshu kairyō** eugenics
子種 **kodane** issue, children, descendants
十種競技 **jisshu kyōgi** decathlon
3 三種神器 **Sanshu (no) Jingi** the Three Sacred Treasures (mirror, sword, and jewels)
下種 **gesu** person of lowly rank, mean person
下種根性 **gesu konjō** mean feelings
4 五種競技 **goshu kyōgi** pentathlon
火種 **hidane** live coals (for kindling)
5 矢種 **yadane** remaining arrows
甲種 **kōshu** grade A
6 多種多様 **tashu-tayō** various, diversified
同種 **dōshu** the same kind, homogeneous
各種 **kakushu** every kind, various types
7 良種 **ryōshu** good breed, thoroughbred
亜種 **ashu** subspecies
別種 **besshu** another kind, distinct species
言種 **i(i)gusa** one's words, remarks
8 育種 **ikushu** (plant) breeding
物種 **monodane** the fundamental thing
9 変種 **henshu** variety, strain; freak of nature
ka(wari)dane a novelty, exceptional case
洋種 **yōshu** Western breed
品種 **hinshu** kind, variety, grade, breed
客種 **kyakudane** quality of the clientele
10 耕種 **kōshu** tilling and planting
原種 **genshu** pure breed; germ
特種 **tokudane** exclusive news, scoop
tokushu special kind/type
純種 **junshu** purebred
11 接種 **sesshu** inoculation, vaccination
採種 **saishu** collecting seeds
菜種 **natane** rapeseed, coleseed, colza
菜種油 **natane abura** rapeseed oil
異種 **ishu** different kind/species
断種 **danshu** (eugenic) sterilization
13 業種 **gyōshu** type of industry, category of business

数種 **sūshu** several kinds
数種類 **sūshurui** several kinds
新種 **shinshu** new type/species
14 種種 **shuju, kusagusa** various
種種相 **shujusō** various aspects/phases
種種様様 **shuju-samazama** all kinds of, diverse
種種雑多 **shuju-zatta** various, every sort of
綿種 **watadane** cottonseed
雑種 **zasshu** of various kinds; mixed breed
15 播種 **hashu** seeding, sowing, planting
噂種 **uwasa (no) tane** source of rumors, subject of gossip
諸種 **shoshu** various/all kinds
16 薬種 **yakushu** drugs, pharmacopoeia
薬種店 **yakushuten** drugstore, apothecary
機種 **kishu** model, type of machine
18 職種 **shokushu** type of occupation
19 艶種 **tsuyadane** love affair/rumor
21 癪種 **shaku (no) tane** cause of offense, peeve
艦種 **kanshu** class of warship

─────── 3 ───────

1 一粒種 **hitotsubudane** an only child
5 白人種 **hakujinshu** white race
6 肉用種 **nikuyōshu** breed of animal raised for meat
9 食人種 **shokujinshu** a cannibal race
11 異人種 **ijinshu** different race
12 短毛種 **tanmōshu** short-haired

─────── 4 ───────

2 人食人種 **hitoku(i) jinshu** cannibals
2 人喰人種 **hitoku(i) jinshu** cannibals
4 予防接種 **yobō sesshu** inoculation
6 近代五種 **kindai goshu** the modern pentathlon
同文同種 **dōbun-dōshu** same script and same race
11 黄色人種 **ōshoku jinshu** the yellow race
13 褐色人種 **kasshoku jinshu** the brown races

稗→稗 5d8.2

稱→称 5d5.8

5d9.2 / 1220

稲 稻 **TŌ, ine, ina-** rice plant

─────── 1 ───────

4 稲刈 **ineka(ri)** rice mowing/reaping
5 稲田 **inada** rice field

6 稲扱 **ineko(ki)** threshing (machine)
稲光 **inabikari** lightning
7 稲作 **inasaku** rice crop
稲車 **inaguruma** cart for loading harvested rice plants onto
8 稲妻 **inazuma** lightning
10 稲荷 **Inari** god of harvests, fox deity
稲荷寿司 **inarizushi** fried tofu stuffed with vinegared rice
15 稲熱病 **imochibyō** rice blight
稲穂 **inaho** ears/heads of rice
18 稲叢 **inamura** rick, stack of rice straw

——————— 2 ———————

4 水稲 **suitō** paddy/wet-land rice
6 早稲 **wase** early-ripening (rice); precocious
10 陸稲 **rikutō, okabo** dry-land rice
12 晩稲 **bantō, okute** late(-maturing) rice

5d9.3

羶 SHŪ, SHU tile flooring, stone pavement

5d9.4 / 1729

穀 穀 KOKU grain, cereals

——————— 1 ———————

8 穀物 **kokumotsu** grain
10 穀倉 **kokusō, kokugura** granary, grain elevator
穀粉 **kokufun** grain flour
11 穀粒 **kokuryū** a grain, kernel
穀断 **kokuda(chi)** abstinence from grains
12 穀象虫 **kokuzō-mushi** rice weevil
15 穀潰 **gokutsubu(shi)** idler, a do-nothing
18 穀類 **kokurui** grains

——————— 2 ———————

4 五穀 **gokoku** the five grains (rice, wheat, *awa* millet, *kibi* millet, beans)
6 米穀 **beikoku** rice
11 脱穀 **dakkoku** threshing
脱穀機 **dakkokuki** threshing machine
13 新穀 **shinkoku** new rice
14 雑穀 **zakkoku** grains
雑穀商 **zakkokushō** grain merchant

——————— 10 ———————

5d10.1

稷 SHOKU, kibi millet

5d10.2 / 1221

穗 穗 SUI, ho ear/head of grain

——————— 1 ———————

6 穂先 **hosaki** tip of an ear/spear/knife/brush
7 穂状 **suijō** shaped like a head of grain
8 穂並 **honami** standing grain
穂波 **honami** waves of grain

——————— 2 ———————

4 刈穂 **ka(ri)ho** harvested ears of rice
5 出穂 **shussui** (grain) coming into ears
7 初穂 **hatsuho** first ears of rice, first harvest
11 接穂 **tsu(gi)ho** grafting, slip, scion
黒穂病 **kurohobyō** smut, blight
12 落穂 **o(chi)bo** fallen (grain) ears, gleanings
落穂拾 **o(chi)bohiro(i)** gleaning; gleaner
13 瑞穂国 **Mizuho(no)kuni** Japan, Land of Vigorous Rice Plants
14 稲穂 **inaho** ears/heads of rice

稻 → 稲 **5d9.2**

5d10.3 / 1750

稼 KA, kase(gu) work, earn (a living)

——————— 1 ———————

2 稼人 **kase(gi)nin** breadwinner; hard worker
4 稼手 **kase(gi)te** breadwinner; hard worker
10 稼高 **kase(gi)daka** earnings
13 稼業 **kagyō** one's trade/occupation
稼働 **kadō** operation, work

——————— 2 ———————

3 山稼 **yamakase(gi)** work in the mountains
4 日稼 **hikase(gi)** day labor
5 出稼 **dekase(gi)** working away from home
6 共稼 **tomokase(gi)** (husband and wife) both working, dual income
8 夜稼 **yokase(gi)** night work; burglary
9 荒稼 **arakase(gi)** a killing (in the stock market), a big haul; robbery
10 旅稼 **tabikase(gi)** work away from home

——————— 3 ———————

8 其日稼 **so(no)hi-kase(gi)** day labor
泥水稼業 **doromizu kagyō** shameful occupation
板間稼 **ita(no)ma kase(gi)** bathhouse thief

5d10.4

裕 YŌ beamish

5d10.5 / 1120

稿 稾

KŌ manuscript, draft; straw

——————— 1 ———————

5 稿本 **kōhon** manuscript
10 稿料 **kōryō** payment for a manuscript

——————— 2 ———————

7 投稿 **tōkō** contribution (to a magazine)
投稿者 **tōkōsha** contributor (to a magazine)
投稿欄 **tōkōran** readers' column
8 画稿 **gakō** a sketch
拙稿 **sekkō** (my) poor manuscript
9 草稿 **sōkō** (rough) draft, notes, manuscript
10 原稿 **genkō** manuscript
原稿用紙 **genkō yōshi** manuscript paper
原稿料 **genkōryō** payment for a manuscript
起稿 **kikō** begin writing, draft
11 寄稿 **kikō** contribute to, write for
寄稿者 **kikōsha** contributor (of articles)
脱稿 **dakkō** finish writing, complete
13 続稿 **zokkō** remaining manuscripts
詩稿 **shikō** draft of a poem
14 遺稿 **ikō** (deceased's) unpublished works
歌稿 **kakō** manuscript of a poem

——————— 3 ———————

5 生原稿 **namagenkō** raw manuscript (not yet typeset)

黎 → **3a10.29**

穀 → 穀 **5d9.4**

——————— 11 ———————

5d11.1

穆

BOKU respectful; mild; beautiful

5d11.2

穄

SHIN, SAN short rice plant

5d11.3

稽 稽

KEI think, consider; stop; reach; bow low

——————— 1 ———————

5 稽古 **keiko** practice, training, drill, rehearsal

稽古台 **keikodai** something/someone to practice on
稽古着 **keikogi** practice/gym suit
9 稽首 **keishu** bowing to the floor

——————— 2 ———————

3 下稽古 **shitageiko** rehearsal, run-through
5 出稽古 **degeiko** giving lessons at the students' homes
代稽古 **daigeiko** act as a substitute teacher
立稽古 **ta(chi)geiko** rehearsal
6 会稽 **kaikei** revenge, vendetta
12 寒稽古 **kangeiko** winter (judo) exercises
無稽 **mukei** unfounded
13 滑稽 **kokkei** comic, funny; joke
滑稽本 **kokkeibon** comic book (Edo period)

——————— 3 ———————

15 舞台稽古 **butai geiko** dress rehearsal

——————— 4 ———————

9 荒唐無稽 **kōtō-mukei** absurdity, nonsense

5d11.4 / 869

穏 穩

ON, oda(yaka) calm, quiet, peaceful, mild, moderate

——————— 1 ———————

6 穏当 **ontō** proper, reasonable, moderate
8 穏和 **onwa** mild, gentle, genial
穏和派 **onwaha** the moderates
穏和論者 **onwaronsha** a moderate
9 穏便 **onbin** gentle, quiet, amicable
10 穏健 **onken** moderate
穏健派 **onkenha** the moderates

——————— 2 ———————

4 不穏 **fuon** unrest, disquiet
不穏当 **fuontō** improper
5 平穏 **heion** calm, peaceful, tranquil
6 安穏 **annon** peaceful, quiet, tranquil
14 静穏 **seion** calm, tranquil

5d11.5 / 656

積

SEKI accumulate; product (in math); size, area, volume **tsu(mu)** heap up, load **tsu(mi)** loading, shipment; capacity **tsu(moru)** be piled up, accumulate; estimate **tsu(mori)** intention; estimate

——————— 1 ———————

2 積入 **tsu(mi)i(reru)** take on (board)
3 積上 **tsu(mi)a(geru)** heap up
4 積切 **tsu(mi)ki(ru)** ship/load completely
積分 **sekibun** integral calculus
積分学 **sekibungaku** integral calculus
積込 **tsu(mi)ko(mu)** load, take on (board)
積木 **tsu(mi)ki** toy blocks; piled timber

積方 **tsu(mi)kata** way of piling/loading
5 積出 **tsu(mi)da(su)** send, ship, forward
積出人 **tsu(mi)da(shi)nin** shipper
積立 **tsu(mi)ta(teru)** save up, amass
積立金 **tsumitatekin** a reserve (fund)
6 積年 **sekinen** (many) years
7 積乱雲 **sekiran'un** cumulonimbus clouds
積戻 **tsu(mi)modo(su)** reship, send back
8 積直 **tsu(mi)nao(su)** reload, pile up again
積送 **sekisō, tsu(mi)oku(ri)** consignment, shipment
積肥 **tsu(mi)goe** compost, manure heap
9 積重 **tsu(mi)kasa(naru)** be piled/stacked up
積卸 **tsu(mi)oro(shi)** loading and unloading; unloading; cargo handling
10 積残 **tsu(mi)noko(su)** omit from a shipment
積荷 **tsu(mi)ni** load, freight, cargo, shipment
積書 **tsu(mori)ga(ki)** written estimate
11 積過 **tsu(mi)su(giru)** overload
積悪 **sekiaku** accumulated sin, series of crimes
積雪 **sekisetsu** fallen snow
12 積善 **sekizen** accumulation of good deeds
積違 **tsu(mori)chiga(i)** incorrect estimate
積換 **tsu(mi)ka(e)** reloading, transshipment
積極 **sekkyoku** positive
積極的 **sekkyokuteki** positive, active
積極性 **sekkyokusei** positiveness
積量 **sekiryō** loadage, carrying capacity
積替 **tsu(mi)ka(e)** reloading, transshipment
積雲 **sekiun** cumulus clouds
13 積置場 **tsu(mi)o(ki)ba** storage/freight yard
積載 **sekisai** lading, loading, carrying
積載量 **sekisairyō** carrying capacity, load
14 積層 **sekisō** lamination, building up layers
積算 **sekisan** integrating (meter)
積読 **tsu(n)doku** acquiring books without reading them
積読主義 **tsu(n)doku shugi** acquiring books without reading them
15 積弊 **sekihei** deep-seated/longstanding evil
16 積積 **tsu(mori)tsu(moru)** keep on piling up

——————— 2 ———————
3 上積 **uwazu(mi)** load/pile on top of
下積 **shitazu(mi)** goods piled underneath; lowest social classes
山積 **yamazu(mi)** big pile
4 心積 **kokorozu(mori)** readiness
6 地積 **chiseki** land area, acreage
7 体積 **taiseki** volume
沖積土 **chūsekido** alluvial soil
沖積期 **chūsekiki** the alluvial epoch
沖積層 **chūsekisō** alluvial stratum
沈積 **chinseki** sedimentation, depositing
見積 **mitsu(moru)** estimate, assess

見積書 **mitsumorisho** written estimate
8 定積 **teiseki** fixed area; constant volume
底積 **sokozu(mi)** goods stowed at the bottom
9 巻積雲 **kensekiun** cirrocumulus clouds
面積 **menseki** area
10 高積雲 **kōsekiun** altocumulus clouds
荷積 **nizu(mi)** loading
容積 **yōseki** capacity, volume
胸積 **munazu(mori)** mental arithmetic; expectation
11 堆積 **taiseki** accumulation, pile, heap
累積 **ruiseki** cumulative
船積 **funazu(mi)** shipment, lading
12 集積 **shūseki** accumulate, amass; integrate
集積回路 **shūseki kairo** integrated circuit
13 微積分 **bisekibun** differential and integral calculus
蓄積 **chikuseki** accumulation, amassing
腹積 **harazu(mori)** anticipating what someone will do; resolve, determination
14 層積雲 **sōsekiun** stratocumulus clouds
16 積積 **tsu(mori)tsu(moru)** keep on piling up
29 鬱積 **usseki** be pent up, be congested

——————— 3 ———————
6 光集積回路 **hikari shūseki kairo** optical integrated circuit
13 微分積分 **bibun-sekibun** differential and integral calculus

穐 → 秋 5d4.1

5d11.6
臻 **SHIN** arrive, reach; gather

——————— 12 ———————
穂 → 穂 5d10.2
稺 → 稚 5d8.1
黏 → 粘 6b5.4

——————— 13 ———————
5d13.1
穡 **SHOKU** harvest

5d13.2

穰 穰 **JŌ** harvest, abundance

———— 2 ————

13 豊穣 **hōjō** abundant harvest

5d13.3

穢 **AI, E, kega(su)** make dirty, defile
kega(reru) be dirty/unclean

———— 1 ————

6 穢多 **eta** old term for "burakumin" (Japanese minority group)

———— 2 ————

6 汚穢 **owai, oai** night soil, muck
汚穢屋 **owaiya** night-soil man
9 浄穢 **jōe** the pure and the profane

5d13.4 / 1314

穫 **KAKU** harvest

———— 2 ————

4 収穫 **shūkaku** harvest
収穫予想 **shūkaku yosō** crop estimate
収穫物 **shūkakubutsu** harvest, crop, yield
収穫高 **shūkakudaka** yield, crop
収穫時 **shūkakuji** time of harvest
収穫祭 **shūkakusai** harvest festival
収穫期 **shūkakuki** harvest time

5d13.5

馥 **FUKU** fragrance

———— 1 ————

8 馥郁 **fukuiku** fragrant, balmy

5d13.6

魏 **GI** high, large

———— 14 ————

穏 → 穏 5d11.4

穢 → 5d13.3

5d14.1

麕 **KIN, noro** roe deer

———— 15 ————

馨 → 4c16.2

———— 17 ————

穰 → 穣 5d13.2

5d17.1

黐 **CHI, mochi** (bird)lime; ilex, holm oak

———— 18 ————

龝 → 秋 5d4.1

————————— 衤 5e —————————

衣	初	衫	表	袒	袂	衲	衽	衿	袖	袢	被	袙
0.1	2.1	3.1	0a8.6	4.1	4.2	4.3	4.4	4.5	5.1	5.2	5.3	5.4

袍	袓	袮	袗	裒	袈	袋	衎	袱	袛	袿	袴	袴
5.5	5.6	4e14.1	5.8	5.9	5.10	5.11	6.1	6.2	5e4.4	6.3	6.4	6.5

袷	裂	装	裁	補	裡	裙	裕	裔	裘	裝	裟	裊
6.6	6.7	6.8	6.9	7.1	2j11.2	7.2	7.3	7.4	7.5	5e6.8	7.6	7.7

裸	裨	補	褂	褄	裼	褐	裾	製	裴	褓	褐	禅
8.1	8.2	8.3	8.4	8.5	8.6	8.7	8.8	8.9	8.10	9.1	5e8.7	5e12.1

褌	複	褊	褪	褞	褥	褫	褪	褸	褶	襀	襖	襍
9.2	9.3	9.4	9.5	10.1	10.2	10.3	11.1	11.2	11.3	11.4	5e13.1	8c6.2

Left margin vertical: **5** 石 立 目 禾 衤 囲 皿 疒 →13

襌	襖	襟	褙	襞	襦	襪	襭	襤	襯	襲	襷	襴
12.1	13.1	13.2	13.3	13.4	14.1	14.2	15.1	15.2	16.1	16.2	17.1	17.2

─────────── 0 ───────────

5e0.1 / 677

衣 **I, E, koromo** garment, clothes
kinu clothing, kimono

─────────── 1 ───────────

4 衣手 **koromode** sleeve
8 衣服 **ifuku** clothes, clothing
9 衣冠 **ikan** nobleman's kimono and headdress
衣冠束帯 **ikan-sokutai** full court dress; Shinto priest's vestments
衣食 **ishoku** food and clothing
衣食住 **ishokujū** food, clothing, and shelter
10 衣桁 **ikō** clothes rack
衣紋 **emon** clothes, one's dress
衣紋掛 **emonka(ke)** hanger/rack (for kimono)
衣料 **iryō** clothing
11 衣魚 **shimi** clothes moth, silverfish, book-worm
12 衣替 **koromoga(e)** seasonal change of clothes
衣装 **ishō** clothes, wardrobe, dress
13 衣鉢 **ihatsu** (assume one's master's) mantle
14 衣裳 **ishō** clothes, wardrobe, dress
衣裳方 **ishōkata** (theater) wardrobe assistant
衣裳持 **ishōmo(chi)** one who has a large wardrobe
17 衣擦 **kinuzu(re)** rustling of clothes
18 衣糧 **iryō** food and clothing
衣類 **irui** clothing

─────────── 2 ───────────

1 一衣帯水 **ichii taisui** narrow strait
3 上衣 **uwagi** coat, jacket
4 天衣無縫 **ten'i-muhō** flawless, perfect
5 囚衣 **shūi** prisoner's clothes
白衣 **hakui, byakue, byakui** white robe, lab coat
6 羽衣 **hagoromo** robe of feathers
汗衣 **kan'i** underwear; sweaty clothes
地衣 **chii** lichen
戎衣 **jūi** armor; military uniform
7 更衣 **kōi** changing one's clothes; lady court attendant **koromogae** seasonal change of clothing
更衣室 **kōishitsu** clothes-changing room
8 法衣 **hōi** vestments, priestly robes
征衣 **seii** military uniform; traveling clothes
9 便衣 **ben'i** ordinary clothes
軍衣 **gun'i** military clothes, uniform
浄衣 **jōi, jōe** pure white robe
狩衣 **ka(ri)ginu** (nobleman's silk garment)

単衣 **tan'i, hitoe** (summer) kimono with no lining
胞衣 **hōi, ena** placenta, afterbirth
10 浴衣 **yukata, yokui** light cotton kimono, bathrobe
浴衣掛 **yukataga(ke)** wearing a yukata
唐衣 **karakoromo, karagoromo** ancient Chinese clothes; strange clothes
夏衣 **natsugoromo** summer clothing
11 脱衣 **datsui** take off one's clothes, undress
脱衣所 **datsuisho, datsuijo** changing/dressing room
黒衣 **kokui** black clothes
粗衣 **soi** coarse/poor clothing
12 着衣 **chakui** dressing (oneself); one's clothes
御衣 **gyoi** imperial clothes
敝衣 **heii** shabby clothes
13 僧衣 **sōi** priest's vestment
14 獄衣 **gokui** prison uniform
15 弊衣 **heii** shabby clothes
16 糖衣 **tōi** sugar coating
糖衣錠 **tōijō** sugar-coated pill
17 濡衣 **nu(re)ginu** wet clothes; false charge
濡衣着 **nu(re)ginu (o) ki(serareru)** be falsely accused
擣衣 **tōi** pounding cloth to make it glossy
18 鶉衣 **uzuragoromo** patched clothes
19 羅衣 **rai** thin kimono

─────────── 3 ───────────

4 手術衣 **shujutsui** operating gown
7 作業衣 **sagyōi** work clothes

─────────── 2 ───────────

5e2.1 / 679

初 **SHO, haji(me)** beginning
haji(mete) for the first time
hatsu-, ui- first **-someru** begin to

─────────── 1 ───────────

1 初一念 **shoichinen** one's original intention
2 初七日 **shonanoka, shonanuka** (religious service on) the seventh day after someone's death
初子 **hatsugo** one's first child
3 初々 **uiui(shii)** innocent, naive, unsophisticated
初口 **shokuchi** beginning
4 初手 **shote** beginning
初日 **hatsuhi** New Year's Day sunrise **shonichi** first/opening day
初日出 **hatsuhi(no)de** New Year's Day sunrise

初心 **shoshin** inexperience; original intention
初心者 **shoshinsha** beginner
5 初出 **shoshutsu** first appearance/occurrence
初生 **shosei** newborn **hatsuna(ri)** first fruits
初生児 **shoseiji** newborn baby
初代 **shodai** the first generation; the founder
初氷 **hatsugōri** first ice of the winter
初号 **shogō** first number/issue (of a magazine)
初句 **shoku** first line (of a poem)
初犯 **shohan** first offense/offender
初冬 **shotō** beginning of winter; tenth lunar month
6 初年 **shonen** first year, early years
初年兵 **shonenhei** new soldier, raw recruit
初年級 **shonenkyū** beginners' class
初任 **shonin** first appointment
初任給 **shoninkyū** starting salary
初老 **shorō** early old age (formerly 40, now about 60)
初回 **shokai** the first time
初旬 **shojun** first ten days of the month
初耳 **hatsumimi** something heard for the first time
7 初更 **shokō** first watch (8–10 p.m.)
初対面 **shotaimen** first meeting
初役 **hatsuyaku** (actor's) first role
初花 **hatsuhana** first flowers of the season
初学者 **shogakusha** beginner, new student
初志 **shoshi** original intention
初売 **hatsuu(ri)** first sale of the new year
初見 **shoken** seeing for the first time
初初 **uiui(shii)** innocent, naive, unsophisticated
8 初受賞 **hatsujushō** winning a prize for the first time
初夜 **shoya** first night; wedding night; first watch (8–10 p.m.)
初版 **shohan** first edition
初空 **hatsuzora, hatsusora** the morning sky on New Year's Day
初歩 **shoho** rudiments, ABCs
初物 **hatsumono** first produce of the season
初物食 **hatsumonogu(i)** novelty seeker
9 初発 **shohatsu** first, initial, incipient
初孫 **uimago, hatsumago** one's first grandchild
初陣 **uijin** one's first campaign, baptism of fire
初盆 **hatsubon** first o-Bon festival after someone's death
初速 **shosoku** initial/muzzle velocity
初段 **shodan** lowest grade/rank
初姿 **hatsusugata** first dress-up (in New Year's kimono)
初星 **hatsuboshi** first star-mark (indicating a win in sumo)

初春 **shoshun** early spring
初音 **hatsune** (bird's) first song
初秋 **shoshū** early autumn
初級 **shokyū** beginners' class
10 初値 **hatsune** first price (of a stock in the new year)
初恋 **hatsukoi** one's first love
初荷 **hatsuni** first cargo/shipment of the new year
初席 **hatsuseki** first variety-show performance of the new year
初校 **shokō** first proofs
初時雨 **hatsushigure** first winter rain
初夏 **shoka** early summer
初航海 **hatsukōkai** maiden voyage
11 初婚 **shokon** one's first marriage
初産 **shosan, shozan, uizan, hatsuzan** one's first childbirth
初産児 **shosanji** one's first(born) child
初産婦 **shosanpu** woman having her first child
初経 **shokei** one's first menstruation
初訳 **shoyaku** first(-ever) translation
初雪 **hatsuyuki** first snow of the season
12 初着 **hatsugi** first dress-up clothes worn in the new year; new clothing worn for the first time
初湯 **hatsuyu** first bath (of the new year)
初場所 **hatsubasho** New Year's grand sumo tournament
初期 **shoki** early period/stage, beginning
初期化 **shokika** initialization
初給 **shokyū** starting salary
初等 **shotō** elementary
初等科 **shotōka** elementary/beginners' course
初診 **shoshin** first medical examination
初診料 **shoshinryō** fee for patient's first visit
13 初夢 **hatsuyume** first dream of the new year
初節句 **hatsuzekku** child's first festival
初詣 **hatsumōde** first shrine/temple visit in the new year
14 初演 **shoen** first performance, premiere
15 初舞台 **hatsubutai** one's stage debut
初潮 **shochō** one's first menstruation
初審 **shoshin** first trial/instance
初穂 **hatsuho** first ears of rice, first harvest
初縁 **shoen** one's first marriage
16 初興行 **hatsukōgyō** first performance, premiere
初頭 **shotō** beginning
17 初霜 **hatsushimo** first frost of the season
18 初顔合 **hatsukaoa(wase)** first meeting

————— 2 —————
4 太初 **taisho** the beginning of the world

5 出初 **dezome** first appearance, debut;
　　　firemen's New Year's demonstrations
　出初式 **dezomeshiki** firemen's New Year's
　　　demonstrations
6 年初 **nensho** beginning of the year
　仮初 **karisome** temporary; trivial
　当初 **tōsho** initial, original; at the beginning
7 売初 **u(ri)zo(me)** placing on sale for the first
　　　time; first New Year's sale
　見初 **miso(meru)** see for the first time; fall in
　　　love at first sight
　初 **uiui(shii)** innocent, naive, unsophisti-
　　　cated
9 咲初 **sa(ki)so(meru)** begin to bloom
　思初 **omo(i)so(meru)** fall in love with
　食初 **ta(be)zo(me), ku(i)zo(me)** weaning
　　　ceremony
10 書初 **ka(ki)zo(me)** first writing of the new
　　　year
12 着初 **kizo(me)** first wearing (of a suit)
　渡初 **wata(ri)zo(me)** bridge-opening
　　　ceremony
　弾初 **hi(ki)zome** the New Year's first
　　　playing of an instrument
　最初 **saisho** the first/beginning
　買初 **ka(i)zo(me)** first purchase of the new
　　　year
13 馴初 **na(re)so(me)** beginning of a romance

———————— 3 ————————

5e3.1

杉

SAN thin kimono

表→   **0a8.6**

———————— 4 ————————

5e4.1

袒

JITSU everyday clothing; underwear

5e4.2

袂

BEI, tamoto sleeve; foot (of a mountain), edge

5e4.3

衲

DŌ, NŌ mend; priest's vestments;
priest

5e4.4

衽　袵

JIN collar, hem
okumi gusset, gore

5e4.5

衿

KIN, eri neck, collar, lapel

———————— 1 ————————

0 V衿 **vīeri, buieri** V-neck (sweater)

———————— 2 ————————

5 半衿 **han'eri** (kimono) neckpiece
13 裏衿 **uraeri** neckband lining

———————— 5 ————————

5e5.1

袖

SHŪ, sode sleeve

———————— 1 ————————

3 袖丈 **sodetake** sleeve length
　袖口 **sodeguchi** edge of a sleeve, cuff
4 袖手 **shūshu** putting one's hands in one's
　　　sleeves; shunning effort
　袖手傍観 **shūshu-bōkan** look on with arms
　　　folded
9 袖垣 **sodegaki** low fence (flanking a gate)
　袖珍本 **shūchinbon** pocket-size book
12 袖無 **sodena(shi)** sleeveless

———————— 2 ————————

3 小袖 **kosode** quilted silk garment
5 半袖 **hansode** short sleeves
　平袖 **hirasode** wide sleeves
6 両袖 **ryōsode** both sleeves
7 角袖 **kakusode** square/bag sleeves;
　　　plainclothes policeman (in Meiji period)
8 長袖 **nagasode** long sleeves
12 筒袖 **tsutsusode** tight sleeve, tight-sleeved
　　　dress
14 領袖 **ryōshū** leader, boss
18 鎧袖一触 **gaishū-isshoku** easy victory

———————— 3 ————————

2 七分袖 **shichibusode** three-quarter sleeves
5 目引袖引 **mehi(ki)-sodehi(ki)** (belittle by)
　　　winking and tugging at (someone's)
　　　sleeve

5e5.2

袢

HAN short summer kimono

———————— 2 ————————

19 襦袢 **juban** underwear (worn under kimono)

───────── 3 ─────────

6 肉襦袢 **nikujuban** tights, leotards
  肌襦袢 **hadajuban** underwear
8 長襦袢 **nagajuban** long underwear
15 膚襦袢 **hadajuban** underwear

5e5.3 / 976

被 **HI** receive; (prefix indicating being acted upon), -ed, -ee **kōmu(ru)** incur, suffer, receive **kabu(ru)** wear, put on (one's head); take (the blame)
kabu(seru) place/pour on top of, cover
kabu(saru) get covered, hang over
ō(u) cover **ō(i)** a cover(ing)

───────── 1 ─────────

5 被写体 **hishatai** subject/object photographed
  被圧迫 **hiappaku** oppressed
7 被告 **hikoku** defendant
  被告人 **hikokunin** defendant
  被告席 **hikokuseki** defendant's chair, the dock
  被災 **hisai** be stricken, suffer from
  被災者 **hisaisha** victim, sufferer
8 被治者 **hichisha** the governed
  被服 **hifuku** clothing
  被物 **kabu(ri)mono** headgear, headdress
9 被保険物 **hihokenbutsu** insured property
  被保護国 **hihogokoku** protectorate, dependency
  被保護者 **hihogosha** ward
  被後見者 **hikōkensha** ward
10 被害 **higai** damage, harm, injury
  被害地 **higaichi** the stricken area
  被害者 **higaisha** victim
14 被疑者 **higisha** a suspect
  被選挙人 **hisenkyonin** person eligible for election
  被選挙権 **hisenkyoken** eligibility for election
18 被覆 **hifuku** covering, coating, insulation
19 被曝 **hibaku** exposure (to radiation)
  被爆 **hibaku** being bombed
  被爆者 **hibakusha** bombing victims

───────── 2 ─────────

3 土被 **tsuchikaburi** (white mushroom, diameter 4–18 cm); overburden, earth cover
4 引被 **hi(k)kabu(ru)** pull over one's head
8 法被 **happi** (workman's) livery coat
11 猫被 **nekokabu(ri)** feigned innocence
12 買被 **ka(i)kabu(ru)** pay too much for; overrate
16 薦被 **komokabu(ri)** saké cask wrapped in straw matting
  頬被 **hōkabu(ri)** mask one's cheeks with a cloth; feign ignorance

───────── 3 ─────────

6 刑事被告 **keiji hikoku** the accused, defendant

5e5.4

袚 **BATSU** warrior's headband

5e5.5

袍 **HŌ** coat

───────── 2 ─────────

15 縕袍 **dotera** padded/quilted kimono
16 褞袍 **dotera** padded/quilted kimono

5e5.6

袒 **TAN** bare one's shoulder; strip to the waist

袮 → 禰 **4e14.1**

5e5.8

袗 **SHIN** thin kimono; embroidery

5e5.9

裊 **horo** hood, top, awning, cover

5e5.10

袈 **KE** (used phonetically)

───────── 1 ─────────

13 袈裟 **kesa** Buddhist priest's surplice draped from left shoulder to right side
  袈裟掛 **kesaga(ke)** hanging/slashed diagonally from the shoulder

───────── 2 ─────────

3 大袈裟 **ōgesa** exaggerated

5e5.11 / 1329

 TAI, fukuro sack, bag, pouch

— 1 —

0 お袋 **(o)fukuro** mom
ビニール袋 **binīru-bukuro** plastic (vinyl) bag
ポリ袋 **pori-bukuro** plastic (polyethlene) bag
2 袋入 **fukuroi(ri)** in bags, sacked, pouched
3 袋小路 **fukurokōji** blind alley, cul-de-sac
5 袋叩 **fukurodata(ki)** gang up on and beat up
6 袋耳 **fukuromimi** retentive memory
8 袋物 **fukuromono** bags and pouches
10 袋帯 **fukuroobi** double-woven obi
14 袋網 **fukuroami** bag/tunnel net
15 袋縫 **fukuronu(i)** double sewing
18 袋織 **fukuroo(ri)** double weaving

— 2 —

4 匂袋 **nioibukuro** sachet
手袋 **tebukuro** gloves, mittens
戸袋 **tobukuro** case into which shutters slide when not in use
5 氷袋 **kōribukuro** ice bag/pack
布袋 **Hotei** (a potbellied god of fortune)
布袋腹 **hoteibara** potbelly, paunch
6 有袋動物 **yūtai dōbutsu** a marsupial
7 状袋 **jōbukuro** envelope
足袋 **tabi** Japanese socks, tabi
足袋屋 **tabiya** tabi seller/shop
9 風袋 **fūtai** tare, weight of the packaging; outward appearance
浮袋 **u(ki)bukuro** air bladder; life preserver, float
革袋 **kawabukuro** leather bag; wineskin
砂袋 **sunabukuro** sandbag; gizzard
胃袋 **ibukuro** stomach
10 郵袋 **yūtai** mailbag
紙袋 **kamibukuro** paper sack/bag
11 蛍袋 **hotarubukuro** bellflower
12 御袋 **ofukuro** one's mom, mama
13 寝袋 **nebukuro** sleeping bag
14 網袋 **amibukuro** net bag
16 薬袋 **yakutai** small paper container for dispensing medicine

— 3 —

4 手提袋 **tesa(ge)bukuro** handbag
8 知恵袋 **chiebukuro** one's close advisers
9 信玄袋 **shingenbukuro** cloth bag
南京袋 **nankinbukuro** gunny sack
11 救命袋 **kyūmeibukuro** escape chute
12 堪忍袋 **kanninbukuro** patience, forbearance
16 頭陀袋 **zudabukuro** (pilgrim's) holdall-bag

— 4 —

6 地下足袋 **jika tabi** split-toed heavy-cloth work shoes

— 6 —

5e6.1

裄 **yuki** sleeve length

— 1 —

3 裄丈 **yukitake** sleeve length and dress length

5e6.2

袱 **FUKU, furoshiki** wrapping kerchief

袵→衽 **5e4.4**

5e6.3

袿 **KEI** garment

5e6.4

袴 **KO, hakama** (divided skirt for men's formal wear)

5e6.5

裃 **kamishimo** (samurai's ceremonial garment)

5e6.6

袷 **KŌ, awase** lined kimono

5e6.7 / 1330

裂 **RETSU, sa(keru/ku)** (intr./tr.) split, tear, rip, burst

— 1 —

5 裂目 **sa(ke)me** rip, split, crack, fissure
6 裂地 **kireji** fabric, cloth, material, piece goods
12 裂開 **rekkai** burst open
13 裂傷 **resshō** laceration

— 2 —

2 八裂 **ya(tsu)za(ki)** tear limb from limb
4 分裂 **bunretsu** dissolution, breakup, division
引裂 **hi(ki)sa(ku)** tear up/off, rip up/open, rend, separate

7 決裂 **ketsuretsu** breakdown, rupture, collapse
9 炸裂 **sakuretsu** explode, burst
炸裂弾 **sakuretsudan** explosive shell
10 破裂 **haretsu** bursting, rupture, explosion
釘裂 **kugiza(ki)** tearing (clothes) on a nail
11 亀裂 **kiretsu** crack, fissure
張裂 **ha(ri)sa(keru)** split open, burst
13 滅裂 **metsuretsu** in chaos, incoherent
鉤裂 **kagiza(ki)** a tear (in one's clothes)
16 縦裂 **tateza(ki)** ripping lengthwise
19 爆裂 **bakuretsu** explosion, blasting
爆裂弾 **bakuretsudan** explosive shell

———— 3 ————

10 核分裂 **kakubunretsu** nuclear fission

———— 4 ————

4 支離滅裂 **shiri-metsuretsu** incoherent, inconsistent, chaotic
5 四分五裂 **shibun-goretsu** disruption, disintegration
14 精神分裂症 **seishin bunretsushō** schizophrenia

5e6.8 / 1328

装 装

SŌ, SHŌ, yosō(u) wear; feign, pretend, disguise oneself as
yosō(i) dress, garb, equipment

———— 1 ————

2 装丁 **sōtei** binding
5 装甲 **sōkō** armor, armor plating
装甲車 **sōkōsha** armored car
7 装身具 **sōshingu** personal accessories
装束 **shōzoku** attire, dress
8 装具 **sōgu** equipment, accouterments
12 装備 **sōbi** equipment
装着 **sōchaku** equip, fit, put, place
装幀 **sōtei** binding
装弾 **sōdan** load (a gun)
13 装填 **sōten** a charge (of gunpowder)
装置 **sōchi** device, apparatus, equipment
装飾 **sōshoku** ornament, decoration
装飾的 **sōshokuteki** ornamental, decorative
装飾品 **sōshokuhin** ornaments, decorations, accessories
装飾音 **sōshokuon** grace note
16 装薬 **sōyaku** charging with gunpowder

———— 2 ————

3 女装 **josō** female attire, drag
5 包装 **hōsō** packaging, packing, wrapping
正装 **seisō** full dress/uniform
白装束 **shiroshōzoku** (clothed) all in white
礼装 **reisō** ceremonial/full dress
6 仮装 **kasō** disguise, fancy dress; converted (cruiser)
仮装舞踏会 **kasō butōkai** masquerade ball

衣装 **ishō** clothes, wardrobe, dress
7 扮装 **funsō** impersonate
改装 **kaisō** remodel, refurbish
男装 **dansō** male attire
8 表装 **hyōsō** mount (a picture); bind (a book)
実装 **jissō** mounting, packaging
服装 **fukusō** dress, attire
服装随意 **fukusō zuii** informal attire
武装 **busō** arms; armed (neutrality)
和装 **wasō** Japanese clothing/binding
9 軍装 **gunsō** soldier's equipment
変装 **hensō** disguise
美装 **bisō** fine dress, rich attire
洋装 **yōsō** Western dress
10 特装 **tokusō** specially equipped
特装版 **tokusōban** specially bound edition
旅装 **ryosō** traveling clothes
11 偽装 **gisō** camouflage
黒装束 **kuroshōzoku** black clothes
略装 **ryakusō** everyday clothes, informal dress
盛装 **seisō** gala dress, resplendent regalia
12 着装 **chakusō** put on, install, attach
軸装 **jikusō** mounting (a scroll)
軽装 **keisō** light dress/equipment
13 塗装 **tosō** painting, coating
新装 **shinsō** new equipment, refurbishing, redecorated
15 儀装 **gisō** ceremonial equipment
舗装 **hosō** pavement, paving
鋪装 **hosō** pavement
19 艤装 **gisō** fitting out a ship, rigging

———— 3 ————

6 再武装 **saibusō** rearmament
安全装置 **anzen sōchi** safety device
8 非武装 **hibusō** demilitarized (zone), unarmed (neutrality)
9 室内装飾 **shitsunai sōshoku** interior decorating
10 核武装 **kakubusō** nuclear arms

5e6.9 / 1123

裁

SAI, saba(ku) pass judgment
ta(tsu) cut out (cloth/leather)

———— 1 ————

4 裁方 **ta(chi)kata** cutting, cut (of one's clothes)
5 裁可 **saika** approval, sanction
7 裁判 **saiban** trial, hearing
裁判長 **saibanchō** presiding judge
裁判官 **saibankan** the judge
裁判所 **saibansho** (law) court
裁判権 **saibanken** jurisdiction
裁決 **saiketsu** decision, ruling
8 裁定 **saitei** decision, ruling, arbitration

裁板 **ta(chi)ita** tailor's cutting board
11 裁断 **saidan** cutting and shearing (cloth); judgment, ruling
裁断師 **saidanshi** cutter, tailor
12 裁量 **sairyō** discretion
15 裁縫 **saihō** sewing, tailoring, dressmaking
ta(chi)nu(i) cutting and sewing

────── 2 ──────
4 公裁 **kōsai** judicial decision
区裁判所 **kusaibansho** local court
6 仲裁 **chūsai** arbitration, mediation
仲裁人 **chūsainin** arbitrator, mediator
仲裁者 **chūsaisha** arbitrator, mediator
地裁 **chisai** district court (short for 地方裁判所)
自裁 **jisai** suicide
7 体裁 **teisai** decency, form, appearance, effect
体裁上 **teisaijō** for sake of appearances
体裁振 **teisaibu(ru)** put on airs, pose
決裁 **kessai** decide upon, approve
8 制裁 **seisai** sanctions, punishment
和裁 **wasai** sewing kimonos
9 勅裁 **chokusai** imperial decision/approval
洋裁 **yōsai** (Western) dressmaking
洋裁師 **yōsaishi** dressmaker
独裁 **dokusai** autocracy, dictatorship
独裁制 **dokusaisei** dictatorship
独裁的 **dokusaiteki** dictatorial
独裁者 **dokusaisha** dictator
独裁政治 **dokusai seiji** dictatorship, autocracy
10 高裁 **kōsai** High Court (short for 高等裁判所)
原裁判 **gensaiban** the original decision/judgment
11 剪裁 **sensai** shear, cut, trim, prune
剪裁機 **sensaiki** shearing machine
12 御裁可 **gosaika** imperial sanction/approval
14 総裁 **sōsai** president, governor
16 親裁 **shinsai** imperial decision

────── 3 ──────
4 不体裁 **futeisai** in bad form, unseemly, improper
5 民事裁判 **minji saiban** civil trial
7 即決裁判 **sokketsu saiban** summary trial
8 宗教裁判 **shūkyō saiban** the Inquisition
9 軍事裁判 **gunji saiban** court-martial
10 家庭裁判所 **katei saibansho** Family Court
12 最高裁 **Saikōsai** Supreme Court
最高裁判所 **Saikō Saibansho** Supreme Court
15 調停裁判 **chōtei saiban** court arbitration
18 簡易裁判所 **kan'i saibansho** summary court

────── 4 ──────
13 鉄拳制裁 **tekken seisai** the law of the fist

────── 7 ──────

5e7.1 / 889

補

HO assist, supplement
ogina(u) supply, make up for, compensate for, offset

────── 1 ──────
0 補する **ho(suru)** appoint, assign
4 補欠 **hoketsu** filling a vacancy
5 補正 **hosei** revision, compensation
6 補任 **honin** appoint
補充 **hojū** supplement, replacement
補充兵 **hojūhei** reservists
補充隊 **hojūtai** the reserves
補色 **hoshoku** complementary color
補回 **hokai** extra innings (in baseball)
補回戦 **hokaisen** game extended into overtime
補血 **hoketsu** replenishing one's blood
補血剤 **hoketsuzai** an antianemic
7 補佐 **hosa** aide, adviser
補助 **hojo** assistance, supplement, subsidy
補助金 **hojokin** subsidy, grant
補角 **hokaku** supplementary angle
補完 **hokan** complement, supplement
補完税 **hokanzei** surtax
補足 **hosoku** supply, replenish, supplement
補足語 **hosokugo** a complement (in grammar)
8 補注 **hochū** supplementary note
補肥 **hohi** supplementary fertilizer
9 補則 **hosoku** supplementary rules
10 補修 **hoshū** repair
補殺 **hosatsu** an assist (in baseball)
補記 **hoki** add/append (to an article)
11 補強 **hokyō** reinforce, shore up
補習 **hoshū** supplementary/continuing (education)
12 補給 **hokyū** supply, replenish
補筆 **hohitsu** add/append to (a work)
補註 **hochū** supplementary note
補間 **hokan** interpolation
13 補填 **hoten** fill, supply (a deficiency), compensate for
14 補遺 **hoi** supplement, addendum, appendix
補導 **hodō** guidance
補綴 **hotetsu** (dental) prosthetics; rewrite; mend **hotei** rewrite (a script)
補語 **hogo** a complement (in grammar)
16 補整 **hosei** manipulation, adjustment
17 補償 **hoshō** compensation, indemnification
補償金 **hoshōkin** indemnity, compensation (money)
補聴器 **hochōki** hearing aid
補講 **hokō** supplementary lecture
18 補職 **hoshoku** appointment (to a post)

5

石
立
目
禾
衤 7←
田
皿
疒

─────────── 2 ───────────
10 候補 **kōho** candidacy
候補生 **kōhosei** cadet
候補地 **kōhochi** proposed site
候補者 **kōhosha** candidate
修補 **shūho** repair
11 訳補 **yakuho** translate adding explanatory
passages
転補 **tenpo** transfer (job assignments)
13 填補 **tenpo** fill up; compensate for, make
good; replenish, complete
試補 **shiho** probationer, beginner
14 増補 **zōho** enlarge, supplement
─────────── 3 ───────────
5 立候補 **rikkōho** stand/run for office,
announce one's candidacy
─────────── 4 ───────────
7 改訂増補 **kaitei-zōho** revised and enlarged

裡→裏 2j11.2

5e7.2
裙
KUN skirt; hem

5e7.3 / 1391
裕
YŪ surplus

─────────── 1 ───────────
13 裕福 **yūfuku** wealth, affluence
─────────── 2 ───────────
7 余裕 **yoyū** surplus, leeway, room, margin
12 富裕 **fuyū** wealthy, affluent
13 寛裕 **kan'yū** magnanimity

5e7.4
裔
EI descendant; border

─────────── 2 ───────────
5 末裔 **matsuei** descendant
9 後裔 **kōei** descendant

5e7.5
裘
KYŪ leather/fur clothing

裝→装 5e6.8

5e7.6
裟
SA (used phonetically)

─────────── 2 ───────────
11 袈裟 **kesa** Buddhist priest's surplice draped
from left shoulder to right side
袈裟掛 **kesaga(ke)** hanging/slashed diagonally from the shoulder
─────────── 3 ───────────
3 大袈裟 **ōgesa** exaggerated

5e7.7
裊
JŌ, tao(yaka) graceful, svelte

─────────── 8 ───────────

5e8.1 / 1536
裸
RA, hadaka naked

─────────── 1 ───────────
1 裸一貫 **hadaka ikkan** with no property but
one's body
2 裸子植物 **rashi shokubutsu** gymnospermous plant
3 裸女 **rajo** nude woman
裸山 **hadakayama** bare mountain/hills
5 裸出 **rashutsu** exposure, denudation
6 裸虫 **hadakamushi** caterpillar
7 裸身 **rashin** nakedness
裸体 **ratai** naked body, nudity
裸体主義 **ratai shugi** nudism
裸体画 **rataiga** nude picture
裸坊 **hadaka(n)bō** naked person
裸麦 **hadakamugi** (a species of) rye
裸足 **hadashi** bare feet, barefooted
8 裸参 **hadakamai(ri)** visiting a shrine naked
(in winter)
10 裸値 **hadakane** net price
裸馬 **hadakauma** unsaddled horse
11 裸婦 **rafu** nude woman
裸眼 **ragan** the naked eye
13 裸電球 **hadaka denkyū** light bulb without a
lampshade
14 裸像 **razō** nude statue
15 裸線 **hadakasen, rasen** bare wire
─────────── 2 ───────────
3 丸裸 **maru hadaka** naked

5 半裸体 **hanratai** seminude
6 全裸 **zenra** stark naked, nude
7 赤裸 **akahadaka** stark naked
　赤裸々 **sekirara** stark naked; frank, outspoken
10 真裸 **ma(p)padaka** stark naked
　素裸 **suhadaka, su(p)padaka** stark naked

5e8.2

禆 **HI** help, supplement

――――――― 1 ―――――――
10 裨益 **hieki** benefit/profit by

5e8.3

裲 **RYŌ** padded sleeveless kimono; robe

――――――― 1 ―――――――
18 裲襠 **uchikake** (a long outer garment)

5e8.4

褂 **KAI** garment

5e8.5

褄 **tsuma** skirt

――――――― 2 ―――――――
4 辻褄 **tsujitsuma** coherence, consistency

5e8.6

褐 **SEKI** bare one's shoulder

5e8.7 / 1623

褐 褐 **KATSU** rough woolen clothing; brown

――――――― 1 ―――――――
6 褐色 **kasshoku** brown
　褐色人種 **kasshoku jinshu** the brown races
9 褐炭 **kattan** brown coal, lignite
――――――― 2 ―――――――
7 赤褐色 **sekkasshoku** reddish brown
9 茶褐色 **chakasshoku** brown
11 淡褐色 **tankasshoku** light brown
　黒褐色 **kokkasshoku** blackish brown
13 暗褐色 **ankasshoku** dark brown

　鉄褐色 **tekkasshoku** iron gray
16 濃褐色 **nōkasshoku** dark brown

5e8.8

裾 **KYO, suso** hem, skirt, cuff; foot of a mountain

――――――― 1 ―――――――
4 裾刈 **susoga(ri)** trim (someone's) hair just above the nape
　裾分 **susowa(ke)** sharing (of a gift)
6 裾回 **susomawa(shi)** hemline (of a kimono)
8 裾物 **susomono** lower-grade goods
9 裾除 **susoyo(ke)** underskirt
11 裾野 **susono** foot of a mountain
13 裾裏 **susoura** hem lining
14 裾模様 **suso moyō** skirt design
　裾綿 **susowata** cotton kimono skirt padding
――――――― 2 ―――――――
3 山裾 **yamasuso** foot of a mountain
14 裳裾 **mosuso** skirt, train

5e8.9 / 428

製 **SEI** make, manufacture; (as suffix) made in/of/by …

――――――― 1 ―――――――
0 製する **sei(suru)** make, manufacture
5 製本 **seihon** bookbinding
　製氷 **seihyō** icemaking
　製氷所 **seihyōsho** ice plant
　製氷機 **seihyōki** ice machine
6 製缶 **seikan** making cans/boilers
　製缶工場 **seikan kōjō** cannery
　製糸 **seishi** silk reeling
　製糸業 **seishigyō** the silk industry
7 製作 **seisaku** manufacturing, production
　製作者 **seisakusha** manufacturer, producer
　製作所 **seisakujo** factory, works, workshop
　製図 **seizu** drafting, drawing, cartography
　製材 **seizai** sawing; lumber
　製材工 **seizaikō** sawyer
　製材所 **seizaisho** sawmill
8 製版 **seihan** platemaking (in printing)
　製版所 **seihanjo** platemaking shop
　製油 **seiyu** oil refining
　製油所 **seiyujo** oil refinery
　製法 **seihō** manufacturing process, recipe
9 製造 **seizō** manufacture
　製造元 **seizōmoto** the manufacturer
　製造者 **seizōsha** manufacturer
　製造業 **seizōgyō** manufacturing industry
　製品 **seihin** product, manufactured goods
　製革 **seikaku** leather making, tanning

5
石 立 目 禾 衤 田 皿 疒 8←

製革所 **seikakujo** tannery
製革業 **seikakugyō** the tanning industry
製茶 **seicha** tea manufacturing
製茶業 **seichagyō** the tea manufacturing industry
製炭 **seitan** charcoal making
製炭業 **seitangyō** the charcoal industry
10 製陶 **seitō** porcelain manufacturing
製陶業 **seitōgyō** the ceramics industry
製紙 **seishi** paper manufacturing
製紙業 **seishigyō** the paper industry
製粉 **seifun** flour milling
製粉所 **seifunjo** flour mill
製粉機 **seifunki** flour mill/grinder
11 製菓 **seika** candymaking
製菓業 **seikagyō** the confectionery industry
製麻 **seima** hemp/jute dressing, flax spinning
12 製帽 **seibō** hat/headgear making
13 製塩 **seien** salt making
製塩業 **seiengyō** the salt industry
製靴 **seika** shoemaking
製靴業 **seikagyō** the shoemaking industry
製鉄 **seitetsu** iron manufacturing
製鉄所 **seitetsujo** ironworks
製鉄業 **seitetsugyō** the iron industry
16 製薬 **seiyaku** manufacturing drugs; manufactured medicine
製薬会社 **seiyaku-gaisha** pharmaceutical company
製糖 **seitō** sugar refining
製糖所 **seitōjo** sugar refinery
製糖業 **seitōgyō** the sugar industry
製錬 **seiren** refining, smelting
製錬所 **seirenjo** refinery, smelting works
製鋼 **seikō** steel manufacturing, steelmaking
製鋼所 **seikōjo** steel plant
20 製麵所 **seimenjo** noodle factory
21 製艦 **seikan** building warships, naval construction
23 製罐 **seikan** making cans/boilers

───────── 2 ─────────

3 上製 **jōsei** superior manufacture/binding
土製 **dosei** earthen, terra cotta
4 内製 **naisei** make in one's own factory (cf. 外注)
毛製品 **mōseihin** woolen goods
手製 **tesei** handmade, homemade
木製 **mokusei** wooden, made of wood
木製品 **mokuseihin** wood products
5 半製品 **hanseihin** semiprocessed goods
未製品 **miseihin** unfinished goods
主製品 **shuseihin** main products
6 再製 **saisei** remanufacture, recondition
全製品 **zenseihin** manufactured product
肉製品 **niku seihin** meat products

自製 **jisei** made by oneself, homemade
7 作製 **sakusei** manufacture
即製 **sokusei** manufacture on the spot
別製 **bessei** special make
乳製品 **nyūseihin** dairy products
私製 **shisei** homemade, private (postcard)
8 官製 **kansei** government-made (postcard)
和製 **wasei** made in Japan
金製 **kinsei** made of gold
9 革製 **kawasei** made of leather
10 既製 **kisei** ready-made
既製服 **kiseifuku** ready-made clothing
既製品 **kiseihin** manufactured/ready-made goods, goods in stock
陶製 **tōsei** ceramic, earthen
剥製 **hakusei** stuffing, stuffed/mounted specimen
特製 **tokusei** special make, deluxe
11 粗製 **sosei** crudely made
粗製品 **soseihin** crude articles
12 創製 **sōsei** invent, create, originate
御製 **gyosei** emperor's poem/composition
極製 **gokusei** the best made
13 新製品 **shinseihin** new product
鉄製 **tessei** made of iron/steel
14 複製 **fukusei** reproduction, duplication
練製品 **ne(ri)seihin** a fish-paste food
綿製品 **menseihin** cotton goods
精製 **seisei** refining; careful manufacture
精製法 **seiseihō** refining process
精製品 **seiseihin** finished goods
精製糖 **seiseitō** refined sugar
銀製 **ginsei** made of silver
銅製 **dōsei** made of copper
15 監製 **kansei** well supervised manufacturing
縫製 **hōsei** sew (by machine)
縫製品 **hōseihin** sewn goods
調製 **chōsei** make, prepare
16 錫製品 **suzu seihin** tinware
鋼製 **kōsei** made of steel
17 擬製 **gisei** imitation, forgery, copy
謹製 **kinsei** carefully made by
18 燻製 **kunsei** smoked (fish)

───────── 3 ─────────

4 日本製 **nihonsei** made in Japan
6 自家製 **jikasei** made at home, home-brewed
7 亜麻製 **amasei** flaxen, linen
8 金属製 **kinzokusei** made of metal
16 機械製 **kikaisei** machine-made
鋼鉄製 **kōtetsusei** made of steel

5e8.10

    HAI long robes

───────── 9 ─────────

5e9.1

裸

HO, HŌ diaper

───────── 2 ─────────

16 裸褓 **kyōhō, mutsuki, oshime** diaper

褐 → 褐 **5e8.7**

襌 → 襌 **5e12.1**

5e9.2

褌

KON, fundoshi loincloth

───────── 2 ─────────

15 緊褌一番 **kinkon-ichiban** gird/brace oneself for

───────── 3 ─────────

19 犢鼻褌 **tokubikon** loincloth

5e9.3 / 916

複

FUKU double, multiple, composite, compound, again

───────── 1 ─────────

2 複十字 **fukujūji** double-crosspiece cross (tuberculosis prevention symbol)

3 複々々線 **fukufukufukusen** six-track rail line
複々線 **fukufukusen** four-track rail line

4 複文 **fukubun** complex sentence
複火山 **fukukazan** compound volcano
複方 **fukuhō** compounded drug (prescription)

5 複本 **fukuhon** a duplicate, copy
複本位 **fukuhon'i** double standard
複本位制 **fukuhon'isei** bimetalism
複母音 **fukuboin** diphthong
複写 **fukusha** copying, duplication; a copy, facsimile
複写紙 **fukushashi** copying paper
複写器 **fukushaki** copier

6 複合 **fukugō** composite, compound, complex
複合語 **fukugōgo** compound word
複式 **fukushiki** double-entry (bookkeeping)
複式学級 **fukushiki gakkyū** combined class (of more than one grade)

7 複利 **fukuri** compound interest
複利法 **fukurihō** the compound interest method

9 複音 **fukuon** (harmonica) with a double row of blowholes

10 複座 **fukuza** two-seater
複座機 **fukuzaki** two-seater airplane

11 複道 **fukudō** double roadways one above the other
複視 **fukushi** double vision
複眼 **fukugan** compound eye (of an insect)

12 複葉 **fukuyō** compound leaf; biplane

13 複数 **fukusū** plural

14 複製 **fukusei** reproduction, duplication
複雑 **fukuzatsu** complicated, complex
複雑化 **fukuzatsuka** complication

15 複線 **fukusen** double track

───────── 2 ─────────

9 重複 **chōfuku, jūfuku** duplication, repetition, overlapping, redundancy

14 複複複線 **fukufukufukusen** six-track rail line
複複線 **fukufukusen** four-track rail line

5e9.4

褊

HEN small, narrow(-minded)

5e9.5

褪

TON, TAI take off (clothes); fade
a(seru), sa(meru) fade, discolor

───────── 1 ─────────

6 褪色 **taishoku** fade, lose color; faded color

9 褪紅色 **taikōshoku** light pink

───────── 10 ─────────

5e10.1

褞

ON (wadded) clothing

───────── 1 ─────────

10 褞袍 **dotera** padded/quilted kimono

5e10.2

褥

JOKU, shitone mattress, futon, cushion

───────── 2 ─────────

11 産褥 **sanjoku** childbed, confinement
産褥熱 **sanjokunetsu** puerperal fever

5e10.3

褫

CHI strip off/away

───────── 1 ─────────

14 褫奪 **chidatsu** strip/deprive of

5

石
立
目
禾
衤 10←
田
皿
疒

5

石 立 目 禾 礻 田 罒 疒

→ 11

— 11 —

5e11.1

襁

KYŌ diaper

— 1 —

14 襁褓 **kyōhō, mutsuki, oshime** diaper

5e11.2

褸

RU, RŌ rags

— 2 —

20 襤褸 **ranru, boro, tsuzure** rags, shreds, tatters

5e11.3

褶

SHŪ, CHŌ folds, pleats

— 1 —

6 褶曲 **shūkyoku** bend into folds, flex

5e11.4

襀

SEKI, hida pleat, fold

— 12 —

襖→襖 **5e13.1**

襍→雑 **8c6.2**

5e12.1

襌 襌

TAN thin kimono; undergarment

— 13 —

5e13.1

襖 襖

Ō coat
fusuma opaque paper sliding door

— 1 —

13 襖障子 **fusuma shōji** opaque paper sliding door

5e13.2 / 1537

襟

KIN, eri neck, collar, lapel

— 1 —
---

0 V襟 **vīeri, buieri** V-neck (sweater)
4 襟元 **erimoto** front of the neck
7 襟足 **eriashi** hairline above the nape
9 襟巻 **erima(ki)** muffler, scarf
　襟首 **erikubi** nape/scruff of the neck
　襟度 **kindo** magnanimity, generosity
10 襟留 **erido(me)** breast pin, brooch
11 襟章 **erishō** (collar/lapel) badge
13 襟腰 **erikoshi** height of the neck
　襟飾 **erikaza(ri)** neckwear (tie, brooch, etc.)
14 襟髪 **erigami** hair at the back of the head/neck
16 襟懐 **kinkai** one's heart, inner thoughts

— 2 —
---

5 半襟 **han'eri** (kimono) neckpiece
　立襟 **ta(chi)eri** stand-up collar
7 折襟 **o(ri)eri** turned-down collar; lapel; lounge suit
10 胸襟 **kyōkin** heart, bosom
12 開襟 **kaikin** open-necked (shirt)
13 裏襟 **uraeri** neckband lining
　詰襟 **tsu(me)eri** stand-up/close-buttoned collar

5e13.3

襠

TŌ robe
machi gusset (in sewing)

— 2 —

13 補襠 **uchikake** (a long outer garment)

5e13.4

襞

HEKI, hida pleat, fold, tuck, crease

— 14 —

5e14.1

襦

JU underwear

— 1 —

10 襦袢 **juban** underwear (worn under kimono)

— 2 —

6 肉襦袢 **nikujuban** tights, leotards
　肌襦袢 **hadajuban** underwear
8 長襦袢 **nagajuban** long underwear
15 膚襦袢 **hadajuban** underwear

5e14.2

襪

BETSU socks

───────────── 15 ─────────────

5e15.1

襭 KETSU, tsumabasa(mu) tuck into (one's obi)

5e15.2

襤 襤 RAN rags

───────────── 1 ─────────────

16 襤褸 **ranru, boro, tsuzure** rags, shreds, tatters

───────────── 16 ─────────────

5e16.1

襯 SHIN underwear

5e16.2 / 1575

襲 SHŪ, oso(u) attack; succeed to

───────────── 1 ─────────────

5 襲用 **shūyō** follow, adopt
6 襲名 **shūmei** succeed to another's (stage) name
7 襲来 **shūrai** invasion, raid, attack
11 襲掛 **oso(i)ka(karu)** pounce upon, attack
15 襲撃 **shūgeki** attack, assault, raid, charge

───────────── 2 ─────────────

5 世襲 **seshū** hereditary (right)
6 因襲 **inshū** custom, convention
7 来襲 **raishū** attack, raid, invasion
8 夜襲 **yashū** night attack
逆襲 **gyakushū** counterattack
奇襲 **kishū** surprise attack
空襲 **kūshū** air raid/strike
9 急襲 **kyūshū** surprise attack, raid
珍襲 **chinshū** treasured, prized
10 猛襲 **mōshū** furious attack, violent assault
11 強襲 **kyōshū** attack, storm
14 熊襲 **Kumaso** (ancient tribe of southern Kyūshū)
15 敵襲 **tekishū** attack by the enemy
踏襲 **tōshū** follow (someone's footsteps)

───────────── 17 ─────────────

5e17.1

襷 tasuki sash/cord for holding up tucked sleeves

5e17.2

襴 RAN (a kind of cloth)

───────────── 2 ─────────────

8 金襴 **kinran** gold brocade

─────────────── 田 **5f** ───────────────

田	町	甲	男	旬	敗	畊	昳	盼	胃	思	畏	毗
0.1	2.1	5f2.1	2.2	2.3	4.1	0a10.13	4.2	5f4.7	4.3	4.4	4.5	4.6

界	畏	畆	卑	畔	畛	畠	留	畝	鬼	畚	畎	畦
4.7	5f4.5	5f5.5	4.8	5.1	5.2	5.3	5.4	5.5	5.6	5.7	6.1	6.2

時	略	累	畢	畧	異	匐	疇	畬	堲	疊	番	畫
6.3	6.4	6.5	6.6	5f6.4	6.7	6.8	5f14.1	7.1	7.2	7.3	7.4	0a8.7

甥	畷	畸	牌	魁	魂	鼻	夥	魅	魃	畿	魄	鳴
7.5	8.1	8.2	2j10.3	9.1	9.2	9.3	0a14.2	10.1	10.2	10.3	10.4	11.1

疊	奮	甌	獸	嬲	戴	魆	壘	翻	魎	魍	疇	疆
5f7.3	11.2	4c13.3	3g12.3	12.1	12.2	12.3	5f7.2	6b12.3	13.1	13.2	14.1	14.2

髀	魑	鼺	壘	疊	魘
14.3	15.1	16.1	5f7.3	5f7.3	2p22.1

───────────── 0 ─────────────

5f0.1 / 35

田 DEN, ta rice field, paddy

───────────── 1 ─────────────

3 田川 **Tagawa** (city, Fukuoka-ken)
4 田夫 **denpu** peasant
田夫野人 **denpu-yajin** a rustic, country bumpkin, yokel

5 田打 **tau(chi)** tilling a paddy field
6 田地 **denchi, denji** paddy field, farmland
田虫 **tamushi** ringworm
8 田舎 **inaka** the country, rural areas
田舎出 **inakade** from the country
田舎回 **inakamawa(ri)** tour of the country, provincial tour
田舎育 **inakasoda(chi)** country-bred
田舎者 **inakamono** person from the country, rustic, rube
田舎風 **inakafū** rustic, country-style
田舎染 **inakajimi(ru)** be countrified
田舎娘 **inakamusume** country girl
田舎家 **inakaya** country house
田舎道 **inakamichi** country road
9 田畑 **tahata** fields and rice paddies
10 田圃 **tanbo** rice field
11 田野 **den'ya** cultivated fields
田紳 **denshin** country gentleman
12 田植 **tau(e)** rice-planting
田植歌 **tau(e) uta** rice-planting song
13 田園 **den'en** fields and gardens; the country, rural areas
田園詩 **den'enshi** pastoral poem
田楽 **dengaku** ritual music and dancing; tofu baked with miso
17 田螺 **tanishi** mud/pond snail

———————— 2 ————————

3 小田 **oda** rice field/paddy
小田原 **Odawara** (city, Kanagawa-ken)
小田原提灯 **odawara-jōchin** collapsible cylindrical paper lantern
小田原評定 **odawara hyōjō** endless debate, fruitless conference
4 屯田 **tonden** colonization
屯田兵 **tondenhei** farmer-soldiers, colonizers
片田舎 **kata-inaka** backwoods, boondocks
公田 **kōden, kuden** public paddy (historical)
水田 **suiden** paddy
5 功田 **kōden** rice-field reward (historical)
半田 **handa** solder
6 羽田 **Haneda** (airport in Tōkyō)
有田焼 **Aritaya(ki)** Arita porcelainware
7 良田 **ryōden** fertile rice field
我田引水 **gaden insui** drawing water for one's own field, promoting one's own interests
8 油田 **yuden** oil field
沼田 **numata** marshy rice field
泥田 **dorota** muddy rice field, paddy
青田 **aota, aoda** green rice field
青田買 **aotaga(i)** buying yet unharvested rice; signing up prospective graduates as employees
9 美田 **biden** good rice field

浅田 **asada** shallow paddy
炭田 **tanden** coalfield
秋田 **Akita** (city, Akita-ken)
秋田犬 **Akita-ken, Akita inu** an Akita (husky-like) dog
秋田県 **Akita-ken** (prefecture)
10 帰田 **kiden** (an official) returning to the farm
桑田 **sōden** mulberry orchard
真田虫 **sanada mushi** tapeworm
真田紐 **sanada himo** braid
竜田姫 **Tatsutahime** the goddess of autumn
11 隅田川 **Sumida-gawa** (river, Tōkyō-to)
乾田 **kanden** dry rice field
12 湿田 **shitsuden** poorly drained paddy wet all year
13 隠田 **kaku(shi)da** unregistered paddy
塩田 **enden** salt field/farm
新田 **shinden** new rice field
14 稲田 **inada** rice field

———————— 3 ————————

3 大牟田 **Ōmuta** (city, Fukuoka-ken)
8 岸和田 **Kishiwada** (city, Ōsaka-fu)
9 荒木田土 **araki-datsuchi** (a reddish clayey soil)
10 高島田 **takashimada** (a traditional hairdo)

———————— 4 ————————

18 臍下丹田 **seika-tanden** center of the abdomen

———————— 2 ————————

5f2.1 / 182

町 **CHŌ** street, town; (unit of length, about 109 m); (unit of area, 3000 tsubo, or about 0.992 hectares) **machi** street, town, quarter

———————— 1 ————————

2 町人 **chōnin** merchant
4 町内 **chōnai** (in the) town, neighborhood
5 町民 **chōmin** townspeople
町外 **machihazu(re)** outskirts of town
町立 **chōritsu** (established by the) town
6 町会 **chōkai** town council, town-block association
町名 **chōmei** town/street name
7 町住 **machizuma(i)** town life
町医者 **machi isha** practicing physician
町村 **chōson** towns and villages, municipality
8 町長 **chōchō** town mayor
町奉行 **machi-bugyō** town magistrate
町制 **chōsei** town organization
町並 **machinami** row of stores and houses along a street
町歩 **chōbu** *chō* (0.992 hectare)
9 町政 **chōsei** town government

10 町家 **chōka** tradesman's/town house
11 町道場 **machi dōjō** martial-arts school in a town
12 町税 **chōzei** town tax
町筋 **machisuji** street

———————— 2 ————————

3 下町 **shitamachi** part of the city near the sea or river, downtown
小町 **komachi** beauty, belle, queen
小町娘 **komachi musume** beauty, belle, queen
4 片町 **katamachi** town with buildings on one side of a road only
5 市町 **shichō** cities and towns
市町村 **shichōson** cities, towns, and villages; municipalities
6 色町 **iromachi** red-light district
7 花町 **hanamachi** section of town where geishas live
9 室町 **Muromachi** (era, 1338–1573)
10 素町人 **suchōnin** common townspeople
12 港町 **minatomachi** port town/city
兜町 **Kabuto-chō** (area of Tōkyō, site of Tōkyō Stock Exchange)
13 裏町 **uramachi** back street, alley
15 横町 **yokochō** side street, lane, alley
19 蟻町 **ari(no)machi** slum

———————— 3 ————————

9 南京町 **Nankinmachi** Chinatown
城下町 **jōkamachi** castle town
屋敷町 **yashiki machi** exclusive residential section
11 宿場町 **shukuba machi** post/hotel town

甼 → 町 5f2.1

5f2.2 / 101

男 **DAN, NAN, otoko** man, male

———————— 1 ————————

1 男一匹 **otoko ippiki** full-grown man
2 男子 **danshi** man, male, boy, son
otoko(no)ko boy
男子用 **danshiyō** for men, men's
3 男工 **dankō** male worker
男女 **danjo, nannyo** men and women
4 男手 **otokode** man's strength; man's handwriting, kanji
5 男世帯 **otokojotai** all-male household
男好 **otokozu(ki)** liked by men; amorous woman
男囚 **danshū** male prisoner

6 男気 **otokogi** chivalrous spirit
otoko(k)ke male, man
男色 **danshoku, nanshoku** sodomy
男向 **otokomu(ki)** for men
7 男坂 **otokozaka** the steeper slope
男狂 **otokoguru(i)** be man-crazy/wanton
男声 **dansei** male voice
男児 **danji** boy, son
男系 **dankei** male line, father's side
8 男泣 **otokona(ki)** weeping in spite of being a man
男性 **dansei** man, male; masculinity
男性美 **danseibi** masculine beauty
男所帯 **otokojotai** all-male household
男妾 **otoko mekake** male paramour
9 男前 **otokomae** good looks, handsome
男持 **otokomo(chi)** men's, for men
男柱 **otokobashira** large pillars on either side of a bridge
男臭 **otokokusa(i)** smelling like a man, masculine
10 男振 **otokobu(ri), otoko(p)pu(ri)** a man's bearing
男帯 **otoko obi** man's obi
男根 **dankon** penis, phallus
11 男娼 **danshō** male prostitute
男盛 **otokozaka(ri)** prime of manhood
12 男尊女卑 **danson-johi** predominance of men over women
男勝 **otokomasa(ri)** strong-minded, spirited
男装 **dansō** male attire
男衆 **otokoshū** manservant
男結 **otokomusu(bi)** men's style of knotting (a sash)
13 男嫌 **otokogira(i)** man-hater
16 男親 **otoko oya** father
17 男優 **dan'yū** actor
男爵 **danshaku** baron
21 男鰥 **otoko yamome** widower

———————— 2 ————————

3 三男 **sannan** third son; three men
大男 **ōotoko** tall/large man
下男 **genan** manservant
小男 **kootoko** short man
山男 **yamaotoko** (back)woodsman, hillbilly; alpinist
5 好男子 **kōdanshi** handsome man
6 年男 **toshiotoko** lucky-bean scatterer (at Setsubun festival)
次男 **jinan** second son
次男坊 **jinanbō** second son
色男 **irootoko** lover, paramour; lady-killer
寺男 **teraotoko** temple sexton
7 作男 **sakuotoko** farm hand
快男子 **kaidanshi** agreeable/straightforward chap

5

石
立
目
禾
衤
田 2←
皿
皿
广

快男児 **kaidanji** a fine fellow
8 長男 **chōnan** eldest son
東男 **azuma otoko** man from eastern Japan
9 美男 **binan** handsome man
美男子 **bidanshi, binanshi** handsome man
10 狼男 **ōkami otoko** wolfman, werewolf
留男 **to(me)otoko** man who stops a quarrel; tout, customer-catcher
11 雪男 **yukiotoko** the abominable snowman, yeti
12 善男善女 **zennan-zennyo** devout men and women
間男 **maotoko** adulterer, secret (male) lover
13 隠男 **kaku(shi)otoko** lover, paramour
14 嫡男 **chakunan** eldest/legitimate son, heir
15 賤男 **shizu(no)o** man of humble birth
17 優男 **yasa-otoko** mild-mannered man, man of delicate features

—————————— 3 ——————————

3 女尊男卑 **joson-danpi** putting women above men
6 伊達男 **dateotoko** a dandy, fop

—————————— 4 ——————————

3 下女下男 **gejo-genan** servants

5f2.3

甸

DEN region around the imperial capital; outskirts

—————————— 4 ——————————

5f4.1

畋

DEN, TEN till, cultivate; hunting

畊 → 耕 0a10.13

5f4.2

畉

FU, tagaya(su) till, cultivate

畍 → 界 5f4.7

5f4.3 / 1268

胃

I stomach

—————————— 1 ——————————

8 胃炎 **ien** stomach inflammation, gastritis

10 胃部 **ibu** stomach region
胃弱 **ijaku** indigestion
胃病 **ibyō** stomach disorder
11 胃液 **ieki** gastric juices
胃袋 **ibukuro** stomach
12 胃散 **isan** medicinal stomach powder
胃痙攣 **ikeiren** stomach convulsions/cramps
胃痛 **itsū** stomachache
13 胃腸 **ichō** stomach and intestines
胃腸病 **ichōbyō** gastrointestinal disorder
胃腸薬 **ichōyaku** stomach and bowel medicine
14 胃酸 **isan** stomach acid
胃酸過多症 **isankatashō** gastric hyperacidity
15 胃潰瘍 **ikaiyō** stomach ulcer
胃熱 **inetsu** gastric fever
16 胃壁 **iheki** stomach lining
17 胃癌 **igan** stomach cancer
19 胃鏡 **ikyō** gastroscope

—————————— 2 ——————————

10 健胃剤 **ken'izai** stomach medicine

5f4.4 / 99

思

SHI, omo(u) think

—————————— 1 ——————————

2 思入 **omo(i)i(ru)** consider, ponder
omo(i)i(re) meditation, reverie; to one's heart's content
思人 **omo(i)bito** sweetheart, lover
思子 **omo(i)go** a favorite child
3 思及 **omo(i)oyo(bu)** think of, hit upon
思上 **omo(i)a(garu)** be conceited
4 思切 **omo(i)ki(ru)** resolve, make up one's mind; resign oneself, give up
omo(i)ki(tta) radical, drastic
思込 **omo(i)ko(mu)** have the idea that, be convinced that; set one's heart on
5 思出 **omo(i)de** memory, remembrance
omo(i)da(su) remember
思出笑 **omo(i)da(shi)wara(u)** smile over a memory
思出話 **omo(i)da(shi)banashi** reminiscences
思弁 **shiben** speculation
思付 **omo(i)tsu(ki)** idea, thought that comes to mind
思存分 **omo(u) zonbun** as much as one pleases
思召 **obo(shi)me(shi)** your wishes/opinion; liking, fancy
思外 **omo(ino)hoka** unexpectedly, more than expected
思巡 **omo(i)megu(rasu)** recall, recollect; think over

思立 **omo(i)ta(tsu)** set one's mind on, plan
6 思合 **omo(i)a(u)** love each other
　　 omo(i)a(waseru) consider together
思考 **shikō** thinking, thought
思考力 **shikōryoku** mental faculties
思返 **omo(i)kae(su)** think over, reconsider
思当 **omo(i)a(taru)** occur to one, think of
思回 **omo(i)mawa(su)** recall, ponder
7 思余 **omo(i)ama(ru)** not know what to do, be unable to contain oneself
思乱 **omo(i)mida(reru)** be distracted with the thought of
思初 **omo(i)so(meru)** fall in love with
8 思事 **omo(i)goto** one's wishes/prayer
思念 **shinen** thought
思直 **omo(i)nao(su)** reconsider, change one's mind
思知 **omo(i)shi(ru)** come to know, realize; repent of
思者 **omo(i)mono** sweetheart
9 思通 **omo(i)dō(ri)** as one likes, to one's satisfaction
思浮 **omo(i)u(kaberu)** recall, hit upon
　　 omo(i)u(kabu) occur to one, come to mind
思春期 **shishunki** puberty
思思 **omo(i)omo(i ni)** as one pleases, each to his liking
10 思残 **omo(i)noko(su)** look back on with regret
思索 **shisaku** thinking, speculation, meditation
思索的 **shisakuteki** speculative, meditative
思起 **omo(i)o(kosu)** remember, recall
思振 **omo(wase)bu(ri)** coquetry; mystification
思案 **shian** thought, consideration, mulling over; plan
思悩 **omo(i)naya(mu)** worry, agonize, be perplexed
思料 **shiryō** thought, consideration
11 思過 **omo(i)su(gosu)** worry too much, be overanxious
思掛 **omo(i)ga(kenai)** unexpected
思寄 **omo(i)yo(ru)** think of, recall
思設 **omo(i)mō(keru)** anticipate, expect
12 思遣 **omo(i)ya(ri)** consideration, sympathy, compassion
思慕 **omo(i)tsuno(ru)** think more and more of
思量 **shiryō** thought, consideration
思惑 **omowaku** thought, intention
　　 omo(i)mado(u) be unable to make up one's mind
思惑師 **omowakushi** speculator
思惑違 **omowakuchiga(i)** disappointment, miscalculation
思惑買 **omowakuga(i)** speculative buying

思焦 **omo(i)koga(reru)** pine for
13 思煩 **omo(i)wazura(u)** worry about, feel anxious
思想 **shisō** thought, idea
思想犯 **shisōhan** dangerous-thought offense
思想界 **shisōkai** world of thought, realm of ideas
思想家 **shisōka** thinker
思詰 **omo(i)tsu(meru)** think hard, brood over
14 思慕 **shibo** yearning, deep affection
15 思慮 **shiryo** thoughtfulness, prudence
思潮 **shichō** trend of thought

────────── 2 ──────────

1 一思 **hitoomo(i)** with one effort, once and for all
3 三思 **sanshi** reflect on, think seriously
千思万考 **senshi-bankō** deep meditation, careful deliberation
4 不思議 **fushigi** wonder, mystery, marvel
片思 **kataomo(i)** unrequited love
5 旧思想 **kyūshisō** old-fashioned/outmoded ideas
6 再思 **saishi** reconsider
7 沈思 **chinshi** meditation, contemplation
8 物思 **monoomo(i)** pensiveness, reverie; anxiety
所思 **shoshi** one's thoughts, opinion
9 後思案 **atojian** afterthought
相思 **sōshi** mutual affection
相思相愛 **sōshi-sōai** mutual love
秋思 **shūshi** the sentimental feeling of fall
思思 **omo(i)omo(i ni)** as one pleases, each to his liking
食思 **shokushi** appetite
食思不振 **shokushi fushin** loss of appetite
11 深思 **shinshi** deep thinking
12 無思慮 **mushiryo** thoughtless, imprudent
13 愁思 **shūshi** worry, distress, grief
意思 **ishi** intent, purpose, mind
14 静思 **seishi** meditation, comtemplation
熟思 **jukushi** careful consideration
15 黙思 **mokushi** contemplation
16 燃思 **mo(eru) omo(i), mo(yuru) omo(i)** burning passion
親思 **oyaomo(i)** affection for one's parents

────────── 3 ──────────

2 七不思議 **nanafushigi** the seven wonders
4 不可思議 **fukashigi** mystery, wonder, miracle
引込思案 **hi(k)ko(mi)jian** conservative, retiring
5 末法思想 **mappō shisō** pessimism due to the decadent-age theory
14 鼻元思案 **hanamoto-jian** superficial view

────────── 4 ──────────

9 神変不思儀 **shinpen-fushigi** miracle, marvel

5

石
立
目
禾
衤
田 4 ←
罒
疒

15 摩可不思議 **maka-fushigi** profound mystery
摩訶不思議 **maka-fushigi** profound mystery

5f4.5

畏 畏

I, oso(reru) fear, be overawed
kashiko(maru) obey respectfully; sit respectfully
kashiko(kumo) graciously, condescendingly

——————— 1 ———————

4 畏友 **iyū** esteemed friend
6 畏多 **oso(re)ō(i)** gracious, august, awe-inspiring
8 畏怖 **ifu** awe, fear, dread
12 畏敬 **ikei** awe and respect, reverence
17 畏縮 **ishuku** cower, quail, be awestruck, shrink from
21 畏懼 **iku** fear, awe

5f4.6

毘

HI, BI help; go into decline, fall into disuse

——————— 1 ———————

7 毘沙門天 **Bishamon-ten** Vaisravana, god of treasure

——————— 2 ———————

10 荼毘 **dabi** cremation

5f4.7 / 454

界 畍

KAI boundary, limits, circle, world

——————— 1 ———————

9 界面 **kaimen** interface, boundary, surface
11 界隈 **kaiwai** neighborhood, vicinity
15 界標 **kaihyō** boundary mark

——————— 2 ———————

3 三界 **sangai** past, present, and future existences
下界 **gekai** this world, here below
4 内界 **naikai** inner world, inward
分界 **bunkai** demarcation, boundary, border
分界線 **bunkaisen** line of demarcation
5 世界 **sekai** the world
世界一 **sekai-ichi** best in the world
世界一周 **sekai isshū** round-the-world trip, circumnavigation
世界人 **sekaijin** citizen of the world, cosmopolitan
世界大戦 **sekai taisen** World War
世界中 **sekaijū** all over the world
世界史 **sekaishi** world history
世界観 **sekaikan** world view

仙界 **senkai** dwelling place of hermits; pure land away from the world
他界 **takai** the next world; die
外界 **gaikai** outside world; physical world; externals
6 肉界 **nikukai** the physical/sensual world
地界 **chikai** boundary
各界 **kakkai, kakukai** every field, various circles
7 学界 **gakkai** academic/scientific world
8 限界 **genkai** limit, boundary; marginal; critical
法界 **hōkai** the universe (in Buddhism)
苦界 **kukai, kugai** the world of suffering; life of prostitution
官界 **kankai** officialdom
9 俗界 **zokkai** the workaday/secular world
浄界 **jōkai** sacred precincts; (Buddhist) paradise
幽界 **yūkai** realm of the dead
政界 **seikai** the political arena
10 冥界 **meikai** hades, realm of the dead
租界 **sokai** (foreign) settlement, concession
財界 **zaikai** financial world
財界人 **zaikaijin** financier, businessman
11 視界 **shikai** field/range of vision, visibility
眼界 **gankai** field/range of vision
12 斯界 **shikai** this field (of endeavor)
13 業界 **gyōkai** the business world, industry, the trade
業界紙 **gyōkaishi** trade paper/journal
楽界 **gakkai** the world of music
14 境界 **kyōkai** boundary, border
境界標 **kyōkaihyō** landmark, boundary stone
境界線 **kyōkaisen** border/boundary line
塵界 **jinkai** this mundane life
磁界 **jikai** magnetic field
15 劇界 **gekikai** the theatrical world, the stage
霊界 **reikai** the spiritual world
18 臨界 **rinkai** critical (temperature)
21 魔界 **makai** world of devils/evil

——————— 3 ———————

2 人間界 **ningenkai** the world of mortals
3 工業界 **kōgyōkai** industrial circles, industry
4 天上界 **tenjōkai** the celestial world, heaven
文学界 **bungakukai** the literary world
分水界 **bunsuikai** watershed, (continental) divide
月世界 **gessekai** the lunar world, the moon
5 生物界 **seibutsukai** plants and animals, life
外交界 **gaikōkai** diplomatic circles
旧世界 **kyūsekai** the Old World
6 全世界 **zensekai** the whole world
自然界 **shizenkai** the realm of nature
7 別世界 **bessekai** another world
医学界 **igakukai** the medical world, medicine

5

石
立
目
禾
礻
⊞
⊞
皿.
疒

→ 4

花柳界 **karyūkai** geisha quarter, red-light district
芸能界 **geinōkai** the entertainment world, show business
社交界 **shakōkai** (high) society
8 事業界 **jigyōkai** industrial/business world
法曹界 **hōsōkai** legal circles, the bench and bar
実世界 **jissekai** the real/outside world
金融界 **kin'yūkai** the financial community
9 俗世界 **zokusekai** the everyday world
前世界 **zensekai** prehistoric ages
美術界 **bijutsukai** the art world
映画界 **eigakai** the cinema/screen world
思想界 **shisōkai** world of thought, realm of ideas
10 差別界 **sabetsukai** world of inequality
教育界 **kyōikukai** (the world of) education
11 動物界 **dōbutsukai** animal kingdom
商業界 **shōgyōkai** the business world
運動界 **undōkai** the sporting world, sports
理学界 **rigakukai, rigakkai** scientific world
現象界 **genshōkai** the phenomenal world
産業界 **sangyōkai** (the) industry
経済界 **keizaikai** financial circles
12 植物界 **shokubutsukai** the plant kingdom
絵画界 **kaigakai** the world of painting
13 新世界 **shinsekai** new world; the New World
新聞界 **shinbunkai** the newspaper world
14 演劇界 **engekikai** (the world of) the theater
読書界 **dokushokai** the reading public
銀世界 **ginsekai** vast silvery/snowy scene
銀行界 **ginkōkai** the banking community
16 儒学界 **jugakkai** Confucianists
機業界 **kigyōkai** the textile world

——————————— 4 ———————————
3 三千世界 **sanzen sekai** the whole world, the universe

畏→畏 **5f4.5**

畆→畝 **5f5.5**

5f4.8 / 1521

卑 卑
HI, iya(shimeru/shimu) despise, look down on **iya(shii)** humble, lowly; base, ignoble, vulgar

——————————— 1 ———————————
3 卑下 **hige** humble oneself
6 卑劣 **hiretsu** mean, contemptible, sneaking

卑劣漢 **hiretsukan** mean bastard, low-down skunk
8 卑陋 **hirō** despicable, vulgar
卑弥呼 **Himiko** female ruler of the early Japanese political federation known as Yamatai (about 3rd century)
卑屈 **hikutsu** mean-spirited, servile
卑怯 **hikyō** cowardly; mean, foul, unfair
卑怯者 **hikyōmono** coward
9 卑俗 **hizoku** vulgar, coarse
12 卑猥 **hiwai** indecent, obscene
14 卑語 **higo** vulgar word/expression
15 卑賤 **hisen** lowly position, obscurity

——————————— 2 ———————————
3 下卑 **gebi** vulgar, coarse
11 野卑 **yahi** vulgar, coarse, boorish
12 尊卑 **sonpi** high and low, aristocrat and plebian

——————————— 4 ———————————
3 女尊男卑 **joson-danpi** putting women above men
7 男尊女卑 **danson-johi** predominance of men over women
8 官尊民卑 **kanson-minpi** exalting the government at the expense of the people

——————————— 5 ———————————

5f5.1 / 1945

畔 畔
HAN, aze, kuro ridge between rice paddies

——————————— 2 ———————————
8 河畔 **kahan** riverside
12 湖畔 **kohan** lakeshore, lakeside

5f5.2

畛
SHIN path/boundary between paddies

5f5.3

畠
hatake, hata (cultivated) field

5f5.4 / 761

留 畄
RYŪ, RU stop; hold fast; detain; keep **to(maru/meru)**, **todo(maru/meru)** (intr./tr.) stop

——————————— 1 ———————————
3 留山 **to(me)yama** mountain where logging is prohibited
5 留立 **to(me)da(te)** dissuade, stop, prevent

5f4.5
5f5.5

6 留任 **ryūnin** remain in office
留守 **rusu** absence, being away from home; looking after the house (while someone is away); neglecting
留守中 **rusuchū** during one's absence
留守宅 **rusutaku** home whose master is away
留守居 **rusui** looking after the house (while someone is away); caretaker
留守番 **rusuban** looking after the house (while someone is away); caretaker
留守番電話 **rusuban denwa** answering machine
7 留別 **ryūbetsu** farewell to those staying
留役 **to(me)yaku** stopping a quarrel; peacemaker
留学 **ryūgaku** studying abroad
留学生 **ryūgakusei** student studying abroad
留学者 **ryūgakusha** person studying abroad
留男 **to(me)otoko** man who stops a quarrel; tout, customer-catcher
8 留具 **to(me)gu** clasp, latch, fastening
留金 **to(me)gane** clasp, latch, fastening
9 留保 **ryūho** reserve, withhold
10 留針 **to(me)bari** pin, safety pin, brooch, hairpin
11 留鳥 **ryūchō** nonmigratory bird
12 留湯 **to(me)yu** (reusing) yesterday's bath water; one's own bath; using a public bath on a pay-by-the-month basis
13 留意 **ryūi** give heed to, be mindful of
留置 **ryūchi** detention, custody, lockup
to(me)o(ku) detain, keep (after school); leave until called for
留置場 **ryūchijō** detention room, police cell
15 留鋲 **to(me)byō** thumbtack

——————— 2 ———————

3 久留米 **Kurume** (city, Fukuoka-ken)
4 勾留 **kōryū** detention, custody
引留 **hi(ki)to(meru)** detain, keep/hold back, stop
5 仕留 **shito(meru)** kill, shoot down (a plane)
打留 **u(chi)to(meru)** kill, shoot/bring down
u(chi)do(me) end (of an entertainment/match)
6 色留 **irodo(me)** color fixing
在留 **zairyū** reside, stay
在留民 **zairyūmin** residents
在留外人 **zairyū gaijin** foreign residents
在留邦人 **zairyū hōjin** Japanese residing abroad
7 抑留 **yokuryū** detention, internment
抑留国 **yokuryūkoku** detaining country
抑留者 **yokuryūsha** detainee, internee
抑留所 **yokuryūjo** detention/internment camp
抑留船 **yokuryūsen** detained/interned ship

局留 **kyokudo(me)** general delivery
8 拘留 **kōryū** detention, custody
拘留状 **kōryūjō** warrant for detention
拘留所 **kōryūjo** detention room, lockup
呼留 **yo(bi)to(meru)** call (to someone) to stop, challenge
歩留 **budo(mari)** yield
居留 **kyoryū** reside
居留民 **kyoryūmin** residents
居留地 **kyoryūchi** settlement, concession
居留守 **irusu** pretend not to be in (to avoid callers)
取留 **to(ri)to(meru)** ascertain, establish; save (a life)
取留無 **to(ri)to(me)na(i)** rambling, fanciful, incoherent, pointless
9 係留 **keiryū** moor, anchor
保留 **horyū** reserve, defer
10 残留 **zanryū** remain behind
逗留 **tōryū** stay, sojourn
逗留客 **tōryūkyaku** guest, visitor, sojourner
帯留 **obido(me)** sash clip
書留 **kakitome** registered mail
ka(ki)to(meru) write down
書留料 **kakitomeryō** registration fee
11 停留 **teiryū** stop, halt
停留所 **teiryūjo** stopping place, (bus) stop
寄留 **kiryū** temporary residence, sojourn
寄留地 **kiryūchi** one's temporary residence
寄留届 **kiryū todo(ke)** notice of temporary domicile
寄留者 **kiryūsha** temporary resident
乾留 **kanryū** dry distillation, carbonization
12 蒸留 **jōryū** distill
13 滞留 **tairyū** stay, sojourn
14 遺留 **iryū** bequeath
遺留分 **iryūbun** heir's legal portion
遺留品 **iryūhin** lost article, article left behind
歌留多 **karuta** playing cards
駅留 **ekido(me)** to-the-station delivery
15 慰留 **iryū** dissuade from resigning
駐留 **chūryū** stationing (of troops)
駐留軍 **chūryūgun** stationed/occupying troops
18 襟留 **erido(me)** breast pin, brooch
19 繋留 **keiryū** mooring, anchorage

——————— 3 ———————

13 靴下留 **kutsushitado(me)** garters

5f5.5 / 1901

 se (unit of area, about 1 are)
une ridge between furrows; rib (in fabric)

——————— 1 ———————

5 畝立 **uneda(te)** building ridges, furrowing

12 畝間 **unema** space between ridges, furrow
18 畝織 **uneori** rep, ribbed fabric

5f5.6 / 1523

鬼

KI, oni demon (with horns and fangs), ogre, devil; "it" in a game of tag; spirits of the dead; (as prefix) a fiend (for work), fanatic; strict, fearsome (boss); abnormally large

————— 1 —————

0 鬼ごっこ **oni(gokko)** tag (the children's game)
2 鬼子 **onigo** child born with teeth or dark hair; unruly child; child unlike its parents
鬼子母神 **Kishibojin, Kishimojin** (goddess of children)
3 鬼才 **kisai** genius, man of remarkable talent
鬼女 **kijo** she-devil; cruel woman
4 鬼火 **onibi** will-o'-the-wisp, ignis fatuus
5 鬼瓦 **onigawara** (gargoyle-like) ridgepole-end tile
6 鬼気 **kiki** ghastly, eerie
鬼百合 **oniyuri** tiger lily
鬼灯 **hōzuki** bladder/ground cherry
8 鬼門 **kimon** unlucky direction (northeast); something/someone which one avoids
9 鬼面 **kimen** devil's face/mask; bluff
鬼神 **kijin, kishin, onigami** fierce god; departed soul
10 鬼将軍 **onishōgun** brave/tough general
鬼畜 **kichiku** devil, brutal man
鬼島 **Oni(ga)shima** the island of ogres
11 鬼婆 **onibaba** witch, hag
12 鬼歯 **oniba** protruding tooth
15 鬼課長 **onikachō** hard-driving boss/section-chief
20 鬼籍 **kiseki** roster of the dead

————— 2 —————

3 小鬼 **kooni** little devil, imp, elf
6 百鬼夜行 **hyakki-yakō, hyakki-yagyō** all sorts of demons roaming about at night; rampant evil, scandal, pandemonium
7 邪鬼 **jaki** a devil, imp, evil spirit
11 悪鬼 **akki** demon, evil spirit
13 債鬼 **saiki** cruel creditor, bill collector
15 餓鬼 **gaki** hungry ghost; little brat
餓鬼大将 **gaki-daishō** dominant child among playmates
餓鬼道 **gakidō** (Buddhist) hell of hungry demons

————— 3 —————

4 天邪鬼 **amanojaku** devil being trampled by temple guardian deities; a contrary/cranky person
6 吸血鬼 **kyūketsuki** vampire

9 神出鬼没 **shinshutsu-kibotsu** elusive, phantom
施餓鬼 **segaki** service for the unmourned dead
10 殺人鬼 **satsujinki** bloodthirsty killer

————— 4 —————

12 葡萄状鬼胎 **budōjō kitai** vesicular/hydatid(iform) mole
14 疑心暗鬼 **gishin-anki** Suspicion creates monsters in the dark. Suspicion feeds on itself.

5f5.7

畚

HON, mokko straw basket (suspended from pole carried by two persons)

————— 6 —————

5f6.1

畎

kesa surplice

5f6.2

畦

KEI, aze ridge between rice paddies **une** ridge between furrows, rib (in fabric)

————— 1 —————

11 畦道 **azemichi** path between rice fields

5f6.3

畤

JI festival grounds

5f6.4 / 841

略 畧

RYAKU abbreviation, abridgment; omission; outline; capture, seize **hobo** roughly, approximately

————— 1 —————

0 略す **ryaku(su)** abbreviate; omit
3 略ぼ **hobo** roughly, approximately
5 略史 **ryakushi** brief history
略号 **ryakugō** abbreviation
略字 **ryakuji** simplified character; abbreviation
6 略伝 **ryakuden** brief biography
略式 **ryakushiki** informal, summary
7 略体 **ryakutai** simplified form (of a character)
略述 **ryakujutsu** brief account, outline
略図 **ryakuzu** rough sketch, outline map
略言 **ryakugen** brief statement, summary
8 略画 **ryakuga** rough sketch

略服 **ryakufuku** everyday clothes, informal dress
略取 **ryakushu** capture, occupation, plunder
9 略叙 **ryakujo** brief account, outline
略略 **hobo** roughly, approximately
10 略書 **ryakusho** abbreviation
略称 **ryakushō** abbreviation
略記 **ryakki** brief account, outline
略記法 **ryakkihō** abridged notation (e.g., 五三 for 五十三)
11 略章 **ryakushō** miniature decoration, medal, ribbon
12 略報 **ryakuhō** brief report
略帽 **ryakubō** ordinary cap
略装 **ryakusō** everyday clothes, informal dress
略筆 **ryakuhitsu** outline, synopsis; simplified character
13 略解 **ryakkai** brief explanation
14 略歴 **ryakureki** brief personal history, résumé
略語 **ryakugo** abbreviation
略説 **ryakusetsu** brief explanation
略奪 **ryakudatsu** pillage, plunder, looting
15 略儀 **ryakugi** informal
19 略譜 **ryakufu** brief genealogy; abbreviated musical notation

──────── 2 ────────

3 大略 **tairyaku** summary, outline; great plan; roughly, approximately
才略 **sairyaku** wise planning, resourcefulness
下略 **geryaku** the rest omitted, ... (in quoting)
4 中略 **chūryaku** omission of a part, ellipsis (...)
方略 **hōryaku** plan
5 史略 **shiryaku** a brief history
7 攻略 **kōryaku** capture, occupy, invade
8 治略 **chiryaku** governance, rulercraft
知略 **chiryaku** resourcefulness
武略 **buryaku** strategy, tactics
9 侵略 **shinryaku** aggression, invasion
侵略的 **shinryakuteki** aggressive
侵略者 **shinryakusha** aggressor, invader
軍略 **gunryaku** strategy, tactics
前略 **zenryaku** first part omitted; (salutation in a letter)
要略 **yōryaku** summary, outline, synopsis
後略 **kōryaku** last part omitted
胆略 **tanryaku** courage and resourcefulness
政略 **seiryaku** political strategy; expedient
政略家 **seiryakuka** political tactician
政略婚 **seiryakukon** marriage of convenience
政略結婚 **seiryaku kekkon** marriage of convenience
省略 **shōryaku** abbreviate, omit
計略 **keiryaku** stratagem, plan, ruse
10 党略 **tōryaku** party policies/platform

殺略 **satsuryaku** killing and robbing
11 疎略 **soryaku** coarse, crude
商略 **shōryaku** business policy
略略 **hobo** roughly, approximately
経略 **keiryaku** govern, rule
粗略 **soryaku** crude, slipshod
12 智略 **chiryaku** resourcefulness, ingenuity
策略 **sakuryaku** stratagem, scheme, tactic
雄略 **Yūryaku** (emperor, 456–479)
13 戦略 **senryaku** strategy
戦略上 **senryakujō** strategic
戦略家 **senryakuka** strategist
詳略 **shōryaku** detailed or sketchy
電略 **denryaku** an abbreviation used in telegrams
14 概略 **gairyaku** outline, summary
奪略 **datsuryaku** plunder, pillage
16 機略 **kiryaku** resourcefulness, expedients
謀略 **bōryaku** stratagem, scheme
18 簡略 **kanryaku** simple, concise

──────── 3 ────────

4 不侵略 **fushinryaku** nonagression

5f6.5 / 1060

累 **RUI** accumulate, pile up; incessantly; encumber

──────── 1 ────────

3 累々 **ruirui(taru)** piled up, in heaps
4 累月 **ruigetsu** for months
累日 **ruijitsu** many days, day after day
5 累世 **ruisei** successive generations; from generation to generation
累代 **ruidai** successive generations; from generation to generation
累加 **ruika** acceleration, progressive increase
累犯 **ruihan** repeated offense
累犯者 **ruihansha** repeat offender
6 累年 **ruinen** successive years; from year to year
累次 **ruiji** successive, repeated
7 累卵危 **ruiran (no) aya(uki)** imminent peril
9 累乗 **ruijō** raising a number to a power
累計 **ruikei** total
10 累進 **ruishin** successive promotions; progressive, graduated
累進税 **ruishinzei** progressive/graduated tax
12 累減 **ruigen** regressive (tax)
14 累増 **ruizō** successive increases
累算 **ruisan** total
16 累積 **ruiseki** cumulative

──────── 2 ────────

9 係累 **keirui** dependents, encumbrances
連累 **renrui** complicity

11 累累 **ruirui(taru)** piled up, in heaps
13 煩累 **hanrui** cares, annoyances
19 繋累 **keirui** encumbrances, dependents

5f6.6

畢 HITSU come to an end

───────── 1 ─────────
5 畢生 **hissei** lifelong

畧 → 略 5f6.4

5f6.7 / 1061

異
I uncommon, strange; difference
koto(naru), koto (ni suru) be different, vary; be unusual

───────── 1 ─────────
2 異人 **ijin** foreigner; different person
異人種 **ijinshu** different race
3 異才 **isai** genius, prodigy
異口同音 **iku-dōon** with one voice, unanimous
4 異文 **ibun** variant reading
異分子 **ibunshi** foreign elements, outsider
異父 **ifu** different father
異心 **ishin** treachery, intrigue
5 異本 **ihon** different edition
異母 **ibo** different mother
異存 **izon** objection
6 異邦 **ihō** foreign country
異邦人 **ihōjin** foreigner, stranger
異色 **ishoku** different color; unique, novel
異同 **idō** difference
異名 **imyō, imei** another name, nickname, alias
7 異体 **itai** different form, variant
異体同心 **itai-dōshin** of one mind, perfect accord
異状 **ijō** something wrong, abnormality
異形 **ikei** heteromorphous
　　igyō grotesque, fantastic
異花受精 **ika jusei** cross-pollination
異図 **ito** ulterior motive
異見 **iken** different opinion; objection
8 異例 **irei** exceptional case; indisposition
異姓 **isei** different surname
異国 **ikoku, kotokuni** foreign country
異国風 **ikokufū** foreign customs
異物 **ibutsu** foreign substance/body
異性 **isei** the opposite sex
9 異俗 **izoku** strange custom

異変 **ihen** accident, disaster, unforeseen occurrence
異風 **ifū** unusual custom; unusual style
異臭 **ishū** offensive smell
10 異郷 **ikyō** foreign country
異教 **ikyō** heathenism, paganism, heresy
異教徒 **ikyōto** heathen, heretic, infidel
異称 **ishō** another name, alias, pseudonym
11 異動 **idō** change, reshuffling
異域 **iiki** a foreign land
異彩 **isai** conspicuous (color), standing out
異常 **ijō** anything unusual, abnormality
12 異朝 **ichō** foreign court; foreign country
13 異義 **igi** different meaning
異腹 **ifuku** born of a different womb/mother
異数 **isū** exceptional, unusual
14 異様 **iyō** strange, outlandish
異端 **itan** heresy
異端者 **itansha** heretic
異種 **ishu** different kind/species
異説 **isetsu** different opinion
異聞 **ibun** another story, strange tale
15 異論 **iron** different opinion; objection
異質 **ishitsu** heterogeneous
18 異類 **irui** different kinds/species
20 異議 **igi** objection, protest

───────── 2 ─────────
3 小異 **shōi** minor difference
6 同異 **dōi** similarities and differences
8 奇異 **kii** strange, odd, singular
怪異 **kaii** mysterious, grotesque; monster
9 変異 **hen'i** mishap, unforeseen event; variation
10 差異 **sai** difference, disparity
特異 **tokui** singular, peculiar, unique
特異性 **tokuisei** singularity, peculiar characteristics
特異質 **tokuishitsu** idiosyncrasy
14 歎異鈔 **Tannishō** (a collection of Buddhist teachings)
15 霊異 **reii** miracle, wonder
22 驚異 **kyōi** wonder, miracle, marvel
驚異的 **kyōiteki** amazing, phenomenal

───────── 3 ─────────
6 同工異曲 **dōkō-ikyoku** superficially different but essentially the same
同名異人 **dōmei-ijin** different person of the same name
同音異義 **dōon-igi** the same pronunciation but different meanings
13 暖冬異変 **dantō ihen** abnormally warm winter

───────── 4 ─────────
3 大同小異 **daidō-shōi** substantially the same, not much different
4 天変地異 **tenpen-chii** cataclysm
8 突然変異 **totsuzen hen'i** mutation

5

石
立
目
禾　　6←
衤
田
皿
疒

5f6.8

匐

FUKU crawl, creep

───── 2 ─────

9 匍匐 **hofuku** crawl, creep

───── 7 ─────

疇 → 疇 5f14.1

5f7.1

畬

YO new field

累 → 5f6.5

5f7.2 / 1694

墨 壘

RUI fort; base (in baseball)

───── 1 ─────

4 塁手 **ruishu** baseman
5 塁打 **ruida** base hit, single
15 塁審 **ruishin** base umpire
16 塁壁 **ruiheki** ramparts, walls

───── 2 ─────

1 一塁 **ichirui** first base
2 二塁 **nirui** second base
3 三塁 **sanrui** third base
　三塁手 **sanruishu** third baseman
　三塁打 **sanruida** three-base hit, triple
5 出塁 **shutsurui** get on base (in baseball)
　本塁 **honrui** base, stronghold; home plate
　本塁打 **honruida** home run
7 走塁 **sōrui** base running
9 城塁 **jōrui** fort
10 残塁 **zanrui** runners left on base
　進塁 **shinrui** advance (to second base)
12 満塁 **manrui** bases loaded
　堅塁 **kenrui** stronghold
　堡塁 **hōrui** fort, stronghold

5f7.3 / 1087

畳 疊疊疊

JŌ repetition; (counter for mats) **tatami** straw mat; (as prefix) folding, collapsible **tata(mu)** fold, fold up; shut; bear in mind; finish off

───── 1 ─────

4 畳水練 **tatami suiren** like practicing swimming on a tatami, useless book learning
5 畳目 **tatamime** fold, crease; the mesh of a tatami
8 畳表 **tatami omote** tatami facing
　畳直 **tata(mi)nao(su)** refold
9 畳屋 **tatamiya** tatami maker/dealer/store
12 畳替 **tatamiga(e)** replace old tatami with new ones
14 畳語 **jōgo** repetition to indicate plurals, etc. (e.g., *hitobito*)
16 畳篤 **jūtoku** serious (illness)
18 畳職 **tatamishoku** tatami maker/dealer

───── 2 ─────

1 一畳 **ichijō** one mat
5 半畳 **hanjō** half mat; heckling
　石畳 **ishidatami** stone pavement/flooring
7 折畳 **o(ri)tata(mu)** fold up
　折畳式 **o(ri)tata(mi)shiki** folding, collapsible
　折畳機 **o(ri)tata(mi)ki** (page-)folding machine
8 青畳 **aodatami** new/green straw mat
9 重畳 **chōjō** one atop another; splendid
　　　 jūjō superimposed

5f7.4 / 185

番

BAN keeping watch; one's turn; number, order **tsuga(u)** pair, mate, copulate **tsuga(i)** pair, couple **tsuga(eru)** (tr.) to mate, pair; fit (an arrow) to (the string)

───── 1 ─────

2 番人 **bannin** watchman, guard
3 番小屋 **bangoya** sentry box
4 番手 **bante** (yarn) count, (sandpaper) number/grade
　番犬 **banken** watchdog
5 番付 **banzu(ke)** graded list, ranking
　番外 **bangai** extra; oversize
　番号 **bangō** number
　番号付 **bangōtsu(ke)** numbering
　番号札 **bangōfuda** numbered (license) plate
　番台 **bandai** bathhouse attendant('s raised seat)
6 番地 **banchi** lot/house number
7 番兵 **banpei** sentry, guard
　番狂 **bankuru(wase)** an upset (of plans)
8 番所 **bansho** sentry box
9 番茶 **bancha** coarse tea
11 番組 **bangumi** program
12 番傘 **bangasa** coarse oilpaper umbrella
16 番頭 **bantō** clerk, (bathhouse) attendant

───── 2 ─────

1 一番 **ichiban** number one, the first; most, best; a game/bout

一番鶏 **ichibandori** first cockcrowing
2 二番 **niban** No. 2, second
二番目 **nibanme** No. 2, second
二番煎 **nibansen(ji)** second brew of tea; rehash
二番線 **nibansen** track No. 2
3 上番 **jōban** on duty
山番 **yamaban** forest ranger
4 辻番 **tsujiban** watchman, guard
水番 **mizuban** irrigation-water watchman
月番 **tsukiban** monthly duty/shift
火番 **hi(no)ban** fire/night watchman
欠番 **ketsuban** missing number
5 出番 **deban** one's turn
本番 **honban** the actual performance (not a dry run)
生番組 **namabangumi** live program
立番 **ta(chi)ban** stand guard; a guard
6 交番 **kōban** police box/stand; alternation
kawa(ri)ban(ko ni) taking turns
当番 **tōban** being on duty
回番 **mawa(ri)ban** taking turns
早番 **hayaban** the first/early shift
7 何番 **nanban** what number
牢番 **rōban** prison guard, jailer
局番 **kyokuban** telephone-exchange number
8 非番 **hiban** off duty
夜番 **yoban, yaban** night watch(man)
泊番 **to(mari)ban** night duty
店番 **miseban** tending store; salesman
所番地 **tokorobanchi** address
門番 **monban** gatekeeper, porter
9 通番号 **tō(shi)bangō** serial number
茶番 **chaban** tea-ceremony assistant; farce, low comedy
茶番劇 **chabangeki** farce, low comedy
庭番 **niwaban** garden watchman; shogun's secret agent
背番号 **sebangō** number on a player's back
10 週番 **shūban** duty for the week
11 張番 **ha(ri)ban** stand watch/lookout; sentinel
12 隔番 **kakuban** alternation, taking turns
検番 **kenban** geisha call-office
順番 **junban** order, one's turn
15 蔵番 **kuraban** warehouse keeper
蝶番 **chōtsugai** (door) hinge, (anatomical) joint
輪番 **rinban** taking turns, in rotation
輪番制 **rinbansei** rotation system

――――――――― 3 ―――――――――
2 十八番 **jūhachiban** Kabuki repertoire of 18 classical pieces; one's forte/hobby, one's favorite (song/topic) **ohako** one's forte/hobby, one's favorite (song/topic)
4 不寝番 **fushinban** night watch

木戸番 **kidoban** gatekeeper
5 玄関番 **genkanban** doorkeeper, porter
6 自身番 **jishinban** (Edo-era) guardhouses
7 見張番 **miha(ri)ban** watch, lookout, guard
9 指南番 **shinanban** instructor, teacher
10 留守番 **rusuban** looking after the house (while someone is away); caretaker
留守番電話 **rusuban denwa** answering machine
15 踏切番 **fumikiriban** railroad crossing gateman

――――――――― 4 ―――――――――
15 緊褌一番 **kinkon-ichiban** gird/brace oneself for

畫 → 画 0a8.7

5f7.5

甥 **SEI, oi** nephew

――――――――― 8 ―――――――――
5f8.1

畷 **TETSU, nawate** path between paddies

5f8.2

畸 **KI** different, strange, crippled

――――――――― 1 ―――――――――
7 畸形 **kikei** deformity, abnormality
畸形児 **kikeiji** deformed child

牌 → 牌 2j10.3

――――――――― 9 ―――――――――
5f9.1

魁 **KAI, sakigake** in the forefront; harbinger

――――――――― 1 ―――――――――
12 魁偉 **kaii** imposing, formidable
――――――――― 2 ―――――――――
5 巨魁 **kyokai** ringleader, chief, boss
7 花魁 **oiran** courtesan, prostitute
9 首魁 **shukai** (ring)leader
12 渠魁 **kyokai** ringleader, chief, boss

5

石
立
目
禾
衤 9←
田
皿
疒

5f9.2 / 1525

魂

KON, tamashii, tama soul, spirit

——————— 1 ———————

6 魂迎 **tamamuka(e)** welcoming the spirits of the dead

9 魂胆 **kontan** soul; ulterior motive

10 魂消 **tamage(ru)** be astonished/flabbergasted

——————— 2 ———————

2 入魂 **jikkon, jukon** intimacy, familiarity

人魂 **hitodama** spirit of a dead person; will-o'-the-wisp

3 亡魂 **bōkon** departed soul, spirit

士魂商才 **shikon-shōsai** samurai in spirit and merchant in business acumen

4 心魂 **shinkon** one's heart

6 気魂 **kikon** spirit

7 肝魂 **kimo(t)tama** pluck, courage, grit

8 招魂 **shōkon** invocation of the spirits of the dead

招魂社 **shōkonsha** shrine to the war dead

招魂祭 **shōkonsai** memorial service; Memorial Day

英魂 **eikon** departed spirit

忠魂 **chūkon** the loyal dead, faithful spirit

忠魂碑 **chūkonhi** monument to the war dead

和魂漢才 **wakon-kansai** Japanese spirit and Chinese learning

9 負魂 **ma(keji)damashii** unyielding spirit, striving to keep ahead of others

面魂 **tsuradamashii** (determined) expression

11 商魂 **shōkon** commercial spirit, salesmanship

13 詩魂 **shikon** poetic sentiment

14 精魂 **seikon** energy, vitality

15 霊魂 **reikon** soul, spirit

霊魂不滅 **reikon fumetsu** immortality of the soul

18 鎮魂 **chinkon** repose of souls

鎮魂曲 **chinkonkyoku** requiem

鎮魂祭 **chinkonsai** services for the deceased

闘魂 **tōkon** fighting spirit

——————— 3 ———————

3 大和魂 **Yamato-damashii** the Japanese spirit

5f9.3 / 813

鼻

BI, hana nose

——————— 1 ———————

3 鼻孔 **bikō** nostril

鼻下 **bika** under the nose   **hana (no) shita** area between nose and mouth, upper lip

鼻下長 **bikachō** amorous man

hana (no) shita (ga) naga(i) easily charmed by women

4 鼻元思案 **hanamoto-jian** superficial view

鼻内 **binai** in the nose

鼻毛 **hanage** nostril hairs

鼻水 **hanamizu** nasal mucus, runny nose

鼻木 **hanagi** (bull's) wooden nose ring

5 鼻汁 **hanashiru** nasal mucus, runny nose

鼻白 **hanajiro(mu)** look disappointed/daunted

6 鼻先 **hanasaki** tip of the nose

鼻血 **hanaji** nosebleed, bloody nose

7 鼻声 **hanagoe, bisei** nasal voice

8 鼻炎 **bien** nasal inflammation

9 鼻風邪 **hanakaze** head cold

鼻茸 **hanatake, biji** nasal polyp

鼻屎 **hanakuso** snot, booger

鼻面 **hanazura** muzzle, snout

鼻柱 **hana(p)pashira, hanabashira** the septum; the bridge of the nose

鼻祖 **biso** founder, originator

鼻音 **bion** nasal sound

10 鼻高々 **hanatakadaka** proudly, triumphantly

鼻骨 **bikotsu** the nasal bone/cartilage

鼻息 **hanaiki, bisoku** breathing through the nose; one's pleasure

鼻紙 **hanagami** paper handkerchief

11 鼻梁 **biryō** bridge of the nose

鼻眼鏡 **hanamegane** pince-nez

12 鼻腔 **bikō** the nasal cavity

鼻筋 **hanasuji** the bridge/line of the nose

13 鼻詰 **hanazu(mari)** nasal congestion

14 鼻摘 **hanatsuma(mi)** disgusting person, outcast

鼻歌 **hanauta** humming, crooning

鼻緒 **hanao** clog/geta thong

鼻綱 **hanazuna** (bull's) nose halter

15 鼻輪 **hanawa** (bull's) nose ring

16 鼻髭 **hanahige** mustache

鼻薬 **hanagusuri** bribe, hush money

17 鼻糞 **hanakuso** snot, booger

——————— 2 ———————

3 小鼻 **kobana** sides of the nose, nostrils

4 手鼻 **tebana** blowing one's nose with one's fingers

5 目鼻 **mehana** eyes and nose; (take) shape

目鼻立 **mehanada(chi)** looks, features

6 耳鼻 **jibi** ear and nose

耳鼻咽喉科 **jibiinkōka** ear, nose, and throat specialty

耳鼻科 **jibika** otorhinology

7 阿鼻叫喚 **abikyōkan** (two of Buddhism's eight hells)

9 造鼻 **zōbi** nasal plastic surgery

段鼻 **danbana** aquiline/Roman nose
10 隆鼻術 **ryūbijutsu** nasal plastic surgery
13 鉤鼻 **kagibana** hooked/aquiline nose
14 酸鼻 **sanbi** horrible, piteous, appalling
19 犢鼻褌 **tokubikon** loincloth
23 鷲鼻 **washibana** aquiline/hooked nose

――――― 3 ―――――

6 団子鼻 **dangobana** flat/pug nose
9 柘榴鼻 **zakuro-bana** swollen red nose, strawberry nose
13 獅子鼻 **shishibana, shishi(p)pana** pug nose

――――― 4 ―――――

8 肥厚性鼻炎 **hikōsei bien** hypertrophic rhinitis

――――― 10 ―――――

夥→ **0a14.2**

5f10.1 / 1526

魅 **MI** charm, enchant, fascinate

――――― 1 ―――――

0 魅する **mi(suru)** charm, enchant, fascinate
1 魅了 **miryō** charm, captivate, hold spellbound
2 魅力 **miryoku** charm, appeal, fascination
魅力的 **miryokuteki** attractive, charming, captivating
12 魅惑 **miwaku** fascination, charm, lure

――――― 2 ―――――

20 魑魅 **chimi** mountain spirits and swamp spirits
魑魅魍魎 **chimimōryō** all kinds of goblins
21 魔魅 **mami** a deceiving/tempting spirit

5f10.2

魃 **HATSU** drought; god of drought

――――― 2 ―――――

3 干魃 **kanbatsu** drought
7 旱魃 **kanbatsu** drought

5f10.3

畿 **KI** capital; capital region

――――― 1 ―――――

4 畿内 **Kinai** the five home provinces around Kyōto

――――― 2 ―――――

6 近畿 **Kinki** the Ōsaka-Kyōto area

5f10.4

魄 **TAKU, HAKU** soul, spirit

――――― 2 ―――――

6 気魄 **kihaku** spirit, vigor
12 落魄 **rakuhaku** straitened circumstances
o(chi)bu(reru) be ruined, be reduced to poverty

――――― 11 ―――――

5f11.1

鴫 **shigi** snipe, sandpiper

疊→畳 **5f7.3**

5f11.2 / 1309

奮 **FUN, furu(u)** be enlivened/invigorated, rouse forth (one's courage); wield; thrive

――――― 1 ―――――

0 奮って **furu(tte)** energetically, heartily
5 奮迅 **funjin** furious/vigorous activity
奮立 **furu(i)ta(tsu)** be stirred/roused
7 奮励 **funrei** strenuous effort
9 奮発 **funpatsu** exertion, strenuous effort; splurge
10 奮進 **funshin** pushing vigorously forward
奮起 **funki** rouse oneself (to action), be inspired
12 奮然 **funzen** resolutely, corageously
13 奮戦 **funsen** hard fighting
16 奮激 **fungeki** be roused/inspired
18 奮闘 **funtō** struggle, strive, fight hard

――――― 2 ―――――

4 亢奮 **kōfun** excitement
9 発奮 **happun** be roused to action
昂奮 **kōfun** get excited
13 感奮 **kanpun** be inspired/moved to action
16 興奮 **kōfun** get excited
興奮剤 **kōfunzai** stimulant

――――― 3 ―――――

13 獅子奮迅 **shishi funjin** great power and speed

甎→甎 **4c13.3**

獣→ **3g12.3**

5

石
立
目
禾
衤
→12 罒
皿
疒

─────────── 12 ───────────

5f12.1

嬲　嫐

JŌ, **nabu(ru)** make sport/fun of, tease, ridicule

─────────── 1 ───────────
8 嬲物 **nabu(ri)mono** laughingstock
10 嬲殺 **nabu(ri)goro(shi)** torture to death

5f12.2

戴

TAI, **itada(ku)** be crowned with; receive, accept

─────────── 1 ───────────
8 戴物 **itada(ki)mono** gift
9 戴冠式 **taikanshiki** coronation
─────────── 2 ───────────
8 押戴 **o(shi)itada(ku)** raise reverently to one's head
11 推戴 **suitai** have as president of
頂戴 **chōdai** accept, receive; please (give me)
頂戴物 **chōdaimono** something received as a gift
─────────── 3 ───────────
4 不倶戴天 **fugutaiten** irreconcilable (enemies)

5f12.3

鼾

KAN, **ibiki** snoring

─────────── 2 ───────────
3 大鼾 **ōibiki** loud snoring
10 高鼾 **takaibiki** loud snoring

─────────── 13 ───────────

壘 → 塁 5f7.2

翻 → 6b12.3

5f13.1

魎

RYŌ spirits of trees and rocks

─────────── 2 ───────────
18 魍魎 **sudama, mōryō** spirits of mountains, streams, trees, and rocks

─────────── 4 ───────────
20 魑魅魍魎 **chimimōryō** all kinds of goblins

5f13.2

魍

MŌ spirits of mountains and streams

─────────── 1 ───────────
18 魍魎 **sudama, mōryō** spirits of mountains, streams, trees, and rocks
─────────── 3 ───────────
20 魑魅魍魎 **chimimōryō** all kinds of goblins

─────────── 14 ───────────

5f14.1

疇　畴

CHŪ before; same kind; field

─────────── 2 ───────────
15 範疇 **hanchū** category

5f14.2

疆

KYŌ boundary

5f14.3

髀　髀

HI thigh, femur

─────────── 1 ───────────
6 髀肉嘆 **hiniku (no) tan** lamenting the lack of opportunity to show one's skill

─────────── 15 ───────────

5f15.1

魑

CHI mountain spirits

─────────── 1 ───────────
15 魑魅 **chimi** mountain spirits and swamp spirits
魑魅魍魎 **chimimōryō** all kinds of goblins

─────────── 16 ───────────

5f16.1

罍

RAI jar (for liquor)

─── 17 ───

疊 → 畳 5f7.3

疊 → 畳 5f7.3

─── 19 ───

厴 → 2p22.1

═══ ⌐ 5g ═══

罘	罠	罟	罥	買	署	罫	罧	罪	罨	罩	蜀	置
4.1	5.1	5.2	7.1	7.2	8.1	8.2	8.3	8.4	8.5	8.6	8.7	8.8

署	罰	罵	罸	罷	罹	爵	絹	羃	羅	羆	羈	鬟
5g8.1	9.1	10.1	5g9.1	10.2	11.1	12.1	13.1	2i13.1	14.1	14.2	17.1	18.1

羇	羈	醬	釁
18.2	19.1	4a25.1	4a25.1

5

石
立
目
禾
ネ
田 7 ←
罒
疒

─── 4 ───

5g4.1

罘

FU rabbit-catching net

─── 5 ───

5g5.1

罠

BIN, MIN, wana trap, snare

5g5.2

罟

KO, ami net

─── 7 ───

5g7.1

罥

RI vilification, vituperation

─── 2 ───

15 罵詈 **bari** abuse, vilification, vituperation
罵詈雑言 **bari-zōgon** abusive language

5g7.2 / 241

買

BAI, ka(u) buy

─── 1 ───

2 買入 **ka(i)i(reru)** purchase, stock up on
3 買上 **ka(i)a(geru)** buy (up/out)
買上品 **ka(i)a(ge)hin** purchases

4 買切 **ka(i)ki(ru)** buy up, reserve, charter
買収 **baishū** purchase; buy off, bribe
買込 **ka(i)ko(mu)** buy, stock up on
買手 **ka(i)te** buyer
買方 **ka(i)kata** buyer; how to buy
5 買出 **ka(i)da(shi)** buy (wholesale), lay in (supplies)
買付 **ka(i)tsu(ke)** buying, purchase
買占 **ka(i)shi(meru)** buy up, corner (the market)
買主 **ka(i)nushi** buyer
6 買気 **ka(i)ki** buying mood, bullishness
7 買戻 **ka(i)modo(su)** buy back, redeem
買初 **ka(i)zo(me)** first purchase of the new year
買言葉 **ka(i)kotoba** harsh retort to harsh words
8 買受 **ka(i)u(keru)** acquire by purchase
買物 **ka(i)mono** shopping, purchase
買取 **ka(i)to(ru)** buy (up), purchase
9 買食 **ka(i)gu(i)** buying and eating (sweets) between meals
10 買値 **ka(i)ne** purchase/bid price
買時 **ka(i)doki** the best time to buy
買被 **ka(i)kabu(ru)** pay too much for; overrate
11 買過 **ka(i)su(giru)** buy too much/many
買控 **ka(i)hika(eru)** refrain from buying
買得 **kaidoku** a good bargain/buy
12 買集 **ka(i)atsu(meru)** buy up
13 買溜 **ka(i)da(me)** hoarding
買置 **ka(i)o(ki)** stocking up on, hoarding
14 買漁 **ka(i)asa(ru)** hunt/shop around for
買煽 **ka(i)ao(ru)** bid up, rig (the market)

─── 2 ───

2 人買 **hitoka(i)** slave trading/trader

3 小買 **koga(i)** buy in small quantities
6 仲買 **nakaga(i)** broking, brokerage
   仲買人 **nakaga(i)nin** broker, agent
7 売買 **baibai** buying and selling, trade, sale
8 非買同盟 **hibai dōmei** boycott
   盲買 **mekuraga(i)** buying sight-unseen
9 故買 **kobai** buy stolen goods, fence
11 掛買 **ka(ke)ga(i)** credit purchase
13 試買 **shibai** trial purchase
17 購買 **kōbai** purchasing
   購買力 **kōbairyoku** purchasing power
   購買者 **kōbaisha** buyer
   購買部 **kōbaibu** cooperative store
   購買組合 **kōbai kumiai** a co-op

——————— 3 ———————

1 一役買 **hitoyaku ka(u)** take on a role/task
6 先物買 **sakimonoga(i)** forward buying; speculation
8 青田買 **aotaga(i)** buying yet unharvested rice; signing up prospective graduates as employees
9 思惑買 **omowakuga(i)** speculative buying
15 歓心買 **kanshin (o) ka(u)** curry favor

——————— 4 ———————

2 人身売買 **jinshin baibai** slave trade
7 売言葉買言葉 **u(ri)kotoba (ni) ka(i)kotoba** (an exchange of) fighting words

——————— 8 ———————

5g8.1 / 860

署　署

SHO government office, (police) station; sign one's name

——————— 1 ———————

6 署名 **shomei** signature
   署名国 **shomeikoku** signatory (country)
   署名捺印 **shomei-natsuin** signature and seal
8 署長 **shochō** government office chief, police precinct head
10 署員 **shoin** office/station staff member

——————— 2 ———————

4 支署 **shisho** branch office, substation
   分署 **bunsho** substation, branch
   公署 **kōsho** government office
5 本署 **honsho** police headquarters; this office
   代署 **daisho** sign for another
6 自署 **jisho** signature, autograph
9 連署 **rensho** joint signature
10 部署 **busho** one's post, duty station
11 副署 **fukusho** countersignature
16 親署 **shinsho** (emperor's) personal signature

——————— 3 ———————

8 官公署 **kankōsho** government and municipal offices

10 消防署 **shōbōsho** fire station
12 税務署 **zeimusho** tax office
19 警察署 **keisatsusho** police station

5g8.2

罫

KEI, KE ruled line

——————— 1 ———————

4 罫引 **keibi(ki)** ruling; ruler
10 罫紙 **keishi** lined/ruled paper
15 罫線 **keisen** ruled line

——————— 2 ———————

15 横罫 **yokokei** horizontal lines

5g8.3

罧

RIN luring fish with a bonfire

5g8.4 / 885

罪

ZAI, tsumi crime, sin, guilt

——————— 1 ———————

2 罪人 **zainin** criminal   **tsumibito** sinner
6 罪名 **zaimei** name of the crime, the charge
7 罪作 **tsumitsuku(ri)** sinfulness; sinner
   罪状 **zaijō** nature of the offense, charges
9 罪科 **zaika** offense, crime; punishment
11 罪過 **zaika** offense, sin, fault
   罪深 **tsumibuka(i)** sinful, guilty, godless
   罪悪 **zaiaku** crime, sin, vice
   罪悪感 **zaiakukan** guilty conscience
   罪實 **zaiseki** liability for a crime
13 罪業 **zaigō** sin
   罪障 **zaishō** sin
   罪障消滅 **zaishō shōmetsu** expiation of one's sins
   罪滅 **tsumihorobo(shi)** atonement, amends, expiation, penance, conscience money
   罪跡 **zaiseki** evidence of guilt
15 罪質 **zaishitsu** nature of the crime/offense

——————— 2 ———————

3 大罪 **daizai** heinous crime, grave sin
   大罪人 **daizainin** great criminal
5 功罪 **kōzai** merits and demerits
   犯罪 **hanzai** crime
   犯罪人 **hanzainin** criminal, offender, convict
   犯罪学 **hanzaigaku** criminology
   犯罪者 **hanzaisha** criminal, offender, convict
6 死罪 **shizai** capital punishment
   伏罪 **fukuzai** plead guilty

同罪 **dōzai** the same crime
有罪 **yūzai** guilty
有罪人 **yūzaijin** guilty person
7 余罪 **yozai** other crimes
8 免罪 **menzai** acquittal, pardon; papal indulgence
免罪符 **menzaifu** an indulgence
服罪 **fukuzai** plead guilty, confess
9 重罪 **jūzai** serious crime, felony
浄罪 **jōzai** purgation (from sins)
10 冤罪 **enzai** false charge
原罪 **genzai** original sin
流罪 **ruzai** exile, banishment
11 堕罪 **dazai** fall into sin
宿罪 **shukuzai** sins of one's previous life
赦罪 **shazai** pardon, absolution
断罪 **danzai** convict, condemn; beheading
斬罪 **zanzai** execution by sword, beheading
問罪 **monzai** accusation, indictment
12 無罪 **muzai** innocent, not guilty
無罪判決 **muzai hanketsu** acquittal
絞罪 **kōzai** (execution by) hanging
軽罪 **keizai** minor offense
13 微罪 **bizai** minor offense
17 聴罪 **chōzai** hearing confessions
聴罪師 **chōzaishi** (Catholic) confessor
謝罪 **shazai** apology
22 贖罪 **shokuzai** atonement, expiation, redemption
———— 3 ————
3 大逆罪 **taigyakuzai, daigyakuzai** treason; parricide
4 不敬罪 **fukeizai** lese majesty
6 死刑罪 **shikeizai** capital offense
汚職罪 **oshokuzai** bribery
8 性犯罪 **sei hanzai** sex crime
9 姦通罪 **kantsūzai** (the crime of) adultery
窃盗罪 **settōzai** theft, larceny
背任罪 **haininzai** breach of trust
10 殺人罪 **satsujinzai** murder
教唆罪 **kyōsazai** (the crime of) incitement
恐喝罪 **kyōkatsuzai** extortion, blackmail
11 偽証罪 **gishōzai** perjury
12 違警罪 **ikeizai** offense against police regulations
無実罪 **mujitsu (no) tsumi** false accusation
詐欺罪 **sagizai** fraud
軽犯罪 **keihanzai** minor offense
16 親告罪 **shinkokuzai** offense subject to prosecution only upon complaint (e.g., defamation)
18 瀆神罪 **tokushinzai** blasphemy, sacrilege, profanity
瀆職罪 **tokushokuzai** bribery, graft
贈賄罪 **zōwaizai** (the crime of) bribery
騒擾罪 **sōjōzai** sedition, rioting

———— 5 ————
11 過失致死罪 **kashitsu chishizai** accidental homicide, manslaughter

5g8.5
罨 **AN** cover
———— 1 ————
8 罨法 **anpō** poultice, compress, pack
———— 2 ————
7 冷罨法 **reianpō** cold compress/pack
12 温罨法 **on'anpō** hot compress

5g8.6
罩 **TŌ** weir; basket for holding fish

5g8.7
蜀 **SHOKU** green caterpillar; Sichuan province (in China)
———— 1 ————
12 蜀葵 **tachiaoi** hollyhock
蜀黍 **morokoshi** millet, sorghum
———— 2 ————
5 玉蜀黍 **tōmorokoshi** corn, maize
11 望蜀 **bōshoku** insatiable

5g8.8 / 426
置 **CHI, o(ku)** put, place, set; leave behind, leave as is **-o(ki)** skipping ..., at intervals of ..., every (other/third day), (five meters) apart
———— 1 ————
0 置いてきぼり **o(itekibori)** leave (someone) behind, slip away
3 置土 **o(ki)tsuchi** earth (from elsewhere) put on top
置土産 **o(ki)miyage** parting gift, souvenir
4 置手紙 **o(ki)tegami** letter left behind
置引 **o(ki)bi(ki)** baggage theft
置火燵 **o(ki)gotatsu** portable brazier
5 置去 **o(ki)za(ri)** desert, leave in the lurch
置字 **o(ki)ji** character skipped over when reading Chinese
置石 **o(ki)ishi** decorative garden stone
6 置行 **o(ki)yu(ku)** leave behind
7 置来 **o(ite) ku(ru)** leave behind
置忘 **o(ki)wasu(reru)** mislay, forget
置床 **o(ki)doko** movable tokonoma alcove

8 置直 **o(ki)nao(su)** replace, transpose, rearrange
置物 **o(ki)mono** ornament; figurehead
置所 **o(ki)dokoro** place to put something
9 置屋 **o(ki)ya** geisha house
置炬燵 **o(ki)gotatsu** portable brazier
10 置時計 **o(ki)dokei** table clock
11 置道 **o(ki)michi** raised road
12 置傘 **o(ki)gasa** spare umbrella kept at one's workplace
置違 **o(ki)chiga(eru)** put in the wrong place
置渡 **o(ki)wata(su)** lay over
置場 **o(ki)ba** place to put something
置換 **o(ki)kae(ru)** replace, transpose, rearrange **chikan** substitute, replace
13 置路 **o(ki)michi** raised road
16 置薬 **o(ki)gusuri** household medicines left by a door-to-door salesman who later collects money for the used portion

———————— 2 ————————

1 一置 **hito(tsu)o(ki)** every other one
4 引置 **inchi** take into custody
心置 **kokoroo(ki naku)** without reserve, frankly
5 仕置 **shio(ki)** punishment; execution
代置 **daichi** replace
存置 **sonchi** retain, maintain
布置 **fuchi** arrangement, grouping, composition
処置 **shochi** disposition, measures, steps
6 安置 **anchi** enshrine
7 位置 **ichi** position, location
対置 **taichi** set opposite/against
床置 **tokoo(ki)** alcove ornament
言置 **i(i)o(ku)** leave word
8 併置 **heichi** juxtapose, place side by side
並置 **heichi** place side by side, juxtapose
拘置 **kōchi** keep in detention, confine, hold
拘置所 **kōchisho** house of detention, prison
定置 **teichi** stationary, fixed
物置 **monoo(ki)** storeroom, shed
放置 **hōchi** let alone, leave as is, leave to chance
取置 **to(tte)o(ki)** set aside, choicest, ace in the hole
9 前置 **maeo(ki)** preface, introduction
前置詞 **zenchishi** preposition
後置詞 **kōchishi** postposition
10 倒置 **tōchi** turning upside down; inversion (of normal word order)
倒置法 **tōchihō** inversion (of normal word order)
差置 **sa(shi)o(ku)** leave, let alone; ignore
書置 **ka(ki)o(ki)** note left behind; will
留置 **ryūchi** detention, custody, lockup
to(me)o(ku) detain, keep (after school); leave until called for
留置場 **ryūchijō** detention room, police cell
配置 **haichi** arrangement, placement, layout
11 措置 **sochi** measure, steps
捨置 **su(te)o(ku)** leave as is, overlook
据置 **su(e)o(ku)** leave as is, let stand
常置 **jōchi** permanent, standing (committee)
設置 **setchi** establishment, founding, institution
転置 **tenchi** transposition
12 廃置 **haichi** abolition and establishment
装置 **sōchi** device, apparatus, equipment
買置 **ka(i)o(ki)** stocking up on, hoarding
13 溜置 **ta(me)o(ku)** store, stock up on
14 聞置 **ki(ki)o(ku)** hear, keep in mind
15 箸置 **hashio(ki)** chopstick rest
16 積置場 **tsu(mi)o(ki)ba** storage/freight yard

———————— 3 ————————

5 未処置 **mishochi** untreated
6 死体置場 **shitai o(ki)ba** morgue
再配置 **saihaichi** reallocate, rearrange
12 廃藩置県 **haihan-chiken** the abolition of clans and establishment of prefectures

———————— 4 ————————

6 安全装置 **anzen sōchi** safety device

———————— 9 ————————

署 → 署 **5g8.1**

5g9.1 / 886

罰 罰 **BATSU** punishment, penalty
BACHI (divine) punishment, retribution

———————— 1 ————————

0 罰する **bas(suru)** punish, penalize
6 罰当 **bachia(tari)** damned, cursed
8 罰杯 **bappai** penalty cup (the loser must drink)
罰金 **bakkin** a fine
9 罰点 **batten** demerit marks
罰則 **bassoku** penal regulations/provisions
10 罰俸 **bappō** docking of salary

———————— 2 ————————

4 天罰 **tenbatsu** divine punishment
5 処罰 **shobatsu** punishment, penalty
6 刑罰 **keibatsu** punishment, penalty
7 体罰 **taibatsu** corporal punishment
9 神罰 **shinbatsu** divine punishment
15 賞罰 **shōbatsu** reward and punishment, praise and censure
17 厳罰 **genbatsu** severe punishment

18 懲罰 **chōbatsu** disciplinary measure, punishment

─────── 4 ───────

9 信賞必罰 **shinshō-hitsubatsu** sure punishment and sure reward

─────── 10 ───────

5g10.1

罵 **BA, nonoshi(ru)** speak ill of, revile, inveigh against

─────── 1 ───────

7 罵声 **basei** jeers, boos, hisses
10 罵倒 **batō** denunciation, condemnation
12 罵詈 **bari** abuse, vilification, vituperation
罵詈雑言 **bari-zōgon** abusive language

─────── 2 ───────

7 冷罵 **reiba** sneer, abuse, revilement
9 面罵 **menba** revile (someone) to his face
11 悪罵 **akuba** vilification, abuse
14 漫罵 **manba** revile, deride, criticize irresponsibly
15 嘲罵 **chōba** taunt, revile, insult

詞 → 罰 **5g9.1**

5g10.2 / 1861

罷 **HI, ya(meru/mu)** (tr./intr.) end, discontinue, stop
maka(ru) leave, withdraw

─────── 1 ───────

5 罷出 **maka(ri)de(ru)** report to, appear before; leave, withdraw
8 罷免 **himen** dismissal (from one's post)
9 罷通 **maka(ri)tō(ru)** force/have one's way, go unchallenged
12 罷越 **maka(ri)ko(su)** go to, visit, call on
罷間違 **maka(ri)machiga(eba)** if worse comes to worst
13 罷業 **higyō** strike, walkout

─────── 2 ───────

7 身罷 **mimaka(ru)** die, pass away
14 総罷業 **sōhigyō** general strike

─────── 4 ───────

14 総同盟罷業 **sōdōmei higyō** general strike

─────── 11 ───────

5g11.1

羅 **RI, kaka(ru)** fall ill to, contract (a disease), catch (the flu)

─────── 12 ───────

5g12.1 / 1923

爵 **SHAKU** peerage, court rank

─────── 1 ───────

7 爵位 **shakui** peerage, court rank

─────── 2 ───────

2 子爵 **shishaku** viscount
4 公爵 **kōshaku** prince, duke
公爵夫人 **kōshaku fujin** princess, duchess
6 有爵 **yūshaku** titled, of the peerage
7 伯爵 **hakushaku** count, earl
男爵 **danshaku** baron
9 侯爵 **kōshaku** marquis, marquess
侯爵夫人 **kōshaku fujin** marchioness
叙爵 **joshaku** conferring a peerage
11 授爵 **jushaku** confer nobility/peerage
15 勲爵 **kunshaku** order of merit and peerage

─────── 13 ───────

5g13.1

絹 **KEN, wana** trap

冪 → 幕 **2i13.1**

─────── 14 ───────

5g14.1 / 1860

羅 **RA** silk gauze, thin silk; (used phonetically)

─────── 1 ───────

5 羅宇 **rao** bamboo pipestem; Laos
6 羅列 **raretsu** marshal, enumerate, cite
羅衣 **rai** thin kimono
8 羅典 **Raten** Latin
10 羅針 **rashin** compass needle
羅針儀 **rashingi** compass
羅針盤 **rashinban** compass
羅馬 **Rōma** Rome
13 羅漢 **rakan** arhat, attainer of Nirvana

─────── 2 ───────

5 甲羅 **kōra** (turtle's) shell
7 伽羅 **kyara** aloes wood (tree or fragrance)
阿羅漢 **arakan** arhat
8 欧羅巴 **Yōroppa** Europe
9 海羅 **funori** (a seaweed, used for laundry starch)

5

石
立
目
禾
衤
田
罒 14←
疒

10 修羅 **shura** Asura (battle-loving Buddhist demon); fighting
   修羅場 **shurajō, shuraba** scene of carnage
   娑羅双樹 **shara sōju** sal tree
11 婆羅門 **Baramon** Brahman
12 森羅万象 **shinra-banshō** all creation, the universe
14 綺羅 **kira** fine clothes
   綺羅星 **kiraboshi** glittering stars
   網羅 **mōra** include, be comprehensive
15 暹羅 **Shamu** Siam
   摩羅 **mara** penis
21 魔羅 **mara** penis

———— 3 ————

1 一帳羅 **itchōra** one's only good clothes
   一張羅 **itchōra** one's only good clothes
4 天麩羅 **tenpura** tempura, Japanese-style fried foods
8 金比羅 **Konpira** (the god of seafarers)
11 曼陀羅 **mandara** mandala, picture of Buddha
   曼荼羅 **mandara** mandala, picture of Buddha

———— 4 ————

7 我武者羅 **gamushara** reckless, daredevil

5g14.2

罷   **HI, higuma, shiguma** brown bear

———— 17 ————

5g17.1

羈   **KI** travel(er)

———— 18 ————

5g18.1

鬟   **KAN, wage** topknot, chignon
      mizura ancient men's hairstyle of looped ponytails

5g18.2

韤   **BETSU** socks

———— 19 ————

5g19.1

羇 羈   **KI** reins; connection

———— 1 ————
11 羈絆 **kihan** yoke, fetters, restraints

———— 2 ————
4 不羈 **fuki** freedom, independence

———— 20 ————

欝 → 鬱 4a25.1

———— 21 ————

欝 → 鬱 4a25.1

———— 5h ————

皿	血	盂	盈	盃	盆	岴	盍	岵	盛	盗	盜	衆
0.1	1.1	3.1	4.1	4a4.11	2o7.6	5h5.1	3b7.9	5.1	6.1	6.2	5h6.2	7.1

峈	盟	盠	盡	監	盤	盬	盪	鹽	欝
7.2	8.1	4n9.3	3r3.1	10.1	10.2	11.1	12.1	3b10.4	4a25.1

———— 0 ————

5h0.1 / 1097

皿   **sara** plate, dish, saucer

———— 1 ————

6 皿回 **saramawa(shi)** dish-spinning trick
9 皿洗 **saraara(i)** dishwashing; dishwasher

———— 2 ————

1 一皿 **hitosara** a plate/dish (of food)
3 小皿 **kozara** small plate, saucer
4 木皿 **kizara** wooden dish
   火皿 **hizara** fire grate; chafing dish; bowl of a pipe
6 灰皿 **haizara** ashtray
8 受皿 **u(ke)zara** saucer
   取皿 **to(ri)zara** serving dish

石 立 目 禾 礻 田 皿 疒

→ 14 皿

────────── 3 ──────────

₄ 手塩皿 **teshiozara** small dish, saucer
₁₁ 菓子皿 **kashizara** cake plate

────────── 1 ──────────

5h1.1 / 789

KETSU, chi blood

血

────────── 1 ──────────

₀ 血だらけ **chi(darake)** bloodstained
₂ 血刀 **chigatana** bloodstained sword
₄ 血友病 **ketsuyūbyō** hemophilia
   血止 **chido(me)** a styptic
₅ 血圧 **ketsuatsu** blood pressure
   血圧計 **ketsuatsukei** sphygmomanometer
   血巡 **chi (no) megu(ri)** circulation of the blood; (quick/slow)-wittedness
   血目 **chime** bloodshot eye
₆ 血気 **kekki** vigor, hot blood
     chi(no)ke -bloodedness, complexion
   血気盛 **kekkizaka(ri)** the prime of one's vigor
   血合 **chia(i)** meat of bloody color
   血肉 **ketsuniku** flesh and blood
   血色 **kesshoku** complexion, color
   血色素 **kesshikiso** hemoglobin
   血汐 **chishio** blood
   血行 **kekkō** circulation of the blood
₇ 血判 **keppan** seal with one's blood
   血沈 **ketchin** precipitation of blood
   血走 **chibashi(ru)** become bloodshot
   血豆 **chimame** blood blister
   血尿 **ketsunyō** bloody urine
₈ 血迷 **chimayo(u)** lose control of oneself; run amok
   血雨 **chi(no)ame** bloodshed
₉ 血便 **ketsuben** bloody stools
   血海 **chi (no) umi** a sea of blood
   血相 **kessō** a look, expression
   血染 **chizo(me)** bloodstained
₁₀ 血涙 **chi (no) namida, ketsurui** tears of blood
   血栓 **kessen** thrombus
   血栓症 **kessenshō** thrombosis
   血脈 **ketsumyaku** blood vessel/relationship
   血書 **kessho** writing in blood
₁₁ 血達磨 **chidaruma** covered with blood
   血道 **chi (no) michi** (women's) dizziness, congestion of the brain, hysterics
   血清 **kessei** (blood) serum
   血液 **ketsueki** blood
   血液型 **ketsuekigata** blood type
   血液像 **ketsuekizō** hemogram
   血祭 **chimatsu(ri)** blood offering (to the war god)

血球 **kekkyū** blood corpuscle
血族 **ketsuzoku** blood relative, kin
血眼 **chimanako** bloodshot eye; frantic
血痕 **kekkon** bloodstain
₁₂ 血斑 **keppan** blood spot
血税 **ketsuzei** conscription; heavy taxation
血統 **kettō** lineage, pedigree, family line
血統書 **kettōsho** pedigree
血筋 **chisuji** blood relationship, lineage
₁₃ 血塊 **kekkai** blood clot, clotted blood
血塗 **chimami(re)** bloodstained
   chinu(ru) smear with blood
血腥 **chinamagusa(i)** smelling of blood, bloody
血煙 **chikemuri** spray of blood
血戦 **kessen** bloody battle
血盟 **ketsumei** blood pledge
血痰 **kettan** bloody phlegm
血続 **chitsuzu(ki)** blood relationship, kin
血路 **ketsuro** a way out, an escape
₁₄ 血管 **kekkan** blood vessel
₁₅ 血漿 **kesshō** (blood) plasma
血潮 **chishio** blood
血縁 **ketsuen** blood relationship/relative
血糊 **chinori** gore, clotted blood
血餅 **keppei** blood clot
₁₆ 血糖 **kettō** blood sugar
血糖値 **kettōchi** blood-sugar level
₁₇ 血膿 **chiumi** bloody pus

────────── 2 ──────────

₄ 止血 **shiketsu** stopping/stanching bleeding
   止血剤 **shiketsuzai** hemostatic drug, styptic agent
   心血 **shinketsu** one's heart's blood, heart and soul
₅ 出血 **shukketsu** bleeding, hemorrhage
   失血 **shikketsu** loss of blood
   生血 **i(ki)chi** lifeblood, blood of a living man/animal   **namachi** blood just shed, blood of a living man/animal
   白血病 **hakketsubyō** leukemia
   白血球 **hakkekkyū** white corpuscles
₆ 多血 **taketsu** sanguine, full-blooded
   多血質 **taketsushitsu** sanguine, hot-blooded
   充血 **jūketsu** become congested/bloodshot
   返血 **kae(ri)chi** blood spurted back (from a stabbing victim onto the assailant)
   汗血 **kanketsu** sweat and blood
   吐血 **toketsu** vomit blood
   吸血 **kyūketsu** sucking blood
   吸血鬼 **kyūketsuki** vampire
₇ 冷血 **reiketsu** cold-blooded; coldhearted
   冷血漢 **reiketsukan** coldhearted person
   赤血球 **sekkekkyū** red corpuscles
   売血 **baiketsu** selling one's blood

5
石
立
目
禾
衤
田
皿 1←
疒

8 受血者 **juketsusha** blood recipient
　放血 **hōketsu** bloodletting
9 造血 **zōketsu** blood making
　造血剤 **zōketsuzai** blood-making medicine
10 高血圧 **kōketsuatsu** high blood pressure
　流血 **ryūketsu** bloodshed
　純血 **junketsu** full-blooded, thoroughbred
11 貧血 **hinketsu** anemia
　貧血症 **hinketsushō** anemia
　混血 **konketsu** racial mixture
　混血児 **konketsuji** person of mixed race, half-breed
　採血 **saiketsu** collect blood
　脳血栓 **nōkessen** cerebral thrombosis
　黒血 **kurochi** blackish/purulent blood
　悪血 **akuchi, oketsu** impure blood
　敗血症 **haiketsushō** blood poisoning
12 温血 **onketsu** warm-blooded (animal)
　喀血 **kakketsu** spitting blood
　無血 **muketsu** bloodless, without bloodshed
　補血 **hoketsu** replenishing one's blood
　補血剤 **hoketsuzai** an antianemic
　給血 **kyūketsu** give blood
　給血者 **kyūketsusha** blood donor
13 溢血 **ikketsu** effusion of blood
　献血 **kenketsu** blood donation
　鉄血 **tekketsu** blood and iron; military preparations
14 膏血 **kōketsu** blood and sweat
　鼻血 **hanaji** nosebleed, bloody nose
15 熱血 **nekketsu** hot blood, fiery zeal, ardor
　熱血漢 **nekketsukan** fervent/hot-blooded man
16 凝血 **gyōketsu** coagulated blood, bloot clot
　壊血病 **kaiketsubyō** scurvy
　輸血 **yuketsu** blood transfusion
17 鮮血 **senketsu** (fresh/still-undried) blood
18 瀉血 **shaketsu** bloodletting
29 鬱血 **ukketsu** blood congestion, engorgement

――――― 3 ―――――

4 内出血 **naishukketsu** internal bleeding/ hemorrhage
　毛細血管 **mōsai kekkan** capillaries
9 肺出血 **haishukketsu** discharge of blood from the lungs
11 脳出血 **nōshukketsu** cerebral hemorrhage
　脳充血 **nōjūketsu** brain congestion
　脳貧血 **nōhinketsu** cerebral anemia
　脳溢血 **nōikketsu** cerebral apoplexy
14 静脈血 **jōmyakuketsu** venous blood

――――― 4 ―――――

4 収縮期血圧 **shūshukuki ketsuatsu** systolic blood pressure
11 眼底出血 **gantei shukketsu** hemorrhage in the fundus of the eye

――――― 3 ―――――

5h3.1

盂　U bowl

――――― 1 ―――――

19 盂蘭盆 **Urabon** o-Bon festival
　盂蘭盆会 **Urabon'e** o-Bon festival

――――― 2 ―――――

13 腎盂 **jin'u** the renal pelvis
　腎盂炎 **jin'uen** pyelitis

――――― 4 ―――――

5h4.1

盈　EI fill, be full

――――― 1 ―――――

11 盈虚 **eikyo** wax and wane
12 盈満 **eiman** be full/ample
17 盈虧 **eiki** waxing and waning, phase (of the moon)

盂 → 杯 4a4.11

盆 → 盆 2o7.6

蚅 → 衄 5h5.1

――――― 5 ―――――

盍 → 3b7.9

5h5.1

衄　蚅　JIKU nosebleed

――――― 6 ―――――

5h6.1 / 719

盛　SEI, JŌ, SHŌ, saka(n) prosperous, energetic　saka(ru) flourish, prosper　mo(ru) heap up; serve (food)

――――― 1 ―――――

3 盛大 **seidai** thriving, grand, magnificent
　盛上 **mo(ri)a(geru)** heap/pile up

盛土 **mo(ri)tsuchi** raising the ground level
4 盛切 **mo(ri)ki(ri)** single helping
5 盛代 **seidai** era of prosperity
盛付 **mo(ri)tsu(keru)** dish up
6 盛年 **seinen** the prime of life
盛会 **seikai** succesful meeting
盛返 **mo(ri)kae(su)** rally, recover
盛名 **seimei** renown, fame
7 盛沢山 **mo(ri)dakusan** many, plenty, varied
盛花 **mo(ri)bana** heaped-up flower arrangement
8 盛事 **seiji** grand undertaking/event
盛典 **seiten** grand/imposing ceremony
盛岡 **Morioka** (city, Iwate-ken)
盛況 **seikyō** prosperity, success, boom
盛者 **shōja** prosperous person
9 盛砂 **mo(ri)zuna** (ceremonial) piles of sand
10 盛衰 **seisui** rise and fall, ups and downs
盛宴 **seien** grand banquet
盛挙 **seikyo** grand undertaking
盛殺 **mo(ri)koro(su)** kill by poisoning
盛時 **seiji** prime of life; era of prosperity/glory   **saka(ri)doki** prosperous/busy time; rutting season
盛夏 **seika** the height of summer
11 盛菓子 **mo(ri)gashi** cakes heaped in a basket
12 盛場 **saka(ri)ba** bustling place, popular resort, amusement center
盛装 **seisō** gala dress, resplendent regalia
14 盛徳 **seitoku** illustrious virtues
15 盛儀 **seigi** grand ceremony
18 盛観 **seikan** grand spectacle

───────── 2 ─────────

1 一盛 **hitomo(ri)** a pile
     hitosaka(ri) temporary prosperity
3 女盛 **onnazaka(ri)** the prime of womanhood
山盛 **yamamo(ri)** heap(ing full)
4 切盛 **ki(ri)mo(ri)** manage, administer, run
水盛 **mizumo(ri)** (using a) carpenter's level
手盛 **temo(ri)** helping oneself (to food); managing for one's own convience; trap, trick
日盛 **hizaka(ri)** midday
5 出盛 **desaka(ri)** best time for, season for   **desaka(ru)** appear in abundance
目盛 **memo(ri)** scale, gradations
6 年盛 **toshizaka(ri)** the prime of life
全盛 **zensei** height of prosperity
全盛期 **zenseiki** golden age, heyday
色盛 **irozaka(ri)** a woman's most (sexually) attractive age
7 花盛 **hanazaka(ri)** in full bloom
男盛 **otokozaka(ri)** prime of manhood
8 若盛 **wakazaka(ri)** the prime/bloom of youth

旺盛 **ōsei** flourishing, in prime condition
9 度盛 **domo(ri)** gradation, scale
食盛 **ta(be)zaka(ri)** the age at which (a boy) has a hearty appetite   **ku(i)zaka(ri)** the right time to eat, the season for
10 隆盛 **ryūsei** prosperous, flourishing, thriving
真盛 **ma(s)saka(ri)** the middle/height of, in full bloom
酒盛 **sakamo(ri)** drinking bout, carousal
娘盛 **musumezaka(ri)** the prime of young womanhood
12 最盛期 **saiseiki** golden age, heyday; the best season for
飯盛 **meshimo(ri)** maidservant at an inn
13 働盛 **hatara(ki)zaka(ri)** prime of one's working life
14 豪盛 **gōsei** great, grand, magnificent
16 燃盛 **mo(e)saka(ru)** be ablaze, burn fiercely
繁盛 **hanjō** prosperity; success

───────── 3 ─────────

4 分別盛 **funbetsuzaka(ri)** age of discretion, mature judgment
6 血気盛 **kekkizaka(ri)** the prime of one's vigor
9 発育盛 **hatsuikuzaka(ri)** period of rapid growth
栄枯盛衰 **eiko-seisui** prosperity and decline, rise and fall

5h6.2 / 1100

                   TŌ, nusu(mu) steal

───────── 1 ─────────

2 盗人 **nusubito, nusutto** thief
4 盗心 **tōshin** propensity to steal, thievishness
5 盗犯 **tōhan** theft, burglary, robbery
6 盗伐 **tōbatsu** illegal logging, timber theft
盗汗 **tōkan, nease** night sweat
7 盗作 **tōsaku** plagiarism
盗見 **nusu(mi)mi(ru)** steal a glance
盗足 **nusu(mi)ashi** walking stealthily
8 盗取 **nusu(mi)to(ru)** steal
9 盗品 **tōhin** stolen goods, loot
盗食 **nusu(mi)gu(i)** eating furtively
10 盗笑 **nusu(mi)wara(i)** laughing in one's sleeve
13 盗賊 **tōzoku** thief, robber, burglar
盗電 **tōden** theft of electricity
14 盗読 **nusu(mi)yo(mi)** surreptitious reading
盗聞 **nusu(mi)gi(ki)** eavesdrop, listen in on
17 盗聴 **tōchō** surreptitious listening, bugging, wiretapping
18 盗癖 **tōheki** kleptomania, larcenousness
盗難 **tōnan** (loss from) theft

───

5

石
立
目
禾
衤
田
皿 6 ←
疒

─────────── 2 ───────────

7 花盗人 **hananusubito** one who steals flowers or cherry-blossom branches

8 夜盗 **yatō** nighttime burglar

怪盗 **kaitō** phantom thief

9 窃盗 **settō** theft, larceny; thief

窃盗犯 **settōhan** thief

窃盗罪 **settōzai** theft, larceny

11 偸盗 **chūtō** theft; thief

強盗 **gōtō** burglar(y), robber(y)

13 剽盗 **hyōtō** (highway) robbery

群盗 **guntō** gang of robbers

─────────── 3 ───────────

4 辻強盗 **tsujigōtō** highway robbery/holdup

─────────── 4 ───────────

8 押込強盗 **o(shi)ko(mi) gōtō** burglar(y)

─────────── 7 ───────────

盗 → 盗 **5h6.2**

5h7.1 / 792

衆   **SHŪ, SHU** multitude, populace

─────────── 1 ───────────

2 衆人 **shūjin** the people/public

3 衆口一致 **shūkō-itchi** unanimous

5 衆生 **shujō** all living things; mankind

衆目 **shūmoku** public attention

8 衆知 **shūchi** the wisdom of many

衆参両院 **shū-san ryōin** both Houses of the Diet

10 衆徒 **shūto** many priests

11 衆望 **shūbō** public confidence, popularity

12 衆評 **shūhyō** public opinion

13 衆愚 **shūgu** the ignorant rabble

衆意 **shūi** the ideas of the people

14 衆寡 **shūka** many vs. few, outnumbered

15 衆論 **shūron** the views of many

20 衆議 **shūgi** public discussion

衆議一決 **shūgi-ikketsu** decided unanimously

衆議院 **Shūgiin** the House of Representatives

─────────── 2 ───────────

3 大衆 **taishū** a crowd; the masses, the general public

大衆化 **taishūka** popularization

大衆向 **taishūmu(ki)** for the general public, popular

大衆性 **taishūsei** popularity

4 公衆 **kōshū** public (telephone, toilet, etc.)

5 民衆 **minshū** people, populace, masses

民衆化 **minshūka** popularization

6 合衆国 **Gasshūkoku** United States

会衆 **kaishū** audience, congregation

有衆 **yūshū** the people/multitude

7 男衆 **otokoshū** manservant

8 若衆 **wakashu** young man

9 俗衆 **zokushū** the mass public, the common herd

連衆 **tsu(re)shu** one's companions/party

13 群衆 **gunshū** crowd, multitude

17 聴衆 **chōshū** audience

18 観衆 **kanshū** audience, spectators

─────────── 3 ───────────

6 全民衆 **zenminshū** all the people

10 烏合衆 **ugō(no)shū** disorderly crowd, mob

5h7.2

略   **KAKU** vomit

─────────── 8 ───────────

5h8.1 / 717

盟   **MEI** oath; alliance

─────────── 1 ───────────

4 盟友 **meiyū** sworn friend, staunch ally

5 盟主 **meishu** the leader, leading power

6 盟休 **meikyū** (students') strike (short for 同盟休校)

盟邦 **meihō** ally

9 盟約 **meiyaku** pledge, pact; alliance

─────────── 2 ───────────

5 加盟 **kamei** join, be affiliated with

加盟国 **kameikoku** member nation, signatory

6 同盟 **dōmei** alliance, league, union

Dōmei Japanese Confederation of Labor (short for 全日本労働総同盟)

同盟国 **dōmeikoku** ally

同盟軍 **dōmeigun** allied armies

血盟 **ketsumei** blood pledge

9 連盟 **renmei** league, federation, union

12 結盟 **ketsumei** pledge

15 締盟 **teimei** conclude a treaty

締盟国 **teimeikoku** treaty signatories

─────────── 3 ───────────

14 総同盟罷業 **sōdōmei higyō** general strike

─────────── 4 ───────────

8 非売同盟 **hibai dōmei** sellers' strike

非買同盟 **hibai dōmei** boycott

12 欧州同盟 **Ōshū Dōmei** the European Union

期成同盟 **kisei dōmei** uniting to carry out

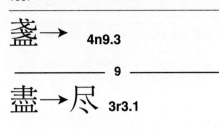 盍→ **4n9.3**

───────── 9 ─────────

盡→尽 **3r3.1**

───────── 10 ─────────

5h10.1 / 1663

監 **KAN** keep watch over

───────── 1 ─────────

6　監守 **kanshu** keeping watch over, custody
　　監守人 **kanshunin** custodian, (forest) ranger
8　監事 **kanji** inspector, supervisor, auditor
　　監房 **kanbō** (prison) cell
9　監査 **kansa** inspection; auditing
　　監査役 **kansayaku** auditor, inspector
10　監修 **kanshū** (editorial) supervision
11　監視 **kanshi** monitor, keep watch over
　　監視者 **kanshisha** guard, caretaker, watch-man
　　監視所 **kanshisho** lookout, guard/observation post
　　監視船 **kanshisen** guard boat, cutter
　　監訳 **kan'yaku** supervision of translation
13　監禁 **kankin** imprison, confine
　　監督 **kantoku** supervision, direction; (movie) director, (team) manager
　　監督下 **kantokuka** under the jurisdiction of
　　監督官 **kantokukan** inspector, superintendent
14　監獄 **kangoku** prison
　　監察 **kansatsu** inspection; inspector, supervisor
　　監察官 **kansatsukan** inspector, police supervisor
　　監製 **kansei** well supervised manufacturing
20　監護 **kango** custody and care

───────── 2 ─────────

3　大監督 **daikantoku** archbishop (Anglican)
4　収監 **shūkan** imprison
6　在監者 **zaikansha** prisoner, inmate
7　学監 **gakkan** dean, school superintendent
8　舎監 **shakan** dormitory superintendent, housemaster
11　脱監 **dakkan** escape from prison, jailbreak
12　統監 **tōkan** supervision; commander, resident-general
14　総監 **sōkan** superintendent-general

5h10.2 / 1098

盤 **BAN** (chess/go) board, tray, platter, basin

───────── 1 ─────────

5　盤台 **bandai** oval basin/tray
　　盤石 **banjaku** huge rock
9　盤面 **banmen** surface of a board/record
10　盤根 **bankon** coiled root
　　盤根錯節 **bankon-sakusetsu** knotty/thorny/complex situation

───────── 2 ─────────

3　大盤石 **daibanjaku** large stone, huge rock
4　中盤戦 **chūbansen** the middle game (in chess and other board games); the midst of an election campaign
　　円盤 **enban** disk; discus
　　円盤投 **enbanna(ge)** the discus throw
　　水盤 **suiban** flower basin
5　石盤 **sekiban** a slate
6　地盤 **jiban** the ground; footing, base, constituency
　　吸盤 **kyūban** sucker (on an octopus)
7　序盤 **joban** opening moves (in go)
　　序盤戦 **jobansen** beginning of a campaign
8　定盤 **jōban** surface plate/table, level block, molding board
9　胎盤 **taiban** placenta, afterbirth
　　音盤 **onban** phonograph record
10　骨盤 **kotsuban** the pelvis
11　基盤 **kiban** base, basis, foundation
　　旋盤 **senban** lathe
　　旋盤工 **senbankō** lathe operator, turner
　　終盤 **shūban** endgame
　　終盤戦 **shūbansen** endgame, final battle
12　落盤 **rakuban** cave-in
13　碁盤 **goban** go board
　　碁盤割 **gobanwa(ri)** partitioned like a checkerboard
　　碁盤縞 **gobanjima** checked/lattice pattern
　　路盤 **roban** roadbed
14　算盤 **soroban** abacus
　　銀盤 **ginban** silver platter; skating rink
16　鍵盤 **kenban** keyboard
21　露盤 **roban** pagoda roof

───────── 3 ─────────

4　文字盤 **mojiban** (clock) dial, (typewriter) keyboard
10　将棋盤 **shōgiban** *shōgi* board, chessboard
　　配電盤 **haidenban** switch panel
14　磁石盤 **jishakuban** (mariner's) compass
19　羅針盤 **rashinban** compass

5

石
立
目
禾
衤
田
罒
皿　10←
疒

———— 11 ————

5h11.1

盥

KAN, tarai washtub, basin

———— 1 ————

6 盥回 taraimawa(shi) feat of spinning a washtub on one's feet; (officeholding) in rotation; detention at one police station after another

———— 2 ————

8 金盥 kanadarai metal basin, washbowl

———— 12 ————

5h12.1

盪 蘯

TŌ, toro(keru) melt; be charmed/captivated
toro(kasu) melt; charm, captivate

———— 2 ————

15 震盪 shintō (cerebral) concussion, shock

———— 3 ————

11 脳振盪 nōshintō cerebral concussion
脳震盪 nōshintō cerebral concussion

———— 20 ————

盬 → 塩 3b10.4

———— 21 ————

欝 → 鬱 4a25.1

———————————— 疒 5i ————————————

疔	疝	疚	疣	疫	疥	疳	疲	病	症	疽	疱	痂
2.1	3.1	3.2	4.1	4.2	4.3	5.1	5.2	5.3	5.4	5.5	5.6	5.7
疸	疼	疹	痃	疾	痀	痍	痕	疵	痔	痊	痒	痤
5.8	5.9	5.10	5.11	5.12	5.13	6.1	6.2	6.3	6.4	6.5	6.6	7.1
痢	痾	瘦	痦	痙	痣	痛	痘	痴	痳	痲	痺	痩
7.2	7.3	5i9.1	7.4	7.5	7.6	7.7	7.8	8.1	8.2	8.3	8.4	8.5
痰	痤	痼	痹	瘦	瘀	瘧	瘍	瘋	癈	瘠	瘤	瘟
8.6	8.7	8.8	5i8.4	9.1	5i13.3	9.2	9.3	9.4	10.1	10.2	10.3	10.4
瘡	瘻	瘭	瘴	瘰	癆	癈	療	癌	癘	瘤	癇	癜
10.5	11.1	11.2	11.3	11.4	12.1	12.2	12.3	12.4	12.5	5i12.6	12.6	13.1
癖	癒	癡	癢	癩	癪	癨	癧	癬	癰	癲		
13.2	13.3	5i8.1	15.1	16.1	16.2	16.3	16.4	17.1	18.1	19.1		

———— 2 ————

5i2.1

疔

CHŌ carbuncle

———— 2 ————

9 面疔 menchō facial cabuncle/boil

———— 3 ————

5i3.1

疝

SEN colic, griping abdominal pain

———— 1 ————

6 疝気 senki lower-abdominal pain, lumbago
12 疝痛 sentsū colic, griping pain

5i3.2

疚

KYŪ (long) illness
yama(shii) be ashamed of, have a guilty conscience

———— 4 ————

5i4.1

疣 疣

YŪ, YU, ibo wart

---------------- 1 ----------------

11 疣痔 **iboji** hemorrhoid
18 疣贅 **yūzei** wart, condyloma

---------------- 2 ----------------

6 汗疣 **asemo** prickly heat, heat rash

5i4.2 / 1319

疫

EKI, YAKU epidemic

---------------- 1 ----------------

7 疫学 **ekigaku** epidemiology
10 疫病 **ekibyō, yakubyō** epidemic, plague
疫病神 **yakubyōgami** god of the plague
12 疫痢 **ekiri** children's dysentery, infant diarrhea

---------------- 2 ----------------

4 牛疫 **gyūeki** cattle plague, rinderpest
6 防疫 **bōeki** prevention of epidemics
8 免疫 **men'eki** immunity (from a disease)
免疫性 **men'ekisei** immunity (from a disease)
11 悪疫 **akueki** plague, pestilence, epidemic
12 検疫 **ken'eki** quarantine
検疫官 **ken'ekikan** quarantine officer
検疫所 **ken'ekisho** quarantine station
16 獣疫 **jūeki** cattle disease

5i4.3

疥

KAI the itch, scabies; malaria
hatake psoriasis, scabies

---------------- 1 ----------------

22 疥癬 **kaisen** itch, scabies, mange

================ 5 ================

5i5.1

疳

KAN child's hysteria; child's intestinal disorder; chancre

---------------- 1 ----------------

10 疳高 **kandaka(i)** high-pitched, shrill

---------------- 2 ----------------

3 下疳 **gekan** chancre

---------------- 4 ----------------

11 軟性下疳 **nansei gekan** soft chancre

5i5.2 / 1321

疲

HI, tsuka(reru) get tired
tsuka(rasu) tire, exhaust

---------------- 1 ----------------

4 疲切 **tsuka(re)ki(ru)** get tired out, be exhausted

7 疲労 **hirō** fatigue
8 疲果 **tsuka(re)ha(teru)** get tired out, be exhausted
15 疲弊 **hihei** impoverishment, exhaustion

---------------- 2 ----------------

6 気疲 **kizuka(re)** mental fatigue, nervous strain
10 倦疲 **u(mi)tsuka(reru)** get tired of, get fed up
旅疲 **tabizuka(re)** travel fatigue

---------------- 3 ----------------

11 眼精疲労 **gansei hirō** eyestrain

5i5.3 / 380

病

BYŌ, HEI, ya(mu/meru) get sick, be ill, suffer from **yamai** illness, disease; bad habit; weakness for

---------------- 1 ----------------

2 病人 **byōnin** sick person, patient, invalid
3 病上 **ya(mi)a(gari)** convalescence
4 病中 **byōchū** during an illness
病友 **byōyū** sick friend; hospital ward-mate
病父 **byōfu** one's invalid father
病犬 **byōken** diseased dog
病欠 **byōketsu** absence due to illness
5 病母 **byōbo** one's invalid mother
病付 **ya(mi)tsu(ku)** be taken ill; be confirmed in a habit
6 病死 **byōshi** death from illness, natural death
病気 **byōki** sickness, illness; sick, ill
病返 **ya(mi)kae(shi)** relapse
病名 **byōmei** name of the disease
病因 **byōin** cause of the disease, etiology
病虫害 **byōchūgai** damage from blight and insects
7 病身 **byōshin** sickly constitution, poor health
病体 **byōtai** sickly constitution, poor health
病状 **byōjō** patient's condition
病兵 **byōhei** sick soldier
病没 **byōbotsu** death from illness, natural death
病床 **byōshō** sickbed
病児 **byōji** sick child
8 病毒 **byōdoku** virus, germ
病舎 **byōsha** infirmary, hospital
病殁 **byōbotsu** death from illness, natural death
病妻 **byōsai** one's invalid wife
病苦 **byōku** suffering from illness
病的 **byōteki** morbid, diseased, abnormal
病者 **byōsha** sick person
9 病臥 **byōga** be sick in bed, be bedridden
病院 **byōin** hospital
病院船 **byōinsen** hospital ship
病変 **byōhen** become morbid
病後 **byōgo** after an illness, convalescence

5

石
立
目
禾
衤
田
皿
疒 5←

病室 **byōshitsu** sickroom, ward, infirmary
10 病原 **byōgen** cause of a disease, etiology
病原体 **byōgentai** pathogen
病原菌 **byōgenkin** pathogenic bacteria, germ
病弱 **byōjaku** delicate constitution
病家 **byōka** patient's home
病害 **byōgai** damage from blight
病根 **byōkon** cause of a disease; root of an evil
病症 **byōshō** nature of a disease
11 病菌 **byōkin** bacteria
病理 **byōri** cause and course of a disease
病理学 **byōrigaku** pathology
病患 **byōkan, ya(mi)wazura(i)** sickness
12 病棟 **byōtō** ward
病間 **byōkan** during an illness
13 病勢 **byōsei** condition of a disease
病源 **byōgen** cause of a disease
病源菌 **byōgenkin** pathogenic bacteria, germ
14 病膏肓 **yamaikōkō** incurable; incorrigible
病歴 **byōreki** patient's case history
病態 **byōtai** patient's condition
15 病弊 **byōhei** an evil, ill effect
18 病軀 **byōku** sickly constitution, poor health
病癖 **byōheki** peculiarity, bad habit
病難 **byōnan** the misfortune of illness
19 病識 **byōshiki** awareness that one is ill
21 病魔 **byōma** demon of ill health, disease

——————————— 2 ———————————

1 一病息災 **ichibyō-sokusai** One who has an illness is careful of his health and lives long.
3 万病 **manbyō** all diseases, any kind of illness
大病 **taibyō** serious illness
5 半病人 **hanbyōnin** sickly person
6 多病 **tabyō** sickly, in frail health
死病 **shibyō** fatal disease
気病 **ki (no) yamai** illness caused by anxiety, neurosis
ki (ni) ya(mu) worry about, brood over
仮病 **kebyō** feigned illness
老病 **rōbyō** infirmities of old age
同病 **dōbyō** the same illness
7 余病 **yobyō** secondary disease, complications
8 奇病 **kibyō** strange disease
性病 **seibyō** sexually-transmitted/venereal disease
9 発病 **hatsubyō** be taken ill
重病 **jūbyō** serious illness
急病 **kyūbyō** sudden illness
急病人 **kyūbyōnin** emergency patient/case
持病 **jibyō** chronic illness
肺病 **haibyō** lung/pulmonary disease
看病 **kanbyō** tending the sick, nursing
胃病 **ibyō** stomach disorder

疫病 **ekibyō, yakubyō** epidemic, plague
疫病神 **yakubyōgami** god of the plague
10 眠病 **nemu(ri)byō** sleeping sickness
疾病 **shippei** disease
11 淋病 **rinbyō** gonorrhea
脳病 **nōbyō** brain disorder
脳病院 **nōbyōin** hospital for brain diseases
眼病 **ganbyō** eye disease
12 無病 **mubyō** well, healthy
無病息災 **mubyō-sokusai** in perfect health
13 傷病 **shōbyō** injury or illness
傷病兵 **shōbyōhei** the sick and wounded (soldiers)
腺病質 **senbyōshitsu** weak constitution
戦病死 **senbyōshi** death from disease contracted at the front
痲病 **rinbyō** gonorrhea
15 避病院 **hibyōin** isolation/quarantine hospital
熱病 **netsubyō** fever
16 憶病 **okubyō** cowardice, timidity
17 臆病 **okubyō** cowardly, timid
臆病者 **okubyōmono** coward
臆病風 **okubyōkaze** panic, loss of nerve
18 難病 **nanbyō** incurable/serious illness
闘病 **tōbyō** struggle against an illness
20 躁病 **sōbyō** mania
21 癩病 **raibyō** leprosy, Hansen's disease

——————————— 3 ———————————

3 山岳病 **sangakubyō** altitude sickness
4 天刑病 **tenkeibyō** leprosy
文明病 **bunmeibyō** a disease of civilization
日射病 **nisshabyō** sunstroke
心臓病 **shinzōbyō** heart disease
5 皮膚病 **hifubyō** skin disease
白血病 **hakketsubyō** leukemia
6 伝染病 **densenbyō** contagious/communicable disease
行路病者 **kōro byōsha** person fallen ill on the road
血友病 **ketsuyūbyō** hemophilia
7 狂犬病 **kyōkenbyō** rabies
花柳病 **karyūbyō** venereal disease
禿頭病 **tokutōbyō** (pathological) baldness
8 枝枯病 **edaga(re)byō** twig blight
金欠病 **kinketsubyō** shortage of money
9 急性病 **kyūseibyō** acute illness
風土病 **fūdobyō** endemic disease
胆石病 **tansekibyō** cholelithiasis, gallstones
神経病 **shinkeibyō** nervous disorder
胃腸病 **ichōbyō** gastrointestinal disorder
10 高山病 **kōzanbyō** mountain/altitude sickness
恙虫病 **tsutsugamushibyō** scrub typhus
原子病 **genshibyō** radiation sickness
流行病 **ryūkōbyō** an epidemic
恐水病 **kyōsuibyō** hydrophobia, rabies

航空病 **kōkūbyō** airsickness
11 婦人病 **fujinbyō** women's diseases/disorders
黄熱病 **ōnetsubyō, kōnetsubyō** yellow fever
黒死病 **kokushibyō** bubonic plague, black death
黒穂病 **kurohobyō** smut, blight
12 象皮病 **zōhibyō** elephantiasis
植物病 **shokubutsubyō** plant disease
紫斑病 **shihanbyō** purpura
13 夢遊病者 **muyūbyōsha** sleepwalker
腎臓病 **jinzōbyō** kidney disease
14 遺伝病 **idenbyō** hereditary disease
稲熱病 **imochibyō** rice blight
精神病 **seishlnbyō** mental illness/disorder
15 舞踏病 **butōbyō** St. Vitus's dance, chorea
潜水病 **sensuibyō** the bends
熱射病 **nesshabyō** heatstroke, sunstroke
熱帯病 **netaibyō** tropical disease
16 壊血病 **kaiketsubyō** scurvy
懐郷病 **kaikyōbyō** nostalgia, homesickness
糖尿病 **tōnyōbyō** diabetes
18 職業病 **shokugyōbyō** occupational disease
20 躁鬱病 **sōutsubyō** manic-depressive psychosis

─────── 4 ───────

5 四百四病 **shihyakushibyō** every kind of disease

5i5.4 / 1318

症 **SHŌ** illness, patient's condition, symptoms

─────── 1 ───────

7 症状 **shōjō** symptoms
8 症例 **shōrei** a case (of cholera)
10 症候 **shōkō** symptom

─────── 2 ───────

7 対症剤 **taishōzai** specific medicine
対症薬 **taishōyaku** specific medicine
8 炎症 **enshō** inflammation
9 重症 **jūshō** serious illness
急症 **kyūshō** sudden illness; emergency case
10 真症 **shinshō** true case (of a disease)
病症 **byōshō** nature of a disease
11 脳症 **nōshō** brain fever
12 無症状 **mushōjō** without symptoms
軽症 **keishō** a mild illness
17 癆症 **rōshō** tabes
18 難症 **nanshō** incurable/serious illness
類症 **ruishō** similar diseases

─────── 3 ───────

4 不妊症 **funinshō** sterility, barrenness
不眠症 **fuminshō** insomnia
不感症 **fukanshō** sexual frigidity

6 多汗症 **takanshō** excessive sweating
気鬱症 **kiutsushō** melancholia, depression
自覚症状 **jikaku shōjō** subjective symptoms, patient's complaints
血栓症 **kessenshō** thrombosis
7 尿毒症 **nyōdokushō** uremia
8 夜尿症 **yanyōshō** bed-wetting
夜盲症 **yamōshō** night blindness
9 狭心症 **kyōshinshō** stricture of the heart, angina pectoris
胆石症 **tansekishō** cholelithiasis, gallstones
神経症 **shinkeishō** nervous disorder
10 既往症 **kiōshō** previous illness, medical history
健忘症 **kenbōshō** forgetfulness, amnesla
原爆症 **genbakushō** illnesses caused by atomic-bomb radiation
珪肺症 **keihaishō** silicosis
恐怖症 **kyōfushō** phobia, morbid fear
11 貧血症 **hinketsushō** anemia
過敏症 **kabinshō** hypersensitivity
脱毛症 **datsumōshō** alopecia, baldness
敗血症 **haiketsushō** blood poisoning
12 硬化症 **kōkashō** sclerosis
13 鼠咬症 **sokōshō** rat-bite fever
農夫症 **nōfushō** farmer's syndrome
適応症 **tekiōshō** diseases for which a medicine is efficacious/indicated
蓄膿症 **chikunōshō** sinusitis
15 憂鬱症 **yūutsushō** melancholia, hypochondria
18 鞭打症 **muchiu(chi)shō** whiplash

─────── 4 ───────

10 骨軟化症 **kotsunankashō** osteomalacia
11 脳軟化症 **nōnankashō** encephalomalacia

─────── 5 ───────

9 胃酸過多症 **isankatashō** gastric hyperacidity
11 動脈硬化症 **dōmyaku kōkashō** arteriosclerosis
14 精神分裂症 **seishin bunretsushō** schizophrenia

─────── 6 ───────

6 早発性痴呆症 **sōhatsusei chihōshō** schizophrenia

5i5.5

疽 **SO** boil, carbuncle

─────── 2 ───────

11 脱疽 **dasso** gangrene
16 壊疽 **eso** gangrene
瘭疽 **hyōso** whitlow, felon, agnail

5
石
立
目
禾
ネ
田
皿
疒 5←

5i5.6

疱　HŌ blister; smallpox

――――――― 2 ―――――――
4 水疱　suihō blister
水疱瘡　mizubōsō chicken pox
9 発疱　happō blister
17 膿疱　nōhō pustule

5i5.7

痂　KA, KE scab, scabies

5i5.8

疸　TAN jaundice

――――――― 2 ―――――――
11 黄疸　ōdan jaundice

5i5.9

疼　TŌ, uzu(ku) ache, smart, throb/tingle with pain, fester

――――――― 1 ―――――――
12 疼痛　tōtsū pain

5i5.10

疹　SHIN measles, rash
CHIN febrile disease

――――――― 2 ―――――――
6 汗疹　asemo prickly heat, heat rash
9 発疹　hasshin, hosshin (break out in) a rash
風疹　fūshin rubella, German measles
11 麻疹　hashika, mashin measles
12 湿疹　shisshin eczema, rash
13 痲疹　mashin measles

――――――― 3 ―――――――
15 蕁麻疹　jinmashin hives

5i5.11

痃　KEN, GEN cramps; chancre

――――――― 1 ―――――――
18 痃癖　kenpeki stiff shoulders

――――――― 2 ―――――――
15 横痃　ōgen, yokone chancre, bubo

5i5.12 / 1812

疾　SHITSU illness, disease; fast, swift
to(ku) fast, swiftly
to(kku ni) already, quite a while ago
yama(shii) feel ashamed, have qualms of conscience

――――――― 1 ―――――――
7 疾走　shissō scamper, run at full speed
8 疾呼　shikko call out, shout
9 疾風　shippū, hayate gale, strong wind
疾風迅雷　shippū-jinrai lightning speed
10 疾病　shippei disease
11 疾患　shikkan disease, ailment
14 疾駆　shikku ride/drive fast, dash along

――――――― 2 ―――――――
6 耳疾　jishitsu ear ailments
8 固疾　koshitsu chronic illness
11 淋疾　rinshitsu gonorrhea
悪疾　akushitsu malignant/virulent disease
眼疾　ganshitsu eye disease
痔疾　jishitsu hemorrhoids
12 廃疾　haishitsu disabled, crippled
13 痼疾　koshitsu chronic illness
17 癈疾　haishitsu disability; chronic illness

5i5.13

痀　KU hunchback; rickets

――――――― 1 ―――――――
16 痀瘻　kuru rickets

――――――― 6 ―――――――

5i6.1

痍　I injury

――――――― 2 ―――――――
12 創痍　sōi a wound
13 傷痍　shōi wound, injury

5i6.2

痕　KON, ato scar, mark; footprint

――――――― 1 ―――――――
13 痕跡　konseki traces, vestiges, evidence
痕跡器官　konseki kikan vestigial organ

――――――― 2 ―――――――
2 刀痕　tōkon sword/saber scar
4 爪痕　tsumeato scratch; pinch mark
6 血痕　kekkon bloodstain

7 条痕　**jōkon** streak
12 弾痕　**dankon** bullet hole/mark
　焼痕　**shōkon** scar from a burn
　痘痕　**abata, tōkon** pockmark
13 傷痕　**shōkon, kizuato** scar
14 墨痕　**bokkon** ink marks; handwriting
15 瘢痕　**hankon** scar

5i6.3

疵

SHI, kizu flaw, blemish, defect

────────── 1 ──────────
5 疵付　**kizutsu(keru)** wound, injure; mar;
　　　　besmirch
8 疵物　**kizumono** defective article; deflowered
　　　　girl
────────── 2 ──────────
4 切疵　**ki(ri)kizu** cut, gash, scar
12 無疵　**mukizu** undamaged, unblemished,
　　　　unhurt
13 搔疵　**ka(ki)kizu** a scratch
　瑕疵　**kashi** defect, flaw

5i6.4

痔

JI hemorrhoids

────────── 1 ──────────
10 痔疾　**jishitsu** hemorrhoids
16 痔瘻　**jirō** anal fistula, hemorrhoid
────────── 2 ──────────
4 切痔　**ki(re)ji** hemorrhoid, anal fistula
5 穴痔　**anaji** anal fistula
9 疣痔　**iboji** hemorrhoid
────────── 4 ──────────
7 吮癰舐痔　**sen'yō shiji** sucking the pus from
　　　　someone's carbuncles and licking his
　　　　hemorrhoids (to curry favor)

5i6.5

痊

SEN heal

5i6.6

痒

YŌ, kayu(garu) itch
kayu(i), kai(i) itchy

────────── 2 ──────────
12 痛痒　**tsūyō** interest, concern
　　　　ita(shi)kayu(shi) delicate, ticklish

歯痒　**hagayu(i)** vexing, irritating
13 搔痒　**sōyō** itching

────────── 4 ──────────
12 隔靴搔痒　**kakka-sōyō** irritation, impatience
　　　　(like trying to scratch an itchy foot
　　　　through the shoe)

────────── 7 ──────────

5i7.1

痤

ZA, enogo swelling in the armpit

────────── 1 ──────────
15 痤瘡　**zasō** acne

5i7.2 / 1811

痢

RI diarrhea

────────── 2 ──────────
3 下痢　**geri** diarrhea
7 赤痢　**sekiri** dysentery
9 疫痢　**ekiri** children's dysentery, infant
　　　　diarrhea

5i7.3

痾

A, yamai (chronic) illness

────────── 2 ──────────
11 宿痾　**shukua** chronic illness

瘦 → 瘦 **5i9.1**

5i7.4

痞

HI, tsukae constipation/costiveness in
chest or intestines

5i7.5

痙

KEI, tsu(ru) have a cramp

────────── 1 ──────────
23 痙攣　**keiren** cramp, spasm, convulsions
────────── 2 ──────────
9 胃痙攣　**ikeiren** stomach convulsions/cramps

5

石
立
目
禾
衤
田
罒
皿

疒 7 ←

5i7.6

痣

SHI, aza birthmark

──────── 2 ────────

11 黒痣 **kuroaza** (facial) mole

5i7.7 / 1320

痛

TSŪ pain **ita(i)** painful
ita(mu) be painful, hurt; be damaged,
spoil **ita(meru)** hurt, pain, afflict
ita(mi) pain, ache

──────── 1 ────────

0 痛がる **ita(garu)** complan of pain
2 痛入 **ita(mi)i(ru)** be grateful
3 痛々 **itaita(shii)** pitiful, pathetic
4 痛切 **tsūsetsu** keen, acute
痛止 **ita(mi)do(me)** painkiller
痛分 **ita(mi)wa(ke)** tie due to injury (sumo)
痛手 **itade** serious wound; hard blow
痛心 **tsūshin** worry
5 痛付 **ita(me)tsu(keru)** rebuke, reprimand
痛打 **tsūda** crushing blow, smash
痛目 **ita(i) me** a painful experience
7 痛快 **tsūkai** keen pleasure, thrill, delight
痛言 **tsūgen** scathing criticism
8 痛事 **itagoto** hard blow, misfortune
痛苦 **tsūku** pain, anguish
ita(mi)kuru(shimu) suffer
9 痛点 **tsūten** point of pain, where it hurts
痛恨 **tsūkon** great sorrow, bitterness
痛恨事 **tsūkonji** matter for deep regret
10 痛烈 **tsūretsu** severe, bitter, scathing
11 痛惜 **tsūseki** great sorrow, deep regret
痛痒 **tsūyō** interest, concern
ita(shi)kayu(shi) delicate, ticklish
12 痛覚 **tsūkaku** sense of pain
痛棒 **tsūbō** harsh criticism
痛痛 **itaita(shii)** pitiful, pathetic
痛飲 **tsūin** drink heavily
13 痛嘆 **tsūtan** bitter regret, grief
15 痛撃 **tsūgeki** severe blow, hard attack
痛憤 **tsūfun** great indignation
痛論 **tsūron** vehement argument

──────── 2 ────────

4 止痛剤 **shitsūzai** painkiller
手痛 **teita(i)** severe, serious, hard, heavy
心痛 **shintsū** mental anguish, heartache
6 耳痛 **jitsū** earache
7 沈痛 **chintsū** sad, sorrowful, grave
足痛 **sokutsū** foot pain
8 苦痛 **kutsū** pain
疝痛 **sentsū** colic, griping pain
9 陣痛 **jintsū** labor (pains)

胃痛 **itsū** stomachache
10 胸痛 **kyōtsū** chest pain
疼痛 **tōtsū** pain
12 無痛 **mutsū** painless
無痛分娩 **mutsū bunben** painless childbirth
悲痛 **hitsū** bitter, grief, sorrow
痛痛 **itaita(shii)** pitiful, pathetic
歯痛 **shitsū, haita** toothache
鈍痛 **dontsū** dull pain
13 腰痛 **yōtsū** lumbago
腹痛 **fukutsū, haraita** stomachache, abdominal pain
16 激痛 **gekitsū** sharp pain
頭痛 **zutsū** headache
18 鎮痛 **chintsū** relieving pain
鎮痛剤 **chintsūzai** painkiller

──────── 3 ────────

4 片腹痛 **katahara-ita(i)** ridiculous, absurd
9 神経痛 **shinkeitsū** neuralgia
11 偏頭痛 **henzutsū, hentōtsū** migraine headache

──────── 5 ────────

10 座骨神経痛 **zakotsu shinkeitsū** sciatic neuralgia

5i7.8 / 1942

痘

TŌ smallpox

──────── 1 ────────

8 痘苗 **tōbyō** vaccine
11 痘痕 **abata, tōkon** pockmark
15 痘瘡 **tōsō** smallpox

──────── 2 ────────

4 水痘 **suitō** chicken pox
牛痘 **gyūtō** cowpox, vaccine
14 種痘 **shutō** vaccination, inoculation

──────── 3 ────────

4 天然痘 **tennentō** smallpox

──────── 8 ────────

5i8.1 / 1813

痴 癡

CHI foolish

──────── 1 ────────

2 痴人 **chijin** fool, idiot
7 痴呆 **chihō** dementia; imbecility
11 痴情 **chijō** blind love, passion, infatuation
13 痴漢 **chikan** molester of women, masher
痴愚 **chigu** stupidity, imbecility
痴話 **chiwa** lovers' talk
痴話喧嘩 **chiwa-genka** lovers' quarrel

14 痴態 **chitai** foolishness, silliness

——————— 2 ———————

5 白痴 **hakuchi** idiot
7 乱痴気騒 **ranchiki sawa(gi)** boisterous merrymaking, spree
9 音痴 **onchi** tone deaf
11 情痴 **jōchi** love foolery
酔痴 **yo(i)shi(reru)** be befuddled/drunk
13 愚痴 **guchi** idle complaint, grumbling
頓痴気 **tonchiki** nincompoop, dope

——————— 4 ———————

6 早発性痴呆症 **sōhatsusei chihōshō** schizo-phrenia

5i8.2

麻 **RIN** gonorrhea; colic

——————— 1 ———————

10 痳病 **rinbyō** gonorrhea

5i8.3

痲 **MA** numbness; pockmarks

——————— 1 ———————

10 痲疹 **mashin** measles
11 痲酔 **masui** anesthesia
13 痲痺 **mahi** paralysis
14 痲瘋 **mafū** leprosy
16 痲薬 **mayaku** narcotics

5i8.4

痺 痹 **HI** palsy
shibi(reru) go numb, tingle, be paralyzed

——————— 1 ———————

16 痺薬 **shibi(re)gusuri** anesthetic

——————— 2 ———————

11 麻痺 **mahi** paralysis
13 痲痺 **mahi** paralysis

——————— 4 ———————

3 小児麻痺 **shōni mahi** infantile paralysis, polio
4 心臓麻痺 **shinzō mahi** heart failure/attack

5i8.5

痿 **I, na(eru)** atrophy, go numb, be paralyzed

5i8.6

痰 **TAN, DAN** sputum, phlegm

——————— 1 ———————

12 痰壺 **tantsubo** spittoon, cuspidor

——————— 2 ———————

6 血痰 **kettan** bloody phlegm
12 喀痰 **kakutan** expectoration; sputum

5i8.7

瘁 **ZUI, SUI** fatigue; become ill

——————— 2 ———————

6 尽瘁 **jinsui** devote all one's efforts to

5i8.8

痼 **KO** chronic illness

——————— 1 ———————

10 痼疾 **koshitsu** chronic illness

痹 → 痺 5i8.4

——————— 9 ———————

5i9.1

瘦 瘦 **SŌ, SHŪ, ya(seru)** become thin

——————— 1 ———————

3 瘦土 **ya(se)tsuchi** barren soil
5 瘦世帯 **ya(se)jotai** poor household
6 瘦地 **ya(se)chi** barren soil, unproductive land
7 瘦身 **sōshin** slender body, thin build
瘦我慢 **ya(se)gaman** endure for sake of pride
瘦形 **ya(se)gata** slender build, skinny
9 瘦面 **ya(se)omote** thin face
10 瘦衰 **ya(se)otoro(eru)** become emaciated, waste away
11 瘦脛 **ya(se)zune** skinny legs
瘦細 **ya(se)hoso(ru)** grow thin, lose weight
12 瘦腕 **ya(se)ude** thin arm; meager income
16 瘦薬 **ya(se)gusuri** reducing drug
18 瘦軀 **sōku** lean figure

——————— 2 ———————

10 夏瘦 **natsuya(se)** loss of weight in summer

瘉 → 癒 5i13.3

5i9.2

瘧 **GYAKU, okori** malaria

5

石
立
目
禾
衤
田
罒
皿

疒 9←

5i9.3

瘍　**YŌ** ulcer, boil, carbuncle

――――― 2 ―――――
13 腫瘍　**shuyō** tumor
15 潰瘍　**kaiyō** ulcer

――――― 3 ―――――
9 胃潰瘍　**ikaiyō** stomach ulcer
13 腸潰瘍　**chōkaiyō** intestinal ulcer

5i9.4

瘋　**FŪ** headache; insanity

――――― 1 ―――――
24 瘋癲　**fūten** lunacy, insanity
――――― 2 ―――――
13 痲瘋　**mafū** leprosy

――――― 10 ―――――

5i10.1

癍　**HAN** scar, mark

――――― 1 ―――――
11 癍痕　**hankon** scar

5i10.2

瘠　**SEKI, ya(seru)** become thin (For compounds, see 痩 5i9.1)

5i10.3

瘤　**RYŪ, kobu** wen, lump, bump, swelling, nodule

――――― 1 ―――――
5 瘤付　**kobutsu(ki)** wen; nuisance; with a child along

――――― 2 ―――――
2 力瘤　**chikarakobu** flexed biceps
10 根瘤　**konryū** root nodules

5i10.4

瘟　**ON** contagious disease

5i10.5

瘡　**SŌ** wound; boil
kasa syphilis

――――― 2 ―――――
10 凍瘡　**tōsō** frostbite, chilblains
12 痤瘡　**zasō** acne
　痘瘡　**tōsō** smallpox

――――― 3 ―――――
4 水疱瘡　**mizubōsō** chicken pox

――――― 11 ―――――

5i11.1

瘻　**RŌ, RU** fistula

――――― 2 ―――――
10 痀瘻　**kuru** rickets
11 痔瘻　**jirō** anal fistula, hemorrhoid

5i11.2

瘭　**HYŌ** whitlow

――――― 1 ―――――
10 瘭疽　**hyōso** whitlow, felon, agnail

5i11.3

瘴　**SHŌ** miasma

――――― 1 ―――――
6 瘴気　**shōki** miasma
17 瘴癘　**shōrei** miasma-caused fever, malaria

5i11.4

瘰　**RUI** swollen neck glands

――――― 1 ―――――
21 瘰癧　**ruireki** scrofula

――――― 12 ―――――

5i12.1

癆　**RŌ** rash; pain; debilitation

――――― 1 ―――――
10 癆症　**rōshō** tabes

5i12.2

癈　**HAI** chronic illness; crippled

───────── 1 ─────────

2 癈人 **haijin** a cripple
7 癈兵 **haihei** disabled soldier
10 癈疾 **haishitsu** disability; chronic illness

5i12.3 / 1322

RYŌ heal, cure

療

───────── 1 ─────────

8 療法 **ryōhō** treatment, therapy, remedy
療治 **ryōji** medical treatment, remedy
15 療養 **ryōyō** medical treatment/care
療養所 **ryōyōjo** sanitarium

───────── 2 ─────────

4 手療治 **teryōji** home treatment, doctoring oneself
7 医療 **iryō** medical treatment, health care; medical
8 治療 **chiryō** medical treatment
治療代 **chiryōdai** medical fees/bill
治療学 **chiryōgaku** therapeutics
治療法 **chiryōhō** method of treatment, remedy
治療所 **chiryōsho** infirmary, clinic
治療師 **chiryōshi** therapist
9 荒療治 **araryōji** drastic/kill-or-cure treatment
施療 **seryō** (give) free medical treatment
12 揉療治 **mo(mi)ryōji** massage
診療 **shinryō** examination and treatment
診療所 **shinryōjo** clinic
15 熱療法 **netsuryōhō** heat therapy

───────── 3 ─────────

4 水治療法 **suichiryōhō** water cure, hydrotherapy
8 物理療法 **butsuriryōhō** physiotherapy
9 指圧療法 **shiatsu ryōhō** finger-pressure treatment, chiropractic
11 転地療養 **tenchi ryōyō** getting away for a change of climate for one's health

5i12.4

GAN cancer

癌

───────── 1 ─────────

13 癌腫 **ganshu** cancer tumor, carcinoma

───────── 2 ─────────

6 舌癌 **zetsugan** cancer of the tongue
7 乳癌 **nyūgan** breast cancer
9 発癌 **hatsugan** cancer-causing, carcinogenic
肺癌 **haigan** lung cancer
胃癌 **igan** stomach cancer

───────── 3 ─────────

2 子宮癌 **shikyūgan** cancer of the uterus
12 喉頭癌 **kōtōgan** cancer of the larynx

5i12.5

REI leprosy; contagious disease

癘

───────── 2 ─────────

16 瘴癘 **shōrei** miasma-caused fever, malaria

癇 → 癇   **5i12.6**

5i12.6

KAN quick temper, irritability, peevishness; nervousness, sensitivity

癇 癇

───────── 1 ─────────

8 癇性 **kanshō** irritability, irascibility
18 癇癖 **kanpeki** hot temper, irritability
21 癇癪 **kanshaku** passion, temper, irritability
癇癪玉 **kanshakudama** fit of anger; firecracker
癇癪持 **kanshakumo(chi)** person with an explosive temper

───────── 2 ─────────

2 子癇 **shikan** eclampsia, pregnancy-caused convulsions
24 癲癇 **tenkan** epilepsy, epileptic fit
癲癇持 **tenkanmo(chi)** an epileptic

───────── 13 ─────────

5i13.1

DEN, namazu leucoderma, piebald skin

癜

5i13.2 / 1490

HEKI, kuse habit, peculiarity

癖

───────── 1 ─────────

4 癖毛 **kusege** curly/kinky hair
8 癖直 **kusenao(shi)** straightening out one's hair

───────── 2 ─────────

1 一癖 **hitokuse** trait, peculiarity; slyness
3 口癖 **kuchiguse** habit of saying, favorite saying
4 手癖 **tekuse** habit of pilfering, sticky fingers
7 足癖 **ashikuse** one's way of walking

5

石
立
目
禾
衤
田
罒
皿
疒 13←

8 其癖 **so(no) kuse** and yet, nevertheless
性癖 **seiheki** disposition, proclivity
10 酒癖 **sakekuse, sakeguse, shuheki** drinking habits
病癖 **byōheki** peculiarity, bad habit
痃癖 **kenpeki** stiff shoulders
11 習癖 **shūheki** habit, peculiarity
悪癖 **akuheki, waruguse** bad habit, vice
盗癖 **tōheki** kleptomania, larcenousness
12 飲癖 **no(mi)kuse** habit of drinking
14 髪癖 **kamikuse** kinkiness, curliness
読癖 **yo(mi)kuse** idiomatic pronunciation (of a compound); peculiar way of reading
15 潔癖 **keppeki** love of cleanliness, fastidiousness
17 癇癖 **kanpeki** hot temper, irritability
18 難癖 **nankuse** a fault, failings

――――――― 3 ―――――――

5 好古癖 **kōkoheki** antiquarianism
8 放浪癖 **hōrōheki** wanderlust
10 浪費癖 **rōhiheki** spendthrift habits
13 蒐集癖 **shūshūheki** collecting habit/mania
14 厭人癖 **enjinheki** misanthropy

5i13.3 / 1600

癒 癒 瘉

YU, **i(yasu)** heal, cure; satisfy, quench; soothe **i(eru)** be healed, recover

――――――― 1 ―――――――

6 癒合 **yugō** agglutination, adhesion, knitting
12 癒着 **yuchaku** adhere, knit together, heal up; too close a relationship (with an organization)

――――――― 2 ―――――――

5 平癒 **heiyu** convalescence
6 全癒 **zen'yu** complete healing
7 快癒 **kaiyu** recovery, convalescence
8 治癒 **chiyu** heal, cure, recover
治癒力 **chiyuryoku** healing/recuperative power
13 腹癒 **harai(se)** revenge, retaliation

――――――― 14 ―――――――

癡 → 痴 5i8.1

――――――― 15 ―――――――

5i15.1

癢

YŌ, **kayu(i)** itchy

――――――― 16 ―――――――

5i16.1

癩

RAI, **kattai** leprosy

――――――― 1 ―――――――

10 癩病 **raibyō** leprosy, Hansen's disease

5i16.2

癪

SHAKU spasm of pain; irritability, temper

――――――― 1 ―――――――

14 癪種 **shaku (no) tane** cause of offense, peeve

――――――― 2 ―――――――

3 小癪 **koshaku** impudent, cheeky
17 癇癪 **kanshaku** passion, temper, irritability
癇癪玉 **kanshakudama** fit of anger; firecracker
癇癪持 **kanshakumo(chi)** person with an explosive temper

5i16.3

癨

KAKU heatstroke, sunstroke

――――――― 1 ―――――――

7 癨乱 **kakuran** heatstroke, sunstroke

5i16.4

癧

REKI scrofula

――――――― 2 ―――――――

16 瘰癧 **ruireki** scrofula

――――――― 17 ―――――――

5i17.1

癬

SEN ringworm

――――――― 2 ―――――――

5 皮癬 **hizen** itch, scabies, mange
白癬 **hakusen** ringworm
9 疥癬 **kaisen** itch, scabies, mange
11 乾癬 **kansen** psoriasis

――――――― 18 ―――――――

5i18.1

癰

YŌ carbuncle

—————————— 2 ——————————

7 吮癰舐痔 **sen'yō shiji** sucking the pus from someone's carbuncles and licking his hemorrhoids (to curry favor)

—————————— 19 ——————————

5i19.1

TEN insanity

癲

—————————— 1 ——————————

17 癲癇 **tenkan** epilepsy, epileptic fit
癲癇持 **tenkanmo(chi)** an epileptic

—————————— 2 ——————————

14 瘋癲 **fūten** lunacy, insanity

—————————————— 糸 6a ——————————————

糸 0.1	礼 6a3.4	幻 0a4.6	系 1.1	幼 2g3.3	紆 3.1	級 3.2	衬 3.3	糾 3.4	紀 3.5	紅 3.6	約 3.7	紡 4.1
紐 4.2	純 4.3	紙 4.4	級 6a3.2	納 4.5	紗 4.6	紕 4.7	紛 4.8	紋 4.9	紜 4.10	紘 4.11	素 4.12	細 5.1
紳 5.2	紬 5.3	紲 5.4	紺 5.5	絆 5.6	組 5.7	紵 5.8	終 5.9	紹 5.10	経 5.11	絃 5.12	給 5.13	絁 5.14
紘 5.15	絅 5.16	紫 5.17	絲 6a0.1	絏 6.1	衍 6.2	絓 6.3	絖 6.4	結 6.5	絡 6.6	給 6.7	絵 6.8	絞 6.9
統 6.10	絶 6.11	絣 6.12	絨 6.13	絢 6.14	紫 6.15	絮 6.16	綉 7.1	綏 7.2	經 6a5.11	絹 7.3	綢 7.4	続 7.5
絳 7.6	綛 7.7	継 7.8	綟 6a8.21	維 8.1	練 8.2	緒 8.3	緋 8.4	絣 6a6.12	綴 8.5	綣 8.6	綏 8.7	綿 8.8
綵 8.9	綾 8.10	綫 8.11	綜 8.12	綻 8.13	綰 8.14	緑 8.15	綺 8.16	緇 8.17	綸 8.18	綪 6a14.3	綽 8.19	総 8.20
綯 8.21	綯 8.22	綱 8.23	綢 8.24	網 8.25	綮 8.26	縄 9.1	練 6a8.2	緒 6a8.3	緘 9.2	緲 9.3	緞 9.4	緝 9.5
緤 9.6	線 9.7	緩 9.8	絹 9.9	緣 9.10	締 9.11	緬 9.12	編 9.13	緦 9.14	縫 9.15	緘 9.16	緊 9.17	幾 4n8.4
縣 6a8.8	緻 10.1	縦 10.2	縛 10.3	縕 10.4	縉 10.5	縡 10.6	緯 10.7	縊 10.8	縞 10.9	縒 10.10	縟 10.11	縡 10.12
縫 6a9.15	繁 10.13	縣 3n6.3	繍 6a13.1	纎 11.1	繈 11.2	縦 6a10.2	縷 11.3	總 6a8.20	標 11.4	繆 11.5	縹 11.6	縵 11.7
績 11.8	縮 11.9	繃 11.10	繋 6a13.4	繁 6a10.13	徹 12.1	繕 12.2	繧 12.3	繚 12.4	繞 12.5	織 12.6	繝 12.7	繙 12.8
畿 5f10.3	繩 6a9.1	繡 13.1	繹 13.2	繰 13.3	繪 6a6.8	繁 13.4	繻 14.1	繽 14.2	繼 14.3	繼 6a7.8	辮 14.4	纇 15.1
纈 15.2	纊 5e15.2	纈 15.3	續 6a7.5	纏 6a16.1	纖 6a11.1	纒 16.1	纓 17.1	纔 17.2	纖 6a11.1	蠹 18.1	纜 22.1	

—————————— 0 ——————————

6a0.1 / 242

SHI, ito thread

糸 絲

—————————— 1 ——————————

2 糸入 **itoi(ri)** (silk/paper) with cotton threads
3 糸口 **itoguchi** thread end; beginning; clue
4 糸切歯 **itoki(ri)ba** eyetooth, canine tooth
5 糸目 **itome** a fine thread

6 糸瓜 **hechima** sponge gourd, loofah
糸印 **itojirushi** thread to make seams conspicuous
糸竹 **itotake** (koto) strings and bamboo (flute), music
7 糸状 **shijō** threadlike, filament
糸杉 **itosugi** cypress
糸車 **itoguruma** spinning wheel
8 糸価 **shika** price of (silk) thread
糸底 **itozoko** bottom rim (of an earthenware cup)
糸取 **itoto(ri)** silk reeling
9 糸巻 **itoma(ki)** spool, reel, bobbin
糸柳 **itoyanagi** weeping willow
10 糸遊 **itoyū** shimmering of heated air
糸姫 **itohime** thread/weaving factory girl
糸屑 **itokuzu** waste thread, ravelings
糸桜 **itozakura** droopy-branch cherry tree
11 糸偏景気 **itohen keiki** textile boom
糸道 **itomichi** samisen playing
16 糸操 **itoayatsu(ri)** manipulating a marionette
糸鋸 **itonoko** fretsaw, jigsaw, scroll saw
18 糸織 **itoo(ri)** (a type of silk cloth)
19 糸繰 **itoku(ri)** reeling, filature; spinner; reel

——————— 2 ———————
1 一糸 **isshi** a string
一糸乱 **isshi mida(renai)** not a thread out of place, airtight (argument)
4 毛糸 **keito** wool yarn, worsted, woolen
5 生糸 **kiito** raw silk
凧糸 **takoito** kite string
白糸 **shiraito** white thread
6 色糸 **iroito** colored thread
7 抜糸 **basshi** take out the stitches
nu(ki)ito drawn thread
8 金糸 **kinshi** gold thread
10 唐糸 **karaito, tōito** foreign thread/yarn
屑糸 **kuzuito** waste threads
紡糸 **bōshi** spinning; yarn
蚕糸 **sanshi** silk thread/yarn
蚕糸業 **sanshigyō** the silk-reeling industry
11 菌糸 **kinshi** mycelium
麻糸 **asaito** linen thread, hemp yarn
細糸 **hosoito** fine thread
紬糸 **tsumugiito** silk thread from waste cocoons
組糸 **ku(mi)ito** braid, plaited thread
釣糸 **tsu(ri)ito** fishing line
12 絓糸 **shikeito, sugaito** raw/unspun silk thread
13 絹糸 **kenshi, kinuito** silk thread
継糸 **tsu(gi)ito** seam threads
節糸 **fushiito** knotted silk
14 墨糸 **sumiito** inked marking string
製糸 **seishi** silk reeling
製糸業 **seishigyō** the silk industry

練糸 **ne(ri)ito** glossed-silk thread
綴糸 **to(ji)ito** binding/basting thread
綿糸 **menshi** cotton thread/yarn
銀糸 **ginshi** silver thread
15 撚糸 **nenshi, yoriito** twisted thread/yarn, twine
横糸 **yokoito** woof
縫糸 **nu(i)ito** sewing thread; suture
16 縦糸 **tateito** warp (vertical thread in weaving)
緯糸 **nukiito** woof
18 繭糸 **kenshi** (cocoon and) silk thread
織糸 **o(ri)ito** weaving thread; strand
鎖糸 **kusariito** yarn interwoven with threads forming a diamond pattern

——————— 3 ———————
4 木綿糸 **momen'ito** cotton thread
5 仕付糸 **shitsu(ke)ito** tacking, basting (thread)
10 紡績糸 **bōsekiito** (cotton) yarn
14 蜘蛛糸 **kumo (no) ito** spider's thread

——————— 1 ———————

 **6a3.4**

 0a4.6

6a1.1 / 908

系

KEI system; lineage, group

——————— 1 ———————
6 系列 **keiretsu** system, series; ownership affiliation, corporate group
7 系図 **keizu** genealogy, family tree
系図学 **keizugaku** genealogy
12 系統 **keitō** system; lineage, descent
系統的 **keitōteki** systematic
系統樹 **keitōju** tree diagram showing evolutionary descent
19 系譜 **keifu** genealogy, family tree

——————— 2 ———————
1 一系 **ikkei** single-family lineage
3 大系 **taikei** outline, overview, survey
女系 **jokei** female line(age), on the mother's side
山系 **sankei** mountain system/range
4 父系 **fukei** male line, patriarchal (family)
日系 **nikkei** of Japanese descent
5 母系 **bokei** maternal line
母系制度 **bokei seido** matriarchal system
母系家族 **bokei kazoku** matriarchal family
正系 **seikei** legitimate lineage, direct descent

白系露人 **hakkei rojin** a White Russian,
　　　Byelorussian
6 同系 **dōkei** affiliated, akin
7 体系 **taikei** system, organization
　体系化 **taikeika** systematize, organize
　体系的 **taikeiteki** systematic
　男系 **dankei** male line, father's side
8 直系 **chokkei** lineal descendant, direct line
　河系 **kakei** river system
10 家系 **kakei** family lineage
　家系図 **kakeizu** family tree
　純系 **junkei** (genetically) pure line
11 庶系 **shokei** illegitimate lineage
12 傍系 **bōkei** collateral family line; affiliated,
　　　subsidiary

———————— 3 ————————
4 太陽系 **taiyōkei** the solar system
6 多産系 **tasankei** the type that bears many
　　　children
9 神経系 **shinkeikei** nervous system
12 循環系 **junkankei** the circulatory system

———————— 4 ————————
3 万世一系 **bansei ikkei** unbroken (imperial)
　　　lineage

———————— 2 ————————

幼→ **2g3.3**

———————— 3 ————————

6a3.1

紆

U bend; crouch

———————— 1 ————————
6 紆曲 **ukyoku** meander
7 紆余 **uyo** meandering; abundant talent
　紆余曲折 **uyo-kyokusetsu** meandering,
　　　twists and turns, complications

6a3.2 / 568

級 級

KYŪ rank, class, grade

———————— 1 ————————
4 級友 **kyūyū** classmate
8 級長 **kyūchō** head/president of the class
13 級数 **kyūsū** series/progression (in math)

———————— 2 ————————
1 一級 **ikkyū** one grade; first class
3 上級 **jōkyū** upper grade, senior
　上級生 **jōkyūsei** upperclassman

下級 **kakyū** lower grade/class, junior,
　　　subordinate
　下級生 **kakyūsei** underclassman
　下級審 **kakyūshin** lower court
　下級職 **kakyūshoku** subordinate post
　分級 **bunkyū** classify
6 全級 **zenkyū** the whole class
　同級 **dōkyū** the same class
　同級生 **dōkyūsei** classmate
7 低級 **teikyū** low-grade, lowbrow, vulgar
　学級 **gakkyū** school class, grade
　初級 **shokyū** beginners' class
8 昇級 **shōkyū** promotion to a higher grade
9 首級 **shukyū** (enemy's) decapitated head
10 高級 **kōkyū** high-grade, high-class; high rank
　高級車 **kōkyūsha** luxury car
　高級品 **kōkyūhin** high-grade goods
　進級 **shinkyū** promotion (to a higher grade)
　特級 **tokkyū** special grade
　特級酒 **tokkyūshu** special-grade saké
11 階級 **kaikyū** (social) class; (military) rank
　船級 **senkyū** (ship's) classification
12 等級 **tōkyū** class, grade, rank

———————— 3 ————————
5 比較級 **hikakukyū** the comparative degree
　　　(in grammar)
7 初年級 **shonenkyū** beginners' class
12 超弩級 **chōdokyū** superdreadnought-class
　等比級数 **tōhi kyūsū** geometric progression
　等差級数 **tōsa kyūsū** arithmetic progression

———————— 4 ————————
4 中産階級 **chūsan kaikyū** middle class
6 有産階級 **yūsan kaikyū** the propertied class
　有閑階級 **yūkan kaikyū** the leisure class
11 第三階級 **dai-san kaikyū** the third estate,
　　　the bourgeoisie
　第四階級 **dai-shi kaikyū** the fourth estate,
　　　the proletariat
12 無産階級 **musan kaikyū** the proletariat
14 複式学級 **fukushiki gakkyū** combined class
　　　(of more than one grade)
15 養護学級 **yōgo gakkyū** class for the
　　　handicapped

6a3.3

紂

CHŪ (Chinese name)

6a3.4 / 1703

糾 紏

KYŪ, tada(su) rectify, clear up
azana(u) twist (rope)

———————— 1 ————————
6 糾合 **kyūgō** rally, muster

6

糸 3←
米
舟
虫
耳
⺮

8 糾明 **kyūmei** study, inquiry; investigation
11 糾問 **kyūmon** close examination, grilling
12 糾弾 **kyūdan** impeach, censure

――――― 2 ―――――
10 紛糾 **funkyū** complication, entanglement
粉糾 **funkyū** complications, entanglements

6a3.5 / 372

紀 **KI** account, narrative, history; (geological) period

――――― 1 ―――――
4 紀元 **kigen** era (of year reckoning)
紀元前 **kigenzen** B.C.
紀元後 **kigengo** A.D.
紀元節 **kigensetsu** Empire Day
6 紀伊 **Kii** (ancient kuni, Wakayama-ken)
紀行 **kikō** account of a journey
紀行文 **kikōbun** account of a journey
9 紀要 **kiyō** bulletin, record, proceedings
紀律 **kiritsu** order, discipline

――――― 2 ―――――
5 世紀 **seiki** century
6 西紀 **seiki** A.D., Christian Era
7 芳紀 **hōki** age (of a young lady)
8 官紀 **kanki** discipline among government officials
9 軍紀 **gunki** military discipline
風紀 **fūki** discipline, public morals
皇紀 **kōki** (...th year of the) imperial era (since Emperor Jinmu's accession in 660 B.C.)
10 党紀 **tōki** party discipline
校紀 **kōki** school discipline/standards
記紀 **Kiki** the Kojiki and Nihonshoki
13 新紀元 **shinkigen** new ear/epoch
14 綱紀 **kōki** official discipline, public order
綱紀粛正 **kōki shukusei** enforcement of discipline among officials

――――― 3 ―――――
1 一世紀 **isseiki** a century; first century
一新紀元 **isshin kigen** a new era
5 半世紀 **hanseiki** half century
9 前世紀 **zenseiki** last century; prehistoric times
11 現世紀 **genseiki** this century
第三紀 **dai-sanki** the Tertiary (geological) period

――――― 4 ―――――
2 二十世紀 **nijisseiki, nijusseiki** the twentieth century

6a3.6 / 820

紅 **KŌ, KU, GU, kurenai** red, crimson
beni rouge, lipstick; red
momi red silk cloth

――――― 1 ―――――
1 紅一点 **kōitten** one red flower in the foliage; the only woman in the group
4 紅毛 **kōmō** red hair
5 紅生姜 **beni shōga** red pickled ginger
紅白 **kōhaku** red and white
紅玉 **kōgyoku** a ruby
6 紅色 **kōshoku** red
紅灯 **kōtō** red lantern; red-light (district)
7 紅花 **benibana** safflower, saffron
9 紅海 **Kōkai** the Red Sea
紅茶 **kōcha** black tea
紅染 **benizo(me)** red-dyed cloth
10 紅差指 **benisa(shi)yubi** the ring finger
紅涙 **kōrui** tears of blood; tears of a beautiful woman
紅唇 **kōshin** red lips
紅梅 **kōbai** red plum blossoms
紅粉 **beniko** powdered rouge
11 紅殻 **benigara** red-ocher rouge
12 紅葉 **kōyō** red (autumn) leaves
momiji maple tree; red (autumn) leaves
紅葉狩 **momijiga(ri)** outing for viewing autumn leaves
13 紅蓮 **guren** red lotus blossom; blazing red
15 紅潮 **kōchō** redden, flush, blush; menstruate
16 紅衛兵 **Kōeihei** the Red Guards (in China)
18 紅顔 **kōgan** rosy cheeks, ruddy face
23 紅鱒 **benimasu** red/sockeye salmon

――――― 2 ―――――
8 退紅色 **taikōshoku** pink
9 浅紅 **senkō** light/pale red, pink
洋紅 **yōkō** carmine, crimson
草紅葉 **kusamomiji** colored grasses of autumn
食紅 **shokubeni** red food coloring
10 真紅 **shinku** crimson
唐紅 **karakurenai** crimson, scarlet
11 淡紅色 **tankōshoku** rose/salmon pink
深紅 **shinku** deep/ruby red, crimson
深紅色 **shinkōshoku** deep/ruby red
12 猩紅熱 **shōkōnetsu** scarlet fever
寒紅梅 **kankōbai** winter red-blossom plum tree
棒紅 **bōbeni** lipstick
14 褪紅色 **taikōshoku** light pink
15 潮紅 **chōkō** flush, redden
16 濃紅色 **nōkōshoku** deep red, crimson
薄紅 **usubeni, usukurenai** pinkish
頬紅 **hōbeni** rouge
17 鮮紅 **senkō** bright red, scarlet

――――― 3 ―――――
6 百日紅 **sarusuberi** crape myrtle, Indian lilac
7 吾木紅 **waremokō** burnet (a flowering herb)
吾亦紅 **waremokō** burnet (a flowering herb)

────────── 4 ──────────

3 千紫万紅 **senshi-bankō** dazzling variety of colors

6a3.7 / 211

約   **YAKU** promise; approximately; curtail; factor (in math)
tsuzu(maru) shrink; be summarized
tsuzu(meru) condense, shorten, curtail

────────── 1 ──────────

0 約する **yaku(suru)** promise; reduce, abbreviate
4 約文 **yakubun** summarize, condense
約分 **yakubun** reduce (a fraction to lowest terms)
約手 **yakute** promissory note (short for 約束手形)
5 約半分 **yaku hanbun** about half
7 約束 **yakusoku** promise; appointment
約束手形 **yakusoku tegata** promissory note
約束事 **yakusokugoto** promise
約言 **yakugen** a contraction; summary
8 約定 **yakujō** promise, agreement
約定書 **yakujōsho** (written) contract/agreement
約定済 **yakujōzu(mi)** promised; engaged; sold
12 約款 **yakkan** agreement, stipulation
14 約説 **yakusetsu** summary
15 約諾 **yakudaku** promise, commitment

────────── 2 ──────────

3 口約 **kōyaku** oral agreement/promise
口約束 **kuchi yakusoku** oral agreement/promise
4 予約 **yoyaku** reservations, booking, advance order, subscription, contract
予約者 **yoyakusha** subscriber
内約 **naiyaku** private/secret agreement
公約 **kōyaku** public commitment/pledge
公約数 **kōyakusū** common divisor
5 民約説 **min'yakusetsu** the social-contract theory
旧約 **kyūyaku** old promise/covenant; the Old Testament
旧約聖書 **Kyūyaku Seisho** the Old Testament
6 先約 **sen'yaku** previous engagement; prior contract
成約 **seiyaku** conclude a contract
7 売約 **baiyaku** sales contract
条約 **jōyaku** treaty
条約国 **jōyakukoku** signatory
8 制約 **seiyaku** restriction, limitation, condition
協約 **kyōyaku** agreement, convention, pact
9 契約 **keiyaku** contract, agreement
契約書 **keiyakusho** contract

前約 **zen'yaku** previous commitment/engagement
括約筋 **katsuyakukin** sphincter (muscle)
要約 **yōyaku** summary
背約 **haiyaku** breach of promise
10 倹約 **ken'yaku** thrift, frugality
倹約家 **ken'yakuka** thrifty person, economizer
特約 **tokuyaku** special contract
特約店 **tokuyakuten** special agent, chain store
破約 **hayaku** breach of contract/promise
11 婚約 **kon'yaku** engagement, betrothal
婚約者 **kon'yakusha** fiancé(e)
密約 **mitsuyaku** secret agreement
規約 **kiyaku** agreement, pact, rules
12 違約 **iyaku** breach of contract, default
違約金 **iyakukin** breach-of-contract penalty
集約 **shūyaku** intensive
集約的 **shūyakuteki** intensive
13 棄約 **kiyaku** break a promise
解約 **kaiyaku** cancellation of a contract
新約 **shin'yaku** the New Testament
新約聖書 **shin'yaku seisho** the New Testament
盟約 **meiyaku** pledge, pact; alliance
節約 **setsuyaku** economizing, saving on
14 誓約 **seiyaku** oath, vow, pledge
誓約者 **seiyakusha** party to a covenant
誓約書 **seiyakusho** written pledge, covenant
15 黙約 **mokuyaku** a tacit agreement
確約 **kakuyaku** definite promise
締約 **teiyaku** (conclude a) treaty
締約国 **teiyakukoku** treaty signatories
18 簡約 **kan'yaku** concise, simplified, abridged

────────── 3 ──────────

6 仮条約 **karijōyaku** provisional treaty

────────── 4 ──────────

4 双務契約 **sōmu keiyaku** bilateral contract
5 平和条約 **heiwa jōyaku** peace treaty
6 安保条約 **anpo jōyaku** security treaty
17 講和条約 **kōwa jōyaku** peace treaty

────────── 4 ──────────

6a4.1 / 1859

紡   **BŌ, tsumu(gu)** spin, make yarn

────────── 1 ──────────

4 紡毛 **bōmō** carded wool
6 紡糸 **bōshi** spinning; yarn
7 紡車 **bōsha, tsumu(gi)guruma** spinning wheel
16 紡錘 **bōsui** spindle
17 紡績 **bōseki** spinning

6

糸 4 ←
米
舟
虫
耳
⺾

紡績工 **bōsekikō** spinner
紡績糸 **bōsekiito** (cotton) yarn
18 紡織 **bōshoku** spinning and weaving

――――――― 2 ―――――――

11 混紡 **konbō** mixed spinning, blended (yarn)
13 絹紡 **kenbō** spun silk
14 綿紡 **menbō** cotton spinning
20 鐘紡 **Kanebō** (company name)

6a4.2

紐 **CHŪ, JŪ, himo** string(s), cord, (shoe)lace, strap

――――――― 1 ―――――――

5 紐付 **himotsu(ki)** with strings attached
8 紐育 **Nyūyōku** New York
9 紐革 **himokawa** strap, thong
10 紐帯 **chūtai** band, bond, tie

――――――― 2 ―――――――

3 下紐 **shitahimo** undersash, belt
9 革紐 **kawahimo** (leather) strap, leash
10 紙紐 **kamihimo** paper twine
13 靴紐 **kutsuhimo** shoelaces
18 顎紐 **agohimo** chin strap

――――――― 3 ―――――――

10 真田紐 **sanada himo** braid

6a4.3 / 965

純 **JUN** pure

――――――― 1 ―――――――

1 純一 **jun'itsu** purity, homogeneity
4 純毛 **junmō** all-wool
純化 **junka** purification
純収益 **junshūeki** net earnings
純文学 **junbungaku** pure literature, belles lettres
純分 **junbun** fineness (of gold)
純分度 **junbundo** fineness (of gold)
純水 **junsui** pure water
純日本風 **jun-Nihon-fū** classical Japanese style
5 純正 **junsei** pure, genuine
純正科学 **junsei kagaku** pure science
純白 **junpaku** pure white
6 純色 **junshoku** pure color
純朴 **junboku** simple and honest
純血 **junketsu** full-blooded, thoroughbred
7 純良 **junryō** pure, genuine
純利 **junri** net profit
純系 **junkei** (genetically) pure line
8 純国産 **junkokusan** all-domestic (product)
純所得 **junshotoku** net income

純金 **junkin** pure/solid gold
9 純美 **junbi** unalloyed beauty
純度 **jundo** purity
純計 **junkei** total excluding duplications
10 純真 **junshin** ingenuous, sincere
純益 **jun'eki** net profit
純粋 **junsui** pure, genuine
11 純理 **junri** pure reason, scientific principle
純理論 **junriron** rationalism
純情 **junjō** pure-minded emotion, naïveté, devotion
12 純量 **junryō** net weight
純然 **junzen** pure, sheer, utter
13 純愛 **jun'ai** pure/Platonic love
純絹 **junken** pure silk
14 純増 **junzō** net increase
純種 **junshu** purebred
純綿 **junmen** all-cotton
純銀 **jungin** pure/solid silver
15 純潔 **junketsu** pure, unsullied, chaste

――――――― 2 ―――――――

4 不純 **fujun** impure
不純物 **fujunbutsu** impurities, foreign matter
6 至純 **shijun** of absolute purity
8 忠純 **chūjun** unswerving loyalty
9 単純 **tanjun** simple
単純化 **tanjunka** simplification
11 清純 **seijun** pure (and innocent)

6a4.4 / 180

紙 **SHI, kami** paper

――――――― 1 ―――――――

0 紙パ **kamipa** paper and pulp (short for 紙パルプ)
1 紙一重 **kami hitoe** paper-thin (difference)
2 紙入 **kamii(re)** purse, wallet
紙子 **kamiko** paper garment
3 紙上 **shijō** on paper; by letter; in the newspapers
4 紙切 **kamiki(re)** scrap of paper
紙片 **shihen** scrap of paper
5 紙包 **kamizutsu(mi)** wrapped in paper
紙芝居 **kamishibai** picture-card show
紙札 **kamifuda** label, tag
7 紙花 **kamibana** paper flowers
8 紙表紙 **kamibyōshi** paper cover, paperback
紙価 **shika** the price of paper
9 紙巻 **kamima(ki)** (cigarette) wound in paper
紙型 **shikei** papier-mâché mold
紙挟 **kamibasa(mi)** folder; clip
紙屋 **kamiya** paper store/dealer
紙面 **shimen** (newspaper) space
紙背 **shihai** reverse side of the paper

10 紙屑 **kamikuzu** waste paper
紙屑拾 **kamikuzuhiro(i)** ragpicker
紙屑籠 **kamikuzukago** wastebasket
紙紐 **kamihimo** paper twine
11 紙帳 **shichō** paper mosquito net
紙袋 **kamibukuro** paper sack/bag
紙細工 **kamizaiku** paper handicrafts
紙粘土 **kaminendo** clay made from newsprint
紙魚 **shimi** clothes moth, silverfish, bookworm
12 紙幅 **shifuku** paper width, space
13 紙数 **shisū** number of pages, space
紙鉄砲 **kamideppō** popgun
14 紙漉 **kamisu(ki)** papermaking
15 紙撚 **koyo(ri)** twisted-paper string
紙器 **shiki** papier-mâché articles
紙幣 **shihei** paper money
紙箱 **kamibako** carton
紙質 **shishitsu** quality of the paper
16 紙縒 **koyo(ri)** twisted-paper string
23 紙鑢 **kamiyasuri** sandpaper, emery paper

――――――― 2 ―――――――

3 上紙 **uwagami** paper cover/wrapping
4 切紙 **ki(ri)kami** cut paper **kirigami** cutting folded paper into figures
手紙 **tegami** letter
5 包紙 **tsutsu(mi)gami** wrapping paper
半紙 **hanshi** common Japanese writing paper, rice paper
本紙 **honshi** this newspaper
生紙 **kigami** unsized paper
外紙 **gaishi** foreign-language newspaper
用紙 **yōshi** form (to be filled out); stationery
台紙 **daishi** (photo) mounting paper, mat
白紙 **hakushi, shirakami** white paper; blank paper, carte blanche; flyleaf, clean slate
6 全紙 **zenshi** the whole sheet/newspaper
色紙 **irogami** colored paper
      shikishi (a type of calligraphy paper)
米紙 **beishi** American newspaper(s)
7 別紙 **besshi** attached sheet, enclosure
延紙 **no(be)gami** paper handkerchief (Edo period)
折紙 **o(ri)gami** the art of paper folding; colored origami paper; authentication, testimonial
折紙付 **o(ri)gamitsu(ki)** certified, genuine
抄紙 **shōshi** papermaking
8 表紙 **hyōshi** cover, binding
厚紙 **atsugami** thick paper, cardboard
油紙 **aburagami, yushi** oiled paper, oilskins
板紙 **itagami** cardboard, pasteboard
和紙 **washi** Japanese paper
金紙 **kingami, kinshi** gold/gilt paper

9 巻紙 **makigami** paper on a roll
洋紙 **yōshi** Western paper
型紙 **katagami** (dressmaking) pattern
草紙 **sōshi** storybook
故紙 **koshi** wastepaper
10 差紙 **sa(shi)gami** summons, official order
帯紙 **obigami** wrapper
唐紙 **karakami** bamboo paper(-covered sliding door)
料紙 **ryōshi** (writing) paper
11 渋紙 **shibukami, shibugami** paper treated with astringent persimmon juice and used for a floor covering
掛紙 **ka(ke)gami** wrapper
張紙 **ha(ri)gami** sticker, (advertising) poster
張紙禁止 **ha(ri)gami kinshi** Post No Bills
12 落紙 **o(toshi)gami** toilet paper
筆紙 **hisshi** pen and paper
証紙 **shōshi** certification sticker/stamp
貼紙 **ha(ri)gami** sticker, poster
間紙 **aigami** sheets inserted to prevent scratches/soiling
13 罫紙 **keishi** lined/ruled paper
継紙 **tsu(gi)gami** patchwork paper
14 漉紙 **koshigami** filter paper
塵紙 **chirigami** coarse (toilet) paper
種紙 **tanegami** (silkworm) egg card
製紙 **seishi** paper manufacturing
製紙業 **seishigyō** the paper industry
鼻紙 **hanagami** paper handkerchief
誓紙 **seishi** written pledge
銀紙 **gingami** silver paper
16 壁紙 **kabegami** wallpaper
薄紙 **usugami** thin paper
磨紙 **miga(ki)gami** sandpaper, emery paper
懐紙 **kaishi** pocket paper hankies; paper for writing poems on
18 濾紙 **roshi, ko(shi)gami** filter paper
19 艶紙 **tsuyagami** glossy paper
21 蠟紙 **rōgami** wax paper

――――――― 3 ―――――――

3 夕刊紙 **yūkanshi** evening paper/edition
千代紙 **chiyogami** colored paper
上表紙 **uwabyōshi** outer cover, (book) jacket
4 五線紙 **gosenshi** music paper
日本紙 **nohonshi** Japanese paper
方眼紙 **hōganshi** graph paper
5 外字紙 **gaijishi** foreign-language newspaper
布表紙 **nunobyōshi** cloth binding
6 西洋紙 **seiyōshi** Western-style (machine-made) paper
羊皮紙 **yōhishi** parchment
吸取紙 **su(i)to(ri)gami** blotting paper
8 表表紙 **omotebyōshi** front cover
画仙紙 **gasenshi** drawing paper

6

糸 4←
米
舟
虫
耳
⺮

画用紙 **gayōshi** drawing paper

9 巻取紙 **ma(ki)to(ri)gami, ma(ki)to(ri)shi** roll of paper

透写紙 **tōshashi** tracing paper

革表紙 **kawabyōshi** leather cover/binding

草双紙 **kusazōshi** storybook with pictures

炭酸紙 **tansanshi** carbon paper

10 書簡紙 **shokanshi** stationery

紙表紙 **kamibyōshi** paper cover, paperback

馬糞紙 **bafunshi** cardboard, strawboard

11 黄表紙 **kibyōshi** Edo-period comic book

12 雁皮紙 **ganpishi** (a type of high-quality paper)

硫酸紙 **ryūsanshi** parchment paper

絵双紙 **ezōshi** picture book

絵草紙 **ezōshi** picture book

13 業界紙 **gyōkaishi** trade paper/journal

障子紙 **shōjigami** shōji paper

新聞紙 **shinbunshi** newspaper (paper)

置手紙 **o(ki)tegami** letter left behind

試験紙 **shikenshi** litmus paper

14 模造紙 **mozōshi** vellum paper

複写紙 **fukushashi** copying paper

16 薬包紙 **yakuhōshi** a paper wrapping for a dose of medicine

磨研紙 **makenshi** emery paper, sandpaper

機関紙 **kikanshi** organization's newspaper

頼信紙 **raishinshi** telegram form/blank

17 擬革紙 **gikakushi** imitation leather

藁半紙 **warabanshi** (a low-grade paper)

19 贋造紙幣 **ganzō shihei** counterfeit currency

蠅取紙 **haeto(ri)gami** flypaper

——————— 4 ———————

6 仮名草紙 **kanazōshi** story book written in kana

7 投票用紙 **tōhyō yōshi** ballot

8 金剛砂紙 **kongōshashi** emery paper

10 原稿用紙 **genkō yōshi** manuscript paper

17 擬羊皮紙 **giyōhishi** parchment paper

級 → 級 **6a3.2**

6a4.5 / 758

納 NŌ, TŌ, NA, NA', NAN, **osa(meru)** pay; supply; accept; store
osa(maru) be paid (in), be supplied; stay (in the stomach); be contented

——————— 1 ———————

2 納入 **nōnyū** pay, deliver, supply

4 納戸 **nando** closet; grayish blue

5 納本 **nōhon** book delivery; presentation copy

納付 **nōfu** payment, delivery

納付金 **nōfukin** contribution

納札 **nōsatsu** votive tablet (left at a temple)

6 納会 **nōkai** the last meeting (of the year/month)

納返 **osa(mari)kae(ru)** be content/nonchalant

7 納豆 **nattō** fermented soybeans

8 納受 **nōju** receipt, acceptance

納杯 **nōhai** the last cup

納采 **nōsai** betrothal gift

納所 **nassho** temple office

納金 **nōkin** payment

9 納品 **nōhin** delivery

納屋 **naya** (storage) shed

10 納骨 **nōkotsu** depositing the (deceased's) ashes

納骨堂 **nōkotsudō** ossuary, crypt

11 納涼 **nōryō** enjoying the evening cool

納得 **nattoku** assent to, be convinced of

12 納棺 **nōkan** placing in the coffin

納期 **nōki** payment date, delivery deadline

納税 **nōzei** payment of taxes

納税者 **nōzeisha** taxpayer

納税額 **nōzeigaku** amount of tax (to be) paid

——————— 2 ———————

3 上納 **jōnō** payment (to the government)

4 不納 **funō** nonpayment, default

収納 **shūnō** receipts; harvest; put in, store

分納 **bunnō** payment/delivery in installments

5 出納 **suitō** receipts and disbursements

出納係 **suitōgakari** cashier; teller

出納簿 **suitōbo** account book

未納 **minō** nonpayment, default, arrears

甘納豆 **amanattō** adzuki-bean candy

代納 **dainō** pay for another; pay in kind

6 全納 **zennō** payment in full

返納 **hennō** return, restoration

7 即納 **sokunō** prompt payment/delivery

別納 **betsunō** another method of payment

延納 **ennō** deferred payment

完納 **kannō** payment/delivery in full

見納 **miosa(me)** last/farewell look

8 奉納 **hōnō** dedication, offering

奉納物 **hōnōbutsu** votive offering

奉納額 **hōnōgaku** votive tablet

受納 **junō** receipt, acceptance

追納 **tsuinō** supplementary payment

物納 **butsunō** payment in kind

物納税 **butsunōzei** tax paid in kind

金納 **kinnō** payment in cash

9 前納 **zennō** prepayment, advance payment

皆納 **kainō** (tax) payment in full

10 帰納 **kinō** induction, recursion

帰納法 **kinōhō** inductive method

帰納的 **kinōteki** inductive (reasoning)

格納 **kakunō** to store, house

格納庫 **kakunōko** hangar

笑納 **shōnō** your acceptance (of my gift)

12 結納 **yuinō** betrothal gift
  結納金 **yuinōkin** engagement gift money
13 滞納 **tainō** delinquency (in payment)
  滞納処分 **tainō shobun** disposition for failure to pay (taxes)
  滞納者 **tainōsha** defaulter, (tax) delinquent
  献納 **kennō** present, donate, dedicate
  献納者 **kennōsha** donor
  献納品 **kennōhin** donation
14 嘉納 **kanō** approve, appreciate; accept with pleasure
  聞納 **ki(ki)osa(me)** the last time (I) heard (him)

─────── 3 ───────

12 御用納 **goyō-osa(me)** year-end office closing

6a4.6

SA, SHA gauze, cloth

─────── 2 ───────

16 薄紗 **hakusa** delicate gauze, gossamer

6a4.7

紕

HI braiding; decoration; error

6a4.8 / 1702

紛

FUN, magi(reru) be mistaken for, be hardly distinguishable; get mixed, disappear among; be diverted **magi(rawasu/rasu)** divert, distract; conceal; evade **magi(rawashii)** ambiguous, misleading **maga(u)** be mistaken for; be confused with

─────── 1 ───────

3 紛々 **funpun** in confusion, conflicting
4 紛込 **magi(re)ko(mu)** be lost among, disappear among
5 紛失 **funshitsu** loss, be missing
6 紛争 **funsō** dispute, strife
7 紛乱 **funran** disorder
9 紛糾 **funkyū** complication, entanglement
12 紛然 **funzen** confused, in a jumble
18 紛擾 **funjō** disorder, trouble, dispute
20 紛議 **fungi** controversy, dissension

─────── 2 ───────

4 内紛 **naifun** internal discord
6 気紛 **kimagu(re)** whimsical, capricious
7 言紛 **i(i)magi(rasu)** evade, quibble
8 苦紛 **kuru(shi)magi(re)** driven by distress, in desperation

取紛 **to(ri)magi(reru)** be in confusion; be busily engaged
9 悔紛 **ku(yashi)magi(re)** out of spite/chagrin
10 紛紛 **funpun** in confusion, conflicting

─────── 3 ───────

13 腹立紛 **harada(chi)magi(re)** a fit of rage

6a4.9 / 1454

紋

MON (family) crest; (textile) pattern

─────── 1 ───────

4 紋切形 **monki(ri)gata** conventional
  紋切型 **monki(ri)gata** conventional
  紋日 **monbi** holiday
5 紋付 **montsu(ki)** clothing bearing one's family crest
6 紋羽二重 **mon habutae** figured habutae
8 紋服 **monpuku** clothing bearing one's family crest
  紋所 **mondokoro** (family) crest
11 紋章 **monshō** crest, coat of arms
  紋章学 **monshōgaku** heraldry
14 紋様 **mon'yō** (textile) pattern

─────── 2 ───────

3 小紋 **komon** fine pattern
4 水紋 **suimon** concentric wavelets, ripples
6 衣紋 **emon** clothes, one's dress
  衣紋掛 **emonka(ke)** hanger/rack (for kimono)
8 波紋 **hamon** ripples; repercussions
  定紋 **jōmon** family crest
9 指紋 **shimon** fingerprints, thumbprint
10 家紋 **kamon** family crest
  書紋 **ka(ki)mon** hand-drawn family crest
11 蛇紋石 **jamonseki** serpentine, ophiolite
12 無紋 **mumon** solid color; without a crest
  斑紋 **hanmon** spot, speckle
13 裏紋 **uramon** informal family crest
15 縫紋 **nu(i)mon** embroidered crest

6a4.10

UN disorder, confusion

6a4.11

KŌ reins; boundary; large

─────── 2 ───────

2 八紘一宇 **hakkō-ichiu** universal brotherhood

6

糸 4←
米
舟
虫
耳
⺮

6a4.12 / 271

素
SO element; beginning
SU naked, uncovered, simple
moto beginning, base

——————— 1 ———————

0 素より **moto(yori)** from the beginning; of course
2 素人 **shirōto** amateur, layman
素人下宿 **shirōto geshuku** boarding house
素人目 **shirōtome** untrained eye
素人芸 **shirōtogei** amateur's skill
素人臭 **shirōtokusa(i)** amateurish
素人離 **shirōtobana(re)** free of amateurishness
素子 **soshi** (electronic) element
3 素干 **subo(shi)** drying in the shade
6 素気 **sokke(nai)** curt, brusque
素地 **sochi** groundwork, the makings of
素行 **sokō** one's conduct, behavior
素因 **soin** contributing factor, cause
素朴 **soboku** simple, artless, ingenuous
素肌 **suhada** bare skin
素早 **subaya(i)** quick, nimble
7 素志 **soshi** original purpose, longstanding aim
素材 **sozai** a material; subject matter
素町人 **suchōnin** common townspeople
素足 **suashi** bare feet, barefooted
8 素直 **sunao** gentle, meek, docile; frank, honest
素知顔 **soshi(ranu) kao** innocent look
素姓 **sujō** birth, lineage, identity
素性 **sujō** birth, lineage, identity
9 素首 **sokubi, so(k)kubi** one's head
素透 **sudō(shi)** transparent, plain-glass (eyeglasses)
素封家 **sohōka** wealthy person/family
素面 **sumen** sober face **shirafu** soberness
10 素浪人 **surōnin** (mere) lordless retainer
素振 **sobu(ri)** manner, bearing, behavior
素破抜 **suppanu(ku)** expose, unmask
11 素描 **sobyō** rough sketch
素粒子 **soryūshi** (subatomic) particle
12 素寒貧 **sukanpin** poverty; pauper
素晴 **suba(rashii)** splendid, magnificent
素焼 **suya(ki)** unglazed pottery, bisque
13 素数 **sosū** a prime (number)
素裸 **suhadaka, su(p)padaka** stark naked
素絹 **soken** coarse silk
14 素語 **sugata(ri)** recital without samisen accompaniment
素読 **sodoku** reading without comprehending
15 素養 **soyō** grounding in, attainments
素敵 **suteki** splendid, marvelous, great
素質 **soshitsu** nature, makeup
16 素樸 **soboku** simple, artless, ingenuous
素懐 **sokai** long-held desire

18 素顔 **sugao** face without makeup; sober face
20 素麺 **sōmen** vermicelli, thin noodles

——————— 2 ———————

4 元素 **genso** (chemical) element
水素 **suiso** hydrogen
水素爆弾 **suiso bakudan** hydrogen bomb
5 弗素 **fusso** fluorine
平素 **heiso** ordinarily; in the past
6 色素 **shikiso** pigment, coloring matter
7 沃素 **yōso** iodine
尿素 **nyōso** urea
8 画素 **gaso** picture element, pixel, dot
毒素 **dokuso** toxin
味素 **Aji(no)moto** monosodium glutamate, MSG
9 要素 **yōso** element, factor
炭素 **tanso** carbon
炭素棒 **tansobō** carbon rod/points
砒素 **hiso** arsenic
臭素 **shūso** bromine
臭素酸 **shūsosan** bromic acid, ... bromate
10 倹素 **kenso** frugal and simple
珪素 **keiso** silicon
11 貧素 **hinso** dire poverty
窒素 **chisso** nitrogen
13 塩素 **enso** chlorine
硼素 **hōso** boron
酵素 **kōso** enzyme
14 酸素 **sanso** oxygen
15 質素 **shisso** simple, plain, frugal
18 簡素 **kanso** plain and simple

——————— 3 ———————

6 血色素 **kesshikiso** hemoglobin
7 抗毒素 **kōdokuso** antitoxin, antidote
9 発酵素 **hakkōso** a ferment, yeast
重水素 **jūsuiso** heavy hydrogen, deuterium
栄養素 **eiyōso** a nutrient
12 葉緑素 **yōryokuso** chlorophyll
17 繊維素 **sen'iso** roughage, fiber, cellulose

——————— 4 ———————

6 同位元素 **dōi genso** isotope
7 含水炭素 **gansuitanso** carbohydrate
9 炭化水素 **tanka suiso** hydrocarbon

——————— 5 ———————

1 一酸化炭素 **issanka tanso** carbon monoxide

——————— 5 ———————

6a5.1 / 695

細
SAI narrow, small, fine **hoso(i)** thin, narrow, slender **hoso(ru)** get thin **hoso(meru)** make narrow **koma(kai/ka)** small, detailed **sasa(yaka)** small

——————— 1 ———————

0 か細い **(ka)boso(i)** slender; delicate

3 細工 **saiku** work(manship); artifice, trick
細工人 **saikunin** craftsman, artisan
細大 **saidai** great and small
細孔 **saikō** small hole, pore
細々 **komagoma** in pieces, in detail
   hosoboso slender; scanty (livelihood)
細小 **saishō** small and fine, minute
4 細毛 **saimō** cilia
細切 **komagi(re)** small pieces of cloth;
   chopped meat
細片 **saihen** chip, splinters
細分 **saibun** subdivide
細心 **saishin** careful, scrupulous
5 細民 **saimin** the poor
細末 **saimatsu** trivia; powder
細字 **saiji** small characters/type
細目 **saimoku** details, particulars
   hosome narrow eyes/opening
6 細糸 **hosoito** fine thread
7 細身 **hosomi** narrow blade, slender build
細別 **saibetsu** subdivide, itemize
細君 **saikun** wife
細見 **saiken** close inspection
8 細長 **hosonaga(i)** long and thin
細事 **saiji** trivia, details
細雨 **saiu** fine/misty rain, drizzle
9 細面 **hosoomote** slender face
細胞 **saibō** cell (in biology)
細胞学 **saibōgaku** cytology
細則 **saisoku** detailed rules, by-laws
10 細部 **saibu** details, particulars
細流 **sairyū** small stream
細帯 **hosoobi** undersash, girdle
細書 **hosoga(ki)** close/fine writing
細記 **saiki** detailed description/account
11 細道 **hosomichi** narrow lane, path
細菌 **saikin** bacteria, germ, microbe
細菌学 **saikingaku** bacteriology, microbiology
細密 **saimitsu** minute, close, miniature
細細 **komagoma** in pieces, in detail
   hosoboso slender; scanty (livelihood)
細粒 **sairyū** granule
細雪 **sasameyuki** light snow(fall)
12 細腕 **hosoude** thin arm; poor ability, slender
   means
細筆 **saihitsu** fine brush; writing small
細評 **saihyō** detailed criticism
13 細微 **saibi** minute, fine, detailed
細腰 **saiyō, hosogoshi** slender hips
細節 **saisetsu** minor details
14 細説 **saisetsu** detailed explanation
15 細論 **sairon** detailed discussion/explanation
16 細緻 **saichi** minute, close, detailed
17 細螺 **kisago, kishago** periwinkle
細謹 **saikin** small defect, slight flaw

───────── 2 ─────────

3 小細工 **kozaiku** handiwork; tricks, wiles
4 不細工 **busaiku** awkward, clumsy, botched;
   homely, plain-looking
毛細血管 **mōsai kekkan** capillaries
仔細 **shisai** reasons, circumstances; significance; details
手細工 **tezaiku** handicraft, handmade
心細 **kokoroboso(i)** forlorn, disheartened
5 皮細工 **kawazaiku** leatherwork
巨細 **kyosai** large and small matters; details
石細工 **ishizaiku** masonry
6 肉細 **nikuboso** light-faced (type)
尖細 **sakiboso** tapering
竹細工 **takezaiku** bamboo handicrafts
7 亜細亜 **Ajia** Asia
卵細胞 **ransaibō** egg cell, ovum
角細工 **tsunozaiku** horn work/carving
貝細工 **kaizaiku** shellwork
8 事細 **kotokoma(ka ni)** minutely, in detail
些細 **sasai** trifling, trivial, slight, insignificant
明細 **meisai** details, particulars
明細書 **meisaisho** detailed statement
委細 **isai** details, particular
金細工 **kinzaiku** goldwork, gold ware
9 俄細工 **niwakazaiku** hastily prepared
革細工 **kawazaiku** leathercraft
単細胞 **tansaibō** single cell
10 紙細工 **kamizaiku** paper handicrafts
11 細細 **komagoma** in pieces, in detail
   hosoboso slender; scanty (livelihood)
13 微細 **bisai** minute, fine, detailed
詳細 **shōsai** details, particulars
零細 **reisai** small, meager
零細農 **reisainō** poor peasant
14 漆細工 **urushizaiku** lacquerware
痩細 **ya(se)hoso(ru)** grow thin, lose weight
網細工 **amizaiku** filigree
精細 **seisai** detailed, precise
銀細工 **ginzaiku** silverwork
銀細工師 **ginzaikushi** silversmith
銅細工 **dōzaiku** copperwork
17 繊細 **sensai** delicate, fine, subtle
21 籐細工 **tōzaiku** rattanwork, canework

───────── 3 ─────────

3 小亜細亜 **Shō-Ajia** Asia Minor
12 象牙細工 **zōgezaiku** ivory work/carving
嵌木細工 **ha(me)kizaiku** inlaid woodwork

6a5.2 / 1109

紳 **SHIN** gentleman

───────── 1 ─────────

3 紳士 **shinshi** gentleman

6
糸 5←
米
舟
虫
耳
ⵜⵜ

紳士用 **shinshiyō** men's, for men
紳士協定 **shinshi kyōtei** gentleman's agreement
紳士服 **shinshifuku** men's clothing
紳士的 **shinshiteki** gentlemanly
紳士道 **shinshidō** the code of a gentleman
紳士録 **shinshiroku** a who's-who, directory
11 紳商 **shinshō** merchant prince

──────── 2 ────────

5 田紳 **denshin** country gentleman
    tau(e) rice-planting
8 非紳士的 **hishinshiteki** ungentlemanly
13 搢紳 **shinshin** high-ranking person
16 縉紳 **shinshin** high official/personage

6a5.3

CHŪ, tsumugi pongee

──────── 1 ────────

6 紬糸 **tsumugiito** silk thread from waste cocoons

6a5.4

SETSU tether

──────── 2 ────────

17 縲紲 **ruisetsu** fetters, bonds

6a5.5 / 1493

KON dark/navy blue

──────── 1 ────────

6 紺色 **kon'iro** dark/navy blue
  紺地 **konji** dark-blue ground (cloth)
8 紺青 **konjō** Prussian blue, ultramarine
9 紺屋 **kon'ya, kōya** dyer, dyer's shop
14 紺碧 **konpeki** deep blue, azure

──────── 2 ────────

7 花紺青 **hana konjō** royal blue
12 紫紺 **shikon** bluish purple
16 濃紺 **nōkon** dark/navy blue

6a5.6

HAN, BAN, hoda(su) tie, bind
kizuna ties, bonds

──────── 1 ────────

12 絆創膏 **bansōkō** adhesive plaster
22 絆纏 **hanten** short coat, vest

──────── 2 ────────

11 脚絆 **kyahan** leggings, gaiters
24 羈絆 **kihan** yoke, fetters, restraints

6a5.7 / 418

SO, kumi group, set, crew, class, company
ku(mu) put together

──────── 1 ────────

0 組する **kumi(suru)** take part in; side with
2 組入 **ku(mi)i(reru)** include, insert
  組子 **ku(mi)ko** member of a squad (of firemen)
3 組上 **ku(mi)a(geru)** compose, make up (a page)
  組下 **kumishita** group member; one's subordinates
4 組天井 **ku(mi)tenjō** fretwork ceiling
  組分 **kumiwa(ke)** sorting, grouping
  組込 **ku(mi)ko(mu)** cut in (in printing)
  組手 **ku(mi)te** joints; karate kata performed with partner
5 組付 **ku(mi)tsu(ku)** grapple with, seize hold of
  組写真 **ku(mi)shashin** composite photograph
  組打 **ku(mi)u(chi)** grapple/wrestle with
  組立 **ku(mi)ta(teru)** construct, assemble
  組立工 **kumita(te)kō** assembler, fitter
  組立工場 **kumita(te) kōjō** assembly/ knockdown plant
  組立式 **kumita(te)shiki** prefab, collapsible
  組立住宅 **kumita(te) jūtaku** prefab housing
6 組曲 **kumikyoku** suite (in music)
  組伏 **ku(mi)fu(seru)** pin/hold (someone) down
  組合 **ku(mi)a(u)** form a partnership; grapple with **kumiai** association, union
  ku(mi)a(waseru) combine; fit together
  ku(mi)a(wase) combination
  組成 **sosei** composition, makeup
  組糸 **ku(mi)ito** braid, plaited thread
8 組長 **kumichō** group leader, foreman
  組物 **kumimono** braid, braiding
12 組換 **ku(mi)ka(eru)** rearrange, recombine
14 組閣 **sokaku** formation of a cabinet
16 組頭 **kumigashira** group leader, foreman
18 組織 **soshiki** organization; tissue

──────── 2 ────────

1 一組 **hitokumi, ichikumi** one class
  hitokumi one set
2 入組 **i(ri)ku(mu)** become complicated
3 三組 **sankumi, mikumi, mi(tsu)gumi** set of three
  大組 **ōgu(mi)** making up (a newspaper)
4 心組 **kokorogu(mi)** intention

5 仕組 **shiku(mi)** construction; contrivance, mechanism; plan
石組 **ishigu(mi)** arrangement of garden rocks
6 気組 **kigu(mi)** readiness, ardor, attitude
再組織 **saisoshiki** reorganization
7 労組 **rōso, rōkumi** labor union (short for 労働組合)
改組 **kaiso** reorganize, reshuffle
8 枠組 **wakugumi** frame, framework; framing
取組 **to(ri)ku(mu)** grapple with
　　 to(ri)kumi (sumo) match
取組合 **to(k)ku(mi)a(u)** grapple, tussle
9 乗組員 **norikumiin** crew
10 骨組 **honegu(mi)** skeleton; framework
12 棒組 **bōgu(mi)** typesetting
腕組 **udegu(mi)** fold one's arms
番組 **bangumi** program
15 隣組 **tonarigumi** neighborhood association
縁組 **engumi** marriage; adoption
編組 **henso** braid; combine

―――― 3 ――――

2 二人組 **niningumi** twosome, duo
3 三人組 **sanningumi** trio, threesome
4 五人組 **goningumi** five-family unit; five-man group
5 生番組 **namabangumi** live program
好取組 **kōtorikumi** good game/match
四人組 **yoningumi** group/gang of four, foursome
6 共済組合 **kyōsai kumiai** mutual aid society
7 労働組合 **rōdō kumiai** labor union
見本組 **mihongu(mi)** specimen page
9 信用組合 **shin'yō kumiai** credit union
10 消防組 **shōbōgumi** fire brigade
11 商業組合 **shōgyō kumiai** trade association
第二組合 **dai-ni kumiai** rival labor union
12 御用組合 **goyō kumiai** company union
結合組織 **ketsugō soshiki** connective tissue
17 購買組合 **kōbai kumiai** a co-op

―――― 4 ――――

14 遺伝子組替 **idenshi kumika(e)** recombinant gene splicing
15 養子縁組 **yōshi engumi** adopting an heir

6a5.8

紵

CHO flax, linen

6a5.9 / 458

終

SHŪ, o(waru/eru) come/bring to an end
o(wari) end, conclusion
tsui (ni) finally, in the end

―――― 1 ――――

1 終了 **shūryō** end, conclusion, completion, expiration
4 終止 **shūshi** come to an end
終止符 **shūshifu** full stop, period, end
終日 **shūjitsu, hinemosu** all day long
5 終末 **shūmatsu** end, conclusion
終末観 **shūmatsukan** eschatology
終生 **shūsei** all one's life, lifelong
終世 **shūsei** all one's life, lifelong
終刊 **shūkan** ceasing publication
終刊号 **shūkangō** final issue
6 終曲 **shūkyoku** finale
終列車 **shūressha** last train
7 終身 **shūshin** for life, lifelong, lifetime
終身刑 **shūshinkei** life sentence
終身官 **shūshinkan** official appointed for life
終決 **shūketsu** settlement, conclusion
終局 **shūkyoku** end, conclusion; endgame
終車 **shūsha** the last bus/train for the day
8 終夜 **shūya, yomosugara** all night long
終夜灯 **shūyatō** nightlight
終始 **shūshi** from beginning to end
終始一貫 **shūshi-ikkan** constant, consistent
9 終点 **shūten** end of the line, last stop, terminus
10 終宵 **shūshō** all night long
終息 **shūsoku** cessation, eradication
終航 **shūkō** last voyage/flight
11 終焉 **shūen** one's last moments, death
12 終着駅 **shūchakueki** terminal station
終極 **shūkyoku** ultimate, final
終期 **shūki** expiration, close, end
終結 **shūketsu** conclusion, termination
13 終業 **shūgyō** close of work/school
終業式 **shūgyōshiki** closing ceremony
終幕 **shūmaku** curtainfall, end, close
終戦 **shūsen** end of the war
終戦後 **shūsengo** after the war
終電 **shūden** the last train/streetcar for the day
終電車 **shūdensha** the last train/streetcar for the day
14 終演 **shūen** end of a performance
終熄 **shūsoku** come to an end
終端 **shūtan** terminus, terminal
15 終審 **shūshin** final trial, last instance
終盤 **shūban** endgame
終盤戦 **shūbansen** endgame, final battle

―――― 2 ――――

6 有終美 **yūshū (no) bi** crowning glory, splendid finish
7 言終 **i(i)owa(ru)** finish speaking
8 始終 **shijū** from first to last, all the while
10 書終 **ka(ki)owa(ru)** finish writing
12 最終 **saishū** the last, the end; final

最終日 **saishūbi** the last day
最終回 **saishūkai** the last time/inning
最終的 **saishūteki** final, ultimate
14 読終 **yo(mi)owa(ru)** finish reading
18 臨終 **rinjū** one's last moments, deathbed

———————— 4 ————————
1 一部始終 **ichibu shijū** full particulars

6a5.10 / 456

紹 **SHŌ** introduce; help; inherit

———————— 1 ————————
4 紹介 **shōkai** introduction, presentation
紹介状 **shōkaijō** letter of introduction
紹介者 **shōkaisha** introducer

———————— 3 ————————
6 自己紹介 **jiko shōkai** introduce oneself

6a5.11 / 548

経 經 圣 **KEI, KYŌ** longitude;
sutra; passage of time;
pass through, via
he(ru) pass, elapse;
pass through **ta(tsu)** pass, elapse, expire

———————— 1 ————————
3 経上 **hea(garu)** climb up, rise
経口 **keikō** via the mouth, oral (medication)
4 経文 **kyōmon** sutras
経水 **keisui** menstruation
経木 **kyōgi** wood shavings, chips
5 経由 **keiyu** via, by way of
経世 **keisei** administration, statecraft
経世家 **keiseika** statesman, administrator
経巡 **hemegu(ru)** wander/travel about
経穴 **keiketsu** spot for acupuncture/
moxybustion
6 経伝 **keiden** writings of saints and sages
経団連 **Keidanren** Federation of Economic
Organizations (Keidanren) (short for 経済
団体連合会)
7 経学 **keigaku** Confucianism
8 経典 **kyōten, keiten** scriptures, sacred books,
sutras
経国 **keikoku** administration, statecraft
9 経度 **keido** longitude
10 経師 **kyōji** scroll/screen mounter, picture
framer
経師屋 **kyōjiya** scroll/screen mounter,
picture framer; philan
経時変化 **keiji henka** change with the
passage of time, aging
経書 **keisho** Confucian classics
11 経過 **keika** lapse, passage of time; progress,

course, developments
経済 **keizai** economy, economics, economical
use
経済人 **keizaijin** economic man
経済力 **keizairyoku** economic strength
経済上 **keizaijō** economically, financially
経済学 **keizaigaku** economics
経済法 **keizaihō** economic laws
経済的 **keizaiteki** economic, financial;
economical
経済界 **keizaikai** financial circles
経済家 **keizaika** economist; thrifty person
経済欄 **keizairan** financial section/columns
経常 **keijō** ordinary, current, working
経常費 **keijōhi** operating costs
経堂 **kyōdō** sutra library
経理 **keiri** accounting
経理士 **keirishi** public accountant
経略 **keiryaku** govern, rule
12 経営 **keiei** manage, operate, run
経営学 **keieigaku** (business) management
経営者 **keieisha** manager, operator
経営費 **keieihi** operating expenses
経営権 **keieiken** right of management
経営難 **keieinan** financial distress
経費 **keihi** expenses, cost
13 経路 **keiro** course, route
14 経歴 **keireki** personal history, career
経綸 **keirin** govern, administer
15 経線 **keisen** meridian, longitude
16 経緯 **keii** longitude and latitude; warp and
woof; particulars **ikisatsu** intricacies,
complications, details
経緯儀 **keiigi** theodolite, altazimuth
18 経験 **keiken** experience
経験的 **keikenteki** experiential, empirical
経験者 **keikensha** experienced person
経験則 **keikensoku** rule of thumb
経験談 **keikendan** account of one's experiences
経験論 **keikenron** empiricism

———————— 2 ————————
4 不経済 **fukeizai** poor economy, waste
五経 **Gokyō** the five classics (of Confucianism)
仏経 **bukkyō** Buddhist sutras
月経 **gekkei** menstruation
月経帯 **gekkeitai** hygienic band, sanitary
napkin
5 未経験 **mikeiken** unexperienced
未経験者 **mikeikensha** person having no
experience
6 西経 **seikei** west longitude
7 初経 **shokei** one's first menstruation
8 東経 **tōkei** east longitude

法経 **hōkei** law and economics
9 神経 **shinkei** nerve
神経学 **shinkeigaku** neurology
神経系 **shinkeikei** nervous system
神経病 **shinkeibyō** nervous disorder
神経症 **shinkeishō** nervous disorder
神経痛 **shinkeitsū** neuralgia
神経戦 **shinkeisen** war of nerves
神経節 **shinkeisetsu** ganglion
神経質 **shinkeishitsu** nervous, high-strung
政経学 **seikeigaku** politics and economics
10 書経 **Shokyō** the Shu Jing (a Confucianist
　　classic)
11 商経 **shokei** commerce and economics
12 無経験 **mukeiken** inexperience
程経 **hodohe(te)** after a while
13 詩経 **Shikyō** the Shijing (a Chinese classic)
14 読経 **dokyō** sutra chanting
説経 **sekkyō** discourse on the sutras
説経節 **sekkyōbushi** sutra-based samisen-
　　accompanied ballads

──────────── 3 ────────────

1 一切経 **Issaikyō** complete collection of
　　Buddhist scriptures
3 大蔵経 **Daizōkyō** The collection of Classic
　　Buddhist Scriptures
6 多角経営 **takaku keiei** diversified manage-
　　ment
8 法華経 **Hokekyō** the Lotus Sutra
10 涅槃経 **Nehangyō** (a Buddhist sutra)
華厳経 **Kegonkyō** the Avatamska sutra
11 視神経 **shishinkei** optic nerve
12 無神経 **mushinkei** insensible to
歯神経 **shishinkei** dental nerve
13 嗅神経 **kyūshinkei** olfactory nerve
17 聴神経 **chōshinkei** auditory nerve

──────────── 4 ────────────

5 末梢神経 **masshō shinkei** peripheral nerves
6 自律神経 **jiritsu shinkei** autonomic nerve
7 阿弥陀経 **Amidakyō** the Sukhavati sutra
10 座骨神経 **zakotsu shinkei** sciatic nerve
座骨神経痛 **zakotsu shinkeitsū** sciatic
　　neuralgia

──────────── 7 ────────────

9 南無妙法蓮華経 **Namu Myōhō Rengekyō**
　　Hail Lotus Sutra

6a5.12

絃 **GEN, ito** strings (on musical instruments)

──────────── 1 ────────────

13 絃楽 **gengaku** string music
絃楽器 **gengakki** stringed instrument

──────────── 2 ────────────

1 一絃琴 **ichigenkin** one-stringed instrument
3 三絃 **sangen** three-stringed instrument;
　　samisen
14 管絃 **kangen** wind and string instruments;
　　music
管絃楽団 **kangen gakudan** orchestra

6a5.13

紿 **TAI** deceive

6a5.14

絁 **SHI** coarse pongee

6a5.15

紘 **KŌ** cotton batting, wadding

6a5.16

絅 **KEI** thin silk

6a5.17

紮 **SATSU, kara(geru)** tie/bundle up; tuck
up

──────────── 2 ────────────

12 結紮 **kessatsu** ligature

──────────── 6 ────────────

絲 → 糸 6a0.1

6a6.1

絏 **SETSU** tether

──────────── 2 ────────────

17 縲絏 **ruisetsu** fetters, bonds

6a6.2

絎 **KŌ, ku(keru)** blindstitch, whip (a
seam)

6

糸 6 ←
米
舟
虫
耳
⺮

6a6.3

結 KA get caught on; be delayed
KAI raw silk thread

──────── 1 ────────

6 絓糸 **shikeito, sugaito** raw/unspun silk thread

6a6.4

絖 KŌ, nume satin (for painting on)

6a6.5 / 485

結 KETSU, KECHI, musu(bu) tie, bind;
conclude (a contract); bear (fruit)
yu(waeru) bind, tie
yu(u), i(u) do up (one's hair)

──────── 1 ────────

1 結了 **ketsuryō** end, be completed
4 結文 **ketsubun** epilog, conclusion
結方 **yu(i)kata** hair style
5 結末 **ketsumatsu** end, conclusion, upshot
結付 **musu(bi)tsu(keru)** tie together, link
結氷 **keppyō** freeze over, form ice
結句 **kekku** conclusion (of a poem); after all
結石 **kesseki** (gall/kidney) stones
結目 **musu(bi)me** knot
6 結合 **ketsugō** union, combination **musu(bi-)
a(waseru)** tie together, combine
結合組織 **ketsugō soshiki** connective tissue
結成 **kessei** formation, organization
7 結束 **kessoku** band together, be united
結尾 **ketsubi** end, conclusion
結局 **kekkyoku** after all, in the end
結社 **kessha** association, society
結言 **ketsugen** conclusion, summary, wrapup
8 結果 **kekka** result, consequence, effect
結実 **ketsujitsu** bear fruit
9 結神 **musu(bi no) kami** Cupid
10 結党 **kettō** formation of a party
結核 **kekkaku** tuberculosis
結核菌 **kekkakukin** tuberculosis germ
結納 **yuinō** betrothal gift
結納金 **yuinōkin** engagement gift money
結託 **kettaku** conspiracy, collusion
11 結婚 **kekkon** marriage
結婚式 **kekkonshiki** wedding
結紮 **kessatsu** ligature
12 結着 **ketchaku** conclusion, settlement
結晶 **kesshō** crystallization; crystal
結晶学 **kesshōgaku** crystallography
結晶核 **kesshōkaku** nucleus of a crystal
結跏趺座 **kekkafuza** sitting in lotus position/
posture

結集 **kesshū** concentrate, marshal together
13 結滞 **kettai** intermittent (pulse)
結腸 **ketchō** the colon
結盟 **ketsumei** pledge
結節 **kessetsu** knot, nodule, tubercle
14 結像 **ketsuzō** image formation
結像面 **ketsuzōmen** focal plane
結髪 **keppatsu** hairdressing, hairdo
結構 **kekkō** fine, good, alright; quite
結膜 **ketsumaku** conjunctiva, inner eyelid
結膜炎 **ketsumakuen** conjunctivitis
結綿 **yu(i)wata** (a traditional hairdo of
unmarried women)
結語 **ketsugo** concluding remarks
15 結審 **kesshin** conclusion of a trial/hearing
結論 **ketsuron** conclusion
19 結願 **kechigan, ketsugan** expiration of a vow
21 結露 **ketsuro** condensation of dew

──────── 2 ────────

4 不結果 **fukekka** failure, poor results
元結 **motoyu(i)** paper cord for tying the hair
5 氷結 **hyōketsu** freeze (over)
好結果 **kōkekka** good results, success
6 団結 **danketsu** unity, solidarity
団結心 **danketsushin** spirit of solidarity
7 妥結 **daketsu** reach agreement
花結 **hanamusu(bi)** rosette
完結 **kanketsu** completion
男結 **otokomusu(bi)** men's style of knotting
(a sash)
8 直結 **chokketsu** direct connection
逆結 **gyakumusu(bi)** granny knot
取結 **to(ri)musu(bu)** conclude (a contract);
act as go-between; curry (favor)
9 連結 **renketsu** coupling, connection;
consolidated
連結器 **renketsuki** coupler
肺結核 **haikekkaku** pulmonary tuberculosis
10 凍結 **tōketsu** freeze
帰結 **kiketsu** conclusion, result, consequence
起結 **kiketsu** beginning and end
秘結 **hiketsu** constipation
11 終結 **shūketsu** conclusion, termination
12 焼結 **shōketsu** sintering
集結 **shūketsu** concentrate, mass (troops)
集結所 **shūketsusho** place of assembly
14 髪結 **kamiyu(i)** hairdressing; hairdresser
髪結床 **kamiyu(i)doko** (Edo) barbershop
15 縁結 **enmusu(bi)** marriage; love knot
締結 **teiketsu** conclude, contract
蝶結 **chōmusu(bi)** bowknot
論結 **ronketsu** conclusion, peroration
16 凝結 **gyōketsu** coagulation, curdling, settling,
congealing, freezing, condensation,
solidification

縦結 **tatemusu(bi)** vertical knot

───────── 3 ─────────

2 二重結婚 **nijū kekkon** bigamy
5 写真結婚 **shashin kekkon** marriage arranged after seeing photos of each other
9 神前結婚 **shinzen kekkon** Shinto wedding
政略結婚 **seiryaku kekkon** marriage of convenience
13 腎臓結石 **jinzō kesseki** kidney stones
14 膀胱結石 **bōkō kesseki** bladder stones

───────── 4 ─────────

3 大同団結 **daidō danketsu** merger, combination
6 自動連結機 **jidō renketsuki** automatic coupler
10 起承転結 **ki-shō-ten-ketsu** introduction, development, turn, and conclusion (rules for composing a Chinese poem)

6a6.6 / 840

絡 **RAKU, kara(mu/maru)** get entangled

───────── 1 ─────────

5 絡付 **kara(mi)tsu(ku)** coil around, cling to
6 絡合 **kara(mi)a(u)** intertwine
19 絡繹 **rakueki** ceaseless traffic

───────── 2 ─────────

9 連絡 **renraku** contact, liaison, communication; get/be in touch
連絡船 **renrakusen** ferryboat
10 脈絡 **myakuraku** logical connection, coherence
12 短絡 **tanraku** short circuit
22 籠絡 **rōraku** cajole, wheedle, entice

6a6.7 / 346

給 **KYŪ** supply
tama(u) give, grant, deign to
-tama(e) (imperative verb suffix)

───────── 1 ─────────

0 給する **kyū(suru)** supply, furnish, grant
3 給与 **kyūyo** allowance, grant, wages
給与金 **kyūyokin** allowance, grant
4 給水 **kyūsui** water supply
給水所 **kyūsuijo** water station
給水栓 **kyūsuisen** faucet, hydrant
給水管 **kyūsuikan** water pipe
5 給仕 **kyūji** wait on; waiter, waitress, bellhop
給付 **kyūfu** present, pay, provide
6 給血 **kyūketsu** give blood
給血者 **kyūketsusha** blood donor
8 給油 **kyūyu** supplying oil, fueling, oiling

給油所 **kyūyusho** filling/gas station
給油船 **kyūyusen** oil tanker
給金 **kyūkin** wages, pay
9 給炭 **kyūtan** supplying coal, coaling
給食 **kyūshoku** providing meals (in school)
10 給料 **kyūryō** pay, wages, salary
給料日 **kyūryōbi** payday
12 給費 **kyūhi** paying (someone's) expenses, a scholarship
給費生 **kyūhisei** student on scholarship
13 給源 **kyūgen** source of supply
給電 **kyūden** supplying electric power
15 給養 **kyūyō** supplies, provisions

───────── 2 ─────────

3 女給 **jokyū** waitress
4 支給 **shikyū** provide, furnish, issue, grant
月給 **gekkyū** (monthly) salary
月給日 **gekkyūbi** payday
月給取 **gekkyūto(ri)** salaried worker
日給 **nikkyū** daily wages
5 本給 **honkyū** basic/regular salary
加給 **kakyū** raising salaries
6 年給 **nenkyū** annual salary
有給 **yūkyū** salaried
有給休暇 **yūkyū kyūka** paid vacation
自給 **jikyū** self-support, self-supplying
自給自足 **jikyū-jisoku** self-sufficiency
7 初給 **shokyū** starting salary
8 供給 **kyōkyū** supply
供給者 **kyōkyūsha** supplier
供給源 **kyōkyūgen** source of supply
受給 **jukyū** receive (payments)
受給者 **jukyūsha** pensioner
官給 **kankyū** government-supplied
官給品 **kankyūhin** government issues
定給 **teikyū** fixed salary/allowance
昇給 **shōkyū** pay raise
9 発給 **hakkyū** issue
10 俸給 **hōkyū** salary
俸給日 **hōkyūbi** payday
高給 **kōkyū** high salary
週給 **shūkyū** weekly pay
時給 **jikyū** payment by the hour
恩給 **onkyū** pension
配給 **haikyū** distribution, rationing
配給米 **haikyūmai** rationed rice
配給所 **haikyūjo** distribution point
配給量 **haikyūryō** a ration
12 減給 **genkyū** salary reduction, pay cut
無給 **mukyū** unpaid, nonsalaried
補給 **hokyū** supply, replenish
14 増給 **zōkyū** salary increase, pay raise
需給 **jukyū** supply and demand
16 薄給 **hakkyū** meager salary

6
糸 6←
米
舟
虫
耳
竹

— 3 —
6 安月給 **yasugekkyū** meager salary
7 初任給 **shoninkyū** starting salary
8 固定給 **koteikyū** fixed salary
10 時間給 **jikankyū** payment by the hour
11 基本給 **kihonkyū** basic salary, base pay
18 職能給 **shokunōkyū** merit pay

6a6.8 / 345

絵 繪　　**KAI, E** picture

— 1 —
2 絵入 **ei(ri)** illustrated, pictorial
4 絵双紙 **ezōshi** picture book
絵文字 **emoji** pictograph
絵心 **egokoro** artistic bent/eye
5 絵本 **ehon** picture book
絵凧 **edako** kite with a picture on it
絵札 **efuda** picture card
6 絵羽 **eba** figured haori coat
絵羽織 **ebaori** figured haori coat
7 絵図 **ezu** drawing, illustration, diagram, plan
絵図面 **ezumen** plan, design
8 絵画 **kaiga** pictures, paintings, drawings
絵画界 **kaigakai** the world of painting
絵画館 **kaigakan** art gallery
絵空言 **esoragoto** a fabrication, fantasy
絵具 **e(no)gu** paints, colors, pigments
9 絵巻 **ema(ki)** picture scroll
絵巻物 **emakimono** picture scroll
絵姿 **esugata** portrait, likeness, picture
絵草紙 **ezōshi** picture book
絵柄 **egara** pattern, design
10 絵捜 **esaga(shi)** picture puzzle
絵師 **eshi** painter, artist
絵書 **eka(ki)** painter, artist
絵馬 **ema** votive tablet (bearing a horse's picture)
11 絵探 **esaga(shi)** picture puzzle
絵描 **eka(ki)** painter, artist
12 絵葉書 **ehagaki** picture postcard
絵筆 **efude** paintbrush
13 絵解 **eto(ki)** explanation of/by a picture
絵絹 **eginu** silk canvas, drawing silk
14 絵像 **ezō** portrait, likeness, picture

— 2 —
3 下絵 **shitae** rough sketch
口絵 **kuchie** frontispiece
5 写絵 **utsu(shi)e** magic-lantern picture; copy picture; shadowgraph
6 色絵 **iroe** colored picture
8 油絵 **aburae** oil painting
泥絵具 **doro e(no)gu** distemper, color wash
押絵 **o(shi)e** pasted-cloth picture

9 透絵 **su(kashi)e** a transparency (picture)
姿絵 **sugatae** portrait
砂絵 **sunae** sand picture
10 挿絵 **sa(shi)e** illustration (in a book)
捜絵 **saga(shi)e** picture puzzle
笑絵 **wara(i)e** comic/pornographic picture
12 焼絵 **ya(ki)e** pyrograph; pyrography
13 塗絵 **nu(ri)e** line drawing for coloring in
蒔絵 **makie** (gold) lacquerwork
絹絵 **kinue** picture on silk
14 漆絵 **urushie** lacquer painting
墨絵 **sumie** India-ink drawing
15 影絵 **kagee** shadow picture, silhouette
踏絵 **fu(mi)e** ikon to be trampled on (to prove one is not a Christian)
16 錦絵 **nishikie** colored woodblock print

— 3 —
3 大和絵 **Yamato-e** medieval picture in Japanese rather than Chinese style
4 水彩絵具 **suisai e(no)gu** watercolors
7 似顔絵 **nigaoe** portrait, likeness
8 武者絵 **mushae** picture of a warrior
金蒔絵 **kinmakie** gold lacquerwork
9 浮世絵 **ukiyoe** (type of Japanese woodblock print)
浮世絵師 **ukiyoeshi** ukiyoe artist
10 高蒔絵 **takamakie** embossed gilt lacquerwork

— 4 —
10 展覧会絵 **Tenrankai (no) e** Pictures at an Exhibition (Mussorgsky, 1874)

6a6.9 / 1452

絞　　**KŌ, shi(meru)** strangle, wring **shi(maru)** be wrung out, be pressed together **shibo(ru)** wring, squeeze, press, milk **shibo(ri)** (camera's) iris diaphragm; throttling; dapple, white-spotted cloth

— 1 —
0 お絞り **(o)shibo(ri)** hot wet towel (in restaurants)
3 絞上 **shibo(ri)a(geru)** gather up (a curtain); squeeze (money) out of
5 絞出 **shibo(ri)da(su)** press/squeeze out
6 絞刑 **kōkei** (execution by) hanging
9 絞首 **kōshu** strangulation, hanging
絞首台 **kōshudai** gallows
絞首刑 **kōshukei** (execution by) hanging
絞染 **shibo(ri)zo(me)** tie-dyeing
10 絞殺 **kōsatsu** strangle to death; hang
13 絞罪 **kōzai** (execution by) hanging

— 2 —
4 引絞 **hi(ki)shibo(ru)** draw back (a bow/curtains) as far as it/they will go; strain (one's voice)
7 豆絞 **mameshibo(ri)** spotted pattern

6a6.10 / 830

統

TŌ, su(beru) govern, control

――――――― 1 ―――――――

1 統一 **tōitsu** unity, unification, uniformity
　統一的 **tōitsuteki** unified, uniform
6 統合 **tōgō** unify, integrate, combine
8 統制 **tōsei** control, regulation
　統制力 **tōseiryoku** control over, power
　統制品 **tōseihin** controlled goods
　統治 **tōchi, tōji** reign, rule
　統治者 **tōchisha, tōjisha** ruler, sovereign
　統治権 **tōchiken** sovereignty
9 統括 **tōkatsu** generalize
　統帥 **tōsui** the high command
　統帥権 **tōsuiken** prerogative of supreme
　　command
　統計 **tōkei** statistics
　統計学 **tōkeigaku** statistics
　統計表 **tōkeihyō** statistical table
　統計的 **tōkeiteki** statistical
11 統率 **tōsotsu** command, lead
　統率者 **tōsotsusha** commander, leader
12 統御 **tōgyo** rule, control, administer
　統覚 **tōkaku** apperception
14 統領 **tōryō** chief, manager, dictator
15 統監 **tōkan** supervision; commander, resident-
　　general
17 統轄 **tōkatsu** control (and jurisdiction)
　統轄者 **tōkatsusha** the one in charge

――――――― 2 ―――――――

1 一統 **ittō** a lineage; bringing under one rule;
　　all (of you)
3 大統領 **daitōryō** president
4 不統一 **futōitsu** disunity
5 正統 **seitō** orthodox, traditional
　正統派 **seitōha** orthodox school, fundamen-
　　talists
6 伝統 **dentō** tradition
　伝統的 **dentōteki** traditional
　血統 **kettō** lineage, pedigree, family line
　血統書 **kettōsho** pedigree
7 系統 **keitō** system; lineage, descent
　系統的 **keitōteki** systematic
　系統樹 **keitōju** tree diagram showing
　　evolutionary descent
8 非統制 **hitōsei** noncontrolled (goods)
9 持統 **Jitō** (empress, 690–697)
　皇統 **kōtō** imperial line
12 無統制 **mutōsei** uncontrolled
14 総統 **sōtō** the Leader/Fuehrer

――――――― 3 ―――――――

8 委任統治 **inin tōchi** mandate
9 信託統治 **shintaku tōchi** trusteeship

11 副大統領 **fukudaitōryō** vice president

6a6.11 / 742

絶

ZETSU, ta(eru) die out, end, fail
ta(yasu) kill off, let die out
ta(tsu) cut off, interrupt; eradicate

――――――― 1 ―――――――

0 絶する **zes(suru)** be beyond (words)
　絶えず **ta(ezu)** constantly, unceasingly;
　　all the time
　絶えざる **ta(ezaru)** unceasing
　絶えて **ta(ete)** (with negative) never, not once
3 絶大 **zetsudai** greatest, immense
5 絶世 **zessei** peerless, unequaled
　絶句 **zekku** stop short, forget one's lines;
　　(Chinese poetry form)
　絶好 **zekkō** splendid, first-rate
6 絶交 **zekkō** sever one's relationship with
　絶交状 **zekkōjō** letter breaking off a
　　relationship
　絶叫 **zekkyō** scream, cry out, shout
7 絶対 **zettai** absolute
　絶対主義 **zettai shugi** absolutism
　絶対的 **zettaiteki** absolute
　絶対者 **zettaisha** the Absolute
　絶対値 **zettaichi** absolute value (in math)
　絶対量 **zettairyō** absolute amount
　絶対絶命 **zettai-zetsumei** desperate situation
　絶妙 **zetsumyō** superb, exquisite
8 絶果 **ta(e)ha(teru)** die out, become extinct
　絶佳 **zekka** superb
　絶命 **zetsumei** death
　絶版 **zeppan** out of print
9 絶美 **zetsubi** of surpassing beauty
　絶海 **zekkai** distant seas
　絶品 **zeppin** superb article, masterpiece
　絶後 **zetsugo** never to be repeated/equaled
　絶食 **zesshoku** fasting
10 絶倒 **zettō** convulsed with laughter
　絶倫 **zetsurin** excellence, superiority
　絶家 **zekke** extinct family
　絶島 **zettō** isolated/desert island
　絶息 **zessoku** breathe one's last, expire
11 絶唱 **zesshō** excellent poem/song
　絶望 **zetsubō** despair
　絶望的 **zetsubōteki** hopeless, desperate
　絶頂 **zetchō** summit, peak, climax
12 絶勝 **zesshō** breathtaking view
　絶景 **zekkei** picturesque scenery
　絶無 **zetsumu** nothing, naught, nil
　絶絶 **ta(e)da(e)** faint, almost exhausted
　絶筆 **zeppitsu** one's last writing
　絶間 **ta(e)ma** interval, pause, gap
　　ta(e)ma(naku) continually, without letup
13 絶滅 **zetsumetsu** eradicate; become extinct

6

糸 6←
米
舟
虫
耳
艹

15 絶縁 **zetsuen** insulation; breaking off a
relationship
絶縁体 **zetsuentai** insulator, nonconductor
絶縁線 **zetsuensen** insulated wire
絶賛 **zessan** praise highly
16 絶壁 **zeppeki** precipice, cliff
22 絶讃 **zessan** praise highly

───────── 2 ─────────

4 中絶 **chūzetsu** interruption, discontinuation,
termination; abortion
6 死絶 **shizetsu** extinction
shi(ni)ta(eru) die out, become extinct
気絶 **kizetsu** faint, pass out
壮絶 **sōzetsu** sublime, magnificent
7 杜絶 **tozetsu** be blocked/obstructed
快絶 **kaizetsu** delightful
8 拒絶 **kyozetsu** refusal, rejection, repudiation
9 冠絶 **kanzetsu** be unique, have no peer
途絶 **toda(eru)** come to a stop
tozetsu suspension, interruption
10 凄絶 **seizetsu** ghastly, gruesome
根絶 **konzetsu, nedaya(shi)** eradication
竜絶蘭 **ryūzetsuran** century plant
11 惨絶 **sanzetsu** brutal
断絶 **danzetsu** become extinct; sever
12 隔絶 **kakuzetsu** be isolated/separated
超絶 **chōzetsu** transcend; excel, surpass
廃絶 **haizetsu** become extinct
絶絶 **ta(e)da(e)** faint, almost exhausted
悶絶 **monzetsu** faint in agony
13 義絶 **gizetsu** disown, break off the relationship
禁絶 **kinzetsu** stamp out, ban
17 謝絶 **shazetsu** refuse, decline

───────── 3 ─────────

8 抱腹絶倒 **hōfuku-zettō** convulsed with
laughter
空前絶後 **kūzen-zetsugo** the first ever and
probably last ever
11 捧腹絶倒 **hōfuku-zettō** convulsed with
laughter
12 絶対絶命 **zettai-zetsumei** desperate situation

───────── 4 ─────────

7 妊娠中絶 **ninshin chūzetsu** abortion

6a6.12

絣 絣 **HŌ, HEI, kasuri** (cloth with
a) splashed pattern

───────── 2 ─────────

5 矢絣 **yagasuri** arrow-feather pattern

6a6.13

絨 **JŪ** wool cloth

───────── 1 ─────────

4 絨毛 **jūmō** (intestinal) villi; (peach) fuzz
12 絨毯 **jūtan** rug, carpet

───────── 3 ─────────

4 天鵞絨 **birōdo** velvet

6a6.14

絢 **KEN** (colorful/beautiful) design

───────── 1 ─────────

21 絢爛 **kenran(taru)** gorgeous, dazzling,
gaudy

6a6.15 / 1389

紫 **SHI, murasaki** purple, violet

───────── 1 ─────────

4 紫水晶 **murasakizuishō** amethyst
5 紫外線 **shigaisen** ultraviolet rays
6 紫色 **murasaki-iro** purple
10 紫宸殿 **Shishinden** Hall for State Ceremonies
11 紫陽花 **ajisai** hydrangea
紫紺 **shikon** bluish purple
12 紫斑病 **shihanbyō** purpura
紫雲 **shiun** auspicious purple clouds
紫雲英 **genge** Chinese milk vetch
13 紫煙 **shien** tobacco smoke
紫電 **shiden** flashes of lightning
19 紫蘇 **shiso** beefsteak plant

───────── 2 ─────────

3 千紫万紅 **senshi-bankō** dazzling variety of
colors
山紫水明 **sanshi-suimei** purple hills and
crystal streams, scenic beauty
7 赤紫 **aka-murasaki** purplish red
赤紫色 **aka-murasaki-iro** purplish red
8 若紫 **wakamurasaki** light purple
11 淡紫色 **tanshishoku** light purple
13 暗紫色 **anshishoku** dark purple
16 濃紫 **komurasaki** deep purple
濃紫色 **nōshishoku** deep purple
薄紫 **usumurasaki** light purple, orchid
18 藤紫 **fujimurasaki** dark lilac, powder blue

6a6.16

絮 **JO** cotton wadding; lengthy, verbose

───────── 1 ─────────

14 絮説 **josetsu** expatiate/enlarge upon

─────── 7 ───────

6a7.1

絤

SHŪ embroidery

6a7.2

綏

SUI peaceful; cheap; grab strap

─────── 1 ───────

13 綏靖 **Suizei** (emperor, 581–549 B.C.)

經→経 6a5.11

6a7.3 / 1261

絹

KEN, kinu silk

─────── 1 ───────

5 絹本 **kenpon** silk cloth/canvas for painting
　絹布 **kenpu** silk (fabric)
6 絹地 **kinuji** silk cloth
　絹糸 **kenshi, kinuito** silk thread
8 絹物 **kinumono** silk goods
10 絹紡 **kenbō** spun silk
　絹針 **kinubari** needle for silk
11 絹張 **kinuba(ri)** silk covered
12 絹絵 **kinue** picture on silk
14 絹綿 **kinuwata** silk floss
17 絹縮 **kinuchiji(mi)** crinkled silk
18 絹織物 **kinuorimono** silk fabrics

─────── 2 ───────

2 人絹 **jinken** artificial silk, rayon
5 本絹 **honken** pure silk
10 純絹 **junken** pure silk
　素絹 **soken** coarse silk
12 絵絹 **eginu** silk canvas, drawing silk
14 練絹 **ne(ri)ginu** glossed silk
16 薄絹 **usuginu** thin/sheer silk

─────── 3 ───────

12 富士絹 **fujiginu** fuji silk

6a7.4

絽

RO silk gauze

6a7.5 / 243

続 續

ZOKU, tsuzu(ku/keru) (intr./tr.) continue

─────── 1 ───────

3 続々 **zokuzoku** successively, one after another
5 続出 **zokushutsu** appear one after another
　続刊 **zokkan** continue publication
6 続行 **zokkō** continuation
7 続投 **zokutō** continue to pitch/rule, remain in office
8 続物 **tsuzu(ki)mono** a serial (story)
9 続発 **zokuhatsu** occur one after another
　続発症 **zokuhatsushō** deuteropathy
　続柄 **tsuzu(ki)gara** family relationship
　続映 **zokuei** continued run (of a movie)
10 続航 **zokkō** continue the voyage, hold to one's course
12 続報 **zokuhō** follow-up report
　続開 **zokkai** resume, continue
14 続演 **zokuen** continued run (of a show)
　続様 **tsuzu(ke)zama** consecutively, in a row
15 続稿 **zokkō** remaining manuscripts
　続編 **zokuhen** sequel
　続篇 **zokuhen** sequel
20 続騰 **zokutō** continued rise (in prices)

─────── 2 ───────

4 手続 **tetsuzu(ki)** procedure, formalities
　引続 **hi(ki)tsuzu(ki)** continuing
5 存続 **sonzoku** continued existence, duration
　永続 **eizoku, nagatsuzu(ki)** perpetuity
　打続 **u(chi)tsuzu(ku)** long, long-continuing
　　u(chi)tsuzu(keru) keep hitting/shooting
　立続 **ta(te)tsuzu(ke)** in succession
6 血続 **chitsuzu(ki)** blood relationship, kin
8 雨続 **amatsuzu(ki), ametsuzu(ki)** rainy spell
9 降続 **fu(ri)tsuzu(ku)** continue to rain/snow
　連続 **renzoku** continuous, consecutive, in a row
　持続 **jizoku** continuation, maintenance
　持続的 **jizokuteki** continuous, lasting
　後続 **kōzoku** succeeding, following
　相続 **sōzoku** inheritance, succession
　相続人 **sōzokunin** heir
　相続争 **sōzoku araso(i)** inheritance dispute
　相続法 **sōzokuhō** inheritance law
　相続者 **sōzokusha** heir
　相続税 **sōzokuzei** inheritance tax
　相続権 **sōzokuken** (right of) inheritance
10 陸続 **rikuzoku** continuously, successively
　家続 **ietsuzu(ki)** row of houses
　書続 **ka(ki)tsuzu(keru)** continue to write
　航続力 **kōzokuryoku** cruising/flying range
　航続距離 **kōzoku kyori** (plane's) range
11 接続 **setsuzoku** connection, joining
　接続詞 **setsuzokushi** a conjunction
　断続 **danzoku** stopping and starting
　断続的 **danzokuteki** intermittent, off-and-on
12 勤続 **kinzoku** long service

6

糸 7←
米
舟
虫
耳
⺮

勤続者 **kinzokusha** person of long service, senior worker
勝続 **ka(chi)tsuzu(ke)** victories in a row
飲続 **no(mi)tsuzu(keru)** keep on drinking
13 続続 **zokuzoku** successively, one after another
継続 **keizoku** continuance
継続的 **keizokuteki** continuous
15 縁続 **entsuzu(ki)** relationship
16 縦続 **jūzoku** concatenation, cascade

──────── 3 ────────

4 不連続 **furenzoku** discontinuity

──────── 4 ────────

10 家督相続 **katoku sōzoku** succession as head of family
13 跡目相続 **atome sōzoku** heirship

6a7.6

絳 **KŌ** red

6a7.7

綷 **kasuri** splashed dyeing pattern
kase reel, skein

6a7.8 / 1025

継 繼 **KEI, tsu(gu)** succeed to, inherit; follow; patch, join together

──────── 1 ────────

2 継子 **keishi** stepchild
4 継切 **tsu(gi)gi(re)** patch
継父 **keifu** stepfather
継手 **tsu(gi)te** joint, coupling, splice
5 継台 **tsu(gi)dai** stock (of a graft)
継立 **tsu(gi)ta(te)** relay
継目 **tsu(gi)me** joint, seam
6 継合 **tsu(gi)a(waseru), tsu(gi)a(wasu)** join/patch/splice together
継当 **tsu(gi)a(te)** patchwork
継糸 **tsu(gi)ito** seam threads
7 継承 **keishō** succession, inheritance
継承者 **keishōsha** successor
継体 **Keitai** (emperor, 507-531)
継走 **keisō** relay race
継足 **tsu(gi)ta(su)** add to, extend
8 継受 **keiju** inheritance
継泳 **keiei** relay swimming
継物 **tsu(gi)mono** patch
9 継室 **keishitsu** second wife
継竿 **tsu(gi)zao** jointed fishing rod
10 継剥 **tsu(gi)ha(gi)** patching; a patch
継紙 **tsu(gi)gami** patchwork paper

12 継歯 **tsu(gi)ha** capped tooth
13 継続 **keizoku** continuance
継続的 **keizokuteki** continuous
継電器 **keidenki** (electrical) relay
14 継端 **tsu(gi)ha** topic to keep the conversation going

──────── 2 ────────

4 中継 **chūkei** (remote broadcast) relay
引継 **hi(ki)tsu(gu)** take/hand over; inherit
5 矢継早 **yatsu(gi)baya (ni)** rapid-fire, in quick succession
世継 **yotsu(gi)** heir, successor
7 言継 **i(i)tsu(gu)** transmit (by word of mouth)
足継 **ashitsu(gi)** footstool
8 受継 **u(ke)tsu(gu)** inherit, succeed to
9 乗継 **no(ri)tsu(gu)** change conveyances, make connections, transfer
後継 **kōkei** succession; successor
後継者 **kōkeisha** successor
10 息継 **ikitsu(gi)** breathing spell, rest
13 跡継 **atotsu(gi)** successor, heir
14 語継 **kata(ri)tsu(gu)** hand down (a story)

──────── 3 ────────

5 生中継 **namachūkei** live (remote) broadcast

綟→綟 6a8.21

──────── 8 ────────

6a8.1 / 1231

維 **I** tie up; rope

──────── 1 ────────

9 維持 **iji** maintenance, support
13 維新 **ishin** (the Meiji) restoration

──────── 2 ────────

17 繊維 **sen'i** fiber, textiles
繊維素 **sen'iso** roughage, fiber, cellulose

──────── 3 ────────

8 治安維持 **chian iji** maintenance of public order
明治維新 **Meiji Ishin** the Meiji Restoration

──────── 4 ────────

6 合成繊維 **gōsei sen'i** synthetic fiber

6a8.2 / 743

練 練 **REN, ne(ru)** knead; train; polish up
ne(reru) be mellowed/mature

──────── 1 ────────

4 練込 **ne(ri)ko(mu)** knead into

6 練合 **ne(ri)a(waseru)** knead together
練糸 **ne(ri)ito** glossed-silk thread
7 練兵 **renpei** (military) drill
練兵場 **renpeijō** parade ground
練乳 **rennyū** condensed milk
8 練直 **ne(ri)nao(su)** polish up, work over
練歩 **ne(ri)aru(ku)** parade, march
練固 **ne(ri)kata(meru)** harden by kneading
練物 **ne(ri)mono** paste (cakes/gems);
procession, (parade) float
9 練香 **ne(ri)kō** pastille
10 練粉 **ne(ri)ko** dough
練馬大根 **Nerima daikon** daikon (grown in
Nerima, Tōkyō), woman's fat legs
11 練達 **rentatsu** skill, dexterity
練習 **renshū** practice, exercise
練習不足 **renshū-busoku** out/lack of training
練習帳 **renshūchō** exercise book, workbook
12 練歯磨 **ne(ri)hamiga(ki)** toothpaste
13 練絹 **ne(ri)ginu** glossed silk
14 練製品 **ne(ri)seihin** a fish-paste food
16 練薬 **ne(ri)gusuri** ointment
練磨 **renma** train, practice, drill

——————— 2 ———————
4 水練 **suiren** swimming practice; (art of)
swimming
手練 **shuren** dexterity, manual skill
teren coaxing, wiles
手練手管 **teren-tekuda** coaxing, wiles,
beguiling
5 未練 **miren** lingering affection
6 老練 **rōren** experienced, veteran
老練家 **rōrenka** expert, veteran
9 洗練 **senren** refine, polish
10 修練 **shūren** training, discipline, drill
猛練習 **mōrenshū** intensive training
教練 **kyōren** (military) drill
訓練 **kunren** training
11 習練 **shūren** practice, training, drill
13 試練 **shiren** trial, test, ordeal
14 熟練 **jukuren** practiced skill, mastery
熟練工 **jukurenkō** skilled workman/
craftsman
精練 **seiren** refining, smelting
精練所 **seirenjo** refinery, smelter
15 調練 **chōren** drill, training
16 操練 **sōren** military exercises, drill

——————— 3 ———————
4 不熟練 **fujukuren** unskilled
9 畑水練 **hatake suiren** (like) learning
swimming on dry land, book learning
10 猛訓練 **mōkunren** hard training
12 畳水練 **tatami suiren** like practicing
swimming on a tatami, useless book
learning

——————— 4 ———————
9 軍事教練 **gunji kyōren** military training

6a8.3 / 862

緒 緒   **SHO, CHO** beginning
o cord, strap, thong
itoguchi thread end; beginning;
clue

——————— 1 ———————
0 緒につく **cho/sho ni tsuku** get underway/
started
7 緒言 **chogen, shogen** preface, foreword
13 緒戦 **shosen, chosen** beginning of a war
15 緒紳 **oji(me)** pouch drawstring
緒論 **shoron, choron** introduction, preface

——————— 2 ———————
1 一緒 **issho** together
3 下緒 **sageo** sword cord
4 内緒 **naisho** secret
内緒事 **naishogoto** a secret
内緒話 **naishobanashi** confidential talk,
whispering
心緒 **shincho** mind, emotions
5 由緒 **yuisho** history, lineage
玉緒 **tama(no)o** bead string; thread of life
9 革緒 **kawao** sword strap; clog thong
10 息緒 **iki(no)o** life
11 情緒 **jōcho** emotion, feelings
14 端緒 **tansho, tancho** beginning, first step, clue
鼻緒 **hanao** clog/geta thong
18 臍緒 **heso(no)o** umbilical cord

——————— 4 ———————
13 詩的情緒 **shiteki jōcho** poetic mood

6a8.4

緋   **HI** scarlet

——————— 1 ———————
18 緋鯉 **higoi** red/gold carp

——————— 3 ———————
12 猩々緋 **shōjōhi** scarlet

絣 → 絣   **6a6.12**

6a8.5

綴   **TEI, tsuzu(ru)** spell; bind; patch; write,
compose **tsuzu(re)** rags, tatters
to(jiru) stitch together, bind, file

——————— 1 ———————
4 綴込 **to(ji)ko(mu)** file away, insert

糸 8 ←
米
舟
虫
耳
艹

6

綴方 **tsuzu(ri)kata** spelling; composition, theme   **to(ji)kata** binding
5 綴本 **to(ji)hon** bound book
綴代 **to(ji)shiro** binding margin
綴目 **to(ji)me, tsuzu(ri)me** seam
6 綴合 **tsuzu(ri)a(waseru)** bind/sew together, fasten, file
綴糸 **to(ji)ito** binding/basting thread
8 綴直 **to(ji)nao(su)** rebind

———————— 2 ————————

6 仮綴 **karito(ji)** temporary binding; paperback
9 点綴 **tentei, tentetsu** be scattered/interspersed here and there
洋綴 **yōto(ji)** Western-style binding
革綴 **kawato(ji)** leather binding
12 補綴 **hotetsu** (dental) prosthetics; rewrite; mend   **hotei** rewrite (a script)
15 横綴 **yokoto(ji)** oblong binding

6a8.6

綣 **KEN** attachment, affection

6a8.7

綬 **JU** cordon, ribbon (on a medal)

———————— 2 ————————

18 藍綬褒章 **ranju hōshō** blue ribbon medal

6a8.8 / 1191

綿 緜 **MEN, wata** cotton

———————— 1 ————————

2 綿入 **watai(re)** padded, quilted
3 綿々 **menmen(taru)** endless, unabating
綿弓 **watayumi** bow-shaped tool for willowing ginned cotton
4 綿毛 **watage** down, fluff, nap
綿火薬 **menkayaku** guncotton
5 綿打 **watau(chi)** cotton willowing
綿布 **menpu** cotton (cloth)
6 綿羊 **men'yō** sheep
綿糸 **menshi** cotton thread/yarn
7 綿抜 **watanu(ki)** unpadded kimono
綿花 **menka** (raw) cotton
8 綿油 **wataabura** cottonseed oil
綿実油 **menjitsuyu** cottonseed oil
綿服 **menpuku** cotton clothes
9 綿津見 **watatsumi** (god of) the sea
綿屋 **wataya** cotton dealer
10 綿紡 **menbō** cotton spinning

11 綿密 **menmitsu** minute, close, meticulous
12 綿帽子 **watabōshi** bride's silk-floss veil
綿棒 **menbō** cotton swab
綿雲 **watagumo** fleecy clouds
14 綿種 **watadane** cottonseed
綿製品 **menseihin** cotton goods
綿綿 **menmen(taru)** endless, unabating
18 綿織物 **men'orimono** cotton goods
19 綿繰 **wataku(ri)** cotton ginning

———————— 2 ————————

4 木綿 **momen** cotton (cloth)
kiwata cotton (plant)
木綿糸 **momen'ito** cotton thread
木綿物 **momenmono** cotton goods/clothing
5 石綿 **ishiwata, sekimen** asbestos
6 米綿 **beimen** American (raw) cotton
9 連綿 **renmen** consecutive, uninterrupted
海綿 **kaimen** sponge
10 真綿 **mawata** silk floss/wadding
純綿 **junmen** all-cotton
12 結綿 **yu(i)wata** (a traditional hairdo of unmarried women)
13 裾綿 **susowata** cotton kimono skirt padding
絹綿 **kinuwata** silk floss
詰綿 **tsu(me)wata** wadding, padding
14 綿綿 **menmen(taru)** endless, unabating
19 繰綿 **ku(ri)wata** ginned cotton
22 纏綿 **tenmen** entanglement, involvement

———————— 3 ————————

10 晒木綿 **sara(shi)momen** bleached cotton cloth
11 脱脂綿 **dasshimen** absorbent cotton

6a8.9

綵 **SAI** colorful

6a8.10

綾 **RYŌ, aya** figured cloth, twill

———————— 1 ————————

8 綾取 **ayato(ri)** play cat's-cradle
16 綾錦 **ayanishiki** twill damask and brocade
18 綾織 **ayao(ri)** twill

6a8.11

綫 **SEN** thread; line

6a8.12

綜 **SŌ** rule over

―――――― 1 ――――――
6 綜合 **sōgō** comprehensive, composite, synthetic
綜合的 **sōgōteki** comprehensive, overall
―――――― 2 ――――――
16 錯綜 **sakusō** complication, intricacy

6a8.13

TAN, hokoro(biru) be torn, come apart at the seams; begin to open
hokoro(baseru) rip (the seams); break into a smile

―――――― 2 ――――――
10 破綻 **hatan** failure, breakdown, bankruptcy

6a8.14

綰

WAN, waga(neru) bend into a loop/hoop

6a8.15 / 537

緑 綠

RYOKU, ROKU, midori green

―――――― 1 ――――――
3 緑土 **ryokudo** green earth
4 緑内障 **ryokunaishō** glaucoma
緑化 **ryokka** tree planting
5 緑玉 **ryokugyoku** emerald
緑玉石 **ryokugyokuseki** emerald
6 緑色 **midori-iro, ryokushoku** green
緑地 **ryokuchi** green tract of land
緑地帯 **ryokuchitai** greenbelt
7 緑豆 **ryokutō** (a variety of green bean)
8 緑林 **ryokurin** (mounted) bandits
緑肥 **ryokuhi** green manure
緑青 **rokushō** verdigris, green/copper rust
緑門 **ryokumon** arch of greenery
9 緑便 **ryokuben** green stools
緑風 **ryokufū** early-summer breeze
緑草 **ryokusō** green grass
緑茶 **ryokucha** green tea
緑柱石 **ryokuchūseki** beryl
10 緑陰 **ryokuin** the shade of trees
緑酒 **ryokushu** green/sweet wine
11 緑野 **ryokuya** green field
緑黄色 **ryokuōshoku** greenish yellow
12 緑葉 **ryokuyō** green leaves
16 緑樹 **ryokuju** green-leaved tree, greenery
19 緑藻 **ryokusō** green algae
―――――― 2 ――――――
6 灰緑色 **kairyokushoku** greenish gray
8 若緑 **wakamidori** fresh verture

青緑 **aomidori** dark green
9 浅緑 **asamidori** light/pale green
10 帯緑 **tairyoku** greenish
11 淡緑色 **tanryokushoku** light green
深緑 **shinryoku, fukamidori** dark green
黄緑色 **ōryokushoku** yellowish green, olive
常緑 **jōryoku** evergreen
常緑樹 **jōryokuju** an evergreen (tree)
12 葉緑素 **yōryokuso** chlorophyll
13 暗緑色 **anryokushoku** dark green
新緑 **shinryoku** fresh verdure
16 濃緑 **nōryoku** dark green
薄緑 **usumidori** light green

6a8.16

綺

KI figured cloth; beautiful

―――――― 1 ――――――
13 綺想曲 **kisōkyoku** capriccio
15 綺談 **kidan** fascinating tale
19 綺麗 **kirei** pretty, beautiful; clean
綺麗事 **kireigoto** glossing over, whitewashing
綺羅 **kira** fine clothes
綺羅星 **kiraboshi** glittering stars

6a8.17

緇

SHI black (clothing); priest

6a8.18

綸

RIN thread, string, line; reign, rule

―――――― 1 ――――――
2 綸子 **rinzu** figured satin
7 綸言 **ringen** emperor's words/mandate
―――――― 2 ――――――
11 経綸 **keirin** govern, administer

綪 → 繢 6a14.3

6a8.19

綽

SHAKU gentle, graceful

―――――― 1 ――――――
6 綽名 **adana** nickname

6a8.20 / 697

総 總
SŌ general, overall
su(beru) control, supervise
fusa tuft, cluster

――――――― -1 ―――――――

0 総じて **sō(jite)** in general
総トン数 **sōtonsū** gross tonnage
2 総二階 **sōnikai** full two-story house
総入歯 **sōi(re)ba** full set of dentures
総力 **sōryoku** all one's might, all-out
総力戦 **sōryokusen** total war
3 総大将 **sōdaishō** commander-in-chief
4 総天然色 **sōtennenshoku** in full (natural) color
総毛立 **sōkeda(tsu)** hair stand on end, have goose flesh
総支出 **sōshishutsu** gross expenditures
総支配人 **sōshihainin** general manager
5 総出 **sōde** all together, in full force
総本山 **sōhonzan** (sect's) head temple
総本店 **sōhonten** head office
総本家 **sōhonke** head family
総仕舞 **sōjimai** closing up, selling out
総代 **sōdai** representative, delegate
総皮 **sōhi, sōgawa** full-leather binding
総司令 **sōshirei** general headquarters, supreme command
総立 **sōda(chi)** everyone standing up together
総目録 **sōmokuroku** complete catalog
6 総合 **sōgō** synthesis, comprehensive
総合大学 **sōgō daigaku** university
総合的 **sōgōteki** comprehensive, overall
総会 **sōkai** general meeting, plenary session
総同盟罷業 **sōdōmei higyō** general strike
総当 **sōa(tari)** round-robin (tournament)
7 総身 **sōmi** the whole body
総体 **sōtai** on the whole
総別 **sōbetsu** in general
総決算 **sōkessan** complete financial statement
総花 **sōbana** gratuities to everyone
総花式 **sōbanashiki** across-the-board (pay raise)
総攻撃 **sōkōgeki** general/all-out offensive
総見 **sōken** go to see in a large group
8 総長 **sōchō** (university) president
総画 **sōkaku** total stroke-count (of a kanji)
総退却 **sōtaikyaku** general retreat
総和 **sōwa** (sum) total
総門 **sōmon** main gate
9 総重量 **sōjūryō** gross weight
総軍 **sōgun** the whole army
総点 **sōten** total points/marks
総括 **sōkatsu** summarize, generalize
総括的 **sōkatsuteki** all-inclusive, overall
総指揮 **sōshiki** supreme command

総指揮官 **sōshikikan** supreme commander
総帥 **sōsui** commander-in-chief
総革 **sōgawa** full-leather binding
総柄 **sōgara** all-patterned (clothes)
総計 **sōkei** (sum) total
総則 **sōsoku** general rules/provisions
10 総高 **sōdaka** total (amount)
総益 **sōeki** gross profit
総益金 **sōekikin** gross profit
総員 **sōin** all hands, in full force
総称 **sōshō** general/generic term
総索引 **sōsakuin** general index
11 総動員 **sōdōin** general mobilization
総勘定 **sōkanjō** final settlement
総掛 **sōga(kari)** concerted effort, all together
総捲 **sōmaku(ri)** general survey/review
総菜 **sōzai** everyday food/side-dish
総崩 **sōkuzu(re)** general rout, collapse
総理 **sōri** prime minister
総理大臣 **sōri daijin** prime minister
総理府 **sōrifu** Prime Minister's Office
総務 **sōmu** general affairs; manager
総務長官 **sōmu chōkan** director-general
総務部長 **sōmu buchō** head of the general affairs department
総務課 **sōmuka** general affairs section
12 総揚 **sōa(ge)** hire all (the geisha)
総量 **sōryō** gross weight
総裁 **sōsai** president, governor
統統 **sōtō** the Leader/Fuehrer
総評 **Sōhyō** General Council of Trade Unions of Japan (short for 日本労働組合総評議会)
13 総勢 **sōzei** the whole army/group
総裏 **sōura** full lining
総裏付 **sōuratsu(ki)** fully lined (coat)
総数 **sōsū** total (number)
総意 **sōi** consensus
総辞職 **sōjishoku** mass resignation
総督 **sōtoku** governor-general
総督府 **sōtokufu** government-general
14 総選挙 **sōsenkyo** general election
総髪 **sōhatsu** hair swept back and tied at the back of the head
総誉 **sōna(me)** sweeping victory
総模様 **sōmoyō** all-patterned (clothes)
総説 **sōsetsu** general remarks
総領 **sōryō** eldest child
総領事 **sōryōji** consul-general
総領事館 **sōryōjikan** consulate-general
総領娘 **sōryō musume** eldest daughter
15 総罷業 **sōhigyō** general strike
総監 **sōkan** superintendent-general
総締 **sōji(me)** total
総論 **sōron** general remarks
17 総覧 **sōran** preside over, control

6
→ 8 糸
米
舟
虫
耳
⺮

総轄 **sōkatsu** general control/supervision
18 総額 **sōgaku** total amount
19 総譜 **sōfu** the full score (sheet music)

────── 2 ──────

3 上総 **Kazusa** (ancient kuni, Chiba-ken)
下総 **Shimousa** (ancient kuni, Chiba-ken)

────── 3 ──────

8 国連総会 **Kokuren Sōkai** UN General
Assembly

6a8.21

REI yellowish green
moji coarse-mesh linen

6a8.22

TŌ, na(u) twist, braid, make (rope)

6a8.23 / 1609

KŌ rope; rule; classification
tsuna rope, cord

────── 1 ──────

4 綱手 **tsunade** mooring/towing rope
綱引 **tsunahi(ki)** tug-of-war
5 綱目 **kōmoku** gist, main points
8 綱具 **tsunagu** rigging
9 綱要 **kōyō** essentials, outline, summary
綱紀 **kōki** official discipline, public order
綱紀粛正 **kōki shukusei** enforcement of
discipline among officials
11 綱常 **kōjō** morality, morals
綱梯子 **tsunabashigo** rope ladder
12 綱渡 **tsunawata(ri)** tightrope walking
14 綱領 **kōryō** plan, program, platform

────── 2 ──────

3 大綱 **ōzuna** hawser, cable **taikō** general
principles; outline, general features
4 太綱 **futozuna** cable, hawser
手綱 **tazuna** reins, bridle
6 帆綱 **hozuna** halyard
8 命綱 **inochizuna** lifeline
9 要綱 **yōkō** outline, general idea/plan
政綱 **seikō** political principles/platform
10 舫綱 **moya(i)zuna** mooring rope/line,
hawser
13 僧綱 **sōgō** (ancient Buddhist ecclesiastical
authority); monk's collar
14 髪綱 **kamizuna** rope made of hair
端綱 **hazuna** (horse's) halter
鼻綱 **hanazuna** (bull's) nose halter
15 横綱 **yokozuna** sumo champion

6a8.24

CHŪ be clothed/wrapped in; tie;
detailed, fine

6a8.25 / 1612

網

MŌ, ami net

────── 1 ──────

0 デジタル網 **dejitaru ami** digital net
4 網元 **amimoto** head of a fishing crew
網戸 **amido** screen door
5 網代 **ajiro** wickerwork
網打 **amiu(chi)** net fishing
網目 **amime** net mesh
7 網状 **mōjō, amijō** netlike, reticular
網形 **amigata** netlike, reticular
8 網版 **amihan** halftone (printing)
10 網針 **amibari** netting needle
11 網袋 **amibukuro** net bag
網細工 **amizaiku** filigree
12 網焼 **amiya(ki)** grilled (steak)
14 網膜 **mōmaku** the retina
19 網羅 **mōra** include, be comprehensive

────── 2 ──────

1 一網打尽 **ichimō dajin** a large catch,
roundup; wholesale arrest
4 天網 **tenmō** heaven's net/vengeance
5 打網 **u(chi)ami** casting net
立網 **ta(te)ami** set net
6 曳網 **hikiami** seine, dragnet
7 投網 **toami** casting net
8 刺網 **sa(shi)ami** gill net
建網 **ta(te)ami** set net
法網 **hōmō** the net/clutches of the law
金網 **kanaami** wire netting, chain-link (fence)
10 流網 **naga(shi)ami** drift net
11 掬網 **suku(i)ami** scoop/dip net
袋網 **fukuroami** bag/tunnel net
鳥網 **toriami** bird-catching net
12 焼網 **ya(ki)ami** toasting/broiling grill
14 漁網 **gyomō** fishing net
15 餅網 **mochiami** net bag for mochi; grate to
toast mochi on
17 霞網 **kasumiami** fine-mesh (bird-catching) net

────── 3 ──────

6 地引網 **jibi(ki)ami** dragnet, seine
地曳網 **jibi(ki)ami** dragnet, seine
8 底引網 **sokobi(ki)ami** dragnet, trawlnet
底曳網 **sokobi(ki)ami** dragnet, trawlnet
9 通信網 **tsūshinmō** communications network
11 救助網 **kyūjoami** (streetcar) cowcatcher;
safety net

6

糸 8 ←
米
舟
虫
耳
⺮

救命網 **kyūmeimō** safety net
情報網 **jōhōmō** intelligence network
13 鉄条網 **tetsujōmō** barbed-wire entanglements
鉄道網 **tetsudōmō** railway network

6a8.26

繋 **KEI** seam between meat and bone; vital spot; halberd sheath

———————— 2 ————————
8 肯綮 **kōkei** (to the) point, (on the) mark

———————— 9 ————————

6a9.1 / 1760

縄 繩 **JŌ, nawa** rope

———————— 1 ————————
4 縄文 **jōmon** (ancient Japanese) straw-rope pattern
9 縄飛 **nawato(bi)** jumping/skipping rope
11 縄張 **nawaba(ri)** rope off; one's domain, bailiwick
縄張争 **nawaba(ri) araso(i)** jurisdictional dispute, turf battle
縄梯子 **nawabashigo** rope ladder
———————— 2 ————————
4 火縄 **hinawa** fuse (cord)
火縄銃 **hinawajū** matchlock, harquebus
6 自縄自縛 **jijō-jibaku** tied up with one's own rope, caught in one's own trap
7 沖縄県 **Okinawa-ken** (prefecture)
投縄 **na(ge)nawa** lasso, lariat
8 泥縄 **doronawa** starting to make a rope to catch a just-discovered burglar, hasty/too-late measures
泥縄式 **doronawashiki** last-minute, eleventh-hour
9 荒縄 **aranawa** straw rope
10 捕縄 **to(ri)nawa** rope for binding criminals
11 麻縄 **asanawa** hemp rope
13 準縄 **junjō** a level and an inked string; norm, criterion
腰縄 **koshinawa** waist cord (for tying prisoners)
14 墨縄 **suminawa** inked marking string
15 標縄 **shimenawa** paper-festooned sacred rope
17 糞縄 **kusobae** bottle-green fly
———————— 3 ————————
1 一筋縄 **hitosujinawa** a piece of rope; ordinary means
8 注連縄 **shimenawa** sacred Shinto rope

練 → 練 **6a8.2**

緒 → 緒 **6a8.3**

6a9.2

緘 **odoshi** the thread/braid (of armor)

6a9.3

緲 **BYŌ** faint, far-off

6a9.4

緞 **DON, TAN** damask

———————— 1 ————————
2 緞子 **donsu** damask
11 緞帳 **donchō** drop curtain; second-rate (actor)

6a9.5

緡 **BIN** string on which coins are threaded

6a9.6

緤 **SETSU, SECHI** leash

6a9.7 / 299

線 **SEN** line

———————— 1 ————————
4 線分 **senbun** line segment
6 線虫 **senchū** eelworm, nematode
線虫学 **senchūgaku** nematology
線虫類 **senchūrui** nematodes
7 線形 **senkei** linear; alignment
線材 **senzai** wire rod
線条 **senjō** filament, streak, line
8 線画 **senga** line drawing
9 線香 **senkō** incense/joss stick
線香代 **senkōdai** (geisha's) time charge
13 線路 **senro** (railroad) track
15 線審 **senshin** linesman (in tennis, etc.)
線輪 **senrin** (electrical) coil

——————————— 2 ———————————

1 一線 **issen** a line
4 内線 **naisen** (telephone) extension; indoor wiring; inner line
五線紙 **gosenshi** music paper
五線譜 **gosenfu** staff notation, score (in music)
切線 **sessen** a tangent (in geometry)
支線 **shisen** branch/feeder line
水線 **suisen** waterline, draft line
火線 **kasen** firing line
5 本線 **honsen** main (railway) line
外線 **gaisen** outside (telephone) line; outside wiring
打線 **dasen** batting lineup
白線 **hakusen** white line
6 死線 **shisen** prison perimeter which one may be shot dead for crossing; the brink of death
曲線 **kyokusen** a curve
曲線美 **kyokusenbi** beautiful curves
伏線 **fukusen** foreshadowing; precautionary measures
全線 **zensen** the whole line, all lines
光線 **kōsen** light (rays/beam)
回線 **kaisen** (electrical) circuit
有線 **yūsen** by wire
有線放送 **yūsen hōsō** broadcasting by wire/cable
7 赤線区域 **akasen kuiki** red-light district
社線 **shasen** private railway line
私線 **shisen** private railway line
8 垂線 **suisen** a perpendicular
直線 **chokusen** straight line
波線 **hasen** wavy line
沿線 **ensen** along the (train) line
弦線 **gensen** (violin) string, catgut
実線 **jissen** solid line
9 点線 **tensen** dotted/perforated line
前線 **zensen** front lines, the front; a (cold) front
活線 **kassen** live wire
弧線 **kosen** arc
単線 **tansen** single line/track
架線 **kasen** aerial wiring
10 流線形 **ryūsenkei** streamlined
流線型 **ryūsenkei** streamlined
埋線 **maisen** underground cable
配線 **haisen** wiring
11 側線 **sokusen** siding, sidetrack; sideline (in field sports)
斜線 **shasen** oblique line
混線 **konsen** getting wires/lines crossed; confusion
基線 **kisen** base line, base (of a triangle)
接線 **sessen** a tangent

脚線美 **kyakusenbi** leg beauty/shapeliness
脱線 **dassen** derailment; digression
視線 **shisen** line of vision, one's eyes/gaze
経線 **keisen** meridian, longitude
断線 **dansen** disconnection, broken wire
雪線 **sessen** snow line
12 傍線 **bōsen** sideline, underline
測線 **sokusen** measuring line
渦線 **uzusen** a spiral
無線 **musen** wireless, radio
無線電信 **musen denshin** radiotelegraph
無線電話 **musen denwa** radiotelephone
琴線 **kinsen** heartstrings
13 腸線 **chōsen** catgut
幹線 **kansen** main/trunk line
戦線 **sensen** battle line, front
稜線 **ryōsen** ridgeline
裸線 **hadakasen, rasen** bare wire
罫線 **keisen** ruled line
路線 **rosen** route, line
跨線橋 **kosenkyō** bridge over railroad tracks
鉄線 **tessen** steel wire
電線 **densen** electric wire/line/cable
14 導線 **dōsen** a lead, conducting wire
複線 **fukusen** double track
銅線 **dōsen** copper wire
15 横線 **ōsen** horizontal line
熱線 **nessen** heat rays; hot wire
16 縦線 **jūsen** vertical line
緯線 **isen** a parallel (of latitude)

——————————— 3 ———————————

1 一直線 **itchokusen** a straight line
2 二番線 **nibansen** track No. 2
子午線 **shigosen** the meridian
3 三味線 **shamisen, samisen** samisen (three-stringed instrument)
三味線弾 **shamisenhi(ki), samisenhi(ki)** samisen player
下降線 **kakōsen** downward curve
4 予防線張 **yobōsen (o) ha(ru)** guard against
切取線 **ki(ri)to(ri)sen** perforated line
双曲線 **sōkyokusen** hyperbola
分水線 **bunsuisen** watershed, (continental) divide
分界線 **bunkaisen** line of demarcation
水平線 **suiheisen** the horizon; horizontal line
5 平行線 **heikōsen** parallel line
正中線 **seichūsen** median line
冬至線 **tōjisen** the Tropic of Capricorn
6 地下線 **chikasen** underground cable/wire
地平線 **chiheisen** the horizon
吃水線 **kissuisen** waterline
宇宙線 **uchūsen** cosmic rays
回帰線 **kaikisen** the tropics (of Cancer and Capricorn); regression line

6

糸 9←
米
舟
虫
耳
⺮

7 対角線 **taikakusen** a diagonal
決勝線 **kesshōsen** goal/finish line
赤外線 **sekigaisen** infrared rays
花火線香 **hanabi senkō** joss-stick fireworks, sparklers; flash-in-the-pan
8 非常線 **hijōsen** cordon
垂直線 **suichokusen** a perpendicular
逆光線 **gyakkōsen** backlighting
送電線 **sōdensen** power lines
抛物線 **hōbutsusen** parabola
空中線 **kūchūsen** antenna
国境線 **kokkyōsen** boundary line, border
放物線 **hōbutsusen** parabola
放射線 **hōshasen** radiation
9 前哨線 **zenshōsen** scouting line
海岸線 **kaigansen** coastline; coastal rail line
待避線 **taihisen** siding, sidetrack
10 既設線 **kisetsusen** lines in operation
陰極線 **inkyokusen** cathode rays
高圧線 **kōatsusen** high-voltage power lines
夏至線 **geshisen** the Tropic of Cancer
蚊取線香 **katori senkō** mosquito-repellent incense
配電線 **haidensen** power line/wire
11 第一線 **dai-issen** the first/front line
12 極前線 **kyokuzensen** polar front
最前線 **saizensen** forefront, front lines
絶縁線 **zetsuensen** insulated wire
紫外線 **shigaisen** ultraviolet rays
等圧線 **tōatsusen** isobar
等高線 **tōkōsen** contour line
13 新幹線 **Shinkansen** New Trunk Line, bullet train
電信線 **denshinsen** telegraph line
電話線 **denwasen** telephone line
14 境界線 **kyōkaisen** border/boundary line
導火線 **dōkasen** fuse; cause, occasion
複々線 **fukufukusen** four-track rail line
16 鋼鉄線 **kōtetsusen** steel wire
17 環状線 **kanjōsen** loop/belt line
18 臨港線 **rinkōsen** harbor railway line
19 警戒線 **keikaisen** police cordon
21 饋電線 **kidensen** feeder (line)

———————— 4 ————————

2 人民戦線 **jinmin sensen** popular front
3 口三味線 **kuchijamisen, kuchizamisen** humming a samisen tune; cajolery
5 北回帰線 **Kita Kaikisen** the Tropic of Cancer
6 有刺鉄線 **yūshi tessen** barbed wire
9 南回帰線 **Minami Kaikisen** the Tropic of Capricorn
12 寒冷前線 **kanrei zensen** cold front
14 複々々線 **fukufukufukusen** six-track rail line

———————— 5 ————————

4 日付変更線 **hizuke henkōsen** the international date line

6a9.8 / 1089

KAN, **yuru(mu)** become loose, abate, slacken **yuru(meru)** loosen, relieve, relax, slacken **yuru(i)** loose; generous; lax; gentle (slope); slow **yuru(yaka)** loose, slack; magnanimous; gentle, easy, slow

———————— 1 ————————

3 緩下剤 **kangezai** laxative
6 緩行 **kankō** go slow
緩行車 **kankōsha** local train
8 緩歩 **kanpo** slow walk
緩和 **kanwa** relieve, ease, alleviate, relax
9 緩急 **kankyū** fast or/and slow; emergency
緩怠 **kantai** laxity, neglect (of duty/courtesy)
10 緩流 **kanryū** gentle current
11 緩球 **kankyū** slow ball
14 緩慢 **kanman** sluggish, slack
15 緩衝 **kanshō** buffer
緩衝国 **kanshōkoku** buffer state
緩衝器 **kanshōki** bumper, shock absorber

———————— 2 ————————

4 手緩 **tenuru(i)** slack, lax, lenient; slow, dilatory
6 弛緩 **chikan, shikan** relaxation, slackening

———————— 3 ————————

15 緊張緩和 **kinchō kanwa** détente

6a9.9

SHŪ spin (thread); bring together; shine

6a9.10 / 1131

EN relation, connection; marriage; fate; veranda **enishi** relation, connection; marriage; fate **fuchi, heri** edge, brink, rim, border **yukari** relation, affinity **yosuga** means, way

———————— 1 ————————

3 縁下 **en(no)shita** under the floor
4 縁切 **enki(ri)** severing of a relationship
縁辺 **enpen** kin; edge, margin
縁引 **enbi(ki)** connection, relation
縁日 **ennichi** festival day, fair
5 縁由 **en'yu** relationship
縁付 **enzu(ku)** get married
enzu(keru) give in marriage
縁台 **endai** bench

6 縁先 **ensaki** edge of the veranda
8 縁定 **ensada(me)** marriage (contract)
縁者 **enja** a relative
縁取 **fuchito(ri)** bordering, hemming
9 縁故 **enko** connection, relation
10 縁起 **engi** history, origin; omen, luck
縁起直 **enginao(shi)** a change of luck
縁起物 **engimono** a lucky charm
縁家 **enka** related family
縁座 **enza** complicity through kinship
11 縁側 **engawa** veranda, porch, balcony
縁組 **engumi** marriage; adoption
12 縁遠 **endō(i)** having dim marriage prospects; far removed from
縁結 **enmusu(bi)** marriage; love knot
13 縁続 **entsuzu(ki)** relationship
縁飾 **fuchikaza(ri)** edging, frill
14 縁語 **engo** related word
15 縁縫 **fuchinu(i)** hemstitching
縁談 **endan** marriage proposal

————— 2 —————

3 川縁 **kawabuchi** riverside
4 不縁 **fuen** divorce; dim marriage prospects; unrealized marriage
内縁 **naien** common-law marriage
5 由縁 **yuen** relationship, reason, way
広縁 **hiroen** broad veranda; eaves
目縁 **mabuchi** eyelid
6 再縁 **saien** remarriage
回縁 **mawa(ri)en** veranda extending around two or more sides of the building
因縁 **innen** fate; connection; origin; pretext
血縁 **ketsuen** blood relationship/relative
竹縁 **takeen** bamboo-floored veranda
7 良縁 **ryōen** good (marital) match
初縁 **shoen** one's first marriage
8 逆縁 **gyakuen** irony of fate
奇縁 **kien** strange fate, curious coincidence
金縁 **kinbuchi** gold-rimmed, gilt-edged
9 俗縁 **zokuen** worldly ties
11 宿縁 **shukuen** karma, fate
黒縁 **kurobuchi** black-rimmed (eyeglasses)
族縁 **zokuen** family ties
悪縁 **akuen** evil fate; unfortunate love
船縁 **funaberi** ship's side, gunwale
12 遠縁 **tōen** distantly related
復縁 **fukuen** reconciliation
落縁 **o(chi)en** low veranda
無縁 **muen** unrelated; with no surviving relatives
無縁仏 **muenbotoke** a deceased having no one to tend his grave
絶縁 **zetsuen** insulation; breaking off a relationship
絶縁体 **zetsuentai** insulator, nonconductor
絶縁線 **zetsuensen** insulated wire

14 腐縁 **kusa(re)en** unpleasant but unseverable relationship
銀縁 **ginbuchi** silver-rimmed
16 薄縁 **usuberi** bordered/thin matting
機縁 **kien** opportunity
17 濡縁 **nu(re)en** open veranda
18 離縁 **rien** divorce, disowning
離縁状 **rienjō** letter of divorce
類縁 **ruien** affinity, kinship
額縁 **gakubuchi** picture frame

————— 3 —————

15 養子縁組 **yōshi engumi** adopting an heir

6a9.11 / 1180

締 **TEI, shi(meru)** tie, tighten; control strictly; shut **shi(maru)** become taut/tight/firm; be thrifty

————— 1 —————

3 締上 **shi(me)a(geru)** tie up
4 締切 **shi(me)ki(ru)** close
　　 shi(me)ki(ri) closing (date), deadline
締込 **shi(me)ko(mu)** shut/lock in
5 締出 **shi(me)da(su)** shut/lock out
締付 **shi(me)tsu(keru)** bind, tighten, throttle; press hard
8 締具 **shi(me)gu** (ski) bindings
締金 **shi(me)gane** clasp, clamp
9 締括 **shi(me)kuku(ru)** tie fast; supervise; round out
締屋 **shi(mari)ya** thrifty person
締約 **teiyaku** (conclude a) treaty
締約国 **teiyakukoku** treaty signatories
10 締高 **shi(me)daka** total
締殺 **shi(me)koro(su)** strangle to death
12 締結 **teiketsu** conclude, contract
13 締盟 **teimei** conclude a treaty
締盟国 **teimeikoku** treaty signatories

————— 2 —————

4 元締 **motoji(me)** manager, boss
引締 **hi(ki)shi(meru)** tighten, stiffen, brace
戸締 **toji(mari)** locking up (for the night)
8 抱締 **da(ki)shi(meru), ida(ki)shi(meru)** embrace closely, cuddle, hug
取締 **to(ri)shima(ru)** manage, oversee
取締役 **torishimariyaku** (company) director
9 音締 **neji(me)** tuning; tune, melody
10 胴締 **dōji(me)** belt, waistband
12 握締 **nigi(ri)shi(meru)** grasp tight
14 緒締 **oji(me)** pouch drawstring
総締 **sōji(me)** total
15 踏締 **fu(mi)shi(meru)** step firmly/cautiously
18 噛締 **ka(mi)shi(meru)** chew well; ponder

————— 3 —————

6 羽交締 **haga(i)ji(me)** pin, full nelson

6

糸 9←
米
舟
虫
耳
⺮

6a9.12

緡 **MEN** fine thread

——————— 1 ———————
6 緡羊 **men'yō** sheep

——————— 2 ———————
17 縮緡 **chirimen** (silk) crepe

6a9.13 / 682

編 **HEN, a(mu)** knit; compile, edit

——————— 1 ———————
2 編入 **hennyū** entry, incorporation
3 編上 **a(mi)a(ge)** lace up (boots)
　編上靴 **a(mi)a(ge)gutsu** lace-up boots
4 編戸 **a(mi)do** braided door
5 編出 **a(mi)da(su)** work out, devise
　編目 **a(mi)me** knitting stitch/mesh
6 編年史 **hennenshi** chronicle, annals
　編年体 **hennentai** chronological order
　編曲 **henkyoku** (musical) arrangement
　編合 **a(mi)a(wasu), a(mi)a(waseru)** knit together
　編成 **hensei** organize, put together
8 編制 **hensei** organize, put together
　編者 **hensha** editor, compiler
　編物 **a(mi)mono** knitting; knitted goods
10 編修 **henshū** editing, compilation
　編針 **a(mi)bari** knitting needle, crochet hook
11 編隊 **hentai** (fly in) formation
　編組 **henso** braid; combine
12 編棒 **a(mi)bō** knitting needle/pin
　編集 **henshū** editing, compilation
　編集長 **henshūchō** editor-in-chief
　編集者 **henshūsha** editor
16 編輯 **henshū** editing, compilation
20 編纂 **hensan** compile, edit

——————— 2 ———————
3 小編 **shōhen** short article/story
4 毛編 **kea(mi)** knitting; knitted (from wool)
　中編 **chūhen** second volume; medium-length (novel)
　手編 **tea(mi)** knit(ting) by hand
5 正編 **seihen** main part (of a book)
6 再編成 **saihensei** reorganization, reshuffle
　全編 **zenpen** the whole book
　名編 **meihen** literary masterpiece
　共編 **kyōhen** joint editorship
7 改編 **kaihen** reorganize, redo
8 長編 **chōhen** long (article), full-length (novel), feature-length (movie)
　表編 **omoteami** plain knitting, stockinet stitch

9 後編 **kōhen** concluding part/volume
10 残編 **zanpen** remaining/extant books
12 短編 **tanpen** short piece/story/film
　雄編 **yūhen** a masterpiece
13 続編 **zokuhen** sequel
14 雑編 **zappen** miscellaneous writings
18 鎖編 **kusaria(mi)** chain stitch

——————— 3 ———————
16 機械編 **kikaia(mi)** machine-knit

6a9.14

縋 **TSUI, suga(ru)** hang/hold on to; depend on, appeal to

——————— 1 ———————
5 縋付 **suga(ri)tsu(ku)** cling to, depend on

——————— 2 ———————
8 追縋 **o(i)suga(ru)** close in on, be hot on the heels of
　取縋 **to(ri)suga(ru)** cling to; entreat
11 寄縋 **yo(ri)suga(ru)** cling to, rely on

6a9.15 / 1349

縫 縫 **HŌ, nu(u)** sew

——————— 1 ———————
3 縫上 **nu(i)a(ge)** a tuck (in a dress)
4 縫込 **nu(i)ko(mu)** sew in, tuck
　縫方 **nu(i)kata** way of sewing; sewer
5 縫代 **nu(i)shiro** margin left for a seam
　縫付 **nu(i)tsu(keru)** sew on
　縫目 **nu(i)me** seam, stitch
6 縫合 **nu(i)a(waseru)** sew up, stitch together
　　hōgō a suture, stitch
　縫返 **nu(i)kae(su)** resew, remake
　縫糸 **nu(i)ito** sewing thread; suture
8 縫直 **nu(i)nao(su)** resew, remake
　縫物 **nu(i)mono** sewing, needlework
　縫物台 **nu(i)monodai** sewing table
　縫取 **nu(i)to(ri)** embroidery
10 縫紋 **nu(i)mon** embroidered crest
　縫針 **nu(i)bari** sewing needle
12 縫揚 **nu(i)a(ge)** a tuck (in a dress)
14 縫模様 **nu(i)moyō** embroidered figures
　縫製 **hōsei** sew (by machine)
　縫製品 **hōseihin** sewn goods
　縫箔 **nu(i)haku** embroidery and foiling

——————— 2 ———————
4 手縫 **tenu(i)** hand-sewn, hand-stitched
6 伏縫 **fu(se)nu(i)** hemming
　仮縫 **karinu(i)** temporary sewing, basting
8 弥縫 **bihō** makeshift, stopgap, temporizing
　弥縫策 **bihōsaku** makeshift, stopgap measure

6
→9 糸
米
舟
虫
耳
⺮

11 袋縫 **fukuronu(i)** double sewing
粗縫 **aranu(i)** basting, tacking
12 裁縫 **saihō** sewing, tailoring, dressmaking
ta(chi)nu(i) cutting and sewing
13 隠縫 **kaku(shi)nu(i)** sewing concealed seams
15 縁縫 **fuchinu(i)** hemstitching

——— 3 ———

11 運針縫 **unshinnu(i)** ordinary stitching

——— 4 ———

4 天衣無縫 **ten'i-muhō** flawless, perfect

6a9.16

緘 **KAN** close, shut, seal

——— 1 ———

0 緘する **kan(suru)** close, shut, seal

——— 2 ———

9 封緘 **fūkan** seal
封緘葉書 **fūkan hagaki** lettercard

6a9.17 / 1290

緊 **KIN** tense, tight

——— 1 ———

4 緊切 **kinsetsu** urgent, pressing
7 緊迫 **kinpaku** tension
9 緊急 **kinkyū** emergency
緊要 **kin'yō** of vital importance
11 緊張 **kinchō** tension
緊張緩和 **kinchō kanwa** détente
緊密 **kinmitsu** close, tight
14 緊褌一番 **kinkon-ichiban** gird/brace oneself for
16 緊縛 **kinbaku** bind tightly
17 緊縮 **kinshuku** contraction; austerity

——— 2 ———

12 喫緊 **kikkin** urgent, pressing, vital

緩 → 4n8.4

緜 → 綿 6a8.8

——— 10 ———

6a10.1

緻 **CHI** fine, close, minute

——— 1 ———

11 緻密 **chimitsu** fine, close, minute, exact

——— 2 ———

5 巧緻 **kōchi** elaborate, finely wrought
11 細緻 **saichi** minute, close, detailed
14 精緻 **seichi** minute, fine, subtle

6a10.2 / 1483

縦 縱 **JŪ, tate** height, length; vertical
hoshiimama self-indulgent
yo(shi) even if

——— 1 ———

5 縦穴 **tateana** pit, vertically dug hole
6 縦列 **jūretsu** file, column, queue
縦糸 **tateito** warp (vertical thread in weaving)
7 縦坑 **tatekō** (mine) shaft, pit
縦走 **jūsō** traverse the length of (a mountain range)
9 縦陣 **jūjin** column (of soldiers)
10 縦射 **jūsha** raking fire, enfilade
縦座標 **tatezahyō** ordinate, y-coordinate
縦書 **tatega(ki)** vertical writing
11 縦隊 **jūtai** column (of soldiers)
縦断 **jūdan** vertical section; traverse, travel along
縦笛 **tatebue** recorder, *shakuhachi*
縦貫 **jūkan** traverse the length of
12 縦割 **tatewa(ri)** slivers
縦揺 **tateyu(re)** (angle of) pitch
縦裂 **tateza(ki)** ripping lengthwise
縦結 **tatemusu(bi)** vertical knot
縦筋 **tatesuji** vertical line/stripe
縦軸 **tatejiku** spindle
13 縦続 **jūzoku** concatenation, cascade
15 縦横 **jūō, tate-yoko** length and breadth, vertical and horizontal
縦横無尽 **jūō-mujin** all around, no end of
縦線 **jūsen** vertical line
16 縦縞 **tatejima** vertical stripes, pinstripes
17 縦覧 **jūran** inspection; reading

——— 2 ———

8 放縦 **hōjū** self-indulgence, debauchery
16 操縦 **sōjū** control, operate, manipulate
操縦士 **sōjūshi** pilot
操縦法 **sōjūhō** manipulation, control
操縦者 **sōjūsha** operator, manipulator; driver, pilot
操縦席 **sōjūseki** cockpit
操縦桿 **sōjūkan** joystick

——— 3 ———

8 奇策縦横 **kisaku-jūō** clever planning

6a10.3 / 1448

縛 縛 **BAKU, shiba(ru)** tie up, bind
imashi(me) bonds, bondage

———————— 1 ————————
3 縛上 **shiba(ri)a(geru)** tie/truss up
5 縛付 **shiba(ri)tsu(keru)** tie/fasten to
9 縛首 **shiba(ri)kubi** (execution by) hanging

———————— 2 ————————
4 収縛 **shūbaku** arrest and tie up
7 束縛 **sokubaku** restraint, constraint, shackles
8 呪縛 **jubaku** a spell
金縛 **kanashiba(ri)** bound hand and foot
10 捕縛 **hobaku** arrest, capture
12 就縛 **shūbaku** catch and tie up
15 緊縛 **kinbaku** bind tightly

———————— 4 ————————
6 自縄自縛 **jijō-jibaku** tied up with one's own rope, caught in one's own trap

6a10.4

緼 **UN, ON** old cotton wadding

———————— 1 ————————
10 緼袍 **dotera** padded/quilted kimono

6a10.5

縉 **SHIN** red silk; insert (a scepter of office into one's obi)

———————— 1 ————————
11 縉紳 **shinshin** high official/personage

6a10.6

縡 **SAI, koto** breath, life

———————— 1 ————————
4 縡切 **kotoki(reru)** breathe one's last, die

6a10.7 / 1054

緯 **I** woof (horizontal thread in weaving); latitude **nuki** woof

———————— 1 ————————
6 緯糸 **nukiito** woof
9 緯度 **ido** latitude
15 緯線 **isen** a parallel (of latitude)

———————— 2 ————————
5 北緯 **hokui** north latitude
9 南緯 **nan'i** south latitude

10 高緯度 **kōido** high/cold latitudes
11 経緯 **keii** longitude and latitude; warp and woof; particulars **ikisatsu** intricacies, complications, details
経緯儀 **keiigi** theodolite, altazimuth

6a10.8

縊 **I, kubi(reru)** strangle/hang oneself

———————— 1 ————————
6 縊死 **ishi** death by strangulation

———————— 2 ————————
7 見縊 **mikubi(ru)** belittle, slight, disparage
9 首縊 **kubikuku(ri)** hang oneself

6a10.9

縞 **KŌ, shima** stripe

———————— 1 ————————
8 縞物 **shimamono** striped cloth
9 縞柄 **shimagara** striped pattern
10 縞馬 **shimauma** zebra
11 縞蛇 **shimahebi** striped snake
14 縞模様 **shimamoyō** striped pattern
18 縞織 **shimaori** woven in stripes

———————— 2 ————————
12 棒縞 **bōjima** stripes
15 横縞 **yokojima** horizontal stripes
16 縦縞 **tatejima** vertical stripes, pinstripes

———————— 3 ————————
10 格子縞 **kōshijima** checkered pattern
13 碁盤縞 **gobanjima** checked/lattice pattern

6a10.10

縒 **SHI, yo(ru)** twist

———————— 2 ————————
10 紙縒 **koyo(ri)** twisted-paper string

6a10.11

縟 **JOKU** decoration

———————— 1 ————————
5 縟礼 **jokurei** tedious formalities, red tape

———————— 3 ————————
16 繁文縟礼 **hanbun-jokurei** tedious formalities, red tape

6a10.12

縺   **REN, motsu(reru)** get tangled, become ensnarled

——— 2 ———
6 舌縺 **shitamotsu(re)** lisp, speech impediment

縫 → 縫 **6a9.15**

6a10.13 / 1292

繁 繁   **HAN** fullness, luxury; frequency **shige(ru)** grow thick/luxuriantly **shige(mi)** thicket **shige(ku)** densely; frequently

——— 1 ———
4 繁文縟礼 **hanbun-jokurei** tedious formalities, red tape
6 繁多 **hanta** busy
 繁忙 **hanbō** busy, pressed
8 繁茂 **hanmo** luxuriant/dense growth
9 繁栄 **han'ei** prosperity
10 繁華 **hanka** flourishing, bustling
 繁華街 **hankagai** busy (shopping/entertainment) area
11 繁盛 **hanjō** prosperity; success
12 繁殖 **hanshoku** breed, multiply
 繁閑 **hankan** busy or slack, hectic or leisurely
14 繁雑 **hanzatsu** complex, intricate
15 繁劇 **hangeki** busyness
18 繁簡 **hankan** simplicity and complexity

——— 2 ———
13 農繁 **nōhan** farmers' busy season
 農繁期 **nōhanki** farmers' busy season
17 頻繁 **hinpan** frequent, incessant

縣 → 県 **3n6.3**

——— 11 ———

繍 → 繡 **6a13.1**

6a11.1 / 1571

繊 纖繊   **SEN** fine, slender

——— 1 ———
4 繊毛 **senmō** fine hairs, cilia
 繊手 **senshu** slender hand

5 繊巧 **senkō** detailed workmanship
7 繊条 **senjō** filament
10 繊弱 **senjaku** frail, delicate
11 繊細 **sensai** delicate, fine, subtle
14 繊維 **sen'i** fiber, textiles
 繊維素 **sen'iso** roughage, fiber, cellulose

——— 2 ———
4 化繊 **kasen** synthetic fiber

——— 3 ———
6 合成繊維 **gōsei sen'i** synthetic fiber

6a11.2

緡   **KYŌ** string (of coins) **mutsuki** child's obi; diaper

縱 → 縦 **6a10.2**

6a11.3

縷   **RU** thread; minute, detailed

——— 1 ———
3 縷々 **ruru** minutely, in detail; continuously

——— 2 ———
1 一縷 **ichiru** a thread, a ray (of hope)

總 → 総 **6a8.20**

6a11.4

縹   **HYŌ, hanada** light indigo/blue

——— 1 ———
12 縹渺 **hyōbyō** hazy; vast

——— 3 ———
9 神韻縹渺 **shin'in-hyōbyō** an undefinable artistic excellence

6a11.5

繆   **BYŪ** error **KYŪ** wrap around; hanging (by the neck)

6a11.6

縲   **RUI** tie up (a criminal)

——— 1 ———
11 縲絏 **ruisetsu** fetters, bonds
12 縲紲 **ruisetsu** fetters, bonds

6a11.7

縵 **MAN** unpatterned silk; loose

6a11.8 / 1117

績 **SEKI** achievements; (silk) spinning

————— 2 —————

5 功績 **kōseki** meritorious service
6 成績 **seiseki** results, (business) performance
　成績表 **seisekihyō** report/score card
7 学績 **gakuseki** student's record
8 事績 **jiseki** achievements, exploits
　治績 **chiseki** (record of one's) administration
　実績 **jisseki** actual results, record of performance
10 紡績 **bōseki** spinning
　紡績工 **bōsekikō** spinner
　紡績糸 **bōsekiito** (cotton) yarn
12 偉績 **iseki** glorious achievements
13 業績 **gyōseki** (business) performance, results, achievement
　戦績 **senseki** war record; score

————— 3 —————

4 不成績 **fuseiseki** poor results/performance
5 好成績 **kōseiseki** good results/record

6a11.9 / 1110

縮 **SHUKU, chiji(maru/mu)** shrink, contract **chiji(mi)** shrinkage; crepe **chiji(meru)** shorten, condense **chiji(rasu/reru)** make/become curly

————— 1 —————

3 縮上 **chiji(mi)a(garu)** shrink, quail, wince
　縮小 **shukushō** reduction, cut
4 縮毛 **chiji(re)ge** curly/kinky/wavy hair
　縮尺 **shukushaku** reduced scale
5 縮写 **shukusha** reduced copy, miniature reproduction
7 縮図 **shukuzu** reduced/scaled-down drawing
8 縮刷 **shukusatsu** print in reduced size
　縮刷版 **shukusatsuban** small-size edition
12 縮減 **shukugen** reduce
15 縮緬 **chirimen** (silk) crepe
18 縮織 **chiji(mi)o(ri)** cotton crepe

————— 2 —————

4 収縮 **shūshuku** contraction, constriction
　収縮期血圧 **shūshukuki ketsuatsu** systolic blood pressure
5 圧縮 **asshuku** compression, compressed (air)
　圧縮機 **asshukuki** compressor
7 伸縮 **shinshuku, no(bi)chiji(mi)** expansion

and contraction; elastic, flexible
　伸縮自在 **shinshuku-jizai** elastic, flexible, telescoping
　伸縮性 **shinshukusei** elasticity
8 委縮 **ishuku** shriveling, contraction, atrophy
9 軍縮 **gunshuku** arms reduction, disarmament
　畏縮 **ishuku** cower, quail, be awestruck, shrink from
10 恐縮 **kyōshuku** be very grateful/sorry
11 萎縮 **ishuku** wither, atrophy; be dispirited
12 減縮 **genshuku** reduction, cutback
　短縮 **tanshuku** shorten, curtail, abridge
13 絹縮 **kinuchiji(mi)** crinkled silk
15 緊縮 **kinshuku** contraction; austerity
16 凝縮 **gyōshuku** condensation
　濃縮 **nōshuku** concentrate, enrich

————— 4 —————

16 操業短縮 **sōgyō tanshuku** curtailed operations

6a11.10

繃 **HŌ** wrap around

————— 1 —————

10 繃帯 **hōtai** bandage

繋 → 繫 6a13.4

繁 → 繁 6a10.13

————— 12 —————

6a12.1

繖 **SAN** parasol; umbrella

6a12.2 / 1140

繕 **ZEN, tsukuro(u)** repair, mend

————— 2 —————

7 身繕 **mizukuro(i)** dress up, groom oneself
　見繕 **mitsukuro(u)** select at one's discretion
　言繕 **i(i)tsukuro(u)** gloss over
8 取繕 **to(ri)tsukuro(u)** repair, patch up, gloss over
10 修繕 **shūzen** repair
12 営繕 **eizen** building and repair, maintenance

6a12.3

繧　UN (a method of dyeing)

――――――― 1 ―――――――
18 繧繝　ungen (a method of dyeing)

6a12.4

繚　RYŌ wrap around; go against

6a12.5

繞　JŌ, NYŌ go around, surround, enclose

――――――― 2 ―――――――
2 之繞掛　shinnyū (o) ka(keru) emphasize, exaggerate
7 囲繞　ijō, inyō surround

6a12.6 / 680

織　SHOKU, SHIKI, o(ru) weave
o(ri) fabric, weave

――――――― 1 ―――――――
2 織子　o(ri)ko weaver, textile worker
3 織工　shokkō weaver, textile worker
　織女　shokujo woman textile worker
4 織元　o(ri)moto textile manufacturer
　織込　o(ri)ko(mu) weave into
　織方　o(ri)kata type of weave; how to weave
5 織出　o(ri)da(su) weave designs into
　織目　o(ri)me texture
6 織合　o(ri)a(waseru) interweave
　織色　o(ri)iro color as woven (undyed)
　織地　o(ri)ji texture; fabric
　織成　o(ri)na(su) weave (a picture)
　織糸　o(ri)ito weaving thread; strand
8 織物　orimono cloth, fabric, textiles
　織物商　orimonoshō draper
　織物業　orimonogyō the textile business
10 織姫　o(ri)hime woman textile worker
14 織模様　o(ri)moyō woven design
16 織機　shokki loom

――――――― 2 ―――――――
4 太織　futoo(ri) coarse silk cloth
　毛織　keo(ri) woolen goods
　毛織物　keorimono woolen goods
　手織　teo(ri) handweaving
5 平織　hiraori plain weave (fabric)
6 羽織　haori Japanese half-coat
　　　hao(ru) put on
　糸織　itoo(ri) (a type of silk cloth)

9 浮織　u(ki)ori weaving with raised figures, brocade
　染織　senshoku dyeing and weaving
10 畝織　uneori rep, ribbed fabric
　紡織　bōshoku spinning and weaving
11 袋織　fukuroo(ri) double weaving
　組織　soshiki organization; tissue
13 絹織物　kinuorimono silk fabrics
　節織　fushio(ri) coarse silk, pongee
14 綿織物　men'orimono cotton goods
　綾織　ayao(ri) twill
16 機織　hatao(ri) weaving, weaver; grasshopper
　機織虫　hatao(ri)mushi grasshopper
　縞織　shimaori woven in stripes
17 縮織　chiji(mi)o(ri) cotton crepe

――――――― 3 ―――――――
6 西陣織　nishijin'o(ri) Nishijin brocade
　再組織　saisoshiki reorganization
7 亜麻織物　ama orimono flax fabrics, linen
9 陣羽織　jinbaori sleeveless coat worn over armor
10 夏羽織　natsubaori summer haori coat
12 絵羽織　ebaori figured haori coat

――――――― 4 ―――――――
12 結合組織　ketsugō soshiki connective tissue

6a12.7

綱　GEN (a method of dyeing)

――――――― 2 ―――――――
18 繧繝　ungen (a method of dyeing)

6a12.8

繙　HAN, HON, himoto(ku) (untie a packaged book and) read

――――――― 1 ―――――――
14 繙読　handoku (open and) read, peruse

畿 → 5f10.3

――――――― 13 ―――――――

繩 → 縄 6a9.1

6a13.1

繍　繡　SHŪ embroidery; brocade

――――――― 2 ―――――――
8 刺繍　shishū embroidery

6
糸 13←
米
舟
虫
耳
⺮

6a13.2

繹

EKI pull out (a thread); ascertain

———— 2 ————

12 絡繹 **rakueki** ceaseless traffic
14 演繹 **en'eki** deduce
演繹法 **en'ekihō** deductive reasoning

6a13.3 / 1654

繰

SŌ, ku(ru) reel, wind; spin (thread); turn (pages); look up (a word); count

———— 1 ————

2 繰入 **ku(ri)i(reru)** transfer (money)
繰入金 **kuriirekin** money/balance transferred
3 繰上 **ku(ri)a(geru)** advance, move up (a date)
繰下 **ku(ri)sa(geru)** move ahead, defer
4 繰込 **ku(ri)ko(mu)** stream into; count in, round up
繰戸 **ku(ri)do** sliding door
5 繰出 **ku(ri)da(su)** pay out (rope); call out (troops); sally forth
繰出梯子 **ku(ri)da(shi)bashigo** extension ladder
繰広 **ku(ri)hiro(geru)** unfold
6 繰合 **ku(ri)a(waseru)** manage, find the time
繰返 **ku(ri)kae(su)** repeat
繰回 **ku(ri)mawa(su)** make shift, roll over (a debt)
7 繰延 **ku(ri)no(be)** postponement, deferment
繰戻 **ku(ri)modo(su)** put back
繰言 **ku(ri)goto** same old story, complaint
11 繰寄 **ku(ri)yo(seru)** draw toward one
12 繰替 **ku(ri)ka(eru)** exchange, swap; divert (money)
繰越 **ku(ri)ko(su)** transfer, carry forward
繰越金 **kurikoshikin** balance brought forward
14 繰綿 **ku(ri)wata** ginned cotton

———— 2 ————

4 爪繰 **tsumagu(ru)** to finger
手繰 **tegu(ri)** spinning by hand; dragnet; procedure, management
　　tagu(ru) reel in (pulling hand over hand)
手繰込 **tagu(ri)ko(mu)** haul in
手繰出 **tagu(ri)da(su)** pay out (a line); trace (a clue)
引繰返 **hi(k)ku(ri)kae(ru)** be overturned, capsize, collapse; be reversed
　　hi(k)ku(ri)kae(su) overturn, turn upside down, turn inside out
6 糸繰 **itoku(ri)** reeling, filature; spinner; reel
7 乳繰 **chichiku(ru)** have a secret love affair
8 金繰 **kanegu(ri)** raising funds
10 差繰 **sa(shi)ku(ru)** manage skillfully
11 勘繰 **kangu(ru)** be suspicious of

船繰 **funaku(ri), funagu(ri)** shipping schedule
12 遣繰 **ya(ri)ku(ri)** makeshift, getting by
遣繰算段 **ya(ri)ku(ri) sandan** getting by, tiding over
煮繰返 **ni(e)ku(ri)kae(ru)** boil, seethe
順繰 **jungu(ri)** in order, in turn
14 綿繰 **wataku(ri)** cotton ginning
18 臍繰 **hesoku(ri)** secret savings
臍繰金 **hesoku(ri)gane** secret savings

———— 3 ————

13 資金繰 **shikingu(ri)** raising funds, generating revenue

繪 → 絵 6a6.8

6a13.4

繋　繋

KEI, tsuna(gu) connect, tie, tether **tsuna(garu)** be connected **kaka(ru)** be tied together; lie at anchor

———— 1 ————

4 繋止 **tsuna(gi)to(meru)** connect; save (a life)
5 繋目 **tsuna(gi)me** joint
6 繋合 **tsuna(gi)a(waseru)** join/tie together
繋争 **keisō** dispute, contention
10 繋留 **keiryū** mooring, anchorage
11 繋累 **keirui** encumbrances, dependents
繋船 **keisen** mooring
13 繋辞 **keiji** copula, link verb

———— 2 ————

9 連繋 **renkei** connection, liaison, contact
18 顔繋 **kaotsuna(gi)** getting acquainted

———— 14 ————

6a14.1

繻

SHU fine silk, satin

———— 1 ————

2 繻子 **shusu** satin

6a14.2

繽

HIN disorder, scattering

6a14.3

繪　縡

kasuri splashed pattern (dyeing/weaving)

繼 → 継 6a7.8

6a14.4

辮

BEN braid, pigtail, queue

——————— 1 ———————
14 辮髮 **benpatsu** pigtail, queue

——————— 15 ———————

6a15.1

纈

KETSU tie-dyeing; purblind

——————— 2 ———————
21 纐纈 **kōketsu** tie-dyeing

6a15.2

纐

KŌ tie-dyeing

——————— 1 ———————
21 纐纈 **kōketsu** tie-dyeing

艦 → 櫼 5e15.2

6a15.3

纘

SAN succeed to, inherit

續 → 続 6a7.5

纏 → 纒 6a16.1

纖 → 繊 6a11.1

——————— 16 ———————

6a16.1

纒 纏

TEN, mato(meru) gather/put together; settle, arrange
mato(maru) be collected/

brought together; take shape; be settled/arranged
matsu(waru) coil around; surround, hang about
mato(u) put on, wear   **mato(i)** (firemen's) standard

——————— 1 ———————
7 纏役 **mato(me)yaku** mediator
纏足 **tensoku** bind one's feet
14 纏綿 **tenmen** entanglement, involvement

——————— 2 ———————
1 一纏 **hitomato(me)** a bunch/bundle
5 半纏 **hanten** short coat
付纏 **tsu(ki)mato(u)** follow about, shadow, tag after
8 取纏 **to(ri)mato(meru)** collect, arrange
11 絆纏 **hanten** short coat, vest

——————— 3 ———————
7 足手纏 **ashitemato(i), ashidemato(i)** hindrance, encumbrance

——————— 17 ———————

6a17.1

纓

EI crown string; breast harness

6a17.2

纔

SAI, wazuka little, slight

纖 → 繊 6a11.1

——————— 18 ———————

6a18.1

纛

TŌ flag, banner

——————— 22 ———————

6a22.1

纜

RAN, tomozuna mooring rope, hawser

——————— 2 ———————
13 解纜 **kairan** sailing, leaving

6

糸 22 ←
米
舟
虫
耳

竹

—————————— 米 **6b** ——————————

米	采	籵	籸	籹	籿	粂	粏	耗	粃	料	粋	粉
0.1	1.1	2.1	6b3.1	3.1	3.2	3.3	4.1	4.2	4.3	4.4	4.5	4.6

氣	粒	粗	粕	粘	釈	断	粧	粭	粭	粭	桐	粟
0a6.8	5.1	5.2	5.3	5.4	5.5	5.6	6.1	6.2	6.3	4i17.1	6.5	6.6

粢	釉	奧	粤	番	歯	粛	梗	糀	粮	粲	梁	精
6.7	6.8	6.9	6.10	5f7.4	6.11	0a11.8	7.1	7.2	6b12.1	7.3	7.4	8.1

粽	粹	椹	糊	粿	粳	麹	模	楠	稼	糖	彝	槽
8.2	6b4.5	9.1	9.2	9.3	9.4	6b13.1	4a10.16	10.1	10.2	10.3	6b12.2	11.1

糠	糞	麋	齢	鞠	糝	糧	彝	翻	麹	釋	糯	糲
11.2	11.3	11.4	11.5	11.6	11.7	12.1	12.2	12.3	13.1	6b5.5	14.1	14.2

飜	鬻	麟
6b12.3	16.1	18.1

───────── 0 ─────────

6b0.1 / 224

米
BEI rice; America, U.S.; meter
kome, yone rice
mētoru meter

───────── 1 ─────────

2 米人 **beijin** an American
4 米中 **Bei-Chū** America and China
米仏 **Bei-Futsu** America and France
米収 **beishū** rice crop/harvest
5 米代 **komedai** money for rice
6 米虫 **kome (no) mushi** rice weevil
7 米寿 **beiju** one's 88th birthday
米作 **beisaku** rice cultivation/crop
米兵 **beihei** U.S. soldier/sailor
米材 **beizai** American timber
米麦 **beibaku** rice and barley; grains
8 米価 **beika** (government-set) rice price
米刺 **komesa(shi)** rice-sampling tool
米油 **komeabura** rice-bran oil
米英 **Bei-Ei** the U.S. and Britain
米国 **Beikoku** the United States
米松 **beimatsu** Douglas/Oregon fir
米所 **komedokoro** rice-producing area
9 米軍 **beigun** U.S. armed forces
米独 **Bei-Doku** the U.S. and Germany
米屋 **komeya** rice dealer
米食 **beishoku** rice diet
米食虫 **komeku(i)mushi** rice weevil; drone, idler
10 米俵 **komedawara** straw rice bag
米倉 **komegura** rice granary
米紙 **beishi** American newspaper(s)
米粉 **komeko, beifun** rice flour
11 米商 **beishō** rice dealer
米菓 **beika** rice crackers
米産 **beisan** rice production
米粒 **kometsubu** grain of rice
米貨 **beika** U.S. currency, the dollar
米問屋 **komedon'ya** rice wholesaler

12 米飯 **beihan** boiled rice
13 米塩 **beien** rice and salt; livelihood
米搗 **kometsu(ki)** rice polishing
米資 **beishi** American capital
14 米穀 **beikoku** American capital
米綿 **beimen** American (raw) cotton
米語 **beigo** American English
米誌 **beishi** American magazine
米銭 **beisen** money for rice
18 米櫃 **komebitsu** rice bin; breadwinner; means of livelihood
米騒動 **kome sōdō** rice riot
21 米艦 **beikan** U.S. warship

───────── 2 ─────────

4 中米 **Chūbei** Central America
反米 **han-Bei** anti-American
日米 **Nichi-Bei** Japan and America, Japan-U.S.
5 北米 **Hokubei** North America
玄米 **genmai** unpolished/unmilled rice
古米 **komai** old/long-stored rice
外米 **gaimai** foreign/imported rice
白米 **hakumai** polished rice
6 全米 **zen-Bei** all-America(n), pan-American
在米 **zai-Bei** in America
有米 **a(ri)mai** rice on hand
7 亜米利加 **Amerika** America
対米 **tai-Bei** toward/with America
8 非米 **hi-Bei** un-American
供米 **kyōmai** delivery of rice (to the government) **kumai** offering of rice to a god
英米 **Ei-Bei** Britain and the U.S.
欧米 **Ō-Bei** Europe and America, the West
金米糖 **konpeitō** confetti (a candy)
9 南米 **Nanbei** South America
洗米 **senmai** washed rice
施米 **semai** rice given as charity
砕米 **kuda(ke)mai** broken rice
10 俸米 **hōmai** rice given in payment for services
屑米 **kuzumai** broken rice
粉米 **kogome** broken rice

11 排米　**hai-Bei** anti-American
黒米　**kurogome** unpolished rice
救米　**suku(i)mai** rice given as charity
12 渡米　**to-Bei** going to America
期米　**kimai** rice for future delivery
焼米　**ya(ki)gome** parched/roasted rice
飯米　**hanmai** food; rice grown for the farm family's own consumption
13 滞米　**tai-Bei** staying in America
新米　**shinmai** new rice; beginner
節米　**setsumai** rice saving/economizing
14 精米　**seimai** polishing/polished rice
15 蔵米　**kuramai** stored rice
駐米　**chū-Bei** resident/stationed in America
16 親米　**shin-Bei** pro-American

─────── 3 ───────

2 人造米　**jinzōmai** artificial rice
3 久留米　**Kurume** (city, Fukuoka-ken)
小作米　**kosakumai** rent paid in rice
4 内地米　**naichimai** homegrown rice
中南米　**Chūnanbei** Central and South America
5 半搗米　**hantsu(ki)mai** half-polished rice
6 年貢米　**nengumai** annual rice tax
早場米　**hayabamai** early rice
7 扶持米　**fuchimai** rice allowance
9 胚芽米　**haigamai** whole rice (with the germ)
10 俸禄米　**hōrokumai** rice given in payment for services
配給米　**haikyūmai** rationed rice
11 黄変米　**ōhenmai** discolored/spoiled rice
救助米　**kyūjomai** dole rice
救援米　**kyūenmai** dole rice
救護米　**kyūgomai** dole rice
14 精白米　**seihakumai** polished rice

─────── 1 ───────

6b1.1
采
HAN separate, divide

─────── 2 ───────

6b2.1
料
dekamētoru decameter, ten meters

─────── 3 ───────

籾 → 籾 **6b3.1**

6b3.1
籾 籾　**momi** unhulled rice; rice hulls, chaff

11 籾殻　**momigara** rice hulls, chaff
14 籾摺　**momisu(ri)** hulling rice

6b3.2
粁
kiromētoru kilometer, km

6b3.3
粂
Kume (used in proper names)

─────── 4 ───────

6b4.1
粐
KO, yonedo (used in proper names)

6b4.2
粍
mirimētoru millimeter

6b4.3
粃
HI, shiina immature ear of grain

─────── 1 ───────

9 粃政　**hisei** misgovernment, misrule
17 粃糠　**hikō** immature ears and bran; useless

6b4.4 / 319
料
RYŌ materials; fee, charge

─────── 1 ───────

6 料地　**ryōchi** preserve, estate
8 料金　**ryōkin** fee, charge, fare
9 料亭　**ryōtei** restaurant
10 料紙　**ryōshi** (writing) paper
11 料理　**ryōri** cooking, cuisine; dish, food
料理人　**ryōrinin** a cook
料理屋　**ryōriya** restaurant
12 料飲　**ryōin** food and drink

─────── 2 ───────

4 手料理　**teryōri** home cooking
5 史料　**shiryō** historical materials/records
6 安料理屋　**yasuryōriya** cheap restaurant
有料　**yūryō** fee-charging, toll (road), pay (toilet)

6

糸
米　4 ←
舟
虫
耳
艹

衣料 **iryō** clothing
7 材料 **zairyō** materials, ingredients; data; factors
見料 **kenryō** (fortuneteller's/admission) fee
8 送料 **sōryō** shipping charges, postage
肥料 **hiryō** manure, fertilizer
9 染料 **senryō** dye, dyestuffs
科料 **karyō, togaryō** minor fine (cf. 過料)
香料 **kōryō** spice; perfume; condolence gift
思料 **shiryō** thought, consideration
食料 **shokuryō** food
食料品 **shokuryōhin** food(stuffs)
食料品店 **shokuryōhinten** grocery store
食料品商 **shokuryōhinshō** grocer
10 借料 **shakuryō** rental fee
原料 **genryō** raw materials
席料 **sekiryō** room/cover charge, admission fee
11 過料 **karyō, ayamachiryō** non-penal fine (cf. 科料)
宿料 **shukuryō** hotel charges
12 御料 **goryō** imperial/crown property
御料地 **goryōchi** imperial estate, crown land
無料 **muryō** without charge, free
給料 **kyūryō** pay, wages, salary
給料日 **kyūryōbi** payday
貸料 **ka(shi)ryō** rent; loan charges
飲料 **inryō** drink, beverage   **no(mi)ryō** the portion (of the drink) for oneself
飲料水 **inryōsui** drinking water
13 塗料 **toryō** paint, paint and varnish
損料 **sonryō** rental charge
節料理 **(o)sechi ryōri** New Year's foods
資料 **shiryō** material, data
飼料 **shiryō** feed, fodder
15 稿料 **kōryō** payment for a manuscript
16 燃料 **nenryō** fuel
18 顔料 **ganryō** pigment; cosmetics

——————— 3 ———————

1 一品料理 **ippin ryōri** dishes à la carte
2 入場料 **nyūjōryō** admission fee
3 下足料 **gesokuryō** footwear-checking charge
下宿料 **geshukuryō** room-and-board charge
口止料 **kuchido(me)ryō** hush money
小作料 **kosakuryō** farm rent
4 中華料理 **chūka ryōri** Chinese cooking/food
水道料 **suidōryō** water charges
手術料 **shujutsuryō** operating fee
手数料 **tesūryō** handling charge, fee
5 弁護料 **bengoryō** attorney's fees
甘味料 **kanmiryō** sweetener
好材料 **kōzairyō** good material/data
広告料 **kōkokuryō** advertising rates

6 会席料理 **kaiseki ryōri** banquet food served on individual trays
返信料 **henshinryō** return postage
7 即席料理 **sokuseki ryōri** quick meal
扶助料 **fujoryō** pension
初診料 **shoshinryō** fee for patient's first visit
8 使用料 **shiyōryō** rental fee
受信料 **jushinryō** (NHK TV) reception fee
受験料 **jukenryō** examination fee
送話料 **sōwaryō** telephone charges
周旋料 **shūsenryō** brokerage, commission
拝観料 **haikanryō** (museum) admission fee
9 保険料 **hokenryō** insurance premium
保管料 **hokanryō** custody/storage fee
通話料 **tsūwaryō** telephone-call charge
染筆料 **senpitsuryō** writing fee
香辛料 **kōshinryō** spices, seasoning
香味料 **kōmiryō** seasoning, condiments
10 倉敷料 **kurashikiryō** storage charges
郵送料 **yūsōryō** postage
原材料 **genzairyō** raw materials
原稿料 **genkōryō** payment for a manuscript
荷揚料 **nia(ge)ryō** landing charges
核燃料 **kakunenryō** nuclear fuel
書留料 **kakitomeryō** registration fee
配達料 **haitatsuryō** delivery charge
11 授業料 **jugyōryō** tuition
宿泊料 **shukuhakuryō** hotel charges
寄宿料 **kishukuryō** boarding expenses
祭祀料 **saishiryō** grant for funeral expenses
12 登記料 **tōkiryō** registration fee
検定料 **kenteiryō** examination fee
筆耕料 **hikkōryō** copying fee
診察料 **shinsatsuryō** medical consultation fee
13 賃借料 **chinshakuryō** rent
電灯料 **dentōryō** electric-lighting charges
電信料 **denshinryō** telegram charges
電報料 **denpōryō** telegram charges
電話料 **denwaryō** telephone charges
14 精進料理 **shōjin ryōri** vegetarian dishes
15 潤筆料 **junpitsuryō** writing/painting fee
慰藉料 **isharyō** consolation money, solatium
慰謝料 **isharyō** consolation money, solatium
調味料 **chōmiryō** condiments, seasonings
17 謄写料 **tōsharyō** copying charge
聴取料 **chōshuryō** radio fee
聴視料 **chōshiryō** television fee
購読料 **kōdokuryō** subscription price/fee
18 観覧料 **kanranryō** admission fee
23 鑑定料 **kanteiryō** expert's/legal fee

——————— 4 ———————

4 水性塗料 **suisei toryō** water-based paint
8 夜光塗料 **yakō toryō** luminous paint
油性塗料 **yusei toryō** oil-based paint
11 清涼飲料 **seiryō inryō** carbonated beverage
12 滋強飲料 **jikyō inryō** tonic drink

6b4.5 / 1708

粋 粹 **SUI** purity, essence; elite, choice; refined, elegant, fashionable, urbane
iki chic, stylish

1

2 粋人 **suijin** man of refined tastes
7 粋狂 **suikyō** caprice, whim

2

3 小粋 **koiki** stylish, tasteful
4 不粋 **busui** lacking in polish, inelegant
5 生粋 **kissui** pure, true
7 抜粋 **bassui** excerpt, extract, selection
8 国粋 **kokusui** national characteristics
国粋主義 **kokusui shugi** ultranationalism
10 純粋 **junsui** pure, genuine
12 無粋 **busui** lacking elegance, unromantic
14 精粋 **seisui** exquisite

6b4.6 / 1701

粉 **FUN, kona, ko** flour, powder
deshimētoru decimeter, tenth of a meter

1

0 粉ミルク **konamiruku** powdered milk
3 粉々 **konagona** into tiny pieces
5 粉本 **funpon** a copy, sketch
粉末 **funmatsu** powder
6 粉米 **kogome** broken rice
7 粉状 **funjō** powder(ed)
粉乳 **funnyū** powdered milk
9 粉茶 **konacha** powdered tea
粉炭 **funtan** powdered coal
konazumi ground charcoal
粉屋 **konaya** flour dealer, miller
粉砕 **funsai** pulverize, crush
粉糾 **funkyū** complications, entanglement
粉食 **funshoku** eating bread products (rather than rice)
10 粉骨 **funkotsu** assiduousness
粉骨砕身 **funkotsu-saishin** do one's utmost
粉粉 **konagona** into tiny pieces
11 粉雪 **konayuki** powder snow
13 粉微塵 **konamijin** tiny fragments
粉飾 **funshoku** makeup; embellishment
16 粉薬 **konagusuri** medicine powder

2

5 汁粉 **shiruko** sweet adzuki-bean soup with rice cake
白粉 **oshiroi** face powder/paint
石粉 **ishiko** stone dust
6 肉粉 **nikufun** powdered meat
米粉 **komeko, beifun** rice flour
7 豆粉 **mame(no)ko** soybean flour
花粉 **kafun** pollen
麦粉 **mugiko** (wheat) flour
8 受粉 **jufun** pollination, fertilization
取粉 **to(ri)ko** rice meal
金粉 **kinpun, kinko** gold dust
9 洗粉 **ara(i)ko** powdered soap
染粉 **so(me)ko** dye, dyestuffs
紅粉 **beniko** powdered rouge
10 捏粉 **ko(ne)ko** dough
脂粉 **shifun** rouge and powder, cosmetics
骨粉 **koppun** bone meal, powdered bone
晒粉 **sara(shi)ko** bleaching powder
砥粉 **to(no)ko** polishing powder
粉粉 **konagona** into tiny pieces
11 授粉 **jufun** pollination
黄粉 **ki(na)ko** soybean flour
魚粉 **gyofun** fish meal
12 葛粉 **kuzuko** arrowroot starch/flour
脹粉 **fuku(rashi)ko** baking powder
13 鉄粉 **teppun** iron filings/powder
14 穀粉 **kokufun** grain flour
製粉 **seifun** flour milling
製粉所 **seifunjo** flour mill
製粉機 **seifunki** flour mill/grinder
練粉 **ne(ri)ko** dough
銀粉 **ginpun** silver dust
16 澱粉 **denpun** starch
澱粉質 **denpunshitsu** starchiness
擂粉木 **su(ri)kogi** wooden pestle
磨粉 **miga(ki)ko** polishing powder
膨粉 **fuku(rashi)ko** baking powder
17 糝粉 **shinko** rice flour; rice-flour dough

3

3 小麦粉 **komugiko** (wheat) flour
4 天瓜粉 **tenkafun** talcum powder
天花粉 **tenkafun** talcum powder
片栗粉 **katakuriko** dogtooth-violet starch
5 白玉粉 **shiratamako** rice flour
10 蚤取粉 **nomito(ri)ko** flea powder
12 歯磨粉 **hamiga(ki)ko** tooth powder
13 煉白粉 **ne(ri)oshiroi** face powder
14 髪洗粉 **kamiara(i)ko** shampoo powder
15 蕎麦粉 **sobako** buckwheat flour

4

6 自花受粉 **jika jufun** self-pollination

氣→気 0a6.8

5

6b5.1 / 1700

粒 **RYŪ, tsubu** a grain; drop(let)

1

2 粒子 **ryūshi** (atomic) particle; grain (in film)

3 粒々 **ryūryū** assiduously
tsubutsubu lumps, grains
5 粒立 **tsubuda(tsu)** become grainy/foamy
7 粒状 **ryūjō** granular, granulated
9 粒食 **ryūshoku** eating rice/wheat in grain
(not flour) form
粒粒辛苦 **ryūryū-shinku** assiduous effort
12 粒揃 **tsubuzoro(i)** uniformly excellent
14 粒選 **tsubuyo(ri)** cull, select
粒銀 **tsubugin** (a small silver coin)

─────────── 2 ───────────

1 一粒 **hitotsubu** a grain
一粒種 **hitotsubudane** an only child
3 大粒 **ōtsubu** a large drop/grain
小粒 **kotsubu** small grain, granule
6 米粒 **kometsubu** grain of rice
8 泡粒 **awatsubu** a bubble
雨粒 **amatsubu** raindrop
9 砂粒 **sunatsubu** grain of sand
10 素粒子 **soryūshi** (subatomic) particle
11 細粒 **sairyū** granule
粒粒 **ryūryū** assiduously
tsubutsubu lumps, grains
粒粒辛苦 **ryūryū-shinku** assiduous effort
12 粟粒 **zokuryū, awatsubu** millet grain
飯粒 **meshitsubu** a grain of boiled rice
13 微粒子 **biryūshi** tiny particle, fine-grained
14 穀粒 **kokuryū** a grain, kernel
17 顆粒 **karyū** grain, granule

─────────── 3 ───────────

7 芥子粒 **keshitsubu** poppy seed; something
tiny

6b5.2 / 1084

粗

SO, ara(i) coarse, rough
ara flaw, defect

─────────── 1 ───────────

3 粗大 **sodai** coarse, rough, bulky
粗大ゴミ **sodai gomi** large-item trash
(discarded washing machines, TV sets,
etc.)
粗々 **araara** roughly, not in detail
4 粗木 **araki** unbarked logs
粗方 **arakata** mostly, roughly, nearly
5 粗末 **somatsu** coarse, plain, crude, rough, rude
粗皮 **arakawa** bark, hull; untanned hide
粗布 **sofu** coarse cloth
粗玉 **aratama** gem in the rough
粗目 **zarame** (brown) crystal sugar
6 粗朶 **soda** twigs, brushwood
粗衣 **soi** coarse/poor clothing
8 粗服 **sofuku** coarse/poor clothing
粗放 **sohō** careless; non-intensive (farming)
粗忽 **sokotsu** carelessness

粗忽者 **sokotsumono** careless/absentminded
person
粗金 **aragane** ore
9 粗削 **arakezu(ri)** rough-planed, rough-hewn
粗造 **arazuku(ri)** rough-wrought
粗品 **soshina, sohin** small gift
粗茶 **socha** (coarse) tea
粗相 **sosō** carelessness, blunder
粗研 **arato(gi)** rough grinding
粗食 **soshoku** coarse food, plain diet
10 粗酒 **soshu** cheap saké
粗砥 **arato** coarse grindstone/whetstone
11 粗野 **soya** rustic, loutish, vulgar
粗彫 **arabo(ri)** rough carving
粗菓 **soka** cakes, refreshments
粗密 **somitsu** coarseness and fineness
粗悪 **soaku** coarse, crude, inferior
粗悪品 **soakuhin** inferior goods
粗略 **soryaku** crude, slipshod
粗粗 **araara** roughly, not in detail
粗笨 **sohon** crude, rough
12 粗筋 **arasuji** outline, summary, synopsis
粗飯 **sohan** plain meal
13 粗塗 **aranu(ri)** rough/first coating (of plaster)
粗鉋 **araganna** foreplane
粗鉱 **sokō** undressed ore
14 粗漏 **sorō** carelessness, oversight
粗製 **sosei** crudely made
粗製品 **soseihin** crude articles
粗雑 **sozatsu** coarse, crude
15 粗暴 **sobō** wild, rough, violent
粗縫 **aranu(i)** basting, tacking
16 粗壁 **arakabe** rough-coated wall
粗糖 **sotō** raw sugar
粗鋼 **sokō** crude steel
粗餐 **sosan** plain meal

─────────── 2 ───────────

11 粗粗 **araara** roughly, not in detail
14 精粗 **seiso** fineness or coarseness

6b5.3

粕

HAKU, kasu (saké) lees, dregs, dross

─────────── 1 ───────────

8 粕取 **kasuto(ri)** low-grade (liquor)
14 粕漬 **kasuzu(ke)** vegetables pickled in saké
lees

─────────── 2 ───────────

10 酒粕 **sakekasu, sakakasu** saké lees
17 糟粕 **sōhaku** lees, dregs

6b5.4 / 1707

粘 黏

NEN, neba(ru) be sticky;
stick to it, persist

——————— 1 ———————

2 粘力 **nenryoku** viscosity; tenacity
3 粘々 **nebaneba** sticky, gooey
粘土 **nendo, nebatsuchi** clay
5 粘付 **nebatsu(ku)** be sticky
6 粘気 **neba(ri)ke** stickiness
8 粘性 **nensei** viscosity
9 粘度 **nendo** viscosity
11 粘液 **nen'eki** mucus
粘液質 **nen'ekishitsu** phlegmatic; mucous
粘強 **neba(ri)zuyo(i)** tenacious, persistent
粘粘 **nebaneba** sticky, gooey
12 粘着 **nenchaku** adhesion
   neba(ri)tsu(ku) be sticky
粘着力 **nenchakuryoku** adhesion, viscosity
13 粘稠 **nenchū, nenchō** thick and viscous
14 粘膜 **nenmaku** mucous membrane
15 粘質 **nenshitsu** viscosity, stickiness

——————— 2 ———————

10 紙粘土 **kaminendo** clay made from newsprint
11 粘粘 **nebaneba** sticky, gooey

6b5.5 / 595

釈 釋
SHAKU explanation

——————— 1 ———————

8 釈迦 **Shaka** Gautama, Buddha
釈迦如来 **Shaka Nyorai** Sakyamuni
釈迦牟尼 **Shakamuni** Sakyamuni, Gautama, Buddha
釈迦象 **shakazō** image of Buddha
釈明 **shakumei** explanation, vindication
釈放 **shakuhō** release, discharge
12 釈尊 **Shakuson** Gautama, Buddha
釈然 **shakuzen** with sudden illumination, well satisfied with (an explanation)
13 釈義 **shakugi** explication, commentary
釈義学 **shakugigaku** exegesis

——————— 2 ———————

6 仮釈放 **karishakuhō** release on parole
会釈 **eshaku** salutation, greeting, bow
7 希釈 **kishaku** dilute
8 注釈 **chūshaku** commentary, annotation
9 保釈 **hoshaku** bail
保釈金 **hoshakukin** bail
10 訓釈 **kunshaku** explanation of the reading and meaning of kanji
12 稀釈 **kishaku** dilution
評釈 **hyōshaku** annotation, commentary
註釈 **chūshaku** annotation, commentary
註釈者 **chūshakusha** annotator, commentator
13 解釈 **kaishaku** interpretation, elucidation
新釈 **shinshaku** new interpretation

14 語釈 **goshaku** explanation of words
17 講釈 **kōshaku** lecture; storytelling
講釈師 **kōshakushi** (professional) storyteller

6b5.6 / 1024

断 斷
DAN decision, judgment; cut off; abstain from **ta(tsu)** cut off; abstain from **kotowa(ru)** decline, refuse; give notice/warning; prohibit

——————— 1 ———————

0 断じる/ずる **dan(jiru/zuru)** conclude, judge
断じて **dan(jite)** decidedly, absolutely
断トツ **dantotsu** right at the top, the unquestioned leader, second to none (short for 断然トップ)
3 断々乎 **dandanko** firm, resolute
4 断切 **ta(chi)ki(ru)** cut off, sever
断片 **danpen** fragment, snippet
断片的 **danpenteki** fragmentary
断水 **dansui** water supply cutoff
5 断乎 **danko** firm, resolute
断末魔 **danmatsuma** one's dying moments
6 断交 **dankō** break off relations with
断行 **dankō** carry out (resolutely)
7 断言 **dangen** assert, declare
8 断念 **dannen** abandon, relinquish
断郊競走 **dankō kyōsō** cross-country race
断定 **dantei** conclusion, decision
断固 **danko** firm, resolute
断物 **ta(chi)mono** foods abstained from
断金 **dankin** warm friendship
9 断面 **danmen** (cross) section
断面図 **danmenzu** cross-sectional view
断食 **danjiki** fasting, fast
10 断案 **dan'an** conclusion, decision
断書 **kotowa(ri)ga(ki)** explanatory note
11 断崖 **dangai** cliff, precipice
断断乎 **dandanko** firm, resolute
12 断割 **ta(chi)wa(ru)** cut apart, split open
断然 **danzen** resolutely, flatly, decidedly
断絶 **danzetsu** become extinct; sever
13 断腸 **danchō** heartbreak
断罪 **danzai** convict, condemn; beheading
断続 **danzoku** stopping and starting
断続的 **danzokuteki** intermittent, off-and-on
14 断髪 **danpatsu** cutting one's hair short
断層 **dansō** (geological) fault; gap
断種 **danshu** (eugenic) sterilization
15 断線 **dansen** disconnection, broken wire
16 断頭 **dantō** beheading
断頭台 **dantōdai** guillotine

——————— 2 ———————

3 寸断 **sundan** cut/tear to pieces
4 不断 **fudan** constant, ceaseless; usually

6

糸
米 5←
舟
虫
耳
⺍

不断着 **fudangi** everyday clothes
予断 **yodan** guess, predict, conclude
中断 **chūdan** break off, interrupt, suspend
切断 **setsudan** cutting, section; cut, sever, amputate
切断面 **setsudanmen** section, cutting plane
切断機 **setsudanki** cutter, cutting machine
5 処断 **shodan** judge, decide; deal with
6 両断 **ryōdan** bisect, break in two
同断 **dōdan** the same as before, ditto
7 即断 **sokudan** prompt decision
判断 **handan** judgment
判断力 **handanryoku** judgment, discernment
決断 **ketsudan** decision, resolve
決断力 **ketsudanryoku** resolution, determination
8 盲断 **mōdan** arbitrary judgment, hasty conclusion
油断 **yudan** inattentiveness, lack of vigilance
英断 **eidan** decisive judgment, resolute step
明断 **meidan** clear/definite judgment
物断 **monoda(chi)** abstinence
武断 **budan** militarism
9 専断 **sendan** deciding/acting on one's own
勇断 **yūdan** resolute decision
速断 **sokudan** hasty conclusion; prompt decision
独断 **dokudan** arbitrary decision; dogmatism
独断専行 **dokudan-senkō** arbitrary action
茶断 **chada(chi)** abstinence from tea
10 酒断 **sakada(chi), sakeda(chi)** swearing off from drinking
破断 **hadan** rupture, break
11 推断 **suidan** infer, deduce, conclude
断断乎 **dandanko** firm, resolute
12 無断 **mudan** unannounced; unauthorized
裁断 **saidan** cutting and shearing (cloth); judgment, ruling
裁断師 **saidanshi** cutter, tailor
診断 **shindan** diagnosis
診断書 **shindansho** medical certificate
間断 **kandan** interruption, pause
13 遮断 **shadan** interception, isolation, cutoff
遮断器 **shadanki** circuit breaker
遮断機 **shadanki** railroad-crossing gate
禁断 **kindan** prohibition; withdrawal (symptoms)
禁断木実 **kindan (no) ko(no)mi** forbidden fruit
聖断 **seidan** imperial decision
14 穀断 **kokuda(chi)** abstinence from grains
截断 **setsudan** cut off, sever
15 横断 **ōdan** cross, traverse
横断歩道 **ōdan hodō** pedestrian crossing
横断者 **ōdansha** street-crossing pedestrians
横断面 **ōdanmen** cross section

論断 **rondan** conclusion, verdict
16 擅断 **sendan** arbitrary decision
憶断 **okudan** conjecture, surmise, guess
縦断 **jūdan** vertical section; traverse, travel along
17 臆断 **okudan** conjecture, supposition, surmise
19 墾断 **rōdan** monopolize
22 轢断 **rekidan** (a train) running over and severing (a body)

──────── 3 ────────

3 大英断 **daieidan** bold decision
4 不決断 **fuketsudan** indecisive, vacillating, irresolute
13 夢判断 **yume handan** interpretation of dreams
14 熟慮断行 **jukuryo-dankō** deliberate and decisive

──────── 4 ────────

5 包皮切断 **hōhi setsudan** circumcision
6 早期診断 **sōki shindan** early diagnosis
7 身上判断 **mi(no)ue handan** telling a person's fortune
10 健康診断 **kenkō shindan** medical examination, physical checkup
殺生禁断 **sesshō kindan** hunting and fishing prohibited
17 優柔不断 **yūjū-fudan** indecisiveness

──────── 6 ────────

6b6.1 / 1699

粧

SHŌ adorn (one's person)

──────── 2 ────────

4 化粧 **keshō** makeup
化粧品 **keshōhin** cosmetics, makeup
9 美粧 **bishō** beautiful makeup
美粧院 **bishōin** beauty parlor, hairdresser's

──────── 3 ────────

3 夕化粧 **yūgeshō** evening makeup
8 厚化粧 **atsugeshō** heavy makeup
13 寝化粧 **negeshō** makeup/toilet before retiring
16 薄化粧 **usugeshō** light makeup

6b6.2

sukumo chaff, rice hulls

6b6.3

hekutomētoru hectometer, hundred meters

糸
→6 米
舟
虫
耳
⺮

6

粝→麪 4i17.1

6b6.5

柌 TŌ unpolished rice

6b6.6

粟 ZOKU, awa millet

——————— 1 ———————
5 粟立 awada(tsu) have gooseflesh
11 粟粒 zokuryū, awatsubu millet grain

——————— 2 ———————
20 罌粟 keshi poppy

——————— 3 ———————
17 濡手粟 nu(re)te (de) awa easy money

6b6.7

粢 SHI millet; rice cakes

6b6.8

釉 YŪ, uwagusuri glaze, enamel

——————— 1 ———————
16 釉薬 uwagusuri glaze, enamel

6b6.9 / 476

奥 奧 Ō, oku interior
oku(maru) extend far back, lie deep in

——————— 1 ———————
0 奥さん oku(san) (your) wife, married lady, ma'am
3 奥山 okuyama mountain recesses
5 奥付 okuzu(ke) colophon
6 奥印 okuin seal of approval
奥地 okuchi the interior, hinterland
奥行 okuyu(ki) depth (vs. height and width)
8 奥底 okusoko, okuzoko depths, bottom
9 奥院 oku(no)in inner sanctuary
奥庭 okuniwa inner garden, back yard
10 奥座敷 okuzashiki inner/back room
11 奥深 okubuka(i) deep, profound
奥許 okuyuru(shi) initiation into the mysteries of

12 奥御殿 okugoten inner palace
奥歯 okuba a molar, back teeth
奥間 oku(no)ma inner room
13 奥義 okugi, ōgi secrets, esoteric mysteries
14 奥様 okusama (your) wife, married lady, ma'am

——————— 2 ———————
3 大奥 ōoku inner palace; harem
山奥 yamaoku deep/back in the mountains
10 陸奥 Mutsu (ancient kuni, Aomori-ken)
胸奥 kyōō one's inmost heart
秘奥 hiō secrets, mysteries
11 深奥 shin'ō esoteric principles, mysteries, secrets

6b6.10

奥 ETSU here; alas

番→ 5f7.4

6b6.11 / 478

歯 齒 SHI, ha tooth

——————— 1 ———————
2 歯入 hai(re) repairing clogs/geta
4 歯牙 shiga teeth
歯切 hagi(re) the feel when biting; articulation hagi(ri) grinding one's teeth; file for cutting cogs
歯止 hado(me) pawl; brake
5 歯石 shiseki dental calculus, tartar
6 歯肉 haniku, shiniku the gums
歯朶 shida fern
7 歯状 shijō tooth-shaped
歯医者 haisha dentist
歯抜 hanu(ke) toothless
歯形 hagata teeth marks/impression
歯応 hagota(e) crispiness felt when sinking one's teeth into
歯車 haguruma gear, cogwheel
8 歯並 hanara(bi), hana(mi) row of teeth, dentition
歯茎 haguki the gums
歯軋 hagishi(ri) grinding one's teeth
9 歯冠 shikan crown of a tooth
歯神経 shishinkei dental nerve
歯音 shion a dental sound (t, s, etc.)
歯科 shika dentistry
歯科医 shikai dentist
10 歯根 shikon root of a tooth

6

糸
米 6←
舟
虫 耳
⺮

11 歯黒 **(o)haguro** tooth blackening
歯痒 **hagayu(i)** vexing, irritating
12 歯痛 **shitsū, haita** toothache
15 歯槽 **shisō** tooth socket
歯槽膿漏 **shisō nōrō** pyorrhea
歯質 **shishitsu** dentin
16 歯磨 **hamiga(ki)** toothpaste
歯磨粉 **hamiga(ki)ko** tooth powder
18 歯嚙 **haga(mi)** grinding one's teeth
歯髄 **shizui** pulp of a tooth
21 歯齦 **shigin** the gums
歯齦炎 **shigin'en** gingivitis

———————— 2 ————————

2 入歯 **i(re)ba** artificial tooth, dentures
3 上歯 **uwaba** upper teeth
下歯 **shitaba** lower teeth
4 切歯 **sesshi** an incisor; gnashing of teeth
切歯扼腕 **sesshi-yakuwan** gnash one's teeth and clench one's arms on the chest (in vexation)
反歯 **soppa** protruding front tooth, buckteeth
犬歯 **kenshi** canine tooth, eyetooth, cuspid
5 出歯 **deba, de(p)pa** protruding tooth, buck-teeth
平歯車 **hirahaguruma** spur gear/wheel
6 臼歯 **kyūshi, usuba** molar
仮歯 **kashi** false tooth
羊歯 **shida, yōshi** fern
羊歯類 **shidarui, yōshirui** ferns
虫歯 **mushiba** decayed tooth, cavity
7 抜歯 **basshi** extraction of a tooth
乳歯 **nyūshi** milk tooth, baby teeth
8 知歯 **chishi** wisdom tooth
金歯 **kinba** gold tooth
門歯 **monshi** incisor, front teeth
9 前歯 **maeba, zenshi** front teeth
10 高歯 **takaba** (clogs/geta with) high supports
差歯 **sa(shi)ba** clog supports; post crown, capped tooth
鬼歯 **oniba** protruding tooth
12 智歯 **chishi** wisdom tooth
皓歯 **kōshi** white/pearly teeth
奥歯 **okuba** a molar, back teeth
13 義歯 **gishi** artificial/false tooth, dentures
継歯 **tsu(gi)ha** capped tooth
14 練歯磨 **ne(ri)hamiga(ki)** toothpaste
16 鋸歯 **nokogiriba, nokoba** saw tooth
鋸歯状 **kyōshijō** sawtooth, serrated
18 鎖歯車 **kusari haguruma** sprocket wheel
24 齲歯 **ushi, mushiba** decayed tooth, caries

———————— 3 ————————

2 八重歯 **yaeba** double tooth, snaggletooth
3 大臼歯 **daikyūshi** molar
5 永久歯 **eikyūshi** permanent tooth
6 糸切歯 **itoki(ri)ba** eyetooth, canine tooth

7 乱杭歯 **ranguiba** irregular teeth
8 味噌歯 **miso(p)pa** decayed baby tooth
知恵歯 **chieba** wisdom tooth
14 総入歯 **sōi(re)ba** full set of dentures

粛→ **0a11.8**

———————— 7 ————————

6b7.1
粳 **KŌ, uruchi** nonglutinous rice

6b7.2
糀 **kōji** malt

粮→糧 **6b12.1**

6b7.3
粲 **SAN** bright, resplendent

6b7.4
粱 **RYŌ** high-quality rice

———————— 8 ————————

6b8.1 / 659
精 精 **SEI, SHŌ** spirit; energy, vitality; semen; precise; refine, polish (rice)
kuwa(shii) in detail, full

———————— 1 ————————

1 精一杯 **sei-ippai** with all one's might
2 精子 **seishi** sperm
精力 **seiryoku** energy, vigor, vitality
精力家 **seiryokuka** energetic person
3 精々 **seizei** to the utmost; at most
4 精分 **seibun** nourishment; vitality
5 精巧 **seikō** exquisite (workmanship), sophisticated (equipment)
精出 **seida(su)** work hard
精白 **seihaku** refine, polish (rice)
精白米 **seihakumai** polished rice
精白糖 **seihakutō** refined sugar
6 精気 **seiki** vitality, spirit

精肉 **seiniku** meat
精米 **seimai** polishing/polished rice
精虫 **seichū** sperm
7 精励 **seirei** diligence
精兵 **seihei, seibyō** elite troops, crack corps
精妙 **seimyō** fine, detailed, subtle
精麦 **seibaku** cleaning/cleaned wheat/barley
8 精舎 **shōja** monastery, convent
精限根限 **seikagi(ri)-konkagi(ri)** with all one's might
精油 **seiyu** refining/refined oil
精油所 **seiyusho** oil refinery
9 精美 **seibi** exquisite beauty
精通 **seitsū** be well versed in
精度 **seido** precision, accuracy
精査 **seisa** close investigation
精神 **seishin** mind, spirit
精神力 **seishinryoku** force of will
精神分析 **seishin bunseki** psychoanalysis
精神分裂症 **seishin bunretsushō** schizophrenia
精神的 **seishinteki** mental, spiritual
精神科 **seishinka** psychiatry
精神病 **seishinbyō** mental illness/disorder
10 精進 **shōjin** diligence, devotion; purification
精進日 **shōjinbi** day of abstinence (from flesh foods)
精進料理 **shōjin ryōri** vegetarian dishes
精進揚 **shōjin'a(ge)** vegetable tempura
精進落 **shōjin'o(chi)** first meat after abstinence
精華 **seika** (quint)essence
精根 **seikon** energy, vitality
精悍 **seikan** intrepid, dauntless
精粋 **seisui** exquisite
11 精液 **seieki** semen, sperm
精彩 **seisai** luster; vitality
精密 **seimitsu** precision
精巣 **seisō** spermary, testicle
精細 **seisai** detailed, precise
精粗 **seiso** fineness or coarseness
12 精勤 **seikin** diligence, good attendance
13 精義 **seigi** exact meaning; detailed exposition
精農 **seinō** hard-working farmer
14 精選 **seisen** careful/choice selection
精製 **seisei** refining; careful manufacture
精製法 **seiseihō** refining process
精製品 **seiseihin** finished goods
精製糖 **seiseitō** refined sugar
精魂 **seikon** energy, vitality
精練 **seiren** refining, smelting
精練所 **seirenjo** refinery, smelter
精精 **seizei** to the utmost; at most
精算 **seisan** exact calculation, (fare) adjustment, settling of accounts
精管 **seikan** seminal duct

精読 **seidoku** reading, carefully
精銅 **seidō** refined copper
15 精確 **seikaku** accurate, precise, exact
精鋭 **seiei** elite, crack (troops), the best
精霊 **seirei** spirit, soul
   shōryō spirit of a dead person
16 精緻 **seichi** minute, fine, subtle
精糖 **seitō** refining/refined sugar
精錬 **seiren** refining, smelting
精錬所 **seirenjo** refinery, smelter
18 精髄 **seizui** (quint)essence
22 精嚢 **seinō** seminal vesicle

---------------- 2 ----------------

4 不精 **bushō** lazy, indolent
不精髭 **bushōhige** stubbly beard
丹精 **tansei** diligence
水精 **suishō** quartz, crystal
木精 **mokusei** wood/methyl alcohol; echo
5 出精 **shussei** diligence, industriousness
7 妖精 **yōsei** fairy, sprite, elf
8 受精 **jusei** fertilization, pollination
10 射精 **shasei** ejaculation, discharge of semen
酒精 **shusei** spirits, alcohol, liquor
11 授精 **jusei** fertilization
眼精疲労 **gansei hirō** eyestrain
12 無精 **bushō** lazy
無精卵 **museiran** unfertilized egg
無精髭 **bushōhige** stubbly beard
14 遺精 **isei** involuntary emission of semen, wet dream
精精 **seizei** to the utmost; at most
16 輸精管 **yuseikan** spermaduct

---------------- 3 ----------------

5 出不精 **debushō** stay-at-home
6 気無精 **kibushō** laziness
12 無酒精 **mushusei** nonalcoholic
筆不精 **fudebushō** negligent in corresponding

---------------- 4 ----------------

6 自家受精 **jika jusei** self-fertilization
11 異花受精 **ika jusei** cross-pollination

6b8.2

粽 **SŌ, chimaki** rice dumplings steamed in bamboo leaves

粹 → 粋   **6b4.5**

---------------- 9 ----------------

6b9.1

糂 **JIN** mixing rice into soup

6

糸
米 9←
舟
虫
耳
⺮

6b9.2

糊 **KO, nori** paste, glue; starch, sizing

———— 1 ————

3 糊口 **kokō** (eke out a) livelihood
5 糊付 **noritsu(ke)** starching; pasting
13 糊塗 **koto** patch up, temporize

———— 2 ————

6 血糊 **chinori** gore, clotted blood
14 模糊 **moko** dim, faint, indistinct

6b9.3

糅 **JŪ** mix

———— 1 ————

5 糅加 **ka(tete) kuwa(ete)** besides, to make matters worse

6b9.4

糎 **senchimētoru** centimeter

麹→麴 6b13.1

———— 10 ————

糢→模 4a10.16

6b10.1

糒 **BI, hoshii** dried boiled rice

6b10.2

糘 **sukumo** chaff, rice hulls

6b10.3 / 1698

糖 **TŌ** sugar

———— 1 ————

4 糖化 **tōka** convert to sugar
糖分 **tōbun** sugar content
6 糖衣 **tōi** sugar coating

糖衣錠 **tōijō** sugar-coated pill
7 糖尿病 **tōnyōbyō** diabetes
11 糖菓 **tōka** candy, sweets
13 糖業 **tōgyō** the sugar industry
14 糖蜜 **tōmitsu** molasses, syrup
15 糖質 **tōshitsu** sugariness
18 糖類 **tōrui** sugars

———— 2 ————

6 血糖 **kettō** blood sugar
血糖値 **kettōchi** blood-sugar level
7 乳糖 **nyūtō** milk sugar, lactose
8 果糖 **katō** fruit sugar, fructose
9 砂糖 **satō** sugar
砂糖大根 **satō daikon** sugar beet
砂糖煮 **satōni** preserved by boiling with sugar, candied
砂糖黍 **satō kibi** sugar cane
11 粗糖 **sotō** raw sugar
12 検糖計 **kentōkei** saccarimeter
無糖 **mutō** sugar-free, unsweetened
14 製糖 **seitō** sugar refining
製糖所 **seitōjo** sugar refinery
製糖業 **seitōgyō** the sugar industry
精糖 **seitō** refining/refined sugar

———— 3 ————

5 甘蔗糖 **kanshotō** cane sugar, sucrose
氷砂糖 **kōrizatō** rock candy, crystal sugar
白砂糖 **shirozatō** white sugar
7 角砂糖 **kakuzatō** sugar cubes
赤砂糖 **akazatō** brown sugar
麦芽糖 **bakugatō** malt sugar, maltose
8 金米糖 **konpeitō** confetti (a candy)
11 甜菜糖 **tensaitō** beet sugar
黒砂糖 **kurozatō** unrefined/brown sugar
転化糖 **tenkatō** inverted sugar
12 葡萄糖 **budōtō** grape sugar, dextrose, glucose
14 精白糖 **seihakutō** refined sugar
精製糖 **seiseitō** refined sugar
16 薄荷糖 **hakkatō** peppermint

彝→彝 6b12.2

———— 11 ————

6b11.1

糟 **SŌ, kasu** saké lees, dregs, dross

———— 1 ————

8 糟取 **kasuto(ri)** low-grade (liquor)
11 糟粕 **sōhaku** lees, dregs
17 糟糠 **sōkō** saké lees and rice bran; plain food
糟糠妻 **sōkō (no) tsuma** wife married in poverty

6

糸
→ 9 米
舟
虫
耳
竹

—————— 2 ——————

8 油糟 **aburakasu** oil cake, the soybean waste after the oil is pressed out

6b11.2

糠   **KŌ, nuka** rice bran

—————— 1 ——————

8 糠油 **nukaabura** rice-bran oil
糠味噌 **nuka miso** rice-bran miso
糠味噌漬 **nukamisozu(ke)** vegetables pickled in rice-bran miso
糠雨 **nukaame** drizzle
12 糠喜 **nukayoroko(bi)** premature rejoicing
13 糠働 **nukabatara(ki)** fruitless effort

—————— 2 ——————

3 小糠雨 **konukaame** fine/drizzling rain
10 枇糠 **hikō** immature ears and bran; useless
17 糟糠 **sōkō** saké lees and rice bran; plain food
糟糠妻 **sōkō (no) tsuma** wife married in poverty

6b11.3

糞   **FUN** excrement, droppings
          kuso shit

—————— 1 ——————

2 糞力 **kusojikara** brute force, great strength
3 糞土 **fundo** black earth; dirt, filth
7 糞尿 **funnyō** feces and urine, excreta
8 糞垂 **kusota(re), kuso(t)ta(re)** (shit-dripping) son-of-a-bitch
糞味噌 **kuso-miso** (confusing) the valuable and the worthless; sweeping denunciation
9 糞便 **funben** excrement, night soil
糞度胸 **kusodokyō** reckless bravery
10 糞真面目 **kusomajime** humorless earnestness
糞勉強 **kusobenkyō** cramming
12 糞落着 **kusoo(chi)tsu(ki)** provokingly calm
13 糞詰 **funzu(mari)** constipation
15 糞縄 **kusobae** bottle-green fly

—————— 2 ——————

2 人糞 **jinpun** human feces, night soil
5 目糞 **mekuso** eye wax/discharge/mucus
10 馬糞 **bafun, maguso** horse manure
馬糞紙 **bafunshi** cardboard, strawboard
11 猫糞 **nekobaba** appropriate/pocket (a found article) as one's own
14 鼻糞 **hanakuso** snot, booger

6b11.4

麋   **BI** reindeer

6b11.5 / 833

齢 齡   **REI, yowai** age

—————— 2 ——————

4 月齢 **getsurei** number of days since the new moon; (infant's) age in months
5 幼齢 **yōrei** young age
6 年齢 **nenrei** age
壮齢 **sōrei** prime of life
老齢 **rōrei** old age
老齢艦 **rōreikan** old warship
7 寿齢 **jurei** long life
余齢 **yorei** one's remaining years
妙齢 **myōrei** youth
学齢 **gakurei** school age
10 高齢 **kōrei** advanced age
高齢者 **kōreisha** elderly person
弱齢 **jakurei** youth
馬齢 **barei** one's age
11 船齢 **senrei** the age of a vessel
13 適齢 **tekirei** the right age
適齢期 **tekireiki** marriageable age
16 樹齢 **jurei** age of a tree
21 艦齢 **kanrei** age of a warship

6b11.6

鞠   **KIKU** nurture, raise; to bend, bow
          mari ball

—————— 1 ——————

10 鞠躬如 **kikkyūjo** (bowing) respectfully
13 鞠靴 **marigutsu** football shoes

—————— 2 ——————

4 手鞠 **temari** (traditional cloth) handball
19 蹴鞠 **kemari** football (historical)

6b11.7

糝   **SHIN, SAN** grains of rice

—————— 1 ——————

10 糝粉 **shinko** rice flour; rice-flour dough

—————— 12 ——————

6b12.1 / 1704

糧 粮   **RYŌ, RŌ, kate** food, provisions

—————— 1 ——————

9 糧食 **ryōshoku** provisions, food
10 糧秣 **ryōmatsu** provisions and fodder

6

糸
米   12←
舟
虫
耳
⺮

11 糧道 **ryōdō** supply of provisions

――――― 2 ―――――

3 口糧 **kōryō** rations
6 衣糧 **iryō** food and clothing
7 兵糧 **hyōrō** provisions, victuals
9 食糧 **shokuryō** food
10 馬糧 **baryō** fodder

6b12.2

彝 彝

I, kanae (type of religious paraphernalia)
tsune unchanging way, law

6b12.3 / 596

翻 飜

HON, hirugae(su) (tr.) turn over; change (one's opinion); wave (a flag)
hirugae(ru) (intr.) turn over; wave, flutter **kobo(su)** overturn, spill

――――― 1 ―――――

7 翻弄 **honrō** trifle with, make sport of
8 翻刻 **honkoku** reprint
10 翻案 **hon'an** an adaptation
11 翻訳 **hon'yaku** translation
翻訳者 **hon'yakusha** translator
翻訳家 **hon'yakuka** translator
翻訳書 **hon'yakusho** a translation
翻訳権 **hon'yakuken** translation rights
12 翻然 **honzen** all of a sudden
13 翻意 **hon'i** change one's mind

――――― 2 ―――――

4 水翻 **mizukobo(shi)** slop basin
15 飜翻 **henpon** fluttering

――――― 13 ―――――

6b13.1

麹 麴

KIKU, kōji malt, yeast

――――― 14 ―――――

釋 → 釈 **6b5.5**

6b14.1

糯

DA, mochigome glutinous rice for making mochi

6b14.2

糲

REI unpolished rice

――――― 2 ―――――

12 斑糲岩 **hanreigan** gabbro

――――― 15 ―――――

飜 → 翻 **6b12.3**

――――― 16 ―――――

6b16.1

鬻

IKU, hisa(gu) sell

――――― 18 ―――――

6b18.1

麟

RIN Chinese-mythological beast associated with wise rule; genius; giraffe; bright, shining

――――― 2 ―――――

19 麒麟 **kirin** giraffe

――――― 舟 **6c** ―――――

舟	舡	舫	航	舩	般	舻	舳	舶	舵	船	舷	舸
0.1	3.1	4.1	4.2	6c5.4	4.3	6c16.1	5.1	5.2	5.3	5.4	5.5	5.6

艀	艇	艘	艙	艝	艚	艟	艢	艨	艤	艪	艦	艫
6.1	6.2	9.1	10.1	11.1	11.2	12.1	4a13.4	13.1	13.2	15.1	15.2	16.1

――――― 0 ―――――

6c0.1 / 1094

舟 舟

SHŪ, fune, funa- boat

――――― 1 ―――――

2 舟人 **funabito** boatman, sailor; passenger
6 舟行 **shūkō** sailing
7 舟足 **funaashi** draft; speed
10 舟遊 **funaaso(bi), shūyū** boating

舟航 **shūkō** sailing, voyage
11 舟運 **shuun** transport by ship
12 舟艇 **shūtei** boat, craft
14 舟歌 **funauta** sailor's song, chantey

─────────── 2 ───────────

4 方舟 **hakobune** (Noah's) ark
6 同舟 **dōshū** in/on the same boat
8 孤舟 **koshū** a single/solitary boat
　 宝舟 **takarabune** (picture of a) treasure ship
9 扁舟 **henshū** small boat, skiff
10 舫舟 **moya(i)bune** moored boat
11 笹舟 **sasabune** toy bamboo-leaf boat
12 渡舟 **wata(shi)bune** ferryboat
　 貸舟 **ka(shi)bune** boat for rent
　 軽舟 **keishū** fast ligh boat, skiff
13 鉄舟 **tesshū** steel boat/pontoon
15 箱舟 **hakobune** (Noah's) ark

─────────── 3 ───────────

3 丸木舟 **marukibune** dugout canoe
10 高瀬舟 **takasebune** flatboat, riverboat

─────────── 4 ───────────

7 呉越同舟 **Go-Etsu dōshū** enemies in the same boat

─────────── 3 ───────────

6c3.1

舡

KŌ boat

─────────── 4 ───────────

6c4.1

舫

HŌ, moya(u) moor, berth

─────────── 1 ───────────

6 舫舟 **moya(i)bune** moored boat
11 舫船 **moya(i)bune** moored ship
14 舫綱 **moya(i)zuna** mooring rope/line, hawser

6c4.2 / 823

航

KŌ navigation

─────────── 1 ───────────

6 航行 **kōkō** navigation, sailing
8 航送 **kōsō** ship (by ship/plane)
　 航空 **kōkū** aviation, flight, aero-
　 航空士 **kōkūshi** aviator
　 航空母艦 **kōkū bokan** aircraft carrier
　 航空写真 **kōkū shashin** aerial photo
　 航空会社 **kōkū-gaisha** airline (company)
　 航空学 **kōkūgaku** aeronautics

航空券 **kōkūken** flight/airplane ticket
航空便 **kōkūbin** airmail
航空家 **kōkūka** aviator
航空病 **kōkūbyō** airsickness
航空隊 **kōkūtai** air force
航空基地 **kōkū kichi** air base
航空術 **kōkūjutsu** aeronautics, aviation
航空船 **kōkūsen** airship, dirigible, blimp
航空路 **kōkūro** air route
航空機 **kōkūki** aircraft, airplane
9 航海 **kōkai** voyage, ocean navigation
　 航海日誌 **kōkai nisshi** ship's log
　 航海者 **kōkaisha** mariner, seaman
　 航海術 **kōkaijutsu** seamanship, navigation
12 航程 **kōtei** distance covered, flight
13 航続力 **kōzokuryoku** cruising/flying range
　 航続距離 **kōzoku kyori** (plane's) range
　 航路 **kōro** (sea) route, course
　 航路標識 **kōro hyōshiki** navigation marker/beacon
　 航跡 **kōseki** wake (of a ship/plane)

─────────── 2 ───────────

4 日航機 **Nikkōki** JAL (Japan Air Lines) plane
欠航 **kekkō** suspension of (ferry) service
5 出航 **shukkō** departure, sailing
巡航 **junkō** cruise
巡航船 **junkōsen** cruiser
6 曳航 **eikō** tow (a ship)
休航 **kyūkō** suspension of ship or airline service
回航 **kaikō** navigation, cruise
舟航 **shūkō** sailing, voyage
7 来航 **raikō** arrival of ships; arrival by ship
初航海 **hatsukōkai** maiden voyage
8 直航 **chokkō** nonstop flight, direct voyage
周航 **shūkō** circumnavigation
往航 **ōkō** outward voyage
9 発航 **hakkō** departure, sailing
南航 **nankō** sail south
通航 **tsūkō** navigate, sail, ply
10 帰航 **kikō** homeward trip/voyage
進航 **shinkō** proceed, sail on
11 運航 **unkō** operate, run (planes, ships)
密航 **mikkō** steal passage, stow away
密航者 **mikkōsha** stowaway
終航 **shūkō** last voyage/flight
12 渡航 **tokō** voyage, passage, sailing, flight
渡航者 **tokōsha** foreign visitor, passenger
就航 **shūkō** be commissioned (a ship)
復航 **fukkō** return voyage/flight
13 溯航 **sokō** go upstream, sail upriver
続航 **zokkō** continue the voyage, hold to one's course
15 潜航 **senkō** cruise underwater, be submerged
潜航艇 **senkōtei** a submarine

─────────────

糸
米
舟　4 ←
虫
耳
竹

18 難航 **nankō** stormy passage, rough going

————— 3 —————

3 大圏航路 **taiken kōro** great-circle route
5 処女航海 **shojo kōkai** maiden voyage

————— 4 —————

9 海外渡航 **kaigai tokō** foreign travel

舩 → 船 6c5.4

6c4.3 / 1096

舩

HAN carry; all, general

————— 2 —————

1 一般 **ippan** general
一般人 **ippannin, ippanjin** an ordinary person
一般化 **ippanka** generalization, popularization
一般的 **ippanteki** general
一般性 **ippansei** generality
3 万般 **banpan** all, every(thing)
6 全般 **zenpan** whole, general, overall
全般的 **zenpanteki** general, overall, across-the-board
先般 **senpan** the other day; some time ago
百般 **hyappan** every kind of, all
各般 **kakuhan** all, every, various
11 過般 **kahan** some time ago, recently
過般来 **kahanrai** for some time
15 諸般 **shohan** various, every

舮 → 艫 6c16.1

————— 5 —————

6c5.1

舳

JIKU, he bow, prow; oar

————— 1 —————

6 舳先 **hesaki** bow, prow

6c5.2 / 1095

舶

HAKU ship

————— 1 —————

5 舶用 **hakuyō** for ships, marine
7 舶来 **hakurai** imported

舶来品 **hakuraihin** imported goods
13 舶載 **hakusai** transport by ship

————— 2 —————

11 船舶 **senpaku** ship, vessel; shipping
船舶法 **senpakuhō** shipping law
船舶業 **senpakugyō** shipping industry

6c5.3

舵

DA, kaji rudder, helm

————— 1 —————

4 舵手 **dashu** helmsman, coxswain
8 舵取 **kajito(ri)** steering; helmsman; guidance; leader
16 舵機 **daki** steering gear, rudder

————— 2 —————

8 取舵 **to(ri)kaji** port (to helm)
9 面舵 **omokaji** turning to starboard
16 操舵 **sōda** steering (of a ship)
操舵手 **sōdashu** helmsman
操舵室 **sōdashitsu** pilothouse

6c5.4 / 376

船 舩

SEN, fune, funa- ship

————— 1 —————

2 船人 **funabito** seaman; passenger
3 船大工 **funadaiku** boatbuilder, shipwright
船小屋 **funagoya** boathouse
4 船中 **senchū** in/aboard the ship
船火事 **funakaji** a fire aboard ship
船方 **funakata** boatman
5 船出 **funade** set sail, put to sea
船外機 **sengaiki** outboard motor
船号 **sengō** ship's name
船台 **sendai** shipbuilding berth
船主 **senshu, funanushi** shipowner
6 船匠 **senshō** shipwright
船守 **funamori** boat watchman
船団 **sendan** fleet, convoy
船成金 **funanarikin** shipping magnate
船虫 **funamushi** sea louse
7 船体 **sentai** hull, ship
船医 **sen'i** ship's doctor
船床 **funadoko** boat's floorboards
船尾 **senbi** the stern, aft
船足 **funaashi** draft; speed
8 船長 **senchō** (ship's) captain
船底 **funazoko, sentei** ship's bottom
船板 **funaita** ship plank/timber
船板塀 **funaitabei** fence made of old ship timbers

船房 **senbō** cabin, stateroom
船具 **funagu, sengu** ship's rigging
9 船乗 **funano(ri)** seaman, sailor
船便 **funabin** sea mail; ship transportation
船首 **senshu** bow, prow
船型 **senkei** type of vessel; model of a ship
船待 **funama(chi)** waiting for a ship
船客 **senkyaku** (ship) passenger
船室 **senshitsu** cabin, stateroom
船幽霊 **funayūrei** a sea spirit
船級 **senkyū** (ship's) classification
10 船倉 **sensō** (ship's) hold, hatch
船遊 **funaaso(bi)** boating
船員 **sen'in** crewman, seaman
船荷 **funani** (ship's) cargo
船荷証券 **funani shōken** bill of lading
船骨 **senkotsu** ribs of a ship
船旅 **funatabi** voyage
11 船側 **sensoku** side of a ship
船側渡 **sensoku-wata(shi)** Free Alongside Ship, ex-ship
船隊 **sentai** fleet
船宿 **funayado** shipping agent; boathouse keeper
船窓 **sensō, funamado** porthole
船梯子 **funabashigo** gangway
船舶 **senpaku** ship, vessel; shipping
船舶法 **senpakuhō** shipping law
船舶業 **senpakugyō** shipping industry
船酔 **funayo(i)** seasickness
船問屋 **funadon'ya** shipping agent
12 船着場 **funatsu(ki)ba** harbor, wharf
船渡 **funawata(shi)** ferry; F.O.B.
船幅 **senpuku** (ship's) beam
船渠 **senkyo** dock
13 船腹 **senpuku** bottoms, cargo space
船賃 **funachin** boat fare; shipping charges
船路 **senro, funaji** course, sea route
14 船歌 **funauta** sailor's song, chantey
船端 **funabata** ship's side, gunwale
15 船影 **sen'ei** signs/sight of a ship
船縁 **funaberi** ship's side, gunwale
船霊 **funadama** ship's guardian deity
16 船橋 **funabashi, senkyō** pontoon bridge; **Funabashi** (city, Chiba-ken)
船積 **funazu(mi)** shipment, lading
17 船齢 **senrei** the age of a vessel
19 船繰 **funaku(ri), funagu(ri)** shipping schedule
20 船籍 **senseki** ship's registry/nationality
船籍港 **sensekikō** ship's port of registry

───────── 2 ─────────

3 大船 **ōbune** big ship
下船 **gesen** disembark, go ashore
小船 **kobune** boat, small craft

4 水船 **mizubune** cistern, water trough; water-supply boat; swamped boat
引船 **hi(ki)bune** tugboat
木船 **mokusen** wooden ship
5 出船 **defune, debune** setting sail; outgoing ship
母船 **bosen** mother ship
外船 **gaisen** foreign ship
用船 **yōsen** chartered ship; chartering a ship
巨船 **kyosen** huge ship
6 曳船 **hikifune, hikibune, eisen** tugboat
全船 **zensen** the whole ship, all the ships
同船 **dōsen** (take) the same ship
帆船 **hansen, hobune** sailing ship, sailboat
回船 **kaisen** barge, cargo vessel
7 助船 **tasu(ke)bune** lifeboat
汽船 **kisen** steamship, steamer
8 泊船 **hakusen** anchoring, berthing
宝船 **takarabune** (picture of a) treasure ship
官船 **kansen** government ship
和船 **wasen** Japanese-style (wooden) ship
9 乗船 **jōsen** get on board, embark
便船 **binsen** available ship
係船 **keisen** mooring, berthing
軍船 **gunsen** warship
南船北馬 **nansen-hokuba** constant traveling, restless wandering
造船 **zōsen** shipbuilding
造船所 **zōsenjo** shipyard
造船業 **zōsengyō** shipbuilding industry
風船 **fūsen** balloon
客船 **kyakusen** passenger ship/boat
砂船 **sunabune** dredging boat
10 郵船 **yūsen** mail boat
帰船 **kisen** return to one's ship
遊船 **yūsen** pleasure boat, yacht
遊船宿 **yūsen'yado** boathouse
荷船 **nibune** freighter; lighter, barge
唐船 **karafune, tōsen** Chinese/foreign ship
破船 **hasen** shipwreck
舫船 **moya(i)bune** moored ship
配船 **haisen** assignment of ships
11 停船 **teisen** stopping (a ship), heave to, quarantine
商船 **shōsen** merchant ship
商船隊 **shōsentai** merchant fleet
商船旗 **shōsenki** merchant flag
脱船 **dassen** desert/jump ship
黒船 **kurofune** the black ships (historical)
救船 **suku(i)bune** rescue ship, lifeboat
12 着船 **chakusen** arrival (of a ship)
湯船 **yubune** bathtub
渡船 **wata(shi)bune, tosen** ferry
渡船場 **tosenba, tosenjō** ferrying place
渡船賃 **tosenchin** ferry charge
廃船 **haisen** scrapped vessel

6

糸
米
舟 5←
虫
耳
⺮

13 傭船 **yōsen** chartered ship; chartering a vessel
鉄船 **tessen** steel ship, an ironclad
14 漁船 **gyosen, ryōsen** fishing boat/vessel
漕船 **ko(gi)bune** rowboat
15 敵船 **tekisen** enemy ship
16 親船 **oyabune** mother ship
18 難船 **nansen** shipwreck, ship in distress
19 繋船 **keisen** mooring
21 艦船 **kansen** warships and other vessels

─────────── 3 ───────────

3 丸木船 **marukibune** dugout canoe
千石船 **sengokubune** large junk (Edo period)
5 平底船 **hirazokobune** flat-bottomed boat
外国船 **gaikokusen** foreign ship
外輪船 **gairinsen** paddlewheel steamer
巡航船 **junkōsen** cruiser
石炭船 **sekitansen** coal ship
6 朱印船 **shuinsen, shuinbune** shogunate-
licensed trading ship
伝馬船 **tenmasen** a lighter, jolly (boat)
帆前船 **homaesen** sailing vessel
帆掛船 **hoka(ke)bune** sailboat
宇宙船 **uchūsen** spaceship
7 冷凍船 **reitōsen** refrigerator ship
沈没船 **chinbotsusen** sunken ship
抑留船 **yokuryūsen** detained/interned ship
社外船 **shagaisen** tramp steamer/vessel
快速船 **kaisokusen** high-speed ship
8 油送船 **yusōsen** oil tanker
油槽船 **yusōsen** oil tanker
定期船 **teikisen** regular(ly scheduled) ship
9 飛行船 **hikōsen** airship, dirigible, blimp
連絡船 **renrakusen** ferryboat
幽霊船 **yūreisen** phantom ship
屋形船 **yakatabune** houseboat, barge,
pleasure boat
砕氷船 **saihyōsen** icebreaker
10 郵便船 **yūbinsen** mail boat
遊覧船 **yūransen** excursion boat
浚渫船 **shunsetsusen** dredger
捕鯨船 **hogeisen** whaling ship
荷足船 **nita(ri)bune** barge, lighter
病院船 **byōinsen** hospital ship
航空船 **kōkūsen** airship, dirigible, blimp
11 運送船 **unsōsen** cargo vessel, freighter
密輸船 **mitsuyusen** smuggling vessel
救助船 **kyūjosen** rescue ship, lifeboat
貨物船 **kamotsusen** freighter
貨客船 **kakyakusen, kakakusen** cargo-and-
passenger ship
12 測量船 **sokuryōsen** surveying ship
蒸気船 **jōkisen** steamship, steamer
給油船 **kyūyusen** oil tanker
14 漂流船 **hyōryūsen** drifting ship, a derelict
15 監視船 **kanshisen** guard boat, cutter

16 機帆船 **kihansen** motor-powered sailing
vessel
輸送船 **yusōsen** transport ship
18 観光船 **kankōsen** excursion ship
難波船 **nanpasen** shipwreck
難破船 **nanpasen** shipwreck
19 蟹工船 **kanikōsen** crab-canning ship
20 護送船 **gosōsen** convoy

─────────── 4 ───────────

5 白河夜船 **Shirakawa yofune** fast asleep
12 御朱印船 **goshuinsen** shogunate-licensed
trading ship

─────────── 5 ───────────

11 軟式飛行船 **nanshiki hikōsen** dirigible,
balloon

6c5.5

舷　　　GEN, **funabata** ship's side, gunwale

─────────── 1 ───────────

6 舷灯 **gentō** running lights
8 舷門 **genmon** gangway
11 舷側 **gensoku** ship's side, broadside
舷窓 **gensō** porthole
舷梯 **gentei** gangway (ladder)

─────────── 2 ───────────

5 左舷 **sagen** port (not starboard)
右舷 **ugen** starboard
12 登舷礼 **tōgenrei** full crew's salute from the
deck

6c5.6

舸　　　KA ship

─────────── 6 ───────────

6c6.1

艀　　　FU, **hashike** lighter

6c6.2 / 1666

艇　　　TEI small boat

─────────── 1 ───────────

7 艇身 **teishin** boat length
8 艇長 **teichō** coxswain; skipper
9 艇首 **teishu** the bow (of a boat)
10 艇員 **teiin** (boat's) crew
11 艇隊 **teitai** flotilla

2
3 小艇 **shōtei** small boat
6 舟艇 **shūtei** boat, craft
7 汽艇 **kitei** (steam) launch
12 短艇 **tantei** boat, lifeboat
14 漕艇 **sōtei** rowing, boating
端艇 **tantei** boat, lighter
20 競艇 **kyōtei** boat race/racing
21 艦艇 **kantei** naval vessels

3
4 水雷艇 **suiraitei** torpedo boat
5 巡視艇 **junshitei** patrol boat
9 飛行艇 **hikōtei** flying boat, seaplane
11 掃海艇 **sōkaitei** minesweeper
救命艇 **kyūmeitei** lifeboat
魚雷艇 **gyoraitei** torpedo boat
14 駆潜艇 **kusentei** submarine chaser
15 潜航艇 **senkōtei** a submarine

9
6c9.1
艘 SŌ, SHŌ (counter for) ships
2
1 一艘 **issō** a ship/vessel

10
6c10.1
艙 SŌ (ship's) hold
1
3 艙口 **sōkō** hatch, hatchway

11
6c11.1
艝 **sori** sled, sleigh
6c11.2
艪 SŌ boat

12
6c12.1
艟 DŌ warship
2
19 艨艟 **mōdō** warship, man-of-war

13
艣 → 櫓 4a13.4

6c13.1
艨 MŌ warship
1
18 艨艟 **mōdō** warship, man-of-war

6c13.2
艤 GI outfitting a ship
1
12 艤装 **gisō** fitting out a ship, rigging

15
6c15.1
艪 RO oar

6c15.2 / 1665
艦 KAN warship
1
3 艦上 **kanjō** aboard (a warship)
6 艦列 **kanretsu** column of warships
7 艦体 **kantai** the hull (of a warship)
艦尾 **kanbi** stern, aft (of a warship)
8 艦長 **kanchō** the captain (of a warship)
9 艦首 **kanshu** the bow (of a warship)
10 艦砲 **kanpō** ship's guns
艦砲射撃 **kanpō shageki** shelling from a naval vessel
11 艦隊 **kantai** fleet, squadron
艦船 **kansen** warships and other vessels
12 艦艇 **kantei** naval vessels
13 艦載 **kansai** carried aboard a warship
艦載機 **kansaiki** carrier-based plane
14 艦種 **kanshu** class of warship
16 艦橋 **kankyō** the bridge (of a warship)
17 艦齢 **kanrei** age of a warship
2
3 大艦 **taikan** large warship
5 母艦 **bokan** mother ship, tender
巨艦 **kyokan** large warship
6 米艦 **beikan** U.S. warship

6
糸
米
舟 15←
虫
耳
⺮

8 建艦 **kenkan** naval construction	
9 軍艦 **gunkan** warship, battleship	
造艦 **zōkan** naval construction	
10 帰艦 **kikan** return to one's warship	
11 脱艦 **dakkan** desertion from a warship	
12 満艦飾 **mankanshoku** full dress, all decked out	
13 戦艦 **senkan** battleship	
鉄艦 **tekkan** ironclad warship	
14 僚艦 **ryōkan** consort ship	
旗艦 **kikan** flagship	
製艦 **seikan** building warships, naval construction	
15 敵艦 **tekikan** enemy ship	
敵艦隊 **teki kantai** enemy fleet	
18 観艦式 **kankanshiki** naval review	

--------------------------- 3 ---------------------------

5 巡洋艦 **jun'yōkan** cruiser
6 老齢艦 **rōreikan** old warship
8 弩弓艦 **dokyūkan** dreadnaught
13 戦闘艦 **sentōkan** battleship
14 駆逐艦 **kuchikukan** destroyer
15 潜水艦 **sensuikan** a submarine
19 警備艦 **keibikan** guard ship

--------------------------- 4 ---------------------------

10 航空母艦 **kōkū bokan** aircraft carrier
15 潜水母艦 **sensui bokan** submarine tender

--------------------------- 16 ---------------------------

6c16.1

艫 舮

RO bow; stern
tomo stern

--------------------------- 虫 6d ---------------------------

虫	虱	虹	虻	蚌	蚋	蚪	蚓	蚊	蚣	蚤	蚕	蚩
0.1	2.1	3.1	3.2	4.1	4.2	4.3	4.4	4.5	4.6	4.7	4.8	4.9
蚜	蚰	蚶	蚵	蛆	蚯	蚫	蛇	蛉	蛄	蛄	蛎	蛋
5.1	5.2	5.3	5.4	5.5	5.6	11a5.4	5.7	5.8	5.9	5.10	6d14.3	5.11
蛍	蛛	蛤	蛒	蛙	蛭	蛞	蛤	蛟	蛔	蜒	蜓	蛮
3n8.2	6.1	6.2	6.3	6.4	6.5	6.6	6.7	6.8	6.9	6.10	6.11	6.12
蜚	蛮	蟒	颪	蛾	蜈	蜊	蜆	蛸	蜂	蜍	蛻	蛹
3k9.27	2j10.1	6.13	6.14	7.1	7.2	7.3	7.4	7.5	7.6	7.7	7.8	7.9
触	蜃	蝿	蜱	蜘	蜥	蝣	蜷	蝎	蜻	蜿	蝋	蜩
7.10	7.11	6d13.1	8.1	8.2	8.3	8.4	8.5	8.6	8.7	8.8	6d15.1	8.9
蜚	颮	蜋	蝌	蝴	蝦	蝟	蝮	蝶	蝗	蝪	蝎	蝸
8.10	8.11	9.1	9.2	9.3	9.4	9.5	9.6	9.7	9.8	9.9	9.10	9.11
蝠	蝉	蟒	蝓	蝙	蟲	蝗	蝾	蟆	蟒	蜈	融	螢
9.12	6d12.3	6d10.3	9.13	9.14	6d2.1	10.1	10.2	3k13.23	10.3	10.4	10.5	3n8.2
螻	蟋	螺	螳	螭	蟒	蟀	蟄	螯	鰲	螽	颺	蟖
11.1	11.2	11.3	6d13.3	11.4	6d10.3	11.5	11.6	11.7	11.8	4i14.1	11.9	12.1
蟠	蟬	蟯	蟲	蠅	蟹	蠍	蟶	蟷	蠖	蟾	蟻	蟹
12.2	12.3	12.4	6d0.1	13.1	6d13.7	6d9.10	13.2	13.3	13.4	13.5	13.6	13.7
蠕	蠑	蠣	觸	飄	颺	蠟	蠢	蠡	飆	蠱	蠋	蠶
14.1	14.2	14.3	6d7.10	14.4	6d14.4	15.1	15.2	15.3	15.4	17.1	17.2	18.1
蠹	蠻	蠶										
3p19.1	2j10.1	6d4.8										

--------------------------- 0 ---------------------------

6d0.1 / 873

虫 蟲

CHŪ, mushi bug, insect

--------------------------- 1 ---------------------------

3 虫干 **mushibo(shi)** airing out (clothes)
虫下 **mushikuda(shi)** medicine for intestinal worms
6 虫気 **mushike** bowel complaint, nervous weakness

7 虫売 **mushiu(ri)** insect peddler
8 虫垂 **chūsui** the (vermiform) appendix
虫垂炎 **chūsuien** appendicitis
虫送 **mushioku(ri)** torch procession to drive away insects
虫押 **mushiosa(e)** medicine for children's irritability
9 虫除 **mushiyo(ke)** insect repellent, charm against insects
虫封 **mushifū(ji)** incantation to prevent intestinal worms in a child
虫食 **mushiku(i)** damage from worms, moth-eaten spot
10 虫害 **chūgai** damage from insects
虫息 **mushi (no) iki** faint breathing, almost dead
11 虫眼鏡 **mushimegane** magnifying glass
12 虫喰 **mushiku(i)** damage from worms, moth-eaten spot
虫媒花 **chūbaika** insect-pollinated flower
虫歯 **mushiba** decayed tooth, cavity
13 虫腹 **mushibara** pain from roundworms
14 虫様突起 **chūyō tokki** the (vermiform) appendix
虫様突起炎 **chūyō tokkien** appendicitis
16 虫薬 **mushigusuri** medicine for intestinal worms
17 虫螻 **mushikera** worm, insect
18 虫類 **chūrui** insects and worms
22 虫籠 **mushikago** insect cage

──── 2 ────

4 毛虫 **kemushi** caterpillar
水虫 **mizumushi** athlete's foot
5 甲虫 **kabutomushi, kōchū** beetle
幼虫 **yōchū** larva
玉虫 **tamamushi** iridescent-winged insect
玉虫色 **tamamushi-iro** iridescent; ambiguous
田虫 **tamushi** ringworm
6 防虫剤 **bōchūzai** insecticide
地虫 **jimushi** grub, ground beetle
回虫 **kaichū** intestinal worm, roundworm
成虫 **seichū** adult insect
米虫 **kome (no) mushi** rice weevil
8 爬虫類 **hachūrui** reptiles
毒虫 **dokumushi** poisonous insect
泣虫 **na(ki)mushi** crybaby
油虫 **aburamushi** aphid; cockroach
苦虫 **nigamushi** (looking as if having bit into) a bitter-tasting bug
松虫 **matsumushi** (a kind of cricket)
青虫 **aomushi** green caterpillar, grub
昆虫 **konchū** insect
昆虫学 **konchūgaku** entomology
9 除虫菊 **jochūgiku** Dalmatian pyrethrum
挟虫 **hasa(mi)mushi** earwig

秋虫 **akimushi** insects heard in autumn
食虫 **shokuchū** insectivore
10 恙虫病 **tsutsugamushibyō** scrub typhus
益虫 **ekichū** beneficial insect
原虫 **genchū** a protozoan
弱虫 **yowamushi** weakling, coward, sissy
害虫 **gaichū** harmful insect, pest
殺虫剤 **satchūzai** insecticide
病虫害 **byōchūgai** damage from blight and insects
11 船虫 **funamushi** sea louse
蚜虫 **aburamushi** plant louse, aphid
蛆虫 **ujimushi** maggot
12 象虫 **zōmushi** weevil, snout beetle
兜虫 **kabutomushi** beetle
蛔虫 **kaichū** intestinal worms
13 條虫 **jōchū** tapeworm
腹虫 **hara (no) mushi** intestinal worms; one's heart, anger
裸虫 **hadakamushi** caterpillar
蛹虫 **yōchū** chrysalis, pupa
鉤虫 **kōchū** hookworm
14 精虫 **seichū** sperm
駆虫剤 **kuchūzai** vermicide, insect repellent
駆虫薬 **kuchūyaku** vermicide, insect repellent
15 線虫 **senchū** eelworm, nematode
線虫学 **senchūgaku** nematology
線虫類 **senchūrui** nematodes
蝗虫 **batta** grasshopper, locust
16 螟虫 **meichū** rice stem borer
17 瓢虫 **tentōmushi** ladybug, ladybird beetle
18 蟯虫 **gyōchū** threadworms, pinworms

──── 3 ────

4 天道虫 **tentōmushi** ladybug, ladybird beetle
尺取虫 **shakuto(ri)mushi** inchworm
木食虫 **kiku(i)mushi** wood borer
5 本食虫 **honku(i)mushi** bookworm
6 米食虫 **komeku(i)mushi** rice weevil; drone, idler
7 貝殻虫 **kaigaramushi** scale (insect/louse)
8 夜光虫 **yakōchū** night-glowing insect
9 南京虫 **nankinmushi** bedbugs
点取虫 **tento(ri)mushi** student who studies just to get good marks, a grind
草鞋虫 **warajimushi** sow bug, wood louse
珊瑚虫 **sangochū** coral insect/polyp
10 真田虫 **sanada mushi** tapeworm
11 寄生虫 **kiseichū** parasitic insects, parasite
14 髪切虫 **kamiki(ri) mushi** long-horned beetle
穀象虫 **kokuzō-mushi** rice weevil
16 機織虫 **hatao(ri)mushi** grasshopper

──── 5 ────

2 十二指腸虫 **jūnishichōchū** hookworm
13 獅子身中虫 **shishi-shinchū (no) mushi** treacherous friend

6

糸
米
舟
虫 0←
耳
⺮

─────── 2 ───────

6d2.1

虱 蝨

SHITSU, shirami louse, lice

─────── 1 ───────

15 虱潰 **shiramitsubu(shi ni)** one by one, thoroughly, with a fine-tooth comb

─────── 2 ───────

7 床虱 **tokojirami** bedbug

─────── 3 ───────

6d3.1

虹

KŌ, niji rainbow

─────── 1 ───────

11 虹彩 **kōsai** iris (of the eye)
23 虹鱒 **nijimasu** rainbow trout

6d3.2

虻

BŌ, abu horsefly

─────── 1 ───────

13 虻蜂取 **abu-hachi to(razu)** trying to catch both a fly and a bee in one swoop of the hand and failing to catch either

─────── 4 ───────

6d4.1

蚌

BŌ, hamaguri clam

6d4.2

蚋

ZEI, buyu, buyo gnat, midge

6d4.3

蚪

TO tadpole, polliwog

─────── 2 ───────

15 蝌蚪 **kato, otamajakushi** tadpole, polliwog

6d4.4

蚓

IN, mimizu earthworm

─────── 2 ───────

11 蚯蚓 **mimizu** earthworm
蚯蚓腫 **mimizuba(re)** welt

6d4.5 / 1876

蚊

ka mosquito

─────── 1 ───────

8 蚊取線香 **katori senkō** mosquito-repellent incense
9 蚊屋 **kaya** mosquito net
蚊柱 **kabashira** column of swarming mosquitoes
10 蚊針 **kabari** fishing fly
11 蚊帳 **kaya, kachō** mosquito net
12 蚊遣 **kaya(ri)** smudge fire to repel mosquitoes
13 蚊鉤 **kabari** fishing fly
18 蚊燻 **kaibu(shi)** smoking out mosquitoes

6d4.6

蚣

KŌ centipede
SHŌ grasshopper

6d4.7

蚤

SŌ early; flea
nomi flea

─────── 1 ───────

8 蚤取 **nomito(ri)** picking fleas; flea powder
蚤取粉 **nomito(ri)ko** flea powder

6d4.8 / 1877

蚕 蠶

SAN, kaiko silkworm

─────── 1 ───────

6 蚕糸 **sanshi** silk thread/yarn
蚕糸業 **sanshigyō** the silk-reeling industry
7 蚕卵 **sanran** silkworm egg
蚕豆 **soramame** broad/fava bean
蚕児 **sanji** silkworm
9 蚕室 **sanshitsu** silkworm-raising room
蚕食 **sanshoku** encroachment, inroads
13 蚕業 **sangyō** sericulture

─────── 2 ───────

9 秋蚕 **shūsan** fall silkworms
15 養蚕 **yōsan** silkworm raising/culture
養蚕地 **yōsanchi** silkworm-raising district
養蚕業 **yōsangyō** silkworm raising, sericulture

6

糸
米
舟
→ 2 虫
耳
⺮

6d4.9

蚩

SHI fool; make a fool of

─────── 5 ───────

6d5.1

蚜

KA plant louse, aphid

─────── 1 ───────

6 蚜虫 **aburamushi** plant louse, aphid

6d5.2

蚰

YŪ, **gejigeji**, **yasude** millipede

─────── 1 ───────

12 蚰蜒 **yūen** winding, serpentine

6d5.3

蚶

KAN ark shell

6d5.4

蛎

REKI longheaded locust

6d5.5

蛆

SO, **uji** maggot

─────── 1 ───────

6 蛆虫 **ujimushi** maggot

6d5.6

蚯

KYŪ, **mimizu** earthworm

─────── 1 ───────

10 蚯蚓 **mimizu** earthworm
　　蚯蚓腫 **mimizuba(re)** welt

蚫 → 鮑 **11a5.4**

6d5.7 / 1875

蛇

JA, DA, **hebi**, **kuchinawa** snake

─────── 1 ───────

3 蛇口 **jaguchi** faucet, tap
5 蛇皮 **hebikawa** snakeskin
　　蛇目 **ja(no)me** bull's-eye design (on an oilpaper umbrella)
　　蛇目傘 **ja(no)megasa** umbrella with a bull's-eye design
6 蛇行 **dakō** meander, zigzag
7 蛇体 **jatai** serpentine
　　蛇足 **dasoku** superfluous (as legs on a snake)
8 蛇毒 **jadoku** snake poison/venom
　　蛇使 **hebitsuka(i)** snake charmer
10 蛇紋石 **jamonseki** serpentine, ophiolite
13 蛇腹 **jabara** accordion-like folds, bellows; cornice
14 蛇管 **jakan** hose
15 蛇蝎 **dakatsu** (detest like) snakes and scorpions

─────── 2 ───────

3 大蛇 **daija, orochi** monster serpent; large snake
8 長蛇 **chōda** long snake; long line of people, long queue
　　毒蛇 **dokuhebi, dokuja** poisonous snake
9 海蛇 **umihebi** sea serpent
16 縞蛇 **shimahebi** striped snake
　　錦蛇 **nishikihebi** rock snake
18 藪蛇 **yabuhebi** stirring up uncecessary trouble

─────── 3 ───────

10 竜頭蛇尾 **ryūtō-dabi** strong start but weak finish
11 眼鏡蛇 **megane hebi** cobra

6d5.8

蛉

REI dragonfly; caterpillar

─────── 2 ───────

14 蜻蛉 **tonbo** dragonfly
　　蜻蛉返 **tonbogae(ri)** somersault

6d5.9

蛄

KO mole cricket

─────── 2 ───────

15 蝦蛄 **shako** squilla (an edible prawn-like creature)
17 螻蛄 **kera, rōko** mole cricket

6d5.10

蛅

ZEN caterpillar

─────── 1 ───────

18 蛅蟖 **kemushi** caterpillar

6

糸
米
舟
虫 5 ←
耳
⺮

蛎→蠣 **6d14.3**

6d5.11

蛋 **TAN** egg

───────── 1 ─────────
5 蛋白 **tanpaku** protein; albumen
蛋白質 **tanpakushitsu** protein; albumen

蛍→ **3n8.2**

───────── 6 ─────────

6d6.1

蛛 **CHU** spider

───────── 2 ─────────
14 蜘蛛 **kumo** spider
蜘蛛糸 **kumo (no) ito** spider's thread
蜘蛛巣 **kumo(no)su** spiderweb

6d6.2

蛯 **ebi** shrimp, prawn

6d6.3

蜉 **FU** (a kind of ant); mayfly

───────── 1 ─────────
14 蜉蝣 **fuyū, kagerō** mayfly, ephemera

6d6.4

蛙 **A, kaeru, kawazu** frog

───────── 1 ─────────
8 蛙泳 **kaeruoyo(gi)** the breast stroke
13 蛙跳 **kaeruto(bi), kawazuto(bi)** leapfrog
───────── 2 ─────────
8 雨蛙 **amagaeru** tree frog
16 蟇蛙 **hikigaeru** toad

6d6.5

蛭 **SHITSU, hiru** leech

6d6.6

蛞 **KATSU, namekuji** slug

───────── 1 ─────────
15 蛞蝓 **namekuji** slug

6d6.7

蛤 **KŌ, hamaguri** clam

6d6.8

蛟 **KŌ, mizuchi** dragon

6d6.9

蛔 **KAI** intestinal worms

───────── 1 ─────────
6 蛔虫 **kaichū** intestinal worms

6d6.10

蜒 **EN** winding, serpentine

───────── 2 ─────────
11 蚰蜒 **yūen** winding, serpentine
14 蜿蜒 **en'en** winding, meandering, serpentine

6d6.11

蜓 **TEI** dragonfly; cicada
TEN lizard

───────── 2 ─────────
14 蜻蜓 **tonbo, yanma** large dragonfly

6d6.12

蛩 **KYŌ** cricket; locust; centipede

蜇→ **3k9.27**

蛮→ **2j10.1**

6d6.13

蜑 **TAN, ebisu** barbarians
ama fisherman; abalone diver

6d6.14

鬮 oroshi wind blowing down from a mountain

────────── 2 ──────────

3 山颪 yamaoroshi wind blowing down a mountain

────────── 7 ──────────

6d7.1

蛾 GA moth

────────── 2 ──────────

8 毒蛾 dokuga Oriental tussock moth

6d7.2

蜈 GO centipede

6d7.3

蜊 RI (a species of) clam

────────── 2 ──────────

9 浅蜊 asari (type of short-necked clam)

6d7.4

蜆 KEN, shijimi corbicula (a freshwater clam)

6d7.5

蛸 蛸 SHŌ, tako octopus

────────── 1 ──────────

2 蛸入道 takonyūdō octopus; bald-headed man
10 蛸配当 takohaitō bogus dividends
12 蛸壺 takotsubo octopus trap; foxhole

6d7.6

蜂 HŌ, hachi bee, wasp

────────── 1 ──────────

8 蜂房 hōbō beehive, apiary
10 蜂起 hōki revolt, uprising
11 蜂巣 hachi (no) su beehive, honeycomb
14 蜂蜜 hachimitsu honey

蜂窩 hōka honeycomb

────────── 2 ──────────

3 山蜂 yamabachi hornet
6 地蜂 jibachi digger wasp
9 虻蜂取 abu-hachi to(razu) trying to catch both a fly and a bee in one swoop of the hand and failing to catch either
11 雀蜂 suzumebachi wasp, hornet
12 雄蜂 obachi drone (bee)
13 働蜂 hatara(ki)bachi worker bee
14 蜜蜂 mitsubachi honeybee
熊蜂 kumabachi hornet
雌蜂 mebachi queen bee
15 養蜂 yōhō beekeeping
養蜂植物 yōhō shokubutsu plants for bees

────────── 3 ──────────

3 女王蜂 joōbachi queen bee

6d7.7

蜍 JO toad

────────── 2 ──────────

19 蟾蜍 hikigaeru toad

6d7.8

蛻 ZEI, monuke (insect's) cast-off skin

6d7.9

蛹 YŌ, sanagi chrysalis, pupa

────────── 1 ──────────

6 蛹虫 yōchū chrysalis, pupa

6d7.10 / 874

触 觸 SHOKU, sawa(ru) touch, feel fu(reru) touch (upon); announce

4 触太鼓 fu(re)daiko drum beating (to herald the start of sumo wrestling)
触文 fu(re)bumi announcement
触込 fu(re)ko(mi) announcement, professing to be
触手 shokushu feeler, tentacle
5 触出 fu(re)da(shi) announcement, professing to be
6 触合 fu(re)a(u) touch, come in contact with
触回 fu(re)mawa(ru) spread (a rumor), bruit about

6

糸
米
舟
虫 7 ←
耳
⺮

7 触角 **shokkaku** feeler, antenna, tentacle
8 触知 **shokuchi** feel, perceive by touch
  触官 **shokkan** tactile organ
9 触発 **shokuhatsu** detonation upon contact
  触発水雷 **shokuhatsu suirai** contact (sea) mine
12 触媒 **shokubai** catalyst
  触覚 **shokkaku** sense of touch
  触診 **shokushin** palpation
13 触感 **shokkan** the feel; sense of touch

——————— 2 ———————

1 一触即発 **isshoku sokuhatsu** touch-and-go, hair-trigger, explosive (situation)
3 口触 **kuchizawa(ri)** taste
4 手触 **tezawa(ri)** the feel, touch
6 気触 **kabu(reru)** have a skin rash; be influenced by, become infected with
  先触 **sakibu(re)** preliminary/previous announcement
  舌触 **shitazawa(ri)** texture (of food)
  肌触 **hadazawa(ri)** the touch/feel
  有触 **a(ri)fu(reta)** commonplace, frequent
7 言触 **i(i)fu(rasu)** start (a rumor), give it out that
8 抵触 **teishoku** conflict with, be contrary to
9 前触 **maebu(re)** advance notice/warning
  牴触 **teishoku** conflict
11 接触 **sesshoku** touch, contact; catalytic
  接触点 **sesshokuten** point of contact/tangency
  接触面 **sesshokumen** contact surface
12 筆触 **hisshoku** touch of the brush/pen
13 感触 **kanshoku** the touch/feel, texture
15 膚触 **hadazawa(ri)** the touch, the feel
18 顔触 **kaobu(re)** personnel, lineup, cast

——————— 3 ———————

14 漆気触 **urushikabure** lacquer poisoning

——————— 4 ———————

18 鎧袖一触 **gaishū-isshoku** easy victory

6d7.11

蜃
SHIN clam

——————— 1 ———————

6 蜃気楼 **shinkirō** mirage

——————— 8 ———————

蝿→蠅 6d13.1

6d8.1

蜱
HI, **dani** tick, mite
mategai razor clam

6d8.2

蜘
CHI spider

——————— 1 ———————

12 蜘蛛 **kumo** spider
  蜘蛛糸 **kumo (no) ito** spider's thread
  蜘蛛巣 **kumo(no)su** spiderweb

6d8.3

蜥
SEKI lizard

——————— 1 ———————

14 蜥蜴 **tokage** lizard

6d8.4

蝣
YŪ mayfly

——————— 2 ———————

12 蜉蝣 **fuyū, kagerō** mayfly, ephemera

6d8.5

蜷
KEN, **nina** marsh snail

6d8.6

蜴
EKI lizard; iridescent beetle

——————— 2 ———————

14 蜥蜴 **tokage** lizard

6d8.7

蜻
SEI dragonfly; mayfly; cicada; cricket

——————— 1 ———————

11 蜻蛉 **tonbo** dragonfly
  蜻蛉返 **tonbogae(ri)** somersault
12 蜻蜓 **tonbo, yanma** large dragonfly

6d8.8

蜿
EN winding, slithering

——————— 1 ———————

12 蜿蜒 **en'en** winding, meandering, serpentine

蝋→蠟 **6d15.1**

6d8.9

蜩
CHŌ, higurashi green/evening cicada

6d8.10

蜚
HI to fly; cockroach, beetle

————— 1 —————
14 蜚語 **higo** wild rumor

6d8.11

颱
TAI typhoon

————— 1 —————
9 颱風 **taifū** typhoon

————————— 9 —————————
6d9.1

螂
RŌ praying mantis; cicada

————— 2 —————
19 蟷螂 **kamakiri, tōrō** praying mantis
蟷螂斧 **tōrō (no) ono** (valiant but) hopeless resistance (like a praying mantis lifting its front legs to block a man's path)

6d9.2

蝌
KA tadpole, polliwog

————— 1 —————
10 蝌蚪 **kato, otamajakushi** tadpole, polliwog

6d9.3

蝴
KO butterfly

————— 1 —————
15 蝴蝶 **kochō** butterfly

6d9.4

蝦
KA, ebi shrimp, prawn, lobster

————— 1 —————
6 蝦夷 **Ezo** Ainu; Hokkaidō
蝦夷松 **Ezo-matsu** silver fir, spruce
蝦夷菊 **Ezo-giku** China aster
11 蝦蛄 **shako** squilla (an edible prawn-like creature)
13 蝦腰 **ebigoshi** bent with age
16 蝦蟇 **gama** toad
蝦蟇口 **gamaguchi** purse
蝦錠 **ebijō** padlock
19 蝦蟹 **ebigani** crawfish, crayfish

————— 2 —————
3 川蝦 **kawaebi** river shrimp, crawfish

————— 3 —————
6 伊勢蝦 **ise-ebi** spiny lobster

6d9.5

蝟
I, harinezumi hedgehog

————— 1 —————
12 蝟集 **ishū** swarm, throng, gather

6d9.6

蝮
FUKU, mamushi (a type of poisonous snake)

6d9.7

蝶
CHŌ butterfly

————— 1 —————
0 蝶ナット **chōnatto** wing nut
蝶ネクタイ **chōnekutai** bow tie
3 蝶々 **chōchō** butterfly
7 蝶貝 **chōgai** pearl oyster
12 蝶番 **chōtsugai** (door) hinge, (anatomical) joint
蝶結 **chōmusu(bi)** bowknot
17 蝶鮫 **chōzame** sturgeon
18 蝶類 **chōrui** butterflies

————— 2 —————
9 胡蝶 **kochō** butterfly
15 蝴蝶 **kochō** butterfly

6d9.8

蝗
KŌ, inago, batta locust, grasshopper

————— 1 —————
6 蝗虫 **batta** grasshopper, locust

6

糸
米
舟
虫 9←
耳
⺮

─────── 2 ───────

9 飛蝗 **batta** grasshopper, locust

6d9.9

蜴 TŌ (a kind of spider)

6d9.10

蝎 蠍 KATSU, sasori scorpion

─────── 1 ───────

10 蝎座 **sasori-za** Scorpio

─────── 2 ───────

11 蛇蝎 **dakatsu** (detest like) snakes and scorpions

6d9.11

蝸 KA snail

─────── 1 ───────

4 蝸牛 **katatsumuri** snail

6d9.12

蝠 FUKU bat

─────── 2 ───────

15 蝙蝠 **kōmori** bat
蝙蝠傘 **kōmorigasa** umbrella

蝉 → 蟬 6d12.3

蟒 → 蠎 6d10.3

6d9.13

蝓 YU slug; snail

─────── 2 ───────

12 蛞蝓 **namekuji** slug

6d9.14

蝙 HEN bat

─────── 1 ───────

15 蝙蝠 **kōmori** bat
蝙蝠傘 **kōmorigasa** umbrella

蟲 → 虫 6d2.1

─────── 10 ───────

6d10.1

蟎 HEI tick, mite; winged ant

6d10.2

蟪 KEI locust; cicada

蟆 → 蟇 3k13.23

6d10.3

蟒 蠎蠎 BŌ, uwabami large snake, anaconda, boa constrictor

6d10.4

螟 MEI rice stem borer

─────── 1 ───────

6 螟虫 **meichū** rice stem borer

6d10.5 / 1588

融 YŪ, to(keru) melt, dissolve

─────── 1 ───────

4 融化 **yūka** deliquesce, soften
6 融合 **yūgō** fusion
8 融和 **yūwa** harmony, reconciliation
9 融点 **yūten** melting point
融通 **yūzū** accommodation, loan; versatility
11 融雪 **yūsetsu** thaw, melting snow
13 融解 **yūkai** fuse, melt, dissolve
融解点 **yūkaiten** melting point
融解熱 **yūkainetsu** heat of fusion
融資 **yūshi** financing, loan

─────── 2 ───────

4 円融 **En'yū** (emperor, 960–984)
8 金融 **kin'yū** money, credit, financing
金融界 **kin'yūkai** the financial community
金融機関 **kin'yū kikan** financial institutions
10 核融合 **kakuyūgō** nuclear fusion
13 溶融 **yōyū** fuse, melt, molten

18 鎔融 **yōyū** fuse, melt, molten
   鎔融点 **yōyūten** melting point

———————— 3 ————————

7 私金融 **shikin'yū** private financing/funds
17 闇金融 **yamikin'yū** illegal lending

螢 → 蛍   **3n8.2**

———————— 11 ————————

6d11.1

螻   **RŌ** mole cricket

———————— 1 ————————

11 螻蛄 **kera, rōko** mole cricket

———————— 2 ————————

6 虫螻 **mushikera** worm, insect

6d11.2

蟋   **SHITSU** cricket; grasshopper

———————— 1 ————————

17 蟋蟀 **kōrogi** cricket; grasshopper

6d11.3

螺   **RA, nishi** spiral shellfish

———————— 1 ————————

2 螺子 **neji** screw; stopcock; (wind-up) spring
11 螺旋 **rasen** spiral, helix
      neji screw; stopcock; (wind-up) spring
   螺旋形 **rasenkei** spiral, helical
13 螺鈿 **raden** mother-of-pearl

———————— 2 ————————

4 木螺旋 **mokuneji** wood screw
5 田螺 **tanishi** mud/pond snail
8 法螺 **hora** trumpet shell; boast, brag
   法螺吹 **horafu(ki)** boaster, braggart
11 細螺 **kisago, kishago** periwinkle

———————— 3 ————————

14 駄法螺 **dabora** bragging

螳 → 蟷   **6d13.3**

6d11.4

蟆   **momu** toad

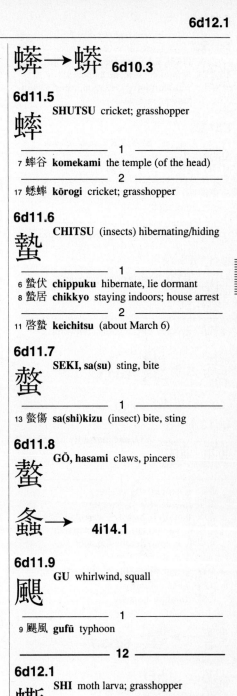

蟒 → 蟒   **6d10.3**

6d11.5

蟀   **SHUTSU** cricket; grasshopper

———————— 1 ————————

7 蟀谷 **komekami** the temple (of the head)

———————— 2 ————————

17 蟋蟀 **kōrogi** cricket; grasshopper

6d11.6

蟄   **CHITSU** (insects) hibernating/hiding

———————— 1 ————————

6 蟄伏 **chippuku** hibernate, lie dormant
8 蟄居 **chikkyo** staying indoors; house arrest

———————— 2 ————————

11 啓蟄 **keichitsu** (about March 6)

6d11.7

螫   **SEKI, sa(su)** sting, bite

———————— 1 ————————

13 螫傷 **sa(shi)kizu** (insect) bite, sting

6d11.8

螯   **GŌ, hasami** claws, pincers

蠢 →   **4i14.1**

6d11.9

颶   **GU** whirlwind, squall

———————— 1 ————————

9 颶風 **gufū** typhoon

———————— 12 ————————

6d12.1

蟖   **SHI** moth larva; grasshopper

———————— 2 ————————

11 蛄蟖 **kemushi** caterpillar
17 蠡蟖 **kirigirisu** grasshopper, katydid, leaf
      cricket

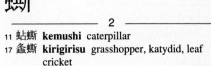

6d12.2

蟠　**HAN, BAN, wadakama(ru)** lie coiled up/around; lurk, be harbored
wadakama(ri) vexation, cares; ill will, grudge; reserve

6d12.3

蟬 蝉　**SEN, ZEN, semi** cicada

──────── 1 ────────
10 蟬時雨　**semishigure** outburst of cicada droning

──────── 2 ────────
8 油蟬　**aburazemi** (a large brown cicada)

6d12.4

蟯　**GYŌ** threadworms, pinworms

──────── 1 ────────
6 蟯虫　**gyōchū** threadworms, pinworms

蟲 → 虫　6d0.1

──────── 13 ────────

6d13.1

蠅 蝿　**YŌ, hae, hai** a fly

──────── 1 ────────
5 蠅打　**haeu(chi)** fly swatter
　蠅叩　**haetata(ki)** fly swatter
8 蠅取　**haeto(ri), haito(ri)** catching flies
　蠅取草　**haeto(ri)gusa** Venus flytrap
　蠅取紙　**haeto(ri)gami** flypaper

──────── 2 ────────
8 青蠅　**aobae** bluebottle fly, blowfly
10 家蠅　**iebae** housefly
　馬蠅　**umabae** horsefly

蠏 → 蟹　6d13.7

蠍 → 蝎　6d9.10

6d13.2

蟶　**TEI** razor clam

6d13.3

蟷 螳　**TŌ** praying mantis

──────── 1 ────────
15 蟷螂　**kamakiri, tōrō** praying mantis
　蟷螂斧　**tōrō (no) ono** (valiant but) hopeless resistance (like a praying mantis lifting its front legs to block a man's path)

6d13.4

蠖　**WAKU, KAKU** inchworm, geometer

6d13.5

蟾　**SEN** toad

──────── 1 ────────
13 蟾蜍　**hikigaeru** toad

6d13.6

蟻　**GI, ari** ant

──────── 1 ────────
6 蟻地獄　**arijigoku** antlion, doodlebug
7 蟻町　**ari(no)machi** slum
9 蟻巻　**arimaki** ant cow, aphid
12 蟻塔　**ari(no)tō** anthill
　蟻塚　**arizuka** anthill
14 蟻酸　**gisan** formic acid

──────── 2 ────────
3 大蟻食　**ōariku(i)** great anteater
5 白蟻　**shiroari** termite
6 羽蟻　**haari** winged ant
　防蟻　**bōgi** termite-proof
9 食蟻獣　**arikui** anteater
11 黒蟻　**kuroari** black ant

6d13.7

蟹 蠏　**KAI, kani** crab

──────── 1 ────────
3 蟹工船　**kanikōsen** crab-canning ship
6 蟹缶　**kanikan** canned crab
　蟹行文字　**kaikō moji/monji** horizontal/ Western writing
8 蟹股　**ganimata** bowlegged
23 蟹罐　**kanikan** canned crab

─────── 2 ───────
12 兜蟹 **kabutogani** horseshoe/king crab
15 蝦蟹 **ebigani** crawfish, crayfish

─────── 3 ───────
10 高足蟹 **takaashigani** giant spider crab
22 鱈場蟹 **tarabagani** king crab

─────── 14 ───────

6d14.1

蠕 ZEN, JU move along like a worm, crawl, squirm

─────── 1 ───────
7 蠕形動物 **zenkei dōbutsu** legless animal
11 蠕動運動 **zendō undō** vermicular motion, peristalsis

6d14.2

蠑 EI newt; turban shell

6d14.3

蠣 蛎 REI oyster

─────── 2 ───────
7 牡蠣 **kaki** oyster

觸 → 触 6d7.10

6d14.4

飄 飇 HYŌ whirlwind; sudden; blown about by the wind **hirugae(ru)** wave, flutter

─────── 1 ───────
3 飄々 **hyōhyō** buoyantly; wandering
10 飄逸 **hyōitsu** buoyant, airy, aloof
12 飄然 **hyōzen** aimlessly, casually

飇 → 飄 6d14.4

─────── 15 ───────

6d15.1

蠟 蝋 RŌ wax

─────── 1 ───────
2 蠟人形 **rōningyō** wax figure

4 蠟引 **rōbi(ki)** waxing
5 蠟石 **rōseki** pagodite, pencil stone
10 蠟紙 **rōgami** wax paper
17 蠟燭 **rōsoku** candle

─────── 2 ───────
5 石蠟 **sekirō** paraffin
9 封蠟 **fūrō** sealing wax
14 蜜蠟 **mitsurō** beeswax

6d15.2

蠢 SHUN, **ugome(ku)** wriggle, squirm

─────── 1 ───────
11 蠢動 **shundō** wriggling, squirming; maneuvering, scheming

6d15.3

蠡 REI be worm-eaten; conch

6d15.4

飆 HYŌ whirlwind

─────── 1 ───────
3 飆々 **hyōhyō** soughing

─────── 17 ───────

6d17.1

蠱 KO worms in grain; lead astray; put a curse on

─────── 1 ───────
12 蠱惑 **kowaku** enchant, fascinate, seduce
蠱惑的 **kowakuteki** alluring

6d17.2

髑 DOKU skull

─────── 1 ───────
21 髑髏 **dokuro, sarekōbe, sharekōbe** skull

─────── 18 ───────

6d18.1

蠵 KEI sea turtle

6
糸
米
舟
虫 18 ←
耳
竹

蠹→蠧 3p19.1

— 19 —

蠻→蛮 2j10.1

— 20 —

蠶→蚕 6d4.8

耳 6e

耳	耶	取	耿	恥	耻	耽	耺	耾	聊	聆	聒	爺
0.1	2.1	2.2	4.1	4.2	6e4.2	4.3	6e12.1	4.4	5.1	5.2	6.1	2o10.6
聘	聖	聢	聡	聚	聟	聨	趣	鵈	聰	聯	聴	聲
7.1	4f9.9	8.1	8.2	8.3	3e9.3	6e11.2	9.1	11.1	6e8.2	11.2	11.3	3p4.4
聳	聱	職	聶	叢	聹	聽	聾					
11.4	11.5	12.1	12.2	12.3	14.1	6e11.3	16.1					

6
糸 米 舟 虫 →0 耳 竹

— 0 —

6e0.1 / 56

耳 **JI, mimi** ear

— 1 —

4 耳元 **mimimoto** close to one's ear
5 耳打 **mimiu(chi)** whisper in (someone's) ear
耳好 **jikō** earhole
耳目 **jimoku** eye and ear; attention, notice
6 耳朶 **mimitabu** earlobe **jida** earlobe, ears
7 耳学問 **mimigakumon** learning acquired by listening
8 耳垂 **mimida(re)** ear discharge
耳底 **jitei** ears
9 耳垢 **mimiaka** earwax
耳科 **jika** otology
10 耳疾 **jishitsu** ear ailments
11 耳寄 **mimiyo(ri)** welcome (news)
耳殻 **jikaku** auricle, external ear
12 耳遠 **mimidō(i)** hard of hearing; strange, uncommon
耳痛 **jitsū** earache
耳順 **jijun** age 60
13 耳障 **mimizawa(ri)** offensive to the ear
耳隠 **mimikaku(shi)** ear-covering hairdo
耳掻 **mimika(ki)** earpick
耳新 **mimiatara(shii)** new, novel
耳飾 **mimikaza(ri)** earring
14 耳漏 **jirō** ear discharge, earwax
耳鳴 **mimina(ri)** ringing in the ears
耳慣 **mimina(reru)** be used to hearing
耳鼻 **jibi** ear and nose
耳鼻咽喉科 **jibiinkōka** ear, nose, and throat specialty
耳鼻科 **jibika** otorhinology
耳語 **jigo** whispering
17 耳擦 **mimikosu(ri)** whispering
耳環 **mimiwa** earring
19 耳鏡 **jikyō** otoscope, ear speculum

— 2 —

3 土耳古 **Toruko** Turkey
小耳 **komimi (ni hasamu)** happen to overhear
4 内耳 **naiji** the inner ear
内耳炎 **naijien** inflammation of the inner ear
中耳 **chūji** the middle ear
中耳炎 **chūjien** otitis media, tympanitis
片耳 **katamimi** one ear
木耳 **kikurage** Jew's-ear (mushroom used in Chinese cooking)
牛耳 **gyūji(ru)** lead, head, control, command, direct
5 外耳 **gaiji** external/outer ear
外耳炎 **gaijien** inflammation of the outer ear, otitis externa
白耳義 **Berugī** Belgium
6 早耳 **hayamimi** quick-eared, in the know
7 初耳 **hatsumimi** something heard for the first time
8 垂耳 **ta(re)mimi** droopy ears, flop-eared
空耳 **soramimi** mishearing; feigned deafness
9 俚耳 **riji** the ears of the rabble/public
俗耳 **zokuji** vulgar ears, attention of the masses
10 馬耳東風 **bajitōfū** utter indifference, turn a deaf ear
11 猫耳 **nekomimi** ear with soft smelly wax
袋耳 **fukuromimi** retentive memory
12 遠耳 **tōmimi** keen ears
13 寝耳水 **nemimi (ni) mizu** a complete surprise
14 聞耳 **ki(ki)mimi** attentive ears

──────── 2 ────────

6e2.1

耶　YA (question mark); (used phonetically)

──────── 1 ────────

19 耶蘇 **Yaso** Jesus
耶蘇教 **yasokyō** Christianity

──────── 2 ────────

6 有耶無耶 **uyamuya** noncommittal

──────── 4 ────────

6 有耶無耶 **uyamuya** noncommittal

6e2.2 / 65

取　SHU, to(ru) take　to(reru) can be taken; come off　(ni) to(tte) to, for, as far as … is concerned

──────── 1 ────────

2 取入 **to(ri)i(reru)** take in, accept, adopt; harvest
　to(ri)i(ru) win (someone's) favor
3 取上 **to(ri)a(geru)** take up, adopt; take away
取下 **to(ri)sa(geru)** withdraw, dismiss
　to(ri)o(rosu) take down
取口 **to(ri)guchi** sumo technique
4 取片付 **to(ri)katazu(keru)** clear away, tidy up
取分 **to(ri)wa(ke)** especially
　to(ri)wa(keru) divide, portion out
　to(ri)bun share, portion
取込 **to(ri)ko(mu)** take in; embezzle; win favor
取込事 **toriko(mi)goto** confusion, busyness
取手 **to(t)te** handle, knob　**to(ri)te** recipient
取引 **torihiki** transaction, deal, business
取引所 **torihikijo, torihikisho** (stock) exchange
取引高 **torihikidaka** volume of business, turnover
取木 **to(ri)ki** layer(ing) (in gardening)
5 取出 **to(ri)da(su)** take/pick out
取仕切 **to(ri)shiki(ru)** run the whole (business)
取代 **to(tte)ka(waru)** take the place of, supersede
取付 **to(ri)tsu(keru)** install; patronize
　to(ri)tsu(ke) (store) which one patronizes; installing; run on a bank
　to(ri)tsu(ku) hold fast to, catch hold of; possess, haunt
　to(ri)tsu(ki), to(t)tsu(ki) the beginning, the first you come to; first impression
取付工事 **to(ri)tsu(ke) kōji** installation work
取外 **to(ri)hazu(su)** remove, dismantle

取去 **to(ri)sa(ru)** take away, remove
取払 **to(ri)hara(u)** remove, clear away
取広 **to(ri)hiro(geru)** enlarge, expand, spread out
取札 **to(ri)fuda** cards to be picked up (in the New Year's card game)
取立 **to(ri)ta(teru)** collect (a debt); appoint; patronize　**to(ri)ta(te)** fresh-picked; collection　**to(ri)ta(tete)** in particular
取立金 **toritatekin** money collected
取皿 **to(ri)zara** serving dish
6 取合 **to(ri)a(u)** take each other's (hand); scramble for; take notice of
　to(ri)a(waseru) put together, assort, match
取次 **to(ri)tsu(gu)** act as agent; transmit, convey
取次店 **toritsugiten** agency, distributor
取次業 **toritsugigyō** agency/commission business
取交 **to(ri)kawa(su)** exchange
　to(ri)ma(zeru) mix, put together
取灰 **to(ri)bai** ashes removed (from an oven)
取返 **to(ri)kae(su)** get back, regain, recover, recoup, catch up on
　to(tte)kae(su) hurry/double back
取扱 **to(ri)atsuka(u)** treat, handle, deal with/in, carry
取扱人 **toriatsukainin** agent, person in charge
取尽 **to(ri)tsuku(su)** take all
取回 **to(ri)mawa(su)** manage, treat
取成 **to(ri)na(shi)** intercession
7 取来 **to(tte) ku(ru)** go get, fetch
取決 **toriki(me)** arrangement, agreement
取沙汰 **to(ri)zata** rumor, gossip
取抑 **to(ri)osa(eru)** catch, capture
取乱 **to(ri)mida(su)** disarrange, mess up; be agitated/perturbed
取囲 **to(ri)kako(mu)** surround, encircle
取材 **shuzai** news gathering, coverage
取戻 **to(ri)modo(su)** take back, regain, recoup, catch up on
取足 **to(ru ni) ta(ranai)** beneath notice, insignificant
8 取直 **to(rimo)nao(sazu)** namely, in other words　**to(ri)nao(su)** recover; retake, regrasp
取逃 **to(ri)ni(gasu)** fail to catch, miss
取押 **to(ri)osa(eru)** catch, capture
取的 **to(ri)teki** minor-rank sumo wrestler
取放題 **to(ri)hōdai** all-you-can-take
取所 **to(ri)dokoro** worth, merit
取取 **to(ri)do(ri)** various
9 取巻 **to(ri)ma(ku)** surround, encircle
　to(ri)ma(ki) follower, hanger-on
取巻連 **to(ri)ma(ki)ren** one's entourage

6
糸
米
舟
虫
耳 2←
竹

取除 **to(ri)nozo(ku)** remove, get rid of
to(ri)no(keru) clear away; make an exception of; set aside
取急 **to(ri)iso(gu)** hurry
取前 **to(ri)mae** share, portion
取持 **to(ri)mo(tsu)** treat, entertain; act as go-between
取柄 **to(ri)e** worth, mention
取計 **to(ri)haka(rau)** manage, arrange
10 取残 **to(ri)noko(su)** leave behind/out
取消 **to(ri)ke(su)** cancel, revoke, rescind
取捌 **to(ri)saba(ku)** manage, settle; judge, try
取殺 **to(ri)koro(su)** curse/haunt to death
取留 **to(ri)to(meru)** ascertain, establish; save (a life)
取留無 **to(ri)to(me)na(i)** rambling, fanciful, incoherent, pointless
取紛 **to(ri)magi(reru)** be in confusion; be busily engaged
取粉 **to(ri)ko** rice meal
11 取運 **to(ri)hako(bu)** start right in on, proceed to
取掛 **to(ri)kaka(ru)** get started on, set about
取捨 **shusha** adoption or rejection
to(ri)su(teru) reject, discard
取得 **shutoku** acquire
to(ri)doku gain, profit
取寄 **to(ri)yo(seru)** send for, order
取崩 **to(ri)kuzu(su)** tear down, demolish; draw down (savings)
取組 **to(ri)ku(mu)** grapple with
to(ri)kumi (sumo) match
取組合 **to(k)ku(mi)a(u)** grapple, tussle
取舵 **to(ri)kaji** port (to helm)
12 取違 **to(ri)chiga(eru)** mistake for, misconstrue
取揃 **to(ri)soro(eru)** put/have all together
取落 **to(ri)o(tosu)** let fall; omit
取極 **to(ri)ki(meru)** arrange, agree upon
取替 **to(ri)ka(eru)** (ex)change, replace
取散 **to(ri)chi(rasu)** strew/scatter about
取敢 **to(ri)a(ezu)** for the present; first of all; immediately
取越 **to(ri)ko(su)** anticipate, do ahead of time
取越苦労 **to(ri)ko(shi)gurō** needless worry
取結 **to(ri)musu(bu)** conclude (a contract); act as go-between; curry (favor)
取集 **to(ri)atsu(meru)** collect, gather
13 取毀 **to(ri)kowa(su)** tear down, demolish
取損 **to(ri)soko(nau)** fail to take/get, miss
取置 **to(tte)o(ki)** set aside, choicest, ace in the hole
取詰 **to(ri)tsu(meru)** drive into a corner; take to task; brood over
14 取様 **to(ri)yō** way of taking, interpretation
15 取澄 **to(ri)su(masu)** put on airs
取締 **to(ri)shima(ru)** manage, oversee

取締役 **torishimariyaku** (company) director
取縋 **to(ri)suga(ru)** cling to; entreat
取調 **to(ri)shira(beru)** investigate, look into
16 取壊 **to(ri)kowa(su)** tear down, demolish
18 取繕 **to(ri)tsukuro(u)** repair, patch up, gloss over
取鎮 **to(ri)shizu(meru)** quiet, quell
取離 **to(ri)hana(su)** let go of, drop
22 取纏 **to(ri)mato(meru)** collect, arrange

──────── 2 ────────

3 下取 **shitado(ri)** trade-in
口取 **kuchito(ri)** groom, horseboy; side dish
4 刈取 **ka(ri)to(ru)** mow, cut down, reap
刈取機 **ka(ri)to(ri)ki** reaper, harvester
切取 **ki(ri)to(ru)** cut off/out
切取線 **ki(ri)to(ri)sen** perforated line
分取 **bunshu** taking a sample
wa(ke)do(ri) apportionment
公取委 **Kōtorii** Fair Trade Commission (short for 公正取引委員会)
手取 **teto(ri)** skillful sumo wrestler; good manager **tedo(ri)** net (profit)
手取早 **te(t)to(ri)baya(i)** quick, rough-and-ready
手取足取 **teto(ri)-ashito(ri)** by the hands and feet, bodily, by main force
手取金 **tedo(ri)kin** take-home pay
引取 **hi(ki)to(ru)** take charge of; take back, claim; leave, retire; die
引取人 **hikitorinin** claimant; caretaker
尺取虫 **shakuto(ri)mushi** inchworm
日取 **hido(ri)** (set) the date, schedule
5 占取 **senshu** pre-occupation, preoccupancy
打取 **u(chi)to(ru)** catch, arrest; kill
只取 **tadato(ri)** get (something) for nothing
好取組 **kōtorikumi** good game/match
6 気取 **kido(ru)** make an affected pose
kedo(ru) suspect, sense
気取屋 **kido(ri)ya** affected person, poseur
色取 **irodo(ru)** add color, paint, makeup
汗取 **aseto(ri)** underwear
汲取 **ku(mi)to(ru)** draw (water), dip up (night soil); take into consideration, make allowances for
汲取便所 **ku(mi)to(ri) benjo** hole-in-the-floor/non-flush toilet
地取 **jido(ri)** layout (of a town)
先取 **senshu** take/score first, preoccupy
sakido(ri) receive in advance; anticipate
吸取 **su(i)to(ru)** suck/blot up, absorb; extort
吸取紙 **su(i)to(ri)gami** blotting paper
名取 **nato(ri)** one who has been given a professional name (in the arts) by one's teacher
早取 **hayato(ri)** snapshot

早取写真 **hayato(ri) shashin** snapshot
糸取 **itoto(ri)** silk reeling
7 位取 **kuraido(ri)** positioning of the ones digit within a number
判取 **hanto(ri)** getting someone to stamp his seal (for receipt or approval)
判取帳 **hanto(ri)chō** receipt/chit book
折取 **o(ri)to(ru)** break off, pick (flowers)
抜取 **nu(ki)to(ru)** pull/take out, extract; pilfer, steal
芥取 **gomito(ri)** dustpan; garbage collector
図取 **zudo(ri)** sketching; sketch, plan
見取 **mito(ru), mi(te)to(ru)** see and understand
見取図 **mito(ri)zu** sketch (map)
足取 **ashido(ri)** one's gait/step; traces, track; trend (of prices)
8 命取 **inochito(ri)** fatal
受取 **u(ke)to(ru)** receive, accept, take **uketo(ri)** receipt, acknowledgment
受取人 **uketorinin** recipient, payee
受取済 **uketorizu(mi)** (payment) received
受取帳 **uketorichō** receipt book
受取証 **uketorishō** receipt, voucher
直取引 **jikitorihiki** spot/cash transaction
空取引 **karatorihiki, kūtorihiki** fictitious transaction
物取 **monoto(ri)** thief
取取 **to(ri)do(ri)** various
9 巻取紙 **ma(ki)to(ri)gami, ma(ki)to(ri)shi** roll of paper
乗取 **no(t)to(ru)** hijack, commandeer, capture, occupy
陣取 **jindo(ru)** encamp, take up positions
点取 **tento(ri)** competition for marks; keeping score
点取虫 **tento(ri)mushi** student who studies just to get good marks, a grind
段取 **dando(ri)** program, plan, arrangements
拭取 **fu(ki)to(ru)** wipe off/away, mop up
草取 **kusato(ri)** weeding
窃取 **sesshu** steal
面取 **mento(ri)** rounding off the corners/edges, beveling, chamfering
看取 **kanshu** perceive, notice, detect **mito(ru)** tend the sick
10 剥取 **ha(gi)to(ru)** strip/tear off; rob of
進取 **shinshu** enterprising
蚊取線香 **katori senkō** mosquito-repellent incense
蚤取 **nomito(ri)** picking fleas; flea powder
蚤取粉 **nomito(ri)ko** flea powder
討取 **u(chi)to(ru)** capture; kill
11 隈取 **kumado(ru)** tint, shade; make up (one's face) **kumado(ri)** shading; makeup
商取引 **shōtorihiki** business transaction

掛取 **ka(ke)to(ri)** bill collection/collector
掛取引 **ka(ke)torihiki** credit transaction
採取 **saishu** gather, pick, harvest, extract
捥取 **mo(gi)to(ru)** break/tear off, wrest from
掃取 **ha(ki)to(ru)** sweep away/off
捩取 **neji(ri)to(ru)** wrench off, wrest from
掬取 **suku(i)to(ru)** scoop up, ladle out
略取 **ryakushu** capture, occupation, plunder
盗取 **nusu(mi)to(ru)** steal
粕取 **kasuto(ri)** low-grade (liquor)
舵取 **kajito(ri)** steering; helmsman; guidance; leader
鳥取 **Tottori** (city, Tottori-ken)
鳥取県 **Tottori-ken** (prefecture)
12 遣取 **ya(ri)to(ri)** give and take, exchange, reciprocate
婿取 **mukoto(ri)** get a husband for one's daughter
婿取娘 **mukoto(ri) musume** daughter whose husband is adopted into her family
買取 **ka(i)to(ru)** buy (up), purchase
詐取 **sashu** fraud, swindle
間取 **mado(ri)** arrangement of the rooms, floor plan
13 鼠取 **nezumito(ri)** rat poison; mousetrap, rattrap
摂取 **sesshu** ingest, take in
搾取 **sakushu** exploitation
嫁取 **yometo(ri)** taking a wife
暇取 **himado(ru)** take a long time, be delayed
暖取 **dan (o) to(ru)** warm oneself (at the fire)
数取 **kazuto(ri)** tally; scorer; counting game
跡取 **atoto(ri)** successor, heir
14 選取 **yo(ri)do(ri)** take one's choice, pick out
摘取 **tsu(mi)to(ru)** pick, pluck
擱取 **tsuka(mi)to(ru)** snatch off, grasp
塵取 **chirito(ri)** dustpan
種取 **taneto(ri)** growing plants for seeds, raising livestock for breeding; news gathering
綾取 **ayato(ri)** play cat's-cradle
読取 **yo(mi)to(ru)** read (someone's mind)
奪取 **uba(i)to(ru)** plunder **dasshu** capture, seize, wrest
聞取 **ki(ki)to(ru)** hear and understand, catch, follow
関取 **sekitori** ranking sumo wrestler
15 横取 **yokodo(ri)** usurp, steal away
縁取 **fuchito(ri)** bordering, hemming
縫取 **nu(i)to(ri)** embroidery
請取 **u(ke)to(ru)** receive, accept
16 鞘取 **sayato(ri)** brokerage
頭取 **tōdori** (bank) president; greenroom manager
17 糟取 **kasuto(ri)** low-grade (liquor)
聴取 **chōshu** listening

聴取者 **chōshusha** (radio) listener
聴取料 **chōshuryō** radio fee
闇取引 **yamitorihiki** black-market dealings, illegal transaction
19 蠅取 **haeto(ri), haito(ri)** catching flies
蠅取草 **haeto(ri)gusa** Venus flytrap
蠅取紙 **haeto(ri)gami** flypaper

——————— 3 ———————
2 人気取 **ninkito(ri)** grandstanding, bid for popularity
4 手玉取 **tedama (ni) to(ru)** lead by the nose, wrap around one's little finger
手間取 **temado(ru)** take time, be delayed
月給取 **gekkyūto(ri)** salaried worker
5 広告取 **kōkokuto(ri)** advertising canvasser
8 事務取扱 **jimu toriatsuka(i)** acting director
注文取 **chūmonto(ri)** taking orders
知行取 **chigyōto(ri)** vassal, daimyo
9 信用取引 **shin'yō torihiki** credit transaction
草履取 **zōrito(ri)** sandal-carrier (servant)
相撲取 **sumōto(ri)** sumo wrestler
虻蜂取 **abu-hachi to(razu)** trying to catch both a fly and a bee in one swoop of the hand and failing to catch either
10 借金取 **shakkinto(ri)** bill collection/collector
真珠取 **shinjuto(ri)** pearl fishing; pearl diver
挙足取 **ageashi (o) to(ru)** find fault, carp at
12 揚足取 **a(ge)ashi (o) to(ru)** find fault, carp at
無理取 **murido(ri)** exaction, extortion
16 機嫌取 **kigento(ri)** pleasing another's humor; flatterer

——————— 4 ———————
4 手取足取 **teto(ri)-ashito(ri)** by the hands and feet, bodily, by main force

——————— 4 ———————

6e4.1

耿 **KŌ** clear; resolute

6e4.2 / 1690

恥 耻 **CHI, haji** shame, disgrace
ha(jiru), ha(zuru) feel shame
ha(jirau) be shy/bashful
ha(zukashii) shy, bashful, ashamed
ha(zubeki) disgraceful, unbecoming

——————— 1 ———————
0 恥ずかしがる **ha(zukashigaru)** be shy/bashful
恥ずかしからぬ **ha(zukashikaranu)** worthy, decent

2 恥入 **ha(ji)i(ru)** feel ashamed
4 恥毛 **chimō** pubic hair
8 恥知 **hajishi(razu)** shameless person
10 恥部 **chibu** the private parts
恥辱 **chijoku** disgrace, humiliation
恥骨 **chikotsu** the pubic bone
恥晒 **hajisara(shi)** a disgrace

——————— 2 ———————
5 生恥 **i(ki)haji** living in dishonor, shame
6 死恥 **shi(ni)haji** shameful death; disgrace not erased by death
気恥 **kiha(zukashii)** embarrassed, ashamed, bashful
7 赤恥 **akahaji** public disgrace
花恥 **hanaha(zukashii)** so beautiful as to put a flower to shame
8 空恥 **soraha(zukashii)** feeling ashamed/shy without knowing why
国恥 **kokuchi** national humiliation
物恥 **monoha(zukashii)** shy, bashful
11 羞恥 **shūchi** shame
羞恥心 **shūchishin** sense of shame
12 無恥 **muchi** shameless, brazen
13 廉恥心 **renchishin** sense of shame/honor

——————— 3 ———————
10 破廉恥 **harenchi** shameless, disgraceful

耻 → 恥 **6e4.2**

6e4.3

耽 **TAN, fuke(ru)** be addicted to, be engrossed in

——————— 1 ———————
9 耽美 **tanbi** estheticism
耽美主義 **tanbi shugi** estheticism
耽美的 **tanbiteki** esthetic
耽美派 **tanbiha** the esthetic school
13 耽溺 **tandeki** addiction, dissipation
14 耽読 **tandoku** read avidly

——————— 3 ———————
8 虎視耽々 **koshi-tantan** with hostile vigilance, waiting one's chance (to pounce)

耺 → 職 **6e12.1**

6e4.4

眈 **KŌ** deaf; whisper

―――――――― 5 ――――――――

6e5.1

聊　RYŌ　ringing in the ears; enjoyment
　　isasa(ka)　a little

―――――――― 2 ――――――――
12 無聊　**buryō**　ennui, tedium, boredom

6e5.2

聆　REI　listen; realizing

―――――――― 6 ――――――――

6e6.1

聒　KATSU　noisy; foolish

爺→　**2o10.6**

―――――――― 7 ――――――――

6e7.1

聘　HEI　invite, summon

―――――――― 1 ――――――――
0 聘する　**hei(suru)**　invite, summon
―――――――― 2 ――――――――
8 招聘　**shōhei**　invite

聖→聖　**4f9.9**

―――――――― 8 ――――――――

6e8.1

璇　shikato　certainly, definitely

6e8.2

聡 聰　SŌ, sato(i)　wise, quick-witted,
　　　　keen (of hearing)

―――――――― 1 ――――――――
8 聡明　**sōmei**　wise, sagacious

6e8.3

聚　SHU, SHŪ　gather together

―――――――― 1 ――――――――
12 聚落　**shūraku**　community, colony
―――――――― 2 ――――――――
18 類聚　**ruijū**　classification by similarity

聟→婿　**3e9.3**

―――――――― 9 ――――――――

聠→聯　**6e11.2**

6e9.1 / 1002

趣　SHU, omomuki　purport, gist; taste,
　　elegance; appearance

―――――――― 1 ――――――――
6 趣向　**shukō**　plan, idea
　　趣旨　**shushi**　purport, meaning, aim, object
8 趣味　**shumi**　interest, liking, tastes; hobby
13 趣意　**shui**　purport, meaning, aim, object
　　趣意書　**shuisho**　prospectus
―――――――― 2 ――――――――
6 多趣味　**tashumi**　many-sided interests
7 没趣味　**bosshumi**　insipid, prosaic, dull
　　妙趣　**myōshu**　beauties, charms
9 風趣　**fūshu**　natural charm, elegance, grace
11 野趣　**yashu**　rural beauty, rustic air
　　情趣　**jōshu**　mood, sentiment; artistic effect
12 無趣味　**mushumi**　lack of taste, vulgarity
13 意趣　**ishu**　malice, vindictiveness
　　意趣返　**ishugae(shi)**　revenge
　　新趣向　**shinshukō**　new idea/contrivance
　　詩趣　**shishu**　poetic beauty, poetry
　　雅趣　**gashu**　elegance, tastefulness, artistry
16 興趣　**kyōshu**　interest
―――――――― 3 ――――――――
7 低回趣味　**teikai shumi**　dilettantism
　　低徊趣味　**teikai shumi**　dilettantism

―――――――― 11 ――――――――

6e11.1

鵄　tobi　kite (the bird)

聰→聡　**6e8.2**

―――――――――――

6

糸
米
舟
虫
耳 11←
竹

6e11.2

聯 聨

REN group, accompaniment (now usually written with 連)

———————— 1 ————————
6 聯合 **rengō** combination, league, coalition
11 聯隊 **rentai** regiment

———————— 2 ————————
14 関聯 **kanren** connection, relation, association

6e11.3 / 1039

聴 聽

CHŌ, ki(ku) hear, listen to

———————— 1 ————————
2 聴力 **chōryoku** hearing ability
8 聴官 **chōkan** auditory organ
聴者 **chōsha** listener
聴取 **chōshu** listening
聴取者 **chōshusha** (radio) listener
聴取料 **chōshuryō** radio fee
9 聴度 **chōdo** audibility
聴神経 **chōshinkei** auditory nerve
聴音 **chōon** hearing, sound detection
聴音器 **chōonki** sound detector
聴音機 **chōonki** sound detector
10 聴従 **chōjū** follow (advice)
11 聴視 **chōshi** listening to and watching
聴視者 **chōshisha** (TV) viewer(s)
聴視料 **chōshiryō** television fee
聴視覚 **chōshikaku** audio-visual
聴許 **chōkyo** permission, approval
12 聴覚 **chōkaku** sense of hearing
聴衆 **chōshū** audience
聴診 **chōshin** auscultation
聴診器 **chōshinki** stethoscope
13 聴罪 **chōzai** hearing confessions
聴罪師 **chōzaishi** (Catholic) confessor
14 聴聞 **chōmon** listening to
聴聞会 **chōmonkai** public hearing
聴聞僧 **chōmonsō** confessor
17 聴講 **chōkō** attendance at a lecture
聴講生 **chōkōsei** auditing student
聴講券 **chōkōken** lecture admittance ticket

———————— 2 ————————
4 幻聴 **genchō** auditory hallucination
公聴会 **kōchōkai** public hearing
5 可聴性 **kachōsei** audibility
7 来聴 **raichō** attend (a lecture)
吹聴 **fuichō** publicize, trumpet, herald
8 拝聴 **haichō** listen to
11 清聴 **seichō** your kind attention (to my talk)
視聴 **shichō** looking and listening, attention

視聴率 **shichōritsu** (TV show popularity) rating
視聴覚 **shichōkaku** audiovisual
盗聴 **tōchō** surreptitious listening, bugging, wiretapping
12 傍聴 **bōchō** hearing, attendance, auditing
傍聴人 **bōchōnin** hearer, auditor, audience
傍聴席 **bōchōseki** seats for the public, visitors' gallery
補聴器 **hochōki** hearing aid
13 傾聴 **keichō** listen (attentively) to
試聴 **shichō** audition
17 謹聴 **kinchō** listen attentively
18 難聴 **nanchō** hard of hearing

聲 → 声 3p4.4

6e11.4

聳

SHŌ, sobi(eru) rise, tower above **sobi(yakasu)** raise, throw back (one's shoulders)

———————— 1 ————————
11 聳動 **shōdō** electrify, startle, shock

6e11.5

聱

GŌ refusal to listen; difficult-to-understand wording

———————— 12 ————————

6e12.1 / 385

職 耺

SHOKU employment, job, occupation, office

———————— 1 ————————
2 職人 **shokunin** craftsman, workman
3 職工 **shokkō** (factory) worker
4 職分 **shokubun** one's duties
6 職印 **shokuin** official seal
職安 **shokuan** (public) employment security office (short for 公共職業安定所)
8 職長 **shokuchō** foreman
職制 **shokusei** office organization
10 職員 **shokuin** personnel, staff (member)
職員室 **shokuinshitsu** staff/teachers' room
職員録 **shokuinroku** list of government officials
職能 **shokunō** function; job performance
職能給 **shokunōkyū** merit pay
11 職階 **shokkai** (civil-service) grade
職階制 **shokkaisei** job-rank system
職域 **shokuiki** occupation, one's post

職務 **shokumu** job, office, duties
職責 **shokuseki** one's duties
12 職場 **shokuba** workplace, job site
職掌 **shokushō** office, duties
13 職業 **shokugyō** occupation, profession
職業安定所 **shokugyō anteisho/jo** (public) employment security office
職業的 **shokugyōteki** professional
職業病 **shokugyōbyō** occupational disease
14 職歴 **shokureki** one's occupational history
職種 **shokushu** type of occupation
15 職権 **shokken** one's official authority

——————— 2 ———————
4 天職 **tenshoku** vocation, calling, lifework
内職 **naishoku** at-home work, side job, cottage industry
公職 **kōshoku** public official
手職 **teshoku** handicraft
5 本職 **honshoku** one's regular occupation; an expert; I
失職 **shisshoku** unemployment
6 休職 **kyūshoku** temporary retirement from office, layoff
同職 **dōshoku** the same occupation, said occupation
汚職 **oshoku** corruption, graft
汚職罪 **oshokuzai** bribery
在職 **zaishoku** hold office, remain in office
当職 **tōshoku** this occupation; one's present duties
有職 **yūshoku** employed **yūsoku, yūshoku** person versed in court and military practices, scholar
有職者 **yūshokusha** employed person
7 住職 **jūshoku** chief priest of a temple
求職 **kyūshoku** job hunting, Situation Wanted
8 非職 **hishoku** retired
奉職 **hōshoku** be in the service of, hold a post
免職 **menshoku** dismissal, discharge
退職 **taishoku** retirement
退職金 **taishokukin** retirement allowance
官職 **kanshoku** government post/service
定職 **teishoku** regular occupation, steady job
9 軍職 **gunshoku** military profession
要職 **yōshoku** important post/office
神職 **shinshoku** Shinto priest(hood)
10 兼職 **kenshoku** concurrent post
座職 **zashoku** sedentary work
殉職 **junshoku** dying in the line of duty
教職 **kyōshoku** the teaching profession
教職者 **kyōshokusha** teacher, clergyman
教職員 **kyōshokuin** faculty, teaching staff
11 停職 **teishoku** suspension from office
現職 **genshoku** present post, incumbent
転職 **tenshoku** change of post/occupation

12 就職 **shūshoku** find employment
就職口 **shūshokuguchi** job opening, employment
就職先 **shūshokusaki** place of employment
就職斡旋 **shūshoku assen** job placement
就職難 **shūshokunan** job shortage
復職 **fukushoku** reinstatement, reappointment
無職 **mushoku** unemployed; no occupation
無職者 **mushokusha** the unemployed
補職 **hoshoku** appointment (to a post)
畳職 **tatamishoku** tatami maker/dealer
閑職 **kanshoku** easy job, sinecure
13 僧職 **sōshoku** (Buddhist) priesthood
適職 **tekishoku** suitable occupation
聖職 **seishoku** ministry, clergy, holy orders
解職 **kaishoku** discharge, dismissal
辞職 **jishoku** resignation, quitting
辞職願 **jishoku nega(i)** letter of resignation
飾職 **kaza(ri)shoku** jewelry maker
14 鳶職 **tobishoku** construction laborer
18 瀆職 **tokushoku** corruption, graft, bribery
瀆職罪 **tokushokuzai** bribery, graft
離職 **rishoku** quit/lose one's job
離職者 **rishokusha** the unemployed
顕職 **kenshoku** important post
19 曠職 **kōshoku** neglecting one's duties
27 黷職 **tokushoku** corruption, graft

——————— 3 ———————
3 下級職 **kakyūshoku** subordinate post
4 手内職 **tenaishoku** manual piecework at home
5 司祭職 **shisaishoku** (Catholic) priesthood
6 名誉職 **meiyoshoku** honary post
10 将軍職 **shōgunshoku** shogunate
14 総辞職 **sōjishoku** mass resignation
管理職 **kanrishoku** administrative position; the management

6e12.2

聶 **JŌ, sasaya(ku)** whisper

6e12.3

叢 **SŌ** congregate, cluster
kusamura thicket, the bush
mura- massing together

——————— 1 ———————
10 叢書 **sōsho** series, library
12 叢雲 **murakumo** cloud masses

——————— 2 ———————
4 木叢 **komura** thicket
6 竹叢 **takamura** bamboo grove/thicket
9 草叢 **kusamura** in the grass

6
糸
米
舟
虫
耳 12←
艹

12 淵叢 **ensō** center, home, cradle of
14 稲叢 **inamura** rick, stack of rice straw
15 論叢 **ronsō** collection of treatises

─────────── 14 ───────────

6e14.1

瞺

NEI noisy; earwax

─────────── 16 ───────────

聽 → 聴 6e11.3

6e16.1

聾

RŌ, tsunbo deaf

─────────── 1 ───────────

0 聾する **rō(suru)** deafen
7 聾学校 **rōgakkō** school for the deaf
10 聾桟敷 **tsunbo sajiki** the upper gallery
11 聾啞 **rōa** deaf and mute
聾啞者 **rōasha** a deaf-mute

─────────── 2 ───────────

4 片聾 **katatsunbo** deaf in one ear
8 金聾 **kanatsunbo** stone-deaf

━━━━━━━━━━ ⺮ 6f ━━━━━━━━━━

竹 0.1	竺 2.1	笈 3.1	筑 3.2	竿 3.3	笋 6f6.14	笑 4.1	笄 6f6.5	笊 4.2	笆 4.3	笏 4.4	笠 5.1	笧 5.2
笹 5.3	笙 5.4	第 5.5	笛 5.6	笨 5.7	笑 5.8	笵 5.9	笳 5.10	笘 5.11	符 5.12	答 5.13	笱 5.14	笥 5.15
筆 6.1	策 6.2	筬 6.3	筋 6.4	笄 6.5	筑 6.6	筏 6.7	笵 6.8	等 6.9	箸 6.10	筌 6.11	答 6.12	筝 6f8.10
筵 6.13	筍 6.14	筒 6.15	筐 6.16	笶 7.1	笙 7.2	節 7.3	笒 6f13.4	笮 7.4	筱 6f11.3	筥 7.5	筮 7.6	筧 7.7
質 7b8.7	箸 6f9.1	箚 8.1	箙 8.2	箝 8.3	箍 8.4	箔 8.5	箕 8.6	算 8.7	箜 8.8	箟 6f8.14	箋 8.9	箏 8.10
箟 8.11	管 8.12	箒 8.13	箘 8.14	箇 8.15	箸 9.1	箴 9.2	範 9.3	節 6f7.3	嵌 3o9.2	箱 9.4	箨 9.5	篁 9.6
箪 6f12.2	箭 9.7	篆 9.8	篇 9.9	匲 9.10	篤 10.1	篩 10.2	篭 6f16.1	篳 10.3	篥 10.4	築 10.5	篡 10.6	篝 10.7
簑 3k10.24	篦 6f8.11	篷 10.8	艊 11.1	簇 11.2	篠 11.3	簍 11.4	簗 11.5	簒 6f10.6	篶 11.6	簀 11.7	簞 12.1	簟 12.2
簀 12.3	簧 12.4	簡 12.5	簫 13.1	簸 13.2	簶 13.3	簿 13.4	籀 13.5	簽 13.6	簷 13.7	簾 13.8	籍 14.1	簇 14.2
簪 14.3	纂 14.4	籌 14.5	籔 3k15.1	籐 15.1	籃 15.2	籤 6f17.2	籠 16.1	籟 16.2	籐 6f15.1	籬 17.1	籤 17.2	籬 18.1

─────────── 0 ───────────

6f0.1 / 129

竹

CHIKU, take bamboo

─────────── 1 ───────────

2 竹子 **take(no)ko** bamboo shoots
竹刀 **shinai** bamboo sword (for kendo)
5 竹矢来 **takeyarai** bamboo palisade
竹皮 **take(no)kawa** bamboo sheath
6 竹光 **takemitsu** bamboo sword

8 竹林 **takebayashi, chikurin** bamboo grove
9 竹垣 **takegaki** bamboo fence/hedge
竹竿 **takezao** bamboo pole
10 竹馬 **takeuma, chikuba** stilts
竹馬友 **chikuba (no) tomo** childhood playmate
11 竹細工 **takezaiku** bamboo handicrafts
12 竹筒 **takezutsu** bamboo tube
13 竹園生 **take (no) sonoo** bamboo garden; the imperial family
14 竹槍 **takeyari** bamboo spear

竹箆 **takebera** bamboo slat/spatula
　　shippei flat bamboo stick for slapping
　　　meditators to keep them awake
竹箆返 **shippeigae(shi)** retaliation, tit for tat
15 竹縁 **takeen** bamboo-floored veranda
18 竹藪 **takeyabu** bamboo grove/thicket
　竹叢 **takamura** bamboo grove/thicket
22 竹籠 **takekago** bamboo basket

————————— 2 —————————

5 石竹 **sekichiku** a pink (the flower)
　石竹色 **sekichiku-iro** pink (the color)
6 糸竹 **itotake** (koto) strings and bamboo (flute),
　　　music
7 夾竹桃 **kyōchikutō** oleander, phlox
8 松竹 **matsutake** New Year's pine-and-
　　　bamboo decorations
　松竹梅 **shō-chiku-bai** pine-bamboo-plum (as
　　　sign of congratulations or to designate
　　　three things of equal rank)
　青竹 **aodake** green bamboo
10 真竹 **madake** (common) bamboo
　破竹 **hachiku** splitting bamboo
11 黒竹 **kurochiku** black bamboo
12 寒竹 **kanchiku** solid bamboo
13 漢竹 **kanchiku** solid bamboo
　群竹 **muratake** stand of bamboo
　筮竹 **zeichiku** divination sticks
19 爆竹 **bakuchiku** firecraker

————————— 3 —————————

4 火吹竹 **hifu(ki)dake** bamboo blowpipe (for
　　　charcoal fires)

————————— 2 —————————

6f2.1

竺

JIKU bamboo

————————— 2 —————————

4 天竺 **Tenjiku** India

————————— 3 —————————

10 唐天竺 **Kara-Tenjiku** China and India

————————— 3 —————————

6f3.1

笈

KYŪ, oi backpack for carrying books

6f3.2

笂

utsubo quiver (for holding arrows)

6f3.3

竿

KAN, sao pole

————————— 1 —————————

16 竿頭 **kantō** top of a pole

————————— 2 —————————

6 竹竿 **takezao** bamboo pole
11 殻竿 **karazao** a flail
　釣竿 **tsu(ri)zao** fishing rod
13 継竿 **tsu(gi)zao** jointed fishing rod

————————— 3 —————————

8 物干竿 **monoho(shi)zao** washline pole

————————— 4 —————————

筝 → 箏 **6f6.14**

6f4.1 / 1235

笑

SHŌ, wara(u) laugh, smile
e(mu) smile

————————— 1 —————————

3 笑上戸 **wara(i)jōgo** one who gets jolly when
　　　drunk; one who laughs readily
4 笑止 **shōshi** laughable, ludicrous
　笑止千万 **shōshi-senban** ridiculous, absurd
5 笑出 **wara(i)da(su)** burst out laughing
6 笑気 **shōki** laughing gas
7 笑声 **wara(i)goe, shōsei** laughter
8 笑事 **wara(i)goto** laughing matter
　笑者 **wara(ware)mono** laughingstock
　笑物 **wara(i)mono** laughingstock, butt of
　　　ridicule
9 笑飛 **wara(i)to(basu)** laugh off/away
　笑草 **wara(i)gusa** topic of amusement
10 笑殺 **shōsatsu** laugh off
　笑納 **shōnō** your acceptance (of my gift)
12 笑割 **e(mi)wa(reru)** crack/split open
　笑絵 **wara(i)e** comic/pornographic picture
13 笑話 **wara(i)banashi, shōwa** funny story
15 笑劇 **shōgeki** farce
17 笑覧 **shōran** your inspection
18 笑顔 **egao, wara(i)gao** smiling face

————————— 2 —————————

1 一笑 **isshō** a laugh/smile
2 人笑 **hitowara(ware)** laughingstock
3 大笑 **ōwara(i), taishō** a big laugh
5 失笑 **shisshō** laugh, burst out laughing
7 作笑 **tsuku(ri)wara(i)** forced laugh
　含笑 **fuku(mi)wara(i)** suppressed laugh,
　　　chuckle, giggle

6

糸
米
舟
虫
耳

⺮ 4 ←

冷笑 **reishō** derisive smile, scornful laugh, sneer
忍笑 **shino(bi)wara(i)** stifled laugh, giggle, chuckle, snickering
8 侮笑 **bushō** derision
泣笑 **na(ki)wara(i)** smile through one's tears
苦笑 **kushō, nigawara(i)** bitter/wry smile
空笑 **sorawara(i)** forced laugh, feigned smile
物笑 **monowara(i)** laughingstock, joke
9 哄笑 **kōshō** loud laughter
10 高笑 **takawara(i)** loud/boisterous laughter
11 盗笑 **nusu(mi)wara(i)** laughing in one's sleeve
12 閔笑 **binshō** smile with pity
13 微笑 **bishō, hohoe(mi)** smile
15 嬌笑 **kyōshō** attractive/charming smile
談笑 **danshō** chat, friendly talk
19 艶笑小説 **enshō shōsetsu** love-comedy story/novel
爆笑 **bakushō** burst out laughing

──────── 3 ────────
9 思出笑 **omo(i)da(shi)wara(u)** smile over a memory
13 微苦笑 **bikushō** wry/bittersweet smile

──────── 4 ────────
10 破顔一笑 **hagan-isshō** break into a grin

笁 → 筭 **6f6.5**

6f4.2

筮

SŌ, zaru bamboo basket

6f4.3

笆

HA thorny bamboo; bamboo fence

6f4.4

笏

KOTSU, shaku wooden slat/spatula carried by court officials as a scepter of office

──────── 5 ────────

6f5.1

笠

RYŪ, kasa bamboo hat; (lamp)shade, hood

──────── 2 ────────
3 小笠原諸島 **Ogasawara-shotō** the Bonin Islands

8 松笠 **matsukasa** pinecone
9 陣笠 **jingasa** (ancient) soldier's helmet; rank and file (of a party)
11 菅笠 **sugegasa** hat woven from sedge

6f5.2

簓

SAKU, shigarami weir

6f5.3

笹

sasa bamboo grass

──────── 1 ────────
6 笹舟 **sasabune** toy bamboo-leaf boat
18 笹藪 **sasayabu** bamboo-grass thicket

6f5.4

笙

SHŌ (a type of reed flute)

6f5.5 / 404

第 才

DAI (prefix for ordinals), No. (1, 2, etc.); a residence; (passing an) examination

──────── 1 ────────
1 第一 **dai-ichi** No. 1, first, best, main
第一人者 **dai-ichininsha** foremost/leading person
第一人称 **dai-ichininshō** first person (in grammar)
第一次 **dai-ichiji** first
第一流 **dai-ichiryū** first-rate
第一義 **dai-ichigi** original meaning; first principles
第一線 **dai-issen** the first/front line
2 第二人称 **dai-nininshō** second person (in grammar)
第二次 **dai-niji** second
第二次的 **dai-nijiteki** secondary
第二組合 **dai-ni kumiai** rival labor union
第二義 **dai-nigi** secondary meaning
第二義的 **dai-nigiteki** of secondary importance
3 第三人称 **dai-sanninshō** third person (in grammar)
第三火 **dai-san (no) hi** nuclear energy
第三国 **dai-sangoku** third country/power
第三国人 **dai-sangokujin** third-country national
第三者 **dai-sansha** third person/party
第三紀 **dai-sanki** the Tertiary (geological) period

第三階級 **dai-san kaikyū** the third estate, the bourgeoisie
4 第五列 **dai-goretsu** fifth column
第六感 **dai-rokkan** sixth sense
5 第四階級 **dai-shi kaikyū** the fourth estate, the proletariat

——— 2 ———
3 及第 **kyūdai** passing (an exam), make the grade
及第点 **kyūdaiten** passing grade
6 次第 **shidai** order, precedence; circumstances; as soon as; according to; gradually
12 登第 **tōdai** pass an examination
落第 **rakudai** failure in an exam
落第生 **rakudaisei** student who failed
落第点 **rakudaiten** failing mark

——— 3 ———
6 安全第一 **anzen dai-ichi** Safety First
11 望次第 **nozo(mi) shidai** as desired, on demand
12 腕次第 **ude-shidai** according to one's ability

——— 4 ———
4 手当次第 **tea(tari) shidai** (whatever is) within reach, haphazardly
12 勝手次第 **katte-shidai** having one's own way

6f5.6 / 1471

笛

TEKI, fue flute, whistle

——— 1 ———
7 笛吹 **fuefu(ki)** flute/fife/clarinet player
笛声 **tekisei** sound of a flute/whistle

——— 2 ———
3 口笛 **kuchibue** whistling
5 号笛 **gōteki** horn, siren, whistle
7 角笛 **tsunobue** huntsman's horn, bugle
汽笛 **kiteki** (steam) whistle, siren
麦笛 **mugibue** wheat-straw whistle
8 牧笛 **bokuteki** shepherd's flute
9 草笛 **kusabue** reed whistle
13 葦笛 **ashibue** reed whistle/flute
鼓笛隊 **kotekitai** drum-and-bugle corps, fife-and-drum band
14 竪笛 **tatebue** recorder, upright flute
銀笛 **ginteki** metal flute
15 横笛 **yokobue** flute, fife
16 縦笛 **tatebue** recorder, *shakuhachi*
19 警笛 **keiteki** alarm whistle, horn
霧笛 **muteki** fog horn

——— 3 ———
8 虎落笛 **mogaribue** sound of the winter wind whistling through a fence

6f5.7

笨

HON rough, coarse, crude; fool

——— 2 ———
11 粗笨 **sohon** crude, rough

6f5.8

笶

SHI arrow

6f5.9

笵

HAN, BON bamboo frame; law

6f5.10

笳

KA reed flute

6f5.11

笪

SEN whip, cane; wooden writing slate

6f5.12 / 505

符

FU sign, mark; amulet

——— 1 ———
2 符丁 **fuchō** mark, symbol, code
5 符号 **fugō** mark, symbol, code
6 符合 **fugō** coincidence, agreement, correspondence
13 符牒 **fuchō** mark, symbol, code
符節 **fusetsu** tally, check

——— 2 ———
4 切符 **kippu** ticket
8 呪符 **jufu** charm, amulet, talisman
9 神符 **shinpu** charm, amulet, talisman
音符 **onpu** (musical) note; the part of a kanji indicating its pronunciation
12 割符 **wa(ri)fu** tally, check
20 護符 **gofu** amulet, talisman

——— 3 ———
4 引用符 **in'yōfu** quotation marks
6 休止符 **kyūshifu** rest (in music)
全音符 **zen'onpu** whole note
7 赤切符 **akagippu** third-class ticket
8 長音符 **chōonpu** long-vowel mark, macron

6

糸
米
舟
虫
耳

⺮ 5 ←

免罪符 **menzaifu** an indulgence
9 通切符 **tō(shi)kippu** through ticket
11 終止符 **shūshifu** full stop, period, end
13 感嘆符 **kantanfu** exclamation point (!)
14 疑問符 **gimonfu** question mark

———————— 4 ————————

2 二分音符 **nibun onpu** half note
八分音符 **hachibu onpu** an eighth note (♪)
5 四分音符 **shibu onpu, shibun onpu** quarter note
8 往復切符 **ōfuku kippu** round trip ticket

6f5.13

答

CHI, muchi whip, cane

———————— 1 ————————

6 笞刑 **chikei** flogging

6f5.14

笴

KA arrow shaft

6f5.15

笥

SHI, SU box; clothes chest

———————— 2 ————————

18 箪笥 **tansu** chest of drawers, dresser

———————— 3 ————————

5 用箪笥 **yōdansu** chest of drawers
9 茶箪笥 **chadansu** tea cupboard/cabinet

———————— 4 ————————

16 整理箪笥 **seiridansu** chest of drawers

———————— 6 ————————

6f6.1 / 130

筆

HITSU, fude writing brush

———————— 1 ————————

2 筆入 **fudei(re)** writing-brush holder
筆力 **hitsuryoku** power of the pen
4 筆不精 **fudebushō** negligent in corresponding
筆太 **fudebuto** bold strokes/lettering
5 筆生 **hissei** copyist, amanuensis
筆付 **fudetsu(ki)** brushwork
筆写 **hissha** copy, transcribe
筆立 **fudeta(te)** writing-brush stand
6 筆先 **fudesaki** brush tip; writings
筆舌 **hitsuzetsu** the pen and the tongue

筆名 **hitsumei** pen name, pseudonym
8 筆法 **hippō** calligraphy technique; manner
筆者 **hissha** the writer/author
9 筆陣 **hitsujin** verbal battle; lineup of writers
筆洗 **hissen** brush-writing receptacle
筆架 **hikka** pen rack
10 筆耕 **hikkō** copy, stencil
筆耕料 **hikkōryō** copying fee
筆書 **(hito)fudega(ki)** writing without redipping the brush into the inkwell
筆致 **hitchi** brush stroke; (writing) style
筆紙 **hisshi** pen and paper
筆記 **hikki** taking notes; notes
筆記者 **hikkisha** copyist
筆記帳 **hikkichō** notebook
12 筆遣 **fudezuka(i)** manner of writing, brush-work
筆塚 **fudezuka** mound made over used writing brushes buried with a memorial service
筆答 **hittō** written reply
筆筒 **fudezutsu** brush case
筆順 **hitsujun** stroke order
13 筆勢 **hissei** brushwork, penmanship
筆禍 **hikka** serious slip of the pen
筆戦 **hissen** a war of the pen
筆意 **hitsui** writing
筆触 **hisshoku** touch of the brush/pen
筆跡 **hisseki** handwriting (specimen)
14 筆墨 **hitsuboku** pen and ink
筆端 **hittan** brush/pen tip; writing/painting style
筆算 **hissan** calculating on paper
15 筆箱 **fudebako** brush/pencil case
筆談 **hitsudan** conversation by writing
16 筆頭 **hittō** brush tip; the first on the list
筆頭書 **hittōsha** head of the household (listed first on the family register)

———————— 2 ————————

1 一筆 **ippitsu, hitofude** a stroke of the pen, a few lines
3 才筆 **saihitsu** literary talent, brilliant style
土筆 **tsukushi** field horsetail
4 毛筆 **mōhitsu** writing/painting brush
文筆 **bunpitsu** literary activity, writing
文筆家 **bunpitsuka** literary man, writer
5 代筆 **daihitsu** write (a letter) for another
加筆 **kahitsu** correct, revise, retouch
古筆 **kohitsu** old writings
用筆 **yōhitsu** brushes used; use of a brush
主筆 **shuhitsu** editor in chief
石筆 **sekihitsu** slate pencil
6 肉筆 **nikuhitsu** one's own handwriting, autograph
同筆 **dōhitsu** the same handwriting
名筆 **meihitsu** excellent calligraphy

6

糸
米
舟
虫
耳
→ 5 ⺮

自筆 **jihitsu** one's own handwriting
7 乱筆 **ranpitsu** hasty writing, scrawl
8 画筆 **gahitsu** artist's brush
毒筆 **dokuhitsu** spiteful/poison pen
直筆 **jikihitsu** in one's own handwriting
　　 chokuhitsu write with brush held upright; write plainly/frankly
拙筆 **seppitsu** poor handwriting
9 俗筆 **zokuhitsu** crude handwriting
染筆料 **senpitsuryō** writing fee
祐筆 **yūhitsu** amanuensis, secretary
10 健筆 **kenpitsu** powerful pen
随筆 **zuihitsu** essay, miscellaneous writings
真筆 **shinpitsu** autograph, one's own handwriting
起筆 **kihitsu** begin to write
宸筆 **shinpitsu** emperor's autograph
能筆 **nōhitsu** calligraphy, skilled penmanship
特筆 **tokuhitsu** make special mention of
特筆大書 **tokuhitsu-taisho** write large, single out
11 偽筆 **gihitsu** forged handwriting/picture
達筆 **tappitsu** good penmanship; speedy writing, flowing style
運筆 **unpitsu** strokes of the brush/pen
執筆 **shippitsu** write (for a magazine)
執筆者 **shippitsusha** writer, contributor
悪筆 **akuhitsu** poor handwriting
略筆 **ryakuhitsu** outline, synopsis; simplified character
細筆 **saihitsu** fine brush; writing small
訳筆 **yakuhitsu** style of translation
12 着筆 **chakuhitsu** begin to write; manner of writing
減筆 **genpitsu** writing abbreviatedly
焼筆 **ya(ki)fude** charcoal (sketching) pencil
無筆 **muhitsu** illiterate, unlettered
硬筆 **kōhitsu** pen or pencil (rather than brush)
補筆 **hohitsu** add/append to (a work)
絵筆 **efude** paintbrush
絶筆 **zeppitsu** one's last writing
13 試筆 **shihitsu** first writing of the new year
鉄筆 **teppitsu** steel/stencil pen, stylus; powerful pen
鉛筆 **enpitsu** pencil
14 漫筆 **manpitsu** random comments/essay
雑筆 **zappitsu** miscellaneous writings
15 潤筆 **junpitsu** painting and writing
潤筆料 **junpitsuryō** writing/painting fee
16 親筆 **shinpitsu** one's own handwriting
17 擱筆 **kakuhitsu** put down one's pen, finish writing
19 麗筆 **reihitsu** beautiful writing

———————— 3 ————————
3 万年筆 **mannenhitsu** fountain pen
6 色鉛筆 **iroenpitsu** colored pencil

6f6.2 / 880

策

SAKU plan, means, measure, policy

———————— 1 ————————
3 策士 **sakushi** tactician, schemer
7 策応 **sakuō** in concert/collusion with
8 策定 **sakutei** devise, formulate (a plan/policy)
11 策動 **sakudō** manipulation, maneuvering
策動家 **sakudōka** schemer
策略 **sakuryaku** stratagem, scheme, tactic
13 策源地 **sakugenchi** base of operations
策戦 **sakusen** (military) operation
16 策謀 **sakubō** stratagem, machinations

———————— 2 ————————
1 一策 **issaku** an idea, a plan
3 万策 **bansaku** every means
上策 **jōsaku** good plan, wisest policy
凡策 **bonsaku** commonplace policy
小策 **shōsaku** pretty trick/artifice
4 方策 **hōsaku** plan
5 失策 **shissaku** blunder, slip, error
6 奸策 **kansaku** sinister scheme
7 良策 **ryōsaku** good plan/policy
対策 **taisaku** (counter)measures
妙策 **myōsaku** ingenious plan
8 画策 **kakusaku** plan, map out; maneuver, scheme
拙策 **sessaku** poor policy, imprudent measure
奇策縦横 **kisaku-jūō** clever planning
国策 **kokusaku** national policy
金策 **kinsaku** means of raising money
9 施策 **shisaku** a measure/policy
政策 **seisaku** policy
10 秘策 **hisaku** secret plan
11 商策 **shōsaku** business policy
術策 **jussaku** stratagem, artifice, tricks
得策 **tokusaku** advantageous policy, wise plan
12 無策 **musaku** resourceless, at a loss
散策 **sansaku** walk, stroll
13 献策 **kensaku** suggest, propose, advise
愚策 **gusaku** foolish/ill-advised plan
詭策 **kisaku** ploy, ruse, trick
15 窮策 **kyūsaku** desperate measure, last resort
論策 **ronsaku** commentary on current topics

———————— 3 ————————
3 万全策 **banzen (no) saku** carefully thought-out plan, prudent policy
4 不得策 **futokusaku** unwise, bad policy, ill-advised
予防策 **yobōsaku** precautionary measures
7 対抗策 **taikōsaku** (counter)measures
対応策 **taiōsaku** (counter)measures
応急策 **ōkyūsaku** emergency/stopgap measure

6

糸
米
舟
虫
耳
⺮ 6 ←

8 弥縫策 **bihōsaku** makeshift, stopgap measure
　具体策 **gutaisaku** specific measures
9 持久策 **jikyūsaku** dilatory tactics
11 救治策 **kyūjisaku** a cure
　救急策 **kyūkyūsaku** emergency measures
　救済策 **kyūsaisaku** relief measure
12 善後策 **zengosaku** remedial measures
18 離間策 **rikansaku** sowing discord

——————————— 4 ———————————

4 水害対策 **suigai taisaku** flood control/relief measures
9 宥和政策 **yūwa seisaku** appeasement policy
15 窮余一策 **kyūyo (no) issaku** last resort

6f6.3

SEI, osa reed, yarn guide (on a loom)

筬

6f6.4 / 1090

筋

KIN muscle, sinews　**suji** muscle, tendon; blood vessel; line; stripe, steak; reason, logic, coherence; plot (of a story); source (of information)

——————————— 1 ———————————

2 筋子 **sujiko** salmon roe
　筋力 **kinryoku** physical strength
5 筋目 **sujime** fold, crease; lineage; logic
6 筋合 **sujia(i)** reason
　筋肉 **kinniku** muscle
　筋交 **sujika(i)** diagonal; brace
　筋向 **sujimu(kai)** diagonally opposite
8 筋金 **sujigane** metal reinforcement
　筋金入 **sujiganei(ri)** hardcore, dyed-in-the-wool
10 筋骨 **kinkotsu, sujibone** sinews and bones
　筋書 **sujiga(ki)** synopsis, outline, plan
11 筋道 **sujimichi** reason, logic, coherence
　筋張 **sujiba(ru)** become stiff/sinewy; be formal
12 筋違 **sujichiga(e)** a cramp
　　　 sujichiga(i) illogical; diagonal
　　　 sujika(i) diagonal; brace

——————————— 2 ———————————

1 一筋 **hitosuji** a line; earnestly, wholeheart-edly
　一筋道 **hitosujimichi** straight road, road with no turnoffs
　一筋縄 **hitosujinawa** a piece of rope; ordinary means
2 二筋道 **futasujimichi** forked road, crossroads
3 川筋 **kawasuji** course of a river
4 太筋 **futosuji** thick line, bar
　毛筋 **kesuji** hairline; a hair

手筋 **tesuji** lines of the palm; aptitude; means, method
心筋 **shinkin** heart muscle, myocardium
心筋梗塞 **shinkin kōsoku** myocardial infarction
5 本筋 **honsuji** plot, main thread (of a story)
6 血筋 **chisuji** blood relationship, lineage
7 伸筋 **shinkin** protractor/extensor muscle
　町筋 **machisuji** street
8 其筋 **so(no) suji** the authorities concerned
　屈筋 **kukkin** flexor muscle
　青筋 **aosuji** blue vein
　金筋 **kinsuji** gold stripes
9 首筋 **kubisuji** nape/scruff of the neck
　通筋 **tō(ri)suji** route, course, road
　客筋 **kyakusuji** quality of the clientele
　背筋 **sesuji** line of the backbone; seam down the back　**haikin** the muscles of the back
　背筋力 **haikinryoku** back-muscle strength
10 家筋 **iesuji** lineage, family pedigree
11 道筋 **michisuji** route, itinerary; reason
　粗筋 **arasuji** outline, summary, synopsis
13 腹筋 **fukkin, fukukin, harasuji** abdominal muscles
　鉄筋 **tekkin** steel reinforcing rods
14 鼻筋 **hanasuji** the bridge/line of the nose
　銀筋 **ginsuji** silver line/stripe
15 横筋 **yokosuji** transversal; horizontal stripes
16 縦筋 **tatesuji** vertical line/stripe
　頸筋 **kubisuji** nape/scruff of the neck

——————————— 3 ———————————

2 二頭筋 **nitōkin** biceps
3 大手筋 **ōtesuji** big traders, major companies
5 玄人筋 **kurōtosuji** professionals
　外交筋 **gaikōsuji** diplomatic sources
8 官辺筋 **kanpensuji** government/official sources
9 括約筋 **katsuyakukin** sphincter (muscle)
　政府筋 **seifusuji** government sources
10 随意筋 **zuiikin** voluntary muscle
　消息筋 **shōsokusuji** well informed sources
11 商売筋 **shōbaisuji** business connections
15 権威筋 **ken'i suji** authoritative sources

——————————— 4 ———————————

4 不随意筋 **fuzuiikin** involuntary muscle

6f6.5

笄 笄

KEI, kōgai ornamental hairpin

6f6.6

筑

CHIKU (ancient koto-like instrument)

────────── 1 ──────────

8 筑波 **Tsukuba** (city and university, Ibaraki-ken)
9 筑前 **Chikuzen** (ancient kuni, Fukuoka-ken)
筑後 **Chikugo** (ancient kuni, Saga-ken)

6f6.7

筏

BATSU, ikada raft

────────── 1 ──────────

10 筏師 **ikadashi** raftsman
12 筏焼 **ikadaya(ki)** split-open fish speared on spits and broiled

6f6.8

筅

SEN bamboo whisk (for tea-making)

────────── 2 ──────────

9 茶筅 **chasen** bamboo tea-ceremony whisk

6f6.9 / 569

等

TŌ class, grade; equal; etc.
hito(shii) equal **-nado** and so forth, etc.
-ra and others, and the like; (plural suffix)

────────── 1 ──────────

3 等々 **tōtō** etc., and so forth
4 等分 **tōbun** (division into) equal parts
等辺 **tōhen** equal sides
等辺三角形 **tōhen sankakkei/sankakukei** equilateral triangle
5 等外 **tōgai** non-winner, also-ran, offgrade
等比 **tōhi** equal ratio
等比級数 **tōhi kyūsū** geometric progression
等圧 **tōatsu** equal pressure
等圧線 **tōatsusen** isobar
等号 **tōgō** equal sign (=)
6 等式 **tōshiki** an equality
7 等身 **tōshin** life-size
等身像 **tōshinzō** life-size statue
等位 **tōi** rank, grade
等角 **tōkaku** equal angles
8 等価 **tōka** equivalence, parity
9 等級 **tōkyū** class, grade, rank
10 等値 **tōchi** equal value
等高線 **tōkōsen** contour line
等差 **tōsa** equal difference; graduated
等差級数 **tōsa kyūsū** arithmetic progression
11 等脚三角形 **tōkyaku sankakkei/sankakukei** isosceles triangle
12 等温 **tōon** isothermal
等量 **tōryō** equivalent
等等 **tōtō** etc., and so forth

等距離 **tōkyori** equidistant
等閑 **tōkan** neglect, disregard
15 等質 **tōshitsu** homogeneous
16 等親 **tōshin** degree of kinship

────────── 2 ──────────

1 一等 **ittō** first class/rank, the most/best
一等兵 **ittōhei** private first-class
一等車 **ittōsha** first-class coach
一等国 **ittōkoku** a first-class power
一等星 **ittōsei** first-magnitude star
一等賞 **ittōshō** first prize
一等親 **ittōshin** first-degree relative, immediate family
2 二等 **nitō** second class; second
二等分 **nitōbun** bisect
二等辺三角形 **nitōhen sankakkei/sankakukei** isosceles triangle
二等賞 **nitōshō** second prize
二等親 **nitōshin** a second-degree relative
3 三等 **santō** third class
三等分 **santōbun** trisect
上等 **jōtō** first-rate, superior
上等品 **jōtōhin** top-quality goods
下等 **katō** low, lower (animals/plants), inferior, base, vulgar
4 不等 **futō** inequality
不等辺 **futōhen** unequal sides
中等 **chūtō** medium/secondary grade, average quality
5 平等 **byōdō** equality, impartiality
6 同等 **dōtō** equal, on a par with
劣等 **rettō** inferiority
劣等感 **rettōkan** inferiority complex
7 我等 **warera** we
何等 **nanra** what, whatever
対等 **taitō** equality, parity
均等 **kintō** equality, uniformity, parity
初等 **shotō** elementary
初等科 **shotōka** elementary/beginners' course
8 郎等 **rōdō** vassals, retainers
彼等 **karera** they
官等 **kantō** official rank, civil-service grade
9 品等 **hintō** grade, rating, quality
相等 **sōtō** equality, equivalence
10 高等 **kōtō** high-grade, high-class
高等学校 **kōtō gakkō** senior high school
高等官 **kōtōkan** senior official
差等 **satō** gradation; difference
特等 **tokutō** special grade
12 減等 **gentō** lowering the class, reduction, mitigation
等等 **tōtō** etc., and so forth
15 勲等 **kuntō** order of merit
16 親等 **shintō** degree of consanguinity/kinship
17 優等 **yūtō** excellence, superiority

6

糸
米
舟
虫
耳

⺮ 6 ←

優等生 **yūtōsei** honors student
優等賞 **yūtōshō** honor prize

——————— 3 ———————
4 不平等 **fubyōdō** unequal

——————— 4 ———————
16 機会均等 **kikai kintō** equal opportunity

6f6.10

筈 **KATSU, hazu** arrow/bow notch; to be expected, surely

——————— 2 ———————
4 手筈 **tehazu** program, plan, arrangements
5 矢筈 **yahazu** nock, notch of an arrow
8 其筈 **so(no) hazu** reasonable, to be expected

6f6.11

筌 **SEN, uke** weir, fish trap

——————— 2 ———————
9 茶筌 **chasen** bamboo tea-ceremony whisk

6f6.12 / 160

答 **TŌ, kota(eru)** answer
kota(e) an answer

——————— 1 ———————
5 答弁 **tōben** reply, explanation, defense
答申 **tōshin** report
答申書 **tōshinsho** report, findings
答礼 **tōrei** return courtesy/salute
答礼使節 **tōrei shisetsu** envoy sent to return courtesies
答礼砲 **tōreihō** gun salute fired in return
10 答案 **tōan** examination paper
答砲 **tōhō** gun salute fired in return
13 答辞 **tōji** formal reply
答電 **tōden** reply telegram/message

——————— 2 ———————
3 口答 **kuchigota(e)** backtalk, retort
kōtō oral reply
口答試問 **kōtō shimon** oral examination/quiz
4 手答 **tegota(e)** response, effect, resistance
6 返答 **hentō** reply
名答 **meitō** excellent/apt answer
回答 **kaitō** reply
7 即答 **sokutō** prompt reply
決答 **kettō** definite answer
応答 **ōtō** answer, reply, response
8 受答 **u(ke)kota(e)** reply, response
直答 **chokutō, jikitō** prompt answer, direct/personal answer

明答 **meitō** definite answer
9 勅答 **chokutō** reply from/to the emperor
速答 **sokutō** prompt reply
11 問答 **mondō** questions and answers
12 無答責 **mutōseki** not liable
筆答 **hittō** written reply
13 解答 **kaitō** answer, solution
14 誤答 **gotō** incorrect answer
15 確答 **kakutō** definite answer
18 贈答 **zōtō** exchange of gifts
贈答品 **zōtōhin** gift, present

——————— 3 ———————
8 押問答 **o(shi)mondō** heated questioning and answering, dispute
13 禅問答 **zen mondō** Zen/incomprehensible dialog

——————— 4 ———————
1 一問一答 **ichimon-ittō** question-and-answer session
6 自問自答 **jimon-jitō** answering one's own question, sololiquy, monolog
13 愚問愚答 **gumon-gutō** silly dialog
15 質疑応答 **shitsugi-ōtō** question-and-answer (session)

筝 → 箏 **6f8.10**

6f6.13

筵 筵 **EN** (bamboo-straw) mat; seat; feast
mushiro (bamboo-straw) mat

——————— 2 ———————
6 帆筵 **homushiro** sail mat
7 花筵 **hana mushiro** floral-pattern mat

6f6.14

筍 笋 **JUN, takenoko** bamboo shoots

——————— 1 ———————
5 筍生活 **takenoko seikatsu** living by selling off one's personal effects
7 筍医者 **takenoko isha** inexperienced doctor

——————— 2 ———————
5 石筍 **sekijun** stalagmite (cf. 鐘乳石)

6f6.15 / 1472

筒 **TŌ, tsutsu** pipe, tube

——————— 1 ———————
4 筒井 **tsutsui** round well

筒井筒　tsutsuizutsu　wall/curb of a round well

6 筒先　tsutsusaki　pipe end, (gun) muzzle, (fireman holding the hose) nozzle

7 筒抜　tsutsunu(ke)　directly, clearly

筒形　tsutsugata　cylindrical, barrel-shaped

9 筒音　tsutsuoto　sound of a gun

10 筒袖　tsutsusode　tight sleeve, tight-sleeved dress

─────── 2 ───────

3 大筒　ōzutsu　cannon

小筒　kozutsu　rifle, small arms; bamboo saké flask

4 井筒　izutsu　well curb/wall

円筒　entō　cylinder

水筒　suitō　water flask, canteen

火筒　hozutsu　gun, firearms

5 矢筒　yazutsu　quiver

6 竹筒　takezutsu　bamboo tube

7 花筒　hanazutsu　flower tube/vase

9 封筒　fūtō　envelope

茶筒　chazutsu　tea canister

12 喞筒　shokutō　pump

筆筒　fudezutsu　brush case

13 煙筒　entō　chimney

─────── 3 ───────

12 弾薬筒　dan'yakutō　cartridge, round

筒井筒　tsutsuizutsu　wall/curb of a round well

17 擲弾筒　tekidantō　grenade launcher

6f6.16

筐　筺　KYŌ, katami　(rectangular) bamboo basket

─────── 1 ───────

7 筐体　kyōtai　housing, case, cabinet, enclosure

─────── 7 ───────

6f7.1

筴　KYŌ insert between; chopsticks
SAKU divining sticks; plan

6f7.2

筮　ZEI divination, augury; divining sticks

─────── 1 ───────

6 筮竹　zeichiku　divination sticks

─────── 2 ───────

2 卜筮　bokuzei　fortunetelling, divination

6f7.3 / 464

節　節　SETSU, SECHI season; occasion; section, paragraph, verse; joint; be moderate in, use sparingly; knot (nautical miles per hour)　fushi joint, knuckle; knot (in wood); melody; point, item

─────── 1 ───────

0 節する　ses(suru)　be moderate in, be sparing of

3 節々　fushibushi　joints; points (in a talk)

4 節分　setsubun　last day of winter

節水　sessui　use water sparingly

5 節付　fushizu(ke)　setting to music

節用　setsuyō　frugality; dictionary

節用集　setsuyōshū　dictionary, manual

節句　sekku　seasonal festival

節句働　sekkubatara(ki)　working on a holiday (to make up for lost time)

節穴　fushiana　knothole

節立　fushi(kure)da(tsu)　be knotty/gnarled/bony

節目　fushime　knot (in wood); turning point

6 節会　sechie　court banquet

節回　fushimawa(shi)　melody

節糸　fushiito　knotted silk

節米　setsumai　rice saving/economizing

7 節季　sekki　end of the year/season

節季仕舞　sekki-jimai　year-end closeout

節季市　sekki-ichi　a year-end fair

8 節供　sekku　seasonal festival

節制　sessei　moderation, temperance

9 節奏　sessō　rhythm

節度　setsudo　rule, standard; moderation

節約　setsuyaku　economizing, saving on

節食　sesshoku　eating in moderation

10 節倹　sekken　economizing, thrift

節酒　sesshu　drinking in moderation

節料理　(o)sechi ryōri　New Year's foods

11 節婦　seppu　faithful wife

12 節博士　fushi hakase　chanting intonation marks

節減　setsugen　curtailing

13 節義　setsugi　fidelity to one's principles

節煙　setsuen　smoking in moderation

節節　fushibushi　joints; points (in a talk)

節電　setsuden　saving on electricity

16 節操　sessō　fidelity, integrity; chastity

18 節織　fushio(ri)　coarse silk, pongee

─────── 2 ───────

1 一節　issetsu　a (Bible) verse, a stanza/passage

3 小節　shōsetsu　minor principles; bar (in music)

4 不節制　fusessei　intemperance, excesses

5 末節　massetsu　trifles, minor details

生節　namabushi　half-dried bonito

礼節　reisetsu　decorum, propriety, politeness

6

糸
米
舟
虫
耳

竹 7

6 此節 **ko(no)setsu** now, at present
当節 **tōsetsu** these days, nowadays
7 臣節 **shinsetsu** loyalty to one's liege
折節 **o(ri)fushi** occasionally
季節 **kisetsu** season, time of year
季節物 **kisetsumono** things in season
季節風 **kisetsufū** seasonal wind, monsoon
初節句 **hatsuzekku** child's first festival
8 使節 **shisetsu** envoy; mission, delegation
使節団 **shisetsudan** mission, delegation
佳節 **kasetsu** auspicious occasion
其節 **so(no) setsu** at that time
苦節 **kusetsu** loyalty under adversity
忠節 **chūsetsu** loyalty, devotion
9 削節 **kezu(ri)bushi** flaked shavings of dried bonito
変節 **hensetsu** defection, apostasy, changing sides
貞節 **teisetsu** fidelity, chastity
音節 **onsetsu** syllable
10 桃節句 **momo (no) sekku** Doll Festival (March 3)
骨節 **kossetsu, honebushi** joint
hone(p)pushi joint; spirit, strong character
時節 **jisetsu** season; the times; opportunity
時節柄 **jisetsugara** in these times
11 清節 **seisetsu** integrity
菊節句 **Kiku (no) Sekku** Chrysanthemum Festival
常節 **tokobushi** abalone, ear shell
章節 **shōsetsu** chapters and sections
細節 **saisetsu** minor details
符節 **fusetsu** tally, check
12 腕節 **ude(p)pushi** muscular strength
晩節 **bansetsu** one's final years
無節制 **musessei** intemperate
無節操 **musessō** inconstant; unchaste
結節 **kessetsu** knot, nodule, tubercle
13 節節 **fushibushi** joints; points (in a talk)
14 関節 **kansetsu** joint
関節炎 **kansetsuen** arthritis
15 調節 **chōsetsu** adjust, control, regulate
17 環節 **kansetsu** segment (of a worm)
18 雛節句 **hina (no) sekku** Girls' Doll Festival (March 3)
23 鰹節 **katsuobushi** dried bonito shavings
鰹節削 **katsuobushi kezu(ri)** plane for making bonito shavings

——————— 3 ———————

1 一音節 **ichionsetsu** one syllable
4 天長節 **Tenchōsetsu** Emperor's Birthday
5 四旬節 **Shijunsetsu** Lent
6 多音節 **taonsetsu** polysyllable

7 肘関節 **hiji kansetsu** elbow joint
8 受難節 **junansetsu** Lent
追分節 **oiwakebushi** packhorse driver's song
股関節 **kokansetsu** hip joint
9 神経節 **shinkeisetsu** ganglion
紀元節 **kigensetsu** Empire Day
10 浪花節 **naniwabushi** samisen-accompanied recital of ancient tales
従属節 **jūzokusetsu** subordinate clause
11 過越節 **Sugikoshi Setsu, Sugikoshi no Iwai** Passover
12 腕関節 **wankansetsu** the wrist joint
14 説経節 **sekkyōbushi** sutra-based samisen-accompanied ballads
15 膝関節 **shitsukansetsu** the knee joint

——————— 4 ———————

8 枝葉末節 **shiyō-massetsu** branches and leaves; unimportant details
12 答礼使節 **tōrei shisetsu** envoy sent to return courtesies
15 盤根錯節 **bankon-sakusetsu** knotty/thorny/complex situation

筶 → 簿 **6f13.4**

6f7.4
筰 **SAKU** bamboo rope

筱 → 篠 **6f11.3**

6f7.5
筥 **KYO** round basket

6f7.6
筩 **TŌ** bamboo tube/flute

6f7.7
筧 **KEN, kakehi, kakei** bamboo pipe, conduit

質 → **7b8.7**

筵→ **6f6.13**

― 8 ―

箸→箸 **6f9.1**

6f8.1

笧 SATSU, TŌ official report/notice

6f8.2

箙 FUKU, ebira quiver (for arrows)

6f8.3

箝 KAN insert (into one's mouth)
kubikase pillory, neck fetter

― 1 ―
3 箝口 kankō keep silent about, gag, hush up
箝口令 kankōrei gag law/order

6f8.4

箍 KO, taga barrel hoop

6f8.5

箔 HAKU foil, leaf, gilt

― 2 ―
8 金箔 kinpaku gold leaf, gilt
14 銀箔 ginpaku silver leaf/foil
15 縫箔 nu(i)haku embroidery and foiling

6f8.6

箕 KI, mi winnowing device

6f8.7 / 747

算 SAN calculate

― 1 ―
0 算する san(suru) number, amount to
2 算入 sannyū count in, include

4 算木 sangi divination/calculation blocks
5 算出 sanshutsu computation, calculation
算用 san'yō computation, calculation
算用数字 san'yō sūji Hindu-Arabic numerals
7 算乱 san (o) mida(su) in utter disorder
8 算法 sanpō arithmetic
算定 santei calculate, estimate
9 算段 sandan contrive, try, manage
11 算術 sanjutsu arithmetic
13 算数 sansū arithmetic, math, calculation
15 算盤 soroban abacus

― 2 ―
4 予算 yosan budget, estimate
予算外 yosangai outside the budget, off-budget
予算案 yosan'an proposed budget
公算 kōsan probability
引算 hi(ki)zan subtraction (in math)
心算 shinsan intention
5 加算 kasan addition (in math)
皮算用 kawazan'yō, kawasan'yō counting one's pelts before catching the raccoons
打算 dasan calculation, self-interest
打算的 dasanteki calculating, mercenary
目算 mokusan expectation, estimate
6 合算 gassan add up, total
成算 seisan prospects of success
7 余算 yosan one's remaining years
決算 kessan settlement (of accounts); liquidation
決算日 kessanbi settlement day
決算報告 kessan hōkoku closing-of-accounts report, financial statement
決算期 kessanki accounting period/term
足算 ta(shi)zan addition (in math)
8 逆算 gyakusan counting backwards/down
和算 wasan Japanese mathematics
9 乗算 jōzan multiplication (in math)
除算 josan division (in math)
速算 sokusan rapid calculation
計算 keisan computation, calculation
計算尺 keisanjaku slide rule
計算係 keisangaka(ri) accountant
計算書 keisansho statement (of account)
計算器 keisanki calculator
計算機 keisanki computer
計算簿 keisanbo account book
10 起算 kisan starting/computed from (a given date)
胸算 munazan mental arithmetic; expectation
胸算用 munazan'yō mental arithmetic; expectation
珠算 shuzan calculation on the abacus
破算 hasan clear the abacus, recalculate
11 運算 unzan mathematical operation, calculation

清算 **seisan** liquidation, settlement
推算 **suisan** calculate, reckon, estimate
掛算 **ka(ke)zan** multiplication (in math)
採算 **saisan** profit
採算割 **saisanwa(re)** below cost
寄算 **yo(se)zan** addition (in math)
球算 **tamazan** calculation on the abacus
累算 **ruisan** total
12 割算 **wa(ri)zan** division (in math)
違算 **isan** miscalculation
減算 **genzan** subtraction (in math)
換算 **kansan** conversion, exchange
換算表 **kansanhyō** conversion table
検算 **kenzan** check the figures, verify the accounts
勝算 **shōsan** chances of success
筆算 **hissan** calculating on paper
13 鼠算 **nezumizan** geometrical progression, multiplying like rats
暗算 **anzan** mental arithmetic
試算 **shisan** test calculation; checking a calculation
電算機 **densanki** computer
14 演算 **enzan** operation (in math)
概算 **gaisan** rough estimate
精算 **seisan** exact calculation, (fare) adjustment, settling of accounts
誤算 **gosan** miscalculation
16 積算 **sekisan** integrating (meter)
18 験算 **kenzan** verification of accounts, checking the figures

——————— 3 ———————
5 未決算 **mikessan** outstanding (accounts)
目子算 **me(no)kozan** measuring by eye; mental arithmetic
8 表計算 **hyōkeisan** spreadsheet
歩合算 **buaizan** calculation of percentage
12 遣繰算段 **ya(ri)ku(ri) sandan** getting by, tiding over
御破算 **gohasan** clearing a soroban; starting afresh
無理算段 **muri-sandan** scrape together (money)
14 総決算 **sōkessan** complete financial statement
21 鶴亀算 **tsurukamezan** solving a system of linear equations (example: How many cranes and how many turtles, given a total of 11 animals and 36 legs?)

——————— 4 ———————
13 損益計算書 **son'eki keisansho** income/profit-and-loss statement

6f8.8

箜 **KU** (a type of harp)

6f8.8

15 箜篌 **kugo** (a type of harp)

箟 → 箘 **6f8.14**

6f8.9

箋 **SEN** paper; label; letter, writing

——————— 2 ———————
5 付箋 **fusen** tag, label
用箋 **yōsen** form, blank, stationery
9 便箋 **binsen** stationery, notepaper

6f8.10

箏 箏 **SŌ** koto

——————— 1 ———————
6 箏曲 **sōkyoku** koto music

6f8.11

箆 箆 **HEI** fine-tooth comb
hera wooden slat/spatula

——————— 1 ———————
12 箆棒 **berabō** absurd; awful, darn

——————— 2 ———————
6 竹箆 **takebera** bamboo slat/spatula
shippei flat bamboo stick for slapping meditators to keep them awake
竹箆返 **shippeigae(shi)** retaliation, tit for tat
12 犂箆 **sukibera** plow blade, plowshare
13 靴箆 **kutsubera** shoehorn

6f8.12 / 328

管 **KAN** control, jurisdiction; pipe, tube; wind instrument **kuda** pipe, tube

——————— 1 ———————
0 ブラウン管 **Buraun-kan** cathode-ray/picture tube
3 管下 **kanka** under the jurisdiction of
管々 **kudakuda(shii)** verbose, tedious
4 管内 **kannai** (area of) jurisdiction
管区 **kanku** district, precinct
5 管外 **kangai** outside the jurisdiction of
7 管状 **kanjō** tubular
管見 **kanken** narrow view; one's views
8 管長 **kanchō** superintendent priest

管制 **kansei** control
管制塔 **kanseitō** control tower
管弦 **kangen** wind and string instruments; music
管弦楽団 **kangen gakudan** orchestra
9 管巻 **kuda (o) ma(ku)** drunkenly babble on
10 管財人 **kanzainin** trustee, administrator
11 管理 **kanri** administration, supervision, control, management
管理人 **kanrinin** manager, superintendent
管理職 **kanrishoku** administrative position; the management
管絃 **kangen** wind and string instruments; music
管絃楽団 **kangen gakudan** orchestra
12 管掌 **kanshō** take/have charge of, manage
13 管楽 **kangaku** wind-instrument music
管楽器 **kangakki** wind instruments
14 管管 **kudakuda(shii)** verbose, tedious
17 管轄 **kankatsu** jurisdiction
管轄違 **kankatsuchiga(i)** lack of jurisdiction

─────── 2 ───────

3 土管 **dokan** earthen pipe, drainage tiles
4 毛管 **mōkan** capillary
水管 **suikan** water pipe/tube
手管 **tekuda** beguiling trick, art, wiles
木管 **mokkan** wooden pipe/bobbin
5 本管 **honkan** main (pipe)
主管 **shukan** be in charge of, supervise, manage(r)
6 気管 **kikan** windpipe, trachea
気管支 **kikanshi** bronchial tubes
気管支炎 **kikanshien** bronchitis
気管炎 **kikan'en** tracheitis
吸管 **kyūkan** suction pipe, siphon
血管 **kekkan** blood vessel
7 卵管 **rankan** Fallopian tubes, oviduct
汽管 **kikan** steam pipe
尿管 **nyōkan** ureter
8 油管 **yukan** oil pipe
弦管 **genkan** wind and string instruments
所管 **shokan** jurisdiction
9 信管 **shinkan** fuse
保管 **hokan** custody, deposit, storage
保管料 **hokanryō** custody/storage fee
軍管区 **gunkanku** military district
音管 **onkan** organ pipe
10 涙管 **ruikan** tear duct
脈管 **myakkan** blood vessel, duct
配管 **haikan** plumbing, piping
11 彩管 **saikan** artist's brush
移管 **ikan** transfer of control/jurisdiction
蛇管 **jakan** hose
12 掌管 **shōkan** manage, handle
13 煙管 **enkan** chimney, flue   **kiseru** tobacco

pipe with metal bowl and mouthpiece and bamboo stem
煙管乗 **kiseruno(ri)** ride a train with tickets only for the first and last stretches of the route
鉄管 **tekkan** iron pipe
鉛管 **enkan** lead pipe, plumbing
雷管 **raikan** blasting/percussion cap, detonator
14 選管 **senkan** election administration (short for 選挙管理委員会)
導管 **dōkan** conduit, pipe, duct, vessel
精管 **seikan** seminal duct
管管 **kudakuda(shii)** verbose, tedious
16 鋼管 **kōkan** steel tubing/pipe

─────── 3 ───────

3 下水管 **gesuikan** sewer/drain (pipe)
4 水道管 **suidōkan** water pipe/main
6 光電管 **kōdenkan** photocell, light sensor
灯火管制 **tōka kansei** lighting control, blackout, brownout
8 送気管 **sōkikan** air pipe/duct
送油管 **sōyukan** oil pipeline
油送管 **yusōkan** (oil) pipeline
放水管 **hōsuikan** drainpipe
9 発射管 **hasshakan** torpedo tube
10 真空管 **shinkūkan** vacuum tube
消化管 **shōkakan** alimentary canal, digestive tract
11 排水管 **haisuikan** drainpipe
排気管 **haikikan** exhaust pipe
12 給水管 **kyūsuikan** water pipe
13 試験管 **shikenkan** test tube
16 輸卵管 **yurankan** oviduct, Fallopian tubes
輸尿管 **yunyōkan** the ureter
輸精管 **yuseikan** spermaduct

─────── 4 ───────

4 毛細血管 **mōsai kekkan** capillaries
手練手管 **teren-tekuda** coaxing, wiles, beguiling

6f8.13

箒   **SŌ, hōki** broom

─────── 2 ───────

4 手箒 **tebōki** hand/whisk broom
6 羽箒 **habōki, hanebōki** feather duster

6f8.14

箘 篏   **KIN** (a type of bamboo); bamboo shoots; dice

6
糸
米
舟
虫
耳
⺮ 8 ←

6f8.15 / 1473

箇 ケ 个   **KA, KO** (counter for inanimate objects)

───── 1 ─────

0 1ヶ年 **ikkanen** one year
3ヶ所 **sankasho** three places
りんご1ヶ **ringo ikko** one apple
7 箇条 **kajō** article, provision, item
箇条書 **kajōga(ki)** an itemization
8 箇所 **kasho** place, part, passage (in a book)

───── 2 ─────

1 一箇 **ikko** one; a piece
3 三箇日 **sanganichi** the first three days of the new year
7 何箇 **nanko** how many (pieces)
何箇月 **nankagetsu** how many months
13 鳩ヶ谷 **Hatogaya** (city, Saitama-ken)

───── 9 ─────

6f9.1

箸 箸   **CHO, CHAKU, hashi** chopsticks

───── 1 ─────

13 箸置 **hashio(ki)** chopstick rest

───── 2 ─────

4 火箸 **hibashi** tongs
7 杉箸 **sugibashi** chopsticks made of sugi wood
11 菜箸 **saibashi** long/serving chopsticks
12 割箸 **wa(ri)bashi** half-split chopsticks
13 塗箸 **nu(ri)bashi** lacquered chopsticks

───── 3 ─────

12 焼火箸 **ya(ke)hibashi** red-hot tongs

6f9.2

箴   **SHIN** needle; warning

───── 1 ─────

7 箴言 **shingen** proverb, aphorism

6f9.3 / 1092

範   **HAN** example, model, pattern; limit

───── 1 ─────

7 範囲 **han'i** extent, scope, range
範囲内 **han'inai** within the limits of
8 範例 **hanrei** example
19 範疇 **hanchū** category

───── 2 ─────

4 文範 **bunpan** model compositions
5 広範 **kōhan** wide(-ranging), extensive
広範囲 **kōhan'i** wide range/scope
8 典範 **tenpan** model, standard; law
9 軌範 **kihan** model, example
軌範的 **kihanteki** model, exemplary
10 師範 **shihan** teacher, instructor
師範学校 **shihan gakkō** normal school, teachers' college
11 規範 **kihan** standard, norm, criterion
規範的 **kihanteki** normative
14 模範 **mohan** model, exemplar
模範生 **mohansei** model student
模範的 **mohanteki** exemplary

節→節 6f7.3

篏→嵌 3o9.2

6f9.4 / 1091

箱   **hako** box

───── 1 ─────

2 箱入 **hakoi(ri)** boxed, in cases
箱入娘 **hakoi(ri) musume** girl who has led a sheltered life
4 箱火鉢 **hako hibachi** box-enclosed brazier
6 箱舟 **hakobune** (Noah's) ark
9 箱乗 **hakono(ri)** riding in the same train car (as the one one wishes to interview)
箱庭 **hakoniwa** miniature garden
箱屋 **hakoya** boxmaker
箱柳 **hakoyanagi** aspen
10 箱師 **hakoshi** train thief
箱宮 **hakomiya** miniature temple
箱根 **Hakone** (resort area near Mt. Fuji)
箱根山 **Hakone-yama** (mountain, Kanagawa-ken)
箱書 **hakoga(ki)** painter's/calligrapher's autograph on the box
箱馬車 **hakobasha** closed carriage
13 箱詰 **hakozume** packed in cases, boxed

───── 2 ─────

3 小箱 **kobako** small box/case
4 文箱 **fubako, fumibako** box/case for letters
手箱 **tebako** case, box
木箱 **kibako** wooden box
5 本箱 **honbako** bookcase
払箱 **(o)hara(i)bako** dismissal, firing

7 折箱 **o(ri)bako** small box made of cardboard or thin wood
乱箱 **mida(re)bako** lidless box for clothes
芥箱 **gomibako** garbage box/bin, waste basket
8 受箱 **u(ke)bako** box for receiving (mail/milk)
宝箱 **takarabako** treasure chest, strongbox
金箱 **kanebako** cashbox, till; source of funds/income
9 重箱 **jūbako** nest of boxes
茶箱 **chabako** tea chest
10 骨箱 **kotsubako** box for the deceased's ashes
紙箱 **kamibako** carton
針箱 **haribako** sewing box
11 巣箱 **subako** nesting box, birdhouse, hive
豚箱 **butabako** police lockup, jail
12 硯箱 **suzuribako** inkstone case
筆箱 **fudebako** brush/pencil case
14 銭箱 **zenibako** cashbox, till
16 薬箱 **kusuribako** medicine chest

───── 3 ─────

3 千両箱 **senryōbako** chest containing a thousand pieces of gold
下駄箱 **getabako** shoe cabinet
5 弁当箱 **bentōbako** lunch box
玉手箱 **tamatebako** treasure chest; Pandora's box
6 百葉箱 **hyakuyōsō, hyakuyōbako** louver-sided box for housing meteorological gauges outdoors
7 投票箱 **tōhyōbako** ballot box
私書箱 **shishobako** post-office box
10 郵便箱 **yūbinbako** mailbox
11 道具箱 **dōgubako** toolbox
救急箱 **kyūkyūbako** first-aid kit
12 貯金箱 **chokinbako** savings box, (piggy) bank
13 献金箱 **kenkinbako** contributions/offertory box
16 整理箱 **seiribako** filing cabinet
17 賽銭箱 **saisenbako** offertory chest

6f9.5

篌

GO (a type of harp)

───── 2 ─────

14 箜篌 **kugo** (a type of harp)

6f9.6

篁

KŌ, takamura bamboo grove

箪 → 簞 **6f12.2**

6f9.7

箭

SEN, ya arrow

───── 2 ─────

3 弓箭 **kyūsen** bows and arrows; arms; war
4 火箭 **kasen, hiya** flaming/incendiary arrow

6f9.8

篆

TEN (a style of kanji used on seals and inscriptions)

───── 1 ─────

5 篆字 **tenji** seal characters
8 篆刻 **tenkoku** seal engraving
10 篆書 **tensho** seal characters

6f9.9

篇

HEN book, volume, edition; chapter, part; (counter for literary works)

───── 2 ─────

3 小篇 **shōhen** short article/story
4 中篇 **chūhen** second volume; medium-length (novel)
6 全篇 **zenpen** the whole book
9 前篇 **zenpen** the first volume/part
後篇 **kōhen** last part, later volume, sequel
12 短篇 **tanpen** short piece/story/film
短篇小説 **tanpen shōsetsu** short story/novel
雄篇 **yūhen** a masterpiece
13 続篇 **zokuhen** sequel
詩篇 **Shihen** (the Book of) Psalms
14 雑篇 **zappen** miscellaneous writings

6f9.10

篋

KYŌ box

───── 10 ─────

6f10.1 / 1883

篤

TOKU, atsu(i) kind, cordial; fervent; serious (illness)

───── 1 ─────

6 篤行 **tokkō** good deed, kind act
7 篤学 **tokugaku** love of learning
篤志 **tokushi** benevolence, charity, zeal
篤志家 **tokushika** benefactor, volunteer
8 篤実 **tokujitsu** sincerity, faithfulness
9 篤信 **tokushin** devotion
13 篤農 **tokunō** exemplary farmer

6

糸
米
舟
虫
耳

⺮ 10 ←

—————— 2 ——————

6 危篤 **kitoku** critically ill, near death
9 重篤 **jūtoku** serious (illness)
17 懇篤 **kontoku** kind, cordial

6f10.2

篩 **SHI, furu(u)** sift, screen
furui sieve, sifting screen

—————— 1 ——————

4 篩分 **furu(i)wa(keru)** screen, sift out

—————— 2 ——————

6 灰篩 **haifurui** ash sieve/sifter

箟 → 籠 **6f16.1**

6f10.3

篳 **HICHI, HITSU** bamboo fence;
brushwood

—————— 1 ——————

16 篳篥 **hichiriki** (type of ceremonial reed flute)

6f10.4

篥 **RIKI** (a type of bamboo)

—————— 2 ——————

16 篳篥 **hichiriki** (type of ceremonial reed flute)

6f10.5 / 1603

築 **CHIKU, kizu(ku), tsu(ku)** build

—————— 1 ——————

3 築上 **kizu(ki)a(geru)** build up
築山 **tsukiyama** mound, artificial hill
6 築地 **tsukiji** reclaimed land
tsuiji roofed mud wall
9 築造 **chikuzō** building, construction
築城 **chikujō** castle construction; fortification
12 築港 **chikkō** harbor construction
築堤 **chikutei** embankment, banking

—————— 2 ——————

7 改築 **kaichiku** rebuild, remodel, alter
8 建築 **kenchiku** building, construction,
architecture
建築学 **kenchikugaku** architecture
建築者 **kenchikusha** builder
建築物 **kenchikubutsu** a building, structure
建築師 **kenchikushi** builder

建築家 **kenchikuka** architect, building
contractor
建築術 **kenchikujutsu** architecture
建築費 **kenchikuhi** construction costs
建築業者 **kenchiku gyōsha** builder
10 修築 **shūchiku** repair (a house)
13 新築 **shinchiku** newly built
14 増築 **zōchiku** build on, extend, enlarge
構築 **kōchiku** construction

6f10.6

簒 簒 **SAN** snatch away, usurp

—————— 1 ——————

14 簒奪 **sandatsu** usurpation

6f10.7

篝 **KŌ** drying coop
kagari bonfire

—————— 1 ——————

4 篝火 **kagaribi** bonfire

簑 → 蓑 **3k10.24**

箆 → 箆 **6f8.11**

6f10.8

篷 **HŌ, toma** woven-rush awning

—————— 11 ——————

6f11.1

簓 **SEN, sasara** bamboo whisk

6f11.2

簇 **ZOKU, SŌ, mura(garu)** congregate

—————— 1 ——————

5 簇生 **zokusei, sōsei** grow in clusters

6f11.3

篠 **SHŌ, shino** (a variety of small
bamboo)

───────────── 1 ─────────────

8 篠突雨 **shinotsu(ku) ame** driving/torrential rain

6f11.4

簍 **RU, RŌ** bamboo basket

6f11.5

籡 **RYŌ, yana** weir, fish trap

篡 → 簒 6f10.6

6f11.6

篶 **EN, kurodake** the black bamboo
suzu slender bamboo

6f11.7

簀 **SAKU, su** rough mat (of bamboo/reeds)

───────────── 1 ─────────────

2 簀子 **su(no)ko** rough-woven mat; slat curtain/blind

───────────── 2 ─────────────

12 葭簀 **yoshizu** reed screen/blind
13 葦簀 **yoshizu** reed screen/blind

───────────── 12 ─────────────

6f12.1

籐 **TEN** woven-bamboo basket

6f12.2

簞 簞 **TAN** (a variety of bamboo); round woven-bamboo lunch box

───────────── 1 ─────────────

11 簞笥 **tansu** chest of drawers, dresser

───────────── 2 ─────────────

5 用簞笥 **yōdansu** chest of drawers
9 茶簞笥 **chadansu** tea cupboard/cabinet
17 瓢簞 **hyōtan** gourd, calabash
瓢簞鯰 **hyōtan namazu** slippery fellow

───────────── 3 ─────────────

8 青瓢簞 **aobyōtan** green calabash/gourd; pale-faced weakling
16 整理簞笥 **seiridansu** chest of drawers

6f12.3

簣 **KI, mokko** earth-carrying basket

───────────── 5 ─────────────

2 九仞功一簣欠 **kyūjin (no) kō (o) ikki (ni) ka(ku)** failure on the verge of success

6f12.4

簧 **KŌ** flute reed

6f12.5 / 1533

簡 **KAN, KEN** simple, brief

───────────── 1 ─────────────

7 簡抜 **kanbatsu** pick out, select
8 簡明 **kanmei** terse, brief, clear
簡易 **kan'i** simple, easy
簡易保険 **kan'i hoken** post-office life insurance
簡易食堂 **kan'i shokudō** fast-food diner
簡易裁判所 **kan'i saibansho** summary court
9 簡便 **kanben** simple, easy, convenient
簡単 **kantan** simple, brief
簡単服 **kantanfuku** simple/light clothing
簡約 **kan'yaku** concise, simplified, abridged
10 簡素 **kanso** plain and simple
11 簡略 **kanryaku** simple, concise
15 簡潔 **kanketsu** concise

───────────── 2 ─────────────

1 了簡 **ryōken** idea; intention; decision, discretion; forgive
了簡違 **ryōkenchiga(i)** mistaken idea; an imprudence
10 書簡 **shokan** letter, note
書簡文 **shokanbun** epistolary style
書簡紙 **shokanshi** stationery
12 貴簡 **kikan** your letter
16 繁簡 **hankan** simplicity and complexity

───────────── 13 ─────────────

6f13.1

簫 **SHŌ** panpipes, flute

6

糸
米
舟
虫
耳

⼍ 13←

6f13.2

簸　**HA, hi(ru)** winnow; fan

6f13.3

籙　**ROKU** quiver, arrow container

———————— 2 ————————
9 胡籙 **yanagui** quiver (for arrows)

6f13.4 / 1450

簿 簒　**BO** record book, ledger, register, list

———————— 1 ————————
10 簿記 **boki** bookkeeping

———————— 2 ————————
6 名簿 **meibo** name list, roster, roll
11 鹵簿 **robo** imperial procession
帳簿 **chōbo** (account) books, book (value)
12 登簿 **tōbo** registration

———————— 3 ————————
2 人名簿 **jinmeibo** name list, directory
4 戸籍簿 **kosekibo** family register
5 出席簿 **shussekibo** roll book, attendance record
出納簿 **suitōbo** account book
出勤簿 **shukkinbo** work attendance record
7 学籍簿 **gakusekibo** school register
9 通信簿 **tsūshinbo** report card
計算簿 **keisanbo** account book
10 家計簿 **kakeibo** household account-book
12 登録簿 **tōrokubo** the register

6f13.5

籀　**CHŪ** (a style of calligraphy)

6f13.6

簽　**SEN** label; signature

———————— 2 ————————
18 題簽 **daisen** (pasted-in insert bearing a book's) title

6f13.7

簷　**EN** eaves

6f13.8

簾　**REN, sudare, su** bamboo/rattan (venetian-type) blind

———————— 2 ————————
12 御簾 **misu** bamboo blind/screen
13 葦簾 **yoshizu** reed screen/blind
暖簾 **noren** shop-entrance curtain; reputation, goodwill
15 鋤簾 **joren** scoop, shovel

———————— 14 ————————

6f14.1 / 1198

籍　**SEKI** (family) register

———————— 2 ————————
2 入籍 **nyūseki** have one's name entered on the family register
4 戸籍 **koseki** family register
戸籍抄本 **koseki shōhon** extract from a family register
戸籍法 **kosekihō** the Family Registration Law
戸籍調 **koseki shira(be)** examine (someone's) family register; take the census
戸籍謄本 **koseki tōhon** copy of a family register
戸籍簿 **kosekibo** family register
5 本籍 **honseki** one's legal domicile
本籍地 **honsekichi** one's legal domicile
史籍 **shiseki** history book, historical work
6 地籍 **chiseki** land register
在籍 **zaiseki** be enrolled
7 兵籍 **heiseki** military register, army roll
臣籍 **shinseki** status as a subject
臣籍降下 **shinseki kōka** (royalty) becoming subjects
学籍 **gakuseki** school register
学籍簿 **gakusekibo** school register
8 版籍 **hanseki** (register of) land and people
典籍 **tenseki** books
送籍 **sōseki** transfer of domicile
国籍 **kokuseki** nationality, citizenship
9 除籍 **joseki** remove a name (from the family register); decommission (a warship)
軍籍 **gunseki** military register, muster roll
10 原籍 **genseki** domicile, permanent address
党籍 **tōseki** registration/membership (in a party)
書籍 **shoseki** books
書籍商 **shosekishō** bookseller, bookstore
書籍業 **shosekigyō** bookselling and publishing business
鬼籍 **kiseki** roster of the dead

6
糸
米
舟
虫
耳
→ 13 ⺮

11 族籍 **zokuseki** class and domicile
移籍 **iseki** transfer of one's domiciliary registration
船籍 **senseki** ship's registry/nationality
船籍港 **sensekikō** ship's port of registry
貫籍 **kanseki** domicile, census registration
転籍 **tenseki** transfer of domicile/registration
12 復籍 **fukuseki** reinstatement as a member; reregistering to one's original domicile
落籍 **rakuseki** no registration (in the census register); buying a geisha her contractual freedom
無籍者 **musekimono** person without registered domicile; vagrant, outcast
13 僧籍 **sōseki** priesthood
漢籍 **kanseki** Chinese book/classics
18 離籍 **riseki** removal of one's name from the official family register

———————— 4 ————————

2 二重国籍 **nijū kokuseki** dual nationality

6f14.2

簱

KI, hata flag, banner

6f14.3

簪

SHIN, kanzashi ornamental hairpin

6f14.4

纂

SAN edit, compile

———————— 2 ————————

14 雑纂 **zassan** miscellaneous collection
15 編纂 **hensan** compile, edit
18 類纂 **ruisan** classified compilation

6f14.5

籌

CHŪ plan

———————— 15 ————————

籔 → 藪 **3k15.1**

6f15.1

籐 籘

TŌ rattan, cane

11 籐細工 **tōzaiku** rattanwork, canework
12 籐椅子 **tōisu** rattan/wickerwork chair

6f15.2

籃

RAN basket

———————— 2 ————————

12 揺籃 **yōran** cradle
揺籃地 **yōran (no) chi** the cradle of, birthplace
揺籃期 **yōranki** infancy

籤 → 籤 **6f17.2**

———————— 16 ————————

6f16.1

籠 篭

RŌ, komo(ru) seclude oneself, hole up; be full of **ko(meru)** put into **kago** (palanquin/carrying) basket, (bird) cage **ko** basket

———————— 1 ————————

4 籠手 **kote** bracer, gauntlet; forearm
5 籠目 **kagome** woven-bamboo pattern
7 籠抜 **kagonu(ke)** swindling (by slipping out the back door)
8 籠居 **rōkyo** stay indoors
9 籠城 **rōjō** be under siege, hole up, be confined
11 籠球 **rōkyū** basketball
12 籠絡 **rōraku** cajole, wheedle, entice

———————— 2 ————————

3 口籠 **kuchigomo(ru)** stammer; mumble
山籠 **yamagomo(ri)** seclude oneself in the moutains; retire to a mountain temple
4 手籠 **tekago** handbasket **tegome** rape
引籠 **hi(ki)komo(ru)** stay indoors, be confined indoors
5 冬籠 **fuyugomo(ri)** stay indoors for the winter, hibernate
立籠 **ta(te)komo(ru)** hole up, remain in seclusion, entrench oneself
6 印籠 **inrō** medicine case, pillbox; seal case
灯籠 **tōrō** (hanging/garden) lantern
灯籠流 **tōrōnaga(shi)** setting votive lanterns afloat
虫籠 **mushikago** insect cage
竹籠 **takekago** bamboo basket
7 身籠 **migomo(ru)** become pregnant
乱籠 **mida(re)kago** clothes basket
花籠 **hanakago** flower basket

6

糸
米
舟
虫
耳

⺮⺮ 16 ←

尾籠 **birō** indelicate, indecent, risqué
言籠 **i(i)ko(meru)** argue (someone) into silence, confute
8 垂籠 **ta(re)ko(meru)** lie/hang over; seclude oneself inside
夜籠 **yogomo(ri)** praying all night (in a temple)
参籠 **sanrō** sequester oneself in a temple/shrine for prayer
雨籠 **amagomo(ri)** rained in, rainbound
10 屑籠 **kuzukago** wastebasket
旅籠 **hatago** inn
旅籠屋 **hatagoya** inn
11 巣籠 **sugomo(ru)** to nest
閉籠 **to(ji)komo(ru)** stay indoors, hole up
鳥籠 **torikago** bird cage
12 揺籠 **yu(ri)kago** cradle
蒸籠 **seirō, seiro** steaming basket
葛籠 **tsuzura** wicker basket
15 駕籠 **kago** palanquin, litter
16 薬籠 **yakurō** medicine chest
薬籠中物 **yakurōchū (no) mono** at one's beck and call

——————— 3 ———————
3 山駕籠 **yamakago** mountain palanquin
4 辻駕籠 **tsujikago** palanquin/litter for hire
手提籠 **tesa(ge)kago** handbasket
6 早駕籠 **hayakago** express palaquin
10 紙屑籠 **kamikuzukago** wastebasket
11 釣灯籠 **tsu(ri)dōrō** hanging lantern

——————— 4 ———————
11 雪見灯籠 **yukimidōrō** ornamental three-legged stone lantern

6f16.2

籟 **RAI** (three-holed) bamboo flute; sound (of the wind)

——————— 2 ———————
8 松籟 **shōrai** soughing of the wind through the pines

籐 → 籘 **6f15.1**

——————— 17 ———————

6f17.1

籥 **YAKU, fue** three-holed flute

6f17.2

籤 籤 **SEN, kuji** written oracle; lottery, raffle

——————— 1 ———————
4 籤引 **kujibi(ki)** drawing lots
8 籤逃 **kujinoga(re)** elimination by lottery
11 籤運 **kujiun** one's luck in lottery

——————— 2 ———————
6 当籤 **tōsen** win (a lottery)
当籤者 **tōsensha** prizewinner
8 抽籤 **chūsen** drawing, lottery
抽籤券 **chūsenken** lottery/raffle ticket
宝籤 **takarakuji** lottery, raffle
空籤 **karakuji** a blank (in a lottery)
12 富籤 **tomikuji** lottery, lottery ticket

——————— 18 ———————

6f18.1

籬 **RI, magaki** bamboo/rough-woven fence

——————— 言 7a ———————

言	計	訃	訂	託	訐	討	訌	記	訓	訖	訊	訪
0.1	2.1	2.2	2.3	3.1	3.2	3.3	3.4	3.5	3.6	3.7	3.8	4.1
訣	訝	許	訥	訛	訟	設	訳	訴	訴	評	註	詛
4.2	7a5.1	4.3	4.4	4.5	4.6	4.7	4.8	5.1	5.2	5.3	7a5.11	5.4
証	詐	詆	詫	診	詔	註	詁	詒	詠	詞	訶	誅
5.5	5.6	5.7	5.8	5.9	5.10	5.11	5.12	5.13	5.14	5.15	5.16	6.1
誄	誠	誂	詩	詫	詰	話	誇	詮	該	詭	詳	詣
6.2	6.3	6.4	6.5	6.6	6.7	6.8	6.9	7a6.14	6.10	6.11	6.12	6.13
詮	詠	詬	詢	試	誣	誤	誑	誘	誥	語	誚	誌
6.14	6.15	6.16	6.17	6.18	7.1	7.2	7.3	7.4	7.5	7.6	7.7	7.8
読	認	諄	説	誨	誦	誕	誠	誓	誰	諫	課	諸
7.9	7.10	7.11	7.12	7.13	7.14	7.15	7.16	7.17	8.1	7a9.1	8.2	8.3

諏	誹	謁	談	請	諍	諾	誼	錠	論	諒	諂	謎
8.4	8.5	8.6	8.7	8.8	8.9	8.10	8.11	8.12	8.13	8.14	8.15	7a9.20
調	諫	諛	諸	謬	諮	譜	諺	謂	諜	謀	謁	謡
8.16	9.1	9.2	7a8.3	9.3	9.4	9.5	7a9.15	9.6	9.7	9.8	7a8.6	9.9
護	諧	諨	諭	諢	諮	諦	譃	諡	諞	謎	諷	謝
9.10	9.11	9.12	9.13	9.14	9.15	9.16	9.17	9.18	9.19	9.20	9.21	10.1
謖	講	謚	詞	謡	諂	謹	謹	謨	諱	謗	謙	謚
10.2	10.3	10.4	4j10.2	7a9.9	10.5	3d10.7	10.6	10.7	10.8	10.9	10.10	7a9.18
謬	謾	謹	謫	謳	謦	鞫	譏	譜	譖	譜	譚	證
11.1	11.2	7a10.6	11.3	11.4	11.5	11.6	12.1	12.2	7a12.3	12.3	12.4	7a5.5
譎	譌	識	警	譯	讓	謀	護	議	譜	譽	譫	譜
12.5	7a4.5	12.6	12.7	7a4.8	13.1	13.2	13.3	13.4	7a12.2	3n10.1	13.5	13.6
譬	辯	讃	讀	譙	讐	讙	讓	讒	讖	钁	讚	
13.7	0a5.30	15.1	7a7.9	16.1	16.2	17.1	7a13.1	17.2	17.3	18.1	7a15.1	

0

7a0.1 / 66

言

GEN, GON, koto word
i(u) say
i(waba) so to speak, as it were

1

0 言いこなす **i(ikonasu)** express well
3 言及 **genkyū, i(i)oyo(bu)** refer to, mention
言上 **gonjō** tell, inform (a superior)
言下 **genka** promptly, readily
言々 **gengen** every word
4 言切 **i(i)ki(ru)** state positively, declare; tell everything
言文一致 **genbun itchi** unification of the written and spoken language
言分 **i(i)bun** one's say; objection
言込 **i(i)ko(meru)** argue (someone) into silence, confute
言方 **i(i)kata** way of saying
5 言左右託 **gen (o) sayū (ni) taku(suru)** equivocate, be noncommittal
言出 **i(i)da(su)** begin to speak, broach
言出屁 **i(i)da(ship)pe, i(i)da(shi)be** The one who brought up the subject must act first. The one who says "What's that smell?" is the one who farted.
言甲斐 **i(i)gai** worth mentioning
言付 **i(i)tsu(keru)** tell (someone to do something); tell on (someone), tattle
kotozu(ke) message
言古 **i(i)furu(shita)** hackneyed, stale
言外 **gengai** unexpressed, implied
言立 **i(i)ta(teru)** state, assert
6 言伏 **i(i)fu(seru)** argue down, confute
言伝 **i(i)tsuta(eru)** hand down (a legend), spread (a rumor) **kotozu(te)** hearsay; message
言合 **i(i)a(u)** quarrel; exchange words
i(i)a(waseru) arrange beforehand
言交 **i(i)kawa(su)** exchange vows/remarks
言争 **i(i)araso(i)** quarrel, altercation
言返 **i(i)kae(su)** talk back, retort
言行 **genkō** words and deeds
言当 **i(i)a(teru)** guess right
言尽 **i(i)tsu(kusu)** tell all, exhaust (a subject)
言回 **i(i)mawa(shi)** expression, phrasing
言成 **i(i)na(ri)** (doing) whatever (someone) says
言成放題 **i(i)na(ri) hōdai** submissive to (someone)
7 言来 **i(i)ki(tari)** legend, tradition
言含 **i(i)fuku(meru)** instruct/brief thoroughly
言抜 **i(i)nu(ke)** excuse, evasion
言改 **i(i)arata(meru)** correct oneself, rephrase
言条 **i(i)jō** although
言言 **gengen** every word
言足 **i(i)ta(su)** add, say further
8 言表 **i(i)ara(wasu)** express
言直 **i(i)nao(su)** rephrase, correct
言逃 **i(i)noga(re)** evasion, excuse
言送 **i(i)oku(ru)** send word
言知 **i(i)shi(renu)** indescribable
言明 **genmei** declaration, (definite) statement
i(i)a(kasu) talk all night
言放 **i(i)hana(tsu)** declare, assert
9 言負 **i(i)ma(keru)** lose an argument
i(i)ma(kasu) confute
言通 **i(i)tō(su)** persist in saying
言草 **i(i)gusa** one's words, remarks
言祝 **kotoho(gu)** congratulate
10 言残 **i(i)noko(su)** leave word; leave unsaid

7

言 0 ←
貝
車
足
酉

言値 **i(i)ne** seller's price
言差 **i(i)sa(su)** stop short (in mid-sentence)
言振 **i(i)bu(ri), i(ip)pu(ri)** way of speaking
言挙 **kotoa(ge)** verbal expression; dispute
言破 **i(i)yabu(ru)** confute, argue down
言紛 **i(i)magi(rasu)** evade, quibble
11 言動 **gendō** speech and conduct
言過 **i(i)su(giru)** overstate, go too far
言渋 **i(i)shibu(ru)** hesitate to say, falter
言淀 **i(i)yodo(mu)** falter in saying, stammer
言掛 **i(i)ka(keru)** speak to; start talking
　　 i(i)ga(kari) false accusation
言捲 **i(i)maku(ru)** argue down, confute
言捨 **i(i)su(teru)** make a parting remark
言張 **i(i)ha(ru)** insist on, maintain
言寄 **i(i)yo(ru)** court, woo
言習 **i(i)nara(washi)** tradition, legend; common saying
言終 **i(i)owa(ru)** finish speaking
言訳 **i(i)wake** excuse, explanation, apology
言責 **genseki** responsibility for what one says
12 言違 **i(i)chiga(eru)** misstate, misspeak
言渡 **i(i)wata(su)** pronounce sentence; order; announce
言換 **i(i)ka(eru)** say in other words
言落 **i(i)o(tosu)** leave unsaid, neglect to mention
言葉 **kotoba** words, expression, language
　　 koto(no)ha words; tanka poem
言葉付 **kotobatsu(ki)** way of speaking
言葉尻 **kotobajiri** end of a word; slip of the tongue
言葉遣 **kotobazuka(i)** wording, expression
言葉質 **kotobajichi** pledge, promise
言募 **i(i)tsuno(ru)** argue with increasing vehemence
言替 **i(i)ka(eru)** say in other words
言散 **i(i)chi(rasu)** say all sorts of things
言開 **i(i)hira(ki)** justification, explanation
13 言損 **i(i)soko(nau)** misspeak; fail to mention
言辞 **genji** words, speech, language
言置 **i(i)o(ku)** leave word
言継 **i(i)tsu(gu)** transmit (by word of mouth)
言触 **i(i)fu(rasu)** start (a rumor), give it out that
言詰 **i(i)tsu(meru)** argue (someone) into a corner, confute
14 言漏 **i(i)mo(rasu)** forget to mention
言暮 **i(i)ku(rasu)** pass the time talking
言様 **i(i)yō** way of saying
言種 **i(i)gusa** one's words, remarks
言誤 **i(i)ayama(ru)** misstate, make a slip
言語 **gengo** language, speech
　　 i(wazu)kata(razu) tacitly
言語学 **gengogaku** linguistics, philology
言説 **gensetsu** remark, statement
言聞 **i(i)ki(kaseru)** tell (someone to do

something), persuade, exhort
15 言慰 **i(i)nagusa(meru)** console
言論 **genron** speech, discussion
言質 **genshitsu, genchi** pledge, promise
言霊 **kotodama** soul/power of language
18 言繕 **i(i)tsukuro(u)** gloss over
言難 **i(i)gata(i)** difficult to say, inexpressible
21 言囃 **i(i)haya(su)** praise; spread (a report)
22 言籠 **i(i)ko(meru)** argue (someone) into silence, confute

──────── 2 ────────

1 一言 **hitokoto, ichigen, ichigon** a word
　一言二言 **hitokoto futakoto** a word or two
2 二言 **futakoto** two words
　　 nigon double-dealing
　二言目 **futakotome** second word; the topic one's talk constantly turns to
3 寸言 **sungen** pithy remark, epigram
　大言壮語 **taigen sōgo** boasting, exaggeration
　口言葉 **kuchi kotoba** spoken/colloquial word(s)
　小言 **kogoto** scolding, faultfinding
4 不言不語 **fugen-fugo** silence
　予言 **yogen** prediction
　　 kanegoto prediction; promise
　予言者 **yogensha** prophet
　切言 **setsugen** urging, earnest persuasion
　片言 **katakoto** baby talk, broken (English)
　　 hengen few words
　片言交 **katakotoma(jiri)** babbling; broken (English)
　片言隻句 **hengen-sekku** few words
　片言隻語 **hengen-sekigo** few words
　公言 **kōgen** declaration, avowal
　方言 **hōgen** dialect
5 巧言 **kōgen** flattery
　巧言令色 **kōgen-reishoku** ingratiating geniality
　失言 **shitsugen** verbal slip/impropriety
　甘言 **kangen** honeyed words, flattery, blarney
　代言 **daigen** speaking for another; lawyer
　他言 **tagon, tagen** tell others, divulge
　付言 **fugen** additional remark, postscript
　用言 **yōgen** declinable word
　広言 **kōgen** bragging, boastful speech
　立言 **ritsugen** expression of one's view, proposal
6 伝言 **dengon** message
　伝言板 **dengonban** message/bulletin board
　合言葉 **a(i)kotoba** password, watchword
　壮言 **sōgen** spirited words
　至言 **shigen** wise saying
　名言 **meigen** wise saying, apt remark
　名言集 **meigenshū** analects
7 里言葉 **sato kotoba** rural dialect; courtesans' language

体言 **taigen** uninflected word
作言 **tsuku(ri)goto** fabrication, lie, fiction
助言 **jogen** advice
助言者 **jogensha** adviser, counselor
抗言 **kōgen** retort, contradiction
狂言 **kyōgen** play, drama; program; Noh
　　farce; trick, sham
狂言自殺 **kyōgen jisatsu** faked suicide
花言葉 **hana kotoba** the language of flowers
売言葉買言葉 **u(ri)kotoba (ni) ka(i)kotoba**
　　(an exchange of) fighting words
序言 **jogen** preface, foreword, introduction
忌言葉 **i(mi)kotoba** tabooed word
言言 **gengen** every word
8 毒言 **dokugen** abusive language
例言 **reigen** explanatory notes
佳言 **kagen** good words
侮言 **bugen** an insult
直言 **chokugen** plain speaking, straight talk
建言 **kengen** petition, proposal
逆言葉 **sakakotoba** word of opposite
　　meaning; word pronounced backwards
泣言 **na(ki)goto** complaint, grievance
苦言 **kugen** frank advice, exhortation
定言 **teigen** categorical proposition
空言 **soragoto, kūgen** falsehood, idle talk
国言葉 **(o)kunikotoba** dialect, vernacular
明言 **meigen** declare, assert
物言 **monoi(u)** speak, talk
放言 **hōgen** talk at random
忠言 **chūgen** good advice
金言 **kingen** wise saying, maxim
9 発言 **hatsugen** utterance, speaking; proposal
発言力 **hatsugenryoku** a voice, a say
発言者 **hatsugensha** speaker
発言権 **hatsugenken** right to speak, a voice
俚言 **rigen** dialect, slang
俗言 **zokugen** colloquial language
前言 **zengen** one's previous remarks
造言 **zōgen** lie, fabrication, false report
造言飛語 **zōgen-higo** false report, wild
　　rumor
通言 **tsūgen** popular saying
通言葉 **tō(ri)kotoba** catchword, jargon, argot,
　　common phrase
浮言 **fugen** unfounded rumor
独言 **hito(ri)goto** talking to oneself; solilo-
　　quy; monolog
宣言 **sengen** declaration, statement
宣言書 **sengensho** declaration, manifesto
祝言 **shūgen** congratulations; celebration;
　　wedding
怨言 **engen, ura(mi)goto** grudge, grievance,
　　reproach
恨言 **ura(mi)goto** grudge, grievance, reproach
悔言 **ku(yami)goto** words of condolence

約言 **yakugen** a contraction; summary
食言 **shokugen** eat one's words; break one's
　　promise
10 高言 **kōgen** boasting
進言 **shingen** advice, proposal
遊言葉 **aso(base)kotoba** word ending with
　　-asobase, characteristic of very polite
　　feminine speech
流言 **ryūgen** false rumor
流言飛語 **ryūgen-higo** rumor, gossip
徒言 **mudagoto** idle talk
格言 **kakugen** saying, proverb, maxim
書言葉 **ka(ki)kotoba** written language
11 虚言 **kyogen** lie, falsehood
過言 **kagon, kagen** exaggeration
添言葉 **so(e)kotoba** advice, encouragement
強言 **shiigoto** talking even though no one
　　wants to listed
得言 **e(mo)i(warenu)** indescribable
略言 **ryakugen** brief statement, summary
断言 **dangen** assert, declare
12 温言 **ongen** kind/gentle words
提言 **teigen** proposal, suggestion
揚言 **yōgen** profess, declare, assert
換言 **kangen (sureba)** in other words
御言 **mikoto** what (your excellency) says
極言 **kyokugen** go so far as to say
無言 **mugon** silent, mute
無言行 **mugon (no) gyō** ascetic silence
無言劇 **mugongeki** pantomime
買言葉 **ka(i)kotoba** harsh retort to harsh
　　words
痛言 **tsūgen** scathing criticism
評言 **hyōgen** (critical) remark
証言 **shōgen** testimony
13 隠言葉 **kaku(shi)kotoba** secret language,
　　argot
献言 **kengen** petition, proposal, memorial
寝言 **negoto** talking in one's sleep
睦言 **mutsugoto** lovers' talk
詫言 **wa(bi)goto** apology
話言葉 **hana(shi)kotoba** spoken language
詳言 **shōgen** detailed explanation
雅言 **gagen** elegant/poetical expression
14 遺言 **yuigon** will, last wishes
遺言状 **yuigonjō** will, testament
遺言者 **yuigonsha** testator
遺言書 **yuigonsho** will, testament
漫言 **mangen, sozo(ro)goto** rambling talk
寡言 **kagen** taciturnity, reticence
概言 **gaigen** general remarks, summary
歌言葉 **uta kotoba** poetic language/wording
緒言 **chogen, shogen** preface, foreword
綸言 **ringen** emperor's words/mandate
誣言 **fugen, bugen** false accusation
誓言 **seigon** oath, vow, pledge

7

言　0 ←

貝
車
跫
酉

雑言 **zōgon** vilification, name-calling
15 褒言葉 **ho(me)kotoba** words of praise, laudatory remarks
戯言 **za(re)goto** joke
確言 **kakugen** state definitely, affirm
箴言 **shingen** proverb, aphorism
16 憾言 **ura(mi)goto** words of regret
諫言 **kangen** remonstrate with, admonish
17 謹言 **kingen** Sincerely/Respectfully yours,
18 贅言 **zeigen** a redundancy, superfluous
題言 **daigen** prefatory phrase, title
19 繰言 **ku(ri)goto** same old story, complaint
20 譫言 **uwagoto** talking deliriously
21 囈言 **uwagoto** talking deliriously
24 讒言 **zangen** false charge, slander

——————— 3 ———————

1 一家言 **ikkagen** one's own opinion, a personal view
4 内祝言 **naishūgen** private wedding
切狂言 **ki(ri)kyōgen** last act
6 当狂言 **a(tari) kyōgen** a hit (play)
早口言葉 **hayakuchi kotoba** tongue twister
9 俄狂言 **niwakakyōgen** mime, farce
通狂言 **tō(shi)kyōgen** (presentation of) a whole play
10 流行言葉 **haya(ri)kotoba** popular expression
能狂言 **nōkyōgen** Noh farce; Noh drama and kyōgen farce
12 御国言葉 **okuni kotoba** dialect, vernacular
替狂言 **ka(wari) kyōgen** next week's/month's program
絵空言 **esoragoto** a fabrication, fantasy

——————— 4 ———————

1 一言二言 **hitokoto futakoto** a word or two
3 三百代言 **sanbyaku daigen** shyster lawyer, pettifogger
5 古義真言宗 **Kogi Shingon shū** the "old meaning" sect of Esoteric Buddhism
11 悪口雑言 **akkō-zōgon** vituperation
13 照葉狂言 **Teriha kyōgen** (a type of Noh entertainment)
新義真言宗 **Shingi Shingon shū** New Shingon religion
15 罵詈雑言 **bari-zōgon** abusive language

——————— 5 ———————

7 売言葉買言葉 **u(ri)kotoba (ni) ka(i)kotoba** (an exchange of) fighting words

——————— 2 ———————

7a2.1 / 340

計

KEI measure, (as suffix) meter, gauge; plan; total
haka(ru) measure, compute
haka(rau) arrange, dispose of, see about

——————— 1 ———————

3 計上 **keijō** add up; appropriate
4 計切 **haka(ri)ki(ru)** give exact measure/weight
計込 **haka(ri)ko(mu)** give overmeasure/overweight
7 計売 **haka(ri)u(ri)** sell by measure/weight
8 計画 **keikaku** plan, project
計画的 **keikakuteki** planned, systematic, intentional
計画者 **keikakusha** planner
計直 **haka(ri)nao(su)** remeasure, reweigh
10 計時 **keiji** timing, clocking
計時係 **keijigaka(ri)** timekeeper
11 計理士 **keirishi** public accountant
計略 **keiryaku** stratagem, plan, ruse
12 計測 **keisoku** measuring, instrumentation
計減 **haka(ri)be(ri)** giving short measure/weight
計量 **keiryō** measure, weigh
計量器 **keiryōki** meter, gauge, scale
13 計数 **keisū** counting, calculation
14 計算 **keisan** computation, calculation
計算尺 **keisanjaku** slide rule
計算係 **keisangaka(ri)** accountant
計算書 **keisansho** statement (of account)
計算器 **keisanki** calculator
計算機 **keisanki** computer
計算簿 **keisanbo** account book
15 計器 **keiki** meter, gauge, instruments

——————— 2 ———————

1 一計 **ikkei** a plan
3 大計 **taikei** long-range plan, farsighted policy
小計 **shōkei** subtotal
4 日計 **nikkei** daily account/expenses; the day's total
5 生計 **seikei** livelihood, living
生計費 **seikeihi** living expenses
主計 **shukei** paymaster, accountant
6 合計 **gōkei** total
会計 **kaikei** accounting; the bill
会計士 **kaikeishi** accountant
奸計 **kankei** evil design, trick
早計 **sōkei** premature, hasty, rash
百計 **hyakkei** every means
7 良計 **ryōkei** good plan, clever scheme
余計 **yokei** more than enough, extra; unneeded, uncalled-for
妙計 **myōkei** wise plan, clever trick
見計 **mihaka(ru), mihaka(rau)** select at one's discretion; time (one's visit)
8 表計算 **hyōkeisan** spreadsheet
奇計 **kikei** ingenious plan
取計 **to(ri)haka(rau)** manage, arrange
9 通計 **tsūkei** total

活計 **kakkei** livelihood, living
姦計 **kankei** evil design, trick
10 家計 **kakei** family finances; livelihood
家計費 **kakeihi** household expenses/budget
家計簿 **kakeibo** household account-book
時計 **tokei** clock, watch, timepiece
時計工 **tokeikō** watchmaker
時計仕掛 **tokei-jika(ke)** clockwork
時計台 **tokeidai** clock stand/tower
時計回 **tokeimawa(ri)** clockwise
時計屋 **tokeiya** watch store, jeweler
時計師 **tokeishi** watchmaker, jeweler
秘計 **hikei** secret plan
純計 **junkei** total excluding duplications
11 推計 **suikei** estimate
術計 **jukkei** stratagem, ruse, trick
密計 **mikkei** secret plan, plot
悪計 **akkei, akukei** evil scheme, plot, trick
累計 **ruikei** total
設計 **sekkei** design, planning
設計図 **sekkeizu** plan, blueprint
設計者 **sekkeisha** designer
12 無計画 **mukeikaku** unplanned, haphazard
統計 **tōkei** statistics
統計学 **tōkeigaku** statistics
統計表 **tōkeihyō** statistical table
統計的 **tōkeiteki** statistical
集計 **shūkei** categorized total, aggregate
13 愚計 **gukei** foolish/my plan
詭計 **kikei** trickery, chicanery, ruse
14 概計 **gaikei** rough estimate
総計 **sōkei** (sum) total
16 謀計 **bōkei** strategem, plot, trick

——————— 3 ———————
4 水圧計 **suiatsukei** water-pressure gauge
水時計 **mizu-dokei** water clock
水量計 **suiryōkei** water meter
日時計 **hidokei** sundial
日照計 **nisshōkei** heliograph
心電計 **shindenkei** electrocardiograph
5 圧力計 **atsuryokukei** pressure gauge
6 気圧計 **kiatsukei** barometer
地震計 **jishinkei** seismometer
光度計 **kōdokei** photometer
血圧計 **ketsuatsukei** sphygmomanometer
7 体温計 **taionkei** (clinical) thermometer
花時計 **hanadokei** flower-bed clock
8 歩度計 **hodokei** pedometer
歩数計 **hosūkei** pedometer
金時計 **kindokei** gold watch
雨量計 **uryōkei** rain gauge
9 速度計 **sokudokei** speedometer
途中計時 **tochū keiji** lap time (in races)
風速計 **fūsokukei** anemometer
柱時計 **hashiradokei** wall clock

砂時計 **sunadokei** hourglass
10 高度計 **kōdokei** altimeter
流量計 **ryūryōkei** flow/current meter
11 掛時計 **ka(ke)dokei** wall clock
乾湿計 **kanshitsukei** hygrometer, humidity
    meter
12 測微計 **sokubikei** micrometer
温度計 **ondokei** thermometer
湿度計 **shitsudokei** hygrometer
寒暖計 **kandankei** thermometer
検流計 **kenryūkei** current gauge, ammeter
検糖計 **kentōkei** saccarimeter
腕時計 **udedokei** wristwatch
晴雨計 **seiukei** barometer
距離計 **kyorikei** range finder
13 損益計算書 **son'eki keisansho** income/
    profit-and-loss statement
腹時計 **haradokei** one's sense of time
置時計 **o(ki)dokei** table clock
電圧計 **den'atsukei** voltmeter
電波計 **denpakei** wave meter
電流計 **denryūkei** ammeter, galvanometer
鳩時計 **hatodokei** cuckoo clock
21 露出計 **roshutsukei** light meter
露光計 **rokōkei** light meter

——————— 4 ———————
3 三十六計 **sanjūrokkei** many plans/strategies
三十六計逃 **sanjūrokkei ni(geru ni**
    shikazu) It's wisest here to run away.
5 目覚時計 **meza(mashi)dokei** alarm clock
6 光高温計 **hikari-kōonkei** optical pyrometer
8 夜光時計 **yakō-dokei** luminous-dial watch
16 懐中時計 **kaichū-dokei** pocket watch

7a2.2

訃   FU report of a death, obituary

——————— 1 ———————
7 訃告 **fukoku** obituary, death notice
9 訃音 **fuin** news of someone's death
12 訃報 **fuhō** news of someone's death

7a2.3 / 1019

訂   TEI correcting

——————— 1 ———————
5 訂正 **teisei** correction, revision
——————— 2 ———————
6 再訂 **saitei** second revision
7 改訂 **kaitei** revision
改訂版 **kaiteiban** revised edition
改訂増補 **kaitei-zōho** revised and enlarged

7

言 2 ←
貝
車
足
酉

10 校訂 **kōtei** revision
　校訂版 **kōteiban** revised edition
13 新訂 **shintei** new revision
　新訂版 **shinteiban** newly revised edition

──────── 3 ────────

7a3.1 / 1636

託

TAKU entrust　**kako(tsu)** complain of, bemoan　**kakotsu(keru)** make a pretext of　**kotozu(keru)** send word, have (someone) deliver

──────── 1 ────────

0 託する **taku(suru)** entrust to, leave in the care of
7 託児所 **takujisho** day nursery
8 託送 **takusō** consignment
9 託宣 **takusen** oracle

──────── 2 ────────

5 付託 **futaku** refer/submit (to a committee)
6 仮託 **kataku** pretext
8 依託 **itaku** request, entrust
　供託 **kyōtaku** deposit
　受託 **jutaku** be entrusted with
　屈託 **kuttaku** be worried/troubled; ennui, boredom
　委託 **itaku** entrust to, put in (someone's) charge
　委託金 **itakukin** money in trust
　委託販売 **itaku hanbai** selling on consignment/commission
9 信託 **shintaku** trust, entrusting
　信託統治 **shintaku tōchi** trusteeship
　負託 **futaku** mandate, trust
　神託 **shintaku** oracle, divine message
10 倚託 **itaku** entrust to
11 寄託 **kitaku** deposit with, entrust to
12 御託 **gotaku** tedious/impertinent talk
　結託 **kettaku** conspiracy, collusion
13 預託 **yotaku** deposit
15 嘱託 **shokutaku** put in charge of, commission; part-time employee
　請託 **seitaku** request, entreat, solicit

──────── 4 ────────

7 言左右託 **gen (o) sayū (ni) taku(suru)** equivocate, be noncommittal

7a3.2

訐

KETSU, aba(ku) divulge, reveal

7a3.3 / 1018

討

TŌ, u(tsu) attack

──────── 1 ────────

2 討入 **u(chi)i(ru)** break into, raid
4 討手 **u(t)te** punitive expedition, pursuers
6 討死 **u(chi)ji(ni)** fall in battle
　討伐 **tōbatsu** subjugation, suppression
　討伐隊 **tōbatsutai** punitive force
8 討果 **u(chi)hata(su)** slay
　討取 **u(chi)to(ru)** capture; kill
13 討滅 **u(chi)horo(bosu)** destroy
14 討漏 **u(chi)mo(rasu)** let escape, fail to kill
15 討論 **tōron** debate, discussion
　討論会 **tōronkai** forum, debate, discussion
20 討議 **tōgi** discussion, deliberation, debate

──────── 2 ────────

4 仇討 **adau(chi)** vendetta, revenge
　手討 **teu(chi)** killing with one's own hand/sword
6 返討 **kae(ri)u(chi)** killing a would-be avenger
8 夜討 **you(chi)** night attack
　追討 **tsuitō** liquidate rebels
　　　　o(i)u(chi) attack the routed enemy
　征討 **seitō** subjugation, pacification
9 相討 **aiu(chi)** striking each other simultaneously
11 掃討 **sōtō** sweeping, clearing, mopping up
12 検討 **kentō** examine, study, look into
　焼討 **ya(ki)u(chi)** attack by burning, set afire
15 敵討 **katakiu(chi)** revenge, vendetta
19 騙討 **dama(shi)u(chi)** sneak attack, foul play

──────── 3 ────────

6 再検討 **saikentō** re-examination, reappraisal, review
　同士討 **dōshiu(chi)** internecine strife

7a3.4

訌

KO confusion, rout

7a3.5 / 371

記

KI write down, note
shiru(su) write/note down

──────── 1 ────────

0 記する **ki(suru)** write down, record, describe
2 記入 **kinyū** entry (in a form/ledger)
5 記号 **kigō** mark, symbol
6 記名 **kimei** register/sign one's name
7 記述 **kijutsu** description, account
8 記事 **kiji** article, report
　記事文 **kijibun** descriptive composition
　記念 **kinen** commemoration, remembrance
　記念切手 **kinen kitte** commemorative stamp
　記念日 **kinenbi** memorial day, anniversary

記念号 **kinengō** commemorative issue (of a magazine)
記念物 **kinenbutsu** souvenir, memento
記念品 **kinenhin** souvenir, memento
記念祭 **kinensai** commoration, anniversary
記念碑 **kinenhi** monument
記念館 **kinenkan** memorial hall
記者 **kisha** newspaper reporter, journalist
記者会見 **kisha kaiken** news/press conference
記者席 **kishaseki** seats for the press
9 記紀 **Kiki** the Kojiki and Nihonshoki
11 記帳 **kichō** entry, registering, signature
記章 **kishō** medal, badge, insignia
13 記数法 **kisūhō** numerical notation
記載 **kisai** record, report, note
14 記銘 **kimei** inscription, engraving
16 記憶 **kioku** memory
記憶力 **kiokuryoku** memory (ability)
記録 **kiroku** record, document(ary)
記録的 **kirokuteki** record(-breaking)
記録係 **kirokugakari** recording secretary

──────── 2 ────────

3 上記 **jōki** the above-mentioned/aforesaid
下記 **kaki** the following
4 手記 **shuki** note, memo
日記 **nikki** diary, journal
日記帳 **nikkichō** diary
5 左記 **saki** the following
付記 **fuki** additional remark, supplementary note
6 伝記 **denki** biography
伝記物 **denkimono** biographical literature
列記 **rekki** enumeration, listing
自記 **jiki** written by oneself, recording (barometer)
7 位記 **iki** diploma of court rank
別記 **bekki** separate paragraph, stated elsewhere
快記録 **kaikiroku** a fine record
私記 **shiki** private record
8 表記 **hyōki** inscription, indication, declaration; orthography
併記 **heiki** write side by side, print together
追記 **tsuiki** postscript, P.S.
注記 **chūki** make entries, write down
実記 **jikki** authentic account, true record
官記 **kanki** written appointment (to an office)
明記 **meiki** clearly state, specify, stipulate
9 軍記 **gunki** war chronicle
軍記物語 **gunki monogatari** war chronicle
前記 **zenki** the above-mentioned
連記 **renki** list
速記 **sokki** shorthand
速記者 **sokkisha** shorthand writer, stenographer

速記術 **sokkijutsu** shorthand, stenography
速記録 **sokkiroku** shorthand notes
後記 **kōki** postscript
単記投票 **tanki tōhyō** voting for one person only
10 既記 **kiki** aforesaid, the above
書記 **shoki** secretary, clerk
　ka(ki)shiru(su) write down, record
書記局 **shokikyoku** secretariat
書記長 **shokichō** chief secretary
書記官 **shokikan** secretary
書記官長 **shokikanchō** chief secretary
特記 **tokki** special mention
11 強記 **kyōki** a good/retentive memory
略記 **ryakki** brief account, outline
略記法 **ryakkihō** abridged notation (e.g., 五三 for 五十三)
細記 **saiki** detailed description/account
転記 **tenki** post, transfer (a bookkeeping entry)
12 登記 **tōki** registration, recording
登記所 **tōkisho** registry (office)
登記料 **tōkiryō** registration fee
無記名 **mukimei** uninscribed (shares), unregistered (bond), blank (endorsement)
補記 **hoki** add/append (to an article)
筆記 **hikki** taking notes; notes
筆記者 **hikkisha** copyist
筆記帳 **hikkichō** notebook
註記 **chūki** make entries, write down
13 暗記 **anki** memorization
暗記物 **ankimono** something to be memorized
戦記 **senki** account of a war
新記録 **shinkiroku** new record
詳記 **shōki** minute description, full account
14 摘記 **tekki** summarize
誤記 **goki** clerical error
銘記 **meiki** bear in mind
雑記 **zakki** miscellaneous notes
雑記帳 **zakkichō** notebook
15 標記 **hyōki** a mark, marking
勲記 **kunki** commendation, diploma
19 簿記 **boki** bookkeeping

──────── 3 ────────

1 一代記 **ichidaiki** a biography
3 三面記事 **sanmen kiji** page-3 news, police news, human-interest stories
丸暗記 **maruanki** learn by heart/rote
4 天然記念物 **tennen kinenbutsu** natural monument
5 古事記 **Kojiki** (Japan's) Ancient Chronicles
6 年代記 **nendaiki** chronicle
9 風土記 **fudoki** description of the natural features of a region, a topography

7

言 3 ←
貝
車
足
酉

音部記号 **onbu kigō** (G) clef
10 従軍記者 **jūgun kisha** war correspondent
旅日記 **tabinikki** travel diary
旅行記 **ryokōki** record of one's trip
11 道中記 **dōchūki** traveler's journal
探検記 **tankenki** account of an expedition
12 創世記 **Sōseiki** Genesis
棒暗記 **bōanki** indiscriminate memorization
評判記 **hyōbanki** book of commentary on artists or celebrities
13 歳時記 **saijiki** almanac
14 漂流記 **hyōryūki** castaway's account of foreign lands

——————— 4 ———————
12 博覧強記 **hakuran-kyōki** extensive reading and retentive memory

7a3.6 / 771

訓 **KUN** Japanese reading of a kanji; teachings, precept

——————— 1 ———————
5 訓令 **kunrei** instructions, directive
訓令式 **kunreishiki** (a system of romanization which differs from Hepburn romanization in such syllables as *shi/si, tsu/tu, cha/tya*)
訓示 **kunji** instruction
7 訓戒 **kunkai** admonition, warning
8 訓育 **kun'iku** education, discipline
9 訓点 **kunten** punctuation marks
11 訓釈 **kunshaku** explanation of the reading and meaning of kanji
12 訓詁 **kunko** exegesis, interpretation
訓詁学 **kunkogaku** exegetics
13 訓義 **kungi** reading and meaning (of a kanji)
訓辞 **kunji** an admonitory speech, instructions
訓話 **kunwa** moral discourse
訓電 **kunden** telegraphed instructions
14 訓導 **kundō** instruct, guide
訓練 **kunren** training
訓読 **kundoku, kun'yo(mi)** native-Japanese reading of a kanji
訓誨 **kunkai** instruct, enlighten
訓誡 **kunkai** admonition, warning

——————— 2 ———————
4 内訓 **naikun** private/secret instructions
5 古訓 **kokun** ancient precept; old reading (of a character)
字訓 **jikun** Japanese/*kun* reading of a kanji
6 回訓 **kaikun** the requested instructions
7 社訓 **shakun** precepts for employees
8 和訓 **wakun** Japanese reading (of a kanji)
9 音訓 **onkun** Chinese and Japanese pronunciations of a kanji
10 猛訓練 **mōkunren** hard training

家訓 **kakun** family precepts
校訓 **kōkun** school precepts/motto
教訓 **kyōkun** lesson, precept, moral
教訓的 **kyōkunteki** instructive, edifying
13 壼訓 **konkun** training in ladylike manners
聖訓 **seikun** sacred teachings
14 遺訓 **ikun** dying injunction
15 請訓 **seikun** request for instructions
18 難訓 **nankun** difficult reading of a kanji

——————— 3 ———————
5 処世訓 **shoseikun** rules for living

7a3.7

訖 **KITSU** come to an end; reach, arrive at; finally

7a3.8

訊 **JIN, tazu(neru)** ask, question, inquire

——————— 1 ———————
11 訊問 **jinmon** questioning, interrogation, cross examination

——————— 3 ———————
4 不審訊問 **fushin jinmon** questioning (by a policeman)
反対訊問 **hantai jinmon** cross-examination

——————— 4 ———————

7a4.1 / 1181

訪 **HŌ, tazu(neru), otozu(reru), to(u)** visit

——————— 1 ———————
4 訪日 **hō-Nichi** visiting Japan
9 訪客 **hōkyaku, hōkaku** visitor, guest
11 訪問 **hōmon** visit
訪問者 **hōmonsha** visitor, caller
訪問販売 **hōmon hanbai** door-to-door sales
訪問着 **hōmongi** woman's semi-formal kimono

——————— 2 ———————
7 来訪 **raihō** visit, call
8 往訪 **ōhō** visit, call on
11 探訪 **tanbō** inquire into, probe
14 歴訪 **rekihō** round/tour of visits

7a4.2

訣 **KETSU** separation, parting; secret

— 1 —
7 訣別 **ketsubetsu** parting, farewell

— 2 —
5 永訣 **eiketsu** farewell forever, death
10 秘訣 **hiketsu** secret, the key to

訏 → 訏 **7a5.1**

7a4.3 / 737

許

KYO, **yuru(su)** permit, allow
moto with, at (someone's house)
-baka(ri) approximately; only; almost; nothing but

— 1 —
5 許可 **kyoka** permission, approval, authorization
　許可制 **kyokasei** license system
　許可証 **kyokashō** a permit, license
7 許否 **kyohi** approval or disapproval
10 許容 **kyoyō** permission, tolerance
11 許婚 **iinazuke** one's betrothed
13 許嫁 **iinazuke** fiancée
15 許諾 **kyodaku** consent, approval

— 2 —
4 允許 **inkyo** permission, license
　公許 **kōkyo** official permission, authorization
　手許 **temoto** at hand; in one's care; ready cash
　心許 **kokorobaka(ri)** trifling, mere token
　kokoromoto(nai) uneasy, apprehensive; unreliable
6 此許 **ko(re)baka(ri)** only this, only this much
8 免許 **menkyo** license, permission
　免許状 **menkyojō** license, certificate, permit
　免許証 **menkyoshō** license, certificate, permit
　其許 **sorebakari** only that, about that much
　官許 **kankyo** government license
　枕許 **makuramoto** bedside
9 爰許 **kokomoto** here; I, me
10 差許 **sa(shi)yuru(su)** permit, allow
　特許 **tokkyo** patent; special permission
　特許庁 **Tokkyochō** Patent Office
　特許状 **tokkyojō** charter, special license
　特許法 **tokkyohō** patent law
　特許品 **tokkyohin** patented article
　特許権 **tokkyoken** patent
12 幾許 **ikubaku** how much/many
　奥許 **okuyuru(shi)** initiation into the mysteries of
14 認許 **ninkyo** consent, recognition
15 黙許 **mokkyo** tacit permission, connivance
16 親許 **oyamoto** one's parents' home
17 聴許 **chōkyo** permission, approval

— 3 —
6 如何許 **ikabaka(ri)** how much
8 其処許 **sokomoto** you
12 無免許 **mumenkyo** without a license

— 4 —
9 専売特許 **senbai tokkyo** patent

7a4.4

訥

TOTSU stutter

— 1 —
5 訥弁 **totsuben** slow/awkward of speech

— 2 —
4 木訥 **bokutotsu** rugged honesty
6 朴訥 **bokutotsu** rugged honesty

7a4.5

訛 譌

KA make a verbal error; have an accent; lie
nama(ru) speak with an accent

— 1 —
7 訛声 **damigoe** thick voice

— 2 —
11 転訛 **tenka** corruption (of a word)

7a4.6 / 1403

訟

SHŌ accuse

— 2 —
12 訴訟 **soshō** lawsuit, litigation
　訴訟人 **soshōnin** plaintiff
　訴訟法 **soshōhō** code of (civil/criminal) procedure

— 3 —
16 壁訴訟 **kabesoshō** grumbling to oneself

— 4 —
5 民事訴訟 **minji soshō** civil suit
6 刑事訴訟 **keiji soshō** criminal action/suit

7a4.7 / 577

設

SETSU, **mō(keru)** provide, prepare, establish, set up

— 1 —
5 設立 **setsuritsu** establishment, founding
　設立者 **setsuritsusha** founder, organizer
8 設定 **settei** establishment, creation
9 設計 **sekkei** design, planning
　設計図 **sekkeizu** plan, blueprint
　設計者 **sekkeisha** designer

7

言 4←
貝
車
足
酉

11 設問 **setsumon** question
12 設備 **setsubi** equipment, facilities, accommodations
　 設営 **setsuei** construction; preparations
13 設置 **setchi** establishment, founding, institution

———————— 2 ————————

4 公設 **kōsetsu** public
5 未設 **misetsu** yet unbuilt, projected
　 布設 **fusetsu** lay (cable/mines), build (a railway/road) (also spelled 敷設)
6 仮設 **kasetsu** temporary construction; (legal) fiction
7 沈設 **chinsetsu** lay (an undersea cable)
　 私設 **shisetsu** private, nongovernmental
8 建設 **kensetsu** construction
　 建設的 **kensetsuteki** constructive
　 建設者 **kensetsusha** builder
　 建設省 **Kensetsushō** Ministry of Construction
　 官設 **kansetsu** government(-established/-run)
9 急設 **kyūsetsu** speedy installation
　 架設 **kasetsu** construction, laying
　 施設 **shisetsu** facilities, institution
　 思設 **omo(i)mō(keru)** anticipate, expect
10 既設 **kisetsu** already built, established, existing
　 既設線 **kisetsusen** lines in operation
　 埋設 **maisetsu** lay (underground cables)
　 特設 **tokusetsu** specially established/installed
11 常設 **jōsetsu** permanent, standing (committee)
12 創設 **sōsetsu** establishment, founding
　 開設 **kaisetsu** establish, inagurate, install
13 新設 **shinsetsu** newly established
14 増設 **zōsetsu** build on, extend, establish/install more
15 敷設 **fusetsu** lay (cable/mines), build (a railway/road) (also spelled 布設)
18 濫設 **ransetsu** establish too many (schools)

———————— 4 ————————

9 軍事施設 **gunji shisetsu** military installations

7a4.8 / 594

訳 譯 **YAKU** translation
wake reason, cause; meaning; circumstances, the case

———————— 1 ————————

0 訳す **yaku(su)** translate
1 訳了 **yakuryō** finish translating
4 訳文 **yakubun** a translation
5 訳出 **yakushutsu** translate
　 訳本 **yakuhon** a translation (of a book)
6 訳合 **wakea(i)** circumstances, matter
7 訳述 **yakujutsu** translate
8 訳注 **yakuchū** translation and annotation

訳者 **yakusha** translator
9 訳柄 **wakegara** reason, circumstances
10 訳書 **yakusho** a translation
12 訳無 **wakena(i)** easy, simple
　 訳補 **yakuho** translate adding explanatory passages
　 訳筆 **yakuhitsu** style of translation
　 訳詞 **yakushi** translation of song lyrics
13 訳解 **yakkai** annotated translation
　 訳詩 **yakushi** translated poem
　 訳載 **yakusai** translate and print (in a magazine)
14 訳語 **yakugo** translated term, an equivalent
　 訳読 **yakudoku** read and translate

———————— 2 ————————

4 内訳 **uchiwake** itemization, breakdown
5 申訳 **mō(shi)wake** excuse, apology
6 全訳 **zen'yaku** complete translation
　 邦訳 **hōyaku** translation into Japanese
　 名訳 **meiyaku** excellent translation
　 共訳 **kyōyaku** joint translation
7 対訳 **taiyaku** bilingual text (with Japanese and English side by side)
　 抄訳 **shōyaku** abridged translation
　 完訳 **kan'yaku** complete translation
　 初訳 **shoyaku** first(-ever) translation
　 言訳 **i(i)wake** excuse, explanation, apology
8 直訳 **chokuyaku** literal translation
　 英訳 **eiyaku** English translation
　 和訳 **wayaku** translation into Japanese
9 通訳 **tsūyaku** interpreting; interpreter
　 通訳官 **tsūyakukan** official interpreter
　 音訳 **on'yaku** transliteration
13 適訳 **tekiyaku** exact translation
　 漢訳 **kan'yaku** translation into classical Chinese
　 意訳 **iyaku** free translation
　 新訳 **shin'yaku** new translation
14 誤訳 **goyaku** mistranslation
15 監訳 **kan'yaku** supervision of translation
　 諸訳 **showake** intricacies, details
18 翻訳 **hon'yaku** translation
　 翻訳者 **hon'yakusha** translator
　 翻訳家 **hon'yakuka** translator
　 翻訳書 **hon'yakusho** a translation
　 翻訳権 **hon'yakuken** translation rights

———————— 3 ————————

3 口語訳 **kōgoyaku** colloquial translation
4 日本訳 **nihon'yaku** Japanese translation
6 自由訳 **jiyūyaku** free translation
9 逐字訳 **chikujiyaku** word-for-word/literal translation
　 逐語訳 **chikugoyaku** word-for-word/literal translation
12 欽定訳聖書 **kinteiyaku seisho** the King James Bible

――― 5 ―――

7a5.1

訝 訝

GA, GE, ibuka(ru) be suspicious of, doubt
ibuka(shii) suspicious, dubious

――― 2 ―――

8 怪訝 **kegen** suspicious, dubious

7a5.2 / 1402

訴

SO, utta(eru) sue; complain of; appeal to

――― 1 ―――

2 訴人 **sonin** suer, plaintiff
6 訴件 **soken** (legal) case
訴因 **soin** cause of action, charge, count
7 訴状 **sojō** petition, (written) complaint
8 訴追 **sotsui** prosecution, indictment
11 訴訟 **soshō** lawsuit, litigation
訴訟人 **soshōnin** plaintiff
訴訟法 **soshōhō** code of (civil/criminal) procedure
15 訴権 **soken** standing/right to sue
19 訴願 **sogan** petition, appeal
訴願人 **sogannin** petitioner, appellant

――― 2 ―――

3 上訴 **jōso** appeal (to a higher court)
4 公訴 **kōso** arraignment, accusation, charge
反訴 **hanso** countersuit, counterclaim
5 主訴 **shuso** main complaint/suit
7 告訴 **kokuso** accuse, charge, bring suit
告訴人 **kokusonin** complainant
応訴 **ōso** countersuit
8 受訴 **juso** (court's) acceptance of a lawsuit
直訴 **jikiso** direct appeal/petition
免訴 **menso** dismissal (of a case), acquittal
追訴 **tsuiso** supplementary lawsuit/indictment
泣訴 **kyūso** appeal, implore
9 哀訴 **aiso** appeal, entreat, implore
10 起訴 **kiso** prosecute, indict; sue, bring action against
起訴状 **kisojō** (written) indictment
11 控訴 **kōso** appeal (to a higher court)
控訴状 **kōsojō** petition of appeal
控訴院 **kōsoin** court of appeal
控訴審 **kōsoshin** appeal trial
控訴権 **kōsoken** right of appeal
強訴 **gōso** direct petition
敗訴 **haiso** losing a suit
12 提訴 **teiso** sue, bring action
勝訴 **shōso** winning a lawsuit
13 愁訴 **shūso** plea, supplication
16 壁訴訟 **kabesoshō** grumbling to oneself
24 讒訴 **zanso** false charge, slander

――― 3 ―――

4 不起訴 **fukiso** nonprosecution, nonindictment
5 民事訴訟 **minji soshō** civil suit
6 刑事訴訟 **keiji soshō** criminal action/suit

7a5.3 / 1028

評

HYŌ criticism, comment

――― 1 ―――

0 評する **hyō(suru)** criticize, comment on
6 評伝 **hyōden** critical biography
7 評判 **hyōban** fame, popularity; rumor, gossip
評判記 **hyōbanki** book of commentary on artists or celebrities
評決 **hyōketsu** verdict
評言 **hyōgen** (critical) remark
8 評価 **hyōka** appraisal
評注 **hyōchū** commentary, annotation
評定 **hyōtei** rating, evaluation
hyōjō conference, council
評者 **hyōsha** critic, reviewer
9 評点 **hyōten** examination marks
11 評釈 **hyōshaku** annotation, commentary
12 評註 **hyōchū** commentary, annotation
14 評語 **hyōgo** critical remark; mark, grade
15 評論 **hyōron** criticism, critique, commentary
評論家 **hyōronka** critic, commentator
20 評議 **hyōgi** confer, discuss, deliberate
評議会 **hyōgikai** council, commission
評議員 **hyōgiin** councilor, trustee

――― 2 ―――

3 寸評 **sunpyō** brief review/commentary
大評判 **daihyōban** sensation, smash
4 不評 **fuhyō** bad reputation, disrepute, unpopularity
不評判 **fuhyōban** bad reputation, disrepute, unpopularity
公評 **kōhyō** fair appraisal; public's opinion
月評 **geppyō** monthly review
5 世評 **sehyō** popular opinion; reputation; rumor
好評 **kōhyō** favorable reception, popularity
6 再評価 **saihyōka** reassessment, re-evaluation
合評 **gappyō** joint review/criticism
妄評 **bōhyō, mōhyō** unfair/savage criticism, excoriation
自評 **jihyō** self-criticism
7 冷評 **reihyō** sarcasm, sneer
批評 **hihyō** criticism, critique, review
批評家 **hihyōka** critic, reviewer
批評眼 **hihyōgan** critical eye
8 定評 **teihyō** acknowledged, recognized
9 風評 **fūhyō** rumor
品評 **hinpyō** criticism, commentary
品評会 **hinpyōkai** competitive exhibition

7

言 5 ←
貝
車
足
酉

10 高評 **kōhyō** your (esteemed) opinion/criticism
週評 **shūhyō** weekly review
時評 **jihyō** (editorial) commentary
書評 **shohyō** book review
書評欄 **shohyōran** book review column/ section
11 悪評 **akuhyō** bad reputation; unfavorable criticism
細評 **saihyō** detailed criticism
12 短評 **tanpyō** short criticism, brief review
衆評 **shūhyō** public opinion
13 適評 **tekihyō** pertinent criticism, apt comment
14 漫評 **manpyō** rambling criticism
総評 **Sōhyō** General Council of Trade Unions of Japan (short for 日本労働組合総評議会)
酷評 **kokuhyō** sharp/harsh criticism
15 論評 **ronpyō** comment, criticism, review
17 講評 **kōhyō** criticism, review

—————————— 3 ——————————

3 下馬評 **gebahyō** outsiders' irresponsible talk, rumor
12 勤務評定 **kinmu hyōtei** job performance appraisal

—————————— 4 ——————————

3 小田原評定 **odawara hyōjō** endless debate, fruitless conference
5 本文批評 **honmon hihyō** textual criticism

註 → 註 7a5.11

7a5.4

詛 **SO, noro(u)** curse

—————————— 2 ——————————

8 呪詛 **juso** curse, imprecation, anathema

7a5.5 / 484

証 證 **SHŌ** proof, evidence; certificate
akashi proof, evidence

—————————— 1 ——————————

0 証する **shō(suru)** prove, certify
2 証人 **shōnin** witness
証人台 **shōnindai** the witness stand/box
証人席 **shōninseki** the witness stand/box
4 証文 **shōmon** deed, bond, in writing
5 証左 **shōsa** evidence, proof
6 証印 **shōin** seal on a document
7 証言 **shōgen** testimony
8 証券 **shōken** securities
証拠 **shōko** evidence, proof

証拠人 **shōkonin** witness
証拠立 **shōkoda(teru)** substantiate, corroborate
証拠物 **shōkobutsu** physical evidence
証明 **shōmei** proof, corroboration
証明書 **shōmeisho** certificate
10 証書 **shōsho** deed, bond, in writing
証紙 **shōshi** certification sticker/stamp
11 証票 **shōhyō** voucher
13 証跡 **shōseki** evidence, traces

—————————— 2 ——————————

3 口証 **kōshō** oral testimony
4 内証 **naishō** secret; internal evidence; one's circumstances
内証事 **naishōgoto** a secret
内証話 **naishōbanashi** confidential talk, whispering
公証 **kōshō** authentication, notarization
公証人 **kōshōnin** notary public
反証 **hanshō** counterevidence
引証 **inshō** quote, cite, adduce
心証 **shinshō** one's impression of; judge's personal opinion of a case
5 弁証法 **benshōhō** dialectic, dialectics
弁証論 **benshōron** apologetics; dialectics
立証 **risshō** prove, establish
6 考証 **kōshō** historical research
8 例証 **reishō** example, illustration
実証 **jisshō** actual proof
実証主義 **jisshō shugi** positivism
実証哲学 **jisshō tetsugaku** positivism
実証論 **jisshōron** positivism
9 信証 **shinshō** evidence, sign
保証 **hoshō** guarantee
保証人 **hoshōnin** guarantor
保証付 **hoshōtsu(ki)** guaranteed
保証金 **hoshōkin** security deposit, key money
査証 **sashō** visa; investigation and attestation
10 挙証 **kyoshō** establishing a fact, proof
書証 **shoshō** documentary evidence
11 偽証 **gishō** false testimony, perjury
偽証罪 **gishōzai** perjury
12 傍証 **bōshō** supporting evidence, corroboration
検証 **kenshō** verification, inspection
13 預証 **azu(kari)shō** (baggage) claim check; (warehouse/deposit) receipt
14 認証 **ninshō** certify, attest, authenticate
15 確証 **kakushō** proof positive, corroboration
論証 **ronshō** demonstration, proof

—————————— 3 ——————————

6 会員証 **kaiinshō** membership certificate/card
有価証券 **yūka shōken** (negotiable) securities
7 学生証 **gakuseishō** student I.D.
8 受取証 **uketorishō** receipt, voucher

受領証 **juryōshō** receipt
免許証 **menkyoshō** license, certificate, permit
10 借用証書 **shakuyō shōsho** bond of debt
11 情況証拠 **jōkyō shōko** circumstantial evidence
船荷証券 **funani shōken** bill of lading
許可証 **kyokashō** a permit, license
13 適任証 **tekininshō** certificate of competence
14 認可証 **ninkashō** permit, license
領収証 **ryōshūshō** receipt

——————— 4 ———————
7 身元保証 **mimoto hoshō** personal references

7a5.6 / 1498

SA, itsuwa(ru) lie, deceive

——————— 1 ———————
8 詐取 **sashu** fraud, swindle
10 詐称 **sashō** misrepresent oneself
11 詐術 **sajutsu** swindling
12 詐欺 **sagi** fraud
詐欺師 **sagishi** swindler, con man
詐欺罪 **sagizai** fraud

7a5.7

TEI vilify, denounce

7a5.8

TA deceive

7a5.9 / 1214

診

SHIN, mi(ru) see (a patient), examine, diagnose

——————— 1 ———————
11 診断 **shindan** diagnosis
診断書 **shindansho** medical certificate
14 診察 **shinsatsu** medical examination
診察日 **shinsatsubi** consultation day
診察券 **shinsatsuken** consultation ticket
診察室 **shinsatsushitsu** room where patients are examined
診察料 **shinsatsuryō** medical consultation fee
17 診療 **shinryō** examination and treatment
診療所 **shinryōjo** clinic

——————— 2 ———————
4 内診 **naishin** internal/pelvic examination
5 代診 **daishin** doctor's assistant

打診 **dashin** percussion, tapping (in medicine); sound/feel out
6 休診 **kyūshin** see no patients, Clinic Closed
宅診 **takushin** consultation at a clinic (rather than a house call)
回診 **kaishin** doctor's hospital rounds
7 来診 **raishin** doctor's visit, house call
初診 **shoshin** first medical examination
初診料 **shoshinryō** fee for patient's first visit
8 受診 **jushin** receive a medical examination
往診 **ōshin** doctor's visit, house call
11 視診 **shishin** (diagnosis by) visual inspection
12 検診 **kenshin** medical examination
検診日 **kenshinbi** medical-examination day
13 触診 **shokushin** palpation
14 誤診 **goshin** misdiagnosis
17 聴診 **chōshin** auscultation
聴診器 **chōshinki** stethoscope

——————— 3 ———————
6 早期診断 **sōki shindan** early diagnosis
10 健康診断 **kenkō shindan** medical examination, physical checkup

7a5.10 / 1885

詔

SHŌ, mikotonori imperial edict

——————— 1 ———————
9 詔勅 **shōchoku** imperial proclamation
10 詔書 **shōsho** imperial edict/rescript

——————— 2 ———————
3 大詔 **taishō** imperial rescript

7a5.11

註 註

CHŪ note, comment, annotation

——————— 1 ———————
10 註記 **chūki** make entries, write down
11 註疏 **chūso** notes, commentary
註釈 **chūshaku** annotation, commentary
註釈者 **chūshakusha** annotator, commentator
13 註解 **chūkai** notes, commentary

——————— 2 ———————
8 受註 **juchū** receive an order for
10 原註 **genchū** the original annotations
校註 **kōchū** proofreading and annotation
11 脚註 **kyakuchū** footnote
12 傍註 **bōchū** marginal notes
補註 **hochū** supplementary note
評註 **hyōchū** commentary, annotation
13 詳註 **shōchū** copious notes/annotation
15 標註 **hyōchū** annotations (in the top margin)
16 頭註 **tōchū** notes at the top of the page

7

言 5←
貝
車
趾
酉

7a5.12

詁

KO reading, interpretation

———————— 2 ————————

10 訓詁 **kunko** exegesis, interpretation
　訓詁学 **kunkogaku** exegetics

7a5.13

詒

I deceive, cheat; give; leave behind

7a5.14 / 1209

詠 咏

EI poem, song; singing; composing
yo(mu) compose, write (a poem)

———————— 1 ————————

5 詠史 **eishi** historical poem, epic
7 詠吟 **eigin** reciting poetry
8 詠物 **eibutsu** nature poem
　詠物詩 **eibutsushi** nature poem
9 詠草 **eisō** draft of a poem
10 詠進 **eishin** presentation of a poem (to the Court)
11 詠唱 **eishō** aria
13 詠嘆 **eitan** exclamation; admiration
14 詠歌 **eika** composition of a poem; (Buddhist) chant
　詠歎 **eitan** exclamation; admiration

———————— 2 ————————

6 近詠 **kin'ei** recent poem
7 吟詠 **gin'ei** sing, recite; (compose a) poem
10 朗詠 **rōei** recite
12 御詠 **gyoei** imperial poem
　御詠歌 **goeika** Buddhist hymn/chant
13 献詠 **ken'ei** dedicate a poem
14 遺詠 **iei** poem by the deceased
　歌詠 **utayo(mi)** poet

7a5.15 / 843

詞

SHI, kotoba words

———————— 1 ————————

8 詞宗 **shisō** literary master
10 詞書 **kotobaga(ki)** foreword; notes
11 詞章 **shishō** poetry and prose
19 詞藻 **shisō** rhetorical embellishments; prose and poetry

———————— 2 ————————

4 弔詞 **chōshi** message of condolence, memorial address

　分詞 **bunshi** participle
5 台詞 **serifu** (actor's) lines, what one says
6 名詞 **meishi** noun
7 助詞 **joshi** a particle (in grammar)
　序詞 **joshi** preface, prolog
8 枕詞 **makurakotoba** prefatory word, set epithet
9 冠詞 **kanshi** article (in grammar)
　品詞 **hinshi** part of speech
　祝詞 **norito** Shinto prayer
　shukushi congratulatory message
11 副詞 **fukushi** adverb
　動詞 **dōshi** verb
　掛詞 **ka(ke)kotoba** play on words
　訳詞 **yakushi** translation of song lyrics
12 賀詞 **gashi** congratulations, greetings
13 数詞 **sūshi** numeral, number word
14 歌詞 **kashi** the lyrics/words (of a song)
　誓詞 **seishi** oath, pledge
15 褒詞 **ho(me)kotoba** words of praise
　賞詞 **shōshi** commendation

———————— 3 ————————

4 不定詞 **futeishi** an infinitive
5 代名詞 **daimeishi** pronoun
　他動詞 **tadōshi** transitive verb
6 自動詞 **jidōshi** intransitive verb
7 助動詞 **jodōshi** auxiliary verb
　形容詞 **keiyōshi** adjective
8 定冠詞 **teikanshi** definite article
9 前置詞 **zenchishi** preposition
　後置詞 **kōchishi** postposition
11 動名詞 **dōmeishi** gerund
　接続詞 **setsuzokushi** a conjunction
　捨台詞 **su(te)zerifu** sharp parting remark
12 間投詞 **kantōshi** an interjection
14 疑問詞 **gimonshi** interrogative word

———————— 4 ————————

7 形容動詞 **keiyōdōshi** quasi-adjective used with -na (e.g., *shizuka, kirei*)
8 固有名詞 **koyū meishi** proper noun
12 集合名詞 **shūgō meishi** collective noun
14 関係副詞 **kankei fukushi** relative adverb

———————— 5 ————————

14 疑問代名詞 **gimon daimeishi** interrogative pronoun
　関係代名詞 **kankei daimeishi** relative pronoun

7a5.16

訶

KA scold, reprove

———————— 2 ————————

15 摩訶不思議 **maka-fushigi** profound mystery

──────── 6 ────────

7a6.1

誄

RUI eulogy

──────── 1 ────────

14 誄歌 **ruika** dirge

7a6.2

誅

CHŪ punish; kill

──────── 2 ────────

4 天誅 **tenchū** heaven's punishment; well-deserved punishment

7a6.3 / 718

誠

SEI, makoto sincerity, fidelity; truth, reality

──────── 1 ────────

0 誠しやか **makoto(shiyaka)** plausible, specious
4 誠心 **seishin** sincerity
　誠心誠意 **seishin-seii** sincerely, wholeheartedly
8 誠実 **seijitsu** sincere, faithful, truthful
　誠忠 **seichū** loyal
13 誠意 **seii** sincerity, good faith

──────── 2 ────────

4 不誠実 **fuseijitsu** insincere, unfaithful, dishonest
　不誠意 **fuseii** insincere, unfaithful, dishonest
　丹誠 **tansei** sincerity; diligence
6 至誠 **shisei** sincerity, heart and soul
7 赤誠 **sekisei** sincerity
8 忠誠 **chūsei** loyalty, allegiance
　忠誠心 **chūseishin** loyalty, devotion, sincerity
15 熱誠 **nessei** earnestness, warmth, emthusiasm, sincerity

──────── 3 ────────

13 誠心誠意 **seishin-seii** sincerely, wholeheartedly

7a6.4

誂

CHŌ, atsura(eru) order (goods)

──────── 1 ────────

6 誂向 **atsura(e)mu(ki)** suitable, made to order

──────── 2 ────────

7 別誂 **betsuatsura(e)** special order, custom-made

7a6.5 / 570

詩

SHI poem, poetry

──────── 1 ────────

2 詩人 **shijin** poet
3 詩才 **shisai** poetic genius
4 詩友 **shiyū** one's friend in poetry
　詩文 **shibun** poetry and prose, literature
　詩心 **shishin** poetic sentiment
5 詩仙 **shisen** great poet
　詩句 **shiku** verse, stanza
6 詩会 **shikai** poetry-writing meeting
7 詩作 **shisaku** write poetry
　詩抄 **shishō** selection of poems
　詩吟 **shigin** reciting Chinese poems
　詩形 **shikei** verse form
　詩学 **shigaku** study of poetry
8 詩味 **shimi** poetic sentiment
　詩宗 **shisō** great poet
　詩的 **shiteki** poetic
　詩的情緒 **shiteki jōcho** poetic mood
9 詩巻 **shikan** a collection of poems
　詩草 **shisō** draft of a poem
11 詩情 **shijō** poetic sentiment
　詩経 **Shikyō** the Shijing (a Chinese classic)
12 詩集 **shishū** a collection of poems
13 詩聖 **shisei** great poet
　詩想 **shisō** thought of a poem
14 詩選 **shisen** poetry anthology
　詩境 **shikyō** the locale of a poem
　詩歌 **shiika, shika** poetry
　詩魂 **shikon** poetic sentiment
15 詩劇 **shigeki** a play in verse
　詩稿 **shikō** draft of a poem
　詩趣 **shishu** poetic beauty, poetry
　詩篇 **Shihen** (the Book of) Psalms
　詩論 **shiron** essay on poetry; poetics
16 詩興 **shikyō** poetic inspiration
　詩壇 **shidan** poetry circles
19 詩藻 **shisō** rhetorical flourishes; prose and poetry

──────── 2 ────────

7 作詩 **sakushi** writing poetry
　狂詩 **kyōshi** comic poem
8 英詩 **eishi** English poem/poetry
9 哀詩 **aishi** elegy
　律詩 **risshi** (a Chinese verse form)
10 唐詩 **tōshi** Tang-dynasty poem
11 訳詩 **yakushi** translated poem
12 短詩 **tanshi** short poem
13 漢詩 **kanshi** Chinese poetry/poem
15 劇詩 **gekishi** dramatic poem/poetry

──────── 3 ────────

3 口語詩 **kōgoshi** poem in colloquial style

7

言 6 ←
貝
車
足
酉

5 田園詩 **den'enshi** pastoral poem
6 近体詩 **kintaishi** modern-style poem
　自由詩 **jiyūshi** free verse
7 即興詩 **sokkyōshi** improvised poem
　抒情詩 **jojōshi** lyric poem/poetry
　吟遊詩人 **gin'yū shijin** troubadour, minstrel
8 押韻詩 **ōinshi** rhyming poem, verse
　定型詩 **teikeishi** poetry in a fixed form
9 叙事詩 **jojishi** epic poem/poetry
　叙情詩 **jojōshi** lyric poem/poetry
10 桂冠詩人 **keikan shijin** poet laureate
12 象徴詩 **shōchōshi** symbolical/symbolist poetry
　無韻詩 **muinshi** blank verse, unrhymed poem
　散文詩 **sanbunshi** prose poem
　詠物詩 **eibutsushi** nature poem
13 新体詩 **shintaishi** new-style poem/poetry

7a6.6

詫
TA apologize; boast; bewail
wa(biru) apologize, make an excuse
wa(bi) apology, excuse

→6 言
貝
車
趴
酉

——————— 1 ———————

7 詫状 **wa(bi)jō** written apology
　詫言 **wa(bi)goto** apology

7a6.7 / 1142

詰
KITSU, tsu(meru) cram, stuff; shorten
-zu(me) packed in (cans/bottles)
tsu(maru) be stopped up, be jammed;
shrink; be cornered **tsu(mu)** be pressed/
packed in **naji(ru)** reprove, rebuke

——————— 1 ———————

4 詰切 **tsu(me)ki(ru)** be always on hand
　詰込 **tsu(me)ko(mu)** cram, stuff, pack in
　詰込主義 **tsu(me)ko(mi) shugi** education emphasizing cramming and memorization rather than understanding
5 詰石 **tsu(me)ishi** foundation stone
6 詰合 **tsu(me)a(waseru)** pack an assortment of
8 詰物 **tsu(me)mono** stuffing, packing, padding
　詰所 **tsu(me)sho** office; guard room; crew's room **tsu(maru) tokoro** that is, after all
9 詰草 **tsumekusa** white Dutch clover
11 詰掛 **tsu(me)ka(keru)** throng to, besiege, crowd
　詰寄 **tsu(me)yo(ru)** draw near, press upon
　詰問 **kitsumon** cross-examination, grilling
12 詰替 **tsu(me)ka(eru)** repack, refill
13 詰腹 **tsu(me)bara** forced harakiri
14 詰綿 **tsu(me)wata** wadding, padding
18 詰襟 **tsu(me)eri** stand-up/close-buttoned collar

——————— 2 ———————

3 大詰 **ōzu(me)** finale, final scene
4 切詰 **ki(ri)tsu(meru)** shorten; reduce, economize, curtail, retrench
　手詰 **tezu(me)** pressing, final
　　tezu(mari) hard up, in a fix
5 氷詰 **kōrizu(me)** packed in ice
　立詰 **ta(chi)zu(me)** keep on standing
　目詰 **mezu(mari)** clogging (of a mesh/filter)
6 気詰 **kizu(mari)** feeling of awkwardness, ill at ease
　缶詰 **kanzume** canned goods
　行詰 **yu(ki)zu(mari), i(ki)zu(mari)** dead end, deadlock, standstill
7 折詰 **o(ri)zu(me)** (food/lunch) packed in a cardboard/thin-wood box
　見詰 **mitsu(meru)** gaze/stare at
　言詰 **i(i)tsu(meru)** argue (someone) into a corner, confute
8 追詰 **o(i)tsu(meru)** corner, drive to the wall, hunt down
　押詰 **o(shi)tsu(meru)** pack in
　突詰 **tsu(ki)tsu(meru)** investigate, get to the bottom of; brood over
　取詰 **to(ri)tsu(meru)** drive into a corner; take to task; brood over
　金詰 **kanezuma(ri), kinzuma(ri)** shortage of money
9 通詰 **kayo(i)tsu(meru)** visit frequently, frequent
　後詰 **gozu(me)** rear guard
　面詰 **menkitsu** reprove (someone) to his face
　思詰 **omo(i)tsu(meru)** think hard, brood over
　食詰 **ku(i)tsu(meru)** become unable to subsist
　食詰者 **ku(i)tsu(me)mono** a down-and-outer
10 差詰 **sa(shi)zu(me)** for the present
　差詰引詰 **sa(shi)tsu(me)-hi(ki)tsu(me)** shooting a flurry of arrows
　息詰 **ikizu(maru)** be stifled, gasp
11 瓶詰 **binzu(me)** bottling; bottled
　張詰 **ha(ri)tsu(meru)** strain, make tense
　理詰 **rizu(me)** persuasion, reasoning
12 煮詰 **nitsu(maru)** be boiled down
13 煎詰 **sen(ji)tsu(meru)** boil down
　腸詰 **chōzu(me)** sausage
14 鼻詰 **hanazu(mari)** nasal congestion
15 膝詰談判 **hizazu(me) danpan** direct/knee-to-knee negotiations
　敷詰 **shi(ki)tsu(meru)** spread all over, cover with
　箱詰 **hakozume** packed in cases, boxed
　論詰 **ronkitsu** refute **ron(ji)tsu(meru)** press an argument home
16 樽詰 **taruzu(me)** barreled, in casks
17 糞詰 **funzu(mari)** constipation

鮨詰 **sushizu(me)** packed like sushi/sardines, jam-packed
18 難詰 **nankitsu** blame, censure

──────── 3 ────────

4 切羽詰 **seppa-tsu(maru)** be driven to the wall, be at one's wit's end, be cornered
5 石子詰 **ishikozu(me)** execution by burying alive under stones
11 雪隠詰 **setchinzu(me)** to (force into a) corner

──────── 4 ────────

10 差詰引詰 **sa(shi)tsu(me)-hi(ki)tsu(me)** shooting a flurry of arrows

7a6.8 / 238

話   **WA, hanashi** talk, conversation, story
     hana(su) speak

──────── 1 ────────

4 話中 **hana(shi)chū** in the midst of speaking; (phone is) busy
　話込 **hana(shi)ko(mu)** have a long talk with
　話手 **hana(shi)te** speaker
　話方 **hana(shi)kata** way of speaking
5 話半分 **hanashi-hanbun** taking a story at half its face value
　話好 **hana(shi)zu(ki)** talkative, chatty
6 話合 **hana(shi)a(u)** talk over, discuss
7 話声 **hana(shi)goe** a voice
　話言葉 **hana(shi)kotoba** spoken language
8 話法 **wahō** speech, parlance
9 話相手 **hanashi aite** someone to talk to; companion
　話柄 **wahei** topic
10 話振 **hana(shi)bu(ri)** manner of speaking
　話家 **hana(shi)ka** storyteller
11 話掛 **hana(shi)ka(keru)** speak to, accost
　話術 **wajutsu** storytelling
16 話頭 **watō** topic, subject
18 話題 **wadai** topic, subject

──────── 2 ────────

1 一話 **hito(tsu)banashi** anecdote, common talk
3 小話 **shōwa, kobanashi** little story, anecdote
4 手話 **shuwa** sign language
5 民話 **minwa** folk tale, folklore
　世話 **sewa** help, assistance; good offices, recommendation; take care of; everyday life
　世話人 **sewanin** go-between, intermediary; sponsor; caretaker
　世話役 **sewayaku** go-between, intermediary; sponsor; caretaker
　白話 **hakuwa** colloquial Chinese
　立話 **ta(chi)banashi** standing and chatting
6 会話 **kaiwa** conversation

7 作話 **tsuku(ri)banashi** made-up story, fabrication, fable
　伽話 **(o)togibanashi** fairy tale
　対話 **taiwa** conversation, dialog
8 長話 **nagabanashi** a long/tedious talk
　例話 **reiwa** illustration
　受話器 **juwaki** (telephone) receiver
　夜話 **yobanashi, yawa** light talk after the day's work is done
　直話 **jikiwa** one's own account, firsthand story
　送話 **sōwa** transmission (of a telephone message)
　送話口 **sōwaguchi** (telephone) mouthpiece
　送話料 **sōwaryō** telephone charges
　送話器 **sōwaki** transmitter
　法話 **hōwa** (Buddhist) sermon
　昔話 **mukashibanashi** old tale, legend
　実話 **jitsuwa** true story
　官話 **Kanwa** the Mandarin language/dialect
9 俗話 **zokuwa** gossip, town talk
　哀話 **aiwa** sad story
　通話 **tsūwa** telephone call/conversation
　通話口 **tsūwaguchi** (telephone) mouthpiece
　通話料 **tsūwaryō** telephone-call charge
　指話 **shiwa** finger language, dactylology
　独話 **dokuwa** talking to oneself; monolog
　茶話 **chabanashi** a chat over tea, gossip
　茶話会 **sawakai, chawakai** tea party
　神話 **shinwa** myth, mythology
　神話学 **shinwagaku** mythology
10 高話 **takabanashi** loud talking
　逸話 **itsuwa** anecdote
　挿話 **sōwa** episode, anecdote
　秘話 **hiwa** secret story, unknown episode
　笑話 **wara(i)banashi, shōwa** funny story
　訓話 **kunwa** moral discourse
11 道話 **dōwa** moral tale, parable
　情話 **jōwa** lover's talk; love story
12 落話 **o(toshi)banashi** story with a comic ending
　寓話 **gūwa** fable, parable, allegory
　悲話 **hiwa** sad story
　童話 **dōwa** children's story, fairy tale
　童話劇 **dōwageki** a play for children
　閑話 **kanwa** quiet/idle talk
13 裏話 **urabanashi** inside story, story behind the story
　腹話術 **fukuwajutsu** ventriloquism
　禅話 **zenwa** a talk on Zen philosophy
　痴話 **chiwa** lovers' talk
　痴話喧嘩 **chiwa-genka** lovers' quarrel
　電話 **denwa** telephone
　電話口 **denwaguchi** telephone (mouthpiece)
　電話局 **denwakyoku** telephone office
　電話室 **denwashitsu** telephone booth
　電話料 **denwaryō** telephone charges

7

言 6 ←
貝
車
足
酉

電話帳 **denwachō** telephone directory
電話線 **denwasen** telephone line
14 説話 **setsuwa** tale, narrative
説話的 **setsuwateki** narrative (style)
雑話 **zatsuwa** idle talk, chitchat
15 噂話 **uwasabanashi** rumor, gossip, hearsay
談話 **danwa** conversation
談話体 **danwatai** colloquial style
談話室 **danwashitsu** parlor, lounge
17 懇話 **konwa** friendly talk, chat
懇話会 **konwakai** social get-together
講話 **kōwa** lecture, a talk
謹話 **kinwa** respectful remarks
20 譬話 **tato(e)banashi** fable, allegory, parable

——————— 3 ———————
3 与太話 **yotabanashi** idle gossip
土産話 **miyagebanashi** story of one's travels
4 内証話 **naishōbanashi** confidential talk, whispering
内緒話 **naishobanashi** confidential talk, whispering
手切話 **tegi(re)banashi** talk of separation
手柄話 **tegarabanashi** bragging of one's exploits
5 世間話 **sekenbanashi** small-talk, chat, gossip
打明話 **u(chi)a(ke)banashi** confidential talk, confession, revealing a secret
打解話 **u(chi)to(ke)banashi** friendly chat, heart-to-heart talk
6 自慢話 **jimanbanashi** boastful talk, bragging
7 身上話 **mi(no)uebanashi** one's life story
赤電話 **akadenwa** public telephone
8 直接話法 **chokusetsu wahō** direct quotation
英会話 **eikaiwa** English conversation
青電話 **aodenwa** public telephone
9 茶飲話 **chano(mi)banashi** a chat over tea, gossip
幽霊話 **yūreibanashi** ghost story
思出話 **omo(i)da(shi)banashi** reminiscences
12 御伽話 **otogibanashi** fairy tale
無駄話 **mudabanashi** idle talk, gossip
13 楽屋話 **gakuyabanashi** backstage talk

——————— 4 ———————
12 無線電話 **musen denwa** radiotelephone

——————— 5 ———————
10 留守番電話 **rusuban denwa** answering machine

7a6.9 / 1629

誇   **KO, hoko(ru)** boast of, be proud of

——————— 1 ———————
3 誇大 **kodai** exaggeration
5 誇示 **koji** display, flaunt

10 誇称 **koshō** exaggeration
11 誇張 **kochō** exaggeration
誇張法 **kochōhō** hyperbole
誇張的 **kochōteki** exaggerated, grandiloquent
18 誇顔 **hoko(ri)gao** triumphant look

——————— 2 ———————
9 咲誇 **sa(ki)hoko(ru)** bloom in full glory
12 勝誇 **ka(chi)hoko(ru)** triumph, exult in victory

詮 → 詮   7a6.14

7a6.10 / 1213

該   **GAI** the said

——————— 1 ———————
6 該当 **gaitō** pertain to, come/fall under
該当者 **gaitōsha** the said person
12 該博 **gaihaku** profound, vast (learning)

——————— 2 ———————
6 当該 **tōgai** the said, relevant

7a6.11

詭   **KI** lie, deceive

——————— 1 ———————
5 詭弁 **kiben** sophistry, logic-chopping
詭弁家 **kibenka** sophist, quibbler
9 詭計 **kikei** trickery, chicanery, ruse
12 詭策 **kisaku** ploy, ruse, trick

7a6.12 / 1577

詳   **SHŌ, kuwa(shii), tsumabi(raka)** detailed, full; familiar with (something)

——————— 1 ———————
6 詳伝 **shōden** detailed biography
7 詳述 **shōjutsu** detailed explanation, full account
詳言 **shōgen** detailed explanation
10 詳記 **shōki** minute description, full account
11 詳密 **shōmitsu** detailed
詳略 **shōryaku** detailed or sketchy
詳細 **shōsai** details, particulars
12 詳報 **shōhō** full/detailed report
詳註 **shōchū** copious notes/annotation
13 詳解 **shōkai** detailed explanation
14 詳説 **shōsetsu** detailed explanation
15 詳論 **shōron** full treatment, detailed exposition

7
→ 6

16 詳録 **shōroku** detailed record

——————— 2 ———————

4 不詳 **fushō** unknown, unidentified
5 未詳 **mishō** unknown, unidentified

7a6.13

詣   **KEI, mō(de), mai(ri)** visit to a temple/shrine

——————— 2 ———————

7 初詣 **hatsumōde** first shrine/temple visit in the new year
8 参詣 **sankei** temple/shrine visit, pilgrimage
9 造詣 **zōkei** scholarship, attainments
  神詣 **kamimō(de)** shrine visiting

7a6.14

詮 詮   **SEN** clarity, reason, truth; investigation; efficacy

——————— 1 ———————

4 詮方 **senkata(naku)** unavoidably, helplessly
10 詮索 **sensaku** search, inquiry
12 詮無 **senna(i)** useless, unavailing
20 詮議 **sengi** discussion, consideration, examination
  詮議立 **sengida(te)** thorough investigation

——————— 2 ———————

8 所詮 **shosen** after all

7a6.15

詼   **KAI** jest

7a6.16

詬   **KŌ** put to shame, revile

7a6.17

詢   **JUN** consult with

7a6.18 / 526

試   **SHI, kokoro(miru), tame(su)** give it a try, try out, attempt

——————— 1 ———————

5 試写 **shisha** preview, private showing
  試用 **shiyō** trial, tryout

6 試合 **shiai** game, match
  試行錯誤 **shikō-sakugo** trial and error
7 試作 **shisaku** trial manufacture
  試売 **shibai** trial sale, test marketing
8 試刷 **shisatsu** proof printing
  試金石 **shikinseki** touchstone; test
9 試乗 **shijō** trial ride, test drive
  試食 **shishoku** sample, taste
10 試射 **shisha** test firing
  試剤 **shizai** reagent
  試案 **shian** draft, tentative plan
11 試運転 **shiunten** trial run
  試掘 **shikutsu** prospecting
  試掘者 **shikutsusha** prospector
  試掘権 **shikutsuken** mining claim
  試斬 **tame(shi)gi(ri)** trying out a new sword
  試問 **shimon** question, interview, test
12 試植 **shishoku** experimental planting
  試補 **shiho** probationer, beginner
  試買 **shibai** trial purchase
  試筆 **shihitsu** first writing of the new year
  試飲 **shiin** sampling, (wine) tasting
14 試演 **shien** rehearsal, preview
  試練 **shiren** trial, test, ordeal
  試算 **shisan** test calculation; checking a calculation
15 試論 **shiron** essay
16 試薬 **shiyaku** reagent
17 試聴 **shichō** audition
18 試験 **shiken** examination, test; experiment, test
  試験地獄 **shiken jigoku** the hell of (entrance) exams
  試験官 **shikenkan** examiner
  試験的 **shikenteki** experimental, tentative
  試験紙 **shikenshi** litmus paper
  試験場 **shikenjō** examination hall; laboratory, proving grounds
  試験管 **shikenkan** test tube

——————— 2 ———————

2 入試 **nyūshi** entrance exam (short for 入学試験)
  力試 **chikaradame(shi)** test of strength/ability
6 再試合 **saishiai** rematch, resumption of a game
  再試験 **saishiken** make-up exam, retesting
7 肝試 **kimodame(shi)** test of courage
8 追試 **tsuishi** follow-up experiment/test; makeup exam
  追試験 **tsuishiken** supplementary/makeup exam
  泥試合 **dorojiai** mudslinging
11 運試 **undame(shi)** try one's luck, take a chance
12 腕試 **udedame(shi)** test of strength/skill

7

言 6 ←
貝
車
足
酉

無試験 **mushiken** without an examination

────────── 3 ──────────

2 入学試験 **nyūgaku shiken** entrance exams
3 口答試問 **kōtō shimon** oral examination/quiz
口頭試問 **kōtō shimon** oral examination
4 五分試 **gobudame(shi)** killing by inches
7 対校試合 **taikō-jiai** interschool match
9 面接試問 **mensetsu shimon** oral examination
12 検定試験 **kentei shiken** (teacher) certification examination
14 模擬試験 **mogi shiken** trial examination

────────── 7 ──────────

7a7.1

諷 **FU, BU, shi(iru)** acuse falsely, slander

────────── 1 ──────────

7 諷告 **bukoku, fukoku** false charge, libel
諷言 **fugen, bugen** false accusation

7a7.2 / 906

誤 誤 **GO, ayama(ru)** err, make a mistake

────────── 1 ──────────

5 誤写 **gosha** error in copying
誤用 **goyō** misuse
誤字 **goji** incorrect character, misprint
6 誤伝 **goden** false report
7 誤判 **gohan** mistrial, miscarriage of justice
9 誤信 **goshin** mistaken belief
10 誤差 **gosa** error, aberration
誤称 **goshō** misnomer
誤記 **goki** clerical error
誤配 **gohai** misdelivery (of mail)
11 誤脱 **godatsu** errors and omissions
誤訳 **goyaku** mistranslation
12 誤報 **gohō** erroneous report/information
誤植 **goshoku** misprint
誤答 **gotō** incorrect answer
誤診 **goshin** misdiagnosis
13 誤解 **gokai** misunderstanding
誤電 **goden** incorrect telegram/telex
14 誤算 **gosan** miscalculation
誤読 **godoku** misreading
誤認 **gonin** mistake, misconception
誤聞 **gobun** mishearing; misinformation
15 誤審 **goshin** error in refereeing
18 誤謬 **gobyū** error
21 誤魔化 **gomaka(su)** cheat, deceive; gloss over; tamper with, doctor

────────── 2 ──────────

5 正誤 **seigo** correction

正誤表 **seigohyō** errata
7 見誤 **miaya(maru)** missee, mistake
言誤 **i(i)ayama(ru)** misstate, make a slip
10 書誤 **ka(ki)ayama(ru)** miswrite
11 過誤 **kago** error
14 読誤 **yo(mi)ayama(ru)** misread
16 錯誤 **sakugo** error

────────── 4 ──────────

13 試行錯誤 **shikō-sakugo** trial and error

7a7.3

誑 **KYŌ, tabura(kasu), taba(karu), tara(su)** deceive, cajole, seduce

────────── 1 ──────────

4 誑込 **tara(shi)ko(mu)** coax into

7a7.4 / 1684

誘 **YŪ, saso(u)** invite; induce; entice, lure
izana(u) invite; lead; entice
obi(ku) lure, entice

────────── 1 ──────────

2 誘入 **saso(i)i(reru), obi(ki)i(reru)** entice, lure into
4 誘水 **saso(i)mizu** pump priming
誘引 **yūin** entice, induce, attract, allure
5 誘出 **saso(i)da(su), obi(ki)da(su)** decoy, lure away
6 誘因 **yūin** enticement, inducement
8 誘拐 **yūkai** kidnapping, abduction
9 誘発 **yūhatsu** induce, give rise to
10 誘起 **yūki** give rise to, lead to, cause
誘致 **yūchi** attract, lure; bring about
11 誘球 **saso(i)dama** a pitch to get the batter to swing at the ball
12 誘惑 **yūwaku** temptation, seduction
誘惑者 **yūwakusha** tempter, seducer
14 誘導 **yūdō** induction; incitement; guidance
誘導体 **yūdōtai** (chemical) derivative
誘導弾 **yūdōdan** guided missile

────────── 2 ──────────

13 勧誘 **kan'yū** solicitation, invitation, canvassing

7a7.5

誥 **KŌ** state, give instructions

7a7.6 / 67

語 **GO** word
kata(ru) talk, relate
kata(rau) converse, chat

1

3 語口 **kata(ri)kuchi** way of talking/narrating
4 語手 **kata(ri)te** narrator, storyteller
5 語末 **gomatsu** word ending
語句 **goku** words and phrases
6 語気 **goki** tone of voice
語合 **kata(ri)a(u)** talk together, chat
7 語呂 **goro** the sound, euphony
語呂合 **goroa(wase)** play on words, pun
語形 **gokei** word form
語学 **gogaku** language learning; linguistics
語学者 **gogakusha** linguist
語尾 **gobi** word ending
語尾変化 **gobi henka** inflection
8 語法 **gohō** phraseology, usage, diction
語明 **kata(ri)a(kasu)** talk all night
語物 **kata(ri)mono** (theme of a) narrative
9 語草 **kata(ri)gusa** topic (of conversation)
10 語部 **kata(ri)be** family of professional reciters
語原 **gogen** derivation, etymology
語原学 **gogengaku** etymology
語根 **gokon** stem, root of a word
語格 **gokaku** grammar
語脈 **gomyaku** interrelationship of words, context
11 語族 **gozoku** a family of languages
語釈 **goshaku** explanation of words
13 語勢 **gosei** stress, emphasis
語彙 **goi** vocabulary
語義 **gogi** meaning of a word
語源 **gogen** derivation, etymology
語幹 **gokan** stem, root of a word
語数 **gosū** number of words
語感 **gokan** connotations of a word; linguistic sense
語意 **goi** meaning of a word
語継 **kata(ri)tsu(gu)** hand down (a story)
語路 **goro** the sound, euphony
語路合 **goroa(wase)** play on words, pun
14 語誌 **goshi** etymology of a word
15 語弊 **gohei** faulty/misleading expression
語調 **gochō** accent, tone, voice
16 語録 **goroku** analects, sayings
語頭 **gotō** beginning of a word

2

1 一語 **ichigo** one word
一語一語 **ichigo-ichigo** word for word
3 土語 **dogo** native tongue, dialect
口語 **kōgo** colloquial language
口語文 **kōgobun** colloquial language
口語体 **kōgotai** colloquial style, colloquialism
口語訳 **kōgoyaku** colloquial translation
口語詩 **kōgoshi** poem in colloquial style
4 冗語 **jōgo** a redundancy, wordiness
文語 **bungo** literary language
文語文 **bungobun** literary language
文語体 **bungotai** literary style
反語 **hango** rhetorical question; irony
5 失語 **shitsugo** inability to speak correctly, forgetting words
古語 **kogo** archaic/obsolete word; old saying
外語 **gaigo** foreign language
用語 **yōgo** term, terminology, vocabulary
主語 **shugo** subject (in grammar)
目語 **mokugo** signal with one's eye
6 死語 **shigo** dead language; obsolete word
伊語 **Igo** Italian language
壮語 **sōgo** boasting, grandiloquence
邦語 **hōgo** vernacular; Japanese language
妄語 **mōgo, bōgo** lie, falsehood
成語 **seigo** set phrase, idiomatic expression
米語 **beigo** American English
耳語 **jigo** whispering
7 述語 **jutsugo** predicate
私語 **shigo** secret talk, whispering
季語 **kigo** word indicating the season (in haiku)
言語 **gengo** language, speech
i(wazu)kata(razu) tacitly
言語学 **gengogaku** linguistics, philology
8 逆語 **saka(sa)kotoba** word of opposite meaning; word pronounced backwards
法語 **hōgo** (Buddhist) sermon
英語 **eigo** the English language
英語版 **eigoban** English-language edition
昔語 **mukashigata(ri)** old story
国語 **kokugo** national/Japanese language
物語 **monogatari** tale, story
和語 **wago** (native) Japanese word
9 飛語 **higo** false report, wild rumor
発語 **hatsugo** speech, utterance; introductory word like "*Sate, …*"
俚語 **rigo** slang, dialect
俗語 **zokugo** colloquial language, slang
勅語 **chokugo** imperial rescript
連語 **rengo** compound word, phrase
逐語的 **chikugoteki** word for word, literal
逐語訳 **chikugoyaku** word-for-word/literal translation
造語 **zōgo** coined word
通語 **tsūgo** jargon, cant
活語 **katsugo** living words; inflected word
独語 **dokugo** talking to oneself, soliloquy, monolog **Dokugo** German language
律語 **ritsugo** verse
客語 **kyakugo, kakugo** object (in grammar)
単語 **tango** word
卑語 **higo** vulgar word/expression
10 原語 **gengo** original word/language
唐語 **kara kotoba** Chinese/foreign language
素語 **sugata(ri)** recital without samisen accompaniment

11 剰語 **jōgo** redundancy
術語 **jutsugo** technical term, terminology
密語 **mitsugo** whispers, confidential talk
梵語 **bongo** Sanskrit
略語 **ryakugo** abbreviation
訳語 **yakugo** translated term, an equivalent
問語 **to(wazu)gata(ri)** voluntary/unasked-for remark
12 蛮語 **bango** barbarian language
弾語 **hi(ki)gata(ri)** reciting while playing (the samisen)
落語 **rakugo** comic storytelling
落語家 **rakugoka** comic storyteller
廃語 **haigo** obsolete word
敬語 **keigo** an honorific, term of respect
補語 **hogo** a complement (in grammar)
畳語 **jōgo** repetition to indicate plurals, etc. (e.g., *hitobito*)
結語 **ketsugo** concluding remarks
評語 **hyōgo** critical remark; mark, grade
13 隠語 **ingo** secret language; argot, jargon
鄙語 **higo** vulgar word/expression
漢語 **kango** Chinese word
夢語 **yumegata(ri)** account of a dream; fantastic story
煩語 **hango** prolix/tedious language
解語 **kaigo** understanding a word
数語 **sūgo** a few words
新語 **shingo** new word, neologism
雅語 **gago** elegant/poetical expression
14 豪語 **gōgo** boasting, bombast, big talk
熟語 **jukugo** word of two or more kanji, compound; phrase
蜚語 **higo** wild rumor
15 標語 **hyōgo** slogan, motto
縁語 **engo** related word
論語 **Rongo** the Analects of Confucius
16 激語 **gekigo** harsh language
18 難語 **nango** word whose meaning is unclear
難語集 **nangoshū** glossary (to an ancient classic)
19 韻語 **ingo** rhyming words
21 囈語 **geigo, tawagoto** nonsense
uwagoto talking deliriously
露語 **rogo** the Russian language

—————————— 3 ——————————

4 文章語 **bunshōgo** literary language
反対語 **hantaigo** antonym
反意語 **han'igo** antonym
日本語 **nihongo** the Japanese language
5 母国語 **bokokugo** one's mother/native tongue
古典語 **kotengo** a classical language
外来語 **gairaigo** word of foreign origin, loanword
外国語 **gaikokugo** foreign language
目的語 **mokutekigo** object (in grammar)

6 合成語 **gōseigo** a compound (word)
同音語 **dōongo** homophone, homonym
同義語 **dōgigo** synonym
同意語 **dōigo** synonym
共通語 **kyōtsūgo** common language
自国語 **jikokugo** one's own language
7 見出語 **mida(shi)go** headword, entry word
8 長物語 **nagamonogatari** a tedious talk
法律語 **hōritsugo** legal term
拉丁語 **Ratengo** Latin
国際語 **kokusaigo** international language
9 活用語 **katsuyōgo** inflected word
派生語 **haseigo** a derivative
10 修飾語 **shūshokugo** modifier
流行語 **ryūkōgo** popular phrase, catchword
11 商用語 **shōyōgo** commercial term
混合語 **kongōgo** word derived/combined from two other words
接尾語 **setsubigo** suffix
接頭語 **settōgo** prefix
常套語 **jōtōgo** hackneyed expression, trite saying
現代語 **gendaigo** modern language
12 補足語 **hosokugo** a complement (in grammar)
13 夢物語 **yume monogatari** account of a dream; fantastic story
寝物語 **nemonogatari** talk while lying in bed
新造語 **shinzōgo** newly coined word
14 慣用語 **kan'yōgo** idiom, colloquial word/phrase
複合語 **fukugōgo** compound word
15 標準語 **hyōjungo** the standard language
膠着語 **kōchakugo** an agglutinative language
敵国語 **tekikokugo** the enemy's language
17 擬声語 **giseigo** onomatopoetic word
18 類音語 **ruiongo** words which sound similar
類義語 **ruigigo** words of similar meaning

—————————— 4 ——————————

1 一語一語 **ichigo-ichigo** word for word
3 大言壮語 **taigen sōgo** boasting, exaggeration
4 不言不語 **fugen-fugo** silence
片言隻語 **hengen-sekigo** few words
7 学術用語 **gakujutsu yōgo** technical term
8 官庁用語 **kanchō yōgo** official jargon
9 専門用語 **senmon yōgo** technical term
軍記物語 **gunki monogatari** war chronicle
造言飛語 **zōgen-higo** false report, wild rumor
10 流言飛語 **ryūgen-higo** rumor, gossip
13 源氏物語 **Genji Monogatari** The Tale of Genji

7a7.7

誚 **SHŌ** censure, blame

7a7.8 / 574

誌 **SHI** write down, chronicle; magazine

——————— 1 ———————
3 誌上 **shijō** in a magazine
4 誌友 **shiyū** fellow subscriber/reader
5 誌代 **shidai** price of a magazine
9 誌面 **shimen** page of a magazine

——————— 2 ———————
5 本誌 **honshi** this magazine
6 地誌 **chishi** topographical description
　米誌 **beishi** American magazine
9 某誌 **bōshi** a certain magazine
10 書誌 **shoshi** bibliography
　書誌学 **shoshigaku** bibliography
13 墓誌 **boshi** epitaph
　墓誌銘 **boshimei** epitaph
14 語誌 **goshi** etymology of a word
　雑誌 **zasshi** magazine

——————— 3 ———————
7 季刊誌 **kikanshi** a quarterly (magazine)
10 週刊誌 **shūkanshi** a weekly (magazine)
11 動物誌 **dōbutsushi** fauna, zoography
12 植物誌 **shokubutsushi** a flora/herbal
16 機関誌 **kikanshi** organization's publication

——————— 4 ———————
3 三号雑誌 **sangō zasshi** short-lived magazine
6 同人雑誌 **dōjin zasshi** literary coterie magazine, small magazine
10 航海日誌 **kōkai nisshi** ship's log
16 機関雑誌 **kikan zasshi** organization's publication

7a7.9 / 244

読 讀 **DOKU, TOKU, TŌ, yo(mu)** read

——————— 1 ———————
0 読みで **yo(mide)** worthwhile reading
　読みこなす **yo(mikonasu)** read and appreciate
1 読了 **dokuryō** finish reading
2 読人 **yo(mi)bito** author of a poem
　読人知 **yo(mi)bito shi(razu)** anonymous (poem)
3 読上 **yo(mi)a(geru)** read aloud/out; finish reading
　読下 **yo(mi)kuda(su)** read it through
4 読切 **yo(mi)ki(ru)** read it through
　読手 **yo(mi)te** reader
　読方 **yo(mi)kata** reading, pronunciation (of a character)
　読心術 **dokushinjutsu** mind reading

5 読本 **tokuhon** reader, book of readings
6 読合 **yo(mi)a(waseru)** read and compare
　読会 **dokkai** reading (of a bill)
　読返 **yo(mi)kae(su)** reread
　読尽 **yo(mi)tsu(kusu)** read it all
8 読直 **yo(mi)nao(su)** reread
　読易 **yo(mi)yasu(i)** easy to read
　読者 **dokusha** reader
　読者層 **dokushasō** class of readers
　読物 **yo(mi)mono** reading matter
　読取 **yo(mi)to(ru)** read (someone's mind)
9 読点 **tōten** comma
　読通 **yo(mi)tō(su)** read it through
　読後 **dokugo** after reading
　読後感 **dokugokan** one's impressions (of a book)
10 読流 **yo(mi)naga(su)** read fluently; skim, glance through
　読振 **yo(mi)bu(ri)** way of reading
　読唇術 **dokushinjutsu** lip reading
　読書 **dokusho** reading
　　yo(mi)ka(ki) reading and writing
　読書人 **dokushojin** (avid) book reader
　読書力 **dokushoryoku** reading ability
　読書会 **dokushokai** reading club
　読書狂 **dokushokyō** bibliophile
　読書室 **dokushoshitsu** reading room
　読書界 **dokushokai** the reading public
　読書家 **dokushoka** (avid) book reader
　読破 **dokuha, yo(mi)yabu(ru)** read it through
11 読過 **dokka** skim through; overlook
　読終 **yo(mi)owa(ru)** finish reading
　読経 **dokyō** sutra chanting
12 読違 **yo(mi)chiga(i)** misreading
　読落 **yo(mi)o(tosu)** overlook in reading
　読替 **yo(mi)ka(eru)** read (a kanji) with a different pronunciation; read (one term) for (another)
13 読解 **yo(mi)to(ku)** decipher
14 読慣 **yo(mi)na(reru)** be used to reading
　読誤 **yo(mi)ayama(ru)** misread
　読誦 **dokushō** read aloud, recite
　読聞 **yo(mi)ki(kasu)** read to (someone)
18 読癖 **yo(mi)kuse** idiomatic pronunciation (of a compound); peculiar way of reading
　読難 **yo(mi)niku(i)** hard to read

——————— 2 ———————
1 一読 **ichidoku** a perusal/reading
5 必読 **hitsudoku** required reading, a must read
　本読 **hon'yo(mi)** good reader; reading the script
　代読 **daidoku** read on behalf of another
　句読 **kutō** punctuation
　句読点 **kutōten** punctuation mark
　立読 **ta(chi)yo(mi)** read while standing (at a magazine rack)

7

言 7←
貝
車
足
酉

6 多読 **tadoku** extensive reading
多読家 **tadokuka** voracious reader, well-read person
再読 **saidoku** reread
会読 **kaidoku** reading-and-discussion meeting
辿読 **tado(ri)yo(mi)** read with difficulty
回読 **kaidoku** read (a book) in turn
7 判読 **handoku** decipher, read, make out
走読 **hashi(ri)yo(mi)** read hurriedly, skim through
抜読 **nu(ki)yo(mi)** read from, read part of
乱読 **randoku** indiscriminate reading
8 拝読 **haidoku** read, note
9 飛読 **to(bi)yo(mi)** read desultorily, skim through
速読 **sokudoku** speed reading
拾読 **hiro(i)yo(mi)** browse through (a book)
音読 **ondoku** reading aloud
　　 on'yo(mi) the Chinese reading of a kanji
秒読 **byōyo(mi)** countdown
10 朗読 **rōdoku** read aloud
素読 **sodoku** reading without comprehending
耽読 **tandoku** read avidly
訓読 **kundoku, kun'yo(mi)** native-Japanese reading of a kanji
11 捧読 **hōdoku** read reverently
盗読 **nusu(mi)yo(mi)** surreptitious reading
訳読 **yakudoku** read and translate
12 復読 **fukudoku** reread, review
棒読 **bōyo(mi)** reading aloud in a monotone; reading Chinese in Chinese word order
13 解読 **kaidoku** decipher, decrypt
愛読 **aidoku** like to read
愛読者 **aidokusha** reader, subscriber
愛読書 **aidokusho** favorite book
14 漫読 **mandoku** browse, read randomly
熟読 **jukudoku** read thoroughly/carefully
精読 **seidoku** reading, carefully
誤読 **godoku** misreading
15 黙読 **mokudoku** read silently
閲読 **etsudoku** perusal, reading
16 積読 **tsu(n)doku** acquiring books without reading them
積読主義 **tsu(n)doku shugi** acquiring books without reading them
17 講読 **kōdoku** read (Shakespeare)
購読 **kōdoku** subscription
購読者 **kōdokusha** subscriber
購読料 **kōdokuryō** subscription price/fee
18 濫読 **randoku** indiscriminate/random reading
繙読 **handoku** (open and) read, peruse
難読 **nandoku** a difficult reading

——————— 4 ———————

12 晴耕雨読 **seikō-udoku** tilling the fields when the sun shines and reading at home when it rains

---

7a7.10 / 738

認

NIN, mito(meru) perceive; recognize; approve
shitata(meru) write, draw up; eat

——————— 1 ———————

5 認可 **ninka** approval
認可証 **ninkashō** permit, license
6 認印 **mito(me)in** personal seal, signet
7 認否 **ninpi** approval or disapproval
8 認知 **ninchi** cognition; acknowledge (as one's offspring)
認定 **nintei** approval, acknowledgment
10 認容 **nin'yō** admit, accept
11 認許 **ninkyo** consent, recognition
12 認証 **ninshō** certify, attest, authenticate
15 認諾 **nindaku** assent to, approve, admit
19 認識 **ninshiki** (re)cognition, perception, knowledge
認識票 **ninshikihyō** identification tag
認識論 **ninshikiron** epistemology

——————— 2 ———————

4 不認可 **funinka** disapproval, rejection
公認 **kōnin** officially authorized, certified
6 自認 **jinin** acknowledge, admit
7 承認 **shōnin** approval
否認 **hinin** deny, repudiate
8 追認 **tsuinin** ratification, confirmation
9 信認 **shinnin** trust and accept, acknowledge
是認 **zenin** approval, sanction
10 容認 **yōnin** admit, approve, accept
14 誤認 **gonin** mistake, misconception
15 黙認 **mokunin** tacit approval/admission
確認 **kakunin** confirm, verify

——————— 3 ———————

6 再確認 **saikakunin** reaffirmation

7a7.11

諄

JUN carefully, earnestly, repeatedly

——————— 1 ———————

3 諄々 **junjun** painstakingly, earnestly

7a7.12 / 400

説

SETSU opinion, theory
ZEI, to(ku) explain; persuade

——————— 1 ———————

3 説及 **to(ki)oyo(bu)** refer to, mention
4 説文 **setsumon** etymology of Chinese characters **Setsumon** (short for 説文解字)
説文解字 **Setsumon Kaiji** (oldest Chinese character dictionary)

説分 **to(ki)wa(keru)** explain carefully
5 説付 **to(ki)tsu(keru)** persuade, talk into
6 説伏 **to(ki)fu(seru)** confute, argue down, convince **seppuku** persuade, convince
7 説述 **setsujutsu** explanation, exposition
8 説法 **seppō** (Buddhist) sermon
説明 **setsumei, to(ki)a(kashi)** explanation
説明文 **setsumeibun** (written) explanation
説明的 **setsumeiteki** explanatory
説明者 **setsumeisha** explainer, exponent
説明書 **setsumeisho** (written) explanation, instructions, manual
10 説起 **to(ki)o(kosu)** begin one's argument/story
説教 **sekkyō** sermon
説教師 **sekkyōshi** preacher
説教壇 **sekkyōdan** pulpit
11 説得 **settoku** persuasion
説得力 **settokuryoku** persuasiveness
説経 **sekkyō** discourse on the sutras
説経節 **sekkyōbushi** sutra-based samisen-accompanied ballads
説問 **setsumon** kanji etymology
12 説落 **to(ki)o(tosu)** win over, talk into
13 説勧 **to(ki)susu(meru)** persuade, urge
説話 **setsuwa** tale, narrative
説話的 **setsuwateki** narrative (style)
14 説聞 **to(ki)ki(kasu)** explain, reason with
16 説諭 **setsuyu** admonish
説 **to(ki)sato(su)** persuade; rebuke

———————— 2 ————————

1 一説 **issetsu** one/another view
2 力説 **rikisetsu** emphasis, stress
3 口説 **kudo(ku)** persuade, entreat, woo, court **kuzetsu** quarrel; curtain lecture
口説落 **kudo(ki)o(tosu)** persuade, talk (someone) into, win over
小説 **shōsetsu** novel, story, fiction
小説家 **shōsetsuka** novelist, (fiction) writer
4 仏説 **bussetsu** Buddha's teachings
辻説法 **tsujiseppō** street preaching
6 伝説 **densetsu** legend
仮説 **kasetsu** hypothesis, tentative theory
妄説 **bōsetsu, mōsetsu** fallacy, false report
同説 **dōsetsu** the same opinion
自説 **jisetsu** one's own view
7 邪説 **jasetsu** heretical doctrine
学説 **gakusetsu** a theory
序説 **josetsu** introduction, preface
図説 **zusetsu** explanatory diagram, illustration
社説 **shasetsu** an editorial
私説 **shisetsu** one's own view
言説 **gensetsu** remark, statement
8 直説法 **chokusetsuhō** indicative mood
卓説 **takusetsu** excellent opinion, enlightened views

逆説 **gyakusetsu** paradox
逆説的 **gyakusetsuteki** paradoxical
実説 **jissetsu** true account
定説 **teisetsu** established/accepted opinion
空説 **kūsetsu** baseless rumor
怪説 **kaisetsu** strange rumor/theory
所説 **shosetsu** one's statement, opinion
9 俗説 **zokusetsu** common saying; folklore
前説 **zensetsu** one's former opinion
通説 **tsūsetsu** common opinion, popular view
風説 **fūsetsu** rumor
浮説 **fusetsu** wild rumor, canard
持説 **jisetsu** pet theory, one's cherished view
巷説 **kōsetsu** rumor, town talk, gossip
珍説 **chinsetsu** strange view, novel theory
約説 **yakusetsu** summary
10 高説 **kōsetsu** (your) valuable opinion/suggestions
遊説 **yūzei** speaking tour, political campaigning
遊説員 **yūzeiin** stumping candidate, election canvassers
流説 **ryūsetsu** rumor, baseless report
11 虚説 **kyosetsu** baseless rumor, false report
略説 **ryakusetsu** brief explanation
異説 **isetsu** different opinion
細説 **saisetsu** detailed explanation
12 絮説 **josetsu** expatiate/enlarge upon
13 解説 **kaisetsu** explanation, commentary
解説者 **kaisetsusha** commentator
愚説 **gusetsu** foolish/my opinion
新説 **shinsetsu** new theory
詳説 **shōsetsu** detailed explanation
14 演説 **enzetsu** speech, address
演説法 **enzetsuhō** elocution, oratory
演説者 **enzetsusha** speaker, orator
演説家 **enzetsuka** speaker, orator
概説 **gaisetsu** general statement, outline
総説 **sōsetsu** general remarks
雑説 **zassetsu** various theories
15 確説 **kakusetsu** established theory
諸説 **shosetsu** various views/accounts
論説 **ronsetsu** dissertation; editorial
16 憶説 **okusetsu** hypothesis, conjecture, surmise
17 臆説 **okusetsu** hypothesis, conjecture
講説 **kōsetsu** explain (by lecture)
18 謬説 **byūsetsu** fallacy, mistaken view, false report

———————— 3 ————————

4 天動説 **tendōsetsu** the Ptolemaic theory
分子説 **bunshisetsu** molecular theory
5 民約説 **min'yakusetsu** the social-contract theory
6 地動説 **chidōsetsu** heliocentric/Copernican theory

7

言 7 ←
貝
車
止
酉

7 私小説 **watakushi shōsetsu** novel narrated in the first person; autobiographical novel
     shishōsetsu autobiographical novel
8 性悪説 **seiakusetsu** the view that human nature is basically evil
     性善説 **seizensetsu** the view that human nature is basically good
9 星雲説 **seiunsetsu** the nebular hypothesis
     神秘説 **shinpisetsu** mysticism
12 悲観説 **hikansetsu** pessimism
13 搔口説 **ka(ki)kudo(ku)** complain of, plead
16 懐疑説 **kaigisetsu** skepticism

—————————— 4 ——————————

3 三文小説 **sanmon shōsetsu** cheap novel
5 立会演説 **ta(chi)a(i) enzetsu** campaign speech in a joint meeting of candidates, debate
8 怪奇小説 **kaiki shōsetsu** mystery/spooky story
11 推理小説 **suiri shōsetsu** detective story, whodunit
     探偵小説 **tantei shōsetsu** detective story
12 短篇小説 **tanpen shōsetsu** short story/novel
     街頭演説 **gaitō enzetsu** street/soapbox speech
19 艶笑小説 **enshō shōsetsu** love-comedy story/novel

7a7.13

誨   **KAI** instruct, enlighten

—————————— 2 ——————————

10 教誨 **kyōkai** exhortation, preaching
     訓誨 **kunkai** instruct, enlighten

7a7.14

誦   **SHŌ, JU** recite, chant

—————————— 1 ——————————

0 誦する **shō(suru)** recite, chant

—————————— 2 ——————————

3 口誦 **kōshō** humming; reading aloud
7 吟誦 **ginshō** recite, chant
8 念誦 **nenju** Buddhist invocation
12 復誦 **fukushō** repeat back (to confirm than an order has been understood)
13 暗誦 **anshō** recite (from memory)
     愛誦 **aishō** love to read
14 歌誦 **kashō** sing (loudly)
     読誦 **dokushō** read aloud, recite

7a7.15 / 1116

誕   **TAN** birth

—————————— 1 ——————————

5 誕生 **tanjō** birth
     誕生日 **tanjōbi** birthday
     誕生石 **tanjōseki** birthstone
     誕生祝 **tanjō iwa(i)** birthday celebration

—————————— 2 ——————————

5 生誕 **seitan** birth
9 降誕 **kōtan** birth, nativity
     荒誕 **kōtan** nonsense
11 虚誕 **kyotan** false, trumped-up
13 聖誕祭 **Seitansai** Christmas

7a7.16

誡   **KAI, imashi(meru)** admonish, rebuke

—————————— 1 ——————————

7 誡告 **kaikoku** warning, caution

—————————— 2 ——————————

2 十誡 **jikkai** the Ten Commandments
10 訓誡 **kunkai** admonition, warning

7a7.17 / 1395

誓   **SEI, chika(u)** swear, pledge, vow

—————————— 1 ——————————

4 誓文 **seimon** written oath
     誓文払 **seimonbara(i)** bargain sale
7 誓言 **seigon** oath, vow, pledge
9 誓約 **seiyaku** oath, vow, pledge
     誓約者 **seiyakusha** party to a covenant
     誓約書 **seiyakusho** written pledge, covenant
10 誓紙 **seishi** written pledge
12 誓詞 **seishi** oath, pledge
19 誓願 **seigan** oath, vow, pledge

—————————— 2 ——————————

8 祈誓 **kisei** vow, oath
9 宣誓 **sensei** oath, vow, pledge
     宣誓式 **senseishiki** administering an oath
     宣誓書 **senseisho** written oath, deposition

—————————— 8 ——————————

7a8.1

誰   **SUI, dare, tare** who

—————————— 1 ——————————

1 誰一人 **dare hitori (mo)** (with negative) no one
7 誰何 **suika** challenge, Who goes there?
8 誰彼 **darekare, tarekare** this or that person; (many) people
9 誰某 **taresore** Mr. So-and-so

諫 → 諌 **7a9.1**

7a8.2 / 488

課

KA lesson; section; levy, impose

───────── 1 ─────────

0 課する **ka(suru)** levy, impose
5 課外 **kagai** extracurricular
課外活動 **kagai katsudō** extracurricular activities
課目 **kamoku** subject (in school), item
8 課長 **kachō** section chief
10 課員 **kain** (member of the) section staff
12 課程 **katei** course, curriculum
課税 **kazei** taxtion
課税品 **kazeihin** taxable/dutiable goods
課税率 **kazeiritsu** tax rate
13 課業 **kagyō** lessons, schoolwork
18 課題 **kadai** subject, theme, topic, problem; (school) assignment

───────── 2 ─────────

4 分課 **bunka** subdivision, section, department
公課 **kōka** taxes
日課 **nikka** daily lessons/work
5 正課 **seika** regular curriculum/course
正課外 **seikagai** extracurricular
6 考課 **kōka** evaluation of someone's record
考課状 **kōkajō** personnel/service record; business report
考課表 **kōkahyō** personnel/service record; business report
7 学課 **gakka** lessons, schoolwork
8 非課税 **hikazei** tax exemption
放課後 **hōkago** after school
10 鬼課長 **onikachō** hard-driving boss/section-chief
15 賦課 **fuka** levy, assessment

───────── 3 ─────────

10 秘書課 **hishoka** secretariat
13 源泉課税 **gensen kazei** taxation at the source, withholding tax
14 総務課 **sōmuka** general affairs section

7a8.3 / 861

諸 諸

SHO- all, various, many, (prefix indicating plural)
moro- various, all, both, every sort of

───────── 1 ─────────

2 諸人 **morobito** everyone
諸子 **shoshi** you all

3 諸刃 **moroha** double-edged
諸々 **moromoro** various, all, every sort of
4 諸元 **shogen** equipment performance figures, specifications
諸元表 **shogenhyō** list of equipment performance figures, specifications
諸氏 **shoshi** you all
諸王 **shoō** all/many kings
諸方 **shohō** all directions
5 諸本 **shohon** various books
諸生 **shosei** students
諸外国 **shogaikoku** foreign countries
諸兄 **shokei** dear friends, gentlemen
諸兄姉 **shokeishi** ladies and gentlemen
6 諸行 **shogyō** all worldly things
諸行無常 **shogyō-mujō** All things change. Nothing lasts.
諸共 **morotomo** all together
諸肌 **morohada** stripped to the waist
諸式 **shoshiki** prices
7 諸君 **shokun** (ladies and) gentlemen, you all
諸芸 **shogei** arts, accomplishments
諸車通行止 **Shosha Tsūkōdo(me)** No Thoroughfare
8 諸事 **shoji** various matters/affairs
諸事万端 **shoji-bantan** everything
諸姉 **shoshi** dear friends, ladies
諸国 **shokoku** all/various countries
諸国行脚 **shokoku angya** walking tour of the country
9 諸侯 **shokō** lords, daimyos
諸派 **shoha** minor (political) parties
諸相 **shosō** various phases/aspects
10 諸家 **shoka** houses; schools of thought
諸島 **shotō** islands
諸般 **shohan** various, every
11 諸道 **shodō** accomplishments
諸掛 **shoka(kari)** expenses
諸訳 **showake** intricacies, details
諸問題 **shomondai** various questions
14 諸種 **shoshu** various/all kinds
諸説 **shosetsu** various views/accounts
諸雑費 **shozappi** miscellaneous expenses
15 諸膚 **morohada** stripped to the waist
諸膝 **morohiza** both knees
諸諸 **moromoro** various, all, every sort of
16 諸賢 **shoken** (ladies and) gentlemen

───────── 2 ─────────

15 諸諸 **moromoro** various, all, every sort of

───────── 3 ─────────

8 東亜諸国 **Tōa shokoku** the countries of East Asia
9 南洋諸島 **Nan'yō-shotō** the South Sea Islands
13 隠岐諸島 **Oki shotō** (group of islands, Shimane-ken)

7

言 8 ←
貝
車
足
酉

───────── 4 ─────────

3 小笠原諸島 **Ogasawara-shotō** the Bonin Islands

7a8.4

諏

SHU, SU consult with

7a8.5

誹

HI speak ill of, slander

───────── 1 ─────────

16 誹諧 **haikai** humorous poem; 17-syllable poem
17 誹謗 **hibō** slander, defame, malign

7a8.6 / 1920

謁 謁

ETSU audience (with someone)

───────── 1 ─────────

0 謁する **es(suru)** have an audience with
7 謁見 **ekken** have an audience with
謁見室 **ekkenshitsu** audience chamber

───────── 2 ─────────

4 内謁 **naietsu** private audience
8 拝謁 **haietsu** an audience (with the emperor)

7a8.7 / 593

談

DAN conversation

───────── 1 ─────────

0 談じる/ずる **dan(jiru/zuru)** discuss, talk
6 談合 **dan(ji)a(u)** confer/negotiate with
dangō consultation, conference
7 談判 **danpan** negotiation, talks
10 談笑 **danshō** chat, friendly talk
13 談義 **dangi** sermon; lecture, scolding
談話 **danwa** conversation
談話体 **danwatai** colloquial style
談話室 **danwashitsu** parlor, lounge
15 談論 **danron** discussion, argument, discourse
談論風発 **danron-fūhatsu** animated conversation

───────── 2 ─────────

4 内談 **naidan** private conversation
冗談 **jōdan** a joke
冗談口 **jōdanguchi** a joke
5 用談 **yōdan** a business talk
示談 **jidan** out-of-court settlement

6 会談 **kaidan** conversation, conference
7 余談 **yodan** digression
対談 **taidan** face-to-face talk, conversation, interview
芸談 **geidan** talk about one's art
快談 **kaidan** pleasant chat
8 長談議 **nagadangi** a long-winded speech
法談 **hōdan** (Buddhist) sermon
奇談 **kidan** strange story, adventure
空談 **kūdan** idle talk, gossip
放談 **hōdan** random/unreserved talk
怪談 **kaidan** ghost story
和談 **wadan** a talk to settle differences
金談 **kindan** request for a loan
9 俗談 **zokudan** chit-chat, gossip
軍談 **gundan** war story
美談 **bidan** praisworthy anecdote/story
要談 **yōdan** important talks/discussion
巷談 **kōdan** town talk, gossip
面談 **mendan** meet and talk with
相談 **sōdan** consult, confer; proposal; arrangements
相談役 **sōdan'yaku** adviser, consultant
相談所 **sōdanjo** consultation office
珍談 **chindan** news, anecdote, piece of gossip
政談 **seidan** political talk; discussion of law cases
10 高談 **kōdan** (your) lofty discourse
座談 **zadan** conversation
座談会 **zadankai** round-table discussion, symposium
破談 **hadan** cancellation, breaking off, rejection
11 商談 **shōdan** business talks/negotiations
強談 **gōdan** importunate demands, vigorous negotiations
密談 **mitsudan** secret/confidential talk
12 猥談 **waidan** indecent talk, dirty story
筆談 **hitsudan** conversation by writing
閑談 **kandan** quiet conversation, chat
13 鼎談 **teidan** three-person conversation, tripartite talks
雅談 **gadan** refined conversation
14 漫談 **mandan** chat, idle talk
漫談家 **mandanka** humorist
熟談 **jukudan** careful discussion/consultation
綺談 **kidan** fascinating tale
雑談 **zatsudan** chitchat, idle conversation
15 劇談 **gekidan** talk on drama; intense negotiating
歓談 **kandan** pleasant chat
縁談 **endan** marriage proposal
17 厳談 **gendan** demand an explanation, protest strongly
懇談 **kondan** cordial conversation, chat

懇談会 **kondankai** get-together, friendly discussion
講談 **kōdan** storytelling, a narrative
講談師 **kōdanshi** (professional) storyteller

───────── 3 ─────────

3 下相談 **shitasōdan** preliminary talks/arrangements
7 体験談 **taikendan** story of one's personal experiences
車中談 **shachūdan** train interview
9 後日談 **gojitsudan** reminiscences
冒険談 **bōkendan** account of one's adventures
11 経験談 **keikendan** account of one's experiences
15 膝詰談判 **hizazu(me) danpan** direct/knee-to-knee negotiations
16 懐古談 **kaikodan** reminiscences

───────── 4 ─────────

3 三者会談 **sansha kaidan** three-party conference
5 主脳会談 **shunō kaidan** summit conference
9 首脳会談 **shunō kaidan** summit conference

7a8.8 / 661

請 請　SEI, SHIN, SHŌ request; invite
ko(u) ask for
u(keru) receive, undertake

───────── 1 ─────────

0 請じる **shō(jiru)** invite, usher in
2 請入 **shō(ji)i(reru)** invite/usher in
請人 **u(ke)nin** guarantor
5 請出 **u(ke)da(su)** redeem, pay off
6 請合 **u(ke)a(u)** undertake; guarantee, vouch for　**u(ke)a(i)** sure, certain, guaranteed
7 請求 **seikyū** demand, request
請求書 **seikyūsho** application, claim, bill
請求額 **seikyūgaku** the amount claimed/billed
請判 **u(ke)han** surety seal
請売 **u(ke)u(ri)** retailing
請戻 **u(ke)modo(shi)** redemption
8 請受 **ko(i)u(keru)** ask and receive
請取 **u(ke)to(ru)** receive, accept
9 請負 **u(ke)o(u)** contract for, undertake
ukeoi contracting
請負人 **ukeoinin** contractor
請負師 **ukeoishi** contractor
請負業 **ukeoigyō** contracting business
10 請書 **u(ke)sho** written acknowledgment
請託 **seitaku** request, entreat, solicit
請訓 **seikun** request for instructions
11 請宿 **u(ke)yado** servants' agency
13 請暇 **seika** requesting a vacation
19 請願 **seigan** petition, application
請願者 **seigansha** petitioner, applicant

請願書 **seigansho** (written) petition

───────── 2 ─────────

3 下請 **shitauke** subcontract
下請負 **shitaukeoi** subcontract
下請業者 **shitauke gyōsha** subcontractor
5 申請 **shinsei** application, petition
申請書 **shinseisho** application, petition
6 安請合 **yasuu(ke)a(i)** be too ready to make a promise/commitment
7 身請 **miu(ke)** redeem, ransom
8 招請 **shōsei** invite
招請国 **shōseikoku** inviting/host nation
店請 **tanau(ke)** surety for a tenant
祈請 **kisei** vow, oath
9 奏請 **sōsei** petition the emperor for approval
要請 **yōsei** demand, call for, require
茶請 **chau(ke)** teacakes
10 起請 **kishō** vow, pledge
起請文 **kishōmon** written pledge, personal contract
11 強請 **kyōsei, gōsei** importune; extort, blackmail
12 普請 **fushin** building, construction
普請場 **fushinba** construction site
13 電請 **densei** ask for instructions by telegram
17 懇請 **konsei** entreaty, earnest request

───────── 3 ─────────

6 仮普請 **karibushin** temporary building
安普請 **yasubushin** flimsy building, jerry-built
11 道普請 **michi bushin** road repair
16 橋普請 **hashi-bushin** bridge construction

7a8.9

諍　SŌ, isaka(i) quarrel, dispute

7a8.10 / 1770

諾　DAKU consent, agree to
ubena(u) agree to

───────── 1 ─────────

3 諾々 **dakudaku** quite willingly
7 諾否 **dakuhi** acceptance or refusal, definite reply

───────── 2 ─────────

4 内諾 **naidaku** informal consent
7 承諾 **shōdaku** consent
即諾 **sokudaku** ready consent
応諾 **ōdaku** consent, accept
快諾 **kaidaku** ready consent
8 受諾 **judaku** accept, agree to
9 約諾 **yakudaku** promise, commitment

7

言
貝　8 ←
車
足
酉

11 許諾 **kyodaku** consent, approval
12 然諾重 **zendaku (o) omo(njiru)** keep one's word
14 認諾 **nindaku** assent to, approve, admit
15 黙諾 **mokudaku** tacit consent
諾諾 **dakudaku** quite willingly

―――――――― 3 ――――――――

4 不承諾 **fushōdaku** nonconsent, refusal
11 唯々諾々 **ii-dakudaku** quite willing, readily, obediently

―――――――― 4 ――――――――

8 事後承諾 **jigo shōdaku** approval after the fact

7a8.11

誼

GI friendship, fellowship; good
yoshi(mi) friendship, fellowship, good will

―――――――― 2 ――――――――

4 友誼 **yūgi** friendship, friendly relations
5 好誼 **kōgi** (your) kindness, favor, friendship
旧誼 **kyūgi** an old friendship
8 厚誼 **kōgi** (your) kindness
11 情誼 **jōgi** friendship, fellowship

7a8.12

諚

JŌ what (you) say, orders, wishes

7a8.13 / 293

論

RON discussion, argument; thesis, dissertation
agetsura(u) discuss, comment on

―――――――― 1 ――――――――

0 論じる/ずる **ron(jiru/zuru)** discuss, argue, comment on, deal with, consider
3 論及 **ronkyū** mention, refer to
4 論文 **ronbun** thesis, essay
5 論弁 **ronben** argument
論功 **ronkō** evaluation of merit
論功行賞 **ronkō kōshō** conferring of honors
論外 **rongai** irrelevant
6 論考 **ronkō** a study
論争 **ronsō** dispute, controversy
論尽 **ron(ji)tsu(kusu)** discuss exhaustively
論旨 **ronshi** point of an argument
7 論判 **ronpan** argument, discussion
論述 **ronjutsu** state, enunciate, set forth
論決 **ronketsu** discuss and decide
論告 **ronkoku** prosecutor's summation
論究 **ronkyū** discuss thoroughly
8 論法 **ronpō** argument, reasoning, logic
論拠 **ronkyo** grounds, basis
論定 **rontei** discuss and determine

論者 **ronsha** disputant; advocate; this writer, I
9 論陣 **ronjin** argument, stating one's case
論点 **ronten** point at issue
論客 **ronkyaku, ronkaku** polemicist
10 論破 **ronpa** refute, argue down
11 論理 **ronri** logic
論理上 **ronrijō** logically (speaking)
論理学 **ronrigaku** logic
論理的 **ronriteki** logical
論断 **rondan** conclusion, verdict
12 論結 **ronketsu** conclusion, peroration
論策 **ronsaku** commentary on current topics
論評 **ronpyō** comment, criticism, review
論証 **ronshō** demonstration, proof
13 論戦 **ronsen** verbal battle, controversy
論詰 **ronkitsu** refute **ron(ji)tsu(meru)** press an argument home
14 論語 **Rongo** the Analects of Confucius
論説 **ronsetsu** dissertation; editorial
論駁 **ronbaku** refute, argue against
15 論敵 **ronteki** opponent (in an argument)
論調 **ronchō** tone of argument
論賛 **ronsan** commentary on the individuals appearing in a biography
論鋒 **ronpō** force of argument, logic
16 論壇 **rondan** world of criticism; rostrum
18 論叢 **ronsō** collection of treatises
論難 **ronnan** censure, criticism, denunciation
論題 **rondai** topic, subject, theme
20 論議 **rongi** discussion, argument

―――――――― 2 ――――――――

3 口論 **kōron** argument, dispute
4 勿論 **mochiron** of course, naturally
公論 **kōron** public opinion; just view
反論 **hanron** counterargument, refutation
5 本論 **honron** main subject/discussion; this subject
弁論 **benron** argument, debate; oral proceedings, pleading
甲論乙駁 **kōron-otsubaku** pros and cons
世論 **seron, yoron** public opinion
世論調査 **seron chōsa, yoron chōsa** (public-opinion) poll
史論 **shiron** historical essay
正論 **seiron** fair/sound argument
立論 **ritsuron** put forth an argument
目論 **mokuro(mi)** plan, project, intention
6 両論 **ryōron** both arguments, both theories
曲論 **kyokuron** sophistry
争論 **sōron** dispute, argument, controversy
汎論 **hanron** outline, summary
至論 **shiron** very convincing argument
名論 **meiron** excellent opinion, sound argument
各論 **kakuron** detailed discussion

7 対論 **tairon** argue face to face
序論 **joron** introduction, preface
私論 **shiron** one's personal view
言論 **genron** speech, discussion
8 非論理的 **hironriteki** illogical, irrational
卓論 **takuron** sound argument
迷論 **meiron** fallacy
法論 **hōron** doctrinal discussion; jurisprudence
定論 **teiron** generally accepted theory/view
空論 **kūron** empty/impractical theory
国論 **kokuron** public opinion/discussion
放論 **hōron** harangue, rant
所論 **shoron** argument
9 俗論 **zokuron** popular opinion, conventional wisdom
通論 **tsūron** outline, introduction
持論 **jiron** one's view, pet opinion
政論 **seiron** political discussion
10 高論 **kōron** (your) exalted opinion
原論 **genron** theory, principles
徒論 **toron** useless argument
党論 **tōron** party's view/platform
時論 **jiron** commentary on current events; current opinion
討論 **tōron** debate, discussion
討論会 **tōronkai** forum, debate, discussion
11 推論 **suiron** reasoning, inference
理論 **riron** theory
理論的 **rironteki** theoretical
理論家 **rironka** theorist
異論 **iron** different opinion; objection
細論 **sairon** detailed discussion/explanation
軟論 **nanron** a weak argument
12 極論 **kyokuron** extreme argument; go so far as to say
無論 **muron** of course, naturally
衆論 **shūron** the views of many
痛論 **tsūron** vehement argument
結論 **ketsuron** conclusion
評論 **hyōron** criticism, critique, commentary
評論家 **hyōronka** critic, commentator
13 愚論 **guron** foolish argument/opinion
詩論 **shiron** essay on poetry; poetics
詳論 **shōron** full treatment, detailed exposition
試論 **shiron** essay
14 概論 **gairon** general remarks, outline, introduction
歌論 **karon** poetry review
緒論 **shoron, choron** introduction, preface
総論 **sōron** general remarks
駁論 **bakuron** refutation, rebuttal
15 暴論 **bōron** irrational/wild argument
熱論 **netsuron** heated argument/discussion
確論 **kakuron** incontrovertible argument,

established theory
談論 **danron** discussion, argument, discourse
談論風発 **danron-fūhatsu** animated conversation
16 激論 **gekiron** heated argument
17 輿論 **yoron** public opinion
輿論調査 **yoron chōsa** public-opinion survey, poll
20 議論 **giron** argument, discussion, controversy
議論好 **gironzu(ki)** argumentative
議論家 **gironka** avid/good debater

──────── 3 ────────

1 一元論 **ichigenron** monism
2 二元論 **nigenron** dualism
3 女権論者 **jokenronsha** feminist
4 文章論 **bunshōron** syntax, grammar
反対論 **hantairon** counterargument, opposing view
水掛論 **mizuka(ke)ron** futile argument
方法論 **hōhōron** methodology
5 本体論 **hontairon** ontology
弁証論 **benshōron** apologetics; dialectics
存在論 **sonzairon** ontology
主観論 **shukanron** subjectivism
目的論 **mokutekiron** teleology
6 多元論 **tagenron** pluralism
多神論 **tashinron** polytheism
汎神論 **hanshinron** pantheism
宇宙論 **uchūron** cosmology
有神論 **yūshinron** theism
7 決定論 **ketteiron** determinism
形式論 **keishikiron** formalism
8 非戦論 **hisenron** pacifism
抽象論 **chūshōron** abstract argument/discussion
実在論 **jitsuzairon** realism
実体論 **jittairon** substantialism, noumenalism
実念論 **jitsunenron** realism
実証論 **jisshōron** positivism
物活論 **bukkatsuron** animism
9 音韻論 **on'inron** phonemics, phonology
10 進化論 **shinkaron** theory of evolution
進化論者 **shinkaronsha** evolutionist
書生論 **shoseiron** impractical argument
純理論 **junriron** rationalism
11 運命論 **unmeiron** fatalism
唯心論 **yuishinron** idealism, spiritualism
唯名論 **yuimeiron** nominalism
唯我論 **yuigaron** solipsism
唯物論 **yuibutsuron** materialism
唯理論 **yuiriron** rationalism
宿命論 **shukumeiron** fatalism
宿命論者 **shukumeironsha** fatalist
理神論 **rishinron** deism
経験論 **keikenron** empiricism

7

言 8 ←
貝
車
足
酉

12 循環論法 **junkan ronpō** a circular argument
量子論 **ryōshiron** quantum theory
無神論 **mushinron** atheism
悲観論 **hikanron** pessimism
悲観論者 **hikanronsha** pessimist
13 感覚論 **kankakuron** sensualism; esthetics
意味論 **imiron** semantics
14 認識論 **ninshikiron** epistemology
16 懐疑論 **kaigiron** skepticism
穏和論者 **onwaronsha** a moderate
18 観念論 **kannenron** idealism (in philosophy)
20 攘夷論 **jōiron** anti-alien policy
懸賞論文 **kenshō ronbun** prize essay

──────── 4 ────────
4 不可知論 **fukachiron** agnosticism

──────── 5 ────────
3 女性解放論 **josei kaihōron** feminism

7a8.14

諒
RYŌ understanding, sympathy; true, sincere

──────── 1 ────────
7 諒承 **ryōshō** acknowledge, understand, note

7a8.15

諂
TEN, hetsura(u) flatter, curry favor

謎 → 謎 7a9.20

7a8.16 / 342

調 調
CHŌ investigate; order, harmony; tune, tone
shira(beru) investigate, check
shira(be) investigation; melody, tune **totono(eru)** prepare, arrange, put in order
totono(u) be prepared/arranged, be in order

──────── 1 ────────
2 調子 **chōshi** tone; mood; condition
調子付 **chōshizu(ku)** warm up to, be elated by, be in high spirits
調子外 **chōshihazu(re)** discord, out of tune
調子者 **chōshimono** person easily elated
5 調号 **chōgō** key signature (in music)
6 調伏 **chōbuku** exorcise; curse
調合 **chōgō** compounding, mixing
調合剤 **chōgōzai** preparation, concoction
調印 **chōin** signing (of a treaty)
調印国 **chōinkoku** a signatory

調色 **chōshoku** mixing colors, toning
調色板 **chōshokuban** palette
7 調車 **shira(be)guruma** belt pulley
8 調直 **shira(be)nao(su)** reinvestigate, reexamine
調味 **chōmi** seasoning, flavoring
調味料 **chōmiryō** condiments, seasonings
調物 **shira(be)mono** matter for inquiry
調和 **chōwa** harmony
9 調律 **chōritsu** tuning
調律師 **chōritsushi** (piano) tuner
調革 **shira(be)gawa** belt (on machinery)
調度 **chōdo** household effects, furnishings
調度品 **chōdohin** household effects, furnishings
調査 **chōsa** investigation, inquiry, survey, research
10 調剤 **chōzai** compounding medicines
調剤師 **chōzaishi** pharmacist
調進 **chōshin** prepare, supply
調書 **chōsho** protocol, record
調教 **chōkyō** break in, train (animals)
調教師 **chōkyōshi** (animal) trainer
調馬 **chōba** horse breaking/training
調馬師 **chōbashi** horse trainer
調馬場 **chōbajō** riding ground
11 調停 **chōtei** arbitration, mediation, conciliation
調停裁判 **chōtei saiban** court arbitration
調達 **chōtatsu, chōdatsu** procure, supply
調理 **chōri** cooking
調理人 **chōrinin** a cook
調理師 **chōrishi** a cook
13 調節 **chōsetsu** adjust, control, regulate
14 調髪 **chōhatsu** barbering
調髪師 **chōhatsushi** barber
調製 **chōsei** make, prepare
調練 **chōren** drill, training
16 調整 **chōsei** adjust, regulate, coordinate

──────── 2 ────────
3 上調子 **uwachōshi, uwajōshi** high pitch, higher key **uwa(t)chōshi** flippant, frivolous, shallow
下調 **shitashira(be)** preliminary investigation; prepare (lessons)
口調 **kuchō** tone, expression
4 不調 **fuchō** failure to agree; out of sorts
不調法 **buchōhō** impoliteness; carelessness; misconduct; awkward, inexperienced
不調和 **fuchōwa** disharmony, disagreement
5 本調子 **honchōshi** proper key (of an instrument); one's regular form
失調 **shitchō** malfunction, lack of coordination
正調 **seichō** traditional tune

好調 **kōchō** good, favorable, satisfactory
6 再調査 **saichōsa** reinvestigation
仮調印 **karichōin** initialing (a treaty)
色調 **shikichō** color tone
同調 **dōchō** alignment; tuning
名調子 **meichōshi** eloquence
7 低調 **teichō** low-pitched; dull, inactive, sluggish (market)
乱調 **ranchō** discord, disorder, confusion; wild (market) fluctuations
乱調子 **ranchōshi** discord, disorder, confusion; wild (market) fluctuations
声調 **seichō** tone of voice
快調 **kaichō** harmony; excellent condition
8 長調 **chōchō** major key, in (C) major
協調 **kyōchō** cooperation, conciliation
逆調 **gyakuchō** adverse, unfavorable
空調 **kūchō** air conditioning (short for 空気調節)
歩調 **hochō** pace, step
取調 **to(ri)shira(beru)** investigate, look into
9 俗調 **zokuchō** popular melody, vulgar music
変調 **henchō** change of tone/key; irregular, abnormal; modulation (in radio)
哀調 **aichō** mournful melody; minor key
品調 **shinashira(be)** stocktaking
単調 **tanchō** monotonous
音調 **onchō** tone, tune, rhythm, euphony
10 高調 **kōchō** high pitch/spirits
高調子 **takachōshi** high pitch; rising stockmarket tone
格調 **kakuchō** tone, style
貢調 **kōchō** pay tribute
11 基調 **kichō** keynote
強調 **kyōchō** emphasis, stress
情調 **jōchō** atmosphere, mood, tone, spirit
移調 **ichō** transpose (musical keys)
軟調 **nanchō** weakness, softness, bearish tone (cf. 堅調)
転調 **tenchō** modulation, changing keys
12 堅調 **kenchō** firmness, bullish tone, rising trend (cf. 軟調)
短調 **tanchō** minor key
無調法 **buchōhō** impolite; clumsy, unaccustomed to
悲調 **hichō** plaintive air, touch of sadness
鈍調 **donchō** dull (market)
順調 **junchō** favorable, smooth, without a hitch
13 楽調 **gakuchō** musical tone
新調 **shinchō** have (clothes) made
14 歌調 **kachō** melody, tune
語調 **gochō** accent, tone, voice
15 論調 **ronchō** tone of argument
16 整調 **seichō** head oarsman

諧調 **kaichō** harmony, euphony

——————— 3 ———————

1 一本調子 **ipponchōshi, ipponjōshi** monotony
2 七五調 **shichigochō** seven-and-five-syllable meter
3 口不調法 **kuchi-buchōhō** awkward in expressing oneself
小手調 **koteshira(be)** tryout, rehearsal
4 戸籍調 **koseki shira(be)** examine (someone's) family register; take the census
5 世論調査 **seron chōsa, yoron chōsa** (public-opinion) poll
6 光変調 **hikari henchō** optical modulation
7 快速調 **kaisokuchō** allegro
8 居中調停 **kyochū-chōtei** mediation, arbitration
国勢調査 **kokusei chōsa** (national) census
9 美文調 **bibunchō** ornate style
12 復古調 **fukkochō** reactionary/revival mood
最好調 **saikōchō** in perfect form
17 輿論調査 **yoron chōsa** public-opinion survey, poll

——————— 4 ———————

9 変ロ長調 **hen-ro chōchō** B-flat major

——————— 9 ———————

7a9.1

諫 諫   **KAN, isa(meru)** remonstrate with, admonish

——————— 1 ———————

4 諫止 **kanshi** dissuade from
6 諫死 **kanshi** commit suicide in protest against
7 諫言 **kangen** remonstrate with, admonish

7a9.2

諛   **YU** flatter

——————— 2 ———————

7 阿諛 **ayu** flattery

諸 → 諸 **7a8.3**

7a9.3

諤   **GAKU** speaking frankly/bluntly

——————— 3 ———————

8 侃々諤々 **kankan-gakugaku** outspoken

7a9.4 / 1769

諮 **SHI, haka(ru)** consult, confer, solicit advice

──────── 1 ────────

11 諮問 **shimon** question, inquiry; question, inquiry; consultive, advisory (body)

7a9.5

諳 **AN, sora(njiru/nzuru)** memorize; recite from memory

諺 → 諺 **7a9.15**

7a9.6

謂 **I, iwa(re)** reason, grounds; origin, history

──────── 2 ────────

8 所謂 **iwayuru** what is called, so-called

7a9.7

諜 **CHŌ** spy out, reconnoiter

──────── 1 ────────

6 諜合 **shime(shi)a(waseru)** prearrange, collude, conspire
8 諜者 **chōja** spy
12 諜報 **chōhō** intelligence, espionage

──────── 2 ────────

6 防諜 **bōchō** counterintelligence
12 間諜 **kanchō** spy

7a9.8 / 1495

謀 **BŌ, MU, haka(ru)** plan, devise; deceive **tabaka(ru)** cheat, take in **hakarigoto** plan, scheme, plot

──────── 1 ────────

4 謀反 **muhon** rebellion, insurrection
謀反人 **muhonnin** rebel, conspirator
9 謀叛 **muhon** rebellion, insurrection
謀叛人 **muhonnin** rebel, conspirator
謀計 **bōkei** strategem, plot, trick
10 謀殺 **bōsatsu** premeditated murder
11 謀略 **bōryaku** strategem, scheme
20 謀議 **bōgi** conferring together; conspiracy

──────── 2 ────────

5 主謀者 **shubōsha** (ring)leader, mastermind

6 共謀 **kyōbō** conspiracy
8 知謀 **chibō** resourcefulness
参謀 **sanbō** staff officer; adviser
参謀長 **sanbōchō** chief of staff
9 首謀 **shubō** plotting; ringleader
首謀者 **shubōsha** ringleader, mastermind
通謀 **tsūbō** conspire with, work in collusion
10 陰謀 **inbō** conspiracy, plot, intrigue
陰謀家 **inbōka** schemer
11 深謀 **shinbō** shrewd planning, deep design
深謀遠慮 **shinbō-enryo** farsighted planning
宿謀 **shukubō** premeditated plot
密謀 **mitsubō** plot, intrigue
12 遠謀 **enbō** forethought, foresight
智謀 **chibō** resourcefulness, ingenuity
無謀 **mubō** incautious, reckless
策謀 **sakubō** strategem, machinations
15 権謀 **kenbō** strategem, scheme, ruse
権謀家 **kenbōka** schemer, maneuverer

謁 → 謁 **7a8.6**

7a9.9 / 1647

謡 謠 **YŌ** song; (Noh) chanting **uta(u)** sing (without accompaniment), chant **utai** Noh chanting

──────── 1 ────────

5 謡本 **utaibon** Noh libretto
6 謡曲 **yōkyoku** Noh song/chant
8 謡物 **utaimono** Noh recitation piece

──────── 2 ────────

5 民謡 **min'yō** folk song
9 俗謡 **zokuyō** popular/folk song
12 童謡 **dōyō** children's song, nursery rhyme
14 歌謡 **kayō** song, ballad
歌謡曲 **kayōkyoku** popular song

7a9.10

諼 **KEN** forget; deceive

7a9.11

諧 **KAI** order, harmony

──────── 1 ────────

9 諧音 **kaion** melody, harmony
15 諧調 **kaichō** harmony, euphony
16 諧謔 **kaigyaku** jest, humor

──────── 2 ────────

5 半諧音 **hankaion** assonance

10 俳諧 **haikai** joke; *haikai*, haiku
俳諧師 **haikaishi** *haikai* poet
15 誹諧 **haikai** humorous poem; 17-syllable
poem

7a9.12

諠

KEN forget; noisy

──────── 1 ────────

9 諠草 **wasuregusa** day lily
17 諠譁 **kenka** quarrel

7a9.13 / 1599

諭 諭

YU, sato(su) admonish,
remonstrate, warn, counsel

──────── 1 ────────

5 諭示 **yushi** admonition, instructions
6 諭旨 **yushi** official suggestion (to a subordinate)
7 諭告 **yukoku** counsel, admonition
11 諭達 **yutatsu** official instructions

──────── 2 ────────

7 告諭 **kokuyu** official notice, proclamation
9 勅諭 **chokuyu** imperial instructions
風諭 **fūyu** hint, indirect suggestion, allegory
10 教諭 **kyōyu** instructor, teacher
14 説諭 **setsuyu** admonish
to(ki)sato(su) persuade; rebuke

7a9.14

諢

KON joke, jest; colloquial

7a9.15

諺 諺

GEN, kotowaza proverb

──────── 1 ────────

4 諺文 **onmon, onmun** Korean script, Hangul

──────── 2 ────────

5 古諺 **kogen** old proverb/adage
9 俚諺 **rigen** folk saying, proverb

7a9.16

諦

TEI clarity, enlightenment
akira(meru) give up, abandon, resign
oneself to

──────── 1 ────────

18 諦観 **teikan** clear vision; resign oneself to

7a9.17

謔

GYAKU jest, sport

──────── 2 ────────

10 俳謔 **haigyaku** joke, funny story
16 諧謔 **kaigyaku** jest, humor

7a9.18

諡 諡

SHI, okurina posthumous
name

──────── 1 ────────

5 諡号 **shigō** posthumous name

7a9.19

諞

HEN flattering, glibness

7a9.20

謎 謎

MEI, nazo riddle, puzzle,
enigma

7a9.21

諷

FŪ hint at, allude to

──────── 1 ────────

0 諷する **fū(suru)** hint, suggest, insinuate
8 諷刺 **fūshi** satire, sarcasm, lampoon
諷刺画 **fūshiga** caricature, cartoon

──────── 10 ────────

7a10.1 / 901

謝

SHA gratitude; apology
ayama(ru) apologize

──────── 1 ────────

0 謝する **sha(suru)** thank; apologize; decline;
refuse; take one's leave
5 謝礼 **sharei** remuneration, honorarium
6 謝肉祭 **shanikusai** carnival
7 謝状 **shajō** letter of thanks/apology
8 謝金 **shakin** monetary gift of thanks
10 謝恩 **shaon** gratitude
謝恩会 **shaonkai** thank-you party, testimonial dinner
12 謝絶 **shazetsu** refuse, decline
13 謝意 **shai** gratitude; apology
謝辞 **shaji** a speech of thanks; apology

7

言
貝　10←
車
足
酉

謝罪 **shazai** apology
謝電 **shaden** telegram of thanks
15 謝儀 **shagi** expression of gratitude

— 2 —

4 月謝 **gessha** monthly tuition
5 代謝 **taisha** metabolism
平謝 **hiraayama(ri)** humble/profuse apology
6 多謝 **tasha** many thanks; a thousand apologies
8 拝謝 **haisha** thank
10 陳謝 **chinsha** apology
11 深謝 **shinsha** heartfelt gratitude, sincere apology
12 報謝 **hōsha** requital of a favor, recompense
13 感謝 **kansha** gratitude, appreciation
感謝状 **kanshajō** letter of thanks
感謝祭 **kanshasai** Thanksgiving
15 慰謝 **isha** consolation, solace
慰謝料 **isharyō** consolation money, solatium
16 薄謝 **hakusha** small token of gratitude

— 3 —

12 無月謝 **mugessha** free tuition

— 4 —

13 新陳代謝 **shinchintaisha** metabolism

7a10.2

謖 **SHOKU** arise

7a10.3 / 783

講 講 **KŌ** lecture, study; club, association

— 1 —

0 講じる/ずる **kō(jiru/zuru)** devise, take (measures); lecture on; study, practice
ねずみ講 **nezumikō** pyramid/chain-letter-type investment/sales organization, Ponzi scheme
4 講中 **kōjū, kōchū** religious association
7 講究 **kōkyū** (specialized) study, research
講社 **kōsha** religious association
8 講和 **kōwa** make peace with
講和条約 **kōwa jōyaku** peace treaty
10 講師 **kōshi** lecturer, instructor
講座 **kōza** course (of lectures); professorship, chair
講書 **kōsho** interpretation of a book
11 講堂 **kōdō** lecture hall
講習 **kōshū** short course, training
講習会 **kōshūkai** short course, class, training conference
講釈 **kōshaku** lecture; storytelling
講釈師 **kōshakushi** (professional) storyteller
12 講評 **kōhyō** criticism, review
13 講義 **kōgi** lecture
講義録 **kōgiroku** lecture transcripts; correspondence course
講話 **kōwa** lecture, a talk
14 講演 **kōen** lecture, address
講演会 **kōenkai** lecture meeting
講演者 **kōensha** lecturer, speaker
講読 **kōdoku** read (Shakespeare)
講説 **kōsetsu** explain (by lecture)
15 講談 **kōdan** storytelling, a narrative
講談師 **kōdanshi** (professional) storyteller
16 講壇 **kōdan** rostrum

— 2 —

5 代講 **daikō** act as a substitute lecturer
6 休講 **kyūkō** lecture cancelled
8 長講 **chōkō** a long talk/lecture
侍講 **jikō** imperial tutor
受講 **jukō** take lectures
受講生 **jukōsei** trainee, seminar participant
10 進講 **shinkō** give a lecture in the presence of the emperor
12 補講 **hokō** supplementary lecture
開講 **kaikō** begin a course of lectures
15 輪講 **rinkō** take turns reading and explaining (a book)
17 聴講 **chōkō** attendance at a lecture
聴講生 **chōkōsei** auditing student
聴講券 **chōkōken** lecture admittance ticket

— 3 —

9 単独講和 **tandoku kōwa** acting on one's own
12 無礼講 **bureikō** free-and-easy get-together

7a10.4

謐 **HITSU** quiet, peaceful

— 2 —

14 静謐 **seihitsu** peace, tranquility

謌→歌 **4j10.2**

謠→謡 **7a9.9**

7a10.5

諂 **TŌ** doubt

— 1 —

11 諂晦 **tōkai** conceal (one's talent/identity)

謹→曄 **3d10.7**

7a10.6 / 1247

謹 謹　KIN, tsutsushi(mu) be respectful

———————— 1 ————————

7 謹呈　**kintei** Respectfully presented, With the compliments of the author

謹告　**kinkoku** respectfully inform

謹言　**kingen** Sincerely/Respectfully yours,

8 謹直　**kinchoku** conscientious

10 謹書　**kinsho** respectfully written

11 謹啓　**kinkei** Dear Sir:, Gentlemen:

12 謹賀新年　**kinga shinnen** Happy New Year

13 謹慎　**kinshin** be on one's best behavior; be confined to one's home

謹話　**kinwa** respectful remarks

14 謹選　**kinsen** respectfully chosen (for you)

謹製　**kinsei** carefully made by

17 謹厳　**kingen** stern, austere, solemn

謹聴　**kinchō** listen attentively

———————— 2 ————————

4 不謹慎　**fukinshin** imprudent, rash

11 細謹　**saikin** small defect, slight flaw

7a10.7

謨　BO plan

———————— 2 ————————

20 護謨　**gomu** rubber

7a10.8

諱　KI hate; avoid; conceal
imina posthumous name; real name

———————— 2 ————————

7 忌諱　**kii, kiki** displeasure, offense

7a10.9

謗　BŌ, soshi(ru) speak ill of, vilify, disparage, slander

———————— 2 ————————

15 誹謗　**hibō** slander, defame, malign

24 讒謗　**zanbō** slander, defamation

譃→ **7a9.17**

7a10.10 / 1687

KEN modesty, humility

謙 謙

———————— 1 ————————

7 謙抑　**ken'yoku** humbling oneself

10 謙称　**kenshō** humble expression

11 謙虚　**kenkyo** modest, humble

12 謙遜　**kenson** modesty, humility

20 謙譲　**kenjō** modesty, humility

———————— 2 ————————

6 孝謙　**Kōken** (empress, 749–758)

謚→謚 **7a9.18**

———————— 11 ————————

7a11.1

謬　BYŪ, ayama(ru) err, be wrong

———————— 1 ————————

14 謬説　**byūsetsu** fallacy, mistaken view, false report

———————— 2 ————————

14 誤謬　**gobyū** error

7a11.2

謾　MAN despise; deceive

謹→謹 **7a10.6**

7a11.3

謫　TAKU accuse, blame, punish

———————— 1 ————————

8 謫居　**takkyo** exile

7a11.4

謳　Ō, uta(u) extol, sing the praises of; state

———————— 1 ————————

14 謳歌　**ōka** glorify, sing the praises of

7

言 11←
貝
車
足
酉

7a11.5

謦 **KEI** clearing one's throat; laughing merrily

——————— 1 ———————

9 謦咳接 **keigai (ni) ses(suru)** have the pleasure of meeting personally

7a11.6

鞫 **KIKU** investigate (a crime)

——————— 12 ———————

7a12.1

譏 **KI, soshi(ru)** denounce, revile

7a12.2 / 1167

譜 譜 **FU** (sheet) music, notes, staff, score; a genealogy; record

——————— 1 ———————

5 譜代 **fudai** successive generations; hereditary vassal
譜代大名 **fudai daimyō** hereditary daimyo
8 譜表 **fuhyō** staff (in music)

——————— 2 ———————

4 氏譜 **shifu** a genealogy
6 年譜 **nenpu** chronological record
7 花譜 **kafu** flower album
系譜 **keifu** genealogy, family tree
8 画譜 **gafu** picture book/album
9 音譜 **onpu** (written) notes, the score
10 家譜 **kafu** a genealogy, family tree
11 略譜 **ryakufu** brief genealogy; abbreviated musical notation
12 棋譜 **kifu** record of a go/shogi game
13 楽譜 **gakufu** musical notation, sheet music, the score
14 総譜 **sōfu** the full score (sheet music)

——————— 3 ———————

4 五線譜 **gosenfu** staff notation, score (in music)

譛→譖 **7a12.3**

7a12.3

譖 譛 **SHIN** slander

7a12.4

譚 **TAN** talk, tale; large(hearted)

證→証 **7a5.5**

7a12.5

譎 **KETSU, itsuwa(ru)** lie, cheat

譌→訛 **7a4.5**

7a12.6 / 681

識 **SHIKI** know, discriminate

——————— 1 ———————

5 識字 **shikiji** literacy
7 識別 **shikibetsu** discrimination, recognition
識見 **shikiken, shikken** knowledge, discernment
8 識者 **shikisha** intelligent/informed people
16 識閾 **shikiiki** threshold of consciousness

——————— 2 ———————

6 多識 **tashiki** well-informed, knowledgeable
先識 **senshiki** prior knowledge
有識 **yūshiki** learned, intellectual
有識者 **yūshikisha** learned person, an intellectual
7 良識 **ryōshiki** good sense
学識 **gakushiki** learning, scholarly attainments
見識 **kenshiki** opinion; discernment, insight; pride, dignity
見識張 **kenshikiba(ru)** assume an air of importance
8 知識 **chishiki** knowledge
知識人 **chishikijin** an intellectual
知識欲 **chishikiyoku** love of learning
物識 **monoshi(ri)** knowledgeable, erudite
9 面識 **menshiki** acquaintance
相識 **sōshiki** acquaintance
10 病識 **byōshiki** awareness that one is ill
11 達識 **tasshiki** insight, farsightedness
唯識 **yuishiki** (Buddhist) spiritualism
常識 **jōshiki** common sense/knowledge
常識的 **jōshikiteki** matter-of-fact, practical

眼識 **ganshiki** discernment, insight
12 博識 **hakushiki** extensive knowledge
智識 **chishiki** knowledge, wisdom
13 意識 **ishiki** consciousness, awareness
意識的 **ishikiteki** consciously
14 認識 **ninshiki** (re)cognition, perception, knowledge
認識票 **ninshikihyō** identification tag
認識論 **ninshikiron** epistemology
15 標識 **hyōshiki** (land)mark, marking, sign, signal, tag
23 鑑識 **kanshiki** discernment, identification
鑑識力 **kanshikiryoku** discernment
鑑識家 **kanshikika** a judge/connoisseur of, appraiser
鑑識眼 **kanshikigan** discerning eye

───────── 3 ─────────

1 一面識 **ichimenshiki** knowing someone by sight, a passing acquaintance
6 自意識 **jiishiki** self-consciousness
7 没常識 **botsujōshiki** lack of common sense
8 非常識 **hijōshiki** lacking common sense, absurd
性知識 **sei chishiki** information on sex
9 美意識 **biishiki** esthetic awareness
12 無意識 **muishiki** unconscious, involuntary
13 新知識 **shinchishiki** up-to-date knowledge

───────── 4 ─────────

4 予備知識 **yobi chishiki** preliminary knowledge, background
10 航路標識 **kōro hyōshiki** navigation marker/ beacon
15 潜在意識 **senzai ishiki** subconscious

7a12.7 / 706

警 KEI, imashi(meru) warn, admonish

───────── 1 ─────────

5 警世 **keisei** warning to the world/public
警世家 **keiseika** prophet, seer
警句 **keiku** epigram, witticism
6 警防 **keibō** preserving order
警防団 **keibōdan** civil defense corps
7 警抜 **keibatsu** extraordinary
警告 **keikoku** warning, admonition
警戒 **keikai** warning, (pre)caution; vigilance
警戒色 **keikaishoku** warning color
警戒線 **keikaisen** police cordon
警戒警報 **keikai keihō** an (air-raid) alert
8 警官 **keikan** policeman
警官隊 **keikantai** police force/squad
9 警乗 **keijō** police (a train)
警乗警察 **keijō keisatsu** railway police

警急 **keikyū** alarm, emergency
10 警部 **keibu** police inspector
警砲 **keihō** warning gun/shot
11 警視 **keishi** police superintendent
警視庁 **Keishichō** Metropolitan Police Agency
警務 **keimu** police affairs
警笛 **keiteki** alarm whistle, horn
12 警備 **keibi** security, guard, defense
警備兵 **keibihei** guard
警備艦 **keibikan** guard ship
警報 **keihō** warning, alarm
警報機 **keihōki** warning device, alarm
警棒 **keibō** policeman's club/nightstick
14 警察 **keisatsu** police
警察力 **keisatsuryoku** police force
警察犬 **keisatsuken** police dog
警察犯 **keisatsuhan** police offense
警察庁 **Keisatsuchō** National Police Agency
警察官 **keisatsukan** police officer
警察署 **keisatsusho** police station
警察権 **keisatsuken** police power
15 警標 **keihyō** warning sign
16 警衛 **keiei** guard, escort, patrol
警醒 **keisei** warn, arouse, awaken
18 警蹕 **keihitsu** heralding
20 警護 **keigo** guard, escort
警鐘 **keishō** alarm/fire bell
22 警邏 **keira** patrol(man)

───────── 2 ─────────

5 巡警 **junkei** patrolman
6 自警 **jikei** self-warning, vigilance; local police
自警団 **jikeidan** vigilance committee, vigilantes
8 夜警 **yakei** night watch(man)
奇警 **kikei** original, witty
11 婦警 **fukei** policewoman
12 違警罪 **ikeizai** offense against police regulations
無警告 **mukeikoku** without warning
無警察 **mukeisatsu** lawlessness, anarchy

───────── 3 ─────────

4 水上警察 **suijō keisatsu** water/harbor police
火災警報 **kasai keihō** fire alarm
9 軍事警察 **gunji keisatsu** military police
11 婦人警官 **fujin keikan** policewoman
19 警戒警報 **keikai keihō** an (air-raid) alert
警乗警察 **keijō keisatsu** railway police

───────── 13 ─────────

譯 → 訳 **7a4.8**

7

言
貝 12←
車
趴
酉

7a13.1 / 1013

譲 讓

JŌ, yuzu(ru) turn over to, transfer, assign; yield to, concede

───────── 1 ─────────

3 譲与 **jōyo** cede, transfer
6 譲合 **yuzu(ri)a(u)** defer/yield to each other, compromise
7 譲位 **jōi** abdication
　 譲状 **yuzu(ri)jō** deed of assignment
8 譲受 **yuzu(ri)u(keru)** obtain by transfer, take over, inherit
　 譲歩 **jōho** concession, compromise
12 譲渡 **jōto** assign, transfer, convey
　　 yuzu(ri)wata(su) turn over to, transfer
　 譲渡人 **jōtonin** assignor, grantor

───────── 2 ─────────

4 互譲 **gojō** mutual concession, compromise, conciliation
　 分譲 **bunjō** selling (land) in lots
　 分譲地 **bunjōchi** a subdivision
8 退譲 **taijō** humility
　 委譲 **ijō** transfer/assign to
12 割譲 **katsujō** cede (territory)
13 禅譲 **zenjō** abdication
　 辞譲 **jijō** decline in favor of someone else
16 親譲 **oyayuzu(ri)** inheritance, heredity
17 謙譲 **kenjō** modesty, humility

7a13.2

譟

SŌ, sawa(gu) shout, be noisy

7a13.3 / 1312

護

GO, mamo(ru) defend, protect

───────── 1 ─────────

7 護身 **goshin** personal protection
　 護身術 **goshinjutsu** art of self-defense
8 護送 **gosō** escort, convoy
　 護送車 **gosōsha** paddy wagon
　 護送船 **gosōsen** convoy
　 護法 **gohō** defense of the law/religion
　 護岸 **gogan** shore/bank protection
　 護岸工事 **gogan kōji** riparian works
　 護国 **gokoku** defense of the country
9 護持 **goji** defend, protect, uphold
11 護符 **gofu** amulet, talisman
15 護摩 **goma** sacred fire
　 護摩灰 **goma(no)hai** thief posing as a fellow traveler
16 護衛 **goei** guard, escort

護衛兵 **goeihei** guard, military escort
17 護謨 **gomu** rubber

───────── 2 ─────────

3 女護島 **nyogo(ga)shima** isle of women
5 弁護 **bengo** defend, plead for
　 弁護人 **bengonin** counsel, defender, advocate
　 弁護士 **bengoshi** lawyer, attorney
　 弁護士会 **bengoshikai** bar association
　 弁護依頼人 **bengo irainin** client
　 弁護者 **bengosha** defender, advocate
　 弁護料 **bengoryō** attorney's fees
　 加護 **kago** divine protection
6 防護 **bōgo** protection, custody
　 守護 **shugo** protection, defense
　 守護神 **shugojin** guardian/tutelary deity, mascot
7 庇護 **higo** protection, patronage
9 保護 **hogo** protect, shelter, take care of
　 保護色 **hogoshoku** protective coloration
　 保護国 **hogokoku** protectorate
　 保護者 **hogosha** protector, guardian
　 保護鳥 **hogochō** protected bird
　 保護貿易 **hogo bōeki** protectionistic trade
　 保護領 **hogoryō** protectorate
　 神護景雲 **Jingo Keiun** (era, 767–769)
　 看護 **kango** tend the sick, care for, nurse
　 看護人 **kangonin** male nurse
　 看護兵 **kangohei** military nurse, medic
　 看護婦 **kangofu** (female) nurse
　 看護婦長 **kangofuchō** head nurse
11 掩護 **engo** covering, protection
　 救護 **kyūgo** relief, aid, rescue
　 救護米 **kyūgomai** dole rice
　 救護所 **kyūgosho** first-aid station
　 救護班 **kyūgohan** relief squad, rescue party
12 援護 **engo** protection, support, relief
13 摂護腺 **setsugosen** prostate gland
　 愛護 **aigo** treat kindly, protect
15 養護 **yōgo** protection, care
　 養護学級 **yōgo gakkyū** class for the handicapped
　 養護学校 **yōgo gakkō** school for the handicapped
　 監護 **kango** custody and care
16 擁護 **yōgo** protect, defend
　 擁護者 **yōgosha** defender, supporter, advocate
19 警護 **keigo** guard, escort

───────── 3 ─────────

10 被保護国 **hihogokoku** protectorate, dependency
　 被保護者 **hihogosha** ward

───────── 4 ─────────

2 人身保護 **jinshin hogo** habeas corpus
4 天平神護 **Tenpyō Jingo** (era, 765–767)

8 国選弁護人 **kokusen bengonin** court-appointed defense counsel
11 動物愛護 **dōbutsu aigo** being kind to animals, animal welfare
17 優生保護法 **Yūsei Hogo Hō** Eugenic Protection Law

7a13.4 / 292

GI deliberation; proposal

議

──────── 1 ────────

0 議する **gi(suru)** discuss, deliberate
1 議了 **giryō** finish discussion, close debate
6 議会 **gikai** parliament, diet, congress
7 議決 **giketsu** decision, resolution
　議決権 **giketsuken** voting rights
8 議長 **gichō** chairman, president
　議事 **giji** proceedings
　議事堂 **gijidō** assembly hall, parliament/diet building
　議事録 **gijiroku** minutes, proceedings
　議定 **gitei, gijō** agreement
　議定書 **giteisho, gijōsho** a protocol
9 議院 **giin** house of a legislature, diet
10 議員 **giin** M.P., dietman, congressman
　議案 **gian** bill, measure
　議席 **giseki** seat in parliament/congress
12 議場 **gijō** the floor (of the legislature)
15 議論 **giron** argument, discussion, controversy
　議論好 **gironzu(ki)** argumentative
　議論家 **gironka** avid/good debater
18 議題 **gidai** topic for discussion, agenda

──────── 2 ────────

1 一議 **ichigi** a word, an opinion, an objection
4 公議 **kōgi** public opinion; just view
5 代議士 **daigishi** member of parliament/congress/diet
　代議員 **daigiin** representative, delegate
　付議 **fugi** bring up, submit, discuss
6 両議院 **ryōgiin** both houses (of parliament/congress)
　再議 **saigi** reconsideration, redeliberation
　合議 **gōgi** consultation, conference
　合議制 **gōgisei** parliamentary system
　会議 **kaigi** conference, meeting
　会議所 **kaigisho** meeting hall, site of a conference
　会議室 **kaigishitsu** meeting/conference room
　会議場 **kaigijō** meeting hall, place of assembly
　会議録 **kaigiroku** minutes, proceedings
　争議 **sōgi** dispute, strife, conflict
　先議権 **sengiken** right to prior consideration
7 決議 **ketsugi** resolution, decision, vote

決議文 **ketsugibun** (written) resolution
決議事項 **ketsugi jikō** agenda, resolutions
決議案 **ketsugian** resolution, proposal
決議権 **ketsugiken** voting right, vote
決議機関 **ketsugi kikan** voting body; party organization, caucus
決議録 **ketsugiroku** minutes (of a meeting)
批議 **higi** criticize, censure, blame
抗議 **kōgi** protest, objection
抗議文 **kōgibun** (written) protest
私議 **shigi** private discussion; backbiting; personal view
8 非議 **higi** criticize, blame
協議 **kyōgi** consultation, conference
協議会 **kyōgikai** conference, council
協議所 **kyōgisho** conference site
協議員 **kyōgiin** delegate, conferee
建議 **kengi** proposal
建議者 **kengisha** proposer
建議案 **kengian** proposition
参議 **sangi** participation in government; councilor
参議院 **Sangiin** House of Councilors
府議会 **fugikai** urban-prefectural assembly
物議 **butsugi** public criticism/discussion
和議 **wagi** peace negotiations, reconciliation; composition (proceedings)
9 発議 **hatsugi** proposal, motion
俗議 **zokugi** popular opinion
院議 **ingi** decision of the House/congress/parliament
軍議 **gungi** war council
県議 **kengi** prefectural assemblyman
県議会 **kengikai** prefectural assembly
10 都議会 **Togikai** Tōkyō Assembly
党議 **tōgi** party policy/conference
紛議 **fungi** controversy, dissension
討議 **tōgi** discussion, deliberation, debate
11 副議長 **fukugichō** vice president/chairman
動議 **dōgi** a (parliamentary) motion
商議 **shōgi** conference, consultation
密議 **mitsugi** secret conference/consultation
常議員 **jōgiin** permanent member; standing committee
異議 **igi** objection, protest
12 提議 **teigi** proposal, motion
朝議 **chōgi** court council
衆議 **shūgi** public discussion
衆議一決 **shūgi-ikketsu** decided unanimously
衆議院 **Shūgiin** the House of Representatives
評議 **hyōgi** confer, discuss, deliberate
評議会 **hyōgikai** council, commission
評議員 **hyōgiin** councilor, trustee
13 稟議 **ringi** decision-making by circular letter (instead of holding a meeting)
群議 **gungi** multitude of opinions

7

言
貝
車
足
酉

13←

幕議 **bakugi** shogunate council
詮議 **sengi** discussion, consideration, examination
詮議立 **sengida(te)** thorough investigation
14 熟議 **jukugi** due deliberation/discussion
閣議 **kakugi** cabinet meeting
15 審議 **shingi** deliberation, consideration
審議会 **shingikai** deliberative assembly, commission, council
横議 **ōgi** arguing persistently
論議 **rongi** discussion, argument
16 凝議 **gyōgi** deliberation, consultation
謀議 **bōgi** conferring together; conspiracy

———————— 3 ————————
4 不思議 **fushigi** wonder, mystery, marvel
8 長談議 **nagadangi** a long-winded speech
府会議員 **fukai giin** urban-prefectural assemblyman

———————— 4 ————————
2 七不思議 **nanafushigi** the seven wonders
3 山猫争議 **yamaneko sōgi** wildcat strike
4 不可思議 **fukashigi** mystery, wonder, miracle
円卓会議 **entaku kaigi** round-table conference
5 主脳会議 **shunō kaigi** summit conference
9 軍事会議 **gunji kaigi** council of war
軍法会議 **gunpō kaigi** court-martial
11 商工会議所 **Shōkō Kaigisho** Chamber of Commerce and Industry
12 御前会議 **gozen kaigi** council held in the presence of the emperor

———————— 5 ————————
4 井戸端会議 **idobata kaigi** well-side gossip
15 摩可不思議 **maka-fushigi** profound mystery
摩訶不思議 **maka-fushigi** profound mystery

譜 → 譜 **7a12.2**

譽 → 誉 **3n10.1**

7a13.5

SEN talking deliriously

譫

———————— 1 ————————
6 譫妄 **senmō** delirium
7 譫言 **uwagoto** talking deliriously

7a13.6

KEN reproach, accuse

譴

———————— 1 ————————
11 譴責 **kenseki** reprimand, rebuke

7a13.7

譬 HI, **tato(eru)** compare, liken to, speak figuratively

———————— 1 ————————
12 譬喩 **hiyu** metaphor, figure of speech
13 譬話 **tato(e)banashi** fable, allegory, parable

———————— 14 ————————

辯 → 弁 **0a5.30**

———————— 15 ————————

7a15.1

讃 讃 SAN praise; inscription on a picture

———————— 1 ————————
7 讃岐 **Sanuki** (ancient kuni, Kagawa-kuni)
9 讃美 **sanbi** praise, glorification
讃美歌 **sanbika** hymn
13 讃嘆 **santan** praise, admiration
讃辞 **sanji** praise
14 讃歌 **sanka** paean, praise

———————— 2 ————————
5 礼讃 **raisan** worship, adore, glorify
6 自讃 **jisan** self-praise
8 画讃 **gasan** legend written over a picture
和讃 **wasan** (Buddhist) hymns of praise
12 絶讃 **zessan** praise highly
15 賞讃 **shōsan** praise, admire

讀 → 読 **7a7.9**

———————— 16 ————————

7a16.1

讌 EN, **utage** party, banquet

7a16.2

讐 讎 SHŪ enemy; revenge

———————— 2 ————————
10 恩讐 **onshū** love and hate
12 復讐 **fukushū** revenge

─────────── 17 ───────────

7a17.1

讙

KAN rejoice; noisy, disputatious

讓 → 譲 **7a13.1**

7a17.2

讒

ZAN speak ill of, defame

─────────── 1 ───────────

7 讒言 **zangen** false charge, slander
12 讒訴 **zanso** false charge, slander
17 讒謗 **zanbō** slander, defamation

7a17.3

讖

SHIN omen, prediction

─────────── 18 ───────────

7a18.1

臠

REN mincemeat
RAN thin
misonawa(su) see, view

─────────── 19 ───────────

讚 → 讃 **7a15.1**

─────────── 貝 7b ───────────

貝	則	財	貶	貢	敗	賎	販	貫	責	貨	貧	貳
0.1	2.1	3.1	3.2	3.3	4.1	7b3.1	4.2	4.3	4.4	4.5	2o9.5	4n3.3

質	貯	貼	貽	費	貰	貢	貴	貿	貸	賀	貳	賎
7b8.7	5.1	5.2	5.3	5.4	5.5	5.6	5.7	5.8	5.9	5.10	4n3.3	7b8.3

賄	賂	賍	賊	賈	貲	賃	資	賑	殯	賭	賠	賜
6.1	6.2	7b15.1	6.3	6.4	6.5	6.6	6.7	7.1	7.2	7b9.1	8.1	8.2

賤	賦	賚	賛	質	賭	賢	賴	賺	賻	購	鵙	贈
8.3	8.4	8.5	8.6	8.7	9.1	9.2	9a7.1	10.1	10.2	10.3	11.1	11.2

贅	贄	殯	贈	贊	贇	韻	牘	贍	嚚	臢	贔	臧
11.3	11.4	11.5	7b11.2	7b8.6	12.1	12.2	12.3	13.1	13.2	14.1	14.2	15.1

贖	覿	鬢	顬
15.2	15.3	17.1	20.1

─────────── 0 ───────────

7b0.1 / 240

貝

kai shellfish, (sea) shell

─────────── 1 ───────────

9 貝柱 **kaibashira** (boiled scallop) adductor muscle
11 貝殻 **kaigara** (sea) shell
貝殻虫 **kaigaramushi** scale (insect/louse)
貝殻追放 **kaigara tsuihō** ostracism
貝殻骨 **kaigarabone** the shoulder blade
貝細工 **kaizaiku** shellwork
12 貝塚 **kaizuka** heap of shells
貝焼 **kaiya(ki)** cooked in the shell
18 貝類 **kairui** shellfish (plural)

─────────── 2 ───────────

5 生貝 **namagai** raw shellfish
7 赤貝 **akagai** ark shell
8 宝貝 **takaragai** cowrie, porcelain shell
青貝 **aogai** limpet; mother-of-pearl
10 烏貝 **karasugai** (a freshwater mussel)
11 鳥貝 **torigai** cockle (shell)
12 貽貝 **igai** (type of hard-shelled mussel)
15 蝶貝 **chōgai** pearl oyster

─────────── 3 ───────────

6 帆立貝 **hotategai** scallop (shell)
10 真珠貝 **shinjugai** pearl oyster
馬刀貝 **mategai** razor clam
28 鸚鵡貝 **ōmugai** chambered nautilus

─────────── 4 ───────────

7 阿古屋貝 **akoyagai** pearl oyster

─────────── 2 ───────────

7b2.1 / 608

則

SOKU, **nori** rule, law
notto(ru) follow, conform to
sunawa(chi) in that case, whereupon

─────────── 1 ───────────

4 則天去私 **sokuten-kyoshi** selfless devotion
　　 to justice

─────────── 2 ───────────

4 天則 **tensoku** nature's law
　 反則 **hansoku** violation of the rules, a foul
5 付則 **fusoku** supplementary provisions,
　　　bylaws
　 正則 **seisoku** regular, systematic, normal,
　　　correct, proper
　 犯則 **hansoku** violation, infraction
　 四則 **shisoku** the four basic arithmetic
　　　operations (+, −, *, /)
6 会則 **kaisoku** rules of a society
7 学則 **gakusoku** school regulations
　 社則 **shasoku** company regulations
8 典則 **tensoku** regulations
　 法則 **hōsoku** law, rule
　 定則 **teisoku** established rule, law
9 変則 **hensoku** irregular, abnormal
　 通則 **tsūsoku** general rule
10 原則 **gensoku** principle, general rule
　 原則的 **gensokuteki** in principle/general
　 党則 **tōsoku** party rules
　 校則 **kōsoku** school regulations
　 教則 **kyōsoku** teaching rules
　 教則本 **kyōsokubon** (music) practice book
11 規則 **kisoku** regulation, rule
　 規則的 **kisokuteki** regular, orderly, system-
　　　atic
　 規則書 **kisokusho** prospectus; regulations
　 細則 **saisoku** detailed rules, by-laws
12 補則 **hosoku** supplementary rules
13 準則 **junsoku** rule, criterion
　 鉄則 **tessoku** hard-and-fast rule
14 獄則 **gokusoku** prison regulations
　 概則 **gaisoku** general rules/principles
　 罰則 **bassoku** penal regulations/provisions
　 総則 **sōsoku** general rules/provisions
　 雑則 **zassoku** miscellaneous rules

─────────── 3 ───────────

4 不規則 **fukisoku** irregular, unsystematic
11 経験則 **keikensoku** rule of thumb

─────────── 3 ───────────

7b3.1 / 553

財 賍

ZAI, SAI money, wealth,
property

─────────── 1 ───────────

0 財テク **zaiteku** sophisticated financial
　　　management
2 財力 **zairyoku** financial resources
5 財用 **zaiyō** uses of property; funds
　 財布 **saifu** purse, pocketbook, wallet
6 財団 **zaidan** foundation, financial group
　 財団法人 **zaidan hōjin** (incorporated)
　　　foundation
8 財宝 **zaihō** wealth, treasure, valuables
　 財物 **zaibutsu** property
9 財政 **zaisei** (public) finances
　 財政上 **zaiseijō** fiscal
　 財政学 **zaiseigaku** (the study of) finance
　 財政家 **zaiseika** financier
　 財界 **zaikai** financial world
　 財界人 **zaikaijin** financier, businessman
11 財務 **zaimu** financial affairs
　 財務官 **zaimukan** finance secretary
　 財産 **zaisan** estate, assets, property
　 財産家 **zaisanka** wealthy person
　 財産税 **zaisanzei** property tax
　 財貨 **zaika** commodities, property
13 財源 **zaigen** revenue source; resourcefulness
14 財閥 **zaibatsu** financial clique

─────────── 2 ───────────

5 巨財 **kyozai** vast fortune
7 余財 **yozai** available funds, spare cash;
　　　remaining fortune
　 私財 **shizai** private funds
9 浄財 **jōzai** money offering, contribution
10 借財 **shakuzai** debt
　 家財 **kazai** household effects, belongings
　 家財道具 **kazai dōgu** household effects
11 理財 **rizai** economy, finance
　 理財学 **rizaigaku** political economy
　 理財家 **rizaika** economist, financier
　 貨財 **kazai** wealth, riches
12 散財 **sanzai** incur expenses; squander
　 殖財 **shokuzai** increasing one's wealth/
　　　fortune, money-making
13 蓄財 **chikuzai** amassing of wealth
　 資財 **shizai** assets, property
14 管財人 **kanzainin** trustee, administrator
15 器財 **kizai** tools

─────────── 3 ───────────

4 文化財 **bunkazai** cultural asset
5 生産財 **seisanzai** producer's goods
6 共有財産 **kyōyū zaisan** community property
10 消費財 **shōhizai** consumer goods
13 資本財 **shihonzai** capital goods

─────────── 4 ───────────

1 一切合財 **issai-gassai** everything, the whole
　　　shebang

—————— 5 ——————

12 無形文化財 **mukei-bunkazai** intangible cultural asset

7b3.2

貶

HEN demote, belittle
kena(su) disparage, speak ill of
otoshi(meru) look down on, scorn

—————— 1 ——————

0 貶する **hen(suru)** demote, relegate, belittle

—————— 2 ——————

15 褒貶 **hōhen** praise and censure, criticism

—————— 4 ——————

13 毀誉褒貶 **kiyo-hōhen** praise and/or criticism

7b3.3 / 1719

貢

KŌ, KU, mitsu(gu) pay tribute; support (financially)

—————— 1 ——————

8 貢物 **mitsu(gi)mono, kōbutsu, kōmotsu** tribute
10 貢進 **kōshin** pay tribute
13 貢献 **kōken** contribution, services
15 貢調 **kōchō** pay tribute
  貢賦 **kōfu** tribute and taxes

—————— 2 ——————

2 入貢 **nyūkō** pay tribute
6 年貢 **nengu** land tax
  年貢米 **nengumai** annual rice tax
10 進貢 **shinkō** pay tribute
12 朝貢 **chōkō** bring tribute

—————— 4 ——————

7b4.1 / 511

敗

HAI, yabu(ru) defeat
yabu(reru) be defeated

—————— 1 ——————

3 敗亡 **haibō** defeat
5 敗北 **haiboku** defeat
6 敗色 **haishoku** signs of impending defeat
  敗因 **haiin** a cause of defeat
  敗血症 **haiketsushō** blood poisoning
7 敗兵 **haihei** routed troops
  敗走 **haisō** rout, flight
8 敗退 **haitai** defeat, setback
  敗者 **haisha** the defeated, loser
9 敗軍 **haigun** defeated army
10 敗残 **haizan** survival after defeat; failure, ruin
  敗残兵 **haizanhei** remnants of a defeated army
  敗将 **haishō** defeated general

12 敗報 **haihō** news of defeat
  敗訴 **haiso** losing a suit
13 敗滅 **haimetsu** crushing defeat
  敗戦 **haisen** lost battle, defeat

—————— 2 ——————

1 一敗 **ippai** one defeat
3 大敗 **taihai** a crushing defeat
4 不敗 **fuhai** invincible, undefeated
5 失敗 **shippai** failure, blunder, mistake
6 全敗 **zenpai** complete defeat
  成敗 **seibai** punish, bring to justice
     seihai success or failure
7 完敗 **kanpai** complete defeat
0 連敗 **renpai** successive defeats, losing streak
11 惨敗 **zanpai** crushing defeat
  惜敗 **sekihai** narrow defeat
12 勝敗 **shōhai** victory or defeat
13 戦敗 **senpai** defeat (in war)
  戦敗国 **senpaikoku** defeated nation
  零敗 **reihai** lose without scoring a point
14 腐敗 **fuhai** decomposition, decay; corrpution
  酸敗 **sanpai** acidify, turn rancid
  酸敗乳 **sanpainyū** sour milk

—————— 3 ——————

6 両成敗 **ryōseibai** punishing both parties

—————— 4 ——————

17 優勝劣敗 **yūshō-reppai** survival of the fittest

賎 → 財   **7b3.1**

7b4.2 / 1048

販

HAN sell

—————— 1 ——————

7 販売 **hanbai** sales, selling
  販売人 **hanbainin** seller, agent
  販売元 **hanbaimoto** selling agency
  販売店 **hanbaiten** shop, store
  販売所 **hanbaisho** shop, store
  販売促進 **hanbai sokushin** sales promotion
9 販促 **hansoku** sales promotion (short for 販売促進)
13 販路 **hanro** market, outlet

—————— 2 ——————

5 市販 **shihan** marketing; commercially available (product)
6 自販機 **jihanki** vending machine (short for 自動販売機)
9 信販 **shinpan** credit sales (short for 信用販売)
  通販 **tsūhan** mail order (short for 通信販売)
10 酒販 **shuhan** liquor sales

言 貝 車 足 酉   7   4←

———————— 3 ————————

1 一手販売 **itte hanbai** sole agency
6 自動販売機 **jidō hanbaiki** vending machine
8 委託販売 **itaku hanbai** selling on consign-
   ment/commission
9 通信販売 **tsūshin hanbai** mail order
11 訪問販売 **hōmon hanbai** door-to-door sales

7b4.3 / 914

貫

KAN pierce, go through; place of
domicile; (unit of weight, about 3.75 kg)
tsuranu(ku) pierce; carry through/out,
attain **nuki** brace, crosspiece

———————— 1 ————————

2 貫入 **kannyū** penetrate
5 貫目 **kanme** (unit of weight, about 3.75 kg)
9 貫首 **kanju** head priest
  貫通 **kantsū** pass through, pierce
    tsuranu(ki)tō(su) carry out (one's will)
10 貫流 **kanryū** flow through
12 貫禄 **kanroku** weight, dignity
15 貫徹 **kantetsu** carry through, attain, realize
20 貫籍 **kanseki** domicile, census registration

———————— 2 ————————

1 一貫 **ikkan** consistency, coherence; (3.75 kg)
4 尺貫法 **shakkanhō** old Japanese system of
   weights and measures
5 打貫 **u(chi)nu(ku)** pierce, shoot through
8 突貫 **tokkan** charge, rush ahead
9 指貫 **yubinu(ki)** thimble
    sashinuki (type of formal garment)
16 縦貫 **jūkan** traverse the length of

———————— 3 ————————

13 裸一貫 **hadaka ikkan** with no property but
   one's body

———————— 4 ————————

9 首尾一貫 **shubi-ikkan** logically consistent,
   coherent
11 終始一貫 **shūshi-ikkan** constant, consistent

7b4.4 / 655

責

SEKI responsibility; censure
se(meru) condemn, censure; torture

———————— 1 ————————

5 責付 **se(me)tsu(keru)** denounce scathingly
  責立 **se(me)ta(teru)** torture; urge
6 責任 **sekinin** responsibility, liability
  責任者 **sekininsha** person in charge
  責任感 **sekininkan** sense of responsibility
8 責苦 **se(me)ku** torture
11 責道具 **se(me)dōgu** instruments of torture
  責務 **sekimu** duty, obligation

———————— 2 ————————

4 文責 **bunseki** responsibility for the wording
   (of an article)
  水責 **mizuze(me)** water torture
  引責 **inseki** assume responsibility for
  火責 **hize(me)** ordeal/torture by fire
5 叱責 **shisseki** reproach, reprimand
6 自責 **jiseki** self-reproach
  自責点 **jisekiten** earned run (in baseball)
7 言責 **genseki** responsibility for what one says
8 免責 **menseki** exemption from responsibility
  呵責 **kashaku** reproach, torment
9 重責 **jūseki** heavy responsibility
  面責 **menseki** reprove (someone) to his face
11 問責 **monseki** censure, reprimand
12 湯責 **yuze(me)** boiling-water torture
  無責任 **musekinin** irresponsibility
13 罪責 **zaiseki** liability for a crime
18 職責 **shokuseki** one's duties
20 譴責 **kenseki** reprimand, rebuke

———————— 3 ————————

6 自賠責 **jibaiseki** auto liability (insurance)
   (short for 自動車損害賠償責任保険)
12 無答責 **mutōseki** not liable

7b4.5 / 752

KA freight; goods, property

———————— 1 ————————

7 貨車 **kasha** freight car
8 貨物 **kamotsu** freight, cargo
  貨物車 **kamotsusha** freight car
  貨物船 **kamotsusen** freighter
  貨物駅 **kamotsueki** freight depot
9 貨客船 **kakyakusen, kakakusen** cargo-and-
    passenger ship
10 貨財 **kazai** wealth, riches
12 貨殖 **kashoku** money-making
15 貨幣 **kahei** money, currency, coin
  貨幣学 **kaheigaku** numismatics

———————— 2 ————————

4 円貨 **enka** yen currency
  日貨 **nikka** Japanese goods/currency
5 外貨 **gaika** foreign currency; imported goods
  外貨債 **gaikasai** foreign-currency bond
6 邦貨 **hōka** Japanese currency; yen
  百貨店 **hyakkaten** department store
  米貨 **beika** U.S. currency, the dollar
7 良貨 **ryōka** good money
8 法貨 **hōka** legal tender
  奇貨 **kika** a curiosity; an opportunity
  英貨 **Eika** British currency; British-made
    goods
  金貨 **kinka** gold coin

7

言 貝 車 跙 酉

→ 4

9 通貨　**tsūka**　currency
10 財貨　**zaika**　commodities, property
11 悪貨　**akka**　bad money
12 硬貨　**kōka**　coin; hard currency
13 滞貨　**taika**　freight congestion, accumulation of stock
14 銭貨　**senka**　coins
　　銀貨　**ginka**　silver coin
　　銅貨　**dōka**　copper coin
　　雑貨　**zakka**　miscellaneous goods, sundries, notions
　　雑貨商　**zakkashō**　general store
15 鋳貨　**chūka**　minting, coinage

——————— 3 ———————
5 白銅貨　**hakudōka**　a nickel (coin)
6 有蓋貨車　**yūgai kasha**　boxcar
12 無蓋貨車　**mugai kasha**　open freight car

貧→貧　**2o9.5**

貳→弐　**4n3.3**

貭→質　**7b8.7**

——————— 5 ———————

7b5.1 / 762

貯　CHO, takuwa(eru)　store, lay in stock, save

——————— 1 ———————
4 貯水　**chosui**　storage of water
　　貯水池　**chosuichi**　reservoir
　　貯水塔　**chosuitō**　water tower
　　貯水量　**chosuiryō**　pondage
8 貯金　**chokin**　savings, deposit
　　貯金通帳　**chokin tsūchō**　bankbook
　　貯金箱　**chokinbako**　savings box, (piggy) bank
9 貯炭　**chotan**　coal storage
　　貯炭所　**chotanjo**　coal yard, coaling station
13 貯蓄　**chochiku**　savings
　　貯蓄心　**chochikushin**　thriftiness
15 貯蔵　**chozō**　storage, preservation
　　貯蔵所　**chozōsho**　storage place
　　貯蔵品　**chozōhin**　stored goods, stock
　　貯蔵室　**chozōshitsu**　storeroom, stockroom

7b5.2

貼　CHŌ, TEN　stick on, affix; (counter for medicine packages)
　　ha(ru)　stick on, paste, affix

——————— 1 ———————
5 貼出　**ha(ri)da(su)**　put up (a notice)
　　貼付　**chōfu, tenpu, ha(ri)tsu(keru)**　stick, paste, affix
　　貼札　**ha(ri)fuda**　placard, poster, label
10 貼紙　**ha(ri)gami**　sticker, poster

——————— 2 ———————
4 切貼　**ki(ri)ba(ri)**　patching (a paper screen)

7b5.3

貽　I　give, bestow; leave behind

——————— 1 ———————
7 貽貝　**igai**　(type of hard-shelled mussel)

7b5.4 / 749

費　HI　expenses, cost
　　tsui(yasu)　spend
　　tsui(eru)　be wasted

——————— 1 ———————
5 費用　**hiyō**　expenses, cost
　　費目　**himoku**　expense item
9 費途　**hito**　expense item
10 費消　**hishō**　spending; embezzlement

——————— 2 ———————
3 工費　**kōhi**　cost of construction
4 冗費　**jōhi**　unnecessary expenses
5 出費　**shuppi**　expenses, disbursements
　　失費　**shippi**　expenses, expenditures
　　巨費　**kyohi**　great cost
6 会費　**kaihi**　membership fee, dues
　　自費　**jihi**　at one's own expense
　　自費出版　**jihi shuppan**　publishing at one's own expense, vanity press
7 乱費　**ranpi**　waste, extravagance
　　学費　**gakuhi**　school expenses
　　村費　**sonpi**　village expenses
　　社費　**shahi**　company expenses
　　私費　**shihi**　private expense, one's own expense
8 実費　**jippi**　actual expense; cost price
　　官費　**kanpi**　government expense
　　官費生　**kanpisei**　government-supported student
　　空費　**kūhi**　waste
　　国費　**kokuhi**　national expenditures, government spending
9 軍費　**gunpi**　military expenditures
　　食費　**shokuhi**　food expenses, board
10 浪費　**rōhi**　waste, squander
　　浪費癖　**rōhiheki**　spendthrift habits
　　消費　**shōhi**　consumption
　　消費力　**shōhiryoku**　consumer buying power
　　消費者　**shōhisha**　consumer

7

言
貝　5 ←
車
足
酉

消費物資 **shōhi busshi** consumer goods
消費高 **shōhidaka** (amount of) consumption
消費財 **shōhizai** consumer goods
消費税 **shōhizei** consumption/excise tax
徒費 **tohi** waste
党費 **tōhi** party expenses/dues
旅費 **ryohi** traveling expenses
11 経費 **keihi** expenses, cost
12 給費 **kyūhi** paying (someone's) expenses, a scholarship
給費生 **kyūhisei** student on scholarship
貸費 **taihi** (student) loan
貸費生 **taihisei** loan-scholarship student
13 戦費 **senpi** war expenditures
歳費 **saihi** annual expenditures
14 雑費 **zappi** miscellaneous expenses
16 燃費 **nenpi** fuel cost; fuel economy (km/liter)
18 濫費 **ranpi** waste, extravagance

———————— 3 ————————

2 人件費 **jinkenhi** personnel expenses
4 予備費 **yobihi** preliminary expenses; reserve/emergency fund
5 出版費 **shuppanhi** publishing costs
生活費 **seikatsuhi** living expenses
生計費 **seikeihi** living expenses
生産費 **seisanhi** production costs
6 交通費 **kōtsūhi** transportation expenses
交際費 **kōsaihi** entertainment expenses
光熱費 **kōnetsuhi** heating and electricity expenses
8 建築費 **kenchikuhi** construction costs
居住費 **kyojūhi** housing expenses
国防費 **kokubōhi** defense expenditures
9 軍事費 **gunjihi** military expenditures
造営費 **zōeihi** construction costs
通信費 **tsūshinhi** postage, communications expenses
宣伝費 **sendenhi** publicity/advertising expenses
10 遊興費 **yūkyōhi** amusement expenses
家計費 **kakeihi** household expenses/budget
教育費 **kyōikuhi** school/education expenses
11 運送費 **unsōhi** transport/shipping expenses
運動費 **undōhi** campaign expenses
運搬費 **unpanhi** transport charges, haulage
経常費 **keijōhi** operating costs
経営費 **keieihi** operating expenses
12 営業費 **eigyōhi** operating expenses
13 滞在費 **taizaihi** living expenses during one's stay
14 選挙費 **senkyohi** campaign expenses
15 諸雑費 **shozappi** miscellaneous expenses
16 操業費 **sōgyōhi** operating expenses
輸送費 **yusōhi** shipping costs
18 臨時費 **rinjihi** contingent expenses

7b5.5

貰

SEI, mora(u) get, obtain, receive; (with verb) have (someone do something), get (someone to do something)

———————— 1 ————————

0 お貰い **(o)mora(i)** beggar
2 貰子 **mora(i)go** adoption; adopted child
4 貰水 **mora(i)mizu** water from a neighbor
貰手 **mora(i)te** receiver, recipient
貰火 **mora(i)bi** catch fire (from a neighboring burning building)
8 貰泣 **mora(i)na(ki)** weeping in sympathy
貰物 **mora(i)mono** present, gift

———————— 2 ————————

8 物貰 **monomora(i)** beggar; sty (on the eyelid)

7b5.6

賁

HI decorate

7b5.7 / 1171

貴

KI valuable; noble; esteemed, your
tatto(i), tōto(i) valuable; noble, exalted
tatto(bu), tōto(bu) value, esteem, respect

———————— 1 ————————

2 貴人 **kijin** nobleman, dignitary
3 貴下 **kika** you
貴女 **kijo, anata** lady, you (feminine)
4 貴公 **kikō** you
貴公子 **kikōshi** young noble
貴方 **kihō, anata** you
5 貴兄 **kikei** you (masculine)
貴台 **kidai** you
貴札 **kisatsu** your letter
6 貴地 **kichi** your place, there
7 貴君 **kikun** you (masculine)
貴社 **kisha** your company
8 貴命 **kimei** your orders/instructions
貴所 **kisho** your place, you
貴金属 **kikinzoku** precious metals
9 貴重 **kichō** valuable, precious
貴重品 **kichōhin** valuables
貴神 **kishin** (gentle)man of rank
10 貴家 **kika** your home
貴書 **kisho** your letter
11 貴婦人 **kifujin** lady
貴族 **kizoku** the nobility
貴族的 **kizokuteki** aristocratic
貴族院 **Kizokuin** the House of Peers/Lords
13 貴僧 **kisō** you (referring to a priest)
貴殿 **kiden** you (masculine)
貴意 **kii** your wishes/request
貴酬 **kishū** reply (to a letter)

14 貴様 **kisama** you (deprecatory)
15 貴賓 **kihin** distinguished guest
貴賓室 **kihinshitsu** room reserved for VIP guests
貴賓席 **kihinseki** seats for the honored guests
貴賤 **kisen** high and low (social rank)
16 貴翰 **kikan** your letter
17 貴覧 **kiran** see, observe (honorific)
18 貴簡 **kikan** your letter
貴顕 **kiken** distinguished personage, dignitaries

───────── 2 ─────────

5 兄貴 **aniki** elder brother; one's senior
8 姉貴 **aneki** elder sister
9 珍貴 **chinki** rare, valuable
10 高貴 **kōki** noble, exalted; valuable
12 尊貴 **sonki** exalted person
富貴 **fūki, fukki** wealth and rank
13 楊貴妃 **Yōkihi** Yang Guifei (beautiful Chinese queen, 719–756)
15 権貴 **kenki** (person of) rank and influence
20 騰貴 **tōki** rise (in prices)

───────── 4 ─────────

8 物価騰貴 **bukka tōki** rise in prices

7b5.8 / 760

BŌ exchange

───────── 1 ─────────

8 貿易 **bōeki** trade, commerce
貿易会社 **bōeki-gaisha** trading firm
貿易風 **bōekifū** trade winds
貿易品 **bōekihin** articles of commerce
貿易商 **bōekishō** trader
貿易場 **bōekijō** foreign market
貿易業 **bōekigyō** the trading business

───────── 2 ─────────

4 片貿易 **kataboeki** one-way/unbalanced trade
11 密貿易 **mitsuboeki** smuggling

───────── 3 ─────────

9 保護貿易 **hogo bōeki** protectionistic trade
11 勘合貿易 **kangō bōeki** licensed trade

7b5.9 / 748

TAI, ka(su) rent out, lend

───────── 1 ─────────

0 貸ボート **ka(shi)bōto** boats for rent, rented boat
3 貸下 **ka(shi)sa(geru)** lend
4 貸元 **ka(shi)moto** financier; boss gambler
貸切 **ka(shi)ki(ri)** reservations, booking

貸切車 **ka(shi)ki(ri)sha** reserved car
貸手 **ka(shi)te** lender, lessor
貸方 **ka(shi)kata** creditor; credit side
5 貸出 **ka(shi)da(su)** lend/hire out
貸本 **ka(shi)hon** book for lending out
貸本屋 **ka(shi)hon'ya** lending library
貸付 **ka(shi)tsu(keru)** lend
貸付金 **kashitsukekin** a loan, advance
貸主 **ka(shi)nushi** lender; landlord
6 貸地 **ka(shi)chi** land/lot for rent
貸自動車 **ka(shi)-jidōsha** rental car
貸舟 **ka(shi)bune** boat for rent
7 貸売 **ka(shi)u(ri)** sale on credit
8 貸店 **ka(shi)mise** store for rent
貸金 **ka(shi)kin** loan
9 貸室 **ka(shi)shitsu** room for rent
10 貸倒 **ka(shi)dao(re)** bad debts
貸借 **taishaku, ka(shi)ka(ri)** lending and borrowing, debit and credit, loan
貸借対照表 **taishakutaishōhyō** balance sheet
貸部屋 **ka(shi)beya** room for rent
貸家 **ka(shi)ie, kashiya** house for rent
貸座敷 **ka(shi)zashiki** brothel
貸席 **ka(shi)seki** hall/rooms for rent; brothel
貸料 **ka(shi)ryō** rent; loan charges
貸馬車 **ka(shi)basha** carriage for hire
12 貸越 **ka(shi)ko(shi)** overdraft
貸費 **taihi** (student) loan
貸費生 **taihisei** loan-scholarship student
貸間 **kashima** room for rent
13 貸賃 **ka(shi)chin** rent, charge

───────── 2 ─────────

2 又貸 **mataga(shi)** lend what one has borrowed, sublet, sublease
4 内貸 **uchiga(shi)** advancing part of a salary
日貸 **higa(shi)** lending by the day
8 店貸 **tanaga(shi)** renting out a house
金貸 **kaneka(shi)** money lending/lender
9 前貸 **maega(shi)** advance payment
10 借貸 **ka(ri)ka(shi)** borrowing and lending, loan
11 転貸 **tentai** sublease
12 間貸 **maga(shi)** renting out a room
13 賃貸 **chintai, chinga(shi)** leasing, renting
賃貸人 **chintainin** lessor
賃貸借 **chintaishaku** leasing, renting

───────── 3 ─────────

10 高利貸 **kōriga(shi)** usury; usurer

7b5.10 / 756

GA congratulations, felicitations

───────── 1 ─────────

0 賀する **ga(suru)** celebrate, congratulate

5 賀正 **gashō** New Year's greetings
7 賀状 **gajō** greeting card
8 賀表 **gahyō** congratulatory card (to the emperor)
10 賀宴 **gaen** banquet
12 賀詞 **gashi** congratulations, greetings
13 賀意 **gai** congratulatory feeling

――――― 2 ―――――

5 加賀 **Kaga** (ancient kuni, Ishikawa-ken)
6 年賀 **nenga** New Year's greetings/visit
　年賀状 **nengajō** New Year's card
　伊賀 **Iga** (ancient kuni, Mie-ken)
7 佐賀 **Saga** (city, Saga-ken)
　佐賀県 **Saga-ken** (prefecture)
8 拝賀 **haiga** greetings, congratulations
　参賀 **sanga** congratulatory palace visit
9 祝賀 **shukuga** celebration; congratulations
　祝賀会 **shukugakai** a celebration
10 恭賀 **kyōga** respectful congratulations
　恭賀新年 **kyōga shinnen** Happy New Year
12 滋賀県 **Shiga-ken** (prefecture)
　朝賀 **chōga** retainers' New Year's greeting to the emperor
15 慶賀 **keiga** congratulation
17 謹賀新年 **kinga shinnen** Happy New Year

――――― 3 ―――――

15 横須賀 **Yokosuka** (city, Kanagawa-ken)

貳→弐 **4n3.3**

――――― 6 ―――――

賎→賤 **7b8.3**

7b6.1 / 1739

賄 **WAI, makana(u)** pay, cover, meet (expenses); provide (meals)

――――― 1 ―――――

13 賄賂 **wairo** bribe, bribery

――――― 2 ―――――

4 収賄 **shūwai** accepting bribes, graft
18 贈賄 **zōwai** bribery
　贈賄罪 **zōwaizai** (the crime of) bribery

――――― 3 ―――――

18 贈収賄 **zōshūwai** bribery

7b6.2

賂 **RO, mainai** bribe

――――― 2 ―――――

13 賄賂 **wairo** bribe, bribery

賍→贓 **7b15.1**

7b6.3 / 1807

賊 **ZOKU** rebel; robber

――――― 1 ―――――

2 賊子 **zokushi** rebel, traitor; rebellious child
6 賊名 **zokumei** (branded as a) rebel/traitor
7 賊臣 **zokushin** rebel, traitor
9 賊軍 **zokugun** rebel army, rebels
10 賊将 **zokushō** insurgent army leader
　賊徒 **zokuto** rebels, traitors
　賊害 **zokugai** harm, kill; destruction caused by bandits

――――― 2 ―――――

3 山賊 **sanzoku** mountain robber, bandit
4 木賊 **tokusa** shave grass, scouring rushes
6 兇賊 **kyōzoku** bandit, a rowdy
8 逆賊 **gyakuzoku** rebel, traitor, insurgent
　国賊 **kokuzoku** traitor, rebel
9 海賊 **kaizoku** pirate
　海賊版 **kaizokuban** pirate edition
10 匪賊 **hizoku** bandit, rebel, outlaw
　烏賊 **ika** squid, cuttlefish
　馬賊 **bazoku** mounted bandits
11 盗賊 **tōzoku** thief, robber, burglar
13 義賊 **gizoku** chivalrous robber

7b6.4

賈 **KO** merchant; buying and selling

7b6.5

賫 **SHI** treasure, assets; pay a fine

7b6.6 / 751

賃 **CHIN** rent, wages, fare, fee

――――― 1 ―――――

3 賃上 **chin'a(ge)** raise in wages
5 賃仕事 **chinshigoto** piecework
8 賃金 **chingin** wages, pay
10 賃借 **chinshaku, chinga(ri)** lease, rent, hire
　賃借人 **chinshakunin** lessee

賃借料 **chinshakuryō** rent
12 賃貸 **chintai, chinga(shi)** leasing, renting
賃貸人 **chintainin** lessor
賃貸借 **chintaishaku** leasing, renting
14 賃銭 **chinsen** wages, pay
賃銀 **chingin** wages, pay
15 賃餅 **chinmochi** rice cakes made to order

――――――― 2 ―――――――

3 工賃 **kōchin** wages, labor costs
4 木賃宿 **kichin'yado** cheap lodging house
7 低賃金 **teichingin** low wages
労賃 **rōchin** wages
車賃 **kurumachin** fare; cartage charge
8 使賃 **tsuka(i)chin** tip for a messenger, errand charge
送賃 **oku(ri)chin** shipping charges
泊賃 **to(mari)chin** hotel charges
店賃 **tanachin** house rent
10 借賃 **ka(ri)chin** the rent
家賃 **yachin** (house) rent
書賃 **ka(ki)chin** writing/copying fee
11 運賃 **unchin** fare; shipping/freight charges
宿賃 **yadochin** hotel charges
船賃 **funachin** boat fare; shipping charges
12 渡賃 **wata(shi)chin** ferry charge
無賃 **muchin** free of charge
無賃乗車 **muchin jōsha** free/stolen ride
雇賃 **yato(i)chin** wages
貸賃 **ka(shi)chin** rent, charge
14 駄賃 **dachin** reward, tip

――――――― 3 ―――――――

4 手間賃 **temachin** wages
7 汽車賃 **kishachin** train fare
車馬賃 **shabachin** fare, transportation expenses
9 乗車賃 **jōshachin** (train) fare
12 渡船賃 **tosenchin** ferry charge
13 電車賃 **denshachin** tramfare, trainfare

7b6.7 / 750

SHI resources, capital, funds

――――――― 1 ―――――――

0 資する **shi(suru)** contribute toward, help to
2 資力 **shiryoku** means, resources, funds
5 資本 **shihon** capital
資本主義 **shihon shugi** capitalism
資本金 **shihonkin** capital
資本家 **shihonka** capitalist, financier
資本財 **shihonzai** capital goods
7 資材 **shizai** materials, supplies
8 資性 **shisei** nature, disposition
資金 **shikin** funds

資金難 **shikinnan** financial difficulty
資金繰 **shikingu(ri)** raising funds, generating revenue
10 資格 **shikaku** qualifications, competence
資料 **shiryō** material, data
資財 **shizai** assets, property
11 資産 **shisan** assets, property
資産家 **shisanka** man of means
13 資源 **shigen** resources
15 資質 **shishitsu** nature, disposition

――――――― 2 ―――――――

4 天資 **tenshi** nature, natural talents
5 出資 **shusshi** investment, financing, contribution
出資金 **shusshikin** investment, capital
外資 **gaishi** foreign capital
巨資 **kyoshi** enormous amount of capital
6 合資 **gōshi** partnership
合資会社 **gōshi-gaisha** limited partnership
有資格者 **yūshikakusha** qualified person
米資 **beishi** American capital
7 投資 **tōshi** investment
学資 **gakushi** school expenses, educational fund/endowment
労資 **rōshi** labor(ers) and capital(ists)
8 英資 **eishi** brilliant qualities, fine character
Eishi British (investment) capital
物資 **busshi** goods, resources
放資 **hōshi** investment
9 軍資 **gunshi** war funds/materiel; campaign funds
軍資金 **gunshikin** war funds; campaign funds
10 遊資 **yūshi** idle capital/funds
家資 **kashi** family property/estate
12 減資 **genshi** reduction of capital
短資 **tanshi** short-term loan (short for 短資金)
無資力 **mushiryoku** without funds
無資本 **mushihon** without capital/funds
無資格 **mushikaku** unqualified
無資格者 **mushikakusha** unqualified/incompetent person
13 嫁資 **kashi** dowry
14 増資 **zōshi** capital increase
16 融資 **yūshi** financing, loan

――――――― 3 ―――――――

4 天然資源 **tennen shigen** natural resources
10 遊休資本 **yūkyū shihon** idle capital
11 運転資金 **unten shikin** working capital, operating funds
17 闇物資 **yamibusshi** black-market goods

――――――― 4 ―――――――

7 見返物資 **mikae(ri) busshi** collateral goods
10 消費物資 **shōhi busshi** consumer goods

————— 7 —————

7b7.1

賑 **SHIN, nigi(wau)** flourish, thrive, be bustling/lively
nigi(yaka) lively, bustling

——— 1 ———
3 賑々 **niginigi(shii)** thriving; merry, gay

——— 2 ———
10 殷賑 **inshin** prosperous, thriving

7b7.2

殞 **IN** fall; die

——— 1 ———
5 殞石 **inseki** meteorite

————— 8 —————

賭 → 賭 **7b9.1**

7b8.1 / 1829

賠 **BAI** indemnify

——— 1 ———
17 賠償 **baishō** reparation, indemnification
賠償金 **baishōkin** indemnities, reparations, damages

——— 2 ———
6 自賠責 **jibaiseki** auto liability (insurance) (short for 自動車損害賠償責任保険)

——— 3 ———
13 損害賠償 **songai baishō** restitution, indemnification, (pay) damages

7b8.2 / 1831

賜 **SHI, tamawa(ru), tama(u)** grant, bestow, confer

——— 1 ———
8 賜杯 **shihai** trophy (from the emperor)
賜物 **tamamono** gift
賜金 **shikin** monetary award
10 賜宴 **shien** court banquet
13 賜暇 **shika** leave of absence, furlough

——— 2 ———
3 下賜 **kashi** imperial grant/gift
10 恩賜 **onshi** gift from the emperor
15 賞賜 **shōshi** reward

7b8.3

賤 賎 **SEN** of low social rank
iya(shimeru) look down on, despise **iya(shii)** low, base, vulgar **shizu** lowly, humble

——— 1 ———
3 賤女 **shizu(no)me** woman of humble birth
5 賤民 **senmin** the lowly
7 賤男 **shizu(no)o** man of humble birth
10 賤家 **shizu(ga)ya** humble cottage, hovel
13 賤業 **sengyō** lowly/shameful occupation

——— 2 ———
3 下賤 **gesen** humble birth/origin
9 卑賤 **hisen** lowly position, obscurity
12 貴賤 **kisen** hight and low (social rank)
13 微賤 **bisen** low rank, humble station, obscurity

7b8.4 / 1808

賦 **FU** tribute; payment, installment; give, confer; prose poem

——— 1 ———
0 賦する **fu(suru)** allot, assign; compose, write
3 賦与 **fuyo** grant, give
5 賦存 **funson** existence, presence (of resources)
賦払 **fubara(i), fuhara(i)** payment by installments
7 賦役 **fueki** compulsory labor, corvée
賦形剤 **fukeizai** excipient, vehicle
12 賦税 **fuzei** taxation
15 賦課 **fuka** levy, assessment

——— 2 ———
4 天賦 **tenpu** natural, inborn
月賦 **geppu** monthly installments
6 年賦 **nenpu** annual installment
10 貢賦 **kōfu** tribute and taxes
12 割賦 **kappu, wa(p)pu** paying in installments

——— 4 ———
11 運否天賦 **unpu-tenpu** trusting to chance

7b8.5

贇 **RAI** gift

賢 → **7b9.2**

7b8.6 / 745

賛 賛 **SAN** praise; agreement; assistance

──────── 1 ────────

6 賛同 **sandō** approval, support
賛成 **sansei** agreement, approbation
賛成者 **sanseisha** approver, supporter
7 賛助 **sanjo** support, backing
賛否 **sanpi** approval or disapproval
9 賛美 **sanbi** praise, glorification
賛美歌 **sanbika** hymn
13 賛嘆 **santan** extol, admire
賛意 **san'i** approval
賛辞 **sanji** praise
14 賛歌 **sanka** paean, praise

──────── 2 ────────

4 不賛成 **fusansei** disapproval, disagreement
5 礼賛 **raisan** worship, adore, glorify
6 自賛 **jisan** self-praise
8 画賛 **gasan** legend written over a picture
協賛 **kyōsan** approve, support, assist
10 称賛 **shōsan** praise
12 絶賛 **zessan** praise highly
15 賞賛 **shōsan** praise, admire
熱賛 **nessan** enthusiastic/wholehearted approval
論賛 **ronsan** commentary on the individuals appearing in a biography
17 翼賛 **yokusan** support, approval

──────── 3 ────────

6 自画賛 **jigasan** praising one's own picture

7b8.7 / 176

質 贋   SHITSU quality, nature; inquire
         SHICHI, CHI hostage; pawn
         tada(su) ask, inquire, verify
         tachi nature, temperament

──────── 1 ────────

2 質入 **shichii(re)** pawning
5 質札 **shichifuda** pawn ticket
6 質朴 **shitsuboku** simple, unsophisticated
8 質券 **shichiken** pawn ticket
質実 **shitsujitsu** plain and simple
質実剛健 **shitsujitsu-gōken** rough-hewn and robust
質店 **shichiten** pawnshop
質的 **shitsuteki** qualitative
質物 **shichimono** pawned article
9 質草 **shichigusa** article for pawning
質屋 **shichiya** pawnshop
10 質流 **shichinaga(re)** unredeemed pawn
質素 **shisso** simple, plain, frugal
11 質商 **shichishō** pawnshop
質問 **shitsumon** question
質問者 **shitsumonsha** questioner
質問書 **shitsumonsho** written inquiry, questionnaire

12 質量 **shitsuryō** mass (in physics); quantity and quality
13 質業 **shichigyō** the pawn business
14 質疑 **shitsugi** question, inquiry
質疑応答 **shitsugi-ōtō** question-and-answer (session)
15 質舗 **shichiho** pawnshop
質権 **shichiken** pledge
16 質樸 **shitsuboku** simple, unsophisticated

──────── 2 ────────

2 入質 **nyūshichi** pawning
人質 **hitojichi** hostage
3 上質 **jōshitsu** fine quality
土質 **doshitsu** nature of the soil
4 木質 **mokushitsu** woody, ligneous
5 本質 **honshitsu** essence
本質的 **honshitsuteki** in substance, essential
6 気質 **katagi, kishitsu** disposition, temperament, spirit
肉質 **nikushitsu** flesh, pulp
同質 **dōshitsu** the same quality/nature, homogeneous
地質 **chishitsu** geology, geological features; nature of the soil
地質 **jishitsu** quality/texture (of cloth)
地質学 **chishitsugaku** geology
地質図 **chishitsuzu** geological map
7 良質 **ryōshitsu** good quality
体質 **taishitsu** physical constitution
対質 **taishitsu** confront (with a witness)
角質 **kakushitsu** horny substance, keratin
角質物 **kakushitsubutsu** horny/keratinous material
均質 **kinshitsu** homogeneous
材質 **zaishitsu** quality (of the material/ lumber)
言質 **genshitsu, genchi** pledge, promise
8 毒質 **dokushitsu** poisonous nature/ingredient
実質 **jisshitsu** substance, essence, quality, content
実質的 **jisshitsuteki** substantial, essential, material, real
物質 **busshitsu** matter, substance
物質的 **busshitsuteki** material, physical
9 変質 **henshitsu** deterioration, degeneration
変質者 **henshitsusha** a pervert/deviant
品質 **hinshitsu** quality
革質 **kakushitsu** leathery
炭質 **tanshitsu** coal quality
音質 **onshitsu** tone quality
10 流質 **ryūshichi** forfeited pawned article
脂質 **shishitsu** fats, lipids
骨質 **kosshitsu** bony tissue
特質 **tokushitsu** characteristic, trait
紙質 **shishitsu** quality of the paper
素質 **soshitsu** nature, makeup

7

言
貝 8←
車
足
酉

11 悪質 **akushitsu** evil, vicious, unscrupulous;
   of poor quality
   異質 **ishitsu** heterogeneous
   粘質 **nenshitsu** viscosity, stickiness
12 媒質 **baishitsu** medium (in physics)
   硬質 **kōshitsu** hard, rigid
   歯質 **shishitsu** dentin
   等質 **tōshitsu** homogeneous
13 罪質 **zaishitsu** nature of the crime/offense
   資質 **shishitsu** nature, disposition
   鉄質 **tesshitsu** ferrous
15 膠質 **kōshitsu** colloid, gelatinous, gluey
16 燃質 **nenshitsu** combustibility
   糖質 **tōshitsu** sugariness
19 麗質 **reishitsu** beauty, charms

——————————— 3 ———————————

6 多肉質 **tanikushitsu** fleshy, pulpy, succulent
   多血質 **taketsushitsu** sanguine, hot-blooded
   有孔質 **yūkōshitsu** porous
7 言葉質 **kotobajichi** pledge, promise
8 侍気質 **samurai katagi** samurai spirit
   昔気質 **mukashi-katagi** old-time spirit, old-
   fashioned
9 胆汁質 **tanjūshitsu** bilious/choleric (temperament)
   神経質 **shinkeishitsu** nervous, high-strung
10 原形質 **genkeishitsu** protoplasm
   娘気質 **musume katagi** the nature of a young
   woman
   脂肪質 **shibōshitsu** fats, lipids
   特異質 **tokuishitsu** idiosyncrasy
11 粘液質 **nen'ekishitsu** phlegmatic; mucous
   蛋白質 **tanpakushitsu** protein; albumen
12 植物質 **shokubutsushitsu** vegetable matter
   琺瑯質 **hōrōshitsu** (tooth) enamel
13 蒲柳質 **horyū (no) shitsu** delicate health
   腺病質 **senbyōshitsu** weak constitution
   鉱物質 **kōbutsushitsu** mineral matter
   電解質 **denkaishitsu** electrolyte
15 憂鬱質 **yūutsushitsu** prone to depression
16 澱粉質 **denpunshitsu** starchiness

——————————— 4 ———————————

5 可塑物質 **kaso busshitsu** plastics
7 抗生物質 **kōsei busshitsu** an antibiotic
11 商売気質 **shōbai katagi** mercenary spirit

——————————— 9 ———————————

7b9.1

賭 賭
TO, ka(keru) bet, wager,
stake, gamble
kake a bet, wager, gamble

——————————— 1 ———————————

0 賭する **to(suru)** bet, wager, stake, risk
   賭マージャン **kakemājan** mahjongg played
   for stakes

8 賭事 **kakegoto** betting, gambling
   賭金 **kakekin** stakes, bet
12 賭博 **tobaku** gambling
13 賭碁 **kakego** go played for stakes

7b9.2 / 1288

賢
KEN, kashiko(i) wise, intelligent
saka(shii) bright, clever, wise
saka(shira) pert, impertinent

——————————— 1 ———————————

2 賢人 **kenjin** wise man, sage, the wise
3 賢才 **kensai** man of ability
4 賢夫人 **kenpujin** wise wife
5 賢母 **kenbo** wise mother
   賢兄 **kenkei** (wise) elder brother/friend
   賢主 **kenshu** wise lord
7 賢弟 **kentei** (wise) younger son/friend
8 賢妻 **kensai** intelligent (house)wife
   賢明 **kenmei** wise, intelligent
   賢者 **kenja** wise man, the wise
   賢所 **Kashikodokoro** Palace Sanctuary
10 賢哲 **kentetsu** wise man, the wise
11 賢婦 **kenpu** wise woman
13 賢愚 **kengu** wise or foolish
14 賢察 **kensatsu** your discernment/understand-
   ing
15 賢慮 **kenryo** (your) wise consideration

——————————— 2 ———————————

2 七賢 **shichiken** the seven wise men (of
   ancient Greece)
3 大賢 **taiken** man of great wisdom, sage
   小賢 **kozaka(shii)** smart(-alecky), crafty,
   shrewd
4 仁賢 **Ninken** (emperor, 488–498)
6 先賢 **senken** ancient sage
9 後賢 **kōken** wise men of the future
11 悪賢 **warugashiko(i)** cunning, sly, crafty, wily
13 猿賢 **sarugashiko(i)** cunning
   聖賢 **seiken** sages, saints
14 遺賢 **iken** able men left out of office
15 諸賢 **shoken** (ladies and) gentlemen

——————————— 3 ———————————

7 良妻賢母 **ryōsai-kenbo** good wife and wise
   mother

賴 → 頼 9a7.1

——————————— 10 ———————————

7b10.1

TAN, REN, suka(su) coax, cajole,
humor

2

9 宥賺 **nada(me)suka(su)** soothe and humor, coax

7b10.2

賻

FU condolence gift

7b10.3 / 1011

購

KŌ, agana(u) buy, purchase

1

2 購入 **kōnyū** purchase
購入者 **kōnyūsha** purchaser, buyer
7 購求 **kōkyū** purchase
10 購書 **kōsho** purchasing/purchased books
12 購買 **kōbai** purchasing
購買力 **kōbairyoku** purchasing power
購買者 **kōbaisha** buyer
購買部 **kōbaibu** cooperative store
購買組合 **kōbai kumiai** a co-op
14 購読 **kōdoku** subscription
購読者 **kōdokusha** subscriber
購読料 **kōdokuryō** subscription price/fee

11

7b11.1

鵙

KEKI, mozu shrike

7b11.2 / 1364

贈 贈

ZŌ, SŌ, oku(ru) give (as a gift), present, bestow

1

3 贈与 **zōyo** gift, donation
贈与者 **zōyosha** donor
贈与物 **zōyobutsu** gift, present
4 贈収賄 **zōshūwai** bribery
5 贈本 **zōhon** gift book, complimentary copy
贈号 **zōgō** posthumous name
7 贈位 **zōi** confer a posthumous court rank
贈呈 **zōtei** presentation, gift
贈呈本 **zōteihon** presentation copy
贈呈式 **zōteishiki** presentation ceremony
贈呈者 **zōteisha** giver, donor
贈呈品 **zōteihin** present, gift
8 贈物 **oku(ri)mono** gift, present
12 贈答 **zōtō** exchange of gifts
贈答品 **zōtōhin** gift, present

---

13 贈賄 **zōwai** bribery
贈賄罪 **zōwaizai** (the crime of) bribery

2

8 受贈 **juzō** receive a gift
受贈者 **juzōsha** recipient (of a gift)
追贈 **tsuizō** posthumous conferment of court rank
10 恵贈 **keizō** receive a gift
11 寄贈 **kizō** donate, present
寄贈者 **kizōsha** donor, contributor
寄贈品 **kizōhin** gift, donation
14 遺贈 **izō** bequest, legacy

7b11.3

贄

SHI, nie an offering, gift

2

5 生贄 **i(ke)nie** sacrificial offering

7b11.4

贅

ZEI luxury, extravagance, redundance, waste; wen, wart; son-in-law

1

6 贅肉 **zeiniku** excess fat
7 贅沢 **zeitaku** luxury, extravagance
贅沢品 **zeitakuhin** luxury item
贅言 **zeigen** a redundancy, superfluous

2

9 疣贅 **yūzei** wart, condyloma

7b11.5

殯

HIN lying in state

1

10 殯宮 **hinkyū** temporary imperial mortuary

12

贈→贈 7b11.2

贊→賛 7b8.6

7b12.1

贇

IN beautiful

7b12.2 / 349

韻 韵　**IN** rhyme; elegant

——————— 1 ———————

4 韻文　**inbun** verse, poetry
5 韻字　**inji** rhyming words
8 韻事　**inji** artistic pursuits
9 韻律　**inritsu** rhythm, meter
10 韻致　**inchi** excellent taste, elegance
11 韻脚　**inkyaku** (metrical) foot
14 韻語　**ingo** rhyming words

——————— 2 ———————

6 気韻　**kiin** grace, elegance
7 余韻　**yoin** lingering tone, reverberation; aftertaste, suggestiveness
8 押韻　**ōin** rhyme
　押韻詩　**ōinshi** rhyming poem, verse
9 風韻　**fūin** grace, tastefulness
　神韻　**shin'in(-hyōbyō)** an undefinable artistic excellence
　神韻縹渺　**shin'in-hyōbyō** an undefinable artistic excellence
　音韻　**on'in** phoneme
　音韻学　**on'ingaku** phonology
　音韻論　**on'inron** phonemics, phonology
11 脚韻　**kyakuin** rhyme
12 無韻詩　**muinshi** blank verse, unrhymed poem
16 頭韻　**tōin** alliteration

7b12.3

牘　**TOKU** writing, letter

——————— 13 ———————

7b13.1

瞻　**SEN** have enough of; add to

7b13.2

罌　**Ō** vase

——————— 1 ———————

12 罌粟　**keshi** poppy

——————— 14 ———————

7b14.1

贐　**JIN, hanamuke** going-away present, parting gift

7b14.2

贔　**HII, HI** favor, patronage

——————— 1 ———————

10 贔屓　**hiiki** favor, partiality, pro-(Japanese)
　贔屓目　**hiikime** viewing favorably

——————— 2 ———————

7 身贔屓　**mibiiki** nepotism

——————— 3 ———————

8 依怙贔屓　**ekohiiki** favoritism, bias

——————— 15 ———————

7b15.1

贓 賍　**ZŌ** stolen goods; acceptance of a bribe

——————— 1 ———————

8 贓物　**zōbutsu** stolen goods
9 贓品　**zōhin, shōhin** stolen goods

7b15.2

贖　**SHOKU, agana(u)** atone for, expiate; redeem, ransom; buy

——————— 1 ———————

8 贖物　**agamono, agana(i)mono** an indemnification; scapegoat, substitute
9 贖宥　**shokuyū** (Catholic) indulgence
13 贖罪　**shokuzai** atonement, expiation, redemption

7b15.3

覿　**TEKI** see, meet

——————— 1 ———————

9 覿面　**tekimen** immediate, prompt

——————— 17 ———————

7b17.1

鬢　**BIN** side locks, sideburns

——————— 2 ———————

3 小鬢　**kobin** side lock (of hair)

——————— 20 ———————

7b20.1

黷　**TOKU** make/become dirty

——————— 1 ———————

18 黷職　**tokushoku** corruption, graft

7

言
貝
→ 12
車
趾
酉

車 7c

車	軋	軌	重	軒	軟	斬	転	軛	衷	軸	軼	軽
0.1	1.1	2.1	0a9.18	3.1	4.1	4.2	4.3	4.4	7c14.2	5.1	5.2	5.3

軫	軻	輌	輅	軽	較	軾	載	輔	輗	輕	皸	輝
5.4	5.5	7c8.1	6.1	6.2	6.3	6.4	6.5	7.1	7.2	7c5.3	7.3	7c7.3

輛	綴	輜	報	輪	輓	輦	輩	輝	輹	輳	輻	輯
8.1	8.2	8.3	7c7.2	8.4	8.5	8.6	8.7	8.8	9.1	9.2	9.3	9.4

輸	轄	轅	輾	轂	轌	轉	轆	轍	轎	轗	轜	轟
9.5	10.1	10.2	10.3	10.4	11.1	7c4.3	11.2	12.1	12.2	13.1	14.1	14.2

轢	轤	轜
15.1	16.1	16.2

0

7c0.1 / 133

車

SHA, kuruma vehicle, car, cart; wheel

1
---

2 車力 **shariki** cartman, dray driver
3 車大工 **kuruma daiku** cartwright
車上 **shajō** aboard (the train/vehicle)
車上荒 **shajōara(shi)** theft from a parked car
4 車内 **shanai** inside the car
車夫 **shafu** rickshaw puller
車中 **shachū** in the car/vehicle
車中談 **shachūdan** train interview
車井戸 **kuruma ido** well with a pulley and rope
車止 **kurumado(me)** Closed to Vehicles; railway buffer stop
車引 **kurumahi(ki)** rickshaw puller
5 車代 **kurumadai** fare; cartage charge
車外 **shagai** outside the car/vehicle
車台 **shadai** chassis
6 車両 **sharyō** vehicles, cars, rolling stock
車地 **shachi** capstan, windlass
7 車体 **shatai** body, chassis
8 車券 **shaken** bicycle-race betting ticket
9 車室 **shashitsu** (train) compartment
車屋 **kurumaya** rickshaw puller/station; cartwright
10 車庫 **shako** garage, carbarn
車座 **kurumaza** sitting in a circle
車馬 **shaba** horses and vehicles
車馬代 **shabadai** traveling expenses
車馬道 **shabadō** road for vehicles and horses
車馬賃 **shabachin** fare, transportation expenses
11 車道 **shadō** roadway
車窓 **shasō** car/train window

車寄 **kurumayo(se)** carriage porch, porte-cochère
12 車掌 **shashō** (train) conductor
車椅子 **kurumaisu** wheelchair
車検 **shaken** auto inspection (certificate)
車軸 **shajiku** axle
13 車賃 **kurumachin** fare; cartage charge
15 車輌 **sharyō** vehicles, cars, rolling stock
車輪 **sharin** wheel

2
---

3 大車輪 **daisharin** hectic activity; large wheel; giant swing (in gymnastics)
下車 **gesha** get off (a train/bus)
口車 **kuchiguruma** cajolery
4 水車 **suisha** water wheel, turbine
手車 **teguruma** handcart
火車 **hi (no) kuruma** fiery chariot of (Buddhist) hell; financial distress
牛車 **gyūsha, ushiguruma** oxcart
gissha (Heian-period) cow carriage
5 外車 **gaisha** foreign car
6 列車 **ressha** train
同車 **dōsha** take the same car, ride together
糸車 **itoguruma** spinning wheel
7 汽車 **kisha** train (drawn by a steam locomotive)
汽車弁当 **kisha bentō** railway lunch
汽車便 **kishabin** (sent) by rail
汽車賃 **kishachin** train fare
8 拍車 **hakusha** a spur
空車 **kūsha, karaguruma** empty car, (taxi) For Hire
肥車 **ko(yashi)guruma, koeguruma** nightsoil cart
肩車 **kataguruma** (give a child a ride) on one's shoulders
9 発車 **hassha** start, departure (of a train)
乗車 **jōsha** get on (a train)
乗車券 **jōshaken** (train) ticket

7

言
貝
車 0 ←
足
酉

乗車賃 **jōshachin** (train) fare
降車 **kōsha** get off (a train)
降車口 **kōshaguchi** gateway for arriving passengers, exit
前車 **zensha** the car ahead
風車 **fūsha** windmill
kazaguruma pinwheel; windmill
洗車 **sensha** car wash
洗車場 **senshajō** car wash
後車 **kōsha** rear car
客車 **kyakusha** passenger coach/train
枢車 **kyūsha** hearse
香車 **kyōsha** spear (a piece in the game shogi)
10 荷車 **niguruma** cart, wagon
砲車 **hōsha** gun carriage
紡車 **bōsha, tsumu(gi)guruma** spinning wheel
配車 **haisha** allocation/dispatching of cars
馬車 **basha** horse-drawn carriage
11 停車 **teisha** stopping a vehicle
停車場 **teishajō, teishaba** railway station; taxi stand
猫車 **nekoguruma** wheelbarrow
終車 **shūsha** the last bus/train for the day
貨車 **kasha** freight car
転車台 **tenshadai** turntable
12 着車 **chakusha** arrival (of a train)
検車 **kensha** vehicle inspection
歯車 **haguruma** gear, cogwheel
13 滑車 **kassha** pulley
愛車 **aisha** one's (cherished) car
戦車 **sensha** tank
戦車隊 **senshatai** tank corps
戦車戦 **senshasen** tank battle/warfare
新車 **shinsha** new car
電車 **densha** electric car, streetcar, train
電車通 **denshadō(ri)** street with a tramway
電車賃 **denshachin** tramfare, trainfare
14 稲車 **inaguruma** cart for loading harvested rice plants onto
15 横車押 **yokoguruma (o) o(su)** be perverse, stubbornly persist (like trying to push a cart at right angles to its wheels)
諸車通行止 **Shosha Tsūkōdo(me)** No Thoroughfare
調車 **shira(be)guruma** belt pulley
踏車 **fu(mi)guruma** treadmill
駐車 **chūsha** parking
駐車場 **chūshajō** parking lot
16 操車 **sōsha** operation (of trains)
操車係 **sōshagakari** train dispatcher
操車場 **sōshajō** switchyard
18 鎖車 **kusariguruma** sprocket wheel
21 轜車 **jisha** hearse

——————— 3 ———————

1 一等車 **ittōsha** first-class coach

一輪車 **ichirinsha** unicycle
2 人力車 **jinrikisha** rickshaw
3 三輪車 **sanrinsha** tricycle, three-wheeled vehicle
大八車 **daihachiguruma** large wagon
上列車 **nobo(ri) ressha** train going toward the capital, up train
下列車 **kuda(ri) ressha** train going away from the capital, down train
4 中古車 **chūkosha** used/secondhand car
辻馬車 **tsujibasha** cab, hansom
手押車 **teo(shi)guruma** pushcart, wheelbarrow
手動車 **shudōsha** handcar
5 平歯車 **hirahaguruma** spur gear/wheel
四輪車 **yonrinsha** four-wheeled vehicle
6 自動車 **jidōsha** motor vehicle, automobile
自転車 **jitensha** bicycle
7 冷房車 **reibōsha** air-conditioned car
冷凍車 **reitōsha** refrigerator car
赤電車 **akadensha** red-lamp car, last streetcar
花電車 **hanadensha** decorated streetcar, (parade) float
乳母車 **ubaguruma** baby carriage/buggy
8 夜汽車 **yogisha** night train
油槽車 **yusōsha** tank car
9 専用車 **sen'yōsha** personal car
乗用車 **jōyōsha** passenger car
急停車 **kyūteisha** sudden stop
指南車 **shinansha** (ancient Chinese) compass vehicle
故障車 **koshōsha** disabled car
食堂車 **shokudōsha** dining car
10 郵便車 **yūbinsha** mail car
高飛車 **takabisha** high-handed, domineering
高級車 **kōkyūsha** luxury car
荷馬車 **nibasha** dray, wagon, cart
11 動滑車 **dōkassha** movable pulley, running block
牽引車 **ken'insha** tractor
梯子車 **hashigosha** (firefighting) ladder truck
救急車 **kyūkyūsha** ambulance
終列車 **shūressha** last train
終電車 **shūdensha** the last train/streetcar for the day
貨物車 **kamotsusha** freight car
雪上車 **setsujōsha** snowmobile
12 揚水車 **yōsuisha** scoop wheel
喫煙車 **kitsuensha** smoking car
御所車 **goshoguruma** canopied ox-drawn carriage
無停車 **muteisha** nonstop
散水車 **sansuisha** street sprinkler truck
装甲車 **sōkōsha** armored car
貸切車 **ka(shi)ki(ri)sha** reserved car
貸馬車 **ka(shi)basha** carriage for hire

7

言
貝
車
酉

→ 0

13 幌馬車 **horobasha** covered wagon/carriage
寝台車 **shindaisha** sleeping car
14 駅馬車 **ekibasha** stagecoach
15 撒水車 **sansuisha, sassuisha** street sprinkler
緩行車 **kankōsha** local train
箱馬車 **hakobasha** closed carriage
霊柩車 **reikyūsha** hearse
16 機関車 **kikansha** locomotive
鋼鉄車 **kōtetsusha** steel (railroad) car
18 観覧車 **kanransha** Ferris wheel
鎖歯車 **kusari haguruma** sprocket wheel
20 護送車 **gosōsha** paddy wagon

--- 4 ---

6 有蓋貨車 **yūgai kasha** boxcar
各駅停車 **kakuekiteisha** local train
7 花自動車 **hana jidōsha** flower-bedecked automobile
9 途中下車 **tochū gesha** stopover, layover
12 無蓋貨車 **mugai kasha** open freight car
無賃乗車 **muchin jōsha** free/stolen ride
貸自動車 **ka(shi)-jidōsha** rental car
軽自動車 **keijidōsha** light car
13 路面電車 **romen densha** streetcar
鉄道馬車 **tetsudō basha** horse-drawn streetcar
14 増発列車 **zōhatsu ressha** extra train

--- 1 ---

7c1.1

軋 **ATSU, kishi(ru), kishime(ku), kishi(mu)** squeak, grate, squeal, creak, screech

--- 1 ---

22 軋轢 **atsureki** friction, discord

--- 2 ---

12 歯軋 **hagishi(ri)** grinding one's teeth

--- 2 ---

7c2.1 / 1787

軌 **KI** wheel track, rut; railway, track; orbit

--- 1 ---

7 軌条 **kijō** rails
11 軌道 **kidō** (railroad) track; orbit
12 軌間 **kikan** (railroad-track) gauge
13 軌跡 **kiseki** locus (in geometry)
15 軌範 **kihan** model, example
軌範的 **kihanteki** model, exemplary

--- 2 ---

4 不軌 **fuki** lawlessness, rebellion
5 広軌 **kōki** broad-gauge (railway)
9 狭軌 **kyōki** narrow gauge

11 常軌 **jōki** usual/proper course
12 無軌道 **mukidō** trackless; erratic, aberrant

重→ **0a9.18**

--- 3 ---

7c3.1 / 1187

軒 **KEN** (counter for buildings)
noki eaves

--- 1 ---

3 軒丈 **nokitake** height of the eaves
軒下 **nokishita** under the eaves
6 軒先 **nokisaki** edge of the eaves; front of the house
軒灯 **kentō** eaves lantern, door light
7 軒別 **kenbetsu** house-to-house
8 軒並 **nokina(mi), nokinara(bi)** row of houses
軒店 **nokimise** small shop under another building's eaves
9 軒昂 **kenkō** rising high; in high spirits
10 軒高 **kenkō** rising high; in high spirits
13 軒数 **kensū** number of houses
軒輊 **kenchi** disparity
14 軒樋 **nokidoi** gutter along the eaves
軒端 **nokibata, nokiba** (edge of) the eaves

--- 2 ---

1 一軒 **ikken** a house
一軒家 **ikken'ya** isolated/freestanding/detached house
2 二軒建 **nikenda(te)** duplex, semidetached (house)

--- 4 ---

7c4.1 / 1788

軟 **NAN, yawa(rakai), yawa(raka)** soft

--- 1 ---

3 軟口蓋 **nankōgai** the soft palate
4 軟毛 **nanmō** soft hairs, down
軟化 **nanka** softening
軟文学 **nanbungaku** light literature
軟水 **nansui** soft water
6 軟式飛行船 **nanshiki hikōsen** dirigible, balloon
軟式庭球 **nanshiki teikyū** softball tennis
軟式野球 **nanshiki yakyū** softball
7 軟体動物 **nantai dōbutsu** mollusk
8 軟泥 **nandei** mud, sludge, ooze
軟性下疳 **nansei gekan** soft chancre
9 軟便 **nanben** soft/loose stools

7

言 貝 車 跙 酉 4←

軟風 **nanpū** gentle breeze
軟派 **nanpa** moderates; a masher
10 軟弱 **nanjaku** weak(-kneed)
軟骨 **nankotsu** cartilage
11 軟球 **nankyū** softball
12 軟着陸 **nanchakuriku** soft landing
13 軟禁 **nankin** house arrest
軟鉄 **nantetsu** soft iron
14 軟膏 **nankō** ointment, salve
15 軟論 **nanron** a weak argument
軟調 **nanchō** weakness, softness, bearish tone (cf. 堅調)

——————— 2 ———————

9 柔軟 **jūnan** soft, supple, flexible
柔軟性 **jūnansei** pliability, suppleness
10 陸軟風 **rikunanpū** land(-to-sea) breeze
骨軟化症 **kotsunankashō** osteomalacia
11 脳軟化症 **nōnankashō** encephalomalacia
12 硬軟 **kōnan** (relative) hardness

7c4.2

斬

ZAN, ki(ru) cut/kill (with a sword)

——————— 1 ———————

6 斬合 **ki(ri)a(i)** crossing swords, fighting with swords
斬奸 **zankan** slaying the wicked
斬奸状 **zankanjō** statement of reasons for slaying (a traitor)
9 斬首 **zanshu** decapitation
ki(ri)kubi a severed head
13 斬新 **zanshin** novel, original, latest
斬罪 **zanzai** execution by sword, beheading

——————— 2 ———————

4 辻斬 **tsujigi(ri)** murder of a passer-by (to try out a new sword)
13 試斬 **tame(shi)gi(ri)** trying out a new sword
15 撫斬 **na(de)gi(ri)** clean sweep, wholesale slaughter

7c4.3 / 433

転　轉

TEN turn; change
koro(bu) tumble, fall down; roll over **koro(garu/geru)** roll, tumble, fall, lie down/about
koro(gasu/basu) roll (a ball), knock down, trip (someone) **utata** more and more, all the more; somehow; indeed

——————— 1 ———————

0 転じる **ten(jiru)** revolve; turn, shift, change; move, be transferred
2 転入 **tennyū** move in, be transferred
3 転々 **tenten** roll; keep changing (jobs), change hands often

4 転化 **tenka** change, be transformed
転化糖 **tenkatō** inverted sugar
転込 **koro(gari)ko(mu), koro(ge)ko(mu)** roll in, come one's way
5 転出 **tenshutsu** move out, be transferred
転写 **tensha** transcribe, transfer, copy
転用 **ten'yō** divert, convert
6 転任 **tennin** change of assignments/personnel
転地 **tenchi** change of air/scene
転地療養 **tenchi ryōyō** getting away for a change of climate for one's health
転向 **tenkō** turn/switch to, convert
転向点 **tenkōten** turning point
転宅 **tentaku** move (to a new address)
転回 **tenkai** rotate, revolve
転成 **tensei** be transformed, change into
7 転身 **tenshin** changing (jobs)
転位 **ten'i** transposition, displacement
転住 **tenjū** move, migrate to
転学 **tengaku** change schools
転売 **tenbai** resale
転車台 **tenshadai** turntable
8 転送 **tensō** transmit, forward (mail)
転注 **tenchū** using a kanji in an extended meaning
転居 **tenkyo** moving, change of address
転炉 **tenro** revolving furnace, converter
9 転変 **tenpen** change, vicissitudes
転音 **ten'on** euphonic change, elision
転科 **tenka** change one's course/major
10 転倒 **tentō** fall down violently, turn upside down, reverse
転借 **tenshaku** sublease
転帰 **tenki** crisis (of an illness)
転進 **tenshin** shift one's position
転校 **tenkō** changing schools
転記 **tenki** post, transfer (a bookkeeping entry)
11 転婆 **(o)tenba** tomboy
転宿 **tenshuku** change lodgings
転移 **ten'i** change, spread, metastasis
転訛 **tenka** corruption (of a word)
転転 **tenten** roll; keep changing (jobs), change hands often
12 転勤 **tenkin** be transferred (to another office)
転換 **tenkan** conversion, changeover; diversion
転換期 **tenkanki** transition period, turning point
転換器 **tenkanki** commutator, switch
転落 **tenraku, koro(ge)o(chiru)** fall, slip down
転属 **tenzoku** be transferred
転期 **tenki** crisis (of an illness)
転補 **tenpo** transfer (job assignments)
転貸 **tentai** sublease
13 転業 **tengyō** change occupations

転義 **tengi** figurative/extended meaning
転嫁 **tenka** shift (the blame/responsibility)
転寝 **koro(bi)ne, utatane** nap, doze
　　　gorone sleep with one's clothes on
転戦 **tensen** take part in various battles
転意 **ten'i** figurative/extended meaning
転置 **tenchi** transposition
転載 **tensai** reproduction, reprinting
転路器 **tenroki** railroad switch
15 転調 **tenchō** modulation, changing keys
16 転機 **tenki** turning point
18 転覆 **tenpuku** overturn, overthrow
転職 **tenshoku** change of post/occupation
19 転轍 **tentetsu** switching, shunting
転轍手 **tentetsushu** switchman, pointsman
転轍機 **tentetsuki** railroad switch
20 転籍 **tenseki** transfer of domicile/registration

─────────── 2 ───────────

1 一転 **itten** a turn, complete change
2 七転八倒 **shichiten-battō, shitten-battō** writhing in agony
七転八起 **nanakoro(bi)ya(oki)** ups and downs of life, Fall seven times and get up eight.
4 反転 **hanten** turn/roll over, reverse directions, invert
円転 **enten(taru)** orotund, smoothly rolling
円転滑脱 **enten-katsudatsu** versatile, all-around, tactful
5 好転 **kōten** a turn for the better
玉転 **tamakoro(gashi)** bowling, bowls
6 気転 **kiten** wits, quick-wittedness
回転 **kaiten** revolve, rotate, swivel
回転木馬 **kaiten mokuba** carrousel
回転儀 **kaitengi** gyroscope
自転 **jiten** rotation
自転車 **jitensha** bicycle
8 退転 **taiten** distraction, backsliding
逆転 **gyakuten** reversal
空転 **kūten** (engine) idling, getting nowhere
9 変転 **henten** changes, vicissitudes
急転 **kyūten** sudden change
急転直下 **kyūten-chokka** sudden change, sudden turn (toward a solution)
急転換 **kyūtenkan** sudden change, rapid switchover
栄転 **eiten** be promoted
10 流転 **ruten** constant change; wandering, vagrancy; reincarnation
11 陽転 **yōten** positive (reaction to a medical test)
動転 **dōten** be surprised/stunned; transition
運転 **unten** operate, run (a machine), drive (a car)
運転士 **untenshi** (ship's) mate, officer
運転手 **untenshu** driver, chauffeur

運転台 **untendai** motorman's seat, driver's cab
運転資金 **unten shikin** working capital, operating funds
捻転 **nenten** twisting, torsion
旋転 **senten** turning, rotation, revolution
移転 **iten** move, change of address
転転 **tenten** roll; keep changing (jobs), change hands often
12 御転婆 **otenba** tomboy
13 寝転 **nekoro(bu)** lie down, throw oneself down
暗転 **anten** scenery change while the stage is unlit
禁転載 **kintensai** Reproduction Prohibited, Copyright
15 横転 **ōten** lateral turn; barrel roll
輪転 **rinten** rotate, revolve
輪転機 **rintenki** rotary press
16 機転 **kiten** quick wit
17 輾転反側 **tenten-hansoku** tossing about (in bed)

─────────── 3 ───────────

1 一回転 **ikkaiten, ichikaiten** one revolution/rotation
3 小機転 **kogiten** quick-witted
4 不退転 **futaiten** determination, firm resolve
6 気分転換 **kibun tenkan** a (refreshing) change, diversion
有為転変 **ui-tenpen** vicissitudes of life
10 起承転結 **ki-shō-ten-ketsu** introduction, development, turn, and conclusion (rules for composing a Chinese poem)
13 腸捻転 **chōnenten** twist in the intestines, volvulus
試運転 **shiunten** trial run

─────────── 4 ───────────

4 心機一転 **shinki-itten** change of attitude

7c4.4

軶

YAKU, kubiki yoke

車　→　轟　7c14.2

─────────── 5 ───────────

7c5.1 / 988

軸

JIKU axis; axle; shaft; (picture) scroll

─────────── 1 ───────────

4 軸木 **jikugi** scroll rod; matchstick; splint

7

言
貝
車　5 ←
足
酉

8 軸受 **jikuu(ke)** bearing
軸物 **jikumono** scroll (picture)
12 軸装 **jikusō** mounting (a scroll)

──────── 2 ────────

4 天軸 **tenjiku** celestial axis
中軸 **chūjiku** axis, pivot, central figure, key man
5 玉軸受 **tamajikuu(ke)** ball bearing
主軸 **shujiku** main shaft/axis
6 同軸 **dōjiku** coaxial
地軸 **chijiku** the earth's axis
7 花軸 **kajiku** flower stalk
車軸 **shajiku** axle
8 長軸 **chōjiku** major axis
枢軸 **sūjiku** pivot, axis, center
枢軸国 **sūjikukoku** the Axis powers
9 巻軸 **kanjiku, ma(ki)jiku** scroll
11 動軸 **dōjiku** live spindle, drive shaft
掛軸 **ka(ke)jiku** hanging scroll
12 短軸 **tanjiku** minor axis
15 横軸 **yokojiku** horizontal shaft; x-axis
16 機軸 **kijiku** axis, axle; plan, contrivance
縦軸 **tatejiku** spindle

──────── 3 ────────

7 対称軸 **taishōjiku** axis of symmetry
13 新機軸 **shinkijiku** new departure; novel idea

7c5.2

軼

ITSU pass by; surpass
TETSU rut

──────── 1 ────────

8 軼事 **itsuji** unknown fact

7c5.3 / 547

軽 輕

KEI, karu(i), karo(yaka) light **karo(njiru)** make light of, slight

──────── 1 ────────

3 軽工業 **keikōgyō** light industry
軽々 **karugaru(shii)** frivolous, rash, thoughtless **karugaru (to)** with ease
軽口 **karuguchi, karukuchi** witty remark; talkative
4 軽文学 **keibungaku** light literature
軽水 **keisui** light water (reactor)
軽少 **keishō** trifling, little
5 軽犯罪 **keihanzai** minor offense
軽石 **karuishi** pumice stone
軽目 **karume** light weight
6 軽気球 **keikikyū** (hot-air/helium) balloon
軽合金 **keigōkin** light alloy
軽自動車 **keijidōsha** light car
軽舟 **keishū** fast ligh boat, skiff

7 軽妙 **keimyō** light and easy, lambent
軽労働 **keirōdō** light work
軽快 **keikai** light, nimble, jaunty, lilting
8 軽佻 **keichō** frivolous, flippant
軽佻浮薄 **keichō-fuhaku** frivolous, flippant
軽侮 **keibu** contempt, disdain
軽油 **keiyu** light oil, gasoline
軽易 **keii** easy, light, simple
軽金属 **keikinzoku** light metals
9 軽重 **keichō, keijū** relative weight, importance
軽便 **keiben** convenient, handy, simple
軽便鉄道 **keiben tetsudō** narrow-gauge railroad
軽浮 **keifu** frivolous, fickle
軽度 **keido** to a slight degree
軽音楽 **keiongaku** light music
軽食 **keishoku** light meal
10 軽挙 **keikyo** rash act, imprudence
軽挙妄動 **keikyo-mōdō** act rashly
軽症 **keishō** a mild illness
11 軽率 **keisotsu** rash, hasty
軽捷 **keishō** agile, nimble
軽視 **keishi** belittle, neglect, scorn
12 軽減 **keigen** reduce, lighten, relieve
軽量 **keiryō** lightweight
軽焼 **karuya(ki)** wafer, cracker
軽装 **keisō** light dress/equipment
軽軽 **karugaru(shii)** frivolous, rash, thoughtless **karugaru (to)** with ease
13 軽業 **karuwaza** acrobatics
軽業師 **karuwazashi** acrobat, tumbler
軽傷 **keishō** minor injury
軽微 **keibi** slight, insignificant
軽罪 **keizai** minor offense
14 軽演劇 **keiengeki** light comedy
軽蔑 **keibetsu** contempt, scorn, disdain
15 軽輩 **keihai** underling, small fry
16 軽薄 **keihaku** insincere, frivolous, fickle
軽薄短小 **keihaku-tanshō** small and light, compact (cf. 重厚長大)
軽機 **keiki** light machine gun
軽機関銃 **keikikanjū** light machine gun
18 軽騎兵 **keikihei** light cavalry(man)
20 軽躁 **keisō** light-headed, thoughtless, flighty

──────── 2 ────────

3 口軽 **kuchigaru** glib, (too) talkative
4 手軽 **tegaru** easy, readily, simple, informal, without ado
心軽 **kokorogaru(i)** rash, giddy, light
5 尻軽 **shirigaru** wanton, loose
6 気軽 **kigaru** lightheartedly, readily, feel free to
7 身軽 **migaru** light, agile, nimble
足軽 **ashigaru** lowest-ranking samurai, foot soldier
9 津軽海峡 **Tsugaru-kaikyō** (strait between Honshū and Hokkaidō)

12 減軽 **genkei** reduction, mitigation
　軽軽 **karugaru(shii)** frivolous, rash,
　　　thoughtless　**karugaru (to)** with ease
13 剽軽 **hyōkin** funny, droll
　剽軽者 **hyōkinmono** jokester, wag

7c5.4

SHIN be sad

――――――― 1 ―――――――

8 軫念 **shinnen** (emperor's) anxiety

7c5.5

KA rough going, difficulties

――――――― 2 ―――――――

20 轗軻不遇 **kanka-fugū** ill fortune and lack of
　public recognition, obscurity

――――――― 6 ―――――――

輌→輛 **7c8.1**

7c6.1

RO, kuruma carriage

7c6.2

軽

CHI lower in front than in back

――――――― 2 ―――――――

10 軒輊 **kenchi** disparity

7c6.3 / 1453

較

KAKU, KŌ, kura(beru) compare

――――――― 1 ―――――――

5 較正 **kōsei** calibration

――――――― 2 ―――――――

5 比較 **hikaku** compare; comparative (litera-
　　　ture)
　比較史 **hikakushi** comparative history
　比較的 **hikakuteki** relative(ly),
　　　comparative(ly)
　比較級 **hikakukyū** the comparative degree
　　　(in grammar)

7c6.4

SHOKU front railing on a carriage (to
hold on to while bowing)

7c6.5 / 1124

載

SAI, no(ru) be recorded, appear (in print)
no(seru) place on top of; load (luggage);
publish, run (an ad)

――――――― 1 ―――――――

16 載録 **sairoku** record, list

――――――― 2 ―――――――

3 千載 **senzai** a thousand years
　千載一遇 **senzai-ichigū** a rare experience,
　　　chance of a lifetime
6 休載 **kyūsai** not be published, not carry
8 所載 **shosai** printed, published
9 連載 **rensai** serialization
10 記載 **kisai** record, report, note
11 混載 **konsai** mixed loading/cargo
　掲載 **keisai** publish, print, carry/run (an ad)
　舶載 **hakusai** transport by ship
　訳載 **yakusai** translate and print (in a
　　　magazine)
　転載 **tensai** reproduction, reprinting
12 満載 **mansai** full load
　搭載 **tōsai** load; embark; mounting (of
　　　electronic components)
　登載 **tōsai** register, record, enter
14 摘載 **tekisai** summarize, give an excerpt
16 積載 **sekisai** lading, loading, carrying
　積載量 **sekisairyō** carrying capacity, load
21 艦載 **kansai** carried aboard a warship
　艦載機 **kansaiki** carrier-based plane

――――――― 3 ―――――――

13 禁転載 **kintensai** Reproduction Prohibited,
　Copyright

――――――― 7 ―――――――

7c7.1

輔

HO help

――――――― 1 ―――――――

7 輔佐 **hosa** assistance; assistant, adviser
12 輔弼 **hohitsu** advise, counsel
14 輔導 **hodō** guidance

7c7.2

CHŌ promptly; easily;
in other words, that is

7

言
貝
車　7←
⻊
酉

輕→軽 **7c5.3**

7c7.3

皸 皵 **KUN, hibi, akagire** rough skin, chapping

皵→皸 **7c7.3**

――――――― 8 ―――――――

7c8.1

輌 輌 **RYŌ** (counter for railroad cars, etc.)

――――――― 2 ―――――――

7 車輌 **sharyō** vehicles, cars, rolling stock

7c8.2

輟 **TETSU** stop; mend

7c8.3

輜 **SHI** wagon, dray; canopied cart

――――――― 1 ―――――――

9 輜重 **shichō** military supplies, logistics

輙→輒 **7c7.2**

7c8.4 / 1164

輪 **RIN** wheel, circle, revolve; (counter for flowers)
wa circle, ring, hoop, loop, wheel

――――――― 1 ―――――――

0 輪ゴム **wagomu** rubber band
4 輪切 **wagi(ri)** round slices
　輪止 **wado(me)** wheel block; linchpin
6 輪伐 **rinbatsu** lumbering area by area
　輪回 **wamawa(shi)** hoop rolling
7 輪作 **rinsaku** crop rotation
　輪状 **rinjō** circular, ring-shaped
　輪抜 **wanu(ke)** jumping through a hoop
　輪投 **wana(ge)** quoits, ringtoss
　輪形 **rinkei, wagata** circle, ring shape
8 輪廻 **rinne** transmigration of souls

9 輪乗 **wano(ri)** riding in a circle
　輪郭 **rinkaku** outline, contours
　輪姦 **rinkan** gang rape
10 輪差 **wasa** loop
11 輪唱 **rinshō** round, canon (in music)
　輪転 **rinten** rotate, revolve
　輪転機 **rintenki** rotary press
12 輪廓 **rinkaku** outline, contours
　輪番 **rinban** taking turns, in rotation
　輪番制 **rinbansei** rotation system
13 輪禍 **rinka** traffic accident
15 輪舞 **rinbu** round dance
　輪蔵 **rinzō** prayer wheel
17 輪講 **rinkō** take turns reading and explaining (a book)

――――――― 2 ―――――――

1 一輪 **ichirin** a flower; a wheel
　一輪車 **ichirinsha** unicycle
　一輪挿 **ichirinza(shi)** a vase for one flower
2 二輪 **nirin** two wheels/flowers
　七輪 **shichirin** earthen charcoal brazier (for cooking)
　九輪 **kurin** nine-ring pagoda spire
3 三輪車 **sanrinsha** tricycle, three-wheeled vehicle
　大輪 **tairin** large wheel; large flower
　口輪 **kuchiwa** muzzle
4 内輪 **uchiwa** family circle, the inside; moderate, conservative (estimate)
　内輪揉 **uchiwamo(me)** internal dissension, family trouble
　五輪大会 **Gorin taikai** Olympic games
　五輪聖火 **Gorin seika** Olympic torch
　五輪旗 **Gorinki** Olympic flag
　片輪 **katawa** deformed, maimed, crippled
　月輪 **tsuki (no) wa** halo around the moon
　　getsurin the moon
　日輪 **nichirin** the sun
5 外輪 **gairin** outer wheel; hubcap
　外輪山 **gairinzan** the outer crater, somma
　外輪船 **gairinsen** paddlewheel steamer
　四輪車 **yonrinsha** four-wheeled vehicle
6 両輪 **ryōrin** two wheels
　年輪 **nenrin** annular (tree) ring
　光輪 **kōrin** halo
7 花輪 **hanawa** wreath, garland
　車輪 **sharin** wheel
8 金輪 **kanawa** metal hoop/band
　金輪際 **konrinzai** never, by no means
9 首輪 **kubiwa** necklace; collar
　前輪 **zenrin, maewa** front wheel
　浮輪 **u(ki)wa** buoyant ring, a float
　指輪 **yubiwa** (finger) ring
　後輪 **kōrin, atowa** rear wheel
　面輪 **omowa** features, looks
11 動輪 **dōrin** driving wheel

埴輪 **haniwa** (4th-7th century clay figurines buried with the dead)
12 渦輪 **uzuwa** whorl, swirl
腕輪 **udewa** bracelet
14 鼻輪 **hanawa** (bull's) nose ring
銀輪 **ginrin** bicycle
15 線輪 **senrin** (electrical) coil
駐輪場 **chūrinjō** bicycle parking lot
16 頸輪 **kubiwa** necklace; collar
18 覆輪 **fukurin** ornamental border/fringe
20 競輪 **keirin** bicycle race/racing

——————— 3 ———————

3 大車輪 **daisharin** hectic activity; large wheel; giant swing (in gymnastics)
8 知恵輪 **chie (no) wa** puzzle ring
13 滑走輪 **kassōrin** landing gear

7c8.5

鞔 BAN pull

——————— 1 ———————

6 鞔近 **bankin** recent, modern

7c8.6

輦 REN palanquin, litter

——————— 1 ———————

5 輦台 **rendai** litter for carrying a traveler across a river
17 輦轂 **renkoku** emperor's carriage
輦轂下 **renkoku (no) moto** the imperial capital

7c8.7 / 1037

輩 HAI fellow, colleague, companion
yakara fellows, gang; family, kin

——————— 1 ———————

5 輩出 **haishutsu** appear one after another

——————— 2 ———————

5 末輩 **mappai** underling; rank and file
6 年輩 **nenpai** age; elderly age
老輩 **rōhai** the aged, old people
同輩 **dōhai** one's equal, comrade, colleague
先輩 **senpai** senior, superior, elder, older graduate
7 我輩 **wagahai** I
吾輩 **wagahai** I, me
8 若輩 **jakuhai** young fellow/people; novice
朋輩 **hōbai** comrade, friend, fellow, mate
9 俗輩 **zokuhai** the vulgar throng, the crowd
後輩 **kōhai** one's junior, younger generation

10 弱輩 **jakuhai** young/inexperienced person
徒輩 **tohai** group, set, companions
党輩 **tōhai** companions, associates
12 傍輩 **hōbai** colleagues under the same teacher or lord, companions
軽輩 **keihai** underling, small fry
14 雑輩 **zappai** rank and file, small fry
16 儕輩 **saihai** colleagues, comrades

——————— 3 ———————

6 同年輩 **dōnenpai** persons of the same age

7c8.8 / 1653

輝 KI, kagaya(ku) shine, gleam, sparkle, be brilliant

——————— 1 ———————

5 輝石 **kiseki** pyroxene, augite
9 輝度 **kido** (degree of) brightness

——————— 2 ———————

6 光輝 **kōki** brightness, splendor
hika(ri)kagaya(ku) shine, sparkle

——————— 9 ———————

7c9.1

輹 FUKU, tokoshibari connection between axle and carriage

7c9.2

輳 SŌ gather, come together

——————— 2 ———————

16 輻輳 **fukusō** influx, rush, congestion

7c9.3

輻 FUKU, ya spoke

——————— 1 ———————

10 輻射 **fukusha** radiate
12 輻湊 **fukusō** influx, rush, congestion
16 輻輳 **fukusō** influx, rush, congestion

7c9.4

輯 SHŪ collect, gather; soften, relent

——————— 1 ———————

16 輯録 **shūroku** record, compile

——————— 2 ———————

15 編輯 **henshū** editing, compilation

7

言 貝 車 足 酉 9←

7c9.5 / 546

輸 輸
YU send, transport

──────── 1 ────────

2 輸入 **yunyū** import
輸入品 **yunyūhin** imports
輸入港 **yunyūkō** port of entry
輸入税 **yunyūzei** import duties/tariff
5 輸出 **yushutsu** export
輸出入 **yushutsunyū** export and import
輸出入品 **yushutsunyūhin** exports and
imports
輸出品 **yushutsuhin** exports
輸出港 **yushutsukō** exporting port
輸出税 **yushutsuzei** export duties/tax
輸出業 **yushutsugyō** export business
6 輸血 **yuketsu** blood transfusion
7 輸卵管 **yurankan** oviduct, Fallopian tubes
輸尿管 **yunyōkan** the ureter
8 輸卒 **yusotsu** transport soldier
輸送 **yusō** transport
輸送船 **yusōsen** transport ship
輸送量 **yusōryō** (volume of freight) traffic
輸送費 **yusōhi** shipping costs
輸送機 **yusōki** transport plane
11 輸液 **yueki** transfusion
14 輸精管 **yuseikan** spermaduct
20 輸贏 **shuei, yuei** victory or defeat

──────── 2 ────────

6 再輸入 **saiyunyū** reimportation
再輸出 **saiyushutsu** re-exportation
8 直輸入 **chokuyunyū, jikiyunyū** direct import
直輸出 **chokuyushutsu, jikiyushutsu** direct
export
逆輸入 **gyakuyunyū** reimportation
逆輸出 **gyakuyushutsu** re-exportation
空輸 **kūyu** air transport
金輸出 **kin yushutsu** export of gold
11 運輸 **un'yu** transport(ation)
運輸省 **Un'yushō** Ministry of Transport
密輸 **mitsuyu** smuggling; contraband
密輸入 **mitsuyunyū** smuggling
密輸出 **mitsuyushutsu** smuggle out/abroad
密輸団 **mitsuyudan** smuggling ring
密輸品 **mitsuyuhin** contraband
密輸船 **mitsuyusen** smuggling vessel
13 禁輸 **kin'yu** embargo on export/import
禁輸品 **kin'yuhin** contraband

──────── 3 ────────

9 軍事輸送 **gunji yusō** military transport

──────── 5 ────────

6 全日本空輸 **Zen Nippon Kūyu** All Nippon
Airways

──────── 10 ────────

7c10.1 / 1186

轄
KATSU control, administration;
a wedge

──────── 2 ────────

4 分轄 **bunkatsu** separate jurisdiction
8 直轄 **chokkatsu** direct control/jurisdiction
所轄 **shokatsu** jurisdiction
12 統轄 **tōkatsu** control (and jurisdiction)
統轄者 **tōkatsusha** the one in charge
14 総轄 **sōkatsu** general control/supervision
管轄 **kankatsu** jurisdiction
管轄違 **kankatsuchiga(i)** lack of jurisdiction

7c10.2

轅
EN, nagae shaft, thill

7c10.3

輾
TEN roll; squeak
kishi(ru) squeak, creak

──────── 1 ────────

11 輾転反側 **tenten-hansoku** tossing about (in
bed)

7c10.4

轂
KOKU, koshiki hub

──────── 2 ────────

15 輦轂 **renkoku** emperor's carriage
輦轂下 **renkoku (no) moto** the imperial
capital

──────── 11 ────────

7c11.1

轌
sori sleigh, sled

轉→転 7c4.3

7c11.2

轆
ROKU pulley

轣 **rokuro** winch, windlass; pulley; potter's
wheel; lathe
23 轆轤首 **rokurokubi** long-necked monster

──────── 2 ────────
23 轣轆 **rekiroku** creaking

──────── 12 ────────

7c12.1

轍
TETSU, wadachi rut, wheel track

──────── 1 ────────
15 轍踏 **tetsu (o) fu(mu)** repeat (another's) past
mistakes
──────── 2 ────────
9 途轍 **totetsu(mo nai)** inordinate, absurd
11 転轍 **tentetsu** switching, shunting
転轍手 **tentetsushu** switchman, pointsman
転轍機 **tentetsuki** railroad switch

7c12.2

轎
KYŌ, kago palanquin, litter

──────── 13 ────────

7c13.1

轗
KAN difficulties

──────── 1 ────────
12 轗軻不遇 **kanka-fugū** ill fortune and lack of
public recognition, obscurity

──────── 14 ────────

7c14.1

轜
JI hearse

──────── 1 ────────
7 轜車 **jisha** hearse

7c14.2

轟 裏
GŌ, todoro(ku) roar, thunder,
reverberate; throb; become
well-known

──────── 1 ────────
3 轟々 **gōgō (to)** thunderously, with a rumble
7 轟沈 **gōchin** sink instantly
9 轟音 **gōon** deafening roar/boom
12 轟然 **gōzen (to)** with a roar, deafeningly

──────── 15 ────────

7c15.1

轢
REKI run over; creak, grate against
hi(ku) run over (a pedestrian)

──────── 1 ────────
6 轢死 **rekishi** be run over and killed
8 轢逃 **hi(ki)ni(ge)** hit-and-run
10 轢倒 **hi(ki)tao(su)** knock down (someone
with a car)
轢殺 **rekisatsu, hi(ki)koro(su)** run over and
kill
11 轢断 **rekidan** (a train) running over and
severing (a body)

──────── 2 ────────
8 軋轢 **atsureki** friction, discord

──────── 16 ────────

7c16.1

轤
RO pulley, windlass

──────── 2 ────────
18 轆轤 **rokuro** winch, windlass; pulley; potter's
wheel; lathe
轆轤首 **rokurokubi** long-necked monster

7c16.2

轣
REKI creaking sound

──────── 1 ────────
18 轣轆 **rekiroku** creaking

──────── **7d** ────────

足	趾	趺	跂	距	跚	跌	跛	跋	跑	跏	距	踐
0.1	4.1	4.2	4.3	5.1	5.2	5.3	5.4	5.5	5.6	5.7	5.8	6.1
跟	跳	跣	路	跨	跡	跪	跫	踈	踉	踊	踉	踂
6.2	6.3	6.4	6.5	6.6	6.7	6.8	6.9	0a11.4	7.1	7.2	7.3	7.4
踝	踘	踏	踐	踪	踠	踞	踵	踴	蹂	蹄	蹻	蹐
8.1	8.2	8.3	7d6.1	8.4	8.5	8.6	9.1	7d7.2	9.2	9.3	9.4	10.1

蹈	蹊	蹌	蹉	蹤	躄	蹟	蹣	蹠	躄	蹼	蹴	蹯
7d8.3	10.2	10.3	10.4	11.1	11.2	11.3	11.4	11.5	11.6	12.1	12.2	12.3

蹲	蹶	躅	躁	躄	躑	躍	躊	躋	躓	躪	齪	躙
12.4	12.5	13.1	13.2	13.3	14.1	14.2	14.3	14.4	15.1	15.2	15.3	16.1

躇	躪
18.1	7d16.1

——————— 0 ———————

7d0.1 / 58

足

SOKU foot, leg, (counter for pairs of footwear); suffice; add **ashi** foot
ta(riru), ta(ru) be enough, suffice
ta(su) add up, add (to)
ta(shi) supplement; help

——————— 1 ———————

0 1足 **issoku** one pair (of shoes/socks)
　　hitoashi a step
2 足入婚 **ashii(re)kon** tentative marriage
3 足下 **ashimoto** gait, pace; at one's feet; (watch your) step **sokka** at one's feet
4 足止 **ashido(me)** keep indoors; induce to stay
　足手繊 **ashitemato(i), ashidemato(i)** hindrance, encumbrance
5 足代 **ashidai** transportation expenses, carfare
　足付 **ashitsu(ki)** gait; having legs
　足立 **Adachi** (surname)
6 足任 **ashimaka(se)** go where one fancies, with no set destination; walk till one's legs tire
　足回 **ashimawa(ri)** chassis
　足早 **ashibaya** quick, swift-footed
7 足形 **ashigata** footprint
　足芸 **ashigei** foot tricks
　足労 **sokurō** trouble of going somewhere
　足利 **Ashikaga** (era, 1392–1573), the Muromachi period; (city, Tochigi-ken)
8 足長 **ashinaga(-ojisan)** Daddy Longlegs
　足並 **ashina(mi)** pace, step
　足拍子 **ashibyōshi** beating time with one's foot
　足拵 **ashigoshira(e)** footgear
　足固 **ashigata(me)** walking practice
　足取 **ashido(ri)** one's gait/step; traces, track; trend (of prices)
9 足首 **ashikubi** ankle
　足前 **ta(shi)mae** supplement; help
　足速 **ashibaya** quick, swift-footed
　足型 **ashigata** shoe last
　足枷 **ashikase** fetters, shackles
　足音 **ashioto** sound of footsteps
10 足部 **sokubu** the foot
　足捌 **ashisaba(ki)** footwork
　足弱 **ashiyowa** slow of foot, weak-legged

11 足掛 **ashiga(kari)** foothold
　　ashika(ke) foothold, pedal, step; counting the first and last fractional (years of a time span) as a whole
　足袋 **tabi** Japanese socks, tabi
　足袋屋 **tabiya** tabi seller/shop
12 足湯 **ashiyu** footbath
　足場 **ashiba** scaffold; foothold; convenience of location
　足痛 **sokutsū** foot pain
　足軽 **ashigaru** lowest-ranking samurai, foot soldier
13 足業 **ashiwaza** footwork; foot tricks
　足溜 **ashida(mari)** stand, foothold; stopping place; center of activity
　足搔 **aga(ku)** paw (the ground/air), wriggle, struggle
　足腰 **ashikoshi** legs and loins
　足継 **ashitsu(gi)** footstool
　足跡 **ashiato** footprint
　足馴 **ashina(rashi)** walking practice
14 足摺 **ashizu(ri)** stamping/scraping one's feet
　足算 **ta(shi)zan** addition (in math)
　足駄 **ashida** high clogs
15 足踏 **ashibu(mi)** step, stamp; treadle; mark time, be at a standstill
16 足頸 **ashikubi** ankle
18 足癖 **ashikuse** one's way of walking
19 足蹴 **ashige** kicking

——————— 2 ———————

1 一足 **issoku** a pair (of shoes) **hitoashi** a step
　一足飛 **issokuto(bi)** at one bound
2 二足 **nisoku** two legs/feet, biped; two pairs (of shoes)
　二足三文 **nisoku-sanmon** a dime a dozen, dirt cheap
　二足踏 **ni (no) ashi (o) fu(mu)** hesitate, think twice
　人足 **hitoashi** pedestrian traffic
　　ninsoku coolie, laborer
3 大足 **ōashi** large feet
　下足 **gesoku** footwear
　下足料 **gesokuryō** footwear-checking charge
　土足 **dosoku** shoes, footwear; feet with shoes on
　土足厳禁 **dosoku genkin** Remove Shoes

小足 **koashi** mincing steps
4 不足 **fusoku** shortage, lack
片足 **kataashi** one leg/foot
手足 **teashi** hands and feet
月足 **tsukita(razu)** premature birth
5 出足 **deashi** start
付足 **tsu(ke)ta(su)** add on, append
用足 **yō (o) ta(su)** do one's business; go to the toilet
右足 **migiashi, usoku** right foot/leg
四足獣 **shisokujū** quadruped
6 多足 **tasoku** many-legged
両足 **ryōashi, ryōsoku** both feet/legs
尤足 **jusoku** sufficiency
舌足 **shitata(razu)** lisping, tongue-tied
早足 **hayaashi** quick pace, fast walking
百足 **mukade** centipede
自足 **jisoku** self-sufficiency
舟足 **funaashi** draft; speed
7 抜足 **nu(ki)ashi (de)** stealthily
抜足差足 **nu(ki)ashi-sa(shi)ashi (de)** stealthily
乱足 **mida(re)ashi** out of step
売足 **u(re)ashi** selling, a sale
忍足 **shino(bi)ashi** stealthy steps
言足 **i(i)ta(su)** add, say further
8 長足 **chōsoku** rapid/giant strides
事足 **kotota(riru), kotota(ru)** suffice
並足 **namiashi** walking pace, slow step
逃足 **ni(ge)ashi** flight; preparation for flight
泥足 **doroashi** muddy feet
定足数 **teisokusū** quorum
物足 **monota(rinai)** unsatisfying, something missing
具足 **gusoku** completeness; armor
具足師 **gusokushi** armorer
取足 **to(ru ni) ta(ranai)** beneath notice, insignificant
9 発足 **hossoku, hassoku** start, inauguration
急足 **iso(gi)ashi** brisk pace, hurried steps
首足 **shusoku** head and feet
前足 **maeashi** forefoot, front leg
風足 **kazaashi** wind speed
浮足 **u(ki)ashi** heels-off-the-ground stance, poised to flee
浮足立 **u(ki)ashida(tsu)** be ready to run away, waver
洗足 **sensoku** washing the feet
後足 **atoashi** hind leg/foot
客足 **kyakuashi** customers, clientele
食足 **ku(i)ta(rinai)** have not eaten enough; be unsatisfied with
10 高足 **kōsoku** best student, leading disciple
高足駄 **takaashida** high clogs/geta
高足蟹 **takaashigani** giant spider crab
差足 **sa(shi)ashi** stealthy steps
逸足 **issoku** swift horse; prodigy

徒足 **mudaashi** a fruitless errand/trip
荷足 **niashi** ballast
荷足船 **nita(ri)bune** barge, lighter
挙足取 **ageashi (o) to(ru)** find fault, carp at
書足 **ka(ki)ta(su)** add (a postscript)
素足 **suashi** bare feet, barefooted
馬足 **uma (no) ashi** poor actor (who plays the legs of a stage horse)
11 探足 **sagu(ri)ashi** groping one's way along
猫足 **nekoashi** carved table-leg
悪足搔 **waruaga(ki)** useless struggling/resistance
盗足 **nusu(mi)ashi** walking stealthily
船足 **funaashi** draft; speed
蛇足 **dasoku** superfluous (as legs on a snake)
12 遠足 **ensoku** excursion, outing, picnic, hike
満足 **manzoku** satisfaction
     mi(chi)ta(riru) be contented
揚足取 **a(ge)ashi (o) to(ru)** find fault, carp at
短足 **tansoku** short legs
補足 **hosoku** supply, replenish, supplement
補足語 **hosokugo** a complement (in grammar)
跑足 **dakuashi** pace, amble
13 義足 **gisoku** artificial leg
禁足 **kinsoku** confinement
裸足 **hadashi** bare feet, barefooted
継足 **tsu(gi)ta(su)** add to, extend
跣足 **hadashi** barefoot, bare feet
飽足 **a(ki)ta(ranai)** be unsatisfying/unsatisfied
14 摺足 **su(ri)ashi** shuffling/sliding one's feet
駆足 **ka(ke)ashi** running, galloping
15 潮足 **shioashi** speed of the tide
17 駿足 **shunsoku** swift horse; person of exceptional talent
18 襟足 **eriashi** hairline above the nape
20 鰐足 **waniashi** frog-footed, pigeon-toed, bowlegged, knock-kneed
22 纏足 **tensoku** bind one's feet
26 驥足 **kisoku** (give full play to) one's talents

───── 3 ─────

3 千鳥足 **chidori-ashi** tottering steps
4 不満足 **fumanzoku** dissatisfaction, displeasure, discontent
手不足 **tebusoku** shorthanded, understaffed
手取足取 **teto(ri)-ashito(ri)** by the hands and feet, bodily, by main force
6 再発足 **saihossoku** start again
地下足袋 **jika tabi** split-toed heavy-cloth work shoes
7 役不足 **yakubusoku** dissatisfaction with one's role
9 扁平足 **henpeisoku** flat feet
11 偏平足 **henpeisoku** flat feet
過不足 **kafusoku** excess or deficiency
12 無駄足 **mudaashi** make a fruitless trip/visit

7

言
貝
車
足 0←
酉

13 寝不足 **nebusoku** lack of sleep
新発足 **shinhossoku** a fresh start
16 頭寒足熱 **zukan-sokunetsu** keeping the head cool and the feet warm

——————— 4 ———————

6 自給自足 **jikyū-jisoku** self-sufficiency
7 抜足差足 **nu(ki)ashi-sa(shi)ashi (de)** stealthily
11 運動不足 **undō-busoku** lack of exercise
14 練習不足 **renshū-busoku** out/lack of training

——————— 6 ———————

1 一挙手一投足 **ikkyoshu-ittōsoku** a slight effort, the least trouble

——————— 4 ———————

7d4.1

趾

SHI foot; footprint

7d4.2

跌

FU foot; calyx; sitting lotus-position/Indian-style

——————— 3 ———————

12 結跏趺座 **kekkafuza** sitting in lotus position/posture

7d4.3

跂

KI, tsumada(tsu) stand on tiptoes

距→ **7d5.8**

——————— 5 ———————

7d5.1

跖

SEKI sole of the foot

7d5.2

跚

SAN stagger, stumble

——————— 2 ———————

18 蹣跚 **mansan** reeling, staggering

7d5.3

跌

TETSU stumble; be excessive

——————— 2 ———————

17 蹉跌 **satetsu** stumbling; failure, setback

7d5.4

跛

HA, HI, bikko lameness, limp
chinba lameness, limp; unmatched pair (of shoes)

——————— 1 ———————

6 跛行 **hakō** limp
跛行景気 **hakō keiki** spotty boom/prosperity

——————— 2 ———————

4 片跛 **katachinba** mismatched (pair of socks); a limp

7d5.5

跋

BATSU, HATSU epilog, postscript; tread; be prevalent

——————— 1 ———————

11 跋渉 **basshō** traverse, rove, hike
跋扈 **bakko** prevalence, rampancy, domination

7d5.6

跑

HŌ, aga(ku) paw the ground, kick
daku trotting

——————— 1 ———————

7 跑足 **dakuashi** pace, amble

7d5.7

跏

KA sitting lotus-position/Indian-style

——————— 2 ———————

12 結跏趺座 **kekkafuza** sitting in lotus position/posture

7d5.8 / 1294

距

KYO distance; spur (in botany)

——————— 1 ———————

10 距骨 **kyokotsu** the anklebone
18 距離 **kyori** distance
距離計 **kyorikei** range finder

——————— 2 ———————

4 中距離 **chūkyori** medium-range, middle-distance
6 近距離 **kinkyori** short distance/range
8 長距離 **chōkyori** long-distance, long-range
10 射距離 **shakyori** range (of a gun/missile)

7

言 貝 車 足 酉

→ 4

12 遠距離 **enkyori** long distance, long-range
測距儀 **sokkyogi** range finder
短距離 **tankyori** short distance, short-range
等距離 **tōkyori** equidistant

——————— 3 ———————

7 走行距離 **sōkō kyori** distance covered (in a given time)
10 航続距離 **kōzoku kyori** (plane's) range
12 着弾距離 **chakudan kyori** range (of a gun)
弾着距離 **danchaku kyori** range (of a gun)

——————— 6 ———————

7d6.1 / 1568

践 踐

SEN step (up to); realize, put into practice

——————— 2 ———————

8 実践 **jissen** in practice
実践的 **jissenteki** practical

7d6.2

跟

KON heel; follow

7d6.3 / 1563

跳

CHŌ, ha(neru), to(bu) leap, spring up, jump, bounce

——————— 1 ———————

3 跳上 **ha(ne)a(garu), to(bi)a(garu)** jump up
跳下 **to(bi)o(ri)** jumping off
5 跳出 **ha(ne)da(su), ha(ne)de(ru), to(bi)de(ru)** spring out
6 跳返 **ha(ne)kae(su)** bounce back, repel
跳回 **ha(ne)mawa(ru), to(bi)mawa(ru), odo(ri)mawa(ru)** jump about, cavort, gambol
8 跳板 **ha(ne)ita, to(bi)ita** springboard
10 跳起 **ha(ne)o(kiru)** jump up, spring to one's feet
11 跳梁 **chōryō** be rampant, dominate
12 跳開橋 **chōkaikyō** drawbridge
13 跳跳 **to(bi)ha(neru)** jump up and down, frisk about
16 跳橋 **ha(ne)bashi** drawbridge
19 跳蹴 **to(bi)ke(ri)** dropkick
21 跳躍 **ha(ne)odo(ru)** prance/frisk about
chōyaku spring, jump, leap
跳躍板 **chōyakuban** springboard

——————— 2 ———————

9 飛跳 **to(bi)hane(ru)** jump up and down, hop
10 馬跳 **umato(bi)** leapfrog

12 幅跳 **habato(bi)** long jump
蛙跳 **kaeruto(bi), kawazuto(bi)** leapfrog
13 跳跳 **to(bi)ha(neru)** jump up and down, frisk about

——————— 3 ———————

3 三段跳 **sandanto(bi)** hop, step, and jump
5 立幅跳 **ta(chi)habato(bi)** standing long jump
7 走高跳 **hashi(ri)takato(bi)** running high jump
走幅跳 **hashi(ri)habato(bi)** running broad jump
12 棒高跳 **bōtakato(bi)** pole vault

7d6.4

跣

SEN, hadashi barefoot

——————— 1 ———————

7 跣足 **hadashi** barefoot, bare feet

7d6.5 / 151

路

RO, -ji, michi road, path, way, street

——————— 1 ———————

3 路上 **rojō** on the road
4 路辺 **rohen** roadside
5 路用 **royō** traveling expenses
6 路次 **roji** on the road/way
路地 **roji** alley, lane, path
7 路床 **roshō** roadbed
9 路面 **romen** road surface
路面電車 **romen densha** streetcar
12 路傍 **robō** roadside, wayside
路程 **rotei** distance, mileage
14 路銀 **rogin** traveling expenses
15 路標 **rohyō** road sign
路盤 **roban** roadbed
路線 **rosen** route, line
16 路頭 **rotō** roadside, wayside

——————— 2 ———————

1 一路 **ichiro** one road; straight
3 川路 **kawaji** course of a river
大路 **ōji** highway, main thoroughfare
小路 **kōji** path, lane, narrow street
山路 **yamaji** mountain road/trail
5 末路 **matsuro** last days, end
正路 **seiro** life's path; escape route
6 曲路 **ma(gari)michi** roundabout road; winding road
行路 **kōro** path, road, course
行路病者 **kōro byōsha** person fallen ill on the road
光路 **kōro** optical path
当路 **tōro** the authorities

7

言 貝 車 足 酉

6 ←

回路 **kairo** (electrical) circuit
血路 **ketsuro** a way out, an escape
7 走路 **sōro** (race) track, course
岐路 **kiro** fork in the road, crossroads
8 迷路 **meiro** maze, labyrinth
退路 **tairo** path of retreat
逃路 **ni(ge)michi** way of escape, loophole
波路 **namiji** sea route/voyage; the sea
径路 **keiro** course, route, process
往路 **ōro** outward journey
空路 **kūro** air route; by air/plane
9 通路 **tsūro** aisle, passageway, path
    kayo(i)ji path, route
活路 **katsuro** means of escape, way out
海路 **kairo, umiji** ocean route, sealane
要路 **yōro** main road/artery; important post, responsible position
10 陸路 **rikuro** (over)land route
険路 **kenro** steep path
帰路 **kiro** the way home/back, return route
恋路 **koiji** love's pathway, romance
進路 **shinro** course, way, route
浦路 **uraji** coastal road
姫路 **Himeji** (city, Hyōgo-ken)
家路 **ieji** one's way home
旅路 **tabiji** journey
航路 **kōro** (sea) route, course
航路標識 **kōro hyōshiki** navigation marker/ beacon
針路 **shinro** course (of a ship)
11 野路 **noji** path across a field
道路 **dōro** road, street, highway
遍路 **henro** pilgrim; pilgrimage
淡路 **Awaji** (ancient kuni, Hyōgo-ken)
淡路島 **Awajishima** (island, Hyōgo-ken)
理路 **riro** reasoning, argument
理路整然 **riro-seizen** well-argued, cogent, logical
悪路 **akuro** bad/dirt road
経路 **keiro** course, route
船路 **senro, funaji** course, sea route
販路 **hanro** market, outlet
転路器 **tenroki** railroad switch
釧路 **Kushiro** (city, Hokkaidō)
12 隘路 **airo** defile, narrow path; bottleneck, impasse
遠路 **enro, tōmichi** long distance/journey, roundabout way
街路 **gairo** street
街路樹 **gairoju** trees along a street
開路 **kairo** open circuit
順路 **junro** the regular route; itinerary
13 夢路 **yumeji** dreamland
置路 **o(ki)michi** raised road
鉄路 **tetsuro** railroad
電路 **denro** electric circuit

14 語路 **goro** the sound, euphony
語路合 **goroa(wase)** play on words, pun
駅路 **ekiro** post road
15 潮路 **shioji** tideway, channel; the sea
線路 **senro** (railroad) track
17 闇路 **yamiji** dark road
18 難路 **nanro** rough/difficult road

————————— 3 —————————

2 丁字路 **teijiro** T-junction of roads/streets
十字路 **jūjiro** crossroads, intersection
八十路 **yasoji** eighty years old
3 三十路 **misoji** age 30
三叉路 **sansaro** Y-junction of roads
4 五十路 **isoji** 50 years; age 50
5 用水路 **yōsuiro** irrigation channel
広小路 **hirokōji** wide/main street
8 並木路 **namiki michi** tree-lined street
放水路 **hōsuiro** drainage canal/channel
10 航空路 **kōkūro** air route
11 排水路 **haisuiro** culvert, sewer system
袋小路 **fukurokōji** blind alley, cul-de-sac
12 短水路 **tansuiro** short course, 25–50 m pool length
13 滑走路 **kassōro** runway

————————— 4 —————————

3 大圏航路 **taiken kōro** great-circle route
12 集積回路 **shūseki kairo** integrated circuit

————————— 5 —————————

6 光集積回路 **hikari shūseki kairo** optical integrated circuit

7d6.6

跨
KO, mata(garu) sit/stand astride, straddle; span
mata(gu) straddle, stride across, step over

————————— 1 —————————

15 跨線橋 **kosenkyō** bridge over railroad tracks

7d6.7 / 1569

跡
SEKI, ato mark, traces, vestiges, remains, ruins

————————— 1 —————————

4 跡切 **togi(reru)** break off, stop, be interrupted
跡切跡切 **togi(re)-togi(re)** intermittent, off-and-on
跡片付 **atokatazu(ke)** straightening up (afterwards)
5 跡目 **atome** successor (as head of family)
跡目相続 **atome sōzoku** heirship
6 跡式 **atoshiki** head of family
7 跡形 **atokata** traces, evidence

8 跡始末 **atoshimatsu** winding-up, settlement, straightening up (afterwards)
跡取 **atoto(ri)** successor, heir
13 跡継 **atotsu(gi)** successor, heir
15 跡敷 **atoshiki** head of family

————— 2 —————

2 人跡 **jinseki** human traces/footsteps
人跡未到 **jinseki-mitō** unexplored
人跡未踏 **jinseki-mitō** unexplored
4 爪跡 **tsumeato** scratch; pinch mark
手跡 **shuseki** handwriting (specimen)
5 失跡 **shisseki** disappear, be missing
史跡 **shiseki** historical landmark
古跡 **koseki, furuato** historic spot, ruins
犯跡 **hanseki** evidences of a crime
旧跡 **kyūseki** historic ruins
6 名跡 **myōseki, meiseki** family name
行跡 **gyōseki** behavior, conduct
7 形跡 **keiseki** traces, signs, evidence
足跡 **ashiato** footprint
8 事跡 **jiseki** evidence, trace, vestige
追跡 **tsuiseki** pursue, track, stalk
追跡者 **tsuisekisha** pursuer
奇跡 **kiseki** miracle
実跡 **jisseki** actual traces, evidence
門跡 **monzeki** (temple headed by a) priest-prince; Honganji Temple
9 城跡 **shiroato** castle ruins/site
荒跡 **a(re)ato** ruins
臭跡 **shūseki** scent, trail
軌跡 **kiseki** locus (in geometry)
10 真跡 **shinseki** one's genuine handwriting
家跡 **ieato** remains of a house; family name
航跡 **kōseki** wake (of a ship/plane)
11 痕跡 **konseki** traces, vestiges, evidence
痕跡器官 **konseki kikan** vestigial organ
12 焼跡 **ya(ke)ato** fire ruins
筆跡 **hisseki** handwriting (specimen)
証跡 **shōseki** evidence, traces
13 傷跡 **kizuato** scar
戦跡 **senseki** old battlefield
罪跡 **zaiseki** evidence of guilt
14 遺跡 **iseki** remains, ruins, relics
15 踏跡 **fu(mi)ato** footprint
踪跡 **sōseki** one's tracks/whereabouts
18 蹤跡 **shōseki** one's traces/whereabouts

————— 3 —————

4 不行跡 **fugyōseki** misconduct, immorality
水茎跡 **mizuguki (no) ato** brush writing, calligraphy
13 跡切跡切 **togi(re)-togi(re)** intermittent, off-and-on

————— 4 —————

6 名所旧跡 **meisho-kyūseki** scenic and historic places

7d6.8

跪 KI, hizamazu(ku) kneel

————— 1 —————

7 跪坐 **kiza** kneel down
8 跪拝 **kihai** kneel and pray

7d6.9

踅 KYŌ sound of footsteps

————— 7 —————

踈 → 疎 0a11.4

7d7.1

跣 TO barefoot

7d7.2 / 1558

踊 踴 YŌ, odo(ru) dance
odo(ri) a dance, dancing

————— 1 —————

2 踊子 **odo(ri)ko** dancer, dancing girl
4 踊込 **odo(ri)ko(mu)** jump/rush into
5 踊出 **odo(ri)da(su)** begin to dance; dance out (into the limelight)
踊字 **odo(ri)ji** character-repetition symbol (e.g., 々 or ゝ)
7 踊狂 **odo(ri)kuru(u)** dance ecstatically
12 踊場 **odo(ri)ba** dance hall/floor; (stairway) landing
20 踊懸 **odo(ri)ka(karu)** spring upon, jump at

————— 2 —————

3 小踊 **koodo(ri)** dancing/jumping for joy
4 手踊 **teodo(ri)** posture dancing
9 盆踊 **Bon odo(ri)** Bon Festival dancing
15 舞踊 **buyō** dancing; dance
ma(i)odo(ru) dance
舞踊劇 **buyōgeki** dance drama

————— 4 —————

8 欣喜雀踊 **kinki-jakuyaku** jump for joy

7d7.3

踉 RŌ, RYŌ stagger

————— 2 —————

17 蹌踉 **yorome(ku)** stagger, totter

7

言 貝 車 足 7←
酉

7d7.4

踘 **KYOKU, segukuma(ru)** stoop, bend over, crouch

———————— 1 ————————

17 踘踖 **kyokuseki** be overmeek/unadventurous

———————— 8 ————————

7d8.1

踝 **KA, kurubushi** ankle

———————— 1 ————————

10 踝骨 **kakotsu** anklebone

7d8.2

踟 **CHI** hesitate

7d8.3 / 1559

踏 蹈 **TŌ, fu(mu)** step on
fu(maeru) stand on, be based on

———————— 1 ————————

2 踏入 **fu(mi)i(reru)** set foot in, tread on
4 踏切 **fu(mi)ki(ru)** cross; take the plunge, take action, make bold to
fumikiri railroad (grade) crossing
踏切番 **fumikiriban** railroad crossing gateman
踏止 **fu(mi)todo(maru)** stand one's ground, hold one's own
踏分 **fu(mi)wa(keru)** push one's way through
踏込 **fu(mi)ko(mu)** step/rush into
5 踏出 **fu(mi)da(su)** step forward, go forth
踏付 **fu(mi)tsu(keru)** trample; oppress; despise
踏外 **fu(mi)hazu(su)** miss one's footing
踏台 **fu(mi)dai** step, footstool, steppingstone
踏石 **fu(mi)ishi** steppingstone
7 踏均 **fu(mi)nara(su)** level by treading, beat (a path)
踏抜 **fu(mi)nu(ku)** step through (the flooring); step on (a nail) and prick one's foot
踏車 **fu(mi)guruma** treadmill
8 踏迷 **fu(mi)mayo(u)** lose one's way
踏拉 **fu(mi)shida(ku)** trample, step on and break
踏固 **fu(mi)kata(meru)** tramp/pack down
踏板 **fu(mi)ita** treadle, pedal, running board
9 踏段 **fu(mi)dan** step, stair
踏荒 **fu(mi)ara(su)** trample, ravage

踏査 **tōsa** survey, field investigation
踏砕 **fu(mi)kuda(ku)** crush underfoot
10 踏倒 **fu(mi)tao(su)** kick over; evade payment
踏消 **fu(mi)ke(su)** stamp out (a fire)
踏殺 **fu(mi)koro(su)** trample to death
11 踏張 **fu(n)ba(ru)** brace one's legs, stand firm, hold out, persist in
12 踏割 **fu(mi)wa(ru)** step on and break
踏違 **fu(mi)chiga(eru)** sprain (one's ankle), misstep
踏堪 **fu(mi)kota(eru)** hold one's own, hold out
踏換 **fu(mi)ka(eru)** shift one's footing
踏越 **fu(mi)ko(eru)** step across, overstep
踏絵 **fu(mi)e** ikon to be trampled on (to prove one is not a Christian)
13 踏跡 **fu(mi)ato** footprint
14 踏鳴 **fu(mi)na(rasu)** stamp noisily
15 踏潰 **fu(mi)tsubu(su)** crush underfoot
踏締 **fu(mi)shi(meru)** step firmly/cautiously
22 踏襲 **tōshū** follow (someone's footsteps)
23 踏躙 **fu(mi)niji(ru)** trample underfoot

———————— 2 ————————

3 土踏 **tsuchifu(mazu)** the arch of the foot
5 未踏 **mitō** untrodden, unexplored
7 麦踏 **mugifu(mi)** treading barley/wheat plants
足踏 **ashibu(mi)** step, stamp; treadle; mark time, be at a standstill
10 値踏 **nebu(mi)** appraisal, valuation
高踏 **kōtō** transcending the mundane
高踏的 **kōtōteki** transcendent
高踏派 **kōtōha** the transcendentalists
14 雑踏 **zattō** hustle and bustle, congestion
15 舞踏 **butō** dancing
舞踏会 **butōkai** ball, dance
舞踏病 **butōbyō** St. Vitus's dance, chorea
舞踏場 **butōjō** dance hall
19 瀬踏 **sebu(mi)** wading to test the depth, trial balloon, sounding out
轍踏 **tetsu (o) fu(mu)** repeat (another's) past mistakes

———————— 3 ————————

2 二足踏 **ni (no) ashi (o) fu(mu)** hesitate, think twice
3 土不踏 **tsuchifumazu** the arch of the foot
12 場数踏 **bakazu (o) fu(mu)** gain experience

———————— 4 ————————

2 人跡未踏 **jinseki-mitō** unexplored
6 仮装舞踏会 **kasō butōkai** masquerade ball
地団駄踏 **jidanda (o) fu(mu)** stamp one's feet

践 → 踐 7d6.1

7d8.4

踪　SŌ footprint, traces, remains

――――― 1 ―――――
13 踪跡 **sōseki** one's tracks/whereabouts
――――― 2 ―――――
5 失踪 **shissō** disappear, be missing

7d8.5

踠　EN, **moga(ku)** writhe, struggle, squirm

7d8.6

踞　KYO, **uzukuma(ru)** crouch

――――― 2 ―――――
19 蹲踞 **sonkyo** crouching

――――――――― 9 ―――――――――

7d9.1

踵　SHŌ, **kakato**, **kubisu** heel

踴 → 踊　7d7.2

7d9.2

蹂　JŪ step on

――――― 1 ―――――
23 蹂躙 **jūrin** trampling upon; infringement, violation
――――― 3 ―――――
2 人権蹂躙 **jinken jūrin** infringement of human rights

7d9.3

蹄　TEI, **hizume** hoof

――――― 1 ―――――
7 蹄状 **teijō** horseshoe/U shape
蹄形 **teikei** horseshoe/U shape
蹄形磁石 **teikei jishaku** horseshoe magnet
13 蹄鉄 **teitetsu** horseshoe
蹄鉄工 **teitetsukō** horseshoer
――――― 2 ―――――
10 馬蹄 **batei** horse's hoof

馬蹄形 **bateikei** horseshoe shape
13 鉄蹄 **tettei** horseshoe

7d9.4

踰　YU go beyond

――――――――― 10 ―――――――――

7d10.1

蹐　SEKI walking gingerly/stealthily

――――― 2 ―――――
14 跼蹐 **kyokuseki** be overmeek/unadventurous

蹈 → 踏　7d8.3

7d10.2

蹊　KEI, **komichi** path

7d10.3

蹌　SŌ stagger; stride imposingly

――――― 1 ―――――
14 蹌踉 **yorome(ku)** stagger, totter

7d10.4

蹉　SA stumble

――――― 1 ―――――
12 蹉跌 **satetsu** stumbling; failure, setback

――――――――― 11 ―――――――――

7d11.1

蹤　SHŌ, **ato** footprints, footsteps

――――― 1 ―――――
13 蹤跡 **shōseki** one's traces/whereabouts

7d11.2

蹕　HITSU one who precedes and clears the road for a nobleman's procession

――――― 2 ―――――
19 警蹕 **keihitsu** heralding

7

言
貝
車
足　11←
酉

7d11.3

蹟

SEKI, SHAKU remains, vestiges

——————— 2 ———————

4 手蹟 **shuseki** handwriting (specimen)
5 史蹟 **shiseki** historical landmark
  古蹟 **koseki** historic spot, ruins
8 事蹟 **jiseki** evidence, trace, vestige
  奇蹟 **kiseki** miracle
14 遺蹟 **iseki** ruins, remains

7d11.4

蹣

MAN stagger

——————— 1 ———————

12 蹣跚 **mansan** reeling, staggering

7d11.5

蹠

SEKI, SHAKU, SHO sole of the foot

——————— 1 ———————

6 蹠行動物 **shokō dōbutsu** a plantigrade
  (animal that walks on the whole sole of
  its foot, as man or bear)

——————— 2 ———————

7 対蹠地 **taisekichi** the antipodes
  対蹠点 **taisekiten** antipode, nadir

7d11.6

蹙

SHUKU become narrow/wrinkled

——————— 2 ———————

24 顰蹙 **hinshuku** frown on, disdain

——————— 12 ———————

7d12.1

蹼

HOKU, mizukaki web(bed foot);
paddle

7d12.2

蹴

SHŪ, SHUKU, ke(ru) kick

——————— 1 ———————

3 蹴上 **kea(geru)** kick up
4 蹴爪 **kezume** spur (on a chicken's foot)

蹴込 **keko(mi)** riser (of a step/entranceway)
5 蹴出 **keda(su)** kick out
  蹴立 **keta(teru)** kick up
6 蹴合 **kea(u)** kick each other
        kea(i) cockfighting
  蹴返 **kekae(su)** kick back
9 蹴飛 **keto(basu)** kick away/out, reject
10 蹴倒 **ketao(su)** kick down/over
  蹴殺 **kekoro(su)** kick to death
  蹴破 **keyabu(ru)** kick open (a door)
11 蹴球 **shūkyū** football
  蹴球場 **shūkyūjō** football/soccer/rugby field
12 蹴落 **keo(tosu)** kick down
  蹴散 **kechi(rasu)** kick around, put to rout
17 蹴鞠 **kemari** football (historical)
22 蹴躓 **ketsumazu(ku)** stumble, trip

——————— 2 ———————

1 一蹴 **isshū** kick; reject
5 石蹴 **ishike(ri)** hopscotch
7 足蹴 **ashige** kicking
13 跳蹴 **to(bi)ke(ri)** dropkick

7d12.3

躇

CHO hesitate

——————— 2 ———————

21 躊躇 **chūcho, tamera(u)** hesitate, be reluctant

7d12.4

蹲

SON, uzukuma(ru), tsukuba(u)
crouch   **tsukuba(i)** crouching; garden
washbasin

——————— 1 ———————

15 蹲踞 **sonkyo** crouching

7d12.5

蹶

KETSU stumble, fall; jump up

——————— 1 ———————

10 蹶起 **kekki** rise up
12 蹶然 **ketsuzen** springing to one's feet

——————— 13 ———————

7d13.1

躅

CHOKU trample, stamp down;
remains

——————— 2 ———————

21 躑躅 **tsutsuji** azalea, rhododendron

——————— 3 ———————
3 山躑躅 **yamatsutsuji** rhododendron

7d13.2

躁

SŌ be clamorous

——————— 1 ———————
10 躁病 **sōbyō** mania
29 躁鬱病 **sōutsubyō** manic-depressive psychosis

——————— 2 ———————
7 狂躁 **kyōsō** mad uproar, frenzy, clamor
12 軽躁 **keisō** light-headed, thoughtless, flighty

7d13.3

躄

BYAKU, HEKI, izari a cripple

——————— 14 ———————

7d14.1

躑

TEKI walk around, paw the ground

——————— 1 ———————
20 躑躅 **tsutsuji** azalea, rhododendron

——————— 2 ———————
3 山躑躅 **yamatsutsuji** rhododendron

7d14.2 / 1560

躍

YAKU, odo(ru) jump, leap, hop

——————— 1 ———————
3 躍上 **odo(ri)a(garu)** jump up, dance for joy
4 躍込 **odo(ri)ko(mu)** jump/rush into
6 躍如 **yakujo** vivid, true to life
10 躍進 **yakushin** advance by leaps and bounds
躍起 **yakki** excitement, franticness, enthusiasm
11 躍動 **yakudō** lively motion
12 躍越 **odo(ri)ko(su)** jump over
20 躍懸 **odo(ri)ka(karu)** spring upon, jump at

1 一躍 **ichiyaku** one bound; in one leap
3 小躍 **koodo(ri)** dancing/jumping for joy
9 飛躍 **hiyaku** leap; activity; rapid progress
飛躍的 **hiyakuteki** rapid, by leaps and bounds
勇躍 **yūyaku** be in high spirits
活躍 **katsuyaku** be active
11 雀躍 **jakuyaku** jump for joy, exult
13 暗躍 **an'yaku** secret maneuvering
跳躍 **ha(ne)odo(ru)** prance/frisk about
chōyaku spring, jump, leap

跳躍板 **chōyakuban** springboard

——————— 3 ———————
3 大活躍 **daikatsuyaku** great/energetic activity

——————— 4 ———————
13 暗中飛躍 **anchū hiyaku** secret maneuvering

7d14.3

躊

CHŪ hesitate

——————— 1 ———————
19 躊躇 **chūcho, tamera(u)** hesitate, be reluctant

7d14.4

躋

SEI climb

——————— 15 ———————

7d15.1

躓

CHI, tsumazu(ku) stumble, trip

——————— 2 ———————
19 蹴躓 **ketsumazu(ku)** stumble, trip

7d15.2

躔

TEN movement of the sun/moon through the heavens

7d15.3

齪

SAKU, SEKU fretful

——————— 2 ———————
24 齷齪 **akuseku, akusaku** fussily, busily

——————— 16 ———————

7d16.1

躙   躪

RIN, niji(ru) edge forward; trample down

——————— 1 ———————
11 躙寄 **niji(ri)yo(ru)** edge/crawl/sidle up to

——————— 2 ———————
15 踏躙 **fu(mi)niji(ru)** trample underfoot
16 蹂躙 **jūrin** trampling upon; infringement, violation

——————— 4 ———————
2 人権蹂躙 **jinken jūrin** infringement of human rights

7

言
貝
車   16 ←
足
酉

─────────── **18** ─────────── | ─────────── **19** ───────────

7d18.1

躡

JŌ step on; put on (shoes)

蹫 → 躪 **7d16.1**

─────────────── 酉 **7e** ───────────────

酉	西	酊	酋	酎	配	酌	酖	酘	酔	酥	酣	酢
0.1	0a6.20	2.1	2o7.1	3.1	3.2	3.3	4.1	4.2	4.3	5.1	5.2	5.3

酡	尊	奠	酵	酬	酩	酪	猷	酷	酸	醒	醅	醇
5.4	2o10.3	2o10.4	6.1	6.2	6.3	6.4	3g9.7	7.1	7.2	7.3	7.4	7.5

酤	醋	醉	醐	醗	醒	醍	醜	醞	醢	醤	醪	醫
8.1	8.2	7e4.3	9.1	7e12.2	9.2	9.3	10.1	10.2	10.3	7e11.2	11.1	2t5.2

醬	醯	醱	釀	醴	醵	醺	釀	釁
11.2	12.1	12.2	13.1	13.2	13.3	14.1	7e13.1	2f24.1

─────────── **0** ───────────

7e0.1

酉

YŪ, tori tenth horary sign (bird)

─────────── **1** ───────────

5 酉市 **tori (no) ichi** year-end fair

西 → **0a6.20**

─────────── **2** ───────────

7e2.1

酊

TEI get drunk

─────── **2** ───────

13 酩酊 **meitei** drunkenness, intoxication

酋 → **2o7.1**

─────────── **3** ───────────

7e3.1

酎

CHŪ saké

─────── **2** ───────

12 焼酎 **shōchū** (a low-grade liquor)

7e3.2 / 515

配

HAI distribute, allot; arrange, place; be together; exile
kuba(ru) distribute, pass out, allocate

─────────── **1** ───────────

0 配する **hai(suru)** allot; arrange; match, mate; exile
3 配下 **haika** followers, subordinates
4 配分 **haibun** distribution, allocation
配水 **haisui** water supply/distribution
5 配本 **haihon** book distribution
配付 **haifu** distribution, apportionment
配布 **haifu** distribution, apportionment
6 配合 **haigō** arrangement, combination
配列 **hairetsu** arrangement, grouping
配色 **haishoku** color scheme/arrangement
配当 **haitō** allotment, share, dividend
配当金 **haitōkin** dividend
7 配役 **haiyaku** cast(ing of roles)
配車 **haisha** allocation/dispatching of cars
8 配送 **haisō** delivery, forwarding
配物 **kuba(ri)mono** gifts
配所 **haisho** place of exile
9 配炭 **haitan** coal distribution
10 配剤 **haizai** compounding (a prescription); (heaven's) disposition
11 配遇 **haigū** combination; spouse
配遇者 **haigūsha** spouse
配達 **haitatsu** deliver
配達人 **haitatsunin** deliveryman
配達先 **haitatsusaki** destination, receiver
配達料 **haitatsuryō** delivery charge
配船 **haisen** assignment of ships
12 配備 **haibi** deployment, disposition
配給 **haikyū** distribution, rationing
配給米 **haikyūmai** rationed rice
配給所 **haikyūjo** distribution point
配給量 **haikyūryō** a ration
13 配意 **haii** consideration, concern
配置 **haichi** arrangement, placement, layout

7

言
貝
車
足
酉

→18

配電 **haiden** distribution of electricity
配電所 **haidensho** power station
配電盤 **haidenban** switch panel
配電線 **haidensen** power line/wire
14 配管 **haikan** plumbing, piping
15 配慮 **hairyo** consideration, care
配線 **haisen** wiring
16 配膳 **haizen** set the table
配膳室 **haizenshitsu** service room, pantry

───────── 2 ─────────

4 勾配 **kōbai** slope, incline, gradient
支配 **shihai** management, control, rule
支配人 **shihainin** manager
支配力 **shihairyoku** one's control/hold over
支配下 **shihaika** under the control of
支配的 **shihaiteki** dominant, overriding
支配者 **shihaisha** ruler, administrator
支配層 **shihaisō** the ruling class
支配権 **shihaiken** control, supremacy
分配 **bunpai** division, sharing, allotment
手配 **tehai, tekuba(ri)** arrangements,
　　preparations; disposition (of troops)
欠配 **keppai** suspension of rations/payments
心配 **shinpai** worry, anxiety, concern
心配事 **shinpaigoto** cares, worries, troubles
心配性 **shinpaishō** worrying disposition
5 目配 **mekuba(se)** give a meaningful look
　　mekuba(ri) be watchful, look about
6 気配 **kehai** sign, indication　**kihai** market
　　trend　**kikuba(ri)** vigilance, attentiveness
年配 **nenpai** age
再配置 **saihaichi** reallocate, rearrange
交配 **kōhai** mating, crossbreeding
宅配便 **takuhaibin** parcel delivery business
8 受配者 **juhaisha** recipient of an allotment
采配 **saihai** flywhisk-like baton of command
9 軍配 **gunbai** strategem, tactics; (ancient)
　　military leader's fan; sumo referee's fan
10 高配 **kōhai** your trouble/assistance
差配 **sahai** conduct of business; management;
　　agency, agent
差配人 **sahainin** landlord's agent
特配 **tokuhai** special ration/dividend, bonus
11 遅配 **chihai** delay in apportioning/delivery
12 減配 **genpai** reduce dividends/rations
復配 **fukuhai** resumption of dividends
無配 **muhai** non-dividend-paying
無配当 **muhaitō** non-dividend-paying
集配 **shūhai** collection and delivery
集配人 **shūhainin** postman
13 蛸配当 **takohaitō** bogus dividends
14 増配 **zōhai** increased dividends/rations
誤配 **gohai** misdelivery (of mail)

───────── 3 ─────────

2 二次配列 **niji hairetsu** secondary arrangement, arrangement on second level
3 三次配列 **sanji hairetsu** tertiary arrangement, arrangement on third level
6 再分配 **saibunpai** redistribution
9 急勾配 **kyūkōbai** steep slope
14 総支配人 **sōshihainin** general manager

7e3.3 / 1863

酌　**SHAKU, ku(mu)** pour (saké); take into
　　consideration

───────── 1 ─────────

6 酌交 **ku(mi)ka(wasu)** pour (saké) for each
　　other
11 酌婦 **shakufu** waitress, barmaid
12 酌量 **shakuryō** consideration, extenuation

───────── 2 ─────────

4 手酌 **tejaku** helping oneself to a drink
9 独酌 **dokushaku** drinking alone
12 媒酌 **baishaku** matchmaking
媒酌人 **baishakunin** matchmaker, go-
between
晩酌 **banshaku** an evening drink (of saké)
13 斟酌 **shinshaku** take into consideration

───────── 4 ─────────

7e4.1

酖　**TAN, fuke(ru)** be addicted to
　　CHIN (a poisonous bird)

───────── 1 ─────────

13 酖溺 **tandeki** addiction, dissipation

7e4.2

　TŌ rebrew, ferment again

7e4.3 / 1709

酔　醉　**SUI, yo(u)** get drunk, be
　　intoxicated; feel (sea)sick

───────── 1 ─────────

0 酔いどれ **yo(idore)** a drunk
4 酔心地 **yo(i)gokochi** pleasant drunken feeling
5 酔生夢死 **suisei-mushi** idle one's life away
酔払 **yo(p)para(i)** a drunk
7 酔余 **suiyo** drunken
酔狂 **suikyō** whimsical, eccentric
　　yo(i)kuru(u) be raving drunk
8 酔歩 **suiho** tipsy/staggering gait
11 酔眼 **suigan** drunken/bleary eyes

7　　言　貝　車　足　酉　4←

12 酔覚 **yo(i)za(me)** sobering up
13 酔漢 **suikan** a drunk
酔痴 **yo(i)shi(reru)** be befuddled/drunk
14 酔態 **suitai** drunkenness
15 酔潰 **yo(i)tsubu(reru)** be dead drunk
16 酔醒 **yo(i)za(me)** sobering up
18 酔顔 **suigan** drunken face/look

——— 2 ———
3 大酔 **taisui** drunken stupor
4 心酔 **shinsui** be fascinated by, ardently admire
心酔者 **shinsuisha** ardent admirer, devotee
5 生酔 **namayo(i)** half-drunk, tipsy
7 乱酔 **ransui** dead drunk
8 泥酔 **deisui** dead drunk
10 陶酔 **tōsui** intoxication; fascination, rapture
11 深酔 **fukayo(i)** get very drunk
麻酔 **masui** anesthesia
麻酔薬 **masuiyaku** an anesthetic/narcotic
悪酔 **waruyo(i)** drink oneself sick; become unpleasant when drunk
船酔 **funayo(i)** seasickness
13 痲酔 **masui** anesthesia

——— 3 ———
2 二日酔 **futsukayo(i)** a hangover

——— 4 ———
6 全身麻酔 **zenshin masui** general anasthesia
7 局部麻酔 **kyokubu masui** local anesthetic

——— 5 ———
7e5.1
酥 SO milk

7e5.2
酣 KAN, takenawa the height/midst of

7e5.3 / 1867
酢 醋 SAKU, su vinegar

——— 1 ———
0 ポン酢 **ponzu** bitter-orange juice
8 酢物 **su(no)mono** vinegared dish
14 酢漬 **suzu(ke)** pickling in vinegar
酢酸 **sakusan** acetic acid
——— 2 ———
5 氷酢酸 **hyōsakusan** glacial acetic acid
8 食酢 **shokusu** (table/edible) vinegar
10 梅酢 **umezu** plum juice/vinegar

7e5.4
酡 TA red from drunkenness

罇→尊 2o10.3
奠→ 2o10.4

——— 6 ———
7e6.1 / 1866
酵 KŌ fermentation; yeast
——— 1 ———
5 酵母 **kōbo** yeast
酵母菌 **kōbokin** yeast fungus
10 酵素 **kōso** enzyme
——— 2 ———
9 発酵 **hakkō** fermentation
発酵素 **hakkōso** a ferment, yeast

7e6.2 / 1864
酬 SHŪ, mukui reward, compensation; retribution
——— 2 ———
7 応酬 **ōshū** reply
12 報酬 **hōshū** remuneration
貴酬 **kishū** reply (to a letter)
13 献酬 **kenshū** exchange of saké cups
——— 3 ———
12 無報酬 **muhōshū** without pay, for free

7e6.3
酩 MEI get drunk
——— 1 ———
9 酩酊 **meitei** drunkenness, intoxication

7e6.4 / 1865
酪 RAKU whey
——— 1 ———
13 酪農 **rakunō** dairy farming
酪農家 **rakunōka** dairy farmer
酪農場 **rakunōjo** dairy farm
14 酪酸 **rakusan** butyric acid

—————— 2 ——————

4 牛酪 **gyūraku** butter
11 乾酪 **kanraku** cheese

献→ **3g9.7**

—————— 7 ——————

7e7.1 / 1711

酷 **KOKU, hido(i), mugo(i)** severe, harsh, cruel, intense

—————— 1 ——————

5 酷目 **hido(i)me** a bitter experience, a hard time
6 酷吏 **kokuri** exacting official
 酷刑 **kokkei** severe punishment
7 酷似 **kokuji** close resemblance
8 酷使 **kokushi** work (someone) hard
10 酷烈 **kokuretsu** intense, rigorous
11 酷遇 **kokugū** maltreatment
12 酷寒 **kokkan** intense/bitter cold
 酷暑 **kokusho** intense/sweltering heat
 酷評 **kokuhyō** sharp/harsh criticism
15 酷熱 **kokunetsu** intense/scorching heat
16 酷薄 **kokuhaku** brutality, inhumanity

—————— 2 ——————

7 冷酷 **reikoku** cruel, callous
8 苛酷 **kakoku** harsh, rigorous, cruel
10 残酷 **zankoku** cruel, brutal
11 過酷 **kakoku** severe, harsh

7e7.2 / 516

酸 **SAN** acid
su(i), su(ppai) sour, tart

—————— 1 ——————

4 酸化 **sanka** oxidation
 酸化物 **sankabutsu** oxide
8 酸味 **sanmi, su(i)mi** acidity, sourness
 酸性 **sansei** acidity
 酸性白土 **sansei hakudo** acid/Kambara clay
 酸性雨 **sanseiu** acid rain
 酸雨 **san'u** acid rain
9 酸度 **sando** acidity
10 酸素 **sanso** oxygen
11 酸敗 **sanpai** acidify, turn rancid
 酸敗乳 **sanpainyū** sour milk
14 酸鼻 **sanbi** horrible, piteous, appalling
15 酸漿 **hōzuki** bladder/ground cherry
18 酸類 **sanrui** acids

—————— 2 ——————

1 一酸化炭素 **issanka tanso** carbon monoxide
4 水酸化物 **suisankabutsu** a hydroxide
7 乳酸 **nyūsan** lactic acid

乳酸菌 **nyūsankin** lactic-acid bacteria
尿酸 **nyōsan** uric acid
辛酸 **shinsan** hardship, privation
8 青酸 **seisan** hydrogen cyanide, prussic acid
 青酸カリ **seisan kari** potassium cyanide
9 耐酸 **taisan** acidproof, acid-resistant
 海酸漿 **umihōzuki** whelk egg capsule (used for child's noisemaker)
 炭酸 **tansan** carbonic acid
 炭酸水 **tansansui** carbonated water
 炭酸紙 **tansanshi** carbon paper
 砒酸 **hisan** arsenic acid, ... arsenate
 胃酸 **isan** stomach acid
 胃酸過多症 **isankatashō** gastric hyperacidity
10 珪酸 **keisan** silicic acid
11 過酸化 **kasanka** (hydrogen) peroxide
12 葉酸 **yōsan** folic acid
 硫酸 **ryūsan** sulfuric acid
 硫酸紙 **ryūsanshi** parchment paper
 硝酸 **shōsan** nitric acid, ... nitrate
 硝酸塩 **shosan'en** a nitrate
 硝酸銀 **shōsangin** silver nitrate
 酢酸 **sakusan** acetic acid
13 塩酸 **ensan** hydrochloric acid
 蓚酸 **shūsan** oxalic acid
 硼酸 **hōsan** boric acid
 酪酸 **rakusan** butyric acid
15 醋酸 **sakusan** acetic acid
17 燐酸 **rinsan** phosphoric acid; (as prefix) ... phosphate
19 蟻酸 **gisan** formic acid

—————— 3 ——————

5 氷酢酸 **hyōsakusan** glacial acetic acid
 氷醋酸 **hyōsakusan** glacial acetic acid
 石炭酸 **sekitansan** carbolic acid, phenol
6 安息酸 **ansokusan** benzoic acid
7 亜砒酸 **ahisan** arsenious acid, ... arsenite
 亜硫酸 **aryūsan** sulfurous acid, ... sulfite
9 枸櫞酸 **kuensan** citric acid
 臭素酸 **shūsosan** bromic acid, ... bromate
10 遊離酸 **yūrisan** free acid
 酒石酸 **shusekisan** tartaric acid
 脂肪酸 **shibōsan** fatty acid
11 過硫酸 **karyūsan** persulfuric acid, (potassium) persulfate

7e7.3

醒 **TEI** hangover

7e7.4

醋 **IN, SHIN** drunken babbling; offer

7

言
貝
車
足
酉   7←

7e7.5

醇　**JUN** pure; kind; sweet saké

——————————— 1 ———————————
4 醇化 **junka** refine, purify
5 醇正 **junsei** pure, proper
6 醇朴 **junboku** simple and honest
9 醇風美俗 **junpū bizoku** good morals and manners

——————————— 2 ———————————
7 芳醇 **hōjun** mellow, rich

——————————— 8 ———————————

7e8.1

酥　**RIN, RAN** remove astringency; bleach in water

——————————— 2 ———————————
8 味酥 **mirin** sweet saké (for seasoning)

7e8.2

醋　**SAKU, su** vinegar

——————————— 1 ———————————
14 醋酸 **sakusan** acetic acid

——————————— 2 ———————————
5 氷醋酸 **hyōsakusan** glacial acetic acid

醉 → 酔　**7e4.3**

——————————— 9 ———————————

7e9.1

醐　**GO** (a kind of butter-cream)

——————————— 2 ———————————
16 醍醐 **Daigo** (emperor, 897–930)
醍醐味 **daigomi** taste, zest, charm; Buddha's gracious teachings

醗 → 醱　**7e12.2**

7e9.2

醒　**SEI, sa(meru)** (intr.) wake up, awaken
　　SEI, sa(masu) (tr.) wake up

——————————— 2 ———————————
11 酔醒 **yo(i)za(me)** sobering up
12 覚醒 **kakusei** awakening
覚醒剤 **kakuseizai** stimulant drugs
16 興醒 **kyōza(mashi), kyōza(me)** dampening the fun, wet blanket
19 警醒 **keisei** warn, arouse, awaken

7e9.3

醍　**DAI** whey

——————————— 1 ———————————
16 醍醐 **Daigo** (emperor, 897–930)
醍醐味 **daigomi** taste, zest, charm; Buddha's gracious teachings

——————————— 10 ———————————

7e10.1 / 1527

醜　**SHŪ, miniku(i)** ugly; indecent

——————————— 1 ———————————
3 醜女 **shūjo, shikome** ugly woman
6 醜交 **shūkō** immoral intercourse
醜名 **shūmei** notoriety, scandal　**shikona** sumo wrestler's professional name
醜行 **shūkō** disgraceful conduct
7 醜状 **shūjō** disgraceful state of affairs
11 醜悪 **shūaku** ugly, abominable, scandalous
13 醜業 **shūgyō** shameful calling, prostitution
醜業婦 **shūgyōfu** prostitute
14 醜態 **shūtai** unseemly sight, disgraceful behavior
醜聞 **shūbun** scandal
醜関係 **shūkankei** illicit liaison
18 醜類 **shūrui** evil/ugly ones

——————————— 2 ———————————
9 美醜 **bishū** beauty or ugliness, appearance

7e10.2

醞　**UN** fermentation, brewing

——————————— 1 ———————————
20 醞醸 **unjō** ferment, brew

7e10.3

醢　**KAI, hishio, shishibishio** salted meat

醤 → 醬 **7e11.2**

─────── 11 ───────

7e11.1

醪

   RŌ, moromi unrefined saké/soy

醫 → 医 **2t5.2**

7e11.2

醬 醤

   SHŌ salted or fermented food

─────── 1 ───────
8 醬油 **shōyu** soy sauce
─────── 2 ───────
5 生醬油 **kijōyu** raw/pure soy sauce

─────── 12 ───────

7e12.1

醯

   KEI vinegar

7e12.2

醱 醗

   HATSU brewing, fermentation

─────── 13 ───────

7e13.1 / 1837

釀 醸

   JŌ, kamo(su) brew; bring about, give rise to

─────── 1 ───────
5 醸出 **kamo(shi)da(su)** cause, bring about
  醸母 **jōbo** yeast
6 醸成 **jōsei** brew; cause, bring about
9 醸造 **jōzō** brewing, distilling
  醸造学 **jōzōgaku** science of brewing
  醸造所 **jōzōsho** brewery, distillery
  醸造酒 **jōzōshu** brewage, liquor
  醸造家 **jōzōka** brewer, distiller
  醸造業 **jōzōgyō** brewing industry
─────── 2 ───────
17 醞醸 **unjō** ferment, brew

7e13.2

醴

   REI sweet saké

7e13.3

醵

   KYO collect/donate contributions

─────── 1 ───────
5 醵出 **kyoshutsu** donation, contribution
8 醵金 **kyokin** donation, contribution

─────── 14 ───────

7e14.1

醺

   KUN get tipsy; smell of liquor

─────── 17 ───────

釀 → 醸 **7e13.1**

─────── 19 ───────

釁 → **2f24.1**

─────── 金 **8a** ───────

金	釗	釛	釟	針	釘	釦	釵	鉈	釩	釧	鈞	欽
0.1	2f0.1	2.1	2.2	2.3	2.4	3.1	2f8.5	3.2	3.3	3.4	3.5	4.1

釸	鈍	鈕	鉄	鈔	釿	鈬	釸	鈑	鈎	釣	鉆	鈿
8a16.1	4.2	4.3	4.4	4.5	4.6	4.7	8a13.3	4.8	8a5.17	4.9	5.1	5.2

鉗	鉢	鈸	銕	鉦	鉋	卯	鉈	鈴	鉉	鈷	鉛	鉱
5.3	5.4	5.5	5.6	5.7	5.8	5.9	5.10	5.11	5.12	5.13	5.14	5.15

鉞	鉤	鉅	銭	銕	銖	銀	銘	銚	銑	銛	鎈	銃
5.16	5.17	5.18	6.1	8a5.6	6.2	6.3	6.4	6.5	6.6	6.7	6.8	6.9

7

言 貝 車 跙 酉   14←

銓	鉾	銅	鋺	鋳	鋪	鋏	鋤	銹	鋹	銹	銪	銷
6.10	6.11	6.12	7.1	7.2	7.3	7.4	7.5	7.6	7.7	7.8	7.9	7.10
鋒	鋭	錐	錘	錬	鉞	錏	錦	錫	錢	錆	綴	錯
7.11	7.12	8.1	8.2	8.3	8.4	8.5	8.6	8.7	8a6.1	8.8	8.9	8.10
錚	錠	錻	錨	鎇	録	錬	鎚	鍵	鋸	鋼	錮	鍾
8.11	8.12	8.13	8.14	8.15	8.16	2j6.3	8a9.10	8.18	8.19	8.20	8.21	9.1
錬	鍖	鍬	鍜	鍛	鍔	鍠	鎰	鍍	鎚	鎹	鍼	鍋
8a8.3	9.2	9.3	9.4	9.5	9.6	9.7	9.8	9.9	9.10	9.11	9.12	9.13
鎔	鎖	鎧	鎗	鎬	鎮	鎛	鎌	鎰	鏈	鏃	鏃	鏘
10.1	10.2	10.3	10.4	10.5	10.6	10.7	10.8	10.9	10.10	11.1	11.2	11.3
鏤	鏐	鏡	鏝	鏥	鏑	鏨	鏖	鏗	鏵	鏜	鐔
11.4	11.5	11.6	11.7	8a7.6	11.8	11.9	11.10	12.1	12.2	12.3	12.4	12.5
鐘	鐙	鐐	鐃	鐡	鐇	鑁	鐶	鐸	鐳	鐫	鐵	鑄
12.6	12.7	12.8	12.9	8a5.6	8a13.5	13.1	13.2	13.3	13.4	13.5	8a5.6	8a7.2
鑠	鑑	鑚	鑞	鑢	鑛	鑷	鑒	鑪	鑵	鑰	鑲	鑷
15.1	15.2	15.3	15.4	15.5	8a5.15	15.6	8a15.2	16.1	2k4.6	17.1	17.2	18.1
鑽	鑼	鑾	钁	鑿
8a15.3	19.1	19.2	20.1	20.2

8

→0 金
食
隹
雷
門

0

8a0.1 / 23

金

KIN gold; metal; money; Friday
KON gold kane money; metal
kana- metal

1

0 サラ金 **sarakin** consumer/no-collateral loan
business (short for サラリーマン金融)
金メダル **kinmedaru** gold medal
1 金一封 **kin'ippū** gift of money (in an envelope)
2 金入 **kanei(re)** purse, wallet; till
金子 **kinsu** money, funds
金力 **kinryoku** the power of money
3 金工 **kinkō** metalwork; metalsmith
金口 **kinguchi, kinkuchi, kinkō** gold-tipped
金山 **kinzan** gold mine **kanayama** mine
4 金仏 **kanabutsu** a metal Buddha
金切声 **kanaki(ri)goe** shrill voice, shriek
金文字 **kinmoji** gold/gilt letters
金欠 **kinketsu** shortage of money
金欠病 **kinketsubyō** shortage of money
5 金本位 **kinhon'i** the gold standard
金本位制 **kinhon'isei** the gold standard
金比羅 **Konpira** (the god of seafarers)
金字 **kinji** gold/gilt letters
金字塔 **kinjitō** a pyramid; a monumental work
金穴 **kinketsu** gold mine; source of money
金玉 **kintama** gold ball; testicles
kingyoku gold and jewels

金主 **kinshu** financial backer
金石 **kinseki** metals and rocks; stone
monument
金石文 **kinsekibun** inscription on a stone
monument
金石学 **kinsekigaku** study of ancient stone
monument inscriptions
金目 **kaneme** (monetary) value
6 金気 **kanake** metalic taste; money
金色 **kinshoku, kin-iro, konjiki** golden color
金色夜叉 **konjiki yasha** usurer
金地金 **kin jigane** gold bullion
金光 **kinpika** glittering
金尽 **kanezu(ku de)** by force of money, at
any cost
金回 **kanemawa(ri)** circulation of money;
financial condition
金糸 **kinshi** gold thread
金米糖 **konpeitō** confetti (a candy)
7 金沢 **Kanazawa** (city, Ishikawa-ken)
金坑 **kinkō** gold mine
金杓子 **kanajakushi** metal ladle, dipper
金利 **kinri** (rate of) interest
金言 **kingen** wise saying, maxim
8 金使 **kanezuka(i)** way of spending money
金券 **kinken** gold certificate, paper money
金建 **kinda(te), kinta(te)** gold basis,
quotations in gold
金廻 **kanemawa(ri)** circulation of money;
financial condition
金波 **kinpa** golden waves

金泥 **kindei, kondei** gold paint/dust
金杯 **kinpai** gold cup/goblet
金肥 **kinpi** store-bought/chemical fertilizer
金的 **kinteki** the bull's-eye
金物 **kanamono** hardware
金物屋 **kanamonoya** hardware store
金具 **kanagu** metal fittings, bracket
9 金冠 **kinkan** gold crown (on a tooth)
金城 **kinjō** impregnable castle
金城鉄壁 **kinjō-teppeki** impregnable castle
金型 **kanagata** (metal) mold, die
金持 **kanemo(chi)** rich person
金挺 **kanateko** crowbar
金品 **kinpin** money or/and valuables
金屏風 **kinbyōbu** gold-leafed folding screen
金相学 **kinsōgaku** metallography
金星 **kinsei** (the planet) Venus
    kinboshi glorious victory
金砂 **kinsha** gold dust
金看板 **kinkanban** gold-lettered sign; slogan
金科玉条 **kinka-gyokujō** a golden rule
10 金剛 **kongō** diamond; strong man; emery
    powder
金剛力 **kongōriki** Herculean strength
金剛石 **kongōseki** diamond
金剛砂紙 **kongōshashi** emery paper
金高 **kindaka** amount of money
金員 **kin'in** money
金庫 **kinko, kanegura** safe, vault; cashbox;
    depository, treasury; rich patron
金庫破 **kinkoyabu(ri)** safe-cracking
金屑 **kanakuzu** scrap metal, filings
金脈 **kinmyaku** gold vein
金時計 **kindokei** gold watch
金扇 **kinsen** gilt (folding) fan
金紙 **kingami, kinshi** gold/gilt paper
金納 **kinnō** payment in cash
金粉 **kinpun, kinko** gold dust
金釘流 **kanakugiryū** a scrawl
11 金側 **kingawa** gold case
金偏景気 **kanehen keiki** metal-industry boom
金掘 **kaneho(ri)** miner
金婚式 **kinkonshiki** golden wedding
    anniversary
金張 **kinba(ri)** gold-plated
金堂 **kondō** (temple's) golden pavilion
金細工 **kinzaiku** goldwork, gold ware
金貨 **kinka** gold coin
金雀児 **enishida** broom, genista (a shrub)
金雀枝 **enishida** broom, genista (a shrub)
金魚 **kingyo** goldfish
金魚草 **kingyosō** snapdragon
金魚屋 **kingyoya** goldfish seller
金魚鉢 **kingyobachi** goldfish bowl
12 金牌 **kinpai** gold medal
金象眼 **kinzōgan** inlaying with gold

金象嵌 **kinzōgan** inlaying with gold
金着 **kinki(se)** gold-plated
金遣 **kanezuka(i)** way of spending money
金満家 **kinmanka** rich man
金壺眼 **kanatsubo manako** large sunken
    eyes (showing anxiety/mistrust)
金属 **kinzoku** metal
金属工業 **kinzoku kōgyō** metalworking
    industry
金属性 **kinzokusei** metallic
金属製 **kinzokusei** made of metal
金棒 **kanabō** iron rod
金棒引 **kanabōhi(ki)** night watchman;
    a gossip
金歯 **kinba** gold tooth
金策 **kinsaku** means of raising money
金筋 **kinsuji** gold stripes
金貸 **kaneka(shi)** money lending/lender
13 金準備 **kin junbi** gold reserves
金塊 **kinkai** gold nugget/bar/bullion
金蒔絵 **kinmakie** gold lacquerwork
金殿 **kinden** golden palace
金殿玉楼 **kinden gyokurō** palatial residence
金槌 **kanazuchi** hammer
金槌頭 **kanazuchi-atama** hard-headed;
    stubborn
金解禁 **kin kaikin** lifting the gold embargo
金盞花 **kinsenka** marigold
金詰 **kanezuma(ri), kinzuma(ri)** shortage of
    money
金鉄 **kintetsu** gold and iron; firmness
金鉱 **kinkō** gold ore/deposits
金鉱脈 **kinkōmyaku** gold vein
14 金鳳花 **kinpōge** buttercup
金髪 **kinpatsu** blond hair
金蔓 **kanezuru** money vine, source of money
金製 **kinsei** made of gold
金網 **kanaami** wire netting, chain-link (fence)
金箔 **kinpaku** gold leaf, gilt
金銭 **kinsen** money
金銀 **kingin** gold and silver
金閣 **kinkaku** golden pavilion
金閣寺 **Kinkakuji** Temple of the Golden
    Pavilion
15 金蔵 **kanegura** treasury; rich patron
金権 **kinken** the power of money, plutocracy
金敷 **kanashi(ki)** anvil
金縁 **kinbuchi** gold-rimmed, gilt-edged
金箱 **kanebako** cashbox, till; source of
    funds/income
金談 **kindan** request for a loan
金輪 **kanawa** metal hoop/band
金輪際 **konrinzai** never, by no means
金鋏 **kanabasami** metal-cutting shears
16 金甌無欠 **kin'ō-muketsu, kinnō-muketsu**
    perfect, unblemished

8

金 0←
食
隹
雺
門

金盥 **kanadarai** metal basin, washbowl
金縛 **kanashiba(ri)** bound hand and foot
金融 **kin'yū** money, credit, financing
金融界 **kin'yūkai** the financial community
金融機関 **kin'yū kikan** financial institutions
金輸出 **kin yushutsu** export of gold
金錆 **kanasabi** rust
17 金環 **kinkan** gold ring; (sun's) corona
金環食 **kinkanshoku** total eclipse of the sun
18 金儲 **kanemō(ke)** moneymaking
金曜 **kin'yō** Friday
金曜日 **kin'yōbi** Friday
金鎖 **kingusari** gold chain
金離 **kanebana(re)** free spending
金額 **kingaku** amount of money
19 金蘭 **kinran** close friendship
金繰 **kanegu(ri)** raising funds
22 金轡 **kanagutsuwa** horse's bit; hush money
金襴 **kinran** gold brocade
金聾 **kanatsunbo** stone-deaf

─────────── 2 ───────────

2 入金 **nyūkin** payment, money received
3 万金 **mankin** immense sum of money
大金 **taikin** large amount of money
大金持 **ōganemochi** very rich man
土金属 **dokinzoku** earth/terrigenous metals
口金 **kuchigane** spinneret, (cake-decorating) tip; (handbag) clasp; bottlecap; (light bulb) base; ferrule
小金 **kogane** small sum of money; small fortune
4 元金 **gankin, motokin** the principal, capital
天金 **tenkin** gilt-topped (book)
内金 **uchikin** partial payment, earnest money
止金 **to(me)gane** clasp, latch
公金 **kōkin** public funds
手金 **tekin** earnest money, deposit
引金 **hi(ki)gane** trigger
心金 **shingane** core bar/grid, mandrel
5 出金 **shukkin** defray, pay; invest money
半金 **hankin** half the amount
代金 **daikin** price, charge, the money/bill
正金 **shōkin** specie, bullion; cash
用金 **yōkin** money for public use; extraordinary levy
打金 **u(chi)gane** (gun) hammer, cock
白金 **hakkin** platinum
礼金 **reikin** honorarium, fee
6 死金 **shi(ni)gane** wastefully spent money; idle capital
年金 **nenkin** annuity, pension
合金 **gōkin** alloy
返金 **henkin** repayment
地金 **jigane** metal, bullion; one's true character
先金 **sakigane** advance payment

行金 **kōkin** bank funds
当金 **tōkin** (paying in) cash
有金 **a(ri)gane** ready cash
成金 **narikin** new rich, parvenu
7 低金利 **teikinri** low interest
冶金 **yakin** metallurgy
冶金学 **yakingaku** metallurgy
即金 **sokkin** (payment in) cash
延金 **no(be)gane** sheet/hammered-out metal; sword, dagger
肘金 **hijigane** hook (of a hook-and-eye fastener)
見金 **mi(se)gane** money to show (that one has money)
利金 **rikin** interest, gains
私金融 **shikin'yū** private financing/funds
8 非金属 **hikinzoku** nonmetallic
送金 **sōkin** remittance
送金額 **sōkingaku** amount remitted
泥金 **deikin** gold paint
拝金 **haikin** worship of money
拝金主義 **haikin shugi** mammonism
拝金宗 **haikinshū** mammonism
官金 **kankin** government funds
板金 **itagane, bankin** sheet metal, metal plate
9 重金属 **jūkinzoku** heavy metals
前金 **maekin, zenkin** advance payment
後金 **atokin, atogane** the remaining amount due
砂金 **sakin, shakin** gold dust, placer gold
10 残金 **zankin** balance, surplus
借金 **shakkin** debt
借金取 **shakkinto(ri)** bill collection/collector
差金 **sakin** difference, margin
  sa(shi)kin partial payment; difference
  sa(shi)gane carpenter's square; instigation; suggestion
遊金 **yūkin** idle money/funds
涙金 **namidakin** consolation money
帯金 **obigane** iron band
座金 **zagane** (metal) washer
唐金 **karakane** bronze
株金 **kabukin** money/investment for a share
胴金 **dōgane** metal clasp
烏金 **karasugane** money lent at daily interest
砲金 **hōkin** gun metal
留金 **to(me)gane** clasp, latch, fastening
純金 **junkin** pure/solid gold
納金 **nōkin** payment
料金 **ryōkin** fee, charge, fare
針金 **harigane** wire
11 基金 **kikin** fund, endowment
掛金 **ka(ke)kin** installment (payment)
  ka(ke)gane latch, hasp
捨金 **su(te)gane** wasted money
彫金 **chōkin** chasing, metal carving

黄金 **ōgon, kogane** gold
黄金色 **ōgonshoku, kogane-iro** gold color
黄金律 **ōgonritsu** the golden rule
現金 **genkin** cash
現金化 **genkinka** convert to cash, cash (a check)
現金払 **genkinbara(i)** cash payment
産金 **sankin** gold mining
粗金 **aragane** ore
断金 **dankin** warm friendship
12 雁金 **karigane** (cry/honk of a) wild goose
換金 **kankin** realize, convert into money
募金 **bokin** fund raising
焼金 **ya(ki)gane** branding/marking iron
税金 **zeikin** tax
給金 **kyūkin** wages, pay
筋金 **sujigane** metal reinforcement
筋金入 **sujiganei(ri)** hardcore, dyed-in-the-wool
貯金 **chokin** savings, deposit
貯金通帳 **chokin tsūchō** bankbook
貯金箱 **chokinbako** savings box, (piggy) bank
貴金属 **kikinzoku** precious metals
貸金 **ka(shi)kin** loan
軽金属 **keikinzoku** light metals
集金 **shūkin** collecting money
集金人 **shūkinnin** bill collector
13 義金 **gikin** donation, contribution
鍍金 **mekki** gilt, plating, galvanizing
損金 **sonkin** financial loss
献金 **kenkin** gift of money, contribution
献金箱 **kenkinbako** contributions/offertory box
聖金曜日 **Seikin'yōbi** Good Friday
試金石 **shikinseki** touchstone; test
賃金 **chingin** wages, pay
資金 **shikin** funds
資金難 **shikinnan** financial difficulty
資金繰 **shikingu(ri)** raising funds, generating revenue
預金 **yokin** deposit, bank account
　　 azu(ke)kin money on deposit
預金者 **yokinsha** depositor
14 端金 **hashi(ta)gane** small change
罰金 **bakkin** a fine
銭金 **zenikane** money
15 賞金 **shōkin** (cash) prize, monetary reward
敷金 **shikikin** (security) deposit
締金 **shi(me)gane** clasp, clamp
賜金 **shikin** monetary award
鋳金 **chūkin** casting
16 賭金 **kakekin** stakes, bet
錬金術 **renkinjutsu** alchemy
頭金 **atamakin** down payment
17 償金 **shōkin** indemnities, reparations, damages
謝金 **shakin** monetary gift of thanks

鍍金 **tokin, mekki** plating, gilding
闇金融 **yamikin'yū** illegal lending
19 贋金 **nisegane** counterfeit money
贋金作 **niseganezuku(ri)** counterfeiter
20 醵金 **kyokin** donation, contribution
29 鬱金色 **ukon-iro** saffron color

──────── 3 ────────

1 一時金 **ichijikin** lump sum
2 入会金 **nyūkaikin** enrollment/admission fee
入学金 **nyūgakukin** entrance/matriculation fee
4 予備金 **yobikin** reserve/emergency fund
弔慰金 **chōikin** condolence money
手切金 **tegi(re)kin** solatium for severing relations
手付金 **tetsu(ke)kin** earnest money, deposit
手取金 **tedo(ri)kin** take-home pay
手提金庫 **tesa(ge)kinko** cash box, portable safe
引当金 **hi(ki)a(te)kin** reserve fund, appropriation
月水金 **ges-sui-kin** Mondays, Wednesdays, and Fridays
5 出資金 **shusshikin** investment, capital
弁償金 **benshōkin** indemnity, reparations
加入金 **kanyūkin** entrance/initiation fee
石部金吉 **Ishibe Kinkichi** man of strict morals
立替金 **ta(te)ka(e)kin** an advance
目腐金 **mekusa(re)gane** pittance
7 身代金 **mi(no)shirokin** ransom money
低賃金 **teichingin** low wages
助成金 **joseikin** subsidy, grant
汞和金 **kōwakin** amalgam
尾錠金 **bijōgane** buckle, clasp
見舞金 **mima(i)kin** money gift to a sick person
8 非鉄金属 **hitetsu kinzoku** nonferrous metals
退職金 **taishokukin** retirement allowance
追徴金 **tsuichōkin** additional collection, supplementary charge
所持金 **shojikin** money on hand
委託金 **itakukin** money in trust
取立金 **toritatekin** money collected
金地金 **kin jigane** gold bullion
9 俄成金 **niwakanarikin** overnight millionaire
保険金 **hokenkin** insurance money
保釈金 **hoshakukin** bail
保証金 **hoshōkin** security deposit, key money
軍用金 **gun'yōkin** war funds; campaign funds
軍資金 **gunshikin** war funds; campaign funds
持参金 **jisankin** dowry
10 借越金 **ka(ri)ko(shi)kin** overdraft, debt balance
冥加金 **myōgakin** votive offering; forced contributions (Edo era)

納付金 **nōfukin** contribution
配当金 **haitōkin** dividend
11 剰余金 **jōyokin** a surplus
過怠金 **kataikin** fine for default
基本金 **kihonkin** endowment fund
寄付金 **kifukin** contributions
常備金 **jōbikin** reserve fund
救済金 **kyūsaikin** relief fund
船成金 **funanarikin** shipping magnate
12 割戻金 **wa(ri)modo(shi)kin** a rebate
違約金 **iyakukin** breach-of-contract penalty
補助金 **hojokin** subsidy, grant
補償金 **hoshōkin** indemnity, compensation
　　(money)
結納金 **yuinōkin** engagement gift money
給与金 **kyūyokin** allowance, grant
貸付金 **kashitsukekin** a loan, advance
軽合金 **keigōkin** light alloy
13 準備金 **junbikin** reserve fund
義捐金 **gienkin** donation, contribution
義援金 **gienkin** donation, contribution
奨学金 **shōgakukin** a scholarship
資本金 **shihonkin** capital
14 総益金 **sōekikin** gross profit
15 養老金 **yōrōkin** old-age pension
賞与金 **shōyokin** bonus
権利金 **kenrikin** key money
慰労金 **irōkin** bonus, gratuity
賠償金 **baishōkin** indemnities, reparations, damages
16 積立金 **tsumitatekin** a reserve (fund)
18 臍繰金 **hesoku(ri)gane** secret savings
19 繰入金 **kuriirekin** money/balance transferred
繰越金 **kurikoshikin** balance brought forward
20 懸賞金 **kenshōkin** prize money, reward

———————— 4 ————————

1 一字千金 **ichiji senkin** great words
一刻千金 **ikkoku senkin** Every minute counts.
一攫千金 **ikkaku senkin** getting rich quick
8 厚生年金 **kōsei nenkin** welfare pension
11 運転資金 **unten shikin** working capital, operating funds
12 街頭募金 **gaitō bokin** street solicitation

———————— 2 ————————

釼 → 刀 **2f0.1**

8a2.1

鈳 **KOKU** gold

8a2.2

鈢 **HACHI, HATSU** forge, temper, anneal

8a2.3 / 341

針 **SHIN, hari** needle

———————— 1 ————————

0 お針 **(o)hari** needlework, sewing; seamstress
3 針女 **harime** seamstress
針小棒大 **shinshō-bōdai** exaggeration
針山 **hariyama** pincushion
5 針仕事 **hari shigoto** needlework, sewing
針目 **harime** seam, stitch
7 針状 **harijō** needle-like
針医 **harii** acupuncturist
針灸 **shinkyū** acupuncture and moxibustion
8 針刺 **harisa(shi)** pincushion
針金 **harigane** wire
10 針師 **harishi** needlemaker; acupuncturist
11 針術 **shinjutsu** acupuncture
12 針葉 **shin'yō** evergreen needles
針葉樹 **shin'yōju** needle-leaf tree, conifer
13 針路 **shinro** course (of a ship)
15 針箱 **haribako** sewing box

———————— 2 ————————

4 方針 **hōshin** compass needle; course, policy
8 長針 **chōshin** the long/minute hand
9 指針 **shishin** compass/indicator needle; guide(line)
待針 **ma(chi)bari** marking pin
秒針 **byōshin** second hand (of a clock)
10 留針 **to(me)bari** pin, safety pin, brooch, hairpin
蚊針 **kabari** fishing fly
11 運針 **unshin** handling the needle
運針縫 **unshinnu(i)** ordinary stitching
釣針 **tsu(ri)bari** fishhook
12 短針 **tanshin** hour hand
検針 **kenshin** checking a meter/gauge
13 絹針 **kinubari** needle for silk
鉤針 **kagibari** hook
14 磁針 **jishin** magnetic needle
網針 **amibari** netting needle
15 編針 **a(mi)bari** knitting needle, crochet hook
縫針 **nu(i)bari** sewing needle
19 羅針 **rashin** compass needle
羅針儀 **rashingi** compass
羅針盤 **rashinban** compass

———————— 3 ————————

3 千人針 **senninbari** soldier's good-luck waistband sewn one stitch each by a thousand women

8 注射針 **chūshabari** hypodermic needle
12 無方針 **muhōshin** without a plan
15 避雷針 **hiraishin** lightning rod

───────── 4 ─────────

11 頂門一針 **chōmon (no) isshin** stinging reproach/admonition (like a needle plunged into the top of one's head)

8a2.4

釘 **TEI, kugi** nail, spike

───────── 1 ─────────

6 釘付 **kugizu(ke)** nailing (down); pegging (a price)
釘目 **kugime** location of the nail
7 釘抜 **kuginu(ki)** nail-puller, claw hammer
12 釘裂 **kugiza(ki)** tearing (clothes) on a nail

───────── 2 ─────────

3 大釘 **ōkugi** large nail, spike
4 犬釘 **inukugi** spike
木釘 **kikugi** wooden peg
7 折釘 **o(re)kugi** broken/hooked nail, screw hook
8 金釘流 **kanakugiryū** a scrawl
13 隠釘 **kaku(shi)kugi** concealed nail

───────── 3 ─────────

4 五寸釘 **gosun kugi** long nail, spike

───────── 3 ─────────

8a3.1

釦 **KŌ, botan** button

───────── 2 ─────────

8 押釦 **o(shi)botan** pushbutton

釼→剣 **2f8.5**

8a3.2

鉇 **SHI** halberd

8a3.3

釵 **SAI, kazashi** ornamental hairpin

8a3.4

釧 **SEN** bracelet

───────── 1 ─────────

13 釧路 **Kushiro** (city, Hokkaidō)

8a3.5 / 1862

釣 **CHŌ, tsu(ru)** fish, angle; lure, entice, take in; (see 吊) hang, suspend
tsu(ri) (rod-and-reel) fishing; change (money returned when the amount paid is greater than the price)

───────── 1 ─────────

0 お釣り **(o)tsu(ri)** change (money returned when the amount paid is greater than the price)
3 釣上 **tsu(ri)a(geru)** fish out, land, raise (one's eyes); keep/jack up (prices)
4 釣天井 **tsu(ri) tenjō** ceiling rigged to fall onto and kill someone
釣込 **tsu(ri)ko(mu)** lure into, entice
釣手 **tsu(ri)te** angler
5 釣出 **tsu(ri)da(su)** fish/draw out
釣台 **tsu(ri)dai** stretcher, litter
6 釣仲間 **tsu(ri) nakama** fishing buddies
釣合 **tsu(ri)a(u)** be in balance, match
tsu(ri)a(i) balance, equilibrium, proportion
釣灯籠 **tsu(ri)dōrō** hanging lantern
釣糸 **tsu(ri)ito** fishing line
7 釣花 **tsu(ri)bana** flowers in a hanging vase
釣床 **tsu(ri)doko** hammock
8 釣具 **tsu(ri)gu** fishing tackle
9 釣竿 **tsu(ri)zao** fishing rod
10 釣師 **tsu(ri)shi** angler
釣針 **tsu(ri)bari** fishhook
11 釣瓶 **tsurube** well bucket
釣瓶打 **tsurubeu(chi)** firing in rapid succession
釣道具 **tsu(ri) dōgu** fishing tackle
釣堀 **tsu(ri)bori** fishpond
釣梯子 **tsu(ri)bashigo** rope ladder
12 釣場 **tsu(ri)ba** fishing spot
釣棚 **tsu(ri)dana** hanging shelf
14 釣銭 **tsu(ri)sen** change (money returned when the amount paid is greater than the price)
16 釣橋 **tsu(ri)bashi** suspension bridge
20 釣鐘 **tsu(ri)gane** hanging bell

───────── 2 ─────────

4 不釣合 **futsuria(i)** unbalanced, disproportionate, ill-matched
友釣 **tomozu(ri)** fishing using decoys
5 穴釣 **anazu(ri)** ice fishing
7 沖釣 **okizu(ri)** offshore fishing
8 夜釣 **yozu(ri)** fishing at night
空釣 **karazu(ri)** fishing without bait
10 陸釣 **okazu(ri)** fishing from the shore
11 魚釣 **uotsu(ri), sakanatsu(ri)** fishing, angling

8

金 3←
食
隹
雨
門

15 撥釣瓶 **ha(ne)tsurube** a well sweep
17 磯釣 **isozu(ri)** fishing from seashore rocks

——————— 4 ———————

8a4.1

欽 **KIN** respect, revere

——————— 1 ———————

8 欽定 **kintei** authorized (by the emperor)
欽定訳聖書 **kinteiyaku seisho** the King
James Bible
欽定憲法 **kintei kenpō** constitution granted
by the emperor
欽明 **Kinmei** (emperor, 539–571)

鈩→鑪 **8a16.1**

8a4.2 / 966

鈍 **DON, nibu(i)** dull, thick, slow-witted,
sluggish, blunt, dim **nibu(ru)** become
dull/blunt, weaken **noro(i)** slow, dull;
doting, flirtatious **nama(ru)** become
dull/blunted **nama(su)** anneal

——————— 1 ———————

3 鈍才 **donsai** dull-witted
6 鈍色 **nibu-iro, nibi-iro** dark gray
鈍行 **donkō** slow (not express) train
鈍百姓 **donbyakushō** dumb farmer
7 鈍角 **donkaku** obtuse angle
8 鈍物 **donbutsu** blockhead, dunce
9 鈍臭 **norokusa(i)** slow, sluggish
10 鈍根 **donkon** slow-witted, inept
11 鈍麻 **donma** dullness
12 鈍痛 **dontsū** dull pain
鈍間 **noroma** slow-witted, stupid
13 鈍感 **donkan** obtuse, thick, insensitive
15 鈍器 **donki** blunt object (used as a weapon)
鈍調 **donchō** dull (market)

——————— 2 ———————

7 利鈍 **ridon** sharp or blunt, bright or dull
11 遅鈍 **chidon** slow-witted, dull, stupid
12 焼鈍 **shōdon, ya(ki)nama(shi)** annealing
13 愚鈍 **gudon** stupid, half-witted, asinine
15 駑鈍 **dodon** dull-witted, doltish
魯鈍 **rodon** stupid, foolish

8a4.3

鈕 **CHŪ, botan** button

8a4.4

鈇 **FU** ax

——————— 1 ———————

13 鈇鉞 **fuetsu** ax; battle-ax

8a4.5

鈔 **SHŌ** write; copy; summarize; confiscate

——————— 3 ———————

14 歎異鈔 **Tannishō** (a collection of Buddhist
teachings)

8a4.6

釿 **KIN** hatchet

8a4.7

鈀 **HAKU, kanagaki, kushiro** hoeing
fork, rake

鈬→鐸 **8a13.3**

8a4.8

鈑 **HAN, itagane** sheet metal

鈎→鉤 **8a5.17**

8a4.9

鈞 **KIN** (unit of weight, about 6 kg);
important position

——————— 5 ———————

8a5.1

鉐 **SEKI, JAKU** brass

8a5.2

鈿 **DEN, kanzashi** ornamental hairpin

8 金 食 隹 雷 門
→ 4

————————— 2 —————————

17 螺鈿 **raden** mother-of-pearl

8a5.3

鉗   **KEN, KAN** pillory; keep (one's mouth) shut

————————— 1 —————————

2 鉗子 **kanshi** forceps

8a5.4 / 1820

鉢   **HACHI, HATSU** bowl, pot; brainpan, crown

————————— 1 —————————

6 鉢合 **hachia(wase)** bump heads; run into
8 鉢物 **hachimono** food served in bowls; potted plant
9 鉢巻 **hachima(ki)** cloth tied around one's head
12 鉢植 **hachiu(e)** potted plant

————————— 2 —————————

3 小鉢 **kobachi** small bowl
4 火鉢 **hibachi** charcoal brazier, hibachi
6 托鉢 **takuhatsu** religious mendicancy; begging priest
   向鉢巻 **mu(kō) hachimaki** rolled towel tied around the head
   衣鉢 **ihatsu** (assume one's master's) mantle
7 乳鉢 **nyūbachi** mortar
9 後鉢巻 **ushi(ro) hachimaki** twisted towel tied around one's head and knotted behind
10 捏鉢 **ko(ne)bachi** kneading trough
11 捨鉢 **su(te)bachi** despair, desperation
   捩鉢巻 **neji(ri)hachima(ki), ne(ji)hachima(ki)** twisted towel tied around one's head
16 擂鉢 **su(ri)bachi** mortar (and pestle)

————————— 3 —————————

4 手洗鉢 **teara(i)bachi** washbasin
8 長火鉢 **nagahibachi** oblong brazier
   金魚鉢 **kingyobachi** goldfish bowl
12 植木鉢 **uekibachi** flowerpot
15 箱火鉢 **hako hibachi** box-enclosed brazier
19 瀬戸鉢 **setobachi** earthenware pot

8a5.5

鈸   **HATSU, HACHI** cymbals

————————— 2 —————————

20 鐃鈸 **nyōhachi** (Buddhist) cymbals

鉄 鐵鐵銕   **TETSU, kurogane** iron

————————— 1 —————————

3 鉄工 **tekkō** ironworker, blacksmith
   鉄工場 **tekkōjō** ironworks
   鉄山 **tetsuzan** iron mine
4 鉄片 **teppen** piece/scrap of iron
   鉄分 **tetsubun** iron content
   鉄火 **tekka** red-hot iron; gambling; swords and guns; fierce temperament
   鉄火巻 **tekkama(ki)** seaweed-wrapped tuna sushi
   鉄火場 **tekkaba** gambling room
   鉄心 **tesshin** iron core; iron/firm will
5 鉄甲 **tekkō** iron armor/helmet
   鉄石 **tesseki** iron and stone; adamant, firm
   鉄石心 **tessekishin** iron/steadfast will
6 鉄色 **tetsu-iro** reddish black, iron blue
   鉄血 **tekketsu** blood and iron; military preparations
   鉄舟 **tesshū** steel boat/pontoon
7 鉄坑 **tekkō** iron mine
   鉄床 **kanatoko** anvil
   鉄材 **tetsuzai** iron/steel material
   鉄条網 **tetsujōmō** barbed-wire entanglements
8 鉄沓 **kanagutsu** horseshoe
   鉄板 **teppan** steel plate; griddle
9 鉄挺 **kanateko** crowbar
   鉄面皮 **tetsumenpi** brazen, impudent
   鉄柵 **tessaku** iron railing/fence
   鉄肺 **tetsu (no) hai** iron lung
   鉄則 **tessoku** hard-and-fast rule
10 鉄剤 **tetsuzai** iron-containing preparation
   鉄索 **tessaku** cable
   鉄拳 **tekken** clenched fist
   鉄拳制裁 **tekken seisai** the law of the fist
   鉄案 **tetsuan** irrevocable decision
   鉄屑 **tetsukuzu** scrap iron
   鉄格子 **tetsugōshi** iron bars, grating
   鉄骨 **tekkotsu** steel frame
   鉄扇 **tessen** iron-ribbed folding fan
   鉄砲 **teppō** gun
   鉄砲傷 **teppō kizu** gunshot wound
   鉄粉 **teppun** iron filings/powder
11 鉄瓶 **tetsubin** iron kettle
   鉄道 **tetsudō** railroad
   鉄道便 **tetsudōbin** transport by rail
   鉄道馬車 **tetsudō basha** horse-drawn streetcar
   鉄道網 **tetsudōmō** railway network
   鉄窓 **tessō** steel-barred (prison) window
   鉄脚 **tekkyaku** iron legs
   鉄船 **tessen** steel ship, an ironclad

8

金 5←
食
隹
雷
門

12 鉄塔 **tettō** steel tower
鉄棒 **tetsubō, kanabō** iron bar/rod; (gymnastics) horizontal bar
鉄棒引 **kanabōhi(ki)** night watchman; a gossip
鉄腕 **tetsuwan** strong untiring arm
鉄兜 **tetsukabuto** steel helmet
鉄扉 **teppi** iron door
鉄筆 **teppitsu** steel/stencil pen, stylus; powerful pen
鉄筋 **tekkin** steel reinforcing rods
13 鉄槌 **tettsui** hammer
鉄褐色 **tekkasshoku** iron gray
鉄路 **tetsuro** railroad
鉄鉱 **tekkō** iron ore
鉄鉱泉 **tekkōsen** rusty-water springs
14 鉄製 **tessei** made of iron/steel
鉄管 **tekkan** iron pipe
15 鉄器 **tekki** ironware, hardware
鉄敷 **kanashi(ki)** anvil
鉄線 **tessen** steel wire
鉄質 **tesshitsu** ferrous
16 鉄壁 **teppeki** iron wall; impregnable fortress
鉄橋 **tekkyō** steel/railroad bridge
鉄蹄 **tettei** horseshoe
鉄錆 **tetsusabi** iron rust
鉄鋼 **tekkō** steel
鉄鋼業 **tekkōgyō** the steel industry
17 鉄鎚 **kanazuchi** hammer
18 鉄鎖 **tessa** iron chain
21 鉄艦 **tekkan** ironclad warship

─────── 2 ───────

3 寸鉄 **suntetsu** small weapon; pithy remark, epigram
4 水鉄砲 **mizudeppō** squirt gun
5 古鉄 **furutetsu** scrap iron
7 豆鉄砲 **mamedeppō** bean/pea shooter, popgun
肘鉄 **hijitetsu** rebuff, rejection
肘鉄砲 **hijideppō** rebuff, rejection
条鉄 **jōtetsu** bar/rod iron
私鉄 **shitetsu** private railway line
8 非鉄金属 **hitetsu kinzoku** nonferrous metals
空鉄砲 **karadeppō** unloaded gun; a blank (cartridge)
国鉄 **Kokutetsu** national railway, JNR (short for 日本国有鉄道)
金鉄 **kintetsu** gold and iron; firmness
9 砂鉄 **satetsu, shatetsu** iron/magnetic sand
10 帯鉄 **obitetsu** band iron
屑鉄 **kuzutetsu** scrap iron
紙鉄砲 **kamideppō** popgun
11 黄鉄鉱 **ōtekkō** iron pyrite, fool's gold
軟鉄 **nantetsu** soft iron
12 満鉄 **Mantetsu** South Manchuria Railway (short for 南満州鉄道)

無鉄砲 **muteppō** reckless, rash
13 電鉄 **dentetsu** electric railway
14 磁鉄 **jitetsu** magnetic iron
磁鉄鉱 **jitekkō** magnetite, loadstone
製鉄 **seitetsu** iron manufacturing
製鉄所 **seitetsujo** ironworks
製鉄業 **seitetsugyō** the iron industry
銑鉄 **sentetsu** pig iron
15 撃鉄 **gekitetsu** rifle/gun hammer
熱鉄 **nettetsu** hot/molten steel
鋳鉄 **chūtetsu, itetsu** cast iron
16 蹄鉄 **teitetsu** horseshoe
蹄鉄工 **teitetsukō** horseshoer
錬鉄 **rentetsu** wrought iron
鋼鉄 **kōtetsu** steel
鋼鉄車 **kōtetsusha** steel (railroad) car
鋼鉄板 **kōtetsuban** steel plate
鋼鉄製 **kōtetsusei** made of steel
鋼鉄線 **kōtetsusen** steel wire
17 鍛鉄 **tantetsu** tempered/wrought iron

─────── 3 ───────

6 地下鉄 **chikatetsu** subway
有刺鉄線 **yūshi tessen** barbed wire
7 亜鉛鉄 **aentetsu** galvanized iron
8 国有鉄道 **kokuyū tetsudō** national railway
金城鉄壁 **kinjō-teppeki** impregnable castle
12 軽便鉄道 **keiben tetsudō** narrow-gauge railroad
13 電磁鉄 **denjitetsu** electromagnet

8a5.7

鉦 **SHŌ, SEI** bell; fermium
kane bell
dora gong

─────── 1 ───────

13 鉦鼓 **shōko** bells and drums

8a5.8

鉋 **HŌ, kanna** (carpenter's) plane

─────── 1 ───────

10 鉋屑 **kannakuzu** wood shavings

─────── 2 ───────

11 粗鉋 **araganna** foreplane

8a5.9

鉚 **RYŪ** gold

8a5.10

鉈 **SHA, nata** hatchet

8
→5 金 食 隹 霊 門

——————— 2 ———————

3 大鉈 **ōnata** big hatchet, ax

8a5.11 / 1822

鈴 **REI, RIN, suzu** bell

——————— 1 ———————

4 鈴木 **Suzuki** (surname)
5 鈴生 **suzuna(ri)** grow in clusters/abundance
19 鈴蘭 **suzuran** lily-of-the-valley

——————— 2 ———————

4 予鈴 **yorei** first bell
8 呼鈴 **yo(bi)rin** door bell, call bell, buzzer
9 風鈴 **fūrin** wind chime
10 振鈴 **shinrei** ringing a (hand) bell
　　馬鈴薯 **bareishoi** (white/Irish) potato
11 啞鈴 **arei** dumbbell
13 電鈴 **denrei** electric bell
14 銀鈴 **ginrei** silver bell

8a5.12

鉉 **GEN, tsuru** handle (on a kettle)

8a5.13

鈷 **KO** cobalt

8a5.14 / 1606

鉛 **EN, namari** lead (the metal)

——————— 1 ———————

3 鉛工 **enkō** plumber
4 鉛中毒 **enchūdoku** lead poisoning
5 鉛白 **enpaku** white lead
6 鉛色 **namari-iro** lead color, gray
8 鉛毒 **endoku** lead poisoning
　　鉛版 **enban** stereotype, printing plate
　　鉛直 **enchoku** perpendicular, plumb
12 鉛筆 **enpitsu** pencil
13 鉛塊 **enkai** lead ingot
　　鉛鉱 **enkō** lead mine/deposits
14 鉛管 **enkan** lead pipe, plumbing
16 鉛錘 **ensui** plumb bob, plummet

——————— 2 ———————

5 白鉛 **hakuen** white lead
6 色鉛筆 **iroenpitsu** colored pencil
7 亜鉛 **aen** zinc
　　亜鉛引 **aenbi(ki)** galvanized

亜鉛末 **aenmatsu** zinc dust
亜鉛版 **aenban** zinc etching
亜鉛板 **aenban** zinc plate
亜鉛華 **aenka** flowers of zinc, zinc oxide
亜鉛鉄 **aentetsu** galvanized iron
11 黒鉛 **kokuen** black lead, graphite
12 測鉛 **sokuen** plumb bob, sounding lead
13 蒼鉛 **sōen** bismuth

8a5.15 / 1604

鉱 鑛 礦 砿 **KŌ** ore

——————— 1 ———————

3 鉱工業 **kōkōgyō** mining and manufacturing
　　鉱山 **kōzan** a mine
　　鉱山業 **kōzangyō** mining
4 鉱夫 **kōfu** miner
　　鉱区 **kōku** mining area/concession
　　鉱水 **kōsui** mineral water
5 鉱石 **kōseki** ore, mineral, (radio) crystal
7 鉱床 **kōshō** ore/mineral deposits
8 鉱毒 **kōdoku** mine pollution, copper poisoning
　　鉱油 **kōyu** mineral oil
　　鉱物 **kōbutsu** mineral
　　鉱物学 **kōbutsugaku** mineralogy
　　鉱物質 **kōbutsushitsu** mineral matter
9 鉱泉 **kōsen** mineral springs
10 鉱脈 **kōmyaku** vein of ore
11 鉱産地 **kōsanchi** mineral-rich area
13 鉱業 **kōgyō** mining
　　鉱滓 **kōsai, kōshi** slag
14 鉱層 **kōsō** ore bed

——————— 2 ———————

8 泥鉱 **deikō** slime ore
　　金鉱 **kinkō** gold ore/deposits
　　金鉱脈 **kinkōmyaku** gold vein
9 洗鉱 **senkō** ore washing
　　炭鉱 **tankō** coal mine
　　砕鉱 **saikō** ore crushing
　　砕鉱機 **saikōki** ore crusher
10 原鉱 **genkō** (raw) ore
11 採鉱 **saikō** mining
　　探鉱 **tankō** prospecting
　　粗鉱 **sokō** undressed ore
13 溶鉱炉 **yōkōro** blast furnace
　　鉄鉱 **tekkō** iron ore
　　鉄鉱泉 **tekkōsen** rusty-water springs
　　鉛鉱 **enkō** lead mine/deposits
14 選鉱 **senkō** ore dressing/sorting
　　銀鉱 **ginkō** silver ore/deposits
　　銅鉱 **dōkō** copper ore
18 鎔鉱炉 **yōkōro** blast furnace

——————— 3 ———————

11 黄鉄鉱 **ōtekkō** iron pyrite, fool's gold

8

金 5 ←
食
隹
雨
門

黄銅鉱 **ōdōkō, kōdōkō** copper pyrite, fool's gold
14 磁鉄鉱 **jitekkō** magnetite, loadstone

8a5.16

鉞
ETSU, masakari battle-ax, broad-ax

——————— 2 ———————

8 斧鉞 **fuetsu** ax
12 鈇鉞 **fuetsu** ax; battle-ax

8a5.17

鉤 鈎
KŌ, kagi hook

——————— 1 ———————

4 鉤手 **kagi(no)te** right-angle bend
6 鉤虫 **kōchū** hookworm
10 鉤針 **kagibari** hook
12 鉤裂 **kagiza(ki)** a tear (in one's clothes)
14 鉤鼻 **kagibana** hooked/aquiline nose

——————— 2 ———————

4 毛鉤 **kebari** (fishing) fly
手鉤 **tekagi** hook
10 蚊鉤 **kabari** fishing fly
11 掛鉤 **ka(ke)kagi** hook

——————— 3 ———————

6 自在鉤 **jizai kagi** height-adjustable hook for hanging a pot over a fire

8a5.18

鉅
KYO big, great

——————— 6 ———————

8a6.1 / 648

銭 錢
SEN money; 1/100 yen
zeni money

——————— 1 ———————

2 銭入 **zenii(re)** purse
8 銭金 **zenikane** money
11 銭貨 **senka** coins
12 銭湯 **sentō** public bath
15 銭箱 **zenibako** cashbox, till
18 銭儲 **zenimō(ke)** money-making

——————— 2 ———————

3 口銭 **kōsen** commission; net profit
小銭 **kozeni** small change, coins
5 古銭 **kosen** old coin

古銭学 **kosengaku** numismatics
6 守銭奴 **shusendo** miser, niggard
米銭 **beisen** money for rice
7 身銭 **mizeni** one's own money
8 追銭 **o(i)sen** additional payment, throwing good money after bad
泡銭 **abukuzeni** ill-gotten/easy money
金銭 **kinsen** money
11 宿銭 **yadosen** hotel charges
悪銭 **akusen** ill-gotten money
釣銭 **tsu(ri)sen** change (money returned when the amount paid is greater than the price)
12 湯銭 **yusen** bathhouse charge
渡銭 **wata(shi)sen** ferry charge
無銭 **musen** without money
無銭旅行 **musen ryokō** penniless travel, hitchhiking
無銭飲食 **musen inshoku** jumping a restaurant bill
13 賃銭 **chinsen** wages, pay
14 端銭 **hasen** small change
銅銭 **dōsen** copper coin
16 橋銭 **hashisen** bridge toll
17 賽銭 **saisen** money offering
賽銭箱 **saisenbako** offertory chest
20 鐚銭 **bitasen** worn/effaced coin

——————— 3 ———————

3 小遣銭 **kozuka(i)sen** spending money
4 木戸銭 **kidosen** admission fee
9 風呂銭 **furosen** bath charge
草鞋銭 **warajisen** traveling money

銕 → 鉄 8a5.6

8a6.2

銖
SHU (unit of weight/currency, one-sixteenth of a *ryō*); percent; small, slight

8a6.3 / 313

銀
GIN, shirogane silver

——————— 1 ———————

0 銀ぶら **gin(bura)** stroll along the Ginza
銀メダル **ginmedaru** silver medal
3 銀山 **ginzan** silver mine
5 銀本位 **ginhon'i** the silver standard
銀世界 **ginsekai** vast silvery/snowy scene
6 銀色 **gin-iro, ginshoku** silver color
銀地 **ginji** silvery background
銀行 **ginkō** bank
銀行券 **ginkōken** bank note

8

→5 金
食
隹
雷
門

銀行界 **ginkōkai** the banking community
銀行員 **ginkōin** bank clerk/employee
銀行家 **ginkōka** banker
銀糸 **ginshi** silver thread
7 銀位 **gin'i** silver fineness/quality
銀坑 **ginkō** silver mine
銀杏 **ginnan** gingko nut　**ichō** gingko tree
8 銀波 **ginpa** silvery waves
銀泥 **gindei** silver paint
銀河 **ginga** the Milky Way
銀杯 **ginpai** silver cup
9 銀砂子 **ginsunago** silver dust
銀盃 **ginpai** silver cup
10 銀流 **ginnaga(shi)** silvering, tinsel
銀座 **ginza** silver mint; the Ginza
銀扇 **ginsen** silver-colored folding fan
銀紙 **gingami** silver paper
銀粉 **ginpun** silver dust
11 銀側 **gingawa** silver case
銀婚式 **ginkonshiki** silver wedding anniversary
銀細工 **ginzaiku** silverwork
銀細工師 **ginzaikushi** silversmith
銀笛 **ginteki** metal flute
銀貨 **ginka** silver coin
12 銀牌 **ginpai** silver medal
銀筋 **ginsuji** silver line/stripe
13 銀塊 **ginkai** silver ingot/bullion
銀幕 **ginmaku** silver screen
銀鈴 **ginrei** silver bell
銀鉱 **ginkō** silver ore/deposits
14 銀髪 **ginpatsu** silvery hair
銀製 **ginsei** made of silver
銀箔 **ginpaku** silver leaf/foil
銀閣 **ginkaku** silver/beautiful building
銀閣寺 **Ginkakuji** (temple in Kyōto)
15 銀器 **ginki** silver utensils
銀盤 **ginban** silver platter; skating rink
銀縁 **ginbuchi** silver-rimmed
銀輪 **ginrin** bicycle
17 銀翼 **gin'yoku** silvery wings

---------------- 2 ----------------

3 工銀 **kōgin** wages, pay
4 水銀 **suigin** mercury
水銀灯 **suigintō** mercury lamp
水銀柱 **suiginchū** column of mercury
日銀 **Nichigin** Bank of Japan (short for 日本銀行)
6 世銀 **Segin** (short for 世界銀行) the World Bank
7 豆銀 **mamegin** (an Edo-era coin)
8 金銀 **kingin** gold and silver
9 洋銀 **yōgin** nickel/German silver
10 純銀 **jungin** pure/solid silver
11 粒銀 **tsubugin** (a small silver coin)

13 賃銀 **chingin** wages, pay
路銀 **rogin** traveling expenses
16 親銀行 **oyaginkō** parent bank
18 燻銀 **ibu(shi)gin** oxidized silver; refined

---------------- 3 ----------------

7 豆板銀 **mameitagin** (an Edo-era coin)
12 硝酸銀 **shōsangin** silver nitrate

8a6.4 / 1552

銘

MEI inscription, signature, name; precept, motto

---------------- 1 ----------------

0 銘じる **mei(jiru)** engrave, impress upon
3 銘々 **meimei** each, apiece
銘々伝 **meimeiden** lives, biographies
5 銘仙 **meisen** (a type of silk)
9 銘茶 **meicha** quality-brand tea
銘柄 **meigara** name, brand, issue (of shares)
10 銘酒 **meishu** special-brand saké
銘酒屋 **meishuya** brothel
銘記 **meiki** bear in mind
11 銘菓 **meika** quality-brand cakes

---------------- 2 ----------------

10 記銘 **kimei** inscription, engraving
12 無銘 **mumei** unsigned, bearing no signature
13 墓銘 **bomei** epitaph
感銘 **kanmei** impression (on one's mind)
14 碑銘 **himei** inscription, epitaph
銘銘 **meimei** each, apiece
銘銘伝 **meimeiden** lives, biographies

---------------- 3 ----------------

10 座右銘 **zayū (no) mei** one's motto
13 墓碑銘 **bohimei** epitaph
墓誌銘 **boshimei** epitaph

---------------- 4 ----------------

5 正真正銘 **shōshin-shōmei** genuine, authentic

8a6.5

銚

CHŌ spade; saké dipper/bottle

8a6.6 / 1905

銑

SEN pig iron

---------------- 1 ----------------

13 銑鉄 **sentetsu** pig iron

8a6.7

銛

SEN, mori harpoon

8a6.8

鋩 **BŌ** point of a sword/halberd

8a6.9 / 829

銃 **JŪ, tsutsu** gun

——————— 1 ———————

3 銃丸 **jūgan** bullet
銃口 **jūkō** (gun) muzzle
銃士 **jūshi** musketeer
4 銃火 **jūka** gunfire
6 銃刑 **jūkei** execution by firing squad
7 銃身 **jūshin** gun barrel
銃把 **jūha** (pistol's) grip
銃声 **jūsei** sound of a gunshot
銃床 **jūshō** stock (of a gun)
銃尾 **jūbi** breech (of a gun)
9 銃後 **jūgo** the home front
銃架 **jūka** gun rest/mount
10 銃剣 **jūken** bayonet
銃剣術 **jūkenjutsu** bayonet fencing
銃殺 **jūsatsu** shoot dead
銃砲 **jūhō** guns, firearms
11 銃猟 **jūryō** hunting
銃眼 **jūgan** gunport, crenel
12 銃創 **jūsō** gunshot wound
銃弾 **jūdan** bullet
13 銃傷 **jūshō** gunshot wound
15 銃撃 **jūgeki** shooting
銃器 **jūki** firearm

——————— 2 ———————

3 小銃 **shōjū** rifle, small arms
10 拳銃 **kenjū** pistol, handgun
11 捧銃 **sasa(ge)tsutsu** Present arms!
猟銃 **ryōjū** hunting gun, shotgun
鳥銃 **chōjū** gun for shooting birds
12 短銃 **tanjū** pistol, handgun
16 機銃 **kijū** machine gun
機銃掃射 **kijū sōsha** machine-gunning
18 騎銃 **kijū** carbine

——————— 3 ———————

2 二連銃 **nirenjū** double-barreled gun
4 火縄銃 **hinawajū** matchlock, harquebus
8 空気銃 **kūkijū** air gun/rifle
9 連発銃 **renpatsujū** repeating firearm
単身銃 **tanshinjū** single-barreled gun
16 機関銃 **kikanjū** machine gun

——————— 4 ———————

9 重機関銃 **jūkikanjū** heavy machine gun
12 軽機関銃 **keikikanjū** light machine gun

8

→ 6 金
食
隹
雨
門

8a6.10

銓 **SEN** scales; weigh, measure

——————— 1 ———————

6 銓考 **senkō** selection, screening
16 銓衡 **senkō** selection, screening

8a6.11

鉾 **BŌ, hoko** halberd

——————— 2 ———————

13 蒲鉾 **kamaboko** boiled fish paste
蒲鉾兵舎 **kamaboko heisha** Quonset hut

8a6.12 / 1605

銅 **DŌ, aka, akagane** copper

——————— 1 ———————

0 銅メダル **dōmedaru** bronze medal
3 銅山 **dōzan** copper mine
6 銅色 **dōshoku** copper-colored
7 銅坑 **dōkō** copper mine
8 銅版 **dōban** copperplate
銅板 **dōban** sheet copper
9 銅臭 **dōshū** mercenary spirit
11 銅細工 **dōzaiku** copperwork
銅貨 **dōka** copper coin
12 銅牌 **dōhai** bronze medal
13 銅鉱 **dōkō** copper ore
14 銅像 **dōzō** bronze statue
銅製 **dōsei** made of copper
銅銭 **dōsen** copper coin
15 銅器 **dōki** copper/bronze utensil
銅線 **dōsen** copper wire
19 銅鏡 **dōkyō** bronze mirror
21 銅鐸 **dōtaku** bronze bell
27 銅鑼 **dora** gong

——————— 2 ———————

4 分銅 **fundō** (counter)weight
5 白銅 **hakudō** nickel
白銅貨 **hakudōka** a nickel (coin)
7 赤銅 **shakudō** gold-copper alloy
赤銅色 **shakudō-iro** brown, bronze, tanned
8 青銅 **seidō, karakane** bronze
青銅色 **seidōshoku** bronze-color
青銅器 **seidōki** bronze ware/tools
和銅 **Wadō** (era, 708–715)
11 黄銅 **ōdō, kōdō** brass
黄銅色 **kōdōshoku** brass yellow
黄銅鉱 **ōdōkō, kōdōkō** copper pyrite, fool's gold

14 精銅 **seidō** refined copper

————————— 3 —————————

13 電気銅 **denkidō** electrolytic copper

————————— 7 —————————

8a7.1

鉖　SAKU, ZAKU, kanahodashi fetters

8a7.2 / 1551

鋳　鑄　CHŪ, i(ru) cast (metal)

————————— 1 —————————

4 鋳込 **iko(mu)** cast (in a mold)
8 鋳直 **inao(su)** recast, recoin
鋳物 **imono** article of cast metal, a casting
鋳金 **chūkin** casting
9 鋳造 **chūzō** casting; minting, coinage
鋳造所 **chūzōsho** mint; foundry
鋳型 **igata** a mold, cast
11 鋳掛 **ika(keru)** recast, mend
鋳掛屋 **ika(ke)ya** tinkerer, tinsmith
鋳貨 **chūka** minting, coinage
13 鋳塊 **chūkai** ingot
鋳鉄 **chūtetsu, itetsu** cast iron
14 鋳像 **chūzō** cast image
15 鋳潰 **itsubu(su)** melt down
16 鋳鋼 **chūkō** casting/cast steel

————————— 2 —————————

6 再鋳 **saichū** recast
7 改鋳 **kaichū** recast, remint
13 新鋳 **shinchū** newly cast/minted
電鋳 **denchū** electrotyping

8a7.3

鋪　HO, shi(ku) lay out, spread, pave

————————— 1 —————————

11 鋪道 **hodō** paved road, pavement
12 鋪装 **hosō** pavement

8a7.4

鋏　KYŌ, hasami scissors; (ticket) punch
yattoko pliers, pincers

————————— 2 —————————

4 木鋏 **kibasami** pruning shears
7 花鋏 **hanabasami** pruning shears
8 金鋏 **kanabasami** metal-cutting shears

————————— 3 —————————

11 剪定鋏 **sentei-basami** pruning shears

8a7.5

鋤　JO, su(ku) till, plow
suki spade, plow

————————— 1 —————————

6 鋤返 **su(ki)kae(su)** plow up, turn over
10 鋤起 **su(ki)o(kosu)** plow up, turn over
12 鋤焼 **sukiya(ki)** sukiyaki
19 鋤簾 **joren** scoop, shovel

8a7.6

銹　鎑　SHŪ, sabi rust, tarnish

————————— 2 —————————

4 不銹鋼 **fushūkō** stainless steel

8a7.7

鋲　byō rivet, (thumb)tack

————————— 1 —————————

5 鋲打 **byōu(chi)** riveting

————————— 2 —————————

8 画鋲 **gabyō** thumbtack
10 留鋲 **to(me)byō** thumbtack

8a7.8

鋹　kazari metal ornament/jewelry

8a7.9

鈋　KA holmium
nie pattern on a sword blade

8a7.10

銷　SHŌ melt, smelt; extinguish

————————— 1 —————————

7 銷沈 **shōchin** dejected, depressed
10 銷夏 **shōka** spending the summer

8a7.11

鋒　HŌ halberd (tip)

————————— 2 —————————

6 舌鋒 **zeppō** tongue

8

金
食　7 ←
隹
電
門

15 論鋒 **ronpō** force of argument, logic
鋭鋒 **eihō** brunt of an attack/argument
16 機鋒 **kihō** point, brunt (of an attack)

8a7.12 / 1371

鋭 鋭
EI, surudo(i) sharp, keen

——————— 1 ———————
6 鋭気 **eiki** spirit, mettle, energy
7 鋭角 **eikaku** acute angle
鋭利 **eiri** sharp, keen
10 鋭敏 **eibin** sharp, keen, acute
13 鋭意 **eii** zealously, diligently
15 鋭鋒 **eihō** brunt of an attack/argument

——————— 2 ———————
6 気鋭 **kiei** spirited, energetic
先鋭 **sen'ei** radical
尖鋭 **sen'ei** acute; radical
尖鋭化 **sen'eika** become acute/radicalized
尖鋭分子 **sen'ei bunshi** radical elements
13 新鋭 **shin'ei** new (and powerful)
14 精鋭 **seiei** elite, crack (troops), the best
17 鮮鋭 **sen'ei** clear, sharp, well-defined

——————— 8 ———————

8a8.1

錐
SUI gimlet; pyramid, cone
kiri gimlet, auger, awl, drill

——————— 1 ———————
7 錐形 **suikei** pyramidal
——————— 2 ———————
4 円錐形 **ensuikei** cone
方錐 **hōsui** square pyramid; square drill
方錐形 **hōsuikei** square pyramid
5 立錐 **rissui** (not enough room to) drive in an awl
7 角錐 **kakusui** pyramid
——————— 3 ———————
3 三角錐 **sankakusui** triangular-base pyramid
22 嚢中錐 **nōchū (no) kiri** Talent will show.

8a8.2 / 1904

錘
SUI, tsumu spindle
omori weight, plumb bob, sinker

——————— 1 ———————
7 錘状 **suijō** spindle-shaped
——————— 2 ———————
10 紡錘 **bōsui** spindle
13 鉛錘 **ensui** plumb bob, plummet

8a8.3 / 1816

錬 錬
REN, ne(ru) forge, temper, refine; polish up; train, drill

——————— 1 ———————
6 錬成 **rensei** training
8 錬金術 **renkinjutsu** alchemy
13 錬鉄 **rentetsu** wrought iron
16 錬鋼 **renkō** wrought steel

——————— 2 ———————
6 百錬 **hyakuren** well tempered/trained
14 製錬 **seiren** refining, smelting
製錬所 **seirenjo** refinery, smelting works
精錬 **seiren** refining, smelting
精錬所 **seirenjo** refinery, smelter
17 鍛錬 **tanren** temper, anneal; train, harden

——————— 3 ———————
6 百戦錬磨 **hyakusen-renma** battle-seasoned, veteran

8a8.4

鉽
BU, buriki tin plate

——————— 1 ———————
2 鉽力 **buriki** tin (plate/sheet)

8a8.5

錏
A, shikoro armor havelock, neck guard (on an ancient battle helmet)

8a8.6

錦
KIN, nishiki brocade

——————— 1 ———————
4 錦木 **nishikigi** winged spindle tree
11 錦蛇 **nishikihebi** rock snake
12 錦御旗 **nishiki (no) mihata** the imperial standard
錦絵 **nishikie** colored woodblock print
——————— 2 ———————
10 唐錦 **karanishiki** Chinese brocade
14 綾錦 **ayanishiki** twill damask and brocade

8a8.7

錫
SEKI, SHAKU, suzu tin

——————— 1 ———————
7 錫杖 **shakujō** priest's staff

14 錫製品 **suzu seihin** tinware

———————— 2 ————————

5 巡錫 **junshaku** preaching tour

錢 → 銭 8a6.1

8a8.8

錆 錆   **SHŌ, sabi** rust
sa(biru) rust, get rusty

———————— 1 ————————

4 錆止 **sabido(me)** anticorrosive, rust preventive

5 錆付 **sabitsu(ku)** rust (together/fast)

6 錆色 **sabi-iro** rust color

———————— 2 ————————

8 金錆 **kanasabi** rust

13 鉄錆 **tetsusabi** iron rust

8a8.9

綴   **TETSU, shikoro** armor havelock, neck guard (on an ancient battle helmet)

8a8.10 / 1199

錯   **SAKU** mix, be in disorder

———————— 1 ————————

7 錯角 **sakkaku** alternate angles

錯乱 **sakuran** distraction, derangement

12 錯覚 **sakkaku** illusion

14 錯綜 **sakusō** complication, intricacy

錯誤 **sakugo** error

錯雑 **sakuzatsu** complication, intricacy

———————— 2 ————————

4 介錯 **kaishaku** assist at harakiri

6 交錯 **kōsaku** mixture, jumble

10 倒錯 **tōsaku** perversion

———————— 3 ————————

13 試行錯誤 **shikō-sakugo** trial and error

15 盤根錯節 **bankon-sakusetsu** knotty/thorny/complex situation

8a8.11

錚   **SŌ** metallic sound

———————— 1 ————————

3 錚々 **sōsō** eminent, outstanding

8a8.12 / 1818

錠   **JŌ** lock, padlock; pill, tablet, (counter for pills)

———————— 1 ————————

9 錠前 **jōmae** a lock

錠前屋 **jōmaeya** locksmith

10 錠剤 **jōzai** tablet, pill

———————— 2 ————————

4 手錠 **tejō** handcuffs

7 尾錠金 **bijōgane** buckle, clasp

9 施錠 **sejō** locking a lock

15 蝦錠 **ebijō** padlock

———————— 3 ————————

9 海老錠 **ebijō** padlock

16 糖衣錠 **tōijō** sugar-coated pill

8a8.13

鋺   **EN, kanamari** metal bowl

8a8.14

錨   **BYŌ, ikari** anchor

———————— 1 ————————

6 錨地 **byōchi** anchorage

8 錨泊 **byōhaku** anchorage

18 錨鎖 **byōsa** (chain) cable, hawser

———————— 2 ————————

7 抜錨 **batsubyō** weigh anchor, set sail

投錨 **tōbyō** drop anchor, lie at anchor

8a8.15

錙   **SHI** (unit of weight); small, slight

8a8.16 / 538

録 録   **ROKU, to(ru)** record

———————— 1 ————————

8 録画 **rokuga** (videotape) recording

9 録音 **rokuon** (sound) recording

録音機 **rokuonki** recorder

———————— 2 ————————

4 収録 **shūroku** collect, record

日録 **nichiroku** journal, daily record

5 付録 **furoku** supplement, appendix

目録 **mokuroku** catalog, list, inventory

8

金 8 ←
食
隹
雷
門

7 抄録 **shōroku** excerpt, abstract, summary
8 追録 **tsuiroku** supplement, postscript, addendum
実録 **jitsuroku** authentic record, true account
10 秘録 **hiroku** secret record/document
記録 **kiroku** record, document(ary)
記録的 **kirokuteki** record(-breaking)
記録係 **kirokugakari** recording secretary
11 採録 **sairoku** record, transcribe
12 登録 **tōroku** registration
登録済 **tōrokuzu(mi)** registered
登録簿 **tōrokubo** the register
街録 **gairoku** recorded man-on-the-street interview (short for 街頭録音)
集録 **shūroku** collect, record, compile
13 詳録 **shōroku** detailed record
載録 **sairoku** record, list
14 漫録 **manroku** random comments
摘録 **tekiroku** summary, précis
語録 **goroku** analects, sayings
雑録 **zatsuroku** miscellaneous notes
16 輯録 **shūroku** record, compile

———————— 3 ————————

2 人名録 **jinmeiroku** name list, directory
6 会議録 **kaigiroku** minutes, proceedings
回想録 **kaisōroku** memoirs
回顧録 **kaikoroku** memoirs, reminiscences
7 住所録 **jūshoroku** address book
決議録 **ketsugiroku** minutes (of a meeting)
芳名録 **hōmeiroku** visitor's book, name list
快記録 **kaikiroku** a fine record
9 速記録 **sokkiroku** shorthand notes
10 随想録 **zuisōroku** occasional thoughts, essays
11 紳士録 **shinshiroku** a who's-who, directory
12 備忘録 **bibōroku** memorandum, notebook
街頭録音 **gaitō rokuon** recorded man-on-the-street interview
13 新記録 **shinkiroku** new record
14 総目録 **sōmokuroku** complete catalog
15 黙示録 **Mokushiroku** Revelations, the Apocalypse
16 興信録 **kōshinroku** directory
17 講義録 **kōgiroku** lecture transcripts; correspondence course
18 職員録 **shokuinroku** list of government officials
20 議事録 **gijiroku** minutes, proceedings

———————— 4 ————————

7 住民登録 **jūmin tōroku** resident registration

錬 → 京 **2j6.3**

鎚 → 鎚 **8a9.10**

8a8.18

鍵 **KEN, kagi** key

———————— 1 ————————

2 鍵子 **kagi(k)ko** latchkey child (who carries a key to school because no one will be home when he returns)
5 鍵穴 **kagiana** keyhole
7 鍵束 **kagitaba** bunch of keys
15 鍵盤 **kenban** keyboard

———————— 2 ————————

6 合鍵 **aikagi** duplicate key; passkey; Keys Made
有鍵楽器 **yūken gakki** keyed (musical) instrument

8a8.19

鋸 **KYO, nokogiri, noko** saw

———————— 1 ————————

10 鋸屑 **nokokuzu** sawdust
12 鋸歯 **nokogiriba, nokoba** saw tooth
鋸歯状 **kyōshijō** sawtooth, serrated
17 鋸鮫 **nokogirizame** saw shark

———————— 2 ————————

3 大鋸 **ōnokogiri** large saw
大鋸屑 **ogakuzu** sawdust
丸鋸 **marunoko** circular/buzz saw
6 糸鋸 **itonoko** fretsaw, jigsaw, scroll saw
10 帯鋸 **obinokogiri, obinoko** band saw

8a8.20 / 1608

鋼 **KŌ, hagane** steel

———————— 1 ————————

7 鋼材 **kōzai** steel (as a material)
8 鋼板 **kōhan, kōban** steel plate
10 鋼索 **kōsaku** cable
13 鋼鉄 **kōtetsu** steel
鋼鉄車 **kōtetsusha** steel (railroad) car
鋼鉄板 **kōtetsuban** steel plate
鋼鉄製 **kōtetsusei** made of steel
鋼鉄線 **kōtetsusen** steel wire
14 鋼製 **kōsei** made of steel
鋼管 **kōkan** steel tubing/pipe

———————— 2 ————————

11 粗鋼 **sokō** crude steel

12 棒鋼　**bōkō**　bar steel
13 鉄鋼　**tekkō**　steel
　　鉄鋼業　**tekkōgyō**　the steel industry
14 製鋼　**seikō**　steel manufacturing, steelmaking
　　製鋼所　**seikōjo**　steel plant
15 鋳鋼　**chūkō**　casting/cast steel
16 錬鋼　**renkō**　wrought steel
17 鍛鋼　**tankō**　forged steel

―――――――― 3 ――――――――

4 不銹鋼　**fushūkō**　stainless steel
5 圧延鋼　**atsuenkō**　rolled steel
9 耐熱鋼　**tainetsukō**　refractory steel
10 特殊鋼　**tokushukō**　special steel

8a8.21

鋼

KO　patch over, plug; tie, bind

―――――――― 2 ――――――――

13 禁錮　**kinko**　imprisonment

―――――――― 9 ――――――――

8a9.1

鍾

SHŌ　gather, collect; (unit of volume, about 80 liters)

―――――――― 1 ――――――――

7 鍾乳石　**shōnyūseki**　stalactite (also spelled 鐘乳石) (cf. 石筍)
　　鍾乳洞　**shōnyūdō**　stalactite cave
13 鍾愛　**shōai**　love dearly

錬→錬　8a8.3

8a9.2

鍖

CHIN　unsatisfactory

8a9.3

鍬

SHŪ, SHŌ, kuwa　hoe

―――――――― 1 ――――――――

2 鍬入　**kuwai(re)**　ground-breaking
6 鍬先　**kuwasaki**　hoe blade
7 鍬形　**kuwagata**　the horns on a traditional Japanese helmet

―――――――― 2 ――――――――

10 馬鍬　**maguwa**　harrow, rake

8a9.4

鍜

KA　armor neck plates

8a9.5 / 1817

鍛

TAN, kita(eru)　forge, temper; train, drill, discipline

―――――――― 1 ――――――――

3 鍛工　**tankō**　metalworker, smith
　　鍛工所　**tankōjo, tankōsho**　foundry
　　鍛上　**kita(e)a(geru)**　become highly trained
7 鍛冶　**kaji**　blacksmith
　　鍛冶屋　**kajiya**　blacksmith
9 鍛造　**tanzō**　forging
11 鍛接　**tansetsu**　forge welding
13 鍛鉄　**tantetsu**　tempered/wrought iron
16 鍛錬　**tanren**　temper, anneal; train, harden
　　鍛鋼　**tankō**　forged steel

―――――――― 2 ――――――――

5 可鍛性　**katansei**　malleability

8a9.6

鍔

GAKU, tsuba　sword guard/hilt; flange

―――――――― 1 ――――――――

7 鍔迫合　**tsubazeria(i)**　close fighting

8a9.7

鍠

KŌ　sound of bells and drums

8a9.8

鍮

CHŪ　brass

―――――――― 2 ――――――――

10 真鍮　**shinchū**　brass

8a9.9

鍍

TO, mekki　plating, gilding

―――――――― 1 ――――――――

8 鍍金　**tokin, mekki**　plating, gilding

8a9.10

鎚　鎚

TSUI, tsuchi　hammer

―――――――― 2 ――――――――

13 鉄鎚　**kanazuchi**　hammer

8

金　9←
食
隹
雷
門

8a9.11

鎹 **kasugai** clamp

8a9.12

鍼 **SHIN, hari** (acupuncture) needle

――――――― 1 ―――――――

7 鍼医者 **hariisha** acupuncturist
鍼灸 **shinkyū** acupuncture and moxibustion
11 鍼術 **shinjutsu** acupuncture

8a9.13

鍋 **KA, nabe** pot, saucepan

――――――― 1 ―――――――

5 鍋尻 **nabejiri** pot's outside bottom
8 鍋底景気 **nabezoko keiki** prolonged recession
鍋物 **nabemono** food served in the pot
12 鍋焼 **nabeya(ki)** boiled in a pot, baked in a casserole
13 鍋蓋 **nabebuta** pot lid
14 鍋墨 **nabezumi** kettle soot

――――――― 2 ―――――――

3 土鍋 **donabe** earthen pot
4 手鍋 **tenabe** pan
牛鍋 **gyūnabe** sukiyaki
5 平鍋 **hiranabe** pan
6 肉鍋 **niku nabe** meat pot; meat served in a pot
10 破鍋 **wa(re)nabe** cracked pot
11 寄鍋 **yo(se)nabe** chowder
12 揚鍋 **a(ge)nabe** frying pan
蒸鍋 **mu(shi)nabe** steamer, casserole

――――――― 3 ―――――――

6 行平鍋 **yukihiranabe** earthenware casserole
13 慈善鍋 **jizennabe** charity pot

――――――― 10 ―――――――

8a10.1

鎔 熔 **YŌ, to(keru)** melt, become molten

――――――― 1 ―――――――

8 鎔岩 **yōgan** lava
鎔岩流 **yōganryū** lava flow
9 鎔点 **yōten** melting point
10 鎔剤 **yōzai** flux
11 鎔接 **yōsetsu** welding

鎔接工 **yōsetsukō** welder
鎔接剤 **yōsetsuzai** welding flux
鎔接機 **yōsetsuki** welding machine
13 鎔解 **yōkai** melt, fuse
鎔解性 **yōkaisei** fusibility
鎔鉱炉 **yōkōro** blast furnace
16 鎔融 **yōyū** fuse, melt, molten
鎔融点 **yōyūten** melting point

――――――― 2 ―――――――

5 可鎔性 **kayōsei** fusibility

8a10.2 / 1819

鎖 **SA** close, shut
kusari chain
to(zasu) close, shut

――――――― 1 ―――――――

4 鎖止 **kusarido(me)** sprocket
6 鎖糸 **kusariito** yarn interwoven with threads forming a diamond pattern
7 鎖状 **sajō** chainlike
鎖車 **kusariguruma** sprocket wheel
8 鎖国 **sakoku** national isolation
10 鎖骨 **sakotsu** the clavicle, collarbone
12 鎖港 **sakō** closing the ports
鎖歯車 **kusari haguruma** sprocket wheel
15 鎖編 **kusaria(mi)** chain stitch
18 鎖題 **kusaridai** composing poems in which the last word of one is the first word of the next

――――――― 2 ―――――――

8 金鎖 **kingusari** gold chain
9 連鎖 **rensa** chain, series
連鎖反応 **rensa hannō** chain reaction
連鎖店 **rensaten** chain store
封鎖 **fūsa** blockade; freeze (assets)
11 閉鎖 **heisa** closing, closure, lockout
13 鉄鎖 **tessa** iron chain
16 錨鎖 **byōsa** (chain) cable, hawser

8a10.3

鎧 **GAI, yoro(u)** put on armor
yoroi (suit of) armor

――――――― 1 ―――――――

4 鎧戸 **yoroido** Venetian blinds
8 鎧板 **yoroiita** louver board, slat
鎧武者 **yoroimusha** warrior in armor
10 鎧袖一触 **gaishū-isshoku** easy victory
11 鎧窓 **yoroimado** louver window

8a10.4

鎗 **SŌ** metallic clanging/ringing; spear

8a10.5

鎬　**KŌ, shinogi** the ridges on the side of a sword blade

——————— 1 ———————

9 鎬削　**shinogi (o) kezu(ru)** fight fiercely

8a10.6 / 1786

鎮　鎭　**CHIN, shizu(meru)** calm, quell
shizu(maru) calm down

——————— 1 ———————

4 鎮火　**chinka** be extinguished
5 鎮圧　**chin'atsu** suppression, quelling
　鎮台　**chindai** garrison
6 鎮守　**chinju** local/tutelary deity
　鎮守府　**chinjufu** naval station
8 鎮定　**chintei** suppress, subdue, pacify
10 鎮座　**chinza** be enshrined
12 鎮痛　**chintsū** relieving pain
　鎮痛剤　**chintsūzai** painkiller
14 鎮静　**chinsei** calm, quiet, soothed
　鎮静剤　**chinseizai** tranquilizer, sedative
　鎮魂　**chinkon** repose of souls
　鎮魂曲　**chinkonkyoku** requiem
　鎮魂祭　**chinkonsai** services for the deceased
15 鎮撫　**chinbu** placate, quell, calm

——————— 2 ———————

4 文鎮　**bunchin** paperweight
6 地鎮祭　**jichinsai** ground-breaking ceremony
8 取鎮　**to(ri)shizu(meru)** quiet, quell
9 重鎮　**jūchin** leader, authority, mainstay
　風鎮　**fūchin** decorative hanging-scroll weight
　神鎮　**kamishizu(maru)** (a god) be quietly present

8a10.7

鏰　**SAKU** wire

——————— 1 ———————

7 鏰条　**sakujō** cable

8a10.8

鎌　鎌　**REN, kama** sickle

——————— 1 ———————

2 鎌入　**kamai(re)** harvesting
9 鎌首　**kamakubi** gooseneck
10 鎌倉　**Kamakura** (city, Kanagawa-ken); (era, 1185–1333)

——————— 2 ———————

3 大鎌　**ōgama** scythe

8a10.9

鎰　**ITSU** (unit of weight)

8a10.10

鏈　**REN, kusari** chain

——————— 11 ———————

8a11.1

鐓　**TAI, ishizuki** ferrule, butt end

8a11.2

鏃　**ZOKU, SOKU, yajiri** arrowhead

8a11.3

鏘　**SŌ** clinking/tinkling sound

8a11.4

鏤　**RU, chiriba(meru)** inlay, set, mount

——————— 1 ———————

10 鏤骨　**rukotsu** painstaking

8a11.5

鏐　**RYŪ** gold

8a11.6 / 863

鏡　**KYŌ, kagami** mirror

——————— 1 ———————

0 お鏡　**(o)kagami** mounded rice-cake offering
5 鏡台　**kyōdai** dressing table
8 鏡板　**kagamiita** panel (board)
12 鏡開　**kagamibira(ki)** cutting the New Year's rice cakes
15 鏡餅　**kagamimochi** mounded rice-cakes

——————— 2 ———————

4 円鏡　**enkyō** round mirror

8

金 11←
食
隹
雷
門

水鏡 **mizu-kagami** reflecting water surface
手鏡 **tekagami** hand mirror; model, example
5 凸鏡 **tokkyō** convex lens
6 耳鏡 **jikyō** otoscope, ear speculum
8 明鏡 **meikyō** clear mirror
明鏡止水 **meikyō-shisui** serene state of mind
9 神鏡 **shinkyō** sacred mirror (one of the three sacred treasures)
胃鏡 **ikyō** gastroscope
10 破鏡 **hakyō** broken mirror; divorce
11 眼鏡 **megane, gankyō** (eye)glasses
眼鏡屋 **meganeya** optician
眼鏡蛇 **megane hebi** cobra
眼鏡橋 **meganebashi** arch bridge
12 検鏡 **kenkyō** microscopic examination
14 銅鏡 **dōkyō** bronze mirror

———— 3 ————

3 万華鏡 **mangekyō, bankakyō** kaleidoscope
4 内視鏡 **naishikyō** endoscope
双眼鏡 **sōgankyō** binoculars
5 凸面鏡 **totsumenkyō** convex mirror/lens
凹面鏡 **ōmenkyō** concave mirror/lens
凹眼鏡 **ōgankyō** concave-lens eyeglasses
平面鏡 **heimenkyō** plane mirror
立体鏡 **rittaikyō** stereoscope
6 老眼鏡 **rōgankyō** eyeglasses for farsightedness
色眼鏡 **iromegane** colored glasses; prejudiced view
近眼鏡 **kingankyō** eyeglasses for nearsightedness
虫眼鏡 **mushimegane** magnifying glass
7 対物鏡 **taibutsukyō** objective lens
8 拡大鏡 **kakudaikyō** magnifying glass
9 単眼鏡 **tangankyō** monocle
11 接眼鏡 **setsugankyō** eyepiece
望遠鏡 **bōenkyō** telescope
雪眼鏡 **yuki megane** snow goggles
12 遠眼鏡 **engankyō** eyeglasses for farsightedness
検眼鏡 **kengankyō** ophthalmoscope
14 鼻眼鏡 **hanamegane** pince-nez
15 潜望鏡 **senbōkyō** periscope
16 懐中鏡 **kaichūkagami** pocket mirror
18 顕微鏡 **kenbikyō** microscope

———— 4 ————

12 超顕微鏡 **chōkenbikyō** ultramicroscope

8a11.7
鏝 **MAN, kote** an iron, flatiron

鏥 → 銹 **8a7.6**

8a11.8
鏑 **TEKI, kabura** arrowhead whistle

———— 1 ————
5 鏑矢 **kaburaya** arrow rigged to buzz as it flies
———— 2 ————
10 流鏑馬 **yabusame** horseback archery

8a11.9
鏨 **SAN** carve, chisel

8a11.10
鏖 **Ō, minagoroshi** massacre
———— 1 ————
10 鏖殺 **ōsatsu** massacre

———— 12 ————

8a12.1
鏗 **KŌ** clinking sound

8a12.2
鐫 **SEN** carve, engrave

8a12.3
鐚 **A, bita** worn/effaced coin
———— 1 ————
1 鐚一文 **bita ichimon** (not even) a farthing/cent
14 鐚銭 **bitasen** worn/effaced coin

8a12.4
鐇 **HAN** hatchet; vanadium

8a12.5
鐔 **TAN, SHIN** sword guard/hilt

8a12.6 / 1821
鐘 **SHŌ, kane** bell

──────────────── 1 ────────────────

7 鐘乳石 **shōnyūseki** stalactite (also spelled 鍾
乳石)

鐘乳洞 **shōnyūdō** stalactite cave

鐘声 **shōsei** sound/ringing of a bell

10 鐘紡 **Kanebō** (company name)

13 鐘楼 **shōrō** bell tower, belfry

15 鐘撞 **kanetsu(ki)** bell ringer/ringing

鐘撞堂 **kanetsu(ki)dō** bell tower, belfry

──────────────── 2 ────────────────

4 弔鐘 **chōshō** funeral bell

5 半鐘 **hanshō** fire bell/alarm

6 早鐘 **hayagane** fire bell/alarm

8 明鐘 **a(ke no) kane** bell tolling daybreak

10 時鐘 **jishō** (ship's) time bell

破鐘 **wa(re)gane** cracked bell

11 梵鐘 **bonshō** temple bell

釣鐘 **tsu(ri)gane** hanging bell

12 晩鐘 **banshō** evening/curfew bell

19 警鐘 **keishō** alarm/fire bell

──────────────── 3 ────────────────

9 除夜鐘 **joya (no) kane** New Year's midnight
bells

8a12.7

鐙   **TŌ, abumi** stirrup

8a12.8

鐐   **RYŌ** silver, platinum; chains, shackles

8a12.9

鐃   **NYŌ, DŌ** bell, gong

──────────────── 1 ────────────────

13 鐃鈸 **nyōhachi** (Buddhist) cymbals

鐵→鉄 **8a5.6**

鐖→鐖 **8a13.5**

──────────────── 13 ────────────────

8a13.1

鑁   **BAN** (used in proper names)

8a13.2

鐶   **KAN** ring

8a13.3

鐸 鈬   **TAKU, nude, nurite, sanaki** hand bell

──────────────── 2 ────────────────

4 木鐸 **bokutaku** bell with a wooden clapper;
leader

14 銅鐸 **dōtaku** bronze bell

8a13.4

鐺   **TŌ, kusari** chain   **kojiri** the tip of a
sheath/scabbard   **kote** an iron, flatiron

8a13.5

鐖 鐖   **yari** spear, lance

鐵→鉄 **8a5.6**

──────────────── 14 ────────────────

鑄→鋳 **8a7.2**

──────────────── 15 ────────────────

8a15.1

鑠   **SHAKU** melt, smelt; radiant

──────────────── 2 ────────────────

20 矍鑠 **kakushaku** (old but) vigorous, hale and
hearty

8a15.2 / 1664

鑑   **KAN, kagami** model, paragon, example;
mirror   **kanga(miru)** take into consideration, in view of; follow (an example)

──────────────── 1 ────────────────

5 鑑札 **kansatsu** a license

7 鑑別 **kanbetsu** discrimination, differentiation

8 鑑定 **kantei** appraisal, expert opinion

鑑定人 **kanteinin** appraiser, expert (witness)

鑑定家 **kanteika** appraiser, expert (witness)

8

金 15←
食
隹
雨
門

鑑定書 **kanteisho** expert's report
鑑定料 **kanteiryō** expert's/legal fee
9 鑑査 **kansa** inspect, evaluate
15 鑑賞 **kanshō** appreciation, enjoyment
鑑賞力 **kanshōryoku** ability to appreciate
鑑賞眼 **kanshōgan** an eye for
19 鑑識 **kanshiki** discernment, identification
鑑識力 **kanshikiryoku** discernment
鑑識家 **kanshikika** a judge/connoisseur of, appraiser
鑑識眼 **kanshikigan** discerning eye

——————— 2 ———————

6 年鑑 **nenkan** yearbook
印鑑 **inkan** one's seal; seal impression
名鑑 **meikan** directory
7 図鑑 **zukan** picture book
8 宝鑑 **hōkan** valued book, handbook
武鑑 **bukan** book of heraldry
門鑑 **monkan** a (gate) pass
10 姫鑑 **hime kagami** a model young lady
11 亀鑑 **kikan** pattern, model, exemplar
12 廃鑑 **haikan** decommissioned warship
無鑑札 **mukansatsu** without a license
15 賞鑑 **shōkan** appreciate, admire

8a15.3

鑽 鑽 **SAN, ki(ru)** bore, drill; twirl a stick into wood to start a fire

——————— 1 ———————
3 鑽孔機 **sankōki** boring machine
——————— 2 ———————
9 研鑽 **kensan** study

8a15.4

鑞 **RŌ, suzu** tin

——————— 2 ———————
5 白鑞 **hakurō** solder; pewter

8a15.5

鑢 **RYO, yasuri** file, rasp

——————— 2 ———————
10 紙鑢 **kamiyasuri** sandpaper, emery paper

鑛 → 鉱 8a5.15

8a15.6

鑣 **HYŌ, kutsuwa** bit (in a horse's mouth)

鑒 → 鑑 8a15.2

——————— 16 ———————

8a16.1

鑪 鈩 **RO** hearth

——————— 17 ———————

鑵 → 缶 2k4.6

8a17.1

鑰 **YAKU** lock

8a17.2

鑲 **JŌ** fit into

——————— 1 ———————
12 鑲嵌 **jōkan** dental inlay

——————— 18 ———————

8a18.1

鑷 **SETSU** tweezers; plucking hair

——————— 1 ———————
2 鑷子 **sesshi** forceps, tweezers

——————— 19 ———————

鑽 → 鑽 8a15.3

8a19.1

鑼 **RA** gong

——————— 2 ———————
14 銅鑼 **dora** gong

8a19.2

鑾 **RAN, suzu** bells (on the emperor's carriage)

— 20 —

8a20.1

鑴

KAKU hoe

8a20.2

鑿

SAKU chisel; drill (a hole); dig out/up
nomi chisel

— 1 —

4 鑿井 **sakusei** well drilling
8 鑿岩機 **sakuganki** rock drill

— 2 —

10 穿鑿 **sensaku** delve into, probe, scrutinize
11 掘鑿 **kussaku** excavation
12 開鑿 **kaisaku** building a road/canal

食 8b

食	飢	飲	飩	飫	飭	飯	飽	飴	飾	飼	蝕	餌
0.1	2.1	4.1	4.2	4.3	4.4	4.5	5.1	5.2	5.3	5.4	6.1	6.2

餃	餅	餉	餓	餔	餒	餝	餘	餐	餠	餮	餞	館
6.3	6.4	6.5	7.1	7.2	7.3	8b5.3	2a5.24	7.4	8b6.4	8.1	8.2	8.3

餡	餬	餮	餽	餾	餾	饗	饅	饉	饑	饒	饌	饋
8.4	9.1	9.2	10.1	10.2	10.3	10.4	11.1	11.2	12.1	12.2	12.3	12.4

饐	饗	饕	饜
12.5	8b10.4	13.1	2p21.1

— 0 —

8b0.1 / 322

食

SHOKU food, eating; (counter for
meals); eclipse JIKI food; eating
ta(beru) eat ku(u/rau) eat, drink;
receive (a blow) ku(eru) can eat
ku(enai) cannot eat; shrewd, cunning
ku(rawasu/wasu) feed; make (someone) eat,
give (someone) a punch), play (someone a trick)
ha(mu) eat, feed on; receive (an allowance)

— 1 —

0 食いちぎる **ku(ichigiru)** bite/tear off
　食いはぐれる **ku(ihagureru)** miss one's
　　meal; lose one's source of livelihood
　食ってかかる **ku(ttekakaru)** lash out at, defy
　食パン **shokupan** (sliced white) bread
2 食入 **ku(i)i(ru)** eat into; encroach upon
　食人種 **shokujinshu** a cannibal race
3 食上 **ku(i)a(geru)** eat (it) all up
　食下 **ku(i)sa(garu)** hang on to, refuse to relent
4 食中 **shokuata(ri)** food poisoning, stomach
　　upset
　食中毒 **shokuchūdoku** food poisoning
　食切 **ku(i)ki(ru)** bite off/through; eat (it) all
　　up
　食止 **ku(i)to(meru)** check, stem, curb, hold
　　back
　食込 **ku(i)ko(mu)** eat into, erode, be deep-
　　rooted **ku(rai)ko(mu)** be put in jail;
　　be forced to bear

　食手 **ku(i)te** eater; glutton
　食方 **ta(be)kata, ku(i)kata** manner of eating
5 食出 **ha(mi)da(su), ha(mi)de(ru)** protrude,
　　project, jut/bulge out, overflow
　食生活 **shokuseikatsu** eating/dietary habits
　食代 **ku(i)shiro** food/board bill
　食付 **ta(be)tsu(keru)** be used to eating
　　ku(i)tsu(ku) bite at/into; hold fast to
　食用 **shokuyō** edible, used for food
　食用油 **shokuyō abura** cooking/edible oil
　食用品 **shokuyōhin** food(stuffs)
　食台 **shokudai** dining table
6 食気 **ku(i)ke, ku(i)ki** appetite
　食休 **shokuyasu(mi)** an after-meal rest
　食合 **ku(i)a(waseru)** combining foods
　　ku(i)a(u) bite each other; fit together
　　exactly, mesh
　食肉 **shokuniku** (edible) meat; flesh-eating
　食肉獣 **shokunikujū** a carnivore
　食肉類 **shokunikurui** carnivorous animals
　食尽 **ku(i)tsu(kusu)** eat up, consume
　食虫 **shokuchū** insectivore
7 食余 **ta(be)ama(su)** not finish one's meal
　食延 **ku(i)no(basu)** stretch out (one's rations),
　　make (supplies) last
　食坊 **ku(ishin)bō** glutton, gourmand
　食扶持 **ku(i)buchi** food/board expenses
　食初 **ta(be)zo(me), ku(i)zo(me)** weaning
　　ceremony
　食言 **shokugen** eat one's words; break one's
　　promise

食足 **ku(i)ta(rinai)** have not eaten enough; be unsatisfied with

8 食事 **shokuji** meal, dining

食事中 **shokujichū** during a meal

食事時 **shokujidoki** mealtime

食券 **shokken** meal ticket

食卓 **shokutaku** dining table

食卓用 **shokutakuyō** for table use

食逃 **ku(i)ni(ge)** run off without paying for what one has eaten

食物 **ta(be)mono, shokumotsu, ku(i)mono** food **ku(wase)mono** a fake; imposter

食放題 **ta(be)hōdai, ku(i)hōdai** eating as much as one pleases, all-you-can-eat

9 食前 **shokuzen** before a meal

食通 **shokutsū** gourmet

食指 **shokushi** the index finger

食指動 **shokushi (ga) ugo(ku)** feel a craving for, want

食品 **shokuhin** food(stuffs)

食品店 **shokuhinten** grocery store

食後 **shokugo** after a meal

食荒 **ku(i)a(rasu)** devour; spoil by eating from; eat a bit of everything

食客 **shokkaku, shokkyaku** a (live-in) dependent

食思 **shokushi** appetite

食思不振 **shokushi fushin** loss of appetite

食紅 **shokubeni** red food coloring

10 食残 **ta(be)noko(su), ku(i)noko(su)** leave half-eaten

食倒 **ku(i)tao(su)** sponge off (someone), eat out of house and home **ku(i)dao(re)** wasting one's money on fine foods

食時 **ta(be)doki** the season for (oysters)

食料 **shokuryō** food

食料品 **shokuryōhin** food(stuffs)

食料品店 **shokuryōhinten** grocery store

食料品商 **shokuryōhinshō** grocer

11 食道 **shokudō** the esophagus

食道楽 **ku(i)dōraku** gourmandizing; epicure

食過 **ta(be)su(gi), ku(i)su(gi)** overeating

食掛 **ta(be)ka(keru), ku(i)ka(keru)** begin to eat **ta(be)ka(ke), ku(i)ka(ke)** half-eaten **ku(tte)ka(karu)** lash out at, defy

食堂 **shokudō** dining hall, cafeteria

食堂車 **shokudōsha** dining car

食習慣 **shokushūkan** eating habits

食欲 **shokuyoku** appetite

食盛 **ta(be)zaka(ri)** the age at which (a boy) has a hearty appetite **ku(i)zaka(ri)** the right time to eat, the season for

食頃 **ta(be)goro, ku(i)goro** the right time to eat, the season for

12 食違 **ku(i)chiga(u)** cross each other; run counter to, differ, clash; go awry

食散 **ku(i)chi(rasu)** eat untidily, eat a bit of everything

食費 **shokuhi** food expenses, board

食酢 **shokusu** (table/edible) vinegar

食間 **shokkan** between meals

13 食傷 **shokushō** be fed up with; suffer food poisoning

食溜 **ku(i)da(me)** stuffing oneself in order to go without eating for some time

食滞 **shokutai** lie heavy/undigested in one's stomach

食滓 **ta(be)kasu** table scraps, leftovers

食塩 **shokuen** table salt

食塩水 **shokuensui** saline solution

食嫌 **ku(wazu)gira(i), ta(bezu)gira(i)** disliking without tasting; prejudice against

食意地 **ku(i)iji** gluttony

食詰 **ku(i)tsu(meru)** become unable to subsist

食詰者 **ku(i)tsu(me)mono** a down-and-outer

14 食様 **ta(be)yō** manner of eating

15 食養生 **shokuyōjō** taking nourishing food, dietary cure

食潰 **ku(i)tsubu(su)** eat away, sponge off (someone)

食器 **shokki** eating utensils

食餌 **shokuji** food (to cure an illness)

16 食膳 **shokuzen** dining table

18 食噛 **ku(i)kaji(ru)** gnaw at, nibble; have a smattering of knowledge

食糧 **shokuryō** food

19 食蟻獣 **arikui** anteater

20 食競 **ta(bek)kura** eating contest

——————— 2 ———————

1 一食 **isshoku** a meal

2 二食 **nishoku, nijiki** two meals (a day)

人食 **hitoku(i)** man-eating, cannibalism

人食人種 **hitoku(i) jinshu** cannibals

3 三食 **sanshoku** three meals (a day)

乞食 **kojiki** beggar

夕食 **yūshoku** supper, evening meal

大食 **taishoku, ōgu(i)** gluttony, voracity; glutton

小食 **shōshoku** eating little/sparingly

小食家 **shōshokuka** light eater

4 水食 **suishoku** erosion

少食 **shōshoku** eating little/sparingly

少食家 **shōshokuka** light eater

木食 **mokujiki** fruit diet

木食虫 **kiku(i)mushi** wood borer

月食 **gesshoku** eclipse of the moon

日食 **nisshoku** solar eclipse

欠食 **kesshoku** go without a meal

5 本食虫 **honku(i)mushi** bookworm

外食 **gaishoku** eating out

主食 **shushoku** a staple food
主食物 **shushokumotsu** a staple food
立食 **ta(chi)gu(i), risshoku** eating while standing
6 気食 **ki (ni) kuwa(nu)** go against the grain, be disagreeable
会食 **kaishoku** dining together; mess
肉食 **nikushoku** meat eating
共食 **tomogu(i)** devouring each other
衣食 **ishoku** food and clothing
衣食住 **ishokujū** food, clothing, and shelter
米食 **beishoku** rice diet
米食虫 **komeku(i)mushi** rice weevil; drone, idler
虫食 **mushiku(i)** damage from worms, moth-eaten spot
7 伴食 **banshoku** eating at the same table
伴食大臣 **banshoku daijin** figurehead minister
何食顔 **naniku(wanu) kao** innocent look
没食子 **mosshokushi, bosshokushi** gallnut
売食 **u(ri)gu(i)** live by selling one's possessions
利食 **rigu(i)** profit taking
8 夜食 **yashoku** supper, night meal
定食 **teishoku** regular meal, table d'hôte
居食 **igu(i)** live in idleness
和食 **washoku** Japanese food
9 侵食 **shinshoku** encroachment; erosion; pitting corrosion
美食 **bishoku** delicious food, lavish diet
美食家 **bishokuka** epicure, gourmet
風食 **fūshoku** weathering, wind erosion
洋食 **yōshoku** Western food
海食 **kaishoku** erosion caused by the sea
草食 **sōshoku** herbivorous
面食 **menku(i)** emphasizing good looks (in choosing a mate)
　　　 menku(rau) be flurried/disconcerted
昼食 **chūshoku** lunch
10 陪食 **baishoku** dining with a superior
遊食 **yūshoku** live in idleness
浸食 **shinshoku** erosion, corrosion
捕食 **hoshoku** prey upon
徒食 **toshoku** life of idleness
座食 **zashoku** live in idleness
粉食 **funshoku** eating bread products (rather than rice)
蚕食 **sanshoku** encroachment, inroads
馬食 **bashoku** eating like a horse
11 偏食 **henshoku** unbalanced diet
貪食 **donshoku, musabo(ri)ku(u), musabo(ri)ku(rau)** eat voraciously, devour
副食 **fukushoku** side dish; supplementary food

副食物 **fukushokubutsu** side dish; supplementary food
過食 **kashoku** overeating
菜食 **saishoku** vegetarian/herbivorous diet
菜食主義 **saishoku shugi** vegetarianism
寄食 **kishoku** be parasitic, sponge off
常食 **jōshoku** daily diet, staple food
悪食 **akushoku, akujiki** eat repulsive things
盗食 **nusu(mi)gu(i)** eating furtively
粒食 **ryūshoku** eating rice/wheat in grain (not flour) form
粗食 **soshoku** coarse food, plain diet
断食 **danjiki** fasting, fast
魚食 **gyoshoku** fish eating
12 減食 **genshoku** cutting down on food; reduced rations
朝食 **chōshoku** breakfast
買食 **ka(i)gu(i)** buying and eating (sweets) between meals
給食 **kyūshoku** providing meals (in school)
絶食 **zesshoku** fasting
軽食 **keishoku** light meal
飲食 **inshoku, no(mi)ku(i)** food and drink, eating and drinking
飲食店 **inshokuten** restaurant
飲食物 **inshokubutsu** food and drink
間食 **kanshoku** eating between meals
13 溜食 **ta(me)gu(i)** eat enough to last a long time
寝食 **shinshoku** food and sleep
節食 **sesshoku** eating in moderation
試食 **shishoku** sample, taste
飽食 **hōshoku** gluttony, engorgement
14 腐食 **fushoku** corrosion
雑食 **zasshoku** omnivorous
15 撮食 **tsuma(mi)gu(i)** eating with the fingers; eating stealthily; corruption, graft
暴食 **bōshoku** gluttony, gorging oneself
餌食 **ejiki** food, bait, prey
16 薬食 **kusurigu(i)** eating (normally forbidden meat) for nutrition
18 糧食 **ryōshoku** provisions, food

――――――― 3 ―――――――

3 大蟻食 **ōariku(i)** great anteater
5 代用食 **daiyōshoku** substitute food
　幼児食 **yōjishoku** baby food
7 冷凍食品 **reitō shokuhin** frozen foods
　初物食 **hatsumonogu(i)** novelty seeker
8 逆捩食 **sakane(ji o) ku(waseru)** retort, criticize in return
　金環食 **kinkanshoku** total eclipse of the sun
9 皆既食 **kaikishoku** total eclipse, totality
10 部分食 **bubunshoku** partial eclipse
　流動食 **ryūdōshoku** liquid diet/food
11 道草食 **michikusa (o) ku(u)** dawdle/loiter along the way

8

 0 ←

12 無駄食 **mudagu(i)** eat between meals; eat but not work, live in idleness
18 簡易食堂 **kan'i shokudō** fast-food diner
離乳食 **rinyūshoku** baby food

━━━━━━ 4 ━━━━━━

1 一泊二食付 **ippaku nishoku-tsu(ki)** with overnight lodging and two meals
4 牛飲馬食 **gyūin-bashoku** heavy eating and drinking
5 生理的食塩水 **seiriteki shokuensui** saline solution
8 河原乞食 **kawara kojiki** actors (and beggars; a term of opprobrium)
10 弱肉強食 **jakuniku-kyōshoku** survival of the fittest
12 無銭飲食 **musen inshoku** jumping a restaurant bill

━━━━━━ 2 ━━━━━━

8b2.1 / 1304

KI, u(eru) starve

飢

━━━━━━ 1 ━━━━━━

6 飢死 **u(e)ji(ni)** starve to death
11 飢渇 **kikatsu** hunger and thirst, starvation
12 飢寒 **kikan** hunger and cold
15 飢餓 **kiga** hunger, starvation
20 飢饉 **kikin** famine

━━━━━━ 4 ━━━━━━

8b4.1 / 323

IN, no(mu) drink

飲 飲

━━━━━━ 1 ━━━━━━

0 飲んだくれ **no(ndakure)** a drunk, heavy drinker
3 飲干 **no(mi)ho(su)** drink (the cup) dry
飲下 **no(mi)kuda(su)** swallow, gulp down
飲口 **no(mi)guchi** spigot, tap
no(mi)kuchi taste, flavor
4 飲込 **no(mi)ko(mu)** swallow; understand; consent to
飲水 **no(mi)mizu** drinking water
飲手 **no(mi)te** heavy drinker
5 飲代 **no(mi)shiro** drinking money
飲用 **in'yō** drinking
飲用水 **in'yōsui** drinking water
6 飲仲間 **no(mi)nakama** drinking buddy
飲回 **no(mi)mawa(su)** pass (the bottle) around
7 飲良 **no(mi)yo(i)** pleasant to drink
飲助 **no(mi)suke** heavy drinker, a souse

飲兵衛 **no(n)bē** heavy drinker
8 飲直 **no(mi)nao(su)** drink again
飲逃 **no(mi)ni(ge)** running off without paying for one's drinks
飲明 **no(mi)a(kasu)** drink all night
飲物 **no(mi)mono** (something to) drink, beverage
9 飲屋 **no(mi)ya** bar, saloon, tavern
飲食 **inshoku, no(mi)ku(i)** food and drink, eating and drinking
飲食店 **inshokuten** restaurant
飲食物 **inshokubutsu** food and drink
10 飲残 **no(mi)noko(ri)** leftover drinks
飲倒 **no(mi)tao(su)** not pay one's bar bill
飲酒 **inshu** drinking (alcohol)
飲酒家 **inshuka** drinker
飲料 **inryō** drink, beverage **no(mi)ryō** the portion (of the drink) for oneself
飲料水 **inryōsui** drinking water
11 飲過 **no(mi)su(giru)** drink too much
飲掛 **no(mi)ka(ke)** half-drunk (cup), half-smoked (cigarette)
13 飲続 **no(mi)tsuzu(keru)** keep on drinking
14 飲歌 **no(meya)uta(e)** carousing, revelry
15 飲潰 **no(mi)tsubu(reru)** get dead drunk
no(mi)tsubu(su) drink (someone) under the table
16 飲薬 **no(mi)gusuri** medicine meant to be ingested
18 飲癖 **no(mi)kuse** habit of drinking

━━━━━━ 2 ━━━━━━

1 一飲 **hitono(mi)** a mouthful; a swallow/sip; an easy prey
3 口飲 **kuchino(mi)** drink from the bottle
4 水飲 **mizuno(mi)** drinking glass/fountain
水飲百姓 **mizuno(mi)-byakushō** poor farmer
牛飲馬食 **gyūin-bashoku** heavy eating and drinking
5 立飲 **ta(chi)no(mi)** drinking while standing
6 吸飲 **kyūin** (opium) smoking
su(i)no(mi) feeding/spout cup
7 乳飲子 **chino(mi)go** suckling infant, babe in arms
乳飲児 **chinomigo** (nursing) infant, baby
9 茶飲 **chano(mi)** teacup; tea lover; tea drinking
茶飲友達 **chano(mi) tomodachi** crony, pal
茶飲茶碗 **chano(mi)jawan** teacup
茶飲話 **chano(mi)banashi** a chat over tea, gossip
10 酒飲 **sakeno(mi)** drinker
料飲 **ryōin** food and drink
11 強飲 **gōin** heavy drinking
12 痛飲 **tsūin** drink heavily
13 滝飲 **takino(mi)** gulping down a drink
溜飲 **ryūin** sour stomach

溜飲下 **ryūin (ga) sa(garu)** feel satisfaction
愛飲 **aiin** like to drink
愛飲者 **aiinsha** habitual drinker
試飲 **shiin** sampling, (wine) tasting
14 豪飲 **gōin** heavy drinking, carousing
15 暴飲 **bōin** heavy/excessive drinking
19 鯨飲 **geiin** drink like a fish, guzzle

―――――――――― 3 ――――――――――
3 大酒飲 **ōzakeno(mi)** heavy drinker
8 固唾飲 **katazu (o) no(mu)** be intensely anxious
11 清涼飲料 **seiryō inryō** carbonated beverage
12 滋強飲料 **jikyō inryō** tonic drink
無銭飲食 **musen inshoku** jumping a restaurant bill
13 煙草飲 **tabakono(mi)** smoker

8b4.2

飩

TON, DON noodles

―――――――――― 2 ――――――――――
19 饂飩 **udon** noodles, udon

8b4.3

飫

YO, O satiety

8b4.4

飭

CHOKU correct, rectify

8b4.5 / 325

飯

HAN, meshi, mama cooked rice; meal, food
ii cooked rice

―――――――――― 1 ――――――――――
0 ご飯 **(go)han** cooked rice; meal, food
5 飯台 **handai** dining table
6 飯米 **hanmai** food; rice grown for the farm family's own consumption
8 飯事 **mamagoto** (children) playing house
飯炊 **meshita(ki)** rice cooking
9 飯屋 **meshiya** eating house
10 飯時 **meshidoki** mealtime
11 飯盒 **hangō** mess kit, eating utensils
飯盛 **meshimo(ri)** maidservant at an inn
飯粒 **meshitsubu** a grain of boiled rice
12 飯場 **hanba** construction camp/bunkhouse
18 飯櫃 **meshibitsu** (wooden) container for boiled rice

―――――――――― 2 ――――――――――
3 夕飯 **yūhan, yūmeshi** evening meal
夕飯時 **yūhandoki** suppertime
干飯 **hoshii** (sun-)dried boiled rice
4 中飯 **chūhan** midday meal, lunch
牛飯 **gyūmeshi** beef and rice
6 早飯 **hayameshi** eating fast/early
米飯 **beihan** boiled rice
7 冷飯 **hi(ya)meshi** cold rice
赤飯 **sekihan, akameshi** (festive) rice with red beans
麦飯 **mugimeshi** boiled barley and rice
8 炊飯器 **suihanki** (electric) rice cooker
炒飯 **chāhan** (Chinese fried-rice dish)
9 茶飯 **chameshi** rice boiled in tea or mixed with soy sauce and saké
茶飯事 **sahanji** everyday occurrence
昼飯 **hirumeshi, chūhan** lunch
10 残飯 **zanpan** left-over rice/food, leftovers
釜飯 **kamameshi** rice dish served in a small pot
11 強飯 **kowameshi** rice with red beans, *sekihan*
乾飯 **kareii, hoshiii** dried boiled rice
粗飯 **sohan** plain meal
12 握飯 **nigi(ri)meshi** rice/sushi ball
御飯 **gohan** boiled rice; a meal
御飯時 **gohandoki** mealtime
御飯蒸 **gohanmu(shi)** rice steamer
朝飯 **asahan, asameshi** breakfast
朝飯前 **asameshimae** (easy enough to do) before breakfast
晩飯 **banmeshi** evening meal, supper
焼飯 **ya(ki)meshi** fried rice
19 鯛飯 **taimeshi** rice with minced sea bream

―――――――――― 3 ――――――――――
1 一膳飯屋 **ichizen meshiya** eatery, diner
4 五目飯 **gomokumeshi** a rice, fish, and vegetable dish
8 物相飯 **mossōmeshi** prison food
12 無駄飯 **mudameshi** eat but not work, live in idleness

―――――――――― 4 ――――――――――
4 日常茶飯事 **nichijō sahanji** an everyday occurrence

―――――――――― 5 ――――――――――

8b5.1 / 1763

飽

HŌ, a(kiru/ku) get (sick and) tired of, have had enough of a(kasu) cloy, satiate, surfeit; tire, bore, make (someone) fed up a(kanu) unwearied of, untiring a(kippoi) fickle, be soon tired of

―――――――――― 1 ――――――――――
0 飽くなき **a(kunaki)** insatiable

飽くまで/くまでも **a(ku) made/ku made mo)** to the last, throughout, strictly
6 飽迄 **a(ku) made, a(ku) made (mo)** to the last, throughout, strictly
7 飽足 **a(ki)ta(ranai)** be unsatisfying/unsatisfied
8 飽性 **a(ki)shō** fickleness, flightiness
飽和 **hōwa** saturation
飽和点 **hōwaten** saturation point
9 飽食 **hōshoku** gluttony, engorgement
12 飽満 **hōman** satiety, satiation
13 飽飽 **a(ki)a(ki)** be weary of, be fed up with

——————— 2 ———————
11 光飽和 **kōhōwa** light saturation
光飽和点 **kōhōwaten** light saturation point
7 見飽 **mia(kiru)** get tired of looking at
11 過飽和 **kahōwa** supersaturation
13 飽飽 **a(ki)a(ki)** be weary of, be fed up with
14 聞飽 **ki(ki)a(kiru)** get tired of hearing

8b5.2

飴 飴

I, ame starch-jelly candy, hard candy

——————— 1 ———————
5 飴玉 **amedama** toffies, taffies, hard candies
6 飴色 **ame-iro** amber, light brown
12 飴棒 **ame(n)bō** lollipop, sucker
18 飴鞭 **ame (to) muchi** incentives and disincentives, carrot-and-stick

——————— 2 ———————
4 水飴 **mizuame** starch syrup

8b5.3 / 979

飾 餝

SHOKU, kaza(ru) decorate, adorn

——————— 1 ———————
5 飾付 **kaza(ri)tsu(ke)** decoration
飾立 **kaza(ri)ta(teru)** adorn, deck out
6 飾気 **kaza(ri)ke** affectation, love of display
8 飾物 **kaza(ri)mono** ornament, decoration; figurehead
9 飾屋 **kaza(ri)ya** jewelry maker
11 飾窓 **kaza(ri)mado** show window
12 飾棚 **kaza(ri)dana** display shelves/case
18 飾職 **kaza(ri)shoku** jewelry maker

——————— 2 ———————
4 文飾 **bunshoku** rhetorical embellishment
5 包飾 **tsutsu(mi)kaza(ri)** ostentation
6 羽飾 **hanekaza(ri)** a feather (in one's lapel)
耳飾 **mimikaza(ri)** earring
8 店飾 **misekaza(ri)** window dressing

服飾 **fukushoku** clothing and accessories, attire
9 首飾 **kubikaza(ri)** necklace
10 修飾 **shūshoku** decorate, adorn; modify (in grammar)
修飾語 **shūshokugo** modifier
胸飾 **munekaza(ri)** brooch
粉飾 **funshoku** makeup; embellishment
11 虚飾 **kyoshoku** ostentation, affectation
窓飾 **madokaza(ri)** window display
12 着飾 **kikaza(ru)** dress up
落飾 **rakushoku** tonsure
装飾 **sōshoku** ornament, decoration
装飾的 **sōshokuteki** ornamental, decorative
装飾品 **sōshokuhin** ornaments, decorations, accessories
装飾音 **sōshokuon** grace note
13 電飾 **denshoku** decorative lighting
14 髪飾 **kamikaza(ri)** hair ornament
15 潤飾 **junshoku** embellishment
縁飾 **fuchikaza(ri)** edging, frill
16 頸飾 **kubikaza(ri)** necklace
18 襟飾 **erikaza(ri)** neckwear (tie, brooch, etc.)

——————— 3 ———————
8 注連飾 **shimekaza(ri)** sacred Shinto rope
12 満艦飾 **mankanshoku** full dress, all decked out

——————— 4 ———————
9 室内装飾 **shitsunai sōshoku** interior decorating

8b5.4 / 1762

飼

SHI, ka(u) raise, keep (animals)

——————— 1 ———————
4 飼犬 **ka(i)inu** pet dog
5 飼主 **ka(i)nushi** (pet) owner, master
8 飼育 **shiiku** raising, breeding
飼育者 **shiikusha** raiser, breeder
9 飼草 **ka(i)gusa** hay
10 飼殺 **ka(i)goro(shi)** keep (a pet) till he dies
飼料 **shiryō** feed, fodder
11 飼猫 **ka(i)neko** pet cat
飼桶 **ka(i)oke** manger
飼鳥 **ka(i)dori** poultry
12 飼葉 **ka(i)ba** fodder
飼葉桶 **ka(i)baoke** manger
13 飼馴 **ka(i)na(rasu)** domesticate, tame
14 飼慣 **ka(i)na(rasu)** domesticate, tame
15 飼養 **shiyō** breeding, raising

——————— 2 ———————
2 子飼 **koga(i)** raising from infancy
4 手飼 **tega(i)** rear, keep (a pet)
牛飼 **ushika(i)** cowherd, cowboy

(margin) 8
→5
金
食
隹
雨
門

6 羊飼 **hitsujika(i)** shepherd, sheepherder
18 鵜飼 **uka(i)** fishing with cormorants

────────── 6 ──────────

8b6.1

蝕　蝕

SHOKU eclipse, occultation; be worm-eaten; be eroded
mushiba(mu) be worm-eaten; gnaw at

────────── 2 ──────────

4 分蝕 **bunshoku** partial eclipse
　水蝕 **suishoku** erosion
　月蝕 **gesshoku** eclipse of the moon
　日蝕 **nisshoku** solar eclipse
6 防蝕 **bōshoku** corrosion-resistant
　防蝕剤 **bōshokuzai** an anticorrosive
9 侵蝕 **shinshoku** encroachment; erosion; pitting corrosion
　風蝕 **fūshoku** weathering, wind erosion
　海蝕 **kaishoku** erosion caused by the sea
10 浸蝕 **shinshoku** erosion, corrosion
14 腐蝕 **fushoku** corrosion

────────── 3 ──────────

9 皆既蝕 **kaikishoku** total eclipse, totality

8b6.2

餌　餌

JI, e, esa feed, food; bait

────────── 1 ──────────

5 餌付 **ezu(ku)** (birds) begin to eat/feed
9 餌食 **ejiki** food, bait, prey

────────── 2 ──────────

5 生餌 **i(ki)e** live bait
　好餌 **kōji** good bait, tempting offer
9 食餌 **shokuji** food (to cure an illness)
11 鳥餌 **torie** bird seed/feed
13 煉餌 **ne(ri)e** paste bait/feed
15 撒餌 **ma(ki)e** scattered food; ground bait
16 擂餌 **su(ri)e** ground food
　薬餌 **yakuji** medicine; medicine and food

8b6.3

餃

KŌ meat-filled dumpling

────────── 1 ──────────

2 餃子 **gyōza** potsticker (pan-fried dumplings stuffed with minced pork and vegetables)

8b6.4

餅　餅　餅

HEI, mochi rice cake

────────── 1 ──────────

6 餅肌 **mochihada** smooth white skin
13 餅搗 **mochitsu(ki)** pounding rice to make mochi
14 餅網 **mochiami** net bag for mochi; grate to toast mochi on
15 餅膚 **mochihada** smooth white skin

────────── 2 ──────────

5 尻餅 **shirimochi** falling on one's behind/fanny
6 血餅 **keppei** blood clot
8 画餅 **gabei** failure, fiasco, (come to) nought
9 柏餅 **kashiwa mochi** rice cake wrapped in an oak leaf
11 菱餅 **hishimochi** colored diamond-shaped rice cakes (for the March 3 Hina-matsuri doll festival)
12 葛餅 **kuzumochi** arrowroot-flour cake
　寒餅 **kanmochi** winter rice cake
　焼餅 **ya(ki)mochi** toasted rice cake; jealousy
13 煎餅 **senbei** (rice) cracker
　煎餅布団 **senbei-buton** thinly stuffed futon/bedding
　賃餅 **chinmochi** rice cakes made to order
17 餡餅 **anmochi** beam-jam-filled rice cake
19 鏡餅 **kagamimochi** mounded rice-cakes

────────── 3 ──────────

7 牡丹餅 **botamochi** rice cake covered with bean jam

8b6.5

餉

SHŌ, karei, kareii dried boiled rice

────────── 2 ──────────

3 夕餉 **yūge** evening meal
9 昼餉 **hiruge** lunch
12 朝餉 **asage** breakfast

────────── 7 ──────────

8b7.1 / 1303

餓

GA, u(eru) starve, be hungry
katsu(eru) be starving for, hunger for

────────── 1 ──────────

6 餓死 **gashi** starve to death
10 餓鬼 **gaki** hungry ghost; little brat
　餓鬼大将 **gaki-daishō** dominant child among playmates
　餓鬼道 **gakidō** (Buddhist) hell of hungry demons

────────── 2 ──────────

9 施餓鬼 **segaki** service for the unmourned dead
10 飢餓 **kiga** hunger, starvation

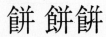

8

金
食　7←
隹
雷
門

8b7.2

舗 HO eat; late-afternoon meal

8b7.3

餒 DAI starve; rot, spoil

餝 → 飾 8b5.3

餘 → 余 2a5.24

8b7.4

餐 SAN eat, drink

───── 2 ─────
4 午餐 gosan luncheon
午餐会 gosankai luncheon
5 正餐 seisan formal dinner, banquet
9 昼餐 chūsan luncheon
11 粗餐 sosan plain meal
12 晩餐 bansan dinner, supper
晩餐会 bansankai dinner party, banquet

───── 8 ─────
餅 → 餅 8b6.4

8b8.1

餤 TAN proceed; offer

8b8.2

餞 SEN, hanamuke farewell banquet/gift

───── 1 ─────
7 餞別 senbetsu farewell gift
───── 2 ─────
4 予餞会 yosenkai farewell party (before graduation is completed)

8b8.3 / 327

館 舘 KAN (large) building, hall
yakata mansion, manor
tate, tachi fort; mansion

───── 1 ─────
4 館内 kannai within the building
8 館長 kanchō director, curator
10 館員 kan'in staff, personnel

───── 2 ─────
4 分館 bunkan annex
公館 kōkan official residence
5 本館 honkan main building; this building
6 会館 kaikan (assembly) hall
7 別館 bekkan annex
学館 gakkan academy, school
8 函館 Hakodate (city, Hokkaidō)
9 洋館 yōkan Western-style building
10 旅館 ryokan inn, hotel
旅館業 ryokangyō the hotel business
11 商館 shōkan trading house, firm
閉館 heikan closing (the hall/building)
12 開館 kaikan opening (of a building)
13 新館 shinkan new building, annex

───── 3 ─────
3 大使館 taishikan embassy
4 公民館 kōminkan public hall, community center
公使館 kōshikan legation
水族館 suizokukan (public) aquarium
5 写真館 shashinkan photo studio
白亜館 Hakuakan the White House
白堊館 Hakuakan the White House
6 迎賓館 geihinkan reception hall, residence for guests
7 体育館 taiikukan gymnasium
図書館 toshokan library
図書館学 toshokangaku library science
図書館長 toshokanchō head librarian
図書館員 toshokan'in library clerk, librarian
8 牧師館 bokushikan rectory, parsonage
9 美術館 bijutsukan art gallery
映画館 eigakan movie theater
10 記念館 kinenkan memorial hall
12 博物館 hakubutsukan museum
絵画館 kaigakan art gallery
14 領事館 ryōjikan consulate
15 隣保館 rinpokan settlement house

───── 4 ─────
14 総領事館 sōryōjikan consulate-general

8b8.4

餡 AN bean jam

───── 1 ─────
0 餡パン anpan bean-jam-filled roll
2 餡子 anko bean jam

15 餡餅 **anmochi** beam-jam-filled rice cake

———————— 9 ————————

8b9.1

餬

KO rice gruel; livelihood

———— 1 ————

3 餬口 **kokō** a living, livelihood

8b9.2

饕

TETSU, musabo(ru) be voracious/
gluttonous/greedy

———————— 10 ————————

8b10.1

餽

KI give, provide

8b10.2

饂

UN noodles

———— 1 ————

13 饂飩 **udon** noodles, udon

8b10.3

餾

RYŪ to steam (rice)

8b10.4

饗 饗

KYŌ banquet

———— 1 ————

0 饗する **kyō(suru)** give a banquet, treat
7 饗応 **kyōō** hold a banquet, wine and dine
10 饗宴 **kyōen** banquet, feast, dinner

———————— 11 ————————

8b11.1

饅

MAN dumpling

———— 1 ————

16 饅頭 **manjū** steamed dumpling (with bean-
jam/meat filling)

———————— 2 ————————

3 土饅頭 **domanjū** grave mound
6 肉饅頭 **niku manjū** meat-filled bun

8b11.2

饉

KIN hunger

———— 2 ————

10 飢饉 **kikin** famine

———————— 12 ————————

8b12.1

饑

KI, u(eru) be hungry, starve

8b12.2

饒

JŌ, yuta(ka) abundant, rich

———— 1 ————

6 饒舌 **jōzetsu** garrulous, talkative
饒舌家 **jōzetsuka** chatterbox

———— 2 ————

13 豊饒 **hōjō** fertile, productive

8b12.3

饌

SEN an offering of food

———— 2 ————

9 神饌 **shinsen** food-and-wine offering to the
gods
13 献饌 **kensen** offering (to a god)

8b12.4

饋

KI give, provide, offer

———— 1 ————

13 饋電線 **kidensen** feeder (line)

8b12.5

饐

I, EI, su(eru) go bad, turn sour, spoil

饗 → 饗 **8b10.4**

8

金
食 12←
隹
雨
門

─────────── 13 ───────────　│　─────────── 14 ───────────

8b13.1

饕　TŌ be greedy/ravenous

饜→　**2p21.1**

─────────── 隹 8c ───────────

隹	隻	隼	售	雀	雄	集	焦	雋	雅	雅	雄	雎
0.1	2.1	2.2	3.1	3.2	4.1	4.2	4.3	4.4	8c5.1	5.1	5.2	5.3

雌	雑	截	奪	雕	虧	雖	雛	難	離	雜	瞿	難
6.1	6.2	6.3	6.4	8.1	9.1	9.2	10.1	10.2	10.3	8c6.2	10.4	8c10.2

雛	耀	羅	讎	罐	觀	軈	羅
8c16.1	12.1	14.1	7a16.2	2k4.6	5c13.7	16.1	17.1

─────────── 0 ───────────

8c0.1

隹　SUI short-tailed bird

─────────── 2 ───────────

8c2.1 / 1311

隻　SEKI (counter for ships); one (of a pair)

─────── 1 ───────

4 隻手 **sekishu** one-armed
11 隻眼 **sekigan** one-eyed
15 隻影 **sekiei** a glimpse/sign/shadow

─────── 2 ───────

1 一隻 **isseki** one ship/boat
一隻眼 **issekigan** discerning eye

─────── 3 ───────

4 片言隻句 **hengen-sekku** few words
片言隻語 **hengen-sekigo** few words

8c2.2

隼　JUN, SHUN, hayabusa falcon

─────────── 3 ───────────

8c3.1

售　SHŪ sell; be popular

8c3.2

雀　JAKU, suzume sparrow

─────────── 1 ───────────

12 雀斑 **sobakasu** freckles
13 雀蜂 **suzumebachi** wasp, hornet
21 雀躍 **jakuyaku** jump for joy, exult

─────────── 2 ───────────

3 孔雀 **kujaku** peacock
6 朱雀 **Suzaku** (emperor, 930–946)
8 金雀児 **enishida** broom, genista (a shrub)
金雀枝 **enishida** broom, genista (a shrub)
11 麻雀 **mājan** mahjong
12 雲雀 **hibari** skylark
16 燕雀 **enjaku** small birds

─────────── 3 ───────────

8 欣喜雀踊 **kinki-jakuyaku** jump for joy
12 着切雀 **ki(ta)ki(ri) suzume** person having only the clothes he is wearing
揚雲雀 **a(ge)hibari** (soaring) skylark

─────────── 4 ───────────

8c4.1 / 1387

雄　YŪ male; brave; great
osu, o-, on- male

─────────── 1 ───────────

0 雄ねじ **o(neji)** male screw, bolt
3 雄大 **yūdai** grand, magnificent
雄々 **oo(shii)** manly, virile, valiant
4 雄犬 **osuinu** male dog
雄牛 **oushi** bull, ox, steer
雄心 **yūshin** heroic spirit, aspiration, ambition
5 雄弁 **yūben** eloquence
6 雄壮 **yūsō** heroic, valiant
雄叫 **otake(bi), osake(bi)** courageous shout, war cry, roar
7 雄花 **obana** male flower
雄志 **yūshi** lofty ambition
雄図 **yūto** ambitious undertaking

8

金
食
隹
雨
門

→13

8 雄松 **omatsu** black pine
雄性 **yūsei** male
9 雄飛 **yūhi** leap, soar; embark on, launch out into
雄勁 **yūkei** pithy, vigorous (style)
雄姿 **yūshi** gallant figure
10 雄健 **yūken** virile, vigorous
雄猛 **yūmō** intrepid, dauntless, brave
雄馬 **ouma** stallion
11 雄略 **Yūryaku** (emperor, 456–479)
雄鳥 **ondori** rooster, male bird
12 雄偉 **yūi** imposing, grand, magnificent
雄渾 **yūkon** vigorous, bold, grand
雄雄 **oo(shii)** manly, virile, valiant
13 雄滝 **odaki** the larger waterfall (of two)
雄蜂 **obachi** drone (bee)
15 雄蕊 **oshibe, yūzui** stamen
雄編 **yūhen** a masterpiece
雄篇 **yūhen** a masterpiece

―――――――――― 2 ――――――――――

6 両雄 **ryōyū** two great men
老雄 **rōyū** old hero
8 英雄 **eiyū** hero
英雄主義 **eiyū shugi** heroism
英雄的 **eiyūteki** heroic
12 雄雄 **oo(shii)** manly, virile, valiant
13 聖雄 **seiyū** holy man, hero saint
群雄 **gun'yū** rival chiefs
群雄割拠 **gun'yū kakkyo** rivalry of local barons
14 雌雄 **shiyū** male and female; (decide) winner and loser, (vie for) supremacy
mesuosu male and female

8c4.2 / 436

集 **SHŪ, atsu(meru)** gather, collect
atsu(maru) gather, come together
tsudo(u) gather, assemble, meet

―――――――――― 1 ――――――――――

3 集大成 **shūtaisei** compilation
4 集中 **shūchū** concentration
5 集札係 **shūsatsugakari** ticket collector
6 集合 **shūgō** gathering, meeting; set (in math)
集合名詞 **shūgō meishi** collective noun
集合的 **shūgōteki** collective
集会 **shūkai** meeting, assembly
集会所 **shūkaijo** meeting place, assembly hall
集会室 **shūkaishitsu** meeting room/hall
集団 **shūdan** group, mass, crowd
集団的 **shūdanteki** collectively
集成 **shūsei** collect, compile
8 集注 **shūchū** concentrating one's attention on
集注本 **shūchūbon** variorum edition
集金 **shūkin** collecting money
集金人 **shūkinnin** bill collector

9 集約 **shūyaku** intensive
集約的 **shūyakuteki** intensive
集計 **shūkei** categorized total, aggregate
10 集荷 **shūka** collection of cargo/freight
集配 **shūhai** collection and delivery
集配人 **shūhainin** postman
11 集魚灯 **shūgyotō** fish-luring light
12 集落 **shūraku** settlement, community, town
集散 **shūsan** collection and distribution
集散地 **shūsanchi** trading center, entrepôt
集結 **shūketsu** concentrate, mass (troops)
集結所 **shūketsusho** place of assembly
13 集塊 **shūkai** mass, cluster
14 集塵器 **shūjinki** dust collector
15 集権 **shūken** centralization of power
16 集積 **shūseki** accumulate, amass; integrate
集積回路 **shūseki kairo** integrated circuit
集録 **shūroku** collect, record, compile

―――――――――― 2 ――――――――――

4 文集 **bunshū** anthology
5 召集 **shōshū** call together, convene
召集令 **shōshūrei** draft call
句集 **kushū** collection of haiku poems
6 全集 **zenshū** complete works
光集積回路 **hikari shūseki kairo** optical integrated circuit
8 招集 **shōshū** call together, convene
呼集 **yo(bi)atsu(meru)** call together, convene
参集 **sanshū** assembling people together
取集 **to(ri)atsu(meru)** collect, gather
9 拾集 **shūshū, hiro(i)atsu(meru)** collect, gather up
10 家集 **kashū** poetry collection
特集 **tokushū** special edition/collection
特集号 **tokushūgō** special issue
11 採集 **saishū** collecting (butterflies)
掃集 **ha(ki)atsu(meru)** sweep up/together
密集 **misshū** crowd/mass together
寄集 **yo(se)atsu(me)** miscellany, motley
yo(ri)atsu(maru) assemble, meet
12 募集 **boshū** recruiting; solicitation
買集 **ka(i)atsu(meru)** buy up
結集 **kesshū** concentrate, marshal together
雲集 **unshū** throng, swarm, crowd
13 掻集 **ka(ki)atsu(meru)** rake together, gather up
群集 **gunshū** crowd, multitude, mob (psychology)
mu(re)atsu(maru) gather in large groups
蒐集 **shūshū** collect, gather, accumulate
蒐集家 **shūshūka** collector
蒐集癖 **shūshūheki** collecting habit/mania
詩集 **shishū** a collection of poems
馳集 **ha(se)atsu(maru)** run/ride together to, flock to
14 選集 **senshū** selection, anthology

8

金
食
隹
雨 4←
門

徴集 **chōshū** levy, recruit, conscript
徴集令 **chōshūrei** order calling up draftees
歌集 **kashū** poetry anthology
駆集 **ka(ri)atsu(meru)** muster, round up
15 撰集 **senshū** anthology
編集 **henshū** editing, compilation
編集長 **henshūchō** editor-in-chief
編集者 **henshūsha** editor
蝟集 **ishū** swarm, throng, gather
16 凝集 **gyōshū** cohesion, condensation, agglutination
凝集力 **gyōshūryoku** cohesive force, cohesion

———————— 3 ————————

3 万葉集 **Man'yōshū** (Japan's oldest anthology of poems)
大募集 **daiboshū** wholesale hiring/solicitation
4 中央集権 **chūō shūken** centralization of government
5 古今集 **Kokinshū** (see preceding entry)
6 名言集 **meigenshū** analects
名歌集 **meikashū** poetry anthology
7 私家集 **shikashū** private/personal collection
9 勅撰集 **chokusenshū** emperor-commissioned anthology of poems
13 節用集 **setsuyōshū** dictionary, manual
18 難語集 **nangoshū** glossary (to an ancient classic)

———————— 4 ————————

12 植物採集 **shokubutsu saishū** plant collecting
20 懸賞募集 **kenshō boshū** prize competition

———————— 5 ————————

5 古今和歌集 **Kokinwakashū** (poetry anthology, early tenth century)

8c4.3 / 999

焦

SHŌ fire; impatience; yearning
ko(geru) get scorched
ko(gasu) scorch, singe; pine for
ko(gareru) pine/yearn for
ase(ru) be in a hurry, be hasty/impatient
ji(reru) fret, be irritated　**ji(rasu)** irritate, nettle, tease

———————— 1 ————————

3 焦土 **shōdo** scorched earth
4 焦心 **shōshin** impatience, anxiousness
5 焦付 **ko(ge)tsu(ku)** get burned/scorched; become uncollectible
6 焦死 **ko(gare)ji(ni)** die from love, pine away
9 焦点 **shōten** focal point, focus
焦茶 **ko(ge)cha** dark brown, umber
焦茶色 **ko(ge)cha-iro** dark brown, umber
焦臭 **ko(ge)kusa(i), kinakusa(i)** smelling burnt
焦眉 **shōbi** urgent, pressing
15 焦慮 **shōryo** impatience, anxiousness

焦熱 **shōnetsu** scorching heat
焦熱地獄 **shōnetsu jigoku** an inferno
17 焦燥 **shōsō** impatience, fretfulness

———————— 2 ————————

7 麦焦 **mugiko(gashi)** parched-barley flour
9 待焦 **ma(chi)ko(gareru)** wait impatiently for
思焦 **omo(i)koga(reru)** pine for
10 恋焦 **ko(i)ko(gareru)** pine for, be desperately in love
11 黒焦 **kuroko(ge)** charred, burned black
12 焼焦 **ya(ke)ko(ge)** burn hole, scorch

8c4.4

隽

SHUN excel

雅 → 雅 8c5.1

———————— 5 ————————

8c5.1 / 1456

雅　雅

GA elegance, gracefulness
miya(bita/biyaka) elegant, refined

———————— 1 ————————

2 雅人 **gajin** man of refined taste
4 雅文 **gabun** elegant/classic style
5 雅号 **gagō** pen name
6 雅名 **gamei** pen name; refined name for
7 雅言 **gagen** elegant/poetical expression
8 雅味 **gami** tastefulness, artistry
9 雅俗 **gazoku** the refined and the vulgar
雅客 **gakaku** man of taste, writer
10 雅致 **gachi** elegance, asthetic effect
雅称 **gashō** pen name; elegant/poetical name for
12 雅量 **garyō** magnanimity
13 雅楽 **gagaku** ancient Japanese court music
14 雅歌 **Gaka** the Song of Solomon
雅語 **gago** elegant/poetical expression
15 雅趣 **gashu** elegance, tastefulness, artistry
雅談 **gadan** refined conversation
16 雅懐 **gakai** esthetic sentiment

———————— 2 ————————

4 文雅 **bunga** elegant, refined, artistic
5 古雅 **koga** classical elegance/grace
8 典雅 **tenga** refined, elegant, classic
9 風雅 **fūga** elegant, refined, tasteful
10 都雅 **toga** elegant, urbane, refined
高雅 **kōga** refined, elegant
12 温雅 **onga** affable and refined, gracious
閑雅 **kanga** refined, elegant; quietude

15 嫻雅 **kanga** refined, elegant
17 優雅 **yūga** elegant, graceful, refined

8c5.2

雉
CHI, kiji pheasant

———————— 1 ————————
2 雉子 **kiji, kigisu** pheasant
———————— 2 ————————
5 白雉 **Hakuchi** (era, 650–672)

8c5.3

睢
SHO osprey

———————— 6 ————————

8c6.1 / 1388

雌
SHI, mesu, me- female

———————— 1 ————————
0 雌ねじ **me(neji)** nut, threaded hole
4 雌犬 **mesuinu** female dog, bitch
雌牛 **meushi** cow
6 雌伏 **shifuku** remain in obscurity, lie low
7 雌花 **mebana** female flower
8 雌性 **shisei** female
10 雌馬 **meuma** mare
11 雌豚 **mebuta** sow
雌鳥 **mendori** hen
12 雌象 **mezō** cow elephant
雌雄 **shiyū** male and female; (decide) winner
and loser, (vie for supremacy)
mesuosu male and female
13 雌蜂 **mebachi** queen bee
14 雌熊 **meguma** female bear
15 雌蕊 **meshibe, shizui** pistil

8c6.2 / 575

雑 雜 襍
ZATSU, ZŌ miscella-
neous, a mix
ma(zeru), maji(eru)
(tr.) mix **ma(zaru/**
jiru) (intr.) mix, mingle

———————— 1 ————————
3 雑巾 **zōkin** wiping cloth, mopping rag
4 雑収入 **zatsushūnyū, zasshūnyū** miscellaneous income
雑文 **zatsubun** literary miscellany
雑木 **zōki, zatsuboku** miscellaneous trees
雑木林 **zōkibayashi, zōbokurin** grove of
trees of various species
5 雑用 **zatsuyō** miscellaneous things to attend to
6 雑多 **zatta** various, all kinds of
雑曲 **zakkyoku** medley; popular song
雑件 **zakken** miscellaneous matters
雑交 **zakkō** crossing (in biology)
雑色 **zasshoku** various colors
7 雑兵 **zappei, zōhyō** common soldiers
雑役 **zatsueki** odd jobs, chores
雑役夫 **zatsuekifu** handyman
雑役婦 **zatsuekifu** maid
雑学 **zatsugaku** knowledge of various
subjects
雑言 **zogon** vilification, name-calling
8 雑事 **zatsuji** miscellaneous affairs
雑念 **zatsunen** idle/worldly thoughts
雑沓 **zattō** hustle and bustle, congestion
雑居 **zakkyo** dwell together
雑居ビル **zakkyobiru** building housing
various businesses
雑炊 **zōsui** porridge of rice and vegetables
雑物 **zatsubutsu** miscellaneous things;
impurities
9 雑品 **zappin** sundries, odds and ends
雑草 **zassō** weeds
雑音 **zatsuon** noise, static
雑則 **zassoku** miscellaneous rules
雑食 **zasshoku** omnivorous
10 雑俳 **zappai** playful literature originating
from haiku
雑株 **zatsukabu, zakkabu** miscellaneous
stocks
雑書 **zassho** miscellaneous books; book on
miscellaneous subjects
雑記 **zakki** miscellaneous notes
雑記帳 **zakkichō** notebook
11 雑婚 **zakkon** intermarriage
雑務 **zatsumu** miscellaneous duties
雑貨 **zakka** miscellaneous goods, sundries,
notions
雑貨商 **zakkashō** general store
雑魚 **zako, jako** small fish/fry
雑魚寝 **zakone** sleep together in a group
12 雑報 **zappō** miscellaneous news
雑煮 **zōni** rice cakes boiled with vegetables
雑然 **zatsuzen** in disorder
雑税 **zatsuzei** miscellaneous taxes
雑筆 **zappitsu** miscellaneous writings
雑費 **zappi** miscellaneous expenses
13 雑感 **zakkan** miscellaneous impressions
雑話 **zatsuwa** idle talk, chitchat
14 雑歌 **zōka** miscellaneous poems
雑種 **zasshu** of various kinds; mixed breed
雑穀 **zakkoku** grains
雑穀商 **zakkokushō** grain merchant
雑誌 **zasshi** magazine

8

金
食
隹 6 ←
雫
門

雑説 **zassetsu** various theories
雑駁 **zappaku** incoherent, desultory
15 雑編 **zappen** miscellaneous writings
雑篇 **zappen** miscellaneous writings
雑談 **zatsudan** chitchat, idle conversation
雑輩 **zappai** rank and file, small fry
雑踏 **zattō** hustle and bustle, congestion
16 雑録 **zatsuroku** miscellaneous notes
18 雑題 **zatsudai** miscellaneous topics
20 雑纂 **zassan** miscellaneous collection

───────── 2 ─────────

3 大雑把 **ōzappa** rough (guess); generous
7 夾雑物 **kyōzatsubutsu** admixture, impurities
乱雑 **ranzatsu** disorder, confusion
11 混雑 **konzatsu** confusion, disorder, congestion
粗雑 **sozatsu** coarse, crude
12 猥雑 **waizatsu** vulgar, disorderly
無雑 **muzatsu** pure, unadulterated
13 煩雑 **hanzatsu** complicated, troublesome
14 複雑 **fukuzatsu** complicated, complex
複雑化 **fukuzatsuka** complication
15 蕪雑 **buzatsu** unpolished, crude
諸雑費 **shozappi** miscellaneous expenses
16 繁雑 **hanzatsu** complex, intricate
錯雑 **sakuzatsu** complication, intricacy

───────── 3 ─────────

3 三号雑誌 **sangō zasshi** short-lived magazine
6 同人雑誌 **dōjin zasshi** literary coterie magazine, small magazine
11 悪口雑言 **akkō-zōgon** vituperation
14 種々雑多 **shuju-zatta** various, every sort of
15 罵詈雑言 **bari-zōgon** abusive language
16 機関雑誌 **kikan zasshi** organization's publication

8c6.3

截

SETSU, ta(tsu) cut

───────── 1 ─────────

11 截断 **setsudan** cut off, sever
12 截然 **setsuzen** distinct, clear, sharp

8c6.4 / 1310

奪

DATSU, uba(u) snatch away, take by force; captivate

───────── 1 ─────────

6 奪合 **uba(i)a(u)** scramble/struggle for
奪返 **uba(i)kae(su)** recapture, take back
奪回 **dakkai** recapture, retake
8 奪取 **uba(i)to(ru)** plunder
dasshu capture, seize, wrest
11 奪掠 **datsuryaku** plunder, pillage

奪略 **datsuryaku** plunder, pillage
15 奪還 **dakkan** recapture, retake

───────── 2 ─────────

3 与奪 **yodatsu** (the power to) give or take away
6 争奪 **sōdatsu** contend/scramble for
争奪戦 **sōdatsusen** contest/scramble/struggle for
9 侵奪 **shindatsu** disseizin, usurpation
10 剥奪 **hakudatsu** deprive/divest of
11 掠奪 **ryakudatsu** plunder, loot, despoil
強奪 **gōdatsu** rob, plunder, hijack, hold up
強奪者 **gōdatsusha** plunderer, robber
強奪物 **gōdatsubutsu** plunder, loot
略奪 **ryakudatsu** pillage, plunder, looting
15 横奪 **ōdatsu** usurp, seize, steal
褫奪 **chidatsu** strip/deprive of
16 簒奪 **sandatsu** usurpation

───────── 3 ─────────

12 換骨奪胎 **kankotsu-dattai** adapt, modify, recast

───────── 4 ─────────

5 生殺与奪 **seisatsu-yodatsu** (the power to) kill or let live

───────── 8 ─────────

8c8.1

雕

CHŌ carve

───────── 9 ─────────

8c9.1

虧

KI lack, lose, wane

───────── 1 ─────────

4 虧月 **kigetsu** waning moon

───────── 2 ─────────

9 盈虧 **eiki** waxing and waning, phase (of the moon)

8c9.2

雖

SUI, iedo(mo) although, even if

───────── 10 ─────────

8c10.1

雛

SŪ, hina chick; (Girls' Festival) doll
hiyoko chick

───────── 1 ─────────

2 雛人形 **hina ningyō** (Girls' Festival) doll

8

金
食
→ 6 隹
帚
門

9 雛型 **hinagata** model, miniature, sample
10 雛遊 **hinaaso(bi)** playing with dolls (arranged on tiers)
11 雛菊 **hinagiku** daisy
雛祭 **hinamatsu(ri)** Girls' Doll Festival (March 3)
雛鳥 **hinadori** chick, fledgling
13 雛節句 **hina (no) sekku** Girls' Doll Festival (March 3)
16 雛壇 **hinadan** tiered stand for displaying dolls

8c10.2 / 557

難 難

NAN difficulty; distress
muzuka(shii), kata(i) difficult
-niku(i), -gata(i) difficult/hard
to …, un…able

───────────── 1 ─────────────

0 難なく **nan(naku)** without difficulty
4 難中難 **nanchū (no) nan** the hardest of all
難文 **nanbun** hard-to-understand passage/style
5 難民 **nanmin** refugees
難句 **nanku** difficult phrase/passage
難字 **nanji** hard-to-learn kanji
6 難曲 **nankyoku** piece which is hard to play/ sing
難件 **nanken** difficult matter/case
難色 **nanshoku** unwillingness, opposition
難行 **nangyō** penance, self-mortification
難行苦行 **nangyō-kugyō** penance, self-mortification
難行道 **nangyōdō** salvation through austerities
7 難役 **nan'yaku** difficult role
難局 **nankyoku** difficult situation, crisis
難攻不落 **nankō-furaku** impregnable
8 難事 **nanji** difficult matter
難波 **nanpa** shipwreck
難波船 **nanpasen** shipwreck
難治 **nanji, nanchi** intractable
難易 **nan'i** (relative) difficulty
難物 **nanbutsu** hard-to-handle person/ problem
難所 **nansho** difficult pass/stage
9 難点 **nanten** difficult point
10 難破 **nanpa** shipwreck
難破船 **nanpasen** shipwreck
難病 **nanbyō** incurable/serious illness
難症 **nanshō** incurable/serious illness
難航 **nankō** stormy passage, rough going
難訓 **nankun** difficult reading of a kanji
11 難渋 **nanjū** suffering, distress, hardship
難球 **nankyū** hard-to-catch batted ball
難産 **nanzan** a difficult delivery/childbirth
難船 **nansen** shipwreck, ship in distress
難問 **nanmon** difficult problem
難問題 **nanmondai** difficult problem

12 難場 **nanba** difficult situation/stage
難無 **nanna(ku)** without difficulty
13 難解 **nankai** hard to understand
難戦 **nansen** hard fighting
難詰 **nankitsu** blame, censure
難路 **nanro** rough/difficult road
14 難語 **nango** word whose meaning is unclear
難語集 **nangoshū** glossary (to an ancient classic)
難読 **nandoku** a difficult reading
難関 **nankan** barrier, obstacle, difficulty
15 難儀 **nangi** difficult, trying
17 難聴 **nanchō** hard of hearing
18 難癖 **nankuse** a fault, failings
難題 **nandai** difficult topic/problem

───────────── 2 ─────────────

1 一難 **ichinan** one difficulty, one danger
3 万難 **bannan** innumerable difficulties, all obstacles
大難 **tainan** great misfortune, calamity
女難 **jonan** trouble with women
小難 **shōnan** small misfortune, mishap
komuzuka(shii) troublesome, finicky
4 止難 **ya(mi)gata(i)** hard to stop, compelling
水難 **suinan** sea disaster, flood, drowning
水難除 **suinan'yo(ke)** charm against drowning
火難 **kanan** fire, conflagration
火難除 **kanan'yo(ke)** charm against fire
6 多難 **tanan** full of difficulties, thorny
気難 **kimuzuka(shii)** hard to please, grouchy
危難 **kinan** danger, distress
至難 **shinan** extreme difficulty
有難 **a(ri)gata(i)** welcome, thankful
a(ri)ga(tō) thank you
有難迷惑 **a(ri)gata-meiwaku** unwelcome favor
有難味 **a(ri)gatami** value, worth
有難涙 **a(ri)gata-namida** tears of gratitude
百難 **hyakunan** all obstacles, all sorts of trouble
7 抑難 **osa(e)gata(i)** irrepressible, uncontrollable
批難 **hinan** criticize, denounce, condemn
困難 **konnan** difficulty, trouble
災難 **sainan** mishap, accident, calamity
忍難 **shino(bi)gata(i)** unbearable
言難 **i(i)gata(i)** difficult to say, inexpressible
8 非難 **hinan** criticize, denounce
受難 **junan** ordeal, sufferings; (Jesus's) Passion
受難日 **junanbi** Good Friday
受難者 **junansha** sufferer
受難週 **junanshū** Passion Week
受難節 **junansetsu** Lent
受難劇 **junangeki** Passion play

8

金
食
隹
雨
門

10←

法難 **hōnan** religious persecution
苦難 **kunan** hardships, adversity
国難 **kokunan** national crisis/disaster
9 急難 **kyūnan** impending danger; sudden disaster
海難 **kainan** sea disaster, shipwreck
後難 **kōnan, gōnan** future trouble, the consequences
度難 **do(shi)gata(i)** beyond saving, incorrigible
10 険難 **kennan** steep; fraught with danger
家難 **kanan** family misfortune
殉難 **junnan** martyrdom
殉難者 **junnansha** martyr, victim
病難 **byōnan** the misfortune of illness
11 得難 **egata(i)** hard to obtain, rare
救難 **kyūnan** rescue, salvage
盗難 **tōnan** (loss from) theft
12 測難 **haka(ri)gata(i)** unfathomable
堪難 **ta(e)gata(i), kora(e)gata(i)** unbearable, intolerable
御難 **gonan** calamity, misfortune
無難 **bunan** safe, acceptable
13 遭難 **sōnan** disaster, accident, mishap, distress
遭難者 **sōnansha** victim, sufferer
14 読難 **yo(mi)niku(i)** hard to read
15 避難 **hinan** refuge, evacuation
避難民 **hinanmin** refugees, evacuees
避難者 **hinansha** refugees, evacuees
避難所 **hinanjo** shelter, place of safety
黙難 **moda(shi)gata(i)** hard to overlook
論難 **ronnan** censure, criticism, denunciation
17 艱難 **kannan** adversity, trials
18 離難 **hana(re)gata(i)** inseparable

─────────── 3 ───────────

2 入学難 **nyūgakunan** difficulty of getting into a school
4 心得難 **kokoroegata(i)** strange, inexplicable
5 生活難 **seikatsunan** economic distress, hard times
7 住宅難 **jūtakunan** housing shortage
11 経営難 **keieinan** financial distress
12 就職難 **shūshokunan** job shortage
無理難題 **muri-nandai** unreasonable demand
13 資金難 **shikinnan** financial difficulty
18 難中難 **nanchū (no) nan** the hardest of all

8c10.3 / 1281

離 离

RI, hana(reru) separate, leave
hana(su) separate, keep apart

─────────── 1 ───────────

3 離山 **rizan** lone mountain; leaving a temple

4 離反 **rihan** estrangement, alienation, breakaway
離水 **risui** (seaplane's) takeoff from water
離日 **rinichi** leave Japan
6 離任 **rinin** quit one's office
離合 **rigō** meeting and parting
7 離別 **ribetsu** separation, divorce
離乳 **rinyū** weaning
離乳食 **rinyūshoku** baby food
離乳期 **rinyūki** the weaning period
離床 **rishō** get up; leave one's sickbed
離村 **rison** rural exodus
8 離京 **rikyō** leaving the capital
10 離陸 **ririku** (airplane) takeoff
離郷 **rikyō** leaving one's home town
離家 **hana(re)ya** detached building
離宮 **rikyū** detached palace
離党 **ritō** secede from a party
離島 **ritō, hana(re)jima** outlying island
離座敷 **hana(re) zashiki** detached room
11 離婚 **rikon** divorce
離脱 **ridatsu** secession, separation, abolition, renunciation
12 離隔 **rikaku** isolation, segregation
離着 **richaku** takeoff and landing
離着陸 **richakuriku** takeoff and landing
離散 **risan** scatter, disperse
離散的 **risanteki** discrete
離間 **rikan** alienation, estrangement
離間策 **rikansaku** sowing discord
13 離業 **hana(re)waza** stunt, feat
離愁 **rishū** the sorrow of parting
15 離縁 **rien** divorce, disowning
離縁状 **rienjō** letter of divorce
17 離礁 **rishō** refloat (a reefbound ship)
18 離職 **rishoku** quit/lose one's job
離職者 **rishokusha** the unemployed
離難 **hana(re)gata(i)** inseparable
離離 **hana(re)bana(re)** separated, scattered, dispersed
20 離籍 **riseki** removal of one's name from the official family register

─────────── 2 ───────────

4 切離 **ki(ri)hana(su)** cut off/apart, sever, separate
支離滅裂 **shiri-metsuretsu** incoherent, inconsistent, chaotic
分離 **bunri** separation, division
分離主義者 **bunri shugisha** separatist, secessionist
手離 **tebana(re) suru** no longer need constant care; be finished and ready to hand over
引離 **hi(ki)hana(su)** pull apart; outdistance
7 別離 **betsuri** parting, separation

乳離 **chibana(re), chichibana(re)** weaning
床離 **tokobana(re)** get out of bed
見離 **mihana(su)** desert, abandon, give up
8 乖離 **kairi** estranged, disparate
明離 **a(ke)hana(reru)** become light, dawn
取離 **to(ri)hana(su)** let go of, drop
金離 **kanebana(re)** free spending
9 飛離 **to(bi)hana(reru)** fly apart; tower above; out of the ordinary
垢離 **kori** purification by ablution
単離 **tanri** isolation (in chemistry)
背離 **hairi** estrangement, alienation
10 陸離 **rikuri** dazzling, brilliant
剥離 **hakuri** come/peel off
遊離 **yūri** isolate, separate
遊離酸 **yūrisan** free acid
流離 **ryūri, sasura(u)** wander, roam
振離 **fu(ri)hana(su)** shake off, break free of
11 脱離 **datsuri** disconnect (oneself) from
12 隔離 **kakuri** isolate, segregate
距離 **kyori** distance
距離計 **kyorikei** range finder
13 電離 **denri** ionization
電離圏 **denriken** ionosphere
18 離離 **hana(re)bana(re)** separated, scattered, dispersed
20 懸離 **ka(ke)hana(reru)** be far apart, differ widely

————————— 3 —————————

2 人間離 **ningenbana(re)** unworldly, superhuman
4 中距離 **chūkyori** medium-range, middle-distance
水垢離 **mizugori** cold-water ablutions
5 世間離 **sekenbana(re)** strange, uncommon; unworldly
6 近距離 **kinkyori** short distance/range
8 長距離 **chōkyori** long-distance, long-range
10 射距離 **shakyori** range (of a gun/missile)
素人離 **shirōtobana(re)** free of amateurishness
12 遠距離 **enkyori** long distance, long-range
短距離 **tankyori** short distance, short-range
等距離 **tōkyori** equidistant
13 愛別離苦 **aibetsuriku** parting from loved ones
15 膚身離 **hadami-hana(sazu)** always kept on one's person, highly treasured

————————— 4 —————————

4 不即不離 **fusoku-furi** neutral, noncommittal
7 走行距離 **sōkō kyori** distance covered (in a given time)
10 航続距離 **kōzoku kyori** (plane's) range
12 着弾距離 **chakudan kyori** range (of a gun)
弾着距離 **danchaku kyori** range (of a gun)

雜 → 雑 **8c6.2**

8c10.4

瞿 **KU** look at; be amazed

————————— 11 —————————

難 → 難 **8c10.2**

雓 → 鸘 **8c16.1**

————————— 12 —————————

8c12.1

耀 耀 **YŌ, kagaya(ku)** shine, sparkle, gleam

————————— 14 —————————

8c14.1

糴 **TEKI, ka(u)** buy (grain)

————————— 15 —————————

讎 → 讐 **7a16.2**

罐 → 缶 **2k4.6**

————————— 16 —————————

觀 → 観 **5c13.7**

8c16.1

鸘 雓 **yagate** presently, soon, by and by

————————— 17 —————————

8c17.1

糶 **CHŌ, u(ru)** sell (grain)
seri auction

8

金
食
隹 17←
雨
門

雨	雫	雪	雲	雾	雷	電	霓	零	需	霆	霄	霊
0.1	3.1	3.2	4.1	4.2	5.1	5.2	5.3	5.4	6.1	6.2	7.1	7.2

震	霍	霖	霏	需	霑	霓	霎	霙	霞	霜	雷	霧
7.3	8.1	8.2	8.3	8.4	8.5	8.6	8.7	8.8	9.1	9.2	10.1	11.1

霆	霰	霸	露	霹	霾	霽	纛	覊	靆	靈	靂	靉
11.2	12.1	4b15.4	13.1	13.2	14.1	14.2	3b16.1	15.1	16.1	8d7.2	16.2	17.1

───────── **0** ─────────

8d0.1 / 30

U, ame, ama- rain

雨

───────── **1** ─────────

3 雨乞 **amago(i)** praying for rain
雨上 **amea(gari), amaa(gari)** after the rain
4 雨天 **uten** rainy weather
雨天順延 **uten-jun'en** in case of rain postponed to the next fair day
雨支度 **amajitaku** preparing for rain
雨水 **amamizu, usui** rainwater
雨戸 **amado** storm door, shutter
5 雨氷 **uhyō** freezing rain
6 雨気 **amake** signs of rain
雨合羽 **amagappa** raincoat
7 雨余 **uyo** after a rainfall
雨声 **usei** the sound of rain
雨季 **uki** the rainy season
8 雨垂 **amada(re)** raindrops, eavesdrops
雨垂石 **amada(re) ishi** dripstone (to catch roof runoff)
雨注 **uchū** shower (arrows) upon
雨空 **amazora** rainy sky
雨具 **amagu** rain gear, rainwear
9 雨飛 **uhi** coming down like rain
雨降 **amefu(ri)** rainfall, rainy weather
雨風 **amekaze** rain and wind
amakaze rainy wind
雨後 **ugo** after a rainfall
11 雨宿 **amayado(ri)** taking shelter from the rain
雨脚 **amaashi, ameashi** speed of a moving rain front; streaks of falling rain
雨粒 **amatsubu** raindrop
12 雨傘 **amagasa** umbrella
雨着 **amagi** raincoat
雨落 **amao(chi)** the place that rainwater strikes in falling from the eaves
雨期 **uki** the rainy season
雨量 **uryō** (amount of) rainfall
雨量計 **uryōkei** rain gauge
雨蛙 **amagaeru** tree frog
雨雲 **amagumo** rain cloud

雨間 **amaai** interval between rains
13 雨催 **amamoyo(i), amemoyo(i)** signs of rain
雨靴 **amagutsu** rubbers, overshoes
雨続 **amatsuzu(ki), ametsuzu(ki)** rainy spell
14 雨滴 **uteki** raindrop
雨漏 **amamo(ri)** leak in the roof
雨模様 **amamoyō, amemoyō** signs of rain
15 雨避 **amayo(ke)** taking shelter from the rain
16 雨曇 **amagumo(ri)** overcast weather
18 雨覆 **amaō(i)** waterproof covering, tarpaulin
19 雨曝 **amazara(shi)** exposed to rain, weather-beaten
21 雨露 **uro** rain and dew
22 雨籠 **amagomo(ri)** rained in, rainbound

───────── **2** ─────────

1 一雨 **hitoame** a shower/rainfall
3 大雨 **ōame, taiu** heavy rainfall, downpour
小雨 **kosame** light rain, drizzle
5 氷雨 **hisame** a cold rain; hail
白雨 **hakuu** shower
6 多雨 **tau** heavy rain
如雨露 **jōro** sprinkling can
血雨 **chi(no)ame** bloodshed
7 冷雨 **reiu** chilly rain
村雨 **murasame** passing shower
快雨 **kaiu** refreshing rain
8 長雨 **nagaame** rain lasting several days
夜雨 **yau** night rain
9 俄雨 **niwakaame** (sudden) shower
降雨 **kōu** rain(fall)
降雨量 **kōuryō** (amount of) rainfall
通雨 **tō(ri)ame** passing shower
風雨 **fūu** wind and rain, rainstorm
春雨 **harusame, shun'u** spring rain; bean-jelly sticks
秋雨 **shūu, akisame** autumn rain
10 涙雨 **namidaame** a light rain; rain falling at a time of sorrow
猛雨 **mōu** heavy rain, downpour
梅雨 **baiu, tsuyu** the rainy season
時雨 **shigure** an off-and-on late-autumn/early-winter rain
11 淫雨 **in'u** prolonged (crop-damaging) rain
涼雨 **ryōu** cooling rain

細雨 **saiu** fine/misty rain, drizzle
12 弾雨 **dan'u** a hail of bullets
寒雨 **kan'u** cold/lonely rain
晴雨 **seiu** rain or shine
晴雨計 **seiukei** barometer
13 慈雨 **jiu** beneficial/welcome rain
微雨 **biu** light rain
煙雨 **en'u** fine/drizzling rain
照雨 **te(ri)ame** a rain during sunshine
雷雨 **raiu** thunderstorm
14 豪雨 **gōu** heavy rain, downpour
漫雨 **sozo(ro)ame** sudden shower
酸雨 **san'u** acid rain
15 横雨 **yokoame** a driving rain
16 霖雨 **rin'u** long rainy spell
17 糠雨 **nukaame** drizzle
19 霧雨 **kirisame** misty rain, drizzle
24 驟雨 **shūu** sudden shower

――――――― 3 ―――――――

2 人工雨 **jinkōu** artificial rain, rainmaking
3 夕時雨 **yūshigure** evening shower
小糠雨 **konukaame** fine/drizzling rain
4 五月雨 **samidare, satsuki ame** early-summer rain
7 初時雨 **hatsushigure** first winter rain
8 空梅雨 **karatsuyu** a dry rainy season
10 流星雨 **ryūseiu** meteor shower
12 晴耕雨読 **seikō-udoku** tilling the fields when the sun shines and reading at home when it rains
14 酸性雨 **sanseiu** acid rain
15 暴風雨 **bōfūu** rainstorm
17 篠突雨 **shinotsu(ku) ame** driving/torrential rain
18 蝉時雨 **semishigure** outburst of cicada droning

――――――― 4 ―――――――

10 砲煙弾雨 **hōen-dan'u** smoke of guns and a hail of shells/bullets

――――――― 3 ―――――――

8d3.1

雫 **shizuku** drop(let), trickle

8d3.2 / 949

雪 雪 **SETSU, yuki** snow
susu(gu), soso(gu) rinse, wash, clear (one's name)

――――――― 1 ―――――――

3 雪上 **setsujō** on the snow
雪上車 **setsujōsha** snowmobile
雪下 **yukio(roshi)** clearing snow off a roof;

snowy wind blowing down a mountain
雪女 **yukionna** snow fairy
雪女郎 **yukijorō** snow fairy
雪山 **yukiyama** snow-covered mountain
4 雪中 **setchū** in/through the snow
雪止 **yukido(me)** barrier against snow, snowshed
雪月花 **setsugekka** snow, moon, and flowers
5 雪白 **seppaku** snow-white
雪玉 **yukidama** snowball
雪目 **yukime** snow blindness
6 雪合戦 **yuki gassen** snowball fight
雪交 **yukima(jiri)** (rain) mixed with snow
7 雪折 **yukio(re)** broken/bent by snow
雪投 **yukina(ge)** throwing snowballs
雪花 **sekka** snowflakes
雪庇 **seppi, yukibisashi** overhanging snow
雪囲 **yukigako(i)** shelter against snow
雪見 **yukimi** snowy scenery
雪見灯籠 **yukimidōrō** ornamental three-legged stone lantern
雪見酒 **yukimizake** drinking saké while viewing snowy scenery
雪男 **yukiotoko** the abominable snowman, yeti
8 雪盲 **setsumō** snow blindness
雪空 **yukizora** snowy sky
雪国 **yukiguni** snow country
雪明 **yukia(kari)** snow light
9 雪降 **yukifu(ri)** snowfall
雪除 **yukiyo(ke)** barrier against snow
雪洞 **bonbori** hand lamp; lampstand
10 雪冤 **setsuen** vindication, exoneration
雪原 **setsugen** field/expanse of snow
雪辱 **setsujoku** vindication, clearing one's name; revenge
雪辱戦 **setsujokusen** return match, a fight for vindication
雪遊 **yukiaso(bi)** playing in the snow
雪害 **setsugai** damage from snow
11 雪達磨 **yuki daruma** snowman
雪道 **yukimichi** snowy road
雪渓 **sekkei** snowy valley
雪眼鏡 **yuki megane** snow goggles
12 雪嵐 **yukiarashi** snowstorm
雪晴 **yukiba(re)** clearing after a snowfall
雪景 **sekkei** snowy scene
雪景色 **yukigeshiki** snowy landscape
雪焼 **yukiya(ke)** tanned by snow-reflected sunlight
雪雲 **yukigumo** snow cloud
13 雪催 **yukimoyo(i)** threatening to snow
雪隠 **setchin** toilet
雪隠詰 **setchinzu(me)** to (force into a) corner
雪搔 **yukika(ki)** snow shovel(ing)/plow(ing)
雪靴 **yukigutsu** snowshoes, snow boots
雪解 **yukige, yukido(ke)** thaw

14 雪模様 **yukimoyō** threatening to snow
雪駄 **setta** leather-soled sandals
15 雪線 **sessen** snow line
16 雪曇 **yukigumo(ri)** threatening to snow

────────── 2 ──────────

3 大雪 **ōyuki, taisetsu** heavy snow
大雪山 **Daisetsuzan** (mountain, Hokkaidō)
小雪 **koyuki** a light snowfall
5 氷雪 **hyōsetsu** ice and snow
白雪 **shirayuki, hakusetsu** (white) snow
白雪姫 **Shirayuki-hime** Snow White (and the Seven Dwarfs)
6 防雪 **bōsetsu** protect against snow
防雪林 **bōsetsurin** snowbreak (forest)
7 吹雪 **fubuki** snowstorm, blizzard
初雪 **hatsuyuki** first snow of the season
9 降雪 **kōsetsu** snow, a snowfall
除雪 **josetsu** snow removal
風雪 **fūsetsu** snowstorm, blizzard
10 残雪 **zansetsu** lingering snow
根雪 **neyuki** lingering snow
粉雪 **konayuki** powder snow
11 淡雪 **awayuki** light snow(fall)
深雪 **shinsetsu** deep snow
排雪 **haisetsu** snow removal
蛍雪 **keisetsu** diligent study (by the light of fireflies and reflection from snow)
蛍雪功 **keisetsu (no) kō** the fruits of diligent study
細雪 **sasameyuki** light snow(fall)
12 着雪 **chakusetsu** accumulation of snow
斑雪 **madara yuki, hadara yuki** snow remaining in spots
13 新雪 **shinsetsu** new-fallen/fresh snow
16 薄雪 **usuyuki** light snow; sugar-coated cookie
薄雪草 **usuyukisō** (a flowering alpine grass)
積雪 **sekisetsu** fallen snow
融雪 **yūsetsu** thaw, melting snow
17 霜雪 **sōsetsu** frost and snow

────────── 3 ──────────

3 万年雪 **mannen'yuki** perpetual snow
7 花吹雪 **hanafubuki** falling cherry blossoms
牡丹雪 **botan yuki** large snowflakes
15 暴風雪 **bōfūsetsu** snowstorm, blizzard

────────── 4 ──────────

8d4.1 / 636

雲

UN, kumo cloud

────────── 1 ──────────

3 雲上 **unjō** above the clouds; the imperial court
雲上人 **unjōbito** a court noble
4 雲丹 **uni** sea urchin

雲水 **unsui** itinerant priest, mendicant
5 雲母 **unmo, kirara** mica, isinglas
雲仙岳 **Unzendake** (mountain, Nagasaki-ken)
6 雲気 **unki** the look of the sky
雲合 **kumoa(i)** the look of the sky
雲行 **kumoyu(ki)** cloud movements; situation
7 雲状 **unjō** cloudlike
雲助 **kumosuke** (cheating) palanquin bearer
雲形 **kumogata, unkei** cloud form
雲形定規 **kumogata jōgi** French curve
8 雲表 **unpyō** above the clouds
雲泥差 **undei (no) sa** a great difference
雲突 **kumotsu(ku)** towering
雲居 **kumoi** the sky; palace; the imperial court
9 雲海 **unkai** a sea of clouds
11 雲脚 **kumoashi** movement of clouds
雲雀 **hibari** skylark
12 雲量 **unryō** (degree of) cloudiness
雲散 **unsan** dispersing like clouds
雲散霧消 **unsan-mushō** vanishing like mist
雲集 **unshū** throng, swarm, crowd
雲間 **kumoma** a break between clouds
13 雲隠 **kumogaku(re)** be hidden behind clouds; disappear
雲煙 **un'en** clouds and smoke; a landscape
15 雲衝 **kumotsu(ku)** towering
雲影 **un'ei** a cloud
16 雲壌 **unjō** clouds and earth; great difference
17 雲霞 **unka** clouds and haze; swarm, throng
19 雲霧 **unmu** clouds and fog

────────── 2 ──────────

4 片雲 **hen'un** a (speck of) cloud
katagumo clouds on one side of the sky only
5 出雲 **Izumo** (ancient kuni, Shimane-ken)
白雲 **shirakumo, hakuun** white/fleecy clouds
6 行雲流水 **kōun-ryūsui** floating clouds and flowing water; taking life easy
7 乱雲 **ran'un** nimbus/rain clouds
妖雲 **yōun** ominous cloud
8 東雲 **shinonome** dawn, daybreak
青雲 **seiun** blue sky; high rank
青雲志 **seiun (no) kokorozashi** ambition for greatness, lofty aspirations
雨雲 **amagumo** rain cloud
9 飛雲 **hiun** fleeting cloud
巻雲 **ma(ki)gumo, ken'in** cirrus clouds
風雲 **fūun** wind and clouds; times of change
kazagumo wind clouds
風雲児 **fūunji** adventurer, soldier of fortune
浮雲 **u(ki)gumo** drifting cloud
星雲 **seiun** nebula
星雲説 **seiunsetsu** the nebular hypothesis
10 凌雲 **ryōun** rising high
11 彩雲 **saiun** glowing clouds

密雲 **mitsuun** thick/dense clouds
黒雲 **kurokumo, kokuun** dark clouds
雪雲 **yukigumo** snow cloud
12 揚雲雀 **a(ge)hibari** (soaring) skylark
紫雲 **shiun** auspicious purple clouds
紫雲英 **genge** Chinese milk vetch
13 暗雲 **an'un** dark clouds
瑞雲 **zuiun** auspicious clouds
愁雲 **shūun** cloud/atmosphere of gloom
戦雲 **sen'un** clouds of war
雷雲 **raiun** thundercloud
14 疑雲 **giun** cloud of suspicion/doubt
層雲 **sōun** stratus clouds
綿雲 **watagumo** fleecy clouds
15 慶雲 **Keiun** (era, 704–708)
横雲 **yokogumo** bank of clouds
16 薄雲 **usugumo** thin/feathery clouds
積雲 **sekiun** cumulus clouds
17 闇雲 **yamikumo (ni)** at random, haphazardly
18 叢雲 **murakumo** cloud masses
24 鱗雲 **urokogumo** cirrocumulus clouds

———————— 3 ————————

2 入道雲 **nyūdōgumo** thunderhead, cumulonimbus cloud
3 上層雲 **jōsōun** upper clouds
8 放射雲 **hōshaun** radioactive cloud
9 巻層雲 **kensōun** cirrostratus clouds
巻積雲 **kensekiun** cirrocumulus clouds
10 高層雲 **kōsōun** altostratus clouds
高積雲 **kōsekiun** altocumulus clouds
原子雲 **genshiun** atomic/mushroom cloud
12 渦星雲 **kaseiun** spiral nebula
14 層積雲 **sōsekiun** stratocumulus clouds
16 積乱雲 **sekiran'un** cumulonimbus clouds

———————— 4 ————————

9 飛行機雲 **hikōkigumo** vapor trail, contrail
神護景雲 **Jingo Keiun** (era, 767–769)

8d4.2 / 1824

FUN fog

雺

———————— 1 ————————

7 雺囲気 **fun'iki** atmosphere, ambience

———————— 5 ————————

8d5.1 / 952

RAI, kaminari, ikazuchi thunder

雷

———————— 1 ————————

4 雷公 **raikō** the god of thunder
雷火 **raika** fire caused by lightning

6 雷同 **raidō** following blindly
雷名 **raimei** illustrious name
8 雷雨 **raiu** thunderstorm
9 雷神 **raijin** the god of thunder
12 雷雲 **raiun** thundercloud
13 雷電 **raiden** thunder and lightning, thunderbolt
14 雷鳴 **raimei** thunder
雷管 **raikan** blasting/percussion cap, detonator
15 雷撃 **raigeki** torpedo attack
雷撃機 **raigekiki** torpedo-carrying plane

———————— 2 ————————

3 万雷 **banrai** thunderous (applause)
4 水雷 **suirai** torpedo; mine
水雷艇 **suiraitei** torpedo boat
5 迅雷 **jinrai** thunderclap; sudden and forceful
6 地雷 **jirai** land mine
百雷 **hyakurai** a hundred thunderclaps
8 空雷 **kūrai** aerial torpedo
9 春雷 **shunrai** spring thunder
11 魚雷 **gyorai** torpedo
魚雷艇 **gyoraitei** torpedo boat
12 遠雷 **enrai** distant thunder
落雷 **rakurai** be struck by lightning
15 避雷針 **hiraishin** lightning rod
熱雷 **netsurai** heat thunderstorm
16 機雷 **kirai** (land/sea) mine
機雷原 **kiraigen** minefield
19 爆雷 **bakurai** depth charge

———————— 3 ————————

5 付和雷同 **fuwa-raidō** follow blindly, echo
9 風神雷神 **fūjin-raijin** the gods of wind and thunder

———————— 4 ————————

10 疾風迅雷 **shippū-jinrai** lightning speed
13 触発水雷 **shokuhatsu suirai** contact (sea) mine

8d5.2 / 108

DEN electricity

電

———————— 1 ————————

2 電子 **denshi** electron   **denshi-** electronic
電子レンジ **denshi renji** microwave oven
電子工学 **denshi kōgaku** electronics
電子式 **denshishiki** electronic
電力 **denryoku** electric power
3 電工 **denkō** electrician
電々 **Denden** Telegraph and Telephone (Co., Ltd.) (short for 電信電話)
4 電化 **denka** electrification
電文 **denbun** telegram
電文体 **denbuntai** telegram-like style

8

金
食
隹
電 5←
門

5 電圧 **den'atsu** voltage
電圧計 **den'atsukei** voltmeter
6 電気 **denki** electricity; electric light
電気版 **denkiban** electrotype
電気炉 **denkiro** electric furnace
電気屋 **denkiya** electrical appliance store/
　dealer
電気浴 **denkiyoku** electric bath
電気量 **denkiryō** amount of electricity
電気銅 **denkidō** electrolytic copper
電休日 **denkyūbi** a no-electricity day
電池 **denchi** battery, dry cell
電光 **denkō** electric light; lightning
電光石火 **denkō-sekka** a flash, an instant
電灯 **dentō** electric light
電灯料 **dentōryō** electric-lighting charges
7 電位 **den'i** (electrical) potential
電車 **densha** electric car, streetcar, train
電車通 **denshadō(ri)** street with a tramway
電車賃 **denshachin** tramfare, trainfare
8 電命 **denmei** telegraphed instructions
電卓 **dentaku** (desktop) calculator (short for
　電子式卓上計算機)
電送 **densō** electrical transmission
電送写真 **densō shashin** telephoto
電波 **denpa** electromagnetic waves, radio
電波計 **denpakei** wave meter
9 電信 **denshin** telegraph, telegram, cable
電信局 **denshinkyoku** telegraph office
電信柱 **denshinbashira** telegraph pole
電信料 **denshinryō** telegram charges
電信術 **denshinjutsu** telegraphy
電信線 **denshinsen** telegraph line
電信機 **denshinki** a telegraph
電弧 **denko** electric arc
電柱 **denchū** telephone/utility pole
10 電流 **denryū** electric current
電流計 **denryūkei** ammeter, galvanometer
電荷 **denka** electrical charge
11 電停 **dentei** streetcar stop
電動 **dendō** electric (not manual)
電動力 **dendōryoku** electromotive force
電動式 **dendōshiki** electric (not manual)
電動機 **dendōki** electric motor
電探 **dentan** radar
電球 **denkyū** light bulb
電略 **denryaku** an abbreviation used in
　telegrams
12 電場 **denba, denjō** electric field
電報 **denpō** telegram
電報料 **denpōryō** telegram charges
電極 **denkyoku** electrode, pole, terminal
電量 **denryō** amount of electricity
13 電源 **dengen** power source
電蓄 **denchiku** gramophone (short for 電気蓄
　音機/器)

電解 **denkai** electrolysis
電解液 **denkaieki** electrolyte
電解質 **denkaishitsu** electrolyte
電話 **denwa** telephone
電話口 **denwaguchi** telephone (mouthpiece)
電話局 **denwakyoku** telephone office
電話室 **denwashitsu** telephone booth
電話料 **denwaryō** telephone charges
電話帳 **denwachō** telephone directory
電話線 **denwasen** telephone line
電路 **denro** electric circuit
電鉄 **dentetsu** electric railway
電鈴 **denrei** electric bell
電飾 **denshoku** decorative lighting
電電 **Denden** Telegraph and Telephone (Co.,
　Ltd.) (short for 電信電話)
14 電磁石 **denjishaku** electromagnet
電磁気 **denjiki** electromagnetic
電磁波 **denjiha** electromagnetic waves
電磁場 **denjiba** electromagnetic field
電磁鉄 **denjitetsu** electromagnet
電算機 **densanki** computer
15 電撃 **dengeki** electric shock; blitzkrieg
電熱 **dennetsu** electric heat
電熱器 **dennetsuki** electric heater
電線 **densen** electric wire/line/cable
電請 **densei** ask for instructions by telegram
電鋳 **denchū** electrotyping
16 電機 **denki** electrical machinery
電機子 **denkishi** armature
18 電離 **denri** ionization
電離圏 **denriken** ionosphere

───────── 2 ─────────

2 入電 **nyūden** message/telegram received
4 弔電 **chōden** telegram of condolence
公電 **kōden** official telegram/dispatch
単3アルカリ電池 **tan san arukari denchi**
　size AA alkali battery
日電 **Nichiden** (short for 日本電気) NEC
　(Corporation)
心電図 **shindenzu** electrocardiogram
心電計 **shindenkei** electrocardiograph
5 市電 **shiden** municipal railway, trolley
外電 **gaiden** foreign cable/dispatch
打電 **daden** send a telegram
6 休電 **kyūden** electricity cut-off, power outage
充電 **jūden** recharge (a battery)
充電器 **jūdenki** charger
返電 **henden** reply telegram
光電池 **kōdenchi** photoelectric cell
光電管 **kōdenkan** photocell, light sensor
7 来電 **raiden** incoming telegram
赤電車 **akadensha** red-lamp car, last streetcar
赤電話 **akadenwa** public telephone
豆電球 **mame-denkyū** miniature light bulb

8
金
食
隹
→ 5
門

花電車 **hanadensha** decorated streetcar, (parade) float
8 送電 **sōden** transmission of electricity
送電線 **sōdensen** power lines
空電 **kūden** (radio) static
国電 **kokuden** national railway electric train, JNR trains (short for 国鉄電車)
青電話 **aodenwa** public telephone
放電 **hōden** electric discharge
9 飛電 **hiden** urgent telegram
発電 **hatsuden** generation of electricity; sending a telegram
発電子 **hatsudenshi** armature
発電力 **hatsudenryoku** power
発電所 **hatsudensho** power plant, generating station
発電機 **hatsudenki** generator, dynamo
変電所 **hendensho** transformer substation
通電 **tsūden** cause an electric current to flow; circular telegram
架電 **kaden** send by wire/fax
祝電 **shukuden** telegram of congratulations
10 既電 **kiden** previous message
陰電子 **indenshi** negatron, electron
陰電気 **indenki** negative electricity
陰電荷 **indenka** negative charge
起電 **kiden** generation of electricity
起電力 **kidenryoku** electromotive force
起電機 **kidenki** electric motor
帯電 **taiden** having an electric charge
帯電体 **taidentai** charged body
荷電 **kaden** electric charge
家電 **kaden** household electrical products/appliances, consumer electronics (short for 家庭用電気製品)
特電 **tokuden** special telegram/dispatch
訓電 **kunden** telegraphed instructions
配電 **haiden** distribution of electricity
配電所 **haidensho** power station
配電盤 **haidenban** switch panel
配電線 **haidensen** power line/wire
11 停電 **teiden** cutoff of electricity, power outage
陽電子 **yōdenshi** positron
陽電気 **yōdenki** positive electricity
陽電荷 **yōdenka** positive charge
乾電池 **kandenchi** dry cell, battery
球電 **kyūden** ball lightning
盗電 **tōden** theft of electricity
終電 **shūden** the last train/streetcar for the day
終電車 **shūdensha** the last train/streetcar for the day
12 着電 **chakuden** telegram received
無電 **muden** wireless, radio
無電放送 **muden hōsō** radio broadcast
超電導 **chōdendō** superconductivity
給電 **kyūden** supplying electric power
紫電 **shiden** flashes of lightning

答電 **tōden** reply telegram/message
13 蓄電 **chikuden** charging with electricity
蓄電池 **chikudenchi** storage battery
蓄電器 **chikudenki** condenser, capacitor
感電 **kanden** electric shock
裸電球 **hadaka denkyū** light bulb without a lampshade
継電器 **keidenki** (electrical) relay
節電 **setsuden** saving on electricity
雷電 **raiden** thunder and lightning, thunderbolt
電電 **Denden** Telegraph and Telephone (Co., Ltd.) (short for 電信電話)
14 漏電 **rōden** leakage of electricity, short circuit
静電気 **seidenki** static electricity
静電気学 **seidenkigaku** electrostatics
静電学 **seidengaku** electrostatics
導電体 **dōdentai** conductor (of electricity)
導電性 **dōdensei** conductivity
導電率 **dōdenritsu** conductivity
誤電 **goden** incorrect telegram/telex
15 熱電対 **netsudentsui** thermocouple
16 親電 **shinden** (emperor's) telegram
17 謝電 **shaden** telegram of thanks
21 饋電線 **kidensen** feeder (line)

─────── 3 ───────
6 光起電力 **hikari-kidenryoku** photoelectromotive force
12 無線電信 **musen denshin** radiotelegraph
無線電話 **musen denwa** radiotelephone
13 路面電車 **romen densha** streetcar
16 懐中電灯 **kaichū dentō** flashlight

─────── 4 ───────
4 水力発電所 **suiryoku hatsudensho** hydro-electric plant
10 留守番電話 **rusuban denwa** answering machine
─────── 5 ───────
10 原子力発電所 **genshiryoku hatsudensho** nuclear power plant

8d5.3

電

HAKU, hyō hail

─────── 1 ───────
10 雹害 **hyōgai** hail damage

─────── 2 ───────
9 降雹 **kōhyō** hailstorm

8d5.4 / 1823

零

REI zero
kobo(reru) (intr.) spill
kobo(su) (tr.) spill

─────── 1 ───────
3 零下 **reika** below zero, subzero

7 零位 **reii** zero (point)
9 零点 **reiten** (a score/temperature of) zero
零度 **reido** zero (degrees), the freezing point
10 零時 **reiji** 12:00 (noon or midnight)
11 零細 **reisai** small, meager
零細農 **reisainō** poor peasant
零敗 **reihai** lose without scoring a point
12 零落 **reiraku** be ruined, go broke

――――― 2 ―――――

12 落零 **o(chi)kobo(re)** (cart-loaded grain) fallen off and left behind, fallen/left behind (academically)

――――― 6 ―――――

8d6.1 / 1416

需

JU request, need, demand

――――― 1 ―――――

5 需用 **juyō** consumption
需用家 **juyōka** consumer, customer
9 需要 **juyō** demand
12 需給 **jukyū** supply and demand

――――― 2 ―――――

4 内需 **naiju** domestic demand
5 必需 **hitsuju** necessary
必需品 **hitsujuhin** necessities, essentials
民需 **minju** private/civilian demand
9 軍需 **gunju** military demand/supplies
軍需工業 **gunju kōgyō** munitions industry
軍需品 **gunjuhin** military supplies, materiel
軍需景気 **gunju keiki** war prosperity
10 特需 **tokuju** emergency/wartime demand

8d6.2

霆

TEI lightning; thunder

――――― 7 ―――――

8d7.1

霄

SHŌ sky

――――― 1 ―――――

16 霄壤 **shōjō** (different as) heaven and earth

8d7.2 / 1168

霊 靈

REI, RYŌ, tama soul, spirit

――――― 1 ―――――

3 霊山 **reizan** sacred mountain

4 霊化 **reika** spiritualization
霊水 **reisui** miracle-working water
霊木 **reiboku** sacred tree
6 霊気 **reiki** feeling of mystery
霊肉一致 **reiniku itchi** oneness of body and soul
霊交術 **reikōjutsu** spiritualism
霊地 **reichi** hallowed ground
霊安室 **reianshitsu** morgue
霊光 **reikō** mysterious light
7 霊位 **reii** (Buddhist) mortuary tablet
霊妙 **reimyō** miraculous, mysterious, wonderful
8 霊長 **reichō** crown of creation, mankind
霊長類 **reichōrui** primates
霊知 **reichi** mystic wisdom
霊宝 **reihō** most precious treasure
霊的 **reiteki** spiritual
霊性 **reisei** divine nature, spirituality
9 霊前 **reizen** before the (deceased's) spirit
霊泉 **reisen** wonder-working fountain/spring
霊草 **reisō** sacred herb
霊屋 **tamaya** mausoleum, ancestral shrine
霊枢 **reikyū** coffin, casket
霊枢車 **reikyūsha** hearse
霊界 **reikai** the spiritual world
10 霊剣 **reiken** wondrous sword
霊峰 **reihō** sacred mountain
11 霊亀 **Reiki** (era, 715–717)
霊域 **reiiki** sacred precincts/ground
霊異 **reii** miracle, wonder
霊鳥 **reichō** sacred bird
12 霊場 **reijō** sacred place, hallowed ground
霊媒 **reibai** a (spiritualistic) medium
13 霊夢 **reimu** inspired dream, vision, revelation
霊殿 **reiden** shrine, mausoleum
霊園 **reien** cemetery park
霊感 **reikan** inspiration
14 霊境 **reikyō** sacred precincts/grounds
霊魂 **reikon** soul, spirit
霊魂不滅 **reikon fumetsu** immortality of the soul
15 霊廟 **reibyō** mausoleum, shrine
16 霊薬 **reiyaku** wonder-working drug, elixir
18 霊験 **reigen(arataka)** wonder-working, marvelously efficacious

――――― 2 ―――――

3 亡霊 **bōrei** departed soul, ghost
山霊 **sanrei** genius loci of a mountain
4 木霊 **kodama** spirit of a tree; echo
心霊 **shinrei** spirit, soul; psychic
心霊学 **shinreigaku** psychics, spiritism
心霊術 **shinreijutsu** spiritualism
5 生霊 **i(ki)ryō** apparition of a living person, wraith

6 死霊 **shiryō** spirit of a dead person
孝霊 **Kōrei** (emperor, 290–215 B.C.)
7 言霊 **kotodama** soul/power of language
8 英霊 **eirei** spirits of the war dead
忠霊塔 **chūreitō** monument to the war dead
9 幽霊 **yūrei** ghost
幽霊屋敷 **yūrei yashiki** haunted house
幽霊船 **yūreisen** phantom ship
幽霊話 **yūreibanashi** ghost story
神霊 **shinrei** spirit
皇霊 **kōrei** spirits of deceased royalty
皇霊殿 **Kōreiden** the Imperial Ancestors' Shrine
11 悪霊 **akuryō, akurei** evil spirit
船霊 **funadama** ship's guardian deity
12 御霊 **mitama** spirit of a dead person
御霊屋 **mitamaya** mausoleum, tomb
13 聖霊 **Seirei** Holy Spirit
14 精霊 **seirei** spirit, soul
shōryō spirit of a dead person
15 慰霊 **irei** repose of the deceased's soul
慰霊祭 **ireisai** memorial service
慰霊塔 **ireitō** cenotaph, memorial tower

————— 3 —————

3 万物霊長 **banbutsu (no) reichō** man, the lord of creation
11 船幽霊 **funayūrei** a sea spirit

8d7.3 / 953

SHIN, **furu(eru/u)** shake, tremble

震

————— 1 —————

3 震上 **furu(e)a(garu)** tremble, shudder
4 震天動地 **shinten-dōchi** (heaven-and-)earth-shaking
5 震央 **shin'ō** epicenter
震付 **furu(i)tsu(ku)** hug with affection
7 震声 **furu(e)goe** tremulous/quavering voice
震災 **shinsai** earthquake disaster
震災地 **shinsaichi** quake-stricken area
9 震度 **shindo** earthquake intensity
10 震害 **shingai** earthquake damage
11 震動 **shindō** tremor, vibration
12 震幅 **shinpuku** seismic amplitude
13 震源 **shingen** epicenter
震源地 **shingenchi** epicenter
16 震撼 **shinkan** shake, tremble
震駭 **shingai** fright, alarm, terror
17 震盪 **shintō** (cerebral) concussion, shock

————— 2 —————

3 大震災 **daishinsai** great earthquake; the 1923 Tōkyō earthquake
4 予震 **yoshin** foreshock, preliminary tremor
6 地震 **jishin** earthquake

地震学 **jishingaku** seismology
地震国 **jishinkoku** earthquake-prone country
地震計 **jishinkei** seismometer
地震帯 **jishintai** earthquake belt/zone
7 身震 **miburu(i)** shiver, tremble, shudder
余震 **yoshin** aftershock
9 耐震 **taishin** earthquake-proof
耐震性 **taishinsei** earthquake resistance, quakeproof
10 弱震 **jakushin** weak earthquake tremor
胴震 **dōburu(i)** shivering, trembling
烈震 **resshin** violent earthquake
11 強震 **kyōshin** violent earthquake
脳震盪 **nōshintō** cerebral concussion
13 微震 **bishin** slight earthquake/tremor
15 横震 **ōshin** horizontal (earthquake) shock
16 激震 **gekishin** severe earthquake

————— 3 —————

3 大地震 **ōjishin, daijishin** major earthquake
8 武者震 **mushaburu(i)** tremble with excitement

————— 4 —————

6 有感地震 **yūkan jishin** earthquake strong enough to feel

————— 6 —————

17 環太平洋地震帯 **kan-Taiheiyō jishintai** circum-Pacific seismic zone

————— 8 —————

8d8.1

KAKU quick, sudden

霍

————— 1 —————

7 霍乱 **kakuran** sunstroke, heatstroke

8d8.2

RIN rain lasting three days or longer

霖

————— 1 —————

8 霖雨 **rin'u** long rainy spell

————— 2 —————

9 秋霖 **shūrin** long rainy spell in autumn

8d8.3

HI rainfall, snowfall

霏

————— 1 —————

3 霏々 **hihi** (falling) thick and fast

8

金
食
隹
罒 8←
門

8d8.4

霈 HAI　heavy rain

8d8.5

霑 TEN, **uruo(su)** wet, moisten
uruo(u) be wet/moistened

————— 2 —————

7 均霑 **kinten** have an equal share in

8d8.6

霓 GEI, **niji** rainbow

8d8.7

霎 SHŌ　light rain; short while

8d8.8

霙 EI, **mizore** sleet

————— 9 —————

8d9.1

霞 KA, **kasumi** haze, mist; dimness of sight
kasu(mu) be hazy; (eyes) grow dim

————— 1 —————

5 霞目 **kasumime** purblind/blurred eyes
9 霞草 **kasumisō** baby's-breath (the flower)
14 霞網 **kasumiami** fine-mesh (bird-catching) net
霞関 **Kasumi(ga)seki** (area of Tōkyō, where government ministries are located)

————— 2 —————

3 夕霞 **yūgasumi** evening mist
9 春霞 **haru-gasumi** spring haze
12 朝霞 **asagasumi** morning mist
雲霞 **unka** clouds and haze; swarm, throng
13 煙霞 **enka** smoke and mist; scenic views

8d9.2 / 948

霜 SŌ, **shimo** frost

————— 1 —————

4 霜月 **shimotsuki** eleventh lunar month
7 霜囲 **shimogako(i)** (straw) covering to protect against frost
8 霜夜 **shimoyo** frosty night
9 霜降 **shimofu(ri)** marbled (meat), salt-and-pepper pattern
霜柱 **shimobashira** ice/frost columns
霜枯 **shimoga(re)** frost-withered, wintry, bleak
霜枯時 **shimoga(re)doki** winter
10 霜害 **sōgai** frost damage
11 霜雪 **sōsetsu** frost and snow
12 霜焼 **shimoya(ke)** frostbite
13 霜解 **shimodo(ke)** thawing

————— 2 —————

3 大霜 **ōshimo** heavy frost
7 初霜 **hatsushimo** first frost of the season
9 降霜 **kōsō** a frost
除霜 **josō** defrosting, deicing
風霜 **fūsō** wind and frost; hardships
星霜 **seisō** years, time
秋霜 **shūsō** autumn frost
秋霜烈日 **shūsō-retsujitsu** withering frost and scorching sun; harsh, severe, exacting
21 露霜 **tsuyujimo** frozen dew

————— 10 —————

8d10.1

霤 RYŪ　raindrops falling from the eaves; eaves

————— 11 —————

8d11.1 / 950

霧 MU, **kiri** fog

————— 1 —————

4 霧中 **muchū** in the fog
霧中信号 **muchū shingō** fog signal
5 霧氷 **muhyō** rime, hoarfrost
7 霧吹 **kirifu(ki)** sprayer, atomizer, vaporizer
8 霧雨 **kirisame** misty rain, drizzle
11 霧笛 **muteki** fog horn
12 霧散 **musan** dissipate, vanish

————— 2 —————

3 川霧 **kawagiri** river fog/mist
夕霧 **yūgiri** evening mist
山霧 **yamagiri** mountain fog
8 夜霧 **yogiri** night fog
9 海霧 **kaimu** sea fog
狭霧 **sagiri** fog, mist
12 朝霧 **asagiri** morning fog
雲霧 **unmu** clouds and fog
13 煙霧 **enmu** mist, fog, smog
15 噴霧器 **funmuki** sprayer, vaporizer

8
金
食
隹
→ 8 雨
門

16 濃霧 **nōmu** dense fog
薄霧 **usugiri** thin mist

───────── 3 ─────────

4 五里霧中 **gori-muchū** in a fog, groping in the dark
12 雲散霧消 **unsan-mushō** vanishing like mist

8d11.2

IN rain lasting ten days or longer

霪

───────── 12 ─────────

8d12.1

SAN, SEN, arare hail

霰

───────── 1 ─────────

12 霰弾 **sandan** buckshot

───────── 13 ─────────

霸 → 覇 4b15.4

8d13.1 / 951

露

RO in the open, exposed; dew; Russia
RŌ open, public   **tsuyu** dew
ara(wa) open, public, frank

───────── 1 ─────────

4 露天 **roten** outdoor, open-air
露天商 **rotenshō** stall/booth keeper
露天掘 **rotenbo(ri)** strip mining
露仏 **Ro-Futsu** Russia and France
5 露出 **roshutsu** (indecent/film) exposure
露出計 **roshutsukei** light meter
露払 **tsuyuhara(i)** herald, forerunner
露台 **rodai** balcony
6 露西亜 **Roshia** Russia
露地 **roji** the bare ground
露光 **rokō** exposure (in photography)
露光計 **rokōkei** light meter
7 露里 **rori** Russian mile, *verst* (1066 m)
露呈 **rotei** exposure, disclosure
露見 **roken** be found out, come to light
8 露命 **romei** transient life
露知 **tsuyushi(razu)** utterly ignorant
露店 **roten** street stall, vending booth
露店商 **rotenshō** stall keeper/vendor
露店街 **rotengai** street of open-air stalls
露国 **Rokoku** Russia
9 露軍 **rogun** the Russian army
露点 **roten** the dew point
露草 **tsuyukusa** dayflower, spiderwort

10 露座 **roza** sitting out in the open
露骨 **rokotsu** open, undisguised, frank; conspicuous; lewd
11 露清 **Ro-Shin** Russia and China
露探 **rotan** Russian spy (in the Russo-Japanese War)
露悪 **roaku** boasting of one's wickedness
12 露場 **rojō** weather measurement site
露営 **roei** bivouac, camping out
露間 **tsuyu(no)ma** a fleeting moment
14 露滴 **roteki** dewdrop
露語 **rogo** the Russian language
15 露盤 **roban** pagoda roof
16 露頭 **rotō** outcrop (of rock)
17 露霜 **tsuyujimo** frozen dew
18 露顕 **roken** be found out, come to light

───────── 2 ─────────

4 日露 **Nichi-Ro** Japan and Russia
5 甘露 **kanro** syrup, nectar, sweetness
甘露煮 **kanroni** sweet dish of boiled fish or shellfish
白露 **Hakuro** White Russia, Belarus
玉露 **gyokuro** refined green tea
6 吐露 **toro** express, voice, speak out
如露 **joro** sprinkling can
7 対露 **tai-Ro** toward/with Russia
8 夜露 **yotsuyu** evening dew
披露 **hirō** announcement
披露会 **hirōkai** (wedding) reception
披露宴 **hirōen** (wedding) reception
松露 **shōro** (a kind of edible mushroom)
雨露 **uro** rain and dew
9 発露 **hatsuro** expression, manifestation
10 流露 **ryūro** disclose, reveal, express
12 朝露 **chōro, asatsuyu** morning dew
結露 **ketsuro** condensation of dew
13 滞露 **tai-Ro** staying in Russia
15 暴露 **bakuro** expose, bring to light
16 親露 **shin-Ro** pro-Russian
19 曝露 **bakuro** expose, bring to light

───────── 3 ─────────

5 白系露人 **hakkei rojin** a White Russian, Belarussian
6 如雨露 **jōro** sprinkling can

───────── 4 ─────────

11 現実暴露 **genjitsu bakuro** disillusionment

8d13.2

霹

HEKI thunderclap

───────── 1 ─────────

24 霹靂 **hekireki** thunderclap, a bolt (from the blue)

8

金
食
隹
雨 13←
門

─────────────── 3 ───────────────

8 青天霹靂 **seiten (no) hekireki** a bolt from
the blue

─────────────── 14 ───────────────

8d14.1

霾

BAI, tsuchifu(ru) wind-blown dust
falling like rain

8d14.2

霽

SEI, ha(reru), ha(rasu) clear up

─────────────── 2 ───────────────

7 見霽 **miharu(kasu)** have a panoramic view

罎 → 壜 3b16.1

─────────────── 15 ───────────────

8d15.1

靆

TAI cloud cover

─────────────── 16 ───────────────

8d16.1

靄

AI, moya mist, haze, fog

─────────────── 2 ───────────────

3 夕靄 **yūmoya** evening haze
12 朝靄 **asamoya** morning haze/mist

靈 → 霊 8d7.2

8d16.2

靂

REKI thunderbolt

─────────────── 2 ───────────────

21 霹靂 **hekireki** thunderclap, a bolt (from the
blue)

─────────────── 4 ───────────────

8 青天霹靂 **seiten (no) hekireki** a bolt from
the blue

─────────────── 17 ───────────────

8d17.1

靉

AI cloudy; rank growth

─────────────── 門 8e ───────────────

| 門 | 鬥 | 閂 | 閃 | 問 | 閊 | 閉 | 閇 | 閊 | 閑 | 間 | 閒 | 閨 |
|0.1|0.2|1.1|2.1|3.1|3.2|3.3|8e3.3|4.1|4.2|4.3|8e4.3|4.4|

| 悶 | 開 | 閔 | 閏 | 閘 | 閙 | 鬧 | 聞 | 閥 | 閣 | 閧 | 閨 | 閤 |
|4.5|4.6|4.7|5.1|5.2|5.3|8e5.3|6.1|6.2|6.3|6.4|6.5|6.6|

| 関 | 閻 | 閲 | 閼 | 閱 | 闇 | 閣 | 鬩 | 闌 | 闇 | 闊 | 関 | 闇 |
|6.7|7.1|7.2|8.1|8.2|8.3|8.4|8.5|9.1|9.2|9.3|9.4|9.5|

| 闐 | 闖 | 鬪 | 闕 | 闔 | 闞 | 關 | 闡 | 闥 | 闢 | 闥 | | |
|9.6|10.1|10.2|10.3|10.4|10.5|8e6.7|12.1|12.2|13.1|18.1| | |

─────────────── 0 ───────────────

8e0.1 / 161

門 门

MON, kado gate

─────────────── 1 ───────────────

2 門人 **monjin** pupil, disciple, follower
3 門下 **monka** one's pupil

門下生 **monkasei** one's pupil
門口 **kadoguchi** front door, entrance
4 門火 **kadobi** funeral/wedding/Obon bonfire
(at the gate)
門戸 **monko** door
5 門出 **kadode** depart, set out
門外 **mongai** outside the gate; outside one's
specialty
門外漢 **mongaikan** outsider; layman

門司 **Moji** (city, Fukuoka-ken)
門札 **monsatsu, kadofuda** nameplate
6 門毎 **kadogoto** at every gate, door-to-door
門地 **monchi** lineage, family status
門先 **kadosaki** front of a house, entrance
門守 **kadomori** gatekeeper
門灯 **montō** gate light
7 門弟 **montei** pupil, disciple
8 門限 **mongen** closing time
門並 **kadona(mi)** row of houses; door to door, at every door
門松 **kadomatsu** New Year's pine-and-bamboo decorations
9 門院 **mon'in** empress dowager
門前 **monzen** before the gate
門前市 **monzen'ichi** throngs of callers outside the gate
門前払 **monzenbara(i)** turning (someone) away at the gate, refusing to see (someone)
門柱 **monchū, monbashira** gatepost
10 門徒 **monto** believer, adherent
12 門違 **kadochiga(i)** calling at the wrong house, barking up the wrong tree
門扉 **monpi** doors of a gate
門番 **monban** gatekeeper, porter
門歯 **monshi** incisor, front teeth
13 門跡 **monzeki** (temple headed by a) priest-prince; Honganji Temple
14 門構 **mongama(e), kadogama(e)** style of a gate
門閥 **monbatsu** lineage, pedigree
16 門衛 **mon'ei** guard, gatekeeper
23 門鑑 **monkan** a (gate) pass

──────── 2 ────────

1 一門 **ichimon** a family/clan
2 入門 **nyūmon** admission, entrance; introduction, handbook, primer
3 三門 **sanmon** large three-door gate
大門 **daimon** large outer gate (of a Buddhist temple) **ōmon** front gate
孔門 **Kōmon** the Confucian school
山門 **sanmon** (two-story) temple gate
4 仏門 **butsumon** Buddhism, priesthood
水門 **suimon** watergate, floodgate, penstock, sluice
火門 **kamon** cannon muzzle
5 正門 **seimon** front gate, main entrance
石門 **sekimon** stone gate
6 朱門 **shumon** red-lacquered gate
同門 **dōmon** fellow student
名門 **meimon** prestigious family/school
7 沙門 **shamon** Buddhist priest
赤門 **akamon** red gate; Tōkyō University
肛門 **kōmon** the anus

肛門科医 **kōmonkai** proctologist
8 長門 **Nagato** (ancient kuni, Yamaguchi-ken)
宗門 **shūmon** sect, religion
宗門改 **shūmon-arata(me)** religious census (Edo era)
板門店 **Hanmonten** Panmunjom
武門 **bumon** military family/class
9 専門 **senmon** specialty
専門化 **senmonka** specialization
専門用語 **senmon yōgo** technical term
専門医 **senmon'i** (medical) specialist
専門学校 **senmon gakkō** professional school
専門店 **senmonten** specialty store
専門的 **senmonteki** professional, technical
専門家 **senmonka** specialist, expert
専門書 **senmonsho** technical books
前門 **zenmon** front gate
海門 **kaimon** strait, channel
洞門 **dōmon** cave entrance
城門 **jōmon** castle gate
後門 **kōmon** back gate/door
幽門 **yūmon** pylorus
肺門 **haimon** hilum of a lung
10 倚門望 **imon (no) bō** a mother's love (leaning on the gate longing for her child's return home)
陰門 **inmon** the vulva
部門 **bumon** field, branch, line; division, section; class, category
桑門 **sōmon** Buddhist priest/monk
家門 **kamon** one's family/clan
宮門 **kyūmon** palace gate
唐門 **karamon** Chinese-style gate
校門 **kōmon** school gate
破門 **hamon** excommunication, expulsion
砲門 **hōmon** muzzle of a gun; gunport, embrasure
鬼門 **kimon** unlucky direction (northeast); something/someone which one avoids
11 舷門 **genmon** gangway
頂門一針 **chōmon (no) isshin** stinging reproach/admonition (like a needle plunged into the top of one's head)
12 港門 **kōmon** harbor entrance
御門 **mikado** palace gate; emperor
開門 **kaimon** opening of the gate
13 僧門 **sōmon** priesthood
裏門 **uramon** back gate
楼門 **rōmon** two-story gate
禅門 **zenmon** entering the Zen priesthood
閘門 **kōmon** lock gate
14 鳴門 **naruto** whirlpool, maelstrom
鳴門海峡 **Naruto-kaikyō** (strait between Shikoku and Awaji island)
獄門 **gokumon** prison gates; display of an executed criminal's decapitated head

8

金
食
隹
雨
門 0←

緑門 **ryokumon** arch of greenery
総門 **sōmon** main gate
関門 **kanmon** gateway, barrier
関門海峡 **Kanmon-kaikyō** (strait between Shimonoseki and Moji)
15 潮門 **chōmon** tide gate
権門 **kenmon** powerful person
16 澳門 **Makao** Macao

—————————— 3 ——————————

2 二王門 **Niōmon** temple gate guarded by Deva statues
入場門 **nyūjōmon** admission gate
3 大手門 **ōtemon** front gate of a castle
4 天安門 **Ten'anmon** Tiananmon, Gate of Heavenly Peace (in Beijing)
仁王門 **Niōmon** temple gate guarded by two fierce Deva king statues
5 生学門 **namagakumon** superficial knowledge
7 邪宗門 **jashūmon** heretical religion
見付門 **mitsukemon** castle lookout gate
8 奉迎門 **hōgeimon** welcome arch
9 冠木門 **kabukimon** gate with overhead crossbar
通用門 **tsūyōmon** side door, service entrance
毘沙門天 **Bishamon-ten** Vaisravana, god of treasure
11 婆羅門 **Baramon** Brahman
12 凱旋門 **gaisenmon** arch of triumph

—————————— 4 ——————————

3 土左衛門 **dozaemon** drowned person

8e0.2

鬥

TŌ fight

—————————— 1 ——————————

8e1.1

閂

SAN, kannuki bolt (on a door/gate)

—————————— 2 ——————————

8e2.1

閃

SEN, hirame(ku) (intr.) flash
hirame(kasu) (tr.) flash, brandish

—————————— 1 ——————————

6 閃光 **senkō** flash

—————————— 2 ——————————

1 一閃 **issen** a flash

—————————— 3 ——————————

8e3.1 / 162

問 向

MON question, problem
to(u) ask, inquire; matter, care about; accuse
to(i), ton question, inquiry

—————————— 1 ——————————

6 問合 **to(i)a(waseru), to(i)a(wasu)** inquire
9 問屋 **ton'ya** wholesaler
11 問掛 **to(i)ka(keru)** (begin to) ask, inquire
問責 **monseki** censure, reprimand
12 問答 **mondō** questions and answers
13 問罪 **monzai** accusation, indictment
14 問語 **to(wazu)gata(ri)** voluntary/unasked-for remark
18 問題 **mondai** problem, question, issue
問題外 **mondaigai** beside the point, irrelevant
問題児 **mondaiji** problem child
問題点 **mondaiten** the point at issue

—————————— 2 ——————————

1 一問一答 **ichimon-ittō** question-and-answer session
3 下問 **kamon** inquire, consult
4 弔問 **chōmon** condolence call/visit
反問 **hanmon** ask in return; cross-examine
6 自問 **jimon** question oneself
自問自答 **jimon-jitō** answering one's own question, sololoquy, monolog
米問屋 **komedon'ya** rice wholesaler
7 別問題 **betsumondai** another question, a different story
学問 **gakumon** learning, scholarship, education, science
8 押問答 **o(shi)mondō** heated questioning and answering, dispute
性問題 **sei mondai** sex problem
9 卸問屋 **oroshiton'ya** wholesaler
拷問 **gōmon** torture
拷問台 **gōmondai** the rack
査問 **samon** inquiry, hearing
査問会 **samonkai** (court of) inquiry, hearing
糾問 **kyūmon** close examination, grilling
10 借問 **shamon, shakumon** inquire
訊問 **jinmon** questioning, interrogation, cross examination
11 船問屋 **funadon'ya** shipping agent
訪問 **hōmon** visit
訪問者 **hōmonsha** visitor, caller
訪問販売 **hōmon hanbai** door-to-door sales
訪問着 **hōmongi** woman's semi-formal kimono
設問 **setsumon** question
12 喚問 **kanmon** summons
尋問 **jinmon** questioning, interrogation
検問 **kenmon** inspect, examine, check

検問所 **kenmonjo** checkpoint
13 禅問答 **zen mondō** Zen/incomprehensible dialog
愚問 **gumon** stupid question
愚問愚答 **gumon-gutō** silly dialog
詰問 **kitsumon** cross-examination, grilling
試問 **shimon** question, interview, test
14 疑問 **gimon** question, doubt
疑問文 **gimonbun** interrogative sentence
疑問代名詞 **gimon daimeishi** interrogative pronoun
疑問符 **gimonfu** question mark
疑問詞 **gimonshi** interrogative word
説問 **setsumon** kanji etymology
15 審問 **shinmon** trial, hearing, inquiry
慰問 **imon** consolation, sympathy
慰問状 **imonjō** letter of condolence
慰問品 **imonhin** comfort articles, amenities
諸問題 **shomondai** various questions
質問 **shitsumon** question
質問者 **shitsumonsha** questioner
質問書 **shitsumonsho** written inquiry, questionnaire
16 諮問 **shimon** question, inquiry; question, inquiry; consultive, advisory (body)
18 難問 **nanmon** difficult problem
難問題 **nanmondai** difficult problem
21 顧問 **komon** adviser
顧問医 **komon'i** medical adviser
顧問官 **komonkan** councilor

——————— 3 ———————
6 死活問題 **shikatsu mondai** a matter of life and death
先決問題 **senketsu mondai** question to be settled first
耳学問 **mimigakumon** learning acquired by listening
7 応用問題 **ōyō mondai** problem to test ability to apply theoretical knowledge
12 御下問 **gokamon** emperor's question

——————— 4 ———————
3 口答試問 **kōtō shimon** oral examination/quiz
口頭試問 **kōtō shimon** oral examination
4 不審訊問 **fushin jinmon** questioning (by a policeman)
反対訊問 **hantai jinmon** cross-examination
9 軍事顧問 **gunji komon** military adviser
面接試問 **mensetsu shimon** oral examination

8e3.2

閊 **tsuka(eru)** be obstructed/clogged, get stuck

8e3.3 / 397

閉 閉 **HEI, shi(meru), to(jiru/zasu)** close, shut
shi(maru) be(come) closed

——————— 1 ———————
3 閉口 **heikō** be dumbfounded
4 閉込 **to(ji)ko(meru)** shut in, confine
6 閉会 **heikai** closing, adjournment
閉廷 **heitei** adjourn court
8 閉店 **heiten** store closing
閉居 **heikyo** stay indoors
9 閉院 **heiin** adjourn the assembly/parliament
10 閉校 **heikō** closing the school
12 閉場 **heijō** closing (the place)
13 閉塞 **heisoku** blockade; obstruction
to(ji)fusa(geru) close up, cover over
16 閉館 **heikan** closing (the hall/building)
18 閉鎖 **heisa** closing, closure, lockout
22 閉籠 **to(ji)komo(ru)** stay indoors, hole up

——————— 2 ———————
9 幽閉 **yūhei** confinement, imprisonment
11 密閉 **mippei** shut tight, seal airtight
12 開閉 **kaihei** opening and closing
a(ke)ta(te) opening and shutting
開閉器 **kaiheiki** make-and-break switch
開閉機 **kaiheiki** circuit breaker
開閉橋 **kaiheikyō** drawbridge
13 腸閉塞 **chōheisoku** intestinal obstruction, ileus

閇 → 閉   8e3.3

8e4.1

閖 **HEI, yu(ru)** shake (while rinsing), pan (for gold)

8e4.2 / 1532

閑 **KAN** leisure

——————— 1 ———————
2 閑人 **kanjin, himajin** man of leisure
4 閑中 **kanchū** during one's free time
閑日月 **kanjitsugetsu** leisure
5 閑古鳥 **kankodori** cuckoo
7 閑却 **kankyaku** neglect, ignore, overlook
8 閑事業 **kanjigyō** useless work
閑居 **kankyo** live in seclusion/leisure
11 閑寂 **kanjaku** quiet, tranquillity
12 閑散 **kansan** leisure; (market) inactivity
13 閑暇 **kanka** leisure, spare time

8
金
食
隹
雨
門 4←

閑話 **kanwa** quiet/idle talk
閑雅 **kanga** refined, elegant; quietude
14 閑静 **kansei** quiet, peaceful
15 閑談 **kandan** quiet conversation, chat
18 閑職 **kanshoku** easy job, sinecure

— 2 —

1 一閑張 **ikkanba(ri)** lacquered papier-mâché
3 小閑 **shōkan** short break/rest, lull
4 少閑 **shōkan** short break/rest, lull
6 休閑 **kyūkan** fallowing
休閑地 **kyūkanchi** land lying fallow
安閑 **ankan** idly **Ankan** (emperor, 531–535)
有閑 **yūkan** having leisure
有閑階級 **yūkan kaikyū** the leisure class
8 長閑 **nodo(ka)** tranquil, mild, balmy
空閑地 **kūkanchi** vacant land
9 幽閑 **yūkan** quiet, leisurely
10 消閑 **shōkan** killing time
11 清閑 **seikan** quiet, tranquil, leisurely
深閑 **shinkan** still, quiet, deserted
12 森閑 **shinkan (to shita)** still, hushed, silent
等閑 **tōkan** neglect, disregard
13 農閑期 **nōkanki** farmers' slack season
16 繁閑 **hakan** busy or slack, hectic or leisurely

— 3 —

4 心長閑 **kokoronodoka** peaceful, at ease

8

金 食 隹 雨 →4 門

8e4.3 / 43

間 間向

KAN interval, space between; (as suffix) between, among **KEN** between, among; (counter for spaces on a go board); (unit of length, about 1.8 m) **aida** interval (of space or time), between, among **ai** interval, between, cross(breed) **ma** space, room; pause, a rest (in music); a room; time, leisure; luck, the situation

— 1 —

0 間もなく **ma(monaku)** presently, in a little while, soon
1 間一髪 **kan ippatsu** a hair's breadth
2 間子 **ai(no)ko** a cross between, halfbreed
3 間々 **mama** often, occasionally
間口 **maguchi** frontage, width
4 間切 **magi(ri)** tacking (in sailing)
間引 **mabi(ki)** thinning out (plants)
間尺合 **mashaku (ni) a(wanai)** not be worth it
間欠 **kanketsu** intermittent
間欠熱 **kanketsunetsu** intermittent fever
5 間代 **madai** room rent
6 間伐 **kanbatsu** thinning out (a forest)
間合 **ma (ni) a(u)** be in time for; serve the purpose, suffice
間色 **kanshoku** a compound color
間近 **majika** nearby, close, affecting one personally
7 間作 **kansaku** intercropping, a catch crop
間延 **mano(bi)** slow, dull-witted
間抜 **manu(ke)** stupid **ma (ga) nu(keru)** be stupid; be out of place/harmony
間抜面 **manu(ke)zura** stupid look
間投詞 **kantōshi** an interjection
間男 **maotoko** adulterer, secret (male) lover
8 間服 **aifuku** between-season wear
間者 **kanja** spy
間取 **mado(ri)** arrangement of the rooms, floor plan
9 間奏曲 **kansōkyoku** interlude
間柄 **aidagara** relationship
間祝 **maiwa(i)** fisherman's coat (given by shipowner to crew to congratulate them on a big catch)
間祝着 **maiwa(i)gi** festive fisherman's kimono
間食 **kanshoku** eating between meals
10 間借 **maga(ri)** renting a room
間借人 **maga(ri)nin** lodger, roomer
間宮海峡 **Mamiya-kaikyō** (strait between Hokkaidō and Sakhalin)
間紙 **aigami** sheets inserted to prevent scratches/soiling
11 間道 **kandō** secret path, side road, shortcut
間接 **kansetsu** indirect
間接税 **kansetsuzei** indirect tax
間脳 **kannō** the interbrain
間断 **kandan** interruption, pause
12 間隔 **kankaku** space, spacing; interval
間隙 **kangeki** gap, opening, crevice
間違 **machiga(u)** be mistaken/wrong **machiga(eru)** mistake
間無 **ma(mo)na(ku)** presently, in a little while, soon
間然 **kanzen** open to criticism
間税 **kanzei** indirect tax
間貸 **maga(shi)** renting out a room
間間 **mama** often, occasionally
13 間際 **magiwa** on the verge of, just before
間数 **kensū** number of *ken* in length **makazu** number of rooms
間歇 **kanketsu** intermittent
間歇熱 **kanketsunetsu** intermittent fever
14 間髪入 **kanhatsu (o) i(rezu)** imminently; immediately
16 間諜 **kanchō** spy

— 2 —

1 一間 **ikken** (1.8 m)
2 人間 **ningen** human being, man
人間工学 **ningen kōgaku** ergonomics
人間学 **ningengaku** anthropology

人間並 **ningenna(mi)** like most people, average, common
人間味 **ningenmi** humanity, human touch
人間性 **ningensei** human nature, humanity
人間界 **ningenkai** the world of mortals
人間業 **ningenwaza** the work of man
人間嫌 **ningengira(i)** misanthropy; misanthrope
人間愛 **ningen'ai** human love
人間離 **ningenbana(re)** unworldly, superhuman
3 大間違 **ōmachiga(i)** big mistake
土間 **doma** room with a dirt floor
小間使 **komazuka(i)** chambermaid
小間物 **komamono** sundry wares, knick-knacks
小間物屋 **komamonoya** haberdashery
山間 **sankan** in the mountains
　　　 yamaai ravine, gorge
山間僻地 **sankan-hekichi** secluded mountain recesses
4 不間 **buma** awkward, clumsy, bungling
中間 **chūkan** middle, midway, intermediate; midterm, interim
中間子 **chūkanshi** meson
中間層 **chūkansō** middle stratum/class
中間駅 **chūkan eki** intermediate station
仏間 **butsuma** Buddhist altar room
切間 **ki(re)ma** interval, break, opening
止間 **ya(mi)ma** lull
反間 **hankan** seeking to cause dissension among the enemy
区間 **kukan** section, interval
手間 **tema** time, labor, trouble; wages
手間仕事 **tema shigoto** tedious work; piecework
手間取 **temado(ru)** take time, be delayed
手間隙 **temahima** labor and time, trouble
手間賃 **temachin** wages
木間 **ko(no)ma** in the trees
5 民間 **minkan** private (not public)
民間人 **minkanjin** private citizen
世間 **seken** the world, people, the public, society, life; rumor, gossip
世間体 **sekentei** decency, respectability, appearances
世間並 **sekenna(mi)** average, ordinary, common
世間知 **sekenshi(razu)** ignorant of the ways of the world
世間的 **sekenteki** worldly, earthly
世間話 **sekenbanashi** small-talk, chat, gossip
世間離 **sekenbana(re)** strange, uncommon; unworldly
広間 **hiroma** hall; spacious room
6 年間 **nenkan** period of a year; during the year

仲間 **nakama** member of a group, mate, fellow　　**chūgen** samurai's attendant
仲間入 **nakama-i(ri)** become one of the group
仲間外 **nakamahazu(re)** being left out
仲間割 **nakamawa(re)** split among friends, internal discord
合間 **a(i)ma** interval
此間 **ko(no) aida** the other day, recently
近間 **chikama** neighborhood, vicinity
行間 **gyōkan** (reading) between the lines
肋間 **rokkan** between the ribs
7 束間 **tsuka(no)ma** brief time, moment
別間 **betsuma** separate/special room
谷間 **tanima, taniai** valley, ravine
坊間 **bōkan** on the market/streets, town (gossip)
床間 **toko(no)ma** alcove (in a Japanese-style room)
8 夜間 **yakan** night, nighttime
其間 **so(no) aida** (in) the meantime/interim
　　　 so(no) kan the situation
波間 **namima** the waves
空間 **kūkan** space　**a(ki)ma** vacant room
居間 **ima** living room
林間学校 **rinkan gakkō** outdoor school, camp
板間 **ita(no)ma** wooden floor
板間稼 **ita(no)ma kase(gi)** bathhouse thief
股間 **kokan** in the crotch
雨間 **amaai** interval between rains
9 俗間 **zokkan** the world/public
透間 **su(ki)ma** crevice, gap, opening, space
浅間山 **Asamayama** (mountain, Nagano-ken, Gunma-ken)
洋間 **yōma** Western-style room
垣間見 **kaimami(ru)** peek in, get a glimpse
狭間 **hazama** interstice; ravine; battlements
巷間 **kōkan** the town, people
茶間 **cha(no)ma** living room
客間 **kyakuma** guest room, parlor
峡間 **kyōkan** between the mountains; ravine, defile
昼間 **hiruma, chūkan** daytime, during the day
眉間 **miken** between the eyebrows
軌間 **kikan** (railroad-track) gauge
食間 **shokkan** between meals
10 借間 **ka(ri)ma** rented room
週間 **shūkan** week
胸間 **kyōkan** breast, chest
胴間声 **dōmagoe** thick/dissonant voice
時間 **jikan** an hour; time
時間表 **jikanhyō** timetable, schedule
時間給 **jikankyū** payment by the hour
畝間 **unema** space between ridges, furrow
病間 **byōkan** during an illness
11 渓間 **keikan** ravine, in the valley
深間 **fukama** depth(s); intimacy

8
金
食
隹
雷
門 4←

12 隙間 **sukima** crevice, opening, gap, space
　隙間風 **sukimakaze** a draft
　幇間 **hōkan** jester; sycophant
　期間 **kikan** term, period
　朝間 **asama** during the morning
　晴間 **ha(re)ma** interval of clear weather
　無間地獄 **muken jigoku** (a Buddhist hell)
　補間 **hokan** interpolation
　絶間 **ta(e)ma** interval, pause, gap
　　　 ta(e)ma(naku) continually, without letup
　奥間 **oku(no)ma** inner room
　貸間 **kashima** room for rent
　鈍間 **noroma** slow-witted, stupid
　雲間 **kumoma** a break between clouds
　間間 **mama** often, occasionally
13 寝間 **nema** bedroom
　寝間着 **nemaki** nightclothes
15 潮間 **shioma** ebb tide
　罷間違 **maka(ri)machiga(eba)** if worse
　　　comes to worst
16 樹間 **jukan** in the trees
18 瞬間 **shunkan** instant, moment
　離間 **rikan** alienation, estrangement
　離間策 **rikansaku** sowing discord
20 欄間 **ranma** transom
21 露間 **tsuyu(no)ma** a fleeting moment

───────── 3 ─────────

1 一週間 **isshūkan** a week
　一瞬間 **isshunkan** a moment, an instant
2 二週間 **nishūkan** two weeks, fortnight
3 大広間 **ōhiroma** grand hall
4 片手間 **katatema** in one's spare time, on the
　　　side
　日本間 **nihonma** Japanese-style room
5 平土間 **hiradoma** pit, orchestra (in a theater)
7 何時間 **nanjikan** how many hours
　応接間 **ōsetsuma** reception room, parlor
8 非人間的 **hiningenteki** inhuman, impersonal
　長時間 **chōjikan** a long time
　実世間 **jisseken** the real/everyday world
　空時間 **a(ki)jikan** open period, spare time
　国際間 **kokusaikan** international
9 俗世間 **zokuseken** this world, secular society
　指呼間 **shiko (no) aida/kan** within hailing
　　　distance
　政府間 **seifukan** government-to-government
10 真人間 **maningen** honest man, good citizen
　真昼間 **ma(p)piruma** broad daylight
　遊仲間 **aso(bi)nakama** playmate
　遊時間 **aso(bi)jikan** playtime, recess
　夏時間 **natsujikan** daylight-saving time
11 釣仲間 **tsu(ri) nakama** fishing buddies
12 惑星間 **wakuseikan** interplanetary
　飲仲間 **no(mi)nakama** drinking buddy
13 数分間 **sūfunkan** for a few minutes, several
　　　minutes

数日間 **sūnichikan** for several days

───────── 4 ─────────

7 走行時間 **sōkō jikan** travel time
9 通用期間 **tsūyō kikan** period of (a ticket's)
　　　validity
12 猶予期間 **yūyo kikan** grace period

閒 → 間 **8e4.3**

8e4.4

閏　**JUN** leap (year); extra; pretending to
　　the throne　**urū** leap (year)

───────── 1 ─────────

6 閏年 **urūdoshi** leap year

8e4.5

悶　**MON, moda(eru)** be in agony

───────── 1 ─────────

3 悶々 **monmon** discontent, anguish
6 悶死 **monshi** die in agony
8 悶苦 **moda(e)kuru(shimu)** writhe in pain
12 悶着 **monchaku** trouble; dispute
　悶絶 **monzetsu** faint in agony

───────── 2 ─────────

7 身悶 **mimoda(e)** writhe
8 苦悶 **kumon** agony, anguish
13 煩悶 **hanmon** worry, anguish
15 憂悶 **yūmon** anguish, mortification

8e4.6 / 396

開　**KAI** opening; development
　　a(ku/keru) (intr./tr.) open
　　hira(keru) be opened, become developed
　　hira(ku) (intr. or tr.) open, develop
hira(ki) opening; difference, margin; (hinged) door

───────── 1 ─────────

3 開口 **kaikō** opening, aperture; beginning
　　　one's speech
　開山 **kaisan** (sect's) founder, originator
4 開化 **kaika** civilization, enlightenment
　　　Kaika (emperor, 158–98 B.C.)
　開方 **kaihō** extraction of roots (in math)
　開戸 **hira(ki)do** hinged door
5 開平 **kaihei** determining the square root
　開広 **a(ke)hiro(geru)** open up/wide
　開庁 **kaichō** opening (of a government office)
　開札 **kaisatsu** opening of bids
　開示 **kaiji** disclose, make public

開立 **kairyū** determining the cube root
6 開会 **kaikai** opening a meeting
開会中 **kaikaichū** during the session
開会日 **kaikaibi** opening day
開会式 **kaikaishiki** opening ceremony
開廷 **kaitei** opening/holding court
7 開花 **kaika** bloom, flower, blossom
開局 **kaikyoku** opening a new office/bureau
8 開直 **hira(ki)nao(ru)** become defiant; turn
    serious
開拓 **kaitaku** opening up land, development
開拓者 **kaitakusha** settler, pioneer
開始 **kaishi** begin, commence, start
開店 **kaiten** opening a new store; opening
    the store for the day
開国 **kaikoku** founding/opening of a country
開明 **kaimei** civilization, enlightenment
開放 **kaihō, a(ke)hana(su)** (fling/leave) open
    a(kep)pana(shi) left open; open, frank
開門 **kaimon** opening of the gate
9 開発 **kaihatsu** development
開巻 **kaikan** opening of a book
開院 **kaiin** opening of a session of parliament;
    opening of a new hospital/institute
開削 **kaisaku** building a road/canal
開通 **kaitsū** opening to traffic
開城 **kaijō** capitulation (of a fortress)
開封 **hira(ki)fū, kaifū** unsealed letter
開祖 **kaiso** (sect) founder, originator
10 開陳 **kaichin** statement
開校 **kaikō** opening a new school
開校式 **kaikōshiki** school opening ceremony
11 開運 **kaiun** improving one's luck
開基 **kaiki** founding; founder
開帳 **kaichō** put a Buddhist image on display;
    run a gambling house
開窓 **hira(ki)mado** casement window
開票 **kaihyō** ballot counting
開票所 **kaihyōjo** ballot-counting place
開眼 **kaigen, kaigan** spiritual awakening;
    consecrating a newly made image
開設 **kaisetsu** establish, inagurate, install
開閉 **kaihei** opening and closing
    a(ke)ta(te) opening and shutting
開閉器 **kaiheiki** make-and-break switch
開閉機 **kaiheiki** circuit breaker
開閉橋 **kaiheikyō** drawbridge
12 開港 **kaikō** opening the port; an open port
開港場 **kaikōjō** open/treaty port
開場 **kaijō** opening
開渠 **kaikyo** open channel
開扉 **kaihi** open the door
13 開業 **kaigyō** opening/starting a business
開業医 **kaigyōi** doctor in private practice
開催 **kaisai** hold (a meeting)
開催中 **kaisaichū** in session

開幕 **kaimaku** opening/raising the curtain
開戦 **kaisen** outbreak of war
開路 **kairo** open circuit
14 開演 **kaien** beginning the performance
16 開墾 **kaikon** clear (land), bring under cultiva-
    tion
開墾地 **kaikonchi** cultivated land
開橋 **kaikyō** opening a new bridge
開館 **kaikan** opening (of a building)
17 開豁 **kaikatsu** open (land); broad(-minded)
開講 **kaikō** begin a course of lectures
18 開襟 **kaikin** open-necked (shirt)
21 開闢 **kaibyaku** (since) the creation
28 開鑿 **kaisaku** building a road/canal

——————— 2 ———————

3 川開 **kawabira(ki)** river festival
山開 **yamabira(ki)** opening a mountain for
    the climbing season
4 切開 **sekkai** incision, section, operation; clear
    (land) **ki(ri)hira(ku)** clear (land), hack
    out (a path)
公開 **kōkai** open to the public
公開状 **kōkaijō** open letter
5 半開 **hankai, hanbira(ki)** semicivilized; half
    open **hanbira(ki)** half open
未開 **mikai** uncivilized, barbarous
未開拓 **mikaitaku** undeveloped, unexploited
未開発 **mikaihatsu** undeveloped
未開墾 **mikaikon** uncultivated
申開 **mō(shi)hira(ku)** explain, justify
打開 **dakai** a break, development, new turn
穴開器 **anaa(ke)ki** punch, perforator
6 両開 **ryōbira(ki)** double(-leafed) door)
再開 **saikai** reopen, resume, reconvene
全開 **zenkai** open fully
7 低開発国 **teikaihatsukoku** less-developed
    countries
序開 **jobira(ki)** beginning, opening
見開 **mihira(ku)** open (one's eyes) wide
    mihira(ki) double-page spread
言開 **i(i)hira(ki)** justification, explanation
8 押開 **o(shi)hira(ku), o(shi)a(keru)** push/
    force open
店開 **misebira(ki)** open shop (for the day);
    go into business
9 背開 **sebira(ki)** slice a fish down its back
10 埒開 **rachi (ga) a(ku)** be settled/concluded
展開 **tenkai** unfold, develop, evolve; deploy,
    fan out; expand (a math expression),
    develop (into a two-dimensional surface)
11 疎開 **sokai** dispersal, removal, evacuation
疎開者 **sokaisha** evacuee
捩開 **ne(ji)a(keru)** wrench/pry open
掘開 **ho(ri)hira(ku)** dig open
12 満開 **mankai** in full bloom

8

金
食
隹
雷
門 4←

散開 **sankai** deploy, fan out
裂開 **rekkai** burst open
13 幕開 **makua(ki), makua(ke)** opening of a
　　play; beginning
新開 **shinkai** newly opened/developed
続開 **zokkai** resume, continue
跳開橋 **chōkaikyō** drawbridge
15 劈開 **hekikai** cleavage (of a gemstone)
蔵開 **kurabira(ki)** first opening of a
　　storehouse in the new year
19 鏡開 **kagamibira(ki)** cutting the New Year's
　　rice cakes

————————— 3 —————————

4 文明開化 **bunmei kaika** civilization and
　　enlightenment
8 非公開 **hikōkai** closed (meeting), closed-door
　　(session)
18 観音開 **kannonbira(ki)** (hinged) double doors

————————— 4 —————————

9 帝王切開 **teiō sekkai** Caesarean section
11 強制疎開 **kyōsei sokai** forced evacuation/
　　removal, eviction

8e4.7

閔

BIN grieve, be sad; pity

————————— 1 —————————

10 閔笑 **binshō** smile with pity
12 閔然 **binzen** pitiful, sad
14 閔察 **binsatsu** compassion, sympathy

————————— 5 —————————

8e5.1

閨

KEI, GYOKU pearly gates

8e5.2

閘

KŌ watergate, lock

————————— 1 —————————

8 閘門 **kōmon** lock gate

8e5.3

鬧　鬧

DŌ be noisy

鬧 → 鬧　8e5.3

————————— 6 —————————

8e6.1 / 64

聞

BUN, MON, ki(ku) hear, listen to; heed;
ask　**ki(koeru)** be heard/audible
ki(koe) reputation, publicity

————————— 1 —————————

0 聞きたがる **ki(kitagaru)** want to hear about,
　　be inquisitive
2 聞入 **ki(ki)i(reru)** accede to, comply with
　　ki(ki)i(ru) listen attentively
3 聞及 **ki(ki)oyo(bu)** hear about, learn of
聞上手 **ki(ki)jōzu** a good listener
聞下手 **ki(ki)beta** a poor listener
4 聞分 **ki(ki)wa(keru)** listen to reason;
　　distinguish between by hearing
聞込 **ki(ki)ko(mu)** hear about, learn
聞手 **ki(ki)te** listener
聞方 **ki(ki)kata** way of hearing/listening
5 聞出 **ki(ki)da(su)** hear, find out about
聞付 **ki(ki)tsu(keru)** hear (the sound of);
　　learn of
聞召 **ki(koshi)me(su)** hear; drink, eat; go
聞古 **ki(ki)furu(shita)** hackneyed, trite
聞外 **ki(ki)hazu(su)** not hear it all, mishear
聞旧 **ki(ki)furu(shita)** hackneyed, trite
6 聞伝 **ki(ki)tsuta(e)** hearsay
聞合 **ki(ki)a(wase)** inquiry
聞返 **ki(ki)kae(su)** ask back
聞尽 **ki(ki)tsuku(su)** hear it all
聞耳 **ki(ki)mimi** attentive ears
7 聞忘 **ki(ki)wasu(reru)** forget to ask about;
　　forget what one hears
聞役 **ki(ki)yaku** one who hears people's
　　complaints
聞辛 **ki(ki)zura(i)** hard to hear/ask
聞糺 **ki(ki)tada(su)** ascertain, verify
8 聞事 **ki(ki)goto** something worth listening to
聞直 **ki(ki)nao(su)** ask/inquire again
聞知 **bunchi, ki(ki)shi(ru)** learn of
聞咎 **ki(ki)toga(meru)** find fault with
聞始 **ki(ki)haji(meru)** begin to hear
聞苦 **ki(ki)guru(shii)** offensive to the ear
聞届 **ki(ki)todo(keru)** grant (a request),
　　accede to
聞物 **ki(ki)mono** something worth hearing,
　　highlight
聞所 **ki(ki)dokoro** the part/point to listen for
聞取 **ki(ki)to(ru)** hear and understand, catch,
　　follow
9 聞洩 **ki(ki)mo(rasu)** miss hearing, not catch
聞栄 **ki(ki)ba(e)** worth listening to
10 聞酒 **ki(ki)zake** wine tasting
聞流 **ki(ki)naga(su)** pay no attention to
聞書 **ki(ki)ga(ki)** (taking) notes

聞納 **ki(ki)osa(me)** the last time (I) heard (him)
11 聞捨 **ki(ki)su(teru)** ignore, overlook
聞悪 **ki(ki)niku(i)** hard to hear; awkward to ask
聞惚 **ki(ki)ho(reru)** listen to with rapt attention
12 聞違 **ki(ki)chiga(eru/u)** mishear, be misinformed
聞落 **ki(ki)o(tosu)** miss hearing, not catch
聞覚 **ki(ki)obo(eru)** learn by ear
13 聞損 **ki(ki)sokona(u)** mishear, not catch
聞置 **ki(ki)o(ku)** hear, keep in mind
聞飽 **ki(ki)a(kiru)** get tired of hearing
聞馴 **ki(ki)na(reru)** get used to hearing
14 聞漏 **ki(ki)mo(rasu)** miss hearing, not catch
聞徳 **ki(ki)doku** worth hearing
聞慣 **ki(ki)na(reru)** get used to hearing
15 聞澄 **ki(ki)su(masu)** listen attentively

———————— 2 ————————

2 人聞 **hitogi(ki)** reputation, respectability
又聞 **matagi(ki)** hearsay, secondhand information
4 凶聞 **kyōbun** bad news
内聞 **naibun** secret, private
仄聞 **sokubun** hear (by chance)
5 未聞 **mimon** not yet heard, unheard of
生聞 **namagi(ki)** smattering of knowledge
令聞 **reibun** good reputation, renown
外聞 **gaibun** reputation, respectability
立聞 **ta(chi)gi(ki)** overhear, eavesdrop
6 伝聞 **denbun** hearsay, report, rumor
名聞 **meibun** fame, honor
百聞一見如 **hyakubun (wa) ikken (ni) shi(kazu)** Seeing for oneself once is better than hearing 100 accounts.
7 余聞 **yobun** rumor, gossip
見聞 **kenbun, kenmon, miki(ki)** information, knowledge, experience
言聞 **i(i)ki(kaseru)** tell (someone to do something), persuade, exhort
8 拝聞 **haibun** listen to, hear
奇聞 **kibun** strange news, anecdote
実聞 **jitsubun** hear with one's own ears
怪聞 **kaibun** strange rumor; scandal
9 奏聞 **sōmon** report to the emperor
風聞 **fūbun** report, rumor
後聞 **kōbun** later information
珍聞 **chinbun** (piece of) news
10 逸聞 **itsubun** something not generally known
11 側聞 **sokubun** hear tell, be told
虚聞 **kyobun** false rumor
探聞 **tanbun** sounding out indirectly
異聞 **ibun** another story, strange tale
盗聞 **nusu(mi)gi(ki)** eavesdrop, listen in on
13 新聞 **shinbun** newspaper

新聞代 **shinbundai** newspaper subscription charge
新聞売 **shinbun'u(ri)** news dealer
新聞社 **shinbunsha** newspaper (company)
新聞界 **shinbunkai** the newspaper world
新聞紙 **shinbunshi** newspaper (paper)
新聞業 **shinbungyō** the newspaper business
14 漏聞 **rōbun** overhear
寡聞 **kabun** little knowledge, ill-informed
誤聞 **gobun** mishearing; misinformation
読聞 **yo(mi)ki(kasu)** read to (someone)
説聞 **to(ki)ki(kasu)** explain, reason with
15 確聞 **kakubun** learn from reliable sources
17 聴聞 **chōmon** listening to
聴聞会 **chōmonkai** public hearing
聴聞僧 **chōmonsō** confessor
醜聞 **shūbun** scandal
19 艶聞 **enbun** love affair/rumor

———————— 3 ————————

7 赤新聞 **akashinbun** yellow journal
8 注文聞 **chūmonki(ki)** taking orders; order taker
12 御用聞 **goyōki(ki)** taking orders
16 壁新聞 **kabe shinbun** wall newspaper/poster

———————— 4 ————————

5 外字新聞 **gaiji shinbun** foreign-language newspaper
6 邦字新聞 **hōji shinbun** Japanese-language newspaper
8 英字新聞 **eiji shinbun** English-language newspaper
9 前代未聞 **zendai-mimon** unprecedented
11 悪徳新聞 **akutoku shinbun** irresponsible/sensationalist newspaper
12 御用新聞 **goyō shinbun** government newspaper

8e6.2 / 1510

BATSU clique, clan, faction

———————— 1 ————————
11 閥族 **batsuzoku** clan, clique
———————— 2 ————————
7 学閥 **gakubatsu** clique of graduates from the same school, old boy network
8 門閥 **monbatsu** lineage, pedigree
9 軍閥 **gunbatsu** military clique, militarist party
派閥 **habatsu** clique, faction
10 党閥 **tōbatsu** faction, clique
財閥 **zaibatsu** financial clique
14 閨閥 **keibatsu** family groupings through marriage
18 藩閥 **hanbatsu** clanship, clannishness

8
金
食
隹
雨
門 6←

8e6.3 / 837

閣 **KAKU** tower, palace; the cabinet

──────── 1 ────────

3 閣下 **kakka** Your Excellency
4 閣内 **kakunai** within the cabinet
5 閣令 **kakurei** cabinet order
閣外 **kakugai** outside the cabinet
10 閣員 **kakuin** member of the cabinet
14 閣僚 **kakuryō** cabinet members
20 閣議 **kakugi** cabinet meeting

──────── 2 ────────

2 入閣 **nyūkaku** enter/join the cabinet
4 内閣 **naikaku** the cabinet
仏閣 **bukkaku** Buddhist temple
5 台閣 **taikaku** tall building; the cabinet
8 金閣 **kinkaku** golden pavilion
金閣寺 **Kinkakuji** Temple of the Golden Pavilion
10 倒閣 **tōkaku** overthrowing the cabinet
高閣 **kōkaku** high building/shelf
11 組閣 **sokaku** formation of a cabinet
13 楼閣 **rōkaku** many-story building, castle
14 銀閣 **ginkaku** silver/beautiful building
銀閣寺 **Ginkakuji** (temple in Kyōto)

──────── 3 ────────

4 天守閣 **tenshukaku** castle tower

──────── 4 ────────

9 連立内閣 **renritsu naikaku** coalition cabinet
12 超然内閣 **chōzen naikaku** non-party government

8e6.4

関 鬨 **KŌ** fight **toki** battle/war cry

──────── 1 ────────

7 鬨声 **toki (no) koe** battle/war cry

──────── 2 ────────

12 勝鬨 **ka(chi)doki** shout of victory

8e6.5

閨 **KEI, neya** bedroom

──────── 1 ────────

7 閨秀 **keishū** accomplished woman
閨秀作家 **keishū sakka** woman writer
8 閨房 **keibō** bedroom, bedchamber
14 閨閥 **keibatsu** family groupings through marriage

──────── 2 ────────

8 空閨 **kūkei** spouseless bedroom

8e6.6

閤 **KŌ** small side gate

──────── 2 ────────

4 太閤 **taikō** the father of an imperial adviser; Toyotomi Hideyoshi

8e6.7 / 398

関 關 **KAN** barrier, (border) checkpoint; relating to, concerning **seki** barrier, (border) checkpoint **kaka(waru)** be related to, have to do with **kaka(wari)** relation, connection

──────── 1 ────────

0 関する **kan(suru)** be related to, concern, involve
関ヶ原 **Sekigahara** decisive battle
3 関与 **kan'yo** participation
関山 **seki (no) yama** the best one can do
4 関心 **kanshin** interest, concern
関心事 **kanshinji** matter of concern
5 関白 **kanpaku** emperor's chief advisor; domineering husband
6 関西 **Kansai** (region including Ōsaka and Kyōto)
関守 **sekimori** barrier keeper
8 関東 **Kantō** (region including Tōkyō)
関知 **kanchi** have to do with
関所 **sekisho** border station, checkpoint
関取 **sekitori** ranking sumo wrestler
関門 **kanmon** gateway, barrier
関門海峡 **Kanmon-kaikyō** (strait between Shimonoseki and Moji)
9 関係 **kankei** relation(ship), connection
関係代名詞 **kankei daimeishi** relative pronoun
関係者 **kankeisha** interested party, those concerned
関係副詞 **kankei fukushi** relative adverb
関連 **kanren** connection, relation, association
12 関税 **kanzei** customs, tariff, duty
関税率 **kanzeiritsu** customs rates/tariff
13 関節 **kansetsu** joint
関節炎 **kansetsuen** arthritis
16 関頭 **kantō** crucial point, crossroads
17 関聯 **kanren** connection, relation, association

──────── 2 ────────

3 大関 **ōzeki** sumo wrestler of second-highest rank
下関 **Shimonoseki** (city, Yamaguchi-ken)
5 玄関 **genkan** entranceway, vestibule, front door

8

金 食 隹 電 → 6 門

玄関払 **genkanbara(i)** refusal to see a visitor
玄関先 **genkansaki** entrance, front door
玄関番 **genkanban** doorkeeper, porter
7 汽関 **kikan** boiler, steam generator
肘関節 **hiji kansetsu** elbow joint
8 股関節 **kokansetsu** hip joint
9 連関 **renkan** relation, association, linkage
通関 **tsūkan** customs clearance
海関 **kaikan** maritime customs
海関税 **kaikanzei** import duties
相関 **sōkan** correlation
相関的 **sōkanteki** interrelated
10 郷関 **kyōkan** one's native place, home town
12 腕関節 **wankansetsu** the wrist joint
無関心 **mukanshin** indifference, unconcern, apathy
無関係 **mukankei** unrelated, irrelevant
税関 **zeikan** customs; customshouse
税関吏 **zeikanri** customs officer/inspector
税関長 **zeikanchō** director of customs
13 摂関 **sekkan** regents and chief advisers
摂関家 **sekkanke** the line of regents and advisers
15 膝関節 **shitsukansetsu** the knee joint
16 機関 **kikan** engine; machinery, organ(ization)
機関士 **kikanshi** (locomotive) engineer
機関手 **kikanshu** (locomotive) engineer
機関車 **kikansha** locomotive
機関室 **kikanshitsu** machine/engine room
機関庫 **kikanko** locomotive shed, roundhouse
機関紙 **kikanshi** organization's newspaper
機関誌 **kikanshi** organization's publication
機関銃 **kikanjū** machine gun
機関雑誌 **kikan zasshi** organization's publication
17 醜関係 **shūkankei** illicit liaison
霞関 **Kasumi(ga)seki** (area of Tōkyō, where government ministries are located)
18 難関 **nankan** barrier, obstacle, difficulty

──────── 3 ────────

3 三角関係 **sankaku kankei** love triangle
4 内玄関 **uchigenkan** side entrance
7 利害関係 **rigai kankei** interests
8 表玄関 **omote genkan** front entrance/door
9 重機関銃 **jūkikanjū** heavy machine gun
亭主関白 **teishu kanpaku** autocratic husband
12 軽機関銃 **keikikanjū** light machine gun
15 熱機関 **netsukikan** heat engine

──────── 4 ────────

4 内燃機関 **nainen kikan** internal-combustion engine
6 交通機関 **kōtsū kikan** transportation facilities
7 決議機関 **ketsugi kikan** voting body; party organization, caucus

8 金融機関 **kin'yū kikan** financial institutions
9 宣伝機関 **senden kikan** propaganda organ
10 娯楽機関 **goraku kikan** recreational facilities
特務機関 **tokumu kikan** military intelligence organization
12 焼玉機関 **ya(ki)dama kikan** hot-bulb/ semidiesel engine

──────── 7 ────────

8e7.1

閭

RYO village

8e7.2 / 1369

閲

ETSU inspection, review, revision

──────── 1 ────────

0 閲する **es(suru)** review, revise
kemi(suru) examine, look over; elapse, pass
7 閲兵 **eppei** inspection of troops, parade, review
14 閲歴 **etsureki** career, personal history
閲読 **etsudoku** perusal, reading
17 閲覧 **etsuran** perusal, inspection, reading
閲覧室 **etsuranshitsu** reading room

──────── 2 ────────

4 内閲 **naietsu** private perusal/inspection
5 巡閲 **jun'etsu** inspection tour
10 校閲 **kōetsu** revise, supervise
12 検閲 **ken'etsu** censorship; inspection (of troops)
検閲官 **ken'etsukan** censor, inspector
16 親閲 **shin'etsu** personal inspection

──────── 8 ────────

8e8.1

閼

A block, stop

──────── 1 ────────

7 閼伽 **aka** (Buddhist) holy water

8e8.2

鬪

GEKI, seme(gu) quarrel

8e8.3

闍

EN eunuch

8

金
食
隹
雨
門 8←

8e8.4

閻 **EN** village (gate)

───── 1 ─────

21 閻魔 **Enma** the King of Hades
閻魔帳 **enmachō** teacher's mark book

8e8.5

閾 **IKI** threshold

───── 1 ─────

10 閾値 **ikichi** threshold (value)

───── 2 ─────

19 識閾 **shikiiki** threshold of consciousness

───── 9 ─────

8e9.1

闌 **RAN, ta(keru)** rise high; be advanced, be well along
takenawa the height/midst of

───── 1 ─────

3 闌干 **rankan** railing, bannister

8e9.2

闍 **TO** watchtower
JA (used phonetically)

8e9.3

闊 濶 **KATSU** wide; broad-minded

───── 1 ─────

11 闊達 **kattatsu** magnanimous, generous

───── 2 ─────

3 久闊 **kyūkatsu** neglecting to keep in touch
久闊叙 **kyūkatsu (o) jo(su)** greet for the first time in a long time
5 広闊 **kōkatsu** spacious, extensive, wide
6 迂闊 **ukatsu** careless, stupid
7 快闊 **kaikatsu** cheerful, lively, merry
13 寛闊 **kankatsu** ample, generous

───── 3 ─────

15 横行闊歩 **ōkō-kappo** swagger around

8e9.4

闃 **GEKI** quiet, still

8e9.5

闇 **AN, yami** darkness; gloom; black market

───── 1 ─────

3 闇々 **yamiyami** without one's knowledge, suddenly, easily
5 闇市 **yamiichi** black market
闇汁 **yamijiru** pot-luck soup to which each participant contributes and which is eaten with the lights out
闇打 **yamiu(chi)** an attack in the darkness; assassination, foul murder
8 闇夜 **yamiyo, an'ya** dark night
闇物資 **yamibusshi** black-market goods
闇取引 **yamitorihiki** black-market dealings, illegal transaction
闇金融 **yamikin'yū** illegal lending
9 闇屋 **yamiya** black marketeer
闇相場 **yamisōba** black-market price
10 闇値 **yamine** black-market price
11 闇商人 **yamishōnin** black marketeer
12 闇雲 **yamikumo (ni)** at random, haphazardly
13 闇路 **yamiji** dark road
17 闇闇 **yamiyami** without one's knowledge, suddenly, easily

───── 2 ─────

3 夕闇 **yūyami** dusk, twilight
10 宵闇 **yoiyami** evening twilight, dusk
11 常闇 **tokoyami** perpetual darkness
12 暁闇 **akatsukiyami** a moonless dawn
無闇 **muyami** thoughtless, rash; excessive; unnecessary
13 暗闇 **kurayami** darkness
17 闇闇 **yamiyami** without one's knowledge, suddenly, easily

───── 3 ─────

10 真暗闇 **makkurayami** utter darkness

8e9.6

関 **KETSU** come to an end; rest

───── 10 ─────

8e10.1

闖 **CHIN** inquire about; sudden entry

───── 1 ─────

2 闖入 **chinnyū** intrusion, forced entry
闖入者 **chinnyūsha** intruder, trespasser

8

金
食
隹
雨

→8 門

8e10.2 / 1511

闘　鬭　斗　　**TŌ, tataka(u)** fight, struggle

──────── 1 ────────

3 闘士 **tōshi** fighter for
闘士型 **tōshigata** the athletic type
4 闘犬 **tōken** dogfight(ing); fighting dog
闘牛 **tōgyū** bullfight(ing); fighting bull
闘牛士 **tōgyūshi** matador, bullfighter
闘牛場 **tōgyūjō** bullring
6 闘争 **tōsō** struggle, conflict; strike
7 闘技 **tōgi** competition, contest, match
闘志 **tōshi** fighting spirit
闘志満々 **tōshi-manman** full of fighting spirit
10 闘将 **tōshō** brave fighter/leader
闘病 **tōbyō** struggle against an illness
14 闘魂 **tōkon** fighting spirit
19 闘鶏 **tōkei** cockfight(ing); fighting cock

──────── 2 ────────

6 死闘 **shitō** life-and-death struggle
争闘 **sōtō** struggle
7 決闘 **kettō** duel
乱闘 **rantō** melee, free-for-all fight
私闘 **shitō** personal feud
8 苦闘 **kutō** bitter struggle, uphill battle
9 春闘 **shuntō** spring labor offensive (short for 春季闘争)
10 健闘 **kentō** put up a good fight, make strenuous efforts
拳闘 **kentō** boxing
格闘 **kakutō** fist fight, scuffle
12 敢闘 **kantō** fight courageously
13 暗闘 **antō** secret enmity/feud
戦闘 **sentō** combat, battle, fighting
戦闘力 **sentōryoku** fighting strength
戦闘服 **sentōfuku** battle dress
戦闘的 **sentōteki** fighting, militant
戦闘員 **sentōin** combatant, combat soldier
戦闘帽 **sentōbō** field cap
戦闘靴 **sentōgutsu** combat boots
戦闘旗 **sentōki** battle flag
戦闘機 **sentōki** fighter (plane)
戦闘艦 **sentōkan** battleship
15 熱闘 **nettō** hard-fought contest
16 激闘 **gekitō** intense fighting, fierce battle
奮闘 **funtō** struggle, strive, fight hard

──────── 3 ────────

8 非戦闘員 **hisentōin** noncombatant

──────── 4 ────────

11 悪戦苦闘 **akusen-kutō** fight desperately

8e10.3

闕　　**KETSU** imperial palace; lack, shortage, gap

──────── 1 ────────

4 闕文 **ketsubun** lacuna
8 闕所 **kessho** confiscation of an estate

8e10.4

闔　　**KŌ** close, shut; door

──────── 1 ────────

8 闔国 **kōkoku** the whole country

8e10.5

闐　　**TEN** be full; drumming, booming

──────── 11 ────────

關 → 関　8e6.7

──────── 12 ────────

8e12.1

闡　　**SEN** make clear

──────── 1 ────────

8 闡明 **senmei** clarify, explain

8e12.2

闥　　**TATSU, TACHI** gate

──────── 13 ────────

8e13.1

闢　　**HEKI, BYAKU** open

──────── 2 ────────

12 開闢 **kaibyaku** (since) the creation

──────── 18 ────────

8e18.1

闥　　**KYŪ, kuji** lottery, raffle

8

金
食
隹
雨
門 18←

─────────── 頁 **9a** ───────────

頁	頂	頃	項	順	須	頓	頒	頒	頌	預	頑	顏
0.1	2.1	2.2	3.1	3.2	3j9.1	4.1	4.2	4.3	4.4	4.5	4.6	5.1

頸	領	頰	頡	頴	頤	賴	煩	頬	頻	頸	穎	頴
9a7.4	5.2	9a7.2	6.1	6.2	6.3	7.1	7.2	7.3	9a8.2	7.4	9a7.5	7.5

頭	頷	顆	頽	類	顎	顏	顋	顕	額	顔	題	類
7.6	7.7	8.1	8.2	9.1	9.2	9.3	9.4	9.5	9.6	9a9.3	9.7	9a9.1

顛	願	顥	顧	囂	顫	鬚	顬	顯	顰	顱	顴	顳
10.1	10.2	12.1	12.2	12.3	13.1	13.2	14.1	9a9.5	15.1	16.1	17.1	18.1

─────────── 0 ───────────

9a0.1

頁

KETSU, pēji page

─────────── 1 ───────────

8 頁岩 **ketsugan** shale

─────────── 2 ───────────

9a2.1 / 1440

頂

CHŌ, itadaki summit, top
itada(ku) be capped with; receive

─────────── 1 ───────────

3 頂上 **chōjō** summit, peak, top, climax
7 頂角 **chōkaku** vertical angle
8 頂垂 **unada(reru)** hang down one's head
　頂門一針 **chōmon (no) isshin** stinging reproach/admonition (like a needle plunged into the top of one's head)
9 頂点 **chōten** zenith, peak, climax
　頂度 **chōdo** exactly
17 頂戴 **chōdai** accept, receive; please (give me)
　頂戴物 **chōdaimono** something received as a gift

─────────── 2 ───────────

3 山頂 **sanchō** summit
4 天頂 **tenchō** zenith
　天頂点 **tenchōten** zenith
　仏頂面 **butchōzura** sour face, pout, scowl
　円頂 **enchō** round top; tonsured head
6 有頂天 **uchōten** ecstasy, rapture
8 押頂 **o(shi)itada(ku)** raise reverently to one's head
10 骨頂 **kotchō** height (of folly)
12 登頂 **tōchō** reach the summit
　絶頂 **zetchō** summit, peak, climax
25 顱頂骨 **rochōkotsu** parietal bone

9a2.2

頃

KEI, koro, -goro time; about, toward
koro(shimo) at that time

─────────── 1 ───────────

4 頃日 **keijitsu** recently, these days
6 頃合 **koroa(i)** suitable time; propriety; moderation

─────────── 2 ───────────

1 一頃 **hitokoro** once, some time ago
4 中頃 **nakagoro** about the middle
　今頃 **imagoro** at about this time
　手頃 **tegoro** handy; suitable; moderate
　日頃 **higoro** usually, always; for a long time
6 年頃 **toshigoro** age; marriageable age
　此頃 **ko(no)goro** these days, lately
　近頃 **chikagoro** recently, nowadays
　先頃 **sakigoro** recently, the other day
7 見頃 **migoro** the best time to see
9 昼頃 **hirugoro** about noon
　食頃 **ta(be)goro, ku(i)goro** the right time to eat, the season for
10 値頃 **negoro** reasonable price

─────────── 3 ───────────

11 常日頃 **tsunehigoro** always, usually

─────────── 3 ───────────

9a3.1 / 1439

項

KŌ item, clause, paragraph; term (in math)
unaji nape of the neck

─────────── 1 ───────────

5 項目 **kōmoku** heading, item
8 項垂 **unada(reru)** hang down one's head

─────────── 2 ───────────

1 一項 **ikkō** an item; a paragraph
6 多項式 **takōshiki** polynomial expression
　各項 **kakkō, kakukō** each item/clause
7 別項 **bekkō** separate/another paragraph
　条項 **jōkō** articles and paragraphs, stipulations

9

→ 0 頁

8 事項 **jikō** matters, facts, items
9 前項 **zenkō** the preceding/foregoing paragraph
　要項 **yōkō** the essential point(s)
　後項 **kōkō** the following paragraph/clause

——————— 4 ———————

7 決議事項 **ketsugi jikō** agenda, resolutions
8 注意事項 **chūi jikō** matter requiring attention; N.B.

9a3.2 / 769

順

JUN order, sequence; obey, follow

——————— 1 ———————

0 ＡＢＣ順 **ē-bī-shī-jun** alphabetic order
3 順々 **junjun** in order, by turns
4 順化 **junka** acclimate
6 順次 **junji** in order, successively; gradually
　順当 **juntō** right, regular, normal
7 順良 **junryō** peaceful, law-abiding
　順位 **jun'i** ranking, standing
　順延 **jun'en** postpone, defer
　順応 **junnō** adapt/conform to
　順応力 **junnōryoku** adaptability
　順応性 **junnōsei** adaptability
　順序 **junjo** order, sequence; procedure
8 順逆 **jungyaku** obedience and disobedience, right and wrong
　順送 **jun'oku(ri)** send/pass on from person to person
9 順風 **junpū** favorable/tail wind
12 順番 **junban** order, one's turn
　順順 **junjun** in order, by turns
13 順路 **junro** the regular route; itinerary
14 順境 **junkyō** favorable circumstances, prosperity
15 順調 **junchō** favorable, smooth, without a hitch
19 順繰 **jungu(ri)** in order, in turn

——————— 2 ———————

3 大順 **ō(kii)jun** decreasing order, largest first
　小順 **chii(sai)jun** increasing order, smallest first
4 不順 **fujun** irregularity; unseasonable
　手順 **tejun** procedure, routine, process
5 打順 **dajun** batting order
6 孝順 **kōjun** obedience, filial piety
　耳順 **jijun** age 60
8 逆順 **gyakujun** in reverse order
　忠順 **chūjun** allegiance, loyalty, obedience
9 柔順 **jūjun** docile, submissive, gentle
10 帰順 **kijun** submission, (rebels') return to allegiance
　従順 **jūjun** submissive, docile, gentle

恭順 **kyōjun** fealty, allegiance
　席順 **sekijun** seating order, precedence
11 道順 **michijun** route, itinerary
12 着順 **chakujun** in order of arrival
　温順 **onjun** gentle, submissive, docile
　筆順 **hitsujun** stroke order
　順順 **junjun** in order, by turns

——————— 3 ———————

4 不従順 **fujūjun** disobedience
5 申込順 **mōshiko(mi)jun** in order of applications received
6 年代順 **nendaijun** chronological order
　先着順 **senchakujun** by order of arrival, in the order of receipt, (on a) first-come-first-served basis
7 身長順 **shinchō-jun** in order of height
8 雨天順延 **uten-jun'en** in case of rain postponed to the next fair day

——————— 4 ———————

4 五十音順 **gojūonjun** in "aiueo" order of the kana alphabet

須 → **3j9.1**

——————— 4 ———————

9a4.1

頓

TON sudden; bow low; stumble; be in order
tomi sudden

——————— 1 ———————

6 頓死 **tonshi** sudden death
7 頓狂 **tonkyō** flurried, hysteric, wild
8 頓知 **tonchi** ready/quick wit
　頓服 **tonpuku** (medicine to) take in one dose
　頓服薬 **tonpukuyaku** drug to be taken once
9 頓首 **tonshu** bow low, kowtow; Your Humble Servant
10 頓挫 **tonza** setback, hitch, impasse
　頓馬 **tonma** fool, nitwit
12 頓着 **tonchaku** be mindful of, care, heed
　頓智 **tonchi** quick/ready wit
13 頓痴気 **tonchiki** nincompoop, dope

——————— 2 ———————

11 停頓 **teiton** standstill, deadlock, stalemate
12 無頓着 **mutonjaku, mutonchaku** indifferent/unattentive to
16 整頓 **seiton** in proper order, neat

9a4.2

頏

KŌ alight, land; throat, neck

9a4.3 / 1850

頒 **HAN, waka(tsu)** divide, distribute

——————— 1 ———————

5 頒布 **hanpu** distribute, circulate
6 頒行 **hankō** distribution, dissemination

9a4.4

頌 **SHŌ** praise, eulogy

——————— 1 ———————

7 頌寿 **shōju** (congratulations on) one's 60th, 70th, 80th, etc. birthday
14 頌徳 **shōtoku** eulogizing someone's virtues
頌徳碑 **shōtokuhi** monument in honor of (someone)
頌歌 **shōka** hymn of praise, anthem
22 頌壽 **shōju** (congratulations on) one's 60th, 70th, 80th, etc. birthday

9a4.5 / 394

預 **YO, azu(keru)** entrust/receive for safekeeping **YO, azu(karu)** entrust/receive for safekeeping

——————— 1 ———————

0 お預け **(o)azu(ke)** putting food before a dog and making him wait for his master's permission to eat; deferring fulfillment of a promise
2 預入 **azu(ke)i(reru)** make a deposit
預人 **azu(kari)nin** person with whom something is entrusted, possessor
5 預主 **azu(kari)nushi** person with whom something is entrusted, possessor
8 預物 **azu(ke)mono** article left in someone's charge
預所 **azu(kari)sho** depository, warehouse
預金 **yokin** deposit, bank account
azu(ke)kin money on deposit
預金者 **yokinsha** depositor
10 預託 **yotaku** deposit
12 預証 **azu(kari)shō** (baggage) claim check; (warehouse/deposit) receipt

——————— 3 ———————

1 一時預場 **ichiji azukarijō** baggage safe-keeping area

9a4.6 / 1848

頑 **GAN, kataku(na)** stubborn, obstinate

——————— 1 ———————

3 頑丈 **ganjō** solid, firm, robust

8 頑迷 **ganmei** bigoted, obstinate
頑固 **ganko** stubborn, obstinate
9 頑是 **ganze(nai)** innocent, artless; helpless
10 頑健 **ganken** strong and robust, in excellent health
頑冥 **ganmei** bigoted, obstinate
11 頑張 **ganba(ru)** persist in, stick to it, hang in there
頑強 **gankyō** stubborn, obstinate, unyielding
13 頑愚 **gangu** stupid and obstinate

——————— 5 ———————

9a5.1

頗 **HA** lean to one side; somewhat **sukobu(ru)** very much, extremely

——————— 2 ———————

11 偏頗 **henpa** partiality, unfair discrimination

頚 → 頸 9a7.4

9a5.2 / 834

領 **RYŌ** govern, rule; territory; neck, collar; (counter for suits of armor)

——————— 1 ———————

3 領土 **ryōdo** territory
4 領内 **ryōnai** (within the) territory
領収 **ryōshū** receipt
領収者 **ryōshūsha** receiver, recipient
領収書 **ryōshūsho** receipt
領収証 **ryōshūshō** receipt
領分 **ryōbun** territory; domain, sphere
領水 **ryōsui** territorial waters
5 領主 **ryōshu** feudal lord
6 領会 **ryōkai** understanding, consent
領地 **ryōchi** territory
領有 **ryōyū** possession
7 領承 **ryōshō** understand, acknowledge, estimate
8 領事 **ryōji** consul
領事館 **ryōjikan** consulate
領空 **ryōkū** territorial airspace
領国 **ryōgoku** daimyo's domain
9 領海 **ryōkai** territorial waters
10 領袖 **ryōshū** leader, boss
11 領域 **ryōiki** territory; domain, field
13 領解 **ryōkai** understanding, consent

——————— 2 ———————

4 仏領 **Futsuryō** French possession/territory
公領 **kōryō** duchy, principality
5 本領 **honryō** characteristic; specialty; duty; proper function; fief

9

→ 4 頁

占領 **senryō** occupation, capture; have all to oneself

占領地 **senryōchi** occupied territory

占領軍 **senryōgun** army of occupation

主領 **shuryō** leader, chief, boss

7 社領 **sharyō** shrine land

8 受領 **juryō** receive, accept

受領者 **juryōsha** recipient

受領高 **juryōdaka** amount received, receipts

受領書 **juryōsho** receipt

受領証 **juryōshō** receipt

拝領 **hairyō** receive (from a superior)

拝領物 **hairyōbutsu** gift (from a superior)

英領 **Eiryō** British territory

所領 **shoryō** territory

9 首領 **shuryō** leader, head, chief, boss

要領 **yōryō** gist, substance, synopsis

独領 **Dokuryō** German territory

10 宰領 **sairyō** management, supervision; manager, supervisor

12 属領 **zokuryō** territory, possession, dependency

統領 **tōryō** chief, manager, dictator

14 総領 **sōryō** eldest child

総領事 **sōryōji** consul-general

総領事館 **sōryōjikan** consulate-general

総領娘 **sōryō musume** eldest daughter

綱領 **kōryō** plan, program, platform

15 横領 **ōryō** misappropriate, embezzle, usurp

16 頭領 **tōryō** leader, chief, dictator

─────── 3 ───────

3 大名領 **daimyōryō** fief

大統領 **daitōryō** president

6 自治領 **jichiryō** self-governing dominion

9 保護領 **hogoryō** protectorate

─────── 4 ───────

4 不得要領 **futoku-yōryō** vague, ambiguous

11 副大統領 **fukudaitōryō** vice president

─────── 6 ───────

頬 → 頰 9a7.2

9a6.1

頡 **KETSU, KITSU** take wing, fly up

9a6.2

頴 **EI** (name of a river in China)

9a6.3

頤 **I, otogai, ago** chin, jaw

─────── 7 ───────

9a7.1 / 1512

頼 賴 **RAI, tano(mu)** ask for, request; entrust to **tano(moshii)** reliable, dependable; promising **tayo(ru)** rely/depend on

─────── 1 ───────

2 頼入 **tano(mi)i(ru)** earnestly request

4 頼込 **tano(mi)ko(mu)** earnestly request

頼少 **tano(mi)suku(nai)** hopeless, helpless, forlorn

9 頼信紙 **raishinshi** telegram form/blank

─────── 2 ───────

2 人頼 **hitodano(mi)** relying on others

又頼 **matadano(mi)** ask for through another

4 心頼 **kokorodano(mi)** dependence, reliance, hope, expectation

8 依頼 **irai** request; entrust; rely on

依頼心 **iraishin** spirit of dependence

空頼 **soradano(mi)** hoping against hope

9 信頼 **shinrai** reliance, trust, confidence

信頼性 **shinraisei** reliability

信頼感 **shinraikan** feeling of trust

神頼 **kamidano(mi)** calling on God when in distress

12 無頼 **burai** villainous

無頼漢 **buraikan** villain, hooligan, outlaw

─────── 4 ───────

5 弁護依頼人 **bengo irainin** client

9a7.2

頬 頰 **KYŌ, hō, hoho** cheek

─────── 1 ───────

0 頬っぺた **ho(ppeta)** cheek

9 頬紅 **hōbeni** rouge

10 頬骨 **hōbone** cheekbone

頬被 **hōkabu(ri)** mask one's cheeks with a cloth; feign ignorance

11 頬張 **hōba(ru)** stuff one's mouth with food

─────── 2 ───────

4 片頬 **katahō** one cheek

9a7.3

頹 **TAI** decline, decay, wane, crumble **kuzuo(reru)** collapse; fall to pieces **nada(re)** avalanche

─────── 1 ───────

4 頹込 **nada(re)ko(mu)** rush/surge into

9

頁 7 ←

12 頽廃 **taihai** decadence, corruption
頽廃的 **taihaiteki** decadent, corrupt
13 頽勢 **taisei** one's declining fortunes

――――――― 2 ―――――――

10 衰頽 **suitai** decline, waning, decay
12 廃頽 **haitai** decay, deterioration, decadence

頻 → 頻 9a8.2

9a7.4

頸 頚
KEI, kubi neck

――――――― 1 ―――――――

4 頸木 **kubiki** yoke
9 頸巻 **kubima(ki)** muffler
10 頸部 **keibu** the neck
頸骨 **keikotsu** neckbones
11 頸動脈 **keidōmyaku** the carotid artery
12 頸椎 **keitsui** the cervical vertebrae
頸筋 **kubisuji** nape/scruff of the neck
13 頸飾 **kubikaza(ri)** necklace
14 頸静脈 **keijōmyaku** the jugular vein
15 頸輪 **kubiwa** necklace; collar

――――――― 2 ―――――――

4 手頸 **tekubi** wrist
6 刎頸交 **funkei (no) maji(wari)** devoted/
lifelong friendship
7 足頸 **ashikubi** ankle
11 猪頸 **ikubi** short and thick neck, bull neck
12 喉頸 **nodokubi** neck, throat

穎 → 頴 9a7.5

9a7.5

頴 穎
EI head of grain; tip; intelligence

――――――― 1 ―――――――

3 頴才 **eisai** gifted, talented
10 頴悟 **eigo** bright, intelligent
11 頴脱 **eidatsu** outstanding ability

9a7.6 / 276

頭
TŌ, ZU, TO, atama, kōbe, kaburi
head
kashira head, leader, top

――――――― 1 ―――――――

0 頭でっかち **atama(dekkachi)** top-heavy

頭ごなし **atama(gonashi)** sweeping,
categorical
3 頭上 **zujō** overhead
頭巾 **zukin** hood, kerchief
4 頭文字 **kashiramoji** initials; capital letter
頭分 **kashirabun** leader, boss, chief
5 頭打 **atamau(chi), zuu(chi)** reach its peak/
ceiling
頭字 **kashiraji** initials, acronym
頭目 **tōmoku** chief, head of, leader
7 頭陀袋 **zudabukuro** (pilgrim's) holdall-bag
頭角現 **tōkaku (o) ara(wasu)** be preeminent
頭囲 **tōi** girth of the head
8 頭注 **tōchū** notes at the top of the page
頭取 **tōdori** (bank) president; greenroom
manager
頭金 **atamakin** down payment
9 頭重 **zuomo** top-heavy; undeferential
頭首 **tōshu** leader, chief, head of
頭垢 **fuke** dandruff
10 頭部 **tōbu** the head
頭株 **atamakabu** leader, top men
頭骨 **tōkotsu** cranial bones, skull
頭書 **tōsho** superscription, headnote;
the above-mentioned
kashiraga(ki) heading
11 頭脳 **zunō** brains, head
12 頭割 **atamawa(ri)** per capita
頭寒足熱 **zukan-sokunetsu** keeping the
head cool and the feet warm
頭痛 **zutsū** headache
頭註 **tōchū** notes at the top of the page
13 頭蓋骨 **zugaikotsu** cranium, skull
頭数 **tōsū, atamakazu** number of persons
14 頭髪 **tōhatsu** hair (on the head)
頭領 **tōryō** leader, chief, dictator
19 頭韻 **tōin** alliteration

――――――― 2 ―――――――

1 一頭 **ittō** a head (of cattle)
一頭地抜 **ittōchi (o) nu(ku)** stand head and
shoulders above others
2 二頭立 **nitōda(te)** two-horse (cart)
二頭筋 **nitōkin** biceps
人頭 **jintō** number of people, population
人頭税 **jintōzei** poll tax
3 三頭政治 **santō seiji** triumvirate
大頭 **ōatama** large head; leader, boss
口頭 **kōtō** oral
口頭試問 **kōtō shimon** oral examination
小頭 **kogashira** subforeman, straw boss
4 毛頭 **mōtō** (not) at all
井頭 **I(no)kashira** (park in Tōkyō)
双頭 **sōtō** double-headed
心頭 **shintō** heart, mind
5 出頭 **shuttō** appear, attend, be present

9

→ 7 頁

巨頭 **kyotō** leading figure, magnate, big name
叩頭 **kōtō** kowtow, bow deeply
台頭 **taitō** rise to prominence, gain strength
石頭 **ishiatama** hard head; stubborn
6 多頭 **tatō** many-headed
両頭 **ryōtō** double-headed
年頭 **nentō** beginning of the year
　　　 toshigashira the oldest person
会頭 **kaitō** president of a society
羊頭狗肉 **yōtō-kuniku** advertising mutton
　　　 but selling dog meat
地頭 **jitō** lord of a manor
先頭 **sentō** (in the) lead, (at the) head
扣頭 **kōtō** kowtow
舌頭 **zettō** tip of the tongue
尖頭 **sentō** peak; cusp; spire
光頭 **kōtō** bald head
7 低頭平身 **teitō heishin** prostrate oneself
没頭 **bottō** be engrossed/absorbed in
赤頭巾 **Akazukin(chan)** Little Red Riding
　　　 Hood
乳頭 **nyūtō** nipple
尾頭付 **okashiratsu(ki)** whole fish
社頭 **shatō** front of a shrine
禿頭 **hageatama, tokutō** bald head
禿頭病 **tokutōbyō** (pathological) baldness
初頭 **shotō** beginning
8 念頭 **nentō** mind
到頭 **tōtō** at last, finally, after all
阜頭 **futō** wharf
波頭 **hatō, namigashira** wave crest, whitecaps
店頭 **tentō** storefront, shop window, store,
　　　 over-the-counter
枕頭 **chintō** bedside
炉頭 **rotō** around the hearth
9 発頭人 **hottōnin** ringleader, originator
巻頭 **kantō** beginning of a book
陣頭 **jintō** at the head of an army
点頭 **tentō** nod
前頭部 **zentōbu** front of the head, forehead
指頭 **shitō** fingertip
咽頭 **intō** pharynx
咽頭炎 **intōen** pharyngitis
後頭 **kōtō** the back of the head
後頭部 **kōtōbu** the back of the head
柱頭 **chūtō** capital (of a column)
冒頭 **bōtō** beginning, opening (paragraph)
音頭 **ondo** leading a song/refrain
竿頭 **kantō** top of a pole
10 座頭 **zagashira** troupe leader
　　　 zatō blind man/musician
教頭 **kyōtō** head teacher
竜頭 **ryūzu** watch stem
竜頭蛇尾 **ryūtō-dabi** strong start but weak
　　　 finish
馬頭観音 **batōkannon** image of the god

Kannon with a horse's head
11 偏頭痛 **henzutsū, hentōtsu** migraine
　　　 headache
亀頭 **kitō** the glans (penis)
埠頭 **futō** wharf, pier
接頭辞 **settōji** prefix
接頭語 **settōgo** prefix
黒頭巾 **kurozukin** black hood
組頭 **kumigashira** group leader, foreman
断頭 **dantō** beheading
断頭台 **dantōdai** guillotine
12 湾頭 **wantō** shore of a bay
渡頭 **totō** ferrying place
喉頭 **kōtō** larynx
喉頭炎 **kōtōen** laryngitis
喉頭癌 **kōtōgan** cancer of the larynx
弾頭 **dantō** warhead
街頭 **gaitō** street
街頭募金 **gaitō bokin** street solicitation
街頭演説 **gaitō enzetsu** street/soapbox speech
街頭録音 **gaitō rokuon** recorded man-on-
　　　 the-street interview
無頭 **mutō** headless
番頭 **bantō** clerk, (bathhouse) attendant
筆頭 **hittō** brush tip; the first on the list
筆頭書 **hittōsha** head of the household
　　　 (listed first on the family register)
13 話頭 **watō** topic, subject
路頭 **rotō** roadside, wayside
14 寡頭政治 **katō seiji** oligarchy
旗頭 **hatagashira** leader, boss
語頭 **gotō** beginning of a word
関頭 **kantō** crucial point, crossroads
駅頭 **ekitō** at the station
15 劈頭 **hekitō** the first, outset
徹頭徹尾 **tettō-tetsubi** thoroughly, through
　　　 and through
膝頭 **hizagashira** kneecap
16 橋頭 **kyōtō** vicinity of a bridge
橋頭堡 **kyōtōhō** bridgehead, beachhead
17 擡頭 **taitō** raise its head, come to the fore, be
　　　 on the rise
檣頭 **shōtō** masthead
19 鶏頭 **keitō** cockscomb (the flower)
20 巌頭 **gantō** top of a rock
饅頭 **manjū** steamed dumpling (with bean-
　　　 jam/meat filling)
21 露頭 **rotō** outcrop (of rock)

──────────── 3 ────────────

3 才槌頭 **saizuchi atama** head with protruding
　　　 forehead and occiput, hammerhead
土饅頭 **domanjū** grave mound
5 出合頭 **dea(i)gashira** upon running into each
　　　 other, upon happening to meet
白髪頭 **shiraga atama** gray(-haired) head
6 肉饅頭 **niku manjū** meat-filled bun

7 坊主頭 **bōzuatama** shaven/close-cropped head
8 金槌頭 **kanazuchi-atama** hard-headed; stubborn
9 茶瓶頭 **chabin atama** bald head
10 核弾頭 **kakudantō** nuclear warhead
11 毬栗頭 **igaguri atama** close-cropped head, burr haircut
12 散切頭 **zangi(ri) atama** cropped head
13 獅子頭 **shishigashira** lion-head mask
16 薬罐頭 **yakan atama** bald head

——— 4 ———
5 平身低頭 **heishin-teitō** prostrate oneself

9a7.7

GAN, unazu(ku) nod (approval)

領

頤→ **9a6.3**

——— 8 ———

9a8.1

顆

KA grain (of rice)

——— 1 ———
11 顆粒 **karyū** grain, granule

9a8.2 / 1847

頻 頻

HIN occur repeatedly
shiki(ri) frequently, repeatedly, incessantly, intently

——— 1 ———
3 頻々 **hinpin** frequent, repeated
5 頻出 **hinshutsu** frequent appearance
9 頻発 **hinpatsu** frequency, frequent occurrence
頻度 **hindo** frequency, rate of occurrence
頻度数 **hindosū** frequency
16 頻繁 **hinpan** frequent, incessant
17 頻頻 **hinpin** frequent, repeated

——— 2 ———
17 頻頻 **hinpin** frequent, repeated

頤→ **9a6.3**

——— 9 ———

9a9.1 / 226

類 類

RUI kind, type, genus; similarity **tagui** kind, sort; match, equal

——— 1 ———
0 類する **rui(suru)** be similar to
2 類人猿 **ruijin'en** anthropoid ape
4 類化 **ruika** assimilate, incorporate
類火 **ruika** a spreading fire
5 類本 **ruihon** similar book
類比 **ruihi** analogy, comparison
類句 **ruiku** similar phrase/haiku
類字 **ruiji** similar kanji
6 類同 **ruidō** similar
類名 **ruimei** generic name
7 類似 **ruiji** similarity, resemblance
類似点 **ruijiten** points of similarity
類似品 **ruijihin** an imitation
類別 **ruibetsu** classify
8 類例 **ruirei** similar example, a parallel
9 類型 **ruikei** type, pattern
類音 **ruion** similar sound/pronunciation
類音語 **ruiongo** words which sound similar
10 類書 **ruisho** books of the same kind
類症 **ruishō** similar diseases
11 類推 **ruisui** (reasoning by) analogy
12 類焼 **ruishō** a spreading fire
13 類義語 **ruigigo** words of similar meaning
14 類概念 **ruigainen** genus, generic concept
類歌 **ruika** similar song
類聚 **ruijū** classification by similarity
15 類縁 **ruien** affinity, kinship
18 類題 **ruidai** (classified by) similar themes; similar question
20 類纂 **ruisan** classified compilation

——— 2 ———
1 一類 **ichirui** same kind; accomplices, companions
2 人類 **jinrui** mankind, man
人類学 **jinruigaku** anthropology
人類猿 **jinruien** anthropoid ape
人類愛 **jinruiai** love for mankind
4 分類 **bunrui** classification
分類学 **bunruigaku** taxonomy
分類表 **bunruihyō** table of classifications
分類法 **bunruihō** system of classification
5 生類 **shōrui, seirui** living creatures
比類 **hirui** a parallel, an equal
6 肉類 **nikurui** meats
同類 **dōrui** the same kind; accomplice
衣類 **irui** clothing
虫類 **chūrui** insects and worms
7 余類 **yorui** remnants of a party/gang
貝類 **kairui** shellfish (plural)
9 連類 **renrui** same kind; accomplice
10 残類 **zanrui** those remaining
部類 **burui** class(ification), category
部類分 **buruiwa(ke)** classification, grouping
畜類 **chikurui** (domestic) animals, livestock

9

→ 7 頁

酒類 **shurui** alcoholic beverages, liquor
党類 **tōrui** faction, partisans, gang
書類 **shorui** documents, papers
11 菌類 **kinrui** fungi
菌類学 **kinruigaku** mycology
異類 **irui** different kinds/species
魚類 **gyorui** fishes
魚類学 **gyoruigaku** ichthyology
鳥類 **chōrui** birds, fowl
鳥類学 **chōruigaku** ornithology
12 着類 **kirui** clothing
無類 **murui** finest, choicest
13 塩類 **enrui** salts
14 種類 **shurul** kind, type, sort
種類別 **shuruibetsu** classification, assortment
穀類 **kokurui** grains
酸類 **sanrui** acids
15 蝶類 **chōrui** butterflies
16 獣類 **jūrui** beasts, animals, brutes
親類 **shinrui** relatives
親類付合 **shinrui-zu(ki)a(i)** association among relatives; intimate association
親類書 **shinruigaki** list of one's relatives
糖類 **tōrui** sugars
17 醜類 **shūrui** evil/ugly ones
19 藻類 **sōrui** water plants, seaweeds
20 蘚類 **senrui** moss, lichen
麺類 **menrui** noodles

—————— 3 ——————

4 双殻類 **sōkakurui** bivalves
5 甲殻類 **kōkakurui** crustaceans
6 全人類 **zenjinrui** all mankind
羊歯類 **shidarui, yōshirui** ferns
8 爬虫類 **hachūrui** reptiles
9 柑橘類 **kankitsurui** citrus fruits
珍無類 **chinmurui** singular, phenomenal, strange
食肉類 **shokunikurui** carnivorous animals
10 哺乳類 **honyūrui** mammal
根菜類 **konsairui** root crops
11 渉禽類 **shōkinrui** wading birds
13 数種類 **sūshurui** several kinds
15 霊長類 **reichōrui** primates
線虫類 **senchūrui** nematodes

—————— 4 ——————

8 担子菌類 **tanshi kinrui** basidiomycetes

9a9.2

顎 顎
GAKU, ago jaw, chin
agito gills

—————— 1 ——————

10 顎骨 **gakkotsu** jawbone
顎紐 **agohimo** chin strap
22 顎鬚 **agohige** beard

—————— 2 ——————

3 上顎 **jōgaku, uwaago** upper jaw; the palate
下顎 **shitaago, kagaku** lower jaw

9a9.3 / 277

顔 顔
GAN, kao face

—————— 1 ——————

5 顔出 **kaoda(shi)** put in an appearance, visit
顔付 **kaotsu(ki)** face, look(s), expression
顔立 **kaoda(chi)** features, looks
6 顔合 **kaoa(wase)** meeting; appearing together
顔色 **kaoiro, ganshoku** complexion; expression
顔汚 **kaoyogo(shi)** disgrace, discredit
顔向 **kaomu(ke)** show one's face
7 顔作 **kaozuku(ri)** makeup
顔役 **kaoyaku** influential man, boss
顔見 **kaomi(se)** show one's face (in public)
顔見知 **kaomishi(ri)** knowing someone by sight, a nodding acquaintance
9 顔負 **kaoma(ke)** be put to shame, be outdone
顔面 **ganmen** the face
10 顔料 **ganryō** pigment; cosmetics
13 顔触 **kaobu(re)** personnel, lineup, cast
19 顔繋 **kaotsuna(gi)** getting acquainted

—————— 2 ——————

3 夕顔 **yūgao** bottle gourd, calabash; moonflower
4 天顔 **tengan** the emperor's countenance
5 幼顔 **osanagao** what one looked like as a baby/tot
古顔 **furugao** familiar face, old-timer
目顔 **megao** a look, expression
6 死顔 **shi(ni)gao** face of a dead person
汗顔 **kangan** sweating from shame
尖顔 **toga(ri)gao** pout
7 作顔 **tsuku(ri)gao** affected look; made-up face
似顔 **nigao** portrait, likeness
似顔絵 **nigaoe** portrait, likeness
対顔 **taigan** face, meet
赤顔 **aka(ra)gao** ruddy/florid face
抜顔 **nu(karanu) kao** a knowing look
呆顔 **aki(re)gao** amazed/dazed look
初顔合 **hatsukaoa(wase)** first meeting
8 厚顔 **kōgan** impudence, effrontery
泣顔 **na(ki)gao** crying/tearful face
拝顔 **haigan** personal meeting
知顔 **shi(ran) kao, shi(ranu) kao** pretending not to know, nonchalant
shi(ri)gao knowing look
9 美顔 **bigan** beautiful face
美顔水 **bigansui** face lotion
美顔術 **biganjutsu** facial treatment

9
頁 9←

紅顔 **kōgan** rosy cheeks, ruddy face
10 真顔 **magao** serious look, straight face
涙顔 **namidagao** tearful face
案顔 **an(ji)gao** worried look
恩顔 **ongan** kindly look, gentle face
破顔 **hagan** broad smile
破顔一笑 **hagan-isshō** break into a grin
竜顔 **ryūgan** the emperor's countenance
素顔 **sugao** face without makeup; sober face
笑顔 **egao, wara(i)gao** smiling face
11 得顔 **e(tari)gao** look of triumph
酔顔 **suigan** drunken face/look
12 温顔 **ongan** kindly face
朝顔 **asagao** morning glory
童顔 **dōgan** childlike/boyish face
13 寝顔 **negao** one's sleeping face
新顔 **shingao** new face, newcomer
誇顔 **hoko(ri)gao** triumphant look
15 横顔 **yokogao** profile, side view, silhouette
憂顔 **ure(i)gao** sorrowful face, troubled look
16 赭顔 **shagan** ruddy face

───────── 3 ─────────
2 人待顔 **hitoma(chi)gao** look of expectation
4 手柄顔 **tegaragao** triumphant look
心得顔 **kokoroegao** a knowing look
6 瓜実顔 **urizanegao** oval/classic face
地蔵顔 **jizōgao** plump cheerful face
自慢顔 **jimangao** boastful look
7 我物顔 **wa(ga)monogao** as if one's own
何食顔 **naniku(wanu) kao** innocent look
8 物知顔 **monoshi(ri)gao** knowing look
所得顔 **tokoroegao** triumph, elation
10 素知顔 **soshi(ranu) kao** innocent look
11 得意顔 **tokuigao** triumphant look

───────── 4 ─────────
10 恵比須顔 **ebisugao** smiling/beaming face

9a9.4

頤 SAI, ago, agito jaw
era gills

9a9.5 / 1170

顕 顯 KEN clear, plain, obvious
ara(wareru) appear, become
evident **ara(wasu)** show,
exhibit, manifest

───────── 1 ─────────
5 顕正 **kenshō** spreading the (religious) truth
顕示 **kenji** show, unveil, reveal
6 顕在 **kenzai** revealed, actual (cf. 潜在)
7 顕花植物 **kenka shokubutsu** flowering plant
8 顕宗 **Kenzō** (emperor, 485–487)
顕官 **kenkan** high official, dignitary

9 顕要 **ken'yō** prominent, important
11 顕著 **kencho** notable, striking, marked
顕現 **kengen** manifestation
12 顕揚 **ken'yō** extol, exalt
顕然 **kenzen** obvious, manifest, clear, conspicuous, prominent
13 顕微鏡 **kenbikyō** microscope
14 顕彰 **kenshō** manifest, exhibit, display
18 顕職 **kenshoku** important post

───────── 2 ─────────
12 超顕微鏡 **chōkenbikyō** ultramicroscope
貴顕 **kiken** distinguished personage, dignitaries
13 隠顕 **inken** appear then disappear (repeatedly)
21 露顕 **roken** be found out, come to light

───────── 3 ─────────
10 破邪顕正 **haja-kenshō** smiting evil and spreading the truth

9a9.6 / 838

額 GAKU amount; framed picture
hitai forehead

───────── 1 ─────────
5 額付 **hitaitsu(ki)** (form of one's) brow, forehead
8 額突 **nukazu(ku)** bow low, kowtow
9 額面 **gakumen** face value, par
13 額際 **hitaigiwa** hairline
15 額縁 **gakubuchi** picture frame

───────── 2 ─────────
3 小額 **shōgaku** small amount
4 少額 **shōgaku** small amount
月額 **getsugaku** monthly amount
5 半額 **hangaku** half the amount/price
巨額 **kyogaku** enormous amount, vast sum
6 多額 **tagaku** large sum/amount
年額 **nengaku** annual amount
全額 **zengaku** the full amount
同額 **dōgaku** the same amount
7 低額 **teigaku** small amount
8 価額 **kagaku** value, amount, price
定額 **teigaku** fixed amount, flat sum
金額 **kingaku** amount of money
9 前額 **zengaku** forehead
扁額 **hengaku** framed picture
10 残額 **zangaku** remaining amount, balance
倍額 **baigaku** double the amount
高額 **kōgaku** large amount
11 猫額 **neko (no) hitai, nekobitai, byōgaku** (small as a) cat's forehead
産額 **sangaku** output, yield, production
12 減額 **gengaku** reduction, cut

14 増額 **zōgaku** increase (the amount)
　総額 **sōgaku** total amount

――――――― 3 ―――――――

4 支出額 **shishutsugaku** (amount of) expenditures
8 奉納額 **hōnōgaku** votive tablet
　送金額 **sōkingaku** amount remitted
　所得額 **shotokugaku** (amount of) income
10 残余額 **zan'yogaku** balance, remainder
　納税額 **nōzeigaku** amount of tax (to be) paid
12 割当額 **wariategaku** allotment
　超過額 **chōkagaku** surplus, excess
　富士額 **fujibitai** hairline resembling the outline of Mt. Fuji
15 請求額 **seikyūgaku** the amount claimed/billed

顔 → 顔 9a9.3

9a9.7 / 354

題   **DAI** subject, topic, theme; title

――――――― 1 ―――――――

0 題する **dai(suru)** entitle
5 題号 **daigō** title
　題句 **daiku** epigraph
　題字 **daiji** prefatory phrase
　題目 **daimoku** title; topic; the Nichiren prayer "*namumyōhōrengekyō*"
6 題名 **daimei** title
7 題材 **daizai** subject matter, theme
　題言 **daigen** prefatory phrase, title
8 題画 **daiga** picture bearing a poem or phrase
13 題意 **daii** meaning of the subject
　題辞 **daiji** prefatory phrase, epigraph
19 題簽 **daisen** (pasted-in insert bearing a book's) title

――――――― 2 ―――――――

4 文題 **bundai** theme, subject
5 出題 **shutsudai** propose a question, set a problem
　本題 **hondai** the main issue/subject
　外題 **gedai** title (of a play); play, piece
　好題目 **kōdaimoku** good topic
　主題 **shudai** theme, subject matter
　主題歌 **shudaika** theme song
6 名題 **nadai** chief actor, star; title of a play
7 即題 **sokudai** subject for improvisation; impromptu composition; (math) problem for immediate solution
　改題 **kaidai** retitle, rename
　季題 **kidai** seasonal theme (in haiku)
8 表題 **hyōdai** title, heading, caption

画題 **gadai** subject/title of a painting
例題 **reidai** example, exercise (in a textbook)
命題 **meidai** proposition, thesis
放題 **-hōdai** (as verb suffix) as much as one pleases, all you can (eat)
9 勅題 **chokudai** theme of the New Year's Imperial Poetry Competition
　首題 **shudai** first topic
10 兼題 **kendai** subject for a poem
11 副題 **fukudai** subtitle, subheading
　探題 **tandai** picking poem themes by lottery; commissioner (historical)
　宿題 **shukudai** homework
　問題 **mondai** problem, question, issue
　問題外 **mondaigai** beside the point, irrelevant
　問題児 **mondaiji** problem child
　問題点 **mondaiten** the point at issue
12 御題 **gyodai** theme of the New Year's imperial poetry contest
　御題目 **odaimoku** Nichiren prayer
　無題 **mudai** untitled
13 解題 **kaidai** bibliographical notes
　話題 **wadai** topic, subject
14 演題 **endai** subject of a speech
　歌題 **kadai** title of a poem
　雑題 **zatsudai** miscellaneous topics
15 標題 **hyōdai** title, heading, caption
　課題 **kadai** subject, theme, topic, problem; (school) assignment
　論題 **rondai** topic, subject, theme
18 鎖題 **kusaridai** composing poems in which the last word of one is the first word of the next
　難題 **nandai** difficult topic/problem
　類題 **ruidai** (classified by) similar themes; similar question
20 議題 **gidai** topic for discussion, agenda

――――――― 3 ―――――――

5 出放題 **dehōdai** free flow; saying whatever comes to mind
　仕放題 **shihōdai** have one's own way
　好放題 **su(ki)hōdai** doing just as one pleases
7 別問題 **betsumondai** another question, a different story
8 性問題 **sei mondai** sex problem
　取放題 **to(ri)hōdai** all-you-can-take
9 荒放題 **a(re)hōdai** left to go to ruin
　食放題 **ta(be)hōdai, ku(i)hōdai** eating as much as one pleases, all-you-can-eat
15 諸問題 **shomondai** various questions
18 難問題 **nanmondai** difficult problem

――――――― 4 ―――――――

6 死活問題 **shikatsu mondai** a matter of life and death

9

頁 9 ←

先決問題 **senketsu mondai** question to be settled first
7 応用問題 **ōyō mondai** problem to test ability to apply theoretical knowledge
言成放題 **i(i)na(ri) hōdai** submissive to (someone)
12 無理難題 **muri-nandai** unreasonable demand

─────────── 10 ───────────

類→類 9a9.1

9a10.1

顛 顛
          TEN overturn; summit; origin

─────────── 1 ───────────
5 顛末 **tenmatsu** circumstances, facts
8 顛沛 **tenpai** stumbling and falling; moment, instant
10 顛倒 **tentō** fall down; turn upside down
18 顛覆 **tenpuku** overturn

─────────── 3 ───────────
5 主客顛倒 **shukaku-tentō** reverse order, putting the cart before the horse
9 造次顛沛 **zōji-tenpai** a moment

9a10.2 / 581

願
         GAN, nega(u) petition, request, desire

─────────── 1 ───────────
2 願力 **ganriki** the power of prayer
3 願下 **nega(i)sa(geru)** withdraw a request
5 願出 **nega(i)de(ru)** apply for
願叶 **nega(ttari)-kana(ttari)** just what one has been wanting
8 願事 **nega(i)goto** one's wish/prayer
10 願書 **gansho** written request, application
11 願掛 **ganga(ke)** say a prayer
願望 **ganbō, ganmō** wish, desire

─────────── 2 ───────────
3 大願 **taigan** ambition, aspiration; earnest wish
4 切願 **setsugan** entreaty, supplication, appeal
心願 **shingan** heartfelt desire; prayer
5 出願 **shutsugan** application
本願 **hongan** long-cherished desire; Amida Buddha's original vow
立願 **ritsugan** offer a prayer (to a god)
7 志願者 **shigansha** applicant, candidate, volunteer, aspirant
志願書 **shigansho** (written) application

8 依願免官 **igan menkan** retirement at one's own request
念願 **nengan** one's heart's desire, earnest wish
祈願 **kigan** a prayer
所願 **shogan** desire, wish, request
9 勅願 **chokugan** imperial prayer
哀願 **aigan** entreat, implore, petition
11 宿願 **shukugan** long-cherished desire
12 満願 **mangan** fulfillment of a vow
悲願 **higan** Buddhist prayer for mankind; earnest wish
結願 **kechigan, ketsugan** expiration of a vow
訴願 **sogan** petition, appeal
訴願人 **sogannin** petitioner, appellant
13 嘆願 **tangan** entreaty, petition
14 歎願 **tangan** petition, appeal
歎願書 **tangansho** written petition
誓願 **seigan** oath, vow, pledge
15 熱願 **netsugan** fervent plea, earnest entreaty
請願 **seigan** petition, application
請願者 **seigansha** petitioner, applicant
請願書 **seigansho** (written) petition
17 懇願 **kongan** entreaty, earnest appeal
懇願者 **kongansha** supplicant, petitioner

─────────── 3 ───────────
2 入学願書 **nyūgaku gansho** application for admission
6 西本願寺 **Nishi Honganji** (main temple, in Kyōto, of Jōdo sect)
13 辞職願 **jishoku nega(i)** letter of resignation

─────────── 4 ───────────
6 自力本願 **jiriki hongan** salvation by works

─────────── 12 ───────────

9a12.1

顥
         KŌ white; clear, bright

9a12.2 / 1554

顧 顧
         KO, kaeri(miru) look back; take into consideration

─────────── 1 ───────────
9 顧客 **kokaku, kokyaku** customer
11 顧問 **komon** adviser
顧問医 **komon'i** medical adviser
顧問官 **komonkan** councilor
15 顧慮 **koryo** regard, consideration

─────────── 2 ───────────
1 一顧 **ikko** (take no) notice of
3 三顧礼 **sanko (no) rei** special confidence (in someone)

5 左顧右眄 **sako-uben** irresolution, vacillation
右顧左眄 **uko-saben** look right and left;
vacillate, waver
四顧 **shiko** look all around
6 回顧 **kaiko** recollect, look back on
回顧的 **kaikoteki** retrospective
回顧録 **kaikoroku** memoirs, reminiscences
9 後顧憂 **kōko (no) ure(i)** anxiety about those
left behind after one is gone
10 恩顧 **onko** favors, patronage
11 眷顧 **kenko** favor, patronage
13 愛顧 **aiko** patronage, favor

——————— 3 ———————
9 軍事顧問 **gunji komon** military adviser

9a12.3
嚻
GŌ, kamabisu(shii) noisy, clamorous

——————— 3 ———————
12 喧々嚻々 **kenken-gōgō** pandemonium

——————— 13 ———————

9a13.1
顫
SEN, furu(eru) tremble

9a13.2
鬚
SHU, hige beard (on the chin)

——————— 2 ———————
8 虎鬚 **torahige** bristly mustache/beard
18 顎鬚 **agohige** beard

——————— 3 ———————
3 山羊鬚 **yagihige** goatee

——————— 14 ———————

9a14.1
顬
JU the temple (side of head)

——————— 2 ———————
27 顳顬 **komekami** the temple(s)

顯 → 顕 9a9.5

——————— 15 ———————
9a15.1
顰
HIN, shika(meru) screw (one's face)
into a frown/scowl/grimace
hiso(meru) knit (one's brow)
hiso(mi) scowl, frown

——————— 1 ———————
9 顰面 **shika(met)tsura, shika(me)zura**
frown, scowl
10 顰倣 **hiso(mi ni) nara(u)** slavishly imitate
18 顰蹙 **hinshuku** frown on, disdain

——————— 16 ———————
9a16.1
顱
RO skull

——————— 1 ———————
11 顱頂骨 **rochōkotsu** parietal bone

——————— 17 ———————
9a17.1
顴
KEN, KAN cheekbone

——————— 1 ———————
10 顴骨 **kankotsu, kenkotsu** cheekbone

——————— 18 ———————
9a18.1
顳
SHŌ the temple (side of head)

——————— 1 ———————
23 顳顬 **komekami** the temple(s)

頁 18←

————————— 馬 **10a** —————————

馬	馭	馳	馴	駄	駁	駮	駅	駆	駛	駈	駐	駝
0.1	2.1	3.1	3.2	4.1	4.2	4.3	4.4	4.5	5.1	10a4.5	5.2	5.3

駘	駒	駟	駕	駑	駻	駱	駮	駭	駢	駿	騁	騂
5.4	5.5	5.6	5.7	5.8	2f4.1	6.2	6.3	6.4	6.5	7.1	7.2	7.3

駸	雛	騏	騎	驗	騒	騨	騙	騰	騷	驃	驂	騾
7.4	8.1	8.2	8.3	8.4	8.5	10a12.3	9.1	4b16.3	10a8.5	11.1	11.2	11.3

驅	驍	驕	驛	驚	驛	驗	驟	羈	驥	驢	驩	驤
10a4.5	12.1	12.2	12.3	12.4	10a4.4	10a8.4	14.1	5g19.1	16.1	16.2	17.1	17.2

驪	驫
19.1	20.1

─────── 0 ───────

10a0.1 / 283

馬

BA, uma, ma horse

─────── 1 ───────

2 馬丁 **batei** groom, footman, stable hand
　馬子 **mago** passenger/pack horse tender
　馬刀貝 **mategai** razor clam
　馬力 **bariki** horsepower
3 馬上 **bajō** on horseback, mounted
　馬小屋 **umagoya** a stable
4 馬匹 **bahitsu** horses
　馬引 **umahi(ki)** pack-horse tender
　馬方 **umakata** pack-horse tender
5 馬市 **umaichi** horse market
　馬主 **bashu** horse owner
6 馬肉 **baniku** horsemeat
　馬印 **umajirushi** (ancient) commander's standard
　馬返 **umagae(shi)** the place on a mountain road too steep to go further on horseback
　馬回 **umamawa(ri)** daimyo's mounted guards
　馬耳東風 **bajitōfū** utter indifference, turn a deaf ear
7 馬身 **bashin** a horse's length
　馬学 **bagaku** hippology
　馬車 **basha** horse-drawn carriage
　馬足 **uma (no) ashi** poor actor (who plays the legs of a stage horse)
8 馬券 **baken** horse-race betting ticket
　馬追 **umao(i)** horse driver; katydid
　馬肥 **umago(yashi)** burr clover, medic
　馬具 **bagu** harness, horse gear
　馬具師 **bagushi** harness maker, saddler
9 馬乗 **umano(ri)** horseback riding
　馬首 **bashu** horse's head
　馬革 **bakaku** horsehide
　馬屋 **umaya** a stable
　馬屋肥 **umayago(e)** horse manure
　馬面 **umazura** horse face
　馬食 **bashoku** eating like a horse
10 馬耕 **bakō** tilling with a horse-drawn harrow
　馬骨 **uma (no) hone** person of unknown origin, stranger, Joe Blow

11 馬術 **bajutsu** horseback riding, dressage
　馬鹿 **baka** fool, idiot, stupid; to a ridiculous degree
　馬脚 **bakyaku** horse's legs; one's true character
12 馬場 **baba** riding ground
13 馬賊 **bazoku** mounted bandits
　馬跳 **umato(bi)** leapfrog
　馬鈴薯 **bareisho** (white/Irish) potato
14 馬銜 **hami** horse's bit
16 馬橇 **basori** horse-drawn sleigh
　馬蹄 **batei** horse's hoof
　馬蹄形 **bateikei** horseshoe shape
　馬頭観音 **batōkannon** image of the god Kannon with a horse's head
17 馬糞 **bafun, maguso** horse manure
　馬糞紙 **bafunshi** cardboard, strawboard
　馬齢 **barei** one's age
　馬鍬 **maguwa** harrow, rake
18 馬糧 **baryō** fodder
19 馬蠅 **umabae** horsefly

─────── 2 ───────

2 人馬 **jinba** men and horses
3 大馬鹿 **ōbaka** big fool
　下馬 **geba** dismount
　下馬評 **gebahyō** outsiders' irresponsible talk, rumor
　弓馬 **kyūba** bow and horse; archery and horsemanship
　小馬 **kouma** pony, colt
　小馬鹿 **kobaka** a fool
4 天馬 **tenba** flying horse, Pegasus
　辻馬車 **tsujibasha** cab, hansom
　犬馬 **kenba** my humble self
　木馬 **mokuba** wooden/rocking/carrousel/ gymnastics horse
　牛馬 **gyūba** horses and cattle/oxen
5 出馬 **shutsuba** ride into battle; go in person; run for election
　生馬 **i(ki)uma** (sharp and wily enough to pluck the eyes out of) a living horse
　穴馬 **anauma** darkhorse, longshot
　尻馬乗 **shiriuma (ni) no(ru)** imitate/follow blindly
　白馬 **hakuba, shirouma** white horse
6 曲馬 **kyokuba** equestrian feats; circus

曲馬団 **kyokubadan** circus troupe
曲馬師 **kyokubashi** circus stunt rider
伝馬 **tenma, denba** post-horse
伝馬船 **tenmasen** a lighter, jolly (boat)
老馬 **rōba** old horse
汗馬 **kanba** sweating horse
名馬 **meiba** fine horse/steed
当馬 **a(te)uma** stallion brought near a mare to
test readiness to mate; stalking horse (for
another candidate); spoiler (candidate)
早馬 **hayauma** post horse, steed
竹馬 **takeuma, chikuba** stilts
竹馬友 **chikuba (no) tomo** childhood
playmate
7 但馬 **Tajima** (ancient kuni, Hyōgo-ken)
対馬 **Tsushima** (island and ancient kuni,
Nagasaki-ken)
対馬海峡 **Tsushima-kaikyō** Tsushima Strait
(between Tsushima and Iki Island)
走馬灯 **sōmatō** (like a) revolving lantern,
kaleidoscopic
牡馬 **ouma** male horse, stallion
車馬 **shaba** horses and vehicles
車馬代 **shabadai** traveling expenses
車馬道 **shabadō** road for vehicles and
horses
車馬賃 **shabachin** fare, transportation
expenses
8 兎馬 **usagiuma** donkey
奔馬 **honba** galloping/runaway horse
河馬 **kaba** hippopotamus
青馬 **aouma** dark horse with a lustrous coat
9 乗馬 **jōba, no(ri)uma** horseback riding;
riding horse
乗馬靴 **jōbagutsu** riding boots
俊馬 **shunme, shunba** fine horse
軍馬 **gunba** warhorse, charger
風馬牛 **fūbagyū** indifferent, of no concern;
widely disparate
海馬 **kaiba** sea horse
荒馬 **arauma** untamed horse
神馬 **shinme** sacred horse
10 荷馬 **niuma** pack/draft horse
荷馬車 **nibasha** dray, wagon, cart
唐馬 **karauma** (ancient) foreign horse
悍馬 **kanba** unruly/mettlesome horse
竜馬 **ryūme** splendid horse/steed
11 野馬 **nouma** wild horse
産馬 **sanba** horse breeding
12 落馬 **rakuba** fall from one's horse
廃馬 **haiba** worn-out horse, jade
替馬 **ka(e)uma** spare horse
斑馬 **madara uma** piebald horse; zebra
絵馬 **ema** votive tablet (bearing a horse's
picture)

貸馬車 **ka(shi)basha** carriage for hire
雄馬 **ouma** stallion
13 催馬楽 **saibara** (type of *gagaku* song)
群馬県 **Gunma-ken** (prefecture)
幌馬車 **horobasha** covered wagon/carriage
愛馬 **aiba** one's favorite horse
意馬心猿 **iba-shin'en** (uncontrollable)
passions
新馬 **shinba** new/unbroken horse
裸馬 **hadakauma** unsaddled horse
頓馬 **tonma** fool, nitwit
14 種馬 **taneuma** stud horse, sire
練馬大根 **Nerima daikon** daikon (grown in
Nerima, Tōkyō); woman's fat legs
雌馬 **meuma** mare
駄馬 **daba** pack horse
駅馬車 **ekibasha** stagecoach
15 鞍馬 **anba** pommel/side horse (gymnastics
apparatus)
暴馬 **aba(re)uma** restive/runaway horse
箱馬車 **hakobasha** closed carriage
調馬 **chōba** horse breaking/training
調馬師 **chōbashi** horse trainer
調馬場 **chōbajō** riding ground
駑馬 **doba** worn-out horse, jade
16 薄馬鹿 **usubaka** fool, simpleton, half-wit
親馬鹿 **oyabaka** overfond parent
縞馬 **shimauma** zebra
17 駿馬 **shunme** fine horse, swift steed
駻馬 **kanba** unruly horse
18 騎馬 **kiba** on horseback, mounted
騎馬戦 **kibasen** cavalry battle
19 羅馬 **Rōma** Rome
20 競馬 **keiba** horse race/racing
競馬馬 **keiba uma** race horse
競馬場 **keibajō** race track
21 騾馬 **raba** mule
26 驢馬 **roba** donkey

──────────── 3 ────────────
4 牛飲馬食 **gyūin-bashoku** heavy eating and
drinking
5 四月馬鹿 **shigatsu baka** April fool
7 対抗馬 **taikōba** rival horse; rival candidate
8 弥次馬 **yajiuma** bystanders, spectators,
crowd of onlookers
9 草競馬 **kusakeiba** local horse race
10 流鏑馬 **yabusame** horseback archery
13 鉄道馬車 **tetsudō basha** horse-drawn
streetcar
20 競馬馬 **keiba uma** race horse

──────────── 4 ────────────
6 回転木馬 **kaiten mokuba** carrousel
9 南船北馬 **nansen-hokuba** constant traveling,
restless wandering

10

馬 0←

—————— 2 ——————

10a2.1

馭

GYO ride/drive (a horse)

—————— 1 ——————

8 馭法 **gyohō** horsemanship
   馭者 **gyosha** driver, coachman

—————— 3 ——————

10a3.1

馳

CHI, ha(seru) run, gallop; win (fame)

—————— 1 ——————

7 馳走 **(go)chisō** feast, treat, entertainment, hospitality
8 馳参 **ha(se)san(jiru)** hurry to
12 馳集 **ha(se)atsu(maru)** run/ride together to, flock to

—————— 2 ——————

9 後馳 **oku(re)ba(se)** belated, last-minute
   背馳 **haichi** be contrary to
12 御馳走 **gochisō** feast, banquet, treat, hospitality

10a3.2

馴

JUN, na(reru) get used to
na(rasu) tame, train

—————— 1 ——————

0 馴れっこ **na(rekko)** used to
4 馴化 **junka** acclimate
6 馴合 **na(re)a(u)** collude; become intimate with
7 馴初 **na(re)so(me)** beginning of a romance
9 馴染 **naji(mi)** familiar
11 馴鹿 **tonakai** reindeer
13 馴馴 **na(re)na(reshii)** (too) familiar

—————— 2 ——————

2 人馴 **hitona(re)** be used to people
3 下馴 **shitanara(shi)** training, warming up
   口馴 **kuchina(rashi)** oral drill
4 不馴 **funa(re)** inexperienced in, unfamiliar with
   手馴 **tena(reru)** get used to, become practiced in
5 世馴 **yona(reru)** get used to the world, become worldly-wise
   幼馴染 **osana najimi** childhood playmate
7 見馴 **mina(reru)** get used to seeing, be familiar to
   足馴 **ashina(rashi)** walking practice
8 昔馴染 **mukashinaji(mi)** old friend

物馴 **monona(reru)** be used to, be experienced in, be at ease in
9 乗馴 **no(ri)na(rasu)** break in (a horse)
12 場馴 **bana(re)** used to (the stage), experience
13 飼馴 **ka(i)na(rasu)** domesticate, tame
   馴馴 **na(re)na(reshii)** (too) familiar
14 聞馴 **ki(ki)na(reru)** get used to hearing
17 磯馴松 **sonarematsu** seashore pine (wind-blown to the contours of the terrain)

—————— 4 ——————

10a4.1 / 1880

駄

DA, TA pack horse; of poor quality

—————— 1 ——————

3 駄々 **dada (o koneru)** wheedle, ask for the impossible
   駄々子 **dada(k)ko** peevish/spoiled child
4 駄文 **dabun** poor piece of writing
5 駄弁 **daben** foolish talk, bunk
   駄句 **daku** poor poem, doggerel
   駄目 **dame** no good
7 駄作 **dasaku** poor work, worthless stuff
8 駄法螺 **dabora** bragging
   駄物 **damono** low-grade goods, trash
10 駄洒落 **dajare** lame pun, corny joke
   駄馬 **daba** pack horse
11 駄菓子 **dagashi** cheap candy
13 駄賃 **dachin** reward, tip

—————— 2 ——————

3 下駄 **geta** clogs
   下駄履住宅 **getaba(ki) jūtaku** apartment building whose first floor is occupied by stores and businesses
   下駄箱 **getabako** shoe cabinet
7 足駄 **ashida** high clogs
10 韋駄天 **Idaten** Skanda, the fleet-footed god
   荷駄 **nida** horseload, pack
11 雪駄 **setta** leather-soled sandals
12 無駄 **muda** futile, useless, wasteful
   無駄口 **mudaguchi** idle talk, prattle
   無駄死 **mudaji(ni)** die in vain
   無駄花 **mudabana** flower which bears no seed/fruit
   無駄足 **mudaashi** make a fruitless trip/visit
   無駄食 **mudagu(i)** eat between meals; eat but not work, live in idleness
   無駄骨 **mudabone** wasted/vain effort
   無駄骨折 **mudaboneo(ri)** wasted/vain effort
   無駄遣 **mudazuka(i)** waste, squander
   無駄飯 **mudameshi** eat but not work, live in idleness
   無駄話 **mudabanashi** idle talk, gossip

14 駄駄 **dada (o koneru)** wheedle, ask for the
impossible
駄駄子 **dada(k)ko** peevish/spoiled child

──────── 3 ────────

6 地団駄踏 **jidanda (o) fu(mu)** stamp one's feet
9 庭下駄 **niwageta** garden clogs
10 高下駄 **takageta** high clogs/geta
高足駄 **takaashida** high clogs/geta
15 駒下駄 **komageta** low clogs

10a4.2

BUN, MON red-maned yellow-eyed
zebra

10a4.3

BAKU speckled, piebald; refutation

──────── 1 ────────

15 駁撃 **bakugeki** argue against, attack, refute
駁論 **bakuron** refutation, rebuttal

──────── 2 ────────

4 反駁 **hanbaku, hanpaku** refutation, rebuttal
5 弁駁 **benpaku** refutation
14 雑駁 **zappaku** incoherent, desultory
15 論駁 **ronbaku** refute, argue against

──────── 4 ────────

5 甲論乙駁 **kōron-otsubaku** pros and cons

10a4.4 / 284

駅 驛

EKI (train) station

──────── 1 ────────

4 駅夫 **ekifu** station hand, porter
駅手 **ekishu** station hand
5 駅弁 **ekiben** box lunch sold at a train station
6 駅伝 **ekiden** post horse, stagecoach; long-
distance relay race
駅伝競走 **ekiden kyōsō** long-distance relay
race
7 駅売 **ekiu(ri)** sold/vendor at a station
8 駅長 **ekichō** stationmaster
駅舎 **ekisha** station building
9 駅前 **ekimae** in front of the station
駅逓 **ekitei** postal service
10 駅員 **ekiin** station employee/staff
駅留 **ekido(me)** to-the-station delivery
駅馬車 **ekibasha** stagecoach
13 駅路 **ekiro** post road
16 駅頭 **ekitō** at the station

──────── 2 ────────

6 各駅 **kakueki** every station

各駅停車 **kakuekiteisha** local train
9 発駅 **hatsueki** starting station
11 宿駅 **shukueki** post town, relay station
12 着駅 **chakueki** destination station

──────── 3 ────────

4 中間駅 **chūkan eki** intermediate station
8 到着駅 **tōchakueki** arrival/destination station
9 通過駅 **tsūka eki** station at which the train
does not stop
11 終着駅 **shūchakueki** terminal station
貨物駅 **kamotsueki** freight depot

10a4.5 / 1882

駆 驅 駈

KU, ka(keru) gallop;
run, rush
ka(ru) drive, spur on

──────── 1 ────────

0 駆けっこ **ka(kekko)** (foot)race
3 駆上 **ka(ke)a(garu)** run up(stairs)
駆下 **ka(ke)o(riru), ka(ke)kuda(ru)** run
down(stairs)
4 駆込 **ka(ke)ko(mu)** rush into, seek refuge in
駆引 **ka(ke)hi(ki)** bargaining, haggling,
maneuvering
5 駆出 **ka(ke)da(su)** rush out, start running
ka(ke)da(shi) beginner
ka(ri)da(su) round up, muster
駆付 **ka(ke)tsu(keru)** rush/hurry to
駆巡 **ka(ke)megu(ru)** run around
駆立 **ka(ri)ta(teru)** round up; spur on
ka(ke)ta(tsu) gallop after, pursue
6 駆回 **ka(ke)mawa(ru), ka(kezuri)mawa(ru)**
run around
駆虫剤 **kuchūzai** vermicide, insect repellent
駆虫薬 **kuchūyaku** vermicide, insect
repellent
7 駆抜 **ka(ke)nu(keru)** run through (a gate)
駆足 **ka(ke)ashi** running, galloping
8 駆使 **kushi** have at one's command
9 駆除 **kujo** exterminate
駆除剤 **kujozai** expellent; insecticide
駆逐 **kuchiku** drive away, expel, get rid of
駆逐艦 **kuchikukan** destroyer
11 駆寄 **ka(ke)yo(ru)** rush up to
12 駆落 **ka(ke)o(chi)** elope
駆集 **ka(ri)atsu(meru)** muster, round up
15 駆潜艇 **kusentei** submarine chaser

──────── 2 ────────

6 先駆 **sakiga(ke)** the lead/initiative
先駆者 **senkusha** forerunner, pioneer
7 抜駆 **nu(ke)ga(ke)** steal a march on, forestall,
scoop
8 長駆 **chōku** ride a great distance, make a long
march
9 前駆 **zenku** vanguard, forerunner, precursor

10

馬 4 ←

10 疾駆 **shikku** ride/drive fast, dash along
12 遠駆 **tōga(ke)** long gallop/march
　朝駆 **asaga(ke)** attack at dawn

─────────── 5 ───────────

10a5.1

駛

SHI, ha(seru) run fast, gallop

駈 → 駆 10a4.5

10a5.2 / 599

駐

CHŪ be resident/stationed in; stop

─────────── 1 ───────────
4 駐屯 **chūton** be stationed/quartered
　駐屯地 **chūtonchi** (army) post
　駐仏 **chū-Futsu** resident/stationed in France
　駐日 **chū-Nichi** resident/stationed in Japan
6 駐在 **chūzai** stay, residence
　駐在所 **chūzaisho** police substation
　駐米 **chū-Bei** resident/stationed in America
7 駐兵 **chūhei** station troops
　駐車 **chūsha** parking
　駐車場 **chūshajō** parking lot
8 駐英 **chū-Ei** resident/stationed in Britain
9 駐独 **chū-Doku** resident/stationed in Germany
10 駐留 **chūryū** stationing (of troops)
　駐留軍 **chūryūgun** stationed/occupying
　　troops
15 駐輪場 **chūrinjō** bicycle parking lot
─────────── 2 ───────────
10 進駐 **shinchū** stationing, occupation
　進駐軍 **shinchūgun** army of occupation
11 常駐 **jōchū** permanently stationed
　移駐 **ichū** move, transfer

10a5.3

駝

DA camel; ostrich

─────────── 1 ───────────
11 駝鳥 **dachō** ostrich
─────────── 2 ───────────
16 駱駝 **rakuda** camel

10a5.4

駘

TAI dull-witted; mild

─────────── 1 ───────────
15 駘蕩 **taitō** mild, genial, balmy (spring
　breezes)

10a5.5

駒

KU, koma colt, pony; (shōgi) chessman;
(samisen) fret, bridge; frame (of a film)

─────────── 1 ───────────
3 駒下駄 **komageta** low clogs
11 駒鳥 **komadori** robin
─────────── 2 ───────────
4 手駒 **tegoma** captured shōgi piece (kept in
　reserve)

10a5.6

駟

SHI four-horse carriage

10a5.7

駑

DO slow/stupid horse

─────────── 1 ───────────
10 駑馬 **doba** worn-out horse, jade
12 駑鈍 **dodon** dull-witted, doltish

10a5.8

駕

GA, KA vehicle

─────────── 1 ───────────
22 駕籠 **kago** palanquin, litter
─────────── 2 ───────────
3 山駕籠 **yamakago** mountain palanquin
4 辻駕籠 **tsujikago** palanquin/litter for hire
6 早駕籠 **hayakago** express palanquin
10 凌駕 **ryōga** surpass, excel, outdo

─────────── 6 ───────────

駲 → 州 2f4.1

10a6.2

駱

RAKU black-maned white horse;
camel

─────────── 1 ───────────
15 駱駝 **rakuda** camel

10a6.3

駮　HAKU mottled, spotted

10a6.4

駭　GAI be surprised

───────── 2 ─────────

15 震駭 **shingai** fright, alarm, terror

10a6.5

駢　HEN, BEN two-horse carriage; line up with

───────── 1 ─────────

21 駢儷体 **benreitai** flowery ancient Chinese prose style

───────── 7 ─────────

10a7.1

駿　SHUN a fine horse; swiftness; excellence

───────── 1 ─────────

7 駿足 **shunsoku** swift horse; person of exceptional talent
8 駿河 **Suruga** (ancient kuni, Shizuoka-ken)
10 駿馬 **shunme** fine horse, swift steed

10a7.2

騁　TEI run fast, gallop; as one pleases

10a7.3

駻　KAN unruly horse

───────── 1 ─────────

10 駻馬 **kanba** unruly horse

10a7.4

駸　SHIN fast, swift

───────── 1 ─────────

3 駸々 **shinshin** rapidly, in great strides

───────── 8 ─────────

10a8.1

騅　SUI gray horse

10a8.2

騏　KI fast horse

───────── 1 ─────────

26 騏驥 **kiki** horse which can run a thousand leagues in a day

10a8.3 / 1881

騎　KI horse riding; (counter for horsemen)

───────── 1 ─────────

3 騎士 **kishi** rider, horseman
　騎士道 **kishidō** knighthood, chivalry
4 騎手 **kishu** rider, jockey
6 騎行 **kikō** go on horseback
7 騎兵 **kihei** cavalry(man)
8 騎虎勢 **kiko (no) ikio(i)** unable to stop/quit
9 騎乗 **kijō** mounted, on horseback
10 騎射 **kisha** equestrian archery
　騎馬 **kiba** on horseback, mounted
　騎馬戦 **kibasen** cavalry battle
14 騎銃 **kijū** carbine

───────── 2 ─────────

1 一騎 **ikki** one horseman
　一騎打 **ikkiu(chi)** man-to-man combat
　一騎当千 **ikki-tōsen** matchless, mighty
10 従騎 **jūki** mounted attendants/retinue
12 軽騎兵 **keikihei** light cavalry(man)
14 槍騎兵 **sōkihei** lancer

10a8.4 / 532

験 驗　KEN effect; testing
　　　GEN beneficial effect
　　　shirushi sign, indication; effect, benefit

───────── 1 ─────────

14 験算 **kenzan** verification of accounts, checking the figures

───────── 2 ─────────

6 先験的 **senkenteki** transcendental, a priori
7 体験 **taiken** experience
　体験談 **taikendan** story of one's personal experiences
8 効験 **kōken** efficacy
　受験 **juken** take an examination
　受験生 **jukensei** student preparing for exams
　受験者 **jukensha** examinee
　受験科 **jukenka** exam-coaching course
　受験料 **jukenryō** examination fee
　受験票 **jukenhyō** examination admission ticket
　実験 **jikken** experiment

10

馬 8←

実験的 **jikkenteki** experimental, empirical
実験者 **jikkensha** experimenter
実験所 **jikkenjo** experiment station
実験室 **jikkenshitsu** laboratory
実験場 **jikkenjō** proving/testing ground
10 修験者 **shugenja** ascetic mountain-dwelling monk
11 経験 **keiken** experience
経験的 **keikenteki** experiential, empirical
経験者 **keikensha** experienced person
経験則 **keikensoku** rule of thumb
経験談 **keikendan** account of one's experiences
経験論 **keikenron** empiricism
13 試験 **shiken** examination, test; experiment, test
試験地獄 **shiken jigoku** the hell of (entrance) exams
試験官 **shikenkan** examiner
試験的 **shikenteki** experimental, tentative
試験紙 **shikenshi** litmus paper
試験場 **shikenjō** examination hall; laboratory, proving grounds
試験管 **shikenkan** test tube
15 霊験 **reigen(arataka)** wonder-working, marvelously efficacious

——————— 3 ———————
5 未経験 **mikeiken** unexperienced
未経験者 **mikeikensha** person having no experience
6 再試験 **saishiken** make-up exam, retesting
8 追試験 **tsuishiken** supplementary/makeup exam
10 核実験 **kakujikken** nuclear testing
12 無経験 **mukeiken** inexperience
無試験 **mushiken** without an examination

——————— 4 ———————
2 入学試験 **nyūgaku shiken** entrance exams
12 検定試験 **kentei shiken** (teacher) certification examination
14 模擬試験 **mogi shiken** trial examination

10a8.5 / 875

騒 騷   SŌ, **sawa(gu)** make a noise/fuss **zawame(ku), zawatsu(ku)** be noisy

——————— 1 ———————
2 騒人 **sōjin** man of letters, poet
3 騒々 **sōzō(shii), zawazawa** noisy, clamorous
5 騒立 **sawa(gi)ta(teru)** raise a big fuss/furor **sawa(gi)ta(tsu)** be agitated
7 騒乱 **sōran** riot, disturbance
9 騒音 **sōon** noise
11 騒動 **sōdō** disturbance, riot
12 騒然 **sōzen** noisy, tumultuous
18 騒擾罪 **sōjōzai** sedition, rioting

——————— 2 ———————
2 人騒 **hitosawa(gase)** false alarm
3 大騒 **ōsawa(gi)** clamor, uproar
4 心騒 **kokorosawa(gi)** uneasiness
5 立騒 **ta(chi)sawa(gu)** raise a din/to-do
6 米騒動 **kome sōdō** rice riot
7 狂騒 **kyōsō** mad uproar, frenzy, clamor
8 空騒 **karasawa(gi)** much ado about nothing
物騒 **bussō** unsettled, troubled, dangerous
monosawa(gashii) noisy, boisterous
10 胸騒 **munasawa(gi)** uneasiness; apprehension
12 喧騒 **kensō** noise, din, clamor
15 潮騒 **shiosai** roar of the sea
18 騒騒 **sōzō(shii), zawazawa** noisy, clamorous

——————— 3 ———————
8 底抜騒 **sokonu(ke) sawa(gi)** boisterous merrymaking
12 御家騒動 **oie sōdō** family quarrel
——————— 4 ———————
7 乱痴気騒 **ranchiki sawa(gi)** boisterous merrymaking, spree

——————— 9 ———————

騨 → 驒 **10a12.3**

10a9.1

騙   HEN, **dama(su/kasu)** deceive, trick, fool, cheat, swindle; humor, soothe, coax **kata(ru)** swindle, cheat; misrepresent

——————— 1 ———————
4 騙込 **dama(shi)ko(mu)** take in, deceive, defraud
6 騙合 **dama(shi)a(i)** cheating each other
10 騙討 **dama(shi)u(chi)** sneak attack, foul play
——————— 3 ———————
2 子供騙 **kodomodama(shi)** childish trick

——————— 10 ———————

騰 → 騰 **4b16.3**

騒 → 騒 **10a8.5**

——————— 11 ———————

10a11.1

驃   HYŌ white horse

10a11.2

驂   **SAN** extra driver/horse

10a11.3

騾   **RA** mule

─────── 1 ───────

10 騾馬 **raba** mule

驅 → 駆 **10a4.5**

─────── 12 ───────

10a12.1

驍   **GYŌ** strong

─────── 1 ───────

9 驍勇 **gyōyū** bravery, valor

10a12.2

驕   **KYŌ, ogo(ru)** be proud/arrogant

─────── 1 ───────

7 驕児 **kyōji** spoiled child
12 驕奢 **kyōsha** luxury, extravagance
13 驕傲 **kyōgō** arrogance, pride

10a12.3

驒 驒   **TAN, TA** dapple-gray horse

─────── 2 ───────

9 飛驒 **Hida** (ancient kuni, Gifu-ken)

10a12.4 / 1778

驚   **KYŌ, odoro(ku)** be surprised/ astonished/frightened
odoro(kasu) surprise, astonish; frighten

─────── 1 ───────

2 驚入 **odoro(ki)i(ru)** be filled with amazement
4 驚天動地 **kyōten-dōchi** earth-shaking, astounding
10 驚倒 **kyōtō** be astounded/amazed
11 驚異 **kyōi** wonder, miracle, marvel

驚異的 **kyōiteki** amazing, phenomenal
12 驚喜 **kyōki** pleasant surprise
驚愕 **kyōgaku** astonishment; alarm, consternation
13 驚嘆 **kyōtan** admiration, wonder

─────── 2 ───────

1 一驚 **ikkyō** surprise, amazement
6 吃驚 **kikkyō, bikkuri** be surprised

─────── 13 ───────

驛 → 駅 **10a4.4**

驗 → 験 **10a8.4**

─────── 14 ───────

10a14.1

驟   **SHŪ** suddenly; run

─────── 1 ───────

8 驟雨 **shūu** sudden shower

─────── 15 ───────

羈 → 羈 **5g19.1**

─────── 16 ───────

10a16.1

驥   **KI** fast horse; talent

─────── 1 ───────

7 驥尾付 **kibi (ni) fu(su)** follow (another's) lead
驥足 **kisoku** (give full play to) one's talents

─────── 2 ───────

18 騏驥 **kiki** horse which can run a thousand leagues in a day

10a16.2

驢   **RO** donkey

─────── 1 ───────

10 驢馬 **roba** donkey

─────── 2 ───────

9 海驢 **ashika** sea lion

馬 16←

───────── 17 ─────────

10a17.1

驩

KAN rejoice, be glad

10a17.2

驤

JŌ, SHŌ raise (one's head)

───────── 19 ─────────

10a19.1

驪

RI, REI black horse

───────── 20 ─────────

10a20.1

馬馬

SHŌ many horses

───────────── 魚 11a ─────────────

魚	魵	魳	魯	鮎	鮃	鮓	鮑	鮒	鮆	鮎	鮪	鮴
0.1	4.1	4.2	4.3	5.1	5.2	5.3	5.4	5.5	5.6	5.7	6.1	6.2

鮭	鮟	鮫	鮑	鮮	鮨	鰤	鮪	鯉	鯁	鯀	鯏	鮹
6.3	6.4	6.5	6.6	6.7	6.8	6.9	7.1	7.2	7.3	7.4	7.5	7.6

鯒	鯑	鯊	鯲	鯡	鯢	鯵	鯤	鯣	鯖	鯔	鯰	鯨
7.7	7.8	7.9	8.1	8.2	8.3	11a11.2	8.4	8.5	8.6	8.7	8.8	8.9

鯱	鯛	鍊	鰍	鮒	蝦	鰐	鰒	鰓	鰭	鰈	鰉	鰷
8.10	8.11	9.1	9.2	9.3	9.4	9.5	9.6	9.7	9.8	9.9	9.10	9.11

鰮	鹹	鹼	鰭	鰤	鰰	鰯	鰭	鰊	鰡	鰮	鱈	鯵
11a10.7	9.12	9.13	9.14	10.1	10.2	10.3	10.4	10.5	10.6	10.7	11.1	11.2

鰾	鱆	鰻	鰊	鰲	鰹	鱈	鱓	鱚	鱏	鱒	鱛	鱠
11.3	11.4	11.5	11.6	4h22.1	12.1	12.2	12.3	12.4	12.5	12.6	12.7	13.1

鱗	鱧	鱠	鱶	鱸
13.2	13.3	13.4	15.1	16.1

→17 馬

───────── 0 ─────────

11a0.1 / 290

魚

GYO, sakana, uo fish

───────── 1 ─────────

4 魚介 **gyokai** fish and shellfish, sea food
　魚心水心 **uogokoro (areba) mizugokoro**
　　helping each other
5 魚市場 **uoichiba** fish market
　魚目 **uo(no)me** corn (on the foot)
6 魚肉 **gyoniku** fish (meat)
　魚灯 **gyotō** fish-luring lights
7 魚卵 **gyoran** fish eggs, roe, spawn
　魚形 **gyokei** fish-like, fish-shaped
8 魚油 **gyoyu** fish oil
　魚河岸 **uogashi** riverside fish market
　魚板 **gyoban** temple's fish-shaped wooden
　　time-gong
　魚肥 **gyohi** fertilizer made from fish
9 魚屋 **sakanaya** fish shop/seller

　魚食 **gyoshoku** fish eating
10 魚粉 **gyofun** fish meal
11 魚道 **gyodō** path regularly taken by a school
　　of fish; fish ladder, fishway
　魚梯 **gyotei** fish ladder, fishway
　魚族 **gyozoku** fishes
　魚眼レンズ **gyogan renzu** fisheye lens
　魚釣 **uotsu(ri), sakanatsu(ri)** fishing, angling
　魚鳥 **gyochō** birds and fishes
13 魚群 **gyogun** school of fish
　魚腹 **gyofuku** fishes' bellies/entrails
　魚雷 **gyorai** torpedo
　魚雷艇 **gyoraitei** torpedo boat
18 魚類 **gyorui** fishes
　魚類学 **gyoruigaku** ichthyology

───────── 2 ─────────

2 人魚 **ningyo** mermaid, merman
3 川魚 **kawauo** river fish
　干魚 **ho(shi)uo, ho(shi)zakana** dried fish
　小魚 **kozakana** small fish, fry, fingerlings
4 公魚 **wakasagi** pond smelt

10

水魚交 **suigyo (no) maji(wari)** intimate friendship
木魚 **mokugyo** wooden temple drum
5 生魚 **namazakana, seigyo** raw/fresh fish
幼魚 **yōgyo** young fish
白魚 **shirauo** whitebait, icefish
6 衣魚 **shimi** clothes moth, silverfish, bookworm
8 怪魚 **kaigyo** strange/monstrous fish
金魚 **kingyo** goldfish
金魚草 **kingyosō** snapdragon
金魚屋 **kingyoya** goldfish seller
金魚鉢 **kingyobachi** goldfish bowl
9 飛魚 **to(bi)uo** flying fish
浮魚 **u(ki)uo** surface fish
活魚 **i(ke)uo** caught fish kept alive in a tank
海魚 **kaigyo** ocean/saltwater fish
肺魚 **haigyo** lungfish
10 紙魚 **shimi** clothes moth, silverfish, bookworm
11 梭魚 **kamasu** barracuda
章魚 **tako** octopus
12 落魚 **o(chi)uo** sweetfish going downstream to spawn; deep-swimming fish; dead fish
焼魚 **ya(ki)zakana** broiled fish
煮魚 **nizakana** fish boiled with soy sauce
集魚灯 **shūgyotō** fish-luring light
13 塩魚 **shiozakana** salted fish
稚魚 **chigyo** young fish, fry, fingerling
14 雑魚 **zako, jako** small fish/fry
雑魚寝 **zakone** sleep together in a group
15 養魚 **yōgyo** fish farming/breeding
養魚池 **yōgyochi** fish/breeding pond
養魚場 **yōgyojō** fish farm/hatchery
17 鮮魚 **sengyo** fresh fish
22 蠹魚 **togyo, shimi** clothes moth, bookworm

───── 3 ─────

3 山椒魚 **sanshōuo** salamander
4 太刀魚 **tachiuo** hairtail, scabbard fish
6 近海魚 **kinkaigyo** coastal/shore fish
7 冷凍魚 **reitōgyo** frozen fish
9 浅海魚 **senkaigyo** shallow-sea fish
秋刀魚 **sanma** mackerel/saury pike
11 淡水魚 **tansuigyo** freshwater fish
深海魚 **shinkaigyo** deep-sea fish
12 遠海魚 **enkaigyo** deep-sea fish
15 熱帯魚 **nettaigyo** tropical fish
20 鹹水魚 **kansuigyo** saltwater fish

───── 4 ─────

11a4.1
鮍 **HŌ, kagamidai** (a kind of sea bream)

11a4.2
鰤 **SHI, kamasu** barracuda

11a4.3
魯 **RO** dull-witted; Russia

───── 1 ─────
12 魯鈍 **rodon** stupid, foolish
───── 2 ─────
12 普魯西 **Puroshia** Prussia

───── 5 ─────

11a5.1
鮖 **kajika** bullhead

11a5.2
鮃 **HEI, hirame** flatfish, flounder, halibut, sole

11a5.3
鮓 **SA, sushi** sushi

11a5.4
鮑 蚫 **HŌ, awabi** abalone

11a5.5
鮒 **FU, funa** (crucian/Prussian) carp

11a5.6
鰶 **konoshiro** gizzard shad

11a5.7
鮎 **DEN, NEN, ayu** (a trout-like fish), sweetfish

───── 1 ─────
8 鮎並 **ainame** rock trout

—————— 2 ——————
12 落鮎 **o(chi)ayu** sweetfish going downstream to spawn

—————— 6 ——————

11a6.1
鮪 **YŪ, maguro** (bluefin) tuna, tunny
shibi tunny, yellowfin tuna

11a6.2
鮴 **gori** bullhead   **mebaru** gopher, rockfish   **mate** razor clam
kochi flathead

11a6.3
鮭 **KAI, KEI, sake, shake** salmon

—————— 2 ——————
13 塩鮭 **shiozake, shiojake** salted salmon

11a6.4
鮟 **AN** anglerfish

—————— 1 ——————
22 鮟鱇 **ankō** anglerfish

11a6.5
鮫 **KŌ, same** shark

—————— 1 ——————
5 鮫皮 **samegawa** sharkskin
6 鮫肌 **samehada** fishskin, dry/scaly skin
15 鮫膚 **samehada** fishskin, dry/scaly skin

—————— 2 ——————
15 蝶鮫 **chōzame** sturgeon
16 鋸鮫 **nokogirizame** saw shark
20 鰐鮫 **wanizame** shark
23 鱏鮫 **chōzame** sturgeon

11a6.6
鮖 **GAI** catfish
hae dace

11a6.7 / 701
鮮 **SEN** fresh, vivid, clear; Korea
aza(yaka) vivid, clear, brilliant, bright, colorful

—————— 1 ——————
4 鮮少 **senshō** (a) few/little
6 鮮肉 **senniku** fresh meat
鮮血 **senketsu** (fresh/still-undried) blood
8 鮮明 **senmei** clear, distinct
9 鮮度 **sendo** (degree of) freshness
鮮紅 **senkō** bright red, scarlet
11 鮮魚 **sengyo** fresh fish
15 鮮鋭 **sen'ei** clear, sharp, well-defined
19 鮮麗 **senrei** resplendent, vivid, bright

—————— 2 ——————
4 不鮮明 **fusenmei** indistinct, blurred
日鮮 **Nis-Sen** Japan and Korea
5 北鮮 **Hokusen** North Korea
生鮮 **seisen** fresh
生鮮度 **seisendo** freshness
12 朝鮮 **Chōsen** Korea
朝鮮人 **Chōsenjin** a Korean
朝鮮人参 **Chōsen ninjin** ginseng
13 新鮮 **shinsen** fresh

—————— 3 ——————
5 北朝鮮 **Kita Chōsen** North Korea

11a6.8
鮨 **SHI, sushi** sushi (raw fish or vegetables with vinegared rice)

—————— 1 ——————
9 鮨屋 **sushiya** sushi shop
13 鮨詰 **sushizu(me)** packed like sushi/sardines, jam-packed

—————— 2 ——————
12 握鮨 **nigi(ri)zushi** sushi ball

11a6.9
鮞 **JI** roe, fish eggs

—————— 7 ——————

11a7.1
鯆 **HO, iruka** dolphin, porpoise

11a7.2
鯉 **RI, koi** carp

—————— 1 ——————
3 鯉口 **koiguchi** mouth of a sword sheath
15 鯉幟 **koinobori** carp streamer (Boys' Festival decoration)

11 → 6 魚 鳥

─────────── 2 ───────────

10 真鯉 **magoi** black carp
14 緋鯉 **higoi** red/gold carp

11a7.3

鯁 **KŌ** fishbones

11a7.4

鯀 **KON** (large mythical fish); (proper name)

11a7.5

鯏 **asari** short-necked clam
ugui dace, chub

11a7.6

鮹 **SHŌ, tako** octopus

11a7.7

鯒 **kochi** flathead

11a7.8

鯑 **kazunoko** herring roe
nishin herring

11a7.9

鯊 **SA, SHA** shark
haze goby

─────────── 8 ───────────

11a8.1

鰌 **dojō** loach

11a8.2

鯡 **HI, nishin** herring

11a8.3

鯢 **GEI** salamander; female whale; small fish; old person's teeth

鯵 → 鰺 **11a11.2**

11a8.4

鯤 **KON** (large mythical fish); roe

11a8.5

鯣 **EKI** red eel   **surume** dried cuttlefish

11a8.6

鯖 鯖 **SEI, saba** mackerel

11a8.7

鯔 **SHI, bora** gray mullet
ina young gray mullet

11a8.8

鯰 **namazu** catfish

─────────── 3 ───────────

17 瓢箪鯰 **hyōtan namazu** slippery fellow

11a8.9 / 700

鯨 **GEI, kujira** whale

─────────── 1 ───────────

4 鯨尺 **kujirajaku** (unit of length, about 37.8 cm)
6 鯨肉 **geiniku** whale meat
8 鯨油 **geiyu** whale oil
10 鯨脂 **geishi** blubber
12 鯨飲 **geiin** drink like a fish, guzzle
13 鯨幕 **kujiramaku** black-and-white curtain/bunting

─────────── 2 ───────────

3 山鯨 **yamakujira** wild-boar meat
10 捕鯨 **hogei** whaling
捕鯨船 **hogeisen** whaling ship

─────────── 3 ───────────

8 長須鯨 **nagasu kujira** razorback whale
抹香鯨 **makkō kujira** sperm whale

11a8.10

鯱 shachi killer whale, orc, grampus
shachihoko fabulous dolphin-like fish

——————— 1 ———————

5 鯱立 shachihokoda(chi) standing on one's hands/head; exerting great effort
11 鯱張 shachikoba(ru), shachihokoba(ru) be stiff and formal

11a8.11

鯛 CHŌ, tai sea bream, porgy

——————— 1 ———————

12 鯛焼 taiya(ki) fish-shaped griddle cake filled with bean jam
鯛飯 taimeshi rice with minced sea bream

——————— 2 ———————

3 大鯛 ōdai red sea bream
7 赤鯛 akadai red sea bream
10 真鯛 madai red sea bream, porgy

——————— 9 ———————

11a9.1

鰊 REN, nishin herring

——————— 3 ———————

7 身欠鰊 mika(ki) nishin dried herring

11a9.2

鰍 SHŪ, kajika bullhead

11a9.3

鯽 SEKI, SHOKU, funa crucian carp, roach

11a9.4

鰕 KA, ebi shrimp, prawn

11a9.5

鰐 GAKU, wani crocodile, alligator

——————— 1 ———————

3 鰐口 waniguchi wide/large mouth; alligator (clip); (temple) gong

5 鰐皮 wanigawa alligator skin
7 鰐足 waniashi frog-footed, pigeon-toed, bowlegged, knock-kneed
17 鰐鮫 wanizame shark

——————— 2 ———————

5 外鰐 sotowani walking with the feet pointing outward, frog-footed

11a9.6

鰒 FUKU, awabi abalone
fugu swellfish

11a9.7

鰓 SAI, era, agito gills

11a9.8

鰆 SHUN, sawara Spanish mackerel

11a9.9

鰈 CHŌ, karei flatfish, turbot

11a9.10

鰉 KŌ swordfish, sailfish
higai (a kind of carp)

11a9.11

鰑 TEI, hishiko anchovy

鰛 → 鰮 11a10.7

11a9.12

鹹 KAN, karei flatfish, turbot
tara cod

11a9.13

鰄 I (a kind of fish)

11a9.14

鰌   **SHŪ, dojō** loach

---------------- 10 ----------------

11a10.1

鰤   **SHI, buri** yellowtail

11a10.2

鰰   **hatahata** sandfish

11a10.3

鰯 鰯   **iwashi** sardine

------------ 2 ------------

7 赤鰯 **aka iwashi** dried/salted sardines

11a10.4

鰭   **KI, hire** fin

------------ 2 ------------

7 尾鰭 **ohire** tail and fin; embellishments, exaggeration   **obire** caudal fin
9 背鰭 **sebire** dorsal fin

11a10.5

鰥   **KAN, yamome** widower, unmarried man

------------ 2 ------------

7 男鰥 **otoko yamome** widower

11a10.6

鰡   **RYŪ, RU** (a type of fish)

11a10.7

鰮 鰮   **iwashi** sardine

---------------- 11 ----------------

11a11.1

鱈 鱈   **tara** cod(fish)

------------ 1 ------------

12 鱈場蟹 **tarabagani** king crab
13 鱈腹 **tarafuku** (eat) to one's heart's content

------------ 2 ------------

3 干鱈 **hidara** dried codfish
12 棒鱈 **bōdara** dried cod

------------ 4 ------------

13 滅多矢鱈 **mettayatara** indiscriminate, frantic

11a11.2

鯵 鰺   **SŌ, aji** horse mackerel

11a11.3

鰾   **HYŌ, fue** (fish's) swim/air bladder

11a11.4

鱆   **SHŌ, tako** octopus

11a11.5

鰻   **MAN, unagi** eel

------------ 1 ------------

3 鰻上 **unaginobo(ri)** rise steadily
5 鰻丼 **unagi donburi, unadon** bowl of eel and rice
9 鰻屋 **unagiya** eel shop

11a11.6

鱇   **KŌ** anglerfish

------------ 2 ------------

17 鮟鱇 **ankō** anglerfish

鰲 → 鼇 4h22.1

---------------- 12 ----------------

11a12.1

鰹   **KEN, katsuo** bonito, skipjack

------------ 1 ------------

4 鰹木 **katsuogi** log on the ridge of a shrine roof

11

魚 12←
鳥

13 鰹節 **katsuobushi** dried bonito shavings
鰹節削 **katsuobushi kezu(ri)** plane for
making bonito shavings

———————— 2 ————————

7 花鰹 **hanagatsuo** dried bonito shavings

11a12.2

鱝 **JIN, ei** ray, skate

11a12.3

鱓 **SEN, utsubo** moray eel
gomame small dried sardines

11a12.4

鱚 **kisu** sillaginoid

11a12.5

鱘 **JIN** sturgeon

———————— 1 ————————

17 鱘鮫 **chōzame** sturgeon

11a12.6

鱒 鱒 **SON, masu** trout

———————— 2 ————————

9 紅鱒 **benimasu** red/sockeye salmon
虹鱒 **nijimasu** rainbow trout

11a12.7

鱛 **eso** lizard fish

———————— 13 ————————

11a13.1

鰟 **SHO, tanago** bitterling

11a13.2

鱗 **RIN, uroko, kokera** scales (on a fish)

———————— 1 ————————

7 鱗状 **rinjō** scale-like, scaly
鱗形 **urokogata** imbricate, scale-like
12 鱗雲 **urokogumo** cirrocumulus clouds

———————— 2 ————————

4 片鱗 **henrin** small part; glimpse, indication
8 逆鱗 **gekirin** the emperor's wrath

11a13.3

鱧 **REI, hamo** pike conger, sea eel

11a13.4

鱠 **KAI, namasu** fish salad seasoned in
vinegar

———————— 15 ————————

11a15.1

鱶 **SHŌ, fuka** shark

———————— 16 ————————

11a16.1

鱸 **RO, suzuki** sea bass

11

→12 魚
鳥

———————— 鳥 11b ————————

鳥	烏	島	梟	鳩	鳲	鳧	鳶	鴃	鳰	鴇	鴎	鴕
0.1	4d6.5	3o7.9	4a7.28	2.1	2.2	2.3	3.1	4.1	4.2	4.3	11b11.3	5.1

鴨	鴉	鴟	鴝	鴒	鴣	蕎	鴛	鴬	鵄	鴿	鵁	鴾
5.2	5.3	5.4	5.5	5.6	5.7	5.8	5.9	11b10.9	11b5.4	6.1	6.2	6.3

鵝	鵞	鵠	鵑	鶉	鵤	鵜	鷲	鵡	鴨	鵲	鶏	鵺
11b7.7	7.1	7.2	7.3	7.4	7.5	7.6	7.7	8.1	8.2	8.3	8.4	8.5

鵡	鵜	鶚	鴨	鷙	鶴	鶸	鶺	鶻	鶏	鶲	鸚	翁鳥
8.6	11b8.1	9.1	9.2	9.3	10.1	10.2	10.3	10.4	11b8.4	10.5	10.6	10.7

鶍	鶯	鷯	鷗	鷗	鷔	鷦	鷭	鷸	鷽	鷺	鸚	鷥
10.8	10.9	11.1	11.2	11.3	11.4	12.1	12.2	12.3	12.4	12.5	13.1	13.2

鸚	鸛	鸞
17.1	17.2	19.1

0

11b0.1 / 285

鳥

CHŌ, tori bird

--- 1 ---

2 鳥人 **chōjin** birdman, aviator
3 鳥小屋 **torigoya** aviary; chicken coop
5 鳥打 **toriu(chi)** shooting birds; cap
鳥打帽 **toriu(chi)bō** cap
鳥目 **torime** night blindness
chōmoku (an ancient coin); money
6 鳥肉 **toriniku** chicken (meat)
鳥羽 **Toba** (emperor, 1107–1124)
鳥肌 **torihada** goose flesh/pimples
7 鳥貝 **torigai** cockle (shell)
8 鳥刺 **torisa(shi)** bird catcher; chicken sashimi
鳥追 **torio(i)** shooing birds away; New Year's minstrel girl
鳥居 **torii** Shinto shrine archway
鳥取 **Tottori** (city, Tottori-ken)
鳥取県 **Tottori-ken** (prefecture)
9 鳥屋 **toya** coop, roost; molting; kabuki actors' greenroom
11 鳥寄 **toriyo(se)** birdcall
12 鳥媒花 **chōbaika** bird-pollinated flower
鳥葬 **chōsō** platform burial (exposing the body to carnivorous birds)
14 鳥網 **toriami** bird-catching net
鳥銃 **chōjū** gun for shooting birds
15 鳥餌 **torie** bird seed/feed
16 鳥獣 **chōjū** birds and animals, wildlife
17 鳥瞰図 **chōkanzu** bird's-eye view
18 鳥類 **chōrui** birds, fowl
鳥類学 **chōruigaku** ornithology
22 鳥籠 **torikago** bird cage

--- 2 ---

3 千鳥 **chidori** thousands of/innumerable birds; plover; flying bird (pattern in family crest); zigzag; (kind of square dance)
千鳥足 **chidori-ashi** tottering steps
千鳥掛 **chidoriga(ke)** catch/cross stitch; crossing
小鳥 **kotori** (small) bird
山鳥 **yamadori** pheasant; mountain bird
4 文鳥 **bunchō** Java sparrow, paddy bird
5 幼鳥 **yōchō** young bird, fledgling
白鳥 **hakuchō** swan

6 朱鳥 **Shuchō** (era, 686–701)
7 花鳥 **kachō** flowers and birds
花鳥風月 **kachō-fūgetsu** the beauties of nature; elegant pursuits
8 夜鳥 **yachō** nocturnal bird
放鳥 **hōchō** setting birds free; bird to be released
怪鳥 **kaichō** strange/ominous bird
9 飛鳥 **hichō** flying bird, bird on the wing
Asuka (era, 593–710)
海鳥 **kaichō, umidori** seabird
珍鳥 **chinchō** rare bird
10 候鳥 **kōchō** bird of passage, migratory bird
都鳥 **miyakodori** plover; gull
益鳥 **ekichō** beneficial bird
猛鳥 **mōchō** bird of prey
害鳥 **gaichō** harmful bird
留鳥 **ryūchō** nonmigratory bird
11 野鳥 **yachō** wild birds
魚鳥 **gyochō** birds and fishes
12 渡鳥 **wata(ri)dori** migratory bird
椋鳥 **mukudori** gray starling; bumpkin, easily duped person
焼鳥 **ya(ki)tori** grilled chicken
雄鳥 **ondori** rooster, male bird
13 禁鳥 **kinchō** protected bird
瑞鳥 **zuichō** bird of good omen
愛鳥 **aichō** pet bird
愛鳥家 **aichōka** bird lover
飼鳥 **ka(i)dori** poultry
14 雌鳥 **mendori** hen
15 窮鳥 **kyūchō** a cornered bird
窮鳥懐入 **kyūchō futokoro (ni) hai(ru)** (like a) bird in distress seeking refuge
霊鳥 **reichō** sacred bird
駝鳥 **dachō** ostrich
駒鳥 **komadori** robin
16 親鳥 **oyadori** parent bird
鴕鳥 **dachō** ostrich
18 雛鳥 **hinadori** chick, fledgling
鵞鳥 **gachō** goose

--- 3 ---

2 七面鳥 **shichimenchō** turkey
4 不死鳥 **fushichō** phoenix
7 尾長鳥 **onagadori** blue magpie; long-tailed bird
9 保護鳥 **hogochō** protected bird
郭公鳥 **kakkōdori** cuckoo
11 啄木鳥 **kitsutsuki** woodpecker

11
魚
鳥 0←

12 極楽鳥 **gokurakuchō** bird of paradise
閑古鳥 **kankodori** cuckoo
13 群千鳥 **mura chidori** flock of plovers

────────── 4 ──────────

1 一石二鳥 **isseki nichō** killing two birds with one stone

烏→ **4d6.5**

島→ **3o7.9**

梟→ **4a7.28**

────────── 2 ──────────

11b2.1

鳩 **KYŪ, hato** dove, pigeon

────────── 1 ──────────

0 鳩ヶ谷 **Hatogaya** (city, Saitama-ken)
3 鳩小屋 **hatogoya** dovecote
5 鳩目 **hatome** eyelet, grommet
6 鳩羽色 **hatoba-iro** bluish gray
7 鳩尾 **kyūbi, mizoochi, mizuochi** solar plexus, pit of the stomach
鳩麦 **hatomugi** adlay, pearl barley
8 鳩舎 **kyūsha** dovecote
9 鳩首 **kyūshu** go into a huddle
鳩派 **hatoha** the doves, soft-liners
10 鳩胸 **hatomune** pigeon-breasted
鳩時計 **hatodokei** cuckoo clock

────────── 2 ──────────

3 山鳩 **yamabato** turtledove
12 斑鳩 **ikaru, ikaruga** grosbeak, Japanese hawfinch

────────── 3 ──────────

5 白子鳩 **shirakobato** collared dove
6 伝書鳩 **denshobato** carrier pigeon
9 軍用鳩 **gun'yōbato** carrier pigeon

11b2.2

鳰 **nio** grebe

11b2.3

鳧 鳬 **FU** wild duck
keri gray-headed lapwing

────────── 3 ──────────

11b3.1

鳶 **EN, tobi, tonbi** kite (the bird); fireman; scaffolding worker

────────── 1 ──────────

3 鳶口 **tobiguchi** fireman's ax/hook
6 鳶色 **tobi-iro** brown, auburn
18 鳶職 **tobishoku** construction laborer

────────── 4 ──────────

11b4.1

鵙 **GEKI, mozu** shrike

────────── 1 ──────────

6 鵙舌 **gekizetsu** barbarian jabbering/tongue

11b4.2

鴆 **CHIN** (a poisonous Chinese bird)

11b4.3

鴇 **HŌ** wild goose; madam of a brothel
toki crested ibis

鴎→鷗 **11b11.3**

────────── 5 ──────────

11b5.1

鴕 **DA** ostrich

────────── 1 ──────────

11 鴕鳥 **dachō** ostrich

11b5.2

鴨 **Ō, kamo** duck, mallard; easily deceived person

────────── 1 ──────────

8 鴨居 **kamoi** lintel

────────── 2 ──────────

3 小鴨 **kogamo** duckling; teal
10 真鴨 **magamo** mallard duck
家鴨 **ahiru** (domestic) duck

────────── 3 ──────────

16 嘴広鴨 **hashibirogamo** spoonbill

11b5.3

鴉　**A, karasu** crow; raven

11b5.4

鵄　鴟　**SHI** kite; owl
tobi kite (the bird)

──────── 1 ────────
7 鴟尾 **shibi** ornamental ridge-end tile

11b5.5

鴥　**ITSU** flying fast (like a hawk), swooping

11b5.6

鴒　**REI** wagtail

──────── 2 ────────
21 鶺鴒 **sekirei** wagtail

11b5.7

鴣　**KO** partridge

──────── 2 ────────
22 鷓鴣 **shako** partridge

11b5.8

鴦　**Ō** female mandarin duck

──────── 2 ────────
16 鴛鴦 **oshidori** mandarin duck (symbol of
harmony and mutual affection)

11b5.9

鴛　**EN** male mandarin duck

──────── 1 ────────
16 鴛鴦 **oshidori** mandarin duck (symbol of
harmony and mutual affection)

鴬 → 鶯 **11b10.9**

──────── 6 ────────

鴩 → 鴟 **11b5.4**

11b6.1

鳩　**KŌ, hato** pigeon

11b6.2

鵁　**KŌ** night heron

11b6.3

鴾　**BŌ, toki** crested ibis

──────── 7 ────────

鵞 → 鵞 **11b7.7**

11b7.1

鶉　**BU, MU** unmottled quail

11b7.2

鵠　鴣　**KOKU, KŌ, kugui** swan

──────── 2 ────────
5 正鵠 **seikoku, seikō** the bull's eye, the mark

11b7.3

鵑　**KEN** cuckoo

──────── 2 ────────
7 杜鵑 **hototogisu** cuckoo

11b7.4

鶉　**JUN, uzura** quail

──────── 1 ────────
6 鶉衣 **uzuragoromo** patched clothes
7 鶉豆 **uzuramame** mottled kidney beans

魚
鳥 7 ←

11b7.5

鵤

ikaru, ikaruga grosbeak, hawfinch

11b7.6

鵜

TEI, u cormorant

─────────── 1 ───────────

5 鵜目鷹目 u(no)me-taka(no)me (de) with a sharp/keen eye
6 鵜匠 ushō, ujō cormorant fisherman
7 鵜呑 uno(mi) swallow whole
13 鵜飼 uka(i) fishing with cormorants

11b7.7

鵞 鵝

GA goose

─────────── 1 ───────────

11 鵞鳥 gachō goose

─────────── 2 ───────────

4 天鵞絨 birōdo velvet

─────────── 8 ───────────

11b8.1

鶫 鶇

TŌ, tsugumi thrush

11b8.2

鵯

HI, hiyodori (brown-eared) bulbul

11b8.3

鵲

JAKU, kasasagi magpie

11b8.4 / 926

鶏 雞

KEI, niwatori chicken, hen, rooster

─────────── 1 ───────────

6 鶏肉 keiniku chicken (meat)
7 鶏卵 keiran chicken egg
8 鶏舎 keisha chicken coop, henhouse
9 鶏冠 keikan cockscomb
13 鶏群 keigun flock of chickens

14 鶏鳴 keimei cockcrow, rooster's crowing
16 鶏頭 keitō cockscomb (the flower)

─────────── 2 ───────────

4 水鶏 kuina rail, mud hen
6 牝鶏 hinkei hen
8 若鶏 wakadori (spring) chicken, pullet
11 晨鶏 shinkei rooster crowing at dawn
15 養鶏 yōkei poultry farming
養鶏家 yōkeika poultry farmer
養鶏場 yōkeijō poultry farm
養鶏業 yōkeigyō poultry farming
18 闘鶏 tōkei cockfight(ing); fighting cock
20 鶤鶏 tōmaru (type of black songbird)

─────────── 3 ───────────

1 一番鶏 ichibandori first cockcrowing

11b8.5

鵺

nue fabulous night bird, chimera

11b8.6

鸚

MU, BU parrot, cockatoo

─────────── 2 ───────────

28 鸚鵡 ōmu parrot
鸚鵡返 ōmugae(shi) parroting
鸚鵡貝 ōmugai chambered nautilus

─────────── 9 ───────────

鶇 → 鶫 **11b8.1**

11b9.1

鶚

GAKU, misago osprey

11b9.2

鶤

UN, tōmaru (type of black songbird)

─────────── 1 ───────────

19 鶤鶏 tōmaru (type of black songbird)

11b9.3

鶩

BOKU, ahiru duck

11

魚
→ 7 鳥

─────────── 10 ───────────

11b10.1

鶴　KAKU, tsuru　crane, stork

─────────── 1 ───────────

1 鶴一声 tsuru (no) hitokoe　the voice of authority
9 鶴首 kakushu　stretching one's neck
11 鶴亀 tsurukame　crane and tortoise; congratulations
　鶴亀算 tsurukamezan　solving a system of linear equations (example: How many cranes and how many turtles, given a total of 11 animals and 36 legs?)
16 鶴嘴 tsuruhashi　pick(ax)

─────────── 2 ───────────

15 舞鶴 Maizuru　(city, Kyōto-fu)

11b10.2

　JAKU, hiwa　siskin, greenfinch; light yellowish green

11b10.3

鶺　SEKI　wagtail

─────────── 1 ───────────

16 鶺鴒 sekirei　wagtail

11b10.4

鶻　KOTSU　falcon, eagle

　11b8.4

11b10.5

鷂　YŌ, haitaka　sparrow hawk

11b10.6

鶲 鷏　TEN, DEN, SHIN, kasui　(a yellow-white mottled songbird)

11b10.7

　hitaki　crested flycatcher, pewee

11b10.8

鷁　GEKI　waterfowl which flies high but not against the wind

11b10.9

鶯 鴬　Ō, uguisu　bush warbler

─────────── 11 ───────────

11b11.1

鷚　RYŪ, hibari　skylark

11b11.2

鷓　SHA　partridge

─────────── 1 ───────────

16 鷓鴣 shako　partridge

11b11.3

鷗 鴎　Ō, kamome　sea gull

11b11.4

鷙　SHI　flying fish

─────────── 12 ───────────

11b12.1

鷦　SHŌ　wren

─────────── 1 ───────────

23 鷦鷯 misosazai　wren

11b12.2

鷭　HAN, ban　water hen, gallinule

11b12.3

鷯　RYŌ　wren

─────────── 2 ───────────

23 鷦鷯 misosazai　wren

11b12.4

ITSU snipe; kingfisher
shigi snipe

11b12.5

SHŪ, washi eagle

―――――――― 1 ――――――――
14 鷲摑 **washizuka(mi)** clutch, grab
鷲鼻 **washibana** aquiline/hooked nose
―――――――― 2 ――――――――
4 犬鷲 **inuwashi** golden eagle

―――――――― 13 ――――――――

11b13.1

鸑
KAKU long-tailed bird; dove
uso bullfinch

11b13.2

鷺
RO, sagi heron

―――――――― 2 ――――――――
8 青鷺 **aosagi** blue heron

―――――――― 17 ――――――――

11b17.1

Ō parrot, parakeet

―――――――― 1 ――――――――
10 鸚哥 **inko** parakeet
19 鸚鵡 **ōmu** parrot
鸚鵡返 **ōmugae(shi)** parroting
鸚鵡貝 **ōmugai** chambered nautilus

11b17.2

鸛
KAN, kōnotori Japanese stork

―――――――― 19 ――――――――

11b19.1

鸞
RAN (a fabulous bird); imperial

―――――――― 2 ――――――――
16 親鸞 **Shinran** (Buddhist priest, 1173–1262)

11

魚
→ 12 鳥

APPENDICES

付　録

The 100 Most Frequent Kanji
最も多く使用されている漢字100

一	日	人	十	大	二	三	会	国	中	年	上	本	五	出	四	行	生	円	同
1	2	3	4	5	6	7	8	9	10	11	12	13	14	15	16	17	18	19	20
月	方	時	用	部	事	六	分	間	者	化	性	長	前	下	地	後	発	家	合
21	22	23	24	25	26	27	28	29	30	31	32	33	34	35	36	37	38	39	40
的	場	業	社	新	八	田	東	七	学	見	作	立	政	物	手	来	京	自	女
41	42	43	44	45	46	47	48	49	50	51	52	53	54	55	56	57	58	59	60
法	入	成	子	主	員	内	体	目	高	所	対	第	動	思	金	議	外	等	世
61	62	63	64	65	66	67	68	69	70	71	72	73	74	75	76	77	78	79	80
名	代	県	府	当	度	気	定	私	山	今	小	多	電	九	力	彼	言	通	知
81	82	83	84	85	86	87	88	89	90	91	92	93	94	95	96	97	98	99	100

The 10 Most Frequent Kanji Used in Family Names
姓氏に最も多く使用されている漢字10

1	2	3	4	5	6	7	8	9	10
田	藤	山	野	川	木	井	村	本	中
ta	TŌ	yama	no	kawa	ki	i	mura	moto	naka
-da	-DŌ		YA	-gawa					

The 10 Most Frequent Kanji Used in Geographic Names
地名に最も多く使用されている漢字10

1	2	3	4	5	6	7	8	9	10
川	田	大	山	野	島	東	津	上	原
kawa	ta	DAI-	yama	no	shima	higashi	tsu	kami	hara
-gawa	-da	TAI-	SAN		-jima	TŌ		ue	-wara
		ō-	-ZAN		TŌ			JŌ	-bara

The 1006 Kanji Taught in Elementary School
("Gakushū Kanji")
学習漢字表 (学年別漢字配当表)

Grade 1 · 第一学年 (80)

一	右	雨	円	王	音	下	火	花	貝	学	気	九	休	玉	金	空	月	犬	見
1	2	3	4	5	6	7	8	9	10	11	12	13	14	15	16	17	18	19	20
五	口	校	左	三	山	子	四	糸	字	耳	七	車	手	十	出	女	小	上	森
21	22	23	24	25	26	27	28	29	30	31	32	33	34	35	36	37	38	39	40
人	水	正	生	青	夕	石	赤	千	川	先	早	草	足	村	大	男	竹	中	虫
41	42	43	44	45	46	47	48	49	50	51	52	53	54	55	56	57	58	59	60
町	天	田	土	二	日	入	年	白	八	百	文	木	本	名	目	立	力	林	六
61	62	63	64	65	66	67	68	69	70	71	72	73	74	75	76	77	78	79	80

Grade 2 · 第二学年 (160)

引	羽	雲	園	遠	何	科	夏	家	歌	画	回	会	海	絵	外	角	楽	活	間
81	82	83	84	85	86	87	88	89	90	91	92	93	94	95	96	97	98	99	100
丸	岩	顔	汽	記	帰	弓	牛	魚	京	強	教	近	兄	形	計	元	言	原	戸
101	102	103	104	105	106	107	108	109	110	111	112	113	114	115	116	117	118	119	120
古	午	後	語	工	公	広	交	光	考	行	高	黄	合	谷	国	黒	今	才	細
121	122	123	124	125	126	127	128	129	130	131	132	133	134	135	136	137	138	139	140
作	算	止	市	矢	姉	思	紙	寺	自	時	室	社	弱	首	秋	週	春	書	少
141	142	143	144	145	146	147	148	149	150	151	152	153	154	155	156	157	158	159	160
場	色	食	心	新	親	図	数	西	声	星	晴	切	雪	船	線	前	組	走	多
161	162	163	164	165	166	167	168	169	170	171	172	173	174	175	176	177	178	179	180
太	体	台	地	池	知	茶	昼	長	鳥	朝	直	通	弟	店	点	電	刀	冬	当
181	182	183	184	185	186	187	188	189	190	191	192	193	194	195	196	197	198	199	200
東	答	頭	同	道	読	内	南	肉	馬	売	買	麦	半	番	父	風	分	聞	米
201	202	203	204	205	206	207	208	209	210	211	212	213	214	215	216	217	218	219	220
万	歩	母	方	北	毎	妹	明	鳴	毛	門	夜	野	友	用	曜	来	里	理	話
221	222	223	224	225	226	227	228	229	230	231	232	233	234	235	236	237	238	239	240

Grade 3 · 第三学年 (200)

悪	安	暗	医	委	意	育	員	院	飲	運	泳	駅	央	横	屋	温	化	荷	界
241	242	243	244	245	246	247	248	249	250	251	252	253	254	255	256	257	258	259	260
開	階	寒	感	漢	館	岸	起	期	客	究	急	級	宮	球	去	橋	業	曲	局
261	262	263	264	265	266	267	268	269	270	271	272	273	274	275	276	277	278	279	280
銀	区	苦	具	君	係	軽	血	決	研	県	庫	湖	向	幸	港	号	根	祭	皿
281	282	283	284	285	286	287	288	289	290	291	292	293	294	295	296	297	298	299	300
仕	死	使	始	指	歯	詩	次	事	持	式	実	写	者	主	守	取	酒	受	州
301	302	303	304	305	306	307	308	309	310	311	312	313	314	315	316	317	318	319	320

拾	終	習	集	住	重	宿	所	暑	助	昭	消	商	章	勝	乗	植	申	身	神
321	322	323	324	325	326	327	328	329	330	331	332	333	334	335	336	337	338	339	340
真	深	進	世	整	昔	全	相	送	想	息	速	族	他	打	対	待	代	第	題
341	342	343	344	345	346	347	348	349	350	351	352	353	354	355	356	357	358	359	360
炭	短	談	着	注	柱	丁	帳	調	追	定	庭	笛	鉄	転	都	度	投	豆	島
361	362	363	364	365	366	367	368	369	370	371	372	373	374	375	376	377	378	379	380
湯	登	等	動	童	農	波	配	倍	箱	畑	発	反	坂	板	皮	悲	美	鼻	筆
381	382	383	384	385	386	387	388	389	390	391	392	393	394	395	396	397	398	399	400
氷	表	秒	病	品	負	部	服	福	物	平	返	勉	放	味	命	面	問	役	薬
401	402	403	404	405	406	407	408	409	410	411	412	413	414	415	416	417	418	419	420
由	油	有	遊	予	羊	洋	葉	陽	様	落	流	旅	両	緑	礼	列	練	路	和
421	422	423	424	425	426	427	428	429	430	431	432	433	434	435	436	437	438	439	440

Grade 4 · 第四学年 (200)

愛	案	以	衣	位	囲	胃	印	英	栄	塩	億	加	果	貨	課	芽	改	械	害
441	442	443	444	445	446	447	448	449	450	451	452	453	454	455	456	457	458	459	460
街	各	覚	完	官	管	関	観	願	希	季	紀	喜	旗	器	機	議	求	泣	救
461	462	463	464	465	466	467	468	469	470	471	472	473	474	475	476	477	478	479	480
給	挙	漁	共	協	鏡	競	極	訓	軍	郡	径	型	景	芸	欠	結	建	健	験
481	482	483	484	485	486	487	488	489	490	491	492	493	494	495	496	497	498	499	500
固	功	好	候	航	康	告	差	菜	最	材	昨	札	刷	殺	察	参	産	散	残
501	502	503	504	505	506	507	508	509	510	511	512	513	514	515	516	517	518	519	520
士	氏	史	司	試	児	治	辞	失	借	種	周	祝	順	初	松	笑	唱	焼	象
521	522	523	524	525	526	527	528	529	530	531	532	533	534	535	536	537	538	539	540
照	賞	臣	信	成	省	清	静	席	積	折	節	説	浅	戦	選	然	争	倉	菓
541	542	543	544	545	546	547	548	549	550	551	552	553	554	555	556	557	558	559	560
束	側	続	卒	孫	帯	隊	達	単	置	仲	貯	兆	腸	低	底	停	的	典	伝
561	562	563	564	565	566	567	568	569	570	571	572	573	574	575	576	577	578	579	580
徒	努	灯	堂	働	特	得	毒	熱	念	敗	梅	博	飯	飛	費	必	票	標	不
581	582	583	584	585	586	587	588	589	590	591	592	593	594	595	596	597	598	599	600
夫	付	府	副	粉	兵	別	辺	変	便	包	法	望	牧	末	満	未	脈	民	無
601	602	603	604	605	606	607	608	609	610	611	612	613	614	615	616	617	618	619	620
約	勇	要	養	浴	利	陸	良	料	量	輪	類	令	冷	例	歴	連	老	労	録
621	622	623	624	625	626	627	628	629	630	631	632	633	634	635	636	637	638	639	640

Grade 5 · 第五学年 (185)

圧	移	因	永	営	衛	易	益	液	演	応	往	桜	恩	可	仮	価	河	過	賀
641	642	643	644	645	646	647	648	649	650	651	652	653	654	655	656	657	658	659	660
快	解	格	確	額	刊	幹	慣	眼	基	寄	規	技	義	逆	久	旧	居	許	境
661	662	663	664	665	666	667	668	669	670	671	672	673	674	675	676	677	678	679	680
均	禁	句	群	経	潔	件	券	険	検	限	現	減	故	個	護	効	厚	耕	鉱
681	682	683	684	685	686	687	688	689	690	691	692	693	694	695	696	697	698	699	700
構	興	講	混	査	再	災	妻	採	際	在	財	罪	雑	酸	賛	支	志	枝	師
701	702	703	704	705	706	707	708	709	710	711	712	713	714	715	716	717	718	719	720

資	飼	示	似	識	質	舎	謝	授	修	述	術	準	序	招	承	証	条	状	常
721	722	723	724	725	726	727	728	729	730	731	732	733	734	735	736	737	738	739	740
情	織	職	制	性	政	勢	精	製	税	責	績	接	設	舌	絶	銭	祖	素	総
741	742	743	744	745	746	747	748	749	750	751	752	753	754	755	756	757	758	759	760
造	像	増	則	測	属	率	損	退	貸	態	団	断	築	張	堤	程	適	敵	統
761	762	763	764	765	766	767	768	769	770	771	772	773	774	775	776	777	778	779	780
銅	導	徳	独	任	燃	能	破	犯	判	版	比	肥	非	備	俵	評	貧	布	婦
781	782	783	784	785	786	787	788	789	790	791	792	793	794	795	796	797	798	799	800
富	武	復	複	仏	編	弁	保	墓	報	豊	防	貿	暴	務	夢	迷	綿	輸	余
801	802	803	804	805	806	807	808	809	810	811	812	813	814	815	816	817	818	819	820
預	容	略	留	領															
821	822	823	824	825															

Grade 6 · 第六学年 (181)

異	遺	域	宇	映	延	沿	我	灰	拡	革	閣	割	株	干	巻	看	簡	危	机
826	827	828	829	830	831	832	833	834	835	836	837	838	839	840	841	842	843	844	845
揮	貴	疑	吸	供	胸	郷	勤	筋	系	敬	警	劇	激	穴	絹	権	憲	源	厳
846	847	848	849	850	851	852	853	854	855	856	857	858	859	860	861	862	863	864	865
己	呼	誤	后	孝	皇	紅	降	鋼	刻	穀	骨	困	砂	座	済	裁	策	冊	蚕
866	867	868	869	870	871	872	873	874	875	876	877	878	879	880	881	882	883	884	885
至	私	姿	視	詞	誌	磁	射	捨	尺	若	樹	収	宗	就	衆	従	縦	縮	熟
886	887	888	889	890	891	892	893	894	895	896	897	898	899	900	901	902	903	904	905
純	処	署	諸	除	将	傷	障	城	蒸	針	仁	垂	推	寸	盛	聖	誠	宣	専
906	907	908	909	910	911	912	913	914	915	916	917	918	919	920	921	922	923	924	925
泉	洗	染	善	奏	窓	創	装	層	操	蔵	臓	存	尊	宅	担	探	誕	段	暖
926	927	928	929	930	931	932	933	934	935	936	937	938	939	940	941	942	943	944	945
値	宙	忠	著	庁	頂	潮	賃	痛	展	討	党	糖	届	難	乳	認	納	脳	派
946	947	948	949	950	951	952	953	954	955	956	957	958	959	960	961	962	963	964	965
拝	背	肺	俳	班	晩	否	批	秘	腹	奮	並	陛	閉	片	補	暮	宝	訪	亡
966	967	968	969	970	971	972	973	974	975	976	977	978	979	980	981	982	983	984	985
忘	棒	枚	幕	密	盟	模	訳	郵	優	幼	欲	翌	乱	卵	覧	裏	律	臨	朗
986	987	988	989	990	991	992	993	994	995	996	997	998	999	1000	1001	1002	1003	1004	1005
論																			
1006																			

The 284 Extra Kanji for Use in Given Names
人名用漢字

丑	丞	乃	之	也	亘	亦	亥	亨	亮
1	2	3	4	5	6	7	8	9	10
伊	伎	伍	伽	佑	伶	侃	侑	倭	倖
11	12	13	14	15	16	17	18	19	20
偲	允	冴	冶	凌	凜	凪	凱	勁	匡
21	22	23	24	25	26	27	28	29	30
卯	叡	叶	只	吾	呂	哉	啄	唄	喬
31	32	33	34	35	36	37	38	39	40
嘉	圭	尭	奈	奎	爽	媛	嬉	孟	宏
41	42	43	44	45	46	47	48	49	50
宥	寅	峻	崚	嵐	嵯	嵩	嶺	巌	巳
51	52	53	54	55	56	57	58	59	60
巴	巽	庄	弘	弥	彗	彦	彪	彬	怜
61	62	63	64	65	66	67	68	69	70
恕	悌	惟	惣	惇	慧	憧	拳	捷	捺
71	72	73	74	75	76	77	78	79	80
敦	斐	魁	於	旦	旭	旺	昂	昌	昴
81	82	83	84	85	86	87	88	89	90
晏	晃	晋	晟	晨	暉	暢	曙	智	朋
91	92	93	94	95	96	97	98	99	100
朔	杏	杜	李	柊	柚	柾	栞	桂	桐
101	102	103	104	105	106	107	108	109	110
栗	梧	梓	梢	梨	椎	椋	椿	楠	楓
111	112	113	114	115	116	117	118	119	120
椰	楊	樺	榛	槙	槻	橘	檀	欣	欽
121	122	123	124	125	126	127	128	129	130
毅	毬	汀	汐	沙	汰	洸	洲	洵	浩
131	132	133	134	135	136	137	138	139	140
淳	渚	渥	湧	滉	漱	澪	熙	熊	燎
141	142	143	144	145	146	147	148	149	150
燦	燿	采	爾	猪	玖	玲	琢	瑛	琳
151	152	153	154	155	156	157	158	159	160
瑚	瑞	瑤	瑳	瑠	璃	甫	皐	皓	眉
161	162	163	164	165	166	167	168	169	170
眸	睦	瞳	瞭	矩	碧	磯	祐	禄	禎
171	172	173	174	175	176	177	178	179	180
秦	稀	稔	稜	穣	竣	靖	笙	笹	紘
181	182	183	184	185	186	187	188	189	190
紗	絃	紬	絢	綺	綜	緋	綾	綸	翔
191	192	193	194	195	196	197	198	199	200
翠	耀	聡	肇	胤	胡	脩	舜	艶	芹
201	202	203	204	205	206	207	208	209	210
芙	苑	茄	茅	茉	茜	莞	莉	菫	菖
211	212	213	214	215	216	217	218	219	220
萌	葵	萩	蕗	蒼	蓉	蓮	蔦	蕉	蕗
221	222	223	224	225	226	227	228	229	230
藤	藍	蘭	虎	虹	蝶	衿	袈	裟	詢
231	232	233	234	235	236	237	238	239	240
誼	諄	諒	赳	輔	辰	迪	遥	遼	邑
241	242	243	244	245	246	247	248	249	250
那	郁	耶	酉	醇	錦	鎌	阿	隼	雛
251	252	253	254	255	256	257	258	259	260
霞	鞠	須	頌	碩	颯	馨	駒	駿	鮎
261	262	263	264	265	266	267	268	269	270
鯉	鯛	鳩	鳳	鴻	鵬	鶴	鷹	鹿	麟
271	272	273	274	275	276	277	278	279	280
麿	黎	黛	亀						
281	282	283	284						

The 100 Most Frequent Surnames
最も多く見られる名字100

1 佐藤 Satō	35 遠藤 Endō	69 島田 Shimada
2 鈴木 Suzuki	36 前田 Maeda	70 宮崎 Miyazaki
3 高橋 Takahashi	37 岡田 Okada	71 菊地 Kikuchi
4 田中 Tanaka	38 近藤 Kondō	72 上田 Ueda
5 伊藤 Itō	39 青木 Aoki	73 桜井 Sakurai
6 渡辺 Watanabe	40 村上 Murakami	74 安藤 Andō
7 小林 Kobayashi	41 金子 Kaneko	75 宮本 Miyamoto
8 中村 Nakamura	42 三浦 Miura	76 大野 Ōno
9 山本 Yamamoto	43 坂本 Sakamoto	77 丸山 Maruyama
10 加藤 Katō	44 福田 Fukuda	78 今井 Imai
11 吉田 Yoshida	45 太田 Ōta	79 大塚 Ōtsuka
12 山田 Yamada	46 田村 Tamura	80 千葉 Chiba
13 斎藤 Saitō	47 小野 Ono	81 菅原 Sugawara
14 佐々木 Sasaki	48 藤井 Fujii	82 村田 Murata
15 山口 Yamaguchi	49 竹内 Takeuchi	83 武田 Takeda
16 松本 Matsumoto	50 中川 Nakagawa	84 新井 Arai
17 木村 Kimura	51 西村 Nishimura	85 野口 Noguchi
18 井上 Inoue	52 松田 Matsuda	86 小山 Koyama
19 清水 Shimizu	53 中野 Nakano	87 増田 Masuda
20 林 Hayashi	54 原田 Harada	88 高田 Takada
21 阿部 Abe	55 和田 Wada	89 平野 Hirano
22 山崎 Yamasaki	56 中山 Nakayama	90 岩崎 Iwasaki
23 池田 Ikeda	57 岡本 Okamoto	91 上野 Ueno
24 中島 Nakajima	58 石田 Ishida	92 佐野 Sano
25 森 Mori	59 小島 Kojima	93 杉山 Sugiyama
26 石川 Ishikawa	60 内田 Uchida	94 谷口 Taniguchi
27 橋本 Hashimoto	61 森田 Morita	95 高野 Takano
28 小川 Ogawa	62 工藤 Kudō	96 松井 Matsui
29 石井 Ishii	63 横山 Yokoyama	97 野村 Nomura
30 長谷川 Hasegawa	64 酒井 Sakai	98 渡部 Watanabe
31 後藤 Gotō	65 柴田 Shibata	99 河野 Kawano
32 斉藤 Saitō	66 原 Hara	100 古川 Furukawa
33 山下 Yamashita	67 藤原 Fujiwara	
34 藤田 Fujita	68 高木 Takagi	

Japanese Nobel Prize Winners
ノーベル賞日本人受賞者

Name (surname, given name) 氏　名		Born–died 生・没年	Field 受賞部門		Year of award 受賞年
湯川秀樹	Yukawa Hideki	1907–1981	物理学	Physics	1949
朝永振一郎	Tomonaga Shin'ichirō	1906–1979	物理学	Physics	1965
川端康成	Kawabata Yasunari	1899–1972	文学	Literature	1968
江崎玲於奈	Esaki Reona	1925–	物理学	Physics	1973
佐藤栄作	Satō Eisaku	1901–1975	平和	Peace	1974
福井謙一	Fukui Ken'ichi	1918–	化学	Chemistry	1981
利根川進	Tonegawa Susumu	1939–	医学生理	Medicine	1987
大江健三郎	Ōe Kenzaburō	1935–	文学	Literature	1994

Japanese Historical Figures
歴史上重要人物

Name (surname, given name) 氏　名		Born–died 生・没年	Title/Historical role 歴史的役割
聖徳太子	Shōtoku Taishi	574–622	Prince
橘諸兄	Tachibana no Moroe	684–757	Court Official
藤原道長	Fujiwara no Michinaga	966–1028	Regent
平清盛	Taira no Kiyomori	1118–1881	Statesman
北条時政	Hōjō no Tokimasa	1138–1215	Regent
源頼朝	Minamoto no Yoritomo	1147–1199	Shōgun
足利尊氏	Ashikaga Takauji	1305–1358	Shōgun
今川欽元	Imagawa Yoshimoto	1519–1560	Daimyō
武田信玄	Takeda Shingen	1521–1573	Daimyō
上杉謙信	Uesugi Kenshin	1530–1578	Daimyō
小田信長	Oda Nobunaga	1534–1582	Statesman
豊臣秀吉	Toyotomi Hideyoshi	1537–1598	Statesman
徳川家康	Tokugawa Ieyasu	1543–1616	Shōgun
伊達政宗	Date Masamune	1567–1636	Warrior
明治天皇	Meiji Tennō	1868–1912	Emperor
昭和天皇	Shōwa Tennō	1901–1989	Emperor

Country Kanji
国名の略称

Most major countries are represented in newspaper headlines and phrases by a single kanji (or katakana), which usually derives from the first kanji of an obsolete phonetic kanji spelling of the country's name. Here is a list of kanji and katakana that represent the names of countries and of the five continents, along with the readings of the kanji and the names of the countries in English in alphabetical order.

阿	A	Africa	朝	Chō	Korea
米	Bei	America, United States	韓	Kan	Korea (South)
			馬	Ma	Malay
亜, ア	A	Asia	満	Man	Manchuria
濠, 豪	Gō	Australia	墨	Boku	Mexico
墺	Ō	Austria	蒙	Mō	Mongolia
白	Haku	Belgium	蘭	Ran	the Netherlands, Holland
伯	Haku	Brazil			
英	Ei	Britain, England	諾	Daku	Norway
			ペ	Pe	Persia
緬	Ben	Burma, Myanmar	比	Hi	Philippines
			波	Ha	Poland
加	Ka	Canada	葡	Po	Portugal
中	Chū	China	普	Fu	Prussia
丁	Tei	Denmark	露, ロ	Ro	Russia
埃, エ	Ai, E	Egypt	ソ	So	Soviet Union
欧	Ō	Europe	西	Sei	Spain
仏	Futsu	France	瑞	Zui	Sweden
独	Doku	Germany	瑞	Zui	Switzerland
希	Gi	Greece	台	Tai	Taiwan
洪	Kō	Hungary	泰	Tai	Thailand
印	In	India	土	To	Turkey
伊	I	Italy	教	Kyō	Vatican
日	Nichi	Japan	越	Etsu	Vietnam

The *Iroha* Kana Sequence
いろは

In addition to the standard *a-i-u-e-o* alphabetical order of the kana characters, there is another arrangement known as the *i-ro-ha*. The *i-ro-ha* arrangement is based on an old poem in which each of the 47 kana characters appears exactly once (including the two obsolete characters ヰ *(w)i* and ヱ *(w)e* but excluding the modern end-of-syllable ン -n):

イ ロ ハ ニ ホ ヘ ト	i-ro-ha ni-ho-he-to
チ リ ヌ ル ヲ	chi-ri-nu-ru (w)o
ワ カ ヨ タ レ ソ	wa-ka yo ta-re so
ツ ネ ナ ラ ム	tsu-ne na-ra-mu
ウ ヰ ノ オ ク ヤ マ	u-(w)i no o-ku-ya-ma
ケ フ コ エ テ	ke-fu ko-e-te
ア サ キ ユ メ ミ シ	a-sa-ki yu-me mi-shi
ヱ ヒ モ セ ス	(w)e-hi mo se-su

The イロハ sequence is used mostly for labeling subheadings or items in a short list, so it is hardly worthwhile to memorize this sequence beyond イロハニホヘト. Another use of the イロハ sequence is in specifying musical keys, where イ = A, ロ = B, ハ = C, ニ = D, ホ = E, ヘ = F, ト = G, a major key is referred to as 長調 *chōchō* and a minor key as 短調 *tanchō*, and sharp is designated by 嬰 *ei* and flat by 変 *hen*: thus, the key of B flat major is 変ロ長調, and C sharp minor is 嬰ハ短調.

A Word about Counters
助数詞

In English, nouns are divided into two types: count nouns, and mass nouns. A count noun is one that has a plural and can be counted, like dog, plan, or mile. A mass noun is one like butter or wheat that has no plural and cannot in itself be counted: instead, one specifies the units in which the mass noun is thought of and counts the units. Thus, one counts 'pats,' 'sticks,' or 'pounds' of butter, and 'grains,' 'bushels,' or 'truckloads' of wheat.

In Japanese, all nouns are mass nouns. That is, to count a Japanese noun, you must specify, by a word known as a "counter" (助数詞 *josūshi*), the unit in which the noun is to be counted. The counter is preceded by a number word, usually from the *ichi-ni-san* series but sometimes, depending on the counter, from the *hito-futa-mi* series. The counter 本 *hon* is used for cylindrical objects like pencils or bottles (*ip-pon, ni-hon, san-bon, …*), 枚 *mai* is used for flat objects like pieces of paper, plates, or panes of glass (*ichi-mai, ni-mai, san-mai, …*), and 冊 *satsu* is used for counting books (*is-satsu, ni-satsu, san-satsu, …*). For many nouns there is more than one counter to choose from: for example, bananas can be counted as individual bananas with 本 *hon* or by the bunch with 房 *fusa*. For nouns for which there is no obvious counter, the trend nowadays is to use the "default" counter つ *tsu* (*hito-tsu, futa-tsu, mit-tsu, …*) or 個 *ko* (*ik-ko, ni-ko, san-ko, …*).

The full story of counters would be a small dictionary in itself, listing one or more counters for each noun and the proper reading(s) for each possible number-counter combination (for example, 100 + 本 = *hyaku* + *hon* → *hyappon*).

The following list illustrates the counters used for a variety of nouns.

account (in bank)	口	*kuchi*	bunch (fruit)	房	*fusa*
acto (of a play)	幕	*maku*	cabbage (head)	玉	*tama*
airplane	機	*ki*	camera	台	*dai*
animal (large)	頭	*tō*	cannon	門	*mon*
animal (small)	匹	*hiki*	car	台	*dai*
article (publication)	編, 本	*hen, hon*	cello	面	*men*
bicycle	台	*dai*	chair	脚	*kyaku*
bird	羽	*wa*	chopsticks (pair)	膳	*zen*
book	冊	*satsu*	comb	枚	*mai*
book (copies)	部	*bu*	computer	台	*dai*
book (set)	巻	*kan*	computer program	本	*hon*
bonsai	鉢	*hachi*	cord, rope	筋	*suji*
bottle	本	*hon*	cow	頭	*tō*
building	棟	*tō*	crime	件	*ken*
bullet, projectile	発, 弾	*hatsu, dan*	desk	脚	*kyaku*

1639

document	通	*tsū*	phylactery	匣	*kyō*	
drink (in cup)	盃	*hai*	piano	台	*dai*	
drum	張	*chō*	pill	錠	*jō*	
egg	粒, 個	*tsubu, ko*	plate	枚	*mai*	
elevator	基	*ki*	poem	篇	*hen*	
engine	基, 台	*ki, dai*	pool	面	*men*	
fan	本	*hon*	projectile, bullet	発, 弾	*hatsu, dan*	
fish	尾, 匹	*bi, hiki*	question	問	*mon*	
film (role)	巻	*kan*	queue	列	*retsu*	
flat objects	枚	*mai*	rabbit	羽	*wa*	
floor (of building)	階	*kai*	railroad car	輛	*ryō*	
food (portion)	人前	*ninmae*	reactor	基	*ki*	
game, match	戦	*sen*	river	条, 筋	*jō, suji*	
gun	挺	*chō*	rocket, missile	発	*hatsu*	
haiku	句	*ku*	rocket base	基	*ki*	
house	軒	*ken*	rope, cord	筋	*suji*	
household	戸	*ko*	scissors	挺	*chō*	
iron, flatiron	挺	*chō*	ship	隻	*seki*	
kanji	字	*ji*	shoes (pair)	足	*soku*	
knife	丁	*chō*	shrine	座, 社	*za, sha*	
letter (character)	字	*ji*	ski	台	*dai*	
letter (document)	通	*tsū*	ski slope	面	*men*	
leaf	葉, 枚	*yō, mai*	song	曲	*kyoku*	
line (of text)	行	*gyō*	stage (theater)	座	*za*	
lodging (overnight stay)	泊	*haku*	stitch, suture	針	*hari*	
long objects	本	*hon*	stock (shares of)	株	*kabu*	
machinery	台	*dai*	stroke (of kanji)	画	*kaku*	
match, game	戦	*sen*	suit	着, 揃い	*chaku, soroi*	
meal	食	*shoku*	sushi (portion)	人前	*ninmae*	
mirror	面	*men*	sword	口	*ku*	
model (experimental)	個	*ko*	telephone	台	*dai*	
movie, video	本	*hon*	television	台	*dai*	
name card	枚	*mai*	temple	寺, 山	*ji, san*	
newspaper	部	*bu*	tennis court	面	*men*	
noh play	番	*ban*	thin objects	枚	*mai*	
novel	編	*hen*	tunnel	本	*hon*	
oar	挺	*chō*	vehicle	台	*dai*	
page (in newspaper)	面	*men*	video, movie	本	*hon*	
paper (sheet)	枚	*mai*	violin	挺	*chō*	
people	人	*nin*	work (opus)	作	*saku*	
pencil	本	*hon*	years (age)	歳, つ	*sai, tsu*	

The Japanese School System
学校制度

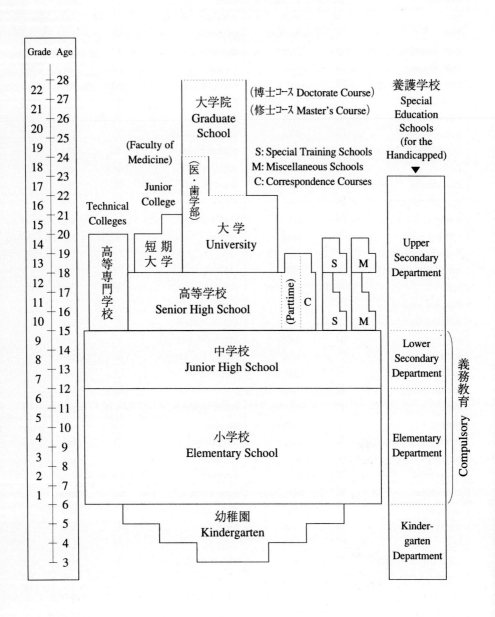

Common Signs
よく見られる標識

女
Onna
Women, Ladies

男
Otoko
Men, Gentlemen

お手洗い
Otearai
Toilet

使用中
Shiyōchū
In Use, Occupied

化粧室
Keshōshitsu
Toilet, Rest Room

押
Osu
Push

引
Hiku
Pull

大人
Otona, Dainin
Adult

小人
Shōnin
Child

子供
Kodomo
Child

案内(所)
Annai(sho/jo)
Information

切符売り場
Kippu uriba
Ticket Counter/Office

窓口
Madoguchi
(Ticket) Window

自動券売機
Jidō kenbaiki
Ticket Vending Machine

両替機
Ryōgaeki
Change Maker

自動販売機
Jidō hanbaiki
Vending Machine

発売中
Hatsubaichū
Now Being Offered
for Sale

売切(れ)
Uriki(re)
Sold Out

調整中
Chōseichū
Under Repair

故障
Koshō
Out of Order

使用禁止
Shiyō kinshi
Do Not Use

精算所
Seisanjo
Fare Adjustment Office

駅
Eki
Station

地下鉄
Chikatetsu
Subway

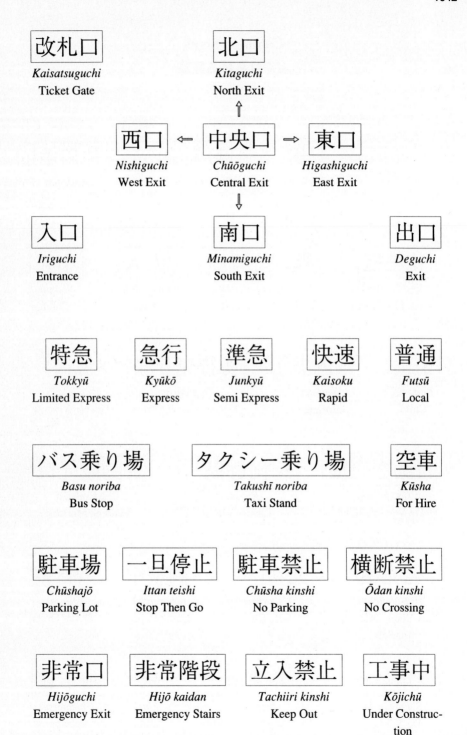

改札口
Kaisatsuguchi
Ticket Gate

北口
Kitaguchi
North Exit

西口
Nishiguchi
West Exit

中央口
Chūōguchi
Central Exit

東口
Higashiguchi
East Exit

入口
Iriguchi
Entrance

南口
Minamiguchi
South Exit

出口
Deguchi
Exit

特急
Tokkyū
Limited Express

急行
Kyūkō
Express

準急
Junkyū
Semi Express

快速
Kaisoku
Rapid

普通
Futsū
Local

バス乗り場
Basu noriba
Bus Stop

タクシー乗り場
Takushī noriba
Taxi Stand

空車
Kūsha
For Hire

駐車場
Chūshajō
Parking Lot

一旦停止
Ittan teishi
Stop Then Go

駐車禁止
Chūsha kinshi
No Parking

横断禁止
Ōdan kinshi
No Crossing

非常口
Hijōguchi
Emergency Exit

非常階段
Hijō kaidan
Emergency Stairs

立入禁止
Tachiiri kinshi
Keep Out

工事中
Kōjichū
Under Construction

注意
Chūi
Caution

足元注意
Ashimoto chūi
Watch Your Step

御注意下さい
Gochūi kudasai
Please Be Careful

…厳禁
… Genkin
… Strictly Prohibited

土足厳禁
Dosoku genkin
Remove Shoes

火気厳禁
Kaki genkin
Caution: Flammable

禁煙
Kin'en
No Smoking

撮影禁止
Satsuei kinshi
No Photographs

危険
Kiken
Danger

定価
Teika
List Price

準備中
Junbichū
Not Open Yet

営業中
Eigyōchū
Open (for Business)

年中無休
Nenjū mukyū
Open Every Day of the Year

定休日
Teikyūbi
Regular Closing Day

本日休業
Honjitsu kyūgyō
Closed Today

飲み水
Nomi-mizu
Drinking Water

飲料水
Inryōsui
Drinking Water

Islands, Cities, Mountains
主な島・都市・山

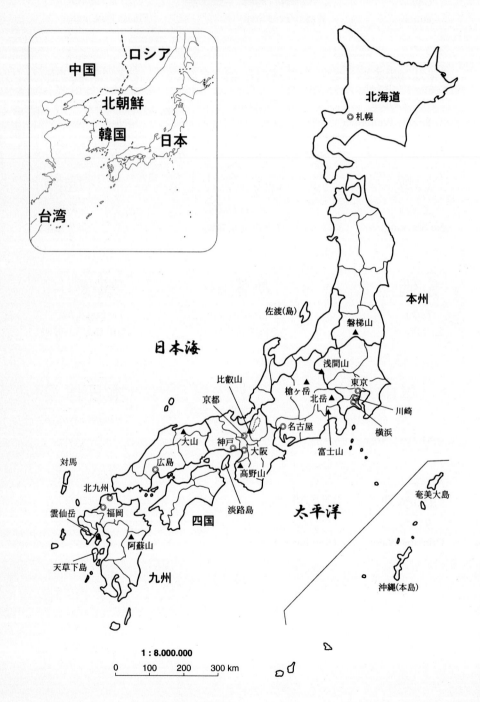

ロシア
中国
北朝鮮
韓国
日本
台湾

北海道
◎札幌

本州

佐渡(島)
磐梯山

日本海

比叡山
浅間山
京都
槍ヶ岳
北岳
東京
名古屋
川崎
大山
神戸
横浜
広島
大阪
富士山
北九州
高野山
雲仙岳
福岡
淡路島
四国
太平洋
奄美大島
天草下島
阿蘇山
九州
対馬
沖縄(本島)

1 : 8.000.000

0   100   200   300 km

1645

主な島　Major Islands

島名　Name		面積 km² Area	府県　Prefecture
本州	Honshū	230,940	
北海道	Hokkaidō	83,520	北海道
九州	Kyūshū	43,000	
四国	Shikoku	18,808	
沖縄 (本島)	Okinawa (Hontō)	1,199	沖　縄
佐渡 (島)	Sado(gashima)	854	新　潟
奄美大島	Amami Ōshima	712	鹿児島
対馬	Tsushima	696	長　崎
天草下島	Amakusa Shimoshima	593	熊　本
淡路島	Awaji-shima	591	兵　庫

主要都市　Cities over One Million (1992)

都市名　Cities over one million		人口 (千人) Population	府県　Prefecture
東京23区	Tōkyō	7,976	東京都
横浜	Yokohama	3,233	神奈川県
大阪	Ōsaka	2,506	大阪府
名古屋	Nagoya	2,098	愛知県
札幌	Sapporo	1,687	北海道
神戸	Kōbe	1,459	兵庫県
京都	Kyōto	1,399	京都府
福岡	Fukuoka	1,205	福岡県
川崎	Kawasaki	1,162	神奈川県
広島	Hiroshima	1,066	広島県
北九州	Kitakyūshū	1,016	福岡県

有名な山　Famous Mountains

山名　Name		標高 m Height	府県　Prefecture
富士山	Fuji-san	3,776	静岡県, 山梨県
北岳	Kita-dake	3,192	山梨県
槍ヶ岳	Yariga-take	3,180	長野県
浅間山	Asama-san	2,568	群馬県, 長野県
磐梯山	Bandai-san	1,819	福島県
大山	Dai-sen	1,729	鳥取県
阿蘇山	Aso-san	1,592	熊本県, 大分県
雲仙岳	Unzen-dake	1,359	長崎県
高野山	Kōya-san	1,000	和歌山県
比叡山	Hiei-zan	848	京都府, 滋賀県

Prefectures *(Ken)*
現在の行政区分

北海道

東北

青森

秋田　岩手

宮城

山形

富山　　福島

北陸　新潟

石川　栃木　　関東

滋賀　福井　長野　群馬　茨城

京都　　　岐阜　埼玉

鳥取　　　　愛知　山梨　千葉

中国　　　　　静岡　東京

島根　兵庫　三重　神奈川

岡山　奈良　中部

広島　　　近畿

山口　徳島　和歌山

愛媛　大阪

福岡　高知　四国

佐賀　大分

長崎　熊本　香川

九州　宮崎

鹿児島

沖縄

1 : 8.000.000

0   100   200   300 km

Prefecture 都 道 府 県			Capital 庁 舎 所 在 地		Area 面積 km²	Population 人口 (千人)
北海道	1 北海道	Hokkaidō	札幌	Sapporo	83 450	5 666
東北 Tōhoku	2 青森	Aomori	青森	Aomori	9 605	1 507
	3 岩手	Iwate	盛岡	Morioka	15 275	1 429
	4 宮城	Miyagi	仙台	Sendai	7 384	2 287
	5 秋田	Akita	秋田	Akita	11 612	1 227
	6 山形	Yamagata	山形	Yamagata	9 323	1 256
	7 福島	Fukushima	福島	Fukushima	13 781	2 130
関東 Kantō	8 茨城	Ibaragi	水戸	Mito	6 093	2 936
	9 栃木	Tochigi	宇都宮	Utsunomiya	6 408	1 969
	10 群馬	Gunma	前橋	Maebashi	6 363	1 991
	11 埼玉	Saitama	浦和	Urawa	3 797	6 612
	12 千葉	Chiba	千葉	Chiba	5 155	5 718
	13 東京	Tōkyō	東京	Tōkyō	2 183	11 573
	14 神奈川	Kanagawa	横浜	Yokohama	2 412	8 104
北陸 Hokuriku	15 新潟	Niigata	新潟	Niigata	12 581	2 484
	16 富山	Toyama	富山	Toyama	4 246	1 124
	17 石川	Ishikawa	金沢	Kanazawa	4 184	1 167
	18 福井	Fukui	福井	Fukui	4 188	823
中部 Chūbu	19 山梨	Yamanashi	甲府	Kōfu	4 465	870
	20 長野	Nagano	長野	Nagano	13 585	2 179
	21 岐阜	Gifu	岐阜	Gifu	10 597	2 090
	22 静岡	Shizuoka	静岡	Shizuoka	7 778	3 718
	23 愛知	Aichi	名古屋	Nagoya	5 147	6 715
近畿 Kinki	24 滋賀	Shiga	大津	Ōtsu	4 017	1 260
	25 三重	Mie	津	Tsu	5 774	1 830
	26 和歌山	Wakayama	和歌山	Wakayama	4 722	1 095
	27 奈良	Nara	奈良	Nara	3 690	1 415
	28 京都	Kyōto	京都	Kyōto	4 612	2 543
	29 大阪	Ōsaka	大阪	Ōsaka	1 890	8 543
	30 兵庫	Hyōgo	神戸	Kōbe	8 384	5 458
中国 Chūgoku	31 鳥取	Tottori	鳥取	Tottori	3 506	618
	32 島根	Shimane	松江	Matsue	6 706	775
	33 岡山	Okayama	岡山	Okayama	7 111	1 944
	34 広島	Hiroshima	広島	Hiroshima	8 473	2 862
	35 山口	Yamaguchi	山口	Yamaguchi	6 109	1 556
四国 Shikoku	36 徳島	Tokushima	徳島	Tokushima	4 143	837
	37 香川	Kagawa	高松	Takamatsu	1 875	1 030
	38 愛媛	Ehime	松山	Matsuyama	5 674	1 525
	39 高知	Kōchi	高知	Kōchi	7 104	826
九州 Kyūshū	40 福岡	Fukuoka	福岡	Fukuoka	4 965	4 849
	41 佐賀	Saga	佐賀	Saga	2 438	883
	42 長崎	Nagasaki	長崎	Nagasaki	4 089	1 557
	43 熊本	Kumamoto	熊本	Kumamoto	7 401	1 859
	44 大分	Ōita	大分	Ōita	6 336	1 241
	45 宮崎	Miyazaki	宮崎	Miyazaki	7 733	1 184
	46 鹿児島	Kagoshima	鹿児島	Kagoshima	9 185	1 792
	47 沖縄	Okinawa	那覇	Naha	2 265	1 267

人口－１９９４年３月３１日現在

Old Provinces *(Kuni)*
近世の行政区分

蝦夷

陸奥
羽後　陸中
羽前　陸前
佐渡　岩代
越後　磐城
下野
越中　上野　常陸
能登
近江　加賀　信濃　武蔵　下総
美作　但馬　丹後　越前　飛騨　上総
備前　因幡　丹波　若狭　甲斐　安房
隠岐　　　　美濃　　駿河　伊豆
伯耆　備中　丹波　　遠江　相模
出雲　　　播磨　摂津　尾張　三河
石見　備後　　　紀　志摩
筑前　安芸　阿波　伊　伊賀
豊前　長門　周　伊予　大和　伊勢
対馬　筑後　防　土佐　河内　伊勢
壱岐　　肥前　淡路　和泉　山城
　　肥後　豊後　讃岐
　　日向　薩摩
　　大隅

1	蝦夷	Ezo	北海道		38	大和	Yamato	奈良
					39	河内	Kawachi	大阪
東山道		**Tōsandō**			40	和泉	Izumi	大阪
2	陸奥	Mutsu	青森・岩手		41	摂津	Settsu	大阪・兵庫
3	羽前	Uzen	山形					
4	羽後	Ugo	秋田・山形		**山陰道**		**San'indō**	
5	陸中	Rikuchū	岩手・秋田		42	丹波	Tanba	京都・兵庫
6	陸前	Rikuzen	岩手・宮城		43	丹後	Tango	京都
7	磐城	Iwaki	宮城・福島		44	但馬	Tajima	兵庫
8	岩代	Iwashiro	福島		45	因幡	Inaba	鳥取
9	下野	Shimotsuke	栃木		46	伯耆	Hōki	鳥取
10	上野	Kōzuke	群馬		47	出雲	Izumo	島根
11	信濃	Shinano	長野		48	石見	Iwami	島根
12	飛騨	Hida	岐阜		49	隠岐	Oki	島根
13	美濃	Mino	岐阜					
14	近江	Ōmi	滋賀		**山陽道**		**San'yōdō**	
					50	播磨	Harima	兵庫
東海道		**Tōkaidō**			51	美作	Mimasaka	岡山
15	常陸	Hitachi	茨城		52	備前	Bizen	岡山
16	下総	Shimōsa	茨城・千葉		53	備中	Bitchū	岡山
17	上総	Kazusa	千葉		54	備後	Bingo	広島
18	安房	Awa	千葉		55	安芸	Aki	広島
19	武蔵	Musashi	埼玉・東京・		56	周防	Suō	山口
			神奈川		57	長門	Nagato	山口
20	相模	Sagami	神奈川					
21	甲斐	Kai	山梨		**南海道**		**Nankaidō**	
22	駿河	Suruga	静岡		58	紀伊	Kii	和歌山・三重
23	伊豆	Izu	静岡		59	淡路	Awaji	兵庫
24	遠江	Tōtōmi	静岡		60	阿波	Awa	徳島
25	三河	Mikawa	愛知		61	讃岐	Sanuki	香川
26	尾張	Owari	愛知		62	伊予	Iyo	愛媛
27	伊勢	Ise	三重		63	土佐	Tosa	高知
28	伊賀	Iga	三重					
29	志摩	Shima	三重		**西海道**		**Saikaidō**	
					64	筑前	Chikuzen	福岡
北陸道		**Hokurikudō**			65	筑後	Chikugo	福岡
30	越後	Echigo	新潟		66	豊前	Buzen	福岡・大分
31	佐渡	Sado	新潟		67	豊後	Bungo	大分
32	越中	Etchū	富山		68	肥前	Hizen	佐賀・長崎
33	能登	Noto	石川		69	肥後	Higo	熊本
34	加賀	Kaga	石川		70	日向	Hyūga	宮崎
35	越前	Echizen	福井		71	大隅	Ōsumi	鹿児島
36	若狭	Wakasa	福井		72	薩摩	Satsuma	鹿児島
					73	壱岐	Iki	長崎
畿内		**Kinai**			74	対馬	Tsushima	長崎
37	山城	Yamashiro	京都					

The Japanese Political System
政治機構
Political Institutions
政治機関

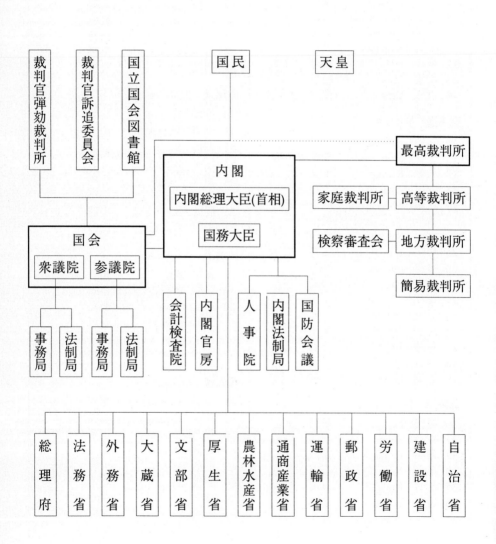

内閣	*Naikaku*	**Cabinet**
内閣総理大臣(首相)	*Naikaku Sōri Daijin (Shushō)*	Prime Minister
国務大臣	*Kokumu Daijin*	Cabinet Ministers
会計検査院	*Kaikei Kensain*	Board of Audit
内閣官房	*Naikaku Kanbō*	Cabinet Secretariat
人事院	*Jinjiin*	National Personnel Authority
内閣法制局	*Naikaku Hōseikyoku*	Cabinet Legislation Bureau
国防会議	*Kokubō Kaigi*	National Defense Council
総理府	*Sōrifu*	Prime Minister's Office
法務省	*Hōmushō*	Ministry of Justice
外務省	*Gaimushō*	Ministry of Foreign Affairs
大蔵省	*Ōkurashō*	Ministry of Finance
文部省	*Monbushō*	Ministry of Education
厚生省	*Kōseishō*	Ministry of Health and Welfare
農林水産省	*Nōrin Suisanshō*	Ministry of Agriculture, Forestry, and Fisheries
通商産業省	*Tsūshō Sangyōshō*	Ministry of International Trade and Industry (MITI)
運輸省	*Un'yushō*	Ministry of Transport
郵政省	*Yūseishō*	Ministry of Posts and Telecommunications
労働省	*Rōdōshō*	Ministry of Labor
建設省	*Kensetsushō*	Ministry of Construction
自治省	*Jichishō*	Ministry of Home Affairs

国会	*Kokkai*	**Diet**
衆議院	*Shūgiin*	House of Representatives
参議院	*Sangiin*	House of Councillors
事務局	*Jimukyoku*	Secretariat
法制局	*Hōseikyoku*	Legislation Bureau
裁判官弾劾裁判所	*Saibankan Dankō Saibansho*	Judges Impeachment Court
裁判官訴追委員会	*Saibankan Sotsui Iinkai*	Judges Indictment Committee
国立国会図書館	*Kokuritsu Kokkai Toshokan*	National Diet Library

最高裁判所	*Saikō Saibansho*	**Supreme Court**
高等裁判所	*Kōtō Saibansho*	High Courts
地方裁判所	*Chihō Saibansho*	District Courts
簡易裁判	*Kan'i Saibansho*	Summary Courts
家庭裁判所	*Katei Saibansho*	Family Courts
検察審査会	*Kensatsu Shinsakai*	Commitees for the Inquest of Prosecution

国民	*Kokumin*	People
天皇	*Tennō*	Emperor

The Japanese Political System
政治機構
Separation of Powers: Legislative, Executive, Judicial
三権分立

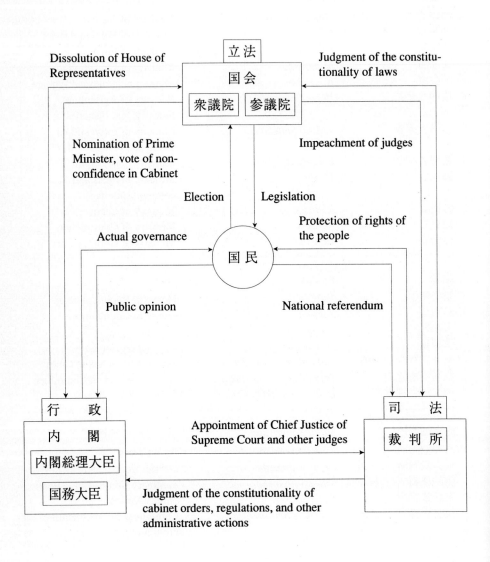

立法	***Rippō***	**Legislative branch**
国会	*Kokkai*	Diet
衆議院	*Shūgiin*	House of Representatives
参議院	*Jinjiin*	House of Councillors

行政	***Gyōsei***	**Executive branch**
内閣	*Naikaku*	Cabinet
内閣総理大臣	*Naikaku Sōri Daijin*	Prime Minister
国務大臣	*Kokumu Daijin*	Cabinet Ministers

司法	***Shihō***	**Judicial branch**
裁判所	*Saibansho*	Courts

国民	*Kokumin*	People

Selected Government Agencies and Quasi-Governmental Organizations
主要官庁及び準官庁

防衛庁	*Bōeichō*	Defence Agency (Prime Minister's office)
経済企画庁	*Keizai Kikakuchō*	Economic Planning Agency (Prime Minister's office)
文化庁	*Bunkachō*	Agency for Cultural Affairs (Ministry of Education)
気象庁	*Kishōchō*	Meteorological Agency (Ministry of Transport)
国際交流基金	*Kokusai Kōryū Kikin*	Japan Foundation (Ministry of Foreign Affairs)
日本国際問題研究所	*Nihon Kokusai Mondai Kenkyūjo*	Japan Institute of International Affairs (Ministry of Foreign Affairs)
青年海外協力隊	*Seinen Kaigai Kyōryoku-tai*	Japan Overseas Cooperation Volunteers (JOCV, often called the Japanese Peace Corps)

Political Parties (since 1945)
主要系統略図

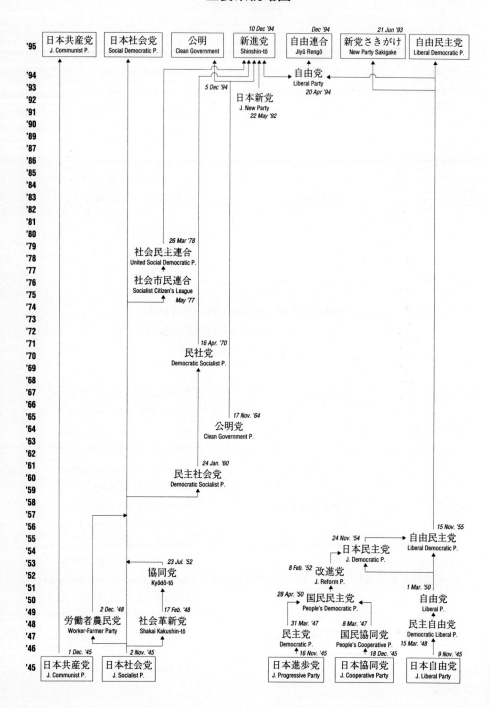

Japanese Postwar Governments
戦後内閣一覧

Prime Minister 総理大臣		Born–died 生・没年		Inauguration 発足年月日		
東久邇稔彦	Higashikuni Naruhiko	1887–1990		17	Aug.	1945
幣原喜重郎	Shidehara Kijūrō	1872–1951		9	Oct.	1945
吉田　茂	Yoshida Shigeru	1878–1967	1st term	22	May	1946
片山　哲	Katayama Tetsu	1887–1978		24	May	1947
芦田　均	Ashida Hitoshi	1887–1959		10	Mar.	1948
吉田　茂	Yoshida Shigeru	1878–1967	2nd term	15	Oct.	1948
			3rd term	16	Feb.	1949
			4th term	30	Oct.	1952
			5th term	21	May	1953
鳩山一郎	Hatoyama Ichirō	1883–1959	1st term	10	Dec.	1954
			2nd term	19	Mar.	1955
			3rd term	22	Nov.	1955
石橋湛山	Ishibashi Tanzan	1884–1973		23	Dec.	1956
岸　信介	Kishi Nobusuke	1896–1987	1st term	25	Feb.	1957
			2nd term	12	June	1958
池田勇人	Ikeda Hayato	1899–1965	1st term	19	July	1960
			2nd term	8	Dec.	1960
			3rd term	9	Dec.	1963
佐藤栄作	Satō Eisaku	1901–1975	1st term	9	Nov.	1964
			2nd term	17	Feb.	1967
			3rd term	14	Jan.	1970
田中角栄	Tanaka Kakuei	1918–1993	1st term	7	July	1972
			2nd term	22	Dec.	1972
三木武夫	Miki Takeo	1907–1988		9	Dec.	1974
福田赳夫	Fukuda Takeo	1905–		24	Dec.	1976
大平正芳	Ōhira Masayoshi	1910–1980	1st term	7	Dec.	1978
			2nd term	9	Nov.	1979
鈴木善幸	Suzuki Zenkō	1911–		17	July	1980
中曽根康弘	Nakasone Yasuhiro	1918–	1st term	27	Nov.	1982
			2nd term	27	Dec.	1983
			3rd term	22	July	1986
竹下　登	Takeshita Noboru	1924–		6	Nov.	1987
宇野宗佑	Uno Sōsuke	1922–		3	June	1989
海部俊樹	Kaifu Toshiki	1931–	1st term	10	Aug.	1989
			2nd term	28	Feb.	1990
宮沢喜一	Miyazawa Kiichi	1919–		5	Nov.	1991
細川護熙	Hosokawa Morihiro	1938–		9	Aug.	1993
羽田　孜	Hata Tsutomu	1935–		28	Apr.	1994
村山富市	Murayama Tomiichi	1924–		30	June	1994

Management Hierarchy
企業及び団体幹部序列

Most large Japanese companies have the legal form of a 株式会社 *kabushiki-gaisha* (limited liability corporation issuing shares of stock). The titles of the management hierarchy differ considerably from company to company, but in general the ranking system is as follows:

XYZ株式会社	*XYZ Kabushiki-Gaisha*	XYZ Co., Ltd.
会長	*Kaichō*	President, Chairman
取締役会長	*Torishimariyaku kaichō*	Chairman of the Board of Directors
社長	*Shachō*	President
副社長	*Fukushachō*	Vice President
代表取締役	*Daihyō torishimariyaku*	Representative Director
専務取締役	*Senmu torishimariyaku*	Executive Director, Senior Managing Director
常務取締役	*Jōmu torishimariyaku*	Managing Director
部長	*Buchō*	Department Head
課長	*Kachō*	Section Chief

These ranks can be members of the board of directors. In this case 締役 *torishimariyaku* is used before or after the rank.

係長	*Kakarichō*	Subsection Chief
作業長	*Sagyōchō*	Supervisor, Foreman
組長	*Kumichō*	Leader, Captain
班長	*Hanchō*	Group Leader (origin of "head honcho")

The prefix 副 *fuku-* on a title means Vice or Sub-, the suffix 代理 *-dairi* means Deputy or Acting, and the suffix 補 *-ho* or 補佐 *-hosa* means Assistant.

有限会社	*yūgen-gaisha*	limited liability company
社長	*Shachō*	President
or 代表取締役	*Daihyō torishimariyaku*	(General) Manager

or 総支配人	*Sōshihainin*	General Manager; Managing Partner
or 社長株主	*Shachō kabunushi*	General Manager; Managing Partner

合名会社	*gōmei-gaisha*	partnership corporation
代表社員	*daihyō shain*	partner associate

個人会社	*kojin-gaisha*	private firm
社主	*shashu*	owner

代理店	*dairiten*	(commercial) agency
取引代理人	*torihiki dairinin*	(commercial) agent

商工会議所	*Shōkō Kaigisho*	Chambers of Commerce
(団体)会頭	*(Dantai) Kaitō*	Chairman
or (団体)会長	*(Dantai) Kaichō*	Chairman
or (団体)理事長	*(Dantai) Rijichō*	Chairman
副会頭	*Fukukaitō*	Vice Chairman
or 副会長	*Fukukaichō*	Vice Chairman
or 副理事長	*Fukurijichō*	Vice Chairman
幹部会員	*Kanbu kaiin*	Member of the Board
常任幹事	*Jōnin kanji*	Chief Executive Director; President
or 専務理事	*Senmu riji*	Chief Executive Director; President
事務総長	*Jimu sōchō*	Secretary General
常務理事	*Jōmu riji*	Deputy Chief Executive Director
事務局長	*Jimukyokuchō*	(Executive) Director
事務局次長	*Jimukyoku jichō*	Deputy (Executive) Director

50 Major Companies
50の主要企業名

1	日本電信電話	*Nippon denshin denwa*	Nippon Telegraph and Telephone Corp.
2	東日本旅客鉄道	*Higashi-Nihon ryokaku tetsudō*	East Japan Railway Co.
3	日立製作所	*Hitachi seisakusho*	Hitachi, Ltd.
4	東芝	*Tōshiba*	Toshiba Corp.
5	トヨタ自動車	*Toyota jidōsha*	Toyota Motor Corp.
6	富士通	*Fujitsū*	Fujitsu Ltd.
7	日本通運	*Nippon tsūun*	Nippon Express Co., Ltd.
8	日産自動車	*Nissan jidōsha*	Nissan Motor Co., Ltd.
9	ヤマト運輸	*Yamato un' yu*	Yamato Transport Co., Ltd.
10	三菱電機	*Mitsubishi denki*	Mitsubishi Electric Corp.
11	松下電器産業	*Matsushita denki sangyō*	Matsushita Electric Industrial Co., Ltd.
12	三菱重工業	*Mitsubishi jūkōgyō*	Mitsubishi Heavy Industries, Ltd.
13	日本電気	*Nippon denki*	NEC Corp.
14	日本電装	*Nippon densō*	Nippondenso Co., Ltd.
15	東京電力	*Tōkyō denryoku*	The Tokyo Electric Power Co., Inc.
16	新日本製鐵	*Shin Nippon seitetsu*	Nippon Steel Corp.
17	本田技研工業	*Honda giken kōgyō*	Honda Motor Co., Ltd.
18	マツダ	*Matsuda*	Mazda Motor Corp.
19	三菱自動車工業	*Mitsubishi jidōsha kōgyō*	Mitsubishi Motors Corp.
20	三洋電機	*San' yō denki*	Sanyo Electric Co., Ltd.
21	関西電力	*Kansai denryoku*	The Kansai Electric Power Co., Inc.
22	ソニー	*Sonī*	Sony Corp.
23	シャープ	*Shāpu*	Sharp Corp.
24	日本鋼管 (NKK)	*Nippon kōkan*	NKK
25	住友金属工業	*Sumitomo kinzoku kōgyō*	Sumitomo Metal Industries, Ltd.
26	日本航空	*Nihon kōkū*	Japan Airlines Co., Ltd.
27	中部電力	*Chūbu denryoku*	The Chubu Electric Power Co., Inc.
28	松下電工	*Matsushita denkō*	Matsushita Electric Works, Ltd.
29	神戸製鋼所	*Kōbe seikōsho*	Kobe Steel, Ltd.
30	ダイエー	*Daiē*	The Daiei, Inc.
31	キャノン	*Kyanon*	Canon Inc.
32	山崎製パン	*Yamazaki seipan*	Yamazaki Baking Co., Ltd.
33	川崎重工業	*Kawasaki jūkōgyō*	Kawasaki Heavy Industries, Ltd.
34	川崎製鉄	*Kawasaki seitetsu*	Kawasaki Steel Corp.
35	旭化成工業	*Asahi kasei kōgyō*	Asahi Chemical Industry Co., Ltd.
36	石川島播磨重工業	*Ishikawajima-Harima jūkōgyō*	Ishikawajima-Harima Heavy Industries Co., Ltd.
37	クボタ	*Kubota*	Kubota Corp.
38	福山通運	*Fukuyama tsūun*	Fukuyama Transporting Co., Ltd.
39	ブリジストン	*Burijisuton*	Bridgestone Corp.
40	西濃運輸	*Seinō un' yu*	Seino Transportation Co., Ltd.
41	イトーヨーカ堂	*Itō-yōkadō*	Ito-Yokado Co., Ltd
42	富士重工業	*Fuji jūkōgyō*	Fuji Heavy Industries Ltd.
43	全日本空輸	*Zen-Nippon kūyu*	All Nippon Airways Co., Ltd.
44	いすゞ自動車	*Isuzu jidōsha*	Isuzu Motors Ltd.
45	住友電気工業	*Sumitomo denki kōgyō*	Sumitomo Electric Industries, Ltd.
46	大日本印刷	*Dai-Nippon insatsu*	Dai Nippon Printing Co., Ltd.
47	鹿島建設	*Kajima kensetsu*	Kajima Corp.
48	凸版印刷	*Toppan insatsu*	Toppan Printing Co., Ltd.
49	富士電機	*Fuji denki*	Fuji Electric Co., Ltd.
50	日本ビクター	*Nihon bikutā*	JVC Ltd.

Major Economic and Labor Organizations
経済団体及び労働組合

主要経済・業界団体　Major Economic Organizations

経済団体連合会 (経団連)　*Keizai Dantai Rengōkai (Keidanren)*　Federation of Economic Organization

日本経営者団体連盟 (日経連)　*Nihon Keieisha Dantai Renmei (Nikkeiren)*　Japan Federation of Employers' Associations

日本中小企業団体連盟　*Nihon Chūshō Kigyō Dantai Renmei*　Japan Federation of Smaller Enterprise

日本工業クラブ　*Nihon Kōgyō Kurabu*　Industrial Club of Japan

日本国際貿易促進協会　*Nihon Kokusai Bōeki Sokushin Kyōkai*　Association for the Promotion of Intenational Trade, Japan

日本貿易振興会 (ジェトロ)　*Nihon Bōeki Shinkōkai (Jetoro)*　Japan External Trade Organization (JETRO)

日本貿易会　*Nihon Bōekikai*　Japan Foreign Trade Council, Inc.

日本輸出入銀行　*Nihon Yushutsunyū Ginkō*　Export-Import Bank of Japan

日本商工会議所　*Nihon Shōkō Kaigisho*　Japan Chamber of Commerce and Industry

経済同友会　*Keizai Dōyūkai*　Japan Association of Corporate Executives

関西経済連合会 (関経連)　*Kansai Keizai Rengōkai (Kankeiren)*　Kansai Economic Federation

日本鉄鋼連盟　*Nihon Tekkō Renmei*　Japan Iron & Steel Federation

日本自動車工業会　*Nihon Jidōsha Kōgyōkai*　Japan Automobile Manufacturers Association (JAMA)

電気事業連合会　*Denki Jigyō Rengōkai*　Federation of Electric Power Companies

電子機械工業会　*Denshi Kikai Kōgyōkai*　Electronic Industries Association of Japan

日本電機工業会　*Nihon Denki Kōgyōkai*　Japan Electrical Manufacturers' Association

日本造船工業会　*Nihon Zōsen Kōgyōkai*　Shipbuilders' Association of Japan

日本損害保険協会　*Nihon Songai Hoken Kyōkai*　Marine and Fire Insurance Association of Japan Inc.

日本出版協会　*Nihon Shuppan Kyōkai*　Japan Publishing Association

日本新聞協会　*Nihon Shinbun Kyōkai*　Japan Newspaper Publishers and Editors Association

労働組合　Labor Federations

日本労働組合総連合会 (連合)　*Nihon Rōdōkumiai Sōrengōkai (Rengō)*　Japan Trade Union Confederation

全国労働組合総連合 (全労連)　*Zenkoku Rōdōkumiai Sōrengō (Zenrōren)*　National Confederation of Trade Unions

全国労働組合連絡協議会 (全労協)　*Zenkoku Rōdōkumiai Renraku Kyōgikai (Zenrōkyō)*　National Trade Union Council

連合 *Rengō* is the labor federation with the largest number of affiliated unions (64), followed by 全労連 *Zenrōren* (17), and 全労協 *Zenrōkyō* (2). Many labor unions are not affiliated with any labor federation.

Periods of Japanese History
日本歴史の時代区分

縄文	**Jōmon**		嘉祥	Kashō	848–851
	ca. 10,000 BC – ca. 300 BC		仁寿	Ninju	851–854
			斉衡	Saikō	854–857
弥生	**Yayoi**		天安	Ten'an	857–859
	ca. 300 BC – 300 AD		貞観	Jōgan	859–877
			元慶	Gangyō	877–885
古代	**Kodai**	ca. 300–1185	仁和	Ninna	885–889
			寛平	Kanpyō	889–898
古墳	**Kofun**	ca. 300–710	昌泰	Shōtai	898–901
飛鳥	**Asuka**	592–645	延喜	Engi	901–923
大化	Taika	645–650	延長	Enchō	923–931
白雉	Hakuchi	650–654	承平	Jōhei	931–938
朱鳥	Shuchō	686	天慶	Tengyō	938–947
大宝	Taihō	701–704	天暦	Tenryaku	947–957
慶雲	Keiun	704–708	天徳	Tentoku	957–961
			応和	Ōwa	961–964
奈良	**Nara**	710–794	康保	Kōhō	964–968
和銅	Wadō	708–715	安和	Anna	968–970
霊亀	Reiki	715–717	天禄	Tenroku	970–973
養老	Yōrō	717–724	天延	Ten'en	973–976
神亀	Jinki	724–729	貞元	Jōgen	976–978
天平	Tenpyō	729–749	天元	Tengen	978–983
天平感宝	Tenpyō-kanpō	749	永観	Eikan	983–985
			寛和	Kanna	985–987
平安	**Heian**	794–1185	永延	Eien	987–989
天平勝宝	Tenpyō-shōhō	749–757	永祚	Eiso	989–990
天平宝字	Tenpyō-hōji	757–765	正暦	Shōryaku	990–995
天平神護	Tenpyō-jingo	765–767	長徳	Chōtoku	995–999
神護景雲	Jingo-keiun	767–770	長保	Chōhō	999–1004
宝亀	Hōki	770–780	寛弘	Kankō	1004–1012
天応	Ten'ō	781–782	長和	Chōwa	1012–1017
延暦	Enryaku	782–806	寛仁	Kannin	1017–1021
大同	Daidō	806–810	治安	Jian	1021–1024
弘仁	Kōnin	810–824	万寿	Manju	1024–1028
天長	Tenchō	824–834	長元	Chōgen	1028–1037
承和	Jōwa	834–848			

長暦	Chōryaku	1037–1040	応保	Ōhō	1161–1163
長久	Chōkyū	1040–1044	長寛	Chōkan	1163–1165
寛徳	Kantoku	1044–1046	永万	Eiman	1165–1166
永承	Eishō	1046–1053	仁安	Nin'an	1166–1169
天喜	Tengi	1053–1058	嘉応	Kaō	1169–1171
康平	Kōhei	1058–1065	承安	Jōan	1171–1175
治暦	Jiryaku	1065–1069	安元	Angen	1175–1177
延久	Enkyū	1069–1074	治承	Jishō	1177–1181
承保	Jōhō	1074–1077	養和	Yōwa	1181–1182
承暦	Jōryaku	1077–1081	寿永	Juci	1182 1185
永保	Eihō	1081–1084	元暦	Genryaku	1184–1185
応徳	Ōtoku	1084–1087	**中世**	**Chūsei**	**1185–1568**
寛治	Kanji	1087–1094	**鎌倉**	**Kamakura**	**1185–1333**
嘉保	Kahō	1094–1096	文治	Bunji	1185–1190
永長	Eichō	1096–1097	建久	Kenkyū	1190–1199
承徳	Jōtoku	1097–1099	正治	Shōji	1199–1201
康和	Kōwa	1099–1104	建仁	Kennin	1201–1204
長治	Chōji	1104–1106	元久	Genkyū	1204–1206
嘉承	Kajō	1106–1108	建永	Ken'ei	1206–1207
天仁	Tennin	1108–1110	承元	Jōgen	1207–1211
天永	Ten'ei	1110–1113	建暦	Kenryaku	1211–1213
永久	Eikyū	1113–1118	建保	Kenpō	1213–1219
元永	Gen'ei	1118–1120	承久	Jōkyū	1219–1222
保安	Hōan	1120–1124	貞応	Jōō	1222–1224
天治	Tenji	1124–1126	元仁	Gennin	1224–1225
大治	Daiji	1126–1131	嘉禄	Karoku	1225–1227
天承	Tenshō	1131–1132	安貞	Antei	1227–1229
長承	Chōshō	1132–1135	寛喜	Kangi	1229–1232
保延	Hōen	1135–1141	貞永	Jōei	1232–1233
永治	Eiji	1141–1142	天福	Tenpuku	1233–1234
康治	Kōji	1142–1144	文暦	Bunryaku	1234–1235
天養	Ten'yō	1144–1145	嘉禎	Katei	1235–1238
久安	Kyūan	1145–1151	暦仁	Ryakunin	1238–1239
仁平	Ninpyō	1151–1154	延応	Enō	1239–1240
久寿	Kyūju	1154–1156	仁治	Ninji	1240–1243
保元	Hōgen	1156–1159	寛元	Kangen	1243–1247
平治	Heiji	1159–1160	宝治	Hōji	1247–1249
永暦	Eiryaku	1160–1161	建長	Kenchō	1249–1256

康元	Kōgen	1256–1257	延文(北)	Enbun	1356–1361
正嘉	Shōka	1257–1259	康安(北)	Kōan	1361–1362
正元	Shōgen	1259–1260	貞治(北)	Jōji	1362–1368
文応	Bun'ō	1260–1261	応安(北)	Ōan	1368–1375
弘長	Kōchō	1261–1264	建徳(南)	Kentoku	1370–1372
文永	Bun'ei	1264–1275	文中(南)	Bunchū	1372–1375
建治	Kenji	1275–1278	永和(北)	Eiwa	1375–1379
弘安	Kōan	1278–1288	天授(南)	Tenju	1375–1381
正応	Shōō	1288–1293	康暦(北)	Kōryaku	1379–1381
永仁	Einin	1293–1299	永徳(北)	Eitoku	1381–1384
正安	Shōan	1299–1302	弘和(南)	Kōwa	1381–1384
乾元	Kengen	1302–1303	至徳(北)	Shitoku	1384–1387
嘉元	Kagen	1303–1306	元中(南)	Genchū	1384–1392
徳治	Tokuji	1306–1308	嘉慶(北)	Kakyō	1387–1389
延慶	Enkyō	1308–1311	康応(北)	Kōō	1389–1390
応長	Ōchō	1311–1312	明徳(北)	Meitoku	1390–1394
正和	Shōwa	1312–1317	応永	Ōei	1394–1428
文保	Bunpō	1317–1319	正長	Shōchō	1428–1429
元応	Gen'ō	1319–1321	永享	Eikyō	1429–1441
元亨	Genkō	1321–1324	嘉吉	Kakitsu	1441–1444
正中	Shōchū	1324–1326	文安	Bunnan	1444–1449
嘉暦	Karyaku	1326–1329	宝徳	Hōtoku	1449–1452
元徳(南)*	Gentoku	1329–1331	享徳	Kyōtoku	1452–1455
元徳(北)*	Gentoku	1331–1332	康正	Kōshō	1455–1457
元弘(南)	Genkō	1331–1334	長禄	Chōroku	1457–1460
			寛正	Kanshō	1460–1466
			文正	Bunshō	1466–1467
室町	**Muromachi**	**1333–1568**	応仁	Ōnin	1467–1469
正慶(北)	Shōkyō	1332–1334	文明	Bunmei	1469–1487
建武(南)	Kenmu	1334–1336	長享	Chōkyō	1487–1489
建武(北)	Kenmu	1334–1338	延徳	Entoku	1489–1492
延元(南)	Engen	1336–1340	明応	Meiō	1492–1501
暦応(北)	Ryakuō	1338–1342	文亀	Bunki	1501–1504
興国(南)	Kōkoku	1340–1346	永正	Eishō	1504–1521
康永(北)	Kōei	1342–1345	大永	Taiei	1521–1528
貞和(北)	Jōwa	1345–1350	享禄	Kyōroku	1528–1532
正平(南)	Shōhei	1346–1370	天文	Tenbun	1532–1555
観応(北)	Kan'ō	1350–1352	弘治	Kōji	1555–1558
文和(北)	Bunna	1352–1356	永禄	Eiroku	1558–1570

近世	**Kinsei**	**1568–1868**		延享	Enkyō	1744–1748
安土桃山	Azuchi-			寛延	Kn'en	1748–1751
	Momoyama	1568–1600		宝暦	Hōreki	1751–1764
元亀	Genki	1570–1573		明和	Meiwa	1764–1772
天正	Tenshō	1573–1592		安永	An'ei	1772–1781
文禄	Bunroku	1592–1596		天明	Tenmei	1781–1789
				寛政	Kansei	1789–1801
江戸/	**Edo =**			享和	Kyōwa	1801–1804
徳川	**Tokugawa**	**1600–1868**		文化	Bunka	1804–1818
慶長	Keichō	1596–1615		文政	Bunsei	1818–1830
元和	Genna	1615–1624		天保	Tenpō	1830–1844
寛永	Kan'ei	1624–1644		弘化	Kōka	1844–1848
正保	Shōhō	1644–1648		嘉永	Kaei	1848–1854
慶安	Keian	1648–1652		安政	Ansei	1854–1860
承応	Jōō	1652–1655		万延	Man'en	1860–1861
明暦	Meireki	1655–1658		文久	Bunkyū	1861–1864
万治	Manji	1658–1661		元治	Genji	1864–1865
寛文	Kanbun	1661–1673		慶応	Keiō	1865–1868
延宝	Enpō	1673–1681				
天和	Tenna	1681–1684		**近代**	**Kindai**	**1868–1945**
貞享	Jōkyō	1684–1688		明治	Meiji	1868–1912
元禄	Genroku	1688–1704		大正	Taishō	1912–1926
宝永	Hōei	1704–1711				
正徳	Shōtoku	1711–1716		**現代**	**Gendai**	**1945–**
享保	Kyōhō	1716–1736		昭和	Shōwa	1926–1989
元文	Genbun	1736–1741		平成	Heisei	1989–
寛保	Kanpō	1741–1744				

* 南朝 = Southern Dynasty 北朝 = Northern Dynasty

Japanese Era Conversion Table
西暦・日本暦対照表

(from Meiji era through 2008) (明治以降)

明治		1898	31	1925	14	1952	27	1982	57
1868	元	1899	32	1926	15	1953	28	1983	58
1869	2	1900	33			1954	29	1984	59
1870	3	1901	34	**昭和**		1955	30	1985	60
1871	4	1902	35	1926	元	1956	31	1986	61
1872	5	1903	36	1927	2	1957	32	1987	62
1873	6	1904	37	1928	3	1958	33	1988	63
1874	7	1905	38	1929	4	1959	34	1989	64
1875	8	1906	39	1930	5	1960	35		
1876	9	1907	40	1931	6	1961	36	**平成**	
1877	10	1908	41	1932	7	1962	37	1989	元
1878	11	1909	42	1933	8	1963	38	1990	2
1879	12	1910	43	1934	9	1964	39	1991	3
1880	13	1911	44	1935	10	1965	40	1992	4
1881	14	1912	45	1936	11	1966	41	1993	5
1882	15			1937	12	1967	42	1994	6
1883	16	**大正**		1938	13	1968	43	1995	7
1884	17	1912	元	1939	14	1969	44	1996	8
1885	18	1913	2	1940	15	1970	45	1997	9
1886	19	1914	3	1941	16	1971	46	1998	10
1887	20	1915	4	1942	17	1972	47	1999	11
1888	21	1916	5	1943	18	1973	48	2000	12
1889	22	1917	6	1944	19	1974	49	2001	13
1890	23	1918	7	1945	20	1975	50	2002	14
1891	24	1919	8	1946	21	1976	51	2003	15
1892	25	1920	9	1947	22	1977	52	2004	16
1893	26	1921	10	1948	23	1978	53	2005	17
1894	27	1922	11	1949	24	1979	54	2006	18
1895	28	1923	12	1950	25	1980	55	2007	19
1896	29	1924	13	1951	26	1981	56	2008	20

The first year of a Japanese era is called 元年 *gannen* rather 1 年 *ichinen* than. The information in this table may be summarized in the following Japanese-to-Western year conversion formulas: 明治 X 年 = 1867 + X; 大正 X 年 = 1911 + X; 昭和 X 年 = 1925 + X; 平成 X 年 = 1988 + X.

National Holidays and Annual Events
日本の祝日と行事

祝日　National Holiday

1月	1日	元日	*Ganjitsu*	New Year's Day
	15日	成人の日	*Seijin no hi*	Coming-of-Age Day
2月	11日	建国記念日	*Kenkoku kinenbi*	National Foundation Day
3月	21日	春分の日	*Shunbun no hi*	Vernal Equinox Day
4月	29日	みどりの日	*Midori no hi*	Greenery Day
5月	3日	憲法記念日	*Kenpō kinenbi*	Constitution Memorial Day
	4日	国民の休日	*Kokumin no Kyūjitsu*	National Holiday
	5日	こどもの日	*Kodomo no hi*	Children's Day
9月	15日	敬老の日	*Keirō no hi*	Respect-for-the-Aged Day
	23日	秋分の日	*Shūbun no hi*	Autumnal Equinox Day
10月	10日	体育の日	*Taiiku no hi*	Health-Sports Day
11月	3日	文化の日	*Bunka no hi*	Culture Day
	23日	勤労感謝の日	*Kinrō kansha no hi*	Labor Thanksgiving Day
12月	23日	天皇誕生日	*Tennō tanjōbi*	Emperor's Birthday

行事　Annual Events

1月	7日	七草がゆ	*Nanakusagayu*	rice gruel containing the seven spring herbs
2月	3日	節分	*Setsubun*	the day before the beginning of spring
3月	3日	ひな祭り	*Hinamatsuri*	Doll's Festival
5月	1日	メーデー	*Mēdē*	May Day
	第2日曜日	母の日	*Haha no hi*	Mother's Day
6月	第3日曜日	父の日	*Chichi no hi*	Father's Day
7月	7日	たなばた	*Tanabata*	Star Festival
	15日	お盆	*Obon*	*Bon* Festival
(8月	15日)	お盆	*Obon*	*Bon* Festival
9月	15日	十五夜	*Jūgoya*	full-moon night
11月	15日	七五三	*Shichi go san*	celebration of a child's growth at three, five and seven years of age
12月	31日	大みそか	*Ōmisoka*	New Year's Eve

30 Famous Shrines
30の有名な神社

気

平・稲・岩　多　　　諏　　　　鹿
　　　　　日　　　　　　　　　日・神・明・靖
　　　　　　　　　　　　熱　　　　鶴
出　　吉　　　　　　　伊　　　　箱
　厳　　　金　春
筥　　　　　　　　生・住
太　　　　　　　　　　熊野本宮
　宇　　　　　　熊・熊
　藤

Name		City/Place		Prefecture	
鹿島神宮	Kashima Jingū	鹿島郡	Kashima-gun	栃木県	Tochigi-ken
気多神社	Keta Jinja	羽咋	Hakui	石川県	Ishikawa-ken
諏訪大社	Suwa Taisha	諏訪	Suwa	長野県	Nagano-ken
日枝神社	Hie Jinja	東京	Tōkyō	東京都	Tōkyō-to
神田神社	Kanda Jinja	東京	Tōkyō	東京都	Tōkyō-to
(神田明神	Kanda Myoujin)				
明治神宮	Meiji Jingū	東京	Tōkyō	東京都	Tōkyō-to
靖国神社	Yasukuni Jinja	東京	Tōkyō	東京都	Tōkyō-to
鶴岡八幡宮	Tsurugaoka Hachiman-gū	鎌倉	Kamakura	神奈川県	Kanagawa-ken
箱根権現	Hakone Gongen	箱根	Hakone	神奈川県	Kanagawa-ken
熱田神宮	Atsuta Jingū	名古屋	Nagoya	愛知県	Aichi-ken
平安神宮	Heian Jingū	京都	Kyōto	京都府	Kyōto-fu
稲荷神社	Inari Jinja	京都	Kyōto	京都府	Kyōto-fu
岩清水八幡宮	Iwashimizu Hachiman-gū	八幡	Yawata	京都府	Kyōto-fu
(男山八幡宮	Otokoyama Hachiman-gū)				
春日大社	Kasuga Taisha	奈良	Nara	奈良県	Nara-ken
生国魂神社	Ikukunitama Jinja	大阪	Ōsaka	大阪府	Ōsaka-fu
(生魂神社	Ikutama Jinja)				
住吉大社	Sumiyoshi Taisha	大阪	Ōsaka	大阪府	Ōsaka-fu
日吉大社	Hie Taisha	大津	Ōtsu	滋賀県	Shiga-ken
	(Hiyoshi Taisha)				
多賀神社	Taga Jinja	多賀	Taga	滋賀県	Shiga-ken
伊勢神宮	Ise Jingū	伊勢	Ise	三重県	Mie-ken
熊野本宮	Kumano Hongū	熊野	Kumano	和歌山県	Wakayama-ken
熊野速玉大社	Kumano Hayatama				
	Taisha	新宮	Shingū	和歌山県	Wakayama-ken
熊野那智大社	Kumano Nachi Taisha	那智勝浦	Nachi Katsuura	和歌山県	Wakayama-ken
(熊野三社	Kumano Sansha <for the three Kumano shrines>)				
厳島神社	Itsukushima Jinja	厳島	Itsukushima	広島県	Hiroshima-ken
吉備津神社	Kibitsu Jinja	岡山	Okayama	岡山県	Okayama-ken
出雲大社	Izumo Taisha	大社	Taisha	島根県	Shimane-ken
金刀比羅宮	Kotohira-gū	琴平	Kotohira	香川県	Kagawa-ken
(金比羅山	Konpira-san)				
筥崎宮	Hakozaki-gū	福岡	Fukuoka	福岡県	Fukuoka-ken
(筥崎八幡宮	Hakozaki Hachiman-gū)				
太宰府天満宮	Dazaifu Tenman-gū	太宰府	Dazaifu	福岡県	Fukuoka-ken
藤崎八幡宮	Fujisaki Hachiman-gū	熊本	Kumamoto	熊本県	Kumamoto-ken
宇佐八幡宮	Usa Hachiman-gū	宇佐	Usa	大分県	Ōita-ken
(宇佐神宮	Usa Jingū)				

Alternative names are given in parentheses under the standard names.

50 Famous Temples
50の有名な寺院

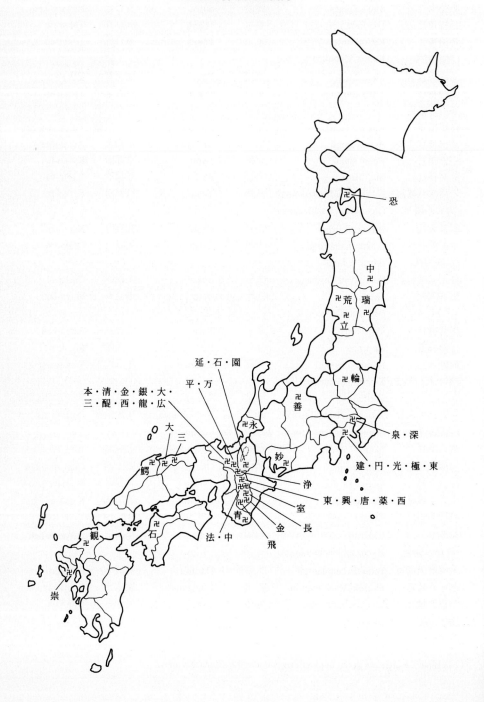

Name		City/Place		Prefecture	
恐山 (菩提寺)	Osorezan (Bodai-ji)	むつ	Mutsu	青森県	Aomori-ken
中尊寺	Chūson-ji	平泉	Hiraizumi	岩手県	Iwate-ken
瑞巌寺	Zuigan-ji	松島	Matsushima	宮城県	Miyagi-ken
荒沢寺	Kōtaku-ji	羽黒	Haguro	山形県	Yamagata-ken
立石寺	Risshaku-ji	山形	Yamagata	山形県	Yamagata-ken
輪王寺	Rinnō-ji	日光	Nikkō	栃木県	Tochigi-ken
泉岳寺	Sengaku-ji	東京	Tōkyō	東京都	Tōkyō-to
深大寺	Jindai-ji	調布	Chōfu	東京都	Tōkyō-to
建長寺	Kenchō-ji	鎌倉	Kamakura	神奈川県	Kanagawa-ken
円覚寺	Engaku-ji	鎌倉	Kamakura	神奈川県	Kanagawa-ken
光明寺	Kōmyō-ji	鎌倉	Kamakura	神奈川県	Kanagawa-ken
極楽寺	Gokuraku-ji	鎌倉	Kamakura	神奈川県	Kanagawa-ken
東慶寺	Tōkei-ji	鎌倉	Kamakura	神奈川県	Kanagawa-ken
永平寺	Eihei-ji	永平寺	Eiheiji	福井県	Fukui-ken
善光寺	Zenkō-ji	長野	Nagano	長野県	Nagano-ken
妙厳寺	Myōgon-ji	豊川	Toyokawa	愛知県	Aichi-ken
本願寺	Hongan-ji	京都	Kyōto	京都府	Kyōto-fu
清水寺	Kiyomizu-dera	京都	Kyōto	京都府	Kyōto-fu
金閣寺	Kinkaku-ji	京都	Kyōto	京都府	Kyōto-fu
銀閣寺	Ginkaku-ji	京都	Kyōto	京都府	Kyōto-fu
大徳寺	Daitoku-ji	京都	Kyōto	京都府	Kyōto-fu
三千院	Sanzen-in	京都	Kyōto	京都府	Kyōto-fu
醍醐寺	Daigo-ji	京都	Kyōto	京都府	Kyōto-fu
西芳寺 (苔寺)	Saihō-ji (Koke-dera)	京都	Kyōto	京都府	Kyōto-fu
龍安寺	Ryōan-ji	京都	Kyōto	京都府	Kyōto-fu
広隆寺	Kōryū-ji	京都	Kyōto	京都府	Kyōto-fu
平等院	Byōdō-in	宇治	Uji	京都府	Kyōto-fu
万福寺	Manpuku-ji	宇治	Uji	京都府	Kyōto-fu
浄瑠璃寺	Jōruri-ji	加茂	Kamo	京都府	Kyōto-fu
東大寺	Tōdai-ji	奈良	Nara	奈良県	Nara-ken
興福寺	Kōfuku-ji	奈良	Nara	奈良県	Nara-ken
唐招提寺	Tōshōdai-ji	奈良	Nara	奈良県	Nara-ken
薬師寺	Yakushi-ji	奈良	Nara	奈良県	Nara-ken
西大寺	Saidai-ji	奈良	Nara	奈良県	Nara-ken
法隆寺	Hōryū-ji	斑鳩	Karuga	奈良県	Nara-ken
中宮寺	Chūgū-ji	斑鳩	Karuga	奈良県	Nara-ken
飛鳥寺	Asuka-dera	明日香	Asuka	奈良県	Nara-ken
長谷寺	Hase-dera	桜井	Sakurai	奈良県	Nara-ken
室生寺	Murō-ji	室生	Murō	奈良県	Nara-ken
金峯山寺	Kinpusen-ji	芳野	Yoshino	奈良県	Nara-ken
延暦寺	Enryaku-ji	大津	Ōtsu	滋賀県	Shiga-ken
石山寺	Ishiyama-dera	大津	Ōtsu	滋賀県	Shiga-ken
園城寺 (三井寺)	Onjō-ji (Mii-dera)	大津	Ōtsu	滋賀県	Shiga-ken
青岸渡寺	Seiganto-ji	那智勝浦	Nachikatsuura	和歌山県	Wakayama-ken
三仏寺	Sanbutsu-ji	三朝	Misasa	鳥取県	Tottori-ken
大山寺	Daisen-ji	大山	Daisen	鳥取県	Tottori-ken
鰐淵寺	Gakuen-ji	平田	Hirata	島根県	Shimane-ken
石手寺	Ishite-ji	松山	Matsuyama	愛媛県	Ehime-ken
観世音寺	Kanzeon-ji	太宰府	Dazaifu	福岡県	Fukuoka-ken
崇福寺	Sōfuku-ji	長崎	Nagasaki	長崎県	Nagasaki-ken

Alternative names are given in parentheses.

The Ten Calendar Signs, the Twelve Horary Signs, and the Sixty-Year Cycle
十干・十二支・干支

The ten calendar signs are a series of ten kanji that originally were used to designate the different days of the ten-day 旬 *jun* periods into which a month is divided. Today this series of kanji, known as the 十干 **jikkan**, is used for distinguishing the different members of any series. For example, in the text of a three-party contract the three parties will typically be referred to as 甲 *kō* ("A"), 乙 *otsu* ("B"), and 丙 *hei* ("C"). The ten kanji of the *jikkan* are divided into two groups of five members each. One group, called 兄 *e*, is associated with the yang (positive) principle, and the other group, called 弟 *to*, is associated with the yin (negative) principle. Each member of these groups is further associated with one of the basic elements wood, fire, earth, metal, water, as presented in the following table.

		兄 *e*				弟 *to*	
木 *ki*	1.	甲	*KŌ*	"A"	2.	乙	*OTSU*	"B"
火 *hi*	3.	丙	*HEI*	"C"	4.	丁	*TEI*	"D"
土 *tsuchi*	5.	戊	*BO*	"E"	6.	己	*KI*	"F"
金 *ka*	7.	庚	*KŌ*	"G"	8.	辛	*SHIN*	"H"
水 *mizu*	9.	壬	*JIN*	"I"	10.	癸	*KI*	"J"

In addition to its *on* reading listed in this table, each kanji has another reading given by its row and column. Thus, 甲 is also referred to as *ki-no-e*, 乙 as *ki-no-to*, 丙 as *hi-no-e*, ..., and 癸 as *mizu-no-to*. (Indeed, this row-and-column nomenclature is needed to avoid confusion between symbols that otherwise have the same pronunciation, *KŌ* or *KI*.)

The twelve horary signs are a series of twelve kanji that were originally used in ancient China to distinguish the twelve months of the year but were later applied to compass directions and times of day (hence "horary" signs), the mid-point kanji 午 *GO* being associated with noon. But the most widespread use of these signs, which are known as the 十二支 **jūnishi**, is in associating successive years with different animals, as in "the year of the rat," "the year of the cow," and so forth. The following list gives the *on* reading, *kun* reading, and animal associated with each kanji of the *jūnishi*, which perhaps should be called the "animal signs."

1.	*SHI*	子	*ne*	rat	7.	*GO*	午	*uma*	horse
2.	*CHŪ*	丑	*ushi*	cow	8.	*MI*	未	*hitsuji*	sheep
3.	*IN*	寅	*tora*	tiger	9.	*SHIN*	申	*saru*	monkey
4.	*BŌ*	卯	*u*	rabbit	10.	*YŪ*	酉	*tori*	bird
5.	*SHIN*	辰	*tatsu*	dragon	11.	*JUTSU*	戌	*inu*	dog
6.	*SHI*	巳	*mi*	serpent	12.	*GAI*	亥	*i*	boar

When the ten-element 十干 *jikkan* series is aligned with the twelve-element 十二支 *jūnishi* series and each series is repeated, we obtain a series of two-kanji combinations known as the 干支 **kanshi** or *eto* (the sixty-year cycle). When this combined *kanshi* series is associated with successive years, it repeats every sixty years (as it must, because 60 is the least common multiple of 10 and 12). This sixty-year *kanshi* is outlined in the following chart, which shows which calendar sign and which horary sign and animal correspond to a given year. Thus, 1984 is a 甲子 *ki-no-e ne* year of the rat, and the year 2001, in the 18th year of the sixty-year cycle, is a 辛巳 *ka-no-to mi* year of the serpent.

干支	1	2	3	4	5	6	7	8	9	10	11	12	13	14	15
十干	甲	乙	丙	丁	戊	己	庚	辛	壬	癸	甲	乙	丙	丁	戊
十二支	子	丑	寅	卯	辰	巳	午	未	申	酉	戌	亥	子	丑	寅
年	1984	'85	'86	'87	'88	'89	'90	'91	'92	'93	'94	'95	'96	'97	'98

干支	16	17	18	19	20	21	22	23	24	25	26	27	28	29	30
十干	己	庚	辛	壬	癸	甲	乙	丙	丁	戊	己	庚	辛	壬	癸
十二支	卯	辰	巳	午	未	申	酉	戌	亥	子	丑	寅	卯	辰	巳
年	1999	'00	'01	'02	'03	'04	'05	'06	'07	'08	'09	'10	'11	'12	'13

干支	31	32	33	34	35	36	37	38	39	40	41	42	43	44	45
十干	甲	乙	丙	丁	戊	己	庚	辛	壬	癸	甲	乙	丙	丁	戊
十二支	午	未	申	酉	戌	亥	子	丑	寅	卯	辰	巳	午	未	申
年	2014	'15	'16	'17	'18	'19	'20	'21	'22	'23	'24	'25	'26	'27	'28

干支	46	47	48	49	50	51	52	53	54	55	56	57	58	59	60
十干	己	庚	辛	壬	癸	甲	乙	丙	丁	戊	己	庚	辛	壬	癸
十二支	酉	戌	亥	子	丑	寅	卯	辰	巳	午	未	申	酉	戌	亥
年	2029	'30	'31	'32	'33	'34	'35	'36	'37	'38	'39	'40	'41	'42	'43

The Eight Divination Signs
八 卦

The eight divination signs, called the 八卦 *hakke*, consist of all eight possible triplets of bars or bar-pairs, analogous to all eight three-place binary numbers 000, 001, 010, 011, 100, 101, 110, 111. They represent the patterns formed by divination sticks used in fortune-telling, and each is associated with a compass direction. Four of these signs appear on the South Korean flag, where they are taken to represent harmony. The following table lists the eight *hakke* signs, along with the kanji for each sign, the kanji's *on* reading, and the direction the sign represents.

☰	乾	*KEN*	northwest	☱	兌	*DA*	west
☲	離	*RI*	south	☳	震	*SHIN*	east
☴	巽	*SON*	southeast	☵	坎	*KAN*	north
☶	艮	*GON*	northeast	☷	坤	*KON*	southwest

Names of Chemical Compounds
化学成分

Chemical nomenclature is systematic, and the following patterns will be handy for figuring out the names of chemical compounds. In these patterns, n stands for a number or number-prefix like 1 = mono-, 2 = di- or bi-, 3 = tri-, 4 = tetra-, 5 = penta-, 6 = hexa-, and X and Y stand for chemical elements like 水素 = hydrogen, 炭素 = carbon, 硝 = 窒素 = nitrogen, 酸素 = oxygen, フッ素 = fluorine, ナトリウム = sodium (natrium), マグネシウム = magnesium, ケイ素 = silicon, リン素 = phosphorus, 硫(黄) = sulfur, 塩素 = chlorine, カリウム = potassium (kalium), カルシウム = calcium, クロム = chromium, マンガン = manganese, 鉄 = iron, ferr-, 銅 = copper, cupr-, 亜鉛 = zinc, ヒ素 = arsenic, 銀 = silver, スズ = tin, stann-, ヨウ素 = iodine, バリウム = barium, 金 = gold, 水銀 = mercury, 鉛 = lead, plumb-. Note the contexts in which the ending -素 is dropped.

PATTERN		EXAMPLE	
X化物	Xide(s)	窒化物	nitride(s)
X化Y	Y Xide	塩化ナトリウム	sodium chloride
nX化Y	Y nXide	2酸化炭素	carbon dioxide
過X化物	perXide(s)	過硫化物	persulfide(s)
過X化Y	Y perXide	過酸化水素	hydrogen peroxide
X酸	Xic acid	硫酸	sulfuric acid
X酸塩	Xate(s)	リン酸塩	phosphate(s)
X酸Y	Y Xate	炭酸カルシウム	calcium carbonate
nX酸Y	Y nXate	2クロム酸ナトリウム	sodium dichromate
過X酸	perXic acid	過ヨウ素酸	periodic acid
過X酸塩	perXate(s)	過炭酸塩	percarbonate(s)
過X酸Y	Y perXate	過塩素酸カリウム	potassium perchlorate
次X酸	hypoXic acid	次リン酸	hypophosphoric acid
次X酸塩	hypoXate(s)	次リン酸塩	hypophosphate(s)
亜X酸	Xous acid	亜硝酸	nitrous acid
亜X酸塩	Xite(s)	亜硝酸塩	nitrite(s)
亜X酸Y	Y Xite	亜硝酸ナトリウム	sodium nitrite
次亜X酸	hypoXous acid	次亜リン酸	hypophosphorous acid
次亜X酸塩	hypoXite(s)	次亜リン酸塩	hypophosphite(s)
次亜X酸Y	Y hypoXite	次亜硫酸ナトリウム	sodium hyposulfite

The 214 Historical Radicals in Comparison with the 79 Radicals

214の伝統的な部首と79の部首を比較

– 1 –			
1	一		—
2	丨		—
3	丶		—
4	丿		—
5	乙		—
6	亅		—
– 2 –			
7	二		—
8	亠	= 2j	亠
9	人, 亻	= 2a	亻
10	儿		—
11	入		—
12	八	= 2o	丷
13	冂	= 2r	冂
14	冖	= 2i	冖
15	冫	= 2b	冫
16	几	= 2s	八
17	凵		—
18	刀, 刂	= 2f	刂
19	力	= 2g	力
20	勹		—
21	匕		—
22	匚	= 2t	匚
23	匸		—
24	十	= 2k	十
25	卜	= 2m	⺊
26	卩	= 2e	卩
27	厂	= 2p	厂
28	厶		—
29	又	= 2h	又
– 3 –			
30	口	= 3d	口
31	囗	= 3s	囗
32	土	= 3b	土
33	士	= 3p	士
34	夂	= 4i	夂
35	夊		—
36	夕		—
37	大		—
38	女	= 3e	女
39	子	= 2c	子
40	宀	= 3m	宀
41	寸		—
42	小	= 3n	⺌
43	尢		—
44	尸, 尸	= 3r	尸
45	屮		—
46	山	= 3o	山
47	川		—
48	工		—
49	己		—
50	巾	= 3f	巾
51	干		—
52	幺		—
53	广	= 3q	广
54	廴	= 2q	辶
55	廾, 廾		—
56	弋	= 4n	戈
57	弓	= 3h	弓
58	彐, ⺕, ⺔		—
59	彡	= 3j	彡
60	彳	= 3i	彳
– 4 –			
61	心, 忄, ⺗	= 4k	心
62	戈	= 4n	戈
63	戶, 戸	= 4m	戸
64	手, 扌	= 3c	扌
65	支	→ 2k	十
66	攴	→ 2m	⺊
67	文	→ 2j	亠
68	斗		—
69	斤		—
70	方	= 4h	方
71	无		—
72	日	= 4c	日
73	曰	→ 3s	囗
74	月	= 4b	月
75	木	= 4a	木
76	欠	= 4j	欠
77	止	→ 2m	⺊
78	歹		—
79	殳	→ 2s	八
80	毋		—
81	比		—
82	毛		—
83	氏		—
84	气		—
85	水, 氵	= 3a	氵
86	火, 灬	= 4d	火
87	爪		—
88	父	→ 2o	丷
89	爻		—
90	爿, 丬	—, 2b	冫
91	片	→ 2j	亠
92	牙		—
93	牛	= 4g	牛
94	犬, 犭	= 3g	犭
– 5 –			
95	玄	→ 2j	亠
96	玉, 王	= 4f	王
97	瓜		—
98	瓦		—
99	甘		—
100	生		—
101	用	→ 2r	冂
102	田	= 5f	田
103	疋, ⺪	→ 2m	⺊
104	疒	= 5i	疒
105	癶		—
106	白	→ 4c	日
107	皮	→ 2h	又
108	皿	= 5h	皿
109	目	= 5c	目
110	矛		—
111	矢		—
112	石	= 5a	石
113	示, 礻	= 4e	礻
114	禸		—
115	禾	= 5d	禾
116	穴	→ 3m	宀
117	立	= 5b	立
– 6 –			
118	竹	= 6f	⺮
119	米	= 6b	米
120	糸, 糹	= 6a	糹
121	缶	→ 2k	十

122	网,罒	= 5g	罒	157	足	= 7d	𧾷	189	高	→ 2j
123	羊	→ 2o		158	身	—		190	髟	→ 3j 彡
124	羽,羽	→ 2b	冫	159	車	= 7c 車		191	鬥	→ 8e 門
125	老	→ 2k	耂	160	辛	→ 5b	立	192	鬯	—
126	而	→ 2r	冂	161	辰	→ 2p	厂	193	鬲	→ 2r 冂
127	耒	—		162	辵,辶	= 2q	辶	194	鬼	→ 5f

－11－

128	耳	= 6e 耳	163	邑,阝	= 2d	阝	195	魚	= 11a	魚
129	聿	—	164	酉	= 7e	酉	196	鳥	= 11b	鳥
130	肉,月	→ 2a 亻,	165	釆	→ 6b	米	197	鹵	→ 2m	
		= 4b 月	166	里	—		198	鹿	→ 3q	广
131	臣	→ 2t 匸					199	麥,麦	→ 4i	攵
132	自	→ 5c 目		**－8－**			200	麻	→ 3q	广

133	全	→ 3b 土	167	金	= 8a	釒
134	臼	—	168	長	—	
135	舌	→ 3d 口	169	門	= 8e	門
136	舛	—	170	阜,阝	→ 2k	耂,

－12－

201	黃,黄	→ 3k	艹
202	黍	→ 5d	禾
203	黑,黒	→ 4d	火
204	黹	—	

137	舟	= 6c 舟		= 2d 阝
138	艮,艮	—	171	隶 → 2b 冫
139	色	→ 2n	172	隹 = 8c 隹
140	艸,⺾	= 3k 艹	173	雨 = 8d 雨
141	虍	→ 2m	174	青,青 → 4b 月
142	虫	= 6d 虫	175	非 —

－13－

205	黽	—
206	鼎	→ 5c 目
207	鼓	→ 3p
208	鼠	—

143	血	→ 5h 皿		**－9－**
144	行	→ 3i 彳	176	面 → 3s 口
145	衣,衤	= 5e 衤	177	革 → 3k 艹
146	西	—	178	韋 → 3d 口

－14－

209	鼻	→ 5f 田
210	齊,斉	→ 2j

－7－

147	見	→ 5c 目	179	韭	—
148	角	→ 2n	180	音	→ 5b 立
149	言	= 7a 訁	181	頁	= 9a 頁
150	谷	→ 2o	182	風	→ 2s 几
151	豆	→ 3d 口	183	飛	—
152	豕	—	184	食	= 8b 飠
153	豸	—	185	首	→ 2o
154	貝	= 7b 貝	186	香	→ 5d 禾

－15－

211	齒,歯	→ 2a 亻,
		→ 6b 米

－10－

155	赤	→ 3b 土	187	馬	= 10a 馬
156	走	→ 3b 土	188	骨	→ 4b 月

－16－

212	龍,竜	→ 5b 立

－17－

213	龜,亀	→ 2n
214	龠	→ 2a 亻

The above table shows the similarities and differences between the historical 214-radical system and our modern 79-radical system. The 214 historical radicals are numbered and listed in order. Correspondence between a historical radical and a modern radical is indicated with an equal sign (=) followed by the name of the modern radical and its standard form. An arrow (→) instead of an equal sign indicates a limited correspondence, and those historical radicals for which there is no corresponding modern radical are marked with a hyphen (—).

上記の表は、伝統的な214部首と、この辞書に使われている79部首の類似点と相違点を示したものである。伝統的な214部首にナンバーを付け、その順序に並べてある。伝統的部首と79部首が一致する場合、イコール (=) で表し、その後に79部首のデスクリプタと標準形が示してある。イコールのかわりに矢印(→)で表されているものは部分的に一致している部首で、一致する79部首がない伝統的な部首はハイフン (—)で示してある。

Sources
参考文献

The tables, lists, and maps in the Appendices have been collected by the authors from many kinds of sources; some are the result of the authors' own research.
The page numbers below refer to those sources that have been essential for preparing the respective table or list.

1634	日本語百科大事典. 金田一春彦編. Tokyo 1988
1636	記者ハンドブック. 7th ed. Tokyo 1994
1640	Statistical Handbook of Japan. Tokyo 1995
1641–1643	The AOTS Nihongo Dictionary for Practical Use. Tokyo 1993
1645, 1646	日本統計年鑑. Tokyo 1995
1650, 1652	Statistical Handbook of Japan. Tokyo 1995
1651, 1653	経済産業用語和英辞典. Tokyo 1995
1654	Data Pal '95 '96. Tokyo 1995
1659	経済産業用語和英辞典. Tokyo 1995

All maps were drawn by Rolf Schlunze, the table "Management Hierarchy" was provided by Brigitte Kubota-Müller, and the layout for all tables, lists, and maps was prepared by Seiko Harada and Rainer Weihs.

ALPHABETICAL INDEX
OF READINGS

音訓索引

– A –

Reading		Kanji	Code
A		丫	0a3.3
		両	0a6.19
		亜	0a7.14
		亞	0a7.14
	阝	阿	2d5.6
	土	埡	3b8.13
	口	哇	3d6.5
		唖	3d8.3
		啞	3d8.3
	女	婀	3e7.4
	宀	窪	3m11.9
	疒	痾	5i7.3
	虫	蛙	6d6.4
	釒	錏	8a8.5
		鎤	8a12.3
	門	閼	8e8.1
	鳥	鴉	11b5.3
ā	口	吖	3d3.2
		嗚	3d10.1
		嗟	3d10.10
		噫	3d13.8
	心	憙	4k12.13
aba(ku)		発	0a9.5
		發	0a9.5
	日	暴	4c11.2
	言	許	7a3.2
abara	月	肋	4b2.1
aba(reru)	日	暴	4c11.2
a(biru)	氵	浴	3a7.18
a(biseru)	氵	浴	3a7.18
abu	虫	虻	6d3.2
abuku	氵	泡	3a5.18
		泡	3a5.18
abumi	釒	鐙	8a12.7
abu(nai)	厃	危	2n4.3
abura	亠	膏	2j12.1
	氵	油	3a5.6
	月	脂	4b6.7
abu(ru)	火	炙	4d4.5
		焙	4d8.1
ada	亻	仇	2a2.4
	彳	徒	3i7.1
ade(yaka)	口	艶	3d16.3
		艶	3d16.3
ae(gu)	口	喘	3d9.11
ae(nai)	攵	敢	4i8.5
a(eru)	亠	齋	2j21.1
		韲	2j21.1
	禾	和	5d3.1
ae(te)	攵	敢	4i8.5
afu(reru)	氵	溢	3a10.19
		溢	3a10.19

Reading		Kanji	Code
aga(ku)	足	跑	7d5.6
aga(meru)	山	崇	3o8.9
agana(u)	貝	購	7b10.3
		贖	7b15.2
a(gari)	卜	上	2m1.1
a(garu)	卜	上	2m1.1
	扌	揚	3c9.5
	丷	挙	3n7.1
		擧	3n7.1
		舉	3n7.1
agata	艹	県	3n6.3
		縣	3n6.3
a(gattari)	卜	上	2m1.1
a(ge)	扌	揚	3c9.5
a(geru)		挙	3n7.1
	卜	上	2m1.1
	扌	揚	3c9.5
		擧	3n7.1
	丷	挙	3n7.1
a(gete)		舉	3n7.1
	扌	擧	3n7.1
	丷	挙	3n7.1
agetsura(u)	言	論	7a8.13
-a(gezu)	卜	上	2m1.1
agito	頁	顎	9a9.2
		顎	9a9.2
		頤	9a9.4
	魚	鰓	11a9.7
ago	月	腮	4b9.5
	頁	頤	9a6.3
		顎	9a9.2
		顎	9a9.2
		頤	9a9.4
agu(mu)	亻	倦	2a8.13
		倦	2a8.13
ahiru	鳥	鶩	11b9.3
AI	阝	阨	2d4.5
		隘	2d10.5
	亠	哀	2j7.4
	土	埃	3b7.6
	扌	挨	3c7.12
	口	噯	3d13.4
		噫	3d13.8
	女	娃	3e6.5
	艹	鞋	3k12.18
		藹	3k16.4
	日	暖	4c13.1
		愛	4i10.1
	欠	欸	4j7.2
		暖	5c13.2
	禾	穢	5d13.3
		靄	8d16.1
		靉	8d17.1
ai	艹	藍	3k15.5

Reading		Kanji	Code
	日	間	8e4.3
	門	間	8e4.3
		閒	8e4.3
ai-	木	相	4a5.3
aida	日	間	8e4.3
	門	間	8e4.3
		閒	8e4.3
aji	口	味	3d5.3
	魚	鯵	11a11.2
		鯵	11a11.2
aji(na)	口	味	3d5.3
aji(wau)		味	3d5.3
aka	氵	淦	3a8.1
		赤	3b4.10
		垢	3b6.3
	釒	銅	8a6.12
akagane	釒	銅	8a6.12
akagire	車	皸	7c7.3
		輝	7c7.3
aka(i)	土	赤	3b4.10
aka(meru)	土	赤	3b4.10
akane	艹	茜	3k6.3
a(kanu)	釒	飽	8b5.1
aka(rameru)			
	土	赤	3b4.10
aka(ramu)	土	赤	3b4.10
	日	明	4c4.1
a(kari)	日	明	4c4.1
aka(rui)		明	4c4.1
aka(rumu)		明	4c4.1
akashi	火	灯	4d2.1
		燈	4d2.1
	言	證	7a5.5
		証	7a5.5
a(kasu)	日	明	4c4.1
	釒	飽	8b5.1
akatsuki	日	暁	4c8.1
		暁	4c8.1
akaza	艹	藜	3k15.6
akebono	日	曙	4c14.2
		曙	4c14.2
a(keru)	宀	空	3m5.12
	日	明	4c4.1
	門	開	8e4.6
aki	禾	稔	5d4.1
		秋	5d4.1
		穐	5d4.1
akina(u)	亠	商	2j9.7
a(kippoi)	釒	飽	8b5.1
akiraka	木	彬	4a7.3
aki(raka)	日	明	4c4.1
akira(meru)			
	言	諦	7a9.16
aki(reru)	口	呆	3d4.13

Reading		Kanji	Code
	心	惘	4k8.15
a(kiru)	亻	倦	2a8.13
		倦	2a8.13
	厂	厭	2p12.1
		靨	2p21.1
	釒	飽	8b5.1
akita(riru)	心	慊	4k10.1
akoga(reru)			
	心	憧	4k12.5
		憬	4k12.7
AKU	亻	偓	2a9.17
	氵	渥	3a9.33
	扌	握	3c9.17
	巾	幄	3f9.4
	尸	齷	3r21.1
	心	悪	4k7.17
		惡	4k7.17
a(ku)	宀	空	3m5.12
	日	明	4c4.1
	釒	飽	8b5.1
	門	開	8e4.6
akubi	艹	缺	4j0.1
	欠	欠	4j0.1
a(kuru)	日	明	4c4.1
akuta	艹	芥	3k4.10
akutsu	土	坏	3b3.4
		埖	3b6.6
Ama	土	遷	3b10.11
ama	尸	尼	3r2.2
	虫	蜑	6d6.13
ama-		天	0a4.21
		雨	8d0.1
ama(eru)		甘	0a5.32
ama(i)		甘	0a5.32
amane(ku)	丷	普	2o10.5
	辶	遍	2q9.16
		遍	2q9.16
ama(njiru)		甘	0a5.32
ama(nzuru)		甘	0a5.32
ama(ri)	亻	余	2a5.24
	釒	餘	2a5.24
ama(ru)	亻	余	2a5.24
	釒	餘	2a5.24
ama(su)	亻	余	2a5.24
	釒	餘	2a5.24
amatsu-		天	0a4.21
amatsusa(e)			
	刂	剰	2f9.1
		剩	2f9.1
ama(ttareru)		甘	0a5.32
ama(yakasu)		甘	0a5.32
ame		天	0a4.21
	釒	飴	8b5.2

Reading		Kanji	Code
		飴	8b5.2
	一	雨	8d0.1
ami	冂	罔	2r6.3
	罒	罔	5g5.2
	糸	網	6a8.25
a(mu)	糸	編	6a9.13
AN	扌	按	3c6.10
	彳	行	3i3.1
	艹	鞍	3k12.19
		菴	3q8.6
	宀	安	3m3.1
		案	3m7.6
	广	庵	3q8.6
	日	晏	4c6.4
		暗	4c9.2
	立	黯	5b16.1
	罒	罨	5g8.5
	言	諳	7a9.5
	食	餡	8b8.4
	門	闇	8e9.5
	魚	鮟	11a6.4
ana	子	孔	2c1.1
	土	坎	3b4.2
	宀	穴	3m2.2
		穴	3m2.2
anado(ru)	亻	侮	2a6.20
		侮	2a6.20
anaga(chi)	弓	強	3h8.3
anagura	宀	窖	3m9.7
ane	女	姐	3e5.5
		姉	3e5.8
ani	口	兄	3d2.9
	艹	豈	3o7.8
aniyome	女	嫂	3e9.1
a(no)	彳	彼	3i5.2
anzu	木	杏	4a3.13
ao	冂	青	4b4.10
	艹	蒼	3k10.22
	月	青	4b4.10
aogiri	木	梧	4a7.9
ao(gu)	亻	仰	2a4.10
	火	煽	4d10.4
		煽	4d10.4
	尸	扇	4m6.1
aoi	艹	葵	3k9.17
ao(i)	冂	青	4b4.10
	月	青	4b4.10
ao(ru)	口	呷	3d5.1
	火	煽	4d10.4
		煽	4d10.4
appare	辶	遖	2q9.11
ara	米	粗	6b5.2
ara(i)	艹	荒	3k6.18
	米	粗	6b5.2

Reading		Kanji	Code
arakaji(me)		予	0a4.12
		豫	0a4.12
ara(ppoi)	艹	荒	3k6.18
ara(rageru)	艹	荒	3k6.18
arare	雨	霰	8d12.1
arashi	山	嵐	3o9.4
araso(i)	ク	争	2n4.2
	ク	争	2n4.2
araso(u)	ク	争	2n4.2
	ク	争	2n4.2
a(rasu)	艹	荒	3k6.18
ara(ta)	立	新	5b8.3
arata(maru)	攵	改	4i3.1
arata(meru)	攵	改	4i3.1
arata(mete)	攵	改	4i3.1
ara(u)	氵	洗	3a6.12
ara(wa)	雨	露	8d13.1
arawa(reru)		表	0a8.6
	王	現	4f7.3
	頁	顕	9a9.5
		顯	9a9.5
arawa(su)		表	0a8.6
	艹	著	3k8.4
		著	3k8.4
ara(wasu)	王	現	4f7.3
	頁	顕	9a9.5
		顯	9a9.5
ara(zu)		非	0a8.1
are	彳	彼	3i5.2
a(re)	艹	荒	3k6.18
a(reru)	艹	荒	3k6.18
ari	虫	蟻	6d13.6
a(ru)	土	在	3b3.8
	月	有	4b2.3
	戈	或	4n4.2
arui(wa)	戈	或	4n4.2
aruji	王	主	4f1.1
		主	4f1.1
aru(ku)	卜	步	3n5.3
		步	3n5.3
asa	广	麻	3q8.3
	月	朝	4b8.12
		朝	4b8.12
Asagara	艹	莇	3k7.6
asahi	日	旭	4c2.6
asa(i)	氵	浅	3a6.4
		淺	3a6.4
asari	魚	鯏	11a7.5
asa(ru)	氵	漁	3a11.1

Reading		Kanji	Code
ase	氵	汗	3a3.6
ase(ru)	隹	焦	8c4.3
a(seru)	衤	褪	5e9.5
ashi	艹	蘆	3k4.3
		芦	3k4.3
		葭	3k9.9
		葦	3k10.21
	月	脚	4b7.3
	足	足	7d0.1
a(shikarazu)			
	心	悪	4k7.17
		惡	4k7.17
ashikase	木	桎	4a6.20
ashinae	宀	蹇	3m14.3
ashita	月	朝	4b8.12
		朝	4b8.12
aso(baseru)	辶	遊	2q8.3
aso(basu)	辶	遊	2q8.3
aso(bu)	辶	遊	2q8.3
ata(eru)		与	0a3.23
		與	0a3.23
atai	亻	価	2a6.3
		價	2a6.3
		値	2a8.30
ataka(mo)	忄	恰	4k6.10
atama	頁	頭	9a7.6
atara(shii)	立	新	5b8.3
ata(ri)	辶	邊	2q2.1
		邊	2q2.1
		辺	2q2.1
a(tari)	ソ	当	3n3.3
		當	3n3.3
a(taru)	ソ	当	3n3.3
		當	3n3.3
atata(ka)	氵	温	3a9.21
		溫	3a9.21
	日	暖	4c9.4
		暖	4c9.4
atata(kai)	氵	温	3a9.21
		溫	3a9.21
	日	暖	4c9.4
		暖	4c9.4
atata(maru)			
	氵	温	3a9.21
		溫	3a9.21
	日	暖	4c9.4
		暖	4c9.4
atata(meru)			
	氵	温	3a9.21
		溫	3a9.21
	日	暖	4c9.4
		暖	4c9.4
a(te)	ソ	当	3n3.3

Reading		Kanji	Code
		當	3n3.3
-ate	宀	宛	3m5.9
a(teru)	亠	充	2j4.5
	宀	宛	3m5.9
	ソ	当	3n3.3
		當	3n3.3
ato	阝	阯	3b4.3
	辶	迹	2q6.6
	土	址	3b4.3
	彳	後	3i6.5
	疒	痕	5i6.2
	足	跡	7d6.7
		蹤	7d11.1
ATSU	厂	圧	2p3.1
		壓	2p3.1
	辶	遏	2q9.6
	扌	握	3c9.18
	日	斡	4c10.3
	車	軋	7c1.1
atsu(i)	厂	厚	2p6.1
	日	暑	4c8.5
		暑	4c8.5
	火	熱	4d11.4
	忄	惇	4k7.12
	⺮	篤	6f10.1
atsuka(u)	扌	扱	3c3.5
		扱	3c3.5
atsu(maru)	隹	集	8c4.2
atsu(meru)	隹	集	8c4.2
atsumono	丷	羹	2o17.1
		羹	2o17.1
atsura(eru)	言	誂	7a6.4
a(u)	亻	合	2a4.18
		会	2a4.19
		會	2a4.19
	辶	逢	2q7.15
		遇	2q9.1
		遭	2q11.2
awa	氵	沫	3a5.5
		泡	3a5.18
		泡	3a5.18
	米	粟	6b6.6
awabi	虫	蚫	11a5.4
	魚	鮑	11a5.4
		鰒	11a9.6
awa(i)	氵	淡	3a8.15
awa(re)	亠	哀	2j7.4
awa(remi)	忄	憐	4k13.4
awa(remu)	亠	哀	2j7.4
	忄	憐	4k13.4
awase	衤	袷	5e6.6
awa(seru)	亻	併	2a6.17
		併	2a6.17
		并	2o4.2

Reading		Kanji	Code
a(waseru)	亻	合	2a4.18
a(wasu)	亻	合	2a4.18
awa(tadashii)			
	忄	慌	4k9.10
awa(teru)	忄	慌	4k9.10
aya	亠	文	2j2.4
		文	2j2.4
	糸	綾	6a8.10
aya(bumu)	厃	危	2n4.3
ayaka(ru)	⺍	肖	3n4.1
ayama(chi)			
	⻌	過	2q9.18
ayama(ru)	言	誤	7a7.2
		誤	7a7.2
		謝	7a10.1
		謬	7a11.1
		謬	7a11.1
ayama(tsu)			
	⻌	過	2q9.18
aya(shige)	忄	怪	4k5.11
	忄	恠	4k5.11
aya(shii)	忄	怪	4k5.11
	忄	恠	4k5.11
aya(shimu)	忄	怪	4k5.11
	忄	恠	4k5.11
ayatsu(ru)	扌	操	3c13.3
ayau(i)	厃	危	2n4.3
ayu	魚	鮎	11a5.7
ayu(mu)	止	歩	3n5.3
	⺌	歩	3n5.3
aza	宀	字	3m2.1
	广	痣	5i7.6
azake(ru)	口	嘲	3d12.2
azami	艹	薊	3k13.2
azamu(ku)	欠	欺	4j8.1
azana	宀	字	3m2.1
azana(u)	糸	糾	6a3.4
		糾	6a3.4
aza(yaka)	魚	鮮	11a6.7
aze	田	畔	5f5.1
		畔	5f5.1
		畦	5f6.2
azu(karu)	頁	預	9a4.5
azu(keru)	頁	預	9a4.5
azuma		東	0a8.9
azusa	木	梓	4a7.5

– B –

Reading		Kanji	Code
BA	女	婆	3e8.9
	艹	芭	3k4.6
	广	廲	3q11.1
	石	碼	5a10.1
	⺲	罵	5g10.1
	馬	馬	10a0.1

Reading		Kanji	Code
ba	土	場	3b9.6
		場	3b9.6
-ba		羽	2b4.5
	氵	羽	2b4.5
babā	女	婆	3e8.9
BACHI	禾	秡	5d5.5
	⺲	罰	5g9.1
		罸	5g9.1
bachi	扌	撥	3c12.11
	木	枹	4a5.16
		桴	4a6.12
BAI	亻	倍	2a8.14
	阝	陪	2d8.3
	土	培	3b8.6
	口	唄	3d7.1
	女	媒	3e9.2
	犭	狽	3g7.1
	彳	徽	3i20.1
	艹	苺	3k5.4
		莓	3k5.4
	士	賣	3p4.3
		売	3p4.3
	木	梅	4a6.27
		楳	4a6.27
		梅	4a6.27
	火	煤	4d9.6
	⺲	買	5g7.2
	貝	賠	7b8.1
	⻗	霾	8d14.1
-baka(ri)	言	許	7a4.3
ba(kasu)	亻	化	2a2.6
ba(keru)	亻	化	2a2.6
BAKU	十	博	2k10.1
	氵	漠	3a10.18
		瀑	3a15.4
	艹	莫	3k7.13
		幕	3k10.19
		驀	3k14.1
		驀	3k17.5
	宀	寞	3m10.4
	日	貉	4c9.10
		暴	4c11.2
		獏	4c13.4
		獏	4c13.4
		曝	4c15.1
	火	爆	4d15.2
	攵	麥	4i4.2
		麦	4i4.2
	心	博	2k10.1
	糸	縛	6a10.3
		縛	6a10.3
	馬	駁	10a4.3
BAN		万	0a3.8
	亻	伴	2a5.4

Reading		Kanji	Code
	刂	判	2f5.2
	虫	蠻	2j10.1
		蛮	2j10.1
	十	卍	2k4.7
	扌	挽	3c7.13
		挽	3c7.13
		播	3c12.8
	巾	幡	3f11.1
		萬	0a3.8
		蕃	3k12.9
	木	板	4a4.21
	日	晩	4c8.3
		晩	4c8.3
	忄	悗	4k7.13
	石	磐	5a10.9
		攀	5a15.2
	田	番	5f7.4
	⽫	盤	5h10.2
	糸	絆	6a5.6
	虫	蟠	6d12.2
	車	鞄	7c8.5
	金	鐉	8a13.1
	鳥	鶚	11b12.2
ban	刂	判	2f5.2
-ban	女	婆	3e8.9
bā(san)			
BATSU		末	0a5.26
	亻	伐	2a4.5
	扌	抜	3c4.10
		抜	3c4.10
	衤	袙	5e5.4
	⺲	罰	5g9.1
		罸	5g9.1
	⺮	筏	6f6.7
	𧾷	跋	7d5.5
	門	閥	8e6.2
batta	虫	蝗	6d9.8
bā(ya)	女	婆	3e8.9
be	阝	部	2d8.15
-be	⻌	邊	2q2.1
		邉	2q2.1
		辺	2q2.1
BEI	口	吠	3d4.1
	木	榠	4a10.21
	衤	袂	5e4.2
		米	0b6.1
BEKI	冖	冖	2i0.1
		冪	2i13.1
	氵	汨	3a4.2
	巾	幎	3f10.3
	目	覓	5c6.8
	⺲	幂	2i13.1
BEN		弁	0a5.30
		黽	0a13.2
	亻	便	2a7.5

Reading		Kanji	Code
		便	2a7.5
		俛	2a7.16
	亠	卞	2j2.1
	⼑	勉	2n8.1
		勉	2n8.1
	氵	湎	3a9.32
	扌	抃	3c4.14
	女	娩	3e7.8
		娩	3e7.8
	艹	鞭	3k15.8
	宀	宀	3m0.1
	日	冕	4c7.9
		冕	4c7.9
	立	辨	0a5.30
		辧	0a5.30
		瓣	0a5.30
	目	眄	5c4.1
	糸	辮	6a14.4
	言	辯	0a5.30
	馬	駢	10a6.5
beni	糸	紅	6a3.6
BETSU	刂	別	2f5.3
	扌	捌	3c7.4
	艹	蔑	3k11.11
	女	鼈	4i20.1
	日	瞥	5c12.5
		瞥	5c12.5
	衤	襪	5e14.2
	⺲	韈	5g18.2
BI	亻	備	2a10.4
	⺍	美	2o7.4
	氵	瀰	3a14.1
		灡	3a17.2
	女	媚	3e9.5
	弓	弥	3h5.2
		彌	3h5.2
		弭	3h6.1
	彳	微	3i10.1
		微	3i10.1
	艹	薇	3k13.13
	宀	寐	3m9.2
	⺲	嵋	3o9.3
	广	麋	3q14.1
		麊	3q14.2
		麋	3q16.2
	尸	尾	3r4.2
	木	枇	4a4.13
		梶	4a7.19
	𤣩	琵	4f8.10
	目	眉	5c4.9
		毘	5f4.6
		鼻	5f9.3
	米	糒	6b10.1
		糜	6b11.4

日 眺 5c6.2
禾 稠 5d8.7
衤 褶 5e11.3
田 町 5f2.1
甼 5f2.1
疒 疔 5i2.1
虫 蜩 6d8.9
蝶 6d9.7
耳 聴 6e11.3
聽 6e11.3
言 誂 7a6.4
調 7a8.16
調 7a8.16
諜 7a9.7
貝 貼 7b5.2
車 輒 7c7.2
輙 7c7.2
足 跳 7d6.3
釒 釣 8a3.5
銚 8a6.5
隹 雕 8c8.1
糴 8c17.1
頁 頂 9a2.1
魚 鯛 11a8.11
鰈 11a9.9
鳥 鳥 11b0.1

CHOKU 阝 陟 2d7.8
隯 2d14.2
力 勅 2g7.1
十 直 2k6.2
扌 挑 3c7.10
挑 3c7.10
攵 敕 2g7.1
禾 稙 5d8.6
足 躑 7d13.1
食 飭 8b4.4

CHU 丶 0a1.3
虫 蛛 6d6.1

CHŪ 丑 0a4.39
中 0a4.40
衷 0a9.9
衷 0a9.9
亻 仲 2a4.7
偸 2a9.13
儔 2a14.3
冫 冲 3a4.5
厂 厨 2p10.1
冂 冑 2r7.2
氵 沖 3a4.5
注 3a5.16
注 3a5.16
扌 抽 3c5.7
巾 幬 3f15.1
犭 狆 3g4.4

宀 宙 3m5.5
广 厨 2p10.1
厨 2p10.1
木 柱 4a5.12
月 肘 4b3.3
冑 4b5.13
昼 4c5.15
晝 4c5.15
心 忠 4k4.6
惆 4k8.14
禾 稠 5d8.7
田 疇 5f14.1
疇 5f14.1
糸 紂 6a3.3
紐 6a4.2
紬 6a5.3
綢 6a8.24
虫 蟲 6d0.1
虫 6d0.1
竹 籀 6f13.5
籌 6f14.5
言 註 7a5.11
註 7a5.11
誅 7a6.2
足 躊 7d14.3
酉 酎 7e3.1
釒 鈕 8a4.3
鑄 8a7.2
鋳 8a7.2
鐳 8a9.8
馬 駐 10a5.2
-chū 中 0a4.40
CHUTSU 火 黜 4d13.8

– D –

DA 亻 儺 2a19.1
阝 陀 2d5.5
隋 2d6.2
丷 兌 2o5.2
氵 沱 3a5.22
土 墬 3b6.10
堕 3b8.14
墮 3b8.14
扌 打 3c2.3
挈 3c5.30
拿 3c5.30
口 唾 3d8.2
女 妥 3e4.9
妥 3e4.9
娜 3e6.3
艹 茶 3k7.17
木 朶 4a2.8
柁 4a5.23
梛 4a6.7

楕 4a9.13
橢 4a9.13
忄 惰 4k9.6
懦 4k14.1
米 糯 6b14.1
舟 舵 6c5.3
虫 蛇 6d5.7
馬 駄 10a4.1
駝 10a5.3
鳥 鴕 11b5.1
DAI 乃 0a2.10
大 0a3.18
才 6f5.5
内 0a4.23
内 0a4.23
亻 代 2a3.3
弟 2o5.1
辶 迺 2q6.10
廼 2q6.10
土 臺 3d2.11
口 台 3d2.11
歹 殆 3d6.21
目 眱 5c5.4
竹 第 6f5.5
酉 醍 7e9.3
食 餒 8b7.3
頁 題 9a9.7
daidai 木 橙 4a12.10
DAKU 氵 濁 3a13.8
扌 搦 3c10.3
言 諾 7a8.10
足 跑 7d5.6
daku 扌 抱 3c5.15
抱 3c5.15
dama(kasu)
馬 騙 10a9.1
dama(ru) 犭 默 4d11.5
火 黙 4d11.5
dama(su) 馬 騙 10a9.1
DAN 斷 6b5.6
几 段 2s7.2
氵 灘 3a19.1
灘 3a19.1
土 壇 3b13.5
弓 弾 3h9.3
弾 3h9.3
艹 葮 3k9.8
口 団 3s3.3
團 3s3.3
木 檀 4a13.11
檀 4a13.11
日 暖 4c9.4
暖 4c9.4
火 煖 4d9.9

罒 男 5f2.2
疒 痰 5i8.6
米 断 6b5.6
言 談 7a8.7
虫 蜱 6d8.1
dani
犭 默 4d11.5
火 黙 4d11.5
言 誰 7a8.1
da(shi) 出 0a5.22
da(su) 出 0a5.22
dāsu 扌 打 3c2.3
-da(te) 辶 建 2q6.2
DATSU 女 姐 3e5.6
犭 獺 3g16.1
艹 韃 3k18.1
月 脱 4b7.8
脱 4b7.8
忄 怛 4k5.8
奞 奪 8c6.4
弟 2o5.1
DE 弟 2o5.1
de 出 0a5.22
DEI 氵 泥 3a5.29
衤 祢 4e14.1
襧 4e14.1
禰 4e14.1
衤 祢 4e14.1
dekaguramu
十 瓲 2k5.2
dekamētoru
米 籵 6b2.1
dekarittoru 立 竍 5b2.1
DEKI 氵 溺 3a10.1
溺 3a10.1
滌 3a11.6
DEN 亻 伝 2a4.14
傳 2a4.14
佃 2a5.2
丷 奠 2o10.4
氵 沺 3a5.2
淀 3a8.23
澱 3a13.2
宀 靛 3m13.6
尸 殿 3r10.1
月 臀 4b13.7
田 田 5f0.1
旬 5f2.3
攵 敀 5f4.1
疒 癜 5i13.1
釒 鈿 8a5.2
雨 電 8d5.2
魚 鮎 11a5.7
鳥 鷆 11b10.6
鷏 11b10.6
de(ru) 出 0a5.22

deshiguramu
砒 2o7.9
deshimētoru
粉 6b4.6
deshirittoru
坌 5b4.2
DO
子 孥 2c5.2
力 努 2g5.6
土 土 3b0.1
口 咄 3d5.9
女 奴 3e2.2
巾 帑 3f5.4
弓 弩 3h5.3
广 度 3q6.1
心 怒 4k5.19
馬 駑 10a5.7
DŌ
亻 働 2a11.1
仂 2a11.1
僮 2a12.3
儂 2a13.3
仝 2r4.2
力 動 2g9.1
厂 耨 2p14.1
辶 道 2q9.14
冂 同 2r4.2
氵 洞 3a6.25
潼 3a12.13
扌 撞 3c12.10
撓 3c12.14
犭 獞 3g14.1
艹 萄 3k8.31
⺌ 堂 3n8.4
木 橈 4a12.15
檘 4a14.2
月 胴 4b6.10
臑 4b14.1
忄 恫 4k6.15
慟 4k11.1
憧 4k12.5
立 童 5b7.3
龍 5b43.1
目 導 5c9.3
瞠 5c11.3
瞳 5c12.2
瞳 5c12.2
衤 裯 5e4.3
舟 艟 6c12.1
金 銅 8a6.12
鐃 8a12.9
門 闈 8e5.3
閙 8e5.3
dobu 氵 溝 3a10.9
dojō 魚 鮡 11a8.1
鰌 11a9.14

do(keru) 辶 退 2q6.3
DOKU 毒 0a8.14
毒 0a8.14
犭 独 3g6.1
獨 3g6.1
虫 髑 6d17.2
言 讀 7a7.9
読 7a7.9
do(ku) 辶 退 2q6.3
domo(ru) 口 吃 3d3.7
DON 亻 貪 2a9.20
土 壜 3b16.1
口 呑 3d4.19
女 嫩 3e11.1
口 団 3s3.3
團 3s3.3
日 曇 4c12.1
糸 緞 6a9.4
金 鈍 8a4.2
食 飩 8b4.2
⻖ 蠶 3b16.1
donburi 丼 0a5.40
-dono 尸 殿 3r10.1
dora 金 鉦 8a5.7
do(re) 亻 何 2a5.21
-dō(ri) 辶 通 2q7.18
doro 氵 泥 3a5.29
doru 弗 0a5.44
DOTSU 月 肭 4b4.4

– E –

E 亻 会 2a4.19
會 2a4.19
依 2a6.1
歪 2m7.4
冂 同 3s3.1
氵 淮 3a8.2
土 壊 3b13.3
壞 3b13.3
口 回 3s3.1
囬 3s3.1
心 恵 4k6.16
惠 4k6.16
禾 穢 5d13.3
衣 衣 5e0.1
糸 絵 6a6.8
繪 6a6.8
e 氵 江 3a3.8
艹 荏 3k6.10
木 柄 4a5.9
食 餌 8b6.2
餌 8b6.2
-e 重 0a9.18
ebi 虫 蛯 6d6.2

蝦 6d9.4
魚 鰕 11a9.4
ebira 箙 6f8.2
ebisu 夷 0a6.24
戈 戎 4n2.4
虫 蝦 6d6.13
Eburi 木 枌 4a2.5
eda 木 枝 4a4.18
edachi 彳 徭 3i10.3
ega(ku) 画 0a8.7
畫 0a8.7
扌 描 3c8.21
egu(ru) 刂 刔 2f6.6
刳 3c4.3
扌 抉 3c4.3
EI 曳 0a6.23
曳 0a6.23
阝 郢 2d7.13
又 叡 2h14.1
亠 嬴 2j18.1
睿 2h14.1
匸 翳 2t15.2
氵 永 3a1.1
泄 3a5.4
泳 3a5.14
洩 3a6.3
瀛 3a16.7
土 塋 3b10.12
口 咏 7a5.14
女 嬰 3e14.3
彳 衛 3i13.3
衛 3i13.3
彡 影 3j12.1
艹 英 3k5.5
⺌ 栄 3n6.1
営 3n9.2
辶 瑿 3p13.1
木 榮 3n6.1
楹 4a9.19
日 映 4c5.1
暎 4c5.1
王 瑛 4f8.6
瑩 4f10.7
瓔 4f17.1
瑛 4f17.1
亠 裔 5e7.4
皿 盈 5h4.1
糸 纓 6a17.1
虫 蠑 6d14.2
言 詠 7a5.14
金 鋭 8a7.12
鋭 8a7.12
食 籝 8b12.5
罒 罋 8d8.8

頁 穎 9a6.2
穎 9a7.5
穎 9a7.5
魚 鱏 11a12.2
ei 口 嘒 3d12.7
Ei-biro
EKI 亠 亦 2j4.4
奕 2j7.2
⺌ 益 2o8.5
氵 液 3a8.29
扌 掖 3c8.29
彳 役 3i4.2
月 腋 4b8.8
日 易 4c4.9
心 懌 4k13.6
疒 疫 5i4.2
糸 繹 6a13.2
虫 蜴 6d8.6
馬 駅 10a4.4
驛 10a4.4
魚 鯣 11a8.5
ekubo 日 靨 4c19.1
e(mu) ⺌ 笑 6f4.1
EN 奄 0a8.10
亻 俺 2a8.25
偃 2a9.18
冖 冤 2i8.3
冤 2i8.3
冤 2i8.3
厂 厭 2p12.1
靨 2p17.1
魘 2p21.1
魘 2p22.1
辶 延 2q5.4
遠 2q10.4
冂 円 2r2.1
氵 沿 3a5.23
淹 3a8.27
淵 3a9.3
渕 3a9.3
淵 3a9.3
湲 3a9.24
演 3a11.13
土 垣 3b6.5
袁 3b7.8
堰 3b9.12
塩 3b10.4
扌 捐 3c7.11
掩 3c8.23
援 3c9.7
援 3c9.7
掾 3c9.12
擐 3c9.18
口 咽 3d6.14
婉 3d12.14

噦 3d16.2		縁 6a9.10	一 富 3m9.5			賻 7b10.2
艶 3d16.3	enju	槐 4a10.9	十 缶 2k4.6		趺 7d4.2
艷 3d16.3	enogo 广	痤 5i7.1	罐 2k4.6	釒 鑵 2k4.6
女 娟 3e7.7	enoki 木	榎 4a10.4	阜 2k6.3	鈇 8a4.4
婉 3e8.5	era 頁	顋 9a9.4	卜 膚 2m13.1	魚 鮒 11a5.5
媛 3e9.4	魚	鰓 11a9.7	步 3n5.3	鳥 鳧 11b2.3
媛 3e9.4	era(bu) 辶	選 2q12.3	彡 負 2n7.1	鳬 11b2.3
嫣 3e11.3	扌	択 3c4.21	丷 父 2o2.3	fu 王 斑 4f8.3
犭 猿 3g10.3		擇 3c4.21	斧 2o6.4	-fu 生 0a5.29
彳 衍 3i6.3		撰 3c12.9	釜 2o8.7	FŪ 夫 0a4.31
艹 苑 3k5.17		撰 3c12.9	釜 2o8.7	冫 馮 2b10.1
燕 3k13.16	era(garu) 亻	偉 2a10.5	普 2o10.5	一 富 3m9.5
蘭 3s10.1	era(i) 亻	偉 2a10.5	几 風 2s7.1	几 風 2s7.1
宀 宛 2i8.3	eri 衤	衿 5e4.5	氵 浮 3a6.11	土 封 3b6.13
宛 3m5.9		襟 5e13.2	浮 3a6.11	宀 富 3m9.5
宴 3m7.3	e(ru) 辶	選 2q12.3	溥 3a10.4	木 楓 4a9.28
丷 爰 3n6.4	犭	獲 3g13.1	土 坿 3b5.7	广 瘋 5i9.4
囗 圓 2r2.1	彳	得 3i8.4	赴 3b6.14	言 諷 7a9.21
園 3s10.1	esa 飠	餌 8b6.2	埠 3b8.5	fuchi 氵 淵 3a9.3
圜 3s13.1		餌 8b6.2	扌 扶 3c4.4	渕 3a9.3
木 檐 4a13.9	eso 魚	鱛 11a12.7	拊 3c5.17	渊 3a9.3
橼 4a15.1	e(tari) 彳	得 3i8.4	阝 附 3d5.10	糸 縁 6a9.10
月 臙 4b16.2	e(te) 彳	得 3i8.4	女 婦 3e8.6	縁 6a9.10
日 曣 4c19.2	ETSU 口	咽 3d6.14	婦 3e8.6	fuda 木 札 4a1.1
火 炎 4d4.4		噎 3d12.6	巾 布 3f2.1	fude 𥫗 筆 6f6.1
焉 4d7.3	口	曰 3s1.1	艹 芙 3k4.4	fue 亻 龠 2a15.5
焰 4d8.5	忄	悦 4k7.15	苻 3k5.18	𥫗 笛 6f5.6
燄 4d8.5		悅 4k7.15	荂 3k6.14	籥 6f17.1
焔 4d8.5	戈	戉 4n1.2	蒲 3k10.8	魚 鰾 11a11.3
焱 4d8.6		越 4n8.2	宀 富 3m9.5	fu(eru) 土 増 3b11.3
煙 4d9.3	米	粤 6b6.10	丷 步 3n5.3	增 3b11.3
烟 4d9.3	言	謁 7a8.6	孵 3n10.5	歹 殖 5c7.4
厱 4d22.1		謁 7a8.6	广 府 3q5.2	fugu 魚 鰒 11a9.6
忄 怨 4k5.20	釒	鉞 8a5.16	腐 3q11.3	fuigo 艹 韛 3k16.11
悁 4k7.8	門	閲 8e7.2	扌 枹 4a5.16	fuigō 艹 韛 3k16.11
皿 鹽 3b10.4			柎 4a5.18	fuji 艹 藤 3k15.3
糸 縁 6a9.10	**–F–**		桴 4a6.12	藤 3k15.3
縁 6a9.10	fīto 口	呎 3d4.12	樺 4a10.5	fujibakama
虫 蜒 6d6.10	FU	不 0a4.2	月 腑 4b8.9	艹 蕳 3k12.16
蜿 6d8.8		夫 0a4.31	攵 敷 4i11.1	fuka 魚 鱶 11a15.1
𥫗 筵 6f6.13		丰 0a4.43	麩 4i12.2	fuka(i) 氵 深 3a8.21
莚 6f6.13		甫 0a7.11	麪 4i12.2	fuka(maru) 氵 深 3a8.21
篶 6f11.6		蕅 0a19.1	忄 怖 4k5.6	fuka(meru) 氵 深 3a8.21
簷 6f13.7		亻 仆 2a2.3	立 婄 5b7.4	fu(kasu) 日 更 0a7.12
言 讌 7a16.1		付 2a3.6	田 昳 5f4.2	更 0a7.12
車 轅 7c10.2		巫 2a5.26	罒 罘 5g4.1	艹 蒸 3k9.19
𧾷 踠 7d8.5		俘 2a6.9	角 觖 6c6.1	fuke(ru) 耳 耽 6e4.3
釒 鉛 8a5.14		俛 2a7.16	虫 蜉 6d6.3	酉 酖 7e4.1
鋺 8a8.13		俯 2a8.35	𥫗 符 6f5.12	fu(keru) 日 更 0a7.12
門 闉 8e8.3		傅 2a10.2	言 訃 7a2.2	更 0a7.12
閻 8e8.4		麩 4i12.2	誣 7a7.1	十 老 2k4.5
鳥 鳶 11b3.1		子 孚 2c4.2	譜 7a12.2	艹 蒸 3k9.19
鴛 11b5.9		阝 附 2d5.4	譜 7a12.2	fuki 艹 芰 3k5.21
enishi 糸 縁 6a9.10		邨 2d6.7	貝 賦 7b8.4	艹 蕗 3k13.4

Reading	Rad.	Kanji	Code
FUKU	亻	伏	2a4.1
	刂	副	2f9.2
	巾	幅	3f9.2
	彳	復	3i9.4
	艹	蔔	3k11.20
	月	服	4b4.6
		腹	4b9.4
	日	覆	4c14.6
		覆	4c14.6
	礻	福	4e9.1
		福	4e9.1
	心	愎	4k9.3
	禾	馥	5d13.5
	木	柮	5e6.2
		複	5e9.3
	田	匐	5f6.8
	虫	蝮	6d9.6
		蝠	6d9.12
	⺮	箙	6f8.2
	車	輹	7c9.1
		輻	7c9.3
	魚	鰒	11a9.6
fu(ku)	氵	潰	3a12.15
	扌	拭	3c6.17
	口	吹	3d4.3
		噴	3d12.8
	艹	葺	3k9.25
fuku(meru)	亻	含	2a5.25
fuku(mu)	亻	含	2a5.25
	口	啣	3i11.1
	彳	衘	3i11.1
fukurahagi	月	腓	4b8.3
fuku(ramasu)			
fuku(ramu)	月	脹	4b8.1
fuku(reru)	月	脹	4b8.1
		膨	4b12.1
fukuro	衤	袋	5e5.11
fukurō	木	梟	4a7.28
fu(maeru)	𧾷	蹈	7d8.3
		踏	7d8.3
fumi	亠	文	2j2.4
		文	2j2.4
	日	書	4c6.6
fumoto	⺊	梺	2m9.3
	木	麓	4a15.9
fu(mu)	𧾷	蹈	7d8.3
		踏	7d8.3
FUN	刂	刎	2f4.3
	丷	分	2o2.1
		分	2o2.1
		坌	2o5.4
		忿	2o6.3
		氛	2o6.7
	氵	汾	3a4.14
		潰	3a12.15
	扌	墳	3b12.1
		扮	3c4.17
	口	吻	3d4.6
		吩	3d4.10
		噴	3d12.8
	艹	芬	3k4.9
	木	粉	4a4.15
	火	焚	4d8.7
	心	憤	4k12.6
		奮	5f11.2
	糸	紛	6a4.8
	米	粉	6b4.6
		糞	6b11.3
		雰	8d4.2
funa	魚	鮒	11a5.5
		鯽	11a9.3
funa-	舟	舟	6c0.1
		舟	6c0.1
		船	6c5.4
		舩	6c5.4
funabata	舟	舷	6c5.5
fundoshi	衤	褌	5e9.2
fune	舟	舟	6c0.1
		舟	6c0.1
		船	6c5.4
		舩	6c5.4
fu(rareru)	扌	振	3c7.14
fu(reru)	扌	振	3c7.14
	犭	狂	3g4.2
	虫	触	6d7.10
		觸	6d7.10
furi	几	風	2s7.1
fu(ri)	扌	振	3c7.14
furoshiki	衤	袱	5e6.2
fu(ru)	阝	降	2d7.7
	扌	振	3c7.14
furu(biru)	艹	古	2k3.1
furu(bokeru)			
	艹	古	2k3.1
furu(eru)	雨	震	8d7.3
	頁	顫	9a13.1
furui	⺮	篩	6f10.2
furu(i)	艹	古	2k3.1
	攵	故	4i5.2
furu(mekashii)			
	艹	古	2k3.1
-furu(su)	艹	古	2k3.1
furu(u)		奮	5f11.2
	⺮	篩	6f10.2
	雨	震	8d7.3
fu(ruu)	扌	振	3c7.14
fusa	尸	房	4m4.2
		房	4m4.2
	糸	総	6a8.20
		總	6a8.20
fusa(garu)	宀	塞	3m10.2
fusa(gu)	宀	塞	3m10.2
	木	欝	4a25.1
		欝	4a25.1
		鬱	4a25.1
fuse(gu)	阝	防	2d4.1
	礻	禦	4e12.2
fu(seru)	亻	伏	2a4.1
		臥	2a7.22
		俯	2a8.35
	⺊	卧	2a7.22
fushi	木	樧	4a12.12
	⺮	節	6f7.3
		節	6f7.3
fu(shite)	亻	伏	2a4.1
fu(su)	亻	伏	2a4.1
		臥	2a7.22
		俯	2a8.35
	⺊	卧	2a7.22
fusu(beru)	火	熏	4d14.1
		燻	4d14.1
fusu(boru)	火	熏	4d14.1
		燻	4d14.1
fusu(buru)	火	熏	4d14.1
		燻	4d14.1
fusuma	亻	衾	2a8.38
		麩	4i12.2
	攵	麩	4i12.2
		麩	4i12.2
	礻	襖	5e13.1
		襖	5e13.1
futa	又	双	2h2.1
		雙	2h2.1
	丷	盖	3k10.15
	艹	蓋	3k10.15
		葢	3k10.15
	屵	屵	3k10.15
futa-	二		0a2.1
futata(bi)	再		0a6.26
futa(tsu)	二		0a2.1
futo(i)	太		0a4.18
futokoro	心	懐	4k13.9
		懷	4k13.9
futo(ru)	太		0a4.18
	月	肥	4b4.5
FUTSU	弗		0a5.44
	黻		0a17.1
	亻	仏	2a2.5
		佛	2a2.5
	氵	沸	3a5.3
	扌	払	3c2.2
		拂	3c2.2
	彳	彿	3i5.1
		彿	3i5.1
	礻	祓	4e5.2
	心	怫	4k5.1
fu(yasu)	土	増	3b11.3
		増	3b11.3
	歹	殖	5c7.4
fuyu	夂	冬	4i2.1

– G –

Reading	Rad.	Kanji	Code
GA	牙		0a4.20
	牙		0a4.28
	瓦		0a5.11
	我		0a7.10
	画		0a8.7
	畫		0a8.7
	亻	伽	2a5.12
		俄	2a7.4
		臥	2a7.22
	⺊	卧	2a7.22
		正	2m3.4
	口	呀	3d4.4
		哦	3d7.2
	女	娥	3e7.1
	彳	衙	3i10.2
	艹	芽	3k5.9
		芽	3k5.9
		莪	3k7.2
	峨	峨	3o7.2
		峩	3o7.2
	虫	蛾	6d7.1
	言	訝	7a5.1
		訝	7a5.1
	貝	賀	7b5.10
	食	餓	8b7.1
	隹	雅	8c5.1
		雅	8c5.1
	馬	駕	10a5.8
	鳥	鵞	11b7.7
		鵞	11b7.7
GA'	亻	合	2a4.18
-gachi	月	勝	4b8.4
		勝	4b8.4
gae(njiru)	月	肯	4b4.11
gae(nzuru)	月	肯	4b4.11
GAI	乂	乂	0a2.11
	孑	孩	2c6.1
	刂	刈	2f2.1
		劓	2f10.2
	力	劾	2g6.1
	亠	亥	2j4.1

Reading	Kanji	Code	Reading	Kanji	Code	Reading	Kanji	Code	Reading	Kanji	Code
	外	2m3.1		諤	7a9.3		訝	7a5.1		芫	3k4.13
	盖	3k10.15		鍔	8a9.6		訝	7a5.1		蒱	3k12.16
	厓	2p6.2		顎	9a9.2	GEI	倪	2a8.12		厳	3n14.1
	凱	2s10.1		顎	9a9.2		迎	2q4.4		广	3q0.1
	涯	3a8.33		額	9a9.6		囈	3d18.4		現	4f7.3
	溉	3a12.3		鰐	11a9.5		貌	3g8.2		愿	4k10.11
	垓	3b6.8		鶚	11b9.1		猊	3g8.2		彦	5b4.4
	咳	3d6.10	gama	蒲	3k10.8		藝	3k4.12		眩	5c5.3
	啀	3d8.16	GAN	丸	0a3.28		芸	3k4.12		眼	5c6.1
	街	3i9.2		元	0a4.5		麑	3q16.1		痃	5i5.11
	艾	3k2.2		含	2a5.25		黥	4d16.1		絃	6a5.12
	蓋	3k10.15		儑	2a9.12		睨	5c8.5		綱	6a12.7
	葢	3k10.15		龕	2a20.3		霓	8d8.6		舷	6c5.5
	害	3m7.4		雁	2p10.3		鯢	11a8.3		言	7a0.1
	屵	3k10.15		厴	2p10.3		鯨	11a8.9		諺	7a9.15
	豈	3o7.8		鴈	2p10.3	gejigeji	蚰	6d5.2		諺	7a9.15
	崖	3o8.11		贗	2p17.2	GEKI	郤	2d7.15		鉉	8a5.12
	嵂	3o8.11		岊	3d9.20		隙	2d10.4		験	10a8.4
	概	4a10.2		芫	3k4.13		隙	2d10.4		驗	10a8.4
	概	4a10.2		莟	3k7.18		劇	2f13.2	GETSU	齧	2a19.4
	橄	4a10.18		岩	3o5.10		逆	2q6.8		嚙	2a19.4
	骸	4b12.7		岸	3o5.11		激	3a13.1		子	2c0.2
	皚	4c11.4		巌	3o17.2		撃	3c11.7		蘖	3k17.4
	慨	4k10.3		巖	3o17.2		撃	3c11.7		月	4b0.1
	慨	4k10.3		瓺	4c11.6		展	3r7.3	GI	伎	2a4.13
	懡	4k10.10		瓺	4c11.6		檄	4a13.1		偽	2a9.2
	碍	5a8.4		玩	4f4.1		戟	4n8.1		僞	2a9.2
	礙	5a8.4		眼	5c6.1		覡	5c9.2		儀	2a13.4
	礚	5a10.6		癌	5i12.4		闃	8e8.2		疑	2m12.1
	睚	5c8.8		頑	9a4.6		関	8e9.4		義	2o11.3
	該	7a6.10		顏	9a7.7		鳨	11b4.1		義	2o14.1
	鎧	8a10.3		顔	9a9.3		鷁	11b10.8		沂	3a4.12
	駭	10a6.4		顔	9a9.3	GEN	元	0a4.5		技	3c4.16
	鮠	11a6.6		願	9a10.2		幻	0a4.6		擬	3c14.2
-ga(kari)	掛	3c8.6	gara	柄	4a5.9		俢	2a9.12		妓	3e4.7
-ga(karu)	掛	3c8.6	-ga(ri)	狩	3g6.5		儼	2a20.1		萱	3k8.26
Gake	岸	3b6.4	-gata	型	3b6.11		儳	2a20.2		宜	3m5.7
gake	岸	3b6.4		形	3j4.1		阮	2d4.3		巇	3o13.3
	崖	3o8.11	-gata(i)	難	8c10.2		限	2d6.1		嶬	3o14.1
	嵂	3o8.11		難	8c10.2		玄	2j3.2		巇	3o17.1
-ga(ke)	掛	3c8.6	GATSU	歹	0a4.14		彦	5b4.4		巍	3o18.2
GAKU	學	3n4.2		月	4b0.1		原	2p8.1		曦	4c16.1
	鄂	2d9.8	-gawa	側	2a9.4		還	2q13.4		祇	4e4.2
	咢	3d6.18	GE	牙	0a4.28		減	3a9.37		祇	4e4.2
	齶	3d21.1		牙	0a4.28		源	3a10.25		犠	4g13.1
	学	3n4.2		偈	2a9.10		拳	3c6.18		犠	4g13.1
	夢	3k9.16		下	2m1.2		拳	3c6.18		欺	4j8.1
	蕚	3k9.16		外	2m3.1		呟	3d5.12		戯	4n11.1
	学	3n4.2		解	4g9.1		嚴	3n14.1		戲	4n11.1
	岳	3o5.12		廨	3q13.1		嫌	3e10.7		礒	5a13.4
	嶽	3o5.12		解	4g9.1		嫌	3e10.7		魏	5d13.6
	楽	4a9.29		夏	4i7.5		嫌	3e10.7		艤	6c13.2
	樂	4a9.29		戲	4n11.1		弦	3h5.1		蟻	6d13.6
	愕	4k9.4		戯	4n11.1		街	3i8.1		誼	7a8.11

Reading	Rad.	Kanji	Code
HACHI	癶	癹	0a5.3
	ハ	八	2o0.1
		八	2o0.1
	扌	捌	3c7.4
	釒	釟	8a2.2
		鉢	8a5.4
		鈸	8a5.5
hachi	虫	蜂	6d7.6
hada	宀	膚	2m13.1
	月	肌	4b2.2
hadaka	衤	裸	5e8.1
hadara	王	斑	4f8.3
hadashi	足	跣	7d6.4
hae	虫	蠅	6d13.1
		蝿	6d13.1
	魚	鮑	11a6.6
ha(e)	艹	栄	3n6.1
	木	榮	3n6.1
ha(eru)		生	0a5.29
	艹	栄	3n6.1
	木	榮	3n6.1
	日	映	4c5.1
		暎	4c5.1
hagane	釒	鋼	8a8.20
ha(gasu)	刂	剥	2f8.4
		剝	2f8.4
hage	禾	禿	5d2.5
hage(masu)	力	勵	2g5.4
		励	2g5.4
hage(mu)	力	勵	2g5.4
		励	2g5.4
ha(geru)	刂	剥	2f8.4
		剝	2f8.4
	禾	禿	5d2.5
hage(shii)	氵	激	3a13.1
	火	烈	4d6.3
hagi	艹	萩	3k9.5
	月	脛	4b7.6
		骭	4b9.12
ha(gu)	刂	剥	2f8.4
		剝	2f8.4
	扌	接	3c8.10
	弓	矧	3h6.3
haguki	口	齶	3d21.1
haguku(mu)			
	亠	育	2j6.4
		毓	2j6.4
hagusa	艹	莠	3k7.11
haha		母	0a5.36
hahaso	木	柞	4a5.13
HAI	亻	佩	2a6.21
		俳	2a8.8
	亠	牌	2j10.3
		牌	2j10.3
	十	孛	2k4.1
	氵	沛	3a5.25
		湃	3a9.10
	土	坏	3b4.4
	扌	抔	3c4.6
		拝	3c5.3
		拜	3c5.3
		排	3c8.8
		擺	3c15.4
	口	吠	3d4.1
	彳	徘	3i8.3
	广	廃	3q9.3
		廢	3q9.3
	木	杯	4a4.11
	月	胚	4b5.8
		肺	4b5.9
		背	4b5.15
	王	珮	4f6.6
		珈	4f8.4
	方	施	4h6.3
	忄	悖	4k6.4
		憊	4k12.11
	石	碚	5a8.3
	禾	稗	5d8.2
		稗	5d8.2
	衤	裴	5e8.10
	皿	盃	4a4.11
	疒	癈	5i12.2
	貝	敗	7b4.1
	車	輩	7c8.7
	酉	配	7e3.2
	雨	需	8d8.4
hai	厂	灰	2p4.1
	虫	蠅	6d13.1
		蝿	6d13.1
hai(ru)		入	0a2.3
haitaka	鳥	鷂	11b10.5
haji	耳	恥	6e4.2
		耻	6e4.2
hajikami	艹	薑	3k13.19
haji(keru)	弓	弾	3h9.3
		彈	3h9.3
haji(ki)	弓	弾	3h9.3
		彈	3h9.3
haji(ku)	弓	弾	3h9.3
		彈	3h9.3
haji(maru)	女	始	3e5.9
haji(me)	衤	初	5e2.1
haji(meru)	女	始	3e5.9
haji(mete)	衤	初	5e2.1
ha(jirau)	耳	恥	6e4.2
		耻	6e4.2
ha(jiru)	⺶	羞	2o9.4
	忄	愧	4k10.6
		慙	4k11.14
		慚	4k11.14
	耳	恥	6e4.2
		耻	6e4.2
haka	艹	墓	3k10.18
hakado(ru)	扌	捗	3c7.10
		捗	3c7.10
hakama	衤	袴	5e6.4
hakana(i)	亻	儚	2a13.7
haka(rau)	言	計	7a2.1
hakari	禾	秤	5d5.4
hakarigoto	言	謀	7a9.8
haka(ru)	氵	測	3a9.4
	口	図	3s4.3
		圖	3s4.3
	日	量	4c8.9
	言	計	7a2.1
		諮	7a9.4
		謀	7a9.8
ha(ke)	扌	捌	3c7.4
hako	冫	函	2b6.3
		凾	2b6.3
	木	椢	4a8.37
	竹	箱	6f9.4
hako(bu)	辶	運	2q9.10
HAKU	亻	伯	2a5.7
		佰	2a6.19
	阝	陌	2d6.3
	刂	剥	2f8.4
		剝	2f8.4
	亠	亳	2j8.4
	十	博	2k10.1
	辶	迫	2q5.5
	氵	泊	3a5.15
	扌	拍	3c5.14
		㧁	3c5.14
		搏	3c10.5
		擘	3c13.7
	巾	帛	3f5.3
	犭	狛	3g5.4
	艹	薄	3k13.11
		蒪	3k13.11
		蘖	4a13.10
	山	岶	3o5.7
	木	栢	4a5.14
		柏	4a5.14
		檗	4a13.10
	月	膊	4b10.2
	日	白	4c1.3
	王	珀	4f5.3
		璞	4f12.1
	忄	博	2k10.1
	甶	魄	5f10.4
	米	粕	6b5.3
	舟	舶	6c5.2
	竹	箔	6f8.5
	釒	鉑	8a4.7
	雨	雹	8d5.3
	馬	駁	10a6.3
ha(ku)	扌	掃	3c8.22
		掃	3c8.22
	口	吐	3d3.1
		喀	3d9.13
		喀	3d9.13
	巾	帚	3f5.5
		帚	3f5.5
	宀	穿	3m7.10
	尸	履	3r12.1
hama	氵	浜	3a7.7
		濱	3a7.7
hamaguri	虫	蚌	6d4.1
		蛤	6d6.7
ha(maru)	山	嵌	3o9.2
	竹	篏	3o9.2
ha(meru)	山	嵌	3o9.2
	竹	篏	3o9.2
hamo	魚	鱧	11a13.3
ha(mu)	食	食	8b0.1
HAN		半	0a5.24
	亻	伴	2a5.4
	阝	阪	2d4.4
	刂	判	2f5.2
	亠	版	2j6.8
	厂	反	2p2.2
		叛	2p7.3
	几	凡	2s1.1
	氵	氾	3a2.3
		泛	3a3.10
		汎	3a3.11
		潘	3a12.8
	土	坂	3b4.7
	扌	拌	3c5.10
		搬	3c10.2
		攀	3c15.5
	巾	帆	3f3.1
		幡	3f12.2
	犭	犯	3g2.1
	艹	范	3k5.14
		蕃	3k12.9
		藩	3k15.4
	木	板	4a4.21
		槃	4a10.30
		樊	4a11.21
	月	胖	4b5.2
		膰	4b12.3
	火	煩	4d9.1
		燔	4d12.3
	王	班	4f6.3

斑 4f8.3
方 播 4h14.1
旛 4h14.1
石 磐 5a10.9
礬 5a15.2
衤 袢 5e5.2
田 畔 5f5.1
畔 5f5.1
疒 瘢 5i10.1
糸 絆 6a5.6
繁 6a10.13
繁 6a10.13
繙 6a12.8
米 釆 6b1.1
舟 般 6c4.3
虫 蟠 6d12.2
竹 笵 6f5.9
範 6f9.3
貝 販 7b4.2
金 鈑 8a4.8
鐇 8a12.4
食 飯 8b4.5
頁 頒 9a4.3
鳥 鷭 11b12.2
han 木 榛 4a10.11
hana 氵 洟 3a6.2
艹 花 3k4.7
花 3k4.7
華 3k7.1
立 端 5b9.2
田 鼻 5f9.3
hanada 糸 縹 6a11.4
hanaha(da) 甚 0a9.10
hanaha(dashii)
甚 0a9.10
hanamuke 貝 贐 7b14.1
食 餞 8b8.2
hana(reru) 亠 离 8c10.3
方 放 4h4.1
隹 離 8c10.3
hanashi 口 咄 3d5.5
噺 3d13.2
言 話 7a6.8
hana(su) 亠 离 8c10.3
方 放 4h4.1
言 話 7a6.8
隹 離 8c10.3
hana(tsu) 方 放 4h4.1
hanawa 土 塙 3b10.3
hana(yagu) 艹 花 3k4.7
花 3k4.7
華 3k7.1
hana(yaka) 艹 花 3k4.7
花 3k4.7
華 3k7.1
hane 羽 2b4.5
冫 羽 2b4.5
十 翅 2k8.4
ha(nekasu) 扌 撥 3c12.11
ha(neru) 刂 刎 2f4.3
扌 撥 3c12.11
⻊ 跳 7d6.3
hani 土 埴 3b8.10
hanzō 木 楾 4a9.15
ha(ppa) 艹 葉 3k9.21
hara 厂 原 2p8.1
月 肚 4b3.1
腹 4b9.4
harai 礻 祓 4e5.2
hara(mu) 子 孕 2c2.1
女 妊 3e4.3
姙 3e4.3
ha(rasu) 月 腫 4b9.1
日 晴 4c8.2
晴 4c8.2
雨 霽 8d14.2
hara(u) 扌 払 3c2.2
拂 3c2.2
礻 祓 4e5.2
禳 4e17.1
harawata 月 腸 4b9.8
膓 4b9.8
ha(re) 日 晴 4c8.2
晴 4c8.2
ha(reru) 月 腫 4b9.1
日 晴 4c8.2
晴 4c8.2
雨 霽 8d14.2
ha(rete) 日 晴 4c8.2
晴 4c8.2
hari 木 梁 4a7.25
金 針 8a2.3
鍼 8a9.12
harinezumi 虫 蝟 6d9.5
haritsuke 石 磔 5a11.2
haru 日 春 4c5.13
ha(ru) 弓 張 3h8.1
貝 貼 7b5.2
haru(ka) 辶 遙 2q10.3
遥 2q10.3
hasa(maru) 扌 挟 3c6.1
挾 3c6.1
hasami 虫 螯 6d11.8
金 鋏 8a7.4
hasa(mu) 丷 剪 2o9.1
翦 2o9.1
扌 挟 3c6.1
挾 3c6.1
挿 3c7.2
插 3c7.2
ha(seru) 馬 馳 10a3.1
駛 10a5.1
hashi 口 嘴 3d13.7
木 橋 4a12.8
立 端 5b9.2
竹 箸 6f9.1
箸 6f9.1
hashibami 木 榛 4a10.11
hashigo 木 梯 4a7.17
hashike 舟 艀 6c6.1
hashira 木 柱 4a5.12
楹 4a9.19
hashi(ri) 土 赱 3b4.9
走 3b4.9
hashi(ru) 十 奔 2k6.5
土 赱 3b4.9
走 3b4.9
hasu 亻 斜 2a9.21
辶 蓮 3k10.31
艹 蓮 3k10.31
蓮 3k10.31
hata 亻 側 2a9.4
傍 2a10.6
巾 幡 3f12.2
木 機 4a12.1
火 畑 4d5.1
方 旗 4h10.1
石 磻 5a13.3
立 端 5b9.2
田 畠 5f5.3
竹 籏 6f14.2
hatahata 魚 鰰 11a10.2
hatake 火 畑 4d5.1
田 畠 5f5.3
疒 疥 5i4.3
hatara(ki) 亻 働 2a11.1
仂 2a11.1
hatara(ku) 亻 働 2a11.1
仂 2a11.1
ha(tashite) 果 0a8.8
ha(tasu) 果 0a8.8
ha(te) 果 0a8.8
ha(teru) 果 0a8.8
ha(teshi) 果 0a8.8
hato 鳥 鳩 11b2.1
鴿 11b6.1
HATSU 癶 0a5.3
発 0a9.5
發 0a9.5
氵 溌 3a12.17
潑 3a12.17
扌 捌 3c7.4
撥 3c12.11
彡 髪 3j11.3
髮 3j11.3
禾 秡 5d5.5
田 魃 5f10.2
⻊ 跋 7d5.5
酉 醗 7e12.2
醱 7e12.2
金 釟 8a2.2
鉢 8a5.4
鈸 8a5.5
hatsu- 衤 初 5e2.1
ha(u) 辶 這 2q7.1
這 2q7.1
hayabusa 隹 隼 8c2.2
haya(i) 辶 速 2q7.4
几 夙 2s4.2
日 早 4c2.1
haya(maru) 日 早 4c2.1
haya(meru)
辶 速 2q7.4
日 早 4c2.1
haya(ru) 辶 逸 2q8.6
逸 2q8.6
hayashi 口 囃 3d18.1
木 林 4a4.1
haya(su) 口 囃 3d18.1
ha(yasu) 生 0a5.29
hazama 石 硲 5a7.7
haze 木 櫨 4a16.2
枦 4a16.2
枦 4a16.2
魚 鯊 11a7.9
ha(zeru) 火 爆 4d15.2
hazu 竹 筈 6f6.10
ha(zubeki) 耳 恥 6e4.2
耻 6e4.2
ha(zukashii)
耳 恥 6e4.2
耻 6e4.2
hazukashi(meru)
厂 辱 2p8.2
⺌ 忝 3n5.4
hazu(mu) 弓 弾 3h9.3
彈 3h9.3
hazu(reru) ⺊ 外 2m3.1
ha(zuru) 耳 恥 6e4.2
耻 6e4.2
hazu(su) ⺊ 外 2m3.1
he 尸 屁 3r4.3
舟 舳 6c5.1
hebi 虫 蛇 6d5.7
HECHI 日 暼 4c12.2
heda(taru) 阝 隔 2d10.2

Reading	Rad.	Kanji	Code
		隔	2d10.2
heda(teru)	阝	隔	2d10.2
		隔	2d10.2
HEI		丙	0a5.21
		秉	0a8.11
	亻	併	2a6.17
		併	2a6.17
	阝	陛	2d7.6
	十	平	2k3.4
		平	2k3.4
	丷	并	204.2
		兵	2o5.6
		並	2o6.1
		瓶	2o9.6
		瓶	2o9.6
	土	坪	3b5.4
		坪	3b5.4
		塀	3b9.11
		塀	3b9.11
	女	娉	3e7.6
		嬖	3e13.2
	巾	幣	3f12.4
		幣	3f12.4
		幣	3f12.4
	艹	萍	3k5.8
		萍	3k8.12
		蔽	3k12.1
		蔽	3k12.1
		薜	3k13.6
	尸	屏	3r6.5
		屏	3r6.5
	木	柄	4a5.9
	火	炳	4d5.2
	攵	敝	4i8.3
		弊	4i11.3
		弊	4i11.3
		斃	4i14.3
	立	竝	2o6.1
	日	睥	5c8.3
	疒	病	5i5.3
	糸	絣	6a6.12
		絣	6a6.12
	虫	蟶	6d10.1
	耳	聘	6e7.1
	竹	箆	6f8.11
		篦	6f8.11
	食	餅	8b6.4
		餅	8b6.4
		餅	8b6.4
	門	閉	8e3.3
		閉	8e3.3
		閇	8e4.1
	魚	鮃	11a5.2
HEKI	亻	僻	2a13.1
	刂	劈	2f13.3
	土	壁	3b13.7
	王	璧	4f13.2
	石	碧	5a9.7
	立	辟	5b8.5
		覕	5b13.1
	衤	襞	5e13.4
	疒	癖	5i13.2
	罒	躄	7d13.3
	雨	霹	8d13.2
	門	闢	8e13.1
heko(masu)		凹	0a5.14
heko(mu)		凹	0a5.14
hekutoguramu			
	日	暊	4c7.16
hekutomētoru			
	米	粨	6b6.3
hekutorittoru			
	立	竡	5b6.2
HEN	亻	偏	2a9.16
		偏	2a9.16
	一	卞	2j2.1
		片	2j2.5
		変	2j7.3
	辶	邊	2q2.1
		邉	2q2.1
		辺	2q2.1
		返	2q4.5
		遍	2q9.16
		遍	2q9.16
	氵	汳	3a4.17
	彳	徧	3i9.5
	月	胼	4b6.5
	夂	變	2j7.3
	忄	愐	4k9.14
	尸	扁	4m5.1
		扁	4m5.1
		翩	4m11.1
	衤	褊	5e9.4
	糸	編	6a9.13
	虫	蝙	6d9.14
	竹	篇	6f9.9
	言	諞	7a9.19
	貝	貶	7b3.2
	馬	駢	10a6.5
		騙	10a9.1
hera	竹	箆	6f8.11
		篦	6f8.11
he(rasu)	氵	減	3a9.37
heri	糸	縁	6a9.10
		緣	6a9.10
herikuda(ru)			
	辶	遜	2q9.4
		遜	2q9.4
he(ru)	又	圣	6a5.11
	厂	歴	2p12.4
		歴	2p12.4
	氵	減	3a9.37
	糸	経	6a5.11
		經	6a5.11
heso	月	臍	4b14.2
		臍	4b14.2
he(su)	氵	減	3a9.37
heta	厂	厤	2p17.1
		蒂	3k11.8
		帶	3k11.8
HETSU	ノ		0a1.2
	日	暼	4c12.2
hetsura(u)	言	諂	7a8.15
hettsui		竈	3m18.1
		竈	3m18.1
hezu(ru)	刂	剥	2f8.4
		剝	2f8.4
HI	匕		0a2.14
	匕		0a2.14
		丕	0a5.2
		非	0a8.1
		飛	0a9.4
		貔	0a11.1
		狉	0a11.1
		翡	0a14.1
	亻	俾	2a8.4
	阝	陂	2d5.3
		鄙	2d11.4
	又	皮	2h3.1
	亠	斐	2j10.4
	匕	比	2m3.5
	辶	避	2q13.3
	匚	匪	2t8.1
	氵	泌	3a5.10
	扌	批	3c4.13
		披	3c5.13
	口	否	3d4.20
		嚊	3d14.2
		嚊	3d19.2
	女	妃	3e3.2
		姵	3e4.6
		婢	3e8.1
	犭	狒	3g5.1
	彳	彼	3i5.2
	艹	菲	3k8.10
		蓖	3k10.13
		鞁	3k11.22
		鞴	3k16.11
	广	庇	3q4.3
		麾	3q16.2
	尸	屁	3r4.3
	木	榧	4a10.29
	月	肥	4b4.5
		朏	4b5.3
		脾	4b8.2
		腓	4b8.3
		臂	4b13.8
	日	棐	4c8.7
	衤	祕	5d5.6
	王	琵	4f8.10
	忄	悲	4k8.18
	尸	扉	4m8.2
		扉	4m8.2
	石	砒	5a4.5
		碑	5a9.2
		碑	5a9.2
	禾	秕	5d4.4
		秘	5d5.6
	衤	被	5e5.3
		裨	5e8.2
	罒	毘	5f4.6
		卑	5f4.8
		卑	5f4.8
		髀	5f14.3
		髀	5f14.3
	罒	羆	5g10.2
		羆	5g14.2
	疒	疲	5i5.2
		痞	5i7.4
		痺	5i8.4
		痹	5i8.4
	糸	紕	6a4.7
		緋	6a8.4
	米	粃	6b4.3
	虫	蜱	6d8.1
		蜚	6d8.10
	言	誹	7a8.5
		譬	7a13.7
	貝	費	7b5.4
		賁	7b5.6
		贔	7b14.2
	足	跛	7d5.4
	雨	霏	8d8.3
	魚	鯡	11a8.2
	鳥	鵯	11b8.2
hi	冫	冰	3a1.2
	阝	陽	2d9.5
	氵	氷	3a1.2
	木	杼	4a4.20
		梭	4a7.11
		桧	4a13.8
		檜	4a13.8
	日	日	4c0.1
	火	火	4d0.1
		灯	4d2.1
		燈	4d2.1

Reading	Rad	Kanji	Code
hibari	鳥	鶲	11b11.1
hibi	十	襻	2k15.1
	車	轡	7c7.3
		輝	7c7.3
hibi(ku)	日	響	4c15.3
		響	4c15.3
HICHI	〜	篳	6f10.3
hida	禩	禩	5e11.4
		襞	5e13.4
hidari	左		0a5.20
hideri	旱		4c3.1
hido(i)	酉	酷	7e7.1
hie	禾	稗	5d8.2
		稗	5d8.2
hi(eru)	冫	冷	2b5.3
higa-	亻	僻	2a13.1
higai	魚	鰄	11a9.10
higa(mu)	亻	僻	2a13.1
higashi	東		0a8.9
hige	彡	髯	3j12.2
		髭	3j13.2
	頁	鬚	9a13.2
higuma	罴	熊	5g14.2
higurashi	虫	蜩	6d8.9
HII	貝	贔	7b14.2
hii(deru)	禾	秀	5d2.4
hiiragi	木	柊	4a5.24
hiji	月	肘	4b3.3
		肱	4b4.9
		臂	4b13.8
Hijiki	木	枡	4a4.5
hijiri	王	聖	4f9.9
		聖	4f9.9
hika(e)	扌	控	3c8.11
hika(eru)	扌	扣	3c3.1
		控	3c8.11
hikagami	月	膕	4b11.6
hikari	丷	光	3n3.2
hika(ru)	丷	光	3n3.2
hi(keru)	弓	引	3h1.1
HIKI	止	疋	2m3.4
hiki	止	疋	2m3.4
	匚	匹	2t2.3
	艹	驀	3k13.23
	虫	蟇	3k13.23
hiki(iru)	玄	率	2j9.1
hiko	彦	彦	5b4.4
		彦	5b4.4
hikobae	艹	蘖	3k17.4
hi(ku)	曳	曳	0a6.23
		曳	0a6.23
	一	牽	2j9.3
	辶	退	2q6.3
	扌	抽	3c5.7
		挽	3c7.13
		挽	3c7.13
	弓	引	3h1.1
		弾	3h9.3
		弾	3h9.3
	艹	惹	3k9.18
	石	碾	5a10.7
	車	轢	7c15.1
hiku(i)	亻	低	2a5.15
	彳	低	2a5.15
hiku(maru)	亻	低	2a5.15
	彳	低	2a5.15
hiku(meru)	亻	低	2a5.15
	彳	低	2a5.15
hima	阝	隙	2d10.4
		隙	2d10.4
	日	暇	4c9.1
hime	女	姫	3e7.11
		姫	3e7.11
		媛	3e9.4
		媛	3e9.4
hi(meru)	礻	祕	5d5.6
	禾	秘	5d5.6
himo	糹	紐	6a4.2
himorogi	月	胙	4b5.4
		膰	4b12.3
himoto(ku)	糸	繙	6a12.8
HIN	宀	稟	2j11.3
		稟	2j11.3
	丷	貧	2o9.5
		貧	2o9.5
	氵	浜	3a7.7
		濱	3a7.7
		瀕	3a16.4
		瀕	3a16.4
	扌	擯	3c14.6
	口	品	3d6.15
		品	3d6.15
		嚬	3d16.1
	女	嬪	3e14.4
	艹	蘋	3k16.6
	宀	賓	3m12.3
		賓	3m12.3
	木	彬	4a7.3
		梹	4a14.3
		檳	4a14.3
	牛	牝	4g2.1
	戈	斌	4n9.4
	糹	繽	6a14.2
	貝	殯	7b11.5
	頁	頻	9a8.2
		頻	9a8.2
		顰	9a15.1
hina	阝	鄙	2d11.4
	隹	雛	8c10.1
hina(biru)	阝	鄙	2d11.4
hine(kuru)	扌	捻	3c8.25
hine(ri)	扌	捻	3c8.25
hine(ru)	扌	捻	3c8.25
hinoe	丙		0a5.21
hinoki	木	桧	4a13.8
	木	檜	4a13.8
hinoto	丁		0a2.4
hira	片		2j2.5
hira-	平		2k3.4
	平		2k3.4
hira(keru)	門	開	8e4.6
hira(ki)	門	開	8e4.6
hira(ku)	扌	拓	3c5.1
	門	開	8e4.6
hirame	魚	鮃	11a5.2
hirame(kasu)	門	閃	8e2.1
hirame(ku)	門	閃	8e2.1
hira(tai)	艹	平	2k3.4
	艹	平	2k3.4
hire	魚	鰭	11a10.4
hiro	寸	尋	3d9.29
		尋	3d9.29
hiro(garu)	扌	拡	3c5.25
		擴	3c5.25
	广	広	3q2.1
		廣	3q2.1
hiro(geru)	扌	拡	3c5.25
		擴	3c5.25
	广	広	3q2.1
		廣	3q2.1
hiro(i)	弓	弘	3h2.1
	广	広	3q2.1
		廣	3q2.1
hiro(maru)	广	広	3q2.1
		廣	3q2.1
hiro(meru)	广	広	3q2.1
		廣	3q2.1
hiro(u)	扌	拾	3c6.14
hiro(yaka)	广	広	3q2.1
		廣	3q2.1
hiru	日	昼	4c5.15
		畫	4c5.15
	虫	蛭	6d6.5
hi(ru)	艹	干	2k1.1
	〜	簛	6f13.2
hirugae(ru)	尸	翩	4m11.1
	米	翻	6b12.3
		籲	6b12.3
	虫	飄	6d14.4
		颺	6d14.4
hirugae(su)	米	翻	6b12.3
		籲	6b12.3
hiru(mu)	忄	怯	4k5.9
hisagi	木	楸	4a9.6
hisago	匏		0a11.2
	瓠		0a12.2
	礻	瓢	4e12.3
hisa(gu)	米	鬻	6b16.1
hisashi	广	庇	3q4.3
		厢	3q9.2
	木	梠	4a7.12
hisa(shii)	久		0a3.7
hishi	艹	菱	3k8.20
		淩	3k11.6
hishi(geru)	扌	拉	3c5.2
hishi(gu)	扌	拉	3c5.2
hishiko	魚	鯷	11a9.11
hishime(ku)	牛	犠	4g8.1
hishio	酉	醢	7e10.3
hishi (to)	牛	犠	4g8.1
hiso(ka)	宀	窃	3m6.5
		竊	3m6.5
		密	3m8.5
	礻	祕	5d5.6
	礻	私	5d2.2
		秘	5d5.6
hiso(maru)	氵	潜	3a12.6
		潛	3a12.6
		潜	3a12.6
hiso(meru)	氵	潜	3a12.6
		潛	3a12.6
		潜	3a12.6
	口	嚬	3d16.1
	頁	顰	9a15.1
hiso(mi)	頁	顰	9a15.1
hiso(mu)	氵	潜	3a12.6
		潛	3a12.6
		潜	3a12.6
hitai	頁	額	9a9.6
hitaki	鳥	鶲	11b10.7
hita(ru)	氵	浸	3a7.17
hita(su)	氵	浸	3a7.17
hito	亻	人	2a0.1
hito-	一		0a1.1
hitoe (ni)	亻	偏	2a9.16
		偏	2a9.16
hitomi	目	睛	5c8.7
		瞳	5c12.2
		瞳	5c12.2
hito(ri)	犭	独	3g6.1
		獨	3g6.1
hito(rideni)	犭	独	3g6.1
		獨	3g6.1

Reading	Kanji	Code
hito(shii)	斉	2j6.5
	齊	2j6.5
	均	3b4.8
	等	6f6.9
hito(tsu)	一	0a1.1
HITSU	必	0a5.16
	疋	2m3.4
	逼	2q9.7
	逼	2q9.7
	匹	2t2.3
	泌	3a5.10
	弼	3h9.2
	畢	5f6.6
	筆	6f6.1
	篳	6f10.3
	謐	7a10.4
	蹕	7d11.2
hitsu	櫃	4a14.5
hitsugi	柩	4a5.31
	棺	4a8.25
hitsuji	未	0a5.27
	羊	2o4.1
hiuchi	燧	4d12.7
hiwa	鷽	11b10.2
hi(ya)	冷	2b5.3
hi(yakasu)	冷	2b5.3
hi(yasu)	冷	2b5.3
hiyodori	鵯	11b8.2
hiyoko	雛	8c10.1
hiza	膝	4b11.4
hizamazu(ku)	跪	7d6.8
hizume	蹄	7d9.3
hizu(mi)	歪	2m7.4
hizu(mu)	歪	2m7.4
HO	甫	0a7.11
	匍	0a9.13
	鯆	0a19.1
	保	2a7.11
	步	3n5.3
	逋	2q7.3
	浦	3a7.2
	埔	3b7.1
	堡	3b9.14
	舗	3b12.4
	舗	3b12.4
	捕	3c7.3
	捗	3c7.10
	捗	3c7.10
	哺	3d7.4
	布	3f2.1
	葡	3k9.30
	蒲	3k10.8
	歩	3n5.3
	圃	3s7.1
	脯	4b7.1
	補	5e7.1
	褓	5e9.1
	輔	7c7.1
	鋪	8a7.3
	舗	8b7.2
	鯆	11a7.1
HO'	法	3a5.20
ho	帆	3f3.1
	火	4d0.1
	穂	5d10.2
	穗	5d10.2
HŌ	勺	0a2.8
	包	0a5.9
	包	0a5.9
	奉	0a8.13
	匏	0a11.2
	仿	2a4.3
	保	2a7.11
	做	2a8.7
	俸	2a8.18
	傍	2a10.6
	邦	2d4.7
	砲	2h8.2
	亨	2j4.2
	烹	2j8.5
	襃	2j13.1
	襃	2j13.1
	襃	2j13.1
	進	2q6.7
	逢	2q7.15
	鳳	2s12.1
	匚	2t0.1
	泙	3a5.13
	泡	3a5.18
	泡	3a5.18
	法	3a5.20
	澎	3a12.4
	垉	3b5.5
	封	3b6.13
	堋	3b8.4
	堡	3b9.14
	報	3b9.16
	抔	3c4.6
	抱	3c5.15
	抱	3c5.15
	抛	3c5.27
	抛	3c5.27
	捧	3c8.12
	呆	3d4.13
	咆	3d5.8
	豊	3d10.15
	豐	3d10.15
	幇	3f9.5
	弸	3h8.2
	彷	3i4.1
	彭	3j9.2
	髱	3j12.3
	芳	3k4.1
	苞	3k5.13
	萌	3k8.11
	萠	3k8.11
	葆	3k9.12
	蒡	3k10.4
	蓬	3k10.32
	蓬	3k10.32
	鞄	3k11.25
	鞄	3k11.25
	宝	3m5.2
	寶	3m5.2
	寶	3m5.2
	峯	3o7.6
	峰	3o7.6
	崩	3o8.7
	崩	3o8.7
	庖	3q5.5
	庖	3q5.5
	鉋	3s11.1
	枋	4a4.3
	枹	4a5.16
	朋	4b4.1
	朋	4b4.1
	胞	4b5.5
	胞	4b5.5
	鵬	4b15.1
	炮	4d5.4
	烽	4d7.1
	焙	4d8.1
	琫	4f8.5
	方	4h0.1
	放	4h4.1
	髣	4h10.2
	麭	4i13.2
	怦	4k5.3
	砲	5a5.3
	砲	5a5.3
	硼	5a8.2
	磅	5a10.4
	袍	5e5.5
	褓	5e9.1
	疱	5i5.6
	絣	6a6.12
	絣	6a6.12
	縫	6a9.15
	縫	6a9.15
	繃	6a11.10
	舫	6c4.1
	蜂	6d7.6
	蚫	11a5.4
	篷	6f10.8
	訪	7a4.1
	跑	7d5.6
	鉋	8a5.8
	鋒	8a7.11
	飽	8b5.1
	魴	11a4.1
	鮑	11a5.4
	鴇	11b4.3
hō	頬	9a7.2
	頰	9a7.2
hobashira	檣	4a13.4
	艢	4a13.4
hobo	略	5f6.4
	畧	5f6.4
hoda	榾	4a10.6
hoda(su)	絆	6a5.6
hodo	程	5d7.2
hodo(keru)	解	4g9.1
	解	4g9.1
hodoko(su)	施	4h5.1
hodo(ku)	解	4g9.1
	解	4g9.1
ho(eru)	吼	3d3.6
	吠	3d4.1
hofu(ru)	屠	3r9.2
	屠	3r9.2
hoga(raka)	朗	4b6.11
	朗	4b6.11
	腺	4b6.11
hoho	頬	9a7.2
	頰	9a7.2
hojiku(ru)	穿	3m7.10
hoji(ru)	穿	3m7.10
hojishi	脯	4b7.1
	腊	4b8.5
hoka	他	2a3.4
	外	2m3.1
hōki	帚	3f5.5
	幕	3f5.5
	箒	6f8.13
hoko	矛	0a5.6
	桙	4a6.25
	槊	4a10.31
	戈	4n0.1
	鉾	8a6.11
hokora	祠	4e5.8
hokori	埃	3b7.6
hokoro(baseru)		
	綻	6a8.13
hokoro(biru)		
	綻	6a8.13

Reading	Kanji	Code
	訝	7a5.1
ibuka(shii) 言	訝	7a5.1
	訝	7a5.1
ibu(ru) 火	熏	4d14.1
	燻	4d14.1
ibu(su) 火	熏	4d14.1
	燻	4d14.1
ICHI	一	0a1.1
士	壱	3p4.2
	壹	3p4.2
戈	式	4n1.1
ichi 亠	市	2j3.1
ichigo 艹	苺	3k5.4
	莓	3k5.4
ichijiru(shii) 艹	著	3k8.4
	著	3k8.4
ida(ku) 扌	抱	3c5.15
	抱	3c5.15
ida(su)	出	0a5.22
ide(ru)	出	0a5.22
ido(mu) 扌	挑	3c6.5
ie 宀	家	3m7.1
iedo(mo) 隹	雖	8c9.2
i(eru) 疒	癒	5i13.3
	癒	5i13.3
	瘉	5i13.3
iga 氵	毬	2b9.1
iga(mu) 口	啀	3d8.16
igurumi 戈	弋	4n0.2
ii 食	飯	8b4.5
i(i)	良	0a7.3
	良	0a7.3
	善	2o10.2
	譱	2o10.2
女	好	3e2.1
iji(kuru) 王	弄	4f3.2
iji(meru) 艹	苛	3k5.30
iji(ru) 王	弄	4f3.2
ikada 木	桴	4a6.12
	槎	4a10.26
竹	筏	6f6.7
ikade 心	怎	4k5.18
ikame(shii) 口	嚴	3n14.1
	厳	3n14.1
ikari 石	碇	5a8.6
	錨	8a8.14
ika(ri) 心	怒	4k5.19
ikaru 鳥	鵤	11b7.5
ika(ru)	忿	2o6.3
口	嗔	3d10.11
心	怒	4k5.19
	愠	4k10.7
目	瞋	5c10.2
ikaruga 鳥	鵤	11b7.5
i(kasu)	生	0a5.29
ikazuchi 雨	雷	8d5.1
ike 氵	池	3a3.4
土	圻	3b6.4
i(keru)	生	0a5.29
氵	活	3a6.16
土	埋	3b7.2
彳	行	3i3.1
IKI 土	域	3b8.3
門	閾	8e8.5
iki 心	息	4k6.17
米	粋	6b4.5
	粹	6b4.5
i(ki)	生	0a5.29
氵	活	3a6.16
ikidō(ru) 心	憤	4k12.6
iki(mu) 心	息	4k6.17
ikio(i) 力	勢	2g11.6
iki(re) 火	熅	4d10.2
i(kiru)	生	0a5.29
氵	活	3a6.16
iko(i) 心	憩	4k12.10
	憇	4k12.10
iko(u) 心	憩	4k12.10
	憇	4k12.10
IKU 阝	郁	2d6.6
亠	育	2j6.4
	毓	2j6.4
火	燠	4d13.2
石	礇	5a13.1
米	鬻	6b16.1
iku- 戈	幾	4n8.4
i(ku) 彳	行	3i3.1
ikusa 宀	軍	2i7.1
戈	戦	4n9.2
	戰	4n9.2
ima 亻	今	2a2.10
ima(da)	未	0a5.27
imashi(me) 戈	戒	4n3.1
糸	縛	6a10.3
	縛	6a10.3
imashi(meru) 戈	戒	4n3.1
言	誡	7a7.16
	警	7a12.7
ima(washii) 心	忌	4k3.4
ima(ya) 亻	今	2a2.10
imi 宀	斎	2j9.6
	齋	2j9.6
i(mi) 心	忌	4k3.4
imina 言	諱	7a10.8
imo 女	妹	3e5.4
艹	芋	3k3.1
	薯	3k14.3
	薯	3k14.3
	藷	3k16.3
	藷	3k16.3
imōto 女	妹	3e5.4
i(mu) 心	忌	4k3.4
IN	允	0a4.13
	尹	0a4.44
阝	院	2d7.9
	陰	2d8.7
	隈	2d10.3
	隠	2d11.3
	隱	2d11.3
卩	印	2e4.1
辶	廴	2q0.1
八	殷	2s8.1
氵	淫	3a8.17
	湮	3a9.11
土	堙	3b9.4
口	咽	3d6.14
	員	3d7.10
	喑	3d9.8
女	姪	3a8.17
	姻	3e6.8
弓	引	3h1.1
艹	茵	3k6.24
	蔭	3k10.10
宀	寅	3m8.4
口	因	3s3.2
	氤	3s7.4
月	胤	4b5.16
心	恚	4k6.21
	愍	4k10.12
立	音	5b4.3
	韵	7b12.2
虫	蚓	6d4.4
貝	殞	7b7.2
	贇	7b12.1
	韻	7b12.2
酉	酳	7e7.4
食	飲	8b4.1
	飮	8b4.1
雨	霪	8d11.2
ina 口	否	3d4.20
魚	鮞	11a8.7
禾	稲	5d9.2
	稻	5d9.2
ina- 禾	稲	5d9.2
	稻	5d9.2
inago 虫	蝗	6d9.8
ina(mu) 口	否	3d4.20
inana(ku) 口	嘶	3d12.1
i(nasu) 彳	往	3i5.6
	徃	3i5.6
ina(ya) 口	否	3d4.20
inchi 口	吋	3d3.3
ine 禾	稲	5d9.2
	稻	5d9.2
inishie 艹	古	2k3.1
inochi 亻	命	2a6.26
inoko 豕	豕	0a7.1
ino(ri) 衤	祈	4e4.3
	祈	4e4.3
ino(ru) 衤	祈	4e4.3
	祈	4e4.3
	祷	4e14.2
	禱	4e14.2
inoshishi 犭	猪	3g8.1
	猪	3g8.1
	猯	3g9.4
	猪	3g8.1
inu 犭	犬	3g0.1
戈	戌	4n2.2
iori 艹	菴	3k8.6
广	庵	3k8.6
	廬	3q16.3
ira(e) 广	応	3q4.2
	應	3q4.2
iraka 艹	薨	3k12.11
i(reru)	入	0a2.3
宀	容	3m7.8
irezumi 火	黥	4d16.1
iri 土	圦	3b2.1
木	杁	4a2.5
iro	色	2n4.1
irodo(ru) 彡	彩	3j8.1
i(ru)	入	0a2.3
	射	0a10.8
灬	煎	2o11.2
女	要	3e6.11
	要	3e6.11
尸	居	3r5.3
火	炒	4d4.3
	熬	4d11.6
金	鋳	8a7.2
	鑄	8a7.2
iruka 魚	鯆	11a7.1
isagiyo(i) 氵	潔	3a12.10
	潔	3a12.10
isago 氵	沙	3a4.13
石	砂	5a4.3
isaka(i) 言	諍	7a8.9
isa(mashii) 力	勇	2g7.3
isa(meru) 言	諫	7a9.1
	諫	7a9.1
isa(mu) 力	勇	2g7.3
isao 力	功	2g3.2
	勲	4d11.3

Reading	Rad.	Char	Code
JIKU	宀	宍	3m4.4
	木	柚	4a5.5
	忄	怵	4k4.1
	皿	岻	5h5.1
		岻	5h5.1
	舟	舳	6c5.1
	竹	竺	6f2.1
	車	軸	7c5.1
JIN	儿	儿	0a2.2
		刃	0a3.22
		刄	0a3.22
		甚	0a9.10
	亻	人	2a0.1
		仁	2a2.8
		仞	2a3.8
		仭	2a3.8
		侭	2a14.2
		儘	2a14.2
	阝	陣	2d7.1
	刂	靭	2f10.4
	辶	迅	2q3.5
	臣	臣	2t4.3
	氵	沈	3a4.9
		沈	3a4.9
		潯	3a12.18
	口	尋	3d9.29
		尋	3d9.29
	艹	靫	2f10.4
		靫	2f10.4
		靭	2f10.4
		荏	3k6.10
		芯	3k7.15
		蕈	3k12.10
		蕁	3k12.13
	士	壬	3p1.1
	广	塵	3q11.4
	尸	尽	3r3.1
	木	椹	4a9.4
	月	腎	4b9.11
	火	燼	4d14.2
	礻	神	4e5.1
		神	4e5.1
	忄	恁	4k6.21
	禾	稔	5d8.5
	礻	衽	5e4.4
		衽	5e4.4
	皿	盡	3r3.1
	米	糂	6b9.1
	訁	訊	7a3.8
	貝	贐	7b14.1
	魚	鱏	11a12.2
		鱘	11a12.5
ji(rasu)	催	焦	8c4.3
ji(reru)	催	焦	8c4.3
JITSU	宀	実	3m5.4
	日	日	4c0.1
		昵	4c5.5
	礻	祉	5e4.1
JO	亻	絞	2h7.1
	阝	除	2d7.10
	力	助	2g5.1
		耡	2g11.2
	又	叙	2h7.1
	氵	汝	3a3.2
	扌	抒	3c4.19
	口	舒	3d9.23
	女	女	3e0.1
		如	3e3.1
	彳	徐	3i7.2
	艹	茹	3k6.7
		茢	3k7.6
	广	序	3q4.4
	攵	敍	2h7.1
	忄	恕	4k6.18
	糹	絮	6a6.16
	虫	蜍	6d7.7
	釒	鋤	8a7.5
JŌ		丈	0a3.26
		丈	0a3.26
		承	0a7.7
		乗	0a9.19
		乘	0a9.19
	亻	仍	2a2.7
		仗	2a3.5
		條	2a11.4
		條	4i4.1
	冫	状	2b5.1
	子	丞	2c4.3
	阝	鄭	2d12.4
		鄭	2d12.4
	刂	剰	2f9.1
		剰	2f9.1
	一	冗	2i2.1
		冗	2i2.1
	亠	襄	2j15.2
		上	2m1.1
		貞	2m7.1
	辶	遶	2q12.2
	氵	浄	3a6.18
		淨	3a6.18
		滌	3a11.6
	土	城	3b6.1
		場	3b9.6
		場	3b9.6
		壌	3b13.4
		壌	3b13.4
	扌	拯	3c5.19
		擾	3c15.1
		攘	3c17.1
	女	娘	3e7.2
		嫋	3e10.2
		嬢	3e13.1
		孃	3e13.1
		嫐	5f12.1
	巾	帖	3f5.2
	犭	狀	2b5.1
	艹	茸	3k6.1
		蒸	3k9.19
		薨	3k12.12
	宀	宂	2i2.1
		定	3m5.8
	丷	常	3n8.3
		靜	4b10.9
	夫	奘	3p7.1
		牂	3p7.1
	木	杖	4a3.5
		橈	4a12.15
	月	静	4b10.9
	日	晟	4c7.5
	火	烝	4d5.7
	礻	祥	4e6.1
		祥	4e6.1
		禳	4e17.1
	攵	条	4i4.1
	忄	情	4k8.9
		情	4k8.9
	戈	成	4n2.1
	禾	穣	5d13.2
		穰	5d13.2
	礻	裊	5e7.7
	田	畳	5f7.3
		疊	5f7.3
		疂	5f7.3
		疊	5f7.3
		嬲	5f12.1
	皿	盛	5h6.1
	糹	縄	6a9.1
		繩	6a9.1
		繞	6a12.5
	耳	聶	6e12.2
	訁	誂	7a8.12
		讓	7a13.1
		譲	7a13.1
	足	躋	7d18.1
	酉	醸	7e13.1
		釀	7e13.1
	釒	錠	8a8.12
		鑲	8a17.2
	食	饒	8b12.2
	馬	驤	10a17.2
jō	扌	搦	3c9.17
JOKU	厂	辱	2p8.2
	氵	潯	3a10.5
	艹	蕁	3k10.30
	礻	褥	5e10.2
	糹	縟	6a10.11
JU		入	0a2.3
		寿	0a7.15
	亻	儒	2a14.1
		从	3i7.3
	子	孺	2c14.1
	又	受	2h6.2
	氵	洳	3a6.9
		濡	3a14.4
	扌	授	3c8.15
	口	呪	3d5.11
		咒	3d5.11
		就	3d9.21
		豎	5b9.5
	女	嬬	3e14.2
	彳	從	3i7.3
		從	3i7.3
	士	壽	0a7.15
		尌	3p9.3
	木	樹	4a12.3
	王	珠	4f6.2
	戈	戍	4n2.3
	立	竪	5b9.5
	礻	襦	5e14.1
	糹	綬	6a8.7
	虫	蠕	6d14.1
	訁	誦	7a7.14
		需	8d6.1
	頁	顬	9a14.1
JŪ		内	0a4.26
		廿	0a4.36
		重	0a9.18
	亻	什	2a2.2
		住	2a5.19
		住	2a5.19
		从	3i7.3
		充	2j4.5
		十	2k0.1
	氵	汁	3a2.1
		渋	3a8.19
		澁	3a8.19
		澀	3a8.19
	扌	拾	3c6.14
		揉	3c9.2
		犰	3g4.3
		獣	3g12.3
		獣	3g12.3
	彳	從	3i7.3
		從	3i7.3
	木	柔	4a5.34
		鞣	4a14.7

	戈 戎	4n2.4
	糸 紐	6a4.2
	絨	6a6.13
	縦	6a10.2
	縱	6a10.2
	米 糅	6b9.3
	足 蹂	7d9.2
	釒 銃	8a6.9
-jū	中	0a4.40
JUKU	土 塾	3b10.7
	口 孰	3d7.14
	弓 粥	3h9.1
	鬻	3h9.1
	火 熟	4d10.5
JUN	冫 准	2b8.1
	十 準	2k11.1
	辶 巡	2q3.3
	遵	2q12.8
	氵 洵	3a6.23
	淳	3a7.19
	潤	3a12.20
	彳 徇	3i6.7
	循	3i9.6
	艹 荀	3k6.22
	木 楯	4a9.3
	月 肫	4b4.3
	日 旬	4c2.5
	殉	4c6.9
	忄 恂	4k6.13
	目 盾	5c4.8
	糸 純	6a4.3
	竹 筍	6f6.14
	笋	6f6.14
	言 詢	7a6.17
	諄	7a7.11
	酉 醇	7e7.5
	隹 隼	8c2.2
	門 閏	8e4.4
	頁 順	9a3.2
	馬 馴	10a3.2
	鳥 鶉	11b7.4
JUTSU	卩 卹	2e6.1
	朮 朮	2k3.3
	辶 述	2q5.3
	彳 術	3i8.2
	術	3i8.2
	忄 怵	4k5.5
	恤	4k6.1
	戈 戍	4n2.2

– K –

KA	ケ	6f8.15
	瓜	0a6.3
	果	0a8.8
	夥	0a14.2
	亻 化	2a2.6
	仮	2a4.15
	假	2a4.15
	伽	2a5.12
	何	2a5.21
	価	2a6.3
	價	2a6.3
	佳	2a6.10
	個	2a8.36
	个	2a8.36
	个	6f8.15
	力 加	2g3.1
	亠 裹	2j12.2
	十 罅	2k15.1
	卜 下	2m1.2
	卦	2m6.1
	厂 厦	3q10.2
	辶 迦	2q5.6
	迦	2q5.6
	遐	2q9.3
	過	2q9.18
	氵 河	3a5.30
	渮	3a8.26
	渦	3a9.36
	土 堝	3b9.8
	口 可	3d2.12
	呵	3d5.13
	哥	3d6.19
	哥	3d7.16
	谺	3d9.24
	嘩	3d10.7
	女 嫁	3e10.6
	弓 彁	3h10.1
	艹 花	3k4.7
	花	3k4.7
	茄	3k5.19
	苛	3k5.30
	華	3k7.1
	荷	3k7.10
	菓	3k8.2
	菥	3k9.6
	葭	3k9.9
	靴	3k10.34
	宀 家	3m7.1
	窠	3m10.5
	寡	3m11.2
	窩	3m11.10
	巛 巣	3o7.1
	嘉	3p11.1
	广 厦	3q10.2
	囗 囮	3s4.4
	木 枷	4a5.19
	柯	4a5.29
	架	4a5.36
	枛	4a6.6
	榎	4a10.4
	樺	4a10.15
	日 暇	4c9.1
	火 火	4d0.1
	ネ 禍	4e9.4
	禍	4e9.4
	王 珈	4f5.4
	珂	4f5.8
	瑕	4f9.2
	夂 夏	4i7.5
	欠 歌	4j10.2
	戈 戈	4n0.1
	石 碬	5a9.3
	禾 禾	5d0.1
	科	5d4.3
	稼	5d10.3
	疒 痂	5i5.7
	糸 絓	6a6.3
	角 舸	6c5.6
	虫 蚜	6d5.1
	蝌	6d9.2
	蝦	6d9.4
	蝸	6d9.11
	竹 笳	6f5.10
	笴	6f5.14
	箇	6f8.15
	言 譁	3d10.7
	謌	4j10.2
	訛	7a4.5
	譌	7a4.5
	訶	7a5.16
	課	7a8.2
	貝 貨	7b4.5
	車 軻	7c5.5
	足 跏	7d5.7
	踝	7d8.1
	釒 銧	8a7.9
	鍜	8a9.4
	鍋	8a9.13
	雨 霞	8d9.1
	頁 顆	9a8.1
	馬 駕	10a5.8
	魚 鰕	11a9.4
KA'	亻 合	2a4.18
	忄 恰	4k6.10
ka	乎	0a5.17
	禾 香	5d4.5
	虫 蚊	6d4.5
-ka	日 日	4c0.1
kaba	木 椛	4a7.14
	樺	4a10.15
kaban	艹 鞄	3k11.25
	鞄	3k11.25
kabane	女 姓	3e5.3
kaba(u)	广 庇	3q4.3
kabe	土 壁	3b13.7
kabi	彳 徽	3i20.1
kabi(ru)	彳 徽	3i20.1
ka(biru)	彳 徽	3i20.1
kabu	艹 蕪	3k12.7
	木 株	4a6.3
kabura	艹 蕪	3k12.7
	釒 鏑	8a11.8
kaburi	頁 頭	9a7.6
kabu(ru)	ネ 被	5e5.3
kabu(saru)	ネ 被	5e5.3
kabu(seru)	ネ 被	5e5.3
kabuto	冂 冑	2r7.2
	日 兜	4c8.16
kachi	彳 徒	3i7.1
ka(chi)	月 勝	4b8.4
	勝	4b8.4
kado	門 門	8e0.1
	勹 角	2n5.1
	广 廉	3q10.1
	木 楞	4a9.12
	門 門	8e0.1
ka(e)-	日 替	4c8.12
kaede	木 楓	4a9.28
kaeri(miru)	目 省	5c4.7
	頁 顧	9a12.2
	顧	9a12.2
kaeru	虫 蛙	6d6.4
kae(ru)	刂 帰	2f8.8
	巾 歸	2f8.8
	日 皈	2f8.8
	辶 返	2q4.5
	還	2q13.4
ka(eru)	亻 代	2a3.3
	亠 変	2j7.3
	扌 換	3c9.15
	換	3c9.15
	日 替	4c8.12
	變	2j7.3
kae(su)	刂 帰	2f8.8
	巾 歸	2f8.8
	日 皈	2f8.8
	辶 返	2q4.5
	孵	3n10.5
kae(tte)	卩 却	2e5.3
	卻	2e5.3
kaga(meru)		
	尸 屈	3r5.2
kagami	釒 鏡	8a11.6
	鑑	8a15.2
kagamidai	魚 鮎	11a4.1

Reading		Kanji	Code
kaga(mu)	尸	屈	3r5.2
kagari	⺮	簳	6f10.7
kagaya(ku)			
	火	燿	4d14.3
	車	輝	7c8.8
	隹	耀	8c12.1
		耀	8c12.1
kage	⻖	陰	2d8.7
	彡	影	3j12.1
	⺾	蔭	3k10.10
kage(ru)	⻖	陰	2d8.7
kagi	釒	鉤	8a5.17
		鈎	8a5.17
		鍵	8a8.18
kagi(ri)	⻖	限	2d6.1
kagi(ru)	⻖	限	2d6.1
	刂	劃	2f12.1
kago	⺮	篭	6f16.1
		籠	6f16.1
	車	轎	7c12.2
ka(gu)	口	嗅	3d10.3
KAI		夬	0a4.37
	亻	介	2a2.9
		勾	2a3.10
		价	2a4.11
		会	2a4.19
		會	2a4.19
		個	2a6.22
		偕	2a9.11
		傀	2a10.3
		儈	2a13.8
	⻖	階	2d9.6
		隗	2d10.1
	刂	刈	2f2.1
	亠	殳	2j8.9
	⺾	乖	2k6.4
	⼧	丐	2m2.3
	⼓	解	4g9.1
	厂	灰	2p4.1
	⻌	迴	2q6.12
		廻	2q6.13
		廻	2q6.13
		邂	2q13.2
	囗	回	3s3.1
	氵	海	3a6.20
		海	3a6.20
		洄	3a6.26
		潰	3a12.14
	土	堺	3b9.5
		塊	3b10.2
		壊	3b13.3
		壞	3b13.3
	扌	拐	3c5.21
		拐	3c5.21
		揩	3c9.6
	口	喎	3d6.19
		喙	3d9.14
		譏	3d14.3
	犭	獪	3g13.2
	彳	徊	3i6.8
		街	3i9.2
	⺾	芥	3k4.10
		茴	3k6.23
		薤	3k13.10
	⼭	嵬	3o10.3
	广	廨	3q13.1
	囗	回	3s3.1
	田		3s3.1
	木	枴	4a5.21
		械	4a7.22
		楖	4a8.37
		楷	4a9.18
		槐	4a10.9
		橙	4a10.18
		橺	4a13.2
		桧	4a13.8
		檜	4a13.8
	月	膾	4b13.6
	日	皆	4c5.14
		晦	4c7.3
		晦	4c7.3
	王	瑰	4f10.2
	牛	解	4g9.1
	攵	改	4i3.1
	忄	快	4k4.2
		怪	4k5.11
		恠	4k5.11
		恢	4k6.3
		恢	4k6.3
		悔	4k6.12
		悔	4k6.12
		楬	4k9.9
		懈	4k13.1
		懐	4k13.9
		懷	4k13.9
	戈	戒	4n3.1
	⺹	掛	5e8.4
	⺳	界	5f4.7
		畍	5f4.7
		魁	5f9.1
	疒	疥	5i4.3
	糹	絓	6a6.3
		絵	6a6.8
		繪	6a6.8
	虫	蛔	6d6.9
		蟹	6d13.7
		蠏	6d13.7
	言	誡	7a6.15
		誨	7a7.13
		誠	7a7.16
		諧	7a9.11
	酉	醢	7e10.3
	門	開	8e4.6
	魚	鮭	11a6.3
		鱠	11a13.4
kai	木	橈	4a12.15
		櫂	4a14.1
	貝	貝	7b0.1
kai(i)	疒	痒	5i6.6
kaiko	虫	蠶	6d4.8
		蚕	6d4.8
kaina	月	腕	4b8.6
kairi	氵	浬	3a7.3
kaji	木	柁	4a5.23
		梶	4a7.19
		楫	4a9.20
	舟	舵	6c5.3
kajika	魚	鮖	11a5.1
		鰍	11a9.2
kaji(ru)	亻	齧	2a19.4
	口	嚙	2a19.4
kakā	女	嬶	3e14.1
kaka(e)	扌	抱	3c5.15
		抱	3c5.15
kaka(eru)	扌	抱	3c5.15
		抱	3c5.15
kaka(geru)	扌	揭	3c8.13
		揭	3c8.13
kakame	口	噤	3d14.2
kakari	亻	係	2a7.8
	扌	掛	3c8.6
ka(kari)	扌	掛	3c8.6
kaka(ru)	亻	係	2a7.8
	⺲	罹	5g11.1
	糹	繋	6a13.4
		繫	6a13.4
ka(karu)	斤	斯	2o10.9
	扌	掛	3c8.6
	木	架	4a5.36
	忄	懸	4k16.2
ka(kasu)	欠	欠	4j0.1
	⺾	缺	4j0.1
kakato	⻊	踵	7d9.1
kakawa(razu)			
	扌	拘	3c5.28
kaka(wari)	門	関	8e6.7
		關	8e6.7
kakawa(ru)	扌	拘	3c5.28
	亻	係	2a7.8
	門	関	8e6.7
		關	8e6.7
kake	貝	賭	7b9.1
		賭	7b9.1
ka(ke)	十	缺	4j0.1
	扌	掛	3c8.6
	欠	欠	4j0.1
kakehi	⺮	筧	6f7.7
kakei	⺮	筧	6f7.7
ka(kera)	十	缺	4j0.1
ka(keru)	十	缺	4j0.1
	⺷	翔	2o10.8
	扌	挂	3c6.7
		掛	3c8.6
	木	架	4a5.36
	欠	欠	4j0.1
	忄	懸	4k16.2
	貝	賭	7b9.1
		賭	7b9.1
	馬	駈	10a4.5
		駆	10a4.5
		驅	10a4.5
kaki	土	垣	3b6.5
		墻	3b13.2
		牆	3b14.6
	木	柿	4a5.25
		枾	4a5.25
	石	磞	5a7.5
ka(ki)-	扌	搔	3c10.11
		搔	3c10.11
kako(mu)	囗	囲	3s4.2
		圍	3s4.2
kako(tsu)	口	喞	3d9.4
	言	託	7a3.1
kakotsu(keru)			
	言	託	7a3.1
kako(u)	囗	囲	3s4.2
		圍	3s4.2
KAKU		画	0a8.7
		畫	0a8.7
		瓠	0a12.2
	⻖	郭	2d7.14
		隔	2d10.2
		隔	2d10.2
	刂	劃	2f12.1
	又	矍	2h18.1
	⺈	角	2n5.1
	土	埆	3b7.5
		塙	3b10.3
		赫	3b11.8
		壑	3b14.4
	扌	拡	3c5.25
		擴	3c5.25
		搰	3c6.6
		掴	3c11.6
		摑	3c11.6

Reading	Rad.	Kanji	Code
		環	4f13.1
	攵	敢	4i8.5
	欠	款	4j8.2
		歓	4j11.1
		歡	4j11.1
		歙	4j13.2
	忄	悍	4k7.4
		患	4k7.18
		悁	4k9.11
		感	4k9.21
		威	4k9.21
		慣	4k11.9
		憾	4k13.3
		懽	4k17.2
	戈	咸	4n5.1
		戡	4n9.1
		鹹	4n16.1
	日	看	5c4.4
		瞰	5c12.1
		観	5c13.7
		觀	5c13.7
	禾	稈	5d7.1
	甶	鼾	5f12.3
	髟	鬟	5g18.1
	皿	監	5h10.1
		盥	5h11.1
	疒	疳	5i5.1
		癇	5i12.6
		癎	5i12.6
	糸	緩	6a9.8
		緘	6a9.16
	舟	艦	6c15.2
	虫	蚶	6d5.3
	竹	篏	3o9.2
		竿	6f3.3
		箝	6f8.3
		管	6f8.12
		簡	6f12.5
	言	諫	7a9.1
		諫	7a9.1
		謹	7a17.1
	貝	貫	7b4.3
	車	轋	7c13.1
	酉	酣	7e5.2
	金	鐶	2k4.6
		鉗	8a5.3
		鐶	8a13.2
		鑑	8a15.2
	食	館	8b8.3
	門	閑	8e4.2
		間	8e4.3
		間	8e4.3
		関	8e6.7
		關	8e6.7
	頁	顴	9a17.1
	馬	騲	10a7.3
		驩	10a17.1
	魚	鹹	11a9.12
		鰥	11a10.5
	鳥	鸛	11b17.2
		鸛	11b17.2
kan-	礻	神	4e5.1
		神	4e5.1
kana-	金	金	8a0.1
kana(deru)		奏	0a9.17
kanae	鬲	鬲	3d7.17
		鼎	5c8.10
	米	彝	6b12.2
		彝	6b12.2
kana(eru)	口	叶	3d2.1
kanagaki	金	釦	8a4.7
kanahodashi			
	金	鉦	8a7.1
kanamari	金	鋺	8a8.13
kaname	女	要	3e6.11
		要	3e6.11
kanara(zu)		必	0a5.16
kanari	木	橄	4a12.4
kana(shii)	心	悲	4k8.18
kana(shimu)			
	心	悲	4k8.18
kana(u)	辶	適	2q11.3
	口	叶	3d2.1
kanba	木	樺	4a10.15
kanba(shii)			
	艹	芳	3k4.1
	日	馨	4c16.2
kane	匚	矩	2t7.1
	金	金	8a0.1
		鉦	8a5.7
		鐘	8a12.6
ka(neru)		兼	2o8.1
kane(te)		予	0a4.12
		豫	0a4.12
kanga(e)	耂	考	2k4.4
kanga(eru)	耂	考	2k4.4
	攵	攷	2k4.4
kanga(miru)			
	金	鑑	8a15.2
kani	虫	蟹	6d13.7
		蠏	6d13.7
kanjiki	木	桐	4a7.20
		橲	4a11.11
kanmuri	冖	冠	2i7.2
kanna	金	鉋	8a5.8
kannagi		覡	5c9.2
kannuki	門	閂	8e1.1
ka(no)	彳	彼	3i5.2
kanoe	广	庚	3q5.1
kanoto	辛	辛	5b2.2
kanzashi	竹	簪	6f14.3
	金	鈿	8a5.2
kao	頁	顔	9a9.3
		顏	9a9.3
kao(ri)	禾	香	5d4.5
kao(ru)	艹	薫	3k13.17
		薰	3k13.17
	日	馨	4c16.2
	禾	香	5d4.5
Kara	广	唐	3q7.3
	日	韓	4c14.3
kara	宀	空	3m5.12
		殼	3p8.1
		殻	3p8.1
karada	身	躰	2a5.6
	亻	体	2a5.6
	匸	躯	3d15.5
	冂	軆	2a5.6
		軀	3d15.5
	月	體	2a5.6
kara(geru)	糸	紮	6a5.17
kara(i)	戈	鹹	4n16.1
	辛	辛	5b2.2
kara(kumo)	辛	辛	5b2.2
kara(maru)	糸	絡	6a6.6
kara(meru)	扌	搦	3c10.3
kara(mu)	糸	絡	6a6.6
karamushi	艹	苧	3k5.20
kara(ppo)	宀	空	3m5.12
karashi	艹	芥	3k4.10
karasu	火	烏	4d6.5
	鳥	鴉	11b5.3
ka(rasu)	氵	涸	3a8.36
	氵	涸	3a8.36
	口	嗄	3d10.5
	木	枯	4a5.26
karatachi	木	枳	4a5.22
kare	彳	彼	3i5.2
	食	餉	8b6.5
karei	魚	鰈	11a9.9
		鹹	11a9.12
kareii	食	餉	8b6.5
ka(reru)	氵	涸	3a8.36
	氵	涸	3a8.36
	口	嗄	3d10.5
	木	枯	4a5.26
kari	亻	仮	2a4.15
		假	2a4.15
	厂	雁	2p10.3
		鳫	2p10.3
		鴈	2p10.3
ka(ri)	亻	借	2a8.22
	犭	狩	3g6.5
		猟	3g8.6
		獵	3g8.6
karigane	厂	雁	2p10.3
		鳫	2p10.3
		鴈	2p10.3
ka(riru)	亻	借	2a8.22
karo(njiru)	車	軽	7c5.3
		軽	7c5.3
karo(ujite)	辛	辛	5b2.2
karo(yaka)	車	軽	7c5.3
		軽	7c5.3
ka(ru)	亻	借	2a8.22
	刂	刈	2f2.1
	犭	狩	3g6.5
	艹	苅	3k4.8
		芟	3k4.11
	馬	駈	10a4.5
		駆	10a4.5
		驅	10a4.5
karu(i)	車	軽	7c5.3
		軽	7c5.3
kasa	亻	傘	2a10.7
	山	嵩	3o10.4
	日	暈	4c9.7
	广	瘡	5i10.5
	艹	笠	6f5.1
kasa(mu)		嵩	3o10.4
kasa(naru)		重	0a9.18
kasa(neru)		重	0a9.18
kasasagi	鳥	鵲	11b8.3
kase	木	枷	4a5.19
		桛	4a6.19
	糸	綛	6a7.7
kase(gu)	禾	稼	5d10.3
kashi	木	橿	4a10.1
		樫	4a12.5
		橿	4a13.5
kashi(geru)	亻	傾	2a11.3
kashi(gu)	亻	傾	2a11.3
kashiko(i)	貝	賢	7b9.2
kashiko(kumo)			
	田	畏	5f4.5
		畏	5f4.5
kashiko(maru)			
	田	畏	5f4.5
		畏	5f4.5
kashima(shii)			
	女	姦	3e6.9
kashira	頁	頭	9a7.6
kashiwa	木	栢	4a5.14
		柏	4a5.14
		槲	4a11.2
		檞	4a13.2

Reading	Rad.	Kanji	Code
kashizu(ku)			
	亻	傅	2a10.2
kasu			
	氵	滓	3a10.16
	米	粕	6b5.3
		糟	6b11.1
ka(su)			
	貝	貸	7b5.9
kasugai	釒	鎹	8a9.11
kasui	鳥	鶍	11b10.6
		鶍	11b10.6
kasu(ka)	亻	微	3i10.1
		微	3i10.1
	凵	幽	3o6.6
kasu(meru)			
	扌	掠	3c8.28
kasumi	雨	霞	8d9.1
kasu(mu)	冖	翳	2t15.2
	雨	霞	8d9.1
kasu(reru)	扌	掠	3c8.28
kasuri	糸	絣	6a6.12
		絣	6a6.12
		綛	6a7.7
		緕	6a14.3
		絣	6a14.3
kasu(ru)	扌	掠	3c8.28
		擦	3c14.5
kata	一	片	2j2.5
	氵	潟	3a12.9
	土	型	3b6.11
	彡	形	3j4.1
	方	方	4h0.1
	尸	肩	4m4.1
		肩	4m4.1
katachi	亻	像	2a12.8
	彡	形	3j4.1
katado(ru)	⺍	象	2n10.1
kata(geru)	亻	傾	2a11.3
kata(i)	土	堅	3b9.13
	口	固	3s5.2
	石	硬	5a7.1
	隹	難	8c10.2
		難	8c10.2
katajike(nai)			
	厂	辱	2p8.2
	⺍	忝	3n5.4
kataki	亻	仇	2a2.4
	攵	敵	4i11.2
kataku(na)	頁	頑	9a4.6
katamari	土	塊	3b10.2
kata(maru)	口	固	3s5.2
kata(meru)	口	固	3s5.2
katami	⺮	筐	6f6.16
		筐	6f6.16
katamu(keru)			
	亻	傾	2a11.3
katamu(ku)	亻	傾	2a11.3
	日	戻	4c4.8
katana	刂	釖	2f0.1
	刀	刀	2f0.1
kata(rau)	言	語	7a7.6
kata(ru)	言	語	7a7.6
	馬	騙	10a9.1
katawara	亻	傍	2a10.6
katawa(ra)	宀	旁	2j8.3
katayo(ru)	亻	偏	2a9.16
		偏	2a9.16
		僻	2a13.1
kate	米	糧	6b12.1
		粮	6b12.1
KATSU	刂	刮	2f6.5
		割	2f10.1
	力	劫	2g6.4
	氵	活	3a6.16
		渇	3a8.13
		渇	3a8.13
		滑	3a10.6
		濶	8e9.3
	扌	括	3c6.12
	口	喝	3d8.8
		喝	3d8.8
	犭	猾	3g10.2
	艹	葛	3k9.22
		葛	3k9.22
	宀	豁	3m14.4
	日	曷	4c5.8
		羯	4c11.5
		鞨	4c14.4
	火	黠	4d14.6
	心	愒	4k9.9
	戈	戛	4n7.1
		戛	4n7.1
	石	碣	5a10.2
	目	瞎	5c10.1
	衤	褐	5e8.7
		褐	5e8.7
	虫	蛞	6d6.6
		蝎	6d9.10
		蠍	6d9.10
	耳	聒	6e6.1
	⺮	筈	6f6.10
	車	轄	7c10.1
	門	闊	8e9.3
ka(tsu)	且	且	0a5.15
	十	克	2k5.1
	扌	搗	3c10.1
	月	勝	4b8.4
		勝	4b8.4
katsu(eru)	飠	餓	8b7.1
katsu(gu)	扌	担	3c5.20
		擔	3c5.20
katsuo	魚	鰹	11a12.1
Katsura	艹	蘰	3k17.3
katsura	又	鬘	2h19.1
	木	桂	4a6.13
katsu(te)		曾	2o9.3
		曽	2o9.3
		嘗	3n11.1
		嘗	3n11.1
kattai	疒	癩	5i16.1
ka(u)	十	支	2k2.1
	氵	沽	3a5.26
		買	5g7.2
	飠	飼	8b5.4
	隹	羅	8c14.1
-ka(u)	亠	交	2j4.3
kawa	川	川	0a3.2
		巛	0a3.2
	亻	側	2a9.4
	又	皮	2h3.1
	氵	河	3a5.30
		革	3k6.2
kawa(kasu)	日	乾	4c7.14
kawa(ku)	氵	渇	3a8.13
		渇	3a8.13
	日	乾	4c7.14
kawara		瓦	0a5.11
	石	磧	5a11.3
ka(waru)	亻	代	2a3.3
	亠	変	2j7.3
	扌	換	3c9.15
		換	3c9.15
	日	替	4c8.12
	女	變	2j7.3
kawa(su)	艹	躱	4a9.32
ka(wasu)	亠	交	2j4.3
kawauso	犭	獺	3g16.1
kawaya	厂	厠	2p9.1
	广	廁	3q7.2
	囗	圂	3s7.2
kawazu	虫	蛙	6d6.4
kaya	艹	茄	3k5.15
		茅	3k5.26
		萱	3k9.26
	木	榧	4a10.29
kayo(u)	辶	通	2q7.18
kayu	弓	粥	3h9.1
		鬻	3h9.1
kayu(garu)	疒	痒	5i6.6
kayu(i)	疒	痒	5i6.6
		癢	5i15.1
kaza-	几	風	2s7.1
kazari	釒	錺	8a7.8
kaza(ru)	飠	餝	8b5.3
		飾	8b5.3
kazashi	釒	釵	8a3.3
kaza(su)	冖	翳	2t15.2
kaze	几	風	2s7.1
kazo(eru)	攵	数	4i9.1
		數	4i9.1
kazu	攵	数	4i9.1
		數	4i9.1
kazunoko	魚	鯑	11a7.8
KE		気	0a6.8
		氣	0a6.8
	亻	化	2a2.6
		仮	2a4.15
		假	2a4.15
	⼘	卦	2m6.1
	巾	希	3f4.1
	艹	花	3k4.7
		花	3k4.7
		華	3k7.1
	宀	家	3m7.1
	忄	怪	4k5.11
		恠	4k5.11
		悔	4k6.12
		悔	4k6.12
		懈	4k13.1
		懸	4k16.2
	禾	稀	5d7.5
		袈	5e5.10
		罫	5g8.2
	疒	痂	5i5.7
ke		毛	0a4.33
		氈	0a12.5
keba	火	煙	4d9.3
		烟	4d9.3
kebu(i)	火	煙	4d9.3
		烟	4d9.3
kebu(ru)	火	煙	4d9.3
		烟	4d9.3
KECHI	糸	結	6a6.5
kedamono	犭	獣	3g12.3
		獸	3g12.3
keda(shi)	⺌	蓋	3k10.15
		蓋	3k10.15
		蓋	3k10.15
	凵	匝	3k10.15
kega(rawashii)			
	氵	汚	3a3.5
kega(reru)	氵	汚	3a3.5
	禾	穢	5d13.3
kega(su)	氵	汚	3a3.5
	禾	穢	5d13.3
KEI		匚	0a2.6
		彐	0a3.15
		互	0a3.15
	亻	係	2a7.8

	偈 2a9.10		烱 4d5.6			鷄 11b8.4		犭	犬 3g0.1
	傾 2a11.3		煢 4d9.14	KEKI	貝	賗 7b11.1			狷 3g7.5
卩	卿 2e10.1	礻	禊 4e9.5	kemono	犭	獸 3g12.3			献 3g9.6
	卿 2e10.1	王	珪 4f6.4			獸 3g12.3			獻 3g9.6
刂	刑 2f4.2		瓊 4f14.1	kemu	火	煙 4d9.3		艹	萱 3k9.26
	刲 2f6.3	攵	敬 4i8.4			烟 4d9.3			蒹 3k10.1
	到 2f7.2	心	惠 4k6.16	kemu(i)	火	煙 4d9.3			繭 3k15.7
	荊 2f7.3		惠 4k6.16			烟 4d9.3		宀	寋 3m11.4
	契 2f7.6		愒 4k9.9	kemuri	火	煙 4d9.3			憲 3m13.2
力	勁 2g7.2		慧 4k11.16			烟 4d9.3			憲 3m13.2
	勍 2g8.1		憬 4k12.7	kemu(ru)	火	煙 4d9.3			審 3m14.1
又	圣 6a5.11		憩 4k12.10			烟 4d9.3			蹇 3m14.3
亠	京 2j6.3		憩 4k12.10	KEN		巻 0a9.11			騫 3m17.1
	京 2j6.3	石	硅 4f6.4			巻 0a9.11		屮	県 3n6.3
宀	夏 2n12.1		磬 5a11.4			豢 0a13.4			縣 3n6.3
丷	亐 2o2.4	立	競 5b15.1		亻	件 2a4.4		山	嶮 3o13.2
辶	迥 2q5.9		競 5b15.1			倪 2a7.9		囗	圈 3s9.1
	逕 3i5.5	目	眑 5c4.6			倦 2a8.13			圈 3s9.1
冂	冂 2r0.1	禾	稽 5d11.3			倦 2a8.13			鹼 3s21.1
	冏 2r5.1		稽 5d11.3			俔 2a8.27			鹼 3s21.1
氵	涇 3a7.12	礻	絓 5e6.3			儉 2a8.27		木	榜 4a8.12
	溪 3a8.16	田	畦 5f6.2			健 2a8.34			検 4a8.28
	溪 3a8.16	罒	罫 5g8.2			劔 2f8.5			檢 4a8.28
土	圭 3b3.2	疒	痙 5i7.5		阝	険 2d8.8			権 4a11.18
	型 3b6.11	糸	系 6a1.1			險 2d8.8			权 4a11.18
	奎 3b6.12		経 6a5.11		刂	券 2f6.10			權 4a11.18
	境 3b11.1		經 6a5.11			券 2f6.10		月	腱 4b8.10
扌	挂 3c6.7		絅 6a5.16			剣 2f8.5			臉 4b13.5
	挈 3c6.19		継 6a7.8			劍 2f8.5		日	乾 4c7.14
	揭 3c8.13		繼 6a7.8			劒 2f8.5			暄 4c9.5
	揭 3c8.13		繋 6a8.26		力	券 2g6.5			間 8e4.3
	携 3c10.4	虫	螢 3n8.2		又	叹 2h7.2		火	黔 4d12.10
	攜 3c10.4		蜈 6d10.2		亠	牽 2j9.3		欠	歉 4j10.1
口	兄 3d2.9		蠛 6d18.1		十	开 2k4.2		心	悁 4k7.8
	啓 3d8.17	竹	笄 6f6.5		卜	虍 2m8.1			惓 4k8.4
	謦 3d13.11		笄 6f6.5		丷	兼 2o8.1			愃 4k9.11
彳	徑 3i5.5	言	計 7a2.1		辶	建 2q6.2			慂 4k9.19
	徑 3i5.5		詣 7a6.13			遣 2q10.2			慊 4k10.1
彡	形 3j4.1		警 7a11.5		氵	涓 3a7.13			慳 4k12.1
艹	荊 2f7.3		警 7a12.7		土	堅 3b9.13			懸 4k16.2
	莖 3k5.23	車	輕 7c5.3			甄 3b11.9		尸	肩 4m4.1
	莖 3k5.23		輕 7c5.3		扌	拳 3c6.18			肩 4m4.1
	薊 3k13.2	足	蹊 7d10.2			拳 3c6.18		石	研 5a4.1
艹	谿 3a8.16	酉	醯 7e12.1			捲 3c8.9			研 5a4.1
	奚 3n7.3	金	鎠 2j6.3			捲 3c8.9			硯 5a7.2
	蛍 3n8.2	門	闑 8e5.1			撿 3c13.4		目	見 5c2.1
广	慶 3q12.8		閨 8e6.5		口	劒 2f8.5			睠 5c6.6
木	枅 4a4.5	頁	頃 9a2.2			喧 3d9.12			瞼 5c13.4
	桂 4a6.13		頚 9a7.4			嗛 3d10.2		罒	羂 5g13.1
	橤 4a12.20		頸 9a7.4		女	妍 3e4.2		广	痃 5i5.11
月	脛 4b7.6	魚	鮭 11a6.3			娟 3e7.7		糸	絢 6a6.14
日	景 4c8.8	鳥	鶏 11b8.4			嫌 3e10.7			絹 6a7.3
	馨 4c16.2					嫌 3e10.7			縖 6a8.6
火	炯 4d5.6					嫌 3e10.7		虫	蜎 6d7.4

	蜷	6d8.5
⺮	筧	6f7.7
	簡	6f12.5
言	諫	7a9.10
	誼	7a9.12
	謙	7a10.10
	謙	7a10.10
	譴	7a13.6
貝	賢	7b9.2
車	軒	7c3.1
釒	釼	2f8.5
	鉗	8a5.3
	鍵	8a8.18
門	間	8e4.3
	間	8e4.3
頁	顕	9a9.5
	顯	9a9.5
	顴	9a17.1
馬	驗	10a8.4
	驗	10a8.4
魚	鰹	11a12.1
鳥	鵑	11b7.3

kena(su) 貝 貶 7b3.2
keri 几 鳧 11b2.3
鳥 鳧 11b2.3
ke(ru) 𧾷 蹴 7d12.2
kesa 罒 眬 5f6.1
keshika(keru)
口 嗾 3d11.4
ke(shikaran)
忄 怪 4k5.11
忄 恠 4k5.11
ke(shikaranu)
忄 怪 4k5.11
忄 恠 4k5.11
ke(su) 氵 消 3a7.16
氵 消 3a7.16
keta 木 桁 4a6.8
KETSU 亅 乚 0a1.4
夬 0a4.37
亻 偈 2a9.10
傑 2a11.6
氵 決 3a4.6
孑 孒 2c0.2
刂 劂 2f12.2
刔 3c4.3
艹 缺 4j0.1
厂 厥 2p10.2
氵 決 3a4.6
潔 3a12.10
潔 3a12.10
扌 抉 3c4.3
犭 獗 3g12.2
艹 蕨 3k12.15

宀	穴	3m2.2
	穴	3m2.2
木	杰	2a11.6
	桔	4a6.16
	桀	4a7.26
日	羯	4c11.5
欠	欠	4j0.1
	歇	4j9.2
石	碣	5a9.4
立	竭	5b9.1
衤	襭	5e15.1
血	血	5h1.1
糸	結	6a6.5
	纈	6a15.1
言	許	7a3.2
	訣	7a4.2
	譎	7a12.5
𧾷	蹶	7d12.5
門	閲	8e9.6
	闕	8e10.3
頁	頁	9a0.1
	頡	9a6.1

kewa(shii) 阝 険 2d8.8
険 2d8.8
屵 嶮 3o13.2
keyaki 木 欅 4a17.1
kezu(ru) 刂 刊 2f3.2
削 2f7.4
削 2f7.4
KI
己 己 0a3.12
气 气 0a4.1
旡 旡 0a4.29
气 気 0a6.8
乇 耗 3p9.1
癸 癸 0a9.2
既 0a10.5
旣 0a10.5
亻 企 2a4.17
倚 2a8.26
僖 2a12.7
刂 剞 2f8.3
帰 2f8.8
亠 棄 2j11.5
弃 2j11.5
艹 卉 2k3.2
厃 危 2n4.3
亀 2n9.1
龜 2n9.1
義 2o14.1
冀 2o14.3
辶 達 2q8.5
几 几 2s0.1
匚 匯 2t11.1
置 2t12.1

氵	汽	3a4.16
	瀜	3a4.16
	淇	3a8.11
土	圻	3b4.5
	起	3b7.11
	埼	3b8.8
	基	3b8.12
	毀	3b10.14
扌	掎	3c8.24
	揆	3c9.3
	揮	3c9.14
口	奇	3d5.17
	竒	3d5.17
	唏	3d7.11
	喟	3d9.9
	敧	3d9.22
	器	3d12.13
	器	3d12.13
	嚚	3d12.13
女	妓	3e4.7
	姫	3e7.11
	姬	3e7.11
	嬉	3e12.3
巾	歸	2f8.8
	希	3f4.1
	豨	3f11.3
彳	徛	3i8.6
	徽	3i14.2
艹	其	3k8.17
	葵	3k9.17
宀	寄	3m8.8
	窺	3m13.3
屵	岐	3o4.1
	豈	3o7.8
	巇	3o17.1
吉	喜	3p9.1
广	麾	3q12.7
	麒	3q16.4
尸	屓	3r7.1
	屓	3r7.1
木	机	4a2.4
	杞	4a3.9
	枳	4a5.22
	棋	4a8.14
	棊	4a8.14
	槻	4a11.4
	機	4a12.1
	櫃	4a14.5
月	肌	4b2.2
	期	4b8.11
	期	4b8.11
	碁	4b8.11
日	畈	2f8.8
	者	4c6.7

	晞	4c7.4
	暉	4c9.6
	暨	4c12.3
火	熙	4d9.11
	熈	4d9.11
	熙	4d9.11
	熹	4d12.9
	燨	4d13.1
礻	祁	4e2.1
	祁	4e2.1
	祈	4e4.3
	祈	4e4.3
	祺	4e8.1
	禧	4e12.1
方	旗	4h10.1
欠	欷	4j7.3
	欲	4j8.3
忄	忌	4k3.4
	悸	4k7.3
	愧	4k10.6
	懻	4k10.10
	憙	4k12.13
戈	幾	4n8.4
石	碕	5a8.5
	磯	5a12.1
立	毅	5b10.1
目	規	5c6.9
	馗	5c6.10
	睢	5c8.1
	瞶	5c12.3
	覬	5c12.9
禾	季	5d2.3
	稀	5d7.5
	稘	5d8.3
田	鬼	5f5.6
	畸	5f8.2
	畿	5f10.3
罒	羈	5g17.1
	羇	5g19.1
糸	紀	6a3.5
	綺	6a8.16
米	氣	0a6.8
⺮	箕	6f8.6
	簣	6f12.3
	簇	6f14.2
言	記	7a3.5
	詭	7a6.11
	諱	7a10.8
	譏	7a12.1
貝	貴	7b5.7
車	軌	7c2.1
	輝	7c8.8
𧾷	跂	7d4.3
	跪	7d6.8

Reading	Rad.	Kanji	Code
	食	飢	8b2.1
		饒	8b10.1
		饑	8b12.1
		饋	8b12.4
	隹	虧	8c9.1
	馬	羈	5g19.1
		騏	10a8.2
		騎	10a8.3
		驥	10a16.1
	魚	鰭	11a10.4
ki	艹	黄	3k8.16
		黄	3k8.16
	木	木	4a0.1
		樹	4a12.3
ki-		生	0a5.29
kiba		牙	0a4.28
		牙	0a4.28
ki(bamu)	艹	黄	3k8.16
		黄	3k8.16
kibi	禾	黍	5d7.6
		稷	5d10.1
kibi(shii)	口	嚴	3n14.1
	厂	厳	3n14.1
KICHI	士	吉	3p3.1
		吉	3p3.1
ki(eru)	氵	消	3a7.16
		消	3a7.16
kihada	艹	蘗	4a13.10
	木	檗	4a13.10
kiji	隹	雉	8c5.2
ki(kasu)	禾	利	5d2.1
ki(koe)	門	聞	8e6.1
ki(koeru)	門	聞	8e6.1
kikori	木	樵	4a12.6
KIKU	扌	掬	3c8.35
	艹	菊	3k8.30
	木	椈	4a8.35
	米	鞠	6b11.6
		麹	6b13.1
		麴	6b13.1
	言	鞫	7a11.6
ki(ku)	力	効	2g6.2
	攵	效	2g6.2
	禾	利	5d2.1
	耳	聴	6e11.3
		聽	6e11.3
	門	聞	8e6.1
ki(mari)	木	極	4a8.11
ki(maru)	氵	決	3a4.6
	氵	決	3a4.6
ki(me)	木	極	4a8.11
ki(meru)	氵	決	3a4.6
	氵	決	3a4.6
kimi	口	君	3d4.23
kimo	月	肝	4b3.2
		胆	4b5.6
		膽	4b5.6
		斤	0a4.3
KIN	亻	今	2a2.10
		衿	2a7.25
		衾	2a8.38
		禽	2a10.8
		僅	2a11.13
		僅	2a11.13
	孑	香	2c6.3
	刂	釁	2f24.1
	力	勤	2g10.1
		勤	2g10.1
	辶	近	2q4.3
	土	均	3b4.8
	扌	掀	3c8.7
		擒	3c12.15
	口	听	3d4.7
		噤	3d13.5
	巾	巾	3f0.1
	艹	芹	3k4.5
		菫	3k8.1
		菌	3k8.32
	宀	窨	3m9.6
	木	權	4a11.15
		橝	4a12.17
	礻	禁	4e8.3
	王	琴	4f8.11
		瑾	4f11.2
	欠	欣	4j4.1
	心	忻	4k4.4
		勲	4k13.11
	目	覲	5c13.8
	禾	齻	5d14.1
	礻	衿	5e4.5
		襟	5e13.2
	糸	緊	6a9.17
	竹	筋	6f6.4
		菌	6f8.14
		筬	6f8.14
	言	謹	7a10.6
		謹	7a10.6
	金	金	8a0.1
		欽	8a4.1
		釿	8a4.6
		鈞	8a4.9
		錦	8a8.6
		饉	8b11.2
kine	木	杵	4a4.9
		甲	0a5.34
kinoko	艹	茸	3k6.1
		蕈	3k12.10
kinoto		乙	0a1.5
kinu	衤	衣	5e0.1
	糸	絹	6a7.3
kinuta	石	砧	5a5.5
		碪	5a5.5
	立	競	5b15.1
		競	5b15.1
kio(u)	立	競	5b15.1
kira(biyaka)			
	火	煌	4d9.7
kira(i)	女	嫌	3e10.7
		嬚	3e10.7
		嫌	3e10.7
kira(meku)	火	煌	4d9.7
ki(rasu)	刂	切	2f2.2
kira(u)	女	嫌	3e10.7
		嫌	3e10.7
		嫌	3e10.7
ki(re)	刂	切	2f2.2
ki(reru)	刂	切	2f2.2
kiri	木	桐	4a6.30
	金	錐	8a8.1
	雨	霧	8d11.1
ki(ri)	刂	切	2f2.2
-ki(ri)	刂	切	2f2.2
kiroguramu			
	瓦	瓩	2k6.6
kiromētoru	米	粁	6b3.2
kirorittoru	立	竏	5b3.1
ki(ru)	刂	切	2f2.2
	羊	着	2o10.1
	艹	著	3k8.4
		著	3k8.4
	木	槎	4a10.26
	車	斬	7c4.2
	金	鑽	8a15.3
		鑽	8a15.3
-ki(ru)	刂	切	2f2.2
kisaki	口	后	3d3.11
kisasage	木	楸	4a9.6
ki(seru)	羊	着	2o10.1
kishi	艹	岸	3o5.11
kishime(ku)			
	車	軋	7c1.1
kishi(mu)	車	軋	7c1.1
kishi(ru)	車	軋	7c1.1
		輾	7c10.3
kiso(u)	立	競	5b15.1
		競	5b15.1
kisu	魚	鱚	11a12.4
kita		北	0a5.5
kita(eru)	金	鍛	8a9.5
kitana(i)	氵	汚	3a3.5
ki(taru)		未	0a7.6
		来	0a7.6
		來	0a7.6
	彳	徠	0a7.6
ki(tasu)		未	0a7.6
		来	0a7.6
	亻	來	0a7.6
	彳	徠	0a7.6
KITSU		乞	0a3.4
		气	0a4.1
	亻	佶	2a6.15
	辶	迄	2q3.4
		迄	2q3.4
	土	吉	3p3.1
	扌	拮	3c6.11
	口	吃	3d3.7
		喫	3d9.7
	屮	屹	3o3.1
	吉	吉	3p3.1
	木	桔	4a6.16
		橘	4a12.11
	言	訖	7a3.7
		詰	7a6.7
	頁	頡	9a6.1
kitsune	犭	狐	3g6.4
-ki(tte no)	刂	切	2f2.2
kiwa	阝	際	2d11.1
kiwa(doi)	阝	際	2d11.1
kiwa(maru)			
	宀	窮	3m12.4
	木	極	4a8.11
kiwa(meru)			
	宀	究	3m4.5
		窮	3m12.4
	木	極	4a8.11
kiwa(mete)	木	極	4a8.11
kiwa(mi)	木	極	4a8.11
kiyo(i)	氵	清	3a8.18
		清	3a8.18
kiyo(maru)	氵	清	3a8.18
kiyo(meru)	氵	浄	3a6.18
		浄	3a6.18
		清	3a8.18
kiyo(raka)	氵	清	3a8.18
		清	3a8.18
kizahashi	阝	陛	2d7.6
		階	2d9.6
kiza(mi)	刂	刻	2f6.7
kiza(mu)	刂	刻	2f6.7
kiza(shi)	氵	兆	2b4.4
		兆	2b4.4
	艹	萌	3k8.11
		萠	3k8.11
kiza(su)	氵	兆	2b4.4
		兆	2b4.4

犭 狒 3g5.2	殻 4b8.13	綱 6a8.23
狡 3g6.6	膠 4b11.3	縞 6a10.9
猴 3g9.1	日 亘 4c2.4	纊 6a15.2
弓 弘 3h2.1	皀 4c3.2	米 粳 6b7.1
彳 行 3i3.1	杲 4c4.3	糠 6b11.2
後 3i6.5	昊 4c4.6	舟 舡 6c3.1
徨 3i9.3	昂 4c5.11	航 6c4.2
衡 3i13.1	昂 4c5.11	虫 虹 6d3.1
艹 苟 3k5.31	晃 4c6.5	蚣 6d4.6
巷 3k6.17	晧 4c7.2	蛤 6d6.7
巷 3k6.17	皋 4c7.12	蛟 6d6.8
荒 3k6.18	皋 4c7.12	蝗 6d9.8
黄 3k8.16	皎 4c7.15	耳 耿 6e4.1
黄 3k8.16	皓 4c8.13	胶 6e4.4
蒿 3k10.25	曠 4c15.2	⺮ 箜 6f9.6
蔻 3k11.17	眖 4c15.2	篝 6f10.7
蔻 3k11.17	火 烘 4d6.2	簧 6f12.4
薨 3k13.22	烋 4d6.4	言 訌 7a6.16
薧 3k14.6	煌 4d9.7	詰 7a7.5
广 宏 3m4.3	煩 4d10.3	講 7a10.3
寇 3m8.10	王 皇 4f5.9	講 7a10.3
窖 3m9.7	牛 犒 4g10.1	貝 貢 7b3.3
⺍ 光 3n3.2	犇 4g11.1	購 7b10.3
⺣ 岬 3o5.5	犇 4g11.1	車 較 7c6.3
峇 3o6.4	攵 效 2g6.2	酉 酵 7e6.1
峴 3o7.3	攷 2k4.4	金 釦 8a3.1
崗 3o8.12	攻 4i3.2	鉱 8a5.15
广 広 3q2.1	心 恒 4k6.5	鑛 8a5.15
廣 3q2.1	恆 4k6.5	鉤 8a5.17
庚 3q5.1	恍 4k6.7	鉤 8a5.17
康 3q8.1	恰 4k6.10	鋼 8a8.20
尸 尻 3r2.1	悾 4k8.7	鍠 8a9.7
木 杠 4a3.8	惶 4k9.7	鎬 8a10.5
杭 4a4.17	慌 4k9.10	鏗 8a12.1
枸 4a5.30	慷 4k11.11	食 餃 8b6.3
栲 4a6.4	石 矼 5a3.1	門 閘 8e5.2
桁 4a6.8	硬 5a7.1	関 8e6.4
格 4a6.17	硜 5a7.4	閧 8e6.4
校 4a6.24	磷 5a12.3	閤 8e6.6
梗 4a7.1	砿 8a5.15	闔 8e10.4
椌 4a8.19	礦 5a15.15	頁 項 9a3.1
槲 4a8.36	目 覸 5c12.8	頏 9a4.2
構 4a10.10	禾 香 5d4.5	顠 9a12.1
構 4a10.10	稿 5d10.5	魚 鮫 11a6.5
槓 4a10.19	稾 5d10.5	鯉 11a7.3
槁 4a10.22	衤 袷 5e6.6	鯝 11a9.10
槹 4a11.12	田 畊 0a10.13	鰥 11a11.6
月 肛 4b3.4	糸 紅 6a3.6	鳥 鴻 11b6.1
胘 4b4.9	紘 6a4.11	鵁 11b6.2
肯 4b4.11	紘 6a5.15	鵠 11b7.2
肴 4b4.12	絎 6a6.2	鵠 11b7.2
胛 4b5.1	絖 6a6.4	kō- 礻 神 4e5.1
胱 4b6.1	絞 6a6.9	神 4e5.1
腔 4b8.7	絳 6a7.6	koba(mu) 扌 拒 3c5.29

kō(bashii) 艹 芳 3k4.1	
馨 4c16.2	
kōbe 日 首 2o7.2	
頁 頭 9a7.6	
ko(biru) 女 媚 3e9.5	
kobo(reru) 氵 溢 3a10.19	
溢 3a10.19	
土 毀 3b10.14	
雩 零 8d5.4	
kobo(su) 氵 溢 3a10.19	
溢 3a10.19	
米 翻 6b12.3	
飜 6b12.3	
雩 零 8d5.4	
kobo(tsu) 土 毀 3b10.14	
kobu 疒 瘤 5i10.3	
kobushi 扌 拳 3c6.18	
拳 3c6.18	
kochi 魚 鮲 11a6.2	
鮦 11a7.7	
kodama 口 谺 3d9.24	
koda(su) 糸 絆 6a5.6	
koe 士 声 3p4.4	
月 肥 4b4.5	
耳 聲 3p4.4	
ko(eru) 土 超 3b9.18	
月 肥 4b4.5	
戈 越 4n8.2	
kōgai ⺮ 筓 6f6.5	
筓 6f6.5	
kogarashi 几 凩 2s4.1	
ko(gareru) 隹 焦 8c4.3	
ko(gasu) 隹 焦 8c4.3	
ko(geru) 隹 焦 8c4.3	
kogo(eru) 冫 凍 2b8.2	
kogo(ru) 冫 凝 2b14.1	
ko(gu) 氵 漕 3a11.7	
kohaze 革 鞐 3k12.20	
kohitsuji ⺷ 羔 2o8.2	
koi 一 恋 2j8.2	
心 戀 2j8.2	
魚 鯉 11a7.2	
ko(i) 氵 濃 3a13.7	
koinega(u) 米 冀 2o14.3	
一 希 3f4.1	
koi(shii) 一 恋 2j8.2	
心 戀 2j8.2	
kōji 米 糀 6b7.2	
麹 6b13.1	
麹 6b13.1	
koji(rasu) 扌 拗 3c5.16	
koji(reru) 扌 拗 3c5.16	
kojiri 金 鐺 8a13.4	
koji(ru) 刂 刔 3c4.3	

Reading	Rad.	Kanji	Code
	扌	抉	3c4.3
koke	艹	苔	3k5.27
kokera	木	柿	4a5.25
		枾	4a5.25
	魚	鱗	11a13.2
ko(keru)	亻	倒	2a8.5
koko		爰	3n6.4
kokono-		九	0a2.15
kokono(tsu)		九	0a2.15
kokoro	忄	心	4k0.1
kokoro(miru)			
	言	試	7a6.18
kokoroyo(ge)	忄	快	4k4.2
kokoroyo(i)	忄	快	4k4.2
kokoroyo(shi)			
	忄	快	4k4.2
kokorozashi			
	士	志	3p4.1
kokoroza(su)			
	士	志	3p4.1
KOKU	⺉	刻	2f6.7
	十	克	2k5.1
	⺈	斛	2n9.2
	丷	谷	2o5.3
	口	告	3d4.18
		剋	3d6.20
		尅	3d6.20
		嚳	3d17.2
	犭	哭	3g6.7
	口	国	3s5.1
		圀	3s5.1
		國	3s5.1
	木	梏	4a7.8
		槲	4a11.2
	火	黒	4d7.2
		黑	4d7.2
	石	石	5a0.1
	禾	穀	5d9.4
		穀	5d9.4
	車	轂	7c10.4
	酉	酷	7e7.1
	釒	鈛	8a2.1
	鳥	鵠	11b7.2
		鵠	11b7.2
ko(ku)	扌	扱	3c3.5
		扱	3c3.5
koma	口	齣	3d17.6
	犭	狛	3g5.4
	馬	駒	10a5.5
koma(ka)	糸	細	6a5.1
koma(kai)	糸	細	6a5.1
komanu(ku)			
	扌	拱	3c6.9
koma(ru)	口	困	3s4.1
koma(yaka)			
	氵	濃	3a13.7
kome	米	米	6b0.1
ko(meru)	辶	込	2q2.3
		込	2q2.3
	竹	篭	6f16.1
		籠	6f16.1
-ko(mi)	辶	込	2q2.3
		込	2q2.3
komichi	足	蹊	7d10.2
komo	艹	菰	3k8.15
		薦	3k13.25
komo(ru)	竹	篭	6f16.1
		籠	6f16.1
ko(mu)	辶	込	2q2.3
		込	2q2.3
komura	月	腓	4b8.3
kōmu(ru)	艹	蒙	3k10.23
KON	礻	被	5e5.3
	亻	今	2a2.10
	宀	衾	2j9.5
	辶	建	2q6.2
	氵	混	3a8.14
		渾	3a9.28
		溷	3a10.28
		滾	3a11.15
	土	坤	3b5.1
		墾	3b13.6
	女	婚	3e8.4
	犭	狠	3g6.3
		献	3g9.6
		獻	3g9.6
	彳	很	3i6.2
	艹	菎	3k8.23
		蒟	3k10.3
	山	崑	3o8.8
	士	壼	3p10.1
	口	困	3s4.1
		圂	3s7.2
	木	根	4a6.5
		梱	4a7.23
		棍	4a8.22
		楛	4a8.23
	日	昆	4c4.10
		昏	4c4.11
	火	焜	4d8.2
	王	瑾	4f9.7
	忄	恨	4k6.2
		悃	4k7.16
		懇	4k13.12
	礻	裩	5e9.2
	田	魂	5f9.2
	疒	痕	5i6.2
	糸	紺	6a5.5
	言	譚	7a9.14
	足	跟	7d6.2
	釒	金	8a0.1
	魚	鯀	11a7.4
		鯤	11a8.4
kona	米	粉	6b4.6
ko(neru)	扌	捏	3c7.6
ko(no)	匕	此	2m4.2
kono(mu)	女	好	3e2.1
	忄	憙	4k12.13
konoshiro	魚	鮗	11a5.6
kōnotori	鳥	鸛	11b17.2
kora(eru)	土	堪	3b9.1
	忄	恔	4k5.13
ko(rasu)	冫	凝	2b14.1
	忄	懲	4k14.3
		懲	4k14.3
kō(rasu)	冫	凍	2b8.2
kore	之		0a2.9
	日	是	4c5.9
ko(re)	匕	此	2m4.2
kori	木	梱	4a7.23
kōri	冫	冰	3a1.2
	氵	氷	3a1.2
ko(riru)	忄	懲	4k14.3
		懲	4k14.3
koro	頁	頃	9a2.2
koro(basu)	車	轉	7c4.3
		転	7c4.3
koro(bu)	車	轉	7c4.3
		転	7c4.3
koro(garu)	車	轉	7c4.3
		転	7c4.3
koro(gasu)	車	轉	7c4.3
		転	7c4.3
koro(geru)	車	轉	7c4.3
		転	7c4.3
kōrogi	艹	蟋	3k9.27
koromo	衤	衣	5e0.1
koro(shimo)			
	頁	頃	9a2.2
koro(su)	木	殺	4a6.35
		殺	4a6.35
		弑	4a8.41
ko(ru)	冫	凝	2b14.1
kō(ru)	冫	凍	2b8.2
		冰	3a1.2
	氵	氷	3a1.2
koshi	舁	輿	2o15.1
	月	腰	4b9.3
koshiki	日	甑	4c13.3
		甑	4c13.3
	車	轂	7c10.4
koshira(eru)			
	扌	拵	3c5.24
ko(su)	氵	漉	3a11.20
		濾	3a15.8
		沪	3a15.8
		滤	3a15.8
	土	超	3b9.18
	戈	越	4n8.2
kosu(i)	犭	狡	3g6.6
kosu(ru)	扌	擦	3c14.5
kota(e)	竹	答	6f6.12
kota(eru)	土	堪	3b9.1
	广	応	3q4.2
		應	3q4.2
	竹	答	6f6.12
kote	釒	鏝	8a11.7
		鎬	8a13.4
koto		事	0a8.15
		事	0a8.15
	王	琴	4f8.11
	糸	縡	6a10.6
	言	言	7a0.1
kotoba	言	詞	7a5.15
kotobuki		寿	0a7.15
		壽	0a7.15
kotogoto(ku)			
	尸	尽	3r3.1
	忄	悉	4k7.19
	皿	盡	3r3.1
kotoho(gu)		寿	0a7.15
	士	壽	0a7.15
koto(naru)	田	異	5f6.7
koto (ni)		殊	0a10.7
koto (ni suru)			
	田	異	5f6.7
kotowari	王	理	4f7.1
kotowa(ru)		断	6b5.6
	米	斷	6b5.6
kotowaza	言	諺	7a9.15
		諺	7a9.15
kotozu(keru)			
	言	託	7a3.1
KOTSU		乞	0a3.4
		兀	0a3.9
	氵	汩	3a4.2
		滑	3a10.6
	木	榾	4a10.6
	月	骨	4b6.14
	忄	忽	4k4.7
		惚	4k8.10
	竹	笏	6f4.4
	鳥	鶻	11b10.4
ko(tta)	冫	凝	2b14.1
ko(u)		乞	0a3.4

	恋 2j8.2	
	丐 2m2.3	
	戀 2j8.2	
	請 7a8.8	
	請 7a8.8	
koushi	犢 4g15.1	
kowa-	声 3p4.4	
	聲 3p4.4	
kowa(gari)	怖 4k5.6	
kowa(garu)		
	怖 4k5.6	
kowa(i)	強 3h8.3	
	怖 4k5.6	
	恐 4k6.19	
	恐 4k6.19	
kowa(reru)	毀 3b10.14	
	壊 3b13.3	
	壞 3b13.3	
kowa(su)	毀 3b10.14	
	壊 3b13.3	
	壞 3b13.3	
ko(yashi)	肥 4b4.5	
ko(yasu)	肥 4b4.5	
koyomi	暦 2p12.3	
	曆 2p12.3	
kōzo	楮 4a9.2	
kozo(tte)	挙 3n7.1	
	擧 3n7.1	
	挙 3n7.1	
kozue	杪 4a4.14	
	梢 4a7.13	
	梢 4a7.13	
KU	九 0a2.15	
	工 0a3.6	
	瓦 0a3.6	
	久 0a3.7	
	佝 2a5.22	
	供 2a6.13	
	倶 2a8.15	
	孔 2c1.1	
	功 2g3.2	
	劬 2g5.5	
	公 2o2.2	
	公 2o2.2	
	区 2t2.1	
	區 2t2.1	
	矩 2t7.1	
	躯 3d15.5	
	垢 3b6.3	
	拘 3c6.4	
	口 3d0.1	
	句 3d2.13	
	吁 3d3.2	
	吼 3d3.6	

	軀 3d15.5	
	狗 3g5.5	
	衢 3i21.1	
	苦 3k5.24	
	蔲 3k11.17	
	蔻 3k11.17	
	宮 3m7.5	
	嫗 3o11.2	
	庫 3q7.1	
	枸 4a5.30	
	枸 4a6.9	
	煦 4d9.13	
	恂 4k5.16	
	倶 4k8.3	
	懼 4k8.3	
	戩 4n18.1	
	痀 5i5.13	
	紅 6a3.6	
	箜 6f8.8	
	貢 7b3.3	
	瞿 8c10.4	
	駈 10a4.5	
	駆 10a4.5	
	驅 10a4.5	
	駒 10a5.5	
KŪ	啌 3d8.6	
	弘 3h2.1	
	空 3m5.12	
	腔 4b8.7	
kuba(ru)	配 7e3.2	
kubi	首 2o7.2	
	頚 9a7.4	
	頸 9a7.4	
kubikase	箝 6f8.3	
kubiki	軛 7c4.4	
kubiki(ru)	剄 2f7.2	
kubi(reru)	括 3c6.12	
	縊 6a10.8	
kubisu	踵 7d9.1	
kubo	凹 0a5.14	
	窪 3m11.9	
kubo(mi)	窪 3m11.9	
kubo(mu)	窪 3m11.9	
kuchi	口 3d0.1	
kuchibashi	喙 3d9.14	
	嘴 3d13.7	
kuchibiru	唇 3d7.12	
	脣 3d7.12	
kuchinashi	梔 4a7.21	
kuchinawa	蛇 6d5.7	
ku(chiru)	朽 4a2.6	
kuda	管 6f8.12	
kuda(keru)	摧 3c11.4	
	砕 5a4.6	

	砕 5a4.6	
	碎 5a4.6	
kuda(keta)	砕 5a4.6	
	砕 5a4.6	
kuda(ku)	摧 3c11.4	
	砕 5a4.6	
	碎 5a4.6	
kudan	件 2a4.4	
kuda(ranai)	下 2m1.2	
kudari	件 2a4.4	
	行 3i3.1	
kuda(ru)	降 2d7.7	
	下 2m1.2	
kuda(sai)	下 2m1.2	
kuda(saru)	下 2m1.2	
kuda(shi)	瀉 3a15.6	
kuda(su)	降 2d7.7	
	下 2m1.2	
kuda(tte)	降 2d7.7	
ku(enai)	食 8b0.1	
ku(eru)	食 8b0.1	
kugi	釘 8a2.4	
kugui	鵠 11b7.2	
	鵠 11b7.2	
kugu(ri)	潜 3a12.6	
	潛 3a12.6	
	潜 3a12.6	
kugu(ru)	潜 3a12.6	
	潛 3a12.6	
	潜 3a12.6	
	潜 3a12.6	
kui	杭 4a3.4	
	杭 4a4.17	
ku(iru)	悔 4k6.12	
	悔 4k6.12	
	懺 4k17.1	
	懺 4k17.1	
kuji	籤 6f17.2	
	籤 6f17.2	
	鬮 8e18.1	
kuji(keru)	挫 3c7.15	
kuji(ku)	挫 3c7.15	
kujira	鯨 11a8.9	
kuji(ru)	刔 3c4.3	
	抉 3c4.3	
ku(keru)	絎 6a6.2	
kuki	茎 3k5.23	
	莖 3k5.23	
kuku(ru)	括 3c6.12	
kuma	隈 2d9.2	
	澳 3a13.4	
	熊 4d10.6	
Kume	粂 6b3.3	
kumi	組 6a5.7	
kumi(suru)	与 0a3.23	
	與 0a3.23	

kumo	雲 8d4.1	
kumo(ru)	曇 4c12.1	
ku(mu)	汲 3a3.7	
	組 6a5.7	
	酌 7e3.3	
KUN	勲 4d11.3	
	君 3d4.23	
	葷 3k9.28	
	薫 3k13.17	
	薰 3k13.17	
	裙 4a7.2	
	勳 4d11.3	
	薫 4d14.1	
	燻 4d14.1	
	裙 5e7.2	
	訓 7a3.6	
	鞋 7c7.3	
	輝 7c7.3	
	醺 7e14.1	
kuni	邦 2d4.7	
	国 3s5.1	
	圀 3s5.1	
	國 3s5.1	
kunugi	椚 4a8.2	
	楜 4a8.37	
	櫟 4a15.3	
	檪 4a15.3	
kura	倉 2a8.37	
	藏 3k12.17	
	蔵 3k12.17	
	鞍 3k12.19	
	岫 3o5.1	
	庫 3q7.1	
	廩 3q13.4	
-kura	競 5b15.1	
	競 5b15.1	
kura(beru)	比 2m3.5	
	較 7c6.3	
kura(gari)	暗 4c9.2	
kurai	位 2a5.1	
-kurai	位 2a5.1	
kura(i)	昏 4c4.11	
	晦 4c7.3	
	暗 4c9.2	
kura(masu)	晦 4c7.3	
	晦 4c7.3	
	暗 4c9.2	
kura(mu)	晦 4c7.3	
	暗 4c9.2	
ku(rashi)	暮 3k11.14	
ku(rasu)	暮 3k11.14	
kura(u)	啖 3d8.10	
	喰 3d9.1	
	嗽 3d12.3	

Reading	Kanji	Code
ku(rau)	食 食	8b0.1
ku(rawasu)	食 食	8b0.1
Kure	⼍ 呉	2o5.7
	呉	2o5.7
kure	木 樽	4a10.5
ku(re)	艹 暮	3k11.14
kurenai	糸 紅	6a3.6
ku(reru)	⼍ 呉	2o5.7
	口 呉	2o5.7
	艹 暮	3k11.14
kuri	木 栗	4a6.32
kurikaeshi kigō		
	々	2n1,1
kuriya	厂 厨	2p10.1
	广 厨	2p10.1
	廚	2p10.1
kuro	火 黒	4d7.2
	黒	4d7.2
	田 畔	5f5.1
	畔	5f5.1
kuro(bamu)	火 黒	4d7.2
	黒	4d7.2
kurodake	⺮ 篶	6f11.6
kurogane	金 銕	8a5.6
	鐵	8a5.6
	鐡	8a5.6
	鉄	8a5.6
kuro(i)	火 黒	4d7.2
	黒	4d7.2
kuro(maru)	火 黒	4d7.2
	黒	4d7.2
kuro(meru)	火 黒	4d7.2
	黒	4d7.2
kuro(zumu)	火 黒	4d7.2
	黒	4d7.2
ku(ru)	耒	0a7.6
	来	0a7.6
	亻 來	0a7.6
	刂 剗	2f6.6
	彳 徠	0a7.6
	糸 繰	6a13.3
kurubushi	足 踝	7d8.1
kuru(i)	犭 狂	3g4.2
kuruma	亻 俥	2a7.2
	車 車	7c0.1
	輅	7c6.1
kurume(ku)	目 眩	5c5.3
kuru(meru)		
	包	0a5.9
	扌 括	3c6.12
kuru(mu)	包	0a5.9
	包	0a5.9
	扌 括	3c6.12
kuru(oshii)	犭 狂	3g4.2
kuru(shigaru)		
	艹 苦	3k5.24
kuru(shii)	艹 苦	3k5.24
kuru(shimeru)		
	艹 苦	3k5.24
kuru(shimu)		
	艹 苦	3k5.24
kuru(u)	犭 狂	3g4.2
kuruwa	阝 郭	2d6.7
	郭	2d7.14
	廓	3q9.1
kuru(waseru)		
	犭 狂	3g4.2
kuru(washii)		
	犭 狂	3g4.2
kuru(wasu)		
	犭 狂	3g4.2
kusa	艸	0a6.14
	艹 草	3k6.13
	禾 種	5d9.1
kusabi	木 楔	4a9.11
kusagi(ru)	耘	0a10.9
kusa(i)	目 臭	5c4.3
	臭	5c4.3
kusame	口 嚔	3d15.3
	嚔	3d15.3
kusamura	耳 叢	6e12.3
kusa(rasu)	广 腐	3q11.3
kusa(reru)	广 腐	3q11.3
kusari	金 鎖	8a10.2
	鏈	8a10.10
	鏑	8a13.4
kusa(ru)	广 腐	3q11.3
kusa(su)	广 腐	3q11.3
kuse	疒 癖	5i13.2
kushami	口 嚔	3d15.3
	嚔	3d15.3
kushi	串	0a7.13
	木 梳	4a7.10
	櫛	4a15.5
	櫛	4a15.5
kushikezu(ru)		
	木 梳	4a7.10
ku(shiki)	口 奇	3d5.17
	竒	3d5.17
ku(shikumo)		
	奇	3d5.17
	竒	3d5.17
kushiro	金 釧	8a4.7
kuso	尸 屎	3r6.1
	米 糞	6b11.3
kusu	木 樟	4a11.10
kusu(beru)	火 薫	4d14.1
	燻	4d14.1
kusu(buru)	火 薫	4d14.1
	燻	4d14.1
kusugu(ru)	扌 擽	3c15.2
kusugu(ttai)		
	扌 擽	3c15.2
kusunoki	木 楠	4a9.25
	樟	4a11.10
kusuri	艹 薬	3k13.15
	薬	3k13.15
kute	氵 湫	3a9.7
KUTSU	亻 倔	2a8.33
	扌 掘	3c8.32
	宀 窟	3m10.6
	屵 崛	3o8.4
	尸 屈	3r5.2
kutsu	氵 沓	3a4.19
	轄	3a13.12
	艹 靴	3k10.34
kutsugae(ru)	日 覆	4c14.6
	覆	4c14.6
kutsugae(su)	覆	4c14.6
	覆	4c14.6
kutsuro(geru)	宀 寛	3m10.3
	寛	3m10.3
kutsuro(gu)	宀 寛	3m10.3
	寛	3m10.3
kutsuwa	口 轡	3d19.2
	啣	3i11.1
	彳 銜	3i11.1
	金 鑣	8a15.6
ku(u)	口 喰	3d9.1
	食 食	8b0.1
kuwa	又 桑	2h8.1
	金 鍬	8a9.3
kuwada(teru)		
	亻 企	2a4.17
kuwa(eru)	力 加	2g3.1
	口 哇	3d6.8
	啣	3i11.1
	彳 銜	3i11.1
kuwa(shii)	禾 精	5d3.2
	精	6b8.1
	言 詳	7a6.12
ku(wasu)	食 食	8b0.1
kuwa(waru)		
	力 加	2g3.1
ku(yamu)	忄 悔	4k6.12
	悔	4k6.12
kuya(shii)	忄 悔	4k6.12
kusu(buru)	火 薫	4d14.1
	燻	4d14.1
kuyu(rasu)	火 薫	4d14.1
	燻	4d14.1
kuzu	艹 葛	3k9.22
	葛	3k9.22
	尸 屑	3r7.4
kuzuo(reru)	頁 頽	9a7.3
kuzu(reru)	崩	3o8.7
	崩	3o8.7
kuzu(shi)	崩	3o8.7
	崩	3o8.7
kuzu(su)	尸 崩	3o8.7
	崩	3o8.7
KYA	亻 伽	2a5.12
	月 脚	4b7.3
KYAKU	卩 却	2e5.3
	卻	2e5.3
	宀 客	3m6.3
	月 脚	4b7.3
	腳	4b11.6
kyan	亻 俠	2a7.7
	俠	2a7.7
KYO	舉	3n7.1
	亻 倨	2a8.31
	卜 虚	2m9.1
	虚	2m9.1
	辶 遽	2q13.5
	匚 巨	2t2.2
	土 去	3b2.2
	墟	3b11.2
	墟	3b11.2
	扌 拠	3c5.26
	據	3c5.26
	拒	3c5.29
	据	3c8.33
	挙	3n7.1
	口 噓	3d11.7
	嘘	3d11.7
	艹 苣	3k5.32
	⺍ 挙	3n7.1
	尸 居	3r5.3
	木 渠	4a8.40
	欅	4a17.1
	火 炬	4d5.5
	禾 秬	5d5.9
	衤 裾	5e8.8
	⺮ 筥	6f7.5
	言 許	7a4.3
	足 距	7d5.8
	踞	7d8.6
	酉 醵	7e13.3
	金 鉅	8a5.18
	鋸	8a8.19
KYŌ	卅	0a3.25

凶 0a4.19	卝共 3k3.3	饗 8b10.4	窮 3m12.4
匈 0a6.10	茨 3k7.3	頁頬 9a7.2	屵岌 3o4.2
兇 0a6.12	恭 3k7.16	頰 9a7.2	广廐 2p12.2
亻夾 2a5.27	蛬 3k9.27	馬驕 10a12.2	廏 2p12.2
供 2a6.13	蕎 3k12.8	驚 10a12.4	木朽 4a2.6
俠 2a7.7	竅 3k12.21 KYOKU	曲 0a6.27	柩 4a5.31
俠 2a7.7	薑 3k13.19	棘 0a12.3	猷 4a9.9
衿 2a7.25	宀竅 3m15.2	氵洫 3a6.7	樛 4a11.9
僑 2a12.5	屵峡 3o6.1	匸亟 3d5.16	日旧 4c1.1
僵 2a13.5	峽 3o6.1	殛 3d9.28	皀 4c3.2
冫況 3a5.21	木杏 4a3.13	彡髯 3j13.1	殷 4c8.15
阝陜 2d7.3	校 4a6.24	艹棘 3k12.2	火炎 4d3.2
郷 2d8.14	框 4a6.31	尸局 3r4.4	休 4d6.4
郷 2d8.14	梟 4a7.28	木桾 4a7.20	王玖 4f3.1
卩卿 2e10.1	橋 4a12.8	極 4a8.11	球 4f7.2
卿 2e10.1	橇 4a12.14	日旭 4c2.6	攵救 4i7.1
刂刔 2g5.2	橿 4a13.5	勖 4c7.6	欠歙 4j12.1
刧 2g5.2	月脇 4b6.3	勗 4c7.6	忄恷 4k6.20
力劫 2g5.2	胸 4b6.9	跼 7d7.4	衤裘 5e7.5
脅 2g8.2	臼皀 4c3.2 KYŪ	九 0a2.15	疒疚 5i3.2
又圣 6a5.11	皎 4c7.15	久 0a3.7	糸級 6a3.2
亠亨 2j4.2	響 4c15.3	及 0a3.24	級 6a3.2
享 2j5.1	響 4c15.3	丘 0a5.12	糾 6a3.4
京 2j6.3	攵教 4i6.1	臼 0a6.4	紏 6a3.4
京 2j6.3	教 4i6.1	亻仇 2a2.4	給 6a6.7
艹協 2k6.1	敬 4i8.4	休 2a4.2	繆 6a11.5
羌 2o6.2	欠歙 4j12.2	翕 2a10.9	虫蚯 6d5.6
姜 2o7.5	忄怯 4k5.9	猷 2a11.18	竹笈 6f3.1
興 2o14.2	愶 4k6.11	氵求 2b5.5	門闂 8e18.1
冂冏 2r5.1	恟 4k6.14	毬 2b9.1	鳥鳩 11b2.1
匚匡 2t4.1	恐 4k6.19	阝邱 2d5.9	
冫況 3a5.21	恐 4k6.19	力舅 2g11.7	**– M –**
洵 3a6.24	立竟 5b6.5	韭 3k9.2 MA	口嘛 3d11.8
土境 3b11.1	競 5b15.1	⺈急 2n7.2	艹蟇 3k13.23
扌挓 3c4.1	競 5b15.1	急 2n7.2	广麻 3q8.3
挟 3c6.1	目眶 5c6.5	厂厩 2p12.2	麼 3q11.1
挾 3c6.1	禾香 5d4.5	廐 2p12.2	摩 3q12.6
拱 3c6.9	衤襁 5e11.1	辶述 2q7.7	麿 3q12.6
口叶 3d2.1	畺 5f14.2	氵汲 3a3.7	磨 3q13.3
兄 3d2.9	糸経 6a5.11	泣 3a5.1	麿 3q13.3
叫 3d3.4	經 6a5.11	赳 3b7.10	魔 3q18.2
叫 3d3.4	繈 6a11.2	扌扱 3c3.5	疒痳 5i8.3
叫 3d3.4	虫蛩 6d6.12	扱 3c3.5	虫蟆 3k13.23
喬 3d9.25	竹筐 6f6.16	摎 3c11.2 ma	日間 8e4.3
競 3d11.10	筐 6f6.16	口吸 3d3.5	目目 5c0.1
矯 3d14.5	笂 6f7.1	咎 3d5.15	門間 8e4.3
嚮 3d15.4	簇 6f9.10	嗅 3d10.3	間 8e4.3
女嬌 3e12.1	言誆 7a7.3	弓弓 3h0.1	馬馬 10a0.1
犭狂 3g4.2	車轎 7c12.2	躬 3h7.1 ma-	亠真 2k8.1
狭 3g6.2	跫 7d6.9	韮 3k9.2	眞 2k8.1
狹 3g6.2	金鐄 2j6.3	舊 4c1.1 maba(ra)	疋疎 0a11.4
弓強 3h8.3	鋏 8a7.4	宀究 3m4.5	疏 0a11.4
彊 3h13.1	鏡 8a11.6	穹 3m5.10 mabata(ku)	目瞬 5c13.1
彳徼 3i13.2	飠饗 8b10.4	宮 3m7.5	瞬 5c13.1

Reading		Kanji	Code
mabayu(i)	目	眩	5c5.3
maboroshi		幻	0a4.6
mabushi	⺾	蔟	3k11.3
mabu(shii)	目	眩	5c5.3
mabu(su)	土	塗	3b10.10
mabuta	目	瞼	5c13.4
machi	彳	街	3i9.2
	礻	禖	5e13.3
	田	町	5f2.1
		甼	5f2.1
mada		未	0a5.27
madara	王	斑	4f8.3
made	⻌	迄	2q3.4
		迄	2q3.4
		辿	2q5.8
mado	宀	窓	3m8.7
		窗	3m8.7
mado(ka)	冂	円	2r2.1
	囗	圓	2r2.1
mado(u)	心	惑	4k8.16
mae		前	2o7.3
maga	礻	禍	4e9.4
		禍	4e9.4
maga(i)	扌	擬	3c14.2
magaki	⺮	籬	6f18.1
ma(garu)		曲	0a6.27
maga(u)	糸	紛	6a4.8
mage	彡	髷	3j13.1
magemono	木	榜	4a8.12
ma(geru)		曲	0a6.27
	木	枉	4a4.2
magi(rasu)	糸	紛	6a4.8
magi(rawashii)			
	糸	紛	6a4.8
magi(rawasu)			
	糸	紛	6a4.8
magi(reru)	糸	紛	6a4.8
mago	子	孫	2c7.1
maguro	魚	鮪	11a6.1
magusa	禾	秣	5d5.1
MAI		毎	0a6.25
	⻌	邁	2q12.7
	土	埋	3b7.2
	女	妹	3e5.4
	⺾	苺	3k5.3
		莓	3k5.4
	木	枚	4a4.4
	日	昧	4c5.2
	王	瑁	4f9.4
	目	眛	5c5.1
mai		舞	0a15.1
mainai	貝	賂	7b6.2
mai(ri)	言	詣	7a6.13
mairu	口	哩	3d7.5
mai(ru)	彡	参	3j5.1
		參	3j5.1
maji(eru)	一	交	2j4.3
	隹	雑	8c6.2
		襍	8c6.2
		雜	8c6.2
majina(i)	口	呪	3d5.11
		咒	3d5.11
majiro(gu)	目	瞬	5c13.1
		瞬	5c13.1
ma(jiru)	一	交	2j4.3
	氵	混	3a8.14
	礻	襍	8c6.2
	隹	雑	8c6.2
		雜	8c6.2
maji(waru)	一	交	2j4.3
makana(u)	貝	賄	7b6.1
maka(ru)	罒	罷	5g10.2
ma(karu)		負	2n7.1
maka(seru)	亻	任	2a4.9
	禾	委	5d3.2
maka(su)	亻	任	2a4.9
	禾	委	5d3.2
ma(kasu)		負	2n7.1
ma(keru)		負	2n7.1
maki		巻	0a9.11
		卷	0a9.11
	⺾	薪	3k13.3
	木	槙	4a10.27
		槇	4a10.27
	牛	牧	4g4.1
makoto	亻	信	2a7.1
	⺾	真	2k8.1
		眞	2k8.1
	宀	実	3m5.4
	言	誠	7a6.3
MAKU		幕	3k10.19
	月	膜	4b10.6
ma(ku)		巻	0a9.11
		卷	0a9.11
	扌	捲	3c8.9
		捲	3c8.9
		撒	3c12.2
		播	3c12.8
	⺾	蒔	3k10.7
makura	木	枕	4a4.8
maku(reru)	扌	捲	3c8.9
		捲	3c8.9
maku(ru)	扌	捲	3c8.9
		捲	3c8.9
mama	亻	侭	2a14.2
		儘	2a14.2
	土	圸	3b3.3
		壔	3b12.3
		壜	3b14.1
	食	飯	8b4.5
mame	豆	豆	3d4.22
		萩	3k8.7
mamegara	其		3k8.17
mami(eru)	見	見	5c2.1
		観	5c13.8
mami(reru)	土	塗	3b10.10
mamo(ru)	宀	守	3m3.2
	言	護	7a13.3
mamushi	虫	蝮	6d9.6
MAN		万	0a3.8
	又	蠻	2h19.1
	十	卍	2k4.7
	氵	満	3a9.25
		滿	3a9.25
		漫	3a11.11
	巾	幔	3f11.1
	⺾	萬	0a3.8
		蔓	3k11.15
		曼	4c7.8
	心	悗	4k7.13
		慢	4k11.8
		瀟	4k14.2
	目	瞞	5c11.2
	糸	縵	6a11.7
	言	謾	7a11.2
		蹣	7d11.4
	金	鏝	8a11.7
	食	饅	8b11.1
	魚	鰻	11a11.5
mana-	女	愛	4i10.1
mana(bu)	子	學	3n4.2
		孝	3n4.2
		学	3n4.2
manaita		俎	2a7.24
	亻	俎	2a7.24
manajiri	目	眥	5c6.7
		眦	5c6.7
		睚	5c8.8
manako		眼	5c6.1
mane(ku)	扌	招	3c5.22
manimani	阝	隨	2d8.10
		随	2d8.10
manji		卍	2k4.7
manuka(reru)			
	刂	免	2n6.1
		免	2n6.1
mare	一	罕	2i5.1
	巾	希	3f4.1
	禾	稀	5d7.5
mari	冫	毬	2b9.1
	米	鞠	6b11.6
maro	广	麿	3q15.2
maro(yaka)			
	冂	円	2r2.1
	囗	圓	2r2.1
maru		丸	0a3.28
maru (de)		丸	0a3.28
maru(i)		丸	0a3.28
	冂	円	2r2.1
	囗	圓	2r2.1
maru(kkoi)		丸	0a3.28
maru(meru)		丸	0a3.28
masa	木	柾	4a5.15
		榲	4a12.13
masakari	戈	戉	4n1.2
	金	鉞	8a5.16
masaki	木	柾	4a5.15
masa (ni)		将	2b8.3
	丬	将	2b8.3
		正	2m3.3
		当	3n3.3
		當	3n3.3
	方	方	4h0.1
masa(ru)	亻	優	2a15.1
	月	勝	4b8.4
		勝	4b8.4
ma(saru)	土	増	3b11.3
		増	3b11.3
masa(shiku)			
	⼇	正	2m3.3
ma(shi)	土	増	3b11.3
		増	3b11.3
mashira	犭	猿	3g10.3
ma(shite)	氵	況	3a5.21
		況	3a5.21
masu		升	0a4.32
	木	桝	4a4.6
		枡	4a4.6
	魚	鱒	11a12.6
		鱒	11a12.6
ma(su)		益	2o8.5
	土	増	3b11.3
		増	3b11.3
masugata	木	櫨	4a16.2
		枦	4a16.2
		枦	4a16.2
mata	亻	俣	2a7.12
	又	又	2h0.1
		又	2h0.1
		叉	2h1.1
	亠	亦	2j4.4
	彳	復	3i9.4
	木	椏	4a8.5
	月	股	4b4.8
		胯	4b6.2

mata(garu) 足 跨 7d6.6
mata(gu) 足 跨 7d6.6
matata(ku) 目 瞬 5c13.1
　　瞬 5c13.1
mata(wa) 又 又 2h0.1
　　又 2h0.1
mate 魚 鮴 11a6.2
mategai 虫 蚶 6d8.1
mato 日 的 4c4.12
　　的 4c4.12
mato(i) 糸 纏 6a16.1
　　纏 6a16.1
mato(maru)
　糸 纏 6a16.1
　　纏 6a16.1
mato(meru)
　糸 纏 6a16.1
　　纏 6a16.1
mato(u) 糸 纏 6a16.1
　　纏 6a16.1
MATSU 末 0a5.26
　氵 沫 3a5.5
　扌 抹 3c5.9
　艹 茉 3k5.6
　　鞋 3k11.21
　禾 秣 5d5.1
matsu 木 松 4a4.16
　　杰 4a4.16
ma(tsu) 亻 俟 2a7.19
　彳 待 3i6.4
　立 竢 2a7.19
matsuge 目 睫 5c8.4
matsu(ri) 礻 祭 4e6.3
matsurigoto
　攵 政 4i5.1
matsu(ru) 礻 祀 4e3.2
　　祭 4e6.3
matsu(waru)
　糸 纏 6a16.1
　　纏 6a16.1
matta(ku) 亻 全 2a4.16
　　全 2a4.16
matto(u suru)
　亻 全 2a4.16
　　全 2a4.16
ma(u) 舞 0a15.1
mawa(ri) 囗 囘 3s3.1
　囗 回 3s3.1
　　囬 3s3.1
mawa(ru) 辶 廻 2q6.13
　　廻 2q6.13
　囗 囘 3s3.1
　囗 回 3s3.1
　　囬 3s3.1

mawa(shi) 囗 囘 3s3.1
　囗 回 3s3.1
　　囬 3s3.1
mawa(su) 辶 廻 2q6.13
　　廻 2q6.13
　囗 囘 3s3.1
　囗 回 3s3.1
　　囬 3s3.1
mayo(i) 辶 迷 2q6.1
mayo(u) 辶 迷 2q6.1
mayo(wasu)
　辶 迷 2q6.1
mayu 艹 繭 3k15.7
　目 眉 5c4.9
mayumi 木 檀 4a13.11
　　檀 4a13.11
mayuzumi 火 黛 4d13.7
ma(zaru) 亠 交 2j4.3
　氵 混 3a8.14
　衤 襍 8c6.2
　隹 雑 8c6.2
　　雜 8c6.2
ma(zeru) 亠 交 2j4.3
　氵 混 3a8.14
　衤 襍 8c6.2
　隹 雑 8c6.2
　　雜 8c6.2
ma(zu) 土 先 3b3.7
mazu(i) 扌 拙 3c5.11
mazu(shii) 貧 2o9.5
　　貧 2o9.5
ME 王 瑪 4f10.1
　石 碼 5a10.1
me 艹 芽 3k5.9
　　芽 3k5.9
　目 目 5c0.1
　　眼 5c6.1
me- 女 女 3e0.1
　牛 牝 4g2.1
　隹 雌 8c6.1
mebaru 魚 鮴 11a6.2
me(deru) 夂 愛 4i10.1
medogi 艹 蓍 3k10.11
megu(mu) 心 恤 4k6.1
　　恵 4k6.16
　　惠 4k6.16
megu(rasu)
　辶 巡 2q3.3
　囗 囘 3s3.1
　囗 回 3s3.1
　　囬 3s3.1
megu(ri) 辶 廻 2q6.13

　　廻 2q6.13
megu(ru) 辶 巡 2q3.3
　　廻 2q6.13
　　廻 2q6.13
　囗 囘 3s3.1
　囗 回 3s3.1
　　囬 3s3.1
MEI 亻 命 2a6.26
　冖 冥 2i8.2
　辶 迷 2q6.1
　夕 名 3d3.12
　口 鳴 3d11.1
　艹 茗 3k6.5
　日 明 4c4.1
　　暝 4c10.2
　目 瞑 5c10.3
　皿 盟 5h8.1
　虫 蟆 6d10.4
　言 謎 7a9.20
　　謎 7a9.20
　酉 酩 7e6.3
　金 銘 8a6.4
mei 女 姪 3e6.6
mekake 立 妾 5b3.2
mekki 金 鍍 8a9.9
mekura 亠 盲 2j6.6
　　盲 2j6.6
meku(ru) 扌 捲 3c8.9
　　捲 3c8.9
MEN 亻 麪 4i17.1
　刂 免 2n6.1
　クノ 免 2n6.1
　氵 湎 3a9.32
　宀 宀 3m0.1
　囗 面 3s6.1
　　麵 4i17.1
　木 棉 4a8.18
　攵 麺 4i17.1
　　麵 4i17.1
　糸 綿 6a8.8
　　緜 6a8.8
　　緬 6a9.12
　米 粬 4i17.1
men 牛 牝 4g2.1
me(ru) 氵 減 3a9.37
meshi 食 飯 8b4.5
meshii 亠 盲 2j6.6
　　盲 2j6.6
mesu 牛 牝 4g2.1
　隹 雌 8c6.1
me(su) 刂 召 2f3.3
meto(ru) 女 娶 3e8.7
mētoru 米 米 6b0.1

METSU 氵 滅 3a10.26
mezura(shii)
　王 珍 4f5.6
　　珎 4f5.6
MI 未 0a5.27
　口 味 3d5.3
　弓 弥 3h5.2
　　彌 3h5.2
　彳 微 3i10.1
　　微 3i10.1
　目 眉 5c4.9
　鬼 魅 5f10.1
mi 巳 0a3.16
　身 0a7.5
　宀 実 3m5.4
　竹 箕 6f8.6
mi- 三 0a3.1
　彳 御 3i9.1
michi 辶 迪 2q5.1
　　廸 2q5.1
　　道 2q9.14
　足 路 7d6.5
michibi(ku)
　辶 迪 2q5.1
　　廸 2q5.1
　　導 5c9.3
mi(chiru) 氵 満 3a9.25
　　滿 3a9.25
mida(ra) 氵 淫 3a8.17
　女 婬 3a8.17
　犭 猥 3g9.2
mida(reru) 口 乱 3d4.21
　　亂 3d4.21
mida(rigamashii)
　犭 猥 3g9.2
mida(ri ni) 亠 妄 2j4.6
　氵 濫 3a15.3
mida(su) 口 乱 3d4.21
　　亂 3d4.21
midori 艹 翠 2k12.2
　　翠 2k12.2
　　翠 2k12.2
　糸 緑 6a8.15
　　緑 6a8.15
mi(eru) 見 5c2.1
miga(ku) 广 磨 3q13.3
　广 磨 3q13.3
migi 口 右 3d2.15
migiri 石 砌 5a4.4
migiwa 氵 汀 3a2.2
mijika(i) 口 短 3d9.27
miji(me) 心 惨 4k8.5
　　惨 4k8.5
mikado 亠 帝 2j7.1

Reading	Rad.	Kanji	Code
	巾	帝	2j7.1
miki	日	幹	4c9.8
mikoto	イ	命	2a6.26
	ハ	尊	2o10.3
		尊	2o10.3
mikotonori	力	勅	2g7.1
	攵	敕	2g7.1
	言	詔	7a5.10
mimaka(ru)			
	艹	薨	3k13.22
mimi	耳	耳	6e0.1
mimizu	虫	蚓	6d4.4
		蚯	6d5.6
MIN		民	0a5.23
	山	岷	3o5.3
	日	明	4c4.1
	目	眠	5c5.2
	罒	罠	5g5.1
mina	イ	僉	2a11.17
	日	皆	4c5.14
minagi(ru)	氵	漲	3a11.5
minagoroshi			
	釒	鏖	8a11.10
minami	十	南	2k7.1
Minamoto	氵	源	3a10.25
minamoto	氵	源	3a10.25
minato	氵	湊	3a9.12
		港	3a9.13
		港	3a9.13
mine	山	岑	3o4.3
		峯	3o7.6
		峰	3o7.6
		嶺	3o14.2
miniku(i)	酉	醜	7e10.1
minna	日	皆	4c5.14
mino	艹	蓑	3k10.24
	⺮	簑	3k10.24
		簔	3k10.24
mino(ru)	宀	実	3m5.4
mio	氵	澪	3a13.6
miriguramu		瓱	0a9.6
mirimētoru			
	米	粍	6b4.2
miririttoru	立	竓	5b4.1
mi(ru)	目	見	5c2.1
		看	5c4.4
		覧	5c12.7
		覧	5c12.7
		観	5c13.7
		觀	5c13.7
	言	診	7a5.9
misago	鳥	鶚	11b9.1
misaki	山	岬	3o5.4
		岫	3o5.5
		崎	3o8.3
		嵜	3o8.3
misao	扌	操	3c13.3
misasagi	阝	陵	2d8.5
mise	广	店	3q5.4
mi(seru)	目	見	5c2.1
misogi	礻	禊	4e9.5
misoka	日	晦	4c7.3
		晦	4c7.3
misonawa(su)			
	言	覽	7a18.1
misona(wasu)			
	日	讐	5c19.1
mi(tasu)	亠	充	2j4.5
	氵	満	3a9.25
		満	3a9.25
mito(meru)	言	認	7a7.10
MITSU	宀	密	3m8.5
		蜜	3m11.7
	木	橘	4a11.16
		橙	4a11.16
mi(tsu)		三	0a3.1
mitsu(gu)	貝	貢	7b3.3
mit(tsu)		三	0a3.1
miya	宀	宮	3m7.5
miya(bita)	隹	雅	8c5.1
		雅	8c5.1
miya(biyaka)			
	隹	雅	8c5.1
		雅	8c5.1
miyako	阝	都	2d8.13
		都	2d8.13
	亠	京	2j6.3
		京	2j6.3
	釒	鐭	2j6.3
mizo	氵	溝	3a10.9
mizore	⻗	霙	8d8.8
mizu	氵	水	3a0.1
	王	瑞	4f9.6
mizuchi	虫	蛟	6d6.8
mizukaki	足	蹼	7d12.1
mizuka(ra)	自	自	5c1.1
mizunoe	壬	壬	3p1.1
mizunoto		癸	0a9.2
mizura	髟	鬟	5g18.1
mizuumi	氵	湖	3a9.8
MO	扌	摸	3c10.13
	女	姆	3e5.2
		姥	3e6.2
		媽	3e10.1
	艹	茂	3k5.7
		摹	3k11.13
	木	楳	3k5.7
		模	4a10.16
mo	土	喪	3b9.20
	艹	藻	3k16.8
	⺳	裳	3n11.2
MŌ	毛	毛	0a4.33
		耗	0a10.12
		耗	0a10.12
	子	孟	2c5.1
	亠	亡	2j1.1
		亡	2j1.1
		妄	2j4.6
		盲	2j6.6
		盲	2j6.6
	耂	耄	2k8.3
	冂	网	2r4.1
		罔	2r6.3
	氵	濛	3a13.9
	犭	猛	3g7.4
	艹	莽	3k6.16
		蒙	3k10.23
	木	檬	4a13.7
	月	朦	4b13.4
	日	曚	4c13.2
	王	望	4f7.6
	目	矇	5c13.3
	罒	魍	5f13.2
	糸	網	6a8.25
	舟	艨	6c13.1
MOCHI		勿	0a4.11
mochi	王	望	4f7.6
	禾	穃	5d17.1
	食	餅	8b6.4
		餅	8b6.4
		餅	8b6.4
mo(chi)	扌	持	3c6.8
mochiawa	艹	朮	2k3.3
mochigome			
	米	糯	6b14.1
mochi(iru)	冂	用	2r3.1
moda(eru)	門	悶	8e4.5
moda(su)	犭	默	4d11.5
	火	默	4d11.5
mō(de)	言	詣	7a6.13
modo(ru)	尸	戻	4m3.1
		戻	4m3.1
modo(su)	尸	戻	4m3.1
		戻	4m3.1
mo(eru)	艹	萌	3k8.11
		萠	3k8.11
	火	燃	4d12.2
moga(ku)	足	踠	7d8.5
mo(geru)	扌	捥	3c8.19
mogi(ru)	扌	捥	3c8.19
	扌	撫	4a12.7
		模	4a10.16
mo(gu)	扌	捥	3c8.19
mogu(ru)	氵	潜	3a12.6
		潜	3a12.6
		潜	3a12.6
mogusa	艹	艾	3k2.2
moji	糸	縺	6a8.21
		縺	6a8.21
moji(ru)	扌	捩	3c8.31
		捩	3c8.31
mō(karu)	イ	儲	2a16.1
		儲	2a16.1
mō(ke)	イ	儲	2a16.1
mō(keru)	イ	儲	2a16.1
		儲	2a16.1
mokko	言	設	7a4.7
	⽥	畚	5f5.7
	⺮	簣	6f12.3
MOKU	氵	沐	3a4.1
	犭	默	4d11.5
	艹	苜	3k5.1
	木	木	4a0.1
	火	默	4d11.5
	目	目	5c0.1
moku	木	杢	4a3.14
mo(mareru)			
	扌	揉	3c9.2
mo(me)	扌	揉	3c9.2
mo(meru)	扌	揉	3c9.2
momi	木	樅	4a11.3
	糸	紅	6a3.6
	米	籾	6b3.1
		籾	6b3.1
momiji	木	椛	4a6.23
		椛	4a7.14
momo	木	桃	4a6.10
	月	股	4b4.8
		腿	4b9.10
		腿	4b9.10
	日	百	4c2.3
momu	虫	蟷	6d11.4
mo(mu)	扌	揉	3c9.2
MON	門	門	8e0.1
	イ	們	2a8.1
	亠	文	2j2.4
		文	2j2.4
	扌	捫	3c8.2
	口	问	8e3.1
	心	懣	4k14.2
	糸	紋	6a4.9
	門	門	8e0.1
		問	8e3.1
		悶	8e4.5
		聞	8e6.1

Reading		Kanji	Code
	馬	駁	10a4.2
monme		勾	0a4.38
mono	日	者	4c4.13
		者	4c4.13
	牛	物	4g4.2
monoimi	宀	斎	2j9.6
		齋	2j9.6
monou(i)	忄	慵	4k11.10
		懶	4k16.1
monuke	虫	蛻	6d7.8
moppa(ra)		専	0a9.16
		專	0a9.16
mo(rasu)	氵	洩	3a6.3
		漏	3a11.19
mora(u)	貝	貰	7b5.5
mo(reru)	氵	洩	3a6.3
		漏	3a11.19
mori	宀	守	3m3.2
	木	杜	4a3.1
		森	4a8.39
	釒	鉎	8a6.7
moro-	訁	諸	7a8.3
		諸	7a8.3
moro(i)	月	脆	4b6.4
moromi	酉	醪	7e11.1
mo(ru)	氵	洩	3a6.3
		漏	3a11.19
	皿	盛	5h6.1
mo(shi)	艹	若	3k5.12
mo(shikuwa)			
	艹	若	3k5.12
mo(su)	火	燃	4d12.2
mō(su)		申	0a5.39
mota(geru)	扌	擡	3c14.7
	女	姚	3c14.7
motai		瓮	2o7.7
motara(su)			
	宀	齎	2j19.1
mota(reru)	几	凭	2s6.1
	口	靠	4g11.1
	牛	靠	4g11.1
mo(taseru)	扌	持	3c6.8
moteaso(bu)			
	扌	挵	3c7.8
	日	翫	4c11.6
		翫	4c11.6
	王	弄	4f3.2
		玩	4f4.1
mo(teru)	扌	持	3c6.8
moto		元	0a4.5
		本	0a5.25
	艹	本	0a5.25
	⺊	下	2m1.2
	土	基	3b8.12
	糸	素	6a4.12
	訁	許	7a4.3
motodori	口	髻	3d13.11
motoi	土	基	3b8.12
moto(meru)			
	氵	求	2b5.5
moto(mu)	氵	求	2b5.5
moto(ru)	彳	很	3i6.2
	忄	忤	4k4.5
		悖	4k6.4
moto(yori)	口	固	3s5.2
MOTSU	氵	没	3a4.15
		沒	3a4.15
	牛	物	4g4.2
mo(tsu)	扌	持	3c6.8
motsu(reru)			
	糸	縺	6a10.12
mot(te)		以	0a5.1
motto(mo)		尤	0a4.20
	日	最	4c8.10
motto(mo-rashii)			
		尤	0a4.20
moya	⻗	靄	8d16.1
mo(yashi)	艹	萌	3k8.11
		萠	3k8.11
mo(yasu)	火	燃	4d12.2
moya(u)	舟	舫	6c4.1
moyō(su)	亻	催	2a11.12
mo(yuru)	火	燃	4d12.2
mozu	貝	鶪	7b11.1
	鳥	鴂	11b4.1
MU		无	0a4.24
		母	0a4.47
		矛	0a5.6
	艹	夢	3k10.14
	木	梦	3k10.14
	火	無	4d8.8
	牛	牟	4g2.2
	夂	務	4i7.6
	戈	武	4n5.3
	訁	謀	7a9.8
	⻗	霧	8d11.1
	鳥	鶩	11b7.1
		鶩	11b8.6
mu	宀	六	2j2.2
mube	宀	宜	3m5.7
muchi	艹	鞭	3k15.8
	⺮	笞	6f5.13
muda	彳	徒	3i7.1
mugi	夂	麥	4i4.2
		麦	4i4.2
mugo(i)	忄	惨	4k8.5
		惨	4k8.5
	酉	酷	7e7.1
mugura	艹	葎	3k9.14
mui	宀	六	2j2.2
mujina	豸	貉	4i10.2
		貉	4i10.2
muka(eru)	辶	迎	2q4.4
		邀	2q13.1
mukashi	艹	昔	3k5.28
muka(u)	口	嚮	3d15.4
		向	3d3.10
mu(kau)	口	向	3d3.10
mu(keru)	刂	剥	2f8.4
		剝	2f8.4
	口	向	3d3.10
muko	土	壻	3e9.3
	女	婿	3e9.3
	耳	聟	3e9.3
mu(kō)	口	向	3d3.10
muku	彡	尨	3j4.2
	木	椋	4a8.31
mu(ku)	刂	剥	2f8.4
		剝	2f8.4
	口	向	3d3.10
mukuge		毳	0a12.5
	艹	葵	3k9.8
	艹	蕣	3k13.21
mukui	酉	酬	7e6.2
muku(iru)	土	報	3b9.16
mukuro	匸	躯	3d15.5
		軀	3d15.5
	月	骸	4b12.7
muna-	木	棟	4a8.3
	月	胸	4b6.9
munagai	艹	鞅	3k11.23
muna(shii)	⺊	虚	2m9.1
		虚	2m9.1
	宀	空	3m5.12
mune	宀	宗	3m5.1
	木	棟	4a8.3
	月	胸	4b6.9
	日	旨	4c2.2
mura	阝	邨	4a3.11
	口	群	3d10.14
		羣	3d10.14
	木	村	4a3.11
	王	斑	4f8.3
mura-	耳	叢	6e12.3
mura(garu)	口	群	3d10.14
		羣	3d10.14
	⺮	簇	6f11.2
murasaki	糸	紫	6a6.15
mu(rasu)	艹	蒸	3k9.19
mu(re)	口	群	3d10.14
		羣	3d10.14
mu(reru)	口	群	3d10.14
		羣	3d10.14
	艹	蒸	3k9.19
muro	宀	室	3m6.4
	木	榁	4a9.21
musabo(ru)			
	亻	貪	2a9.20
	食	饕	8b9.2
muse(bu)		旡	0a4.29
	口	咽	3d6.14
		噎	3d12.6
mu(seru)	口	噎	3d12.6
mushi	虫	蟲	6d0.1
		虫	6d0.1
mushiba	亻	齲	2a22.1
mushiba(mu)			
	食	蝕	8b6.1
		蝕	8b6.1
mushiro	艹	蓆	3k10.29
		莚	6f6.13
	⺮	筵	6f6.13
mushi(ro)	宀	寧	3m11.8
		寧	3m11.8
mushi(ru)	扌	挘	3c6.3
	⺌	毟	3n5.1
mu(su)	艹	蒸	3k9.19
musu(bu)	扌	掬	3c8.35
	糸	結	6a6.5
musume	女	娘	3e7.2
mu(tsu)	宀	六	2j2.2
mutsuki	糸	繦	6a11.2
mutsu(majii)			
	日	睦	5c8.6
mut(tsu)	宀	六	2j2.2
muzuka(shii)	隹	難	8c10.2
		難	8c10.2
MYAKU	月	脈	4b6.8
		脈	4b6.8
		脉	4b6.8
MYŌ	亻	命	2a6.26
	宀	冥	2i8.2
	口	名	3d3.12
	女	妙	3e4.5
	艹	苗	3k5.2
		茗	3k6.5
	日	明	4c4.1

– N –

Reading		Kanji	Code
NA	亻	儺	2a19.1
	阝	那	2d4.6
		那	2d4.6
	艹	南	2k7.1
	扌	拿	3c5.30
		拿	3c5.30
	木	奈	4e3.3

Reading	El.	Kanji	Code
natsu(ku)	心	懷	4k13.9
		懷	4k13.9
natsume		棗	0a12.4
na(u)	糸	絢	6a8.22
nawa	艹	苗	3k5.2
	糸	繩	6a9.1
		繩	6a9.1
nawate	田	畷	5f8.1
naya(masu)			
	心	惱	4k7.11
		惱	4k7.11
naya(mu)	心	惱	4k7.11
		惱	4k7.11
nayo(yaka)	女	嫋	3e10.2
nazo	言	謎	7a9.20
		謎	7a9.20
nazora(eru)			
	艹	準	2k11.1
nazuna	艹	薺	3k14.5
NE	氵	涅	3a7.8
		涅	3a7.8
	礻	祢	4e14.1
		襧	4e14.1
		禰	4e14.1
	礻	祢	4e14.1
ne	亻	値	2a8.30
	子	子	2c0.1
	宀	寢	3m10.1
		寢	3m10.1
	艹	嶺	3o14.2
	木	根	4a6.5
	立	音	5b4.3
neba(ru)	禾	黏	6b5.4
	米	粘	6b5.4
nebu(ru)	口	舐	3d7.15
nega(u)	頁	願	9a10.2
negi	艹	葱	3k9.20
negira(u)	力	勞	3n4.3
		労	3n4.3
	牛	犒	4g10.1
negura	土	壚	3b10.9
NEI	亻	佞	2a5.20
		侫	2a5.20
	氵	濘	3a14.6
	口	嚀	3d14.4
	宀	寧	3m11.8
		寧	3m11.8
	木	檸	4a14.2
	耳	聹	6e14.1
neji(keru)	扌	拗	3c5.16
neji(kureru)	扌	拗	3c5.16
neji(reru)	扌	捻	3c8.25
		捩	3c8.31
		捩	3c8.31
neji(ru)	扌	拗	3c5.16
		捻	3c8.25
		捩	3c8.31
		捩	3c8.31
ne(kasu)	宀	寢	3m10.1
		寢	3m10.1
neko	犭	猫	3g8.5
nemu(i)	目	眠	5c5.2
nemunoki	木	楺	4a8.23
nemu(ru)	目	眠	5c5.2
nemu(tai)	目	眠	5c5.2
NEN		冉	0a5.43
		冉	0a5.43
		年	0a6.16
	亻	念	2a6.24
	扌	拈	3c5.23
		捻	3c8.25
		撚	3c12.6
	木	棯	4a8.29
	火	然	4d8.10
		燃	4d12.2
	禾	稔	5d8.5
	禾	黏	6b5.4
	米	粘	6b5.4
	魚	鮎	11a5.7
nengo(ro)	心	懇	4k13.12
nera(u)	犭	狙	3g5.3
ne(reru)	糸	練	6a8.2
		練	6a8.2
ne(ri)	火	煉	4d9.2
		煉	4d9.2
ne(ru)	辶	邌	2q15.1
	宀	寢	3m10.1
		寢	3m10.1
	火	煉	4d9.2
		煉	4d9.2
	立	焙	5b7.4
	糸	練	6a8.2
		練	6a8.2
	金	鍊	8a8.3
		錬	8a8.3
nē(san)	女	姉	3e5.8
neta(mu)	女	妬	3e5.1
	心	恪	4k7.6
NETSU	氵	涅	3a7.8
		涅	3a7.8
	扌	捏	3c7.6
	火	熱	4d11.4
neya	門	閨	8e6.5
nē(ya)	女	姉	3e5.8
nezumi		鼠	0a13.1
		鼡	0a13.1
NI	二	二	0a2.1
		爾	0a14.3
	亻	仁	2a2.8
	儿	兒	4c3.3
	⺌	尔	0a14.3
	尸	尼	3r2.2
	日	児	4c3.3
	戈	弍	4n2.5
		貳	4n3.3
		貳	4n3.3
		弐	4n3.3
ni		丹	0a4.34
		丹	0a4.34
	艹	荷	3k7.10
	火	煮	4d8.9
		煮	4d8.9
nibu(i)	金	鈍	8a4.2
nibu(ru)	金	鈍	8a4.2
NICHI	日	日	4c0.1
nie	牛	牲	4g5.1
	貝	贄	7b11.3
	金	錵	8a7.9
ni(eru)	火	煮	4d8.9
		煮	4d8.9
niga(i)	艹	苦	3k5.24
niga(ru)	艹	苦	3k5.24
ni(gasu)	辶	迯	2q6.5
		逃	2q6.5
nige(gamu)	口	齝	3d17.5
ni(geru)	辶	迯	2q6.5
		逃	2q6.5
nigi(ri)	扌	握	3c9.17
nigi(ru)	扌	握	3c9.17
nigi(wau)	貝	賑	7b7.1
nigi(yaka)	貝	賑	7b7.1
nigo(ri)	氵	濁	3a13.8
nigo(ru)	氵	濁	3a13.8
nigo(su)	氵	濁	3a13.8
nii-	立	新	5b8.3
niji	虫	虹	6d3.1
	雨	霓	8d8.6
niji(mu)	氵	滲	3a11.17
niji(ru)	足	躙	7d16.1
		躙	7d16.1
nijū	廿	廿	0a4.36
(ni) ka(kete wa)			
	扌	掛	3c8.6
nikawa	月	膠	4b11.3
nikibi	又	皰	2h8.2
NIKU	亻	肉	2a4.20
niku(garu)	心	憎	4k11.7
		憎	4k11.7
niku(i)	心	憎	4k11.7
		憎	4k11.7
-niku(i)	心	惡	4k7.17
		悪	4k7.17
	隹	難	8c10.2
		難	8c10.2
niku(mu)	心	憎	4k11.7
		憎	4k11.7
niku(rashii)			
	心	憎	4k11.7
		憎	4k11.7
niku(shimi)			
	心	憎	4k11.7
		憎	4k11.7
NIN	儿	儿	0a2.2
		刃	0a3.22
		刄	0a3.22
	亻	人	2a0.1
		仁	2a2.8
		任	2a4.9
	女	妊	3e4.3
		姙	3e4.3
	艹	荵	3k7.15
	士	壬	3p1.1
	心	忍	4k3.3
		忍	4k3.3
	言	認	7a7.10
nina	虫	蜷	6d8.5
nina(u)	扌	担	3c5.20
		擔	3c5.20
nio	鳥	鳰	11b2.2
nio(i)	勹	匂	0a4.7
	日	臭	5c4.3
		臭	5c4.3
(ni) oi(te)	方	於	4h4.2
(ni) o(keru)	方	於	4h4.2
nio(u)	勹	匂	0a4.7
nira	⼀	韭	3k9.2
	艹	韮	3k9.2
	艹	薤	3k13.10
nira(gu)	氵	淬	3a8.32
	火	焠	4d8.3
nira(mu)	目	睨	5c8.5
nire	木	楡	4a9.26
nire(gamu)	口	齝	3d17.5
ni(ru)	亻	似	2a5.11
	火	煮	4d8.9
		煮	4d8.9
nise	亻	偽	2a9.2
		僞	2a9.2
	厂	贋	2p17.2
ni(seru)	亻	似	2a5.11
nishi		西	0a6.20
	虫	螺	6d11.3
nishiki	金	錦	8a8.6
nishin	魚	鯡	11a7.8
		鰊	11a8.2
		鰊	11a9.1

Reading	Rad	Kanji	Code
(ni) to(tte)	耳	取	6e2.2
(ni) tsu(ite)		就	3d9.21
(ni) tsu(rete)	辶	連	2q7.2
niwa	广	庭	3q6.3
niwaka	亻	俄	2a7.4
niwa(ka)	亻	俄	2a7.4
niwatori	鳥	鶏	11b8.4
		鶏	11b8.4
ni(yasu)	火	煮	4d8.9
		煮	4d8.9
no		之	0a2.9
		乃	0a2.10
		野	0a11.5
	辶	迺	2q6.10
		迺	2q6.10
	圡	埜	0a11.5
NŌ	亻	儂	2a13.3
	宀	嚢	3d19.3
	厂	農	2p11.1
	氵	濃	3a13.7
	口	嚢	3d19.3
	月	能	4b6.15
		脳	4b7.7
		脳	4b7.7
		膿	4b13.2
	日	嚢	4c17.1
	王	瑙	4f8.7
	忄	悩	4k7.11
		悩	4k7.11
	石	碯	4f8.7
	礻	衲	5e4.3
	糸	納	6a4.5
nō	口	喃	3d9.18
no(basu)	亻	伸	2a5.3
	辶	延	2q5.4
no(be)	辶	延	2q5.4
no(beru)	阝	陳	2d8.2
	辶	述	2q5.3
	辶	延	2q5.4
	宀	宣	3m6.2
no(biru)	亻	伸	2a5.3
	辶	延	2q5.4
no(biyaka)	亻	伸	2a5.3
nobori	巾	幟	3f12.1
nobo(ri)	上	上	2m1.1
nobo(ru)	上	上	2m1.1
	阝	登	3d9.26
	日	昇	4c4.5
nobo(seru)	上	上	2m1.1
nobo(su)	上	上	2m1.1
nochi	彳	後	3i6.5
nodo	口	咽	3d6.14
		喉	3d9.6
noga(reru)	辶	逃	2q6.5
		逃	2q6.5
no(gasu)	辶	逃	2q6.5
		逃	2q6.5
nogi	艹	芒	3k3.2
	禾	禾	5d0.1
no(keru)	阝	除	2d7.10
	辶	退	2q6.3
noki	木	檐	4a13.9
	車	軒	7c3.1
no(kkaru)		乗	0a9.19
		乗	0a9.19
noko	金	鋸	8a8.19
nokogiri	金	鋸	8a8.19
noko(ri)		残	0a10.11
	戈	残	0a10.11
noko(ru)		残	0a10.11
	戈	残	0a10.11
noko(su)		残	0a10.11
	戈	残	0a10.11
	辶	遺	2q12.4
no(ku)	辶	退	2q6.3
nomi	虫	蚤	6d4.7
	金	鑿	8a20.2
no(mu)	口	呑	3d4.19
	食	飲	8b4.1
		飲	8b4.1
nonoshi(ru)	罒	罵	5g10.1
nori	丷	典	2o6.5
	氵	法	3a5.20
	米	糊	6b9.2
	貝	則	7b2.1
noro	禾	黐	5d14.1
noro(i)	金	鈍	8a4.2
noroshi	火	烽	4d7.1
noro(u)	口	呪	3d5.11
		咒	3d5.11
	言	詛	7a5.4
no(ru)		乗	0a9.19
		乗	0a9.19
	車	載	7c6.5
no(seru)		乗	0a9.19
		乗	0a9.19
	車	載	7c6.5
noshi	火	熨	4d11.2
no(su)	亻	伸	2a5.3
	火	熨	4d11.2
notto(ru)	貝	則	7b2.1
nozo(ite)	阝	除	2d7.10
nozo(ku)	阝	除	2d7.10
	目	覗	5c7.3
nozo(mashii)			
	王	望	4f7.6
nozo(mu)	臣	臨	2t15.1
	王	望	4f7.6
NU	女	奴	3e2.2
nude	金	釖	8a13.3
		鐸	8a13.3
nue	鳥	鵺	11b8.5
nu(gasu)	月	脱	4b7.8
		脱	4b7.8
nu(geru)	月	脱	4b7.8
nu(gu)	月	脱	4b7.8
		脱	4b7.8
nugu(u)	扌	拭	3c6.17
nuka	米	糠	6b11.2
nu(karu)	扌	抜	3c4.10
		抜	3c4.10
nu(kasu)	扌	抜	3c4.10
		抜	3c4.10
nu(keru)	扌	抜	3c4.10
		抜	3c4.10
nuki	糸	緯	6a10.7
	貝	貫	7b4.3
-nu(ki)	扌	抜	3c4.10
		抜	3c4.10
nuki(nderu)	扌	擢	3c14.3
		擢	3c14.3
nu(ku)	扌	抜	3c4.10
		抜	3c4.10
		抽	3c5.7
nuku(i)	氵	温	3a9.21
		温	3a9.21
nuku(maru)	氵	温	3a9.21
		温	3a9.21
nuku(meru)	氵	温	3a9.21
		温	3a9.21
nuku(mi)	氵	温	3a9.21
		温	3a9.21
nukumo(ri)	氵	温	3a9.21
		温	3a9.21
numa	氵	沼	3a5.24
nume	糸	絖	6a6.4
nunawa	艹	蒓	3k5.15
nuno	巾	布	3f2.1
nu(rasu)	氵	濡	3a14.4
nu(reru)	氵	濡	3a14.4
nurite	金	釖	8a13.3
		鐸	8a13.3
nu(ru)	圡	塗	3b10.10
nusa	巾	幣	3f12.4
		幣	3f12.4
		幣	3f12.4
nushi	王	主	4f1.1
		主	4f1.1
nusu(mu)	亻	偸	2a9.13
	宀	窈	3m6.5
		竊	3m6.5
	皿	盗	5h6.2
		盗	5h6.2
nuta	氵	泏	3a3.1
	圡	垈	3b5.10
nu(u)		縒	0a12.1
	糸	縫	6a9.15
		縫	6a9.15
NYAKU	艹	若	3k5.12
		蒻	3k10.6
NYO	女	女	3e0.1
		如	3e3.1
NYŪ	辶	遶	2q12.2
	女	女	3e0.1
	尸	尿	3r4.1
	糸	繞	6a12.5
	金	鐃	8a12.9
NYŪ		入	0a2.3
	丷	乳	3n4.4
	木	柔	4a5.34

– O –

Reading	Rad	Kanji	Code
O	阝	阿	2d5.6
	氵	汚	3a3.5
		淤	3a8.9
	圡	塢	3b10.1
	口	唹	3d8.7
		嗚	3d10.1
	火	烏	4d6.5
	方	於	4h4.2
	禾	和	5d3.1
	食	飫	8b4.3
o	艹	苧	3k5.20
	尸	尾	3r4.2
	糸	緒	6a8.3
		緒	6a8.3
o-	彳	御	3i9.1
	丷	小	3n0.1
	牛	牡	4g3.1
		雄	8c4.1
Ō	尢	尢	0a3.21
		凹	0a5.14
		央	0a5.33
		殃	0a9.8
	宀	甕	2j16.1
	丷	瓮	2o7.7
		翁	2o8.6
		翁	2o8.6
	几	鳳	2s9.1
	匚	區	2t6.1
		毆	2t6.1
	氵	汪	3a4.3
		決	3a5.8

泓 3a5.19
澳 3a13.4
土 埦 3b8.7
墺 3b13.1
扌 押 3c5.5
拗 3c5.16
口 嘔 3d11.9
甌 3d13.12
嚶 3d17.1
女 姶 3e6.7
媼 3e10.5
嫗 3e11.6
彳 往 3i5.6
徃 3i5.6
艹 黄 3k8.16
黃 3k8.16
蓊 3k10.27
鞅 3k11.23
广 応 3q4.2
應 3q4.2
鷹 3q21.1
木 枉 4a4.2
桜 4a6.15
櫻 4a6.15
横 4a11.13
橫 4a11.13
日 旺 4c4.2
王 王 4f0.1
皇 4f5.9
欠 欧 4j4.2
歐 4j4.2
心 怏 4k5.2
懊 4k13.2
禾 秧 5d5.3
衤 襖 5e13.1
襖 5e13.1
米 奥 6b6.9
奧 6b6.9
言 謳 7a11.4
貝 罌 7b13.2
金 鏖 8a11.10
鳥 鴨 11b5.2
鴦 11b5.8
鶯 11b10.9
鶯 11b10.9
鴎 11b11.3
鷗 11b11.3
鸚 11b17.1
ō- 大 0a3.18
obashima 木 欄 4a16.4
欄 4a16.4
obi 巾 帯 3f7.1
帶 3f7.1
obi(eru) 心 怯 4k5.9
obi(ku) 言 誘 7a7.4
o(biru) 巾 帯 3f7.1
帶 3f7.1
obitada(shii) 夥 0a14.2
obiya(kasu) 刂 刦 2g5.2
刧 2g5.2
力 劫 2g5.2
脅 2g8.2
obo(eru) ⺍ 覚 3n9.3
目 覺 3n9.3
obo(ezu) ⺍ 覚 3n9.3
目 覺 3n9.3
obo(rasu) 氵 溺 3a10.1
溺 3a10.1
obo(reru) 氵 溺 3a10.1
溺 3a10.1
oboro 月 朧 4b16.1
obo(shii) ⺍ 覚 3n9.3
目 覺 3n9.3
o(busaru) ⺈ 負 2n7.1
o(buu) ⺈ 負 2n7.1
o(chi) 艹 落 3k9.13
ōchi 木 楝 4a9.1
樗 4a11.5
ochii(ru) 阝 陥 2d7.11
陷 2d7.11
o(chiru) 艹 落 3k9.13
oda(teru) 火 煽 4d10.4
煽 4d10.4
oda(yaka) 禾 穏 5d11.4
穩 5d11.4
odo(kasu) 力 脅 2g8.2
口 嚇 3d14.1
odo(ri) 足 踴 7d7.2
踊 7d7.2
odoriji ⺈ 々 2n1.1
odoro(kasu)
馬 驚 10a12.4
odoro(ku) 心 愕 4k9.4
馬 驚 10a12.4
odo(ru) 足 踴 7d7.2
踊 7d7.2
躍 7d14.2
odoshi 糸 縅 6a9.2
odo(su) 力 脅 2g8.2
口 嚇 3d14.1
戈 威 4n5.2
o(eru) 糸 終 6a5.9
oga(mu) 拜 3c5.3
扌 拝 3c5.3
ogi 艹 荻 3k7.8
蒹 3k10.1
ōgi 戸 扇 4m6.1
ogina(u) 衤 補 5e7.1
ōgo 木 朸 4a2.2
ogo(ru) 日 奢 4c8.17
馬 驕 10a12.2
ogoso(ka) 口 嚴 3n14.1
⺍ 厳 3n14.1
ohitsuji ⺍ 羝 2o9.7
oi 田 甥 5f7.5
竹 笈 6f3.1
o(i) 十 老 2k4.5
ō(i) 多 0a6.5
夛 0a6.5
日 覆 4c14.6
覆 4c14.6
衤 被 5e5.3
ō(inaru) 大 0a3.18
ō(i ni) 大 0a3.18
oi(raku) 十 老 2k4.5
o(iru) 十 老 2k4.5
ojika 广 麌 3q15.1
ōjika 广 麈 3q13.2
o(jikeru) 心 怖 4k5.6
o(jiru) 心 怖 4k5.6
oka 丘 0a5.12
阝 邱 2d5.9
陸 2d8.4
冂 岡 2r6.2
土 堽 2r6.2
(o)kage 阝 陰 2d8.7
ōkami 犭 狼 3g7.3
(o)kā(san) 母 0a5.36
oka(su) 亻 侵 2a7.15
犭 犯 3g2.1
日 冒 4c5.6
冐 4c5.6
oke 木 桶 4a7.18
okera 十 朮 2k3.3
oki 冫 冲 3a4.5
氵 沖 3a4.5
火 燠 4d13.2
-o(ki) 罒 置 5g8.8
ō(kii) 大 0a3.18
okina ⺍ 翁 2o8.6
翁 2o8.6
o(kiru) 土 起 3b7.11
okite 扌 掟 3c8.18
okona(u) 彳 行 3i3.1
okori 疒 瘧 5i9.2
oko(ru) ⺍ 興 2o14.2
心 怒 4k5.19
o(koru) 土 起 3b7.11
oko(su) ⺍ 興 2o14.2
火 熾 4d12.5
o(kosu) 土 起 3b7.11
okota(ru) 心 怠 4k5.21
惰 4k9.6
懈 4k13.1
懶 4k16.1
OKU 亻 億 2a13.6
億 2a13.6
尸 屋 3r6.3
木 檍 4a13.6
月 臆 4b13.3
心 憶 4k13.5
憶 4k13.5
oku 米 奥 6b6.9
奧 6b6.9
o(ku) 扌 措 3c8.20
擱 3c14.11
罒 置 5g8.8
okubi 口 噫 3d13.8
oku(maru) 米 奥 6b6.9
奧 6b6.9
okumi 衤 衽 5e4.4
袵 5e4.4
oku(rasu) 辶 遅 2q9.17
遲 2q9.17
oku(reru) 辶 遅 2q9.17
遲 2q9.17
彳 後 3i6.5
okurina 言 諡 7a9.18
謚 7a9.18
oku(ru) 辶 送 2q6.9
貝 贈 7b11.2
贈 7b11.2
(o)kyan 亻 俠 2a7.7
侠 2a7.7
(o)mai(ri) 彡 参 3j5.1
參 3j5.1
(o)ma(ke) ⺈ 負 2n7.1
(o)mawa(ri-san)
辶 巡 2q3.3
omi 匚 臣 2t4.3
omo 口 面 3s6.1
王 主 4f1.1
主 4f1.1
omo(i) 重 0a9.18
omokage 亻 俤 2a7.18
omo(mi) 重 0a9.18
omomuki 耳 趣 6e9.1
omomu(ku)
土 赴 3b6.14
omomu(ro) 彳 徐 3i7.2
omone(ru) 阝 阿 2d5.6
omo(njiru) 重 0a9.18
omonmi(ru)
心 惟 4k8.1
omonpaka(ri)
⺊ 慮 2m13.2

Reading	Rad.	Kanji	Code
omo(nzuru)		重	0a9.18
omori	釒	錘	8a8.2
omo(sa)		重	0a9.18
omo(tai)		重	0a9.18
omote		表	0a8.6
	口	面	3s6.1
omo(u)	亻	侖	2a6.25
	心	惟	4k8.1
		想	4k9.18
		憶	4k13.5
		憶	4k13.5
	田	思	5f4.4
ōmu(no)	木	概	4a10.2
		概	4a10.2
ON	阝	陰	2d8.7
		隠	2d11.3
		隠	2d11.3
	辶	遠	2q10.4
	氵	温	3a9.21
		温	3a9.21
	艹	薀	3k13.12
	心	怨	4k5.20
		恩	4k6.23
		慍	4k10.7
	立	音	5b4.3
	禾	穏	5d11.4
		穏	5d11.4
	衤	褞	5e10.1
	疒	瘟	5i10.4
	糸	縕	6a10.4
on-	彳	御	3i9.1
	牛	牡	4g3.1
	隹	雄	8c4.1
ōna	女	媼	3e10.5
ona(ji)	亻	仝	2r4.2
	冂	同	2r4.2
(o)naka	月	腹	4b9.4
onamomi	艹	葹	3k9.11
onara	尸	屁	3r4.3
o(nbu)	⺈	負	2n7.1
(o)nē(san)	女	姉	3e5.8
oni	田	鬼	5f5.6
(o)nii(san)	口	兄	3d2.9
onna	女	女	3e0.1
ono	斤	斧	2o6.4
onono(ku)	心	慄	4k10.5
	戈	戦	4n9.2
		戦	4n9.2
onoono	夂	各	4i3.3
onore		己	0a3.12
ono(zukara)			
	日	自	5c1.1
ono(zuto)	日	自	5c1.1
ore	亻	俺	2a8.25
o(reru)	扌	折	3c4.7
ori	氵	澱	3a13.2
	扌	折	3c4.7
	木	檻	4a15.4
o(ri)	糸	織	6a12.6
o(riru)	阝	降	2d7.7
		下	2m1.2
oro(ka)	心	愚	4k9.15
oro(kashii)		愚	4k9.15
oroshi	卩	卸	2e7.1
	虫	颪	6d6.14
oroso(ka)		疎	0a11.4
		疎	0a11.4
oro(su)	卩	卸	2e7.1
o(rosu)	阝	降	2d7.7
		下	2m1.2
o(ru)	扌	折	3c4.7
	糸	織	6a12.6
osa		長	0a8.2
	⺮	筬	6f6.3
o(sae)	扌	押	3c5.5
osa(eru)	扌	抑	3c4.12
o(saeru)	扌	押	3c5.5
osa(maru)	亻	修	2a8.11
	又	収	2h2.2
	氵	治	3a5.28
	攵	収	2h2.2
	糸	納	6a4.5
osa(meru)	亻	修	2a8.11
	又	収	2h2.2
	氵	治	3a5.28
	攵	収	2h2.2
	糸	納	6a4.5
osana(i)	力	幼	2g3.3
ōse	亻	仰	2a4.10
ō(seru)		果	0a8.8
oshi	口	唖	3d8.3
		啞	3d8.3
		暗	3d9.8
o(shi)	扌	押	3c5.5
oshi(e)	攵	教	4i6.1
		教	4i6.1
oshi(eru)	攵	教	4i6.1
		教	4i6.1
o(shii)	心	惜	4k8.11
o(shimu)		惜	4k8.11
o(shite)	扌	押	3c5.5
oso(i)	辶	遅	2q9.17
		遅	2q9.17
oso(raku)	心	恐	4k6.19
		恐	4k6.19
osore	虍	虞	2m11.1
		虞	2m11.1
oso(re)	心	恐	4k6.19
		恐	4k6.19
oso(reru)	心	慌	4k5.5
		怖	4k5.6
		恐	4k6.19
		恐	4k6.19
		惧	4k8.3
		懼	4k8.3
	田	畏	5f4.5
		畏	5f4.5
oso(roshii)	心	恐	4k6.19
		恐	4k6.19
oso(u)	衤	襲	5e16.2
oso(waru)	攵	教	4i6.1
		教	4i6.1
os(sharu)	亻	仰	2a4.10
osu	牛	牡	4g3.1
	隹	雄	8c4.1
o(su)	厂	圧	2p3.1
		壓	2p3.1
	扌	押	3c5.5
		推	3c8.1
		捘	3c8.17
(o)taka(ku)	亠	高	2j8.6
		高	2j8.6
oto	立	音	5b4.3
otogai	頁	頤	9a6.3
otoko	田	男	5f2.2
otori	口	囮	3s4.4
ōtori	月	鵬	4b15.1
otoro(eru)	亠	衰	2j8.1
oto(ru)		劣	3n3.4
(o)tō(san)		父	2o2.3
o(toshi)		落	3k9.13
otoshii(reru)			
	阝	陥	2d7.11
		陥	2d7.11
otoshi(meru)			
	貝	貶	7b3.2
o(tosu)		落	3k9.13
otōto		弟	2o5.1
otozu(reru)	言	訪	7a4.1
OTSU		乙	0a1.5
	木	榲	4a10.14
	月	膃	4b10.4
o(tte)	辶	追	2q6.4
otto		夫	0a4.31
o(u)		生	0a5.29
	⺈	負	2n7.1
	辶	追	2q6.4
		逐	2q7.6
ō(u)	艹	蔽	3k12.1
		蔽	3k12.1
	日	覆	4c14.6
		覆	4c14.6
	衤	被	5e5.3
o(wari)	糸	終	6a5.9
o(waru)	糸	終	6a5.9
o(waseru)		負	2n7.1
oya		親	5b11.1
ōyake		公	2o2.2
		公	2o2.2
oyo(bi)		及	0a3.24
oyo(bosu)		及	0a3.24
oyo(bu)		及	0a3.24
oyo(gu)	氵	泳	3a5.14
		泗	3a5.31
		游	3a8.10
oyo(so)	几	凡	2s1.1

– P –

Reading	Rad.	Kanji	Code
pai	宀	牌	2j10.3
		牌	2j10.3
pēji	頁	頁	9a0.1
PON	木	椪	4a8.33
pondo	口	听	3d4.7
	石	磅	5a10.4

– R –

Reading	Rad.	Kanji	Code
RA	辶	邏	2q19.1
	扌	拉	3c5.2
	口	喇	3d9.3
	艹	蓏	3k12.3
		蘿	3k19.1
	衤	裸	5e8.1
	罒	羅	5g14.1
	虫	螺	6d11.3
	釒	鑼	8a19.1
	馬	騾	10a11.3
-ra	⺾	等	6f6.9
RACHI	土	埒	3b7.4
		埓	3b7.4
RAI	禾	耒	0a6.21
		耒	0a7.6
		来	0a7.6
	亻	來	0a7.6
		儡	2a15.3
	彳	徠	0a7.6
	艹	莱	3k8.3
		萊	3k8.3
		蕾	3k13.18
		藾	3k16.5
	广	麗	3q16.5
	木	檑	4a15.6
	礻	礼	4e1.1
		禮	4e1.1
	心	懶	4k16.1
	石	磊	5a10.8
	田	畾	5f16.1

Reading	Kanji	Code	Reading	Kanji	Code	Reading	Kanji	Code	Reading	Kanji	Code
	癩	5i16.1		捋	3c7.9		驪	10a19.1	renji	檋	4a17.2
	籟	6f16.2		喇	3d9.3		鱧	11a13.3	RETSU	列	2b6.1
	賚	7b8.5		辣	5b9.6		鴒	11b5.6		列	2f4.4
	頼	9a7.1	REI	令	2a3.9	REKI	暦	2p12.3		洌	3a6.8
	雷	8d5.1		伶	2a5.17		曆	2p12.3		捩	3c8.31
	賴	9a7.1		例	2a6.7		歴	2p12.4		捩	3c8.31
RAKU	洛	3a6.13		儷	2a19.2		歷	2p12.4		劣	3n3.4
	落	3k9.13		齢	6b11.5		瀝	3a16.9		烈	4d6.3
	楽	4a9.29		冷	2b5.3		鬲	3d7.17		裂	5e6.7
	樂	4a9.29		勵	2g5.4		櫟	4a15.3	RI	吏	0a6.22
	烙	4d6.1		励	2g5.4		櫟	4a15.3		吏	0a6.22
	珞	4f6.5		羚	2o9.8		櫪	4a16.3		里	0a7.9
	犖	4g10.2		厲	2p12.5		礫	5a15.1		俚	2a7.6
	絡	6a6.6		邐	2q15.1		癧	5i16.4		俐	4k7.2
	酪	7e6.4		黎	3a10.29		蜥	6d5.4		裏	2j11.2
	駱	10a6.2		澪	3a13.6		轢	7c15.1		离	8c10.3
RAN	儖	2a15.2		捩	3c8.31		轣	7c16.2		浬	3a7.3
	卵	2e5.2		捩	3c8.31		靂	8d16.2		漓	3a10.22
	濫	3a15.3		唳	3d8.15	REN	恋	2j8.2		哩	3d7.5
	瀾	3a17.4		唳	3d8.15		連	2q7.2		貍	3g7.2
	攬	3c22.1		苓	3k5.22		蓮	3k10.31		狸	3g7.2
	乱	3d4.21		荔	3k6.21		匲	2t13.1		莉	3k7.5
	嫐	3e8.10		藜	3k15.6		漣	3a10.27		莅	3k7.9
	孄	3e16.1		嶺	3o14.2		漣	3a10.27		履	3r12.1
	藍	3k15.5		麗	3q16.5		濂	3a13.11		李	4a2.7
	蘭	3k16.9		囹	3s5.3		激	3a17.1		梨	4a7.24
	蘭	3k16.9		櫺	4a17.2		攣	3c19.3		理	4f7.1
	亂	3d4.21		礼	4e1.1		奩	2t13.1		璃	4f10.5
	嵐	3o9.4		禮	4e1.1		嗹	3d10.12		犂	4g8.2
	欒	3o19.1		隷	4e11.1		蓮	3k10.31		犁	4g8.2
	欄	4a16.4		隸	4e11.1		蓮	3k10.31		犛	4g11.2
	欄	4a16.4		玲	4f5.7		斂	3k17.1		氂	4i14.2
	欒	4a19.1		犁	4g8.2		廉	3q10.1		悧	4k7.2
	欖	4a22.1		犂	4g8.2		楝	4a9.1		利	5d2.1
	燗	4d12.8		怜	4k5.10		煉	4d9.2		裡	2j11.2
	燗	4d12.8		戻	4m3.1		煉	4d9.2		罹	5g7.1
	爛	4d17.1		戾	4m3.1		斂	4i13.1		羅	5g11.1
	懶	4k16.1		砺	5a14.1		戀	2j8.2		痢	5i7.2
	覧	5c12.7		礪	5a14.1		憐	4k13.4		蜊	6d7.3
	覽	5c12.7		癘	5i12.5		練	6a8.2		籬	6f18.1
	矕	5c19.1		綟	6a8.21		練	6a8.2		離	8c10.3
	襤	5e15.2		綟	6a8.21		縺	6a10.12		驪	10a19.1
	襴	5e17.2		齢	6b11.5		聯	6e11.2		鯉	11a7.2
	纜	5e15.2		櫺	6b14.2		聯	6e11.2	RICHI	律	3i6.1
	纜	6a22.1		蛉	6d5.8		簾	6f13.8	RIKI	力	2g0.1
	籃	6f15.2		蛎	6d14.3		臁	7a18.1		簗	6f10.4
	蘭	7a18.1		蠣	6d14.3		賺	7b10.1	riki(mu)	力	2g0.1
	酣	7e8.1		蠡	6d15.3		輦	7c8.6	RIKU	陸	2d8.4
	鑾	8a19.2		聆	6e5.2		錬	8a8.3		勠	2g11.3
	闌	8e9.1		醴	7e13.2		錬	8a8.3		六	2j2.2
	鸞	11b19.1		鈴	8a5.11		鎌	8a10.8		淕	3a8.12
RATSU	剌	2f7.1		零	8d5.4		鎌	8a10.8		蓼	3k11.10
	溂	3a9.5		靈	8d7.2		鏈	8a10.10		戮	4n11.3
	拉	3c5.2		靈	8d7.2		鰊	11a9.1	RIN	倫	2a6.25

倫 2a8.28	臚 4b16.4	臘 4b15.3	畄 5f5.4
凜 2b13.1	髏 4b17.1	朧 4b16.1	瘻 5i11.1
凛 2b13.1	炉 4d4.2	弄 4f3.2	縷 6a11.3
鄰 2d13.1	爐 4d4.2	瑯 4f9.1	簍 6f11.4
隣 2d13.1	絽 6a7.4	琅 4f9.1	鏤 8a11.4
吝 2j5.2	艪 6c15.1	瓏 4f16.1	鰡 11a10.6
稟 2j11.3	艫 6c16.1	褸 5e11.2	羸 2j17.1
凛 2j11.3	舮 6c16.1	癆 5i11.1 **RUI**	涙 3a7.21
厘 2p7.1	賂 7b6.2	癆 5i12.1	涙 3a7.21
臨 2t15.1	輅 7c6.1	糧 6b12.1	泪 3a7.21
淋 3a8.6	轤 7c16.1	粮 6b12.1	檑 4a11.11
淪 3a8.28	路 7d6.5	蜋 6d9.1	累 5f6.5
蒜 3k8.8	鑪 8a16.1	螻 6d11.1	塁 5f7.2
藺 3k16.10	鈩 8a16.1	蠟 6d15.1	壘 5f7.2
廩 3q13.4	露 8d13.1	蜡 6d15.1	瘰 5i11.4
林 4a4.1	顱 9a16.1	聾 6e16.1	縲 6a11.6
檎 4a8.30	驢 10a16.2	簍 6f11.4	誄 7a6.1
燐 4d13.4	魯 11a4.3	篭 6f16.1	類 9a9.1
琳 4f8.2	鱸 11a16.1	籠 6f16.1	類 9a9.1
恪 4k7.6	鷺 11b13.2	踉 7d7.3 **RYAKU**	曆 2p12.3
懍 4k13.8 **RŌ**	僂 2a11.5	醪 7e11.1	暦 2p12.3
罧 5g8.3	陋 2d6.4	鑞 8a15.4	掠 3c8.28
痳 5i8.2	郎 2d6.5	露 8d13.1	擽 3c15.2
綸 6a8.18	郎 2d6.5 **ROKU**	陸 2d8.4	略 5f6.4
麟 6b18.1	隴 2d16.1	勒 2g9.2	畧 5f6.4
輪 7c8.4	勞 3n4.3	六 2j2.2 **RYO**	侶 2a7.13
躙 7d16.1	老 2k4.5	溚 3a8.12	虜 2m11.2
躪 7d16.1	浪 3a7.5	漉 3a11.20	虜 2m11.2
酩 7e8.1	漏 3a11.19	鹿 3q8.5	慮 2m13.2
鈴 8a5.11	潦 3a12.16	麓 4a15.9	呂 3d4.16
霖 8d8.2	壟 3b16.2	肋 4b2.1	梠 4a7.12
鱗 11a13.2	挊 3c7.8	禄 4e8.2	膂 4b10.8
RITSU	撈 3c12.5	祿 4e8.2	旅 4h6.4
率 2j9.1	咾 3d6.4	碌 5a8.8	鑢 8a15.5
律 3i6.1	哰 3d7.6	綠 6a8.15	閭 8e7.1
葎 3k9.14	婁 3e8.8	緑 6a8.15 **RYŌ**	兩 0a6.11
栗 4a6.32	狼 3g7.3	簏 6f13.3	両 0a6.11
慄 4k10.5	莨 3k7.4	轆 7c11.2	艮 0a7.3
立 5b0.1	蒗 3k13.5	録 8a8.16	良 0a7.3
rittoru	蘢 3k16.2	錄 8a8.16	令 2a3.9
立 5b0.1	牢 3m4.2 **RON**	侖 2a6.25	倆 2a8.3
RO	労 3n4.3	崙 3o8.10	僚 2a12.4
侶 2a7.13	廊 3q8.4	崘 3o8.10	凌 2b8.5
園 2m9.2	廊 3q8.4	論 7a8.13	涼 3a8.31
盧 2m14.1	柆 4a5.2 **RU**	僂 2a11.5	了 2c0.3
潴 3a11.16	榔 4a9.5	流 3a7.10	陵 2d8.5
濾 3a15.8	榔 4a9.5	婁 3e8.8	亮 2j7.6
沪 3a15.8	楼 4a9.10	屢 3r11.1	遼 2q12.5
滤 3a15.8	樓 4a9.10	屡 3r11.1	遼 2q12.5
瀘 3a16.8	槞 4a10.8	琉 4f7.5	涼 3a8.31
呂 3d4.16	朗 4b6.11	瑠 4f10.3	漁 3a11.1
蘆 3k4.3	朗 4b6.11	璢 4f10.3	撩 3c12.12
芦 3k4.3	朖 4b6.11	褸 5e11.2	喨 3d9.17
蕗 3k13.4	臘 4b15.3	留 5f5.4	猟 3g8.6
廬 3q16.3			
櫓 4a15.2			
櫚 4a15.8			

Reading	Rad	Kanji	Code
	戈	哉	4n5.4
		栽	4n6.1
		歳	4n9.5
	石	砌	5a4.4
		砕	5a4.6
		碎	5a4.6
		砦	5a6.1
	目	皆	5c6.7
		眦	5c6.7
	禾	裁	5e6.9
	糸	細	6a5.1
		綵	6a8.9
		縡	6a10.6
		纔	6a17.2
	貝	財	7b3.1
		賍	7b3.1
	車	載	7c6.5
	釒	釵	8a3.3
	頁	顋	9a9.4
	魚	鰓	11a9.7
sai	月	骱	4b10.10
saina(mu)		苛	3k5.30
saiwa(i)	士	幸	3b5.9
saji		匕	0a2.14
		匕	0a2.14
		匙	4c7.13
saka	阝	阪	2d4.4
	士	坂	3b4.7
saka-	辶	逆	2q6.8
	氵	酒	3a7.1
saka(eru)		栄	3n6.1
	禾	榮	3n6.1
sakai	土	堺	3b9.5
		境	3b11.1
sakaki	木	榊	4a10.3
		榊	4a10.3
saka(n)	冫	壮	2b4.2
	皿	盛	5h6.1
		壯	2b4.2
sakana	月	肴	4b4.12
	魚	魚	11a0.1
sakanobo(ru)			
	辶	遡	3a10.2
		遡	3a10.2
	氵	泝	3a5.11
		溯	3a10.2
sakara(u)	忄	忤	4k4.5
saka(rau)	辶	逆	2q6.8
saka(ru)	皿	盛	5h6.1
saka(shii)	貝	賢	7b9.2
saka(shira)	貝	賢	7b9.2
sakazuki	木	杯	4a4.11
	皿	盃	4a4.11
sake	氵	酒	3a7.1
	魚	鮭	11a6.3
sake(bu)	口	叫	3d3.4
		叫	3d3.4
		叫	3d3.4
		吅	3d3.4
sa(keru)	辶	避	2q13.3
	衤	裂	5e6.7
saki	土	先	3b3.7
		埼	3b8.8
		嚮	3d15.4
	山	崎	3o8.3
		嵜	3o8.3
		曩	4c17.1
sakigake	甲	魁	5f9,1
sako	辶	迮	2q7.17
SAKU		冊	0a5.42
		冊	0a5.42
		冊	0a5.42
		册	0a5.42
	亻	作	2a5.10
	刂	削	2f7.4
		削	2f7.4
	十	索	2k8.2
	扌	搾	3c10.9
	口	咋	3d5.7
		噴	3d11.6
	艹	蒴	3k10.2
	宀	窄	3m7.11
	木	柵	4a5.4
		柵	4a5.4
		柞	4a5.13
		槊	4a10.31
	月	朔	4b6.12
	日	昨	4c5.3
	火	炸	4d5.3
	竹	筰	6f5.2
		策	6f6.2
		筴	6f7.1
		笮	6f7.4
		簀	6f11.7
	阝	醋	7d15.3
	酉	醋	7e5.3
		酢	7e5.3
		醋	7e8.2
	釒	鋜	8a7.1
		錯	8a8.10
		鑠	8a10.7
		鑿	8a20.2
sa(ku)	刂	割	2f10.1
		劈	2f13.3
	口	咲	3d6.12
	衤	裂	5e6.7
sakura	木	桜	4a6.15
		櫻	4a6.15
sama	木	様	4a10.25
		様	4a10.25
-sama	木	様	4a10.25
		様	4a10.25
sa(masu)	冫	冷	2b5.3
		覚	3n9.3
	目	覚	3n9.3
	酉	醒	7e9.2
samata(geru)			
	女	妨	3e4.1
same	魚	鮫	11a6.5
sa(meru)	冫	冷	2b5.3
		覚	3n9.3
	目	覺	3n9.3
	衤	褪	5e9.5
	酉	醒	7e9.2
samu(i)	宀	寒	3m9.3
		寒	3m9.3
samurai	亻	侍	2a6.11
SAN		三	0a3.1
	亻	傘	2a10.7
	刂	删	2f5.1
	亠	産	5b6.4
	氵	汕	3a3.3
		潸	3a12.7
	扌	撒	3c12.2
		攢	3c19.2
		攢	3c19.2
	彡	彡	3j0.1
		参	3j5.1
		參	3j5.1
	艹	芟	3k4.11
		蒜	3k10.5
	宀	竄	3m15.1
	山	山	3o0.1
		嶄	3o11.3
	木	桟	4a6.1
		棧	4a6.1
	火	燦	4d13.3
		爨	4d26.1
	王	珊	4f5.1
	攵	散	4i8.1
	忄	惨	4k8.5
		惨	4k8.5
		懺	4k17.1
		懺	4k17.1
	戈	弍	4n3.4
	立	産	5b6.4
	禾	穇	5d11.2
	衤	衫	5e3.1
	糸	繖	6a12.1
		纘	6a15.3
		粲	6b7.3
		糝	6b11.7
	虫	蠶	6d4.8
		蚕	6d4.8
		算	6f8.7
		纂	6f10.6
		纂	6f10.6
		纂	6f14.4
	言	讃	7a15.1
		讚	7a15.1
	貝	贊	7b8.6
		賛	7b8.6
	阝	跚	7d5.2
	酉	酸	7e7.2
	釒	鏨	8a11.9
		鑽	8a15.3
		鑽	8a15.3
	飠	餐	8b7.4
	雨	霰	8d12.1
	門	閂	8e1.1
	馬	驂	10a11.2
sanaga(ra)	宀	宛	3m5.9
sanagi	虫	蛹	6d7.9
sanaki	釒	釸	8a13.3
		鐸	8a13.3
sane	宀	実	3m5.4
	木	核	4a6.22
		核	4a6.22
sao	木	棹	4a8.38
		竿	6f3.3
sara		更	0a7.12
		更	0a7.12
	皿	皿	5h0.1
sara(naru)		更	0a7.12
		更	0a7.12
sara (ni)		更	0a7.12
		更	0a7.12
sara(shi)	日	晒	4c6.1
		曬	4c6.1
sara(su)	日	晒	4c6.1
		曬	4c6.1
		曝	4c15.1
sara(u)	氵	浚	3a7.11
		潃	3a14.7
	扌	攫	3c20.2
sa(redo)	火	然	4d8.10
sa(ri to wa)			
	火	然	4d8.10
saru		申	0a5.39
	犭	猿	3g10.3
sa(ru)	土	去	3b2.10
	火	然	4d8.10
sasa	竹	笹	6f5.3
sasa(eru)	十	支	2k2.1
sasa(geru)	扌	捧	3c8.12
	犭	献	3g9.6
		獻	3g9.6

Reading		Kanji	Code
sasara	⺮	籭	6f11.1
sa(saru)	刂	刺	2f6.2
sasa(yaka)	糸	細	6a5.1
sasaya(ku)	口	囁	3d18.5
	耳	囁	6e12.2
sa(shi)-	丷	差	2o8.4
sa(shi de)	丷	差	2o8.4
sashigane	匚	矩	2t7.1
sashihasa(mu)	扌	挟	3c6.1
		挾	3c6.1
sashimane(ku)	广	麾	3q12.7
sasori	虫	蝎	6d9.10
		蠍	6d9.10
saso(u)	口	唆	3d6.2
	言	誘	7a7.4
sa(su)		射	0a10.8
	刂	刺	2f6.2
	丷	差	2o8.4
	氵	注	3a5.16
	氵	注	3a5.16
	扌	指	3c6.15
	扌	挿	3c7.2
	扌	插	3c7.2
	虫	螫	6d11.7
sasuga	辶	遉	2q9.12
sasu(ru)	广	摩	3q12.6
	厂	摩	3q12.6
sate	亻	偖	2a9.3
	扌	拟	3c3.4
		拟	3c3.6
sato		里	0a7.9
sato(i)	耳	聡	6e8.2
		聰	6e8.2
sato(ri)	忄	悟	4k7.5
sato(ru)		覚	3n9.3
	忄	悟	4k7.5
	目	覺	3n9.3
sato(su)	言	諭	7a9.13
		諭	7a9.13
SATSU		冊	0a5.42
		冊	0a5.42
		册	0a5.42
		册	0a5.42
	刂	利	2f6.8
		刷	2f6.9
	扌	扎	3c1.1
		拶	3c6.13
		撒	3c12.2
		撮	3c12.13
		擦	3c14.5
	⺾	薩	3k13.14
		薩	3k13.14
	宀	察	3m11.6
	木	札	4a1.1
		殺	4a6.35
		殺	4a6.35
	立	颯	5b9.4
	糸	絷	6a5.17
	⺮	箚	6f8.1
sat(to)	立	颯	5b9.4
sawa	氵	沢	3a4.18
		澤	3a4.18
sawa(gu)	言	譟	7a13.2
	馬	騒	10a8.5
		騷	10a8.5
sawara	木	椹	4a9.4
	魚	鰆	11a9.8
sawa(ru)	阝	障	2d11.2
	虫	触	6d7.10
		觸	6d7.10
sawa(yaka)		爽	0a11.7
saya	⺾	莢	3k7.3
	月	鞘	4b12.8
		鞘	4b12.8
sazanami	氵	漣	3a10.27
		漣	3a10.27
sazo	口	嘸	3d12.4
sazu(karu)	扌	授	3c8.15
sazu(keru)	扌	授	3c8.15
SE		世	0a5.37
		世	0a5.37
	力	勢	2g11.6
	⺾	卋	0a5.37
		卋	0a5.37
	方	施	4h5.1
se	氵	瀬	3a16.3
		瀬	3a16.3
	月	背	4b5.15
		脊	4b6.13
	⺗	歃	5f5.5
		歃	5f5.5
seba(maru)	犭	狭	3g6.2
		狹	3g6.2
seba(meru)	犭	狭	3g6.2
		狹	3g6.2
SECHI	糸	繰	6a9.6
	⺮	節	6f7.3
		節	6f7.3
segare	亻	倅	2a8.29
		倅	2a8.29
	忄	悴	4k8.12
		悴	4k8.12
segukuma(ru)			
		蹐	7d7.4
SEI		井	0a4.46
		生	0a5.29
		世	0a5.37
		世	0a5.37
		西	0a6.20
	亻	倩	2a8.20
		儕	2a14.4
	氵	凄	2b8.4
	刂	制	2f6.1
	力	勢	2g11.6
		斉	2j6.5
		齊	2j6.5
		齋	2j19.1
		齎	2j21.1
		齏	2j21.1
	⺾	丗	0a5.37
		卋	0a5.37
		正	2m3.3
	辶	逝	2q7.8
		逝	2q7.8
	門	靑	4b4.10
	氵	凄	2b8.4
		清	3a8.18
		清	3a8.18
		済	3a8.30
		濟	3a8.30
		瀞	3a16.2
		瀞	3a16.2
	土	堺	3e9.3
	扌	掣	3c8.37
		撕	3c12.4
		擥	3c14.4
		擠	3c14.9
	口	嘶	3d12.1
	女	姓	3e5.3
		婿	3e9.3
	弓	彁	3h10.1
	彳	征	3i5.3
	⺾	萋	3k8.19
		菁	3k8.24
		薺	3k14.5
	宀	窄	3m6.6
		静	4b10.9
		青	3p4.4
	口	圊	3s8.1
	木	栖	4a6.2
		柹	4a6.23
		棲	4a8.16
	月	靑	4b4.10
		腥	4b9.7
		静	4b10.9
		臍	4b14.2
		臍	4b14.2
	日	星	4c5.7
		晟	4c7.5
		晴	4c8.2
		晴	4c8.2
	王	聖	4f9.9
	牛	牲	4g5.1
	方	旌	4h7.1
	攵	政	4i5.1
		整	4i12.3
	忄	性	4k5.4
		懐	4k8.6
		情	4k8.9
		情	4k8.9
		惺	4k9.8
	戈	成	4n2.1
		歳	4n9.5
	石	砌	5a4.4
	立	靖	5b8.1
		靖	5b8.1
	目	省	5c4.7
		睛	5c8.7
	衤	製	5e8.9
	田	甥	5f7.5
	皿	盛	5h6.1
	米	精	6b8.1
		精	6b8.1
	虫	蜻	6d8.7
	耳	聟	3e9.3
		聲	3p4.4
		聖	4f9.9
	⺮	筬	6f6.3
	言	誠	7a6.3
		誓	7a7.17
		請	7a8.8
		請	7a8.8
	貝	貰	7b5.5
	足	躋	7d14.4
	酉	醒	7e9.2
	金	鉦	8a5.7
	雨	霽	8d14.2
	魚	鯖	11a8.6
		鯖	11a8.6
sei	月	背	4b5.15
SEKI	夕	夕	0a3.14
		斥	0a5.18
	力	勣	2g11.4
	辶	迹	2q6.6
	氵	汐	3a3.9
		淅	3a8.7
		潟	3a12.9
	土	赤	3b4.10
	口	齣	3d17.6
	女	媳	3e10.3
		昔	3k5.28
		蓆	3k10.29
		藉	3k14.2
	宀	寂	3m8.2

	疒 疵 5i6.3	shibatata(ku)			虍 虐 2m7.3		⺈ 0a2.12
	痞 5i7.6		日 瞬 5c13.1	shijimi	虫 蜆 6d7.4	shime(ppoi)	
	糸 糸 6a0.1	shibe ⺾ 蘂 3k12.14	瞬 5c13.1	shijū	皿 卌 0a5.41		氵 湿 3a9.22
	絲 6a0.1	蕋 3k12.14	shika	广 鹿 3q8.5		濕 3a9.22
	紙 6a4.4	蕋 3k12.14		火 然 4d8.10	shime(ru) 氵 湿 3a9.22
	絶 6a5.14	蕊 3k12.14	shikabane 尸 尸 3r0.1		濕 3a9.22
	紫 6a6.15	榮 3k12.14		屍 3r6.2	shi(meru) 卜 占 2m3.2
	緇 6a8.17	shibi 魚 鮨 11a6.1	shika(meru)	糸 絞 6a6.9
	縒 6a10.10	shibi(reru) 疒 痹 5i8.4		頁 顰 9a15.1	締 6a9.11
米 粢 6b6.7		痹 5i8.4	shika(mo) 冂 而 2r4.3	門 閂 8e3.3
	齒 6b6.11	shibo(mu) 氵 凋 2b8.6	shika(raba) 火 然 4d8.10	閉 8e3.3
虫 蟖 6d4.9		凋 2b8.6	shika(redomo)	shime(shi) ⺬ 示 4e0.1
	蟖 6d12.1	⺾ 萎 3k8.18		火 然 4d8.10	shime(su) 氵 湿 3a9.22
⺮ 笑 6f5.8		shibo(ri) 糸 絞 6a6.9	shika(ri)	火 然 4d8.10		濕 3a9.22
	筒 6f5.15	shibo(ru) 扌 搾 3c10.9	shika(ru) 口 叱 3d2.2	⺬ 示 4e0.1
	篩 6f10.2	糸 絞 6a6.9		呵 3d5.13	shime(te) ⺈ 0a2.12
言 詞 7a5.15		shibu 氵 渋 3a8.19		火 然 4d8.10	⺈ 0a2.12
	詩 7a6.5	澁 3a8.19	shika(rubeki)	shime(yaka)
	試 7a6.18	澀 3a8.19		火 然 4d8.10	
	誌 7a7.8	shibu(i) 氵 渋 3a8.19	shika(ru ni) 火 然 4d8.10	氵 湿 3a9.22
	諮 7a9.4	澁 3a8.19	shika(shi) 火 然 4d8.10	濕 3a9.22
	諡 7a9.18	澀 3a8.19	shika(shite)	shi(mi) 木 染 4a5.35
	諡 7a9.18	shibu(ru) 氵 渋 3a8.19	冂 而 2r4.3	shi(miru) 氵 凍 2b8.2
貝 貲 7b6.5		澁 3a8.19	shikato 耳 聢 6e8.1	氵 滲 3a11.17
	資 7b6.7	澀 3a8.19	shika (to) 石 確 5a10.3	木 染 4a5.35
	賜 7b8.2	SHICHI 七 0a2.13	shi(kazu) 女 如 3e3.1	shimo 卜 下 2m1.2
	贄 7b11.3	貝 質 7b8.7	SHIKI ⺈ 色 2n4.1	⺷ 霜 8d9.2
車 輜 7c8.3		賈 7b8.7	戈 式 4n3.2	shimobe イ 僕 2a12.1
卩 趾 7d4.1		shide 木 椣 4a8.13	糸 織 6a12.6	SHIN 申 0a5.39
金 鉇 8a3.2		shigarami 木 栅 4a5.4	言 識 7a12.6	身 0a7.5
	鎺 8a8.15	栅 4a5.4	shikigawara 瓦 甋 0a16.1	斟 0a13.5
食 飼 8b5.4		⺮ 箍 6f5.2	shikimi 木 樒 4a7.4	イ 伸 2a5.3
隹 雌 8c6.1		shige(ku) 糸 繁 6a10.13	梱 4a7.23	信 2a7.1
馬 駛 10a5.1		繁 6a10.13	橂 4a11.16	侵 2a7.15
	駟 10a5.6	shige(mi) 糸 繁 6a10.13	橂 4a11.16	齔 2a15.6
魚 鰤 11a4.2		繁 6a10.13	shiki(ri) 頁 頻 9a8.2	⺾ 真 2k8.1
	鮨 11a6.8	shige(ru) ⺾ 茂 3k5.7	頻 9a8.2	眞 2k8.1
	鯔 11a8.7	木 栬 3k5.7	shikoro 金 錏 8a8.5	厂 辰 2p5.1
	鰤 11a10.1	糸 繁 6a10.13	錣 8a8.9	辶 進 2q8.1
鳥 鴬 11b5.4		shigi 罒 鴫 5f11.1	shiko(ru) 氵 凝 2b14.1	臣 2t4.3
	鴎 11b5.4	鳥 鷸 11b12.4	shi(ku) 女 如 3e3.1	氵 沁 3a4.4
	鷙 11b11.4	shigo(ki) 扌 扱 3c3.5	⺾ 若 3k5.12	津 3a6.1
shiawa(se) イ 倖 2a8.23		扱 3c3.5	攵 敷 4i11.1	浸 3a7.17
土 幸 3b5.9		shigo(ku) 扌 扱 3c3.5	金 鋪 8a7.3	清 3a8.18
shiba ⺾ 芝 3k2.1		扱 3c3.5	shima 氵 洲 3a6.10	清 3a8.18
木 柴 4a6.33		shiguma 罒 羆 5g14.2	屮 島 3o7.9	深 3a8.21
shibara(ku) 日 暫 4c11.3		SHII 木 弒 4a8.41	嶋 3o7.9	潯 3a10.10
shiba(ru) 糸 縛 6a10.3		shii 木 椎 4a8.1	嵩 3o7.9	滲 3a11.17
	縛 6a10.3	shiina 耒 秕 5d4.4	糸 縞 6a10.9	瀋 3a15.5
shibashiba		米 粃 6b4.3	shi(maru) 糸 絞 6a6.9	扌 抻 3c5.6
尸 屢 3r11.1		shi(iru) 弓 強 3h8.3	締 6a9.11	振 3c7.14
	屢 3r11.1	言 誣 7a7.1	門 閂 8e3.3	揤 3c10.7
shibata(ku) 日 瞬 5c13.1		shiita(geru) 虍 虐 2m7.3	閉 8e3.3	口 呻 3d5.2
	瞬 5c13.1		shime ⺈ 0a2.12	哂 3d6.1
					唇 3d7.12

Reading	Radical	Kanji	Code
		嗔	3d10.11
	女	娠	3e7.10
	艹	芯	3k4.2
		蓁	3k10.17
		蔘	3k11.18
		薪	3k13.3
	宀	宸	3m7.13
		寝	3m10.1
		寢	3m10.1
		審	3m12.1
	山	岑	3o4.3
	木	森	4a8.39
		榛	4a10.11
		槇	4a10.27
		槙	4a10.27
	月	脣	3d7.12
	日	晋	4c6.8
		晉	4c6.8
		晨	4c7.7
	ネ	神	4e5.1
		神	4e5.1
	忄	心	4k0.1
		忱	4k4.3
		怎	4k5.18
		慎	4k10.4
		愼	4k10.4
	立	辛	5b2.2
		新	5b8.3
		親	5b11.1
	目	瞋	5c10.2
	禾	秦	5d5.10
		穆	5d11.2
		臻	5d11.6
	ネ	袗	5e5.8
		襯	5e16.1
	田	畛	5f5.2
	疒	疹	5i5.10
	糸	紳	6a5.2
		縉	6a10.5
	米	糂	6b11.7
	虫	蜃	6d7.11
	竹	箴	6f9.2
		簪	6f14.3
	言	診	7a5.9
		請	7a8.8
		請	7a8.8
		譖	7a12.3
		譛	7a12.3
		識	7a17.3
	貝	賑	7b7.1
	車	軫	7c5.4
	酉	酳	7e7.4
	金	針	8a2.3
		鍼	8a9.12
		鐔	8a12.5
	雨	震	8d7.3
	馬	駸	10a7.4
	鳥	鷐	11b10.6
		鷐	11b10.6
shina	口	品	3d6.15
		品	3d6.15
	禾	科	5d4.3
shina(biru)	艹	萎	3k8.18
shina(u)	扌	撓	3c12.14
shingari	尸	殿	3r10.1
shino	竹	篠	6f11.3
shino(baseru)			
	忄	忍	4k3.3
		忍	4k3.3
shino(bi)	忄	忍	4k3.3
		忍	4k3.3
shinobu	艹	荵	3k7.15
shino(bu)	亻	偲	2a9.7
	忄	忍	4k3.3
		忍	4k3.3
shinogi	金	鎬	8a10.5
shino(gu)	冫	凌	2b8.5
shi(nu)		死	0a6.6
	又	殳	2h6.3
shio	氵	汐	3a3.9
		潮	3a12.1
	土	塩	3b10.4
	皿	鹽	3b10.4
shio(reru)	艹	萎	3k8.18
shiori	木	栞	4a6.34
		栞	4a6.34
shira	日	白	4c1.3
shira-	日	白	4c1.3
shira(be)	言	調	7a8.16
		調	7a8.16
shira(beru)	言	調	7a8.16
		調	7a8.16
shirami	虫	虱	6d2.1
		蝨	6d2.1
shira(mu)	日	白	4c1.3
shi(rase)		知	3d5.14
shiri	尸	尻	3r2.1
	月	臀	4b13.7
shirigai	火	韉	4d14.4
shirizo(keru)		斥	0a5.18
	辶	退	2q6.3
shirizo(ku)	辶	退	2q6.3
shiro	亻	代	2a3.3
	土	城	3b6.1
	日	白	4c1.3
shirogane	金	銀	8a6.3
shiro(i)	日	白	4c1.3
shiru	氵	汁	3a2.1
shi(ru)	口	知	3d5.14
shirube	木	標	4a11.8
	日	導	5c9.3
shirushi	卩	印	2e4.1
	彳	徴	3i11.2
		徵	3i11.2
	木	標	4a11.8
	馬	験	10a8.4
		驗	10a8.4
shiru(su)	言	記	7a3.5
shishi	犭	獅	3g10.1
	宀	宍	3m4.4
shishibishio			
	酉	醢	7e10.3
shis(suru)		失	0a5.28
shita	卜	下	2m1.2
	口	舌	3d3.9
shitaga(eru)	亻	从	3i7.3
	彳	従	3i7.3
		從	3i7.3
shitaga(tte)	亻	从	3i7.3
	彳	従	3i7.3
		從	3i7.3
shitaga(u)	亻	从	3i7.3
	阝	随	2d8.10
		隨	2d8.10
	彳	従	3i7.3
		從	3i7.3
shitami	氵	渭	3a9.19
shita(shii)	立	親	5b11.1
shita(shimu)			
	立	親	5b11.1
shitata(meru)			
	言	認	7a7.10
shitata(ru)	氵	滴	3a11.14
shita(u)	艹	慕	3k11.12
shita(washii)			
	艹	慕	3k11.12
shitomi	艹	蔀	3k10.4
shitone	艹	茵	3k6.24
		蓐	3k10.30
shito(yaka)	氵	淑	3a8.5
SHITSU		失	0a5.28
	阝	隲	2d14.1
		隲	2d14.2
	氵	湿	3a9.22
		濕	3a9.22
		漆	3a11.10
	土	執	3b8.15
	口	叱	3d2.2
	女	嫉	3e10.8
	宀	室	3m6.4
	木	桎	4a6.20
		櫛	4a15.5
		櫛	4a15.5
	月	膝	4b11.4
	王	瑟	4f9.10
	忄	悉	4k7.19
	疒	疾	5i5.12
	虫	虱	6d2.1
		蝨	6d2.1
		蛭	6d6.5
		蟋	6d11.2
	貝	質	7b8.7
		質	7b8.7
shitsuke	王	躾	4f12.2
shitsu(keru)			
	王	躾	4f12.2
shiwa	又	皺	2h13.1
shiwabuki	口	咳	3d6.10
shiwaga(reru)			
	口	嗄	3d10.5
shiwa(i)	亠	吝	2j5.2
shizu	艹	静	4b10.9
	月	静	4b10.9
	貝	賤	7b8.3
		賎	7b8.3
shizu(ka)	艹	静	4b10.9
	月	静	4b10.9
shizuku	氵	滴	3a11.14
	雨	雫	8d3.1
shizu(maru)			
	艹	静	4b10.9
	月	静	4b10.9
	金	鎮	8a10.6
		鎭	8a10.6
shizu(meru)			
	氵	沈	3a4.9
	艹	静	4b10.9
	月	静	4b10.9
	金	鎮	8a10.6
		鎭	8a10.6
shizu(mu)	氵	沈	3a4.9
		淪	3a8.28
SHO		且	0a5.15
	卜	正	2m3.4
		処	4i2.2
	氵	渚	3a9.1
		渚	3a9.1
		湑	3a9.19
	土	墅	3b11.6
	艹	苴	3k5.11
		蔗	3k11.19
		薯	3k14.3
		藷	3k14.3

言 請 7a8.8
足 踵 7d9.1
蹤 7d11.1
酉 醬 7e11.2
醬 7e11.2
金 鈔 8a4.5
鉦 8a5.7
銷 8a7.10
錆 8a8.8
鍺 8a8.8
鍾 8a9.1
鍬 8a9.3
鐘 8a12.6
食 餇 8b6.5
隹 焦 8c4.3
宀 宵 8d7.1
霄 8d8.7
頁 頌 9a4.4
顠 9a18.1
馬 驤 10a17.2
驫 10a20.1
魚 鮹 11a7.6
鱆 11a11.4
鱰 11a15.1
鳥 鷉 11b12.1

SHOKU
ク 色 2n4.1
土 埴 3b8.10
嗇 3b10.13
扌 拭 3c6.17
口 喞 3d9.4
嘱 3d12.11
囑 3d12.11
宀 寔 3m9.4
尸 属 3r9.1
屬 3r9.1
木 植 4a8.32
日 昃 4c4.8
火 燭 4d13.5
衤 褥 4e10.1
歹 殖 5c7.4
矚 5c21.1
禾 稙 5d8.6
稷 5d10.1
穡 5d13.1
罒 蜀 5g8.7
糸 織 6a12.6
虫 触 6d7.10
觸 6d7.10
耳 職 6e12.1
耘 6e12.1
言 謖 7a10.2
貝 贖 7b15.2
車 軾 7c6.4
食 食 8b0.1

餝 8b5.3
飾 8b5.3
蝕 8b6.1
蝕 8b6.1
魚 鯽 11a9.3

SHU
朱 0a6.13
殊 0a10.7
鼠 0a13.1
亻 侏 2a6.4
修 2a8.11
首 2o7.2
几 殳 2s2.1
氵 洙 3a6.6
酒 3a7.1
土 趣 3b14.5
扌 手 3c0.1
掫 3c8.34
撞 3c12.10
女 娵 3e8.2
娶 3e8.7
犭 狩 3g6.5
彡 須 3j9.1
艹 茱 3k6.4
蒐 3k8.6
宀 守 3m3.2
⺌ 甶 0a13.1
广 麈 3q13.2
木 棕 4a8.24
椶 4a8.24
月 腫 4b9.1
腴 4b10.1
王 主 4f1.1
主 4f1.1
珠 4f6.2
禾 種 5d9.1
氀 5d9.3
皿 衆 5h7.1
糸 繻 6a14.1
耳 取 6e2.2
聚 6e8.3
趣 6e9.1
言 諏 7a8.4
金 銖 8a6.2
頁 鬚 9a13.2

SHŪ
冊 0a5.41
禾 0a6.1
亻 修 2a8.11
脩 2a9.6
刂 州 2f4.1
又 收 2h2.2
皺 2h13.1
丷 酋 2o7.1
酉 2o7.1
羞 2o9.4

辶 週 2q8.7
遒 2q9.15
酒 2q9.15
冂 周 2r6.1
周 2r6.1
氵 泗 3a5.31
洲 3a6.10
渋 3a8.19
澁 3a8.19
澀 3a8.19
湫 3a9.7
溲 3a10.3
土 執 3b8.15
扌 拾 3c6.14
揖 3c9.9
摺 3c11.3
摺 3c11.3
口 啾 3d9.5
就 3d9.21
艹 萩 3k8.6
萩 3k9.5
葺 3k9.25
蒩 3k10.9
蒐 3k10.12
宀 宗 3m5.1
口 囚 3s2.1
木 柊 4a5.24
楸 4a9.6
楫 4a9.20
楢 4a9.23
楢 4a9.23
月 腹 4b10.1
日 習 4c7.11
習 4c7.11
火 鍬 4d14.4
衤 祝 4e5.5
祝 4e5.5
王 主 4f1.1
主 4f1.1
攵 收 2h2.2
螽 4i14.1
忄 愀 4k9.2
愁 4k9.16
目 臭 5c4.3
臭 5c4.3
禾 秀 5d2.4
穐 5d4.1
秋 5d4.1
穐 5d4.1
氀 5d9.3
衤 袖 5e5.1
褶 5e11.3
襲 5e16.2
皿 衆 5h7.1

疒 瘦 5i9.1
瘦 5i9.1
糸 終 6a5.9
綉 6a7.1
絹 6a9.9
繍 6a13.1
繍 6a13.1
舟 舟 6c0.1
舟 6c0.1
耳 聚 6e8.3
言 讐 7a16.2
車 輯 7c9.4
足 蹴 7d12.2
酉 酬 7e6.2
醜 7e10.1
金 銹 8a7.6
鏥 8a7.6
鍬 8a9.3
隹 雔 7a16.2
售 8c3.1
集 8c4.2
馬 駶 2f4.1
騶 10a14.1
魚 鰍 11a9.2
鮋 11a9.14
鳥 鷲 11b12.5

SHUKU
粛 0a11.8
蕭 0a11.8
亻 俶 2a8.6
倏 2a8.9
又 叔 2h6.1
几 夙 2s4.2
氵 淑 3a8.5
弓 粥 3h9.1
鬻 3h9.1
艹 菽 3k8.7
蓿 3k11.16
宀 宿 3m8.3
衤 祝 4e5.5
祝 4e5.5
糸 縮 6a11.9
足 蹙 7d11.6
蹴 7d12.2

SHUN
亻 俊 2a7.10
儁 2a13.2
又 皴 2h10.1
辶 逡 2q7.12
氵 浚 3a7.11
濬 3a14.7
艹 蓴 3k11.7
蕣 3k13.21
山 舜 3n10.2
峻 3o7.4
日 春 4c5.13

Reading	Kanji	Code
sō	然	4d8.10
soba	側	2a9.4
	傍	2a10.6
sobada(teru)		
	欹	4j8.3
sobada(tsu)		
	岻	3o6.2
sobi(eru)	聳	6e11.4
sobi(yakasu)		
	聳	6e11.4
soda(chi)	育	2j6.4
	毓	2j6.4
soda(te)	育	2j6.4
	毓	2j6.4
soda(teru)	育	2j6.4
	毓	2j6.4
soda(tsu)	育	2j6.4
	毓	2j6.4
sode	袖	5e5.1
so(eru)	添	3a8.22
so(geru)	削	2f7.4
	削	2f7.4
	殺	4a6.35
	殺	4a6.35
sogi	矧	4a4.15
so(gu)	削	2f7.4
	削	2f7.4
	殺	4a6.35
	殺	4a6.35
soko	底	3q5.3
	楹	4a8.37
soko(nau)	損	3c10.12
-soko(nau)	損	3c10.12
soko(neru)	損	3c10.12
SOKU	束	0a7.8
	促	2a7.3
	側	2a9.4
	即	2e5.1
	即	2e5.1
	仄	2p2.1
	速	2q7.4
	測	3a9.4
	捉	3c7.1
	唧	3d9.4
	簇	3k11.3
	塞	3m10.2
	熄	4d10.1
	息	4k6.17
	惻	4k9.1
	則	7b2.1
	足	7d0.1
	鼳	7d15.3
	鏃	8a11.2
soma	杣	4a3.3
so(maru)	染	4a5.35
so(me)	染	4a5.35
so(meru)	染	4a5.35
-someru	初	5e2.1
somosomo	抑	3c4.12
somu(keru)	背	4b5.15
somu(ku)	舛	0a6.17
	乖	2k6.4
	叛	2p7.3
	背	4b5.15
SON	存	2c3.1
	孫	2c7.1
	邨	4a3.11
	尊	2o10.3
	尊	2o10.3
	巽	2o10.7
	巽	2o10.7
	遜	2q9.4
	遜	2q9.4
	墫	4a12.19
	拵	3c5.24
	損	3c10.12
	噂	3d12.5
	噂	3d12.10
	噂	3d12.10
	村	4a3.11
	樽	4a12.19
	樽	4a12.19
	忖	4k3.1
	蹲	7d12.4
	鱒	11a12.6
	鱒	11a12.6
sona(eru)	供	2a6.13
	備	2a10.4
	具	5c3.1
	具	5c3.1
sona(waru)	備	2a10.4
	具	5c3.1
	具	5c3.1
sone(mu)	嫉	3e10.8
sono	薗	3s10.1
	囿	3s6.2
	園	3s10.1
	其	2o6.6
sora	空	3m5.12
	昊	4c4.6
sora(njiru)	諳	7a9.5
sora(nzuru)	諳	7a9.5
so(rasu)	反	2p2.2
	逸	2q8.6
	逸	2q8.6
sore	其	2o6.6
so(re)	夫	0a4.31
soregashi	某	4a5.33
so(reru)	逸	2q8.6
	逸	2q8.6
sori	橇	4a12.14
	膤	4b11.1
	艝	6c11.1
	轌	7c11.1
-sōrō	候	2a8.10
soro(eru)	揃	3c9.16
soro(i)	揃	3c9.16
soro(u)	揃	3c9.16
so(ru)	剃	2f7.5
	反	2p2.2
soshi(ru)	謗	7a10.9
	譏	7a12.1
sō(shite)	然	4d8.10
soso(gu)	注	3a5.16
	注	3a5.16
	濯	3a14.5
	濯	3a14.5
	潅	3a17.3
	灌	3a17.3
	雪	8d3.2
	雪	8d3.2
sosonoka(su)		
	唆	3d7.8
soto	外	2m3.1
SOTSU	卒	2j6.2
	卒	2j6.2
	率	2j9.1
	埣	3b8.9
	猝	3g8.8
so(u)	副	2f9.2
	沿	3a5.23
	添	3a8.22
soyo(gu)	戦	4n9.2
	戦	4n9.2
sozo(ro)	漫	3a11.11
SU	寿	0a7.15
	子	2c0.1
	須	3j9.1
	菆	3k8.6
	稣	3k16.1
	蘇	3k16.1
	守	3m3.2
	壽	0a7.15
	主	4f1.1
	主	4f1.1
	数	4i9.1
	數	4i9.1
	素	6a4.12
	笥	6f5.15
	諏	7a8.4
su	州	2f4.1
	洲	3a6.10
	巣	3n8.1
	巣	3n8.1
	樸	4a11.17
	鬆	4a14.6
	簀	6f11.7
	簾	6f13.8
	醋	7e5.3
	酢	7e5.3
	醋	7e8.2
	駟	2f4.1
SŪ	芻	0a10.6
	阪	2d8.9
	鄒	2d10.6
	皺	2h13.1
	趨	3b14.5
	蒭	0a10.6
	菘	3k8.9
	崇	3o8.9
	嵩	3o10.4
	枢	4a4.22
	樞	4a4.22
	数	4i9.1
	數	4i9.1
	雛	8c10.1
Subaru	昴	4c5.12
sube	術	3i8.2
	術	3i8.2
subeka(raku)		
	須	3j9.1
sube(kkoi)	滑	3a10.6
sube(ru)	辷	2q1.1
	滑	3a10.6
su(beru)	統	6a6.10
	総	6a8.20
	總	6a8.20
sube(te)	凡	2s1.1
	渾	3a9.28
subo(maru)	窄	3m7.11
subo(meru)		
	窄	3m7.11
subo(mu)	窄	3m7.11
sudare	簾	6f13.8
sude (ni)	既	0a10.5
	既	0a10.5
sue	末	0a5.26
su(eru)	据	3c8.33
	籃	8b12.5
sugame	眇	5c4.2
suga(ru)	縋	6a9.14
sugata	姿	3e6.10
suge	菅	3k8.27
sugi	杉	4a3.2
	椙	4a8.21

Reading	Rad.	Kanji	Code
su(giru)	⻌	過	2q9.18
sugo(i)	⺡	凄	2b8.4
	⺡	凄	2b8.4
sugo(mu)	⺡	凄	2b8.4
	⺡	凄	2b8.4
su(gosu)	⻌	過	2q9.18
su(gu)	⺾	直	2k6.2
sugu(reru)	亻	傑	2a11.6
		優	2a15.1
	木	杰	2a11.6
	月	勝	4b8.4
		勝	4b8.4
sugu(ru)	⻌	選	2q12.3
SUI	乂	乂	0a3.30
		出	0a5.22
		垂	0a8.12
		彗	0a11.9
	阝	陲	2d8.1
		隧	2d12.1
	亠	衰	2j8.1
	⺾	翠	2k12.2
		翠	2k12.2
		翠	2k12.2
	⻌	遂	2q9.13
		邃	2q14.2
	⺡	水	3a0.1
	扌	推	3c8.1
		捶	3c8.3
	口	吹	3d4.3
	巾	帥	3f6.1
	⺾	萃	3k8.29
	木	榱	4a10.23
	月	膵	4b11.5
	火	炊	4d4.1
		燧	4d12.7
	木	祟	4e5.9
	心	悴	4k8.12
		忰	4k8.12
	目	眭	5c8.1
		睡	5c8.2
	禾	穂	5d10.2
		穗	5d10.2
	疒	瘁	5i8.7
	糸	綏	6a7.2
	米	粋	6b4.5
		粹	6b4.5
	言	誰	7a8.1
	酉	醉	7e4.3
		醉	7e4.3
	金	錐	8a8.1
		錘	8a8.2
	隹	隹	8c0.1
		雖	8c9.2
	馬	騅	10a8.1
su(i)	酉	酸	7e7.2
suji	⺾	筋	6f6.4
su(kasazu)			
	⻌	透	2q7.10
su(kashi)	⻌	透	2q7.10
su(kasu)	⻌	透	2q7.10
suka(su)	貝	賺	7b10.1
suke	力	助	2g5.1
	弓	弼	3h9.2
su(keru)	⻌	透	2q7.10
suki		未	0a6.21
		耒	0a11.3
	阝	隙	2d10.4
		隙	2d10.4
	力	耡	2g11.2
	牛	犁	4g8.2
		犂	4g8.2
	金	鋤	8a7.5
su(ki)	女	好	3e2.1
sukobu(ru)			
	頁	頗	9a5.1
suko(shi)	⺌	少	3n1.1
suko(yaka)	亻	健	2a8.34
su(ku)	力	耡	2g11.2
	⻌	透	2q7.10
	⺡	漉	3a11.20
	女	好	3e2.1
	⺍	空	3m5.12
	金	鋤	8a7.5
suku(meru)			
		竦	5b7.1
sukumo	米	粏	6b6.2
		稼	6b10.2
suku(mu)	立	竦	5b7.1
		尠	3n10.3
suku(nai)	⺌	少	3n1.1
suku(u)	扌	抔	3c4.6
		掬	3c8.35
	木	樕	4a11.17
	攵	救	4i7.1
su(kuu)	⺾	巣	3n8.1
	木	巣	3n8.1
su(mai)	亻	住	2a5.19
		住	2a5.19
su(manai)	⺡	済	3a8.30
		済	3a8.30
su(masu)	⺡	清	3a8.18
		清	3a8.18
		済	3a8.30
		済	3a8.30
		澄	3a12.11
		激	3a12.11
su(mau)	亻	住	2a5.19
		住	2a5.19
sumi	阝	隅	2d9.1
	⺈	角	2n5.1
	土	墨	3b11.4
		墨	3b11.4
	山	炭	3o6.5
		炭	3o6.5
su(mi)	⺡	済	3a8.30
		済	3a8.30
sumi(kko)	阝	隅	2d9.1
su(mimasen)			
	⺡	済	3a8.30
		済	3a8.30
sumire	⺾	菫	3k8.1
sumi(yaka)			
	⻌	速	2q7.4
sumomo	木	李	4a2.7
su(mu)	亻	住	2a5.19
		住	2a5.19
	⺡	済	3a8.30
		済	3a8.30
		澄	3a12.11
		激	3a12.11
	木	棲	4a8.16
SUN	寸	寸	0a3.17
suna	⺡	沙	3a4.13
	石	砂	5a4.3
sunawachi	⻌	逎	2q6.10
		逎	2q6.10
sunawa(chi)	乃	乃	0a2.10
	阝	即	2e5.1
		即	2e5.1
	貝	則	7b2.1
sune	月	脛	4b7.6
		臑	4b14.1
su(neru)	扌	拗	3c5.16
su(ppai)	酉	酸	7e7.2
suppon	黽	鼈	4i20.1
su(reru)	扌	擦	3c14.5
su(ru)	刂	刷	2f6.9
		剃	2f7.5
	扌	掏	3c8.36
		摺	3c11.3
		摺	3c11.3
		擂	3c13.2
		擦	3c14.5
	广	磨	3q13.3
		磨	3q13.3
	火	為	4d5.8
		爲	4d5.8
surudo(i)	金	鋭	8a7.12
		鋭	8a7.12
surume	魚	鯣	11a8.5
susa(bi)	⻌	遊	2q8.3
susa(bu)	⺾	荒	3k6.18
susa(majii)	⺡	凄	2b8.4
		凄	2b8.4
susa(mu)	⺾	荒	3k6.18
sushi	魚	鮓	11a5.3
		鮨	11a6.8
suso	衤	裾	5e8.8
susu	火	煤	4d9.6
susu(gu)	⺡	漱	3a11.4
		濯	3a14.5
		濯	3a14.5
	口	嗽	3d11.3
	雨	雪	8d3.2
		雪	8d3.2
susuki	⺾	芒	3k3.2
		薄	3k13.11
		荳	3k13.11
susu(meru)		奨	3n10.4
	力	勧	2g11.1
		勸	2g11.1
	⻌	進	2q8.1
	犭	獎	3n10.4
	⺾	薦	3k13.25
	⺌	奨	3n10.4
	心	憑	4k10.15
		慫	4k11.15
susu(mu)	⻌	迪	2q5.1
		廸	2q5.1
		進	2q8.1
susu(ru)	口	啜	3d8.11
	欠	歠	4j9.1
suta(reru)	广	廃	3q9.3
		廢	3q9.3
suta(ru)	广	廃	3q9.3
		廢	3q9.3
su(teru)	亠	棄	2j11.5
		弃	2j11.5
	扌	捨	3c8.26
		捨	3c8.26
su(u)	口	吸	3d3.5
		吮	3d4.11
suwa(ru)	土	坐	3b4.11
	广	座	3q7.2
su(waru)	扌	据	3c8.33
suzu	⺾	篶	6f11.6
	金	鈴	8a5.11
		錫	8a8.7
		鑯	8a15.4
		鑾	8a19.2
suzuki	魚	鱸	11a16.1
suzume	隹	雀	8c3.2
suzu(mu)	⺡	涼	3a8.31
		凉	3a8.31
suzuri	石	硯	5a7.2
suzu(shii)	⺡	涼	3a8.31

Reading	Rad.	Kanji	Code
	氵	涼	3a8.31

– T –

Reading	Rad.	Kanji	Code
TA		太	0a4.18
		多	0a6.5
		夛	0a6.5
	亻	他	2a3.4
		佗	2a6.14
		佗	2a6.14
	丷	朶	2o5.5
	氵	汰	3a4.8
	土	埵	3b8.2
	口	咤	3d6.6
		咤	3d6.6
	宀	它	3m2.3
	木	躱	4a9.32
	言	詑	7a5.8
		詫	7a6.6
	酉	酡	7e5.4
	馬	駄	10a4.1
		驒	10a12.3
		驒	10a12.3
ta	田	田	5f0.1
ta-	扌	手	3c0.1
taba		束	0a7.8
tabaka(ru)	言	謀	7a9.8
taba(karu)	言	誑	7a7.3
tabako	艹	莨	3k7.4
taba(neru)		束	0a7.8
ta(beru)	食	食	8b0.1
tabi	广	度	3q6.1
	方	旅	4h6.4
tabo	髟	髱	3j12.3
tabu	木	橅	4a8.34
tabura(kasu)			
	言	誑	7a7.3
tabusa	口	謦	3d13.11
TACHI	門	闥	8e12.2
tachi	口	舘	8b8.3
	貝	質	7b8.7
		貭	7b8.7
	食	館	8b8.3
-tachi	辶	達	2q9.8
		達	2q9.8
tachibana	木	橘	4a12.11
tachima(chi)			
	心	忽	4k4.7
tada	亠	啻	2j10.2
	口	只	3d2.8
		唯	3d8.1
	彳	徒	3i7.1
tada(chi ni)			
	十	直	2k6.2
tada(reru)	火	爛	4d17.1
tada(shi)	亻	但	2a5.14
tada(shii)	亅	正	2m3.3
tada(su)		正	2m3.3
	扌	擶	3c15.3
	糸	糾	6a3.4
		紏	6a3.4
	貝	質	7b8.7
		貭	7b8.7
tadayo(u)	氵	漂	3a11.9
tade	艹	蓼	3k11.10
tado(ru)	辶	辿	2q3.1
		辿	2q3.1
tae	木	栲	4a6.4
tae(naru)	女	妙	3e4.5
tae(ru)	土	堪	3b9.1
ta(eru)	冂	耐	2r7.1
	木	橾	4a11.17
	糸	絶	6a6.11
tafu	木	榑	4a8.34
taga	竹	箍	6f8.4
taga(eru)	辶	違	2q10.5
taga(i)		互	0a4.15
taga(u)		舛	0a6.17
	辶	違	2q10.5
tagaya(su)		耕	0a10.13
		畊	0a10.13
		畉	5f4.2
tagi(ru)	氵	滾	3a11.15
tagui	亻	倫	2a8.28
		比	2m3.5
	貝	類	9a9.1
		類	9a9.1
TAI		大	0a3.18
		太	0a4.18
		夛	0a7.2
		躰	2a5.6
	亻	代	2a3.3
		体	2a5.6
	彡	隶	2b6.2
	阝	隊	2d9.7
		隊	2d9.7
	一	対	2j5.5
	辶	退	2q6.3
		逮	2q8.2
	冂	耐	2r7.1
	氵	泰	3a5.34
		滞	3a10.14
		滞	3a10.14
	土	堆	3b8.1
		臺	3d2.11
	扌	擡	3c14.7
	口	體	2a5.6
		台	3d2.11
		殆	3d6.21
	女	姚	3c14.7
	巾	帯	3f7.1
		帶	3f7.1
	彳	待	3i6.4
	艹	苔	3k5.27
		蒂	3k11.8
		帯	3k11.8
		臺	3k14.4
	山	岱	3o5.13
	月	體	2a5.6
		胎	4b5.10
		腿	4b9.10
		腿	4b9.10
	日	替	4c8.12
	火	黛	4d13.7
	王	對	2j5.5
		玳	4f5.5
	心	怠	4k5.21
		態	4k10.14
	石	碓	5a8.1
	衤	袋	5e5.11
		褪	5e9.5
	田	戴	5f12.2
	糸	給	6a5.13
	虫	颱	6d8.11
	貝	貸	7b5.9
	釒	鐓	8a11.1
	雨	靆	8d15.1
	頁	頽	9a7.3
	馬	駘	10a5.4
tai	魚	鯛	11a8.11
-tai	广	度	3q6.1
tai(ra)	亠	平	2k3.4
		平	2k3.4
taka	亠	高	2j8.6
		髙	2j8.6
	广	鷹	3q21.1
taka(buru)	亠	高	2j8.6
		髙	2j8.6
taka(ga)		高	2j8.6
		髙	2j8.6
taka(i)	亠	高	2j8.6
		髙	2j8.6
taka(maru)	亠	高	2j8.6
		髙	2j8.6
taka(meru)	亠	高	2j8.6
		髙	2j8.6
takamura	竹	篁	6f9.6
takara	宀	宝	3m5.2
		寳	3m5.2
		寶	3m5.2
taka(raka)	亠	高	2j8.6
		髙	2j8.6
take		丈	0a3.26
		丈	0a3.26
	艹	茸	3k6.1
		蕈	3k12.10
	山	岳	3o5.12
		嶽	3o5.12
	竹	竹	6f0.1
takenawa	酉	酣	7e5.2
	門	闌	8e9.1
takenoko	竹	筍	6f6.14
		笋	6f6.14
take(ru)	口	嗜	3d6.3
ta(keru)	長	長	0a8.2
	犭	猛	3g7.4
	門	闌	8e9.1
taki	氵	滝	3a10.8
		瀧	3a10.8
takigi	艹	薪	3k13.3
tako	几	凧	2s3.1
	月	胅	4b5.7
	虫	蛸	6d7.5
		蛸	6d7.5
	魚	鮹	11a7.6
		鱆	11a11.4
TAKU	亻	倬	2a8.32
	卜	卓	2m6.2
	氵	沢	3a4.18
		澤	3a4.18
		濯	3a14.5
		濯	3a14.5
	土	坼	3b5.6
	扌	托	3c3.3
		択	3c4.21
		擇	3c4.21
		拓	3c5.1
		拆	3c5.12
		擢	3c14.3
		擢	3c14.3
	口	啄	3d8.4
		啄	3d8.4
		啅	3d8.13
	宀	宅	3m3.4
	广	度	3q6.1
	木	柝	4a5.10
	王	琢	4f8.1
		琢	4f8.1
	戈	戳	4n14.1
	石	磔	5a11.2
	田	魄	5f10.4
	言	託	7a3.1
		謫	7a11.3
	釒	鈬	8a13.3
		鐸	8a13.3
ta(ku)	火	炊	4d4.1
		焚	4d8.7

takuma(shii)
　[辶] 逞 2q7.13
takumi 工 0a3.6
　互 0a3.6
　[匚] 匠 2t4.2
taku(mi) 巧 0a5.7
taku(ramu) [亻] 企 2a4.17
takuwa(eru)
　[艹] 蓄 3k10.16
　[貝] 貯 7b5.1
tama [辶] 適 2q11.3
　[弓] 弾 3h9.3
　彈 3h9.3
　[王] 玉 4f0.2
　珠 4f6.2
　球 4f7.2
　璧 4f13.2
　[田] 魂 5f9.2
　[需] 靈 8d7.2
　霊 8d7.2
-tama(e) [糸] 給 6a6.7
tamago [卩] 卵 2e5.2
tamaki [王] 環 4f13.1
　環 4f13.1
tama(ni) [亻] 偶 2a9.1
tama(ranai) [土] 堪 3b9.1
tama(ri) [氵] 溜 3a10.11
　溜 3a10.11
tama(ru) [氵] 溜 3a10.11
　溜 3a10.11
　[土] 堪 3b9.1
tamashii [田] 魂 5f9.2
tamatama [亻] 偶 2a9.1
tama(u) [糸] 給 6a6.7
　[貝] 賜 7b8.2
tamawa(ru) [貝] 賜 7b8.2
tame [火] 為 4d5.8
　爲 4d5.8
ta(me) [氵] 溜 3a10.11
　溜 3a10.11
ta(meru) [氵] 溜 3a10.11
　溜 3a10.11
　[口] 矯 3d14.5
tameshi [亻] 例 2a6.7
tame(su) [言] 試 7a6.18
tami 民 0a5.23
　[一] 岷 2j6.7
tamoto [衤] 袂 5e4.2
tamo(tsu) [亻] 保 2a7.11
tamuro 屯 0a4.35
TAN 丹 0a4.34
　丹 0a4.34
　丼 0a5.40
　象 0a9.1

　[亻] 貪 2a9.20
　[阝] 鄲 2d12.5
　[亠] 亶 2j11.4
　[十] 覃 2k10.3
　[厂] 反 2p2.2
　[八] 段 2s7.2
　[虫] 淡 3a8.15
　湛 3a9.2
　湍 3a9.20
　湯 3a9.23
　潭 3a12.12
　澹 3a13.10
　灘 3a19.1
　灘 3a19.1
　[土] 坦 3b5.8
　堪 3b9.1
　赧 3b9.17
　壇 3b16.1
　[扌] 担 3c5.20
　擔 3c5.20
　探 3c8.16
　搏 3c11.1
　攤 3c19.1
　[口] 啖 3d8.10
　啗 3d8.14
　短 3d9.27
　嘆 3d10.8
　嘆 3d10.8
　嗽 3d12.3
　殫 3d13.13
　單 3n6.2
　[犭] 猯 3g9.4
　[⺍] 単 3n6.2
　[⺌] 炭 3o6.5
　炭 3o6.5
　[木] 椴 4a9.7
　槫 4a11.6
　檀 4a13.11
　檀 4a13.11
　[月] 胆 4b5.6
　膽 4b5.6
　[日] 旦 4c1.2
　靼 4c10.5
　[火] 毯 4d8.11
　[欠] 歎 4j10.3
　[心] 怛 4k5.8
　博 4k11.3
　憚 4k12.4
　憺 4k13.10
　[立] 站 5b5.2
　端 5b9.2
　[目] 眈 5c4.5
　[衤] 袒 5e5.6
　禅 5e12.1

　禅 5e12.1
　[疒] 疸 5i5.8
　痰 5i8.6
　[糸] 綻 6a8.13
　緞 6a9.4
　[虫] 蛋 6d5.11
　蜑 6d6.13
　[耳] 耽 6e4.3
　[⺮] 箪 6f12.2
　箪 6f12.2
　[言] 誕 7a7.15
　譚 7a12.4
　[貝] 賺 7b10.1
　[酉] 酖 7c4.1
　[金] 鍛 8a9.5
　鐔 8a12.5
　[食] 餤 8b8.1
　[雨] 蠶 3b16.1
　[馬] 驒 10a12.3
　驒 10a12.3
tana [山] 岊 3o2.1
　[木] 棚 4a8.10
tana- [广] 店 3q5.4
tanago [魚] 鱮 11a13.1
tanagokoro [⺌] 掌 3n9.4
tane [月] 胤 4b5.16
　[禾] 種 5d9.1
tani [⺷] 谷 2o5.3
tano(moshii)
　[貝] 賴 9a7.1
　頼 9a7.1
tano(mu) [貝] 賴 9a7.1
　頼 9a7.1
tano(shii) [木] 楽 4a9.29
　樂 4a9.29
　[心] 愉 4k9.13
　愉 4k9.13
tanoshi(mu)
　[木] 楽 4a9.29
　樂 4a9.29
tanuki [犭] 狸 3g7.2
　狸 3g7.2
Tao [土] 埓 3b6.6
tao [山] 嶋 3o10.1
tao(reru) [亻] 倒 2a8.5
　[攵] 斃 4i14.3
tao(su) [亻] 倒 2a8.5
tao(yaka) [女] 嫋 3e10.2
tara [魚] 鹹 11a9.12
　鱈 11a11.1
　鱈 11a11.1
tarai [皿] 盥 5h11.1

tara(su) [言] 誑 7a7.3
ta(rasu) 垂 0a8.12
tare 垂 0a8.12
　[言] 誰 7a8.1
ta(reru) 垂 0a8.12
ta(riru) [足] 足 7d0.1
taru [木] 樽 4a12.19
　樽 4a12.19
　壿 4a12.19
ta(ru) [足] 足 7d0.1
taruki [木] 桷 4a7.16
　榱 4a10.23
taru(mu) [弓] 弛 3h3.1
ta(chi) [足] 足 7d0.1
tashika [心] 慥 4k10.9
tashi(ka) [石] 確 5a10.3
tashi(kameru)
tashina(meru)
　[石] 確 5a10.3
　[宀] 窘 3m9.6
tashina(mi) [口] 嗜 3d10.4
tashina(mu)
　[口] 嗜 3d10.4
ta(su) [足] 足 7d0.1
tasu(karu) [力] 助 2g5.1
tasu(keru) [力] 助 2g5.1
　[扌] 扶 3c4.4
　援 3c9.7
　援 3c9.7
tasuki [衤] 襷 5e17.1
tata(eru) [氵] 湛 3a9.2
　[禾] 称 5d5.8
　稱 5d5.8
tataka(u) 斗 8e10.2
　[戈] 戦 4n9.2
　戰 4n9.2
　[門] 闘 8e10.2
　鬪 8e10.2
tata(ku) [扌] 扣 3c3.1
　[口] 叩 3d2.3
　敲 3d11.11
tatami [田] 畳 5f7.3
　疊 5f7.3
　疉 5f7.3
tata(mu) [田] 畳 5f7.3
　疊 5f7.3
　疉 5f7.3
tata(ru) [衤] 祟 4e5.9
tatazu(mai) [亻] 佇 2a5.16
tatazu(mu) [亻] 佇 2a5.16
tate [口] 舘 8b8.3
　[匚] 豎 5b9.5

Reading	Kanji	Code
tonga(ru)	尖	3n3.1
tono	殿	3r10.1
tora	乕	2m6.3
	虎	2m6.3
	寅	3m8.4
tora(eru)	捉	3c7.1
to(raeru)	捕	3c7.3
torawa(reru)		
	囚	3s2.1
to(rawareru)		
	捕	3c7.3
to(reru)	取	6e2.2
tori	禽	2a10.8
	酉	7e0.1
	鳥	11b0.1
tō(ri)	通	2q7.18
toride	砦	5a6.1
toriko	俘	2a6.9
	虜	2m11.2
	虜	2m11.2
toro	瀞	3a16.2
	瀞	3a16.2
toro(kasu)	蕩	3k12.4
	盪	5h12.1
	蘯	5h12.1
toro(keru)	蕩	3k12.4
	盪	5h12.1
	蘯	5h12.1
to(ru)	執	3b8.15
	捕	3c7.3
	採	3c8.14
	採	3c8.14
	撮	3c12.13
	取	6e2.2
	錄	8a8.16
	録	8a8.16
tō(ru)	透	2q7.10
	通	2q7.18
toshi	年	0a6.16
	歳	4n9.5
tō(su)	透	2q7.10
	通	2q7.18
tote(mo)	迚	2q4.1
tōto(bu)	尊	2o10.3
	尊	2o10.3
	貴	7b5.7
tōto(i)	尊	2o10.3
	尊	2o10.3
	貴	7b5.7
tōto(mu)	尊	2o10.3
	尊	2o10.3
totono(eru)	整	4i12.3
	調	7a8.16
	調	7a8.16
totono(u)	整	4i12.3
	調	7a8.16
	調	7a8.16
TOTSU	凸	0a5.13
	吶	3d4.5
	咄	3d5.5
	突	3m5.11
	突	3m5.11
	杤	4a5.8
	訥	7a4.4
totsu(gu)	嫁	3e10.6
to(u)	向	8e3.1
	訪	7a4.1
	問	8e3.1
toyo-	豊	3d10.15
	豊	3d10.15
to(zasu)	鎖	8a10.2
	閂	8e3.3
	閉	8e3.3
TSU	都	2d8.13
	都	2d8.13
	通	2q7.18
tsu	津	3a6.1
TSŪ	通	2q7.18
	痛	5i7.7
tsuba	唾	3d8.2
	鍔	8a9.6
tsubaki	唾	3d8.2
	椿	4a9.16
tsubame	燕	3k13.16
tsubasa	翼	2o15.2
	翼	2o15.2
tsubo	坪	3b5.4
	坪	3b5.4
	壷	3p9.2
	壺	3p9.2
tsubo(maru)		
	窄	3m7.11
tsubo(meru)		
	窄	3m7.11
tsubomi	莟	3k7.18
	蕾	3k13.18
tsubone	局	3r4.4
tsubu	粒	6b5.1
tsubu(reru)	潰	3a12.14
tsubu(ru)	瞑	5c10.3
tsubusa (ni)		
	具	5c3.1
	具	5c3.1
tsubu(su)	潰	3a12.14
tsubute	礫	5a15.1
tsubuya(ku)		
	呟	3d5.12
tsuchi	土	3b0.1
	椎	4a8.1
	槌	4a9.27
	槌	4a9.27
	鎚	8a9.10
	鎚	8a9.10
tsuchifu(ru)		
	霾	8d14.1
tsuchika(u)	培	3b8.6
tsuchinoe	戊	4n1.3
tsuchinoto	己	0a3.12
tsudo(u)	集	8c4.2
tsue	杖	4a3.5
	枴	4a5.21
tsuga	栂	4a5.7
tsuga(eru)	番	5f7.4
tsuga(i)	番	5f7.4
tsuga(u)	番	5f7.4
tsu(geru)	告	3d4.18
tsugi	次	2b4.1
tsugomori	晦	4c7.3
	晦	4c7.3
tsu(gu)	次	2b4.1
	注	3a5.16
	注	3a5.16
	接	3c8.10
	椄	4a8.15
	継	6a7.8
	繼	6a7.8
tsugumi	鶫	11b8.1
	鶫	11b8.1
tsugu(mu)	拑	3c5.8
tsuguna(u)	償	2a15.4
TSUI	対	2j5.5
	對	2j5.5
	追	2q6.4
	墜	3b11.7
	椎	4a8.1
	槌	4a9.27
	槌	4a9.27
	縋	6a9.14
	鎚	8a9.10
tsuiba(mu)	啄	3d8.4
	啄	3d8.4
tsuide	序	3q4.4
tsui(eru)	潰	3a12.14
tsui(eru)	費	7b5.4
tsui (ni)	遂	2q9.13
	終	6a5.9
tsuitachi	朔	4b6.12
tsui(yasu)	費	7b5.4
tsuji	辻	2q2.2
	辻	2q2.2
tsuka	束	0a7.8
	塚	3b9.10
	塚	3b9.10
	柄	4a5.9
	欟	4a21.1
	欟	4a21.1
tsukae	痞	5i7.4
tsuka(eru)	仕	2a3.2
	支	2k2.1
	閊	8e3.2
tsuka(i)	使	2a6.2
	使	2a6.2
tsuka(maeru)		
	捕	3c7.3
	掴	3c11.6
	摑	3c11.6
tsuka(maru)		
	捕	3c7.3
	掴	3c11.6
	摑	3c11.6
tsuka(maseru)		
	掴	3c11.6
	摑	3c11.6
tsuka(mi)	掴	3c11.6
	摑	3c11.6
tsuka(mu)	掴	3c11.6
	摑	3c11.6
	攪	3c20.2
tsuka(neru)	束	0a7.8
tsuka(rasu)		
	疲	5i5.2
tsuka(reru)		
	疲	5i5.2
tsu(kareru)	憑	4k12.12
tsu(karu)	浸	3a7.17
	漬	3a11.12
tsukasa	司	3d2.14
tsukasado(ru)		
	司	3d2.14
	掌	3n9.4
tsu(kasu)	尽	3r3.1
	盡	3r3.1
tsuka(u)	使	2a6.2
	使	2a6.2
	遣	2q10.2
tsuka(wasu)		
	遣	2q10.2
tsu(keru)	付	2a3.6
	附	2d5.4
	着	2o10.1
	漬	3a11.12
	就	3d9.21
tsuki	坏	3b4.4
	槻	4a11.4
	櫬	4a24.1

Reading		Kanji	Code
	月	月	4b0.1
tsu(kiru)	尸	尽	3r3.1
	皿	盡	3r3.1
tsu(ku)	亻	付	2a3.6
		傅	2a10.2
	阝	附	2d5.4
	卩	即	2e5.1
		卽	2e5.1
	卜	點	2m7.2
		点	2m7.2
		奌	2m7.2
	丷	着	2o10.1
	扌	搗	3c10.1
		撞	3c12.10
		擣	3c14.8
	口	吐	3d3.1
		就	3d9.21
	宀	突	3m5.11
		突	3m5.11
	心	憑	4k12.12
	⺮	築	6f10.5
tsukuba(i)	𧾷	蹲	7d12.4
tsukuba(u)	𧾷	蹲	7d12.4
tsukuda	亻	佃	2a5.2
tsukue	木	机	4a2.4
tsukuri	亠	旁	2j8.3
tsukuro(u)	糹	繕	6a12.2
tsuku(ru)	亻	作	2a5.10
	辶	造	2q7.11
tsu(kusu)	尸	尽	3r3.1
	心	悉	4k7.19
	皿	盡	3r3.1
tsuma	女	妻	3e5.10
	衤	褄	5e8.5
tsuma-	爪	爪	0a4.9
tsumabasa(mu)			
	衤	襀	5e15.1
tsumabi(raka)			
	宀	審	3m12.1
	言	詳	7a6.12
tsumada(tsu)			
	𧾷	跂	7d4.3
tsuma(mi)	扌	撮	3c12.13
tsuma(mu)	扌	抓	3c4.8
		摘	3c11.5
		撮	3c12.13
tsu(maru)	言	詰	7a6.7
tsuma(shii)	亻	倹	2a8.27
		儉	2a8.27
tsumazu(ku)			
	𧾷	躓	7d15.1
tsume	爪	爪	0a4.9
tsu(meru)	言	詰	7a6.7
tsume(tai)	冫	冷	2b5.3
tsumi	罒	罪	5g8.4
tsu(mi)	禾	積	5d11.5
tsu(mori)	禾	積	5d11.5
tsu(moru)	禾	積	5d11.5
tsumu	金	錘	8a8.2
tsu(mu)	扌	摘	3c11.5
	禾	積	5d11.5
	言	詰	7a6.7
tsumugi	糹	紬	6a5.3
tsumu(gu)	糹	紡	6a4.1
tsuna	糹	綱	6a8.23
tsuna(garu)			
	糹	繋	6a13.4
		繋	6a13.4
tsuna(gu)	糹	繋	6a13.4
		繋	6a13.4
tsunbo	耳	聾	6e16.1
tsune	丷	常	3n8.3
	米	彝	6b12.2
		彝	6b12.2
tsune (ni)	心	恒	4k6.5
		恆	4k6.5
tsune(ru)	扌	抓	3c4.8
tsuno	𠂊	角	2n5.1
tsuno(ru)	艹	募	3k9.23
tsunza(ku)	刂	劈	2f13.3
tsura	口	面	3s6.1
tsura(i)	立	辛	5b2.2
tsura(naru)	刂	列	2f4.4
	辶	連	2q7.2
tsura(neru)	刂	列	2f4.4
	辶	連	2q7.2
tsuranu(ku)	貝	貫	7b4.3
tsuratsura	亻	倩	2a8.20
tsu(re)	辶	連	2q7.2
tsu(reru)	辶	連	2q7.2
tsu(ri)	金	釣	8a3.5
tsuru	弓	弦	3h5.1
	艹	蔓	3k11.15
	宀	崔	3m8.1
	金	鉉	8a5.12
	鳥	鶴	11b10.1
tsu(ru)	口	吊	3d3.8
	疒	痙	5i7.5
	金	釣	8a3.5
tsurugi	亻	劔	2f8.5
	刂	剣	2f8.5
		劍	2f8.5
		劒	2f8.5
	口	剱	2f8.5
	金	釼	2f8.5
tsuru(shi)	口	吊	3d3.8
tsuru(su)	口	吊	3d3.8
tsusa	木	楮	4a12.16
tsuta	艹	蔦	3k11.1
		蘿	3k19.1
tsuta(eru)	亻	伝	2a4.14
		傳	2a4.14
tsuta(u)	亻	伝	2a4.14
		傳	2a4.14
tsuta(waru)	亻	伝	2a4.14
		傳	2a4.14
tsuto	彡	髦	3j12.3
	艹	苞	3k5.13
tsuto(maru)			
	力	勤	2g10.1
		勤	2g10.1
tsuto(meru)			
	力	努	2g5.6
		勤	2g10.1
		勤	2g10.1
	勹	勉	2n8.1
		勉	2n8.1
	女	務	4i7.6
tsutsu	石	砲	5a5.3
		砲	5a5.3
	⺮	筒	6f6.15
	金	銃	8a6.9
tsutsuga	丷	恙	2o8.3
tsutsu(ku)	宀	突	3m5.11
		突	3m5.11
tsutsu(mashii)			
	心	慎	4k10.4
		愼	4k10.4
tsutsumi	阝	陂	2d5.3
	土	坡	3b5.3
		堤	3b9.7
tsutsu(mi)		包	0a5.9
		包	0a5.9
tsutsu(mu)		包	0a5.9
		包	0a5.9
tsutsushi(mu)			
	心	慎	4k10.4
		愼	4k10.4
	言	謹	7a10.6
		謹	7a10.6
tsuwamono			
	丷	兵	2o5.6
tsuya	口	艶	3d16.3
		艷	3d16.3
tsuya(meku)			
	口	艶	3d16.3
		艷	3d16.3
tsuya(ppoi)	口	艶	3d16.3
		艷	3d16.3
tsuyo(i)	弓	強	3h8.3
tsuyo(maru)			
	弓	強	3h8.3
tsuyo(meru)			
	弓	強	3h8.3
tsuyu	氵	汁	3a2.1
		液	3a8.29
	雨	露	8d13.1
tsuzu(keru)			
	糹	続	6a7.5
		續	6a7.5
tsuzu(ku)	糹	続	6a7.5
		續	6a7.5
tsuzu(maru)			
	糹	約	6a3.7
tsuzuma(yaka)			
	亻	倹	2a8.27
		儉	2a8.27
tsuzu(meru)			
	糹	約	6a3.7
tsuzumi	壴	鼓	3p10.2
		皷	3p10.2
tsuzura	艹	葛	3k9.22
		葛	3k9.22
tsuzu(re)	糹	綴	6a8.5
tsuzu(ru)	糹	綴	6a8.5

– U –

Reading		Kanji	Code
U		于	0a3.20
		羽	2b4.5
		禹	0a9.14
	亻	佑	2a5.8
		傴	2a11.15
		齲	2a22.1
	冫	羽	2b4.5
	辶	迂	2q3.2
		迂	2q3.2
	扌	扔	3c6.4
	口	右	3d2.15
		吁	3d3.2
	女	嫗	3e11.6
	艹	芋	3k3.1
	宀	宇	3m3.3
	木	栩	4a6.25
	月	有	4b2.3
		胡	4b5.12
	火	烏	4d6.5
		燠	4d13.2
	皿	盂	5h3.1
	糹	紆	6a3.1
	雨	雨	8d0.1
u	卩	卯	2e3.1
		夘	2e3.1
	鳥	鵜	11b7.6
uba	女	姥	3e6.2
uba(u)	亻	奪	8c6.4
ubena(u)	言	諾	7a8.10

Reading		Kanji	Code
ubu	亠	産	5b6.4
	立	産	5b6.4
uchi		内	0a4.23
		内	0a4.23
		中	0a4.40
u(daru)	艹	茹	3k6.7
udatsu	木	梲	4a7.29
		梲	4a7.29
ude	月	腕	4b8.6
u(deru)	艹	茹	3k6.7
ue	卜	上	2m1.1
u(eru)	木	植	4a8.32
	飠	飢	8b2.1
		餓	8b7.1
		饉	8b12.1
ugai	口	嗽	3d11.3
uga(tsu)	宀	穿	3m7.10
ugo(kasu)	力	動	2g9.1
ugo(ku)	力	動	2g9.1
ugome(ku)	虫	蠢	6d15.2
ugui	魚	鮖	11a7.5
uguisu	鳥	鶯	11b10.9
		鶯	11b10.9
UI	艹	菌	3k6.23
ui-	衤	初	5e2.1
u(i)	夊	憂	4i12.1
u(ita)	氵	浮	3a6.11
		浮	3a6.11
uji		氏	0a4.25
	虫	蛆	6d5.5
u(kaberu)	氵	浮	3a6.11
		浮	3a6.11
u(kabu)	氵	浮	3a6.11
		浮	3a6.11
ukaga(i)	亻	伺	2a5.23
ukaga(u)	亻	伺	2a5.23
	亻	倪	2a7.9
	宀	窺	3m13.3
u(kanu)	氵	浮	3a6.11
		浮	3a6.11
u(kareru)	氵	浮	3a6.11
		浮	3a6.11
u(karu)	又	受	2h6.2
u(kasareru)			
	氵	浮	3a6.11
		浮	3a6.11
u(kasu)	氵	浮	3a6.11
		浮	3a6.11
uke	⺮	筌	6f6.11
u(ke)	又	受	2h6.2
u(keru)	又	受	2h6.2
	亠	享	2j5.1
	言	請	7a8.8

Reading		Kanji	Code
		請	7a8.8
uketamawa(ru)		承	0a7.7
u(ki)	氵	浮	3a6.11
		浮	3a6.11
ukikusa	艹	萍	3k8.12
u(ku)	氵	浮	3a6.11
		浮	3a6.11
uma	艹	午	2k2.2
	馬	馬	10a0.1
uma(i)	甘	甘	0a5.32
	日	旨	4c2.2
u(mareru)	生	生	0a5.29
	亠	産	5b6.4
	立	産	5b6.4
u(maru)	土	埋	3b7.2
umaya	厂	厩	2p12.2
		廐	2p12.2
	广	廏	2p12.2
		廐	2p12.2
ume	木	梅	4a6.27
		楳	4a6.27
		梅	4a6.27
ume(ku)	口	呻	3d5.2
u(meru)	土	埋	3b7.2
umi	氵	海	3a6.20
		海	3a6.20
	月	膿	4b13.2
u(moreru)	土	埋	3b7.2
u(mu)		生	0a5.29
	亻	倦	2a8.13
		倦	2a8.13
	亠	産	5b6.4
	月	膿	4b13.2
	火	熟	4d10.5
ure(shii)	女	嬉	3e12.3
ure(u)	女	憂	4i12.1
UN		云	0a4.4
		耘	0a10.9
	辶	運	2q9.10
	艹	蘊	3k13.12
		蘊	3k16.7
	日	暈	4c9.7
	火	熅	4d10.2
	心	慍	4k10.7
	糸	紜	6a4.10
		縕	6a10.4
		繧	6a12.3
	酉	醞	7e10.2
	飠	饂	8b10.2
	雲	雲	8d4.1
	鳥	鶤	11b9.2
unaga(su)	亻	促	2a7.3
unagi	魚	鰻	11a11.5

Reading		Kanji	Code
unaji	頁	項	9a3.1
una(ru)	口	唸	3d8.12
unasa(reru)			
	厂	魘	2p22.1
unazu(ku)	頁	頷	9a7.7
une	田	畝	5f5.5
		畝	5f5.5
		畦	5f6.2
uo	魚	魚	11a0.1
ura	亠	裏	2j11.2
	氵	浦	3a7.2
		裡	2j11.2
ura(meshii)			
	心	怨	4k5.20
		恨	4k6.2
ura(mu)	心	怨	4k5.20
		恨	4k6.2
		憂	4k10.7
		憾	4k13.3
urana(u)	卜	卜	2m0.1
		占	2m3.2
urara(ka)	广	麗	3q16.5
uraya(mashigaru)			
	羊	羨	2o11.4
uraya(mashii)			
		羨	2o11.4
uraya(mu)		羨	2o11.4
ure(e)	夊	憂	4i12.1
ure(eru)	夊	憂	4i12.1
	心	愁	4k9.16
ure(i)	夊	憂	4i12.1
	心	愁	4k9.16
u(reru)	士	賣	3p4.3
		売	3p4.3
	火	熟	4d10.5
ure(shii)	女	嬉	3e12.3
ure(u)	女	憂	4i12.1
uri		瓜	0a6.3
uro	卜	虚	2m9.1
		虚	2m9.1
uroko	魚	鱗	11a13.2
u(ru)	氵	沽	3a5.26
	彳	得	3i8.4
		賣	3p4.3
		売	3p4.3
	隹	羅	8c17.1
urū	門	閏	8e4.4
uruchi	米	粳	6b7.1
uru(mu)	氵	潤	3a12.20
uruo(i)	氵	潤	3a12.20
uruo(su)	氵	潤	3a12.20
	雨	霑	8d8.5
uruo(u)	氵	潤	3a12.20
	雨	霑	8d8.5

Reading		Kanji	Code
urusa(i)	火	煩	4d9.1
urushi	氵	漆	3a11.10
uruwa(shii)			
	广	麗	3q16.5
usagi		兔	0a8.5
	刂	兎	0a8.5
	勹	兔	0a8.5
	艹	莵	0a8.5
u(seru)		失	0a5.28
ushi		丑	0a4.39
	牛	牛	4g0.1
ushina(u)		失	0a5.28
ushio	氵	潮	3a12.1
ushi(ro)	彳	後	3i6.5
uso	口	嘘	3d11.7
		噓	3d11.7
	犭	獺	3g16.1
	鳥	鶯	11b13.1
usobu(ku)	口	嘯	3d13.1
usu		臼	0a6.4
	石	碓	5a8.1
usu(i)	艹	薄	3k13.11
		薀	3k13.11
usu(maru)	艹	薄	3k13.11
		薀	3k13.11
usu(meru)	艹	薄	3k13.11
		薀	3k13.11
usu(ppera)			
	艹	薄	3k13.11
		薀	3k13.11
usu(ragu)	艹	薄	3k13.11
		薀	3k13.11
usu(reru)	艹	薄	3k13.11
		薀	3k13.11
usutsu(ku)		舂	0a11.6
uta	口	唄	3d7.1
	欠	歌	4j10.2
	言	謌	4j10.2
utaga(u)	卜	疑	2m12.1
utaga(washii)			
	卜	疑	2m12.1
utage	宀	宴	3m7.3
	言	讌	7a16.1
utagu(ru)	卜	疑	2m12.1
utai	言	謡	7a9.9
		謠	7a9.9
utata	車	轉	7c4.3
		転	7c4.3
uta(u)	欠	歌	4j10.2
	言	謌	4j10.2
		謡	7a9.9
		謠	7a9.9
		謳	7a11.4
utena	土	臺	3d2.11

Reading		Kanji	Code
	口	台	3d2.11
uto(i)		疎	0a11.4
	足	疎	0a11.4
uto(mashii)		疎	0a11.4
	足	疎	0a11.4
uto(mu)		疎	0a11.4
	足	疎	0a11.4
uto(njiru)		疎	0a11.4
	足	疎	0a11.4
UTSU	艹	蔚	3k11.2
	木	欝	4a25.1
		欝	4a25.1
		鬱	4a25.1
		鬱	4a25.1
	火	熨	4d11.2
u(tsu)	亻	伐	2a4.5
	扌	打	3c2.3
		抔	3c4.14
		拍	3c5.14
		挏	3c5.14
		搏	3c10.5
		撃	3c11.7
		撃	3c11.7
		撲	3c12.1
		攄	3c14.8
	言	討	7a3.3
utsubari	木	梁	4a7.25
utsubo	刂	靭	2f10.4
	艹	靫	2f10.4
		靫	2f10.4
		靭	2f10.4
	竹	筬	6f3.2
	魚	鰧	11a12.3
utsuke	宀	空	3m5.12
utsuku(shii)			
	䒑	美	2o7.4
utsumu(keru)			
	亻	俯	2a8.35
utsumu(ku)			
	亻	俯	2a8.35
utsu(ro)	宀	空	3m5.12
utsu(rou)	禾	移	5d6.1
utsu(ru)	宀	写	2i3.1
		寫	2i3.1
	辶	遷	2q12.1
	彳	徙	3i8.5
	宀	寫	2i3.1
	日	映	4c5.1
		映	4c5.1
	禾	移	5d6.1
utsu(su)	宀	写	2i3.1
		寫	2i3.1
	彳	徙	3i8.5
	宀	寫	2i3.1
	日	映	4c5.1
		暎	4c5.1
utsutsu	王	現	4f7.3
utsuwa	口	器	3d12.13
		器	3d12.13
		器	3d12.13
utta(eru)	言	訴	7a5.2
uwa-		上	2m1.1
uwabami	虫	蟒	6d10.3
		蟒	6d10.3
		蟒	6d10.3
uwagusuri	米	釉	6b6.8
u(waru)	木	植	4a8.32
uwasa	口	噂	3d12.10
		噂	3d12.10
uyama(u)	攵	敬	4i8.4
uyauya(shii)			
	䒑	恭	3k7.16
uzu	氵	渦	3a9.36
uzu(ku)	疒	疼	5i5.9
uzukuma(ru)			
	足	踞	7d8.6
		蹲	7d12.4
uzu(maru)	土	埋	3b7.2
uzu(meru)	土	埋	3b7.2
uzu(moreru)			
	土	埋	3b7.2
uzura	鳥	鶉	11b7.4
uzutaka(i)	土	堆	3b8.1

– W –

Reading		Kanji	Code
WA	亻	倭	2a8.16
	口	咊	3d8.5
	艹	萬	3k9.24
	宀	窪	3m11.9
	禾	和	5d3.1
	言	話	7a6.8
wa		我	0a7.10
	王	環	4f13.1
		環	4f13.1
	車	輪	7c8.4
-wa		羽	2b4.5
	氵	羽	2b4.5
wa(bi)	亻	佗	2a6.14
		佗	2a6.14
	言	詫	7a6.6
wa(biru)	亻	佗	2a6.14
		佗	2a6.14
	言	詫	7a6.6
		佗	2a6.14
wadachi	車	轍	7c12.1
wadakama(ri)		蟠	6d12.2

Reading		Kanji	Code
wadakama(ru)			
	虫	蟠	6d12.2
waga	口	吾	3d4.17
wa(ga)		我	0a7.10
waga(neru)			
	糸	縮	6a8.14
wage		鬟	5g18.1
WAI	阝	隈	2d9.2
		歪	2m7.4
	氵	淮	3a8.2
	犭	猥	3g9.2
	艹	薈	3k13.24
	火	煨	4d9.4
	禾	矮	5d8.8
	貝	賄	7b6.1
waka(chi)	刂	分	2f5.3
waka(i)	女	嫩	3e11.1
	艹	若	3k5.12
waka(reru)	刂	別	2f5.3
		分	2o2.1
wa(kareru)		分	2o2.1
waka(ru)	刂	判	2f5.2
	角	解	4g9.1
	角	解	4g9.1
		分	2o2.1
		分	2o2.1
wa(karu)	刂	分	2o2.1
		分	2o2.1
wa(kasu)	氵	沸	3a5.3
waka(tsu)	刂	別	2f5.3
	頁	頒	9a4.3
wa(katsu)		分	2o2.1
		分	2o2.1
wake	言	譯	7a4.8
		訳	7a4.8
wa(keru)	刂	別	2f5.3
		分	2o2.1
		分	2o2.1
wa(kete)	刂	別	2f5.3
waki	月	脇	4b6.3
		腋	4b8.8
wakima(eru)		弁	0a5.30
		辨	0a5.30
		辦	0a5.30
		瓣	0a5.30
	言	辯	0a5.30
WAKU	心	惑	4k8.16
	戈	或	4n4.2
	虫	蠖	6d13.4
waku	木	枠	4a4.19
wa(ku)	氵	沸	3a5.3
		湧	3a9.31
		涌	3a9.31
wame(ku)	口	喚	3d9.19
WAN	氵	湾	3a9.15
		灣	3a9.15

Reading		Kanji	Code
	土	垸	3b8.7
	扌	捥	3c8.19
	弓	弯	3h19.1
		彎	3h19.1
	木	椀	4a8.26
	月	腕	4b8.6
	石	碗	5a8.7
	糸	綰	6a8.14
wana		罠	5g5.1
		罻	5g13.1
wanana(ku)			
	戈	戦	4n9.2
		戰	4n9.2
wani	魚	鰐	11a9.5
wara	艹	藁	3k14.6
	禾	稈	5d7.1
warabe		童	5b7.3
warabi	艹	蕨	3k12.15
wara(u)	竹	笑	6f4.1
warawa	女	妾	5b3.2
ware		我	0a7.10
	口	吾	3d4.17
wa(reru)	刂	割	2f10.1
wari	刂	割	2f10.1
wa(ru)	刂	割	2f10.1
waru(i)	心	悪	4k7.17
		悪	4k7.17
washi	亻	儂	2a13.3
	鳥	鷲	11b12.5
wasu(reru)			
	一	忘	2j5.4
		忘	2j5.4
wata	木	棉	4a8.18
	月	腸	4b9.8
		腸	4b9.8
	糸	綿	6a8.8
		緜	6a8.8
watakushi	禾	私	5d2.2
wata(ru)		互	0a6.2
		互	0a6.2
	氵	渡	3a9.35
	日	亘	4c2.4
wata(su)	氵	渡	3a9.35
waza		業	0a13.3
	扌	技	3c4.16
waza(to)	心	態	4k10.14
wazawai	木	禍	4e9.4
		禍	4e9.4
wazawa(i)	火	災	4d3.3
wazuka	糸	纔	6a17.2
	亻	僅	2a11.13
wazu(ka)		僅	2a11.13
wazura(u)	火	煩	4d9.1
	心	患	4k7.18

Reading	Kanji	Code
	癒	5i13.3
虫	蝓	6d9.13
言	諛	7a9.2
言	諭	7a9.13
言	諭	7a9.13
車	輸	7c9.5
車	輸	7c9.5
𧾷	踰	7d9.4
yu 氵	湯	3a9.23
YŪ	尤	0a4.20
	由	0a5.35
	鼬	0a18.1
亻	佑	2a5.8
	攸	2a5.13
	侑	2a6.5
	優	2a15.1
阝	郵	2d8.12
力	勇	2g7.3
	勦	2g15.1
又	友	2h2.3
辶	遊	2q8.3
氵	油	3a5.6
	游	3a8.10
	湧	3a9.31
	涌	3a9.31
口	右	3d2.15
	邑	3d4.15
犭	猶	3g9.5
	猷	3g9.7
	猷	3g9.7
艹	莠	3k7.11
	蕕	3k12.5
宀	宥	3m6.1
	幽	3o6.6
口	囿	3s6.2
木	柚	4a5.5
	楢	4a7.6
	楢	4a9.23
	楢	4a9.23
月	有	4b2.3
	肬	5i4.1
火	熊	4d10.6
礻	祐	4e5.3
	祐	4e5.3
攵	憂	4i12.1
忄	悒	4k7.9
	悠	4k7.20
礻	裕	5e7.3
疒	疣	5i4.1
米	釉	6b6.8
虫	蚰	6d5.2
	蝣	6d8.4
	融	6d10.5
言	誘	7a7.4

Reading	Kanji	Code
	酉 7e0.1	
	雄 8c4.1	
魚	鮪 11a6.1	
yū	夕 0a3.14	
yubari 尸	尿 3r4.1	
yubazu 弓	弭 3h6.1	
yū(be)	夕 0a3.14	
yubi 扌	指 3c6.15	
yuda(neru)	委 5d3.2	
yu(daru) 艹	茹 3k6.7	
yu(deru) 艹	茹 3k6.7	
yue 攵	故 4i5.2	
yuga(meru)	歪 2m7.4	
yuga(mi)	歪 2m7.4	
yuga(mu)	歪 2m7.4	
YUI	由 0a5.35	
	遺 2q12.4	
	唯 3d8.1	
yuka 广	床 3q4.1	
木	林 3q4.1	
yukari 糸	縁 6a9.10	
	縁 6a9.10	
yuka(shii) 广	床 3q4.1	
木	林 3q4.1	
yuki 礻	裄 5e6.1	
	雪 8d3.2	
	雪 8d3.2	
yu(ku)	之 0a2.9	
辶	逝 2q7.8	
	逝 2q7.8	
彳	行 3i3.1	
	徃 3i5.6	
	徃 3i5.6	
yume 艹	夢 3k10.14	
木	梦 3k10.14	
yumi 弓	弓 3h0.1	
yu(ragu) 扌	揺 3c9.8	
	搖 3c9.8	
yu(rameku) 扌	揺 3c9.8	
	搖 3c9.8	
	揺 3c9.8	
yu(reru) 扌	揺 3c9.8	
	搖 3c9.8	
yuri 山	峠 3o5.2	
yu(ru) 扌	揺 3c9.8	
	搖 3c9.8	
門	閔 8e4.1	
yuruga(se) 忄	忽 4k4.7	
yu(rugasu) 扌	揺 3c9.8	
	搖 3c9.8	
yu(rugu) 扌	揺 3c9.8	
	搖 3c9.8	
yuru(i) 糸	緩 6a9.8	
yuru(meru) 弓	弛 3h3.1	
糸	緩 6a9.8	

Reading	Kanji	Code
yuru(mu) 弓	弛 3h3.1	
糸	緩 6a9.8	
yuru(su) 攵	赦 4i7.3	
言	許 7a4.3	
yuru(yaka) 糸	緩 6a9.8	
yu(saburu) 扌	揺 3c9.8	
	搖 3c9.8	
yu(suburu) 扌	揺 3c9.8	
	搖 3c9.8	
yusu(gu) 氵	濯 3a14.5	
氵	濯 3a14.5	
yu(suru) 扌	揺 3c9.8	
	搖 3c9.8	
yuta(ka) 口	豊 3d10.16	
	豐 3d10.15	
食	饒 8b12.2	
yu(u) 糸	結 6a6.5	
yu(waeru) 糸	結 6a6.5	
yuzu 木	柚 4a5.5	
yuzu(ru) 言	譲 7a13.1	
	讓 7a13.1	

– Z –

Reading	Kanji	Code
ZA 土	坐 3b4.11	
扌	挫 3c7.15	
艹	莝 3k10.28	
广	座 3q7.2	
疒	痤 5i7.1	
ZAI 刂	剤 2f8.6	
	劑 2f8.6	
土	在 3b3.8	
木	材 4a3.7	
	杁 4a3.7	
罒	罪 5g8.4	
貝	財 7b3.1	
	賍 7b3.1	
ZAKU 釒	鉐 8a7.1	
zama 木	様 4a10.25	
	樣 4a10.25	
ZAN	残 0a10.11	
土	塹 3b11.5	
宀	竄 3m15.1	
山	嶄 3o11.3	
	巉 3o18.1	
木	槧 4a11.20	
日	暫 4c11.3	
忄	惨 4k8.5	
	慘 4k8.5	
	慙 4k11.14	
	慚 4k11.14	
	懺 4k17.1	
	懺 4k17.1	
戈	残 0a10.11	
	戔 4n4.1	

Reading	Kanji	Code
言	讒	7a17.2
車	斬	7c4.2
za(reru) 戈	戯	4n11.1
	戲	4n11.1
zaru 竹	笊	6f4.2
ZATSU 礻	襍	8c6.2
隹	雑	8c6.2
	雜	8c6.2
zawame(ku) 馬	騒	10a8.5
	騷	10a8.5
zawatsu(ku)		
馬	騒	10a8.5
	騷	10a8.5
ZE 日	是	4c5.9
ZEI	毳	0a12.5
口	噬	3d13.6
木	柄	4a4.7
	橇	4a12.14
月	脆	4b6.4
禾	税	5d7.4
虫	蜹	6d4.2
	蛻	6d7.8
竹	筮	6f7.2
言	説	7a7.12
貝	贅	7b11.4
ZEN	冉	0a5.43
	冉	0a5.43
亻	全	2a4.16
	全	2a4.16
阝	鄯	2d12.3
⸌	前	2o7.3
	善	2o10.2
	蕎	2o10.2
氵	漸	3a11.2
口	喘	3d9.11
彡	髯	3j12.2
艹	苒	3k5.3
月	膳	4b12.2
火	然	4d8.10
礻	禅	4e9.2
	禪	4e9.2
糸	繕	6a12.2
虫	鮎	6d5.10
	蝉	6d12.3
	蟬	6d12.3
	蠕	6d14.1
zeni 釒	銭	8a6.1
	錢	8a6.1
zenmai 艹	薇	3k13.13
ZETSU 口	舌	3d3.9
糸	絶	6a6.11
ZŌ 爿	爿	0a4.10
亻	像	2a12.8

OTHER TITLES BY THE SAME AUTHORS

W. Hadamitzky, M. Spahn
Kanji and Kana. Handbook and Dictionary of the Japanese Writing System
Rutland (Vermont) and Tokyo: Tuttle 1981
German edition by Langenscheidt, Berlin; French edition by Maisonneuve, Paris

W. Hadamitzky, M. Spahn
A Guide to Writing Kanji & Kana. Book 1,2
Rutland (Vermont) and Tokyo: Tuttle 1991

W. Hadamitzky, K. Fujie-Winter (2: Y. Watanabe-Rögner)
Langenscheidts Praktisches Lehrbuch Japanisch. Band 1.2
Berlin: Langenscheidt 1987–1990

W. Hadamitzky, M. Kocks
Bibliography of Japan. German-Language Publications on Japan
Series A: Monographs, Periodicals and Maps. Series B: Articles. 1477-1985.
Ca. 10 volumes; Volumes in print: A 1–3/1 "Monographs, Periodicals and Maps 1477–1970".
München: Saur 1990–

W. Hadamitzky, M. Spahn, and others
MacSUNRISE Script 2000. Kanji and Kana Learning System.
Release 3.1: 1 CD-ROM + 2 floppy disks + manual
(Japanese–English/Deutsch/Français/Español/Portugues/Magyar/Italiano)
Berlin: JAPAN Media 1995

W. Hadamitzky, M. Spahn, and others
MacSUNRISE Kanji Dictionary. With Kanji and Compound Look-up via Any Grapheme
Release 1.3: 1 CD-ROM + 2 floppy disks + manual
(English/German–Japanese and Japanese–English/German)
Berlin: JAPAN Media 1995

W. Hadamitzky, J. Ruminski
The SUNRISE Japan Tour. Travel, Culture, and Language
1 CD-ROM for Macintosh and Windows
(English and German)
Berlin: JAPAN Media 1996

MARK SPAHN   WOLFGANG HADAMITZKY

Mark Spahn has a background in mathematics, engineering, and computer science. He has worked in Japan as a teacher, computer magazine writer, programmer, and translator. He presently resides in the United States, where he is active as a technical translator and consultant.

Wolfgang Hadamitzky is a librarian of the East Asia section of the Berlin State Library. He has worked in Oslo and Tokyo on the staff of the German Cultural Institute (Goethe-Institute).

Kimiko Winter studied English literature at Waseda University and graduated from Freie Universität Berlin with a master's degree in ethnology. She has been on the editorial staff of several Japanese language textbooks. Besides translating she teaches Japanese at various organizations.

The 79 Radicals (without variants)
79 の部首 (異体をのぞく)

2	イ	冫	孑	阝	卩	刂	力	又	宀	亠
	a	b	c	d	e	f	g	h	i	j
	十	艹	夂	丷	厂	辶	冂	几	匚	
	k	m	n	o	p	q	r	s	t	

3	氵	土	扌	口	女	巾	犭	弓	彳	彡
	a	b	c	d	e	f	g	h	i	j
	艹	宀	丷	屮	青	广	尸	口		
	k	m	n	o	p	q	r	s		

4	木	月	日	火	礻	王	牛	方	攵	欠
	a	b	c	d	e	f	g	h	i	j
	心	戸	戈							
	k	m	n							

5	石	立	目	禾	衤	罒	罒	皿	疒	
	a	b	c	d	e	f	g	h	i	

6	糸	米	舟	虫	耳	竹				
	a	b	c	d	e	f				

7	言	貝	車	足	酉					
	a	b	c	d	e					

8	金	食	隹	雨	門					
	a	b	c	d	e					

9	頁		10	馬		11	魚	鳥
	a			a			a	b

Characters which have no radical are listed under the pseudo-radical 0a.
部首をもたない漢字は疑似部首の 0a 部に収録。